6/01

2001
Second Edition

Weather America

A Thirty-Year Summary
of
Statistical Weather Data
and Rankings

Grey House
Publishing

LAKEVILLE, CT 06039

PUBLISHER: Leslie Mackenzie
EDITOR: David Garoogian
EDITORIAL DIRECTOR: Laura Mars
MARKET RESEARCH: Jessica Moody
GRAPHIC DESIGN: Deb Fletcher
CARTOGRAPHER: North Arrow Cartographic Design
PRODUCTION: Stacey Curtis, Michael Marturana

Grey House Publishing, Inc.
Pocket Knife Square
Lakeville, CT 06039
860.435.0868
FAX 860.435.6613
www.greyhouse.com
e-mail: books@greyhouse.com

First edition published 1996
Second edition published 2000

Printed in the USA

ISBN 1-891482-29-7   softcover
ISBN 0-930956-10-X   hardcover

Table of Contents
Weather America

Section Four: Appendices

Grey House Publishing
Statistical & Demographic Reference Books

Grey House Publishing is proud to announce that our business, health and education directories will be available in Online Databases by Fall 2000. Subscribers can access their subscription to our comprehensive databases via the Internet and do customized searches that instantly target the segment of each market that is right for them. Visit www.greyhouse.com and explore the subscription site, free of charge, or call 800-562-2139 for more information.

America's Top-Rated Cities, 2000

America's Top-Rated Cities provides current, comprehensive statistical information in one easy-to-use source on 76 cities which have been cited as the best for business and living in the U.S. Previously published by Universal Reference, this four-volume set offers a concise social, business, economic, demographic and environmental profile of each city, including brief evaluative comments. Comparisons with MSA and U.S. figures are shown and a special section with comparative statistics is also included. Each of the four volumes covers a specific region of the country: Southern, Western, Central and Eastern. This outstanding source of information will be widely used in any reference collection.

4 Volume Set	ISBN 1-891482-50-5	1,528 pages	softcover	$195.00
Vol. 1: Southern	ISBN 1-891482-51-3	387 pages	softcover	$59.95
Vol. 2: Western	ISBN 1-891482-52-1	383 pages	softcover	$59.95
Vol. 3: Central	ISBN 1-891482-53-X	375 pages	softcover	$59.95
Vol. 4: Eastern	ISBN 1-891482-54-8	383 pages	softcover	$59.95

Crime in America's Top-Rated Cities, 2000

This brand new volume includes over 20 years of crime statistics in all major crime categories: violent crimes, property crimes and total crime. *Crime in America's Top-Rated Cities* is arranged alphabetically by city and covers the 76 cities listed in *America's Top-Rated Cities, 2000*. It offers details that compare the number of crimes and crime rates for the city, suburbs and metro area and national crime trends for violent, property and total crimes. This handbook also contains important statistics on Anti-Crime Programs, Crime Risk, Crime Statistics, Hate Crimes, Illegal Drugs, Law Enforcement, Correctional Facilities and much more. Designed for people who are relocating, business professionals, general researchers, the press, law enforcement officials and students of criminal justice, this would be a well-used addition to the reference collection of public, academic and special libraries.

ISBN 1-891482-84-X	841 pages	softcover	$155.00
ISBN 1-891482-85-8	841 pages	hardcover	$180.00

America's Top-Rated Smaller Cities, 2000

A perfect companion to *America's Top-Rated Cities*, *America's Top-Rated Smaller Cities* provides a current, comprehensive business and living profile of smaller cities (population 25,000-99,999) that have been cited as the best for business and living in the United States. This one volume provides important statistical data on the Business and Living Environment of 60 "top" cities. Presented with each-of-use in mind, *America's Top-Rated Smaller Cities*, is arranged alphabetically by city. Each city report includes a Historical Background, an Overview of the State Finances and statistical details on Employment and Earnings, Household Income, Unemployment Rate, Population Characteristics, Taxes, Cost of Living, Education, Health Care, Public Safety, Recreation, Media, Air and Water Quality, and much more. *America's Top-Rated Smaller Cities* offers a reliable, one-stop source for statistical data that, before now, could only be found scattered in hundreds of sources.

ISBN 1-891482-65-3	968 pages	softcover	$160.00
ISBN 1-891482-66-1	968 pages	hardcover	$185.00

Health & Environment in America's Top-Rated Cities, 2001

This comprehensive publication provides critical health and environmental statistics for the 76 top-rated cities listed in *America's Top-Rated Cities*. Diverse topics are covered for each city, such as children's well being, infant mortality, air pollutants and death rates. From health and environmental protection agencies to school classrooms and libraries, this fact-filled handbook continues to educate the public through providing the most accurate and current health and environmental statistics for 76 top-rated cities.

ISBN 1-891482-92-0	800 pages	softcover	$155.00
ISBN 1-891482-93-9	800 pages	hardcover	$180.00

Working Americans, 1880-1999 Volume I: The Working Class

This brand new reference work focuses on the lifestyles and economic life of the American working class from 1880 to 1999. Family Profiles include real data on Income & Job Descriptions, Selected Prices of the Times, Annual Income, Annual Budget of Individuals, Family Finances & Budget, Life at Work, Life at Home, Life in the Community, Working Conditions, Cost of Living, Amusements and much more. You'll also find Economic Profiles with Average Wages of other Professions, a selection of Typical Pricing, Key Events and Inventions, Historical Snapshots, News Profiles, Articles from Local Media and Illustrations. This volume contains 72 Family Profiles that cover 34 occupations, and more than 25 ethnic groups. Geographically, the text travels the entire country, from the East Coast to Hawaii, to provide comprehensive coverage of the social and economic life of working class families available nowhere else. This interesting and useful compilation of portraits of the working class during the last 120 years will be an important addition to any high school, public or academic library reference collection.

ISBN 1-891482-81-5   *558 pages*   *hardcover*   *$125.00*

Working Americans, 1880-1999 Volume II: The Middle Class

ISBN 1-891482-72-6   *600 pages*   *hardcover*   *$125.00*

The Value of a Dollar – Millennium Edition

A guide to practical economy, *The Value of a Dollar* records the actual prices of thousands of items that consumers purchased from the Civil War to the present, along with facts about investment options and income opportunities. The first edition, published by Gale Research in 1994, covered the period of 1860 to 1989. This second edition has been completely redesigned and revised and now contains two new chapters, 1990-1994 and 1995-1999. Each 5-year chapter includes a Historical Snapshot, Consumer Expenditures, Investments, Selected Income, Income/Standard Jobs, Food Basket, Standard Prices and Miscellany. This interesting and useful publication will be widely used in any reference collection.

ISBN 1-891482-49-1   *660 pages*   *hardcover*   *$125.00*

The Comparative Guide to American Elementary & Secondary Schools

This comprehensive volume offers a snapshot profile of each public school district in the United States that serves 2,500 or more students. You'll find important contact information for each school district (name, address, phone number and web site) plus Grades Served, the Numbers of Students and Teachers and the Number of Regular, Special Education, Alternative and Vocational Schools in the district. Also, *The Comparative Guide to Elementary & Secondary Schools* provides important statistics to help evaluate educational programs, including Student/Classroom Teacher Ratios, Number of Librarians, Number of Guidance Counselors, District Expenditures per student and a National Socioeconomic Indicator for the district.

ISBN 1-884925-63-4   *774 pages*   *softcover*   *$85.00*

The Comparative Guide to American Suburbs

This unique reference focuses on the individual and suburban communities within each of the 50 largest metro areas. You'll find profiles of over 1,800 suburban communities with a 10,000+ population, a selection of Statistics on Population, Geography, the Economy, Safety, Housing and Education, plus details on Local Newspapers, Chambers of Commerce, School Districts and Place Name Origins. For each metro area, a Ranking Table is included that compares the suburbs in six critical indicators: Per Capita Income, Unemployment Rate, New Housing Permits, Median Home Prices and Crime Rates for Violent and Property Crimes. *The Comparative Guide to American Suburbs* is conveniently arranged by metro area. For anyone looking to relocate, as well as those doing preliminary market research, this volume is a must-have reference.

ISBN 1-884925-61-8   *816 pages*   *softcover*   *$85.00*

To preview any of our Directories for 30 days, please call toll-free
(800) 562-2139 or fax to (860) 435-3004

INTRODUCTION

Weather America, now in its second edition, is a reference source that organizes, analyzes and ranks key U.S. weather data for the last 30 years. Unique among dozens of weather data publications, Grey House Publishing's *Weather America*, formally published by Toucan Valley Publications, provides the most comprehensive and useful compilation of weather data and statistics available.

Almost all weather data originates from the National Oceanic and Atmospheric Administration (NOAA), and more specifically within NOAA, the National Climatic Data Center, (NCDC) in Asheville, NC. NCDC organizes over 10,000 weather stations across the country, and, on a regular basis, collects, compiles, edits, and adjusts climatological data, and then publishes it in a number of regular serial publications.

Because our editors worked directly from the government's raw data files, we were able to create a reference that stands out from other weather books in several significant ways:

- **Coverage**: *Weather America* includes data for nearly 4,000 weather stations, thousands more than the several hundred places covered by most other books.

- **Detail**: *Weather America* computes more data elements for more places than any other source, including the Federal government; see Section Three below for more specifics.

- **Currency**: *Weather America* uses the most recent data available. Traditionally 30 years of weather data is collected and presented every 10 years (e.g. 1951-1980, 1961-1990, etc.). Because more recent data exists, this edition is based on data from 1970-1999, the most recent thirty year period for which complete year data is available.

- **Organization**: Not only are the tables concise and easy to use, unlike many Federal publications, but *Weather America* presents all the data in a meaningful context:

Section One: Weather Rankings
Now easily accessed in the front of the book, these National and State tables include detailed temperature, precipitation and snowfall data.

Section Two: Major Storm Events
New to this edition, this 44-page section summarizes major storms by both various storm criteria (type, fatalities, injuries, damage amounts), and by state. It offers information on over 2,000 storms from 1995-1999.

Section Three: State Chapters
Organized alphabetically by state, each chapter contains detailed tables on both National Weather Service (NWS) and Cooperative weather stations. NWS stations contain 30 climatological data elements, 17 more than last edition. Cooperative stations contain 16 data elements, 3 more than last edition. Preceding the weather station data is a narrative of the state's climatological conditions, listings of weather stations by county, city (new to this edition) and elevation. Readers will find a new, detailed map of each state that includes station names, counties, and cities.

This edition's format separates data from National Weather Service stations (those operated by professional meteorologists), and data from Cooperative weather stations, which are primarily manned by volunteers. Not only are there more data elements charted — extreme temperatures, thunderstorm days, foggy days, sky cover, humidity, dew points, and wind speeds — but each National Weather Service station table is preceded by a narrative that details specific geographical and topographical information — important to that station's reading.

Section Four: Appendices
New to this edition are the following four appendices:

Appendix A includes national, regional and state climate centers that include complete contact information with web sites and contact names.
Appendix B provides period of record information for National Weather Service stations.
Appendix C is a map that shows the location of NEXRAD's 153 Doppler Radar Stations in the United States.
Appendix D contains an explanation of the data found in the weather station tables.

Weather America's innovations and supplemental resources combine to create a source of choice for researchers looking for basic climatic data for places across the United States.

Author's Note — Adapted from Introduction to the first edition, by Alfred N. Garwood

Inclusion Criteria — How the Data and Stations Were Selected

There were two central goals in the preparation of *Weather America*. The first was to select those data elements which would have the broadest possible use by the greatest range of potential users. For most of the National Weather Service stations there is a substantial quantity and variety of climatological data that is collected, however for the majority of stations the data is more limited. After evaluating the available data set, the editors chose nine temperature measures, five precipitation measures, and heating and cooling degree days — sixteen key data elements that are widely requested and are believed to be of the greatest general interest.

The second goal was to provide data for as many weather stations as possible. Although there are over 10,000 stations, not every station collects data for both precipitation and temperature, and even among those that do, the data is not always complete for the last thirty years. As the editors used a different methodology than that of NCDC to compute data, a formal data sufficiency criteria was devised and applied to the source tapes in order to select stations for inclusion. See Appendix D for explanation of data.

Organization

The main body of *Weather America* is composed of 50 state sections (weather information for the District of Columbia is interfiled by station name in the Maryland and Virginia sections). Each section starts off with a narrative description of the climatic conditions of the state.

Following the state narrative is a state map with the location of weather stations, counties, and major cities clearly marked.

This is followed by three indexes to the data tables. The first index is by the name of the county (or county equivalent) in which the station is located. The second index lists the major cities and the distance, in miles, to all weather stations within a 20-mile radius. The third index is by station elevation.

The indexes are followed by tables for each National Weather Service station along with a brief climactic narrative. Tables covering each Cooperative Station complete the chapter.

Sources of the Data

The data in *Weather America* is compiled from several sources. The majority comes from the original National Climactic Data Center computer tapes (TD-3220 Summary of Month Co-Operative). This data was used to create the entire table for each Cooperative station and part of each National Weather Service station. The remainder of the data for each NWS station comes from the International Station Meteorological Climate Summary, Version 4.0, September 1996, which is also available from the NCDC.

The storm events come from the NCDC Storm Events Database which is accessible over the Internet at http://www4.ncdc.noaa.gov/cgi-win/wwcgi.dll?wwevent~storms.

NCDC has two main classes or types of weather stations; first order stations which are staffed by professional meteorologists (there are approximately 300 such stations) and cooperative stations which are staffed by volunteers. In *Weather America* all first order stations operated by the National Weather Service are included, as well as every cooperative station that met our selection criteria.

Methodology

Weather America is based on an arithmetic average of all available data for a specific data element at a given station. For example, the average maximum daily high temperature during July for Alma, Michigan, was abstracted from NCDC source tapes for the thirty Julys, starting in July, 1970 and ending in July, 1999. These thirty figures were then summed and divided by thirty to produce an arithmetic average. As might be expected, there were not thirty values for every data element on every table. For a variety of reasons, NCDC data is sometimes incomplete. See Appendix D for explanation of data.

Potential cautions in using *Weather America*

First, as with any statistical reference work of this type, users need to be aware of the source of the data. The information here comes from NOAA, and it is the most comprehensive and reliable core data available. Although it is the best, it is not perfect. Most weather stations are staffed by volunteers, times of observation sometimes vary, stations occasionally are moved (especially over a thirty year period), equipment is changed or upgraded, and all of these factors affect the uniformity of the data. *Weather America* does not attempt to correct for these factors, and is not intended for either climatologists or atmospheric scientists. Users with concerns about data collection and reporting protocols are both referred to NCDC technical documentation, and also, they are perhaps better served by using the original computer tapes themselves as well.

Second, users need to be aware of the methodology here which is described above and in Appendix D. Although this methodology has produced fully satisfactory results, it is not directly compatible with other methodologies, hence variances in the results published here and those which appear in other publications will doubtlessly arise.

Third, is the trap of that informal logical fallacy known as "hasty generalization," and its corollaries. This may involve presuming the future will be like the past (specifically, next year will be an average year), or it may involve misunderstanding the limitations of an arithmetic average, but more interestingly, it may involve those mistakes made most innocently by generalizing informally on too broad a basis. As weather is highly localized, the data should be taken in that context. A weather station collects data about climatic conditions at that spot, and that spot may or may not be an effective paradigm for an entire town or area. For example, the weather station in Burlington, Vermont is located at the airport about 3 miles east of the center of town. Most of Burlington is a lot closer to Lake Champlain, and that should mean to a careful user that there could be a significant difference between the temperature readings gathered at the weather station and readings that might be gathered at City Hall downtown. How much would this difference be? How could it be estimated? There are no answers here for these sorts of questions, but it is important for users of this book to raise them for themselves. (It is interesting to note that similar situations abound across the country. For example, compare different readings for the multiple stations in San Francisco, CA or for those around New York City.)

Our source of data has been consistent, so has our methodology. The data has been computed and reported consistently as well. As a result, the *Weather America* should prove valuable to the careful and informed reader.

Weather Station Rankings

Highest Annual Extreme Maximum Temperature					
Rank	**Station Name**	**°F**	**Rank**	**Station Name**	**°F**
1	Death Valley, CA	129	44	Tempe A S U, AZ	119
2	Gold Rock Ranch, CA	*127*	44	Weatherford, TX	119
3	Bullhead City, AZ	*126*	44	Wikieup, AZ	*119*
3	Mecca Fire Station, CA	126	44	Willow Creek 1 NW, CA	119
3	Palm Springs Thermal Airport, CA	126	44	Yuma Valley, AZ	*119*
3	Tacna 3 NE, AZ	126	56	Daggett Barstow-Daggett Airport, CA	118
7	Buckeye, AZ	125	56	Organ Pipe Cactus Nat'l Mon., AZ	118
7	Laveen 3 SSE, AZ	125	56	Paducah, TX	118
7	Litchfield Park, AZ	125	56	Trona, CA	118
7	Willow Beach, AZ	125	56	Truscott 3 W, TX	118
11	Alamo Dam, AZ	*124*	56	Tucson Magnetic Observatory, AZ	*118*
11	Maricopa 4 N, AZ	124	56	Vernon, TX	118
11	Parker, AZ	124	63	Ajo, AZ	117
11	Yuma Citrus Station, AZ	124	63	Aspermont, TX	117
11	Yuma Int'l Airport, AZ	*124*	63	Chandler Heights, AZ	117
11	Yuma Proving Ground, AZ	124	63	Chico University Farm, CA	117
17	Blythe Riverside Co. Airport, CA	123	63	Childress Municipal Airport, TX	117
17	Casa Grande Nat'l Monument, AZ	123	63	Childs, AZ	117
17	Palm Springs, CA	123	63	Fort Stockton, TX	117
17	Parker Reservoir, CA	123	63	Mangum, OK	117
21	Bartlett Dam, AZ	122	63	Montezuma Castle Nat'l Monument, AZ	117
21	Blythe, CA	122	63	Munday, TX	117
21	Borrego Desert Park, CA	122	63	Orland, CA	117
21	El Centro 2 SSW, CA	122	63	Pecos, TX	117
21	Gila Bend, AZ	122	63	Pelton Dam, OR	117
21	Iron Mountain, CA	122	63	Roosevelt 1 WNW, AZ	117
21	Phoenix Sky Harbor Int'l Arpt., AZ	122	63	Saint George, UT	117
21	Youngtown, AZ	122	63	San Bernardino Co. Hospital, CA	117
29	Bouse, AZ	121	63	Tucson Int'l Airport, AZ	117
29	Brawley 2 SW, CA	121	63	Twentynine Palms, CA	117
29	Imperial, CA	121	63	Valley of Fire State Park, NV	117
29	Needles Airport, CA	121	63	Wichita Falls Municipal Airport, TX	117
29	Wickenburg, AZ	121	63	Willows 6 W, CA	117
34	Beaver Dam, AZ	120	63	Wink Winkler Co. Airport, TX	117
34	Casa Grande, AZ	*120*	85	Boulder City, NV	116
34	Castle Hot Springs, AZ	120	85	Canoga Park Pierce College, CA	116
34	Eagle Mountain, CA	120	85	Cascabel, AZ	116
34	Henshaw Dam, CA	120	85	Chattanooga 3 NE, OK	116
34	Monahans, TX	120	85	Clifton, AZ	116
34	Phantom Ranch, AZ	120	85	Falcon Dam, TX	116
34	Stewart Mountain, AZ	120	85	Gail, TX	116
34	Wahweap, AZ	120	85	Healdsburg, CA	116
34	Yucca 1 NNE, AZ	120	85	Hobart Municipal Airport, OK	116
44	Eloy 4 NE, AZ	*119*	85	Hollis, OK	116
44	Florence, AZ	119	85	Jayton, TX	116
44	Guthrie, TX	119	85	Las Vegas McCarran Int'l Arpt., NV	116
44	Hayfield Pumping Plant, CA	119	85	Maljamar 4 SE, NM	116
44	Inyokern, CA	119	85	Matador, TX	116
44	Kofa Mine, AZ	*119*	85	Memphis, TX	116
44	Quanah 5 SE, TX	119	85	Midland 4 ENE, TX	116

Lowest Annual Extreme Maximum Temperature

Rank	Station Name	°F	Rank	Station Name	°F
1	Saint Paul Island Airport, AK	66	40	Slide Mountain, NY	88
2	Mauna Loa Slope Observatory, HI	71	40	Talkeetna State Airport, AK	88
3	Mount Washington, NH	72	40	Tonsina, AK	88
4	Cold Bay Airport, AK	76	54	Auke Bay, AK	89
4	Glen Alps, AK	*76*	54	Cordova, AK	89
6	Barrow W. Post-W. Rogers Airport, AK	79	54	Kulani Camp 79, HI	89
7	Haleakala Ranger Station 338, HI	80	54	McGrath Airport, AK	89
8	Dillingham Airport, AK	*81*	54	Olga 2 SE, WA	89
8	Homer Airport, AK	81	54	Ookala 223, HI	*89*
8	Wolf Creek Pass 1 E, CO	81	54	Rainier Paradise Ranger Station, WA	89
11	Anchorage Int'l Airport, AK	82	54	Rico, CO	89
11	Kodiak State USCG Base, AK	82	54	Whites Crossing, AK	89
13	Grandfather Mountain, NC	83	54	Wolf Canyon, NM	89
13	Palmer IAS, AK	83	64	Beaver Falls, AK	90
13	Taylor Park, CO	83	64	Big Delta Allen AAF, AK	90
16	Bethel Airport, AK	84	64	Blaine, WA	90
16	Cabin Creek, CO	84	64	Coupeville 1 S, WA	90
16	Cooper Lake Project, AK	84	64	Crater Lake Nat'l Park Hdqtrs., OR	90
16	Intricate Bay, AK	84	64	Gascon, NM	90
16	Mount Mansfield, VT	84	64	Grant, CO	90
21	Climax, CO	85	64	Grant Grove, CA	90
21	Dillon 1 E, CO	85	64	Greer, AZ	90
21	King Salmon Airport, AK	85	64	Hermit 7 ESE, CO	90
21	Kotzebue Ralph Wein Memorial, AK	85	64	Juneau Int'l Airport, AK	90
21	Matanuska AES, AK	85	64	Kanalohuluhulu 1075, HI	90
21	Sugarloaf Reservoir, CO	85	64	Lihue Airport, HI	90
27	Kenai Municipal Airport, AK	86	64	Red River, NM	90
27	Nome Municipal Airport, AK	86	64	Spicer, CO	90
27	Port Alsworth, AK	86	64	Stillwater Reservoir, NY	90
27	Ruxton Park, CO	86	64	Yampa, CO	90
27	Valdez WSO, AK	*86*	81	Bodie, CA	91
32	Eureka, CA	87	81	Bright Angel Ranger Station, AZ	*91*
32	Grand Lake 6 SSW, CO	87	81	Center 4 SSW, CO	91
32	Kailua 446, HI	87	81	Del Norte 2 E, CO	91
32	Kitoi Bay, AK	87	81	Eagle Nest, NM	91
32	Seward, AK	87	81	First Conn Lake, NH	91
32	Silver Lake Brighton, UT	87	81	Green Mountain Dam, CO	91
32	Wasilla 3 S, AK	87	81	Highlands, NC	91
32	Yakutat State Airport, AK	87	81	Lodgepole, CA	91
40	Annette Island Airport, AK	88	81	Moran 5 WNW, WY	91
40	Antero Reservoir, CO	88	81	Mystic Lake, MT	91
40	Crested Butte, CO	88	81	Old Forge, NY	91
40	Gulkana Intermediate Field, AK	88	81	Opihihale 2 24.1, HI	91
40	Huntington Lake, CA	88	81	Ouray, CO	91
40	Kainaliu 73.2, HI	88	81	Pinedale, WY	91
40	Lake George 8 SW, CO	88	81	Tahoe City, CA	91
40	Little Port Walter, AK	88	81	Tanana R.M. Calhoun Mem. Arpt., AK	91
40	Northway Airport, AK	88	98	Alta 1 NNW, WY	92
40	Silverton, CO	*88*	98	Banner Elk, NC	92
40	Sitka Japonski Airport, AK	88	98	Blowing Rock 1 NW, NC	92

Highest Annual Mean Maximum Temperature

Rank	Station Name	°F	Rank	Station Name	°F
1	Death Valley, CA	90.6	49	McAllen Miller Int'l Airport, TX	84.8
2	Mecca Fire Station, CA	89.9	52	Honolulu Int'l Airport, HI	84.7
3	Gila Bend, AZ	89.2	52	Puukohola Heiau 98.1, HI	84.7
4	Palm Springs, CA	88.9	54	Stewart Mountain, AZ	84.6
5	Buckeye, AZ	88.7	54	Weslaco 2 E, TX	84.6
6	Bullhead City, AZ	88.5	56	Eagle Mountain, CA	84.5
7	Palm Springs Thermal Airport, CA	88.4	56	Fort Myers Page Field, FL	84.5
8	El Centro 2 SSW, CA	88.3	56	McCook, TX	84.5
9	Brawley 2 SW, CA	88.1	56	Punta Gorda 4 ESE, FL	84.5
9	Litchfield Park, AZ	88.1	56	Raymondville, TX	84.5
11	Casa Grande Nat'l Monument, AZ	88.0	56	Waikiki 717.2, HI	84.5
11	Yuma Int'l Airport, AZ	88.0	62	Mountain Lake, FL	84.4
13	Parker, AZ	87.9	62	Wickenburg, AZ	84.4
14	Blythe, CA	87.8	64	Hayfield Pumping Plant, CA	84.3
15	Imperial, CA	87.7	64	Hialeah, FL	84.3
16	Blythe Riverside Co. Airport, CA	87.6	64	Kahului Airport, HI	84.3
16	Gold Rock Ranch, CA	87.6	64	Wauchula, FL	84.3
16	Tacna 3 NE, AZ	87.6	68	Kofa Mine, AZ	84.2
19	Borrego Desert Park, CA	87.5	69	Canal Point USDA, FL	84.1
19	Yuma Proving Ground, AZ	87.5	69	Tavernier, FL	84.1
21	Yuma Citrus Station, AZ	87.2	69	Wikieup, AZ	84.1
22	Presidio, TX	87.1	72	Bartow, FL	84.0
23	Casa Grande, AZ	86.8	72	Belle Glade Exp. Station, FL	84.0
23	Maricopa 4 N, AZ	86.8	72	Twentynine Palms, CA	84.0
23	Tempe A S U, AZ	86.8	75	Arcadia, FL	83.9
26	Youngtown, AZ	86.6	75	Fort Drum 5 NW, FL	83.9
27	Iron Mountain, CA	86.5	75	Hebbronville, TX	83.9
27	Willow Beach, AZ	86.5	75	Tucson Camp Ave. Exp. Farm, AZ	83.9
29	Alamo Dam, AZ	86.4	79	Flamingo Ranger Station, FL	83.8
29	Bouse, AZ	86.4	79	Tucson NWSO, AZ	83.8
29	Eloy 4 NE, AZ	86.4	81	Falfurrias, TX	83.7
29	Zapata 3 SW, TX	86.4	81	Lake Alfred Exp. Station, FL	83.7
33	Laveen 3 SSE, AZ	86.3	81	Lakeland Linder Airport, FL	83.7
33	Needles Airport, CA	86.3	84	Clewiston U.S. Engineers, FL	83.6
33	Organ Pipe Cactus Nat'l Mon., AZ	86.3	84	Moore Haven Lock 1, FL	83.6
33	Phoenix Sky Harbor Int'l Arpt., AZ	86.3	84	Plant City, FL	83.6
37	Florence, AZ	86.1	84	Saint Leo, FL	83.6
38	Parker Reservoir, CA	86.0	88	Avon Park 2 W, FL	83.5
39	Rio Grande City 1 SE, TX	85.8	88	Kissimmee 2, FL	83.5
40	Laredo 2, TX	85.7	90	Charlotte 5 NNW, TX	83.4
40	Tamiami Trail 40 Mile Bend, FL	85.7	90	Fort Lauderdale, FL	83.4
42	Falcon Dam, TX	85.6	90	Miami Int'l Airport, FL	83.4
43	Myakka River State Park, FL	85.3	90	Tilden 4 SSE, TX	83.4
44	Candelaria, TX	85.1	90	Tucson Magnetic Observatory, AZ	83.4
44	Naples, FL	85.1	95	Castle Hot Springs, AZ	83.3
46	South Phoenix, AZ	85.0	95	Fort Pierce, FL	83.3
47	Archbold Bio Station, FL	84.9	97	Alice, TX	83.2
47	Immokalee 3 NNW, FL	84.9	97	Harlingen, TX	83.2
49	Bartlett Dam, AZ	84.8	97	Parrish, FL	83.2
49	Chandler Heights, AZ	84.8	97	Stuart 1 S, FL	83.2

Lowest Annual Mean Maximum Temperature

Rank	Station Name	°F	Rank	Station Name	°F
1	Barrow W. Post-W. Rogers Airport, AK	15.6	51	Duluth Int'l Airport, MN	47.9
2	Kotzebue Ralph Wein Memorial, AK	28.0	52	First Conn Lake, NH	48.1
3	Bettles Field, AK	31.6	52	International Falls Int'l Arpt., MN	48.1
4	Northway Airport, AK	33.4	54	Auke Bay, AK	48.2
5	Mount Washington, NH	33.6	54	Cabin Creek, CO	48.2
5	Nome Municipal Airport, AK	33.6	54	Crater Lake Nat'l Park Hdqtrs., OR	48.2
7	Tanana R.M. Calhoun Mem. Arpt., AK	34.7	57	Hancock Houghton Co. Airport, MI	48.3
8	McGrath Airport, AK	35.8	57	Warroad, MN	48.3
9	Eielson Field, AK	36.2	57	Winton Power Plant, MN	*48.3*
9	Snowshoe Lake, AK	36.2	60	Red Lake Indian Agency, MN	48.5
11	Bethel Airport, AK	36.4	60	Silver Lake Brighton, UT	48.5
12	North Pole, AK	36.7	62	Whitefish Point, MI	48.6
13	Big Delta Allen AAF, AK	37.3	63	Hibbing Chisholm-Hibbing Airport, MN	48.7
13	Fairbanks Int'l Airport, AK	37.3	63	Petersburg 2 N, ND	48.7
15	Gulkana Intermediate Field, AK	37.5	63	Taylor Park, CO	48.7
16	College Observatory, AK	37.9	66	Fort Kent, ME	48.8
17	Tonsina, AK	38.3	66	Pembina, ND	48.8
18	University Exp. Station, AK	38.7	68	Caribou Municipal Airport, ME	48.9
19	Saint Paul Island Airport, AK	39.0	68	Cavalier 7 NW, ND	48.9
20	Old Edgerton, AK	*39.4*	68	Sugarloaf Reservoir, CO	*48.9*
21	Dillingham Airport, AK	*39.9*	71	Superior, WI	49.0
22	Glen Alps, AK	*40.2*	71	Van Buren 2, ME	*49.0*
23	Mount Mansfield, VT	41.6	73	Marquette County Airport, MI	49.1
24	Kenai Municipal Airport, AK	42.1	73	Tower 3 S, MN	49.1
25	King Salmon Airport, AK	42.2	75	Edmore 1 NW, ND	49.2
26	Whites Crossing, AK	42.7	75	Little Port Walter, AK	49.2
27	Anchorage Int'l Airport, AK	43.1	77	Bottineau, ND	49.3
27	Cold Bay Airport, AK	43.1	77	Brassua Dam, ME	49.3
29	Climax, CO	43.2	77	Hebgen Dam, MT	49.3
29	Talkeetna State Airport, AK	43.2	77	Saint Germain 2 E, WI	49.3
31	Intricate Bay, AK	44.0	77	Two Harbors, MN	49.3
32	Port Alsworth, AK	44.1	82	Sault Ste Marie Sanderson Field, MI	49.5
33	Palmer IAS, AK	44.4	82	Willow City, ND	49.5
33	Valdez WSO, AK	*44.4*	84	Long Falls Dam, ME	49.6
35	Homer Airport, AK	44.5	84	Ripogenus Dam, ME	*49.6*
36	Matanuska AES, AK	44.6	86	Sitka Japonski Airport, AK	49.7
37	Rainier Paradise Ranger Station, WA	44.7	87	Fortuna 1 W, ND	49.8
38	Cooper Lake Project, AK	44.9	87	Jackman, ME	49.8
39	Seward, AK	45.3	87	Pinkham Notch, NH	49.8
40	Kitoi Bay, AK	45.9	87	Sharon, ND	49.8
41	Wasilla 3 S, AK	46.1	91	Devils Lake KDLR, ND	49.9
41	Wolf Creek Pass 1 E, CO	*46.1*	91	Government Camp, OR	49.9
43	Yakutat State Airport, AK	46.3	91	Hansboro 4 NNE, ND	49.9
44	Cordova, AK	46.5	91	Ironwood, MI	49.9
45	Rolla 3 NW, ND	46.8	91	Rangeley, ME	49.9
46	Kodiak State USCG Base, AK	46.9	91	Ruxton Park, CO	49.9
47	Grand Marais, MN	47.2	97	Argyle 4 E, MN	50.0
47	Langdon Exp. Farm, ND	47.2	97	Fosston 1 E, MN	50.0
49	Duluth Harbor Station, MN	47.4	97	Herman, MI	50.0
50	Juneau Int'l Airport, AK	47.5	97	Leeds, ND	50.0

Highest Annual Mean Temperature					
Rank	**Station Name**	**°F**	**Rank**	**Station Name**	**°F**
1	Key West Int'l Airport, FL	78.0	51	Bartow, FL	73.2
2	Tavernier, FL	*77.8*	51	Belle Glade Exp. Station, FL	73.2
3	Honolulu Int'l Airport, HI	77.5	51	Lakeland Linder Airport, FL	*73.2*
4	Waikiki 717.2, HI	76.7	54	McCook, TX	73.1
5	Miami Int'l Airport, FL	76.6	54	Venice, FL	*73.1*
6	Hialeah, FL	76.4	56	Harlingen, TX	73.0
6	Miami Beach, FL	76.4	56	Parker, AZ	73.0
8	Death Valley, CA	76.3	58	Kofa Mine, AZ	*72.9*
9	Tamiami Trail 40 Mile Bend, FL	*76.0*	59	Kissimmee 2, FL	72.8
10	Kahului Airport, HI	75.9	59	Tampa Int'l Airport, FL	72.8
11	Lihue Airport, HI	75.8	59	Wauchula, FL	72.8
12	Fort Lauderdale, FL	75.7	62	Borrego Desert Park, CA	72.7
13	West Palm Beach Int'l Airport, FL	75.3	62	El Centro 2 SSW, CA	72.7
14	Waimanalo Exp. Farm, HI	75.2	62	Manoa Lyon Arboretum, HI	*72.7*
15	Flamingo Ranger Station, FL	74.9	62	Mecca Fire Station, CA	72.7
15	Fort Myers Page Field, FL	74.9	62	Mountain Lake, FL	72.7
17	Naples, FL	74.8	62	Ookala 223, HI	*72.7*
18	McAllen Miller Int'l Airport, TX	*74.7*	62	Orlando Int'l Airport, FL	*72.7*
18	Molokai Airport, HI	74.7	69	Bradenton 5 ESE, FL	72.6
20	Yuma Int'l Airport, AZ	*74.6*	69	Fort Drum 5 NW, FL	*72.6*
21	Stuart 1 S, FL	74.5	69	Tarpon Springs Sewage Plant, FL	72.6
21	Zapata 3 SW, TX	74.5	72	Plant City, FL	72.5
23	Gold Rock Ranch, CA	*74.4*	72	Saint Leo, FL	72.5
24	Clewiston U.S. Engineers, FL	*74.3*	72	Vero Beach, FL	72.5
24	Hana Airport 355, HI	74.3	75	Melbourne Regional Airport, FL	72.4
24	Weslaco 2 E, TX	74.3	75	Parrish, FL	72.4
27	Hilo International Airport, HI	74.1	77	Arcadia, FL	72.3
27	Saint Petersburg, FL	74.1	77	Avon Park 2 W, FL	72.3
29	Brownsville Int'l Airport, TX	74.0	77	Willow Beach, AZ	72.3
29	Bullhead City, AZ	*74.0*	80	Palm Springs Thermal Airport, CA	72.2
29	Parker Reservoir, CA	74.0	81	Blythe, CA	72.1
29	Yuma Proving Ground, AZ	74.0	81	Lake Alfred Exp. Station, FL	72.1
33	Phoenix Sky Harbor Int'l Arpt., AZ	73.9	83	Archbold Bio Station, FL	72.0
34	Eagle Mountain, CA	73.8	83	Brawley 2 SW, CA	72.0
34	Immokalee 3 NNW, FL	73.8	83	Hebbronville, TX	72.0
34	Palm Springs, CA	73.8	86	Alice, TX	71.9
34	Punta Gorda 4 ESE, FL	73.8	86	Clermont 7 S, FL	71.9
38	Canal Point USDA, FL	73.7	86	Corpus Christi Int'l Airport, TX	71.9
38	Falcon Dam, TX	73.7	86	Falfurrias, TX	71.9
38	Iron Mountain, CA	73.7	90	Chapman Ranch, TX	71.8
38	Laredo 2, TX	73.7	90	Crystal City, TX	71.8
42	Gila Bend, AZ	73.6	90	Robstown, TX	71.8
42	Needles Airport, CA	73.6	90	Youngtown, AZ	71.8
44	Blythe Riverside Co. Airport, CA	73.5	94	Brooksville Chin Hill, FL	*71.6*
44	Rio Grande City 1 SE, TX	73.5	94	Port Mansfield, TX	*71.6*
46	Imperial, CA	73.4	94	Titusville, FL	71.6
46	Moore Haven Lock 1, FL	73.4	97	Buckeye, AZ	71.5
48	Fort Pierce, FL	73.3	97	Yuma Citrus Station, AZ	71.5
48	Myakka River State Park, FL	73.3	99	Sanford Experiment Station, FL	71.4
48	Raymondville, TX	73.3	100	Litchfield Park, AZ	71.3

Rank	Station Name	°F	Rank	Station Name	°F
1	Barrow W. Post-W. Rogers Airport, AK	10.2	51	Hebgen Dam, MT	36.5
2	Kotzebue Ralph Wein Memorial, AK	21.9	51	Moose, WY	36.5
3	Northway Airport, AK	22.5	51	Moran 5 WNW, WY	36.5
4	Bettles Field, AK	22.6	54	Silver Lake Brighton, UT	36.6
5	Snowshoe Lake, AK	23.5	54	Spicer, CO	36.6
6	Tanana R.M. Calhoun Mem. Arpt., AK	25.0	54	Wasilla 3 S, AK	36.6
7	North Pole, AK	25.3	57	Grand Lake 1 NW, CO	36.8
8	McGrath Airport, AK	26.1	58	Rolla 3 NW, ND	37.0
9	Nome Municipal Airport, AK	26.6	59	First Conn Lake, NH	37.1
10	Eielson Field, AK	26.7	59	Fontenelle Dam, WY	37.1
10	Tonsina, AK	26.7	61	Pembina, ND	37.2
12	Mount Washington, NH	27.0	62	International Falls Int'l Arpt., MN	37.3
13	Fairbanks Int'l Airport, AK	27.5	62	Rainier Paradise Ranger Station, WA	37.3
13	Gulkana Intermediate Field, AK	27.5	64	Cooper Lake Project, AK	37.4
15	University Exp. Station, AK	27.9	64	Van Buren 2, ME	*37.4*
16	College Observatory, AK	28.0	64	Walden, CO	37.4
17	Old Edgerton, AK	*28.3*	67	Grouse, ID	*37.5*
18	Big Delta Allen AAF, AK	28.4	67	Petersburg 2 N, ND	37.5
19	Bethel Airport, AK	29.6	67	Warren, ID	37.5
20	Climax, CO	30.7	67	Willow City, ND	37.5
21	Taylor Park, CO	32.0	71	Fort Kent, ME	37.6
22	Whites Crossing, AK	32.1	71	Warroad, MN	37.6
23	Glen Alps, AK	*33.3*	73	Crater Lake Nat'l Park Hdqtrs., OR	37.7
24	Wolf Creek Pass 1 E, CO	*33.5*	73	Edmore 1 NW, ND	37.7
25	Dillingham Airport, AK	*33.8*	75	Bodie, CA	37.8
25	Hermit 7 ESE, CO	33.8	75	Gunnison 3 SW, CO	37.8
25	Snake River, WY	33.8	75	Hibbing Chisholm-Hibbing Airport, MN	37.8
25	Talkeetna State Airport, AK	33.8	75	Sage 4 NNW, WY	*37.8*
29	Crested Butte, CO	33.9	79	Winton Power Plant, MN	*37.9*
30	Kenai Municipal Airport, AK	34.2	80	Bottineau, ND	38.0
31	King Salmon Airport, AK	34.3	80	Homer Airport, AK	38.0
32	Mount Mansfield, VT	34.4	82	Cavalier 7 NW, ND	38.1
33	Sugarloaf Reservoir, CO	*34.6*	82	Cochetopa Creek, CO	38.1
34	Saint Paul Island Airport, AK	34.8	82	Lake George 8 SW, CO	38.1
35	Port Alsworth, AK	34.9	82	Stanley 3 NNW, ND	38.1
35	Silverton, CO	*34.9*	82	Upham 3 N, ND	38.1
37	Intricate Bay, AK	35.3	87	Argyle 4 E, MN	38.2
38	Dillon 1 E, CO	35.5	87	Hansboro 4 NNE, ND	38.2
39	Antero Reservoir, CO	35.6	87	Powers Lake 1 N, ND	38.2
40	Matanuska AES, AK	35.7	90	Cass Lake, MN	38.3
40	Tower 3 S, MN	35.7	90	Jackman, ME	38.3
42	Palmer IAS, AK	35.8	90	Meredith, CO	*38.3*
42	Wisdom, MT	35.8	90	Rangeley, ME	38.3
44	Dixie, ID	*35.9*	94	Cold Bay Airport, AK	38.4
44	Ruxton Park, CO	35.9	94	Fortuna 1 W, ND	38.4
46	Pinedale, WY	36.0	94	Leeds, ND	38.4
47	Cabin Creek, CO	36.1	94	Red Lake Indian Agency, MN	38.4
48	Grand Lake 6 SSW, CO	36.3	98	Bowbells, ND	38.5
49	Anchorage Int'l Airport, AK	36.4	98	Tioga 1 E, ND	38.5
49	Langdon Exp. Farm, ND	36.4	100	Bergland Dam, MI	38.6

Lowest Annual Mean Temperature

Highest Annual Mean Minimum Temperature

Rank	Station Name	°F	Rank	Station Name	°F
1	Key West Int'l Airport, FL	73.2	50	Belle Glade Exp. Station, FL	62.3
2	Miami Beach, FL	71.6	50	Point Comfort, TX	62.3
3	Tavernier, FL	*71.5*	53	Bradenton 5 ESE, FL	62.1
4	Lihue Airport, HI	70.3	53	Raymondville, TX	62.1
5	Honolulu Int'l Airport, HI	70.2	55	Death Valley, CA	62.0
6	Miami Int'l Airport, FL	69.7	55	Freeport 2 NW, TX	62.0
7	Waimanalo Exp. Farm, HI	69.4	55	Kissimmee 2, FL	62.0
8	Waikiki 717.2, HI	68.9	55	Parker Reservoir, CA	62.0
9	Hialeah, FL	68.4	59	Falcon Dam, TX	61.9
10	Fort Lauderdale, FL	68.0	60	Clermont 7 S, FL	61.7
11	Hana Airport 355, HI	67.9	61	Kofa Mine, AZ	*61.6*
12	Kahului Airport, HI	67.5	61	Laredo 2, TX	61.6
13	West Palm Beach Int'l Airport, FL	67.4	61	McCook, TX	61.6
14	Molokai Airport, HI	67.3	61	Parrish, FL	61.6
15	Saint Petersburg, FL	66.7	61	Robstown, TX	61.6
16	Hilo International Airport, HI	66.6	66	New Orleans Audubon, LA	61.5
16	Ookala 223, HI	*66.6*	66	Phoenix Sky Harbor Int'l Arpt., AZ	61.5
18	Manoa Lyon Arboretum, HI	*66.3*	68	Daytona Beach Regional Airport, FL	61.4
18	Tamiami Trail 40 Mile Bend, FL	*66.3*	68	Jacksonville Beach, FL	*61.4*
20	Flamingo Ranger Station, FL	66.0	68	Plant City, FL	61.4
21	Stuart 1 S, FL	65.7	68	Saint Leo, FL	61.4
22	Fort Myers Page Field, FL	65.2	68	Titusville, FL	61.4
22	Galveston, TX	65.2	73	Fort Drum 5 NW, FL	*61.3*
24	Clewiston U.S. Engineers, FL	*65.1*	73	Palacios Municipal Airport, TX	61.3
25	Brownsville Int'l Airport, TX	64.9	75	Myakka River State Park, FL	61.2
25	Port Mansfield, TX	64.9	75	Wauchula, FL	61.2
27	McAllen Miller Int'l Airport, TX	*64.5*	75	Yuma Int'l Airport, AZ	*61.2*
28	Naples, FL	64.4	78	Avon Park 2 W, FL	61.1
29	Weslaco 2 E, TX	63.9	78	Rio Grande City 1 SE, TX	61.1
30	Tampa Int'l Airport, FL	63.6	80	Brooksville Chin Hill, FL	*61.0*
31	Rockport, TX	63.5	80	Gold Rock Ranch, CA	*61.0*
32	Venice, FL	*63.4*	82	Hackberry 8 SSW, LA	60.9
33	Canal Point USDA, FL	63.3	82	Mountain Lake, FL	60.9
33	Fort Pierce, FL	63.3	82	Needles Airport, CA	60.9
35	Melbourne Regional Airport, FL	63.2	85	Iron Mountain, CA	60.8
36	Punta Gorda 4 ESE, FL	63.1	85	Opihihale 2 24.1, HI	60.8
37	Eagle Mountain, CA	63.0	87	Sanford Experiment Station, FL	60.7
37	Moore Haven Lock 1, FL	63.0	88	Alice, TX	60.6
39	Harlingen, TX	62.8	88	Arcadia, FL	60.6
40	Aransas Wildlife Refuge, TX	62.7	88	Crystal City, TX	60.6
41	Chapman Ranch, TX	62.6	88	Houston William P. Hobby Airport, TX	60.6
41	Immokalee 3 NNW, FL	62.6	92	Lake Alfred Exp. Station, FL	60.5
41	Lakeland Linder Airport, FL	*62.6*	93	Lisbon, FL	60.4
41	Tarpon Springs Sewage Plant, FL	62.6	93	Saint Augustine, FL	*60.4*
41	Zapata 3 SW, TX	62.6	93	Yuma Proving Ground, AZ	60.4
46	Corpus Christi Int'l Airport, TX	62.5	96	Victoria Regional Airport, TX	60.3
46	Matagorda 2, TX	62.5	97	Falfurrias, TX	60.2
46	Orlando Int'l Airport, FL	*62.5*	98	Hebbronville, TX	60.0
46	Vero Beach, FL	62.5	99	Apalachicola Municipal Airport, FL	59.9
50	Bartow, FL	62.3	99	Brunswick Malcolm McKinnon Arpt., GA	59.9

Lowest Annual Mean Minimum Temperature

Rank	Station Name	°F	Rank	Station Name	°F
1	Barrow W. Post-W. Rogers Airport, AK	4.8	51	Bethel Airport, AK	22.6
2	Snowshoe Lake, AK	10.7	52	Eagle Nest, NM	22.8
3	Northway Airport, AK	11.6	53	Lake George 8 SW, CO	23.0
4	Bettles Field, AK	13.5	54	Steamboat Springs, CO	23.1
5	North Pole, AK	13.9	55	Jackson, WY	23.2
6	Tonsina, AK	15.0	56	Alamosa Bergman Field, CO	23.4
7	Tanana R.M. Calhoun Mem. Arpt., AK	15.2	57	Center 4 SSW, CO	23.5
7	Taylor Park, CO	15.2	57	Woodruff, UT	23.5
9	Kotzebue Ralph Wein Memorial, AK	15.8	59	Afton, WY	23.7
10	Hermit 7 ESE, CO	15.9	59	Cimarron, CO	23.7
11	McGrath Airport, AK	16.5	61	Hebgen Dam, MT	23.8
12	University Exp. Station, AK	17.0	62	Yellow Pine 7 S, ID	*23.9*
13	Eielson Field, AK	17.1	63	Cabin Creek, CO	24.0
14	Old Edgerton, AK	*17.2*	64	Red River, NM	24.1
15	Gulkana Intermediate Field, AK	17.4	65	Bridgeport, CA	24.2
15	Silverton, CO	*17.4*	66	Polebridge, MT	*24.3*
17	Crested Butte, CO	17.5	66	Talkeetna State Airport, AK	24.3
17	Snake River, WY	17.5	66	Telluride 4 WNW, CO	24.3
19	Fairbanks Int'l Airport, AK	17.8	66	Wolf Canyon, NM	24.3
20	College Observatory, AK	18.0	70	Boca, CA	24.4
21	Climax, CO	18.1	70	Seneca, OR	24.4
22	Antero Reservoir, CO	18.5	72	Grant, CO	24.5
23	Bodie, CA	19.4	73	Bailey, CO	24.6
24	Big Delta Allen AAF, AK	19.5	73	Silver Lake Brighton, UT	24.6
25	Nome Municipal Airport, AK	19.6	75	Chama, NM	24.7
26	Wisdom, MT	19.8	75	Green Mountain Dam, CO	24.7
27	Dillon 1 E, CO	20.1	77	Chilly Barton Flat, ID	24.9
28	Cochetopa Creek, CO	20.3	78	Tierra Amarilla 4 N, NM	*25.0*
28	Gunnison 3 SW, CO	20.3	79	Saguache, CO	25.2
28	Mount Washington, NH	20.3	79	Upham 3 N, ND	25.2
28	Sugarloaf Reservoir, CO	*20.3*	79	Yampa, CO	25.2
32	Pinedale, WY	20.4	82	Cheesman, CO	25.3
33	Grand Lake 1 NW, CO	20.7	82	Manassa, CO	25.3
33	Sage 4 NNW, WY	*20.7*	82	Willow City, ND	25.3
35	Wolf Creek Pass 1 E, CO	*20.9*	85	Blanca, CO	25.4
36	Fontenelle Dam, WY	21.0	85	Fort Valley, AZ	25.4
37	Dixie, ID	*21.1*	87	Lima, MT	25.5
38	Moose, WY	21.2	87	New Meadows Ranger Station, ID	*25.5*
39	Meredith, CO	*21.3*	87	Opheim 10 N, MT	25.5
40	Whites Crossing, AK	21.4	87	Sula 3 ENE, MT	25.5
41	Grouse, ID	*21.5*	87	Ten Sleep 16 SSE, WY	25.5
42	Ruxton Park, CO	21.9	87	Westcliffe, CO	25.5
42	Walden, CO	21.9	93	Langdon Exp. Farm, ND	25.6
42	Warren, ID	21.9	93	Pembina, ND	25.6
45	Grand Lake 6 SSW, CO	22.0	95	Austin 3 S, OR	25.7
45	Spicer, CO	22.0	95	Butte Bert Mooney Airport, MT	25.7
47	Moran 5 WNW, WY	22.1	95	Hamer 4 NW, ID	*25.7*
48	Lake City, CO	22.2	95	Port Alsworth, AK	25.7
49	Rico, CO	22.3	99	Van Buren 2, ME	*25.9*
49	Tower 3 S, MN	22.3	100	Fairfield Ranger Station, ID	*26.0*

Highest Annual Extreme Minimum Temperature

Rank	Station Name	°F	Rank	Station Name	°F
1	Hilo International Airport, HI	54	46	Yuma Citrus Station, AZ	25
2	Honolulu Int'l Airport, HI	53	52	Berkeley, CA	*24*
2	Lihue Airport, HI	53	52	Flamingo Ranger Station, FL	24
4	Lahaina 361, HI	52	52	Richmond, CA	24
5	Hana Airport 355, HI	51	52	Saint Petersburg, FL	24
5	Kailua 446, HI	51	52	Salinas Municipal Airport, CA	24
5	Ookala 223, HI	*51*	52	Salinas 2, CA	24
8	Kahului Airport, HI	50	52	San Francisco Int'l Airport, CA	24
8	Naalehu 14, HI	50	52	San Gabriel Fire Dept., CA	24
10	Manoa Lyon Arboretum, HI	*49*	60	Moore Haven Lock 1, FL	23
10	Opihihale 2 24.1, HI	49	60	Palm Springs, CA	23
10	Waimanalo Exp. Farm, HI	49	60	Pasadena, CA	23
13	Kainaliu 73.2, HI	48	60	Punta Gorda 4 ESE, FL	23
14	Molokai Airport, HI	46	60	Redlands, CA	23
14	Waikiki 717.2, HI	46	60	San Francisco Mission, CA	23
16	Key West Int'l Airport, FL	41	60	Stuart 1 S, FL	23
16	Puukohola Heiau 98.1, HI	*41*	60	Venice, FL	*23*
18	Tavernier, FL	*35*	60	Vero Beach, FL	23
19	Santa Monica Pier, CA	34	60	Yuma Proving Ground, AZ	23
20	Los Angeles Int'l Airport, CA	33	70	Gold Rock Ranch, CA	*22*
20	San Diego Lindbergh Field, CA	33	70	Hollywood-Burbank Airport, CA	22
20	U.C.L.A., CA	33	70	Iron Mountain, CA	22
23	Miami Beach, FL	32	70	Morro Bay Fire Dept., CA	22
24	Hawaii Volcano Nat'l Park HQ 54, HI	31	70	Pomona Cal Poly, CA	*22*
25	Los Angeles Civic Center, CA	30	70	Riverside Citrus Exp. Station, CA	22
25	Miami Int'l Airport, FL	30	70	Riverside Fire Station 3, CA	22
25	Newport Beach, CA	30	70	Yuma Valley, AZ	*22*
25	Oxnard, CA	30	78	Bartlett Dam, AZ	21
25	Santa Ana Fire Station, CA	30	78	Belle Glade Exp. Station, FL	21
30	Kanalohuluhulu 1075, HI	29	78	Imperial, CA	21
31	Chula Vista, CA	28	78	Newark, CA	21
31	Fort Lauderdale, FL	28	78	Roosevelt 1 WNW, AZ	21
31	Haleakala Ranger Station 338, HI	28	78	San Bernardino Co. Hospital, CA	21
31	Hialeah, FL	28	78	Tempe A S U, AZ	21
31	Kulani Camp 79, HI	28	78	Visalia, CA	21
31	Long Beach Daugherty Field, CA	28	78	Willow Beach, AZ	21
31	Tamiami Trail 40 Mile Bend, FL	28	87	Bartow, FL	20
38	Fort Myers Page Field, FL	*27*	87	Blythe Riverside Co. Airport, CA	20
38	Laguna Beach, CA	27	87	Borrego Desert Park, CA	20
38	Oceanside Marina, CA	27	87	Bradenton 5 ESE, FL	20
38	Torrance Municipal Airport, CA	27	87	Fort Ross, CA	20
38	West Palm Beach Int'l Airport, FL	27	87	Immokalee 3 NNW, FL	20
43	Clewiston U.S. Engineers, FL	26	87	Lakeland Linder Airport, FL	*20*
43	Naples, FL	26	87	Lompoc, CA	20
43	Tustin Irvine Ranch, CA	26	87	Monterey, CA	20
46	Canal Point USDA, FL	25	87	Palo Alto, CA	20
46	Eagle Mountain, CA	25	87	San Gregorio 2 SE, CA	20
46	Kofa Mine, AZ	*25*	87	Santa Barbara Municipal Airport, CA	*20*
46	Parker Reservoir, CA	25	87	Santa Maria Public Airport, CA	20
46	Santa Paula, CA	25	87	Vista 2 NNE, CA	20

Lowest Annual Extreme Minimum Temperature

Rank	Station Name	°F	Rank	Station Name	°F
1	Tanana R.M. Calhoun Mem. Arpt., AK	-76	42	Tioga 1 E, ND	-50
2	McGrath Airport, AK	-75	42	Whites Crossing, AK	-50
3	Northway Airport, AK	-71	42	Williston Sloulin Int'l Airport, ND	-50
4	Bettles Field, AK	-70	42	Worland Municipal Airport, WY	-50
5	North Pole, AK	-67	55	Baudette Int'l Airport, MN	-49
6	Eielson Field, AK	-64	55	Content 3 SSE, MT	-49
7	Fairbanks Int'l Airport, AK	-60	55	Dixie, ID	*-49*
7	Snowshoe Lake, AK	-60	55	Kotzebue Ralph Wein Memorial, AK	-49
7	Taylor Park, CO	-60	55	Mizpah 4 NNW, MT	-49
7	Tonsina, AK	-60	55	Pinedale, WY	-49
7	Tower 3 S, MN	-60	55	Plevna, MT	-49
7	University Exp. Station, AK	-60	55	Rest Lake, WI	-49
13	Big Delta Allen AAF, AK	-59	55	Sandy Lake Dam Libby, MN	-49
14	Old Edgerton, AK	*-58*	55	Towner 2 NE, ND	-49
15	College Observatory, AK	-57	55	Willow City, ND	-49
15	Gulkana Intermediate Field, AK	-57	66	Argyle 4 E, MN	-48
17	Port Alsworth, AK	-55	66	Bethel Airport, AK	-48
17	Wisdom, MT	-55	66	Cass Lake, MN	-48
19	Brainerd, MN	-54	66	Clearmont 5 SW, WY	-48
19	Ingomar 14 NE, MT	-54	66	Culbertson, MT	-48
19	Loma 1 WNW, MT	-54	66	Devils Tower 2, WY	-48
19	Nome Municipal Airport, AK	-54	66	Elk City 1 NE, ID	-48
23	Barrow W. Post-W. Rogers Airport, AK	-53	66	Gordon, WI	-48
23	Dillingham Airport, AK	*-53*	66	Hamer 4 NW, ID	-48
23	Fosston 1 E, MN	-53	66	Joplin, MT	*-48*
23	Moose Lake 1 SSE, MN	-53	66	King Salmon Airport, AK	-48
27	Busby, MT	-52	66	Lincoln Ranger Station, MT	-48
27	Butte Bert Mooney Airport, MT	-52	66	Mahnomen 1 W, MN	-48
27	Chester, MT	-52	66	Milaca 1 ENE, MN	-48
27	Itasca Univ. of Minnesota, MN	-52	66	Minocqua Dam, WI	-48
27	Mora, MN	-52	66	Opheim 10 N, MT	-48
27	Old Forge, NY	-52	66	Polebridge, MT	*-48*
27	Redstone, MT	-52	66	Powers Lake 1 N, ND	-48
27	Wright 4 NW, MN	-52	66	Saco 1 NNW, MT	-48
35	Antero Reservoir, CO	-51	66	Seneca, OR	-48
35	Big Falls, MN	-51	66	Sun River 4 S, MT	-48
35	Malta 35 S, MT	*-51*	66	Talkeetna State Airport, AK	-48
35	Park Rapids Municipal Airport, MN	-51	66	Upham 3 N, ND	-48
35	Ridgeway 1 S, MT	-51	89	Augusta, MT	-47
35	Sage 4 NNW, WY	*-51*	89	Babb 6 NE, MT	-47
35	Ten Sleep 16 SSE, WY	-51	89	Broadus, MT	-47
42	Big Sandy, MT	-50	89	Cody 21 SW, WY	-47
42	Cotton, MN	-50	89	Crested Butte, CO	-47
42	Denton 1 NNE, MT	-50	89	Eagle Nest, NM	-47
42	Havre City-County Airport, MT	-50	89	Elkader 5 SSW, IA	-47
42	Hibbing Chisholm-Hibbing Airport, MN	-50	89	Huntley Experiment Station, MT	*-47*
42	Hysham 25 SSE, MT	-50	89	Idaho Falls 46 W, ID	-47
42	Intricate Bay, AK	-50	89	Jump River 3 E, WI	-47
42	Jackson, WY	-50	89	Kenai Municipal Airport, AK	-47
42	Spicer, CO	-50	89	North Pelican, WI	-47

Highest July Mean Maximum Temperature

Rank	Station Name	°F	Rank	Station Name	°F
1	Death Valley, CA	115.2	50	Stewart Mountain, AZ	103.6
2	Bullhead City, AZ	*111.6*	52	Kofa Mine, AZ	103.5
3	Willow Beach, AZ	110.4	53	Inyokern, CA	102.8
4	Gila Bend, AZ	109.0	54	Castle Hot Springs, AZ	102.5
5	Buckeye, AZ	108.9	55	Saint George, UT	102.4
6	Needles Airport, CA	108.7	55	South Phoenix, AZ	102.4
7	Mecca Fire Station, CA	108.5	55	Yucca 1 NNE, AZ	102.4
8	Blythe, CA	108.4	58	Ajo, AZ	*102.3*
8	Blythe Riverside Co. Airport, CA	108.4	59	Roosevelt 1 WNW, AZ	102.1
10	Iron Mountain, CA	108.3	60	Childs, AZ	102.0
10	Palm Springs, CA	108.3	61	Boulder City, NV	101.9
10	Parker, AZ	108.3	61	Desert Nat'l Wildlife Range, NV	101.9
13	Litchfield Park, AZ	108.0	63	Tucson Magnetic Observatory, AZ	*101.0*
14	Bouse, AZ	107.8	64	Montezuma Castle Nat'l Monument, AZ	100.8
15	Casa Grande Nat'l Monument, AZ	107.7	65	Pahrump, NV	100.6
16	Alamo Dam, AZ	*107.5*	65	Presidio, TX	100.6
16	Parker Reservoir, CA	107.5	65	Tucson Camp Ave. Exp. Farm, AZ	100.6
18	Gold Rock Ranch, CA	*107.3*	68	Laredo 2, TX	100.5
19	Borrego Desert Park, CA	107.2	68	Tucson NWSO, AZ	100.5
20	El Centro 2 SSW, CA	107.1	70	San Carlos Reservoir, AZ	100.3
21	Maricopa 4 N, AZ	107.0	71	Moab, UT	99.9
21	Yuma Int'l Airport, AZ	107.0	72	Tucson Int'l Airport, AZ	99.7
23	Brawley 2 SW, CA	106.8	73	Candelaria, TX	99.6
24	Palm Springs Thermal Airport, CA	106.5	73	Dewey, UT	99.6
24	Yuma Proving Ground, AZ	106.5	73	Falcon Dam, TX	99.6
26	Imperial, CA	106.2	76	Clifton, AZ	99.5
27	Tacna 3 NE, AZ	106.1	76	Three Rivers Edison 1, CA	99.5
28	Casa Grande, AZ	106.0	78	Zion National Park, UT	99.3
28	Phoenix Sky Harbor Int'l Arpt., AZ	106.0	79	Cascabel, AZ	99.2
30	Youngtown, AZ	105.9	79	Friant Government Camp, CA	99.2
31	Phantom Ranch, AZ	105.8	79	Hanksville, UT	99.2
31	Twentynine Palms, CA	105.8	82	Anvil Ranch, AZ	99.1
31	Yuma Citrus Station, AZ	105.8	82	Coalinga, CA	99.1
34	Beaver Dam, AZ	*105.6*	82	Zapata 3 SW, TX	99.1
35	Tempe A S U, AZ	105.5	85	Rio Grande City 1 SE, TX	98.9
36	Laveen 3 SSE, AZ	105.4	85	Wasco, CA	98.9
37	Valley of Fire State Park, NV	105.2	87	La Verkin, UT	98.8
38	Wikieup, AZ	*105.0*	88	Chattanooga 3 NE, OK	98.6
38	Yuma Valley, AZ	*105.0*	88	Ysleta, TX	98.6
40	Bartlett Dam, AZ	104.9	90	Mangum, OK	98.5
40	Florence, AZ	104.9	90	Monahans, TX	98.5
42	Eloy 4 NE, AZ	104.8	90	Pecos, TX	98.5
42	Trona, CA	104.8	93	Pahranagat Wildlife Refuge, NV	98.4
44	Eagle Mountain, CA	104.6	94	Fort Thomas 2 SW, AZ	98.3
45	Chandler Heights, AZ	104.4	95	Bakersfield Meadows Field, CA	98.2
45	Daggett Barstow-Daggett Airport, CA	104.4	95	Elsinore, CA	98.2
45	Wickenburg, AZ	104.4	95	Independence, CA	98.2
48	Hayfield Pumping Plant, CA	104.1	95	Porterville, CA	98.2
48	Las Vegas McCarran Int'l Arpt., NV	104.1	95	Safford Agricultural Center, AZ	98.2
50	Organ Pipe Cactus Nat'l Mon., AZ	103.6	100	Corcoran Irrigation District, CA	98.1

Lowest July Mean Maximum Temperature

Rank	Station Name	°F	Rank	Station Name	°F
1	Barrow W. Post-W. Rogers Airport, AK	46.4	50	Port Alsworth, AK	67.5
2	Saint Paul Island Airport, AK	50.2	50	Tillamook 1 W, OR	67.5
3	Mount Washington, NH	54.2	53	Government Camp, OR	67.6
4	Cold Bay Airport, AK	55.2	53	San Francisco Mission, CA	67.6
5	Mauna Loa Slope Observatory, HI	56.4	53	Seaside, OR	67.6
6	Nome Municipal Airport, AK	58.5	56	Astoria Clatsop County Airport, OR	67.7
7	Glen Alps, AK	*58.6*	57	Gold Beach Ranger Station, OR	67.9
8	Kotzebue Ralph Wein Memorial, AK	59.8	57	Talkeetna State Airport, AK	67.9
9	Yakutat State Airport, AK	60.1	59	Port Orford 2, OR	68.0
10	Kodiak State USCG Base, AK	60.4	60	Brookings, OR	68.1
11	Rainier Paradise Ranger Station, WA	60.7	61	Quillayute Airport, WA	68.2
12	Kitoi Bay, AK	60.8	62	Aberdeen, WA	68.3
13	Homer Airport, AK	60.9	63	Port Angeles, WA	68.5
14	Sitka Japonski Airport, AK	61.0	64	Cabin Creek, CO	68.6
15	Dillingham Airport, AK	*61.4*	64	Gulkana Intermediate Field, AK	68.6
16	Seward, AK	61.8	64	Monterey, CA	68.6
17	Cordova, AK	61.9	67	Orick Prairie Creek Park, CA	68.9
18	Kenai Municipal Airport, AK	62.0	68	Scotia, CA	69.0
19	Little Port Walter, AK	62.2	69	Whites Crossing, AK	69.1
20	Valdez WSO, AK	62.4	70	McGrath Airport, AK	69.2
21	Eureka, CA	62.8	71	Honeyman State Park, OR	69.3
22	Bethel Airport, AK	63.1	72	Grand Marais, MN	69.5
23	King Salmon Airport, AK	63.7	72	Santa Monica Pier, CA	69.5
24	Annette Island Airport, AK	64.2	72	Tonsina, AK	69.5
24	Juneau Int'l Airport, AK	64.2	75	San Gregorio 2 SE, CA	69.6
26	Half Moon Bay, CA	64.4	76	Otis 2 NE, OR	69.7
27	Beaver Falls, AK	*64.5*	76	Wasilla 3 S, AK	69.7
28	Climax, CO	64.7	78	Grandfather Mountain, NC	69.8
29	Newport, OR	64.8	78	Old Edgerton, AK	69.8
30	Kulani Camp 79, HI	65.1	80	Olga 2 SE, WA	69.9
31	Anchorage Int'l Airport, AK	65.3	81	Cloverdale, OR	70.0
32	Auke Bay, AK	65.5	82	Northway Airport, AK	70.1
32	Crescent City 3 NNW, CA	65.5	83	Clearwater, WA	70.3
32	Haleakala Ranger Station 338, HI	65.5	84	Bettles Field, AK	70.5
32	Morro Bay Fire Dept., CA	65.5	84	Kanalohuluhulu 1075, HI	70.5
32	Mount Mansfield, VT	65.5	86	Berkeley, CA	*70.6*
37	Intricate Bay, AK	65.6	86	Big Delta Allen AAF, AK	70.6
38	Cooper Lake Project, AK	65.7	88	Coupeville 1 S, WA	70.8
38	Long Beach Exp. Station, WA	65.7	88	Ruxton Park, CO	70.8
40	Wolf Creek Pass 1 E, CO	65.9	90	Bellingham Int'l Airport, WA	70.9
41	Fort Bragg 5 N, CA	66.1	91	Taylor Park, CO	71.1
42	Fort Ross, CA	66.4	92	Salinas Municipal Airport, CA	71.2
43	North Bend Municipal Airport, OR	66.5	92	Sugarloaf Reservoir, CO	71.2
44	Klamath, CA	66.7	94	Eielson Field, AK	71.4
45	Bandon 2 NNE, OR	66.8	94	Hawaii Volcano Nat'l Park HQ 54, HI	71.4
46	Palmer IAS, AK	66.9	94	Salinas 2, CA	71.4
46	Snowshoe Lake, AK	66.9	97	Richmond, CA	71.6
48	Matanuska AES, AK	67.2	97	Silver Lake Brighton, UT	71.6
49	Hoquiam Airport, WA	67.3	99	Aberdeen 20 NNE, WA	71.7
50	Crater Lake Nat'l Park Hdqtrs., OR	67.5	99	Anacortes, WA	71.7

Highest January Mean Minimum Temperature

Rank	Station Name	°F	Rank	Station Name	°F
1	Honolulu Int'l Airport, HI	65.4	50	Los Angeles Civic Center, CA	49.5
1	Lihue Airport, HI	65.4	52	McAllen Miller Int'l Airport, TX	*49.4*
3	Key West Int'l Airport, FL	65.1	52	Myakka River State Park, FL	49.4
4	Waimanalo Exp. Farm, HI	64.6	52	Weslaco 2 E, TX	49.4
5	Waikiki 717.2, HI	64.5	55	Clermont 7 S, FL	49.3
6	Hana Airport 355, HI	64.3	55	Plant City, FL	49.3
7	Lahaina 361, HI	*64.1*	57	Arcadia, FL	49.0
7	Ookala 223, HI	*64.1*	57	Mountain Lake, FL	49.0
9	Hilo International Airport, HI	63.6	59	Orlando Int'l Airport, FL	*48.9*
10	Kahului Airport, HI	63.5	60	Saint Leo, FL	48.7
10	Molokai Airport, HI	63.5	61	Los Angeles Int'l Airport, CA	48.6
12	Tavernier, FL	63.3	62	Brooksville Chin Hill, FL	48.5
13	Miami Beach, FL	63.0	62	Port Mansfield, TX	48.5
14	Manoa Lyon Arboretum, HI	*62.5*	64	Titusville, FL	48.3
15	Naalehu 14, HI	*62.3*	65	Newport Beach, CA	48.1
16	Miami Int'l Airport, FL	60.1	66	Galveston, TX	48.0
17	Fort Lauderdale, FL	58.6	66	Harlingen, TX	48.0
18	Hialeah, FL	58.5	68	Avon Park 2 W, FL	47.7
19	Opihihale 2 24.1, HI	57.5	68	Sanford Experiment Station, FL	47.7
20	West Palm Beach Int'l Airport, FL	57.1	70	Archbold Bio Station, FL	47.6
21	Tamiami Trail 40 Mile Bend, FL	57.0	71	Daytona Beach Regional Airport, FL	47.5
22	Flamingo Ranger Station, FL	56.0	72	Lake Alfred Exp. Station, FL	47.1
23	Stuart 1 S, FL	55.1	72	Raymondville, TX	47.1
24	Saint Petersburg, FL	54.3	74	Chapman Ranch, TX	46.8
25	Clewiston U.S. Engineers, FL	54.2	75	Lisbon, FL	46.7
26	Fort Myers Page Field, FL	54.1	76	Santa Ana Fire Station, CA	46.6
27	Naples, FL	54.0	77	Corpus Christi Int'l Airport, TX	46.4
28	Canal Point USDA, FL	52.9	77	Kanalohuluhulu 1075, HI	46.4
29	Immokalee 3 NNW, FL	52.0	77	San Francisco Mission, CA	46.4
30	Belle Glade Exp. Station, FL	51.9	80	Kofa Mine, AZ	46.3
31	Fort Pierce, FL	51.7	80	Zapata 3 SW, TX	46.3
31	Punta Gorda 4 ESE, FL	51.7	82	Rockport, TX	46.2
33	Moore Haven Lock 1, FL	51.6	82	Torrance Municipal Airport, CA	46.2
34	Melbourne Regional Airport, FL	51.2	84	Gold Rock Ranch, CA	*46.1*
35	Venice, FL	51.0	85	Jacksonville Beach, FL	46.0
36	Brownsville Int'l Airport, TX	50.7	85	McCook, TX	46.0
37	Tampa Int'l Airport, FL	50.6	85	Saint Augustine, FL	*46.0*
37	Vero Beach, FL	50.6	88	Long Beach Daugherty Field, CA	45.9
39	Lakeland Linder Airport, FL	50.4	88	Matagorda 2, TX	45.9
40	Santa Monica Pier, CA	50.3	90	Chula Vista, CA	45.7
41	U.C.L.A., CA	50.2	91	Aransas Wildlife Refuge, TX	45.6
42	Bartow, FL	50.1	91	Ocala, FL	45.6
42	Fort Drum 5 NW, FL	50.1	93	Eagle Mountain, CA	45.4
42	Tarpon Springs Sewage Plant, FL	50.1	93	Falcon Dam, TX	45.4
45	Bradenton 5 ESE, FL	50.0	93	Oxnard, CA	45.4
45	Parrish, FL	50.0	96	Point Comfort, TX	45.3
47	Kissimmee 2, FL	49.8	96	Yuma Int'l Airport, AZ	45.3
48	San Diego Lindbergh Field, CA	49.7	98	New Orleans Audubon, LA	45.2
48	Wauchula, FL	49.7	99	Freeport 2 NW, TX	45.1
50	Hawaii Volcano Nat'l Park HQ 54, HI	49.5	100	Oceanside Marina, CA	44.8

	Lowest January Mean Minimum Temperature					
Rank	**Station Name**	**°F**		**Rank**	**Station Name**	**°F**
1	Northway Airport, AK	-26.3		51	Red Lake Falls, MN	-5.9
2	North Pole, AK	-21.1		52	Gordon, WI	-5.8
3	Barrow W. Post-W. Rogers Airport, AK	-19.6		52	Powers Lake 1 N, ND	-5.8
4	Bettles Field, AK	-19.5		54	Crookston NW Exp. Station, MN	-5.6
5	Snowshoe Lake, AK	-18.6		54	Mora, MN	-5.6
6	Eielson Field, AK	-18.0		54	Park Rapids Municipal Airport, MN	-5.6
7	Tanana R.M. Calhoun Mem. Arpt., AK	-17.4		57	Hibbing Chisholm-Hibbing Airport, MN	-5.5
8	Fairbanks Int'l Airport, AK	-17.3		58	Wadena 3 S, MN	-5.3
9	McGrath Airport, AK	-17.1		59	Mahnomen 1 W, MN	-5.1
10	University Exp. Station, AK	-14.8		60	Rolla 3 NW, ND	-5.0
11	Tonsina, AK	-13.5		60	Tioga 1 E, ND	-5.0
12	Gulkana Intermediate Field, AK	-13.0		62	Grand Forks Int'l Airport, ND	-4.8
13	College Observatory, AK	-12.7		62	Isle 12 N, MN	-4.8
14	Taylor Park, CO	-12.2		62	Leech Lake Dam, MN	-4.8
15	Old Edgerton, AK	-11.8		62	Rugby, ND	-4.8
16	Tower 3 S, MN	-11.1		66	Cochetopa Creek, CO	-4.7
17	Big Delta Allen AAF, AK	-10.3		66	Grand Rapids Forestry Lab, MN	-4.7
18	Cass Lake, MN	-9.6		66	McVille, ND	-4.7
19	Pembina, ND	-9.4		66	Silverton, CO	-4.7
20	Warroad, MN	-9.2		70	Pine River Dam, MN	-4.6
21	Upham 3 N, ND	-9.1		70	Valley City 3 NNW, ND	-4.6
21	Willow City, ND	-9.1		72	Fortuna 1 W, ND	-4.5
23	Big Falls, MN	*-8.8*		72	Westby, MT	-4.5
23	Kotzebue Ralph Wein Memorial, AK	-8.8		74	Sharon, ND	-4.4
25	Argyle 4 E, MN	-8.7		75	Oakes 2 S, ND	-4.3
26	International Falls Int'l Arpt., MN	-8.5		75	Stanley 3 NNW, ND	-4.3
27	Langdon Exp. Farm, ND	-8.4		77	Bowbells, ND	-4.2
28	Fosston 1 E, MN	-7.9		78	Mount Washington, NH	-4.1
29	Baudette Int'l Airport, MN	-7.8		79	Grafton, ND	-4.0
29	Petersburg 2 N, ND	-7.8		80	Colgate, ND	-3.9
29	Van Buren 2, ME	-7.8		80	Drake 9 NE, ND	-3.9
32	Edmore 1 NW, ND	-7.6		82	Cooperstown, ND	-3.8
33	Itasca Univ. of Minnesota, MN	-7.2		82	Sandy Lake Dam Libby, MN	*-3.8*
33	Red Lake Indian Agency, MN	-7.2		82	Solon Springs, WI	-3.8
33	Winton Power Plant, MN	*-7.2*		85	Antero Reservoir, CO	-3.7
36	Bottineau, ND	-7.1		85	Wright 4 NW, MN	-3.7
36	Brainerd, MN	-7.1		87	Ada, MN	-3.6
36	Cotton, MN	-7.1		87	La Moure, ND	-3.6
36	Hermit 7 ESE, CO	-7.1		87	Whites Crossing, AK	-3.6
40	Cavalier 7 NW, ND	-6.9		90	Hillsboro 3 N, ND	-3.5
40	Towner 2 NE, ND	-6.9		90	Kenmare 1 WSW, ND	-3.5
42	Agassiz Refuge, MN	-6.7		92	Wildrose 3 NW, ND	-3.4
42	Squa Pan Dam, ME	-6.7		93	Alamosa Bergman Field, CO	-3.3
44	McHenry 3 W, ND	-6.6		93	Max, ND	-3.3
45	Hansboro 4 NNE, ND	-6.5		95	Devils Lake KDLR, ND	-3.2
46	Crested Butte, CO	-6.3		95	Fergus Falls, MN	-3.2
47	Fort Kent, ME	-6.2		95	Garrison 1 NNW, ND	-3.2
47	Westhope, ND	-6.2		95	Moose Lake 1 SSE, MN	-3.2
49	Leeds, ND	-6.1		99	Carrington 4 N, ND	-3.1
50	Gunnison 3 SW, CO	-6.0		99	Foxboro, WI	-3.1

Highest Number of Days Annually Maximum Temperature ≥ 90°F

Rank	Station Name	Days	Rank	Station Name	Days
1	Death Valley, CA	190	50	Eagle Mountain, CA	154
2	Gila Bend, AZ	187	52	Hayfield Pumping Plant, CA	153
2	Mecca Fire Station, CA	187	52	Kofa Mine, AZ	*153*
4	Buckeye, AZ	183	52	Tucson NWSO, AZ	153
5	Bullhead City, AZ	*182*	52	Twentynine Palms, CA	153
5	Casa Grande Nat'l Monument, AZ	182	56	Tucson Camp Ave. Exp. Farm, AZ	152
7	Palm Springs, CA	180	57	Raymondville, TX	150
7	Presidio, TX	180	57	Tilden 4 SSE, TX	150
9	Palm Springs Thermal Airport, CA	179	59	Hebbronville, TX	149
10	Litchfield Park, AZ	177	59	Tucson Magnetic Observatory, AZ	*149*
10	Parker, AZ	177	61	Weslaco 2 E, TX	148
12	El Centro 2 SSW, CA	176	62	Eagle Pass, TX	147
12	Tacna 3 NE, AZ	176	62	Myakka River State Park, FL	147
12	Yuma Int'l Airport, AZ	*176*	62	Phantom Ranch, AZ	*147*
12	Zapata 3 SW, TX	176	65	Falfurrias, TX	146
16	Brawley 2 SW, CA	175	66	Anvil Ranch, AZ	144
16	Casa Grande, AZ	*175*	66	Castle Hot Springs, AZ	144
18	Blythe Riverside Co. Airport, CA	174	66	Tucson Int'l Airport, AZ	144
18	Maricopa 4 N, AZ	174	69	Crystal City, TX	142
20	Blythe, CA	173	70	Beaver Dam, AZ	141
20	Gold Rock Ranch, CA	*173*	70	Langtry, TX	141
20	Rio Grande City 1 SE, TX	173	72	Alice, TX	140
20	Yuma Proving Ground, AZ	173	72	Charlotte 5 NNW, TX	140
24	Borrego Desert Park, CA	172	72	Pecos, TX	140
24	Imperial, CA	172	75	Valley of Fire State Park, NV	139
24	Tempe A S U, AZ	172	76	Cascabel, AZ	138
27	Falcon Dam, TX	171	76	Dilley, TX	*138*
27	Laveen 3 SSE, AZ	171	78	Archbold Bio Station, FL	137
27	Youngtown, AZ	171	78	Daggett Barstow-Daggett Airport, CA	137
30	Alamo Dam, AZ	*170*	78	Trona, CA	137
30	Bouse, AZ	170	81	Roosevelt 1 WNW, AZ	136
30	Eloy 4 NE, AZ	*170*	82	Ajo, AZ	135
30	Laredo 2, TX	170	83	Childs, AZ	134
30	Phoenix Sky Harbor Int'l Arpt., AZ	170	83	Monahans, TX	134
35	Florence, AZ	169	85	Inyokern, CA	133
36	Iron Mountain, CA	168	85	Yucca 1 NNE, AZ	133
36	Willow Beach, AZ	168	87	Amistad Dam, TX	132
36	Yuma Citrus Station, AZ	168	87	Las Vegas McCarran Int'l Arpt., NV	132
39	Organ Pipe Cactus Nat'l Mon., AZ	167	89	Clifton, AZ	*131*
39	Parker Reservoir, CA	167	89	Harlingen, TX	131
41	Needles Airport, CA	166	89	San Carlos Reservoir, AZ	131
42	South Phoenix, AZ	163	92	Safford Agricultural Center, AZ	130
43	Chandler Heights, AZ	162	93	Del Rio Int'l Airport, TX	129
44	Candelaria, TX	160	93	Floresville, TX	129
45	McAllen Miller Int'l Airport, TX	*158*	93	Goliad, TX	129
46	McCook, TX	157	93	Tamiami Trail 40 Mile Bend, FL	*129*
47	Stewart Mountain, AZ	156	97	Fort Thomas 2 SW, AZ	128
47	Wickenburg, AZ	156	97	Montezuma Castle Nat'l Monument, AZ	128
49	Wikieup, AZ	*155*	97	Mountain Lake, FL	128
50	Bartlett Dam, AZ	154	100	Mathis 4 SSW, TX	127

Highest Number of Days Annually Maximum Temperature ≤ 32°F

Rank	Station Name	Days	Rank	Station Name	Days
1	Barrow W. Post-W. Rogers Airport, AK	250	50	Hansboro 4 NNE, ND	102
2	Kotzebue Ralph Wein Memorial, AK	197	50	Leeds, ND	102
3	Bettles Field, AK	181	53	Grafton, ND	101
4	Tanana R.M. Calhoun Mem. Arpt., AK	173	53	Hancock Houghton Co. Airport, MI	101
5	Nome Municipal Airport, AK	169	53	Marquette County Airport, MI	101
6	Northway Airport, AK	167	56	Devils Lake KDLR, ND	100
7	Mount Washington, NH	166	56	Mahnomen 1 W, MN	100
8	Eielson Field, AK	157	56	Park Rapids Municipal Airport, MN	100
8	North Pole, AK	157	56	Red Lake Falls, MN	100
10	Fairbanks Int'l Airport, AK	156	56	Upham 3 N, ND	100
11	McGrath Airport, AK	155	61	First Conn Lake, NH	99
12	College Observatory, AK	154	61	Fortuna 1 W, ND	99
13	University Exp. Station, AK	153	61	Glen Alps, AK	*99*
14	Big Delta Allen AAF, AK	150	61	Grand Forks Univ. NWS, ND	99
15	Snowshoe Lake, AK	146	61	Herman, MI	99
16	Gulkana Intermediate Field, AK	142	61	Itasca Univ. of Minnesota, MN	99
17	Tonsina, AK	138	61	Towner 2 NE, ND	99
18	Bethel Airport, AK	137	61	Wadena 3 S, MN	99
19	Mount Mansfield, VT	133	61	Westhope, ND	99
20	Old Edgerton, AK	*128*	70	Carrington, ND	98
21	Whites Crossing, AK	*121*	70	Cass Lake, MN	98
22	Langdon Exp. Farm, ND	117	70	Hillsboro 3 N, ND	98
23	Rolla 3 NW, ND	115	70	Palmer IAS, AK	98
24	Petersburg 2 N, ND	112	70	Rugby, ND	98
24	Talkeetna State Airport, AK	112	70	Saint Germain 2 E, WI	98
26	Dillingham Airport, AK	*110*	70	Stanley 3 NNW, ND	98
26	Edmore 1 NW, ND	110	70	Walker Ah Gwah Ching, MN	98
26	International Falls Int'l Arpt., MN	110	78	Bowbells, ND	97
26	Pembina, ND	110	78	Cotton, MN	97
30	Bottineau, ND	109	78	Fargo Hector Field, ND	97
30	Cavalier 7 NW, ND	109	78	Hebgen Dam, MT	97
30	Warroad, MN	109	78	Ironwood, MI	97
33	Anchorage Int'l Airport, AK	108	78	Powers Lake 1 N, ND	97
34	Duluth Int'l Airport, MN	107	78	Tioga 1 E, ND	97
34	Winton Power Plant, MN	*107*	85	Caribou Municipal Airport, ME	96
36	Argyle 4 E, MN	106	85	Colgate, ND	96
36	Climax, CO	106	85	Cooperstown, ND	96
36	Crookston NW Exp. Station, MN	106	85	Grand Rapids Forestry Lab, MN	96
36	Hibbing Chisholm-Hibbing Airport, MN	106	85	Max, ND	96
36	Sharon, ND	106	85	Rainbow Reservoir Lake Tomaha, WI	96
41	McVille, ND	*105*	85	Rest Lake, WI	96
42	Kenai Municipal Airport, AK	104	85	Willow Reservoir, WI	96
42	Red Lake Indian Agency, MN	104	93	Alexandria Chandler Field, MN	95
42	Tower 3 S, MN	104	93	Bergland Dam, MI	95
42	Willow City, ND	104	93	Fergus Falls, MN	95
46	Agassiz Refuge, MN	103	93	Fort Kent, ME	95
46	Fosston 1 E, MN	103	93	Isle 12 N, MN	95
46	Grand Forks Int'l Airport, ND	103	93	Leech Lake Dam, MN	95
46	McHenry 3 W, ND	103	93	Matanuska AES, AK	95
50	Baudette Int'l Airport, MN	102	93	Minocqua Dam, WI	95

Highest Number of Days Annually Minimum Temperature ≤ 32°F

Rank	Station Name	Days	Rank	Station Name	Days
1	Barrow W. Post-W. Rogers Airport, AK	317	48	Mount Washington, NH	243
2	Bodie, CA	304	52	Cabin Creek, CO	242
3	Snake River, WY	*296*	52	Woodruff, UT	242
4	Hermit 7 ESE, CO	290	54	Bailey, CO	241
5	Silverton, CO	*285*	54	Cimarron, CO	241
6	Warren, ID	282	54	Old Edgerton, AK	*241*
7	Dixie, ID	*280*	54	Silver Lake Brighton, UT	241
8	Wisdom, MT	277	58	Eagle Nest, NM	240
9	Climax, CO	276	58	Sula 3 ENE, MT	240
9	Crested Butte, CO	276	60	Lake City, CO	239
11	Dillon 1 E, CO	274	60	Telluride 4 WNW, CO	239
12	Boca, CA	273	62	Afton, WY	238
12	Grand Lake 1 NW, CO	273	62	Chama, NM	238
12	Taylor Park, CO	273	62	Luna Ranger Station, NM	238
15	Snowshoe Lake, AK	269	65	Bettles Field, AK	237
15	Sugarloaf Reservoir, CO	269	65	Nome Municipal Airport, AK	237
17	Rico, CO	267	67	Gulkana Intermediate Field, AK	236
18	Antero Reservoir, CO	266	68	Cascade 1 NW, ID	235
19	Spicer, CO	264	68	Tanana R.M. Calhoun Mem. Arpt., AK	235
19	Tonsina, AK	264	68	Ukiah, OR	235
21	Pinedale, WY	262	71	Libby 32 SSE, MT	234
22	Walden, CO	261	72	Lake George 8 SW, CO	233
23	Ruxton Park, CO	260	72	Ochoco Ranger Station, OR	233
24	Cochetopa Creek, CO	259	74	Bryce Canyon Nat'l Park Hdqtrs., UT	232
24	Sage 4 NNW, WY	*259*	74	Cheesman, CO	232
26	Meredith, CO	258	74	College Observatory, AK	232
27	Fort Valley, AZ	257	74	Hebgen Dam, MT	232
27	Yellow Pine 7 S, ID	*257*	74	McCall, ID	232
29	Seneca, OR	256	74	Tahoe Valley FAA Airport, CA	232
30	Wolf Creek Pass 1 E, CO	*255*	74	University Exp. Station, AK	232
31	Gunnison 3 SW, CO	252	81	Chilly Barton Flat, ID	231
31	Moose, WY	252	81	Encampment 10 ESE, WY	231
33	Austin 3 S, OR	251	81	Green Mountain Dam, CO	231
33	Bridgeport, CA	251	84	Lima, MT	230
33	Fontenelle Dam, WY	251	84	Lodgepole, CA	230
33	Wolf Canyon, NM	251	84	Panguitch, UT	230
37	Moran 5 WNW, WY	250	87	Dulce, NM	229
38	Grand Lake 6 SSW, CO	248	87	Sprague River 1 NW, OR	229
38	Jackson, WY	248	87	Truckee Ranger Station, CA	229
38	Polebridge, MT	*248*	90	McGrath Airport, AK	228
41	Crater Lake Nat'l Park Hdqtrs., OR	247	90	Yampa, CO	228
42	Grant, CO	246	92	Alamosa Bergman Field, CO	227
42	Northway Airport, AK	246	92	Lakeview, MT	227
44	Kotzebue Ralph Wein Memorial, AK	245	92	McGaffey 5 SE, NM	227
44	North Pole, AK	245	92	Tierra Amarilla 4 N, NM	227
44	Red River, NM	245	96	Saguache, CO	226
47	Steamboat Springs, CO	244	96	Tower 3 S, MN	226
48	Donner Memorial State Park, CA	243	98	Rainier Paradise Ranger Station, WA	225
48	Elk City 1 NE, ID	243	98	Whites Crossing, AK	225
48	Grouse, ID	*243*	100	Bethel Airport, AK	224

Highest Number of Days Annually Minimum Temperature ≤ 0°F

Rank	Station Name	Days	Rank	Station Name	Days
1	Barrow W. Post-W. Rogers Airport, AK	170	50	Fosston 1 E, MN	59
2	Northway Airport, AK	135	50	Gunnison 3 SW, CO	59
3	Bettles Field, AK	127	50	Itasca Univ. of Minnesota, MN	59
4	North Pole, AK	124	50	McHenry 3 W, ND	59
5	Snowshoe Lake, AK	123	55	First Conn Lake, NH	58
6	Tanana R.M. Calhoun Mem. Arpt., AK	116	55	Rolla 3 NW, ND	58
7	Eielson Field, AK	114	55	Towner 2 NE, ND	58
7	Fairbanks Int'l Airport, AK	114	58	Crookston NW Exp. Station, MN	57
7	Kotzebue Ralph Wein Memorial, AK	114	58	Red Lake Falls, MN	57
10	McGrath Airport, AK	112	58	Talkeetna State Airport, AK	57
11	University Exp. Station, AK	108	61	Climax, CO	56
12	Tonsina, AK	105	61	Grand Forks Int'l Airport, ND	56
13	College Observatory, AK	102	61	Powers Lake 1 N, ND	56
14	Gulkana Intermediate Field, AK	100	61	Tioga 1 E, ND	56
15	Taylor Park, CO	95	61	Westhope, ND	56
16	Old Edgerton, AK	*92*	66	Fontenelle Dam, WY	55
17	Big Delta Allen AAF, AK	89	66	Hibbing Chisholm-Hibbing Airport, MN	55
18	Hermit 7 ESE, CO	82	66	Jackman, ME	55
19	Nome Municipal Airport, AK	81	66	McVille, ND	*55*
20	Crested Butte, CO	76	66	Moose, WY	55
21	Silverton, CO	*73*	66	Rangeley, ME	55
22	Tower 3 S, MN	71	66	Sage 4 NNW, WY	*55*
22	Whites Crossing, AK	71	73	Bowbells, ND	54
24	Langdon Exp. Farm, ND	70	73	Gordon, WI	54
24	Pembina, ND	70	73	Grafton, ND	54
26	Argyle 4 E, MN	67	73	Grand Rapids Forestry Lab, MN	54
26	Bethel Airport, AK	67	73	Mahnomen 1 W, MN	54
28	Antero Reservoir, CO	66	73	Park Rapids Municipal Airport, MN	54
28	Snake River, WY	66	73	Sharon, ND	54
28	Willow City, ND	66	73	Stanley 3 NNW, ND	54
31	Mount Washington, NH	65	73	Valley City 3 NNW, ND	54
31	Squa Pan Dam, ME	65	73	Wadena 3 S, MN	54
31	Warroad, MN	65	83	Big Falls, MN	53
34	Cass Lake, MN	64	83	Brainerd, MN	53
34	Edmore 1 NW, ND	64	83	Drake 9 NE, ND	53
34	Upham 3 N, ND	64	83	Lake City, CO	53
34	Van Buren 2, ME	64	83	Long Lake Dam, WI	53
38	International Falls Int'l Arpt., MN	63	83	Pinedale, WY	53
38	Petersburg 2 N, ND	63	83	Ripogenus Dam, ME	*53*
40	Baudette Int'l Airport, MN	62	83	Rugby, ND	53
40	Cavalier 7 NW, ND	62	83	West Burke, VT	53
40	Fort Kent, ME	62	92	Brassua Dam, ME	52
43	Bottineau, ND	61	92	Colgate, ND	52
43	Cochetopa Creek, CO	61	92	Cooperstown, ND	52
43	Hansboro 4 NNE, ND	61	92	Hillsboro 3 N, ND	52
43	Red Lake Indian Agency, MN	61	92	Isle 12 N, MN	52
47	Cotton, MN	60	92	Kenmare 1 WSW, ND	52
47	Leeds, ND	60	92	Leech Lake Dam, MN	52
47	Winton Power Plant, MN	*60*	92	Max, ND	52
50	Agassiz Refuge, MN	59	92	Opheim 10 N, MT	52

Highest Number of Annual Heating Degree Days

Rank	Station Name	Num.	Rank	Station Name	Num.
1	Barrow W. Post-W. Rogers Airport, AK	19,942	51	Anchorage Int'l Airport, AK	10,353
2	Kotzebue Ralph Wein Memorial, AK	15,645	52	Rolla 3 NW, ND	10,344
3	Bettles Field, AK	15,454	53	Moose, WY	10,313
3	Northway Airport, AK	15,454	54	Moran 5 WNW, WY	10,311
5	Snowshoe Lake, AK	15,069	55	Hebgen Dam, MT	10,309
6	Tanana R.M. Calhoun Mem. Arpt., AK	14,556	56	Silver Lake Brighton, UT	10,283
7	North Pole, AK	14,420	57	Spicer, CO	10,276
8	McGrath Airport, AK	14,115	58	Wasilla 3 S, AK	10,275
9	Eielson Field, AK	13,956	59	Willow City, ND	10,262
10	Nome Municipal Airport, AK	13,916	60	International Falls Int'l Arpt., MN	10,253
11	Tonsina, AK	13,909	61	Petersburg 2 N, ND	10,234
12	Mount Washington, NH	13,782	62	Warroad, MN	10,216
13	Fairbanks Int'l Airport, AK	13,663	63	Grand Lake 1 NW, CO	10,190
14	Gulkana Intermediate Field, AK	13,620	64	Edmore 1 NW, ND	10,181
15	University Exp. Station, AK	13,503	65	First Conn Lake, NH	10,178
16	College Observatory, AK	13,480	66	Fontenelle Dam, WY	10,166
17	Old Edgerton, AK	*13,298*	67	Van Buren 2, ME	*10,118*
18	Big Delta Allen AAF, AK	13,297	68	Fort Kent, ME	10,078
19	Bethel Airport, AK	12,849	69	Bottineau, ND	10,073
20	Climax, CO	12,436	70	Upham 3 N, ND	10,061
21	Taylor Park, CO	11,962	71	Winton Power Plant, MN	*10,057*
22	Whites Crossing, AK	11,943	72	Rainier Paradise Ranger Station, WA	10,049
23	Glen Alps, AK	*11,477*	73	Cavalier 7 NW, ND	10,033
24	Wolf Creek Pass 1 E, CO	*11,397*	74	Argyle 4 E, MN	10,020
25	Talkeetna State Airport, AK	11,311	75	Hibbing Chisholm-Hibbing Airport, MN	10,005
26	Snake River, WY	11,303	76	Hansboro 4 NNE, ND	9,984
27	Hermit 7 ESE, CO	11,299	76	Walden, CO	9,984
28	Dillingham Airport, AK	*11,271*	78	Stanley 3 NNW, ND	9,979
29	Crested Butte, CO	11,252	79	Cass Lake, MN	9,973
30	Kenai Municipal Airport, AK	11,155	79	Powers Lake 1 N, ND	9,973
31	King Salmon Airport, AK	11,124	81	Cooper Lake Project, AK	9,959
32	Mount Mansfield, VT	11,083	82	Grouse, ID	*9,946*
33	Sugarloaf Reservoir, CO	*10,980*	83	Red Lake Indian Agency, MN	9,940
34	Saint Paul Island Airport, AK	10,914	84	Warren, ID	9,939
35	Silverton, CO	*10,880*	85	Leeds, ND	9,935
36	Port Alsworth, AK	10,879	86	Fortuna 1 W, ND	9,917
37	Intricate Bay, AK	10,747	87	Crater Lake Nat'l Park Hdqtrs., OR	9,892
38	Tower 3 S, MN	10,733	87	Tioga 1 E, ND	9,892
39	Dillon 1 E, CO	10,650	89	McHenry 3 W, ND	9,865
40	Antero Reservoir, CO	10,619	90	Sage 4 NNW, WY	*9,862*
41	Matanuska AES, AK	10,609	91	Bowbells, ND	9,860
42	Wisdom, MT	10,582	92	Towner 2 NE, ND	9,855
43	Langdon Exp. Farm, ND	10,580	93	Gunnison 3 SW, CO	9,835
44	Palmer IAS, AK	10,574	94	Fosston 1 E, MN	9,831
45	Dixie, ID	*10,514*	95	Bodie, CA	9,821
46	Ruxton Park, CO	10,513	96	Jackman, ME	9,792
47	Pinedale, WY	10,502	97	Homer Airport, AK	9,765
48	Cabin Creek, CO	10,442	98	Rangeley, ME	9,762
49	Pembina, ND	10,361	99	Itasca Univ. of Minnesota, MN	9,753
50	Grand Lake 6 SSW, CO	10,357	100	Bergland Dam, MI	9,750

Lowest Number of Annual Heating Degree Days

Rank	Station Name	Num.	Rank	Station Name	Num.
1	Key West Int'l Airport, FL	61	51	Raymondville, TX	789
2	Tavernier, FL	*81*	52	Yuma Int'l Airport, AZ	*791*
3	Miami Beach, FL	130	53	Daytona Beach Regional Airport, FL	797
4	Miami Int'l Airport, FL	151	54	Gold Rock Ranch, CA	*826*
5	Hialeah, FL	155	55	Lisbon, FL	830
6	Tamiami Trail 40 Mile Bend, FL	*168*	56	Palm Springs, CA	836
7	Fort Lauderdale, FL	172	57	Ocala, FL	841
8	Flamingo Ranger Station, FL	191	58	Port Mansfield, TX	*863*
9	West Palm Beach Int'l Airport, FL	238	59	McCook, TX	864
10	Naples, FL	249	60	Chapman Ranch, TX	865
11	Stuart 1 S, FL	255	61	Imperial, CA	866
12	Fort Myers Page Field, FL	303	62	Falcon Dam, TX	875
13	Canal Point USDA, FL	308	63	Weeki Wachee, FL	891
14	Immokalee 3 NNW, FL	323	64	Los Angeles Civic Center, CA	892
15	Clewiston U.S. Engineers, FL	*335*	65	Yuma Proving Ground, AZ	905
16	Punta Gorda 4 ESE, FL	374	66	Rio Grande City 1 SE, TX	910
17	Belle Glade Exp. Station, FL	380	67	Corpus Christi Int'l Airport, TX	924
18	Saint Petersburg, FL	403	68	Inverness 3 SE, FL	929
19	Fort Pierce, FL	414	69	Saint Augustine, FL	*933*
20	Moore Haven Lock 1, FL	424	70	Laredo 2, TX	953
21	Fort Drum 5 NW, FL	*446*	71	Rockport, TX	964
22	Myakka River State Park, FL	450	72	Borrego Desert Park, CA	967
23	Vero Beach, FL	479	73	El Centro 2 SSW, CA	978
24	Bartow, FL	483	74	Alice, TX	988
25	Venice, FL	*490*	75	Eagle Mountain, CA	992
26	Kissimmee 2, FL	497	76	Robstown, TX	1,003
27	Wauchula, FL	505	77	Kofa Mine, AZ	1,009
28	Lakeland Linder Airport, FL	*514*	78	Aransas Wildlife Refuge, TX	1,016
29	Arcadia, FL	523	79	San Diego Lindbergh Field, CA	1,018
30	Mountain Lake, FL	526	80	Phoenix Sky Harbor Int'l Arpt., AZ	1,019
31	Melbourne Regional Airport, FL	529	81	Hebbronville, TX	1,025
32	Parrish, FL	543	82	Usher Tower, FL	1,029
33	Bradenton 5 ESE, FL	544	83	Falfurrias, TX	1,032
34	Plant City, FL	562	84	Point Comfort, TX	1,035
35	Tarpon Springs Sewage Plant, FL	566	85	Santa Ana Fire Station, CA	1,036
36	Archbold Bio Station, FL	577	86	Gila Bend, AZ	1,039
37	Orlando Int'l Airport, FL	*578*	87	Mecca Fire Station, CA	1,042
38	Saint Leo, FL	580	88	Goliad, TX	1,045
39	Tampa Int'l Airport, FL	582	89	Matagorda 2, TX	1,054
40	Avon Park 2 W, FL	590	90	Jacksonville Beach, FL	*1,059*
41	Brownsville Int'l Airport, TX	603	91	Brawley 2 SW, CA	1,067
42	Clermont 7 S, FL	617	92	Crystal City, TX	1,073
43	Weslaco 2 E, TX	631	93	Blythe Riverside Co. Airport, CA	1,078
44	Brooksville Chin Hill, FL	*655*	94	Bullhead City, AZ	*1,085*
45	Lake Alfred Exp. Station, FL	662	94	Palm Springs Thermal Airport, CA	1,085
45	McAllen Miller Int'l Airport, TX	*662*	96	Iron Mountain, CA	1,097
47	Titusville, FL	663	97	Galveston, TX	1,108
48	Sanford Experiment Station, FL	704	98	Parker Reservoir, CA	1,114
49	Zapata 3 SW, TX	751	99	Mathis 4 SSW, TX	1,116
50	Harlingen, TX	767	100	Parker, AZ	1,120

Highest Number of Annual Cooling Degree Days

Rank	Station Name	Num.	Rank	Station Name	Num.
1	Death Valley, CA	5,338	51	Clewiston U.S. Engineers, FL	*3,905*
2	Key West Int'l Airport, FL	4,926	52	Tempe A S U, AZ	3,887
3	Tavernier, FL	*4,899*	53	Palm Springs Thermal Airport, CA	3,883
4	Honolulu Int'l Airport, HI	4,738	54	Litchfield Park, AZ	*3,869*
5	Yuma Int'l Airport, AZ	*4,623*	55	Brawley 2 SW, CA	3,831
6	Hialeah, FL	4,586	56	Buckeye, AZ	3,810
7	Phoenix Sky Harbor Int'l Arpt., AZ	4,556	57	Waimanalo Exp. Farm, HI	3,807
8	Parker Reservoir, CA	4,545	58	Punta Gorda 4 ESE, FL	3,805
9	Miami Int'l Airport, FL	4,543	59	Crystal City, TX	3,794
10	Needles Airport, CA	4,528	60	Laveen 3 SSE, AZ	3,792
11	Bullhead City, AZ	4,517	61	Falfurrias, TX	3,789
12	Waikiki 717.2, HI	4,490	62	Saint Petersburg, FL	3,770
13	McAllen Miller Int'l Airport, TX	*4,485*	63	Hebbronville, TX	3,765
14	Gold Rock Ranch, CA	*4,481*	64	Lakeland Linder Airport, FL	*3,762*
15	Miami Beach, FL	4,462	65	Yuma Citrus Station, AZ	3,752
16	Zapata 3 SW, TX	*4,441*	66	Alamo Dam, AZ	3,742
17	Iron Mountain, CA	4,434	67	Presidio, TX	3,721
18	Tamiami Trail 40 Mile Bend, FL	*4,412*	68	Alice, TX	3,702
19	Yuma Proving Ground, AZ	4,384	69	Bouse, AZ	3,690
20	Laredo 2, TX	4,370	70	Immokalee 3 NNW, FL	3,671
21	Blythe Riverside Co. Airport, CA	4,368	71	Bartow, FL	3,659
22	Gila Bend, AZ	4,363	72	Canal Point USDA, FL	3,657
23	Falcon Dam, TX	4,316	73	Casa Grande, AZ	3,656
24	Eagle Mountain, CA	4,315	73	Tacna 3 NE, AZ	3,656
25	Fort Lauderdale, FL	4,295	75	Myakka River State Park, FL	3,652
26	Palm Springs, CA	4,282	76	Eagle Pass, TX	3,643
27	Rio Grande City 1 SE, TX	4,265	77	Robstown, TX	3,642
28	Willow Beach, AZ	4,185	78	Venice, FL	*3,637*
29	Parker, AZ	4,175	79	Moore Haven Lock 1, FL	3,629
30	Weslaco 2 E, TX	4,173	80	Maricopa 4 N, AZ	3,610
31	Puukohola Heiau 98.1, HI	4,167	81	Chandler Heights, AZ	3,607
32	Kahului Airport, HI	4,146	81	Molokai Airport, HI	3,607
33	West Palm Beach Int'l Airport, FL	4,139	83	Tilden 4 SSE, TX	3,605
34	Fort Myers Page Field, FL	*4,098*	84	Valley of Fire State Park, NV	3,593
34	McCook, TX	4,098	85	Tucson NWSO, AZ	3,587
36	Honolulu Observatory 702.2, HI	4,081	86	Tampa Int'l Airport, FL	3,575
37	Kofa Mine, AZ	4,063	87	Casa Grande Nat'l Monument, AZ	3,569
38	Brownsville Int'l Airport, TX	4,059	88	Tarpon Springs Sewage Plant, FL	3,563
39	Mecca Fire Station, CA	4,052	89	Goliad, TX	3,561
40	Imperial, CA	4,047	90	Fort Pierce, FL	3,559
41	Raymondville, TX	4,028	91	Bartlett Dam, AZ	3,553
42	El Centro 2 SSW, CA	4,021	92	Corpus Christi Int'l Airport, TX	3,531
43	Blythe, CA	3,992	93	Florence, AZ	3,519
43	Youngtown, AZ	3,992	94	Bradenton 5 ESE, FL	3,518
45	Lihue Airport, HI	3,988	95	Charlotte 5 NNW, TX	3,515
46	Flamingo Ranger Station, FL	3,977	96	Orlando Int'l Airport, FL	3,507
47	Naples, FL	3,953	97	Belle Glade Exp. Station, FL	3,490
48	Harlingen, TX	3,945	98	Saint Leo, FL	3,487
49	Stuart 1 S, FL	3,944	99	Hana Airport 355, HI	3,479
50	Borrego Desert Park, CA	3,933	100	Rockport, TX	3,473

Rank	Station Name	Num.	Rank	Station Name	Num.
	Lowest Number of Annual Cooling Degree Days				
1	Barrow W. Post-W. Rogers Airport, AK	0	49	Port Alsworth, AK	4
1	Cabin Creek, CO	0	49	Wasilla 3 S, AK	4
1	Climax, CO	0	53	Bandon 2 NNE, OR	5
1	Cold Bay Airport, AK	0	53	Eureka, CA	5
1	Crested Butte, CO	0	53	Kotzebue Ralph Wein Memorial, AK	5
1	Dillon 1 E, CO	0	53	Kulani Camp 79, HI	5
1	Glen Alps, AK	0	53	North Bend Municipal Airport, OR	5
1	Grand Lake 6 SSW, CO	0	53	Silver Lake Brighton, UT	5
1	Haleakala Ranger Station 338, HI	0	59	Gulkana Intermediate Field, AK	6
1	Hermit 7 ESE, CO	0	59	Telluride 4 WNW, CO	6
1	Homer Airport, AK	0	59	Wisdom, MT	6
1	Kenai Municipal Airport, AK	0	62	Crater Lake Nat'l Park Hdqtrs., OR	7
1	Little Port Walter, AK	0	62	Dixie, ID	*7*
1	Mount Washington, NH	0	62	Fort Bragg 5 N, CA	7
1	Red River, NM	0	62	Lake George 8 SW, CO	7
1	Rico, CO	0	62	Pinedale, WY	7
1	Saint Paul Island Airport, AK	0	62	Warren, ID	7
1	Silverton, CO	*0*	68	Crescent City 3 NNW, CA	8
1	Snowshoe Lake, AK	0	68	Klamath, CA	8
1	Spicer, CO	0	68	Seward, AK	8
1	Sugarloaf Reservoir, CO	0	71	Auke Bay, AK	9
1	Taylor Park, CO	0	71	Lake City, CO	9
1	Wolf Creek Pass 1 E, CO	*0*	71	Newport, OR	9
1	Yakutat State Airport, AK	0	71	Talkeetna State Airport, AK	9
25	Antero Reservoir, CO	1	71	Twin Lakes, CA	*9*
25	Cooper Lake Project, AK	1	76	Fort Ross, CA	*10*
25	Cordova, AK	1	76	Gascon, NM	10
25	Dillingham Airport, AK	1	76	Meredith, CO	10
25	Intricate Bay, AK	1	76	Orick Prairie Creek Park, CA	*10*
25	King Salmon Airport, AK	1	76	Whites Crossing, AK	10
25	Ruxton Park, CO	1	81	Bailey, CO	11
25	Sitka Japonski Airport, AK	1	81	Gold Beach Ranger Station, OR	*11*
25	Snake River, WY	1	81	Port Orford 2, OR	11
25	Tonsina, AK	1	84	Green Mountain Dam, CO	13
25	Wolf Canyon, NM	1	85	Half Moon Bay, CA	14
36	Anchorage Int'l Airport, AK	2	85	Tillamook 1 W, OR	14
36	Bethel Airport, AK	2	85	Yampa, CO	14
36	Bodie, CA	2	88	Greer, AZ	15
36	Grant, CO	2	88	Long Beach Exp. Station, WA	15
36	Kitoi Bay, AK	2	88	Northway Airport, AK	15
36	Palmer IAS, AK	2	91	Center 4 SSW, CO	16
36	Valdez WSO, AK	2	91	Hebgen Dam, MT	16
36	Walden, CO	2	91	Honeyman State Park, OR	*16*
44	Grand Lake 1 NW, CO	3	91	Moran 5 WNW, WY	16
44	Juneau Int'l Airport, AK	3	95	Beaver Falls, AK	*17*
44	Kodiak State USCG Base, AK	3	95	Gunnison 3 SW, CO	*17*
44	Matanuska AES, AK	3	95	Libby 32 SSE, MT	17
44	Nome Municipal Airport, AK	3	95	Olga 2 SE, WA	17
49	Eagle Nest, NM	4	99	Coupeville 1 S, WA	18
49	Old Edgerton, AK	*4*	99	Yellow Pine 7 S, ID	*18*

Highest Annual Precipitation

Rank	Station Name	Inches	Rank	Station Name	Inches
1	Little Port Walter, AK	226.75	51	Brookings, OR	74.73
2	Yakutat State Airport, AK	157.46	52	Port Orford 2, OR	74.53
3	Manoa Lyon Arboretum, HI	*153.49*	53	Lake Spaulding, CA	74.52
4	Beaver Falls, AK	147.90	54	Clayton 1 SSW, GA	73.78
5	Aberdeen 20 NNE, WA	136.27	55	Honeyman State Park, OR	73.09
6	Hilo International Airport, HI	126.21	56	Three Lynx, OR	72.93
7	Kailua 446, HI	124.13	57	Coweeta Exp. Station, NC	72.43
8	Ookala 223, HI	*123.63*	58	Concrete Ppl. Fish Station, WA	71.79
9	Forks 1 E, WA	122.14	59	Marion Frks. Fish Hatchery, OR	71.50
10	Rainier Paradise Ranger Station, WA	119.43	60	Helen, GA	*71.36*
11	Cougar 6 E, WA	117.51	61	Saucier Experiment Forest, MS	71.11
12	Clearwater, WA	114.63	62	Seward, AK	71.09
13	Grays River Hatchery, WA	110.85	63	Newport, OR	70.27
14	Baring, WA	110.62	64	Thibodaux 3 ESE, LA	*70.24*
15	Kulani Camp 79, HI	109.07	65	Milton Experiment Station, FL	70.20
16	Hawaii Volcano Nat'l Park HQ 54, HI	107.94	66	Elma, WA	69.60
17	Quillayute Airport, WA	102.44	67	Richardson Gr. State Park, CA	69.56
18	Mount Washington, NH	102.43	68	Valdez WSO, AK	*69.02*
19	Upper Baker Dam, WA	100.90	69	Hoquiam Airport, WA	68.92
20	Annette Island Airport, AK	100.65	70	Corvallis Water Bureau, OR	68.77
21	Cedar Lake, WA	100.00	71	Robertsdale 5 NE, AL	68.71
22	Otis 2 NE, OR	99.03	72	Blowing Rock 1 NW, NC	68.70
23	Cordova, AK	96.84	73	Falls City 2, OR	68.67
24	Tillamook 1 W, OR	91.46	74	Bowman Dam, CA	68.62
25	Cushman Powerhouse 2, WA	90.91	75	Fairhope 2 NE, AL	68.50
26	Detroit Dam, OR	90.61	76	Bay Minette 3 NNW, AL	68.21
27	Tidewater 2 SW, OR	90.33	77	Woodville 4 ESE, MS	68.19
28	Government Camp, OR	89.45	78	Pascagoula 3 NE, MS	67.99
29	Highlands, NC	87.85	79	Astoria Clatsop County Airport, OR	67.75
30	Palmer 3 ESE, WA	87.11	80	De Sabla, CA	67.62
31	Skamania Fish Hatchery, WA	87.02	81	Glenoma, WA	67.61
32	Sitka Japonski Airport, AK	85.84	82	Crater Lake Nat'l Park Hdqtrs., OR	67.37
33	Aberdeen, WA	85.31	83	Oberlin Fire Tower, LA	67.35
34	Scotts Mills 9 SE, OR	84.13	84	Mobile Regional Airport, AL	67.08
35	Cloverdale, OR	83.40	85	De Funiak Springs, FL	67.06
36	Illahe, OR	82.28	86	Brewton 3 SSE, AL	67.03
37	Long Beach Exp. Station, WA	81.72	87	Crescent City 3 NNW, CA	67.00
37	Strawberry Valley, CA	81.72	88	Leaburg 1 SW, OR	66.91
39	Headworks Ptld. Wtr. Bur., OR	80.77	89	Orick Prairie Creek Park, CA	66.85
40	Klamath, CA	80.26	90	Kitoi Bay, AK	66.64
41	Gold Beach Ranger Station, OR	80.15	91	Merrill, MS	66.46
42	Newhalem, WA	79.98	92	Lemolo Lake 3 NNW, OR	*66.30*
43	Diablo Dam, WA	79.59	93	Shelton, WA	66.28
44	Hana Airport 355, HI	79.41	94	Galliano, LA	66.23
45	Bonneville Dam, OR	78.26	95	Panama City 5 NE, FL	66.07
46	Mount Mansfield, VT	77.88	96	Brevard, NC	*66.04*
47	Belknap Springs 8 N, OR	76.88	96	Gulfport Municipal, MS	66.04
48	Seaside, OR	76.61	98	Andrews, NC	65.96
49	Kodiak State USCG Base, AK	76.41	99	Hialeah, FL	65.92
50	Caesars Head, SC	75.53	100	Amite, LA	65.89

Lowest Annual Precipitation

Rank	Station Name	Inches	Rank	Station Name	Inches
1	Death Valley, CA	2.38	51	Bakersfield Meadows Field, CA	6.51
2	El Centro 2 SSW, CA	2.96	51	Boulder City, NV	6.51
3	Imperial, CA	3.06	53	Pahranagat Wildlife Refuge, NV	6.53
4	Yuma Valley, AZ	*3.15*	54	Eskdale, UT	6.54
5	Brawley 2 SW, CA	3.17	55	Mexican Hat, UT	6.65
6	Yuma Int'l Airport, AZ	*3.34*	56	Bullhead City, AZ	*6.72*
7	Mecca Fire Station, CA	3.38	57	Mojave, CA	6.74
8	Palm Springs Thermal Airport, CA	3.65	58	Page, AZ	6.75
9	Iron Mountain, CA	3.81	59	Basin, WY	6.76
10	Yuma Proving Ground, AZ	3.87	59	Lovell, WY	6.76
11	Yuma Citrus Station, AZ	3.92	61	Wahweap, AZ	6.78
12	Barrow W. Post-W. Rogers Airport, AK	4.03	62	Wah Wah Ranch, UT	6.81
13	Blythe, CA	4.06	63	Valley of Fire State Park, NV	6.83
14	Blythe Riverside Co. Airport, CA	4.08	64	Wildrose Ranger Station, CA	6.84
15	Gold Rock Ranch, CA	*4.10*	65	Randsburg, CA	6.88
16	Daggett Barstow-Daggett Airport, CA	4.22	66	Priest Rapids Dam, WA	6.89
17	Tacna 3 NE, AZ	4.30	67	Center 4 SSW, CO	6.95
17	Trona, CA	4.30	68	Gila Bend, AZ	7.03
19	Eagle Mountain, CA	4.39	69	Borrego Desert Park, CA	7.04
20	Silverpeak, NV	4.48	70	Myton, UT	7.05
21	Las Vegas McCarran Int'l Arpt., NV	4.52	71	Partoun, UT	7.11
22	Hayfield Pumping Plant, CA	4.56	72	Grand View 2 W, ID	7.17
23	Twentynine Palms, CA	4.59	73	Sunnyside, WA	7.19
24	Desert Nat'l Wildlife Range, NV	4.80	74	Smokey Valley, NV	7.28
25	Wendover USAF Auxiliary Field, UT	4.84	75	Kofa Mine, AZ	7.30
26	Inyokern, CA	4.86	76	Ouray 4 NE, UT	7.31
27	Bishop Airport, CA	5.05	77	Roosevelt, UT	7.32
28	Pahrump, NV	5.12	78	Alamosa Bergman Field, CO	7.37
29	Dyer, NV	5.18	78	Wasco, CA	7.37
30	Palm Springs, CA	5.20	80	Fontenelle Dam, WY	7.43
31	Needles Airport, CA	5.21	81	Palmdale, CA	7.44
32	Fallon Experiment Station, NV	5.24	82	Clark 3 NE, WY	7.47
33	Parker, AZ	5.25	83	Richland, WA	7.48
34	Lovelock Derby Field, NV	*5.32*	84	Haiwee, CA	7.49
35	Yerington, NV	5.36	85	Reno Cannon Int'l Airport, NV	7.51
36	Independence, CA	5.39	86	Golconda, NV	7.63
37	Deaver, WY	5.49	87	Emblem, WY	7.65
38	Lahontan Dam, NV	5.50	88	Capitol Reef Nat'l Park, UT	7.66
39	Willow Beach, AZ	5.65	89	Corcoran Irrigation District, CA	7.67
40	Tonopah Airport, NV	5.72	90	Ephrata Airport, WA	7.70
41	Hanksville, UT	5.75	91	Beaver Dam, AZ	7.76
42	Lovelock, NV	5.80	92	Challis, ID	7.77
43	Bouse, AZ	5.95	93	Castle Dale, UT	7.80
44	Mina, NV	5.97	94	Bruneau, ID	7.81
45	El Mirage, CA	6.03	95	Maricopa 4 N, AZ	7.86
46	Beatty 8 N, NV	6.28	96	Worland Municipal Airport, WY	7.89
46	Callao, UT	6.28	97	Lancaster Gen. Wm. Fox Field, CA	*7.90*
48	Victorville Pumping Plant, CA	6.30	98	Ajo, AZ	7.91
49	Parker Reservoir, CA	6.34	99	Worland, WY	7.92
50	Buttonwillow, CA	6.36	100	Pavillion, WY	7.93

Highest Number of Days Annually With ≥ 0.1″ Precipitation

Rank	Station Name	Days	Rank	Station Name	Days
1	Manoa Lyon Arboretum, HI	*207*	50	Mud Mountain Dam, WA	126
2	Little Port Walter, AK	202	52	Belknap Springs 8 N, OR	125
3	Hilo International Airport, HI	194	53	Diablo Dam, WA	124
4	Yakutat State Airport, AK	187	53	Newport, OR	124
5	Beaver Falls, AK	175	53	Snoqualmie Falls, WA	124
6	Annette Island Airport, AK	169	56	Landsburg, WA	123
7	Hawaii Volcano Nat'l Park HQ 54, HI	*165*	56	Leaburg 1 SW, OR	123
7	Sitka Japonski Airport, AK	165	56	Little Valley, NY	123
9	Mount Washington, NH	160	56	Newhalem, WA	*123*
10	Cordova, AK	159	60	Boonville 2 SSW, NY	121
11	Hana Airport 355, HI	*158*	60	Lacomb 3 NNE, OR	*121*
12	Rainier Paradise Ranger Station, WA	156	60	Marion Frks. Fish Hatchery, OR	121
13	Forks 1 E, WA	154	60	Terra Alta 1, WV	121
14	Kulani Camp 79, HI	*152*	64	Buckley 1 NE, WA	120
15	Aberdeen 20 NNE, WA	151	65	Estacada 2 SE, OR	119
15	Mount Mansfield, VT	151	65	Oakville, WA	*119*
17	Cedar Lake, WA	150	67	Battle Ground, WA	*118*
17	Grays River Hatchery, WA	150	67	Foster Dam, OR	118
17	Ookala 223, HI	*150*	69	Canaan Valley, WV	117
17	Palmer 3 ESE, WA	150	69	Monroe, WA	117
21	Auke Bay, AK	*149*	71	North Bend Municipal Airport, OR	116
21	Clearwater, WA	149	71	Rowlesburg 1, WV	116
23	Quillayute Airport, WA	146	71	Shelton, WA	116
24	Tillamook 1 W, OR	145	74	Lemolo Lake 3 NNW, OR	*115*
25	Juneau Int'l Airport, AK	143	74	Longview, WA	115
26	Otis 2 NE, OR	*142*	74	Old Forge, NY	115
26	Upper Baker Dam, WA	142	74	Seward, AK	115
28	Headworks Ptld. Wtr. Bur., OR	141	74	Stillwater Reservoir, NY	115
29	Cougar 6 E, WA	140	79	Clatskanie, OR	114
29	Kitoi Bay, AK	140	79	Colden 1 N, NY	114
29	Long Beach Exp. Station, WA	140	79	Cushman Powerhouse 2, WA	114
32	Government Camp, OR	139	79	Stayton, OR	114
33	Aberdeen, WA	135	83	Crater Lake Nat'l Park Hdqtrs., OR	113
33	Cloverdale, OR	135	84	Idleyld Park 4 NE, OR	112
33	Detroit Dam, OR	135	84	Vernonia 2, OR	112
33	Scotts Mills 9 SE, OR	135	86	Bayard, WV	111
33	Skamania Fish Hatchery, WA	135	86	Honeyman State Park, OR	111
38	Concrete Ppl. Fish Station, WA	134	86	Lookout Point Dam, OR	111
39	Startup 1 E, WA	133	86	Port Orford 2, OR	111
39	Valdez WSO, AK	*133*	86	Silverton, OR	111
41	Three Lynx, OR	131	91	Allegany State Park, NY	110
42	Glenoma, WA	130	91	Centralia, WA	110
42	Kodiak State USCG Base, AK	130	91	Corry, PA	110
42	Seaside, OR	130	91	Corvallis Water Bureau, OR	110
42	Tidewater 2 SW, OR	130	91	Warsaw 6 SW, NY	110
46	Bonneville Dam, OR	129	96	Bandon 2 NNE, OR	109
47	Elma, WA	128	96	Ebensburg Sewage Plant, PA	109
47	Hoquiam Airport, WA	128	96	McMillin Reservoir, WA	109
49	Astoria Clatsop County Airport, OR	127	96	Packwood, WA	*109*
50	Cascadia, OR	126	100	Chasm Falls, NY	*108*

Lowest Number of Days Annually With ≥ 0.1" Precipitation

Rank	Station Name	Days	Rank	Station Name	Days
1	Death Valley, CA	5	45	Lovelock Derby Field, NV	*16*
2	Yuma Valley, AZ	*6*	45	Valley of Fire State Park, NV	16
3	Blythe Riverside Co. Airport, CA	7	45	Wendover USAF Auxiliary Field, UT	16
3	Brawley 2 SW, CA	7	45	Yerington, NV	16
3	El Centro 2 SSW, CA	7	55	Borrego Desert Park, CA	17
3	Imperial, CA	7	55	Buckeye, AZ	17
3	Mecca Fire Station, CA	7	55	Deaver, WY	17
3	Yuma Citrus Station, AZ	7	55	Gila Bend, AZ	17
3	Yuma Int'l Airport, AZ	*7*	55	Haiwee, CA	17
3	Yuma Proving Ground, AZ	7	55	Litchfield Park, AZ	17
11	Blythe, CA	*8*	55	Mountain Pass, CA	*17*
11	Gold Rock Ranch, CA	*8*	55	Tonopah Airport, NV	17
11	Palm Springs Thermal Airport, CA	8	63	Bakersfield Meadows Field, CA	18
14	Eagle Mountain, CA	9	63	Beatty 8 N, NV	18
15	Inyokern, CA	10	63	Buttonwillow, CA	18
15	Palm Springs, CA	10	63	Hanksville, UT	18
15	Trona, CA	10	63	Santa Monica Pier, CA	18
15	Twentynine Palms, CA	10	63	Yucca 1 NNE, AZ	18
19	Barrow W. Post-W. Rogers Airport, AK	11	69	Callao, UT	19
19	Hayfield Pumping Plant, CA	11	69	Maricopa 4 N, AZ	19
19	Iron Mountain, CA	11	69	Mitchell Caverns, CA	19
19	Tacna 3 NE, AZ	11	69	Pahranagat Wildlife Refuge, NV	19
23	Independence, CA	12	69	Phoenix Sky Harbor Int'l Arpt., AZ	19
24	Daggett Barstow-Daggett Airport, CA	13	74	Bridgeport, CA	20
24	Desert Nat'l Wildlife Range, NV	13	74	Casa Grande, AZ	20
24	Lahaina 361, HI	13	74	Chula Vista, CA	20
24	Needles Airport, CA	13	74	Eskdale, UT	20
24	Parker, AZ	13	74	Myton, UT	20
24	Parker Reservoir, CA	13	74	Organ Pipe Cactus Nat'l Mon., AZ	20
24	Silverpeak, NV	13	74	Page, AZ	20
31	Bishop Airport, CA	14	74	Pavillion, WY	20
31	Bouse, AZ	14	74	San Diego Lindbergh Field, CA	20
31	Dyer, NV	14	74	Searchlight, NV	20
31	Las Vegas McCarran Int'l Arpt., NV	14	74	Wahweap, AZ	20
31	Pahrump, NV	14	74	Youngtown, AZ	20
31	Randsburg, CA	14	86	Alamo Dam, AZ	*21*
31	Willow Beach, AZ	14	86	Basin, WY	21
38	Fallon Experiment Station, NV	15	86	Center 4 SSW, CO	21
38	Kofa Mine, AZ	15	86	Coalinga, CA	21
38	Mina, NV	15	86	Laveen 3 SSE, AZ	21
38	Mojave, CA	15	86	Long Beach Daugherty Field, CA	21
38	Palmdale, CA	15	86	Lovelock, NV	21
38	Victorville Pumping Plant, CA	15	86	Priest Rapids Dam, WA	21
38	Wildrose Ranger Station, CA	15	86	Riverside Fire Station 3, CA	21
45	Ajo, AZ	16	86	Sheffield, TX	21
45	Boulder City, NV	16	86	South Phoenix, AZ	21
45	Bullhead City, AZ	*16*	86	Tempe A S U, AZ	21
45	El Mirage, CA	16	98	Bosque Del Apache, NM	22
45	Lahontan Dam, NV	16	98	Casa Grande Nat'l Monument, AZ	22
45	Lancaster Gen. Wm. Fox Field, CA	*16*	98	Chandler Heights, AZ	22

Highest Number of Days Annually With ≥ 1.0″ Precipitation

Rank	Station Name	Days	Rank	Station Name	Days
1	Little Port Walter, AK	79	41	Palmer 3 ESE, WA	23
2	Yakutat State Airport, AK	53	41	Reserve, LA	23
3	Aberdeen 20 NNE, WA	48	41	Scotts Mills 9 SE, OR	23
4	Beaver Falls, AK	47	41	Tryon, NC	23
5	Manoa Lyon Arboretum, HI	*44*	55	Baton Rouge Ryan Airport, LA	22
6	Forks 1 E, WA	42	55	Bay Minette 3 NNW, AL	22
7	Clearwater, WA	40	55	Bogalusa, LA	22
8	Cougar 6 E, WA	39	55	Brewton 3 SSE, AL	22
8	Rainier Paradise Ranger Station, WA	39	55	Cave Junction 1 WNW, OR	22
10	Grays River Hatchery, WA	35	55	Covington 4 NNW, LA	22
11	Upper Baker Dam, WA	33	55	Diablo Dam, WA	22
12	Ookala 223, HI	*32*	55	Gulfport Municipal, MS	22
13	Baring, WA	*31*	55	Hamilton 3 S, AL	22
13	Illahe, OR	31	55	Houma, LA	22
13	Otis 2 NE, OR	31	55	McComb Pike County Airport, MS	22
13	Quillayute Airport, WA	31	55	New Orleans Audubon, LA	22
17	Cedar Lake, WA	30	55	Oberlin Fire Tower, LA	22
17	Cushman Powerhouse 2, WA	30	55	Pisgah Forest 1 N, NC	22
17	Hilo International Airport, HI	30	55	Richardson Gr. State Park, CA	22
20	Annette Island Airport, AK	29	55	Robertsdale 5 NE, AL	22
20	Strawberry Valley, CA	29	55	Thibodaux 3 ESE, LA	*22*
22	Klamath, CA	28	55	Woodville 4 ESE, MS	22
23	Cordova, AK	27	55	Yazoo City 5 NNE, MS	22
23	Government Camp, OR	27	74	Bankhead Lock & Dam, AL	21
23	Highlands, NC	27	74	Bienville 3 NE, LA	21
23	Mount Washington, NH	27	74	Bunkie, LA	21
27	Lake Spaulding, CA	26	74	Carville 2 SW, LA	21
27	Tidewater 2 SW, OR	26	74	Chatom, AL	21
29	Clayton 1 SSW, GA	25	74	Crossett 2 SSE, AR	21
29	Detroit Dam, OR	25	74	De Funiak Springs, FL	21
29	Helen, GA	*25*	74	De Quincy, LA	*21*
29	Kulani Camp 79, HI	25	74	Donaldsonville 4 SW, LA	21
33	Brevard, NC	*24*	74	Evergreen, AL	21
33	Caesars Head, SC	24	74	Fairhope 2 NE, AL	21
33	Coweeta Exp. Station, NC	24	74	Forest 3 S, MS	21
33	Mobile Regional Airport, AL	24	74	Galliano, LA	21
33	Picayune, MS	24	74	Hialeah, FL	21
33	Saucier Experiment Forest, MS	24	74	Homer 3 SSW, LA	21
33	Skamania Fish Hatchery, WA	24	74	LSU Ben Hur Farm, LA	21
33	Tillamook 1 W, OR	24	74	Moorhead, MS	21
41	Aberdeen, WA	23	74	Newhalem, WA	*21*
41	Amite, LA	23	74	Pascagoula 3 NE, MS	21
41	Brookings, OR	23	74	Pelahatchie, MS	*21*
41	Cloverdale, OR	23	74	Port Orford 2, OR	21
41	De Sabla, CA	23	74	Rolling Fork, MS	21
41	Franklin 3 NW, LA	23	74	Saint Bernard, LA	21
41	Franklinton 3 SW, LA	23	74	Sam Rayburn Dam, TX	21
41	Hawaii Volcano Nat'l Park HQ 54, HI	23	74	Shasta Dam, CA	21
41	Merrill, MS	23	74	Thomasville, AL	21
41	New Orleans Int'l Airport, LA	23	74	Waynesboro 2 W, MS	21

Highest Annual Snowfall

Rank	Station Name	Inches	Rank	Station Name	Inches
1	Rainier Paradise Ranger Station, WA	702.7	51	Gaylord, MI	149.4
2	Crater Lake Nat'l Park Hdqtrs., OR	488.1	52	Bright Angel Ranger Station, AZ	*147.1*
3	Wolf Creek Pass 1 E, CO	*435.6*	53	Alberta Ford, MI	*147.0*
4	Silver Lake Brighton, UT	428.6	54	Spicer, CO	*145.6*
5	Twin Lakes, CA	*394.8*	55	Ouray, CO	145.3
6	Valdez WSO, AK	*327.8*	56	Grand Lake 1 NW, CO	142.5
7	Mount Washington, NH	315.4	57	Mineral, CA	141.9
8	Snake River, WY	275.9	58	Plain, WA	140.3
9	Climax, CO	271.0	59	Gascon, NM	139.4
10	Government Camp, OR	256.7	60	McCall, ID	138.9
11	Holden Village, WA	254.3	61	Gurney, WI	138.7
12	Lake Spaulding, CA	247.0	62	Talkeetna State Airport, AK	137.3
13	Lodgepole, CA	237.5	63	Stehekin 4 NW, WA	136.2
14	Herman, MI	235.9	64	Canaan Valley, WV	*134.8*
15	Bowman Dam, CA	228.2	65	Pinkham Notch, NH	*133.9*
16	Old Forge, NY	226.7	66	Whitefish Point, MI	132.7
17	Crested Butte, CO	223.9	67	Sugarloaf Reservoir, CO	*132.4*
18	Hancock Houghton Co. Airport, MI	222.6	68	Champion Van Riper Park, MI	*131.7*
19	Mount Mansfield, VT	222.0	69	Sault Ste Marie Sanderson Field, MI	131.2
20	Lemolo Lake 3 NNW, OR	*221.4*	70	Cabin Creek, CO	*129.7*
21	Boonville 2 SSW, NY	218.6	71	Howard Prairie Dam, OR	128.8
22	Telluride 4 WNW, CO	205.8	72	Elk City 1 NE, ID	128.6
23	Truckee Ranger Station, CA	203.4	73	Wolf Canyon, NM	128.4
24	Dixie, ID	197.1	74	Wanakena Ranger School, NY	128.0
25	Lead, SD	193.0	75	Little Valley, NY	127.9
26	Stillwater Reservoir, NY	190.8	76	Chester, CA	126.0
27	Donner Memorial State Park, CA	188.8	77	Tully Heiberg Forest, NY	125.2
28	Grant Grove, CA	186.9	78	Lowville, NY	125.1
29	Manzanita Lake, CA	180.2	79	Pine View Dam, UT	125.0
30	Marquette County Airport, MI	179.8	80	Ray Brook, NY	124.5
31	Yakutat State Airport, AK	178.5	81	Mazama, WA	122.8
32	Ironwood, MI	177.1	82	Corry, PA	121.6
33	Bergland Dam, MI	176.4	83	Hayden, CO	121.4
34	Steamboat Springs, CO	173.3	84	Chasm Falls, NY	*121.2*
35	Tahoe City, CA	172.3	85	Petoskey, MI	120.6
36	Moose, WY	170.8	86	Syracuse Hancock Int'l Airport, NY	120.2
37	Glen Alps, AK	*169.4*	87	Marquette WBO, MI	118.2
38	Rico, CO	167.7	88	Rangeley, ME	*118.0*
39	Powell, ID	*166.0*	89	Vallecito Dam, CO	117.6
40	Red River, NM	164.9	89	Yampa, CO	117.6
41	Warren, ID	160.1	91	Boyne Falls, MI	116.3
42	Silverton, CO	*159.4*	92	Cherry Valley 2 NNE, NY	116.1
43	Terra Alta 1, WV	157.8	92	Cordova, AK	116.1
44	Colden 1 N, NY	157.5	94	Frankfort, MI	115.7
45	Oswego East, NY	153.3	95	Dillon 1 E, CO	115.5
46	Lindbergh Lake, MT	152.7	96	Pellston Emmet County Airport, MI	114.9
47	Ruxton Park, CO	152.0	97	Calaveras Big Trees, CA	114.8
48	First Conn Lake, NH	151.4	98	Newberry 3 S, MI	114.7
48	Maple City, MI	151.4	99	Caribou Municipal Airport, ME	113.7
50	Grand Marais 2 E, MI	150.4	100	Meadville 1 S, PA	111.2

Lowest Annual Snowfall

Rank	Station Name	Inches	Rank	Station Name	Inches
1	Arcadia, FL	0.0	1	Melbourne Regional Airport, FL	0.0
1	Bartow, FL	0.0	1	Miami Beach, FL	0.0
1	Blythe, CA	0.0	1	Molokai Airport, HI	0.0
1	Bouse, AZ	0.0	1	Moore Haven Lock 1, FL	0.0
1	Bradenton 5 ESE, FL	0.0	1	Naalehu 14, HI	0.0
1	Brawley 2 SW, CA	0.0	1	Naples, FL	0.0
1	Brooksville Chin Hill, FL	0.0	1	Newport Beach, CA	0.0
1	Buckeye, AZ	0.0	1	Ojai, CA	0.0
1	Bullhead City, AZ	*0.0*	1	Ookala 223, HI	*0.0*
1	Buttonwillow, CA	0.0	1	Opihihale 2 24.1, HI	0.0
1	Cachuma Lake, CA	0.0	1	Palo Alto, CA	0.0
1	Canal Point USDA, FL	0.0	1	Parker, AZ	0.0
1	Casa Grande Nat'l Monument, AZ	0.0	1	Plant City, FL	0.0
1	Chandler Heights, AZ	0.0	1	Port Mansfield, TX	0.0
1	Clewiston U.S. Engineers, FL	0.0	1	Punta Gorda 4 ESE, FL	0.0
1	Cross City 2 WNW, FL	0.0	1	Puukohola Heiau 98.1, HI	*0.0*
1	El Centro 2 SSW, CA	0.0	1	Raymondville, TX	0.0
1	Falfurrias, TX	0.0	1	Riverside Fire Station 3, CA	0.0
1	Flamingo Ranger Station, FL	0.0	1	Salinas 2, CA	0.0
1	Fort Lauderdale, FL	0.0	1	San Bernardino Co. Hospital, CA	0.0
1	Fort Myers Page Field, FL	*0.0*	1	San Gabriel Fire Dept., CA	0.0
1	Friant Government Camp, CA	0.0	1	San Luis Obispo Polytech, CA	0.0
1	Gila Bend, AZ	0.0	1	Sanford Experiment Station, FL	0.0
1	Haleakala Ranger Station 338, HI	0.0	1	Santa Ana Fire Station, CA	0.0
1	Hana Airport 355, HI	0.0	1	Santa Barbara Municipal Airport, CA	*0.0*
1	Hawaii Volcano Nat'l Park HQ 54, HI	0.0	1	Santa Monica Pier, CA	0.0
1	Hialeah, FL	0.0	1	Santa Paula, CA	0.0
1	Hilo International Airport, HI	0.0	1	Sheffield, TX	0.0
1	Honolulu Int'l Airport, HI	0.0	1	South Phoenix, AZ	0.0
1	Honolulu Observatory 702.2, HI	0.0	1	Stuart 1 S, FL	0.0
1	Immokalee 3 NNW, FL	0.0	1	Tamiami Trail 40 Mile Bend, FL	0.0
1	Imperial, CA	0.0	1	Tarpon Springs Sewage Plant, FL	0.0
1	Inverness 3 SE, FL	0.0	1	Tavernier, FL	0.0
1	Iron Mountain, CA	0.0	1	Three Rivers Edison 1, CA	*0.0*
1	Kahului Airport, HI	0.0	1	Tracy Pumping Plant, CA	0.0
1	Kailua 446, HI	0.0	1	Waikiki 717.2, HI	0.0
1	Kainaliu 73.2, HI	0.0	1	Waimanalo Exp. Farm, HI	0.0
1	Kanalohuluhulu 1075, HI	0.0	1	Watsonville Waterworks, CA	0.0
1	Key West Int'l Airport, FL	0.0	1	Weeki Wachee, FL	0.0
1	Kissimmee 2, FL	0.0	1	Yuma Citrus Station, AZ	0.0
1	Kulani Camp 79, HI	0.0	1	Yuma Valley, AZ	*0.0*
1	Laguna Beach, CA	0.0			
1	Lahaina 361, HI	0.0			
1	Laveen 3 SSE, AZ	0.0			
1	Lemon Cove, CA	0.0			
1	Lihue Airport, HI	0.0			
1	Litchfield Park, AZ	0.0			
1	Los Banos Det. Reservation, CA	0.0			
1	Manoa Lyon Arboretum, HI	*0.0*			
1	Mecca Fire Station, CA	0.0			

247 stations were tied with trace amounts.

Highest Number of Days Annually With ≥ 1.0″ Snow Depth

Rank	Station Name	Days	Rank	Station Name	Days
1	Rainier Paradise Ranger Station, WA	262	49	Lemolo Lake 3 NNW, OR	*151*
2	Barrow W. Post–W. Rogers Airport, AK	247	52	Alberta Ford, MI	*149*
3	Crater Lake Nat'l Park Hdqtrs., OR	238	52	Squa Pan Dam, ME	149
4	Silver Lake Brighton, UT	222	54	Ironwood, MI	148
5	Climax, CO	217	54	Ouray, CO	148
6	Bettles Field, AK	215	56	Grant Grove, CA	147
6	Kotzebue Ralph Wein Memorial, AK	215	56	McCall, ID	147
8	Mount Mansfield, VT	205	56	Mellen 4 NE, WI	147
9	Snowshoe Lake, AK	201	56	West Glacier, MT	147
10	McGrath Airport, AK	200	56	Yellow Pine 7 S, ID	147
10	Tanana R.M. Calhoun Mem. Arpt., AK	200	61	Kenai Municipal Airport, AK	146
10	Tonsina, AK	200	61	Winton Power Plant, MN	*146*
13	College Observatory, AK	199	63	Boonville 2 SSW, NY	144
14	Snake River, WY	197	63	Lakeview, MT	*144*
15	North Pole, AK	196	63	Minocqua Dam, WI	144
16	Northway Airport, AK	194	63	Rainbow Reservoir Lake Tomaha, WI	*144*
16	Talkeetna State Airport, AK	194	63	Sugarloaf Reservoir, CO	*144*
18	Fairbanks Int'l Airport, AK	192	68	Bright Angel Ranger Station, AZ	*143*
19	Dixie, ID	*188*	68	Elk City 1 NE, ID	143
20	Mount Washington, NH	187	68	Manzanita Lake, CA	143
20	Nome Municipal Airport, AK	187	71	Duluth Int'l Airport, MN	142
22	Old Edgerton, AK	*186*	71	Pinkham Notch, NH	142
23	Big Delta Allen AAF, AK	184	73	Cloquet, MN	141
23	Gulkana Intermediate Field, AK	184	73	Van Buren 2, ME	141
25	University Exp. Station, AK	181	73	Whitefish Point, MI	141
26	Eielson Field, AK	*179*	76	Cooper Lake Project, AK	140
27	Valdez WSO, AK	*178*	76	Donner Memorial State Park, CA	140
27	Whites Crossing, AK	*178*	76	Fort Kent, ME	*140*
29	Moran 5 WNW, WY	172	76	International Falls Int'l Arpt., MN	140
30	Hebgen Dam, MT	171	76	Lake Spaulding, CA	140
30	Holden Village, WA	171	76	Powell, ID	*140*
32	Crested Butte, CO	167	76	Yampa, CO	140
32	Lodgepole, CA	167	83	Caribou Municipal Airport, ME	139
32	Warren, ID	167	83	Laona 6 SW, WI	139
35	Lindbergh Lake, MT	165	83	Libby 32 SSE, MT	139
35	Moose, WY	165	83	Marquette WBO, MI	139
37	Grand Lake 1 NW, CO	164	83	Mazama, WA	139
38	Herman, MI	162	83	Old Forge, NY	*139*
39	Government Camp, OR	161	83	Stillwater Reservoir, NY	*139*
40	Bethel Airport, AK	160	83	Truckee Ranger Station, CA	139
41	Alta 1 NNW, WY	159	91	Ashton, ID	138
42	First Conn Lake, NH	158	91	Grand Marais 2 E, MI	138
43	Bergland Dam, MI	155	91	Sault Ste Marie Sanderson Field, MI	138
43	Champion Van Riper Park, MI	155	91	Seeley Lake Ranger Station, MT	*138*
43	Marquette County Airport, MI	155	91	Steamboat Springs, CO	138
46	Dillingham Airport, AK	*154*	96	Rico, CO	137
47	Grant, CO	153	97	Chasm Falls, NY	*136*
47	Silverton, CO	*153*	97	Dillon 1 E, CO	136
49	Anchorage Int'l Airport, AK	151	97	Gordon, WI	136
49	Hancock Houghton Co. Airport, MI	151	97	Itasca Univ. of Minnesota, MN	136

Note: See Appendix D for explanation of data.

Annual Extreme Maximum Temperature

Highest			Lowest		
Rank	**Station Name**	**°F**	**Rank**	**Station Name**	**°F**
1	Jasper	*108*	1	Clayton	101
2	Bankhead Lock & Dam	107	1	Fairhope 2 NE	101
2	Greensboro	107	3	Robertsdale 5 NE	102
2	Hamilton 3 S	107	4	Bay Minette 3 NNW	103
2	Heflin	107	4	Geneva 2	*103*
2	Selma	107	4	Haleyville	103
2	Winfield 2 SW	*107*	4	Mobile Regional Airport	103
8	Anniston Calhoun Co. Airport	106	4	Russellville 2	103
8	Ashland 3 SE	106	4	Sand Mountain Substation	103
8	Birmingham Municipal Airport	106	4	Troy	103
8	Chatom	106	4	Whatley	103
8	Livingston	106	12	Alexander City	104
8	Moulton 2	106	12	Andalusia 3 W	104
14	Centreville WSMO	*105*	12	Belle Mina 2 N	104
14	Childersburg Water Plant	105	12	Brewton 3 SSE	104
14	Demopolis Lock & Dam	105	12	Camden 3 NW	104
14	Eufaula Wildlife Refuge	105	12	Clanton	104
14	Evergreen	105	12	Enterprise 5 NNW	104
14	Gainesville Lock	105	12	Huntsville Airport	104
14	Greenville	105	12	Lafayette 2 W	*104*
14	Headland	105	12	Marion Junction 2 NE	104
14	Highland Home	105	12	Montgomery Dannelly Field	104
14	Muscle Shoals Regional Airport	105	12	Sylacauga 4 NE	*104*
14	Oneonta	105	12	Thomasville	104
14	Saint Bernard	105	12	Thorsby Exp. Station	104

Annual Mean Maximum Temperature

Highest			Lowest		
Rank	**Station Name**	**°F**	**Rank**	**Station Name**	**°F**
1	Brewton 3 SSE	78.3	1	Valley Head	69.5
2	Chatom	78.1	2	Sand Mountain Substation	69.7
3	Whatley	77.7	3	Haleyville	70.7
4	Andalusia 3 W	77.4	4	Russellville 2	70.8
4	Bay Minette 3 NNW	77.4	5	Huntsville Airport	71.2
4	Robertsdale 5 NE	77.4	6	Belle Mina 2 N	71.4
7	Greenville	*77.3*	7	Muscle Shoals Regional Airport	71.6
7	Mobile Regional Airport	77.3	7	Oneonta	71.6
9	Headland	77.1	9	Ashland 3 SE	71.8
10	Fairhope 2 NE	76.9	10	Heflin	72.2
11	Geneva 2	*76.8*	11	Jasper	*72.5*
12	Selma	76.7	11	Saint Bernard	72.5
13	Eufaula Wildlife Refuge	76.5	13	Moulton 2	72.6
14	Childersburg Water Plant	76.3	14	Winfield 2 SW	*72.9*
14	Greensboro	76.3	15	Anniston Calhoun Co. Airport	73.3
14	Montgomery Dannelly Field	76.3	16	Birmingham Municipal Airport	73.4
14	Thomasville	76.3	16	Hamilton 3 S	73.4
18	Camden 3 NW	76.2	18	Vernon 2 N	73.5
18	Evergreen	76.2	19	Thorsby Exp. Station	73.6
20	Livingston	76.1	20	Centreville WSMO	*74.0*
21	Troy	76.0	21	Clanton	74.1
22	Enterprise 5 NNW	75.8	22	Bankhead Lock & Dam	74.3
23	Highland Home	75.6	23	Gainesville Lock	74.4
24	Clayton	75.5	24	Marion Junction 2 NE	74.5
24	Union Springs 9 S	75.5	25	Alexander City	74.6

Annual Mean Temperature

	Highest			Lowest	
Rank	Station Name	°F	Rank	Station Name	°F
1	Mobile Regional Airport	67.4	1	Valley Head	57.1
2	Fairhope 2 NE	67.0	2	Russellville 2	58.6
3	Bay Minette 3 NNW	66.9	3	Sand Mountain Substation	58.9
4	Robertsdale 5 NE	66.3	4	Hamilton 3 S	59.3
5	Selma	65.6	5	Heflin	59.5
6	Greenville	*65.5*	5	Saint Bernard	59.5
7	Enterprise 5 NNW	65.4	7	Winfield 2 SW	*59.7*
8	Chatom	*65.3*	8	Haleyville	59.8
9	Brewton 3 SSE	65.1	9	Belle Mina 2 N	59.9
9	Geneva 2	*65.1*	10	Jasper	*60.0*
9	Headland	65.1	10	Oneonta	60.0
9	Montgomery Dannelly Field	65.1	12	Ashland 3 SE	60.2
13	Troy	64.8	13	Huntsville Airport	60.6
14	Evergreen	64.6	13	Vernon 2 N	60.6
14	Greensboro	64.6	15	Muscle Shoals Regional Airport	60.8
16	Whatley	64.5	16	Moulton 2	61.3
17	Thomasville	64.3	17	Sylacauga 4 NE	*61.6*
18	Eufaula Wildlife Refuge	64.2	18	Bankhead Lock & Dam	61.8
19	Andalusia 3 W	64.1	19	Clanton	62.1
19	Clayton	64.1	20	Alexander City	62.3
21	Highland Home	64.0	20	Anniston Calhoun Co. Airport	62.3
22	Camden 3 NW	63.9	20	Thorsby Exp. Station	62.3
22	Tuscaloosa Municipal Airport	63.9	23	Birmingham Municipal Airport	62.4
24	Union Springs 9 S	63.6	24	Centreville WSMO	*62.6*
25	Livingston	63.3	25	Lafayette 2 W	*62.7*

Annual Mean Minimum Temperature

	Highest			Lowest	
Rank	Station Name	°F	Rank	Station Name	°F
1	Mobile Regional Airport	57.4	1	Valley Head	44.7
2	Fairhope 2 NE	56.9	2	Hamilton 3 S	45.2
3	Bay Minette 3 NNW	56.3	3	Russellville 2	46.3
4	Robertsdale 5 NE	55.2	3	Saint Bernard	46.3
5	Enterprise 5 NNW	55.0	5	Winfield 2 SW	*46.4*
6	Selma	54.4	6	Heflin	46.8
7	Montgomery Dannelly Field	53.9	7	Jasper	*47.5*
8	Greenville	53.7	8	Vernon 2 N	47.6
9	Troy	53.6	9	Sand Mountain Substation	48.0
10	Geneva 2	*53.5*	10	Oneonta	48.3
11	Headland	53.1	11	Ashland 3 SE	48.4
12	Evergreen	52.9	11	Belle Mina 2 N	48.4
12	Greensboro	52.9	11	Sylacauga 4 NE	*48.4*
14	Clayton	52.7	14	Haleyville	48.9
15	Tuscaloosa Municipal Airport	52.6	15	Bankhead Lock & Dam	49.3
16	Chatom	52.4	16	Alexander City	50.0
17	Highland Home	52.3	16	Clanton	50.0
18	Thomasville	52.2	16	Huntsville Airport	50.0
19	Brewton 3 SSE	52.0	16	Moulton 2	50.0
19	Eufaula Wildlife Refuge	52.0	20	Childersburg Water Plant	50.1
21	Union Springs 9 S	51.7	20	Muscle Shoals Regional Airport	50.1
22	Camden 3 NW	51.5	22	Lafayette 2 W	*50.4*
23	Gainesville Lock	51.4	23	Livingston	50.6
24	Birmingham Municipal Airport	51.3	24	Andalusia 3 W	50.7
24	Whatley	51.3	25	Thorsby Exp. Station	50.9

Annual Extreme Minimum Temperature

	Highest			Lowest	
Rank	Station Name	°F	Rank	Station Name	°F
1	Eufaula Wildlife Refuge	5	1	Belle Mina 2 N	-14
1	Fairhope 2 NE	5	1	Russellville 2	-14
3	Brewton 3 SSE	3	1	Valley Head	-14
3	Mobile Regional Airport	3	4	Moulton 2	-13
3	Robertsdale 5 NE	3	4	Sand Mountain Substation	-13
6	Bay Minette 3 NNW	2	6	Hamilton 3 S	-12
6	Geneva 2	*2*	7	Huntsville Airport	-11
8	Chatom	1	7	Muscle Shoals Regional Airport	-11
9	Andalusia 3 W	0	9	Heflin	-10
9	Camden 3 NW	0	9	Jasper	*-10*
9	Evergreen	0	9	Saint Bernard	-10
9	Headland	0	12	Haleyville	-9
9	Montgomery Dannelly Field	0	13	Oneonta	-8
9	Selma	0	13	Vernon 2 N	-8
15	Enterprise 5 NNW	-1	13	Winfield 2 SW	*-8*
15	Greenville	-1	16	Ashland 3 SE	-7
15	Marion Junction 2 NE	-1	16	Lafayette 2 W	*-7*
15	Thomasville	-1	18	Alexander City	-6
15	Troy	-1	18	Birmingham Municipal Airport	-6
15	Tuscaloosa Municipal Airport	-1	18	Centreville WSMO	*-6*
21	Demopolis Lock & Dam	-2	18	Clayton	-6
21	Gainesville Lock	-2	22	Anniston Calhoun Co. Airport	-5
21	Greensboro	-2	22	Bankhead Lock & Dam	-5
21	Union Springs 9 S	-2	24	Childersburg Water Plant	-4
21	Whatley	-2	24	Clanton	-4

July Mean Maximum Temperature

	Highest			Lowest	
Rank	Station Name	°F	Rank	Station Name	°F
1	Greensboro	92.7	1	Sand Mountain Substation	87.6
2	Chatom	92.6	2	Valley Head	87.7
3	Childersburg Water Plant	92.3	3	Ashland 3 SE	88.0
4	Livingston	92.2	4	Haleyville	88.7
5	Greenville	92.1	5	Russellville 2	89.0
5	Selma	92.1	6	Huntsville Airport	89.4
7	Bankhead Lock & Dam	92.0	6	Oneonta	89.4
7	Tuscaloosa Municipal Airport	92.0	8	Heflin	89.8
7	Whatley	92.0	9	Jasper	89.9
10	Brewton 3 SSE	91.8	9	Thorsby Exp. Station	89.9
10	Camden 3 NW	91.8	11	Belle Mina 2 N	90.0
10	Eufaula Wildlife Refuge	91.8	11	Clayton	90.0
10	Headland	91.8	13	Enterprise 5 NNW	90.2
10	Montgomery Dannelly Field	91.8	13	Fairhope 2 NE	90.2
15	Andalusia 3 W	91.4	15	Anniston Calhoun Co. Airport	90.3
15	Demopolis Lock & Dam	91.4	15	Moulton 2	90.3
15	Thomasville	91.4	17	Saint Bernard	90.4
18	Gainesville Lock	91.2	18	Bay Minette 3 NNW	90.5
18	Hamilton 3 S	91.2	18	Birmingham Municipal Airport	90.5
18	Vernon 2 N	91.2	18	Lafayette 2 W	90.5
21	Mobile Regional Airport	91.1	21	Clanton	90.6
22	Alexander City	90.9	21	Evergreen	90.6
22	Sylacauga 4 NE	*90.9*	21	Muscle Shoals Regional Airport	90.6
24	Marion Junction 2 NE	90.8	21	Robertsdale 5 NE	90.6
24	Union Springs 9 S	90.8	21	Troy	90.6

January Mean Minimum Temperature

Highest			Lowest		
Rank	Station Name	°F	Rank	Station Name	°F
1	Mobile Regional Airport	40.5	1	Hamilton 3 S	25.9
2	Fairhope 2 NE	40.2	2	Valley Head	26.0
3	Bay Minette 3 NNW	40.1	3	Winfield 2 SW	26.8
4	Robertsdale 5 NE	38.7	4	Russellville 2	27.6
5	Enterprise 5 NNW	37.9	4	Saint Bernard	27.6
6	Selma	37.5	6	Heflin	28.4
7	Greenville	37.3	6	Vernon 2 N	28.4
8	Troy	36.5	8	Jasper	28.5
9	Brewton 3 SSE	36.1	9	Sand Mountain Substation	28.9
9	Headland	36.1	10	Haleyville	29.3
11	Montgomery Dannelly Field	36.0	11	Belle Mina 2 N	29.4
12	Geneva 2	35.6	11	Oneonta	29.4
13	Chatom	35.4	13	Muscle Shoals Regional Airport	30.0
13	Evergreen	35.4	14	Ashland 3 SE	30.3
15	Clayton	35.2	15	Huntsville Airport	30.4
16	Greensboro	35.0	16	Bankhead Lock & Dam	30.8
17	Eufaula Wildlife Refuge	34.7	17	Moulton 2	31.0
18	Highland Home	34.4	18	Clanton	31.4
18	Whatley	34.4	19	Alexander City	31.7
20	Andalusia 3 W	34.2	19	Sylacauga 4 NE	31.7
20	Thomasville	34.2	21	Livingston	32.1
22	Union Springs 9 S	34.0	22	Centreville WSMO	32.2
23	Camden 3 NW	33.9	23	Gainesville Lock	32.5
24	Tuscaloosa Municipal Airport	33.8	24	Birmingham Municipal Airport	32.6
25	Anniston Calhoun Co. Airport	32.9	24	Childersburg Water Plant	32.6

Number of Annual Heating Degree Days

Highest			Lowest		
Rank	Station Name	Num.	Rank	Station Name	Num.
1	Valley Head	3,974	1	Mobile Regional Airport	1,634
2	Russellville 2	3,643	2	Bay Minette 3 NNW	1,643
3	Hamilton 3 S	3,538	3	Fairhope 2 NE	1,667
4	Sand Mountain Substation	3,519	4	Robertsdale 5 NE	1,787
5	Winfield 2 SW	3,429	5	Enterprise 5 NNW	1,974
6	Saint Bernard	3,393	6	Greenville	1,990
7	Heflin	3,392	7	Brewton 3 SSE	2,004
8	Belle Mina 2 N	3,377	8	Geneva 2	2,034
9	Haleyville	3,353	9	Chatom	2,036
10	Oneonta	3,323	10	Selma	2,058
11	Jasper	3,302	11	Headland	2,064
12	Vernon 2 N	3,217	12	Troy	2,116
13	Huntsville Airport	3,215	13	Montgomery Dannelly Field	2,159
14	Muscle Shoals Regional Airport	3,198	14	Whatley	2,179
15	Ashland 3 SE	3,113	15	Evergreen	2,180
16	Moulton 2	3,027	16	Clayton	2,245
17	Bankhead Lock & Dam	2,909	17	Andalusia 3 W	2,250
18	Sylacauga 4 NE	2,816	18	Eufaula Wildlife Refuge	2,278
19	Clanton	2,788	19	Greensboro	2,301
20	Birmingham Municipal Airport	2,784	20	Thomasville	2,314
21	Anniston Calhoun Co. Airport	2,764	21	Highland Home	2,324
22	Alexander City	2,725	22	Camden 3 NW	2,379
23	Thorsby Exp. Station	2,690	23	Union Springs 9 S	2,437
24	Centreville WSMO	2,685	24	Tuscaloosa Municipal Airport	2,508
25	Gainesville Lock	2,681	25	Childersburg Water Plant	2,516

Number of Annual Cooling Degree Days

	Highest				Lowest	
Rank	Station Name	Num.		Rank	Station Name	Num.
1	Mobile Regional Airport	2,539		1	Valley Head	1,231
2	Fairhope 2 NE	2,473		2	Sand Mountain Substation	1,421
3	Bay Minette 3 NNW	2,421		3	Russellville 2	1,445
4	Greenville	2,357		4	Ashland 3 SE	1,464
5	Montgomery Dannelly Field	2,338		5	Saint Bernard	1,495
6	Selma	2,335		6	Heflin	1,522
7	Greensboro	2,323		7	Winfield 2 SW	1,605
8	Robertsdale 5 NE	2,317		8	Haleyville	1,614
9	Chatom	*2,258*		8	Oneonta	1,614
10	Tuscaloosa Municipal Airport	2,252		10	Hamilton 3 S	1,643
11	Enterprise 5 NNW	2,244		11	Vernon 2 N	1,653
12	Headland	2,196		12	Jasper	*1,663*
13	Geneva 2	2,192		13	Belle Mina 2 N	1,677
14	Thomasville	2,190		14	Sylacauga 4 NE	1,681
15	Camden 3 NW	2,153		15	Huntsville Airport	1,767
16	Troy	2,147		16	Lafayette 2 W	*1,810*
17	Eufaula Wildlife Refuge	2,124		17	Thorsby Exp. Station	1,820
18	Evergreen	2,118		18	Moulton 2	1,825
19	Brewton 3 SSE	2,109		19	Bankhead Lock & Dam	1,844
20	Livingston	2,082		20	Alexander City	1,848
21	Andalusia 3 W	2,076		21	Clanton	*1,857*
21	Whatley	2,076		22	Muscle Shoals Regional Airport	*1,875*
23	Gainesville Lock	2,064		23	Anniston Calhoun Co. Airport	1,885
24	Demopolis Lock & Dam	2,049		24	Centreville WSMO	1,929
25	Highland Home	2,037		25	Marion Junction 2 NE	1,978

Annual Precipitation

	Highest				Lowest	
Rank	Station Name	Inches		Rank	Station Name	Inches
1	Robertsdale 5 NE	68.71		1	Eufaula Wildlife Refuge	52.22
2	Fairhope 2 NE	68.50		2	Anniston Calhoun Co. Airport	52.33
3	Bay Minette 3 NNW	68.21		3	Selma	53.13
4	Mobile Regional Airport	67.08		4	Clayton	53.32
5	Brewton 3 SSE	67.03		5	Birmingham Municipal Airport	54.03
6	Chatom	64.91		6	Gainesville Lock	54.52
7	Evergreen	64.57		7	Troy	54.57
8	Whatley	63.93		8	Montgomery Dannelly Field	55.12
9	Haleyville	62.84		9	Marion Junction 2 NE	55.19
10	Andalusia 3 W	62.74		10	Sand Mountain Substation	55.29
11	Hamilton 3 S	61.02		11	Belle Mina 2 N	55.56
12	Vernon 2 N	60.51		12	Demopolis Lock & Dam	55.70
13	Bankhead Lock & Dam	60.44		13	Union Springs 9 S	55.99
14	Clanton	60.35		14	Livingston	56.08
15	Saint Bernard	60.12		15	Sylacauga 4 NE	*56.34*
16	Thomasville	60.10		16	Muscle Shoals Regional Airport	56.40
17	Winfield 2 SW	60.07		17	Highland Home	56.74
18	Geneva 2	*59.81*		18	Tuscaloosa Municipal Airport	57.12
19	Jasper	59.61		19	Lafayette 2 W	57.16
20	Centreville WSMO	*59.47*		20	Childersburg Water Plant	57.28
21	Ashland 3 SE	59.28		21	Greensboro	57.35
22	Moulton 2	58.88		22	Alexander City	57.43
23	Oneonta	58.45		23	Russellville 2	57.47
24	Valley Head	58.29		24	Camden 3 NW	57.55
25	Greenville	58.09		25	Thorsby Exp. Station	57.76

Number of Days Annually With ≥ 0.1″ Precipitation

	Highest			Lowest	
Rank	Station Name	Days	Rank	Station Name	Days
1	Moulton 2	88	1	Livingston	67
2	Bay Minette 3 NNW	87	2	Clayton	*69*
3	Brewton 3 SSE	86	3	Eufaula Wildlife Refuge	71
3	Valley Head	86	4	Troy	73
5	Haleyville	85	5	Chatom	74
5	Sand Mountain Substation	85	5	Gainesville Lock	74
7	Ashland 3 SE	84	7	Enterprise 5 NNW	75
7	Evergreen	84	7	Montgomery Dannelly Field	75
7	Jasper	*84*	7	Union Springs 9 S	75
7	Oneonta	84	10	Greenville	76
11	Alexander City	83	10	Selma	76
11	Andalusia 3 W	83	12	Camden 3 NW	77
11	Bankhead Lock & Dam	83	12	Greensboro	77
11	Belle Mina 2 N	83	12	Heflin	*77*
11	Hamilton 3 S	83	12	Russellville 2	77
11	Lafayette 2 W	*83*	12	Whatley	*77*
11	Marion Junction 2 NE	83	17	Geneva 2	*78*
11	Mobile Regional Airport	83	18	Anniston Calhoun Co. Airport	79
11	Robertsdale 5 NE	83	18	Centreville WSMO	*79*
20	Childersburg Water Plant	82	18	Demopolis Lock & Dam	79
20	Huntsville Airport	82	18	Highland Home	79
20	Sylacauga 4 NE	*82*	18	Thomasville	79
20	Winfield 2 SW	82	18	Thorsby Exp. Station	79
24	Birmingham Municipal Airport	81	24	Clanton	80
24	Fairhope 2 NE	81	24	Headland	80

Number of Days Annually With ≥ 1.0″ Precipitation

	Highest			Lowest	
Rank	Station Name	Days	Rank	Station Name	Days
1	Mobile Regional Airport	24	1	Anniston Calhoun Co. Airport	13
2	Bay Minette 3 NNW	22	2	Belle Mina 2 N	15
2	Brewton 3 SSE	22	2	Eufaula Wildlife Refuge	15
2	Hamilton 3 S	22	2	Union Springs 9 S	15
2	Robertsdale 5 NE	22	5	Childersburg Water Plant	16
6	Bankhead Lock & Dam	21	5	Montgomery Dannelly Field	16
6	Chatom	21	5	Oneonta	16
6	Evergreen	21	5	Sand Mountain Substation	16
6	Fairhope 2 NE	21	5	Selma	16
6	Thomasville	21	5	Troy	16
6	Whatley	21	11	Birmingham Municipal Airport	17
6	Winfield 2 SW	21	11	Clayton	*17*
13	Clanton	20	11	Headland	17
13	Greensboro	20	11	Highland Home	17
13	Haleyville	20	11	Lafayette 2 W	17
13	Huntsville Airport	20	11	Muscle Shoals Regional Airport	17
13	Jasper	20	11	Russellville 2	17
13	Vernon 2 N	20	11	Valley Head	17
19	Alexander City	19	19	Enterprise 5 NNW	18
19	Andalusia 3 W	19	19	Gainesville Lock	18
19	Ashland 3 SE	19	19	Saint Bernard	18
19	Camden 3 NW	19	22	Alexander City	19
19	Centreville WSMO	*19*	22	Andalusia 3 W	19
19	Demopolis Lock & Dam	19	22	Ashland 3 SE	19
19	Geneva 2	*19*	22	Camden 3 NW	19

Annual Snowfall

Highest			Lowest		
Rank	Station Name	Inches	Rank	Station Name	Inches
1	Valley Head	6.0	1	Bankhead Lock & Dam	Trace
2	Moulton 2	2.9	1	Fairhope 2 NE	Trace
3	Huntsville Airport	2.7	1	Marion Junction 2 NE	Trace
4	Muscle Shoals Regional Airport	*2.3*	4	Demopolis Lock & Dam	0.1
5	Ashland 3 SE	2.2	4	Robertsdale 5 NE	0.1
5	Belle Mina 2 N	2.2	6	Andalusia 3 W	0.2
7	Heflin	2.0	6	Brewton 3 SSE	0.2
7	Oneonta	2.0	6	Chatom	0.2
9	Birmingham Municipal Airport	1.6	6	Headland	0.2
9	Hamilton 3 S	1.6	10	Camden 3 NW	0.3
11	Anniston Calhoun Co. Airport	1.5	10	Greensboro	0.3
11	Haleyville	1.5	10	Lafayette 2 W	0.3
13	Centreville WSMO	*1.2*	10	Mobile Regional Airport	0.3
13	Sand Mountain Substation	1.2	10	Selma	0.3
13	Union Springs 9 S	1.2	15	Bay Minette 3 NNW	0.4
13	Winfield 2 SW	1.2	15	Evergreen	0.4
17	Highland Home	1.0	15	Gainesville Lock	0.4
17	Jasper	1.0	15	Greenville	0.4
17	Saint Bernard	1.0	15	Montgomery Dannelly Field	0.4
20	Clanton	0.9	15	Thomasville	0.4
20	Russellville 2	0.9	21	Alexander City	0.5
20	Sylacauga 4 NE	*0.9*	21	Enterprise 5 NNW	0.5
23	Childersburg Water Plant	0.7	21	Tuscaloosa Municipal Airport	0.5
23	Livingston	0.7	24	Clayton	0.6
23	Troy	0.7	24	Eufaula Wildlife Refuge	0.6

Note: See Appendix D for explanation of data.

Annual Extreme Maximum Temperature

	Highest				Lowest	
Rank	**Station Name**	**°F**		**Rank**	**Station Name**	**°F**
1	North Pole	95		1	Saint Paul Island Airport	66
1	Snowshoe Lake	95		2	Cold Bay Airport	76
3	College Observatory	94		2	Glen Alps	*76*
3	Fairbanks Int'l Airport	94		4	Barrow W. Post-W. Rogers Airport	79
5	Bettles Field	93		5	Dillingham Airport	*81*
5	University Exp. Station	93		5	Homer Airport	81
7	Eielson Field	92		7	Anchorage Int'l Airport	82
7	Old Edgerton	*92*		7	Kodiak State USCG Base	82
9	Tanana R.M. Calhoun Mem. Arpt.	91		9	Palmer IAS	83
10	Beaver Falls	90		10	Bethel Airport	84
10	Big Delta Allen AAF	90		10	Cooper Lake Project	84
10	Juneau Int'l Airport	90		10	Intricate Bay	84
13	Auke Bay	89		13	King Salmon Airport	85
13	Cordova	89		13	Kotzebue Ralph Wein Memorial	85
13	McGrath Airport	89		13	Matanuska AES	85
13	Whites Crossing	89		16	Kenai Municipal Airport	86
17	Annette Island Airport	88		16	Nome Municipal Airport	86
17	Gulkana Intermediate Field	88		16	Port Alsworth	86
17	Little Port Walter	88		16	Valdez WSO	*86*
17	Northway Airport	88		20	Kitoi Bay	87
17	Sitka Japonski Airport	88		20	Seward	87
17	Talkeetna State Airport	88		20	Wasilla 3 S	87
17	Tonsina	88		20	Yakutat State Airport	87
24	Kitoi Bay	87		24	Annette Island Airport	88
24	Seward	87		24	Gulkana Intermediate Field	88

Annual Mean Maximum Temperature

	Highest				Lowest	
Rank	**Station Name**	**°F**		**Rank**	**Station Name**	**°F**
1	Annette Island Airport	51.5		1	Barrow W. Post-W. Rogers Airport	15.6
2	Beaver Falls	*50.5*		2	Kotzebue Ralph Wein Memorial	28.0
3	Sitka Japonski Airport	49.7		3	Bettles Field	31.6
4	Little Port Walter	49.2		4	Northway Airport	33.4
5	Auke Bay	48.2		5	Nome Municipal Airport	33.6
6	Juneau Int'l Airport	47.5		6	Tanana R.M. Calhoun Mem. Arpt.	34.7
7	Kodiak State USCG Base	46.9		7	McGrath Airport	35.8
8	Cordova	46.5		8	Eielson Field	36.2
9	Yakutat State Airport	46.3		8	Snowshoe Lake	36.2
10	Wasilla 3 S	46.1		10	Bethel Airport	36.4
11	Kitoi Bay	45.9		11	North Pole	36.7
12	Seward	45.3		12	Big Delta Allen AAF	37.3
13	Cooper Lake Project	44.9		12	Fairbanks Int'l Airport	37.3
14	Matanuska AES	44.6		14	Gulkana Intermediate Field	37.5
15	Homer Airport	44.5		15	College Observatory	37.9
16	Palmer IAS	44.4		16	Tonsina	38.3
16	Valdez WSO	*44.4*		17	University Exp. Station	38.7
18	Port Alsworth	44.1		18	Saint Paul Island Airport	39.0
19	Intricate Bay	44.0		19	Old Edgerton	*39.4*
20	Talkeetna State Airport	43.2		20	Dillingham Airport	*39.9*
21	Anchorage Int'l Airport	43.1		21	Glen Alps	*40.2*
21	Cold Bay Airport	43.1		22	Kenai Municipal Airport	42.1
23	Whites Crossing	42.7		23	King Salmon Airport	42.2
24	King Salmon Airport	42.2		24	Whites Crossing	42.7
25	Kenai Municipal Airport	42.1		25	Anchorage Int'l Airport	43.1

Annual Mean Temperature

	Highest				Lowest	
Rank	Station Name	°F		Rank	Station Name	°F
1	Annette Island Airport	46.1		1	Barrow W. Post-W. Rogers Airport	10.2
2	Sitka Japonski Airport	44.9		2	Kotzebue Ralph Wein Memorial	21.9
3	Beaver Falls	*44.8*		3	Northway Airport	22.5
4	Little Port Walter	43.6		4	Bettles Field	22.6
5	Auke Bay	42.2		5	Snowshoe Lake	23.5
6	Juneau Int'l Airport	41.4		6	Tanana R.M. Calhoun Mem. Arpt.	25.0
7	Kodiak State USCG Base	41.2		7	North Pole	25.3
8	Kitoi Bay	39.9		8	McGrath Airport	26.1
9	Seward	39.8		9	Nome Municipal Airport	26.6
10	Yakutat State Airport	39.7		10	Eielson Field	26.7
11	Cordova	39.0		10	Tonsina	26.7
12	Valdez WSO	*38.6*		12	Fairbanks Int'l Airport	27.5
13	Cold Bay Airport	38.4		12	Gulkana Intermediate Field	27.5
14	Homer Airport	38.0		14	University Exp. Station	27.9
15	Cooper Lake Project	37.4		15	College Observatory	28.0
16	Wasilla 3 S	36.6		16	Old Edgerton	*28.3*
17	Anchorage Int'l Airport	36.4		17	Big Delta Allen AAF	28.4
18	Palmer IAS	35.8		18	Bethel Airport	29.6
19	Matanuska AES	35.7		19	Whites Crossing	32.1
20	Intricate Bay	35.3		20	Glen Alps	*33.3*
21	Port Alsworth	34.9		21	Dillingham Airport	*33.8*
22	Saint Paul Island Airport	34.8		21	Talkeetna State Airport	33.8
23	King Salmon Airport	34.3		23	Kenai Municipal Airport	34.2
24	Kenai Municipal Airport	34.2		24	King Salmon Airport	34.3
25	Dillingham Airport	*33.8*		25	Saint Paul Island Airport	34.8

Annual Mean Minimum Temperature

	Highest				Lowest	
Rank	Station Name	°F		Rank	Station Name	°F
1	Annette Island Airport	40.7		1	Barrow W. Post-W. Rogers Airport	4.8
2	Sitka Japonski Airport	40.0		2	Snowshoe Lake	10.7
3	Beaver Falls	*39.0*		3	Northway Airport	11.6
4	Little Port Walter	37.9		4	Bettles Field	13.5
5	Auke Bay	36.1		5	North Pole	13.9
6	Kodiak State USCG Base	35.5		6	Tonsina	15.0
7	Juneau Int'l Airport	35.3		7	Tanana R.M. Calhoun Mem. Arpt.	15.2
8	Seward	34.3		8	Kotzebue Ralph Wein Memorial	15.8
9	Kitoi Bay	33.8		9	McGrath Airport	16.5
10	Cold Bay Airport	33.7		10	University Exp. Station	17.0
11	Yakutat State Airport	33.1		11	Eielson Field	17.1
12	Valdez WSO	*32.7*		12	Old Edgerton	*17.2*
13	Cordova	31.4		13	Gulkana Intermediate Field	17.4
13	Homer Airport	31.4		14	Fairbanks Int'l Airport	17.8
15	Saint Paul Island Airport	30.7		15	College Observatory	18.0
16	Cooper Lake Project	29.9		16	Big Delta Allen AAF	19.5
17	Anchorage Int'l Airport	29.6		17	Nome Municipal Airport	19.6
18	Dillingham Airport	*27.8*		18	Whites Crossing	21.4
19	Palmer IAS	27.2		19	Bethel Airport	22.6
20	Wasilla 3 S	27.1		20	Talkeetna State Airport	24.3
21	Matanuska AES	26.7		21	Port Alsworth	25.7
22	Glen Alps	*26.5*		22	Kenai Municipal Airport	26.2
22	Intricate Bay	26.5		23	King Salmon Airport	26.3
24	King Salmon Airport	26.3		24	Glen Alps	*26.5*
25	Kenai Municipal Airport	26.2		24	Intricate Bay	26.5

Annual Extreme Minimum Temperature

	Highest			Lowest	
Rank	Station Name	°F	Rank	Station Name	°F
1	Little Port Walter	4	1	Tanana R.M. Calhoun Mem. Arpt.	-76
2	Sitka Japonski Airport	0	2	McGrath Airport	-75
3	Beaver Falls	-2	3	Northway Airport	-71
4	Annette Island Airport	-3	4	Bettles Field	-70
5	Cold Bay Airport	-13	5	North Pole	-67
6	Kodiak State USCG Base	-16	6	Eielson Field	-64
7	Saint Paul Island Airport	-19	7	Fairbanks Int'l Airport	-60
7	Seward	-19	7	Snowshoe Lake	-60
9	Kitoi Bay	-20	7	Tonsina	-60
9	Valdez WSO	*-20*	7	University Exp. Station	-60
11	Yakutat State Airport	-21	11	Big Delta Allen AAF	-59
12	Juneau Int'l Airport	-22	12	Old Edgerton	*-58*
13	Homer Airport	-24	13	College Observatory	-57
14	Cooper Lake Project	-26	13	Gulkana Intermediate Field	-57
15	Cordova	-30	15	Port Alsworth	-55
16	Auke Bay	-33	16	Nome Municipal Airport	-54
17	Anchorage Int'l Airport	-34	17	Barrow W. Post-W. Rogers Airport	-53
18	Glen Alps	*-37*	17	Dillingham Airport	*-53*
18	Palmer IAS	-37	19	Intricate Bay	-50
20	Matanuska AES	-41	19	Whites Crossing	-50
21	Wasilla 3 S	-42	21	Kotzebue Ralph Wein Memorial	-49
22	Kenai Municipal Airport	-47	22	Bethel Airport	-48
23	Bethel Airport	-48	22	King Salmon Airport	-48
23	King Salmon Airport	-48	22	Talkeetna State Airport	-48
23	Talkeetna State Airport	-48	25	Kenai Municipal Airport	-47

July Mean Maximum Temperature

	Highest			Lowest	
Rank	Station Name	°F	Rank	Station Name	°F
1	University Exp. Station	73.9	1	Barrow W. Post-W. Rogers Airport	46.4
2	College Observatory	73.4	2	Saint Paul Island Airport	50.2
3	Fairbanks Int'l Airport	73.2	3	Cold Bay Airport	55.2
4	North Pole	73.1	4	Nome Municipal Airport	58.5
5	Tanana R.M. Calhoun Mem. Arpt.	72.2	5	Glen Alps	*58.6*
6	Eielson Field	71.4	6	Kotzebue Ralph Wein Memorial	59.8
7	Big Delta Allen AAF	70.6	7	Yakutat State Airport	60.1
8	Bettles Field	70.5	8	Kodiak State USCG Base	60.4
9	Northway Airport	70.1	9	Kitoi Bay	60.8
10	Old Edgerton	69.8	10	Homer Airport	60.9
11	Wasilla 3 S	69.7	11	Sitka Japonski Airport	61.0
12	Tonsina	69.5	12	Dillingham Airport	*61.4*
13	McGrath Airport	69.2	13	Seward	61.8
14	Whites Crossing	69.1	14	Cordova	61.9
15	Gulkana Intermediate Field	68.6	15	Kenai Municipal Airport	62.0
16	Talkeetna State Airport	67.9	16	Little Port Walter	62.2
17	Port Alsworth	67.5	17	Valdez WSO	62.4
18	Matanuska AES	67.2	18	Bethel Airport	63.1
19	Palmer IAS	66.9	19	King Salmon Airport	63.7
19	Snowshoe Lake	66.9	20	Annette Island Airport	64.2
21	Cooper Lake Project	65.7	20	Juneau Int'l Airport	64.2
22	Intricate Bay	65.6	22	Beaver Falls	*64.5*
23	Auke Bay	65.5	23	Anchorage Int'l Airport	65.3
24	Anchorage Int'l Airport	65.3	24	Auke Bay	65.5
25	Beaver Falls	*64.5*	25	Intricate Bay	65.6

January Mean Minimum Temperature

	Highest				Lowest	
Rank	**Station Name**	**°F**		**Rank**	**Station Name**	**°F**
1	Sitka Japonski Airport	30.7		1	Northway Airport	-26.3
2	Annette Island Airport	30.4		2	North Pole	-21.1
3	Little Port Walter	28.9		3	Barrow W. Post-W. Rogers Airport	-19.6
4	Beaver Falls	27.7		4	Bettles Field	-19.5
5	Kodiak State USCG Base	26.4		5	Snowshoe Lake	-18.6
6	Kitoi Bay	24.1		6	Eielson Field	-18.0
7	Cold Bay Airport	23.7		7	Tanana R.M. Calhoun Mem. Arpt.	-17.4
8	Auke Bay	22.2		8	Fairbanks Int'l Airport	-17.3
9	Saint Paul Island Airport	21.6		9	McGrath Airport	-17.1
10	Seward	21.3		10	University Exp. Station	-14.8
11	Juneau Int'l Airport	20.5		11	Tonsina	-13.5
12	Yakutat State Airport	19.8		12	Gulkana Intermediate Field	-13.0
13	Valdez WSO	*19.1*		13	College Observatory	-12.7
14	Homer Airport	17.5		14	Old Edgerton	-11.8
15	Cordova	16.8		15	Big Delta Allen AAF	-10.3
16	Cooper Lake Project	14.5		16	Kotzebue Ralph Wein Memorial	-8.8
17	Glen Alps	*13.2*		17	Whites Crossing	-3.6
18	Dillingham Airport	10.8		18	Nome Municipal Airport	-2.3
19	Anchorage Int'l Airport	9.4		19	Bethel Airport	-0.1
20	Intricate Bay	8.6		20	Talkeetna State Airport	1.9
21	King Salmon Airport	8.2		21	Kenai Municipal Airport	5.3
22	Wasilla 3 S	6.8		21	Matanuska AES	5.3
23	Palmer IAS	6.4		23	Port Alsworth	6.1
24	Port Alsworth	6.1		24	Palmer IAS	6.4
25	Kenai Municipal Airport	5.3		25	Wasilla 3 S	6.8

Number of Annual Heating Degree Days

	Highest				Lowest	
Rank	**Station Name**	**Num.**		**Rank**	**Station Name**	**Num.**
1	Barrow W. Post-W. Rogers Airport	19,942		1	Annette Island Airport	6,826
2	Kotzebue Ralph Wein Memorial	15,645		2	Sitka Japonski Airport	7,240
3	Bettles Field	15,454		3	Beaver Falls	*7,304*
3	Northway Airport	15,454		4	Little Port Walter	7,733
5	Snowshoe Lake	15,069		5	Auke Bay	8,237
6	Tanana R.M. Calhoun Mem. Arpt.	14,556		6	Juneau Int'l Airport	8,512
7	North Pole	14,420		7	Kodiak State USCG Base	8,582
8	McGrath Airport	14,115		8	Kitoi Bay	9,079
9	Eielson Field	13,956		9	Seward	9,094
10	Nome Municipal Airport	13,916		10	Yakutat State Airport	9,145
11	Tonsina	13,909		11	Cordova	9,400
12	Fairbanks Int'l Airport	13,663		12	Valdez WSO	*9,547*
13	Gulkana Intermediate Field	13,620		13	Cold Bay Airport	9,610
14	University Exp. Station	13,503		14	Homer Airport	9,765
15	College Observatory	13,480		15	Cooper Lake Project	9,959
16	Old Edgerton	*13,298*		16	Wasilla 3 S	10,275
17	Big Delta Allen AAF	13,297		17	Anchorage Int'l Airport	10,353
18	Bethel Airport	12,849		18	Palmer IAS	10,574
19	Whites Crossing	11,943		19	Matanuska AES	10,609
20	Glen Alps	*11,477*		20	Intricate Bay	10,747
21	Talkeetna State Airport	11,311		21	Port Alsworth	10,879
22	Dillingham Airport	*11,271*		22	Saint Paul Island Airport	10,914
23	Kenai Municipal Airport	11,155		23	King Salmon Airport	11,124
24	King Salmon Airport	11,124		24	Kenai Municipal Airport	11,155
25	Saint Paul Island Airport	10,914		25	Dillingham Airport	*11,271*

Number of Annual Cooling Degree Days

	Highest			Lowest	
Rank	**Station Name**	**Num.**	**Rank**	**Station Name**	**Num.**
1	Fairbanks Int'l Airport	80	1	Barrow W. Post-W. Rogers Airport	0
2	College Observatory	65	1	Cold Bay Airport	0
3	University Exp. Station	55	1	Glen Alps	0
4	Eielson Field	53	1	Homer Airport	0
5	Bettles Field	47	1	Kenai Municipal Airport	0
6	Tanana R.M. Calhoun Mem. Arpt.	44	1	Little Port Walter	0
7	Big Delta Allen AAF	*35*	1	Saint Paul Island Airport	0
7	North Pole	35	1	Snowshoe Lake	0
9	McGrath Airport	23	1	Yakutat State Airport	0
10	Annette Island Airport	19	10	Cooper Lake Project	1
11	Beaver Falls	*17*	10	Cordova	1
12	Northway Airport	15	10	Dillingham Airport	1
13	Whites Crossing	10	10	Intricate Bay	1
14	Auke Bay	9	10	King Salmon Airport	1
14	Talkeetna State Airport	9	10	Sitka Japonski Airport	1
16	Seward	8	10	Tonsina	1
17	Gulkana Intermediate Field	6	17	Anchorage Int'l Airport	2
18	Kotzebue Ralph Wein Memorial	5	17	Bethel Airport	2
19	Old Edgerton	*4*	17	Kitoi Bay	2
19	Port Alsworth	4	17	Palmer IAS	2
19	Wasilla 3 S	4	17	Valdez WSO	2
22	Juneau Int'l Airport	3	22	Juneau Int'l Airport	3
22	Kodiak State USCG Base	3	22	Kodiak State USCG Base	3
22	Matanuska AES	3	22	Matanuska AES	3
22	Nome Municipal Airport	3	22	Nome Municipal Airport	3

Annual Precipitation

	Highest			Lowest	
Rank	**Station Name**	**Inches**	**Rank**	**Station Name**	**Inches**
1	Little Port Walter	226.75	1	Barrow W. Post-W. Rogers Airport	4.03
2	Yakutat State Airport	157.46	2	Northway Airport	9.18
3	Beaver Falls	147.90	3	Kotzebue Ralph Wein Memorial	9.87
4	Annette Island Airport	100.65	4	Fairbanks Int'l Airport	10.51
5	Cordova	96.84	5	North Pole	10.78
6	Sitka Japonski Airport	85.84	6	Old Edgerton	*11.00*
7	Kodiak State USCG Base	76.41	7	Gulkana Intermediate Field	11.33
8	Seward	71.09	8	Eielson Field	11.57
9	Valdez WSO	*69.02*	9	College Observatory	11.83
10	Kitoi Bay	66.64	10	Big Delta Allen AAF	11.96
11	Auke Bay	63.88	11	Snowshoe Lake	12.04
12	Juneau Int'l Airport	58.04	12	University Exp. Station	12.18
13	Cold Bay Airport	39.01	13	Tonsina	12.38
14	Intricate Bay	35.27	14	Tanana R.M. Calhoun Mem. Arpt.	12.48
15	Cooper Lake Project	31.33	15	Port Alsworth	13.30
16	Talkeetna State Airport	28.53	16	Bettles Field	13.88
17	Glen Alps	*27.30*	17	Matanuska AES	14.94
18	Dillingham Airport	*25.76*	18	Palmer IAS	15.55
19	Homer Airport	25.29	19	Anchorage Int'l Airport	16.02
20	Saint Paul Island Airport	22.96	20	Bethel Airport	16.05
21	Whites Crossing	22.10	21	Nome Municipal Airport	16.21
22	King Salmon Airport	19.38	22	Wasilla 3 S	16.82
23	Kenai Municipal Airport	19.06	23	McGrath Airport	17.49
24	McGrath Airport	17.49	24	Kenai Municipal Airport	19.06
25	Wasilla 3 S	16.82	25	King Salmon Airport	19.38

Number of Days Annually With ≥ 0.1″ Precipitation

	Highest			Lowest	
Rank	Station Name	Days	Rank	Station Name	Days
1	Little Port Walter	202	1	Barrow W. Post-W. Rogers Airport	11
2	Yakutat State Airport	187	2	Northway Airport	29
3	Beaver Falls	175	3	Kotzebue Ralph Wein Memorial	31
4	Annette Island Airport	169	4	Fairbanks Int'l Airport	32
5	Sitka Japonski Airport	165	4	North Pole	32
6	Cordova	159	6	Old Edgerton	*33*
7	Auke Bay	*149*	7	Eielson Field	35
8	Juneau Int'l Airport	143	8	Big Delta Allen AAF	36
9	Kitoi Bay	140	8	Gulkana Intermediate Field	36
10	Valdez WSO	*133*	8	Snowshoe Lake	36
11	Kodiak State USCG Base	130	11	University Exp. Station	37
12	Seward	115	12	College Observatory	38
13	Cold Bay Airport	106	13	Tonsina	39
14	Intricate Bay	84	14	Tanana R.M. Calhoun Mem. Arpt.	40
15	Talkeetna State Airport	76	15	Port Alsworth	42
16	Glen Alps	*73*	16	Bettles Field	43
17	Homer Airport	72	17	Palmer IAS	47
18	Saint Paul Island Airport	70	18	Bethel Airport	48
19	Dillingham Airport	*66*	18	Matanuska AES	48
20	Cooper Lake Project	*62*	18	Nome Municipal Airport	48
20	King Salmon Airport	62	21	Anchorage Int'l Airport	49
22	Whites Crossing	57	22	Wasilla 3 S	*52*
23	Kenai Municipal Airport	55	23	McGrath Airport	53
24	McGrath Airport	53	24	Kenai Municipal Airport	55
25	Wasilla 3 S	*52*	25	Whites Crossing	57

Number of Days Annually With ≥ 1.0″ Precipitation

	Highest			Lowest	
Rank	Station Name	Days	Rank	Station Name	Days
1	Little Port Walter	79	1	Anchorage Int'l Airport	0
2	Yakutat State Airport	53	1	Barrow W. Post-W. Rogers Airport	0
3	Beaver Falls	47	1	Bethel Airport	0
4	Annette Island Airport	29	1	Bettles Field	0
5	Cordova	27	1	Big Delta Allen AAF	0
6	Seward	19	1	College Observatory	0
7	Kodiak State USCG Base	18	1	Eielson Field	0
7	Sitka Japonski Airport	18	1	Fairbanks Int'l Airport	0
9	Valdez WSO	*16*	1	Gulkana Intermediate Field	0
10	Kitoi Bay	13	1	Homer Airport	0
11	Auke Bay	9	1	Kenai Municipal Airport	0
12	Juneau Int'l Airport	7	1	King Salmon Airport	0
13	Cooper Lake Project	4	1	Kotzebue Ralph Wein Memorial	0
13	Intricate Bay	4	1	Matanuska AES	0
15	Cold Bay Airport	3	1	McGrath Airport	0
16	Dillingham Airport	*2*	1	Nome Municipal Airport	0
16	Talkeetna State Airport	2	1	North Pole	0
16	Whites Crossing	2	1	Northway Airport	0
19	Glen Alps	*1*	1	Old Edgerton	*0*
20	Anchorage Int'l Airport	0	1	Palmer IAS	0
20	Barrow W. Post-W. Rogers Airport	0	1	Port Alsworth	0
20	Bethel Airport	0	1	Saint Paul Island Airport	0
20	Bettles Field	0	1	Snowshoe Lake	0
20	Big Delta Allen AAF	0	1	Tanana R.M. Calhoun Mem. Arpt.	0
20	College Observatory	0	1	Tonsina	0

Annual Snowfall

	Highest			Lowest	
Rank	**Station Name**	**Inches**	**Rank**	**Station Name**	**Inches**
1	Valdez WSO	*327.8*	1	Barrow W. Post-W. Rogers Airport	28.1
2	Yakutat State Airport	178.5	2	Sitka Japonski Airport	37.3
3	Glen Alps	*169.4*	3	Northway Airport	38.7
4	Talkeetna State Airport	137.3	4	Annette Island Airport	43.7
5	Cordova	116.1	5	Tanana R.M. Calhoun Mem. Arpt.	46.3
6	Little Port Walter	109.7	6	King Salmon Airport	46.8
7	McGrath Airport	98.1	7	Kotzebue Ralph Wein Memorial	48.8
8	Juneau Int'l Airport	95.3	8	Old Edgerton	*49.0*
9	Dillingham Airport	*92.8*	9	Big Delta Allen AAF	*49.9*
10	Auke Bay	89.6	10	Matanuska AES	50.3
11	Bettles Field	88.3	11	Bethel Airport	51.6
12	Cooper Lake Project	88.2	12	University Exp. Station	51.7
13	Port Alsworth	*78.1*	13	Snowshoe Lake	53.1
14	Whites Crossing	*74.9*	14	North Pole	55.2
15	Seward	*74.8*	15	Wasilla 3 S	*56.4*
16	Eielson Field	74.7	16	Saint Paul Island Airport	56.8
17	Kodiak State USCG Base	72.3	17	Gulkana Intermediate Field	57.1
18	Cold Bay Airport	71.1	18	Homer Airport	60.5
19	Fairbanks Int'l Airport	70.7	18	Kenai Municipal Airport	60.5
19	Intricate Bay	70.7	20	Palmer IAS	62.2
21	Anchorage Int'l Airport	69.3	21	Beaver Falls	*64.4*
22	College Observatory	69.1	22	Tonsina	64.8
23	Kitoi Bay	66.9	23	Nome Municipal Airport	66.2
24	Nome Municipal Airport	66.2	24	Kitoi Bay	66.9
25	Tonsina	64.8	25	College Observatory	69.1

Note: See Appendix D for explanation of data.

Annual Extreme Maximum Temperature

	Highest				Lowest	
Rank	**Station Name**	**°F**		**Rank**	**Station Name**	**°F**
1	Bullhead City	*126*		1	Greer	90
1	Tacna 3 NE	126		2	Bright Angel Ranger Station	*91*
3	Buckeye	125		3	Flagstaff Pulliam Airport	97
3	Laveen 3 SSE	125		3	Springerville	97
3	Litchfield Park	125		5	Betatakin	98
3	Willow Beach	125		5	Blue Ridge Ranger Station	98
7	Alamo Dam	*124*		5	Fort Valley	98
7	Maricopa 4 N	124		5	Kitt Peak	98
7	Parker	124		5	McNary 2 N	98
7	Yuma Citrus Station	124		5	Show Low Municipal Airport	98
7	Yuma Int'l Airport	*124*		11	Sunset Crater Nat'l Monument	99
7	Yuma Proving Ground	124		12	Heber Ranger Station	100
13	Casa Grande Nat'l Monument	123		12	Williams	100
14	Bartlett Dam	122		14	Portal 4 SW	101
14	Gila Bend	122		14	Snowflake 15 W	101
14	Phoenix Sky Harbor Int'l Arpt.	122		16	Snowflake	102
14	Youngtown	122		16	Whiteriver 1 SW	102
18	Bouse	121		18	Black River Pumps	103
18	Wickenburg	121		18	Prescott	103
20	Beaver Dam	120		18	Saint Johns	103
20	Casa Grande	*120*		21	Canyon De Chelly	104
20	Castle Hot Springs	120		21	Jerome	104
20	Phantom Ranch	120		23	Chino Valley	105
20	Stewart Mountain	120		23	Coronado Nat'l Monument Hdqtrs.	105
20	Wahweap	120		23	Pleasant Valley Ranger Station	105

Annual Mean Maximum Temperature

	Highest				Lowest	
Rank	**Station Name**	**°F**		**Rank**	**Station Name**	**°F**
1	Gila Bend	89.2		1	Bright Angel Ranger Station	*55.9*
2	Buckeye	88.7		2	Greer	58.0
3	Bullhead City	*88.5*		3	Fort Valley	61.1
4	Litchfield Park	88.1		4	Flagstaff Pulliam Airport	61.3
5	Casa Grande Nat'l Monument	88.0		5	Betatakin	61.5
5	Yuma Int'l Airport	*88.0*		6	McNary 2 N	62.5
7	Parker	87.9		7	Sunset Crater Nat'l Monument	63.3
8	Tacna 3 NE	87.6		7	Williams	63.3
9	Yuma Proving Ground	87.5		9	Kitt Peak	64.8
10	Yuma Citrus Station	87.2		10	Springerville	65.3
11	Casa Grande	*86.8*		11	Show Low Municipal Airport	65.7
11	Maricopa 4 N	86.8		12	Snowflake 15 W	66.4
11	Tempe A S U	86.8		13	Teec Nos Pos	67.8
14	Youngtown	86.6		14	Black River Pumps	67.9
15	Willow Beach	86.5		15	Canyon De Chelly	68.7
16	Alamo Dam	*86.4*		16	Prescott	68.8
16	Bouse	86.4		16	Sanders	68.8
16	Eloy 4 NE	*86.4*		18	Colorado City	69.4
19	Laveen 3 SSE	86.3		18	Jerome	69.4
19	Organ Pipe Cactus Nat'l Mon.	86.3		20	Snowflake	69.6
19	Phoenix Sky Harbor Int'l Arpt.	86.3		21	Page	69.7
22	Florence	86.1		22	Saint Johns	69.8
23	South Phoenix	85.0		23	Winslow Municipal Airport	70.3
24	Bartlett Dam	84.8		24	Seligman	70.5
24	Chandler Heights	84.8		25	Petrified Forest Nat'l Park	70.6

Annual Mean Temperature

	Highest			Lowest	
Rank	Station Name	°F	Rank	Station Name	°F
1	Yuma Int'l Airport	*74.6*	1	Bright Angel Ranger Station	*42.9*
2	Bullhead City	*74.0*	2	Fort Valley	43.3
2	Yuma Proving Ground	74.0	3	Greer	44.1
4	Phoenix Sky Harbor Int'l Arpt.	73.9	4	Sunset Crater Nat'l Monument	45.8
5	Gila Bend	73.6	5	Flagstaff Pulliam Airport	46.1
6	Parker	73.0	6	McNary 2 N	47.6
7	Kofa Mine	*72.9*	7	Springerville	48.1
8	Willow Beach	72.3	8	Bctatakin	49.8
9	Youngtown	71.8	9	Williams	49.9
10	Buckeye	71.5	10	Show Low Municipal Airport	51.7
10	Yuma Citrus Station	71.5	11	Snowflake 15 W	51.8
12	Litchfield Park	71.3	12	Sanders	52.1
13	Laveen 3 SSE	71.2	13	Black River Pumps	52.3
13	Tempe A S U	71.2	14	Walnut Creek	52.7
15	Tucson NWSO	70.9	15	Snowflake	52.9
16	Alamo Dam	*70.6*	16	Canyon De Chelly	53.0
16	Bartlett Dam	70.6	17	Seligman	53.3
18	Casa Grande	*70.5*	18	Pleasant Valley Ranger Station	53.5
18	Florence	70.5	18	Saint Johns	53.5
20	Tacna 3 NE	70.4	20	Prescott	53.8
21	Organ Pipe Cactus Nat'l Mon.	70.3	21	Portal 4 SW	54.1
22	Bouse	70.2	22	Teec Nos Pos	54.6
23	Chandler Heights	70.1	23	Petrified Forest Nat'l Park	54.7
23	Eloy 4 NE	*70.1*	23	Pipe Springs Nat'l Monument	54.7
25	Casa Grande Nat'l Monument	69.9	25	Kitt Peak	55.1

Annual Mean Minimum Temperature

	Highest			Lowest	
Rank	Station Name	°F	Rank	Station Name	°F
1	Kofa Mine	*61.6*	1	Fort Valley	25.4
2	Phoenix Sky Harbor Int'l Arpt.	61.5	2	Sunset Crater Nat'l Monument	28.2
3	Yuma Int'l Airport	*61.2*	3	Bright Angel Ranger Station	*29.7*
4	Yuma Proving Ground	60.4	4	Greer	30.3
5	Bullhead City	*59.4*	5	Flagstaff Pulliam Airport	30.9
6	Superior	58.2	5	Springerville	30.9
7	Parker	58.1	7	McNary 2 N	32.6
7	Willow Beach	58.1	8	Walnut Creek	34.6
9	Gila Bend	58.0	9	Pleasant Valley Ranger Station	35.2
9	Tucson NWSO	58.0	10	Sanders	35.4
11	Youngtown	57.0	11	Seligman	36.1
12	Bartlett Dam	56.4	11	Snowflake	36.1
13	Laveen 3 SSE	56.1	13	Williams	36.4
14	Phantom Ranch	56.0	14	Black River Pumps	36.7
15	Castle Hot Springs	55.7	15	Saint Johns	37.1
15	Yuma Citrus Station	55.7	16	Snowflake 15 W	37.2
17	Tempe A S U	55.6	17	Canyon De Chelly	37.3
18	Chandler Heights	55.4	18	Portal 4 SW	37.4
19	Tucson Int'l Airport	54.9	19	Show Low Municipal Airport	37.6
20	Alamo Dam	*54.8*	20	Betatakin	38.1
20	Florence	54.8	21	Pipe Springs Nat'l Monument	38.4
22	Roosevelt 1 WNW	54.7	22	Petrified Forest Nat'l Park	38.7
23	Litchfield Park	54.5	23	Payson	38.8
23	South Phoenix	54.5	23	Prescott	38.8
25	Buckeye	54.3	25	Hillside 4 NNE	39.6

Annual Extreme Minimum Temperature

	Highest				Lowest	
Rank	**Station Name**	**°F**		**Rank**	**Station Name**	**°F**
1	Kofa Mine	*25*		1	Fort Valley	-33
1	Yuma Citrus Station	25		2	Saint Johns	-29
3	Yuma Proving Ground	23		2	Snowflake	-29
4	Yuma Valley	*22*		4	Sunset Crater Nat'l Monument	-28
5	Bartlett Dam	21		5	Petrified Forest Nat'l Park	-27
5	Roosevelt 1 WNW	21		6	Show Low Municipal Airport	-25
5	Tempe A S U	21		6	Snowflake 15 W	-25
5	Willow Beach	21		6	Springerville	-25
9	Youngtown	20		9	Canyon De Chelly	-24
10	Alamo Dam	*19*		9	Greer	-24
10	Organ Pipe Cactus Nat'l Mon.	19		9	Heber Ranger Station	-24
10	Phoenix Sky Harbor Int'l Arpt.	19		12	Bright Angel Ranger Station	*-23*
10	Superior	19		12	Flagstaff Pulliam Airport	-23
10	Tucson NWSO	19		12	Sanders	-23
15	Litchfield Park	18		15	Blue Ridge Ranger Station	-22
16	Castle Hot Springs	17		15	Pleasant Valley Ranger Station	-22
16	Gila Bend	17		17	Black River Pumps	-20
16	Parker	17		18	McNary 2 N	-19
16	Stewart Mountain	17		19	Teec Nos Pos	-18
20	Laveen 3 SSE	16		20	Walnut Creek	-15
20	South Phoenix	16		20	Winslow Municipal Airport	-15
20	Tucson Int'l Airport	16		22	Betatakin	-14
23	Casa Grande	*15*		23	Pipe Springs Nat'l Monument	-13
23	Tucson Magnetic Observatory	*15*		23	Williams	-13
25	Chandler Heights	14		25	Seligman	-12

July Mean Maximum Temperature

	Highest				Lowest	
Rank	**Station Name**	**°F**		**Rank**	**Station Name**	**°F**
1	Bullhead City	*111.6*		1	Greer	75.4
2	Willow Beach	110.4		2	Bright Angel Ranger Station	77.0
3	Gila Bend	109.0		3	Kitt Peak	81.0
4	Buckeye	108.9		3	McNary 2 N	81.0
5	Parker	108.3		5	Fort Valley	81.3
6	Litchfield Park	108.0		6	Flagstaff Pulliam Airport	82.2
7	Bouse	107.8		6	Springerville	82.2
8	Casa Grande Nat'l Monument	107.7		8	Blue Ridge Ranger Station	82.8
9	Alamo Dam	*107.5*		9	Williams	82.9
10	Maricopa 4 N	107.0		10	Sunset Crater Nat'l Monument	84.3
10	Yuma Int'l Airport	107.0		11	Heber Ranger Station	84.6
12	Yuma Proving Ground	106.5		12	Betatakin	85.1
13	Tacna 3 NE	106.1		13	Show Low Municipal Airport	85.8
14	Casa Grande	106.0		14	Portal 4 SW	86.2
14	Phoenix Sky Harbor Int'l Arpt.	106.0		15	Black River Pumps	87.3
16	Youngtown	105.9		16	Snowflake 15 W	87.5
17	Phantom Ranch	105.8		17	Prescott	88.3
17	Yuma Citrus Station	105.8		18	Chiricahua Nat'l Monument	88.7
19	Beaver Dam	*105.6*		19	Canelo 1 NW	88.9
20	Tempe A S U	105.5		20	Whiteriver 1 SW	89.3
21	Laveen 3 SSE	105.4		21	Saint Johns	89.7
22	Wikieup	*105.0*		22	Coronado Nat'l Monument Hdqtrs.	89.8
22	Yuma Valley	*105.0*		23	Snowflake	89.9
24	Bartlett Dam	104.9		24	Pleasant Valley Ranger Station	90.3
24	Florence	104.9		25	Jerome	90.5

January Mean Minimum Temperature

	Highest			Lowest	
Rank	Station Name	°F	Rank	Station Name	°F
1	Kofa Mine	46.3	1	Fort Valley	10.9
2	Yuma Int'l Airport	45.3	2	Sunset Crater Nat'l Monument	12.5
3	Ajo	*44.6*	3	Greer	15.7
4	Phoenix Sky Harbor Int'l Arpt.	43.6	4	Springerville	15.9
5	Yuma Proving Ground	43.5	5	Bright Angel Ranger Station	16.2
6	Bullhead City	*43.1*	6	Flagstaff Pulliam Airport	16.4
7	Superior	42.4	7	McNary 2 N	18.2
8	Tucson NWSO	41.7	8	Sanders	18.4
9	Bartlett Dam	40.5	9	Canyon De Chelly	18.6
9	Gila Bend	40.5	10	Saint Johns	19.4
11	Parker	40.3	11	Snowflake	19.7
12	Castle Hot Springs	40.2	12	Snowflake 15 W	19.8
12	Yuma Citrus Station	40.2	13	Show Low Municipal Airport	20.5
12	Yuma Valley	*40.2*	14	Betatakin	20.6
15	Youngtown	39.9	15	Black River Pumps	20.7
16	Tempe A S U	39.2	16	Teec Nos Pos	21.0
17	Organ Pipe Cactus Nat'l Mon.	39.1	17	Petrified Forest Nat'l Park	21.1
17	Willow Beach	39.1	17	Winslow Municipal Airport	21.1
19	South Phoenix	39.0	19	Pleasant Valley Ranger Station	21.2
19	Tucson Int'l Airport	39.0	20	Walnut Creek	21.3
21	Laveen 3 SSE	38.9	21	Pipe Springs Nat'l Monument	21.6
22	Chandler Heights	38.7	22	Seligman	22.3
23	Florence	38.6	22	Williams	22.3
24	Roosevelt 1 WNW	37.7	24	Prescott	23.0
25	Litchfield Park	37.6	25	Portal 4 SW	23.2

Number of Annual Heating Degree Days

	Highest			Lowest	
Rank	Station Name	Num.	Rank	Station Name	Num.
1	Bright Angel Ranger Station	*8,013*	1	Yuma Int'l Airport	*791*
2	Fort Valley	7,863	2	Yuma Proving Ground	905
3	Greer	7,531	3	Kofa Mine	1,009
4	Sunset Crater Nat'l Monument	7,062	4	Phoenix Sky Harbor Int'l Arpt.	1,019
5	Flagstaff Pulliam Airport	6,925	5	Gila Bend	1,039
6	McNary 2 N	6,380	6	Bullhead City	*1,085*
7	Springerville	6,205	7	Parker	1,120
8	Betatakin	5,978	8	Yuma Citrus Station	1,186
9	Williams	5,717	9	Tucson NWSO	1,238
10	Snowflake 15 W	5,337	10	Youngtown	1,243
11	Show Low Municipal Airport	5,303	11	Organ Pipe Cactus Nat'l Mon.	1,260
12	Sanders	5,273	12	Tempe A S U	1,276
13	Canyon De Chelly	5,143	13	Buckeye	1,287
14	Black River Pumps	5,089	14	Laveen 3 SSE	1,338
15	Snowflake	4,987	15	Litchfield Park	1,347
16	Walnut Creek	4,939	16	South Phoenix	1,364
17	Teec Nos Pos	4,899	17	Bartlett Dam	1,380
18	Saint Johns	4,849	18	Willow Beach	1,402
19	Seligman	4,802	19	Florence	1,404
20	Pleasant Valley Ranger Station	4,688	20	Castle Hot Springs	1,429
21	Prescott	4,683	21	Tacna 3 NE	1,435
22	Pipe Springs Nat'l Monument	4,666	22	Casa Grande	*1,452*
23	Winslow Municipal Airport	4,644	23	Eloy 4 NE	*1,461*
24	Petrified Forest Nat'l Park	4,638	24	Chandler Heights	1,497
25	Colorado City	4,532	25	Tucson Int'l Airport	1,545

Number of Annual Cooling Degree Days

	Highest			Lowest	
Rank	Station Name	Num.	Rank	Station Name	Num.
1	Yuma Int'l Airport	4,623	1	Greer	15
2	Phoenix Sky Harbor Int'l Arpt.	4,556	2	Bright Angel Ranger Station	26
3	Bullhead City	4,517	3	Fort Valley	39
4	Yuma Proving Ground	4,384	4	McNary 2 N	109
5	Gila Bend	4,363	5	Flagstaff Pulliam Airport	134
6	Willow Beach	4,185	6	Springerville	145
7	Parker	4,175	7	Sunset Crater Nat'l Monument	146
8	Kofa Mine	4,063	8	Williams	296
9	Youngtown	3,992	9	Portal 4 SW	489
10	Tempe A S U	3,887	10	Betatakin	538
11	Litchfield Park	3,869	11	Show Low Municipal Airport	570
12	Buckeye	3,810	12	Walnut Creek	573
13	Laveen 3 SSE	3,792	13	Black River Pumps	592
14	Yuma Citrus Station	3,752	14	Pleasant Valley Ranger Station	614
15	Alamo Dam	3,742	15	Snowflake 15 W	636
16	Bouse	3,690	16	Kitt Peak	645
17	Casa Grande	3,656	17	Snowflake	686
17	Tacna 3 NE	3,656	18	Seligman	699
19	Maricopa 4 N	3,610	19	Sanders	705
20	Chandler Heights	3,607	20	Saint Johns	734
21	Tucson NWSO	3,587	21	Prescott	765
22	Casa Grande Nat'l Monument	3,569	22	Payson	930
23	Bartlett Dam	3,553	23	Canyon De Chelly	941
24	Florence	3,519	24	Petrified Forest Nat'l Park	991
25	Phantom Ranch	3,408	25	Canelo 1 NW	998

Annual Precipitation

	Highest			Lowest	
Rank	Station Name	Inches	Rank	Station Name	Inches
1	McNary 2 N	28.34	1	Yuma Valley	3.15
2	Bright Angel Ranger Station	26.05	2	Yuma Int'l Airport	3.34
3	Oracle 2 SE	24.79	3	Yuma Proving Ground	3.87
4	Kitt Peak	24.07	4	Yuma Citrus Station	3.92
5	Flagstaff Pulliam Airport	23.22	5	Tacna 3 NE	4.30
6	Santa Rita Exp. Range	23.21	6	Parker	5.25
7	Greer	22.99	7	Willow Beach	5.65
8	Fort Valley	22.34	8	Bouse	5.95
9	Payson	22.22	9	Bullhead City	6.72
10	Pleasant Valley Ranger Station	22.05	10	Page	6.75
11	Williams	21.41	11	Wahweap	6.78
12	Portal 4 SW	21.37	12	Gila Bend	7.03
13	Coronado Nat'l Monument Hdqtrs.	20.76	13	Kofa Mine	7.30
14	Blue Ridge Ranger Station	20.56	14	Beaver Dam	7.76
15	Chiricahua Nat'l Monument	20.55	15	Maricopa 4 N	7.86
16	Superior	20.36	16	Ajo	7.91
17	Jerome	19.83	17	Winslow Municipal Airport	7.97
18	Black River Pumps	19.75	18	Buckeye	8.13
19	Whiteriver 1 SW	19.69	19	Yucca 1 NNE	8.14
20	Childs	19.48	20	Teec Nos Pos	8.16
21	Prescott	19.31	21	Phoenix Sky Harbor Int'l Arpt.	8.29
22	Miami	19.29	22	Laveen 3 SSE	8.56
23	Sedona Ranger Station	19.16	23	Litchfield Park	8.76
24	Heber Ranger Station	19.00	24	Wupatki Nat'l Monument	8.98
25	Nogales 6 N	18.52	25	South Phoenix	9.02

Number of Days Annually With ≥ 0.1″ Precipitation

	Highest			Lowest	
Rank	**Station Name**	**Days**	**Rank**	**Station Name**	**Days**
1	Greer	60	1	Yuma Valley	*6*
1	McNary 2 N	60	2	Yuma Citrus Station	7
3	Black River Pumps	51	2	Yuma Int'l Airport	*7*
4	Bright Angel Ranger Station	*50*	2	Yuma Proving Ground	7
4	Flagstaff Pulliam Airport	50	5	Tacna 3 NE	11
6	Pleasant Valley Ranger Station	48	6	Parker	13
6	Portal 4 SW	48	7	Bouse	14
6	Williams	48	7	Willow Beach	14
9	Fort Valley	46	9	Kofa Mine	15
9	Oracle 2 SE	46	10	Ajo	16
11	Payson	44	10	Bullhead City	*16*
11	Santa Rita Exp. Range	44	12	Buckeye	17
13	Chiricahua Nat'l Monument	43	12	Gila Bend	17
13	Coronado Nat'l Monument Hdqtrs.	43	12	Litchfield Park	17
15	Jerome	42	15	Yucca 1 NNE	18
15	Sunset Crater Nat'l Monument	42	16	Maricopa 4 N	19
17	Blue Ridge Ranger Station	41	16	Phoenix Sky Harbor Int'l Arpt.	19
17	Childs	41	18	Casa Grande	20
17	Kitt Peak	41	18	Organ Pipe Cactus Nat'l Mon.	20
17	Nogales 6 N	41	18	Page	20
17	Show Low Municipal Airport	41	18	Wahweap	20
22	Whiteriver 1 SW	40	18	Youngtown	20
23	Canelo 1 NW	39	23	Alamo Dam	*21*
23	Miami	39	23	Laveen 3 SSE	21
23	Prescott	39	23	South Phoenix	21

Number of Days Annually With ≥ 1.0″ Precipitation

	Highest			Lowest	
Rank	**Station Name**	**Days**	**Rank**	**Station Name**	**Days**
1	Oracle 2 SE	8	1	Ajo	0
2	McNary 2 N	6	1	Alamo Dam	*0*
3	Superior	5	1	Anvil Ranch	0
4	Jerome	4	1	Beaver Creek Ranger Station	0
4	Kitt Peak	4	1	Beaver Dam	0
6	Bright Angel Ranger Station	*3*	1	Betatakin	0
6	Castle Hot Springs	3	1	Bouse	0
6	Flagstaff Pulliam Airport	3	1	Bowie	0
6	Heber Ranger Station	3	1	Buckeye	0
6	Hillside 4 NNE	3	1	Bullhead City	*0*
6	Payson	3	1	Canyon De Chelly	0
6	Pleasant Valley Ranger Station	3	1	Casa Grande Nat'l Monument	0
6	Santa Rita Exp. Range	3	1	Chandler Heights	0
14	Blue Ridge Ranger Station	2	1	Chino Valley	0
14	Canelo 1 NW	2	1	Clifton	0
14	Childs	2	1	Colorado City	0
14	Chiricahua Nat'l Monument	2	1	Duncan	0
14	Coronado Nat'l Monument Hdqtrs.	2	1	Eloy 4 NE	0
14	Douglas	*2*	1	Florence	0
14	Douglas Bisbee-Douglas Int'l	2	1	Fort Thomas 2 SW	0
14	Greer	2	1	Gila Bend	0
14	Miami	2	1	Kingman 2	*0*
14	Nogales 6 N	2	1	Kofa Mine	0
14	Portal 4 SW	2	1	Laveen 3 SSE	0
14	Prescott	2	1	Litchfield Park	0

Annual Snowfall

	Highest			Lowest	
Rank	**Station Name**	**Inches**	**Rank**	**Station Name**	**Inches**
1	Bright Angel Ranger Station	*147.1*	1	Bouse	0.0
2	Flagstaff Pulliam Airport	*111.1*	1	Buckeye	0.0
3	McNary 2 N	*87.6*	1	Bullhead City	*0.0*
4	Fort Valley	79.3	1	Casa Grande Nat'l Monument	0.0
5	Williams	72.8	1	Chandler Heights	0.0
6	Sunset Crater Nat'l Monument	*65.0*	1	Gila Bend	0.0
7	Betatakin	*53.7*	1	Laveen 3 SSE	0.0
8	Blue Ridge Ranger Station	*52.8*	1	Litchfield Park	0.0
9	Heber Ranger Station	*36.9*	1	Parker	0.0
10	Show Low Municipal Airport	28.3	1	South Phoenix	0.0
11	Payson	24.8	1	Yuma Citrus Station	0.0
12	Colorado City	22.2	1	Yuma Valley	*0.0*
13	Prescott	20.0	13	Ajo	Trace
14	Kitt Peak	17.3	13	Bartlett Dam	Trace
15	Snowflake 15 W	*16.5*	13	Casa Grande	Trace
16	Snowflake	16.1	13	Clifton	*Trace*
17	Saint Johns	13.7	13	Douglas	*Trace*
18	Whiteriver 1 SW	13.3	13	Eloy 4 NE	Trace
19	Oracle 2 SE	12.4	13	Florence	Trace
20	Winslow Municipal Airport	10.4	13	Kofa Mine	Trace
21	Jerome	9.9	13	Maricopa 4 N	Trace
22	Pipe Springs Nat'l Monument	8.9	13	Organ Pipe Cactus Nat'l Mon.	Trace
23	Chiricahua Nat'l Monument	8.1	13	Phoenix Sky Harbor Int'l Arpt.	Trace
24	Seligman	8.0	13	Roosevelt 1 WNW	Trace
25	Black River Pumps	7.5	13	Stewart Mountain	Trace

Note: *See Appendix D for explanation of data.*

Annual Extreme Maximum Temperature

	Highest				Lowest	
Rank	**Station Name**	**°F**		**Rank**	**Station Name**	**°F**
1	Hot Springs 1 NNE	115		1	Deer	*102*
2	Alicia	113		2	Bentonville 4 S	105
3	Batesville Lock & Dam 1	112		2	Brinkley Airport	105
3	Beedeville 4 NE	112		2	Camden 1	105
3	Benton	112		2	Crossett 2 SSE	105
3	Blue Mountain Dam	112		2	Eudora	105
3	Cabot 4 SW	112		2	Keo	105
3	Little Rock Adams Field	112		2	Rohwer 2 NNE	105
9	Batesville Livestock	111		2	Stuttgart 9 ESE	105
9	Blakely Mountain Dam	111		10	Arkadelphia 2 N	106
9	Calico Rock 2 WSW	111		10	Arkansas Post	106
9	Conway	111		10	Clarendon	*106*
9	Gilbert	111		10	Keiser	106
9	Greenbrier	*111*		10	Marianna 2 S	106
9	Greers Ferry Dam	111		10	Portland	*106*
9	Waldron	111		10	Warren 2 WSW	106
17	Alum Fork	110		10	West Memphis	106
17	Dardanelle	110		10	Wynne	106
17	Eureka Springs 3 WNW	110		19	Dermott 3 NE	107
17	Lead Hill	110		19	Dumas	107
17	Malvern	110		19	Fayetteville Exp. Station	107
17	Mammoth Spring	110		19	Harrison FAA Airport	107
17	Mountain View	110		19	Helena	107
17	Nimrod Dam	110		19	Jonesboro 4 N	107
17	North Little Rock Airport	*110*		19	Mena	107

Annual Mean Maximum Temperature

	Highest				Lowest	
Rank	**Station Name**	**°F**		**Rank**	**Station Name**	**°F**
1	Portland	*75.6*		1	Deer	*63.7*
2	El Dorado Goodwin Field	75.0		2	Bentonville 4 S	67.8
3	Magnolia 3 N	74.9		3	Harrison FAA Airport	68.0
4	Crossett 2 SSE	74.5		4	Fayetteville Exp. Station	68.5
4	Dequeen	74.5		5	Mountain Home 1 NNW	69.5
4	Prescott	74.5		6	Gravette	69.9
7	Camden 1	74.4		7	Keiser	70.0
7	Dumas	74.4		8	Newport	70.2
7	Eudora	74.4		9	Jonesboro 4 N	70.3
10	Dermott 3 NE	74.3		9	Pocahontas 1	70.3
11	Arkadelphia 2 N	74.2		11	Corning	70.4
11	Benton	74.2		11	Mammoth Spring	70.4
11	Waldron	74.2		13	Blytheville	70.5
14	Malvern	74.0		13	Mountain View	70.5
15	Hot Springs 1 NNE	73.6		15	Mena	70.7
16	Arkansas Post	73.5		16	Greers Ferry Dam	70.8
16	Warren 2 WSW	73.5		17	Brinkley Airport	71.1
18	Hope 3 NE	73.4		17	Lead Hill	71.1
18	Monticello 3 SW	73.4		19	Batesville Lock & Dam 1	71.2
20	Conway	73.3		20	Nimrod Dam	71.3
20	Pine Bluff	73.3		20	North Little Rock Airport	*71.3*
22	Searcy	73.2		22	Beedeville 4 NE	71.4
23	Alum Fork	73.1		22	Calico Rock 2 WSW	71.4
23	Dardanelle	73.1		24	Cabot 4 SW	71.6
23	Rohwer 2 NNE	73.1		24	Stuttgart 9 ESE	71.6

Annual Mean Temperature

	Highest			Lowest	
Rank	**Station Name**	**°F**	**Rank**	**Station Name**	**°F**
1	Portland	*64.1*	1	Deer	*54.4*
2	Dumas	63.7	2	Bentonville 4 S	56.3
2	Eudora	63.7	3	Mammoth Spring	57.6
4	El Dorado Goodwin Field	63.6	4	Fayetteville Exp. Station	57.8
5	Arkansas Post	63.3	4	Harrison FAA Airport	57.8
5	Magnolia 3 N	63.3	6	Calico Rock 2 WSW	58.0
7	Prescott	63.2	6	Mountain Home 1 NNW	58.0
8	Dermott 3 NE	63.1	8	Gravette	58.3
9	Pine Bluff	62.6	9	Gilbert	58.4
10	Camden 1	62.4	9	Lead Hill	58.4
11	Arkadelphia 2 N	62.3	11	Mountain View	58.5
11	Rohwer 2 NNE	62.3	12	Evening Shade 1 NNE	58.8
13	Little Rock Adams Field	62.2	12	Mount Ida 3 SE	58.8
14	Dequeen	62.1	14	Greers Ferry Dam	59.0
15	Des Arc	62.0	15	Clarksville	*59.2*
15	Keo	62.0	16	Nimrod Dam	59.3
15	Monticello 3 SW	62.0	17	Blakely Mountain Dam	*59.4*
15	North Little Rock Airport	*62.0*	17	Mena	59.4
15	Warren 2 WSW	62.0	17	Pocahontas 1	59.4
20	Benton	61.9	20	Keiser	59.6
20	Conway	61.9	21	Corning	59.7
22	Crossett 2 SSE	61.8	22	Batesville Lock & Dam 1	59.8
22	Hot Springs 1 NNE	61.8	23	Greenbrier	*59.9*
22	Saint Charles	*61.8*	24	Jonesboro 4 N	60.1
25	Alum Fork	61.7	25	Blue Mountain Dam	60.2

Annual Mean Minimum Temperature

	Highest			Lowest	
Rank	**Station Name**	**°F**	**Rank**	**Station Name**	**°F**
1	Arkansas Post	53.0	1	Gilbert	44.3
1	Dumas	53.0	2	Calico Rock 2 WSW	44.5
3	Eudora	52.9	3	Bentonville 4 S	44.7
4	North Little Rock Airport	*52.5*	4	Mammoth Spring	44.8
5	Portland	*52.4*	5	Deer	*45.0*
6	El Dorado Goodwin Field	52.1	6	Evening Shade 1 NNE	45.5
6	Keo	52.1	7	Lead Hill	45.7
8	Dermott 3 NE	51.9	8	Mount Ida 3 SE	45.8
8	Prescott	51.9	9	Mountain Home 1 NNW	46.4
10	Pine Bluff	51.8	10	Blakely Mountain Dam	*46.5*
11	Little Rock Adams Field	51.7	10	Clarksville	*46.5*
12	Des Arc	51.6	10	Mountain View	46.5
12	Magnolia 3 N	51.6	13	Gravette	46.6
12	Stuttgart 9 ESE	51.6	14	Fayetteville Exp. Station	47.1
15	Rohwer 2 NNE	51.4	14	Greers Ferry Dam	47.1
16	West Memphis	51.3	16	Nimrod Dam	47.3
17	Blytheville	51.1	17	Harrison FAA Airport	47.5
17	Helena	51.1	18	Greenbrier	*47.7*
19	Clarendon	*50.9*	19	Mena	48.0
19	Saint Charles	*50.9*	19	Waldron	48.0
21	Marianna 2 S	50.8	21	Batesville Lock & Dam 1	48.3
22	Nashville	50.6	21	Pocahontas 1	48.3
23	Monticello 3 SW	50.5	23	Murfreesboro 5 SW	48.4
23	Wynne	50.5	24	Batesville Livestock	48.6
25	Arkadelphia 2 N	50.4	24	Blue Mountain Dam	48.6

Annual Extreme Minimum Temperature

	Highest				Lowest	
Rank	Station Name	°F		Rank	Station Name	°F
1	Eudora	3		1	Deer	*-20*
2	Arkansas Post	1		2	Gilbert	-18
2	Camden 1	1		3	Mammoth Spring	-17
2	Dermott 3 NE	1		3	Newport	-17
2	Dumas	1		5	Bentonville 4 S	-16
2	El Dorado Goodwin Field	1		5	Gravette	-16
2	Hope 3 NE	1		7	Calico Rock 2 WSW	-15
2	Pine Bluff	1		7	Eureka Springs 3 WNW	-15
9	Arkadelphia 2 N	0		7	Evening Shade 1 NNE	-15
9	Blakely Mountain Dam	0		7	Lead Hill	-15
9	Crossett 2 SSE	0		7	Pocahontas 1	-15
9	Portland	*0*		12	Blytheville	-14
9	Prescott	0		12	Mountain Home 1 NNW	-14
9	Rohwer 2 NNE	0		14	Corning	-13
9	Warren 2 WSW	0		14	Fayetteville Exp. Station	-13
16	Keo	-2		14	Harrison FAA Airport	-13
16	Leola	*-2*		17	Mountain View	-12
16	Little Rock Adams Field	-2		18	Batesville Livestock	-11
16	Malvern	-2		18	Batesville Lock & Dam 1	-11
16	Murfreesboro 5 SW	-2		18	Clarksville	*-11*
16	Saint Charles	-2		18	Jonesboro 4 N	-11
22	Alum Fork	-3		22	Alicia	-10
22	Benton	-3		22	Fort Smith Regional Airport	-10
22	Blue Mountain Dam	-3		24	Keiser	-9
22	Dequeen	-3		24	Waldron	-9

July Mean Maximum Temperature

	Highest				Lowest	
Rank	Station Name	°F		Rank	Station Name	°F
1	Hot Springs 1 NNE	94.3		1	Deer	*83.8*
2	Searcy	93.7		2	Bentonville 4 S	88.9
2	Waldron	93.7		3	Harrison FAA Airport	89.0
4	Alicia	93.6		4	Fayetteville Exp. Station	89.4
5	Dermott 3 NE	93.5		5	Mena	90.0
6	Evening Shade 1 NNE	93.3		6	Eureka Springs 3 WNW	90.5
7	Blue Mountain Dam	93.2		7	Mountain Home 1 NNW	90.8
7	Conway	93.2		8	Cabot 4 SW	91.0
7	Dardanelle	93.2		8	Keo	91.0
7	Dequeen	93.2		10	Gravette	91.2
7	Subiaco	93.2		10	Murfreesboro 5 SW	91.2
12	Malvern	93.1		12	Brinkley Airport	91.4
12	Portland	93.1		12	Stuttgart 9 ESE	91.4
14	Batesville Lock & Dam 1	93.0		12	West Memphis	91.4
14	Benton	93.0		15	Keiser	91.5
16	Arkadelphia 2 N	92.9		16	Clarendon	*91.6*
16	Beedeville 4 NE	92.9		16	Mammoth Spring	91.6
16	Des Arc	92.9		18	Greers Ferry Dam	91.7
16	Fort Smith Regional Airport	92.9		18	Helena	91.7
20	Batesville Livestock	92.8		18	Monticello 3 SW	91.7
20	Prescott	92.8		18	Mount Ida 3 SE	91.7
22	Calico Rock 2 WSW	92.7		18	Mountain View	91.7
22	Clarksville	*92.7*		23	Jonesboro 4 N	91.8
22	Dumas	92.7		23	Marianna 2 S	91.8
22	Little Rock Adams Field	92.7		23	Nashville	91.8

January Mean Minimum Temperature

	Highest			Lowest	
Rank	Station Name	°F	Rank	Station Name	°F
1	Dumas	33.0	1	Bentonville 4 S	22.0
2	Eudora	32.9	1	Deer	*22.0*
3	El Dorado Goodwin Field	32.7	3	Mammoth Spring	22.4
3	Magnolia 3 N	32.7	4	Gilbert	23.2
5	Arkansas Post	32.5	5	Calico Rock 2 WSW	23.9
6	Portland	32.1	6	Lead Hill	24.0
6	Prescott	32.1	6	Mountain Home 1 NNW	24.0
8	Dermott 3 NE	31.9	8	Clarksville	*24.1*
9	Keo	31.3	8	Evening Shade 1 NNE	24.1
9	Rohwer 2 NNE	31.3	10	Mountain View	24.3
11	Clarendon	*31.1*	11	Fayetteville Exp. Station	24.4
11	Pine Bluff	31.1	11	Gravette	24.4
13	Arkadelphia 2 N	30.5	13	Greers Ferry Dam	25.2
13	Little Rock Adams Field	30.5	14	Harrison FAA Airport	25.3
13	North Little Rock Airport	*30.5*	14	Mount Ida 3 SE	25.3
16	Des Arc	30.4	16	Eureka Springs 3 WNW	25.9
17	Stuttgart 9 ESE	30.3	16	Nimrod Dam	25.9
17	Warren 2 WSW	30.3	18	Pocahontas 1	26.0
19	Camden 1	30.2	19	Batesville Lock & Dam 1	26.4
19	Leola	30.2	20	Blakely Mountain Dam	26.5
21	Monticello 3 SW	30.1	20	Corning	26.5
21	Nashville	30.1	22	Waldron	26.6
23	Alum Fork	29.9	23	Fort Smith Regional Airport	26.8
23	Saint Charles	29.9	24	Blue Mountain Dam	27.2
25	Crossett 2 SSE	29.8	25	Batesville Livestock	27.3

Number of Annual Heating Degree Days

	Highest			Lowest	
Rank	Station Name	Num.	Rank	Station Name	Num.
1	Deer	*4,765*	1	Portland	*2,528*
2	Bentonville 4 S	4,394	2	El Dorado Goodwin Field	2,611
3	Mammoth Spring	4,051	3	Magnolia 3 N	2,614
4	Fayetteville Exp. Station	4,027	4	Dumas	2,623
5	Harrison FAA Airport	3,990	5	Eudora	2,667
6	Mountain Home 1 NNW	3,984	6	Prescott	2,691
7	Calico Rock 2 WSW	3,905	7	Arkansas Post	2,723
8	Mountain View	3,893	8	Dermott 3 NE	2,822
9	Gravette	3,891	9	Arkadelphia 2 N	2,876
10	Lead Hill	3,857	10	Camden 1	2,888
11	Gilbert	3,793	11	Pine Bluff	2,927
12	Greers Ferry Dam	3,757	12	Crossett 2 SSE	2,953
13	Evening Shade 1 NNE	3,754	13	Benton	2,961
14	Clarksville	*3,738*	14	Warren 2 WSW	2,966
15	Mount Ida 3 SE	3,732	15	Monticello 3 SW	2,973
16	Pocahontas 1	3,709	16	Rohwer 2 NNE	2,974
17	Keiser	3,692	17	Dequeen	2,978
18	Corning	3,664	18	Malvern	2,994
19	Nimrod Dam	3,626	19	Keo	3,010
20	Batesville Lock & Dam 1	3,606	20	Alum Fork	3,016
21	Newport	3,561	21	Nashville	3,034
22	Jonesboro 4 N	3,560	22	Little Rock Adams Field	3,045
23	Blakely Mountain Dam	*3,539*	23	Clarendon	*3,077*
24	Mena	3,511	24	Conway	3,085
25	Blue Mountain Dam	3,493	25	Des Arc	3,089

Number of Annual Cooling Degree Days

	Highest			Lowest	
Rank	Station Name	Num.	Rank	Station Name	Num.
1	Portland	2,382	1	Deer	1,027
2	Eudora	2,323	2	Bentonville 4 S	1,343
3	Dermott 3 NE	2,322	3	Calico Rock 2 WSW	1,461
4	Dumas	2,261	4	Mammoth Spring	1,465
5	El Dorado Goodwin Field	2,244	5	Lead Hill	1,510
6	Arkansas Post	2,224	6	Harrison FAA Airport	1,514
7	Little Rock Adams Field	2,186	7	Gilbert	1,519
8	Helena	2,167	7	Mena	1,519
9	Magnolia 3 N	2,158	9	Fayetteville Exp. Station	1,534
10	Pine Bluff	2,146	10	Mountain Home 1 NNW	1,541
11	North Little Rock Airport	2,143	11	Gravette	1,563
12	Rohwer 2 NNE	2,138	12	Mount Ida 3 SE	1,586
13	Prescott	2,135	13	Blakely Mountain Dam	*1,612*
14	Des Arc	*2,130*	14	Evening Shade 1 NNE	1,655
15	Saint Charles	*2,126*	15	Mountain View	1,682
16	Stuttgart 9 ESE	2,094	16	Greenbrier	1,699
17	Searcy	2,093	17	Murfreesboro 5 SW	1,712
18	Conway	2,092	18	Nimrod Dam	1,727
18	Hot Springs 1 NNE	2,092	19	Greers Ferry Dam	1,729
20	Blytheville	2,072	20	Cabot 4 SW	1,765
21	Keo	2,061	21	Pocahontas 1	1,771
22	Camden 1	2,045	22	Batesville Lock & Dam 1	1,817
23	Fort Smith Regional Airport	2,036	23	Crossett 2 SSE	*1,842*
24	Arkadelphia 2 N	2,029	24	Waldron	*1,848*
25	Alicia	2,025	25	Keiser	1,875

Annual Precipitation

	Highest			Lowest	
Rank	Station Name	Inches	Rank	Station Name	Inches
1	Mena	58.51	1	Fort Smith Regional Airport	43.92
2	Mount Ida 3 SE	58.07	2	Lead Hill	44.62
3	Crossett 2 SSE	57.94	3	Mammoth Spring	44.92
4	Hot Springs 1 NNE	57.58	4	Gilbert	45.24
5	Portland	57.44	5	Mountain Home 1 NNW	45.35
6	Blakely Mountain Dam	56.85	6	Harrison FAA Airport	45.45
7	Murfreesboro 5 SW	56.59	7	Alicia	45.74
8	Eudora	56.58	8	Fayetteville Exp. Station	45.79
9	Malvern	56.42	9	Eureka Springs 3 WNW	46.28
10	Prescott	56.11	10	Calico Rock 2 WSW	46.31
11	Alum Fork	55.41	11	Subiaco	46.65
12	Monticello 3 SW	55.26	12	Jonesboro 4 N	46.73
13	Warren 2 WSW	55.22	13	Bentonville 4 S	47.07
14	Dequeen	54.93	14	Blue Mountain Dam	47.11
15	Hope 3 NE	54.56	15	Batesville Livestock	47.21
16	Deer	*54.49*	16	Gravette	47.30
17	Helena	54.22	17	Keo	47.69
18	Nashville	54.17	18	Corning	47.98
19	Dermott 3 NE	54.11	19	Clarksville	*48.18*
20	El Dorado Goodwin Field	54.09	20	Batesville Lock & Dam 1	48.31
21	Leola	*54.01*	21	Wynne	48.67
22	Benton	53.66	22	Evening Shade 1 NNE	48.78
23	Arkadelphia 2 N	53.41	23	Beedeville 4 NE	48.84
24	Pine Bluff	53.33	24	Pocahontas 1	48.97
25	Marianna 2 S	53.23	25	Conway	49.13

Number of Days Annually With ≥ 0.1″ Precipitation

	Highest			Lowest	
Rank	**Station Name**	**Days**	**Rank**	**Station Name**	**Days**
1	Hot Springs 1 NNE	78	1	Beedeville 4 NE	60
2	West Memphis	77	2	Saint Charles	63
3	Alum Fork	76	3	Fort Smith Regional Airport	65
3	Deer	*76*	4	Alicia	67
3	Dermott 3 NE	76	4	Arkansas Post	67
3	Mena	76	4	Batesville Livestock	67
3	Mount Ida 3 SE	76	4	Dumas	67
8	Crossett 2 SSE	75	8	Gravette	68
8	Evening Shade 1 NNE	75	8	Mammoth Spring	68
8	Keiser	75	8	Stuttgart 9 ESE	68
8	Pine Bluff	75	11	Arkadelphia 2 N	69
8	Prescott	75	11	Blakely Mountain Dam	69
13	Blytheville	74	11	Des Arc	*69*
13	Camden 1	74	11	Fayetteville Exp. Station	69
13	Malvern	74	11	Greenbrier	*69*
13	Marianna 2 S	74	11	Keo	69
13	Monticello 3 SW	74	17	Benton	70
13	Murfreesboro 5 SW	74	17	Blue Mountain Dam	70
19	Cabot 4 SW	73	17	Helena	70
19	Clarksville	*73*	17	Jonesboro 4 N	70
19	Corning	73	17	Leola	*70*
19	Little Rock Adams Field	73	17	Mountain Home 1 NNW	70
19	Newport	73	17	Nimrod Dam	70
19	Warren 2 WSW	73	17	North Little Rock Airport	*70*
25	Batesville Lock & Dam 1	72	17	Portland	*70*

Number of Days Annually With ≥ 1.0″ Precipitation

	Highest			Lowest	
Rank	**Station Name**	**Days**	**Rank**	**Station Name**	**Days**
1	Crossett 2 SSE	21	1	Batesville Livestock	13
2	Arkansas Post	19	1	Corning	13
2	Benton	19	1	Eureka Springs 3 WNW	13
2	Dequeen	19	1	Lead Hill	13
2	Dumas	19	1	Mammoth Spring	13
2	Eudora	19	1	Mountain Home 1 NNW	13
2	Hope 3 NE	19	7	Alicia	14
2	Hot Springs 1 NNE	19	7	Blue Mountain Dam	14
2	Malvern	19	7	Blytheville	14
2	Mount Ida 3 SE	19	7	Evening Shade 1 NNE	14
2	Nashville	19	7	Fayetteville Exp. Station	14
2	Portland	19	7	Fort Smith Regional Airport	14
2	Prescott	19	7	Gilbert	14
2	Rohwer 2 NNE	19	7	Harrison FAA Airport	14
2	Warren 2 WSW	19	7	Keo	14
16	Alum Fork	18	7	Mountain View	14
16	Blakely Mountain Dam	18	7	Newport	14
16	Camden 1	18	7	Stuttgart 9 ESE	14
16	Dermott 3 NE	18	7	Subiaco	14
16	El Dorado Goodwin Field	18	20	Bentonville 4 S	15
16	Greenbrier	*18*	20	Clarksville	*15*
16	Helena	18	20	Dardanelle	15
16	Mena	18	20	Des Arc	*15*
16	Monticello 3 SW	18	20	Jonesboro 4 N	15
16	Murfreesboro 5 SW	18	20	Keiser	15

Annual Snowfall

	Highest			Lowest	
Rank	**Station Name**	**Inches**	**Rank**	**Station Name**	**Inches**
1	Gravette	16.2	1	Eudora	Trace
2	Eureka Springs 3 WNW	14.9	1	Rohwer 2 NNE	Trace
3	Deer	*13.9*	3	Monticello 3 SW	0.7
4	Harrison FAA Airport	13.5	4	Crossett 2 SSE	0.8
5	Mountain Home 1 NNW	11.4	5	Clarendon	*1.0*
6	Bentonville 4 S	*10.4*	6	El Dorado Goodwin Field	1.1
7	Pocahontas 1	10.1	6	Helena	*1.1*
8	Corning	9.9	8	Dequeen	*1.2*
9	Evening Shade 1 NNE	*9.6*	8	Keiser	*1.2*
10	Batesville Livestock	7.6	10	Stuttgart 9 ESE	*1.3*
10	Waldron	7.6	10	Warren 2 WSW	*1.3*
12	Batesville Lock & Dam 1	7.2	12	Camden 1	1.6
13	Fort Smith Regional Airport	6.6	13	Dermott 3 NE	1.7
14	Gilbert	6.5	14	Blakely Mountain Dam	*1.8*
15	Fayetteville Exp. Station	6.3	14	West Memphis	*1.8*
16	North Little Rock Airport	*5.9*	16	Hot Springs 1 NNE	*1.9*
17	Calico Rock 2 WSW	*5.7*	16	Marianna 2 S	*1.9*
18	Mammoth Spring	*5.4*	16	Pine Bluff	*1.9*
19	Mountain View	*5.3*	16	Saint Charles	*1.9*
20	Newport	*5.2*	20	Arkadelphia 2 N	2.0
21	Jonesboro 4 N	5.1	20	Dumas	2.0
22	Blue Mountain Dam	4.9	20	Magnolia 3 N	2.0
22	Mount Ida 3 SE	4.9	23	Des Arc	*2.1*
24	Cabot 4 SW	4.7	23	Hope 3 NE	*2.1*
25	Alicia	*4.6*	23	Murfreesboro 5 SW	*2.1*

Note: See Appendix D for explanation of data.

Annual Extreme Maximum Temperature

	Highest				Lowest	
Rank	Station Name	°F		Rank	Station Name	°F
1	Death Valley	129		1	Eureka	87
2	Gold Rock Ranch	*127*		2	Huntington Lake	88
3	Mecca Fire Station	126		3	Grant Grove	90
3	Palm Springs Thermal Airport	126		4	Bodie	91
5	Blythe Riverside Co. Airport	123		4	Lodgepole	91
5	Palm Springs	123		4	Tahoe City	91
5	Parker Reservoir	123		7	Crescent City 3 NNW	93
8	Blythe	122		7	Fort Ross	93
8	Borrego Desert Park	122		9	Big Bear Lake	94
8	El Centro 2 SSW	122		9	Fort Bragg 5 N	94
8	Iron Mountain	122		9	Half Moon Bay	94
12	Brawley 2 SW	121		9	Klamath	94
12	Imperial	121		13	Twin Lakes	95
12	Needles Airport	121		14	Manzanita Lake	96
15	Eagle Mountain	120		15	Bowman Dam	98
15	Henshaw Dam	120		15	Bridgeport	98
17	Hayfield Pumping Plant	119		15	Orick Prairie Creek Park	98
17	Inyokern	119		15	Scotia	98
17	Willow Creek 1 NW	119		19	Boca	99
20	Daggett Barstow-Daggett Airport	118		19	Donner Memorial State Park	99
20	Trona	118		19	Mount Wilson 2	99
22	Chico University Farm	117		19	San Gregorio 2 SE	99
22	Orland	117		19	Santa Monica Pier	99
22	San Bernardino Co. Hospital	117		19	Tahoe Valley FAA Airport	99
22	Twentynine Palms	117		19	Truckee Ranger Station	99

Annual Mean Maximum Temperature

	Highest				Lowest	
Rank	Station Name	°F		Rank	Station Name	°F
1	Death Valley	90.6		1	Twin Lakes	*52.6*
2	Mecca Fire Station	89.9		2	Lodgepole	54.8
3	Palm Springs	88.9		3	Bodie	56.3
4	Palm Springs Thermal Airport	88.4		3	Grant Grove	56.3
5	El Centro 2 SSW	88.3		5	Huntington Lake	56.8
6	Brawley 2 SW	88.1		5	Tahoe City	56.8
7	Blythe	87.8		7	Manzanita Lake	57.6
8	Imperial	87.7		8	Tahoe Valley FAA Airport	58.1
9	Blythe Riverside Co. Airport	87.6		9	Mineral	58.5
9	Gold Rock Ranch	*87.6*		10	Donner Memorial State Park	58.6
11	Borrego Desert Park	87.5		11	Eureka	59.2
12	Iron Mountain	86.5		12	Truckee Ranger Station	59.3
13	Needles Airport	86.3		13	Jess Valley	60.0
14	Parker Reservoir	86.0		14	Termo 1 E	60.1
15	Eagle Mountain	84.5		15	Bowman Dam	*60.2*
16	Hayfield Pumping Plant	84.3		16	Crescent City 3 NNW	60.5
17	Twentynine Palms	84.0		17	Calaveras Big Trees	60.7
18	Daggett Barstow-Daggett Airport	81.6		17	Yosemite Nat'l Park S. Entrance	60.7
19	Canoga Park Pierce College	81.1		19	Canyon Dam	60.9
19	Trona	81.1		20	Fort Bragg 5 N	61.0
21	Inyokern	80.8		20	Klamath	61.0
22	Elsinore	*80.7*		22	Cedarville	61.1
23	Riverside Fire Station 3	80.2		23	Boca	61.6
24	San Bernardino Co. Hospital	79.7		24	Fort Bidwell	61.7
25	Redlands	79.2		24	Lake Spaulding	61.7

Annual Mean Temperature

	Highest				Lowest	
Rank	Station Name	°F		Rank	Station Name	°F
1	Death Valley	76.3		1	Bodie	37.8
2	Gold Rock Ranch	*74.4*		2	Twin Lakes	*40.7*
3	Parker Reservoir	74.0		3	Lodgepole	41.6
4	Eagle Mountain	73.8		4	Donner Memorial State Park	42.9
4	Palm Springs	73.8		4	Tahoe Valley FAA Airport	42.9
6	Iron Mountain	73.7		6	Boca	43.0
7	Needles Airport	73.6		7	Bridgeport	43.4
8	Blythe Riverside Co. Airport	73.5		8	Tahoe City	43.8
9	Imperial	73.4		8	Truckee Ranger Station	43.8
10	Borrego Desert Park	72.7		10	Termo 1 E	44.2
10	El Centro 2 SSW	72.7		11	Manzanita Lake	44.5
10	Mecca Fire Station	72.7		12	Mineral	44.8
13	Palm Springs Thermal Airport	72.2		13	Jess Valley	45.7
14	Blythe	72.1		14	Huntington Lake	45.8
15	Brawley 2 SW	72.0		15	Alturas	46.0
16	Hayfield Pumping Plant	69.8		16	Grant Grove	46.6
17	Daggett Barstow-Daggett Airport	68.0		17	Chester	46.7
18	Twentynine Palms	67.9		18	Big Bear Lake	47.2
19	Trona	67.8		19	Burney	*47.3*
20	Los Angeles Civic Center	66.6		20	Canyon Dam	47.5
21	Riverside Fire Station 3	65.7		21	Lake Spaulding	47.8
21	San Bernardino Co. Hospital	65.7		22	Fort Bidwell	47.9
23	Bakersfield Meadows Field	65.6		23	Cedarville	48.2
23	San Gabriel Fire Dept.	65.6		24	Yosemite Nat'l Park S. Entrance	48.4
25	Pasadena	65.4		25	Bowman Dam	*48.9*

Annual Mean Minimum Temperature

	Highest				Lowest	
Rank	Station Name	°F		Rank	Station Name	°F
1	Eagle Mountain	63.0		1	Bodie	19.4
2	Death Valley	62.0		2	Bridgeport	24.2
2	Parker Reservoir	62.0		3	Boca	24.4
4	Gold Rock Ranch	*61.0*		4	Donner Memorial State Park	27.1
5	Needles Airport	60.9		5	Tahoe Valley FAA Airport	27.7
6	Iron Mountain	60.8		6	Termo 1 E	28.2
7	Blythe Riverside Co. Airport	59.4		6	Truckee Ranger Station	28.2
8	Imperial	59.0		8	Lodgepole	28.4
9	Palm Springs	58.8		9	Twin Lakes	*28.8*
10	San Diego Lindbergh Field	58.0		10	Alturas	29.4
11	Borrego Desert Park	57.9		11	Burney	*29.5*
12	Los Angeles Civic Center	57.5		12	Tahoe City	30.8
13	El Centro 2 SSW	57.1		13	Mineral	30.9
14	Blythe	56.3		14	Chester	31.3
14	Santa Monica Pier	*56.3*		15	Jess Valley	31.4
16	Los Angeles Int'l Airport	56.1		16	Manzanita Lake	31.5
17	Palm Springs Thermal Airport	56.0		17	Big Bear Lake	32.2
18	Brawley 2 SW	55.8		18	Lake Spaulding	33.8
19	Newport Beach	55.6		19	Canyon Dam	34.0
20	Mecca Fire Station	55.4		19	Fort Bidwell	34.0
20	U.C.L.A.	55.4		21	Hat Creek	34.2
22	Hayfield Pumping Plant	55.2		22	Huntington Lake	34.6
22	Long Beach Daugherty Field	55.2		23	Doyle 4 SSE	34.9
24	Chula Vista	54.8		24	McCloud	35.0
24	Santa Ana Fire Station	54.8		25	Cedarville	35.3

Annual Extreme Minimum Temperature

	Highest				Lowest	
Rank	**Station Name**	**°F**		**Rank**	**Station Name**	**°F**
1	Santa Monica Pier	34		1	Boca	-43
2	Los Angeles Int'l Airport	33		2	Termo 1 E	-40
2	San Diego Lindbergh Field	33		3	Alturas	-34
2	U.C.L.A.	33		4	Bodie	-33
5	Los Angeles Civic Center	30		5	Bridgeport	-31
5	Newport Beach	30		6	Tahoe Valley FAA Airport	-29
5	Oxnard	30		7	Cedarville	-28
5	Santa Ana Fire Station	30		7	Jess Valley	-28
9	Chula Vista	28		9	Donner Memorial State Park	-27
9	Long Beach Daugherty Field	28		10	Adin Ranger Station	-26
11	Laguna Beach	27		10	Burney	*-26*
11	Oceanside Marina	27		10	Fort Bidwell	-26
11	Torrance Municipal Airport	27		13	Big Bear Lake	-25
14	Tustin Irvine Ranch	26		13	Doyle 4 SSE	-25
15	Eagle Mountain	25		15	Truckee Ranger Station	-22
15	Parker Reservoir	25		16	Hat Creek	*-20*
15	Santa Paula	25		17	Twin Lakes	-17
18	Berkeley	*24*		18	Chester	-16
18	Richmond	24		18	Lodgepole	-16
18	Salinas Municipal Airport	24		18	Tahoe City	-16
18	Salinas 2	24		21	Canyon Dam	-14
18	San Francisco Int'l Airport	24		21	Lake Spaulding	-14
18	San Gabriel Fire Dept.	24		23	Manzanita Lake	-13
24	Palm Springs	23		23	Mount Shasta	-13
24	Pasadena	23		25	McCloud	-12

July Mean Maximum Temperature

	Highest				Lowest	
Rank	**Station Name**	**°F**		**Rank**	**Station Name**	**°F**
1	Death Valley	115.2		1	Eureka	62.8
2	Needles Airport	108.7		2	Half Moon Bay	64.4
3	Mecca Fire Station	108.5		3	Crescent City 3 NNW	65.5
4	Blythe	108.4		3	Morro Bay Fire Dept.	65.5
4	Blythe Riverside Co. Airport	108.4		5	Fort Bragg 5 N	66.1
6	Iron Mountain	108.3		6	Fort Ross	66.4
6	Palm Springs	108.3		7	Klamath	66.7
8	Parker Reservoir	107.5		8	San Francisco Mission	67.6
9	Gold Rock Ranch	*107.3*		9	Monterey	68.6
10	Borrego Desert Park	107.2		10	Orick Prairie Creek Park	68.9
11	El Centro 2 SSW	107.1		11	Scotia	69.0
12	Brawley 2 SW	106.8		12	Santa Monica Pier	69.5
13	Palm Springs Thermal Airport	106.5		13	San Gregorio 2 SE	69.6
14	Imperial	106.2		14	Berkeley	*70.6*
15	Twentynine Palms	105.8		15	Salinas Municipal Airport	71.2
16	Trona	104.8		16	Salinas 2	71.4
17	Eagle Mountain	104.6		17	Richmond	71.6
18	Daggett Barstow-Daggett Airport	104.4		18	Newport Beach	71.7
19	Hayfield Pumping Plant	104.1		18	Watsonville Waterworks	71.7
20	Inyokern	102.8		20	Twin Lakes	71.9
21	Three Rivers Edison 1	99.5		21	San Francisco Int'l Airport	72.0
22	Friant Government Camp	99.2		22	Oceanside Marina	72.3
23	Coalinga	99.1		23	Santa Maria Public Airport	73.5
24	Wasco	98.9		24	Huntington Lake	73.8
25	Bakersfield Meadows Field	98.2		25	Chula Vista	74.2

January Mean Minimum Temperature

	Highest			Lowest	
Rank	Station Name	°F	Rank	Station Name	°F
1	Santa Monica Pier	50.3	1	Bodie	5.9
2	U.C.L.A.	50.2	2	Bridgeport	9.1
3	San Diego Lindbergh Field	49.7	3	Boca	10.8
4	Los Angeles Civic Center	49.5	4	Donner Memorial State Park	14.4
5	Los Angeles Int'l Airport	48.6	5	Termo 1 E	14.9
6	Newport Beach	48.1	6	Lodgepole	15.7
7	Santa Ana Fire Station	46.6	7	Truckee Ranger Station	15.8
8	San Francisco Mission	46.4	8	Tahoe Valley FAA Airport	16.2
9	Torrance Municipal Airport	46.2	9	Alturas	17.1
10	Gold Rock Ranch	*46.1*	10	Twin Lakes	18.1
11	Long Beach Daugherty Field	45.9	11	Burney	*18.2*
12	Chula Vista	45.7	12	Jess Valley	19.4
13	Eagle Mountain	45.4	13	Tahoe City	19.8
13	Oxnard	45.4	14	Chester	19.9
15	Oceanside Marina	44.8	15	Cedarville	20.1
16	Berkeley	44.3	16	Fort Bidwell	20.3
16	Vista 2 NNE	44.3	17	Big Bear Lake	20.7
18	Pasadena	44.1	18	Manzanita Lake	21.2
19	Monterey	43.9	19	Mineral	21.8
19	Palm Springs	43.9	20	Bishop Airport	22.4
21	Borrego Desert Park	43.6	21	Hat Creek	22.6
22	Half Moon Bay	43.3	22	Doyle 4 SSE	22.9
22	Iron Mountain	43.3	23	Canyon Dam	23.0
24	Parker Reservoir	43.0	24	Lake Spaulding	24.4
25	San Francisco Int'l Airport	42.9	25	McCloud	24.5

Number of Annual Heating Degree Days

	Highest			Lowest	
Rank	Station Name	Num.	Rank	Station Name	Num.
1	Bodie	9,821	1	Gold Rock Ranch	*826*
2	Twin Lakes	*8,784*	2	Palm Springs	836
3	Lodgepole	8,456	3	Imperial	866
4	Donner Memorial State Park	8,014	4	Los Angeles Civic Center	892
5	Tahoe Valley FAA Airport	7,981	5	Borrego Desert Park	967
6	Boca	7,955	6	El Centro 2 SSW	978
7	Bridgeport	7,834	7	Eagle Mountain	992
8	Truckee Ranger Station	7,701	8	San Diego Lindbergh Field	1,018
9	Tahoe City	7,657	9	Santa Ana Fire Station	1,036
10	Termo 1 E	7,608	10	Mecca Fire Station	1,042
11	Manzanita Lake	7,444	11	Brawley 2 SW	1,067
12	Mineral	7,351	12	Blythe Riverside Co. Airport	1,078
13	Jess Valley	7,104	13	Palm Springs Thermal Airport	1,085
14	Alturas	7,001	14	Iron Mountain	1,097
15	Huntington Lake	6,959	15	Parker Reservoir	1,114
16	Grant Grove	6,746	16	Death Valley	1,145
17	Chester	6,715	17	Long Beach Daugherty Field	1,166
18	Burney	*6,533*	18	Needles Airport	1,179
19	Canyon Dam	6,501	19	San Gabriel Fire Dept.	1,204
20	Big Bear Lake	6,492	20	Blythe	1,227
21	Cedarville	6,475	21	Los Angeles Int'l Airport	1,231
22	Fort Bidwell	6,408	22	U.C.L.A.	1,262
23	Lake Spaulding	6,330	23	Pasadena	1,277
24	Yosemite Nat'l Park S. Entrance	6,139	24	Torrance Municipal Airport	1,330
25	Bowman Dam	*6,039*	25	Riverside Fire Station 3	1,414

Number of Annual Cooling Degree Days

	Highest			Lowest	
Rank	Station Name	Num.	Rank	Station Name	Num.
1	Death Valley	5,338	1	Bodie	2
2	Parker Reservoir	4,545	2	Eureka	5
3	Needles Airport	4,528	3	Fort Bragg 5 N	7
4	Gold Rock Ranch	*4,481*	4	Crescent City 3 NNW	8
5	Iron Mountain	4,434	4	Klamath	8
6	Blythe Riverside Co. Airport	4,368	6	Twin Lakes	*9*
7	Eagle Mountain	4,315	7	Fort Ross	*10*
8	Palm Springs	4,282	7	Orick Prairie Creek Park	*10*
9	Mecca Fire Station	4,052	9	Half Moon Bay	14
10	Imperial	4,047	10	Lodgepole	20
11	El Centro 2 SSW	4,021	11	San Gregorio 2 SE	27
12	Blythe	3,992	12	Scotia	29
13	Borrego Desert Park	3,933	13	Boca	30
14	Palm Springs Thermal Airport	3,883	14	Tahoe City	32
15	Brawley 2 SW	3,831	15	Tahoe Valley FAA Airport	33
16	Trona	3,395	16	Donner Memorial State Park	42
17	Hayfield Pumping Plant	3,308	17	Huntington Lake	43
18	Twentynine Palms	3,069	18	Bridgeport	47
19	Daggett Barstow-Daggett Airport	3,067	19	Mineral	56
20	Inyokern	2,330	20	Morro Bay Fire Dept.	59
21	Bakersfield Meadows Field	2,210	21	Big Bear Lake	71
22	Coalinga	2,160	22	Manzanita Lake	73
23	Porterville	2,129	23	Truckee Ranger Station	76
24	Fresno Air Terminal	2,106	24	Monterey	98
25	Ash Mountain	2,067	25	Termo 1 E	108

Annual Precipitation

	Highest			Lowest	
Rank	Station Name	Inches	Rank	Station Name	Inches
1	Strawberry Valley	81.72	1	Death Valley	2.38
2	Klamath	80.26	2	El Centro 2 SSW	2.96
3	Lake Spaulding	74.52	3	Imperial	3.06
4	Richardson Gr. State Park	69.56	4	Brawley 2 SW	3.17
5	Bowman Dam	68.62	5	Mecca Fire Station	3.38
6	De Sabla	67.62	6	Palm Springs Thermal Airport	3.65
7	Crescent City 3 NNW	67.00	7	Iron Mountain	3.81
8	Orick Prairie Creek Park	66.85	8	Blythe	4.06
9	Shasta Dam	64.12	9	Blythe Riverside Co. Airport	4.08
10	Whiskeytown Reservoir	63.78	10	Gold Rock Ranch	*4.10*
11	Nevada City	59.39	11	Daggett Barstow-Daggett Airport	4.22
12	Mineral	57.11	12	Trona	4.30
13	Paradise	56.51	13	Eagle Mountain	4.39
14	Calaveras Big Trees	55.66	14	Hayfield Pumping Plant	4.56
15	Willow Creek 1 NW	55.40	15	Twentynine Palms	4.59
16	Orleans	53.88	16	Inyokern	4.86
17	Grass Valley 2	53.31	17	Bishop Airport	5.05
18	Willits 1 NE	50.75	18	Palm Springs	5.20
19	McCloud	49.50	19	Needles Airport	5.21
20	Scotia	49.04	20	Independence	5.39
21	Kentfield	48.72	21	El Mirage	6.03
22	Ben Lomond 4	48.70	22	Victorville Pumping Plant	6.30
23	Colfax	48.40	23	Parker Reservoir	6.34
24	Twin Lakes	47.89	24	Buttonwillow	6.36
25	Tiger Creek	47.24	25	Bakersfield Meadows Field	6.51

Number of Days Annually With ≥ 0.1″ Precipitation

	Highest			Lowest	
Rank	**Station Name**	**Days**	**Rank**	**Station Name**	**Days**
1	Klamath	99	1	Death Valley	5
2	Orick Prairie Creek Park	*88*	2	Blythe Riverside Co. Airport	7
3	Richardson Gr. State Park	77	2	Brawley 2 SW	7
3	Scotia	77	2	El Centro 2 SSW	7
5	Orleans	76	2	Imperial	7
6	Eureka	74	2	Mecca Fire Station	7
6	Lake Spaulding	74	7	Blythe	*8*
6	Manzanita Lake	74	7	Gold Rock Ranch	*8*
9	Mineral	73	7	Palm Springs Thermal Airport	8
10	Strawberry Valley	72	10	Eagle Mountain	9
11	Fort Bragg 5 N	67	11	Inyokern	10
11	McCloud	67	11	Palm Springs	10
11	Willits 1 NE	*67*	11	Trona	10
14	Twin Lakes	66	11	Twentynine Palms	10
15	De Sabla	65	15	Hayfield Pumping Plant	11
15	Huntington Lake	*65*	15	Iron Mountain	11
15	Nevada City	65	17	Independence	12
15	Shasta Dam	65	18	Daggett Barstow-Daggett Airport	13
15	Whiskeytown Reservoir	65	18	Needles Airport	13
20	Bowman Dam	63	18	Parker Reservoir	13
21	Mount Shasta	62	21	Bishop Airport	14
22	Calaveras Big Trees	61	21	Randsburg	14
22	Paradise	61	23	Mojave	15
22	Potter Valley P H	61	23	Palmdale	15
22	Trinity River Hatchery	*61*	23	Victorville Pumping Plant	15

Number of Days Annually With ≥ 1.0″ Precipitation

	Highest			Lowest	
Rank	**Station Name**	**Days**	**Rank**	**Station Name**	**Days**
1	Strawberry Valley	29	1	Adin Ranger Station	0
2	Klamath	28	1	Alturas	0
3	Lake Spaulding	26	1	Antioch Pump Plant 3	0
4	De Sabla	23	1	Bakersfield Meadows Field	0
5	Richardson Gr. State Park	22	1	Bishop Airport	0
6	Shasta Dam	21	1	Blythe	0
6	Whiskeytown Reservoir	21	1	Blythe Riverside Co. Airport	0
8	Bowman Dam	20	1	Bodie	*0*
8	Nevada City	20	1	Borrego Desert Park	0
8	Orick Prairie Creek Park	*20*	1	Brawley 2 SW	0
11	Paradise	19	1	Bridgeport	0
12	Calaveras Big Trees	18	1	Buttonwillow	0
12	Willits 1 NE	18	1	Cedarville	0
14	Grass Valley 2	17	1	Chula Vista	0
14	Kentfield	17	1	Coalinga	0
16	Colfax	16	1	Corcoran Irrigation District	0
16	McCloud	16	1	Daggett Barstow-Daggett Airport	0
16	Mineral	16	1	Death Valley	0
16	Orleans	16	1	Eagle Mountain	0
20	Cherry Valley Dam	*15*	1	El Centro 2 SSW	0
20	Huntington Lake	*15*	1	El Mirage	0
20	Tiger Creek	15	1	Fort Bidwell	0
23	Ben Lomond 4	14	1	Fresno Air Terminal	0
23	Grant Grove	14	1	Gold Rock Ranch	*0*
23	Healdsburg	14	1	Haiwee	0

Annual Snowfall

	Highest				Lowest	
Rank	**Station Name**	**Inches**		**Rank**	**Station Name**	**Inches**
1	Twin Lakes	*394.8*		1	Blythe	0.0
2	Lake Spaulding	247.0		1	Brawley 2 SW	0.0
3	Lodgepole	237.5		1	Buttonwillow	0.0
4	Bowman Dam	228.2		1	Cachuma Lake	0.0
5	Truckee Ranger Station	203.4		1	El Centro 2 SSW	0.0
6	Donner Memorial State Park	188.8		1	Friant Government Camp	0.0
7	Grant Grove	186.9		1	Imperial	0.0
8	Manzanita Lake	180.2		1	Iron Mountain	0.0
9	Tahoe City	172.3		1	Laguna Beach	0.0
10	Mineral	141.9		1	Lemon Cove	0.0
11	Chester	126.0		1	Los Banos Det. Reservation	0.0
12	Calaveras Big Trees	114.8		1	Mecca Fire Station	0.0
13	Cherry Valley Dam	108.7		1	Newport Beach	0.0
14	Canyon Dam	106.3		1	Ojai	0.0
15	Strawberry Valley	99.8		1	Palo Alto	0.0
16	Boca	88.2		1	Riverside Fire Station 3	0.0
17	Mount Shasta	84.8		1	Salinas 2	0.0
18	Jess Valley	72.3		1	San Bernardino Co. Hospital	0.0
19	Big Bear Lake	*65.3*		1	San Gabriel Fire Dept.	0.0
20	McCloud	64.5		1	San Luis Obispo Polytech	0.0
21	Fort Bidwell	53.2		1	Santa Ana Fire Station	0.0
22	Adin Ranger Station	*45.1*		1	Santa Barbara Municipal Airport	*0.0*
23	Yosemite Nat'l Park HQ	*45.0*		1	Santa Monica Pier	0.0
24	Hetch Hetchy	*44.6*		1	Santa Paula	0.0
25	Bridgeport	*38.6*		1	Three Rivers Edison 1	*0.0*

Note: See Appendix D for explanation of data.

Annual Extreme Maximum Temperature

	Highest			Lowest	
Rank	Station Name	°F	Rank	Station Name	°F
1	Las Animas	112	1	Wolf Creek Pass 1 E	81
2	Springfield 7 WSW	111	2	Taylor Park	83
3	La Junta 4 NNE	*110*	3	Cabin Creek	84
3	Sterling	110	4	Climax	85
3	Uravan	110	4	Dillon 1 E	85
6	Holly	109	4	Sugarloaf Reservoir	85
6	Holyoke	109	7	Ruxton Park	86
6	Sedgwick 5 S	109	8	Grand Lake 6 SSW	87
6	Wray 2 E	*109*	9	Antero Reservoir	88
10	Cherry Creek Dam	108	9	Crested Butte	88
10	Kit Carson	*108*	9	Lake George 8 SW	88
10	Leroy 5 WSW	*108*	9	Silverton	*88*
10	Palisade	108	13	Rico	89
10	Pueblo Memorial Airport	108	14	Grant	90
10	Walsh 1 W	108	14	Hermit 7 ESE	90
16	Akron 4 E	*107*	14	Spicer	90
16	Cheyenne Wells	107	14	Yampa	90
16	Fort Morgan	107	18	Center 4 SSW	91
16	Lamar	107	18	Del Norte 2 E	91
16	Tacony 10 SE	107	18	Green Mountain Dam	91
21	Byers 5 ENE	106	18	Ouray	91
21	Fruita 1 W	106	22	Grand Lake 1 NW	92
21	Greeley	106	22	Gunnison 3 SW	92
21	Longmont 2 ESE	106	22	Vallecito Dam	92
21	Rocky Ford 2 SE	106	25	Blanca	93

Annual Mean Maximum Temperature

	Highest			Lowest	
Rank	Station Name	°F	Rank	Station Name	°F
1	Las Animas	70.8	1	Climax	43.2
2	Rocky Ford 2 SE	70.4	2	Wolf Creek Pass 1 E	*46.1*
3	La Junta 4 NNE	*69.2*	3	Cabin Creek	48.2
4	Holly	69.1	4	Taylor Park	48.7
5	Lamar	68.9	5	Sugarloaf Reservoir	*48.9*
5	Springfield 7 WSW	68.9	6	Ruxton Park	49.9
7	Uravan	68.8	7	Crested Butte	50.3
8	Pueblo Memorial Airport	68.7	8	Grand Lake 6 SSW	50.6
9	Walsh 1 W	68.1	9	Dillon 1 E	50.9
10	Tacony 10 SE	67.8	10	Spicer	51.1
10	Wray 2 E	*67.8*	11	Hermit 7 ESE	51.6
12	Palisade	67.4	12	Silverton	*52.3*
13	Trinidad Las Animas Co. Airport	67.1	13	Antero Reservoir	52.7
14	Trinidad	66.9	14	Walden	52.8
15	Cheyenne Wells	66.5	15	Grand Lake 1 NW	52.9
15	Walsenburg	66.5	16	Lake George 8 SW	53.1
17	Kit Carson	66.4	17	Grant	53.4
18	Fruita 1 W	66.3	18	Yampa	53.5
19	Grand Junction 6 ESE	65.7	19	Green Mountain Dam	53.6
19	Grand Junction Walker Field	65.7	20	Rico	54.9
21	Cherry Creek Dam	*65.6*	21	Gunnison 3 SW	55.2
22	Brighton 1 NE	*65.1*	21	Meredith	*55.2*
23	Kassler	64.9	23	Steamboat Springs	55.4
24	Paonia 1 SW	64.8	24	Lake City	55.7
25	Byers 5 ENE	64.7	25	Cochetopa Creek	55.9

Annual Mean Temperature

	Highest				Lowest	
Rank	**Station Name**	**°F**		**Rank**	**Station Name**	**°F**
1	Palisade	54.5		1	Climax	30.7
2	Las Animas	54.3		2	Taylor Park	32.0
3	La Junta 4 NNE	*54.1*		3	Wolf Creek Pass 1 E	*33.5*
4	Springfield 7 WSW	53.6		4	Hermit 7 ESE	33.8
5	Walsh 1 W	53.5		5	Crested Butte	33.9
6	Lamar	53.4		6	Sugarloaf Reservoir	*34.6*
6	Rocky Ford 2 SE	53.4		7	Silverton	*34.9*
8	Grand Junction 6 ESE	53.0		8	Dillon 1 E	35.5
8	Grand Junction Walker Field	53.0		9	Antero Reservoir	35.6
8	Holly	53.0		10	Ruxton Park	35.9
8	Uravan	53.0		11	Cabin Creek	36.1
12	Pueblo Memorial Airport	52.4		12	Grand Lake 6 SSW	36.3
13	Trinidad	52.1		13	Spicer	36.6
14	Trinidad Las Animas Co. Airport	51.9		14	Grand Lake 1 NW	36.8
15	Cheyenne Wells	51.8		15	Walden	37.4
15	Colorado National Monument	*51.8*		16	Gunnison 3 SW	37.8
15	Walsenburg	51.8		17	Cochetopa Creek	38.1
18	Tacony 10 SE	51.7		17	Lake George 8 SW	38.1
18	Wray 2 E	*51.7*		19	Meredith	*38.3*
20	Denver Stapleton Int'l Airport	50.7		20	Rico	38.6
21	Kit Carson	*50.4*		21	Lake City	38.9
22	Fruita 1 W	50.3		22	Grant	39.0
22	Sedgwick 5 S	50.3		23	Green Mountain Dam	39.2
24	Greeley	50.2		24	Steamboat Springs	39.3
25	Kassler	50.1		25	Yampa	39.4

Annual Mean Minimum Temperature

	Highest				Lowest	
Rank	**Station Name**	**°F**		**Rank**	**Station Name**	**°F**
1	Palisade	41.5		1	Taylor Park	15.2
2	Grand Junction Walker Field	40.2		2	Hermit 7 ESE	15.9
3	Grand Junction 6 ESE	40.1		3	Silverton	*17.4*
4	Colorado National Monument	*39.4*		4	Crested Butte	17.5
5	La Junta 4 NNE	*38.9*		5	Climax	18.1
6	Walsh 1 W	38.8		6	Antero Reservoir	18.5
7	Springfield 7 WSW	38.2		7	Dillon 1 E	20.1
8	Lamar	37.9		8	Cochetopa Creek	20.3
9	Las Animas	37.7		8	Gunnison 3 SW	20.3
10	Trinidad	37.2		8	Sugarloaf Reservoir	*20.3*
11	Uravan	37.1		11	Grand Lake 1 NW	20.7
12	Cheyenne Wells	37.0		12	Wolf Creek Pass 1 E	*20.9*
12	Walsenburg	37.0		13	Meredith	*21.3*
14	Denver Stapleton Int'l Airport	36.9		14	Ruxton Park	21.9
14	Holly	36.9		14	Walden	21.9
16	Trinidad Las Animas Co. Airport	36.5		16	Grand Lake 6 SSW	22.0
17	Sedgwick 5 S	36.4		16	Spicer	22.0
18	Rocky Ford 2 SE	36.3		18	Lake City	22.2
19	Lakewood	36.2		19	Rico	22.3
20	Pueblo Memorial Airport	36.0		20	Lake George 8 SW	23.0
21	Holyoke	35.9		21	Steamboat Springs	23.1
22	Akron Washington Co. Airport	*35.8*		22	Alamosa Bergman Field	23.4
22	Greeley	35.8		23	Center 4 SSW	23.5
22	Mesa Verde	35.8		24	Cimarron	23.7
25	Fort Collins	35.7		25	Cabin Creek	24.0

Annual Extreme Minimum Temperature

	Highest				Lowest	
Rank	Station Name	°F		Rank	Station Name	°F
1	Colorado National Monument	-12		1	Taylor Park	-60
1	Palisade	-12		2	Antero Reservoir	-51
3	Mesa Verde	-15		3	Spicer	-50
3	Uravan	-15		4	Crested Butte	-47
5	Grand Junction Walker Field	-18		4	Walden	-47
6	Ouray	-19		6	Green Mountain Dam	-46
7	Cedaredge	*-20*		7	Hermit 7 ESE	-45
7	Trinidad	-20		8	Hayden	-44
9	Grand Junction 6 ESE	-21		8	Steamboat Springs	-44
9	La Junta 4 NNE	*-21*		10	Lake George 8 SW	-43
9	Montrose 2	-21		11	Alamosa Bergman Field	-42
9	Yellow Jacket 2 W	-21		11	Grand Lake 6 SSW	-42
13	Lamar	-23		13	Browns Park Refuge	-41
13	Springfield 7 WSW	-23		13	Center 4 SSW	-41
15	Colorado Springs Muni Airport	-24		13	Westcliffe	-41
15	Great Sand Dunes Nat'l Monument	-24		16	Cochetopa Creek	-40
15	Trinidad Las Animas Co. Airport	-24		16	Gunnison 3 SW	-40
18	Akron Washington Co. Airport	*-25*		16	Wolf Creek Pass 1 E	-40
18	Buena Vista	-25		19	Silverton	*-39*
18	Denver Stapleton Int'l Airport	-25		20	Blanca	-38
18	Greeley	-25		20	Lake City	-38
18	Lakewood	-25		20	Meredith	-38
18	Leroy 5 WSW	*-25*		23	Grand Lake 1 NW	-37
18	Rocky Ford 2 SE	-25		23	Sugarloaf Reservoir	-37
18	Walsh 1 W	-25		25	Cimarron	-36

July Mean Maximum Temperature

	Highest				Lowest	
Rank	Station Name	°F		Rank	Station Name	°F
1	Las Animas	95.2		1	Climax	64.7
2	Uravan	94.8		2	Wolf Creek Pass 1 E	65.9
3	La Junta 4 NNE	94.6		3	Cabin Creek	68.6
4	Palisade	94.3		4	Ruxton Park	70.8
5	Holly	93.9		5	Taylor Park	71.1
6	Rocky Ford 2 SE	93.4		6	Sugarloaf Reservoir	71.2
7	Grand Junction Walker Field	93.1		7	Dillon 1 E	73.2
7	Lamar	93.1		8	Silverton	73.3
9	Pueblo Memorial Airport	92.8		9	Grand Lake 6 SSW	74.1
10	Fruita 1 W	92.6		10	Crested Butte	74.2
11	Grand Junction 6 ESE	92.1		11	Rico	74.7
12	Springfield 7 WSW	91.6		12	Hermit 7 ESE	74.8
12	Tacony 10 SE	91.6		13	Spicer	74.9
12	Walsh 1 W	91.6		14	Grant	75.4
12	Wray 2 E	91.6		15	Antero Reservoir	75.6
16	Colorado National Monument	91.3		15	Lake George 8 SW	75.6
17	Kit Carson	91.1		17	Grand Lake 1 NW	75.7
18	Cheyenne Wells	90.8		18	Yampa	76.4
19	Dinosaur Nat'l Monument	90.5		19	Lake City	76.6
20	Fort Morgan	90.2		20	Telluride 4 WNW	77.6
20	Paonia 1 SW	90.2		21	Ouray	77.7
22	Sterling	90.1		22	Walden	77.9
23	Byers 5 ENE	89.7		23	Green Mountain Dam	78.1
23	Cherry Creek Dam	89.7		24	Bailey	78.2
25	Sedgwick 5 S	89.5		25	Del Norte 2 E	78.3

January Mean Minimum Temperature

Highest			Lowest		
Rank	**Station Name**	**°F**	**Rank**	**Station Name**	**°F**
1	Walsenburg	20.6	1	Taylor Park	-12.2
2	Palisade	19.1	2	Hermit 7 ESE	-7.1
2	Trinidad	19.1	3	Crested Butte	-6.3
4	Colorado National Monument	18.1	4	Gunnison 3 SW	-6.0
5	Springfield 7 WSW	17.9	5	Cochetopa Creek	-4.7
6	Mesa Verde	17.7	5	Silverton	-4.7
7	Lakewood	17.6	7	Antero Reservoir	-3.7
8	Denver Stapleton Int'l Airport	17.1	8	Alamosa Bergman Field	-3.3
8	Walsh 1 W	17.1	9	Center 4 SSW	-2.8
10	Parker 6 E	17.0	10	Lake City	-2.1
11	Trinidad Las Animas Co. Airport	16.9	11	Lake George 8 SW	-1.7
12	Grand Junction 6 ESE	16.8	12	Climax	0.6
13	Colorado Springs Muni Airport	16.5	13	Grand Lake 6 SSW	0.8
13	Grand Junction Walker Field	16.5	14	Cimarron	1.1
15	Cheyenne Wells	16.0	15	Blanca	1.2
16	La Junta 4 NNE	15.7	16	Dillon 1 E	1.3
17	Fort Collins	15.4	17	Manassa	1.6
17	Uravan	15.4	18	Meredith	*1.9*
19	Yellow Jacket 2 W	15.2	19	Saguache	2.3
20	Kassler	15.0	20	Steamboat Springs	2.6
21	Greeley	14.6	20	Sugarloaf Reservoir	*2.6*
22	Cedaredge	*14.5*	22	Grand Lake 1 NW	3.3
23	Akron Washington Co. Airport	14.4	23	Wolf Creek Pass 1 E	3.4
23	Lamar	14.4	24	Green Mountain Dam	4.1
25	Las Animas	14.3	25	Eagle County Airport	*4.7*

Number of Annual Heating Degree Days

Highest			Lowest		
Rank	**Station Name**	**Num.**	**Rank**	**Station Name**	**Num.**
1	Climax	12,436	1	Palisade	5,049
2	Taylor Park	11,962	2	Springfield 7 WSW	5,089
3	Wolf Creek Pass 1 E	*11,397*	3	Las Animas	5,107
4	Hermit 7 ESE	11,299	4	La Junta 4 NNE	*5,213*
5	Crested Butte	11,252	4	Trinidad	5,213
6	Sugarloaf Reservoir	*10,980*	6	Rocky Ford 2 SE	5,224
7	Silverton	*10,880*	7	Walsh 1 W	5,226
8	Dillon 1 E	10,650	8	Walsenburg	5,306
9	Antero Reservoir	10,619	9	Uravan	5,314
10	Ruxton Park	10,513	10	Lamar	5,348
11	Cabin Creek	10,442	11	Grand Junction 6 ESE	5,431
12	Grand Lake 6 SSW	10,357	12	Trinidad Las Animas Co. Airport	5,448
13	Spicer	10,276	13	Holly	5,469
14	Grand Lake 1 NW	10,190	14	Pueblo Memorial Airport	5,485
15	Walden	9,984	15	Grand Junction Walker Field	5,491
16	Gunnison 3 SW	9,835	16	Tacony 10 SE	5,616
17	Cochetopa Creek	9,730	17	Cheyenne Wells	5,633
18	Lake George 8 SW	9,720	18	Colorado National Monument	*5,724*
19	Meredith	*9,651*	19	Wray 2 E	*5,776*
20	Rico	9,533	20	Denver Stapleton Int'l Airport	5,840
21	Lake City	9,416	21	Paonia 1 SW	5,984
22	Grant	9,405	22	Kassler	6,001
23	Green Mountain Dam	9,333	23	Greeley	6,006
24	Steamboat Springs	9,305	24	Brighton 1 NE	*6,014*
25	Yampa	9,255	25	Fruita 1 W	6,023

Number of Annual Cooling Degree Days

	Highest			Lowest	
Rank	Station Name	Num.	Rank	Station Name	Num.
1	La Junta 4 NNE	*1,326*	1	Cabin Creek	0
2	Las Animas	1,324	1	Climax	0
3	Palisade	1,316	1	Crested Butte	0
4	Holly	1,204	1	Dillon 1 E	0
5	Grand Junction Walker Field	1,194	1	Grand Lake 6 SSW	0
6	Lamar	1,192	1	Hermit 7 ESE	0
7	Grand Junction 6 ESE	1,171	1	Rico	0
8	Walsh 1 W	1,140	1	Silverton	*0*
9	Rocky Ford 2 SE	1,099	1	Spicer	0
10	Springfield 7 WSW	1,078	1	Sugarloaf Reservoir	0
11	Uravan	1,052	1	Taylor Park	0
12	Colorado National Monument	*988*	1	Wolf Creek Pass 1 E	*0*
13	Wray 2 E	*984*	13	Antero Reservoir	1
14	Pueblo Memorial Airport	947	13	Ruxton Park	1
15	Cheyenne Wells	938	15	Grant	2
16	Fort Morgan	900	15	Walden	2
17	Kit Carson	*883*	17	Grand Lake 1 NW	3
18	Sterling	881	18	Telluride 4 WNW	6
19	Tacony 10 SE	871	19	Lake George 8 SW	7
20	Sedgwick 5 S	859	20	Lake City	9
21	Fruita 1 W	*774*	21	Meredith	10
22	Holyoke	771	22	Bailey	11
23	Denver Stapleton Int'l Airport	758	23	Green Mountain Dam	13
24	Trinidad Las Animas Co. Airport	754	24	Yampa	14
25	Akron Washington Co. Airport	*738*	25	Center 4 SSW	16

Annual Precipitation

	Highest			Lowest	
Rank	Station Name	Inches	Rank	Station Name	Inches
1	Wolf Creek Pass 1 E	47.46	1	Center 4 SSW	6.95
2	Vallecito Dam	27.76	2	Alamosa Bergman Field	7.37
3	Rico	27.06	3	Manassa	7.96
4	Silverton	25.05	4	Saguache	8.28
5	Ouray	24.56	5	Browns Park Refuge	8.64
6	Ruxton Park	24.47	6	Grand Junction Walker Field	8.99
7	Steamboat Springs	24.13	7	Grand Junction 6 ESE	9.05
8	Crested Butte	23.95	8	Blanca	9.23
9	Telluride 4 WNW	23.56	9	Fruita 1 W	9.28
10	Climax	22.85	10	Montrose 2	9.81
11	Grand Lake 1 NW	20.73	11	Gunnison 3 SW	10.05
12	Evergreen	19.48	12	Antero Reservoir	10.11
13	Cabin Creek	19.46	13	Buena Vista	10.22
14	Fort Lewis	19.16	14	Del Norte 2 E	10.42
15	Mesa Verde	18.68	15	Palisade	10.84
16	Holyoke	18.19	16	Eagle County Airport	*10.86*
17	Cherry Creek Dam	18.12	17	Colorado National Monument	11.27
18	Sedgwick 5 S	18.07	17	Tacony 10 SE	11.27
19	Kassler	17.93	19	Walden	11.58
20	Walsh 1 W	17.87	20	Great Sand Dunes Nat'l Monument	11.64
21	Wray 2 E	17.62	21	Cochetopa Creek	11.66
22	Leroy 5 WSW	17.57	22	La Junta 4 NNE	*11.80*
23	Walsenburg	17.44	23	Dinosaur Nat'l Monument	11.82
24	Colorado Springs Muni Airport	17.40	23	Rocky Ford 2 SE	11.82
25	Cheesman	17.34	25	Pueblo Memorial Airport	12.29

Number of Days Annually With ≥ 0.1″ Precipitation

	Highest			Lowest	
Rank	**Station Name**	**Days**	**Rank**	**Station Name**	**Days**
1	Wolf Creek Pass 1 E	*92*	1	Center 4 SSW	21
2	Climax	77	2	Alamosa Bergman Field	25
3	Silverton	*75*	3	Fruita 1 W	26
3	Steamboat Springs	75	3	Manassa	26
5	Rico	74	5	Browns Park Refuge	27
6	Crested Butte	73	5	Saguache	27
6	Ouray	73	5	Tacony 10 SE	27
6	Telluride 4 WNW	73	8	Blanca	28
9	Taylor Park	68	8	Grand Junction Walker Field	28
10	Grand Lake 1 NW	67	10	La Junta 4 NNE	*29*
11	Vallecito Dam	65	10	Rocky Ford 2 SE	29
12	Ruxton Park	61	12	Antero Reservoir	30
13	Cabin Creek	59	12	Grand Junction 6 ESE	30
14	Hayden	55	14	Buena Vista	31
14	Yampa	55	14	Las Animas	31
16	Altenbern	53	14	Montrose 2	31
17	Green Mountain Dam	51	17	Pueblo Memorial Airport	32
18	Mesa Verde	50	18	Del Norte 2 E	33
18	Spicer	50	18	Fort Morgan	33
20	Bailey	49	18	Gunnison 3 SW	33
20	Dillon 1 E	49	21	Kit Carson	*34*
20	Grant	49	21	New Raymer	34
20	Paonia 1 SW	49	21	Palisade	34
24	Evergreen	48	24	Brighton 1 NE	*35*
24	Fort Lewis	48	24	Eagle County Airport	*35*

Number of Days Annually With ≥ 1.0″ Precipitation

	Highest			Lowest	
Rank	**Station Name**	**Days**	**Rank**	**Station Name**	**Days**
1	Wolf Creek Pass 1 E	10	1	Alamosa Bergman Field	0
2	Cheyenne Wells	4	1	Altenbern	0
2	Flagler 5 NNE	4	1	Antero Reservoir	0
2	Holyoke	4	1	Bailey	0
2	Kit Carson	4	1	Blanca	0
2	Vallecito Dam	4	1	Browns Park Refuge	0
2	Walsh 1 W	4	1	Buena Vista	0
8	Colorado Springs Muni Airport	3	1	Cabin Creek	0
8	Holly	3	1	Cedaredge	*0*
8	Ruxton Park	3	1	Center 4 SSW	0
8	Sedgwick 5 S	3	1	Cheesman	0
8	Sterling	3	1	Cimarron	0
8	Wray 2 E	3	1	Climax	0
14	Akron 4 E	*2*	1	Cochetopa Creek	0
14	Akron Washington Co. Airport	*2*	1	Colorado National Monument	0
14	Lakewood	2	1	Crested Butte	0
14	Leroy 5 WSW	2	1	Del Norte 2 E	0
14	New Raymer	2	1	Dillon 1 E	0
14	Waterdale	2	1	Dinosaur Nat'l Monument	0
20	Brighton 1 NE	*1*	1	Eagle County Airport	*0*
20	Byers 5 ENE	1	1	Fort Lewis	0
20	Cherry Creek Dam	1	1	Fort Morgan	0
20	Denver Stapleton Int'l Airport	1	1	Fruita 1 W	0
20	Evergreen	1	1	Grand Junction 6 ESE	0
20	Fort Collins	1	1	Grand Junction Walker Field	0

Annual Snowfall

Highest			Lowest		
Rank	Station Name	Inches	Rank	Station Name	Inches
1	Wolf Creek Pass 1 E	*435.6*	1	Palisade	*12.9*
2	Climax	271.0	2	Grand Junction 6 ESE	*13.0*
3	Crested Butte	223.9	3	Grand Junction Walker Field	21.9
4	Telluride 4 WNW	205.8	4	Las Animas	22.0
5	Steamboat Springs	173.3	5	Saguache	*23.6*
6	Rico	167.7	6	Walsh 1 W	24.3
7	Silverton	*159.4*	7	Fort Morgan	24.7
8	Ruxton Park	152.0	8	Cheyenne Wells	25.0
9	Spicer	*145.6*	9	Sterling	*25.5*
10	Ouray	145.3	10	Rocky Ford 2 SE	25.7
11	Grand Lake 1 NW	142.5	11	Holly	26.6
12	Sugarloaf Reservoir	*132.4*	12	Colorado National Monument	*27.4*
13	Cabin Creek	*129.7*	13	Tacony 10 SE	29.0
14	Hayden	121.4	14	Lamar	29.8
15	Vallecito Dam	117.6	15	La Junta 4 NNE	*29.9*
15	Yampa	117.6	16	Manassa	*30.2*
17	Dillon 1 E	115.5	17	Wray 2 E	*30.3*
18	Walsenburg	100.2	18	Blanca	31.3
18	Westcliffe	100.2	19	Buena Vista	*32.5*
20	Grant	98.7	20	Alamosa Bergman Field	32.8
21	Meredith	*87.8*	21	Longmont 2 ESE	33.4
22	Evergreen	*87.5*	22	Holyoke	*33.6*
23	Bailey	*86.7*	23	Springfield 7 WSW	33.7
24	Lake City	83.8	24	Pueblo Memorial Airport	34.1
25	Mesa Verde	83.6	25	New Raymer	35.3

Note: See Appendix D for explanation of data.

Annual Extreme Maximum Temperature

	Highest				Lowest	
Rank	**Station Name**	**°F**		**Rank**	**Station Name**	**°F**
1	Danbury	*106*		1	Norfolk 2 SW	92
2	Mount Carmel	*103*		2	Shepaug Dam	95
3	Hartford Brainard Field	102		3	Bridgeport Sikorsky Memorial	100
3	Middletown 4 W	102		3	Burlington	100
3	Stamford 5 N	102		3	Falls Village	100
6	Bulls Bridge Dam	101		3	Mansfield Hollow Lake	100
6	Groton	101		3	West Thompson Lake	100
6	Hartford Bradley Int'l Airport	101		3	Wigwam Reservoir	*100*
6	Norwich Public Util. Plant	101		9	Bulls Bridge Dam	101
10	Bridgeport Sikorsky Memorial	100		9	Groton	101
10	Burlington	100		9	Hartford Bradley Int'l Airport	101
10	Falls Village	100		9	Norwich Public Util. Plant	101
10	Mansfield Hollow Lake	100		13	Hartford Brainard Field	102
10	West Thompson Lake	100		13	Middletown 4 W	102
10	Wigwam Reservoir	*100*		13	Stamford 5 N	102
16	Shepaug Dam	95		16	Mount Carmel	*103*
17	Norfolk 2 SW	92		17	Danbury	*106*

Annual Mean Maximum Temperature

	Highest				Lowest	
Rank	**Station Name**	**°F**		**Rank**	**Station Name**	**°F**
1	Stamford 5 N	62.5		1	Norfolk 2 SW	53.8
2	Norwich Public Util. Plant	61.2		2	Shepaug Dam	*57.8*
3	Mount Carmel	*61.0*		3	West Thompson Lake	*59.2*
4	Hartford Bradley Int'l Airport	60.5		4	Burlington	59.3
5	Danbury	*60.4*		5	Groton	59.4
6	Bulls Bridge Dam	60.2		6	Mansfield Hollow Lake	*59.8*
6	Hartford Brainard Field	60.2		7	Bridgeport Sikorsky Memorial	59.9
8	Falls Village	60.1		7	Wigwam Reservoir	*59.9*
9	Middletown 4 W	60.0		9	Middletown 4 W	60.0
10	Bridgeport Sikorsky Memorial	59.9		10	Falls Village	60.1
10	Wigwam Reservoir	*59.9*		11	Bulls Bridge Dam	60.2
12	Mansfield Hollow Lake	*59.8*		11	Hartford Brainard Field	60.2
13	Groton	59.4		13	Danbury	*60.4*
14	Burlington	59.3		14	Hartford Bradley Int'l Airport	60.5
15	West Thompson Lake	*59.2*		15	Mount Carmel	*61.0*
16	Shepaug Dam	*57.8*		16	Norwich Public Util. Plant	61.2
17	Norfolk 2 SW	53.8		17	Stamford 5 N	62.5

Annual Mean Temperature

Rank	Station Name (Highest)	°F		Rank	Station Name (Lowest)	°F
1	Bridgeport Sikorsky Memorial	52.1		1	Norfolk 2 SW	44.7
2	Stamford 5 N	51.5		2	Shepaug Dam	*47.4*
3	Mount Carmel	*50.9*		3	Wigwam Reservoir	*47.9*
4	Norwich Public Util. Plant	*50.7*		4	Falls Village	48.0
5	Middletown 4 W	50.6		5	Mansfield Hollow Lake	*48.2*
6	Groton	50.3		6	Burlington	48.4
6	Hartford Bradley Int'l Airport	50.3		7	Bulls Bridge Dam	48.9
8	Hartford Brainard Field	50.1		8	Danbury	*50.0*
9	Danbury	*50.0*		9	Hartford Brainard Field	50.1
10	Bulls Bridge Dam	48.9		10	Groton	50.3
11	Burlington	48.4		10	Hartford Bradley Int'l Airport	50.3
12	Mansfield Hollow Lake	*48.2*		12	Middletown 4 W	50.6
13	Falls Village	48.0		13	Norwich Public Util. Plant	*50.7*
14	Wigwam Reservoir	*47.9*		14	Mount Carmel	*50.9*
15	Shepaug Dam	*47.4*		15	Stamford 5 N	51.5
16	Norfolk 2 SW	44.7		16	Bridgeport Sikorsky Memorial	52.1

Annual Mean Minimum Temperature

Rank	Station Name (Highest)	°F		Rank	Station Name (Lowest)	°F
1	Bridgeport Sikorsky Memorial	44.3		1	Norfolk 2 SW	35.5
2	Groton	41.2		2	Wigwam Reservoir	*35.9*
2	Middletown 4 W	41.2		3	Falls Village	36.0
4	Mount Carmel	*40.8*		4	Mansfield Hollow Lake	*36.6*
5	Stamford 5 N	40.4		5	Shepaug Dam	*37.0*
6	Norwich Public Util. Plant	40.1		6	Bulls Bridge Dam	37.6
7	Hartford Bradley Int'l Airport	40.0		6	Burlington	37.6
8	Hartford Brainard Field	39.9		8	Danbury	*39.6*
9	Danbury	*39.6*		9	Hartford Brainard Field	39.9
10	Bulls Bridge Dam	37.6		10	Hartford Bradley Int'l Airport	40.0
10	Burlington	37.6		11	Norwich Public Util. Plant	40.1
12	Shepaug Dam	*37.0*		12	Stamford 5 N	40.4
13	Mansfield Hollow Lake	*36.6*		13	Mount Carmel	*40.8*
14	Falls Village	36.0		14	Groton	41.2
15	Wigwam Reservoir	*35.9*		14	Middletown 4 W	41.2
16	Norfolk 2 SW	35.5		16	Bridgeport Sikorsky Memorial	44.3

Annual Extreme Minimum Temperature

	Highest				Lowest	
Rank	**Station Name**	**°F**		**Rank**	**Station Name**	**°F**
1	Bridgeport Sikorsky Memorial	-7		1	Falls Village	-27
2	Groton	-13		2	Bulls Bridge Dam	-24
3	Middletown 4 W	-14		2	Shepaug Dam	-24
4	Hartford Brainard Field	-15		4	Mansfield Hollow Lake	-23
4	Mount Carmel	*-15*		4	West Thompson Lake	-23
6	Norwich Public Util. Plant	-17		6	Hartford Bradley Int'l Airport	-21
7	Burlington	-18		6	Norfolk 2 SW	-21
7	Danbury	*-18*		6	Wigwam Reservoir	*-21*
7	Stamford 5 N	-18		9	Burlington	-18
10	Hartford Bradley Int'l Airport	-21		9	Danbury	*-18*
10	Norfolk 2 SW	-21		9	Stamford 5 N	-18
10	Wigwam Reservoir	*-21*		12	Norwich Public Util. Plant	-17
13	Mansfield Hollow Lake	-23		13	Hartford Brainard Field	-15
13	West Thompson Lake	-23		13	Mount Carmel	*-15*
15	Bulls Bridge Dam	-24		15	Middletown 4 W	-14
15	Shepaug Dam	-24		16	Groton	-13
17	Falls Village	-27		17	Bridgeport Sikorsky Memorial	-7

July Mean Maximum Temperature

	Highest				Lowest	
Rank	**Station Name**	**°F**		**Rank**	**Station Name**	**°F**
1	Stamford 5 N	85.4		1	Norfolk 2 SW	77.7
2	Hartford Bradley Int'l Airport	85.1		2	Shepaug Dam	79.9
3	Danbury	84.2		3	Groton	80.7
4	Falls Village	84.0		4	Bridgeport Sikorsky Memorial	82.1
4	Middletown 4 W	84.0		5	Burlington	82.6
4	Mount Carmel	84.0		5	West Thompson Lake	82.6
7	Bulls Bridge Dam	83.8		7	Mansfield Hollow Lake	82.7
8	Hartford Brainard Field	83.7		8	Wigwam Reservoir	*83.3*
9	Norwich Public Util. Plant	83.4		9	Norwich Public Util. Plant	83.4
10	Wigwam Reservoir	*83.3*		10	Hartford Brainard Field	83.7
11	Mansfield Hollow Lake	82.7		11	Bulls Bridge Dam	83.8
12	Burlington	82.6		12	Falls Village	84.0
12	West Thompson Lake	82.6		12	Middletown 4 W	84.0
14	Bridgeport Sikorsky Memorial	82.1		12	Mount Carmel	84.0
15	Groton	80.7		15	Danbury	84.2
16	Shepaug Dam	79.9		16	Hartford Bradley Int'l Airport	85.1
17	Norfolk 2 SW	77.7		17	Stamford 5 N	85.4

January Mean Minimum Temperature

	Highest				Lowest	
Rank	Station Name	°F		Rank	Station Name	°F
1	Bridgeport Sikorsky Memorial	22.7		1	Norfolk 2 SW	11.7
2	Groton	19.6		2	West Thompson Lake	*11.9*
2	Middletown 4 W	19.6		3	Falls Village	13.0
4	Mount Carmel	19.1		4	Mansfield Hollow Lake	13.6
5	Stamford 5 N	18.9		4	Shepaug Dam	13.6
6	Norwich Public Util. Plant	18.3		6	Wigwam Reservoir	13.7
7	Danbury	*17.4*		7	Burlington	14.3
8	Hartford Bradley Int'l Airport	16.9		8	Bulls Bridge Dam	14.9
9	Hartford Brainard Field	16.7		9	Hartford Brainard Field	16.7
10	Bulls Bridge Dam	14.9		10	Hartford Bradley Int'l Airport	16.9
11	Burlington	14.3		11	Danbury	*17.4*
12	Wigwam Reservoir	13.7		12	Norwich Public Util. Plant	18.3
13	Mansfield Hollow Lake	13.6		13	Stamford 5 N	18.9
13	Shepaug Dam	13.6		14	Mount Carmel	19.1
15	Falls Village	13.0		15	Groton	19.6
16	West Thompson Lake	*11.9*		15	Middletown 4 W	19.6
17	Norfolk 2 SW	11.7		17	Bridgeport Sikorsky Memorial	22.7

Number of Annual Heating Degree Days

	Highest				Lowest	
Rank	Station Name	Num.		Rank	Station Name	Num.
1	Norfolk 2 SW	7,628		1	Bridgeport Sikorsky Memorial	5,405
2	Shepaug Dam	*6,728*		2	Stamford 5 N	5,590
3	Wigwam Reservoir	*6,611*		3	Mount Carmel	*5,757*
4	Falls Village	6,610		4	Norwich Public Util. Plant	*5,782*
5	Mansfield Hollow Lake	*6,529*		5	Groton	5,824
6	Burlington	6,485		6	Middletown 4 W	5,866
7	Bulls Bridge Dam	6,344		7	Hartford Bradley Int'l Airport	6,048
8	Hartford Brainard Field	6,084		8	Danbury	*6,062*
9	Danbury	*6,062*		9	Hartford Brainard Field	6,084
10	Hartford Bradley Int'l Airport	6,048		10	Bulls Bridge Dam	6,344
11	Middletown 4 W	5,866		11	Burlington	6,485
12	Groton	5,824		12	Mansfield Hollow Lake	*6,529*
13	Norwich Public Util. Plant	*5,782*		13	Falls Village	6,610
14	Mount Carmel	*5,757*		14	Wigwam Reservoir	*6,611*
15	Stamford 5 N	5,590		15	Shepaug Dam	*6,728*
16	Bridgeport Sikorsky Memorial	5,405		16	Norfolk 2 SW	7,628

Number of Annual Cooling Degree Days

	Highest			Lowest	
Rank	**Station Name**	**Num.**	**Rank**	**Station Name**	**Num.**
1	Bridgeport Sikorsky Memorial	814	1	Norfolk 2 SW	324
2	Stamford 5 N	799	2	Shepaug Dam	*410*
3	Middletown 4 W	*781*	3	Mansfield Hollow Lake	*525*
4	Mount Carmel	*768*	4	Wigwam Reservoir	*528*
5	Hartford Bradley Int'l Airport	763	5	Falls Village	557
6	Hartford Brainard Field	751	6	Burlington	560
7	Danbury	*738*	7	Groton	588
8	Norwich Public Util. Plant	702	8	Bulls Bridge Dam	599
9	Bulls Bridge Dam	599	9	Norwich Public Util. Plant	702
10	Groton	588	10	Danbury	*738*
11	Burlington	560	11	Hartford Brainard Field	751
12	Falls Village	557	12	Hartford Bradley Int'l Airport	763
13	Wigwam Reservoir	*528*	13	Mount Carmel	*768*
14	Mansfield Hollow Lake	*525*	14	Middletown 4 W	*781*
15	Shepaug Dam	*410*	15	Stamford 5 N	799
16	Norfolk 2 SW	324	16	Bridgeport Sikorsky Memorial	814

Annual Precipitation

	Highest			Lowest	
Rank	**Station Name**	**Inches**	**Rank**	**Station Name**	**Inches**
1	Norfolk 2 SW	53.49	1	Bridgeport Sikorsky Memorial	43.76
2	Mount Carmel	*52.75*	2	Hartford Brainard Field	44.39
3	Stamford 5 N	52.65	3	Falls Village	45.16
4	Norwich Public Util. Plant	52.54	4	Hartford Bradley Int'l Airport	45.96
5	Middletown 4 W	52.29	5	Bulls Bridge Dam	47.53
6	Danbury	*51.99*	6	Groton	48.43
7	Burlington	51.83	7	Shepaug Dam	50.14
8	Mansfield Hollow Lake	51.08	8	Wigwam Reservoir	*50.76*
9	West Thompson Lake	51.06	9	West Thompson Lake	51.06
10	Wigwam Reservoir	*50.76*	10	Mansfield Hollow Lake	51.08
11	Shepaug Dam	50.14	11	Burlington	51.83
12	Groton	48.43	12	Danbury	*51.99*
13	Bulls Bridge Dam	47.53	13	Middletown 4 W	52.29
14	Hartford Bradley Int'l Airport	45.96	14	Norwich Public Util. Plant	52.54
15	Falls Village	45.16	15	Stamford 5 N	52.65
16	Hartford Brainard Field	44.39	16	Mount Carmel	*52.75*
17	Bridgeport Sikorsky Memorial	43.76	17	Norfolk 2 SW	53.49

Number of Days Annually With ≥ 0.1″ Precipitation

Highest			Lowest		
Rank	Station Name	Days	Rank	Station Name	Days
1	Norfolk 2 SW	92	1	Hartford Brainard Field	72
2	Shepaug Dam	88	2	Bridgeport Sikorsky Memorial	77
3	Falls Village	85	3	Burlington	79
4	Bulls Bridge Dam	84	3	Groton	79
4	Mansfield Hollow Lake	84	5	Norwich Public Util. Plant	80
6	Danbury	*82*	5	Stamford 5 N	*80*
6	Middletown 4 W	82	5	West Thompson Lake	80
8	Hartford Bradley Int'l Airport	81	8	Hartford Bradley Int'l Airport	81
8	Mount Carmel	*81*	8	Mount Carmel	*81*
8	Wigwam Reservoir	*81*	8	Wigwam Reservoir	*81*
11	Norwich Public Util. Plant	80	11	Danbury	*82*
11	Stamford 5 N	*80*	11	Middletown 4 W	82
11	West Thompson Lake	80	13	Bulls Bridge Dam	84
14	Burlington	79	13	Mansfield Hollow Lake	84
14	Groton	79	15	Falls Village	85
16	Bridgeport Sikorsky Memorial	77	16	Shepaug Dam	88
17	Hartford Brainard Field	72	17	Norfolk 2 SW	92

Number of Days Annually With ≥ 1.0″ Precipitation

Highest			Lowest		
Rank	Station Name	Days	Rank	Station Name	Days
1	Mount Carmel	*14*	1	Bridgeport Sikorsky Memorial	12
2	Danbury	*13*	1	Bulls Bridge Dam	12
2	Mansfield Hollow Lake	13	1	Burlington	12
2	Middletown 4 W	13	1	Falls Village	12
2	Norwich Public Util. Plant	13	1	Groton	12
2	Stamford 5 N	13	1	Hartford Bradley Int'l Airport	12
2	West Thompson Lake	13	1	Hartford Brainard Field	12
8	Bridgeport Sikorsky Memorial	12	1	Norfolk 2 SW	12
8	Bulls Bridge Dam	12	1	Shepaug Dam	12
8	Burlington	12	1	Wigwam Reservoir	*12*
8	Falls Village	12	11	Danbury	*13*
8	Groton	12	11	Mansfield Hollow Lake	13
8	Hartford Bradley Int'l Airport	12	11	Middletown 4 W	13
8	Hartford Brainard Field	12	11	Norwich Public Util. Plant	13
8	Norfolk 2 SW	12	11	Stamford 5 N	13
8	Shepaug Dam	12	11	West Thompson Lake	13
8	Wigwam Reservoir	*12*	17	Mount Carmel	*14*

Annual Snowfall

	Highest			Lowest	
Rank	**Station Name**	**Inches**	**Rank**	**Station Name**	**Inches**
1	Norfolk 2 SW	87.7	1	Groton	21.1
2	Shepaug Dam	49.9	2	Bridgeport Sikorsky Memorial	*24.8*
3	Hartford Bradley Int'l Airport	44.9	3	Mount Carmel	*29.0*
4	Danbury	*39.6*	4	Stamford 5 N	*29.4*
5	West Thompson Lake	36.8	5	Mansfield Hollow Lake	32.0
6	Middletown 4 W	34.1	6	Middletown 4 W	34.1
7	Mansfield Hollow Lake	32.0	7	West Thompson Lake	36.8
8	Stamford 5 N	*29.4*	8	Danbury	*39.6*
9	Mount Carmel	*29.0*	9	Hartford Bradley Int'l Airport	44.9
10	Bridgeport Sikorsky Memorial	*24.8*	10	Shepaug Dam	49.9
11	Groton	21.1	11	Norfolk 2 SW	87.7

Note: *See Appendix D for explanation of data.*

Annual Extreme Maximum Temperature

	Highest			Lowest	
Rank	Station Name	°F	Rank	Station Name	°F
1	Newark University Farm	105	1	Wilmington Airport	100
2	Dover	102	1	Wilmington Porter Reservior	100
2	Lewes	102	3	Georgetown 5 SW	101
4	Georgetown 5 SW	101	4	Dover	102
5	Wilmington Airport	100	4	Lewes	102
5	Wilmington Porter Reservior	100	6	Newark University Farm	105

Annual Mean Maximum Temperature

	Highest			Lowest	
Rank	Station Name	°F	Rank	Station Name	°F
1	Dover	66.5	1	Wilmington Porter Reservior	62.9
2	Lewes	65.9	2	Wilmington Airport	64.0
3	Newark University Farm	65.7	3	Georgetown 5 SW	65.5
4	Georgetown 5 SW	65.5	4	Newark University Farm	65.7
5	Wilmington Airport	64.0	5	Lewes	65.9
6	Wilmington Porter Reservior	62.9	6	Dover	66.5

Annual Mean Temperature

	Highest			Lowest	
Rank	Station Name	°F	Rank	Station Name	°F
1	Lewes	56.9	1	Wilmington Porter Reservior	54.1
2	Dover	56.6	2	Wilmington Airport	54.6
3	Georgetown 5 SW	55.1	3	Newark University Farm	54.9
4	Newark University Farm	54.9	4	Georgetown 5 SW	55.1
5	Wilmington Airport	54.6	5	Dover	56.6
6	Wilmington Porter Reservior	54.1	6	Lewes	56.9

Annual Mean Minimum Temperature

	Highest			Lowest	
Rank	Station Name	°F	Rank	Station Name	°F
1	Lewes	47.9	1	Newark University Farm	44.1
2	Dover	46.7	2	Georgetown 5 SW	44.6
3	Wilmington Airport	45.3	3	Wilmington Porter Reservior	45.2
4	Wilmington Porter Reservior	45.2	4	Wilmington Airport	45.3
5	Georgetown 5 SW	44.6	5	Dover	46.7
6	Newark University Farm	44.1	6	Lewes	47.9

Annual Extreme Minimum Temperature

	Highest			Lowest	
Rank	Station Name	°F	Rank	Station Name	°F
1	Dover	-5	1	Wilmington Airport	-14
2	Wilmington Porter Reservior	-9	2	Georgetown 5 SW	-13
3	Newark University Farm	-10	3	Lewes	-11
4	Lewes	-11	4	Newark University Farm	-10
5	Georgetown 5 SW	-13	5	Wilmington Porter Reservior	-9
6	Wilmington Airport	-14	6	Dover	-5

July Mean Maximum Temperature

Highest			Lowest		
Rank	Station Name	°F	Rank	Station Name	°F
1	Dover	87.6	1	Wilmington Porter Reservior	85.1
1	Newark University Farm	87.6	2	Lewes	85.9
3	Georgetown 5 SW	86.6	3	Wilmington Airport	86.2
4	Wilmington Airport	86.2	4	Georgetown 5 SW	86.6
5	Lewes	85.9	5	Dover	87.6
6	Wilmington Porter Reservior	85.1	5	Newark University Farm	87.6

January Mean Minimum Temperature

Highest			Lowest		
Rank	Station Name	°F	Rank	Station Name	°F
1	Lewes	27.9	1	Newark University Farm	23.5
2	Dover	26.4	1	Wilmington Airport	23.5
3	Georgetown 5 SW	24.3	3	Wilmington Porter Reservior	23.6
4	Wilmington Porter Reservior	23.6	4	Georgetown 5 SW	24.3
5	Newark University Farm	23.5	5	Dover	26.4
5	Wilmington Airport	23.5	6	Lewes	27.9

Number of Annual Heating Degree Days

Highest			Lowest		
Rank	Station Name	Num.	Rank	Station Name	Num.
1	Wilmington Porter Reservior	4,949	1	Lewes	4,123
2	Wilmington Airport	4,833	2	Dover	4,257
3	Newark University Farm	4,721	3	Georgetown 5 SW	4,630
4	Georgetown 5 SW	4,630	4	Newark University Farm	4,721
5	Dover	4,257	5	Wilmington Airport	4,833
6	Lewes	4,123	6	Wilmington Porter Reservior	4,949

Number of Annual Cooling Degree Days

Highest			Lowest		
Rank	Station Name	Num.	Rank	Station Name	Num.
1	Lewes	1,395	1	Georgetown 5 SW	*1,139*
2	Dover	1,329	2	Wilmington Porter Reservior	1,142
3	Newark University Farm	1,189	3	Wilmington Airport	1,174
4	Wilmington Airport	1,174	4	Newark University Farm	1,189
5	Wilmington Porter Reservior	1,142	5	Dover	1,329
6	Georgetown 5 SW	*1,139*	6	Lewes	1,395

Annual Precipitation

Highest			Lowest		
Rank	Station Name	Inches	Rank	Station Name	Inches
1	Wilmington Porter Reservior	49.02	1	Wilmington Airport	42.59
2	Lewes	45.87	2	Georgetown 5 SW	44.99
3	Dover	45.75	3	Newark University Farm	45.08
4	Newark University Farm	45.08	4	Dover	45.75
5	Georgetown 5 SW	44.99	5	Lewes	45.87
6	Wilmington Airport	42.59	6	Wilmington Porter Reservior	49.02

Number of Days Annually With ≥ 0.1″ Precipitation

	Highest			Lowest	
Rank	Station Name	Days	Rank	Station Name	Days
1	Wilmington Porter Reservior	79	1	Wilmington Airport	72
2	Dover	78	2	Lewes	75
3	Georgetown 5 SW	*76*	3	Georgetown 5 SW	*76*
3	Newark University Farm	76	3	Newark University Farm	76
5	Lewes	75	5	Dover	78
6	Wilmington Airport	72	6	Wilmington Porter Reservior	79

Number of Days Annually With ≥ 1.0″ Precipitation

	Highest			Lowest	
Rank	Station Name	Days	Rank	Station Name	Days
1	Georgetown 5 SW	*13*	1	Dover	12
1	Lewes	13	1	Newark University Farm	12
1	Wilmington Porter Reservior	13	1	Wilmington Airport	12
4	Dover	12	4	Georgetown 5 SW	*13*
4	Newark University Farm	12	4	Lewes	13
4	Wilmington Airport	12	4	Wilmington Porter Reservior	13

Annual Snowfall

	Highest			Lowest	
Rank	Station Name	Inches	Rank	Station Name	Inches
1	Wilmington Airport	18.7	1	Lewes	10.4
2	Wilmington Porter Reservior	14.9	2	Newark University Farm	11.6
3	Dover	14.0	3	Georgetown 5 SW	*12.2*
4	Georgetown 5 SW	*12.2*	4	Dover	14.0
5	Newark University Farm	11.6	5	Wilmington Porter Reservior	14.9
6	Lewes	10.4	6	Wilmington Airport	18.7

Note: See Appendix D for explanation of data.

Annual Extreme Maximum Temperature

	Highest			Lowest	
Rank	**Station Name**	**°F**	**Rank**	**Station Name**	**°F**
1	High Springs	107	1	Tavernier	*97*
2	Live Oak	106	2	Belle Glade Exp. Station	98
2	Pensacola Regional Airport	106	2	Key West Int'l Airport	98
4	De Funiak Springs	*105*	2	Miami Beach	98
4	Lakeland Linder Airport	*105*	2	Miami Int'l Airport	98
4	Mountain Lake	105	6	Fort Lauderdale	99
4	Myakka River State Park	105	6	Naples	99
4	Ocala	105	6	Tampa Int'l Airport	99
4	Usher Tower	105	6	Vero Beach	99
10	Arcadia	104	6	West Palm Beach Int'l Airport	99
10	Brooksville Chin Hill	104	11	Bradenton 5 ESE	100
10	Chipley 3 E	104	11	Canal Point USDA	100
10	Flamingo Ranger Station	104	11	Hialeah	100
10	La Belle	*104*	11	Saint Petersburg	100
10	Lake Alfred Exp. Station	104	11	Venice	*100*
10	Lake City 2 E	104	11	Weeki Wachee	100
10	Mayo	104	17	Avon Park 2 W	101
10	Perry	104	17	Clermont 7 S	101
19	Apalachicola Municipal Airport	103	17	Clewiston U.S. Engineers	101
19	Archbold Bio Station	103	17	Cross City 2 WNW	101
19	Bartow	103	17	Fort Pierce	101
19	Fort Myers Page Field	*103*	17	Immokalee 3 NNW	101
19	Jacksonville Beach	103	17	Inverness 3 SE	101
19	Jacksonville Int'l Airport	103	17	Kissimmee 2	101
19	Jasper	103	17	Lisbon	101

Annual Mean Maximum Temperature

	Highest			Lowest	
Rank	**Station Name**	**°F**	**Rank**	**Station Name**	**°F**
1	Tamiami Trail 40 Mile Bend	*85.7*	1	Fernandina Beach	77.0
2	Myakka River State Park	85.3	1	Pensacola Regional Airport	77.0
3	Naples	85.1	3	Apalachicola Municipal Airport	77.2
4	Archbold Bio Station	84.9	4	Jacksonville Beach	*77.6*
4	Immokalee 3 NNW	84.9	5	Chipley 3 E	77.8
6	Fort Myers Page Field	84.5	5	Panama City 5 NE	77.8
6	Punta Gorda 4 ESE	84.5	7	Monticello 3 W	78.0
8	Mountain Lake	84.4	8	Milton Experiment Station	78.1
9	Hialeah	84.3	8	Quincy 3 SSW	78.1
9	Wauchula	84.3	10	De Funiak Springs	78.6
11	Canal Point USDA	84.1	11	Saint Augustine	*79.2*
11	Tavernier	*84.1*	12	Jacksonville Int'l Airport	79.3
13	Bartow	84.0	13	Cross City 2 WNW	*79.4*
13	Belle Glade Exp. Station	84.0	13	Jasper	79.4
15	Arcadia	83.9	13	Lake City 2 E	79.4
15	Fort Drum 5 NW	*83.9*	16	Tallahassee Municipal Airport	79.5
17	Flamingo Ranger Station	83.8	17	Daytona Beach Regional Airport	80.3
18	Lake Alfred Exp. Station	83.7	18	Mayo	80.4
18	Lakeland Linder Airport	*83.7*	19	Miami Beach	81.1
20	Clewiston U.S. Engineers	*83.6*	20	Lisbon	81.3
20	Moore Haven Lock 1	83.6	21	Saint Petersburg	81.4
20	Plant City	83.6	22	Melbourne Regional Airport	81.6
20	Saint Leo	83.6	22	Perry	81.6
24	Avon Park 2 W	83.5	24	Live Oak	81.7
24	Kissimmee 2	83.5	24	Usher Tower	81.7

Annual Mean Temperature

	Highest			Lowest	
Rank	**Station Name**	**°F**	**Rank**	**Station Name**	**°F**
1	Key West Int'l Airport	78.0	1	Chipley 3 E	66.1
2	Tavernier	*77.8*	1	Monticello 3 W	66.1
3	Miami Int'l Airport	76.6	3	De Funiak Springs	66.4
4	Hialeah	76.4	4	Milton Experiment Station	66.8
4	Miami Beach	76.4	5	Panama City 5 NE	66.9
6	Tamiami Trail 40 Mile Bend	*76.0*	6	Jasper	67.0
7	Fort Lauderdale	75.7	6	Quincy 3 SSW	67.0
8	West Palm Beach Int'l Airport	75.3	8	Tallahassee Municipal Airport	67.4
9	Flamingo Ranger Station	74.9	9	Cross City 2 WNW	*67.7*
9	Fort Myers Page Field	74.9	10	Pensacola Regional Airport	68.1
11	Naples	74.8	11	Lake City 2 E	68.2
12	Stuart 1 S	74.5	12	Mayo	68.3
13	Clewiston U.S. Engineers	*74.3*	13	Fernandina Beach	68.4
14	Saint Petersburg	74.1	14	Jacksonville Int'l Airport	68.5
15	Immokalee 3 NNW	73.8	15	Apalachicola Municipal Airport	68.6
15	Punta Gorda 4 ESE	73.8	16	Perry	69.0
17	Canal Point USDA	73.7	17	High Springs	69.2
18	Moore Haven Lock 1	73.4	18	Live Oak	69.4
19	Fort Pierce	73.3	19	Jacksonville Beach	*69.5*
19	Myakka River State Park	73.3	20	Usher Tower	69.6
21	Bartow	73.2	21	Saint Augustine	*69.8*
21	Belle Glade Exp. Station	73.2	22	Inverness 3 SE	70.4
21	Lakeland Linder Airport	*73.2*	22	Weeki Wachee	70.4
24	Venice	*73.1*	24	Ocala	70.8
25	Kissimmee 2	72.8	25	Daytona Beach Regional Airport	70.9

Annual Mean Minimum Temperature

	Highest			Lowest	
Rank	**Station Name**	**°F**	**Rank**	**Station Name**	**°F**
1	Key West Int'l Airport	73.2	1	De Funiak Springs	54.2
2	Miami Beach	71.6	1	Monticello 3 W	54.2
3	Tavernier	*71.5*	3	Chipley 3 E	54.3
4	Miami Int'l Airport	69.7	4	Jasper	54.6
5	Hialeah	68.4	5	Tallahassee Municipal Airport	55.3
6	Fort Lauderdale	68.0	6	Milton Experiment Station	55.5
7	West Palm Beach Int'l Airport	67.4	7	Cross City 2 WNW	*55.8*
8	Saint Petersburg	66.7	8	Quincy 3 SSW	55.9
9	Tamiami Trail 40 Mile Bend	*66.3*	9	Panama City 5 NE	56.0
10	Flamingo Ranger Station	66.0	10	High Springs	56.2
11	Stuart 1 S	65.7	10	Mayo	56.2
12	Fort Myers Page Field	65.2	10	Perry	56.2
13	Clewiston U.S. Engineers	*65.1*	13	Live Oak	57.0
14	Naples	64.4	14	Lake City 2 E	57.1
15	Tampa Int'l Airport	63.6	15	Usher Tower	57.4
16	Venice	*63.4*	16	Jacksonville Int'l Airport	57.7
17	Canal Point USDA	63.3	17	Weeki Wachee	58.4
17	Fort Pierce	63.3	18	Inverness 3 SE	58.7
19	Melbourne Regional Airport	63.2	19	Ocala	58.8
20	Punta Gorda 4 ESE	63.1	20	Archbold Bio Station	59.1
21	Moore Haven Lock 1	63.0	21	Pensacola Regional Airport	59.2
22	Immokalee 3 NNW	62.6	22	Apalachicola Municipal Airport	59.9
22	Lakeland Linder Airport	*62.6*	22	Fernandina Beach	59.9
22	Tarpon Springs Sewage Plant	62.6	24	Lisbon	60.4
25	Orlando Int'l Airport	*62.5*	24	Saint Augustine	*60.4*

Annual Extreme Minimum Temperature

	Highest			Lowest	
Rank	Station Name	°F	Rank	Station Name	°F
1	Key West Int'l Airport	41	1	Quincy 3 SSW	0
2	Tavernier	*35*	2	Chipley 3 E	2
3	Miami Beach	32	3	De Funiak Springs	*3*
4	Miami Int'l Airport	30	3	Milton Experiment Station	3
5	Fort Lauderdale	28	5	Fernandina Beach	4
5	Hialeah	28	5	Jasper	4
5	Tamiami Trail 40 Mile Bend	28	5	Monticello 3 W	4
8	Fort Myers Page Field	*27*	8	Pensacola Regional Airport	5
8	West Palm Beach Int'l Airport	27	9	Live Oak	6
10	Clewiston U.S. Engineers	26	9	Panama City 5 NE	6
10	Naples	26	9	Tallahassee Municipal Airport	6
12	Canal Point USDA	25	12	Jacksonville Int'l Airport	7
13	Flamingo Ranger Station	24	12	Lake City 2 E	7
13	Saint Petersburg	24	12	Mayo	7
15	Moore Haven Lock 1	23	12	Perry	7
15	Punta Gorda 4 ESE	23	16	High Springs	*8*
15	Stuart 1 S	23	17	Apalachicola Municipal Airport	9
15	Venice	*23*	17	Usher Tower	9
15	Vero Beach	23	19	Cross City 2 WNW	10
20	Belle Glade Exp. Station	21	19	Saint Augustine	*10*
21	Bartow	20	21	Ocala	11
21	Bradenton 5 ESE	20	22	Archbold Bio Station	13
21	Immokalee 3 NNW	20	22	Brooksville Chin Hill	13
21	Lakeland Linder Airport	*20*	22	Weeki Wachee	13
21	Wauchula	20	25	Jacksonville Beach	14

July Mean Maximum Temperature

	Highest			Lowest	
Rank	Station Name	°F	Rank	Station Name	°F
1	Live Oak	93.1	1	Miami Beach	87.4
2	Archbold Bio Station	93.0	2	Flamingo Ranger Station	89.3
2	Myakka River State Park	93.0	2	Key West Int'l Airport	89.3
4	Lakeland Linder Airport	92.9	4	Fort Lauderdale	89.5
5	Lake Alfred Exp. Station	92.8	5	Apalachicola Municipal Airport	89.7
5	Mountain Lake	92.8	5	Miami Int'l Airport	89.7
7	Perry	92.7	7	Jacksonville Beach	89.8
8	High Springs	92.5	8	Fernandina Beach	89.9
9	Saint Leo	92.4	8	Panama City 5 NE	89.9
9	Wauchula	92.4	10	Stuart 1 S	90.0
11	Bartow	92.3	11	West Palm Beach Int'l Airport	90.1
11	Ocala	92.3	12	Cross City 2 WNW	*90.4*
13	Mayo	92.2	12	Vero Beach	90.4
13	Punta Gorda 4 ESE	92.2	14	Daytona Beach Regional Airport	90.5
13	Tamiami Trail 40 Mile Bend	92.2	14	Melbourne Regional Airport	90.5
16	Jacksonville Int'l Airport	92.1	14	Pensacola Regional Airport	90.5
17	Sanford Experiment Station	92.0	17	Monticello 3 W	90.6
18	Orlando Int'l Airport	91.9	17	Saint Augustine	90.6
18	Usher Tower	91.9	17	Saint Petersburg	90.6
20	Arcadia	91.8	20	Brooksville Chin Hill	90.7
20	Avon Park 2 W	91.8	20	Quincy 3 SSW	90.7
20	Canal Point USDA	91.8	20	Tampa Int'l Airport	90.7
20	Clewiston U.S. Engineers	91.8	23	Hialeah	90.8
20	De Funiak Springs	91.8	24	Tavernier	*90.9*
20	Kissimmee 2	91.8	25	Venice	*91.0*

January Mean Minimum Temperature

	Highest			Lowest	
Rank	**Station Name**	**°F**	**Rank**	**Station Name**	**°F**
1	Key West Int'l Airport	65.1	1	Chipley 3 E	37.6
2	Tavernier	63.3	2	Monticello 3 W	37.8
3	Miami Beach	63.0	3	De Funiak Springs	38.2
4	Miami Int'l Airport	60.1	4	Jasper	38.4
5	Fort Lauderdale	58.6	5	Milton Experiment Station	39.1
6	Hialeah	58.5	5	Tallahassee Municipal Airport	39.1
7	West Palm Beach Int'l Airport	57.1	7	Panama City 5 NE	39.7
8	Tamiami Trail 40 Mile Bend	57.0	8	Cross City 2 WNW	39.8
9	Flamingo Ranger Station	56.0	8	Quincy 3 SSW	39.8
10	Stuart 1 S	55.1	10	High Springs	40.2
11	Saint Petersburg	54.3	10	Mayo	40.2
12	Clewiston U.S. Engineers	54.2	12	Perry	41.4
13	Fort Myers Page Field	54.1	13	Jacksonville Int'l Airport	41.8
14	Naples	54.0	13	Lake City 2 E	41.8
15	Canal Point USDA	52.9	15	Live Oak	42.1
16	Immokalee 3 NNW	52.0	16	Pensacola Regional Airport	42.6
17	Belle Glade Exp. Station	51.9	17	Fernandina Beach	43.2
18	Fort Pierce	51.7	18	Usher Tower	43.4
18	Punta Gorda 4 ESE	51.7	19	Apalachicola Municipal Airport	44.1
20	Moore Haven Lock 1	51.6	19	Inverness 3 SE	44.1
21	Melbourne Regional Airport	51.2	21	Weeki Wachee	44.5
22	Venice	51.0	22	Ocala	45.6
23	Tampa Int'l Airport	50.6	23	Jacksonville Beach	46.0
23	Vero Beach	50.6	23	Saint Augustine	*46.0*
25	Lakeland Linder Airport	50.4	25	Lisbon	46.7

Number of Annual Heating Degree Days

	Highest			Lowest	
Rank	**Station Name**	**Num.**	**Rank**	**Station Name**	**Num.**
1	Chipley 3 E	1,867	1	Key West Int'l Airport	61
2	Monticello 3 W	1,767	2	Tavernier	*81*
3	De Funiak Springs	1,730	3	Miami Beach	130
4	Milton Experiment Station	1,710	4	Miami Int'l Airport	151
5	Panama City 5 NE	1,608	5	Hialeah	155
6	Quincy 3 SSW	1,602	6	Tamiami Trail 40 Mile Bend	*168*
7	Tallahassee Municipal Airport	1,592	7	Fort Lauderdale	172
8	Jasper	1,591	8	Flamingo Ranger Station	191
9	Pensacola Regional Airport	1,472	9	West Palm Beach Int'l Airport	238
10	Mayo	1,394	10	Naples	249
11	Cross City 2 WNW	*1,391*	11	Stuart 1 S	255
12	Lake City 2 E	1,333	12	Fort Myers Page Field	303
13	Jacksonville Int'l Airport	1,325	13	Canal Point USDA	308
14	Fernandina Beach	1,297	14	Immokalee 3 NNW	323
15	Apalachicola Municipal Airport	1,277	15	Clewiston U.S. Engineers	*335*
16	Perry	1,210	16	Punta Gorda 4 ESE	374
17	Live Oak	1,173	17	Belle Glade Exp. Station	380
18	High Springs	*1,139*	18	Saint Petersburg	403
19	Jacksonville Beach	*1,059*	19	Fort Pierce	414
20	Usher Tower	1,029	20	Moore Haven Lock 1	424
21	Saint Augustine	*933*	21	Fort Drum 5 NW	*446*
22	Inverness 3 SE	929	22	Myakka River State Park	450
23	Weeki Wachee	891	23	Vero Beach	479
24	Ocala	841	24	Bartow	483
25	Lisbon	830	25	Venice	*490*

Number of Annual Cooling Degree Days

	Highest			Lowest	
Rank	**Station Name**	**Num.**	**Rank**	**Station Name**	**Num.**
1	Key West Int'l Airport	4,926	1	Monticello 3 W	2,314
2	Tavernier	*4,899*	2	Chipley 3 E	2,345
3	Hialeah	4,586	3	De Funiak Springs	*2,365*
4	Miami Int'l Airport	4,543	4	Panama City 5 NE	2,399
5	Miami Beach	4,462	5	Jasper	2,440
6	Tamiami Trail 40 Mile Bend	*4,412*	6	Quincy 3 SSW	2,474
7	Fort Lauderdale	4,295	7	Milton Experiment Station	2,475
8	West Palm Beach Int'l Airport	4,139	8	Cross City 2 WNW	*2,499*
9	Fort Myers Page Field	*4,098*	9	Tallahassee Municipal Airport	2,627
10	Flamingo Ranger Station	3,977	10	Fernandina Beach	2,677
11	Naples	3,953	10	Lake City 2 E	2,677
12	Stuart 1 S	3,944	12	Pensacola Regional Airport	2,690
13	Clewiston U.S. Engineers	*3,905*	13	Apalachicola Municipal Airport	2,721
14	Punta Gorda 4 ESE	3,805	14	Gainesville Regional Airport	*2,729*
15	Saint Petersburg	3,770	15	Mayo	2,744
16	Lakeland Linder Airport	*3,762*	16	Jacksonville Int'l Airport	2,750
17	Immokalee 3 NNW	3,671	17	Perry	2,751
18	Bartow	3,659	18	Saint Augustine	2,781
19	Canal Point USDA	3,657	19	High Springs	2,801
20	Myakka River State Park	3,652	20	Jacksonville Beach	*2,810*
21	Venice	*3,637*	21	Usher Tower	2,834
22	Moore Haven Lock 1	3,629	22	Inverness 3 SE	2,916
23	Tampa Int'l Airport	3,575	23	Live Oak	2,919
24	Tarpon Springs Sewage Plant	3,563	24	Daytona Beach Regional Airport	3,015
25	Fort Pierce	3,559	25	Lisbon	3,036

Annual Precipitation

	Highest			Lowest	
Rank	**Station Name**	**Inches**	**Rank**	**Station Name**	**Inches**
1	Milton Experiment Station	70.20	1	Key West Int'l Airport	39.32
2	De Funiak Springs	67.06	2	Tavernier	44.82
3	Panama City 5 NE	66.07	3	Tampa Int'l Airport	45.07
4	Hialeah	65.92	4	Clewiston U.S. Engineers	45.79
5	Pensacola Regional Airport	65.18	5	Miami Beach	46.75
6	Tallahassee Municipal Airport	64.31	6	Moore Haven Lock 1	47.05
7	Fort Lauderdale	64.13	7	Flamingo Ranger Station	47.81
8	West Palm Beach Int'l Airport	61.81	7	Saint Augustine	*47.81*
9	Stuart 1 S	60.34	9	Melbourne Regional Airport	48.16
10	Usher Tower	60.31	10	Kissimmee 2	48.34
11	Myakka River State Park	59.11	11	Mountain Lake	48.52
12	Cross City 2 WNW	59.03	12	Lisbon	48.88
13	Perry	58.97	13	Daytona Beach Regional Airport	48.92
14	Chipley 3 E	58.61	14	Venice	49.23
15	Monticello 3 W	58.41	15	Saint Petersburg	49.29
16	Miami Int'l Airport	58.00	16	Orlando Int'l Airport	*49.70*
17	Quincy 3 SSW	57.20	17	Arcadia	49.82
18	Apalachicola Municipal Airport	56.91	18	Avon Park 2 W	49.86
19	Vero Beach	55.71	19	Punta Gorda 4 ESE	50.01
20	Mayo	55.59	20	Immokalee 3 NNW	50.08
21	Fort Myers Page Field	54.86	21	Lakeland Linder Airport	*50.11*
22	High Springs	54.58	22	Clermont 7 S	50.32
23	Saint Leo	54.29	23	Lake Alfred Exp. Station	50.60
24	Bradenton 5 ESE	54.27	24	Ocala	50.68
25	Lake City 2 E	54.15	25	Fernandina Beach	50.87

Number of Days Annually With ≥ 0.1″ Precipitation

	Highest			Lowest	
Rank	Station Name	Days	Rank	Station Name	Days
1	Stuart 1 S	94	1	Fort Drum 5 NW	60
2	Hialeah	92	2	Tavernier	*61*
3	West Palm Beach Int'l Airport	89	3	Key West Int'l Airport	62
4	Fort Lauderdale	88	3	La Belle	62
5	Miami Int'l Airport	86	5	Weeki Wachee	65
6	De Funiak Springs	85	6	Arcadia	66
7	Milton Experiment Station	84	6	Clewiston U.S. Engineers	66
7	Usher Tower	84	8	Tampa Int'l Airport	67
7	Vero Beach	84	9	Saint Petersburg	69
10	Titusville	82	9	Sanford Experiment Station	*69*
11	Fort Pierce	81	9	Venice	69
11	Panama City 5 NE	81	12	Parrish	70
11	Perry	81	13	Brooksville Chin Hill	71
14	Tallahassee Municipal Airport	80	13	Flamingo Ranger Station	71
15	Belle Glade Exp. Station	79	13	Miami Beach	71
15	Chipley 3 E	79	16	Apalachicola Municipal Airport	72
17	Cross City 2 WNW	78	16	Daytona Beach Regional Airport	72
17	Jacksonville Int'l Airport	78	16	Live Oak	72
17	Myakka River State Park	78	16	Melbourne Regional Airport	72
17	Ocala	78	16	Moore Haven Lock 1	72
21	Canal Point USDA	77	16	Saint Augustine	*72*
21	High Springs	77	16	Tarpon Springs Sewage Plant	72
21	Immokalee 3 NNW	77	23	Avon Park 2 W	73
21	Lake City 2 E	77	23	Lake Alfred Exp. Station	73
21	Mayo	77	23	Wauchula	73

Number of Days Annually With ≥ 1.0″ Precipitation

	Highest			Lowest	
Rank	Station Name	Days	Rank	Station Name	Days
1	De Funiak Springs	21	1	Flamingo Ranger Station	11
1	Hialeah	21	1	Key West Int'l Airport	11
3	Milton Experiment Station	20	3	Saint Augustine	*13*
3	Myakka River State Park	20	3	Tamiami Trail 40 Mile Bend	13
3	Panama City 5 NE	20	5	Clewiston U.S. Engineers	14
6	Archbold Bio Station	19	5	Moore Haven Lock 1	14
6	Cross City 2 WNW	19	5	Tavernier	14
6	Fort Lauderdale	19	8	Belle Glade Exp. Station	15
6	Pensacola Regional Airport	19	8	Clermont 7 S	15
6	Perry	19	8	Daytona Beach Regional Airport	15
6	Tallahassee Municipal Airport	19	8	Fernandina Beach	15
6	Usher Tower	19	8	Jacksonville Int'l Airport	15
6	West Palm Beach Int'l Airport	19	8	Kissimmee 2	15
14	Bradenton 5 ESE	18	8	La Belle	15
14	Chipley 3 E	18	8	Melbourne Regional Airport	15
14	High Springs	18	8	Miami Beach	15
14	Mayo	18	8	Ocala	15
14	Parrish	18	8	Punta Gorda 4 ESE	15
14	Saint Leo	18	8	Tampa Int'l Airport	15
14	Stuart 1 S	18	8	Vero Beach	15
14	Tarpon Springs Sewage Plant	18	21	Fort Drum 5 NW	16
22	Apalachicola Municipal Airport	17	21	Fort Myers Page Field	16
22	Arcadia	17	21	Fort Pierce	16
22	Avon Park 2 W	17	21	Inverness 3 SE	16
22	Bartow	17	21	Jacksonville Beach	16

Annual Snowfall

Rank	Station Name	Inches		Rank	Station Name	Inches
	Highest				**Lowest**	
1	Milton Experiment Station	0.2		1	Arcadia	0.0
2	Live Oak	0.1		1	Bartow	0.0
3	Apalachicola Municipal Airport	Trace		1	Bradenton 5 ESE	0.0
3	Archbold Bio Station	Trace		1	Brooksville Chin Hill	0.0
3	Avon Park 2 W	Trace		1	Canal Point USDA	0.0
3	Belle Glade Exp. Station	Trace		1	Clewiston U.S. Engineers	0.0
3	Chipley 3 E	Trace		1	Cross City 2 WNW	0.0
3	Clermont 7 S	Trace		1	Flamingo Ranger Station	0.0
3	Daytona Beach Regional Airport	Trace		1	Fort Lauderdale	0.0
3	De Funiak Springs	Trace		1	Fort Myers Page Field	*0.0*
3	Fernandina Beach	Trace		1	Hialeah	0.0
3	Fort Drum 5 NW	Trace		1	Immokalee 3 NNW	0.0
3	Fort Pierce	Trace		1	Inverness 3 SE	0.0
3	High Springs	Trace		1	Key West Int'l Airport	0.0
3	Jacksonville Beach	Trace		1	Kissimmee 2	0.0
3	Jacksonville Int'l Airport	Trace		1	Melbourne Regional Airport	0.0
3	Jasper	Trace		1	Miami Beach	0.0
3	La Belle	Trace		1	Moore Haven Lock 1	0.0
3	Lake Alfred Exp. Station	Trace		1	Naples	0.0
3	Lake City 2 E	Trace		1	Plant City	0.0
3	Lakeland Linder Airport	*Trace*		1	Punta Gorda 4 ESE	0.0
3	Lisbon	Trace		1	Sanford Experiment Station	0.0
3	Mayo	Trace		1	Stuart 1 S	0.0
3	Miami Int'l Airport	Trace		1	Tamiami Trail 40 Mile Bend	0.0
3	Monticello 3 W	Trace		1	Tarpon Springs Sewage Plant	0.0

Note: See Appendix D for explanation of data.

Annual Extreme Maximum Temperature

	Highest				Lowest	
Rank	Station Name	°F		Rank	Station Name	°F
1	Fort Stewart	110		1	Blairsville Exp. Station	97
2	Brooklet 1 W	109		2	Clayton 1 SSW	98
2	Dublin	109		3	Helen	*100*
2	Milledgeville	109		4	Cornelia	101
2	Thomaston 2 S	109		4	Dahlonega 1 W	101
6	Augusta Bush Field	108		6	Ashburn 3 ENE	102
6	Hartwell	108		6	Experiment	102
6	Macon Regional Airport	108		6	La Grange	102
6	Warrenton	108		9	Carrollton	103
6	Waycross 4 NE	108		9	Dalton	103
6	Waynesboro 2 NE	108		9	Gainesville	103
12	Albany 3 SE	107		9	Jasper 1 NNW	103
12	Athens Municipal Airport	107		9	Monticello	103
12	Camilla 3 SE	107		9	Newnan 4 NE	103
12	Eastman 1 W	107		9	Plains SW Georgia Exp. Station	103
12	Irwinton 4 WNW	107		16	Brunswick Malcolm McKinnon Arpt.	104
12	Jesup 8 S	107		16	Cartersville	104
12	Sandersville	107		16	Cedartown 3 NE	104
12	Siloam 3 N	107		16	Columbus Metropolitan Airport	104
12	Swainsboro	107		16	Dallas 7 NE	104
21	Appling 2 NW	106		16	Fitzgerald	104
21	Cordele	106		16	Homerville 3 WSW	104
21	Douglas	106		16	Moultrie 2 ESE	104
21	Elberton 2 N	106		16	Nahunta 3 E	104
21	Folkston 9 SW	106		16	Rome	104

Annual Mean Maximum Temperature

	Highest				Lowest	
Rank	Station Name	°F		Rank	Station Name	°F
1	Folkston 9 SW	81.2		1	Blairsville Exp. Station	67.5
2	Waycross 4 NE	79.9		2	Jasper 1 NNW	68.6
3	Jesup 8 S	79.0		3	Cornelia	68.8
4	Fort Stewart	78.9		4	Dahlonega 1 W	69.0
5	Quitman 2 NW	78.8		5	Clayton 1 SSW	69.4
6	Camilla 3 SE	78.7		6	Gainesville	70.1
6	Homerville 3 WSW	78.7		7	Helen	*70.4*
8	Cordele	78.6		7	Lafayette 5 SW	70.4
9	Surrency 2 WNW	78.5		9	Dalton	71.0
10	Douglas	78.4		9	Rome	71.0
10	Moultrie 2 ESE	78.4		11	Dallas 7 NE	71.3
12	Albany 3 SE	78.0		12	Calhoun Exp. Station	71.7
12	Alma Bacon County Airport	78.0		13	Toccoa	71.9
12	Glennville	78.0		14	Atlanta Hartsfield Int'l Arpt.	72.0
15	Cuthbert	77.8		15	Cartersville	72.2
16	Swainsboro	77.6		15	Experiment	72.2
17	Hawkinsville	*77.5*		17	Commerce 4 NNW	72.3
18	Irwinton 4 WNW	*77.3*		18	Athens Municipal Airport	72.6
19	Dublin	77.2		18	Winder 1 SSE	72.6
19	Savannah Int'l Airport	77.2		20	Carrollton	72.7
21	Fitzgerald	77.1		21	Covington	72.8
22	Brooklet 1 W	77.0		21	Elberton 2 N	72.8
22	Louisville 1 E	77.0		21	Hartwell	72.8
24	Eastman 1 W	76.8		24	Cedartown 3 NE	73.0
25	Thomaston 2 S	76.7		24	Univ. of GA Plant Science Farm	73.0

Annual Mean Temperature

	Highest				Lowest	
Rank	Station Name	°F		Rank	Station Name	°F
1	Folkston 9 SW	68.5		1	Blairsville Exp. Station	55.2
2	Brunswick Malcolm McKinnon Arpt.	67.8		2	Clayton 1 SSW	56.9
3	Fort Stewart	67.7		3	Dahlonega 1 W	57.3
4	Alma Bacon County Airport	67.1		4	Cornelia	57.9
4	Camilla 3 SE	67.1		5	Jasper 1 NNW	58.4
4	Sapelo Island	67.1		5	Lafayette 5 SW	58.4
7	Moultrie 2 ESE	67.0		7	Helen	*58.5*
8	Glennville	66.9		8	Dallas 7 NE	59.2
8	Savannah Int'l Airport	66.9		9	Rome	59.4
10	Cordele	66.7		10	Calhoun Exp. Station	59.5
11	Jesup 8 S	66.6		11	Dalton	59.7
12	Quitman 2 NW	66.5		12	Gainesville	59.8
13	Cuthbert	66.4		13	Elberton 2 N	60.1
13	Fitzgerald	66.4		14	Commerce 4 NNW	60.5
15	Homerville 3 WSW	66.2		15	Carrollton	60.6
15	Waycross 4 NE	66.2		16	Cartersville	60.8
17	Surrency 2 WNW	66.0		16	Toccoa	60.8
18	Brooklet 1 W	65.9		16	Winder 1 SSE	60.8
18	Tifton Exp. Station	65.9		19	Cedartown 3 NE	61.0
20	Douglas	65.7		20	Experiment	61.2
21	Swainsboro	65.6		21	Washington 2 ESE	61.3
22	Albany 3 SE	65.4		22	Appling 2 NW	61.5
23	Columbus Metropolitan Airport	65.3		23	Covington	61.7
24	Ashburn 3 ENE	*65.2*		23	Newnan 4 NE	61.7
25	Eastman 1 W	65.1		23	Univ. of GA Plant Science Farm	61.7

Annual Mean Minimum Temperature

	Highest				Lowest	
Rank	Station Name	°F		Rank	Station Name	°F
1	Brunswick Malcolm McKinnon Arpt.	59.9		1	Blairsville Exp. Station	42.7
2	Sapelo Island	57.9		2	Clayton 1 SSW	44.4
3	Fort Stewart	56.5		3	Dahlonega 1 W	45.6
4	Savannah Int'l Airport	56.4		4	Lafayette 5 SW	46.4
5	Alma Bacon County Airport	56.2		5	Helen	*46.6*
6	Folkston 9 SW	55.8		6	Cornelia	46.9
7	Glennville	55.7		7	Dallas 7 NE	47.1
8	Fitzgerald	55.6		8	Elberton 2 N	47.3
8	Moultrie 2 ESE	55.6		9	Calhoun Exp. Station	47.4
10	Camilla 3 SE	55.5		10	Rome	47.8
11	Nahunta 3 E	*55.1*		11	Jasper 1 NNW	48.0
11	Tifton Exp. Station	55.1		12	Carrollton	48.4
13	Cuthbert	55.0		13	Appling 2 NW	48.5
14	Cordele	54.8		13	Dalton	48.5
15	Brooklet 1 W	54.7		15	Commerce 4 NNW	48.6
16	Columbus Metropolitan Airport	54.6		16	Cedartown 3 NE	48.9
17	Ashburn 3 ENE	*54.3*		17	Winder 1 SSE	49.1
18	Quitman 2 NW	54.1		18	Cartersville	49.4
19	Jesup 8 S	54.0		18	Gainesville	49.4
20	Homerville 3 WSW	53.7		20	Milledgeville	49.5
21	Surrency 2 WNW	53.5		20	Washington 2 ESE	49.5
21	Swainsboro	53.5		22	Toccoa	49.7
23	Eastman 1 W	53.4		23	Newnan 4 NE	49.9
24	Macon Regional Airport	53.2		23	Waynesboro 2 NE	49.9
25	Douglas	52.9		25	Warrenton	50.1

Annual Extreme Minimum Temperature

	Highest				Lowest	
Rank	Station Name	°F		Rank	Station Name	°F
1	Fitzgerald	8		1	Blairsville Exp. Station	-16
2	Brunswick Malcolm McKinnon Arpt.	6		2	Jasper 1 NNW	-14
3	Folkston 9 SW	5		3	Lafayette 5 SW	-13
4	Homerville 3 WSW	3		4	Dahlonega 1 W	-12
4	Jesup 8 S	3		4	Dallas 7 NE	-12
4	Nahunta 3 E	3		4	Helen	*-12*
4	Quitman 2 NW	3		7	Clayton 1 SSW	-11
4	Sapelo Island	3		8	Calhoun Exp. Station	-10
4	Savannah Int'l Airport	3		8	Cornelia	-10
10	Camilla 3 SE	2		8	Dalton	-10
10	Waycross 4 NE	*2*		11	Carrollton	-9
12	Albany 3 SE	1		11	Cartersville	-9
12	Ashburn 3 ENE	1		11	Cedartown 3 NE	-9
12	Brooklet 1 W	1		11	Rome	-9
12	Douglas	1		15	Atlanta Hartsfield Int'l Arpt.	-8
12	Glennville	1		15	Experiment	-8
12	Surrency 2 WNW	1		15	Gainesville	-8
18	Dublin	0		15	Newnan 4 NE	-8
18	Fort Stewart	0		15	West Point	-8
18	Moultrie 2 ESE	0		15	Winder 1 SSE	-8
18	Tifton Exp. Station	0		21	Covington	-7
22	Alma Bacon County Airport	-1		21	Monticello	-7
22	Augusta Bush Field	-1		21	Siloam 3 N	-7
22	Univ. of GA Plant Science Farm	-1		24	Macon Regional Airport	-6
22	Waynesboro 2 NE	-1		25	Commerce 4 NNW	-5

July Mean Maximum Temperature

	Highest				Lowest	
Rank	Station Name	°F		Rank	Station Name	°F
1	Cordele	94.2		1	Blairsville Exp. Station	84.6
1	Folkston 9 SW	94.2		2	Clayton 1 SSW	85.3
1	Waycross 4 NE	94.2		3	Cornelia	85.9
4	Dublin	94.0		4	Dahlonega 1 W	86.3
5	Fort Stewart	93.3		5	Jasper 1 NNW	86.5
5	Jesup 8 S	93.3		6	Helen	*86.8*
7	Douglas	93.2		7	Gainesville	87.3
7	Hawkinsville	93.2		8	Rome	87.8
9	Swainsboro	92.9		9	Carrollton	88.9
10	Irwinton 4 WNW	92.8		9	Lafayette 5 SW	88.9
11	Milledgeville	92.7		11	Experiment	89.0
12	Glennville	92.6		11	Toccoa	89.0
12	Homerville 3 WSW	92.6		13	Dallas 7 NE	89.2
12	Louisville 1 E	92.6		13	Dalton	89.2
12	Macon Regional Airport	92.6		15	Atlanta Hartsfield Int'l Arpt.	89.3
16	Albany 3 SE	92.5		16	Cartersville	89.4
16	Augusta Bush Field	92.5		17	Newnan 4 NE	89.6
18	Camilla 3 SE	92.4		17	Winder 1 SSE	89.6
18	Surrency 2 WNW	92.4		19	Elberton 2 N	89.8
20	Cuthbert	92.3		20	Cedartown 3 NE	90.0
20	Moultrie 2 ESE	92.3		20	Commerce 4 NNW	90.0
22	Brooklet 1 W	92.2		20	Covington	90.0
22	Savannah Int'l Airport	92.2		23	Brunswick Malcolm McKinnon Arpt.	90.1
24	Fitzgerald	92.0		23	Calhoun Exp. Station	90.1
24	Quitman 2 NW	92.0		25	Hartwell	90.3

January Mean Minimum Temperature

	Highest				Lowest	
Rank	Station Name	°F		Rank	Station Name	°F
1	Brunswick Malcolm McKinnon Arpt.	42.6		1	Blairsville Exp. Station	24.4
2	Sapelo Island	41.2		2	Clayton 1 SSW	27.7
3	Alma Bacon County Airport	40.6		3	Lafayette 5 SW	27.8
3	Folkston 9 SW	40.6		4	Dahlonega 1 W	27.9
5	Fort Stewart	40.4		5	Calhoun Exp. Station	28.4
6	Moultrie 2 ESE	39.7		5	Dallas 7 NE	28.4
7	Camilla 3 SE	39.3		7	Cornelia	29.1
8	Glennville	39.1		7	Dalton	29.1
8	Savannah Int'l Airport	39.1		9	Rome	29.2
10	Nahunta 3 E	*39.0*		10	Jasper 1 NNW	29.8
11	Fitzgerald	38.9		11	Elberton 2 N	30.0
12	Homerville 3 WSW	38.4		11	Helen	*30.0*
13	Brooklet 1 W	38.3		13	Commerce 4 NNW	30.4
13	Cuthbert	38.3		14	Appling 2 NW	30.7
15	Jesup 8 S	38.2		15	Carrollton	30.9
16	Surrency 2 WNW	38.0		16	Gainesville	31.1
17	Cordele	37.9		17	Washington 2 ESE	31.2
17	Tifton Exp. Station	37.9		18	Cedartown 3 NE	31.4
19	Quitman 2 NW	37.7		19	Milledgeville	31.7
20	Swainsboro	37.1		20	Cartersville	31.8
21	Ashburn 3 ENE	36.8		20	Winder 1 SSE	31.8
22	Columbus Metropolitan Airport	36.5		22	West Point	31.9
23	Eastman 1 W	36.1		23	Toccoa	32.0
24	Douglas	36.0		24	Experiment	32.2
24	Louisville 1 E	36.0		24	Warrenton	32.2

Number of Annual Heating Degree Days

	Highest				Lowest	
Rank	Station Name	Num.		Rank	Station Name	Num.
1	Blairsville Exp. Station	4,293		1	Folkston 9 SW	1,306
2	Dahlonega 1 W	3,770		2	Brunswick Malcolm McKinnon Arpt.	1,490
3	Clayton 1 SSW	3,746		3	Fort Stewart	1,514
4	Lafayette 5 SW	3,637		4	Sapelo Island	1,563
5	Cornelia	3,595		5	Alma Bacon County Airport	1,599
6	Jasper 1 NNW	3,533		6	Moultrie 2 ESE	1,619
7	Dallas 7 NE	3,447		7	Camilla 3 SE	1,644
8	Dalton	3,402		8	Glennville	1,698
9	Calhoun Exp. Station	3,401		9	Jesup 8 S	1,699
10	Helen	*3,393*		10	Quitman 2 NW	1,726
11	Rome	3,347		11	Homerville 3 WSW	1,735
12	Gainesville	3,209		12	Savannah Int'l Airport	1,742
13	Elberton 2 N	3,189		13	Surrency 2 WNW	1,772
14	Commerce 4 NNW	3,115		14	Cuthbert	1,808
15	Cartersville	3,025		15	Cordele	1,820
16	Cedartown 3 NE	3,010		16	Fitzgerald	1,827
17	Toccoa	2,972		17	Brooklet 1 W	1,863
18	Carrollton	2,965		18	Waycross 4 NE	1,876
19	Winder 1 SSE	2,952		19	Tifton Exp. Station	1,897
20	Washington 2 ESE	2,950		20	Douglas	1,977
21	Appling 2 NW	2,907		21	Swainsboro	1,981
22	Experiment	2,895		22	Irwinton 4 WNW	*2,041*
23	Univ. of GA Plant Science Farm	2,851		23	Ashburn 3 ENE	*2,042*
24	Covington	2,837		24	Albany 3 SE	2,072
25	Athens Municipal Airport	2,792		25	Eastman 1 W	2,107

Number of Annual Cooling Degree Days

	Highest			Lowest	
Rank	Station Name	Num.	Rank	Station Name	Num.
1	Folkston 9 SW	2,783	1	Blairsville Exp. Station	844
2	Fort Stewart	2,657	2	Clayton 1 SSW	931
3	Cordele	2,653	3	Dahlonega 1 W	1,061
4	Brunswick Malcolm McKinnon Arpt.	2,633	4	Cornelia	1,177
5	Savannah Int'l Airport	2,572	5	Helen	*1,223*
6	Camilla 3 SE	2,551	6	Jasper 1 NNW	1,245
7	Alma Bacon County Airport	2,515	7	Lafayette 5 SW	1,345
8	Moultrie 2 ESE	2,513	8	Rome	1,419
9	Glennville	2,488	9	Dallas 7 NE	1,493
10	Waycross 4 NE	2,465	10	Elberton 2 N	1,502
11	Cuthbert	2,444	11	Carrollton	1,504
12	Sapelo Island	2,433	12	Calhoun Exp. Station	1,509
13	Columbus Metropolitan Airport	2,396	13	Gainesville	1,546
14	Douglas	2,373	14	Winder 1 SSE	1,563
15	Fitzgerald	2,365	15	Toccoa	1,587
16	Quitman 2 NW	2,363	16	Commerce 4 NNW	1,613
17	Jesup 8 S	2,361	17	Experiment	1,627
18	Brooklet 1 W	2,354	18	Newnan 4 NE	1,645
19	Swainsboro	2,349	19	Cartersville	1,650
20	Albany 3 SE	2,348	20	Dalton	1,653
21	Tifton Exp. Station	2,336	21	Cedartown 3 NE	1,666
22	Eastman 1 W	2,282	22	Appling 2 NW	1,735
23	Macon Regional Airport	2,278	23	Hartwell	1,768
24	Surrency 2 WNW	2,267	24	Univ. of GA Plant Science Farm	1,769
25	Ashburn 3 ENE	*2,258*	25	Washington 2 ESE	1,781

Annual Precipitation

	Highest			Lowest	
Rank	Station Name	Inches	Rank	Station Name	Inches
1	Clayton 1 SSW	73.78	1	Cartersville	42.99
2	Helen	*71.36*	2	Augusta Bush Field	44.62
3	Dahlonega 1 W	64.84	3	Macon Regional Airport	45.16
4	Toccoa	61.07	4	Swainsboro	45.40
5	Jasper 1 NNW	60.43	5	Fitzgerald	46.02
6	Cornelia	60.36	6	Irwinton 4 WNW	46.31
7	Lafayette 5 SW	58.50	7	Cordele	46.37
8	Blairsville Exp. Station	58.33	8	Louisville 1 E	46.51
9	Dalton	56.62	9	Hawkinsville	46.77
10	Rome	56.21	10	Milledgeville	46.84
11	Gainesville	54.97	11	Sandersville	46.88
12	Dallas 7 NE	54.49	12	Washington 2 ESE	46.94
13	Calhoun Exp. Station	53.96	13	Tifton Exp. Station	47.32
14	La Grange	53.87	14	Surrency 2 WNW	47.33
15	Albany 3 SE	53.61	15	Waynesboro 2 NE	47.48
15	Carrollton	53.61	16	Appling 2 NW	47.51
17	Cedartown 3 NE	53.60	17	Dublin	47.55
18	Quitman 2 NW	53.49	18	Brooklet 1 W	47.57
19	Camilla 3 SE	53.15	19	Eastman 1 W	47.58
20	Homerville 3 WSW	53.14	20	Siloam 3 N	47.59
21	Cuthbert	53.01	21	Monticello	47.64
22	Folkston 9 SW	52.92	22	Glennville	47.90
23	Newnan 4 NE	52.80	23	Athens Municipal Airport	48.01
24	Sapelo Island	52.59	24	Brunswick Malcolm McKinnon Arpt.	48.45
25	Commerce 4 NNW	52.29	25	Ashburn 3 ENE	48.76

Number of Days Annually With ≥ 0.1″ Precipitation

	Highest			Lowest	
Rank	**Station Name**	**Days**	**Rank**	**Station Name**	**Days**
1	Clayton 1 SSW	95	1	Quitman 2 NW	*56*
2	Blairsville Exp. Station	94	2	Cartersville	*60*
3	Helen	*93*	3	Swainsboro	65
4	Dahlonega 1 W	88	4	Waynesboro 2 NE	66
4	Jasper 1 NNW	88	5	Nahunta 3 E	67
6	Dalton	85	6	Irwinton 4 WNW	*68*
6	Toccoa	85	7	Fitzgerald	69
8	Gainesville	84	8	Brunswick Malcolm McKinnon Arpt.	70
8	Lafayette 5 SW	84	8	Hawkinsville	70
8	Rome	84	8	Jesup 8 S	70
11	Cornelia	83	8	Milledgeville	70
11	Dallas 7 NE	83	8	Talbotton	70
13	Calhoun Exp. Station	81	8	Warrenton	70
14	Commerce 4 NNW	80	14	Ashburn 3 ENE	71
15	Cedartown 3 NE	79	14	Augusta Bush Field	71
15	Douglas	79	14	Cordele	71
15	Experiment	79	14	Louisville 1 E	71
15	Newnan 4 NE	79	14	Monticello	71
19	Elberton 2 N	78	19	Appling 2 NW	72
19	La Grange	78	19	Macon Regional Airport	72
21	Carrollton	77	19	Sandersville	72
21	Univ. of GA Plant Science Farm	77	19	Savannah Int'l Airport	72
23	Albany 3 SE	76	19	Surrency 2 WNW	72
23	Brooklet 1 W	76	19	Thomaston 2 S	72
23	Covington	76	19	Tifton Exp. Station	72

Number of Days Annually With ≥ 1.0″ Precipitation

	Highest			Lowest	
Rank	**Station Name**	**Days**	**Rank**	**Station Name**	**Days**
1	Clayton 1 SSW	25	1	Augusta Bush Field	12
1	Helen	*25*	1	Milledgeville	12
3	Dahlonega 1 W	20	3	Athens Municipal Airport	13
4	Toccoa	19	3	Dublin	13
5	Dalton	18	3	Fitzgerald	13
5	Jasper 1 NNW	18	3	Glennville	13
5	Lafayette 5 SW	18	3	Louisville 1 E	13
8	Albany 3 SE	17	3	Macon Regional Airport	13
8	Camilla 3 SE	17	3	Siloam 3 N	13
8	Cornelia	17	3	Univ. of GA Plant Science Farm	13
8	Hartwell	17	3	Waynesboro 2 NE	13
8	La Grange	17	12	Appling 2 NW	14
8	Moultrie 2 ESE	17	12	Atlanta Hartsfield Int'l Arpt.	14
8	Quitman 2 NW	*17*	12	Brooklet 1 W	14
8	Talbotton	17	12	Calhoun Exp. Station	14
16	Alma Bacon County Airport	16	12	Cartersville	*14*
16	Blairsville Exp. Station	16	12	Cordele	14
16	Cuthbert	16	12	Covington	14
16	Dallas 7 NE	16	12	Elberton 2 N	14
16	Douglas	16	12	Experiment	14
16	Fort Stewart	16	12	Hawkinsville	14
16	Homerville 3 WSW	16	12	Irwinton 4 WNW	*14*
16	Waycross 4 NE	16	12	Monticello	14
16	West Point	16	12	Rome	14
25	Ashburn 3 ENE	15	12	Sandersville	14

Annual Snowfall

Rank	Highest — Station Name	Inches	Rank	Lowest — Station Name	Inches
1	Blairsville Exp. Station	*4.5*	1	Fitzgerald	Trace
2	Clayton 1 SSW	3.6	1	Folkston 9 SW	Trace
3	Dallas 7 NE	3.4	1	Homerville 3 WSW	Trace
4	Athens Municipal Airport	2.7	1	Moultrie 2 ESE	Trace
5	Cedartown 3 NE	2.6	1	Nahunta 3 E	Trace
5	Toccoa	2.6	1	Tifton Exp. Station	Trace
7	Atlanta Hartsfield Int'l Arpt.	2.4	1	Waycross 4 NE	Trace
8	Dalton	2.3	8	Albany 3 SE	0.1
9	Gainesville	2.1	8	Ashburn 3 ENE	0.1
10	Lafayette 5 SW	*2.0*	8	Brunswick Malcolm McKinnon Arpt.	0.1
11	Jasper 1 NNW	1.9	8	Camilla 3 SE	0.1
12	Calhoun Exp. Station	*1.7*	8	Cordele	0.1
12	Newnan 4 NE	1.7	8	Eastman 1 W	0.1
12	Siloam 3 N	1.7	8	Elberton 2 N	0.1
15	Hartwell	1.4	8	Fort Stewart	0.1
16	Augusta Bush Field	1.3	8	Glennville	0.1
16	Dahlonega 1 W	1.3	8	Washington 2 ESE	0.1
16	Rome	1.3	8	West Point	0.1
19	Commerce 4 NNW	1.2	19	Alma Bacon County Airport	0.2
19	Covington	1.2	19	Carrollton	0.2
19	Macon Regional Airport	1.2	19	Douglas	0.2
22	Cartersville	1.1	19	Jesup 8 S	0.2
22	Thomaston 2 S	1.1	19	Quitman 2 NW	0.2
24	Monticello	1.0	19	Sapelo Island	0.2
25	Sandersville	0.9	19	Surrency 2 WNW	0.2

Note: See Appendix D for explanation of data.

Annual Extreme Maximum Temperature

	Highest				Lowest	
Rank	**Station Name**	**°F**		**Rank**	**Station Name**	**°F**
1	Puukohola Heiau 98.1	*98*		1	Mauna Loa Slope Observatory	71
2	Kahului Airport	97		2	Haleakala Ranger Station 338	80
2	Lahaina 361	97		3	Kailua 446	87
4	Manoa Lyon Arboretum	*96*		4	Kainaliu 73.2	88
4	Molokai Airport	96		5	Kulani Camp 79	89
6	Honolulu Int'l Airport	95		5	Ookala 223	*89*
6	Waikiki 717.2	95		7	Kanalohuluhulu 1075	90
6	Waimanalo Exp. Farm	95		7	Lihue Airport	90
9	Hana Airport 355	94		9	Opihihale 2 24.1	91
10	Hawaii Volcano Nat'l Park HQ 54	93		10	Hawaii Volcano Nat'l Park HQ 54	93
10	Hilo International Airport	93		10	Hilo International Airport	93
10	Naalehu 14	93		10	Naalehu 14	93
13	Opihihale 2 24.1	91		13	Hana Airport 355	94
14	Kanalohuluhulu 1075	90		14	Honolulu Int'l Airport	95
14	Lihue Airport	90		14	Waikiki 717.2	95
16	Kulani Camp 79	89		14	Waimanalo Exp. Farm	95
16	Ookala 223	*89*		17	Manoa Lyon Arboretum	*96*
18	Kainaliu 73.2	88		17	Molokai Airport	96
19	Kailua 446	87		19	Kahului Airport	97
20	Haleakala Ranger Station 338	80		19	Lahaina 361	97
21	Mauna Loa Slope Observatory	71		21	Puukohola Heiau 98.1	*98*

Annual Mean Maximum Temperature

	Highest				Lowest	
Rank	**Station Name**	**°F**		**Rank**	**Station Name**	**°F**
1	Honolulu Int'l Airport	84.7		1	Haleakala Ranger Station 338	62.6
1	Puukohola Heiau 98.1	*84.7*		2	Kulani Camp 79	63.6
3	Waikiki 717.2	84.5		3	Kanalohuluhulu 1075	67.2
4	Kahului Airport	84.3		4	Hawaii Volcano Nat'l Park HQ 54	69.5
5	Molokai Airport	82.0		5	Ookala 223	*78.7*
6	Hilo International Airport	81.5		6	Opihihale 2 24.1	78.8
7	Lihue Airport	81.2		7	Manoa Lyon Arboretum	*79.1*
8	Waimanalo Exp. Farm	81.0		8	Hana Airport 355	80.6
9	Hana Airport 355	80.6		9	Waimanalo Exp. Farm	81.0
10	Manoa Lyon Arboretum	*79.1*		10	Lihue Airport	81.2
11	Opihihale 2 24.1	78.8		11	Hilo International Airport	81.5
12	Ookala 223	*78.7*		12	Molokai Airport	82.0
13	Hawaii Volcano Nat'l Park HQ 54	69.5		13	Kahului Airport	84.3
14	Kanalohuluhulu 1075	67.2		14	Waikiki 717.2	84.5
15	Kulani Camp 79	63.6		15	Honolulu Int'l Airport	84.7
16	Haleakala Ranger Station 338	62.6		15	Puukohola Heiau 98.1	*84.7*

Annual Mean Temperature

	Highest			Lowest	
Rank	Station Name	°F	Rank	Station Name	°F
1	Honolulu Int'l Airport	77.5	1	Haleakala Ranger Station 338	53.6
2	Waikiki 717.2	76.7	2	Kulani Camp 79	55.4
3	Kahului Airport	75.9	3	Kanalohuluhulu 1075	59.1
4	Lihue Airport	75.8	4	Hawaii Volcano Nat'l Park HQ 54	61.1
5	Waimanalo Exp. Farm	75.2	5	Opihihale 2 24.1	69.8
6	Molokai Airport	74.7	6	Manoa Lyon Arboretum	*72.7*
7	Hana Airport 355	74.3	6	Ookala 223	*72.7*
8	Hilo International Airport	74.1	8	Hilo International Airport	74.1
9	Manoa Lyon Arboretum	*72.7*	9	Hana Airport 355	74.3
9	Ookala 223	*72.7*	10	Molokai Airport	74.7
11	Opihihale 2 24.1	69.8	11	Waimanalo Exp. Farm	75.2
12	Hawaii Volcano Nat'l Park HQ 54	61.1	12	Lihue Airport	75.8
13	Kanalohuluhulu 1075	59.1	13	Kahului Airport	75.9
14	Kulani Camp 79	55.4	14	Waikiki 717.2	76.7
15	Haleakala Ranger Station 338	53.6	15	Honolulu Int'l Airport	77.5

Annual Mean Minimum Temperature

	Highest			Lowest	
Rank	Station Name	°F	Rank	Station Name	°F
1	Lihue Airport	70.3	1	Haleakala Ranger Station 338	44.7
2	Honolulu Int'l Airport	70.2	2	Kulani Camp 79	47.2
3	Waimanalo Exp. Farm	69.4	3	Kanalohuluhulu 1075	50.9
4	Waikiki 717.2	68.9	4	Hawaii Volcano Nat'l Park HQ 54	52.6
5	Hana Airport 355	67.9	5	Opihihale 2 24.1	60.8
6	Kahului Airport	67.5	6	Manoa Lyon Arboretum	*66.3*
7	Molokai Airport	67.3	7	Hilo International Airport	66.6
8	Hilo International Airport	66.6	7	Ookala 223	*66.6*
8	Ookala 223	*66.6*	9	Molokai Airport	67.3
10	Manoa Lyon Arboretum	*66.3*	10	Kahului Airport	67.5
11	Opihihale 2 24.1	60.8	11	Hana Airport 355	67.9
12	Hawaii Volcano Nat'l Park HQ 54	52.6	12	Waikiki 717.2	68.9
13	Kanalohuluhulu 1075	50.9	13	Waimanalo Exp. Farm	69.4
14	Kulani Camp 79	47.2	14	Honolulu Int'l Airport	70.2
15	Haleakala Ranger Station 338	44.7	15	Lihue Airport	70.3

Annual Extreme Minimum Temperature

	Highest				Lowest	
Rank	Station Name	°F		Rank	Station Name	°F
1	Hilo International Airport	54		1	Mauna Loa Slope Observatory	19
2	Honolulu Int'l Airport	53		2	Haleakala Ranger Station 338	28
2	Lihue Airport	53		2	Kulani Camp 79	28
4	Lahaina 361	52		4	Kanalohuluhulu 1075	29
5	Hana Airport 355	51		5	Hawaii Volcano Nat'l Park HQ 54	31
5	Kailua 446	51		6	Puukohola Heiau 98.1	*41*
5	Ookala 223	*51*		7	Molokai Airport	46
8	Kahului Airport	50		7	Waikiki 717.2	46
8	Naalehu 14	50		9	Kainaliu 73.2	48
10	Manoa Lyon Arboretum	*49*		10	Manoa Lyon Arboretum	*49*
10	Opihihale 2 24.1	49		10	Opihihale 2 24.1	49
10	Waimanalo Exp. Farm	49		10	Waimanalo Exp. Farm	49
13	Kainaliu 73.2	48		13	Kahului Airport	50
14	Molokai Airport	46		13	Naalehu 14	50
14	Waikiki 717.2	46		15	Hana Airport 355	51
16	Puukohola Heiau 98.1	*41*		15	Kailua 446	51
17	Hawaii Volcano Nat'l Park HQ 54	31		15	Ookala 223	*51*
18	Kanalohuluhulu 1075	29		18	Lahaina 361	52
19	Haleakala Ranger Station 338	28		19	Honolulu Int'l Airport	53
19	Kulani Camp 79	28		19	Lihue Airport	53
21	Mauna Loa Slope Observatory	19		21	Hilo International Airport	54

July Mean Maximum Temperature

	Highest				Lowest	
Rank	Station Name	°F		Rank	Station Name	°F
1	Honolulu Int'l Airport	87.9		1	Mauna Loa Slope Observatory	56.4
2	Honolulu Observatory 702.2	*87.8*		2	Kulani Camp 79	65.1
3	Lahaina 361	*87.6*		3	Haleakala Ranger Station 338	65.5
4	Waikiki 717.2	87.2		4	Kanalohuluhulu 1075	70.5
5	Puukohola Heiau 98.1	*87.1*		5	Hawaii Volcano Nat'l Park HQ 54	71.4
6	Kahului Airport	86.9		6	Manoa Lyon Arboretum	*79.9*
7	Molokai Airport	84.7		7	Opihihale 2 24.1	80.2
8	Lihue Airport	83.9		8	Ookala 223	*80.3*
9	Waimanalo Exp. Farm	83.4		9	Hana Airport 355	82.4
10	Hilo International Airport	83.0		10	Hilo International Airport	83.0
11	Hana Airport 355	82.4		11	Waimanalo Exp. Farm	83.4
12	Ookala 223	*80.3*		12	Lihue Airport	83.9
13	Opihihale 2 24.1	80.2		13	Molokai Airport	84.7
14	Manoa Lyon Arboretum	*79.9*		14	Kahului Airport	86.9
15	Hawaii Volcano Nat'l Park HQ 54	71.4		15	Puukohola Heiau 98.1	*87.1*
16	Kanalohuluhulu 1075	70.5		16	Waikiki 717.2	87.2
17	Haleakala Ranger Station 338	65.5		17	Lahaina 361	*87.6*
18	Kulani Camp 79	65.1		18	Honolulu Observatory 702.2	*87.8*
19	Mauna Loa Slope Observatory	56.4		19	Honolulu Int'l Airport	87.9

January Mean Minimum Temperature

	Highest				Lowest	
Rank	Station Name	°F		Rank	Station Name	°F
1	Honolulu Int'l Airport	65.4		1	Mauna Loa Slope Observatory	*34.1*
1	Lihue Airport	65.4		2	Haleakala Ranger Station 338	42.1
3	Waimanalo Exp. Farm	64.6		3	Kulani Camp 79	43.0
4	Waikiki 717.2	64.5		4	Kanalohuluhulu 1075	46.4
5	Hana Airport 355	64.3		5	Hawaii Volcano Nat'l Park HQ 54	49.5
6	Lahaina 361	*64.1*		6	Opihihale 2 24.1	57.5
6	Ookala 223	*64.1*		7	Naalehu 14	*62.3*
8	Hilo International Airport	63.6		8	Manoa Lyon Arboretum	*62.5*
9	Kahului Airport	63.5		9	Kahului Airport	63.5
9	Molokai Airport	63.5		9	Molokai Airport	63.5
11	Manoa Lyon Arboretum	*62.5*		11	Hilo International Airport	63.6
12	Naalehu 14	*62.3*		12	Lahaina 361	*64.1*
13	Opihihale 2 24.1	57.5		12	Ookala 223	*64.1*
14	Hawaii Volcano Nat'l Park HQ 54	49.5		14	Hana Airport 355	64.3
15	Kanalohuluhulu 1075	46.4		15	Waikiki 717.2	64.5
16	Kulani Camp 79	43.0		16	Waimanalo Exp. Farm	64.6
17	Haleakala Ranger Station 338	42.1		17	Honolulu Int'l Airport	65.4
18	Mauna Loa Slope Observatory	*34.1*		17	Lihue Airport	65.4

Number of Annual Heating Degree Days

No stations had heating degree days.

Number of Annual Cooling Degree Days

	Highest				Lowest	
Rank	Station Name	Num.		Rank	Station Name	Num.
1	Honolulu Int'l Airport	4,738		1	Haleakala Ranger Station 338	0
2	Waikiki 717.2	4,490		2	Kulani Camp 79	5
3	Puukohola Heiau 98.1	4,167		3	Kanalohuluhulu 1075	26
4	Kahului Airport	4,146		4	Hawaii Volcano Nat'l Park HQ 54	86
5	Honolulu Observatory 702.2	4,081		5	Opihihale 2 24.1	2,026
6	Lihue Airport	3,988		6	Naalehu 14	*2,821*
7	Waimanalo Exp. Farm	3,807		7	Manoa Lyon Arboretum	2,976
8	Molokai Airport	3,607		8	Hilo International Airport	3,430
9	Hana Airport 355	3,479		9	Hana Airport 355	3,479
10	Hilo International Airport	3,430		10	Molokai Airport	3,607
11	Manoa Lyon Arboretum	2,976		11	Waimanalo Exp. Farm	3,807
12	Naalehu 14	*2,821*		12	Lihue Airport	3,988
13	Opihihale 2 24.1	2,026		13	Honolulu Observatory 702.2	4,081
14	Hawaii Volcano Nat'l Park HQ 54	86		14	Kahului Airport	4,146
15	Kanalohuluhulu 1075	26		15	Puukohola Heiau 98.1	4,167
16	Kulani Camp 79	5		16	Waikiki 717.2	4,490
17	Haleakala Ranger Station 338	0		17	Honolulu Int'l Airport	4,738

Annual Precipitation

	Highest			Lowest	
Rank	**Station Name**	**Inches**	**Rank**	**Station Name**	**Inches**
1	Manoa Lyon Arboretum	*153.49*	1	Puukohola Heiau 98.1	*11.33*
2	Hilo International Airport	126.21	2	Lahaina 361	13.77
3	Kailua 446	124.13	3	Honolulu Observatory 702.2	18.22
4	Ookala 223	*123.63*	4	Honolulu Int'l Airport	18.54
5	Kulani Camp 79	109.07	5	Mauna Loa Slope Observatory	18.84
6	Hawaii Volcano Nat'l Park HQ 54	107.94	6	Kahului Airport	19.08
7	Hana Airport 355	79.41	7	Waikiki 717.2	22.59
8	Kanalohuluhulu 1075	62.99	8	Molokai Airport	24.73
9	Kainaliu 73.2	54.79	9	Opihihale 2 24.1	38.71
10	Haleakala Ranger Station 338	54.30	10	Lihue Airport	40.29
11	Naalehu 14	48.44	11	Waimanalo Exp. Farm	43.36
12	Waimanalo Exp. Farm	43.36	12	Naalehu 14	48.44
13	Lihue Airport	40.29	13	Haleakala Ranger Station 338	54.30
14	Opihihale 2 24.1	38.71	14	Kainaliu 73.2	54.79
15	Molokai Airport	24.73	15	Kanalohuluhulu 1075	62.99
16	Waikiki 717.2	22.59	16	Hana Airport 355	79.41
17	Kahului Airport	19.08	17	Hawaii Volcano Nat'l Park HQ 54	107.94
18	Mauna Loa Slope Observatory	18.84	18	Kulani Camp 79	109.07
19	Honolulu Int'l Airport	18.54	19	Ookala 223	*123.63*
20	Honolulu Observatory 702.2	18.22	20	Kailua 446	124.13
21	Lahaina 361	13.77	21	Hilo International Airport	126.21
22	Puukohola Heiau 98.1	*11.33*	22	Manoa Lyon Arboretum	*153.49*

Number of Days Annually With ≥ 0.1" Precipitation

	Highest			Lowest	
Rank	**Station Name**	**Days**	**Rank**	**Station Name**	**Days**
1	Manoa Lyon Arboretum	*207*	1	Lahaina 361	13
2	Hilo International Airport	194	2	Mauna Loa Slope Observatory	*22*
3	Hawaii Volcano Nat'l Park HQ 54	*165*	3	Honolulu Observatory 702.2	30
4	Hana Airport 355	*158*	4	Honolulu Int'l Airport	31
5	Kulani Camp 79	*152*	5	Kahului Airport	34
6	Ookala 223	*150*	6	Waikiki 717.2	38
7	Kanalohuluhulu 1075	92	7	Molokai Airport	47
8	Opihihale 2 24.1	79	8	Naalehu 14	*65*
9	Lihue Airport	75	9	Kainaliu 73.2	*66*
10	Haleakala Ranger Station 338	73	10	Waimanalo Exp. Farm	72
11	Waimanalo Exp. Farm	72	11	Haleakala Ranger Station 338	73
12	Kainaliu 73.2	*66*	12	Lihue Airport	75
13	Naalehu 14	*65*	13	Opihihale 2 24.1	79
14	Molokai Airport	47	14	Kanalohuluhulu 1075	92
15	Waikiki 717.2	38	15	Ookala 223	*150*
16	Kahului Airport	34	16	Kulani Camp 79	*152*
17	Honolulu Int'l Airport	31	17	Hana Airport 355	*158*
18	Honolulu Observatory 702.2	30	18	Hawaii Volcano Nat'l Park HQ 54	*165*
19	Mauna Loa Slope Observatory	*22*	19	Hilo International Airport	194
20	Lahaina 361	13	20	Manoa Lyon Arboretum	*207*

Number of Days Annually With ≥ 1.0″ Precipitation

	Highest			Lowest	
Rank	**Station Name**	**Days**	**Rank**	**Station Name**	**Days**
1	Manoa Lyon Arboretum	*44*	1	Mauna Loa Slope Observatory	0
2	Ookala 223	*32*	2	Lahaina 361	2
3	Hilo International Airport	30	2	Puukohola Heiau 98.1	*2*
4	Kulani Camp 79	25	4	Molokai Airport	4
5	Hawaii Volcano Nat'l Park HQ 54	23	5	Kahului Airport	5
6	Kailua 446	*20*	6	Honolulu Int'l Airport	6
7	Hana Airport 355	15	6	Honolulu Observatory 702.2	6
7	Kanalohuluhulu 1075	15	6	Waikiki 717.2	6
9	Haleakala Ranger Station 338	11	9	Kainaliu 73.2	8
9	Naalehu 14	11	9	Lihue Airport	8
9	Waimanalo Exp. Farm	11	9	Opihihale 2 24.1	8
12	Kainaliu 73.2	8	12	Haleakala Ranger Station 338	11
12	Lihue Airport	8	12	Naalehu 14	11
12	Opihihale 2 24.1	8	12	Waimanalo Exp. Farm	11
15	Honolulu Int'l Airport	6	15	Hana Airport 355	15
15	Honolulu Observatory 702.2	6	15	Kanalohuluhulu 1075	15
15	Waikiki 717.2	6	17	Kailua 446	*20*
18	Kahului Airport	5	18	Hawaii Volcano Nat'l Park HQ 54	23
19	Molokai Airport	4	19	Kulani Camp 79	25
20	Lahaina 361	2	20	Hilo International Airport	30
20	Puukohola Heiau 98.1	*2*	21	Ookala 223	*32*
22	Mauna Loa Slope Observatory	0	22	Manoa Lyon Arboretum	*44*

Annual Snowfall

	Highest			Lowest	
Rank	**Station Name**	**Inches**	**Rank**	**Station Name**	**Inches**
1	Haleakala Ranger Station 338	0.0	1	Haleakala Ranger Station 338	0.0
1	Hana Airport 355	0.0	1	Hana Airport 355	0.0
1	Hawaii Volcano Nat'l Park HQ 54	0.0	1	Hawaii Volcano Nat'l Park HQ 54	0.0
1	Hilo International Airport	0.0	1	Hilo International Airport	0.0
1	Honolulu Int'l Airport	0.0	1	Honolulu Int'l Airport	0.0
1	Honolulu Observatory 702.2	0.0	1	Honolulu Observatory 702.2	0.0
1	Kahului Airport	0.0	1	Kahului Airport	0.0
1	Kailua 446	0.0	1	Kailua 446	0.0
1	Kainaliu 73.2	0.0	1	Kainaliu 73.2	0.0
1	Kanalohuluhulu 1075	0.0	1	Kanalohuluhulu 1075	0.0
1	Kulani Camp 79	0.0	1	Kulani Camp 79	0.0
1	Lahaina 361	0.0	1	Lahaina 361	0.0
1	Lihue Airport	0.0	1	Lihue Airport	0.0
1	Manoa Lyon Arboretum	*0.0*	1	Manoa Lyon Arboretum	*0.0*
1	Molokai Airport	0.0	1	Molokai Airport	0.0
1	Naalehu 14	0.0	1	Naalehu 14	0.0
1	Ookala 223	*0.0*	1	Ookala 223	*0.0*
1	Opihihale 2 24.1	0.0	1	Opihihale 2 24.1	0.0
1	Puukohola Heiau 98.1	*0.0*	1	Puukohola Heiau 98.1	*0.0*
1	Waikiki 717.2	0.0	1	Waikiki 717.2	0.0
1	Waimanalo Exp. Farm	0.0	1	Waimanalo Exp. Farm	0.0

Note: See Appendix D for explanation of data.

Annual Extreme Maximum Temperature

	Highest				Lowest	
Rank	Station Name	°F		Rank	Station Name	°F
1	Swan Falls P H	115		1	Driggs	92
2	Brownlee Dam	113		2	Dixie	*94*
3	Mountain Home	112		2	Grouse	*94*
4	Bruneau	111		2	Lifton Pumping Station	94
4	Malta 4 ESE	111		5	Chilly Barton Flat	95
6	Dworshak Fish Hatchery	110		5	Tetonia Experiment Station	95
7	Boise Air Terminal	109		7	Ashton	96
7	Boise Lucky Peak Dam	109		7	Idaho Falls 16 SE	96
7	Caldwell	109		7	Winchester	96
7	Emmett 2 E	109		7	Yellow Pine 7 S	96
7	Lewiston Airport	109		11	Cascade 1 NW	97
7	Payette	109		11	Warren	97
7	Shoshone 1 WNW	109		13	Cottonwood 2 WSW	*98*
7	Shoup	109		13	Dubois Experiment Station	98
15	Arrowrock Dam	108		15	Fairfield Ranger Station	99
15	Grand View 2 W	108		15	Mackay USFS	99
15	Jerome	108		15	McCall	99
15	Massacre Rocks State Park	*108*		18	Arbon 2 NW	100
19	Cambridge	107		18	Challis	*100*
19	Fenn Ranger Station	107		18	Craters of the Moon	100
21	Boise 7 N	106		18	Gibbonsville	*100*
21	Hazelton	106		18	Grace	100
21	Kellogg Shoshone Airport	106		18	Hill City 1 W	100
21	Minidoka Dam	106		18	Priest River Exp. Station	100
21	Parma Experiment Station	106		18	Saint Anthony 1 WNW	100

Annual Mean Maximum Temperature

	Highest				Lowest	
Rank	Station Name	°F		Rank	Station Name	°F
1	Swan Falls P H	68.1		1	Dixie	*50.8*
2	Bruneau	66.6		2	Warren	53.1
3	Grand View 2 W	66.3		3	Grouse	*53.5*
4	Brownlee Dam	65.7		4	Lifton Pumping Station	54.1
5	Payette	65.6		5	Driggs	54.2
6	Caldwell	65.3		5	Idaho Falls 16 SE	54.2
7	Emmett 2 E	64.3		7	Ashton	54.3
8	Mountain Home	64.1		7	Winchester	54.3
9	Parma Experiment Station	63.9		9	Cascade 1 NW	54.4
10	Dworshak Fish Hatchery	63.8		10	Chilly Barton Flat	54.7
11	Deer Flat Dam	63.7		11	Yellow Pine 7 S	*54.9*
12	Massacre Rocks State Park	*63.3*		12	McCall	55.0
13	Lewiston Airport	63.2		13	Dubois Experiment Station	55.2
14	Boise Air Terminal	63.0		14	Priest River Exp. Station	55.4
15	Jerome	62.7		15	Bayview Model Basin	55.6
16	Shoshone 1 WNW	62.6		15	Saint Anthony 1 WNW	55.6
17	Malta 4 ESE	62.4		17	Cottonwood 2 WSW	*55.7*
18	Castleford 2 N	62.2		17	Craters of the Moon	*55.7*
19	Hazelton	61.8		17	Wallace Woodland Park	55.7
20	Cambridge	61.6		20	Mackay USFS	56.1
21	Burley Municipal Airport	61.2		21	Elk River 1 S	56.2
22	Arrowrock Dam	61.1		21	Powell	56.2
22	Reynolds	61.1		23	Elk City 1 NE	56.3
24	Fenn Ranger Station	61.0		23	Gibbonsville	*56.3*
25	Malad City	60.9		23	Swan Valley 2 E	56.3

Annual Mean Temperature

	Highest			Lowest	
Rank	Station Name	°F	Rank	Station Name	°F
1	Swan Falls P H	55.2	1	Dixie	35.9
2	Brownlee Dam	54.0	2	Grouse	37.5
3	Lewiston Airport	52.8	2	Warren	37.5
4	Bruneau	52.5	4	Yellow Pine 7 S	39.4
5	Caldwell	52.1	5	Chilly Barton Flat	39.8
6	Dworshak Fish Hatchery	52.0	6	Cascade 1 NW	40.5
7	Grand View 2 W	51.9	6	Driggs	40.5
8	Deer Flat Dam	51.6	8	Idaho Falls 16 SE	41.1
8	Payette	51.6	8	New Meadows Ranger Station	41.1
10	Boise Air Terminal	51.2	10	McCall	41.2
11	Emmett 2 E	51.1	11	Elk City 1 NE	41.3
12	Mountain Home	50.6	11	Lifton Pumping Station	41.3
13	Parma Experiment Station	49.9	11	Saint Anthony 1 WNW	41.3
14	Boise 7 N	49.5	14	Hill City 1 W	41.4
15	Fenn Ranger Station	49.2	15	Mackay USFS	41.6
15	Jerome	49.2	16	Ashton	41.7
17	Massacre Rocks State Park	49.1	17	Fairfield Ranger Station	41.8
18	Arrowrock Dam	49.0	18	Gibbonsville	41.9
18	Shoshone 1 WNW	49.0	19	Swan Valley 2 E	42.0
20	Castleford 2 N	48.9	20	Hamer 4 NW	42.1
21	Burley Municipal Airport	48.5	21	Idaho Falls 46 W	42.2
22	Hazelton	48.3	22	Picabo	42.5
22	Oakley	48.3	23	Powell	42.7
24	Cambridge	48.0	24	Craters of the Moon	42.9
25	Minidoka Dam	47.9	25	Dubois Experiment Station	43.2

Annual Mean Minimum Temperature

	Highest			Lowest	
Rank	Station Name	°F	Rank	Station Name	°F
1	Lewiston Airport	42.4	1	Dixie	21.1
2	Swan Falls P H	42.3	2	Grouse	21.5
3	Brownlee Dam	42.1	3	Warren	21.9
4	Dworshak Fish Hatchery	40.2	4	Yellow Pine 7 S	23.9
5	Boise Air Terminal	39.3	5	Chilly Barton Flat	24.9
5	Deer Flat Dam	39.3	6	New Meadows Ranger Station	25.5
7	Caldwell	38.9	7	Hamer 4 NW	25.7
8	Boise 7 N	38.3	8	Fairfield Ranger Station	26.0
8	Bruneau	38.3	9	Elk City 1 NE	26.2
10	Emmett 2 E	37.9	10	Hill City 1 W	26.4
11	Payette	37.6	11	Cascade 1 NW	26.6
12	Grand View 2 W	37.5	12	Driggs	26.7
13	Fenn Ranger Station	37.3	13	Saint Anthony 1 WNW	26.9
14	Mountain Home	37.0	14	Mackay USFS	27.1
15	Arrowrock Dam	36.8	14	Picabo	27.1
16	Saint Maries 1 W	36.1	16	Idaho Falls 46 W	27.3
17	Moscow University of Idaho	36.0	16	McCall	27.3
17	Oakley	36.0	18	Gibbonsville	27.5
19	Parma Experiment Station	35.9	19	Swan Valley 2 E	27.7
20	Burley Municipal Airport	35.7	20	Idaho Falls 16 SE	28.0
20	Jerome	35.7	21	Lifton Pumping Station	28.5
22	Castleford 2 N	35.6	22	Lowman	28.6
22	Kellogg Shoshone Airport	35.6	23	Idaho City	28.8
24	American Falls 3 NW	35.4	24	Ashton	29.0
24	Shoshone 1 WNW	35.4	25	Grace	29.1

Annual Extreme Minimum Temperature

Highest			Lowest		
Rank	**Station Name**	**°F**	**Rank**	**Station Name**	**°F**
1	Dworshak Fish Hatchery	-11	1	Dixie	*-49*
2	Brownlee Dam	-13	2	Elk City 1 NE	-48
2	Fenn Ranger Station	-13	2	Hamer 4 NW	-48
4	Bayview Model Basin	-15	4	Idaho Falls 46 W	-47
5	Lewiston Airport	-16	5	New Meadows Ranger Station	-45
6	Boise Lucky Peak Dam	-17	5	Tetonia Experiment Station	-45
7	Arrowrock Dam	-18	5	Warren	-45
8	Kellogg Shoshone Airport	-20	8	Swan Valley 2 E	-43
9	Swan Falls P H	-21	9	Fairfield Ranger Station	-42
10	Bonners Ferry	-22	9	Grouse	*-42*
10	Deer Flat Dam	-22	9	Hill City 1 W	-42
10	Emmett 2 E	-22	9	Idaho Falls 16 SE	-42
10	Reynolds	-22	13	Lifton Pumping Station	-41
10	Sandpoint Exp. Station	-22	14	Driggs	-40
15	Boise 7 N	*-23*	14	Grace	-40
15	Grangeville	-23	14	Saint Anthony 1 WNW	-40
15	Hazelton	-23	17	Aberdeen Experiment Station	-38
15	Payette	-23	17	Idaho Falls Fanning Airport	*-38*
15	Twin Falls 6 E	-23	19	Arbon 2 NW	*-37*
20	Caldwell	-24	19	Chilly Barton Flat	-37
20	Jerome	-24	19	Craters of the Moon	-37
20	Oakley	-24	19	Picabo	-37
20	Porthill	-24	23	Cascade 1 NW	-36
20	Saint Maries 1 W	-24	23	Gibbonsville	*-36*
25	Boise Air Terminal	-25	23	Richfield	-36

July Mean Maximum Temperature

Highest			Lowest		
Rank	**Station Name**	**°F**	**Rank**	**Station Name**	**°F**
1	Swan Falls P H	95.3	1	Dixie	74.3
2	Brownlee Dam	94.0	2	Winchester	76.0
3	Bruneau	93.0	3	Warren	76.3
4	Caldwell	92.5	4	Cottonwood 2 WSW	*77.5*
5	Grand View 2 W	92.0	5	Bayview Model Basin	78.4
6	Mountain Home	91.7	6	Wallace Woodland Park	79.3
6	Payette	91.7	7	Grouse	*79.4*
8	Shoshone 1 WNW	91.5	8	Idaho Falls 16 SE	79.6
9	Massacre Rocks State Park	*90.9*	8	Yellow Pine 7 S	79.6
10	Parma Experiment Station	90.7	10	Nezperce	79.7
11	Emmett 2 E	90.6	11	Elk City 1 NE	79.8
12	Cambridge	90.5	11	Elk River 1 S	79.8
13	Jerome	90.3	13	Driggs	79.9
14	Boise Air Terminal	89.9	14	McCall	80.2
15	Boise Lucky Peak Dam	89.6	15	Potlatch 3 NNE	80.3
16	Shoup	89.2	16	Sandpoint Exp. Station	80.6
17	Malad City	89.0	17	Cascade 1 NW	80.7
18	Malta 4 ESE	88.9	18	Lifton Pumping Station	80.8
19	Arrowrock Dam	88.8	19	Grangeville	80.9
19	Dworshak Fish Hatchery	88.8	20	Ashton	81.1
21	Lewiston Airport	88.5	21	Chilly Barton Flat	81.2
22	Hazelton	88.4	22	Porthill	81.3
23	Deer Flat Dam	88.0	22	Priest River Exp. Station	81.3
24	Salmon	87.9	24	Cabinet Gorge	82.0
25	Boise 7 N	87.7	24	Saint Anthony 1 WNW	82.0

January Mean Minimum Temperature

	Highest				Lowest	
Rank	Station Name	°F		Rank	Station Name	°F
1	Lewiston Airport	27.9		1	Grouse	-0.2
2	Dworshak Fish Hatchery	26.4		2	Hamer 4 NW	3.2
3	Swan Falls P H	24.8		3	Dixie	4.2
4	Fenn Ranger Station	24.1		4	Chilly Barton Flat	4.8
5	Brownlee Dam	23.6		5	Idaho Falls 46 W	5.2
6	Saint Maries 1 W	23.3		6	Fairfield Ranger Station	6.0
7	Moscow University of Idaho	23.2		7	Mackay USFS	6.2
8	Cottonwood 2 WSW	*22.9*		8	Lifton Pumping Station	6.5
9	Bruneau	22.6		9	Picabo	7.1
10	Boise Air Terminal	22.4		10	Hill City 1 W	7.3
10	Grangeville	22.4		11	Warren	7.5
12	Deer Flat Dam	22.3		12	Driggs	7.7
13	Kellogg Shoshone Airport	21.8		13	Saint Anthony 1 WNW	7.9
13	Potlatch 3 NNE	21.8		14	New Meadows Ranger Station	*8.2*
15	Boise 7 N	21.7		15	Gibbonsville	8.7
15	Emmett 2 E	21.7		16	Yellow Pine 7 S	9.0
15	Nezperce	21.7		17	Idaho Falls Fanning Airport	*10.2*
18	Bayview Model Basin	21.6		18	Cascade 1 NW	10.3
18	Grand View 2 W	21.6		19	Ashton	10.5
20	Caldwell	21.5		19	Challis	10.5
21	Cabinet Gorge	21.4		19	Craters of the Moon	10.5
21	Sandpoint Exp. Station	21.4		22	Swan Valley 2 E	10.6
23	Mountain Home	20.8		23	Idaho Falls 16 SE	11.1
24	Arrowrock Dam	20.1		24	Grace	11.2
24	Bonners Ferry	20.1		25	Dubois Experiment Station	11.3

Number of Annual Heating Degree Days

	Highest				Lowest	
Rank	Station Name	Num.		Rank	Station Name	Num.
1	Dixie	*10,514*		1	Swan Falls P H	4,781
2	Grouse	*9,946*		2	Brownlee Dam	5,143
3	Warren	9,939		3	Lewiston Airport	5,153
4	Yellow Pine 7 S	*9,265*		4	Bruneau	5,325
5	Chilly Barton Flat	9,142		5	Dworshak Fish Hatchery	5,333
6	Driggs	8,927		6	Grand View 2 W	5,450
7	Cascade 1 NW	8,912		7	Deer Flat Dam	5,499
8	New Meadows Ranger Station	*8,725*		8	Caldwell	5,506
9	Saint Anthony 1 WNW	8,682		9	Payette	5,584
10	Idaho Falls 16 SE	8,675		10	Emmett 2 E	5,684
11	Lifton Pumping Station	8,668		11	Boise Air Terminal	5,735
12	McCall	8,653		12	Mountain Home	5,983
13	Hill City 1 W	8,651		13	Parma Experiment Station	6,058
14	Elk City 1 NE	8,615		14	Fenn Ranger Station	6,107
15	Mackay USFS	*8,568*		15	Boise 7 N	6,225
16	Fairfield Ranger Station	*8,548*		16	Castleford 2 N	6,236
17	Ashton	8,519		17	Jerome	6,321
18	Idaho Falls 46 W	8,492		18	Massacre Rocks State Park	*6,323*
19	Hamer 4 NW	*8,474*		19	Arrowrock Dam	6,388
20	Gibbonsville	*8,456*		20	Oakley	6,391
21	Swan Valley 2 E	8,392		21	Burley Municipal Airport	6,409
22	Picabo	8,318		22	Shoshone 1 WNW	6,480
23	Craters of the Moon	*8,256*		23	Hazelton	6,529
24	Dubois Experiment Station	8,169		24	Reynolds	6,610
25	Powell	8,146		25	Moscow University of Idaho	6,624

Number of Annual Cooling Degree Days

	Highest			Lowest	
Rank	Station Name	Num.	Rank	Station Name	Num.
1	Swan Falls P H	1,295	1	Dixie	*7*
2	Brownlee Dam	1,250	1	Warren	7
3	Caldwell	888	3	Yellow Pine 7 S	*18*
4	Mountain Home	868	4	Grouse	*23*
5	Bruneau	850	5	Elk City 1 NE	49
6	Payette	844	6	Cascade 1 NW	58
7	Boise Air Terminal	800	6	McCall	58
7	Lewiston Airport	800	8	Driggs	59
9	Grand View 2 W	796	9	Idaho Falls 16 SE	60
10	Shoshone 1 WNW	761	10	Chilly Barton Flat	65
11	Dworshak Fish Hatchery	721	11	Winchester	87
12	Deer Flat Dam	717	12	Saint Anthony 1 WNW	106
13	Emmett 2 E	701	13	Potlatch 3 NNE	107
14	Jerome	664	14	Lowman	113
15	Massacre Rocks State Park	662	15	Powell	119
16	Arrowrock Dam	659	16	Bayview Model Basin	124
16	Boise 7 N	659	17	Ashton	126
18	Parma Experiment Station	648	18	Elk River 1 S	*131*
19	Cambridge	619	18	Mackay USFS	*131*
20	Hazelton	544	18	Swan Valley 2 E	131
21	Minidoka Dam	538	21	Gibbonsville	*134*
22	Burley Municipal Airport	519	22	Hill City 1 W	138
23	American Falls 3 NW	513	22	Priest River Exp. Station	138
24	Paul 1 ENE	484	24	Lifton Pumping Station	139
25	Castleford 2 N	481	25	Fairfield Ranger Station	*167*

Annual Precipitation

	Highest			Lowest	
Rank	Station Name	Inches	Rank	Station Name	Inches
1	Wallace Woodland Park	39.85	1	Grand View 2 W	7.17
2	Powell	39.23	2	Challis	7.77
3	Fenn Ranger Station	39.13	3	Bruneau	7.81
4	Elk River 1 S	36.53	4	Chilly Barton Flat	8.10
5	Sandpoint Exp. Station	34.37	5	Swan Falls P H	8.49
6	Kellogg Shoshone Airport	32.56	6	Idaho Falls 46 W	8.90
7	Cabinet Gorge	32.38	7	Aberdeen Experiment Station	9.42
8	Priest River Exp. Station	31.54	8	Mackay USFS	9.85
9	Elk City 1 NE	31.32	9	Hamer 4 NW	9.88
10	Saint Maries 1 W	30.59	10	Paul 1 ENE	9.92
11	Moscow University of Idaho	27.63	11	Minidoka Dam	10.10
12	McCall	27.60	12	Salmon	10.22
13	Yellow Pine 7 S	27.54	13	Deer Flat Dam	10.26
14	Dixie	27.21	14	Burley Municipal Airport	10.42
15	Potlatch 3 NNE	26.64	15	Hollister	10.52
16	Lowman	*26.21*	16	Shoshone 1 WNW	10.53
17	Warren	25.98	17	Castleford 2 N	10.60
18	Dworshak Fish Hatchery	25.82	18	Hazelton	10.67
19	Bayview Model Basin	25.46	19	Mountain Home	10.88
20	New Meadows Ranger Station	25.14	20	Jerome	10.99
21	Winchester	24.91	20	Reynolds	10.99
22	Idaho City	24.54	22	Idaho Falls Fanning Airport	*11.12*
23	Grangeville	24.19	23	Twin Falls 6 E	11.17
24	Cascade 1 NW	22.97	24	Payette	11.22
25	Cottonwood 2 WSW	*22.88*	25	Richfield	11.33

Number of Days Annually With ≥ 0.1″ Precipitation

	Highest			Lowest	
Rank	Station Name	Days	Rank	Station Name	Days
1	Powell	104	1	Bruneau	*26*
2	Wallace Woodland Park	102	1	Challis	*26*
3	Fenn Ranger Station	97	1	Grand View 2 W	26
4	Kellogg Shoshone Airport	*93*	4	Chilly Barton Flat	27
5	Elk River 1 S	92	5	Hollister	28
6	Elk City 1 NE	89	5	Mackay USFS	28
7	Cabinet Gorge	87	7	Idaho Falls 46 W	29
8	Sandpoint Exp. Station	85	8	Paul 1 ENE	30
9	Dixie	*83*	8	Swan Falls P H	30
9	Priest River Exp. Station	83	10	Hamer 4 NW	32
11	Dworshak Fish Hatchery	79	11	Deer Flat Dam	33
11	McCall	79	11	Minidoka Dam	33
13	Moscow University of Idaho	76	13	Aberdeen Experiment Station	34
14	Potlatch 3 NNE	75	13	Burley Municipal Airport	34
15	Bayview Model Basin	*74*	13	Reynolds	34
15	Winchester	74	13	Salmon	34
17	Saint Maries 1 W	73	13	Shoshone 1 WNW	34
17	Yellow Pine 7 S	*73*	18	Castleford 2 N	35
19	Porthill	68	18	Fort Hall 1 NNE	*35*
20	Grangeville	67	18	Idaho Falls Fanning Airport	*35*
20	Lowman	*67*	18	Massacre Rocks State Park	*35*
20	Warren	67	18	Mountain Home	35
23	Cascade 1 NW	65	18	Richfield	35
23	Nezperce	65	18	Twin Falls 6 E	35
25	Bonners Ferry	64	25	Hazelton	36

Number of Days Annually With ≥ 1.0″ Precipitation

	Highest			Lowest	
Rank	Station Name	Days	Rank	Station Name	Days
1	Sandpoint Exp. Station	4	1	Aberdeen Experiment Station	0
1	Wallace Woodland Park	4	1	American Falls 3 NW	0
3	Elk River 1 S	3	1	Arbon 2 NW	0
3	Powell	3	1	Arrowrock Dam	0
3	Priest River Exp. Station	3	1	Ashton	0
6	Fenn Ranger Station	2	1	Boise 7 N	0
7	Bayview Model Basin	1	1	Boise Air Terminal	0
7	Cabinet Gorge	1	1	Boise Lucky Peak Dam	0
7	Cottonwood 2 WSW	*1*	1	Bonners Ferry	0
7	Lowman	*1*	1	Brownlee Dam	0
7	Saint Maries 1 W	1	1	Bruneau	0
12	Aberdeen Experiment Station	0	1	Burley Municipal Airport	0
12	American Falls 3 NW	0	1	Caldwell	0
12	Arbon 2 NW	0	1	Cambridge	0
12	Arrowrock Dam	0	1	Cascade 1 NW	0
12	Ashton	0	1	Castleford 2 N	0
12	Boise 7 N	0	1	Challis	0
12	Boise Air Terminal	0	1	Chilly Barton Flat	0
12	Boise Lucky Peak Dam	0	1	Craters of the Moon	0
12	Bonners Ferry	0	1	Deer Flat Dam	0
12	Brownlee Dam	0	1	Dixie	0
12	Bruneau	0	1	Driggs	0
12	Burley Municipal Airport	0	1	Dubois Experiment Station	0
12	Caldwell	0	1	Dworshak Fish Hatchery	0
12	Cambridge	0	1	Elk City 1 NE	0

Annual Snowfall

	Highest			Lowest	
Rank	**Station Name**	**Inches**	**Rank**	**Station Name**	**Inches**
1	Dixie	197.1	1	Swan Falls P H	*4.0*
2	Powell	*166.0*	2	Lewiston Airport	12.6
3	Warren	160.1	3	Caldwell	*14.5*
4	McCall	138.9	4	Castleford 2 N	*15.5*
5	Elk City 1 NE	128.6	5	Parma Experiment Station	15.9
6	Yellow Pine 7 S	108.8	6	Hazelton	*16.0*
7	Ashton	101.0	7	Brownlee Dam	*16.7*
8	Elk River 1 S	100.2	7	Paul 1 ENE	*16.7*
9	Winchester	94.4	9	Challis	*16.9*
10	Craters of the Moon	*91.9*	10	Boise Air Terminal	19.3
11	Cascade 1 NW	89.2	11	Burley Municipal Airport	22.7
12	Gibbonsville	*86.2*	12	Minidoka Dam	22.9
13	Driggs	*84.1*	13	Fort Hall 1 NNE	*24.7*
14	Wallace Woodland Park	78.8	14	Idaho Falls 46 W	26.2
15	Idaho Falls 16 SE	78.7	15	Oakley	27.1
16	Priest River Exp. Station	74.5	16	American Falls 3 NW	*27.6*
17	Idaho City	*74.1*	17	Twin Falls 6 E	28.8
18	New Meadows Ranger Station	72.6	18	Salmon	28.9
19	Cabinet Gorge	67.8	19	Hamer 4 NW	33.3
20	Fairfield Ranger Station	*66.3*	20	Arrowrock Dam	37.2
21	Bonners Ferry	62.7	21	Bayview Model Basin	*37.9*
22	Sandpoint Exp. Station	62.1	21	Lifton Pumping Station	37.9
23	Swan Valley 2 E	*60.7*	23	Idaho Falls Fanning Airport	*38.4*
24	Boise 7 N	55.5	24	Malad City	39.6
25	Fenn Ranger Station	52.5	25	Potlatch 3 NNE	*42.8*

Note: See Appendix D for explanation of data.

Annual Extreme Maximum Temperature

	Highest			Lowest	
Rank	**Station Name**	**°F**	**Rank**	**Station Name**	**°F**
1	Piper City	108	1	Stockton 3 NNE	99
1	Sparta 1 W	108	2	Freeport Waste Water Plant	101
3	Kankakee Metro Wastewater	*107*	2	Paw Paw 2 NW	101
3	Palestine 2 W	107	4	Charleston	102
5	Alton Melvin Price Lock & Dam	106	4	Danville	102
5	Chicago Midway Airport	106	4	Dixon Springs Agr. Center	102
5	Decatur	106	4	Fulton Lock & Dam 13	102
5	Du Quoin 4 SE	106	4	Galesburg	102
5	Havana 4 NNE	106	4	Mount Carroll	102
5	Nashville 4 NE	106	4	Rosiclare 5 NW	102
11	Albion	105	4	Springfield Capital Airport	102
11	Belleville Scott AFB	105	4	Waukegan	102
11	Brookport Dam 52	105	4	Windsor	102
11	Carlinville	105	14	Aledo	103
11	Flora 5 NW	105	14	Aurora	103
11	Greater Peoria Airport	105	14	Carbondale Sewage Plant	*103*
11	Harrisburg	105	14	Chenoa	103
11	Hillsboro	105	14	De Kalb	103
11	La Harpe	105	14	Dixon 1 NW	103
11	Marengo	105	14	Effingham	*103*
11	Morrison	105	14	Galva	103
11	Princeville	105	14	Geneseo	103
11	Quincy Muni Baldwin Field	105	14	Golden	103
11	Rantoul Chanute AFB	105	14	Jacksonville 2 E	103
11	Salem Leckrone Airport	105	14	Lacon 1 N	103

Annual Mean Maximum Temperature

	Highest			Lowest	
Rank	**Station Name**	**°F**	**Rank**	**Station Name**	**°F**
1	Dixon Springs Agr. Center	68.1	1	Stockton 3 NNE	56.4
2	Brookport Dam 52	68.0	1	Waukegan	56.4
3	Harrisburg	67.7	3	Paw Paw 2 NW	57.0
4	Cairo WSO City	67.5	4	Freeport Waste Water Plant	57.4
5	Rosiclare 5 NW	67.3	5	Rockford Greater Rockford Arpt.	57.9
6	Anna 2 NNE	67.2	6	Fulton Lock & Dam 13	58.1
7	Belleville Scott AFB	66.9	7	De Kalb	58.5
8	Albion	66.8	7	Dixon 1 NW	58.5
8	Sparta 1 W	66.8	9	Marengo	58.6
10	Du Quoin 4 SE	66.6	9	Park Forest	58.6
11	Carbondale Sewage Plant	66.4	11	Chicago O'Hare Int'l Airport	58.7
12	Flora 5 NW	66.0	11	Mount Carroll	58.7
13	Salem Leckrone Airport	65.8	13	Galva	59.1
14	McLeansboro 2 ENE	65.7	14	Aurora	59.4
15	Hillsboro	65.6	14	Walnut	59.4
15	Waterloo	65.6	16	Chicago Midway Airport	59.5
17	Fairfield Radio WFIW	65.4	17	Galesburg	59.6
17	Nashville 4 NE	65.4	17	Geneseo	59.6
17	Olney 2 S	65.4	17	Morrison	59.6
20	Mount Vernon-Outland Airport	65.0	20	Chicago University	*59.8*
21	Marion 4 NNE	64.9	21	Moline Quad City Airport	60.0
21	Palestine 2 W	64.9	22	Watseka 2 NW	60.3
23	Carlinville	64.3	23	Princeville	60.4
24	Tuscola	64.1	24	Aledo	60.5
25	Virden	64.0	24	Peru	60.5

Annual Mean Temperature

	Highest				Lowest	
Rank	**Station Name**	**°F**		**Rank**	**Station Name**	**°F**
1	Cairo WSO City	58.5		1	Mount Carroll	46.8
2	Brookport Dam 52	57.6		1	Stockton 3 NNE	46.8
3	Dixon Springs Agr. Center	57.4		3	Freeport Waste Water Plant	47.1
4	Harrisburg	56.9		4	Paw Paw 2 NW	47.2
5	Anna 2 NNE	56.8		4	Waukegan	47.2
6	Albion	56.6		6	Marengo	47.7
7	Sparta 1 W	56.2		7	Rockford Greater Rockford Arpt.	48.0
8	Belleville Scott AFB	55.9		8	Dixon 1 NW	48.3
8	Du Quoin 4 SE	55.9		9	De Kalb	48.7
8	Rosiclare 5 NW	55.9		10	Morrison	48.8
11	Nashville 4 NE	55.6		11	Aurora	48.9
12	Waterloo	55.5		11	Fulton Lock & Dam 13	48.9
13	Salem Leckrone Airport	55.3		13	Princeville	49.2
14	Carbondale Sewage Plant	55.1		13	Walnut	49.2
15	Flora 5 NW	55.0		15	Galva	49.3
15	Olney 2 S	55.0		15	Park Forest	49.3
17	Fairfield Radio WFIW	54.8		17	Chicago O'Hare Int'l Airport	49.5
17	McLeansboro 2 ENE	54.8		18	Hennepin Power Plant	49.6
17	Palestine 2 W	54.8		19	Peru	49.9
20	Hillsboro	54.7		19	Watseka 2 NW	49.9
21	Alton Melvin Price Lock & Dam	54.4		21	Geneseo	50.0
21	Mount Vernon-Outland Airport	54.4		21	Kankakee Metro Wastewater	*50.0*
23	Marion 4 NNE	54.3		21	Moline Quad City Airport	50.0
24	Carlinville	54.0		24	Minonk	50.1
25	Virden	53.8		25	Aledo	50.3

Annual Mean Minimum Temperature

	Highest				Lowest	
Rank	**Station Name**	**°F**		**Rank**	**Station Name**	**°F**
1	Cairo WSO City	49.5		1	Mount Carroll	34.9
2	Brookport Dam 52	47.1		2	Marengo	36.7
3	Dixon Springs Agr. Center	46.6		3	Freeport Waste Water Plant	36.8
4	Albion	46.3		4	Stockton 3 NNE	37.2
4	Anna 2 NNE	46.3		5	Paw Paw 2 NW	37.4
6	Harrisburg	45.9		6	Morrison	37.9
7	Nashville 4 NE	45.7		6	Princeville	37.9
8	Sparta 1 W	45.6		6	Waukegan	37.9
9	Waterloo	45.4		9	Dixon 1 NW	38.0
10	Du Quoin 4 SE	45.1		10	Rockford Greater Rockford Arpt.	38.1
11	Alton Melvin Price Lock & Dam	44.9		11	Hennepin Power Plant	38.2
12	Belleville Scott AFB	44.8		12	Aurora	38.5
13	Salem Leckrone Airport	44.7		13	De Kalb	38.8
14	Olney 2 S	44.6		14	Walnut	38.9
14	Palestine 2 W	44.6		15	Kankakee Metro Wastewater	*39.3*
14	Rosiclare 5 NW	44.6		15	Minonk	39.3
17	Fairfield Radio WFIW	44.2		15	Peru	39.3
18	Flora 5 NW	44.0		15	Wheaton 3 SE	39.3
19	Charleston	43.9		19	Galva	39.4
20	Carbondale Sewage Plant	43.8		20	Fulton Lock & Dam 13	39.5
20	Hillsboro	43.8		20	Watseka 2 NW	39.5
20	McLeansboro 2 ENE	43.8		22	La Harpe	39.6
20	Mount Vernon-Outland Airport	43.8		23	Piper City	39.8
24	Carlinville	43.7		24	Moline Quad City Airport	39.9
24	Marion 4 NNE	43.7		25	Park Forest	40.0

Annual Extreme Minimum Temperature

	Highest			Lowest	
Rank	Station Name	°F	Rank	Station Name	°F
1	Cairo WSO City	*-12*	1	Paw Paw 2 NW	-33
2	Alton Melvin Price Lock & Dam	-16	2	Havana 4 NNE	-30
2	Sparta 1 W	-16	2	Hennepin Power Plant	-30
4	Anna 2 NNE	-17	2	Mount Carroll	-30
5	Waterloo	-18	2	Stockton 3 NNE	-30
6	Carlinville	-19	6	Kankakee Metro Wastewater	*-29*
7	Albion	*-20*	6	Marengo	-29
7	Dixon Springs Agr. Center	-20	8	Aledo	-28
7	Du Quoin 4 SE	-20	8	Moline Quad City Airport	-28
7	White Hall 1 E	-20	8	Morrison	-28
11	Brookport Dam 52	-21	8	Newton 6 SSE	-28
11	Hillsboro	-21	8	Watseka 2 NW	-28
11	Jacksonville 2 E	-21	13	Belleville Scott AFB	-27
11	McLeansboro 2 ENE	-21	13	Charleston	-27
11	Mount Vernon-Outland Airport	-21	13	Chicago O'Hare Int'l Airport	-27
11	Nashville 4 NE	-21	13	De Kalb	-27
11	Pana 3 E	-21	13	Dixon 1 NW	-27
11	Rushville	-21	13	Freeport Waste Water Plant	-27
11	Springfield Capital Airport	-21	13	Lacon 1 N	-27
20	Harrisburg	-22	13	Park Forest	-27
20	Marion 4 NNE	-22	13	Rantoul Chanute AFB	-27
20	Paris Waterworks	-22	13	Rockford Greater Rockford Arpt.	-27
20	Quincy Muni Baldwin Field	-22	13	Walnut	-27
20	Rosiclare 5 NW	-22	13	Waukegan	-27
20	Virden	-22	25	Aurora	-26

July Mean Maximum Temperature

	Highest			Lowest	
Rank	Station Name	°F	Rank	Station Name	°F
1	Harrisburg	90.2	1	Waukegan	81.4
2	Albion	90.0	2	Stockton 3 NNE	82.0
3	Cairo WSO City	89.7	3	Paw Paw 2 NW	82.9
3	Du Quoin 4 SE	89.7	4	Freeport Waste Water Plant	83.8
5	Belleville Scott AFB	89.6	4	Park Forest	83.8
5	Sparta 1 W	89.6	6	Dixon 1 NW	83.9
7	Brookport Dam 52	89.5	6	Fulton Lock & Dam 13	83.9
7	Hillsboro	89.5	6	Rockford Greater Rockford Arpt.	83.9
9	Flora 5 NW	89.2	9	Chicago O'Hare Int'l Airport	84.3
10	Salem Leckrone Airport	89.1	10	Chicago University	*84.5*
11	Dixon Springs Agr. Center	89.0	10	De Kalb	84.5
12	Anna 2 NNE	88.9	12	Mount Carroll	84.7
12	McLeansboro 2 ENE	88.9	13	Aurora	84.8
12	Waterloo	88.9	13	Watseka 2 NW	84.8
15	Carbondale Sewage Plant	88.6	15	Chicago Midway Airport	84.9
16	Nashville 4 NE	88.4	15	Galesburg	84.9
16	Olney 2 S	88.4	17	Galva	85.0
18	Havana 4 NNE	88.3	17	Marengo	85.0
18	Mount Vernon-Outland Airport	88.3	17	Princeville	85.0
20	Fairfield Radio WFIW	88.2	20	Pontiac	85.1
20	Tuscola	88.2	20	Walnut	85.1
22	Alton Melvin Price Lock & Dam	88.1	22	Morrison	85.3
22	Palestine 2 W	88.1	22	Urbana	85.3
24	Carlinville	88.0	24	Hoopeston 1 NE	85.4
24	Rosiclare 5 NW	88.0	24	Ottawa 5 SW	85.4

January Mean Minimum Temperature

	Highest				Lowest	
Rank	Station Name	°F		Rank	Station Name	°F
1	Cairo WSO City	25.9		1	Mount Carroll	7.5
2	Brookport Dam 52	24.5		2	Stockton 3 NNE	8.8
3	Dixon Springs Agr. Center	24.2		3	Freeport Waste Water Plant	9.0
4	Anna 2 NNE	23.3		4	Dixon 1 NW	9.7
5	Albion	23.0		4	Marengo	9.7
6	Harrisburg	22.6		6	Morrison	10.1
7	Rosiclare 5 NW	22.3		7	Paw Paw 2 NW	10.2
8	Sparta 1 W	21.9		8	Rockford Greater Rockford Arpt.	10.5
9	Belleville Scott AFB	21.7		9	Hennepin Power Plant	10.6
10	Du Quoin 4 SE	21.5		9	Walnut	10.6
11	Nashville 4 NE	21.4		11	Fulton Lock & Dam 13	10.8
12	Fairfield Radio WFIW	21.0		12	De Kalb	10.9
13	Waterloo	20.9		13	Princeville	11.1
14	Carbondale Sewage Plant	20.8		14	Aurora	11.4
15	Flora 5 NW	20.6		15	Galva	11.8
15	Olney 2 S	20.6		16	Moline Quad City Airport	12.0
17	Salem Leckrone Airport	20.5		17	Peru	12.2
18	Palestine 2 W	20.4		17	Waukegan	12.2
19	McLeansboro 2 ENE	20.3		19	Geneseo	12.3
20	Marion 4 NNE	20.0		20	La Harpe	12.7
21	Mount Vernon-Outland Airport	19.6		20	Minonk	12.7
22	Hillsboro	18.8		22	Kankakee Metro Wastewater	12.9
23	Alton Melvin Price Lock & Dam	18.7		23	Galesburg	13.1
23	Charleston	18.7		24	Park Forest	13.2
25	Windsor	18.6		25	Aledo	13.4

Number of Annual Heating Degree Days

	Highest				Lowest	
Rank	Station Name	Num.		Rank	Station Name	Num.
1	Stockton 3 NNE	7,190		1	Cairo WSO City	3,997
2	Mount Carroll	7,165		2	Brookport Dam 52	4,129
3	Freeport Waste Water Plant	7,129		3	Dixon Springs Agr. Center	4,144
4	Paw Paw 2 NW	7,077		4	Anna 2 NNE	4,328
5	Waukegan	7,032		5	Harrisburg	4,381
6	Marengo	6,991		6	Rosiclare 5 NW	4,466
7	Rockford Greater Rockford Arpt.	6,881		7	Albion	4,511
8	Dixon 1 NW	6,793		8	Sparta 1 W	4,565
9	De Kalb	6,692		9	Belleville Scott AFB	4,599
10	Morrison	6,648		10	Du Quoin 4 SE	4,643
11	Fulton Lock & Dam 13	6,646		11	Nashville 4 NE	4,723
12	Aurora	6,575		12	Waterloo	4,778
13	Walnut	6,567		13	Carbondale Sewage Plant	4,797
14	Galva	6,540		14	Salem Leckrone Airport	4,818
15	Park Forest	6,483		15	Flora 5 NW	4,841
16	Princeville	6,461		16	Olney 2 S	4,856
17	Chicago O'Hare Int'l Airport	6,427		17	Fairfield Radio WFIW	4,868
18	Hennepin Power Plant	6,409		18	Palestine 2 W	4,910
19	Geneseo	6,383		19	McLeansboro 2 ENE	4,916
20	Moline Quad City Airport	6,369		20	Marion 4 NNE	4,996
21	Peru	6,328		21	Hillsboro	4,999
22	Kankakee Metro Wastewater	*6,294*		22	Mount Vernon-Outland Airport	5,027
23	Minonk	6,281		23	Alton Melvin Price Lock & Dam	5,121
24	Watseka 2 NW	6,273		24	Carlinville	5,157
25	Galesburg	6,256		25	Windsor	5,230

Number of Annual Cooling Degree Days

	Highest			Lowest	
Rank	**Station Name**	**Num.**	**Rank**	**Station Name**	**Num.**
1	Cairo WSO City	1,716	1	Mount Carroll	625
2	Albion	1,579	2	Waukegan	646
3	Dixon Springs Agr. Center	1,542	3	Stockton 3 NNE	648
4	Brookport Dam 52	1,527	4	Paw Paw 2 NW	690
5	Harrisburg	1,478	5	Freeport Waste Water Plant	710
6	Sparta 1 W	1,463	6	Princeville	733
7	Anna 2 NNE	1,460	7	Dixon 1 NW	753
8	Waterloo	1,455	8	Marengo	766
9	Hillsboro	1,452	9	Rockford Greater Rockford Arpt.	800
10	Du Quoin 4 SE	1,422	10	Aurora	827
11	Belleville Scott AFB	1,417	11	De Kalb	840
12	Alton Melvin Price Lock & Dam	1,405	12	Morrison	842
12	Nashville 4 NE	1,405	13	Chicago O'Hare Int'l Airport	850
14	Salem Leckrone Airport	1,401	14	Fulton Lock & Dam 13	859
15	Flora 5 NW	1,350	15	Walnut	880
16	Olney 2 S	1,336	16	Watseka 2 NW	887
17	Palestine 2 W	1,331	17	Park Forest	888
18	Virden	1,310	18	Hennepin Power Plant	894
19	McLeansboro 2 ENE	1,308	19	Kankakee Metro Wastewater	914
20	Carbondale Sewage Plant	*1,280*	20	Peru	934
21	Carlinville	1,272	21	Galva	944
22	Fairfield Radio WFIW	1,264	22	Minonk	952
23	Tuscola	1,259	23	Aledo	958
24	Rosiclare 5 NW	1,258	24	Pontiac	966
25	Windsor	1,239	25	Ottawa 5 SW	976

Annual Precipitation

	Highest			Lowest	
Rank	**Station Name**	**Inches**	**Rank**	**Station Name**	**Inches**
1	Rosiclare 5 NW	48.82	1	Waukegan	34.10
2	Anna 2 NNE	48.28	2	Freeport Waste Water Plant	34.52
3	Dixon Springs Agr. Center	48.22	3	Fulton Lock & Dam 13	34.70
4	Cairo WSO City	48.16	4	Chenoa	34.99
5	Brookport Dam 52	48.04	5	Stockton 3 NNE	35.15
6	Marion 4 NNE	47.01	6	Hennepin Power Plant	*35.26*
7	Harrisburg	45.70	7	Springfield Capital Airport	35.85
8	Carbondale Sewage Plant	45.33	8	Mason City 1 W	35.89
9	Albion	44.86	9	Marengo	36.00
10	Fairfield Radio WFIW	44.69	10	Aledo	36.12
11	Olney 2 S	44.45	11	White Hall 1 E	36.19
12	McLeansboro 2 ENE	43.95	12	Ottawa 5 SW	36.20
13	Du Quoin 4 SE	43.86	13	Pontiac	36.44
14	Sparta 1 W	42.18	14	Rockford Greater Rockford Arpt.	36.45
15	Flora 5 NW	42.16	15	Chicago O'Hare Int'l Airport	36.59
16	Palestine 2 W	42.12	16	Greater Peoria Airport	36.65
17	Salem Leckrone Airport	42.09	17	Piper City	36.80
18	Mount Vernon-Outland Airport	41.89	18	Hoopeston 1 NE	37.02
19	Effingham	41.36	19	Paw Paw 2 NW	37.11
20	Waterloo	41.32	20	Virden	37.13
21	Paris Waterworks	41.31	20	Walnut	37.13
22	Danville	41.11	22	Dixon 1 NW	37.21
23	Charleston	41.01	23	Geneseo	37.61
24	Urbana	40.99	24	De Kalb	37.69
25	Tuscola	40.79	24	Mount Carroll	37.69

Number of Days Annually With ≥ 0.1″ Precipitation

	Highest			Lowest	
Rank	Station Name	Days	Rank	Station Name	Days
1	Marion 4 NNE	80	1	Fulton Lock & Dam 13	63
2	Brookport Dam 52	78	1	Rushville	63
2	Carbondale Sewage Plant	78	3	Freeport Waste Water Plant	65
2	Dixon Springs Agr. Center	78	3	Virden	65
2	Fairfield Radio WFIW	78	5	Aledo	67
2	McLeansboro 2 ENE	78	5	Belleville Scott AFB	67
2	Paris Waterworks	78	5	Moweaqua	*67*
8	Anna 2 NNE	77	5	Springfield Capital Airport	67
8	Danville	77	5	Waukegan	67
8	Rosiclare 5 NW	77	5	White Hall 1 E	67
11	Harrisburg	76	11	Geneseo	68
11	Urbana	76	11	Jerseyville 2 SW	68
13	Chicago University	*75*	11	Ottawa 5 SW	68
13	Flora 5 NW	75	11	Rockford Greater Rockford Arpt.	68
13	Olney 2 S	75	11	Stockton 3 NNE	68
13	Pana 3 E	75	16	Decatur	69
13	Tuscola	75	16	Jacksonville 2 E	69
18	Charleston	74	16	Lincoln	69
18	Effingham	*74*	16	Mason City 1 W	69
18	Minonk	*74*	16	Moline Quad City Airport	69
18	Mount Vernon-Outland Airport	74	16	Pontiac	69
18	Palestine 2 W	74	16	Quincy Muni Baldwin Field	69
18	Salem Leckrone Airport	74	16	Sparta 1 W	69
24	Cairo WSO City	73	16	Waterloo	69
24	Chicago Midway Airport	73	25	Albion	*70*

Number of Days Annually With ≥ 1.0″ Precipitation

	Highest			Lowest	
Rank	Station Name	Days	Rank	Station Name	Days
1	Cairo WSO City	14	1	Pontiac	6
2	Albion	13	2	De Kalb	7
2	Anna 2 NNE	13	2	Walnut	7
2	Brookport Dam 52	13	2	Waukegan	7
2	Dixon Springs Agr. Center	13	5	Aledo	8
2	Du Quoin 4 SE	13	5	Chenoa	8
7	Carbondale Sewage Plant	12	5	Chicago University	*8*
7	Fairfield Radio WFIW	12	5	Dixon 1 NW	8
7	Harrisburg	12	5	Freeport Waste Water Plant	8
7	Marion 4 NNE	12	5	Fulton Lock & Dam 13	8
7	Mount Vernon-Outland Airport	12	5	Kankakee Metro Wastewater	*8*
7	Olney 2 S	12	5	Lincoln	8
7	Rosiclare 5 NW	12	5	Marengo	8
14	Effingham	*11*	5	Monmouth	8
14	Flora 5 NW	11	5	Morrison	8
14	Galva	11	5	Mount Carroll	8
14	Jacksonville 2 E	11	5	Ottawa 5 SW	8
14	McLeansboro 2 ENE	11	5	Park Forest	8
14	Pana 3 E	11	5	Paw Paw 2 NW	8
14	Quincy Muni Baldwin Field	11	5	Rockford Greater Rockford Arpt.	8
14	Rantoul Chanute AFB	11	21	Aurora	9
14	Rushville	11	21	Carlinville	9
14	Waterloo	11	21	Chicago Midway Airport	9
24	Alton Melvin Price Lock & Dam	10	21	Chicago O'Hare Int'l Airport	9
24	Belleville Scott AFB	10	21	Danville	9

Annual Snowfall

	Highest			Lowest	
Rank	Station Name	Inches	Rank	Station Name	Inches
1	Chicago Midway Airport	42.8	1	Flora 5 NW	*8.3*
2	Waukegan	37.9	2	Brookport Dam 52	8.6
3	Rockford Greater Rockford Arpt.	37.4	3	Cairo WSO City	9.6
4	Chicago O'Hare Int'l Airport	37.3	4	Dixon Springs Agr. Center	9.7
5	Marengo	*36.9*	5	Albion	*10.3*
6	Dixon 1 NW	34.2	6	Rosiclare 5 NW	10.7
7	De Kalb	34.0	7	Olney 2 S	*13.3*
7	Morrison	34.0	8	Harrisburg	*13.6*
9	Moline Quad City Airport	33.8	9	Du Quoin 4 SE	*13.7*
10	Mount Carroll	32.9	9	Salem Leckrone Airport	13.7
10	Walnut	32.9	11	Carbondale Sewage Plant	*13.8*
12	Wheaton 3 SE	32.5	12	Waterloo	14.6
13	Stockton 3 NNE	*32.4*	13	Anna 2 NNE	14.7
14	Freeport Waste Water Plant	32.0	14	Newton 6 SSE	14.8
15	Park Forest	*30.8*	14	Sparta 1 W	14.8
16	Paw Paw 2 NW	*30.2*	16	Fairfield Radio WFIW	15.2
17	Havana 4 NNE	30.1	17	Belleville Scott AFB	16.1
18	Aurora	29.7	18	McLeansboro 2 ENE	16.3
19	Galva	28.6	18	Nashville 4 NE	16.3
20	Monmouth	28.2	20	Jerseyville 2 SW	16.8
20	Paris Waterworks	28.2	21	Mount Vernon-Outland Airport	*17.3*
22	Aledo	28.1	22	Fulton Lock & Dam 13	*17.7*
22	Minonk	28.1	22	Mattoon	17.7
22	Piper City	28.1	24	Hoopeston 1 NE	17.8
25	Geneseo	27.1	25	Rushville	17.9

Note: See Appendix D for explanation of data.

Annual Extreme Maximum Temperature

	Highest			Lowest	
Rank	Station Name	°F	Rank	Station Name	°F
1	Fort Wayne Baer Field	106	1	Cambridge City 3 N	100
1	Vevay	106	1	Richmond Water Works	100
3	Delphi 3 S	105	1	Valparaiso Waterworks	100
3	Frankfort Disposal Plant	105	4	Angola	*101*
3	Hobart 2 WNW	105	4	Greensburg	101
3	Wanatah 2 WNW	105	4	La Porte	101
3	West Lafayette Purdue Univ. Arpt.	*105*	4	Martinsville 2 SW	101
8	Berne	104	4	New Whiteland	*101*
8	Bloomington Indiana Univ.	104	4	Spencer	101
8	Bluffton 1 N	104	4	Winchester Airport 3E	101
8	Crane Naval Depot	104	11	Dubois S Ind. Forage Farm	102
8	English 4 S	104	11	Elwood Wastewater Plant	102
8	Indianapolis SE Side	104	11	Evansville Museum	*102*
8	Kentland	*104*	11	Evansville Regional Airport	102
8	Kokomo 3 WSW	104	11	Farmland 5 NNW	102
8	Lafayette 8 S	104	11	Goshen College	102
8	Lagrange Sewage Plant	104	11	Muncie	102
8	Lowell	104	11	Oaklandon Geist Reservoir	102
8	Madison Sewage Plant	104	11	Oolitic Purdue Exp. Farm	102
8	Rensselaer	104	11	Portland 1 SW	*102*
8	Rockville	104	11	Princeton 1 W	102
8	Seymour 2 N	104	11	Saint Meinrad	102
8	South Bend Michiana Regional	104	11	Shoals Hiway 50 Bridge	102
8	Washington	104	11	Terre Haute Indiana State	*102*
8	Whitestown	104	11	Winamac 2 SSE	102

Annual Mean Maximum Temperature

	Highest			Lowest	
Rank	Station Name	°F	Rank	Station Name	°F
1	Evansville Museum	*67.7*	1	Angola	*57.3*
2	English 4 S	66.9	2	Lagrange Sewage Plant	57.9
3	Saint Meinrad	66.6	3	La Porte	58.4
4	Vevay	66.5	4	Wanatah 2 WNW	58.8
5	Evansville Regional Airport	66.3	5	Columbia City	58.9
6	Crane Naval Depot	*66.0*	5	South Bend Michiana Regional	58.9
6	Tell City	66.0	7	Bluffton 1 N	59.1
8	Madison Sewage Plant	65.9	7	Rochester	59.1
8	Washington	65.9	9	Warsaw	*59.2*
10	Mount Vernon	65.8	10	Valparaiso Waterworks	59.3
11	Paoli	65.7	11	Goshen College	59.4
12	Salem	65.6	11	Hartford City 4 ESE	*59.4*
13	Princeton 1 W	65.2	13	Kokomo 3 WSW	59.5
14	Scottsburg	65.1	13	Lowell	59.5
15	Shoals Hiway 50 Bridge	64.7	15	Fort Wayne Baer Field	59.7
16	Dubois S Ind. Forage Farm	64.1	15	Winchester Airport 3E	59.7
16	Rockville	64.1	17	Portland 1 SW	*59.8*
18	Brookville	63.7	18	Rensselaer	59.9
19	Seymour 2 N	63.6	18	Winamac 2 SSE	59.9
19	Terre Haute Indiana State	*63.6*	20	Farmland 5 NNW	60.2
21	Oolitic Purdue Exp. Farm	63.5	20	Marion 2 N	60.2
22	Bloomington Indiana Univ.	63.4	20	West Lafayette 6 NW	60.2
23	Columbus	63.3	23	Anderson Sewage Plant	60.5
24	Martinsville 2 SW	62.7	23	Cambridge City 3 N	60.5
25	Spencer	62.5	23	Lafayette 8 S	60.5

Annual Mean Temperature

	Highest			Lowest	
Rank	Station Name	°F	Rank	Station Name	°F
1	Evansville Museum	*57.7*	1	Angola	*47.4*
2	Evansville Regional Airport	56.2	2	Lagrange Sewage Plant	48.2
3	Saint Meinrad	56.1	3	Columbia City	48.7
3	Washington	56.1	4	Wanatah 2 WNW	48.8
5	Tell City	55.9	5	Lowell	49.1
6	Mount Vernon	55.8	5	Rochester	49.1
7	Madison Sewage Plant	55.6	7	Kokomo 3 WSW	49.3
8	Crane Naval Depot	*55.5*	8	Bluffton 1 N	49.4
8	Princeton 1 W	55.5	9	Portland 1 SW	*49.6*
8	Vevay	55.5	9	Warsaw	*49.6*
11	Salem	54.7	11	Cambridge City 3 N	49.7
12	English 4 S	54.5	12	Hartford City 4 ESE	*49.8*
13	Scottsburg	54.0	12	La Porte	49.8
14	Dubois S Ind. Forage Farm	53.8	14	Farmland 5 NNW	49.9
14	Paoli	53.8	14	Valparaiso Waterworks	49.9
16	Bloomington Indiana Univ.	53.5	16	South Bend Michiana Regional	50.0
17	Rockville	53.4	16	Winamac 2 SSE	50.0
18	Shoals Hiway 50 Bridge	53.2	18	Elwood Wastewater Plant	50.1
19	Terre Haute Indiana State	*52.9*	18	Goshen College	50.1
20	Columbus	52.8	18	Marion 2 N	50.1
21	Indianapolis Int'l Airport	52.7	18	Rensselaer	50.1
22	Greensburg	52.6	22	Fort Wayne Baer Field	50.2
23	Greencastle 1 SE	52.5	22	New Castle 4 N	50.2
23	Seymour 2 N	52.5	24	West Lafayette 6 NW	50.3
25	Oolitic Purdue Exp. Farm	52.3	24	Winchester Airport 3E	50.3

Annual Mean Minimum Temperature

	Highest			Lowest	
Rank	Station Name	°F	Rank	Station Name	°F
1	Evansville Museum	*47.6*	1	Angola	*37.5*
2	Washington	46.2	2	Lagrange Sewage Plant	38.5
3	Evansville Regional Airport	45.9	3	Columbia City	38.6
4	Mount Vernon	45.7	4	Lowell	38.7
4	Princeton 1 W	45.7	4	Wanatah 2 WNW	38.7
4	Tell City	45.7	6	Cambridge City 3 N	38.8
7	Saint Meinrad	45.5	7	Kokomo 3 WSW	39.0
8	Madison Sewage Plant	45.3	8	Rochester	39.1
9	Crane Naval Depot	*45.0*	9	Portland 1 SW	*39.3*
10	Vevay	44.4	10	Elwood Wastewater Plant	39.4
11	Salem	43.8	11	Farmland 5 NNW	39.5
12	Bloomington Indiana Univ.	43.5	12	Bluffton 1 N	39.6
12	Dubois S Ind. Forage Farm	43.5	13	New Castle 4 N	39.8
14	Indianapolis Int'l Airport	43.0	13	Spencer	39.8
15	Greensburg	42.9	15	Warsaw	*39.9*
16	Scottsburg	42.8	16	Brookville	40.0
17	Rockville	42.7	16	Marion 2 N	40.0
18	Greencastle 1 SE	42.6	16	Winamac 2 SSE	40.0
19	Anderson Sewage Plant	42.3	19	Hartford City 4 ESE	*40.2*
19	Indianapolis SE Side	42.3	19	Hobart 2 WNW	40.2
21	Columbus	42.2	21	Lafayette 8 S	40.3
22	Terre Haute Indiana State	*42.1*	21	Rensselaer	40.3
23	English 4 S	41.9	21	West Lafayette 6 NW	40.3
23	Paoli	41.9	24	Valparaiso Waterworks	40.4
25	Berne	41.7	25	Richmond Water Works	40.5

Annual Extreme Minimum Temperature

	Highest				Lowest	
Rank	**Station Name**	**°F**		**Rank**	**Station Name**	**°F**
1	Mount Vernon	-16		1	New Whiteland	-36
2	Evansville Museum	*-17*		2	Martinsville 2 SW	-35
2	Tell City	-17		3	Spencer	-33
4	Madison Sewage Plant	-18		4	Scottsburg	-32
5	Princeton 1 W	-19		5	Brookville	-31
5	Washington	-19		5	Cambridge City 3 N	-31
7	Bloomington Indiana Univ.	-21		5	English 4 S	-31
7	Evansville Regional Airport	-21		8	Greenfield	-29
7	South Bend Michiana Regional	-21		8	Hobart 2 WNW	-29
10	Fort Wayne Baer Field	-22		8	Muncie	-29
10	Indianapolis SE Side	-22		8	Oolitic Purdue Exp. Farm	-29
10	Lagrange Sewage Plant	-22		8	Paoli	-29
13	Crane Naval Depot	-23		8	Portland 1 SW	*-29*
13	Greencastle 1 SE	-23		8	Salem	-29
13	La Porte	-23		8	Winamac 2 SSE	-29
13	Marion 2 N	-23		16	Lowell	-28
13	Oaklandon Geist Reservoir	-23		16	Rushville Sewage Plant	-28
13	Seymour 2 N	-23		18	Angola	*-27*
13	Shoals Hiway 50 Bridge	-23		18	Indianapolis Int'l Airport	-27
13	West Lafayette Purdue Univ. Arpt.	*-23*		18	Richmond Water Works	-27
21	Anderson Sewage Plant	-24		18	Whitestown	-27
21	Berne	-24		22	Columbus	-26
21	Bluffton 1 N	-24		22	Frankfort Disposal Plant	-26
21	Columbia City	-24		22	Hartford City 4 ESE	*-26*
21	Delphi 3 S	-24		22	Kokomo 3 WSW	-26

July Mean Maximum Temperature

	Highest				Lowest	
Rank	**Station Name**	**°F**		**Rank**	**Station Name**	**°F**
1	Evansville Museum	*89.7*		1	Angola	82.1
2	Evansville Regional Airport	88.9		2	Lagrange Sewage Plant	82.9
3	Vevay	88.5		3	La Porte	83.0
4	Mount Vernon	88.4		3	Warsaw	83.0
5	Washington	88.3		5	Columbia City	83.3
6	Princeton 1 W	88.2		5	Valparaiso Waterworks	83.3
7	English 4 S	88.1		5	Winchester Airport 3E	83.3
8	Paoli	87.9		8	Hartford City 4 ESE	*83.4*
9	Crane Naval Depot	87.8		8	South Bend Michiana Regional	83.4
9	Tell City	87.8		8	Wanatah 2 WNW	83.4
11	Scottsburg	87.5		11	Cambridge City 3 N	83.5
12	Rockville	87.4		12	Winamac 2 SSE	83.6
13	Saint Meinrad	87.3		13	Anderson Sewage Plant	83.7
13	Terre Haute Indiana State	87.3		13	Bluffton 1 N	83.7
15	Madison Sewage Plant	87.2		15	Rochester	83.9
16	Salem	87.0		16	Kokomo 3 WSW	84.0
17	Brookville	86.9		16	New Castle 4 N	84.0
18	North Vernon 1 NW	*86.8*		16	Portland 1 SW	*84.0*
18	Shoals Hiway 50 Bridge	86.8		19	Goshen College	84.1
20	Greencastle 1 SE	86.2		19	West Lafayette 6 NW	84.1
20	West Lafayette Purdue Univ. Arpt.	*86.2*		21	Farmland 5 NNW	84.2
22	Bloomington Indiana Univ.	86.1		22	Frankfort Disposal Plant	84.4
23	Columbus	86.0		22	Lowell	84.4
23	Dubois S Ind. Forage Farm	86.0		22	Oaklandon Geist Reservoir	84.4
25	Kentland	85.9		22	Rushville Sewage Plant	84.4

January Mean Minimum Temperature

	Highest				Lowest	
Rank	Station Name	°F		Rank	Station Name	°F
1	Evansville Museum	24.4		1	Lowell	12.9
2	Madison Sewage Plant	23.3		2	Wanatah 2 WNW	13.4
2	Tell City	23.3		3	Angola	13.5
4	Saint Meinrad	23.2		4	Rochester	14.1
5	Washington	23.1		5	Kokomo 3 WSW	14.2
6	Evansville Regional Airport	22.9		5	Lagrange Sewage Plant	14.2
7	Vevay	22.7		7	Columbia City	14.3
8	Mount Vernon	22.3		8	Winamac 2 SSE	14.4
9	Salem	22.0		9	Warsaw	14.7
10	Crane Naval Depot	21.5		9	West Lafayette 6 NW	14.7
10	Princeton 1 W	21.5		11	Hartford City 4 ESE	14.8
12	North Vernon 1 NW	*21.2*		11	Lafayette 8 S	14.8
13	English 4 S	20.8		13	Bluffton 1 N	15.1
14	Dubois S Ind. Forage Farm	19.8		13	Kentland	15.1
14	Scottsburg	19.8		15	Elwood Wastewater Plant	15.2
16	Bloomington Indiana Univ.	19.3		16	Cambridge City 3 N	15.3
17	Paoli	19.2		16	Rensselaer	15.3
18	Greensburg	19.1		16	Valparaiso Waterworks	15.3
19	Seymour 2 N	18.9		19	Farmland 5 NNW	15.4
19	Shoals Hiway 50 Bridge	18.9		20	Hobart 2 WNW	15.5
21	Anderson Sewage Plant	18.7		21	Portland 1 SW	*15.6*
22	Columbus	18.6		22	La Porte	15.8
23	Indianapolis Int'l Airport	18.4		22	Whitestown	15.8
24	Martinsville 2 SW	18.0		24	Marion 2 N	16.0
25	Indianapolis SE Side	17.9		24	New Castle 4 N	16.0

Number of Annual Heating Degree Days

	Highest				Lowest	
Rank	Station Name	Num.		Rank	Station Name	Num.
1	Angola	*6,933*		1	Evansville Museum	*4,188*
2	Lagrange Sewage Plant	6,713		2	Saint Meinrad	4,446
3	Wanatah 2 WNW	6,569		3	Washington	4,554
4	Columbia City	6,524		4	Evansville Regional Airport	4,568
5	Lowell	6,508		5	Madison Sewage Plant	4,569
6	Rochester	6,467		6	Tell City	4,590
7	Kokomo 3 WSW	6,414		7	Vevay	4,626
8	Bluffton 1 N	6,389		8	Crane Naval Depot	*4,646*
9	Portland 1 SW	*6,308*		9	Mount Vernon	4,665
10	Warsaw	*6,289*		10	Princeton 1 W	4,754
11	La Porte	6,263		11	Salem	4,798
12	Rensselaer	6,240		12	English 4 S	4,813
13	Farmland 5 NNW	6,222		13	Paoli	5,088
14	Hartford City 4 ESE	*6,220*		14	Scottsburg	5,099
15	Cambridge City 3 N	6,204		15	Dubois S Ind. Forage Farm	5,113
15	Valparaiso Waterworks	6,204		16	Bloomington Indiana Univ.	5,238
17	South Bend Michiana Regional	6,203		17	Shoals Hiway 50 Bridge	5,246
18	Winamac 2 SSE	6,197		18	Rockville	5,252
19	Goshen College	6,168		19	Columbus	5,389
20	Marion 2 N	6,167		20	Seymour 2 N	5,403
21	West Lafayette 6 NW	6,151		21	Terre Haute Indiana State	*5,420*
22	Elwood Wastewater Plant	6,142		22	Greensburg	5,443
23	Fort Wayne Baer Field	6,141		23	Indianapolis Int'l Airport	5,467
24	Hobart 2 WNW	6,124		24	Oolitic Purdue Exp. Farm	5,479
25	Lafayette 8 S	6,109		25	Greencastle 1 SE	5,551

Number of Annual Cooling Degree Days

	Highest			Lowest	
Rank	**Station Name**	**Num.**	**Rank**	**Station Name**	**Num.**
1	Evansville Museum	*1,687*	1	Angola	631
2	Evansville Regional Airport	1,477	2	Cambridge City 3 N	703
3	Washington	1,418	3	Columbia City	715
4	Princeton 1 W	1,413	4	Lagrange Sewage Plant	716
5	Mount Vernon	1,407	5	Wanatah 2 WNW	768
6	Tell City	1,402	6	New Castle 4 N	794
7	Crane Naval Depot	*1,323*	7	Rochester	798
8	Vevay	1,312	8	Warsaw	801
9	Saint Meinrad	1,308	9	Kokomo 3 WSW	806
10	Madison Sewage Plant	1,241	10	Valparaiso Waterworks	809
11	Scottsburg	1,189	11	Portland 1 SW	816
12	Dubois S Ind. Forage Farm	1,188	12	Lowell	822
13	Rockville	1,179	13	Bluffton 1 N	828
14	Paoli	1,168	14	Spencer	834
15	Salem	1,160	15	La Porte	838
16	Terre Haute Indiana State	*1,156*	16	Winchester Airport 3E	845
17	Bloomington Indiana Univ.	1,154	17	Elwood Wastewater Plant	849
18	Greencastle 1 SE	1,097	17	Goshen College	849
19	Indianapolis Int'l Airport	1,089	19	South Bend Michiana Regional	850
20	Columbus	1,083	20	Farmland 5 NNW	851
21	English 4 S	1,082	21	Winamac 2 SSE	855
22	Shoals Hiway 50 Bridge	1,073	22	Hartford City 4 ESE	*859*
23	Greensburg	1,067	23	Richmond Water Works	861
24	Greenfield	1,037	24	Marion 2 N	876
24	West Lafayette Purdue Univ. Arpt.	*1,037*	25	Fort Wayne Baer Field	877

Annual Precipitation

	Highest			Lowest	
Rank	**Station Name**	**Inches**	**Rank**	**Station Name**	**Inches**
1	English 4 S	49.55	1	West Lafayette Purdue Univ. Arpt.	*36.32*
2	Tell City	48.17	2	Fort Wayne Baer Field	36.52
3	Crane Naval Depot	47.55	3	Bluffton 1 N	36.60
4	Paoli	47.49	4	Goshen College	36.65
5	Dubois S Ind. Forage Farm	47.35	5	Lagrange Sewage Plant	36.71
6	Shoals Hiway 50 Bridge	47.31	6	Warsaw	36.77
7	Saint Meinrad	46.40	7	Lafayette 8 S	36.88
8	Evansville Museum	*46.24*	8	Portland 1 SW	37.13
9	Princeton 1 W	46.01	8	West Lafayette 6 NW	37.13
10	Mount Vernon	45.73	10	Angola	*37.29*
11	Seymour 2 N	45.64	11	Winchester Airport 3E	37.48
12	Salem	*45.58*	12	Winamac 2 SSE	37.50
13	Spencer	45.51	13	Farmland 5 NNW	37.51
14	Madison Sewage Plant	45.49	13	Hartford City 4 ESE	*37.51*
15	Washington	45.45	15	Hobart 2 WNW	37.82
16	Vevay	44.82	16	Wanatah 2 WNW	38.01
17	Bloomington Indiana Univ.	44.72	17	Delphi 3 S	38.06
18	Scottsburg	44.68	18	Muncie	38.34
19	Rockville	44.52	19	Columbia City	38.35
20	Oolitic Purdue Exp. Farm	44.49	20	Berne	38.41
21	Evansville Regional Airport	44.23	21	Rochester	38.48
22	Greencastle 1 SE	43.95	22	Kentland	*38.58*
23	Greenfield	43.41	23	Marion 2 N	38.80
24	North Vernon 1 NW	*43.40*	23	Rensselaer	38.80
25	Greensburg	43.25	25	Richmond Water Works	39.40

Number of Days Annually With ≥ 0.1″ Precipitation

	Highest			Lowest	
Rank	**Station Name**	**Days**	**Rank**	**Station Name**	**Days**
1	Seymour 2 N	86	1	West Lafayette Purdue Univ. Arpt.	*69*
2	English 4 S	84	2	Crane Naval Depot	71
2	La Porte	84	2	Delphi 3 S	71
4	Kokomo 3 WSW	83	2	West Lafayette 6 NW	71
4	Madison Sewage Plant	83	5	Hobart 2 WNW	72
4	South Bend Michiana Regional	83	5	Lafayette 8 S	72
4	Vevay	83	7	Hartford City 4 ESE	*74*
8	Cambridge City 3 N	82	7	Indianapolis SE Side	74
8	Greenfield	82	7	Rensselaer	*74*
8	Salem	82	7	Wanatah 2 WNW	74
8	Scottsburg	82	7	Warsaw	*74*
8	Shoals Hiway 50 Bridge	82	7	Winchester Airport 3E	*74*
13	Brookville	81	13	Fort Wayne Baer Field	75
13	Columbia City	81	13	Goshen College	75
13	Dubois S Ind. Forage Farm	81	13	Kentland	*75*
13	Greensburg	81	13	North Vernon 1 NW	75
13	Oaklandon Geist Reservoir	81	13	Portland 1 SW	75
13	Valparaiso Waterworks	81	18	Evansville Regional Airport	76
13	Whitestown	81	18	Farmland 5 NNW	76
20	Anderson Sewage Plant	80	18	Princeton 1 W	76
20	Berne	80	18	Winamac 2 SSE	76
20	Paoli	*80*	22	Angola	*77*
23	Bloomington Indiana Univ.	79	22	Columbus	77
23	Frankfort Disposal Plant	79	22	Indianapolis Int'l Airport	77
23	Saint Meinrad	79	22	Marion 2 N	77

Number of Days Annually With ≥ 1.0″ Precipitation

	Highest			Lowest	
Rank	**Station Name**	**Days**	**Rank**	**Station Name**	**Days**
1	Crane Naval Depot	14	1	Anderson Sewage Plant	7
2	Mount Vernon	13	1	Berne	7
2	Paoli	*13*	1	Bluffton 1 N	7
2	Washington	13	1	Elwood Wastewater Plant	7
5	Bloomington Indiana Univ.	12	1	Fort Wayne Baer Field	7
5	Dubois S Ind. Forage Farm	12	1	Lafayette 8 S	7
5	English 4 S	12	1	Lagrange Sewage Plant	7
5	Evansville Museum	*12*	1	Muncie	7
5	Madison Sewage Plant	12	1	West Lafayette Purdue Univ. Arpt.	*7*
5	Princeton 1 W	12	10	Angola	*8*
5	Rockville	12	10	Columbia City	8
5	Saint Meinrad	12	10	Delphi 3 S	8
5	Salem	12	10	Farmland 5 NNW	8
5	Scottsburg	12	10	Frankfort Disposal Plant	8
5	Shoals Hiway 50 Bridge	12	10	Goshen College	8
5	Tell City	12	10	Hartford City 4 ESE	*8*
5	Vevay	12	10	Hobart 2 WNW	8
18	Evansville Regional Airport	11	10	Indianapolis SE Side	8
18	Greencastle 1 SE	11	10	Marion 2 N	8
18	North Vernon 1 NW	11	10	New Castle 4 N	8
18	Oolitic Purdue Exp. Farm	11	10	Rensselaer	8
18	Rushville Sewage Plant	11	10	Richmond Water Works	8
18	Seymour 2 N	11	10	Rochester	8
18	Terre Haute Indiana State	*11*	10	South Bend Michiana Regional	8
25	Brookville	10	10	Wanatah 2 WNW	8

Annual Snowfall

	Highest			Lowest	
Rank	Station Name	Inches	Rank	Station Name	Inches
1	South Bend Michiana Regional	76.6	1	Tell City	*9.2*
2	La Porte	*61.5*	2	Saint Meinrad	*9.7*
3	Wanatah 2 WNW	44.5	3	Washington	11.5
4	Kokomo 3 WSW	43.1	4	Columbus	*13.1*
5	Valparaiso Waterworks	39.8	5	Mount Vernon	13.7
6	Lagrange Sewage Plant	38.7	6	Evansville Museum	*13.8*
7	Goshen College	38.2	7	Evansville Regional Airport	14.8
8	Fort Wayne Baer Field	34.8	8	Madison Sewage Plant	*15.3*
9	Angola	*33.6*	8	Oolitic Purdue Exp. Farm	15.3
10	Lowell	33.1	10	Shoals Hiway 50 Bridge	15.6
11	Rochester	*32.5*	11	Rushville Sewage Plant	16.1
12	Columbia City	31.5	12	Rockville	16.3
13	Berne	30.7	12	Winchester Airport 3E	*16.3*
14	Bluffton 1 N	27.9	14	Scottsburg	16.7
15	Hobart 2 WNW	*27.4*	15	Spencer	*16.9*
16	Greencastle 1 SE	27.3	16	Martinsville 2 SW	*17.7*
17	Kentland	*26.7*	17	Anderson Sewage Plant	*17.8*
18	Indianapolis Int'l Airport	26.4	18	Greensburg	18.0
19	Marion 2 N	26.2	18	Salem	18.0
20	Hartford City 4 ESE	*26.0*	20	Vevay	18.6
21	Winamac 2 SSE	25.8	21	Richmond Water Works	18.7
22	Farmland 5 NNW	25.7	22	Delphi 3 S	20.5
23	Frankfort Disposal Plant	25.6	23	Portland 1 SW	21.0
23	Muncie	*25.6*	24	West Lafayette 6 NW	21.5
25	Whitestown	25.4	25	West Lafayette Purdue Univ. Arpt.	*21.6*

Note: See Appendix D for explanation of data.

Annual Extreme Maximum Temperature

	Highest				Lowest	
Rank	Station Name	°F		Rank	Station Name	°F
1	Red Oak	109		1	Cresco 1 NE	100
1	Sidney	109		2	Clinton 1	101
3	Clarinda	108		2	Dubuque Regional Airport	101
3	Des Moines Airport	108		2	Forest City 2 NNE	101
3	Dubuque Lock & Dam 11	108		2	Lake Park	101
3	Eldora	108		2	Storm Lake 2 E	101
3	Glenwood 3 SW	108		7	Ames 8 WSW	102
3	Keosauqua	108		7	Anamosa 1 WNW	102
3	Rock Rapids	108		7	Clarion	102
3	Sioux City Municipal Airport	108		7	Decorah	102
11	Centerville	107		7	Emmetsburg	102
11	Hawarden	107		7	Estherville 2 N	102
11	Iowa Falls	107		7	Grundy Center	102
11	Jefferson	107		7	Guttenberg Lock & Dam 10	102
11	Knoxville	107		7	Manchester 2	*102*
11	Leon 6 ESE	107		7	Milford 4 NW	102
11	Shenandoah	107		7	Northwood	102
11	Sigourney	107		7	Osage	102
19	Albia 3 NNE	106		7	Sac City	102
19	Ankeny	106		7	Sanborn	102
19	Audubon 1 SSE	106		7	Sheldon	102
19	Bloomfield 1 WNW	106		7	Sioux Rapids 4 E	*102*
19	Boone	106		7	Swea City 1 NE	102
19	Columbus Junction 2 SSW	106		7	Waukon 1 NNE	102
19	Corning	106		25	Bellevue Lock & Dam 12	103

Annual Mean Maximum Temperature

	Highest				Lowest	
Rank	Station Name	°F		Rank	Station Name	°F
1	Keosauqua	63.0		1	Cresco 1 NE	54.0
2	Sidney	62.8		2	Lake Park	54.6
3	Shenandoah	62.6		3	Estherville 2 N	55.0
4	Glenwood 3 SW	62.5		3	Waukon 1 NNE	55.0
4	Keokuk	62.5		5	Northwood	55.3
4	Red Oak	62.5		6	Sibley 5 NNE	55.4
7	Bloomfield 1 WNW	62.1		7	Mason City Municipal Airport	55.5
8	Bedford	61.7		7	Milford 4 NW	55.5
8	Washington	61.7		9	Forest City 2 NNE	55.7
10	Clarinda	61.5		10	Sanborn	55.8
10	Leon 6 ESE	61.5		11	Osage	55.9
12	Albia 3 NNE	61.4		12	Dubuque Regional Airport	56.0
13	Iowa City	61.3		12	New Hampton	56.0
14	Fairfield	61.2		12	Swea City 1 NE	56.0
14	Fort Madison	61.2		15	Mason City	56.1
14	Logan	61.2		15	Storm Lake 2 E	56.1
17	Centerville	*61.1*		17	Clarion	56.2
17	Chariton 1 E	61.1		18	Decorah	56.3
17	Greenfield	61.1		18	Oelwein 2 S	56.3
20	Columbus Junction 2 SSW	61.0		20	Hampton	56.4
20	Indianola	61.0		20	Sheldon	56.4
20	Muscatine	61.0		20	Tripoli	56.4
23	Knoxville	60.9		23	Algona 3 W	56.5
23	Onawa 3 NW	60.9		23	Fayette	56.5
25	Mount Pleasant 1 SSW	60.8		23	Grundy Center	56.5

Annual Mean Temperature

	Highest				Lowest	
Rank	Station Name	°F		Rank	Station Name	°F
1	Keokuk	52.8		1	Cresco 1 NE	43.8
2	Sidney	52.1		2	Lake Park	44.4
3	Keosauqua	51.8		2	Sibley 5 NNE	44.4
4	Bloomfield 1 WNW	51.6		4	Estherville 2 N	44.5
4	Fort Madison	51.6		5	Northwood	45.3
6	Shenandoah	51.5		5	Sanborn	45.3
6	Washington	51.5		7	Mason City Municipal Airport	45.4
8	Iowa City	51.4		7	Milford 4 NW	45.4
9	Albia 3 NNE	51.1		7	Rock Rapids	45.4
9	Burlington Radio KBUR	51.1		10	Clarion	45.6
11	Bedford	51.0		10	Forest City 2 NNE	45.6
11	Fairfield	51.0		10	Mason City	45.6
11	Red Oak	51.0		10	Storm Lake 2 E	45.6
14	Glenwood 3 SW	50.9		10	Waukon 1 NNE	45.6
14	Knoxville	50.9		15	Fayette	45.7
14	Muscatine	50.9		15	Sheldon	45.7
17	Mount Pleasant 1 SSW	50.8		15	Swea City 1 NE	45.7
17	Ottumwa Industrial Airport	50.8		18	Pocahontas	46.0
19	Columbus Junction 2 SSW	50.6		18	Sioux Rapids 4 E	46.0
20	Clarinda	50.5		20	Manchester 2	*46.1*
21	Greenfield	50.4		20	Tripoli	46.1
22	Des Moines Airport	50.2		22	Cherokee	46.2
22	Le Claire Lock & Dam 14	50.2		23	Algona 3 W	46.3
22	Leon 6 ESE	50.2		23	Decorah	46.3
22	Mount Ayr 4 SW	*50.2*		23	Grundy Center	46.3

Annual Mean Minimum Temperature

	Highest				Lowest	
Rank	Station Name	°F		Rank	Station Name	°F
1	Keokuk	43.2		1	Cresco 1 NE	33.5
2	Fort Madison	42.0		1	Sibley 5 NNE	33.5
3	Burlington Radio KBUR	41.8		3	Rock Rapids	33.7
4	Iowa City	41.4		4	Estherville 2 N	34.0
4	Ottumwa Industrial Airport	41.4		5	Lake Park	34.2
6	Centerville	*41.3*		6	Cherokee	34.6
7	Le Claire Lock & Dam 14	41.2		7	Fayette	34.8
7	Sidney	41.2		7	Sanborn	34.8
7	Washington	41.2		7	Sheldon	34.8
10	Bloomfield 1 WNW	41.1		10	Elkader 5 SSW	35.0
11	Mount Pleasant 1 SSW	40.9		10	Mason City	35.0
12	Albia 3 NNE	40.8		10	Pocahontas	35.0
12	Fairfield	40.8		13	Clarion	35.1
12	Knoxville	40.8		13	Milford 4 NW	35.1
12	Muscatine	40.8		13	Storm Lake 2 E	35.1
16	Keosauqua	40.6		16	Mason City Municipal Airport	35.2
17	Des Moines Airport	40.5		16	Northwood	35.2
18	Dubuque Lock & Dam 11	40.4		18	Sioux Rapids 4 E	35.3
18	Shenandoah	40.4		19	Manchester 2	*35.4*
20	Columbus Junction 2 SSW	40.3		19	Swea City 1 NE	35.4
21	Bedford	40.1		21	Grinnell 3 SW	35.5
22	Clinton 1	40.0		22	Boone	35.6
22	Sigourney	40.0		22	Forest City 2 NNE	35.6
24	Greenfield	39.8		24	Tripoli	35.8
24	Mount Ayr 4 SW	39.8		25	Sioux Center 2 SE	35.9

Annual Extreme Minimum Temperature

Highest			Lowest		
Rank	**Station Name**	**°F**	**Rank**	**Station Name**	**°F**
1	Keokuk	-22	1	Elkader 5 SSW	-47
2	Fort Madison	-23	2	Decorah	-41
3	Beaconsfield	-25	3	Fayette	-40
3	Centerville	-25	4	Chariton 1 E	-38
3	Clarinda	-25	4	Guttenberg Lock & Dam 10	-38
3	Sidney	-25	6	Anamosa 1 WNW	-37
7	Burlington Radio KBUR	-26	6	Atlantic 1 NE	-37
7	Creston 2 SW	-26	8	Cresco 1 NE	-36
7	Des Moines Airport	-26	8	Leon 6 ESE	-36
7	Greenfield	-26	10	Belle Plaine	-35
7	Iowa City	-26	10	Boone	-35
7	Rockwell City	-26	10	Cascade	-35
7	Shenandoah	-26	10	Cherokee	-35
7	Sioux City Municipal Airport	-26	10	Grinnell 3 SW	-35
7	Washington	-26	10	Guthrie Center	-35
16	Castana Experiment Farm	-27	10	Indianola	-35
16	Denison	-27	10	Le Mars	-35
16	Jefferson	-27	10	Marshalltown	-35
16	Mount Pleasant 1 SSW	-27	19	Ankeny	-34
16	Onawa 3 NW	-27	19	Bedford	-34
16	Ottumwa Industrial Airport	-27	19	Bellevue Lock & Dam 12	-34
16	Sigourney	-27	19	Maquoketa 3 S	-34
16	Storm Lake 2 E	-27	19	Muscatine	-34
24	Ames 8 WSW	-28	19	Toledo	-34
24	Cedar Rapids Municipal Airport	-28	19	Waukon 1 NNE	-34

July Mean Maximum Temperature

Highest			Lowest		
Rank	**Station Name**	**°F**	**Rank**	**Station Name**	**°F**
1	Keosauqua	88.4	1	Waukon 1 NNE	81.5
2	Red Oak	88.2	2	Cresco 1 NE	81.6
3	Sidney	87.9	3	Dubuque Regional Airport	82.2
4	Shenandoah	87.8	4	Estherville 2 N	82.5
5	Washington	87.7	5	Lake Park	82.7
6	Glenwood 3 SW	87.6	5	Oelwein 2 S	82.7
6	Iowa City	87.6	5	Sibley 5 NNE	82.7
6	Keokuk	87.6	8	New Hampton	82.8
9	Fairfield	87.4	9	Osage	82.9
9	Logan	87.4	9	Storm Lake 2 E	82.9
11	Bloomfield 1 WNW	87.3	11	Forest City 2 NNE	83.0
11	Leon 6 ESE	87.3	12	Grundy Center	83.2
13	Knoxville	87.2	12	Northwood	83.2
14	Jefferson	87.1	12	Sanborn	83.2
15	Centerville	*87.0*	15	Decorah	83.3
15	Clarinda	87.0	15	Hampton	83.3
17	Onawa 3 NW	86.9	15	Tripoli	83.3
18	Albia 3 NNE	86.8	18	Fayette	83.4
18	Bedford	86.8	18	Manchester 2	*83.4*
20	Chariton 1 E	86.7	18	Mason City Municipal Airport	83.4
20	Columbus Junction 2 SSW	86.7	18	Milford 4 NW	83.4
22	Fort Madison	86.6	18	Swea City 1 NE	83.4
22	Greenfield	86.6	23	Clarion	83.5
22	Le Mars	86.6	23	Mason City	83.5
22	Osceola	86.6	23	Sheldon	83.5

January Mean Minimum Temperature

	Highest				Lowest	
Rank	**Station Name**	**°F**		**Rank**	**Station Name**	**°F**
1	Keokuk	16.1		1	Rock Rapids	2.6
2	Centerville	14.1		2	Cresco 1 NE	2.7
2	Fort Madison	14.1		3	Lake Park	2.9
4	Burlington Radio KBUR	14.0		4	Sibley 5 NNE	3.2
5	Albia 3 NNE	13.9		5	Estherville 2 N	3.5
6	Bloomfield 1 WNW	13.8		6	Northwood	4.0
7	Keosauqua	13.7		7	Sanborn	4.1
8	Sidney	13.5		8	Milford 4 NW	4.2
9	Washington	13.3		9	Clarion	4.4
10	Mount Pleasant 1 SSW	13.1		9	Forest City 2 NNE	4.4
11	Iowa City	13.0		9	Mason City	4.4
12	Ottumwa Industrial Airport	12.8		12	Sheldon	4.6
13	Fairfield	12.7		13	Cherokee	4.7
14	Muscatine	12.6		13	Mason City Municipal Airport	4.7
14	Shenandoah	12.6		15	Pocahontas	5.0
16	Knoxville	12.5		16	Swea City 1 NE	5.1
17	Columbus Junction 2 SSW	12.4		16	Tripoli	5.1
18	Bedford	12.2		18	Fayette	5.2
18	Le Claire Lock & Dam 14	12.2		19	Storm Lake 2 E	5.4
20	Leon 6 ESE	12.1		20	Boone	5.7
21	Clarinda	12.0		20	Sioux Rapids 4 E	5.7
21	Mount Ayr 4 SW	12.0		22	Algona 3 W	5.8
23	Clinton 1	11.9		23	Charles City	5.9
24	Red Oak	11.8		23	Decorah	5.9
25	Beaconsfield	11.7		23	Emmetsburg	5.9

Number of Annual Heating Degree Days

	Highest				Lowest	
Rank	**Station Name**	**Num.**		**Rank**	**Station Name**	**Num.**
1	Cresco 1 NE	8,173		1	Keokuk	5,578
2	Lake Park	8,043		2	Keosauqua	5,832
3	Sibley 5 NNE	7,998		3	Sidney	5,841
4	Estherville 2 N	7,990		4	Bloomfield 1 WNW	5,859
5	Rock Rapids	7,817		5	Fort Madison	5,892
6	Northwood	7,789		6	Washington	5,980
7	Sanborn	7,774		7	Shenandoah	5,982
8	Milford 4 NW	7,755		8	Albia 3 NNE	6,018
9	Mason City Municipal Airport	7,749		9	Burlington Radio KBUR	6,027
10	Mason City	7,680		10	Iowa City	6,034
11	Clarion	7,674		11	Mount Pleasant 1 SSW	6,073
12	Forest City 2 NNE	7,654		12	Bedford	6,074
13	Swea City 1 NE	7,646		13	Fairfield	6,096
14	Sheldon	7,639		14	Muscatine	6,119
15	Storm Lake 2 E	7,635		14	Red Oak	6,119
16	Fayette	7,581		16	Knoxville	6,153
16	Waukon 1 NNE	7,581		17	Columbus Junction 2 SSW	6,156
18	Pocahontas	7,578		17	Glenwood 3 SW	6,156
19	Cherokee	7,538		19	Ottumwa Industrial Airport	6,176
20	Sioux Rapids 4 E	7,533		20	Clarinda	6,223
21	Tripoli	7,483		21	Greenfield	6,242
22	Osage	7,460		22	Mount Ayr 4 SW	*6,249*
23	Algona 3 W	7,451		23	Leon 6 ESE	6,277
24	Grundy Center	7,437		24	Creston 2 SW	6,332
25	Manchester 2	*7,436*		25	Clinton 1	6,336

Number of Annual Cooling Degree Days

	Highest			Lowest	
Rank	Station Name	Num.	Rank	Station Name	Num.
1	Keokuk	1,237	1	Cresco 1 NE	532
2	Iowa City	1,204	2	Sibley 5 NNE	545
3	Sidney	1,180	3	Waukon 1 NNE	606
4	Fort Madison	1,171	4	Estherville 2 N	612
5	Shenandoah	1,166	5	Fayette	626
6	Keosauqua	1,155	6	Lake Park	635
7	Washington	1,151	7	Mason City	660
8	Bloomfield 1 WNW	1,134	7	Northwood	660
9	Ottumwa Industrial Airport	1,132	9	Manchester 2	662
10	Knoxville	1,126	9	Milford 4 NW	662
11	Burlington Radio KBUR	1,124	11	Tripoli	667
12	Fairfield	1,113	12	Storm Lake 2 E	669
12	Red Oak	1,113	13	Sheldon	672
14	Muscatine	1,106	14	Forest City 2 NNE	678
15	Glenwood 3 SW	1,092	15	Mason City Municipal Airport	680
16	Bedford	1,076	16	Sanborn	683
17	Des Moines Airport	1,065	17	Elkader 5 SSW	688
18	Le Claire Lock & Dam 14	1,042	18	Sioux Rapids 4 E	699
19	Albia 3 NNE	1,037	19	Dubuque Regional Airport	706
19	Newton	1,037	20	Hampton	709
21	Columbus Junction 2 SSW	1,034	21	Clarion	714
22	Jefferson	1,031	22	Charles City	715
23	Logan	1,022	23	Grinnell 3 SW	716
24	Greenfield	1,017	24	Maquoketa 3 S	720
25	Onawa 3 NW	1,012	24	Oelwein 2 S	720

Annual Precipitation

	Highest			Lowest	
Rank	Station Name	Inches	Rank	Station Name	Inches
1	Keosauqua	39.14	1	Sioux City Municipal Airport	26.15
2	Fort Madison	39.05	2	Le Mars	26.56
3	Bloomfield 1 WNW	38.64	3	Hawarden	26.92
4	Burlington Radio KBUR	38.20	4	Rock Rapids	27.23
5	Columbus Junction 2 SSW	38.13	5	Sibley 5 NNE	28.24
6	Albia 3 NNE	37.81	6	Sanborn	28.27
7	Keokuk	37.79	7	Estherville 2 N	28.33
8	Mount Pleasant 1 SSW	37.78	8	Lake Park	28.60
9	Leon 6 ESE	37.56	9	Sioux Center 2 SE	28.77
10	Iowa City	37.39	10	Cherokee	29.23
11	Centerville	*37.18*	11	Sheldon	29.42
12	Tipton 4 NE	37.16	12	Milford 4 NW	29.62
13	Oskaloosa	37.15	13	Mapleton 2	30.16
14	Chariton 1 E	37.10	14	Onawa 3 NW	30.22
15	Rathbun Dam	37.05	15	Ida Grove 5 NW	30.26
16	Fairfield	37.01	16	Primghar	30.39
17	Williamsburg	36.91	17	Algona 3 W	30.44
18	Muscatine	36.86	18	Swea City 1 NE	30.49
19	Cedar Rapids 1	36.76	19	Denison	30.58
20	Grinnell 3 SW	36.61	20	Castana Experiment Farm	30.84
21	Clarinda	36.60	21	Emmetsburg	31.18
22	Red Oak	36.59	22	Sioux Rapids 4 E	31.34
23	Boone	36.54	23	Waukon 1 NNE	31.44
24	Marshalltown	36.51	24	Rockwell City	31.52
25	New Hampton	36.37	25	Forest City 2 NNE	31.96

Number of Days Annually With ≥ 0.1″ Precipitation

	Highest			Lowest	
Rank	**Station Name**	**Days**	**Rank**	**Station Name**	**Days**
1	Dubuque Regional Airport	72	1	Hawarden	51
1	Keosauqua	72	2	Le Mars	52
3	Columbus Junction 2 SSW	71	2	Sioux City Municipal Airport	52
3	Mount Pleasant 1 SSW	71	4	Estherville 2 N	53
5	Fort Madison	70	5	Lake Park	54
5	Tripoli	70	5	Milford 4 NW	54
7	Bloomfield 1 WNW	69	7	Castana Experiment Farm	55
7	Burlington Radio KBUR	69	7	Cherokee	55
7	Clinton 1	69	7	Ida Grove 5 NW	55
7	Fairfield	69	7	Rock Rapids	55
7	Fayette	69	7	Sioux Center 2 SE	55
12	Albia 3 NNE	68	12	Primghar	56
12	Cedar Rapids 1	68	12	Sanborn	56
12	Grinnell 3 SW	68	12	Sibley 5 NNE	56
12	Maquoketa 3 S	68	15	Forest City 2 NNE	57
12	Oelwein 2 S	68	15	Glenwood 3 SW	57
12	Tipton 4 NE	68	15	Oakland 2 SW	57
18	Anamosa 1 WNW	67	15	Onawa 3 NW	57
18	Boone	67	15	Sioux Rapids 4 E	57
18	Decorah	67	15	Storm Lake 2 E	57
18	Guttenberg Lock & Dam 10	67	21	Algona 3 W	58
18	Iowa City	67	21	Emmetsburg	58
18	Keokuk	67	21	Mount Ayr 4 SW	58
18	Marshalltown	67	21	Perry	58
18	New Hampton	67	21	Rockwell City	58

Number of Days Annually With ≥ 1.0″ Precipitation

	Highest			Lowest	
Rank	**Station Name**	**Days**	**Rank**	**Station Name**	**Days**
1	Bedford	11	1	Le Mars	5
1	Red Oak	11	1	Sioux Center 2 SE	5
3	Beaconsfield	10	3	Algona 3 W	6
3	Burlington Radio KBUR	10	3	Allison	6
3	Fort Madison	10	3	Cedar Rapids Municipal Airport	6
3	Keokuk	10	3	Clinton 1	6
3	Keosauqua	10	3	Dubuque Regional Airport	6
3	Marshalltown	10	3	Elkader 5 SSW	6
3	Mount Pleasant 1 SSW	10	3	Fort Dodge	6
3	Shenandoah	10	3	Guttenberg Lock & Dam 10	6
3	Sidney	10	3	Hampton	6
12	Albia 3 NNE	9	3	Hawarden	6
12	Ames 8 WSW	9	3	Pocahontas	6
12	Anamosa 1 WNW	9	3	Rock Rapids	6
12	Bloomfield 1 WNW	9	3	Sheldon	6
12	Clarinda	9	3	Sibley 5 NNE	6
12	Colo	9	3	Swea City 1 NE	6
12	Corning	9	3	Washington	6
12	Cresco 1 NE	9	3	Waterloo Municipal Airport	6
12	Des Moines Airport	9	3	Waukon 1 NNE	6
12	Grundy Center	9	21	Ankeny	7
12	Guthrie Center	9	21	Bellevue Lock & Dam 12	7
12	Mount Ayr 4 SW	9	21	Boone	7
12	Sigourney	9	21	Cedar Rapids 1	7
12	Tripoli	9	21	Charles City	7

Annual Snowfall

	Highest			Lowest	
Rank	**Station Name**	**Inches**	**Rank**	**Station Name**	**Inches**
1	Dubuque Regional Airport	43.8	1	Fort Madison	*18.1*
2	Cresco 1 NE	41.7	2	Mount Ayr 4 SW	*18.6*
3	Mason City Municipal Airport	40.5	3	Rathbun Dam	*18.7*
4	Fayette	40.4	4	Keokuk	*21.1*
5	Sanborn	40.0	5	Washington	22.8
6	New Hampton	39.7	6	Perry	*23.0*
7	Decorah	39.4	7	Centerville	23.4
8	Forest City 2 NNE	39.0	8	Glenwood 3 SW	23.8
9	Columbus Junction 2 SSW	38.9	9	Beaconsfield	24.1
10	Northwood	38.6	9	Knoxville	*24.1*
11	Lake Park	38.4	11	Tipton 4 NE	*24.2*
12	Grundy Center	38.3	12	Shenandoah	24.4
13	Swea City 1 NE	*37.8*	13	Anamosa 1 WNW	*24.6*
14	Charles City	37.7	13	Corning	24.6
14	Sioux Center 2 SE	37.7	15	Bedford	*24.7*
16	Sheldon	37.3	16	Atlantic 1 NE	*25.2*
17	Sibley 5 NNE	37.2	16	Indianola	25.2
18	Elkader 5 SSW	36.2	18	Osceola	*25.4*
18	Fort Dodge	36.2	19	Ankeny	25.8
20	Denison	36.1	19	Clarinda	25.8
21	Tripoli	36.0	19	Mount Pleasant 1 SSW	25.8
22	Algona 3 W	35.8	22	Burlington Radio KBUR	25.9
22	Storm Lake 2 E	35.8	23	Oakland 2 SW	26.0
24	Osage	35.7	24	Leon 6 ESE	26.3
25	Des Moines Airport	*35.5*	25	Chariton 1 E	26.5

Note: See Appendix D for explanation of data.

Annual Extreme Maximum Temperature

	Highest			Lowest	
Rank	Station Name	°F	Rank	Station Name	°F
1	Council Grove Lake	114	1	Troy 2 E	106
1	Liberal	114	2	Tribune 1 W	107
1	Ness City	114	3	Garden City Exp. Station	108
1	Russell Municipal Airport	114	3	Goodland Renner Field	108
5	Alton 6 ESE	*113*	3	John Redmond Lake	108
5	Cottonwood Falls	113	3	Lawrence	108
5	Hays 1 S	113	3	Leavenworth	108
5	Healy	113	3	Lovewell Lake	108
5	Medicine Lodge	*113*	3	Oakley 4 W	*108*
5	Minneapolis	*113*	3	Olathe 3 E	108
5	Plainville 4 WNW	*113*	11	Atchison	109
5	Webster Dam	113	11	Atwood 2 SW	109
13	Abilene 1 W	112	11	Cimarron	109
13	Ashland	112	11	Columbus 1 SW	109
13	Beloit	112	11	Concordia Blosser Muni Airport	109
13	Bison	112	11	El Dorado	109
13	Ellsworth	*112*	11	Hoxie	109
13	Eskridge	*112*	11	Iola 1 W	109
13	Eureka	112	11	Marion Lake	109
13	Fall River Lake	112	11	McDonald	109
13	Florence	112	11	Mound Valley 3 WSW	109
13	Hugoton	112	11	Ottawa	109
13	Kingman	112	11	Quinter	109
13	Kirwin Dam	112	11	Wamego	109
13	Lakin	112	11	Washington	109

Annual Mean Maximum Temperature

	Highest			Lowest	
Rank	Station Name	°F	Rank	Station Name	°F
1	Liberal	71.0	1	Lovewell Lake	63.7
2	Meade	70.8	2	Mankato	63.8
3	Anthony	70.5	3	Marysville	64.2
3	Medicine Lodge	70.5	4	Belleville	64.3
5	Coldwater	70.3	4	Troy 2 E	64.3
6	Ashland	70.2	6	Colby 1 SW	64.4
7	Elkhart	70.0	6	Goodland Renner Field	64.4
8	Syracuse	69.8	6	Perry Lake	64.4
8	Ulysses	69.8	9	Concordia Blosser Muni Airport	64.5
10	Winfield 1	69.6	9	Norton Dam	*64.5*
11	Kingman	69.5	11	Centralia	64.6
11	Norwich	69.5	12	Eskridge	*64.8*
11	Sedan	69.5	12	Tuttle Creek Lake	64.8
14	Pratt 4 W	69.3	14	Atchison	64.9
14	Sublette	69.3	14	Glen Elder Lake	64.9
16	Hugoton	69.2	16	Council Grove Lake	65.0
16	Independence	69.2	16	Pomona Lake	65.0
18	Great Bend	69.0	18	Atwood 2 SW	65.2
18	Howard 5 NE	69.0	18	Milford Lake	65.2
20	Eureka	68.8	18	Olathe 3 E	65.2
21	Hudson	68.7	21	McDonald	65.3
21	Ness City	68.7	21	Topeka Municipal Airport	65.3
23	Cimarron	68.6	23	Oskaloosa	65.4
23	Sharon Springs	68.6	23	Quinter	65.4
25	Mound Valley 3 WSW	68.5	25	Marion Lake	65.5

Annual Mean Temperature

	Highest			Lowest	
Rank	Station Name	°F	Rank	Station Name	°F
1	Anthony	58.5	1	Colby 1 SW	50.4
2	Norwich	58.0	2	Atwood 2 SW	50.7
3	Independence	57.8	3	Norton Dam	50.9
4	Winfield 1	57.7	4	Goodland Renner Field	51.0
5	Coldwater	57.5	5	Lovewell Lake	51.4
6	Fort Scott	57.3	6	Kirwin Dam	51.5
7	Medicine Lodge	57.2	7	Mankato	51.6
7	Sedan	57.2	8	McDonald	51.7
9	Columbus 1 SW	57.1	9	Saint Francis	52.0
9	Girard	57.1	9	Tribune 1 W	52.0
9	Kingman	57.1	9	Winona	52.0
12	Iola 1 W	57.0	12	Oberlin	52.1
13	Howard 5 NE	56.9	13	Leoti 1 W	52.3
13	Liberal	56.9	13	Norton 9 SSE	52.3
15	Eureka	56.8	13	Quinter	52.3
15	Hudson	56.8	16	Glen Elder Lake	52.4
15	Mound Valley 3 WSW	56.8	16	Oakley 4 W	52.4
18	El Dorado	56.7	18	Marysville	52.5
19	Great Bend	56.6	18	Webster Dam	52.5
19	Parsons 2 NW	56.6	20	Belleville	52.8
19	Yates Center	56.6	21	Garden City Exp. Station	52.9
22	Meade	56.4	21	Phillipsburg	52.9
22	Newton 2 SW	56.4	21	Tuttle Creek Lake	52.9
22	Wellington	56.4	24	Wakeeney	53.0
22	Wichita Mid-Continent Airport	56.4	25	Russell Springs 4 W	53.1

Annual Mean Minimum Temperature

	Highest			Lowest	
Rank	Station Name	°F	Rank	Station Name	°F
1	Fort Scott	46.5	1	Atwood 2 SW	36.1
2	Anthony	46.4	2	Colby 1 SW	36.2
2	Norwich	46.4	3	Tribune 1 W	36.6
4	Independence	46.3	4	Norton Dam	37.3
5	Girard	46.2	4	Saint Francis	37.3
5	Iola 1 W	46.2	6	Goodland Renner Field	37.4
7	Columbus 1 SW	46.1	6	Kirwin Dam	37.4
8	Lawrence	46.0	8	Oberlin	37.6
9	Winfield 1	45.9	9	Leoti 1 W	37.7
10	Parsons 2 NW	45.7	9	Russell Springs 4 W	37.7
11	Yates Center	45.4	11	McDonald	38.0
12	Chanute Martin Johnson Airport	45.3	12	Syracuse	38.2
13	El Dorado	45.2	12	Winona	38.2
13	Wichita Mid-Continent Airport	45.2	14	Webster Dam	38.5
15	Olathe 3 E	45.1	15	Norton 9 SSE	38.6
16	Newton 2 SW	45.0	16	Oakley 4 W	38.7
16	Ottawa	45.0	17	Garden City Exp. Station	38.8
18	Garnett 1 E	44.9	18	Alton 6 ESE	38.9
18	Mound Valley 3 WSW	44.9	19	Scott City	39.0
18	Sedan	44.9	19	Ulysses	39.0
21	Eureka	44.8	21	Lovewell Lake	39.1
21	Howard 5 NE	44.8	21	Phillipsburg	39.1
23	Hudson	44.7	21	Quinter	39.1
23	Kingman	44.7	24	Healy	39.2
25	Paola	44.6	24	Hoxie	39.2

Annual Extreme Minimum Temperature

	Highest				Lowest	
Rank	**Station Name**	**°F**		**Rank**	**Station Name**	**°F**
1	Liberal	-13		1	Atwood 2 SW	-34
2	Anthony	*-15*		2	Colby 1 SW	-32
2	Norwich	-15		3	Alton 6 ESE	-31
2	Wellington	-15		3	Oberlin	-31
5	Columbus 1 SW	-16		3	Saint Francis	-31
5	Independence	-16		6	Kirwin Dam	-30
7	Chanute Martin Johnson Airport	-17		7	Lovewell Lake	-29
7	Coldwater	-17		7	Plainville 4 WNW	*-29*
7	Howard 5 NE	-17		7	Washington	-29
7	Kingman	-17		10	Ellsworth	*-28*
7	Meade	-17		10	Hoxie	-28
7	Parsons 2 NW	-17		10	Norton Dam	*-28*
13	El Dorado	-18		10	Phillipsburg	*-28*
13	Elk City Lake	*-18*		10	Tuttle Creek Lake	-28
13	Fall River Lake	-18		15	Glen Elder Lake	-27
13	Fort Scott	-18		15	Goodland Renner Field	-27
13	Girard	-18		15	Horton	-27
13	Hudson	-18		15	Leavenworth	-27
13	Hugoton	-18		15	Lincoln 1 ESE	-27
13	Sterling	-18		15	Marysville	-27
13	Toronto Lake	-18		15	Mound City	-27
22	Ashland	-19		15	Norton 9 SSE	-27
22	Eureka	-19		15	Russell Springs 4 W	-27
22	Garden City Municipal Airport	-19		15	Ulysses	-27
22	Hutchinson 10 SW	-19		25	Beloit	-26

July Mean Maximum Temperature

	Highest				Lowest	
Rank	**Station Name**	**°F**		**Rank**	**Station Name**	**°F**
1	Anthony	95.5		1	Troy 2 E	88.3
2	Medicine Lodge	95.0		2	Olathe 3 E	88.9
3	Lincoln 1 ESE	94.9		3	Atchison	89.1
3	Norwich	94.9		4	Perry Lake	89.2
5	Liberal	94.8		5	Goodland Renner Field	89.4
6	Meade	94.7		5	Pomona Lake	89.4
7	Ashland	94.6		5	Topeka Municipal Airport	89.4
7	Kingman	94.6		8	Eskridge	89.5
9	Hudson	94.3		9	Centralia	89.7
10	Bison	94.2		10	Lovewell Lake	89.8
11	Great Bend	94.1		11	Colby 1 SW	89.9
12	Minneapolis	94.0		11	Council Grove Lake	89.9
13	Coldwater	93.9		11	John Redmond Lake	89.9
14	Ness City	93.8		11	Marysville	89.9
14	Syracuse	93.8		15	Tuttle Creek Lake	90.0
14	Ulysses	93.8		16	Belleville	90.1
17	Pratt 4 W	93.7		16	Leavenworth	90.1
18	Elkhart	93.6		18	Holton 1 S	90.2
19	Alton 6 ESE	93.5		18	Oskaloosa	90.2
19	Ellsworth	93.5		20	Mankato	90.4
21	Phillipsburg	*93.4*		20	Milford Lake	90.4
21	Wellington	93.4		20	Oakley 4 W	90.4
21	Winfield 1	93.4		23	Fall River Lake	90.5
24	Abilene 1 W	93.3		24	McDonald	90.6
24	Garden City Municipal Airport	93.3		24	Paola	90.6

January Mean Minimum Temperature

	Highest				Lowest	
Rank	Station Name	°F		Rank	Station Name	°F
1	Anthony	22.7		1	Kirwin Dam	12.0
2	Columbus 1 SW	22.3		2	Norton Dam	12.2
3	Norwich	22.2		3	Atwood 2 SW	12.7
4	Independence	21.7		3	Lovewell Lake	12.7
5	Girard	21.5		5	Mankato	12.8
6	Iola 1 W	21.1		6	Colby 1 SW	13.0
6	Winfield 1	21.1		7	Webster Dam	13.1
8	Fort Scott	21.0		8	Marysville	13.4
9	Parsons 2 NW	20.9		8	Phillipsburg	*13.4*
10	Yates Center	20.8		10	Alton 6 ESE	13.5
11	Coldwater	20.6		11	Glen Elder Lake	13.6
12	Chanute Martin Johnson Airport	20.5		12	Syracuse	13.7
13	Hudson	20.2		13	Russell Springs 4 W	14.0
13	Kingman	20.2		13	Tuttle Creek Lake	14.0
13	Lawrence	20.2		15	Oberlin	14.1
16	Howard 5 NE	20.1		16	Tribune 1 W	14.2
16	Mound Valley 3 WSW	20.1		17	Garden City Exp. Station	14.5
18	El Dorado	19.9		17	Hays 1 S	14.5
18	Eureka	19.9		17	Norton 9 SSE	14.5
18	Liberal	19.9		17	Saint Francis	14.5
18	Wichita Mid-Continent Airport	19.9		21	Leoti 1 W	14.9
22	Garnett 1 E	19.8		21	Lincoln 1 ESE	14.9
22	Great Bend	19.8		23	Belleville	15.1
24	Newton 2 SW	19.7		24	Healy	15.2
24	Sedan	19.7		25	McDonald	15.4

Number of Annual Heating Degree Days

	Highest				Lowest	
Rank	Station Name	Num.		Rank	Station Name	Num.
1	Colby 1 SW	6,198		1	Anthony	*4,177*
2	Atwood 2 SW	6,113		2	Independence	4,231
3	Norton Dam	*6,086*		3	Norwich	4,294
4	Mankato	5,981		4	Winfield 1	4,305
5	Lovewell Lake	5,979		5	Coldwater	4,344
6	Goodland Renner Field	5,944		6	Columbus 1 SW	4,345
7	Kirwin Dam	*5,930*		7	Sedan	4,395
8	McDonald	5,791		8	Girard	4,409
9	Marysville	5,765		9	Iola 1 W	4,418
10	Glen Elder Lake	5,749		10	Howard 5 NE	4,434
11	Oberlin	5,745		11	Fort Scott	4,451
12	Saint Francis	5,740		12	Mound Valley 3 WSW	4,476
13	Winona	5,736		13	Medicine Lodge	4,485
14	Webster Dam	5,723		14	Liberal	4,487
15	Norton 9 SSE	5,704		15	Yates Center	4,495
16	Quinter	5,696		16	Eureka	4,502
17	Phillipsburg	*5,678*		17	Parsons 2 NW	4,512
18	Tribune 1 W	5,668		18	Kingman	4,525
19	Leoti 1 W	5,647		19	El Dorado	4,530
20	Belleville	5,613		20	Chanute Martin Johnson Airport	4,614
20	Tuttle Creek Lake	5,613		21	Hudson	4,616
22	Oakley 4 W	5,570		22	Garnett 1 E	4,625
23	Wakeeney	5,561		23	Meade	4,628
24	Alton 6 ESE	5,514		24	Pratt 4 W	4,639
25	Garden City Exp. Station	5,504		25	Great Bend	4,655

Number of Annual Cooling Degree Days

Rank	Station Name (Highest)	Num.	Rank	Station Name (Lowest)	Num.
1	Anthony	1,907	1	Goodland Renner Field	940
2	Norwich	1,880	2	Colby 1 SW	964
3	Hudson	1,779	3	Atwood 2 SW	977
4	Kingman	1,762	4	McDonald	1,015
5	Winfield 1	1,759	4	Tribune 1 W	1,015
6	Medicine Lodge	*1,746*	6	Saint Francis	1,030
7	Independence	1,742	7	Oakley 4 W	*1,050*
8	Coldwater	1,741	8	Leoti 1 W	1,067
9	Wichita Mid-Continent Airport	1,724	9	Winona	1,092
10	Newton 2 SW	1,710	10	Norton Dam	*1,102*
11	Wellington	1,706	11	Oberlin	1,116
12	Fort Scott	1,705	12	Lovewell Lake	1,138
13	Great Bend	1,696	13	Mankato	1,162
14	Sedan	1,678	14	Quinter	1,172
15	Abilene 1 W	1,676	15	Norton 9 SSE	1,188
16	Minneapolis	*1,662*	16	Hoxie	1,207
17	Salina Municipal Airport	*1,657*	17	Plainville 4 WNW	*1,225*
18	McPherson	1,643	18	Eskridge	*1,226*
19	Lawrence	1,638	19	Garden City Exp. Station	1,231
20	Eureka	1,632	20	Scott City	1,236
21	Howard 5 NE	1,629	21	Russell Springs 4 W	1,245
21	Sterling	1,629	22	Healy	1,268
23	Iola 1 W	1,628	23	Belleville	1,276
24	Clay Center	1,627	24	Sharon Springs	1,277
25	Liberal	1,624	24	Webster Dam	1,277

Annual Precipitation

Rank	Station Name (Highest)	Inches	Rank	Station Name (Lowest)	Inches
1	Girard	46.00	1	Syracuse	16.56
2	Mound Valley 3 WSW	45.53	2	Tribune 1 W	17.29
3	Columbus 1 SW	44.57	3	Ulysses	17.34
4	Fort Scott	44.15	4	Saint Francis	18.01
5	Independence	43.52	5	Hugoton	18.31
6	Yates Center	42.22	6	Leoti 1 W	18.41
7	Chanute Martin Johnson Airport	42.17	7	Lakin	18.62
8	Parsons 2 NW	42.11	8	Elkhart	18.72
9	Mound City	42.08	9	Russell Springs 4 W	18.74
10	Iola 1 W	42.05	10	Garden City Exp. Station	18.77
11	Elk City Lake	41.83	11	Sublette	19.20
12	Paola	41.14	12	Liberal	19.48
13	Garnett 1 E	40.77	13	Oakley 4 W	19.55
14	Sedan	40.63	14	Goodland Renner Field	19.58
15	Leavenworth	40.59	15	Winona	19.71
16	Olathe 3 E	40.38	16	Sharon Springs	19.87
17	Lawrence	39.91	17	Garden City Municipal Airport	20.16
18	Ottawa	39.43	18	Scott City	20.69
19	Oskaloosa	38.50	19	Colby 1 SW	20.82
20	Toronto Lake	38.29	20	Healy	21.37
21	Holton 1 S	38.22	21	Hoxie	21.58
22	Atchison	37.74	22	McDonald	21.77
23	Eureka	37.73	23	Ness City	21.85
24	Troy 2 E	37.68	24	Dodge City Municipal Airport	21.96
25	Howard 5 NE	37.62	25	Meade	22.00

Number of Days Annually With ≥ 0.1″ Precipitation

	Highest			Lowest	
Rank	**Station Name**	**Days**	**Rank**	**Station Name**	**Days**
1	Fort Scott	67	1	Ulysses	34
1	Paola	67	2	Hugoton	35
3	Mound City	66	2	Syracuse	35
4	Columbus 1 SW	65	4	Sublette	36
4	Olathe 3 E	65	4	Tribune 1 W	36
4	Ottawa	65	6	Lakin	37
7	Girard	63	6	Russell Springs 4 W	37
7	Horton	63	8	Elkhart	*38*
7	Independence	63	8	Garden City Exp. Station	38
7	Yates Center	63	8	Goodland Renner Field	38
11	Atchison	62	8	Liberal	38
11	Chanute Martin Johnson Airport	62	8	Winona	*38*
11	Iola 1 W	62	13	Colby 1 SW	39
11	Lawrence	62	13	Garden City Municipal Airport	39
11	Leavenworth	*62*	15	Healy	40
11	Mound Valley 3 WSW	62	15	Leoti 1 W	40
11	Oskaloosa	62	15	Meade	40
11	Pomona Lake	62	15	Oakley 4 W	40
11	Troy 2 E	62	19	Ness City	41
20	Eureka	61	19	Saint Francis	41
20	Holton 1 S	61	19	Scott City	41
20	Parsons 2 NW	61	22	Coldwater	42
23	Centralia	60	22	Sharon Springs	42
23	Eskridge	*60*	24	Dodge City Municipal Airport	43
23	Garnett 1 E	60	24	Kirwin Dam	43

Number of Days Annually With ≥ 1.0″ Precipitation

	Highest			Lowest	
Rank	**Station Name**	**Days**	**Rank**	**Station Name**	**Days**
1	Girard	14	1	Saint Francis	2
1	Mound Valley 3 WSW	14	2	Elkhart	3
3	Independence	13	2	Hoxie	3
3	Yates Center	13	2	Hugoton	3
5	Chanute Martin Johnson Airport	12	2	Leoti 1 W	3
5	Columbus 1 SW	12	2	Oakley 4 W	3
5	Cottonwood Falls	12	2	Russell Springs 4 W	3
5	Garnett 1 E	12	2	Tribune 1 W	3
5	Holton 1 S	12	2	Ulysses	3
5	Olathe 3 E	12	10	Bison	4
5	Parsons 2 NW	12	10	Colby 1 SW	4
5	Pomona Lake	12	10	Garden City Exp. Station	4
13	Elk City Lake	*11*	10	Garden City Municipal Airport	4
13	Eskridge	*11*	10	Goodland Renner Field	4
13	Eureka	11	10	Hays 1 S	4
13	Fall River Lake	11	10	Healy	4
13	Florence	11	10	Lakin	4
13	Fort Scott	11	10	Liberal	4
13	Herington	11	10	McDonald	4
13	Iola 1 W	11	10	Oberlin	4
13	Lawrence	11	10	Quinter	4
13	Leavenworth	*11*	10	Scott City	4
13	Mound City	11	10	Sharon Springs	4
13	Oskaloosa	11	10	Sublette	4
13	Ottawa	11	10	Syracuse	4

Annual Snowfall

	Highest			Lowest	
Rank	**Station Name**	**Inches**	**Rank**	**Station Name**	**Inches**
1	McDonald	46.0	1	Girard	*6.0*
2	Goodland Renner Field	42.5	2	Parsons 2 NW	*9.0*
3	Centralia	35.0	3	Tuttle Creek Lake	*10.1*
4	Saint Francis	34.5	4	Ashland	*10.6*
5	Oberlin	32.5	5	Kanopolis Lake	*10.8*
6	Colby 1 SW	30.7	6	Winfield 1	*10.9*
7	Atwood 2 SW	*29.9*	7	Columbus 1 SW	11.0
8	Scott City	27.9	7	Newton 2 SW	*11.0*
8	Winona	*27.9*	9	Norwich	*11.1*
10	Hoxie	*26.9*	9	Sedan	11.1
11	Wakeeney	*26.7*	11	El Dorado	*11.3*
12	Leoti 1 W	*26.6*	12	Milford Lake	11.4
13	Norton 9 SSE	26.5	13	Independence	*12.1*
14	Healy	26.4	14	Wellington	13.3
14	Sharon Springs	26.4	15	Howard 5 NE	13.6
16	Oakley 4 W	26.2	15	Marysville	*13.6*
17	Tribune 1 W	26.0	17	Anthony	*13.7*
18	Mankato	*25.3*	18	Abilene 1 W	*13.9*
19	Herington	25.1	19	Mound City	14.0
20	Russell Municipal Airport	*24.8*	20	Chanute Martin Johnson Airport	*14.2*
21	Quinter	*24.7*	21	Kingman	14.7
22	Russell Springs 4 W	24.2	22	Cottonwood Falls	15.0
23	Plainville 4 WNW	23.8	22	Medicine Lodge	*15.0*
24	Concordia Blosser Muni Airport	*22.6*	24	Fort Scott	15.2
25	Bison	22.5	24	Sterling	*15.2*

Note: See Appendix D for explanation of data.

Annual Extreme Maximum Temperature

Highest			Lowest		
Rank	Station Name	°F	Rank	Station Name	°F
1	Nolin River Lake	109	1	Baxter	101
2	Bowling Green Warren Co. Airport	*107*	1	Gray Hawk	*101*
2	Gilbertsville Kentucky Dam	107	1	London-Carbin Airport	101
2	Hodgenville-Lincoln	107	1	Manchester 4 W	101
2	Rough River Lake	107	1	Williamsburg	101
2	West Liberty	107	6	Barbourville	102
7	Barren River Lake	106	6	Berea College	102
7	Bernheim Forest	106	6	Henderson 7 SSW	102
7	Louisville Standiford Field	106	6	Mount Vernon	102
10	Ashland	105	6	Scottsville 3 SSW	102
10	Bardstown 5 E	*105*	6	Somerset 2 N	102
10	Bradfordsville	105	6	Summer Shade	102
10	Carrollton Lock 1	105	13	Cincinnati Covington Airport	103
10	Farmers 2 S	105	13	Danville	103
10	Glasgow	105	13	Falmouth	*103*
10	Greensburg	105	13	Frankfort Lock 4	103
10	Maysville Sewage Plant	105	13	Leitchfield 2 N	103
10	Murray	105	13	Lexington Bluegrass Field	103
10	Paducah Walker Boat Yard	*105*	13	Mayfield Radio Wngo	103
10	Princeton 1 SE	105	13	Monticello 3 NE	103
10	Shelbyville 1 E	105	21	Bardwell 2 E	104
22	Bardwell 2 E	104	21	Beaver Dam	104
22	Beaver Dam	104	21	Dix Dam	104
22	Dix Dam	104	21	Grayson 3 SW	104
22	Grayson 3 SW	104	21	Hopkinsville	*104*

Annual Mean Maximum Temperature

Highest			Lowest		
Rank	Station Name	°F	Rank	Station Name	°F
1	Gilbertsville Kentucky Dam	70.6	1	Cincinnati Covington Airport	63.4
2	Lovelaceville	69.4	2	Gray Hawk	*64.6*
2	Mayfield Radio Wngo	69.4	3	Lexington Bluegrass Field	64.8
4	Bernheim Forest	69.2	4	Falmouth	*64.9*
4	Princeton 1 SE	69.2	5	Warsaw Markland Dam	65.2
6	Madisonville	69.1	6	Williamstown 3 W	65.3
7	Bardwell 2 E	68.8	7	Maysville Sewage Plant	65.4
7	Murray	68.8	8	Shelbyville 1 E	65.5
9	Barren River Lake	68.7	9	Danville	65.6
10	Beaver Dam	68.5	10	Frankfort Lock 4	66.0
11	Mammoth Cave	68.4	10	Grayson 3 SW	66.0
12	Glasgow	68.3	12	Farmers 2 S	66.5
12	Greensburg	68.3	12	Louisville Standiford Field	66.5
14	Manchester 4 W	68.2	12	Mount Vernon	66.5
15	Barbourville	68.1	15	Baxter	66.7
15	Nolin River Lake	68.1	16	Ashland	66.8
17	Paducah Barkley Field	67.9	16	London-Carbin Airport	66.8
18	Bowling Green Warren Co. Airport	*67.8*	18	Carrollton Lock 1	66.9
18	Paducah Walker Boat Yard	*67.8*	18	Leitchfield 2 N	66.9
20	Hodgenville-Lincoln	67.7	18	Rough River Lake	66.9
20	Hopkinsville	*67.7*	18	Somerset 2 N	66.9
20	Monticello 3 NE	67.7	22	West Liberty	67.0
20	Scottsville 3 SSW	67.7	23	Bardstown 5 E	*67.3*
20	Summer Shade	67.7	23	Dix Dam	67.3
20	Williamsburg	67.7	25	Berea College	67.4

Annual Mean Temperature

	Highest				Lowest	
Rank	**Station Name**	**°F**		**Rank**	**Station Name**	**°F**
1	Gilbertsville Kentucky Dam	59.8		1	Gray Hawk	*52.3*
2	Murray	58.6		2	Grayson 3 SW	52.9
3	Princeton 1 SE	58.3		3	Shelbyville 1 E	53.0
4	Mayfield Radio Wngo	58.2		4	Falmouth	*53.1*
5	Scottsville 3 SSW	58.1		5	Ashland	53.2
6	Lovelaceville	58.0		5	West Liberty	*53.2*
6	Madisonville	58.0		7	Cincinnati Covington Airport	53.6
8	Bardwell 2 E	57.8		8	Warsaw Markland Dam	53.7
9	Paducah Barkley Field	57.6		9	Maysville Sewage Plant	53.8
10	Beaver Dam	57.4		10	Frankfort Lock 4	54.3
10	Glasgow	57.4		11	Rough River Lake	54.4
10	Paducah Walker Boat Yard	*57.4*		12	Farmers 2 S	54.7
13	Henderson 7 SSW	57.2		13	Baxter	55.0
14	Barren River Lake	57.1		14	Danville	55.2
14	Berea College	57.1		14	Lexington Bluegrass Field	55.2
14	Bernheim Forest	57.1		14	Nolin River Lake	55.2
14	Bowling Green Warren Co. Airport	*57.1*		14	Williamstown 3 W	55.2
18	Dix Dam	57.0		18	Bradfordsville	55.4
19	Louisville Standiford Field	56.9		18	Manchester 4 W	55.4
20	Mammoth Cave	56.8		20	Mount Vernon	55.5
21	Hodgenville-Lincoln	56.7		21	Barbourville	55.6
21	Summer Shade	56.7		21	Leitchfield 2 N	55.6
23	Hopkinsville	*56.5*		23	Williamsburg	55.7
24	Monticello 3 NE	56.4		24	Carrollton Lock 1	55.8
25	Bardstown 5 E	*56.3*		25	Somerset 2 N	55.9

Annual Mean Minimum Temperature

	Highest				Lowest	
Rank	**Station Name**	**°F**		**Rank**	**Station Name**	**°F**
1	Gilbertsville Kentucky Dam	48.9		1	West Liberty	*39.4*
2	Scottsville 3 SSW	48.4		2	Ashland	39.6
3	Murray	48.3		2	Grayson 3 SW	39.6
4	Princeton 1 SE	47.4		4	Gray Hawk	*40.0*
5	Louisville Standiford Field	47.3		5	Shelbyville 1 E	40.5
5	Paducah Barkley Field	47.3		6	Falmouth	*41.2*
7	Mayfield Radio Wngo	46.9		7	Rough River Lake	41.9
7	Paducah Walker Boat Yard	*46.9*		8	Maysville Sewage Plant	42.2
9	Henderson 7 SSW	46.8		8	Warsaw Markland Dam	42.2
9	Madisonville	46.8		10	Nolin River Lake	42.3
11	Bardwell 2 E	46.7		11	Frankfort Lock 4	42.5
11	Berea College	46.7		11	Manchester 4 W	42.5
13	Dix Dam	46.6		13	Farmers 2 S	42.7
14	Glasgow	46.5		14	Barbourville	43.0
15	Bowling Green Warren Co. Airport	*46.4*		15	Bradfordsville	43.2
16	Beaver Dam	46.3		16	Baxter	43.3
16	Lovelaceville	46.3		17	Williamsburg	43.5
18	Hodgenville-Lincoln	45.6		18	Cincinnati Covington Airport	43.8
18	Summer Shade	45.6		19	Greensburg	44.3
20	Barren River Lake	45.5		20	Leitchfield 2 N	44.4
20	Lexington Bluegrass Field	45.5		20	Mount Vernon	44.4
22	Bardstown 5 E	*45.2*		22	Carrollton Lock 1	44.7
22	Hopkinsville	*45.2*		23	Danville	44.8
22	Mammoth Cave	45.2		24	Somerset 2 N	44.9
25	London-Carbin Airport	45.1		25	Bernheim Forest	45.0

Annual Extreme Minimum Temperature

Highest				Lowest		
Rank	**Station Name**	**°F**		**Rank**	**Station Name**	**°F**
1	Paducah Walker Boat Yard	*-12*		1	Shelbyville 1 E	-37
2	Bowling Green Warren Co. Airport	*-15*		2	Gray Hawk	*-35*
2	Gilbertsville Kentucky Dam	-15		3	Somerset 2 N	-32
2	Paducah Barkley Field	-15		4	Grayson 3 SW	-31
5	Murray	-16		5	Falmouth	*-30*
6	Dix Dam	-18		5	Manchester 4 W	*-30*
6	Mayfield Radio Wngo	-18		5	West Liberty	*-30*
6	Princeton 1 SE	-18		8	Frankfort Lock 4	-27
6	Scottsville 3 SSW	-18		8	Leitchfield 2 N	-27
10	Barren River Lake	-19		8	Rough River Lake	-27
10	Baxter	-19		11	Bardstown 5 E	*-26*
10	Glasgow	-19		11	Farmers 2 S	-26
10	Greensburg	-19		11	Summer Shade	-26
10	Hopkinsville	*-19*		14	Ashland	*-25*
15	Danville	-20		14	Cincinnati Covington Airport	-25
15	Henderson 7 SSW	-20		14	Hodgenville-Lincoln	-25
15	Lexington Bluegrass Field	-20		14	London-Carbin Airport	-25
15	Madisonville	-20		14	Maysville Sewage Plant	-25
15	Mammoth Cave	-20		19	Beaver Dam	-24
15	Nolin River Lake	-20		19	Bernheim Forest	-24
21	Bardwell 2 E	-21		19	Mount Vernon	-24
21	Berea College	-21		22	Lovelaceville	-23
21	Williamsburg	*-21*		22	Monticello 3 NE	-23
24	Barbourville	-22		22	Warsaw Markland Dam	-23
24	Bradfordsville	-22		22	Williamstown 3 W	-23

July Mean Maximum Temperature

Highest				Lowest		
Rank	**Station Name**	**°F**		**Rank**	**Station Name**	**°F**
1	Gilbertsville Kentucky Dam	92.6		1	Gray Hawk	84.8
2	Lovelaceville	90.7		2	Cincinnati Covington Airport	85.8
3	Paducah Walker Boat Yard	*90.3*		3	Baxter	86.0
4	Bardwell 2 E	90.2		3	Lexington Bluegrass Field	86.0
5	Madisonville	90.0		5	London-Carbin Airport	86.2
6	Murray	89.8		5	Manchester 4 W	86.2
6	Princeton 1 SE	89.8		5	Mount Vernon	86.2
8	Barren River Lake	89.7		5	Williamstown 3 W	86.2
9	Bernheim Forest	89.6		9	Somerset 2 N	86.3
10	Mayfield Radio Wngo	89.5		10	Danville	86.4
10	Paducah Barkley Field	89.5		11	Grayson 3 SW	86.7
12	Nolin River Lake	89.4		11	Monticello 3 NE	86.7
13	Bowling Green Warren Co. Airport	89.2		13	Falmouth	86.8
13	Greensburg	89.2		14	Scottsville 3 SSW	86.9
15	Hopkinsville	*89.1*		14	Warsaw Markland Dam	86.9
16	Glasgow	88.8		14	Williamsburg	86.9
17	Rough River Lake	88.7		17	Berea College	87.1
18	Beaver Dam	88.6		18	Carrollton Lock 1	87.2
19	Henderson 7 SSW	88.4		18	Maysville Sewage Plant	87.2
20	Bradfordsville	88.3		18	Shelbyville 1 E	87.2
21	Mammoth Cave	88.2		18	Summer Shade	87.2
22	Ashland	88.0		22	West Liberty	87.3
22	Louisville Standiford Field	88.0		23	Barbourville	87.4
24	Bardstown 5 E	87.9		23	Dix Dam	87.4
25	Farmers 2 S	87.5		23	Hodgenville-Lincoln	87.4

January Mean Minimum Temperature

	Highest				Lowest	
Rank	**Station Name**	**°F**		**Rank**	**Station Name**	**°F**
1	Scottsville 3 SSW	27.0		1	Ashland	18.6
2	Murray	26.6		2	West Liberty	18.8
3	Gilbertsville Kentucky Dam	26.4		3	Falmouth	19.1
4	Berea College	25.9		3	Shelbyville 1 E	19.1
5	Glasgow	25.7		5	Grayson 3 SW	19.6
6	Dix Dam	25.6		6	Rough River Lake	20.0
7	Mayfield Radio Wngo	25.5		7	Warsaw Markland Dam	20.2
8	Monticello 3 NE	25.3		8	Gray Hawk	20.5
8	Princeton 1 SE	25.3		9	Cincinnati Covington Airport	20.7
10	Lovelaceville	25.0		10	Maysville Sewage Plant	20.9
10	Somerset 2 N	25.0		11	Nolin River Lake	21.2
12	Louisville Standiford Field	24.8		12	Frankfort Lock 4	21.3
12	Summer Shade	24.8		13	Farmers 2 S	22.2
14	Madisonville	24.7		14	Bradfordsville	22.5
14	Paducah Barkley Field	24.7		14	Williamstown 3 W	22.5
16	Beaver Dam	24.6		16	Barbourville	22.7
16	Bowling Green Warren Co. Airport	24.6		17	Hopkinsville	*22.8*
18	Bardwell 2 E	24.5		18	Leitchfield 2 N	22.9
18	London-Carbin Airport	24.5		19	Danville	23.0
20	Henderson 7 SSW	24.4		19	Manchester 4 W	23.0
20	Mammoth Cave	24.4		21	Greensburg	23.1
22	Hodgenville-Lincoln	24.2		22	Carrollton Lock 1	23.2
23	Bardstown 5 E	*24.1*		23	Lexington Bluegrass Field	23.5
24	Barren River Lake	23.9		24	Mount Vernon	23.6
24	Paducah Walker Boat Yard	23.9		25	Baxter	23.7

Number of Annual Heating Degree Days

	Highest				Lowest	
Rank	**Station Name**	**Num.**		**Rank**	**Station Name**	**Num.**
1	Gray Hawk	*5,280*		1	Gilbertsville Kentucky Dam	3,683
2	Shelbyville 1 E	5,244		2	Scottsville 3 SSW	3,841
3	Falmouth	*5,234*		3	Murray	3,873
4	Grayson 3 SW	5,221		4	Mayfield Radio Wngo	3,906
5	Ashland	5,158		5	Princeton 1 SE	3,907
6	Cincinnati Covington Airport	5,136		6	Lovelaceville	4,000
7	West Liberty	*5,108*		7	Madisonville	4,021
8	Warsaw Markland Dam	5,047		8	Bardwell 2 E	4,050
9	Maysville Sewage Plant	5,035		9	Glasgow	4,069
10	Rough River Lake	4,900		10	Berea College	4,090
11	Frankfort Lock 4	4,897		11	Beaver Dam	4,095
12	Farmers 2 S	4,762		12	Paducah Barkley Field	4,145
13	Lexington Bluegrass Field	4,669		13	Mammoth Cave	4,151
14	Danville	4,653		14	Dix Dam	4,159
15	Williamstown 3 W	4,650		15	Bernheim Forest	4,160
16	Nolin River Lake	4,639		16	Summer Shade	4,174
17	Bradfordsville	4,602		17	Bowling Green Warren Co. Airport	*4,211*
18	Baxter	4,535		17	Hodgenville-Lincoln	4,211
19	Mount Vernon	4,505		19	Henderson 7 SSW	4,217
20	Leitchfield 2 N	4,495		20	Barren River Lake	4,227
21	Carrollton Lock 1	4,457		21	Monticello 3 NE	4,232
22	Barbourville	4,431		22	Paducah Walker Boat Yard	*4,243*
23	Greensburg	4,403		23	London-Carbin Airport	4,304
24	Manchester 4 W	4,401		24	Louisville Standiford Field	4,308
25	Williamsburg	4,395		25	Somerset 2 N	4,310

Number of Annual Cooling Degree Days

	Highest				Lowest	
Rank	Station Name	Num.		Rank	Station Name	Num.
1	Gilbertsville Kentucky Dam	*1,924*		1	Gray Hawk	782
2	Murray	1,656		2	Grayson 3 SW	895
3	Madisonville	1,624		3	West Liberty	900
4	Princeton 1 SE	1,623		4	Ashland	958
5	Lovelaceville	1,599		5	Shelbyville 1 E	975
6	Paducah Barkley Field	1,598		6	Manchester 4 W	*989*
7	Paducah Walker Boat Yard	*1,596*		7	Baxter	1,001
8	Mayfield Radio Wngo	1,589		8	Falmouth	*1,039*
9	Bardwell 2 E	1,554		9	Warsaw Markland Dam	1,075
10	Louisville Standiford Field	1,531		10	Frankfort Lock 4	1,085
11	Barren River Lake	1,510		11	Maysville Sewage Plant	1,097
12	Glasgow	1,500		12	Barbourville	1,115
13	Henderson 7 SSW	1,481		13	Cincinnati Covington Airport	1,117
14	Bernheim Forest	1,467		14	Williamsburg	1,118
15	Bowling Green Warren Co. Airport	*1,447*		15	Mount Vernon	1,119
16	Beaver Dam	1,445		15	Rough River Lake	1,119
17	Scottsville 3 SSW	1,442		17	Farmers 2 S	1,134
18	Greensburg	1,358		18	Somerset 2 N	1,141
18	Hopkinsville	*1,358*		19	Jackson Julian Carroll Airport	1,181
20	Dix Dam	1,349		20	Monticello 3 NE	1,182
21	Berea College	1,326		21	London-Carbin Airport	*1,190*
22	Mammoth Cave	1,312		22	Bradfordsville	1,200
23	Summer Shade	1,291		22	Nolin River Lake	1,200
24	Hodgenville-Lincoln	1,286		24	Leitchfield 2 N	1,225
25	Bardstown 5 E	*1,270*		25	Williamstown 3 W	1,226

Annual Precipitation

	Highest				Lowest	
Rank	Station Name	Inches		Rank	Station Name	Inches
1	Murray	55.75		1	Cincinnati Covington Airport	42.45
2	Glasgow	54.27		2	Grayson 3 SW	42.82
3	Greensburg	53.40		3	Falmouth	42.99
3	Scottsville 3 SSW	53.40		4	Ashland	43.10
5	Bradfordsville	52.99		5	Frankfort Lock 4	43.55
6	Mount Vernon	52.56		6	Warsaw Markland Dam	44.19
7	Mammoth Cave	52.36		7	West Liberty	44.29
8	Bardwell 2 E	51.93		8	Henderson 7 SSW	44.69
9	Mayfield Radio Wngo	51.91		9	Carrollton Lock 1	44.74
10	Hodgenville-Lincoln	51.63		10	Louisville Standiford Field	44.75
11	Barren River Lake	51.59		11	Williamstown 3 W	44.98
12	Nolin River Lake	51.57		12	Maysville Sewage Plant	45.16
13	Hopkinsville	51.54		13	Lexington Bluegrass Field	46.08
14	Baxter	51.51		14	Paducah Walker Boat Yard	46.29
15	Princeton 1 SE	51.50		15	Dix Dam	46.53
16	Bardstown 5 E	*51.43*		16	Berea College	47.12
17	Bowling Green Warren Co. Airport	*51.41*		17	London-Carbin Airport	47.23
18	Somerset 2 N	51.34		18	Farmers 2 S	47.35
19	Monticello 3 NE	51.23		19	Madisonville	48.23
20	Barbourville	51.15		20	Shelbyville 1 E	48.26
21	Williamsburg	51.14		21	Rough River Lake	48.40
22	Summer Shade	50.94		22	Beaver Dam	48.76
23	Manchester 4 W	50.92		23	Paducah Barkley Field	49.09
24	Gilbertsville Kentucky Dam	50.69		24	Lovelaceville	49.12
25	Bernheim Forest	50.47		25	Danville	49.32

Number of Days Annually With ≥ 0.1″ Precipitation

	Highest			Lowest	
Rank	**Station Name**	**Days**	**Rank**	**Station Name**	**Days**
1	Baxter	96	1	Mayfield Radio Wngo	76
2	Barbourville	92	1	Paducah Barkley Field	76
2	Mount Vernon	92	1	Paducah Walker Boat Yard	*76*
2	Williamsburg	92	4	Gilbertsville Kentucky Dam	77
5	Manchester 4 W	91	4	Lovelaceville	77
6	Monticello 3 NE	90	6	Beaver Dam	78
6	Scottsville 3 SSW	90	6	Frankfort Lock 4	78
8	Ashland	*88*	6	Henderson 7 SSW	78
8	Glasgow	88	6	Rough River Lake	78
8	Somerset 2 N	88	10	Bardwell 2 E	79
11	Farmers 2 S	87	10	Falmouth	79
11	Grayson 3 SW	87	10	Hodgenville-Lincoln	79
11	Nolin River Lake	87	13	Carrollton Lock 1	80
14	Bradfordsville	86	13	Madisonville	80
14	Greensburg	86	13	Warsaw Markland Dam	80
14	Maysville Sewage Plant	86	16	Bernheim Forest	81
14	Williamstown 3 W	86	16	Louisville Standiford Field	81
18	Bardstown 5 E	*85*	16	Mammoth Cave	81
18	Barren River Lake	85	19	Dix Dam	*82*
18	Berea College	*85*	19	Leitchfield 2 N	82
18	Bowling Green Warren Co. Airport	*85*	19	Lexington Bluegrass Field	82
18	Gray Hawk	*85*	19	Murray	82
18	London-Carbin Airport	85	23	Cincinnati Covington Airport	83
18	Summer Shade	85	23	Princeton 1 SE	83
18	West Liberty	85	23	Shelbyville 1 E	83

Number of Days Annually With ≥ 1.0″ Precipitation

	Highest			Lowest	
Rank	**Station Name**	**Days**	**Rank**	**Station Name**	**Days**
1	Bardwell 2 E	15	1	Ashland	10
2	Bardstown 5 E	14	2	Cincinnati Covington Airport	11
2	Bowling Green Warren Co. Airport	*14*	2	Grayson 3 SW	11
2	Hopkinsville	14	2	Williamstown 3 W	11
2	Mayfield Radio Wngo	14	5	Barbourville	12
2	Murray	14	5	Berea College	12
7	Barren River Lake	13	5	Bradfordsville	12
7	Baxter	13	5	Carrollton Lock 1	12
7	Beaver Dam	13	5	Danville	12
7	Bernheim Forest	13	5	Dix Dam	12
7	Farmers 2 S	13	5	Falmouth	12
7	Gilbertsville Kentucky Dam	13	5	Frankfort Lock 4	12
7	Glasgow	13	5	Gray Hawk	*12*
7	Greensburg	13	5	Henderson 7 SSW	12
7	Hodgenville-Lincoln	13	5	London-Carbin Airport	12
7	Leitchfield 2 N	13	5	Louisville Standiford Field	12
7	Lexington Bluegrass Field	13	5	Maysville Sewage Plant	12
7	Lovelaceville	13	5	Monticello 3 NE	12
7	Madisonville	13	5	Mount Vernon	12
7	Mammoth Cave	13	5	Paducah Barkley Field	12
7	Manchester 4 W	13	5	Scottsville 3 SSW	12
7	Nolin River Lake	13	5	Somerset 2 N	12
7	Paducah Walker Boat Yard	*13*	5	Summer Shade	12
7	Princeton 1 SE	13	5	Warsaw Markland Dam	12
7	Rough River Lake	13	5	West Liberty	12

Annual Snowfall

Highest			Lowest		
Rank	Station Name	Inches	Rank	Station Name	Inches
1	Cincinnati Covington Airport	23.6	1	Rough River Lake	*6.9*
2	Williamstown 3 W	18.5	2	Madisonville	*7.0*
3	Mount Vernon	17.3	3	Barren River Lake	7.6
4	Monticello 3 NE	16.6	4	Hodgenville-Lincoln	*8.0*
5	Gray Hawk	*16.0*	5	Bernheim Forest	*8.6*
6	Lexington Bluegrass Field	15.9	6	Hopkinsville	9.7
7	Henderson 7 SSW	15.2	7	Falmouth	*10.2*
8	Louisville Standiford Field	15.0	7	Paducah Barkley Field	10.2
9	London-Carbin Airport	*14.7*	9	Bowling Green Warren Co. Airport	*10.4*
10	Grayson 3 SW	14.6	9	Murray	*10.4*
11	Princeton 1 SE	13.8	9	Somerset 2 N	*10.4*
12	Mammoth Cave	12.5	12	Scottsville 3 SSW	10.7
13	Danville	12.0	13	Summer Shade	11.3
13	Shelbyville 1 E	12.0	14	Warsaw Markland Dam	11.4
15	Carrollton Lock 1	11.9	15	Glasgow	11.6
15	Manchester 4 W	*11.9*	16	Bardwell 2 E	11.8
17	Bardwell 2 E	11.8	16	Leitchfield 2 N	*11.8*
17	Leitchfield 2 N	*11.8*	18	Carrollton Lock 1	11.9
19	Glasgow	11.6	18	Manchester 4 W	*11.9*
20	Warsaw Markland Dam	11.4	20	Danville	12.0
21	Summer Shade	11.3	20	Shelbyville 1 E	12.0
22	Scottsville 3 SSW	10.7	22	Mammoth Cave	12.5
23	Bowling Green Warren Co. Airport	*10.4*	23	Princeton 1 SE	13.8
23	Murray	*10.4*	24	Grayson 3 SW	14.6
23	Somerset 2 N	*10.4*	25	London-Carbin Airport	*14.7*

Note: See Appendix D for explanation of data.

Annual Extreme Maximum Temperature

	Highest				Lowest	
Rank	**Station Name**	**°F**		**Rank**	**Station Name**	**°F**
1	Plain Dealing	112		1	Carville 2 SW	100
2	Rosepine Research Station	*110*		1	Donaldsonville 4 SW	100
3	Bienville 3 NE	109		1	Franklin 3 NW	100
3	Ruston Louisiana Tech	109		1	Galliano	100
3	Winnfield 2 W	109		1	Houma	100
6	Ashland	108		1	Jeanerette 5 NW	*100*
6	Calhoun Research Station	108		7	Baton Rouge Ryan Airport	101
6	Leesville	108		7	Jennings	101
6	Logansport 4 ENE	*108*		7	New Iberia	101
6	Red River Research Station	*108*		7	New Roads 5 ESE	101
6	Shreveport Regional Airport	108		7	Reserve	101
12	Alexandria	107		7	Saint Bernard	101
12	Minden	107		7	Thibodaux 3 ESE	*101*
12	Natchitoches	107		14	Clinton 5 SE	*102*
15	De Ridder	106		14	Crowley 2 NE	102
15	LSU Dean Lee Research Station	*106*		14	LSU Ben Hur Farm	102
15	Winnsboro 5 SSE	106		14	Lafayette Regional Airport	102
18	Bastrop	105		14	Lake Charles Municipal Airport	102
18	Bogalusa	105		14	Morgan City	102
18	Boyce 3 WNW	*105*		14	New Orleans Audubon	102
18	Bunkie	105		14	New Orleans Int'l Airport	102
18	De Quincy	*105*		14	Rockefeller Wildlife Refuge	102
18	Elizabeth	105		14	Saint Joseph 3 N	102
18	Homer 3 SSW	105		24	Covington 4 NNW	103
18	Many	105		24	Hackberry 8 SSW	103

Annual Mean Maximum Temperature

	Highest				Lowest	
Rank	**Station Name**	**°F**		**Rank**	**Station Name**	**°F**
1	Thibodaux 3 ESE	*78.7*		1	Lake Providence	74.4
2	New Orleans Audubon	78.6		2	Homer 3 SSW	74.7
2	Saint Bernard	78.6		3	Tallulah	75.0
4	Grand Coteau	78.5		4	Plain Dealing	75.3
5	Amite	78.3		5	Minden	75.5
5	Covington 4 NNW	78.3		6	Ruston Louisiana Tech	75.6
7	Franklinton 3 SW	78.1		7	Ashland	75.7
8	Donaldsonville 4 SW	78.0		7	Bienville 3 NE	75.7
8	Houma	78.0		7	Monroe Regional Airport	75.7
10	New Orleans Int'l Airport	77.9		10	Calhoun Research Station	75.9
11	Baton Rouge Ryan Airport	77.8		11	Winnsboro 5 SSE	76.0
11	Carville 2 SW	77.8		12	Saint Joseph 3 N	76.2
11	Elizabeth	77.8		12	Shreveport Regional Airport	76.2
11	Lafayette Regional Airport	77.8		14	Bastrop	76.3
11	New Iberia	77.8		14	Hackberry 8 SSW	76.3
11	Reserve	77.8		14	Jonesville Locks	76.3
11	Slidell	77.8		17	Red River Research Station	*76.4*
18	Bogalusa	77.7		18	Many	76.5
18	De Quincy	*77.7*		19	Clinton 5 SE	*76.7*
18	LSU Ben Hur Farm	77.7		20	Jeanerette 5 NW	*76.9*
18	Rosepine Research Station	*77.7*		20	LSU Dean Lee Research Station	*76.9*
22	Franklin 3 NW	77.5		20	New Roads 5 ESE	*76.9*
22	Galliano	77.5		20	Winnfield 2 W	76.9
22	Lake Charles Municipal Airport	77.5		24	Alexandria	77.0
25	De Ridder	77.4		24	Boyce 3 WNW	*77.0*

Annual Mean Temperature

	Highest			Lowest	
Rank	**Station Name**	**°F**	**Rank**	**Station Name**	**°F**
1	New Orleans Audubon	70.0	1	Plain Dealing	62.9
2	Saint Bernard	69.1	2	Homer 3 SSW	63.2
3	Hackberry 8 SSW	68.7	3	Ashland	63.5
4	Galliano	68.6	4	Calhoun Research Station	64.0
4	New Orleans Int'l Airport	68.6	4	Minden	64.0
6	Houma	68.5	4	Ruston Louisiana Tech	64.0
6	Thibodaux 3 ESE	*68.5*	7	Tallulah	64.2
8	Rockefeller Wildlife Refuge	68.4	8	Bienville 3 NE	64.3
9	Morgan City	68.3	9	Lake Providence	64.4
10	Lafayette Regional Airport	68.2	9	Many	64.4
11	Franklin 3 NW	68.1	11	Red River Research Station	*64.7*
11	Lake Charles Municipal Airport	68.1	12	Winnfield 2 W	64.8
11	New Iberia	68.1	13	Logansport 4 ENE	*64.9*
14	Donaldsonville 4 SW	68.0	13	Winnsboro 5 SSE	64.9
15	Carville 2 SW	67.8	15	Bastrop	65.0
15	Grand Coteau	67.8	16	Monroe Regional Airport	65.1
17	Reserve	67.7	17	Shreveport Regional Airport	65.3
18	Baton Rouge Ryan Airport	67.6	18	Saint Joseph 3 N	65.6
18	Slidell	67.6	19	Leesville	65.7
20	Crowley 2 NE	67.3	20	Clinton 5 SE	*65.8*
20	Jeanerette 5 NW	*67.3*	21	Jonesville Locks	65.9
20	Jennings	67.3	21	Natchitoches	65.9
23	Oberlin Fire Tower	67.2	21	Rosepine Research Station	*65.9*
24	Covington 4 NNW	67.0	24	Franklinton 3 SW	66.0
24	LSU Ben Hur Farm	67.0	24	LSU Dean Lee Research Station	*66.0*

Annual Mean Minimum Temperature

	Highest			Lowest	
Rank	**Station Name**	**°F**	**Rank**	**Station Name**	**°F**
1	New Orleans Audubon	61.5	1	Plain Dealing	50.5
2	Hackberry 8 SSW	60.9	2	Ashland	51.4
3	Galliano	59.7	3	Homer 3 SSW	51.7
4	Rockefeller Wildlife Refuge	59.6	4	Calhoun Research Station	52.2
4	Saint Bernard	59.6	4	Many	52.2
6	Morgan City	59.4	6	Ruston Louisiana Tech	52.3
7	New Orleans Int'l Airport	59.3	7	Minden	52.4
8	Houma	59.0	8	Logansport 4 ENE	*52.5*
9	Franklin 3 NW	58.7	9	Winnfield 2 W	52.7
9	Lake Charles Municipal Airport	58.7	10	Bienville 3 NE	52.9
11	Lafayette Regional Airport	58.6	11	Red River Research Station	*53.1*
12	New Iberia	58.4	12	Tallulah	53.4
12	Thibodaux 3 ESE	*58.4*	13	Bastrop	53.7
14	Donaldsonville 4 SW	58.1	14	Franklinton 3 SW	53.9
15	Carville 2 SW	57.9	14	Winnsboro 5 SSE	53.9
16	Jeanerette 5 NW	*57.6*	16	Leesville	54.0
17	Jennings	57.5	16	Rosepine Research Station	*54.0*
17	Reserve	57.5	18	Lake Providence	54.3
19	Baton Rouge Ryan Airport	57.4	19	Shreveport Regional Airport	54.4
19	Crowley 2 NE	57.4	20	Monroe Regional Airport	54.5
21	Slidell	57.3	21	Elizabeth	54.6
22	Grand Coteau	57.2	22	De Quincy	*54.7*
23	Oberlin Fire Tower	56.9	22	Natchitoches	54.7
24	Boyce 3 WNW	*56.7*	24	Clinton 5 SE	*54.9*
25	LSU Ben Hur Farm	56.3	24	Saint Joseph 3 N	54.9

Annual Extreme Minimum Temperature

	Highest			Lowest	
Rank	**Station Name**	**°F**	**Rank**	**Station Name**	**°F**
1	Hackberry 8 SSW	12	1	Logansport 4 ENE	*0*
1	New Orleans Audubon	12	1	Plain Dealing	0
3	Lake Charles Municipal Airport	11	1	Ruston Louisiana Tech	0
3	New Orleans Int'l Airport	11	4	Clinton 5 SE	*1*
5	Carville 2 SW	10	4	Homer 3 SSW	1
5	Franklin 3 NW	10	6	Ashland	2
5	Galliano	10	6	Bienville 3 NE	2
5	Houma	10	6	Minden	2
5	Jeanerette 5 NW	*10*	9	Bastrop	*3*
5	Jennings	10	9	Many	3
5	Morgan City	10	9	Red River Research Station	*3*
5	Rockefeller Wildlife Refuge	10	9	Tallulah	3
5	Saint Bernard	10	13	Calhoun Research Station	4
14	Crowley 2 NE	9	13	Lake Providence	4
14	De Quincy	*9*	13	Monroe Regional Airport	4
14	Donaldsonville 4 SW	9	16	Amite	5
14	LSU Ben Hur Farm	9	16	Natchitoches	5
14	Lafayette Regional Airport	9	16	Saint Joseph 3 N	5
14	New Iberia	9	16	Shreveport Regional Airport	5
14	Reserve	9	16	Winnfield 2 W	5
14	Thibodaux 3 ESE	*9*	16	Winnsboro 5 SSE	5
22	Baton Rouge Ryan Airport	8	22	Bogalusa	6
22	Bunkie	8	22	Franklinton 3 SW	6
22	Elizabeth	8	22	Leesville	6
22	Grand Coteau	8	22	Rosepine Research Station	*6*

July Mean Maximum Temperature

	Highest			Lowest	
Rank	**Station Name**	**°F**	**Rank**	**Station Name**	**°F**
1	Red River Research Station	*93.9*	1	Morgan City	89.8
2	Logansport 4 ENE	*93.6*	2	Franklin 3 NW	90.0
2	Natchitoches	93.6	2	Galliano	90.0
4	Bastrop	93.4	4	Hackberry 8 SSW	90.1
5	Boyce 3 WNW	*93.2*	5	Jeanerette 5 NW	*90.2*
5	Rosepine Research Station	*93.2*	6	Rockefeller Wildlife Refuge	90.3
5	Shreveport Regional Airport	93.2	7	Houma	90.6
8	Bienville 3 NE	93.1	8	Jennings	90.7
8	Calhoun Research Station	93.1	9	Crowley 2 NE	90.9
10	Leesville	92.9	9	Lake Charles Municipal Airport	90.9
10	Plain Dealing	92.9	11	New Orleans Int'l Airport	91.0
10	Ruston Louisiana Tech	92.9	11	New Roads 5 ESE	91.0
10	Winnsboro 5 SSE	92.9	13	Clinton 5 SE	*91.1*
14	Franklinton 3 SW	92.8	13	Donaldsonville 4 SW	91.1
15	Alexandria	92.7	13	Lafayette Regional Airport	91.1
15	Ashland	92.7	13	New Iberia	91.1
15	Elizabeth	92.7	13	Slidell	91.1
18	LSU Dean Lee Research Station	*92.6*	18	Carville 2 SW	91.2
18	Many	92.6	18	Reserve	91.2
18	Monroe Regional Airport	92.6	20	Baton Rouge Ryan Airport	91.3
21	Minden	92.5	20	LSU Ben Hur Farm	91.3
21	Winnfield 2 W	92.5	20	Saint Bernard	91.3
23	Amite	92.3	23	New Orleans Audubon	91.4
23	De Quincy	*92.3*	23	Thibodaux 3 ESE	*91.4*
23	Saint Joseph 3 N	92.3	25	Covington 4 NNW	91.6

January Mean Minimum Temperature

	Highest				Lowest	
Rank	Station Name	°F		Rank	Station Name	°F
1	New Orleans Audubon	45.2		1	Plain Dealing	31.1
2	Galliano	43.3		2	Homer 3 SSW	32.6
2	Saint Bernard	43.3		3	Ashland	32.7
4	Hackberry 8 SSW	43.2		4	Minden	32.8
5	New Orleans Int'l Airport	43.0		5	Calhoun Research Station	33.3
6	Houma	42.7		5	Ruston Louisiana Tech	33.3
7	Franklin 3 NW	42.6		7	Red River Research Station	*33.5*
8	Morgan City	42.5		8	Many	33.8
8	Rockefeller Wildlife Refuge	42.5		9	Logansport 4 ENE	*34.3*
10	Lake Charles Municipal Airport	42.0		9	Tallulah	34.3
11	Lafayette Regional Airport	41.9		11	Bienville 3 NE	34.5
12	Thibodaux 3 ESE	*41.8*		12	Bastrop	34.6
13	New Iberia	41.4		12	Lake Providence	34.6
14	Donaldsonville 4 SW	41.3		14	Winnfield 2 W	35.1
15	Grand Coteau	41.0		14	Winnsboro 5 SSE	35.1
16	Reserve	40.8		16	Monroe Regional Airport	35.6
17	Jeanerette 5 NW	*40.7*		16	Shreveport Regional Airport	35.6
18	Baton Rouge Ryan Airport	40.6		18	Rosepine Research Station	*35.8*
18	Carville 2 SW	40.6		19	Natchitoches	36.1
18	Slidell	40.6		20	Saint Joseph 3 N	36.3
21	Jennings	40.4		21	Leesville	36.6
22	Oberlin Fire Tower	40.1		22	Clinton 5 SE	*36.8*
23	Crowley 2 NE	40.0		22	Elizabeth	36.8
24	Covington 4 NNW	39.6		22	Jonesville Locks	36.8
24	LSU Ben Hur Farm	39.6		25	LSU Dean Lee Research Station	*36.9*

Number of Annual Heating Degree Days

	Highest				Lowest	
Rank	Station Name	Num.		Rank	Station Name	Num.
1	Plain Dealing	2,738		1	New Orleans Audubon	1,187
2	Homer 3 SSW	2,653		2	Saint Bernard	1,292
3	Ashland	2,560		3	Galliano	1,323
4	Minden	2,536		4	Houma	1,370
5	Calhoun Research Station	2,514		5	Thibodaux 3 ESE	*1,380*
6	Lake Providence	2,474		6	New Orleans Int'l Airport	1,396
7	Ruston Louisiana Tech	2,472		7	Morgan City	1,405
8	Tallulah	2,458		8	Franklin 3 NW	1,440
9	Bienville 3 NE	2,408		8	Hackberry 8 SSW	1,440
10	Red River Research Station	*2,406*		10	Rockefeller Wildlife Refuge	1,453
11	Many	2,365		11	New Iberia	1,500
12	Winnsboro 5 SSE	2,341		12	Lake Charles Municipal Airport	1,513
13	Bastrop	2,333		13	Lafayette Regional Airport	1,515
14	Monroe Regional Airport	2,315		14	Donaldsonville 4 SW	1,531
15	Logansport 4 ENE	*2,255*		15	Carville 2 SW	1,540
16	Shreveport Regional Airport	2,224		16	Grand Coteau	1,553
17	Winnfield 2 W	2,220		17	Reserve	1,554
18	Saint Joseph 3 N	2,178		18	Slidell	1,598
19	Natchitoches	2,115		19	Baton Rouge Ryan Airport	1,637
20	Jonesville Locks	2,079		20	Jeanerette 5 NW	*1,639*
21	Leesville	2,059		21	Covington 4 NNW	1,644
22	LSU Dean Lee Research Station	*2,030*		22	Crowley 2 NE	1,700
23	Rosepine Research Station	*2,015*		23	Jennings	1,707
24	Clinton 5 SE	*1,962*		24	Oberlin Fire Tower	1,712
25	Alexandria	1,941		25	LSU Ben Hur Farm	1,727

Number of Annual Cooling Degree Days

	Highest			Lowest	
Rank	Station Name	Num.	Rank	Station Name	Num.
1	New Orleans Audubon	3,183	1	Homer 3 SSW	2,117
2	Hackberry 8 SSW	2,951	2	Plain Dealing	2,167
3	Saint Bernard	2,886	3	Ashland	2,185
4	New Orleans Int'l Airport	2,858	4	Ruston Louisiana Tech	2,257
5	Rockefeller Wildlife Refuge	2,829	5	Bienville 3 NE	2,278
6	Lake Charles Municipal Airport	2,813	6	Many	2,282
7	Houma	2,798	7	Minden	2,289
8	Lafayette Regional Airport	2,795	8	Calhoun Research Station	2,308
9	Thibodaux 3 ESE	2,789	9	Tallulah	2,316
10	New Iberia	2,778	10	Winnfield 2 W	2,336
11	Grand Coteau	2,750	11	Logansport 4 ENE	*2,346*
12	Galliano	2,731	12	Lake Providence	2,375
13	Crowley 2 NE	2,726	13	Clinton 5 SE	2,385
14	Morgan City	2,721	14	Bastrop	2,398
15	Baton Rouge Ryan Airport	2,718	15	Red River Research Station	2,445
16	Donaldsonville 4 SW	2,697	16	Franklinton 3 SW	2,450
17	Carville 2 SW	2,685	17	Leesville	2,451
18	Boyce 3 WNW	2,681	18	Rosepine Research Station	2,471
19	Alexandria	2,680	19	Winnsboro 5 SSE	2,474
20	Slidell	2,673	20	De Quincy	*2,477*
21	Franklin 3 NW	2,665	21	Amite	2,493
22	Reserve	2,650	22	Covington 4 NNW	2,498
23	LSU Ben Hur Farm	2,620	23	New Roads 5 ESE	2,507
24	Oberlin Fire Tower	2,614	24	Elizabeth	2,508
25	Jennings	2,595	25	Shreveport Regional Airport	2,512

Annual Precipitation

	Highest			Lowest	
Rank	Station Name	Inches	Rank	Station Name	Inches
1	Thibodaux 3 ESE	*70.24*	1	Logansport 4 ENE	*50.52*
2	Oberlin Fire Tower	67.35	2	Shreveport Regional Airport	50.74
3	Galliano	66.23	3	Red River Research Station	*51.27*
4	Amite	65.89	4	Plain Dealing	52.82
5	Franklin 3 NW	65.83	5	Monroe Regional Airport	53.00
6	Morgan City	65.77	6	Ashland	54.23
7	Franklinton 3 SW	65.57	7	Ruston Louisiana Tech	54.67
8	Reserve	65.08	8	Minden	54.82
9	New Orleans Int'l Airport	64.54	9	Many	54.97
10	Bogalusa	64.46	10	Homer 3 SSW	55.05
11	Covington 4 NNW	64.34	11	Calhoun Research Station	55.12
12	Elizabeth	64.16	12	Natchitoches	55.20
13	New Orleans Audubon	64.08	13	Saint Joseph 3 N	56.66
14	Saint Bernard	63.89	14	Winnsboro 5 SSE	56.71
15	Houma	63.79	15	Bastrop	57.15
16	Clinton 5 SE	*63.75*	16	Lake Charles Municipal Airport	57.41
17	Baton Rouge Ryan Airport	63.62	17	Leesville	57.62
18	Grand Coteau	63.59	18	Tallulah	58.47
19	Slidell	62.97	19	Jonesville Locks	58.93
20	Bunkie	62.84	20	Rosepine Research Station	59.09
21	Jeanerette 5 NW	62.70	21	Boyce 3 WNW	*59.11*
22	Lafayette Regional Airport	62.48	22	Lake Providence	59.14
23	Rockefeller Wildlife Refuge	62.44	23	Winnfield 2 W	59.58
24	New Roads 5 ESE	62.40	24	Hackberry 8 SSW	59.73
25	Donaldsonville 4 SW	61.82	25	Jennings	60.58

Number of Days Annually With ≥ 0.1″ Precipitation

	Highest			Lowest	
Rank	Station Name	Days	Rank	Station Name	Days
1	Thibodaux 3 ESE	*86*	1	Red River Research Station	*67*
2	Franklinton 3 SW	84	1	Shreveport Regional Airport	67
3	New Orleans Audubon	83	3	Logansport 4 ENE	*68*
4	Franklin 3 NW	82	4	Lake Charles Municipal Airport	71
5	Amite	81	4	Monroe Regional Airport	71
5	Jeanerette 5 NW	81	4	Plain Dealing	71
5	LSU Ben Hur Farm	81	4	Winnsboro 5 SSE	71
5	Lafayette Regional Airport	81	8	Ashland	72
5	Oberlin Fire Tower	81	8	Boyce 3 WNW	*72*
10	Clinton 5 SE	*80*	8	Calhoun Research Station	72
10	Donaldsonville 4 SW	80	8	Many	72
10	Houma	80	8	Rockefeller Wildlife Refuge	72
10	Morgan City	80	13	Bastrop	73
10	New Orleans Int'l Airport	80	13	Bunkie	73
10	Reserve	80	13	Hackberry 8 SSW	73
10	Slidell	80	13	Homer 3 SSW	73
17	De Quincy	*79*	13	Lake Providence	73
17	Galliano	79	13	Minden	73
17	New Roads 5 ESE	79	13	Natchitoches	73
20	Baton Rouge Ryan Airport	78	13	Ruston Louisiana Tech	73
20	Bogalusa	78	13	Saint Joseph 3 N	73
20	Carville 2 SW	78	22	Alexandria	74
20	Covington 4 NNW	78	22	Jonesville Locks	74
20	Crowley 2 NE	78	22	Tallulah	74
20	Grand Coteau	78	22	Winnfield 2 W	74

Number of Days Annually With ≥ 1.0″ Precipitation

	Highest			Lowest	
Rank	Station Name	Days	Rank	Station Name	Days
1	Amite	23	1	Red River Research Station	*16*
1	Franklin 3 NW	23	1	Shreveport Regional Airport	16
1	Franklinton 3 SW	23	3	Lake Charles Municipal Airport	17
1	New Orleans Int'l Airport	23	3	Logansport 4 ENE	*17*
1	Reserve	23	5	Ashland	18
6	Baton Rouge Ryan Airport	22	5	Calhoun Research Station	18
6	Bogalusa	22	5	Jeanerette 5 NW	18
6	Covington 4 NNW	22	5	Monroe Regional Airport	18
6	Houma	22	5	Plain Dealing	18
6	New Orleans Audubon	22	5	Tallulah	18
6	Oberlin Fire Tower	22	5	Winnfield 2 W	18
6	Thibodaux 3 ESE	*22*	5	Winnsboro 5 SSE	18
13	Bienville 3 NE	21	13	Alexandria	19
13	Bunkie	21	13	Hackberry 8 SSW	19
13	Carville 2 SW	21	13	Jennings	19
13	De Quincy	*21*	13	LSU Dean Lee Research Station	*19*
13	Donaldsonville 4 SW	21	13	Lake Providence	19
13	Galliano	21	13	Leesville	19
13	Homer 3 SSW	21	13	Many	19
13	LSU Ben Hur Farm	21	13	Minden	19
13	Saint Bernard	21	13	Natchitoches	19
22	Bastrop	20	13	New Iberia	19
22	Boyce 3 WNW	*20*	13	Rosepine Research Station	19
22	Clinton 5 SE	*20*	13	Saint Joseph 3 N	19
22	Crowley 2 NE	20	25	Bastrop	20

Annual Snowfall

	Highest			Lowest	
Rank	**Station Name**	**Inches**	**Rank**	**Station Name**	**Inches**
1	Shreveport Regional Airport	1.4	1	Bunkie	Trace
2	Plain Dealing	1.2	1	Crowley 2 NE	Trace
3	Ashland	1.0	1	De Quincy	*Trace*
3	Monroe Regional Airport	1.0	1	Donaldsonville 4 SW	Trace
3	Winnfield 2 W	1.0	1	Franklin 3 NW	Trace
6	Homer 3 SSW	0.8	1	Galliano	Trace
6	Lake Providence	0.8	1	Grand Coteau	Trace
8	Calhoun Research Station	0.6	1	Jeanerette 5 NW	Trace
8	Logansport 4 ENE	*0.6*	1	Jennings	Trace
8	Minden	0.6	1	Jonesville Locks	*Trace*
8	Natchitoches	0.6	1	LSU Ben Hur Farm	Trace
12	Bienville 3 NE	*0.5*	1	Lafayette Regional Airport	Trace
12	Ruston Louisiana Tech	0.5	1	Morgan City	Trace
14	Saint Joseph 3 N	0.4	1	New Iberia	Trace
15	Alexandria	0.3	1	New Orleans Audubon	Trace
15	Bastrop	*0.3*	1	New Orleans Int'l Airport	Trace
15	Bogalusa	0.3	1	New Roads 5 ESE	Trace
15	Franklinton 3 SW	0.3	1	Oberlin Fire Tower	Trace
15	Many	0.3	1	Rosepine Research Station	Trace
15	Red River Research Station	*0.3*	1	Saint Bernard	Trace
21	Amite	0.2	1	Thibodaux 3 ESE	*Trace*
21	Baton Rouge Ryan Airport	*0.2*	22	Boyce 3 WNW	*0.1*
21	Covington 4 NNW	0.2	22	Carville 2 SW	0.1
21	Elizabeth	0.2	22	Clinton 5 SE	*0.1*
21	LSU Dean Lee Research Station	*0.2*	22	De Ridder	0.1

Note: See Appendix D for explanation of data.

Annual Extreme Maximum Temperature

	Highest			Lowest	
Rank	**Station Name**	**°F**	**Rank**	**Station Name**	**°F**
1	Jonesboro	104	1	Rangeley	93
2	Gardiner	103	2	Fort Kent	94
2	Portland Int'l Jetport	103	3	Van Buren 2	*95*
4	Bangor Airport	*102*	4	Belfast	96
4	East Hiram	102	4	Bridgewater	96
4	Orono	102	4	Caribou Municipal Airport	96
7	Farmington	101	4	Dover-Foxcroft	*96*
7	Grand Lake Stream	101	4	Middle Dam	96
7	Newcastle	101	4	Presque Isle	96
7	Sanford 2 NNW	101	4	Squa Pan Dam	96
7	Waterville Treatment Plant	101	4	West Rockport 1 NNW	*96*
12	Bridgton 3 NW	*100*	12	Brassua Dam	97
12	Lewiston	100	12	Corinna	97
12	Madison	100	12	Jackman	97
12	Millinocket	100	12	Ripogenus Dam	*97*
12	Rumford 1 SSE	100	16	Augusta Airport	98
17	Houlton Int'l Airport	99	16	Eastport	98
18	Augusta Airport	98	16	Long Falls Dam	98
18	Eastport	98	16	Springfield	98
18	Long Falls Dam	98	16	Vanceboro 2	98
18	Springfield	98	16	West Buxton 2 NNW	98
18	Vanceboro 2	98	22	Houlton Int'l Airport	99
18	West Buxton 2 NNW	98	23	Bridgton 3 NW	*100*
24	Brassua Dam	97	23	Lewiston	100
24	Corinna	97	23	Madison	100

Annual Mean Maximum Temperature

	Highest			Lowest	
Rank	**Station Name**	**°F**	**Rank**	**Station Name**	**°F**
1	Sanford 2 NNW	58.7	1	Fort Kent	48.8
2	Waterville Treatment Plant	57.1	2	Caribou Municipal Airport	48.9
3	West Buxton 2 NNW	56.2	3	Van Buren 2	*49.0*
4	Belfast	56.0	4	Brassua Dam	49.3
5	Lewiston	55.7	5	Long Falls Dam	49.6
6	Gardiner	55.4	5	Ripogenus Dam	*49.6*
7	East Hiram	55.3	7	Jackman	49.8
8	Portland Int'l Jetport	55.2	8	Rangeley	49.9
9	Bridgton 3 NW	54.7	9	Middle Dam	50.1
10	Augusta Airport	54.5	10	Presque Isle	50.5
10	Newcastle	54.5	11	Houlton Int'l Airport	51.2
12	Rumford 1 SSE	54.4	12	Bridgewater	51.3
13	Orono	54.2	13	Dover-Foxcroft	*51.8*
14	Corinna	54.1	13	Millinocket	51.8
14	Vanceboro 2	54.1	15	Eastport	52.1
16	Madison	53.6	16	Springfield	52.6
17	Bangor Airport	*53.5*	17	Jonesboro	52.9
18	Grand Lake Stream	53.3	18	Farmington	53.2
19	Farmington	53.2	18	West Rockport 1 NNW	*53.2*
19	West Rockport 1 NNW	*53.2*	20	Grand Lake Stream	53.3
21	Jonesboro	52.9	21	Bangor Airport	*53.5*
22	Springfield	52.6	22	Madison	53.6
23	Eastport	52.1	23	Corinna	54.1
24	Dover-Foxcroft	*51.8*	23	Vanceboro 2	54.1
24	Millinocket	51.8	25	Orono	54.2

Annual Mean Temperature

	Highest			Lowest	
Rank	**Station Name**	**°F**	**Rank**	**Station Name**	**°F**
1	Sanford 2 NNW	47.1	1	Van Buren 2	*37.4*
2	Lewiston	46.6	2	Fort Kent	37.6
3	Portland Int'l Jetport	45.8	3	Jackman	38.3
4	Augusta Airport	45.7	3	Rangeley	38.3
5	Newcastle	45.6	5	Brassua Dam	38.7
6	Belfast	45.5	6	Ripogenus Dam	*38.8*
7	Waterville Treatment Plant	45.4	7	Middle Dam	39.0
8	Gardiner	44.6	8	Caribou Municipal Airport	39.3
9	West Rockport 1 NNW	*44.4*	8	Long Falls Dam	39.3
10	Bangor Airport	*44.1*	10	Bridgewater	39.9
10	West Buxton 2 NNW	44.1	11	Houlton Int'l Airport	40.0
12	Rumford 1 SSE	44.0	12	Presque Isle	40.4
13	Orono	43.9	13	Dover-Foxcroft	*40.9*
14	Eastport	43.8	14	Farmington	41.2
15	Bridgton 3 NW	43.2	15	Millinocket	41.7
16	East Hiram	43.0	15	Springfield	41.7
17	Jonesboro	42.8	17	Grand Lake Stream	42.1
18	Madison	42.4	18	Corinna	42.3
18	Vanceboro 2	42.4	19	Madison	42.4
20	Corinna	42.3	19	Vanceboro 2	42.4
21	Grand Lake Stream	42.1	21	Jonesboro	42.8
22	Millinocket	41.7	22	East Hiram	43.0
22	Springfield	41.7	23	Bridgton 3 NW	43.2
24	Farmington	41.2	24	Eastport	43.8
25	Dover-Foxcroft	*40.9*	25	Orono	43.9

Annual Mean Minimum Temperature

	Highest			Lowest	
Rank	**Station Name**	**°F**	**Rank**	**Station Name**	**°F**
1	Lewiston	37.5	1	Van Buren 2	*25.9*
2	Augusta Airport	36.9	2	Fort Kent	26.3
3	Newcastle	36.7	3	Jackman	26.7
4	Portland Int'l Jetport	36.4	3	Rangeley	26.7
5	Sanford 2 NNW	35.5	5	Middle Dam	27.8
5	West Rockport 1 NNW	*35.5*	6	Brassua Dam	28.1
7	Eastport	35.4	6	Ripogenus Dam	*28.1*
8	Belfast	34.9	8	Bridgewater	28.5
9	Bangor Airport	*34.8*	9	Houlton Int'l Airport	28.8
10	Gardiner	33.8	10	Long Falls Dam	28.9
11	Waterville Treatment Plant	33.7	11	Farmington	29.1
12	Orono	33.6	12	Caribou Municipal Airport	29.6
12	Rumford 1 SSE	33.6	13	Dover-Foxcroft	*29.9*
14	Jonesboro	32.7	14	Presque Isle	30.3
15	West Buxton 2 NNW	32.0	15	Corinna	30.5
16	Bridgton 3 NW	31.7	16	East Hiram	30.6
17	Millinocket	31.5	17	Springfield	30.7
18	Madison	31.2	17	Vanceboro 2	30.7
19	Grand Lake Stream	30.8	19	Grand Lake Stream	30.8
20	Springfield	30.7	20	Madison	31.2
20	Vanceboro 2	30.7	21	Millinocket	31.5
22	East Hiram	30.6	22	Bridgton 3 NW	31.7
23	Corinna	30.5	23	West Buxton 2 NNW	32.0
24	Presque Isle	30.3	24	Jonesboro	32.7
25	Dover-Foxcroft	*29.9*	25	Orono	33.6

Annual Extreme Minimum Temperature

	Highest				Lowest	
Rank	Station Name	°F		Rank	Station Name	°F
1	Eastport	-16		1	Van Buren 2	-47
2	Augusta Airport	-19		2	Rangeley	-45
3	Newcastle	-20		3	Jackman	-44
4	Sanford 2 NNW	-25		3	Squa Pan Dam	-44
4	West Rockport 1 NNW	*-25*		5	Bridgewater	-43
6	Jonesboro	-26		6	Houlton Int'l Airport	-41
6	Orono	-26		7	Farmington	-39
6	Portland Int'l Jetport	-26		7	Madison	-39
9	Belfast	-27		9	Corinna	-38
10	Bangor Airport	*-28*		9	Fort Kent	-38
10	Bridgton 3 NW	-28		9	Ripogenus Dam	*-38*
10	Grand Lake Stream	-28		12	Brassua Dam	-37
10	Lewiston	-28		12	Long Falls Dam	-37
14	Dover-Foxcroft	*-31*		14	Rumford 1 SSE	-36
14	Springfield	-31		15	East Hiram	-35
16	Waterville Treatment Plant	-32		15	Millinocket	-35
17	Caribou Municipal Airport	-33		15	Presque Isle	-35
18	Gardiner	-34		15	Vanceboro 2	-35
18	Middle Dam	-34		19	Gardiner	-34
18	West Buxton 2 NNW	-34		19	Middle Dam	-34
21	East Hiram	-35		19	West Buxton 2 NNW	-34
21	Millinocket	-35		22	Caribou Municipal Airport	-33
21	Presque Isle	-35		23	Waterville Treatment Plant	-32
21	Vanceboro 2	-35		24	Dover-Foxcroft	*-31*
25	Rumford 1 SSE	-36		24	Springfield	-31

July Mean Maximum Temperature

	Highest				Lowest	
Rank	Station Name	°F		Rank	Station Name	°F
1	Sanford 2 NNW	83.2		1	Eastport	74.0
2	Waterville Treatment Plant	82.2		2	Long Falls Dam	75.3
3	Lewiston	81.3		3	Brassua Dam	75.5
4	Orono	80.8		4	Jonesboro	75.6
5	East Hiram	80.3		5	Middle Dam	75.8
5	West Buxton 2 NNW	80.3		6	Rangeley	76.0
7	Gardiner	80.2		7	Fort Kent	76.3
8	Vanceboro 2	80.1		7	Jackman	76.3
9	Belfast	79.9		7	Van Buren 2	76.3
9	Rumford 1 SSE	79.9		10	West Rockport 1 NNW	*76.4*
11	Corinna	79.7		11	Caribou Municipal Airport	76.6
12	Augusta Airport	79.6		12	Ripogenus Dam	*76.8*
13	Portland Int'l Jetport	79.2		13	Presque Isle	78.0
14	Bridgton 3 NW	79.1		14	Squa Pan Dam	*78.1*
14	Madison	79.1		15	Dover-Foxcroft	*78.3*
16	Houlton Int'l Airport	78.9		15	Springfield	78.3
17	Grand Lake Stream	78.8		17	Newcastle	78.5
18	Bangor Airport	*78.7*		18	Bridgewater	78.6
18	Farmington	78.7		18	Millinocket	78.6
20	Bridgewater	78.6		20	Bangor Airport	*78.7*
20	Millinocket	78.6		20	Farmington	78.7
22	Newcastle	78.5		22	Grand Lake Stream	78.8
23	Dover-Foxcroft	*78.3*		23	Houlton Int'l Airport	78.9
23	Springfield	78.3		24	Bridgton 3 NW	79.1
25	Squa Pan Dam	*78.1*		24	Madison	79.1

January Mean Minimum Temperature

	Highest				Lowest	
Rank	Station Name	°F		Rank	Station Name	°F
1	Eastport	13.4		1	Van Buren 2	-7.8
2	Newcastle	12.7		2	Squa Pan Dam	-6.7
3	Portland Int'l Jetport	12.2		3	Fort Kent	-6.2
4	Lewiston	11.5		4	Rangeley	-2.5
4	Sanford 2 NNW	11.5		5	Jackman	-2.0
6	Augusta Airport	10.9		6	Ripogenus Dam	-1.8
7	Belfast	10.5		7	Brassua Dam	-1.3
8	West Rockport 1 NNW	*10.2*		8	Bridgewater	-0.8
9	Orono	8.3		9	Caribou Municipal Airport	-0.4
10	Bangor Airport	*7.9*		10	Middle Dam	-0.3
11	Jonesboro	7.4		11	Houlton Int'l Airport	0.0
12	Waterville Treatment Plant	7.2		12	Farmington	0.8
13	Rumford 1 SSE	6.7		13	Corinna	1.1
14	Gardiner	6.2		13	Long Falls Dam	1.1
15	West Buxton 2 NNW	6.1		15	Presque Isle	1.2
16	Bridgton 3 NW	4.8		16	Dover-Foxcroft	*2.1*
17	East Hiram	3.8		17	Madison	2.4
18	Grand Lake Stream	3.5		17	Millinocket	2.4
19	Vanceboro 2	3.3		19	Springfield	2.9
20	Springfield	2.9		20	Vanceboro 2	3.3
21	Madison	2.4		21	Grand Lake Stream	3.5
21	Millinocket	2.4		22	East Hiram	3.8
23	Dover-Foxcroft	*2.1*		23	Bridgton 3 NW	4.8
24	Presque Isle	1.2		24	West Buxton 2 NNW	6.1
25	Corinna	1.1		25	Gardiner	6.2

Number of Annual Heating Degree Days

	Highest				Lowest	
Rank	Station Name	Num.		Rank	Station Name	Num.
1	Van Buren 2	*10,118*		1	Sanford 2 NNW	6,913
2	Fort Kent	10,078		2	Lewiston	7,119
3	Jackman	9,792		3	Portland Int'l Jetport	7,253
4	Rangeley	9,762		4	Newcastle	7,288
5	Brassua Dam	9,647		5	Belfast	7,305
6	Ripogenus Dam	*9,623*		6	Augusta Airport	7,358
7	Middle Dam	9,532		7	Waterville Treatment Plant	7,443
8	Caribou Municipal Airport	9,488		8	West Rockport 1 NNW	*7,680*
9	Long Falls Dam	9,434		9	Gardiner	7,687
10	Houlton Int'l Airport	9,258		10	Eastport	7,725
11	Bridgewater	9,249		11	West Buxton 2 NNW	7,830
12	Presque Isle	9,112		12	Bangor Airport	*7,838*
13	Dover-Foxcroft	*8,911*		13	Rumford 1 SSE	7,898
14	Farmington	8,814		14	Orono	7,904
15	Millinocket	8,712		15	Bridgton 3 NW	8,114
16	Springfield	8,663		16	Jonesboro	8,145
17	Grand Lake Stream	8,502		17	East Hiram	8,223
18	Corinna	8,444		18	Vanceboro 2	8,409
19	Madison	8,416		19	Madison	8,416
20	Vanceboro 2	8,409		20	Corinna	8,444
21	East Hiram	8,223		21	Grand Lake Stream	8,502
22	Jonesboro	8,145		22	Springfield	8,663
23	Bridgton 3 NW	8,114		23	Millinocket	8,712
24	Orono	7,904		24	Farmington	8,814
25	Rumford 1 SSE	7,898		25	Dover-Foxcroft	*8,911*

Number of Annual Cooling Degree Days

	Highest			Lowest	
Rank	Station Name	Num.	Rank	Station Name	Num.
1	Lewiston	538	1	Eastport	98
2	Sanford 2 NNW	506	2	Rangeley	128
3	Augusta Airport	427	3	Jackman	138
4	Waterville Treatment Plant	396	4	Jonesboro	147
5	Portland Int'l Jetport	378	5	Middle Dam	151
6	Bangor Airport	*365*	6	Brassua Dam	156
7	Gardiner	358	6	Long Falls Dam	156
8	Rumford 1 SSE	355	8	Fort Kent	167
9	West Buxton 2 NNW	318	9	Van Buren 2	174
10	Newcastle	312	10	Ripogenus Dam	*178*
11	Orono	309	11	Caribou Municipal Airport	195
12	Millinocket	306	12	Bridgewater	198
13	Corinna	285	13	Dover-Foxcroft	215
13	East Hiram	285	14	Farmington	220
15	Belfast	279	15	Houlton Int'l Airport	*227*
16	Madison	277	16	Grand Lake Stream	240
17	West Rockport 1 NNW	267	17	Bridgton 3 NW	243
18	Springfield	263	18	Presque Isle	246
19	Vanceboro 2	262	19	Vanceboro 2	262
20	Presque Isle	246	20	Springfield	263
21	Bridgton 3 NW	243	21	West Rockport 1 NNW	267
22	Grand Lake Stream	240	22	Madison	277
23	Houlton Int'l Airport	*227*	23	Belfast	279
24	Farmington	220	24	Corinna	285
25	Dover-Foxcroft	215	24	East Hiram	285

Annual Precipitation

	Highest			Lowest	
Rank	Station Name	Inches	Rank	Station Name	Inches
1	Jonesboro	51.20	1	Presque Isle	35.32
2	West Rockport 1 NNW	*51.19*	2	Fort Kent	36.46
3	Sanford 2 NNW	48.43	3	Squa Pan Dam	37.19
4	East Hiram	48.35	4	Middle Dam	37.31
5	Bridgton 3 NW	47.85	5	Van Buren 2	37.35
6	Belfast	47.71	6	Caribou Municipal Airport	37.42
7	Newcastle	46.83	7	Jackman	39.08
8	Farmington	46.35	8	Houlton Int'l Airport	39.19
9	Springfield	46.14	9	Madison	39.43
10	West Buxton 2 NNW	46.11	10	Ripogenus Dam	*39.61*
11	Portland Int'l Jetport	45.87	11	Long Falls Dam	39.71
12	Lewiston	45.66	12	Bangor Airport	*39.80*
13	Grand Lake Stream	44.67	13	Orono	40.13
14	Rumford 1 SSE	44.63	14	Rangeley	40.56
15	Eastport	44.62	15	Waterville Treatment Plant	41.17
16	Vanceboro 2	44.31	16	Brassua Dam	41.29
17	Dover-Foxcroft	*43.93*	17	Augusta Airport	41.99
18	Gardiner	43.79	18	Bridgewater	42.16
19	Corinna	42.89	19	Millinocket	42.35
20	Millinocket	42.35	20	Corinna	42.89
21	Bridgewater	42.16	21	Gardiner	43.79
22	Augusta Airport	41.99	22	Dover-Foxcroft	*43.93*
23	Brassua Dam	41.29	23	Vanceboro 2	44.31
24	Waterville Treatment Plant	41.17	24	Eastport	44.62
25	Rangeley	40.56	25	Rumford 1 SSE	44.63

Number of Days Annually With ≥ 0.1″ Precipitation

	Highest			Lowest	
Rank	**Station Name**	**Days**	**Rank**	**Station Name**	**Days**
1	Ripogenus Dam	*92*	1	Belfast	*73*
1	Springfield	92	2	Gardiner	76
3	Jackman	91	3	Portland Int'l Jetport	77
4	Brassua Dam	90	3	Waterville Treatment Plant	77
5	Dover-Foxcroft	*89*	5	Augusta Airport	78
6	Bridgewater	88	5	West Buxton 2 NNW	78
7	Caribou Municipal Airport	87	7	Eastport	80
7	Millinocket	87	7	Squa Pan Dam	80
7	Van Buren 2	87	9	Bangor Airport	*81*
10	Corinna	86	9	Orono	81
10	Fort Kent	86	9	West Rockport 1 NNW	*81*
12	East Hiram	85	12	Bridgton 3 NW	*82*
12	Farmington	85	12	Lewiston	82
12	Houlton Int'l Airport	85	12	Rumford 1 SSE	82
12	Middle Dam	85	12	Sanford 2 NNW	82
12	Rangeley	*85*	16	Long Falls Dam	83
12	Vanceboro 2	85	16	Madison	83
18	Grand Lake Stream	84	16	Newcastle	83
18	Jonesboro	84	16	Presque Isle	83
20	Long Falls Dam	83	20	Grand Lake Stream	84
20	Madison	83	20	Jonesboro	84
20	Newcastle	83	22	East Hiram	85
20	Presque Isle	83	22	Farmington	85
24	Bridgton 3 NW	*82*	22	Houlton Int'l Airport	85
24	Lewiston	82	22	Middle Dam	85

Number of Days Annually With ≥ 1.0″ Precipitation

	Highest			Lowest	
Rank	**Station Name**	**Days**	**Rank**	**Station Name**	**Days**
1	Jonesboro	13	1	Caribou Municipal Airport	3
2	Augusta Airport	12	1	Squa Pan Dam	3
2	Belfast	12	3	Presque Isle	4
2	Bridgewater	12	4	Fort Kent	5
2	Bridgton 3 NW	12	4	Ripogenus Dam	*5*
2	East Hiram	12	4	Van Buren 2	5
2	Eastport	12	7	Jackman	6
2	Farmington	12	7	Middle Dam	6
2	Gardiner	12	7	Rangeley	6
2	Grand Lake Stream	12	10	Houlton Int'l Airport	7
2	Lewiston	12	11	Brassua Dam	8
2	Newcastle	12	12	Dover-Foxcroft	*10*
2	Portland Int'l Jetport	12	12	Long Falls Dam	10
2	Rumford 1 SSE	12	12	Madison	10
2	Sanford 2 NNW	12	12	Millinocket	10
2	Springfield	12	12	Vanceboro 2	10
2	West Buxton 2 NNW	12	17	Bangor Airport	*11*
2	West Rockport 1 NNW	*12*	17	Corinna	11
19	Bangor Airport	*11*	17	Orono	11
19	Corinna	11	17	Waterville Treatment Plant	11
19	Orono	11	21	Augusta Airport	12
19	Waterville Treatment Plant	11	21	Belfast	12
23	Dover-Foxcroft	*10*	21	Bridgewater	12
23	Long Falls Dam	10	21	Bridgton 3 NW	12
23	Madison	10	21	East Hiram	12

Annual Snowfall

	Highest			Lowest	
Rank	**Station Name**	**Inches**	**Rank**	**Station Name**	**Inches**
1	Rangeley	*118.0*	1	Waterville Treatment Plant	*59.7*
2	Caribou Municipal Airport	113.7	2	Gardiner	*60.0*
3	Long Falls Dam	109.7	3	Eastport	61.5
4	Ripogenus Dam	*108.6*	4	Jonesboro	66.2
5	Brassua Dam	108.5	5	Portland Int'l Jetport	66.5
6	Jackman	108.2	6	Bangor Airport	*69.2*
7	Springfield	107.6	7	Lewiston	69.8
8	Squa Pan Dam	102.7	8	Augusta Airport	71.7
9	Dover-Foxcroft	*99.1*	9	Orono	72.2
10	Houlton Int'l Airport	96.4	10	Corinna	72.6
11	Fort Kent	95.7	11	Newcastle	72.7
12	Millinocket	91.5	12	Vanceboro 2	75.7
13	Bridgewater	*90.3*	13	Bridgton 3 NW	*76.8*
14	Presque Isle	88.7	14	Madison	77.8
15	Van Buren 2	88.5	15	East Hiram	78.6
16	Farmington	87.8	16	Rumford 1 SSE	85.4
17	Rumford 1 SSE	85.4	17	Farmington	87.8
18	East Hiram	78.6	18	Van Buren 2	88.5
19	Madison	77.8	19	Presque Isle	88.7
20	Bridgton 3 NW	*76.8*	20	Bridgewater	*90.3*
21	Vanceboro 2	75.7	21	Millinocket	91.5
22	Newcastle	72.7	22	Fort Kent	95.7
23	Corinna	72.6	23	Houlton Int'l Airport	96.4
24	Orono	72.2	24	Dover-Foxcroft	*99.1*
25	Augusta Airport	71.7	25	Squa Pan Dam	102.7

Note: See Appendix D for explanation of data.

Annual Extreme Maximum Temperature

	Highest				Lowest	
Rank	Station Name	°F		Rank	Station Name	°F
1	Frederick Police	106		1	Frostburg 2	96
2	Baltimore City	105		2	Oakland 1 SE	97
2	Baltimore-Washington Int'l Arpt.	105		3	Catoctin Mountain Park	98
2	Dalecarlia Reservoir	105		4	Aberdeen Phillips Field	100
5	College Park	*104*		4	Salisbury	100
5	Cumberland 2	*104*		6	Chestertown	101
5	Glenn Dale Bell Station	104		6	Rockville 1 NE	101
5	Laurel 3 W	104		6	Royal Oak 2 SSW	101
5	National Arboretum	104		6	Savage River Dam	101
10	Beltsville	103		10	Assateague Island	102
10	Benson Police Barracks	*103*		10	Hancock	102
10	Clarksville 3 NNE	103		10	Salisbury Wicomico Co. Airport	102
10	Emmitsburg 2 SE	103		10	Snow Hill 4 N	102
10	La Plata 1 W	103		10	Upper Marlboro 3 NNW	102
10	Unionville	103		10	Woodstock	102
16	Assateague Island	102		16	Beltsville	103
16	Hancock	102		16	Benson Police Barracks	*103*
16	Salisbury Wicomico Co. Airport	102		16	Clarksville 3 NNE	103
16	Snow Hill 4 N	102		16	Emmitsburg 2 SE	103
16	Upper Marlboro 3 NNW	102		16	La Plata 1 W	103
16	Woodstock	102		16	Unionville	103
22	Chestertown	101		22	College Park	*104*
22	Rockville 1 NE	101		22	Cumberland 2	*104*
22	Royal Oak 2 SSW	101		22	Glenn Dale Bell Station	104
22	Savage River Dam	101		22	Laurel 3 W	104

Annual Mean Maximum Temperature

	Highest				Lowest	
Rank	Station Name	°F		Rank	Station Name	°F
1	Dalecarlia Reservoir	68.0		1	Frostburg 2	57.2
2	Glenn Dale Bell Station	67.7		2	Savage River Dam	59.4
2	Salisbury	67.7		3	Oakland 1 SE	59.5
4	Snow Hill 4 N	67.4		4	Catoctin Mountain Park	60.2
5	Baltimore City	66.8		5	Hancock	63.6
5	National Arboretum	66.8		6	Emmitsburg 2 SE	64.1
7	College Park	*66.6*		7	Unionville	64.4
8	Benson Police Barracks	*66.5*		8	Assateague Island	64.9
8	La Plata 1 W	66.5		9	Beltsville	65.2
8	Salisbury Wicomico Co. Airport	66.5		10	Chestertown	65.3
11	Frederick Police	*66.3*		11	Baltimore-Washington Int'l Arpt.	65.4
11	Royal Oak 2 SSW	66.3		12	Woodstock	65.5
13	Clarksville 3 NNE	65.9		13	Rockville 1 NE	65.6
13	Laurel 3 W	65.9		14	Cumberland 2	*65.8*
13	Upper Marlboro 3 NNW	65.9		15	Clarksville 3 NNE	65.9
16	Cumberland 2	*65.8*		15	Laurel 3 W	65.9
17	Rockville 1 NE	65.6		15	Upper Marlboro 3 NNW	65.9
18	Woodstock	65.5		18	Frederick Police	*66.3*
19	Baltimore-Washington Int'l Arpt.	65.4		18	Royal Oak 2 SSW	66.3
20	Chestertown	65.3		20	Benson Police Barracks	*66.5*
21	Beltsville	65.2		20	La Plata 1 W	66.5
22	Assateague Island	64.9		20	Salisbury Wicomico Co. Airport	66.5
23	Unionville	64.4		23	College Park	*66.6*
24	Emmitsburg 2 SE	64.1		24	Baltimore City	66.8
25	Hancock	63.6		24	National Arboretum	66.8

Annual Mean Temperature

	Highest			Lowest	
Rank	**Station Name**	**°F**	**Rank**	**Station Name**	**°F**
1	Baltimore City	58.7	1	Frostburg 2	47.8
2	Salisbury	57.7	2	Oakland 1 SE	48.4
3	Royal Oak 2 SSW	57.3	3	Savage River Dam	49.0
4	Snow Hill 4 N	56.8	4	Catoctin Mountain Park	51.6
5	College Park	*56.5*	5	Hancock	52.2
5	Dalecarlia Reservoir	56.5	6	Unionville	52.5
7	Assateague Island	56.4	7	Emmitsburg 2 SE	52.9
7	Salisbury Wicomico Co. Airport	56.4	8	Cumberland 2	*53.8*
9	La Plata 1 W	56.3	9	Clarksville 3 NNE	54.0
10	Frederick Police	*56.2*	10	Beltsville	54.5
11	National Arboretum	56.1	10	Woodstock	54.5
12	Laurel 3 W	56.0	12	Upper Marlboro 3 NNW	54.6
13	Baltimore-Washington Int'l Arpt.	55.6	13	Rockville 1 NE	54.9
14	Chestertown	55.5	14	Benson Police Barracks	*55.2*
15	Glenn Dale Bell Station	55.4	15	Glenn Dale Bell Station	55.4
16	Benson Police Barracks	*55.2*	16	Chestertown	55.5
17	Rockville 1 NE	54.9	17	Baltimore-Washington Int'l Arpt.	55.6
18	Upper Marlboro 3 NNW	54.6	18	Laurel 3 W	56.0
19	Beltsville	54.5	19	National Arboretum	56.1
19	Woodstock	54.5	20	Frederick Police	*56.2*
21	Clarksville 3 NNE	54.0	21	La Plata 1 W	56.3
22	Cumberland 2	*53.8*	22	Assateague Island	56.4
23	Emmitsburg 2 SE	52.9	22	Salisbury Wicomico Co. Airport	56.4
24	Unionville	52.5	24	College Park	*56.5*
25	Hancock	52.2	24	Dalecarlia Reservoir	56.5

Annual Mean Minimum Temperature

	Highest			Lowest	
Rank	**Station Name**	**°F**	**Rank**	**Station Name**	**°F**
1	Baltimore City	50.6	1	Oakland 1 SE	37.2
2	Royal Oak 2 SSW	48.2	2	Frostburg 2	38.3
3	Assateague Island	47.9	3	Savage River Dam	38.4
4	Salisbury	47.6	4	Unionville	40.5
5	College Park	*46.4*	5	Hancock	40.7
6	Laurel 3 W	46.2	6	Cumberland 2	*41.8*
6	Salisbury Wicomico Co. Airport	46.2	6	Emmitsburg 2 SE	41.8
8	La Plata 1 W	46.1	8	Clarksville 3 NNE	41.9
9	Frederick Police	*46.0*	9	Catoctin Mountain Park	42.9
9	Snow Hill 4 N	46.0	10	Glenn Dale Bell Station	43.0
11	Baltimore-Washington Int'l Arpt.	45.7	11	Upper Marlboro 3 NNW	43.3
12	Chestertown	45.6	12	Woodstock	43.6
13	National Arboretum	45.3	13	Beltsville	43.7
14	Dalecarlia Reservoir	44.8	14	Benson Police Barracks	*43.9*
15	Rockville 1 NE	44.1	15	Rockville 1 NE	44.1
16	Benson Police Barracks	*43.9*	16	Dalecarlia Reservoir	44.8
17	Beltsville	43.7	17	National Arboretum	45.3
18	Woodstock	43.6	18	Chestertown	45.6
19	Upper Marlboro 3 NNW	43.3	19	Baltimore-Washington Int'l Arpt.	45.7
20	Glenn Dale Bell Station	43.0	20	Frederick Police	*46.0*
21	Catoctin Mountain Park	42.9	20	Snow Hill 4 N	46.0
22	Clarksville 3 NNE	41.9	22	La Plata 1 W	46.1
23	Cumberland 2	*41.8*	23	Laurel 3 W	46.2
23	Emmitsburg 2 SE	41.8	23	Salisbury Wicomico Co. Airport	46.2
25	Hancock	40.7	25	College Park	*46.4*

Annual Extreme Minimum Temperature

	Highest				Lowest	
Rank	**Station Name**	**°F**		**Rank**	**Station Name**	**°F**
1	Assateague Island	-2		1	Emmitsburg 2 SE	-27
1	Salisbury	-2		1	Hancock	-27
3	Baltimore City	-4		3	Frostburg 2	-26
4	Snow Hill 4 N	-5		4	Oakland 1 SE	-25
5	Royal Oak 2 SSW	-6		5	Savage River Dam	-22
5	Salisbury Wicomico Co. Airport	-6		5	Unionville	-22
7	Baltimore-Washington Int'l Arpt.	-7		7	Catoctin Mountain Park	-18
7	Chestertown	-7		7	Clarksville 3 NNE	-18
7	College Park	*-7*		9	Benson Police Barracks	*-16*
10	La Plata 1 W	-8		10	Cumberland 2	*-14*
11	Frederick Police	*-10*		11	Rockville 1 NE	-13
11	National Arboretum	-10		11	Woodstock	-13
13	Dalecarlia Reservoir	-11		13	Aberdeen Phillips Field	-12
13	Glenn Dale Bell Station	-11		13	Beltsville	-12
15	Aberdeen Phillips Field	-12		13	Laurel 3 W	-12
15	Beltsville	-12		13	Upper Marlboro 3 NNW	-12
15	Laurel 3 W	-12		17	Dalecarlia Reservoir	-11
15	Upper Marlboro 3 NNW	-12		17	Glenn Dale Bell Station	-11
19	Rockville 1 NE	-13		19	Frederick Police	*-10*
19	Woodstock	-13		19	National Arboretum	-10
21	Cumberland 2	*-14*		21	La Plata 1 W	-8
22	Benson Police Barracks	*-16*		22	Baltimore-Washington Int'l Arpt.	-7
23	Catoctin Mountain Park	-18		22	Chestertown	-7
23	Clarksville 3 NNE	-18		22	College Park	*-7*
25	Savage River Dam	-22		25	Royal Oak 2 SSW	-6

July Mean Maximum Temperature

	Highest				Lowest	
Rank	**Station Name**	**°F**		**Rank**	**Station Name**	**°F**
1	Baltimore City	89.4		1	Frostburg 2	79.1
2	Dalecarlia Reservoir	89.2		2	Oakland 1 SE	79.5
3	Frederick Police	88.9		3	Catoctin Mountain Park	80.6
4	College Park	88.6		4	Savage River Dam	80.9
4	Glenn Dale Bell Station	88.6		5	Assateague Island	83.8
6	National Arboretum	88.4		6	La Plata 1 W	85.2
7	Laurel 3 W	88.2		7	Hancock	85.3
8	Cumberland 2	*88.1*		8	Emmitsburg 2 SE	86.0
9	Benson Police Barracks	*88.0*		9	Unionville	86.2
10	Baltimore-Washington Int'l Arpt.	87.7		10	Aberdeen Phillips Field	*86.8*
11	Clarksville 3 NNE	87.6		11	Rockville 1 NE	86.9
11	Woodstock	87.6		12	Salisbury Wicomico Co. Airport	87.1
13	Chestertown	87.4		12	Snow Hill 4 N	87.1
13	Salisbury	87.4		12	Upper Marlboro 3 NNW	87.1
15	Royal Oak 2 SSW	87.3		15	Beltsville	87.2
16	Beltsville	87.2		16	Royal Oak 2 SSW	87.3
17	Salisbury Wicomico Co. Airport	87.1		17	Chestertown	87.4
17	Snow Hill 4 N	87.1		17	Salisbury	87.4
17	Upper Marlboro 3 NNW	87.1		19	Clarksville 3 NNE	87.6
20	Rockville 1 NE	86.9		19	Woodstock	87.6
21	Aberdeen Phillips Field	*86.8*		21	Baltimore-Washington Int'l Arpt.	87.7
22	Unionville	86.2		22	Benson Police Barracks	*88.0*
23	Emmitsburg 2 SE	86.0		23	Cumberland 2	*88.1*
24	Hancock	85.3		24	Laurel 3 W	88.2
25	La Plata 1 W	85.2		25	National Arboretum	88.4

January Mean Minimum Temperature

	Highest			Lowest	
Rank	Station Name	°F	Rank	Station Name	°F
1	Baltimore City	29.2	1	Oakland 1 SE	17.3
2	Salisbury	28.1	2	Frostburg 2	17.6
3	Assateague Island	27.7	3	Savage River Dam	17.9
4	Royal Oak 2 SSW	27.5	4	Unionville	19.8
5	Snow Hill 4 N	27.1	5	Hancock	20.2
6	Salisbury Wicomico Co. Airport	26.5	6	Cumberland 2	*20.9*
7	La Plata 1 W	25.5	7	Catoctin Mountain Park	21.0
8	College Park	25.1	8	Emmitsburg 2 SE	21.1
9	Frederick Police	*24.9*	9	Clarksville 3 NNE	21.7
10	Baltimore-Washington Int'l Arpt.	24.7	10	Upper Marlboro 3 NNW	22.2
10	Chestertown	24.7	11	Beltsville	22.3
12	Laurel 3 W	24.4	12	Benson Police Barracks	22.4
12	National Arboretum	24.4	13	Glenn Dale Bell Station	22.9
14	Rockville 1 NE	23.8	14	Woodstock	23.1
15	Dalecarlia Reservoir	23.6	15	Dalecarlia Reservoir	23.6
16	Woodstock	23.1	16	Rockville 1 NE	23.8
17	Glenn Dale Bell Station	22.9	17	Laurel 3 W	24.4
18	Benson Police Barracks	22.4	17	National Arboretum	24.4
19	Beltsville	22.3	19	Baltimore-Washington Int'l Arpt.	24.7
20	Upper Marlboro 3 NNW	22.2	19	Chestertown	24.7
21	Clarksville 3 NNE	21.7	21	Frederick Police	*24.9*
22	Emmitsburg 2 SE	21.1	22	College Park	25.1
23	Catoctin Mountain Park	21.0	23	La Plata 1 W	25.5
24	Cumberland 2	*20.9*	24	Salisbury Wicomico Co. Airport	26.5
25	Hancock	20.2	25	Snow Hill 4 N	27.1

Number of Annual Heating Degree Days

	Highest			Lowest	
Rank	Station Name	Num.	Rank	Station Name	Num.
1	Frostburg 2	6,582	1	Salisbury	3,914
2	Oakland 1 SE	6,323	2	Baltimore City	3,929
3	Savage River Dam	6,233	3	Royal Oak 2 SSW	4,093
4	Catoctin Mountain Park	5,507	4	Snow Hill 4 N	4,129
5	Hancock	5,395	5	Assateague Island	4,161
6	Unionville	5,328	6	La Plata 1 W	4,237
7	Emmitsburg 2 SE	5,186	7	Salisbury Wicomico Co. Airport	4,289
8	Cumberland 2	*5,013*	8	Dalecarlia Reservoir	4,357
9	Clarksville 3 NNE	4,938	9	College Park	*4,398*
10	Beltsville	4,840	10	National Arboretum	4,446
11	Woodstock	4,796	11	Frederick Police	*4,453*
12	Upper Marlboro 3 NNW	4,773	12	Laurel 3 W	4,491
13	Rockville 1 NE	4,675	13	Glenn Dale Bell Station	4,558
14	Benson Police Barracks	*4,651*	14	Baltimore-Washington Int'l Arpt.	4,578
15	Chestertown	4,597	15	Chestertown	4,597
16	Baltimore-Washington Int'l Arpt.	4,578	16	Benson Police Barracks	*4,651*
17	Glenn Dale Bell Station	4,558	17	Rockville 1 NE	4,675
18	Laurel 3 W	4,491	18	Upper Marlboro 3 NNW	4,773
19	Frederick Police	*4,453*	19	Woodstock	4,796
20	National Arboretum	4,446	20	Beltsville	4,840
21	College Park	*4,398*	21	Clarksville 3 NNE	4,938
22	Dalecarlia Reservoir	4,357	22	Cumberland 2	*5,013*
23	Salisbury Wicomico Co. Airport	4,289	23	Emmitsburg 2 SE	5,186
24	La Plata 1 W	4,237	24	Unionville	5,328
25	Assateague Island	4,161	25	Hancock	5,395

Number of Annual Cooling Degree Days

	Highest			Lowest	
Rank	Station Name	Num.	Rank	Station Name	Num.
1	Baltimore City	1,811	1	Oakland 1 SE	393
2	College Park	*1,454*	2	Frostburg 2	418
3	Royal Oak 2 SSW	1,406	3	Savage River Dam	508
4	Salisbury	1,395	4	Catoctin Mountain Park	749
5	Laurel 3 W	1,394	5	Hancock	*868*
6	Frederick Police	1,383	6	Unionville	*904*
7	Dalecarlia Reservoir	1,378	7	Emmitsburg 2 SE	929
8	National Arboretum	1,322	8	Cumberland 2	1,037
9	Snow Hill 4 N	1,296	9	Clarksville 3 NNE	*1,049*
10	Chestertown	1,293	10	Upper Marlboro 3 NNW	1,131
11	Baltimore-Washington Int'l Arpt.	1,276	11	Woodstock	1,160
12	Benson Police Barracks	*1,274*	12	Rockville 1 NE	1,167
13	Salisbury Wicomico Co. Airport	1,260	13	Glenn Dale Bell Station	1,177
14	Assateague Island	1,187	14	La Plata 1 W	*1,179*
15	Beltsville	1,182	15	Beltsville	1,182
16	La Plata 1 W	*1,179*	16	Assateague Island	1,187
17	Glenn Dale Bell Station	1,177	17	Salisbury Wicomico Co. Airport	1,260
18	Rockville 1 NE	1,167	18	Benson Police Barracks	*1,274*
19	Woodstock	1,160	19	Baltimore-Washington Int'l Arpt.	1,276
20	Upper Marlboro 3 NNW	1,131	20	Chestertown	1,293
21	Clarksville 3 NNE	*1,049*	21	Snow Hill 4 N	1,296
22	Cumberland 2	1,037	22	National Arboretum	1,322
23	Emmitsburg 2 SE	929	23	Dalecarlia Reservoir	1,378
24	Unionville	*904*	24	Frederick Police	1,383
25	Hancock	*868*	25	Laurel 3 W	1,394

Annual Precipitation

	Highest			Lowest	
Rank	Station Name	Inches	Rank	Station Name	Inches
1	Benson Police Barracks	*49.53*	1	Cumberland 2	*37.00*
2	Catoctin Mountain Park	49.32	2	Hancock	39.00
3	Oakland 1 SE	47.47	3	Savage River Dam	39.57
4	Salisbury Wicomico Co. Airport	47.01	4	Frederick Police	40.31
5	Laurel 3 W	46.41	5	Baltimore-Washington Int'l Arpt.	41.71
6	Woodstock	45.87	6	Unionville	42.92
7	Salisbury	45.82	7	Rockville 1 NE	43.24
8	Snow Hill 4 N	45.80	8	Baltimore City	*43.33*
9	Royal Oak 2 SSW	45.68	9	Assateague Island	43.44
10	Emmitsburg 2 SE	45.54	10	National Arboretum	43.75
11	Clarksville 3 NNE	45.45	10	Upper Marlboro 3 NNW	43.75
12	Dalecarlia Reservoir	45.17	12	Beltsville	44.05
13	Frostburg 2	44.93	13	College Park	*44.15*
14	Glenn Dale Bell Station	44.69	14	Aberdeen Phillips Field	44.36
15	Chestertown	44.58	15	La Plata 1 W	44.51
16	La Plata 1 W	44.51	16	Chestertown	44.58
17	Aberdeen Phillips Field	44.36	17	Glenn Dale Bell Station	44.69
18	College Park	*44.15*	18	Frostburg 2	44.93
19	Beltsville	44.05	19	Dalecarlia Reservoir	45.17
20	National Arboretum	43.75	20	Clarksville 3 NNE	45.45
20	Upper Marlboro 3 NNW	43.75	21	Emmitsburg 2 SE	45.54
22	Assateague Island	43.44	22	Royal Oak 2 SSW	45.68
23	Baltimore City	*43.33*	23	Snow Hill 4 N	45.80
24	Rockville 1 NE	43.24	24	Salisbury	45.82
25	Unionville	42.92	25	Woodstock	45.87

Number of Days Annually With ≥ 0.1″ Precipitation

	Highest			Lowest	
Rank	Station Name	Days	Rank	Station Name	Days
1	Oakland 1 SE	104	1	Aberdeen Phillips Field	*52*
2	Frostburg 2	91	2	Assateague Island	*72*
3	Emmitsburg 2 SE	85	2	College Park	*72*
3	Savage River Dam	85	4	Baltimore City	*73*
5	Benson Police Barracks	*84*	4	Baltimore-Washington Int'l Arpt.	73
6	Catoctin Mountain Park	83	6	La Plata 1 W	74
7	Dalecarlia Reservoir	81	7	Hancock	75
7	Laurel 3 W	81	8	Beltsville	*76*
9	Upper Marlboro 3 NNW	79	8	Chestertown	76
9	Woodstock	79	8	Glenn Dale Bell Station	76
11	National Arboretum	78	8	Rockville 1 NE	76
11	Salisbury	78	8	Royal Oak 2 SSW	76
13	Clarksville 3 NNE	77	8	Salisbury Wicomico Co. Airport	76
13	Cumberland 2	*77*	8	Snow Hill 4 N	76
13	Frederick Police	77	8	Unionville	76
16	Beltsville	*76*	16	Clarksville 3 NNE	77
16	Chestertown	76	16	Cumberland 2	*77*
16	Glenn Dale Bell Station	76	16	Frederick Police	77
16	Rockville 1 NE	76	19	National Arboretum	78
16	Royal Oak 2 SSW	76	19	Salisbury	78
16	Salisbury Wicomico Co. Airport	76	21	Upper Marlboro 3 NNW	79
16	Snow Hill 4 N	76	21	Woodstock	79
16	Unionville	76	23	Dalecarlia Reservoir	81
24	Hancock	75	23	Laurel 3 W	81
25	La Plata 1 W	74	25	Catoctin Mountain Park	83

Number of Days Annually With ≥ 1.0″ Precipitation

	Highest			Lowest	
Rank	Station Name	Days	Rank	Station Name	Days
1	Benson Police Barracks	*13*	1	Hancock	9
1	La Plata 1 W	13	1	Oakland 1 SE	9
1	Salisbury	13	1	Savage River Dam	9
1	Salisbury Wicomico Co. Airport	13	4	College Park	*10*
1	Snow Hill 4 N	13	5	Beltsville	11
6	Aberdeen Phillips Field	12	5	Cumberland 2	*11*
6	Assateague Island	12	5	Frederick Police	11
6	Baltimore City	*12*	5	Frostburg 2	11
6	Baltimore-Washington Int'l Arpt.	12	5	National Arboretum	11
6	Catoctin Mountain Park	12	10	Aberdeen Phillips Field	12
6	Chestertown	12	10	Assateague Island	12
6	Clarksville 3 NNE	12	10	Baltimore City	*12*
6	Dalecarlia Reservoir	12	10	Baltimore-Washington Int'l Arpt.	12
6	Emmitsburg 2 SE	12	10	Catoctin Mountain Park	12
6	Glenn Dale Bell Station	12	10	Chestertown	12
6	Laurel 3 W	12	10	Clarksville 3 NNE	12
6	Rockville 1 NE	12	10	Dalecarlia Reservoir	12
6	Royal Oak 2 SSW	12	10	Emmitsburg 2 SE	12
6	Unionville	12	10	Glenn Dale Bell Station	12
6	Upper Marlboro 3 NNW	12	10	Laurel 3 W	12
6	Woodstock	12	10	Rockville 1 NE	12
22	Beltsville	11	10	Royal Oak 2 SSW	12
22	Cumberland 2	*11*	10	Unionville	12
22	Frederick Police	11	10	Upper Marlboro 3 NNW	12
22	Frostburg 2	11	10	Woodstock	12

Annual Snowfall

Highest			Lowest		
Rank	Station Name	Inches	Rank	Station Name	Inches
1	Oakland 1 SE	95.9	1	Salisbury	*3.8*
2	Frostburg 2	94.1	2	Assateague Island	*5.0*
3	Catoctin Mountain Park	33.0	3	Dalecarlia Reservoir	*7.6*
4	Cumberland 2	*32.4*	4	Aberdeen Phillips Field	*9.5*
5	Emmitsburg 2 SE	31.7	5	Salisbury Wicomico Co. Airport	11.0
6	Savage River Dam	*25.3*	6	Snow Hill 4 N	11.5
7	Woodstock	22.8	7	National Arboretum	*12.8*
8	Hancock	22.4	8	Beltsville	*13.6*
9	Clarksville 3 NNE	20.4	8	Royal Oak 2 SSW	13.6
10	Unionville	*19.5*	10	Glenn Dale Bell Station	14.1
11	Frederick Police	*18.5*	11	College Park	*14.5*
12	Baltimore-Washington Int'l Arpt.	17.8	12	Upper Marlboro 3 NNW	15.0
13	Rockville 1 NE	*16.5*	13	Chestertown	15.6
14	Chestertown	15.6	13	La Plata 1 W	15.6
14	La Plata 1 W	15.6	15	Rockville 1 NE	*16.5*
16	Upper Marlboro 3 NNW	15.0	16	Baltimore-Washington Int'l Arpt.	17.8
17	College Park	*14.5*	17	Frederick Police	*18.5*
18	Glenn Dale Bell Station	14.1	18	Unionville	*19.5*
19	Beltsville	*13.6*	19	Clarksville 3 NNE	20.4
19	Royal Oak 2 SSW	13.6	20	Hancock	22.4
21	National Arboretum	*12.8*	21	Woodstock	22.8
22	Snow Hill 4 N	11.5	22	Savage River Dam	*25.3*
23	Salisbury Wicomico Co. Airport	11.0	23	Emmitsburg 2 SE	31.7
24	Aberdeen Phillips Field	*9.5*	24	Cumberland 2	*32.4*
25	Dalecarlia Reservoir	*7.6*	25	Catoctin Mountain Park	33.0

Note: See Appendix D for explanation of data.

Annual Extreme Maximum Temperature

	Highest				Lowest	
Rank	Station Name	°F		Rank	Station Name	°F
1	New Bedford	107		1	Edgartown	96
2	Peabody	*105*		1	Worcester Municipal Airport	96
2	Reading	105		3	Birch Hill Dam	97
4	West Medway	104		3	Knightville Dam	97
5	Haverhill	103		5	Barre Falls Dam	98
6	Boston Logan Int'l Airport	102		5	Buffumville Lake	98
6	Middleton	102		7	Amherst	99
6	Rochester	102		7	East Brimfield Lake	99
6	Taunton	102		7	Great Barrington Airport	*99*
6	Walpole 2	102		7	Tully Lake	99
11	Bedford	101		11	East Wareham	100
11	Brockton	101		11	Hingham	100
11	Lawrence	101		13	Bedford	101
11	Milton Blue Hill Observatory	101		13	Brockton	101
11	Plymouth-Kingston	101		13	Lawrence	101
16	East Wareham	100		13	Milton Blue Hill Observatory	101
16	Hingham	100		13	Plymouth-Kingston	101
18	Amherst	99		18	Boston Logan Int'l Airport	102
18	East Brimfield Lake	99		18	Middleton	102
18	Great Barrington Airport	*99*		18	Rochester	102
18	Tully Lake	99		18	Taunton	102
22	Barre Falls Dam	98		18	Walpole 2	102
22	Buffumville Lake	98		23	Haverhill	103
24	Birch Hill Dam	97		24	West Medway	104
24	Knightville Dam	97		25	Peabody	*105*

Annual Mean Maximum Temperature

	Highest				Lowest	
Rank	Station Name	°F		Rank	Station Name	°F
1	West Medway	60.7		1	Worcester Municipal Airport	55.8
2	Brockton	60.6		2	Great Barrington Airport	*57.1*
3	Taunton	60.4		2	Tully Lake	*57.1*
4	Amherst	60.2		4	Milton Blue Hill Observatory	57.6
4	Middleton	60.2		5	East Brimfield Lake	58.2
6	Rochester	59.9		5	East Wareham	58.2
6	Walpole 2	59.9		7	Edgartown	58.7
8	Haverhill	59.7		7	Peabody	*58.7*
8	New Bedford	59.7		9	Lawrence	59.1
8	Plymouth-Kingston	59.7		10	Boston Logan Int'l Airport	59.3
11	Bedford	59.4		10	Hingham	59.3
12	Boston Logan Int'l Airport	59.3		10	Reading	59.3
12	Hingham	59.3		13	Bedford	59.4
12	Reading	59.3		14	Haverhill	59.7
15	Lawrence	59.1		14	New Bedford	59.7
16	Edgartown	58.7		14	Plymouth-Kingston	59.7
16	Peabody	*58.7*		17	Rochester	59.9
18	East Brimfield Lake	58.2		17	Walpole 2	59.9
18	East Wareham	58.2		19	Amherst	60.2
20	Milton Blue Hill Observatory	57.6		19	Middleton	60.2
21	Great Barrington Airport	*57.1*		21	Taunton	60.4
21	Tully Lake	*57.1*		22	Brockton	60.6
23	Worcester Municipal Airport	55.8		23	West Medway	60.7

Annual Mean Temperature

	Highest				Lowest	
Rank	**Station Name**	**°F**		**Rank**	**Station Name**	**°F**
1	New Bedford	51.9		1	Great Barrington Airport	*45.4*
2	Boston Logan Int'l Airport	51.6		2	Tully Lake	*45.5*
3	Edgartown	50.4		3	East Brimfield Lake	47.1
4	Hingham	50.0		4	Worcester Municipal Airport	47.2
4	Rochester	50.0		5	Amherst	48.4
6	Walpole 2	49.9		5	West Medway	48.4
7	Middleton	49.8		7	Reading	48.6
8	Brockton	49.7		8	Bedford	48.8
9	East Wareham	49.6		9	Milton Blue Hill Observatory	49.0
9	Peabody	*49.6*		10	Haverhill	49.1
11	Taunton	49.5		11	Lawrence	49.3
12	Plymouth-Kingston	49.4		12	Plymouth-Kingston	49.4
13	Lawrence	49.3		13	Taunton	49.5
14	Haverhill	49.1		14	East Wareham	49.6
15	Milton Blue Hill Observatory	49.0		14	Peabody	*49.6*
16	Bedford	48.8		16	Brockton	49.7
17	Reading	48.6		17	Middleton	49.8
18	Amherst	48.4		18	Walpole 2	49.9
18	West Medway	48.4		19	Hingham	50.0
20	Worcester Municipal Airport	47.2		19	Rochester	50.0
21	East Brimfield Lake	47.1		21	Edgartown	50.4
22	Tully Lake	*45.5*		22	Boston Logan Int'l Airport	51.6
23	Great Barrington Airport	*45.4*		23	New Bedford	51.9

Annual Mean Minimum Temperature

	Highest				Lowest	
Rank	**Station Name**	**°F**		**Rank**	**Station Name**	**°F**
1	New Bedford	44.1		1	Great Barrington Airport	*33.7*
2	Boston Logan Int'l Airport	43.9		2	Tully Lake	*33.9*
3	Edgartown	42.1		3	East Brimfield Lake	35.9
4	East Wareham	40.9		4	West Medway	36.0
5	Hingham	40.7		5	Amherst	36.5
6	Peabody	*40.4*		6	Reading	37.9
7	Milton Blue Hill Observatory	40.3		7	Bedford	38.1
8	Rochester	40.1		8	Haverhill	38.4
9	Walpole 2	39.8		9	Worcester Municipal Airport	38.5
10	Middleton	39.4		10	Taunton	38.6
11	Lawrence	39.3		11	Brockton	38.9
12	Plymouth-Kingston	39.1		12	Plymouth-Kingston	39.1
13	Brockton	38.9		13	Lawrence	39.3
14	Taunton	38.6		14	Middleton	39.4
15	Worcester Municipal Airport	38.5		15	Walpole 2	39.8
16	Haverhill	38.4		16	Rochester	40.1
17	Bedford	38.1		17	Milton Blue Hill Observatory	40.3
18	Reading	37.9		18	Peabody	*40.4*
19	Amherst	36.5		19	Hingham	40.7
20	West Medway	36.0		20	East Wareham	40.9
21	East Brimfield Lake	35.9		21	Edgartown	42.1
22	Tully Lake	*33.9*		22	Boston Logan Int'l Airport	43.9
23	Great Barrington Airport	*33.7*		23	New Bedford	44.1

Annual Extreme Minimum Temperature

	Highest				Lowest	
Rank	**Station Name**	**°F**		**Rank**	**Station Name**	**°F**
1	Edgartown	-5		1	Birch Hill Dam	-31
2	Boston Logan Int'l Airport	-7		2	Amherst	-29
2	New Bedford	-7		3	Buffumville Lake	-28
4	Milton Blue Hill Observatory	-12		4	East Brimfield Lake	-27
4	Peabody	*-12*		4	Great Barrington Airport	*-27*
4	Rochester	-12		4	Tully Lake	-27
7	Hingham	-13		7	Barre Falls Dam	-25
7	Worcester Municipal Airport	-13		7	Knightville Dam	-25
9	Brockton	-15		9	West Medway	-23
9	East Wareham	-15		10	Middleton	-22
11	Bedford	-19		11	Haverhill	-21
11	Plymouth-Kingston	-19		12	Lawrence	-20
11	Reading	-19		12	Taunton	-20
11	Walpole 2	-19		14	Bedford	-19
15	Lawrence	-20		14	Plymouth-Kingston	-19
15	Taunton	-20		14	Reading	-19
17	Haverhill	-21		14	Walpole 2	-19
18	Middleton	-22		18	Brockton	-15
19	West Medway	-23		18	East Wareham	-15
20	Barre Falls Dam	-25		20	Hingham	-13
20	Knightville Dam	-25		20	Worcester Municipal Airport	-13
22	East Brimfield Lake	-27		22	Milton Blue Hill Observatory	-12
22	Great Barrington Airport	*-27*		22	Peabody	*-12*
22	Tully Lake	-27		22	Rochester	-12
25	Buffumville Lake	-28		25	Boston Logan Int'l Airport	-7

July Mean Maximum Temperature

	Highest				Lowest	
Rank	**Station Name**	**°F**		**Rank**	**Station Name**	**°F**
1	Amherst	84.1		1	Edgartown	78.8
2	West Medway	84.0		2	Worcester Municipal Airport	79.4
3	Haverhill	83.8		3	Barre Falls Dam	79.7
4	Taunton	83.3		4	East Wareham	80.0
5	Brockton	83.2		5	Birch Hill Dam	81.0
6	Lawrence	83.0		6	Milton Blue Hill Observatory	81.1
6	Middleton	83.0		7	Great Barrington Airport	*81.4*
8	Walpole 2	82.9		8	Buffumville Lake	81.5
9	Bedford	82.8		9	Knightville Dam	81.6
9	Peabody	*82.8*		10	Hingham	81.7
11	Reading	82.6		11	East Brimfield Lake	82.0
11	Tully Lake	82.6		12	New Bedford	82.1
13	Boston Logan Int'l Airport	82.4		12	Plymouth-Kingston	82.1
13	Rochester	82.4		14	Boston Logan Int'l Airport	82.4
15	New Bedford	82.1		14	Rochester	82.4
15	Plymouth-Kingston	82.1		16	Reading	82.6
17	East Brimfield Lake	82.0		16	Tully Lake	82.6
18	Hingham	81.7		18	Bedford	82.8
19	Knightville Dam	81.6		18	Peabody	*82.8*
20	Buffumville Lake	81.5		20	Walpole 2	82.9
21	Great Barrington Airport	*81.4*		21	Lawrence	83.0
22	Milton Blue Hill Observatory	81.1		21	Middleton	83.0
23	Birch Hill Dam	81.0		23	Brockton	83.2
24	East Wareham	80.0		24	Taunton	83.3
25	Barre Falls Dam	79.7		25	Haverhill	83.8

January Mean Minimum Temperature

	Highest				Lowest	
Rank	Station Name	°F		Rank	Station Name	°F
1	New Bedford	22.7		1	Birch Hill Dam	6.6
2	Edgartown	22.2		2	Tully Lake	7.9
3	Boston Logan Int'l Airport	22.0		3	Knightville Dam	9.0
4	East Wareham	19.6		4	Barre Falls Dam	10.0
5	Hingham	19.4		5	Buffumville Lake	10.3
6	Peabody	18.4		6	Great Barrington Airport	10.9
7	Rochester	18.1		7	East Brimfield Lake	11.9
8	Milton Blue Hill Observatory	17.9		8	Amherst	12.7
8	Walpole 2	17.9		9	West Medway	12.8
10	Brockton	17.6		10	Lawrence	15.4
11	Plymouth-Kingston	17.4		10	Reading	15.4
12	Taunton	17.0		12	Bedford	15.5
13	Middleton	16.8		13	Worcester Municipal Airport	15.6
14	Haverhill	15.8		14	Haverhill	15.8
15	Worcester Municipal Airport	15.6		15	Middleton	16.8
16	Bedford	15.5		16	Taunton	17.0
17	Lawrence	15.4		17	Plymouth-Kingston	17.4
17	Reading	15.4		18	Brockton	17.6
19	West Medway	12.8		19	Milton Blue Hill Observatory	17.9
20	Amherst	12.7		19	Walpole 2	17.9
21	East Brimfield Lake	11.9		21	Rochester	18.1
22	Great Barrington Airport	10.9		22	Peabody	18.4
23	Buffumville Lake	10.3		23	Hingham	19.4
24	Barre Falls Dam	10.0		24	East Wareham	19.6
25	Knightville Dam	9.0		25	Boston Logan Int'l Airport	22.0

Number of Annual Heating Degree Days

	Highest				Lowest	
Rank	Station Name	Num.		Rank	Station Name	Num.
1	Tully Lake	7,443		1	New Bedford	5,472
2	Great Barrington Airport	7,393		2	Boston Logan Int'l Airport	5,574
3	East Brimfield Lake	6,907		3	Edgartown	5,687
4	Worcester Municipal Airport	6,850		4	Hingham	5,960
5	Amherst	6,549		5	Rochester	5,970
6	West Medway	6,522		6	East Wareham	6,066
7	Reading	6,444		7	Brockton	6,071
8	Bedford	6,390		8	Walpole 2	6,073
9	Haverhill	6,356		9	Middleton	6,086
10	Milton Blue Hill Observatory	6,324		10	Plymouth-Kingston	6,144
11	Lawrence	6,296		11	Taunton	6,161
12	Peabody	6,173		12	Peabody	6,173
13	Taunton	6,161		13	Lawrence	6,296
14	Plymouth-Kingston	6,144		14	Milton Blue Hill Observatory	6,324
15	Middleton	6,086		15	Haverhill	6,356
16	Walpole 2	6,073		16	Bedford	6,390
17	Brockton	6,071		17	Reading	6,444
18	East Wareham	6,066		18	West Medway	6,522
19	Rochester	5,970		19	Amherst	6,549
20	Hingham	5,960		20	Worcester Municipal Airport	6,850
21	Edgartown	5,687		21	East Brimfield Lake	6,907
22	Boston Logan Int'l Airport	5,574		22	Great Barrington Airport	7,393
23	New Bedford	5,472		23	Tully Lake	7,443

Number of Annual Cooling Degree Days

	Highest			Lowest	
Rank	**Station Name**	**Num.**	**Rank**	**Station Name**	**Num.**
1	Boston Logan Int'l Airport	804	1	Great Barrington Airport	388
2	New Bedford	769	2	East Brimfield Lake	458
3	Peabody	*692*	3	Worcester Municipal Airport	461
4	Walpole 2	661	4	Edgartown	488
5	Rochester	660	5	East Wareham	548
6	Lawrence	654	6	Amherst	569
7	Middleton	651	6	Haverhill	569
8	Brockton	649	8	Reading	575
9	Taunton	633	9	Bedford	578
10	Hingham	604	9	West Medway	578
11	Plymouth-Kingston	592	11	Milton Blue Hill Observatory	586
12	Milton Blue Hill Observatory	586	12	Plymouth-Kingston	592
13	Bedford	578	13	Hingham	604
13	West Medway	578	14	Taunton	633
15	Reading	575	15	Brockton	649
16	Amherst	569	16	Middleton	651
16	Haverhill	569	17	Lawrence	654
18	East Wareham	548	18	Rochester	660
19	Edgartown	488	19	Walpole 2	661
20	Worcester Municipal Airport	461	20	Peabody	*692*
21	East Brimfield Lake	458	21	New Bedford	769
22	Great Barrington Airport	388	22	Boston Logan Int'l Airport	804

Annual Precipitation

	Highest			Lowest	
Rank	**Station Name**	**Inches**	**Rank**	**Station Name**	**Inches**
1	Milton Blue Hill Observatory	51.12	1	Boston Logan Int'l Airport	42.40
2	Plymouth-Kingston	50.66	2	Lawrence	44.46
3	New Bedford	50.64	3	Birch Hill Dam	44.67
4	Hingham	49.76	4	Middleton	44.89
5	Rochester	49.64	5	Barre Falls Dam	45.17
6	Worcester Municipal Airport	48.83	6	Amherst	45.19
7	Buffumville Lake	48.74	7	Tully Lake	45.76
8	East Wareham	48.60	8	Edgartown	46.18
9	West Medway	48.57	9	Haverhill	46.52
10	Taunton	48.21	10	Walpole 2	46.70
11	Knightville Dam	48.14	11	Bedford	46.75
12	Reading	48.11	12	East Brimfield Lake	47.24
13	Brockton	48.09	13	Great Barrington Airport	*47.29*
14	Peabody	*47.31*	14	Peabody	*47.31*
15	Great Barrington Airport	*47.29*	15	Brockton	48.09
16	East Brimfield Lake	47.24	16	Reading	48.11
17	Bedford	46.75	17	Knightville Dam	48.14
18	Walpole 2	46.70	18	Taunton	48.21
19	Haverhill	46.52	19	West Medway	48.57
20	Edgartown	46.18	20	East Wareham	48.60
21	Tully Lake	45.76	21	Buffumville Lake	48.74
22	Amherst	45.19	22	Worcester Municipal Airport	48.83
23	Barre Falls Dam	45.17	23	Rochester	49.64
24	Middleton	44.89	24	Hingham	49.76
25	Birch Hill Dam	44.67	25	New Bedford	50.64

Number of Days Annually With ≥ 0.1″ Precipitation

	Highest			Lowest	
Rank	Station Name	Days	Rank	Station Name	Days
1	Great Barrington Airport	*89*	1	Brockton	76
2	Barre Falls Dam	88	1	Lawrence	*76*
3	Milton Blue Hill Observatory	87	3	Boston Logan Int'l Airport	77
4	East Brimfield Lake	86	3	West Medway	77
5	Plymouth-Kingston	84	5	Walpole 2	78
5	Tully Lake	84	6	East Wareham	79
7	Birch Hill Dam	83	6	Edgartown	79
7	Buffumville Lake	83	6	Knightville Dam	79
7	New Bedford	83	6	Middleton	79
7	Reading	83	10	Amherst	80
11	Bedford	81	10	Haverhill	80
11	Worcester Municipal Airport	81	10	Hingham	80
13	Amherst	80	10	Peabody	*80*
13	Haverhill	80	10	Rochester	80
13	Hingham	80	10	Taunton	80
13	Peabody	*80*	16	Bedford	81
13	Rochester	80	16	Worcester Municipal Airport	81
13	Taunton	80	18	Birch Hill Dam	83
19	East Wareham	79	18	Buffumville Lake	83
19	Edgartown	79	18	New Bedford	83
19	Knightville Dam	79	18	Reading	83
19	Middleton	79	22	Plymouth-Kingston	84
23	Walpole 2	78	22	Tully Lake	84
24	Boston Logan Int'l Airport	77	24	East Brimfield Lake	86
24	West Medway	77	25	Milton Blue Hill Observatory	87

Number of Days Annually With ≥ 1.0″ Precipitation

	Highest			Lowest	
Rank	Station Name	Days	Rank	Station Name	Days
1	Amherst	13	1	Great Barrington Airport	*11*
1	Barre Falls Dam	13	2	Bedford	12
1	East Wareham	13	2	Birch Hill Dam	12
1	Rochester	13	2	Boston Logan Int'l Airport	12
1	Worcester Municipal Airport	13	2	Brockton	12
6	Bedford	12	2	Buffumville Lake	12
6	Birch Hill Dam	12	2	East Brimfield Lake	12
6	Boston Logan Int'l Airport	12	2	Edgartown	12
6	Brockton	12	2	Haverhill	12
6	Buffumville Lake	12	2	Hingham	12
6	East Brimfield Lake	12	2	Knightville Dam	12
6	Edgartown	12	2	Lawrence	*12*
6	Haverhill	12	2	Middleton	12
6	Hingham	12	2	Milton Blue Hill Observatory	12
6	Knightville Dam	12	2	New Bedford	12
6	Lawrence	*12*	2	Peabody	*12*
6	Middleton	12	2	Plymouth-Kingston	12
6	Milton Blue Hill Observatory	12	2	Reading	12
6	New Bedford	12	2	Taunton	12
6	Peabody	*12*	2	Tully Lake	12
6	Plymouth-Kingston	12	2	Walpole 2	12
6	Reading	12	2	West Medway	12
6	Taunton	12	23	Amherst	13
6	Tully Lake	12	23	Barre Falls Dam	13
6	Walpole 2	12	23	East Wareham	13

Annual Snowfall						

Highest				Lowest		
Rank	**Station Name**	**Inches**		**Rank**	**Station Name**	**Inches**
1	Worcester Municipal Airport	*60.2*		1	East Wareham	32.6
2	Reading	58.8		2	New Bedford	33.0
3	Milton Blue Hill Observatory	57.9		3	Taunton	33.2
4	Barre Falls Dam	55.1		4	Plymouth-Kingston	37.0
5	East Brimfield Lake	54.6		5	Amherst	39.3
6	Bedford	54.5		6	West Medway	41.4
7	Tully Lake	53.1		7	Middleton	*41.7*
8	Haverhill	52.2		8	Boston Logan Int'l Airport	42.1
9	Birch Hill Dam	49.2		9	Knightville Dam	*42.4*
10	Walpole 2	46.5		10	Buffumville Lake	*42.9*
11	Hingham	46.0		11	Lawrence	43.7
12	Peabody	*45.8*		12	Peabody	*45.8*
13	Lawrence	43.7		13	Hingham	46.0
14	Buffumville Lake	*42.9*		14	Walpole 2	46.5
15	Knightville Dam	*42.4*		15	Birch Hill Dam	49.2
16	Boston Logan Int'l Airport	42.1		16	Haverhill	52.2
17	Middleton	*41.7*		17	Tully Lake	53.1
18	West Medway	41.4		18	Bedford	54.5
19	Amherst	39.3		19	East Brimfield Lake	54.6
20	Plymouth-Kingston	37.0		20	Barre Falls Dam	55.1
21	Taunton	33.2		21	Milton Blue Hill Observatory	57.9
22	New Bedford	33.0		22	Reading	58.8
23	East Wareham	32.6		23	Worcester Municipal Airport	*60.2*

Note: See Appendix D for explanation of data.

Annual Extreme Maximum Temperature

	Highest				Lowest	
Rank	Station Name	°F		Rank	Station Name	°F
1	Monroe	106		1	Fayette 4 SW	93
2	Grosse Pointe Farms	105		2	Saint James 2 S Beaver Island	94
3	Adrian 2 NNE	104		3	Cross Village	95
3	Benton Harbor Ross Field	104		3	Frankfort	95
3	Dearborn	104		3	Grand Haven Fire Dept.	95
3	Detroit Metropolitan Airport	104		6	Herman	96
3	Hillsdale	104		6	Montague 4 NW	96
3	Marquette WBO	104		6	Petoskey	96
3	Pontiac State Hospital	104		6	Whitefish Point	96
10	Alma	103		10	Gaylord	97
10	Alpena Phelps Collins Airport	103		10	Hart	97
10	Detroit City Airport	*103*		10	Ironwood	97
10	Dowagiac 1 W	103		10	Newberry 3 S	97
10	Eau Claire 4 NE	103		10	Sault Ste Marie Sanderson Field	97
10	Gull Lake Biological Station	103		10	South Haven	97
10	Houghton Lake Airport	103		16	Bergland Dam	98
10	Ionia 2 SSW	103		16	Champion Van Riper Park	98
10	Jackson Reynolds Field	103		16	Cheboygan	98
10	Midland	103		16	Detour Village	98
10	Mio Hydro Plant	103		16	East Jordan	98
10	Saginaw Tri City Int'l Airport	103		16	Muskegon County Airport	98
10	Three Rivers	103		16	Stambaugh 2 SSE	98
10	West Branch 3 SE	103		23	Boyne Falls	99
24	Coldwater State School	102		23	Cadillac	99
24	Detroit WBAP Willow	102		23	Grand Marais 2 E	99

Annual Mean Maximum Temperature

	Highest				Lowest	
Rank	Station Name	°F		Rank	Station Name	°F
1	Gull Lake Biological Station	59.4		1	Hancock Houghton Co. Airport	48.3
2	Dearborn	59.3		2	Whitefish Point	48.6
2	Three Rivers	59.3		3	Marquette County Airport	49.1
4	Detroit WBAP Willow	59.2		4	Sault Ste Marie Sanderson Field	49.5
4	Monroe	59.2		5	Ironwood	49.9
6	Dowagiac 1 W	59.0		6	Herman	50.0
7	Grosse Pointe Farms	58.9		7	Bergland Dam	50.2
8	Adrian 2 NNE	58.8		8	Fayette 4 SW	50.5
8	Eau Claire 4 NE	58.8		8	Newberry 3 S	50.5
10	Benton Harbor Ross Field	58.7		10	Detour Village	50.6
11	Ann Arbor Univ. of Michigan	58.5		11	Marquette WBO	50.7
12	Battle Creek	58.4		12	Stambaugh 2 SSE	51.2
12	Detroit Metropolitan Airport	58.4		13	Saint James 2 S Beaver Island	*51.3*
14	Holland	58.3		14	Alberta Ford	*51.4*
15	Detroit City Airport	*58.1*		14	Grand Marais 2 E	51.4
16	Allegan 5 NE	58.0		16	Champion Van Riper Park	51.5
16	Hastings	58.0		17	Alpena Wastewater Plant	52.2
16	Saint Johns	58.0		18	Cheboygan	52.4
19	Pontiac State Hospital	57.9		18	Petoskey	52.4
20	Bloomingdale	57.8		20	Cross Village	52.9
20	Midland	57.8		21	Cadillac	53.0
22	Caro Regional Center	*57.7*		21	Pellston Emmet County Airport	53.0
22	Coldwater State School	57.7		23	Frankfort	53.2
22	Ionia 2 SSW	57.7		23	Iron Mountain-Kingsford WWTP	53.2
25	Greenville 2 NNE	57.5		23	Vanderbilt 11 ENE	53.2

Annual Mean Temperature

	Highest				Lowest	
Rank	Station Name	°F		Rank	Station Name	°F
1	Detroit City Airport	*50.4*		1	Bergland Dam	38.6
2	Grosse Pointe Farms	50.2		2	Champion Van Riper Park	38.9
3	Detroit WBAP Willow	50.0		3	Stambaugh 2 SSE	39.0
4	Monroe	49.9		4	Herman	39.4
5	Eau Claire 4 NE	49.8		5	Ironwood	39.5
6	Dearborn	49.4		5	Marquette County Airport	39.5
7	Ann Arbor Univ. of Michigan	49.3		7	Sault Ste Marie Sanderson Field	40.0
7	Gull Lake Biological Station	49.3		8	Whitefish Point	40.4
9	Detroit Metropolitan Airport	49.2		9	Alberta Ford	*40.5*
10	Benton Harbor Ross Field	49.1		10	Hancock Houghton Co. Airport	40.6
10	South Haven	49.1		11	Vanderbilt 11 ENE	40.8
12	Three Rivers	48.8		12	Newberry 3 S	41.0
13	Grand Haven Fire Dept.	48.7		13	Grand Marais 2 E	41.5
13	Holland	48.7		14	Iron Mountain-Kingsford WWTP	41.9
15	Dowagiac 1 W	48.5		15	Grayling	42.0
15	Pontiac State Hospital	48.5		16	Detour Village	42.1
17	Battle Creek	48.3		17	Stephenson 8 WNW	42.2
18	Jackson Reynolds Field	48.2		18	Houghton Lake 6 WSW	42.5
19	Adrian 2 NNE	48.0		19	Cadillac	42.6
19	Midland	48.0		19	Pellston Emmet County Airport	42.6
19	Port Huron	48.0		19	Seney Wildlife Refuge	*42.6*
22	Coldwater State School	47.8		22	Marquette WBO	42.7
22	Saint Johns	47.8		23	Fayette 4 SW	42.8
24	Grand Rapids Int'l Airport	47.7		23	Lake City Exp. Farm	42.8
25	Allegan 5 NE	47.5		25	Cheboygan	43.0

Annual Mean Minimum Temperature

	Highest				Lowest	
Rank	Station Name	°F		Rank	Station Name	°F
1	Detroit City Airport	*42.6*		1	Champion Van Riper Park	26.3
2	Grosse Pointe Farms	41.4		2	Stambaugh 2 SSE	26.6
3	South Haven	41.3		3	Bergland Dam	26.9
4	Grand Haven Fire Dept.	40.9		4	Vanderbilt 11 ENE	28.5
5	Detroit WBAP Willow	40.8		5	Herman	28.8
5	Eau Claire 4 NE	40.8		6	Ironwood	29.0
7	Monroe	40.6		7	Alberta Ford	*29.6*
8	Ann Arbor Univ. of Michigan	40.0		8	Marquette County Airport	29.8
8	Detroit Metropolitan Airport	40.0		9	Grayling	30.4
10	Dearborn	39.4		9	Sault Ste Marie Sanderson Field	30.4
11	Benton Harbor Ross Field	39.3		11	Iron Mountain-Kingsford WWTP	30.5
12	Gull Lake Biological Station	39.2		12	Stephenson 8 WNW	30.7
13	Port Huron	39.1		13	Houghton Lake 6 WSW	30.8
14	Holland	39.0		14	Newberry 3 S	31.4
14	Pontiac State Hospital	39.0		15	Grand Marais 2 E	31.6
16	Muskegon County Airport	38.8		16	Lake City Exp. Farm	31.9
17	Jackson Reynolds Field	38.7		16	Seney Wildlife Refuge	*31.9*
18	Grand Rapids Int'l Airport	38.3		18	Whitefish Point	32.1
18	Three Rivers	38.3		19	Cadillac	32.2
20	Battle Creek	38.1		19	Pellston Emmet County Airport	32.2
20	Midland	38.1		21	Mio Hydro Plant	32.5
20	Saginaw Tri City Int'l Airport	38.1		22	Alpena Phelps Collins Airport	32.8
23	Flint Bishop Airport	38.0		22	Baldwin	*32.8*
24	Coldwater State School	37.9		22	Hancock Houghton Co. Airport	32.8
24	Dowagiac 1 W	37.9		25	Gaylord	32.9

Annual Extreme Minimum Temperature

	Highest				Lowest	
Rank	Station Name	°F		Rank	Station Name	°F
1	Grand Haven Fire Dept.	-11		1	Stambaugh 2 SSE	-45
2	South Haven	-14		1	Stephenson 8 WNW	-45
3	Frankfort	-15		3	Champion Van Riper Park	-44
4	Benton Harbor Ross Field	-17		4	Vanderbilt 11 ENE	-43
4	Detroit City Airport	*-17*		5	Grayling	-42
4	Grosse Pointe Farms	-17		6	East Jordan	-41
7	Holland	-18		6	Ironwood	-41
7	Monroe	-18		6	Seney Wildlife Refuge	-41
9	Harbor Beach 1 SSE	-19		9	Bergland Dam	-40
9	Midland	-19		9	Hale Loud Dam	-40
9	Mount Pleasant University	*-19*		9	Herman	-40
9	Muskegon County Airport	-19		12	Detour Village	-39
9	Port Huron	-19		12	Iron Mountain-Kingsford WWTP	-39
14	Bad Axe	-20		14	Alberta Ford	*-38*
14	Battle Creek	-20		14	Baldwin	-38
14	Dearborn	-20		14	Houghton Lake 6 WSW	-38
14	Detroit WBAP Willow	-20		14	Mio Hydro Plant	-38
14	East Lansing 4 S	-20		18	Alpena Phelps Collins Airport	-37
14	Gull Lake Biological Station	-20		18	Gaylord	-37
14	Jackson Reynolds Field	-20		18	Pellston Emmet County Airport	-37
21	Detroit Metropolitan Airport	-21		18	Traverse City Cherry Capital	-37
21	Ionia 2 SSW	-21		22	Sault Ste Marie Sanderson Field	-36
21	Pontiac State Hospital	*-21*		23	Boyne Falls	-35
24	Adrian 2 NNE	-22		23	Lake City Exp. Farm	-35
24	Alma	-22		23	Onaway State Park	-35

July Mean Maximum Temperature

	Highest				Lowest	
Rank	Station Name	°F		Rank	Station Name	°F
1	Monroe	85.2		1	Whitefish Point	71.9
2	Gull Lake Biological Station	84.5		2	Fayette 4 SW	75.2
3	Dearborn	84.4		3	Hancock Houghton Co. Airport	75.7
3	Detroit WBAP Willow	84.4		3	Marquette WBO	75.7
5	Three Rivers	84.2		3	Saint James 2 S Beaver Island	75.7
6	Caro Regional Center	*84.1*		6	Sault Ste Marie Sanderson Field	75.8
7	Midland	84.0		7	Grand Marais 2 E	75.9
8	Grosse Pointe Farms	83.9		8	Petoskey	76.0
9	Dowagiac 1 W	83.6		9	Detour Village	76.1
9	Eau Claire 4 NE	83.6		10	Marquette County Airport	76.4
9	Saint Johns	83.6		11	Newberry 3 S	76.6
12	Adrian 2 NNE	83.5		12	Herman	76.8
12	Detroit Metropolitan Airport	83.5		13	Cross Village	76.9
12	Greenville 2 NNE	83.5		13	Ironwood	76.9
12	Ionia 2 SSW	83.5		15	Alpena Wastewater Plant	77.2
16	Ann Arbor Univ. of Michigan	83.4		15	Frankfort	77.2
16	Detroit City Airport	*83.4*		17	Bergland Dam	77.7
16	Pontiac State Hospital	83.4		17	Cheboygan	77.7
19	Alma	83.3		19	Stambaugh 2 SSE	77.9
20	Allegan 5 NE	83.1		20	Harbor Beach 1 SSE	78.0
20	Battle Creek	83.1		21	Alberta Ford	78.6
20	Gladwin	83.1		21	Champion Van Riper Park	78.6
23	Hastings	83.0		23	Cadillac	79.0
24	Holland	82.9		24	South Haven	79.2
25	Jackson Reynolds Field	82.8		25	Pellston Emmet County Airport	79.3

January Mean Minimum Temperature

	Highest				Lowest	
Rank	Station Name	°F		Rank	Station Name	°F
1	Detroit City Airport	*19.1*		1	Stambaugh 2 SSE	-2.2
2	Grand Haven Fire Dept.	19.0		2	Bergland Dam	-0.8
2	South Haven	19.0		3	Ironwood	-0.4
4	Grosse Pointe Farms	18.2		4	Champion Van Riper Park	0.0
5	Benton Harbor Ross Field	17.6		5	Iron Mountain-Kingsford WWTP	1.4
6	Holland	17.4		6	Stephenson 8 WNW	2.7
6	Muskegon County Airport	17.4		7	Alberta Ford	3.0
8	Detroit WBAP Willow	17.3		8	Herman	3.1
9	Eau Claire 4 NE	16.9		9	Marquette County Airport	3.7
10	Detroit Metropolitan Airport	16.7		10	Sault Ste Marie Sanderson Field	4.8
10	Frankfort	16.7		11	Vanderbilt 11 ENE	4.9
12	Monroe	16.6		12	Seney Wildlife Refuge	*6.3*
13	Ann Arbor Univ. of Michigan	16.5		13	Grayling	6.5
14	Montague 4 NW	16.4		14	Newberry 3 S	7.2
15	Dearborn	16.2		15	Houghton Lake 6 WSW	7.6
16	Port Huron	16.1		16	Detour Village	7.7
17	Gull Lake Biological Station	15.7		17	Mio Hydro Plant	8.3
17	Pontiac State Hospital	15.7		17	Pellston Emmet County Airport	8.3
19	Grand Rapids Int'l Airport	15.5		17	West Branch 3 SE	8.3
19	Hart	15.5		20	Lake City Exp. Farm	8.5
21	Jackson Reynolds Field	15.4		21	Hancock Houghton Co. Airport	8.6
21	Midland	15.4		22	Cheboygan	8.9
23	Battle Creek	15.2		23	Houghton Lake Airport	9.3
23	Three Rivers	15.2		24	Cadillac	9.4
25	Adrian 2 NNE	15.0		24	Hale Loud Dam	9.4

Number of Annual Heating Degree Days

	Highest				Lowest	
Rank	Station Name	Num.		Rank	Station Name	Num.
1	Bergland Dam	9,750		1	Detroit City Airport	*6,128*
2	Champion Van Riper Park	9,594		2	Grosse Pointe Farms	6,134
3	Stambaugh 2 SSE	9,591		3	Detroit WBAP Willow	6,186
4	Ironwood	9,459		4	Eau Claire 4 NE	6,247
5	Marquette County Airport	9,444		5	Monroe	6,287
6	Herman	9,442		6	South Haven	6,296
7	Sault Ste Marie Sanderson Field	9,177		7	Dearborn	6,379
8	Alberta Ford	*9,118*		8	Gull Lake Biological Station	6,382
9	Hancock Houghton Co. Airport	9,030		9	Ann Arbor Univ. of Michigan	6,387
10	Whitefish Point	8,971		10	Detroit Metropolitan Airport	6,389
11	Vanderbilt 11 ENE	8,957		11	Benton Harbor Ross Field	6,395
12	Newberry 3 S	8,856		12	Grand Haven Fire Dept.	6,444
13	Iron Mountain-Kingsford WWTP	8,679		13	Three Rivers	6,494
14	Grand Marais 2 E	8,669		14	Holland	6,514
15	Grayling	8,583		15	Dowagiac 1 W	6,598
16	Stephenson 8 WNW	8,511		16	Pontiac State Hospital	6,623
17	Detour Village	8,476		17	Battle Creek	6,640
18	Houghton Lake 6 WSW	8,392		18	Adrian 2 NNE	6,685
19	Pellston Emmet County Airport	8,363		19	Jackson Reynolds Field	6,719
20	Cadillac	8,359		20	Port Huron	6,740
21	Seney Wildlife Refuge	*8,358*		21	Midland	6,773
22	Marquette WBO	8,315		22	Coldwater State School	6,774
23	Lake City Exp. Farm	8,285		23	Saint Johns	6,820
24	Cheboygan	8,212		24	Grand Rapids Int'l Airport	6,837
25	Fayette 4 SW	8,194		25	Allegan 5 NE	6,857

Number of Annual Cooling Degree Days

Highest			Lowest		
Rank	Station Name	Num.	Rank	Station Name	Num.
1	Monroe	933	1	Whitefish Point	115
2	Detroit City Airport	*902*	2	Sault Ste Marie Sanderson Field	158
3	Detroit WBAP Willow	860	3	Stambaugh 2 SSE	174
4	Eau Claire 4 NE	855	4	Champion Van Riper Park	180
5	Grosse Pointe Farms	842	5	Bergland Dam	205
6	Gull Lake Biological Station	801	6	Newberry 3 S	208
7	Detroit Metropolitan Airport	775	7	Grand Marais 2 E	213
8	Dearborn	765	8	Herman	219
9	Ann Arbor Univ. of Michigan	758	9	Saint James 2 S Beaver Island	*237*
10	Pontiac State Hospital	724	10	Fayette 4 SW	*240*
11	Three Rivers	706	11	Detour Village	243
12	Midland	700	12	Marquette County Airport	244
13	Holland	689	13	Ironwood	250
14	Benton Harbor Ross Field	672	14	Hancock Houghton Co. Airport	252
15	Dowagiac 1 W	671	15	Vanderbilt 11 ENE	278
16	Port Huron	662	16	Lake City Exp. Farm	292
17	South Haven	661	17	Marquette WBO	295
18	Grand Haven Fire Dept.	*659*	18	Houghton Lake 6 WSW	296
19	Jackson Reynolds Field	656	19	Cross Village	298
20	Grand Rapids Int'l Airport	646	20	Alberta Ford	*299*
21	Battle Creek	640	20	Petoskey	299
22	Coldwater State School	638	22	Cheboygan	300
23	Saint Johns	619	23	Stephenson 8 WNW	306
24	Adrian 2 NNE	607	24	Grayling	310
25	Hastings	601	25	Pellston Emmet County Airport	314

Annual Precipitation

Highest			Lowest		
Rank	Station Name	Inches	Rank	Station Name	Inches
1	Dowagiac 1 W	39.97	1	Mio Hydro Plant	26.75
2	Allegan 5 NE	39.88	2	Cross Village	28.24
3	Bloomingdale	39.58	3	Alpena Wastewater Plant	28.50
4	Gull Lake Biological Station	38.29	4	Alpena Phelps Collins Airport	28.52
5	Herman	38.26	5	Houghton Lake Airport	28.62
6	Bergland Dam	38.17	6	Hale Loud Dam	28.74
7	Hillsdale	37.30	7	Fayette 4 SW	28.86
8	Grand Rapids Int'l Airport	37.23	8	Grand Marais 2 E	28.95
9	Benton Harbor Ross Field	36.63	9	Houghton Lake 6 WSW	29.39
10	Three Rivers	36.61	10	Iron Mountain-Kingsford WWTP	29.90
11	Gaylord	36.53	11	Cheboygan	29.93
12	Marquette County Airport	36.47	12	Detour Village	30.06
13	Eau Claire 4 NE	36.40	13	Pontiac State Hospital	30.21
14	Hart	35.94	14	Marquette WBO	30.29
15	Ionia 2 SSW	35.82	15	Jackson Reynolds Field	30.54
16	Coldwater State School	35.80	16	West Branch 3 SE	30.57
17	Holland	35.68	17	Stambaugh 2 SSE	30.58
18	Hastings	35.41	18	Midland	30.62
19	South Haven	*35.38*	18	Onaway State Park	30.62
20	Frankfort	35.24	20	East Tawas	30.68
21	Sault Ste Marie Sanderson Field	35.17	21	Seney Wildlife Refuge	30.71
22	Battle Creek	35.03	22	Lapeer WWTP	30.76
23	Adrian 2 NNE	34.98	23	Lake City Exp. Farm	30.92
24	Ann Arbor Univ. of Michigan	34.86	24	East Lansing 4 S	30.93
25	Greenville 2 NNE	34.70	25	Port Huron	31.06

Number of Days Annually With ≥ 0.1″ Precipitation

	Highest			Lowest	
Rank	**Station Name**	**Days**	**Rank**	**Station Name**	**Days**
1	Bergland Dam	95	1	Midland	64
1	Gaylord	95	2	Mount Pleasant University	*65*
3	Herman	93	3	Hale Loud Dam	67
4	Hancock Houghton Co. Airport	89	4	Alma	68
4	Maple City	89	4	Alpena Phelps Collins Airport	68
4	Whitefish Point	*89*	4	Iron Mountain-Kingsford WWTP	*68*
7	Bloomingdale	88	4	Pontiac State Hospital	68
7	Dowagiac 1 W	88	4	Saint James 2 S Beaver Island	*68*
7	Sault Ste Marie Sanderson Field	88	4	Seney Wildlife Refuge	68
10	Boyne Falls	86	4	West Branch 3 SE	68
11	Allegan 5 NE	85	11	Cheboygan	69
11	Frankfort	85	11	East Lansing 4 S	69
13	Hillsdale	84	11	Fayette 4 SW	*69*
14	Harbor Beach 1 SSE	83	11	Houghton Lake 6 WSW	69
15	Gull Lake Biological Station	82	11	Lapeer WWTP	69
16	Eau Claire 4 NE	81	11	Mio Hydro Plant	69
16	Hart	81	11	Montague 4 NW	*69*
16	Ironwood	81	18	Alpena Wastewater Plant	70
16	Marquette County Airport	81	18	Cross Village	70
20	East Jordan	80	18	Detroit WBAP Willow	70
21	Benton Harbor Ross Field	*79*	18	East Tawas	*70*
21	Pellston Emmet County Airport	79	18	Gladwin	*70*
23	Champion Van Riper Park	78	18	Houghton Lake Airport	70
23	Detour Village	78	18	Jackson Reynolds Field	70
23	South Haven	*78*	18	Lansing Capital City Airport	70

Number of Days Annually With ≥ 1.0″ Precipitation

	Highest			Lowest	
Rank	**Station Name**	**Days**	**Rank**	**Station Name**	**Days**
1	Grand Rapids Int'l Airport	9	1	Cross Village	2
1	Gull Lake Biological Station	9	1	Pontiac State Hospital	2
3	Battle Creek	8	3	Alpena Phelps Collins Airport	3
3	Benton Harbor Ross Field	8	3	Cheboygan	3
3	Bloomingdale	8	3	Detour Village	3
3	Dowagiac 1 W	8	3	Fayette 4 SW	*3*
3	Eau Claire 4 NE	8	3	Gaylord	3
3	Marquette County Airport	8	3	Hancock Houghton Co. Airport	3
9	Adrian 2 NNE	7	3	Houghton Lake 6 WSW	3
9	Allegan 5 NE	7	3	Mio Hydro Plant	3
9	Alma	7	3	Onaway State Park	3
9	Herman	7	3	Petoskey	3
9	Holland	7	3	Port Huron	3
9	Ionia 2 SSW	7	14	Alpena Wastewater Plant	4
9	Montague 4 NW	*7*	14	Bad Axe	4
9	Mount Pleasant University	7	14	Boyne Falls	4
9	South Haven	*7*	14	Cadillac	4
9	Stephenson 8 WNW	7	14	Caro Regional Center	4
9	Three Rivers	7	14	East Jordan	4
20	Alberta Ford	*6*	14	East Lansing 4 S	4
20	Baldwin	6	14	Flint Bishop Airport	4
20	Bergland Dam	6	14	Hale Loud Dam	4
20	Charlotte	6	14	Harbor Beach 1 SSE	4
20	Coldwater State School	6	14	Houghton Lake Airport	4
20	Gladwin	6	14	Jackson Reynolds Field	4

Annual Snowfall							
Highest				**Lowest**			
Rank	**Station Name**	**Inches**		**Rank**	**Station Name**	**Inches**	
1	Herman	235.9		1	Grosse Pointe Farms	26.4	
2	Hancock Houghton Co. Airport	222.6		2	Adrian 2 NNE	*30.1*	
3	Marquette County Airport	179.8		3	Pontiac State Hospital	*31.3*	
4	Ironwood	177.1		4	Three Rivers	32.6	
5	Bergland Dam	176.4		5	Dearborn	33.0	
6	Maple City	151.4		6	Port Huron	*34.2*	
7	Grand Marais 2 E	150.4		7	Detroit WBAP Willow	35.5	
8	Gaylord	149.4		8	Caro Regional Center	35.8	
9	Alberta Ford	*147.0*		9	Lapeer WWTP	*36.3*	
10	Whitefish Point	132.7		10	East Lansing 4 S	*37.3*	
11	Champion Van Riper Park	*131.7*		11	Jackson Reynolds Field	39.1	
12	Sault Ste Marie Sanderson Field	131.2		12	Alma	40.2	
13	Petoskey	120.6		13	Detroit Metropolitan Airport	43.2	
14	Marquette WBO	118.2		14	Hale Loud Dam	43.7	
15	Boyne Falls	116.3		15	Saginaw Tri City Int'l Airport	44.8	
16	Frankfort	115.7		16	Saint Johns	45.3	
17	Pellston Emmet County Airport	114.9		17	Charlotte	47.8	
18	Newberry 3 S	114.7		18	Flint Bishop Airport	48.1	
19	Grayling	*106.5*		19	Gladwin	*50.2*	
20	Muskegon County Airport	105.9		20	Mio Hydro Plant	*50.4*	
21	East Jordan	104.8		21	Ionia 2 SSW	51.1	
22	Seney Wildlife Refuge	*101.2*		22	West Branch 3 SE	51.2	
23	Vanderbilt 11 ENE	97.8		23	Hillsdale	51.3	
24	Traverse City Cherry Capital	96.8		24	Bad Axe	51.7	
25	Onaway State Park	92.9		24	Battle Creek	51.7	

Note: See Appendix D for explanation of data.

Annual Extreme Maximum Temperature

	Highest				Lowest	
Rank	**Station Name**	**°F**		**Rank**	**Station Name**	**°F**
1	Madison Sewage Plant	110		1	Grand Marais	94
1	Montevideo 1 SW	110		2	Duluth Harbor Station	97
3	Browns Valley	*109*		2	Duluth Int'l Airport	97
3	Marshall	*109*		4	Tower 3 S	98
5	Artichoke Lake	108		4	Two Harbors	98
5	Canby	108		6	Agassiz Refuge	99
7	Chaska	107		6	International Falls Int'l Arpt.	99
7	Milan 1 NW	107		6	Isle 12 N	99
7	Redwood Falls Muni Airport	107		6	Pokegama Dam	99
10	Lamberton SW Exp. Station	106		10	Austin 3 S	100
10	Luverne	106		10	Cotton	100
10	Pipestone	106		10	Fairmont	100
10	Stewart	106		10	Grand Rapids Forestry Lab	100
10	Stillwater 1 SE	106		10	Hibbing Chisholm-Hibbing Airport	100
10	Wheaton	106		10	Leech Lake Dam	100
16	Ada	105		10	Red Lake Indian Agency	100
16	Argyle 4 E	105		10	Winton Power Plant	*100*
16	Buffalo	105		10	Wright 4 NW	100
16	Gaylord	105		19	Baudette Int'l Airport	101
16	Jordan 1 S	105		19	Big Falls	101
16	Lake Wilson	*105*		19	Cloquet	101
16	Minneapolis-St Paul Int'l Arpt.	105		19	Itasca Univ. of Minnesota	101
16	New Ulm 2 SE	105		19	Moose Lake 1 SSE	101
16	Rosemount Agr. Exp. Station	105		19	Park Rapids Municipal Airport	101
16	Rothsay	105		19	Preston	101

Annual Mean Maximum Temperature

	Highest				Lowest	
Rank	**Station Name**	**°F**		**Rank**	**Station Name**	**°F**
1	Madison Sewage Plant	*57.2*		1	Grand Marais	47.2
2	Luverne	57.0		2	Duluth Harbor Station	47.4
3	Chaska	56.9		3	Duluth Int'l Airport	47.9
4	New Ulm 2 SE	56.2		4	International Falls Int'l Arpt.	48.1
4	Stillwater 1 SE	56.2		5	Warroad	48.3
6	Canby	56.1		5	Winton Power Plant	*48.3*
6	Owatonna	56.1		7	Red Lake Indian Agency	48.5
6	Saint James Filtration Plant	56.1		8	Hibbing Chisholm-Hibbing Airport	48.7
6	Zumbrota	56.1		9	Tower 3 S	49.1
10	Saint Peter 2 SW	56.0		10	Two Harbors	49.3
11	Preston	55.9		11	Argyle 4 E	50.0
12	Rosemount Agr. Exp. Station	55.6		11	Fosston 1 E	50.0
12	Wheaton	55.6		11	Wadena 3 S	50.0
12	Windom	55.6		14	Cass Lake	50.2
15	Montevideo 1 SW	55.5		15	Agassiz Refuge	50.3
15	Redwood Falls Muni Airport	55.5		16	Isle 12 N	50.4
17	Marshall	*55.4*		16	Walker Ah Gwah Ching	50.4
18	Gaylord	55.3		18	Baudette Int'l Airport	50.6
18	Milan 1 NW	55.3		19	Crookston NW Exp. Station	50.7
18	Pipestone	55.3		19	Itasca Univ. of Minnesota	50.7
18	Stewart	55.3		21	Red Lake Falls	50.9
22	Lake Wilson	*55.2*		21	Wright 4 NW	50.9
22	Lamberton SW Exp. Station	55.2		23	Cloquet	51.3
22	Saint Paul	55.2		23	Fergus Falls	51.3
25	Fairmont	55.1		23	Mahnomen 1 W	51.3

Annual Mean Temperature

	Highest			Lowest	
Rank	**Station Name**	**°F**	**Rank**	**Station Name**	**°F**
1	Chaska	46.2	1	Tower 3 S	35.7
2	New Ulm 2 SE	45.8	2	International Falls Int'l Arpt.	37.3
3	Saint Paul	45.7	3	Warroad	37.6
3	Stillwater 1 SE	45.7	4	Hibbing Chisholm-Hibbing Airport	37.8
5	Luverne	45.6	5	Winton Power Plant	*37.9*
5	Owatonna	45.6	6	Argyle 4 E	38.2
5	Redwood Falls Muni Airport	45.6	7	Cass Lake	38.3
5	Saint James Filtration Plant	45.6	8	Red Lake Indian Agency	38.4
9	Madison Sewage Plant	*45.5*	9	Duluth Int'l Airport	38.7
10	Fairmont	45.4	9	Fosston 1 E	38.7
11	Saint Peter 2 SW	45.3	11	Itasca Univ. of Minnesota	38.8
12	Canby	45.2	12	Baudette Int'l Airport	39.0
12	Minneapolis-St Paul Int'l Arpt.	45.2	13	Agassiz Refuge	39.1
14	Gaylord	45.0	13	Grand Marais	39.1
14	Marshall	*45.0*	15	Wadena 3 S	39.4
16	Austin 3 S	44.9	16	Wright 4 NW	39.6
16	Farmington 3 NW	44.9	17	Isle 12 N	39.8
16	Rosemount Agr. Exp. Station	44.9	18	Grand Rapids Forestry Lab	39.9
16	Windom	44.9	18	Red Lake Falls	*39.9*
16	Zumbrota	44.9	20	Crookston NW Exp. Station	40.0
21	Forest Lake 5 NE	44.7	20	Park Rapids Municipal Airport	40.0
21	Lake Wilson	*44.7*	22	Cloquet	40.1
21	Stewart	44.7	23	Brainerd	*40.3*
24	Albert Lea 3 SE	44.6	23	Duluth Harbor Station	40.3
24	Montevideo 1 SW	44.6	23	Mahnomen 1 W	40.3

Annual Mean Minimum Temperature

	Highest			Lowest	
Rank	**Station Name**	**°F**	**Rank**	**Station Name**	**°F**
1	Saint Paul	36.1	1	Tower 3 S	22.3
2	Minneapolis-St Paul Int'l Arpt.	35.8	2	Cass Lake	26.3
3	Fairmont	35.7	3	Argyle 4 E	26.4
3	Redwood Falls Muni Airport	35.7	4	International Falls Int'l Arpt.	26.5
5	Chaska	35.4	5	Warroad	26.8
6	New Ulm 2 SE	35.3	6	Hibbing Chisholm-Hibbing Airport	26.9
7	Stillwater 1 SE	35.2	6	Itasca Univ. of Minnesota	26.9
8	Saint James Filtration Plant	35.0	8	Baudette Int'l Airport	27.4
9	Austin 3 S	34.9	8	Fosston 1 E	27.4
9	Owatonna	34.9	8	Winton Power Plant	*27.4*
11	Farmington 3 NW	34.8	11	Agassiz Refuge	27.9
12	Gaylord	34.7	12	Brainerd	28.2
13	Forest Lake 5 NE	34.6	12	Red Lake Indian Agency	28.2
14	Marshall	34.5	12	Wright 4 NW	28.2
15	Albert Lea 3 SE	34.4	15	Moose Lake 1 SSE	28.3
15	Saint Peter 2 SW	34.4	15	Mora	28.3
17	Canby	34.3	17	Grand Rapids Forestry Lab	28.4
18	Lake Wilson	*34.2*	18	Park Rapids Municipal Airport	28.5
18	Luverne	34.2	19	Wadena 3 S	28.7
18	Rochester Municipal Airport	34.2	20	Cloquet	28.8
18	Stewart	34.2	21	Red Lake Falls	*28.9*
18	Windom	34.2	22	Isle 12 N	29.2
18	Winnebago	34.2	22	Pine River Dam	29.2
24	Caledonia	34.1	24	Crookston NW Exp. Station	29.3
24	Rosemount Agr. Exp. Station	34.1	24	Leech Lake Dam	29.3

Annual Extreme Minimum Temperature

	Highest				Lowest	
Rank	Station Name	°F		Rank	Station Name	°F
1	Lake Wilson	*-29*		1	Tower 3 S	-60
2	Marshall	-30		2	Brainerd	-54
2	Saint James Filtration Plant	-30		3	Fosston 1 E	-53
2	Worthington 2 NNE	-30		3	Moose Lake 1 SSE	-53
5	Canby	-31		5	Itasca Univ. of Minnesota	-52
6	Saint Paul	-32		5	Mora	-52
6	Springfield 1 NW	-32		5	Wright 4 NW	-52
6	Tracy	-32		8	Big Falls	-51
6	Winnebago	-32		8	Park Rapids Municipal Airport	-51
10	Albert Lea 3 SE	-33		10	Cotton	-50
10	Fairmont	-33		10	Hibbing Chisholm-Hibbing Airport	-50
10	Grand Marais	-33		12	Baudette Int'l Airport	-49
10	Wheaton	-33		12	Sandy Lake Dam Libby	-49
14	Gaylord	-34		14	Argyle 4 E	-48
14	Lamberton SW Exp. Station	-34		14	Cass Lake	-48
14	Minneapolis-St Paul Int'l Arpt.	-34		14	Mahnomen 1 W	-48
14	Redwood Falls Muni Airport	-34		14	Milaca 1 ENE	-48
18	Austin 3 S	-35		18	Pine River Dam	-47
18	Benson	-35		19	Agassiz Refuge	-46
18	Caledonia	-35		19	Isle 12 N	-46
18	Glenwood 2 WNW	*-35*		19	Leech Lake Dam	-46
18	Grand Meadow	-35		19	Red Lake Falls	-46
18	Owatonna	-35		19	Warroad	-46
18	Rochester Municipal Airport	-35		24	Crookston NW Exp. Station	-45
18	Stewart	-35		24	Gull Lake Dam	-45

July Mean Maximum Temperature

	Highest				Lowest	
Rank	Station Name	°F		Rank	Station Name	°F
1	Madison Sewage Plant	85.8		1	Grand Marais	69.5
2	Canby	85.5		2	Two Harbors	74.0
2	Chaska	85.5		3	Duluth Harbor Station	74.2
4	Wheaton	85.1		4	Duluth Int'l Airport	76.2
5	Browns Valley	84.9		5	Hibbing Chisholm-Hibbing Airport	77.2
5	Luverne	84.9		6	Tower 3 S	77.5
5	Stillwater 1 SE	84.9		7	Red Lake Indian Agency	77.7
8	Milan 1 NW	84.6		8	Winton Power Plant	*78.1*
8	Redwood Falls Muni Airport	84.6		9	International Falls Int'l Arpt.	78.2
10	Gaylord	84.4		10	Cotton	78.5
10	Montevideo 1 SW	84.4		10	Warroad	78.5
10	Stewart	84.4		12	Wadena 3 S	78.6
13	Owatonna	84.3		13	Isle 12 N	78.7
14	Windom	84.2		14	Walker Ah Gwah Ching	79.1
15	Pipestone	84.1		14	Wright 4 NW	79.1
16	New Ulm 2 SE	84.0		16	Cass Lake	79.4
16	Saint Peter 2 SW	84.0		17	Fosston 1 E	79.8
18	Saint James Filtration Plant	83.9		17	Leech Lake Dam	79.8
18	Santiago 3 E	83.9		19	Itasca Univ. of Minnesota	79.9
20	Little Falls 1 N	83.8		19	Pokegama Dam	79.9
20	Zumbrota	83.8		21	Agassiz Refuge	80.1
22	Litchfield	83.7		21	Baudette Int'l Airport	80.1
22	Marshall	*83.7*		21	Sandy Lake Dam Libby	80.1
22	Melrose	83.7		24	Cloquet	80.3
22	Rosemount Agr. Exp. Station	83.7		24	Grand Rapids Forestry Lab	80.3

January Mean Minimum Temperature

	Highest			Lowest	
Rank	Station Name	°F	Rank	Station Name	°F
1	Saint Paul	5.0	1	Tower 3 S	-11.1
2	Grand Marais	4.7	2	Cass Lake	-9.6
2	Two Harbors	4.7	3	Warroad	-9.2
4	Fairmont	4.4	4	Big Falls	*-8.8*
5	Lake Wilson	*4.0*	5	Argyle 4 E	-8.7
5	Luverne	4.0	6	International Falls Int'l Arpt.	-8.5
5	Minneapolis-St Paul Int'l Arpt.	4.0	7	Fosston 1 E	-7.9
5	Saint James Filtration Plant	4.0	8	Baudette Int'l Airport	-7.8
9	Owatonna	3.8	9	Itasca Univ. of Minnesota	-7.2
10	Austin 3 S	3.7	9	Red Lake Indian Agency	-7.2
10	Caledonia	3.7	9	Winton Power Plant	*-7.2*
10	New Ulm 2 SE	3.7	12	Brainerd	-7.1
10	Redwood Falls Muni Airport	3.7	12	Cotton	-7.1
14	Chaska	3.6	14	Agassiz Refuge	-6.7
15	Farmington 3 NW	3.3	15	Red Lake Falls	-5.9
15	Rochester Municipal Airport	3.3	16	Crookston NW Exp. Station	-5.6
17	Canby	3.2	16	Mora	-5.6
17	Stillwater 1 SE	3.2	16	Park Rapids Municipal Airport	-5.6
17	Windom	3.2	19	Hibbing Chisholm-Hibbing Airport	-5.5
20	Duluth Harbor Station	3.0	20	Wadena 3 S	-5.3
20	Marshall	3.0	21	Mahnomen 1 W	-5.1
22	Albert Lea 3 SE	2.9	22	Isle 12 N	-4.8
22	Worthington 2 NNE	2.9	22	Leech Lake Dam	-4.8
24	Gaylord	2.7	24	Grand Rapids Forestry Lab	-4.7
24	Preston	2.7	25	Pine River Dam	-4.6

Number of Annual Heating Degree Days

	Highest			Lowest	
Rank	Station Name	Num.	Rank	Station Name	Num.
1	Tower 3 S	10,733	1	Chaska	7,561
2	International Falls Int'l Arpt.	10,253	2	New Ulm 2 SE	7,653
3	Warroad	10,216	3	Stillwater 1 SE	7,682
4	Winton Power Plant	*10,057*	4	Saint Paul	7,685
5	Argyle 4 E	10,020	5	Luverne	7,693
6	Hibbing Chisholm-Hibbing Airport	10,005	6	Saint James Filtration Plant	7,723
7	Cass Lake	9,973	7	Owatonna	7,739
8	Red Lake Indian Agency	9,940	8	Redwood Falls Muni Airport	7,748
9	Fosston 1 E	9,831	9	Fairmont	7,750
10	Itasca Univ. of Minnesota	9,753	10	Madison Sewage Plant	*7,774*
11	Baudette Int'l Airport	9,707	11	Saint Peter 2 SW	7,816
12	Agassiz Refuge	9,700	12	Minneapolis-St Paul Int'l Arpt.	7,836
13	Duluth Int'l Airport	9,685	13	Austin 3 S	7,838
14	Wadena 3 S	9,576	14	Zumbrota	7,878
15	Crookston NW Exp. Station	9,506	15	Farmington 3 NW	7,882
16	Red Lake Falls	*9,479*	16	Rosemount Agr. Exp. Station	7,894
17	Park Rapids Municipal Airport	9,422	17	Canby	7,898
17	Wright 4 NW	9,422	18	Gaylord	7,901
19	Grand Marais	9,415	19	Marshall	*7,921*
20	Isle 12 N	9,407	20	Windom	7,932
21	Grand Rapids Forestry Lab	9,387	21	Forest Lake 5 NE	7,937
22	Mahnomen 1 W	9,346	21	Lake Wilson	*7,937*
23	Brainerd	*9,281*	23	Preston	7,958
24	Cloquet	9,266	24	Caledonia	*7,979*
25	Leech Lake Dam	9,238	25	Albert Lea 3 SE	7,992

Number of Annual Cooling Degree Days

	Highest				Lowest	
Rank	Station Name	Num.		Rank	Station Name	Num.
1	Chaska	814		1	Grand Marais	67
2	Madison Sewage Plant	*792*		2	Tower 3 S	143
3	Stillwater 1 SE	766		3	Two Harbors	165
4	Redwood Falls Muni Airport	759		4	Hibbing Chisholm-Hibbing Airport	194
5	Owatonna	757		5	Duluth Int'l Airport	209
6	Saint Paul	745		6	International Falls Int'l Arpt.	247
7	Canby	744		7	Wright 4 NW	250
8	Saint Peter 2 SW	739		8	Duluth Harbor Station	*253*
9	Marshall	*732*		9	Cloquet	276
10	Saint James Filtration Plant	729		10	Itasca Univ. of Minnesota	290
11	Gaylord	728		11	Fosston 1 E	303
12	Fairmont	726		12	Moose Lake 1 SSE	309
13	Minneapolis-St Paul Int'l Arpt.	722		13	Warroad	311
14	Wheaton	717		14	Red Lake Indian Agency	323
15	Stewart	715		15	Wadena 3 S	325
16	New Ulm 2 SE	711		16	Cass Lake	328
17	Montevideo 1 SW	701		17	Isle 12 N	329
18	Luverne	699		18	Grand Rapids Forestry Lab	332
19	Browns Valley	695		19	Baudette Int'l Airport	346
20	Forest Lake 5 NE	690		20	Mora	350
21	Tracy	674		21	Leech Lake Dam	354
22	Benson	671		22	Argyle 4 E	362
23	Rosemount Agr. Exp. Station	670		23	Brainerd	373
23	Windom	670		24	Walker Ah Gwah Ching	375
25	Farmington 3 NW	668		25	Agassiz Refuge	386

Annual Precipitation

	Highest				Lowest	
Rank	Station Name	Inches		Rank	Station Name	Inches
1	Caledonia	35.05		1	Argyle 4 E	19.76
2	Rosemount Agr. Exp. Station	34.70		2	Crookston NW Exp. Station	20.63
3	Waseca Exp. Station	34.60		3	Warroad	21.89
4	Grand Meadow	34.42		4	Agassiz Refuge	21.90
5	Preston	33.96		5	Baudette Int'l Airport	22.20
6	Stillwater 1 SE	33.86		6	Wheaton	22.40
7	Zumbrota	33.29		7	Browns Valley	*22.51*
8	Albert Lea 3 SE	32.96		8	Red Lake Indian Agency	22.56
9	Saint Paul	32.59		9	Red Lake Falls	22.81
10	New London	*32.15*		10	Rothsay	22.93
11	Cedar	31.81		11	Fergus Falls	23.46
12	Forest Lake 5 NE	31.77		12	Ada	23.66
13	Faribault	31.73		13	Mahnomen 1 W	23.69
14	Cloquet	31.68		14	International Falls Int'l Arpt.	23.92
15	Austin 3 S	*31.64*		15	Artichoke Lake	24.03
16	Owatonna	31.62		16	Glenwood 2 WNW	24.71
17	Farmington 3 NW	31.52		17	Fosston 1 E	24.78
18	Fairmont	31.44		18	Madison Sewage Plant	24.79
19	Rochester Municipal Airport	31.17		19	Milan 1 NW	24.94
20	Winnebago	31.00		20	Grand Marais	25.19
21	Chaska	30.92		21	Morris WC Exp. Station	25.47
22	Santiago 3 E	30.89		22	Leech Lake Dam	25.49
23	Duluth Int'l Airport	30.88		23	Duluth Harbor Station	*25.76*
24	Two Harbors	30.46		24	Canby	25.85
25	Moose Lake 1 SSE	29.68		25	Marshall	25.87

Number of Days Annually With ≥ 0.1″ Precipitation

	Highest			Lowest	
Rank	**Station Name**	**Days**	**Rank**	**Station Name**	**Days**
1	Rosemount Agr. Exp. Station	69	1	Crookston NW Exp. Station	43
2	Waseca Exp. Station	68	2	Red Lake Indian Agency	47
3	Forest Lake 5 NE	66	3	Agassiz Refuge	48
3	Winton Power Plant	*66*	3	Argyle 4 E	48
5	Cloquet	65	3	Wheaton	48
5	Farmington 3 NW	65	6	Browns Valley	*49*
5	Zumbrota	65	6	Fergus Falls	49
8	Albert Lea 3 SE	64	6	Rothsay	49
8	Caledonia	64	9	Ada	*50*
8	Cedar	64	9	Red Lake Falls	*50*
8	Duluth Int'l Airport	64	9	Warroad	50
8	Grand Meadow	64	12	Artichoke Lake	51
8	Grand Rapids Forestry Lab	64	12	Baudette Int'l Airport	51
8	New London	*64*	12	Canby	51
8	Wright 4 NW	64	12	Glenwood 2 WNW	*51*
16	Faribault	63	12	Madison Sewage Plant	51
16	Minneapolis-St Paul Int'l Arpt.	63	12	Marshall	51
16	Moose Lake 1 SSE	63	12	Milan 1 NW	51
16	Owatonna	63	19	Lake Wilson	*52*
16	Preston	63	19	Lamberton SW Exp. Station	52
16	Rochester Municipal Airport	63	19	Morris WC Exp. Station	52
16	Two Harbors	63	19	Pipestone	52
23	Stillwater 1 SE	62	23	Alexandria Chandler Field	53
23	Tower 3 S	62	23	Gaylord	53
23	Winnebago	62	23	Litchfield	53

Number of Days Annually With ≥ 1.0″ Precipitation

	Highest			Lowest	
Rank	**Station Name**	**Days**	**Rank**	**Station Name**	**Days**
1	Rosemount Agr. Exp. Station	9	1	Argyle 4 E	3
2	Austin 3 S	*8*	1	Browns Valley	*3*
2	Springfield 1 NW	8	1	Mahnomen 1 W	3
2	Stillwater 1 SE	8	1	Warroad	3
5	Albert Lea 3 SE	7	5	Artichoke Lake	4
5	Caledonia	7	5	Baudette Int'l Airport	4
5	Cedar	7	5	Big Falls	4
5	Fairmont	7	5	Cass Lake	4
5	Faribault	7	5	Cotton	4
5	Gaylord	7	5	Crookston NW Exp. Station	4
5	Grand Meadow	7	5	Duluth Int'l Airport	4
5	Marshall	7	5	Fergus Falls	4
5	New London	*7*	5	Fosston 1 E	4
5	New Ulm 2 SE	7	5	International Falls Int'l Arpt.	4
5	Saint James Filtration Plant	*7*	5	Leech Lake Dam	4
5	Santiago 3 E	7	5	Red Lake Falls	*4*
5	Waseca Exp. Station	7	5	Red Lake Indian Agency	4
5	Windom	7	5	Wheaton	4
5	Winnebago	7	5	Winton Power Plant	*4*
5	Zumbrota	7	20	Agassiz Refuge	5
21	Ada	*6*	20	Benson	5
21	Alexandria Chandler Field	6	20	Duluth Harbor Station	*5*
21	Brainerd	6	20	Glenwood 2 WNW	5
21	Buffalo	6	20	Grand Marais	5
21	Cambridge State Hosp	6	20	Grand Rapids Forestry Lab	5

Annual Snowfall

	Highest			Lowest	
Rank	**Station Name**	**Inches**	**Rank**	**Station Name**	**Inches**
1	Duluth Int'l Airport	83.3	1	Saint Peter 2 SW	*30.7*
2	International Falls Int'l Arpt.	71.0	2	Pipestone	*34.0*
3	Tower 3 S	68.3	3	Redwood Falls Muni Airport	34.7
4	Cloquet	65.4	4	Glenwood 2 WNW	*36.1*
5	Hibbing Chisholm-Hibbing Airport	62.0	5	Madison Sewage Plant	*37.6*
6	Wright 4 NW	59.2	6	Crookston NW Exp. Station	38.9
7	Big Falls	58.2	7	Worthington 2 NNE	*39.0*
8	Ottertail	57.2	8	Cambridge State Hosp	*39.4*
9	Sandy Lake Dam Libby	*57.0*	8	Hutchinson 1 N	39.4
10	Grand Rapids Forestry Lab	56.7	10	Agassiz Refuge	39.5
11	Minneapolis-St Paul Int'l Arpt.	55.1	11	Gaylord	39.9
12	Waseca Exp. Station	54.7	12	Artichoke Lake	40.0
13	Cedar	53.4	13	Milaca 1 ENE	*40.2*
14	New London	*52.7*	13	Wheaton	*40.2*
15	Saint Paul	51.8	15	Moose Lake 1 SSE	40.5
16	Grand Marais	51.6	16	Albert Lea 3 SE	40.7
17	Long Prairie	51.2	17	Argyle 4 E	40.8
17	Rochester Municipal Airport	51.2	17	Saint James Filtration Plant	*40.8*
19	Cotton	*50.6*	19	Owatonna	40.9
20	Collegeville Saint John	50.3	20	Benson	41.4
21	Itasca Univ. of Minnesota	49.7	21	Fosston 1 E	41.6
22	Red Lake Falls	49.2	21	Preston	*41.6*
23	Park Rapids Municipal Airport	48.9	23	Lamberton SW Exp. Station	41.7
24	Little Falls 1 N	48.8	23	Melrose	41.7
25	Stewart	48.7	25	Marshall	42.1

Note: See Appendix D for explanation of data.

Annual Extreme Maximum Temperature

	Highest				Lowest	
Rank	Station Name	°F		Rank	Station Name	°F
1	Fulton 3 W	108		1	Natchez	101
1	Greenville	108		1	Port Gibson 3 NE	101
1	Hickory Flat	108		3	Brookhaven City	102
1	Ripley	108		3	Collins	102
1	State University	108		3	Hattiesburg 5 SW	102
6	Belzoni	107		3	Saucier Experiment Forest	102
6	Corinth City	107		3	Vicksburg Military Park	102
6	Meridian Key Field	107		8	Gulfport Municipal	103
6	Moorhead	107		8	Liberty 5 W	103
10	Batesville 2 SW	106		8	McComb Pike County Airport	103
10	Booneville	106		8	Philadelphia 1 WSW	103
10	Hernando 5 S	106		8	Picayune	103
10	Holly Springs 4 N	106		8	Poplarville Experiment Station	103
10	Jackson Thompson Field	106		8	Woodville 4 ESE	103
10	Water Valley 1 NNE	106		15	Aberdeen	104
10	Waynesboro 2 W	*106*		15	Calhoun City 2 NW	104
10	Yazoo City 5 NNE	106		15	Canton	*104*
18	Carthage 3 SW	105		15	D Lo 2 SW	104
18	Clarksdale	105		15	Eupora 2 E	104
18	Columbia	105		15	Forest 3 S	104
18	Greenwood Leflore Airport	105		15	Grenada 5 NNE	104
18	Houston	105		15	Kipling	*104*
18	Independence 1 W	105		15	Laurel	104
18	Kosciusko	105		15	Lexington 2 NNW	104
18	Merrill	105		15	Louisville	104

Annual Mean Maximum Temperature

	Highest				Lowest	
Rank	Station Name	°F		Rank	Station Name	°F
1	Merrill	78.1		1	Holly Springs 4 N	70.6
2	Columbia	78.0		1	Independence 1 W	70.6
2	Picayune	78.0		3	Booneville	70.7
4	Saucier Experiment Forest	77.9		4	Ripley	70.9
5	Poplarville Experiment Station	77.8		5	Tunica 2	71.6
6	Waynesboro 2 W	77.4		6	Hernando 5 S	71.9
7	Tylertown 2 WNW	77.3		6	Pontotoc Experiment Station	71.9
8	Woodville 4 ESE	77.2		8	Clarksdale	72.0
9	Gulfport Municipal	77.1		9	University	72.2
9	Pelahatchie	*77.1*		10	Batesville 2 SW	72.4
9	Richton 3 SSE	77.1		10	Houston	72.4
12	McComb Pike County Airport	77.0		12	Louisville	72.8
12	Monticello	77.0		12	Winona 5 E	72.8
12	Vicksburg Military Park	77.0		14	Corinth City	72.9
15	Hattiesburg 5 SW	76.9		14	Water Valley 1 NNE	72.9
16	Natchez	76.8		16	Hickory Flat	73.1
17	Collins	76.4		16	Stoneville Exp. Station	73.1
17	Meridian Key Field	76.4		18	Tupelo C D Lemons Airport	73.2
17	Pascagoula 3 NE	76.4		19	Grenada 5 NNE	73.4
20	Liberty 5 W	76.3		20	State University	73.5
21	Forest 3 S	76.1		21	Fulton 3 W	73.9
21	Jackson Thompson Field	76.1		22	Aberdeen	74.0
21	Laurel	76.1		23	Greenwood Leflore Airport	74.2
21	Quitman 1 N	76.1		23	Moorhead	74.2
25	Brookhaven City	75.9		25	Calhoun City 2 NW	74.3

Annual Mean Temperature

	Highest				Lowest	
Rank	**Station Name**	**°F**		**Rank**	**Station Name**	**°F**
1	Gulfport Municipal	68.0		1	Holly Springs 4 N	59.2
2	Pascagoula 3 NE	67.4		2	Ripley	59.4
2	Saucier Experiment Forest	67.4		3	Independence 1 W	59.9
4	Poplarville Experiment Station	66.9		4	Booneville	60.1
5	Picayune	66.8		5	Winona 5 E	60.2
6	Natchez	66.3		6	University	60.4
6	Woodville 4 ESE	66.3		7	Batesville 2 SW	60.6
8	Columbia	66.2		8	Houston	60.7
8	Tylertown 2 WNW	66.2		9	Water Valley 1 NNE	60.8
10	Hattiesburg 5 SW	65.7		10	Pontotoc Experiment Station	60.9
11	McComb Pike County Airport	65.4		11	Corinth City	61.3
12	Vicksburg Military Park	65.3		11	Hickory Flat	61.3
13	Collins	65.1		13	Tunica 2	61.4
14	Yazoo City 5 NNE	64.9		14	Grenada 5 NNE	61.7
15	Merrill	*64.8*		14	Hernando 5 S	61.7
16	Jackson Thompson Field	64.7		14	Tupelo C D Lemons Airport	61.7
17	Pelahatchie	*64.6*		17	Louisville	61.9
17	Waynesboro 2 W	64.6		18	Fulton 3 W	62.0
19	Laurel	64.5		19	Clarksdale	62.1
19	Meridian Key Field	64.5		20	Calhoun City 2 NW	62.3
19	Monticello	64.5		20	Kosciusko	62.3
22	Brookhaven City	64.3		22	State University	62.5
22	Richton 3 SSE	64.3		23	Eupora 2 E	62.6
24	Moorhead	64.2		24	Lexington 2 NNW	62.7
25	Greenville	64.1		25	Aberdeen	62.9

Annual Mean Minimum Temperature

	Highest				Lowest	
Rank	**Station Name**	**°F**		**Rank**	**Station Name**	**°F**
1	Gulfport Municipal	58.9		1	Winona 5 E	47.6
2	Pascagoula 3 NE	58.4		2	Holly Springs 4 N	47.7
3	Saucier Experiment Forest	57.0		3	Ripley	47.9
4	Poplarville Experiment Station	55.9		4	University	48.6
5	Natchez	55.7		5	Batesville 2 SW	48.8
6	Picayune	55.5		5	Water Valley 1 NNE	48.8
7	Woodville 4 ESE	55.4		7	Houston	49.0
8	Tylertown 2 WNW	55.1		8	Independence 1 W	49.2
9	Columbia	54.4		9	Hickory Flat	49.4
10	Hattiesburg 5 SW	54.3		10	Booneville	49.5
10	Yazoo City 5 NNE	54.3		11	Corinth City	49.6
12	Moorhead	54.2		12	Pontotoc Experiment Station	49.7
13	Collins	53.8		13	Kosciusko	49.9
13	McComb Pike County Airport	53.8		14	Grenada 5 NNE	50.0
15	Vicksburg Military Park	53.6		15	Fulton 3 W	50.1
16	Greenville	53.3		15	Tupelo C D Lemons Airport	50.1
16	Greenwood Leflore Airport	53.3		17	Calhoun City 2 NW	50.3
16	Jackson Thompson Field	53.3		17	Eupora 2 E	50.3
19	Belzoni	52.9		19	D Lo 2 SW	50.5
19	Laurel	52.9		20	Carthage 3 SW	50.6
21	Stoneville Exp. Station	52.8		21	Kipling	*50.7*
22	Brookhaven City	52.7		22	Lexington 2 NNW	50.8
23	Meridian Key Field	52.4		23	Louisville	51.0
24	Oakley Experiment Station	52.3		23	Newton Experiment Station	51.0
24	Rolling Fork	*52.3*		25	Quitman 1 N	51.1

Annual Extreme Minimum Temperature

	Highest			Lowest	
Rank	Station Name	°F	Rank	Station Name	°F
1	Picayune	7	1	University	-13
2	Pascagoula 3 NE	6	2	Corinth City	-10
3	Monticello	5	2	Hickory Flat	-10
3	Natchez	5	2	Ripley	-10
5	Columbia	4	5	Fulton 3 W	-9
5	Gulfport Municipal	4	6	Batesville 2 SW	-8
5	Hattiesburg 5 SW	4	6	Booneville	-8
5	Saucier Experiment Forest	4	6	Calhoun City 2 NW	-8
5	Woodville 4 ESE	4	6	Independence 1 W	-8
10	Brookhaven City	3	6	State University	-8
10	Laurel	3	6	Water Valley 1 NNE	-8
10	Liberty 5 W	3	12	Pontotoc Experiment Station	-7
10	Poplarville Experiment Station	3	13	Hernando 5 S	-6
10	Richton 3 SSE	3	13	Holly Springs 4 N	-6
10	Stoneville Exp. Station	*3*	13	Merrill	*-6*
10	Tylertown 2 WNW	3	13	Tupelo C D Lemons Airport	-6
17	Collins	2	13	Winona 5 E	-6
17	Jackson Thompson Field	2	18	Aberdeen	-5
17	McComb Pike County Airport	2	18	Houston	-5
17	Meridian Key Field	2	20	Eupora 2 E	-4
17	Vicksburg Military Park	2	20	Grenada 5 NNE	-4
17	Yazoo City 5 NNE	2	20	Lexington 2 NNW	-4
23	Belzoni	1	20	Tunica 2	-4
23	Canton	*1*	24	Kipling	*-3*
23	Oakley Experiment Station	1	24	Louisville	-3

July Mean Maximum Temperature

	Highest			Lowest	
Rank	Station Name	°F	Rank	Station Name	°F
1	Greenville	92.9	1	Booneville	89.4
2	Belzoni	92.8	2	Louisville	89.5
3	Canton	92.7	3	Holly Springs 4 N	89.6
3	Columbia	92.7	3	Independence 1 W	89.6
5	Monticello	92.6	3	Winona 5 E	89.6
5	Pelahatchie	*92.6*	6	Pascagoula 3 NE	89.8
5	Rolling Fork	*92.6*	7	Ripley	90.3
8	Merrill	92.5	8	Water Valley 1 NNE	90.4
9	Meridian Key Field	92.4	9	Pontotoc Experiment Station	90.5
9	Yazoo City 5 NNE	92.4	10	Collins	90.7
11	Moorhead	92.3	10	Houston	90.7
12	Jackson Thompson Field	92.2	10	Lexington 2 NNW	90.7
13	Corinth City	92.0	13	Hernando 5 S	90.8
13	Vicksburg Military Park	92.0	14	Brookhaven City	90.9
13	Waynesboro 2 W	92.0	14	Philadelphia 1 WSW	90.9
16	Carthage 3 SW	91.9	14	University	90.9
17	Fulton 3 W	91.8	17	Batesville 2 SW	91.0
17	Greenwood Leflore Airport	91.8	17	Woodville 4 ESE	91.0
17	Newton Experiment Station	91.8	19	Gulfport Municipal	91.1
17	Oakley Experiment Station	91.8	19	Kipling	91.1
17	Quitman 1 N	91.8	19	Tylertown 2 WNW	91.1
22	Hattiesburg 5 SW	91.7	22	D Lo 2 SW	91.2
22	Kosciusko	91.7	22	Natchez	91.2
22	McComb Pike County Airport	91.7	22	Port Gibson 3 NE	91.2
22	Tunica 2	91.7	25	Forest 3 S	91.3

January Mean Minimum Temperature

	Highest				Lowest	
Rank	**Station Name**	**°F**		**Rank**	**Station Name**	**°F**
1	Gulfport Municipal	42.2		1	Holly Springs 4 N	27.4
2	Pascagoula 3 NE	41.3		2	Ripley	27.6
3	Saucier Experiment Forest	40.9		3	University	28.2
4	Poplarville Experiment Station	39.4		3	Water Valley 1 NNE	28.2
5	Picayune	38.9		5	Winona 5 E	28.6
6	Woodville 4 ESE	38.7		6	Batesville 2 SW	28.7
7	Natchez	38.6		7	Booneville	28.9
7	Tylertown 2 WNW	38.6		7	Independence 1 W	28.9
9	Columbia	37.2		9	Pontotoc Experiment Station	29.4
10	McComb Pike County Airport	36.8		10	Corinth City	29.5
11	Hattiesburg 5 SW	36.6		11	Houston	29.9
12	Collins	36.3		12	Hickory Flat	30.0
13	Laurel	35.5		13	Tunica 2	30.1
14	Yazoo City 5 NNE	35.4		14	Grenada 5 NNE	30.2
15	Vicksburg Military Park	35.3		15	Hernando 5 S	30.7
15	Waynesboro 2 W	35.3		16	Tupelo C D Lemons Airport	30.8
17	Brookhaven City	35.1		17	Kosciusko	30.9
17	Merrill	35.1		18	Calhoun City 2 NW	31.0
19	Jackson Thompson Field	34.8		19	Clarksdale	31.2
20	Liberty 5 W	34.5		20	Fulton 3 W	31.4
20	Meridian Key Field	34.5		20	State University	31.4
22	Moorhead	34.4		22	Louisville	31.6
23	Monticello	34.3		23	Carthage 3 SW	32.1
24	Pelahatchie	*34.2*		24	Eupora 2 E	32.2
25	Richton 3 SSE	34.1		25	D Lo 2 SW	32.4

Number of Annual Heating Degree Days

	Highest				Lowest	
Rank	**Station Name**	**Num.**		**Rank**	**Station Name**	**Num.**
1	Holly Springs 4 N	3,625		1	Gulfport Municipal	1,475
2	Ripley	3,607		2	Saucier Experiment Forest	1,537
3	Independence 1 W	3,466		3	Pascagoula 3 NE	1,607
4	Booneville	3,384		4	Picayune	1,698
5	University	3,360		5	Poplarville Experiment Station	1,699
6	Batesville 2 SW	3,298		6	Woodville 4 ESE	1,806
7	Winona 5 E	3,247		7	Tylertown 2 WNW	1,818
8	Water Valley 1 NNE	3,230		8	Natchez	1,876
9	Tunica 2	3,212		9	Columbia	1,927
10	Pontotoc Experiment Station	3,211		10	McComb Pike County Airport	2,019
11	Houston	3,198		11	Hattiesburg 5 SW	2,039
12	Corinth City	3,156		12	Collins	2,057
13	Hickory Flat	3,089		13	Vicksburg Military Park	2,111
14	Clarksdale	3,064		14	Merrill	*2,143*
15	Hernando 5 S	3,054		15	Waynesboro 2 W	2,175
16	Tupelo C D Lemons Airport	3,028		16	Pelahatchie	*2,239*
17	Grenada 5 NNE	2,995		17	Brookhaven City	2,259
18	Fulton 3 W	2,874		18	Laurel	2,261
19	Louisville	2,871		19	Richton 3 SSE	2,273
20	State University	2,850		20	Monticello	2,315
21	Stoneville Exp. Station	2,847		21	Meridian Key Field	2,320
22	Kosciusko	2,833		22	Jackson Thompson Field	2,333
23	Calhoun City 2 NW	2,787		23	Liberty 5 W	2,344
24	Aberdeen	2,692		24	Yazoo City 5 NNE	2,345
25	Eupora 2 E	2,689		25	Forest 3 S	2,384

Number of Annual Cooling Degree Days

	Highest			Lowest	
Rank	Station Name	Num.	Rank	Station Name	Num.
1	Gulfport Municipal	2,646	1	Winona 5 E	1,627
2	Saucier Experiment Forest	2,555	2	Holly Springs 4 N	1,663
3	Columbia	2,470	3	Ripley	1,672
4	Yazoo City 5 NNE	2,457	4	Independence 1 W	1,703
5	Poplarville Experiment Station	2,453	5	Booneville	1,739
6	Natchez	2,436	6	Houston	*1,746*
7	Woodville 4 ESE	2,424	7	Pontotoc Experiment Station	1,844
8	Hattiesburg 5 SW	2,406	8	Hickory Flat	1,850
9	Moorhead	2,402	9	Water Valley 1 NNE	1,852
9	Pascagoula 3 NE	2,402	10	Batesville 2 SW	1,855
11	Picayune	2,395	11	Grenada 5 NNE	1,868
12	Tylertown 2 WNW	2,380	12	Louisville	1,892
13	Belzoni	2,361	13	University	1,898
14	Jackson Thompson Field	2,354	14	Lexington 2 NNW	1,919
15	Vicksburg Military Park	2,340	15	Fulton 3 W	1,927
16	McComb Pike County Airport	2,327	16	Calhoun City 2 NW	1,930
17	Greenwood Leflore Airport	2,324	17	Corinth City	1,934
18	Greenville	2,318	18	Eupora 2 E	1,961
19	Monticello	2,271	19	Hernando 5 S	1,970
20	Rolling Fork	2,270	20	Kipling	*1,975*
21	Meridian Key Field	2,256	21	Tupelo C D Lemons Airport	1,987
22	Collins	2,233	22	Kosciusko	2,009
23	Canton	*2,226*	23	Newton Experiment Station	2,011
24	Stoneville Exp. Station	2,218	24	Forest 3 S	2,035
25	Oakley Experiment Station	2,216	24	Tunica 2	2,035

Annual Precipitation

	Highest			Lowest	
Rank	Station Name	Inches	Rank	Station Name	Inches
1	Saucier Experiment Forest	71.11	1	Stoneville Exp. Station	52.75
2	Woodville 4 ESE	68.19	2	Independence 1 W	52.90
3	Pascagoula 3 NE	67.99	3	Greenville	54.26
4	Merrill	66.46	4	Tunica 2	54.32
5	Gulfport Municipal	66.04	5	Clarksdale	54.42
6	McComb Pike County Airport	64.88	6	Greenwood Leflore Airport	54.50
7	Picayune	64.62	7	Hernando 5 S	55.49
8	Tylertown 2 WNW	64.33	8	Aberdeen	55.69
9	Columbia	64.29	9	Calhoun City 2 NW	55.97
10	Poplarville Experiment Station	63.77	10	Rolling Fork	55.98
11	Liberty 5 W	62.80	11	Kipling	*56.06*
12	Hattiesburg 5 SW	62.63	12	Jackson Thompson Field	56.14
13	Natchez	62.42	13	Lexington 2 NNW	56.23
14	Forest 3 S	62.32	14	Batesville 2 SW	56.26
15	Monticello	62.20	15	State University	56.35
16	Brookhaven City	61.90	16	Quitman 1 N	56.45
17	Pelahatchie	*61.18*	17	Moorhead	56.51
18	Kosciusko	61.04	18	Canton	*56.54*
19	Richton 3 SSE	60.75	19	Tupelo C D Lemons Airport	56.57
20	Fulton 3 W	60.57	20	Corinth City	56.69
21	D Lo 2 SW	60.22	21	Oakley Experiment Station	57.21
22	Yazoo City 5 NNE	59.90	22	Winona 5 E	57.31
23	Collins	59.72	23	Carthage 3 SW	57.52
24	Louisville	59.63	24	Newton Experiment Station	57.68
25	Port Gibson 3 NE	59.34	25	Holly Springs 4 N	57.76

Number of Days Annually With ≥ 0.1″ Precipitation

	Highest			Lowest	
Rank	**Station Name**	**Days**	**Rank**	**Station Name**	**Days**
1	Saucier Experiment Forest	86	1	Greenville	69
2	Poplarville Experiment Station	85	2	Calhoun City 2 NW	*71*
3	Woodville 4 ESE	84	2	Moorhead	71
4	Columbia	83	2	Rolling Fork	71
4	Fulton 3 W	83	5	Belzoni	72
4	Ripley	83	5	Greenwood Leflore Airport	72
7	Booneville	82	5	Stoneville Exp. Station	72
7	McComb Pike County Airport	82	8	Batesville 2 SW	73
7	Picayune	82	8	Canton	*73*
10	Merrill	81	8	Lexington 2 NNW	73
10	Pontotoc Experiment Station	81	8	Quitman 1 N	73
10	Tupelo C D Lemons Airport	81	8	Tunica 2	73
10	Tylertown 2 WNW	81	8	Vicksburg Military Park	73
14	Brookhaven City	80	14	Clarksdale	74
14	Carthage 3 SW	80	14	Eupora 2 E	74
14	Corinth City	80	14	Oakley Experiment Station	74
14	Gulfport Municipal	80	17	Jackson Thompson Field	75
14	Hickory Flat	80	17	Liberty 5 W	75
14	Pelahatchie	*80*	17	Pascagoula 3 NE	75
14	Richton 3 SSE	80	17	Port Gibson 3 NE	75
14	State University	80	17	Winona 5 E	75
14	University	80	17	Yazoo City 5 NNE	75
23	Aberdeen	79	23	Hernando 5 S	76
23	Forest 3 S	79	23	Kipling	*76*
23	Holly Springs 4 N	79	23	Louisville	76

Number of Days Annually With ≥ 1.0″ Precipitation

	Highest			Lowest	
Rank	**Station Name**	**Days**	**Rank**	**Station Name**	**Days**
1	Picayune	24	1	Corinth City	17
1	Saucier Experiment Forest	24	1	Independence 1 W	17
3	Merrill	23	1	Winona 5 E	17
4	Gulfport Municipal	22	4	Aberdeen	18
4	McComb Pike County Airport	22	4	Greenwood Leflore Airport	18
4	Woodville 4 ESE	22	4	Hernando 5 S	18
4	Yazoo City 5 NNE	22	4	Kipling	*18*
8	Forest 3 S	21	4	Lexington 2 NNW	18
8	Moorhead	21	4	Newton Experiment Station	18
8	Pascagoula 3 NE	21	4	Quitman 1 N	18
8	Pelahatchie	*21*	4	Ripley	18
8	Rolling Fork	21	4	State University	18
8	Waynesboro 2 W	21	4	Tunica 2	18
14	Belzoni	20	4	Tupelo C D Lemons Airport	18
14	Brookhaven City	20	4	University	18
14	Collins	20	4	Water Valley 1 NNE	18
14	Columbia	20	17	Batesville 2 SW	19
14	Grenada 5 NNE	20	17	Booneville	19
14	Hattiesburg 5 SW	20	17	Calhoun City 2 NW	19
14	Hickory Flat	20	17	Canton	*19*
14	Louisville	20	17	Carthage 3 SW	19
14	Meridian Key Field	20	17	Clarksdale	19
14	Natchez	20	17	D Lo 2 SW	19
14	Oakley Experiment Station	20	17	Eupora 2 E	19
14	Pontotoc Experiment Station	20	17	Fulton 3 W	19

Annual Snowfall

Highest			Lowest		
Rank	**Station Name**	**Inches**	**Rank**	**Station Name**	**Inches**
1	Hickory Flat	3.5	1	Belzoni	Trace
2	Hernando 5 S	3.1	1	Gulfport Municipal	Trace
3	Water Valley 1 NNE	2.8	1	Laurel	Trace
4	Corinth City	2.6	1	Liberty 5 W	Trace
5	Independence 1 W	2.5	1	Pascagoula 3 NE	Trace
6	Booneville	2.4	1	Pelahatchie	*Trace*
7	Ripley	2.3	1	Saucier Experiment Forest	Trace
8	University	2.2	1	Woodville 4 ESE	Trace
9	Holly Springs 4 N	2.1	1	Yazoo City 5 NNE	Trace
10	Tunica 2	1.8	10	Picayune	0.1
11	Tupelo C D Lemons Airport	1.7	11	McComb Pike County Airport	0.2
12	Houston	1.6	11	Merrill	0.2
13	Fulton 3 W	1.5	11	Monticello	0.2
14	Clarksdale	1.4	11	Poplarville Experiment Station	0.2
15	Calhoun City 2 NW	1.1	11	Rolling Fork	0.2
15	Moorhead	1.1	11	Tylertown 2 WNW	0.2
15	Stoneville Exp. Station	1.1	17	Brookhaven City	0.3
18	Aberdeen	1.0	17	Collins	0.3
18	Batesville 2 SW	*1.0*	17	Columbia	0.3
18	Kosciusko	*1.0*	17	Greenville	0.3
18	Winona 5 E	1.0	17	Hattiesburg 5 SW	0.3
22	Greenwood Leflore Airport	0.8	17	Vicksburg Military Park	0.3
22	Pontotoc Experiment Station	0.8	17	Waynesboro 2 W	0.3
24	Eupora 2 E	0.7	24	D Lo 2 SW	0.4
24	Grenada 5 NNE	0.7	24	Forest 3 S	0.4

Note: See Appendix D for explanation of data.

Annual Extreme Maximum Temperature

	Highest				Lowest	
Rank	**Station Name**	**°F**		**Rank**	**Station Name**	**°F**
1	Appleton City	112		1	Marble Hill	104
1	Kennett Radio KBOA	112		1	Mountain Grove 2 N	104
3	Butler	111		3	Advance 1 S	105
3	Columbia Regional Airport	111		3	Cape Girardeau Municipal Airport	105
3	Freedom	111		3	Farmington	105
3	Pomme De Terre Dam	111		3	Kirksville	105
3	Steelville 2 N	111		3	Marshfield	105
8	Arcadia	*110*		8	Cassville Ranger Station	106
8	Boonville	110		8	Galena 1 SW	106
8	Canton Lock & Dam 20	110		8	Jackson	106
8	Carrollton	110		8	Mansfield	*106*
8	Clearwater Dam	110		8	Monett 4 SW	*106*
8	Doniphan	110		8	Mount Vernon M U SW Center	106
8	Jefferson City Water Plant	110		8	New Madrid	106
8	Nevada Water Plant	110		8	Portageville	106
8	Osceola	110		8	Steffenville	106
8	Princeton 6 SW	110		8	Willow Springs Radio KUKU	106
8	Sweet Springs	110		18	Anderson	107
8	Vienna 2 WNW	110		18	Bethany	107
8	Wappapello Dam	110		18	Bolivar 1 NE	107
21	Billings 2 N	*109*		18	Caruthersville	107
21	Brookfield	109		18	Clinton	107
21	Buffalo 3 S	109		18	Lakeside	107
21	California	109		18	Lamar	107
21	Dora	109		18	Maryville 2 E	107

Annual Mean Maximum Temperature

	Highest				Lowest	
Rank	**Station Name**	**°F**		**Rank**	**Station Name**	**°F**
1	Kennett Radio KBOA	70.5		1	Conception	61.9
2	Doniphan	69.6		1	Kirksville	61.9
3	Ozark Beach	69.5		3	Maryville 2 E	62.0
4	Neosho	69.3		4	Princeton 6 SW	62.2
5	Caruthersville	68.8		5	Hannibal Water Works	62.4
5	Jackson	68.8		6	Bethany	62.6
7	Waynesville 2 W	68.6		6	Grant City	62.6
8	Anderson	68.4		6	Spickard	62.6
8	Dora	68.4		9	Hamilton 2 W	62.9
10	Galena 1 SW	68.3		10	Canton Lock & Dam 20	63.4
10	Wappapello Dam	*68.3*		10	Steffenville	63.4
12	New Madrid	68.2		12	Brunswick	63.6
13	Marble Hill	68.1		13	Saverton Lock & Dam 22	63.7
13	Portageville	68.1		14	Kansas City Int'l Airport	63.8
15	Clearwater Dam	*68.0*		15	Brookfield	64.1
15	Nevada Water Plant	68.0		15	Fulton	64.1
17	Lockwood	67.9		15	Mexico	64.1
17	Union	67.9		18	Salisbury	64.2
19	Joplin Municipal Airport	67.8		19	Columbia Regional Airport	64.3
20	Advance 1 S	67.7		20	Lexington 3 NE	64.4
20	West Plains	67.7		21	Vandalia	64.6
22	Arcadia	*67.5*		22	Boonville	64.7
23	Butler	67.4		22	Sedalia Water Plant	64.7
23	Cape Girardeau Municipal Airport	67.4		24	Moberly	64.8
23	Osceola	67.4		25	Windsor	65.0

Annual Mean Temperature

	Highest			Lowest	
Rank	Station Name	°F	Rank	Station Name	°F
1	Kennett Radio KBOA	59.2	1	Maryville 2 E	50.4
2	Caruthersville	58.7	2	Hamilton 2 W	51.0
3	Portageville	58.4	3	Conception	51.3
4	New Madrid	58.0	3	Spickard	51.3
5	Jackson	57.6	5	Princeton 6 SW	51.5
6	Joplin Municipal Airport	57.5	6	Bethany	51.9
7	Cape Girardeau Municipal Airport	57.4	6	Grant City	*51.9*
7	Wappapello Dam	*57.4*	6	Kirksville	51.9
9	Neosho	57.1	9	Hannibal Water Works	52.7
10	Lockwood	56.8	9	Steffenville	52.7
11	Anderson	56.6	11	Brunswick	52.9
12	Advance 1 S	56.4	11	Mexico	52.9
12	Osceola	56.4	13	Canton Lock & Dam 20	53.1
14	Doniphan	56.3	13	Steelville 2 N	53.1
15	California	56.2	15	Sedalia Water Plant	53.2
15	Lebanon 2 W	56.2	16	Fulton	53.4
15	Nevada Water Plant	56.2	16	Salisbury	53.4
15	Saint Louis Lambert Int'l Arpt.	56.2	18	Brookfield	53.7
19	Stockton Dam	56.1	18	Vandalia	53.7
20	Marble Hill	56.0	18	Windsor	53.7
20	Monett 4 SW	*56.0*	21	Lexington 3 NE	53.8
20	Ozark Beach	56.0	22	Saverton Lock & Dam 22	53.9
20	Springfield Regional Airport	56.0	23	Kansas City Int'l Airport	54.0
24	Butler	55.9	24	Farmington	54.1
24	Summersville	*55.9*	24	Vienna 2 WNW	54.1

Annual Mean Minimum Temperature

	Highest			Lowest	
Rank	Station Name	°F	Rank	Station Name	°F
1	Portageville	48.7	1	Maryville 2 E	38.6
2	Caruthersville	48.4	2	Hamilton 2 W	39.1
3	Kennett Radio KBOA	47.9	3	Steelville 2 N	39.3
4	New Madrid	47.7	4	Spickard	40.0
5	Cape Girardeau Municipal Airport	47.3	5	Conception	40.6
6	Joplin Municipal Airport	47.2	6	Princeton 6 SW	40.7
7	Saint Louis Lambert Int'l Arpt.	46.7	7	Bethany	41.1
8	Wappapello Dam	*46.5*	7	Grant City	*41.1*
9	Jackson	46.4	9	Sedalia Water Plant	41.7
10	Lockwood	45.8	10	Kirksville	41.8
11	Monett 4 SW	*45.7*	10	Mexico	41.8
12	Rolla Univ. of Missouri	45.5	12	Fredericktown	41.9
13	California	45.4	13	Steffenville	42.1
13	Stockton Dam	45.4	14	Brunswick	42.2
15	Marshfield	45.3	14	Vienna 2 WNW	42.2
15	Osceola	45.3	14	Waynesville 2 W	42.2
17	Springfield Regional Airport	45.2	17	Mansfield	*42.3*
18	Advance 1 S	45.1	17	Windsor	42.3
19	Lebanon 2 W	45.0	19	Ozark Beach	42.5
20	Neosho	44.9	19	Salisbury	42.5
21	Anderson	44.7	21	Elsberry 1 S	42.6
21	Lamar	44.7	21	Fulton	42.6
23	Buffalo 3 S	44.5	23	Clinton	42.7
23	Eldon	44.5	23	Farmington	42.7
23	Moberly	44.5	25	Bolivar 1 NE	42.8

Annual Extreme Minimum Temperature

Highest			Lowest		
Rank	Station Name	°F	Rank	Station Name	°F
1	Kennett Radio KBOA	-12	1	Maryville 2 E	-32
2	Caruthersville	-13	2	Clinton	-31
3	New Madrid	-14	2	Steelville 2 N	-31
4	Joplin Municipal Airport	-15	4	Spickard	-30
4	Lakeside	-15	5	Bethany	-29
4	Ozark Beach	-15	6	Buffalo 3 S	-28
4	Portageville	-15	6	Eldon	-28
4	Wappapello Dam	-15	6	Salisbury	-28
9	Monett 4 SW	*-16*	6	Sedalia Water Plant	-28
9	Willow Springs Radio KUKU	-16	10	Grant City	-27
11	Billings 2 N	*-17*	10	Hamilton 2 W	-27
11	Lockwood	-17	10	Vienna 2 WNW	-27
11	Springfield Regional Airport	-17	13	Butler	-26
14	Cape Girardeau Municipal Airport	-18	13	Princeton 6 SW	-26
14	Clearwater Dam	-18	13	Steffenville	-26
14	Lamar	-18	13	Union	-26
14	Mount Vernon M U SW Center	-18	17	Brunswick	-25
14	Neosho	-18	17	Lees Summit Reed Wildlife Refuge	-25
14	Saint Louis Lambert Int'l Arpt.	-18	17	Mansfield	*-25*
14	Stockton Dam	-18	17	Mexico	-25
14	West Plains	-18	17	Nevada Water Plant	-25
22	Bolivar 1 NE	-19	17	Osceola	-25
22	Doniphan	-19	17	Waynesville 2 W	-25
22	Lebanon 2 W	-19	24	Brookfield	-24
22	Mountain Grove 2 N	-19	24	Carrollton	-24

July Mean Maximum Temperature

Highest			Lowest		
Rank	Station Name	°F	Rank	Station Name	°F
1	Kennett Radio KBOA	92.8	1	Kirksville	86.9
2	Doniphan	91.8	2	Hannibal Water Works	87.0
3	Jackson	91.5	3	Princeton 6 SW	87.1
4	Nevada Water Plant	91.3	4	Conception	87.6
4	Ozark Beach	91.3	4	Maryville 2 E	87.6
6	New Madrid	91.2	6	Brunswick	87.7
6	Wappapello Dam	91.2	7	Grant City	87.8
8	Clearwater Dam	91.0	8	Fulton	87.9
9	Osceola	90.9	8	Mountain Grove 2 N	87.9
10	Appleton City	90.8	10	Farmington	88.0
10	Neosho	90.8	10	Steffenville	88.0
10	Union	90.8	12	Hamilton 2 W	88.1
13	Butler	90.7	13	Spickard	88.2
14	Sweet Springs	90.6	14	Bethany	88.3
15	Caruthersville	90.5	15	Licking 4 N	88.4
15	Lockwood	90.5	15	Marshfield	88.4
17	Joplin Municipal Airport	90.4	15	Salisbury	88.4
17	Pomme De Terre Dam	90.4	18	Cassville Ranger Station	*88.5*
19	Carrollton	90.3	18	Columbia Regional Airport	88.5
19	Clinton	90.3	20	Brookfield	88.6
19	Portageville	90.3	20	Monett 4 SW	*88.6*
22	California	90.2	20	Versailles	88.6
22	Cape Girardeau Municipal Airport	90.2	23	Billings 2 N	88.7
22	Stockton Dam	90.2	23	Canton Lock & Dam 20	88.7
25	Advance 1 S	90.1	23	Saverton Lock & Dam 22	88.7

January Mean Minimum Temperature

	Highest				Lowest	
Rank	Station Name	°F		Rank	Station Name	°F
1	Portageville	26.0		1	Maryville 2 E	11.5
2	Caruthersville	25.6		2	Hamilton 2 W	12.2
3	Kennett Radio KBOA	25.4		3	Spickard	13.0
4	New Madrid	24.7		4	Conception	13.2
5	Cape Girardeau Municipal Airport	23.4		5	Grant City	13.8
5	Joplin Municipal Airport	23.4		6	Bethany	14.0
7	Advance 1 S	23.0		7	Princeton 6 SW	14.3
7	Jackson	23.0		8	Kirksville	15.3
9	Monett 4 SW	22.1		9	Mexico	15.5
10	Anderson	21.9		10	Steffenville	15.6
11	Lockwood	21.8		11	Brunswick	15.9
11	Neosho	21.8		11	Hannibal Water Works	15.9
13	Willow Springs Radio KUKU	21.7		13	Steelville 2 N	16.0
14	Springfield Regional Airport	21.6		14	Canton Lock & Dam 20	16.1
15	Lebanon 2 W	21.5		14	Sedalia Water Plant	16.1
15	Summersville	21.5		14	Windsor	16.1
15	Wappapello Dam	*21.5*		17	Salisbury	16.2
18	Marble Hill	21.3		18	Brookfield	16.7
18	Rolla Univ. of Missouri	21.3		18	Lexington 3 NE	16.7
18	West Plains	21.3		20	Clinton	17.1
21	Marshfield	21.2		21	Elsberry 1 S	17.2
21	Saint Louis Lambert Int'l Arpt.	21.2		22	Vandalia	17.3
23	Buffalo 3 S	21.1		23	Lees Summit Reed Wildlife Refuge	17.5
24	Mountain Grove 2 N	20.8		23	Saverton Lock & Dam 22	17.5
25	Arcadia	*20.7*		25	Fulton	17.6

Number of Annual Heating Degree Days

	Highest				Lowest	
Rank	Station Name	Num.		Rank	Station Name	Num.
1	Maryville 2 E	6,246		1	Kennett Radio KBOA	3,823
2	Hamilton 2 W	6,053		2	Caruthersville	3,917
3	Conception	6,020		3	Portageville	3,997
4	Spickard	5,978		4	New Madrid	4,154
5	Princeton 6 SW	5,865		5	Jackson	4,213
6	Bethany	5,847		6	Joplin Municipal Airport	4,241
7	Grant City	*5,811*		7	Neosho	4,245
8	Kirksville	5,767		8	Wappapello Dam	*4,268*
9	Hannibal Water Works	5,582		9	Anderson	4,278
10	Steffenville	5,549		10	Cape Girardeau Municipal Airport	4,295
11	Mexico	5,519		11	Lockwood	4,402
12	Canton Lock & Dam 20	5,512		12	Ozark Beach	4,433
13	Brunswick	5,485		13	Advance 1 S	4,457
14	Sedalia Water Plant	5,387		14	Doniphan	4,458
15	Salisbury	5,378		15	Summersville	*4,469*
16	Brookfield	5,321		16	Marble Hill	4,479
17	Fulton	5,310		17	Galena 1 SW	4,494
17	Steelville 2 N	5,310		17	West Plains	4,494
19	Lexington 3 NE	5,291		19	Lebanon 2 W	4,508
20	Saverton Lock & Dam 22	5,288		19	Monett 4 SW	*4,508*
21	Vandalia	5,274		21	Willow Springs Radio KUKU	4,527
22	Kansas City Int'l Airport	5,267		22	Dora	4,532
23	Windsor	5,264		23	Osceola	4,545
24	Boonville	5,179		24	Arcadia	*4,560*
25	Carrollton	5,156		25	Springfield Regional Airport	4,561

Number of Annual Cooling Degree Days

	Highest			Lowest	
Rank	**Station Name**	**Num.**	**Rank**	**Station Name**	**Num.**
1	Kennett Radio KBOA	1,844	1	Princeton 6 SW	1,025
2	Portageville	1,747	2	Maryville 2 E	1,032
3	New Madrid	1,728	3	Hamilton 2 W	1,056
4	Caruthersville	1,708	4	Steelville 2 N	1,057
5	Saint Louis Lambert Int'l Arpt.	1,668	5	Spickard	1,073
6	Joplin Municipal Airport	1,667	6	Kirksville	1,084
7	Jackson	1,651	7	Mansfield	*1,095*
8	Cape Girardeau Municipal Airport	1,641	8	Conception	1,105
9	Stockton Dam	1,554	9	Grant City	*1,119*
10	Osceola	1,545	10	Brunswick	1,133
11	Lockwood	1,540	11	Bethany	1,134
12	Butler	1,528	12	Farmington	1,155
13	California	1,505	13	Sedalia Water Plant	1,163
14	Nevada Water Plant	1,474	14	Fulton	1,167
15	Moberly	1,462	15	Mountain Grove 2 N	1,189
16	Union	1,457	16	Licking 4 N	1,195
17	Neosho	1,456	17	Arcadia	*1,196*
18	Clearwater Dam	*1,434*	18	Waynesville 2 W	1,203
19	Rolla Univ. of Missouri	1,428	19	Vienna 2 WNW	1,209
19	Sweet Springs	1,428	20	Fredericktown	1,212
21	Springfield Regional Airport	1,421	21	Hannibal Water Works	1,217
22	Doniphan	1,420	22	Steffenville	1,218
23	Advance 1 S	1,417	23	Salisbury	1,227
23	Boonville	1,417	24	Lexington 3 NE	1,228
25	Carrollton	1,416	25	Freedom	1,236

Annual Precipitation

	Highest			Lowest	
Rank	**Station Name**	**Inches**	**Rank**	**Station Name**	**Inches**
1	New Madrid	50.24	1	Grant City	35.06
2	Caruthersville	50.16	2	Maryville 2 E	36.07
3	Doniphan	49.71	3	Princeton 6 SW	36.28
4	Kennett Radio KBOA	49.69	4	Steffenville	36.71
5	Marble Hill	48.62	5	Conception	37.09
6	Lamar	48.49	6	Spickard	37.12
7	Wappapello Dam	47.93	7	Hamilton 2 W	37.17
8	Arcadia	*47.90*	8	Kirksville	37.86
9	Jackson	47.73	9	Saverton Lock & Dam 22	37.94
10	Portageville	47.58	10	Bethany	37.97
11	Advance 1 S	46.96	11	Elsberry 1 S	38.36
12	Cape Girardeau Municipal Airport	46.94	12	Brunswick	38.66
13	West Plains	46.57	12	Kansas City Int'l Airport	38.66
14	Lockwood	46.43	14	Saint Louis Lambert Int'l Arpt.	38.71
15	Clearwater Dam	46.26	15	Canton Lock & Dam 20	38.94
16	Joplin Municipal Airport	46.23	16	New Franklin 1 W	39.01
17	Monett 4 SW	*46.08*	17	Jefferson City Water Plant	39.81
18	Cassville Ranger Station	45.94	18	Vandalia	39.82
19	Neosho	45.92	19	Brookfield	39.85
20	Mountain Grove 2 N	45.88	20	Mexico	40.28
21	Bolivar 1 NE	45.83	21	California	40.31
22	Licking 4 N	45.52	22	Moberly	40.34
23	Galena 1 SW	45.49	23	Lexington 3 NE	40.36
24	Mount Vernon M U SW Center	45.47	24	Columbia Regional Airport	40.42
25	Fredericktown	45.39	25	Hannibal Water Works	40.64

Number of Days Annually With ≥ 0.1″ Precipitation

	Highest			Lowest	
Rank	**Station Name**	**Days**	**Rank**	**Station Name**	**Days**
1	Caruthersville	76	1	Grant City	61
1	Marble Hill	76	1	Kirksville	61
3	Arcadia	*75*	1	Summersville	61
3	Cape Girardeau Municipal Airport	75	4	Cassville Ranger Station	62
3	Jackson	75	4	Dora	*62*
6	Doniphan	74	6	Bethany	63
6	Kennett Radio KBOA	74	7	Conception	64
6	Licking 4 N	74	7	Eldon	64
6	New Madrid	74	7	Maryville 2 E	64
6	Portageville	74	7	Willow Springs Radio KUKU	64
6	Union	74	11	Hamilton 2 W	65
6	Waynesville 2 W	74	11	Kansas City Int'l Airport	65
13	Mexico	73	11	Pomme De Terre Dam	65
13	Rolla Univ. of Missouri	73	11	Spickard	65
15	Elsberry 1 S	72	11	Steffenville	65
15	Farmington	72	16	Anderson	66
15	Lamar	72	16	Appleton City	66
15	West Plains	72	16	Billings 2 N	*66*
19	Advance 1 S	71	16	Lebanon 2 W	66
19	Fulton	71	16	Princeton 6 SW	66
19	Hannibal Water Works	71	16	Vandalia	*66*
19	Marshfield	71	22	Brunswick	67
19	Mountain Grove 2 N	71	22	California	67
19	Salisbury	71	22	Carrollton	67
19	Springfield Regional Airport	71	22	Columbia Regional Airport	67

Number of Days Annually With ≥ 1.0″ Precipitation

	Highest			Lowest	
Rank	**Station Name**	**Days**	**Rank**	**Station Name**	**Days**
1	New Madrid	15	1	Canton Lock & Dam 20	8
2	Advance 1 S	14	1	Kansas City Int'l Airport	8
2	Doniphan	14	1	Princeton 6 SW	8
2	Dora	14	4	Appleton City	9
2	Kennett Radio KBOA	14	4	Brunswick	9
2	Wappapello Dam	14	4	Carrollton	9
7	Caruthersville	13	4	Conception	9
7	Fredericktown	13	4	Hamilton 2 W	9
7	Galena 1 SW	13	4	Lexington 3 NE	9
7	Jackson	13	4	Pomme De Terre Dam	9
7	Lamar	13	4	Saint Louis Lambert Int'l Arpt.	9
7	Licking 4 N	13	4	Spickard	9
7	Mansfield	13	13	Bethany	10
7	Marble Hill	13	13	Billings 2 N	10
7	Mount Vernon M U SW Center	13	13	Brookfield	10
7	Neosho	13	13	Columbia Regional Airport	10
7	Nevada Water Plant	13	13	Eldon	10
7	Ozark Beach	13	13	Elsberry 1 S	10
7	West Plains	13	13	Grant City	10
20	Anderson	12	13	Jefferson City Water Plant	10
20	Boonville	12	13	Kirksville	10
20	Cape Girardeau Municipal Airport	12	13	Lakeside	10
20	Cassville Ranger Station	12	13	Lebanon 2 W	10
20	Clearwater Dam	12	13	Lees Summit Reed Wildlife Refuge	10
20	Joplin Municipal Airport	12	13	Mexico	10

Annual Snowfall

	Highest				Lowest	
Rank	**Station Name**	**Inches**		**Rank**	**Station Name**	**Inches**
1	Bethany	25.5		1	New Madrid	*4.3*
2	Columbia Regional Airport	*25.3*		2	Caruthersville	*4.9*
3	Grant City	23.8		3	Wappapello Dam	*6.3*
4	Sweet Springs	23.6		4	Stockton Dam	*8.4*
5	Carrollton	22.8		5	Kennett Radio KBOA	8.8
5	Hannibal Water Works	22.8		6	Portageville	9.7
7	Fulton	22.7		7	Advance 1 S	9.8
8	Mexico	22.5		8	Butler	*10.0*
9	Boonville	22.0		8	Hamilton 2 W	*10.0*
10	Conception	21.9		10	Ozark Beach	10.3
11	Saint Louis Lambert Int'l Arpt.	21.6		11	Cassville Ranger Station	*10.9*
12	Salisbury	21.2		11	Willow Springs Radio KUKU	*10.9*
13	Steffenville	20.7		13	Lakeside	*11.1*
14	Rolla Univ. of Missouri	*20.4*		14	Saverton Lock & Dam 22	*11.4*
15	Elsberry 1 S	20.2		15	Sedalia Water Plant	*11.8*
15	Waynesville 2 W	20.2		16	Doniphan	12.1
17	Kansas City Int'l Airport	20.1		17	West Plains	12.5
18	Springfield Regional Airport	20.0		18	Dora	12.7
19	Kirksville	19.9		18	Lamar	*12.7*
20	Vandalia	*19.6*		20	Monett 4 SW	*12.8*
21	Lexington 3 NE	18.7		20	Neosho	12.8
22	Billings 2 N	18.5		22	California	13.0
22	Moberly	*18.5*		22	Cape Girardeau Municipal Airport	13.0
24	Union	18.4		24	Farmington	*13.1*
25	Vienna 2 WNW	17.5		24	Joplin Municipal Airport	13.1

Note: See Appendix D for explanation of data.

Annual Extreme Maximum Temperature

	Highest				Lowest	
Rank	Station Name	°F		Rank	Station Name	°F
1	Brandenberg	111		1	Mystic Lake	91
1	Loma 1 WNW	111		2	Hebgen Dam	92
1	Terry	111		2	Lennep 5 SW	92
4	Brockway 3 WSW	110		4	Melville 4 W	93
4	Glendive	110		4	Wisdom	93
4	Miles City Municipal Airport	110		6	Lakeview	94
4	Mizpah 4 NNW	110		6	Lima	94
4	Plevna	110		8	Alder 17 S	95
4	Redstone	110		8	Wilsall 8 ENE	95
10	Biddle 8 SW	109		10	Ennis	96
10	Circle	109		10	Libby 32 SSE	96
10	Cohagen	109		10	Neihart 8 NNW	96
10	Culbertson	109		13	Babb 6 NE	97
10	Jordan	109		13	Bozeman Montana State Univ.	97
10	Malta 35 S	109		13	Butte Bert Mooney Airport	97
10	Powderville 8 NNE	109		13	Creston	97
10	Roundup	*109*		13	Del Bonita	97
10	Savage	109		13	Martinsdale 3 NNW	97
10	Wibaux 2 E	109		13	Philipsburg Ranger Station	97
20	Birney	108		13	Polebridge	*97*
20	Bredette	108		13	Red Lodge 2 N	97
20	Broadus	108		13	Twin Bridges	97
20	Fort Assinniboine	108		23	Bozeman 6 W Exp. Farm	98
20	Glasgow Int'l Airport	108		23	Divide	98
20	Hysham 25 SSE	108		23	Gibson Dam	98

Annual Mean Maximum Temperature

	Highest				Lowest	
Rank	Station Name	°F		Rank	Station Name	°F
1	Yellowtail Dam	63.7		1	Hebgen Dam	49.3
2	Billings Water Plant	63.0		2	Lennep 5 SW	51.4
3	Birney	62.1		3	Opheim 12 SSE	51.6
4	Roundup	*61.6*		3	Wisdom	51.6
5	Hysham	61.1		5	Westby	*52.3*
6	Columbus	60.9		6	Del Bonita	52.6
6	Forsyth	*60.9*		6	Lindbergh Lake	52.6
8	Joliet	60.8		6	Mystic Lake	52.6
8	Thompson Falls	60.8		6	Opheim 10 N	52.6
8	Wyola 1 SW	60.8		10	Lima	52.9
11	Bridger 1 S	*60.6*		11	Bredette	53.2
11	Melstone	60.6		11	Cut Bank Municipal Airport	53.2
13	Brandenberg	60.4		13	Butte Bert Mooney Airport	53.3
13	Grass Range	60.4		13	West Glacier	53.3
15	Big Timber	60.3		15	Austin 1 W	53.4
15	Fort Benton	60.3		16	Hungry Horse Dam	53.5
17	Flatwillow 4 ENE	60.2		16	Libby 32 SSE	53.5
17	Loma 1 WNW	60.2		16	Melville 4 W	53.5
17	Mosby 2 ENE	*60.2*		19	Polebridge	53.7
17	Powderville 8 NNE	60.2		20	Raymond Border Station	53.8
21	Ingomar 14 NE	60.0		21	Divide	53.9
21	Jordan	*60.0*		22	Judith Gap 13 E	54.1
23	Rapelje 4 S	59.9		23	Gibson Dam	54.2
24	Superior	59.8		23	Wilsall 8 ENE	54.2
25	Biddle 8 SW	59.7		25	Alder 17 S	54.3

Annual Mean Temperature

Rank	Highest Station Name	°F	Rank	Lowest Station Name	°F
1	Yellowtail Dam	50.9	1	Wisdom	35.8
2	Billings Water Plant	48.5	2	Hebgen Dam	36.5
3	Holter Dam	47.9	3	Opheim 12 SSE	38.9
3	Thompson Falls	47.9	4	Polebridge	*39.0*
5	Roundup	*47.4*	5	Opheim 10 N	39.1
6	Billings Logan Int'l Airport	47.3	6	Lima	39.2
7	Melstone	47.1	7	Lennep 5 SW	39.3
8	Hysham	47.0	8	Butte Bert Mooney Airport	39.5
8	Norris Madison Pump HS	47.0	9	Westby	*39.9*
10	Big Timber	46.8	10	Libby 32 SSE	40.4
10	Bridger 1 S	*46.8*	11	Del Bonita	40.6
10	Forsyth	*46.8*	12	Redstone	40.7
10	Superior	46.8	13	Divide	40.9
14	Mosby 2 ENE	*46.6*	13	Melville 4 W	40.9
15	Polson Kerr Dam	46.4	15	Judith Gap 13 E	41.0
16	Birney	46.3	15	Lincoln Ranger Station	41.0
16	Colstrip	46.3	17	Raymond Border Station	41.2
16	Joliet	46.3	18	Cut Bank Municipal Airport	41.3
16	Libby 1 NE	46.3	18	Seeley Lake Ranger Station	41.3
20	Columbus	46.2	20	Wilsall 8 ENE	41.4
20	Miles City Municipal Airport	46.2	21	Alder 17 S	41.5
22	Brandenberg	46.1	21	Forks 4 NNE	*41.5*
22	Darby	46.1	21	Lindbergh Lake	41.5
22	Flatwillow 4 ENE	46.1	21	Sula 3 ENE	41.5
25	Fort Benton	46.0	25	Austin 1 W	41.6

Annual Mean Minimum Temperature

Rank	Highest Station Name	°F	Rank	Lowest Station Name	°F
1	Yellowtail Dam	38.0	1	Wisdom	19.8
2	Holter Dam	36.7	2	Hebgen Dam	23.8
3	Billings Logan Int'l Airport	36.0	3	Polebridge	*24.3*
4	Norris Madison Pump HS	35.8	4	Lima	25.5
5	Polson Kerr Dam	35.7	4	Opheim 10 N	25.5
6	Thompson Falls	35.0	4	Sula 3 ENE	25.5
7	Miles City Municipal Airport	34.3	7	Butte Bert Mooney Airport	25.7
8	Billings Water Plant	34.0	8	Opheim 12 SSE	26.2
9	Superior	33.9	9	Redstone	26.5
10	Saint Ignatius	33.8	10	Lincoln Ranger Station	27.0
11	Livingston Mission Field	33.6	11	Lennep 5 SW	27.2
11	Missoula 2 NE	33.6	12	Denton 1 NNE	27.4
13	Melstone	33.5	12	Libby 32 SSE	27.4
14	Canyon Ferry Dam	33.4	12	Westby	*27.4*
15	Big Timber	33.3	15	Simpson 6 NW	27.5
16	Eureka Ranger Station	33.2	16	Chester	27.7
16	Roundup	33.2	16	Saco 1 NNW	27.7
18	Heron 2 NW	33.1	18	Divide	27.8
18	Libby 1 NE	33.1	18	Judith Gap 13 E	27.8
20	Choteau	33.0	18	Seeley Lake Ranger Station	27.8
20	Mosby 2 ENE	*33.0*	21	Culbertson	27.9
22	Colstrip	32.9	21	Philipsburg Ranger Station	27.9
22	Fort Peck Power Plant	32.9	23	Boulder	28.2
22	Glendive	32.9	23	Cascade 20 SSE	28.2
22	Great Falls Int'l Airport	32.9	23	Conrad	28.2

Annual Extreme Minimum Temperature

Highest				Lowest		
Rank	**Station Name**	**°F**		**Rank**	**Station Name**	**°F**
1	Polson Kerr Dam	-22		1	Wisdom	-55
2	Hungry Horse Dam	-26		2	Ingomar 14 NE	-54
3	Superior	-28		2	Loma 1 WNW	-54
4	Missoula 2 NE	-30		4	Busby	-52
4	Missoula Johnson-Bell Field	-30		4	Butte Bert Mooney Airport	-52
4	Norris Madison Pump HS	-30		4	Chester	-52
4	Saint Ignatius	-30		4	Redstone	-52
4	Thompson Falls	-30		8	Malta 35 S	*-51*
9	Hamilton	-31		8	Ridgeway 1 S	-51
9	Libby 1 NE	*-31*		10	Big Sandy	-50
11	Billings Logan Int'l Airport	-32		10	Denton 1 NNE	-50
11	Bozeman Montana State Univ.	-32		10	Havre City-County Airport	-50
11	Canyon Ferry Dam	*-32*		10	Hysham 25 SSE	-50
11	Ennis	-32		14	Content 3 SSE	-49
11	West Glacier	-32		14	Mizpah 4 NNW	-49
11	Western Agr. Research Station	-32		14	Plevna	-49
11	Yellowtail Dam	-32		17	Culbertson	-48
18	Creston	-33		17	Joplin	*-48*
18	Heron 2 NW	-33		17	Lincoln Ranger Station	-48
18	Trout Creek Ranger Station	-33		17	Opheim 10 N	-48
21	Darby	-34		17	Polebridge	*-48*
22	Divide	-35		17	Saco 1 NNW	-48
22	Eureka Ranger Station	-35		17	Sun River 4 S	-48
22	Fairfield	-35		24	Augusta	-47
22	Stevensville	-35		24	Babb 6 NE	-47

July Mean Maximum Temperature

Highest				Lowest		
Rank	**Station Name**	**°F**		**Rank**	**Station Name**	**°F**
1	Powderville 8 NNE	89.9		1	Mystic Lake	74.7
1	Yellowtail Dam	89.9		2	Lennep 5 SW	75.5
3	Birney	89.5		3	Melville 4 W	75.6
4	Mizpah 4 NNW	89.3		4	Babb 6 NE	75.7
5	Brandenberg	89.1		5	Lakeview	76.0
6	Jordan	88.8		6	Del Bonita	76.2
7	Billings Water Plant	88.3		7	Gibson Dam	76.9
7	Plevna	88.3		8	Judith Gap 13 E	77.1
9	Forsyth	*88.2*		9	Cut Bank Municipal Airport	77.7
9	Glendive	88.2		9	Hebgen Dam	77.7
11	Ingomar 14 NE	88.1		9	Lindbergh Lake	77.7
12	Hysham	87.8		12	Libby 32 SSE	77.8
12	Miles City Municipal Airport	87.8		12	Wisdom	77.8
12	Mosby 2 ENE	87.8		14	Wilsall 8 ENE	78.2
15	Melstone	87.7		15	Neihart 8 NNW	78.4
16	Terry	87.5		16	Polebridge	78.5
17	Busby	87.3		17	Red Lodge 2 N	78.6
18	Cohagen	87.2		17	West Glacier	78.6
18	Hysham 25 SSE	87.2		19	Divide	78.7
18	Roundup	*87.2*		20	Alder 17 S	78.9
21	Savage	87.1		20	Austin 1 W	78.9
22	Bridger 1 S	87.0		22	Lima	79.2
23	Loma 1 WNW	86.9		22	Philipsburg Ranger Station	79.2
23	Thompson Falls	86.9		24	Martinsdale 3 NNW	*79.4*
25	Biddle 8 SW	86.8		25	Butte Bert Mooney Airport	79.5

January Mean Minimum Temperature

	Highest			Lowest	
Rank	**Station Name**	**°F**	**Rank**	**Station Name**	**°F**
1	Thompson Falls	21.1	1	Westby	-4.5
2	Polson Kerr Dam	20.2	2	Opheim 10 N	-2.9
3	Heron 2 NW	19.7	3	Redstone	-2.7
4	Trout Creek Ranger Station	19.6	4	Opheim 12 SSE	-2.1
5	Superior	19.5	5	Saco 1 NNW	-1.7
6	Norris Madison Pump HS	19.2	6	Culbertson	-1.6
7	Saint Ignatius	18.8	7	Raymond Border Station	-1.1
8	Holter Dam	18.6	8	Medicine Lake 3 SE	-1.0
9	Darby	18.3	9	Lakeview	*-0.5*
10	Yellowtail Dam	18.0	10	Terry	0.5
11	Libby 1 NE	17.9	11	Forks 4 NNE	0.7
12	Livingston Mission Field	17.8	12	Malta 7 E	1.1
13	Hamilton	17.4	13	Simpson 6 NW	1.3
14	Missoula 2 NE	17.3	14	Bredette	1.4
15	Stevensville	16.9	15	Glasgow Int'l Airport	1.5
16	Mystic Lake	16.8	16	Wibaux 2 E	1.6
17	Missoula Johnson-Bell Field	16.3	17	Wisdom	1.7
18	Hungry Horse Dam	15.9	18	Vida 6 NE	2.2
19	Big Timber	15.8	19	Sidney	2.4
20	West Glacier	15.3	20	Hebgen Dam	2.7
21	Creston	15.1	20	Mizpah 4 NNW	2.7
22	Eureka Ranger Station	15.0	22	Plevna	2.9
23	Ennis	14.9	23	Circle	3.1
24	Billings Logan Int'l Airport	14.6	24	Savage	3.2
25	Philipsburg Ranger Station	14.0	25	Chester	3.5

Number of Annual Heating Degree Days

	Highest			Lowest	
Rank	**Station Name**	**Num.**	**Rank**	**Station Name**	**Num.**
1	Wisdom	10,582	1	Yellowtail Dam	5,883
2	Hebgen Dam	10,309	2	Billings Water Plant	6,503
3	Opheim 12 SSE	9,655	3	Thompson Falls	6,516
4	Opheim 10 N	9,612	4	Holter Dam	6,559
5	Polebridge	*9,433*	5	Superior	6,829
5	Westby	*9,433*	6	Norris Madison Pump HS	6,846
7	Lima	9,364	7	Roundup	*6,854*
8	Lennep 5 SW	9,322	8	Big Timber	6,921
9	Butte Bert Mooney Airport	9,276	9	Billings Logan Int'l Airport	6,958
10	Redstone	9,132	10	Polson Kerr Dam	6,984
11	Raymond Border Station	9,001	11	Bridger 1 S	*7,009*
12	Libby 32 SSE	8,907	12	Melstone	7,026
13	Del Bonita	8,900	13	Darby	7,035
14	Forks 4 NNE	*8,867*	14	Libby 1 NE	7,041
15	Bredette	8,838	15	Hysham	7,050
16	Divide	8,780	16	Trout Creek Ranger Station	7,053
17	Melville 4 W	8,747	17	Saint Ignatius	7,083
18	Judith Gap 13 E	8,742	18	Joliet	7,102
18	Saco 1 NNW	8,742	19	Hamilton	7,132
20	Lincoln Ranger Station	8,735	20	Columbus	7,140
21	Simpson 6 NW	*8,700*	21	Western Agr. Research Station	7,150
22	Cut Bank Municipal Airport	8,684	22	Forsyth	*7,153*
23	Culbertson	8,666	23	Livingston Mission Field	7,181
24	Seeley Lake Ranger Station	8,653	24	Cascade 5 S	7,202
25	Medicine Lake 3 SE	8,649	25	Fort Benton	7,211

Number of Annual Cooling Degree Days

	Highest			Lowest	
Rank	**Station Name**	**Num.**	**Rank**	**Station Name**	**Num.**
1	Yellowtail Dam	855	1	Wisdom	6
2	Miles City Municipal Airport	806	2	Hebgen Dam	16
3	Glendive	743	3	Libby 32 SSE	17
4	Powderville 8 NNE	726	4	Polebridge	32
5	Mizpah 4 NNW	696	5	Lennep 5 SW	38
6	Fort Peck Power Plant	663	5	Sula 3 ENE	38
6	Savage	663	7	Lima	43
8	Jordan	636	8	Gibson Dam	59
9	Billings Logan Int'l Airport	628	9	Lincoln Ranger Station	60
10	Forsyth	626	10	Philipsburg Ranger Station	61
11	Billings Water Plant	621	11	Melville 4 W	63
12	Birney	610	12	Divide	76
13	Brandenberg	608	13	Wilsall 8 ENE	77
13	Melstone	608	14	Alder 17 S	78
15	Plevna	604	14	Butte Bert Mooney Airport	78
16	Terry	600	16	Cascade 20 SSE	81
17	Hysham	586	17	Martinsdale 3 NNW	*84*
18	Circle	578	18	Judith Gap 13 E	86
19	Broadus	575	19	Seeley Lake Ranger Station	91
20	Sidney	568	20	Lindbergh Lake	100
21	Biddle 8 SW	551	21	Austin 1 W	105
22	Ingomar 14 NE	547	22	Neihart 8 NNW	107
23	Glasgow Int'l Airport	544	22	Twin Bridges	107
24	Hinsdale 4 SW	530	24	Virginia City	109
25	Cohagen	528	24	West Glacier	109

Annual Precipitation

	Highest			Lowest	
Rank	**Station Name**	**Inches**	**Rank**	**Station Name**	**Inches**
1	Heron 2 NW	*33.44*	1	Twin Bridges	9.89
2	Hebgen Dam	*29.35*	2	Joplin	10.33
3	Trout Creek Ranger Station	29.33	3	Choteau	*10.36*
4	West Glacier	*28.58*	4	Glasgow Int'l Airport	*10.57*
5	Lindbergh Lake	26.45	5	Tiber Dam	10.71
6	Red Lodge 2 N	*25.77*	6	Townsend	10.75
7	Mystic Lake	*25.09*	7	Simpson 6 NW	10.88
8	Libby 32 SSE	24.72	8	Chester	11.05
9	Thompson Falls	*22.45*	9	Fort Peck Power Plant	*11.18*
10	Neihart 8 NNW	21.43	10	Gildford	11.23
11	Polebridge	21.20	11	Havre City-County Airport	*11.42*
12	Seeley Lake Ranger Station	21.10	12	Helena Airport ASOS	*11.44*
13	Wilsall 8 ENE	21.05	13	Brockway 3 WSW	11.47
14	Lakeview	19.86	13	Rock Springs	11.47
15	Bozeman Montana State Univ.	*18.96*	15	Canyon Ferry Dam	11.53
16	Lincoln Ranger Station	18.87	16	Boulder	11.66
17	Libby 1 NE	18.65	17	Opheim 12 SSE	11.85
18	Raynesford 2 NNW	18.44	18	Wisdom	11.87
19	Lewistown Municipal Airport	17.98	19	Saco 1 NNW	11.88
20	Melville 4 W	17.80	20	Content 3 SSE	12.04
21	Norris Madison Pump HS	*17.45*	21	Holter Dam	12.17
22	Stanford	17.27	22	Ingomar 14 NE	12.23
23	Ekalaka	17.16	22	Opheim 10 N	12.23
23	Missoula 2 NE	17.16	24	Cohagen	12.26
25	Wyola 1 SW	17.12	25	Conrad	12.30

Number of Days Annually With ≥ 0.1″ Precipitation

	Highest			Lowest	
Rank	Station Name	Days	Rank	Station Name	Days
1	Heron 2 NW	92	1	Glasgow Int'l Airport	28
2	Hebgen Dam	88	1	Tiber Dam	28
3	Lindbergh Lake	*84*	3	Brockway 3 WSW	29
3	West Glacier	84	3	Fort Peck Power Plant	29
5	Trout Creek Ranger Station	82	5	Choteau	30
6	Hungry Horse Dam	81	5	Gildford	30
7	Mystic Lake	75	5	Joplin	30
8	Libby 32 SSE	74	5	Opheim 12 SSE	30
9	Thompson Falls	69	5	Rock Springs	30
10	Polebridge	66	5	Saco 1 NNW	30
11	Seeley Lake Ranger Station	65	5	Simpson 6 NW	30
12	Creston	64	12	Cut Bank Municipal Airport	31
13	Wilsall 8 ENE	62	12	Twin Bridges	31
14	Lincoln Ranger Station	61	14	Dillon	32
15	Neihart 8 NNW	60	14	Forks 4 NNE	*32*
16	Red Lodge 2 N	59	14	Malta 35 S	32
17	Libby 1 NE	57	14	Malta 7 E	32
18	Kalispell Airport	55	14	Opheim 10 N	32
19	Bozeman Montana State Univ.	54	14	Savage	32
19	Lennep 5 SW	54	14	Townsend	32
21	Austin 1 W	53	14	Vida 6 NE	32
21	Sula 3 ENE	53	22	Canyon Ferry Dam	33
23	Darby	52	22	Chester	33
23	Fortine 1 N	*52*	22	Fairfield	33
23	Missoula 2 NE	52	22	Holter Dam	33

Number of Days Annually With ≥ 1.0″ Precipitation

	Highest			Lowest	
Rank	Station Name	Days	Rank	Station Name	Days
1	Heron 2 NW	3	1	Alder 17 S	0
2	Babb 6 NE	2	1	Austin 1 W	0
2	Big Sandy	2	1	Biddle 8 SW	0
2	Carlyle 12 NW	2	1	Billings Logan Int'l Airport	0
2	Culbertson	2	1	Billings Water Plant	0
2	Del Bonita	2	1	Birney	0
2	Hinsdale 4 SW	2	1	Boulder	0
2	Neihart 8 NNW	2	1	Bozeman 6 W Exp. Farm	0
2	Red Lodge 2 N	2	1	Bozeman Gallatin Field	0
2	Sweetgrass	2	1	Bozeman Montana State Univ.	0
2	Trout Creek Ranger Station	2	1	Brandenberg	0
2	Westby	2	1	Bredette	0
13	Augusta	1	1	Broadus	0
13	Big Timber	1	1	Busby	0
13	Bridger 1 S	*1*	1	Butte Bert Mooney Airport	0
13	Brockway 3 WSW	1	1	Canyon Ferry Dam	0
13	Columbus	1	1	Cascade 20 SSE	0
13	Ekalaka	1	1	Cascade 5 S	0
13	Forks 4 NNE	*1*	1	Chester	0
13	Forsyth	*1*	1	Choteau	0
13	Fort Peck Power Plant	1	1	Circle	0
13	Geraldine	1	1	Cohagen	0
13	Gibson Dam	1	1	Colstrip	0
13	Gildford	1	1	Conrad	0
13	Goldbutte 7 N	1	1	Content 3 SSE	*0*

Annual Snowfall

	Highest			Lowest	
Rank	Station Name	Inches	Rank	Station Name	Inches
1	Lindbergh Lake	152.7	1	Mosby 2 ENE	*26.2*
2	Wilsall 8 ENE	104.3	2	Forks 4 NNE	*28.6*
3	Libby 32 SSE	98.4	3	Birney	*29.1*
4	Del Bonita	68.9	4	Westby	*29.3*
5	Raynesford 2 NNW	*64.2*	5	Mizpah 4 NNW	29.4
6	Joliet	58.1	6	Cohagen	31.0
7	Hysham 25 SSE	57.5	7	Malta 35 S	*35.8*
8	Missoula 2 NE	56.0	8	Ingomar 14 NE	38.9
9	Alder 17 S	*55.4*	8	Ridgeway 1 S	*38.9*
10	Carlyle 12 NW	49.7	10	Hysham	*40.3*
11	Bozeman Gallatin Field	*44.4*	11	Drummond	41.4
12	Brandenberg	44.1	12	Biddle 8 SW	*42.1*
13	Ryegate 18 NNW	43.1	13	Ryegate 18 NNW	43.1
14	Biddle 8 SW	*42.1*	14	Brandenberg	44.1
15	Drummond	41.4	15	Bozeman Gallatin Field	*44.4*
16	Hysham	*40.3*	16	Carlyle 12 NW	49.7
17	Ingomar 14 NE	38.9	17	Alder 17 S	*55.4*
17	Ridgeway 1 S	*38.9*	18	Missoula 2 NE	56.0
19	Malta 35 S	*35.8*	19	Hysham 25 SSE	57.5
20	Cohagen	31.0	20	Joliet	58.1
21	Mizpah 4 NNW	29.4	21	Raynesford 2 NNW	*64.2*
22	Westby	*29.3*	22	Del Bonita	68.9
23	Birney	*29.1*	23	Libby 32 SSE	98.4
24	Forks 4 NNE	*28.6*	24	Wilsall 8 ENE	104.3
25	Mosby 2 ENE	*26.2*	25	Lindbergh Lake	152.7

Note: See Appendix D for explanation of data.

Annual Extreme Maximum Temperature

	Highest				Lowest	
Rank	**Station Name**	**°F**		**Rank**	**Station Name**	**°F**
1	Valentine Miller Field	114		1	Dalton	103
2	Beaver City	112		2	Crescent Lake Nat'l Wildlife Ref	104
2	Fairbury	112		2	Harrisburg 10 NW	104
4	Cambridge	111		2	Harrison	104
4	Red Cloud	111		2	Madison 2 W	104
6	Alliance 1 WNW	110		6	Central City	105
6	Ashland 2	110		6	Fairmont	105
6	Auburn 5 ESE	110		6	Hyannis	*105*
6	Benkelman	110		6	Kimball 2 N	105
6	Columbus 3 NE	110		6	Loup City	105
6	Curtis 3 NNE	*110*		6	North Loup	105
6	Enders Lake	110		6	Oakdale	105
6	Grand Island Airport	110		6	Saint Paul 4 N	105
6	Hay Springs	*110*		6	Stanton	105
6	Hebron	110		15	Albion 1 N	106
6	Hershey 5 SSE	*110*		15	Arthur	106
6	O'Neill	110		15	Big Springs	106
6	Omaha Eppley Airfield	110		15	Broken Bow 2 W	106
6	Pawnee City	110		15	Clarkson	106
6	Springview	110		15	Crete	106
6	Tekamah	110		15	David City	106
6	Trenton Dam	110		15	Ellsworth 15 NNE	106
23	Anselmo 2 SE	109		15	Ewing	106
23	Atkinson	109		15	Geneva	106
23	Brewster	109		15	Mullen 21 NW	106

Annual Mean Maximum Temperature

	Highest				Lowest	
Rank	**Station Name**	**°F**		**Rank**	**Station Name**	**°F**
1	Beaver City	68.4		1	Harrison	57.3
2	Benkelman	66.0		2	Gavins Point Dam	*58.2*
3	Cambridge	65.8		3	Northeast Nebraska Exp. Station	58.3
3	Lodgepole	65.8		4	Springview	59.0
5	Pawnee City	65.3		5	Oakdale	59.7
6	Bridgeport	65.2		6	Ellsworth 15 NNE	59.8
7	Madrid	65.1		7	Hemingford	59.9
7	Superior	65.1		7	West Point	59.9
9	Curtis 3 NNE	*64.9*		9	Omaha WSFO	60.0
9	Trenton Dam	64.9		10	Mullen 21 NW	*60.1*
11	Culbertson	64.8		10	Newport	60.1
11	Imperial	64.8		12	Norfolk Karl Stefan Mem. Arpt.	60.2
13	Falls City Brenner Field	64.5		12	O'Neill	60.2
13	Minden	64.5		14	Blair	60.4
15	McCook	64.4		15	Clarkson	60.5
16	Red Cloud	64.2		16	Albion 1 N	60.6
17	Auburn 5 ESE	63.8		16	Madison 2 W	60.6
17	Enders Lake	*63.8*		18	Atkinson	60.8
19	Oshkosh	63.7		18	Valentine Miller Field	60.8
20	Medicine Creek Dam	63.6		18	Wakefield	60.8
21	Crete	63.5		21	Ainsworth	60.9
22	Harlan County Lake	63.4		21	Brewster	*60.9*
22	Hebron	63.4		21	Butte	60.9
22	Kingsley Dam	63.4		21	Columbus 3 NE	60.9
25	Fairbury	63.3		21	David City	60.9

Annual Mean Temperature

	Highest			Lowest	
Rank	**Station Name**	**°F**	**Rank**	**Station Name**	**°F**
1	Pawnee City	53.8	1	Harrison	44.3
2	Beaver City	53.1	2	Agate 3 E	*45.4*
2	Superior	53.1	3	Ellsworth 15 NNE	46.2
4	Falls City Brenner Field	52.7	4	Mullen 21 NW	*46.6*
5	Auburn 5 ESE	52.5	4	Northeast Nebraska Exp. Station	46.6
6	Crete	52.1	6	Hay Springs 12 S	46.7
7	Seward	52.0	7	Harrisburg 10 NW	46.9
8	Central City	51.8	7	Sidney 6 NNW	46.9
8	Geneva	51.8	9	Hay Springs	47.0
10	Minden	51.7	10	Valentine Miller Field	47.1
11	Hebron	51.6	11	Springview	47.2
11	Lincoln	51.6	12	Alliance 1 WNW	47.3
13	Cambridge	51.5	13	Brewster	*47.4*
14	Fremont	51.3	13	Gavins Point Dam	*47.4*
15	Fairbury	51.2	15	Hemingford	47.5
15	Fairmont	51.2	15	Kimball 2 N	47.5
15	Tecumseh	51.2	17	Oakdale	47.6
18	Hastings 4 N	51.1	18	Arthur	47.7
18	Imperial	51.1	18	Crescent Lake Nat'l Wildlife Ref	47.7
18	McCook	51.1	18	Merriman	47.7
18	York	51.1	21	Mitchell 5 E	*47.8*
22	Benkelman	51.0	22	Broken Bow 2 W	48.1
22	Lincoln Municipal Airport	51.0	22	Chadron Municipal Airport	48.1
22	Syracuse	51.0	22	O'Neill	48.1
25	Weeping Water	50.9	25	Albion 1 N	48.2

Annual Mean Minimum Temperature

	Highest			Lowest	
Rank	**Station Name**	**°F**	**Rank**	**Station Name**	**°F**
1	Pawnee City	42.3	1	Agate 3 E	*28.8*
2	Lincoln	41.4	2	Harrison	31.3
3	Auburn 5 ESE	41.2	3	Hay Springs 12 S	31.7
4	Superior	41.1	4	Harrisburg 10 NW	32.1
5	Falls City Brenner Field	41.0	5	Sidney 6 NNW	32.5
6	Omaha WSFO	40.8	6	Ellsworth 15 NNE	32.6
6	Seward	40.8	7	Mullen 21 NW	*33.0*
8	Crete	40.7	8	Hay Springs	33.1
9	Geneva	40.6	9	Kimball 2 N	33.2
10	Central City	40.3	10	Alliance 1 WNW	33.3
11	Fremont	39.9	10	Crescent Lake Nat'l Wildlife Ref	33.3
12	Hebron	39.8	12	Valentine Miller Field	33.4
12	Nebraska City	39.8	13	Mitchell 5 E	33.7
12	Omaha Eppley Airfield	39.8	13	Oshkosh	33.7
12	York	39.8	15	Arthur	33.8
16	Weeping Water	39.5	16	Brewster	*33.9*
17	Columbus 3 NE	39.4	17	Enders Lake	*34.2*
17	Lincoln Municipal Airport	39.4	18	Dalton	34.3
17	Tecumseh	39.4	18	Scottsbluff County Airport	34.3
20	Fairmont	39.3	20	Merriman	34.4
20	Hastings 4 N	39.3	21	Chadron Municipal Airport	34.5
22	Fairbury	39.0	21	North Platte Lee Bird Field	34.5
22	Syracuse	39.0	21	Wallace 2 W	34.5
24	Blair	38.9	24	Broken Bow 2 W	34.6
24	Minden	38.9	25	Anselmo 2 SE	34.7

Annual Extreme Minimum Temperature

	Highest				Lowest	
Rank	Station Name	°F		Rank	Station Name	°F
1	Hastings 4 N	-23		1	Oshkosh	-47
1	Nebraska City	-23		2	Crescent Lake Nat'l Wildlife Ref	-46
1	Omaha Eppley Airfield	-23		3	Agate 3 E	-44
4	Blair	-24		3	Harrisburg 10 NW	-44
4	Columbus 3 NE	-24		5	Alliance 1 WNW	-42
4	York	-24		5	Bridgeport	-42
7	Crete	-25		5	Ellsworth 15 NNE	-42
7	Kingsley Dam	-25		5	Hay Springs 12 S	-42
7	Omaha WSFO	-25		5	Scottsbluff County Airport	-42
7	Pawnee City	-25		10	Mitchell 5 E	-41
11	Central City	-26		11	Chadron Municipal Airport	-40
11	Fairbury	-26		12	Clay Center	-39
11	Fairmont	-26		12	Harrison	-39
11	Geneva	-26		12	Sidney 6 NNW	-39
11	Grand Island Airport	-26		12	Valentine Miller Field	-39
11	Hebron	-26		16	Enders Lake	-38
11	Loup City	-26		17	Big Springs	-37
11	Tekamah	-26		18	Merriman	-36
19	Auburn 5 ESE	-27		18	North Platte Exp. Farm	-36
19	Canaday Steam Plant	-27		18	Ogallala	-36
19	David City	-27		18	Red Cloud	-36
19	Fremont	-27		22	Brewster	-35
19	Hartington	-27		22	Cambridge	-35
19	Hayes Center	-27		22	Harlan County Lake	-35
19	Lincoln	*-27*		22	Hemingford	-35

July Mean Maximum Temperature

	Highest				Lowest	
Rank	Station Name	°F		Rank	Station Name	°F
1	Beaver City	93.9		1	Harrison	84.4
2	Lodgepole	91.7		2	Northeast Nebraska Exp. Station	85.3
3	Madrid	91.4		3	Ellsworth 15 NNE	85.6
4	Benkelman	91.2		4	Omaha WSFO	85.7
5	Bridgeport	90.9		5	Oakdale	85.8
6	Pawnee City	90.7		6	North Loup	85.9
7	Superior	90.6		7	Hemingford	86.1
8	Red Cloud	90.5		8	Blair	86.2
9	Culbertson	90.4		9	Gavins Point Dam	86.3
10	Cambridge	90.2		10	Harrisburg 10 NW	86.4
10	Curtis 3 NNE	90.2		10	Hay Springs	86.4
12	Falls City Brenner Field	90.1		10	Mullen 21 NW	86.4
12	Trenton Dam	90.1		10	Saint Paul 4 N	86.4
14	McCook	90.0		14	Hyannis	*86.5*
15	Imperial	89.8		14	Springview	86.5
16	Ogallala	89.7		16	Broken Bow 2 W	86.7
17	Hebron	89.6		17	West Point	86.8
17	Minden	89.6		18	Arthur	86.9
19	Enders Lake	89.5		18	Clarkson	86.9
19	Harlan County Lake	89.5		18	Crescent Lake Nat'l Wildlife Ref	86.9
21	Lincoln Municipal Airport	89.4		18	Mitchell 5 E	86.9
22	Seward	89.3		18	Norfolk Karl Stefan Mem. Arpt.	86.9
23	Fairbury	89.2		18	Valentine Lakes Game Refuge	86.9
23	Kingsley Dam	89.2		24	Albion 1 N	87.0
23	Syracuse	89.2		24	Ewing	87.0

January Mean Minimum Temperature

	Highest				Lowest	
Rank	**Station Name**	**°F**		**Rank**	**Station Name**	**°F**
1	Pawnee City	15.6		1	Northeast Nebraska Exp. Station	6.0
2	Kingsley Dam	15.1		2	Valentine Miller Field	7.2
3	Superior	15.0		3	Gavins Point Dam	7.3
4	Falls City Brenner Field	14.9		4	Agate 3 E	*7.6*
5	Imperial	14.4		4	Oakdale	7.6
6	Dalton	14.2		6	Brewster	8.2
7	Geneva	14.0		7	Osmond	8.4
8	Crete	13.9		8	Greeley	8.6
8	Hayes Center	13.9		8	West Point	8.6
8	Lincoln	13.9		10	Loup City	8.7
8	McCook	13.9		10	Madison 2 W	8.7
12	Auburn 5 ESE	13.7		10	Wakefield	8.7
12	Central City	13.7		13	Albion 1 N	8.9
12	Lodgepole	13.7		13	Ellsworth 15 NNE	8.9
12	Seward	13.7		15	Hay Springs 12 S	9.0
16	Hemingford	13.6		15	O'Neill	9.0
17	Hastings 4 N	13.3		17	Springview	9.1
18	Minden	13.2		18	Ewing	9.2
19	Holdrege	13.1		18	Harrison	9.2
20	Beaver City	12.9		20	Mullen 21 NW	9.3
20	Hebron	12.9		21	Clarkson	9.4
20	Kimball 2 N	12.9		22	Crescent Lake Nat'l Wildlife Ref	9.6
20	Madrid	12.9		22	Mead 6 S	9.6
24	York	12.8		22	Newport	9.6
25	Cambridge	12.6		25	Anselmo 2 SE	9.7

Number of Annual Heating Degree Days

	Highest				Lowest	
Rank	**Station Name**	**Num.**		**Rank**	**Station Name**	**Num.**
1	Harrison	7,865		1	Pawnee City	5,386
2	Agate 3 E	*7,455*		2	Beaver City	5,541
3	Northeast Nebraska Exp. Station	7,385		3	Superior	5,550
4	Ellsworth 15 NNE	7,313		4	Falls City Brenner Field	5,639
5	Mullen 21 NW	*7,228*		5	Auburn 5 ESE	5,742
6	Valentine Miller Field	7,213		6	Crete	5,781
7	Gavins Point Dam	*7,203*		7	Geneva	5,849
8	Springview	7,189		8	Minden	5,872
9	Hay Springs 12 S	7,145		9	Central City	5,874
10	Brewster	*7,078*		10	Seward	5,882
11	Oakdale	7,068		11	Cambridge	5,892
12	Hay Springs	7,051		12	Imperial	5,955
13	Sidney 6 NNW	7,033		13	Lincoln	5,989
14	Alliance 1 WNW	7,016		14	Hebron	6,003
15	Harrisburg 10 NW	6,992		15	McCook	6,010
16	O'Neill	6,982		16	Kingsley Dam	6,029
17	Merriman	6,974		17	Fairmont	6,043
18	Newport	6,925		18	Fremont	6,054
19	Arthur	6,905		19	Benkelman	6,064
20	Hemingford	6,896		20	Lodgepole	6,067
21	Albion 1 N	6,879		21	Fairbury	6,073
22	Chadron Municipal Airport	6,867		22	Hastings 4 N	6,080
23	West Point	6,847		23	Trenton Dam	6,082
24	Madison 2 W	6,833		24	Tecumseh	6,105
25	Crescent Lake Nat'l Wildlife Ref	6,819		25	Madrid	6,110

Number of Annual Cooling Degree Days

	Highest			Lowest	
Rank	Station Name	Num.	Rank	Station Name	Num.
1	Pawnee City	1,398	1	Harrison	428
2	Superior	1,338	2	Agate 3 E	437
3	Beaver City	1,321	3	Harrisburg 10 NW	503
4	Auburn 5 ESE	1,314	4	Sidney 6 NNW	555
5	Lincoln	*1,271*	5	Ellsworth 15 NNE	566
6	Seward	1,247	6	Dalton	567
7	Falls City Brenner Field	1,217	7	Hay Springs 12 S	571
8	Lincoln Municipal Airport	1,195	8	Kimball 2 N	573
9	Hebron	1,193	9	Hay Springs	575
10	Crete	1,181	10	Mullen 21 NW	632
11	Tecumseh	1,179	11	Hemingford	638
12	Fremont	1,176	12	Mitchell 5 E	*642*
13	Syracuse	1,170	13	Crescent Lake Nat'l Wildlife Ref	643
14	Columbus 3 NE	1,164	14	Alliance 1 WNW	667
15	York	1,159	15	Arthur	709
16	Central City	1,154	16	Broken Bow 2 W	710
17	Geneva	1,128	17	Big Springs	718
18	Minden	1,126	18	Valentine Lakes Game Refuge	742
19	Fairbury	1,121	19	Scottsbluff County Airport	746
20	Omaha WSFO	1,105	20	Oshkosh	753
21	Ashland 2	1,095	21	Northeast Nebraska Exp. Station	768
22	Hastings 4 N	1,089	21	Wallace 2 W	768
23	Omaha Eppley Airfield	1,088	23	Anselmo 2 SE	771
24	Niobrara	1,086	23	Merriman	771
25	Fairmont	1,082	25	Brewster	*774*

Annual Precipitation

	Highest			Lowest	
Rank	Station Name	Inches	Rank	Station Name	Inches
1	Falls City Brenner Field	35.23	1	Mitchell 5 E	13.36
2	Wahoo	34.10	2	Agate 3 E	13.99
3	Nebraska City	33.89	3	Harrisburg 10 NW	14.95
4	Weeping Water	33.71	4	Alliance 1 WNW	15.73
5	Auburn 5 ESE	32.55	5	Sidney 6 NNW	16.05
5	Tecumseh	32.55	6	Bridgeport	16.24
7	Pawnee City	32.25	6	Scottsbluff County Airport	16.24
8	Fairbury	31.00	8	Chadron Municipal Airport	16.65
9	Syracuse	30.63	9	Hay Springs 12 S	16.79
10	Blair	30.27	10	Crescent Lake Nat'l Wildlife Ref	16.98
10	Omaha Eppley Airfield	30.27	10	Oshkosh	16.98
12	Omaha WSFO	30.25	12	Hemingford	17.04
13	Lincoln	30.18	13	Big Springs	17.09
14	Ashland 2	30.11	13	Kimball 2 N	17.09
15	West Point	30.06	15	Harrison	17.32
16	Tekamah	30.03	16	Ellsworth 15 NNE	18.06
17	Fremont	30.02	17	Lodgepole	18.42
18	David City	29.98	18	Merriman	18.47
19	Geneva	29.93	19	Arthur	18.62
20	Hebron	29.86	20	Wallace 2 W	18.70
21	Walthill	29.64	21	Ogallala	18.76
22	Crete	29.63	22	Kingsley Dam	19.03
23	Clarkson	29.15	23	Dalton	19.17
24	Aurora	29.10	24	Hershey 5 SSE	*19.29*
25	Stanton	29.01	25	Valentine Miller Field	19.35

Number of Days Annually With ≥ 0.1″ Precipitation

	Highest			Lowest	
Rank	Station Name	Days	Rank	Station Name	Days
1	Wahoo	68	1	Mitchell 5 E	34
2	Tecumseh	60	2	Agate 3 E	*35*
3	Falls City Brenner Field	58	3	Enders Lake	37
3	Nebraska City	58	3	Oshkosh	37
5	Auburn 5 ESE	57	5	Alliance 1 WNW	38
5	Weeping Water	57	5	Big Springs	38
7	David City	56	5	Bridgeport	38
7	Omaha Eppley Airfield	56	5	Chadron Municipal Airport	38
7	Omaha WSFO	56	9	Crescent Lake Nat'l Wildlife Ref	39
7	Syracuse	56	9	Sidney 6 NNW	39
7	West Point	56	11	Brewster	*40*
12	Blair	55	11	Curtis 3 NNE	40
12	Fairbury	55	11	Harrisburg 10 NW	40
12	Fremont	55	11	Hay Springs 12 S	40
12	Tekamah	55	11	Hemingford	40
12	Wakefield	55	11	Imperial	40
17	Ashland 2	54	11	Madrid	40
17	Stanton	54	11	Medicine Creek Dam	40
19	Aurora	53	11	Ogallala	40
19	Columbus 3 NE	53	11	Wallace 2 W	40
19	Lincoln Municipal Airport	53	21	Arthur	41
19	York	53	21	Benkelman	41
23	Albion 1 N	52	21	Ellsworth 15 NNE	41
23	Atkinson	52	21	Hershey 5 SSE	*41*
23	Crete	52	21	Hyannis	*41*

Number of Days Annually With ≥ 1.0″ Precipitation

	Highest			Lowest	
Rank	Station Name	Days	Rank	Station Name	Days
1	Clarkson	9	1	Agate 3 E	1
1	David City	9	1	Big Springs	1
1	Falls City Brenner Field	9	1	Chadron Municipal Airport	1
1	Lincoln	9	1	Harrisburg 10 NW	1
1	Nebraska City	9	1	Harrison	1
1	Stanton	9	1	Hay Springs 12 S	1
1	Tecumseh	9	1	Kimball 2 N	1
1	Wahoo	9	1	Mitchell 5 E	1
9	Auburn 5 ESE	8	1	Scottsbluff County Airport	1
9	Blair	8	10	Arthur	2
9	Crete	8	10	Crescent Lake Nat'l Wildlife Ref	2
9	Fremont	8	10	Hay Springs	2
9	Pawnee City	8	10	Hemingford	2
9	Superior	8	10	Lodgepole	2
9	Syracuse	8	10	Sidney 6 NNW	2
9	Tekamah	8	16	Alliance 1 WNW	3
9	Weeping Water	8	16	Benkelman	3
9	West Point	8	16	Bridgeport	3
19	Albion 1 N	7	16	Dalton	3
19	Ashland 2	7	16	Ellsworth 15 NNE	3
19	Aurora	7	16	Kingsley Dam	3
19	Butte	7	16	Merriman	3
19	Fairmont	7	16	North Platte Exp. Farm	3
19	Greeley	7	16	North Platte Lee Bird Field	3
19	Loup City	7	16	Oshkosh	3

Annual Snowfall

	Highest			Lowest	
Rank	**Station Name**	**Inches**	**Rank**	**Station Name**	**Inches**
1	Mullen 21 NW	59.3	1	Canaday Steam Plant	*18.5*
2	Hemingford	51.5	2	Harlan County Lake	*18.6*
3	Harrison	51.4	3	Medicine Creek Dam	*18.7*
4	Dalton	50.6	4	Mead 6 S	19.4
5	Harrisburg 10 NW	49.6	5	Red Cloud	*20.0*
6	Kimball 2 N	45.6	6	Falls City Brenner Field	21.0
7	Newport	45.5	7	Pawnee City	*21.4*
8	Scottsbluff County Airport	45.1	8	Central City	22.6
9	Valentine Lakes Game Refuge	41.1	9	Crete	23.2
10	Ainsworth	40.8	10	Seward	23.4
11	Chadron Municipal Airport	40.6	11	Lincoln	23.8
12	Bridgeport	39.7	12	Ashland 2	23.9
13	Hay Springs 12 S	39.0	13	Syracuse	24.3
13	Madrid	39.0	14	Geneva	24.5
15	Anselmo 2 SE	37.9	15	Northeast Nebraska Exp. Station	*24.9*
15	Valentine Miller Field	37.9	15	Sidney 6 NNW	*24.9*
17	Atkinson	37.4	17	Madison 2 W	25.0
18	Hayes Center	36.9	18	Columbus 3 NE	25.3
19	Wakefield	36.7	19	Hebron	25.8
20	Kingsley Dam	36.4	20	Superior	26.0
21	Wahoo	36.2	21	Oshkosh	26.2
22	Ellsworth 15 NNE	36.1	22	Fairbury	26.4
23	Springview	35.9	23	Blair	*26.5*
24	Lodgepole	*35.8*	24	Curtis 3 NNE	*26.7*
24	Loup City	35.8	24	Omaha Eppley Airfield	*26.7*

Note: See Appendix D for explanation of data.

Annual Extreme Maximum Temperature

Highest			Lowest		
Rank	Station Name	°F	Rank	Station Name	°F
1	Valley of Fire State Park	117	1	Snowball Ranch	93
2	Boulder City	116	2	Arthur 4 NW	95
2	Las Vegas McCarran Int'l Arpt.	116	2	Glenbrook	95
4	Desert Nat'l Wildlife Range	115	4	Eureka	98
4	Pahrump	115	5	Austin	99
6	Beatty 8 N	112	5	McGill	99
6	Pahranagat Wildlife Refuge	112	5	Wells	99
8	Searchlight	111	8	Ruby Lake	100
8	Silverpeak	111	9	Beowawe Univ. of Nevada Ranch	101
10	Lake Valley Steward	110	9	Ely Yelland Field	101
11	Battle Mountain	109	11	Lund	102
11	Caliente	109	11	Pioche	102
11	Virginia City	109	11	Smokey Valley	102
14	Beowawe	108	14	Carson City	103
14	Lahontan Dam	108	14	Tonopah Airport	103
14	Mina	108	16	Fallon Experiment Station	104
14	Rye Patch Dam	108	16	Paradise Valley 1 NW	104
14	Winnemucca Municipal Airport	108	18	Dyer	105
19	Denio	107	18	Orovada 3 W	105
19	Elko Municipal Airport	107	18	Reno Cannon Int'l Airport	105
19	Leonard Creek Ranch	107	18	Yerington	105
19	Lovelock	107	22	Golconda	106
19	Lovelock Derby Field	107	23	Denio	107
19	Minden	107	23	Elko Municipal Airport	107
25	Golconda	106	23	Leonard Creek Ranch	107

Annual Mean Maximum Temperature

Highest			Lowest		
Rank	Station Name	°F	Rank	Station Name	°F
1	Valley of Fire State Park	80.4	1	Arthur 4 NW	57.2
2	Las Vegas McCarran Int'l Arpt.	79.8	2	Glenbrook	58.4
3	Desert Nat'l Wildlife Range	78.7	3	Snowball Ranch	59.1
4	Pahrump	78.3	4	Eureka	59.5
5	Boulder City	78.2	5	Virginia City	59.6
6	Searchlight	75.4	5	Wells	59.6
7	Pahranagat Wildlife Refuge	75.0	7	Lake Valley Steward	60.3
8	Beatty 8 N	74.4	8	McGill	60.4
9	Silverpeak	71.2	9	Ruby Lake	61.2
10	Caliente	70.6	10	Ely Yelland Field	61.5
11	Dyer	69.3	11	Austin	61.7
12	Mina	69.2	12	Elko Municipal Airport	62.1
13	Yerington	68.5	13	Beowawe Univ. of Nevada Ranch	62.8
14	Lahontan Dam	68.4	14	Pioche	63.1
15	Rye Patch Dam	67.9	15	Orovada 3 W	64.1
16	Lovelock Derby Field	67.5	15	Paradise Valley 1 NW	64.1
17	Lovelock	67.3	17	Beowawe	64.4
18	Minden	67.1	18	Denio	64.6
19	Fallon Experiment Station	67.0	18	Lund	64.6
19	Reno Cannon Int'l Airport	67.0	20	Leonard Creek Ranch	65.2
21	Battle Mountain	66.4	21	Golconda	65.6
21	Tonopah Airport	66.4	22	Winnemucca Municipal Airport	65.9
23	Smokey Valley	66.3	23	Carson City	66.0
24	Carson City	66.0	24	Smokey Valley	66.3
25	Winnemucca Municipal Airport	65.9	25	Battle Mountain	66.4

Annual Mean Temperature

	Highest			Lowest	
Rank	**Station Name**	**°F**	**Rank**	**Station Name**	**°F**
1	Valley of Fire State Park	*68.9*	1	Arthur 4 NW	44.1
2	Boulder City	67.5	1	Snowball Ranch	44.1
3	Las Vegas McCarran Int'l Arpt.	67.3	3	Wells	44.3
4	Searchlight	63.6	4	Ely Yelland Field	44.8
5	Desert Nat'l Wildlife Range	62.7	5	Elko Municipal Airport	46.4
6	Pahrump	61.9	5	Eureka	46.4
7	Pahranagat Wildlife Refuge	*59.4*	7	Glenbrook	46.5
8	Beatty 8 N	*58.9*	8	McGill	46.7
9	Silverpeak	55.3	9	Beowawe Univ. of Nevada Ranch	*46.8*
10	Lahontan Dam	*55.0*	9	Ruby Lake	*46.8*
11	Mina	54.8	11	Paradise Valley 1 NW	47.6
12	Caliente	53.5	12	Lund	47.9
13	Yerington	52.3	13	Beowawe	48.0
14	Dyer	52.0	14	Austin	48.3
15	Lovelock	51.6	15	Lake Valley Steward	48.6
16	Tonopah Airport	51.5	16	Orovada 3 W	49.0
17	Lovelock Derby Field	*51.3*	17	Minden	49.2
18	Fallon Experiment Station	51.2	17	Winnemucca Municipal Airport	49.2
18	Leonard Creek Ranch	51.2	19	Virginia City	49.3
20	Reno Cannon Int'l Airport	51.0	20	Battle Mountain	49.6
21	Pioche	50.8	20	Denio	49.6
22	Rye Patch Dam	*50.5*	22	Smokey Valley	49.9
23	Carson City	50.3	23	Carson City	50.3
23	Golconda	50.3	23	Golconda	50.3
25	Smokey Valley	49.9	25	Rye Patch Dam	*50.5*

Annual Mean Minimum Temperature

	Highest			Lowest	
Rank	**Station Name**	**°F**	**Rank**	**Station Name**	**°F**
1	Valley of Fire State Park	*57.4*	1	Ely Yelland Field	27.9
2	Boulder City	56.8	2	Wells	28.9
3	Las Vegas McCarran Int'l Arpt.	54.9	3	Snowball Ranch	29.1
4	Searchlight	51.8	4	Elko Municipal Airport	30.6
5	Desert Nat'l Wildlife Range	46.6	5	Beowawe Univ. of Nevada Ranch	*30.7*
6	Pahrump	45.5	6	Arthur 4 NW	30.8
7	Pahranagat Wildlife Refuge	*43.7*	7	Paradise Valley 1 NW	31.0
8	Beatty 8 N	*43.5*	8	Lund	31.1
9	Lahontan Dam	*41.5*	8	Minden	31.1
10	Mina	40.5	10	Beowawe	31.6
11	Silverpeak	39.3	11	Ruby Lake	32.3
12	Virginia City	38.9	12	Winnemucca Municipal Airport	32.5
13	Pioche	38.5	13	Battle Mountain	32.6
14	Leonard Creek Ranch	37.3	14	McGill	32.9
15	Lake Valley Steward	36.9	15	Rye Patch Dam	*33.1*
16	Tonopah Airport	36.6	16	Eureka	33.2
17	Caliente	36.4	17	Smokey Valley	33.4
18	Yerington	36.0	18	Orovada 3 W	33.8
19	Lovelock	35.9	19	Denio	34.5
20	Fallon Experiment Station	35.4	19	Glenbrook	34.5
21	Golconda	35.0	21	Carson City	34.6
21	Lovelock Derby Field	*35.0*	21	Dyer	34.6
21	Reno Cannon Int'l Airport	35.0	23	Austin	34.7
24	Austin	34.7	24	Golconda	35.0
25	Carson City	34.6	24	Lovelock Derby Field	*35.0*

Annual Extreme Minimum Temperature

	Highest				Lowest	
Rank	Station Name	°F		Rank	Station Name	°F
1	Valley of Fire State Park	12		1	Beowawe	-43
2	Las Vegas McCarran Int'l Arpt.	11		2	Battle Mountain	-39
3	Searchlight	8		3	Winnemucca Municipal Airport	-37
4	Boulder City	4		4	Wells	-36
5	Beatty 8 N	2		5	Elko Municipal Airport	-33
6	Desert Nat'l Wildlife Range	0		5	Golconda	-33
7	Pahranagat Wildlife Refuge	-1		5	Orovada 3 W	-33
8	Pahrump	-2		8	Paradise Valley 1 NW	-32
9	Glenbrook	-10		9	Beowawe Univ. of Nevada Ranch	-31
9	Tonopah Airport	-10		9	Smokey Valley	-31
11	Virginia City	-11		11	Ely Yelland Field	-30
12	Lake Valley Steward	-13		12	Ruby Lake	-29
13	Pioche	-15		13	Lovelock Derby Field	-28
14	Reno Cannon Int'l Airport	-16		14	Fallon Experiment Station	-27
15	Lahontan Dam	-17		15	Arthur 4 NW	-26
16	Lund	-18		16	Denio	-25
17	Austin	-19		17	Minden	-24
17	Caliente	-19		17	Snowball Ranch	-24
17	Leonard Creek Ranch	-19		19	Dyer	-23
20	Eureka	-21		19	Lovelock	-23
20	McGill	-21		19	Mina	-23
22	Carson City	-22		19	Rye Patch Dam	-23
22	Silverpeak	-22		19	Yerington	-23
24	Dyer	-23		24	Carson City	-22
24	Lovelock	-23		24	Silverpeak	-22

July Mean Maximum Temperature

	Highest				Lowest	
Rank	Station Name	°F		Rank	Station Name	°F
1	Valley of Fire State Park	105.2		1	Glenbrook	78.4
2	Las Vegas McCarran Int'l Arpt.	104.1		2	Snowball Ranch	81.4
3	Boulder City	101.9		3	Arthur 4 NW	82.1
3	Desert Nat'l Wildlife Range	101.9		4	Virginia City	82.8
5	Pahrump	100.6		5	Eureka	85.0
6	Pahranagat Wildlife Refuge	98.4		6	Lake Valley Steward	85.1
7	Searchlight	97.8		7	McGill	85.4
8	Silverpeak	97.0		8	Wells	86.5
9	Beatty 8 N	96.6		9	Pioche	86.7
10	Caliente	95.1		9	Ruby Lake	86.7
11	Lovelock Derby Field	94.4		11	Austin	87.2
11	Mina	94.4		11	Ely Yelland Field	87.2
13	Rye Patch Dam	94.1		13	Beowawe Univ. of Nevada Ranch	87.3
14	Lahontan Dam	93.9		14	Lund	88.6
15	Battle Mountain	93.6		15	Carson City	89.0
16	Dyer	92.9		16	Elko Municipal Airport	89.6
17	Winnemucca Municipal Airport	92.8		17	Paradise Valley 1 NW	89.8
18	Golconda	92.5		18	Minden	90.0
19	Lovelock	92.4		19	Orovada 3 W	90.2
20	Leonard Creek Ranch	92.0		20	Fallon Experiment Station	90.5
21	Yerington	91.9		21	Denio	90.9
22	Beowawe	91.5		22	Smokey Valley	91.0
23	Reno Cannon Int'l Airport	91.2		23	Reno Cannon Int'l Airport	91.2
23	Tonopah Airport	91.2		23	Tonopah Airport	91.2
25	Smokey Valley	91.0		25	Beowawe	91.5

January Mean Minimum Temperature

Highest			Lowest		
Rank	**Station Name**	**°F**	**Rank**	**Station Name**	**°F**
1	Boulder City	39.2	1	Ely Yelland Field	10.3
2	Valley of Fire State Park	38.1	2	Wells	11.9
3	Searchlight	36.2	3	Beowawe Univ. of Nevada Ranch	13.9
4	Las Vegas McCarran Int'l Arpt.	35.3	3	Snowball Ranch	13.9
5	Desert Nat'l Wildlife Range	29.4	5	Elko Municipal Airport	14.1
6	Beatty 8 N	29.0	6	Arthur 4 NW	14.5
7	Pahrump	27.7	7	Lund	14.6
8	Pahranagat Wildlife Refuge	26.8	8	Beowawe	14.8
9	Glenbrook	23.8	9	Ruby Lake	14.9
10	Virginia City	23.7	10	McGill	15.9
11	Lahontan Dam	23.1	10	Smokey Valley	15.9
12	Mina	23.0	12	Paradise Valley 1 NW	17.0
13	Pioche	21.7	13	Battle Mountain	17.3
13	Reno Cannon Int'l Airport	21.7	13	Eureka	17.3
15	Carson City	21.4	15	Dyer	17.4
15	Denio	21.4	16	Lovelock Derby Field	17.6
17	Leonard Creek Ranch	20.5	16	Minden	17.6
18	Yerington	20.2	18	Rye Patch Dam	17.7
19	Austin	20.1	19	Winnemucca Municipal Airport	18.3
19	Lake Valley Steward	20.1	20	Caliente	18.8
21	Fallon Experiment Station	19.8	20	Silverpeak	18.8
21	Golconda	19.8	22	Lovelock	19.3
21	Orovada 3 W	19.8	23	Tonopah Airport	19.5
24	Tonopah Airport	19.5	24	Fallon Experiment Station	19.8
25	Lovelock	19.3	24	Golconda	19.8

Number of Annual Heating Degree Days

Highest			Lowest		
Rank	**Station Name**	**Num.**	**Rank**	**Station Name**	**Num.**
1	Arthur 4 NW	7,691	1	Valley of Fire State Park	*2,042*
2	Wells	7,672	2	Boulder City	2,117
3	Snowball Ranch	7,594	3	Las Vegas McCarran Int'l Arpt.	2,240
4	Ely Yelland Field	7,495	4	Searchlight	2,693
5	Elko Municipal Airport	7,046	5	Desert Nat'l Wildlife Range	2,901
6	Eureka	7,027	6	Pahrump	3,064
7	McGill	6,951	7	Beatty 8 N	*3,514*
8	Ruby Lake	*6,878*	8	Pahranagat Wildlife Refuge	*3,597*
9	Beowawe Univ. of Nevada Ranch	*6,836*	9	Lahontan Dam	*4,786*
10	Glenbrook	6,764	10	Mina	4,792
11	Paradise Valley 1 NW	6,582	11	Silverpeak	4,809
12	Beowawe	6,578	12	Caliente	5,020
13	Lund	6,478	13	Yerington	5,216
14	Austin	6,457	14	Dyer	5,340
15	Lake Valley Steward	6,374	15	Lovelock	5,501
16	Orovada 3 W	6,239	16	Fallon Experiment Station	5,510
17	Winnemucca Municipal Airport	6,208	17	Reno Cannon Int'l Airport	5,531
18	Virginia City	6,153	18	Tonopah Airport	5,539
19	Battle Mountain	6,124	19	Carson City	5,663
20	Denio	6,060	20	Leonard Creek Ranch	5,689
21	Minden	6,012	21	Pioche	5,708
22	Smokey Valley	*5,990*	22	Lovelock Derby Field	*5,709*
23	Golconda	*5,926*	23	Rye Patch Dam	*5,819*
24	Rye Patch Dam	*5,819*	24	Golconda	*5,926*
25	Lovelock Derby Field	*5,709*	25	Smokey Valley	*5,990*

Number of Annual Cooling Degree Days

	Highest			Lowest	
Rank	**Station Name**	**Num.**	**Rank**	**Station Name**	**Num.**
1	Valley of Fire State Park	3,593	1	Glenbrook	79
2	Las Vegas McCarran Int'l Arpt.	3,248	2	Snowball Ranch	80
3	Boulder City	3,234	3	Arthur 4 NW	156
4	Searchlight	2,303	4	Ely Yelland Field	213
5	Desert Nat'l Wildlife Range	2,172	5	Wells	216
6	Pahrump	2,011	6	Beowawe Univ. of Nevada Ranch	290
7	Pahranagat Wildlife Refuge	1,732	7	Eureka	318
8	Beatty 8 N	1,479	8	Paradise Valley 1 NW	321
9	Silverpeak	1,308	9	Minden	333
10	Lahontan Dam	*1,276*	10	Elko Municipal Airport	334
11	Mina	1,208	11	Lund	337
12	Caliente	964	11	Ruby Lake	337
13	Lovelock Derby Field	*794*	13	McGill	372
14	Leonard Creek Ranch	764	14	Carson City	407
15	Tonopah Airport	745	15	Beowawe	439
16	Yerington	713	16	Orovada 3 W	451
17	Dyer	708	17	Lake Valley Steward	463
18	Golconda	*669*	18	Austin	*470*
18	Lovelock	669	19	Virginia City	519
20	Rye Patch Dam	*639*	20	Winnemucca Municipal Airport	524
21	Pioche	636	21	Denio	539
22	Battle Mountain	609	22	Reno Cannon Int'l Airport	581
23	Fallon Experiment Station	592	23	Smokey Valley	584
24	Smokey Valley	584	24	Fallon Experiment Station	592
25	Reno Cannon Int'l Airport	581	25	Battle Mountain	609

Annual Precipitation

	Highest			Lowest	
Rank	**Station Name**	**Inches**	**Rank**	**Station Name**	**Inches**
1	Glenbrook	17.44	1	Silverpeak	4.48
2	Lake Valley Steward	15.56	2	Las Vegas McCarran Int'l Arpt.	4.52
3	Arthur 4 NW	14.91	3	Desert Nat'l Wildlife Range	4.80
4	Virginia City	14.51	4	Pahrump	5.12
5	Austin	14.34	5	Dyer	5.18
6	Pioche	14.01	6	Fallon Experiment Station	5.24
7	Ruby Lake	13.89	7	Lovelock Derby Field	*5.32*
8	Eureka	12.23	8	Yerington	5.36
9	Beowawe Univ. of Nevada Ranch	*11.20*	9	Lahontan Dam	5.50
10	Lund	11.05	10	Tonopah Airport	5.72
11	Paradise Valley 1 NW	10.84	11	Lovelock	5.80
12	Orovada 3 W	10.58	12	Mina	5.97
13	Carson City	10.55	13	Beatty 8 N	6.28
14	Wells	10.42	14	Boulder City	6.51
15	Ely Yelland Field	9.98	15	Pahranagat Wildlife Refuge	6.53
16	Denio	9.94	16	Valley of Fire State Park	6.83
17	Elko Municipal Airport	9.79	17	Smokey Valley	7.28
18	Caliente	9.76	18	Reno Cannon Int'l Airport	7.51
19	Leonard Creek Ranch	9.45	19	Golconda	7.63
20	Snowball Ranch	8.87	20	Winnemucca Municipal Airport	8.28
21	Beowawe	8.82	21	Searchlight	8.34
22	Rye Patch Dam	8.74	22	Minden	8.53
23	Battle Mountain	8.70	23	McGill	8.69
24	McGill	8.69	24	Battle Mountain	8.70
25	Minden	8.53	25	Rye Patch Dam	8.74

Number of Days Annually With ≥ 0.1″ Precipitation

	Highest			Lowest	
Rank	**Station Name**	**Days**	**Rank**	**Station Name**	**Days**
1	Arthur 4 NW	45	1	Desert Nat'l Wildlife Range	13
2	Lake Valley Steward	*40*	1	Silverpeak	13
2	Ruby Lake	40	3	Dyer	14
4	Austin	39	3	Las Vegas McCarran Int'l Arpt.	14
5	Glenbrook	38	3	Pahrump	14
6	Beowawe Univ. of Nevada Ranch	*37*	6	Fallon Experiment Station	15
7	Virginia City	36	6	Mina	15
8	Pioche	35	8	Boulder City	16
9	Paradise Valley 1 NW	34	8	Lahontan Dam	16
10	Denio	33	8	Lovelock Derby Field	*16*
10	Wells	33	8	Valley of Fire State Park	16
12	Elko Municipal Airport	32	8	Yerington	16
12	Eureka	32	13	Tonopah Airport	17
12	Orovada 3 W	32	14	Beatty 8 N	18
15	Leonard Creek Ranch	31	15	Pahranagat Wildlife Refuge	19
16	Ely Yelland Field	30	16	Searchlight	20
17	Lund	28	17	Lovelock	21
17	Rye Patch Dam	28	18	Reno Cannon Int'l Airport	22
17	Winnemucca Municipal Airport	28	18	Smokey Valley	22
20	Beowawe	*27*	20	Minden	23
20	Caliente	27	21	Carson City	24
20	Snowball Ranch	27	21	McGill	24
23	Battle Mountain	26	23	Battle Mountain	26
23	Golconda	26	23	Golconda	26
25	Carson City	24	25	Beowawe	*27*

Number of Days Annually With ≥ 1.0″ Precipitation

	Highest			Lowest	
Rank	**Station Name**	**Days**	**Rank**	**Station Name**	**Days**
1	Glenbrook	3	1	Arthur 4 NW	0
2	Arthur 4 NW	0	1	Austin	0
2	Austin	0	1	Battle Mountain	0
2	Battle Mountain	0	1	Beatty 8 N	0
2	Beatty 8 N	0	1	Beowawe	0
2	Beowawe	0	1	Beowawe Univ. of Nevada Ranch	*0*
2	Beowawe Univ. of Nevada Ranch	*0*	1	Boulder City	0
2	Boulder City	0	1	Caliente	0
2	Caliente	0	1	Carson City	0
2	Carson City	0	1	Denio	0
2	Denio	0	1	Desert Nat'l Wildlife Range	0
2	Desert Nat'l Wildlife Range	0	1	Dyer	0
2	Dyer	0	1	Elko Municipal Airport	0
2	Elko Municipal Airport	0	1	Ely Yelland Field	0
2	Ely Yelland Field	0	1	Eureka	0
2	Eureka	0	1	Fallon Experiment Station	0
2	Fallon Experiment Station	0	1	Golconda	0
2	Golconda	0	1	Lahontan Dam	0
2	Lahontan Dam	0	1	Lake Valley Steward	0
2	Lake Valley Steward	0	1	Las Vegas McCarran Int'l Arpt.	0
2	Las Vegas McCarran Int'l Arpt.	0	1	Leonard Creek Ranch	0
2	Leonard Creek Ranch	0	1	Lovelock	0
2	Lovelock	0	1	Lovelock Derby Field	*0*
2	Lovelock Derby Field	*0*	1	Lund	0
2	Lund	0	1	McGill	0

	Annual Snowfall				

Highest			**Lowest**		
Rank	**Station Name**	**Inches**	**Rank**	**Station Name**	**Inches**
1	Austin	79.9	1	Boulder City	Trace
2	Virginia City	64.7	1	Pahrump	Trace
3	Glenbrook	*63.2*	3	Valley of Fire State Park	*0.3*
4	Ely Yelland Field	50.8	4	Desert Nat'l Wildlife Range	0.5
5	Ruby Lake	*49.4*	5	Searchlight	0.6
6	Wells	48.1	6	Las Vegas McCarran Int'l Arpt.	1.0
7	Eureka	*47.7*	7	Pahranagat Wildlife Refuge	1.7
8	Arthur 4 NW	*47.6*	8	Beatty 8 N	*2.5*
9	Snowball Ranch	43.9	9	Silverpeak	*2.9*
10	Elko Municipal Airport	37.2	10	Yerington	*4.9*
11	Paradise Valley 1 NW	*26.3*	11	Fallon Experiment Station	*7.6*
12	Reno Cannon Int'l Airport	23.4	12	Lovelock Derby Field	*7.7*
13	Winnemucca Municipal Airport	*22.2*	13	Lovelock	*9.0*
14	Denio	*21.0*	14	Dyer	9.9
15	Battle Mountain	20.0	15	Mina	12.0
16	Beowawe	*17.5*	16	Carson City	*16.2*
17	Orovada 3 W	*16.7*	16	Tonopah Airport	16.2
18	Carson City	*16.2*	18	Orovada 3 W	*16.7*
18	Tonopah Airport	16.2	19	Beowawe	*17.5*
20	Mina	12.0	20	Battle Mountain	20.0
21	Dyer	9.9	21	Denio	*21.0*
22	Lovelock	*9.0*	22	Winnemucca Municipal Airport	*22.2*
23	Lovelock Derby Field	*7.7*	23	Reno Cannon Int'l Airport	23.4
24	Fallon Experiment Station	*7.6*	24	Paradise Valley 1 NW	*26.3*
25	Yerington	*4.9*	25	Elko Municipal Airport	37.2

Note: See Appendix D for explanation of data.

Annual Extreme Maximum Temperature

	Highest				Lowest	
Rank	Station Name	°F		Rank	Station Name	°F
1	Greenland	*104*		1	Mount Washington	72
2	Hanover	103		2	First Conn Lake	91
2	North Conway	*103*		3	Pinkham Notch	93
4	Durham	102		4	Benton 5 SW	95
5	Concord Municipal Airport	101		4	Colebrook	95
6	Epping	100		4	Lancaster	95
6	Nashua 2 NNW	100		7	Grafton	97
8	Keene	99		8	Berlin	*98*
8	Monroe 5 NNE	*99*		8	Mount Sunapee	98
10	Berlin	*98*		8	Plymouth	98
10	Mount Sunapee	98		8	Tamworth 3	*98*
10	Plymouth	98		12	Keene	99
10	Tamworth 3	*98*		12	Monroe 5 NNE	*99*
14	Grafton	97		14	Epping	100
15	Benton 5 SW	95		14	Nashua 2 NNW	100
15	Colebrook	95		16	Concord Municipal Airport	101
15	Lancaster	95		17	Durham	102
18	Pinkham Notch	93		18	Hanover	103
19	First Conn Lake	91		18	North Conway	*103*
20	Mount Washington	72		20	Greenland	*104*

Annual Mean Maximum Temperature

	Highest				Lowest	
Rank	Station Name	°F		Rank	Station Name	°F
1	Durham	58.9		1	Mount Washington	33.6
1	Greenland	*58.9*		2	First Conn Lake	48.1
3	Epping	58.5		3	Pinkham Notch	49.8
3	Nashua 2 NNW	58.5		4	Colebrook	52.1
5	Keene	58.4		5	Monroe 5 NNE	*53.1*
6	Concord Municipal Airport	57.4		6	Benton 5 SW	53.2
7	Hanover	56.7		7	Berlin	*53.4*
8	North Conway	*56.3*		8	Lancaster	54.1
9	Mount Sunapee	55.3		9	Plymouth	54.6
10	Grafton	54.8		9	Tamworth 3	*54.6*
11	Plymouth	54.6		11	Grafton	54.8
11	Tamworth 3	*54.6*		12	Mount Sunapee	55.3
13	Lancaster	54.1		13	North Conway	*56.3*
14	Berlin	*53.4*		14	Hanover	56.7
15	Benton 5 SW	53.2		15	Concord Municipal Airport	57.4
16	Monroe 5 NNE	*53.1*		16	Keene	58.4
17	Colebrook	52.1		17	Epping	58.5
18	Pinkham Notch	49.8		17	Nashua 2 NNW	58.5
19	First Conn Lake	48.1		19	Durham	58.9
20	Mount Washington	33.6		19	Greenland	*58.9*

Annual Mean Temperature

	Highest			Lowest	
Rank	**Station Name**	**°F**	**Rank**	**Station Name**	**°F**
1	Greenland	47.9	1	Mount Washington	27.0
2	Nashua 2 NNW	47.3	2	First Conn Lake	37.1
3	Durham	47.2	3	Pinkham Notch	39.7
4	Epping	47.1	4	Colebrook	40.6
5	Keene	46.5	5	Lancaster	41.9
6	Concord Municipal Airport	45.6	5	Monroe 5 NNE	41.9
6	Hanover	45.6	7	Berlin	42.2
8	Mount Sunapee	45.5	8	Plymouth	42.4
9	North Conway	44.7	8	Tamworth 3	42.4
10	Benton 5 SW	43.0	10	Grafton	42.5
11	Grafton	42.5	11	Benton 5 SW	43.0
12	Plymouth	42.4	12	North Conway	44.7
12	Tamworth 3	42.4	13	Mount Sunapee	45.5
14	Berlin	42.2	14	Concord Municipal Airport	45.6
15	Lancaster	41.9	14	Hanover	45.6
15	Monroe 5 NNE	41.9	16	Keene	46.5
17	Colebrook	40.6	17	Epping	47.1
18	Pinkham Notch	39.7	18	Durham	47.2
19	First Conn Lake	37.1	19	Nashua 2 NNW	47.3
20	Mount Washington	27.0	20	Greenland	47.9

Annual Mean Minimum Temperature

	Highest			Lowest	
Rank	**Station Name**	**°F**	**Rank**	**Station Name**	**°F**
1	Greenland	36.8	1	Mount Washington	20.3
2	Nashua 2 NNW	35.9	2	First Conn Lake	26.1
3	Epping	35.6	3	Colebrook	28.9
3	Mount Sunapee	35.6	4	Pinkham Notch	29.5
5	Durham	35.5	5	Lancaster	29.6
6	Hanover	34.6	6	Grafton	30.1
6	Keene	34.6	6	Plymouth	30.1
8	Concord Municipal Airport	33.8	6	Tamworth 3	30.1
9	North Conway	33.0	9	Monroe 5 NNE	30.7
10	Benton 5 SW	32.6	10	Berlin	30.9
11	Berlin	30.9	11	Benton 5 SW	32.6
12	Monroe 5 NNE	30.7	12	North Conway	33.0
13	Grafton	30.1	13	Concord Municipal Airport	33.8
13	Plymouth	30.1	14	Hanover	34.6
13	Tamworth 3	30.1	14	Keene	34.6
16	Lancaster	29.6	16	Durham	35.5
17	Pinkham Notch	29.5	17	Epping	35.6
18	Colebrook	28.9	17	Mount Sunapee	35.6
19	First Conn Lake	26.1	19	Nashua 2 NNW	35.9
20	Mount Washington	20.3	20	Greenland	36.8

Annual Extreme Minimum Temperature

	Highest				Lowest	
Rank	Station Name	°F		Rank	Station Name	°F
1	Mount Sunapee	-23		1	First Conn Lake	-44
2	Nashua 2 NNW	-24		1	Mount Washington	-44
3	Greenland	*-26*		3	Colebrook	-40
4	Hanover	-27		3	Grafton	-40
4	Keene	-27		3	Lancaster	-40
6	Pinkham Notch	-28		6	Monroe 5 NNE	*-36*
7	Benton 5 SW	-29		7	Plymouth	-35
7	Epping	-29		8	Concord Municipal Airport	-33
7	North Conway	*-29*		9	Berlin	*-32*
7	Tamworth 3	*-29*		10	Durham	-30
11	Durham	-30		11	Benton 5 SW	-29
12	Berlin	*-32*		11	Epping	-29
13	Concord Municipal Airport	-33		11	North Conway	*-29*
14	Plymouth	-35		11	Tamworth 3	*-29*
15	Monroe 5 NNE	*-36*		15	Pinkham Notch	-28
16	Colebrook	-40		16	Hanover	-27
16	Grafton	-40		16	Keene	-27
16	Lancaster	-40		18	Greenland	*-26*
19	First Conn Lake	-44		19	Nashua 2 NNW	-24
19	Mount Washington	-44		20	Mount Sunapee	-23

July Mean Maximum Temperature

	Highest				Lowest	
Rank	Station Name	°F		Rank	Station Name	°F
1	Durham	83.4		1	Mount Washington	54.2
2	Keene	83.2		2	First Conn Lake	73.7
3	Epping	83.1		3	Pinkham Notch	74.1
4	Greenland	82.9		4	Colebrook	77.5
5	Hanover	82.8		5	Benton 5 SW	78.0
6	Concord Municipal Airport	82.7		6	Berlin	78.9
7	Nashua 2 NNW	82.6		7	Monroe 5 NNE	*79.6*
8	North Conway	81.8		7	Mount Sunapee	79.6
9	Plymouth	80.2		9	Grafton	79.9
10	Grafton	79.9		9	Lancaster	79.9
10	Lancaster	79.9		9	Tamworth 3	*79.9*
10	Tamworth 3	*79.9*		12	Plymouth	80.2
13	Monroe 5 NNE	*79.6*		13	North Conway	81.8
13	Mount Sunapee	79.6		14	Nashua 2 NNW	82.6
15	Berlin	78.9		15	Concord Municipal Airport	82.7
16	Benton 5 SW	78.0		16	Hanover	82.8
17	Colebrook	77.5		17	Greenland	82.9
18	Pinkham Notch	74.1		18	Epping	83.1
19	First Conn Lake	73.7		19	Keene	83.2
20	Mount Washington	54.2		20	Durham	83.4

January Mean Minimum Temperature

Highest			Lowest		
Rank	Station Name	°F	Rank	Station Name	°F
1	Greenland	14.8	1	Mount Washington	-4.1
2	Epping	12.6	2	First Conn Lake	-3.0
3	Durham	12.3	3	Colebrook	1.1
4	Nashua 2 NNW	12.1	4	Monroe 5 NNE	2.1
5	Mount Sunapee	12.0	5	Lancaster	2.2
6	Keene	10.4	6	Berlin	3.9
7	Concord Municipal Airport	8.8	7	Pinkham Notch	4.1
8	Hanover	8.3	8	Grafton	4.6
9	Benton 5 SW	7.3	8	Plymouth	4.6
9	North Conway	*7.3*	10	Tamworth 3	*4.7*
11	Tamworth 3	*4.7*	11	Benton 5 SW	7.3
12	Grafton	4.6	11	North Conway	*7.3*
12	Plymouth	4.6	13	Hanover	8.3
14	Pinkham Notch	4.1	14	Concord Municipal Airport	8.8
15	Berlin	3.9	15	Keene	10.4
16	Lancaster	2.2	16	Mount Sunapee	12.0
17	Monroe 5 NNE	2.1	17	Nashua 2 NNW	12.1
18	Colebrook	1.1	18	Durham	12.3
19	First Conn Lake	-3.0	19	Epping	12.6
20	Mount Washington	-4.1	20	Greenland	14.8

Number of Annual Heating Degree Days

Highest			Lowest		
Rank	Station Name	Num.	Rank	Station Name	Num.
1	Mount Washington	13,782	1	Greenland	*6,641*
2	First Conn Lake	10,178	2	Durham	6,858
3	Pinkham Notch	9,231	3	Nashua 2 NNW	6,869
4	Colebrook	8,989	4	Epping	6,909
5	Monroe 5 NNE	*8,608*	5	Keene	7,111
6	Lancaster	8,581	6	Mount Sunapee	7,383
7	Berlin	*8,489*	7	Concord Municipal Airport	7,421
8	Plymouth	8,391	8	Hanover	7,433
9	Tamworth 3	*8,378*	9	North Conway	*7,701*
10	Grafton	8,359	10	Benton 5 SW	8,185
11	Benton 5 SW	8,185	11	Grafton	8,359
12	North Conway	*7,701*	12	Tamworth 3	*8,378*
13	Hanover	7,433	13	Plymouth	8,391
14	Concord Municipal Airport	7,421	14	Berlin	*8,489*
15	Mount Sunapee	7,383	15	Lancaster	8,581
16	Keene	7,111	16	Monroe 5 NNE	*8,608*
17	Epping	6,909	17	Colebrook	8,989
18	Nashua 2 NNW	6,869	18	Pinkham Notch	9,231
19	Durham	6,858	19	First Conn Lake	10,178
20	Greenland	*6,641*	20	Mount Washington	13,782

Number of Annual Cooling Degree Days

	Highest			Lowest	
Rank	Station Name	Num.	Rank	Station Name	Num.
1	Nashua 2 NNW	523	1	Mount Washington	0
2	Greenland	492	2	First Conn Lake	94
3	Durham	491	3	Pinkham Notch	114
4	Hanover	490	4	Colebrook	193
5	Epping	489	5	Grafton	231
6	Keene	462	6	Tamworth 3	233
7	Concord Municipal Airport	457	7	Plymouth	242
8	North Conway	418	8	Lancaster	243
9	Mount Sunapee	399	9	Benton 5 SW	247
10	Monroe 5 NNE	296	10	Berlin	277
11	Berlin	277	11	Monroe 5 NNE	296
12	Benton 5 SW	247	12	Mount Sunapee	399
13	Lancaster	243	13	North Conway	418
14	Plymouth	242	14	Concord Municipal Airport	457
15	Tamworth 3	233	15	Keene	462
16	Grafton	231	16	Epping	489
17	Colebrook	193	17	Hanover	490
18	Pinkham Notch	114	18	Durham	491
19	First Conn Lake	94	19	Greenland	492
20	Mount Washington	0	20	Nashua 2 NNW	523

Annual Precipitation

	Highest			Lowest	
Rank	Station Name	Inches	Rank	Station Name	Inches
1	Mount Washington	102.43	1	Monroe 5 NNE	*36.36*
2	Pinkham Notch	58.85	2	Concord Municipal Airport	37.49
3	Tamworth 3	*50.63*	3	Lancaster	37.59
4	North Conway	*47.93*	4	Benton 5 SW	38.12
5	Greenland	47.76	5	Hanover	38.36
6	Nashua 2 NNW	45.03	6	Colebrook	40.02
7	First Conn Lake	44.76	7	Grafton	40.07
8	Plymouth	44.55	8	Berlin	40.28
9	Epping	44.42	9	Keene	41.10
10	Mount Sunapee	43.65	10	Durham	42.60
11	Durham	42.60	11	Mount Sunapee	43.65
12	Keene	41.10	12	Epping	44.42
13	Berlin	40.28	13	Plymouth	44.55
14	Grafton	40.07	14	First Conn Lake	44.76
15	Colebrook	40.02	15	Nashua 2 NNW	45.03
16	Hanover	38.36	16	Greenland	47.76
17	Benton 5 SW	38.12	17	North Conway	*47.93*
18	Lancaster	37.59	18	Tamworth 3	*50.63*
19	Concord Municipal Airport	37.49	19	Pinkham Notch	58.85
20	Monroe 5 NNE	*36.36*	20	Mount Washington	102.43

Number of Days Annually With ≥ 0.1″ Precipitation

	Highest			Lowest	
Rank	**Station Name**	**Days**	**Rank**	**Station Name**	**Days**
1	Mount Washington	160	1	Concord Municipal Airport	77
2	First Conn Lake	*105*	1	Grafton	77
3	Pinkham Notch	102	3	Hanover	78
4	Colebrook	90	4	Durham	79
5	Lancaster	89	4	Greenland	*79*
6	Tamworth 3	*88*	4	Mount Sunapee	79
7	Plymouth	86	7	Epping	80
8	Berlin	*85*	8	Keene	81
8	Monroe 5 NNE	*85*	8	Nashua 2 NNW	81
8	North Conway	*85*	10	Benton 5 SW	84
11	Benton 5 SW	84	11	Berlin	*85*
12	Keene	81	11	Monroe 5 NNE	*85*
12	Nashua 2 NNW	81	11	North Conway	*85*
14	Epping	80	14	Plymouth	86
15	Durham	79	15	Tamworth 3	*88*
15	Greenland	*79*	16	Lancaster	89
15	Mount Sunapee	79	17	Colebrook	90
18	Hanover	78	18	Pinkham Notch	102
19	Concord Municipal Airport	77	19	First Conn Lake	*105*
19	Grafton	77	20	Mount Washington	160

Number of Days Annually With ≥ 1.0″ Precipitation

	Highest			Lowest	
Rank	**Station Name**	**Days**	**Rank**	**Station Name**	**Days**
1	Mount Washington	27	1	Monroe 5 NNE	*5*
2	Pinkham Notch	14	2	Colebrook	6
3	Durham	12	2	First Conn Lake	6
3	Epping	12	2	Hanover	6
3	Greenland	*12*	2	Lancaster	6
3	Mount Sunapee	12	6	Benton 5 SW	7
3	Nashua 2 NNW	12	7	Berlin	9
3	North Conway	*12*	7	Grafton	9
3	Plymouth	12	9	Keene	10
3	Tamworth 3	*12*	10	Concord Municipal Airport	11
11	Concord Municipal Airport	11	11	Durham	12
12	Keene	10	11	Epping	12
13	Berlin	9	11	Greenland	*12*
13	Grafton	9	11	Mount Sunapee	12
15	Benton 5 SW	7	11	Nashua 2 NNW	12
16	Colebrook	6	11	North Conway	*12*
16	First Conn Lake	6	11	Plymouth	12
16	Hanover	6	11	Tamworth 3	*12*
16	Lancaster	6	19	Pinkham Notch	14
20	Monroe 5 NNE	*5*	20	Mount Washington	27

		Annual Snowfall				
	Highest				**Lowest**	
Rank	**Station Name**	**Inches**		**Rank**	**Station Name**	**Inches**
1	Mount Washington	315.4		1	Durham	49.7
2	First Conn Lake	151.4		2	Greenland	*53.4*
3	Pinkham Notch	*133.9*		3	Keene	54.5
4	Colebrook	*88.5*		4	Epping	56.2
5	North Conway	*84.2*		5	Nashua 2 NNW	*56.4*
6	Berlin	82.6		6	Hanover	63.8
7	Tamworth 3	*82.0*		7	Concord Municipal Airport	63.9
8	Grafton	78.9		8	Monroe 5 NNE	*65.8*
9	Plymouth	75.2		9	Benton 5 SW	69.7
10	Mount Sunapee	*72.5*		10	Lancaster	70.9
11	Lancaster	70.9		11	Mount Sunapee	*72.5*
12	Benton 5 SW	69.7		12	Plymouth	75.2
13	Monroe 5 NNE	*65.8*		13	Grafton	78.9
14	Concord Municipal Airport	63.9		14	Tamworth 3	*82.0*
15	Hanover	63.8		15	Berlin	82.6
16	Nashua 2 NNW	*56.4*		16	North Conway	*84.2*
17	Epping	56.2		17	Colebrook	*88.5*
18	Keene	54.5		18	Pinkham Notch	*133.9*
19	Greenland	*53.4*		19	First Conn Lake	151.4
20	Durham	49.7		20	Mount Washington	315.4

Note: See Appendix D for explanation of data.

Annual Extreme Maximum Temperature

	Highest				Lowest	
Rank	Station Name	°F		Rank	Station Name	°F
1	Newark Int'l Airport	105		1	Long Valley	99
1	Toms River	105		2	Boonton 1 SE	100
3	Flemington 5 NNW	104		2	Cape May 2 NW	100
3	Pemberton	104		2	Charlotteburg Reservoir	100
3	Plainfield	104		2	Seabrook Farms	*100*
3	Tuckerton	*104*		6	Atlantic City Int'l Airport	101
7	Belleplain State Forest	103		6	Essex Fells Serv Bldg	101
7	Canoe Brook	103		6	Glassboro 2 W	101
7	Indian Mills 2 W	103		6	Millville Municipal Airport	101
7	Lambertville	103		6	Newton Saint Pauls Abbey	101
7	Little Falls	103		11	Atlantic City State Marina	102
7	New Brunswick 3 SE	103		11	Cranford	102
7	Somerville 3 NW	103		11	Hightstown 2 W	102
14	Atlantic City State Marina	102		11	Woodstown	102
14	Cranford	102		15	Belleplain State Forest	103
14	Hightstown 2 W	102		15	Canoe Brook	103
14	Woodstown	102		15	Indian Mills 2 W	103
18	Atlantic City Int'l Airport	101		15	Lambertville	103
18	Essex Fells Serv Bldg	101		15	Little Falls	103
18	Glassboro 2 W	101		15	New Brunswick 3 SE	103
18	Millville Municipal Airport	101		15	Somerville 3 NW	103
18	Newton Saint Pauls Abbey	101		22	Flemington 5 NNW	104
23	Boonton 1 SE	100		22	Pemberton	104
23	Cape May 2 NW	100		22	Plainfield	104
23	Charlotteburg Reservoir	100		22	Tuckerton	*104*

Annual Mean Maximum Temperature

	Highest				Lowest	
Rank	Station Name	°F		Rank	Station Name	°F
1	Belleplain State Forest	66.3		1	Newton Saint Pauls Abbey	59.4
2	Woodstown	65.8		2	Charlotteburg Reservoir	59.7
3	Indian Mills 2 W	65.4		3	Long Valley	60.0
3	Pemberton	65.4		4	Boonton 1 SE	60.9
5	Lambertville	64.6		5	Atlantic City State Marina	61.0
6	Toms River	64.4		6	Essex Fells Serv Bldg	61.7
7	Cranford	64.3		6	Somerville 3 NW	61.7
7	Millville Municipal Airport	64.3		8	Little Falls	62.3
9	Seabrook Farms	*64.0*		9	New Brunswick 3 SE	62.4
9	Tuckerton	*64.0*		10	Canoe Brook	62.5
11	Atlantic City Int'l Airport	63.7		10	Flemington 5 NNW	62.5
12	Glassboro 2 W	63.5		12	Hightstown 2 W	62.8
12	Plainfield	63.5		13	Cape May 2 NW	62.9
14	Newark Int'l Airport	63.4		14	Newark Int'l Airport	63.4
15	Cape May 2 NW	62.9		15	Glassboro 2 W	63.5
16	Hightstown 2 W	62.8		15	Plainfield	63.5
17	Canoe Brook	62.5		17	Atlantic City Int'l Airport	63.7
17	Flemington 5 NNW	62.5		18	Seabrook Farms	*64.0*
19	New Brunswick 3 SE	62.4		18	Tuckerton	*64.0*
20	Little Falls	62.3		20	Cranford	64.3
21	Essex Fells Serv Bldg	61.7		20	Millville Municipal Airport	64.3
21	Somerville 3 NW	61.7		22	Toms River	64.4
23	Atlantic City State Marina	61.0		23	Lambertville	64.6
24	Boonton 1 SE	60.9		24	Indian Mills 2 W	65.4
25	Long Valley	60.0		24	Pemberton	65.4

Annual Mean Temperature

	Highest				Lowest	
Rank	Station Name	°F		Rank	Station Name	°F
1	Newark Int'l Airport	55.1		1	Newton Saint Pauls Abbey	48.2
2	Cape May 2 NW	55.0		2	Charlotteburg Reservoir	48.6
3	Woodstown	54.9		3	Long Valley	48.9
4	Atlantic City State Marina	54.8		4	Boonton 1 SE	50.7
5	Belleplain State Forest	54.7		5	Somerville 3 NW	50.8
6	Millville Municipal Airport	54.5		6	Essex Fells Serv Bldg	*51.0*
7	Seabrook Farms	*54.4*		7	Flemington 5 NNW	51.1
8	Glassboro 2 W	54.1		8	Canoe Brook	51.3
9	Tuckerton	*54.0*		9	Little Falls	52.3
10	Pemberton	53.9		10	New Brunswick 3 SE	52.5
11	Indian Mills 2 W	53.8		11	Hightstown 2 W	52.6
12	Atlantic City Int'l Airport	53.6		12	Toms River	53.0
13	Lambertville	53.3		13	Cranford	53.2
13	Plainfield	53.3		14	Lambertville	53.3
15	Cranford	53.2		14	Plainfield	53.3
16	Toms River	53.0		16	Atlantic City Int'l Airport	53.6
17	Hightstown 2 W	52.6		17	Indian Mills 2 W	53.8
18	New Brunswick 3 SE	52.5		18	Pemberton	53.9
19	Little Falls	52.3		19	Tuckerton	*54.0*
20	Canoe Brook	51.3		20	Glassboro 2 W	54.1
21	Flemington 5 NNW	51.1		21	Seabrook Farms	*54.4*
22	Essex Fells Serv Bldg	*51.0*		22	Millville Municipal Airport	54.5
23	Somerville 3 NW	50.8		23	Belleplain State Forest	54.7
24	Boonton 1 SE	50.7		24	Atlantic City State Marina	54.8
25	Long Valley	48.9		25	Woodstown	54.9

Annual Mean Minimum Temperature

	Highest				Lowest	
Rank	Station Name	°F		Rank	Station Name	°F
1	Atlantic City State Marina	48.5		1	Newton Saint Pauls Abbey	36.9
2	Cape May 2 NW	47.0		2	Charlotteburg Reservoir	37.4
3	Newark Int'l Airport	46.8		3	Long Valley	37.7
4	Glassboro 2 W	44.8		4	Flemington 5 NNW	39.8
5	Seabrook Farms	*44.7*		5	Somerville 3 NW	39.9
6	Millville Municipal Airport	44.6		6	Canoe Brook	40.2
7	Woodstown	44.1		6	Essex Fells Serv Bldg	40.2
8	Tuckerton	*44.0*		8	Boonton 1 SE	40.4
9	Atlantic City Int'l Airport	43.4		9	Toms River	41.7
10	Plainfield	43.1		10	Cranford	42.0
11	Belleplain State Forest	43.0		10	Lambertville	42.0
12	New Brunswick 3 SE	42.5		12	Indian Mills 2 W	42.1
13	Hightstown 2 W	42.4		13	Pemberton	42.2
14	Little Falls	42.3		14	Little Falls	42.3
15	Pemberton	42.2		15	Hightstown 2 W	42.4
16	Indian Mills 2 W	42.1		16	New Brunswick 3 SE	42.5
17	Cranford	42.0		17	Belleplain State Forest	43.0
17	Lambertville	42.0		18	Plainfield	43.1
19	Toms River	41.7		19	Atlantic City Int'l Airport	43.4
20	Boonton 1 SE	40.4		20	Tuckerton	*44.0*
21	Canoe Brook	40.2		21	Woodstown	44.1
21	Essex Fells Serv Bldg	40.2		22	Millville Municipal Airport	44.6
23	Somerville 3 NW	39.9		23	Seabrook Farms	*44.7*
24	Flemington 5 NNW	39.8		24	Glassboro 2 W	44.8
25	Long Valley	37.7		25	Newark Int'l Airport	46.8

Annual Extreme Minimum Temperature

	Highest				Lowest	
Rank	Station Name	°F		Rank	Station Name	°F
1	Cape May 2 NW	-2		1	Newton Saint Pauls Abbey	-26
2	Atlantic City State Marina	-3		2	Charlotteburg Reservoir	-24
3	Tuckerton	*-7*		3	Toms River	-19
4	Glassboro 2 W	-8		4	Flemington 5 NNW	-18
4	Newark Int'l Airport	-8		4	Indian Mills 2 W	-18
4	Plainfield	-8		4	Long Valley	-18
7	Cranford	-10		7	Pemberton	-17
7	Little Falls	-10		8	Somerville 3 NW	-16
7	Millville Municipal Airport	-10		9	Boonton 1 SE	-15
10	Atlantic City Int'l Airport	-11		9	Canoe Brook	-15
10	Lambertville	-11		11	Belleplain State Forest	-14
12	Hightstown 2 W	-12		11	Essex Fells Serv Bldg	-14
13	New Brunswick 3 SE	-13		13	New Brunswick 3 SE	-13
13	Seabrook Farms	*-13*		13	Seabrook Farms	*-13*
13	Woodstown	-13		13	Woodstown	-13
16	Belleplain State Forest	-14		16	Hightstown 2 W	-12
16	Essex Fells Serv Bldg	-14		17	Atlantic City Int'l Airport	-11
18	Boonton 1 SE	-15		17	Lambertville	-11
18	Canoe Brook	-15		19	Cranford	-10
20	Somerville 3 NW	-16		19	Little Falls	-10
21	Pemberton	-17		19	Millville Municipal Airport	-10
22	Flemington 5 NNW	-18		22	Glassboro 2 W	-8
22	Indian Mills 2 W	-18		22	Newark Int'l Airport	-8
22	Long Valley	-18		22	Plainfield	-8
25	Toms River	-19		25	Tuckerton	*-7*

July Mean Maximum Temperature

	Highest				Lowest	
Rank	Station Name	°F		Rank	Station Name	°F
1	Woodstown	88.2		1	Atlantic City State Marina	80.6
2	Lambertville	87.6		2	Long Valley	81.9
3	Indian Mills 2 W	87.5		3	Charlotteburg Reservoir	82.6
4	Cranford	87.0		4	Newton Saint Pauls Abbey	83.0
4	Pemberton	87.0		5	Cape May 2 NW	83.7
6	Belleplain State Forest	86.7		6	Boonton 1 SE	83.9
7	Plainfield	86.6		7	Essex Fells Serv Bldg	84.7
8	Newark Int'l Airport	86.5		8	Somerville 3 NW	85.0
9	Toms River	86.3		9	Atlantic City Int'l Airport	85.1
10	Millville Municipal Airport	86.0		10	New Brunswick 3 SE	85.2
11	Flemington 5 NNW	85.9		11	Hightstown 2 W	85.5
11	Seabrook Farms	*85.9*		11	Tuckerton	*85.5*
13	Glassboro 2 W	85.8		13	Canoe Brook	85.6
13	Little Falls	85.8		14	Glassboro 2 W	85.8
15	Canoe Brook	85.6		14	Little Falls	85.8
16	Hightstown 2 W	85.5		16	Flemington 5 NNW	85.9
16	Tuckerton	*85.5*		16	Seabrook Farms	*85.9*
18	New Brunswick 3 SE	85.2		18	Millville Municipal Airport	86.0
19	Atlantic City Int'l Airport	85.1		19	Toms River	86.3
20	Somerville 3 NW	85.0		20	Newark Int'l Airport	86.5
21	Essex Fells Serv Bldg	84.7		21	Plainfield	86.6
22	Boonton 1 SE	83.9		22	Belleplain State Forest	86.7
23	Cape May 2 NW	83.7		23	Cranford	87.0
24	Newton Saint Pauls Abbey	83.0		23	Pemberton	87.0
25	Charlotteburg Reservoir	82.6		25	Indian Mills 2 W	87.5

January Mean Minimum Temperature

	Highest				Lowest	
Rank	Station Name	°F		Rank	Station Name	°F
1	Atlantic City State Marina	27.9		1	Newton Saint Pauls Abbey	14.2
2	Cape May 2 NW	27.0		2	Charlotteburg Reservoir	15.6
3	Newark Int'l Airport	24.3		3	Long Valley	16.6
4	Seabrook Farms	*24.1*		4	Boonton 1 SE	17.9
5	Millville Municipal Airport	24.0		4	Canoe Brook	17.9
6	Woodstown	23.7		6	Flemington 5 NNW	18.2
7	Belleplain State Forest	23.2		7	Somerville 3 NW	18.3
7	Glassboro 2 W	23.2		8	Essex Fells Serv Bldg	18.6
9	Atlantic City Int'l Airport	23.1		9	Little Falls	20.1
10	Tuckerton	22.9		10	Toms River	20.8
11	Plainfield	22.3		11	New Brunswick 3 SE	21.0
12	Pemberton	22.0		12	Lambertville	21.1
13	Indian Mills 2 W	21.8		13	Cranford	21.4
14	Cranford	21.4		13	Hightstown 2 W	21.4
14	Hightstown 2 W	21.4		15	Indian Mills 2 W	21.8
16	Lambertville	21.1		16	Pemberton	22.0
17	New Brunswick 3 SE	21.0		17	Plainfield	22.3
18	Toms River	20.8		18	Tuckerton	22.9
19	Little Falls	20.1		19	Atlantic City Int'l Airport	23.1
20	Essex Fells Serv Bldg	18.6		20	Belleplain State Forest	23.2
21	Somerville 3 NW	18.3		20	Glassboro 2 W	23.2
22	Flemington 5 NNW	18.2		22	Woodstown	23.7
23	Boonton 1 SE	17.9		23	Millville Municipal Airport	24.0
23	Canoe Brook	17.9		24	Seabrook Farms	*24.1*
25	Long Valley	16.6		25	Newark Int'l Airport	24.3

Number of Annual Heating Degree Days

	Highest				Lowest	
Rank	Station Name	Num.		Rank	Station Name	Num.
1	Newton Saint Pauls Abbey	6,561		1	Atlantic City State Marina	4,549
2	Charlotteburg Reservoir	6,404		2	Cape May 2 NW	4,570
3	Long Valley	6,261		3	Belleplain State Forest	4,686
4	Boonton 1 SE	5,853		4	Woodstown	4,720
5	Somerville 3 NW	5,812		5	Newark Int'l Airport	4,758
6	Essex Fells Serv Bldg	*5,745*		6	Millville Municipal Airport	4,828
7	Flemington 5 NNW	5,739		7	Seabrook Farms	*4,846*
8	Canoe Brook	5,735		8	Tuckerton	*4,931*
9	Little Falls	5,469		9	Pemberton	4,941
10	New Brunswick 3 SE	5,364		10	Glassboro 2 W	4,943
11	Hightstown 2 W	5,305		11	Indian Mills 2 W	4,999
12	Toms River	5,169		12	Atlantic City Int'l Airport	5,028
13	Lambertville	5,161		13	Cranford	5,141
14	Plainfield	5,153		14	Plainfield	5,153
15	Cranford	5,141		15	Lambertville	5,161
16	Atlantic City Int'l Airport	5,028		16	Toms River	5,169
17	Indian Mills 2 W	4,999		17	Hightstown 2 W	5,305
18	Glassboro 2 W	4,943		18	New Brunswick 3 SE	5,364
19	Pemberton	4,941		19	Little Falls	5,469
20	Tuckerton	*4,931*		20	Canoe Brook	5,735
21	Seabrook Farms	*4,846*		21	Flemington 5 NNW	5,739
22	Millville Municipal Airport	4,828		22	Essex Fells Serv Bldg	*5,745*
23	Newark Int'l Airport	4,758		23	Somerville 3 NW	5,812
24	Woodstown	4,720		24	Boonton 1 SE	5,853
25	Belleplain State Forest	4,686		25	Long Valley	6,261

Number of Annual Cooling Degree Days

Rank	Station Name	Num.		Rank	Station Name	Num.
	Highest				**Lowest**	
1	Newark Int'l Airport	1,309		1	Long Valley	507
2	Woodstown	1,188		2	Charlotteburg Reservoir	535
3	Seabrook Farms	*1,133*		3	Newton Saint Pauls Abbey	559
4	Millville Municipal Airport	1,121		4	Essex Fells Serv Bldg	749
5	Glassboro 2 W	1,105		5	Boonton 1 SE	*754*
6	Tuckerton	*1,075*		6	Somerville 3 NW	756
7	Cape May 2 NW	1,074		7	Flemington 5 NNW	814
8	Belleplain State Forest	1,038		8	Canoe Brook	860
9	Indian Mills 2 W	1,035		9	Hightstown 2 W	908
10	Lambertville	1,022		10	New Brunswick 3 SE	918
11	Pemberton	*1,012*		11	Toms River	937
12	Plainfield	1,011		12	Little Falls	954
13	Atlantic City State Marina	1,001		13	Cranford	965
14	Atlantic City Int'l Airport	999		14	Atlantic City Int'l Airport	999
15	Cranford	965		15	Atlantic City State Marina	1,001
16	Little Falls	954		16	Plainfield	1,011
17	Toms River	937		17	Pemberton	*1,012*
18	New Brunswick 3 SE	918		18	Lambertville	1,022
19	Hightstown 2 W	908		19	Indian Mills 2 W	1,035
20	Canoe Brook	860		20	Belleplain State Forest	1,038
21	Flemington 5 NNW	814		21	Cape May 2 NW	1,074
22	Somerville 3 NW	756		22	Tuckerton	*1,075*
23	Boonton 1 SE	*754*		23	Glassboro 2 W	1,105
24	Essex Fells Serv Bldg	749		24	Millville Municipal Airport	1,121
25	Newton Saint Pauls Abbey	559		25	Seabrook Farms	*1,133*

Annual Precipitation

Rank	Station Name	Inches		Rank	Station Name	Inches
	Highest				**Lowest**	
1	Long Valley	53.28		1	Atlantic City State Marina	37.82
2	Charlotteburg Reservoir	53.22		2	Atlantic City Int'l Airport	40.32
3	Essex Fells Serv Bldg	51.72		3	Cape May 2 NW	41.22
4	Little Falls	51.69		4	Millville Municipal Airport	43.29
5	Canoe Brook	51.47		5	Belleplain State Forest	44.32
6	Cranford	50.93		6	Seabrook Farms	*44.69*
7	Boonton 1 SE	50.82		7	Tuckerton	*45.32*
8	Flemington 5 NNW	49.58		8	Woodstown	45.49
9	Plainfield	49.50		9	Glassboro 2 W	45.63
10	Lambertville	48.97		10	Newark Int'l Airport	45.98
11	New Brunswick 3 SE	48.66		11	Indian Mills 2 W	46.84
12	Toms River	48.63		12	Newton Saint Pauls Abbey	47.25
13	Somerville 3 NW	48.14		13	Hightstown 2 W	47.30
14	Pemberton	*47.37*		14	Pemberton	*47.37*
15	Hightstown 2 W	47.30		15	Somerville 3 NW	48.14
16	Newton Saint Pauls Abbey	47.25		16	Toms River	48.63
17	Indian Mills 2 W	46.84		17	New Brunswick 3 SE	48.66
18	Newark Int'l Airport	45.98		18	Lambertville	48.97
19	Glassboro 2 W	45.63		19	Plainfield	49.50
20	Woodstown	45.49		20	Flemington 5 NNW	49.58
21	Tuckerton	*45.32*		21	Boonton 1 SE	50.82
22	Seabrook Farms	*44.69*		22	Cranford	50.93
23	Belleplain State Forest	44.32		23	Canoe Brook	51.47
24	Millville Municipal Airport	43.29		24	Little Falls	51.69
25	Cape May 2 NW	41.22		25	Essex Fells Serv Bldg	51.72

Number of Days Annually With ≥ 0.1″ Precipitation

	Highest			Lowest	
Rank	**Station Name**	**Days**	**Rank**	**Station Name**	**Days**
1	Long Valley	84	1	Atlantic City State Marina	70
2	Cranford	82	2	Millville Municipal Airport	72
2	Lambertville	82	3	Belleplain State Forest	73
2	Plainfield	82	3	Cape May 2 NW	73
2	Somerville 3 NW	82	5	Atlantic City Int'l Airport	74
6	Boonton 1 SE	81	5	Tuckerton	*74*
6	Newton Saint Pauls Abbey	81	7	Seabrook Farms	75
8	Charlotteburg Reservoir	80	7	Woodstown	75
8	Flemington 5 NNW	80	9	Essex Fells Serv Bldg	76
8	Hightstown 2 W	80	10	Glassboro 2 W	77
8	Little Falls	80	10	Indian Mills 2 W	77
8	Toms River	80	10	Newark Int'l Airport	77
13	Canoe Brook	79	13	Canoe Brook	79
13	New Brunswick 3 SE	79	13	New Brunswick 3 SE	79
13	Pemberton	*79*	13	Pemberton	*79*
16	Glassboro 2 W	77	16	Charlotteburg Reservoir	80
16	Indian Mills 2 W	77	16	Flemington 5 NNW	80
16	Newark Int'l Airport	77	16	Hightstown 2 W	80
19	Essex Fells Serv Bldg	76	16	Little Falls	80
20	Seabrook Farms	*75*	16	Toms River	80
20	Woodstown	75	21	Boonton 1 SE	81
22	Atlantic City Int'l Airport	74	21	Newton Saint Pauls Abbey	81
22	Tuckerton	*74*	23	Cranford	82
24	Belleplain State Forest	73	23	Lambertville	82
24	Cape May 2 NW	73	23	Plainfield	82

Number of Days Annually With ≥ 1.0″ Precipitation

	Highest			Lowest	
Rank	**Station Name**	**Days**	**Rank**	**Station Name**	**Days**
1	Charlotteburg Reservoir	16	1	Atlantic City State Marina	11
2	Boonton 1 SE	14	1	Newton Saint Pauls Abbey	11
2	Essex Fells Serv Bldg	14	1	Somerville 3 NW	11
2	Long Valley	14	4	Atlantic City Int'l Airport	12
5	Belleplain State Forest	13	4	Canoe Brook	12
5	Cranford	13	4	Cape May 2 NW	12
5	Flemington 5 NNW	13	4	Glassboro 2 W	12
5	Hightstown 2 W	13	4	Indian Mills 2 W	12
5	Lambertville	13	4	Millville Municipal Airport	12
5	Little Falls	13	4	Newark Int'l Airport	12
5	New Brunswick 3 SE	13	4	Seabrook Farms	*12*
5	Pemberton	*13*	4	Tuckerton	*12*
5	Plainfield	13	4	Woodstown	12
5	Toms River	13	14	Belleplain State Forest	13
15	Atlantic City Int'l Airport	12	14	Cranford	13
15	Canoe Brook	12	14	Flemington 5 NNW	13
15	Cape May 2 NW	12	14	Hightstown 2 W	13
15	Glassboro 2 W	12	14	Lambertville	13
15	Indian Mills 2 W	12	14	Little Falls	13
15	Millville Municipal Airport	12	14	New Brunswick 3 SE	13
15	Newark Int'l Airport	12	14	Pemberton	*13*
15	Seabrook Farms	*12*	14	Plainfield	13
15	Tuckerton	*12*	14	Toms River	13
15	Woodstown	12	24	Boonton 1 SE	14
25	Atlantic City State Marina	11	24	Essex Fells Serv Bldg	14

Annual Snowfall

	Highest			Lowest	
Rank	**Station Name**	**Inches**	**Rank**	**Station Name**	**Inches**
1	Newton Saint Pauls Abbey	37.8	1	Belleplain State Forest	*9.5*
2	Charlotteburg Reservoir	34.5	2	Millville Municipal Airport	13.2
3	Long Valley	33.7	3	Atlantic City Int'l Airport	*13.3*
4	Flemington 5 NNW	28.8	4	Cape May 2 NW	13.5
5	Boonton 1 SE	*28.2*	5	Woodstown	16.5
6	Somerville 3 NW	27.5	6	Essex Fells Serv Bldg	*16.7*
7	Plainfield	26.6	7	Pemberton	16.9
8	New Brunswick 3 SE	26.4	8	Indian Mills 2 W	17.2
9	Canoe Brook	25.6	9	Tuckerton	*17.9*
10	Newark Int'l Airport	24.9	10	Lambertville	20.4
11	Hightstown 2 W	22.0	11	Cranford	20.6
12	Cranford	20.6	12	Hightstown 2 W	22.0
13	Lambertville	20.4	13	Newark Int'l Airport	24.9
14	Tuckerton	*17.9*	14	Canoe Brook	25.6
15	Indian Mills 2 W	17.2	15	New Brunswick 3 SE	26.4
16	Pemberton	16.9	16	Plainfield	26.6
17	Essex Fells Serv Bldg	*16.7*	17	Somerville 3 NW	27.5
18	Woodstown	16.5	18	Boonton 1 SE	*28.2*
19	Cape May 2 NW	13.5	19	Flemington 5 NNW	28.8
20	Atlantic City Int'l Airport	*13.3*	20	Long Valley	33.7
21	Millville Municipal Airport	13.2	21	Charlotteburg Reservoir	34.5
22	Belleplain State Forest	*9.5*	22	Newton Saint Pauls Abbey	37.8

Note: See Appendix D for explanation of data.

Annual Extreme Maximum Temperature

	Highest				Lowest	
Rank	Station Name	°F		Rank	Station Name	°F
1	Maljamar 4 SE	116		1	Wolf Canyon	89
2	Tatum	115		2	Gascon	90
3	Bitter Lakes Wildlife Refuge	114		2	Red River	90
3	Carlsbad	114		4	Eagle Nest	91
3	Conchas Dam	114		5	Chama	92
3	Hobbs	114		5	Lake Maloya	92
3	Lordsburg 4 SE	114		7	McGaffey 5 SE	94
3	Roswell Industrial Airpark	114		8	Los Alamos	95
9	Artesia 6 S	113		8	Tierra Amarilla 4 N	95
9	Bernardo	113		10	Dulce	97
9	Carlsbad Cavern City Air Term	113		10	Luna Ranger Station	97
9	Hatch 5 NW	113		10	Ocate 2 NW	97
13	Elida	112		10	Raton Filter Plant	97
14	Bosque Del Apache	111		10	Taos	97
14	Caballo Dam	111		15	Des Moines	98
14	Columbus	111		15	El Vado Dam	98
14	Elephant Butte Dam	111		15	Mountain Park	98
14	Jal	111		18	Cimarron 4 SW	99
14	Sumner Lake	111		18	El Rito	99
14	White Sands Nat'l Monument	111		18	Las Vegas Municipal Airport	99
21	Alamogordo	110		18	Santa Fe 2	99
21	Animas	110		18	Star Lake	99
21	Carlsbad Caverns	110		23	Abiquiu Dam	100
21	Clovis	110		23	Clines Corners 7 SE	100
21	Hachita	110		23	Cuba	100

Annual Mean Maximum Temperature

	Highest				Lowest	
Rank	Station Name	°F		Rank	Station Name	°F
1	Jal	79.0		1	Wolf Canyon	55.8
2	Columbus	78.2		2	Red River	56.0
2	Hatch 5 NW	78.2		3	Eagle Nest	57.2
4	Carlsbad	78.1		4	Chama	58.1
5	Lordsburg 4 SE	77.9		4	Gascon	58.1
5	White Sands Nat'l Monument	77.9		6	McGaffey 5 SE	58.9
7	Carlsbad Cavern City Air Term	77.4		7	Lake Maloya	59.0
8	Animas	77.2		8	Los Alamos	59.8
8	Hachita	77.2		9	Tierra Amarilla 4 N	60.2
10	Maljamar 4 SE	77.0		10	El Vado Dam	62.1
10	Orogrande	77.0		11	Ocate 2 NW	62.5
10	State University	77.0		12	Raton Filter Plant	62.7
13	Redrock 1 NNE	76.9		12	Taos	62.7
14	Bosque Del Apache	76.8		14	Dulce	62.9
15	Caballo Dam	76.6		15	Sandia Park	63.3
16	Hobbs	76.5		16	Des Moines	63.4
17	Artesia 6 S	76.3		16	El Rito	63.4
17	Bitter Lakes Wildlife Refuge	76.3		18	Clines Corners 7 SE	63.6
19	Jornada Experiment Range	76.2		19	El Morro Nat'l Monument	64.2
20	Alamogordo	75.9		20	Abiquiu Dam	64.3
21	Roswell Industrial Airpark	75.3		20	Las Vegas Municipal Airport	64.3
21	Tularosa	75.3		20	Star Lake	64.3
23	Bernardo	74.9		23	Santa Fe 2	64.4
24	Elephant Butte Dam	74.6		24	Cimarron 4 SW	64.9
25	Aleman Ranch	74.4		24	Pecos National Monument	64.9

Annual Mean Temperature

Highest			Lowest		
Rank	**Station Name**	**°F**	**Rank**	**Station Name**	**°F**
1	Jal	63.7	1	Eagle Nest	40.1
2	Columbus	62.9	1	Red River	40.1
3	Carlsbad	62.8	1	Wolf Canyon	40.1
3	Carlsbad Cavern City Air Term	62.8	4	Chama	41.4
5	Hobbs	62.2	5	Tierra Amarilla 4 N	*42.6*
6	Alamogordo	61.7	6	McGaffey 5 SE	42.7
7	Carlsbad Caverns	61.5	7	Lake Maloya	43.6
7	State University	61.5	8	Gascon	43.8
9	Orogrande	61.3	9	Dulce	44.8
10	Elephant Butte Dam	61.0	10	El Vado Dam	44.9
10	Roswell Industrial Airpark	61.0	11	Ocate 2 NW	46.3
12	Maljamar 4 SE	60.6	12	Luna Ranger Station	46.4
13	Caballo Dam	60.5	13	Taos	46.8
14	Hachita	60.4	14	El Morro Nat'l Monument	47.6
14	Tularosa	*60.4*	14	Star Lake	47.6
16	Animas	60.2	16	Los Alamos	47.8
17	Hatch 5 NW	60.0	17	Gallup Sen Clarke Field	*48.5*
17	Lordsburg 4 SE	60.0	18	Fence Lake	48.6
19	White Sands Nat'l Monument	59.6	19	Maxwell 3 NW	48.7
20	Artesia 6 S	59.3	20	El Rito	48.9
21	Redrock 1 NNE	59.2	21	Cimarron 4 SW	49.0
22	Bitter Lakes Wildlife Refuge	*58.8*	22	Pecos National Monument	49.2
23	Conchas Dam	58.7	23	Raton Filter Plant	49.3
23	San Jon	58.7	23	Sandia Park	49.3
25	Tucumcari 4 NE	58.6	23	Valmora	49.3

Annual Mean Minimum Temperature

Highest			Lowest		
Rank	**Station Name**	**°F**	**Rank**	**Station Name**	**°F**
1	Carlsbad Caverns	49.6	1	Eagle Nest	22.8
2	Jal	48.4	2	Red River	24.1
3	Carlsbad Cavern City Air Term	48.1	3	Wolf Canyon	24.3
4	Hobbs	47.8	4	Chama	24.7
5	Alamogordo	47.5	5	Tierra Amarilla 4 N	*25.0*
5	Carlsbad	47.5	6	McGaffey 5 SE	26.3
5	Columbus	47.5	7	Dulce	26.6
8	Elephant Butte Dam	47.4	8	Luna Ranger Station	26.8
9	Roswell Industrial Airpark	46.6	9	El Vado Dam	27.5
10	State University	46.0	10	Lake Maloya	28.0
11	Orogrande	45.5	11	Gascon	29.4
12	Tularosa	45.4	12	Ocate 2 NW	30.0
13	Caballo Dam	44.4	13	Taos	30.7
14	Maljamar 4 SE	44.3	14	Star Lake	30.9
15	Conchas Dam	44.2	15	El Morro Nat'l Monument	31.0
16	San Jon	43.9	16	Fence Lake	31.3
17	Tucumcari 4 NE	43.7	16	Gallup Sen Clarke Field	*31.3*
18	Hachita	43.5	18	Maxwell 3 NW	31.5
19	Animas	43.3	19	Valmora	32.0
20	Albuquerque Int'l Airport	43.1	20	Chaco Canyon Nat'l Monument	32.1
21	Clovis	42.9	21	Cimarron 4 SW	33.0
22	Portales	42.7	21	Springer	33.0
23	Elida	42.6	23	Grants Milan Muni Airport	33.1
24	Santa Rosa	42.5	24	Pecos National Monument	33.3
25	Crossroads 2	42.4	25	Stanley 1 NNE	33.5

Annual Extreme Minimum Temperature

	Highest				Lowest	
Rank	**Station Name**	**°F**		**Rank**	**Station Name**	**°F**
1	Carlsbad Caverns	2		1	Eagle Nest	-47
1	Columbus	2		2	El Vado Dam	-45
1	Elephant Butte Dam	2		3	Fence Lake	-40
1	Hatch 5 NW	2		4	Tierra Amarilla 4 N	-39
1	Orogrande	2		5	Cuba	-38
6	Alamogordo	0		5	Dulce	-38
6	Caballo Dam	0		5	Star Lake	-38
6	Faywood	0		8	Chaco Canyon Nat'l Monument	-37
6	Tularosa	0		8	Estancia 7 NE	-37
10	Hobbs	-2		10	Red River	-36
11	Glenwood	-3		10	Wolf Canyon	-36
11	Redrock 1 NNE	-3		12	Alcalde	-34
13	Carlsbad Cavern City Air Term	-4		12	Gallup Sen Clarke Field	-34
13	Fort Bayard	-4		14	Grants Milan Muni Airport	-33
13	State University	-4		14	Torreon Navajo Mission	-33
16	Hillsboro	-5		16	El Morro Nat'l Monument	-32
16	Mountain Park	-5		16	Luna Ranger Station	-32
18	Aleman Ranch	-6		16	McGaffey 5 SE	-32
18	Carlsbad	-6		19	Ocate 2 NW	-31
20	Clovis	-7		20	Chama	-30
21	Jal	-8		20	Lake Maloya	-30
21	Maljamar 4 SE	-8		20	Stanley 1 NNE	-30
23	Hachita	-9		20	Valmora	-30
23	Roswell Industrial Airpark	-9		24	Clines Corners 7 SE	-29
23	White Signal	-9		24	Pedernal 4 E	-29

July Mean Maximum Temperature

	Highest				Lowest	
Rank	**Station Name**	**°F**		**Rank**	**Station Name**	**°F**
1	White Sands Nat'l Monument	96.9		1	Gascon	75.1
2	Lordsburg 4 SE	96.0		2	Wolf Canyon	75.7
3	Bosque Del Apache	95.7		3	Red River	76.2
3	Columbus	95.7		4	Eagle Nest	77.4
5	Bernardo	95.6		5	Lake Maloya	78.6
6	Carlsbad	95.5		6	McGaffey 5 SE	79.9
7	Carlsbad Cavern City Air Term	95.3		7	Chama	80.3
7	Hatch 5 NW	95.3		8	Los Alamos	80.5
7	Maljamar 4 SE	95.3		9	Mountain Park	80.9
10	Orogrande	95.2		9	Ocate 2 NW	80.9
11	Bitter Lakes Wildlife Refuge	95.1		11	Tierra Amarilla 4 N	82.0
11	Caballo Dam	95.1		12	Raton Filter Plant	82.5
11	Jal	95.1		13	Las Vegas Municipal Airport	83.1
14	Jornada Experiment Range	94.9		14	Des Moines	83.2
15	Redrock 1 NNE	94.7		14	Luna Ranger Station	83.2
15	State University	94.7		16	Cimarron 4 SW	83.5
17	Animas	94.4		16	Clines Corners 7 SE	83.5
18	Hachita	94.2		18	Sandia Park	84.0
19	Roswell Industrial Airpark	94.0		19	Capitan	84.2
20	Alamogordo	93.7		20	Pecos National Monument	84.4
20	Artesia 6 S	93.7		21	El Rito	84.5
22	Elephant Butte Dam	93.5		22	Dulce	84.8
23	Conchas Dam	93.4		22	El Morro Nat'l Monument	84.8
23	Hobbs	93.4		22	El Vado Dam	84.8
23	San Jon	93.4		25	Cuba	84.9

January Mean Minimum Temperature

Highest			Lowest		
Rank	**Station Name**	**°F**	**Rank**	**Station Name**	**°F**
1	Carlsbad Caverns	32.4	1	Eagle Nest	1.0
2	Alamogordo	29.7	2	Tierra Amarilla 4 N	3.8
3	Columbus	29.5	3	Chama	4.7
4	Hobbs	29.0	4	Red River	6.0
5	Elephant Butte Dam	28.7	5	El Vado Dam	6.3
6	Carlsbad Cavern City Air Term	28.5	6	Dulce	6.8
7	Jal	28.3	7	Wolf Canyon	7.5
8	State University	28.2	8	McGaffey 5 SE	8.1
9	Tularosa	28.0	9	Lake Maloya	8.6
10	Carlsbad	27.9	10	Taos	9.2
11	Orogrande	27.5	11	Star Lake	10.3
12	Hachita	26.7	12	Maxwell 3 NW	11.6
13	Animas	26.6	13	Luna Ranger Station	12.2
14	Faywood	26.2	14	Chaco Canyon Nat'l Monument	12.8
14	Roswell Industrial Airpark	26.2	15	Springer	13.2
16	Caballo Dam	25.8	16	Gallup Sen Clarke Field	13.3
16	Fort Bayard	25.8	17	El Morro Nat'l Monument	13.4
18	Mountain Park	25.6	18	Ocate 2 NW	13.9
19	Glenwood	25.4	18	Valmora	13.9
20	Redrock 1 NNE	25.3	20	Grants Milan Muni Airport	14.9
21	Lordsburg 4 SE	25.0	21	Fence Lake	15.2
21	Maljamar 4 SE	25.0	21	Torreon Navajo Mission	15.2
23	Santa Rosa	24.8	23	Pecos National Monument	15.4
24	Hillsboro	24.5	24	Aztec Ruins Nat'l Monument	15.8
25	Aleman Ranch	24.3	24	Cimarron 4 SW	15.8

Number of Annual Heating Degree Days

Highest			Lowest		
Rank	**Station Name**	**Num.**	**Rank**	**Station Name**	**Num.**
1	Eagle Nest	9,004	1	Jal	2,529
2	Red River	9,003	2	Columbus	2,677
3	Wolf Canyon	9,001	3	Carlsbad	*2,766*
4	Chama	8,513	4	Hobbs	2,789
5	Tierra Amarilla 4 N	*8,107*	5	Carlsbad Cavern City Air Term	2,812
6	McGaffey 5 SE	8,092	6	Carlsbad Caverns	2,834
7	Lake Maloya	7,751	7	Alamogordo	2,874
8	Gascon	7,660	8	State University	2,929
9	El Vado Dam	7,404	9	Orogrande	3,016
10	Dulce	7,385	10	Tularosa	*3,084*
11	Ocate 2 NW	6,804	11	Elephant Butte Dam	3,117
12	Taos	6,797	12	Hachita	3,129
13	Luna Ranger Station	6,753	13	Animas	3,164
14	Star Lake	6,606	14	Caballo Dam	3,197
15	El Morro Nat'l Monument	6,452	15	Maljamar 4 SE	3,207
16	Los Alamos	6,433	16	Hatch 5 NW	3,220
17	Gallup Sen Clarke Field	*6,297*	17	Roswell Industrial Airpark	3,223
18	Fence Lake	6,176	18	Lordsburg 4 SE	3,336
19	Maxwell 3 NW	6,148	19	Redrock 1 NNE	3,394
20	Chaco Canyon Nat'l Monument	6,098	20	White Sands Nat'l Monument	3,512
21	El Rito	6,068	21	Artesia 6 S	3,548
22	Pecos National Monument	5,990	22	Faywood	3,594
23	Cimarron 4 SW	5,986	23	Santa Rosa	3,665
24	Stanley 1 NNE	5,958	24	Aleman Ranch	3,680
25	Des Moines	*5,955*	25	Crossroads 2	*3,696*

Number of Annual Cooling Degree Days

	Highest			Lowest	
Rank	**Station Name**	**Num.**	**Rank**	**Station Name**	**Num.**
1	Jal	2,166	1	Red River	0
2	Carlsbad Cavern City Air Term	2,155	2	Wolf Canyon	1
3	Carlsbad	2,149	3	Eagle Nest	4
4	Columbus	2,123	4	Gascon	10
5	Hobbs	1,949	5	Chama	21
6	Roswell Industrial Airpark	1,885	6	Lake Maloya	31
7	Maljamar 4 SE	1,858	7	McGaffey 5 SE	34
8	State University	1,855	8	Tierra Amarilla 4 N	*37*
9	Alamogordo	1,822	9	Luna Ranger Station	64
10	Orogrande	1,796	10	Ocate 2 NW	74
11	Elephant Butte Dam	1,786	11	Dulce	133
12	Carlsbad Caverns	1,734	12	El Vado Dam	168
13	Caballo Dam	1,704	13	El Morro Nat'l Monument	211
14	Lordsburg 4 SE	1,667	14	Cimarron 4 SW	220
15	Bitter Lakes Wildlife Refuge	*1,666*	15	Los Alamos	247
16	White Sands Nat'l Monument	1,651	16	Taos	251
17	Artesia 6 S	1,627	17	Sandia Park	263
18	Hachita	1,600	18	Fence Lake	272
19	Conchas Dam	1,586	19	Pecos National Monument	305
20	San Jon	1,584	20	Valmora	312
21	Animas	1,557	21	El Rito	319
22	Tularosa	1,531	22	Raton Filter Plant	323
23	Hatch 5 NW	*1,508*	23	Las Vegas Municipal Airport	326
24	Tucumcari 4 NE	1,476	24	Capitan	337
25	Bernardo	*1,457*	25	Maxwell 3 NW	340

Annual Precipitation

	Highest			Lowest	
Rank	**Station Name**	**Inches**	**Rank**	**Station Name**	**Inches**
1	Lake Maloya	24.63	1	Fruitland 3 E	8.32
2	Gascon	24.33	2	Bernardo	8.80
2	Wolf Canyon	24.33	3	Bloomfield 3 SE	9.25
4	Chama	22.78	4	Albuquerque Int'l Airport	9.39
5	Red River	22.02	5	Chaco Canyon Nat'l Monument	9.44
6	Mountain Park	21.42	6	Bosque Del Apache	9.62
7	McGaffey 5 SE	20.33	7	State University	9.65
8	Sandia Park	19.76	8	Los Lunas 3 SSW	9.74
9	Cameron	19.20	9	Star Lake	9.90
10	Los Alamos	18.97	10	Columbus	10.05
11	Clines Corners 7 SE	18.57	11	Socorro	10.07
12	Ocate 2 NW	18.55	12	Abiquiu Dam	10.11
13	Clovis	18.44	13	White Sands Nat'l Monument	10.20
14	San Jon	18.40	14	Elephant Butte Dam	10.38
15	Raton Filter Plant	18.28	15	Alcalde	10.43
16	Ragland 3 SSW	18.20	16	Laguna	10.59
17	Las Vegas Municipal Airport	18.10	17	Torreon Navajo Mission	10.72
18	Mimbres Ranger Station	18.06	18	Aztec Ruins Nat'l Monument	10.75
19	Hobbs	18.01	19	Hatch 5 NW	10.76
20	Dulce	17.90	20	Caballo Dam	10.93
21	Valmora	17.87	21	Grants Milan Muni Airport	10.99
22	Capitan	*17.86*	22	Aleman Ranch	11.21
22	Des Moines	*17.86*	23	Tularosa	11.22
24	Cimarron 4 SW	17.68	24	Jornada Experiment Range	11.23
25	Jemez Springs	17.59	25	Hachita	11.48

Number of Days Annually With ≥ 0.1″ Precipitation

	Highest			Lowest	
Rank	**Station Name**	**Days**	**Rank**	**Station Name**	**Days**
1	Red River	65	1	Bosque Del Apache	22
2	Wolf Canyon	63	2	Bernardo	24
3	Chama	61	2	State University	24
3	Lake Maloya	61	4	Elephant Butte Dam	25
5	Gascon	55	4	Jal	25
6	McGaffey 5 SE	51	4	Los Lunas 3 SSW	25
7	Clines Corners 7 SE	50	4	Socorro	25
7	Dulce	50	8	Alcalde	26
9	Mountain Park	49	8	Bitter Lakes Wildlife Refuge	26
10	Jemez Springs	48	8	Carlsbad	26
11	El Vado Dam	47	11	Carlsbad Cavern City Air Term	27
11	Sandia Park	47	11	Columbus	27
13	Los Alamos	46	11	Laguna	27
13	Raton Filter Plant	46	11	Orogrande	*27*
13	Tierra Amarilla 4 N	46	15	Bloomfield 3 SE	28
16	Capitan	*45*	15	Chaco Canyon Nat'l Monument	28
16	Eagle Nest	45	15	Fruitland 3 E	28
16	Ocate 2 NW	45	15	Hatch 5 NW	*28*
19	El Morro Nat'l Monument	44	15	Jornada Experiment Range	28
19	Luna Ranger Station	44	15	Pedernal 4 E	28
19	Pecos National Monument	44	15	Roswell Industrial Airpark	28
22	Fence Lake	43	15	White Sands Nat'l Monument	28
22	Gila Hot Springs	43	23	Albuquerque Int'l Airport	29
22	Gran Quivira Nat'l Monument	43	23	Animas	29
25	Cimarron 4 SW	42	23	Artesia 6 S	29

Number of Days Annually With ≥ 1.0″ Precipitation

	Highest			Lowest	
Rank	**Station Name**	**Days**	**Rank**	**Station Name**	**Days**
1	Hobbs	5	1	Abiquiu Dam	0
1	Jal	5	1	Alamogordo	0
1	Tatum	5	1	Albuquerque Int'l Airport	0
4	Clovis	4	1	Alcalde	0
4	Clovis 13 N	4	1	Aleman Ranch	0
4	Crossroads 2	4	1	Animas	0
4	Elida	4	1	Aztec Ruins Nat'l Monument	0
4	Lake Maloya	4	1	Bernardo	0
4	Maljamar 4 SE	4	1	Bloomfield 3 SE	0
4	Ragland 3 SSW	4	1	Bosque Del Apache	0
11	Amistad 5 SSW	3	1	Carrizozo 1 SW	0
11	Cameron	3	1	Chaco Canyon Nat'l Monument	0
11	Dilia	3	1	Chama	0
11	Maxwell 3 NW	3	1	Cliff 11 SE	0
11	Melrose	3	1	Columbus	0
11	Ocate 2 NW	3	1	Cuba	0
11	Pasamonte	3	1	Dulce	0
11	Portales	3	1	Eagle Nest	0
11	San Jon	3	1	El Morro Nat'l Monument	0
11	Springer	3	1	El Rito	0
11	Tucumcari 4 NE	3	1	El Vado Dam	0
11	Valmora	3	1	Elephant Butte Dam	0
23	Bell Ranch	2	1	Estancia 7 NE	0
23	Bitter Lakes Wildlife Refuge	2	1	Faywood	0
23	Carlsbad	2	1	Fence Lake	0

Annual Snowfall

	Highest			Lowest	
Rank	**Station Name**	**Inches**	**Rank**	**Station Name**	**Inches**
1	Red River	164.9	1	Caballo Dam	1.1
2	Gascon	139.4	1	Glenwood	1.1
3	Wolf Canyon	128.4	3	Tularosa	1.4
4	Chama	107.5	4	Columbus	2.5
5	Lake Maloya	106.0	5	Carlsbad	2.7
6	Sandia Park	64.4	6	Elephant Butte Dam	2.9
6	Tierra Amarilla 4 N	64.4	7	Jornada Experiment Range	3.1
8	Eagle Nest	62.9	8	Redrock 1 NNE	3.2
9	Los Alamos	58.9	9	Faywood	3.3
10	Dulce	55.8	9	White Sands Nat'l Monument	3.3
11	El Morro Nat'l Monument	52.2	11	Hatch 5 NW	3.6
12	Clines Corners 7 SE	43.3	12	Jal	3.9
13	Cimarron 4 SW	41.5	12	Orogrande	3.9
14	El Vado Dam	41.1	14	Crossroads 2	4.0
15	Las Vegas Municipal Airport	39.5	14	Lordsburg 4 SE	4.0
16	Ocate 2 NW	39.3	14	State University	4.0
17	Des Moines	36.7	17	Alamogordo	4.3
18	Taos	36.1	17	Cliff 11 SE	4.3
19	Raton Filter Plant	35.5	19	Bernardo	4.5
20	El Rito	32.7	19	Fort Bayard	4.5
20	Gallup Sen Clarke Field	32.7	21	Bosque Del Apache	5.0
22	Jemez Springs	32.2	22	Carlsbad Caverns	5.2
23	Dilia	31.2	22	Hachita	5.2
24	Valmora	31.1	24	Animas	5.7
25	Fence Lake	29.2	25	Los Lunas 3 SSW	5.8

Note: See Appendix D for explanation of data.

Annual Extreme Maximum Temperature

	Highest			Lowest	
Rank	**Station Name**	**°F**	**Rank**	**Station Name**	**°F**
1	Dobbs Ferry Ardsley	104	1	Slide Mountain	88
1	New York Central Park Observatory	104	2	Stillwater Reservoir	90
3	Glenham	*103*	3	Old Forge	91
3	New York Avenue V Brooklyn	103	4	Cherry Valley 2 NNE	93
3	New York Laguardia Airport	103	4	Grafton	93
3	Poughkeepsie Dutchess Co. Arpt.	103	4	Tully Heiberg Forest	93
7	Bridgehampton	102	7	Boonville 2 SSW	94
7	Elmira	102	7	Indian Lake 2 SW	94
7	New York JFK Int'l Airport	102	7	Lake Placid 2 S	94
7	Patchogue 2 N	102	10	Chasm Falls	*95*
7	West Point	102	10	Conklingville Dam	*95*
12	Albion 2 NE	101	10	Fredonia	95
12	Aurora Research Farm	101	10	Gloversville	95
12	Bath	101	10	Oswego East	95
12	Hudson Correctionl Facility	101	10	Wanakena Ranger School	95
12	Middletown 2 NW	101	10	Watertown Airport	95
12	Troy Lock & Dam	101	17	Alfred	96
18	Chazy	100	17	Batavia	96
18	Cortland	100	17	Colden 1 N	96
18	Dansville	100	17	Little Valley	96
18	Glens Falls Airport	100	17	Norwich	96
18	Lockport 2 SE	100	17	Ray Brook	96
18	Massena Airport	100	17	Utica Oneida County Airport	96
18	Peru 2 WSW	100	24	Allegany State Park	97
18	Port Jervis	100	24	Angelica	97

Annual Mean Maximum Temperature

	Highest			Lowest	
Rank	**Station Name**	**°F**	**Rank**	**Station Name**	**°F**
1	New York Central Park Observatory	62.6	1	Slide Mountain	50.0
2	Dobbs Ferry Ardsley	62.5	2	Stillwater Reservoir	50.8
3	New York Avenue V Brooklyn	62.3	3	Boonville 2 SSW	51.1
4	Riverhead Research Farm	61.9	3	Indian Lake 2 SW	51.1
5	New York Laguardia Airport	61.8	5	Old Forge	51.3
5	Patchogue 2 N	61.8	6	Tully Heiberg Forest	51.9
5	Setauket Strong	61.8	7	Ray Brook	52.0
8	West Point	61.7	8	Lake Placid 2 S	52.2
9	Glenham	*61.6*	9	Wanakena Ranger School	52.8
10	New York JFK Int'l Airport	61.2	10	Chasm Falls	*53.2*
11	Port Jervis	60.8	10	Dannemora	53.2
12	Middletown 2 NW	60.7	12	Warsaw 6 SW	*53.3*
13	Hudson Correctionl Facility	60.4	13	Lowville	53.4
14	Poughkeepsie Dutchess Co. Arpt.	60.1	14	Canton 4 SE	53.6
15	Walden 1 ESE	59.7	15	Massena Airport	53.9
16	Bridgehampton	59.4	16	Cherry Valley 2 NNE	54.0
16	White Plains Westchester Co Arpt.	*59.4*	17	Grafton	54.3
18	Yorktown Heights 1 W	59.2	17	Lawrenceville 3 SW	54.3
19	Saratoga Springs 4 SW	58.6	19	Binghamton Edwin A. Link Field	54.5
19	Troy Lock & Dam	58.6	19	Franklinville	54.5
21	Dansville	58.5	21	Chazy	54.7
22	Elmira	58.3	22	Watertown	54.9
23	Whitehall	58.0	22	Watertown Airport	54.9
24	Glens Falls Farm	57.9	24	Conklingville Dam	*55.0*
25	Albany County Airport	57.8	24	Little Valley	55.0

Annual Mean Temperature

	Highest			Lowest	
Rank	**Station Name**	**°F**	**Rank**	**Station Name**	**°F**
1	New York Avenue V Brooklyn	55.1	1	Old Forge	39.9
1	New York Central Park Observatory	55.1	2	Indian Lake 2 SW	40.2
3	New York Laguardia Airport	55.0	3	Stillwater Reservoir	40.6
4	New York JFK Int'l Airport	54.2	4	Ray Brook	40.7
5	Dobbs Ferry Ardsley	53.2	5	Lake Placid 2 S	40.9
5	Riverhead Research Farm	53.2	6	Slide Mountain	41.0
5	Setauket Strong	53.2	7	Wanakena Ranger School	41.5
8	Patchogue 2 N	52.1	8	Boonville 2 SSW	42.2
9	West Point	52.0	9	Chasm Falls	*42.4*
10	Bridgehampton	51.1	10	Canton 4 SE	43.2
10	Glenham	*51.1*	10	Tully Heiberg Forest	43.2
12	White Plains Westchester Co. Arpt.	*51.0*	12	Lowville	43.3
13	Middletown 2 NW	50.9	13	Franklinville	43.5
14	Port Jervis	50.1	14	Dannemora	43.7
15	Yorktown Heights 1 W	50.0	14	Massena Airport	43.7
16	Hudson Correctionl Facility	49.5	16	Gouverneur 3 NW	44.0
17	Poughkeepsie Dutchess Co. Arpt.	49.3	17	Warsaw 6 SW	*44.1*
18	Fredonia	49.2	18	Bolivar	44.3
19	Troy Lock & Dam	48.8	18	Chazy	44.3
20	Mohonk Lake	48.7	20	Lawrenceville 3 SW	44.4
20	Westfield 2 SSE	48.7	21	Allegany State Park	44.5
22	Albion 2 NE	48.5	22	Little Valley	44.6
23	Sodus Center	48.4	23	Cherry Valley 2 NNE	44.7
23	Walden 1 ESE	48.4	24	Conklingville Dam	*44.9*
25	Canandaigua 3 S	48.3	24	Watertown Airport	44.9

Annual Mean Minimum Temperature

	Highest			Lowest	
Rank	**Station Name**	**°F**	**Rank**	**Station Name**	**°F**
1	New York Laguardia Airport	48.0	1	Old Forge	28.4
2	New York Avenue V Brooklyn	47.8	2	Indian Lake 2 SW	29.2
3	New York Central Park Observatory	47.5	2	Ray Brook	29.2
4	New York JFK Int'l Airport	47.1	4	Lake Placid 2 S	29.5
5	Setauket Strong	44.5	5	Wanakena Ranger School	30.3
6	Riverhead Research Farm	44.4	6	Stillwater Reservoir	30.4
7	Dobbs Ferry Ardsley	43.8	7	Chasm Falls	*31.5*
8	Bridgehampton	42.7	8	Slide Mountain	32.0
9	White Plains Westchester Co. Arpt.	*42.6*	9	Franklinville	32.4
10	Patchogue 2 N	42.4	10	Canton 4 SE	32.8
11	West Point	42.3	11	Gouverneur 3 NW	32.9
12	Middletown 2 NW	41.1	12	Bolivar	33.0
12	Westfield 2 SSE	41.1	13	Lowville	33.2
14	Yorktown Heights 1 W	40.8	14	Boonville 2 SSW	33.3
15	Fredonia	40.7	15	Massena Airport	33.5
16	Glenham	*40.5*	16	Allegany State Park	33.6
16	Mohonk Lake	40.5	17	Angelica	33.7
18	Buffalo Int'l Airport	39.9	18	Alfred	33.8
19	Oswego East	39.7	19	Chazy	33.9
20	Albion 2 NE	39.3	20	Little Valley	34.1
20	Port Jervis	39.3	21	Bath	34.2
22	Canandaigua 3 S	39.1	22	Dannemora	34.3
22	Sodus Center	39.1	23	Lawrenceville 3 SW	34.4
24	Rochester Int'l Airport	39.0	24	Cooperstown	34.5
25	Lockport 2 SE	38.9	24	Glens Falls Farm	34.5

Annual Extreme Minimum Temperature

	Highest				Lowest	
Rank	**Station Name**	**°F**		**Rank**	**Station Name**	**°F**
1	New York Central Park Observatory	-2		1	Old Forge	-52
1	New York JFK Int'l Airport	-2		2	Gouverneur 3 NW	-45
3	New York Laguardia Airport	-3		3	Chazy	-44
4	New York Avenue V Brooklyn	-4		3	Stillwater Reservoir	-44
4	Setauket Strong	-4		5	Watertown Airport	-43
6	Riverhead Research Farm	-8		6	Chasm Falls	*-42*
7	Dobbs Ferry Ardsley	-10		7	Wanakena Ranger School	-41
7	White Plains Westchester Co Arpt.	*-10*		8	Canton 4 SE	-40
9	Bridgehampton	-11		9	Massena Airport	-38
10	Patchogue 2 N	-13		9	Whitehall	-38
11	West Point	-15		11	Lake Placid 2 S	-37
11	Yorktown Heights 1 W	-15		12	Franklinville	-36
13	Geneva Research Farm	-16		12	Indian Lake 2 SW	-36
13	Glenham	*-16*		14	Glens Falls Airport	-35
13	Lockport 4 NE	*-16*		14	Lowville	-35
16	Canandaigua 3 S	-17		14	Ray Brook	-35
16	Fredonia	-17		17	Bolivar	-34
18	Binghamton Edwin A. Link Field	-18		17	Dannemora	-34
18	Buffalo Int'l Airport	-18		17	Glens Falls Farm	-34
18	Cortland	-18		17	Lawrenceville 3 SW	-34
21	Lockport 2 SE	-19		17	Peru 2 WSW	-34
21	Mohonk Lake	-19		17	Watertown	-34
21	Port Jervis	-19		23	Angelica	-33
21	Rochester Int'l Airport	-19		23	Boonville 2 SSW	-33
21	Westfield 2 SSE	-19		23	Saratoga Springs 4 SW	-33

July Mean Maximum Temperature

	Highest				Lowest	
Rank	**Station Name**	**°F**		**Rank**	**Station Name**	**°F**
1	West Point	86.1		1	Slide Mountain	71.8
2	Glenham	85.7		2	Stillwater Reservoir	75.1
3	Dobbs Ferry Ardsley	85.6		3	Indian Lake 2 SW	75.3
4	New York Central Park Observatory	85.5		4	Boonville 2 SSW	75.9
5	Hudson Correctionl Facility	84.8		4	Old Forge	75.9
5	New York Avenue V Brooklyn	84.8		6	Tully Heiberg Forest	76.0
7	New York Laguardia Airport	84.7		7	Lake Placid 2 S	76.6
7	Whitehall	84.7		8	Ray Brook	77.0
9	Port Jervis	84.5		9	Warsaw 6 SW	*77.4*
10	Riverhead Research Farm	84.2		10	Wanakena Ranger School	77.7
11	Saratoga Springs 4 SW	84.0		11	Franklinville	78.1
12	Middletown 2 NW	83.9		12	Cherry Valley 2 NNE	78.2
12	Troy Lock & Dam	83.9		13	Grafton	78.4
14	Poughkeepsie Dutchess Co. Arpt.	83.8		14	Allegany State Park	78.5
15	Patchogue 2 N	83.4		15	Bolivar	78.6
16	Setauket Strong	83.3		16	Binghamton Edwin A. Link Field	78.8
17	Walden 1 ESE	83.2		16	Chasm Falls	*78.8*
18	Glens Falls Farm	83.0		16	Little Valley	78.8
18	New York JFK Int'l Airport	83.0		19	Conklingville Dam	*79.0*
20	Albany County Airport	82.7		19	Dannemora	79.0
20	Dansville	82.7		19	Lowville	79.0
22	Elmira	82.6		22	Colden 1 N	79.1
23	Albion 2 NE	82.5		23	Canton 4 SE	79.3
24	White Plains Westchester Co Arpt.	82.4		24	Watertown Airport	79.4
25	Yorktown Heights 1 W	82.2		25	Alfred	79.6

January Mean Minimum Temperature

Highest				Lowest		
Rank	**Station Name**	**°F**		**Rank**	**Station Name**	**°F**
1	New York Laguardia Airport	26.3		1	Old Forge	1.4
2	New York Avenue V Brooklyn	26.1		2	Stillwater Reservoir	1.5
3	New York Central Park Observatory	26.0		3	Indian Lake 2 SW	3.1
3	New York JFK Int'l Airport	26.0		4	Wanakena Ranger School	3.2
5	Setauket Strong	24.4		5	Canton 4 SE	3.9
6	Riverhead Research Farm	24.2		6	Massena Airport	4.0
7	Bridgehampton	22.9		6	Ray Brook	4.0
7	Dobbs Ferry Ardsley	22.9		8	Lake Placid 2 S	4.1
9	Patchogue 2 N	21.5		9	Chasm Falls	*4.7*
10	White Plains Westchester Co Arpt.	21.0		10	Gouverneur 3 NW	5.5
11	West Point	20.0		11	Chazy	6.0
12	Fredonia	18.9		12	Lawrenceville 3 SW	6.4
13	Westfield 2 SSE	18.4		13	Lowville	6.6
14	Yorktown Heights 1 W	18.0		14	Dannemora	7.4
15	Middletown 2 NW	17.9		14	Glens Falls Airport	7.4
16	Buffalo Int'l Airport	17.6		14	Ogdensburg 4 NE	*7.4*
17	Port Jervis	17.1		17	Boonville 2 SSW	7.6
18	Albion 2 NE	17.0		18	Peru 2 WSW	7.9
19	Mohonk Lake	16.9		19	Conklingville Dam	*8.3*
19	Sodus Center	16.9		20	Glens Falls Farm	8.8
21	Rochester Int'l Airport	16.8		21	Watertown	9.0
22	Lockport 2 SE	16.6		22	Watertown Airport	9.3
23	Canandaigua 3 S	16.5		23	Slide Mountain	9.4
24	Lockport 4 NE	*16.4*		24	Whitehall	9.9
24	Oswego East	16.4		25	Gloversville	10.2

Number of Annual Heating Degree Days

Highest				Lowest		
Rank	**Station Name**	**Num.**		**Rank**	**Station Name**	**Num.**
1	Old Forge	9,191		1	New York Avenue V Brooklyn	4,693
2	Indian Lake 2 SW	9,082		2	New York Central Park Observatory	4,702
3	Stillwater Reservoir	8,972		3	New York Laguardia Airport	4,726
4	Ray Brook	8,966		4	New York JFK Int'l Airport	4,833
5	Lake Placid 2 S	8,848		5	Setauket Strong	5,054
6	Slide Mountain	8,735		6	Riverhead Research Farm	5,082
7	Wanakena Ranger School	8,674		7	Dobbs Ferry Ardsley	5,159
8	Boonville 2 SSW	8,432		8	Patchogue 2 N	5,375
9	Chasm Falls	*8,416*		9	West Point	5,523
10	Canton 4 SE	8,239		10	Bridgehampton	5,586
11	Lowville	8,117		11	White Plains Westchester Co Arpt.	*5,719*
12	Tully Heiberg Forest	8,093		12	Middletown 2 NW	5,798
13	Massena Airport	8,092		13	Glenham	*5,872*
14	Dannemora	8,015		14	Port Jervis	6,031
15	Franklinville	7,961		15	Yorktown Heights 1 W	6,033
16	Gouverneur 3 NW	7,910		16	Hudson Correctionl Facility	6,239
17	Lawrenceville 3 SW	7,880		17	Fredonia	6,264
18	Chazy	7,832		18	Poughkeepsie Dutchess Co. Arpt.	6,267
19	Warsaw 6 SW	*7,815*		19	Mohonk Lake	6,419
20	Bolivar	7,678		20	Westfield 2 SSE	6,430
21	Cherry Valley 2 NNE	7,636		21	Walden 1 ESE	6,535
22	Allegany State Park	7,633		22	Troy Lock & Dam	6,538
23	Peru 2 WSW	7,622		23	Sodus Center	6,543
24	Watertown Airport	7,616		24	Albion 2 NE	6,546
25	Little Valley	7,614		25	Canandaigua 3 S	6,589

Number of Annual Cooling Degree Days

	Highest				Lowest	
Rank	Station Name	Num.		Rank	Station Name	Num.
1	New York Laguardia Airport	1,228		1	Slide Mountain	94
2	New York Central Park Observatory	1,206		2	Indian Lake 2 SW	134
3	New York Avenue V Brooklyn	1,180		3	Old Forge	144
4	New York JFK Int'l Airport	1,027		4	Lake Placid 2 S	161
5	Dobbs Ferry Ardsley	939		5	Stillwater Reservoir	178
6	Glenham	*937*		6	Ray Brook	192
7	Riverhead Research Farm	903		7	Franklinville	226
8	West Point	895		8	Wanakena Ranger School	227
9	Setauket Strong	856		9	Boonville 2 SSW	229
10	Patchogue 2 N	812		10	Allegany State Park	249
11	Middletown 2 NW	794		10	Angelica	249
12	White Plains Westchester Co Arpt.	776		12	Tully Heiberg Forest	259
13	Troy Lock & Dam	733		13	Bolivar	263
14	Port Jervis	726		14	Little Valley	278
15	Yorktown Heights 1 W	696		15	Alfred	281
16	Hudson Correctionl Facility	683		16	Warsaw 6 SW	289
17	Albion 2 NE	661		17	Lowville	303
17	Whitehall	661		18	Colden 1 N	319
19	Poughkeepsie Dutchess Co. Arpt.	645		19	Cherry Valley 2 NNE	326
20	Westfield 2 SSE	637		19	Cooperstown	326
21	Mohonk Lake	627		21	Grafton	335
22	Fredonia	622		22	Dannemora	345
23	Canandaigua 3 S	616		23	Bath	346
24	Bridgehampton	608		24	Conklingville Dam	348
25	Saratoga Springs 4 SW	602		25	Gouverneur 3 NW	357

Annual Precipitation

	Highest				Lowest	
Rank	Station Name	Inches		Rank	Station Name	Inches
1	Slide Mountain	63.61		1	Peru 2 WSW	30.84
2	Boonville 2 SSW	59.83		2	Dansville	31.40
3	Dobbs Ferry Ardsley	51.74		3	Bath	31.96
4	Yorktown Heights 1 W	50.96		4	Geneva Research Farm	33.43
5	Mohonk Lake	50.51		5	Canandaigua 3 S	33.57
6	Old Forge	50.47		6	Rochester Int'l Airport	33.98
7	West Point	50.03		7	Watertown Airport	34.25
8	White Plains Westchester Co Arpt.	*49.95*		8	Elmira	34.80
9	Patchogue 2 N	49.90		8	Ogdensburg 4 NE	34.80
10	Little Valley	49.25		10	Batavia	35.55
11	New York Central Park Observatory	49.16		11	Albion 2 NE	35.71
12	Stillwater Reservoir	49.01		11	Massena Airport	35.71
13	Colden 1 N	48.20		13	Lawrenceville 3 SW	36.40
14	Bridgehampton	47.88		14	Lockport 4 NE	*36.84*
15	Riverhead Research Farm	46.62		15	Ithaca Cornell University	36.85
16	Walton	46.35		16	Angelica	37.08
17	Westfield 2 SSE	46.23		17	Canton 4 SE	37.15
18	Grafton	46.17		18	Lockport 2 SE	37.22
19	Conklingville Dam	45.95		19	Aurora Research Farm	37.33
20	New York Avenue V Brooklyn	45.93		20	Gouverneur 3 NW	37.46
21	Glenham	*45.74*		21	Troy Lock & Dam	37.58
22	Port Jervis	45.67		22	Dannemora	37.96
23	Setauket Strong	45.60		23	Alfred	38.02
24	Tully Heiberg Forest	45.57		24	Albany County Airport	38.05
25	Allegany State Park	45.51		25	Glens Falls Airport	38.08

Number of Days Annually With ≥ 0.1″ Precipitation

	Highest			Lowest	
Rank	**Station Name**	**Days**	**Rank**	**Station Name**	**Days**
1	Little Valley	123	1	Peru 2 WSW	*69*
2	Boonville 2 SSW	121	2	Bath	73
3	Old Forge	115	3	New York JFK Int'l Airport	74
3	Stillwater Reservoir	115	3	Setauket Strong	*74*
5	Colden 1 N	114	5	New York Avenue V Brooklyn	75
6	Allegany State Park	110	5	New York Laguardia Airport	75
6	Warsaw 6 SW	110	7	Dansville	76
8	Chasm Falls	*108*	7	Hudson Correctionl Facility	76
9	Tully Heiberg Forest	105	7	Riverhead Research Farm	76
10	Wanakena Ranger School	104	10	Bridgehampton	77
11	Oswego East	101	11	Elmira	78
11	Slide Mountain	101	11	Glenham	*78*
11	Utica Oneida County Airport	101	11	Middletown 2 NW	78
14	Franklinville	99	11	Poughkeepsie Dutchess Co. Arpt.	78
15	Grafton	97	11	Troy Lock & Dam	78
15	Watertown	97	11	White Plains Westchester Co Arpt.	*78*
15	Westfield 2 SSE	97	17	Albany County Airport	79
18	Cherry Valley 2 NNE	96	18	Canandaigua 3 S	80
18	Fredonia	96	18	Geneva Research Farm	80
18	Ray Brook	96	18	Glens Falls Airport	80
18	Walton	96	18	New York Central Park Observatory	80
22	Bolivar	94	18	Ogdensburg 4 NE	80
22	Lake Placid 2 S	94	23	Port Jervis	81
24	Buffalo Int'l Airport	93	23	Saratoga Springs 4 SW	81
24	Syracuse Hancock Int'l Airport	93	23	Walden 1 ESE	81

Number of Days Annually With ≥ 1.0″ Precipitation

	Highest			Lowest	
Rank	**Station Name**	**Days**	**Rank**	**Station Name**	**Days**
1	Slide Mountain	15	1	Watertown Airport	2
1	Yorktown Heights 1 W	15	2	Albion 2 NE	*3*
3	Boonville 2 SSW	13	2	Canandaigua 3 S	3
3	Mohonk Lake	13	2	Ogdensburg 4 NE	3
3	White Plains Westchester Co Arpt.	*13*	5	Aurora Research Farm	4
6	Bridgehampton	12	5	Lawrenceville 3 SW	4
6	Conklingville Dam	12	5	Lockport 4 NE	*4*
6	Dobbs Ferry Ardsley	12	5	Massena Airport	4
6	Glenham	*12*	5	Oswego East	4
6	New York Avenue V Brooklyn	12	5	Rochester Int'l Airport	4
6	New York Central Park Observatory	12	11	Alfred	5
6	New York JFK Int'l Airport	12	11	Angelica	5
6	New York Laguardia Airport	12	11	Batavia	5
6	Patchogue 2 N	12	11	Bath	5
6	Port Jervis	12	11	Cortland	5
6	Riverhead Research Farm	12	11	Dansville	5
6	Setauket Strong	12	11	Franklinville	5
6	West Point	12	11	Geneva Research Farm	5
19	Glens Falls Farm	11	11	Gouverneur 3 NW	5
19	Hudson Correctionl Facility	11	11	Ithaca Cornell University	5
19	Middletown 2 NW	11	11	Lockport 2 SE	5
19	Saratoga Springs 4 SW	11	11	Ray Brook	5
19	Walden 1 ESE	11	11	Sodus Center	5
24	Cherry Valley 2 NNE	10	24	Allegany State Park	6
24	Gloversville	10	24	Binghamton Edwin A. Link Field	6

Annual Snowfall

	Highest			Lowest	
Rank	**Station Name**	**Inches**	**Rank**	**Station Name**	**Inches**
1	Old Forge	226.7	1	Setauket Strong	*11.6*
2	Boonville 2 SSW	218.6	2	New York JFK Int'l Airport	20.5
3	Stillwater Reservoir	190.8	3	New York Central Park Observatory	21.2
4	Colden 1 N	157.5	4	New York Avenue V Brooklyn	21.5
5	Oswego East	153.3	5	New York Laguardia Airport	22.6
6	Wanakena Ranger School	128.0	6	Bridgehampton	24.2
7	Little Valley	127.9	7	Riverhead Research Farm	25.7
8	Tully Heiberg Forest	125.2	8	White Plains Westchester Co Arpt.	*29.3*
9	Lowville	125.1	9	West Point	*30.4*
10	Ray Brook	124.5	10	Patchogue 2 N	30.5
11	Chasm Falls	*121.2*	11	Dobbs Ferry Ardsley	31.2
12	Syracuse Hancock Int'l Airport	120.2	12	Poughkeepsie Dutchess Co. Arpt.	34.5
13	Cherry Valley 2 NNE	116.1	13	Glenham	*36.7*
14	Watertown	110.8	14	Walden 1 ESE	38.0
15	Warsaw 6 SW	*109.9*	14	Yorktown Heights 1 W	38.0
16	Slide Mountain	101.8	16	Troy Lock & Dam	*41.1*
17	Franklinville	*101.1*	17	Port Jervis	42.0
18	Rochester Int'l Airport	99.5	18	Elmira	42.7
19	Utica Oneida County Airport	98.5	19	Bath	46.7
20	Walton	95.9	20	Dansville	47.2
21	Buffalo Int'l Airport	95.7	21	Chazy	*56.0*
22	Cortland	91.3	22	Peru 2 WSW	*58.4*
23	Watertown Airport	91.1	23	Angelica	59.1
24	Canton 4 SE	90.9	24	Aurora Research Farm	61.8
25	Sodus Center	89.3	25	Albany County Airport	62.1

Note: See Appendix D for explanation of data.

Annual Extreme Maximum Temperature

	Highest				Lowest	
Rank	**Station Name**	**°F**		**Rank**	**Station Name**	**°F**
1	Dunn 4 NW	108		1	Grandfather Mountain	83
2	Albemarle	107		2	Highlands	91
2	Concord	107		3	Banner Elk	92
2	Forest City 6 SW	*107*		3	Blowing Rock 1 NW	92
2	Hamlet	107		5	Transou	93
2	Jackson Springs 5 WNW	107		6	Celo 2 S	95
2	Laurinburg	107		6	Waynesville 1 E	95
2	Monroe 4 SE	107		8	Canton 1 SW	*96*
2	Sanford 8 NE	107		8	Cape Hatteras NWS Bldg	96
2	Wadesboro	107		8	Jefferson 2 E	96
11	Chapel Hill 2 W	106		11	Brevard	*97*
11	Goldsboro Seymour Johnson AFB	106		11	Coweeta Exp. Station	97
11	Statesville 2 NNE	106		11	Pisgah Forest 1 N	97
14	Asheboro 2 W	105		14	Cullowhee	98
14	Burlington Fire Station 5	105		15	Andrews	99
14	Fayetteville	105		15	Asheville	99
14	Jackson	105		15	Black Mountain 2 W	99
14	Lenoir	105		15	Edenton	99
14	Lewiston	105		15	Fletcher 3 W	99
14	Lexington	105		15	Franklin 3 W	99
14	Lincolnton 4 W	105		15	Murphy 2 NE	99
14	Raleigh-Durham Airport	105		22	Asheville Regional Airport	100
14	Salisbury	105		22	Bent Creek	100
14	Shelby 2 NNE	105		22	Marshall	100
14	Siler City 2 N	105		22	Morehead City 2 WNW	100

Annual Mean Maximum Temperature

	Highest				Lowest	
Rank	**Station Name**	**°F**		**Rank**	**Station Name**	**°F**
1	Willard 4 SW	74.7		1	Grandfather Mountain	53.5
2	Laurinburg	74.5		2	Blowing Rock 1 NW	58.6
3	Kinston Agr. Research Center	74.3		3	Banner Elk	60.8
4	Longwood	74.1		4	Highlands	61.3
4	Whiteville 7 NW	74.1		5	Transou	62.5
4	Wilmington Airport	74.1		6	Jefferson 2 E	63.0
7	Wilmington 7 N	74.0		7	Celo 2 S	64.5
8	Southport 5 N	*73.6*		8	Canton 1 SW	*65.8*
9	Hamlet	73.5		9	Fletcher 3 W	66.6
10	New Bern Craven Co. Reg. Airport	*73.2*		10	Asheville	66.7
11	Plymouth 5 E	73.1		11	Asheville Regional Airport	67.0
12	Lumberton	*73.0*		12	Waynesville 1 E	67.1
12	Sanford 8 NE	73.0		13	Marshall	67.2
14	Clinton 2 NE	72.8		14	Pisgah Forest 1 N	67.3
14	Morehead City 2 WNW	72.8		15	Coweeta Exp. Station	67.5
16	Goldsboro Seymour Johnson AFB	72.7		16	Bent Creek	67.6
17	Fayetteville	72.6		16	Hendersonville 1 NE	67.6
17	Smithfield	72.6		18	Black Mountain 2 W	68.0
17	Tarboro 1 S	72.6		18	Waterville 2	68.0
20	Wadesboro	72.3		20	Brevard	*68.1*
21	Dunn 4 NW	72.2		21	Reidsville 2 NW	68.2
21	Greenville	72.2		22	Danbury 1 NW	68.3
21	Kinston 5 SE	72.2		23	Oconaluftee	68.5
21	Lewiston	72.2		24	Cullowhee	68.6
21	Monroe 4 SE	72.2		24	Greensboro Airport	68.6

Annual Mean Temperature

	Highest				Lowest	
Rank	Station Name	°F		Rank	Station Name	°F
1	Wilmington Airport	63.8		1	Grandfather Mountain	46.2
2	Cedar Island	63.2		2	Blowing Rock 1 NW	49.3
2	Morehead City 2 WNW	63.2		3	Banner Elk	49.9
4	New Bern Craven Co. Reg. Airport	*62.9*		4	Transou	50.5
5	Cape Hatteras NWS Bldg	62.8		5	Highlands	51.2
5	Willard 4 SW	62.8		6	Jefferson 2 E	51.6
5	Wilmington 7 N	62.8		7	Celo 2 S	51.9
8	Laurinburg	62.5		8	Canton 1 SW	*53.5*
9	Kinston Agr. Research Center	62.4		9	Oconaluftee	53.7
10	Aurora 6 N	*62.3*		10	Waynesville 1 E	54.1
10	Southport 5 N	*62.3*		11	Pisgah Forest 1 N	54.2
12	Whiteville 7 NW	62.1		12	Fletcher 3 W	54.6
13	Goldsboro Seymour Johnson AFB	62.0		13	Coweeta Exp. Station	54.7
14	Longwood	61.9		14	Marshall	55.0
15	Edenton	61.7		15	Andrews	55.5
16	Belhaven 5 SE	61.5		16	Bent Creek	55.6
16	Clinton 2 NE	61.5		17	Black Mountain 2 W	55.7
18	Plymouth 5 E	61.3		17	Brevard	*55.7*
18	Wadesboro	61.3		19	Asheville Regional Airport	55.8
20	Elizabeth City	61.2		20	North Wilkesboro	55.9
21	Fayetteville	61.1		21	Murphy 2 NE	56.0
22	Williamston 1 E	61.0		22	Franklin 3 W	56.1
23	Greenville	60.9		23	Cullowhee	56.2
24	Monroe 4 SE	60.8		24	Hendersonville 1 NE	56.3
25	Gastonia	60.7		24	W Kerr Scott Reservoir	56.3

Annual Mean Minimum Temperature

	Highest				Lowest	
Rank	Station Name	°F		Rank	Station Name	°F
1	Cape Hatteras NWS Bldg	55.6		1	Transou	38.5
2	Cedar Island	54.5		2	Grandfather Mountain	38.8
3	Morehead City 2 WNW	53.6		2	Oconaluftee	38.8
4	Wilmington Airport	53.5		4	Banner Elk	39.0
5	Aurora 6 N	*52.8*		5	Celo 2 S	39.2
6	New Bern Craven Co. Reg. Airport	*52.6*		6	Blowing Rock 1 NW	40.0
7	Edenton	51.9		7	Jefferson 2 E	40.1
8	Belhaven 5 SE	51.5		8	Highlands	41.0
9	Wilmington 7 N	51.4		9	Pisgah Forest 1 N	41.1
10	Goldsboro Seymour Johnson AFB	51.3		9	Waynesville 1 E	41.1
11	Southport 5 N	*51.0*		11	Canton 1 SW	*41.2*
12	Elizabeth City	50.8		12	Coweeta Exp. Station	41.8
12	Willard 4 SW	50.8		13	Andrews	42.2
14	Laurinburg	50.5		14	Fletcher 3 W	42.6
15	Charlotte Douglas Int'l Airport	50.4		15	Marshall	42.8
15	Kinston Agr. Research Center	50.4		15	North Wilkesboro	42.8
15	Wadesboro	50.4		17	Murphy 2 NE	43.0
18	Williamston 1 E	50.2		18	Brevard	*43.2*
19	Clinton 2 NE	50.1		19	Black Mountain 2 W	43.3
19	Whiteville 7 NW	50.1		19	Franklin 3 W	43.3
21	Greenville	49.6		21	W Kerr Scott Reservoir	43.5
21	Longwood	49.6		22	Bent Creek	43.6
21	Raleigh State University	49.6		23	Cullowhee	43.7
24	Fayetteville	49.5		24	Louisburg	43.8
24	Plymouth 5 E	49.5		25	Danbury 1 NW	44.4

Annual Extreme Minimum Temperature

	Highest			Lowest	
Rank	Station Name	°F	Rank	Station Name	°F
1	Cape Hatteras NWS Bldg	6	1	Grandfather Mountain	-32
2	Williamston 1 E	4	2	Banner Elk	-31
3	Cedar Island	2	3	Blowing Rock 1 NW	-24
4	Goldsboro Seymour Johnson AFB	1	3	Transou	-24
4	Morehead City 2 WNW	1	5	Oconaluftee	-23
6	Wilmington 7 N	0	6	Waynesville 1 E	-22
6	Wilmington Airport	0	7	Canton 1 SW	*-20*
8	Aurora 6 N	*-1*	8	Andrews	-19
8	Fayetteville	-1	8	Cullowhee	-19
10	Clinton 2 NE	-2	8	Highlands	-19
10	Elizabeth City	-2	11	Coweeta Exp. Station	-18
10	Kinston 5 SE	-2	11	Marshall	-18
10	Kinston Agr. Research Center	-2	13	Asheville	-17
10	Lumberton	-2	13	Waterville 2	-17
10	Whiteville 7 NW	-2	15	Asheville Regional Airport	-16
16	Elizabethtown Lock 2	-3	15	Bent Creek	-16
16	Laurinburg	-3	15	Celo 2 S	-16
16	Roanoke Rapids	-3	15	Fletcher 3 W	-16
16	Sanford 8 NE	-3	15	Murphy 2 NE	-16
16	Southport 5 N	-3	20	Brevard	*-15*
21	Dunn 4 NW	-4	20	Franklin 3 W	-15
21	Edenton	-4	20	Jefferson 2 E	-15
21	Greenville	-4	20	Pisgah Forest 1 N	-15
21	Longwood	-4	24	Black Mountain 2 W	-14
21	New Bern Craven Co. Reg. Airport	*-4*	24	Hendersonville 1 NE	-14

July Mean Maximum Temperature

	Highest			Lowest	
Rank	Station Name	°F	Rank	Station Name	°F
1	Laurinburg	91.7	1	Grandfather Mountain	69.8
2	Hamlet	91.4	2	Blowing Rock 1 NW	76.5
3	Sanford 8 NE	91.1	3	Banner Elk	77.5
4	Goldsboro Seymour Johnson AFB	90.7	4	Highlands	77.9
4	Kinston Agr. Research Center	90.7	5	Transou	80.6
4	Tarboro 1 S	90.7	6	Jefferson 2 E	80.9
7	Fayetteville	90.6	7	Celo 2 S	81.0
7	Smithfield	90.6	8	Canton 1 SW	*82.7*
7	Whiteville 7 NW	90.6	9	Waynesville 1 E	83.5
10	Concord	90.5	10	Coweeta Exp. Station	83.8
11	Wadesboro	90.4	11	Brevard	83.9
11	Wilson 3 SW	90.4	12	Pisgah Forest 1 N	84.1
13	Willard 4 SW	90.3	13	Fletcher 3 W	84.3
14	Burlington Fire Station 5	90.2	14	Asheville Regional Airport	84.5
14	Plymouth 5 E	90.2	14	Bent Creek	84.5
16	Clinton 2 NE	90.1	16	Black Mountain 2 W	84.7
16	Jackson	90.1	16	Marshall	84.7
16	Lewiston	90.1	18	Asheville	84.8
16	Lumberton	90.1	19	Hendersonville 1 NE	84.9
20	Greenville	90.0	20	Cullowhee	85.0
20	Wilmington 7 N	90.0	21	Cape Hatteras NWS Bldg	85.4
22	Wilmington Airport	89.9	22	Andrews	85.5
23	Lexington	89.8	23	Oconaluftee	85.6
23	Longwood	89.8	24	Franklin 3 W	85.8
25	Dunn 4 NW	89.7	25	Murphy 2 NE	86.1

January Mean Minimum Temperature

	Highest				Lowest	
Rank	Station Name	°F		Rank	Station Name	°F
1	Cape Hatteras NWS Bldg	38.3		1	Grandfather Mountain	19.9
2	Cedar Island	36.4		2	Blowing Rock 1 NW	20.7
3	Wilmington Airport	35.6		3	Banner Elk	20.9
4	Morehead City 2 WNW	35.3		4	Oconaluftee	21.0
5	New Bern Craven Co. Reg. Airport	*34.2*		5	Transou	21.1
6	Aurora 6 N	33.7		6	Celo 2 S	21.5
7	Edenton	33.5		7	Jefferson 2 E	22.6
8	Willard 4 SW	33.3		8	Canton 1 SW	*23.2*
8	Wilmington 7 N	33.3		9	Pisgah Forest 1 N	23.3
10	Kinston Agr. Research Center	32.8		10	North Wilkesboro	23.6
11	Goldsboro Seymour Johnson AFB	32.7		11	Andrews	23.8
12	Belhaven 5 SE	32.5		12	Highlands	24.0
13	Whiteville 7 NW	32.4		12	W Kerr Scott Reservoir	24.0
14	Elizabethtown Lock 2	*32.3*		12	Waynesville 1 E	24.0
15	Longwood	32.2		15	Coweeta Exp. Station	24.2
16	Laurinburg	32.1		16	Fletcher 3 W	24.7
16	Southport 5 N	32.1		16	Louisburg	24.7
18	Williamston 1 E	32.0		16	Marshall	24.7
19	Elizabeth City	31.9		19	Brevard	25.4
20	Plymouth 5 E	31.8		19	Murphy 2 NE	25.4
21	Clinton 2 NE	31.7		21	Danbury 1 NW	25.5
22	Charlotte Douglas Int'l Airport	31.2		21	Franklin 3 W	25.5
22	Monroe 4 SE	31.2		23	Black Mountain 2 W	25.8
24	Wadesboro	31.1		24	Mount Airy 2 W	25.9
25	Raleigh 4 SW	31.0		25	Forest City 6 SW	*26.0*

Number of Annual Heating Degree Days

	Highest				Lowest	
Rank	Station Name	Num.		Rank	Station Name	Num.
1	Grandfather Mountain	6,821		1	Wilmington Airport	2,394
2	Blowing Rock 1 NW	5,881		2	Morehead City 2 WNW	2,421
3	Banner Elk	5,616		3	Cape Hatteras NWS Bldg	2,492
4	Transou	5,517		4	Cedar Island	2,509
5	Jefferson 2 E	5,239		5	Willard 4 SW	2,545
6	Highlands	5,234		6	New Bern Craven Co. Reg. Airport	*2,588*
7	Celo 2 S	5,092		7	Wilmington 7 N	2,602
8	Oconaluftee	4,674		8	Southport 5 N	*2,660*
9	Canton 1 SW	*4,658*		9	Kinston Agr. Research Center	2,688
10	Pisgah Forest 1 N	4,512		10	Laurinburg	2,738
11	Waynesville 1 E	4,460		11	Longwood	2,750
12	Fletcher 3 W	4,436		12	Whiteville 7 NW	2,760
13	Marshall	4,347		13	Aurora 6 N	*2,761*
14	Coweeta Exp. Station	4,306		14	Edenton	2,849
15	North Wilkesboro	4,291		15	Goldsboro Seymour Johnson AFB	2,909
16	Andrews	4,238		16	Plymouth 5 E	2,926
17	W Kerr Scott Reservoir	4,198		17	Belhaven 5 SE	2,944
18	Danbury 1 NW	4,164		18	Clinton 2 NE	2,967
19	Asheville Regional Airport	4,142		19	Elizabeth City	2,998
20	Bent Creek	4,138		20	Wadesboro	3,025
20	Murphy 2 NE	4,138		21	Williamston 1 E	3,036
22	Brevard	*4,088*		22	Monroe 4 SE	3,079
23	Black Mountain 2 W	4,066		23	Tryon	3,095
24	Mount Airy 2 W	4,038		24	Lumberton	*3,109*
25	Franklin 3 W	4,032		25	Fayetteville	3,110

Number of Annual Cooling Degree Days

	Highest			Lowest	
Rank	**Station Name**	**Num.**	**Rank**	**Station Name**	**Num.**
1	Wilmington Airport	2,065	1	Grandfather Mountain	67
2	New Bern Craven Co. Reg. Airport	*2,009*	2	Banner Elk	250
3	Goldsboro Seymour Johnson AFB	2,001	3	Blowing Rock 1 NW	280
4	Cedar Island	1,986	4	Highlands	284
5	Laurinburg	1,936	5	Transou	364
6	Kinston Agr. Research Center	1,911	6	Celo 2 S	455
7	Morehead City 2 WNW	1,896	7	Jefferson 2 E	457
8	Wilmington 7 N	1,892	8	Waynesville 1 E	630
9	Aurora 6 N	1,890	9	Pisgah Forest 1 N	680
10	Willard 4 SW	1,867	10	Oconaluftee	684
11	Wadesboro	1,841	11	Coweeta Exp. Station	691
12	Whiteville 7 NW	1,823	12	Fletcher 3 W	765
13	Cape Hatteras NWS Bldg	1,817	13	Black Mountain 2 W	773
14	Clinton 2 NE	1,803	14	Brevard	*798*
15	Fayetteville	1,797	15	Marshall	836
16	Southport 5 N	*1,793*	16	Bent Creek	860
17	Belhaven 5 SE	1,780	17	Andrews	890
18	Greenville	1,775	18	Cullowhee	896
19	Elizabeth City	1,774	19	Asheville Regional Airport	906
20	Charlotte Douglas Int'l Airport	1,767	19	Franklin 3 W	906
21	Longwood	1,765	21	Murphy 2 NE	976
22	Plymouth 5 E	1,760	22	Asheville	1,002
23	Edenton	1,749	22	Hendersonville 1 NE	1,002
24	Gastonia	1,723	24	Waterville 2	1,130
25	Lewiston	1,719	25	Danbury 1 NW	1,138

Annual Precipitation

	Highest			Lowest	
Rank	**Station Name**	**Inches**	**Rank**	**Station Name**	**Inches**
1	Highlands	87.85	1	Asheville	37.37
2	Coweeta Exp. Station	72.43	2	Marshall	40.14
3	Blowing Rock 1 NW	68.70	3	Canton 1 SW	*42.38*
4	Brevard	*66.04*	4	Raleigh-Durham Airport	42.94
5	Andrews	65.96	5	Salisbury	43.19
6	Tryon	65.58	6	Greensboro Airport	43.27
7	Pisgah Forest 1 N	64.91	7	Charlotte Douglas Int'l Airport	43.56
8	Grandfather Mountain	63.46	8	Tarboro 1 S	45.02
9	Southport 5 N	60.97	9	Burlington Fire Station 5	45.39
10	Tapoco	60.04	10	Gastonia	45.43
11	Celo 2 S	59.22	11	Oxford 1 E	*45.45*
12	Wilmington 7 N	58.28	12	Lexington	45.65
13	Oconaluftee	57.97	13	Jackson	45.66
14	Cape Hatteras NWS Bldg	57.72	14	Yadkinville 6 E	45.81
15	Cedar Island	57.70	15	Roanoke Rapids	46.04
16	Morehead City 2 WNW	57.50	16	Statesville 2 NNE	46.14
17	Wilmington Airport	57.03	17	Raleigh 4 SW	46.27
18	Transou	56.92	18	High Point	46.34
19	Hendersonville 1 NE	56.60	19	Roxboro 7 ESE	46.38
20	Murphy 2 NE	56.43	20	Raleigh State University	46.49
21	Franklin 3 W	54.51	21	Fayetteville	46.71
22	Longwood	54.47	22	Asheboro 2 W	46.98
23	New Bern Craven Co. Reg. Airport	*54.13*	22	Asheville Regional Airport	46.98
24	Marion 2 NW	53.92	22	Reidsville 2 NW	46.98
25	Willard 4 SW	53.81	25	Louisburg	47.14

Number of Days Annually With ≥ 0.1″ Precipitation

	Highest			Lowest	
Rank	**Station Name**	**Days**	**Rank**	**Station Name**	**Days**
1	Highlands	108	1	Elizabethtown Lock 2	68
2	Grandfather Mountain	106	1	Salisbury	68
3	Andrews	104	3	Gastonia	72
4	Blowing Rock 1 NW	99	4	Albemarle	73
4	Tapoco	99	4	Greensboro Airport	73
6	Waterville 2	98	4	Louisburg	73
7	Banner Elk	97	4	Raleigh-Durham Airport	73
7	Coweeta Exp. Station	97	8	Arcola	74
7	Oconaluftee	97	8	Charlotte Douglas Int'l Airport	74
10	Murphy 2 NE	96	8	Lumberton	74
11	Franklin 3 W	95	8	Shelby 2 NNE	74
11	Pisgah Forest 1 N	95	12	Burlington Fire Station 5	75
13	Celo 2 S	94	12	Laurinburg	75
13	Cullowhee	94	12	Lewiston	75
15	Brevard	*91*	12	Lexington	75
16	Transou	89	12	Raleigh 4 SW	75
16	Tryon	89	12	Roxboro 7 ESE	75
16	Waynesville 1 E	89	12	Sanford 8 NE	*75*
19	Marshall	*88*	12	Siler City 2 N	75
20	Fletcher 3 W	87	12	Tarboro 1 S	75
21	Cedar Island	86	21	Asheville	76
22	Hendersonville 1 NE	85	21	Chapel Hill 2 W	76
22	North Wilkesboro	85	21	Dunn 4 NW	76
24	W Kerr Scott Reservoir	84	21	Jackson	76
25	Black Mountain 2 W	82	21	Oxford 1 E	*76*

Number of Days Annually With ≥ 1.0″ Precipitation

	Highest			Lowest	
Rank	**Station Name**	**Days**	**Rank**	**Station Name**	**Days**
1	Highlands	27	1	Marshall	8
2	Brevard	*24*	2	Asheville	10
2	Coweeta Exp. Station	24	2	Canton 1 SW	*10*
4	Tryon	23	4	Banner Elk	11
5	Pisgah Forest 1 N	22	5	Asheboro 2 W	12
6	Andrews	20	5	Asheville Regional Airport	12
6	Blowing Rock 1 NW	20	5	Bent Creek	12
8	Southport 5 N	19	5	Black Mountain 2 W	12
9	Celo 2 S	17	5	Burlington Fire Station 5	12
9	Tapoco	17	5	Chapel Hill 2 W	12
11	Cape Hatteras NWS Bldg	16	5	Charlotte Douglas Int'l Airport	12
11	Cedar Island	16	5	Cullowhee	12
11	Grandfather Mountain	16	5	Danbury 1 NW	12
11	Hendersonville 1 NE	16	5	Gastonia	12
11	Kinston Agr. Research Center	16	5	Greensboro Airport	12
11	Longwood	16	5	High Point	12
11	New Bern Craven Co. Reg. Airport	*16*	5	Jefferson 2 E	12
11	W Kerr Scott Reservoir	16	5	Lexington	12
11	Willard 4 SW	16	5	Monroe 4 SE	12
11	Wilmington 7 N	16	5	Mount Airy 2 W	12
11	Wilmington Airport	16	5	North Wilkesboro	12
22	Morehead City 2 WNW	15	5	Oxford 1 E	*12*
22	Murphy 2 NE	15	5	Raleigh 4 SW	12
22	Oconaluftee	15	5	Raleigh State University	12
22	Plymouth 5 E	15	5	Raleigh-Durham Airport	12

Annual Snowfall

	Highest			Lowest	
Rank	**Station Name**	**Inches**	**Rank**	**Station Name**	**Inches**
1	Grandfather Mountain	57.8	1	Elizabeth City	*Trace*
2	Banner Elk	42.6	2	Gastonia	*0.4*
3	Blowing Rock 1 NW	30.0	3	Aurora 6 N	*0.9*
4	Transou	24.7	4	Elizabethtown Lock 2	*1.0*
5	Jefferson 2 E	18.1	4	Roanoke Rapids	*1.0*
6	Celo 2 S	16.7	4	Southport 5 N	1.0
7	Highlands	16.2	7	Kinston Agr. Research Center	1.1
8	Marshall	15.7	8	Fayetteville	1.2
9	Waynesville 1 E	14.5	9	Hamlet	1.4
10	Asheville	13.3	10	Morehead City 2 WNW	1.6
11	Asheville Regional Airport	13.2	11	Longwood	*1.7*
12	Fletcher 3 W	10.2	12	Cape Hatteras NWS Bldg	2.0
12	W Kerr Scott Reservoir	10.2	12	Lumberton	2.0
14	Mount Airy 2 W	9.8	12	Wilmington Airport	2.0
15	Marion 2 NW	*9.6*	15	Kinston 5 SE	2.1
15	North Wilkesboro	9.6	16	Burlington Fire Station 5	*2.2*
17	Brevard	*9.3*	17	Dunn 4 NW	*2.3*
17	Cullowhee	9.3	17	Laurinburg	2.3
17	Pisgah Forest 1 N	9.3	17	Wilmington 7 N	2.3
17	Reidsville 2 NW	9.3	20	New Bern Craven Co. Reg. Airport	*2.4*
21	Black Mountain 2 W	*9.1*	21	Cedar Island	2.6
22	Hendersonville 1 NE	9.0	21	Whiteville 7 NW	2.6
22	Yadkinville 6 E	9.0	23	Clinton 2 NE	2.7
24	Roxboro 7 ESE	8.5	24	Jackson Springs 5 WNW	*2.9*
25	Danbury 1 NW	*8.4*	24	Louisburg	2.9

Note: See Appendix D for explanation of data.

Annual Extreme Maximum Temperature

	Highest				Lowest	
Rank	**Station Name**	**°F**		**Rank**	**Station Name**	**°F**
1	Hettinger	111		1	Rolla 3 NW	100
2	Dickinson Exp. Station	110		2	Bottineau	101
2	Fort Yates 4 SW	110		2	Sharon	101
2	Medora	110		4	Hansboro 4 NNE	102
2	Trotters 3 SSE	110		4	Petersburg 2 N	102
2	Watford City 14 S	110		6	Cavalier 7 NW	103
7	Bismarck Municipal Airport	109		6	Devils Lake KDLR	103
7	Dickinson Municipal Airport	109		6	Langdon Exp. Farm	103
7	Fairfield	109		6	Minot Experiment Station	103
7	Foxholm 7 N	109		6	Powers Lake 1 N	103
7	Gackle	109		6	Westhope	103
7	Jamestown State Hospital	109		12	Bowbells	104
7	Oakes 2 S	109		12	Butte	104
7	Williston Sloulin Int'l Airport	109		12	Cooperstown	104
15	Beulah 1 W	108		12	Grafton	104
15	Drake 9 NE	108		12	Grand Forks Int'l Airport	104
15	Dunn Center 2 SW	108		12	McVille	104
15	Ellendale	108		12	Pembina	104
15	Fullerton 1 ESE	108		12	Richardton Abbey	104
15	Jamestown Municipal Airport	108		12	Valley City 3 NNW	104
15	La Moure	108		12	Wildrose 3 NW	104
15	Mott	108		22	Carson	105
15	Napoleon	108		22	Fortuna 1 W	105
15	Pretty Rock	108		22	Garrison 1 NNW	105
15	Tioga 1 E	108		22	Grand Forks Univ. NWS	105

Annual Mean Maximum Temperature

	Highest				Lowest	
Rank	**Station Name**	**°F**		**Rank**	**Station Name**	**°F**
1	Medora	58.8		1	Rolla 3 NW	46.8
2	Watford City 14 S	57.7		2	Langdon Exp. Farm	47.2
3	Fort Yates 4 SW	56.7		3	Petersburg 2 N	48.7
4	Pretty Rock	55.4		4	Pembina	48.8
5	New England	55.3		5	Cavalier 7 NW	48.9
5	Williston Exp. Farm	55.3		6	Edmore 1 NW	49.2
7	Mott	55.2		7	Bottineau	49.3
8	Washburn	55.1		8	Willow City	49.5
9	Amidon	55.0		9	Fortuna 1 W	49.8
9	Hettinger	55.0		9	Sharon	49.8
11	Ellendale	54.8		11	Devils Lake KDLR	49.9
12	Bowman	54.7		11	Hansboro 4 NNE	49.9
12	Fullerton 1 ESE	54.7		13	Leeds	50.0
12	Keene 3 S	54.7		13	McHenry 3 W	50.0
15	Beulah 1 W	54.6		15	Stanley 3 NNW	50.1
15	Trotters 3 SSE	54.6		16	Powers Lake 1 N	50.2
17	Dickinson Exp. Station	54.4		17	Bowbells	50.4
17	Dickinson Municipal Airport	54.4		17	Carrington	50.4
17	Dunn Center 2 SW	54.4		19	Grand Forks Int'l Airport	50.5
20	McLeod 3 E	54.3		20	Tioga 1 E	50.7
21	Bismarck Municipal Airport	54.0		20	Wildrose 3 NW	50.7
21	New Salem 5 NW	54.0		22	Max	50.9
23	Richardton Abbey	53.9		22	Minot Experiment Station	50.9
23	Williston Sloulin Int'l Airport	53.9		22	Upham 3 N	50.9
25	Center 4 SE	53.8		25	McVille	51.1

Annual Mean Temperature

	Highest			Lowest	
Rank	**Station Name**	**°F**	**Rank**	**Station Name**	**°F**
1	Fort Yates 4 SW	45.1	1	Langdon Exp. Farm	36.4
2	Medora	44.7	2	Rolla 3 NW	37.0
3	Watford City 14 S	44.1	3	Pembina	37.2
4	Richardton Abbey	43.1	4	Petersburg 2 N	37.5
4	Wahpeton 3 N	43.1	4	Willow City	37.5
4	Washburn	43.1	6	Edmore 1 NW	37.7
4	Williston Exp. Farm	43.1	7	Bottineau	38.0
8	Amidon	43.0	8	Cavalier 7 NW	38.1
8	Ellendale	43.0	8	Stanley 3 NNW	38.1
8	New England	43.0	8	Upham 3 N	38.1
8	Pretty Rock	43.0	11	Hansboro 4 NNE	38.2
12	Trotters 3 SSE	42.8	11	Powers Lake 1 N	38.2
13	Dickinson Municipal Airport	42.7	13	Fortuna 1 W	38.4
14	Bowman	42.6	13	Leeds	38.4
14	Fullerton 1 ESE	42.6	15	Bowbells	38.5
14	McLeod 3 E	42.6	15	Tioga 1 E	38.5
17	Hettinger	42.5	17	McHenry 3 W	38.7
18	Mott	42.4	18	Towner 2 NE	38.8
19	Dunn Center 2 SW	42.3	19	Wildrose 3 NW	39.1
20	Butte	42.2	20	Kenmare 1 WSW	39.3
21	Gackle	42.1	21	Sharon	39.4
21	Hankinson	*42.1*	21	Westhope	39.4
21	Jamestown State Hospital	42.1	23	Max	39.5
21	Keene 3 S	42.1	24	Valley City 3 NNW	39.6
25	Bismarck Municipal Airport	42.0	25	Carrington	39.7

Annual Mean Minimum Temperature

	Highest			Lowest	
Rank	**Station Name**	**°F**	**Rank**	**Station Name**	**°F**
1	Fort Yates 4 SW	33.5	1	Upham 3 N	25.2
2	Wahpeton 3 N	32.4	2	Willow City	25.3
3	Richardton Abbey	32.1	3	Langdon Exp. Farm	25.6
4	Minot FAA Airport	31.4	3	Pembina	25.6
5	Dickinson Municipal Airport	31.1	5	Edmore 1 NW	26.1
5	Ellendale	31.1	5	Powers Lake 1 N	26.1
5	Fargo Hector Field	31.1	5	Stanley 3 NNW	26.1
5	Jamestown State Hospital	31.1	8	Petersburg 2 N	26.3
5	Washburn	31.1	8	Tioga 1 E	26.3
10	Amidon	31.0	8	Towner 2 NE	26.3
10	Trotters 3 SSE	31.0	11	Hansboro 4 NNE	26.4
12	Gackle	30.9	12	Bowbells	26.6
12	Jamestown Municipal Airport	30.9	13	Bottineau	26.7
12	McLeod 3 E	30.9	14	Fortuna 1 W	26.9
15	Butte	30.8	14	Leeds	26.9
15	Williston Exp. Farm	30.8	16	Rolla 3 NW	27.2
17	Grand Forks Univ. NWS	30.7	17	Cavalier 7 NW	27.3
17	McClusky	30.7	17	McHenry 3 W	27.3
19	Fullerton 1 ESE	30.6	19	Kenmare 1 WSW	27.4
19	New England	30.6	20	Wildrose 3 NW	27.6
19	Pretty Rock	30.6	21	Dickinson Exp. Station	27.7
22	Bowman	30.5	21	Westhope	27.7
22	Forman 5 SSE	30.5	23	Valley City 3 NNW	27.8
22	Medora	30.5	24	Max	28.0
22	Watford City 14 S	30.5	25	Tuttle	*28.1*

Annual Extreme Minimum Temperature

	Highest				Lowest	
Rank	**Station Name**	**°F**		**Rank**	**Station Name**	**°F**
1	Richardton Abbey	-33		1	Tioga 1 E	-50
2	Dickinson Municipal Airport	-34		1	Williston Sloulin Int'l Airport	-50
2	Hankinson	*-34*		3	Towner 2 NE	-49
2	McClusky	-34		3	Willow City	-49
2	Washburn	*-34*		5	Powers Lake 1 N	-48
6	Underwood	-35		5	Upham 3 N	-48
7	Bowman	-36		7	Rugby	-47
7	Carrington	-36		7	Stanley 3 NNW	-47
7	Minot FAA Airport	-36		9	Beulah 1 W	-46
7	Wahpeton 3 N	-36		9	Edmore 1 NW	-46
11	Devils Lake KDLR	*-37*		11	Fort Yates 4 SW	-45
11	Ellendale	-37		11	Fortuna 1 W	-45
11	Gackle	-37		11	Hansboro 4 NNE	-45
11	Hillsboro 3 N	-37		11	Oakes 2 S	-45
11	Jamestown Municipal Airport	-37		11	Watford City 14 S	-45
11	New England	-37		16	Fullerton 1 ESE	-44
11	Trotters 3 SSE	-37		16	Medora	-44
18	Butte	-38		16	Petersburg 2 N	-44
18	Cooperstown	-38		16	Valley City 3 NNW	-44
18	Dunn Center 2 SW	-38		16	Westhope	-44
18	Fairfield	-38		21	Bismarck Municipal Airport	-43
18	Mandan Experiment Station	-38		21	Drake 9 NE	-43
18	Max	-38		21	Keene 3 S	-43
18	Turtle Lake	-38		21	Rolla 3 NW	-43
25	Carrington 4 N	-39		25	Garrison 1 NNW	*-42*

July Mean Maximum Temperature

	Highest				Lowest	
Rank	**Station Name**	**°F**		**Rank**	**Station Name**	**°F**
1	Medora	87.3		1	Rolla 3 NW	75.8
2	Watford City 14 S	86.8		2	Langdon Exp. Farm	77.4
3	Fort Yates 4 SW	85.8		3	Cavalier 7 NW	78.8
4	Ellendale	85.2		4	Petersburg 2 N	79.1
5	Fullerton 1 ESE	85.1		5	Sharon	79.4
6	Pretty Rock	84.9		6	Bottineau	79.6
6	Williston Exp. Farm	84.9		7	Fortuna 1 W	79.7
8	Hankinson	*84.5*		7	Pembina	79.7
8	Washburn	84.5		9	Hansboro 4 NNE	79.8
10	Oakes 2 S	84.4		9	Powers Lake 1 N	79.8
10	Wahpeton 3 N	84.4		11	Edmore 1 NW	79.9
12	Beulah 1 W	84.3		11	Stanley 3 NNW	79.9
12	McLeod 3 E	84.3		13	Willow City	80.0
14	Bismarck Municipal Airport	84.2		14	Devils Lake KDLR	80.1
15	Butte	84.1		15	Carrington	80.2
15	Jamestown State Hospital	84.1		16	Leeds	80.3
17	Williston Sloulin Int'l Airport	84.0		17	Wildrose 3 NW	80.4
18	Forman 5 SSE	83.8		18	Bowbells	80.5
18	Lisbon	83.8		19	Kenmare 1 WSW	80.6
18	New England	83.8		20	McHenry 3 W	80.7
18	New Salem 5 NW	83.8		20	Minot Experiment Station	80.7
22	Hettinger	83.7		22	Tioga 1 E	80.9
22	Keene 3 S	83.7		23	Westhope	81.1
22	Trotters 3 SSE	83.7		24	Grand Forks Int'l Airport	81.2
25	Dunn Center 2 SW	83.6		24	Upham 3 N	81.2

January Mean Minimum Temperature

	Highest				Lowest	
Rank	**Station Name**	**°F**		**Rank**	**Station Name**	**°F**
1	Dickinson Municipal Airport	4.2		1	Pembina	-9.4
2	Bowman	4.1		2	Upham 3 N	-9.1
2	Richardton Abbey	4.1		2	Willow City	-9.1
4	Amidon	4.0		4	Langdon Exp. Farm	-8.4
5	Medora	3.7		5	Petersburg 2 N	-7.8
5	Trotters 3 SSE	3.7		6	Edmore 1 NW	-7.6
7	Fort Yates 4 SW	3.5		7	Bottineau	-7.1
8	Hettinger	3.4		8	Cavalier 7 NW	-6.9
9	New England	3.3		8	Towner 2 NE	-6.9
10	Pretty Rock	2.7		10	McHenry 3 W	-6.6
11	Fairfield	2.4		11	Hansboro 4 NNE	-6.5
12	Watford City 14 S	1.4		12	Westhope	-6.2
13	Mott	1.2		13	Leeds	-6.1
14	Washburn	1.1		14	Powers Lake 1 N	-5.8
15	Williston Exp. Farm	0.9		15	Rolla 3 NW	-5.0
16	Dunn Center 2 SW	0.8		15	Tioga 1 E	-5.0
17	Minot FAA Airport	0.5		17	Grand Forks Int'l Airport	-4.8
18	Underwood	0.4		17	Rugby	-4.8
19	New Salem 5 NW	0.3		19	McVille	-4.7
20	Carson	0.1		20	Valley City 3 NNW	-4.6
21	Ellendale	0.0		21	Fortuna 1 W	-4.5
21	Keene 3 S	0.0		22	Sharon	-4.4
23	Dickinson Exp. Station	-0.2		23	Oakes 2 S	-4.3
24	Butte	-0.4		23	Stanley 3 NNW	-4.3
25	Center 4 SE	-0.5		25	Bowbells	-4.2

Number of Annual Heating Degree Days

	Highest				Lowest	
Rank	**Station Name**	**Num.**		**Rank**	**Station Name**	**Num.**
1	Langdon Exp. Farm	10,580		1	Fort Yates 4 SW	7,882
2	Pembina	10,361		2	Medora	7,903
3	Rolla 3 NW	10,344		3	Watford City 14 S	8,112
4	Willow City	10,262		4	New England	8,370
5	Petersburg 2 N	10,234		5	Amidon	8,401
6	Edmore 1 NW	10,181		5	Richardton Abbey	8,401
7	Bottineau	10,073		7	Pretty Rock	8,427
8	Upham 3 N	10,061		8	Washburn	8,429
9	Cavalier 7 NW	10,033		9	Trotters 3 SSE	8,457
10	Hansboro 4 NNE	9,984		10	Williston Exp. Farm	8,465
11	Stanley 3 NNW	9,979		11	Dickinson Municipal Airport	8,476
12	Powers Lake 1 N	9,973		12	Bowman	8,498
13	Leeds	9,935		13	Ellendale	8,522
14	Fortuna 1 W	9,917		14	Hettinger	8,550
15	Tioga 1 E	9,892		15	Wahpeton 3 N	8,562
16	McHenry 3 W	9,865		16	Mott	8,606
17	Bowbells	9,860		17	Fullerton 1 ESE	8,636
18	Towner 2 NE	9,855		18	Dunn Center 2 SW	8,667
19	Wildrose 3 NW	9,656		19	McLeod 3 E	8,690
20	Sharon	9,608		20	Keene 3 S	8,735
20	Westhope	9,608		21	Bismarck Municipal Airport	8,769
22	Max	9,596		22	Butte	8,785
23	Kenmare 1 WSW	9,583		23	New Salem 5 NW	8,808
24	McVille	*9,553*		24	Jamestown State Hospital	8,813
25	Valley City 3 NNW	9,530		25	Underwood	8,822

Number of Annual Cooling Degree Days

	Highest			Lowest	
Rank	**Station Name**	**Num.**	**Rank**	**Station Name**	**Num.**
1	Fort Yates 4 SW	754	1	Rolla 3 NW	233
2	Wahpeton 3 N	666	2	Langdon Exp. Farm	248
3	Medora	622	3	Stanley 3 NNW	283
4	McLeod 3 E	620	4	Hansboro 4 NNE	299
5	Ellendale	612	5	Bowbells	304
5	Watford City 14 S	612	6	Cavalier 7 NW	308
7	Grafton	595	6	Pembina	308
8	Williston Exp. Farm	594	8	Fortuna 1 W	309
9	Forman 5 SSE	587	9	Powers Lake 1 N	310
10	Butte	573	10	Edmore 1 NW	312
11	Jamestown State Hospital	565	11	Petersburg 2 N	318
12	Fargo Hector Field	563	12	Willow City	326
13	Oakes 2 S	549	13	Bottineau	328
14	Jamestown Municipal Airport	548	14	Wildrose 3 NW	333
15	Grand Forks Univ. NWS	547	15	Kenmare 1 WSW	338
16	Fullerton 1 ESE	544	16	Leeds	339
17	Gackle	542	17	Tioga 1 E	345
18	McClusky	540	18	Upham 3 N	355
19	Washburn	*537*	19	Towner 2 NE	364
20	Lisbon	527	20	Sharon	368
21	Underwood	524	21	McHenry 3 W	371
22	Amidon	517	22	Wishek	373
22	Pretty Rock	517	23	Garrison 1 NNW	377
22	Richardton Abbey	517	24	Turtle Lake	379
25	Dunn Center 2 SW	516	25	Valley City 3 NNW	383

Annual Precipitation

	Highest			Lowest	
Rank	**Station Name**	**Inches**	**Rank**	**Station Name**	**Inches**
1	Wahpeton 3 N	21.81	1	Williston Sloulin Int'l Airport	14.09
2	Hankinson	*21.80*	2	Fort Yates 4 SW	14.11
3	La Moure	21.51	3	Wildrose 3 NW	14.49
4	Ellendale	21.41	4	Fortuna 1 W	*14.51*
5	Sharon	21.28	5	Tioga 1 E	14.57
6	Fullerton 1 ESE	21.07	6	Trotters 3 SSE	14.86
7	Fargo Hector Field	20.59	7	Crosby	14.90
8	Cooperstown	20.38	8	Williston Exp. Farm	14.98
9	Forman 5 SSE	20.37	9	Amidon	15.04
10	McLeod 3 E	20.24	10	Fairfield	15.16
11	Hillsboro 3 N	20.21	10	Medora	15.16
12	Lisbon	20.12	12	Watford City 14 S	15.49
13	Petersburg 2 N	20.01	13	Bowman	15.60
14	Stanley 3 NNW	20.00	14	Hettinger	15.65
15	McHenry 3 W	19.67	15	Garrison 1 NNW	15.78
16	Grand Forks Univ. NWS	19.58	16	Keene 3 S	15.91
17	Carrington 4 N	19.57	17	Drake 9 NE	16.10
18	Oakes 2 S	*19.49*	18	Powers Lake 1 N	16.12
19	Grand Forks Int'l Airport	19.40	19	Dickinson Municipal Airport	16.42
20	McVille	*18.99*	20	New England	16.48
21	Devils Lake KDLR	18.97	21	Butte	16.52
22	Valley City 3 NNW	18.83	22	Beulah 1 W	16.59
23	Napoleon	18.81	23	Foxholm 7 N	16.62
24	Minot Experiment Station	18.75	24	Bismarck Municipal Airport	16.63
24	Minot FAA Airport	18.75	25	Carson	16.64

Number of Days Annually With ≥ 0.1″ Precipitation

	Highest			Lowest	
Rank	**Station Name**	**Days**	**Rank**	**Station Name**	**Days**
1	Hankinson	*50*	1	Fort Yates 4 SW	33
1	Stanley 3 NNW	50	2	Medora	35
3	Sharon	49	2	Wildrose 3 NW	35
4	Ellendale	47	2	Williston Exp. Farm	35
4	Fullerton 1 ESE	47	2	Williston Sloulin Int'l Airport	35
4	Petersburg 2 N	47	6	Drake 9 NE	36
7	Carrington	46	6	Foxholm 7 N	36
7	Grand Forks Int'l Airport	46	8	Bismarck Municipal Airport	37
7	Hillsboro 3 N	46	8	Fairfield	37
7	La Moure	46	8	Garrison 1 NNW	*37*
7	McHenry 3 W	46	8	Hettinger	37
7	Minot Experiment Station	46	8	Trotters 3 SSE	37
7	Wahpeton 3 N	46	8	Watford City 14 S	37
14	Cooperstown	45	8	Westhope	37
14	Pembina	45	15	Butte	38
16	Bottineau	44	15	Crosby	38
16	Devils Lake KDLR	44	15	Mandan Experiment Station	38
16	Fargo Hector Field	44	15	Pretty Rock	38
16	Grafton	44	15	Tioga 1 E	38
16	Grand Forks Univ. NWS	44	15	Towner 2 NE	38
16	Lisbon	*44*	15	Washburn	38
16	New Salem 5 NW	44	22	Amidon	39
16	Rolla 3 NW	44	22	Ashley	39
24	Forman 5 SSE	43	22	Bowbells	39
24	Hansboro 4 NNE	43	22	Center 4 SE	39

Number of Days Annually With ≥ 1.0″ Precipitation

	Highest			Lowest	
Rank	**Station Name**	**Days**	**Rank**	**Station Name**	**Days**
1	Ellendale	6	1	Bismarck Municipal Airport	0
2	Fargo Hector Field	5	1	Williston Sloulin Int'l Airport	0
2	Fullerton 1 ESE	5	3	Amidon	1
2	Oakes 2 S	*5*	3	Beulah 1 W	1
2	Wahpeton 3 N	5	3	Bowman	1
6	Forman 5 SSE	4	3	Butte	1
6	Hankinson	*4*	3	Center 4 SE	1
6	Hillsboro 3 N	4	3	Crosby	1
6	Jamestown State Hospital	4	3	Dickinson Exp. Station	1
6	Pembina	4	3	Dickinson Municipal Airport	1
6	Rugby	4	3	Dunn Center 2 SW	1
6	Valley City 3 NNW	4	3	Fairfield	1
13	Ashley	3	3	Fort Yates 4 SW	1
13	Bowbells	3	3	Keene 3 S	1
13	Cavalier 7 NW	3	3	Kenmare 1 WSW	1
13	Cooperstown	3	3	McClusky	1
13	Edmore 1 NW	3	3	Medora	1
13	Grafton	3	3	Mott	1
13	Grand Forks Univ. NWS	3	3	Napoleon	1
13	Hansboro 4 NNE	3	3	Tioga 1 E	1
13	La Moure	3	3	Towner 2 NE	1
13	Langdon Exp. Farm	3	3	Trotters 3 SSE	1
13	McLeod 3 E	3	3	Turtle Lake	1
13	Minot Experiment Station	3	3	Underwood	1
13	New England	3	3	Wildrose 3 NW	1

Annual Snowfall

Highest				Lowest		
Rank	**Station Name**	**Inches**		**Rank**	**Station Name**	**Inches**
1	Bowman	56.5		1	McLeod 3 E	*25.1*
2	Minot Experiment Station	50.9		2	Fort Yates 4 SW	27.7
3	Bismarck Municipal Airport	50.5		3	Wahpeton 3 N	29.2
4	Pretty Rock	49.7		4	Ashley	29.8
5	Upham 3 N	48.9		5	Pembina	*30.7*
6	Stanley 3 NNW	48.7		6	Beulah 1 W	*31.3*
7	Minot FAA Airport	48.6		7	Center 4 SE	31.7
8	McHenry 3 W	47.4		7	Williston Exp. Farm	31.7
9	Fargo Hector Field	46.2		9	Medora	31.9
10	Napoleon	46.1		10	Edmore 1 NW	32.1
11	Carrington	45.4		11	Colgate	*32.2*
12	Max	44.9		12	Butte	*32.5*
13	Richardton Abbey	44.0		13	Fairfield	32.6
14	Grand Forks Int'l Airport	43.8		14	Watford City 14 S	33.7
15	New Salem 5 NW	43.6		15	Forman 5 SSE	33.8
16	New England	*43.5*		15	Trotters 3 SSE	33.8
17	McClusky	43.2		17	Turtle Lake	*34.3*
17	Williston Sloulin Int'l Airport	43.2		18	Hettinger	35.0
19	Velva	*42.8*		19	Wildrose 3 NW	35.1
20	Wishek	*42.6*		20	Dickinson Municipal Airport	35.4
21	Washburn	*42.1*		20	Drake 9 NE	35.4
22	Kenmare 1 WSW	42.0		20	Valley City 3 NNW	35.4
22	La Moure	*42.0*		23	Mott	35.7
24	Sharon	41.9		24	Dickinson Exp. Station	*36.4*
25	Bottineau	41.5		25	Tioga 1 E	37.0

Note: See Appendix D for explanation of data.

Annual Extreme Maximum Temperature

	Highest				Lowest	
Rank	Station Name	°F		Rank	Station Name	°F
1	Chilo Meldahl Lock & Dam	107		1	Washington Court House	97
1	Cincinnati Fernbank	107		2	Painesville 4 NW	98
3	Chillicothe Mound City	105		3	Centerburg 2 SE	99
3	Cincinnati Lunken Airport	105		3	Wilmington 3 N	99
3	Gallipolis	105		5	Ashland 2 SW	100
3	Hoytville 2 NE	105		5	Barnesville	100
3	Napoleon	105		5	Chardon	100
3	Tiffin	105		5	Columbus Valley Crossing	100
9	Bowling Green WWTP	104		5	Dorset	100
9	Cleveland Hopkins Int'l Airport	104		5	Fredericktown 4 S	100
9	Dayton MCD	104		5	Hannibal Lock & Dam	100
9	Defiance	104		5	Hillsboro	100
9	Elyria 3 E	104		5	Hiram	100
9	Findlay Airport	104		5	Lima WWTP	100
9	Findlay WPCC	104		5	Mansfield 5 W	100
9	Fremont	104		5	Newark Water Works	100
9	Greenville Water Plant	104		5	Put-In-Bay	100
9	Kenton	104		5	Springfield New Water Works	100
9	Milford	104		5	Youngstown Municipal Airport	100
9	Montpelier	104		20	Akron-Canton Regional Airport	101
9	Oberlin	104		20	Bellefontaine	101
9	Paulding	104		20	Cadiz	101
9	Portsmouth Sciotoville	104		20	Canfield 1 S	101
9	Toledo Express Airport	104		20	Circleville	101
9	Upper Sandusky	104		20	Columbus-Port Columbus Int'l	101

Annual Mean Maximum Temperature

	Highest				Lowest	
Rank	Station Name	°F		Rank	Station Name	°F
1	Gallipolis	66.8		1	Chardon	57.2
2	Portsmouth Sciotoville	65.3		2	Put-In-Bay	57.6
3	Waverly	65.2		3	Dorset	57.8
4	Cincinnati Fernbank	64.6		4	Sandusky	58.2
4	Cincinnati Lunken Airport	64.6		5	Hiram	58.3
4	Marietta WWTP	64.6		5	Youngstown Municipal Airport	58.3
7	Chilo Meldahl Lock & Dam	64.4		7	Findlay Airport	58.7
8	Chillicothe Mound City	63.8		7	Mansfield Lahm Municipal Airport	58.7
8	Milford	63.8		7	Wooster Exp. Station	58.7
10	Ripley Exp. Farm	63.6		10	Fremont	58.8
11	Jackson 3 NW	63.5		10	Mansfield 5 W	58.8
11	McConnelsville Lock 7	63.5		10	Montpelier	58.8
13	Cambridge	63.4		10	Norwalk WWTP	58.8
13	Circleville	63.4		14	Bucyrus	58.9
15	Columbus Valley Crossing	63.1		14	Painesville 4 NW	58.9
16	Dayton MCD	63.0		16	Cleveland Hopkins Int'l Airport	59.0
17	New Lexington 2 NW	62.9		16	Toledo Express Airport	59.0
17	Westerville	62.9		18	Findlay WPCC	59.1
19	Franklin	62.7		19	Akron-Canton Regional Airport	59.2
19	Irwin	62.7		19	Ashland 2 SW	59.2
21	Hannibal Lock & Dam	62.5		19	Centerburg 2 SE	59.2
22	Mineral Ridge Water Works	62.2		19	Paulding	59.2
22	Xenia 6 SSE	62.2		23	Hoytville 2 NE	59.3
24	Newark Water Works	62.1		24	Coshocton Agr. Res. Station	59.4
25	Coshocton WPC Plant	62.0		25	Defiance	59.5

Annual Mean Temperature

	Highest				Lowest	
Rank	Station Name	°F		Rank	Station Name	°F
1	Gallipolis	55.0		1	Chardon	46.9
2	Cincinnati Lunken Airport	54.7		2	Dorset	47.4
3	Portsmouth Sciotoville	54.4		3	Montpelier	48.0
4	Marietta WWTP	53.8		4	Fredericktown 4 S	48.3
5	Chilo Meldahl Lock & Dam	53.6		5	Canfield 1 S	48.6
5	Cincinnati Fernbank	53.6		5	Paulding	48.6
5	Dayton MCD	53.6		7	Mansfield 5 W	48.7
8	Ripley Exp. Farm	53.0		7	Warren 3 S	48.7
8	Waverly	53.0		9	Ashland 2 SW	48.8
10	Circleville	52.9		9	Youngstown Municipal Airport	48.8
11	Columbus Valley Crossing	52.8		11	Bucyrus	48.9
12	Chillicothe Mound City	52.5		11	Hiram	48.9
12	Washington Court House	52.5		13	Hoytville 2 NE	49.0
14	Cambridge	52.4		14	Toledo Express Airport	49.1
15	Columbus-Port Columbus Int'l	52.3		15	Chippewa Lake	49.2
15	Hillsboro	52.3		15	Defiance	49.2
15	Milford	52.3		15	Norwalk WWTP	49.2
18	Jackson 3 NW	52.1		15	Wooster Exp. Station	49.2
19	Dayton Int'l Airport	52.0		19	Centerburg 2 SE	49.3
19	Westerville	52.0		19	Danville 2 W	49.3
19	Xenia 6 SSE	52.0		19	Fremont	49.3
22	Steubenville	51.9		19	Wauseon Water Plant	49.3
23	Franklin	51.8		23	Millport 2 NW	49.4
23	Hannibal Lock & Dam	51.8		23	Oberlin	49.4
23	Zanesville Municipal Airport	51.8		25	Greenville Water Plant	49.6

Annual Mean Minimum Temperature

	Highest				Lowest	
Rank	Station Name	°F		Rank	Station Name	°F
1	Cincinnati Lunken Airport	44.8		1	Chardon	36.7
2	Dayton MCD	44.2		2	Fredericktown 4 S	36.9
3	Put-In-Bay	43.4		3	Dorset	37.0
4	Portsmouth Sciotoville	43.3		4	Montpelier	37.1
5	Gallipolis	43.0		5	Canfield 1 S	37.2
5	Marietta WWTP	43.0		6	Warren 3 S	37.3
5	Washington Court House	43.0		7	Danville 2 W	37.4
8	Chilo Meldahl Lock & Dam	42.8		8	Millport 2 NW	37.8
8	Hillsboro	42.8		9	Paulding	37.9
10	Columbus-Port Columbus Int'l	42.6		10	Ashland 2 SW	38.3
10	Painesville 4 NW	42.6		11	Mansfield 5 W	38.6
12	Cincinnati Fernbank	42.5		12	Greenville Water Plant	38.7
13	Circleville	42.4		12	Hoytville 2 NE	38.7
13	Columbus Valley Crossing	42.4		12	Oberlin	38.7
13	Dayton Int'l Airport	42.4		15	Chippewa Lake	38.8
16	Ripley Exp. Farm	42.3		15	Defiance	38.8
17	Sandusky	42.2		17	Bucyrus	38.9
18	Steubenville	42.1		17	Eaton	38.9
19	Lima WWTP	42.0		19	Wauseon Water Plant	39.0
20	Xenia 6 SSE	41.8		20	Delaware	39.1
20	Zanesville Municipal Airport	41.8		20	New Philadelphia	39.1
22	Celina 3 NE	41.7		22	New Lexington 2 NW	39.2
23	Coshocton Agr. Res. Station	41.5		22	Toledo Express Airport	39.2
24	Cadiz	41.4		24	Barnesville	39.3
24	Cambridge	41.4		24	McConnelsville Lock 7	39.3

Annual Extreme Minimum Temperature

	Highest				Lowest	
Rank	Station Name	°F		Rank	Station Name	°F
1	Put-In-Bay	-18		1	Danville 2 W	-35
2	Painesville 4 NW	-19		1	New Lexington 2 NW	-35
3	Bowling Green WWTP	-20		3	Millport 2 NW	-34
3	Cleveland Hopkins Int'l Airport	-20		4	Eaton	-33
3	Findlay Airport	-20		4	Greenville Water Plant	-33
3	Findlay WPCC	-20		6	Cambridge	-32
3	Fremont	*-20*		6	McConnelsville Lock 7	-32
3	Sandusky	-20		8	Waverly	-31
3	Toledo Express Airport	-20		9	Fredericktown 4 S	*-30*
10	Dayton MCD	-21		10	Centerburg 2 SE	-29
10	Lima WWTP	-21		10	Chillicothe Mound City	-29
10	Norwalk WWTP	-21		10	Portsmouth Sciotoville	-29
10	Pandora	-21		13	Columbus Valley Crossing	-28
10	Tiffin	-21		13	Delaware	-28
15	Chilo Meldahl Lock & Dam	-22		13	Dorset	-28
15	Cincinnati Lunken Airport	-22		13	Gallipolis	-28
15	Circleville	-22		13	Irwin	-28
15	Columbus-Port Columbus Int'l	-22		13	Jackson 3 NW	*-28*
15	Defiance	-22		13	Ripley Exp. Farm	-28
15	Elyria 3 E	-22		13	Xenia 6 SSE	-28
15	Hoytville 2 NE	-22		21	Bellefontaine	-27
15	Kenton	-22		21	Philo 3 SW	-27
15	Mansfield Lahm Municipal Airport	-22		21	Washington Court House	-27
15	New Philadelphia	-22		21	Westerville	-27
15	Steubenville	-22		25	Bucyrus	-26

July Mean Maximum Temperature

	Highest				Lowest	
Rank	Station Name	°F		Rank	Station Name	°F
1	Gallipolis	87.4		1	Chardon	80.1
2	Dayton MCD	87.3		2	Dorset	81.2
3	Cincinnati Lunken Airport	86.8		3	Painesville 4 NW	81.4
3	Milford	86.8		4	Hiram	81.6
5	Portsmouth Sciotoville	86.7		5	Philo 3 SW	81.7
6	Cincinnati Fernbank	86.6		6	Wooster Exp. Station	81.8
7	Waverly	86.5		7	Mansfield 5 W	81.9
8	Chillicothe Mound City	86.2		7	Youngstown Municipal Airport	81.9
8	Chilo Meldahl Lock & Dam	86.2		9	Coshocton Agr. Res. Station	82.0
10	Marietta WWTP	85.8		10	Barnesville	82.1
11	Mineral Ridge Water Works	85.7		10	Mansfield Lahm Municipal Airport	82.1
12	Irwin	85.6		12	Centerburg 2 SE	82.3
13	Circleville	85.5		12	Put-In-Bay	82.3
13	Franklin	85.5		12	Sandusky	82.3
15	Columbus Valley Crossing	85.3		15	Akron-Canton Regional Airport	82.4
15	Westerville	85.3		15	Cleveland Hopkins Int'l Airport	82.4
17	Ripley Exp. Farm	85.2		17	Norwalk WWTP	82.6
17	Van Wert 1 S	85.2		17	Washington Court House	82.6
19	Cambridge	85.1		19	Cadiz	82.7
19	Dayton Int'l Airport	85.1		20	Findlay Airport	82.8
19	Kenton	85.1		21	Canfield 1 S	82.9
19	London	85.1		22	Chippewa Lake	83.0
23	McConnelsville Lock 7	85.0		23	Ashland 2 SW	83.1
23	Napoleon	85.0		23	Bucyrus	83.1
25	Newark Water Works	84.9		23	Fredericktown 4 S	83.1

January Mean Minimum Temperature

Highest				Lowest		
Rank	**Station Name**	**°F**		**Rank**	**Station Name**	**°F**
1	Gallipolis	22.4		1	Montpelier	13.3
2	Cincinnati Lunken Airport	22.2		2	Fredericktown 4 S	13.5
3	Marietta WWTP	22.1		3	Paulding	13.7
3	Portsmouth Sciotoville	22.1		4	Chardon	14.1
5	Circleville	20.8		5	Dorset	14.6
6	Chilo Meldahl Lock & Dam	20.4		6	Defiance	14.7
6	Dayton MCD	20.4		7	Greenville Water Plant	15.0
8	Steubenville	20.3		7	Hoytville 2 NE	15.0
8	Washington Court House	20.3		9	Napoleon	15.2
10	Cincinnati Fernbank	*20.2*		10	Wauseon Water Plant	15.3
10	Ripley Exp. Farm	20.2		11	Eaton	15.4
12	Cambridge	20.1		11	Mansfield 5 W	15.4
12	Painesville 4 NW	20.1		13	Ashland 2 SW	15.5
12	Zanesville Municipal Airport	20.1		14	Centerburg 2 SE	15.6
15	Columbus Valley Crossing	20.0		15	Marion 2 N	15.8
16	Columbus-Port Columbus Int'l	19.9		16	Kenton	15.9
16	Hillsboro	19.9		16	Warren 3 S	15.9
18	Hannibal Lock & Dam	*19.6*		18	Bucyrus	16.0
18	Philo 3 SW	19.6		18	Danville 2 W	16.0
20	Xenia 6 SSE	19.3		18	Fremont	16.0
21	Waverly	19.2		18	Toledo Express Airport	16.0
22	Cadiz	19.1		22	Oberlin	16.1
22	Chillicothe Mound City	19.1		23	Bowling Green WWTP	16.2
22	Jackson 3 NW	*19.1*		23	Delaware	16.2
22	Newark Water Works	19.1		25	Canfield 1 S	16.3

Number of Annual Heating Degree Days

Highest				Lowest		
Rank	**Station Name**	**Num.**		**Rank**	**Station Name**	**Num.**
1	Chardon	6,934		1	Gallipolis	4,673
2	Dorset	6,809		2	Cincinnati Lunken Airport	4,839
3	Montpelier	6,745		3	Portsmouth Sciotoville	4,860
4	Paulding	6,576		4	Marietta WWTP	4,984
5	Fredericktown 4 S	6,542		5	Chilo Meldahl Lock & Dam	5,083
6	Ashland 2 SW	6,457		6	Cincinnati Fernbank	*5,126*
7	Hoytville 2 NE	6,456		7	Waverly	5,238
8	Defiance	6,444		8	Ripley Exp. Farm	5,245
9	Mansfield 5 W	6,440		9	Circleville	5,275
10	Bucyrus	6,435		10	Dayton MCD	5,292
11	Toledo Express Airport	6,413		11	Columbus Valley Crossing	5,318
12	Canfield 1 S	6,410		12	Cambridge	5,348
13	Youngstown Municipal Airport	6,386		13	Washington Court House	5,362
14	Warren 3 S	6,382		14	Hillsboro	5,414
15	Hiram	6,372		15	Chillicothe Mound City	5,422
16	Fremont	6,371		16	Jackson 3 NW	*5,451*
17	Norwalk WWTP	6,359		17	Xenia 6 SSE	5,464
18	Wauseon Water Plant	6,346		18	Steubenville	5,484
19	Centerburg 2 SE	6,297		19	Columbus-Port Columbus Int'l	5,491
20	Oberlin	6,287		20	Milford	5,495
21	Chippewa Lake	6,284		21	Hannibal Lock & Dam	*5,520*
22	Greenville Water Plant	6,271		22	Zanesville Municipal Airport	5,525
23	Wooster Exp. Station	6,261		23	Westerville	5,528
24	Napoleon	*6,259*		24	Franklin	5,604
25	Danville 2 W	6,240		25	Dayton Int'l Airport	5,616

Number of Annual Cooling Degree Days

	Highest			Lowest	
Rank	**Station Name**	**Num.**	**Rank**	**Station Name**	**Num.**
1	Dayton MCD	1,283	1	Chardon	468
2	Cincinnati Lunken Airport	1,215	2	Dorset	514
3	Gallipolis	1,156	3	Canfield 1 S	*552*
4	Chilo Meldahl Lock & Dam	1,079	4	Fredericktown 4 S	571
5	Cincinnati Fernbank	1,076	5	Warren 3 S	581
6	Portsmouth Sciotoville	1,030	6	Millport 2 NW	595
7	Marietta WWTP	1,018	7	Youngstown Municipal Airport	599
8	Milford	1,016	8	Danville 2 W	613
9	Columbus-Port Columbus Int'l	991	9	Mansfield 5 W	619
10	Chillicothe Mound City	988	10	Ashland 2 SW	622
11	Ripley Exp. Farm	981	11	Hiram	633
12	Dayton Int'l Airport	974	12	Wooster Exp. Station	635
13	Westerville	971	13	Chippewa Lake	666
14	Lima WWTP	968	14	Philo 3 SW	671
15	Circleville	965	15	Barnesville	679
16	Columbus Valley Crossing	954	16	Mansfield Lahm Municipal Airport	698
17	Waverly	943	17	Montpelier	700
18	Celina 3 NE	937	18	Oberlin	705
19	Cambridge	919	19	Bucyrus	706
20	Washington Court House	915	20	Centerburg 2 SE	711
21	Kenton	911	21	Akron-Canton Regional Airport	716
22	Van Wert 1 S	910	22	Paulding	717
23	Franklin	903	23	New Lexington 2 NW	731
24	Hillsboro	895	24	Hoytville 2 NE	740
25	Put-In-Bay	*892*	24	Norwalk WWTP	740

Annual Precipitation

	Highest			Lowest	
Rank	**Station Name**	**Inches**	**Rank**	**Station Name**	**Inches**
1	Cincinnati Fernbank	*47.43*	1	Bowling Green WWTP	33.14
2	Chardon	47.01	2	Toledo Express Airport	33.23
3	Ripley Exp. Farm	45.33	3	Hoytville 2 NE	33.89
4	Milford	44.72	4	Sandusky	34.19
5	Barnesville	44.34	5	Paulding	34.29
6	Hillsboro	43.33	6	Wauseon Water Plant	34.59
7	Dorset	43.30	7	Findlay Airport	34.68
8	Chilo Meldahl Lock & Dam	43.05	8	Put-In-Bay	34.79
8	Mansfield Lahm Municipal Airport	43.05	9	Napoleon	34.81
10	McConnelsville Lock 7	42.96	10	Kenton	35.47
11	Marietta WWTP	42.20	11	Pandora	35.63
12	Hiram	41.91	12	Defiance	35.64
13	Cincinnati Lunken Airport	41.89	13	Montpelier	35.82
14	Newark Water Works	41.86	14	Upper Sandusky	36.03
15	New Lexington 2 NW	41.74	15	Fremont	36.04
16	Portsmouth Sciotoville	41.39	16	Oberlin	36.32
17	Danville 2 W	41.21	17	Marysville	36.37
18	Jackson 3 NW	*41.13*	18	Van Wert 1 S	36.52
19	Wilmington 3 N	41.12	19	Celina 3 NE	36.56
20	Coshocton WPC Plant	40.96	20	Norwalk WWTP	36.62
21	Centerburg 2 SE	40.89	21	Tiffin	36.75
22	New Philadelphia	40.88	22	Bellefontaine	36.92
23	Cadiz	40.86	23	Findlay WPCC	36.95
24	Gallipolis	40.66	24	Philo 3 SW	37.03
25	Steubenville	40.37	25	Coshocton Agr. Res. Station	37.04

Number of Days Annually With ≥ 0.1″ Precipitation

	Highest			Lowest	
Rank	**Station Name**	**Days**	**Rank**	**Station Name**	**Days**
1	Chardon	107	1	Put-In-Bay	69
2	Dorset	99	2	Paulding	70
3	Hiram	97	3	Lancaster 2 NW	*71*
4	Barnesville	90	4	Irwin	*72*
4	Millport 2 NW	90	4	Sandusky	72
4	New Lexington 2 NW	90	6	Bowling Green WWTP	73
7	Chippewa Lake	89	6	Findlay Airport	73
7	Cincinnati Fernbank	*89*	6	Hoytville 2 NE	73
7	Marietta WWTP	89	9	Coshocton Agr. Res. Station	75
7	McConnelsville Lock 7	89	9	Springfield New Water Works	75
7	Milford	89	9	Wauseon Water Plant	75
12	Cadiz	88	12	Chillicothe Mound City	76
12	Steubenville	88	12	Chilo Meldahl Lock & Dam	76
14	Cleveland Hopkins Int'l Airport	87	12	Greenville Water Plant	76
14	Coshocton WPC Plant	87	12	Napoleon	76
14	Elyria 3 E	87	12	Toledo Express Airport	76
14	Ripley Exp. Farm	87	17	Dayton MCD	77
18	Gallipolis	86	17	Defiance	77
18	Newark Water Works	86	17	Eaton	77
18	Painesville 4 NW	86	17	London	77
18	Warren 3 S	86	17	Pandora	77
22	Cambridge	85	22	Circleville	78
22	Jackson 3 NW	*85*	22	Columbus Valley Crossing	78
22	Portsmouth Sciotoville	85	22	Delaware	78
25	Akron-Canton Regional Airport	84	22	Kenton	78

Number of Days Annually With ≥ 1.0″ Precipitation

	Highest			Lowest	
Rank	**Station Name**	**Days**	**Rank**	**Station Name**	**Days**
1	Cincinnati Fernbank	*14*	1	Elyria 3 E	4
2	Chilo Meldahl Lock & Dam	12	1	Mineral Ridge Water Works	4
2	Ripley Exp. Farm	12	3	Bowling Green WWTP	5
4	Portsmouth Sciotoville	11	3	Cadiz	5
4	Urbana WWTP	11	3	Canfield 1 S	5
6	Chillicothe Mound City	10	3	Findlay Airport	5
6	Cincinnati Lunken Airport	10	3	Hiram	5
6	Eaton	10	3	Hoytville 2 NE	5
6	Hillsboro	10	3	Millport 2 NW	5
6	Milford	10	3	Napoleon	5
6	Wilmington 3 N	10	3	Norwalk WWTP	5
12	Barnesville	9	3	Oberlin	5
12	Centerburg 2 SE	9	3	Painesville 4 NW	5
12	Dayton MCD	9	3	Pandora	5
12	Fredericktown 4 S	9	3	Put-In-Bay	5
12	Mansfield Lahm Municipal Airport	9	3	Sandusky	5
12	McConnelsville Lock 7	9	3	Toledo Express Airport	5
12	Waverly	9	3	Wauseon Water Plant	5
12	Xenia 6 SSE	9	19	Celina 3 NE	6
20	Chardon	8	19	Chippewa Lake	6
20	Danville 2 W	8	19	Cleveland Hopkins Int'l Airport	6
20	Dayton Int'l Airport	8	19	Dorset	6
20	Franklin	8	19	Findlay WPCC	6
20	Gallipolis	8	19	Fremont	6
20	Greenville Water Plant	8	19	Kenton	6

Annual Snowfall

Rank	Station Name	Inches		Rank	Station Name	Inches
Highest				**Lowest**		
1	Chardon	97.0		1	Cincinnati Lunken Airport	13.2
2	Dorset	73.1		2	Portsmouth Sciotoville	13.3
3	Hiram	61.6		3	Gallipolis	*14.2*
4	Cleveland Hopkins Int'l Airport	61.0		4	Circleville	14.9
5	Youngstown Municipal Airport	54.7		5	Dayton MCD	15.7
6	Akron-Canton Regional Airport	46.9		6	Milford	*15.9*
7	Elyria 3 E	43.6		7	Bellefontaine	*17.8*
8	Mansfield Lahm Municipal Airport	43.3		8	Chillicothe Mound City	*17.9*
9	Oberlin	*41.4*		9	Cambridge	18.4
10	Chippewa Lake	39.8		10	Columbus Valley Crossing	19.3
11	Toledo Express Airport	37.2		11	Westerville	19.6
12	Danville 2 W	35.5		12	Paulding	*19.7*
13	Painesville 4 NW	*34.8*		12	Put-In-Bay	*19.7*
14	Mineral Ridge Water Works	34.5		14	Marysville	20.2
15	Ashland 2 SW	34.0		15	Hillsboro	20.5
16	Montpelier	*33.9*		16	Newark Water Works	20.6
16	Warren 3 S	33.9		17	Delaware	20.7
18	Celina 3 NE	33.1		18	Defiance	20.8
19	Barnesville	32.9		19	McConnelsville Lock 7	21.2
20	Cadiz	*32.3*		20	Fredericktown 4 S	*21.4*
21	Wooster Exp. Station	31.7		21	Ripley Exp. Farm	21.5
22	Pandora	30.7		22	Greenville Water Plant	*21.7*
23	Millport 2 NW	30.2		23	Bowling Green WWTP	21.9
24	Van Wert 1 S	*29.8*		24	Zanesville Municipal Airport	22.5
25	New Philadelphia	29.7		25	Coshocton WPC Plant	22.7

Note: See Appendix D for explanation of data.

Annual Extreme Maximum Temperature

Highest			Lowest		
Rank	Station Name	°F	Rank	Station Name	°F
1	Mangum	117	1	Ada	108
2	Chattanooga 3 NE	116	1	Broken Bow Dam	108
2	Hobart Municipal Airport	116	1	Kansas 1 ESE	108
2	Hollis	116	1	Kenton	108
2	Ponca City Municipal Airport	116	1	Pryor	108
6	Altus Irrigation Research Station	115	1	Sallisaw 2 NW	108
6	Buffalo	115	1	Stilwell 5 NNW	108
6	Clinton	115	8	Boise City 2 E	109
6	Frederick	115	8	Claremore 2 ENE	109
6	Hammon 3 SSW	115	8	Geary	109
6	Mutual	115	8	Hanna	109
6	Waurika	115	8	Lake Eufaula	109
13	Altus Dam	114	8	Okemah	109
13	Blackwell	*114*	8	Okmulgee Water Works	109
13	Healdton	114	8	Seminole	109
13	Hugo	114	8	Spavinaw	109
13	Perry	114	8	Wagoner	109
18	Alva	*113*	8	Watonga	109
18	Beaver	113	19	Anadarko 3 E	110
18	Billings	113	19	Arnett	110
18	Carnegie 5 NE	113	19	Blanchard 2 SSW	*110*
18	Gate	113	19	Cushing	110
18	Guthrie 5 S	113	19	El Reno 1 N	110
18	Helena 1 SSE	113	19	Enid	110
18	Jefferson	113	19	Fort Supply 3 SE	110

Annual Mean Maximum Temperature

Highest			Lowest		
Rank	Station Name	°F	Rank	Station Name	°F
1	Waurika	76.2	1	Arnett	69.2
2	Altus Irrigation Research Station	76.1	2	Miami	69.5
2	Chattanooga 3 NE	76.1	3	Billings	70.0
2	Mangum	76.1	3	Claremore 2 ENE	70.0
5	Hollis	76.0	3	Vinita 2 N	70.0
6	Ardmore	75.0	6	Goodwell Research Station	70.1
7	Frederick	74.9	6	Helena 1 SSE	70.1
7	Healdton	*74.9*	6	Kansas 1 ESE	70.1
7	Hugo	74.9	6	Ponca City Municipal Airport	70.1
10	Marietta	74.6	10	Fort Supply 3 SE	*70.2*
10	Tuskahoma	74.6	10	Stilwell 5 NNW	70.2
12	Idabel	74.4	12	Mutual	70.3
12	Pauls Valley 4 WSW	74.4	12	Pryor	70.3
14	Madill	74.3	14	Kenton	70.4
15	Buffalo	74.2	15	Blackwell	*70.5*
15	Chickasha Experiment Station	74.2	15	Cushing	70.5
17	Broken Bow Dam	74.1	17	Beaver	70.7
17	Seminole	74.1	17	Nowata	70.7
19	Carnegie 5 NE	73.7	17	Stillwater 2 W	70.7
19	McCurtain 1 SE	73.7	20	Gage Airport	*70.8*
21	Purcell 5 SW	73.6	21	Hooker	70.9
22	Clinton	73.5	22	Boise City 2 E	71.0
22	Erick	73.5	22	Oklahoma City Int'l Airport	71.0
24	Duncan	73.4	22	Tulsa Int'l Airport	71.0
25	Bristow	73.3	25	Geary	71.2

Annual Mean Temperature

Highest			Lowest		
Rank	**Station Name**	**°F**	**Rank**	**Station Name**	**°F**
1	Ardmore	63.9	1	Kenton	55.1
2	Waurika	63.5	2	Goodwell Research Station	55.4
3	Hugo	63.4	3	Boise City 2 E	55.6
4	Marietta	63.2	4	Beaver	56.1
5	Madill	63.1	5	Hooker	56.3
6	Chattanooga 3 NE	62.5	6	Arnett	56.6
7	Altus Irrigation Research Station	62.4	7	Fort Supply 3 SE	*57.2*
8	Healdton	*62.3*	8	Gage Airport	*57.4*
8	McCurtain 1 SE	62.3	9	Mutual	57.5
8	Seminole	62.3	10	Miami	57.6
8	Tuskahoma	62.3	11	Helena 1 SSE	57.7
12	Frederick	62.2	12	Hammon 3 SSW	58.0
13	Pauls Valley 4 WSW	62.1	13	Gate	58.2
14	Idabel	62.0	14	Billings	58.4
14	Mangum	62.0	14	Claremore 2 ENE	58.4
16	Duncan	61.8	14	Freedom	58.4
17	Hollis	61.7	14	Pryor	58.4
18	Chickasha Experiment Station	61.6	18	Vinita 2 N	58.6
19	Okemah	61.5	19	Taloga	58.8
20	Ada	61.3	20	Blackwell	*59.0*
20	Broken Bow Dam	61.3	21	Nowata	*59.1*
20	Hanna	61.3	21	Stillwater 2 W	59.1
20	Holdenville	*61.3*	23	Kansas 1 ESE	59.2
20	McAlester Municipal Airport	61.3	23	Ponca City Municipal Airport	59.2
25	Purcell 5 SW	61.2	25	Pawhuska	59.3

Annual Mean Minimum Temperature

Highest			Lowest		
Rank	**Station Name**	**°F**	**Rank**	**Station Name**	**°F**
1	Ardmore	52.7	1	Kenton	39.8
2	Hugo	51.8	2	Boise City 2 E	40.1
2	Madill	51.8	3	Goodwell Research Station	40.6
4	Marietta	51.7	4	Beaver	41.4
5	McCurtain 1 SE	50.8	5	Hooker	41.7
5	Waurika	50.8	6	Arnett	43.9
7	Okemah	50.5	6	Gage Airport	*43.9*
8	Seminole	50.4	8	Fort Supply 3 SE	44.1
9	McAlester Municipal Airport	50.3	9	Freedom	44.2
10	Duncan	50.2	10	Hammon 3 SSW	44.3
11	Muskogee	50.1	11	Buffalo	44.6
11	Spavinaw	50.1	12	Gate	44.7
11	Tulsa Int'l Airport	50.1	12	Mutual	44.7
14	Tuskahoma	49.9	14	Helena 1 SSE	45.2
14	Wagoner	49.9	15	Taloga	45.3
16	Lake Eufaula	*49.8*	16	Miami	45.6
16	Pauls Valley 4 WSW	49.8	17	Erick	45.9
18	Hanna	49.7	18	Waynoka 3 S	46.0
18	Holdenville	*49.7*	19	Pryor	46.4
20	Healdton	*49.6*	20	Alva	*46.7*
20	Idabel	49.6	20	Billings	46.7
22	Ada	49.5	20	Claremore 2 ENE	46.7
22	Blanchard 2 SSW	49.5	23	Cherokee	46.8
22	Chandler 1	49.5	24	Jefferson	46.9
25	Frederick	49.4	25	Elk City	47.1

Annual Extreme Minimum Temperature

	Highest			Lowest	
Rank	**Station Name**	**°F**	**Rank**	**Station Name**	**°F**
1	Broken Bow Dam	0	1	Gate	-25
2	Idabel	-2	2	Kenton	-22
3	Hugo	-4	3	Hooker	-21
4	Smithville	-6	3	Spavinaw	-21
4	Wichita Mtn Wildlife Refuge	-6	5	Claremore 2 ENE	-20
6	Duncan	-7	5	Pryor	-20
7	Ada	-8	7	Vinita 2 N	-19
7	Ardmore	-8	8	Beaver	-18
7	Lake Eufaula	-8	8	Perry	-18
7	Madill	-8	8	Stillwater 2 W	-18
7	Marietta	-8	11	Anadarko 3 E	-17
7	Oklahoma City Int'l Airport	-8	11	Barnsdall	-17
13	Cushing	-9	11	Freedom	-17
13	Erick	-9	11	Taloga	-17
13	Hobart Municipal Airport	-9	15	Boise City 2 E	-16
13	McCurtain 1 SE	-9	15	Hammon 3 SSW	-16
13	Muskogee	-9	15	Jefferson	-16
13	Okemah	-9	15	Mannford 6 NW	-16
13	Sallisaw 2 NW	-9	19	Bartlesville F. Phillips Field	-15
13	Seminole	-9	19	Billings	-15
21	Altus Dam	-10	19	Cherokee	-15
21	Altus Irrigation Research Station	-10	19	Gage Airport	*-15*
21	Enid	-10	19	Hanna	-15
21	Healdton	-10	19	Helena 1 SSE	-15
21	Hollis	-10	19	Kingfisher 2 SE	-15

July Mean Maximum Temperature

	Highest			Lowest	
Rank	**Station Name**	**°F**	**Rank**	**Station Name**	**°F**
1	Chattanooga 3 NE	98.6	1	Kansas 1 ESE	90.9
2	Mangum	98.5	1	Stilwell 5 NNW	90.9
3	Buffalo	97.9	3	Miami	91.6
4	Altus Irrigation Research Station	97.7	4	Vinita 2 N	91.8
5	Hollis	97.5	5	Kenton	91.9
6	Frederick	97.4	5	Smithville	91.9
7	Cherokee	97.1	7	Tahlequah	92.2
8	Alva	*96.9*	8	Pryor	92.3
8	Clinton	96.9	9	Arnett	92.4
8	Waurika	96.9	9	Claremore 2 ENE	92.4
11	Freedom	96.3	11	Spavinaw	92.5
11	Jefferson	96.3	12	McAlester Municipal Airport	92.6
11	Okeene	96.3	13	Boise City 2 E	92.7
14	Altus Dam	96.2	13	Meeker 4 W	92.7
15	Carnegie 5 NE	96.0	15	Cushing	92.8
15	Healdton	96.0	15	Wagoner	92.8
15	Waynoka 3 S	96.0	17	Idabel	93.0
18	Taloga	95.8	17	Pawhuska	93.0
19	Weatherford	95.7	19	Ada	93.1
20	Chickasha Experiment Station	95.6	19	Fort Supply 3 SE	93.1
21	Erick	95.5	19	Goodwell Research Station	93.1
21	Guthrie 5 S	95.5	19	Lake Eufaula	*93.1*
23	Gate	95.4	19	Stillwater 2 W	93.1
23	Kingfisher 2 SE	95.4	24	Oklahoma City Int'l Airport	93.2
25	Hobart Municipal Airport	95.3	24	Webbers Falls 5 WSW	93.2

January Mean Minimum Temperature

Highest			Lowest		
Rank	**Station Name**	**°F**	**Rank**	**Station Name**	**°F**
1	Hugo	31.4	1	Beaver	17.1
2	Ardmore	30.7	2	Goodwell Research Station	18.2
3	Marietta	30.1	3	Kenton	18.4
4	Madill	29.9	4	Hooker	18.9
5	McCurtain 1 SE	29.1	5	Boise City 2 E	19.0
6	Idabel	28.9	6	Freedom	19.4
7	Tuskahoma	28.7	7	Fort Supply 3 SE	19.7
8	Waurika	28.4	7	Gage Airport	19.7
9	Okemah	28.2	9	Arnett	20.2
10	Ada	27.9	10	Hammon 3 SSW	20.6
11	Pauls Valley 4 WSW	27.7	11	Buffalo	20.7
11	Seminole	27.7	12	Helena 1 SSE	20.8
13	Broken Bow Dam	27.5	13	Mutual	21.1
13	Hanna	27.5	14	Gate	21.2
15	McAlester Municipal Airport	27.4	15	Miami	21.6
16	Blanchard 2 SSW	27.3	16	Taloga	21.8
16	Healdton	27.3	17	Waynoka 3 S	22.0
16	Holdenville	27.3	18	Claremore 2 ENE	22.1
19	Duncan	27.2	19	Cherokee	22.2
19	Muskogee	27.2	20	Pryor	22.4
21	Spavinaw	27.0	21	Billings	22.7
22	Sallisaw 2 NW	26.8	21	Jefferson	22.7
22	Smithville	26.8	21	Stillwater 2 W	22.7
22	Wagoner	26.8	24	Alva	*22.9*
25	Frederick	26.6	24	Pawhuska	22.9

Number of Annual Heating Degree Days

Highest			Lowest		
Rank	**Station Name**	**Num.**	**Rank**	**Station Name**	**Num.**
1	Beaver	4,768	1	Hugo	2,703
2	Goodwell Research Station	4,767	2	Ardmore	2,715
3	Kenton	4,693	3	Marietta	2,815
4	Hooker	4,572	4	Waurika	2,827
5	Boise City 2 E	4,558	5	Madill	2,853
6	Arnett	4,522	6	Idabel	2,976
7	Fort Supply 3 SE	*4,431*	7	Tuskahoma	2,993
8	Helena 1 SSE	4,394	8	McCurtain 1 SE	3,040
9	Mutual	4,389	9	Healdton	*3,079*
10	Gage Airport	*4,376*	10	Seminole	3,114
11	Freedom	4,242	11	Pauls Valley 4 WSW	3,116
12	Gate	4,228	12	Altus Irrigation Research Station	3,134
13	Hammon 3 SSW	4,222	13	Broken Bow Dam	3,139
14	Miami	4,190	14	Chattanooga 3 NE	3,149
15	Billings	4,187	15	Frederick	3,192
16	Claremore 2 ENE	4,086	16	Ada	3,195
17	Ponca City Municipal Airport	4,039	17	Duncan	3,215
18	Blackwell	*4,027*	18	Okemah	3,237
18	Pryor	4,027	19	Holdenville	*3,247*
20	Taloga	3,998	20	Hanna	3,248
21	Waynoka 3 S	3,973	21	Mangum	3,262
22	Buffalo	3,969	22	Hollis	3,275
23	Alva	*3,952*	23	McAlester Municipal Airport	3,297
24	Cherokee	3,943	24	Chickasha Experiment Station	3,326
25	Stillwater 2 W	3,941	25	Sallisaw 2 NW	3,335

Number of Annual Cooling Degree Days

	Highest			Lowest	
Rank	Station Name	Num.	Rank	Station Name	Num.
1	Waurika	2,453	1	Kenton	1,183
2	Chattanooga 3 NE	2,390	2	Boise City 2 E	1,251
3	Ardmore	2,358	3	Goodwell Research Station	1,389
4	Marietta	2,338	4	Hooker	1,526
5	Altus Irrigation Research Station	2,334	5	Arnett	1,539
6	Madill	2,283	6	Smithville	*1,582*
7	Altus Dam	2,258	7	Miami	1,603
8	Frederick	2,237	8	Beaver	1,620
9	Mangum	2,228	9	Fort Supply 3 SE	1,639
10	Guthrie 5 S	2,220	10	Stilwell 5 NNW	1,640
11	Hugo	2,218	11	Pryor	1,670
12	Seminole	2,216	12	Kansas 1 ESE	1,679
13	Healdton	*2,204*	13	Gage Airport	*1,700*
14	Chickasha Experiment Station	2,189	14	Hammon 3 SSW	1,708
15	McCurtain 1 SE	2,180	15	Mutual	1,720
16	Clinton	2,174	16	Vinita 2 N	1,758
17	Cherokee	2,172	17	Tahlequah	1,787
18	Carnegie 5 NE	2,167	18	Gate	1,794
19	Duncan	2,146	19	Claremore 2 ENE	1,800
20	Hollis	2,139	20	Okmulgee Water Works	1,819
21	Perry	2,135	21	Elk City	1,850
22	Tuskahoma	2,132	21	Nowata	1,850
23	Hobart Municipal Airport	*2,131*	23	Taloga	1,851
24	Okemah	2,128	24	Billings	1,862
25	Tulsa Int'l Airport	2,121	25	Helena 1 SSE	1,867

Annual Precipitation

	Highest			Lowest	
Rank	Station Name	Inches	Rank	Station Name	Inches
1	Smithville	56.18	1	Goodwell Research Station	16.81
2	Broken Bow Dam	54.64	2	Kenton	17.06
3	Tuskahoma	50.52	3	Hooker	18.01
4	Idabel	50.05	4	Boise City 2 E	18.19
5	Stilwell 5 NNW	49.94	5	Beaver	21.29
6	McCurtain 1 SE	49.02	6	Gage Airport	*21.48*
7	Kansas 1 ESE	48.59	7	Gate	22.37
8	Tahlequah	48.13	8	Fort Supply 3 SE	24.03
9	Hugo	47.49	9	Arnett	24.80
10	Sallisaw 2 NW	46.68	10	Freedom	25.52
11	Webbers Falls 5 WSW	46.43	10	Hollis	25.52
12	Lake Eufaula	45.76	12	Erick	25.68
13	McAlester Municipal Airport	45.56	13	Mutual	25.73
14	Hanna	45.33	14	Buffalo	26.13
15	Vinita 2 N	45.03	15	Waynoka 3 S	26.63
15	Wagoner	45.03	16	Alva	*26.93*
17	Spavinaw	44.25	17	Hammon 3 SSW	27.49
18	Muskogee	44.17	18	Mangum	27.90
19	Miami	44.01	19	Hobart Municipal Airport	28.01
20	Pryor	43.86	20	Altus Irrigation Research Station	28.41
21	Claremore 2 ENE	43.70	21	Elk City	28.48
22	Okmulgee Water Works	43.45	21	Taloga	28.48
23	Pawhuska	43.31	23	Geary	28.80
24	Madill	42.43	24	Altus Dam	28.94
25	Barnsdall	42.30	25	Weatherford	29.45

Number of Days Annually With ≥ 0.1″ Precipitation

	Highest			Lowest	
Rank	Station Name	Days	Rank	Station Name	Days
1	Kansas 1 ESE	71	1	Goodwell Research Station	34
1	Stilwell 5 NNW	71	2	Hooker	36
3	Broken Bow Dam	70	2	Kenton	36
4	McCurtain 1 SE	68	4	Boise City 2 E	37
4	Smithville	68	5	Beaver	39
4	Tuskahoma	68	6	Gage Airport	*40*
7	Tahlequah	67	7	Gate	41
8	Idabel	66	7	Geary	41
9	Hugo	65	7	Hollis	41
10	Claremore 2 ENE	64	10	Mangum	42
10	Webbers Falls 5 WSW	64	11	Altus Irrigation Research Station	43
12	Lake Eufaula	63	11	Arnett	43
12	McAlester Municipal Airport	63	11	Elk City	43
14	Miami	62	11	Erick	43
14	Muskogee	62	11	Freedom	43
14	Pawhuska	62	11	Hammon 3 SSW	43
14	Spavinaw	62	11	Waynoka 3 S	43
14	Vinita 2 N	62	18	Cherokee	44
14	Wagoner	62	18	Fort Supply 3 SE	44
20	Hanna	61	18	Frederick	44
20	Purcell 5 SW	61	18	Mutual	44
22	Barnsdall	60	18	Taloga	44
22	Mannford 6 NW	60	18	Waurika	44
22	Nowata	60	24	Altus Dam	45
22	Pryor	60	24	Anadarko 3 E	45

Number of Days Annually With ≥ 1.0″ Precipitation

	Highest			Lowest	
Rank	Station Name	Days	Rank	Station Name	Days
1	Smithville	19	1	Boise City 2 E	3
2	Broken Bow Dam	18	1	Hooker	3
2	Hugo	18	1	Kenton	3
2	Tuskahoma	18	4	Beaver	4
5	Idabel	17	4	Gage Airport	*4*
5	Kansas 1 ESE	17	4	Goodwell Research Station	4
5	Sallisaw 2 NW	17	7	Gate	5
8	McCurtain 1 SE	16	8	Fort Supply 3 SE	6
8	Stilwell 5 NNW	16	8	Freedom	6
10	Barnsdall	15	8	Hollis	6
10	Hanna	15	11	Altus Dam	7
10	McAlester Municipal Airport	15	11	Altus Irrigation Research Station	7
10	Seminole	15	11	Erick	7
10	Webbers Falls 5 WSW	15	11	Mutual	7
15	Ada	14	15	Alva	*8*
15	Healdton	14	15	Arnett	8
15	Lake Eufaula	14	15	Buffalo	8
15	Madill	14	15	Hobart Municipal Airport	8
15	Muskogee	14	15	Mangum	8
15	Okemah	14	15	Watonga	8
15	Okmulgee Water Works	14	15	Waynoka 3 S	8
15	Pryor	14	22	Billings	9
15	Purcell 5 SW	14	22	Chattanooga 3 NE	9
15	Tahlequah	14	22	Cherokee	9
25	Ardmore	13	22	Clinton	9

Annual Snowfall

	Highest			Lowest	
Rank	**Station Name**	**Inches**	**Rank**	**Station Name**	**Inches**
1	Boise City 2 E	31.6	1	Idabel	*1.6*
2	Kenton	*22.8*	2	Chattanooga 3 NE	*2.1*
3	Gate	21.9	3	Hugo	*2.4*
4	Hooker	18.6	3	Wichita Mtn Wildlife Refuge	*2.4*
5	Helena 1 SSE	18.2	5	Ardmore	*2.9*
6	Gage Airport	*16.0*	6	Duncan	*3.0*
7	Taloga	15.8	7	Mangum	*3.1*
8	Goodwell Research Station	14.2	8	Smithville	*3.2*
9	Fort Supply 3 SE	14.0	8	Waurika	*3.2*
10	Mutual	13.9	10	Lake Eufaula	*3.3*
11	Kansas 1 ESE	13.8	10	Madill	*3.3*
12	Buffalo	*13.1*	12	Meeker 4 W	*3.5*
13	Cherokee	*12.9*	13	Frederick	*3.6*
14	Vinita 2 N	12.2	13	Healdton	*3.6*
15	Watonga	12.0	15	Seminole	*3.7*
15	Waynoka 3 S	*12.0*	16	Kingfisher 2 SE	*4.1*
17	Stilwell 5 NNW	11.9	16	Tuskahoma	4.1
18	Erick	10.3	18	Ada	*4.5*
19	Bartlesville F. Phillips Field	10.0	18	Marietta	*4.5*
20	Ralston	9.9	20	Geary	*4.6*
21	Pawhuska	9.7	21	Altus Dam	*5.0*
22	Claremore 2 ENE	9.2	21	Okemah	*5.0*
23	Arnett	*9.1*	23	Hollis	5.1
23	Barnsdall	*9.1*	24	Cushing	*5.3*
23	Billings	9.1	25	Holdenville	*5.5*

Note: See Appendix D for explanation of data.

Annual Extreme Maximum Temperature

	Highest				Lowest	
Rank	**Station Name**	**°F**		**Rank**	**Station Name**	**°F**
1	Pelton Dam	117		1	Crater Lake Nat'l Park Hdqtrs.	90
2	Medford Jackson County Airport	114		2	Port Orford 2	93
3	Lost Creek Dam	112		3	North Bend Municipal Airport	95
4	Arlington	111		4	Astoria Clatsop County Airport	96
4	Pendleton Br. Exp. Station	111		4	Newport	96
4	Pendleton Municipal Airport	111		6	Hart Mountain Refuge	98
4	Pilot Rock 1 SE	111		6	Mason Dam	98
4	Ruch	111		6	Seneca	98
9	Cave Junction 1 WNW	110		9	Brothers	99
9	Illahe	*110*		9	Honeyman State Park	99
9	Monument 2	110		9	Otis 2 NE	99
9	Ontario	110		9	Scotts Mills 9 SE	99
9	Prospect 2 SW	110		13	Bandon 2 NNE	100
9	Riddle	110		13	Howard Prairie Dam	100
15	Dufur	109		13	Paisley	100
15	Grants Pass	109		16	Austin 3 S	101
15	Madras	109		16	Lemolo Lake 3 NNW	*101*
15	Medford Experiment Station	109		16	Ochoco Ranger Station	101
15	Milton Freewater	109		16	Wickiup Dam	101
15	Roseburg KQEN	109		20	Barnes Station	102
15	Sisters	109		20	Bend	102
15	Toketee Falls	109		20	Coquille City	102
23	Ashland	108		20	Gold Beach Ranger Station	102
23	Burns Junction	*108*		20	Lakeview 2 NNW	102
23	Corvallis State Univ	108		20	Long Creek	102

Annual Mean Maximum Temperature

	Highest				Lowest	
Rank	**Station Name**	**°F**		**Rank**	**Station Name**	**°F**
1	Pelton Dam	69.1		1	Crater Lake Nat'l Park Hdqtrs.	48.2
2	Ruch	68.7		2	Government Camp	49.9
3	Grants Pass	68.3		3	Seneca	55.8
4	Illahe	67.5		4	Scotts Mills 9 SE	56.5
4	Medford Jackson County Airport	67.5		5	Howard Prairie Dam	56.6
6	Cave Junction 1 WNW	67.3		6	Austin 3 S	57.3
7	Lost Creek Dam	66.9		7	Mason Dam	57.5
8	Medford Experiment Station	*66.4*		7	Wickiup Dam	57.5
9	Riddle	66.2		9	Hart Mountain Refuge	*58.1*
10	Elkton 3 SW	*66.0*		9	Ochoco Ranger Station	58.1
10	Roseburg KQEN	66.0		11	Newport	58.2
12	Ashland	65.7		12	Marion Frks. Fish Hatchery	58.3
13	Powers	65.6		13	Astoria Clatsop County Airport	58.5
14	Prospect 2 SW	65.5		13	Brothers	58.5
15	Arlington	65.4		15	Ukiah	58.9
15	Boardman	65.4		16	Condon	59.0
15	Burns Junction	*65.4*		16	Otis 2 NE	59.0
18	Ontario	65.2		18	Long Creek	59.4
18	Rome 2 NW	65.2		18	Three Lynx	59.4
20	Drain	65.0		20	Lakeview 2 NNW	59.5
20	Owyhee Dam	65.0		20	Moro	59.5
22	Vale	64.8		20	Tillamook 1 W	59.5
23	Hermiston 1 SE	*64.6*		23	Baker Municipal Airport	59.6
23	Madras	64.6		23	Belknap Springs 8 N	59.6
23	McDermitt 26 N	64.6		25	Clatskanie	59.8

Annual Mean Temperature

	Highest			Lowest	
Rank	**Station Name**	**°F**	**Rank**	**Station Name**	**°F**
1	Illahe	55.5	1	Crater Lake Nat'l Park Hdqtrs.	37.7
2	Elkton 3 SW	*55.0*	2	Seneca	40.2
3	Roseburg KQEN	54.9	3	Austin 3 S	41.5
4	Grants Pass	54.8	4	Government Camp	42.1
5	Arlington	54.7	5	Ukiah	43.3
5	Oregon City	54.7	6	Mason Dam	43.4
7	Medford Jackson County Airport	54.5	6	Ochoco Ranger Station	43.4
7	Portland KGW TV	*54.5*	8	Brothers	43.7
9	Riddle	54.3	9	Hart Mountain Refuge	*43.9*
10	Brookings	54.1	9	Wickiup Dam	43.9
10	Portland Int'l Airport	54.1	11	Howard Prairie Dam	44.0
12	Powers	53.9	12	Sprague River 1 NW	*44.5*
13	Ruch	53.8	13	Enterprise 20 NNE	45.2
13	Troutdale Airport	*53.8*	14	Silver Lake Ranger Station	*45.6*
15	Milton Freewater	53.7	14	Sisters	*45.6*
15	Tidewater 2 SW	*53.7*	16	Paulina	45.7
17	Cave Junction 1 WNW	53.6	17	Baker Municipal Airport	46.0
17	Drain	53.6	17	Barnes Station	46.0
19	Boardman	53.4	17	Wallowa	46.0
20	Gold Beach Ranger Station	*53.3*	20	Long Creek	46.2
21	Lookout Point Dam	53.2	21	Bend	46.4
22	Pelton Dam	53.1	21	Drewsey	46.4
22	Port Orford 2	53.1	21	Halfway	46.4
24	Bonneville Dam	53.0	24	Lakeview 2 NNW	46.6
25	Forest Grove	52.9	25	Marion Frks. Fish Hatchery	46.7

Annual Mean Minimum Temperature

	Highest			Lowest	
Rank	**Station Name**	**°F**	**Rank**	**Station Name**	**°F**
1	Brookings	46.4	1	Seneca	24.4
2	Portland KGW TV	*46.3*	2	Austin 3 S	25.7
3	North Bend Municipal Airport	45.7	3	Crater Lake Nat'l Park Hdqtrs.	27.1
4	Gold Beach Ranger Station	*45.6*	4	Ukiah	27.7
5	Port Orford 2	45.4	5	Sprague River 1 NW	*27.8*
6	Portland Int'l Airport	45.2	6	Ochoco Ranger Station	28.6
7	Bonneville Dam	44.9	7	Brothers	28.8
8	Oregon City	44.8	8	Mason Dam	29.2
9	Arlington	44.0	8	Paulina	29.2
9	Elkton 3 SW	*44.0*	10	Hart Mountain Refuge	*29.7*
9	Troutdale Airport	*44.0*	11	Enterprise 20 NNE	29.9
12	Bandon 2 NNE	43.9	12	Sisters	*30.2*
12	Newport	43.9	12	Wickiup Dam	30.2
14	Seaside	43.8	14	Drewsey	30.6
15	Astoria Clatsop County Airport	43.7	15	Silver Lake Ranger Station	*30.7*
15	Honeyman State Park	*43.7*	16	Rockville 5 N	31.1
15	Lookout Point Dam	43.7	17	Alkali Lake	*31.2*
15	Tidewater 2 SW	*43.7*	18	Barnes Station	31.3
19	Roseburg KQEN	43.6	19	Howard Prairie Dam	31.4
20	Illahe	43.4	20	Prineville 4 NW	31.5
21	Silverton	43.3	21	Halfway	31.7
22	Cloverdale	43.1	22	Wallowa	31.9
22	Milton Freewater	43.1	23	McDermitt 26 N	32.3
24	Headworks Ptld. Wtr. Bur.	43.0	24	Baker Municipal Airport	32.4
25	Estacada 2 SE	42.9	25	Bend	32.7

Annual Extreme Minimum Temperature

	Highest				Lowest	
Rank	Station Name	°F		Rank	Station Name	°F
1	Brookings	18		1	Seneca	-48
2	Gold Beach Ranger Station	16		2	Mason Dam	-40
3	Port Orford 2	13		3	Baker Municipal Airport	-39
4	Cloverdale	9		4	Paulina	-38
4	Honeyman State Park	9		4	Ukiah	-38
6	Bandon 2 NNE	8		6	Austin 3 S	-37
6	Coquille City	8		7	Drewsey	-36
6	Portland Int'l Airport	8		8	Prineville 4 NW	-34
6	Portland KGW TV	*8*		9	Alkali Lake	*-33*
10	Astoria Clatsop County Airport	6		9	Enterprise 20 NNE	-33
10	Bonneville Dam	6		9	Rockville 5 N	-33
10	Estacada 2 SE	6		9	Silver Lake Ranger Station	-33
10	Illahe	*6*		13	Burns Junction	*-32*
10	Oregon City	6		13	Hart Mountain Refuge	-32
15	Detroit Dam	5		13	Riverside 7 SSW	-32
15	Headworks Ptld. Wtr. Bur.	5		13	Sprague River 1 NW	-32
15	Powers	5		17	Elgin	-31
15	Seaside	5		17	Halfway	-31
15	Tidewater 2 SW	*5*		19	Barnes Station	-30
20	Otis 2 NE	4		19	Brothers	-30
20	Tillamook 1 W	4		19	McDermitt 26 N	-30
22	Lookout Point Dam	3		22	Beulah	-29
22	Riddle	3		22	Madras	-29
22	Roseburg KQEN	3		24	Paisley	-28
25	Corvallis Water Bureau	2		24	Redmond Roberts Field	-28

July Mean Maximum Temperature

	Highest				Lowest	
Rank	Station Name	°F		Rank	Station Name	°F
1	Ontario	94.1		1	Newport	64.8
2	Pelton Dam	93.8		2	North Bend Municipal Airport	66.5
3	Vale	93.3		3	Bandon 2 NNE	66.8
4	Huntington	92.3		4	Crater Lake Nat'l Park Hdqtrs.	67.5
5	Burns Junction	91.9		4	Tillamook 1 W	67.5
6	Owyhee Dam	91.8		6	Government Camp	67.6
7	Rome 2 NW	91.4		6	Seaside	67.6
8	McDermitt 26 N	91.1		8	Astoria Clatsop County Airport	67.7
9	Arlington	90.9		9	Gold Beach Ranger Station	67.9
10	Monument 2	*90.8*		10	Port Orford 2	68.0
11	Malheur Branch Exp. Station	90.6		11	Brookings	68.1
11	Medford Jackson County Airport	90.6		12	Honeyman State Park	69.3
13	Nyssa	90.5		13	Otis 2 NE	69.7
14	Ruch	90.0		14	Cloverdale	70.0
15	Grants Pass	89.7		15	Coquille City	71.9
16	Riverside 7 SSW	89.6		15	Scotts Mills 9 SE	71.9
17	Boardman	89.5		17	Clatskanie	73.6
18	Beulah	89.4		18	Tidewater 2 SW	74.8
19	Cave Junction 1 WNW	89.2		19	Vernonia 2	75.4
20	Drewsey	88.9		20	Three Lynx	77.2
21	Lost Creek Dam	88.7		21	Detroit Dam	77.7
22	Pilot Rock 1 SE	88.3		22	Cascadia	78.2
23	Milton Freewater	88.1		23	Corvallis Water Bureau	78.3
23	Pendleton Br. Exp. Station	88.1		24	Powers	78.4
23	Rockville 5 N	88.1		25	Bonneville Dam	78.6

January Mean Minimum Temperature

Highest			Lowest		
Rank	**Station Name**	**°F**	**Rank**	**Station Name**	**°F**
1	Brookings	41.8	1	Seneca	9.9
2	Gold Beach Ranger Station	*41.0*	2	Austin 3 S	11.2
3	Port Orford 2	39.9	3	Mason Dam	12.7
4	North Bend Municipal Airport	39.8	4	Drewsey	14.7
5	Bandon 2 NNE	38.7	5	Ukiah	15.1
6	Newport	38.6	6	Halfway	15.4
7	Cloverdale	37.6	7	Beulah	16.4
7	Honeyman State Park	37.6	8	Enterprise 20 NNE	16.8
9	Seaside	37.5	9	Paulina	17.0
10	Elkton 3 SW	36.9	10	Ochoco Ranger Station	17.1
11	Astoria Clatsop County Airport	36.7	10	Sprague River 1 NW	17.1
11	Otis 2 NE	36.7	12	Baker Municipal Airport	17.2
13	Tidewater 2 SW	36.6	13	Brothers	17.7
14	Illahe	36.5	14	Wickiup Dam	17.9
15	Portland KGW TV	36.4	15	Crater Lake Nat'l Park Hdqtrs.	18.0
15	Tillamook 1 W	36.4	16	Rome 2 NW	18.3
17	Coquille City	35.9	17	Burns Junction	18.4
18	Oregon City	35.6	18	Rockville 5 N	18.6
19	Roseburg KQEN	35.2	18	Wallowa	18.6
20	Powers	34.9	20	Vale	18.7
21	Lookout Point Dam	34.8	21	Alkali Lake	19.0
22	Riddle	34.7	21	McDermitt 26 N	19.0
23	Portland Int'l Airport	34.6	23	Barnes Station	19.1
24	Estacada 2 SE	34.5	23	Malheur Branch Exp. Station	19.1
24	Headworks Ptld. Wtr. Bur.	34.5	25	Hart Mountain Refuge	19.2

Number of Annual Heating Degree Days

Highest			Lowest		
Rank	**Station Name**	**Num.**	**Rank**	**Station Name**	**Num.**
1	Crater Lake Nat'l Park Hdqtrs.	9,892	1	Illahe	3,910
2	Seneca	8,998	2	Elkton 3 SW	*3,918*
3	Austin 3 S	8,546	3	Brookings	3,946
4	Government Camp	8,320	4	Roseburg KQEN	4,099
5	Mason Dam	7,911	5	Powers	4,130
6	Ukiah	7,897	6	Oregon City	4,135
7	Ochoco Ranger Station	7,881	7	Tidewater 2 SW	*4,158*
8	Brothers	7,812	8	Portland KGW TV	*4,169*
9	Wickiup Dam	7,709	9	Gold Beach Ranger Station	*4,185*
10	Hart Mountain Refuge	*7,691*	9	Riddle	4,185
11	Howard Prairie Dam	7,651	11	Grants Pass	4,226
12	Sprague River 1 NW	*7,492*	12	Port Orford 2	4,261
13	Enterprise 20 NNE	7,267	13	Portland Int'l Airport	4,301
14	Silver Lake Ranger Station	*7,155*	14	Drain	4,374
15	Paulina	7,128	14	Troutdale Airport	*4,374*
16	Sisters	*7,127*	16	Coquille City	4,375
17	Baker Municipal Airport	7,093	17	North Bend Municipal Airport	4,378
18	Barnes Station	7,042	18	Medford Jackson County Airport	4,472
19	Wallowa	7,027	19	Lookout Point Dam	4,490
20	Drewsey	7,020	20	Ruch	4,503
21	Halfway	6,967	21	Cave Junction 1 WNW	4,521
22	Long Creek	*6,922*	22	Bandon 2 NNE	4,566
23	Lakeview 2 NNW	6,909	23	McMinnville	4,587
24	Bend	6,849	24	Bonneville Dam	4,633
25	Rockville 5 N	6,817	25	Honeyman State Park	*4,641*

Number of Annual Cooling Degree Days

	Highest			Lowest	
Rank	Station Name	Num.	Rank	Station Name	Num.
1	Huntington	1,044	1	Bandon 2 NNE	5
2	Arlington	1,010	1	North Bend Municipal Airport	5
3	Nyssa	866	3	Crater Lake Nat'l Park Hdqtrs.	7
4	Ontario	864	4	Newport	9
5	Milton Freewater	824	5	Gold Beach Ranger Station	*11*
6	Vale	814	5	Port Orford 2	11
7	Owyhee Dam	787	7	Tillamook 1 W	14
8	Boardman	773	8	Honeyman State Park	*16*
9	Malheur Branch Exp. Station	765	9	Astoria Clatsop County Airport	21
10	Medford Jackson County Airport	762	10	Seaside	22
11	Burns Junction	707	11	Coquille City	23
12	Hermiston 1 SE	*705*	12	Cloverdale	24
13	Pelton Dam	692	12	Otis 2 NE	24
14	Pendleton Municipal Airport	620	14	Seneca	30
15	Grants Pass	573	15	Austin 3 S	54
16	Illahe	*570*	15	Brookings	54
17	Roseburg KQEN	515	17	Ukiah	62
18	Pilot Rock 1 SE	514	18	Government Camp	66
19	Ruch	*503*	19	Vernonia 2	76
20	Rome 2 NW	492	20	Hart Mountain Refuge	*95*
21	Cave Junction 1 WNW	484	20	Howard Prairie Dam	95
22	Pendleton Br. Exp. Station	476	22	Sprague River 1 NW	*96*
23	Beulah	*473*	23	Ochoco Ranger Station	99
24	Oregon City	472	24	Wickiup Dam	106
25	Lost Creek Dam	466	25	Clatskanie	117

Annual Precipitation

	Highest			Lowest	
Rank	Station Name	Inches	Rank	Station Name	Inches
1	Otis 2 NE	99.03	1	Rome 2 NW	8.32
2	Tillamook 1 W	91.46	2	Alkali Lake	*8.44*
3	Detroit Dam	90.61	3	Redmond Roberts Field	8.52
4	Tidewater 2 SW	90.33	4	Boardman	8.71
5	Government Camp	89.45	5	Burns Junction	*8.87*
6	Scotts Mills 9 SE	84.13	6	Arlington	9.22
7	Cloverdale	83.40	7	Brothers	9.36
8	Illahe	82.28	8	Ontario	9.69
9	Headworks Ptld. Wtr. Bur.	80.77	9	Silver Lake Ranger Station	9.75
10	Gold Beach Ranger Station	80.15	10	McDermitt 26 N	9.82
11	Bonneville Dam	78.26	11	Owyhee Dam	9.98
12	Belknap Springs 8 N	76.88	12	Riverside 7 SSW	10.16
13	Seaside	76.61	13	Vale	10.32
14	Brookings	74.73	14	Madras	10.33
15	Port Orford 2	74.53	15	Drewsey	10.50
16	Honeyman State Park	73.09	16	Malheur Branch Exp. Station	10.54
17	Three Lynx	72.93	17	Hermiston 1 SE	*10.57*
18	Marion Frks. Fish Hatchery	71.50	18	Prineville 4 NW	10.64
19	Newport	70.27	19	Baker Municipal Airport	10.70
20	Corvallis Water Bureau	68.77	19	Nyssa	10.70
21	Falls City 2	68.67	21	Paisley	10.84
22	Astoria Clatsop County Airport	67.75	21	Pelton Dam	10.84
23	Crater Lake Nat'l Park Hdqtrs.	67.37	23	Paulina	11.43
24	Leaburg 1 SW	66.91	24	Mitchell 2 NW	*11.45*
25	Lemolo Lake 3 NNW	*66.30*	25	Moro	11.53

Number of Days Annually With ≥ 0.1″ Precipitation

	Highest			Lowest	
Rank	Station Name	Days	Rank	Station Name	Days
1	Tillamook 1 W	145	1	Alkali Lake	27
2	Otis 2 NE	142	1	Redmond Roberts Field	27
3	Headworks Ptld. Wtr. Bur.	141	3	Rome 2 NW	28
4	Government Camp	139	4	Brothers	29
5	Cloverdale	135	4	Silver Lake Ranger Station	29
5	Detroit Dam	135	6	Arlington	30
5	Scotts Mills 9 SE	135	6	Boardman	30
8	Three Lynx	131	6	McDermitt 26 N	30
9	Seaside	130	9	Hermiston 1 SE	31
9	Tidewater 2 SW	130	10	Burns Junction	32
11	Bonneville Dam	129	10	Madras	32
12	Astoria Clatsop County Airport	127	10	Paisley	32
13	Cascadia	126	10	Pelton Dam	32
14	Belknap Springs 8 N	125	14	Baker Municipal Airport	33
15	Newport	124	14	Ontario	33
16	Leaburg 1 SW	123	16	Malheur Branch Exp. Station	34
17	Lacomb 3 NNE	121	16	Malin 5 E	34
17	Marion Frks. Fish Hatchery	121	16	Owyhee Dam	34
19	Estacada 2 SE	119	16	Prineville 4 NW	34
20	Foster Dam	118	20	Beulah	35
21	North Bend Municipal Airport	116	20	Riverside 7 SSW	35
22	Lemolo Lake 3 NNW	115	20	Vale	35
23	Clatskanie	114	23	Bend	36
23	Stayton	114	23	Hart Mountain Refuge	36
25	Crater Lake Nat'l Park Hdqtrs.	113	23	Sisters	36

Number of Days Annually With ≥ 1.0″ Precipitation

	Highest			Lowest	
Rank	Station Name	Days	Rank	Station Name	Days
1	Illahe	31	1	Alkali Lake	0
1	Otis 2 NE	31	1	Antelope 1 NW	0
3	Government Camp	27	1	Arlington	0
4	Tidewater 2 SW	26	1	Ashland	0
5	Detroit Dam	25	1	Austin 3 S	0
6	Tillamook 1 W	24	1	Baker Municipal Airport	0
7	Brookings	23	1	Barnes Station	0
7	Cloverdale	23	1	Bend	0
7	Scotts Mills 9 SE	23	1	Beulah	0
10	Cave Junction 1 WNW	22	1	Boardman	0
11	Port Orford 2	21	1	Brothers	0
12	Belknap Springs 8 N	20	1	Burns Junction	0
12	Bonneville Dam	20	1	Condon	0
14	Corvallis Water Bureau	19	1	Drewsey	0
14	Falls City 2	19	1	Dufur	0
14	Headworks Ptld. Wtr. Bur.	19	1	Elgin	0
14	Seaside	19	1	Enterprise 20 NNE	0
18	Crater Lake Nat'l Park Hdqtrs.	18	1	Fossil	0
18	Marion Frks. Fish Hatchery	18	1	Hart Mountain Refuge	0
20	Newport	17	1	Heppner	0
21	Honeyman State Park	16	1	Hermiston 1 SE	0
21	Powers	16	1	Huntington	0
23	Astoria Clatsop County Airport	15	1	John Day	0
23	Idleyld Park 4 NE	15	1	Kent	0
23	Leaburg 1 SW	15	1	Klamath Falls 2 SSW	0

Annual Snowfall

	Highest			Lowest	
Rank	**Station Name**	**Inches**	**Rank**	**Station Name**	**Inches**
1	Crater Lake Nat'l Park Hdqtrs.	488.1	1	Gold Beach Ranger Station	0.2
2	Government Camp	256.7	1	Port Orford 2	0.2
3	Lemolo Lake 3 NNW	*221.4*	3	Seaside	0.4
4	Howard Prairie Dam	128.8	4	Bandon 2 NNE	0.5
5	Austin 3 S	92.0	4	Brookings	0.5
6	Marion Frks. Fish Hatchery	88.7	4	Coquille City	0.5
7	Wickiup Dam	82.8	7	Honeyman State Park	0.9
8	Halfway	73.1	8	Cloverdale	1.0
9	Scotts Mills 9 SE	66.3	8	Newport	1.0
10	Belknap Springs 8 N	64.9	10	North Bend Municipal Airport	1.1
11	Lakeview 2 NNW	55.6	11	Elkton 3 SW	1.2
12	Elgin	50.3	12	Roseburg KQEN	1.3
13	Barnes Station	45.5	13	North Willamette Exp. Station	1.4
14	Hart Mountain Refuge	*45.1*	13	Otis 2 NE	1.4
15	Ochoco Ranger Station	43.3	13	Tidewater 2 SW	*1.4*
16	Sprague River 1 NW	*41.2*	13	Tillamook 1 W	1.4
17	Wallowa	40.6	17	Foster Dam	1.6
18	Mason Dam	*38.0*	18	Fern Ridge Dam	1.7
19	Long Creek	35.9	19	Lookout Point Dam	1.9
20	Prospect 2 SW	33.3	19	Powers	1.9
21	Hood River Exp. Station	32.8	21	Drain	2.1
22	Toketee Falls	32.7	21	Oregon City	2.1
23	Bend	32.2	21	Stayton	*2.1*
23	Ukiah	32.2	24	Beaverton 2 SSW	*2.2*
25	Malin 5 E	32.1	24	Grants Pass	2.2

Note: See Appendix D for explanation of data.

Annual Extreme Maximum Temperature

	Highest				Lowest	
Rank	Station Name	°F		Rank	Station Name	°F
1	Laurelton Center	105		1	Tobyhanna	94
1	Montgomery Lock & Dam	105		2	Corry	95
1	Selinsgrove 2 S	*105*		2	Pleasant Mount 1 W	95
4	Confluence 1 SW Dam	104		2	Ridgway	95
4	Raystown Lake 2	*104*		5	Francis E Walter Dam	96
4	Shippensburg	104		5	Kane 1 NNE	96
7	Chambersburg 1 ESE	103		7	Bradford Regional Airport	*97*
7	Marcus Hook	103		7	Montrose	97
7	Millville 2 SW	*103*		7	Philipsburg Mid-State Airport	*97*
7	Philadelphia Int'l Airport	103		10	Bradford 4 SW Res. 5	98
7	Pittsburgh Int'l Airport	103		10	Dubois FAA Airport	98
7	Putneyville 2 SE Dam	103		10	Ebensburg Sewage Plant	98
7	Williamsport Airport	103		10	Hawley 1 E	98
14	Biglerville	102		14	Altoona 3 W	99
14	Butler 2 SW	102		14	Brookville Sewage Plant	*99*
14	Donora 1 SW	102		14	Franklin	99
14	Landisville 2 NW	102		14	Holtwood	99
14	Lebanon 2 W	102		14	Indiana 3 SE	99
14	Lewistown	102		14	Mercer	99
14	Reading 4 NNW	102		20	Clarion 3 SW	100
14	Slippery Rock 1 SSW	102		20	Erie Int'l Airport	100
14	State College	102		20	Matamoras	*100*
14	Stroudsburg	*102*		20	Meadville 1 S	100
14	Towanda 1 ESE	102		20	New Castle 1 N	100
14	Uniontown 1 NE	102		20	Titusville Water Works	100

Annual Mean Maximum Temperature

	Highest				Lowest	
Rank	Station Name	°F		Rank	Station Name	°F
1	York 3 SSW Pumping Station	64.7		1	Bradford Regional Airport	*53.2*
2	Donora 1 SW	64.3		2	Pleasant Mount 1 W	53.5
3	Philadelphia Int'l Airport	64.2		3	Montrose	55.0
4	Marcus Hook	63.9		4	Kane 1 NNE	55.2
5	Landisville 2 NW	63.6		5	Bradford 4 SW Res. 5	55.5
5	Laurelton Center	63.6		5	Philipsburg Mid-State Airport	*55.5*
7	Uniontown 1 NE	62.7		7	Tobyhanna	*55.6*
8	Stroudsburg	62.5		8	Dubois FAA Airport	55.8
9	Reading 4 NNW	62.4		9	Francis E Walter Dam	*56.1*
9	Waynesburg 1 E	62.4		10	Erie Int'l Airport	56.6
11	Chambersburg 1 ESE	62.3		11	Corry	57.2
12	Lebanon 2 W	62.1		12	Ridgway	57.3
12	Montgomery Lock & Dam	62.1		13	Titusville Water Works	57.5
12	Shippensburg	62.1		14	Altoona 3 W	57.8
15	Holtwood	61.9		14	Hawley 1 E	57.8
16	Lewistown	61.7		16	Meadville 1 S	57.9
17	Biglerville	61.6		17	Jamestown 2 NW	58.3
17	Confluence 1 SW Dam	61.6		18	Warren	58.4
19	Salina 3 W	61.5		18	Wilkes-Barre Scranton Airport	58.4
20	New Castle 1 N	61.3		20	State College	58.7
21	Allentown A-B-E Int'l Airport	61.2		21	Emporium	59.0
22	Bloserville 1 N	61.1		21	Franklin	59.0
22	Ford City 4 S Dam	61.1		21	Putneyville 2 SE Dam	59.0
24	Matamoras	*60.8*		24	Brookville Sewage Plant	*59.2*
25	Indiana 3 SE	60.7		24	Stevenson Dam	59.2

Annual Mean Temperature

	Highest				Lowest	
Rank	Station Name	°F		Rank	Station Name	°F
1	Marcus Hook	56.3		1	Pleasant Mount 1 W	43.3
2	Philadelphia Int'l Airport	55.3		2	Bradford Regional Airport	*43.6*
3	Holtwood	53.2		3	Kane 1 NNE	43.7
3	York 3 SSW Pumping Station	53.2		4	Bradford 4 SW Res. 5	44.5
5	Donora 1 SW	53.1		5	Francis E Walter Dam	*45.0*
6	Landisville 2 NW	52.5		6	Montrose	45.1
7	Shippensburg	52.3		7	Tobyhanna	*45.4*
8	Chambersburg 1 ESE	52.0		8	Ridgway	45.6
8	Reading 4 NNW	52.0		9	Philipsburg Mid-State Airport	*46.1*
10	Montgomery Lock & Dam	51.9		9	Titusville Water Works	46.1
11	Allentown A-B-E Int'l Airport	51.6		11	Hawley 1 E	46.5
12	Lebanon 2 W	*51.5*		12	Dubois FAA Airport	47.1
13	Bloserville 1 N	51.3		13	Corry	47.2
14	Biglerville	51.1		14	Meadville 1 S	47.3
14	Laurelton Center	51.1		15	Slippery Rock 1 SSW	47.4
14	Lewistown	51.1		16	Emporium	47.5
14	Uniontown 1 NE	51.1		17	Ebensburg Sewage Plant	47.6
18	Pittsburgh Int'l Airport	51.0		18	Jamestown 2 NW	47.7
18	Stroudsburg	51.0		18	Putneyville 2 SE Dam	47.7
20	Williamsport Airport	50.4		20	Brookville Sewage Plant	*47.8*
21	Waynesburg 1 E	50.2		20	Warren	47.8
22	Indiana 3 SE	49.9		22	Stevenson Dam	47.9
22	New Castle 1 N	49.9		23	Altoona 3 W	48.3
22	Raystown Lake 2	*49.9*		24	Clarion 3 SW	48.4
22	Selinsgrove 2 S	*49.9*		24	Franklin	48.4

Annual Mean Minimum Temperature

	Highest				Lowest	
Rank	Station Name	°F		Rank	Station Name	°F
1	Marcus Hook	48.6		1	Kane 1 NNE	32.2
2	Philadelphia Int'l Airport	46.3		2	Pleasant Mount 1 W	33.0
3	Holtwood	44.6		3	Bradford 4 SW Res. 5	33.4
4	Shippensburg	42.4		4	Francis E Walter Dam	*33.8*
5	Allentown A-B-E Int'l Airport	42.0		4	Ridgway	33.8
6	Donora 1 SW	41.8		6	Bradford Regional Airport	*34.0*
7	Chambersburg 1 ESE	41.7		7	Titusville Water Works	34.6
8	Montgomery Lock & Dam	41.6		8	Montrose	35.0
8	York 3 SSW Pumping Station	41.6		9	Tobyhanna	*35.1*
10	Pittsburgh Int'l Airport	41.5		10	Hawley 1 E	35.2
11	Landisville 2 NW	41.4		10	Slippery Rock 1 SSW	35.2
11	Reading 4 NNW	41.4		12	Ebensburg Sewage Plant	35.7
13	Bloserville 1 N	41.3		13	Emporium	35.9
14	Erie Int'l Airport	41.1		14	Brookville Sewage Plant	*36.3*
15	Lebanon 2 W	*40.9*		15	Putneyville 2 SE Dam	36.4
16	Biglerville	40.6		16	Confluence 1 SW Dam	36.5
16	Williamsport Airport	40.6		16	Philipsburg Mid-State Airport	*36.5*
18	Lewistown	40.4		18	Meadville 1 S	36.7
18	Wilkes-Barre Scranton Airport	40.4		18	Stevenson Dam	36.7
20	State College	39.5		20	Clarion 3 SW	36.9
21	Stroudsburg	39.4		20	Jamestown 2 NW	36.9
21	Uniontown 1 NE	39.4		22	Corry	37.1
23	Selinsgrove 2 S	*39.3*		22	Greenville 2 NE	37.1
24	Raystown Lake 2	*39.2*		22	Warren	37.1
25	Indiana 3 SE	39.1		25	Butler 2 SW	37.3

Annual Extreme Minimum Temperature

	Highest			Lowest	
Rank	Station Name	°F	Rank	Station Name	°F
1	Marcus Hook	-4	1	Bradford 4 SW Res. 5	-36
2	Philadelphia Int'l Airport	-7	2	Kane 1 NNE	-35
3	Holtwood	-9	3	Warren	-34
4	Allentown A-B-E Int'l Airport	-15	4	Brookville Sewage Plant	*-32*
4	Raystown Lake 2	*-15*	4	Mercer	-32
6	Shippensburg	-16	6	Hawley 1 E	-31
7	Lewistown	-17	6	Ridgway	-31
7	Millville 2 SW	*-17*	6	Titusville Water Works	-31
9	Biglerville	-18	9	Bradford Regional Airport	*-30*
9	Erie Int'l Airport	-18	9	Confluence 1 SW Dam	-30
9	Matamoras	*-18*	9	Corry	-30
9	Montgomery Lock & Dam	-18	9	Salina 3 W	-30
9	State College	-18	13	Ford City 4 S Dam	-29
14	Bloserville 1 N	-19	13	Montrose	-29
14	Donora 1 SW	-19	15	Ebensburg Sewage Plant	-28
14	Stroudsburg	*-19*	15	Emporium	-28
17	Altoona 3 W	-20	15	Francis E Walter Dam	-28
17	Butler 2 SW	-20	15	Putneyville 2 SE Dam	-28
17	Reading 4 NNW	-20	15	Slippery Rock 1 SSW	-28
17	Williamsport Airport	-20	20	Jamestown 2 NW	-27
21	Chambersburg 1 ESE	-21	20	New Castle 1 N	-27
21	Wilkes-Barre Scranton Airport	-21	20	Towanda 1 ESE	-27
21	York 3 SSW Pumping Station	-21	23	Dubois FAA Airport	-26
24	Franklin	-22	23	Greenville 2 NE	-26
24	Laurelton Center	-22	23	Selinsgrove 2 S	*-26*

July Mean Maximum Temperature

	Highest			Lowest	
Rank	Station Name	°F	Rank	Station Name	°F
1	Marcus Hook	87.4	1	Pleasant Mount 1 W	76.8
2	Laurelton Center	86.9	2	Bradford Regional Airport	77.0
2	Philadelphia Int'l Airport	86.9	3	Philipsburg Mid-State Airport	78.2
2	York 3 SSW Pumping Station	86.9	3	Tobyhanna	78.2
5	Stroudsburg	86.7	5	Bradford 4 SW Res. 5	78.5
6	Landisville 2 NW	86.0	5	Kane 1 NNE	78.5
7	Donora 1 SW	85.6	7	Montrose	78.7
8	Harrisburg Capital City Airport	*85.5*	8	Dubois FAA Airport	78.9
9	Reading 4 NNW	85.3	8	Francis E Walter Dam	78.9
9	Shippensburg	85.3	10	Erie Int'l Airport	79.3
11	Chambersburg 1 ESE	85.0	11	Ridgway	79.8
12	Lebanon 2 W	84.9	12	Corry	80.0
13	Lewistown	84.8	12	Hawley 1 E	80.0
14	Allentown A-B-E Int'l Airport	84.6	14	Altoona 3 W	80.7
14	Holtwood	84.6	15	Titusville Water Works	80.9
16	Biglerville	84.5	16	Meadville 1 S	81.1
17	Matamoras	*84.2*	17	Ebensburg Sewage Plant	81.3
17	Montgomery Lock & Dam	84.2	18	Brookville Sewage Plant	*81.4*
17	Uniontown 1 NE	84.2	19	Mercer	81.6
20	Bloserville 1 N	84.1	20	Jamestown 2 NW	81.7
20	Selinsgrove 2 S	*84.1*	20	State College	81.7
22	Confluence 1 SW Dam	84.0	22	Wilkes-Barre Scranton Airport	81.9
23	New Castle 1 N	83.9	23	Putneyville 2 SE Dam	82.0
24	Waynesburg 1 E	83.7	24	Slippery Rock 1 SSW	82.1
24	Williamsport Airport	83.7	24	Warren	82.1

January Mean Minimum Temperature

	Highest				Lowest	
Rank	**Station Name**	**°F**		**Rank**	**Station Name**	**°F**
1	Marcus Hook	27.4		1	Pleasant Mount 1 W	10.2
2	Philadelphia Int'l Airport	24.4		2	Bradford 4 SW Res. 5	11.0
3	Holtwood	22.4		3	Kane 1 NNE	11.2
4	Harrisburg Capital City Airport	*22.0*		4	Francis E Walter Dam	*11.4*
5	Donora 1 SW	21.2		5	Bradford Regional Airport	*12.2*
6	Shippensburg	21.0		6	Montrose	12.3
7	Montgomery Lock & Dam	20.7		7	Hawley 1 E	12.5
8	York 3 SSW Pumping Station	20.6		8	Ridgway	13.0
9	Landisville 2 NW	20.4		9	Titusville Water Works	13.1
10	Chambersburg 1 ESE	20.3		10	Tobyhanna	*13.3*
11	Allentown A-B-E Int'l Airport	20.1		11	Slippery Rock 1 SSW	13.9
12	Bloserville 1 N	19.9		12	Emporium	14.3
13	Lebanon 2 W	19.8		12	Jamestown 2 NW	14.3
14	Pittsburgh Int'l Airport	19.7		14	Millville 2 SW	*14.4*
14	Uniontown 1 NE	19.7		15	Philipsburg Mid-State Airport	14.9
16	Lewistown	19.5		16	Greenville 2 NE	15.0
16	Reading 4 NNW	19.5		17	Putneyville 2 SE Dam	15.1
18	Erie Int'l Airport	19.1		18	Meadville 1 S	15.2
19	Biglerville	19.0		18	Stevenson Dam	15.2
20	Wilkes-Barre Scranton Airport	18.3		20	Corry	15.4
21	Indiana 3 SE	18.2		21	Brookville Sewage Plant	15.5
21	Stroudsburg	18.2		22	Ebensburg Sewage Plant	15.6
21	Williamsport Airport	18.2		23	Towanda 1 ESE	15.7
24	Raystown Lake 2	*17.9*		24	Confluence 1 SW Dam	15.8
25	Waynesburg 1 E	17.8		25	Clarion 3 SW	16.0

Number of Annual Heating Degree Days

	Highest				Lowest	
Rank	**Station Name**	**Num.**		**Rank**	**Station Name**	**Num.**
1	Pleasant Mount 1 W	8,023		1	Marcus Hook	4,460
2	Bradford Regional Airport	*7,910*		2	Philadelphia Int'l Airport	4,709
3	Kane 1 NNE	7,860		3	Donora 1 SW	5,158
4	Bradford 4 SW Res. 5	7,628		4	York 3 SSW Pumping Station	5,172
5	Montrose	7,521		5	Holtwood	5,199
6	Francis E Walter Dam	*7,477*		6	Landisville 2 NW	5,342
7	Tobyhanna	*7,334*		7	Shippensburg	5,454
8	Ridgway	7,265		8	Montgomery Lock & Dam	5,465
9	Titusville Water Works	7,164		9	Chambersburg 1 ESE	5,492
10	Philipsburg Mid-State Airport	*7,130*		10	Reading 4 NNW	5,561
11	Hawley 1 E	7,016		11	Lebanon 2 W	*5,612*
12	Dubois FAA Airport	6,838		12	Allentown A-B-E Int'l Airport	5,622
13	Corry	6,816		13	Uniontown 1 NE	5,691
14	Meadville 1 S	6,789		14	Bloserville 1 N	5,696
15	Emporium	6,762		15	Lewistown	5,721
16	Slippery Rock 1 SSW	6,742		16	Laurelton Center	5,746
17	Jamestown 2 NW	6,720		17	Biglerville	5,762
18	Warren	6,684		18	Pittsburgh Int'l Airport	5,771
19	Putneyville 2 SE Dam	6,668		19	Stroudsburg	5,787
20	Stevenson Dam	6,625		20	Waynesburg 1 E	5,904
21	Ebensburg Sewage Plant	6,601		21	Indiana 3 SE	5,958
22	Brookville Sewage Plant	*6,594*		22	Williamsport Airport	5,966
23	Greenville 2 NE	6,522		23	Raystown Lake 2	*6,044*
24	Clarion 3 SW	6,499		24	New Castle 1 N	6,054
25	Franklin	6,496		25	Salina 3 W	6,059

Number of Annual Cooling Degree Days

	Highest			Lowest	
Rank	Station Name	Num.	Rank	Station Name	Num.
1	Marcus Hook	1,360	1	Kane 1 NNE	205
2	Philadelphia Int'l Airport	1,290	2	Pleasant Mount 1 W	223
3	Holtwood	1,021	3	Bradford Regional Airport	*233*
4	York 3 SSW Pumping Station	991	4	Bradford 4 SW Res. 5	243
5	Shippensburg	961	5	Tobyhanna	*271*
6	Landisville 2 NW	938	6	Ridgway	274
7	Reading 4 NNW	937	7	Francis E Walter Dam	*279*
8	Donora 1 SW	935	8	Philipsburg Mid-State Airport	*325*
9	Chambersburg 1 ESE	898	9	Montrose	341
10	Allentown A-B-E Int'l Airport	876	10	Hawley 1 E	390
11	Montgomery Lock & Dam	823	10	Titusville Water Works	390
12	Stroudsburg	819	12	Ebensburg Sewage Plant	403
13	Biglerville	816	13	Brookville Sewage Plant	*408*
14	Bloserville 1 N	805	14	Corry	421
15	Laurelton Center	796	15	Dubois FAA Airport	*433*
16	Pittsburgh Int'l Airport	790	16	Slippery Rock 1 SSW	440
17	Lebanon 2 W	785	17	Meadville 1 S	464
18	Williamsport Airport	752	18	Emporium	476
19	Lewistown	735	19	Mercer	488
20	Selinsgrove 2 S	718	20	Putneyville 2 SE Dam	501
21	Ford City 4 S Dam	699	21	Warren	522
22	Uniontown 1 NE	695	22	Stevenson Dam	523
23	Erie Int'l Airport	670	23	Jamestown 2 NW	527
24	Raystown Lake 2	662	24	Altoona 3 W	536
25	Wilkes-Barre Scranton Airport	654	25	Salina 3 W	546

Annual Precipitation

	Highest			Lowest	
Rank	Station Name	Inches	Rank	Station Name	Inches
1	Tobyhanna	*50.04*	1	Towanda 1 ESE	34.36
2	Ebensburg Sewage Plant	50.02	2	Montgomery Lock & Dam	37.29
3	Stroudsburg	49.90	3	Wilkes-Barre Scranton Airport	37.42
4	Pleasant Mount 1 W	48.57	4	Donora 1 SW	37.44
5	Corry	47.68	5	Pittsburgh Int'l Airport	37.76
6	Bradford Regional Airport	*47.45*	6	Holtwood	37.80
7	Indiana 3 SE	47.38	7	Raystown Lake 2	*37.91*
8	Bradford 4 SW Res. 5	46.87	8	New Castle 1 N	38.64
9	Clarion 3 SW	46.80	9	Greenville 2 NE	39.61
10	Kane 1 NNE	46.79	10	State College	39.80
11	Francis E Walter Dam	46.41	11	Shippensburg	39.96
12	Brookville Sewage Plant	*45.95*	12	Waynesburg 1 E	39.99
13	Confluence 1 SW Dam	45.55	13	Marcus Hook	40.15
14	Warren	45.44	14	Ford City 4 S Dam	40.90
15	Allentown A-B-E Int'l Airport	45.09	15	Salina 3 W	41.24
16	Laurelton Center	45.06	16	Hawley 1 E	41.26
17	Matamoras	*44.94*	17	Jamestown 2 NW	41.29
18	Reading 4 NNW	44.71	18	Lewistown	41.32
19	Putneyville 2 SE Dam	44.67	19	Chambersburg 1 ESE	41.57
20	Titusville Water Works	44.64	20	Williamsport Airport	41.59
21	Meadville 1 S	44.56	21	Selinsgrove 2 S	*41.61*
22	Montrose	44.09	22	Philadelphia Int'l Airport	41.86
23	Biglerville	44.02	23	Emporium	41.89
24	Dubois FAA Airport	43.90	24	Bloserville 1 N	42.06
25	Lebanon 2 W	43.86	25	Stevenson Dam	42.30

Number of Days Annually With ≥ 0.1″ Precipitation

	Highest			Lowest	
Rank	**Station Name**	**Days**	**Rank**	**Station Name**	**Days**
1	Corry	110	1	Marcus Hook	64
2	Ebensburg Sewage Plant	109	2	Holtwood	72
3	Bradford 4 SW Res. 5	107	3	Towanda 1 ESE	74
3	Bradford Regional Airport	*107*	4	Philadelphia Int'l Airport	75
5	Kane 1 NNE	106	5	Raystown Lake 2	*76*
6	Warren	103	6	Bloserville 1 N	77
7	Confluence 1 SW Dam	100	6	Shippensburg	77
8	Titusville Water Works	99	6	York 3 SSW Pumping Station	77
9	Indiana 3 SE	98	9	Biglerville	78
9	Meadville 1 S	98	9	Landisville 2 NW	78
11	Clarion 3 SW	97	11	Chambersburg 1 ESE	79
11	Uniontown 1 NE	97	11	Hawley 1 E	79
13	Brookville Sewage Plant	*96*	11	Lebanon 2 W	*79*
13	Dubois FAA Airport	96	11	Wilkes-Barre Scranton Airport	79
13	Putneyville 2 SE Dam	96	15	Allentown A-B-E Int'l Airport	80
13	Ridgway	96	15	Francis E Walter Dam	*80*
17	Franklin	95	15	Lewistown	80
18	Erie Int'l Airport	94	15	Reading 4 NNW	80
19	Jamestown 2 NW	93	15	Selinsgrove 2 S	*80*
19	Montrose	93	15	Williamsport Airport	80
19	Pleasant Mount 1 W	93	21	Matamoras	*81*
19	Slippery Rock 1 SSW	93	21	Tobyhanna	81
23	Emporium	92	23	Laurelton Center	83
23	Salina 3 W	92	23	State College	83
23	Stevenson Dam	92	25	Donora 1 SW	84

Number of Days Annually With ≥ 1.0″ Precipitation

	Highest			Lowest	
Rank	**Station Name**	**Days**	**Rank**	**Station Name**	**Days**
1	Stroudsburg	13	1	Erie Int'l Airport	5
2	Biglerville	12	1	Greenville 2 NE	5
2	Laurelton Center	12	1	Jamestown 2 NW	5
2	Marcus Hook	12	1	Montgomery Lock & Dam	5
2	Matamoras	*12*	1	New Castle 1 N	5
2	Philadelphia Int'l Airport	12	1	Pittsburgh Int'l Airport	5
2	Tobyhanna	12	7	Titusville Water Works	6
2	York 3 SSW Pumping Station	12	8	Butler 2 SW	7
9	Allentown A-B-E Int'l Airport	11	8	Corry	7
9	Bloserville 1 N	11	8	Emporium	7
9	Chambersburg 1 ESE	11	8	Ford City 4 S Dam	7
9	Holtwood	11	8	Franklin	7
9	Landisville 2 NW	11	8	Meadville 1 S	7
9	Lebanon 2 W	11	8	Mercer	7
9	Pleasant Mount 1 W	11	8	Warren	7
9	Reading 4 NNW	11	8	Waynesburg 1 E	7
9	Selinsgrove 2 S	*11*	17	Clarion 3 SW	8
9	Shippensburg	11	17	Donora 1 SW	8
9	Williamsport Airport	11	17	Dubois FAA Airport	8
20	Altoona 3 W	10	17	Kane 1 NNE	8
20	Confluence 1 SW Dam	10	17	Millville 2 SW	*8*
20	Ebensburg Sewage Plant	10	17	Montrose	8
20	Francis E Walter Dam	10	17	Philipsburg Mid-State Airport	8
20	Hawley 1 E	10	17	Raystown Lake 2	*8*
20	Lewistown	10	17	Salina 3 W	8

Annual Snowfall

	Highest			Lowest	
Rank	**Station Name**	**Inches**	**Rank**	**Station Name**	**Inches**
1	Corry	121.6	1	Montgomery Lock & Dam	*16.3*
2	Meadville 1 S	111.2	2	Philadelphia Int'l Airport	18.3
3	Ebensburg Sewage Plant	99.2	3	Bloserville 1 N	*21.2*
4	Kane 1 NNE	89.8	4	Landisville 2 NW	23.6
5	Erie Int'l Airport	89.6	5	York 3 SSW Pumping Station	24.8
6	Bradford Regional Airport	*89.3*	6	Biglerville	25.5
7	Montrose	89.1	7	New Castle 1 N	*26.4*
8	Bradford 4 SW Res. 5	82.6	8	Salina 3 W	*29.5*
9	Titusville Water Works	74.0	9	Allentown A-B-E Int'l Airport	30.6
10	Pleasant Mount 1 W	72.4	9	Waynesburg 1 E	30.6
11	Jamestown 2 NW	68.2	11	Chambersburg 1 ESE	31.4
12	Tobyhanna	*66.4*	12	Ford City 4 S Dam	31.9
13	Warren	63.7	12	Selinsgrove 2 S	*31.9*
14	Confluence 1 SW Dam	59.2	14	Matamoras	*32.0*
15	Dubois FAA Airport	*58.9*	15	Butler 2 SW	*34.9*
16	Franklin	*54.4*	16	Stroudsburg	35.2
17	Greenville 2 NE	*53.8*	17	Shippensburg	35.6
18	Indiana 3 SE	53.5	18	Stevenson Dam	36.3
19	Ridgway	53.2	19	Clarion 3 SW	36.4
20	Mercer	50.1	20	Putneyville 2 SE Dam	36.7
21	Philipsburg Mid-State Airport	*50.0*	21	Altoona 3 W	*36.8*
22	State College	48.8	22	Emporium	*38.3*
23	Francis E Walter Dam	48.1	23	Towanda 1 ESE	40.2
24	Brookville Sewage Plant	*47.3*	24	Williamsport Airport	40.4
25	Wilkes-Barre Scranton Airport	47.2	25	Slippery Rock 1 SSW	41.1

Note: See Appendix D for explanation of data.

Annual Extreme Maximum Temperature

Highest			Lowest		
Rank	Station Name	°F	Rank	Station Name	°F
1	Providence T F Green State Arpt.	104	1	North Foster 1 E	*97*
2	Kingston	100	2	Newport Rose	98
3	Newport Rose	98	3	Kingston	100
4	North Foster 1 E	*97*	4	Providence T F Green State Arpt.	104

Annual Mean Maximum Temperature

Highest			Lowest		
Rank	Station Name	°F	Rank	Station Name	°F
1	Kingston	60.6	1	North Foster 1 E	*58.4*
2	Providence T F Green State Arpt.	60.2	2	Newport Rose	58.8
3	Newport Rose	58.8	3	Providence T F Green State Arpt.	60.2
4	North Foster 1 E	*58.4*	4	Kingston	60.6

Annual Mean Temperature

Highest			Lowest		
Rank	Station Name	°F	Rank	Station Name	°F
1	Newport Rose	51.1	1	North Foster 1 E	*48.5*
1	Providence T F Green State Arpt.	51.1	2	Kingston	49.9
3	Kingston	49.9	3	Newport Rose	51.1
4	North Foster 1 E	*48.5*	3	Providence T F Green State Arpt.	51.1

Annual Mean Minimum Temperature

Highest			Lowest		
Rank	Station Name	°F	Rank	Station Name	°F
1	Newport Rose	43.3	1	North Foster 1 E	*38.5*
2	Providence T F Green State Arpt.	41.9	2	Kingston	39.2
3	Kingston	39.2	3	Providence T F Green State Arpt.	41.9
4	North Foster 1 E	*38.5*	4	Newport Rose	43.3

Annual Extreme Minimum Temperature

Highest			Lowest		
Rank	Station Name	°F	Rank	Station Name	°F
1	Newport Rose	-9	1	Kingston	-21
2	Providence T F Green State Arpt.	-13	2	North Foster 1 E	*-15*
3	North Foster 1 E	*-15*	3	Providence T F Green State Arpt.	-13
4	Kingston	-21	4	Newport Rose	-9

July Mean Maximum Temperature

Highest			Lowest		
Rank	**Station Name**	**°F**	**Rank**	**Station Name**	**°F**
1	Providence T F Green State Arpt.	82.7	1	Newport Rose	78.6
2	Kingston	81.9	2	North Foster 1 E	*80.7*
3	North Foster 1 E	*80.7*	3	Kingston	81.9
4	Newport Rose	78.6	4	Providence T F Green State Arpt.	82.7

January Mean Minimum Temperature

Highest			Lowest		
Rank	**Station Name**	**°F**	**Rank**	**Station Name**	**°F**
1	Newport Rose	23.0	1	North Foster 1 E	*16.6*
2	Providence T F Green State Arpt.	20.0	2	Kingston	18.6
3	Kingston	18.6	3	Providence T F Green State Arpt.	20.0
4	North Foster 1 E	*16.6*	4	Newport Rose	23.0

Number of Annual Heating Degree Days

Highest			Lowest		
Rank	**Station Name**	**Num.**	**Rank**	**Station Name**	**Num.**
1	North Foster 1 E	*6,422*	1	Newport Rose	5,509
2	Kingston	5,936	2	Providence T F Green State Arpt.	5,707
3	Providence T F Green State Arpt.	5,707	3	Kingston	5,936
4	Newport Rose	5,509	4	North Foster 1 E	*6,422*

Number of Annual Cooling Degree Days

Highest			Lowest		
Rank	**Station Name**	**Num.**	**Rank**	**Station Name**	**Num.**
1	Providence T F Green State Arpt.	753	1	North Foster 1 E	505
2	Kingston	557	2	Newport Rose	543
3	Newport Rose	543	3	Kingston	557
4	North Foster 1 E	505	4	Providence T F Green State Arpt.	753

Annual Precipitation

Highest			Lowest		
Rank	**Station Name**	**Inches**	**Rank**	**Station Name**	**Inches**
1	North Foster 1 E	*52.90*	1	Newport Rose	46.09
2	Kingston	51.67	2	Providence T F Green State Arpt.	46.43
3	Providence T F Green State Arpt.	46.43	3	Kingston	51.67
4	Newport Rose	46.09	4	North Foster 1 E	*52.90*

Number of Days Annually With ≥ 0.1″ Precipitation

	Highest			Lowest	
Rank	**Station Name**	**Days**	**Rank**	**Station Name**	**Days**
1	North Foster 1 E	*83*	1	Newport Rose	78
2	Kingston	79	2	Kingston	79
2	Providence T F Green State Arpt.	79	2	Providence T F Green State Arpt.	79
4	Newport Rose	78	4	North Foster 1 E	*83*

Number of Days Annually With ≥ 1.0″ Precipitation

	Highest			Lowest	
Rank	**Station Name**	**Days**	**Rank**	**Station Name**	**Days**
1	North Foster 1 E	*15*	1	Newport Rose	12
2	Kingston	13	1	Providence T F Green State Arpt.	12
3	Newport Rose	12	3	Kingston	13
3	Providence T F Green State Arpt.	12	4	North Foster 1 E	*15*

Annual Snowfall

	Highest			Lowest	
Rank	**Station Name**	**Inches**	**Rank**	**Station Name**	**Inches**
1	North Foster 1 E	*55.5*	1	Kingston	29.0
2	Providence T F Green State Arpt.	32.9	2	Providence T F Green State Arpt.	32.9
3	Kingston	29.0	3	North Foster 1 E	*55.5*

Note: See Appendix D for explanation of data.

Annual Extreme Maximum Temperature

	Highest				Lowest	
Rank	Station Name	°F		Rank	Station Name	°F
1	Aiken 4 NE	*109*		1	Caesars Head	99
1	Clark Hill 1 W	109		2	Brookgreen Gardens	103
1	Saluda	109		3	Beaufort 7 SW	104
4	Blackville 3 W	108		3	Camden 3 W	104
4	Darlington	108		3	Charleston City	104
4	Kingstree 1 SE	108		3	Clemson University	104
4	Manning	108		3	Greenville-Spartanbrg Airport	104
4	Newberry	108		3	Pinopolis Dam	*104*
4	Yemassee	108		3	Summerville	104
10	Bamberg	107		3	West Pelzer 2 W	104
10	Cheraw	107		11	Charleston Int'l Airport	105
10	Columbia Metro Airport	107		11	Conway	105
10	Hampton	107		11	Florence 8 NE	105
10	Hilton Head	107		11	Lake City 2 SE	*105*
10	Johnston 4 SW	107		11	Pickens	105
10	Laurens	107		11	Ridgeland 5 NE	105
10	McColl 3 NNW	107		11	Santuck	105
10	Parr	107		11	Sumter	105
10	Pelion 4 NW	107		11	Union 8 SW	105
20	Anderson	106		11	Walhalla	105
20	Anderson County Airport	106		21	Anderson	106
20	Bishopville 8 NNW	106		21	Anderson County Airport	106
20	Calhoun Falls	106		21	Bishopville 8 NNW	106
20	Chester 1 NW	106		21	Calhoun Falls	106
20	Dillon	106		21	Chester 1 NW	106

Annual Mean Maximum Temperature

	Highest				Lowest	
Rank	Station Name	°F		Rank	Station Name	°F
1	Yemassee	77.8		1	Caesars Head	63.3
2	Hampton	77.5		2	Greenville-Spartanbrg Airport	70.9
3	Aiken 4 NE	77.1		3	Ninety Nine Islands	71.5
4	Blackville 3 W	77.0		4	Walhalla	71.6
5	Ridgeland 5 NE	76.7		5	Pickens	71.7
6	Georgetown 2 E	76.2		6	Winthrop University	71.8
6	Manning	76.2		7	Clemson University	71.9
8	Beaufort 7 SW	76.1		8	West Pelzer 2 W	72.3
9	Charleston Int'l Airport	75.9		9	Anderson County Airport	72.5
10	Bamberg	75.7		9	Union 8 SW	72.5
10	Hilton Head	75.7		11	Camden 3 W	72.6
12	Darlington	75.6		12	Greenwood 3 SW	72.7
12	Orangeburg 2	75.6		12	Santuck	72.7
12	Summerville	75.6		14	Chester 1 NW	72.8
15	Columbia Metro Airport	75.5		15	Cheraw	72.9
15	Kingstree 1 SE	75.5		16	Laurens	73.1
17	Sumter	75.4		17	Little Mountain	73.3
18	Clark Hill 1 W	75.3		17	Winnsboro	73.3
18	Pinopolis Dam	*75.3*		19	Calhoun Falls	73.4
20	Pelion 4 NW	75.2		19	Charleston City	73.4
21	Brookgreen Gardens	75.1		21	Bishopville 8 NNW	73.7
21	Conway	75.1		21	Pageland	73.7
21	Lake City 2 SE	75.1		21	Sandhill Research Elgin	73.7
21	Newberry	75.1		24	Johnston 4 SW	73.8
25	Parr	75.0		25	Dillon	73.9

Annual Mean Temperature

	Highest				Lowest	
Rank	**Station Name**	**°F**		**Rank**	**Station Name**	**°F**
1	Beaufort 7 SW	66.8		1	Caesars Head	54.5
2	Charleston City	66.7		2	Ninety Nine Islands	58.7
3	Hilton Head	*66.0*		3	Union 8 SW	59.2
4	Charleston Int'l Airport	65.9		4	Walhalla	59.3
4	Hampton	65.9		5	Laurens	60.0
6	Ridgeland 5 NE	65.5		6	Greenville-Spartanbrg Airport	60.2
7	Georgetown 2 E	65.3		6	Greenwood 3 SW	60.2
8	Yemassee	64.9		8	Camden 3 W	60.3
9	Bamberg	64.4		8	Clemson University	60.3
9	Blackville 3 W	64.4		10	Pickens	60.5
11	Brookgreen Gardens	64.3		11	West Pelzer 2 W	60.8
12	Aiken 4 NE	*64.1*		12	Cheraw	60.9
13	Conway	64.0		12	Chester 1 NW	60.9
13	Florence City County Airport	64.0		14	Anderson	61.3
13	Summerville	64.0		15	Calhoun Falls	61.5
16	Pinopolis Dam	*63.9*		15	Saluda	61.5
17	Orangeburg 2	63.8		15	Winthrop University	61.5
18	Darlington	63.7		18	Santuck	61.6
19	Columbia Metro Airport	63.5		18	Winnsboro	61.6
20	Manning	63.4		20	Anderson County Airport	61.8
21	Sumter	63.2		20	Bishopville 8 NNW	61.8
22	Lake City 2 SE	63.0		20	Johnston 4 SW	61.8
22	Pelion 4 NW	63.0		23	Parr	61.9
24	Florence 8 NE	62.8		24	Dillon	62.0
24	McColl 3 NNW	62.8		25	Clark Hill 1 W	62.1

Annual Mean Minimum Temperature

	Highest				Lowest	
Rank	**Station Name**	**°F**		**Rank**	**Station Name**	**°F**
1	Charleston City	59.9		1	Caesars Head	45.7
2	Beaufort 7 SW	57.4		2	Ninety Nine Islands	45.8
3	Hilton Head	*56.3*		2	Union 8 SW	45.8
4	Charleston Int'l Airport	55.8		4	Laurens	46.8
5	Georgetown 2 E	54.3		5	Walhalla	47.0
6	Hampton	54.2		6	Greenwood 3 SW	47.7
6	Ridgeland 5 NE	54.2		7	Camden 3 W	48.0
8	Brookgreen Gardens	53.4		8	Saluda	48.5
9	Florence City County Airport	53.2		9	Anderson	48.7
10	Bamberg	53.1		9	Clemson University	48.7
11	Conway	52.8		11	Parr	48.8
12	Pinopolis Dam	*52.5*		12	Cheraw	48.9
13	Summerville	52.3		12	Chester 1 NW	48.9
14	Orangeburg 2	52.0		12	Clark Hill 1 W	48.9
15	Little Mountain	51.9		15	West Pelzer 2 W	49.2
15	Yemassee	51.9		16	Pickens	49.3
17	Darlington	51.8		17	Greenville-Spartanbrg Airport	49.4
18	Blackville 3 W	51.7		18	Calhoun Falls	49.5
19	Columbia Metro Airport	51.6		18	Kingstree 1 SE	49.5
20	Florence 8 NE	51.5		20	Johnston 4 SW	49.6
21	McColl 3 NNW	51.1		21	Bishopville 8 NNW	49.9
21	Sandhill Research Elgin	51.1		21	Winnsboro	49.9
21	Winthrop University	51.1		23	Dillon	50.0
24	Anderson County Airport	51.0		24	Newberry	50.1
24	Sumter	51.0		25	Santuck	50.4

Annual Extreme Minimum Temperature

Highest			Lowest		
Rank	Station Name	°F	Rank	Station Name	°F
1	Charleston City	10	1	Caesars Head	-20
2	Pinopolis Dam	*8*	2	Anderson County Airport	-6
3	Charleston Int'l Airport	6	2	Pickens	-6
3	Georgetown 2 E	6	4	Anderson	-5
5	Beaufort 7 SW	5	4	McColl 3 NNW	-5
6	Brookgreen Gardens	4	4	Walhalla	-5
6	Conway	4	7	Aiken 4 NE	*-4*
6	Hilton Head	4	7	Darlington	-4
6	Summerville	4	7	Greenville-Spartanbrg Airport	-4
10	Pageland	3	7	Ninety Nine Islands	-4
11	Bamberg	2	7	Santuck	-4
11	Lake City 2 SE	*2*	7	West Pelzer 2 W	-4
11	Orangeburg 2	2	7	Winthrop University	-4
11	Ridgeland 5 NE	2	14	Camden 3 W	-3
11	Sumter	2	14	Chester 1 NW	-3
16	Florence 8 NE	1	14	Clemson University	-3
16	Hampton	1	17	Bishopville 8 NNW	-2
18	Cheraw	0	17	Calhoun Falls	-2
18	Florence City County Airport	0	17	Clark Hill 1 W	-2
18	Kingstree 1 SE	0	17	Greenwood 3 SW	-2
18	Manning	0	17	Johnston 4 SW	-2
18	Parr	0	17	Laurens	-2
18	Yemassee	0	17	Little Mountain	-2
24	Blackville 3 W	-1	17	Pelion 4 NW	-2
24	Columbia Metro Airport	-1	17	Saluda	-2

July Mean Maximum Temperature

Highest			Lowest		
Rank	Station Name	°F	Rank	Station Name	°F
1	Aiken 4 NE	93.5	1	Caesars Head	79.7
2	Manning	93.2	2	Charleston City	88.5
3	Clark Hill 1 W	93.0	3	Walhalla	88.7
4	Yemassee	92.9	4	Greenville-Spartanbrg Airport	89.1
5	Parr	92.7	4	Pickens	89.1
5	Saluda	92.7	6	Ninety Nine Islands	89.3
7	Columbia Metro Airport	92.5	7	Camden 3 W	89.4
7	Hampton	92.5	8	Hilton Head	89.5
7	Newberry	92.5	9	Clemson University	89.8
10	Blackville 3 W	92.4	10	Winthrop University	90.0
11	Darlington	92.1	11	West Pelzer 2 W	90.4
11	Kingstree 1 SE	92.1	12	Anderson County Airport	90.5
13	Orangeburg 2	91.9	12	Beaufort 7 SW	90.5
13	Sumter	91.9	12	Brookgreen Gardens	90.5
15	Johnston 4 SW	91.8	12	Little Mountain	90.5
15	Lake City 2 SE	91.8	16	Chester 1 NW	90.6
15	Pinopolis Dam	*91.8*	16	Santuck	90.6
15	Ridgeland 5 NE	91.8	18	Bishopville 8 NNW	90.7
19	McColl 3 NNW	91.7	18	Cheraw	90.7
20	Laurens	91.5	18	Georgetown 2 E	90.7
20	Pelion 4 NW	91.5	18	Union 8 SW	90.7
22	Bamberg	91.4	22	Greenwood 3 SW	90.8
22	Calhoun Falls	91.4	22	Pageland	90.8
24	Florence City County Airport	91.3	22	Summerville	90.8
25	Anderson	91.2	25	Conway	90.9

January Mean Minimum Temperature

Highest			Lowest		
Rank	Station Name	°F	Rank	Station Name	°F
1	Charleston City	42.1	1	Caesars Head	27.1
2	Beaufort 7 SW	40.2	2	Ninety Nine Islands	27.2
3	Hilton Head	39.1	3	Union 8 SW	27.3
4	Charleston Int'l Airport	38.1	4	Laurens	28.4
5	Georgetown 2 E	37.5	5	Camden 3 W	29.1
6	Hampton	37.3	6	Greenwood 3 SW	29.5
7	Ridgeland 5 NE	37.2	7	Cheraw	29.7
8	Bamberg	36.1	8	Clemson University	29.8
8	Brookgreen Gardens	36.1	8	Walhalla	29.8
10	Florence City County Airport	35.4	10	Saluda	29.9
10	Yemassee	35.4	11	Chester 1 NW	30.3
12	Blackville 3 W	35.0	12	Clark Hill 1 W	30.5
13	Pinopolis Dam	*34.8*	13	Parr	30.6
14	Summerville	34.6	14	Greenville-Spartanbrg Airport	30.7
15	Conway	34.4	14	West Pelzer 2 W	30.7
16	Little Mountain	34.2	16	Anderson	30.8
17	Darlington	34.1	17	Pickens	30.9
17	Orangeburg 2	34.1	17	Winnsboro	30.9
19	Aiken 4 NE	33.5	19	Bishopville 8 NNW	31.2
20	Sumter	33.4	20	Calhoun Falls	31.3
21	Columbia Metro Airport	33.3	21	Dillon	31.6
22	Pelion 4 NW	33.1	21	Johnston 4 SW	31.6
23	Lake City 2 SE	33.0	23	Kingstree 1 SE	31.7
24	McColl 3 NNW	32.8	24	Pageland	32.2
25	Florence 8 NE	32.7	24	Sandhill Research Elgin	32.2

Number of Annual Heating Degree Days

Highest			Lowest		
Rank	Station Name	Num.	Rank	Station Name	Num.
1	Caesars Head	4,373	1	Beaufort 7 SW	1,687
2	Ninety Nine Islands	3,567	2	Charleston City	1,728
3	Union 8 SW	3,483	3	Hilton Head	*1,776*
4	Laurens	3,331	4	Hampton	1,898
5	Walhalla	3,280	5	Ridgeland 5 NE	1,925
6	Greenwood 3 SW	3,243	6	Charleston Int'l Airport	1,946
7	Greenville-Spartanbrg Airport	3,220	7	Georgetown 2 E	1,952
8	Camden 3 W	3,189	8	Yemassee	2,072
9	Clemson University	3,171	9	Blackville 3 W	2,184
10	Cheraw	3,120	10	Bamberg	2,207
11	Chester 1 NW	3,089	11	Brookgreen Gardens	2,209
12	West Pelzer 2 W	3,086	12	Summerville	2,310
13	Pickens	3,068	13	Aiken 4 NE	*2,350*
14	Saluda	3,012	14	Pinopolis Dam	*2,356*
15	Calhoun Falls	2,982	15	Conway	2,363
16	Winnsboro	2,950	16	Florence City County Airport	2,405
17	Winthrop University	2,949	17	Orangeburg 2	2,411
18	Anderson	2,913	18	Darlington	2,429
19	Santuck	2,893	19	Manning	2,515
20	Anderson County Airport	2,890	20	Sumter	2,526
21	Dillon	2,883	21	Columbia Metro Airport	2,550
22	Bishopville 8 NNW	2,880	22	Pelion 4 NW	2,576
23	Parr	2,874	23	Lake City 2 SE	2,608
24	Johnston 4 SW	2,866	24	Little Mountain	2,643
25	Clark Hill 1 W	2,814	25	McColl 3 NNW	2,672

Number of Annual Cooling Degree Days

	Highest			Lowest	
Rank	**Station Name**	**Num.**	**Rank**	**Station Name**	**Num.**
1	Beaufort 7 SW	2,478	1	Caesars Head	664
2	Charleston City	2,455	2	Walhalla	1,339
3	Charleston Int'l Airport	2,417	3	Ninety Nine Islands	1,363
4	Hampton	2,384	4	Union 8 SW	1,518
5	Hilton Head	*2,313*	5	Pickens	1,563
6	Ridgeland 5 NE	2,242	6	Greenville-Spartanbrg Airport	1,605
7	Georgetown 2 E	*2,187*	7	Clemson University	1,608
8	Aiken 4 NE	2,185	8	Greenwood 3 SW	1,625
9	Florence City County Airport	2,168	9	Camden 3 W	1,630
10	Yemassee	2,166	9	Laurens	1,630
11	Columbia Metro Airport	2,144	11	Chester 1 NW	1,661
12	Conway	2,139	12	West Pelzer 2 W	1,691
13	Orangeburg 2	2,136	13	Anderson	1,730
14	Bamberg	2,132	14	Santuck	1,781
15	Darlington	2,103	15	Cheraw	1,799
16	Blackville 3 W	2,102	16	Anderson County Airport	1,802
17	Summerville	2,096	17	Winthrop University	1,825
18	Manning	2,083	18	Calhoun Falls	1,855
19	Brookgreen Gardens	2,076	18	Little Mountain	1,855
20	Florence 8 NE	2,050	20	Johnston 4 SW	1,859
21	Pelion 4 NW	1,988	21	Parr	1,868
22	Lake City 2 SE	*1,982*	22	Bishopville 8 NNW	1,876
23	Newberry	1,973	23	Winnsboro	1,878
24	Kingstree 1 SE	1,944	24	Clark Hill 1 W	1,902
24	Sandhill Research Elgin	1,944	25	Pageland	1,906

Annual Precipitation

	Highest			Lowest	
Rank	**Station Name**	**Inches**	**Rank**	**Station Name**	**Inches**
1	Caesars Head	75.53	1	McColl 3 NNW	38.41
2	Walhalla	60.53	2	Florence City County Airport	44.95
3	Georgetown 2 E	56.23	3	Bishopville 8 NNW	45.29
4	Pickens	56.22	4	Parr	45.72
5	Brookgreen Gardens	54.47	5	Winnsboro	45.82
6	Clemson University	54.08	6	Santuck	46.46
7	Aiken 4 NE	53.64	7	Greenwood 3 SW	46.52
8	Hilton Head	53.54	8	Camden 3 W	46.61
9	Conway	53.40	9	Charleston City	46.63
9	Summerville	53.40	10	Darlington	46.68
11	Yemassee	52.42	11	Clark Hill 1 W	46.78
12	Charleston Int'l Airport	51.52	12	Anderson County Airport	46.81
13	West Pelzer 2 W	51.25	13	Dillon	46.87
14	Pelion 4 NW	51.18	14	Sandhill Research Elgin	46.98
15	Ridgeland 5 NE	51.14	15	Florence 8 NE	47.19
16	Anderson	51.03	16	Blackville 3 W	47.35
17	Pinopolis Dam	*50.57*	17	Laurens	47.50
18	Greenville-Spartanbrg Airport	50.33	18	Orangeburg 2	47.56
19	Kingstree 1 SE	50.01	19	Cheraw	47.72
20	Beaufort 7 SW	49.92	20	Chester 1 NW	47.76
21	Lake City 2 SE	49.53	21	Calhoun Falls	47.82
22	Union 8 SW	49.43	22	Saluda	48.02
23	Newberry	49.27	23	Hampton	48.32
24	Pageland	49.03	24	Winthrop University	48.38
25	Manning	49.02	25	Little Mountain	48.49

Number of Days Annually With ≥ 0.1″ Precipitation

	Highest			Lowest	
Rank	Station Name	Days	Rank	Station Name	Days
1	Caesars Head	96	1	McColl 3 NNW	66
2	Walhalla	86	2	Charleston City	68
3	Clemson University	83	3	Parr	69
4	Pickens	82	4	Newberry	71
5	Aiken 4 NE	81	4	Winnsboro	71
6	Brookgreen Gardens	80	6	Clark Hill 1 W	72
6	Kingstree 1 SE	80	6	Lake City 2 SE	72
6	Manning	*80*	6	Little Mountain	72
6	Summerville	80	6	Saluda	72
10	Conway	79	10	Chester 1 NW	73
10	Greenville-Spartanbrg Airport	79	10	Georgetown 2 E	73
10	Pelion 4 NW	79	10	Hilton Head	73
10	West Pelzer 2 W	79	10	Johnston 4 SW	73
14	Anderson	78	10	Orangeburg 2	73
14	Ridgeland 5 NE	78	10	Yemassee	*73*
16	Bamberg	77	16	Bishopville 8 NNW	74
16	Charleston Int'l Airport	77	16	Calhoun Falls	74
16	Darlington	77	16	Columbia Metro Airport	74
16	Ninety Nine Islands	77	19	Beaufort 7 SW	75
16	Pinopolis Dam	*77*	19	Blackville 3 W	75
16	Santuck	77	19	Camden 3 W	75
16	Winthrop University	77	19	Cheraw	75
23	Anderson County Airport	76	19	Florence 8 NE	75
23	Dillon	76	19	Florence City County Airport	75
23	Laurens	*76*	19	Greenwood 3 SW	75

Number of Days Annually With ≥ 1.0″ Precipitation

	Highest			Lowest	
Rank	Station Name	Days	Rank	Station Name	Days
1	Caesars Head	24	1	Bishopville 8 NNW	12
2	Walhalla	19	1	Laurens	*12*
3	Aiken 4 NE	17	1	McColl 3 NNW	12
3	Brookgreen Gardens	17	1	Ninety Nine Islands	12
3	Pickens	17	5	Anderson County Airport	13
6	Beaufort 7 SW	16	5	Calhoun Falls	13
6	Charleston Int'l Airport	16	5	Camden 3 W	13
6	Conway	16	5	Clark Hill 1 W	13
6	Georgetown 2 E	16	5	Florence City County Airport	13
6	Hilton Head	16	5	Greenville-Spartanbrg Airport	13
6	Pelion 4 NW	16	5	Greenwood 3 SW	13
6	Summerville	16	5	Parr	13
13	Cheraw	15	5	Saluda	13
13	Clemson University	15	5	Sandhill Research Elgin	13
13	Kingstree 1 SE	15	5	Santuck	13
13	Lake City 2 SE	15	5	West Pelzer 2 W	13
13	Pinopolis Dam	*15*	5	Winnsboro	13
13	Ridgeland 5 NE	15	5	Winthrop University	13
13	Sumter	15	19	Anderson	14
13	Union 8 SW	15	19	Bamberg	14
13	Yemassee	15	19	Blackville 3 W	14
22	Anderson	14	19	Charleston City	14
22	Bamberg	14	19	Chester 1 NW	14
22	Blackville 3 W	14	19	Columbia Metro Airport	14
22	Charleston City	14	19	Darlington	14

Annual Snowfall

Highest			Lowest		
Rank	**Station Name**	**Inches**	**Rank**	**Station Name**	**Inches**
1	Caesars Head	*8.7*	1	Hilton Head	Trace
2	Greenville-Spartanbrg Airport	5.7	1	Pinopolis Dam	*Trace*
3	Walhalla	4.5	3	Yemassee	0.1
4	Clemson University	3.5	4	Sumter	0.2
4	Santuck	3.5	5	Georgetown 2 E	0.3
4	Winthrop University	3.5	6	Beaufort 7 SW	0.4
7	West Pelzer 2 W	3.4	6	Clark Hill 1 W	*0.4*
8	Ninety Nine Islands	3.1	6	Sandhill Research Elgin	0.4
9	Pickens	*3.0*	9	Orangeburg 2	0.5
10	Chester 1 NW	2.8	9	Ridgeland 5 NE	0.5
11	Anderson County Airport	2.7	11	Hampton	0.8
11	Florence City County Airport	2.7	12	Blackville 3 W	0.9
13	Greenwood 3 SW	2.4	12	Charleston Int'l Airport	0.9
13	Little Mountain	2.4	12	Parr	0.9
15	Cheraw	2.3	12	Summerville	0.9
15	Laurens	2.3	16	Aiken 4 NE	*1.0*
17	Lake City 2 SE	2.2	16	Conway	1.0
17	Union 8 SW	2.2	18	Camden 3 W	1.1
19	Columbia Metro Airport	2.0	18	Darlington	1.1
20	Bishopville 8 NNW	1.9	18	Pelion 4 NW	1.1
21	Johnston 4 SW	1.8	21	Brookgreen Gardens	1.2
21	Kingstree 1 SE	1.8	21	Calhoun Falls	1.2
21	McColl 3 NNW	1.8	21	Florence 8 NE	1.2
21	Newberry	1.8	24	Bamberg	1.3
25	Dillon	1.7	24	Pageland	1.3

Note: See Appendix D for explanation of data.

Annual Extreme Maximum Temperature

	Highest				Lowest	
Rank	**Station Name**	**°F**		**Rank**	**Station Name**	**°F**
1	Ludlow 3 SSE	115		1	Lead	98
2	Maurine 10 SW	*114*		2	Custer	99
2	Oahe Dam	114		3	Mount Rushmore Nat'l Memorial	100
2	Oelrichs	114		3	Pactola Dam	*100*
2	Pierre Municipal Airport	114		5	Deadwood	101
2	Porcupine 11 N	114		6	Brookings 2 NE	103
7	Academy 2 NE	112		6	Clear Lake	103
7	Cedar Butte 1 NE	112		6	Summit 1 W	103
7	Forestburg 3 NE	112		9	Waubay Nat'l Wildlife Refuge	104
7	Gann Valley 4 NW	112		10	Castlewood	105
7	Kennebec	112		10	Flandreau	105
7	Oral	112		10	Madison 2 SE	105
7	Ralph 1 N	112		10	Spearfish Airport	105
14	Cottonwood 2 E	111		10	Watertown Municipal Airport	105
14	Dupree 15 SSE	111		15	Bonesteel	106
14	Faulkton 1 NW	111		15	Clark	106
14	Highmore 1 W	111		15	Columbia 8 N	106
14	Highmore 23 N	111		15	De Smet	106
14	Hot Springs	111		15	Mobridge	106
14	Interior 3 NE	111		20	Alexandria	107
14	Stephan 1 ENE	111		20	Bison	107
14	White Lake	111		20	Canton 4 WNW	107
23	Belle Fourche	110		20	Centerville 6 SE	107
23	Camp Crook	110		20	Fort Meade	107
23	Gregory	110		20	Lemmon	107

Annual Mean Maximum Temperature

	Highest				Lowest	
Rank	**Station Name**	**°F**		**Rank**	**Station Name**	**°F**
1	Interior 3 NE	63.2		1	Summit 1 W	52.7
2	Hot Springs	63.1		2	Brookings 2 NE	53.3
3	Oral	*62.7*		3	Webster	53.6
4	Cedar Butte 1 NE	62.5		4	Watertown Municipal Airport	53.9
5	Winner	62.3		5	Clear Lake	54.1
6	Oelrichs	62.0		5	Columbia 8 N	54.1
7	Porcupine 11 N	61.9		5	Waubay Nat'l Wildlife Refuge	54.1
8	Ardmore 2 N	61.8		8	Clark	54.2
8	Long Valley	61.8		9	Flandreau	54.4
8	Vermillion 2 SE	61.8		10	Eureka	54.6
11	Belle Fourche	61.6		11	Selby	54.7
11	Wood	61.6		12	Lead	54.9
13	Wasta	61.5		13	Leola	55.0
14	Gregory	61.4		13	Madison 2 SE	55.0
15	Kennebec	61.3		15	Aberdeen Regional Airport	55.1
15	Wagner	61.3		15	Gettysburg	55.1
17	Cottonwood 2 E	60.9		17	Castlewood	55.2
18	Armour	60.5		17	Pactola Dam	55.2
19	Fort Meade	60.4		17	Sisseton	55.2
20	Academy 2 NE	60.3		20	Mobridge	55.3
20	Harrington	60.3		21	Britton	55.4
20	Rapid City 4 NW	60.3		22	Lemmon	55.6
23	Murdo	60.1		22	Mellette	55.6
23	Pickstown	60.1		24	Custer	55.8
25	Mission 14 S	59.9		25	De Smet	55.9

Annual Mean Temperature

	Highest				Lowest	
Rank	Station Name	°F		Rank	Station Name	°F
1	Interior 3 NE	50.2		1	Pactola Dam	41.4
2	Winner	49.9		2	Summit 1 W	41.5
3	Wagner	49.6		3	Brookings 2 NE	42.4
4	Vermillion 2 SE	49.4		4	Columbia 8 N	42.7
5	Cedar Butte 1 NE	49.2		4	Eureka	42.7
6	Pickstown	48.7		6	Webster	42.9
6	Wood	48.7		7	Selby	43.0
8	Armour	48.4		7	Watertown Municipal Airport	43.0
8	Long Valley	48.4		9	Custer	43.1
10	Tyndall	48.3		9	Mellette	43.1
11	Hot Springs	48.2		11	Flandreau	43.2
12	Gregory	48.1		11	Waubay Nat'l Wildlife Refuge	43.2
12	Kennebec	48.1		13	Castlewood	43.3
14	Alexandria	47.9		13	Ipswich	43.3
14	Fort Meade	47.9		13	Leola	43.3
14	Menno	47.9		16	Clark	43.5
17	Oelrichs	47.8		17	Gettysburg	43.6
17	Wasta	47.8		18	Aberdeen Regional Airport	43.7
19	Yankton 2 E	47.7		18	Ralph 1 N	43.7
20	Academy 2 NE	47.6		20	Britton	43.8
20	Bonesteel	47.6		20	Clear Lake	43.8
22	Murdo	47.5		20	Deadwood	43.8
23	Belle Fourche	47.4		20	Lemmon	43.8
23	Oral	*47.4*		20	Redfield 2 NE	43.8
23	Rapid City 4 NW	47.4		25	Ludlow 3 SSE	43.9

Annual Mean Minimum Temperature

	Highest				Lowest	
Rank	Station Name	°F		Rank	Station Name	°F
1	Wagner	37.7		1	Pactola Dam	27.5
2	Winner	37.4		2	Ralph 1 N	29.7
3	Pickstown	37.3		3	Custer	30.2
4	Interior 3 NE	37.1		4	Ardmore 2 N	30.4
5	Tyndall	36.9		4	Summit 1 W	30.4
5	Vermillion 2 SE	36.9		6	Ipswich	30.5
7	Alexandria	36.8		7	Camp Crook	30.6
8	Wessington Springs	36.7		7	Mellette	30.6
9	Armour	36.3		9	Eureka	30.8
10	Menno	36.0		10	Redig 11 NE	31.0
11	Mount Rushmore Nat'l Memorial	35.9		11	Castlewood	31.2
11	Yankton 2 E	35.9		11	Columbia 8 N	31.2
13	Cedar Butte 1 NE	35.8		11	Zeona 10 SSW	*31.2*
14	Bonesteel	35.7		14	Ludlow 3 SSE	31.3
14	Wood	35.7		14	Selby	31.3
16	Pierre Municipal Airport	35.4		16	Brookings 2 NE	31.4
17	Fort Meade	35.3		16	Deadwood	31.4
18	Mitchell 2 N	35.2		18	Leola	31.5
18	Oahe Dam	*35.2*		18	Pollock	31.5
18	White Lake	35.2		20	Maurine 10 SW	*31.6*
21	Canton 4 WNW	35.1		21	Highmore 23 N	31.7
22	Spearfish Airport	35.0		21	Redfield 2 NE	31.7
23	Kennebec	34.9		23	Cottonwood 2 E	31.8
23	Long Valley	34.9		24	Lemmon	31.9
23	Murdo	34.9		25	Flandreau	32.0

Annual Extreme Minimum Temperature

	Highest				Lowest	
Rank	**Station Name**	**°F**		**Rank**	**Station Name**	**°F**
1	Pickstown	-26		1	Pollock	-47
2	Murdo	-29		1	Redfield 2 NE	-47
2	Rapid City 4 NW	-29		3	Camp Crook	-46
2	Wagner	-29		4	Aberdeen Regional Airport	-45
2	Winner	-29		4	Columbia 8 N	-45
6	Bonesteel	-30		4	Mellette	-45
6	Cedar Butte 1 NE	-30		4	Porcupine 11 N	-45
6	Deadwood	-30		8	Belle Fourche	-44
6	Fort Meade	-30		8	Castlewood	-44
10	Interior 3 NE	-31		8	Gann Valley 4 NW	-44
10	Marion	-31		11	Ardmore 2 N	-43
10	Mission 14 S	-31		11	Oral	-43
10	Mount Rushmore Nat'l Memorial	-31		11	Waubay Nat'l Wildlife Refuge	-43
10	Rapid City Regional Airport	-31		11	Zeona 10 SSW	*-43*
10	Spearfish Airport	-31		15	Eureka	-41
10	Tyndall	-31		15	Huron Regional Airport	-41
10	Yankton 2 E	-31		17	Britton	-40
18	Academy 2 NE	-32		17	Flandreau	-40
18	Armour	-32		17	Forestburg 3 NE	-40
18	Mission	-32		17	Highmore 1 W	-40
18	Wessington Springs	-32		17	Ipswich	-40
18	White Lake	-32		17	Mitchell 2 N	-40
18	Wood	*-32*		17	Ralph 1 N	-40
24	Centerville 6 SE	-33		17	Stephan 1 ENE	-40
24	Clear Lake	-33		17	Summit 1 W	-40

July Mean Maximum Temperature

	Highest				Lowest	
Rank	**Station Name**	**°F**		**Rank**	**Station Name**	**°F**
1	Interior 3 NE	90.8		1	Pactola Dam	78.5
2	Cedar Butte 1 NE	90.7		2	Lead	79.0
2	Kennebec	90.7		3	Custer	79.3
4	Winner	90.1		4	Mount Rushmore Nat'l Memorial	80.6
5	Oelrichs	90.0		5	Deadwood	81.0
6	Wagner	89.9		6	Brookings 2 NE	81.9
7	Oral	89.6		7	Summit 1 W	82.0
8	Wood	89.3		8	Clear Lake	82.7
9	Pierre Municipal Airport	89.2		9	Flandreau	82.8
9	Porcupine 11 N	89.2		10	Clark	83.4
11	Ardmore 2 N	89.0		10	Madison 2 SE	83.4
11	Wasta	89.0		12	Waubay Nat'l Wildlife Refuge	83.5
13	Cottonwood 2 E	88.8		13	Webster	83.6
14	Armour	88.7		14	Watertown Municipal Airport	83.7
14	Hot Springs	88.7		15	Lemmon	84.1
14	Vermillion 2 SE	88.7		16	Castlewood	84.3
17	Murdo	88.6		16	Columbia 8 N	84.3
18	Gregory	88.5		16	Spearfish Airport	84.3
18	Long Valley	88.5		19	Wentworth 2 WNW	84.4
18	Oahe Dam	88.5		20	Mobridge	84.5
21	Onida 4 NW	88.4		20	Sisseton	84.5
22	Academy 2 NE	88.2		22	Selby	84.6
22	Milesville 5 NE	88.2		23	De Smet	84.7
22	Stephan 1 ENE	88.2		23	Gettysburg	84.7
25	White Lake	88.1		23	Ludlow 3 SSE	84.7

January Mean Minimum Temperature

	Highest				Lowest	
Rank	**Station Name**	**°F**		**Rank**	**Station Name**	**°F**
1	Mount Rushmore Nat'l Memorial	16.3		1	Columbia 8 N	-1.8
2	Lead	14.3		2	Mellette	-1.6
3	Spearfish Airport	13.2		3	Britton	-0.8
4	Fort Meade	12.7		4	Redfield 2 NE	-0.7
5	Interior 3 NE	12.4		5	Summit 1 W	-0.6
6	Hot Springs	11.6		6	Castlewood	-0.4
6	Rapid City 4 NW	11.6		7	Flandreau	-0.2
8	Deadwood	11.1		8	Brookings 2 NE	-0.1
8	Rapid City Regional Airport	11.1		8	Eureka	-0.1
8	Winner	11.1		8	Ipswich	-0.1
11	Long Valley	10.8		11	Pollock	0.0
11	Oelrichs	10.8		12	Webster	0.1
13	Custer	10.4		13	Watertown Municipal Airport	0.3
14	Belle Fourche	10.0		14	Aberdeen Regional Airport	0.5
15	Oral	9.9		14	Waubay Nat'l Wildlife Refuge	0.5
16	Cedar Butte 1 NE	9.7		16	Leola	0.9
17	Wagner	9.6		16	Selby	0.9
18	Wood	9.4		18	Clark	1.1
19	Pickstown	9.1		19	Sisseton	1.8
20	Pactola Dam	8.6		20	Highmore 23 N	2.2
21	Mission 14 S	8.5		21	Gettysburg	2.3
22	Murdo	8.4		22	Clear Lake	2.4
23	Porcupine 11 N	8.3		23	Madison 2 SE	2.5
23	Wasta	8.3		24	Mobridge	2.8
25	Mission	8.1		25	Faulkton 1 NW	2.9

Number of Annual Heating Degree Days

	Highest				Lowest	
Rank	**Station Name**	**Num.**		**Rank**	**Station Name**	**Num.**
1	Summit 1 W	8,919		1	Interior 3 NE	6,368
2	Pactola Dam	*8,649*		2	Winner	6,505
3	Brookings 2 NE	8,646		3	Wagner	6,650
4	Columbia 8 N	8,636		4	Cedar Butte 1 NE	6,675
5	Eureka	8,589		5	Hot Springs	6,679
6	Webster	8,563		5	Vermillion 2 SE	6,679
7	Mellette	8,539		7	Long Valley	6,799
8	Selby	8,517		8	Pickstown	6,809
9	Watertown Municipal Airport	8,509		9	Wood	6,812
10	Waubay Nat'l Wildlife Refuge	8,454		10	Fort Meade	6,851
11	Leola	8,415		11	Armour	6,912
12	Castlewood	8,409		12	Oelrichs	6,925
13	Flandreau	8,408		13	Rapid City 4 NW	6,929
14	Ipswich	8,400		14	Gregory	6,938
15	Clark	8,371		15	Tyndall	6,948
16	Britton	8,356		16	Belle Fourche	6,968
17	Redfield 2 NE	8,334		17	Oral	*6,976*
18	Gettysburg	8,330		18	Wasta	6,991
19	Aberdeen Regional Airport	8,318		19	Menno	7,061
20	Clear Lake	8,239		20	Kennebec	7,083
21	Pollock	8,236		21	Alexandria	7,089
22	Lemmon	8,172		22	Bonesteel	7,105
23	McIntosh 6 SE	8,130		23	Academy 2 NE	7,113
24	Ralph 1 N	8,123		24	Yankton 2 E	7,114
25	Custer	8,119		25	Spearfish Airport	7,135

Number of Annual Cooling Degree Days

	Highest			Lowest	
Rank	**Station Name**	**Num.**	**Rank**	**Station Name**	**Num.**
1	Interior 3 NE	1,097	1	Pactola Dam	133
2	Vermillion 2 SE	1,091	2	Custer	234
3	Wagner	1,083	3	Lead	308
4	Winner	1,071	4	Deadwood	321
5	Kennebec	991	5	Summit 1 W	449
6	Armour	985	6	Mount Rushmore Nat'l Memorial	469
7	Tyndall	976	7	Redig 11 NE	485
8	Cedar Butte 1 NE	971	8	Brookings 2 NE	486
9	Pickstown	961	9	Ralph 1 N	491
10	Alexandria	941	10	Ludlow 3 SSE	495
11	Pierre Municipal Airport	938	11	Castlewood	534
12	Yankton 2 E	936	12	Camp Crook	539
13	Menno	921	13	Columbia 8 N	543
14	Wessington Springs	912	14	Ipswich	554
15	Wood	*898*	15	Eureka	556
16	Oahe Dam	*894*	16	Flandreau	557
17	White Lake	867	17	Lemmon	568
18	Murdo	861	18	Rapid City 4 NW	575
19	Mitchell 2 N	856	18	Selby	575
20	Gregory	853	20	Leola	576
21	Kirley 6 N	833	21	Spearfish Airport	*578*
22	Forestburg 3 NE	823	22	Clark	579
23	Wasta	811	22	Clear Lake	579
24	Academy 2 NE	809	24	Waubay Nat'l Wildlife Refuge	591
25	Onida 4 NW	802	25	Watertown Municipal Airport	*593*

Annual Precipitation

	Highest			Lowest	
Rank	**Station Name**	**Inches**	**Rank**	**Station Name**	**Inches**
1	Lead	29.98	1	Camp Crook	14.48
2	Deadwood	28.65	2	Oahe Dam	14.95
3	Bonesteel	26.76	3	Zeona 10 SSW	15.52
4	Clear Lake	26.08	4	Newell	15.55
5	Gregory	26.07	5	Redig 11 NE	15.73
6	Wagner	25.64	6	Ralph 1 N	16.15
7	Vermillion 2 SE	25.59	7	McIntosh 6 SE	16.59
8	Madison 2 SE	25.09	8	Oral	16.71
9	Marion	24.98	8	Rapid City Regional Airport	16.71
10	Centerville 6 SE	24.79	10	Ludlow 3 SSE	16.87
11	Wentworth 2 WNW	24.77	11	Ardmore 2 N	16.97
12	Sioux Falls Foss Field	24.70	12	Mobridge	17.07
12	Yankton 2 E	24.70	13	Oelrichs	17.10
14	Tyndall	24.13	14	Wasta	17.12
15	De Smet	23.86	15	Hot Springs	17.28
16	Armour	23.82	16	Porcupine 11 N	17.38
17	Winner	23.78	17	Dupree 15 SSE	17.40
18	Howard	23.69	18	Cottonwood 2 E	17.43
19	Castlewood	23.66	19	Faith	17.50
20	Flandreau	23.63	20	Pollock	17.60
21	Canton 4 WNW	23.52	21	Bison	17.67
22	Pickstown	23.44	22	Dupree	17.72
23	Menno	23.33	23	Selby	17.74
24	Academy 2 NE	23.18	24	Interior 3 NE	17.95
24	Summit 1 W	23.18	25	Maurine 10 SW	*17.97*

Number of Days Annually With ≥ 0.1″ Precipitation

	Highest			Lowest	
Rank	Station Name	Days	Rank	Station Name	Days
1	Lead	70	1	Oahe Dam	28
2	Deadwood	63	2	Camp Crook	35
3	Gregory	54	3	Ludlow 3 SSE	38
4	Clear Lake	52	3	McIntosh 6 SE	38
4	Marion	52	3	Mobridge	38
4	Tyndall	52	3	Newell	38
4	Wentworth 2 WNW	52	3	Ralph 1 N	38
4	Winner	52	3	Redig 11 NE	38
9	Howard	51	3	Selby	38
9	Madison 2 SE	51	3	Zeona 10 SSW	*38*
9	Mount Rushmore Nat'l Memorial	51	11	Cottonwood 2 E	39
9	Wagner	51	11	Dupree 15 SSE	39
13	Castlewood	50	11	Eureka	39
13	Centerville 6 SE	50	11	Faith	39
13	Highmore 1 W	50	11	Pollock	39
13	Menno	50	11	Rapid City Regional Airport	39
13	Summit 1 W	50	17	Gettysburg	40
18	Academy 2 NE	49	17	Highmore 23 N	40
18	Clark	49	17	Hot Springs	40
18	De Smet	49	17	Interior 3 NE	40
18	Forestburg 3 NE	49	17	Milesville 5 NE	40
18	Sioux Falls Foss Field	49	17	Porcupine 11 N	40
18	Sisseton	49	17	Redfield 2 NE	40
18	Spearfish Airport	49	17	Wasta	40
25	Armour	48	25	Columbia 8 N	41

Number of Days Annually With ≥ 1.0″ Precipitation

	Highest			Lowest	
Rank	Station Name	Days	Rank	Station Name	Days
1	Bonesteel	8	1	Ardmore 2 N	1
1	Marion	8	1	Camp Crook	1
3	Gregory	7	1	Dupree	1
4	Academy 2 NE	6	1	Maurine 10 SW	*1*
4	Clear Lake	6	1	Oahe Dam	1
4	Flandreau	6	1	Oelrichs	1
4	Highmore 1 W	6	7	Belle Fourche	2
4	Madison 2 SE	6	7	Bison	2
4	Mitchell 2 N	6	7	Custer	2
4	Sioux Falls Foss Field	6	7	Highmore 23 N	2
4	Vermillion 2 SE	6	7	Interior 3 NE	2
4	Wagner	6	7	Kirley 6 N	2
4	Wessington Springs	6	7	Leola	2
14	Alexandria	5	7	Ludlow 3 SSE	2
14	Brookings 2 NE	5	7	McIntosh 6 SE	2
14	Canton 4 WNW	5	7	Milesville 5 NE	2
14	Castlewood	5	7	Mobridge	2
14	Centerville 6 SE	5	7	Newell	2
14	De Smet	5	7	Onida 4 NW	2
14	Mellette	5	7	Oral	2
14	Menno	5	7	Ralph 1 N	2
14	Pickstown	5	7	Rapid City 4 NW	2
14	Redfield 2 NE	5	7	Rapid City Regional Airport	2
14	Tyndall	5	7	Redig 11 NE	2
14	Wentworth 2 WNW	5	7	Zeona 10 SSW	2

Annual Snowfall

Highest			Lowest		
Rank	**Station Name**	**Inches**	**Rank**	**Station Name**	**Inches**
1	Lead	193.0	1	Pickstown	22.7
2	Deadwood	101.8	2	Interior 3 NE	*25.1*
3	Spearfish Airport	*65.3*	3	Castlewood	27.0
4	Mount Rushmore Nat'l Memorial	56.2	4	Gann Valley 4 NW	27.3
5	Redig 11 NE	51.8	5	Canton 4 WNW	28.3
6	Milesville 5 NE	50.3	6	White Lake	28.6
7	Clear Lake	50.1	7	Centerville 6 SE	29.7
8	Harrington	49.3	7	Oral	*29.7*
9	Pactola Dam	*48.9*	9	Yankton 2 E	30.5
10	Summit 1 W	47.4	10	Alexandria	30.6
11	Winner	46.8	11	Watertown Municipal Airport	*31.2*
12	Faith	46.4	12	Vermillion 2 SE	31.9
13	Oelrichs	45.4	13	Flandreau	32.4
14	Ardmore 2 N	44.9	14	Porcupine 11 N	*32.5*
14	Leola	*44.9*	15	Redfield 2 NE	*32.6*
16	Gregory	*44.4*	16	Tyndall	32.7
17	Academy 2 NE	44.2	17	Ipswich	32.9
18	Highmore 1 W	43.7	17	Pierre Municipal Airport	32.9
19	Kirley 6 N	42.6	19	Selby	33.0
20	Onida 4 NW	42.5	20	Wasta	33.1
21	Rapid City Regional Airport	42.4	21	Clark	33.2
22	Huron Regional Airport	42.3	22	Bison	*33.4*
23	Sisseton	41.8	22	Hot Springs	33.4
24	Bonesteel	41.5	22	Kennebec	33.4
25	Long Valley	41.4	25	Forestburg 3 NE	33.6

Note: See Appendix D for explanation of data.

Annual Extreme Maximum Temperature

	Highest			Lowest	
Rank	Station Name	°F	Rank	Station Name	°F
1	Livingston Radio WLIV	108	1	Monteagle	97
1	Memphis Int'l Airport	108	2	Gatlinburg 2 SW	98
3	Dayton	107	3	Rogersville 1 NE	99
3	Pikeville	107	4	Greeneville Exp. Station	100
3	Rockwood 2	107	4	Newport 1 NW	100
3	Savannah 6 SW	107	6	Bristol Tri-City Airport	101
7	Covington 1 W	106	6	Crossville Exp. Station	101
7	Murfreesboro 5 N	106	6	Crossville Memorial Airport	101
7	Woodbury 1 WNW	106	6	Kingsport	101
10	Athens	105	6	Milan Experiment Station	*101*
10	Bolivar Waterworks	105	6	Tullahoma	101
10	Brownsville	105	12	Copperhill	102
10	Chattanooga Lovell Field	105	12	Dresden	102
10	Clarksville Sewage Plant	105	12	Knoxville McGhee Tyson Airport	102
10	Cleveland Filter Plant	105	12	Martin Univ. of Tennessee	102
10	Columbia 3 WNW	105	12	Portland Sewage Plant	102
10	Dickson	105	12	Sevierville 1 SE	102
10	Franklin Sewage Plant	105	12	Tazewell	102
10	Jackson McKellar-Sipes Reg. Arpt.	105	19	Allardt	103
10	Lebanon 3 W	105	19	Centerville Water Plant	103
10	Nashville Int'l Airport	105	19	Fayetteville Water Plant	103
10	Paris 2 NW	105	19	Huntingdon Water Plant	103
10	Pulaski Water Plant	105	19	Jackson Exp. Station	103
10	Samburg Wildlife Refuge	105	19	Kingston Springs	103
10	Selmer	105	19	Lawrenceburg Filter Plant	103

Annual Mean Maximum Temperature

	Highest			Lowest	
Rank	Station Name	°F	Rank	Station Name	°F
1	Savannah 6 SW	72.8	1	Crossville Exp. Station	65.0
2	Memphis Int'l Airport	72.0	2	Crossville Memorial Airport	65.6
2	Pulaski Water Plant	72.0	3	Allardt	65.7
4	Centerville Water Plant	71.6	4	Monteagle	65.8
5	Woodbury 1 WNW	71.1	5	Bristol Tri-City Airport	66.9
6	Shelbyville Water Dept.	71.0	5	Tazewell	66.9
7	Jackson McKellar-Sipes Reg. Arpt.	70.9	7	Springfield Exp. Station	67.7
8	Selmer	70.8	8	Paris 2 NW	67.8
9	Chattanooga Lovell Field	70.7	8	Portland Sewage Plant	67.8
10	Bolivar Waterworks	70.5	10	Gatlinburg 2 SW	68.0
10	Brownsville	70.5	11	Cookeville	68.2
10	Pikeville	70.5	11	Union City	68.2
13	Covington 1 W	70.3	13	Dover 1 W	68.4
13	Fayetteville Water Plant	70.3	14	Greeneville Exp. Station	68.6
13	Lawrenceburg Filter Plant	70.3	14	Rockwood 2	68.6
16	Franklin Sewage Plant	70.2	14	Rogersville 1 NE	68.6
17	Waynesboro	70.1	14	Smithville 2 SE	68.6
18	McMinnville	70.0	18	Dresden	68.8
19	Cleveland Filter Plant	69.9	19	Newport 1 NW	68.9
19	Dayton	69.9	19	Oak Ridge	68.9
19	Dyersburg Municipal Airport	69.9	19	Samburg Wildlife Refuge	*68.9*
19	Nashville Int'l Airport	69.9	22	Kingsport	69.1
19	Waverly	*69.9*	23	Knoxville McGhee Tyson Airport	69.2
24	Clarksville Sewage Plant	69.7	23	Lafayette	69.2
24	Lebanon 3 W	69.7	23	Livingston Radio WLIV	69.2

Annual Mean Temperature

	Highest			Lowest	
Rank	**Station Name**	**°F**	**Rank**	**Station Name**	**°F**
1	Memphis Int'l Airport	62.6	1	Crossville Exp. Station	53.8
2	Savannah 6 SW	60.8	2	Tazewell	54.1
3	Dyersburg Municipal Airport	60.6	3	Gatlinburg 2 SW	55.3
4	Brownsville	60.2	4	Allardt	55.4
5	Jackson McKellar-Sipes Reg. Arpt.	60.1	5	Crossville Memorial Airport	55.5
6	Pulaski Water Plant	60.0	6	Greeneville Exp. Station	55.8
7	Chattanooga Lovell Field	59.9	7	Bristol Tri-City Airport	55.9
8	Covington 1 W	59.7	8	Monteagle	56.4
9	Bolivar Waterworks	59.5	8	Rockwood 2	56.4
10	Nashville Int'l Airport	59.4	8	Smithville 2 SE	56.4
10	Shelbyville Water Dept.	59.4	8	Springfield Exp. Station	56.4
12	Jackson Exp. Station	59.3	12	Cookeville	56.5
13	Selmer	59.1	13	Kingston Springs	56.7
14	McMinnville	58.9	13	Rogersville 1 NE	56.7
15	Knoxville McGhee Tyson Airport	58.8	15	Sevierville 1 SE	56.8
16	Lawrenceburg Filter Plant	58.6	16	Copperhill	*56.9*
16	Tullahoma	58.6	17	Newport 1 NW	57.0
18	Dayton	58.5	17	Paris 2 NW	57.0
18	Lafayette	58.5	17	Waynesboro	57.0
20	Pikeville	58.4	20	Dover 1 W	57.1
21	Cleveland Filter Plant	58.2	21	Waverly	*57.2*
21	Fayetteville Water Plant	58.2	22	Lebanon 3 W	57.3
21	Samburg Wildlife Refuge	*58.2*	22	Lewisburg Exp. Station	57.3
21	Woodbury 1 WNW	58.2	24	Portland Sewage Plant	57.4
25	Centerville Water Plant	58.1	24	Union City	57.4

Annual Mean Minimum Temperature

	Highest			Lowest	
Rank	**Station Name**	**°F**	**Rank**	**Station Name**	**°F**
1	Memphis Int'l Airport	53.2	1	Tazewell	41.2
2	Dyersburg Municipal Airport	51.2	2	Gatlinburg 2 SW	42.5
3	Brownsville	49.8	3	Crossville Exp. Station	42.7
4	Jackson McKellar-Sipes Reg. Arpt.	49.3	4	Greeneville Exp. Station	42.9
5	Chattanooga Lovell Field	49.1	5	Kingston Springs	44.0
5	Jackson Exp. Station	49.1	5	Waynesboro	44.0
7	Covington 1 W	49.0	7	Copperhill	*44.1*
8	Nashville Int'l Airport	48.9	7	Smithville 2 SE	44.1
9	Savannah 6 SW	48.8	9	Sevierville 1 SE	44.2
10	Bolivar Waterworks	48.4	10	Rockwood 2	44.3
10	Knoxville McGhee Tyson Airport	48.4	11	Centerville Water Plant	44.5
12	Pulaski Water Plant	48.0	11	Waverly	*44.5*
13	Lafayette	47.7	13	Cookeville	44.7
13	McMinnville	47.7	14	Bristol Tri-City Airport	44.8
13	Shelbyville Water Dept.	47.7	15	Lebanon 3 W	44.9
16	Tullahoma	47.6	15	Newport 1 NW	44.9
17	Samburg Wildlife Refuge	*47.3*	15	Rogersville 1 NE	44.9
18	Selmer	47.2	18	Allardt	45.1
19	Dayton	47.1	18	Lewisburg Exp. Station	45.1
20	Monteagle	47.0	18	Springfield Exp. Station	45.1
21	Dresden	46.9	21	Woodbury 1 WNW	45.2
21	Lawrenceburg Filter Plant	46.9	22	Crossville Memorial Airport	45.4
21	Portland Sewage Plant	46.9	23	Columbia 3 WNW	45.6
24	Martin Univ. of Tennessee	46.8	24	Athens	45.7
25	Dickson	46.6	25	Dover 1 W	45.8

Annual Extreme Minimum Temperature

	Highest			Lowest	
Rank	**Station Name**	**°F**	**Rank**	**Station Name**	**°F**
1	Memphis Int'l Airport	-4	1	Greeneville Exp. Station	-29
2	Brownsville	-10	2	Woodbury 1 WNW	-28
2	Chattanooga Lovell Field	-10	3	Allardt	-27
2	Covington 1 W	-10	4	Centerville Water Plant	-26
2	Jackson Exp. Station	-10	5	Crossville Exp. Station	-25
2	Jackson McKellar-Sipes Reg. Arpt.	-10	5	Livingston Radio WLIV	-25
2	Rockwood 2	-10	7	Knoxville McGhee Tyson Airport	-24
8	Bolivar Waterworks	-11	7	Sevierville 1 SE	-24
9	Dyersburg Municipal Airport	-12	7	Smithville 2 SE	-24
10	Murfreesboro 5 N	-13	7	Tazewell	-24
10	Savannah 6 SW	-13	7	Waverly	-24
12	Huntingdon Water Plant	-14	12	Dickson	-23
12	Lawrenceburg Filter Plant	-14	12	Kingston Springs	-23
12	Lenoir City	-14	12	Newport 1 NW	-23
12	Selmer	-14	12	Rogersville 1 NE	-23
12	Union City	-14	16	Cookeville	-22
17	Clarksville Sewage Plant	-15	17	Bristol Tri-City Airport	-21
17	Dayton	-15	17	Crossville Memorial Airport	-21
17	Dover 1 W	-15	17	Franklin Sewage Plant	-21
17	Martin Univ. of Tennessee	-15	20	Columbia 3 WNW	-20
17	Samburg Wildlife Refuge	-15	20	Fayetteville Water Plant	-20
22	Athens	-16	20	Lebanon 3 W	-20
22	Cleveland Filter Plant	-16	20	Lewisburg Exp. Station	-20
22	Copperhill	-16	20	Milan Experiment Station	*-20*
22	Paris 2 NW	-16	20	Monteagle	-20

July Mean Maximum Temperature

	Highest			Lowest	
Rank	**Station Name**	**°F**	**Rank**	**Station Name**	**°F**
1	Memphis Int'l Airport	91.6	1	Allardt	83.7
2	Covington 1 W	91.2	1	Monteagle	83.7
3	Savannah 6 SW	91.1	3	Crossville Memorial Airport	84.0
4	Jackson McKellar-Sipes Reg. Arpt.	90.9	4	Crossville Exp. Station	84.1
5	Dyersburg Municipal Airport	90.6	5	Gatlinburg 2 SW	84.8
6	Brownsville	90.4	6	Bristol Tri-City Airport	85.4
6	Clarksville Sewage Plant	90.4	7	Tazewell	86.1
8	Samburg Wildlife Refuge	*90.3*	8	Rogersville 1 NE	87.1
9	Selmer	90.2	9	Greeneville Exp. Station	87.2
10	Martin Univ. of Tennessee	90.1	10	Cookeville	87.4
10	Pulaski Water Plant	90.1	11	Rockwood 2	87.5
12	Bolivar Waterworks	89.9	12	Kingsport	87.6
12	Lebanon 3 W	89.9	12	Newport 1 NW	87.6
14	Chattanooga Lovell Field	89.8	12	Tullahoma	87.6
14	Franklin Sewage Plant	89.8	15	Sevierville 1 SE	87.7
16	Centerville Water Plant	89.7	16	Smithville 2 SE	87.8
16	Huntingdon Water Plant	89.7	17	Copperhill	*87.9*
18	Nashville Int'l Airport	89.6	17	Livingston Radio WLIV	87.9
18	Shelbyville Water Dept.	89.6	19	Knoxville McGhee Tyson Airport	88.0
20	Waverly	*89.5*	20	Paris 2 NW	88.1
20	Woodbury 1 WNW	89.5	21	McMinnville	88.2
22	Milan Experiment Station	89.4	21	Oak Ridge	88.2
23	Dresden	89.3	23	Lawrenceburg Filter Plant	88.3
23	Fayetteville Water Plant	89.3	23	Portland Sewage Plant	88.3
23	Murfreesboro 5 N	89.3	25	Dover 1 W	88.4

January Mean Minimum Temperature

Highest			Lowest		
Rank	Station Name	°F	Rank	Station Name	°F
1	Memphis Int'l Airport	31.6	1	Tazewell	21.7
2	Chattanooga Lovell Field	29.6	2	Crossville Exp. Station	22.1
3	Dyersburg Municipal Airport	29.3	3	Waverly	23.1
4	McMinnville	29.0	4	Kingston Springs	23.3
5	Savannah 6 SW	28.8	5	Springfield Exp. Station	23.8
6	Knoxville McGhee Tyson Airport	28.7	6	Greeneville Exp. Station	23.9
7	Pulaski Water Plant	28.6	7	Dover 1 W	24.0
8	Shelbyville Water Dept.	28.4	7	Lebanon 3 W	24.0
8	Tullahoma	28.4	9	Clarksville Sewage Plant	24.3
10	Brownsville	28.2	9	Waynesboro	24.3
10	Dayton	28.2	11	Dresden	24.5
12	Pikeville	28.0	11	Martin Univ. of Tennessee	24.5
13	Jackson McKellar-Sipes Reg. Arpt.	27.9	13	Paris 2 NW	24.6
13	Kingsport	27.9	13	Union City	24.6
13	Nashville Int'l Airport	27.9	15	Gatlinburg 2 SW	24.7
16	Jackson Exp. Station	27.8	16	Milan Experiment Station	24.8
17	Bolivar Waterworks	27.7	17	Centerville Water Plant	24.9
18	Lawrenceburg Filter Plant	27.6	17	Samburg Wildlife Refuge	24.9
19	Covington 1 W	27.5	17	Smithville 2 SE	24.9
20	Cleveland Filter Plant	27.4	20	Cookeville	25.0
21	Lafayette	27.1	21	Portland Sewage Plant	25.1
22	Livingston Radio WLIV	26.9	21	Rockwood 2	25.1
22	Monteagle	26.9	23	Columbia 3 WNW	25.4
22	Selmer	26.9	23	Huntingdon Water Plant	25.4
25	Fayetteville Water Plant	26.7	23	Lewisburg Exp. Station	25.4

Number of Annual Heating Degree Days

Highest			Lowest		
Rank	Station Name	Num.	Rank	Station Name	Num.
1	Tazewell	4,803	1	Memphis Int'l Airport	2,997
2	Crossville Exp. Station	4,776	2	Savannah 6 SW	3,185
3	Springfield Exp. Station	4,352	3	Pulaski Water Plant	3,334
4	Greeneville Exp. Station	4,336	4	Chattanooga Lovell Field	3,393
5	Crossville Memorial Airport	4,321	5	Dyersburg Municipal Airport	3,404
6	Allardt	4,308	6	Jackson McKellar-Sipes Reg. Arpt.	3,478
7	Gatlinburg 2 SW	4,278	7	Shelbyville Water Dept.	3,499
8	Bristol Tri-City Airport	4,257	8	Brownsville	3,505
9	Kingston Springs	4,228	9	McMinnville	3,549
10	Cookeville	4,209	10	Bolivar Waterworks	3,573
11	Smithville 2 SE	4,205	11	Lawrenceburg Filter Plant	3,592
12	Paris 2 NW	4,188	12	Nashville Int'l Airport	3,616
13	Rockwood 2	4,180	13	Tullahoma	3,629
14	Union City	4,159	14	Dayton	3,633
15	Dover 1 W	4,158	14	Knoxville McGhee Tyson Airport	3,633
16	Waverly	*4,152*	16	Covington 1 W	3,634
17	Lebanon 3 W	4,135	17	Pikeville	3,645
18	Portland Sewage Plant	4,096	18	Selmer	3,648
19	Waynesboro	4,086	19	Jackson Exp. Station	3,662
20	Monteagle	4,084	20	Cleveland Filter Plant	3,724
21	Lewisburg Exp. Station	4,063	21	Lafayette	3,743
22	Newport 1 NW	4,046	22	Woodbury 1 WNW	3,751
23	Dresden	4,043	23	Centerville Water Plant	3,767
23	Sevierville 1 SE	4,043	24	Kingsport	3,793
25	Clarksville Sewage Plant	4,036	25	Fayetteville Water Plant	3,802

Number of Annual Cooling Degree Days

Highest				Lowest		
Rank	Station Name	Num.		Rank	Station Name	Num.
1	Memphis Int'l Airport	2,279		1	Crossville Exp. Station	855
2	Dyersburg Municipal Airport	1,931		2	Gatlinburg 2 SW	869
3	Covington 1 W	1,858		3	Allardt	936
4	Brownsville	1,848		4	Crossville Memorial Airport	984
5	Jackson McKellar-Sipes Reg. Arpt.	1,829		5	Tazewell	989
6	Savannah 6 SW	1,821		6	Greeneville Exp. Station	1,031
7	Jackson Exp. Station	1,740		7	Bristol Tri-City Airport	1,046
8	Nashville Int'l Airport	1,737		8	Monteagle	1,065
9	Bolivar Waterworks	1,724		9	Copperhill	*1,109*
10	Chattanooga Lovell Field	1,709		10	Rogersville 1 NE	1,151
11	Selmer	1,682		11	Rockwood 2	1,182
12	Pulaski Water Plant	1,636		12	Smithville 2 SE	1,190
13	Dresden	1,593		13	Cookeville	1,216
14	Clarksville Sewage Plant	1,584		14	Newport 1 NW	1,249
14	Shelbyville Water Dept.	1,584		15	Kingsport	1,288
16	Martin Univ. of Tennessee	1,581		16	Sevierville 1 SE	1,293
17	Milan Experiment Station	*1,578*		17	Waynesboro	1,315
18	Lafayette	1,549		18	Springfield Exp. Station	1,349
19	Union City	1,538		19	Columbia 3 WNW	1,352
20	Huntingdon Water Plant	1,535		20	Kingston Springs	1,356
21	Portland Sewage Plant	1,525		21	Pikeville	1,361
22	Lenoir City	1,519		22	Athens	1,363
22	Waverly	*1,519*		23	Livingston Radio WLIV	1,366
24	Knoxville McGhee Tyson Airport	1,512		24	Dayton	1,382
25	Murfreesboro 5 N	1,487		25	Tullahoma	1,384

Annual Precipitation

Highest				Lowest		
Rank	Station Name	Inches		Rank	Station Name	Inches
1	Monteagle	63.61		1	Bristol Tri-City Airport	41.27
2	Waynesboro	60.83		2	Greeneville Exp. Station	43.57
3	Copperhill	60.75		3	Sevierville 1 SE	43.77
4	Crossville Exp. Station	60.59		4	Kingsport	44.51
5	Rockwood 2	60.56		5	Newport 1 NW	44.81
6	Lawrenceburg Filter Plant	60.32		6	Rogersville 1 NE	45.23
7	Tullahoma	59.95		7	Knoxville McGhee Tyson Airport	48.08
8	Savannah 6 SW	59.32		8	Nashville Int'l Airport	48.16
9	Dayton	58.42		9	Dyersburg Municipal Airport	50.94
10	Athens	58.38		10	Springfield Exp. Station	51.22
11	Selmer	58.05		11	Samburg Wildlife Refuge	51.55
12	Cookeville	57.77		12	Clarksville Sewage Plant	52.10
13	Crossville Memorial Airport	57.50		13	Union City	52.44
14	Woodbury 1 WNW	57.36		14	Tazewell	52.45
15	Shelbyville Water Dept.	57.14		15	Livingston Radio WLIV	52.55
16	Gatlinburg 2 SW	57.03		16	Kingston Springs	52.68
17	Lafayette	56.55		17	Lenoir City	52.85
18	Pulaski Water Plant	56.52		18	Portland Sewage Plant	52.96
19	Smithville 2 SE	56.32		19	Dover 1 W	53.36
20	Waverly	56.26		20	Martin Univ. of Tennessee	53.50
21	Fayetteville Water Plant	56.11		21	Brownsville	53.64
22	Dickson	55.96		22	Covington 1 W	53.72
23	Columbia 3 WNW	55.93		23	McMinnville	53.86
23	Lewisburg Exp. Station	55.93		24	Franklin Sewage Plant	54.26
25	Cleveland Filter Plant	55.78		25	Paris 2 NW	54.28

Number of Days Annually With ≥ 0.1″ Precipitation

	Highest			Lowest	
Rank	**Station Name**	**Days**	**Rank**	**Station Name**	**Days**
1	Gatlinburg 2 SW	101	1	Samburg Wildlife Refuge	69
2	Crossville Exp. Station	98	2	Dyersburg Municipal Airport	73
3	Monteagle	*97*	3	Rogersville 1 NE	74
4	Crossville Memorial Airport	96	4	Waverly	75
5	Allardt	95	5	Memphis Int'l Airport	76
5	Cookeville	95	6	Brownsville	77
7	Tazewell	94	7	Covington 1 W	78
8	Smithville 2 SE	93	7	Jackson McKellar-Sipes Reg. Arpt.	78
9	Tullahoma	92	9	Bolivar Waterworks	79
9	Woodbury 1 WNW	92	9	Union City	79
11	Athens	91	11	Dresden	80
11	Dayton	91	11	Jackson Exp. Station	80
11	Kingsport	91	11	Martin Univ. of Tennessee	80
11	Lenoir City	91	11	Savannah 6 SW	80
11	Oak Ridge	91	15	Dickson	81
11	Rockwood 2	91	15	Huntingdon Water Plant	81
17	Newport 1 NW	90	15	Kingston Springs	81
18	Bristol Tri-City Airport	89	15	Lafayette	81
18	Copperhill	89	15	Milan Experiment Station	*81*
18	McMinnville	89	15	Sevierville 1 SE	81
21	Cleveland Filter Plant	88	15	Springfield Exp. Station	81
21	Pikeville	*88*	22	Dover 1 W	82
23	Fayetteville Water Plant	87	22	Nashville Int'l Airport	82
23	Greeneville Exp. Station	87	22	Paris 2 NW	82
25	Shelbyville Water Dept.	86	22	Pulaski Water Plant	82

Number of Days Annually With ≥ 1.0″ Precipitation

	Highest			Lowest	
Rank	**Station Name**	**Days**	**Rank**	**Station Name**	**Days**
1	Lawrenceburg Filter Plant	19	1	Bristol Tri-City Airport	10
1	Rockwood 2	19	1	Greeneville Exp. Station	10
1	Waynesboro	19	3	Newport 1 NW	11
4	Jackson McKellar-Sipes Reg. Arpt.	18	4	Dyersburg Municipal Airport	12
4	Lafayette	18	4	Kingsport	12
4	Monteagle	18	4	Knoxville McGhee Tyson Airport	12
4	Savannah 6 SW	18	4	Rogersville 1 NE	12
4	Selmer	18	4	Sevierville 1 SE	12
9	Athens	17	9	Clarksville Sewage Plant	13
9	Covington 1 W	17	9	Lenoir City	13
9	Crossville Exp. Station	17	9	Livingston Radio WLIV	13
9	Dayton	17	9	Nashville Int'l Airport	13
9	Dresden	17	9	Portland Sewage Plant	13
9	Jackson Exp. Station	17	9	Smithville 2 SE	13
9	Martin Univ. of Tennessee	17	9	Tazewell	13
9	Memphis Int'l Airport	17	9	Union City	13
9	Pulaski Water Plant	17	17	Allardt	14
9	Waverly	17	17	Cleveland Filter Plant	14
19	Bolivar Waterworks	16	17	Dover 1 W	14
19	Chattanooga Lovell Field	16	17	McMinnville	14
19	Cookeville	16	17	Oak Ridge	14
19	Copperhill	16	17	Paris 2 NW	14
19	Dickson	16	17	Pikeville	14
19	Franklin Sewage Plant	16	17	Samburg Wildlife Refuge	14
19	Shelbyville Water Dept.	16	17	Springfield Exp. Station	14

Annual Snowfall

	Highest			Lowest	
Rank	Station Name	Inches	Rank	Station Name	Inches
1	Tazewell	16.7	1	Cleveland Filter Plant	*1.6*
2	Allardt	15.8	2	Bolivar Waterworks	*1.9*
3	Crossville Exp. Station	15.3	2	Waynesboro	1.9
4	Bristol Tri-City Airport	15.1	4	Selmer	*2.5*
5	Kingsport	12.1	5	Centerville Water Plant	2.6
6	Crossville Memorial Airport	12.0	5	Pulaski Water Plant	*2.6*
7	Greeneville Exp. Station	10.4	5	Savannah 6 SW	*2.6*
8	Knoxville McGhee Tyson Airport	10.0	8	Columbia 3 WNW	2.8
9	Springfield Exp. Station	9.9	9	Fayetteville Water Plant	3.1
10	Gatlinburg 2 SW	9.7	9	Lewisburg Exp. Station	*3.1*
10	Newport 1 NW	9.7	11	Kingston Springs	*3.2*
12	Lafayette	*9.3*	12	Murfreesboro 5 N	*3.3*
12	Union City	9.3	13	Copperhill	3.4
14	Oak Ridge	9.2	14	Franklin Sewage Plant	*3.5*
15	Milan Experiment Station	*8.7*	14	Rockwood 2	*3.5*
16	Livingston Radio WLIV	*8.6*	16	Jackson Exp. Station	3.8
16	Nashville Int'l Airport	8.6	17	Memphis Int'l Airport	4.0
18	Lenoir City	8.2	18	Dayton	4.4
19	Cookeville	7.9	19	Lawrenceburg Filter Plant	4.6
20	Paris 2 NW	7.3	19	Martin Univ. of Tennessee	4.6
21	Dover 1 W	7.2	19	Portland Sewage Plant	4.6
22	Rogersville 1 NE	*7.0*	19	Tullahoma	*4.6*
23	Athens	6.6	23	Chattanooga Lovell Field	4.7
23	Dyersburg Municipal Airport	6.6	24	Huntingdon Water Plant	4.8
25	McMinnville	6.5	24	Shelbyville Water Dept.	4.8

Note: See Appendix D for explanation of data.

Annual Extreme Maximum Temperature

Highest				Lowest		
Rank	**Station Name**	**°F**		**Rank**	**Station Name**	**°F**
1	Monahans	120		1	Palacios Municipal Airport	99
2	Guthrie	119		2	Rockport	100
2	Quanah 5 SE	119		3	Angleton 2 W	101
2	Weatherford	119		3	Freeport 2 NW	101
5	Paducah	118		3	Matagorda 2	101
5	Truscott 3 W	118		3	Port Mansfield	101
5	Vernon	118		7	Aransas Wildlife Refuge	*102*
8	Aspermont	117		7	Chapman Ranch	102
8	Childress Municipal Airport	117		7	Galveston	102
8	Fort Stockton	117		10	Anahuac	103
8	Munday	117		10	Chisos Basin	103
8	Pecos	117		10	Houston William P. Hobby Airport	103
8	Wichita Falls Municipal Airport	117		10	Liberty	103
8	Wink Winkler Co. Airport	117		10	Port Arthur Jefferson County	103
15	Falcon Dam	116		10	Sugar Land	103
15	Gail	116		16	Danevang 1 W	104
15	Jayton	116		16	Flatonia	104
15	Matador	116		16	Mount Locke	104
15	Memphis	116		16	New Gulf	104
15	Midland 4 ENE	116		16	Thompsons 3 WSW	*104*
15	Midland Regional Air Terminal	116		21	Boerne	105
15	Penwell	116		21	Harlingen	105
15	Rio Grande City 1 SE	116		21	Kerrville 3 NNE	*105*
15	Zapata 3 SW	116		21	Lexington	105
25	Bowie	115		21	Texarkana	105

Annual Mean Maximum Temperature

Highest				Lowest		
Rank	**Station Name**	**°F**		**Rank**	**Station Name**	**°F**
1	Presidio	87.1		1	Follett	69.1
2	Zapata 3 SW	86.4		2	Stratford	69.5
3	Rio Grande City 1 SE	85.8		3	Perryton	69.6
4	Laredo 2	85.7		4	Dumas	69.7
5	Falcon Dam	85.6		4	Pampa 2	69.7
6	Candelaria	85.1		6	Dalhart Municipal Airport	69.8
7	McAllen Miller Int'l Airport	*84.8*		6	Mount Locke	69.8
8	Weslaco 2 E	84.6		8	Amarillo Int'l Airport	70.2
9	McCook	84.5		8	Claude	70.2
9	Raymondville	84.5		8	Miami	70.2
11	Hebbronville	83.9		11	Friona	70.7
12	Falfurrias	83.7		12	Hereford	70.8
13	Charlotte 5 NNW	83.4		13	Silverton	70.9
13	Tilden 4 SSE	83.4		14	Dimmitt 2 N	71.0
15	Alice	83.2		15	Lipscomb	71.2
15	Harlingen	83.2		16	Olton	71.5
17	Brownsville Int'l Airport	83.1		17	Panhandle	71.6
17	Crystal City	83.1		17	Tulia	71.6
19	Goliad	82.9		19	Gruver	71.7
20	Eagle Pass	82.6		20	Borger	71.8
21	Dilley	82.2		20	Bravo	71.8
22	Robstown	81.9		20	Plainview	71.8
23	Floresville	81.8		23	Floydada	71.9
23	Langtry	81.8		24	Shamrock 2	72.2
23	Mathis 4 SSW	81.8		25	Muleshoe 1	72.5

Annual Mean Temperature

	Highest				Lowest	
Rank	**Station Name**	**°F**		**Rank**	**Station Name**	**°F**
1	McAllen Miller Int'l Airport	*74.7*		1	Stratford	54.7
2	Zapata 3 SW	74.5		2	Perryton	54.9
3	Weslaco 2 E	74.3		3	Dalhart Municipal Airport	55.3
4	Brownsville Int'l Airport	74.0		4	Dimmitt 2 N	55.7
5	Falcon Dam	73.7		5	Dumas	55.9
5	Laredo 2	73.7		6	Follett	56.1
7	Rio Grande City 1 SE	73.5		7	Bravo	56.2
8	Raymondville	73.3		7	Friona	56.2
9	McCook	73.1		9	Claude	56.3
10	Harlingen	73.0		9	Hereford	56.3
11	Hebbronville	72.0		9	Lipscomb	56.3
12	Alice	71.9		12	Pampa 2	56.6
12	Corpus Christi Int'l Airport	71.9		13	Miami	56.7
12	Falfurrias	71.9		13	Muleshoe 1	56.7
15	Chapman Ranch	71.8		15	Amarillo Int'l Airport	56.8
15	Crystal City	71.8		15	Gruver	56.8
15	Robstown	71.8		15	Olton	56.8
18	Port Mansfield	*71.6*		18	Silverton	56.9
19	Rockport	71.3		19	Tulia	57.2
20	Goliad	71.2		20	Panhandle	57.4
21	Charlotte 5 NNW	70.9		21	Mount Locke	57.8
21	Mathis 4 SSW	70.9		22	Morton	58.0
21	Point Comfort	70.9		23	Littlefield 2 NW	58.1
21	Tilden 4 SSE	70.9		24	Floydada	58.2
25	Aransas Wildlife Refuge	*70.8*		25	Borger	58.3

Annual Mean Minimum Temperature

	Highest				Lowest	
Rank	**Station Name**	**°F**		**Rank**	**Station Name**	**°F**
1	Galveston	65.2		1	Stratford	39.9
2	Brownsville Int'l Airport	64.9		2	Dimmitt 2 N	40.3
2	Port Mansfield	64.9		2	Perryton	40.3
4	McAllen Miller Int'l Airport	*64.5*		4	Bravo	40.5
5	Weslaco 2 E	63.9		5	Dalhart Municipal Airport	40.8
6	Rockport	63.5		5	Muleshoe 1	40.8
7	Harlingen	62.8		7	Lipscomb	41.3
8	Aransas Wildlife Refuge	62.7		8	Friona	41.7
9	Chapman Ranch	62.6		9	Hereford	41.8
9	Zapata 3 SW	62.6		10	Gruver	41.9
11	Corpus Christi Int'l Airport	62.5		11	Dumas	42.1
11	Matagorda 2	62.5		11	Olton	42.1
13	Point Comfort	62.3		13	Claude	42.3
14	Raymondville	62.1		14	Silverton	42.8
15	Freeport 2 NW	62.0		14	Tulia	42.8
16	Falcon Dam	61.9		16	Morton	42.9
17	Laredo 2	61.6		17	Marfa 2	43.0
17	McCook	61.6		18	Panhandle	43.1
17	Robstown	61.6		19	Follett	43.2
20	Palacios Municipal Airport	61.3		19	Miami	43.2
21	Rio Grande City 1 SE	61.1		21	Amarillo Int'l Airport	43.3
22	Alice	60.6		21	Littlefield 2 NW	43.3
22	Crystal City	60.6		23	Levelland	43.4
22	Houston William P. Hobby Airport	60.6		23	Pampa 2	43.4
25	Victoria Regional Airport	60.3		25	Spearman	43.8

Annual Extreme Minimum Temperature

Highest			Lowest		
Rank	Station Name	°F	Rank	Station Name	°F
1	McAllen Miller Int'l Airport	*18*	1	Lipscomb	-18
2	Brownsville Int'l Airport	16	2	Perryton	-17
2	Weslaco 2 E	16	3	Glen Rose 2 W	-15
4	Falcon Dam	15	3	Quanah 5 SE	-15
4	Harlingen	15	5	Dalhart Municipal Airport	-14
4	Port Mansfield	15	5	Stratford	-14
4	Raymondville	15	7	Canadian	-13
4	Rio Grande City 1 SE	15	7	Follett	-13
4	Zapata 3 SW	*15*	7	Gruver	-13
10	Galveston	14	7	Shamrock 2	-13
10	McCook	14	11	Amarillo Int'l Airport	-12
12	Corpus Christi Int'l Airport	13	11	Anson	*-12*
12	Falfurrias	13	11	Bravo	-12
12	Freeport 2 NW	13	11	Penwell	-12
12	Presidio	13	15	Bowie	-11
16	Alice	*12*	15	Canyon	-11
16	Chapman Ranch	12	15	Clarendon Municipal Airport	-11
16	Dilley	*12*	15	Dumas	-11
16	Eagle Pass	12	15	Miami	-11
16	Hebbronville	12	15	Midland Regional Air Terminal	-11
16	Port Arthur Jefferson County	12	15	Muleshoe 1	-11
16	Robstown	12	15	Spearman	-11
16	Rockport	12	15	Throckmorton	-11
24	Crystal City	11	24	Friona	-10
24	Laredo 2	11	24	Guthrie	-10

July Mean Maximum Temperature

Highest			Lowest		
Rank	Station Name	°F	Rank	Station Name	°F
1	Presidio	100.6	1	Mount Locke	82.9
2	Laredo 2	100.5	2	Chisos Basin	84.1
3	Candelaria	99.6	3	Galveston	88.2
3	Falcon Dam	99.6	4	Port Mansfield	88.3
5	Zapata 3 SW	99.1	5	Alpine	89.2
6	Rio Grande City 1 SE	98.9	6	Marfa 2	89.6
7	Ysleta	98.6	7	Friona	90.1
8	Monahans	98.5	7	Palacios Municipal Airport	90.1
8	Pecos	98.5	9	Aransas Wildlife Refuge	90.2
10	Eagle Pass	97.9	9	Marathon	90.2
10	Tilden 4 SSE	97.9	9	Olton	90.2
12	Vernon	97.8	12	Rockport	90.5
13	Langtry	97.7	13	Dalhart Municipal Airport	90.7
14	Glen Rose 2 W	97.6	13	Dimmitt 2 N	90.7
14	Wichita Falls Municipal Airport	97.6	15	Hereford	90.8
16	Aspermont	97.5	16	Matagorda 2	90.9
16	Bridgeport	97.5	16	Silverton	90.9
16	Dilley	97.5	18	Amarillo Int'l Airport	91.0
16	Lake Kemp	*97.5*	18	Claude	91.0
16	Munday	97.5	20	Bravo	91.2
21	Paint Rock	97.4	20	Morton	91.2
22	Truscott 3 W	97.3	20	Tulia	91.2
23	Guthrie	97.2	23	Stratford	91.3
24	Cleburne	97.0	24	Plainview	91.4
24	Mineral Wells Municipal Airport	*97.0*	25	Pampa 2	91.5

January Mean Minimum Temperature

Highest			Lowest		
Rank	**Station Name**	**°F**	**Rank**	**Station Name**	**°F**
1	Brownsville Int'l Airport	50.7	1	Lipscomb	17.2
2	McAllen Miller Int'l Airport	*49.4*	1	Perryton	17.2
2	Weslaco 2 E	49.4	3	Stratford	18.4
4	Port Mansfield	48.5	4	Dalhart Municipal Airport	19.7
5	Galveston	48.0	5	Gruver	19.8
5	Harlingen	48.0	6	Muleshoe 1	19.9
7	Raymondville	47.1	7	Follett	20.0
8	Chapman Ranch	46.8	8	Bravo	20.3
9	Corpus Christi Int'l Airport	46.4	8	Dimmitt 2 N	20.3
10	Zapata 3 SW	46.3	10	Miami	20.4
11	Rockport	46.2	11	Dumas	20.6
12	McCook	46.0	12	Claude	20.8
13	Matagorda 2	45.9	13	Hereford	21.2
14	Aransas Wildlife Refuge	45.6	13	Silverton	21.2
15	Falcon Dam	45.4	15	Pampa 2	21.5
16	Point Comfort	45.3	16	Canadian	21.6
17	Freeport 2 NW	45.1	16	Friona	21.6
18	Robstown	44.8	16	Olton	21.6
19	Palacios Municipal Airport	44.3	19	Amarillo Int'l Airport	21.8
19	Rio Grande City 1 SE	44.3	19	Panhandle	21.8
21	Alice	44.1	21	Spearman	22.1
22	Falfurrias	43.7	21	Tulia	22.1
22	Houston William P. Hobby Airport	43.7	23	Clarendon Municipal Airport	22.3
22	Laredo 2	43.7	24	Littlefield 2 NW	22.5
25	Mathis 4 SSW	43.5	25	Shamrock 2	22.9

Number of Annual Heating Degree Days

Highest			Lowest		
Rank	**Station Name**	**Num.**	**Rank**	**Station Name**	**Num.**
1	Perryton	4,916	1	Brownsville Int'l Airport	603
2	Stratford	4,818	2	Weslaco 2 E	631
3	Lipscomb	4,660	3	McAllen Miller Int'l Airport	*662*
4	Dalhart Municipal Airport	4,598	4	Zapata 3 SW	751
5	Follett	4,589	5	Harlingen	767
6	Dumas	4,574	6	Raymondville	789
7	Dimmitt 2 N	4,445	7	Port Mansfield	*863*
8	Miami	4,442	8	McCook	864
9	Pampa 2	4,405	9	Chapman Ranch	865
10	Claude	4,396	10	Falcon Dam	875
11	Gruver	4,375	11	Rio Grande City 1 SE	910
12	Hereford	4,338	12	Corpus Christi Int'l Airport	924
13	Friona	4,295	13	Laredo 2	953
14	Bravo	4,287	14	Rockport	964
15	Amarillo Int'l Airport	4,268	15	Alice	988
16	Muleshoe 1	4,231	16	Robstown	1,003
17	Silverton	4,218	17	Aransas Wildlife Refuge	1,016
18	Olton	4,123	18	Hebbronville	1,025
19	Tulia	4,120	19	Falfurrias	1,032
20	Panhandle	4,106	20	Point Comfort	1,035
21	Spearman	3,948	21	Goliad	1,045
22	Clarendon Municipal Airport	3,934	22	Matagorda 2	1,054
23	Floydada	3,920	23	Crystal City	1,073
24	Borger	3,903	24	Galveston	1,108
25	Shamrock 2	3,897	25	Mathis 4 SSW	1,116

Number of Annual Cooling Degree Days

	Highest			Lowest	
Rank	**Station Name**	**Num.**	**Rank**	**Station Name**	**Num.**
1	McAllen Miller Int'l Airport	*4,485*	1	Mount Locke	851
2	Zapata 3 SW	*4,441*	2	Stratford	1,154
3	Laredo 2	4,370	3	Bravo	1,171
4	Falcon Dam	4,316	4	Dimmitt 2 N	1,177
5	Rio Grande City 1 SE	4,265	5	Friona	1,189
6	Weslaco 2 E	4,173	6	Dalhart Municipal Airport	1,195
7	McCook	4,098	7	Marfa 2	1,251
8	Brownsville Int'l Airport	4,059	8	Chisos Basin	1,278
9	Raymondville	4,028	9	Olton	1,288
10	Harlingen	3,945	10	Claude	*1,340*
11	Crystal City	3,794	11	Hereford	1,341
12	Falfurrias	3,789	12	Muleshoe 1	1,350
13	Hebbronville	3,765	13	Perryton	1,351
14	Presidio	3,721	14	Dumas	1,368
15	Alice	3,702	15	Tulia	1,386
16	Eagle Pass	3,643	16	Amarillo Int'l Airport	1,399
17	Robstown	3,642	17	Silverton	1,408
18	Tilden 4 SSE	3,605	18	Follett	1,417
19	Goliad	3,561	18	Morton	1,417
20	Corpus Christi Int'l Airport	3,531	20	Panhandle	1,425
21	Charlotte 5 NNW	3,515	21	Gruver	1,437
22	Rockport	3,473	22	Pampa 2	1,451
23	Chapman Ranch	3,469	23	Littlefield 2 NW	1,456
24	Point Comfort	3,454	24	Miami	1,540
25	Dilley	*3,443*	25	Sierra Blanca 2 E	1,563

Annual Precipitation

	Highest			Lowest	
Rank	**Station Name**	**Inches**	**Rank**	**Station Name**	**Inches**
1	Liberty	61.13	1	El Paso Int'l Airport	9.38
2	Sam Rayburn Dam	60.27	2	Ysleta	*9.71*
3	Port Arthur Jefferson County	60.11	3	Presidio	11.08
4	Angleton 2 W	58.37	4	Pecos	11.81
5	Town Bluff Dam	54.81	5	Sierra Blanca 2 E	12.20
6	Anahuac	54.72	6	Wink Winkler Co. Airport	13.10
7	Cleveland	54.57	7	Candelaria	13.11
8	Toledo Bend Dam	*54.51*	8	Penwell	13.29
9	Houston William P. Hobby Airport	54.02	9	Monahans	13.39
10	Center	52.57	10	Fort Stockton	14.35
11	Livingston 2 NNE	51.47	11	Balmorhea	14.42
12	Coldspring 5 SSW	51.40	11	Panther Junction	14.42
13	Carthage	51.08	13	McCamey	14.62
14	Texarkana	51.01	14	Midland Regional Air Terminal	14.82
15	Freeport 2 NW	50.98	15	Langtry	14.90
16	Marshall	50.79	15	Marathon	14.90
17	Sugar Land	50.00	17	Midland 4 ENE	14.91
18	Conroe	49.15	18	Sheffield	15.02
19	Nacogdoches	48.82	19	Andrews	15.04
20	Mount Pleasant	48.31	20	Sanderson	15.15
21	Henderson	48.09	21	Crane	15.49
21	Rusk	48.09	22	Bakersfield	15.58
23	Houston Bush Intercontinental	47.86	23	Marfa 2	16.09
24	Groveton	47.76	24	Muleshoe 1	17.19
25	Huntsville	47.60	25	Garden City 1 E	17.32

Number of Days Annually With ≥ 0.1″ Precipitation

	Highest			Lowest	
Rank	Station Name	Days	Rank	Station Name	Days
1	Liberty	75	1	Sheffield	21
1	Sam Rayburn Dam	75	2	Presidio	22
3	Cleveland	73	3	Midland 4 ENE	23
4	Anahuac	71	3	Pecos	23
4	Center	71	5	El Paso Int'l Airport	24
4	Port Arthur Jefferson County	71	5	Monahans	24
4	Toledo Bend Dam	71	5	Wink Winkler Co. Airport	24
4	Town Bluff Dam	71	8	Langtry	25
9	Angleton 2 W	70	8	Penwell	25
9	Texarkana	70	8	Ysleta	25
11	Coldspring 5 SSW	69	11	McCamey	26
12	Houston William P. Hobby Airport	68	12	Crane	27
12	Livingston 2 NNE	68	13	Balmorhea	28
14	Carthage	67	13	Candelaria	28
14	Marshall	67	13	Fort Stockton	28
14	Nacogdoches	67	13	Midland Regional Air Terminal	28
17	Conroe	66	13	Sanderson	28
17	Huntsville	66	18	Bakersfield	29
17	Lufkin FAA Airport	66	18	Marathon	29
17	Sugar Land	66	18	Panther Junction	29
21	Freeport 2 NW	65	18	Sierra Blanca 2 E	29
21	Pilot Point	65	22	Andrews	30
23	Columbus	64	22	Garden City 1 E	30
23	Crockett	64	22	Ozona 1 SSW	30
23	Gilmer 2 W	64	25	Del Rio Int'l Airport	31

Number of Days Annually With ≥ 1.0″ Precipitation

	Highest			Lowest	
Rank	Station Name	Days	Rank	Station Name	Days
1	Sam Rayburn Dam	21	1	El Paso Int'l Airport	0
2	Marshall	19	1	Ysleta	0
2	Port Arthur Jefferson County	19	3	Pecos	1
4	Center	18	3	Presidio	1
4	Liberty	18	5	Alpine	2
4	Toledo Bend Dam	18	5	Balmorhea	2
7	Carthage	17	5	Candelaria	2
7	Cleveland	17	5	Crane	2
7	Mount Pleasant	17	5	Fort Stockton	2
7	Rusk	17	5	Hereford	2
7	Town Bluff Dam	17	5	Langtry	2
12	Anahuac	16	5	McCamey	2
12	Angleton 2 W	16	5	Midland Regional Air Terminal	2
12	Coldspring 5 SSW	16	5	Monahans	2
12	Houston William P. Hobby Airport	16	5	Muleshoe 1	2
12	Livingston 2 NNE	16	5	Penwell	2
12	Pilot Point	16	5	Sanderson	2
12	Texarkana	16	5	Sierra Blanca 2 E	2
19	Clarksville 2 NE	15	5	Wink Winkler Co. Airport	2
19	Conroe	15	20	Andrews	3
19	Daingerfield 9 S	15	20	Bakersfield	3
19	Danevang 1 W	15	20	Childress Municipal Airport	3
19	Groveton	15	20	Chisos Basin	3
19	Hallettsville 2 N	15	20	Gruver	3
19	Henderson	15	20	Marathon	3

Annual Snowfall

Highest			Lowest		
Rank	**Station Name**	**Inches**	**Rank**	**Station Name**	**Inches**
1	Borger	23.9	1	Falfurrias	0.0
2	Spearman	22.5	1	Port Mansfield	0.0
3	Perryton	20.9	1	Raymondville	0.0
4	Follett	20.4	1	Sheffield	0.0
5	Pampa 2	20.3	5	Alice	Trace
6	Panhandle	20.2	5	Anahuac	Trace
7	Stratford	19.7	5	Angleton 2 W	Trace
8	Dalhart Municipal Airport	19.0	5	Aransas Wildlife Refuge	Trace
9	Lipscomb	17.8	5	Beeville 5 NE	Trace
10	Amarillo Int'l Airport	17.4	5	Brownsville Int'l Airport	Trace
11	Miami	*16.7*	5	Candelaria	Trace
12	Friona	16.2	5	Chapman Ranch	Trace
13	Gruver	*15.9*	5	Charlotte 5 NNW	Trace
14	Tulia	15.0	5	Columbus	Trace
15	Dumas	14.6	5	Conroe	Trace
16	Hereford	*13.6*	5	Corpus Christi Int'l Airport	Trace
17	Claude	*12.0*	5	Danevang 1 W	Trace
18	Silverton	11.7	5	Dilley	*Trace*
19	Canyon	11.4	5	Falcon Dam	Trace
20	Plainview	11.0	5	Fredericksburg	*Trace*
21	Dimmitt 2 N	*10.4*	5	Freeport 2 NW	Trace
22	Lubbock Regional Airport	10.1	5	Galveston	Trace
23	Levelland	10.0	5	Goldthwaite 1 WSW	*Trace*
24	Muleshoe 1	9.6	5	Gonzales 1 N	Trace
25	Matador	9.5	5	Harlingen	Trace

Note: See Appendix D for explanation of data.

Annual Extreme Maximum Temperature

	Highest				Lowest	
Rank	Station Name	°F		Rank	Station Name	°F
1	Saint George	117		1	Silver Lake Brighton	87
2	Hanksville	114		2	Woodruff	94
2	Moab	114		3	Bryce Canyon Nat'l Park Hdqtrs.	95
4	Dewey	113		4	Boulder	96
4	La Verkin	113		4	Laketown	96
4	Zion National Park	113		4	Monticello	96
7	Mexican Hat	110		4	Neola	96
7	Nephi	110		8	Altamont	97
9	Deseret	109		8	Deer Creek Dam	97
9	Dugway	109		10	Koosharem	98
9	Fish Springs Refuge	109		10	Manti	98
12	Bluff	108		10	Mountain Dell Dam	*98*
12	Delta FAA Airport	108		10	Pine View Dam	98
12	Ephraim Sorensens Field	108		10	Wanship Dam	98
12	Kanab	108		15	Alton	99
12	Oak City	108		15	Echo Dam	99
17	Canyonlands The Needle	107		15	Snake Creek Powerhouse	99
17	Dinosaur Nat'l Mon. Quarry Area	107		15	Tropic	99
17	Kanosh	107		19	Cedar Point	100
17	Milford Airport	*107*		19	Fairfield	100
17	Ouray 4 NE	107		19	Flaming Gorge	100
17	Partoun	107		19	Morgan Como Springs	100
17	Veyo Powerhouse	107		23	Logan Utah State University	101
24	Cottonwood Weir	106		23	Panguitch	101
24	Jensen	106		25	Blanding	102

Annual Mean Maximum Temperature

	Highest				Lowest	
Rank	Station Name	°F		Rank	Station Name	°F
1	Saint George	78.3		1	Silver Lake Brighton	48.5
2	La Verkin	75.9		2	Woodruff	54.9
3	Zion National Park	75.2		3	Laketown	56.0
4	Moab	72.8		4	Bryce Canyon Nat'l Park Hdqtrs.	56.2
5	Mexican Hat	71.6		5	Altamont	57.1
6	Dewey	71.0		6	Pine View Dam	57.7
6	Hanksville	71.0		7	Neola	58.4
8	Bluff	70.2		8	Logan Utah State University	58.7
9	Kanab	69.8		9	Snake Creek Powerhouse	58.9
10	Orderville	68.6		10	Flaming Gorge	59.2
10	Veyo Powerhouse	68.6		10	Monticello	59.2
12	Canyonlands The Needle	68.3		12	Deer Creek Dam	59.4
12	Wah Wah Ranch	68.3		13	Logan 5 SW Exp. Farm	59.7
14	Eskdale	66.7		13	Logan Radio KVNU	59.7
15	Black Rock	66.6		15	Echo Dam	60.1
16	Capitol Reef Nat'l Park	66.5		16	Cedar Point	60.3
16	Partoun	66.5		17	Wanship Dam	60.4
18	Oak City	66.3		18	Koosharem	*60.6*
19	Fish Springs Refuge	66.2		19	Richmond	60.7
20	Deseret	66.1		20	Alton	60.8
21	Enterprise Airport	65.8		21	Mountain Dell Dam	*61.0*
21	New Harmony	65.8		22	Vernal Municipal Airport	61.1
23	Escalante	65.7		23	Heber	61.3
23	Ibapah	65.7		23	Manti	61.3
23	Kanosh	65.7		25	Boulder	61.4

Annual Mean Temperature

	Highest			Lowest	
Rank	**Station Name**	**°F**	**Rank**	**Station Name**	**°F**
1	Saint George	62.9	1	Silver Lake Brighton	36.6
2	Zion National Park	61.2	2	Woodruff	39.3
3	La Verkin	60.4	3	Bryce Canyon Nat'l Park Hdqtrs.	41.4
4	Moab	57.3	4	Laketown	42.6
5	Mexican Hat	56.3	5	Altamont	43.4
6	Veyo Powerhouse	55.2	6	Pine View Dam	43.6
7	Kanab	54.6	6	Snake Creek Powerhouse	43.6
8	Capitol Reef Nat'l Park	53.8	8	Deer Creek Dam	43.8
8	Dewey	53.8	8	Koosharem	*43.8*
10	Bluff	53.7	10	Flaming Gorge	44.1
11	Hanksville	53.5	11	Wanship Dam	44.4
12	Canyonlands The Needle	53.3	12	Panguitch	44.9
12	Cottonwood Weir	53.3	13	Echo Dam	45.1
14	Fish Springs Refuge	52.9	13	Neola	45.1
14	Oak City	52.9	15	Heber	45.4
16	Canyonlands The Neck	52.7	16	Logan 5 SW Exp. Farm	45.5
17	Kanosh	52.5	17	Alton	45.8
17	Salt Lake City Int'l Airport	52.5	17	Monticello	45.8
19	Orderville	52.2	19	Vernal Municipal Airport	46.0
20	Wendover USAF Auxiliary Field	52.1	20	Jensen	46.1
21	Ogden Pioneer P H	52.0	20	Myton	46.1
22	Farmington USU Field Station	51.8	22	Moroni	46.3
22	New Harmony	51.8	23	Logan Radio KVNU	46.5
24	Spanish Fork Power House	51.6	24	Roosevelt	46.6
25	Pleasant Grove	51.5	25	Morgan Como Springs	46.7

Annual Mean Minimum Temperature

	Highest			Lowest	
Rank	**Station Name**	**°F**	**Rank**	**Station Name**	**°F**
1	Saint George	47.5	1	Woodruff	23.5
2	Zion National Park	47.2	2	Silver Lake Brighton	24.6
3	La Verkin	44.9	3	Bryce Canyon Nat'l Park Hdqtrs.	26.5
4	Cottonwood Weir	42.6	4	Panguitch	26.9
5	Wendover USAF Auxiliary Field	42.1	5	Koosharem	*27.1*
6	Canyonlands The Neck	41.8	6	Ibapah	27.9
6	Moab	41.8	7	Deer Creek Dam	28.2
6	Veyo Powerhouse	41.8	7	Snake Creek Powerhouse	28.2
9	Capitol Reef Nat'l Park	41.1	9	Wanship Dam	28.4
9	Mexican Hat	41.1	10	Flaming Gorge	28.9
9	Salt Lake City Int'l Airport	41.1	11	Laketown	29.2
12	Ogden Pioneer P H	40.8	12	Pine View Dam	29.5
13	Fish Springs Refuge	39.5	13	Altamont	29.6
13	Oak City	39.5	13	Heber	29.6
15	Tooele	39.4	15	Jensen	29.7
16	Kanab	39.2	16	Enterprise Airport	29.9
17	Kanosh	39.1	17	Echo Dam	30.1
18	Farmington USU Field Station	39.0	18	Moroni	30.3
18	Spanish Fork Power House	39.0	19	Myton	30.4
20	Pleasant Grove	38.8	19	Roosevelt	30.4
21	Canyonlands The Needle	38.3	21	Fairfield	30.7
21	Ogden Sugar Factory	38.3	22	Alton	30.8
23	New Harmony	37.7	23	Vernal Municipal Airport	31.0
24	Natural Bridges Nat'l Monument	37.6	24	Circleville	31.1
25	Blanding	37.4	25	Morgan Como Springs	31.2

Annual Extreme Minimum Temperature

	Highest				Lowest	
Rank	**Station Name**	**°F**		**Rank**	**Station Name**	**°F**
1	La Verkin	1		1	Roosevelt	-47
1	Saint George	1		2	Woodruff	-46
3	Veyo Powerhouse	-3		3	Logan 5 SW Exp. Farm	-44
4	Zion National Park	-5		4	Ouray 4 NE	-43
5	Capitol Reef Nat'l Park	-9		5	Dinosaur Nat'l Mon. Quarry Area	-40
6	Kanab	-10		5	Jensen	-40
7	Cottonwood Weir	-12		7	Deer Creek Dam	-39
7	Ogden Pioneer P H	-12		7	Myton	-39
9	Canyonlands The Neck	-13		7	Pine View Dam	-39
9	Moab	-13		10	Scipio	*-38*
11	Blanding	-14		10	Vernal Municipal Airport	-38
11	Escalante	-14		12	Black Rock	-37
11	Farmington USU Field Station	-14		12	Wanship Dam	-37
11	Natural Bridges Nat'l Monument	-14		14	Fairfield	-36
11	Timpanogos Cave	-14		14	Flaming Gorge	-36
16	Salt Lake City Int'l Airport	-15		14	Heber	-36
17	Canyonlands The Needle	-16		17	Marysvale	-35
17	Mexican Hat	-16		17	Milford Airport	*-35*
17	Tooele	-16		19	Echo Dam	-34
20	Boulder	-17		19	Enterprise Airport	-34
20	Pleasant Grove	-17		19	Ephraim Sorensens Field	-34
22	Ogden Sugar Factory	-18		19	Laketown	-34
22	Tropic	-18		19	Snake Creek Powerhouse	-34
22	Wendover USAF Auxiliary Field	-18		24	Hanksville	-33
25	Fish Springs Refuge	-19		24	Morgan Como Springs	-33

July Mean Maximum Temperature

	Highest				Lowest	
Rank	**Station Name**	**°F**		**Rank**	**Station Name**	**°F**
1	Saint George	102.4		1	Silver Lake Brighton	71.6
2	Moab	99.9		2	Bryce Canyon Nat'l Park Hdqtrs.	79.4
3	Dewey	99.6		3	Woodruff	81.2
4	Zion National Park	99.3		4	Laketown	82.0
5	Hanksville	99.2		5	Altamont	82.7
6	La Verkin	98.8		6	Alton	83.3
7	Mexican Hat	97.7		7	Monticello	84.1
8	Bluff	95.4		8	Koosharem	84.4
9	Canyonlands The Needle	95.0		9	Boulder	84.5
10	Dugway	94.5		9	Neola	84.5
11	Deseret	94.4		9	Snake Creek Powerhouse	84.5
11	Dinosaur Nat'l Mon. Quarry Area	94.4		12	Flaming Gorge	85.2
11	Fish Springs Refuge	94.4		13	Tropic	85.3
14	Wah Wah Ranch	94.2		14	Deer Creek Dam	85.5
15	Oak City	94.1		14	Pine View Dam	85.5
15	Partoun	94.1		16	Cedar Point	85.8
17	Ouray 4 NE	94.0		17	Manti	86.0
18	Eskdale	92.7		18	Panguitch	86.2
19	Delta FAA Airport	92.6		19	Wanship Dam	86.3
20	Black Rock	92.5		20	Logan Utah State University	86.5
21	Kanab	92.4		21	Echo Dam	86.9
22	Kanosh	92.2		22	Heber	87.2
22	Milford Airport	92.2		22	Logan 5 SW Exp. Farm	87.2
24	Nephi	92.1		24	Ferron	87.5
24	Salt Lake City Int'l Airport	92.1		25	Parowan Power Plant	87.8

January Mean Minimum Temperature

	Highest			Lowest	
Rank	**Station Name**	**°F**	**Rank**	**Station Name**	**°F**
1	Zion National Park	29.0	1	Woodruff	3.1
2	Saint George	28.8	2	Ouray 4 NE	3.3
3	La Verkin	27.2	3	Myton	3.6
4	Veyo Powerhouse	25.6	4	Jensen	3.7
5	Kanab	23.0	5	Roosevelt	4.1
6	Cottonwood Weir	22.0	6	Dinosaur Nat'l Mon. Quarry Area	4.8
7	Salt Lake City Int'l Airport	21.3	7	Altamont	6.8
8	Ogden Pioneer P H	20.9	8	Vernal Municipal Airport	6.9
9	New Harmony	20.8	9	Pine View Dam	7.8
10	Farmington USU Field Station	20.4	10	Castle Dale	8.2
11	Spanish Fork Power House	20.2	10	Neola	8.2
12	Pleasant Grove	20.1	12	Deer Creek Dam	8.7
13	Canyonlands The Neck	20.0	13	Silver Lake Brighton	9.1
14	Mexican Hat	19.9	14	Panguitch	9.2
15	Tooele	19.7	15	Flaming Gorge	9.5
16	Oak City	19.6	16	Koosharem	9.6
17	Moab	19.5	17	Bryce Canyon Nat'l Park Hdqtrs.	9.8
18	Timpanogos Cave	19.3	18	Heber	10.3
18	Wendover USAF Auxiliary Field	19.3	19	Snake Creek Powerhouse	10.8
20	Capitol Reef Nat'l Park	19.1	20	Logan 5 SW Exp. Farm	10.9
21	Cedar City Municipal Airport	18.6	21	Wanship Dam	11.1
21	Orderville	18.6	22	Hanksville	11.2
23	Kanosh	18.5	23	Echo Dam	11.3
24	Natural Bridges Nat'l Monument	18.4	24	Ferron	11.4
25	Blanding	18.2	24	Moroni	11.4

Number of Annual Heating Degree Days

	Highest			Lowest	
Rank	**Station Name**	**Num.**	**Rank**	**Station Name**	**Num.**
1	Silver Lake Brighton	10,283	1	Saint George	3,030
2	Woodruff	9,326	2	Zion National Park	3,347
3	Bryce Canyon Nat'l Park Hdqtrs.	8,559	3	La Verkin	3,387
4	Laketown	8,168	4	Moab	4,410
5	Altamont	8,004	5	Veyo Powerhouse	4,511
6	Pine View Dam	7,938	6	Kanab	4,596
7	Snake Creek Powerhouse	7,822	7	Mexican Hat	4,610
8	Deer Creek Dam	7,767	8	Bluff	5,114
9	Flaming Gorge	7,741	9	Capitol Reef Nat'l Park	5,130
10	Koosharem	*7,721*	10	Orderville	5,240
11	Wanship Dam	7,584	11	Dewey	5,298
12	Neola	7,508	12	Canyonlands The Needle	5,355
13	Echo Dam	7,405	13	Cottonwood Weir	5,382
14	Panguitch	7,386	14	New Harmony	5,405
15	Logan 5 SW Exp. Farm	7,375	15	Hanksville	5,418
16	Myton	7,314	16	Oak City	5,506
17	Vernal Municipal Airport	7,295	17	Kanosh	5,538
18	Heber	7,274	18	Salt Lake City Int'l Airport	5,550
19	Jensen	7,271	19	Canyonlands The Neck	5,556
20	Roosevelt	7,181	20	Fish Springs Refuge	5,583
21	Monticello	7,151	21	Pleasant Grove	5,647
22	Logan Radio KVNU	7,122	22	Farmington USU Field Station	5,649
23	Alton	7,038	23	Ogden Pioneer P H	5,652
24	Moroni	7,011	24	Spanish Fork Power House	5,670
25	Ouray 4 NE	*6,982*	25	Wah Wah Ranch	5,728

Number of Annual Cooling Degree Days

Highest			Lowest		
Rank	Station Name	Num.	Rank	Station Name	Num.
1	Saint George	2,515	1	Silver Lake Brighton	5
2	Zion National Park	2,065	2	Woodruff	39
3	La Verkin	1,946	3	Bryce Canyon Nat'l Park Hdqtrs.	45
4	Moab	1,752	4	Laketown	123
5	Mexican Hat	1,591	5	Snake Creek Powerhouse	139
6	Hanksville	1,341	6	Alton	141
7	Dewey	1,314	7	Deer Creek Dam	143
8	Cottonwood Weir	1,251	8	Panguitch	157
9	Fish Springs Refuge	1,244	9	Wanship Dam	185
10	Wendover USAF Auxiliary Field	1,205	10	Flaming Gorge	208
11	Oak City	1,194	11	Altamont	220
12	Canyonlands The Needle	1,184	12	Pine View Dam	250
13	Salt Lake City Int'l Airport	1,145	13	Monticello	251
14	Bluff	1,136	14	Echo Dam	252
15	Canyonlands The Neck	1,132	15	Heber	260
15	Capitol Reef Nat'l Park	1,132	16	Tropic	287
17	Kanosh	1,083	17	Moroni	307
18	Ogden Pioneer P H	1,046	18	Ibapah	309
19	Dugway	1,038	19	Circleville	335
20	Veyo Powerhouse	1,037	20	Marysvale	336
21	Farmington USU Field Station	998	21	Neola	352
22	Tooele	959	22	Cedar Point	353
23	Ogden Sugar Factory	941	23	Logan 5 SW Exp. Farm	374
24	Kanab	935	24	Fairfield	380
25	Spanish Fork Power House	922	25	Morgan Como Springs	386

Annual Precipitation

Highest			Lowest		
Rank	Station Name	Inches	Rank	Station Name	Inches
1	Silver Lake Brighton	43.85	1	Wendover USAF Auxiliary Field	4.84
2	Pine View Dam	32.59	2	Hanksville	5.75
3	Cottonwood Weir	26.27	3	Callao	6.28
4	Timpanogos Cave	25.66	4	Eskdale	6.54
5	Mountain Dell Dam	*24.40*	5	Mexican Hat	6.65
6	Ogden Pioneer P H	23.91	6	Wah Wah Ranch	6.81
7	Farmington USU Field Station	23.40	7	Myton	7.05
8	Deer Creek Dam	23.35	8	Partoun	7.11
9	Snake Creek Powerhouse	22.33	9	Ouray 4 NE	7.31
10	Spanish Fork Power House	21.74	10	Roosevelt	7.32
11	Richmond	20.49	11	Capitol Reef Nat'l Park	7.66
12	Logan Utah State University	20.15	12	Castle Dale	7.80
13	Tooele	19.82	13	Bluff	8.01
14	Morgan Como Springs	19.23	14	Marysvale	8.19
15	Logan 5 SW Exp. Farm	19.03	15	Fish Springs Refuge	8.24
16	Ogden Sugar Factory	18.55	16	Delta FAA Airport	8.38
17	Santaquin Chlorinator	18.30	17	Jensen	8.45
18	New Harmony	18.13	18	Richfield Radio KSVC	8.52
19	Corinne	18.01	19	Canyonlands The Needle	8.55
20	Logan Radio KVNU	17.94	20	Dugway	8.60
21	Pleasant Grove	17.54	21	Ferron	8.63
22	Johnson Pass	17.43	22	Deseret	8.69
23	Salt Lake City Int'l Airport	16.62	23	Vernal Municipal Airport	8.77
23	Wanship Dam	16.62	24	Saint George	8.81
25	Alton	16.55	25	Circleville	9.04

Number of Days Annually With ≥ 0.1″ Precipitation

	Highest			Lowest	
Rank	Station Name	Days	Rank	Station Name	Days
1	Silver Lake Brighton	93	1	Wendover USAF Auxiliary Field	16
2	Pine View Dam	67	2	Hanksville	18
3	Mountain Dell Dam	*60*	3	Callao	19
4	Snake Creek Powerhouse	59	4	Eskdale	20
4	Timpanogos Cave	59	4	Myton	20
6	Cottonwood Weir	58	6	Ouray 4 NE	22
7	Logan Utah State University	56	7	Capitol Reef Nat'l Park	23
8	Ogden Pioneer P H	55	7	Mexican Hat	23
8	Richmond	55	7	Partoun	*23*
8	Spanish Fork Power House	55	7	Wah Wah Ranch	23
11	Deer Creek Dam	54	11	Castle Dale	24
11	Morgan Como Springs	54	12	Bluff	25
13	Farmington USU Field Station	53	12	Roosevelt	25
13	Logan 5 SW Exp. Farm	53	12	Saint George	25
15	Wanship Dam	52	15	Deseret	26
16	Logan Radio KVNU	51	15	Moab	26
16	Pleasant Grove	51	17	Canyonlands The Neck	27
18	Tooele	49	17	Canyonlands The Needle	*27*
19	Echo Dam	48	17	Delta FAA Airport	27
19	Nephi	48	17	Ferron	27
21	Corinne	47	17	Fish Springs Refuge	27
21	Heber	47	17	Ibapah	*27*
23	Fillmore	46	17	Richfield Radio KSVC	27
23	Johnson Pass	*46*	17	Vernal Municipal Airport	27
23	Levan	46	25	Black Rock	28

Number of Days Annually With ≥ 1.0″ Precipitation

	Highest			Lowest	
Rank	Station Name	Days	Rank	Station Name	Days
1	Pine View Dam	8	1	Altamont	0
2	Silver Lake Brighton	7	1	Alton	0
3	New Harmony	3	1	Black Rock	0
4	Cottonwood Weir	2	1	Blanding	0
4	Deer Creek Dam	2	1	Bluff	0
4	Timpanogos Cave	2	1	Boulder	0
7	Farmington USU Field Station	1	1	Bryce Canyon Nat'l Park Hdqtrs.	0
7	Mountain Dell Dam	*1*	1	Callao	0
7	Ogden Pioneer P H	1	1	Canyonlands The Neck	0
7	Veyo Powerhouse	1	1	Canyonlands The Needle	0
11	Altamont	0	1	Capitol Reef Nat'l Park	0
11	Alton	0	1	Castle Dale	0
11	Black Rock	0	1	Cedar City Municipal Airport	0
11	Blanding	0	1	Cedar Point	0
11	Bluff	0	1	Circleville	0
11	Boulder	0	1	Corinne	0
11	Bryce Canyon Nat'l Park Hdqtrs.	0	1	Delta FAA Airport	0
11	Callao	0	1	Deseret	0
11	Canyonlands The Neck	0	1	Dewey	0
11	Canyonlands The Needle	0	1	Dinosaur Nat'l Mon. Quarry Area	0
11	Capitol Reef Nat'l Park	0	1	Dugway	0
11	Castle Dale	0	1	Echo Dam	0
11	Cedar City Municipal Airport	0	1	Enterprise Airport	0
11	Cedar Point	0	1	Ephraim Sorensens Field	0
11	Circleville	0	1	Escalante	0

Annual Snowfall

	Highest				Lowest	
Rank	**Station Name**	**Inches**		**Rank**	**Station Name**	**Inches**
1	Silver Lake Brighton	428.6		1	Saint George	*2.0*
2	Pine View Dam	125.0		2	La Verkin	3.2
3	Cottonwood Weir	*104.7*		3	Veyo Powerhouse	*4.5*
4	Alton	*92.5*		4	Hanksville	*5.0*
5	Bryce Canyon Nat'l Park Hdqtrs.	*88.6*		5	Zion National Park	6.8
6	Tooele	86.5		6	Bluff	*9.8*
7	Kanosh	*82.4*		7	Dewey	*10.1*
8	Fillmore	81.6		8	Callao	*10.6*
9	Cedar Point	76.8		9	Canyonlands The Needle	*14.0*
10	Timpanogos Cave	*75.7*		9	Fish Springs Refuge	14.0
11	Morgan Como Springs	75.1		9	Myton	*14.0*
12	Echo Dam	73.9		12	Eskdale	*14.5*
13	Johnson Pass	*72.4*		13	Dugway	14.7
14	Heber	71.7		14	Capitol Reef Nat'l Park	15.7
15	Parowan Power Plant	69.7		15	Marysvale	*15.9*
16	Monticello	69.4		16	Ouray 4 NE	*16.3*
17	Richmond	68.8		17	Deseret	18.3
18	Spanish Fork Power House	*67.5*		18	Roosevelt	*19.4*
19	Logan Utah State University	64.3		19	Castle Dale	19.6
20	Salt Lake City Int'l Airport	62.9		20	Thiokol Plant 78	*21.6*
21	Flaming Gorge	60.5		21	Dinosaur Nat'l Mon. Quarry Area	21.9
22	Manti	59.6		22	Jensen	22.6
23	Santaquin Chlorinator	*57.5*		23	Tropic	*23.0*
24	Nephi	*55.8*		24	Canyonlands The Neck	23.2
25	Laketown	*54.1*		24	Circleville	23.2

Note: See Appendix D for explanation of data.

Annual Extreme Maximum Temperature

Highest				Lowest		
Rank	**Station Name**	**°F**		**Rank**	**Station Name**	**°F**
1	Bellows Falls	100		1	Mount Mansfield	84
1	Burlington Int'l Airport	100		2	Enosburg Falls	95
1	Cornwall	*100*		3	Newport	96
1	Vernon	100		3	West Burke	96
5	Chelsea	99		5	Montpelier Airport	97
5	Saint Johnsbury	99		6	Cavendish	98
5	South Hero	99		6	Readsboro 1 SE	98
8	Cavendish	98		6	Rochester	98
8	Readsboro 1 SE	98		6	Rutland	98
8	Rochester	98		10	Chelsea	99
8	Rutland	98		10	Saint Johnsbury	99
12	Montpelier Airport	97		10	South Hero	99
13	Newport	96		13	Bellows Falls	100
13	West Burke	96		13	Burlington Int'l Airport	100
15	Enosburg Falls	95		13	Cornwall	*100*
16	Mount Mansfield	84		13	Vernon	100

Annual Mean Maximum Temperature

Highest				Lowest		
Rank	**Station Name**	**°F**		**Rank**	**Station Name**	**°F**
1	Vernon	58.5		1	Mount Mansfield	41.6
2	Rutland	57.2		2	West Burke	52.1
3	Bellows Falls	56.4		3	Montpelier Airport	52.3
4	Saint Johnsbury	56.1		4	Newport	53.7
5	Cornwall	*55.9*		5	Chelsea	54.2
6	Cavendish	55.5		6	Burlington Int'l Airport	54.5
7	Enosburg Falls	55.3		6	South Hero	54.5
8	Rochester	55.0		8	Readsboro 1 SE	54.8
9	Readsboro 1 SE	54.8		9	Rochester	55.0
10	Burlington Int'l Airport	54.5		10	Enosburg Falls	55.3
10	South Hero	54.5		11	Cavendish	55.5
12	Chelsea	54.2		12	Cornwall	*55.9*
13	Newport	53.7		13	Saint Johnsbury	56.1
14	Montpelier Airport	52.3		14	Bellows Falls	56.4
15	West Burke	52.1		15	Rutland	57.2
16	Mount Mansfield	41.6		16	Vernon	58.5

Annual Mean Temperature

	Highest				Lowest	
Rank	Station Name	°F		Rank	Station Name	°F
1	Vernon	47.0		1	Mount Mansfield	34.4
2	Rutland	46.3		2	West Burke	39.3
3	Bellows Falls	45.8		3	Chelsea	41.2
3	South Hero	45.8		4	Montpelier Airport	42.8
5	Cornwall	*45.7*		5	Rochester	42.9
6	Burlington Int'l Airport	45.2		6	Newport	43.0
7	Saint Johnsbury	44.7		7	Cavendish	43.6
8	Enosburg Falls	44.0		8	Readsboro 1 SE	43.8
9	Readsboro 1 SE	43.8		9	Enosburg Falls	44.0
10	Cavendish	43.6		10	Saint Johnsbury	44.7
11	Newport	43.0		11	Burlington Int'l Airport	45.2
12	Rochester	42.9		12	Cornwall	*45.7*
13	Montpelier Airport	42.8		13	Bellows Falls	45.8
14	Chelsea	41.2		13	South Hero	45.8
15	West Burke	39.3		15	Rutland	46.3
16	Mount Mansfield	34.4		16	Vernon	47.0

Annual Mean Minimum Temperature

	Highest				Lowest	
Rank	Station Name	°F		Rank	Station Name	°F
1	South Hero	37.1		1	West Burke	26.4
2	Burlington Int'l Airport	35.8		2	Mount Mansfield	27.1
3	Cornwall	*35.4*		3	Chelsea	28.2
3	Vernon	35.4		4	Rochester	30.7
5	Rutland	35.3		5	Cavendish	31.7
6	Bellows Falls	35.1		6	Newport	32.2
7	Saint Johnsbury	33.3		7	Enosburg Falls	32.6
8	Montpelier Airport	33.1		8	Readsboro 1 SE	32.7
9	Readsboro 1 SE	32.7		9	Montpelier Airport	33.1
10	Enosburg Falls	32.6		10	Saint Johnsbury	33.3
11	Newport	32.2		11	Bellows Falls	35.1
12	Cavendish	31.7		12	Rutland	35.3
13	Rochester	30.7		13	Cornwall	*35.4*
14	Chelsea	28.2		13	Vernon	35.4
15	Mount Mansfield	27.1		15	Burlington Int'l Airport	35.8
16	West Burke	26.4		16	South Hero	37.1

Annual Extreme Minimum Temperature

	Highest				Lowest	
Rank	Station Name	°F		Rank	Station Name	°F
1	Bellows Falls	-23		1	Enosburg Falls	-41
2	Readsboro 1 SE	-25		2	Mount Mansfield	-38
2	Vernon	-25		2	Newport	-38
4	Burlington Int'l Airport	-30		2	West Burke	-38
4	Cornwall	*-30*		5	Cavendish	-36
6	South Hero	-31		5	Chelsea	-36
7	Rochester	-32		5	Rutland	-36
7	Saint Johnsbury	-32		8	Montpelier Airport	-34
9	Montpelier Airport	-34		9	Rochester	-32
10	Cavendish	-36		9	Saint Johnsbury	-32
10	Chelsea	-36		11	South Hero	-31
10	Rutland	-36		12	Burlington Int'l Airport	-30
13	Mount Mansfield	-38		12	Cornwall	*-30*
13	Newport	-38		14	Readsboro 1 SE	-25
13	West Burke	-38		14	Vernon	-25
16	Enosburg Falls	-41		16	Bellows Falls	-23

July Mean Maximum Temperature

	Highest				Lowest	
Rank	Station Name	°F		Rank	Station Name	°F
1	Vernon	83.8		1	Mount Mansfield	65.5
2	Saint Johnsbury	82.3		2	Montpelier Airport	78.5
3	Rutland	82.1		3	West Burke	79.1
4	Cornwall	81.8		4	Readsboro 1 SE	79.4
5	Bellows Falls	81.7		5	Rochester	79.7
6	Burlington Int'l Airport	81.2		6	Newport	79.8
7	Cavendish	81.0		7	Chelsea	79.9
8	South Hero	80.9		8	Enosburg Falls	80.4
9	Enosburg Falls	80.4		9	South Hero	80.9
10	Chelsea	79.9		10	Cavendish	81.0
11	Newport	79.8		11	Burlington Int'l Airport	81.2
12	Rochester	79.7		12	Bellows Falls	81.7
13	Readsboro 1 SE	79.4		13	Cornwall	81.8
14	West Burke	79.1		14	Rutland	82.1
15	Montpelier Airport	78.5		15	Saint Johnsbury	82.3
16	Mount Mansfield	65.5		16	Vernon	83.8

January Mean Minimum Temperature

	Highest				Lowest	
Rank	Station Name	°F		Rank	Station Name	°F
1	Rutland	10.8		1	West Burke	-1.8
2	Vernon	10.0		2	Chelsea	0.7
3	South Hero	9.9		3	Mount Mansfield	1.1
4	Cornwall	9.6		4	Newport	4.3
5	Bellows Falls	9.2		5	Enosburg Falls	5.0
6	Readsboro 1 SE	9.0		5	Rochester	5.0
7	Burlington Int'l Airport	8.7		7	Cavendish	5.7
8	Montpelier Airport	6.9		8	Saint Johnsbury	6.5
9	Saint Johnsbury	6.5		9	Montpelier Airport	6.9
10	Cavendish	5.7		10	Burlington Int'l Airport	8.7
11	Enosburg Falls	5.0		11	Readsboro 1 SE	9.0
11	Rochester	5.0		12	Bellows Falls	9.2
13	Newport	4.3		13	Cornwall	9.6
14	Mount Mansfield	1.1		14	South Hero	9.9
15	Chelsea	0.7		15	Vernon	10.0
16	West Burke	-1.8		16	Rutland	10.8

Number of Annual Heating Degree Days

	Highest				Lowest	
Rank	Station Name	Num.		Rank	Station Name	Num.
1	Mount Mansfield	11,083		1	Vernon	7,014
2	West Burke	9,465		2	Rutland	7,172
3	Chelsea	8,789		3	Bellows Falls	7,367
4	Montpelier Airport	8,301		4	Cornwall	*7,406*
5	Newport	8,264		5	South Hero	7,408
6	Rochester	8,209		6	Burlington Int'l Airport	7,629
7	Cavendish	8,011		7	Saint Johnsbury	7,733
8	Enosburg Falls	7,925		8	Readsboro 1 SE	7,909
9	Readsboro 1 SE	7,909		9	Enosburg Falls	7,925
10	Saint Johnsbury	7,733		10	Cavendish	8,011
11	Burlington Int'l Airport	7,629		11	Rochester	8,209
12	South Hero	7,408		12	Newport	8,264
13	Cornwall	*7,406*		13	Montpelier Airport	8,301
14	Bellows Falls	7,367		14	Chelsea	8,789
15	Rutland	7,172		15	West Burke	9,465
16	Vernon	7,014		16	Mount Mansfield	11,083

Number of Annual Cooling Degree Days

	Highest			Lowest	
Rank	**Station Name**	**Num.**	**Rank**	**Station Name**	**Num.**
1	Vernon	579	1	Mount Mansfield	25
2	South Hero	523	2	West Burke	188
3	Burlington Int'l Airport	505	3	Chelsea	194
4	Bellows Falls	*475*	4	Rochester	244
5	Cornwall	*455*	5	Readsboro 1 SE	*263*
6	Saint Johnsbury	428	6	Montpelier Airport	*283*
7	Rutland	424	7	Cavendish	316
8	Enosburg Falls	371	8	Newport	341
9	Newport	341	9	Enosburg Falls	371
10	Cavendish	316	10	Rutland	424
11	Montpelier Airport	*283*	11	Saint Johnsbury	428
12	Readsboro 1 SE	*263*	12	Cornwall	*455*
13	Rochester	244	13	Bellows Falls	*475*
14	Chelsea	194	14	Burlington Int'l Airport	505
15	West Burke	188	15	South Hero	523
16	Mount Mansfield	25	16	Vernon	579

Annual Precipitation

	Highest			Lowest	
Rank	**Station Name**	**Inches**	**Rank**	**Station Name**	**Inches**
1	Mount Mansfield	77.88	1	South Hero	32.59
2	Readsboro 1 SE	50.97	2	Montpelier Airport	35.50
3	Rochester	47.42	3	Burlington Int'l Airport	35.82
4	Vernon	47.04	4	Cornwall	*36.04*
5	Cavendish	45.65	5	Saint Johnsbury	38.15
6	Enosburg Falls	43.48	6	Chelsea	38.40
7	West Burke	42.12	7	Rutland	38.63
8	Newport	40.55	8	Bellows Falls	40.33
9	Bellows Falls	40.33	9	Newport	40.55
10	Rutland	38.63	10	West Burke	42.12
11	Chelsea	38.40	11	Enosburg Falls	43.48
12	Saint Johnsbury	38.15	12	Cavendish	45.65
13	Cornwall	*36.04*	13	Vernon	47.04
14	Burlington Int'l Airport	35.82	14	Rochester	47.42
15	Montpelier Airport	35.50	15	Readsboro 1 SE	50.97
16	South Hero	32.59	16	Mount Mansfield	77.88

Number of Days Annually With ≥ 0.1″ Precipitation

Highest			Lowest		
Rank	Station Name	Days	Rank	Station Name	Days
1	Mount Mansfield	151	1	South Hero	74
2	Enosburg Falls	*105*	2	Cornwall	*78*
3	Newport	97	3	Bellows Falls	81
3	West Burke	97	3	Burlington Int'l Airport	81
5	Rochester	93	3	Montpelier Airport	81
6	Readsboro 1 SE	*92*	6	Rutland	*82*
7	Cavendish	85	7	Vernon	83
7	Saint Johnsbury	85	8	Chelsea	84
9	Chelsea	84	9	Cavendish	85
10	Vernon	83	9	Saint Johnsbury	85
11	Rutland	*82*	11	Readsboro 1 SE	*92*
12	Bellows Falls	81	12	Rochester	93
12	Burlington Int'l Airport	81	13	Newport	97
12	Montpelier Airport	81	13	West Burke	97
15	Cornwall	*78*	15	Enosburg Falls	*105*
16	South Hero	74	16	Mount Mansfield	151

Number of Days Annually With ≥ 1.0″ Precipitation

Highest			Lowest		
Rank	Station Name	Days	Rank	Station Name	Days
1	Mount Mansfield	18	1	Burlington Int'l Airport	5
2	Readsboro 1 SE	13	1	Cornwall	*5*
3	Bellows Falls	12	1	Montpelier Airport	5
3	Cavendish	12	1	Newport	5
3	Rochester	12	1	Rutland	5
3	Vernon	12	1	South Hero	5
7	Chelsea	8	1	West Burke	5
8	Enosburg Falls	7	8	Saint Johnsbury	6
9	Saint Johnsbury	6	9	Enosburg Falls	7
10	Burlington Int'l Airport	5	10	Chelsea	8
10	Cornwall	*5*	11	Bellows Falls	12
10	Montpelier Airport	5	11	Cavendish	12
10	Newport	5	11	Rochester	12
10	Rutland	5	11	Vernon	12
10	South Hero	5	15	Readsboro 1 SE	13
10	West Burke	5	16	Mount Mansfield	18

Annual Snowfall

	Highest				Lowest	
Rank	**Station Name**	**Inches**		**Rank**	**Station Name**	**Inches**
1	Mount Mansfield	222.0		1	South Hero	50.6
2	Montpelier Airport	97.9		2	Vernon	*56.6*
2	Newport	97.9		3	Cornwall	*63.1*
4	West Burke	95.4		4	Rutland	65.4
5	Enosburg Falls	91.9		5	Bellows Falls	66.7
6	Cavendish	90.0		6	Readsboro 1 SE	*78.9*
7	Saint Johnsbury	88.3		7	Chelsea	80.3
8	Rochester	87.8		8	Burlington Int'l Airport	81.6
9	Burlington Int'l Airport	81.6		9	Rochester	87.8
10	Chelsea	80.3		10	Saint Johnsbury	88.3
11	Readsboro 1 SE	*78.9*		11	Cavendish	90.0
12	Bellows Falls	66.7		12	Enosburg Falls	91.9
13	Rutland	65.4		13	West Burke	95.4
14	Cornwall	*63.1*		14	Montpelier Airport	97.9
15	Vernon	*56.6*		14	Newport	97.9
16	South Hero	50.6		16	Mount Mansfield	222.0

Note: See Appendix D for explanation of data.

Annual Extreme Maximum Temperature

	Highest			Lowest	
Rank	Station Name	°F	Rank	Station Name	°F
1	Charlottesville 2 W	105	1	Burkes Garden	94
1	Dale Enterprise	105	1	Wise 3 E	94
1	Danville	105	3	Big Meadows	95
1	Farmville 2 N	105	4	Floyd 2 NE	97
1	John H. Kerr Dam	105	4	Galax Radio WBRF	97
1	Langley AFB	105	6	Wytheville 1 S	98
1	Lincoln	105	7	Blacksburg WSO	99
1	Luray 5 E	105	7	Mount Weather	99
1	Richmond R.E. Byrd Int'l Airport	105	7	Painter 2 W	99
1	Roanoke Woodrum Airport	105	7	Pulaski	99
1	Tye River 1 SE	105	11	Abingdon 3 S	100
1	Washington DC National Airport	105	11	Bedford	100
1	Woodstock 2 NE	105	11	Hot Springs	*100*
14	Buchanan	*104*	11	Lexington	100
14	Corbin	104	11	Staffordsville 3 ENE	100
14	Holland 1 E	104	11	Stuart	*100*
14	Norfolk Int'l Airport	104	11	Suffolk Lake Kilby	100
14	Warrenton 3 SE	104	18	Pennington Gap	101
14	Washington DC Dulles Int'l Arpt.	104	19	Back Bay Wildlife Refuge	102
14	West Point 2 NW	104	19	Chatham	102
14	Williamsburg 2 N	104	19	Grundy	102
22	Appomattox	103	19	Lawrenceville 3 E	102
22	Ashland	103	19	Louisa	102
22	Camp Pickett	103	19	Lynchburg Municipal Airport	102
22	Charlotte Court House	103	19	Philpott Dam 2	102

Annual Mean Maximum Temperature

	Highest			Lowest	
Rank	Station Name	°F	Rank	Station Name	°F
1	Lawrenceville 3 E	70.4	1	Big Meadows	55.9
2	Danville	70.1	2	Mount Weather	58.9
2	Williamsburg 2 N	70.1	3	Burkes Garden	60.4
4	Holland 1 E	70.0	4	Blacksburg WSO	63.2
5	John H. Kerr Dam	69.8	4	Hot Springs	63.2
5	West Point 2 NW	69.8	6	Wise 3 E	63.7
7	Farmville 2 N	69.5	7	Floyd 2 NE	63.8
7	Walkerton 2 NW	69.5	8	Galax Radio WBRF	64.1
9	Suffolk Lake Kilby	69.3	9	Dale Enterprise	65.0
10	Richmond R.E. Byrd Int'l Airport	69.2	10	Pulaski	65.1
11	Camp Pickett	68.9	10	Staffordsville 3 ENE	65.1
12	Norfolk Int'l Airport	68.8	12	Wytheville 1 S	65.2
12	Warsaw 2 NW	68.8	13	Warrenton 3 SE	65.5
14	Buchanan	*68.6*	14	Washington DC Dulles Int'l Arpt.	65.6
15	Charlotte Court House	68.2	15	Luray 5 E	65.9
15	Chatham	68.2	15	Piedmont Research Station	65.9
15	Grundy	68.2	17	Corbin	66.7
18	Tye River 1 SE	68.1	17	Stuart	66.7
19	Ashland	67.9	19	Lynchburg Municipal Airport	66.8
19	Louisa	67.9	19	Rocky Mount	66.8
19	Pennington Gap	67.9	21	Abingdon 3 S	66.9
22	Philpott Dam 2	67.8	21	Roanoke Woodrum Airport	66.9
23	Langley AFB	67.6	23	Charlottesville 2 W	67.0
24	Painter 2 W	67.5	23	Washington DC National Airport	67.0
25	Lexington	67.3	25	Appomattox	67.1

Annual Mean Temperature

	Highest			Lowest	
Rank	**Station Name**	**°F**	**Rank**	**Station Name**	**°F**
1	Norfolk Int'l Airport	60.2	1	Big Meadows	46.6
2	Langley AFB	59.6	2	Burkes Garden	49.1
3	Suffolk Lake Kilby	59.3	3	Mount Weather	51.0
4	Williamsburg 2 N	58.7	4	Hot Springs	51.4
5	Holland 1 E	58.6	5	Blacksburg WSO	51.5
6	West Point 2 NW	58.4	6	Floyd 2 NE	51.6
7	John H. Kerr Dam	58.3	7	Galax Radio WBRF	52.4
7	Richmond R.E. Byrd Int'l Airport	58.3	8	Wytheville 1 S	52.6
9	Danville	58.2	9	Pulaski	53.0
9	Painter 2 W	58.2	10	Luray 5 E	53.1
9	Washington DC National Airport	58.2	11	Staffordsville 3 ENE	53.3
12	Warsaw 2 NW	58.0	12	Dale Enterprise	53.5
13	Walkerton 2 NW	57.9	13	Wise 3 E	53.6
14	Lawrenceville 3 E	57.8	14	Abingdon 3 S	54.4
15	Farmville 2 N	57.2	14	Washington DC Dulles Int'l Arpt.	54.4
16	Ashland	56.9	16	Woodstock 2 NE	54.5
17	Charlottesville 2 W	56.7	17	Chatham	*54.6*
18	Bedford	56.5	17	Warrenton 3 SE	54.6
18	Buchanan	*56.5*	19	Pennington Gap	55.0
18	Charlotte Court House	56.5	20	Grundy	55.3
21	Camp Pickett	56.4	20	Lexington	55.3
22	Lynchburg Municipal Airport	56.3	22	Piedmont Research Station	55.4
22	Roanoke Woodrum Airport	56.3	23	Rocky Mount	55.5
22	Tye River 1 SE	56.3	24	Appomattox	55.6
25	Philpott Dam 2	56.1	25	Lincoln	55.7

Annual Mean Minimum Temperature

	Highest			Lowest	
Rank	**Station Name**	**°F**	**Rank**	**Station Name**	**°F**
1	Langley AFB	51.6	1	Big Meadows	37.2
1	Norfolk Int'l Airport	51.6	2	Burkes Garden	37.8
3	Washington DC National Airport	49.5	3	Floyd 2 NE	39.3
4	Suffolk Lake Kilby	49.2	4	Blacksburg WSO	39.6
5	Painter 2 W	48.9	4	Hot Springs	39.6
6	Richmond R.E. Byrd Int'l Airport	47.4	6	Wytheville 1 S	40.0
7	Williamsburg 2 N	47.3	7	Luray 5 E	40.2
8	Holland 1 E	47.2	8	Galax Radio WBRF	40.6
9	Warsaw 2 NW	47.1	9	Pulaski	40.8
9	West Point 2 NW	47.1	10	Chatham	*41.0*
11	John H. Kerr Dam	46.8	11	Staffordsville 3 ENE	41.5
12	Charlottesville 2 W	46.3	12	Abingdon 3 S	41.8
12	Danville	46.3	13	Dale Enterprise	41.9
14	Walkerton 2 NW	46.2	13	Woodstock 2 NE	41.9
15	Bedford	46.0	15	Pennington Gap	42.0
16	Ashland	45.8	16	Grundy	42.3
16	Lynchburg Municipal Airport	45.8	17	Mount Weather	42.9
18	Roanoke Woodrum Airport	45.7	18	Washington DC Dulles Int'l Arpt.	43.0
19	Stuart	45.3	19	Lexington	43.2
20	Lawrenceville 3 E	45.1	20	Wise 3 E	43.6
21	Charlotte Court House	44.8	21	Warrenton 3 SE	43.7
21	Corbin	44.8	22	Camp Pickett	43.8
21	Farmville 2 N	44.8	23	Lincoln	44.0
24	Piedmont Research Station	44.7	24	Louisa	44.1
25	Buchanan	*44.4*	25	Appomattox	44.2

Annual Extreme Minimum Temperature

	Highest				Lowest	
Rank	Station Name	°F		Rank	Station Name	°F
1	Painter 2 W	-1		1	Big Meadows	-29
2	Langley AFB	-3		2	Burkes Garden	-26
2	Norfolk Int'l Airport	-3		3	Pennington Gap	-25
4	Danville	-5		4	Wise 3 E	-24
4	Holland 1 E	-5		5	Abingdon 3 S	-21
4	John H. Kerr Dam	-5		5	Louisa	-21
4	Suffolk Lake Kilby	-5		7	Hot Springs	-20
4	Washington DC National Airport	-5		7	Wytheville 1 S	-20
9	Warsaw 2 NW	-6		9	Floyd 2 NE	-19
10	West Point 2 NW	-7		10	Blacksburg WSO	-18
10	Williamsburg 2 N	-7		10	Galax Radio WBRF	-18
12	Charlotte Court House	-8		10	Staffordsville 3 ENE	-18
12	Richmond R.E. Byrd Int'l Airport	-8		10	Washington DC Dulles Int'l Arpt.	-18
14	Chatham	-9		14	Woodstock 2 NE	-17
14	Farmville 2 N	-9		15	Pulaski	-16
16	Bedford	-10		16	Lexington	-15
16	Charlottesville 2 W	-10		16	Mount Weather	-15
16	Lawrenceville 3 E	-10		18	Appomattox	-14
16	Lincoln	-10		18	Grundy	-14
16	Lynchburg Municipal Airport	-10		18	Luray 5 E	-14
16	Philpott Dam 2	-10		21	Buchanan	*-13*
16	Tye River 1 SE	-10		21	Dale Enterprise	-13
23	Ashland	-11		21	Stuart	*-13*
23	Back Bay Wildlife Refuge	-11		24	Camp Pickett	-12
23	Corbin	-11		24	Walkerton 2 NW	-12

July Mean Maximum Temperature

	Highest				Lowest	
Rank	Station Name	°F		Rank	Station Name	°F
1	Danville	90.1		1	Big Meadows	75.5
2	West Point 2 NW	89.5		2	Burkes Garden	78.9
3	John H. Kerr Dam	89.3		3	Mount Weather	80.5
4	Richmond R.E. Byrd Int'l Airport	89.2		4	Wise 3 E	81.4
5	Farmville 2 N	89.1		5	Floyd 2 NE	82.0
6	Lawrenceville 3 E	89.0		6	Blacksburg WSO	82.8
6	Williamsburg 2 N	89.0		7	Galax Radio WBRF	82.9
8	Warsaw 2 NW	88.8		8	Hot Springs	83.4
9	Holland 1 E	88.7		9	Pulaski	84.0
9	Walkerton 2 NW	88.7		9	Staffordsville 3 ENE	84.0
9	Washington DC National Airport	88.7		11	Wytheville 1 S	84.3
12	Camp Pickett	88.5		12	Abingdon 3 S	85.4
13	Lincoln	88.2		13	Bedford	85.8
14	Buchanan	88.1		13	Stuart	85.8
14	Suffolk Lake Kilby	88.1		15	Luray 5 E	86.0
16	Woodstock 2 NE	88.0		16	Dale Enterprise	86.1
17	Norfolk Int'l Airport	87.9		16	Warrenton 3 SE	86.1
18	Charlotte Court House	87.6		18	Pennington Gap	86.4
19	Washington DC Dulles Int'l Arpt.	87.5		19	Piedmont Research Station	86.5
20	Chatham	87.4		20	Lexington	86.6
20	Louisa	87.4		20	Lynchburg Municipal Airport	86.6
22	Ashland	87.3		20	Rocky Mount	86.6
22	Charlottesville 2 W	87.3		23	Langley AFB	86.7
22	Grundy	87.3		24	Philpott Dam 2	87.0
22	Tye River 1 SE	87.3		25	Back Bay Wildlife Refuge	*87.1*

January Mean Minimum Temperature

Highest			Lowest		
Rank	**Station Name**	**°F**	**Rank**	**Station Name**	**°F**
1	Norfolk Int'l Airport	32.2	1	Big Meadows	16.6
2	Langley AFB	31.9	2	Luray 5 E	19.9
3	Suffolk Lake Kilby	30.0	3	Burkes Garden	20.1
4	Painter 2 W	29.8	4	Blacksburg WSO	20.2
5	Holland 1 E	28.1	5	Hot Springs	20.3
6	Washington DC National Airport	28.0	6	Mount Weather	20.8
7	Williamsburg 2 N	27.9	7	Floyd 2 NE	21.5
8	Warsaw 2 NW	27.5	8	Woodstock 2 NE	22.0
8	West Point 2 NW	27.5	9	Dale Enterprise	22.1
10	John H. Kerr Dam	27.3	10	Washington DC Dulles Int'l Arpt.	22.2
10	Richmond R.E. Byrd Int'l Airport	27.3	10	Wytheville 1 S	22.2
12	Bedford	27.1	12	Galax Radio WBRF	22.4
13	Danville	26.7	13	Chatham	22.6
13	Lawrenceville 3 E	26.7	14	Pulaski	22.9
15	Stuart	26.5	14	Warrenton 3 SE	22.9
16	Roanoke Woodrum Airport	26.3	16	Grundy	23.2
17	Charlottesville 2 W	26.1	16	Pennington Gap	23.2
17	Walkerton 2 NW	26.1	16	Staffordsville 3 ENE	23.2
19	Lynchburg Municipal Airport	26.0	19	Piedmont Research Station	23.6
20	Buchanan	25.7	20	Lincoln	23.7
21	Ashland	25.6	21	Corbin	23.9
22	Rocky Mount	25.3	21	Lexington	23.9
23	Charlotte Court House	25.2	23	Camp Pickett	24.1
23	Farmville 2 N	25.2	24	Wise 3 E	24.2
25	Philpott Dam 2	25.0	25	Appomattox	24.3

Number of Annual Heating Degree Days

Highest			Lowest		
Rank	**Station Name**	**Num.**	**Rank**	**Station Name**	**Num.**
1	Big Meadows	6,835	1	Norfolk Int'l Airport	3,304
2	Burkes Garden	5,965	2	Langley AFB	3,451
3	Mount Weather	5,740	3	Suffolk Lake Kilby	3,470
4	Hot Springs	5,474	4	Williamsburg 2 N	3,634
5	Blacksburg WSO	5,440	5	Holland 1 E	3,654
6	Floyd 2 NE	5,277	6	Painter 2 W	3,741
7	Galax Radio WBRF	5,069	7	West Point 2 NW	3,752
8	Luray 5 E	5,053	8	John H. Kerr Dam	3,800
9	Wytheville 1 S	5,050	9	Lawrenceville 3 E	3,810
10	Dale Enterprise	4,979	10	Richmond R.E. Byrd Int'l Airport	3,834
11	Pulaski	4,950	11	Danville	3,874
12	Washington DC Dulles Int'l Arpt.	4,876	12	Warsaw 2 NW	3,878
13	Staffordsville 3 ENE	4,850	13	Walkerton 2 NW	3,911
14	Woodstock 2 NE	4,735	14	Washington DC National Airport	3,954
15	Warrenton 3 SE	4,726	15	Farmville 2 N	4,044
16	Wise 3 E	4,698	16	Bedford	4,079
17	Chatham	*4,630*	17	Ashland	4,123
18	Abingdon 3 S	4,572	18	Buchanan	*4,158*
19	Piedmont Research Station	4,552	19	Charlottesville 2 W	4,179
20	Grundy	4,492	20	Stuart	4,201
21	Pennington Gap	4,487	21	Charlotte Court House	4,208
22	Lincoln	4,479	22	Lynchburg Municipal Airport	4,231
23	Corbin	4,462	23	Roanoke Woodrum Airport	4,238
24	Lexington	4,446	24	Tye River 1 SE	4,252
25	Appomattox	4,427	25	Philpott Dam 2	4,258

Number of Annual Cooling Degree Days

	Highest			Lowest	
Rank	**Station Name**	**Num.**	**Rank**	**Station Name**	**Num.**
1	Norfolk Int'l Airport	1,707	1	Big Meadows	219
2	Langley AFB	1,640	2	Burkes Garden	288
3	Washington DC National Airport	1,615	3	Floyd 2 NE	514
4	Danville	1,543	4	Galax Radio WBRF	587
5	Richmond R.E. Byrd Int'l Airport	1,531	5	Blacksburg WSO	637
6	West Point 2 NW	1,529	6	Wytheville 1 S	642
7	John H. Kerr Dam	1,516	7	Hot Springs	*647*
8	Suffolk Lake Kilby	1,499	8	Pulaski	686
9	Williamsburg 2 N	1,459	9	Wise 3 E	696
10	Warsaw 2 NW	1,453	10	Staffordsville 3 ENE	740
11	Walkerton 2 NW	1,448	11	Mount Weather	778
12	Painter 2 W	1,445	12	Abingdon 3 S	832
13	Holland 1 E	1,444	13	Luray 5 E	841
14	Farmville 2 N	1,319	14	Dale Enterprise	923
15	Lawrenceville 3 E	1,315	15	Chatham	943
16	Ashland	1,278	15	Pennington Gap	943
17	Charlottesville 2 W	1,260	17	Lexington	1,012
18	Charlotte Court House	1,252	17	Woodstock 2 NE	1,012
19	Buchanan	*1,248*	19	Warrenton 3 SE	1,064
20	Camp Pickett	1,246	20	Grundy	1,082
21	Corbin	1,218	21	Rocky Mount	1,101
22	Roanoke Woodrum Airport	1,210	22	Stuart	*1,110*
23	Lynchburg Municipal Airport	1,204	23	Bedford	1,119
24	Lincoln	1,188	24	Washington DC Dulles Int'l Arpt.	1,145
25	Tye River 1 SE	1,176	25	Appomattox	1,158

Annual Precipitation

	Highest			Lowest	
Rank	**Station Name**	**Inches**	**Rank**	**Station Name**	**Inches**
1	Big Meadows	55.07	1	Dale Enterprise	35.89
2	Stuart	52.01	2	Woodstock 2 NE	37.53
3	Philpott Dam 2	51.09	3	Wytheville 1 S	37.65
4	Pennington Gap	49.41	4	Pulaski	37.66
5	Charlottesville 2 W	48.98	5	Washington DC National Airport	39.30
6	Holland 1 E	48.78	6	Staffordsville 3 ENE	39.38
7	Williamsburg 2 N	48.62	7	Lexington	39.66
8	Suffolk Lake Kilby	48.39	8	Floyd 2 NE	41.00
9	Langley AFB	47.63	9	Luray 5 E	41.53
10	Abingdon 3 S	47.56	10	Washington DC Dulles Int'l Arpt.	41.85
11	Wise 3 E	46.96	11	Roanoke Woodrum Airport	42.52
12	Rocky Mount	46.73	12	Hot Springs	42.60
13	Camp Pickett	46.16	13	Lincoln	42.73
14	Lawrenceville 3 E	45.99	14	Blacksburg WSO	42.75
15	Tye River 1 SE	45.83	15	Painter 2 W	43.06
16	Grundy	45.73	16	Lynchburg Municipal Airport	43.10
17	Appomattox	45.68	16	Walkerton 2 NW	43.10
18	Back Bay Wildlife Refuge	45.66	18	Buchanan	*43.13*
19	Burkes Garden	45.63	19	Mount Weather	43.15
20	Charlotte Court House	45.47	20	Warrenton 3 SE	43.42
21	Norfolk Int'l Airport	45.24	21	Richmond R.E. Byrd Int'l Airport	43.43
22	Chatham	45.18	22	Warsaw 2 NW	43.46
23	West Point 2 NW	45.10	23	Louisa	43.85
24	Danville	45.02	24	Galax Radio WBRF	43.93
25	Bedford	44.86	25	John H. Kerr Dam	44.03

Number of Days Annually With ≥ 0.1″ Precipitation

	Highest			Lowest	
Rank	Station Name	Days	Rank	Station Name	Days
1	Abingdon 3 S	98	1	Back Bay Wildlife Refuge	*62*
2	Wise 3 E	96	2	Floyd 2 NE	70
3	Burkes Garden	94	2	Lincoln	*70*
4	Grundy	92	4	Painter 2 W	71
5	Blacksburg WSO	90	5	Washington DC National Airport	72
6	Pennington Gap	*87*	6	Dale Enterprise	73
7	Stuart	83	6	Lexington	73
8	Big Meadows	81	6	Louisa	73
8	Buchanan	*81*	6	Luray 5 E	73
8	Philpott Dam 2	81	10	John H. Kerr Dam	74
11	Hot Springs	80	10	Pulaski	74
11	Staffordsville 3 ENE	80	12	Roanoke Woodrum Airport	75
11	Williamsburg 2 N	80	12	Warsaw 2 NW	75
14	Bedford	79	14	Appomattox	76
14	Holland 1 E	79	14	Charlotte Court House	76
14	Rocky Mount	79	14	Corbin	76
14	Tye River 1 SE	79	14	Galax Radio WBRF	76
18	Camp Pickett	78	14	Langley AFB	76
18	Chatham	78	14	Lawrenceville 3 E	76
18	Walkerton 2 NW	78	14	Lynchburg Municipal Airport	76
18	Woodstock 2 NE	78	14	Mount Weather	76
22	Ashland	77	14	Norfolk Int'l Airport	76
22	Charlottesville 2 W	77	14	Piedmont Research Station	76
22	Danville	77	14	Richmond R.E. Byrd Int'l Airport	76
22	Farmville 2 N	77	14	Suffolk Lake Kilby	76

Number of Days Annually With ≥ 1.0″ Precipitation

	Highest			Lowest	
Rank	Station Name	Days	Rank	Station Name	Days
1	Holland 1 E	14	1	Woodstock 2 NE	8
1	Philpott Dam 2	14	2	Dale Enterprise	9
1	Stuart	14	2	Staffordsville 3 ENE	9
1	Suffolk Lake Kilby	14	2	Wytheville 1 S	9
5	Big Meadows	13	5	Blacksburg WSO	10
5	Langley AFB	13	5	Grundy	10
5	Lawrenceville 3 E	13	5	Pulaski	10
5	Norfolk Int'l Airport	13	5	Washington DC National Airport	10
5	Williamsburg 2 N	13	9	Back Bay Wildlife Refuge	11
10	Abingdon 3 S	12	9	Mount Weather	11
10	Appomattox	12	9	Roanoke Woodrum Airport	11
10	Ashland	12	9	West Point 2 NW	11
10	Bedford	12	13	Abingdon 3 S	12
10	Buchanan	*12*	13	Appomattox	12
10	Burkes Garden	12	13	Ashland	12
10	Camp Pickett	12	13	Bedford	12
10	Charlotte Court House	12	13	Buchanan	*12*
10	Charlottesville 2 W	12	13	Burkes Garden	12
10	Chatham	12	13	Camp Pickett	12
10	Corbin	12	13	Charlotte Court House	12
10	Danville	12	13	Charlottesville 2 W	12
10	Farmville 2 N	12	13	Chatham	12
10	Floyd 2 NE	12	13	Corbin	12
10	Galax Radio WBRF	12	13	Danville	12
10	Hot Springs	12	13	Farmville 2 N	12

Annual Snowfall

	Highest			Lowest	
Rank	**Station Name**	**Inches**	**Rank**	**Station Name**	**Inches**
1	Burkes Garden	51.8	1	Back Bay Wildlife Refuge	*3.6*
2	Wise 3 E	51.0	2	Philpott Dam 2	*5.0*
3	Big Meadows	42.9	3	Suffolk Lake Kilby	6.2
4	Hot Springs	*28.4*	4	Holland 1 E	6.3
5	Dale Enterprise	24.5	5	Chatham	*6.4*
6	Woodstock 2 NE	22.9	6	Williamsburg 2 N	6.8
7	Blacksburg WSO	22.4	7	Langley AFB	7.1
8	Staffordsville 3 ENE	21.2	8	Painter 2 W	7.5
9	Luray 5 E	21.0	9	Norfolk Int'l Airport	7.6
10	Washington DC Dulles Int'l Arpt.	20.8	10	Charlotte Court House	8.0
10	Wytheville 1 S	20.8	11	Camp Pickett	*8.7*
12	Roanoke Woodrum Airport	20.5	12	Lawrenceville 3 E	8.8
13	Floyd 2 NE	20.4	13	West Point 2 NW	10.1
14	Grundy	20.0	14	Walkerton 2 NW	10.5
15	Lincoln	19.4	15	Richmond R.E. Byrd Int'l Airport	11.7
16	Galax Radio WBRF	19.1	16	Stuart	*12.1*
17	Charlottesville 2 W	18.7	17	Appomattox	13.4
18	Piedmont Research Station	18.3	18	Corbin	13.7
19	Ashland	18.0	19	Farmville 2 N	14.1
20	Mount Weather	*17.9*	20	Lexington	14.2
21	Warrenton 3 SE	17.7	21	Washington DC National Airport	14.6
22	Lynchburg Municipal Airport	*17.6*	22	Warsaw 2 NW	15.0
23	Rocky Mount	16.9	23	Bedford	15.1
24	Louisa	16.8	24	Abingdon 3 S	15.4
25	Pennington Gap	16.3	25	Pulaski	*15.5*

Note: See Appendix D for explanation of data.

Annual Extreme Maximum Temperature

	Highest			Lowest	
Rank	**Station Name**	**°F**	**Rank**	**Station Name**	**°F**
1	Walla Walla City County Airport	*114*	1	Olga 2 SE	89
2	Smyrna	113	1	Rainier Paradise Ranger Station	89
3	Priest Rapids Dam	112	3	Blaine	90
4	The Dalles Municipal Airport	111	3	Coupeville 1 S	90
5	Chief Joseph Dam	110	5	Anacortes	93
5	Connell 1 W	110	5	Port Townsend	*93*
5	Dayton 1 WSW	110	7	Bellingham Int'l Airport	94
5	Kennewick	110	7	Everett	94
5	Sunnyside	110	7	Mount Vernon 3 WNW	94
5	Whitman Mission	110	7	Port Angeles	94
5	Yakima Air Terminal	110	11	Sedro Woolley	95
12	Hatton 9 SE	109	12	Seattle Portage Bay	*96*
12	Richland	109	13	Cushman Powerhouse 2	*97*
14	Ephrata Airport	108	13	Elwha Ranger Station	97
14	Glenoma	108	15	Clearbrook	98
14	Lacrosse	108	15	Clearwater	98
14	Longview	108	15	Grapeview 3 SW	*98*
14	Wenatchee Pangborn Field	108	15	Hoquiam Airport	98
19	Coulee Dam 1 SW	107	15	Mud Mountain Dam	98
19	Hartline	107	20	Concrete Ppl. Fish Station	99
19	Leavenworth 3 S	107	20	Holden Village	99
19	Lind 3 NE	107	20	Long Beach Exp. Station	99
19	McNary Dam	107	20	Puyallup 2 W Exp. Station	*99*
19	Methow 2 S	107	20	Quillayute Airport	99
19	Northport	107	20	Snoqualmie Falls	99

Annual Mean Maximum Temperature

	Highest			Lowest	
Rank	**Station Name**	**°F**	**Rank**	**Station Name**	**°F**
1	Kennewick	65.7	1	Rainier Paradise Ranger Station	44.7
2	Priest Rapids Dam	65.6	2	Holden Village	52.9
3	Sunnyside	65.4	3	Cedar Lake	55.6
4	Smyrna	65.3	3	Mazama	55.6
5	Richland	65.1	3	Republic	55.6
6	The Dalles Municipal Airport	65.0	6	Boundary Dam	*56.0*
6	Wapato	65.0	7	Appleton	56.4
8	Whitman Mission	64.6	7	Upper Baker Dam	56.4
9	McNary Dam	64.1	9	Ross Dam	56.5
10	Connell 1 W	*63.7*	10	Elwha Ranger Station	56.7
10	Walla Walla City County Airport	*63.7*	11	Port Angeles	56.8
12	Yakima Air Terminal	63.0	12	Aberdeen 20 NNE	57.0
13	Wenatchee	62.9	13	Blaine	57.3
14	Eltopia 8 WSW	*62.8*	14	Cle Elum	57.4
14	Hatton 9 SE	62.8	14	Newhalem	57.4
16	Dayton 1 WSW	62.6	14	Pullman 2 NW	57.4
16	Lacrosse	62.6	14	Quillayute Airport	57.4
18	Wenatchee Exp. Station	*62.3*	14	Wellpinit	*57.4*
19	Chief Joseph Dam	62.2	19	Bellingham Int'l Airport	57.5
20	Lind 3 NE	62.1	19	Diablo Dam	57.5
20	Toledo Winlock Muni Airport	62.1	19	Spokane Int'l Airport	57.5
22	Elma	62.0	22	Hoquiam Airport	57.6
22	Ephrata Airport	62.0	22	Olga 2 SE	57.6
24	Centralia	61.9	24	Baring	57.7
24	Puyallup 2 W Exp. Station	*61.9*	24	Mud Mountain Dam	57.7

Annual Mean Temperature

Highest			Lowest		
Rank	**Station Name**	**°F**	**Rank**	**Station Name**	**°F**
1	Priest Rapids Dam	*55.1*	1	Rainier Paradise Ranger Station	37.3
2	The Dalles Municipal Airport	54.3	2	Holden Village	41.0
3	Kennewick	54.1	3	Republic	43.4
4	McNary Dam	53.8	4	Mazama	43.8
4	Walla Walla City County Airport	*53.8*	5	Boundary Dam	*45.0*
6	Richland	53.6	6	Winthrop 1 WSW	45.3
7	Seattle Portage Bay	*53.2*	7	Newport	45.6
8	Centralia	52.5	7	Plain	45.6
8	Sunnyside	52.5	9	Appleton	46.2
10	Wapato	52.4	9	Harrington 1 NW	46.2
11	Seattle-Tacoma Int'l Airport	52.3	9	Wilbur	46.2
11	Smyrna	52.3	12	Cle Elum	46.4
13	Wenatchee	52.2	13	Chewelah	46.7
14	Longview	51.9	14	Rosalia	46.9
15	Elma	51.7	14	Wellpinit	*46.9*
16	Puyallup 2 W Exp. Station	*51.6*	16	Pullman 2 NW	47.2
16	Shelton	51.6	17	Cedar Lake	47.4
16	Toledo Winlock Muni Airport	51.6	17	Spokane Int'l Airport	47.4
19	Whitman Mission	51.5	19	Ellensburg	47.5
20	Connell 1 W	*51.4*	20	Leavenworth 3 S	47.7
20	Cushman Powerhouse 2	*51.4*	20	Methow 2 S	47.7
20	Ephrata Airport	51.4	22	Upper Baker Dam	47.8
20	Monroe	51.4	23	Colfax	*48.0*
20	Port Townsend	*51.4*	23	Ritzville 1 SSE	48.0
25	Battle Ground	51.3	25	Northport	48.1

Annual Mean Minimum Temperature

Highest			Lowest		
Rank	**Station Name**	**°F**	**Rank**	**Station Name**	**°F**
1	Seattle Portage Bay	*46.0*	1	Holden Village	29.1
2	Seattle-Tacoma Int'l Airport	44.8	2	Rainier Paradise Ranger Station	29.9
3	Port Townsend	*44.6*	3	Republic	31.2
3	Priest Rapids Dam	*44.6*	3	Winthrop 1 WSW	31.2
5	Hoquiam Airport	44.5	5	Mazama	31.9
6	Walla Walla City County Airport	*43.9*	6	Plain	33.3
7	Aberdeen	43.5	7	Newport	33.4
7	Anacortes	43.5	8	Chewelah	33.5
7	The Dalles Municipal Airport	43.5	9	Wilbur	33.9
10	McNary Dam	43.4	10	Boundary Dam	*34.0*
11	Centralia	43.0	11	Leavenworth 3 S	34.1
12	Everett	42.9	12	Harrington 1 NW	34.2
13	Long Beach Exp. Station	42.8	13	Methow 2 S	34.5
13	Olga 2 SE	42.8	14	Odessa	34.8
15	Bellingham Int'l Airport	42.6	15	Ellensburg	35.2
15	Grapeview 3 SW	*42.6*	16	Cle Elum	35.3
17	Cougar 6 E	42.5	17	Rosalia	35.6
17	Kennewick	42.5	18	Northport	35.8
17	Shelton	42.5	18	Saint John	35.8
20	Cushman Powerhouse 2	*42.4*	20	Appleton	35.9
20	Port Angeles	42.4	20	Ritzville 1 SSE	35.9
22	Longview	42.3	22	Colfax	*36.3*
22	Monroe	42.3	23	Wellpinit	*36.4*
24	Sedro Woolley	42.2	24	Yakima Air Terminal	36.5
25	Richland	42.1	25	Pullman 2 NW	36.9

Annual Extreme Minimum Temperature

	Highest				Lowest	
Rank	Station Name	°F		Rank	Station Name	°F
1	Cushman Powerhouse 2	*11*		1	Newport	-33
1	Port Townsend	*11*		2	Lacrosse	-30
1	Seattle Portage Bay	*11*		2	Mazama	-30
4	Aberdeen	10		2	Winthrop 1 WSW	-30
5	Grapeview 3 SW	*9*		5	Chewelah	-29
5	Hoquiam Airport	9		5	Odessa	-29
7	Anacortes	8		5	Republic	-29
7	Elwha Ranger Station	8		8	Ellensburg	-28
7	Forks 1 E	8		8	Saint John	-28
7	Sedro Woolley	8		10	Leavenworth 3 S	-26
11	Quillayute Airport	7		11	Holden Village	-25
11	Seattle-Tacoma Int'l Airport	7		11	Rosalia	-25
13	Port Angeles	6		11	Wellpinit	*-25*
13	Shelton	6		14	Cle Elum	-24
15	Coupeville 1 S	5		14	Harrington 1 NW	-24
16	Clearwater	4		14	Plain	-24
16	Concrete Ppl. Fish Station	4		14	Pullman 2 NW	-24
16	Longview	4		14	Smyrna	-24
19	Aberdeen 20 NNE	3		14	Spokane Int'l Airport	-24
20	Cougar 6 E	2		20	Boundary Dam	*-23*
20	Elma	2		20	Wilbur	-23
20	Grays River Hatchery	2		22	Lind 3 NE	-22
20	Mud Mountain Dam	2		22	Quincy 1 S	-22
20	Newhalem	2		22	Whitman Mission	-22
20	Skamania Fish Hatchery	2		25	Dayton 1 WSW	-21

July Mean Maximum Temperature

	Highest				Lowest	
Rank	Station Name	°F		Rank	Station Name	°F
1	Priest Rapids Dam	91.0		1	Rainier Paradise Ranger Station	60.7
2	Smyrna	90.7		2	Long Beach Exp. Station	65.7
3	Kennewick	90.2		3	Hoquiam Airport	67.3
4	Sunnyside	89.4		4	Quillayute Airport	68.2
4	Wapato	89.4		5	Aberdeen	68.3
6	Walla Walla City County Airport	*89.3*		6	Port Angeles	68.5
7	Connell 1 W	89.2		7	Olga 2 SE	69.9
8	Richland	89.1		8	Clearwater	70.3
9	Chief Joseph Dam	89.0		9	Coupeville 1 S	70.8
10	Whitman Mission	88.9		10	Bellingham Int'l Airport	70.9
11	Hatton 9 SE	88.8		11	Aberdeen 20 NNE	71.7
12	Ephrata Airport	88.3		11	Anacortes	71.7
12	Lacrosse	88.3		11	Blaine	71.7
12	Wenatchee	88.3		11	Cedar Lake	71.7
15	Lind 3 NE	88.2		11	Port Townsend	71.7
16	McNary Dam	88.1		16	Mud Mountain Dam	72.3
16	The Dalles Municipal Airport	88.1		17	Grays River Hatchery	72.6
18	Methow 2 S	87.8		17	Mount Vernon 3 WNW	72.6
19	Hartline	87.2		19	Elwha Ranger Station	72.7
19	Wenatchee Exp. Station	87.2		20	Forks 1 E	72.8
19	Yakima Air Terminal	87.2		21	Everett	72.9
22	Leavenworth 3 S	87.1		22	Palmer 3 ESE	73.3
23	Northport	86.9		22	Upper Baker Dam	73.3
24	Wenatchee Pangborn Field	86.8		24	Sedro Woolley	73.6
25	Dayton 1 WSW	86.6		25	Baring	74.3

January Mean Minimum Temperature

	Highest				Lowest	
Rank	Station Name	°F		Rank	Station Name	°F
1	Hoquiam Airport	37.3		1	Winthrop 1 WSW	12.4
2	Port Townsend	37.1		2	Mazama	12.7
3	Seattle Portage Bay	36.8		3	Holden Village	15.0
4	Seattle-Tacoma Int'l Airport	36.0		4	Republic	15.1
5	Long Beach Exp. Station	35.8		5	Methow 2 S	15.6
6	Aberdeen	35.6		6	Boundary Dam	17.6
7	Olga 2 SE	35.3		6	Leavenworth 3 S	17.6
8	Coupeville 1 S	34.8		8	Chewelah	18.3
9	Cushman Powerhouse 2	34.6		9	Wilbur	18.6
9	Quillayute Airport	34.6		10	Ellensburg	19.4
11	Anacortes	34.5		11	Newport	19.6
11	Clearwater	34.5		12	Odessa	19.7
13	Centralia	34.4		13	Plain	19.9
13	Grapeview 3 SW	*34.4*		14	Chief Joseph Dam	20.2
15	Port Angeles	34.3		14	Hartline	20.2
16	Forks 1 E	34.2		14	Quincy 1 S	20.2
17	Shelton	34.1		17	Harrington 1 NW	20.4
18	Elma	33.9		18	Wellpinit	20.6
19	Longview	33.7		19	Rainier Paradise Ranger Station	20.7
19	Mount Vernon 3 WNW	33.7		20	Northport	20.8
21	Everett	33.6		21	Cle Elum	21.0
22	Snoqualmie Falls	33.4		22	Wenatchee Exp. Station	21.2
23	Buckley 1 NE	33.2		23	Ephrata Airport	21.5
23	Sedro Woolley	33.2		24	Spokane Int'l Airport	21.6
23	Startup 1 E	33.2		25	Coulee Dam 1 SW	21.7

Number of Annual Heating Degree Days

	Highest				Lowest	
Rank	Station Name	Num.		Rank	Station Name	Num.
1	Rainier Paradise Ranger Station	10,049		1	Seattle Portage Bay	*4,387*
2	Holden Village	8,707		2	The Dalles Municipal Airport	4,654
3	Republic	7,930		3	Centralia	4,696
4	Mazama	7,913		4	Priest Rapids Dam	*4,702*
5	Boundary Dam	*7,401*		5	Seattle-Tacoma Int'l Airport	4,722
6	Winthrop 1 WSW	7,398		6	Kennewick	4,777
7	Newport	7,201		7	McNary Dam	4,808
8	Plain	7,163		8	Longview	4,840
9	Wilbur	7,092		9	Richland	4,889
10	Harrington 1 NW	7,040		10	Walla Walla City County Airport	*4,905*
11	Appleton	6,993		11	Port Townsend	*4,910*
12	Cle Elum	6,940		12	Elma	4,923
13	Wellpinit	*6,909*		13	Puyallup 2 W Exp. Station	*4,946*
14	Chewelah	6,874		13	Toledo Winlock Muni Airport	*4,946*
15	Rosalia	6,789		15	Shelton	4,971
16	Spokane Int'l Airport	6,752		16	Cushman Powerhouse 2	*4,988*
17	Methow 2 S	6,719		17	Monroe	4,996
18	Pullman 2 NW	6,685		18	Hoquiam Airport	5,023
19	Ellensburg	6,649		19	Grapeview 3 SW	*5,028*
20	Leavenworth 3 S	6,630		20	Vancouver 4 NNE	5,091
21	Ritzville 1 SSE	6,552		21	Anacortes	5,098
22	Stehekin 4 NW	6,491		22	Battle Ground	5,101
23	Northport	6,480		23	Everett	5,111
24	Odessa	6,464		24	Aberdeen	5,119
25	Cedar Lake	6,424		25	Sedro Woolley	5,144

Number of Annual Cooling Degree Days

	Highest			Lowest	
Rank	**Station Name**	**Num.**	**Rank**	**Station Name**	**Num.**
1	Priest Rapids Dam	1,162	1	Long Beach Exp. Station	15
2	Kennewick	919	2	Olga 2 SE	17
3	Walla Walla City County Airport	*917*	3	Coupeville 1 S	18
4	The Dalles Municipal Airport	854	4	Quillayute Airport	23
5	Ephrata Airport	848	4	Rainier Paradise Ranger Station	*23*
6	Wenatchee	846	6	Clearwater	25
7	McNary Dam	818	7	Blaine	28
8	Richland	815	8	Port Angeles	30
9	Smyrna	811	9	Hoquiam Airport	37
10	Chief Joseph Dam	803	10	Mount Vernon 3 WNW	41
11	Wapato	774	11	Anacortes	54
12	Sunnyside	756	12	Aberdeen	57
13	Wenatchee Pangborn Field	750	13	Bellingham Int'l Airport	*58*
14	Coulee Dam 1 SW	705	13	Port Townsend	58
15	Hatton 9 SE	701	15	Aberdeen 20 NNE	61
16	Chelan	635	15	Holden Village	61
17	Connell 1 W	*625*	17	Grays River Hatchery	71
18	Quincy 1 S	591	18	Forks 1 E	73
19	Hartline	*581*	19	Sedro Woolley	79
20	Dayton 1 WSW	578	20	Elwha Ranger Station	83
21	Wenatchee Exp. Station	577	21	Clearbrook	89
22	Lind 3 NE	524	22	Cedar Lake	91
23	Methow 2 S	517	23	Upper Baker Dam	98
24	Whitman Mission	516	24	Everett	106
25	Eltopia 8 WSW	477	25	Baring	108

Annual Precipitation

	Highest			Lowest	
Rank	**Station Name**	**Inches**	**Rank**	**Station Name**	**Inches**
1	Aberdeen 20 NNE	136.27	1	Priest Rapids Dam	6.89
2	Forks 1 E	122.14	2	Sunnyside	7.19
3	Rainier Paradise Ranger Station	119.43	3	Richland	7.48
4	Cougar 6 E	117.51	4	Ephrata Airport	7.70
5	Clearwater	114.63	5	Kennewick	7.96
6	Grays River Hatchery	110.85	6	Smyrna	8.00
7	Baring	110.62	7	Wapato	8.12
8	Quillayute Airport	102.44	8	McNary Dam	8.13
9	Upper Baker Dam	100.90	8	Quincy 1 S	8.13
10	Cedar Lake	100.00	10	Moxee City 10 E	8.26
11	Cushman Powerhouse 2	90.91	11	Yakima Air Terminal	8.33
12	Palmer 3 ESE	87.11	12	Wenatchee Pangborn Field	8.58
13	Skamania Fish Hatchery	87.02	13	Connell 1 W	8.60
14	Aberdeen	85.31	14	Eltopia 8 WSW	*8.85*
15	Long Beach Exp. Station	81.72	15	Ellensburg	9.20
16	Newhalem	79.98	15	Wenatchee	9.20
17	Diablo Dam	79.59	17	Lind 3 NE	9.96
18	Concrete Ppl. Fish Station	71.79	18	Wenatchee Exp. Station	*10.47*
19	Elma	69.60	19	Hatton 9 SE	10.52
20	Hoquiam Airport	68.92	20	Odessa	10.72
21	Glenoma	67.61	21	Chief Joseph Dam	10.88
22	Shelton	66.28	22	Coulee Dam 1 SW	11.15
23	Startup 1 E	65.22	23	Chelan	11.32
24	Snoqualmie Falls	62.23	24	Ritzville 1 SSE	12.27
25	Packwood	58.40	25	Wilbur	12.99

Number of Days Annually With ≥ 0.1″ Precipitation

	Highest			Lowest	
Rank	Station Name	Days	Rank	Station Name	Days
1	Rainier Paradise Ranger Station	156	1	Priest Rapids Dam	21
2	Forks 1 E	154	2	Sunnyside	23
3	Aberdeen 20 NNE	151	3	Richland	26
4	Cedar Lake	150	4	Ephrata Airport	27
4	Grays River Hatchery	150	4	Wapato	27
4	Palmer 3 ESE	150	6	Connell 1 W	28
7	Clearwater	149	6	Kennewick	28
8	Quillayute Airport	146	6	McNary Dam	28
9	Upper Baker Dam	142	6	Moxee City 10 E	28
10	Cougar 6 E	140	6	Quincy 1 S	28
10	Long Beach Exp. Station	140	6	Smyrna	28
12	Aberdeen	135	6	Wenatchee Pangborn Field	28
12	Skamania Fish Hatchery	135	6	Yakima Air Terminal	28
14	Concrete Ppl. Fish Station	134	14	Wenatchee	29
15	Startup 1 E	133	15	Hartline	30
16	Glenoma	130	16	Ellensburg	31
17	Elma	128	16	Eltopia 8 WSW	31
17	Hoquiam Airport	128	18	Chelan	33
19	Mud Mountain Dam	126	18	Wenatchee Exp. Station	33
20	Diablo Dam	124	20	Chief Joseph Dam	34
20	Snoqualmie Falls	124	21	Lind 3 NE	35
22	Landsburg	123	22	Hatton 9 SE	36
22	Newhalem	123	23	Coulee Dam 1 SW	38
24	Buckley 1 NE	120	23	Odessa	38
25	Oakville	119	25	Methow 2 S	39

Number of Days Annually With ≥ 1.0″ Precipitation

	Highest			Lowest	
Rank	Station Name	Days	Rank	Station Name	Days
1	Aberdeen 20 NNE	48	1	Boundary Dam	0
2	Forks 1 E	42	1	Chelan	0
3	Clearwater	40	1	Chewelah	0
4	Cougar 6 E	39	1	Chief Joseph Dam	0
4	Rainier Paradise Ranger Station	39	1	Colfax	0
6	Grays River Hatchery	35	1	Connell 1 W	0
7	Upper Baker Dam	33	1	Coulee Dam 1 SW	0
8	Baring	31	1	Coupeville 1 S	0
8	Quillayute Airport	31	1	Dayton 1 WSW	0
10	Cedar Lake	30	1	Ellensburg	0
10	Cushman Powerhouse 2	30	1	Eltopia 8 WSW	0
12	Skamania Fish Hatchery	24	1	Ephrata Airport	0
13	Aberdeen	23	1	Harrington 1 NW	0
13	Palmer 3 ESE	23	1	Hartline	0
15	Diablo Dam	22	1	Hatton 9 SE	0
16	Newhalem	21	1	Kennewick	0
17	Long Beach Exp. Station	20	1	Lacrosse	0
18	Elma	17	1	Lind 3 NE	0
19	Concrete Ppl. Fish Station	16	1	McNary Dam	0
19	Shelton	16	1	Methow 2 S	0
21	Hoquiam Airport	15	1	Moxee City 10 E	0
22	Elwha Ranger Station	14	1	Northport	0
23	Glenoma	13	1	Odessa	0
23	Ross Dam	13	1	Port Townsend	0
23	Startup 1 E	13	1	Priest Rapids Dam	0

Annual Snowfall

Highest			Lowest		
Rank	**Station Name**	**Inches**	**Rank**	**Station Name**	**Inches**
1	Rainier Paradise Ranger Station	702.7	1	Port Angeles	*1.0*
2	Holden Village	254.3	2	Long Beach Exp. Station	1.5
3	Plain	140.3	3	Aberdeen	*1.9*
4	Stehekin 4 NW	136.2	3	Clearwater	*1.9*
5	Mazama	122.8	5	Everett	2.3
6	Leavenworth 3 S	91.6	6	Mount Vernon 3 WNW	*2.6*
7	Cle Elum	86.0	7	Centralia	2.9
8	Appleton	79.7	8	Port Townsend	*3.0*
9	Winthrop 1 WSW	65.4	9	Longview	3.3
10	Boundary Dam	*59.9*	10	Hoquiam Airport	3.5
11	Newport	57.1	11	Anacortes	*4.2*
12	Baring	55.1	11	Shelton	4.2
13	Cedar Lake	53.6	13	Vancouver 4 NNE	*4.8*
14	Northport	52.2	14	Battle Ground	*4.9*
15	Upper Baker Dam	49.5	14	Seattle Portage Bay	*4.9*
16	Diablo Dam	*46.4*	16	Oakville	*5.2*
17	Republic	45.2	17	Grapeview 3 SW	*5.3*
18	Spokane Int'l Airport	43.8	17	Puyallup 2 W Exp. Station	*5.3*
19	Chewelah	38.5	19	Connell 1 W	*5.5*
20	Wenatchee Exp. Station	*36.0*	19	Monroe	5.5
21	Newhalem	*35.4*	21	Grays River Hatchery	5.8
22	Pullman 2 NW	34.8	22	Olga 2 SE	5.9
23	Wenatchee Pangborn Field	33.6	23	Coupeville 1 S	*6.0*
24	Chelan	31.3	24	Elma	6.6
25	Colfax	*28.8*	24	McMillin Reservoir	6.6

Note: See Appendix D for explanation of data.

Annual Extreme Maximum Temperature

	Highest				Lowest	
Rank	Station Name	°F		Rank	Station Name	°F
1	Martinsburg Eastern WV Reg. Arpt.	107		1	Flat Top	92
1	Ripley	107		2	Bayard	94
3	Creston	106		2	Summersville Lake	94
3	Mathias	106		4	Oak Hill	95
3	Moorefield 2 SSE	106		4	Terra Alta 1	95
6	Kearneysville	*105*		6	Beckley Memorial Airport	96
6	Parkersburg WSO	105		6	Beckley Virginia Hospital	96
6	Wardensville R M Farm	105		6	Bluefield Mercer Co. Airport	96
9	Cacapon State Park 2	*104*		6	Buckeye	96
9	Charleston Kanawha Airport	104		6	Buckhannon	96
9	Glenville 1 ENE	104		6	Union 3 SSE	96
9	Weston	104		12	Athens	97
13	Hamlin	103		12	Canaan Valley	97
13	Middlebourne 3 ESE	103		14	Clarksburg 1	98
13	Romney 1 SW	103		14	Kopperston	*98*
13	Spencer 4 S	103		14	Lewisburg 3 N	98
13	West Union 2	*103*		17	Bluestone Lake	99
18	Gassaway	102		17	Elkins-Randolph Co. Airport	99
18	Hogsett R.C. Byrd Dam	102		17	Moundsville	*99*
18	Huntington Tri-State Airport	102		17	Seneca State Forest 1 N	99
18	Parkersburg Wood County Airport	102		21	Dunlow 1 SW	100
18	Winfield Locks	102		21	Fairmont	100
23	Franklin 2 NE	101		21	Morgantown Lock & Dam	100
23	Logan	*101*		21	Morgantown Municipal Airport	100
23	London Locks	101		21	Pineville	100

Annual Mean Maximum Temperature

	Highest				Lowest	
Rank	Station Name	°F		Rank	Station Name	°F
1	Logan	*67.3*		1	Flat Top	57.6
2	Gassaway	67.0		2	Terra Alta 1	57.7
3	Madison	66.9		3	Canaan Valley	58.1
4	Moorefield 2 SSE	66.8		4	Bayard	58.7
5	Ripley	66.7		5	Beckley Memorial Airport	61.0
6	Hamlin	66.6		6	Bluefield Mercer Co. Airport	61.4
7	Charleston Kanawha Airport	65.9		6	Parsons 1 NE	61.4
8	Creston	65.8		8	Elkins-Randolph Co. Airport	61.5
8	London Locks	65.8		8	Seneca State Forest 1 N	61.5
10	Winfield Locks	65.7		10	Rowlesburg 1	61.6
11	Huntington Tri-State Airport	65.6		11	Buckeye	61.7
12	Spencer 4 S	65.5		12	Beckley Virginia Hospital	61.8
13	Glenville 1 ENE	65.4		13	Summersville Lake	61.9
13	Hogsett R.C. Byrd Dam	65.4		14	Fairmont	62.6
13	Pineville	65.4		14	Morgantown Municipal Airport	62.6
16	Weston	64.9		14	Oak Hill	62.6
16	White Sulphur Springs	64.9		17	Cacapon State Park 2	*63.0*
18	Dunlow 1 SW	64.8		18	Morgantown Lock & Dam	63.3
18	Romney 1 SW	64.8		19	Clarksburg 1	63.4
20	Martinsburg Eastern WV Reg. Arpt.	64.6		20	Mathias	63.5
21	Franklin 2 NE	64.5		20	Union 3 SSE	63.5
22	Wardensville R M Farm	64.4		22	Kearneysville	*63.6*
23	Parkersburg WSO	64.3		22	Lewisburg 3 N	63.6
24	Bluestone Lake	64.2		22	Parkersburg Wood County Airport	63.6
25	Athens	63.9		22	West Union 2	*63.6*

Annual Mean Temperature

	Highest				Lowest	
Rank	Station Name	°F		Rank	Station Name	°F
1	Logan	*56.2*		1	Canaan Valley	46.7
2	Huntington Tri-State Airport	55.5		2	Bayard	47.6
3	Charleston Kanawha Airport	55.3		3	Seneca State Forest 1 N	48.0
3	London Locks	55.3		4	Terra Alta 1	48.5
5	Winfield Locks	54.6		5	Flat Top	48.8
6	Gassaway	54.5		6	Buckeye	49.3
7	Ripley	54.4		7	Elkins-Randolph Co. Airport	49.5
8	Madison	54.3		8	Parsons 1 NE	50.0
9	Moorefield 2 SSE	54.2		9	Beckley Virginia Hospital	50.5
10	Dunlow 1 SW	54.1		10	Rowlesburg 1	50.6
11	Martinsburg Eastern WV Reg. Arpt.	54.0		11	Summersville Lake	51.0
12	Parkersburg Wood County Airport	53.9		12	Mathias	51.2
13	Parkersburg WSO	53.8		13	West Union 2	*51.4*
14	Hamlin	53.7		14	Beckley Memorial Airport	51.5
15	Hogsett R.C. Byrd Dam	53.6		14	Union 3 SSE	51.5
16	Pineville	53.5		16	Buckhannon	51.7
17	Bluestone Lake	53.2		16	Oak Hill	51.7
18	Spencer 4 S	52.9		16	Wardensville R M Farm	51.7
19	Morgantown Municipal Airport	52.8		19	Franklin 2 NE	51.8
20	Bluefield Mercer Co. Airport	52.7		20	Fairmont	51.9
20	Creston	52.7		20	Lewisburg 3 N	51.9
20	Glenville 1 ENE	52.7		22	Clarksburg 1	52.0
23	Romney 1 SW	52.6		23	Kearneysville	*52.1*
24	Morgantown Lock & Dam	52.5		24	Cacapon State Park 2	*52.2*
24	Moundsville	*52.5*		24	Weston	52.2

Annual Mean Minimum Temperature

	Highest				Lowest	
Rank	Station Name	°F		Rank	Station Name	°F
1	Huntington Tri-State Airport	45.4		1	Seneca State Forest 1 N	34.5
2	Logan	*45.0*		2	Canaan Valley	35.3
3	London Locks	44.8		3	Bayard	36.4
4	Charleston Kanawha Airport	44.7		4	Buckeye	36.9
5	Bluefield Mercer Co. Airport	44.1		5	Elkins-Randolph Co. Airport	37.4
5	Parkersburg Wood County Airport	44.1		6	Parsons 1 NE	38.7
7	Winfield Locks	43.5		7	Wardensville R M Farm	38.9
8	Dunlow 1 SW	43.3		8	Franklin 2 NE	39.0
8	Martinsburg Eastern WV Reg. Arpt.	43.3		8	Mathias	39.0
8	Parkersburg WSO	43.3		10	Beckley Virginia Hospital	39.1
11	Morgantown Municipal Airport	42.9		11	West Union 2	*39.2*
12	Bluestone Lake	42.1		12	Terra Alta 1	39.3
13	Beckley Memorial Airport	42.0		13	Rowlesburg 1	39.5
13	Gassaway	42.0		13	Union 3 SSE	39.5
13	Ripley	42.0		13	Weston	39.5
16	Hogsett R.C. Byrd Dam	41.7		16	Buckhannon	39.6
17	Madison	41.6		17	Creston	39.7
17	Moorefield 2 SSE	41.6		18	White Sulphur Springs	39.8
17	Morgantown Lock & Dam	41.6		19	Glenville 1 ENE	39.9
20	Pineville	41.5		20	Flat Top	40.1
21	Cacapon State Park 2	*41.4*		20	Lewisburg 3 N	40.1
22	Fairmont	41.1		20	Summersville Lake	40.1
22	Kopperston	*41.1*		23	Romney 1 SW	40.3
22	Moundsville	*41.1*		23	Spencer 4 S	40.3
25	Middlebourne 3 ESE	40.9		25	Clarksburg 1	40.6

Annual Extreme Minimum Temperature

	Highest				Lowest	
Rank	Station Name	°F		Rank	Station Name	°F
1	Logan	*-15*		1	Middlebourne 3 ESE	-34
2	Charleston Kanawha Airport	-16		2	West Union 2	*-33*
2	London Locks	-16		3	Spencer 4 S	-31
4	Bluestone Lake	-17		4	Buckhannon	-30
4	Pineville	-17		4	Creston	-30
4	Romney 1 SW	-17		6	Flat Top	-28
4	Wardensville R M Farm	-17		6	Hamlin	-28
8	Martinsburg Eastern WV Reg. Arpt.	-18		6	Ripley	-28
8	Winfield Locks	-18		9	Canaan Valley	-27
10	Kopperston	*-19*		10	Buckeye	*-26*
11	Dunlow 1 SW	-20		10	Cacapon State Park 2	*-26*
11	Franklin 2 NE	-20		10	Parkersburg WSO	-26
11	Mathias	-20		10	Union 3 SSE	-26
11	Moorefield 2 SSE	-20		14	Glenville 1 ENE	-25
11	Morgantown Municipal Airport	-20		14	Madison	-25
11	Moundsville	*-20*		14	Seneca State Forest 1 N	-25
11	Oak Hill	-20		14	Terra Alta 1	-25
11	Parsons 1 NE	-20		18	Clarksburg 1	-24
11	Summersville Lake	-20		18	Elkins-Randolph Co. Airport	-24
11	White Sulphur Springs	-20		18	Hogsett R.C. Byrd Dam	-24
21	Bluefield Mercer Co. Airport	-21		18	Parkersburg Wood County Airport	-24
21	Fairmont	-21		18	Weston	-24
21	Huntington Tri-State Airport	-21		23	Bayard	-23
21	Kearneysville	*-21*		23	Beckley Virginia Hospital	-23
21	Morgantown Lock & Dam	-21		25	Athens	-22

July Mean Maximum Temperature

	Highest				Lowest	
Rank	Station Name	°F		Rank	Station Name	°F
1	Logan	87.6		1	Flat Top	76.8
2	Ripley	87.5		2	Terra Alta 1	77.6
3	Moorefield 2 SSE	87.4		3	Canaan Valley	77.7
4	Martinsburg Eastern WV Reg. Arpt.	87.2		4	Bayard	79.2
5	Madison	87.1		5	Bluefield Mercer Co. Airport	79.3
6	Hamlin	86.9		6	Beckley Virginia Hospital	79.6
7	Creston	86.8		7	Beckley Memorial Airport	80.0
7	Romney 1 SW	86.8		8	Elkins-Randolph Co. Airport	81.1
9	Hogsett R.C. Byrd Dam	86.7		9	Summersville Lake	81.4
10	Gassaway	86.2		10	Parsons 1 NE	81.8
10	Winfield Locks	86.2		11	Rowlesburg 1	81.9
12	Spencer 4 S	86.1		11	Seneca State Forest 1 N	81.9
13	Charleston Kanawha Airport	86.0		13	Buckeye	82.0
13	Huntington Tri-State Airport	86.0		14	Athens	82.1
15	Parkersburg WSO	85.9		15	Oak Hill	82.3
16	Glenville 1 ENE	85.8		16	Union 3 SSE	82.9
16	London Locks	85.8		17	Kopperston	*83.3*
16	Weston	85.8		18	Buckhannon	83.4
19	Moundsville	85.7		19	Fairmont	83.5
19	Wardensville R M Farm	85.7		19	Lewisburg 3 N	83.5
21	Kearneysville	*85.6*		21	Morgantown Municipal Airport	83.7
22	Cacapon State Park 2	85.4		22	Franklin 2 NE	83.8
23	Pineville	85.2		23	Mathias	83.9
24	Middlebourne 3 ESE	84.6		23	Morgantown Lock & Dam	83.9
25	Bluestone Lake	84.5		25	West Union 2	*84.1*

January Mean Minimum Temperature

	Highest				Lowest	
Rank	**Station Name**	**°F**		**Rank**	**Station Name**	**°F**
1	Logan	25.8		1	Seneca State Forest 1 N	14.9
2	London Locks	24.8		2	Canaan Valley	15.9
3	Huntington Tri-State Airport	24.6		3	Buckeye	16.1
4	Charleston Kanawha Airport	24.5		4	Bayard	17.2
5	Bluefield Mercer Co. Airport	23.9		5	Elkins-Randolph Co. Airport	17.8
6	Dunlow 1 SW	23.8		6	Terra Alta 1	18.1
7	Winfield Locks	23.1		7	Wardensville R M Farm	18.3
8	Gassaway	22.6		8	Parsons 1 NE	18.4
9	Bluestone Lake	22.4		9	West Union 2	*18.9*
9	Parkersburg Wood County Airport	22.4		10	Flat Top	19.1
11	Morgantown Municipal Airport	22.3		11	Creston	19.2
12	Parkersburg WSO	22.2		12	Rowlesburg 1	19.3
13	Kopperston	*22.1*		13	Glenville 1 ENE	19.5
13	Martinsburg Eastern WV Reg. Arpt.	22.1		14	Buckhannon	19.6
15	Athens	22.0		15	Moundsville	*19.7*
16	Beckley Memorial Airport	21.9		16	Kearneysville	19.8
16	Pineville	21.9		16	Mathias	19.8
18	Ripley	21.8		16	Weston	19.8
19	Madison	21.5		19	Romney 1 SW	19.9
20	Moorefield 2 SSE	21.2		20	Summersville Lake	20.0
21	Morgantown Lock & Dam	21.1		21	Beckley Virginia Hospital	20.1
22	Lewisburg 3 N	21.0		21	Cacapon State Park 2	20.1
22	White Sulphur Springs	21.0		23	Middlebourne 3 ESE	20.2
24	Hogsett R.C. Byrd Dam	20.9		24	Franklin 2 NE	20.4
24	Union 3 SSE	20.9		25	Hamlin	20.5

Number of Annual Heating Degree Days

	Highest				Lowest	
Rank	**Station Name**	**Num.**		**Rank**	**Station Name**	**Num.**
1	Canaan Valley	6,764		1	Logan	*4,356*
2	Bayard	6,534		2	Huntington Tri-State Airport	4,522
3	Seneca State Forest 1 N	6,410		3	Charleston Kanawha Airport	4,529
4	Terra Alta 1	6,291		4	London Locks	4,533
5	Flat Top	6,159		5	Gassaway	4,653
6	Buckeye	6,080		6	Winfield Locks	4,734
7	Elkins-Randolph Co. Airport	5,981		7	Dunlow 1 SW	4,774
8	Parsons 1 NE	5,909		8	Ripley	4,791
9	Rowlesburg 1	5,739		9	Madison	4,827
10	Beckley Virginia Hospital	5,589		10	Moorefield 2 SSE	4,837
11	West Union 2	*5,573*		11	Parkersburg Wood County Airport	4,963
12	Summersville Lake	5,560		12	Hamlin	4,973
13	Wardensville R M Farm	5,508		13	Pineville	4,981
14	Mathias	5,505		14	Martinsburg Eastern WV Reg. Arpt.	4,987
15	Kearneysville	*5,432*		15	Bluefield Mercer Co. Airport	4,998
16	Cacapon State Park 2	*5,428*		16	Parkersburg WSO	5,011
17	Fairmont	5,423		17	Hogsett R.C. Byrd Dam	5,021
18	Clarksburg 1	5,411		18	Bluestone Lake	5,045
19	Buckhannon	5,400		19	Athens	5,078
20	Oak Hill	5,376		20	Kopperston	*5,105*
21	Union 3 SSE	5,364		21	Spencer 4 S	5,181
22	Beckley Memorial Airport	5,363		22	White Sulphur Springs	5,204
23	Weston	5,352		23	Morgantown Municipal Airport	5,223
24	Moundsville	*5,350*		24	Morgantown Lock & Dam	5,236
25	Lewisburg 3 N	5,333		25	Glenville 1 ENE	5,246

Number of Annual Cooling Degree Days

	Highest			Lowest	
Rank	**Station Name**	**Num.**	**Rank**	**Station Name**	**Num.**
1	Logan	1,282	1	Canaan Valley	*222*
2	Huntington Tri-State Airport	1,189	2	Bayard	320
3	London Locks	1,144	3	Seneca State Forest 1 N	348
4	Charleston Kanawha Airport	1,139	4	Terra Alta 1	388
5	Martinsburg Eastern WV Reg. Arpt.	1,090	5	Beckley Virginia Hospital	418
6	Winfield Locks	1,079	6	Flat Top	419
7	Parkersburg WSO	1,075	7	Elkins-Randolph Co. Airport	459
8	Madison	1,049	8	Buckeye	484
9	Parkersburg Wood County Airport	1,030	9	Parsons 1 NE	571
10	Moorefield 2 SSE	1,018	10	Summersville Lake	574
11	Hogsett R.C. Byrd Dam	1,013	11	Union 3 SSE	588
12	Ripley	1,009	12	Beckley Memorial Airport	592
13	Hamlin	1,007	13	Athens	594
14	Creston	988	13	Franklin 2 NE	594
15	Gassaway	973	15	Mathias	*605*
16	Moundsville	*923*	15	Rowlesburg 1	605
16	Pineville	923	17	Oak Hill	613
18	Glenville 1 ENE	909	18	White Sulphur Springs	634
19	Romney 1 SW	903	19	Lewisburg 3 N	650
20	Cacapon State Park 2	888	20	Buckhannon	*657*
21	Spencer 4 S	884	21	Bluefield Mercer Co. Airport	666
22	Morgantown Municipal Airport	873	22	West Union 2	*719*
23	Kearneysville	*869*	23	Fairmont	735
24	Dunlow 1 SW	862	24	Wardensville R M Farm	785
25	Bluestone Lake	852	25	Weston	817

Annual Precipitation

	Highest			Lowest	
Rank	**Station Name**	**Inches**	**Rank**	**Station Name**	**Inches**
1	Rowlesburg 1	55.88	1	Moorefield 2 SSE	32.85
1	Terra Alta 1	55.88	2	Franklin 2 NE	35.38
3	Parsons 1 NE	52.14	3	Wardensville R M Farm	35.41
4	Canaan Valley	*51.71*	4	Romney 1 SW	35.64
5	Kopperston	*50.99*	5	Union 3 SSE	35.90
6	Weston	50.86	6	Athens	36.90
7	Bayard	49.42	7	Bluestone Lake	37.49
8	Gassaway	49.06	8	Mathias	37.64
9	Buckhannon	48.89	9	Cacapon State Park 2	*38.83*
10	Seneca State Forest 1 N	48.14	10	Beckley Virginia Hospital	39.39
11	Madison	47.72	11	Martinsburg Eastern WV Reg. Arpt.	39.41
12	Summersville Lake	47.24	12	Bluefield Mercer Co. Airport	39.54
13	Logan	*47.08*	13	White Sulphur Springs	40.27
14	West Union 2	*46.41*	14	Kearneysville	*40.36*
15	Pineville	46.04	15	Parkersburg WSO	40.63
16	Creston	45.97	16	Lewisburg 3 N	40.74
16	Oak Hill	45.97	17	Hogsett R.C. Byrd Dam	40.93
18	Elkins-Randolph Co. Airport	45.95	18	Beckley Memorial Airport	41.50
19	Dunlow 1 SW	45.94	19	Moundsville	41.60
20	Fairmont	45.81	20	Winfield Locks	41.75
20	Glenville 1 ENE	45.81	21	Huntington Tri-State Airport	42.30
22	Flat Top	45.77	22	Morgantown Municipal Airport	42.59
23	Spencer 4 S	45.73	23	Parkersburg Wood County Airport	42.84
24	Buckeye	45.68	24	Morgantown Lock & Dam	43.25
25	Middlebourne 3 ESE	45.31	25	Charleston Kanawha Airport	44.07

Number of Days Annually With ≥ 0.1″ Precipitation

	Highest			Lowest	
Rank	**Station Name**	**Days**	**Rank**	**Station Name**	**Days**
1	Terra Alta 1	121	1	Moorefield 2 SSE	70
2	Canaan Valley	117	2	Wardensville R M Farm	71
3	Rowlesburg 1	116	3	Franklin 2 NE	73
4	Bayard	111	4	Cacapon State Park 2	*74*
5	Parsons 1 NE	108	5	Martinsburg Eastern WV Reg. Arpt.	76
6	Weston	106	5	Union 3 SSE	76
7	Elkins-Randolph Co. Airport	105	7	Kearneysville	*77*
8	Gassaway	103	7	Mathias	77
8	Oak Hill	103	9	Romney 1 SW	78
10	Buckhannon	102	10	Athens	79
10	Kopperston	*102*	11	Lewisburg 3 N	*82*
12	Middlebourne 3 ESE	99	12	Bluestone Lake	84
12	Summersville Lake	99	12	White Sulphur Springs	84
14	Clarksburg 1	98	14	Bluefield Mercer Co. Airport	85
15	Madison	97	15	Hogsett R.C. Byrd Dam	86
16	Flat Top	96	15	Parkersburg WSO	86
16	London Locks	96	15	Winfield Locks	86
16	Ripley	96	18	Huntington Tri-State Airport	87
19	Creston	*95*	19	Beckley Virginia Hospital	89
19	Fairmont	95	19	Hamlin	89
19	Logan	*95*	21	Dunlow 1 SW	90
19	Morgantown Lock & Dam	95	22	Moundsville	*91*
19	Pineville	95	22	Parkersburg Wood County Airport	91
19	Seneca State Forest 1 N	95	24	Beckley Memorial Airport	92
19	Spencer 4 S	95	24	Buckeye	92

Number of Days Annually With ≥ 1.0″ Precipitation

	Highest			Lowest	
Rank	**Station Name**	**Days**	**Rank**	**Station Name**	**Days**
1	Rowlesburg 1	13	1	Beckley Memorial Airport	5
2	Buckeye	12	2	Athens	6
2	Kopperston	*12*	2	Beckley Virginia Hospital	6
2	Seneca State Forest 1 N	12	2	Elkins-Randolph Co. Airport	6
2	Terra Alta 1	12	2	Morgantown Municipal Airport	6
6	Creston	11	6	Charleston Kanawha Airport	7
6	Flat Top	11	6	Franklin 2 NE	7
6	Lewisburg 3 N	11	6	Moundsville	7
6	Madison	11	6	Oak Hill	7
6	Middlebourne 3 ESE	11	6	Parkersburg WSO	7
6	Ripley	11	11	Bluefield Mercer Co. Airport	8
6	West Union 2	*11*	11	Bluestone Lake	8
6	White Sulphur Springs	11	11	Canaan Valley	8
14	Buckhannon	10	11	Fairmont	8
14	Dunlow 1 SW	10	11	Glenville 1 ENE	8
14	Gassaway	10	11	Hamlin	8
14	Logan	*10*	11	Moorefield 2 SSE	8
14	Parsons 1 NE	10	11	Morgantown Lock & Dam	8
14	Pineville	10	11	Romney 1 SW	8
14	Spencer 4 S	10	11	Union 3 SSE	8
14	Summersville Lake	10	21	Bayard	9
14	Weston	10	21	Cacapon State Park 2	*9*
23	Bayard	9	21	Clarksburg 1	9
23	Cacapon State Park 2	*9*	21	Hogsett R.C. Byrd Dam	9
23	Clarksburg 1	9	21	Huntington Tri-State Airport	9

Annual Snowfall

Highest			Lowest		
Rank	Station Name	Inches	Rank	Station Name	Inches
1	Terra Alta 1	157.8	1	Winfield Locks	*14.1*
2	Canaan Valley	*134.8*	2	Logan	*16.9*
3	Bayard	94.7	3	Parkersburg WSO	*17.6*
4	Elkins-Randolph Co. Airport	79.8	4	Ripley	18.3
5	Seneca State Forest 1 N	64.1	5	Madison	19.7
6	Flat Top	63.4	6	Kearneysville	*19.8*
7	Beckley Memorial Airport	60.1	7	Dunlow 1 SW	*20.2*
8	Rowlesburg 1	55.5	8	Bluestone Lake	21.1
9	Parsons 1 NE	*54.3*	9	White Sulphur Springs	*21.3*
10	Buckhannon	51.7	10	Gassaway	*22.1*
11	Summersville Lake	*44.1*	11	Pineville	22.9
12	Oak Hill	43.3	12	Glenville 1 ENE	23.5
13	Buckeye	41.2	13	Hamlin	23.7
14	Weston	40.2	13	Moorefield 2 SSE	*23.7*
15	Charleston Kanawha Airport	38.5	15	Parkersburg Wood County Airport	24.6
16	Fairmont	37.7	16	Middlebourne 3 ESE	24.9
17	Mathias	36.2	17	Union 3 SSE	*25.4*
18	Beckley Virginia Hospital	*34.7*	18	Martinsburg Eastern WV Reg. Arpt.	25.8
19	Athens	*31.7*	19	Huntington Tri-State Airport	26.2
20	Bluefield Mercer Co. Airport	31.4	20	Wardensville R M Farm	27.2
21	Morgantown Municipal Airport	30.4	21	Clarksburg 1	*27.3*
22	Franklin 2 NE	28.6	22	Romney 1 SW	27.5
23	Lewisburg 3 N	*28.5*	23	Spencer 4 S	*28.2*
24	Spencer 4 S	*28.2*	24	Lewisburg 3 N	*28.5*
25	Romney 1 SW	27.5	25	Franklin 2 NE	28.6

Note: See Appendix D for explanation of data.

Annual Extreme Maximum Temperature

	Highest			Lowest	
Rank	Station Name	°F	Rank	Station Name	°F
1	Genoa Dam 8	109	1	Laona 6 SW	92
1	Waukesha	*109*	2	Washington Island	94
3	Arboretum Univ. Wisconsin	108	3	Antigo	*96*
3	La Crosse Municipal Airport	108	3	Goodman	96
3	Milwaukee Mt. Mary College	108	3	North Pelican	96
3	Sheboygan	108	3	Rainbow Reservoir Lake Tomaha	96
7	Wisconsin Rapids	107	7	Minocqua Dam	97
8	Clintonville	106	7	Rest Lake	97
8	Lake Geneva	106	7	Saint Germain 2 E	97
8	Port Washington	106	7	Two Rivers	97
11	Blair	105	7	Willow Reservoir	97
11	Burlington	105	12	Long Lake Dam	*98*
11	Ellsworth 1 E	*105*	12	Medford	98
11	Hancock Exp. Farm	105	12	Mellen 4 NE	98
11	Hartford 2 W	105	12	Oconto 4 W	98
11	Necedah	105	16	Gurney	99
11	New London	105	16	Jump River 3 E	99
11	Saint Croix Falls	105	16	Prentice 2	99
11	Waupaca	105	16	Sturgeon Bay Exp. Farm	99
11	West Bend	105	20	Alma Dam 4	100
21	Bloomer	104	20	Beaver Dam	100
21	Eau Claire County Airport	104	20	Bowler	100
21	Foxboro	104	20	Grantsburg	100
21	Kenosha	104	20	Holcombe	100
21	Lake Mills	104	20	Lakewood 3 NE	100

Annual Mean Maximum Temperature

	Highest			Lowest	
Rank	Station Name	°F	Rank	Station Name	°F
1	Prairie Du Chien	59.1	1	Superior	49.0
2	Lake Geneva	58.3	2	Saint Germain 2 E	49.3
3	Beloit	57.9	3	Willow Reservoir	50.1
4	Lake Mills	57.8	4	Rainbow Reservoir Lake Tomaha	50.3
4	Milwaukee Mt. Mary College	57.8	5	Laona 6 SW	50.4
6	Arboretum Univ. Wisconsin	57.3	6	Minocqua Dam	50.6
6	Richland Center	57.3	6	Rest Lake	50.6
6	Whitewater	57.3	8	North Pelican	50.9
9	Brodhead	57.2	9	Prentice 2	51.0
9	Lynxville Dam 9	57.2	10	Bayfield 6 N	51.1
9	Necedah	57.2	10	Long Lake Dam	*51.1*
12	Platteville	57.0	12	Mellen 4 NE	51.2
13	Darlington	56.9	13	Medford	51.3
14	Fort Atkinson	56.8	14	Goodman	*51.4*
14	Portage	56.8	14	Washington Island	51.4
16	Dalton	56.7	16	Owen 3 W	51.5
17	La Crosse Municipal Airport	56.6	17	Two Rivers	51.6
17	Watertown	56.6	18	Antigo	*51.8*
19	Beaver Dam	56.5	18	Foxboro	51.8
19	Waukesha	*56.5*	18	Gurney	51.8
21	Madison Regional Airport	56.4	18	Rhinelander	51.8
21	Mauston 1 SE	56.4	22	Gordon	52.1
23	Genoa Dam 8	56.3	23	Amery	52.5
24	Baraboo	56.2	24	Ashland Exp. Farm	*52.6*
24	Burlington	56.2	24	Grantsburg	52.6

Annual Mean Temperature

	Highest				Lowest	
Rank	Station Name	°F		Rank	Station Name	°F
1	Milwaukee Mt. Mary College	48.8		1	Rainbow Reservoir Lake Tomaha	38.9
2	Lake Geneva	48.5		2	Long Lake Dam	*39.1*
3	Prairie Du Chien	48.4		3	Willow Reservoir	39.2
4	Beloit	48.2		4	Minocqua Dam	39.4
5	Lynxville Dam 9	47.9		5	Gordon	39.6
6	Waukesha	*47.4*		5	North Pelican	39.6
7	Lake Mills	47.3		5	Saint Germain 2 E	39.6
8	Milwaukee Gen. Mitchell Field	47.2		8	Foxboro	39.7
9	Genoa Dam 8	47.1		9	Prentice 2	39.8
10	Racine	47.0		10	Mellen 4 NE	40.0
11	Platteville	46.9		10	Superior	40.0
11	Sheboygan	46.9		12	Rest Lake	40.1
11	Whitewater	46.9		13	Laona 6 SW	40.4
14	La Crosse Municipal Airport	46.8		13	Solon Springs	40.4
15	Kenosha	46.7		15	Goodman	*40.5*
15	Watertown	46.7		16	Rhinelander	40.8
17	Beaver Dam	46.5		17	Antigo	*41.0*
17	Fort Atkinson	46.5		18	Medford	41.1
19	Alma Dam 4	46.4		19	Jump River 3 E	41.2
20	Burlington	46.3		19	Merrill	41.2
20	Darlington	46.3		19	Owen 3 W	41.2
20	Oconomowoc	46.3		22	Ashland Exp. Farm	*41.3*
20	Prairie Du Sac 2 N	*46.3*		22	Gurney	41.3
24	Dalton	46.2		24	Bayfield 6 N	41.5
25	Brodhead	46.1		24	Lakewood 3 NE	41.5

Annual Mean Minimum Temperature

	Highest				Lowest	
Rank	Station Name	°F		Rank	Station Name	°F
1	Milwaukee Mt. Mary College	39.6		1	Long Lake Dam	*27.0*
2	Racine	39.3		2	Gordon	27.1
3	Milwaukee Gen. Mitchell Field	39.1		3	Foxboro	27.5
4	Lake Geneva	38.6		3	Rainbow Reservoir Lake Tomaha	27.5
4	Sheboygan	38.6		5	Solon Springs	27.9
6	Beloit	38.5		6	Minocqua Dam	28.2
6	Kenosha	38.5		6	Willow Reservoir	28.2
6	Lynxville Dam 9	38.5		8	North Pelican	28.3
9	Waukesha	*38.3*		9	Prentice 2	28.5
10	Genoa Dam 8	37.8		10	Mellen 4 NE	28.8
10	Port Washington	37.8		11	Rest Lake	29.5
12	Prairie Du Chien	37.7		12	Goodman	*29.6*
13	Alma Dam 4	37.1		12	Lakewood 3 NE	29.6
13	Fond Du Lac	37.1		14	Jump River 3 E	29.7
15	La Crosse Municipal Airport	36.9		14	Merrill	29.7
16	Lake Mills	36.8		16	Rhinelander	29.8
16	Platteville	36.8		17	Saint Germain 2 E	29.9
16	Watertown	36.8		18	Ashland Exp. Farm	*30.0*
19	Manitowoc	36.6		18	Weyerhauser	30.0
19	Prairie Du Sac 2 N	*36.6*		20	Antigo	*30.1*
21	Beaver Dam	36.5		21	Laona 6 SW	30.4
21	Two Rivers	36.5		22	Danbury	30.6
23	Oconomowoc	36.4		22	Grantsburg	30.6
24	Burlington	36.3		24	Gurney	30.7
24	Lancaster 4 WSW	36.3		25	Medford	30.8

Annual Extreme Minimum Temperature

	Highest			Lowest	
Rank	Station Name	°F	Rank	Station Name	°F
1	Beloit	-26	1	Rest Lake	-49
1	Milwaukee Gen. Mitchell Field	-26	2	Gordon	-48
1	Milwaukee Mt. Mary College	-26	2	Minocqua Dam	-48
1	Sheboygan	-26	4	Jump River 3 E	-47
1	Two Rivers	-26	4	North Pelican	-47
6	Burlington	-27	4	Prentice 2	-47
6	Lake Geneva	-27	4	Ridgeland 1 NNE	-47
6	Manitowoc	-27	4	Solon Springs	-47
6	Washington Island	-27	9	Amery	-46
6	Whitewater	-27	9	Mcllcn 4 NE	-46
11	Green Bay Int'l Airport	-28	11	Blair	-45
11	Waukesha	*-28*	11	Foxboro	-45
13	Appleton	-29	11	Holcombe	-45
13	Lake Mills	-29	11	Long Lake Dam	*-45*
13	Madison Regional Airport	-29	11	Merrill	-45
13	Oconomowoc	-29	11	Willow Reservoir	-45
13	Plymouth	-29	17	Breed 6 SSE	-44
13	Port Washington	-29	17	Danbury	-44
13	Sturgeon Bay Exp. Farm	-29	17	Luck	-44
20	Chilton	-30	17	Spooner Experiment Farm	-44
20	Darlington	-30	21	Bloomer	-43
20	Marinette	-30	21	Lakewood 3 NE	-43
20	Oshkosh	-30	21	Rice Lake Municipal Airport	-43
20	West Bend	-30	21	Saint Croix Falls	-43
25	Beaver Dam	-31	21	Saint Germain 2 E	-43

July Mean Maximum Temperature

	Highest			Lowest	
Rank	Station Name	°F	Rank	Station Name	°F
1	Prairie Du Chien	85.7	1	Two Rivers	75.1
2	Lake Geneva	85.1	2	Saint Germain 2 E	75.4
3	Lake Mills	84.8	3	Laona 6 SW	75.7
4	Milwaukee Mt. Mary College	84.7	4	Washington Island	76.1
5	Necedah	84.6	5	Superior	76.4
6	La Crosse Municipal Airport	84.4	6	North Pelican	76.9
7	Richland Center	84.3	7	Rest Lake	77.1
8	Lynxville Dam 9	84.2	8	Rainbow Reservoir Lake Tomaha	77.2
9	Beloit	83.9	9	Willow Reservoir	77.4
10	Arboretum Univ. Wisconsin	83.8	10	Bayfield 6 N	77.6
11	Brodhead	83.5	10	Minocqua Dam	77.6
11	Menomonie	83.5	12	Prentice 2	77.8
11	Whitewater	83.5	13	Gurney	78.1
14	Platteville	83.4	13	Long Lake Dam	78.1
14	Saint Croix Falls	83.4	15	Goodman	*78.3*
16	Dalton	83.3	15	Port Washington	78.3
16	Darlington	83.3	17	Mellen 4 NE	78.7
16	Fort Atkinson	83.3	18	Medford	78.9
16	Trempealeau Dam 6	83.3	19	Rhinelander	79.0
16	Watertown	83.3	20	Kenosha	79.1
16	Waukesha	83.3	21	Racine	79.2
22	Portage	83.2	22	Owen 3 W	79.3
23	Genoa Dam 8	83.1	22	Sturgeon Bay Exp. Farm	79.3
24	Madison Regional Airport	83.0	24	Antigo	*79.4*
25	Montello	82.9	25	Jump River 3 E	79.6

January Mean Minimum Temperature

Highest			Lowest		
Rank	Station Name	°F	Rank	Station Name	°F
1	Milwaukee Mt. Mary College	13.3	1	Gordon	-5.8
2	Milwaukee Gen. Mitchell Field	13.1	2	Solon Springs	-3.8
3	Sheboygan	13.0	3	Foxboro	-3.1
4	Kenosha	12.7	4	Prentice 2	-3.0
5	Racine	12.4	5	Willow Reservoir	-2.9
6	Port Washington	12.1	6	Long Lake Dam	-2.7
7	Lake Geneva	11.9	7	Grantsburg	-2.4
8	Two Rivers	11.2	7	Rainbow Reservoir Lake Tomaha	-2.4
9	Beloit	11.1	9	Mellen 4 NE	-1.9
10	Manitowoc	10.5	10	Minocqua Dam	-1.7
11	Waukesha	*10.4*	11	Danbury	-1.6
12	Washington Island	9.9	12	Amery	-1.3
12	West Bend	9.9	12	North Pelican	-1.3
14	Plymouth	9.8	14	Saint Croix Falls	-1.2
15	Burlington	9.3	15	Jump River 3 E	-1.0
15	Whitewater	9.3	15	Rhinelander	-1.0
17	Sturgeon Bay Exp. Farm	9.1	17	Rice Lake Municipal Airport	-0.9
18	Beaver Dam	8.8	17	Weyerhauser	-0.9
19	Fond Du Lac	8.6	19	Owen 3 W	-0.8
19	Lake Mills	8.6	20	Ridgeland 1 NNE	-0.7
21	Marinette	8.5	21	Rest Lake	-0.6
22	Watertown	8.4	22	Merrill	-0.5
23	Platteville	8.3	22	Spooner Experiment Farm	-0.5
23	Prairie Du Chien	8.3	24	Medford	-0.4
25	Chilton	8.1	25	Saint Germain 2 E	-0.2

Number of Annual Heating Degree Days

Highest			Lowest		
Rank	Station Name	Num.	Rank	Station Name	Num.
1	Rainbow Reservoir Lake Tomaha	9,627	1	Milwaukee Mt. Mary College	6,661
2	Long Lake Dam	*9,586*	2	Lake Geneva	6,767
3	Willow Reservoir	9,542	3	Prairie Du Chien	6,815
4	Gordon	9,464	4	Beloit	6,820
5	Minocqua Dam	9,459	5	Lynxville Dam 9	6,971
6	Foxboro	9,385	6	Waukesha	*7,032*
7	Saint Germain 2 E	9,371	7	Racine	7,033
8	North Pelican	9,364	7	Sheboygan	7,033
9	Prentice 2	9,351	9	Milwaukee Gen. Mitchell Field	7,041
10	Mellen 4 NE	9,317	10	Lake Mills	7,063
11	Superior	9,256	11	Kenosha	7,083
12	Rest Lake	9,242	12	Whitewater	7,167
13	Solon Springs	9,225	13	Genoa Dam 8	7,176
14	Goodman	*9,082*	14	Platteville	7,201
15	Laona 6 SW	9,064	15	Watertown	7,249
16	Rhinelander	9,026	16	Beaver Dam	7,282
17	Antigo	*8,954*	17	Fort Atkinson	7,304
18	Medford	8,953	18	Burlington	7,325
19	Owen 3 W	8,938	19	La Crosse Municipal Airport	7,334
20	Merrill	8,906	20	Oconomowoc	7,336
21	Jump River 3 E	8,887	21	Port Washington	7,357
22	Ashland Exp. Farm	*8,857*	22	Darlington	7,362
23	Gurney	8,847	23	Dalton	7,392
24	Grantsburg	8,835	24	Brodhead	7,401
25	Danbury	8,798	25	Prairie Du Sac 2 N	*7,403*

Number of Annual Cooling Degree Days

	Highest			Lowest	
Rank	**Station Name**	**Num.**	**Rank**	**Station Name**	**Num.**
1	Milwaukee Mt. Mary College	876	1	Laona 6 SW	188
2	Prairie Du Chien	872	2	Rainbow Reservoir Lake Tomaha	*200*
3	Lake Geneva	857	3	North Pelican	203
4	Lynxville Dam 9	851	4	Willow Reservoir	*213*
5	La Crosse Municipal Airport	834	5	Foxboro	223
6	Genoa Dam 8	779	6	Minocqua Dam	224
7	Waukesha	*767*	7	Long Lake Dam	*228*
8	Beloit	761	7	Saint Germain 2 E	228
9	Lake Mills	*738*	9	Rest Lake	244
10	Alma Dam 4	734	10	Prentice 2	246
11	Platteville	708	11	Washington Island	249
12	Trempealeau Dam 6	695	12	Bayfield 6 N	259
13	Prairie Du Sac 2 N	*694*	13	Superior	260
14	Milwaukee Gen. Mitchell Field	681	14	Two Rivers	265
15	Watertown	663	15	Antigo	*267*
16	Necedah	653	16	Gordon	288
17	Fond Du Lac	641	17	Lakewood 3 NE	298
18	Dalton	639	17	Mellen 4 NE	298
18	Darlington	639	19	Gurney	306
20	Appleton	635	20	Rhinelander	317
21	Portage	633	21	Jump River 3 E	319
22	Fort Atkinson	632	22	Merrill	321
23	Oconomowoc	629	23	Ashland Exp. Farm	*327*
24	Whitewater	628	24	Solon Springs	329
25	River Falls	625	25	Rosholt 9 NNE	341

Annual Precipitation

	Highest			Lowest	
Rank	**Station Name**	**Inches**	**Rank**	**Station Name**	**Inches**
1	Viroqua 2 S	49.33	1	Washington Island	28.43
2	Lake Geneva	36.85	2	Green Bay Int'l Airport	29.10
3	Arboretum Univ. Wisconsin	36.45	3	Fond Du Lac	29.75
4	Plymouth	36.31	4	Appleton	29.92
5	Dodgeville	35.95	5	Spooner Experiment Farm	29.94
6	Platteville	35.83	6	Manitowoc	29.95
7	Beloit	35.25	7	Two Rivers	30.02
8	Richland Center	35.24	8	Goodman	*30.30*
9	Brodhead	35.18	9	Ashland Exp. Farm	30.40
10	Racine	35.06	10	Danbury	30.50
11	Darlington	35.02	11	Menomonie	30.55
12	Ellsworth 1 E	*34.93*	12	Willow Reservoir	30.74
13	Alma Dam 4	34.58	13	River Falls	30.76
14	Gurney	34.56	14	Antigo	30.77
15	Waukesha	*34.55*	15	Prairie Du Sac 2 N	30.85
16	Kenosha	34.46	16	Superior	30.86
17	Portage	34.32	17	Foxboro	30.90
18	Milwaukee Gen. Mitchell Field	34.29	18	Prentice 2	30.94
19	Lake Mills	34.24	19	New London	*30.99*
20	Watertown	34.15	20	North Pelican	31.02
21	Blair	34.04	21	Saint Croix Falls	31.08
22	Fairchild Ranger Station	33.98	22	Solon Springs	31.14
23	Montello	33.82	23	Shawano 2 SSW	31.26
24	Burlington	33.77	24	Bowler	31.33
25	Lancaster 4 WSW	33.76	25	Chilton	31.37

Number of Days Annually With ≥ 0.1″ Precipitation

	Highest			Lowest	
Rank	Station Name	Days	Rank	Station Name	Days
1	Gurney	78	1	Bowler	56
2	Mellen 4 NE	75	2	Ashland Exp. Farm	59
3	Long Lake Dam	74	2	Goodman	*59*
3	Rainbow Reservoir Lake Tomaha	74	2	Holcombe	59
5	Bayfield 6 N	73	5	Fairchild Ranger Station	60
5	Saint Germain 2 E	73	6	Appleton	61
5	Sturgeon Bay Exp. Farm	73	6	Foxboro	61
8	Dodgeville	72	6	Menomonie	61
8	Lake Geneva	72	6	Milwaukee Mt. Mary College	61
8	Laona 6 SW	72	6	Solon Springs	*61*
8	Rhinelander	72	11	Neillsville 3 SW	62
8	Weyerhauser	*72*	11	Prairie Du Sac 2 N	62
13	Marinette	71	11	Spooner Experiment Farm	62
13	Mather 3 NW	71	14	Amery	63
13	Medford	71	14	Bloomer	63
13	Minocqua Dam	71	14	Genoa Dam 8	63
13	North Pelican	71	14	Green Bay Int'l Airport	63
13	Plymouth	71	14	Port Washington	63
19	Arlington Univ. Farm	70	14	Rice Lake Municipal Airport	63
19	Lakewood 3 NE	70	14	River Falls	63
19	Merrill	70	21	Danbury	64
19	Stevens Point	70	21	Eau Claire County Airport	64
23	Beaver Dam	69	21	Fond Du Lac	64
23	Breed 6 SSE	69	21	Germantown	64
23	Cumberland	69	21	Jump River 3 E	64

Number of Days Annually With ≥ 1.0″ Precipitation

	Highest			Lowest	
Rank	Station Name	Days	Rank	Station Name	Days
1	Bloomer	9	1	Ashland Exp. Farm	4
1	Lakewood 3 NE	9	1	North Pelican	4
3	Arboretum Univ. Wisconsin	8	3	Amery	5
3	Beloit	8	3	Appleton	5
3	Lancaster 4 WSW	8	3	Chilton	5
3	Marshfield Exp. Farm	8	3	Eau Claire County Airport	5
3	Plymouth	8	3	Foxboro	5
3	Rice Lake Municipal Airport	8	3	Germantown	5
3	Viroqua 2 S	8	3	Green Bay Int'l Airport	5
10	Bayfield 6 N	7	3	Gurney	5
10	Bowler	7	3	Hancock Exp. Farm	5
10	Breed 6 SSE	7	3	Hartford 2 W	5
10	Brodhead	7	3	Horicon	5
10	Charmany Farm	7	3	Mather 3 NW	5
10	Clintonville	7	3	Medford	5
10	Cumberland	7	3	Menomonie	5
10	Fort Atkinson	7	3	Minocqua Dam	5
10	Holcombe	7	3	River Falls	5
10	Lake Geneva	7	3	Saint Germain 2 E	5
10	Lynxville Dam 9	7	3	Sheboygan	5
10	Milwaukee Gen. Mitchell Field	7	3	Solon Springs	5
10	Oconto 4 W	7	3	Stevens Point	5
10	Platteville	7	3	Sturgeon Bay Exp. Farm	5
10	Prairie Du Chien	7	3	Superior	5
10	Richland Center	7	3	Two Rivers	5

Annual Snowfall

	Highest			Lowest	
Rank	**Station Name**	**Inches**	**Rank**	**Station Name**	**Inches**
1	Gurney	138.7	1	Prairie Du Sac 2 N	25.4
2	Minocqua Dam	110.5	2	Beloit	*28.1*
3	Mellen 4 NE	100.9	3	Whitewater	30.5
4	Bayfield 6 N	96.4	4	Genoa Dam 8	30.9
5	Rest Lake	81.0	5	Necedah	31.3
6	Laona 6 SW	72.7	6	Two Rivers	*32.9*
7	Long Lake Dam	*66.7*	7	Brodhead	*33.4*
8	Lakewood 3 NE	64.7	8	Lynxville Dam 9	*34.1*
9	Saint Germain 2 E	*63.2*	9	Charmany Farm	35.3
10	Plymouth	60.4	10	Burlington	35.8
11	North Pelican	*60.3*	11	Port Washington	36.4
12	Antigo	59.6	12	Arlington Univ. Farm	36.8
13	Luck	*58.7*	13	Hartford 2 W	37.0
14	Rainbow Reservoir Lake Tomaha	*58.1*	14	Kenosha	37.4
15	Ashland Exp. Farm	57.5	15	Alma Dam 4	*37.5*
16	Wausau Municipal Airport	57.2	16	Horicon	37.7
17	Breed 6 SSE	56.4	17	Beaver Dam	38.1
18	Gordon	55.6	17	Fort Atkinson	38.1
19	Jump River 3 E	55.4	17	Portage	*38.1*
20	Prentice 2	54.9	20	Darlington	38.2
21	Marinette	*54.7*	21	Milwaukee Mt. Mary College	38.3
22	Solon Springs	54.6	22	Lake Mills	38.7
23	Cumberland	54.2	23	Watertown	39.0
24	Goodman	*54.1*	24	Platteville	39.6
25	Hancock Exp. Farm	53.5	25	Oconomowoc	39.7

Note: See Appendix D for explanation of data.

Annual Extreme Maximum Temperature

	Highest				Lowest	
Rank	**Station Name**	**°F**		**Rank**	**Station Name**	**°F**
1	Basin	115		1	Moran 5 WNW	91
1	Diversion Dam	115		1	Pinedale	91
3	Colony	112		3	Alta 1 NNW	92
4	Torrington Exp. Farm	111		3	Elk Mountain	92
5	Redbird	110		5	Buffalo Bill Dam	93
6	La Grange	109		5	Moose	93
6	Yoder 2 WSW	109		5	Mountain View	93
8	Devils Tower 2	108		5	Snake River	93
8	Leiter 9 N	108		9	Laramie General Brees Field	94
8	Weston 1 E	108		9	Sage 4 NNW	*94*
11	Dull Center 1 SE	107		11	Afton	95
11	Gillette 6 SE	107		11	Burris	95
11	Glenrock 5 ESE	107		11	Fontenelle Dam	95
11	Kaycee	107		14	Rock Springs Airport	96
11	Rochelle 3 E	107		15	Bitter Creek 4 NE	97
11	Wheatland 4 N	107		15	Rawlins Municipal Airport	97
11	Worland Municipal Airport	107		17	Bates Creek 2	98
18	Buffalo	106		17	Cheyenne Municipal Airport	98
18	Sheridan County Airport	106		17	Jackson	98
18	Sheridan Field Station	106		17	Pavillion	98
18	Worland	106		17	Saratoga	98
22	Billy Creek	105		22	Cody 21 SW	99
22	Boysen Dam	105		22	Double Four Ranch	99
22	Clark 3 NE	105		22	Encampment 10 ESE	99
22	Deaver	105		22	Evanston 1 E	99

Annual Mean Maximum Temperature

	Highest				Lowest	
Rank	**Station Name**	**°F**		**Rank**	**Station Name**	**°F**
1	Yoder 2 WSW	64.3		1	Snake River	50.0
2	Wheatland 4 N	63.7		2	Moran 5 WNW	50.8
3	Torrington Exp. Farm	63.6		3	Pinedale	51.4
4	La Grange	62.6		4	Moose	51.7
5	Phillips	62.3		5	Alta 1 NNW	52.2
6	Carpenter	62.0		6	Fontenelle Dam	53.0
7	Redbird	61.8		7	Elk Mountain	53.6
8	Chugwater	61.3		8	Laramie General Brees Field	54.2
8	Glenrock 5 ESE	61.3		9	Jackson	54.3
10	Dull Center 1 SE	61.0		10	Afton	*54.7*
10	Kaycee	61.0		11	Sage 4 NNW	*54.8*
12	Clark 3 NE	60.9		12	Encampment 10 ESE	54.9
13	Albin	60.8		13	Rock Springs Airport	55.0
13	Basin	60.8		14	Rawlins Municipal Airport	55.2
13	Ten Sleep 4 NE	60.8		15	Evanston 1 E	55.4
16	Worland Municipal Airport	60.4		15	Mountain View	55.4
17	Deaver	60.2		17	Sundance	56.5
17	Devils Tower 2	60.2		18	Double Four Ranch	56.6
17	Weston 1 E	60.2		19	Bitter Creek 4 NE	56.8
20	Archer	60.1		20	Saratoga	56.9
21	Worland	60.0		21	Gillette 6 SE	57.4
22	Boysen Dam	*59.8*		22	Bates Creek 2	57.5
22	Newcastle	59.8		22	Black Mountain	57.5
24	Rochelle 3 E	59.6		22	Burris	57.5
25	Buffalo	59.3		25	Clearmont 5 SW	57.6

Annual Mean Temperature

	Highest			Lowest	
Rank	**Station Name**	**°F**	**Rank**	**Station Name**	**°F**
1	Wheatland 4 N	49.0	1	Snake River	33.8
2	Yoder 2 WSW	48.5	2	Pinedale	36.0
3	Phillips	48.1	3	Moose	36.5
4	Glenrock 5 ESE	47.9	3	Moran 5 WNW	36.5
5	Ten Sleep 4 NE	47.6	5	Fontenelle Dam	37.1
5	Torrington Exp. Farm	47.6	6	Sage 4 NNW	*37.8*
7	La Grange	47.4	7	Jackson	38.8
8	Albin	47.3	8	Afton	*39.3*
9	Carpenter	47.2	9	Alta 1 NNW	*39.6*
10	Boysen Dam	*46.9*	10	Encampment 10 ESE	40.6
11	Colony	46.8	10	Laramie General Brees Field	40.6
11	Dull Center 1 SE	46.8	12	Evanston 1 E	41.2
11	Newcastle	46.8	13	Bitter Creek 4 NE	41.6
14	Chugwater	46.6	13	Elk Mountain	41.6
14	Redbird	46.6	15	Mountain View	41.7
16	Leiter 9 N	46.5	16	Ten Sleep 16 SSE	42.1
17	Sybille Research Unit	46.3	17	Riverton	42.7
18	Cody	46.1	18	Double Four Ranch	42.8
19	Worland Municipal Airport	46.0	19	Rawlins Municipal Airport	42.9
20	Black Mountain	45.7	19	Rock Springs Airport	42.9
20	Cheyenne Municipal Airport	45.7	21	Clearmont 5 SW	43.1
22	Archer	45.6	21	Saratoga	43.1
22	Basin	45.6	23	Burris	43.3
22	Buffalo	45.6	24	Cody 21 SW	43.9
25	Casper Int'l Airport	45.5	25	Sheridan Field Station	44.1

Annual Mean Minimum Temperature

	Highest			Lowest	
Rank	**Station Name**	**°F**	**Rank**	**Station Name**	**°F**
1	Colony	34.5	1	Snake River	17.5
2	Glenrock 5 ESE	34.4	2	Pinedale	20.4
3	Ten Sleep 4 NE	34.3	3	Sage 4 NNW	*20.7*
4	Wheatland 4 N	34.1	4	Fontenelle Dam	21.0
5	Black Mountain	34.0	5	Moose	21.2
6	Boysen Dam	33.9	6	Moran 5 WNW	22.1
6	Newcastle	33.9	7	Jackson	23.2
8	Phillips	33.8	8	Afton	23.7
9	Albin	33.7	9	Ten Sleep 16 SSE	25.5
9	Leiter 9 N	33.7	10	Encampment 10 ESE	26.3
11	Cody	33.6	11	Bitter Creek 4 NE	26.4
12	Cheyenne Municipal Airport	33.4	12	Riverton	26.5
13	Sybille Research Unit	33.2	13	Evanston 1 E	26.9
14	Yoder 2 WSW	32.8	14	Alta 1 NNW	*27.0*
15	Gillette 6 SE	32.6	14	Laramie General Brees Field	27.0
16	Dull Center 1 SE	32.5	16	Mountain View	27.9
17	Carpenter	32.3	17	Clearmont 5 SW	28.5
18	La Grange	32.2	18	Devils Tower 2	28.6
19	Casper Int'l Airport	32.0	19	Double Four Ranch	28.9
20	Buffalo	31.9	19	Sheridan Field Station	28.9
20	Chugwater	31.9	21	Burris	29.1
20	Lander Hunt Field	31.9	22	Saratoga	29.2
23	Bates Creek 2	31.8	23	Deaver	29.3
23	Sundance	31.8	24	Clark 3 NE	29.5
25	Torrington Exp. Farm	31.6	24	Diversion Dam	29.5

Annual Extreme Minimum Temperature

	Highest				Lowest	
Rank	Station Name	°F		Rank	Station Name	°F
1	Cheyenne Municipal Airport	-29		1	Sage 4 NNW	*-51*
1	Rock Springs Airport	-29		1	Ten Sleep 16 SSE	-51
3	Archer	-30		3	Jackson	-50
3	Sybille Research Unit	-30		3	Worland Municipal Airport	-50
5	Albin	-31		5	Pinedale	-49
5	Carpenter	-31		6	Clearmont 5 SW	-48
5	Evanston 1 E	-31		6	Devils Tower 2	-48
8	Mountain View	-33		8	Cody 21 SW	-47
8	Phillips	-33		8	Redbird	-47
10	Ten Sleep 4 NE	-34		8	Rochelle 3 E	-47
11	Buffalo	-35		8	Weston 1 E	-47
11	Chugwater	-35		12	Afton	-46
11	La Grange	-35		12	Bitter Creek 4 NE	-46
11	Newcastle	-35		12	Fontenelle Dam	-46
15	Black Mountain	-36		12	Moose	-46
15	Buffalo Bill Dam	-36		12	Riverton	-46
15	Colony	-36		12	Snake River	-46
15	Elk Mountain	-36		18	Burris	-45
15	Leiter 9 N	-36		18	Dillinger	-45
15	Rawlins Municipal Airport	-36		18	Moran 5 WNW	-45
21	Cody	-37		21	Clark 3 NE	-44
21	Emblem	-37		21	Diversion Dam	-44
21	Gillette 6 SE	-37		21	Encampment 10 ESE	-44
21	Lander Hunt Field	-37		21	Sheridan Field Station	-44
21	Sheridan County Airport	-37		21	Worland	-44

July Mean Maximum Temperature

	Highest				Lowest	
Rank	Station Name	°F		Rank	Station Name	°F
1	Basin	90.0		1	Buffalo Bill Dam	74.4
2	Boysen Dam	89.8		2	Snake River	76.7
3	Worland Municipal Airport	89.6		3	Pinedale	77.4
3	Yoder 2 WSW	89.6		4	Moran 5 WNW	77.8
5	Redbird	89.4		5	Alta 1 NNW	78.3
5	Worland	89.4		6	Encampment 10 ESE	78.4
7	Dull Center 1 SE	89.3		7	Elk Mountain	79.0
8	Torrington Exp. Farm	89.1		7	Moose	79.0
9	Glenrock 5 ESE	88.7		9	Laramie General Brees Field	79.4
10	Wheatland 4 N	88.6		10	Mountain View	80.0
11	La Grange	88.3		11	Burris	80.8
11	Riverton	88.3		12	Afton	80.9
13	Rochelle 3 E	88.1		13	Double Four Ranch	81.4
14	Deaver	87.8		13	Fontenelle Dam	81.4
15	Leiter 9 N	87.7		15	Evanston 1 E	81.5
15	Newcastle	87.7		16	Cody 21 SW	81.7
17	Casper Int'l Airport	87.4		16	Jackson	81.7
17	Colony	87.4		18	Sage 4 NNW	81.8
17	Kaycee	87.4		19	Cheyenne Municipal Airport	82.1
20	Weston 1 E	87.2		20	Saratoga	82.3
21	Ten Sleep 16 SSE	87.0		21	Rock Springs Airport	82.7
22	Ten Sleep 4 NE	86.9		21	Sundance	82.7
23	Dillinger	86.8		23	Rawlins Municipal Airport	82.8
24	Phillips	86.7		24	Bates Creek 2	83.4
25	Devils Tower 2	86.6		25	Bitter Creek 4 NE	83.5

January Mean Minimum Temperature

	Highest				Lowest	
Rank	**Station Name**	**°F**		**Rank**	**Station Name**	**°F**
1	Buffalo Bill Dam	*19.5*		1	Ten Sleep 16 SSE	-2.5
2	Phillips	16.3		2	Fontenelle Dam	-2.2
3	Glenrock 5 ESE	16.0		3	Sage 4 NNW	-1.7
4	Cheyenne Municipal Airport	15.8		4	Snake River	-1.2
4	Chugwater	15.8		5	Riverton	-0.7
4	Sybille Research Unit	15.8		6	Pinedale	-0.3
4	Wheatland 4 N	15.8		7	Moose	0.6
8	Albin	14.9		8	Moran 5 WNW	1.7
9	Black Mountain	14.3		9	Basin	2.1
9	Cody 21 SW	14.3		10	Worland	2.2
11	Yoder 2 WSW	14.1		11	Worland Municipal Airport	3.2
12	Elk Mountain	13.8		12	Devils Tower 2	4.4
13	Archer	13.4		13	Clearmont 5 SW	4.6
13	Double Four Ranch	13.4		13	Deaver	4.6
15	Carpenter	13.3		13	Lovell	4.6
16	Cody	13.2		16	Afton	4.7
17	La Grange	13.0		17	Jackson	5.0
18	Casper Int'l Airport	12.5		18	Sheridan Field Station	5.3
19	Rawlins Municipal Airport	12.4		19	Upton	5.5
19	Ten Sleep 4 NE	12.4		20	Boysen Dam	6.3
21	Rock Springs Airport	11.6		21	Clark 3 NE	6.7
22	Bates Creek 2	11.4		21	Emblem	6.7
22	Colony	11.4		23	Kaycee	6.8
24	Dull Center 1 SE	11.1		24	Bitter Creek 4 NE	7.0
24	Mountain View	11.1		24	Dillinger	7.0

Number of Annual Heating Degree Days

	Highest				Lowest	
Rank	**Station Name**	**Num.**		**Rank**	**Station Name**	**Num.**
1	Snake River	11,303		1	Wheatland 4 N	6,305
2	Pinedale	10,502		2	Yoder 2 WSW	6,479
3	Moose	10,313		3	Phillips	6,539
4	Moran 5 WNW	10,311		4	Glenrock 5 ESE	6,725
5	Fontenelle Dam	10,166		5	Albin	6,814
6	Sage 4 NNW	*9,862*		6	Torrington Exp. Farm	6,824
7	Jackson	9,491		7	Carpenter	6,825
8	Afton	*9,323*		7	Ten Sleep 4 NE	6,825
9	Alta 1 NNW	*9,242*		9	La Grange	6,828
10	Laramie General Brees Field	8,846		10	Chugwater	6,952
11	Encampment 10 ESE	8,828		11	Sybille Research Unit	7,097
12	Evanston 1 E	8,644		12	Dull Center 1 SE	7,147
13	Ten Sleep 16 SSE	8,549		13	Newcastle	7,177
14	Bitter Creek 4 NE	8,548		14	Cody	7,186
15	Elk Mountain	8,505		15	Colony	7,220
16	Mountain View	8,473		16	Cheyenne Municipal Airport	7,222
17	Riverton	8,412		17	Redbird	7,263
18	Clearmont 5 SW	8,188		18	Leiter 9 N	7,264
19	Rock Springs Airport	8,182		19	Archer	7,277
20	Rawlins Municipal Airport	8,151		20	Boysen Dam	*7,304*
21	Double Four Ranch	8,109		21	Buffalo	7,447
22	Saratoga	8,044		22	Kaycee	7,455
23	Upton	7,954		23	Casper Int'l Airport	7,475
24	Burris	7,937		24	Black Mountain	7,482
24	Sheridan Field Station	7,937		25	Clark 3 NE	7,487

Number of Annual Cooling Degree Days

	Highest			Lowest	
Rank	Station Name	Num.	Rank	Station Name	Num.
1	Boysen Dam	*806*	1	Snake River	1
2	Colony	714	2	Pinedale	7
3	Worland Municipal Airport	679	3	Moran 5 WNW	16
4	Newcastle	672	4	Moose	21
5	Redbird	671	5	Encampment 10 ESE	27
6	Leiter 9 N	664	6	Sage 4 NNW	28
7	Basin	631	7	Jackson	40
8	Worland	627	8	Afton	45
9	Dull Center 1 SE	591	9	Laramie General Brees Field	52
10	Wheatland 4 N	590	10	Elk Mountain	59
11	Torrington Exp. Farm	579	11	Fontenelle Dam	66
12	Glenrock 5 ESE	576	12	Evanston 1 E	70
13	Ten Sleep 4 NE	567	13	Alta 1 NNW	72
13	Yoder 2 WSW	567	14	Mountain View	83
15	Upton	541	15	Double Four Ranch	84
16	Black Mountain	537	16	Burris	125
17	Buffalo	511	17	Bitter Creek 4 NE	136
17	La Grange	511	18	Saratoga	142
19	Weston 1 E	496	19	Cody 21 SW	159
20	Lander Hunt Field	492	20	Rawlins Municipal Airport	218
21	Kaycee	483	21	Rock Springs Airport	236
21	Rochelle 3 E	483	22	Ten Sleep 16 SSE	278
23	Dillinger	481	23	Archer	293
24	Phillips	477	24	Clearmont 5 SW	300
25	Gillette 6 SE	473	25	Cheyenne Municipal Airport	308

Annual Precipitation

	Highest			Lowest	
Rank	Station Name	Inches	Rank	Station Name	Inches
1	Snake River	31.89	1	Deaver	5.49
2	Moran 5 WNW	25.50	2	Basin	6.76
3	Alta 1 NNW	25.36	2	Lovell	6.76
4	Moose	21.69	4	Fontenelle Dam	7.43
5	Sundance	18.70	5	Clark 3 NE	7.47
6	Albin	18.63	6	Emblem	7.65
7	Afton	18.30	7	Worland Municipal Airport	7.89
8	Devils Tower 2	17.63	8	Worland	7.92
9	Gillette 6 SE	17.16	9	Pavillion	7.93
10	Jackson	16.97	10	Riverton	8.69
11	La Grange	16.86	11	Burris	9.11
12	Archer	16.56	12	Heart Mountain	9.23
13	Sybille Research Unit	15.98	13	Mountain View	9.27
14	Newcastle	15.96	14	Diversion Dam	9.31
15	Chugwater	15.72	15	Boysen Dam	9.38
16	Double Four Ranch	15.47	16	Rock Springs Airport	9.46
17	Phillips	15.42	17	Rawlins Municipal Airport	9.78
18	Cheyenne Municipal Airport	15.41	18	Cody 12 SE	10.17
19	Leiter 9 N	15.39	19	Saratoga	10.28
20	Redbird	15.38	20	Cody	10.83
21	Upton	14.97	21	Buffalo Bill Dam	10.97
22	Colony	14.93	22	Laramie General Brees Field	11.28
23	Sheridan County Airport	14.81	23	Pinedale	11.41
24	Dillinger	14.69	24	Evanston 1 E	11.43
25	Yoder 2 WSW	14.61	25	Glenrock 5 ESE	12.31

Number of Days Annually With ≥ 0.1″ Precipitation

	Highest			Lowest	
Rank	Station Name	Days	Rank	Station Name	Days
1	Snake River	92	1	Deaver	17
2	Moran 5 WNW	80	2	Pavillion	20
3	Alta 1 NNW	74	3	Basin	21
4	Moose	65	4	Riverton	22
5	Afton	56	5	Emblem	23
6	Jackson	54	5	Lovell	23
7	Albin	48	5	Worland Municipal Airport	23
7	Encampment 10 ESE	48	8	Clark 3 NE	*24*
7	Sundance	48	8	Worland	24
10	Devils Tower 2	44	10	Boysen Dam	25
10	Double Four Ranch	44	10	Diversion Dam	25
10	Gillette 6 SE	44	10	Fontenelle Dam	25
13	La Grange	43	13	Burris	27
13	Leiter 9 N	43	14	Heart Mountain	28
13	Newcastle	43	15	Rock Springs Airport	29
13	Sheridan County Airport	43	16	Buffalo Bill Dam	30
17	Archer	42	16	Mountain View	30
17	Chugwater	42	18	Cody 12 SE	*31*
17	Sybille Research Unit	42	18	Glenrock 5 ESE	31
20	Phillips	41	20	Rawlins Municipal Airport	32
21	Cheyenne Municipal Airport	40	21	Laramie General Brees Field	33
21	Clearmont 5 SW	40	21	Saratoga	33
21	Dillinger	40	21	Wheatland 4 N	33
21	Sheridan Field Station	40	24	Billy Creek	34
21	Ten Sleep 4 NE	40	24	Cody	34

Number of Days Annually With ≥ 1.0″ Precipitation

	Highest			Lowest	
Rank	Station Name	Days	Rank	Station Name	Days
1	Yoder 2 WSW	2	1	Afton	0
2	Archer	1	1	Albin	0
2	Chugwater	1	1	Alta 1 NNW	0
2	Colony	1	1	Basin	0
2	Devils Tower 2	1	1	Bates Creek 2	0
2	Gillette 6 SE	1	1	Billy Creek	0
2	La Grange	1	1	Bitter Creek 4 NE	*0*
2	Sundance	1	1	Black Mountain	0
9	Afton	0	1	Boysen Dam	0
9	Albin	0	1	Buffalo	0
9	Alta 1 NNW	0	1	Buffalo Bill Dam	0
9	Basin	0	1	Burris	0
9	Bates Creek 2	0	1	Carpenter	0
9	Billy Creek	0	1	Casper Int'l Airport	0
9	Bitter Creek 4 NE	*0*	1	Cheyenne Municipal Airport	0
9	Black Mountain	0	1	Clark 3 NE	0
9	Boysen Dam	0	1	Clearmont 5 SW	0
9	Buffalo	0	1	Cody	0
9	Buffalo Bill Dam	0	1	Cody 12 SE	*0*
9	Burris	0	1	Cody 21 SW	0
9	Carpenter	0	1	Deaver	0
9	Casper Int'l Airport	0	1	Dillinger	0
9	Cheyenne Municipal Airport	0	1	Diversion Dam	0
9	Clark 3 NE	0	1	Double Four Ranch	0
9	Clearmont 5 SW	0	1	Dull Center 1 SE	0

Annual Snowfall

	Highest			Lowest	
Rank	**Station Name**	**Inches**	**Rank**	**Station Name**	**Inches**
1	Snake River	275.9	1	Deaver	*10.9*
2	Moose	170.8	2	Emblem	*14.2*
3	Alta 1 NNW	109.4	3	Lovell	*18.8*
4	Lander Hunt Field	106.9	4	Basin	19.3
5	Elk Mountain	86.4	5	Clark 3 NE	*25.1*
6	Casper Int'l Airport	85.6	6	Worland Municipal Airport	31.6
7	Bates Creek 2	83.8	7	Torrington Exp. Farm	*33.0*
8	Albin	83.2	8	Riverton	*33.4*
9	Sundance	82.5	9	Carpenter	34.7
10	Sybille Research Unit	78.3	10	Colony	36.4
11	Sheridan County Airport	75.6	11	Mountain View	*39.6*
12	Jackson	*75.5*	12	Newcastle	*39.7*
13	Afton	*75.4*	13	Wheatland 4 N	40.4
14	Encampment 10 ESE	*73.9*	14	Weston 1 E	40.7
15	Chugwater	72.7	15	Rochelle 3 E	40.9
16	Double Four Ranch	72.1	16	Dillinger	*41.9*
17	Pinedale	69.9	17	Kaycee	42.4
18	Gillette 6 SE	65.3	18	Billy Creek	44.9
19	Ten Sleep 16 SSE	62.4	19	Clearmont 5 SW	45.6
20	Saratoga	62.3	20	Cody	*46.5*
21	La Grange	62.1	21	Upton	*46.9*
22	Black Mountain	*62.0*	22	Rock Springs Airport	47.7
23	Cheyenne Municipal Airport	59.6	23	Yoder 2 WSW	48.0
24	Leiter 9 N	57.9	24	Archer	49.6
25	Ten Sleep 4 NE	57.0	25	Cody 21 SW	50.1

Note: See Appendix D for explanation of data.

100 Storms With The Greatest Number of Fatalities: 1995-1999

Rank	Location or County	Date	Type	Mag.	Fatalities	Injuries	Property Damage ($mil.)	Crop Damage ($mil.)
1	Oak Grove, AL	04/08/98	Tornado	F5	32	258	200.0	2.2
2	Jarrell, TX	05/27/97	Tornado	F5	27	12	40.0	0.1
3	Intercession City, FL	02/23/98	Tornado	F3	25	145	50.0	0.0
4	All of Indiana, IN	07/13/95	Heat Wave	na	14	0	1.0	0.0
5	Eastern North Carolina, NC	09/14/99	Hurricane Floyd	105 mph	13	0	410.6	413.6
6	Longwood, FL	02/23/98	Tornado	F3	12	36	30.0	0.0
7	Amber, OK	05/03/99	Tornado	F5	12	39	90.0	0.0
8	Del City, OK	05/03/99	Tornado	F4	12	234	450.0	0.0
9	Bexar Co., TX	10/17/98	Flood	na	11	600	8.0	0.1
10	Moore, OK	05/03/99	Tornado	F5	11	293	450.0	0.0
11	Murrayville, GA	03/20/98	Tornado	F3	10	96	15.0	0.0
12	Kansas City, MO	10/04/98	Flash Flood	na	9	0	20.0	0.0
13	Val Verde Co., TX	08/23/98	Flash Flood	na	9	150	40.0	0.1
14	Central Georgia, GA	10/05/95	Thunderstorm Winds	na	8	7	75.0	50.0
15	North Central Oregon, OR	09/25/99	High Wind	na	8	33	1.0	0.0
16	Northern Oregon, OR	02/06/96	Flood	na	7	0	400.0	0.0
17	Southeastern Pennsylvania, PA	01/07/96	Blizzard	na	7	0	18.9	0.0
18	Carter Co., TN	01/07/98	Flood	na	7	0	20.0	0.0
19	Bossier City, LA	04/03/99	Tornado	F4	7	90	6.6	0.0
20	Joppa to Guntersville, AL	02/16/95	Tornado	F0	6	130	5.0	0.0
21	Delaware Co., NY	01/19/96	Flash Flood	na	6	0	9.3	0.0
22	Spencer, SD	05/30/98	Tornado	F4	6	150	17.0	0.4
23	Caldwell Co., TX	10/17/98	Flood	na	6	500	20.0	0.1
24	Peck, KS	05/03/99	Tornado	F4	6	150	140.0	0.0
25	Bemis, TN	01/17/99	Tornado	F4	6	106	10.0	0.0
26	Halifax Co., NC	01/15/95	Flood/Flash Flood	na	5	0	2.5	0.0
27	Fox, AR	04/14/96	Tornado	F4	5	5	2.5	0.0
28	Southern Coast/Umpqua Basin, OR	11/17/96	Flood	na	5	6	42.0	0.4
29	Southern Sacramento Valley, CA	12/11/97	Fog	na	5	26	1.5	0.0
30	S. Central/SE Colorado, CO	10/24/97	Blizzard	na	5	2	1.2	0.0
31	Ft. Collins, CO	07/28/97	Flash Flood	na	5	40	190.0	0.0
32	Pendleton Co., KY	03/01/97	Flood	na	5	0	35.0	0.0
33	Grosse Pt. Farms, MI	07/02/97	Thunderstorm Winds	92 mph	5	8	10.0	0.0
34	Noble Co., OH	06/27/98	Flash Flood	na	5	0	10.0	10.0
35	Marion Jct., AL	03/06/96	Tornado	F3	4	40	8.0	0.0
36	Eastern North Carolina, NC	09/04/96	Hurricane Fran	100 mph	4	4	792.1	0.0
37	Northern Virginia, VA	01/19/96	Flood	na	4	0	15.0	0.0
38	Elba, AL	03/08/98	Flash Flood	na	4	0	105.0	0.0
39	Guadalupe Co., TX	10/17/98	Flood	na	4	500	5.0	0.1
40	Southeastern Wisconsin, WI	11/10/98	High Wind	na	4	14	10.3	1.5
41	Blue Ash, OH	04/09/99	Tornado	F4	4	65	82.0	0.0
42	Crawfordsville, IN	05/13/95	Tornado	F2	3	5	3.5	0.0
43	Piney To, TN	05/18/95	Tornado	F4	3	32	4.6	0.0
44	All of Iowa, IA	07/12/95	Heat Wave	na	3	0	3.8	0.0
45	North/SW New Jersey, NJ	01/07/96	Blizzard	na	3	0	18.8	0.0
46	Southeastern Pennsylvania, PA	01/19/96	Flood	na	3	3	42.3	0.0
47	Southeastern South Dakota, SD	11/14/96	Ice Storm	na	3	50	2.0	0.0
48	El Paso Co., TX	01/17/96	High Wind	86 mph	3	0	10.0	0.0
49	Mecklenburg Co., NC	07/23/97	Flash Flood	na	3	0	8.5	0.0
50	Western Tennessee, TN	03/01/97	Flood	na	3	0	19.7	0.1
51	Northern Utah, UT	03/31/97	Winter Storm	na	3	60	2.0	0.0
52	All of Utah, UT	01/11/97	Blizzard	na	3	50	40.0	0.0
53	Winter Garden, FL	02/22/98	Tornado	F3	3	70	15.0	0.0
54	Baldwinsville, NY	09/07/98	Thunderstorm Winds	na	3	7	90.0	0.0
55	Clifton, TN	04/16/98	Tornado	F4	3	6	4.0	0.0

Rank	Location or County	Date	Type	Mag.	Fatalities	Injuries	Property Damage ($mil.)	Crop Damage ($mil.)
56	Southeastern Texas, TX	09/07/98	Tropical Storm Frances	na	3	0	287.1	0.0
57	Montgomery Co., PA	09/16/99	Flash Flood	na	3	8	12.0	0.0
58	Roscommon Co., MI	07/13/95	Thunderstorm Winds	na	2	0	50.0	0.0
59	Southern Minnesota, MN	07/10/95	Heat Wave	na	2	0	2.0	0.0
60	Eastern Florida Panhandle, FL	08/02/95	Hurricane Erin	na	2	0	1.0	0.0
61	Western North Carolina, NC	10/05/95	High Wind	na	2	10	15.0	0.0
62	Northwest California, CA	12/11/95	High Wind	na	2	0	4.8	0.0
63	Montgomery, AL	03/06/96	Tornado	F2	2	17	1.5	0.0
64	Sylamore, AR	04/14/96	Tornado	F4	2	30	5.0	0.0
65	Ft. Smith, AR	04/21/96	Tornado	F2	2	40	150.0	0.0
66	St. Paul, AR	04/21/96	Tornado	F3	2	6	1.0	0.0
67	Schoharie Co., NY	01/19/96	Flood	na	2	0	12.0	0.0
68	Pender Co., NC	09/05/96	Hurricane Fran	na	2	0	180.0	46.0
69	Southwestern Ohio, OH	01/06/96	Winter Storm	na	2	0	14.2	0.0
70	Southeast, PA	06/12/96	Flash Flood	na	2	0	14.5	0.0
71	Montgomery Co., PA	09/08/96	Flash Flood	na	2	0	20.0	0.0
72	All of Vermont, VT	01/19/96	Flood	na	2	0	2.8	0.0
73	Augusta Co., VA	09/06/96	Flash Flood	na	2	0	2.0	0.5
74	Randolph Co., WV	05/16/96	Flash Flood	na	2	0	1.5	0.0
75	Southeastern Colorado, CO	10/24/97	Blizzard	na	2	0	1.0	0.0
76	Owen Co., KY	03/01/97	Flash Flood	na	2	0	2.1	0.0
77	Southwestern Louisiana, LA	01/12/97	Ice Storm	na	2	15	11.8	0.0
78	Western Nevada, NV	01/01/97	Flood	na	2	50	640.0	0.0
79	South Central North Dakota, ND	03/21/97	Flood	na	2	1	3.0	0.0
80	Southern North Dakota, ND	04/04/97	Blizzard	na	2	16	44.7	0.0
81	South/NW North Dakota, ND	01/09/97	Blizzard	na	2	45	55.0	0.0
82	Southeastern North Dakota, ND	01/15/97	Blizzard	na	2	10	6.3	0.0
83	Adams Co., OH	03/01/97	Flash Flood	na	2	0	8.0	0.0
84	Hays Co., TX	06/08/97	Flood	na	2	7	2.5	0.0
85	Bandera Co., TX	06/21/97	Flood	na	2	20	5.0	1.0
86	Llano Co., TX	02/20/97	Flood	na	2	0	2.0	0.0
87	Moody, AL	04/08/98	Tornado	F2	2	12	2.0	0.0
88	Northwestern California, CA	02/02/98	Flood	na	2	0	4.3	7.8
89	Orange Co., CA	02/23/98	Flood	na	2	2	29.7	0.2
90	Central/Southern San Joaquin Valley, CA	11/14/98	Fog	na	2	78	1.4	0.0
91	Central San Joaquin Valley, CA	12/20/98	Ice Storm	na	2	0	1.0	0.0
92	Northwestern Florida, FL	09/02/98	Hurricane Earl	70 mph	2	2	6.0	0.0
93	Southern Florida, FL	11/04/98	Tropical Storm Mitch	na	2	65	30.0	20.0
94	Cleveland, GA	03/20/98	Tornado	F3	2	75	5.0	0.0
95	Pembroke, GA	04/09/98	Tornado	F3	2	16	2.2	0.0
96	Overland Park, KS	10/04/98	Flash Flood	na	2	0	8.0	0.0
97	East Central Kentucky, KY	02/03/98	Heavy Snow	na	2	1	10.0	0.0
98	Glasgow, KY	04/16/98	Tornado	F3	2	9	10.0	0.0
99	Cannon Falls, MN	06/26/98	Flash Flood	na	2	0	1.5	0.0
100	Hattiesburg, MS	06/05/98	Thunderstorm Winds	na	2	45	1.0	0.0

Note: Storms with less than one million dollars of property damage are excluded.

100 Storms With The Greatest Number of Injuries: 1995-1999

Rank	Location or County	Date	Type	Mag.	Fatalities	Injuries	Property Damage ($mil.)	Crop Damage ($mil.)
1	Comal Co., TX	10/17/98	Flood	na	2	800	50.0	0.0
2	Comal/Guadalupe/Gonzales/De Witt Co., TX	10/17/98	Flood	na	0	750	268.0	1.5
3	Bexar Co., TX	10/17/98	Flood	na	11	600	8.0	0.1
4	Bexar/Guadalupe/Wilson/Karnes Co., TX	10/17/98	Flood	na	0	550	66.0	0.2
5	Caldwell Co., TX	10/17/98	Flood	na	6	500	20.0	0.1
6	Guadalupe Co., TX	10/17/98	Flood	na	4	500	5.0	0.1
7	De Witt Co., TX	10/18/98	Flood	na	0	500	5.0	1.0
8	Lavaca Co., TX	10/18/98	Flood	na	0	300	3.0	0.5
9	Moore, OK	05/03/99	Tornado	F5	11	293	450.0	0.0
10	Oak Grove, AL	04/08/98	Tornado	F5	32	258	200.0	2.2
11	Del City, OK	05/03/99	Tornado	F4	12	234	450.0	0.0
12	Spencer, SD	05/30/98	Tornado	F4	6	150	17.0	0.4
13	Val Verde Co., TX	08/23/98	Flash Flood	na	9	150	40.0	0.1
14	Peck, KS	05/03/99	Tornado	F4	6	150	140.0	0.0
15	Intercession City, FL	02/23/98	Tornado	F3	25	145	50.0	0.0
16	Joppa to Guntersville, AL	02/16/95	Tornado	F0	6	130	5.0	0.0
17	Hays/Caldwell/Gonzales Co., TX	10/17/98	Flood	na	0	125	62.0	0.6
18	Bemis, TN	01/17/99	Tornado	F4	6	106	10.0	0.0
19	Bexar Co., TX	10/17/98	Flood	na	0	100	8.0	0.0
20	Bastrop Co., TX	10/17/98	Flood	na	0	100	3.0	0.1
21	Wilson Co., TX	10/18/98	Flood	na	0	100	35.0	0.1
22	Somerset Co., NJ	09/16/99	Flash Flood	na	2	100	358.0	0.0
23	Murrayville, GA	03/20/98	Tornado	F3	10	96	15.0	0.0
24	Highland Park, MI	07/02/97	Tornado	F2	0	90	90.0	0.0
25	Bossier City, LA	04/03/99	Tornado	F4	7	90	6.6	0.0
26	Grimes, IA	06/29/98	Tornado	F2	0	83	10.0	0.0
27	Salt Lake City, UT	08/11/99	Tornado	F2	1	80	170.0	0.5
28	Central/Southern San Joaquin Valley, CA	11/14/98	Fog	na	2	78	1.4	0.0
29	Cleveland, GA	03/20/98	Tornado	F3	2	75	5.0	0.0
30	Middlesex Co., NJ	09/16/99	Flash Flood	na	0	72	28.0	0.0
31	Winter Garden, FL	02/22/98	Tornado	F3	3	70	15.0	0.0
32	Ushers, NY	05/31/98	Tornado	F3	0	68	60.0	0.0
33	Southern Florida, FL	11/04/98	Tropical Storm Mitch	na	2	65	30.0	20.0
34	Blue Ash, OH	04/09/99	Tornado	F4	4	65	82.0	0.0
35	Brockton, MA	05/21/96	Thunderstorm Winds	104 mph	0	60	4.0	0.0
36	Northern Utah, UT	03/31/97	Winter Storm	na	3	60	2.0	0.0
37	Nashville, TN	04/16/98	Tornado	F3	1	60	100.0	0.0
38	Limestone, AL	05/18/95	Tornado	F4	1	55	5.0	0.0
39	Slim Butte, SD	06/04/99	Tornado	F2	1	54	3.2	0.0
40	Sand Lake, MI	05/31/98	Thunderstorm Winds	na	0	53	49.3	20.0
41	Brevard Co., FL	07/01/98	Wild/Forest Fire	na	0	52	200.0	0.0
42	San Angelo, TX	05/28/95	Thunderstorm Winds	86 mph	0	50	60.0	0.0
43	Southeastern South Dakota, SD	11/14/96	Ice Storm	na	3	50	2.0	0.0
44	Western Nevada, NV	01/01/97	Flood	na	2	50	640.0	0.0
45	S.W. of Cleveland, TN	03/29/97	Tornado	F3	0	50	3.2	0.0
46	Medina Co., TX	06/22/97	Flood	na	1	50	13.0	0.1
47	Uvalde Co., TX	06/22/97	Flood	na	0	50	1.0	0.1
48	All of Utah, UT	01/11/97	Blizzard	na	3	50	40.0	0.0
49	Carnegie, PA	06/02/98	Tornado	F1	0	50	13.0	0.0
50	Real/Uvalde/Zavala Co., TX	08/23/98	Flood	na	0	50	1.4	0.0
51	Travis Co., TX	10/17/98	Flash Flood	na	1	50	1.5	0.1
52	Travis Co., TX	10/17/98	Flood	na	0	50	1.0	0.0
53	Comal Co., TX	10/17/98	Flood	na	0	50	8.0	0.1
54	De Witt Co., TX	10/17/98	Flood	na	0	50	1.0	0.0
55	Caldwell Co., TX	10/17/98	Flood	na	0	50	30.0	0.0

Rank	Location or County	Date	Type	Mag.	Fatalities	Injuries	Property Damage ($mil.)	Crop Damage ($mil.)
56	Lavaca Co., TX	10/17/98	Flood	na	0	50	2.0	0.1
57	Van Buren, AR	04/21/96	Tornado	F3	0	49	150.0	0.0
58	Big Spring, TX	05/10/96	Hail	5.00 in.	0	48	30.0	0.0
59	Radcliff, KY	05/14/95	Thunderstorm Winds	na	0	46	5.0	0.0
60	Ipava to Lewistown, IL	05/13/95	Tornado	F4	0	45	6.0	0.0
61	South/NW North Dakota, ND	01/09/97	Blizzard	na	2	45	55.0	0.0
62	Hattiesburg, MS	06/05/98	Thunderstorm Winds	na	2	45	1.0	0.0
63	Chattanooga, TN	03/29/97	Tornado	F3	0	44	45.0	0.0
64	Covington, LA	11/21/97	Tornado	F2	0	43	3.5	0.0
65	Marion Jct., AL	03/06/96	Tornado	F3	4	40	8.0	0.0
66	Ft. Smith, AR	04/21/96	Tornado	F2	2	40	150.0	0.0
67	Ft. Collins, CO	07/28/97	Flash Flood	na	5	40	190.0	0.0
68	Real Co., TX	06/21/97	Flood	na	0	40	1.0	0.1
69	Des Moines, IA	06/29/98	Thunderstorm Winds	120 mph	0	40	40.0	0.0
70	Amber, OK	05/03/99	Tornado	F5	12	39	90.0	0.0
71	Pentwater, MI	05/31/98	Thunderstorm Winds	na	0	37	4.0	0.0
72	Albany, GA	11/07/95	Tornado	F2	0	36	10.0	0.0
73	Longwood, FL	02/23/98	Tornado	F3	12	36	30.0	0.0
74	North Central Oregon, OR	09/25/99	High Wind	na	8	33	1.0	0.0
75	Piney To, TN	05/18/95	Tornado	F4	3	32	4.6	0.0
76	New Smyrna Beach, FL	11/02/97	Tornado	F3	0	32	14.0	0.0
77	Sylamore, AR	04/14/96	Tornado	F4	2	30	5.0	0.0
78	Shreveport, LA	01/23/96	Tornado	F2	0	30	5.0	0.0
79	Western Utah, UT	12/01/96	Winter Storm	na	0	30	1.0	0.0
80	Hebron, MS	04/14/99	Tornado	F3	1	30	4.0	0.0
81	Niantic, IL	04/19/96	Tornado	F3	0	29	9.0	0.0
82	Sumner Co., TN	05/18/95	Tornado	F2	0	28	3.0	0.0
83	Washington, IA	05/15/98	Tornado	F3	0	28	9.0	0.0
84	Drayton, GA	04/15/99	Tornado	F3	0	28	10.0	0.0
85	Mayodan, NC	03/20/98	Tornado	F3	2	27	34.0	0.0
86	Wendell, NC	04/15/96	Tornado	F1	0	26	3.0	0.0
87	Southern Sacramento Valley, CA	12/11/97	Fog	na	5	26	1.5	0.0
88	Tremont, IL	05/13/95	Tornado	F3	0	25	4.0	0.0
89	Hays Co., TX	10/17/98	Flood	na	0	25	4.0	0.0
90	Scottsbluff, NE	06/27/99	Hail	2.75 in.	0	25	55.0	2.0
91	Jessamine Co., KY	05/18/95	Thunderstorm Winds	na	0	24	5.0	0.0
92	Southeastern California, CA	12/09/98	High Wind	93 mph	0	24	1.0	0.0
93	Howard City, MI	05/31/98	Thunderstorm Winds	na	0	23	14.0	0.0
94	Seven Springs, NC	01/07/95	Tornado	F1	0	22	1.5	0.0
95	De Kalb, TX	05/04/99	Tornado	F3	0	22	125.0	0.0
96	Deerfield, TN	04/16/98	Tornado	F5	0	21	4.0	0.0
97	Summerfield, FL	01/07/95	Tornado	F2	1	20	2.8	0.0
98	Cumberland Co., TN	05/18/95	Tornado	F3	0	20	2.0	0.0
99	Northeastern Utah, UT	10/24/96	Winter Storm	na	0	20	1.0	0.0
100	Bandera Co., TX	06/21/97	Flood	na	2	20	5.0	1.0

Note: Storms with less than one million dollars of property damage are excluded.

100 Storms With The Greatest Property Damage: 1995-1999

Rank	Location or County	Date	Type	Mag.	Fatal.	Inj.	Property Damage ($mil.)	Crop Damage ($mil.)
1	Grand Forks, ND	04/18/97	Flood	na	0	0	3,000.0	0.0
2	Eastern North Carolina, NC	09/15/99	Hurricane Floyd	na	0	0	3,000.0	500.0
3	Southeast Louisiana, LA	05/08/95	Heavy Rain/Severe Weather	na	0	0	2,500.0	0.0
4	Northwest Florida, FL	10/03/95	Hurricane Opal	na	1	0	2,100.0	5.0
5	North Central Texas, TX	05/05/95	Severe Thunderstorm	na	0	0	1,200.0	0.0
6	Northwest Florida, FL	10/04/95	Hurricane Opal	na	0	0	1,000.0	0.0
7	Eastern North Carolina, NC	09/04/96	Hurricane Fran	100 mph	4	4	792.1	0.0
8	Western Nevada, NV	01/01/97	Flood	na	2	50	640.0	0.0
9	Pearl River/Hancock/Harrison/Jackson Co., MS	09/27/98	Hurricane Georges	117 mph	0	0	602.0	0.0
10	West Polk Co., MN	04/17/97	Flood	na	0	0	600.0	0.0
11	Bowling Green, KY	04/16/98	Hail	2.75 in.	0	0	510.0	0.0
12	Moore, OK	05/03/99	Tornado	F5	11	293	450.0	0.0
13	Del City, OK	05/03/99	Tornado	F4	12	234	450.0	0.0
14	Eastern North Carolina, NC	09/14/99	Hurricane Floyd	105 mph	13	0	410.6	413.6
15	Northern Oregon, OR	02/06/96	Flood	na	7	0	400.0	0.0
16	Northwestern Florida, FL	03/10/98	Flood	na	0	0	367.0	0.0
17	Somerset Co., NJ	09/16/99	Flash Flood	na	2	100	358.0	0.0
18	North Central California, CA	01/01/97	Flood	na	0	2	330.0	0.0
19	All of Maine, ME	01/05/98	Ice Storm	na	1	0	304.0	0.0
20	Southeastern Texas, TX	09/07/98	Tropical Storm Frances	na	3	0	287.1	0.0
21	Comal/Guadalupe/Gonzales/De Witt Co., TX	10/17/98	Flood	na	0	750	268.0	1.5
22	Coastal Palm Beach/Broward/Dade Co., FL	10/14/99	Hurricane Irene	93 mph	0	4	262.0	338.0
23	Coastal Dade/Monroe Co./Lower Keys, FL	09/25/98	Hurricane Georges	120+ mph	0	0	255.0	15.0
24	Northwest Florida, FL	08/03/95	Hurricane Erin	101 mph	0	0	230.0	5.0
25	Dale/Henry/Geneva/Houston Co., AL	03/08/98	Flood	na	0	0	230.0	0.0
26	Tarrant Co., TX	04/29/95	Hailstorm	na	0	0	220.0	0.0
27	New Hanover Co., NC	09/05/96	Hurricane Fran	110 mph	0	0	200.0	1.0
28	Temple, TX	04/19/96	Hail	4.50 in.	0	0	200.0	0.0
29	Oak Grove, AL	04/08/98	Tornado	F5	32	258	200.0	2.2
30	Brevard Co., FL	07/01/98	Wild/Forest Fire	na	0	52	200.0	0.0
31	Southern Sierra Nevada Mountains, CA	01/01/97	Flood	na	1	0	190.0	0.0
32	Ft. Collins, CO	07/28/97	Flash Flood	na	5	40	190.0	0.0
33	Pender Co., NC	09/05/96	Hurricane Fran	na	2	0	180.0	46.0
34	Miami Intl. Airport, FL	02/02/98	Tornado	F2	0	0	175.0	0.0
35	Southwestern Alabama, AL	09/25/98	Hurricane Georges	91 mph	1	0	174.1	5.0
36	Salt Lake City, UT	08/11/99	Tornado	F2	1	80	170.0	0.5
37	Southwestern Georgia, GA	03/08/98	Flood	na	1	1	161.0	0.0
38	Ft. Smith, AR	04/21/96	Tornado	F2	2	40	150.0	0.0
39	Van Buren, AR	04/21/96	Tornado	F3	0	49	150.0	0.0
40	Cass Co., ND	04/16/97	Flood	na	0	0	150.0	0.0
41	Volusia Co., FL	07/01/98	Wild/Forest Fire	na	0	11	150.0	0.0
42	Eastern North Carolina, NC	07/12/96	Hurricane Bertha	108 mph	1	10	140.2	127.0
43	Peck, KS	05/03/99	Tornado	F4	6	150	140.0	0.0
44	Northwestern Florida, FL	09/25/98	Hurricane Georges	na	0	0	135.0	0.0
45	Lakewood, CO	08/11/97	Flash Flood	na	0	0	128.0	0.0
46	Northeastern Kentucky, KY	03/02/97	Flood	na	1	0	125.0	0.0
47	De Kalb, TX	05/04/99	Tornado	F3	0	22	125.0	0.0
48	Thornton, CO	05/22/96	Hail	1.25 in.	0	0	120.0	0.0
49	Nicollet, MN	03/29/98	Tornado	F3	1	0	120.0	0.0
50	Pender/Brunswick/New Hanover Co., NC	09/15/99	Hurricane Floyd	90 mph	0	0	109.0	4.0
51	Elba, AL	03/08/98	Flash Flood	na	4	0	105.0	0.0
52	Eastern North Dakota, ND	04/05/97	Blizzard	na	1	0	102.0	0.0
53	Phoenix, AZ	08/14/96	Thunderstorm Winds	na	0	0	100.0	0.0
54	Brooks, KY	05/28/96	Tornado	F4	0	10	100.0	0.0
55	Punxsutawney, PA	07/19/96	Flash Flood	na	0	0	100.0	0.0

Rank	Location or County	Date	Type	Mag.	Fatal.	Inj.	Property Damage ($mil.)	Crop Damage ($mil.)
56	Cass Co., ND	04/08/97	Flood	na	0	0	100.0	0.0
57	Nashville, TN	04/16/98	Tornado	F3	1	60	100.0	0.0
58	Dade/Broward/Palm Beach Co., FL	10/15/99	Flash Flood	na	0	0	100.0	200.0
59	Benson/Ramsey Co., ND	09/01/99	Flood	na	0	0	100.0	0.0
60	Eastern Alabama, AL	10/04/95	Hurricane Opal	98 mph	2	0	100.0	10.0
61	Southeastern Virginia, VA	09/15/99	Hurricane Floyd	100 mph	1	0	99.3	42.3
62	Eastern North Dakota, ND	04/04/97	Ice Storm	na	0	0	96.0	0.0
63	Highland Park, MI	07/02/97	Tornado	F2	0	90	90.0	0.0
64	Baldwinsville, NY	09/07/98	Thunderstorm Winds	na	3	7	90.0	0.0
65	Amber, OK	05/03/99	Tornado	F5	12	39	90.0	0.0
66	Buckley Field NAS, CO	10/16/98	Hail	2.00 in.	0	0	87.8	0.0
67	Jefferson Co., KY	03/01/97	Flood	na	1	0	85.0	0.0
68	Odessa, TX	05/26/99	Hail	2.75 in.	0	0	85.0	0.0
69	Blue Ash, OH	04/09/99	Tornado	F4	4	65	82.0	0.0
70	Fargo, ND	07/04/99	Thunderstorm Winds	91 mph	0	0	80.0	0.0
71	Northern Virginia, VA	09/06/96	River Flood	na	0	0	78.7	26.8
72	Fox Point, WI	06/21/97	Flash Flood	na	0	0	78.7	0.0
73	S. Coast/Rogue Basin/S. Central OR, OR	01/01/97	Flood	na	0	0	76.6	13.4
74	Hamilton Co., NY	07/15/95	Thunderstorm Winds	na	0	0	75.0	0.0
75	Central Georgia, GA	10/05/95	Thunderstorm Winds	na	8	7	75.0	50.0
76	Shippenville, PA	07/19/96	Flash Flood	na	1	1	75.0	0.0
77	Southeastern Virginia, VA	02/04/98	Coastal Flooding	na	0	0	75.0	0.0
78	Clarksville, TN	01/22/99	Tornado	F3	0	5	72.7	0.0
79	Wayne/Perry/Greene/Stone/George Co., MS	09/25/98	Hurricane Georges	na	0	0	72.0	0.0
80	Cedar Park, TX	05/27/97	Tornado	F3	0	15	70.0	0.0
81	Carmel, CA	09/08/99	Wild/Forest Fire	na	0	0	66.9	0.0
82	Bexar/Guadalupe/Wilson/Karnes Co., TX	10/17/98	Flood	na	0	550	66.0	0.2
83	Hays/Caldwell/Gonzales Co., TX	10/17/98	Flood	na	0	125	62.0	0.6
84	Northwestern Florida, FL	09/28/98	Hurricane Georges	60 mph	0	1	61.9	0.0
85	East Central Florida, FL	09/14/99	Hurricane Floyd	70 mph	0	0	61.0	0.0
86	Southwestern Alabama, AL	07/18/97	Hurricane Danny	100 mph	1	0	60.5	2.5
87	San Angelo, TX	05/28/95	Thunderstorm Winds	86 mph	0	50	60.0	0.0
88	Northwestern California, CA	12/09/95	Winter Storm/High Winds	na	1	15	60.0	5.0
89	North Central Maryland, MD	01/19/96	Flood	na	0	0	60.0	0.0
90	Southern Indiana, IN	03/02/97	Flood	na	0	0	60.0	0.0
91	Ushers, NY	05/31/98	Tornado	F3	0	68	60.0	0.0
92	Palm Beach Co., FL	10/15/99	Flash Flood	na	0	0	60.0	65.0
93	Sparks, OK	05/03/99	Tornado	F3	0	13	60.0	0.0
94	Southeastern Nebraska, NE	10/25/97	Heavy Snow	na	0	0	56.5	1.6
95	South/NW North Dakota, ND	01/09/97	Blizzard	na	2	45	55.0	0.0
96	Scottsbluff, NE	06/27/99	Hail	2.75 in.	0	25	55.0	2.0
97	Estell Manor, NJ	08/20/97	Flash Flood	na	0	0	54.0	0.0
98	Garden City, KS	07/01/99	Hail	4.00 in.	0	0	53.0	0.0
99	Space Coast/Treasure Coast, FL	10/15/99	Hurricane Irene	70 mph	0	0	51.0	0.0
100	Los Angeles Basin, CA	01/04/95	Flood/Flash Flood	na	1	0	50.0	0.0

Major Storm Events by State: 1995-1999

Location or County	Date	Type	Mag.	Fatalities	Injuries	Property Damage ($mil.)	Crop Damage ($mil.)
			ALABAMA				
Athens	05/03/97	Tornado	F2	0	12	2.3	0.0
Baldwin Co.	03/08/98	Flood	na	0	0	1.0	0.0
Covington Co.	03/08/98	Flood	na	0	0	6.0	0.0
Dale/Henry/Geneva/Houston Co.	03/08/98	Flood	na	0	0	230.0	0.0
Eastern Alabama	10/04/95	Hurricane Opal	98 mph	2	0	100.0	10.0
Echo	10/24/97	Tornado	F1	0	0	1.0	0.0
Elba	03/08/98	Flash Flood	na	4	0	105.0	0.0
Elba	09/28/98	Flash Flood	na	0	0	2.5	15.0
Enterprise	09/29/98	Tornado	F1	0	0	1.5	0.0
Escambia Co.	03/08/98	Flood	na	0	0	1.5	0.0
Huntsville	06/28/99	Flash Flood	na	1	1	1.5	0.0
Jackson Municipal Airport	03/18/96	Tornado	F1	0	15	1.0	0.0
Joppa to Guntersville	02/16/95	Tornado	F0	6	130	5.0	0.0
Lee Co.	06/28/99	Flash Flood	na	0	0	1.5	0.0
Limestone	05/18/95	Tornado	F4	1	55	5.0	0.0
Madison Co.	06/06/95	Thunderstorm Winds	na	0	0	1.0	0.0
Marion Jct.	03/06/96	Tornado	F3	4	40	8.0	0.0
Mobile Co.	03/08/98	Flood	na	0	0	1.0	0.0
Montgomery	03/06/96	Tornado	F1	0	0	1.2	0.0
Montgomery	03/06/96	Thunderstorm Winds	75 mph	0	0	1.2	0.0
Montgomery	03/06/96	Tornado	F2	2	17	1.5	0.0
Moody	04/08/98	Tornado	F2	2	12	2.0	0.0
N. Central/NW Alabama	12/23/98	Ice Storm	na	1	0	14.4	0.0
Oak Grove	04/08/98	Tornado	F5	32	258	200.0	2.2
Opp	04/17/98	Tornado	F1	0	0	1.0	0.0
Rainsville	04/22/97	Tornado	F2	0	10	2.2	0.0
S. and S.W. Alabama/N.W. Florida	10/03/95	Hurricane Opal	90 mph	0	0	48.0	4.0
Samson	09/28/98	Flash Flood	na	0	0	1.5	0.0
Saraland	11/21/97	Tornado	F3	0	0	2.0	0.0
Southeast Alabama	10/04/95	Hurricane Opal	na	0	0	20.0	10.0
Southwest Alabama	08/03/95	Hurricane Erin	100+ mph	0	0	25.0	1.0
Southwestern Alabama	07/18/97	Hurricane Danny	100 mph	1	0	60.5	2.5
Southwestern Alabama	09/25/98	Hurricane Georges	91 mph	1	0	174.1	5.0
Talladega Co.	02/10/95	Flash Flood	na	0	0	5.0	0.0
Tuscaloosa	01/24/97	Tornado	F2	1	10	5.0	0.0
Washington Co.	06/05/98	Thunderstorm Winds	92 mph	0	0	1.5	0.0
			ALASKA				
Big Lake	06/02/96	Wild/Forest Fire	na	0	0	10.0	0.0
Fairbanks	06/08/97	Thunderstorm Winds	58 mph	0	0	2.0	0.0
Juneau	10/20/98	Flood	na	0	0	2.3	0.0
Kenai River	09/02/95	River Flood	na	0	0	10.0	0.0
Southern Mainland	09/18/95	Heavy Rain/High Wind	na	0	0	7.5	0.0
St. Lawrence Is./Bering Strait	10/28/96	Storm Surge	na	0	0	1.0	0.0
Tanana Valley	07/24/97	Flood	na	0	0	1.2	0.0
			ARIZONA				
Chandler	09/14/99	Thunderstorm Winds	86 mph	0	2	5.0	0.0
Cornville	03/06/95	Flood	na	0	0	1.3	0.0
Grand Canyon Arpt.	07/14/99	Flash Flood	na	0	4	2.5	0.0
Littlefield	03/11/95	Flood	na	0	0	1.6	0.0
Mesa	09/19/99	Thunderstorm Winds	104 mph	0	2	30.0	0.0
Northeastern Arizona	01/04/95	Heavy Rain	na	0	0	5.0	0.0
Phoenix	08/14/96	Thunderstorm Winds	na	0	0	100.0	0.0
Phoenix	09/14/99	Thunderstorm Winds	75 mph	0	0	2.0	0.0

Location or County	Date	Type	Mag.	Fatalities	Injuries	Property Damage ($mil.)	Crop Damage ($mil.)
ARIZONA *(cont.)*							
Prescott	09/15/99	Hail	2.75 in.	0	2	18.0	0.0
Tucson	07/15/99	Flash Flood	na	0	0	10.0	0.0
Tucson	08/07/95	Thunderstorm Winds	74 mph	0	2	4.1	0.0
Tucson	08/11/95	Thunderstorm Winds	na	0	0	5.0	0.0
ARKANSAS							
Amity	03/05/99	Tornado	F3	0	0	2.0	0.0
Ashley/Chicot Co.	12/22/98	Ice Storm	na	0	0	1.8	0.0
Clay/Craighead/Poinsett/Mississippi Co.	03/01/97	Flood	na	0	0	1.7	0.0
Datto	01/21/99	Tornado	F2	0	0	8.0	0.0
El Dorado	02/10/98	Thunderstorm Winds	81 mph	0	1	1.0	0.0
El Dorado	07/20/95	Lightning	na	0	0	5.0	0.0
Fayetteville	04/22/96	Hail	1.75 in.	0	0	9.0	0.0
Fox	04/14/96	Tornado	F4	5	5	2.5	0.0
Ft. Smith	04/21/96	Tornado	F2	2	40	150.0	0.0
Ft. Smith	12/03/99	Tornado	F1	0	0	5.0	0.0
Hope	03/01/97	Tornado	F2	0	0	1.0	0.0
Hope	03/01/97	Tornado	F3	0	2	2.0	0.0
Knobel	01/21/99	Tornado	F4	0	0	1.0	0.0
Lowell	09/30/95	Thunderstorm Winds	na	0	1	3.5	0.0
Magnolia	04/04/97	Flash Flood	na	0	0	11.0	0.0
Malvern	04/27/98	Lightning	na	0	0	2.2	0.0
Malvern	09/26/96	Tornado	F2	0	15	2.1	0.0
Melbourne	03/05/96	Tornado	F3	0	2	1.0	0.0
Okolona	05/27/96	Tornado	F3	0	0	1.8	0.0
Pocahontas	04/05/99	Tornado	F2	0	0	2.0	0.0
Rogers	02/20/97	Thunderstorm Winds	na	0	0	1.0	0.0
Sidney	03/05/96	Tornado	F3	0	0	1.5	0.0
St. Paul	04/21/96	Tornado	F3	2	6	1.0	0.0
Sylamore	04/14/96	Tornado	F4	2	30	5.0	0.0
Texarkana	05/28/98	Flash Flood	na	0	0	1.1	0.0
Van Buren	04/21/96	Tornado	F3	0	49	150.0	0.0
Whitehall	01/21/99	Tornado	F1	0	4	2.0	0.0
Yellville	04/22/96	Tornado	F2	0	6	1.0	0.0
CALIFORNIA							
Alameda Co.	12/12/95	High Wind	na	0	0	1.0	0.0
Alameda Co.	12/12/95	High Wind	na	0	0	5.0	0.0
American River	01/01/97	Flash Flood	na	0	0	10.0	0.0
American River	01/24/97	Flash Flood	na	0	0	5.0	0.0
Apple Valley	07/11/99	Flash Flood	na	0	0	1.0	0.0
Bakersfield	02/01/98	Heavy Rain	na	0	0	12.5	5.4
Bella Vista	10/16/99	Wild/Forest Fire	na	0	4	22.2	0.0
Big Sur	10/18/96	Wild/Forest Fire	na	0	0	12.3	0.0
Cambria	10/07/96	Wild/Forest Fire	na	0	3	4.5	1.0
Cantil	09/03/97	Flash Flood	na	0	4	5.0	0.0
Capitola	10/28/99	Storm Surge	na	2	2	1.0	0.0
Carmel	09/08/99	Wild/Forest Fire	na	0	0	66.9	0.0
Central Portion of Orange Co.	12/06/97	Flood	na	0	0	17.7	0.0
Central San Joaquin Valley	01/03/97	Flood	na	0	0	3.5	15.0
Central San Joaquin Valley	01/15/98	Flood	na	0	0	5.3	0.0
Central San Joaquin Valley	12/20/98	Ice Storm	na	2	0	1.0	0.0
Central/Southern San Joaquin Valley	02/07/98	Flood	na	0	0	2.5	1.0
Central/Southern San Joaquin Valley	11/14/98	Fog	na	2	78	1.4	0.0
Clear Lake/Southern Lake County	02/02/98	Flood	na	0	0	15.0	0.0
Denny	10/01/99	Wild/Forest Fire	na	0	0	1.3	0.0
Escalon	05/05/98	Flash Flood	na	0	0	1.6	0.0
Forest Falls	07/11/99	Flash Flood	na	1	5	6.0	0.0

Location or County	Date	Type	Mag.	Fatalities	Injuries	Property Damage ($mil.)	Crop Damage ($mil.)
		CALIFORNIA (cont.)					
Forest Falls	07/13/99	Flash Flood	na	0	0	2.0	0.0
Forest Falls	09/04/97	Flash Flood	na	0	2	3.4	0.0
Fresno	02/01/98	Heavy Rain	na	0	0	1.6	1.8
Fresno	05/19/97	Lightning	na	0	0	1.5	0.3
Fresno	08/06/97	Wild/Forest Fire	na	0	0	1.9	0.0
Harmony Grove	10/21/96	Wild/Forest Fire	na	0	6	37.4	0.0
Hemet	08/31/98	Wild/Forest Fire	na	0	0	4.5	0.0
Humboldt Co.	12/29/95	Flood	na	0	0	7.0	0.0
Kern County Desert	12/22/96	High Wind	63 mph	0	0	1.7	0.0
Lake Arrowhead	08/28/99	Wild/Forest Fire	na	0	6	2.0	0.0
Lake Isabella	08/31/98	Wild/Forest Fire	na	0	1	1.0	0.0
Lemon Heights	10/21/96	Wild/Forest Fire	na	0	0	3.0	0.0
Los Angeles Basin	01/04/95	Flood/Flash Flood	na	1	0	50.0	0.0
Malibu	10/21/96	Wild/Forest Fire	na	0	16	1.5	0.0
Manzanita Lake	07/30/97	Wild/Forest Fire	na	0	0	2.0	10.0
Marysville	10/16/99	Wild/Forest Fire	na	0	6	3.5	0.0
Merced	02/01/98	Heavy Rain	na	0	0	2.0	1.4
Merced	03/25/98	Flood	na	0	0	9.6	1.5
Mojave	01/25/95	Flash Flood	na	0	0	5.0	0.5
Monterey Co.	03/10/95	Flash Flood	na	0	0	20.0	0.0
Moonridge	07/12/99	Flash Flood	na	0	0	1.0	0.0
N. Sacramento/Cent. Sacramento Vly.	02/02/98	Flood	na	0	0	20.8	6.5
Napa Co.	03/10/95	Flood	na	0	0	1.0	1.0
North Central California	01/01/97	Flood	na	0	2	330.0	0.0
Northwest California	01/23/96	Flood	na	0	0	1.0	0.0
Northwest California	12/11/95	High Wind	na	2	0	4.8	0.0
Northwestern California	02/02/98	Flood	na	2	0	4.3	7.8
Northwestern California	02/09/99	High Wind	69 mph	0	0	1.0	0.0
Northwestern California	11/29/98	High Wind	86 mph	0	0	1.8	0.0
Northwestern California	12/09/95	Winter Storm/High Winds	na	1	15	60.0	5.0
Oakland	12/05/96	Heavy Rain	na	0	0	1.0	0.0
Oakland	12/05/96	Heavy Rain	na	0	0	1.0	0.0
Onyx	08/08/97	Wild/Forest Fire	na	0	0	3.0	0.0
Orange Co.	02/06/98	Urban/Small Stream Flood	na	0	0	4.2	0.2
Orange Co.	02/23/98	Flood	na	2	2	29.7	0.2
Petaluma	02/02/98	Flash Flood	na	0	0	2.0	0.0
Piru	08/05/97	Wild/Forest Fire	na	0	0	5.0	0.0
Rancho Santa Fe	01/10/95	Flood/Flash Flood	na	0	0	5.0	5.0
Redding	09/26/99	Wild/Forest Fire	na	0	1	4.5	0.0
Redding	10/01/99	Wild/Forest Fire	na	0	4	13.3	0.0
Redwood Coast	01/01/97	Flood	na	0	0	30.3	0.0
Redwood Coast	12/07/96	Flood	na	0	0	7.0	0.0
Rio Nido	02/03/98	Flash Flood	na	0	0	5.0	0.0
SW Portion of San Bernardino Co.	02/23/98	Flood	na	0	0	35.9	14.1
Sacramento	01/22/97	Flash Flood	na	0	0	1.5	0.0
San Bernardino	10/07/97	Flash Flood	na	0	0	2.5	0.0
San Francisco Co.	12/12/95	High Wind	na	0	0	1.0	0.0
San Francisco Co.	12/12/95	High Wind	na	0	0	15.0	5.0
Santa Barbara	12/31/95	High Wind	75 mph	0	0	5.5	7.0
Santa Rosa	12/05/98	Tornado	F1	0	0	1.0	0.0
Siskiyou/Modoc Co. exc. Surprise Vly.	01/01/97	Flood	na	0	0	11.0	0.0
Sonoma Co.	03/09/95	Flood	na	0	0	3.5	0.5
South Portion of Marin Co.	02/06/98	Flood	na	0	0	1.5	0.5
Southeastern California	12/09/98	High Wind	93 mph	0	24	1.0	0.0
Southern Sacramento Valley	12/11/97	Fog	na	5	26	1.5	0.0
Southern San Joaquin Valley	02/23/98	Flood	na	0	0	18.0	0.0

Location or County	Date	Type	Mag.	Fatalities	Injuries	Property Damage ($mil.)	Crop Damage ($mil.)
		CALIFORNIA (*cont.*)					
Southern Sierra Nevada Mountains	01/01/97	Flood	na	1	0	190.0	0.0
Southern Sierra Nevada Mountains	01/23/97	Heavy Rain	na	0	0	2.1	0.0
Southern Sierra Nevada-West Slopes	05/16/96	Flood	na	0	0	5.0	0.0
Stockton	04/01/96	Thunderstorm Winds	na	0	0	1.0	0.0
Sunnyvale	05/05/98	Tornado	F2	0	1	3.8	0.0
Tulare County Mountains	01/02/97	Flood	na	0	0	1.6	0.0
Upper Trinity River	01/01/97	Flood	na	0	0	5.0	0.0
Valley Center	08/01/97	Wild/Forest Fire	na	0	0	1.7	0.0
Ventura	01/10/95	Flood/Flash Flood	na	0	0	50.0	50.0
Visalia	02/01/98	Heavy Rain	na	0	0	13.9	1.5
West Portion of Riverside Co.	02/23/98	Flood	na	0	0	8.2	4.2
West Portion of San Diego Co.	02/23/98	Flood	na	0	0	10.3	6.9
West Portion of. Monterey Co.	02/06/98	Flash Flood	na	0	0	10.0	0.0
Wilton	01/02/97	Flash Flood	na	1	0	2.4	0.0
Yuba Co.	09/27/97	Wild/Forest Fire	na	0	0	15.0	0.0
Yucaipa	07/11/99	Flash Flood	na	0	0	1.5	0.0
		COLORADO					
Atwood	07/30/97	Flood	na	0	0	12.9	0.0
Aurora	06/14/99	Hail	1.00 in.	0	0	35.0	0.0
Bayfield	04/29/99	Thunderstorm Winds	100 mph	0	0	1.0	0.0
Broomfield	07/12/96	Hail	1.25 in.	0	0	1.0	0.0
Brush	05/22/98	Hail	1.50 in.	0	2	2.2	1.0
Buckley Field NAS	10/16/98	Hail	2.00 in.	0	0	87.8	0.0
Colorado Springs	07/24/96	Hail	0.75 in.	0	0	8.7	0.0
Denver	06/23/97	Lightning	na	0	0	1.0	0.0
Denver	08/10/99	Urban/Small Stream Flood	na	0	0	1.0	0.0
East Central Colorado	06/02/95	Flash Flood	na	0	0	1.0	0.0
Franktown	06/11/99	Hail	1.75 in.	0	3	3.0	0.0
Ft. Collins	07/28/97	Flash Flood	na	5	40	190.0	0.0
Genoa	05/31/99	Tornado	F3	0	0	4.0	0.0
Greeley	05/27/97	Hail	1.00 in.	0	0	2.0	0.0
Greeley	06/23/97	Hail	1.50 in.	0	0	3.1	0.0
Hotchkiss	05/02/98	Flash Flood	na	0	0	1.4	0.1
Lakewood	08/11/97	Flash Flood	na	0	0	128.0	0.0
Manitou Springs	04/29/99	Flash Flood	na	0	0	28.0	0.0
N. Central/NE Colorado	02/02/99	High Wind	127 mph	0	0	3.0	0.0
N. Central/NE Colorado	04/08/99	High Wind	115 mph	0	0	7.2	0.0
N. Central/NE Colorado	04/09/99	High Wind	98 mph	0	0	13.8	0.0
N. Central/NE Colorado	10/29/96	High Wind	101 mph	1	5	5.2	0.0
Pueblo	07/09/96	Flash Flood	na	0	5	2.0	0.2
Pueblo	08/11/97	Urban/Small Stream Flood	na	0	0	25.0	0.0
Pueblo Co.	06/03/95	Flash Flood	na	0	0	17.0	0.0
Rangely	09/20/97	Hail	4.00 in.	0	0	1.0	0.0
Ridgeway	07/31/99	Flash Flood	na	0	0	1.2	0.0
S. Central/SE Colorado	10/24/97	Blizzard	na	5	2	1.2	0.0
Southeastern Colorado	04/30/99	Flood	na	0	0	25.1	0.0
Southeastern Colorado	05/01/99	Flood	na	0	0	4.1	3.6
Southeastern Colorado	10/24/97	Blizzard	na	2	0	1.0	0.0
Thornton	05/22/96	Hail	1.25 in.	0	0	120.0	0.0
Weldona	07/29/97	Flash Flood	na	0	0	2.0	0.0
Yuma	06/22/98	Hail	2.75 in.	0	0	1.0	0.0
		CONNECTICUT					
Fairfield Co.	09/16/99	Flood	na	0	0	1.3	0.0
Hartford/Tolland/Windham Co.	04/01/97	Heavy Snow	na	0	0	1.0	0.0
Hartford/Tolland/Windham Co.	12/07/96	Heavy Snow	na	0	0	6.0	0.0
Litchfield Co.	03/31/97	Winter Storm	na	0	0	1.0	0.0

Location or County	Date	Type	Mag.	Fatalities	Injuries	Property Damage ($mil.)	Crop Damage ($mil.)
		CONNECTICUT *(cont.)*					
Litchfield Co.	09/16/99	Flood	na	0	0	1.1	0.0
N. Central/NE Connecticut	11/12/95	High Wind	na	0	0	1.0	0.0
New Haven Co.	04/16/96	Flash Flood	na	0	0	1.5	0.0
S. Fairfield/S. New Haven Co.	10/19/96	High Wind	58 mph	1	2	2.0	0.0
Waterbury	07/03/96	Tornado	F1	0	0	2.0	0.0
		DELAWARE					
Dewey Beach	11/11/95	Thunderstorm Winds	75 mph	0	0	1.0	0.0
Dover	06/26/98	Thunderstorm Winds	81 mph	0	0	1.5	0.0
Inland Sussex Co./Delaware Beaches	01/07/96	Coastal Flooding/Erosion	na	0	0	2.0	0.0
Kent Co./Inland Sussex Co./Beaches	01/06/96	Winter Storm	na	0	0	1.0	0.0
Kent Co./Inland Sussex Co./Beaches	01/28/98	Coastal Flooding/Erosion	na	0	0	1.3	0.0
Kent Co./Inland Sussex Co./Beaches	02/04/98	Coastal Flooding/Erosion	na	0	5	1.7	0.0
New Castle Co.	01/07/96	Blizzard	na	0	0	1.0	0.0
New Castle Co.	09/16/99	Flash Flood	na	2	1	8.0	0.0
		DISTRICT OF COLUMBIA					
District of Columbia	01/20/96	Flood	na	0	0	10.0	0.0
		FLORIDA					
Arcadia	03/19/98	River Flood	na	0	0	1.0	0.0
Arcadia	03/20/98	River Flood	na	0	0	3.8	0.0
Bartow Airport	11/08/95	Tornado	F0	0	0	1.1	0.0
Bradenton	01/23/98	Flood	na	0	0	1.2	0.0
Bradenton	10/31/97	Urban/Small Stream Flood	na	0	0	2.0	0.0
Brevard Co.	07/01/98	Wild/Forest Fire	na	0	52	200.0	0.0
Brooksville	12/18/97	River Flood	na	0	0	1.5	0.0
Broward Co.	10/15/99	Flash Flood	na	0	0	45.0	25.0
Coastal Dade/Monroe Co./Lower Keys	09/25/98	Hurricane Georges	120+ mph	0	0	255.0	15.0
Coastal Palm Beach/Broward/Dade Co.	10/14/99	Hurricane Irene	93 mph	0	4	262.0	338.0
Dade/Broward/Palm Beach Co.	10/15/99	Flash Flood	na	0	0	100.0	200.0
Daytona Beach	02/22/98	Tornado	F2	1	3	4.0	0.0
Desoto/Sarasota/Charlotte/Lee Co.	06/23/95	Flood	na	0	0	10.0	0.0
Duval Co.	09/15/99	Hurricane Floyd	46 mph	0	0	1.0	0.0
East Broward Co.	06/08/99	Flash Flood	na	0	0	1.0	0.0
East Broward/East Dade Co.	06/22/95	Flash Flood	na	0	0	1.5	0.0
East Central Florida	09/14/99	Hurricane Floyd	70 mph	0	0	61.0	0.0
Eastern Florida Panhandle	08/02/95	Hurricane Erin	na	2	0	1.0	0.0
Edgewater	10/07/96	Tornado	F2	0	0	2.4	0.0
Escambia Co.	03/08/98	Flood	na	0	0	1.5	0.0
Ft. Pierce	03/09/98	Tornado	F1	0	0	3.2	0.0
Haines City	12/27/97	Tornado	F2	0	18	6.0	0.0
Hillsborough Co.	12/13/97	Flood	na	0	0	1.5	0.0
Holder	01/02/98	River Flood	na	0	0	2.0	0.0
Holley	03/03/99	Tornado	F1	0	0	1.0	0.0
Holmes Beach	03/14/99	Lightning	na	0	0	3.5	0.0
Holmes Co.	09/29/98	Flash Flood	na	0	0	1.2	0.0
Holopaw	04/30/96	Tornado	F0	0	0	1.0	0.0
Hudson	01/02/98	Storm Surge	na	0	0	1.8	0.0
Hudson	01/02/99	Storm Surge	na	0	0	1.8	0.0
Indian Rocks Beach	10/27/97	Tornado	F1	0	4	4.5	0.0
Intercession City	02/23/98	Tornado	F3	25	145	50.0	0.0
Jacksonville	02/02/96	Tornado	F2	0	0	2.8	0.0
Jacksonville	05/27/97	Thunderstorm Winds	108 mph	0	0	2.0	0.0
Key Largo	11/04/98	Tornado	F2	0	20	25.0	0.0
Lake Wales	03/09/98	Tornado	F2	0	4	2.0	0.0
Lake Wales	03/30/96	Hail	4.50 in.	0	0	24.0	0.0
Lakeland	03/30/96	Hail	1.75 in.	0	0	1.5	0.0

Location or County	Date	Type	Mag.	Fatalities	Injuries	Property Damage ($mil.)	Crop Damage ($mil.)
		FLORIDA (cont.)					
Lakeland	05/21/99	Tornado	F1	0	0	1.0	0.0
Lee Co.	09/01/95	Flood	na	0	0	1.3	0.0
Lee Co.	10/05/95	Flood	na	0	0	5.0	0.0
Longwood	02/23/98	Tornado	F3	12	36	30.0	0.0
Lower Keys-Coastal	10/03/95	Hurricane Opal	na	0	0	4.0	0.0
Manatee Co.	04/26/97	Flood	na	0	0	2.9	0.0
Marathon	02/02/98	Tornado	F1	0	0	20.0	0.0
Martin Co.	10/17/95	Flood	na	0	0	4.0	9.0
Melbourne	08/02/95	Flash Flood	na	0	0	3.0	0.0
Miami	02/13/95	Thunderstorm Winds	99 mph	0	0	5.0	0.0
Miami Intl. Airport	01/03/96	Tornado	F1	0	9	1.2	0.0
Miami Intl. Airport	02/02/98	Tornado	F2	0	0	175.0	0.0
Miramar	02/02/98	Tornado	F1	0	0	30.0	0.0
Monroe Co.	10/14/99	Hurricane Irene	na	0	0	13.4	0.0
Nassau Co.	09/15/99	Hurricane Floyd	na	0	0	2.5	0.0
New Smyrna Beach	11/02/97	Tornado	F3	0	32	14.0	0.0
North Central Florida	03/01/98	Flood	na	0	0	25.5	0.0
Northwest Florida	08/03/95	Hurricane Erin	101 mph	0	0	230.0	5.0
Northwest Florida	10/03/95	Hurricane Opal	na	1	0	2,100.0	5.0
Northwest Florida	10/04/95	Hurricane Opal	na	0	0	1,000.0	0.0
Northwestern Florida	03/10/98	Flood	na	0	0	367.0	0.0
Northwestern Florida	09/02/98	Hurricane Earl	70 mph	2	2	6.0	0.0
Northwestern Florida	09/25/98	Hurricane Georges	na	0	0	135.0	0.0
Northwestern Florida	09/28/98	Hurricane Georges	60 mph	0	1	61.9	0.0
Okaloosa Co.	03/08/98	Flood	na	0	0	1.0	0.0
Okaloosa Co.	06/06/98	Thunderstorm Winds	70 mph	0	0	4.0	0.0
Okeechobee	03/09/98	Tornado	F1	0	10	5.4	0.0
Orlando	04/06/95	Thunderstorm Winds	na	0	0	2.5	0.0
Orlando Intl. Arpt.	02/23/98	Tornado	F3	0	5	5.0	0.0
Osteen	02/23/98	Tornado	F3	1	0	1.0	0.0
Palatka	04/24/95	Tornado	F2	0	5	1.1	0.0
Palm Beach Co.	10/15/99	Flash Flood	na	0	0	60.0	65.0
Palm Beach Gardens	01/02/99	Flash Flood	na	0	0	1.9	0.0
Palm Beach/Hendry/Glades Co.	10/16/95	Flood	na	0	0	3.0	45.0
Panama City Beach	01/02/99	Tornado	F2	0	7	4.0	0.0
Pasco Co.	03/19/98	Flood	na	0	0	1.5	0.0
Pasco Co.	12/13/97	Flood	na	0	0	2.9	0.5
Plant City	09/26/97	Flood	na	1	1	5.3	0.0
Port Canaveral	02/23/98	Tornado	F1	0	0	1.0	0.0
Port Canaveral	09/02/98	Tornado	F1	0	1	6.0	0.0
Port St Lucie	04/15/99	Wild/Forest Fire	na	0	0	10.0	0.0
Riviera Beach	01/02/99	Tornado	F1	0	0	5.9	0.0
Sarasota	11/13/97	Flood	na	0	0	2.3	0.0
Seminole Co.	07/01/98	Wild/Forest Fire	na	0	2	30.0	0.0
South Portion of Bay Co.	05/07/99	Flash Flood	na	0	0	4.0	0.0
Southern Florida	11/04/98	Tropical Storm Mitch	na	2	65	30.0	20.0
Space Coast/Treasure Coast	10/15/99	Hurricane Irene	70 mph	0	0	51.0	0.0
St. Cloud	12/27/97	Tornado	F1	0	0	1.5	0.0
St. Johns Co.	09/15/99	Hurricane Floyd	67 mph	0	0	3.0	0.0
St. Lucie Co.	10/17/95	Flood	na	0	0	4.0	0.0
Summerfield	01/07/95	Tornado	F2	1	20	2.8	0.0
Sunrise Golf Village	06/16/97	Tornado	F1	0	1	1.0	0.0
Tampa	03/09/98	Thunderstorm Winds	na	0	0	1.0	0.0
Tampa	12/13/97	River Flood	na	0	0	1.1	0.0
Trilby	12/15/97	River Flood	na	0	0	1.1	0.0
Vero Beach	06/01/97	Lightning	na	0	0	1.0	0.0

Location or County	Date	Type	Mag.	Fatalities	Injuries	Property Damage ($mil.)	Crop Damage ($mil.)
		FLORIDA *(cont.)*					
Volusia Co.	07/01/98	Wild/Forest Fire	na	0	11	150.0	0.0
West Central & Southwest FL	08/02/95	Hurricane Erin	70 mph	0	1	2.0	0.0
West Central & Southwest FL	08/23/95	Tropical Storm Jerry	na	0	0	4.0	15.0
West Central Florida	01/09/96	Damaging Freeze	na	0	0	8.0	0.0
West Central Florida	09/02/98	Hurricane Earl	49 mph	0	2	1.1	0.0
West Central Florida	10/07/96	Tropical Storm Josephine	na	0	1	44.6	0.0
Winter Garden	02/22/98	Tornado	F3	3	70	15.0	0.0
		GEORGIA					
Albany	11/07/95	Tornado	F2	0	36	10.0	0.0
Bulloch/Effingham/Screven Co.	08/25/95	Flash Flood	na	0	0	1.5	0.0
Central Georgia	10/05/95	Thunderstorm Winds	na	8	7	75.0	50.0
Chatham Co.	09/03/98	Thunderstorm Winds	63 mph	0	0	1.2	0.0
Chatham/Effingham Co.	06/29/99	Flood	na	0	0	7.0	0.0
Cleveland	03/20/98	Tornado	F3	2	75	5.0	0.0
Cleveland	11/08/96	Tornado	F0	0	0	1.0	0.0
Douglasville	08/11/96	Flash Flood	na	0	0	1.0	0.0
Drayton	04/15/99	Tornado	F3	0	28	10.0	0.0
Dunwoody	04/08/98	Tornado	F2	1	0	25.0	0.0
Effingham Co.	08/25/95	Flash Flood	na	0	0	2.0	0.0
Goeshen	03/07/96	Thunderstorm Winds	86 mph	0	0	2.0	0.0
Greensboro	01/07/98	Thunderstorm Winds	na	0	0	2.0	0.0
Hinesville	04/09/98	Tornado	F2	1	7	38.0	0.0
Jonesboro	01/24/96	Thunderstorm Winds	na	0	0	2.0	0.0
Murrayville	03/20/98	Tornado	F3	10	96	15.0	0.0
Norcross	04/08/98	Tornado	F2	0	10	50.0	0.0
Pembroke	04/09/98	Tornado	F3	2	16	2.2	0.0
Powder Springs	06/30/99	Flash Flood	na	0	0	1.2	0.0
Rabun Co.	10/05/95	High Wind	na	0	0	5.0	0.0
Red Rock	03/06/96	Tornado	F2	0	0	6.0	2.0
Sandy Spgs	07/06/99	Lightning	na	0	0	1.0	0.0
Sandy Springs	04/08/98	Tornado	F1	0	4	10.0	0.0
Savannah	07/05/96	Flash Flood	na	0	2	1.0	0.0
Smyrna	04/08/98	Tornado	F2	0	0	15.0	0.0
Southeastern Georgia	03/01/98	Flood	na	0	0	3.5	0.0
Southwestern Georgia	03/08/98	Flood	na	1	1	161.0	0.0
Thomson	04/22/97	Thunderstorm Winds	92 mph	0	0	2.7	0.0
Waycross	01/02/99	Thunderstorm Winds	na	0	0	2.2	0.0
Wrens	03/07/96	Tornado	F1	0	5	1.0	0.0
		HAWAII					
Island of Hawaii	02/24/97	High Wind	104 mph	0	0	2.1	2.0
Oahu	11/05/96	Heavy Rain/High Surf	na	0	0	13.5	1.5
Waikoloa/S. Kohala	09/08/96	Flash Flood	na	0	0	1.0	0.0
		IDAHO					
Boise	08/22/95	Flash Flood	na	0	0	5.0	0.0
Eastern Idaho	06/01/97	Flood	na	0	0	50.0	0.0
Florida Panhandle	02/08/96	Flood	na	0	1	44.0	0.0
Northern Idaho	05/01/97	Flood	na	0	0	4.0	0.0
Northwestern Idaho	02/02/99	High Wind	na	0	0	3.0	0.0
Northwestern Idaho	06/01/97	Flood	na	0	0	4.0	0.0
Northwestern Idaho	11/16/96	Heavy Snow	na	0	0	6.0	0.0
Pocatello	05/26/95	Heavy Rain	na	0	0	50.0	0.0
Pocatello	06/17/97	Lightning	na	0	0	1.0	0.0
Pocatello	08/12/97	Hail	1.75 in.	0	0	1.0	0.0
Troy	02/24/99	Flood	na	0	0	1.0	0.0

Location or County	Date	Type	Mag.	Fatalities	Injuries	Property Damage ($mil.)	Crop Damage ($mil.)
		ILLINOIS					
Albany	05/09/95	Tornado	F3	0	0	2.0	0.0
Armington	04/19/96	Tornado	F2	0	0	1.0	0.0
Ashland	04/08/99	Tornado	F1	1	6	1.7	0.0
Bald Bluff	04/19/96	Tornado	F1	0	0	4.0	0.0
Bethany	04/07/98	Hail	2.00 in.	0	0	7.0	0.0
Bishop Hill	04/19/96	Tornado	F1	0	4	10.0	0.0
Camden	03/27/98	Thunderstorm Winds	60 mph	0	2	1.0	0.0
Cantrall	05/09/95	Tornado	F3	0	6	10.0	0.0
Carmi Muni. Arpt.	04/19/96	Tornado	F1	0	0	1.0	0.0
Cass Co.	05/08/96	Flash Flood	na	0	0	2.0	0.0
Cass Co.	05/16/95	Flood	na	0	0	1.0	0.0
Cass Co.	06/01/95	Flood	na	0	0	1.0	0.0
Chadwick	06/23/96	Thunderstorm Winds	104 mph	0	0	1.0	0.0
Coles/Shelby Co.	06/01/99	Flash Flood	na	0	0	3.0	0.0
Cook Co.	07/17/96	Flash Flood	na	0	0	44.7	0.0
De Witt Co.	06/29/98	Thunderstorm Winds	110 mph	0	0	1.0	0.0
Decatur	04/18/96	Tornado	F1	0	9	1.5	0.0
Flora	04/15/98	Tornado	F2	0	8	2.1	0.0
Forsyth	05/13/95	Thunderstorm Winds	na	0	0	1.4	0.0
Fox Lake	04/19/96	Thunderstorm Winds	na	0	2	5.0	0.0
Galva	04/19/96	Tornado	F0	0	4	10.0	0.0
Glendale Heights	06/06/95	Thunderstorm Winds	na	0	0	1.5	0.0
Grundy Co.	07/17/96	Flash Flood	na	0	0	1.0	16.0
Hamilton	04/08/99	Tornado	F3	0	4	10.0	0.0
Harrisburg	04/28/96	Flash Flood	na	0	0	1.5	0.0
Harrisburg	05/10/96	Flash Flood	na	0	0	1.5	0.0
Ipava to Lewistown	05/13/95	Tornado	F4	0	45	6.0	0.0
Kendall Co.	07/17/96	Flash Flood	na	0	0	1.5	0.0
Knox Co.	06/29/98	Thunderstorm Winds	60 mph	0	2	1.0	0.0
Lincoln	04/29/98	Flash Flood	na	0	0	1.0	0.5
Lincoln	05/09/95	Hail	2.25 in.	0	0	12.0	0.0
Logan Co.	05/16/95	Flash Flood	na	0	0	2.0	0.0
Logan Co.	06/28/98	Thunderstorm Winds	79 mph	0	1	1.0	0.0
Madison Co.	05/16/95	Flash Flood	na	0	0	2.0	0.0
Marion	05/10/96	Flash Flood	na	0	0	1.0	0.0
Marquette Hgts.	06/29/98	Tornado	F1	0	0	1.0	0.0
Mattoon	03/28/98	Tornado	F2	0	3	3.0	0.0
McLean	04/19/96	Tornado	F3	0	0	1.0	0.0
McLean Co.	06/29/98	Thunderstorm Winds	81 mph	0	0	1.1	0.0
Menard Co.	05/08/96	Flash Flood	na	0	0	1.0	0.0
Monticello	04/19/96	Tornado	F1	0	1	1.0	0.0
Murphysboro	04/19/96	Thunderstorm Winds	na	0	0	1.0	0.0
Neponset	05/09/95	Tornado	F3	0	0	3.0	0.0
Niantic	04/19/96	Tornado	F3	0	29	9.0	0.0
Niota	05/13/95	Tornado	F4	0	7	10.0	0.0
Northwestern Illinois	04/06/97	High Wind	62 mph	0	0	1.6	0.0
Odin	04/19/96	Tornado	F2	0	7	7.0	0.0
Oquawka	04/19/96	Tornado	F0	0	0	4.0	0.0
Pearl City	04/19/96	Thunderstorm Winds	104 mph	0	0	1.2	0.0
Peoria Co.	06/29/98	Thunderstorm Winds	66 mph	0	4	1.1	0.4
Piopolis	04/19/96	Tornado	F3	0	0	2.8	0.0
Savoy	04/19/96	Tornado	F3	0	12	9.0	0.0
Scott/Pike/Greene/Calhoun/Jersey Co.	05/09/95	River Flood	na	0	0	15.0	12.0
South Pekin	05/09/95	Tornado	F1	0	2	1.0	0.0
South and Central DuPage Co.	07/17/96	Flash Flood	na	0	0	4.4	0.0
South and Central Kane Co.	07/17/96	Flash Flood	na	0	0	14.5	0.0

Location or County	Date	Type	Mag.	Fatalities	Injuries	Property Damage ($mil.)	Crop Damage ($mil.)
ILLINOIS *(cont.)*							
Southeastern Illinois	03/01/97	Flood	na	0	0	2.5	0.0
Southwestern Illinois	06/01/95	River Flood	na	0	0	1.9	0.0
St. Augustine	05/13/95	Tornado	F2	0	2	1.6	0.0
St. Clair Co.	05/16/95	Flash Flood	na	0	0	1.8	0.0
Tazewell Co.	06/29/98	Thunderstorm Winds	96 mph	0	0	2.0	1.0
Tower Hill	06/01/99	Tornado	F2	0	4	2.0	0.0
Tremont	05/13/95	Tornado	F3	0	25	4.0	0.0
Wabash/White Co.	05/01/96	Flood	na	0	0	1.0	0.0
Warsaw	04/08/99	Tornado	F2	0	0	5.0	0.0
West Frankfort	04/28/96	Flash Flood	na	0	0	3.0	0.0
West Frankfort	05/10/96	Flash Flood	na	0	0	8.0	0.0
Williamsfield	06/29/98	Tornado	F1	0	1	2.0	0.0
Zion	04/19/96	Tornado	F2	0	2	6.6	0.0
INDIANA							
All of Indiana	07/13/95	Heat Wave	na	14	0	1.0	0.0
Angola Airport	05/18/97	Tornado	F0	0	0	10.0	0.0
Bartholomew/Martin/Lawrence/Jackson Co.	01/22/99	Flood	na	0	0	5.0	0.0
Boone/Marion Co.	01/22/99	Flood	na	0	0	1.0	0.0
Carroll/Tippecanoe/Howard Co.	01/22/99	Flood	na	0	0	14.0	0.0
Central Portion of Owen Co.	06/28/98	Flash Flood	na	0	0	4.0	0.0
Crawfordsville	05/13/95	Tornado	F2	3	5	3.5	0.0
Cumberland	06/11/98	Tornado	F3	0	3	1.5	0.0
Dearborn/Ohio/Switzerland Co.	03/02/97	Flood	na	0	0	6.0	0.0
East Central Indiana	01/21/99	Flood	na	0	0	19.0	0.0
Elwood	06/11/98	Tornado	F1	0	0	1.0	0.0
Fairmount	06/11/98	Tornado	F1	0	0	1.0	0.0
Frankfort	07/17/96	Thunderstorm Winds	na	0	6	2.0	0.0
Franklin/Dearborn Co.	04/29/96	Flood	na	0	0	1.0	0.0
Gibson/Pike Co.	05/01/96	Flood	na	0	0	1.0	0.0
Gibson/Posey Co.	05/01/96	Flood	na	0	0	1.2	0.0
Greenfield	06/11/98	Tornado	F4	0	1	1.1	0.0
Greensburg	04/20/96	Tornado	F1	0	0	1.2	0.0
Greentown	06/11/98	Tornado	F3	0	8	5.0	0.0
Huntington	07/22/98	Flood	na	0	0	1.5	0.5
Huntington County	07/18/96	Flash Flood	na	0	0	7.0	0.1
Lagrange	05/18/97	Tornado	F0	0	1	1.5	0.0
Lebanon	05/14/95	Tornado	F2	0	5	2.0	0.0
Marion	08/04/98	Flood	na	0	0	1.0	0.5
Mooresville	04/19/96	Tornado	F1	0	5	2.0	0.0
Mooresville	04/19/96	Tornado	F1	0	0	2.0	0.0
Near Ligonier	05/18/97	Thunderstorm Winds	na	0	0	4.0	0.0
Peru	07/22/98	Flood	na	0	0	1.0	0.5
Posey/Vanderburgh/Warrick/Spencer Co.	03/02/97	Flood	na	0	0	2.5	0.0
Princeton	05/03/96	Hail	3.00 in.	0	0	1.5	0.5
Rexville	04/09/99	Tornado	F3	0	2	1.4	0.0
Ripley	06/11/98	Tornado	F2	0	1	1.0	0.1
Seymour	05/08/96	Tornado	F2	0	0	1.3	0.0
Shipshewana	05/18/97	Thunderstorm Winds	na	0	0	1.5	0.0
Southern Indiana	03/02/97	Flood	na	0	0	60.0	0.0
Southwestern Indiana	01/06/96	Winter Storm	na	0	0	1.1	0.0
Southwestern Indiana	01/22/99	Flood	na	0	0	9.0	0.0
Southwestern Indiana	04/29/96	Flood	na	0	0	1.5	0.0
Stone Lake	05/18/97	Tornado	F0	0	1	1.5	0.0
Wabash	07/22/98	Flood	na	0	0	6.0	2.0

Location or County	Date	Type	Mag.	Fatalities	Injuries	Property Damage ($mil.)	Crop Damage ($mil.)
		IOWA					
Algona	05/15/98	Tornado	F2	0	0	1.0	0.0
All of Iowa	07/12/95	Heat Wave	na	3	0	3.8	0.0
Altoona	06/29/98	Thunderstorm Winds	92 mph	0	0	3.0	0.1
Atlantic	06/14/98	Flood	na	0	0	2.0	1.2
Bayard	05/27/95	Tornado	F4	0	1	2.0	0.0
Bridgewater	04/08/99	Tornado	F4	0	2	1.0	0.0
Buchanan Co.	06/18/98	Thunderstorm Winds	na	0	0	1.8	0.0
Buchanan/Delaware Counties Co.	07/27/95	Tornado	F3	0	0	1.0	0.3
Carroll to Fonda	05/27/95	Tornado	F4	0	0	3.0	0.0
Central Iowa	01/04/98	Ice Storm	na	0	0	1.0	0.0
Central Iowa	03/07/98	Heavy Snow	na	1	0	2.0	0.0
Central Iowa	04/12/98	High Wind	62 mph	0	0	2.5	0.0
Central Iowa	05/16/99	Flood	na	0	0	7.5	0.8
Central Iowa	05/21/99	Flood	na	0	0	1.4	0.2
Central Iowa	06/09/99	Flood	na	0	0	1.8	2.7
Central Iowa	06/18/98	Flood	na	0	0	8.6	0.4
Central Iowa	07/02/99	Flood	na	0	0	1.7	0.9
Central Iowa	11/10/98	High Wind	70 mph	1	0	17.3	0.2
Clayton Co.	05/16/99	Flash Flood	na	0	0	1.5	0.0
Clayton Co.	07/27/95	Thunderstorm Winds	86 mph	0	0	2.5	0.2
Climbing Hill	05/28/98	Hail	1.75 in.	0	0	1.4	1.0
Clinton	05/10/96	Thunderstorm Winds	104 mph	0	0	1.0	0.0
Clinton	05/10/96	Tornado	F1	0	0	1.0	0.0
Council Bluffs	08/07/99	Flash Flood	na	0	0	4.0	0.0
Creston	04/08/99	Tornado	F4	0	1	2.0	0.0
Creston to Perry	05/27/95	Tornado	F4	0	2	3.0	0.0
Cumberland	06/21/97	Thunderstorm Winds	69 mph	0	0	1.1	0.0
Denison	06/21/96	Flash Flood	na	0	0	11.0	0.1
Des Moines	06/18/98	Flash Flood	na	0	0	1.0	0.0
Des Moines	06/29/98	Thunderstorm Winds	120 mph	0	40	40.0	0.0
Des Moines	06/29/98	Thunderstorm Winds	100 mph	0	0	4.0	0.2
Dubuque	05/17/99	Flash Flood	na	0	0	16.0	0.0
Dunkerton	05/16/99	Flash Flood	na	0	0	1.2	0.0
Dyersville	05/16/99	Flash Flood	na	0	0	5.0	0.0
East Central Iowa	04/06/97	High Wind	68 mph	0	0	2.5	0.0
Fayette Co.	05/16/99	Flash Flood	na	0	0	2.0	0.0
Fayette/Clayton Co.	05/17/99	Flood	na	0	0	5.0	0.5
Forest City	06/22/97	Hail	3.50 in.	0	0	1.5	0.1
Granger	06/29/98	Thunderstorm Winds	100 mph	0	0	5.0	0.4
Grimes	06/29/98	Tornado	F2	0	83	10.0	0.0
Hamilton/Boone/Story/Jasper/Mahaska Co.	06/17/96	Flood	na	0	0	1.0	0.5
Harrison Co.	06/21/96	Flood	na	0	0	7.5	24.0
Harrison Co.	07/16/96	Flood	na	0	0	1.5	8.0
Hills	05/15/98	Tornado	F3	0	17	6.0	0.0
Iowa City	05/18/97	Hail	2.75 in.	0	0	40.0	0.0
Johnson Co.	06/29/98	Thunderstorm Winds	na	0	12	30.7	14.0
Johnston	06/29/98	Thunderstorm Winds	120 mph	0	0	10.0	0.0
Knoxville	06/21/97	Thunderstorm Winds	100 mph	0	0	1.0	0.0
Lohrville	05/30/98	Hail	2.75 in.	0	1	1.0	0.0
Louisa Co.	06/29/98	Thunderstorm Winds	81 mph	1	1	1.0	0.0
Manly	07/19/99	Flash Flood	na	0	0	1.1	0.2
Mason City	07/19/99	Flash Flood	na	0	0	1.0	0.1
Missouri Valley	05/16/99	Tornado	F3	2	16	1.9	0.0
Mitchell/Howard/Floyd/Chickasaw Co.	07/19/99	Flood	na	0	0	1.5	0.4
Monona Co.	07/16/96	Flood	na	0	0	1.5	27.0
Monticello	07/27/95	Thunderstorm Winds	86 mph	0	0	1.5	0.0

Location or County	Date	Type	Mag.	Fatalities	Injuries	Property Damage ($mil.)	Crop Damage ($mil.)
		IOWA (*cont.*)					
Muscatine Co.	06/29/98	Thunderstorm Winds	90 mph	0	10	1.5	0.0
Nodaway	04/08/99	Tornado	F4	0	1	1.0	0.0
North Central Iowa	04/06/97	High Wind	63 mph	0	0	1.8	0.0
North Central Iowa	07/19/99	Flood	na	0	0	2.8	1.7
Northeastern Iowa	06/24/98	Flood	na	0	0	1.2	0.3
Northeastern Iowa	11/10/98	High Wind	90 mph	0	2	1.4	0.0
Parkview	05/10/96	Thunderstorm Winds	98 mph	0	0	1.0	0.0
Prairie City	04/08/99	Tornado	F2	0	1	1.0	0.0
Saylorville	06/29/98	Thunderstorm Winds	79 mph	0	0	2.0	0.0
Sioux City	07/02/99	Flash Flood	na	0	2	8.0	0.0
Sioux City	07/16/96	Flash Flood	na	0	0	1.0	0.0
Sioux/Plymouth/Cherokee/Woodbury/Ida Co.	06/19/96	Flood	na	0	0	1.3	3.5
South Central Iowa	04/10/97	Heavy Snow	na	0	0	1.6	0.0
South Central Iowa	06/14/98	Flood	na	0	0	5.4	0.6
South Central Iowa	10/26/97	Heavy Snow	na	0	0	25.0	65.0
Southern Iowa	05/13/97	Frost/Freeze	na	0	0	1.0	0.1
Southwestern Iowa	07/10/95	Heat Wave	na	0	0	2.4	0.0
Southwestern Iowa	10/25/97	Heavy Snow	na	0	0	7.9	0.9
Stockton	05/09/95	Tornado	F3	0	0	3.0	0.0
Story City	06/16/96	Flash Flood	na	0	0	1.5	0.1
Toledo	06/29/98	Thunderstorm Winds	79 mph	0	0	1.0	0.1
Urbandale	06/29/98	Thunderstorm Winds	70 mph	0	0	2.0	0.0
Washington	05/15/98	Tornado	F3	0	28	9.0	0.0
Washington Co.	06/29/98	Thunderstorm Winds	96 mph	0	0	21.0	0.0
Waterloo	07/02/99	Flash Flood	na	0	0	1.0	0.2
West Des Moines	06/29/98	Thunderstorm Winds	70 mph	0	0	2.0	0.0
		KANSAS					
Arkansas City	04/28/96	Thunderstorm Winds	92 mph	0	0	1.5	0.0
Baldwin City	05/16/95	Tornado	F1	0	0	1.0	0.0
Baxter Springs	04/28/96	Thunderstorm Winds	84 mph	0	0	5.0	0.0
Bourbon Co.	09/13/98	Flood	na	0	0	1.0	0.9
Buhler	05/04/99	Tornado	F1	0	0	1.0	0.0
Buhler	05/04/99	Tornado	F1	0	0	1.0	0.0
Burlington	11/01/98	Flash Flood	na	0	0	1.0	0.0
Caldwell	06/13/98	Thunderstorm Winds	70 mph	0	0	1.0	0.0
Central Kansas	03/16/98	Ice Storm	na	0	0	1.0	0.0
Charleston	05/15/95	Thunderstorm Winds	104 mph	0	0	2.0	0.0
Cullison	08/02/96	Thunderstorm Winds	127 mph	0	0	2.0	0.0
Dighton	05/09/96	Hail	1.75 in.	0	0	1.8	0.7
Dodge City	05/23/98	Hail	2.50 in.	0	0	6.0	0.0
Dodge City	09/12/97	Flash Flood	na	0	0	2.0	0.0
Emporia	11/01/98	Flash Flood	na	0	0	2.5	0.0
Erie	06/29/98	Thunderstorm Winds	70 mph	0	0	1.0	0.0
Franklin Co.	05/16/95	Flash Flood	na	0	0	5.0	0.5
Garden City	05/16/95	Hail	4.50 in.	0	0	4.9	0.0
Garden City	07/01/99	Hail	4.00 in.	0	0	53.0	0.0
Globe	05/16/95	Thunderstorm Winds	81 mph	0	0	1.8	0.1
Gove	05/16/95	Hail	1.75 in.	0	0	2.5	0.0
Grainfield	05/22/95	Hail	2.50 in.	0	0	2.5	0.0
Haviland	08/02/96	Thunderstorm Winds	100 mph	0	0	2.0	1.0
Holcomb	06/12/97	Thunderstorm Winds	na	0	0	1.0	0.0
Independence	06/08/98	Hail	1.50 in.	0	0	1.0	0.0
Independence	06/08/98	Thunderstorm Winds	60 mph	0	0	1.0	0.0
Kansas City	10/04/98	Flash Flood	na	0	0	2.0	0.0
Kinsley	08/02/96	Thunderstorm Winds	81 mph	0	0	1.6	0.0
Larned	08/02/96	Thunderstorm Winds	115 mph	0	1	3.2	0.0

Location or County	Date	Type	Mag.	Fatalities	Injuries	Property Damage ($mil.)	Crop Damage ($mil.)
			KANSAS *(cont.)*				
Lawrence	03/24/97	Hail	1.75 in.	0	0	1.0	0.0
Lawrence	06/05/96	Flash Flood	na	0	3	2.0	0.2
Lawrence	10/04/98	Flash Flood	na	0	5	1.1	0.0
Lawrence	11/01/98	Flash Flood	na	0	0	2.5	0.0
Le Roy	04/21/96	Hail	2.75 in.	0	0	1.0	0.0
Lewis	08/02/96	Thunderstorm Winds	104 mph	0	0	1.8	0.0
Liberal	10/01/98	Flash Flood	na	0	0	1.0	0.0
Minneola	08/20/97	Hail	4.50 in.	0	0	2.0	0.0
Missler	05/24/98	Thunderstorm Winds	81 mph	0	0	1.6	0.2
Mullinville	06/11/96	Thunderstorm Winds	109 mph	0	0	1.5	0.0
Ness City	05/09/96	Hail	1.75 in.	0	0	1.2	0.7
Ness City	06/21/96	Thunderstorm Winds	60 mph	0	0	1.4	0.0
North Central Kansas	10/25/97	Winter Storm	na	0	0	3.0	0.5
North Half Osage Co.	05/16/95	Flash Flood	na	0	0	1.5	0.5
Northeast and Northcentral Kansas	09/22/95	Extreme Cold	na	0	0	25.0	0.0
Northeastern Kansas	10/22/96	Heavy Snow	na	0	0	3.5	0.0
Northwestern Kansas	10/25/97	Blizzard	na	0	1	5.0	0.0
Norton	06/03/99	Tornado	F3	0	0	1.0	0.0
Ottawa	08/26/98	Thunderstorm Winds	69 mph	0	0	1.3	2.0
Ottawa	11/01/98	Flash Flood	na	0	0	2.5	0.0
Overland Park	10/04/98	Flash Flood	na	2	0	8.0	0.0
Peck	05/03/99	Tornado	F4	6	150	140.0	0.0
Perry	05/18/97	Hail	2.75 in.	0	0	1.0	0.0
Perth	05/25/97	Tornado	F2	0	0	1.8	0.0
Protection	07/23/96	Hail	4.00 in.	0	0	1.5	1.0
Rush Center	05/16/99	Hail	1.75 in.	0	0	2.4	0.0
Sabetha	06/13/98	Tornado	F2	0	0	3.5	0.0
Scott City	05/16/99	Thunderstorm Winds	82 mph	0	0	1.5	0.0
Southeastern Kansas	01/01/99	Winter Storm	na	0	0	1.9	0.0
Southeastern Kansas	11/01/98	Flood	na	1	2	31.9	0.0
Southwestern Kansas	03/16/98	Ice Storm	na	0	0	1.2	0.0
Southwestern Kansas	03/16/98	Ice Storm	na	0	0	1.2	0.0
Sublette	05/26/96	Tornado	F3	0	0	2.0	0.1
Tonganoxie	10/04/98	Flash Flood	na	0	0	2.0	0.0
Ulysses	06/21/96	Thunderstorm Winds	na	0	2	1.0	0.0
Wakarusa	05/16/95	Flash Flood	na	0	0	1.0	0.0
Wellington	04/28/96	Thunderstorm Winds	109 mph	0	0	7.0	0.0
Wellington	06/13/98	Hail	1.75 in.	0	0	2.0	0.0
Wellington	06/13/98	Hail	1.75 in.	0	0	1.0	0.0
Wichita	04/05/99	Tornado	F0	0	0	2.0	0.0
Wichita	07/10/98	Thunderstorm Winds	92 mph	0	0	3.0	0.0
Wyandotte Co.	06/28/99	Flash Flood	na	0	0	1.0	0.0
Yocemento	10/16/98	Tornado	F3	0	1	1.2	0.0
			KENTUCKY				
Belfry	05/05/96	Flash Flood	na	0	0	1.0	0.0
Berea	04/20/96	Tornado	F2	0	10	12.8	0.0
Bonnieville	03/28/97	Tornado	F3	1	14	1.4	0.0
Bowling Green	04/16/98	Hail	2.75 in.	0	0	510.0	0.0
Boyd Co.	03/02/97	Flood	na	0	0	1.0	0.0
Boyd Co.	07/31/96	Flash Flood	na	0	0	3.0	0.0
Bracken Co.	03/01/97	Flash Flood	na	0	0	1.0	0.0
Brooks	05/28/96	Tornado	F4	0	10	100.0	0.0
Butler/Edmonson/Hart Co.	03/01/97	Flood	na	0	0	3.0	0.0
Campton	06/16/97	Flash Flood	na	0	0	1.0	4.0
Cane Valley	03/28/97	Tornado	F3	0	7	3.0	0.0
Carroll Co.	08/07/95	Flash Flood	na	0	0	1.0	0.0

Location or County	Date	Type	Mag.	Fatalities	Injuries	Property Damage ($mil.)	Crop Damage ($mil.)
		KENTUCKY *(cont.)*					
Carter Co.	03/01/97	Flash Flood	na	0	0	1.0	0.0
Carter Co.	03/01/97	Flood	na	0	0	2.5	0.0
Carter Co.	05/18/95	Thunderstorm Winds	na	0	1	1.0	0.0
Columbia	05/18/95	Flash Flood	na	0	0	5.0	5.0
Dunnville	04/16/98	Thunderstorm Winds	92 mph	0	0	5.0	0.0
East Bernstat	05/18/95	Tornado	F2	0	0	5.0	0.0
East Central Kentucky	02/03/98	Heavy Snow	na	2	1	10.0	0.0
Elliott Co.	05/18/95	Thunderstorm Winds	na	0	2	1.0	0.0
Fayette Co.	03/01/97	Flash Flood	na	0	0	1.1	0.0
Fleming/Bath/Rowan Co.	03/01/97	Flood	na	0	0	5.0	0.0
Fox Creek	05/28/96	Tornado	F2	0	1	1.0	0.0
Frankfort	05/14/95	Thunderstorm Winds	na	0	0	5.0	0.0
Frenchburg	03/01/97	Flash Flood	na	0	0	1.0	0.0
Frenchburg	03/01/97	Flash Flood	na	0	0	1.0	0.0
Glasgow	01/24/97	Tornado	F2	0	2	1.8	0.0
Glasgow	04/16/98	Tornado	F3	2	9	10.0	0.0
Grant Co.	03/01/97	Flash Flood	na	0	0	1.0	0.0
Greenup Co.	03/01/97	Flood	na	0	0	3.5	0.0
Greenup Co.	03/02/97	Flash Flood	na	0	0	1.0	0.0
Greenup Co.	07/31/96	Flash Flood	na	0	0	2.5	0.0
Hardin/Bullitt/Nelson Co.	03/01/97	Flood	na	0	0	28.5	0.0
Harrison/Bourbon/Nicholas Co.	03/01/97	Flood	na	1	0	8.4	0.0
Henderson/Daviess/Mclean Co.	03/01/97	Flood	na	0	0	19.5	0.0
Hopkinsville	03/01/97	Flash Flood	na	0	0	40.0	0.0
Independence	06/30/96	Flash Flood	na	0	0	1.0	0.0
Independence	07/01/96	Flash Flood	na	0	0	1.0	0.0
Jamestown	03/28/97	Tornado	F0	0	0	1.0	0.0
Jefferson Co.	03/01/97	Flood	na	1	0	85.0	0.0
Jessamine Co.	05/18/95	Thunderstorm Winds	na	0	24	5.0	0.0
Lawrence Co.	03/01/97	Flash Flood	na	0	0	1.0	0.0
Liberty	05/13/95	Flash Flood	na	0	0	5.0	0.0
Louisville	05/03/96	Hail	2.75 in.	0	0	20.0	0.0
Magnolia	03/28/97	Tornado	F3	0	1	3.0	0.0
Marion Co.	05/14/95	Hail	2.75 in.	0	0	5.0	0.0
McKinney	04/20/96	Tornado	F2	0	7	1.5	0.0
Mercer Co.	05/18/95	Tornado	F2	0	8	5.0	0.0
Mt. Sterling	05/18/95	Thunderstorm Winds	na	0	0	5.0	0.0
Mt. Washington	05/28/96	Tornado	F3	0	0	1.0	0.0
Northeastern Kentucky	01/06/96	Winter Storm	na	0	0	2.9	0.0
Northeastern Kentucky	03/02/97	Flood	na	1	0	9.7	0.0
Northeastern Kentucky	03/02/97	Flood	na	0	0	25.0	0.0
Northeastern Kentucky	03/02/97	Flood	na	1	0	125.0	0.0
Northwestern Kentucky	03/01/97	Flood	na	0	0	2.4	0.0
Owen Co.	03/01/97	Flash Flood	na	2	0	2.1	0.0
Pendleton Co.	03/01/97	Flash Flood	na	0	0	10.0	0.0
Pendleton Co.	03/01/97	Flood	na	5	0	35.0	0.0
Portland	04/16/98	Tornado	F3	0	0	3.0	0.0
Radcliff	05/14/95	Thunderstorm Winds	na	0	46	5.0	0.0
Rineyville	03/28/97	Tornado	F1	0	0	2.0	0.0
Salvisa	05/18/95	Tornado	F2	0	0	5.0	0.0
Sandy Hook	03/01/97	Flash Flood	na	0	0	1.1	0.0
Scott Co.	03/01/97	Flash Flood	na	0	0	1.8	0.0
Shelby Co.	03/01/97	Flash Flood	na	1	0	1.2	0.0
Somerset	01/17/99	Thunderstorm Winds	na	0	0	1.0	0.0
Southeastern Kentucky	04/17/98	Flood	na	0	0	1.7	0.0
Southwestern Kentucky	03/01/97	Flood	na	0	0	1.5	0.0

Location or County	Date	Type	Mag.	Fatalities	Injuries	Property Damage ($mil.)	Crop Damage ($mil.)
		KENTUCKY (*cont.*)					
Southwestern Kentucky	03/01/97	Flood	na	0	0	1.0	0.0
Southwestern Kentucky	03/01/97	Flood	na	0	0	5.0	0.0
Stanton	03/02/97	Tornado	F0	0	0	1.2	0.0
Stanton	06/16/97	Flash Flood	na	0	1	3.3	1.7
Summer Shade	03/28/97	Tornado	F2	1	6	1.0	0.0
Trenton	01/17/99	Thunderstorm Winds	100 mph	0	3	1.5	0.0
Union	06/30/96	Flash Flood	na	0	0	1.0	0.0
Union	07/01/96	Flash Flood	na	0	0	1.0	0.0
Vine Grove	05/14/95	Thunderstorm Winds	na	0	0	50.0	0.0
Western Half	07/19/96	Flash Flood	na	0	0	1.0	1.2
Winchester	05/18/95	Thunderstorm Winds	na	0	3	50.0	0.0
Wisdom	04/16/98	Tornado	F2	1	0	5.0	0.0
		LOUISIANA					
Alexandria	01/21/99	Tornado	F2	0	1	1.0	0.0
Athens	04/03/99	Tornado	F3	0	0	1.5	0.0
Basile	09/11/98	Tornado	F1	0	3	2.0	0.0
Bossier City	04/03/99	Tornado	F4	7	90	6.6	0.0
Bossier City	04/22/95	Hail	4.50 in.	0	0	50.0	0.0
Charenton	08/02/98	Thunderstorm Winds	na	0	0	6.0	0.0
Converse	02/10/98	Thunderstorm Winds	115 mph	0	0	5.0	0.0
Coushatta	02/10/98	Thunderstorm Winds	115 mph	0	0	6.0	0.0
Covington	11/21/97	Tornado	F2	0	43	3.5	0.0
Jeanerette	03/02/99	Tornado	F1	0	2	2.0	0.0
Lafayette	11/21/97	Tornado	F1	0	1	3.5	0.0
Lake Charles	12/03/97	Thunderstorm Winds	na	0	0	1.5	0.0
Mansfield	02/10/98	Thunderstorm Winds	104 mph	0	3	4.0	0.0
Midland	09/11/98	Tornado	F0	0	2	5.0	0.0
Monroe	05/27/97	Thunderstorm Winds	115 mph	0	0	3.0	0.0
Natchitoches	02/10/98	Thunderstorm Winds	115 mph	0	0	3.0	0.0
New Iberia	01/02/99	Tornado	F1	0	0	1.5	0.0
North Shreveport	04/22/97	Thunderstorm Winds	115 mph	0	0	10.0	0.0
Northeastern Louisiana	12/22/98	Ice Storm	na	0	0	4.1	0.0
Northwestern Louisiana	12/22/98	Ice Storm	na	1	0	1.0	0.0
Pt. Coupee/Iberville/W. Baton Rouge	03/07/96	Extreme Cold	na	0	0	7.2	0.0
Ringgold	02/10/98	Thunderstorm Winds	81 mph	0	2	1.0	0.0
Shreveport	01/23/96	Tornado	F2	0	30	5.0	0.0
Shreveport	04/22/95	Hail	4.50 in.	0	0	50.0	0.0
Shreveport Regional Arpt.	01/01/99	Tornado	F2	0	1	1.0	0.0
Shreveport Regional Arpt.	04/03/99	Tornado	F4	0	12	1.2	0.0
Simsboro	11/30/96	Tornado	F2	1	9	2.0	0.0
Slidell	05/08/95	Tornado	F1	0	0	1.5	0.0
Southeast Louisiana	05/08/95	Hvy Rain/Severe Weather	na	0	0	2,500.0	0.0
Southeastern Louisiana	07/17/97	Hurricane Danny	96 mph	0	0	5.0	0.0
Southeastern Louisiana	09/10/98	Tropical Storm Frances	na	0	0	31.5	0.0
Southeastern Louisiana	09/27/98	Hurricane Georges	82 mph	0	0	30.0	0.0
Southeastern Louisiana	10/05/96	Coastal Flooding	na	0	0	5.4	0.0
Southwestern Louisiana	01/12/97	Ice Storm	na	2	15	11.8	0.0
Southwestern Louisiana	09/09/98	Tropical Storm Frances	na	0	3	21.0	0.0
St. Landry	02/26/98	Tornado	F1	0	0	1.0	0.0
Summerfield	04/03/99	Tornado	F3	0	0	3.5	0.0
Union Co.	03/02/97	Flood	na	0	0	2.0	0.0
Vernon/Beauregard Co.	02/01/99	Flood	na	0	0	1.5	0.0
Ville Platte	02/26/98	Thunderstorm Winds	na	0	2	2.0	0.0
Vivian	06/13/97	Thunderstorm Winds	104 mph	0	1	2.0	0.0

Location or County	Date	Type	Mag.	Fatalities	Injuries	Property Damage ($mil.)	Crop Damage ($mil.)
MAINE							
All of Maine	01/05/98	Ice Storm	na	1	0	304.0	0.0
Allens Mills	06/18/98	Flash Flood	na	0	0	1.5	0.0
Central Maine	01/05/98	Heavy Snow	na	0	0	7.0	0.0
Cumberland Co.	10/21/96	Flood	na	1	0	14.9	0.0
Oxford Co.	10/21/96	Flood	na	0	0	1.1	0.0
Southwestern Maine	04/16/96	Flood	na	0	0	2.3	0.0
York Co.	10/20/96	Flood	na	0	0	10.2	0.0
York and Coastal Cumberland Co.	01/24/98	Ice Storm	na	0	0	9.0	0.0
MARYLAND							
Allegany Co.	01/19/96	Flash Flood	na	0	0	7.0	0.0
Along the Chesapeake	09/06/96	Storm Surge	na	0	0	1.4	0.0
Along the Potomac	09/06/96	Storm Surge	na	0	0	1.6	0.0
Anne Arundel Co.	09/16/99	Flash Flood	na	0	0	2.0	0.0
Baltimore Co.	08/26/99	Flash Flood	na	0	0	2.5	0.0
Caroline Co.	09/16/99	Flash Flood	na	0	1	3.2	0.0
Cecil Co.	09/16/99	Flash Flood	na	0	2	3.0	0.0
Cheverly	05/18/95	Tornado	F1	0	2	2.0	0.0
E. Portion of Washington Co.	06/18/96	Flash Flood	na	0	0	1.0	0.0
Easton	06/26/97	Lightning	na	0	5	1.0	0.0
Friendsville	06/02/98	Tornado	F2	0	0	1.0	0.0
Frostburg	06/02/98	Tornado	F4	0	5	5.0	0.2
Gamber	07/19/96	Tornado	F3	0	3	5.0	0.0
Harford Co.	09/16/99	Flash Flood	na	0	15	2.6	0.0
Inland Worcester Co./MD Beaches	01/27/98	Coastal Flooding	na	0	0	1.5	0.0
Inland Worcester Co./MD Beaches	02/04/98	Coastal Flooding	na	0	0	1.5	0.0
Kent Co.	09/16/99	Flash Flood	na	0	0	1.0	0.0
N. Portion of Frederick Co.	06/19/96	Flash Flood	na	1	0	5.0	0.0
North Central Maryland	01/19/96	Flood	na	0	0	60.0	0.0
North Central Maryland	09/06/96	River Flood	na	0	0	10.7	0.2
Northwestern Maryland	01/14/99	Ice Storm	na	0	0	3.1	0.0
Oakland	01/19/96	Flash Flood	na	0	0	3.0	0.0
Ocean City	11/11/95	Thunderstorm Winds	na	0	0	1.0	0.0
Oxon Hill	06/24/96	Thunderstorm Winds	76 mph	0	0	1.2	0.0
Queen Anne's Co.	09/16/99	Flash Flood	na	0	2	4.0	0.0
Southeast Maryland	09/06/96	Hurricane Fran	35 mph	0	0	1.0	0.0
Southeastern Maryland	12/23/98	Ice Storm	na	0	0	5.0	0.0
Talbot Co.	09/16/99	Flash Flood	na	0	0	3.5	0.0
Temple Hills	10/05/95	Tornado	F2	0	3	5.0	0.0
Washington Co.	01/19/96	Flash Flood	na	0	0	1.0	0.0
West Portion	06/19/96	Flash Flood	na	0	0	1.0	0.0
Westernport	06/27/95	Flood/Flash Flood	na	0	0	1.3	0.0
MASSACHUSETTS							
Berkshire Co.	03/31/97	Winter Storm	na	0	0	1.0	0.0
Boston Metro Area	10/21/96	Flash Flood	na	0	0	10.0	0.0
Brockton	05/21/96	Thunderstorm Winds	104 mph	0	60	4.0	0.0
Leverett	06/13/96	Flash Flood	na	0	0	1.8	0.0
Monterey	07/03/97	Tornado	F2	0	0	1.5	0.0
Southeastern Massachusetts	01/07/96	Heavy Snow	na	0	0	32.0	0.0
Southeastern Massachusetts	04/01/97	Heavy Snow	na	0	1	10.0	0.0
Southeastern Massachusetts	12/07/96	Heavy Snow	na	0	0	14.9	0.0
West Otis	07/03/97	Tornado	F2	0	0	1.5	0.0
Worcester	05/31/98	Thunderstorm Winds	92 mph	0	0	10.0	0.0
MICHIGAN							
Adrian	04/12/96	Hail	1.00 in.	0	0	1.0	0.0
Adrian	04/12/96	Thunderstorm Winds	69 mph	0	0	1.0	0.0

Location or County	Date	Type	Mag.	Fatalities	Injuries	Property Damage ($mil.)	Crop Damage ($mil.)
		MICHIGAN *(cont.)*					
Allegan Co.	06/20/97	Flash Flood	na	0	4	2.0	5.0
Ann Arbor	07/21/98	Thunderstorm Winds	75 mph	0	0	4.5	0.0
Bay City	05/31/98	Thunderstorm Winds	81 mph	0	0	1.0	0.0
Big Rapids	10/06/98	Tornado	F1	0	12	1.2	0.0
Branch	05/31/98	Thunderstorm Winds	na	0	0	1.1	0.0
Brighton	08/10/98	Lightning	na	0	0	1.5	0.0
Bronson	04/12/96	Hail	1.75 in.	0	0	1.0	0.0
Clayton	04/12/96	Hail	1.50 in.	0	1	1.0	0.0
Clio	07/02/97	Tornado	F3	1	1	3.8	0.0
Comins	07/03/99	Tornado	F2	0	2	1.5	0.0
Frankenmuth	06/21/96	Tornado	F3	0	0	5.0	0.0
Freeland	05/31/98	Thunderstorm Winds	86 mph	0	0	1.0	0.0
Gaylord	09/26/98	Thunderstorm Winds	109 mph	0	15	12.0	0.0
Georgetown Twp.	12/05/95	High Wind	52 mph	0	2	1.0	0.0
Grand Haven	05/31/98	Thunderstorm Winds	na	1	20	34.6	10.0
Grosse Pt. Farms	07/02/97	Thunderstorm Winds	92 mph	5	8	10.0	0.0
Highland Park	07/02/97	Tornado	F2	0	90	90.0	0.0
Holly	07/02/97	Tornado	F1	1	0	2.0	0.0
Howard City	05/31/98	Thunderstorm Winds	na	0	23	14.0	0.0
Hudson	04/12/96	Thunderstorm Winds	60 mph	0	0	1.0	0.0
Ishpeming	06/21/95	Lightning/Fire	na	0	0	5.0	0.0
Livonia	07/02/97	Thunderstorm Winds	81 mph	0	0	2.0	0.0
Ludington	05/31/98	Thunderstorm Winds	na	0	5	1.0	0.0
Midland Co.	06/21/96	Flash Flood	na	0	0	1.0	0.0
Montague	05/31/98	Thunderstorm Winds	na	0	2	24.2	5.0
Mt. Clemens	07/21/98	Thunderstorm Winds	81 mph	0	1	1.4	0.0
Muskegon	05/29/98	Thunderstorm Winds	na	0	0	1.0	0.0
N. Half of Lapeer Co.	06/21/96	Flash Flood	na	0	0	5.8	0.0
N. Half of Saginaw Co.	06/21/96	Flash Flood	na	0	0	1.0	0.0
N. Half of St. Clair Co.	06/22/96	Flash Flood	na	0	0	2.5	0.0
Niles	08/25/98	Tornado	F1	0	0	1.1	0.0
Ottawa Co.	06/20/97	Flash Flood	na	0	2	1.3	0.0
Pentwater	05/31/98	Thunderstorm Winds	na	0	37	4.0	0.0
Plymouth	07/21/98	Thunderstorm Winds	69 mph	0	0	3.2	0.0
Reading	04/12/96	Hail	2.00 in.	0	0	2.0	0.0
Redford	07/21/98	Thunderstorm Winds	78 mph	0	0	18.0	0.0
Romeo	07/02/97	Tornado	F0	0	6	30.0	0.0
Roscommon Co.	07/13/95	Thunderstorm Winds	na	2	0	50.0	0.0
Sand Lake	05/31/98	Thunderstorm Winds	na	0	53	49.3	20.0
South Half of Berrien Co.	05/09/96	Flash Flood	na	0	0	5.4	0.0
Southeastern Michigan	01/12/99	Snow	na	0	3	1.7	0.0
Southeastern Michigan	02/17/98	Flood	na	0	0	1.1	0.0
Southeastern Michigan	03/13/97	Ice Storm	na	0	0	19.0	0.0
Southeastern Michigan	04/06/97	High Wind	81 mph	0	1	1.1	0.0
Southeastern Michigan	11/10/98	High Wind	70 mph	0	0	1.1	0.0
Southern Half of Bay Co.	06/21/96	Flash Flood	na	1	0	2.2	0.0
Southwestern Michigan	04/06/97	High Wind	na	0	0	5.0	0.0
Southwestern Michigan	10/26/97	Heavy Snow	na	0	0	1.2	0.0
Sterling Heights	07/07/96	Thunderstorm Winds	109 mph	0	1	3.0	0.0
Sterling Hgts.	07/02/97	Thunderstorm Winds	81 mph	0	0	1.0	0.0
Taylor	07/21/98	Thunderstorm Winds	71 mph	0	0	4.5	0.0
Tuscola Co.	05/21/96	Flood	na	0	0	1.0	0.0
Tuscola Co.	06/21/96	Flash Flood	na	0	0	6.5	0.0
Warren	07/21/98	Thunderstorm Winds	81 mph	0	0	5.8	0.0
Washtenaw/Wayne/Lenawee/Monroe Co.	01/11/99	Extreme Cold	na	0	0	1.2	0.0
Woodland Park	05/31/98	Thunderstorm Winds	na	0	0	1.2	0.0

Location or County	Date	Type	Mag.	Fatalities	Injuries	Property Damage ($mil.)	Crop Damage ($mil.)
		MINNESOTA					
Apple Valley	05/30/98	Thunderstorm Winds	75 mph	0	0	2.8	0.0
Austin	06/27/98	Thunderstorm Winds	70 mph	0	0	1.9	0.0
Austin	06/27/98	Thunderstorm Winds	70 mph	0	0	3.2	0.2
Austin Airport	06/27/98	Thunderstorm Winds	93 mph	0	0	1.5	0.1
Bloomington	05/15/98	Hail	0.75 in.	0	0	3.0	0.0
Brainerd	07/13/97	Lightning	na	0	0	1.5	0.0
Brainerd	09/25/98	Thunderstorm Winds	90 mph	0	0	1.0	0.0
Burnsville	05/30/98	Thunderstorm Winds	92 mph	0	7	35.0	0.0
Cambridge	07/21/95	Tornado	F1	0	3	1.5	0.0
Cannon Falls	06/26/98	Flash Flood	na	2	0	1.5	0.0
Chaska	05/30/98	Thunderstorm Winds	70 mph	0	2	2.3	0.0
Clay Co.	04/16/97	Flood	na	0	0	25.0	0.0
Cleveland	03/29/98	Tornado	F2	0	2	20.0	0.0
Clinton	05/17/96	Tornado	F3	0	0	1.5	0.0
Comfrey	03/29/98	Tornado	F4	1	16	45.0	0.0
Dodge Center	05/19/96	Thunderstorm Winds	69 mph	0	0	8.5	0.0
Duluth	08/23/98	Hail	3.50 in.	0	0	50.0	0.0
Eagan	05/30/98	Thunderstorm Winds	86 mph	0	1	6.0	0.0
Eitzen	05/18/96	Hail	2.75 in.	0	2	1.0	0.5
Grant Co.	04/09/97	Flood	na	0	0	3.0	0.0
Hallock	07/09/95	Tornado	F1	0	8	3.0	0.0
Haydenville	10/08/97	Thunderstorm Winds	63 mph	0	1	1.0	0.0
International Falls	05/15/98	Hail	3.00 in.	0	0	3.0	0.0
Kittson Co.	04/21/97	Flood	na	0	0	5.0	0.0
Lakeville	05/19/96	Thunderstorm Winds	81 mph	0	0	4.5	0.0
Lastrup	09/18/97	Tornado	F3	1	1	1.7	0.0
Lewiston	07/08/99	Tornado	F2	0	2	2.0	0.0
Lonsdale	03/29/98	Tornado	F2	0	0	20.0	0.0
Mankato	05/15/98	Thunderstorm Winds	70 mph	0	0	1.0	0.0
Monticello	07/01/97	Thunderstorm Winds	109 mph	0	0	20.0	0.0
New Ulm	07/20/98	Thunderstorm Winds	96 mph	0	0	7.0	4.0
New York Mills	09/25/98	Thunderstorm Winds	na	0	0	4.0	0.0
Nicollet	03/29/98	Tornado	F3	1	0	120.0	0.0
Nicollet	07/20/98	Thunderstorm Winds	92 mph	0	0	4.0	8.0
Norman Co.	04/05/97	Flood	na	0	0	20.0	0.0
Norman Co.	04/17/97	Flood	na	0	0	10.0	0.0
Northwestern Minnesota	04/04/97	Ice Storm	na	0	0	18.0	0.0
Northwestern Minnesota	04/05/97	Blizzard	na	0	3	25.0	0.0
Oak Center	05/19/96	Thunderstorm Winds	86 mph	0	0	12.0	0.0
Oakdale	06/25/98	Thunderstorm Winds	81 mph	0	0	1.0	0.0
Olivia	06/18/98	Tornado	F1	0	0	1.0	0.0
Ottertail	09/25/98	Thunderstorm Winds	na	0	0	2.0	0.0
Owatonna	05/19/96	Thunderstorm Winds	81 mph	0	0	5.0	0.0
Portions of W. Central MN	07/13/95	Thunderstorm Winds	92 mph	0	6	15.0	16.0
Prior Lake	05/30/98	Thunderstorm Winds	98 mph	0	0	4.3	0.0
Rochester	08/09/99	Hail	1.75 in.	0	0	1.2	0.0
Rochester	08/09/99	Hail	1.00 in.	0	0	1.0	0.0
Rochester	08/09/99	Hail	1.25 in.	0	0	1.5	0.0
Southern Minnesota	07/10/95	Heat Wave	na	2	0	2.0	0.0
Southwestern Minnesota	11/14/96	Ice Storm	na	0	0	13.0	0.0
Stillwater	06/26/98	Thunderstorm Winds	92 mph	0	0	1.0	0.0
Tracy	07/27/95	Thunderstorm Winds	na	0	0	1.0	0.0
Waseca	05/19/96	Thunderstorm Winds	99 mph	0	0	4.0	0.0
Wells	05/19/96	Thunderstorm Winds	86 mph	0	0	1.5	0.0
West Marshall Co.	04/19/97	Flood	na	0	0	10.0	0.0
West Polk Co.	04/17/97	Flood	na	0	0	600.0	0.0

Location or County	Date	Type	Mag.	Fatalities	Injuries	Property Damage ($mil.)	Crop Damage ($mil.)
			MINNESOTA (*cont.*)				
Westbrook	03/29/98	Tornado	F3	0	3	30.0	0.0
Wilkin Co.	04/05/97	Flood	na	0	0	20.0	0.0
Wilkin Co.	04/13/97	Flood	na	0	0	20.0	0.0
Woodbury	05/19/96	Hail	1.50 in.	0	0	1.7	0.0
Woodbury	05/30/98	Thunderstorm Winds	86 mph	0	0	3.5	0.0
			MISSISSIPPI				
Brandon	03/05/96	Hail	1.75 in.	0	0	1.0	0.0
Central Mississippi	02/01/96	Ice Storm	na	0	0	3.0	0.0
Central Mississippi	12/22/98	Ice Storm	na	0	0	16.6	0.0
Columbia	06/18/97	Flash Flood	na	0	0	15.0	0.0
De Soto Co.	06/05/98	Thunderstorm Winds	75 mph	0	0	2.5	0.0
Greene Co.	06/05/98	Thunderstorm Winds	81 mph	0	0	1.4	0.1
Hattiesburg	03/18/96	Hail	1.75 in.	0	0	2.0	0.0
Hattiesburg	03/18/96	Hail	2.75 in.	0	0	2.0	0.0
Hattiesburg	06/05/98	Thunderstorm Winds	na	2	45	1.0	0.0
Hebron	04/14/99	Tornado	F3	1	30	4.0	0.0
Jackson	06/01/96	Thunderstorm Winds	98 mph	0	0	1.2	0.0
Lexington	06/10/97	Flash Flood	na	0	0	10.0	0.0
Moss	04/14/99	Tornado	F3	0	3	2.0	0.0
Natchez	02/26/98	Thunderstorm Winds	81 mph	0	4	30.0	0.0
Pearl	03/31/96	Hail	3.00 in.	0	0	10.0	0.0
Pearl River/Hancock/Harrison/Jackson Co.	09/27/98	Hurricane Georges	117 mph	0	0	602.0	0.0
Southern Mississippi	09/27/98	High Wind	na	0	0	2.7	0.0
Southwestern Mississippi	03/09/97	Flood	na	0	0	7.3	0.0
Terry	03/18/96	Hail	2.75 in.	0	0	1.0	0.0
Valley Park	01/18/95	Thunderstorm Winds	na	0	0	1.0	0.0
Walnut Grove	02/21/97	Tornado	F2	0	0	1.5	0.0
Wayne/Perry/Greene/Stone/George Co.	09/25/98	Hurricane Georges	na	0	0	72.0	0.0
			MISSOURI				
Billings	04/28/96	Thunderstorm Winds	81 mph	0	2	2.5	0.0
Columbia	11/10/98	Tornado	F3	0	16	6.0	0.0
Gladstone	04/16/95	Hail	3.25 in.	0	0	2.0	0.0
Harrisonville	04/16/95	Hail	1.75 in.	0	0	3.0	0.2
Jackson Co.	10/23/96	Heavy Snow	na	0	0	1.0	0.0
Jefferson City	08/07/99	Thunderstorm Winds	81 mph	0	0	1.0	0.0
Joplin	04/28/96	Tornado	F1	0	12	12.0	0.0
Joplin	04/28/96	Tornado	F1	0	0	1.0	0.0
Kansas City	10/04/98	Flash Flood	na	9	0	20.0	0.0
La Belle	04/08/99	Tornado	F2	0	2	2.1	0.0
Laclede Co.	11/10/95	Tornado	F2	0	0	3.0	0.0
Lee's Summit	05/26/96	Thunderstorm Winds	119 mph	0	9	10.0	0.0
Linn	04/08/99	Tornado	F1	0	0	1.0	0.0
Madison Co.	04/03/99	Flash Flood	na	1	0	6.0	0.0
Maryland Hgts	04/13/98	Tornado	F1	0	1	2.5	0.0
Monett	04/28/96	Thunderstorm Winds	81 mph	0	0	1.0	0.0
Mosby	10/04/98	Flash Flood	na	0	0	4.0	0.0
Nevada	05/17/95	Tornado	F3	0	9	7.0	0.0
New Cambria	04/08/99	Tornado	F2	0	2	1.0	0.4
North/Central/W. Central Missouri	05/07/95	River Flood	na	0	0	2.8	2.0
Northeastern Missouri	01/18/95	Heavy Snow	na	0	0	2.4	0.0
Northwestern Missouri	04/10/97	Heavy Snow	na	0	2	9.8	0.0
Owensville	06/06/97	Hail	2.00 in.	0	0	1.0	0.0
Perryville	04/19/96	Tornado	F3	0	0	5.0	0.0
Platte City	10/04/98	Flash Flood	na	0	0	4.0	0.0
Rogersville	05/07/95	Thunderstorm Winds	na	0	0	1.0	0.0
Silver Lake	02/27/99	Hail	2.00 in.	0	0	6.0	0.0

Location or County	Date	Type	Mag.	Fatalities	Injuries	Property Damage ($mil.)	Crop Damage ($mil.)
		MISSOURI *(cont.)*					
Southeastern Missouri	07/26/98	Flood	na	0	0	2.3	6.2
Southwestern Missouri	01/01/99	Winter Storm	na	0	0	2.7	0.0
St. James	06/01/99	Tornado	F3	0	0	3.5	0.0
		MONTANA					
Billings	07/04/98	Hail	1.75 in.	0	0	4.0	1.0
Billings	07/31/98	Hail	1.25 in.	0	0	8.0	1.0
Chinnok	06/19/95	Hail	1.75 in.	0	0	1.0	0.0
Culbertson	07/04/98	Flash Flood	na	0	0	1.0	0.3
Glasgow	07/21/99	Hail	4.50 in.	0	0	1.5	0.1
Huntley	07/04/98	Hail	2.50 in.	0	0	2.0	0.0
Lewistown	08/14/99	Tornado	F2	0	3	4.0	0.0
Libby	07/21/97	Thunderstorm Winds	81 mph	0	2	1.5	0.0
Miles City	07/04/98	Flash Flood	na	0	0	1.0	0.0
NW Chinook Zone/N. Central Montana	03/11/96	Flood	na	0	0	1.5	0.0
Northwestern Montana	03/24/95	Winter Storm	na	0	0	5.0	0.0
Northwestern Montana	05/01/97	Flood	na	0	0	2.2	0.0
Outlook	10/31/99	Wild/Forest Fire	na	0	0	6.0	0.0
Wolf Pt.	10/31/99	Wild/Forest Fire	na	0	0	5.0	0.0
		NEBRASKA					
Arlington	08/06/99	Flash Flood	na	0	0	4.0	0.0
Beatrice	05/08/96	Tornado	F2	0	15	12.0	0.0
Bellevue	05/16/95	Hail	3.00 in.	0	0	20.0	0.0
Brownson	06/26/99	Hail	2.75 in.	0	0	6.0	20.0
Bushnell	05/24/97	Flash Flood	na	0	0	1.0	0.5
Carleton	05/29/98	Thunderstorm Winds	75 mph	0	0	1.0	0.2
Cedar Co.	07/16/96	Flood	na	0	0	1.0	0.0
Columbus	05/15/99	Hail	2.75 in.	0	0	7.5	0.0
Columbus	06/23/98	Tornado	F2	0	17	4.0	0.5
Dodge Co.	08/04/96	Flood	na	0	0	1.7	5.2
Eastern Nebraska	07/19/99	Excessive Heat	na	2	0	3.3	0.0
Elm Creek	09/25/98	Thunderstorm Winds	100 mph	0	5	2.4	2.0
Gilead	05/08/96	Tornado	F1	0	0	2.0	0.5
Grand Island	08/05/95	Hail	1.75 in.	0	0	1.0	0.0
Grand Island	08/05/95	Hail	2.00 in.	0	0	1.5	0.5
Hayes Co.	08/28/99	Flash Flood	na	0	0	2.0	0.0
Holdrege	05/21/98	Hail	2.75 in.	0	0	1.0	0.7
Hooper	06/20/96	Hail	2.75 in.	0	0	10.0	12.0
Imperial	08/21/97	Hail	2.75 in.	0	0	1.0	1.5
Imperial	08/21/97	Hail	1.75 in.	0	0	1.0	1.5
Jackson	07/16/96	Flash Flood	na	0	0	1.0	0.0
Johnstown	06/30/97	Hail	2.00 in.	0	0	1.2	3.4
Kimball	06/25/97	Hail	1.75 in.	0	0	1.0	6.0
Lincoln Airport	05/22/96	Thunderstorm Winds	83 mph	0	0	1.4	0.0
Maywood	06/25/97	Hail	1.75 in.	0	0	3.0	0.0
Northwestern Nebraska	04/04/97	Blizzard	na	0	0	5.0	0.0
O'Neill	06/19/96	Tornado	F2	0	0	1.0	0.0
O'Neill	08/14/97	Hail	2.00 in.	0	0	1.0	0.5
Offutt AFB	06/24/97	Flood	na	0	0	1.0	0.0
Omaha	08/07/99	Flash Flood	na	1	0	11.0	0.0
Ord	06/03/99	Tornado	F3	0	0	1.5	1.0
Panama	05/08/96	Flash Flood	na	0	0	1.5	0.0
Plattsmouth	07/28/96	Hail	1.50 in.	0	0	1.0	0.2
Ponca	07/02/99	Flash Flood	na	0	0	1.0	0.0
Potter	05/25/97	Flood	na	0	0	2.0	0.5
Scottsbluff	06/27/99	Hail	2.75 in.	0	25	55.0	2.0
South Sioux City	07/16/96	Thunderstorm Winds	81 mph	0	0	3.0	3.0

Location or County	Date	Type	Mag.	Fatalities	Injuries	Property Damage ($mil.)	Crop Damage ($mil.)
		NEBRASKA (*cont.*)					
Southeastern Nebraska	10/25/97	Winter Storm	na	0	0	15.0	1.5
Southeastern Nebraska	10/25/97	Heavy Snow	na	0	0	56.5	1.6
Southwest Portion of Lincoln Co.	08/28/99	Flash Flood	na	0	2	1.0	0.0
Wallace	06/25/97	Hail	1.75 in.	0	0	1.5	1.5
Wellfleet	06/25/97	Hail	1.75 in.	0	0	1.5	1.4
		NEVADA					
Boulder City	08/10/97	Flash Flood	na	0	1	4.5	0.0
Henderson	07/09/98	Lightning	na	0	0	1.5	0.0
Henderson	08/10/97	Flash Flood	na	1	4	4.0	0.0
Lake Tahoe-Truckee	03/09/95	Flood	na	0	0	1.5	0.0
Las Vegas	07/08/99	Flash Flood	na	1	0	25.0	0.0
Las Vegas	07/20/98	Heavy Rain	na	0	0	11.0	0.0
Mead Lake	07/19/98	Thunderstorm Winds	na	0	0	1.2	0.0
Pahrump	09/03/97	Flash Flood	na	0	0	2.7	0.0
Storey Co.	03/10/95	Flash Flood	na	0	0	2.5	0.0
Western Nevada	01/01/97	Flood	na	2	50	640.0	0.0
Western Nevada	03/20/95	Heavy Snow/ High Winds/Flood	na	0	0	1.5	0.0
		NEW HAMPSHIRE					
Bradford	07/09/97	Lightning	na	0	0	3.0	0.0
Cheshire/Hillsborough Co.	01/07/98	Ice Storm	na	0	0	1.0	0.0
Cheshire/Hillsborough Co.	12/07/96	Heavy Snow	na	1	0	1.5	0.0
Grafton Co.	10/21/96	Flood	na	0	0	1.0	0.0
Lempster	10/21/96	Flash Flood	na	0	0	1.0	0.0
Merrimack Co.	10/20/96	Flood	na	0	0	2.2	0.0
North/Central New Hampshire	01/07/98	Ice Storm	na	0	1	26.8	0.0
Piermont	06/27/98	Flood	na	1	1	1.5	0.0
Rockingham Co.	10/20/96	Flood	na	0	0	4.8	0.0
Strafford Co.	10/20/96	Flood	na	0	0	1.8	0.0
		NEW JERSEY					
All of New Jersey	09/16/99	High Wind	62 mph	0	2	4.0	0.0
Beach Haven	08/20/99	Tornado	F2	0	1	4.2	0.0
Bergen Co.	09/16/99	Flood	na	2	0	17.5	0.0
Burlington Co.	09/16/99	Flash Flood	na	0	0	7.0	0.0
Camden Co.	09/16/99	Flash Flood	na	0	0	7.0	0.0
Cumberland Co.	09/16/99	Heavy Rain	na	0	0	1.0	0.0
E. Cape May/E. Atlantic/E. Ocean Co.	09/16/99	Hurricane Floyd	na	0	0	1.1	0.0
Essex Co.	07/24/97	Flood	na	0	0	3.0	0.0
Essex Co.	09/16/99	Flood	na	0	0	7.3	0.0
Estell Manor	08/20/97	Flash Flood	na	0	0	54.0	0.0
Gloucester Co.	09/16/99	Flash Flood	na	0	0	5.0	0.0
Hunterdon Co.	09/16/99	Flash Flood	na	0	3	8.5	0.0
Hunterdon Co.	10/19/96	Flash Flood	na	0	0	1.0	0.0
Lake Hiawatha	06/20/95	Thunderstorm Winds	70 mph	0	0	1.0	0.0
Linden Airport	09/07/98	Thunderstorm Winds	73 mph	0	0	3.0	0.0
Mercer Co.	09/16/99	Flash Flood	na	0	5	32.0	0.0
Middlesex Co.	09/07/98	Thunderstorm Winds	69 mph	0	1	1.8	0.0
Middlesex Co.	09/16/99	Flash Flood	na	0	72	28.0	0.0
Middlesex Co.	10/19/96	Flash Flood	na	0	1	2.7	0.0
Millburn	10/19/96	Flood	na	0	0	5.0	0.0
Monmouth Co.	09/16/99	Flash Flood	na	0	0	7.5	0.0
Morris Co.	09/16/99	Flash Flood	na	0	6	30.0	0.0
Morris Co.	10/19/96	Flash Flood	na	0	0	1.0	0.0
North/SW New Jersey	01/07/96	Blizzard	na	3	0	18.8	0.0
Northeastern New Jersey	01/19/96	Flood	na	0	0	3.0	0.0
Northwestern New Jersey	01/19/96	Flood	na	0	1	10.7	0.0

Location or County	Date	Type	Mag.	Fatalities	Injuries	Property Damage ($mil.)	Crop Damage ($mil.)
NEW JERSEY (cont.)							
Ocean Co.	09/16/99	Flash Flood	na	0	0	5.5	0.0
Passaic Co.	09/16/99	Flood	na	1	0	6.0	0.0
Plainfield	09/07/98	Tornado	F0	0	0	1.5	0.0
Rahway	06/03/95	Lightning	na	0	0	2.0	0.0
Salem Co.	09/16/99	Flash Flood	na	1	0	5.0	0.0
Sea Breeze	08/20/97	Flood	na	0	0	2.1	0.0
Somerset Co.	09/07/98	Thunderstorm Winds	70 mph	0	1	2.6	0.0
Somerset Co.	09/16/99	Flash Flood	na	2	100	358.0	0.0
Somerset Co.	10/19/96	Flash Flood	na	0	0	31.0	0.0
South/SE New Jersey	01/07/96	Winter Storm	na	1	0	2.4	0.0
Southeastern New Jersey	01/07/96	Coastal Flooding/Erosion	na	0	0	14.2	0.0
Southeastern New Jersey	01/28/98	Coastal Flooding/Erosion	na	0	0	15.0	0.0
Southeastern New Jersey	02/04/98	Coastal Flooding/Erosion	na	0	0	17.0	0.0
Springfield	10/19/96	Flood	na	0	0	4.3	0.0
Sussex Co.	09/16/99	Flash Flood	na	0	0	2.5	0.0
Sykesville	06/22/96	Thunderstorm Winds	na	0	0	11.0	1.0
Thorofare	07/08/96	Thunderstorm Winds	79 mph	0	0	1.1	0.1
Union Co.	09/16/99	Flood	na	0	0	4.2	0.0
Warren Co.	09/16/99	Flash Flood	na	0	0	7.0	0.0
Western	06/12/96	Flash Flood	na	0	0	8.0	0.0
NEW MEXICO							
Albuquerque	06/16/99	Flash Flood	na	0	0	1.2	0.0
Artesia	05/06/95	Hail	1.75 in.	0	0	1.5	0.0
Artesia	05/06/95	Hail	1.75 in.	0	0	1.5	0.0
Central New Mexico	04/24/97	Winter Storm	na	0	0	1.5	1.2
Cimarron	07/25/96	Tornado	F2	0	5	1.6	0.0
Curry Co.	05/06/95	Thunderstorm Winds	86 mph	0	0	1.5	0.0
Hobbs	05/28/97	Hail	2.50 in.	0	0	27.0	0.0
Lama	05/06/96	Wild/Forest Fire	na	0	0	1.5	0.0
Las Cruces	06/07/97	Hail	1.50 in.	0	0	3.5	0.0
Los Chavez	05/24/99	Thunderstorm Winds	81 mph	0	2	1.2	0.0
Northeastern New Mexico	12/21/97	Winter Storm	na	0	0	2.5	4.0
Rio Rancho	07/29/99	Flash Flood	na	0	0	1.0	0.0
Truth Or Consequence	06/29/96	Flash Flood	na	0	0	1.0	0.0
NEW YORK							
Albany Co.	07/15/95	Thunderstorm Winds	na	0	0	1.0	0.0
Albany Co.	09/16/99	Flood	na	0	0	2.2	0.0
Allegany Co.	01/19/96	Flood	na	0	0	1.0	0.0
Arcade	06/26/98	Flash Flood	na	0	0	4.5	0.0
Baldwinsville	09/07/98	Thunderstorm Winds	na	3	7	90.0	0.0
Broome Co.	01/19/96	Flash Flood	na	0	0	7.9	0.0
Cato	09/07/98	Thunderstorm Winds	na	0	0	5.0	1.0
Cattaraugus Co.	01/19/96	Flood	na	0	0	2.5	0.0
Cayuga Co.	01/19/96	Flash Flood	na	1	0	1.4	0.0
Chemung Co.	01/19/96	Flash Flood	na	0	0	17.8	0.0
Chemung Co.	11/08/96	Flash Flood	na	0	0	1.5	0.0
Chenango Co.	01/19/96	Flash Flood	na	0	0	7.9	0.0
Clinton Co.	06/27/98	Flood	na	0	0	7.0	0.0
Clinton Co.	07/01/98	Flash Flood	na	0	0	2.0	0.0
Clinton Co.	11/09/96	Flash Flood	na	0	0	23.0	0.0
Cortland Co.	01/19/96	Flash Flood	na	0	0	5.7	0.0
Delaware Co.	01/19/96	Flash Flood	na	6	0	9.3	0.0
Delaware Co.	07/04/99	Flash Flood	na	0	0	1.5	0.5
Deposit	05/31/98	Tornado	F3	0	0	1.0	0.0
East Central New York	03/06/97	High Wind	na	0	1	4.2	0.0
East Central New York	03/31/97	Winter Storm	na	0	0	7.8	0.0

Location or County	Date	Type	Mag.	Fatalities	Injuries	Property Damage ($mil.)	Crop Damage ($mil.)
		NEW YORK *(cont.)*					
East Central New York	09/16/99	High Wind	na	0	0	3.7	0.0
East Portion of Essex Co.	08/11/98	Flash Flood	na	0	0	1.0	0.0
Eastern Essex Co.	09/16/99	High Wind	na	0	0	2.0	0.0
Erie/Genesee/Wyoming Co.	07/08/98	Flood	na	2	0	1.6	0.1
Essex Co	10/21/95	Flood	na	0	0	2.0	0.0
Essex Co.	06/27/98	Flood	na	0	0	5.0	0.0
Essex Co.	07/01/98	Flash Flood	na	0	0	1.0	0.0
Essex Co.	11/09/96	Flash Flood	na	0	0	9.0	0.0
Gloversville	09/07/98	Thunderstorm Winds	69 mph	0	0	1.0	0.0
Gowanda	06/26/98	Flash Flood	na	0	0	2.5	0.0
Greene Co.	09/16/99	Flood	na	0	0	3.0	0.0
Greene Co.	10/21/95	Flash Flood	na	0	0	2.0	0.0
Greene Co.	10/21/95	Flood	na	0	0	1.0	0.0
Hamilton Co.	07/15/95	Thunderstorm Winds	na	0	0	75.0	0.0
Herkimer Co.	07/15/95	Thunderstorm Winds	na	0	0	10.0	0.0
Hudson to East Hillsdale	05/29/95	Tornado	F2	0	5	10.0	0.0
Jefferson Co.	01/19/96	Flood	na	0	0	1.0	0.0
Jefferson Co.	07/15/95	Thunderstorm Winds	na	0	0	15.0	0.0
Jefferson/Lewis Co.	01/08/98	Ice Storm	na	0	0	12.0	0.0
Kings Co.	10/19/96	Flood	na	0	0	1.5	0.0
Lewis Co.	07/15/95	Thunderstorm Winds	na	0	0	15.0	0.0
Lynbrook	09/07/98	Tornado	F2	0	6	1.0	0.0
Lyons	09/07/98	Thunderstorm Winds	na	0	0	5.0	0.5
Macedon	09/06/98	Thunderstorm Winds	na	0	0	5.0	0.0
Madison Co.	01/19/96	Flash Flood	na	0	0	1.5	0.0
Mattituck	08/08/99	Tornado	F2	0	1	1.0	0.0
Monroe/Wayne Co.	03/04/99	Blizzard	na	0	0	2.5	0.0
Montezuma	09/07/98	Thunderstorm Winds	na	0	3	20.0	0.0
Montgomery Co.	01/19/96	Flood	na	0	0	4.0	0.0
N. Herkimer/S. Herkimer Co.	01/19/96	Flood	na	0	0	4.0	0.0
N. Saratoga/S. Saratoga Co.	01/19/96	Flood	na	0	0	10.0	0.0
Nassau Co.	09/07/98	Thunderstorm Winds	75 mph	0	0	2.5	0.0
New York City and Long Island	10/19/96	Coastal Flooding	na	0	0	11.5	0.0
Niagara Falls	01/08/98	Flash Flood	na	0	0	1.0	0.0
Northeastern New York	01/06/98	Ice Storm	na	1	0	11.0	0.0
Northeastern New York	01/19/96	Flood	na	0	0	6.5	0.0
Northeastern New York	11/09/96	Flood	na	0	0	2.0	0.0
Northwestern New York	02/22/97	High Wind	70 mph	1	1	1.7	0.0
Northwestern New York	02/27/97	High Wind	81 mph	0	9	1.2	0.0
Northwestern New York	03/04/99	Heavy Snow	na	0	0	2.9	0.0
Northwestern New York	03/06/99	Heavy Snow	na	0	0	2.7	0.0
Oneida	09/07/98	Thunderstorm Winds	na	0	0	5.0	0.0
Oneida Co.	07/04/99	Flash Flood	na	0	0	2.5	0.0
Oneida Co.	07/15/95	Thunderstorm Winds	na	0	0	20.0	0.0
Onondaga Co.	01/19/96	Flash Flood	na	0	0	7.6	0.0
Ontario Co.	01/19/96	Flood	na	0	0	2.2	0.0
Orange Co.	09/16/99	Flood	na	0	0	1.7	0.0
Orangeville Center	06/02/98	Tornado	F2	0	0	1.0	0.0
Otsego Co.	01/19/96	Flash Flood	na	0	0	5.4	0.0
Pittsford	09/06/98	Thunderstorm Winds	na	0	0	1.2	0.0
Port Douglass	06/25/98	Flash Flood	na	0	0	1.0	0.0
Putnam Co.	09/16/99	Flood	na	0	0	1.9	0.0
Queens Co.	10/19/96	Flood	na	0	0	3.6	0.0
Rensselaer Co.	07/26/95	Flash Flood	na	0	0	1.0	0.0
Rensselaer Co.	09/16/99	Flood	na	0	0	1.5	0.0
Reynolds	05/31/98	Tornado	F2	0	0	10.0	0.2

Location or County	Date	Type	Mag.	Fatalities	Injuries	Property Damage ($mil.)	Crop Damage ($mil.)
NEW YORK (*cont.*)							
Rochester Airport	09/06/98	Thunderstorm Winds	90 mph	0	1	20.0	2.0
Rockland Co.	09/16/99	Flood	na	1	0	4.4	0.0
Schoharie Co.	01/19/96	Flood	na	2	0	12.0	0.0
Schuyler Co.	01/19/96	Flash Flood	na	0	0	1.5	0.0
Shelby	09/06/98	Thunderstorm Winds	na	0	0	5.0	5.0
St. Lawrence Co.	07/15/95	Thunderstorm Winds	na	0	0	34.0	0.0
Steuben Co.	01/19/96	Flash Flood	na	0	0	4.4	0.0
Steuben Co.	11/08/96	Flash Flood	na	0	0	14.4	0.0
Sullivan Co.	01/19/96	Flash Flood	na	0	0	8.7	0.0
Tioga Co.	01/19/96	Flash Flood	na	0	0	4.5	0.0
Tompkins Co.	01/19/96	Flash Flood	na	0	0	19.0	0.0
Ushers	05/31/98	Tornado	F3	0	68	60.0	0.0
Verona	09/07/98	Thunderstorm Winds	na	0	0	10.0	0.0
Vestal	05/31/98	Tornado	F3	0	12	1.5	0.0
Victor	09/07/98	Thunderstorm Winds	na	0	0	1.0	0.0
W. Columbia/E. Columbia Co.	01/19/96	Flood	na	0	0	4.0	0.0
W. Dutchess/E. Dutchess Co.	01/19/96	Flood	na	0	0	7.0	0.0
W. Rensselaer/E. Rensselaer Co.	01/19/96	Flood	na	0	0	6.0	0.0
W. Schenectady/E. Schenectady Co.	01/19/96	Flood	na	1	0	6.0	0.0
Warren Co.	01/19/96	Flood	na	0	0	3.0	0.0
Warren Co.	07/15/95	Thunderstorm Winds	na	0	0	10.0	0.0
Washington Co.	01/19/96	Flood	na	0	0	1.5	0.0
West Seneca	01/18/96	Flash Flood	na	0	0	1.0	0.5
Westchester Co.	09/16/99	Flood	na	0	0	6.6	0.0
Western Albany/Eastern Albany Co.	01/19/96	Flood	na	0	0	4.0	0.0
Western Greene/Eastern Greene Co.	01/19/96	Flood	na	0	0	10.0	0.0
Western Ulster/Eastern Ulster Co.	01/19/96	Flood	na	0	0	10.0	0.0
Yates Co.	01/19/96	Flash Flood	na	0	0	7.9	0.0
NORTH CAROLINA							
Albemarle	09/29/99	Tornado	F2	0	0	3.0	0.0
Allenstand	07/06/99	Flash Flood	na	0	0	3.0	3.0
Asheville Airport	09/11/97	Hail	2.00 in.	0	0	1.0	4.0
Bakersville	01/07/98	Flash Flood	na	0	0	5.0	0.0
Bladen Co.	09/05/96	High Wind	81 mph	1	0	20.0	20.0
Bolton	09/15/99	Flood	na	1	1	30.0	10.0
Brunswick Co.	07/12/96	Hurricane Bertha	101 mph	0	0	2.0	9.0
Brunswick Co.	08/26/98	Hurricane Bonnie	93 mph	0	0	35.0	64.0
Brunswick Co.	09/05/96	Hurricane Fran	109 mph	0	0	5.0	2.0
Buncombe Co.	01/07/98	Flood	na	0	0	1.0	0.0
Cabarrus Co.	07/23/97	Flash Flood	na	0	4	3.0	2.0
Charlotte	05/24/96	Hail	2.50 in.	0	0	1.0	0.0
Chimney Rock	09/04/96	Flash Flood	na	0	0	3.0	0.0
Clemmons	05/07/98	Tornado	F3	0	5	50.0	0.0
Columbus Co.	09/05/96	High Wind	86 mph	0	1	18.0	18.0
Dudley Shoals	05/07/98	Tornado	F4	0	2	1.1	0.0
Eastern North Carolina	02/03/98	Winter Storm	na	0	0	22.1	0.0
Eastern North Carolina	06/18/96	Tropical Storm Arthur	na	0	0	1.0	0.0
Eastern North Carolina	07/12/96	Hurricane Bertha	108 mph	1	10	140.2	127.0
Eastern North Carolina	08/26/98	Hurricane Bonnie	na	0	0	6.4	117.0
Eastern North Carolina	09/01/99	Tropical Storm Dennis	na	0	0	21.3	39.8
Eastern North Carolina	09/04/96	Hurricane Fran	100 mph	4	4	792.1	0.0
Eastern North Carolina	09/14/99	Hurricane Floyd	105 mph	13	0	410.6	413.6
Eastern North Carolina	09/15/99	Hurricane Floyd	na	0	0	3,000.0	500.0
Eden	07/04/97	Lightning	na	0	0	1.5	0.0
Goldsboro	07/05/97	Hail	1.75 in.	0	0	2.0	0.0
Halifax Co.	01/15/95	Flood/Flash Flood	na	5	0	2.5	0.0

Location or County	Date	Type	Mag.	Fatalities	Injuries	Property Damage ($mil.)	Crop Damage ($mil.)
NORTH CAROLINA (cont.)							
Hargetts	04/15/99	Tornado	F2	0	8	2.0	0.0
Harmony	05/07/98	Tornado	F1	0	0	1.0	0.0
Henderson	10/27/95	Tornado	F2	0	0	10.0	0.0
Hertford Co.	09/15/99	Flood	na	0	0	7.0	12.5
Holden Beach	09/09/95	Coastal Flooding	na	0	0	1.2	0.0
Jacksonville	08/01/96	Lightning	na	0	0	2.0	0.0
Johnston	01/07/95	Thunderstorm Winds	na	1	2	1.5	0.0
Kannapolis	08/27/95	Flash Flood	na	0	0	1.5	0.0
Kelly	09/15/99	Flood	na	0	0	10.0	0.0
Kenansville	04/15/99	Tornado	F2	0	11	4.0	0.0
Kinston	09/16/96	Tornado	F2	0	1	1.0	0.0
Lake Lure	09/04/96	Flash Flood	na	0	0	2.0	0.0
Lenoir Co.	09/13/96	Flood	na	0	0	9.0	24.0
Marion	06/02/97	Hail	2.00 in.	0	0	2.0	0.0
Mayodan	03/20/98	Tornado	F3	2	27	34.0	0.0
Mecklenburg Co.	07/20/98	Lightning	na	0	0	1.0	0.0
Mecklenburg Co.	07/23/97	Flash Flood	na	3	0	8.5	0.0
Mt. Sterling	07/01/97	Heavy Rain	na	0	3	4.0	0.0
N.E. Raleigh	08/27/95	Flash Flood	na	0	0	6.0	0.0
New Hanover Co.	07/12/96	Hurricane Bertha	92 mph	0	0	18.0	1.0
New Hanover Co.	08/26/98	Hurricane Bonnie	100 mph	0	0	26.2	0.0
New Hanover Co.	09/05/96	Hurricane Fran	110 mph	0	0	200.0	1.0
Newton	05/24/96	Hail	1.75 in.	0	0	10.0	0.0
Northampton Co.	09/16/99	Flood	na	0	0	1.2	20.3
Northeastern North Carolina	08/26/98	Hurricane Bonnie	93 mph	1	0	13.4	0.0
Northeastern North Carolina	09/05/96	Hurricane Fran	55 mph	0	0	1.0	0.0
Northeastern North Carolina	09/15/99	Hurricane Floyd	64 mph	0	0	12.0	63.4
Oak City	06/03/98	Hail	2.75 in.	0	0	1.0	2.0
Pender Co.	07/12/96	Hurricane Bertha	105 mph	0	0	7.0	7.5
Pender Co.	08/26/98	Hurricane Bonnie	98 mph	0	0	11.0	6.1
Pender Co.	09/05/96	Hurricane Fran	na	2	0	180.0	46.0
Pender/Brunswick/New Hanover Co.	09/15/99	Hurricane Floyd	90 mph	0	0	109.0	4.0
Penderlea	08/05/97	Thunderstorm Winds	na	0	0	1.0	2.8
Pilot	04/15/96	Tornado	F2	0	5	1.0	0.0
Plumtree	01/07/98	Flash Flood	na	0	0	5.5	0.0
Richlands	04/15/99	Tornado	F1	0	7	2.0	0.0
Robeson Co.	09/05/96	High Wind	73 mph	0	2	24.0	33.0
Rockingham Co.	06/28/95	Flash Flood	na	0	1	1.2	0.0
Rosman	01/07/98	Flash Flood	na	0	10	1.5	0.0
Sand Hill	09/16/96	Tornado	F1	0	1	1.0	0.0
Seven Springs	01/07/95	Tornado	F1	0	22	1.5	0.0
Southeastern North Carolina	03/23/95	Hail	1.75 in.	0	0	6.0	0.0
Sylva	05/24/96	Hail	1.75 in.	0	0	1.0	0.0
Vale	05/24/96	Hail	1.00 in.	0	0	1.0	0.0
Wendell	04/15/96	Tornado	F1	0	26	3.0	0.0
Western North Carolina	01/09/97	Ice Storm	na	0	0	2.0	0.0
Western North Carolina	02/02/96	Ice Storm	na	0	0	50.0	0.0
Western North Carolina	02/02/96	Ice Storm	na	0	0	10.0	0.0
Western North Carolina	10/05/95	High Wind	na	2	10	15.0	0.0
NORTH DAKOTA							
Benson/Ramsey Co.	04/21/97	Flood	na	0	1	20.0	0.0
Benson/Ramsey Co.	07/23/97	Flood	na	0	0	4.0	4.0
Benson/Ramsey Co.	09/01/99	Flood	na	0	0	100.0	0.0
Bismarck	05/16/96	Thunderstorm Winds	79 mph	0	0	3.2	0.0
Bismarck	06/25/99	Thunderstorm Winds	90 mph	0	0	2.0	0.0
Cass Co.	04/02/97	Flood	na	0	0	10.0	0.0

Location or County	Date	Type	Mag.	Fatalities	Injuries	Property Damage ($mil.)	Crop Damage ($mil.)
		NORTH DAKOTA (cont.)					
Cass Co.	04/08/97	Flood	na	0	0	100.0	0.0
Cass Co.	04/16/97	Flood	na	0	0	150.0	0.0
Cooperstown	08/02/97	Hail	2.75 in.	0	1	5.0	2.0
Crystal	06/06/99	Tornado	F4	0	0	1.0	0.0
Dickinson	08/15/99	Hail	3.00 in.	0	0	2.0	0.0
Eastern North Dakota	04/04/97	Ice Storm	na	0	0	96.0	0.0
Eastern North Dakota	04/05/97	Blizzard	na	1	0	102.0	0.0
Edmunds	06/25/99	Thunderstorm Winds	102 mph	0	0	2.0	0.0
Fargo	07/04/99	Thunderstorm Winds	91 mph	0	0	80.0	0.0
Ft. Ransom	08/15/99	Tornado	F2	0	0	1.2	0.0
Grand Forks	04/18/97	Flood	na	0	0	3,000.0	0.0
Grand Forks	07/21/96	Hail	1.75 in.	0	0	10.0	0.1
Jamestown	08/31/97	Hail	4.50 in.	0	0	10.0	0.0
Keene	08/18/95	Hail	4.50 in.	0	5	2.0	0.0
Mandan	05/16/96	Thunderstorm Winds	81 mph	0	0	1.3	0.0
Mandan	06/25/99	Thunderstorm Winds	90 mph	1	0	2.0	0.0
Marion to Prospect	08/08/95	Flash Flood	na	0	0	1.2	0.1
Melville	06/25/99	Thunderstorm Winds	100 mph	0	0	10.0	0.0
Michigan	06/27/97	Hail	2.75 in.	0	0	10.0	0.0
Minot	08/18/95	Hail	1.50 in.	0	3	40.0	10.0
Pembina Co.	04/21/97	Flood	na	0	0	20.0	0.0
Raleigh	05/16/96	Thunderstorm Winds	81 mph	0	0	1.5	0.0
Richland Co.	04/05/97	Flood	na	0	0	50.0	0.0
Richland Co.	04/13/97	Flood	na	0	0	25.0	0.0
South Central North Dakota	03/21/97	Flood	na	2	1	3.0	0.0
South/NW North Dakota	01/09/97	Blizzard	na	2	45	55.0	0.0
Southeastern North Dakota	01/15/97	Blizzard	na	2	10	6.3	0.0
Southeastern North Dakota	01/21/97	Blizzard	na	0	10	6.3	0.0
Southern North Dakota	01/04/97	Blizzard	na	0	10	6.5	0.0
Southern North Dakota	04/04/97	Blizzard	na	2	16	44.7	0.0
Traill Co.	04/17/97	Flood	na	0	0	10.0	0.0
Tuttle	06/25/99	Thunderstorm Winds	110 mph	0	0	5.0	0.0
Vermilion	08/09/95	Flash Flood	na	0	0	3.6	0.1
Walsh Co.	04/03/97	Flood	na	0	0	1.0	0.0
Walsh Co.	04/19/97	Flood	na	0	0	10.0	0.0
West Fargo	07/04/99	Thunderstorm Winds	na	0	0	5.0	0.0
Western North Dakota	10/31/99	High Wind	74 mph	0	0	2.5	4.9
		OHIO					
Adams Co.	03/01/97	Flash Flood	na	2	0	8.0	0.0
Adams Co.	03/01/97	Flood	na	0	0	1.0	0.0
Adams Co.	05/15/96	Flood	na	0	0	1.0	0.0
Bay View	04/09/98	Storm Surge	na	0	0	1.0	0.0
Belmont Co.	06/28/98	Flood	na	1	0	5.0	5.0
Blue Ash	04/09/99	Tornado	F4	4	65	82.0	0.0
Brown Co.	03/01/97	Flash Flood	na	1	0	2.0	0.0
Buckeye Lake	05/08/96	Flash Flood	na	0	0	1.0	0.0
Carey	06/27/98	Lightning	na	0	0	2.0	0.0
Chippewa On The Lake	07/09/99	Thunderstorm Winds	na	0	0	1.1	0.0
Circleville	10/13/99	Tornado	F3	0	6	4.0	0.0
Clarksville	04/09/99	Thunderstorm Winds	115 mph	0	0	1.0	0.0
Columbiana/Jefferson/Belmont/Monroe Co.	01/19/96	Flood	na	0	0	3.7	0.0
Copley Center	05/29/95	Tornado	na	0	0	1.5	0.0
Coshocton Co.	06/27/98	Flood	na	0	0	5.0	10.0
Cuyahoga Co.	04/12/96	Thunderstorm Winds	83 mph	1	1	1.0	0.0
Dublin	01/05/97	Thunderstorm Winds	98 mph	0	1	1.0	0.0
East Central Ohio	01/20/95	Heavy Snow	na	0	8	1.0	0.0

Location or County	Date	Type	Mag.	Fatalities	Injuries	Property Damage ($mil.)	Crop Damage ($mil.)
		OHIO *(cont.)*					
Franklin Co.	06/29/98	Flash Flood	na	0	0	1.0	0.0
Guernsey Co.	06/27/98	Flood	na	0	0	5.0	14.0
Hamilton Co.	04/16/98	Flood	na	0	0	4.0	0.0
Hamilton/Clermont/Brown/Adams/Scioto Co.	03/02/97	Flood	na	0	0	15.0	0.0
Hancock Co.	06/01/97	Flood	na	0	5	1.0	0.0
Hanover Twp.	01/05/97	Thunderstorm Winds	98 mph	0	0	1.0	0.0
Hocking Co.	03/02/97	Flash Flood	na	0	0	1.0	0.0
Hocking Co.	03/02/97	Flood	na	0	0	1.0	0.0
Huron Co.	08/25/98	Flood	na	0	0	1.0	0.0
Jackson Co.	03/01/97	Flash Flood	na	0	0	3.5	0.0
Jefferson Co.	06/29/98	Flash Flood	na	0	0	5.0	0.0
Knox Co.	06/27/98	Flood	na	0	0	3.0	1.0
Knox Co.	06/27/98	Flood	na	0	0	3.0	0.5
Lawrence Co.	03/01/97	Flash Flood	na	0	0	2.0	0.0
Lawrence Co.	03/02/97	Flash Flood	na	0	0	1.0	0.0
Lawrence Co.	03/02/97	Flood	na	0	0	2.0	0.0
Licking Co.	07/26/97	Flash Flood	na	0	0	2.0	0.0
Loveland Park	04/09/99	Tornado	F1	0	0	3.0	0.0
Maineville	04/09/99	Tornado	F2	0	0	2.5	0.0
Meigs Co.	03/02/97	Flood	na	0	0	1.5	0.0
Meigs Co.	05/14/95	Flash Flood	na	0	0	3.0	0.0
Meigs Co.	06/28/98	Flash Flood	na	1	0	3.0	0.0
Middlefield	05/29/95	Tornado	na	0	4	1.0	0.0
Monroe Co.	06/27/98	Flood	na	0	0	5.0	10.0
Morrow Co.	06/27/98	Flood	na	0	0	1.5	0.2
Morrow Co.	06/27/98	Flood	na	0	0	1.5	0.2
Moscow	07/02/97	Tornado	F3	0	0	2.0	0.0
Muskingum Co.	06/27/98	Flood	na	0	0	10.0	14.0
Noble Co.	06/27/98	Flash Flood	na	5	0	10.0	10.0
North Portion	06/28/98	Flash Flood	na	0	0	4.0	0.0
North/Northeast Ohio	02/02/96	Extreme Cold	na	1	0	3.4	0.0
North/Northeast Ohio	10/30/96	High Wind	79 mph	1	2	5.2	2.2
Northeastern Ohio	01/02/96	Heavy Snow	na	0	0	3.3	0.0
Northeastern Ohio	01/07/96	Heavy Snow	na	0	1	1.1	0.0
Northeastern Ohio	01/14/99	Heavy Snow	na	0	0	1.0	0.0
Northeastern Ohio	11/09/96	Heavy Snow	na	0	13	21.0	0.0
Ottawa Co.	06/24/98	Thunderstorm Winds	92 mph	0	0	3.0	1.0
Paulding Co.	05/17/96	Flood	na	0	0	1.0	0.0
Perry Co.	06/28/98	Flash Flood	na	0	0	2.0	0.0
Pike Co.	03/02/97	Flash Flood	na	1	0	1.5	0.0
Port Clinton	04/09/98	Storm Surge	na	0	0	2.0	0.0
Port Clinton	06/24/98	Tornado	F2	0	13	20.0	5.0
Richland Co.	06/27/98	Flood	na	0	0	1.0	0.5
Sandusky Co.	06/24/98	Thunderstorm Winds	na	0	0	2.0	1.0
Scioto Co.	03/01/97	Flash Flood	na	0	0	3.0	0.0
Southwestern Ohio	01/06/96	Winter Storm	na	2	0	14.2	0.0
Southwestern Ohio	01/23/96	Flood	na	0	0	5.0	0.0
Southwestern Ohio	06/01/97	Flood	na	0	0	1.0	0.0
Stark Co.	06/30/98	Thunderstorm Winds	70 mph	0	0	1.0	0.0
Tuscarawas Co.	06/28/98	Flood	na	0	0	20.0	0.0
Union Co.	06/01/97	Flash Flood	na	0	0	3.0	0.0
Warren Co.	04/16/98	Flood	na	0	0	2.0	0.0
Washington Co.	06/27/98	Flash Flood	na	1	0	10.0	0.0
Washington/Meigs/Gallia/Lawrence Co.	01/20/96	Flood	na	0	0	1.7	0.0
West Manchester	11/07/96	Thunderstorm Winds	86 mph	0	0	1.0	0.0
West/Southwest Ohio	02/01/96	Extreme Cold	na	0	0	1.2	0.0

Location or County	Date	Type	Mag.	Fatalities	Injuries	Property Damage ($mil.)	Crop Damage ($mil.)
OHIO *(cont.)*							
Westport	07/08/95	Thunderstorm Winds	100 mph	0	1	2.0	0.0
Williams Co.	05/17/96	Flash Flood	na	0	0	3.0	0.2
Woodsfield	03/01/97	Flash Flood	na	0	0	3.0	0.0
OKLAHOMA							
Addington	06/10/95	Lightning	na	0	0	5.0	0.0
Altus AFB	06/03/95	Thunderstorm Winds	82 mph	0	0	5.0	0.0
Altus Muni. Arpt.	05/31/99	Thunderstorm Winds	na	0	0	1.2	0.0
Amber	05/03/99	Tornado	F5	12	39	90.0	0.0
Beaver	09/12/99	Thunderstorm Winds	81 mph	0	0	8.0	0.0
Blanchard	05/03/99	Tornado	F4	1	17	10.0	0.0
Carrier	04/21/99	Tornado	F2	0	0	1.5	0.0
Checotah	06/01/99	Tornado	F1	0	0	1.6	0.0
Choctaw	05/03/99	Tornado	F2	0	4	3.2	0.0
Cimarron/Texas Co.	10/25/97	Blizzard	na	1	0	1.5	7.0
Crescent	05/03/99	Tornado	F4	1	13	10.0	0.0
Crescent	05/03/99	Tornado	F3	0	13	10.0	0.0
Del City	05/03/99	Tornado	F4	12	234	450.0	0.0
Dover	05/03/99	Tornado	F4	1	11	2.5	0.0
Ft. Gibson	06/01/99	Tornado	F1	0	0	2.0	0.0
Garfield Co.	07/19/97	Flash Flood	na	0	0	1.0	0.0
Gene Autry	09/10/99	Thunderstorm Winds	102 mph	0	0	2.0	0.0
Guthrie	09/21/98	Thunderstorm Winds	na	0	5	3.5	0.0
Hennessey	04/21/99	Hail	2.75 in.	0	0	1.0	0.0
Hollis and vicinity	06/03/95	Flash Flood	na	0	0	5.0	0.0
Hulbert	06/01/99	Tornado	F3	2	5	1.5	0.0
Indiahoma	05/31/99	Thunderstorm Winds	na	0	3	5.0	0.0
Jones	09/21/98	Thunderstorm Winds	na	1	10	2.0	0.0
Lamont	05/24/98	Tornado	F3	0	0	2.0	0.0
Moore	05/03/99	Tornado	F5	11	293	450.0	0.0
Moore	10/04/98	Tornado	F2	0	0	2.0	0.0
Moore/Oklahoma City	07/23/95	Thunderstorm Winds	na	0	2	50.0	0.0
Oklahoma City	06/13/98	Tornado	F2	0	17	1.0	0.0
Oklahoma City	07/02/96	Thunderstorm Winds	na	0	0	2.0	0.0
Pauls Valley	03/18/98	Thunderstorm Winds	na	0	0	2.5	0.0
Pawnee	10/04/98	Thunderstorm Winds	na	0	0	1.0	0.0
Perry	05/03/99	Tornado	F2	0	10	3.0	0.0
Poteau	01/21/99	Hail	1.75 in.	0	0	2.6	0.0
S. Seminole	06/09/95	Tornado	F2	0	0	5.0	0.0
Sapulpa	05/03/99	Tornado	F1	0	0	6.5	0.0
Shawnee	10/04/98	Thunderstorm Winds	na	0	0	1.5	0.0
Shawnee	10/04/98	Thunderstorm Winds	na	0	0	1.0	0.0
Shawnee	10/04/98	Tornado	F3	0	1	1.5	0.0
Sparks	05/03/99	Tornado	F3	0	13	60.0	0.0
Tulsa	05/03/99	Tornado	F1	0	0	2.0	0.0
Union City	06/03/95	Thunderstorm Winds	na	0	0	5.0	0.0
Vinita	05/04/99	Flash Flood	na	0	0	4.0	0.0
OREGON							
Bend	06/29/97	Lightning	na	0	0	1.5	0.0
Bend	07/09/98	Hail	1.75 in.	0	0	2.0	0.0
Gilliam Morrow Co.	07/09/95	Hail	1.00 in.	0	0	20.0	30.0
Lincoln City	01/15/96	Thunderstorm Winds	na	0	0	1.5	0.0
Medford Airport	07/29/96	Thunderstorm Winds	69 mph	0	0	3.5	0.0
North Central Oregon	09/25/99	High Wind	na	8	33	1.0	0.0
North and Central Oregon Coast	11/25/99	Flood	na	0	0	4.7	0.0
Northeast Oregon	01/01/97	Flood	na	0	0	2.7	0.0
Northeast Oregon	01/01/97	Flood	na	0	0	9.9	0.0

Location or County	Date	Type	Mag.	Fatalities	Injuries	Property Damage ($mil.)	Crop Damage ($mil.)
OREGON *(cont.)*							
Northern Oregon	02/06/96	Flood	na	7	0	400.0	0.0
Northern Oregon	12/11/95	High Wind	na	1	0	10.0	0.0
Northwestern Oregon	01/11/98	Ice Storm	na	1	0	1.0	0.0
Northwestern Oregon	11/18/96	Flood	na	0	0	3.2	0.0
Northwestern Oregon	12/27/98	Flood	na	0	0	2.0	0.0
Nyssa	06/17/97	Thunderstorm Winds	na	0	0	3.0	0.0
Oakridge	08/24/96	Wild/Forest Fire	na	0	0	1.7	0.0
Oakridge	09/01/96	Wild/Forest Fire	na	0	0	1.7	0.0
S. Coast/Rogue Basin/S. Central OR	01/01/97	Flood	na	0	0	76.6	13.4
Southern Coast/Rogue Basin	12/07/96	Flood	na	0	0	8.0	0.0
Southern Coast/Umpqua Basin	11/17/96	Flood	na	5	6	42.0	0.4
PENNSYLVANIA							
Allegheny Co.	06/30/98	Thunderstorm Winds	85 mph	0	10	41.0	0.0
Allegheny Co.	07/28/99	Flash Flood	na	0	0	1.0	0.0
Beaver/Allegheny Co.	01/19/96	Flood	na	0	0	9.6	0.0
Berks Co.	09/16/99	Flash Flood	na	0	0	1.0	0.0
Braddock	08/02/95	Lightning	na	0	0	5.0	0.0
Bradford	08/20/99	Flash Flood	na	0	1	25.0	0.0
Bradford Co.	01/19/96	Flash Flood	na	0	0	21.1	0.0
Bucks Co.	09/16/99	Flash Flood	na	0	15	22.0	0.0
Bustleton	06/01/98	Tornado	F2	0	0	1.8	0.0
Carnegie	06/02/98	Tornado	F1	0	50	13.0	0.0
Central	07/04/95	Flood/Flash Flood	na	0	1	8.0	0.0
Chester Co.	09/16/99	Flash Flood	na	1	1	3.0	0.0
Clarion/Allegheny/Armstrong Co.	01/19/96	Flood	na	0	0	4.3	0.0
Crawford Co.	07/09/99	Thunderstorm Winds	na	0	0	1.4	0.0
Crawford Co.	07/19/96	Flash Flood	na	0	0	1.5	0.0
Delaware Co.	09/16/99	Flash Flood	na	1	14	15.0	0.0
East Porrtion of Union Co.	09/07/99	Flash Flood	na	0	0	10.0	0.0
Elliottsville	06/02/98	Tornado	F2	0	0	3.0	2.0
Evansville	05/31/98	Tornado	F3	0	7	1.4	0.0
Franklin	07/19/96	Flash Flood	na	0	0	50.0	0.0
Freedom	06/19/96	Flash Flood	na	0	0	7.5	0.0
Harmony	01/19/96	Flash Flood	na	0	0	1.3	0.0
Harrisburg	07/16/95	Thunderstorm Winds	79 mph	0	0	1.0	0.0
Homer City	01/19/96	Flash Flood	na	0	0	2.0	0.0
Honey Brook	11/26/99	Tornado	F1	0	12	3.0	0.0
Lackawanna Co.	01/19/96	Flash Flood	na	0	0	19.5	0.0
Lancaster Co.	04/09/95	Thunderstorm Winds	na	0	0	1.0	0.0
Lancaster Co.	09/16/99	Flash Flood	na	0	0	1.6	0.0
Loganton	06/20/96	Thunderstorm Winds	na	0	0	15.0	0.0
Luzerne Co.	01/19/96	Flash Flood	na	0	0	21.3	0.0
McKeesport	06/19/96	Flash Flood	na	0	0	3.0	0.0
Meshoppen	06/02/98	Tornado	F3	2	15	2.2	0.0
Montgomery Co.	09/08/96	Flash Flood	na	2	0	20.0	0.0
Montgomery Co.	09/16/99	Flash Flood	na	3	8	12.0	0.0
Murrysville	06/30/98	Thunderstorm Winds	na	0	0	1.0	0.0
N. Erie/S. Erie/Crawford Co.	11/09/96	Heavy Snow	na	0	0	4.0	0.0
Northeastern Pennsylvania	11/02/99	High Wind	na	0	0	1.4	0.0
Northern Portion of Erie Co.	09/17/96	Flash Flood	na	0	0	5.0	0.0
Pecks Pond	05/31/98	Tornado	F3	0	2	1.0	0.0
Philadelphia Co.	09/16/99	Flash Flood	na	1	0	4.2	0.0
Pike Co.	01/19/96	Flash Flood	na	0	0	23.0	0.0
Pitcairn	07/01/97	Flash Flood	na	1	0	10.0	0.0
Punxsutawney	07/19/96	Flash Flood	na	0	0	100.0	0.0
Salisbury	05/31/98	Tornado	F3	1	15	4.0	0.0

Location or County	Date	Type	Mag.	Fatalities	Injuries	Property Damage ($mil.)	Crop Damage ($mil.)
PENNSYLVANIA *(cont.)*							
Shippenville	07/19/96	Flash Flood	na	1	1	75.0	0.0
Southeast	06/12/96	Flash Flood	na	2	0	14.5	0.0
Southeast Portion of Lycoming Co.	09/07/99	Flash Flood	na	0	0	1.0	0.0
Southeastern Pennsylvania	01/07/96	Blizzard	na	7	0	18.9	0.0
Southeastern Pennsylvania	01/19/96	Flood	na	3	3	42.3	0.0
Southeastern Pennsylvania	09/16/99	High Wind	58 mph	0	0	2.8	0.0
Southwestern Pennsylvania	01/19/96	Flood	na	0	0	12.7	0.0
St. Thomas	06/18/96	Flash Flood	na	0	0	1.0	0.0
Susquehanna Co.	01/19/96	Flash Flood	na	0	0	9.9	0.0
Wayne Co.	01/19/96	Flash Flood	na	0	0	17.9	0.0
Wayne/Lackawanna/Luzerne/Pike Co.	09/16/99	High Wind	na	0	0	2.5	0.0
Wellsboro	11/08/96	Flash Flood	na	0	0	2.5	0.0
Wyoming Co.	01/19/96	Flash Flood	na	0	0	20.1	0.0
SOUTH CAROLINA							
Abbeville/Calhoun	08/26/95	Flood/Flash Flood	na	0	0	1.0	0.0
Anderson Co. Arpt.	09/16/96	Tornado	F1	0	0	1.0	0.0
Conway	11/07/95	Tornado	F2	0	0	1.5	0.0
Dillon Co.	09/05/96	High Wind	71 mph	0	1	1.5	5.0
Easley	01/07/98	Tornado	F2	0	4	3.0	0.0
Edgefield	05/07/98	Tornado	F3	1	9	1.0	0.0
Greenville Co.	08/26/95	Flash Flood	na	1	5	5.0	0.0
Horry Co.	08/26/98	Hurricane Bonnie	82 mph	0	0	3.8	0.0
Horry Co.	09/05/96	Hurricane Fran	81 mph	1	0	1.0	19.8
Kershaw Co.	01/06/95	Thunderstorm Winds	na	0	0	1.5	0.0
Ladson	05/10/98	Tornado	F2	1	7	5.0	0.0
Laurens Co.	08/27/95	Flood	na	0	0	2.0	0.0
Mauldin/Simpsonville	08/26/95	Flood	na	0	0	1.5	0.0
Moncks Corner	09/03/98	Tornado	F2	0	9	2.8	0.0
Near Ballentine	01/06/95	Tornado	F1	0	0	10.0	0.0
Northwestern South Carolina	01/02/99	Ice Storm	na	0	0	20.0	0.0
Piedmont	09/16/96	Tornado	F1	0	0	1.0	0.0
Saluda	04/24/99	Hail	2.75 in.	0	2	2.0	2.0
Sandy Springs	09/16/96	Tornado	F2	0	2	3.0	0.0
Simpsonville	08/27/95	Flash Flood	na	0	0	2.0	0.0
Southern South Carolina	09/15/99	Hurricane Floyd	85 mph	0	0	17.0	0.0
Spartanburg	08/14/98	Flash Flood	na	0	0	2.5	0.0
Spartanburg	08/20/99	Hail	1.75 in.	0	0	1.0	0.0
Spartanburg	08/20/99	Hail	3.50 in.	0	0	9.0	0.0
Spartanburg Co.	08/26/95	Flash Flood	na	0	0	1.0	0.0
Spartanburg Co.	08/27/95	Flash Flood	na	1	3	1.0	0.0
Spartanburg Co.	08/27/95	Flood	na	0	0	2.0	0.0
Starr	05/25/96	Lightning	na	0	0	5.0	0.0
Statewide	08/28/95	Tropical Storm Jerry	na	0	0	10.0	0.1
Woodruff-Enoree	08/27/95	Flash Flood	na	0	0	1.0	0.0
SOUTH DAKOTA							
Alexandria	06/20/97	Thunderstorm Winds	90 mph	0	3	1.2	0.0
Armour	06/20/97	Thunderstorm Winds	81 mph	0	0	1.0	0.0
Belle Fourche	07/05/98	Hail	4.00 in.	0	3	3.0	0.0
Brookings Co.	05/15/98	High Wind	49 mph	0	0	1.0	0.0
Central South Dakota	01/11/95	Ice/High Wind	na	0	0	3.5	0.0
Central and Northeast SD	10/23/95	Heavy Snow/High Winds	na	0	0	1.7	0.0
East Central South Dakota	04/19/95	Flood	na	0	0	1.5	0.2
East Central South Dakota	05/01/95	Flood	na	0	0	2.0	2.0
Farmer	05/30/98	Tornado	F3	0	0	1.0	0.1
Hartford	07/13/97	Hail	4.50 in.	0	0	2.0	2.0
Huron	08/24/98	Thunderstorm Winds	83 mph	0	0	1.0	0.0

Location or County	Date	Type	Mag.	Fatalities	Injuries	Property Damage ($mil.)	Crop Damage ($mil.)
SOUTH DAKOTA (cont.)							
Northeastern South Dakota	05/11/98	Flood	na	0	0	3.8	0.0
Platte	07/06/98	Hail	1.75 in.	0	0	1.0	2.2
Rapid City Airport	07/06/96	Thunderstorm Winds	na	0	0	1.0	5.0
Salem	09/02/95	Hail	4.50 in.	0	0	2.0	0.3
Slim Butte	06/04/99	Tornado	F2	1	54	3.2	0.0
South Central S. Dakota	10/23/95	Heavy Snow	na	1	1	10.0	0.0
Southeastern South Dakota	11/14/96	Ice Storm	na	3	50	2.0	0.0
Spencer	05/30/98	Tornado	F4	6	150	17.0	0.4
Western South Dakota	04/05/97	Blizzard	na	0	0	50.0	0.0
Western South Dakota	10/26/96	Winter Storm	na	0	0	1.1	0.0
TENNESSEE							
Alamo	01/17/99	Tornado	F3	0	4	1.6	0.0
Alcoa	08/01/95	Thunderstorm Winds	99 mph	0	0	1.0	0.0
Atwood	03/01/97	Tornado	F2	0	0	2.0	0.0
Barnesville	04/20/96	Tornado	F2	0	12	1.2	0.0
Bemis	01/17/99	Tornado	F4	6	106	10.0	0.0
Blount Co.	07/04/97	Thunderstorm Winds	115 mph	0	0	1.0	0.0
Blue Goose	01/17/99	Thunderstorm Winds	na	1	4	2.6	0.0
Brush Creek	01/24/97	Tornado	F2	0	6	1.0	0.0
Byrdstown	04/16/98	Tornado	F3	0	4	10.0	1.0
Camden	01/22/99	Tornado	F3	1	5	1.0	0.0
Carter Co.	01/07/98	Flood	na	7	0	20.0	0.0
Central Tennessee	02/03/98	Heavy Snow	na	0	0	5.0	0.0
Central Tennessee	12/23/98	Winter Storm	na	0	11	1.5	0.0
Chattanooga	03/29/97	Tornado	F3	0	44	45.0	0.0
Cheatham Co.	03/02/97	Flash Flood	na	0	0	1.0	0.0
Chic	03/01/97	Tornado	F4	0	15	2.0	0.0
Clarksville	01/22/99	Tornado	F3	0	5	72.7	0.0
Clifton	04/16/98	Tornado	F4	3	6	4.0	0.0
Columbia	01/17/99	Thunderstorm Winds	na	0	0	4.0	0.0
Culleoka	04/16/98	Tornado	F3	0	8	4.0	0.0
Cumberland Co.	05/18/95	Tornado	F3	0	20	2.0	0.0
Deerfield	04/16/98	Tornado	F5	0	21	4.0	0.0
East Ridge	06/10/99	Lightning	na	0	0	1.0	0.0
Eastern Tennessee	01/27/98	Winter Storm	na	1	0	1.0	0.0
Eastern Tennessee	10/05/95	High Wind	na	0	0	2.0	0.0
Gallatin	05/05/99	Tornado	F2	0	17	1.0	0.0
Green Hill	04/16/98	Tornado	F2	0	0	1.0	0.0
Green Hill	04/16/98	Tornado	F2	0	0	3.0	0.0
Halls	01/17/99	Tornado	F2	0	11	2.0	0.0
Kingsport	05/25/98	Thunderstorm Winds	na	0	0	1.5	0.0
Lawrenceburg	07/13/98	Flash Flood	na	2	20	4.0	0.0
Lexington	05/05/99	Thunderstorm Winds	na	0	0	1.0	0.0
Livingston	03/16/96	Tornado	F2	0	1	5.5	0.0
Maryville	05/23/99	Lightning	na	0	0	6.0	0.0
Memphis	06/05/98	Thunderstorm Winds	na	0	1	1.0	0.0
Mercer	01/17/99	Tornado	F3	0	0	25.0	0.0
Murfreesboro	01/24/97	Tornado	F4	0	18	4.7	0.0
Nashville	04/16/98	Tornado	F3	1	60	100.0	0.0
Nashville Metro Arpt.	05/05/99	Thunderstorm Winds	99 mph	0	0	2.7	0.0
Piney To	05/18/95	Tornado	F4	3	32	4.6	0.0
Red Bank	08/11/96	Flash Flood	na	0	0	2.0	0.0
S.W. of Cleveland	03/29/97	Tornado	F3	0	50	3.2	0.0
Sevier Co.	09/01/95	Thunderstorm Winds	na	0	0	2.0	0.0
Sevierville	07/27/99	Wind/Wave	na	0	0	1.0	0.0
Smithville	05/18/95	Hail	1.75 in.	0	0	1.5	0.0

Location or County	Date	Type	Mag.	Fatalities	Injuries	Property Damage ($mil.)	Crop Damage ($mil.)
TENNESSEE (*cont.*)							
Smyrna	06/02/98	Tornado	F1	0	0	1.6	0.0
Sumner Co.	05/18/95	Tornado	F2	0	28	3.0	0.0
Vine	01/24/97	Tornado	F2	0	0	2.0	0.0
Western Tennessee	03/01/97	Flood	na	3	0	19.7	0.1
Western Tennessee	04/11/95	High Wind	na	0	4	1.0	0.0
Yokley	04/16/98	Tornado	F4	0	1	1.0	0.0
TEXAS							
Abilene	06/07/96	Hail	3.00 in.	0	0	1.0	0.0
Abilene Muni. Arpt.	06/16/97	Thunderstorm Winds	81 mph	0	0	2.0	0.1
Aledo	05/05/95	Hail	2.75 in.	0	0	4.0	0.0
Allison	06/08/95	Tornado	F4	0	0	2.0	1.0
Alpine	10/01/95	Hail	2.00 in.	0	0	3.0	0.0
Amarillo	05/15/97	Hail	1.25 in.	0	0	2.0	0.0
Amarillo	05/25/99	Hail	2.75 in.	0	0	1.0	0.0
Amarillo	05/25/99	Hail	2.75 in.	0	0	5.7	0.0
Amarillo	05/25/99	Hail	2.75 in.	0	0	2.5	0.0
Andrews	04/28/99	Hail	1.75 in.	0	0	5.0	0.0
Andrews	06/04/95	Hail	3.50 in.	0	0	6.0	0.0
Austin	09/07/95	Thunderstorm Winds	na	0	7	3.0	0.0
Bandera Co.	06/21/97	Flood	na	2	20	5.0	1.0
Bastrop Co.	10/17/98	Flood	na	0	100	3.0	0.1
Bastrop/Fayette Co.	10/17/98	Flood	na	0	15	8.2	0.1
Baytown	02/10/98	Tornado	F1	0	4	3.0	0.0
Baytown	07/28/97	Lightning	na	0	0	5.0	0.0
Bedford	03/24/96	Hail	2.50 in.	0	0	25.0	0.0
Bedford	03/24/96	Hail	1.75 in.	0	0	15.0	0.0
Bell Co.	06/27/95	Severe Thunderstorms	na	0	0	1.5	0.0
Bexar Co.	06/22/97	Flood	na	0	10	3.0	0.0
Bexar Co.	10/17/98	Flood	na	11	600	8.0	0.1
Bexar Co.	10/17/98	Flood	na	0	100	8.0	0.0
Bexar/Guadalupe/Wilson/Karnes Co.	10/17/98	Flood	na	0	550	66.0	0.2
Big Spring	04/03/95	Hail	2.75 in.	0	0	20.0	0.0
Big Spring	05/10/96	Hail	5.00 in.	0	48	30.0	0.0
Blackwell	06/12/97	Thunderstorm Winds	86 mph	0	0	1.0	0.0
Blanco Co.	06/22/97	Flood	na	0	0	1.0	0.1
Buna	02/10/98	Tornado	F1	0	0	1.0	0.0
Burnet Co.	06/22/97	Flood	na	0	0	1.0	0.0
Caldwell	10/17/98	Tornado	F2	0	0	1.5	0.0
Caldwell Co.	10/17/98	Flood	na	6	500	20.0	0.1
Caldwell Co.	10/17/98	Flood	na	0	50	30.0	0.0
Canton	04/19/95	Hail	2.75 in.	0	0	3.0	0.0
Canyon	06/10/99	Hail	2.75 in.	0	0	8.0	0.0
Cedar Park	05/27/97	Tornado	F3	0	15	70.0	0.0
Central Portion of Harris Co.	09/18/96	Flash Flood	na	0	0	1.5	0.0
Childress	05/22/96	Hail	2.50 in.	0	0	3.0	0.1
College Station	01/22/99	Hail	4.50 in.	0	0	10.0	0.0
Comal Co.	06/22/97	Flood	na	0	10	2.0	0.0
Comal Co.	10/17/98	Flood	na	2	800	50.0	0.0
Comal Co.	10/17/98	Flood	na	0	50	8.0	0.1
Comal/Guadalupe/Gonzales/De Witt Co.	10/17/98	Flood	na	0	750	268.0	1.5
Corpus Christi	03/28/99	Thunderstorm Winds	68 mph	0	0	5.5	0.2
Dalhart	06/11/99	Hail	2.00 in.	0	0	1.5	0.2
Dallas	03/25/95	Hail	2.00 in.	0	0	20.0	0.0
Dallas	04/19/95	Tornado	F1	0	8	6.0	0.0
Dallas	05/02/99	Lightning	na	0	0	1.2	0.0
Dallas	10/21/96	Tornado	F1	0	7	3.0	0.0

Location or County	Date	Type	Mag.	Fatalities	Injuries	Property Damage ($mil.)	Crop Damage ($mil.)
			TEXAS (cont.)				
De Kalb	05/04/99	Tornado	F3	0	22	125.0	0.0
De Leon	09/14/96	Tornado	F1	0	0	1.0	0.0
De Witt Co.	10/17/98	Flood	na	0	50	1.0	0.0
De Witt Co.	10/18/98	Flood	na	0	500	5.0	1.0
Decatur	05/08/98	Hail	2.00 in.	0	0	2.0	0.0
Del Rio	05/07/95	Hail	2.75 in.	0	0	6.6	0.0
Denton	04/22/97	Thunderstorm Winds	na	0	0	2.0	0.0
Denton	08/11/96	Thunderstorm Winds	70 mph	0	0	1.0	0.0
Denver City	06/02/96	Hail	4.00 in.	0	1	2.5	0.0
Devine	02/10/98	Hail	2.75 in.	0	0	10.0	0.0
Devine	02/10/98	Thunderstorm Winds	na	0	0	10.0	0.0
Duncanville	03/25/95	Hail	1.75 in.	0	0	10.0	0.0
Dyess AFB	07/12/98	Thunderstorm Winds	na	0	0	3.3	0.0
Egypt	06/20/96	Hail	4.50 in.	0	0	5.0	5.0
El Paso Co.	01/17/96	High Wind	86 mph	3	0	10.0	0.0
Eldorado	11/06/96	Hail	2.75 in.	0	0	4.5	4.0
Etoile	02/10/98	Thunderstorm Winds	100 mph	0	2	3.0	0.0
Evadale	01/02/99	Tornado	F2	1	10	1.2	0.0
Fort Stockton	06/23/95	Hail	2.75 in.	0	0	2.5	0.0
Fort Worth	04/19/95	Tornado	F2	0	0	4.0	0.0
Friona	06/01/95	Tornado	F3	0	12	24.0	0.0
Ft. Worth	10/21/96	Hail	2.00 in.	0	0	1.0	0.0
Fulshear	06/11/95	Thunderstorm Winds	na	0	0	1.0	0.0
Gaines Co.	04/30/99	Flash Flood	na	0	0	2.0	0.0
Garland	03/25/95	Hail	1.75 in.	0	0	10.0	0.0
Gilmer	01/06/98	Hail	4.50 in.	0	0	1.0	0.0
Gilmer	01/06/98	Hail	1.75 in.	0	0	1.1	0.0
Goldthwaite	02/20/97	Flash Flood	na	0	0	2.0	0.0
Granbury	05/27/99	Hail	4.50 in.	0	0	5.0	0.0
Grapevine	03/24/96	Hail	1.75 in.	0	0	15.0	0.0
Gray Co.	06/01/95	Tornado	F4	0	7	30.0	0.0
Grayson Co.	04/29/95	Hailstorm	na	0	0	20.0	0.0
Guadalupe Co.	10/17/98	Flood	na	4	500	5.0	0.1
Hamilton	02/20/97	Flash Flood	na	0	0	2.3	0.0
Hamlin	06/20/98	Hail	2.50 in.	0	0	1.0	0.0
Hamlin	06/20/98	Thunderstorm Winds	81 mph	0	0	1.0	0.0
Hardin/Jefferson/Orange Co.	01/12/97	Ice Storm	na	1	20	18.0	0.0
Harper	05/11/99	Tornado	F3	0	0	1.0	0.1
Hays Co.	06/08/97	Flood	na	2	7	2.5	0.0
Hays Co.	10/17/98	Flood	na	0	25	4.0	0.0
Hays/Caldwell/Gonzales Co.	10/17/98	Flood	na	0	125	62.0	0.6
Hemphill	02/10/98	Thunderstorm Winds	115 mph	0	0	16.0	0.0
Houston	12/18/95	Thunderstorm Winds	na	0	0	1.0	0.0
Hutto	09/07/95	Thunderstorm Winds	na	0	0	1.0	0.0
Irving	06/06/96	Thunderstorm Winds	82 mph	0	0	10.0	0.0
Jack Co.	10/05/96	Coastal Flooding	na	0	0	1.0	0.0
Jarrell	05/27/97	Tornado	F5	27	12	40.0	0.1
Jefferson/Orange Co.	09/09/98	Tropical Storm Frances	na	0	0	7.0	0.0
Jolly	08/17/97	Thunderstorm Winds	na	0	2	2.2	0.0
Kellerville	06/08/95	Tornado	F4	0	0	8.0	2.0
Kellerville	06/11/97	Tornado	F3	0	13	1.7	0.0
Kendall Co.	06/22/97	Flood	na	0	5	5.0	1.0
Kilgore	05/04/99	Tornado	F2	0	0	6.0	0.0
Kilgore	05/04/99	Tornado	F2	0	2	19.0	0.0
Kimble/Mason Co.	10/28/96	Flood	na	0	0	3.0	0.1
Lakeway	05/27/97	Tornado	F4	1	5	15.0	0.0

Location or County	Date	Type	Mag.	Fatalities	Injuries	Property Damage ($mil.)	Crop Damage ($mil.)
			TEXAS (*cont.*)				
Lavaca Co.	04/10/97	Flash Flood	na	1	0	1.0	0.0
Lavaca Co.	10/17/98	Flood	na	0	50	2.0	0.1
Lavaca Co.	10/18/98	Flood	na	0	300	3.0	0.5
Levelland	05/25/99	Hail	2.75 in.	0	0	20.0	0.5
Livingston	02/10/98	Thunderstorm Winds	135 mph	0	0	14.0	3.7
Llano Co.	02/20/97	Flood	na	2	0	2.0	0.0
Llano Co.	06/22/97	Flood	na	0	0	5.0	0.1
Longview	01/06/98	Hail	4.50 in.	0	0	1.0	0.0
Lubbock	05/25/96	Hail	1.75 in.	0	0	1.0	0.0
Lubbock	04/10/97	Hail	1.75 in.	0	0	18.0	0.0
Lubbock	04/10/97	Hail	1.75 in.	0	0	12.0	0.0
Lubbock Co.	06/22/99	Flash Flood	na	0	0	2.0	0.0
Lufkin	02/10/98	Thunderstorm Winds	86 mph	0	0	2.5	0.0
Lynn Co.	06/11/99	Thunderstorm Winds	na	0	0	1.4	2.0
Mabank	03/02/97	Thunderstorm Winds	na	0	1	1.5	0.0
Macune	02/10/98	Thunderstorm Winds	115 mph	0	0	15.0	0.0
Markham	12/17/95	Tornado	F0	0	0	1.0	0.0
Mason	06/22/97	Flood	na	0	0	2.0	1.0
Medina Co.	06/22/97	Flood	na	1	50	13.0	0.1
Mertzon	05/29/96	Thunderstorm Winds	92 mph	0	0	10.0	0.1
Mesquite	03/25/95	Hail	2.75 in.	0	0	20.0	0.0
Midland	09/24/95	Hail	1.75 in.	0	0	2.5	0.0
Midland	04/13/99	Hail	1.75 in.	0	0	8.0	0.0
Midland	04/13/99	Thunderstorm Winds	81 mph	0	0	3.0	0.0
Mt. Pleasant	06/13/97	Thunderstorm Winds	115 mph	0	1	1.5	0.0
Navarro Co.	04/29/95	Hailstorm	na	0	0	1.0	0.0
Newton Co.	02/01/99	Flood	na	0	0	1.0	0.0
North Central Texas	05/05/95	Severe Thunderstorm	na	0	0	1,200.0	0.0
North Richland Hills	05/07/95	Tornado	F1	0	4	3.3	0.0
North Richland Hills	03/24/96	Hail	1.75 in.	0	0	15.0	0.0
Northeast Dallas	03/25/95	Hail	1.75 in.	0	0	10.0	0.0
Northwestern Texas	05/01/96	Drought	na	0	0	2.4	12.0
Northwestern Texas	06/01/96	Drought	na	0	0	2.4	12.0
Northwestern Texas	08/01/96	Drought	na	0	0	12.6	189.6
Northwestern Texas	01/29/99	Winter Storm	na	0	0	8.5	0.0
Odessa	05/26/99	Hail	2.75 in.	0	0	85.0	0.0
Parmer/Castro Co.	04/24/97	Extreme Cold	na	0	0	2.0	0.4
Parmer/Castro/Swisher/Bailey/Lamb Co.	01/29/99	Winter Storm	na	0	0	1.5	0.0
Pasadena	01/27/97	Tornado	F1	0	0	12.0	0.0
Payne Springs	03/02/97	Thunderstorm Winds	na	0	0	1.7	0.0
Plainview	05/08/98	Hail	1.75 in.	0	0	5.0	0.0
Presidio	07/24/96	Thunderstorm Winds	100 mph	0	0	1.0	0.0
Real Co.	06/21/97	Flood	na	0	40	1.0	0.1
Real/Uvalde/Zavala Co.	08/23/98	Flood	na	0	50	1.4	0.0
Runnels/San Saba/Kimble/Mason Co.	06/21/97	Flood	na	0	0	2.0	1.0
San Angelo	05/28/95	Hail	1.75 in.	0	0	5.0	0.0
San Angelo	05/28/95	Hail	1.75 in.	0	0	5.0	0.1
San Angelo	05/28/95	Thunderstorm Winds	86 mph	0	50	60.0	0.0
San Angelo	05/28/95	Hail	4.00 in.	0	10	20.0	0.0
San Angelo	05/28/95	Hail	4.50 in.	0	10	25.0	0.0
Seagraves	05/08/97	Hail	3.00 in.	0	0	2.5	0.5
Segovia	06/21/97	Flood	na	0	0	5.0	2.0
Seminole	04/30/99	Hail	2.00 in.	0	0	8.0	0.0
Sheffield	06/05/99	Hail	4.00 in.	0	0	1.8	0.0
Sheppard AFB	06/09/98	Hail	2.00 in.	0	2	1.0	0.0
Snyder	06/10/99	Hail	1.75 in.	0	0	4.0	0.0

Location or County	Date	Type	Mag.	Fatalities	Injuries	Property Damage ($mil.)	Crop Damage ($mil.)
		TEXAS (*cont.*)					
Sour Lake	05/29/96	Thunderstorm Winds	na	0	1	1.1	0.0
South Central Texas	02/01/96	Winter Storm	na	0	0	1.5	0.0
South Dallas	03/25/95	Hail	1.75 in.	0	0	10.0	0.0
Southeastern Texas	08/01/98	Drought	na	0	0	23.0	167.9
Southeastern Texas	09/07/98	Tropical Storm Frances	na	3	0	287.1	0.0
Southern Half Llano Co.	05/29/95	Flash Flood	na	0	2	2.5	0.0
Southwestern Texas	05/01/96	Drought	na	0	0	20.0	40.0
Southwestern Texas	06/01/96	Drought	na	0	0	20.0	40.0
Southwestern Texas	07/01/96	Drought	na	0	0	20.0	40.0
Southwestern Texas	08/01/96	Drought	na	0	0	20.0	40.0
Southwestern Texas	09/01/96	Drought	na	0	0	12.0	20.0
Southwestern Texas	10/01/96	Drought	na	0	0	10.0	20.0
Southwestern Texas	11/01/96	Drought	na	0	0	8.0	15.0
Southwestern Texas	12/01/96	Drought	na	0	0	8.0	15.0
Southwestern Texas	01/01/97	Drought	na	0	0	8.0	15.0
Southwestern Texas	01/07/97	Winter Storm	na	0	0	5.0	0.1
Southwestern Texas	01/11/97	Winter Storm	na	0	0	1.0	0.0
Southwestern Texas	02/01/97	Drought	na	0	0	6.0	12.0
Southwestern Texas	03/01/97	Drought	na	0	0	4.0	10.0
Southwestern Texas	04/01/97	Drought	na	0	0	3.0	8.0
Southwestern Texas	05/01/97	Drought	na	0	0	2.0	6.0
Sugarland	02/16/98	Tornado	F1	0	4	3.7	0.0
Sugarland	10/23/97	Tornado	F1	0	0	1.1	0.0
Sunset	05/07/95	Tornado	F3	1	11	2.0	0.0
Sweetwater	05/31/95	Thunderstorm Winds	na	0	1	1.0	0.0
Tarrant Co.	04/29/95	Hailstorm	na	0	0	220.0	0.0
Temple	04/19/96	Hail	4.50 in.	0	0	200.0	0.0
Tenaha	02/10/98	Thunderstorm Winds	92 mph	0	0	8.0	0.0
Texarkana	05/28/98	Flash Flood	na	0	2	1.1	0.0
Texas	10/05/96	Coastal Flooding	na	0	0	20.0	0.0
Texas City	06/04/96	Lightning	na	0	0	2.0	0.0
Tool	03/02/97	Thunderstorm Winds	na	0	0	3.0	0.0
Travis Co.	06/22/97	Flood	na	0	0	1.0	0.0
Travis Co.	10/17/98	Flash Flood	na	1	50	1.5	0.1
Travis Co.	10/17/98	Flood	na	0	50	1.0	0.0
Uvalde Co.	06/22/97	Flood	na	0	50	1.0	0.1
Uvalde/Zavala/Dimmit Co.	10/28/96	Flood	na	0	0	15.0	40.0
Val Verde Co.	08/23/98	Flash Flood	na	9	150	40.0	0.1
Val Verde/Kinney/Maverick/Zavala Co.	06/01/97	Drought	na	0	0	1.0	4.0
Veribest	05/26/98	Tornado	F1	0	2	1.3	0.5
Vernon	09/15/95	Thunderstorm Winds	na	0	0	5.0	0.0
Wall	05/10/96	Tornado	F1	0	0	1.0	0.0
Wilson Co.	10/18/98	Flood	na	0	100	35.0	0.1
Windom	08/20/97	Thunderstorm Winds	100 mph	0	1	1.1	0.0
		UTAH					
All of Utah	01/11/97	Blizzard	na	3	50	40.0	0.0
Draper	05/15/97	Flash Flood	na	0	0	1.2	0.0
Northeastern Utah	10/24/96	Winter Storm	na	0	20	1.0	0.0
Northern Utah	03/31/97	Winter Storm	na	3	60	2.0	0.0
Northwestern Utah	02/24/97	High Wind	108 mph	0	3	4.2	0.0
Northwestern Utah	04/02/97	High Wind	101 mph	0	20	4.2	0.0
Northwestern Utah	04/22/99	High Wind	na	0	0	11.1	0.1
Salt Lake City	08/11/99	Tornado	F2	1	80	170.0	0.5
St. George	01/03/97	Flash Flood	na	0	11	5.0	0.0
St. George Municipal	11/21/96	Flash Flood	na	0	2	5.0	0.0
Tooele Co.	06/05/95	High Wind	na	0	10	15.0	1.0

Location or County	Date	Type	Mag.	Fatalities	Injuries	Property Damage ($mil.)	Crop Damage ($mil.)
		UTAH *(cont.)*					
West Jordan	06/09/98	Heavy Rain	na	0	0	1.5	0.0
Western Utah	12/01/96	Winter Storm	na	0	30	1.0	0.0
		VERMONT					
Addison Co.	06/27/98	Flash Flood	na	0	0	5.0	0.5
Addison Co.	07/01/98	Flash Flood	na	0	0	1.0	0.0
Addison Co.	07/01/98	Flood	na	0	0	1.0	0.0
All of Vermont	01/19/96	Flood	na	2	0	2.8	0.0
Bennington/Windham Co.	03/31/97	Winter Storm	na	0	0	1.5	0.0
Caledonia Co.	08/04/95	Flood	na	0	0	1.0	0.0
Caledonia Co.	08/11/98	Flash Flood	na	0	0	1.0	0.0
Chittenden Co.	07/01/98	Flash Flood	na	0	0	1.0	0.0
Chittenden Co.	07/01/98	Flood	na	0	0	1.0	0.0
Chittenden Co.	08/11/98	Flash Flood	na	0	0	2.0	0.0
Franklin Co.	07/15/97	Flash Flood	na	0	0	8.0	0.0
Franklin Co.	08/11/98	Flash Flood	na	0	0	1.0	0.0
Grafton	06/13/96	Flash Flood	na	0	0	1.0	0.0
Lamoille Co.	08/04/95	Flood	na	1	1	2.0	0.0
Northwestern Vermont	01/06/98	Ice Storm	na	0	1	5.7	0.0
Orange Co.	06/27/98	Flash Flood	na	0	0	2.0	0.0
Washington Co.	06/27/98	Flash Flood	na	0	0	5.0	0.2
Washington Co.	08/04/95	Flood	na	0	0	1.5	0.0
West Portion of Orleans Co.	07/15/97	Flash Flood	na	0	0	2.0	0.0
Windsor Co.	06/27/98	Flash Flood	na	0	0	1.0	0.0
		VIRGINIA					
Aldie	04/23/99	Hail	1.50 in.	0	0	2.0	0.0
Alleghany Co.	01/19/96	Flash Flood	na	0	0	3.5	0.0
Appomattox Co.	09/06/96	Flash Flood	na	0	0	1.0	0.1
Arcola	04/23/99	Hail	1.75 in.	0	0	3.0	0.0
Augusta Co.	09/06/96	Flash Flood	na	2	0	2.0	0.5
Bath Co.	01/18/96	Flash Flood	na	0	0	6.5	0.0
Berryville	04/23/99	Hail	1.75 in.	0	0	1.0	0.0
Botetourt Co.	01/19/96	Flash Flood	na	0	0	1.6	0.0
Boyce	04/23/99	Hail	1.75 in.	0	0	1.0	0.0
Burke	04/23/99	Hail	1.25 in.	0	0	3.0	0.0
Campbell Co.	06/22/95	Flash Flood	na	1	2	1.0	0.3
Campbell Co.	09/06/96	Flash Flood	na	0	0	1.3	0.5
Centreville	04/23/99	Hail	1.75 in.	0	0	3.0	0.0
Centreville	06/24/96	Tornado	F2	0	1	4.0	0.0
Chantilly	04/23/99	Hail	1.25 in.	0	0	2.0	0.0
Charlotte Co.	09/06/96	Flash Flood	na	0	0	1.2	0.3
Chesterfield Co.	09/16/99	Flood	na	0	0	3.0	0.0
Clifton	04/23/99	Hail	1.75 in.	0	0	2.0	0.0
Colonial Heights	09/16/99	Flood	na	0	0	1.2	0.0
Danville	06/08/95	Thunderstorm Winds	na	0	0	1.1	0.0
Dickenson/Buchanan Co.	01/27/98	Heavy Snow	na	0	0	1.5	0.0
E. Portion Bedford Co.	06/22/95	Flash Flood	na	1	1	2.0	0.1
East/Southeast Virginia	12/23/98	Ice Storm	na	0	0	20.0	0.0
Fairfax	04/23/99	Hail	1.00 in.	0	0	2.0	0.0
Frederick Co.	01/19/96	Flash Flood	na	0	0	2.0	0.0
Ft. Belvoir	04/23/99	Hail	1.25 in.	0	0	1.0	0.0
Greene Co.	06/27/95	Flood/Flash Flood	na	0	0	1.9	0.2
Greensville Co.	09/16/99	Flood	na	1	0	1.2	0.8
Halifax Co.	09/06/96	Flash Flood	na	0	0	7.0	1.0
Hampton	05/01/97	Hail	2.75 in.	0	0	1.0	0.0
Hampton	09/04/99	Tornado	F2	0	6	7.7	0.0
Haymarket	04/23/99	Hail	1.75 in.	0	0	1.0	0.0

Location or County	Date	Type	Mag.	Fatalities	Injuries	Property Damage ($mil.)	Crop Damage ($mil.)
VIRGINIA (*cont.*)							
Henry/Pittsylvania/Halifax/Charlotte Co.	09/05/96	High Wind	na	0	0	2.0	0.1
Highland Co.	09/06/96	Flash Flood	na	1	0	1.0	0.0
Lorton	04/23/99	Hail	2.75 in.	0	0	2.0	0.0
Loudoun Co.	01/19/96	Flash Flood	na	0	0	1.0	0.0
Madison Co.	06/27/95	Flood/Flash Flood	na	1	0	3.5	36.0
Manassas	04/23/99	Hail	1.25 in.	0	0	2.0	0.0
Middleburg	04/23/99	Hail	2.75 in.	0	0	2.0	0.0
Nelson Co.	09/06/96	Flash Flood	na	0	0	1.0	0.0
Newport News	05/01/97	Hail	1.75 in.	0	0	1.0	0.0
Norfolk	05/01/97	Hail	1.75 in.	0	2	10.0	0.0
Northern Virginia	01/19/96	Flood	na	4	0	15.0	0.0
Northern Virginia	09/06/96	River Flood	na	0	0	78.7	26.8
Orange Co.	06/27/95	Flood/Flash Flood	na	0	0	3.0	1.7
Pittsylvania Co.	09/06/96	Flash Flood	na	1	0	4.3	0.4
Pittsylvania/Halifax Co.	09/03/96	Flood	na	0	0	9.0	5.4
Prince Georges Co.	09/16/99	Flood	na	0	0	1.4	0.9
Rockbridge Co.	01/18/96	Flash Flood	na	0	0	1.6	0.0
Rockbridge Co.	09/06/96	Flash Flood	na	0	0	2.8	0.0
Rockingham Co.	01/19/96	Flash Flood	na	0	0	7.0	0.0
Rockingham Co.	09/06/96	Flash Flood	na	0	0	4.0	2.5
Shenandoah Co.	01/19/96	Flash Flood	na	0	0	27.0	0.0
Shenandoah Co.	09/06/96	Flash Flood	na	0	0	1.0	1.2
Southeastern Virginia	01/27/98	Coastal Flooding	na	0	0	1.5	0.0
Southeastern Virginia	02/04/98	Coastal Flooding	na	0	0	75.0	0.0
Southeastern Virginia	08/26/98	Hurricane Bonnie	104 mph	0	4	23.5	3.1
Southeastern Virginia	09/15/99	Hurricane Floyd	100 mph	1	0	99.3	42.3
Southwest Portion of Fairfax Co.	06/24/96	Thunderstorm Winds	na	0	0	1.0	0.0
Springfield	04/23/99	Hail	1.75 in.	0	0	1.0	0.0
Springfield	04/23/99	Hail	2.50 in.	0	0	1.0	0.0
Stafford	04/23/99	Hail	1.75 in.	0	0	1.0	0.0
Sussex Co.	09/16/99	Flood	na	0	0	4.4	1.0
Upperville	04/23/99	Hail	1.50 in.	0	0	1.0	0.0
Virginia Beach	05/01/97	Hail	1.75 in.	0	0	5.0	0.0
Warren Co.	01/19/96	Flash Flood	na	0	0	2.0	0.0
Warren Co.	09/06/96	Flash Flood	na	0	0	6.0	0.5
Waynesboro	06/10/95	Tornado	F1	0	0	2.0	0.0
Winchester	04/23/99	Hail	2.75 in.	0	0	2.5	0.0
Winchester Arpt.	04/23/99	Hail	1.75 in.	0	0	1.5	0.0
Winchester Arpt.	04/23/99	Hail	3.50 in.	0	0	3.0	0.0
Woodbridge	04/23/99	Hail	1.00 in.	0	0	1.0	0.0
WASHINGTON							
Chelan	08/02/98	Wild/Forest Fire	na	0	0	10.0	80.0
Everett/Seattle/Tacoma	01/01/97	Flood	na	1	0	20.0	0.0
Hoodsport	03/25/99	Heavy Rain	na	0	0	5.0	0.0
King Co.	03/01/99	Heavy Rain	na	0	0	5.5	0.0
Lilliwaup	03/01/99	Heavy Rain	na	0	0	10.2	0.0
Montesano	03/15/97	Heavy Rain	na	0	0	1.2	0.0
North Central Washington	02/02/99	High Wind	na	0	0	4.0	0.0
North Central Washington	12/28/96	Heavy Snow	na	0	0	30.0	0.0
Ocean Shrs	03/03/99	Storm Surge	na	0	0	1.0	0.0
Okanogan Co.	07/09/95	Hail	1.50 in.	0	0	10.0	15.0
Republic	05/26/98	Flood	na	0	0	3.5	0.0
Seattle-Tacoma Intl.	12/29/96	Heavy Rain	na	0	0	31.5	0.0
Spokane Co.	11/19/96	Ice Storm	na	1	0	1.3	5.7
Thurston Co.	03/30/99	Heavy Rain	na	0	0	7.0	0.0
W. Central/NW Washington	03/02/99	High Wind	70 mph	1	0	3.0	0.0

Location or County	Date	Type	Mag.	Fatalities	Injuries	Property Damage ($mil.)	Crop Damage ($mil.)
WASHINGTON (cont.)							
W. Central/NW Washington	11/23/98	High Wind	76 mph	0	0	6.5	0.0
West Central Washington	03/20/97	Flood	na	0	0	1.2	0.0
Western Washington	11/28/95	Flood/Heavy Rain	na	0	0	10.0	0.0
WEST VIRGINIA							
Barbour Co.	05/16/96	Flash Flood	na	0	0	1.0	0.0
Braxton Co.	07/31/96	Flash Flood	na	0	0	1.5	0.0
Cabell Co.	03/02/97	Flash Flood	na	0	0	1.0	0.0
Charleston	06/02/98	Thunderstorm Winds	na	0	0	3.0	0.0
Charleston	06/02/98	Hail	1.50 in.	0	0	2.0	0.0
Charleston	06/02/98	Hail	2.00 in.	0	0	6.0	0.0
Cross Lanes	06/02/98	Hail	1.75 in.	0	0	1.0	0.0
Glade Farms	06/02/98	Tornado	F2	0	0	5.0	2.0
Hancock/Brooke/Ohio/Marshall/Wetzel Co.	01/19/96	Flood	na	0	0	7.5	0.0
Hardy Co.	01/19/96	Flash Flood	na	0	0	9.5	0.0
Jackson Co.	06/28/98	Flash Flood	na	0	0	4.0	0.0
Kanawha Co.	03/01/97	Flash Flood	na	0	0	3.5	0.0
Kanawha Co.	03/02/97	Flash Flood	na	0	0	1.0	0.0
Logan Co.	05/15/96	Flash Flood	na	1	0	3.5	0.0
Marion Co.	06/28/98	Flash Flood	na	0	0	5.0	0.0
Mercer/Summers/Monroe/Greenbrier Co.	02/06/98	Heavy Snow	na	0	0	1.7	0.0
Northeastern West Virginia	01/19/96	Flood	na	0	0	4.5	0.0
Northeastern West Virginia	01/19/96	Flood	na	0	0	20.0	0.1
Northeastern West Virginia	09/06/96	River Flood	na	0	0	16.5	0.9
Northwestern West Virginia	01/20/96	Flood	na	0	0	1.0	0.0
Pendleton Co.	01/19/96	Flash Flood	na	0	0	10.0	0.0
Pendleton Co.	09/06/96	Flash Flood	na	1	0	1.0	0.0
Philippi	04/23/99	Hail	1.50 in.	0	0	2.0	0.0
Piedmont-Keyser	06/27/95	Flood/Flash Flood	na	0	0	1.1	0.0
Preston/Tucker Co.	01/19/96	Flood	na	0	0	2.4	0.0
Randolph Co.	05/16/96	Flash Flood	na	2	0	1.5	0.0
Roane Co.	03/01/97	Flash Flood	na	0	0	1.5	0.0
S. Portion Mercer Co.	06/28/95	Flash Flood	na	0	0	6.2	0.6
Sissonville	06/28/98	Flash Flood	na	2	0	5.0	0.0
Southeastern West Virginia	01/27/98	Heavy Snow	na	2	1	12.5	0.0
Southwestern West Virginia	02/03/98	Winter Storm	na	0	4	5.5	0.0
Summers/Monroe/Greenbrier Co.	01/19/96	Flood	na	0	0	4.1	0.0
Wayne Co.	03/01/97	Flash Flood	na	0	0	2.0	0.0
Wetzel Co.	06/30/98	Flash Flood	na	0	0	10.0	0.0
Wood Co.	06/28/98	Flash Flood	na	0	0	4.0	0.0
WISCONSIN							
Belgium	06/18/96	Flash Flood	na	0	0	1.0	0.0
Beloit	08/24/98	Lightning	na	0	0	3.5	0.0
Benton	05/15/98	Tornado	F2	0	11	1.7	0.1
Berlin	08/03/97	Thunderstorm Winds	na	0	0	1.0	5.0
Brookfield	08/06/98	Flash Flood	na	2	1	17.3	0.0
Browntown	07/18/96	Flash Flood	na	0	1	6.0	6.0
Cashton	06/18/98	Thunderstorm Winds	69 mph	0	0	1.0	0.0
Columbia Co.	05/31/98	Thunderstorm Winds	na	0	1	3.6	0.2
Connorsville	05/19/96	Thunderstorm Winds	81 mph	0	0	2.2	0.0
Dane Co.	05/31/98	Thunderstorm Winds	100 mph	0	2	3.1	0.1
Dane Co.	06/17/96	Flood	na	0	0	3.0	10.0
Dodge Co.	05/31/98	Thunderstorm Winds	128 mph	0	8	3.7	0.0
Douglas Co.	07/25/99	Flash Flood	na	0	0	2.0	0.0
Egg Harbor	08/23/98	Tornado	F3	0	2	4.7	1.7
Elkhorn	07/21/98	Thunderstorm Winds	100 mph	0	12	1.9	0.1
Florence	07/15/99	Flash Flood	na	0	0	1.5	0.0

Location or County	Date	Type	Mag.	Fatalities	Injuries	Property Damage ($mil.)	Crop Damage ($mil.)
			WISCONSIN *(cont.)*				
Fond Du Lac Co.	05/31/98	Thunderstorm Winds	83 mph	0	1	2.0	0.0
Fox Point	06/21/97	Flash Flood	na	0	0	78.7	0.0
Germantown	06/21/97	Flash Flood	na	0	0	2.7	0.0
Hager City	06/29/96	Thunderstorm Winds	81 mph	0	0	3.5	0.0
Hudson	05/19/96	Thunderstorm Winds	98 mph	0	0	2.5	0.0
Janesville	08/05/98	Flash Flood	na	0	1	1.5	0.1
Jefferson Co.	05/31/98	Thunderstorm Winds	na	0	8	2.7	0.2
Lake Geneva	07/20/98	Thunderstorm Winds	100 mph	0	2	1.5	0.0
Madison	06/17/96	Flash Flood	na	0	0	4.0	0.0
Menomonee Falls	06/21/97	Flash Flood	na	0	0	5.3	1.2
Mequon	06/21/97	Flash Flood	na	0	0	3.6	0.0
Meridean	05/15/98	Tornado	F1	0	1	1.9	0.0
Milwaukee	07/21/97	Lightning	na	0	0	1.0	0.0
Milwaukee Co.	05/31/98	Thunderstorm Winds	100 mph	0	0	19.2	0.0
Mondovi	07/08/99	Tornado	F1	0	3	1.0	0.0
Monona	06/17/96	Flash Flood	na	0	0	1.6	0.0
Mukwonago	10/29/96	Hail	2.00 in.	0	0	1.2	0.0
Northeastern Wisconsin	11/10/98	High Wind	73 mph	1	1	1.0	0.0
Nutterville	07/16/97	Tornado	F2	0	0	1.0	3.0
Oakfield	07/18/96	Tornado	F5	0	12	39.5	0.9
Ozaukee Co.	05/31/98	Thunderstorm Winds	na	0	4	3.4	0.3
Ozaukee Co.	06/18/96	Flood	na	0	0	3.9	3.0
Pleasant Prairie	04/19/96	Thunderstorm Winds	na	0	0	1.1	0.0
Porcupine	05/19/96	Thunderstorm Winds	86 mph	0	0	4.5	0.0
Port Washington	06/18/96	Flash Flood	na	0	0	5.3	0.0
River Falls	05/19/96	Thunderstorm Winds	86 mph	0	0	1.0	0.0
Roberts	05/19/96	Thunderstorm Winds	81 mph	0	0	2.7	0.3
Rock Co.	06/18/96	Flood	na	0	0	1.0	17.5
S. Central/SW Wisconsin	11/10/98	High Wind	93 mph	1	2	1.7	0.0
Sheboygan	08/06/98	Flash Flood	na	0	0	40.0	0.0
Southeastern Wisconsin	11/10/98	High Wind	na	4	14	10.3	1.5
Southwestern Wisconsin	04/03/97	Flood	na	0	0	1.0	0.0
Twin Lakes	07/18/97	Thunderstorm Winds	na	0	9	1.0	0.0
Vilas Co.	07/30/99	Thunderstorm Winds	67 mph	2	0	1.0	0.0
Washington Co.	05/31/98	Thunderstorm Winds	105 mph	1	2	8.5	0.1
Waukesha Co.	05/31/98	Thunderstorm Winds	81 mph	0	0	6.7	0.0
Wauwatosa	08/06/98	Flash Flood	na	0	1	22.1	0.0
			WYOMING				
Albin	07/13/96	Hail	1.25 in.	0	0	1.0	0.0
Central Wyoming	10/15/98	Winter Storm	na	0	0	1.0	0.0
Cheyenne	07/13/96	Hail	1.50 in.	0	0	4.0	0.0
Cheyenne	07/31/96	Hail	2.50 in.	0	0	3.4	0.0
Cheyenne	08/29/96	Hail	1.75 in.	0	0	2.4	0.0
Southeastern Wyoming	04/04/97	Blizzard	na	0	0	5.0	0.0
Yoder	06/26/99	Hail	2.75 in.	0	0	1.2	0.5

Note: Storms with less than one million dollars of property damage are excluded.

ALABAMA

PHYSICAL FEATURES. The surface of Alabama rises as a rolling plain from the Gulf of Mexico in the southwest to foothills in the central part of the State. Thence there is a rise to the Appalachian Mountains which extend into the northeastern counties. Ridges from the Appalachians extend southward through the eastern counties, with elevations along these ridges as much as 600 to 800 feet above sea level in the southeast. The general elevation of the high northeastern area is about 800 feet above sea level, but some mountain summits rise to over 2,000 feet, the highest (Mount Cheaha in southwestern Cleburne County) being 2,407 feet.

GENERAL CLIMATE. The climate is temperate, becoming largely subtropical near the coast. The summers are long, hot, and humid, with little day-to-day temperature change. In the northeastern counties, higher altitudes help make the summer nights more comfortable. From late June through middle August, approximately a third of the evenings are made comfortable by local afternoon thundershowers which bring cool breezes over the areas where they occur.

In the coldest months of December, January, and February, there are frequent shifts between mild air, which has been moistened and warmed by the Gulf, and dry, cool continental air. Severely cold weather seldom occurs. Even in the northern third of the State, temperatures of zero or lower are rare and occur only when there is snow on the ground. Since cold air on clear nights collects in low places, there is considerable irregularity in the distribution of the last spring or first fall freezes in all sections.

PRECIPITATION. Precipitation is nearly all in the form of rain. Snow falls in the northern counties on an average of about twice each winter. The average fall in that area is only about three inches per year, and since this includes unusually heavy snows in a few individual winters, some winters have little or none. From late June through the first half of August, nearly all precipitation is from local thundershowers which occur mostly in the afternoons. During late August and in September, summer conditions of atmospheric temperature and moisture persist, but thundershowers become less frequent. However, late night and early morning thundershowers, characteristic of late summer on the coast, continue in the coastal counties until mid-September. Rains during October are nearly always from showers or thundershowers occurring ahead of temperature drops. Such changes become more frequent and more pronounced as winter approaches. Dry, sunny weather prevails most of the time in September and October, but from August through early October, heavy general rain may occur with a tropical disturbance or hurricane moving inland from the Gulf of Mexico. Since summer rain is heavier near the coast than elsewhere and winter rain is heavier in the north, the middle areas of the State get somewhat less precipitation for the year as a whole than the other areas.

Droughts may occur any time during the growing season from late April through October. Relatively long periods with little or no rain are more likely to occur in late summer and autumn than at any other time, while a secondary maximum of such periods occurs in May and June. Severe local droughts occur nearly every year, but severe statewide droughts are practically unknown.

Rivers in Alabama overflow about once a year on an average. Most floods occur from rains in late winter and early spring, with March the month of greatest flood frequency. The lower Tombigbee overflows most often, and in some stretches may stay over the banks most of the time in wet winter and spring seasons.

STORMS. Nearly all tornadoes occur during the season from November through early May. The greatest frequency is in March and April. The area covered by the average tornado is small. Destructive tropical hurricanes visit the coastal area on an average of about once in seven years between July and November. Windstorm damage may occur in local thundersqualls any time of the year.

Thunderstorms in the north and central sections occur on an average of one day each month in winter, on about 13 days in July, and on about 60 days during the year. Almost all the hail that falls in Alabama occurs in the period from February through May, although in the northern counties there are rare occurrences of damaging hail in June.

Heavy fog occurs mostly in winter. It occurs on an average of five days per year in Birmingham, eight days per year in Montgomery, and 31 days per year in Mobile, near the coast.

WINDS. In winter, winds from a northerly direction are most frequent. In summer, the wind is quite variable, but most often comes from southerly directions.

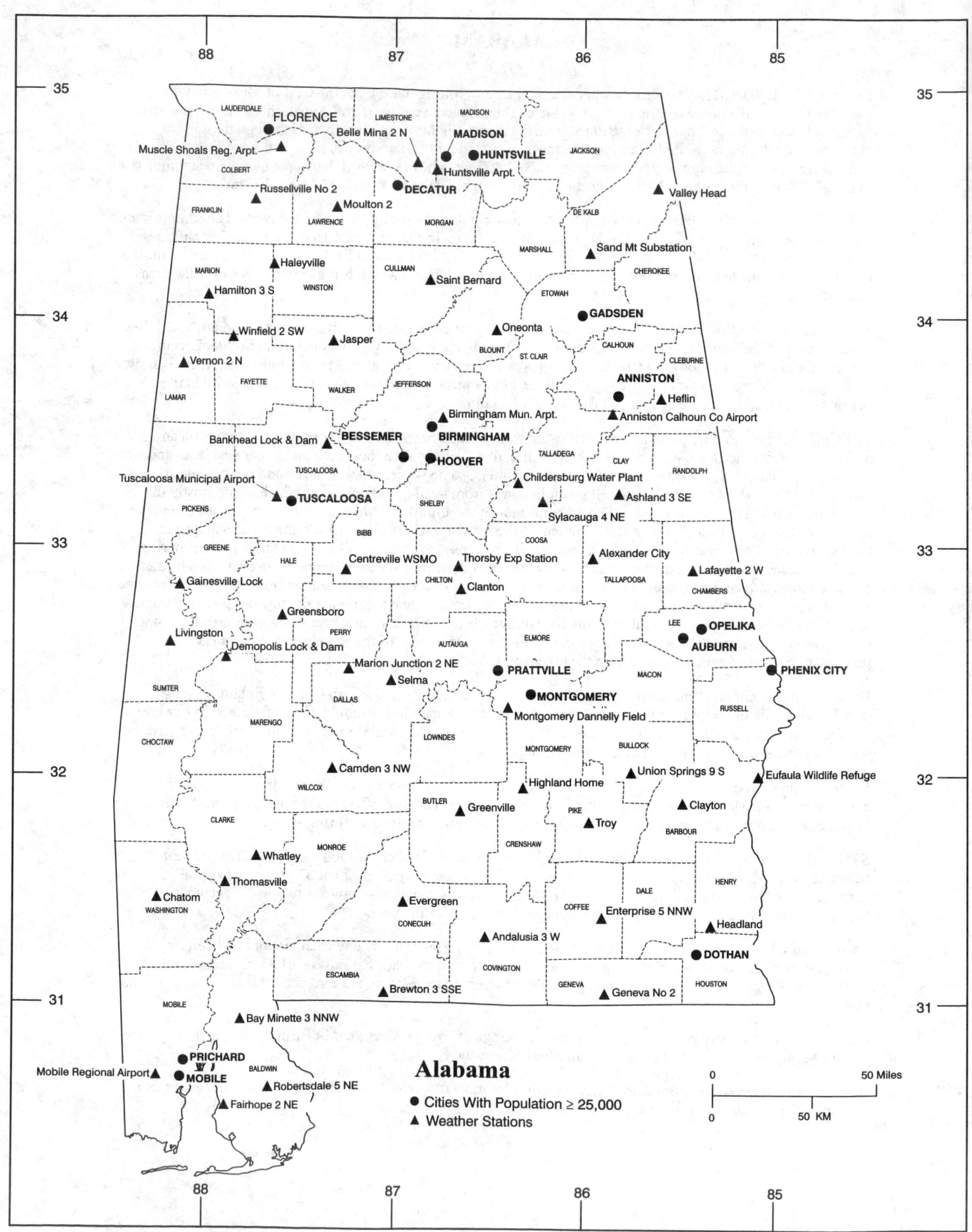

LAUDERDALE
FLORENCE
Belle Mina 2 N
LIMESTONE
MADISON
MADISON
HUNTSVILLE
JACKSON
Muscle Shoals Reg. Arpt.
Huntsville Arpt.
COLBERT
Russellville No 2
DECATUR
FRANKLIN
MORGAN
Moulton 2
LAWRENCE
Valley Head
DE KALB
MARSHALL
Sand Mt Substation
Haleyville
MARION
CULLMAN
Saint Bernard
CHEROKEE
Hamilton 3 S
WINSTON
ETOWAH
Winfield 2 SW
Jasper
Oneonta
GADSDEN
CALHOUN
Vernon 2 N
BLOUNT
ST. CLAIR
CLEBURNE
FAYETTE
ANNISTON
JEFFERSON
Heflin
LAMAR
WALKER
Birmingham Mun. Arpt.
Anniston Calhoun Co Airport
Bankhead Lock & Dam
BESSEMER
BIRMINGHAM
TALLADEGA
CLAY
TUSCALOOSA
HOOVER
RANDOLPH
Tuscaloosa Municipal Airport
Childersburg Water Plant
TUSCALOOSA
SHELBY
Ashland 3 SE
PICKENS
Sylacauga 4 NE
BIBB
Centreville WSMO
Thorsby Exp Station
COOSA
GREENE
Alexander City
HALE
CHILTON
Clanton
TALLAPOOSA
Lafayette 2 W
Gainesville Lock
CHAMBERS
Greensboro
LEE
OPELIKA
Livingston
PERRY
AUTAUGA
ELMORE
AUBURN
Demopolis Lock & Dam
Marion Junction 2 NE
PRATTVILLE
PHENIX CITY
SUMTER
Selma
MACON
DALLAS
MONTGOMERY
RUSSELL
CHOCTAW
MARENGO
LOWNDES
Montgomery Dannelly Field
MONTGOMERY
BULLOCK
Camden 3 NW
Union Springs 9 S
Eufaula Wildlife Refuge
WILCOX
Highland Home
PIKE
Clayton
CLARKE
BUTLER
Greenville
Troy
BARBOUR
Whatley
MONROE
CRENSHAW
HENRY
Thomasville
DALE
Chatom
Evergreen
COFFEE
Enterprise 5 NNW
WASHINGTON
CONECUH
Headland
Andalusia 3 W
COVINGTON
DOTHAN
Brewton 3 SSE
GENEVA
HOUSTON
MOBILE
ESCAMBIA
Geneva No 2
Bay Minette 3 NNW
PRICHARD
BALDWIN
Mobile Regional Airport
MOBILE
Robertsdale 5 NE
Fairhope 2 NE

Alabama

● Cities With Population ≥ 25,000
▲ Weather Stations

0   50 Miles

0   50 KM

Alabama Weather Stations by County

County	Station Name
Baldwin	Bay Minette 3 NNW
	Fairhope 2 NE
	Robertsdale 5 NE
Barbour	Clayton
	Eufaula Wildlife Refuge
Bibb	Centreville WSMO
Blount	Oneonta
Bullock	Union Springs 9 S
Butler	Greenville
Calhoun	Anniston Calhoun Co. Airport
Chambers	Lafayette 2 W
Chilton	Clanton
	Thorsby Exp. Station
Clarke	Thomasville
	Whatley
Clay	Ashland 3 SE
Cleburne	Heflin
Coffee	Enterprise 5 NNW
Colbert	Muscle Shoals Regional Airport
Conecuh	Evergreen
Covington	Andalusia 3 W
Crenshaw	Highland Home
Cullman	Saint Bernard
Dallas	Marion Junction 2 NE
	Selma
Dekalb	Sand Mountain Substation
	Valley Head
Escambia	Brewton 3 SSE
Fayette	Winfield 2 SW
Franklin	Russellville 2
Geneva	Geneva 2
Greene	Gainesville Lock
Hale	Greensboro
Henry	Headland
Jefferson	Birmingham Municipal Airport
Lamar	Vernon 2 N

County	Station Name
Lawrence	Moulton 2
Limestone	Belle Mina 2 N
Madison	Huntsville Airport
Marengo	Demopolis Lock & Dam
Marion	Haleyville
	Hamilton 3 S
Mobile	Mobile Regional Airport
Montgomery	Montgomery Dannelly Field
Pike	Troy
Sumter	Livingston
Talladega	Childersburg Water Plant
	Sylacauga 4 NE
Tallapoosa	Alexander City
Tuscaloosa	Bankhead Lock & Dam
	Tuscaloosa Municipal Airport
Walker	Jasper
Washington	Chatom
Wilcox	Camden 3 NW

Alabama Weather Stations by City

City	Station Name	Miles
Anniston	Anniston Calhoun Co. Airport	6
	Heflin	13
Bessemer	Birmingham Municipal Airport	17
Birmingham	Birmingham Municipal Airport	4
Decatur	Belle Mina 2 N	9
	Huntsville Airport	13
	Moulton 2	19
Dothan	Headland	10
Florence	Muscle Shoals Regional Airport	6
Gadsden	Sand Mountain Substation	19
Hoover	Birmingham Municipal Airport	13
Huntsville	Belle Mina 2 N	17
	Huntsville Airport	12
Madison	Belle Mina 2 N	8
	Huntsville Airport	5
Mobile	Fairhope 2 NE	17
	Mobile Regional Airport	8
Montgomery	Montgomery Dannelly Field	8
Opelika	Lafayette 2 W	18
	West Point, GA	19
Phenix City	Columbus Metropolitan Airport, GA	5
Prattville	Montgomery Dannelly Field	12
Prichard	Fairhope 2 NE	19
	Mobile Regional Airport	10
Tuscaloosa	Tuscaloosa Municipal Airport	5

Note: Miles is the distance between the geographic center of the city and the weather station.

Alabama Weather Stations by Elevation

Feet	Station Name
1,194	Sand Mountain Substation
1,059	Valley Head
1,007	Ashland 3 SE
918	Haleyville
869	Oneonta
849	Heflin
830	Russellville 2
797	Saint Bernard
738	Lafayette 2 W
679	Thorsby Exp. Station
643	Moulton 2
639	Alexander City
623	Huntsville Airport
620	Birmingham Municipal Airport
610	Anniston Calhoun Co. Airport
606	Clanton
597	Belle Mina 2 N
593	Highland Home
541	Troy
538	Muscle Shoals Regional Airport
498	Clayton
488	Sylacauga 4 NE
485	Jasper
469	Enterprise 5 NNW
469	Greenville
465	Winfield 2 SW
456	Centreville WSMO
439	Union Springs 9 S
433	Hamilton 3 S
416	Childersburg Water Plant
403	Thomasville
367	Headland
288	Evergreen
282	Chatom
278	Bankhead Lock & Dam
275	Bay Minette 3 NNW
262	Vernon 2 N
249	Andalusia 3 W
232	Camden 3 NW
219	Greensboro
213	Eufaula Wildlife Refuge
213	Mobile Regional Airport
200	Marion Junction 2 NE
200	Montgomery Dannelly Field
173	Robertsdale 5 NE
167	Tuscaloosa Municipal Airport
167	Whatley
144	Geneva 2
144	Selma
127	Livingston
124	Gainesville Lock
98	Demopolis Lock & Dam
82	Brewton 3 SSE
22	Fairhope 2 NE

Birmingham Municipal Airport

Birmingham is located in a hilly area of north-central Alabama in the foothills of the Appalachians about 300 miles inland from the Gulf of Mexico. There is a series of southwest to northeast valleys and ridges in the area.

The city is far enough inland to be protected from destructive tropical hurricanes, yet close enough that the Gulf has a pronounced modifying effect on the climate.

Although summers are long and hot, they are not generally excessively hot. On a typical mid-summer day, the temperature will be nearly 70 degrees at daybreak, approach 90 degrees at mid-day, and level off in the low 90s during the afternoon. It is not unusual for the temperature to remain below 100 degrees for several years in a row. However, every few years an extended heat wave will bring temperatures over 100 degrees. July is normally the hottest month but there is little difference from mid-June to mid-August. Rather persistent high humidity adds to the summer discomfort.

January is normally the coldest month but there is not much difference from mid-December to mid-February. Overall, winters are relatively mild. Even in cold spells, it is unusual for the temperature to remain below freezing all day. Sub-zero cold is extremely rare. Extremely low temperatures almost always occur under clear skies after a snowfall.

Snowfall is erratic. Sometimes there is a two- or three-year span with no measurable snow. On rare occasions, there may be a two to four inch snowstorm. The snow usually melts quickly. Even one or two inches of snow can effectively shut down this sunbelt city because of the hilly terrain, the wetness of the snow, and the unfamiliarity of motorists driving on snow and ice.

Birmingham is blessed with abundant rainfall. It is fairly well distributed throughout the year. However, some of the wetter winter months, plus March and July, have twice the rainfall of October, the driest month. Summer rainfall is almost entirely from scattered afternoon and early evening thunderstorms. Serious droughts are rare and most dry spells are not severe.

The stormiest time of the year with the greatest risk of severe thunderstorms and tornadoes is in spring, especially in March and April.

In a normal year, the last 32 degree minimum temperature in the spring is in mid to late March and the first in autumn is in early November.

Birmingham Municipal Airport *Jefferson County*   Elevation: 620 ft.   Latitude: 33° 34' N   Longitude: 86° 45' W

	JAN	FEB	MAR	APR	MAY	JUN	JUL	AUG	SEP	OCT	NOV	DEC	YEAR
Mean Maximum Temp. (°F)	52.6	58.0	66.4	74.3	81.0	87.4	90.5	90.0	84.8	74.8	64.5	56.4	73.4
Mean Temp. (°F)	42.6	46.8	54.5	61.7	69.5	76.7	80.4	79.7	74.1	63.0	53.2	46.2	62.4
Mean Minimum Temp. (°F)	32.6	35.6	42.7	49.1	57.9	65.9	70.2	69.3	63.4	51.1	41.9	35.9	51.3
Extreme Maximum Temp. (°F)	77	83	89	92	96	100	106	103	100	91	85	79	106
Extreme Minimum Temp. (°F)	-6	4	2	26	36	44	54	52	39	28	13	1	-6
Days Maximum Temp. ≥ 90°F	0	0	0	0	2	11	19	17	8	0	0	0	57
Days Maximum Temp. ≤ 32°F	2	0	0	0	0	0	0	0	0	0	0	1	3
Days Minimum Temp. ≤ 32°F	17	12	5	1	0	0	0	0	0	0	6	14	55
Days Minimum Temp. ≤ 0°F	0	0	0	0	0	0	0	0	0	0	0	0	0
Heating Degree Days (base 65°F)	688	508	334	148	29	1	0	0	10	128	357	581	2,784
Cooling Degree Days (base 65°F)	1	3	17	54	181	368	498	477	290	78	9	4	1,980
Mean Precipitation (in.)	5.34	4.22	6.13	4.58	4.88	3.80	5.04	3.64	4.03	3.42	4.43	4.52	54.03
Maximum Precipitation (in.)	11.0	17.7	15.8	13.8	11.1	8.4	13.7	10.8	10.4	11.9	15.3	14.0	76.5
Minimum Precipitation (in.)	1.1	1.1	1.7	0.4	1.1	0.7	0.3	0.4	trace	0.1	0.4	0.8	39.2
Maximum 24-hr. Precipitation (in.)	4.1	5.3	6.9	4.6	3.8	3.8	5.5	3.3	3.7	6.9	4.4	4.5	6.9
Days With ≥ 0.1" Precipitation	8	7	8	6	7	7	8	6	5	5	7	7	81
Days With ≥ 1.0" Precipitation	2	1	2	2	2	1	1	1	1	1	2	1	17
Mean Snowfall (in.)	0.7	0.1	0.6	0.2	trace	trace	trace	0.0	trace	trace	trace	trace	1.6
Maximum Snowfall (in.)	7	2	13	5	0	0	0	0	0	trace	1	8	13
Maximum 24-hr. Snowfall (in.)	5	2	10	5	0	0	0	0	0	trace	1	8	10
Days With ≥ 1.0" Snow Depth	0	0	0	0	0	0	0	0	0	0	0	0	0
Thunderstorm Days	2	2	4	5	7	8	12	9	4	1	2	1	57
Foggy Days	15	13	13	11	14	13	15	15	14	14	13	14	164
Predominant Sky Cover	OVR	OVR	OVR	OVR	SCT	SCT	SCT	SCT	CLR	CLR	OVR	OVR	OVR
Mean Relative Humidity 7am (%)	82	81	78	76	76	78	81	82	81	82	82	82	80
Mean Relative Humidity 4pm (%)	57	53	48	46	51	54	58	55	54	50	52	58	53
Mean Dewpoint (°F)	33	36	41	49	58	66	69	68	62	51	42	36	51
Prevailing Wind Direction	N	N	S	S	S	NE	S	NE	NE	NE	N	N	NE
Prevailing Wind Speed (mph)	9	9	10	10	9	6	7	6	6	6	9	9	8
Maximum Wind Gust (mph)	66	61	69	71	89	59	61	66	52	43	66	53	89

Huntsville Airport

Huntsville has a temperate climate. Summers are characterized by warm and humid weather, with rather frequent thunderstorms. Winters are usually rather cool, but vary considerably from one year to the next.

The city of Huntsville is almost surrounded by the foothills of the Appalachian Mountains. The Tennessee River winds its way westward about seven miles to the south of the city, and the broad, fertile Tennessee River Valley, with flat to gently rolling terrain, extends to the west. The weather station is located at the Huntsville-Madison County Airport, which is 11 miles southwest of the center of Huntsville. Mountain ridges, with elevations from 1,200 to 1,600 feet above sea level, are located some 14 miles to the northeast, east, and southeast of the airport.

Cold air masses from the continent are predominant over the area during the winter season, but, at times, mild air from the Gulf of Mexico spreads northward to Huntsville or beyond, and may persist for several days. December through March account for about 43 percent of the normal annual precipitation. Severely cold weather seldom occurs.

In the transition from winter to spring, appearances of warm, moist air in place of the cold air become more frequent, and the greatest variety of weather usually occurs during this season. Spring season thunderstorms in the vicinity of the boundary between warm and cold air masses are likely to be accompanied by locally severe weather conditions.

Day to day weather changes in the summer season are rather small, other than the occurrence of thunderstorms that provide relief from the heat on about one-third of the days. Temperatures frequently rise to 90 degrees or higher, but reach 100 degrees only on rare occasions.

During the fall the weather is usually dry and pleasant. The air masses are cooler in the lower levels and the thunderstorm activity of summer decreases sharply. A major departure from the relatively dry weather of fall is an occasional rainy spell of one or more days.

Precipitation amounts for the drier months of the fall are appreciably less than for the relatively wet season in winter. However, with the exception of an infrequent long dry spell, precipitation provides adequate moisture for plant growth throughout the year. Precipitation is mostly in the form of rain, but snow can be expected each winter. The growing season is 214 days. The average date for the last occurrence of freezing temperatures in the spring is late March and the average date of the first freeze is late October.

Huntsville Airport *Madison County*   Elevation: 623 ft.   Latitude: 34° 39' N   Longitude: 86° 47' W

	JAN	FEB	MAR	APR	MAY	JUN	JUL	AUG	SEP	OCT	NOV	DEC	YEAR
Mean Maximum Temp. (°F)	49.0	54.4	63.1	72.2	79.3	86.3	89.4	89.0	83.3	72.9	61.9	53.2	71.2
Mean Temp. (°F)	39.7	44.2	52.2	60.5	68.4	75.8	79.4	78.5	72.5	61.3	51.2	43.6	60.6
Mean Minimum Temp. (°F)	30.4	33.9	41.2	48.7	57.4	65.3	69.3	68.0	61.7	49.6	40.5	34.0	50.0
Extreme Maximum Temp. (°F)	76	83	85	90	96	101	104	103	101	90	83	79	104
Extreme Minimum Temp. (°F)	-11	1	6	26	36	45	54	52	40	29	15	-3	-11
Days Maximum Temp. ≥ 90°F	0	0	0	0	1	9	16	15	6	0	0	0	47
Days Maximum Temp. ≤ 32°F	3	1	0	0	0	0	0	0	0	0	0	1	5
Days Minimum Temp. ≤ 32°F	18	13	6	1	0	0	0	0	0	0	8	15	61
Days Minimum Temp. ≤ 0°F	0	0	0	0	0	0	0	0	0	0	0	0	0
Heating Degree Days (base 65°F)	777	583	398	173	38	1	0	0	17	159	412	657	3,215
Cooling Degree Days (base 65°F)	0	1	10	43	160	344	467	435	248	52	5	2	1,767
Mean Precipitation (in.)	5.43	4.95	6.74	4.56	5.29	4.27	4.44	3.42	4.29	3.70	5.06	5.63	57.78
Maximum Precipitation (in.)	10.9	10.1	17.0	12.5	11.9	15.0	14.8	9.8	9.8	12.1	11.5	18.7	73.6
Minimum Precipitation (in.)	1.3	0.6	1.6	0.4	1.5	0.2	0.8	0.7	0.5	trace	0.6	0.8	41.8
Maximum 24-hr. Precipitation (in.)	4.8	4.0	5.2	3.8	4.6	4.5	3.8	4.3	3.9	4.9	3.3	9.1	9.1
Days With ≥ 0.1" Precipitation	8	7	8	7	7	6	7	6	6	5	7	8	82
Days With ≥ 1.0" Precipitation	2	2	2	2	2	1	1	1	2	1	2	2	20
Mean Snowfall (in.)	1.4	0.7	0.4	trace	trace	trace	0.0	trace	0.0	trace	trace	0.2	2.7
Maximum Snowfall (in.)	10	7	7	trace	0	0	0	0	0	trace	4	21	24
Maximum 24-hr. Snowfall (in.)	7	4	5	trace	0	0	0	0	0	trace	4	16	16
Days With ≥ 1.0" Snow Depth	1	1	0	0	0	0	0	0	0	0	0	0	2
Thunderstorm Days	1	2	4	5	7	8	10	8	4	2	2	1	54
Foggy Days	13	11	11	8	12	13	16	17	15	13	12	13	154
Predominant Sky Cover	OVR	OVR	OVR	OVR	OVR	OVR	OVR	OVR	OVR	OVR	OVR	OVR	OVR
Mean Relative Humidity 7am (%)	82	81	79	78	79	81	84	86	85	86	84	81	82
Mean Relative Humidity 4pm (%)	60	56	51	46	51	53	56	55	54	51	55	60	54
Mean Dewpoint (°F)	30	33	39	47	57	65	69	68	62	50	41	33	50
Prevailing Wind Direction	ESE	ESE	SE	SE	ESE	ESE	SE	ESE	ESE	ESE	ESE	SE	ESE
Prevailing Wind Speed (mph)	9	9	10	10	8	7	7	7	8	8	9	10	9
Maximum Wind Gust (mph)	62	58	70	59	69	67	63	58	52	54	94	54	94

Mobile Regional Airport

Mobile is located at the head of Mobile Bay and approximately 30 miles from the Gulf of Mexico. Its weather is influenced to a considerable extent by the Gulf.

The summers are consistently warm, but temperatures are seldom as high as they are at inland stations. Normally, in summer, the day begins in the low 70s and the temperature rises rapidly before noon to the high 80s or low 90s, when it is checked by the onset of the sea breeze. On the rare occasions when northerly winds prevail throughout the day, temperatures may reach the high 90s or rise slightly above 100 degrees.

Winter weather is usually mild except for occasional invasions of cold air that last about three days. January is the coldest month in the year. Unusual winters may produce readings that require extensive protective measures as some citrus fruit is grown in the area and outdoor nurseries are numerous.

Based on the 1951-1980 period, the average first occurrence of 32 degrees Fahrenheit in the fall is November 26 and the average last occurrence in the spring is February 27.

The yearly rainfall is among the highest in the United States. It is fairly evenly distributed throughout the year with a slight maximum at the height of the summer thunderstorm season and a slight minimum during the late fall. Rainfall is usually of the shower type and long periods of continuous rain are rare.

Frontal thunderstorms may occur in any month of the year. There may be a thunderstorm every other day in July and August. The summer storms are usually not too violent and seldom produce hail.

The area is subject to hurricanes from the West Indies, the western Caribbean, and the Gulf of Mexico.

Mobile Regional Airport *Mobile County*   Elevation: 213 ft.   Latitude: 30° 41' N   Longitude: 88° 15' W

	JAN	FEB	MAR	APR	MAY	JUN	JUL	AUG	SEP	OCT	NOV	DEC	YEAR
Mean Maximum Temp. (°F)	60.4	64.3	71.0	77.6	84.2	89.4	91.1	90.7	87.0	79.1	70.1	63.3	77.3
Mean Temp. (°F)	50.4	53.8	60.6	66.9	74.1	80.0	82.1	81.8	77.9	68.3	59.5	53.3	67.4
Mean Minimum Temp. (°F)	40.5	43.2	50.1	56.1	64.0	70.6	73.1	72.9	68.8	57.5	48.8	43.2	57.4
Extreme Maximum Temp. (°F)	79	82	87	94	96	100	103	100	99	92	87	81	103
Extreme Minimum Temp. (°F)	3	11	21	32	44	49	63	60	47	30	24	8	3
Days Maximum Temp. ≥ 90°F	0	0	0	0	3	16	22	21	11	1	0	0	74
Days Maximum Temp. ≤ 32°F	0	0	0	0	0	0	0	0	0	0	0	0	0
Days Minimum Temp. ≤ 32°F	8	5	1	0	0	0	0	0	0	0	1	6	21
Days Minimum Temp. ≤ 0°F	0	0	0	0	0	0	0	0	0	0	0	0	0
Heating Degree Days (base 65°F)	454	321	177	53	2	0	0	0	1	47	202	377	1,634
Cooling Degree Days (base 65°F)	5	11	43	104	283	447	531	524	381	152	41	17	2,539
Mean Precipitation (in.)	5.78	5.23	7.25	5.04	6.32	5.15	6.71	6.39	5.98	3.42	5.08	4.73	67.08
Maximum Precipitation (in.)	16.1	11.9	13.5	17.7	15.1	13.1	19.3	15.2	14.0	13.2	13.6	11.4	86.6
Minimum Precipitation (in.)	1.0	1.3	0.6	0.5	0.4	1.2	1.7	1.5	0.6	trace	0.3	1.3	42.3
Maximum 24-hr. Precipitation (in.)	4.9	5.4	7.1	13.0+	8.0	6.1	4.2	5.6	8.2	5.0	7.0	4.7	13.0+
Days With ≥ 0.1" Precipitation	8	6	7	5	7	7	10	9	8	4	6	6	83
Days With ≥ 1.0" Precipitation	2	2	3	2	2	2	2	2	2	1	2	2	24
Mean Snowfall (in.)	trace	0.2	0.1	trace	trace	0.0	trace	0.0	0.0	0.0	0.0	trace	0.3
Maximum Snowfall (in.)	4	4	3	trace	0	0	0	0	0	0	trace	3	4
Maximum 24-hr. Snowfall (in.)	4	4	2	trace	0	0	0	0	0	0	trace	3	4
Days With ≥ 1.0" Snow Depth	0	0	0	0	0	0	0	0	0	0	0	0	0
Thunderstorm Days	2	2	5	5	7	12	18	14	7	2	2	2	78
Foggy Days	15	13	16	15	14	9	10	13	13	12	13	14	157
Predominant Sky Cover	OVR	OVR	OVR	OVR	SCT	SCT	BRK	SCT	SCT	CLR	CLR	OVR	OVR
Mean Relative Humidity 7am (%)	84	85	83	82	81	82	85	86	86	84	84	84	84
Mean Relative Humidity 4pm (%)	60	58	55	54	57	62	67	65	61	55	58	62	60
Mean Dewpoint (°F)	41	44	49	55	63	70	72	72	67	57	48	43	57
Prevailing Wind Direction	N	N	S	S	S	S	S	NE	NE	NE	N	N	N
Prevailing Wind Speed (mph)	13	13	12	12	10	9	8	8	9	8	12	12	10
Maximum Wind Gust (mph)	48	61	55	61	62	67	64	74	97	59	58	56	97

Montgomery Dannelly Field

Montgomery is located in a gently rolling area of Alabama with no local topographic features which appreciably influence weather and climate. The National Weather Service Office is on the north side of Dannelly Field which is located about 6 airline miles south-southwest of the downtown bend in the Alabama River. Surrounding terrain is rather level with long gentle slopes toward the northeast and east.

During the months of June through September, inclusive, temperature and humidity conditions generally show little change from day to day. During the coldest months, December, January, and February, there are frequent shifts between mild and moist air from the Gulf of Mexico and dry, cool continental air.

From late June through the first half of August, nearly all precipitation is from local, mostly afternoon, thunderstorms, and there are apt to be considerable differences in day-to-day amounts of rainfall in different parts of the Montgomery area. In late August and in September, summer conditions of temperature and humidity persist as air continues to drift in from the Gulf, but local thunderstorms become less frequent because of the shortening of the days and the decrease in heat received from the sun. As this late summer season progresses, the local thunderstorms give way to thunderstorms which occur with cold fronts and occasional general rains associated with storms on the Gulf.

All types and intensities of rain, except the local thunderstorms of summer, may occur at any time from December through March or early April. Floods in the rivers are correspondingly most frequent during this period.

Most rain from late April through early June is in the form of showers or thunderstorms occurring in advance of approaching cool fronts, which become weaker and less frequent as summer approaches. It is during this spring season, and during the late summer and early autumn, that droughts sometimes occur.

Snow in Montgomery is important only as a curiosity.

Montgomery Dannelly Field *Montgomery County*   Elevation: 200 ft.   Latitude: 32° 18' N   Longitude: 86° 24' W

	JAN	FEB	MAR	APR	MAY	JUN	JUL	AUG	SEP	OCT	NOV	DEC	YEAR
Mean Maximum Temp. (°F)	57.1	61.6	69.4	76.5	83.3	89.5	91.8	91.4	87.4	78.2	68.4	60.6	76.3
Mean Temp. (°F)	46.6	50.4	57.7	64.3	72.0	78.8	81.8	81.2	76.7	65.8	56.4	49.7	65.1
Mean Minimum Temp. (°F)	36.0	39.1	45.9	52.1	60.6	68.0	71.6	71.0	65.9	53.3	44.2	38.7	53.9
Extreme Maximum Temp. (°F)	81	84	89	91	96	103	102	104	101	95	87	85	104
Extreme Minimum Temp. (°F)	0	10	17	28	40	49	61	56	42	29	18	5	0
Days Maximum Temp. ≥ 90°F	0	0	0	0	4	17	23	22	13	1	0	0	80
Days Maximum Temp. ≤ 32°F	0	0	0	0	0	0	0	0	0	0	0	0	0
Days Minimum Temp. ≤ 32°F	13	8	2	0	0	0	0	0	0	0	4	10	37
Days Minimum Temp. ≤ 0°F	0	0	0	0	0	0	0	0	0	0	0	0	0
Heating Degree Days (base 65°F)	568	411	245	92	8	0	0	0	3	79	275	478	2,159
Cooling Degree Days (base 65°F)	2	6	26	78	240	427	535	522	355	115	23	9	2,338
Mean Precipitation (in.)	5.00	5.51	6.49	4.39	4.23	4.32	5.45	3.68	4.04	2.72	4.35	4.94	55.12
Maximum Precipitation (in.)	16.5	13.4	16.8	15.6	23.1	14.4	11.9	10.4	10.6	9.1	21.3	11.3	135.
Minimum Precipitation (in.)	0.7	1.8	1.9	0.5	0.7	0.3	1.6	0.8	0.4	trace	0.3	1.4	26.8
Maximum 24-hr. Precipitation (in.)	4.2	5.5	7.9	4.5	5.2	3.9	3.8	5.4	8.7	4.0	8.2	3.9	8.7
Days With ≥ 0.1" Precipitation	8	6	7	5	6	6	9	6	5	4	6	7	75
Days With ≥ 1.0" Precipitation	1	2	2	1	1	1	2	1	1	1	1	2	16
Mean Snowfall (in.)	0.2	0.1	0.1	trace	trace	0.0	0.0	0.0	0.0	trace	trace	trace	0.4
Maximum Snowfall (in.)	6	3	4	1	0	0	0	0	0	trace	trace	1	6
Maximum 24-hr. Snowfall (in.)	3	3	4	1	0	0	0	0	0	trace	trace	1	4
Days With ≥ 1.0" Snow Depth	0	0	0	0	0	0	0	0	0	0	0	0	0
Thunderstorm Days	2	2	5	5	6	9	12	9	4	1	2	2	59
Foggy Days	14	11	12	11	15	13	15	17	16	16	14	14	168
Predominant Sky Cover	OVR	OVR	OVR	CLR	OVR	SCT	SCT	SCT	CLR	CLR	CLR	OVR	OVR
Mean Relative Humidity 7am (%)	83	82	81	80	80	81	84	86	85	86	86	84	83
Mean Relative Humidity 4pm (%)	56	51	48	46	51	54	59	56	55	50	52	56	53
Mean Dewpoint (°F)	37	39	45	52	61	67	71	70	65	54	45	39	54
Prevailing Wind Direction	NW	NW	S	S	S	SW	SW	E	E	E	NW	NW	E
Prevailing Wind Speed (mph)	10	10	10	9	7	7	7	6	7	7	9	10	8
Maximum Wind Gust (mph)	48	66	64	67	60	60	55	53	64	62	56	48	67

Alexander City *Tallapoosa County*   Elevation: 639 ft.   Latitude: 32° 57' N   Longitude: 85° 57' W

	JAN	FEB	MAR	APR	MAY	JUN	JUL	AUG	SEP	OCT	NOV	DEC	YEAR
Mean Maximum Temp. (°F)	54.6	59.4	67.8	75.5	81.8	88.0	90.9	89.9	85.6	76.5	66.7	58.3	74.6
Mean Temp. (°F)	43.2	46.8	54.6	61.8	69.3	76.4	79.9	78.9	73.9	63.0	53.7	46.5	62.3
Mean Minimum Temp. (°F)	31.7	34.1	41.3	48.1	56.8	64.9	68.9	67.8	62.1	49.5	40.6	34.6	50.0
Extreme Maximum Temp. (°F)	80	81	89	92	96	102	104	102	99	93	85	81	104
Extreme Minimum Temp. (°F)	-6	5	12	27	35	42	55	54	38	26	14	-1	-6
Days Maximum Temp. ≥ 90°F	0	0	0	0	3	13	20	18	9	1	0	0	64
Days Maximum Temp. ≤ 32°F	1	0	0	0	0	0	0	0	0	0	0	0	1
Days Minimum Temp. ≤ 32°F	18	14	6	1	0	0	0	0	0	0	7	15	61
Days Minimum Temp. ≤ 0°F	0	0	0	0	0	0	0	0	0	0	0	0	0
Heating Degree Days (base 65°F)	671	510	329	141	26	1	0	0	10	121	344	572	2,725
Cooling Degree Days (base 65°F)	0	1	12	46	165	353	479	442	272	66	9	3	1,848
Mean Precipitation (in.)	6.02	5.27	6.66	4.65	4.33	4.49	5.42	4.22	3.83	3.23	4.34	4.97	57.43
Days With ≥ 0.1" Precipitation	9	7	8	6	7	7	9	7	6	4	6	7	83
Days With ≥ 1.0" Precipitation	2	2	2	2	1	1	2	1	1	1	2	2	19
Mean Snowfall (in.)	0.2	trace	0.2	trace	0.0	0.0	0.0	0.0	0.0	0.0	0.0	0.1	0.5
Days With ≥ 1.0" Snow Depth	0	0	0	0	0	0	0	0	0	0	0	0	0

Andalusia 3 W *Covington County*   Elevation: 249 ft.   Latitude: 31° 18' N   Longitude: 86° 31' W

	JAN	FEB	MAR	APR	MAY	JUN	JUL	AUG	SEP	OCT	NOV	DEC	YEAR
Mean Maximum Temp. (°F)	59.6	63.8	71.6	78.5	84.5	89.8	91.4	90.7	87.2	78.6	69.6	62.8	77.4
Mean Temp. (°F)	47.1	50.1	57.0	63.3	70.4	77.2	79.7	79.1	75.0	64.3	55.4	50.0	64.1
Mean Minimum Temp. (°F)	34.2	36.2	42.4	48.1	56.4	64.6	67.8	67.4	62.8	50.2	41.7	36.6	50.7
Extreme Maximum Temp. (°F)	80	83	89	94	98	104	103	103	100	92	87	84	104
Extreme Minimum Temp. (°F)	0	10	16	27	34	44	54	55	39	28	16	2	0
Days Maximum Temp. ≥ 90°F	0	0	0	1	5	18	23	21	12	1	0	0	81
Days Maximum Temp. ≤ 32°F	0	0	0	0	0	0	0	0	0	0	0	0	0
Days Minimum Temp. ≤ 32°F	15	12	6	1	0	0	0	0	0	1	7	13	55
Days Minimum Temp. ≤ 0°F	0	0	0	0	0	0	0	0	0	0	0	0	0
Heating Degree Days (base 65°F)	551	424	266	113	15	0	0	0	6	104	301	470	2,250
Cooling Degree Days (base 65°F)	2	8	27	67	198	387	477	461	316	103	20	10	2,076
Mean Precipitation (in.)	5.91	5.49	7.36	4.53	4.97	5.63	6.51	4.99	4.71	3.30	4.58	4.76	62.74
Days With ≥ 0.1" Precipitation	8	7	8	5	6	8	10	8	6	4	6	7	83
Days With ≥ 1.0" Precipitation	2	2	3	1	2	2	2	1	1	1	1	1	19
Mean Snowfall (in.)	trace	0.0	0.2	0.0	0.0	0.0	0.0	0.0	0.0	0.0	0.0	0.0	0.2
Days With ≥ 1.0" Snow Depth	0	0	0	0	0	0	0	0	0	0	0	0	0

Anniston Calhoun Co. Airport *Calhoun County*   Elevation: 610 ft.   Latitude: 33° 35' N   Longitude: 85° 51' W

	JAN	FEB	MAR	APR	MAY	JUN	JUL	AUG	SEP	OCT	NOV	DEC	YEAR
Mean Maximum Temp. (°F)	52.7	57.9	66.4	74.4	81.0	87.3	90.3	89.6	84.2	74.5	64.7	56.7	73.3
Mean Temp. (°F)	42.8	46.8	54.6	61.9	69.5	76.6	80.1	79.4	73.6	62.6	53.1	46.2	62.3
Mean Minimum Temp. (°F)	32.9	35.5	42.8	49.4	58.0	65.8	69.7	69.1	63.1	50.6	41.5	35.7	51.2
Extreme Maximum Temp. (°F)	78	84	89	92	96	101	105	106	99	91	88	79	106
Extreme Minimum Temp. (°F)	-5	8	12	27	35	42	55	52	40	28	14	3	-5
Days Maximum Temp. ≥ 90°F	0	0	0	0	3	11	19	17	7	0	0	0	57
Days Maximum Temp. ≤ 32°F	1	0	0	0	0	0	0	0	0	0	0	0	1
Days Minimum Temp. ≤ 32°F	16	12	5	1	0	0	0	0	0	1	7	13	55
Days Minimum Temp. ≤ 0°F	0	0	0	0	0	0	0	0	0	0	0	0	0
Heating Degree Days (base 65°F)	681	510	330	140	25	0	0	0	10	131	359	578	2,764
Cooling Degree Days (base 65°F)	0	1	15	50	175	359	483	457	266	67	9	3	1,885
Mean Precipitation (in.)	5.21	4.80	6.43	4.84	4.14	4.17	4.57	3.48	3.35	3.07	4.05	4.22	52.33
Days With ≥ 0.1" Precipitation	8	7	8	6	7	7	8	6	5	4	6	7	79
Days With ≥ 1.0" Precipitation	1	1	2	1	1	1	1	1	1	1	1	1	13
Mean Snowfall (in.)	0.6	0.4	0.5	trace	trace	trace	trace	0.0	0.0	trace	trace	trace	1.5
Days With ≥ 1.0" Snow Depth	0	0	0	0	0	0	0	0	0	0	0	0	0

Ashland 3 SE *Clay County*   Elevation: 1,007 ft.   Latitude: 33° 14' N   Longitude: 85° 49' W

	JAN	FEB	MAR	APR	MAY	JUN	JUL	AUG	SEP	OCT	NOV	DEC	YEAR
Mean Maximum Temp. (°F)	52.0	56.9	65.0	73.0	79.1	85.1	88.0	87.3	82.7	73.2	63.9	55.7	71.8
Mean Temp. (°F)	41.1	44.9	52.5	59.7	67.0	74.0	77.5	76.7	71.3	60.6	51.9	44.7	60.2
Mean Minimum Temp. (°F)	30.3	32.8	39.9	46.3	55.0	62.7	66.9	66.0	59.9	47.9	39.8	33.6	48.4
Extreme Maximum Temp. (°F)	77	80	86	91	94	98	106	99	96	89	83	76	106
Extreme Minimum Temp. (°F)	-7	1	8	23	34	43	54	51	37	27	11	1	-7
Days Maximum Temp. ≥ 90°F	0	0	0	0	0	6	12	9	3	0	0	0	30
Days Maximum Temp. ≤ 32°F	2	1	0	0	0	0	0	0	0	0	0	1	4
Days Minimum Temp. ≤ 32°F	19	15	7	2	0	0	0	0	0	1	8	16	68
Days Minimum Temp. ≤ 0°F	0	0	0	0	0	0	0	0	0	0	0	0	0
Heating Degree Days (base 65°F)	733	562	389	181	45	2	0	0	18	168	391	624	3,113
Cooling Degree Days (base 65°F)	0	1	8	25	118	284	403	377	205	39	3	1	1,464
Mean Precipitation (in.)	6.07	5.75	7.35	4.69	4.66	4.63	5.16	3.91	3.75	3.78	4.46	5.07	59.28
Days With ≥ 0.1" Precipitation	9	7	8	7	7	7	8	6	6	5	7	7	84
Days With ≥ 1.0" Precipitation	2	2	2	2	2	1	2	1	1	1	1	2	19
Mean Snowfall (in.)	0.8	0.4	0.6	0.2	0.0	0.0	0.0	0.0	0.0	trace	trace	0.2	2.2
Days With ≥ 1.0" Snow Depth	1	0	0	0	0	0	0	0	0	0	0	0	1

Bankhead Lock & Dam *Tuscaloosa County*   Elevation: 278 ft.   Latitude: 33° 27' N   Longitude: 87° 21' W

	JAN	FEB	MAR	APR	MAY	JUN	JUL	AUG	SEP	OCT	NOV	DEC	YEAR
Mean Maximum Temp. (°F)	52.9	58.0	66.6	74.8	82.2	89.1	92.0	91.3	86.2	75.9	65.5	56.8	74.3
Mean Temp. (°F)	41.8	45.5	53.4	60.9	69.2	76.5	80.1	79.4	73.9	62.7	53.1	45.5	61.8
Mean Minimum Temp. (°F)	30.8	32.9	40.1	47.0	56.1	63.9	68.2	67.4	61.6	49.4	40.6	34.1	49.3
Extreme Maximum Temp. (°F)	80	82	87	94	98	101	107	105	101	95	86	80	107
Extreme Minimum Temp. (°F)	-5	4	14	25	36	41	51	52	34	25	16	0	-5
Days Maximum Temp. ≥ 90°F	0	0	0	0	3	15	22	21	10	0	0	0	71
Days Maximum Temp. ≤ 32°F	1	0	0	0	0	0	0	0	0	0	0	1	2
Days Minimum Temp. ≤ 32°F	18	14	7	2	0	0	0	0	0	0	7	15	63
Days Minimum Temp. ≤ 0°F	0	0	0	0	0	0	0	0	0	0	0	0	0
Heating Degree Days (base 65°F)	712	545	363	162	27	1	0	0	11	129	359	600	2,909
Cooling Degree Days (base 65°F)	0	1	10	43	160	352	478	456	274	62	7	1	1,844
Mean Precipitation (in.)	6.38	5.13	6.69	4.99	4.97	4.64	5.60	3.76	3.77	4.30	4.77	5.44	60.44
Days With ≥ 0.1" Precipitation	9	7	8	6	6	7	8	7	6	5	7	7	83
Days With ≥ 1.0" Precipitation	2	2	2	1	2	2	2	1	1	2	2	2	21
Mean Snowfall (in.)	trace	trace	0.0	0.0	0.0	0.0	0.0	0.0	0.0	0.0	0.0	trace	trace
Days With ≥ 1.0" Snow Depth	0	0	0	0	0	0	0	0	0	0	0	0	0

Bay Minette 3 NNW *Baldwin County*   Elevation: 275 ft.   Latitude: 30° 56' N   Longitude: 87° 48' W

	JAN	FEB	MAR	APR	MAY	JUN	JUL	AUG	SEP	OCT	NOV	DEC	YEAR
Mean Maximum Temp. (°F)	60.6	65.3	72.1	78.3	84.4	89.0	90.5	90.1	86.8	79.0	69.9	63.4	77.4
Mean Temp. (°F)	50.4	54.0	60.5	66.6	73.5	79.0	80.9	80.6	77.0	67.8	59.3	53.1	66.9
Mean Minimum Temp. (°F)	40.1	42.6	48.9	54.9	62.7	68.8	71.3	70.9	67.0	56.7	48.6	42.8	56.3
Extreme Maximum Temp. (°F)	80	83	88	93	95	101	103	100	100	92	86	82	103
Extreme Minimum Temp. (°F)	2	13	16	28	42	51	60	58	42	31	21	7	2
Days Maximum Temp. ≥ 90°F	0	0	0	0	4	15	20	19	10	1	0	0	69
Days Maximum Temp. ≤ 32°F	0	0	0	0	0	0	0	0	0	0	0	0	0
Days Minimum Temp. ≤ 32°F	8	6	1	0	0	0	0	0	0	0	2	7	24
Days Minimum Temp. ≤ 0°F	0	0	0	0	0	0	0	0	0	0	0	0	0
Heating Degree Days (base 65°F)	455	316	177	55	3	0	0	0	2	50	204	381	1,643
Cooling Degree Days (base 65°F)	5	13	46	106	275	426	502	491	357	141	41	18	2,421
Mean Precipitation (in.)	6.23	5.06	6.88	4.78	5.99	5.63	8.24	6.28	5.75	3.24	5.00	5.13	68.21
Days With ≥ 0.1" Precipitation	8	7	8	5	7	8	11	10	7	4	6	6	87
Days With ≥ 1.0" Precipitation	2	2	2	1	2	2	2	2	2	1	2	2	22
Mean Snowfall (in.)	0.1	0.2	0.1	0.0	0.0	0.0	0.0	0.0	0.0	0.0	0.0	trace	0.4
Days With ≥ 1.0" Snow Depth	0	0	0	0	0	0	0	0	0	0	0	0	0

Belle Mina 2 N *Limestone County*   Elevation: 597 ft.   Latitude: 34° 41' N   Longitude: 86° 53' W

	JAN	FEB	MAR	APR	MAY	JUN	JUL	AUG	SEP	OCT	NOV	DEC	YEAR
Mean Maximum Temp. (°F)	48.9	54.1	63.0	72.3	79.7	86.5	90.0	89.5	84.1	73.7	62.5	52.8	71.4
Mean Temp. (°F)	39.2	43.1	51.3	59.9	68.0	75.3	79.0	77.8	71.9	60.5	50.7	42.6	59.9
Mean Minimum Temp. (°F)	29.4	32.1	39.5	47.3	56.3	64.1	68.0	66.0	59.7	47.3	38.9	32.2	48.4
Extreme Maximum Temp. (°F)	75	81	85	90	97	100	104	103	101	92	84	80	104
Extreme Minimum Temp. (°F)	-14	0	7	26	35	42	53	51	38	27	12	-5	-14
Days Maximum Temp. ≥ 90°F	0	0	0	0	2	10	18	16	7	0	0	0	53
Days Maximum Temp. ≤ 32°F	3	1	0	0	0	0	0	0	0	0	0	1	5
Days Minimum Temp. ≤ 32°F	20	15	8	1	0	0	0	0	0	1	9	17	71
Days Minimum Temp. ≤ 0°F	0	0	0	0	0	0	0	0	0	0	0	0	0
Heating Degree Days (base 65°F)	794	611	425	189	43	1	0	0	20	177	427	690	3,377
Cooling Degree Days (base 65°F)	0	0	7	38	149	329	457	414	230	47	5	1	1,677
Mean Precipitation (in.)	5.36	4.58	6.34	4.42	4.61	4.46	4.39	3.30	3.91	3.68	4.92	5.59	55.56
Days With ≥ 0.1" Precipitation	8	7	8	7	7	7	7	6	6	5	7	8	83
Days With ≥ 1.0" Precipitation	1	1	2	1	1	1	1	1	1	1	2	2	15
Mean Snowfall (in.)	1.0	0.6	0.4	trace	0.0	0.0	0.0	0.0	0.0	0.0	trace	0.2	2.2
Days With ≥ 1.0" Snow Depth	0	0	0	0	0	0	0	0	0	0	0	0	0

Brewton 3 SSE *Escambia County*   Elevation: 82 ft.   Latitude: 31° 03' N   Longitude: 87° 03' W

	JAN	FEB	MAR	APR	MAY	JUN	JUL	AUG	SEP	OCT	NOV	DEC	YEAR
Mean Maximum Temp. (°F)	61.3	65.8	73.0	79.3	85.5	90.2	91.8	91.2	87.4	79.2	70.5	63.9	78.3
Mean Temp. (°F)	48.7	52.0	58.9	64.6	71.6	77.7	80.3	79.6	75.5	65.0	56.6	51.3	65.1
Mean Minimum Temp. (°F)	36.1	38.2	44.7	49.8	57.7	65.1	68.7	68.0	63.5	50.8	42.6	38.5	52.0
Extreme Maximum Temp. (°F)	82	84	91	94	98	104	103	101	101	92	88	84	104
Extreme Minimum Temp. (°F)	3	11	10	28	34	44	55	54	39	27	16	9	3
Days Maximum Temp. ≥ 90°F	0	0	0	1	7	17	23	22	13	2	0	0	85
Days Maximum Temp. ≤ 32°F	0	0	0	0	0	0	0	0	0	0	0	0	0
Days Minimum Temp. ≤ 32°F	14	10	5	1	0	0	0	0	0	1	7	12	50
Days Minimum Temp. ≤ 0°F	0	0	0	0	0	0	0	0	0	0	0	0	0
Heating Degree Days (base 65°F)	506	369	220	92	10	0	0	0	5	96	272	434	2,004
Cooling Degree Days (base 65°F)	5	9	31	77	208	380	478	459	316	108	25	13	2,109
Mean Precipitation (in.)	6.20	5.71	7.21	4.44	5.75	6.28	7.16	5.85	5.38	3.36	4.89	4.80	67.03
Days With ≥ 0.1" Precipitation	8	7	7	5	7	9	11	9	7	4	6	6	86
Days With ≥ 1.0" Precipitation	2	2	2	2	2	2	2	2	2	1	2	1	22
Mean Snowfall (in.)	trace	0.2	trace	0.0	0.0	0.0	0.0	0.0	0.0	0.0	0.0	trace	0.2
Days With ≥ 1.0" Snow Depth	0	0	0	0	0	0	0	0	0	0	0	0	0

Camden 3 NW *Wilcox County*   Elevation: 232 ft.   Latitude: 32° 02' N   Longitude: 87° 19' W

	JAN	FEB	MAR	APR	MAY	JUN	JUL	AUG	SEP	OCT	NOV	DEC	YEAR
Mean Maximum Temp. (°F)	56.7	61.5	70.2	77.3	83.6	89.6	91.8	91.0	87.4	77.6	67.5	59.8	76.2
Mean Temp. (°F)	45.4	49.2	57.1	63.9	71.1	77.6	80.1	79.4	75.2	64.4	54.8	48.0	63.9
Mean Minimum Temp. (°F)	33.9	36.7	44.0	50.4	58.6	65.7	68.5	68.0	62.9	51.1	42.1	36.2	51.5
Extreme Maximum Temp. (°F)	79	83	89	94	95	102	104	103	102	94	86	82	104
Extreme Minimum Temp. (°F)	0	7	15	26	35	45	52	55	42	29	13	4	0
Days Maximum Temp. ≥ 90°F	0	0	0	0	4	17	23	22	13	1	0	0	80
Days Maximum Temp. ≤ 32°F	0	0	0	0	0	0	0	0	0	0	0	0	0
Days Minimum Temp. ≤ 32°F	15	10	4	1	0	0	0	0	0	0	6	13	49
Days Minimum Temp. ≤ 0°F	0	0	0	0	0	0	0	0	0	0	0	0	0
Heating Degree Days (base 65°F)	601	446	263	104	14	0	0	0	7	103	315	526	2,379
Cooling Degree Days (base 65°F)	2	6	28	77	226	402	492	473	326	98	17	6	2,153
Mean Precipitation (in.)	5.92	5.30	6.65	4.50	4.77	4.36	5.65	4.06	3.63	2.84	4.74	5.13	57.55
Days With ≥ 0.1" Precipitation	8	7	7	6	7	6	8	6	5	4	6	7	77
Days With ≥ 1.0" Precipitation	2	2	2	1	2	1	2	1	1	1	2	2	19
Mean Snowfall (in.)	trace	trace	0.2	0.0	0.0	0.0	0.0	0.0	0.0	0.0	0.0	0.1	0.3
Days With ≥ 1.0" Snow Depth	0	0	0	0	0	0	0	0	0	0	0	0	0

Centreville WSMO *Bibb County*   Elevation: 456 ft.   Latitude: 32° 54' N   Longitude: 87° 15' W

	JAN	FEB	MAR	APR	MAY	JUN	JUL	AUG	SEP	OCT	NOV	DEC	YEAR
Mean Maximum Temp. (°F)	53.6	59.3	67.5	75.0	81.3	87.9	90.7	89.9	84.9	75.1	65.9	57.3	74.0
Mean Temp. (°F)	42.9	47.8	55.0	62.1	69.8	76.9	80.1	79.3	73.8	62.8	54.1	46.3	62.6
Mean Minimum Temp. (°F)	32.2	36.2	42.6	49.2	58.2	65.8	69.5	68.6	62.6	50.5	42.2	35.4	51.1
Extreme Maximum Temp. (°F)	80	82	89	92	96	100	105	101	100	91	84	82	105
Extreme Minimum Temp. (°F)	-6	5	14	27	38	48	58	56	38	29	17	1	-6
Days Maximum Temp. ≥ 90°F	0	0	0	0	2	12	19	18	8	0	0	0	59
Days Maximum Temp. ≤ 32°F	1	0	0	0	0	0	0	0	0	0	0	0	1
Days Minimum Temp. ≤ 32°F	17	11	6	1	0	0	0	0	0	0	6	14	55
Days Minimum Temp. ≤ 0°F	0	0	0	0	0	0	0	0	0	0	0	0	0
Heating Degree Days (base 65°F)	678	483	319	134	22	0	0	0	10	129	333	577	2,685
Cooling Degree Days (base 65°F)	1	3	18	55	179	364	479	455	284	75	12	4	1,929
Mean Precipitation (in.)	6.07	5.63	6.94	5.13	4.32	4.49	5.21	4.13	4.33	3.51	4.89	4.82	59.47
Days With ≥ 0.1" Precipitation	8	7	7	6	7	7	8	6	6	4	6	7	79
Days With ≥ 1.0" Precipitation	2	2	3	2	1	1	2	1	1	1	2	1	19
Mean Snowfall (in.)	0.6	trace	0.5	0.1	0.0	0.0	0.0	0.0	0.0	trace	trace	trace	1.2
Days With ≥ 1.0" Snow Depth	0	0	0	0	0	0	0	0	0	0	0	0	0

Chatom *Washington County*   Elevation: 282 ft.   Latitude: 31° 28' N   Longitude: 88° 15' W

	JAN	FEB	MAR	APR	MAY	JUN	JUL	AUG	SEP	OCT	NOV	DEC	YEAR
Mean Maximum Temp. (°F)	59.5	64.8	72.4	79.2	85.5	90.1	92.6	91.8	88.3	79.7	69.8	63.1	78.1
Mean Temp. (°F)	47.5	51.7	58.6	65.2	72.6	78.0	80.7	80.1	75.8	66.0	56.4	50.6	65.3
Mean Minimum Temp. (°F)	35.4	38.5	44.7	51.1	59.5	66.0	68.8	68.1	63.2	52.3	43.1	38.1	52.4
Extreme Maximum Temp. (°F)	82	88	92	93	102	103	106	103	101	97	88	84	106
Extreme Minimum Temp. (°F)	1	9	14	28	40	43	56	49	36	29	14	4	1
Days Maximum Temp. ≥ 90°F	0	0	0	1	7	17	24	24	14	2	0	0	89
Days Maximum Temp. ≤ 32°F	0	0	0	0	0	0	0	0	0	0	0	0	0
Days Minimum Temp. ≤ 32°F	13	8	4	1	0	0	0	0	0	0	5	11	42
Days Minimum Temp. ≤ 0°F	0	0	0	0	0	0	0	0	0	0	0	0	0
Heating Degree Days (base 65°F)	542	376	225	80	7	0	0	0	5	74	275	452	2,036
Cooling Degree Days (base 65°F)	3	8	27	89	250	406	512	485	334	114	21	9	2,258
Mean Precipitation (in.)	6.88	6.02	6.95	5.26	5.63	4.60	5.99	4.71	4.88	3.51	4.93	5.55	64.91
Days With ≥ 0.1" Precipitation	7	6	7	5	6	7	8	7	5	4	6	6	74
Days With ≥ 1.0" Precipitation	2	2	2	2	2	1	2	1	2	1	2	2	21
Mean Snowfall (in.)	trace	trace	0.2	0.0	0.0	0.0	0.0	0.0	0.0	0.0	0.0	trace	0.2
Days With ≥ 1.0" Snow Depth	0	0	0	0	0	0	0	0	0	0	0	0	0

Childersburg Water Plant *Talladega County*   Elevation: 416 ft.   Latitude: 33° 17' N   Longitude: 86° 21' W

	JAN	FEB	MAR	APR	MAY	JUN	JUL	AUG	SEP	OCT	NOV	DEC	YEAR
Mean Maximum Temp. (°F)	56.4	61.6	70.3	77.5	83.4	89.6	92.3	91.6	87.1	77.8	68.0	59.9	76.3
Mean Temp. (°F)	44.6	48.4	56.2	62.9	70.1	77.0	80.4	79.4	74.2	63.4	54.4	47.6	63.2
Mean Minimum Temp. (°F)	32.6	35.1	42.1	48.3	56.7	64.4	68.4	67.1	61.3	48.8	40.7	35.3	50.1
Extreme Maximum Temp. (°F)	80	84	89	92	97	102	105	103	99	93	86	83	105
Extreme Minimum Temp. (°F)	-4	4	7	25	35	43	52	50	36	22	14	3	-4
Days Maximum Temp. ≥ 90°F	0	0	0	0	4	17	24	22	12	1	0	0	80
Days Maximum Temp. ≤ 32°F	0	0	0	0	0	0	0	0	0	0	0	0	0
Days Minimum Temp. ≤ 32°F	16	13	7	2	0	0	0	0	0	1	8	14	61
Days Minimum Temp. ≤ 0°F	0	0	0	0	0	0	0	0	0	0	0	0	0
Heating Degree Days (base 65°F)	629	466	286	123	22	1	0	0	9	116	327	537	2,516
Cooling Degree Days (base 65°F)	1	4	21	66	192	374	492	456	281	77	13	5	1,982
Mean Precipitation (in.)	6.14	5.51	6.85	5.14	4.43	4.08	4.76	3.85	4.11	3.41	4.13	4.87	57.28
Days With ≥ 0.1" Precipitation	9	7	8	7	7	7	8	6	5	5	6	7	82
Days With ≥ 1.0" Precipitation	2	2	2	2	1	1	1	1	1	1	1	1	16
Mean Snowfall (in.)	0.3	trace	0.4	0.0	0.0	0.0	0.0	0.0	0.0	trace	0.0	trace	0.7
Days With ≥ 1.0" Snow Depth	0	0	0	0	0	0	0	0	0	0	0	0	0

Clanton *Chilton County*   Elevation: 606 ft.   Latitude: 32° 49' N   Longitude: 86° 39' W

	JAN	FEB	MAR	APR	MAY	JUN	JUL	AUG	SEP	OCT	NOV	DEC	YEAR
Mean Maximum Temp. (°F)	53.5	58.7	67.1	75.1	81.6	87.7	90.6	89.8	85.7	76.0	65.9	57.6	74.1
Mean Temp. (°F)	42.5	46.4	54.3	61.8	69.3	76.2	79.6	78.6	73.7	62.9	53.2	46.3	62.1
Mean Minimum Temp. (°F)	31.4	34.0	41.6	48.4	56.9	64.7	68.5	67.3	61.7	49.8	40.5	35.0	50.0
Extreme Maximum Temp. (°F)	78	82	89	89	95	103	104	103	101	92	86	80	104
Extreme Minimum Temp. (°F)	-4	5	10	28	36	43	56	53	40	29	15	3	-4
Days Maximum Temp. ≥ 90°F	0	0	0	0	2	11	19	17	9	1	0	0	59
Days Maximum Temp. ≤ 32°F	1	0	0	0	0	0	0	0	0	0	0	0	1
Days Minimum Temp. ≤ 32°F	18	14	6	1	0	0	0	0	0	0	8	15	62
Days Minimum Temp. ≤ 0°F	0	0	0	0	0	0	0	0	0	0	0	0	0
Heating Degree Days (base 65°F)	693	521	338	141	26	1	0	0	10	125	358	575	2,788
Cooling Degree Days (base 65°F)	1	1	15	50	172	352	473	435	270	75	10	3	1,857
Mean Precipitation (in.)	5.80	5.36	7.08	5.80	4.51	4.05	5.79	4.13	4.54	3.42	4.76	5.11	60.35
Days With ≥ 0.1" Precipitation	8	7	8	6	7	7	8	7	5	4	6	7	80
Days With ≥ 1.0" Precipitation	2	2	3	2	1	1	2	1	2	1	2	1	20
Mean Snowfall (in.)	0.3	trace	0.6	0.0	0.0	0.0	0.0	0.0	0.0	0.0	0.0	trace	0.9
Days With ≥ 1.0" Snow Depth	0	0	0	0	0	0	0	0	0	0	0	0	0

Clayton *Barbour County*   Elevation: 498 ft.   Latitude: 31° 53' N   Longitude: 85° 29' W

	JAN	FEB	MAR	APR	MAY	JUN	JUL	AUG	SEP	OCT	NOV	DEC	YEAR
Mean Maximum Temp. (°F)	56.7	61.2	69.1	76.1	82.3	87.8	90.0	89.5	86.1	77.4	68.5	60.7	75.5
Mean Temp. (°F)	46.0	49.6	57.1	63.6	71.0	77.1	79.6	79.0	75.1	65.2	56.7	49.4	64.1
Mean Minimum Temp. (°F)	35.2	37.8	45.0	51.1	59.6	66.3	69.0	68.5	64.1	53.0	44.8	38.0	52.7
Extreme Maximum Temp. (°F)	82	83	88	94	97	101	101	101	98	93	87	84	101
Extreme Minimum Temp. (°F)	-6	11	13	27	36	49	57	57	42	31	17	5	-6
Days Maximum Temp. ≥ 90°F	0	0	0	0	2	11	18	16	9	1	0	0	57
Days Maximum Temp. ≤ 32°F	1	0	0	0	0	0	0	0	0	0	0	0	1
Days Minimum Temp. ≤ 32°F	13	9	3	0	0	0	0	0	0	0	4	10	39
Days Minimum Temp. ≤ 0°F	0	0	0	0	0	0	0	0	0	0	0	0	0
Heating Degree Days (base 65°F)	585	435	265	109	12	0	0	0	4	87	265	483	2,245
Cooling Degree Days (base 65°F)	1	6	26	69	209	377	472	449	304	97	22	4	2,036
Mean Precipitation (in.)	5.05	5.07	6.65	3.83	3.99	4.88	5.27	4.09	3.61	2.83	3.88	4.17	53.32
Days With ≥ 0.1" Precipitation	7	6	7	5	6	6	8	6	5	3	5	5	69
Days With ≥ 1.0" Precipitation	2	2	2	1	1	2	2	1	1	1	1	1	17
Mean Snowfall (in.)	trace	0.4	0.0	0.0	0.0	0.0	0.0	0.0	0.0	0.0	0.0	0.2	0.6
Days With ≥ 1.0" Snow Depth	0	0	0	0	0	0	0	0	0	0	0	0	0

Demopolis Lock & Dam *Marengo County*   Elevation: 98 ft.   Latitude: 32° 31' N   Longitude: 87° 53' W

	JAN	FEB	MAR	APR	MAY	JUN	JUL	AUG	SEP	OCT	NOV	DEC	YEAR
Mean Maximum Temp. (°F)	55.1	59.9	68.2	75.7	82.5	88.8	91.4	90.9	86.3	76.8	67.0	58.8	75.1
Mean Temp. (°F)	44.1	47.9	55.7	62.6	70.5	77.3	80.3	79.7	74.8	63.6	54.1	47.1	63.1
Mean Minimum Temp. (°F)	32.9	36.0	43.2	49.7	58.4	65.7	69.2	68.5	63.2	50.3	41.2	35.3	51.1
Extreme Maximum Temp. (°F)	80	85	89	92	98	103	105	103	101	93	86	82	105
Extreme Minimum Temp. (°F)	-2	6	16	25	40	42	57	53	41	29	17	4	-2
Days Maximum Temp. ≥ 90°F	0	0	0	0	3	14	21	20	11	1	0	0	70
Days Maximum Temp. ≤ 32°F	1	0	0	0	0	0	0	0	0	0	0	0	1
Days Minimum Temp. ≤ 32°F	16	11	4	1	0	0	0	0	0	1	7	15	55
Days Minimum Temp. ≤ 0°F	0	0	0	0	0	0	0	0	0	0	0	0	0
Heating Degree Days (base 65°F)	645	480	302	128	19	0	0	0	8	119	333	555	2,589
Cooling Degree Days (base 65°F)	2	6	21	64	205	382	490	471	303	86	13	6	2,049
Mean Precipitation (in.)	6.09	4.91	6.51	4.88	4.50	3.59	5.01	3.64	3.81	3.77	4.47	4.52	55.70
Days With ≥ 0.1" Precipitation	9	7	7	6	7	6	8	6	6	4	6	7	79
Days With ≥ 1.0" Precipitation	2	2	3	2	2	1	1	1	1	1	2	1	19
Mean Snowfall (in.)	trace	0.0	0.1	0.0	0.0	0.0	0.0	0.0	0.0	0.0	0.0	0.0	0.1
Days With ≥ 1.0" Snow Depth	0	0	0	0	0	0	0	0	0	0	0	0	0

Enterprise 5 NNW *Coffee County*   Elevation: 469 ft.   Latitude: 31° 23' N   Longitude: 85° 54' W

	JAN	FEB	MAR	APR	MAY	JUN	JUL	AUG	SEP	OCT	NOV	DEC	YEAR
Mean Maximum Temp. (°F)	57.7	61.8	69.7	76.3	82.8	88.1	90.2	89.4	86.4	77.6	68.8	61.2	75.8
Mean Temp. (°F)	47.8	51.2	58.5	64.8	72.1	78.1	80.5	79.8	76.3	66.7	58.2	51.1	65.4
Mean Minimum Temp. (°F)	37.9	40.4	47.3	53.2	61.4	68.0	70.7	70.3	66.2	55.7	47.5	40.9	55.0
Extreme Maximum Temp. (°F)	80	82	88	93	96	101	104	101	100	92	86	82	104
Extreme Minimum Temp. (°F)	-1	10	17	30	40	49	62	59	45	32	18	6	-1
Days Maximum Temp. ≥ 90°F	0	0	0	0	3	12	19	16	9	1	0	0	60
Days Maximum Temp. ≤ 32°F	0	0	0	0	0	0	0	0	0	0	0	0	0
Days Minimum Temp. ≤ 32°F	10	7	2	0	0	0	0	0	0	0	2	7	28
Days Minimum Temp. ≤ 0°F	0	0	0	0	0	0	0	0	0	0	0	0	0
Heating Degree Days (base 65°F)	530	392	224	88	9	0	0	0	2	66	228	435	1,974
Cooling Degree Days (base 65°F)	2	9	32	86	244	408	491	469	338	125	32	8	2,244
Mean Precipitation (in.)	6.19	5.32	6.62	4.08	4.69	5.16	6.25	3.95	3.65	2.97	4.24	4.66	57.78
Days With ≥ 0.1" Precipitation	7	6	7	6	6	7	9	7	5	4	5	6	75
Days With ≥ 1.0" Precipitation	2	2	2	1	1	2	1	1	1	1	2	2	18
Mean Snowfall (in.)	0.2	0.3	0.0	0.0	0.0	0.0	0.0	0.0	0.0	0.0	0.0	trace	0.5
Days With ≥ 1.0" Snow Depth	0	0	0	0	0	0	0	0	0	0	0	0	0

Eufaula Wildlife Refuge *Barbour County*   Elevation: 213 ft.   Latitude: 32° 00' N   Longitude: 85° 05' W

	JAN	FEB	MAR	APR	MAY	JUN	JUL	AUG	SEP	OCT	NOV	DEC	YEAR
Mean Maximum Temp. (°F)	57.7	62.2	70.0	76.8	83.3	89.5	91.8	91.0	87.3	78.0	69.1	61.1	76.5
Mean Temp. (°F)	46.2	49.8	57.2	63.3	70.8	77.7	80.7	79.9	75.6	64.5	55.9	49.3	64.2
Mean Minimum Temp. (°F)	34.7	37.3	44.3	49.7	58.3	65.8	69.4	68.7	63.9	51.0	42.8	37.4	52.0
Extreme Maximum Temp. (°F)	81	82	89	93	96	105	104	103	101	94	90	82	105
Extreme Minimum Temp. (°F)	5	8	17	27	36	44	55	57	40	26	14	8	5
Days Maximum Temp. ≥ 90°F	0	0	0	0	4	16	22	21	12	2	0	0	77
Days Maximum Temp. ≤ 32°F	0	0	0	0	0	0	0	0	0	0	0	0	0
Days Minimum Temp. ≤ 32°F	15	11	4	1	0	0	0	0	0	1	6	12	50
Days Minimum Temp. ≤ 0°F	0	0	0	0	0	0	0	0	0	0	0	0	0
Heating Degree Days (base 65°F)	577	429	260	113	17	0	0	0	4	101	291	486	2,278
Cooling Degree Days (base 65°F)	2	6	26	63	208	397	501	475	320	100	21	5	2,124
Mean Precipitation (in.)	5.41	4.74	6.48	3.93	3.77	4.29	5.01	3.52	3.26	3.05	4.13	4.63	52.22
Days With ≥ 0.1" Precipitation	8	6	7	5	6	6	8	6	5	3	5	6	71
Days With ≥ 1.0" Precipitation	2	2	2	1	1	1	1	1	1	1	1	1	15
Mean Snowfall (in.)	0.2	0.3	0.1	0.0	0.0	0.0	0.0	0.0	0.0	0.0	0.0	trace	0.6
Days With ≥ 1.0" Snow Depth	0	0	0	0	0	0	0	0	0	0	0	0	0

Evergreen *Conecuh County*   Elevation: 288 ft.   Latitude: 31° 27' N   Longitude: 86° 57' W

	JAN	FEB	MAR	APR	MAY	JUN	JUL	AUG	SEP	OCT	NOV	DEC	YEAR
Mean Maximum Temp. (°F)	58.1	62.8	70.4	76.6	83.1	88.3	90.6	90.2	86.6	78.1	68.7	61.3	76.2
Mean Temp. (°F)	46.8	50.4	57.5	63.6	71.4	77.6	80.3	79.9	75.8	65.8	56.6	49.8	64.6
Mean Minimum Temp. (°F)	35.4	37.8	44.6	50.6	59.6	66.9	70.1	69.5	65.0	53.1	44.0	38.3	52.9
Extreme Maximum Temp. (°F)	80	84	89	94	96	105	104	102	98	96	87	83	105
Extreme Minimum Temp. (°F)	0	9	16	28	42	47	62	57	43	31	18	6	0
Days Maximum Temp. ≥ 90°F	0	0	0	0	3	12	19	19	10	1	0	0	64
Days Maximum Temp. ≤ 32°F	0	0	0	0	0	0	0	0	0	0	0	0	0
Days Minimum Temp. ≤ 32°F	14	10	4	0	0	0	0	0	0	0	5	12	45
Days Minimum Temp. ≤ 0°F	0	0	0	0	0	0	0	0	0	0	0	0	0
Heating Degree Days (base 65°F)	561	414	254	107	14	0	0	0	4	81	271	474	2,180
Cooling Degree Days (base 65°F)	2	8	27	72	216	387	479	466	320	110	22	9	2,118
Mean Precipitation (in.)	6.52	5.75	7.48	5.11	5.37	5.62	6.79	4.62	4.71	2.86	4.54	5.20	64.57
Days With ≥ 0.1" Precipitation	8	7	8	6	7	8	10	8	6	4	6	6	84
Days With ≥ 1.0" Precipitation	2	2	3	2	2	2	2	1	1	1	1	2	21
Mean Snowfall (in.)	0.2	0.0	0.2	0.0	0.0	0.0	0.0	0.0	0.0	0.0	0.0	trace	0.4
Days With ≥ 1.0" Snow Depth	0	0	0	0	0	0	0	0	0	0	0	0	0

Fairhope 2 NE *Baldwin County*   Elevation: 22 ft.   Latitude: 30° 33' N   Longitude: 87° 53' W

	JAN	FEB	MAR	APR	MAY	JUN	JUL	AUG	SEP	OCT	NOV	DEC	YEAR
Mean Maximum Temp. (°F)	60.4	63.9	70.3	76.9	83.4	88.5	90.2	90.1	87.0	79.1	70.3	63.2	76.9
Mean Temp. (°F)	50.3	53.3	60.0	66.3	73.3	79.3	81.5	81.1	77.5	68.1	59.6	53.1	67.0
Mean Minimum Temp. (°F)	40.2	42.7	49.7	55.7	63.2	70.1	72.7	72.0	68.0	57.1	48.9	42.9	56.9
Extreme Maximum Temp. (°F)	79	87	85	91	96	98	101	100	97	92	91	82	101
Extreme Minimum Temp. (°F)	5	14	21	34	45	52	63	60	47	33	23	9	5
Days Maximum Temp. ≥ 90°F	0	0	0	0	2	12	20	20	10	1	0	0	65
Days Maximum Temp. ≤ 32°F	0	0	0	0	0	0	0	0	0	0	0	0	0
Days Minimum Temp. ≤ 32°F	9	5	1	0	0	0	0	0	0	0	1	6	22
Days Minimum Temp. ≤ 0°F	0	0	0	0	0	0	0	0	0	0	0	0	0
Heating Degree Days (base 65°F)	458	334	186	58	3	0	0	0	2	47	197	382	1,667
Cooling Degree Days (base 65°F)	6	10	35	94	267	434	524	513	377	152	43	18	2,473
Mean Precipitation (in.)	6.15	5.58	6.82	4.55	5.68	6.12	7.95	6.52	5.84	3.79	5.04	4.46	68.50
Days With ≥ 0.1" Precipitation	7	6	7	5	6	8	10	9	7	4	6	6	81
Days With ≥ 1.0" Precipitation	2	2	2	1	2	2	2	2	1	2	1	21
Mean Snowfall (in.)	trace	trace	trace	0.0	0.0	0.0	0.0	0.0	0.0	0.0	0.0	0.0	trace
Days With ≥ 1.0" Snow Depth	0	0	0	0	0	0	0	0	0	0	0	0	0

Gainesville Lock *Greene County*   Elevation: 124 ft.   Latitude: 32° 50' N   Longitude: 88° 08' W

	JAN	FEB	MAR	APR	MAY	JUN	JUL	AUG	SEP	OCT	NOV	DEC	YEAR
Mean Maximum Temp. (°F)	53.7	58.9	67.2	75.0	81.8	88.3	91.2	90.7	86.1	76.2	65.9	57.5	74.4
Mean Temp. (°F)	43.1	47.2	55.2	62.6	70.4	77.4	80.8	80.2	74.9	63.4	53.6	46.5	62.9
Mean Minimum Temp. (°F)	32.5	35.4	43.1	49.9	58.9	66.6	70.4	69.6	63.6	50.6	41.3	35.4	51.4
Extreme Maximum Temp. (°F)	81	85	87	92	97	101	105	103	102	94	86	83	105
Extreme Minimum Temp. (°F)	-2	9	15	29	38	42	57	55	41	30	17	2	-2
Days Maximum Temp. ≥ 90°F	0	0	0	0	3	13	21	20	10	1	0	0	68
Days Maximum Temp. ≤ 32°F	1	0	0	0	0	0	0	0	0	0	0	0	1
Days Minimum Temp. ≤ 32°F	17	12	4	0	0	0	0	0	0	0	7	15	55
Days Minimum Temp. ≤ 0°F	0	0	0	0	0	0	0	0	0	0	0	0	0
Heating Degree Days (base 65°F)	671	501	315	129	21	1	0	0	8	118	347	570	2,681
Cooling Degree Days (base 65°F)	1	4	17	60	198	386	509	490	307	78	10	4	2,064
Mean Precipitation (in.)	5.79	4.88	6.59	5.44	4.52	4.18	4.07	3.02	3.57	3.33	4.32	4.81	54.52
Days With ≥ 0.1" Precipitation	8	6	7	6	7	6	7	6	5	4	6	6	74
Days With ≥ 1.0" Precipitation	2	2	2	2	1	1	1	1	1	1	2	2	18
Mean Snowfall (in.)	0.4	trace	trace	trace	0.0	0.0	0.0	0.0	0.0	0.0	trace	trace	0.4
Days With ≥ 1.0" Snow Depth	0	0	0	0	0	0	0	0	0	0	0	0	0

Geneva 2 *Geneva County*   Elevation: 144 ft.   Latitude: 31° 03' N   Longitude: 85° 53' W

	JAN	FEB	MAR	APR	MAY	JUN	JUL	AUG	SEP	OCT	NOV	DEC	YEAR
Mean Maximum Temp. (°F)	58.8	63.7	70.8	77.2	83.7	88.9	90.7	90.0	86.6	78.4	70.2	62.2	76.8
Mean Temp. (°F)	47.2	51.6	58.5	64.6	71.9	78.2	80.5	79.8	75.8	65.6	57.7	50.4	65.1
Mean Minimum Temp. (°F)	35.6	39.4	46.0	51.9	60.1	67.4	70.3	69.6	64.9	52.8	45.1	38.6	53.5
Extreme Maximum Temp. (°F)	80	84	88	94	95	102	103	101	96	92	86	84	103
Extreme Minimum Temp. (°F)	2	11	18	30	41	44	61	57	43	31	21	7	2
Days Maximum Temp. ≥ 90°F	0	0	0	0	4	15	21	19	10	1	0	0	70
Days Maximum Temp. ≤ 32°F	0	0	0	0	0	0	0	0	0	0	0	0	0
Days Minimum Temp. ≤ 32°F	14	8	3	0	0	0	0	0	0	0	4	11	40
Days Minimum Temp. ≤ 0°F	0	0	0	0	0	0	0	0	0	0	0	0	0
Heating Degree Days (base 65°F)	546	382	228	89	9	0	0	0	3	83	241	453	2,034
Cooling Degree Days (base 65°F)	3	11	31	79	231	399	487	467	328	115	31	10	2,192
Mean Precipitation (in.)	6.63	5.54	6.60	3.92	4.58	5.24	5.91	4.74	4.22	3.35	5.05	4.03	59.81
Days With ≥ 0.1" Precipitation	8	7	7	5	6	7	9	8	6	4	5	6	78
Days With ≥ 1.0" Precipitation	2	2	2	1	2	2	2	1	1	1	2	1	19
Mean Snowfall (in.)	na	trace	0.0	0.0	0.0	0.0	0.0	0.0	0.0	0.0	0.0	0.0	na
Days With ≥ 1.0" Snow Depth	na	0	0	0	0	0	0	0	0	0	0	0	na

Greensboro *Hale County*   Elevation: 219 ft.   Latitude: 32° 42' N   Longitude: 87° 35' W

	JAN	FEB	MAR	APR	MAY	JUN	JUL	AUG	SEP	OCT	NOV	DEC	YEAR
Mean Maximum Temp. (°F)	55.8	61.1	69.7	77.3	83.9	90.2	92.7	92.2	87.5	77.8	67.3	59.4	76.3
Mean Temp. (°F)	45.4	49.7	57.0	64.1	71.8	78.7	81.7	81.2	76.2	65.2	55.4	48.8	64.6
Mean Minimum Temp. (°F)	35.0	38.2	44.3	50.7	59.6	67.2	70.7	70.1	64.8	52.6	43.4	38.0	52.9
Extreme Maximum Temp. (°F)	80	85	91	94	98	102	107	102	103	93	85	81	107
Extreme Minimum Temp. (°F)	-2	7	10	28	40	47	58	56	42	28	15	2	-2
Days Maximum Temp. ≥ 90°F	0	0	0	0	5	18	25	23	12	1	0	0	84
Days Maximum Temp. ≤ 32°F	1	0	0	0	0	0	0	0	0	0	0	0	1
Days Minimum Temp. ≤ 32°F	14	8	4	1	0	0	0	0	0	0	5	11	43
Days Minimum Temp. ≤ 0°F	0	0	0	0	0	0	0	0	0	0	0	0	0
Heating Degree Days (base 65°F)	603	431	265	99	10	0	0	0	5	87	298	503	2,301
Cooling Degree Days (base 65°F)	2	6	26	78	239	433	542	521	346	108	17	5	2,323
Mean Precipitation (in.)	6.02	5.44	6.53	5.29	4.58	4.02	5.43	3.53	3.89	3.56	4.30	4.76	57.35
Days With ≥ 0.1" Precipitation	8	6	7	6	7	6	8	5	6	5	6	7	77
Days With ≥ 1.0" Precipitation	2	2	3	2	1	1	2	1	1	1	2	2	20
Mean Snowfall (in.)	0.2	trace	trace	0.1	0.0	0.0	0.0	0.0	0.0	0.0	0.0	trace	0.3
Days With ≥ 1.0" Snow Depth	0	0	0	0	0	0	0	0	0	0	0	0	0

Greenville *Butler County*   Elevation: 469 ft.   Latitude: 31° 51' N   Longitude: 86° 39' W

	JAN	FEB	MAR	APR	MAY	JUN	JUL	AUG	SEP	OCT	NOV	DEC	YEAR
Mean Maximum Temp. (°F)	58.9	62.9	71.0	78.0	84.6	89.7	92.1	91.5	87.8	78.9	69.7	62.0	77.3
Mean Temp. (°F)	48.4	51.0	58.3	64.9	72.2	78.3	81.0	80.4	76.6	66.6	57.7	50.8	65.5
Mean Minimum Temp. (°F)	37.3	39.1	45.6	51.7	59.8	66.8	69.9	69.3	65.2	54.2	45.7	39.5	53.7
Extreme Maximum Temp. (°F)	80	85	89	96	98	105	105	101	101	96	91	84	105
Extreme Minimum Temp. (°F)	-1	9	15	28	38	49	58	50	39	30	11	5	-1
Days Maximum Temp. ≥ 90°F	0	0	0	1	5	17	24	22	14	1	0	0	84
Days Maximum Temp. ≤ 32°F	0	0	0	0	0	0	0	0	0	0	0	0	0
Days Minimum Temp. ≤ 32°F	11	9	3	0	0	0	0	0	0	0	4	9	36
Days Minimum Temp. ≤ 0°F	0	0	0	0	0	0	0	0	0	0	0	0	0
Heating Degree Days (base 65°F)	512	395	232	85	9	0	0	0	3	67	241	446	1,990
Cooling Degree Days (base 65°F)	2	9	36	92	253	418	515	498	355	136	32	11	2,357
Mean Precipitation (in.)	6.01	5.39	6.63	4.27	4.17	5.21	5.67	4.48	4.21	2.80	4.46	4.79	58.09
Days With ≥ 0.1" Precipitation	8	7	7	6	6	7	8	6	5	4	6	6	76
Days With ≥ 1.0" Precipitation	2	2	2	1	1	2	2	1	1	1	2	2	19
Mean Snowfall (in.)	trace	0.2	0.1	0.0	0.0	0.0	0.0	0.0	0.0	0.0	0.0	0.1	0.4
Days With ≥ 1.0" Snow Depth	0	0	0	0	0	0	0	0	0	0	0	0	0

Haleyville *Marion County*   Elevation: 918 ft.   Latitude: 34° 14' N   Longitude: 87° 38' W

	JAN	FEB	MAR	APR	MAY	JUN	JUL	AUG	SEP	OCT	NOV	DEC	YEAR
Mean Maximum Temp. (°F)	48.9	54.0	62.9	71.8	78.6	85.3	88.7	88.5	83.1	72.6	61.3	52.7	70.7
Mean Temp. (°F)	39.1	43.1	51.7	59.9	67.5	74.6	78.1	77.6	72.0	60.7	50.7	42.9	59.8
Mean Minimum Temp. (°F)	29.3	32.2	40.6	47.9	56.4	63.9	67.5	66.6	60.8	48.8	40.0	33.0	48.9
Extreme Maximum Temp. (°F)	76	79	84	90	93	100	103	101	99	91	85	76	103
Extreme Minimum Temp. (°F)	-9	-3	8	25	37	45	50	50	34	25	11	-7	-9
Days Maximum Temp. ≥ 90°F	0	0	0	0	0	6	15	13	6	0	0	0	40
Days Maximum Temp. ≤ 32°F	3	1	0	0	0	0	0	0	0	0	0	1	5
Days Minimum Temp. ≤ 32°F	20	14	7	2	0	0	0	0	0	1	8	15	67
Days Minimum Temp. ≤ 0°F	0	0	0	0	0	0	0	0	0	0	0	0	0
Heating Degree Days (base 65°F)	796	612	411	187	45	2	0	0	21	171	428	680	3,353
Cooling Degree Days (base 65°F)	0	0	8	39	132	302	428	414	238	48	4	1	1,614
Mean Precipitation (in.)	5.94	5.34	6.90	5.31	6.11	4.81	4.85	3.71	4.70	3.76	5.48	5.93	62.84
Days With ≥ 0.1" Precipitation	8	7	9	7	8	7	8	5	6	5	7	8	85
Days With ≥ 1.0" Precipitation	2	2	2	2	2	2	1	1	1	1	2	2	20
Mean Snowfall (in.)	0.7	0.3	0.3	trace	0.0	0.0	0.0	0.0	0.0	trace	trace	0.2	1.5
Days With ≥ 1.0" Snow Depth	0	0	0	0	0	0	0	0	0	0	0	0	0

Hamilton 3 S *Marion County*   Elevation: 433 ft.   Latitude: 34° 06' N   Longitude: 87° 59' W

	JAN	FEB	MAR	APR	MAY	JUN	JUL	AUG	SEP	OCT	NOV	DEC	YEAR
Mean Maximum Temp. (°F)	51.1	56.6	65.8	74.6	81.3	87.8	91.2	91.0	85.9	75.5	64.4	55.2	73.4
Mean Temp. (°F)	38.5	42.4	50.7	58.5	66.8	74.5	78.6	77.8	72.0	59.9	49.8	42.3	59.3
Mean Minimum Temp. (°F)	25.9	28.2	35.5	42.4	52.3	61.1	66.0	64.5	57.9	44.2	35.2	29.3	45.2
Extreme Maximum Temp. (°F)	78	87	88	95	98	102	107	106	102	95	87	81	107
Extreme Minimum Temp. (°F)	-12	0	5	21	30	37	48	46	35	24	9	-5	-12
Days Maximum Temp. ≥ 90°F	0	0	0	0	3	13	21	20	11	1	0	0	69
Days Maximum Temp. ≤ 32°F	2	1	0	0	0	0	0	0	0	0	0	1	4
Days Minimum Temp. ≤ 32°F	23	20	14	7	0	0	0	0	0	5	14	20	103
Days Minimum Temp. ≤ 0°F	0	0	0	0	0	0	0	0	0	0	0	0	0
Heating Degree Days (base 65°F)	815	632	445	218	56	3	0	0	22	195	453	699	3,538
Cooling Degree Days (base 65°F)	0	1	8	33	130	312	449	419	238	48	4	1	1,643
Mean Precipitation (in.)	5.63	5.15	6.49	5.46	6.11	4.65	4.76	3.64	4.49	3.60	5.16	5.88	61.02
Days With ≥ 0.1" Precipitation	8	7	8	7	7	7	7	6	6	5	7	8	83
Days With ≥ 1.0" Precipitation	2	2	2	2	2	2	2	1	2	1	2	2	22
Mean Snowfall (in.)	0.7	0.7	0.2	trace	0.0	0.0	0.0	0.0	0.0	trace	trace	trace	1.6
Days With ≥ 1.0" Snow Depth	1	1	0	0	0	0	0	0	0	0	0	0	2

Headland *Henry County*   Elevation: 367 ft.   Latitude: 31° 21' N   Longitude: 85° 20' W

	JAN	FEB	MAR	APR	MAY	JUN	JUL	AUG	SEP	OCT	NOV	DEC	YEAR
Mean Maximum Temp. (°F)	58.3	62.8	70.5	77.7	84.7	90.1	91.8	91.2	87.6	78.8	69.4	62.0	77.1
Mean Temp. (°F)	47.1	50.8	58.4	65.1	72.9	78.6	80.5	79.6	75.6	65.5	57.1	50.3	65.1
Mean Minimum Temp. (°F)	36.1	38.8	46.3	52.4	60.6	67.0	69.2	68.1	63.6	52.2	44.8	38.6	53.1
Extreme Maximum Temp. (°F)	80	83	89	94	100	104	105	102	101	93	88	83	105
Extreme Minimum Temp. (°F)	0	10	12	30	41	50	59	57	40	30	15	5	0
Days Maximum Temp. ≥ 90°F	0	0	0	1	6	18	23	23	13	1	0	0	85
Days Maximum Temp. ≤ 32°F	0	0	0	0	0	0	0	0	0	0	0	0	0
Days Minimum Temp. ≤ 32°F	13	8	2	0	0	0	0	0	0	0	3	9	35
Days Minimum Temp. ≤ 0°F	0	0	0	0	0	0	0	0	0	0	0	0	0
Heating Degree Days (base 65°F)	552	400	228	83	7	0	0	0	3	79	256	456	2,064
Cooling Degree Days (base 65°F)	1	8	31	85	254	419	490	460	315	102	25	6	2,196
Mean Precipitation (in.)	6.48	5.37	6.44	3.95	4.36	5.07	6.19	4.51	4.07	3.29	4.07	4.18	57.98
Days With ≥ 0.1" Precipitation	8	7	8	5	6	8	10	7	6	4	5	6	80
Days With ≥ 1.0" Precipitation	2	2	2	1	1	2	2	1	1	1	1	1	17
Mean Snowfall (in.)	0.1	0.1	trace	0.0	0.0	0.0	0.0	0.0	0.0	0.0	0.0	trace	0.2
Days With ≥ 1.0" Snow Depth	0	0	0	0	0	0	0	0	0	0	0	0	0

Heflin *Cleburne County*   Elevation: 849 ft.   Latitude: 33° 39' N   Longitude: 85° 36' W

	JAN	FEB	MAR	APR	MAY	JUN	JUL	AUG	SEP	OCT	NOV	DEC	YEAR
Mean Maximum Temp. (°F)	50.9	56.0	64.8	73.1	79.7	86.3	89.8	89.0	83.9	73.9	63.9	54.8	72.2
Mean Temp. (°F)	39.7	43.4	51.3	58.7	66.4	74.1	78.2	77.2	71.6	59.7	50.5	43.3	59.5
Mean Minimum Temp. (°F)	28.4	30.7	37.8	44.2	53.0	61.9	66.6	65.3	59.3	45.4	37.1	31.7	46.8
Extreme Maximum Temp. (°F)	76	80	87	90	95	98	107	105	98	91	87	78	107
Extreme Minimum Temp. (°F)	-3	1	8	22	30	39	50	51	37	22	10	-10	-10
Days Maximum Temp. ≥ 90°F	0	0	0	0	1	8	17	15	6	0	0	0	47
Days Maximum Temp. ≤ 32°F	2	1	0	0	0	0	0	0	0	0	0	1	4
Days Minimum Temp. ≤ 32°F	21	17	10	3	0	0	0	0	0	3	11	17	82
Days Minimum Temp. ≤ 0°F	0	0	0	0	0	0	0	0	0	0	0	0	0
Heating Degree Days (base 65°F)	780	605	423	209	59	3	0	0	19	193	433	668	3,392
Cooling Degree Days (base 65°F)	0	0	6	26	116	293	429	392	219	37	3	1	1,522
Mean Precipitation (in.)	6.04	5.43	7.09	5.09	4.69	4.75	5.09	3.13	3.86	3.29	4.51	4.81	57.78
Days With ≥ 0.1" Precipitation	8	6	8	6	7	7	7	5	6	4	6	7	77
Days With ≥ 1.0" Precipitation	2	2	2	2	2	2	1	1	1	1	2	1	19
Mean Snowfall (in.)	0.8	0.2	0.6	0.2	0.0	0.0	0.0	0.0	0.0	trace	0.0	0.2	2.0
Days With ≥ 1.0" Snow Depth	0	0	0	0	0	0	0	0	0	0	0	0	0

Highland Home *Crenshaw County*   Elevation: 593 ft.   Latitude: 31° 57' N   Longitude: 86° 19' W

	JAN	FEB	MAR	APR	MAY	JUN	JUL	AUG	SEP	OCT	NOV	DEC	YEAR
Mean Maximum Temp. (°F)	56.1	61.1	69.0	76.1	82.9	88.3	90.7	90.1	86.7	77.7	68.1	60.1	75.6
Mean Temp. (°F)	45.3	49.3	56.7	63.4	70.9	77.1	79.9	79.3	75.3	65.2	56.1	49.0	64.0
Mean Minimum Temp. (°F)	34.4	37.5	44.4	50.6	58.9	65.9	69.1	68.5	63.8	52.6	44.0	37.7	52.3
Extreme Maximum Temp. (°F)	79	83	87	94	96	104	105	101	102	93	88	81	105
Extreme Minimum Temp. (°F)	-3	7	14	24	40	45	61	56	42	29	18	4	-3
Days Maximum Temp. ≥ 90°F	0	0	0	0	3	14	20	19	12	1	0	0	69
Days Maximum Temp. ≤ 32°F	1	0	0	0	0	0	0	0	0	0	0	0	1
Days Minimum Temp. ≤ 32°F	14	10	3	0	0	0	0	0	0	0	4	11	42
Days Minimum Temp. ≤ 0°F	0	0	0	0	0	0	0	0	0	0	0	0	0
Heating Degree Days (base 65°F)	608	440	274	114	15	0	0	0	6	89	280	498	2,324
Cooling Degree Days (base 65°F)	1	5	23	67	207	376	470	454	309	101	18	6	2,037
Mean Precipitation (in.)	5.54	5.53	7.02	4.39	4.28	4.92	4.93	4.31	3.95	2.89	4.45	4.53	56.74
Days With ≥ 0.1" Precipitation	8	7	8	6	6	7	9	7	5	4	6	6	79
Days With ≥ 1.0" Precipitation	2	2	2	1	1	2	1	1	1	1	1	2	17
Mean Snowfall (in.)	0.2	0.5	0.3	trace	0.0	0.0	0.0	0.0	0.0	0.0	0.0	trace	1.0
Days With ≥ 1.0" Snow Depth	0	0	0	0	0	0	0	0	0	0	0	0	0

Jasper *Walker County*　Elevation: 485 ft.　Latitude: 33° 54' N　Longitude: 87° 19' W

	JAN	FEB	MAR	APR	MAY	JUN	JUL	AUG	SEP	OCT	NOV	DEC	YEAR
Mean Maximum Temp. (°F)	51.1	56.2	65.8	73.8	79.7	86.6	89.9	89.6	84.5	74.1	63.3	55.5	72.5
Mean Temp. (°F)	39.8	43.7	51.9	59.4	67.1	74.7	78.7	78.0	72.2	60.5	50.3	43.9	60.0
Mean Minimum Temp. (°F)	28.5	31.1	38.0	45.0	54.4	62.7	67.5	66.3	59.8	46.9	37.3	32.3	47.5
Extreme Maximum Temp. (°F)	76	84	88	89	94	99	108	103	100	92	83	78	108
Extreme Minimum Temp. (°F)	-10	2	6	25	31	41	51	52	36	26	10	5	-10
Days Maximum Temp. ≥ 90°F	0	0	0	0	1	9	17	16	7	0	0	0	50
Days Maximum Temp. ≤ 32°F	2	1	0	0	0	0	0	0	0	0	0	0	3
Days Minimum Temp. ≤ 32°F	20	16	10	3	0	0	0	0	0	2	11	17	79
Days Minimum Temp. ≤ 0°F	0	0	0	0	0	0	0	0	0	0	0	0	0
Heating Degree Days (base 65°F)	775	596	407	193	51	2	0	0	17	176	437	648	3,302
Cooling Degree Days (base 65°F)	0	1	9	30	136	311	450	427	241	51	4	3	1,663
Mean Precipitation (in.)	5.96	5.08	6.68	5.21	5.27	4.60	5.10	3.16	4.22	3.99	4.41	5.93	59.61
Days With ≥ 0.1" Precipitation	9	7	8	6	7	7	8	6	6	5	7	8	84
Days With ≥ 1.0" Precipitation	2	2	2	2	2	2	2	1	1	1	1	2	20
Mean Snowfall (in.)	0.4	0.3	0.3	trace	0.0	0.0	0.0	0.0	0.0	0.0	0.0	trace	1.0
Days With ≥ 1.0" Snow Depth	0	0	0	0	0	0	0	0	0	0	0	0	0

Lafayette 2 W *Chambers County*　Elevation: 738 ft.　Latitude: 32° 54' N　Longitude: 85° 26' W

	JAN	FEB	MAR	APR	MAY	JUN	JUL	AUG	SEP	OCT	NOV	DEC	YEAR
Mean Maximum Temp. (°F)	55.2	60.4	69.1	76.4	82.5	88.5	90.5	89.8	85.5	76.3	66.7	58.6	75.0
Mean Temp. (°F)	44.0	47.9	55.9	62.6	69.7	76.4	79.2	78.5	73.7	63.2	54.4	46.9	62.7
Mean Minimum Temp. (°F)	32.7	35.5	42.6	48.8	56.9	64.3	67.9	67.0	61.9	50.1	42.0	35.2	50.4
Extreme Maximum Temp. (°F)	79	82	89	93	97	103	104	102	99	94	84	81	104
Extreme Minimum Temp. (°F)	-7	3	8	26	35	43	53	55	38	28	14	0	-7
Days Maximum Temp. ≥ 90°F	0	0	0	0	4	14	19	18	9	0	0	0	64
Days Maximum Temp. ≤ 32°F	1	0	0	0	0	0	0	0	0	0	0	0	1
Days Minimum Temp. ≤ 32°F	17	11	6	1	0	0	0	0	0	1	6	14	56
Days Minimum Temp. ≤ 0°F	0	0	0	0	0	0	0	0	0	0	0	0	0
Heating Degree Days (base 65°F)	646	477	292	123	24	1	0	0	8	122	324	556	2,573
Cooling Degree Days (base 65°F)	0	3	15	51	176	350	449	425	257	72	10	2	1,810
Mean Precipitation (in.)	5.62	5.56	6.71	4.97	4.60	4.26	5.66	3.79	3.81	3.06	3.99	5.13	57.16
Days With ≥ 0.1" Precipitation	8	7	8	6	7	7	9	7	6	5	6	7	83
Days With ≥ 1.0" Precipitation	2	2	2	1	1	1	2	1	1	1	1	2	17
Mean Snowfall (in.)	0.2	0.1	trace	trace	0.0	0.0	0.0	0.0	0.0	0.0	trace	trace	0.3
Days With ≥ 1.0" Snow Depth	0	0	0	0	0	0	0	0	0	0	0	0	0

Livingston *Sumter County*　Elevation: 127 ft.　Latitude: 32° 35' N　Longitude: 88° 11' W

	JAN	FEB	MAR	APR	MAY	JUN	JUL	AUG	SEP	OCT	NOV	DEC	YEAR
Mean Maximum Temp. (°F)	55.6	61.2	69.2	76.6	83.2	89.8	92.2	91.6	87.4	77.9	68.2	59.6	76.1
Mean Temp. (°F)	43.9	48.2	55.9	62.9	70.6	77.7	80.7	79.8	74.8	63.8	54.4	47.3	63.3
Mean Minimum Temp. (°F)	32.1	35.1	42.6	49.2	57.9	65.6	69.1	68.0	62.2	49.7	40.5	35.0	50.6
Extreme Maximum Temp. (°F)	80	85	89	95	97	102	106	105	103	95	87	88	106
Extreme Minimum Temp. (°F)	-3	7	16	27	36	42	56	52	35	27	13	2	-3
Days Maximum Temp. ≥ 90°F	0	0	0	0	4	17	23	23	12	1	0	0	80
Days Maximum Temp. ≤ 32°F	1	0	0	0	0	0	0	0	0	0	0	0	1
Days Minimum Temp. ≤ 32°F	17	12	5	1	0	0	0	0	0	1	7	14	57
Days Minimum Temp. ≤ 0°F	0	0	0	0	0	0	0	0	0	0	0	0	0
Heating Degree Days (base 65°F)	649	472	295	123	15	0	0	0	8	114	325	547	2,548
Cooling Degree Days (base 65°F)	1	6	20	67	202	396	501	480	304	87	13	5	2,082
Mean Precipitation (in.)	5.58	4.78	6.30	5.27	4.47	4.02	5.45	3.44	3.32	3.91	4.49	5.05	56.08
Days With ≥ 0.1" Precipitation	7	6	7	5	6	6	7	5	4	3	5	6	67
Days With ≥ 1.0" Precipitation	2	2	3	2	1	1	2	1	1	1	2	1	19
Mean Snowfall (in.)	0.4	trace	0.2	0.1	0.0	0.0	0.0	0.0	0.0	0.0	0.0	trace	0.7
Days With ≥ 1.0" Snow Depth	0	0	0	0	0	0	0	0	0	0	0	0	0

Marion Junction 2 NE *Dallas County*　Elevation: 200 ft.　Latitude: 32° 28' N　Longitude: 87° 14' W

	JAN	FEB	MAR	APR	MAY	JUN	JUL	AUG	SEP	OCT	NOV	DEC	YEAR
Mean Maximum Temp. (°F)	54.6	59.3	67.5	74.9	81.8	88.1	90.8	90.1	86.0	76.3	66.6	58.2	74.5
Mean Temp. (°F)	43.7	47.6	55.4	62.3	70.2	77.2	80.2	79.4	74.4	63.3	53.9	46.8	62.9
Mean Minimum Temp. (°F)	32.8	35.8	43.2	49.7	58.5	66.2	69.6	68.6	62.8	50.4	41.1	35.3	51.2
Extreme Maximum Temp. (°F)	79	82	87	90	95	102	104	100	100	92	86	83	104
Extreme Minimum Temp. (°F)	-1	9	14	30	39	40	58	56	38	29	16	0	-1
Days Maximum Temp. ≥ 90°F	0	0	0	0	3	13	21	18	10	0	0	0	65
Days Maximum Temp. ≤ 32°F	1	0	0	0	0	0	0	0	0	0	0	0	1
Days Minimum Temp. ≤ 32°F	17	12	5	0	0	0	0	0	0	0	7	14	55
Days Minimum Temp. ≤ 0°F	0	0	0	0	0	0	0	0	0	0	0	0	0
Heating Degree Days (base 65°F)	654	488	310	132	21	0	0	0	9	121	340	562	2,637
Cooling Degree Days (base 65°F)	1	3	17	55	193	378	485	458	290	81	13	4	1,978
Mean Precipitation (in.)	5.79	4.76	6.50	4.79	4.16	4.55	5.12	3.43	3.83	3.09	4.18	4.99	55.19
Days With ≥ 0.1" Precipitation	9	7	8	6	7	7	8	6	6	5	7	7	83
Days With ≥ 1.0" Precipitation	2	1	2	2	1	2	2	1	1	1	2	2	19
Mean Snowfall (in.)	trace	trace	trace	0.0	0.0	0.0	0.0	0.0	0.0	0.0	0.0	trace	trace
Days With ≥ 1.0" Snow Depth	0	0	0	0	0	0	0	0	0	0	0	0	0

Moulton 2 *Lawrence County*   Elevation: 643 ft.   Latitude: 34° 29' N   Longitude: 87° 18' W

	JAN	FEB	MAR	APR	MAY	JUN	JUL	AUG	SEP	OCT	NOV	DEC	YEAR
Mean Maximum Temp. (°F)	50.8	56.1	65.1	74.0	80.6	87.0	90.3	90.1	84.8	74.3	63.2	54.8	72.6
Mean Temp. (°F)	41.0	45.1	53.3	61.5	69.0	76.1	79.7	78.8	73.2	61.8	52.0	44.7	61.3
Mean Minimum Temp. (°F)	31.0	34.1	41.6	48.8	57.4	65.1	69.0	67.4	61.5	49.3	40.8	34.6	50.0
Extreme Maximum Temp. (°F)	77	85	86	90	94	101	106	103	102	92	84	79	106
Extreme Minimum Temp. (°F)	-13	0	8	24	33	44	53	50	37	26	12	-5	-13
Days Maximum Temp. ≥ 90°F	0	0	0	0	2	10	18	18	8	0	0	0	56
Days Maximum Temp. ≤ 32°F	2	1	0	0	0	0	0	0	0	0	0	1	4
Days Minimum Temp. ≤ 32°F	18	14	7	2	0	0	0	0	0	1	8	14	64
Days Minimum Temp. ≤ 0°F	0	0	0	0	0	0	0	0	0	0	0	0	0
Heating Degree Days (base 65°F)	739	557	367	155	32	1	0	0	14	149	390	623	3,027
Cooling Degree Days (base 65°F)	0	2	14	56	170	347	471	440	258	59	6	2	1,825
Mean Precipitation (in.)	5.72	4.99	6.67	4.78	5.47	4.61	4.17	3.29	4.28	3.89	5.16	5.85	58.88
Days With ≥ 0.1" Precipitation	9	8	9	7	8	8	7	6	6	5	7	8	88
Days With ≥ 1.0" Precipitation	2	2	2	2	2	1	1	1	1	1	2	2	19
Mean Snowfall (in.)	1.4	0.9	0.4	trace	0.0	0.0	0.0	0.0	0.0	trace	trace	0.2	2.9
Days With ≥ 1.0" Snow Depth	1	1	0	0	0	0	0	0	0	0	0	0	2

Muscle Shoals Regional Airport *Colbert County*   Elevation: 538 ft.   Latitude: 34° 45' N   Longitude: 87° 36' W

	JAN	FEB	MAR	APR	MAY	JUN	JUL	AUG	SEP	OCT	NOV	DEC	YEAR
Mean Maximum Temp. (°F)	48.6	54.3	63.6	72.8	79.6	87.3	90.6	89.9	83.8	73.1	62.4	53.1	71.6
Mean Temp. (°F)	39.3	44.0	52.6	61.0	68.4	76.4	80.1	79.0	72.9	61.2	51.7	43.5	60.8
Mean Minimum Temp. (°F)	30.0	33.6	41.6	49.1	57.2	65.4	69.6	68.0	62.0	49.3	40.9	33.9	50.1
Extreme Maximum Temp. (°F)	78	80	85	92	94	101	105	104	101	91	82	76	105
Extreme Minimum Temp. (°F)	-11	8	12	27	36	44	53	53	39	28	13	-5	-11
Days Maximum Temp. ≥ 90°F	0	0	0	0	2	12	19	17	7	0	0	0	57
Days Maximum Temp. ≤ 32°F	3	1	0	0	0	0	0	0	0	0	0	1	5
Days Minimum Temp. ≤ 32°F	20	14	5	1	0	0	0	0	0	0	7	15	62
Days Minimum Temp. ≤ 0°F	0	0	0	0	0	0	0	0	0	0	0	0	0
Heating Degree Days (base 65°F)	789	588	386	164	36	0	0	0	18	158	399	660	3,198
Cooling Degree Days (base 65°F)	*0*	*1*	10	52	*157*	*368*	*501*	467	*260*	*52*	6	*1*	1,875
Mean Precipitation (in.)	4.67	4.60	6.29	4.51	5.49	4.75	4.51	3.05	4.48	3.43	5.01	5.61	56.40
Days With ≥ 0.1" Precipitation	7	6	8	7	7	7	7	5	6	5	7	8	80
Days With ≥ 1.0" Precipitation	1	1	2	1	2	2	1	1	1	1	2	2	17
Mean Snowfall (in.)	0.9	0.9	0.3	trace	*trace*	*trace*	*0.0*	*0.0*	*0.0*	*0.0*	*trace*	*0.2*	*2.3*
Days With ≥ 1.0" Snow Depth	1	1	0	0	*0*	*0*	*0*	*0*	*0*	*0*	*0*	*0*	*2*

Oneonta *Blount County*   Elevation: 869 ft.   Latitude: 33° 57' N   Longitude: 86° 28' W

	JAN	FEB	MAR	APR	MAY	JUN	JUL	AUG	SEP	OCT	NOV	DEC	YEAR
Mean Maximum Temp. (°F)	50.2	55.1	63.8	72.2	79.3	85.8	89.4	88.8	83.7	73.4	63.1	54.3	71.6
Mean Temp. (°F)	39.8	43.5	51.6	59.3	67.3	74.7	78.6	77.8	72.1	60.4	51.2	43.4	60.0
Mean Minimum Temp. (°F)	29.4	32.0	39.4	46.3	55.2	63.5	67.8	66.7	60.4	47.4	39.2	32.5	48.3
Extreme Maximum Temp. (°F)	75	82	87	89	93	100	105	103	100	91	85	77	105
Extreme Minimum Temp. (°F)	-8	0	8	24	33	41	52	51	38	25	11	-3	-8
Days Maximum Temp. ≥ 90°F	0	0	0	0	1	8	17	15	7	0	0	0	48
Days Maximum Temp. ≤ 32°F	2	1	0	0	0	0	0	0	0	0	0	1	4
Days Minimum Temp. ≤ 32°F	20	16	9	2	0	0	0	0	0	2	9	17	75
Days Minimum Temp. ≤ 0°F	0	0	0	0	0	0	0	0	0	0	0	0	0
Heating Degree Days (base 65°F)	774	601	415	201	50	3	0	0	20	179	415	665	3,323
Cooling Degree Days (base 65°F)	0	1	8	33	133	307	440	408	231	46	5	2	1,614
Mean Precipitation (in.)	6.02	5.21	6.36	5.31	4.77	4.66	5.31	3.26	4.46	3.68	4.46	4.95	58.45
Days With ≥ 0.1" Precipitation	9	7	8	7	7	7	7	6	6	5	7	8	84
Days With ≥ 1.0" Precipitation	2	2	2	2	1	1	1	1	1	1	1	1	16
Mean Snowfall (in.)	0.9	0.3	0.7	0.0	0.0	0.0	0.0	0.0	0.0	0.0	trace	0.1	2.0
Days With ≥ 1.0" Snow Depth	0	0	0	0	0	0	0	0	0	0	0	0	0

Robertsdale 5 NE *Baldwin County*   Elevation: 173 ft.   Latitude: 30° 38' N   Longitude: 87° 39' W

	JAN	FEB	MAR	APR	MAY	JUN	JUL	AUG	SEP	OCT	NOV	DEC	YEAR
Mean Maximum Temp. (°F)	60.8	64.5	70.9	77.1	83.9	88.8	90.6	90.3	87.3	79.6	70.9	63.7	77.4
Mean Temp. (°F)	49.7	52.8	59.3	65.3	72.6	78.7	81.0	80.6	77.0	67.3	58.9	52.4	66.3
Mean Minimum Temp. (°F)	38.7	41.1	47.6	53.6	61.3	68.4	71.3	70.8	66.6	55.0	46.8	41.0	55.2
Extreme Maximum Temp. (°F)	80	83	86	94	98	102	101	102	99	92	88	82	102
Extreme Minimum Temp. (°F)	3	12	20	31	41	49	57	57	45	31	21	9	3
Days Maximum Temp. ≥ 90°F	0	0	0	0	3	14	21	20	11	1	0	0	70
Days Maximum Temp. ≤ 32°F	0	0	0	0	0	0	0	0	0	0	0	0	0
Days Minimum Temp. ≤ 32°F	11	6	2	0	0	0	0	0	0	0	2	8	29
Days Minimum Temp. ≤ 0°F	0	0	0	0	0	0	0	0	0	0	0	0	0
Heating Degree Days (base 65°F)	476	348	205	75	6	0	0	0	3	59	216	399	1,787
Cooling Degree Days (base 65°F)	6	11	32	80	243	411	501	493	355	134	36	15	2,317
Mean Precipitation (in.)	6.19	5.15	7.10	4.53	5.15	5.63	8.41	6.97	6.25	3.89	5.38	4.06	68.71
Days With ≥ 0.1" Precipitation	8	6	7	5	6	7	11	10	7	4	6	6	83
Days With ≥ 1.0" Precipitation	2	2	2	1	2	2	3	2	2	1	2	1	22
Mean Snowfall (in.)	trace	0.1	trace	0.0	0.0	0.0	0.0	0.0	0.0	0.0	0.0	trace	0.1
Days With ≥ 1.0" Snow Depth	0	0	0	0	0	0	0	0	0	0	0	0	0

Russellville 2 *Franklin County*   Elevation: 830 ft.   Latitude: 34° 31' N   Longitude: 87° 44' W

	JAN	FEB	MAR	APR	MAY	JUN	JUL	AUG	SEP	OCT	NOV	DEC	YEAR
Mean Maximum Temp. (°F)	49.1	53.7	62.6	71.4	78.6	85.5	89.0	88.7	83.4	72.7	62.0	53.1	70.8
Mean Temp. (°F)	38.5	41.9	50.0	57.9	65.8	73.4	77.4	76.5	70.8	58.9	49.7	42.1	58.6
Mean Minimum Temp. (°F)	27.6	29.9	37.4	44.3	53.0	61.2	65.8	64.4	58.2	45.1	37.2	30.9	46.3
Extreme Maximum Temp. (°F)	78	84	84	88	93	99	103	103	100	91	84	77	103
Extreme Minimum Temp. (°F)	-14	-1	5	22	31	39	45	50	35	24	10	-7	-14
Days Maximum Temp. ≥ 90°F	0	0	0	0	1	7	15	14	6	0	0	0	43
Days Maximum Temp. ≤ 32°F	3	2	0	0	0	0	0	0	0	0	0	1	6
Days Minimum Temp. ≤ 32°F	21	17	11	4	0	0	0	0	0	3	11	18	85
Days Minimum Temp. ≤ 0°F	0	0	0	0	0	0	0	0	0	0	0	0	0
Heating Degree Days (base 65°F)	816	648	464	235	70	5	0	0	27	215	457	706	3,643
Cooling Degree Days (base 65°F)	0	1	6	26	108	275	405	377	208	35	3	1	1,445
Mean Precipitation (in.)	5.35	4.81	6.45	5.07	5.91	4.22	4.61	2.99	4.13	3.72	4.87	5.34	57.47
Days With ≥ 0.1" Precipitation	7	6	8	6	7	7	7	5	5	5	7	7	77
Days With ≥ 1.0" Precipitation	1	1	2	2	2	1	1	1	1	1	2	2	17
Mean Snowfall (in.)	0.6	0.2	trace	0.0	0.0	0.0	0.0	0.0	0.0	0.0	trace	0.1	0.9
Days With ≥ 1.0" Snow Depth	*0*	0	0	0	0	0	0	0	0	0	0	0	*0*

Saint Bernard *Cullman County*   Elevation: 797 ft.   Latitude: 34° 10' N   Longitude: 86° 49' W

	JAN	FEB	MAR	APR	MAY	JUN	JUL	AUG	SEP	OCT	NOV	DEC	YEAR
Mean Maximum Temp. (°F)	50.8	55.9	65.0	73.7	80.3	86.7	90.4	89.9	84.6	74.3	63.9	54.8	72.5
Mean Temp. (°F)	39.3	43.3	51.5	59.3	67.0	74.0	77.9	77.1	71.2	59.9	50.5	42.7	59.5
Mean Minimum Temp. (°F)	27.6	30.5	37.8	44.9	53.6	61.2	65.4	64.2	57.8	45.3	37.0	30.6	46.3
Extreme Maximum Temp. (°F)	76	85	88	90	95	100	105	103	101	92	87	80	105
Extreme Minimum Temp. (°F)	-10	1	5	21	32	40	50	48	34	21	10	-5	-10
Days Maximum Temp. ≥ 90°F	0	0	0	0	2	10	18	17	7	0	0	0	54
Days Maximum Temp. ≤ 32°F	2	1	0	0	0	0	0	0	0	0	0	1	4
Days Minimum Temp. ≤ 32°F	21	17	10	4	0	0	0	0	0	3	11	18	84
Days Minimum Temp. ≤ 0°F	0	0	0	0	0	0	0	0	0	0	0	0	0
Heating Degree Days (base 65°F)	792	609	420	197	48	3	0	0	21	187	430	686	3,393
Cooling Degree Days (base 65°F)	0	1	7	32	119	281	417	392	206	36	3	1	1,495
Mean Precipitation (in.)	5.84	5.46	6.57	5.01	5.14	4.57	4.92	3.42	4.93	3.91	4.59	5.76	60.12
Days With ≥ 0.1" Precipitation	8	7	*8*	6	7	7	7	6	6	5	6	8	*81*
Days With ≥ 1.0" Precipitation	2	2	2	2	2	1	1	1	2	1	1	1	18
Mean Snowfall (in.)	0.5	0.2	0.3	trace	0.0	0.0	0.0	0.0	0.0	0.0	trace	trace	1.0
Days With ≥ 1.0" Snow Depth	0	0	0	0	0	0	0	0	0	0	0	0	0

Sand Mountain Substation *Dekalb County*   Elevation: 1,194 ft.   Latitude: 34° 17' N   Longitude: 85° 58' W

	JAN	FEB	MAR	APR	MAY	JUN	JUL	AUG	SEP	OCT	NOV	DEC	YEAR
Mean Maximum Temp. (°F)	48.2	53.1	61.8	70.4	77.3	84.1	87.6	87.2	82.0	71.8	61.1	52.0	69.7
Mean Temp. (°F)	38.6	42.5	50.8	58.6	66.4	73.6	77.1	76.3	70.7	59.6	50.2	42.2	58.9
Mean Minimum Temp. (°F)	28.9	31.8	39.7	46.9	55.5	63.2	66.6	65.3	59.3	47.4	39.3	32.3	48.0
Extreme Maximum Temp. (°F)	74	79	85	88	90	97	103	103	97	89	83	76	103
Extreme Minimum Temp. (°F)	-13	0	11	24	35	41	51	50	35	23	10	-4	-13
Days Maximum Temp. ≥ 90°F	0	0	0	0	0	5	12	9	4	0	0	0	30
Days Maximum Temp. ≤ 32°F	3	1	0	0	0	0	0	0	0	0	0	1	5
Days Minimum Temp. ≤ 32°F	19	15	8	2	0	0	0	0	0	2	9	17	72
Days Minimum Temp. ≤ 0°F	0	0	0	0	0	0	0	0	0	0	0	0	0
Heating Degree Days (base 65°F)	812	629	439	215	60	4	0	0	25	193	441	701	3,519
Cooling Degree Days (base 65°F)	0	0	6	28	111	276	397	365	197	37	3	1	1,421
Mean Precipitation (in.)	5.46	5.22	6.11	4.82	4.38	4.05	4.51	3.50	4.43	3.30	4.36	5.15	55.29
Days With ≥ 0.1" Precipitation	9	7	9	7	7	7	7	6	6	5	7	8	85
Days With ≥ 1.0" Precipitation	1	2	2	2	1	1	1	1	1	1	1	2	16
Mean Snowfall (in.)	0.8	0.4	trace	0.0	0.0	0.0	0.0	0.0	0.0	0.0	trace	trace	1.2
Days With ≥ 1.0" Snow Depth	0	0	0	0	0	0	0	0	0	0	0	0	0

Selma *Dallas County*   Elevation: 144 ft.   Latitude: 32° 25' N   Longitude: 87° 01' W

	JAN	FEB	MAR	APR	MAY	JUN	JUL	AUG	SEP	OCT	NOV	DEC	YEAR
Mean Maximum Temp. (°F)	57.4	62.2	70.3	77.2	84.1	89.9	92.1	91.7	87.6	78.2	68.5	60.7	76.7
Mean Temp. (°F)	47.6	51.1	58.5	65.0	72.7	79.2	82.0	81.4	76.8	66.2	56.7	49.8	65.6
Mean Minimum Temp. (°F)	37.5	40.0	46.7	52.6	61.2	68.5	71.7	71.0	66.0	54.0	44.8	38.9	54.4
Extreme Maximum Temp. (°F)	80	83	88	93	96	103	107	103	102	93	89	83	107
Extreme Minimum Temp. (°F)	0	12	18	31	42	42	61	57	46	33	18	6	0
Days Maximum Temp. ≥ 90°F	0	0	0	1	5	17	24	22	13	1	0	0	83
Days Maximum Temp. ≤ 32°F	0	0	0	0	0	0	0	0	0	0	0	0	0
Days Minimum Temp. ≤ 32°F	11	7	2	0	0	0	0	0	0	0	3	10	33
Days Minimum Temp. ≤ 0°F	0	0	0	0	0	0	0	0	0	0	0	0	0
Heating Degree Days (base 65°F)	539	390	227	84	7	0	0	0	3	71	263	474	2,058
Cooling Degree Days (base 65°F)	3	7	29	78	247	435	536	515	351	111	18	5	2,335
Mean Precipitation (in.)	5.61	4.97	6.72	4.33	3.85	4.21	4.40	3.82	3.83	2.78	4.03	4.58	53.13
Days With ≥ 0.1" Precipitation	8	7	7	5	6	7	8	6	5	4	6	7	76
Days With ≥ 1.0" Precipitation	2	2	2	2	1	1	1	1	1	1	1	1	16
Mean Snowfall (in.)	0.3	trace	0.0	trace	0.0	0.0	0.0	0.0	0.0	0.0	0.0	trace	0.3
Days With ≥ 1.0" Snow Depth	0	0	0	0	0	0	0	0	0	0	0	0	0

Sylacauga 4 NE *Talladega County*   Elevation: 488 ft.   Latitude: 33° 12' N   Longitude: 86° 13' W

	JAN	FEB	MAR	APR	MAY	JUN	JUL	AUG	SEP	OCT	NOV	DEC	YEAR
Mean Maximum Temp. (°F)	55.6	60.1	68.0	75.3	82.5	87.9	90.9	90.5	85.8	76.6	66.6	58.1	74.8
Mean Temp. (°F)	43.6	47.1	54.4	60.7	68.8	75.3	78.6	77.9	72.7	62.1	52.7	46.0	61.6
Mean Minimum Temp. (°F)	31.7	34.0	40.8	46.0	55.0	62.6	66.2	65.2	59.5	47.6	38.8	33.8	48.4
Extreme Maximum Temp. (°F)	81	81	90	91	99	100	102	104	98	92	86	79	104
Extreme Minimum Temp. (°F)	-4	5	10	25	33	42	51	48	35	23	14	3	-4
Days Maximum Temp. ≥ 90°F	0	0	0	0	3	12	20	19	9	1	0	0	64
Days Maximum Temp. ≤ 32°F	1	0	0	0	0	0	0	0	0	0	0	0	1
Days Minimum Temp. ≤ 32°F	18	14	8	3	0	0	0	0	0	3	10	15	71
Days Minimum Temp. ≤ 0°F	0	0	0	0	0	0	0	0	0	0	0	0	0
Heating Degree Days (base 65°F)	656	502	335	171	33	2	0	0	15	144	372	586	2,816
Cooling Degree Days (base 65°F)	0	2	14	43	157	322	436	405	236	56	7	3	1,681
Mean Precipitation (in.)	5.72	5.39	6.16	4.54	3.76	4.44	5.15	3.96	4.13	3.38	4.53	5.18	56.34
Days With ≥ 0.1" Precipitation	8	7	8	6	7	7	8	7	6	5	6	7	82
Days With ≥ 1.0" Precipitation	2	2	2	2	1	1	2	1	1	1	2	2	19
Mean Snowfall (in.)	0.3	0.1	0.4	0.1	0.0	0.0	0.0	0.0	0.0	trace	0.0	trace	0.9
Days With ≥ 1.0" Snow Depth	0	0	0	0	0	0	0	0	0	0	0	0	0

Thomasville *Clarke County*   Elevation: 403 ft.   Latitude: 31° 32' N   Longitude: 87° 53' W

	JAN	FEB	MAR	APR	MAY	JUN	JUL	AUG	SEP	OCT	NOV	DEC	YEAR
Mean Maximum Temp. (°F)	57.2	61.9	69.9	77.0	83.3	89.2	91.4	91.2	87.5	78.2	68.2	60.3	76.3
Mean Temp. (°F)	45.7	49.5	57.0	63.9	71.4	77.9	80.6	80.2	75.7	65.1	55.7	48.7	64.3
Mean Minimum Temp. (°F)	34.2	36.9	44.1	50.8	59.3	66.6	69.7	69.1	63.9	52.1	43.2	37.0	52.2
Extreme Maximum Temp. (°F)	79	82	89	94	97	102	104	102	104	96	88	82	104
Extreme Minimum Temp. (°F)	-1	9	14	28	41	46	57	56	42	29	16	4	-1
Days Maximum Temp. ≥ 90°F	0	0	0	0	4	16	23	22	13	2	0	0	80
Days Maximum Temp. ≤ 32°F	0	0	0	0	0	0	0	0	0	0	0	0	0
Days Minimum Temp. ≤ 32°F	15	11	4	0	0	0	0	0	0	0	5	13	48
Days Minimum Temp. ≤ 0°F	0	0	0	0	0	0	0	0	0	0	0	0	0
Heating Degree Days (base 65°F)	594	438	266	106	13	0	0	0	6	91	293	507	2,314
Cooling Degree Days (base 65°F)	2	7	25	75	223	403	500	489	331	106	21	8	2,190
Mean Precipitation (in.)	6.19	5.13	7.09	4.63	4.79	4.90	6.17	3.96	4.08	3.00	5.09	5.07	60.10
Days With ≥ 0.1" Precipitation	8	7	7	6	7	7	9	6	5	4	6	7	79
Days With ≥ 1.0" Precipitation	2	2	2	2	2	2	2	1	1	1	2	2	21
Mean Snowfall (in.)	trace	trace	0.4	0.0	0.0	0.0	0.0	0.0	0.0	0.0	0.0	trace	0.4
Days With ≥ 1.0" Snow Depth	0	0	0	0	0	0	0	0	0	0	0	0	0

Thorsby Exp. Station *Chilton County*   Elevation: 679 ft.   Latitude: 32° 55' N   Longitude: 86° 40' W

	JAN	FEB	MAR	APR	MAY	JUN	JUL	AUG	SEP	OCT	NOV	DEC	YEAR
Mean Maximum Temp. (°F)	53.4	58.5	66.8	74.7	81.3	87.6	89.9	89.1	84.7	75.3	65.1	57.2	73.6
Mean Temp. (°F)	43.1	47.1	54.9	62.1	69.6	76.5	79.2	78.3	73.5	63.0	53.5	46.5	62.3
Mean Minimum Temp. (°F)	32.6	35.5	43.0	49.4	57.9	65.4	68.6	67.4	62.3	50.6	41.8	35.8	50.9
Extreme Maximum Temp. (°F)	78	80	89	91	97	99	104	102	100	92	85	81	104
Extreme Minimum Temp. (°F)	-4	5	12	28	39	44	57	55	42	31	15	1	-4
Days Maximum Temp. ≥ 90°F	0	0	0	0	2	11	17	15	7	0	0	0	52
Days Maximum Temp. ≤ 32°F	1	0	0	0	0	0	0	0	0	0	0	0	1
Days Minimum Temp. ≤ 32°F	17	11	4	1	0	0	0	0	0	0	6	13	52
Days Minimum Temp. ≤ 0°F	0	0	0	0	0	0	0	0	0	0	0	0	0
Heating Degree Days (base 65°F)	674	503	319	133	20	0	0	0	9	115	348	569	2,690
Cooling Degree Days (base 65°F)	0	2	13	43	168	355	462	435	267	64	8	3	1,820
Mean Precipitation (in.)	6.21	5.29	6.89	5.04	4.17	4.17	5.42	3.98	4.20	3.18	4.42	4.79	57.76
Days With ≥ 0.1" Precipitation	9	7	8	6	7	6	8	6	6	4	6	6	79
Days With ≥ 1.0" Precipitation	2	2	3	2	1	1	2	1	1	1	2	1	19
Mean Snowfall (in.)	trace	trace	0.5	0.1	0.0	0.0	0.0	0.0	0.0	0.0	0.0	trace	0.6
Days With ≥ 1.0" Snow Depth	0	0	0	0	0	0	0	0	0	0	0	0	0

Troy *Pike County*   Elevation: 541 ft.   Latitude: 31° 48' N   Longitude: 85° 58' W

	JAN	FEB	MAR	APR	MAY	JUN	JUL	AUG	SEP	OCT	NOV	DEC	YEAR
Mean Maximum Temp. (°F)	57.7	62.1	69.9	76.9	83.2	88.6	90.6	90.1	86.6	77.5	68.2	60.5	76.0
Mean Temp. (°F)	47.1	50.6	57.7	64.2	71.6	77.7	80.4	80.0	76.1	65.9	56.7	49.9	64.8
Mean Minimum Temp. (°F)	36.5	39.0	45.5	51.5	59.9	66.8	70.1	69.7	65.4	54.2	45.2	39.2	53.6
Extreme Maximum Temp. (°F)	79	82	88	92	98	102	103	100	102	91	87	81	103
Extreme Minimum Temp. (°F)	-1	10	13	30	38	48	58	57	42	31	17	5	-1
Days Maximum Temp. ≥ 90°F	0	0	0	0	3	14	20	19	9	1	0	0	66
Days Maximum Temp. ≤ 32°F	0	0	0	0	0	0	0	0	0	0	0	0	0
Days Minimum Temp. ≤ 32°F	12	8	3	0	0	0	0	0	0	0	4	9	36
Days Minimum Temp. ≤ 0°F	0	0	0	0	0	0	0	0	0	0	0	0	0
Heating Degree Days (base 65°F)	549	406	244	95	11	0	0	0	3	76	264	468	2,116
Cooling Degree Days (base 65°F)	1	7	23	69	218	393	494	480	331	107	19	5	2,147
Mean Precipitation (in.)	5.11	4.93	6.66	4.14	3.86	4.96	5.85	3.78	3.48	3.06	4.38	4.36	54.57
Days With ≥ 0.1" Precipitation	7	6	7	5	6	7	9	6	5	4	5	6	73
Days With ≥ 1.0" Precipitation	1	2	2	1	1	2	2	1	1	1	1	1	16
Mean Snowfall (in.)	0.1	0.4	0.1	0.0	0.0	0.0	0.0	0.0	0.0	0.0	0.0	0.1	0.7
Days With ≥ 1.0" Snow Depth	0	0	0	0	0	0	0	0	0	0	0	0	0

Tuscaloosa Municipal Airport *Tuscaloosa County*   Elevation: 167 ft.   Latitude: 33° 13' N   Longitude: 87° 37' W

	JAN	FEB	MAR	APR	MAY	JUN	JUL	AUG	SEP	OCT	NOV	DEC	YEAR
Mean Maximum Temp. (°F)	54.1	59.6	68.3	76.0	82.7	88.9	92.0	91.4	86.7	76.9	66.0	58.0	75.1
Mean Temp. (°F)	44.0	48.2	56.2	63.3	71.3	78.2	81.8	81.2	75.8	64.4	54.2	47.5	63.9
Mean Minimum Temp. (°F)	33.8	36.8	44.1	50.7	59.9	67.4	71.7	70.9	64.9	52.0	42.5	37.0	52.6
Extreme Maximum Temp. (°F)	79	84	90	94	96	101	105	104	102	94	86	82	105
Extreme Minimum Temp. (°F)	-1	7	12	29	36	45	58	56	42	30	15	2	-1
Days Maximum Temp. ≥ 90°F	0	0	0	0	4	15	22	22	11	1	0	0	75
Days Maximum Temp. ≤ 32°F	1	0	0	0	0	0	0	0	0	0	0	0	1
Days Minimum Temp. ≤ 32°F	16	11	4	0	0	0	0	0	0	0	6	13	50
Days Minimum Temp. ≤ 0°F	0	0	0	0	0	0	0	0	0	0	0	0	0
Heating Degree Days (base 65°F)	646	470	288	113	16	0	0	0	5	100	330	540	2,508
Cooling Degree Days (base 65°F)	2	5	23	70	228	411	540	519	337	96	15	6	2,252
Mean Precipitation (in.)	5.64	4.99	6.33	5.01	4.67	4.23	5.52	4.00	3.53	3.59	4.69	4.92	57.12
Days With ≥ 0.1" Precipitation	8	7	8	6	7	6	8	6	5	5	7	7	80
Days With ≥ 1.0" Precipitation	2	2	2	2	2	1	2	1	1	1	2	1	19
Mean Snowfall (in.)	0.3	trace	0.2	trace	trace	0.0	0.0	0.0	0.0	0.0	trace	trace	0.5
Days With ≥ 1.0" Snow Depth	0	0	0	0	0	0	0	0	0	0	0	0	0

Union Springs 9 S *Bullock County*   Elevation: 439 ft.   Latitude: 32° 01' N   Longitude: 85° 45' W

	JAN	FEB	MAR	APR	MAY	JUN	JUL	AUG	SEP	OCT	NOV	DEC	YEAR
Mean Maximum Temp. (°F)	56.2	60.9	68.7	76.0	82.7	88.6	90.8	90.1	86.4	77.2	68.0	59.9	75.5
Mean Temp. (°F)	45.1	48.7	55.9	62.7	70.3	77.5	80.3	79.4	75.1	64.4	55.4	48.2	63.6
Mean Minimum Temp. (°F)	34.0	36.4	43.1	49.3	57.9	66.3	69.8	68.7	63.8	51.6	42.8	36.5	51.7
Extreme Maximum Temp. (°F)	80	83	90	92	96	104	104	101	100	92	88	83	104
Extreme Minimum Temp. (°F)	-2	8	15	29	39	44	60	56	43	29	16	5	-2
Days Maximum Temp. ≥ 90°F	0	0	0	0	3	14	21	19	10	1	0	0	68
Days Maximum Temp. ≤ 32°F	1	0	0	0	0	0	0	0	0	0	0	0	1
Days Minimum Temp. ≤ 32°F	16	12	5	1	0	0	0	0	0	0	6	13	53
Days Minimum Temp. ≤ 0°F	0	0	0	0	0	0	0	0	0	0	0	0	0
Heating Degree Days (base 65°F)	614	460	294	126	18	0	0	0	6	100	300	519	2,437
Cooling Degree Days (base 65°F)	2	6	19	57	188	386	489	457	301	92	19	4	2,020
Mean Precipitation (in.)	5.41	4.84	6.62	4.22	4.16	5.26	5.42	3.70	4.12	3.15	4.50	4.59	55.99
Days With ≥ 0.1" Precipitation	8	6	7	5	6	7	8	7	6	4	5	6	75
Days With ≥ 1.0" Precipitation	1	2	2	1	1	1	1	1	2	1	1	1	15
Mean Snowfall (in.)	0.3	0.5	0.2	0.0	0.0	0.0	0.0	0.0	0.0	0.0	0.0	0.2	1.2
Days With ≥ 1.0" Snow Depth	0	0	0	0	0	0	0	0	0	0	0	0	0

Valley Head *Dekalb County*   Elevation: 1,059 ft.   Latitude: 34° 34' N   Longitude: 85° 37' W

	JAN	FEB	MAR	APR	MAY	JUN	JUL	AUG	SEP	OCT	NOV	DEC	YEAR
Mean Maximum Temp. (°F)	47.7	52.6	61.3	70.2	77.2	84.0	87.7	87.0	81.8	71.8	61.3	51.9	69.5
Mean Temp. (°F)	36.9	40.3	48.2	56.1	64.3	72.0	76.1	75.3	69.5	57.9	48.4	40.5	57.1
Mean Minimum Temp. (°F)	26.0	27.9	35.1	41.9	51.4	60.0	64.5	63.6	57.2	44.0	35.5	29.0	44.7
Extreme Maximum Temp. (°F)	74	78	84	89	92	98	104	104	98	88	84	76	104
Extreme Minimum Temp. (°F)	-14	-3	2	19	29	37	46	48	31	21	8	-4	-14
Days Maximum Temp. ≥ 90°F	0	0	0	0	0	4	12	9	3	0	0	0	28
Days Maximum Temp. ≤ 32°F	3	1	0	0	0	0	0	0	0	0	0	1	5
Days Minimum Temp. ≤ 32°F	22	19	14	6	0	0	0	0	0	5	14	20	100
Days Minimum Temp. ≤ 0°F	1	0	0	0	0	0	0	0	0	0	0	0	1
Heating Degree Days (base 65°F)	865	691	517	276	94	9	0	1	36	237	494	754	3,974
Cooling Degree Days (base 65°F)	0	0	2	12	83	236	368	333	171	24	2	0	1,231
Mean Precipitation (in.)	5.93	5.65	6.61	4.79	4.73	4.22	5.22	3.47	4.28	3.40	4.81	5.18	58.29
Days With ≥ 0.1" Precipitation	9	7	9	7	7	7	8	6	6	5	7	8	86
Days With ≥ 1.0" Precipitation	1	2	2	2	2	1	2	1	1	1	1	1	17
Mean Snowfall (in.)	2.4	1.7	1.0	0.4	0.0	0.0	0.0	0.0	0.0	trace	0.1	0.4	6.0
Days With ≥ 1.0" Snow Depth	2	1	0	0	0	0	0	0	0	0	0	0	3

Vernon 2 N *Lamar County*   Elevation: 262 ft.   Latitude: 33° 48' N   Longitude: 88° 07' W

	JAN	FEB	MAR	APR	MAY	JUN	JUL	AUG	SEP	OCT	NOV	DEC	YEAR
Mean Maximum Temp. (°F)	51.6	57.3	66.2	74.8	81.5	87.8	91.2	90.7	85.4	75.2	64.3	55.6	73.5
Mean Temp. (°F)	40.0	44.4	52.6	60.2	68.2	75.5	79.3	78.4	72.5	60.8	51.3	43.6	60.6
Mean Minimum Temp. (°F)	28.4	31.5	38.9	45.7	54.9	63.2	67.3	66.0	59.6	46.4	38.3	31.5	47.6
Extreme Maximum Temp. (°F)	78	85	89	94	95	101	105	103	100	92	85	81	105
Extreme Minimum Temp. (°F)	-8	1	6	20	30	41	50	46	36	21	9	-3	-8
Days Maximum Temp. ≥ 90°F	0	0	0	0	3	12	20	20	9	0	0	0	64
Days Maximum Temp. ≤ 32°F	2	1	0	0	0	0	0	0	0	0	0	1	4
Days Minimum Temp. ≤ 32°F	21	16	10	4	0	0	0	0	0	3	11	18	83
Days Minimum Temp. ≤ 0°F	0	0	0	0	0	0	0	0	0	0	0	0	0
Heating Degree Days (base 65°F)	768	577	387	180	41	2	0	0	19	174	410	659	3,217
Cooling Degree Days (base 65°F)	0	2	7	33	140	313	444	421	236	49	6	2	1,653
Mean Precipitation (in.)	6.20	5.12	6.92	5.59	5.59	4.25	4.94	3.23	4.02	3.59	5.40	5.66	60.51
Days With ≥ 0.1" Precipitation	8	7	8	6	7	7	7	5	5	5	7	8	80
Days With ≥ 1.0" Precipitation	2	2	2	2	2	1	2	1	1	1	2	2	20
Mean Snowfall (in.)	0.5	trace	0.2	trace	0.0	0.0	0.0	0.0	0.0	trace	trace	trace	0.7
Days With ≥ 1.0" Snow Depth	0	0	0	0	0	0	0	0	0	0	0	0	0

Whatley *Clarke County* Elevation: 167 ft.   Latitude: 31° 39' N   Longitude: 87° 43' W

	JAN	FEB	MAR	APR	MAY	JUN	JUL	AUG	SEP	OCT	NOV	DEC	YEAR
Mean Maximum Temp. (°F)	59.4	64.5	71.8	78.2	84.5	89.9	92.0	91.7	88.0	79.7	70.0	62.6	77.7
Mean Temp. (°F)	47.0	50.7	57.5	63.8	71.0	77.6	80.1	80.0	75.7	65.3	56.0	49.9	64.5
Mean Minimum Temp. (°F)	34.4	37.0	43.1	49.2	57.5	65.2	68.5	68.3	63.2	50.9	41.8	36.9	51.3
Extreme Maximum Temp. (°F)	82	83	92	92	98	101	103	101	101	95	87	83	103
Extreme Minimum Temp. (°F)	-2	6	13	26	34	40	54	53	38	25	15	2	-2
Days Maximum Temp. ≥ 90°F	0	0	0	0	5	18	23	23	14	2	0	0	85
Days Maximum Temp. ≤ 32°F	0	0	0	0	0	0	0	0	0	0	0	0	0
Days Minimum Temp. ≤ 32°F	15	10	5	1	0	0	0	0	0	1	6	12	50
Days Minimum Temp. ≤ 0°F	0	0	0	0	0	0	0	0	0	0	0	0	0
Heating Degree Days (base 65°F)	567	402	251	100	14	0	0	0	5	85	283	472	2,179
Cooling Degree Days (base 65°F)	2	6	23	69	209	376	472	468	318	105	18	10	2,076
Mean Precipitation (in.)	6.66	5.72	7.81	4.96	5.36	5.45	5.88	4.21	4.36	3.08	4.72	5.72	63.93
Days With ≥ 0.1" Precipitation	8	7	6	6	6	7	9	7	5	4	6	6	77
Days With ≥ 1.0" Precipitation	2	2	2	2	2	2	2	1	1	1	2	2	21
Mean Snowfall (in.)	0.2	0.1	0.2	trace	0.0	0.0	0.0	0.0	0.0	0.0	0.0	0.1	0.6
Days With ≥ 1.0" Snow Depth	0	0	0	0	0	0	0	0	0	0	0	0	0

Winfield 2 SW *Fayette County*   Elevation: 465 ft.   Latitude: 33° 55' N   Longitude: 87° 51' W

	JAN	FEB	MAR	APR	MAY	JUN	JUL	AUG	SEP	OCT	NOV	DEC	YEAR
Mean Maximum Temp. (°F)	50.8	56.3	64.9	73.6	80.6	87.4	90.8	90.5	85.2	74.7	64.6	55.1	72.9
Mean Temp. (°F)	38.8	43.2	51.0	59.1	67.4	75.0	78.8	77.9	71.9	59.9	50.7	42.5	59.7
Mean Minimum Temp. (°F)	26.8	30.1	37.0	44.5	54.1	62.6	66.7	65.2	58.5	44.9	36.8	29.8	46.4
Extreme Maximum Temp. (°F)	76	84	86	94	95	101	107	103	101	91	85	79	107
Extreme Minimum Temp. (°F)	-8	1	6	22	35	40	51	49	36	23	11	-3	-8
Days Maximum Temp. ≥ 90°F	0	0	0	0	2	12	20	19	9	0	0	0	62
Days Maximum Temp. ≤ 32°F	2	1	0	0	0	0	0	0	0	0	0	1	4
Days Minimum Temp. ≤ 32°F	22	18	12	4	0	0	0	0	0	3	12	19	90
Days Minimum Temp. ≤ 0°F	0	0	0	0	0	0	0	0	0	0	0	0	0
Heating Degree Days (base 65°F)	805	610	432	200	49	2	0	0	19	194	426	692	3,429
Cooling Degree Days (base 65°F)	0	2	7	30	129	308	434	412	233	46	3	1	1,605
Mean Precipitation (in.)	6.24	5.11	6.64	5.14	5.67	4.80	4.86	3.25	3.80	3.64	5.17	5.75	60.07
Days With ≥ 0.1" Precipitation	8	7	8	6	7	7	8	5	6	5	7	8	82
Days With ≥ 1.0" Precipitation	2	2	2	2	2	2	2	1	1	1	2	2	21
Mean Snowfall (in.)	0.7	0.3	0.2	0.0	0.0	0.0	0.0	0.0	0.0	trace	trace	trace	1.2
Days With ≥ 1.0" Snow Depth	0	0	0	0	0	0	0	0	0	0	0	0	0

Note: See Appendix D for explanation of data.

ALASKA

PHYSICAL FEATURES. Alaska is the westernmost extension of the North American continent. Its east-west span covers a distance of 2,000 miles, and from north to south a distance of 1,100 miles. The state's coastline, 33,000 miles in length, is 50 percent longer than that of the conterminous U.S. In addition to the Aleutian Islands, hundreds of other islands are found along the northern coast of the Gulf of Alaska, the Alaska Peninsula, and the Bering Sea Coast. Alaska contains 375 million acres of land, and over 3 million lakes.

The two longest mountain ranges are the Brooks Range which separates the Arctic region from the interior, and the Alaska-Aleutian Range, which extends westward along the Alaska Peninsula and the Aleutian Islands, and northward about 200 miles from the Peninsula, then eastward to Canada. Other shorter but important ranges are the Chugach Mountains which form a rim to the central north Gulf of Alaska, and the Wrangell Mountains lying to the northeast of the Chugach Range and south of the Alaska Range. Both of these shorter ranges merge with the St. Elias Mountains, extending southeastward through Canada and across southeastern Alaska as the Coast Range. Numerous peaks in excess of 10,000 feet are found in all but the Brooks Range. The highest peak (20,320 feet above sea level) in the North American continent, Mt. McKinley, is found in Alaska, and several others tower above 16,000 feet.

Permafrost is a major factor in the geography of Alaska. It is defined as a layer of soil at variable depths beneath the surface of the earth in which the temperature has been below freezing continuously from a few to several thousands of years. It exists where summer heating fails to penetrate to the base of the layer of frozen ground. Permafrost covers most of the northern third of the State. Discontinuous or isolated patches also exist over the central portion in an overall area covering nearly a third of the State. No permafrost exists in the south-central and southern coastal portions, including southeastern Alaska, the Alaska Peninsula, and the Aleutian chain.

GENERAL CLIMATE. The geographical features already mentioned have a significant effect on Alaska's climate, which falls into four major zones. The climate zones are: (1) a Maritime Zone which includes southeastern Alaska, the South Coast, and southwestern islands, (2) a transition zone between marine and continental influences (this zone is difficult to define but generally comprises a very narrow band along the southern portion of the Copper River and the northern extreme of the South Coast—specifically the Chugach Mountains, Cook Inlet, Bristol Bay, and the coastal regions of the West-Central Division), (3) a continental zone made up of the remainders of the Copper River and West-Central Divisions, and the Interior Basin, and (4) an Arctic zone.

PRECIPITATION. In the maritime zone a coastal mountain range coupled with plentiful moisture produces annual precipitation amounts up to 200 inches in the southeastern panhandle, and up to 150 inches along the northern coast of the Gulf of Alaska. Amounts taper to near 60 inches on the southern side of the Alaska Range in the Peninsula and Aleutian Island sections. Precipitation amounts decrease rapidly to the north, with an average of 12 inches in the continental zone and less than 6 inches in the Arctic Region.

Snowfall makes up a large portion of the total annual precipitation.. Total snow depths on the ground are controlled by the temperature of an area. Fortunately, most of the areas of heavy snow have relatively mild temperatures which prevent total depths from becoming excessive.

TEMPERATURE. Mean annual temperatures in Alaska range from the low 40s under the maritime influence in the south to a chilly 10 degrees along the Arctic Slope north of the Brooks Mountain Range. The greatest seasonal temperature contrast between seasons is found in the central and eastern portion of the Continental Interior. In this area summer heating produces average maximum temperatures in the upper 70s with extreme readings in the 90s. In winter the lack of sunshine permits radiation to lower temperatures to the minus 50s and occasionally colder for two or three weeks at a time. Average winter minimums in this area are 20 to 30 degrees below zero. Elsewhere in the State, temperature contrasts are much more moderate. In the maritime zone the summer to winter range of average temperatures is from near 60 to the 20s. In the transition zone, temperatures range from the low 60s to near zero, except for the colder northern coastal region of the West-Central Division, where the range is from the mid 50s to near 10 below zero. The Arctic slope has a range extending from the upper 40s to 20 below zero.

Winter temperatures play a principal role in the flow of most of Alaska's rivers. Usually beginning in late October and extending into May (and sometimes early June for the northernmost streams), thick layers of ice form, permitting passage with all types of heavy equipment. Several rivers cease to flow completely during the coldest months.

WIND. A normal storm track along the Aleutian Island chain, the Alaska Peninsula and all of the coastal area of the Gulf of Alaska exposes these parts of the State to a large majority of the storms crossing the north Pacific, resulting in a variety of wind problems. Direct exposure to the wind of the storms themselves results in the frequent occurrence of winds in excess of 50 m.p.h. during all but the summer months, and on occasion even then for the land areas along the storm track. Wind velocities approaching 100 m.p.h. are not common but do occur, usually associated with mountainous terrain and narrow passes.

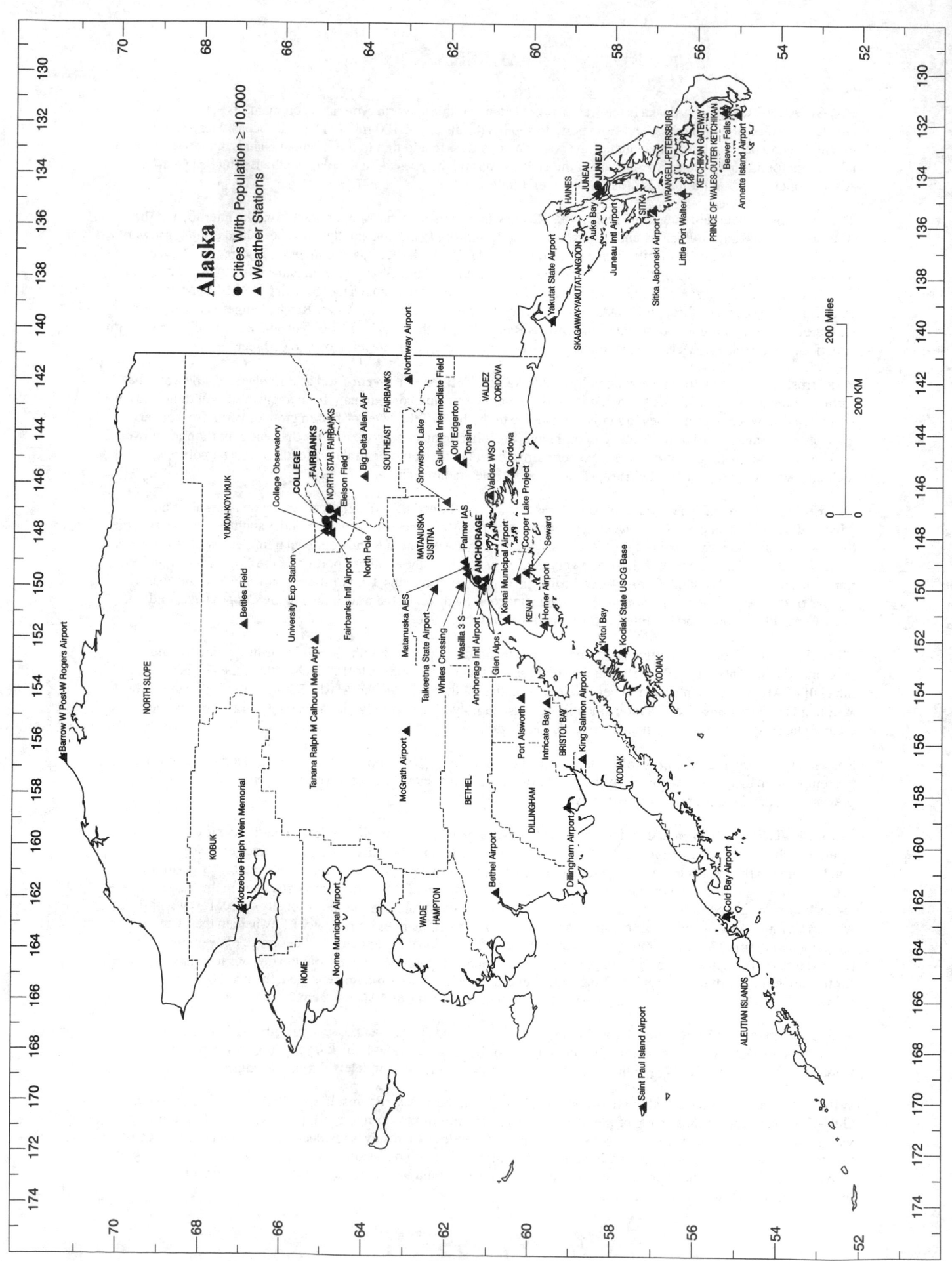

Alaska

● Cities With Population ≥ 10,000
▲ Weather Stations

Alaska Weather Stations by Division

Division	Station Name
Arctic Drainage	Barrow W. Post-W. Rogers Airport
	Kotzebue Ralph Wein Memorial
Bristol Bay	Dillingham Airport
	Intricate Bay
	King Salmon Airport
	Port Alsworth
Cook Inlet	Anchorage Int'l Airport
	Glen Alps
	Homer Airport
	Kenai Municipal Airport
	Matanuska AES
	Palmer IAS
	Talkeetna State Airport
	Wasilla 3 S
	Whites Crossing
Copper River	Gulkana Intermediate Field
	Old Edgerton
	Snowshoe Lake
	Tonsina
Interior Basin	Bettles Field
	Big Delta Allen AAF
	College Observatory
	Eielson Field
	Fairbanks Int'l Airport
	McGrath Airport
	North Pole
	Northway Airport
	Tanana R.M. Calhoun Mem. Arpt.
	University Exp. Station
South Coast	Cooper Lake Project
	Cordova
	Kitoi Bay
	Kodiak State USCG Base
	Seward
	Valdez WSO
	Yakutat State Airport
Southeastern	Annette Island Airport
	Auke Bay
	Beaver Falls
	Juneau Int'l Airport
	Little Port Walter
	Sitka Japonski Airport
Southwestern	Cold Bay Airport
Southwestern Islands	Saint Paul Island Airport
West Central	Bethel Airport
	Nome Municipal Airport

Alaska Weather Stations by City

City	Station Name	Miles
Anchorage	Anchorage Int'l Airport	7
	Glen Alps	8
College	College Observatory	1
	Fairbanks Int'l Airport	3
	North Pole	16
	University Exp. Station	1
Fairbanks	College Observatory	4
	Fairbanks Int'l Airport	4
	North Pole	13
	University Exp. Station	4
Juneau	Auke Bay	4
	Juneau Int'l Airport	2

Note: Miles is the distance between the geographic center of the city and the weather station.

Alaska Weather Stations by Elevation

Feet	Station Name
2,299	Snowshoe Lake
2,257	Glen Alps
1,712	Northway Airport
1,574	Tonsina
1,568	Gulkana Intermediate Field
1,318	Old Edgerton
1,266	Big Delta Allen AAF
643	Bettles Field
620	College Observatory
544	Eielson Field
472	North Pole
472	University Exp. Station
442	Cooper Lake Project
433	Fairbanks Int'l Airport
344	Talkeetna State Airport
341	McGrath Airport
269	Whites Crossing
259	Port Alsworth
229	Tanana R.M. Calhoun Mem. Arpt.
223	Palmer IAS
167	Intricate Bay
147	Matanuska AES
124	Bethel Airport
111	Anchorage Int'l Airport
108	Annette Island Airport
95	Cold Bay Airport
88	Homer Airport
85	Dillingham Airport
85	Kenai Municipal Airport
72	Seward
49	Wasilla 3 S
45	King Salmon Airport
39	Auke Bay
39	Cordova
36	Sitka Japonski Airport
32	Beaver Falls
29	Barrow W. Post-W. Rogers Airport
26	Yakutat State Airport
22	Valdez WSO
19	Saint Paul Island Airport
13	Kitoi Bay
13	Kodiak State USCG Base
13	Little Port Walter
13	Nome Municipal Airport
9	Juneau Int'l Airport
9	Kotzebue Ralph Wein Memorial

Anchorage Int'l Airport

Anchorage is in a broad valley with adjacent narrow bodies of water. Cook Inlet, including Knik Arm and Turnagain Arm, lies approximately 2 miles to the west, north, and south. The terrain rises gradually to the east for about 10 miles, Beyond this area, the Chugach Mountains acts as a barrier to the influx of warm, moist air from the Gulf of Alaska, so the average annual precipitation is only 10 to 15 percent of that at stations located on the Gulf of Alaska side of the Chugach Range. The Alaska Mountain Range lies in a long arc from southwest, through northwest, to northeast, approximately 100 miles distant from Anchorage. During the winter, this range is an effective barrier to the influx of very cold air from the north side of the range.

The four seasons are well marked in Anchorage. In the summer, high temperatures average about 60 degrees and low temperatures nearly 50 degrees. On summer days, temperatures on the east side of Anchorage may be about 10 degrees warmer than the official airport readings. Rain increases after mid-June. About two-thirds of the days in July and August are cloudy and one-third have rain.

Autumn is brief, beginning in early September and ending in mid-October. Temperatures begin to fall in September with snow becoming more frequent in October.

Winter can be considered as mid-October to early April when streams and lakes are frozen. Temperatures steadily decrease into January when the highs are near 20 degrees and lows near five degrees. On cold winter nights, temperatures on the east side of Anchorage may be 10-20 degrees lower than airport readings on the west side. Most winter precipitation is snow, but rain may occur on a few days.

Annual snowfall varies from about 70 inches on the west side to about 90 inches on the east side of Anchorage at low elevations. Along the Chugach Mountains, snow totals increase steadily with increasing elevations and winter arrives a month earlier and stays a month longer at the 1,000 to 2,000 foot level.

Spring begins in late April and May when days are warm and sunny, nights are cool, and precipitation is exceedingly small. Foliage turns green by late May.

The wind in Anchorage is generally light. However, on several days each winter, strong northerly winds, up to 90 mph, affect the entire Anchorage area.

The average occurrence of the first snow is mid-October, but has occurred as early as mid-September. The average date of the last snow is mid-April, but has occurred as late as early May. The growing season is about 125 days. Average occurrence of the last temperature of 32 degrees in spring is mid-May and the first in fall is mid-September. Daylight varies from about 19 hours in late June to 6 hours in late December with 12 hours of daylight occurring in late September and late March.

Anchorage Int'l Airport *Cook Inlet Division*   Elevation: 111 ft.   Latitude: 61° 11' N   Longitude: 150° 00' W

	JAN	FEB	MAR	APR	MAY	JUN	JUL	AUG	SEP	OCT	NOV	DEC	YEAR
Mean Maximum Temp. (°F)	22.1	25.9	33.8	43.8	55.0	62.2	65.3	63.2	54.9	39.9	27.5	23.3	43.1
Mean Temp. (°F)	15.8	19.1	26.3	36.5	47.2	54.8	58.6	56.6	48.3	34.2	21.8	17.3	36.4
Mean Minimum Temp. (°F)	9.4	12.2	18.8	29.1	39.3	47.4	51.9	49.8	41.7	28.5	16.0	11.3	29.6
Extreme Maximum Temp. (°F)	49	48	51	65	76	80	82	82	71	61	53	48	82
Extreme Minimum Temp. (°F)	-34	-28	-24	-4	25	34	39	31	19	-3	-15	-24	-34
Days Maximum Temp. ≥ 90°F	na	na	na	na	na	na	na	na	na	na	na	na	na
Days Maximum Temp. ≤ 32°F	24	19	12	2	0	0	0	0	0	5	21	25	108
Days Minimum Temp. ≤ 32°F	30	27	29	20	3	0	0	0	3	20	29	30	191
Days Minimum Temp. ≤ 0°F	9	7	2	0	0	0	0	0	0	0	3	7	28
Heating Degree Days (base 65°F)	1,522	1,292	1,193	849	546	299	192	256	494	947	1,291	1,472	10,353
Cooling Degree Days (base 65°F)	0	0	0	0	0	0	2	0	0	0	0	0	2
Mean Precipitation (in.)	0.67	0.74	0.64	0.52	0.69	1.04	1.68	2.94	2.80	2.12	1.09	1.09	16.02
Maximum Precipitation (in.)	2.7	3.1	2.8	1.9	1.9	3.4	4.4	9.8	6.6	4.1	2.8	2.7	27.5
Minimum Precipitation (in.)	trace	0.1	trace	trace	trace	0.2	0.4	0.3	0.8	0.3	0.1	0.1	8.1
Maximum 24-hr. Precipitation (in.)	1.1	1.2	1.3	0.8	1.0	1.6	2.0	2.7	1.3	1.6	1.2	1.4	2.7
Days With ≥ 0.1" Precipitation	2	3	2	2	2	3	5	8	8	6	4	4	49
Days With ≥ 1.0" Precipitation	0	0	0	0	0	0	0	0	0	0	0	0	0
Mean Snowfall (in.)	8.8	11.1	10.0	4.1	trace	0.0	0.0	trace	0.2	8.4	11.6	15.1	69.3
Maximum Snowfall (in.)	28	49	31	28	4	0	0	0	5	27	39	42	172
Maximum 24-hr. Snowfall (in.)	8	12	14	8	4	0	0	0	3	9	11	16	16
Days With ≥ 1.0" Snow Depth	29	26	28	12	0	0	0	0	0	7	21	28	151
Thunderstorm Days	0	0	0	0	< 1	< 1	< 1	< 1	< 1	0	0	0	2
Foggy Days	11	9	5	4	1	2	4	5	6	7	10	12	76
Predominant Sky Cover	OVR	OVR	OVR	OVR	OVR	OVR	OVR	OVR	OVR	OVR	OVR	OVR	OVR
Mean Relative Humidity 6am (%)	74	74	72	75	73	74	80	84	84	78	78	78	77
Mean Relative Humidity 3pm (%)	73	67	57	54	50	55	62	64	64	67	74	76	64
Mean Dewpoint (°F)	8	11	15	25	34	43	49	48	41	27	15	10	27
Prevailing Wind Direction	N	N	N	N	SSE	SSE	SSE	SSE	SSE	N	N	N	N
Prevailing Wind Speed (mph)	9	9	8	7	13	13	12	10	10	8	8	8	9
Maximum Wind Gust (mph)	73	74	75	51	48	46	40	54	53	60	63	62	75

Barrow W. Post-W. Rogers Airport

Barrow is the most northerly First-Order station operated by the National Weather Service. Although this station generally records one of the lowest mean temperatures for the winter months, the surrounding topography prevents the establishment of the lowest minima for the state. With the Arctic Ocean to the north, east, and west, and level tundra stretching 200 miles to the south, there are no natural wind barriers to assist in stilling the wind, permitting the lowering of temperatures by radiation, and no downslope drainage area to aid the flow of cold air to lower levels. Consequently, temperature inversions in the lower levels of the atmosphere are not as marked as those observed at stations in the central interior.

Temperatures at this northern station remain below the freezing point through most of the year, with the daily maxima reaching higher than 32 degrees on an average of only 109 days a year. Freezing temperatures have been observed every month of the year. February is generally the coldest month and March temperatures are but little higher than those observed in the winter months. In April, temperatures begin a general upward trend, with May becoming the definite transitional period from winter to the summer season. July is the warmest month of the year and the frequency of minimum temperatures of 32 degrees or less are about one day out of two for July and August. During late July or early August, the Arctic Ocean is usually ice-free for the first time in summer. September marks the end of the short summer is and by November about half of the daily mean temperatures are zero or below.

At 12:50 p.m. on November 18, the sun dips below the horizon and is not seen again until 11:51 a.m. on January 24. Then the amount of possible sunshine each day increases by never less than 9 minutes per day. By 1:06 a.m. on May 10th the possible sunshine has increased to 24 hours per day. The sun remains visible from that time to August 2, when it again sets for 1 hour and 25 minutes. The decrease in hours of sunshine is as rapid as the increase. The occurrence of cloudiness, precipitation, and heavy fog build up to a maximum along with the hours of sunshine. Maximum cloudiness does continue into the fall months, although the amount of sunshine, precipitation, and fog are on the decrease. Since an accurate estimate of cloudiness cannot be made under conditions of darkness, of cloudiness for that time is not recorded. However, it probably approximates that observed during late winter and spring months.

Variation of wind speed during the year is small, with the fall months being windiest. Extreme winds in the upper 40s and low 50s have been recorded for all months.

Barrow W. Post-W. Rogers Arpt. *Arctic Drainage Div.*   Elevation: 29 ft.   Latitude: 71° 17' N   Longitude: 156° 46' W

	JAN	FEB	MAR	APR	MAY	JUN	JUL	AUG	SEP	OCT	NOV	DEC	YEAR
Mean Maximum Temp. (°F)	-7.8	-10.0	-7.9	6.2	25.0	39.3	46.4	43.4	34.5	18.7	4.5	-4.9	15.6
Mean Temp. (°F)	-13.7	-16.0	-14.2	-0.7	20.3	34.8	40.4	38.6	31.0	14.0	-1.1	-10.9	10.2
Mean Minimum Temp. (°F)	-19.6	-22.1	-20.5	-7.5	15.6	30.3	34.3	33.8	27.4	9.2	-6.7	-16.8	4.8
Extreme Maximum Temp. (°F)	36	36	34	38	47	72	79	74	62	41	35	32	79
Extreme Minimum Temp. (°F)	-53	-52	-52	-38	-19	12	25	21	1	-32	-38	-51	-53
Days Maximum Temp. ≥ 90°F	na	na	na	na	na	na	na	na	na	na	na	na	na
Days Maximum Temp. ≤ 32°F	31	28	31	29	25	3	0	1	12	29	30	31	250
Days Minimum Temp. ≤ 32°F	31	28	31	30	31	23	12	15	24	31	30	31	317
Days Minimum Temp. ≤ 0°F	30	27	30	23	2	0	0	0	0	8	21	29	170
Heating Degree Days (base 65°F)	2,444	2,293	2,461	1,970	1,378	900	756	811	1,014	1,575	1,984	2,356	19,942
Cooling Degree Days (base 65°F)	0	0	0	0	0	0	0	0	0	0	0	0	0
Mean Precipitation (in.)	0.11	0.12	0.09	0.12	0.12	0.29	0.81	1.02	0.67	0.38	0.17	0.13	4.03
Maximum Precipitation (in.)	1.0	0.8	1.5	1.4	0.5	1.1	3.2	2.8	1.6	1.4	1.1	0.8	9.8
Minimum Precipitation (in.)	trace	trace	trace	trace	trace	trace	0.1	0.1	trace	0.1	trace	trace	1.8
Maximum 24-hr. Precipitation (in.)	0.5	0.3	0.7	0.4	0.3	0.8	1.3	0.8	0.6	0.4	0.4	0.2	1.3
Days With ≥ 0.1" Precipitation	0	0	0	0	0	1	3	4	2	1	0	0	11
Days With ≥ 1.0" Precipitation	0	0	0	0	0	0	0	0	0	0	0	0	0
Mean Snowfall (in.)	1.8	1.8	1.7	2.1	1.6	0.8	0.2	0.8	4.8	7.1	3.3	2.1	28.1
Maximum Snowfall (in.)	12	9	16	15	7	4	4	4	16	15	13	9	62
Maximum 24-hr. Snowfall (in.)	5	3	7	4	4	3	3	2	5	5	4	3	7
Days With ≥ 1.0" Snow Depth	31	28	31	30	27	3	0	0	8	28	30	31	247
Thunderstorm Days	< 1	< 1	< 1	0	0	< 1	< 1	< 1	0	0	< 1	< 1	1
Foggy Days	14	14	13	14	20	22	23	24	20	17	15	14	210
Predominant Sky Cover	CLR	CLR	CLR	OVR	OVR	OVR	OVR	OVR	OVR	OVR	OVR	OVR	OVR
Mean Relative Humidity 6am (%)	68	67	66	74	87	91	92	94	92	85	77	70	81
Mean Relative Humidity 3pm (%)	68	67	67	73	83	86	85	87	87	84	77	70	78
Mean Dewpoint (°F)	-20	-23	-21	-6	17	31	36	35	28	12	-7	-18	6
Prevailing Wind Direction	ENE	ENE	ENE	ENE	ENE	E	E	E	ENE	ENE	ENE	ENE	ENE
Prevailing Wind Speed (mph)	14	13	14	14	15	14	14	15	15	16	15	14	14
Maximum Wind Gust (mph)	58	74	56	48	41	43	55	48	66	55	53	67	74

Fairbanks Int'l Airport

Fairbanks is located in the Tanana Valley, in the interior of Alaska. It has a distinctly continental climate, with large variation of temperature from winter to summer.

The sun is above the horizon from 18 to 21 hours during June and July. During this period, daily average maximum temperatures reach the lower 70s. Temperatures of 80 degrees or higher occur on about 10 days each summer. In contrast, from November to early March, when the period of daylight ranges from 10 to less than 4 hours per day, the lowest temperature readings normally fall below zero quite regularly. Low temperatures of -40 degrees or colder occur each winter. The range of temperatures in summer is comparatively low, from the lower 30s to the mid 90s. In winter, this range is larger, from about 65 below to 45 degrees above. This large winter range of temperature reflects the great difference between frigid weather associated with dry northerly airflow from the Arctic to mild temperatures associated with southerly airflow from the Gulf of Alaska, accompanied by chinook winds off the Alaska Range, 80 miles to the south of Fairbanks.

Snow cover is persistent in Fairbanks, without interruption, from October through April. Snowfalls of four inches or more in a day occur only three times during winter. Blizzard conditions are almost never seen. Precipitation normally reaches a minimum in spring, and a maximum in August, when rainfall is common. During summer, thunderstorms occur in Fairbanks on an average of about eight days.

There are rolling hills reaching elevations up to 2,000 feet above Fairbanks to the north and east of the city. During winter, the uplands are often warmer than Fairbanks. During summer, the uplands are a few degrees cooler than the city. Precipitation in the uplands around Fairbanks is heavier than it is in the city by roughly 20 to 50 percent. Fairbanks exhibits an urban heat island, especially during winter. Low lying areas nearby, such as the community of North Pole, are often colder than the city.

During winter, with temperatures of -20 degrees or colder, ice fog frequently forms in the city. Cold snaps accompanied by ice fog generally last about a week, but can last three weeks in unusual situations. The fog is almost always less than 300 feet deep, so that the surrounding uplands are usually in the clear, with warmer temperatures. Visibility in the ice fog is sometimes quite low.

Hardy vegetables and grains grow luxuriantly. Freezing of local rivers normally begins in the first week of October, with ice normally supporting a persons weight by October 27. Rivers remain frozen and safe for travel until early April. Breakup usually occurs in the first week of May.

Fairbanks Int'l Airport *Interior Basin Division*   Elevation: 433 ft.   Latitude: 64° 49' N   Longitude: 147° 51' W

	JAN	FEB	MAR	APR	MAY	JUN	JUL	AUG	SEP	OCT	NOV	DEC	YEAR
Mean Maximum Temp. (°F)	-0.5	8.0	25.0	43.6	61.0	70.7	73.2	66.5	54.3	31.2	11.3	2.9	37.3
Mean Temp. (°F)	-8.9	-2.8	12.2	32.6	49.8	60.2	63.1	57.0	45.1	24.1	3.2	-5.3	27.5
Mean Minimum Temp. (°F)	-17.3	-13.6	-0.7	21.6	38.5	49.7	53.1	47.4	35.9	17.0	-4.9	-13.6	17.8
Extreme Maximum Temp. (°F)	50	47	56	73	88	94	94	93	78	64	49	45	94
Extreme Minimum Temp. (°F)	-60	-58	-43	-24	11	33	39	27	3	-27	-46	-53	-60
Days Maximum Temp. ≥ 90°F	na	na	na	na	na	na	na	na	na	na	na	na	na
Days Maximum Temp. ≤ 32°F	30	26	21	5	0	0	0	0	0	16	28	30	156
Days Minimum Temp. ≤ 32°F	31	28	31	26	5	0	0	0	9	29	30	31	220
Days Minimum Temp. ≤ 0°F	26	22	16	2	0	0	0	0	0	4	19	25	114
Heating Degree Days (base 65°F)	2,294	1,915	1,633	965	466	162	92	250	590	1,261	1,853	2,182	13,663
Cooling Degree Days (base 65°F)	0	0	0	0	1	30	41	8	0	0	0	0	80
Mean Precipitation (in.)	0.49	0.37	0.29	0.22	0.59	1.46	1.75	1.70	1.10	0.95	0.78	0.81	10.51
Maximum Precipitation (in.)	2.4	1.8	2.2	0.9	1.7	3.5	4.9	6.2	3.0	2.2	3.3	3.2	18.5
Minimum Precipitation (in.)	trace	trace	trace	trace	0.1	0.2	0.3	0.4	0.1	0.1	trace	trace	5.5
Maximum 24-hr. Precipitation (in.)	0.8	0.9	1.0	0.5	0.8	1.4	1.8	3.4	1.2	0.8	0.8	0.9	3.4
Days With ≥ 0.1" Precipitation	2	1	1	1	2	4	5	5	3	3	3	2	32
Days With ≥ 1.0" Precipitation	0	0	0	0	0	0	0	0	0	0	0	0	0
Mean Snowfall (in.)	9.5	7.5	5.3	2.6	0.6	trace	trace	trace	2.3	12.7	15.1	15.1	70.7
Maximum Snowfall (in.)	40	43	30	12	14	0	0	trace	24	26	54	51	146
Maximum 24-hr. Snowfall (in.)	10	16	13	6	9	0	0	trace	8	10	15	13	16
Days With ≥ 1.0" Snow Depth	31	28	31	21	1	0	0	0	1	18	30	31	192
Thunderstorm Days	1	< 1	0	< 1	< 1	3	3	1	< 1	< 1	< 1	< 1	8
Foggy Days	13	9	4	2	2	2	5	7	6	8	9	12	79
Predominant Sky Cover	OVR	OVR	OVR	OVR	OVR	OVR	OVR	OVR	OVR	OVR	OVR	OVR	OVR
Mean Relative Humidity 6am (%)	70	68	69	70	64	71	80	87	85	81	74	72	74
Mean Relative Humidity 3pm (%)	70	64	54	46	38	44	51	55	56	69	74	72	58
Mean Dewpoint (°F)	-13	-11	1	17	31	44	50	47	35	19	-1	-13	17
Prevailing Wind Direction	N	N	N	N	N	SW	SW	SW	N	N	N	N	N
Prevailing Wind Speed (mph)	6	6	7	8	8	10	9	9	7	7	6	6	7
Maximum Wind Gust (mph)	47	40	46	40	44	48	63	54	51	40	46	38	63

Juneau Int'l Airport

Juneau lies well within the area of maritime influences which prevail over the coastal areas of southeastern Alaska, and is in the path of most storms that cross the Gulf of Alaska. Consequently, the area has little sunshine, generally moderate temperatures, and abundant precipitation. There are intervals, however, sometimes lasting for several days at a stretch, during which clear skies prevail. The rugged terrain creates considerable variations in both temperature and precipitation within relatively short distances.

Temperature variations, both daily and seasonal, are usually limited. There are, however, periods of comparatively severe cold, which usually start with strong northerly winds, and are most often caused by the flow of cold air from northwestern Canada through nearby mountain passes and over the Juneau ice field. During such periods strong, gusty winds, known locally as Taku Winds, often occur especially in downtown Juneau, Douglas, and other local areas.During periods of calm or light winds, temperature differences within short distances are frequently very pronounced. Variations in local sunlight and air drainage patterns produce wide differences in temperatures particularly between upland or sloping areas and areas of low, flat terrain. Juneau International Airport, located on low, flat terrain formed by the Mendenhall River delta, and in the path of drainage air from the Mendenhall Glacier, averages about 10 days a year with minimum readings below zero. Downtown Juneau, located on a sloping portion of a rugged mountain area, experiences on the average only about one day each year with minimum readings below zero. At the airport the growing season averages 146 days, from May 4 to September 28, while the downtown average is 181 days, from April 22 to October 21.

The months of February to June mark the period of lightest precipitation, with monthly averages of about three inches. After June the monthly amounts increase gradually, reaching an average of 7.71 inches in October. Due to the rugged topography, precipitation throughout the year tends to vary greatly within short distances. At the Juneau Airport, yearly precipitation is 53 inches while downtown, only eight miles away, it is 93 inches.

Although a trace of snow has fallen as early as September 9, first falls usually occur in the latter part of October, and sometimes not until the first part of December. On the average there is very little accumulation on the ground at low levels until the last of November, although at higher elevations, and particularly on mountain tops, a cover is usually established in early October. Ice accumulations are frequent problems in the Juneau area during the winter months.

Juneau Int'l Airport *Southeastern Division*   Elevation: 9 ft.   Latitude: 58° 21' N   Longitude: 134° 35' W

	JAN	FEB	MAR	APR	MAY	JUN	JUL	AUG	SEP	OCT	NOV	DEC	YEAR
Mean Maximum Temp. (°F)	30.5	34.4	39.5	48.2	55.6	61.5	64.2	63.0	56.0	47.0	37.7	32.7	47.5
Mean Temp. (°F)	25.5	29.1	33.6	40.9	47.9	53.8	56.6	55.6	49.9	42.3	33.3	28.4	41.4
Mean Minimum Temp. (°F)	20.5	23.7	27.7	33.5	40.2	46.0	49.1	48.2	43.7	37.7	28.9	24.1	35.3
Extreme Maximum Temp. (°F)	55	57	61	72	76	85	90	83	73	61	55	54	90
Extreme Minimum Temp. (°F)	-22	-11	-15	16	25	31	38	34	23	11	-2	-10	-22
Days Maximum Temp. ≥ 90°F	na	na	na	na	na	na	na	na	na	na	na	na	na
Days Maximum Temp. ≤ 32°F	15	9	3	0	0	0	0	0	0	0	6	12	45
Days Minimum Temp. ≤ 32°F	24	21	21	12	2	0	0	0	1	7	18	22	128
Days Minimum Temp. ≤ 0°F	3	1	0	0	0	0	0	0	0	0	0	2	6
Heating Degree Days (base 65°F)	1,216	1,008	965	717	522	331	254	284	447	696	944	1,128	8,512
Cooling Degree Days (base 65°F)	0	0	0	0	0	1	2	0	0	0	0	0	3
Mean Precipitation (in.)	4.73	4.08	3.45	2.93	3.51	3.27	4.09	5.42	7.57	8.25	5.38	5.36	58.04
Maximum Precipitation (in.)	9.1	8.2	6.5	5.3	9.2	6.0	7.9	12.3	15.1	15.3	11.2	9.9	85.1
Minimum Precipitation (in.)	0.9	0.1	0.6	0.9	1.4	1.1	1.1	0.6	2.3	2.7	1.1	0.5	37.7
Maximum 24-hr. Precipitation (in.)	2.1	2.7	1.7	1.9	2.1	1.9	1.6	2.5	2.7	2.2	3.2	2.3	3.2
Days With ≥ 0.1" Precipitation	12	10	11	9	10	9	10	12	16	18	13	13	143
Days With ≥ 1.0" Precipitation	1	1	0	0	0	0	0	1	1	1	1	1	7
Mean Snowfall (in.)	29.0	17.8	11.6	1.1	trace	trace	0.0	0.0	trace	1.0	13.4	21.4	95.3
Maximum Snowfall (in.)	69	86	51	46	1	0	0	0	trace	16	70	55	212
Maximum 24-hr. Snowfall (in.)	20	24	18	21	1	0	0	0	trace	9	17	20	24
Days With ≥ 1.0" Snow Depth	22	17	14	2	0	0	0	0	0	0	8	17	80
Thunderstorm Days	< 1	0	0	0	0	< 1	< 1	< 1	< 1	0	< 1	0	1
Foggy Days	9	8	7	5	5	5	9	11	13	11	10	10	103
Predominant Sky Cover	OVR	OVR	OVR	OVR	OVR	OVR	OVR	OVR	OVR	OVR	OVR	OVR	OVR
Mean Relative Humidity 6am (%)	82	83	85	88	88	87	88	91	93	90	86	85	87
Mean Relative Humidity 3pm (%)	79	74	69	63	62	64	70	73	78	80	81	83	73
Mean Dewpoint (°F)	20	23	26	32	39	45	49	49	45	38	29	24	35
Prevailing Wind Direction	ESE	ESE	ESE	ESE	ESE	ESE	N	N	ESE	ESE	ESE	ESE	ESE
Prevailing Wind Speed (mph)	15	15	15	14	14	13	6	6	15	15	15	15	13
Maximum Wind Gust (mph)	54	69	54	61	54	46	47	48	69	71	92	64	92

Nome Municipal Airport

The weather station at Nome is located at Nome Field, approximately 1 mile northwest of the city. Low, marshy flats lie between the station and Norton Sound to the south, exposing the station to winds from the southeast through the west. A series of foothills, with heights of 500 to 1,200 feet, extend from northwest through north to east at a distance of from four to eight miles. The terrain increases in ruggedness and height farther north, with the Kigluaik Mountains reaching a height of 5,000 feet at a distance of 30 miles. The ground along the coastal flats is swampy during the summer months, but is permanently frozen below a depth of two to three feet. Vegetation in the Nome area consists mostly of grass and numerous small flowering plants.

The moderating influence of the open water of Norton Sound is effective only from early June to about the middle of November. Storms moving through this area during these months result in extended periods of cloudiness and rain. There is a nearly continuous cloud cover during July and August. During the summer months the daily temperature range is very slight. The freezing of Norton Sound in November causes a rather abrupt change from a maritime to a continental climate. The majority of low pressure systems during this period take a path south of Nome, resulting in strong easterly winds, accompanied by frequent blizzards, with the winds later becoming northerly and reaching Nome across the colder frozen areas of northern Alaska.

Temperatures generally remain well below freezing from the middle of November to the latter part of April, with January usually the coldest month of the year. Temperatures usually begin to rise near the end of February and continue to rise until they reach a maximum in July.

Precipitation reaches its maximum during the late summer months and drops to a minimum in April and May. Snow begins to fall in September, but usually does not accumulate on the ground until the first part of November. The snow cover decreases rapidly in April and May, and normally disappears by the middle of June. Snow depths in Nome have exceeded 70 inches.

Severe windstorms do occur with winds over 70 mph recorded several times. Strong winds during the winter months when there is snow cover produce blowing snow conditions that severely hinder transportation in the area.

Nome Municipal Airport *West Central Division*   Elevation: 13 ft.   Latitude: 64° 31' N   Longitude: 165° 27' W

	JAN	FEB	MAR	APR	MAY	JUN	JUL	AUG	SEP	OCT	NOV	DEC	YEAR
Mean Maximum Temp. (°F)	13.3	13.4	17.6	26.6	43.3	53.8	58.5	56.1	48.6	33.7	23.0	15.3	33.6
Mean Temp. (°F)	5.5	5.2	9.0	19.2	36.9	46.8	52.2	50.3	42.5	27.9	16.6	7.6	26.6
Mean Minimum Temp. (°F)	-2.3	-3.0	0.4	11.7	30.4	39.7	45.8	44.4	36.3	22.1	10.1	-0.1	19.6
Extreme Maximum Temp. (°F)	43	48	43	51	78	80	86	81	71	54	45	42	86
Extreme Minimum Temp. (°F)	-54	-42	-46	-24	-6	23	30	26	9	-6	-27	-40	-54
Days Maximum Temp. ≥ 90°F	na	na	na	na	na	na	na	na	na	na	na	na	na
Days Maximum Temp. ≤ 32°F	28	25	27	20	4	0	0	0	0	13	24	28	169
Days Minimum Temp. ≤ 32°F	31	28	31	29	18	3	0	1	10	26	29	31	237
Days Minimum Temp. ≤ 0°F	17	16	15	8	0	0	0	0	0	1	8	16	81
Heating Degree Days (base 65°F)	1,843	1,688	1,732	1,369	865	541	392	450	669	1,142	1,448	1,777	13,916
Cooling Degree Days (base 65°F)	0	0	0	0	0	1	2	0	0	0	0	0	3
Mean Precipitation (in.)	0.83	0.72	0.60	0.66	0.73	1.14	2.13	3.15	2.44	1.56	1.27	0.98	16.21
Maximum Precipitation (in.)	2.1	2.1	1.9	2.1	2.0	4.1	4.7	7.8	7.5	3.8	4.4	2.2	24.3
Minimum Precipitation (in.)	trace	trace	trace	trace	trace	trace	0.3	0.4	0.4	trace	trace	trace	7.4
Maximum 24-hr. Precipitation (in.)	1.1	0.6	0.5	0.6	0.8	1.4	1.7	2.4	1.3	1.5	0.8	0.7	2.4
Days With ≥ 0.1" Precipitation	3	3	2	2	3	3	5	8	7	5	4	3	48
Days With ≥ 1.0" Precipitation	0	0	0	0	0	0	0	0	0	0	0	0	0
Mean Snowfall (in.)	10.1	8.4	7.1	6.8	2.5	0.2	0.0	trace	0.4	5.4	13.5	11.8	66.2
Maximum Snowfall (in.)	24	23	20	23	10	3	0	trace	4	14	31	30	102
Maximum 24-hr. Snowfall (in.)	7	8	5	6	5	2	0	trace	2	6	9	8	9
Days With ≥ 1.0" Snow Depth	30	28	31	28	10	0	0	0	0	7	23	30	187
Thunderstorm Days	< 1	< 1	0	0	< 1	< 1	< 1	< 1	0	0	0	< 1	2
Foggy Days	10	7	9	9	10	12	16	15	8	7	8	9	120
Predominant Sky Cover	OVR	OVR	OVR	OVR	OVR	OVR	OVR	OVR	OVR	OVR	OVR	OVR	OVR
Mean Relative Humidity 6am (%)	75	73	74	79	80	81	86	88	84	80	77	75	79
Mean Relative Humidity 3pm (%)	75	71	70	74	73	74	79	79	73	73	76	74	74
Mean Dewpoint (°F)	0	-1	1	13	29	39	46	45	36	23	10	1	20
Prevailing Wind Direction	E	E	NE	E	E	WSW	WSW	SW	N	N	ENE	E	N
Prevailing Wind Speed (mph)	16	15	14	14	13	12	12	13	9	9	15	16	13
Maximum Wind Gust (mph)	67	66	60	58	53	45	49	56	59	69	69	71	71

Annette Island Airport *Southeastern Division*   Elevation: 108 ft.   Latitude: 55° 03' N   Longitude: 131° 34' W

	JAN	FEB	MAR	APR	MAY	JUN	JUL	AUG	SEP	OCT	NOV	DEC	YEAR
Mean Maximum Temp. (°F)	39.7	42.1	44.9	50.0	55.8	60.5	64.2	64.7	59.6	51.5	44.2	40.6	51.5
Mean Temp. (°F)	35.1	37.3	39.6	43.9	49.5	54.4	58.3	58.7	53.8	46.6	39.6	36.3	46.1
Mean Minimum Temp. (°F)	30.4	32.5	34.3	37.7	43.1	48.3	52.3	52.6	48.0	41.8	34.9	32.0	40.7
Extreme Maximum Temp. (°F)	61	65	64	82	84	86	88	88	82	67	67	57	88
Extreme Minimum Temp. (°F)	1	5	13	26	31	38	40	40	33	18	-3	3	-3
Days Maximum Temp. ≥ 90°F	na	na	na	na	na	na	na	na	na	na	na	na	na
Days Maximum Temp. ≤ 32°F	5	2	0	0	0	0	0	0	0	0	1	3	11
Days Minimum Temp. ≤ 32°F	17	13	11	4	0	0	0	0	0	2	10	14	71
Days Minimum Temp. ≤ 0°F	0	0	0	0	0	0	0	0	0	0	0	0	0
Heating Degree Days (base 65°F)	919	776	779	627	474	313	209	199	329	563	756	882	6,826
Cooling Degree Days (base 65°F)	0	0	0	0	1	3	6	8	1	0	0	0	19
Mean Precipitation (in.)	9.61	8.11	7.76	7.38	5.91	4.78	4.19	6.01	9.51	14.04	11.92	11.43	100.65
Days With ≥ 0.1" Precipitation	16	15	15	13	12	10	9	10	14	19	18	18	169
Days With ≥ 1.0" Precipitation	3	2	2	2	1	1	1	2	3	5	4	3	29
Mean Snowfall (in.)	11.0	10.0	7.1	2.6	trace	trace	0.0	0.0	0.0	0.1	3.6	9.3	43.7
Days With ≥ 1.0" Snow Depth	8	6	2	0	0	0	0	0	0	0	2	5	23

Auke Bay *Southeastern Division*   Elevation: 39 ft.   Latitude: 58° 23' N   Longitude: 134° 38' W

	JAN	FEB	MAR	APR	MAY	JUN	JUL	AUG	SEP	OCT	NOV	DEC	YEAR
Mean Maximum Temp. (°F)	30.5	35.1	40.7	49.3	57.0	63.0	65.5	64.2	56.9	47.0	37.0	32.4	48.2
Mean Temp. (°F)	26.4	30.0	34.7	41.5	48.8	54.8	57.8	56.8	50.8	42.7	33.3	28.8	42.2
Mean Minimum Temp. (°F)	22.2	24.8	28.6	33.7	40.5	46.6	50.0	49.4	44.7	38.3	29.5	25.1	36.1
Extreme Maximum Temp. (°F)	55	58	58	71	78	85	89	82	73	61	54	51	89
Extreme Minimum Temp. (°F)	-11	-12	-8	17	27	32	41	37	27	13	-33	-8	-33
Days Maximum Temp. ≥ 90°F	na	na	na	na	na	na	na	na	na	na	na	na	na
Days Maximum Temp. ≤ 32°F	15	8	2	0	0	0	0	0	0	0	6	12	43
Days Minimum Temp. ≤ 32°F	25	21	21	11	1	0	0	0	1	5	18	24	127
Days Minimum Temp. ≤ 0°F	2	1	0	0	0	0	0	0	0	0	0	1	4
Heating Degree Days (base 65°F)	1,191	982	934	699	497	299	221	249	419	685	946	1,115	8,237
Cooling Degree Days (base 65°F)	0	0	0	0	0	2	5	2	0	0	0	0	9
Mean Precipitation (in.)	4.99	3.88	3.40	2.99	4.02	4.19	5.06	6.58	8.90	9.36	5.35	5.16	63.88
Days With ≥ 0.1" Precipitation	12	10	11	9	11	10	11	13	16	*19*	13	14	*149*
Days With ≥ 1.0" Precipitation	1	0	0	0	0	0	1	1	2	2	1	1	9
Mean Snowfall (in.)	27.3	16.7	10.1	1.1	trace	0.0	0.0	0.0	trace	0.7	12.4	21.3	89.6
Days With ≥ 1.0" Snow Depth	25	21	18	4	0	0	0	0	0	0	10	19	97

Beaver Falls *Southeastern Division*   Elevation: 32 ft.   Latitude: 55° 23' N   Longitude: 131° 28' W

	JAN	FEB	MAR	APR	MAY	JUN	JUL	AUG	SEP	OCT	NOV	DEC	YEAR
Mean Maximum Temp. (°F)	36.7	40.2	43.9	49.6	56.0	*61.2*	*64.5*	64.7	59.2	50.3	42.1	38.1	*50.5*
Mean Temp. (°F)	32.2	35.1	38.1	42.6	48.6	*54.1*	*58.0*	58.3	53.4	45.4	37.7	33.9	*44.8*
Mean Minimum Temp. (°F)	27.7	30.0	32.2	35.6	41.0	46.9	*51.4*	52.0	47.6	40.7	33.3	29.7	*39.0*
Extreme Maximum Temp. (°F)	55	63	67	80	86	88	88	90	78	67	61	53	90
Extreme Minimum Temp. (°F)	2	-2	10	21	30	35	40	37	32	17	0	3	-2
Days Maximum Temp. ≥ 90°F	na	na	na	na	na	na	na	na	na	na	na	na	na
Days Maximum Temp. ≤ 32°F	6	2	0	0	0	0	0	0	0	0	2	4	14
Days Minimum Temp. ≤ 32°F	20	17	15	6	0	0	0	0	0	2	11	19	90
Days Minimum Temp. ≤ 0°F	0	0	0	0	0	0	0	0	0	0	0	0	0
Heating Degree Days (base 65°F)	1,010	839	828	665	503	*323*	*219*	207	341	600	813	956	*7,304*
Cooling Degree Days (base 65°F)	0	*0*	0	0	0	*3*	*8*	6	0	*0*	*0*	*0*	*17*
Mean Precipitation (in.)	14.73	11.76	11.95	9.57	7.71	6.18	5.21	8.83	15.20	22.40	17.38	16.98	147.90
Days With ≥ 0.1" Precipitation	16	14	16	14	13	11	10	11	14	20	18	18	175
Days With ≥ 1.0" Precipitation	5	4	4	3	2	1	1	3	5	7	6	6	47
Mean Snowfall (in.)	*18.5*	*17.4*	7.1	1.5	trace	0.0	0.0	0.0	0.0	trace	*5.3*	*14.6*	*64.4*
Days With ≥ 1.0" Snow Depth	*16*	*13*	10	2	0	0	0	0	0	0	*4*	11	*56*

Bethel Airport *West Central Division*   Elevation: 124 ft.   Latitude: 60° 47' N   Longitude: 161° 50' W

	JAN	FEB	MAR	APR	MAY	JUN	JUL	AUG	SEP	OCT	NOV	DEC	YEAR
Mean Maximum Temp. (°F)	12.0	13.6	21.8	33.1	49.7	59.4	63.1	59.7	51.7	35.1	23.2	14.9	36.4
Mean Temp. (°F)	5.9	7.0	14.2	25.5	41.2	51.1	55.7	53.3	45.1	29.6	17.4	8.6	29.6
Mean Minimum Temp. (°F)	-0.1	0.4	6.6	17.8	32.7	42.8	48.2	46.9	38.5	24.1	11.5	2.3	22.6
Extreme Maximum Temp. (°F)	45	46	46	60	80	83	83	84	72	56	48	44	84
Extreme Minimum Temp. (°F)	-48	-39	-36	-20	8	30	37	28	18	-4	-24	-37	-48
Days Maximum Temp. ≥ 90°F	na	na	na	na	na	na	na	na	na	na	na	na	na
Days Maximum Temp. ≤ 32°F	25	22	21	12	1	0	0	0	0	11	21	24	137
Days Minimum Temp. ≤ 32°F	31	28	31	28	15	1	0	0	6	26	28	30	224
Days Minimum Temp. ≤ 0°F	15	14	12	4	0	0	0	0	0	1	6	15	67
Heating Degree Days (base 65°F)	1,830	1,637	1,571	1,179	731	411	284	356	590	1,090	1,424	1,746	12,849
Cooling Degree Days (base 65°F)	0	0	0	0	0	0	2	0	0	0	0	0	2
Mean Precipitation (in.)	0.58	0.50	0.66	0.66	0.88	1.57	2.04	2.97	2.23	1.48	1.34	1.14	16.05
Days With ≥ 0.1" Precipitation	2	1	2	2	3	5	6	9	7	4	4	3	48
Days With ≥ 1.0" Precipitation	0	0	0	0	0	0	0	0	0	0	0	0	0
Mean Snowfall (in.)	6.4	5.2	7.7	4.8	1.8	trace	trace	0.0	0.4	4.0	10.5	10.8	51.6
Days With ≥ 1.0" Snow Depth	30	26	28	18	3	0	0	0	0	5	22	28	160

Bettles Field *Interior Basin Division*   Elevation: 643 ft.   Latitude: 66° 55' N   Longitude: 151° 31' W

	JAN	FEB	MAR	APR	MAY	JUN	JUL	AUG	SEP	OCT	NOV	DEC	YEAR
Mean Maximum Temp. (°F)	-3.9	1.0	15.7	33.2	54.7	68.0	70.5	63.0	48.5	24.5	5.3	-1.0	31.6
Mean Temp. (°F)	-11.7	-8.6	4.1	22.3	44.8	57.8	60.3	53.6	40.4	18.0	-1.7	-8.4	22.6
Mean Minimum Temp. (°F)	-19.5	-18.1	-7.6	11.3	34.8	47.5	50.1	44.1	32.3	11.4	-8.8	-15.8	13.5
Extreme Maximum Temp. (°F)	48	40	45	63	86	92	93	88	75	50	45	35	93
Extreme Minimum Temp. (°F)	-70	-64	-55	-37	-7	31	32	22	0	-35	-57	-59	-70
Days Maximum Temp. ≥ 90°F	na	na	na	na	na	na	na	na	na	na	na	na	na
Days Maximum Temp. ≤ 32°F	30	27	27	13	0	0	0	0	1	23	29	31	181
Days Minimum Temp. ≤ 32°F	31	27	31	28	12	0	0	2	15	30	30	31	237
Days Minimum Temp. ≤ 0°F	24	22	21	7	0	0	0	0	0	7	21	25	127
Heating Degree Days (base 65°F)	2,382	2,080	1,887	1,276	621	228	164	351	731	1,453	2,003	2,278	15,454
Cooling Degree Days (base 65°F)	0	0	0	0	1	20	23	3	0	0	0	0	47
Mean Precipitation (in.)	0.77	0.63	0.55	0.38	0.85	1.44	2.08	2.51	1.75	1.10	0.90	0.92	13.88
Days With ≥ 0.1" Precipitation	2	2	2	1	3	5	6	7	5	4	3	3	43
Days With ≥ 1.0" Precipitation	0	0	0	0	0	0	0	0	0	0	0	0	0
Mean Snowfall (in.)	13.5	10.1	9.9	5.6	0.9	trace	0.0	trace	2.6	13.6	14.4	17.7	88.3
Days With ≥ 1.0" Snow Depth	31	27	31	30	9	0	0	0	2	24	30	31	215

Big Delta Allen AAF *Interior Basin Division*   Elevation: 1,266 ft.   Latitude: 64° 00' N   Longitude: 145° 43' W

	JAN	FEB	MAR	APR	MAY	JUN	JUL	AUG	SEP	OCT	NOV	DEC	YEAR
Mean Maximum Temp. (°F)	3.9	10.8	25.3	42.4	58.2	67.0	70.6	65.0	53.2	30.9	13.3	6.8	37.3
Mean Temp. (°F)	-3.2	1.9	14.3	32.1	48.0	57.2	60.9	55.7	44.4	23.9	6.2	-0.4	28.4
Mean Minimum Temp. (°F)	-10.3	-6.8	3.2	21.7	37.9	47.3	51.1	46.2	35.5	16.9	-0.9	-7.7	19.5
Extreme Maximum Temp. (°F)	48	47	58	72	85	90	88	90	74	62	52	55	90
Extreme Minimum Temp. (°F)	-59	-52	-46	-27	11	30	32	23	-2	-39	-47	-58	-59
Days Maximum Temp. ≥ 90°F	na	na	na	na	na	na	na	na	na	na	na	na	na
Days Maximum Temp. ≤ 32°F	28	24	19	6	0	0	0	0	1	17	27	28	150
Days Minimum Temp. ≤ 32°F	30	27	29	24	7	0	0	1	10	27	29	30	214
Days Minimum Temp. ≤ 0°F	19	16	13	2	0	0	0	0	0	4	15	20	89
Heating Degree Days (base 65°F)	2,114	1,781	1,567	981	520	235	139	291	612	1,266	1,763	2,028	13,297
Cooling Degree Days (base 65°F)	0	0	0	0	*1*	9	16	9	0	0	0	0	*35*
Mean Precipitation (in.)	0.32	0.41	0.21	0.21	0.82	2.44	2.74	2.02	1.04	0.76	0.61	0.38	11.96
Days With ≥ 0.1" Precipitation	1	1	1	1	2	7	7	6	3	3	2	2	36
Days With ≥ 1.0" Precipitation	0	0	0	0	0	0	0	0	0	0	0	0	0
Mean Snowfall (in.)	5.1	5.9	3.5	2.7	*1.0*	trace	0.0	trace	2.4	11.8	11.1	6.4	*49.9*
Days With ≥ 1.0" Snow Depth	30	27	29	19	2	0	0	0	2	19	27	29	184

Cold Bay Airport *Southwestern Division*   Elevation: 95 ft.   Latitude: 55° 12' N   Longitude: 162° 43' W

	JAN	FEB	MAR	APR	MAY	JUN	JUL	AUG	SEP	OCT	NOV	DEC	YEAR
Mean Maximum Temp. (°F)	32.9	32.2	35.1	38.1	44.9	50.8	55.2	56.1	52.4	44.9	39.2	35.4	43.1
Mean Temp. (°F)	28.3	27.5	30.0	33.5	39.9	46.0	50.7	51.8	47.8	40.0	34.6	30.9	38.4
Mean Minimum Temp. (°F)	23.7	22.7	24.9	28.8	34.9	41.1	46.2	47.4	43.1	35.1	29.9	26.3	33.7
Extreme Maximum Temp. (°F)	51	50	56	54	67	72	71	74	76	58	59	54	76
Extreme Minimum Temp. (°F)	-8	-5	-13	4	18	30	33	32	26	6	10	-1	-13
Days Maximum Temp. ≥ 90°F	na	na	na	na	na	na	na	na	na	na	na	na	na
Days Maximum Temp. ≤ 32°F	12	11	8	5	0	0	0	0	0	1	4	9	50
Days Minimum Temp. ≤ 32°F	24	23	24	20	9	1	0	0	1	9	19	22	152
Days Minimum Temp. ≤ 0°F	1	0	1	0	0	0	0	0	0	0	0	0	2
Heating Degree Days (base 65°F)	1,131	1,054	1,078	939	771	564	437	402	510	767	906	1,051	9,610
Cooling Degree Days (base 65°F)	0	0	0	0	0	0	0	0	0	0	0	0	0
Mean Precipitation (in.)	3.01	2.48	2.40	2.28	2.57	2.71	2.51	3.51	4.61	4.39	4.48	4.06	39.01
Days With ≥ 0.1" Precipitation	8	7	8	7	7	7	7	10	11	11	12	11	106
Days With ≥ 1.0" Precipitation	0	0	0	0	0	0	0	0	1	1	0	1	3
Mean Snowfall (in.)	12.4	12.5	12.8	6.8	1.8	trace	trace	trace	trace	3.0	9.2	12.6	71.1
Days With ≥ 1.0" Snow Depth	16	15	12	7	1	0	0	0	0	1	8	15	75

College Observatory *Interior Basin Division*   Elevation: 620 ft.   Latitude: 64° 52' N   Longitude: 147° 50' W

	JAN	FEB	MAR	APR	MAY	JUN	JUL	AUG	SEP	OCT	NOV	DEC	YEAR
Mean Maximum Temp. (°F)	2.0	9.4	25.6	43.3	61.0	70.6	73.4	67.1	54.5	31.7	12.1	4.6	37.9
Mean Temp. (°F)	-5.3	-0.1	13.8	31.6	48.6	58.8	61.9	56.3	44.2	23.8	4.8	-2.7	28.0
Mean Minimum Temp. (°F)	-12.7	-9.5	2.0	19.8	36.0	46.9	50.5	45.4	33.9	15.9	-2.5	-9.9	18.0
Extreme Maximum Temp. (°F)	47	49	57	70	86	94	92	93	77	64	49	44	94
Extreme Minimum Temp. (°F)	-57	-52	-36	-24	9	29	35	24	5	-27	-45	-54	-57
Days Maximum Temp. ≥ 90°F	na	na	na	na	na	na	na	na	na	na	na	na	na
Days Maximum Temp. ≤ 32°F	29	25	20	6	0	0	0	0	1	16	28	29	154
Days Minimum Temp. ≤ 32°F	31	28	31	28	10	0	0	1	12	30	30	31	232
Days Minimum Temp. ≤ 0°F	22	19	14	3	0	0	0	0	0	4	17	23	102
Heating Degree Days (base 65°F)	2,180	1,837	1,583	996	504	198	120	273	616	1,270	1,804	2,099	13,480
Cooling Degree Days (base 65°F)	0	0	0	0	1	22	34	8	0	0	0	0	65
Mean Precipitation (in.)	0.55	0.45	0.34	0.22	0.57	1.74	1.94	1.87	1.30	1.05	0.90	0.90	11.83
Days With ≥ 0.1" Precipitation	2	2	1	1	2	5	6	6	4	3	3	3	38
Days With ≥ 1.0" Precipitation	0	0	0	0	0	0	0	0	0	0	0	0	0
Mean Snowfall (in.)	9.0	7.3	5.7	2.9	0.4	trace	0.0	0.0	2.0	12.9	14.8	14.1	69.1
Days With ≥ 1.0" Snow Depth	31	28	31	25	2	0	0	0	1	20	30	31	199

Cooper Lake Project *South Coast Division*   Elevation: 442 ft.   Latitude: 60° 23' N   Longitude: 149° 40' W

	JAN	FEB	MAR	APR	MAY	JUN	JUL	AUG	SEP	OCT	NOV	DEC	YEAR
Mean Maximum Temp. (°F)	26.8	29.0	35.6	44.3	53.8	61.7	65.7	64.0	53.8	41.8	33.4	29.2	44.9
Mean Temp. (°F)	20.7	21.8	27.1	36.0	44.6	52.0	56.7	55.5	47.1	36.2	28.0	23.6	37.4
Mean Minimum Temp. (°F)	14.5	14.5	18.6	27.6	35.6	42.3	47.6	47.0	40.3	30.5	22.5	18.0	29.9
Extreme Maximum Temp. (°F)	49	51	51	64	73	84	83	81	70	60	52	55	84
Extreme Minimum Temp. (°F)	-25	-26	-25	-6	20	30	37	33	20	5	-7	-10	-26
Days Maximum Temp. ≥ 90°F	na	na	na	na	na	na	na	na	na	na	na	na	na
Days Maximum Temp. ≤ 32°F	16	13	9	1	0	0	0	0	0	3	11	15	68
Days Minimum Temp. ≤ 32°F	27	25	27	22	6	0	0	0	3	17	24	27	178
Days Minimum Temp. ≤ 0°F	6	5	3	0	0	0	0	0	0	0	0	2	16
Heating Degree Days (base 65°F)	1,369	1,214	1,166	864	626	383	253	288	531	885	1,104	1,276	9,959
Cooling Degree Days (base 65°F)	0	0	0	0	0	0	1	0	0	0	0	0	1
Mean Precipitation (in.)	2.67	2.33	1.38	1.32	0.93	0.93	1.35	2.97	5.65	4.95	3.17	3.68	31.33
Days With ≥ 0.1" Precipitation	5	5	3	3	2	3	4	6	9	9	6	7	62
Days With ≥ 1.0" Precipitation	0	0	0	0	0	0	0	0	1	1	1	1	4
Mean Snowfall (in.)	13.2	16.0	11.7	4.1	trace	trace	0.0	0.0	trace	5.8	14.5	22.9	88.2
Days With ≥ 1.0" Snow Depth	28	24	28	16	1	0	0	0	0	4	15	24	140

Cordova *South Coast Division*   Elevation: 39 ft.   Latitude: 60° 30' N   Longitude: 145° 30' W

	JAN	FEB	MAR	APR	MAY	JUN	JUL	AUG	SEP	OCT	NOV	DEC	YEAR
Mean Maximum Temp. (°F)	31.4	35.0	39.0	45.5	52.8	58.4	61.9	61.7	56.2	46.4	36.7	32.8	46.5
Mean Temp. (°F)	24.1	27.1	31.0	37.6	44.9	50.9	54.6	53.9	48.2	39.4	29.9	26.1	39.0
Mean Minimum Temp. (°F)	16.8	19.2	22.9	29.7	37.0	43.3	47.3	46.1	40.2	32.4	23.0	19.3	31.4
Extreme Maximum Temp. (°F)	55	58	57	67	78	84	89	86	74	61	53	53	89
Extreme Minimum Temp. (°F)	-30	-23	-23	-2	19	31	33	29	20	-1	-10	-18	-30
Days Maximum Temp. ≥ 90°F	na	na	na	na	na	na	na	na	na	na	na	na	na
Days Maximum Temp. ≤ 32°F	14	9	4	1	0	0	0	0	0	0	8	12	48
Days Minimum Temp. ≤ 32°F	25	21	24	19	6	0	0	0	5	14	22	25	161
Days Minimum Temp. ≤ 0°F	6	4	1	0	0	0	0	0	0	0	1	4	16
Heating Degree Days (base 65°F)	1,260	1,063	1,047	816	616	416	316	337	497	786	1,046	1,200	9,400
Cooling Degree Days (base 65°F)	0	0	0	0	0	0	1	0	0	0	0	0	1
Mean Precipitation (in.)	7.11	6.78	6.31	5.89	6.21	5.52	5.66	9.64	14.27	12.46	7.35	9.64	96.84
Days With ≥ 0.1" Precipitation	12	11	12	12	14	12	12	14	17	17	12	14	159
Days With ≥ 1.0" Precipitation	2	2	2	1	1	1	1	3	5	4	2	3	27
Mean Snowfall (in.)	21.3	18.7	23.8	9.8	0.4	trace	0.0	trace	trace	2.4	12.6	27.1	116.1
Days With ≥ 1.0" Snow Depth	24	21	24	12	1	0	0	0	0	1	12	23	118

Dillingham Airport *Bristol Bay Division*   Elevation: 85 ft.   Latitude: 59° 03' N   Longitude: 158° 31' W

	JAN	FEB	MAR	APR	MAY	JUN	JUL	AUG	SEP	OCT	NOV	DEC	YEAR
Mean Maximum Temp. (°F)	21.8	21.6	28.9	37.5	49.3	57.4	*61.4*	59.7	*52.8*	39.0	*27.8*	21.4	*39.9*
Mean Temp. (°F)	16.4	15.4	22.7	31.5	42.6	50.6	*55.1*	53.8	*47.1*	33.1	*22.3*	15.7	*33.8*
Mean Minimum Temp. (°F)	10.8	9.2	16.4	25.3	35.8	43.8	*48.7*	47.8	*41.3*	27.2	*16.8*	10.1	*27.8*
Extreme Maximum Temp. (°F)	44	47	47	55	77	79	*81*	80	73	55	46	51	*81*
Extreme Minimum Temp. (°F)	-53	-35	-30	-17	16	29	*36*	32	21	0	-19	-27	*-53*
Days Maximum Temp. ≥ 90°F	na	na	na	na	na	na	na	na	na	na	na	na	na
Days Maximum Temp. ≤ 32°F	22	20	16	5	0	0	*0*	0	0	7	18	22	*110*
Days Minimum Temp. ≤ 32°F	29	26	29	24	8	0	*0*	0	4	21	26	29	*196*
Days Minimum Temp. ≤ 0°F	8	9	4	1	0	0	*0*	0	0	0	3	9	*34*
Heating Degree Days (base 65°F)	1,504	1,396	1,304	1,000	688	426	*302*	342	*532*	981	*1,274*	1,522	*11,271*
Cooling Degree Days (base 65°F)	0	0	0	0	0	0	1	0	0	0	0	0	1
Mean Precipitation (in.)	*1.73*	*1.11*	*1.52*	*1.07*	1.38	1.90	2.93	3.79	3.78	2.29	2.32	*1.94*	25.76
Days With ≥ 0.1" Precipitation	*5*	3	4	*3*	4	6	7	8	8	6	6	6	66
Days With ≥ 1.0" Precipitation	*0*	0	0	0	*0*	*0*	*0*	1	1	0	*0*	0	2
Mean Snowfall (in.)	19.8	12.1	15.9	6.5	0.5	trace	*0.0*	*0.0*	*trace*	2.5	16.4	19.1	*92.8*
Days With ≥ 1.0" Snow Depth	29	28	28	18	3	0	*0*	0	0	3	18	27	*154*

Eielson Field *Interior Basin Division*   Elevation: 544 ft.   Latitude: 64° 40' N   Longitude: 147° 06' W

	JAN	FEB	MAR	APR	MAY	JUN	JUL	AUG	SEP	OCT	NOV	DEC	YEAR
Mean Maximum Temp. (°F)	-2.0	6.6	24.2	42.6	59.7	69.3	71.4	65.7	54.0	30.5	10.2	1.7	36.2
Mean Temp. (°F)	-10.0	-3.6	11.6	31.6	48.8	58.9	61.7	56.3	44.7	23.3	2.6	-6.1	26.7
Mean Minimum Temp. (°F)	-18.0	-13.8	-1.1	20.6	37.8	48.4	51.9	46.9	35.3	16.1	-5.0	-13.9	17.1
Extreme Maximum Temp. (°F)	49	50	56	74	84	92	92	91	79	64	50	48	92
Extreme Minimum Temp. (°F)	-64	-54	-49	-23	9	27	34	22	5	-36	-45	-53	-64
Days Maximum Temp. ≥ 90°F	na	na	na	na	na	na	na	na	na	na	na	na	na
Days Maximum Temp. ≤ 32°F	29	26	22	6	0	0	0	0	1	17	27	29	157
Days Minimum Temp. ≤ 32°F	31	28	31	26	6	0	0	1	10	28	30	30	221
Days Minimum Temp. ≤ 0°F	26	21	16	3	0	0	0	0	0	4	19	25	114
Heating Degree Days (base 65°F)	2,327	1,939	1,652	994	496	194	119	269	602	1,285	1,870	2,209	13,956
Cooling Degree Days (base 65°F)	0	0	0	0	1	19	26	7	0	0	0	0	53
Mean Precipitation (in.)	0.38	0.30	0.32	0.22	0.66	1.75	2.27	2.16	1.25	0.96	0.73	0.57	11.57
Days With ≥ 0.1" Precipitation	1	1	1	1	2	5	7	6	4	3	2	2	35
Days With ≥ 1.0" Precipitation	0	0	0	0	0	0	0	0	0	0	0	0	0
Mean Snowfall (in.)	9.1	7.2	6.5	3.7	1.1	trace	trace	trace	2.6	14.1	17.1	13.3	74.7
Days With ≥ 1.0" Snow Depth	29	27	*30*	14	0	0	0	0	1	18	29	31	*179*

Glen Alps *Cook Inlet Division*   Elevation: 2,257 ft.   Latitude: 61° 06' N   Longitude: 149° 41' W

	JAN	FEB	MAR	APR	MAY	JUN	JUL	AUG	SEP	OCT	NOV	DEC	YEAR
Mean Maximum Temp. (°F)	26.6	26.6	31.2	38.1	47.0	55.7	58.6	57.1	49.0	37.1	28.8	26.3	40.2
Mean Temp. (°F)	19.7	18.9	23.5	31.0	40.4	48.3	51.9	50.5	42.7	30.8	22.2	19.6	33.3
Mean Minimum Temp. (°F)	13.2	11.5	15.9	23.9	33.7	40.9	45.3	43.9	36.4	24.4	15.4	13.0	26.5
Extreme Maximum Temp. (°F)	44	55	55	55	69	76	75	75	65	55	51	46	76
Extreme Minimum Temp. (°F)	-37	-34	-15	-9	16	30	28	28	9	-4	-19	-23	-37
Days Maximum Temp. ≥ 90°F	na	na	na	na	na	na	na	na	na	na	na	na	na
Days Maximum Temp. ≤ 32°F	18	18	14	4	0	0	0	0	0	7	17	21	99
Days Minimum Temp. ≤ 32°F	31	28	31	27	12	0	0	0	7	25	29	31	221
Days Minimum Temp. ≤ 0°F	6	6	3	1	0	0	0	0	0	0	3	5	24
Heating Degree Days (base 65°F)	1,400	1,297	1,279	1,013	756	493	398	443	662	1,054	1,280	1,402	11,477
Cooling Degree Days (base 65°F)	0	0	0	0	0	0	0	0	0	0	0	0	0
Mean Precipitation (in.)	1.84	1.84	1.65	1.22	1.10	1.53	2.31	3.32	4.28	3.12	2.36	2.73	27.30
Days With ≥ 0.1" Precipitation	5	5	5	4	4	5	6	8	9	8	6	8	73
Days With ≥ 1.0" Precipitation	0	0	0	0	0	0	0	0	1	0	0	0	1
Mean Snowfall (in.)	21.8	25.3	24.0	13.3	2.8	trace	0.0	0.0	1.2	19.1	26.5	35.4	169.4
Days With ≥ 1.0" Snow Depth	na	na	na	na	na	0	0	0	1	na	na	na	na

Gulkana Intermediate Field *Copper River Division*   Elevation: 1,568 ft.   Latitude: 62° 09' N   Longitude: 145° 27' W

	JAN	FEB	MAR	APR	MAY	JUN	JUL	AUG	SEP	OCT	NOV	DEC	YEAR
Mean Maximum Temp. (°F)	3.0	13.8	28.4	42.3	55.8	65.0	68.6	64.9	53.7	34.5	13.6	6.1	37.5
Mean Temp. (°F)	-5.0	3.5	15.8	31.3	44.5	53.6	57.5	53.8	43.7	26.7	6.1	-1.8	27.5
Mean Minimum Temp. (°F)	-13.0	-6.9	3.2	20.3	33.1	42.1	46.4	42.6	33.6	18.8	-1.4	-9.6	17.4
Extreme Maximum Temp. (°F)	43	43	51	67	78	87	88	88	74	58	46	49	88
Extreme Minimum Temp. (°F)	-57	-51	-48	-27	14	26	29	20	2	-23	-44	-52	-57
Days Maximum Temp. ≥ 90°F	na	na	na	na	na	na	na	na	na	na	na	na	na
Days Maximum Temp. ≤ 32°F	29	24	18	3	0	0	0	0	1	12	27	28	142
Days Minimum Temp. ≤ 32°F	31	28	31	27	14	1	0	3	14	26	30	31	236
Days Minimum Temp. ≤ 0°F	23	18	14	2	0	0	0	0	0	3	17	23	100
Heating Degree Days (base 65°F)	2,172	1,736	1,520	1,005	629	337	229	342	634	1,182	1,765	2,069	13,620
Cooling Degree Days (base 65°F)	0	0	0	0	0	1	3	2	0	0	0	0	6
Mean Precipitation (in.)	0.44	0.53	0.36	0.22	0.59	1.53	1.83	1.73	1.42	1.00	0.69	0.99	11.33
Days With ≥ 0.1" Precipitation	1	2	1	1	2	5	5	5	5	4	2	3	36
Days With ≥ 1.0" Precipitation	0	0	0	0	0	0	0	0	0	0	0	0	0
Mean Snowfall (in.)	7.3	8.6	6.1	3.3	0.7	trace	trace	trace	1.4	8.9	9.2	11.6	57.1
Days With ≥ 1.0" Snow Depth	31	28	31	20	1	0	0	0	1	15	27	30	184

Homer Airport *Cook Inlet Division*   Elevation: 88 ft.   Latitude: 59° 39' N   Longitude: 151° 29' W

	JAN	FEB	MAR	APR	MAY	JUN	JUL	AUG	SEP	OCT	NOV	DEC	YEAR
Mean Maximum Temp. (°F)	29.2	31.4	36.4	43.3	50.6	57.0	60.9	60.7	54.8	44.0	35.1	31.2	44.5
Mean Temp. (°F)	23.4	24.9	29.6	36.3	43.6	49.9	54.1	53.7	47.9	37.7	29.3	25.3	38.0
Mean Minimum Temp. (°F)	17.5	18.4	22.7	29.3	36.7	42.9	47.1	46.7	40.9	31.3	23.4	19.4	31.4
Extreme Maximum Temp. (°F)	51	50	53	60	71	75	81	75	69	58	52	49	81
Extreme Minimum Temp. (°F)	-24	-19	-21	3	25	27	35	33	23	2	-7	-12	-24
Days Maximum Temp. ≥ 90°F	na	na	na	na	na	na	na	na	na	na	na	na	na
Days Maximum Temp. ≤ 32°F	16	13	7	1	0	0	0	0	0	2	10	15	64
Days Minimum Temp. ≤ 32°F	27	25	26	21	6	0	0	0	3	17	25	27	177
Days Minimum Temp. ≤ 0°F	4	2	1	0	0	0	0	0	0	0	0	2	9
Heating Degree Days (base 65°F)	1,284	1,126	1,092	853	655	445	333	342	507	840	1,065	1,223	9,765
Cooling Degree Days (base 65°F)	0	0	0	0	0	0	0	0	0	0	0	0	0
Mean Precipitation (in.)	2.60	2.09	1.85	1.24	1.08	0.96	1.40	2.32	3.33	2.80	2.77	2.85	25.29
Days With ≥ 0.1" Precipitation	7	6	5	4	3	3	5	7	9	8	7	8	72
Days With ≥ 1.0" Precipitation	0	0	0	0	0	0	0	0	0	0	0	0	0
Mean Snowfall (in.)	9.9	12.3	10.0	3.5	0.4	0.0	0.0	0.0	trace	2.9	8.2	13.3	60.5
Days With ≥ 1.0" Snow Depth	22	18	18	7	0	0	0	0	0	2	10	21	98

Intricate Bay *Bristol Bay Division*   Elevation: 167 ft.   Latitude: 59° 34' N   Longitude: 154° 28' W

	JAN	FEB	MAR	APR	MAY	JUN	JUL	AUG	SEP	OCT	NOV	DEC	YEAR
Mean Maximum Temp. (°F)	25.1	26.0	33.4	41.9	53.2	61.6	65.6	63.4	55.3	42.3	33.0	26.9	44.0
Mean Temp. (°F)	16.8	17.1	23.9	32.8	43.5	51.5	56.0	54.4	47.3	35.0	25.9	19.3	35.3
Mean Minimum Temp. (°F)	8.6	8.1	14.3	23.7	33.6	41.3	46.3	45.4	39.2	27.7	18.8	11.6	26.5
Extreme Maximum Temp. (°F)	60	53	54	61	79	82	84	78	71	62	53	49	84
Extreme Minimum Temp. (°F)	-43	-50	-47	-20	3	26	29	27	10	-5	-16	-29	-50
Days Maximum Temp. ≥ 90°F	na	na	na	na	na	na	na	na	na	na	na	na	na
Days Maximum Temp. ≤ 32°F	16	15	10	3	0	0	0	0	0	3	12	16	75
Days Minimum Temp. ≤ 32°F	27	25	27	23	13	3	0	1	6	20	26	28	199
Days Minimum Temp. ≤ 0°F	11	11	7	2	0	0	0	0	0	0	3	9	43
Heating Degree Days (base 65°F)	1,489	1,351	1,269	958	661	399	274	321	524	922	1,166	1,413	10,747
Cooling Degree Days (base 65°F)	0	0	0	0	0	0	1	0	0	0	0	0	1
Mean Precipitation (in.)	2.80	2.51	2.22	2.37	2.53	1.77	2.27	4.11	4.37	3.72	3.30	3.30	35.27
Days With ≥ 0.1" Precipitation	6	6	5	6	7	5	6	10	10	8	7	8	84
Days With ≥ 1.0" Precipitation	0	0	0	0	0	0	0	1	1	1	1	0	4
Mean Snowfall (in.)	10.6	11.0	9.4	5.8	1.5	trace	0.0	0.0	trace	4.1	10.2	18.1	70.7
Days With ≥ 1.0" Snow Depth	23	19	20	10	1	0	0	0	0	3	14	26	116

Kenai Municipal Airport *Cook Inlet Division* Elevation: 85 ft. Latitude: 60° 34' N Longitude: 151° 15' W

	JAN	FEB	MAR	APR	MAY	JUN	JUL	AUG	SEP	OCT	NOV	DEC	YEAR
Mean Maximum Temp. (°F)	21.2	25.9	32.9	42.4	52.7	58.5	62.0	61.6	54.7	41.0	28.9	23.3	42.1
Mean Temp. (°F)	13.2	16.7	23.7	34.5	44.4	50.8	54.9	53.9	46.8	34.0	21.5	15.8	34.2
Mean Minimum Temp. (°F)	5.3	7.5	14.4	26.5	35.9	43.1	47.8	46.2	38.9	27.0	14.2	8.2	26.2
Extreme Maximum Temp. (°F)	43	47	51	62	77	79	85	86	69	58	48	46	86
Extreme Minimum Temp. (°F)	-47	-37	-41	-17	22	28	34	24	16	-12	-27	-36	-47
Days Maximum Temp. ≥ 90°F	na	na	na	na	na	na	na	na	na	na	na	na	na
Days Maximum Temp. ≤ 32°F	23	19	13	3	0	0	0	0	0	4	18	24	104
Days Minimum Temp. ≤ 32°F	30	27	29	24	8	0	0	0	6	21	28	30	203
Days Minimum Temp. ≤ 0°F	12	10	6	1	0	0	0	0	0	1	6	10	46
Heating Degree Days (base 65°F)	1,604	1,359	1,275	909	633	418	306	337	540	953	1,298	1,523	11,155
Cooling Degree Days (base 65°F)	0	0	0	0	0	0	0	0	0	0	0	0	0
Mean Precipitation (in.)	1.00	0.93	0.82	0.69	0.98	1.12	1.73	2.64	3.30	2.71	1.65	1.49	19.06
Days With ≥ 0.1" Precipitation	3	3	3	2	3	3	5	7	9	7	5	5	55
Days With ≥ 1.0" Precipitation	0	0	0	0	0	0	0	0	0	0	0	0	0
Mean Snowfall (in.)	9.0	9.3	8.0	2.7	0.2	trace	trace	0.0	0.1	6.1	11.1	14.0	60.5
Days With ≥ 1.0" Snow Depth	29	26	27	14	0	0	0	0	0	5	19	26	146

King Salmon Airport *Bristol Bay Division* Elevation: 45 ft. Latitude: 58° 41' N Longitude: 156° 39' W

	JAN	FEB	MAR	APR	MAY	JUN	JUL	AUG	SEP	OCT	NOV	DEC	YEAR
Mean Maximum Temp. (°F)	22.6	23.6	32.0	41.0	52.2	59.5	63.7	62.0	54.9	40.3	30.4	24.5	42.2
Mean Temp. (°F)	15.4	15.6	23.6	32.9	43.4	50.7	55.4	54.4	47.4	32.9	23.0	16.6	34.3
Mean Minimum Temp. (°F)	8.2	7.5	15.1	24.6	34.6	41.7	47.0	46.8	39.7	25.4	15.6	8.7	26.3
Extreme Maximum Temp. (°F)	50	57	55	64	80	83	85	80	74	58	56	48	85
Extreme Minimum Temp. (°F)	-48	-41	-42	-15	14	29	33	25	15	-12	-28	-37	-48
Days Maximum Temp. ≥ 90°F	na	na	na	na	na	na	na	na	na	na	na	na	na
Days Maximum Temp. ≤ 32°F	18	16	12	5	0	0	0	0	0	6	15	18	90
Days Minimum Temp. ≤ 32°F	28	25	27	24	10	0	0	0	6	22	26	28	196
Days Minimum Temp. ≤ 0°F	11	11	6	1	0	0	0	0	0	1	6	11	47
Heating Degree Days (base 65°F)	1,533	1,393	1,279	957	662	424	292	321	523	989	1,254	1,497	11,124
Cooling Degree Days (base 65°F)	0	0	0	0	0	0	1	0	0	0	0	0	1
Mean Precipitation (in.)	1.01	0.71	0.84	0.98	1.32	1.67	2.14	2.96	2.75	2.10	1.49	1.41	19.38
Days With ≥ 0.1" Precipitation	4	2	3	4	5	6	6	9	8	6	5	4	62
Days With ≥ 1.0" Precipitation	0	0	0	0	0	0	0	0	0	0	0	0	0
Mean Snowfall (in.)	9.6	6.0	6.2	4.6	0.8	trace	0.0	trace	trace	3.3	6.4	9.9	46.8
Days With ≥ 1.0" Snow Depth	19	16	14	6	0	0	0	0	0	3	12	20	90

Kitoi Bay *South Coast Division* Elevation: 13 ft. Latitude: 58° 11' N Longitude: 152° 21' W

	JAN	FEB	MAR	APR	MAY	JUN	JUL	AUG	SEP	OCT	NOV	DEC	YEAR
Mean Maximum Temp. (°F)	33.7	34.3	38.6	43.0	49.4	55.8	60.8	62.2	55.6	45.5	37.8	34.1	45.9
Mean Temp. (°F)	28.9	29.0	32.3	36.6	42.8	49.4	54.3	54.9	49.1	39.4	32.8	29.1	39.9
Mean Minimum Temp. (°F)	24.1	23.6	25.8	30.1	36.3	42.9	47.6	47.6	42.4	33.3	27.8	23.9	33.8
Extreme Maximum Temp. (°F)	50	54	56	60	76	87	82	83	71	62	54	51	87
Extreme Minimum Temp. (°F)	-20	-6	-6	2	20	28	37	32	25	10	7	-2	-20
Days Maximum Temp. ≥ 90°F	na	na	na	na	na	na	na	na	na	na	na	na	na
Days Maximum Temp. ≤ 32°F	10	8	4	1	0	0	0	0	0	1	5	11	40
Days Minimum Temp. ≤ 32°F	25	22	24	19	7	0	0	0	2	15	23	26	163
Days Minimum Temp. ≤ 0°F	1	1	0	0	0	0	0	0	0	0	0	0	2
Heating Degree Days (base 65°F)	1,112	1,012	1,009	846	680	463	326	306	472	788	958	1,107	9,079
Cooling Degree Days (base 65°F)	0	0	0	0	0	0	1	1	0	0	0	0	2
Mean Precipitation (in.)	6.89	5.20	4.61	5.26	5.71	4.57	3.77	5.28	6.76	6.50	5.65	6.44	66.64
Days With ≥ 0.1" Precipitation	13	11	11	13	14	10	9	10	12	12	11	14	140
Days With ≥ 1.0" Precipitation	2	1	0	0	1	1	1	1	2	2	1	1	13
Mean Snowfall (in.)	14.7	14.0	9.3	4.0	0.2	0.0	0.0	0.0	trace	1.2	6.8	16.7	66.9
Days With ≥ 1.0" Snow Depth	18	16	13	6	1	0	0	0	0	1	6	18	79

Kodiak State USCG Base *South Coast Division* Elevation: 13 ft. Latitude: 57° 45' N Longitude: 152° 30' W

	JAN	FEB	MAR	APR	MAY	JUN	JUL	AUG	SEP	OCT	NOV	DEC	YEAR
Mean Maximum Temp. (°F)	35.9	35.6	39.4	43.7	49.9	55.9	60.4	61.9	56.4	47.2	39.9	36.6	46.9
Mean Temp. (°F)	31.2	30.4	33.9	38.2	44.3	50.1	54.7	55.4	50.0	40.9	34.6	31.3	41.2
Mean Minimum Temp. (°F)	26.4	25.1	28.3	32.7	38.6	44.3	48.9	48.8	43.5	34.5	29.3	25.9	35.5
Extreme Maximum Temp. (°F)	48	55	53	62	76	82	82	79	73	62	54	56	82
Extreme Minimum Temp. (°F)	-16	-8	1	7	28	31	38	34	26	10	2	-2	-16
Days Maximum Temp. ≥ 90°F	na	na	na	na	na	na	na	na	na	na	na	na	na
Days Maximum Temp. ≤ 32°F	6	7	3	1	0	0	0	0	0	1	4	7	29
Days Minimum Temp. ≤ 32°F	20	20	21	12	3	0	0	0	1	12	19	23	131
Days Minimum Temp. ≤ 0°F	0	1	0	0	0	0	0	0	0	0	0	0	1
Heating Degree Days (base 65°F)	1,042	971	959	798	635	441	315	292	444	741	905	1,039	8,582
Cooling Degree Days (base 65°F)	0	0	0	0	0	1	1	1	0	0	0	0	3
Mean Precipitation (in.)	8.73	5.72	5.32	5.57	6.11	5.43	4.23	4.53	8.04	8.35	6.66	7.72	76.41
Days With ≥ 0.1" Precipitation	13	11	11	12	11	10	8	8	12	11	11	12	130
Days With ≥ 1.0" Precipitation	2	1	1	1	1	1	1	1	3	2	2	2	18
Mean Snowfall (in.)	13.9	15.5	10.7	7.0	0.2	0.0	0.0	trace	trace	1.8	7.4	15.8	72.3
Days With ≥ 1.0" Snow Depth	10	13	8	3	0	0	0	0	0	1	4	12	51

Kotzebue Ralph Wein Mem. *Arctic Drainage Division*   Elevation: 9 ft.   Latitude: 66° 53' N   Longitude: 162° 36' W

	JAN	FEB	MAR	APR	MAY	JUN	JUL	AUG	SEP	OCT	NOV	DEC	YEAR
Mean Maximum Temp. (°F)	4.3	3.8	8.5	20.6	38.4	50.7	59.8	56.7	46.5	27.5	13.6	6.0	28.0
Mean Temp. (°F)	-2.3	-3.2	0.3	12.0	31.9	44.8	54.7	52.0	41.8	23.0	8.4	-0.5	21.9
Mean Minimum Temp. (°F)	-8.8	-10.2	-7.8	3.3	25.4	38.8	49.6	47.4	37.1	18.5	3.1	-7.0	15.8
Extreme Maximum Temp. (°F)	37	40	39	48	70	85	84	75	69	51	38	37	85
Extreme Minimum Temp. (°F)	-49	-49	-45	-30	-11	24	30	29	13	-19	-27	-47	-49
Days Maximum Temp. ≥ 90°F	na	na	na	na	na	na	na	na	na	na	na	na	na
Days Maximum Temp. ≤ 32°F	30	27	30	23	8	0	0	0	1	20	28	30	197
Days Minimum Temp. ≤ 32°F	31	28	31	30	24	5	0	0	7	28	30	31	245
Days Minimum Temp. ≤ 0°F	21	20	21	14	1	0	0	0	0	2	13	22	114
Heating Degree Days (base 65°F)	2,086	1,928	2,005	1,587	1,018	602	315	395	689	1,294	1,695	2,031	15,645
Cooling Degree Days (base 65°F)	0	0	0	0	0	2	3	0	0	0	0	0	5
Mean Precipitation (in.)	0.51	0.41	0.39	0.41	0.32	0.56	1.41	1.94	1.66	0.96	0.71	0.59	9.87
Days With ≥ 0.1" Precipitation	2	1	1	1	1	2	4	6	5	3	3	2	31
Days With ≥ 1.0" Precipitation	0	0	0	0	0	0	0	0	0	0	0	0	0
Mean Snowfall (in.)	7.3	5.0	5.3	4.4	1.2	trace	trace	trace	1.0	6.9	9.0	8.7	48.8
Days With ≥ 1.0" Snow Depth	31	28	31	30	20	0	0	0	1	16	27	31	215

Little Port Walter *Southeastern Division*   Elevation: 13 ft.   Latitude: 56° 23' N   Longitude: 134° 39' W

	JAN	FEB	MAR	APR	MAY	JUN	JUL	AUG	SEP	OCT	NOV	DEC	YEAR
Mean Maximum Temp. (°F)	37.3	39.3	42.3	47.3	53.1	58.8	62.2	62.3	56.9	49.5	42.2	38.8	49.2
Mean Temp. (°F)	33.1	34.6	36.9	40.9	46.1	51.6	55.5	55.6	51.0	44.6	37.9	34.7	43.6
Mean Minimum Temp. (°F)	28.9	30.0	31.5	34.5	39.0	44.4	48.7	48.9	45.1	39.6	33.5	30.5	37.9
Extreme Maximum Temp. (°F)	54	58	57	66	72	80	79	88	73	61	57	52	88
Extreme Minimum Temp. (°F)	4	7	11	24	29	34	37	40	31	23	4	4	4
Days Maximum Temp. ≥ 90°F	na	na	na	na	na	na	na	na	na	na	na	na	na
Days Maximum Temp. ≤ 32°F	6	4	1	0	0	0	0	0	0	0	2	4	17
Days Minimum Temp. ≤ 32°F	21	18	19	10	2	0	0	0	0	3	13	19	105
Days Minimum Temp. ≤ 0°F	0	0	0	0	0	0	0	0	0	0	0	0	0
Heating Degree Days (base 65°F)	982	851	863	716	579	395	287	284	413	625	805	933	7,733
Cooling Degree Days (base 65°F)	0	0	0	0	0	0	0	0	0	0	0	0	0
Mean Precipitation (in.)	23.61	19.35	17.93	14.83	12.38	8.20	8.02	13.18	22.20	33.78	27.90	25.37	226.75
Days With ≥ 0.1" Precipitation	20	17	19	17	14	11	10	12	17	23	21	21	202
Days With ≥ 1.0" Precipitation	8	8	6	5	4	3	3	4	8	11	10	9	79
Mean Snowfall (in.)	29.6	24.1	15.4	2.0	trace	0.0	0.0	0.0	0.0	0.3	12.4	25.9	109.7
Days With ≥ 1.0" Snow Depth	22	18	17	7	1	0	0	0	0	0	7	19	91

Matanuska AES *Cook Inlet Division*   Elevation: 147 ft.   Latitude: 61° 34' N   Longitude: 149° 16' W

	JAN	FEB	MAR	APR	MAY	JUN	JUL	AUG	SEP	OCT	NOV	DEC	YEAR
Mean Maximum Temp. (°F)	22.1	27.1	35.8	46.5	58.0	64.6	67.2	65.1	56.2	41.5	28.1	23.4	44.6
Mean Temp. (°F)	13.7	18.3	26.6	37.2	47.4	54.7	58.1	55.9	47.5	33.5	20.1	15.3	35.7
Mean Minimum Temp. (°F)	5.3	9.5	17.3	27.7	36.7	44.7	48.9	46.7	38.7	25.5	12.0	7.1	26.7
Extreme Maximum Temp. (°F)	50	54	58	68	78	83	85	81	72	67	55	52	85
Extreme Minimum Temp. (°F)	-40	-41	-28	-6	19	33	37	28	15	-11	-26	-31	-41
Days Maximum Temp. ≥ 90°F	na	na	na	na	na	na	na	na	na	na	na	na	na
Days Maximum Temp. ≤ 32°F	22	17	9	1	0	0	0	0	0	5	19	22	95
Days Minimum Temp. ≤ 32°F	30	27	29	22	7	0	0	0	6	23	29	30	203
Days Minimum Temp. ≤ 0°F	12	9	3	0	0	0	0	0	0	1	7	11	43
Heating Degree Days (base 65°F)	1,586	1,313	1,185	829	540	304	209	276	518	970	1,342	1,537	10,609
Cooling Degree Days (base 65°F)	0	0	0	0	0	1	2	0	0	0	0	0	3
Mean Precipitation (in.)	0.69	0.68	0.47	0.43	0.71	1.38	2.16	2.33	2.42	1.52	0.96	1.19	14.94
Days With ≥ 0.1" Precipitation	2	2	2	2	2	5	7	7	7	5	3	4	48
Days With ≥ 1.0" Precipitation	0	0	0	0	0	0	0	0	0	0	0	0	0
Mean Snowfall (in.)	7.5	8.6	6.1	2.1	trace	0.0	0.0	0.0	trace	4.9	8.9	12.2	50.3
Days With ≥ 1.0" Snow Depth	*19*	*18*	16	3	0	0	0	0	0	6	17	*21*	*100*

McGrath Airport *Interior Basin Division*   Elevation: 341 ft.   Latitude: 62° 57' N   Longitude: 155° 36' W

	JAN	FEB	MAR	APR	MAY	JUN	JUL	AUG	SEP	OCT	NOV	DEC	YEAR
Mean Maximum Temp. (°F)	0.8	9.5	24.1	39.2	56.3	66.7	69.2	63.7	52.6	31.2	12.8	3.4	35.8
Mean Temp. (°F)	-8.2	-2.0	10.9	28.3	46.0	56.2	59.6	54.7	44.2	24.5	4.9	-5.2	26.1
Mean Minimum Temp. (°F)	-17.1	-13.5	-2.4	17.3	35.6	45.6	49.8	45.7	35.7	17.8	-3.1	-13.8	16.5
Extreme Maximum Temp. (°F)	43	50	55	64	82	88	89	89	75	57	49	49	89
Extreme Minimum Temp. (°F)	-75	-61	-49	-40	6	30	33	25	2	-28	-53	-59	-75
Days Maximum Temp. ≥ 90°F	na	na	na	na	na	na	na	na	na	na	na	na	na
Days Maximum Temp. ≤ 32°F	29	25	22	7	0	0	0	0	0	16	27	29	155
Days Minimum Temp. ≤ 32°F	31	28	31	28	10	0	0	1	10	28	30	31	228
Days Minimum Temp. ≤ 0°F	24	21	18	4	0	0	0	0	0	4	18	23	112
Heating Degree Days (base 65°F)	2,269	1,894	1,674	1,096	586	263	174	313	617	1,249	1,802	2,178	14,115
Cooling Degree Days (base 65°F)	0	0	0	0	0	6	15	2	0	0	0	0	23
Mean Precipitation (in.)	0.96	0.74	0.83	0.68	1.02	1.51	2.25	2.72	2.28	1.49	1.48	1.53	17.49
Days With ≥ 0.1" Precipitation	3	2	3	2	3	5	7	8	7	4	4	5	53
Days With ≥ 1.0" Precipitation	0	0	0	0	0	0	0	0	0	0	0	0	0
Mean Snowfall (in.)	14.3	10.5	11.4	5.9	1.1	trace	trace	0.0	1.3	11.3	20.2	22.1	98.1
Days With ≥ 1.0" Snow Depth	31	28	31	28	4	0	0	0	1	16	30	31	200

North Pole *Interior Basin Division*   Elevation: 472 ft.   Latitude: 64° 45' N   Longitude: 147° 20' W

	JAN	FEB	MAR	APR	MAY	JUN	JUL	AUG	SEP	OCT	NOV	DEC	YEAR
Mean Maximum Temp. (°F)	-2.8	7.9	26.4	44.1	60.8	70.5	73.1	66.3	54.0	30.6	9.5	0.1	36.7
Mean Temp. (°F)	-12.0	-4.1	11.6	30.7	47.4	57.7	60.8	54.8	43.1	22.3	0.5	-8.9	25.3
Mean Minimum Temp. (°F)	-21.1	-16.1	-3.3	17.2	33.9	44.8	48.5	43.3	32.1	14.1	-8.6	-17.8	13.9
Extreme Maximum Temp. (°F)	50	49	60	76	86	95	90	90	77	64	50	47	95
Extreme Minimum Temp. (°F)	-67	-59	-52	-32	6	25	31	21	-1	-41	-51	-62	-67
Days Maximum Temp. ≥ 90°F	na	na	na	na	na	na	na	na	na	na	na	na	na
Days Maximum Temp. ≤ 32°F	30	26	20	5	0	0	0	0	1	17	28	30	157
Days Minimum Temp. ≤ 32°F	31	28	31	28	15	1	0	3	17	30	30	31	245
Days Minimum Temp. ≤ 0°F	27	22	18	4	0	0	0	0	0	5	22	26	124
Heating Degree Days (base 65°F)	2,385	1,951	1,653	1,024	539	223	138	312	653	1,316	1,936	2,290	14,420
Cooling Degree Days (base 65°F)	0	0	0	0	0	12	19	4	0	0	0	0	35
Mean Precipitation (in.)	0.59	0.37	0.55	0.30	0.55	1.42	1.65	1.56	1.10	0.96	0.88	0.85	10.78
Days With ≥ 0.1" Precipitation	2	1	1	1	2	4	4	5	4	3	3	2	32
Days With ≥ 1.0" Precipitation	0	0	0	0	0	0	0	0	0	0	0	0	0
Mean Snowfall (in.)	7.4	5.1	3.8	2.4	0.4	trace	0.0	0.0	1.3	10.7	12.8	11.3	55.2
Days With ≥ 1.0" Snow Depth	31	28	30	22	2	0	0	0	1	21	30	31	196

Northway Airport *Interior Basin Division*   Elevation: 1,712 ft.   Latitude: 62° 58' N   Longitude: 141° 56' W

	JAN	FEB	MAR	APR	MAY	JUN	JUL	AUG	SEP	OCT	NOV	DEC	YEAR
Mean Maximum Temp. (°F)	-9.8	2.4	24.4	43.0	57.5	66.6	70.1	65.3	52.4	29.0	5.1	-5.8	33.4
Mean Temp. (°F)	-18.1	-9.1	8.3	29.3	45.4	55.3	59.2	54.2	41.7	20.8	-3.2	-13.9	22.5
Mean Minimum Temp. (°F)	-26.3	-20.6	-7.8	15.5	33.2	43.9	48.2	43.0	30.9	12.6	-11.5	-22.0	11.6
Extreme Maximum Temp. (°F)	35	39	53	70	85	87	86	88	79	67	42	51	88
Extreme Minimum Temp. (°F)	-68	-71	-54	-34	13	28	32	12	-6	-36	-55	-62	-71
Days Maximum Temp. ≥ 90°F	na	na	na	na	na	na	na	na	na	na	na	na	na
Days Maximum Temp. ≤ 32°F	31	28	22	4	0	0	0	0	1	20	30	31	167
Days Minimum Temp. ≤ 32°F	31	28	31	29	15	1	0	1	18	31	30	31	246
Days Minimum Temp. ≤ 0°F	29	25	21	3	0	0	0	0	0	5	23	29	135
Heating Degree Days (base 65°F)	2,580	2,093	1,754	1,064	603	289	182	333	694	1,364	2,047	2,451	15,454
Cooling Degree Days (base 65°F)	0	0	0	0	0	5	6	4	0	0	0	0	15
Mean Precipitation (in.)	0.24	0.22	0.20	0.21	0.99	1.74	2.33	1.35	0.82	0.51	0.31	0.26	9.18
Days With ≥ 0.1" Precipitation	1	1	1	1	3	5	6	5	3	1	1	1	29
Days With ≥ 1.0" Precipitation	0	0	0	0	0	0	0	0	0	0	0	0	0
Mean Snowfall (in.)	5.3	4.6	3.6	1.8	1.0	trace	trace	0.1	1.6	7.4	7.3	6.0	38.7
Days With ≥ 1.0" Snow Depth	31	28	31	23	1	0	0	0	1	19	29	31	194

Old Edgerton *Copper River Division*   Elevation: 1,318 ft.   Latitude: 61° 48' N   Longitude: 144° 59' W

	JAN	FEB	MAR	APR	MAY	JUN	JUL	AUG	SEP	OCT	NOV	DEC	YEAR
Mean Maximum Temp. (°F)	6.3	15.2	30.4	44.5	57.7	66.6	69.8	66.1	54.8	36.8	16.1	8.7	39.4
Mean Temp. (°F)	-2.8	4.2	17.7	32.6	44.8	53.5	57.1	53.6	43.7	28.5	7.4	-0.2	28.3
Mean Minimum Temp. (°F)	-11.8	-6.8	5.0	20.7	31.9	40.3	44.4	41.1	32.5	20.1	-1.4	-9.2	17.2
Extreme Maximum Temp. (°F)	46	46	55	68	77	92	88	88	77	60	46	45	92
Extreme Minimum Temp. (°F)	-58	-52	-45	-26	12	25	30	20	-1	-25	-45	-56	-58
Days Maximum Temp. ≥ 90°F	na	na	na	na	na	na	na	na	na	na	na	na	na
Days Maximum Temp. ≤ 32°F	27	23	14	2	0	0	0	0	0	10	25	27	128
Days Minimum Temp. ≤ 32°F	31	28	31	28	17	2	0	4	14	27	29	30	241
Days Minimum Temp. ≤ 0°F	22	18	11	1	0	0	0	0	0	3	16	21	92
Heating Degree Days (base 65°F)	2,102	1,716	1,460	966	619	339	239	347	633	1,126	1,728	2,023	13,298
Cooling Degree Days (base 65°F)	0	0	0	0	0	1	2	1	0	0	0	0	4
Mean Precipitation (in.)	0.56	0.59	0.29	0.15	0.51	1.42	1.89	1.50	1.40	1.06	0.83	0.80	11.00
Days With ≥ 0.1" Precipitation	2	2	1	0	1	4	5	5	4	3	3	3	33
Days With ≥ 1.0" Precipitation	0	0	0	0	0	0	0	0	0	0	0	0	0
Mean Snowfall (in.)	6.4	7.7	4.0	1.7	0.2	trace	trace	0.0	1.7	7.7	10.2	9.4	49.0
Days With ≥ 1.0" Snow Depth	31	28	31	21	1	0	0	0	2	14	28	30	186

Palmer IAS *Cook Inlet Division*   Elevation: 223 ft.   Latitude: 61° 36' N   Longitude: 149° 06' W

	JAN	FEB	MAR	APR	MAY	JUN	JUL	AUG	SEP	OCT	NOV	DEC	YEAR
Mean Maximum Temp. (°F)	21.7	26.9	35.4	46.0	57.8	64.4	66.9	64.7	56.2	41.2	27.9	23.4	44.4
Mean Temp. (°F)	14.1	18.4	26.2	37.0	47.7	54.8	57.9	55.8	47.7	33.5	20.3	15.9	35.8
Mean Minimum Temp. (°F)	6.4	9.9	17.0	27.9	37.5	45.2	48.9	46.9	39.2	25.8	12.7	8.4	27.2
Extreme Maximum Temp. (°F)	50	54	56	66	77	83	83	82	73	63	54	52	83
Extreme Minimum Temp. (°F)	-37	-32	-25	-8	22	34	36	28	15	-8	-26	-30	-37
Days Maximum Temp. ≥ 90°F	na	na	na	na	na	na	na	na	na	na	na	na	na
Days Maximum Temp. ≤ 32°F	22	17	10	2	0	0	0	0	0	5	19	23	98
Days Minimum Temp. ≤ 32°F	30	27	29	22	5	0	0	0	4	23	29	30	199
Days Minimum Temp. ≤ 0°F	12	8	3	0	0	0	0	0	0	1	6	10	40
Heating Degree Days (base 65°F)	1,576	1,311	1,196	835	530	300	214	279	512	969	1,334	1,518	10,574
Cooling Degree Days (base 65°F)	0	0	0	0	0	0	1	1	0	0	0	0	2
Mean Precipitation (in.)	0.83	0.84	0.72	0.46	0.64	1.30	2.04	2.21	2.55	1.72	1.06	1.18	15.55
Days With ≥ 0.1" Precipitation	2	3	2	2	2	4	6	6	7	5	4	4	47
Days With ≥ 1.0" Precipitation	0	0	0	0	0	0	0	0	0	0	0	0	0
Mean Snowfall (in.)	8.5	11.0	8.8	3.3	0.1	0.0	0.0	0.0	trace	7.0	9.4	14.1	62.2
Days With ≥ 1.0" Snow Depth	24	23	20	5	0	0	0	0	0	8	20	26	126

Port Alsworth *Bristol Bay Division* Elevation: 259 ft. Latitude: 60° 12' N Longitude: 154° 18' W

	JAN	FEB	MAR	APR	MAY	JUN	JUL	AUG	SEP	OCT	NOV	DEC	YEAR
Mean Maximum Temp. (°F)	23.1	25.7	34.0	43.7	55.3	63.8	67.5	64.9	55.6	41.1	30.8	24.3	44.1
Mean Temp. (°F)	14.9	15.8	23.2	33.9	44.9	52.9	57.1	55.2	47.2	34.0	23.7	16.6	34.9
Mean Minimum Temp. (°F)	6.1	5.9	12.4	24.0	34.4	42.0	46.6	45.5	38.7	26.9	16.6	8.9	25.7
Extreme Maximum Temp. (°F)	53	54	56	64	81	85	86	83	74	62	55	50	86
Extreme Minimum Temp. (°F)	-53	-55	-48	-18	14	20	25	25	13	-7	-24	-36	-55
Days Maximum Temp. ≥ 90°F	na	na	na	na	na	na	na	na	na	na	na	na	na
Days Maximum Temp. ≤ 32°F	18	16	11	3	0	0	0	0	0	5	14	18	85
Days Minimum Temp. ≤ 32°F	28	25	27	23	12	2	0	1	6	21	26	27	198
Days Minimum Temp. ≤ 0°F	12	12	8	2	0	0	0	0	0	0	4	11	49
Heating Degree Days (base 65°F)	1,551	1,387	1,290	928	617	357	240	297	528	954	1,232	1,498	10,879
Cooling Degree Days (base 65°F)	0	0	0	0	0	1	2	1	0	0	0	0	4
Mean Precipitation (in.)	0.74	0.57	0.65	0.51	0.48	0.97	1.38	2.16	2.08	1.41	1.26	1.09	13.30
Days With ≥ 0.1" Precipitation	3	2	2	2	2	3	4	6	6	5	4	3	42
Days With ≥ 1.0" Precipitation	0	0	0	0	0	0	0	0	0	0	0	0	0
Mean Snowfall (in.)	*13.7*	*9.8*	11.3	5.1	0.2	0.0	0.0	0.0	trace	*4.4*	*14.9*	18.7	*78.1*
Days With ≥ 1.0" Snow Depth	22	17	19	8	0	0	0	0	0	4	17	24	111

Saint Paul Island Arpt. *Southwestern Islands Division* Elevation: 19 ft. Latitude: 57° 10' N Longitude: 170° 13' W

	JAN	FEB	MAR	APR	MAY	JUN	JUL	AUG	SEP	OCT	NOV	DEC	YEAR
Mean Maximum Temp. (°F)	29.9	27.0	28.8	32.7	39.7	46.2	50.2	51.5	49.1	42.5	37.2	32.9	39.0
Mean Temp. (°F)	25.7	22.6	24.1	28.3	35.6	41.9	46.6	48.2	44.9	38.3	33.1	28.7	34.8
Mean Minimum Temp. (°F)	21.6	18.4	19.3	23.9	31.4	37.5	42.9	44.9	40.7	34.1	29.0	24.6	30.7
Extreme Maximum Temp. (°F)	44	42	50	49	59	61	63	66	61	53	48	44	66
Extreme Minimum Temp. (°F)	-14	-16	-19	-8	8	16	29	29	22	12	4	-3	-19
Days Maximum Temp. ≥ 90°F	na	na	na	na	na	na	na	na	na	na	na	na	na
Days Maximum Temp. ≤ 32°F	16	16	18	12	2	0	0	0	0	1	5	12	82
Days Minimum Temp. ≤ 32°F	25	25	28	26	17	3	0	0	3	12	20	24	183
Days Minimum Temp. ≤ 0°F	1	3	2	0	0	0	0	0	0	0	0	0	6
Heating Degree Days (base 65°F)	1,211	1,193	1,262	1,095	905	687	564	514	596	820	949	1,118	10,914
Cooling Degree Days (base 65°F)	0	0	0	0	0	0	0	0	0	0	0	0	0
Mean Precipitation (in.)	1.69	1.22	1.14	1.12	1.22	1.38	1.90	2.92	2.78	2.69	2.80	2.10	22.96
Days With ≥ 0.1" Precipitation	5	4	4	3	4	4	6	8	8	8	9	7	70
Days With ≥ 1.0" Precipitation	0	0	0	0	0	0	0	0	0	0	0	0	0
Mean Snowfall (in.)	9.8	9.0	10.1	6.3	2.1	trace	0.0	0.0	trace	2.3	7.5	9.7	56.8
Days With ≥ 1.0" Snow Depth	20	20	25	19	7	1	0	0	0	2	9	18	121

Seward *South Coast Division* Elevation: 72 ft. Latitude: 60° 06' N Longitude: 149° 26' W

	JAN	FEB	MAR	APR	MAY	JUN	JUL	AUG	SEP	OCT	NOV	DEC	YEAR
Mean Maximum Temp. (°F)	30.6	32.2	37.5	43.9	51.6	57.8	61.8	61.3	54.8	44.1	35.7	32.1	45.3
Mean Temp. (°F)	26.0	26.9	31.9	38.0	45.4	51.7	56.0	55.4	49.2	39.3	31.0	27.3	39.8
Mean Minimum Temp. (°F)	21.3	21.6	26.2	32.1	39.1	45.5	50.2	49.4	43.5	34.4	26.2	22.5	34.3
Extreme Maximum Temp. (°F)	51	51	53	65	76	84	87	86	73	59	58	48	87
Extreme Minimum Temp. (°F)	-15	-15	-6	1	27	35	40	35	30	8	-2	-19	-19
Days Maximum Temp. ≥ 90°F	na	na	na	na	na	na	na	na	na	na	na	na	na
Days Maximum Temp. ≤ 32°F	13	12	5	1	0	0	0	0	0	2	8	13	54
Days Minimum Temp. ≤ 32°F	24	22	24	14	1	0	0	0	1	10	23	25	144
Days Minimum Temp. ≤ 0°F	1	1	0	0	0	0	0	0	0	0	0	1	3
Heating Degree Days (base 65°F)	1,200	1,070	1,020	803	602	395	277	294	468	792	1,013	1,160	9,094
Cooling Degree Days (base 65°F)	0	0	0	0	0	1	4	3	0	0	0	0	8
Mean Precipitation (in.)	7.04	5.85	4.18	4.92	4.71	2.33	2.19	5.51	10.32	9.75	6.81	7.48	71.09
Days With ≥ 0.1" Precipitation	10	10	9	9	9	6	6	10	13	13	9	11	115
Days With ≥ 1.0" Precipitation	2	2	1	1	1	0	0	1	4	3	2	2	19
Mean Snowfall (in.)	*12.1*	14.9	11.3	6.0	0.3	0.0	0.0	0.0	trace	1.9	8.8	19.5	*74.8*
Days With ≥ 1.0" Snow Depth	20	18	17	7	0	0	0	0	0	1	8	19	90

Sitka Japonski Airport *Southeastern Division* Elevation: 36 ft. Latitude: 57° 04' N Longitude: 135° 21' W

	JAN	FEB	MAR	APR	MAY	JUN	JUL	AUG	SEP	OCT	NOV	DEC	YEAR
Mean Maximum Temp. (°F)	39.0	40.6	43.6	48.4	53.1	57.5	61.0	62.0	58.1	50.4	43.2	39.9	49.7
Mean Temp. (°F)	34.8	36.0	38.5	42.6	47.4	52.3	56.2	57.1	53.0	46.0	39.1	36.1	44.9
Mean Minimum Temp. (°F)	30.7	31.3	33.3	36.7	41.7	47.1	51.3	52.0	47.8	41.6	34.9	32.2	40.0
Extreme Maximum Temp. (°F)	58	60	58	76	76	79	88	83	77	65	65	57	88
Extreme Minimum Temp. (°F)	0	4	11	25	30	37	42	41	33	20	2	1	0
Days Maximum Temp. ≥ 90°F	na	na	na	na	na	na	na	na	na	na	na	na	na
Days Maximum Temp. ≤ 32°F	5	3	1	0	0	0	0	0	0	0	2	3	14
Days Minimum Temp. ≤ 32°F	16	14	12	5	0	0	0	0	0	2	9	13	71
Days Minimum Temp. ≤ 0°F	0	0	0	0	0	0	0	0	0	0	0	0	0
Heating Degree Days (base 65°F)	928	814	815	666	539	375	267	240	354	581	771	890	7,240
Cooling Degree Days (base 65°F)	0	0	0	0	0	0	0	1	0	0	0	0	0
Mean Precipitation (in.)	7.90	6.26	5.98	4.68	4.39	3.37	3.69	6.23	11.33	14.01	9.16	8.84	85.84
Days With ≥ 0.1" Precipitation	15	12	14	12	11	9	10	12	16	21	16	17	165
Days With ≥ 1.0" Precipitation	2	1	1	0	1	0	0	1	4	4	2	2	18
Mean Snowfall (in.)	10.2	7.8	5.8	1.3	trace	0.0	0.0	0.0	trace	0.4	4.3	7.5	37.3
Days With ≥ 1.0" Snow Depth	10	8	5	0	0	0	0	0	0	0	4	9	36

Snowshoe Lake *Copper River Division*   Elevation: 2,299 ft.   Latitude: 62° 02' N   Longitude: 146° 42' W

	JAN	FEB	MAR	APR	MAY	JUN	JUL	AUG	SEP	OCT	NOV	DEC	YEAR
Mean Maximum Temp. (°F)	2.2	14.6	27.9	40.4	52.8	62.5	66.9	63.1	51.6	33.5	13.9	5.0	36.2
Mean Temp. (°F)	-8.2	0.6	10.4	25.2	40.0	49.3	53.5	49.6	39.1	22.8	3.9	-4.4	23.5
Mean Minimum Temp. (°F)	-18.6	-13.4	-7.4	9.9	27.2	36.1	40.1	36.1	26.6	12.1	-6.3	-13.8	10.7
Extreme Maximum Temp. (°F)	40	43	50	62	76	95	86	88	74	58	44	43	95
Extreme Minimum Temp. (°F)	-60	-56	-52	-30	2	19	23	-6	-13	-29	-50	-54	-60
Days Maximum Temp. ≥ 90°F	na	na	na	na	na	na	na	na	na	na	na	na	na
Days Maximum Temp. ≤ 32°F	28	25	18	5	0	0	0	0	1	13	27	29	146
Days Minimum Temp. ≤ 32°F	29	27	29	29	24	8	4	10	22	28	29	30	269
Days Minimum Temp. ≤ 0°F	25	22	20	6	0	0	0	0	0	5	21	24	123
Heating Degree Days (base 65°F)	2,272	1,818	1,689	1,186	768	465	349	470	770	1,300	1,831	2,151	15,069
Cooling Degree Days (base 65°F)	0	0	0	0	0	0	0	0	0	0	0	0	0
Mean Precipitation (in.)	0.45	0.53	0.43	0.24	0.67	2.20	2.30	1.60	0.98	0.96	0.80	0.88	12.04
Days With ≥ 0.1" Precipitation	1	2	1	1	2	6	7	5	3	3	2	3	36
Days With ≥ 1.0" Precipitation	0	0	0	0	0	0	0	0	0	0	0	0	0
Mean Snowfall (in.)	6.3	6.3	4.6	3.3	1.7	trace	0.0	trace	1.6	9.5	8.7	11.1	53.1
Days With ≥ 1.0" Snow Depth	30	28	30	29	5	0	0	0	1	18	29	31	201

Talkeetna State Airport *Cook Inlet Division*   Elevation: 344 ft.   Latitude: 62° 19' N   Longitude: 150° 06' W

	JAN	FEB	MAR	APR	MAY	JUN	JUL	AUG	SEP	OCT	NOV	DEC	YEAR
Mean Maximum Temp. (°F)	19.5	25.7	34.0	44.4	56.9	65.2	67.9	64.5	55.1	38.7	25.5	20.8	43.2
Mean Temp. (°F)	10.7	15.4	22.7	34.0	45.9	55.1	58.9	55.5	46.2	31.0	17.4	12.5	33.8
Mean Minimum Temp. (°F)	1.9	5.1	11.2	23.6	34.8	44.9	49.8	46.5	37.2	23.3	9.2	4.1	24.3
Extreme Maximum Temp. (°F)	43	51	54	64	80	87	88	85	74	59	50	54	88
Extreme Minimum Temp. (°F)	-48	-45	-41	-16	19	30	36	25	11	-16	-34	-45	-48
Days Maximum Temp. ≥ 90°F	na	na	na	na	na	na	na	na	na	na	na	na	na
Days Maximum Temp. ≤ 32°F	25	19	12	2	0	0	0	0	0	6	22	26	112
Days Minimum Temp. ≤ 32°F	31	28	31	27	12	0	0	0	7	25	29	31	221
Days Minimum Temp. ≤ 0°F	14	11	7	1	0	0	0	0	0	2	9	13	57
Heating Degree Days (base 65°F)	1,680	1,395	1,306	923	586	292	188	288	558	1,046	1,423	1,626	11,311
Cooling Degree Days (base 65°F)	0	0	0	0	0	3	5	1	0	0	0	0	9
Mean Precipitation (in.)	1.37	1.28	1.27	1.27	1.67	2.56	3.27	4.61	4.37	3.15	1.69	2.02	28.53
Days With ≥ 0.1" Precipitation	4	3	4	4	6	7	9	10	10	8	5	6	76
Days With ≥ 1.0" Precipitation	0	0	0	0	0	0	0	1	1	0	0	0	2
Mean Snowfall (in.)	21.6	19.4	19.3	9.6	0.8	trace	0.0	0.0	0.5	15.1	22.4	28.6	137.3
Days With ≥ 1.0" Snow Depth	31	28	31	28	4	0	0	0	0	13	28	31	194

Tanana R.M. Calhoun Mem. Arpt. *Interior Basin Div.*   Elevation: 229 ft.   Latitude: 65° 10' N   Longitude: 152° 06' W

	JAN	FEB	MAR	APR	MAY	JUN	JUL	AUG	SEP	OCT	NOV	DEC	YEAR
Mean Maximum Temp. (°F)	-2.1	4.3	20.2	38.8	58.9	69.9	72.2	65.2	51.7	28.5	8.7	0.7	34.7
Mean Temp. (°F)	-9.8	-5.3	8.1	27.0	46.5	57.9	60.9	55.0	42.9	21.7	1.7	-6.9	25.0
Mean Minimum Temp. (°F)	-17.4	-14.8	-4.1	15.2	34.3	46.0	49.7	44.6	34.1	14.8	-5.4	-14.5	15.2
Extreme Maximum Temp. (°F)	41	38	50	63	84	91	90	86	75	56	45	42	91
Extreme Minimum Temp. (°F)	-76	-64	-54	-37	3	26	32	22	4	-23	-53	-59	-76
Days Maximum Temp. ≥ 90°F	na	na	na	na	na	na	na	na	na	na	na	na	na
Days Maximum Temp. ≤ 32°F	31	28	26	8	0	0	0	0	1	19	29	31	173
Days Minimum Temp. ≤ 32°F	31	28	31	27	12	1	0	2	13	29	30	31	235
Days Minimum Temp. ≤ 0°F	24	21	18	5	0	0	0	0	0	5	19	24	116
Heating Degree Days (base 65°F)	2,321	1,984	1,762	1,133	568	219	139	308	656	1,337	1,898	2,231	14,556
Cooling Degree Days (base 65°F)	0	0	0	0	0	17	23	4	0	0	0	0	44
Mean Precipitation (in.)	0.53	0.48	0.49	0.32	0.50	1.53	2.19	2.50	1.59	0.87	0.70	0.78	12.48
Days With ≥ 0.1" Precipitation	2	2	2	1	2	4	6	8	5	3	2	3	40
Days With ≥ 1.0" Precipitation	0	0	0	0	0	0	0	0	0	0	0	0	0
Mean Snowfall (in.)	5.8	6.0	5.8	2.2	0.4	trace	0.0	0.0	0.7	7.1	8.2	10.1	46.3
Days With ≥ 1.0" Snow Depth	31	28	31	26	3	0	0	0	0	20	30	31	200

Tonsina *Copper River Division*   Elevation: 1,574 ft.   Latitude: 61° 39' N   Longitude: 145° 10' W

	JAN	FEB	MAR	APR	MAY	JUN	JUL	AUG	SEP	OCT	NOV	DEC	YEAR
Mean Maximum Temp. (°F)	3.6	14.9	29.7	43.6	56.1	66.0	69.5	65.6	54.0	35.3	14.8	6.6	38.3
Mean Temp. (°F)	-5.0	3.4	14.9	30.6	43.0	52.1	56.1	52.0	41.8	26.2	6.4	-1.7	26.7
Mean Minimum Temp. (°F)	-13.5	-8.2	0.3	17.6	29.9	38.1	42.7	38.4	29.5	17.1	-1.9	-9.9	15.0
Extreme Maximum Temp. (°F)	45	46	52	64	79	88	87	88	79	58	47	50	88
Extreme Minimum Temp. (°F)	-60	-49	-45	-24	13	20	26	17	-1	-23	-42	-52	-60
Days Maximum Temp. ≥ 90°F	na	na	na	na	na	na	na	na	na	na	na	na	na
Days Maximum Temp. ≤ 32°F	29	23	17	2	0	0	0	0	0	11	27	29	138
Days Minimum Temp. ≤ 32°F	31	28	31	29	22	5	1	7	20	29	30	31	264
Days Minimum Temp. ≤ 0°F	24	19	15	3	0	0	0	0	0	4	17	23	105
Heating Degree Days (base 65°F)	2,169	1,739	1,547	1,025	675	381	270	395	690	1,196	1,755	2,067	13,909
Cooling Degree Days (base 65°F)	0	0	0	0	0	0	1	0	0	0	0	0	1
Mean Precipitation (in.)	0.81	0.84	0.46	0.27	0.50	1.26	1.74	1.43	1.32	1.31	1.16	1.28	12.38
Days With ≥ 0.1" Precipitation	3	3	2	1	1	4	5	5	4	4	3	4	39
Days With ≥ 1.0" Precipitation	0	0	0	0	0	0	0	0	0	0	0	0	0
Mean Snowfall (in.)	9.0	9.6	5.8	2.8	0.2	0.0	0.0	0.0	0.9	9.5	12.9	14.1	64.8
Days With ≥ 1.0" Snow Depth	31	28	31	28	4	0	0	0	1	17	29	31	200

University Exp. Station *Interior Basin Division*   Elevation: 472 ft.   Latitude: 64° 51' N   Longitude: 147° 52' W

	JAN	FEB	MAR	APR	MAY	JUN	JUL	AUG	SEP	OCT	NOV	DEC	YEAR
Mean Maximum Temp. (°F)	2.3	10.7	27.3	44.9	61.9	71.3	73.9	67.5	55.5	32.6	12.2	4.7	38.7
Mean Temp. (°F)	-6.3	0.0	14.2	32.1	48.6	58.7	61.8	56.2	44.6	24.2	4.0	-3.6	27.9
Mean Minimum Temp. (°F)	-14.8	-10.6	1.1	19.3	35.3	46.0	49.7	44.8	33.7	15.8	-4.2	-11.9	17.0
Extreme Maximum Temp. (°F)	47	57	58	76	85	93	91	89	77	63	50	44	93
Extreme Minimum Temp. (°F)	-60	-54	-37	-24	9	23	35	25	5	-34	-49	-58	-60
Days Maximum Temp. ≥ 90°F	na	na	na	na	na	na	na	na	na	na	na	na	na
Days Maximum Temp. ≤ 32°F	30	25	19	5	0	0	0	0	0	15	29	30	153
Days Minimum Temp. ≤ 32°F	31	28	31	28	11	0	0	1	12	29	30	31	232
Days Minimum Temp. ≤ 0°F	24	19	15	3	0	0	0	0	0	4	19	24	108
Heating Degree Days (base 65°F)	2,210	1,836	1,570	981	502	197	116	272	605	1,259	1,828	2,127	13,503
Cooling Degree Days (base 65°F)	0	0	0	0	1	19	29	6	0	0	0	0	55
Mean Precipitation (in.)	0.52	0.38	0.35	0.18	0.57	1.76	2.03	2.01	1.28	0.91	1.39	0.80	12.18
Days With ≥ 0.1" Precipitation	2	1	1	1	2	5	6	6	4	3	3	3	37
Days With ≥ 1.0" Precipitation	0	0	0	0	0	0	0	0	0	0	0	0	0
Mean Snowfall (in.)	7.5	5.0	4.0	1.3	0.2	0.0	0.0	0.0	1.1	9.5	11.2	11.9	51.7
Days With ≥ 1.0" Snow Depth	29	27	30	18	0	0	0	0	1	17	29	30	181

Valdez WSO *South Coast Division*   Elevation: 22 ft.   Latitude: 61° 08' N   Longitude: 146° 21' W

	JAN	FEB	MAR	APR	MAY	JUN	JUL	AUG	SEP	OCT	NOV	DEC	YEAR
Mean Maximum Temp. (°F)	28.0	30.2	36.3	44.6	53.2	59.7	62.4	60.7	53.2	43.0	32.5	29.0	44.4
Mean Temp. (°F)	23.6	25.3	30.4	37.8	46.1	52.5	55.5	53.8	47.2	38.3	28.1	24.7	38.6
Mean Minimum Temp. (°F)	19.1	20.2	24.5	31.0	38.9	45.3	48.5	46.8	41.0	33.5	23.6	20.2	32.7
Extreme Maximum Temp. (°F)	46	52	53	62	78	86	85	82	74	58	50	52	86
Extreme Minimum Temp. (°F)	-20	-10	-6	5	21	31	33	32	25	8	1	-7	-20
Days Maximum Temp. ≥ 90°F	na	na	na	na	na	na	na	na	na	na	na	na	na
Days Maximum Temp. ≤ 32°F	19	14	6	1	0	0	0	0	0	1	13	19	73
Days Minimum Temp. ≤ 32°F	29	27	29	17	1	0	0	0	1	12	27	30	173
Days Minimum Temp. ≤ 0°F	1	1	0	0	0	0	0	0	0	0	0	1	3
Heating Degree Days (base 65°F)	1,278	1,119	1,064	809	580	368	291	342	529	822	1,100	1,245	9,547
Cooling Degree Days (base 65°F)	0	0	0	0	0	0	2	0	0	0	0	0	2
Mean Precipitation (in.)	6.38	5.61	4.74	3.54	3.12	3.02	3.89	6.77	9.88	8.56	5.48	8.03	69.02
Days With ≥ 0.1" Precipitation	12	10	10	9	9	8	10	12	16	14	10	13	133
Days With ≥ 1.0" Precipitation	1	2	1	1	0	0	0	2	3	2	1	3	16
Mean Snowfall (in.)	63.0	56.5	56.4	22.2	1.2	0.0	0.0	0.0	0.4	11.5	41.0	75.6	327.8
Days With ≥ 1.0" Snow Depth	31	28	31	27	4	0	0	0	0	3	24	30	178

Wasilla 3 S *Cook Inlet Division*   Elevation: 49 ft.   Latitude: 61° 32' N   Longitude: 149° 26' W

	JAN	FEB	MAR	APR	MAY	JUN	JUL	AUG	SEP	OCT	NOV	DEC	YEAR
Mean Maximum Temp. (°F)	22.6	27.6	36.8	48.2	60.0	66.9	69.7	67.4	58.5	42.4	28.4	24.3	46.1
Mean Temp. (°F)	14.7	19.1	27.4	38.0	48.1	55.5	59.2	56.9	48.7	34.4	20.7	16.5	36.6
Mean Minimum Temp. (°F)	6.8	10.5	18.0	27.7	36.2	44.0	48.7	46.4	38.8	26.3	13.0	8.6	27.1
Extreme Maximum Temp. (°F)	50	52	54	68	78	82	87	83	74	62	56	51	87
Extreme Minimum Temp. (°F)	-40	-42	-30	-8	22	31	32	27	14	-11	-25	-30	-42
Days Maximum Temp. ≥ 90°F	na	na	na	na	na	na	na	na	na	na	na	na	na
Days Maximum Temp. ≤ 32°F	21	17	8	1	0	0	0	0	0	4	19	21	91
Days Minimum Temp. ≤ 32°F	29	26	29	23	8	0	0	0	6	22	28	30	201
Days Minimum Temp. ≤ 0°F	11	8	3	0	0	0	0	0	0	1	6	9	38
Heating Degree Days (base 65°F)	1,556	1,292	1,158	805	517	279	174	245	484	943	1,322	1,500	10,275
Cooling Degree Days (base 65°F)	0	0	0	0	0	1	2	1	0	0	0	0	4
Mean Precipitation (in.)	0.62	0.78	0.58	0.48	0.80	1.59	2.29	2.57	2.88	1.95	1.20	1.08	16.82
Days With ≥ 0.1" Precipitation	2	3	2	2	3	5	7	7	8	5	4	4	52
Days With ≥ 1.0" Precipitation	0	0	0	0	0	0	0	0	0	0	0	0	0
Mean Snowfall (in.)	9.0	8.0	6.3	3.0	0.2	0.0	0.0	0.0	trace	5.3	10.3	14.3	56.4
Days With ≥ 1.0" Snow Depth	na	na	13	3	0	0	0	0	0	4	na	na	na

Whites Crossing *Cook Inlet Division*   Elevation: 269 ft.   Latitude: 61° 42' N   Longitude: 150° 00' W

	JAN	FEB	MAR	APR	MAY	JUN	JUL	AUG	SEP	OCT	NOV	DEC	YEAR
Mean Maximum Temp. (°F)	15.3	22.8	34.6	46.1	59.0	66.6	69.1	65.9	56.0	38.2	22.3	16.5	42.7
Mean Temp. (°F)	5.9	10.9	21.0	34.0	46.4	55.1	58.9	55.7	46.1	29.6	13.4	7.9	32.1
Mean Minimum Temp. (°F)	-3.6	-1.1	7.3	21.8	33.8	43.5	48.6	45.4	36.2	21.0	4.4	-0.7	21.4
Extreme Maximum Temp. (°F)	47	46	54	65	82	88	89	83	76	59	50	48	89
Extreme Minimum Temp. (°F)	-50	-48	-36	-21	16	28	31	22	5	-20	-40	-42	-50
Days Maximum Temp. ≥ 90°F	na	na	na	na	na	na	na	na	na	na	na	na	na
Days Maximum Temp. ≤ 32°F	27	22	11	1	0	0	0	0	0	8	25	27	121
Days Minimum Temp. ≤ 32°F	31	28	30	26	13	1	0	1	10	26	29	30	225
Days Minimum Temp. ≤ 0°F	16	13	10	2	0	0	0	0	0	2	12	16	71
Heating Degree Days (base 65°F)	1,830	1,526	1,359	924	570	294	191	284	560	1,091	1,544	1,770	11,943
Cooling Degree Days (base 65°F)	0	0	0	0	0	3	6	1	0	0	0	0	10
Mean Precipitation (in.)	0.99	0.88	0.82	0.95	1.11	1.54	2.11	3.29	3.54	3.25	1.65	1.97	22.10
Days With ≥ 0.1" Precipitation	3	3	3	3	3	4	6	7	8	7	5	5	57
Days With ≥ 1.0" Precipitation	0	0	0	0	0	0	0	0	1	1	0	0	2
Mean Snowfall (in.)	9.7	10.2	8.4	2.9	trace	0.0	0.0	0.0	0.3	9.2	14.9	19.3	74.9
Days With ≥ 1.0" Snow Depth	29	28	30	23	1	0	0	0	0	10	26	31	178

Yakutat State Airport *South Coast Division*   Elevation: 26 ft.   Latitude: 59° 31' N   Longitude: 139° 38' W

	JAN	FEB	MAR	APR	MAY	JUN	JUL	AUG	SEP	OCT	NOV	DEC	YEAR
Mean Maximum Temp. (°F)	32.1	35.8	39.3	45.0	51.0	56.5	60.1	60.3	55.7	47.3	38.2	33.8	46.3
Mean Temp. (°F)	26.0	28.9	32.0	37.5	44.2	50.2	54.2	53.7	48.4	41.0	32.1	28.1	39.7
Mean Minimum Temp. (°F)	19.8	21.9	24.6	30.0	37.2	43.8	48.3	47.1	41.0	34.8	25.9	22.3	33.1
Extreme Maximum Temp. (°F)	55	54	59	71	78	87	83	84	73	61	55	50	87
Extreme Minimum Temp. (°F)	-21	-20	-20	5	21	29	36	29	21	7	-3	-14	-21
Days Maximum Temp. ≥ 90°F	na	na	na	na	na	na	na	na	na	na	na	na	na
Days Maximum Temp. ≤ 32°F	14	8	3	0	0	0	0	0	0	0	6	11	42
Days Minimum Temp. ≤ 32°F	24	22	23	20	6	0	0	0	5	11	21	24	156
Days Minimum Temp. ≤ 0°F	3	2	1	0	0	0	0	0	0	0	0	2	8
Heating Degree Days (base 65°F)	1,203	1,014	1,017	818	640	438	327	343	492	736	980	1,137	9,145
Cooling Degree Days (base 65°F)	0	0	0	0	0	0	0	0	0	0	0	0	0
Mean Precipitation (in.)	12.98	11.03	11.56	10.40	9.66	7.04	7.79	13.14	20.53	23.01	14.96	15.36	157.46
Days With ≥ 0.1" Precipitation	17	14	16	15	14	11	12	14	18	21	17	18	187
Days With ≥ 1.0" Precipitation	4	4	3	3	3	2	2	5	7	9	6	5	53
Mean Snowfall (in.)	37.1	31.4	32.6	15.8	1.0	trace	0.0	0.0	trace	5.6	21.9	33.1	178.5
Days With ≥ 1.0" Snow Depth	25	21	23	13	2	0	0	0	0	2	13	24	123

Note: See Appendix D for explanation of data.

ARIZONA

PHYSICAL FEATURES. Arizona covers 113,909 square miles, with about 350 square miles of water surface. The State can be divided into three main topographical areas: (1) the northeastern portion is a high plateau averaging between 5,000 and 7,000 feet in elevation; (2) running diagonally from the southeastern to the northwestern corners of the State is a mountainous region with maximum elevations between about 9,000 and 12,000 feet above mean sea level; (3) the southwestern third of the State is made up of low mountain ranges and desert valleys. From the White Mountain area across the Mogollon Rim to the San Francisco Peaks is an unbroken stand of Ponderosa pine. The Kaibab plateau north of the Grand Canyon continues this timbered strip into southern Utah. The highest point in the State is Humphreys Peak with an elevation of 12,611 feet, located just northwest of Flagstaff. Baldy Peak, in the White Mountains of eastern Arizona, is the second highest in the State with an elevation of 11,490 feet.

The higher elevations of the State, running diagonally from the southeast to the northwest, average between 25 and 30 inches of precipitation (rain plus melted snow) annually, while the desert southwest has averages as low as three or four inches per year. The desert valleys of southwestern Arizona are an extension of the Sonora Desert of Mexico, with elevations as low as about 100 feet above sea level in the Lower Colorado River Valley. The plateau country in the northeastern corner of the State receives approximately 10 inches of precipitation annually. Higher ridges here are covered with junipers and pinon trees.

Nearly the entire State is in the Colorado River drainage basin emptying into the Gulf of California. The world-famed Grand Canyon lies within the State, extending from the junction of the Little Colorado with the main stream southwestward for approximately 217 miles. The Grand Canyon varies in width from four to 18 miles, and depths from the rim to the river bed range from 2,700 to as much as 5,700 feet. This is an outstanding example of arid or semiarid land erosion by a major river whose source is in a more rainy area.

GENERAL CLIMATE. Cold air masses from Canada sometimes penetrate into the State bringing temperatures well below zero in the high plateau and mountainous regions of central and northern Arizona. Great extremes occur between day and night temperatures throughout Arizona. The daily range between maximum and minimum temperatures sometimes runs as high as 50 to 60°F. during drier portions of the year. During winter months, daytime temperatures may average 70°F., with night temperatures often falling to freezing or slightly below in lower desert valleys. In the summer the pine-clad forests in the central part of the State may have afternoon temperatures of 80°F., while night temperatures drop to 35 to 40°F.

PRECIPITATION. Precipitation throughout Arizona is governed to a great extent by elevation and the season of the year. From November through March, storm systems from the Pacific Ocean cross the State. These winter storms occur frequently in the higher mountains of the central and northern parts of the State and sometimes bring with them heavy snows. Snow accumulation may reach depths of 100 inches or more during the winter. The gradual melting of this snow during the spring serves to maintain a supply of water in the main rivers of the State. Reservoirs on these streams supply water to the desert areas in the lower Salt River Valley and the lower Gila River Valley areas.

Summer rainfall begins early in July and usually extends to mid-September. Moisture-bearing winds sweep into Arizona from the southeast, with their source region in the Gulf of Mexico. Summer rains occur in the form of thundershowers which are caused, to a great extent, by excessive heating of the ground and the lifting of moisture-laden air along main mountain ranges. Thus, the heaviest thundershowers are usually found in mountainous regions of the central and southeastern portions of Arizona. These thunderstorms are often accompanied by strong winds and brief periods of blowing dust prior to the onset of rain. Hail occurs rather infrequently.

The average number of days with measurable precipitation per year varies from 72 in the Flagstaff region to 34 in Phoenix, 50 in Tucson, 53 in Winslow, and 15 in Yuma. A large portion of Arizona is included in the semiarid region of the United States. Long periods often occur with little or no precipitation. The air is generally dry and clear, with relatively low humidity and a high percentage of sunshine. April, May, and June are the months with the greatest number of clear days, while July and August, as well as December, January, and February have the cloudiest weather and lowest percent of sunshine. Humidities, while low when compared to most other states, are higher throughout much of Arizona during July and August, which is the thunderstorm season. Annual average humidity values, based on four readings per day, show Flagstaff with 55 percent, Phoenix 38 percent, Tucson 38 percent, Winslow 46 percent, and Yuma 33 percent. Yearly averages of percent of possible sunshine show Phoenix with 86 percent, Tucson 86 percent, and Yuma 92 percent. Due to high temperatures, the dryness of the air, and the high percentage of sunshine, evaporation rates in Arizona are high. Mean annual lake evaporation varies from about 80 inches in the southwestern corner of the State to about 50 inches in the northeastern corner. Phoenix averages about 72 inches and Tucson 70 inches per year.

The length of the growing season (period between freezes) varies tremendously over Arizona, averaging less than 3 months in some of the elevated areas of northern and eastern portions of the State. On the other hand, lower desert valleys sometimes have two or three years in succession without freezes.

Flood conditions occur infrequently, although heavy thundershowers during July and August at times cause flash floods that do considerable local damage. Floods on main rivers are mostly limited to the upper basins. Heaviest runoff usually occurs in connection with the arrival of tropical air over Arizona, which had its origin in hurricanes that dissipated in or off the west coast of Mexico. Heavy rains associated with these systems usually occur during August or September. High winds accompanying heavy thunderstorms during July and August sometimes reach peak gusts of about 100 miles per hour in local areas. Tornado funnels have been reported in Arizona.

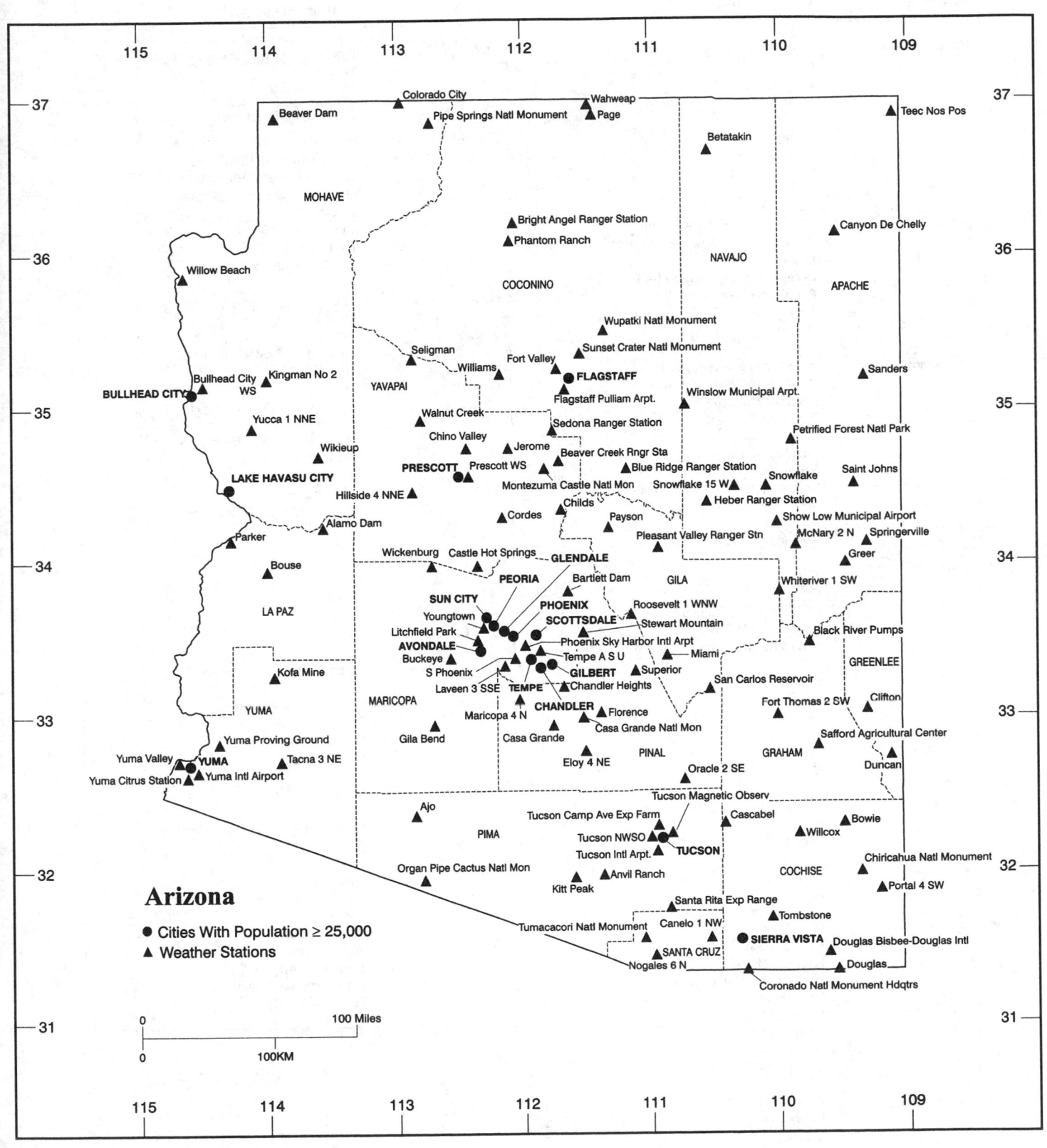

Arizona

● Cities With Population ≥ 25,000
▲ Weather Stations

Arizona Weather Stations by County

County	Station Name
Apache	Canyon De Chelly
	Greer
	McNary 2 N
	Saint Johns
	Sanders
	Springerville
	Teec Nos Pos
Cochise	Bowie
	Cascabel
	Chiricahua Nat'l Monument
	Coronado Nat'l Monument Hdqtrs.
	Douglas
	Douglas Bisbee-Douglas Int'l
	Portal 4 SW
	Tombstone
	Willcox
Coconino	Blue Ridge Ranger Station
	Bright Angel Ranger Station
	Flagstaff Pulliam Airport
	Fort Valley
	Page
	Phantom Ranch
	Sedona Ranger Station
	Sunset Crater Nat'l Monument
	Wahweap
	Williams
	Wupatki Nat'l Monument
Gila	Miami
	Payson
	Pleasant Valley Ranger Station
	Roosevelt 1 WNW
	San Carlos Reservoir
Graham	Black River Pumps
	Fort Thomas 2 SW
	Safford Agricultural Center
Greenlee	Clifton
	Duncan
La Paz	Alamo Dam
	Bouse
	Parker
Maricopa	Bartlett Dam
	Buckeye
	Chandler Heights
	Gila Bend
	Laveen 3 SSE
	Litchfield Park
	Phoenix Sky Harbor Int'l Arpt.
	South Phoenix
	Stewart Mountain
	Tempe A S U
	Wickenburg
	Youngtown
Mohave	Beaver Dam
	Bullhead City
	Colorado City
	Kingman 2

County	Station Name
Mohave (cont.)	Pipe Springs Nat'l Monument
	Wikieup
	Willow Beach
	Yucca 1 NNE
Navajo	Betatakin
	Heber Ranger Station
	Petrified Forest Nat'l Park
	Show Low Municipal Airport
	Snowflake
	Snowflake 15 W
	Whiteriver 1 SW
	Winslow Municipal Airport
Pima	Ajo
	Anvil Ranch
	Kitt Peak
	Organ Pipe Cactus Nat'l Mon.
	Santa Rita Exp. Range
	Sasabe
	Tucson Camp Ave. Exp. Farm
	Tucson Int'l Airport
	Tucson Magnetic Observatory
	Tucson NWSO
Pinal	Casa Grande
	Casa Grande Nat'l Monument
	Eloy 4 NE
	Florence
	Maricopa 4 N
	Oracle 2 SE
	Superior
Santa Cruz	Canelo 1 NW
	Nogales 6 N
	Tumacacori Nat'l Monument
Yavapai	Beaver Creek Ranger Station
	Castle Hot Springs
	Childs
	Chino Valley
	Cordes
	Hillside 4 NNE
	Jerome
	Montezuma Castle Nat'l Monument
	Prescott
	Seligman
	Walnut Creek
Yuma	Kofa Mine
	Tacna 3 NE
	Yuma Citrus Station
	Yuma Int'l Airport
	Yuma Proving Ground
	Yuma Valley

Arizona Weather Stations by City

City	Station Name	Miles
Avondale	Buckeye	14
	Laveen 3 SSE	13
	Litchfield Park	5
	South Phoenix	16
	Youngtown	12
Bullhead City	Bullhead City	3
Chandler	Chandler Heights	13
	Laveen 3 SSE	16
	Maricopa 4 N	17
	Phoenix Sky Harbor Int'l Arpt.	11
	South Phoenix	12
	Tempe A S U	8
Flagstaff	Flagstaff Pulliam Airport	5
	Fort Valley	7
	Sunset Crater Nat'l Monument	12
Gilbert	Chandler Heights	12
	Phoenix Sky Harbor Int'l Arpt.	13
	South Phoenix	16
	Stewart Mountain	20
	Tempe A S U	9
Glendale	Laveen 3 SSE	16
	Litchfield Park	11
	Phoenix Sky Harbor Int'l Arpt.	14
	South Phoenix	15
	Tempe A S U	18
	Youngtown	7
Lake Havasu City	Parker Reservoir, CA	16
Mesa	Chandler Heights	16
	Phoenix Sky Harbor Int'l Arpt.	11
	South Phoenix	16
	Stewart Mountain	18
	Tempe A S U	8
Peoria	Laveen 3 SSE	19
	Litchfield Park	10
	Phoenix Sky Harbor Int'l Arpt.	18
	South Phoenix	18
	Youngtown	4
Phoenix	Laveen 3 SSE	14
	Litchfield Park	16
	Phoenix Sky Harbor Int'l Arpt.	8
	South Phoenix	10
	Tempe A S U	11
	Youngtown	14
Prescott	Chino Valley	14
	Prescott	2
Scottsdale	Laveen 3 SSE	20
	Phoenix Sky Harbor Int'l Arpt.	7
	South Phoenix	14
	Tempe A S U	8
Sierra Vista	Canelo 1 NW	14
	Coronado Nat'l Monument Hdqtrs.	14
	Tombstone	18

City	Station Name	Miles
Sun City	Litchfield Park	9
	Youngtown	2
Tempe	Chandler Heights	19
	Laveen 3 SSE	14
	Maricopa 4 N	20
	Phoenix Sky Harbor Int'l Arpt.	5
	South Phoenix	8
	Tempe A S U	2
Tucson	Tucson Camp Ave. Exp. Farm	5
	Tucson Magnetic Observatory	5
	Tucson NWSO	3
	Tucson Int'l Airport	6
Yuma	Yuma Citrus Station	5
	Yuma Proving Ground	17
	Yuma Valley	5
	Yuma Int'l Airport	3
	Gold Rock Ranch, CA	19

Note: Miles is the distance between the geographic center of the city and the weather station.

Arizona Weather Stations by Elevation

Feet	Station Name	Feet	Station Name
8,487	Greer	3,316	Hillside 4 NNE
8,398	Bright Angel Ranger Station	3,264	Tumacacori Nat'l Monument
7,345	Fort Valley	3,179	Montezuma Castle Nat'l Monument
7,339	McNary 2 N	3,143	Cascabel
7,283	Betatakin	2,952	Safford Agricultural Center
7,034	Springerville	2,798	Fort Thomas 2 SW
6,991	Flagstaff Pulliam Airport	2,798	Superior
6,978	Sunset Crater Nat'l Monument	2,749	Anvil Ranch
6,879	Blue Ridge Ranger Station	2,647	Childs
6,788	Kitt Peak	2,568	Phantom Ranch
6,748	Williams	2,545	Tucson Int'l Airport
6,587	Heber Ranger Station	2,529	San Carlos Reservoir
6,410	Show Low Municipal Airport	2,522	Tucson Magnetic Observatory
6,079	Snowflake 15 W	2,477	Tucson NWSO
6,040	Black River Pumps	2,329	Tucson Camp Ave. Exp. Farm
5,853	Sanders	2,204	Roosevelt 1 WNW
5,787	Saint Johns	2,093	Wickenburg
5,639	Snowflake	2,007	Wikieup
5,606	Canyon De Chelly	1,988	Castle Hot Springs
5,442	Petrified Forest Nat'l Park	1,948	Yucca 1 NNE
5,387	Portal 4 SW	1,873	Beaver Dam
5,298	Chiricahua Nat'l Monument	1,797	Ajo
5,288	Teec Nos Pos	1,774	Kofa Mine
5,249	Seligman	1,676	Organ Pipe Cactus Nat'l Mon.
5,239	Coronado Nat'l Monument Hdqtrs.	1,646	Bartlett Dam
5,203	Prescott	1,541	Eloy 4 NE
5,118	Whiteriver 1 SW	1,502	Florence
5,088	Walnut Creek	1,459	Casa Grande
5,049	Pleasant Valley Ranger Station	1,423	Chandler Heights
5,009	Canelo 1 NW	1,420	Stewart Mountain
5,009	Colorado City	1,417	Casa Grande Nat'l Monument
4,947	Jerome	1,289	Alamo Dam
4,917	Pipe Springs Nat'l Monument	1,167	Tempe A S U
4,911	Payson	1,158	Maricopa 4 N
4,908	Wupatki Nat'l Monument	1,154	South Phoenix
4,888	Winslow Municipal Airport	1,131	Youngtown
4,747	Chino Valley	1,112	Laveen 3 SSE
4,609	Tombstone	1,105	Phoenix Sky Harbor Int'l Arpt.
4,507	Oracle 2 SE	1,026	Litchfield Park
4,297	Santa Rita Exp. Range	921	Bouse
4,268	Page	889	Buckeye
4,219	Sedona Ranger Station	738	Willow Beach
4,173	Willcox	734	Gila Bend
4,097	Douglas Bisbee-Douglas Int'l	538	Bullhead City
4,038	Douglas	410	Parker
3,818	Beaver Creek Ranger Station	321	Tacna 3 NE
3,769	Bowie	321	Yuma Proving Ground
3,769	Cordes	203	Yuma Int'l Airport
3,727	Wahweap	190	Yuma Citrus Station
3,658	Duncan	118	Yuma Valley
3,589	Sasabe		
3,559	Miami		
3,559	Nogales 6 N		
3,536	Kingman 2		
3,517	Clifton		

Flagstaff Pulliam Airport

Flagstaff, elevation 7,000 feet, is situated on a volcanic plateau at the base of the highest mountains in Arizona. The climate may be classified as vigorous with cold winters, mild, pleasantly cool summers, moderate humidity, and considerable diurnal temperature change. Only limited farming exists due to the short growing season. The stormy months are January, February, March, July, and August.

The average first occurrence of 32 degrees Fahrenheit in the fall is September 21 and the average last occurrence in the spring is June 13.

Temperatures in Flagstaff are characteristic of high altitude climates. The average daily range of temperature is relatively high, especially in the winter months, October to March, as a result of extensive snow cover and clear skies. Winter minimum temperatures frequently reach zero or below and temperatures of -25 degrees or less have occurred. Summer maximum temperatures are often above 80 degrees and occasionally, temperatures have exceeded 95 degrees.

The Flagstaff area is semi-arid. Several months have recorded little or no precipitation. Over 90 consecutive days without measurable precipitation have occurred. Annual precipitation ranges from less than 10 inches to more than 35 inches. Winter snowfalls can be heavy, exceeding 100 inches during one month and over 200 inches during the winter season. However, accumulations are quite variable from year to year. Some winter months may experience little or no snow and the winter season has produced total snow accumulations of less than 12 inches.

Flagstaff Pulliam Airport *Coconino County*   Elevation: 6,991 ft.   Latitude: 35° 08' N   Longitude: 111° 40' W

	JAN	FEB	MAR	APR	MAY	JUN	JUL	AUG	SEP	OCT	NOV	DEC	YEAR
Mean Maximum Temp. (°F)	42.8	45.7	50.3	58.1	67.5	78.5	82.2	79.7	73.5	63.2	51.1	43.5	61.3
Mean Temp. (°F)	29.6	32.3	36.5	42.6	50.7	59.9	66.1	64.5	57.6	47.1	36.7	30.0	46.1
Mean Minimum Temp. (°F)	16.4	18.8	22.8	27.1	33.9	41.3	50.0	49.1	41.5	30.9	22.3	16.5	30.9
Extreme Maximum Temp. (°F)	66	71	73	80	87	96	97	92	89	85	74	67	97
Extreme Minimum Temp. (°F)	-22	-23	-10	-2	14	23	33	33	23	-2	-6	-23	-23
Days Maximum Temp. ≥ 90°F	0	0	0	0	0	2	2	1	0	0	0	0	5
Days Maximum Temp. ≤ 32°F	4	2	1	0	0	0	0	0	0	0	1	4	12
Days Minimum Temp. ≤ 32°F	31	28	29	25	13	3	0	0	3	19	28	30	209
Days Minimum Temp. ≤ 0°F	2	1	0	0	0	0	0	0	0	0	0	2	5
Heating Degree Days (base 65°F)	1,090	918	875	666	436	171	29	51	220	549	842	1,078	6,925
Cooling Degree Days (base 65°F)	0	0	0	0	0	21	66	44	3	0	0	0	134
Mean Precipitation (in.)	2.17	2.52	2.75	1.32	0.80	0.41	2.48	2.96	2.24	1.81	1.87	1.89	23.22
Maximum Precipitation (in.)	9.5	10.0	6.8	5.6	4.1	2.9	6.6	8.1	6.8	9.9	6.6	7.3	36.6
Minimum Precipitation (in.)	0	trace	trace	trace	trace	0	trace	0.3	trace	trace	trace	trace	10.4
Maximum 24-hr. Precipitation (in.)	1.8	3.9	2.8	1.7	1.1	2.4	2.5	3.0	2.8	2.4	3.2	2.9	3.9
Days With ≥ 0.1" Precipitation	5	5	6	3	2	1	6	7	4	3	4	4	50
Days With ≥ 1.0" Precipitation	0	1	0	0	0	0	0	1	1	0	0	0	3
Mean Snowfall (in.)	22.2	20.6	*27.1*	9.7	1.2	*trace*	trace	trace	trace	*2.7*	*12.7*	14.9	*111.1*
Maximum Snowfall (in.)	63	46	79	58	8	trace	0	0	2	25	41	86	184
Maximum 24-hr. Snowfall (in.)	16	21	26	11	7	trace	0	0	2	10	18	27	27
Days With ≥ 1.0" Snow Depth	*16*	14	*10*	*4*	*0*	*0*	*0*	na	na	na	5	12	na
Thunderstorm Days	< 1	1	1	2	5	5	18	18	9	3	1	< 1	63
Foggy Days	10	8	8	4	2	< 1	1	2	3	4	6	8	56
Predominant Sky Cover	CLR	CLR	CLR	CLR	CLR	CLR	BRK	BRK	CLR	CLR	CLR	CLR	CLR
Mean Relative Humidity 5am (%)	75	75	73	67	64	55	70	79	75	71	72	73	71
Mean Relative Humidity 5pm (%)	52	46	43	32	28	21	38	44	37	35	44	51	39
Mean Dewpoint (°F)	16	18	19	21	25	28	44	46	38	27	20	16	27
Prevailing Wind Direction	NE	SW	SW	SW	SW	SW	SW	SW	SW	NE	NE	NE	SW
Prevailing Wind Speed (mph)	8	9	10	10	10	10	8	8	8	7	8	7	9
Maximum Wind Gust (mph)	53	47	49	55	66	51	44	62	46	52	69	49	69

Phoenix Sky Harbor Int'l Arpt.

Phoenix is located in the Salt River Valley at an elevation of about 1,100 feet. The valley is oval shaped and flat except for scattered precipitous mountains rising a few hundred to as much as 1,500 feet above the valley floor. Sky Harbor Airport, where the weather observations are taken, is in the southern part of the city. Six miles to the south of the airport are the South Mountains rising to 2,500 feet. Eighteen miles southwest, the Estrella Mountains rise to 4,500 feet, and 30 miles to the west are the White Tank Mountains rising to 4,100 feet. The Superstition Mountains, over 30 miles to the east, rise to as much as 5,000 feet. The valley, though located in the Sonora Desert, supports large acreages of cotton, citrus, and other agriculture along with one of the largest urban populations in the United States. The water supply for this complex desert community is partly from reservoirs on the impounded Salt and Verde Rivers, and partly from a large underground water table.

Temperatures range from very hot in summer to mild in winter. Many winter days reach over 70 degrees and typical high temperatures in the middle of the winter are in the 60s. The climate becomes less attractive in the summer. The normal high temperature is over 90 degrees from early May through early October, and over 100 degrees from early June through early September. Many days each summer will exceed 110 degrees in the afternoon and remain above 85 degrees all night.

Indeed, the climate is very dry. Annual precipitation is only about seven inches, and afternoon humidities range from about 30 percent in winter to only about 10 percent in June. Rain comes mostly in two seasons. From about Thanksgiving to early April there are periodic rains from Pacific storms. Moisture from the south and southeast results in a summer thunderstorm peak in July and August. Usually the break from extreme dryness in June to the onset of thunderstorms in early July is very abrupt. Afternoon humidities suddenly double to about 20 percent, which with the great heat, gives a feeling of mugginess. Fog is rare, occurring about once per winter, and is unknown in the other seasons.

The valley is characterized by light winds. High winds associated with thunderstorms occur periodically in the summer. These occasionally create duststorms which move large distances across the deserts. Strong thunderstorm winds occur any month of the year, but are rare outside the summer months. Persistent strong winds of 30 mph or more are rare except for two or three events in an average spring due to Pacific storms.

The average first occurrence of 32 degrees Fahrenheit in the fall is December 13 and the average last occurrence in the spring is February 7.

Phoenix Sky Harbor Int'l Arpt. *Maricopa County*   Elevation: 1,105 ft.   Latitude: 33° 27' N   Longitude: 111° 59' W

	JAN	FEB	MAR	APR	MAY	JUN	JUL	AUG	SEP	OCT	NOV	DEC	YEAR
Mean Maximum Temp. (°F)	66.7	71.4	76.3	84.7	93.7	103.8	106.0	104.2	99.1	88.2	75.2	66.5	86.3
Mean Temp. (°F)	55.2	59.4	64.0	71.3	80.3	89.8	94.1	92.7	87.0	75.7	62.8	55.1	73.9
Mean Minimum Temp. (°F)	43.6	47.4	51.6	57.7	66.7	75.7	82.2	81.2	74.9	63.2	50.4	43.7	61.5
Extreme Maximum Temp. (°F)	88	92	100	105	113	122	121	116	112	107	93	86	122
Extreme Minimum Temp. (°F)	19	28	30	39	45	56	68	68	55	34	31	26	19
Days Maximum Temp. ≥ 90°F	0	0	2	10	23	29	31	31	28	15	1	0	170
Days Maximum Temp. ≤ 32°F	0	0	0	0	0	0	0	0	0	0	0	0	0
Days Minimum Temp. ≤ 32°F	2	0	0	0	0	0	0	0	0	0	0	1	3
Days Minimum Temp. ≤ 0°F	0	0	0	0	0	0	0	0	0	0	0	0	0
Heating Degree Days (base 65°F)	300	167	97	29	1	0	0	0	0	11	113	301	1,019
Cooling Degree Days (base 65°F)	2	21	82	258	512	764	911	887	685	369	64	1	4,556
Mean Precipitation (in.)	0.83	0.78	1.05	0.25	0.16	0.08	1.00	0.96	0.84	0.70	0.72	0.92	8.29
Maximum Precipitation (in.)	5.2	2.2	3.2	1.9	1.1	1.7	5.1	5.6	3.4	4.4	3.0	4.0	15.2
Minimum Precipitation (in.)	0	0	0	0	0	0	trace	trace	0	0	0	0	2.8
Maximum 24-hr. Precipitation (in.)	1.2	1.5	2.0	0.7	0.9	1.4	1.9	2.7	2.4	2.3	1.6	1.4	2.7
Days With ≥ 0.1" Precipitation	2	2	3	1	0	0	2	2	2	1	2	2	19
Days With ≥ 1.0" Precipitation	0	0	0	0	0	0	0	0	0	0	0	0	0
Mean Snowfall (in.)	trace	trace	trace	0.0	trace	0.0	0.0	0.0	0.0	trace	0.0	trace	trace
Maximum Snowfall (in.)	trace	trace	0	0	0	0	0	0	0	0	0	trace	trace
Maximum 24-hr. Snowfall (in.)	trace	trace	0	0	0	0	0	0	0	0	0	trace	trace
Days With ≥ 1.0" Snow Depth	0	0	0	0	0	0	0	0	0	0	0	0	0
Thunderstorm Days	< 1	1	1	1	1	1	6	7	4	1	1	< 1	24
Foggy Days	2	1	1	< 1	< 1	0	< 1	< 1	< 1	< 1	1	2	7
Predominant Sky Cover	CLR	CLR	CLR	CLR	CLR	CLR	CLR	CLR	CLR	CLR	CLR	CLR	CLR
Mean Relative Humidity 5am (%)	68	63	57	45	37	33	46	53	50	52	59	66	52
Mean Relative Humidity 5pm (%)	34	28	25	17	14	12	21	24	23	23	28	35	24
Mean Dewpoint (°F)	33	33	34	33	36	40	56	59	52	43	36	33	41
Prevailing Wind Direction	E	E	E	E	E	W	W	E	E	E	E	E	E
Prevailing Wind Speed (mph)	6	7	7	7	7	9	8	7	7	7	6	6	7
Maximum Wind Gust (mph)	60	54	52	49	59	73	86	78	61	61	60	68	86

Tucson Int'l Airport

Tucson lies at the foot of the Catalina Mountains, north of the airport. The area within about 15 miles of the airport station is flat or gently rolling, with many dry washes. The soil is sandy, and vegetation is mostly brush, cacti, and small trees. Rugged mountains encircle the valley. The mountains to the north, east, and south rise to over 5,000 feet above the airport. The western hills and mountains range from 500 to 4,000 feet.

The climate of Tucson is characterized by a long hot season, from April to October. Temperatures above 90 degrees prevail from May through September. Temperatures of 100 degrees or higher average 41 days annually, including 14 days each for June and July, but these extreme temperatures are moderated by low relative humidities. The temperature range is large, averaging 30 degrees or more a day.

More than 50 percent of the annual precipitation falls between July 1 and September 15, and over 20 percent falls from December through March. During the summer, scattered convective or orographic showers and thunderstorms often fill dry washes to overflowing. On occasion, brief, torrential downpours cause destructive flash floods in the Tucson area. Hail rarely occurs in thunderstorms. The December through March precipitation occurs as prolonged rainstorms that replenish the ground water. During these storms, snow often falls on the higher mountains, but snow in Tucson is infrequent. From the first of the year, the humidity decreases steadily until the summer thunderstorm season, when it shows a marked increase. From mid- September, the end of the thunderstorm season, the humidity decreases again until late November. Occasionally during the summer, humidities are high enough to produce discomfort, but only for short periods. During the hot season, humidity values sometimes fall below five percent.

Tucson lies in the zone receiving more sunshine than any other section of the United States. Cloudless days are commonplace, and average cloudiness is low.

Surface winds are generally light, with no major seasonal changes in velocity or direction. Occasional duststorms occur in areas where the ground has been disturbed. During the spring, winds may briefly be strong enough to cause some damage to trees and buildings. Usually local winds tend to be in the southeast quadrant during the night and early morning hours. Highest velocities usually occur with winds from the southwest and east to south.

Based on the 1951-1980 period, the average first occurrence of 32 degrees Fahrenheit in the fall is November 29 and the average last occurrence in the spring is February 28.

Tucson Int'l Airport *Pima County*   Elevation: 2,545 ft.   Latitude: 32° 08' N   Longitude: 110° 57' W

	JAN	FEB	MAR	APR	MAY	JUN	JUL	AUG	SEP	OCT	NOV	DEC	YEAR
Mean Maximum Temp. (°F)	65.0	68.9	73.5	81.3	90.2	100.3	99.7	97.6	93.9	84.3	73.1	65.1	82.7
Mean Temp. (°F)	52.0	55.4	59.5	65.9	74.5	84.3	86.7	85.2	80.8	70.6	59.2	52.2	68.9
Mean Minimum Temp. (°F)	39.0	41.9	45.4	50.4	58.7	68.2	73.7	72.7	67.6	56.8	45.3	39.3	54.9
Extreme Maximum Temp. (°F)	87	89	99	104	107	117	114	112	107	102	93	83	117
Extreme Minimum Temp. (°F)	17	23	22	33	40	50	59	63	53	26	24	16	16
Days Maximum Temp. ≥ 90°F	0	0	1	5	18	29	29	29	24	9	0	0	144
Days Maximum Temp. ≤ 32°F	0	0	0	0	0	0	0	0	0	0	0	0	0
Days Minimum Temp. ≤ 32°F	5	2	1	0	0	0	0	0	0	0	1	5	14
Days Minimum Temp. ≤ 0°F	0	0	0	0	0	0	0	0	0	0	0	0	0
Heating Degree Days (base 65°F)	396	267	191	75	7	0	0	0	0	32	187	390	1,545
Cooling Degree Days (base 65°F)	0	5	28	129	336	600	691	647	497	224	23	1	3,181
Mean Precipitation (in.)	0.98	0.88	0.82	0.29	0.24	0.20	2.10	2.29	1.57	1.10	0.63	1.04	12.14
Maximum Precipitation (in.)	4.8	2.9	2.3	1.7	1.1	1.5	6.2	7.9	5.1	5.0	1.9	5.0	21.9
Minimum Precipitation (in.)	0	0	0	0	0	0	trace	0.2	0	0	0	0	5.3
Maximum 24-hr. Precipitation (in.)	1.3	1.3	1.2	0.7	0.5	1.3	3.9	2.5	2.8	3.0	1.6	2.1	3.9
Days With ≥ 0.1" Precipitation	3	2	3	1	1	1	5	5	3	2	2	3	31
Days With ≥ 1.0" Precipitation	0	0	0	0	0	0	0	0	0	0	0	0	0
Mean Snowfall (in.)	0.3	0.2	0.2	trace	trace	0.0	trace	trace	trace	trace	trace	0.4	1.1
Maximum Snowfall (in.)	5	4	6	2	0	0	0	0	0	0	6	7	8
Maximum 24-hr. Snowfall (in.)	4	2	4	2	0	0	0	0	0	0	6	7	7
Days With ≥ 1.0" Snow Depth	0	0	0	0	0	0	0	0	0	0	0	0	0
Thunderstorm Days	< 1	< 1	1	1	2	3	14	14	6	2	< 1	< 1	43
Foggy Days	1	1	< 1	< 1	< 1	0	< 1	< 1	< 1	< 1	< 1	1	3
Predominant Sky Cover	CLR	CLR	CLR	CLR	CLR	CLR	OVR	CLR	CLR	CLR	CLR	CLR	CLR
Mean Relative Humidity 5am (%)	63	59	53	42	35	32	57	65	55	52	55	62	52
Mean Relative Humidity 5pm (%)	32	26	22	15	13	13	28	32	26	24	27	34	25
Mean Dewpoint (°F)	29	28	28	27	30	36	56	58	50	39	31	29	37
Prevailing Wind Direction	SE	SE	SE	SE	SE	SE	SE	SE	SE	SE	SE	SE	SE
Prevailing Wind Speed (mph)	8	8	8	8	8	8	9	8	9	9	8	8	8
Maximum Wind Gust (mph)	55	48	53	55	55	58	81	76	71	49	51	47	81

Winslow Municipal Airport

Winslow is located in the Little Colorado River Valley. The adjacent terrain rises gradually in all directions except to the north-northwest along the river. The White Mountain area, 100 miles to the southeast, rises to over 11,000 feet. To the south and west the Mogollon Rim averages very close to 8,000 feet above sea level, while 60 miles to the northwest the San Francisco Peaks rise to 12,655 feet.

The surrounding high terrain has a considerable effect upon the climate and weather of the Winslow area. It acts as a barrier to the movement of low-level moist air currents, as well as to cold wintertime air masses from the plains states. As a consequence, the climate is very dry and relatively mild for the latitude and elevation.

The elevation of Winslow and the generally clear skies tend to create a large diurnal temperature variation during all seasons. Below-zero readings occur during the winter months about one year in three. Daytime temperatures over 70 degrees have been recorded during all winter months. Summer days are warm with temperatures of 90 degrees or higher occurring frequently from late May to mid-September. Because of the extremely low humidity, however, the high daytime temperatures are quite comfortable. The air cools rapidly after sunset so that nights are generally cool during the summer months.

Monthly and annual precipitation is extremely variable in amount. Moist air carried aloft over the surrounding mountains from the Gulf of Mexico and the Pacific Ocean during the summer and early fall helps produce the major portion of the annual precipitation. The lifting of the moist air over the mountains and the intense surface heating of the sparsely covered lower elevations causes considerable thunderstorm activity during this summer period. Snowfall during the winter is generally light, and because of warm daytime temperatures, it soon melts. The annual snowfall is about 10 inches, but occasionally a winter season will pass with only a trace being recorded. With the annual precipitation averaging about seven inches, agricultural activity in the vicinity of Winslow is restricted to small irrigated tracts.

More than 270 days during the year are clear or only partly cloudy. The average growing period is 186 days.

During the spring months, occasional high winds pick up considerable dust. During the late fall and winter months the prevailing wind direction is from the southeast, while in the spring and summer months the winds blow primarily from the southwest. Destructive weather such as tornadoes and ice storms rarely occur.

Winslow Municipal Airport *Navajo County*   Elevation: 4,888 ft.   Latitude: 35° 02' N   Longitude: 110° 43' W

	JAN	FEB	MAR	APR	MAY	JUN	JUL	AUG	SEP	OCT	NOV	DEC	YEAR
Mean Maximum Temp. (°F)	46.8	54.3	61.4	69.4	78.8	89.9	92.9	90.1	83.2	71.6	58.1	46.8	70.3
Mean Temp. (°F)	34.0	39.9	46.2	53.0	62.0	72.0	77.5	75.6	68.0	55.8	43.4	33.9	55.1
Mean Minimum Temp. (°F)	21.1	25.4	30.9	36.6	45.2	54.1	62.0	61.1	52.8	39.9	28.7	20.9	39.9
Extreme Maximum Temp. (°F)	75	76	85	90	98	106	109	103	98	93	80	71	109
Extreme Minimum Temp. (°F)	-15	-3	7	16	25	35	44	45	31	13	0	-11	-15
Days Maximum Temp. ≥ 90°F	0	0	0	0	2	17	23	18	5	0	0	0	65
Days Maximum Temp. ≤ 32°F	3	0	0	0	0	0	0	0	0	0	0	3	6
Days Minimum Temp. ≤ 32°F	29	23	18	9	1	0	0	0	0	6	21	28	135
Days Minimum Temp. ≤ 0°F	1	0	0	0	0	0	0	0	0	0	0	1	2
Heating Degree Days (base 65°F)	955	703	577	355	127	11	0	1	31	286	640	958	4,644
Cooling Degree Days (base 65°F)	0	0	0	4	45	222	376	331	125	5	0	0	1,108
Mean Precipitation (in.)	0.47	0.53	0.59	0.27	0.36	0.29	1.18	1.30	1.05	0.85	0.54	0.54	7.97
Maximum Precipitation (in.)	1.4	2.0	2.1	1.2	1.4	3.2	2.7	4.8	2.5	5.6	1.7	3.7	12.3
Minimum Precipitation (in.)	0	trace	0	trace	0	0	0	0.1	0	0	trace	trace	4.5
Maximum 24-hr. Precipitation (in.)	0.5	0.7	0.6	0.4	0.9	1.8	1.1	2.1	1.2	2.2	0.7	1.3	2.2
Days With ≥ 0.1" Precipitation	2	2	2	1	1	1	3	3	2	2	2	2	23
Days With ≥ 1.0" Precipitation	0	0	0	0	0	0	0	0	0	0	0	0	0
Mean Snowfall (in.)	2.3	2.0	2.1	0.5	trace	0.0	0.0	0.0	0.0	0.2	0.7	2.6	10.4
Maximum Snowfall (in.)	11	11	11	5	1	0	0	0	0	8	7	40	40
Maximum 24-hr. Snowfall (in.)	5	8	5	3	1	0	0	0	0	7	3	15	15
Days With ≥ 1.0" Snow Depth	3	1	1	0	0	0	0	0	0	0	0	3	8
Thunderstorm Days	< 1	< 1	< 1	1	2	3	11	11	5	1	< 1	< 1	34
Foggy Days	2	1	1	< 1	< 1	< 1	< 1	< 1	< 1	1	1	3	9
Predominant Sky Cover	CLR	CLR	CLR	CLR	CLR	CLR	SCT	CLR	CLR	CLR	CLR	CLR	CLR
Mean Relative Humidity 5am (%)	76	69	60	51	44	38	57	64	59	59	66	73	60
Mean Relative Humidity 5pm (%)	47	34	25	19	16	14	26	29	25	26	33	47	29
Mean Dewpoint (°F)	18	19	19	20	24	29	46	48	40	30	22	18	28
Prevailing Wind Direction	SW	SW	SW	SW	SW	SW	SW	SW	SW	SW	SW	SE	SW
Prevailing Wind Speed (mph)	10	12	14	15	14	14	12	10	12	10	10	7	12
Maximum Wind Gust (mph)	53	58	73	73	74	68	56	66	52	54	55	59	74

Yuma Int'l Airport

Yuma has a desert climate. Winter is a period of mostly clear skies and abundant sunshine. Yuma records a higher percentage of sunshine than any other place in the United States. Even in December and January, Yuma averages more than eight hours of sunshine a day. Summers in the lower Colorado River Valley are long and hot. Afternoon temperatures reach at least 100 degrees on the average, from June 4 to September 24, and at least 105 degrees from June 22 to August 26. Extremes over 120 degrees have occurred. From mid July to mid September, moisture-laden air from the Gulf of California frequently invades the area. The water content of the air is higher than might be expected over a desert area.

Precipitation in the Yuma area is sparce. Normal annual precipitation is under three inches. The wettest years have produced less than 12 inches and the driest years less than one inch. Snow is rare in the Yuma area but amounts under two inches in a winter season have been recorded.

Yuma Int'l Airport *Yuma County*   Elevation: 203 ft.   Latitude: 32° 40' N   Longitude: 114° 36' W

	JAN	FEB	MAR	APR	MAY	JUN	JUL	AUG	SEP	OCT	NOV	DEC	YEAR
Mean Maximum Temp. (°F)	68.7	74.5	79.0	86.5	94.0	104.1	107.0	105.7	100.9	90.2	77.0	68.3	88.0
Mean Temp. (°F)	57.0	61.3	65.5	71.9	79.2	88.6	93.7	92.9	87.6	76.7	64.2	56.7	74.6
Mean Minimum Temp. (°F)	45.3	48.0	52.1	57.3	64.5	73.0	80.5	80.2	74.2	63.1	51.3	45.0	61.2
Extreme Maximum Temp. (°F)	88	97	100	107	116	122	124	120	116	112	97	84	124
Extreme Minimum Temp. (°F)	24	5	34	41	49	56	66	68	56	35	35	29	5
Days Maximum Temp. ≥ 90°F	0	0	3	12	23	29	31	31	28	18	1	0	176
Days Maximum Temp. ≤ 32°F	0	0	0	0	0	0	0	0	0	0	0	0	0
Days Minimum Temp. ≤ 32°F	1	0	0	0	0	0	0	0	0	0	0	1	2
Days Minimum Temp. ≤ 0°F	0	0	0	0	0	0	0	0	0	0	0	0	0
Heating Degree Days (base 65°F)	244	125	64	16	1	0	0	0	0	5	83	253	791
Cooling Degree Days (base 65°F)	3	37	101	279	479	726	907	899	707	403	80	2	4,623
Mean Precipitation (in.)	0.41	0.30	0.32	0.09	0.05	0.02	0.26	0.70	0.27	0.29	0.16	0.47	3.34
Maximum Precipitation (in.)	2.8	1.8	1.6	1.2	0.4	0.3	2.5	3.4	2.5	2.7	1.7	2.1	6.8
Minimum Precipitation (in.)	0	0	0	0	0	0	0	0	0	0	0	0	0.3
Maximum 24-hr. Precipitation (in.)	1.6	1.2	0.7	1.1	0.4	0.2	2.5	3.4	2.4	2.2	1.4	1.8	3.4
Days With ≥ 0.1" Precipitation	1	1	1	0	0	0	0	1	1	1	0	1	7
Days With ≥ 1.0" Precipitation	0	0	0	0	0	0	0	0	0	0	0	0	0
Mean Snowfall (in.)	0.0	trace	0.0	0.0	0.0	0.0	0.0	0.0	0.0	0.0	0.0	0.0	trace
Maximum Snowfall (in.)	0	0	0	0	0	0	0	0	0	0	0	trace	trace
Maximum 24-hr. Snowfall (in.)	0	0	0	0	0	0	0	0	0	0	0	trace	trace
Days With ≥ 1.0" Snow Depth	0	0	0	0	0	0	0	0	0	0	0	0	0
Thunderstorm Days	< 1	< 1	< 1	< 1	< 1	< 1	2	2	1	1	< 1	< 1	6
Foggy Days	1	< 1	0	< 1	0	0	< 1	< 1	< 1	< 1	< 1	1	2
Predominant Sky Cover	CLR	CLR	CLR	CLR	CLR	CLR	CLR	CLR	CLR	CLR	CLR	CLR	CLR
Mean Relative Humidity 5am (%)	55	52	49	45	42	39	48	55	55	52	51	53	50
Mean Relative Humidity 5pm (%)	28	22	18	15	14	13	21	24	22	21	24	29	21
Mean Dewpoint (°F)	29	30	31	33	38	44	58	61	55	44	34	29	40
Prevailing Wind Direction	N	N	W	W	S	SSE	SSE	SSE	SSE	N	N	N	N
Prevailing Wind Speed (mph)	10	10	10	10	9	12	13	12	10	8	9	9	10
Maximum Wind Gust (mph)	43	40	43	40	40	44	58	67	76	43	43	46	76

Ajo *Pima County*   Elevation: 1,797 ft.   Latitude: 32° 22' N   Longitude: 112° 52' W

	JAN	FEB	MAR	APR	MAY	JUN	JUL	AUG	SEP	OCT	NOV	DEC	YEAR
Mean Maximum Temp. (°F)	64.8	69.6	73.9	81.2	na	99.7	102.3	100.8	96.8	86.5	na	na	na
Mean Temp. (°F)	54.7	58.9	62.9	69.2	na	86.8	90.6	89.1	85.0	75.2	na	na	na
Mean Minimum Temp. (°F)	44.6	48.3	51.7	57.0	na	73.9	78.9	77.4	73.2	63.8	na	na	na
Extreme Maximum Temp. (°F)	85	90	98	102	111	115	117	115	111	107	93	88	117
Extreme Minimum Temp. (°F)	5	27	27	35	38	52	58	62	52	32	33	5	5
Days Maximum Temp. ≥ 90°F	0	0	1	6	14	26	26	27	22	12	1	0	135
Days Maximum Temp. ≤ 32°F	0	0	0	0	0	0	0	0	0	0	0	0	0
Days Minimum Temp. ≤ 32°F	1	0	0	0	0	0	0	0	0	0	0	1	2
Days Minimum Temp. ≤ 0°F	0	0	0	0	0	0	0	0	0	0	0	0	0
Heating Degree Days (base 65°F)	316	186	127	49	na	0	0	0	0	16	na	na	na
Cooling Degree Days (base 65°F)	na	25	69	204	na	655	na	766	na	349	na	na	na
Mean Precipitation (in.)	0.64	0.68	0.82	0.24	0.15	0.05	0.79	1.74	0.86	0.57	0.47	0.90	7.91
Days With ≥ 0.1" Precipitation	1	1	2	1	0	0	2	3	2	1	1	2	16
Days With ≥ 1.0" Precipitation	0	0	0	0	0	0	0	0	0	0	0	0	0
Mean Snowfall (in.)	trace	0.0	0.0	0.0	0.0	0.0	0.0	0.0	0.0	0.0	0.0	trace	trace
Days With ≥ 1.0" Snow Depth	0	0	0	0	0	0	0	0	0	0	0	0	0

Alamo Dam *La Paz County*   Elevation: 1,289 ft.   Latitude: 34° 14' N   Longitude: 113° 35' W

	JAN	FEB	MAR	APR	MAY	JUN	JUL	AUG	SEP	OCT	NOV	DEC	YEAR
Mean Maximum Temp. (°F)	65.1	70.3	75.8	84.6	93.4	104.1	107.5	105.9	100.1	89.4	75.3	65.8	86.4
Mean Temp. (°F)	50.8	55.3	60.3	68.0	76.8	86.5	92.1	90.9	84.2	72.5	59.2	50.8	70.6
Mean Minimum Temp. (°F)	36.4	40.2	44.8	51.4	60.1	68.9	76.7	75.9	68.4	55.7	43.1	35.8	54.8
Extreme Maximum Temp. (°F)	81	88	97	105	114	123	124	119	115	110	96	84	124
Extreme Minimum Temp. (°F)	23	21	21	32	38	45	58	59	50	36	26	19	19
Days Maximum Temp. ≥ 90°F	0	0	2	10	23	29	30	31	28	16	1	0	170
Days Maximum Temp. ≤ 32°F	0	0	0	0	0	0	0	0	0	0	0	0	0
Days Minimum Temp. ≤ 32°F	8	2	0	0	0	0	0	0	0	0	1	9	20
Days Minimum Temp. ≤ 0°F	0	0	0	0	0	0	0	0	0	0	0	0	0
Heating Degree Days (base 65°F)	434	271	164	51	5	0	0	0	0	15	185	433	1,558
Cooling Degree Days (base 65°F)	0	2	28	152	388	647	847	824	583	252	19	0	3,742
Mean Precipitation (in.)	1.18	1.15	1.02	0.33	0.18	0.03	0.71	1.47	1.03	0.52	0.67	0.76	9.05
Days With ≥ 0.1" Precipitation	3	3	2	1	1	0	2	3	2	1	1	2	21
Days With ≥ 1.0" Precipitation	0	0	0	0	0	0	0	0	0	0	0	0	0
Mean Snowfall (in.)	trace	0.1	0.0	0.0	0.0	0.0	0.0	0.0	0.0	0.0	trace	0.0	0.1
Days With ≥ 1.0" Snow Depth	0	0	0	0	0	0	0	0	0	0	0	0	0

Anvil Ranch *Pima County*   Elevation: 2,749 ft.   Latitude: 31° 59' N   Longitude: 111° 23' W

	JAN	FEB	MAR	APR	MAY	JUN	JUL	AUG	SEP	OCT	NOV	DEC	YEAR
Mean Maximum Temp. (°F)	65.8	69.6	74.3	81.5	89.7	99.5	99.1	96.8	93.8	84.8	74.1	65.8	82.9
Mean Temp. (°F)	49.5	52.8	57.2	62.9	71.2	80.9	84.6	82.7	77.8	67.4	56.4	49.6	66.1
Mean Minimum Temp. (°F)	33.1	36.0	40.0	44.1	52.6	62.2	70.0	68.6	61.8	49.9	38.7	33.3	49.2
Extreme Maximum Temp. (°F)	89	97	97	102	106	115	111	109	106	102	94	86	115
Extreme Minimum Temp. (°F)	10	11	17	24	33	38	52	53	41	20	15	11	10
Days Maximum Temp. ≥ 90°F	0	0	1	5	17	28	30	29	24	9	1	0	144
Days Maximum Temp. ≤ 32°F	0	0	0	0	0	0	0	0	0	0	0	0	0
Days Minimum Temp. ≤ 32°F	14	9	4	1	0	0	0	0	0	1	6	14	49
Days Minimum Temp. ≤ 0°F	0	0	0	0	0	0	0	0	0	0	0	0	0
Heating Degree Days (base 65°F)	474	337	245	112	15	0	0	0	0	51	257	471	1,962
Cooling Degree Days (base 65°F)	0	1	7	63	216	479	606	551	389	130	7	0	2,449
Mean Precipitation (in.)	0.84	0.81	0.79	0.21	0.24	0.30	2.56	2.62	1.52	1.03	0.53	1.08	12.53
Days With ≥ 0.1" Precipitation	2	2	2	1	1	1	6	6	3	2	1	2	29
Days With ≥ 1.0" Precipitation	0	0	0	0	0	0	0	0	0	0	0	0	0
Mean Snowfall (in.)	0.0	trace	trace	0.0	0.0	0.0	0.0	0.0	0.0	0.0	0.0	0.2	0.2
Days With ≥ 1.0" Snow Depth	0	0	0	0	0	0	0	0	0	0	0	0	0

Bartlett Dam *Maricopa County*   Elevation: 1,646 ft.   Latitude: 33° 49' N   Longitude: 111° 39' W

	JAN	FEB	MAR	APR	MAY	JUN	JUL	AUG	SEP	OCT	NOV	DEC	YEAR
Mean Maximum Temp. (°F)	65.4	70.1	73.7	81.9	91.1	101.9	104.9	103.1	97.8	86.9	74.3	66.0	84.8
Mean Temp. (°F)	53.0	56.8	60.0	66.8	75.2	85.1	89.8	88.8	83.7	73.0	60.8	53.8	70.6
Mean Minimum Temp. (°F)	40.5	43.4	46.3	51.7	59.2	68.2	74.7	74.6	69.4	59.1	47.6	41.6	56.4
Extreme Maximum Temp. (°F)	88	90	97	103	111	120	122	115	111	109	95	87	122
Extreme Minimum Temp. (°F)	21	22	26	34	43	46	57	59	48	36	28	22	21
Days Maximum Temp. ≥ 90°F	0	0	1	7	19	28	30	29	26	13	1	0	154
Days Maximum Temp. ≤ 32°F	0	0	0	0	0	0	0	0	0	0	0	0	0
Days Minimum Temp. ≤ 32°F	2	1	0	0	0	0	0	0	0	0	1	2	6
Days Minimum Temp. ≤ 0°F	0	0	0	0	0	0	0	0	0	0	0	0	0
Heating Degree Days (base 65°F)	367	234	186	70	7	0	0	0	0	21	153	342	1,380
Cooling Degree Days (base 65°F)	0	10	38	147	335	594	773	753	573	285	43	2	3,553
Mean Precipitation (in.)	1.82	1.84	2.25	0.65	0.33	0.24	1.36	1.79	1.45	1.21	1.25	1.65	15.84
Days With ≥ 0.1" Precipitation	3	3	4	2	1	0	3	4	3	2	2	3	30
Days With ≥ 1.0" Precipitation	0	0	1	0	0	0	0	0	0	0	0	0	1
Mean Snowfall (in.)	0.0	trace	trace	0.0	0.0	0.0	0.0	0.0	0.0	0.0	0.0	trace	trace
Days With ≥ 1.0" Snow Depth	0	0	0	0	0	0	0	0	0	0	0	0	0

Beaver Creek Ranger Station *Yavapai County*   Elevation: 3,818 ft.   Latitude: 34° 40' N   Longitude: 111° 43' W

	JAN	FEB	MAR	APR	MAY	JUN	JUL	AUG	SEP	OCT	NOV	DEC	YEAR
Mean Maximum Temp. (°F)	57.4	61.9	*66.1*	74.8	*82.3*	93.6	96.4	*93.8*	88.3	78.1	*65.9*	*56.7*	*76.3*
Mean Temp. (°F)	43.6	47.7	*51.9*	59.4	*66.9*	77.2	81.4	*79.3*	73.2	62.4	*50.4*	*43.2*	*61.4*
Mean Minimum Temp. (°F)	29.8	33.5	*37.6*	44.0	*51.5*	60.8	66.2	*64.7*	58.2	46.6	*34.9*	29.6	*46.4*
Extreme Maximum Temp. (°F)	81	83	87	95	105	111	109	107	106	98	85	78	111
Extreme Minimum Temp. (°F)	5	11	18	19	32	36	52	50	35	22	15	3	3
Days Maximum Temp. ≥ 90°F	0	0	0	1	5	20	26	23	12	3	0	0	90
Days Maximum Temp. ≤ 32°F	0	0	0	0	0	0	0	0	0	0	0	0	0
Days Minimum Temp. ≤ 32°F	20	11	6	2	0	0	0	0	0	1	10	19	69
Days Minimum Temp. ≤ 0°F	0	0	0	0	0	0	0	0	0	0	0	0	0
Heating Degree Days (base 65°F)	655	482	*401*	187	*54*	2	0	*0*	7	127	*430*	*668*	*3,013*
Cooling Degree Days (base 65°F)	*0*	0	*2*	37	*135*	*384*	513	*458*	*263*	50	*0*	na	na
Mean Precipitation (in.)	1.48	1.63	2.11	0.95	0.48	0.18	1.69	2.16	2.07	1.34	1.25	1.42	16.76
Days With ≥ 0.1" Precipitation	3	4	4	2	1	1	3	4	3	3	2	3	33
Days With ≥ 1.0" Precipitation	0	0	0	0	0	0	0	0	0	0	0	0	0
Mean Snowfall (in.)	0.7	0.4	0.2	0.2	0.0	0.0	0.0	0.0	0.0	0.0	trace	0.8	2.3
Days With ≥ 1.0" Snow Depth	0	0	0	0	0	0	0	0	0	0	0	0	0

Beaver Dam *Mohave County*   Elevation: 1,873 ft.   Latitude: 36° 54' N   Longitude: 113° 57' W

	JAN	FEB	MAR	APR	MAY	JUN	JUL	AUG	SEP	OCT	NOV	DEC	YEAR
Mean Maximum Temp. (°F)	57.8	64.1	70.8	79.4	89.6	100.5	*105.6*	103.3	95.5	83.2	68.0	58.5	*81.4*
Mean Temp. (°F)	45.1	50.2	55.7	62.7	72.5	82.1	*88.1*	86.5	78.9	67.1	53.6	45.3	*65.7*
Mean Minimum Temp. (°F)	32.5	36.2	40.6	45.9	55.3	63.7	*70.6*	69.8	62.3	50.9	39.1	32.1	*49.9*
Extreme Maximum Temp. (°F)	78	87	91	101	109	117	120	115	110	106	89	77	120
Extreme Minimum Temp. (°F)	12	14	19	27	33	42	52	51	37	27	15	4	4
Days Maximum Temp. ≥ 90°F	0	0	0	4	17	28	30	30	24	8	0	0	141
Days Maximum Temp. ≤ 32°F	0	0	0	0	0	0	0	0	0	0	0	0	0
Days Minimum Temp. ≤ 32°F	16	8	4	1	0	0	0	0	0	0	6	16	51
Days Minimum Temp. ≤ 0°F	0	0	0	0	0	0	0	0	0	0	0	0	0
Heating Degree Days (base 65°F)	608	412	291	125	22	1	*0*	0	2	67	339	604	*2,471*
Cooling Degree Days (base 65°F)	0	1	*11*	78	266	*514*	*721*	*689*	*425*	*132*	*4*	0	*2,841*
Mean Precipitation (in.)	1.02	0.94	1.12	0.37	0.35	0.17	0.60	0.69	0.52	0.71	0.71	0.56	7.76
Days With ≥ 0.1" Precipitation	3	3	4	1	1	1	2	2	2	2	2	2	25
Days With ≥ 1.0" Precipitation	0	0	0	0	0	0	0	0	0	0	0	0	0
Mean Snowfall (in.)	0.2	*trace*	*0.0*	0.0	0.0	0.0	0.0	0.0	0.0	0.0	trace	trace	*0.2*
Days With ≥ 1.0" Snow Depth	*0*	*0*	*0*	0	0	0	0	0	0	0	*0*	0	*0*

Betatakin *Navajo County*   Elevation: 7,283 ft.   Latitude: 36° 41' N   Longitude: 110° 32' W

	JAN	FEB	MAR	APR	MAY	JUN	JUL	AUG	SEP	OCT	NOV	DEC	YEAR
Mean Maximum Temp. (°F)	39.4	43.6	50.5	59.4	69.7	80.8	85.1	82.4	74.9	63.0	48.7	40.2	61.5
Mean Temp. (°F)	30.0	33.8	39.4	46.6	56.2	66.8	71.8	69.6	62.7	51.5	38.7	30.9	49.8
Mean Minimum Temp. (°F)	20.6	23.9	28.2	33.7	42.7	52.7	58.4	56.8	50.3	39.8	28.7	21.5	38.1
Extreme Maximum Temp. (°F)	61	69	76	80	89	96	98	95	91	82	70	60	98
Extreme Minimum Temp. (°F)	-11	-14	4	8	21	32	43	40	31	13	-2	-14	-14
Days Maximum Temp. ≥ 90°F	0	0	0	0	0	3	7	3	0	0	0	0	13
Days Maximum Temp. ≤ 32°F	6	3	0	0	0	0	0	0	0	0	2	5	16
Days Minimum Temp. ≤ 32°F	30	25	23	13	3	0	0	0	0	6	20	29	149
Days Minimum Temp. ≤ 0°F	0	0	0	0	0	0	0	0	0	0	0	0	0
Heating Degree Days (base 65°F)	1,077	875	788	546	273	56	2	9	105	414	782	1,051	5,978
Cooling Degree Days (base 65°F)	0	0	0	0	9	112	217	159	40	1	0	0	538
Mean Precipitation (in.)	1.14	1.04	1.13	0.86	0.57	0.34	1.30	1.73	1.29	1.35	1.23	1.07	13.05
Days With ≥ 0.1" Precipitation	4	3	4	3	1	1	4	5	3	3	3	3	37
Days With ≥ 1.0" Precipitation	0	0	0	0	0	0	0	0	0	0	0	0	0
Mean Snowfall (in.)	12.5	9.7	6.6	4.8	0.8	trace	0.0	0.0	trace	0.6	7.3	*11.4*	*53.7*
Days With ≥ 1.0" Snow Depth	*17*	*14*	5	2	0	0	0	0	0	0	*3*	*11*	*52*

Black River Pumps *Graham County*   Elevation: 6,040 ft.   Latitude: 33° 29' N   Longitude: 109° 45' W

	JAN	FEB	MAR	APR	MAY	JUN	JUL	AUG	SEP	OCT	NOV	DEC	YEAR
Mean Maximum Temp. (°F)	49.0	52.7	57.5	65.7	75.2	85.8	87.3	84.3	79.4	69.8	57.8	50.1	67.9
Mean Temp. (°F)	34.9	38.4	42.3	48.8	57.7	67.7	71.7	69.9	64.4	54.1	42.5	35.6	52.3
Mean Minimum Temp. (°F)	20.7	24.0	27.1	31.8	40.1	49.5	56.1	55.6	49.3	38.4	27.0	21.0	36.7
Extreme Maximum Temp. (°F)	70	75	79	84	95	103	102	99	94	94	79	72	103
Extreme Minimum Temp. (°F)	-20	-3	6	12	19	26	44	43	34	14	-2	-19	-20
Days Maximum Temp. ≥ 90°F	0	0	0	0	0	10	12	4	1	0	0	0	27
Days Maximum Temp. ≤ 32°F	1	0	0	0	0	0	0	0	0	0	0	1	2
Days Minimum Temp. ≤ 32°F	29	26	26	17	3	0	0	0	0	7	24	29	161
Days Minimum Temp. ≤ 0°F	1	0	0	0	0	0	0	0	0	0	0	1	2
Heating Degree Days (base 65°F)	926	744	695	479	228	34	1	4	67	336	670	905	5,089
Cooling Degree Days (base 65°F)	0	0	0	0	9	126	216	177	57	7	0	0	592
Mean Precipitation (in.)	1.70	1.68	1.63	0.69	0.62	0.67	3.38	3.09	1.86	1.67	1.24	1.52	19.75
Days With ≥ 0.1" Precipitation	4	5	5	2	2	2	8	8	4	4	3	4	51
Days With ≥ 1.0" Precipitation	0	0	0	0	0	0	1	0	0	0	0	0	1
Mean Snowfall (in.)	2.5	2.1	0.6	1.2	0.0	0.0	0.0	0.0	0.0	trace	0.3	0.8	7.5
Days With ≥ 1.0" Snow Depth	0	0	*0*	0	0	0	0	0	0	0	0	0	*0*

Blue Ridge Ranger Station *Coconino County*   Elevation: 6,879 ft.   Latitude: 34° 37' N   Longitude: 111° 11' W

	JAN	FEB	MAR	APR	MAY	JUN	JUL	AUG	SEP	OCT	NOV	DEC	YEAR
Mean Maximum Temp. (°F)	na	na	52.4	59.8	68.7	79.4	82.8	80.2	74.6	64.5	na	na	na
Mean Temp. (°F)	na	na	37.4	43.7	52.2	61.5	67.4	65.3	58.8	47.9	na	na	na
Mean Minimum Temp. (°F)	na	17.4	22.5	27.6	35.8	43.3	52.0	50.4	43.0	31.3	na	na	na
Extreme Maximum Temp. (°F)	66	71	74	81	91	95	98	93	89	85	75	71	98
Extreme Minimum Temp. (°F)	-22	-16	-5	-2	12	26	33	28	19	-1	-8	-21	-22
Days Maximum Temp. ≥ 90°F	0	0	0	0	0	2	3	1	0	0	0	0	6
Days Maximum Temp. ≤ 32°F	2	1	1	0	0	0	0	0	0	0	1	2	7
Days Minimum Temp. ≤ 32°F	25	23	25	21	11	3	0	0	2	17	22	25	174
Days Minimum Temp. ≤ 0°F	2	1	0	0	0	0	0	0	0	0	0	2	5
Heating Degree Days (base 65°F)	na	na	849	633	390	139	18	40	188	523	na	na	na
Cooling Degree Days (base 65°F)	na	na	0	0	2	39	99	61	9	0	na	na	na
Mean Precipitation (in.)	1.82	1.88	2.17	1.01	0.74	0.41	2.30	3.06	2.02	1.74	1.58	1.83	20.56
Days With ≥ 0.1" Precipitation	3	3	4	3	2	1	6	7	4	3	2	3	41
Days With ≥ 1.0" Precipitation	0	0	0	0	0	0	0	1	0	1	0	0	2
Mean Snowfall (in.)	9.8	11.4	10.3	6.9	0.2	0.0	0.0	0.0	0.0	0.2	5.7	8.3	52.8
Days With ≥ 1.0" Snow Depth	na	na	2	1	0	0	0	0	0	0	0	3	na

Bouse *La Paz County*   Elevation: 921 ft.   Latitude: 33° 57' N   Longitude: 114° 01' W

	JAN	FEB	MAR	APR	MAY	JUN	JUL	AUG	SEP	OCT	NOV	DEC	YEAR
Mean Maximum Temp. (°F)	65.3	71.1	76.8	85.1	94.0	104.3	107.8	105.7	99.6	87.8	74.2	65.0	86.4
Mean Temp. (°F)	50.5	55.5	60.7	67.8	76.7	86.1	92.3	90.7	83.4	70.9	57.8	50.0	70.2
Mean Minimum Temp. (°F)	35.6	39.9	44.6	50.4	59.3	67.8	76.8	75.6	67.2	54.0	41.4	35.0	54.0
Extreme Maximum Temp. (°F)	87	92	96	103	115	120	121	117	117	109	94	83	121
Extreme Minimum Temp. (°F)	11	22	22	32	37	49	60	56	45	24	22	17	11
Days Maximum Temp. ≥ 90°F	0	0	2	10	24	29	31	31	28	14	1	0	170
Days Maximum Temp. ≤ 32°F	0	0	0	0	0	0	0	0	0	0	0	0	0
Days Minimum Temp. ≤ 32°F	11	4	1	0	0	0	0	0	0	0	3	12	31
Days Minimum Temp. ≤ 0°F	0	0	0	0	0	0	0	0	0	0	0	0	0
Heating Degree Days (base 65°F)	444	265	157	47	4	0	0	0	0	29	219	458	1,623
Cooling Degree Days (base 65°F)	0	4	30	159	389	640	849	821	568	218	12	0	3,690
Mean Precipitation (in.)	0.71	0.77	0.70	0.19	0.12	0.05	0.52	0.98	0.65	0.36	0.37	0.53	5.95
Days With ≥ 0.1" Precipitation	2	2	2	1	0	0	1	2	1	1	1	1	14
Days With ≥ 1.0" Precipitation	0	0	0	0	0	0	0	0	0	0	0	0	0
Mean Snowfall (in.)	0.0	0.0	0.0	0.0	0.0	0.0	0.0	0.0	0.0	0.0	0.0	0.0	0.0
Days With ≥ 1.0" Snow Depth	0	0	0	0	0	0	0	0	0	0	0	0	0

Bowie *Cochise County*   Elevation: 3,769 ft.   Latitude: 32° 19' N   Longitude: 109° 29' W

	JAN	FEB	MAR	APR	MAY	JUN	JUL	AUG	SEP	OCT	NOV	DEC	YEAR
Mean Maximum Temp. (°F)	60.3	65.6	71.8	79.6	87.9	97.4	97.1	94.3	90.1	80.2	68.9	60.3	79.4
Mean Temp. (°F)	45.9	50.3	55.4	62.0	70.3	79.6	82.3	80.1	75.0	64.3	53.0	45.8	63.7
Mean Minimum Temp. (°F)	31.6	34.9	39.1	44.4	52.8	61.7	67.5	65.8	59.8	48.3	37.1	31.3	47.8
Extreme Maximum Temp. (°F)	78	84	92	97	104	111	109	107	108	96	86	77	111
Extreme Minimum Temp. (°F)	11	15	19	27	33	36	55	44	44	24	18	3	3
Days Maximum Temp. ≥ 90°F	0	0	0	2	13	28	28	27	18	3	0	0	119
Days Maximum Temp. ≤ 32°F	0	0	0	0	0	0	0	0	0	0	0	0	0
Days Minimum Temp. ≤ 32°F	18	10	5	2	0	0	0	0	0	1	8	19	63
Days Minimum Temp. ≤ 0°F	0	0	0	0	0	0	0	0	0	0	0	0	0
Heating Degree Days (base 65°F)	584	409	293	123	16	0	0	0	2	87	355	589	2,458
Cooling Degree Days (base 65°F)	0	0	4	47	203	451	544	479	317	73	1	0	2,119
Mean Precipitation (in.)	1.02	0.87	0.70	0.28	0.41	0.35	2.14	2.19	1.08	1.27	0.73	1.26	12.30
Days With ≥ 0.1" Precipitation	3	3	2	1	1	1	5	5	3	3	2	3	32
Days With ≥ 1.0" Precipitation	0	0	0	0	0	0	0	0	0	0	0	0	0
Mean Snowfall (in.)	0.5	0.3	0.3	trace	0.0	0.0	0.0	0.0	0.0	0.0	0.2	0.7	2.0
Days With ≥ 1.0" Snow Depth	0	0	0	0	0	0	0	0	0	0	0	0	0

Bright Angel Ranger Station *Coconino County*   Elevation: 8,398 ft.   Latitude: 36° 13' N   Longitude: 112° 04' W

	JAN	FEB	MAR	APR	MAY	JUN	JUL	AUG	SEP	OCT	NOV	DEC	YEAR
Mean Maximum Temp. (°F)	38.3	40.2	44.5	51.6	61.2	72.9	77.0	74.2	68.0	57.4	45.9	40.1	55.9
Mean Temp. (°F)	27.3	28.7	32.8	39.0	47.1	56.6	61.8	60.1	53.9	43.9	34.4	28.5	42.9
Mean Minimum Temp. (°F)	16.2	17.2	20.9	26.3	32.9	40.3	46.6	45.9	39.8	30.3	22.9	16.8	29.7
Extreme Maximum Temp. (°F)	63	62	65	74	80	88	91	90	84	82	65	68	91
Extreme Minimum Temp. (°F)	-18	-23	-4	3	12	22	27	31	22	7	-2	-22	-23
Days Maximum Temp. ≥ 90°F	0	0	0	0	0	0	0	0	0	0	0	0	0
Days Maximum Temp. ≤ 32°F	9	5	2	1	0	0	0	0	0	0	3	5	25
Days Minimum Temp. ≤ 32°F	31	28	29	24	15	4	0	0	4	19	27	31	212
Days Minimum Temp. ≤ 0°F	1	1	0	0	0	0	0	0	0	0	0	1	3
Heating Degree Days (base 65°F)	1,162	1,017	993	773	548	250	108	152	326	648	911	1,125	8,013
Cooling Degree Days (base 65°F)	0	0	0	0	0	0	4	16	6	0	0	0	26
Mean Precipitation (in.)	4.08	3.65	3.68	1.55	0.87	0.44	1.88	2.16	1.77	1.71	1.79	2.47	26.05
Days With ≥ 0.1" Precipitation	7	6	6	4	2	1	4	5	4	3	3	5	50
Days With ≥ 1.0" Precipitation	1	1	1	0	0	0	0	0	0	0	0	0	3
Mean Snowfall (in.)	36.4	27.9	28.3	12.9	2.3	0.2	0.0	0.0	0.0	3.3	15.2	20.6	147.1
Days With ≥ 1.0" Snow Depth	30	28	29	15	4	0	0	0	0	1	11	25	143

Buckeye *Maricopa County*   Elevation: 889 ft.   Latitude: 33° 23' N   Longitude: 112° 35' W

	JAN	FEB	MAR	APR	MAY	JUN	JUL	AUG	SEP	OCT	NOV	DEC	YEAR
Mean Maximum Temp. (°F)	68.4	74.0	79.1	87.8	96.0	106.4	108.9	106.8	101.2	90.3	77.3	68.4	88.7
Mean Temp. (°F)	52.9	57.5	62.2	69.2	77.3	86.6	92.3	90.8	84.1	72.4	59.9	52.8	71.5
Mean Minimum Temp. (°F)	37.2	41.0	45.3	50.5	58.6	66.8	75.8	74.8	67.1	54.3	42.6	37.1	54.3
Extreme Maximum Temp. (°F)	86	92	99	106	115	122	125	119	113	108	93	85	125
Extreme Minimum Temp. (°F)	18	23	26	32	36	42	60	59	46	26	23	12	12
Days Maximum Temp. ≥ 90°F	0	0	3	14	26	30	31	31	29	18	1	0	183
Days Maximum Temp. ≤ 32°F	0	0	0	0	0	0	0	0	0	0	0	0	0
Days Minimum Temp. ≤ 32°F	8	3	0	0	0	0	0	0	0	0	2	8	21
Days Minimum Temp. ≤ 0°F	0	0	0	0	0	0	0	0	0	0	0	0	0
Heating Degree Days (base 65°F)	370	210	119	32	2	0	0	0	0	17	165	372	1,287
Cooling Degree Days (base 65°F)	0	8	38	190	402	651	841	818	584	254	23	1	3,810
Mean Precipitation (in.)	0.79	0.78	1.07	0.26	0.16	0.02	0.73	1.22	0.92	0.58	0.66	0.94	8.13
Days With ≥ 0.1" Precipitation	2	2	3	1	0	0	2	2	1	1	1	2	17
Days With ≥ 1.0" Precipitation	0	0	0	0	0	0	0	0	0	0	0	0	0
Mean Snowfall (in.)	0.0	0.0	0.0	0.0	0.0	0.0	0.0	0.0	0.0	0.0	0.0	0.0	0.0
Days With ≥ 1.0" Snow Depth	0	0	0	0	0	0	0	0	0	0	0	0	0

Bullhead City *Mohave County*   Elevation: 538 ft.   Latitude: 35° 08' N   Longitude: 114° 34' W

	JAN	FEB	MAR	APR	MAY	JUN	JUL	AUG	SEP	OCT	NOV	DEC	YEAR
Mean Maximum Temp. (°F)	65.3	71.2	78.6	87.7	97.0	107.3	111.6	109.9	102.9	90.7	75.0	65.4	88.5
Mean Temp. (°F)	54.2	58.8	64.3	72.0	80.9	90.0	95.3	94.5	87.2	75.0	62.1	53.9	74.0
Mean Minimum Temp. (°F)	43.1	46.3	50.0	56.2	64.8	72.7	78.9	79.1	71.5	59.4	49.1	42.4	59.4
Extreme Maximum Temp. (°F)	79	93	99	106	118	126	126	122	117	111	94	88	126
Extreme Minimum Temp. (°F)	25	28	33	40	47	50	64	60	54	na	31	24	na
Days Maximum Temp. ≥ 90°F	0	0	3	13	26	30	31	31	29	19	0	0	182
Days Maximum Temp. ≤ 32°F	0	0	0	0	0	0	0	0	0	0	0	0	0
Days Minimum Temp. ≤ 32°F	1	0	0	0	0	0	0	0	0	0	0	1	2
Days Minimum Temp. ≤ 0°F	0	0	0	0	0	0	0	0	0	0	0	0	0
Heating Degree Days (base 65°F)	330	183	84	20	1	0	0	0	0	6	122	339	1,085
Cooling Degree Days (base 65°F)	1	15	72	243	507	757	951	931	674	320	45	1	4,517
Mean Precipitation (in.)	1.17	1.14	1.08	0.20	0.10	0.02	0.37	0.71	0.45	0.39	0.49	0.60	6.72
Days With ≥ 0.1" Precipitation	3	2	3	1	0	0	1	1	1	1	1	2	16
Days With ≥ 1.0" Precipitation	0	0	0	0	0	0	0	0	0	0	0	0	0
Mean Snowfall (in.)	0.0	0.0	0.0	0.0	0.0	0.0	0.0	0.0	0.0	0.0	0.0	0.0	0.0
Days With ≥ 1.0" Snow Depth	0	0	0	0	0	0	0	0	0	0	0	0	0

Canelo 1 NW *Santa Cruz County*   Elevation: 5,009 ft.   Latitude: 31° 34' N   Longitude: 110° 32' W

	JAN	FEB	MAR	APR	MAY	JUN	JUL	AUG	SEP	OCT	NOV	DEC	YEAR
Mean Maximum Temp. (°F)	58.1	61.7	66.1	73.3	81.2	90.7	88.9	86.2	83.6	75.7	65.9	58.4	74.1
Mean Temp. (°F)	43.0	45.7	49.5	55.3	63.0	72.1	74.7	72.7	68.6	59.4	49.6	43.5	58.1
Mean Minimum Temp. (°F)	27.9	29.8	32.9	37.2	44.8	53.5	60.5	59.2	53.6	43.1	33.3	28.5	42.0
Extreme Maximum Temp. (°F)	79	81	88	94	100	106	103	99	96	92	84	77	106
Extreme Minimum Tcmp. (°F)	3	7	13	11	24	35	45	48	38	16	11	-4	-4
Days Maximum Temp. ≥ 90°F	0	0	0	0	3	17	15	7	3	0	0	0	45
Days Maximum Temp. ≤ 32°F	0	0	0	0	0	0	0	0	0	0	0	0	0
Days Minimum Temp. ≤ 32°F	23	18	15	8	1	0	0	0	0	3	14	22	104
Days Minimum Temp. ≤ 0°F	0	0	0	0	0	0	0	0	0	0	0	0	0
Heating Degree Days (base 65°F)	674	537	473	288	97	5	0	0	13	182	456	659	3,384
Cooling Degree Days (base 65°F)	0	0	0	5	51	232	310	252	133	15	0	0	998
Mean Precipitation (in.)	1.39	1.17	1.11	0.49	0.24	0.46	3.72	3.67	1.81	1.19	0.89	1.42	17.56
Days With ≥ 0.1" Precipitation	3	3	3	1	1	1	8	8	4	2	2	3	39
Days With ≥ 1.0" Precipitation	0	0	0	0	0	0	1	1	0	0	0	0	2
Mean Snowfall (in.)	0.0	trace	0.3	0.1	0.0	0.0	0.0	0.0	0.0	0.0	trace	0.4	0.8
Days With ≥ 1.0" Snow Depth	0	0	0	0	0	0	0	0	0	0	0	0	0

Canyon De Chelly *Apache County*   Elevation: 5,606 ft.   Latitude: 36° 09' N   Longitude: 109° 32' W

	JAN	FEB	MAR	APR	MAY	JUN	JUL	AUG	SEP	OCT	NOV	DEC	YEAR
Mean Maximum Temp. (°F)	44.1	51.3	60.1	68.4	77.5	88.3	91.6	88.8	82.3	70.6	55.9	45.1	68.7
Mean Temp. (°F)	31.4	37.3	44.7	51.6	60.3	69.6	75.3	73.4	65.7	53.7	41.4	31.7	53.0
Mean Minimum Temp. (°F)	18.6	23.4	29.3	34.8	42.9	50.9	58.9	57.9	49.1	36.9	26.8	18.3	37.3
Extreme Maximum Temp. (°F)	70	72	85	90	97	104	104	101	99	88	79	67	104
Extreme Minimum Temp. (°F)	-24	-11	7	13	22	31	39	38	23	15	-3	-14	-24
Days Maximum Temp. ≥ 90°F	0	0	0	0	1	14	21	14	3	0	0	0	53
Days Maximum Temp. ≤ 32°F	3	1	0	0	0	0	0	0	0	0	0	3	7
Days Minimum Temp. ≤ 32°F	29	25	21	12	2	0	0	0	0	9	23	28	149
Days Minimum Temp. ≤ 0°F	1	0	0	0	0	0	0	0	0	0	0	1	2
Heating Degree Days (base 65°F)	1,034	775	622	397	164	24	0	1	56	343	702	1,025	5,143
Cooling Degree Days (base 65°F)	0	0	0	2	31	186	342	287	91	2	0	0	941
Mean Precipitation (in.)	0.80	0.65	0.66	0.58	0.58	0.34	1.10	1.34	0.94	1.02	0.82	0.68	9.51
Days With ≥ 0.1" Precipitation	2	2	3	1	2	1	3	4	3	3	2	2	28
Days With ≥ 1.0" Precipitation	0	0	0	0	0	0	0	0	0	0	0	0	0
Mean Snowfall (in.)	2.0	1.1	0.9	0.2	0.0	0.0	0.0	0.0	0.0	0.1	0.5	1.8	6.6
Days With ≥ 1.0" Snow Depth	0	0	0	0	0	0	0	0	0	0	0	1	1

Casa Grande *Pinal County*   Elevation: 1,459 ft.   Latitude: 32° 57' N   Longitude: 111° 46' W

	JAN	FEB	MAR	APR	MAY	JUN	JUL	AUG	SEP	OCT	NOV	DEC	YEAR
Mean Maximum Temp. (°F)	67.1	71.8	77.3	86.1	94.9	104.7	106.0	103.7	99.1	88.3	76.0	66.5	86.8
Mean Temp. (°F)	52.2	56.1	61.0	68.0	76.7	86.0	90.8	89.1	83.4	71.6	59.4	51.7	70.5
Mean Minimum Temp. (°F)	37.3	40.2	44.6	49.9	58.5	67.3	75.5	74.3	67.5	54.8	42.6	37.0	54.1
Extreme Maximum Temp. (°F)	86	97	101	105	113	119	120	115	112	108	95	87	120
Extreme Minimum Temp. (°F)	19	23	24	29	36	46	56	57	47	29	22	15	15
Days Maximum Temp. ≥ 90°F	0	0	2	12	25	30	31	31	28	15	1	0	175
Days Maximum Temp. ≤ 32°F	0	0	0	0	0	0	0	0	0	0	0	0	0
Days Minimum Temp. ≤ 32°F	8	4	1	0	0	0	0	0	0	0	2	7	22
Days Minimum Temp. ≤ 0°F	0	0	0	0	0	0	0	0	0	0	0	0	0
Heating Degree Days (base 65°F)	390	250	153	46	3	0	0	0	0	24	182	404	1,452
Cooling Degree Days (base 65°F)	0	6	38	168	393	640	799	767	573	244	27	1	3,656
Mean Precipitation (in.)	0.77	0.84	1.01	0.27	0.19	0.10	0.82	1.97	0.86	0.76	0.73	1.00	9.32
Days With ≥ 0.1" Precipitation	2	2	2	1	1	0	2	3	2	2	1	2	20
Days With ≥ 1.0" Precipitation	0	0	0	0	0	0	0	1	0	0	0	0	1
Mean Snowfall (in.)	0.0	0.0	0.0	0.0	0.0	0.0	0.0	0.0	0.0	0.0	0.0	trace	trace
Days With ≥ 1.0" Snow Depth	0	0	0	0	0	0	0	0	0	0	0	0	0

Casa Grande Nat'l Monument *Pinal County*   Elevation: 1,417 ft.   Latitude: 33° 00' N   Longitude: 111° 32' W

	JAN	FEB	MAR	APR	MAY	JUN	JUL	AUG	SEP	OCT	NOV	DEC	YEAR
Mean Maximum Temp. (°F)	67.7	72.6	78.0	86.9	96.3	106.1	107.7	105.6	100.7	90.1	76.9	67.4	88.0
Mean Temp. (°F)	51.3	55.3	60.0	66.9	76.0	85.2	90.6	89.1	83.2	71.5	58.6	51.2	69.9
Mean Minimum Temp. (°F)	34.9	37.8	42.0	46.8	55.6	64.3	73.5	72.7	65.7	52.9	40.3	34.8	51.8
Extreme Maximum Temp. (°F)	87	92	100	106	116	123	123	120	115	111	96	86	123
Extreme Minimum Temp. (°F)	15	11	21	29	32	44	58	49	37	25	20	15	11
Days Maximum Temp. ≥ 90°F	0	0	3	13	26	30	31	31	29	18	1	0	182
Days Maximum Temp. ≤ 32°F	0	0	0	0	0	0	0	0	0	0	0	0	0
Days Minimum Temp. ≤ 32°F	13	6	3	0	0	0	0	0	0	0	4	13	39
Days Minimum Temp. ≤ 0°F	0	0	0	0	0	0	0	0	0	0	0	0	0
Heating Degree Days (base 65°F)	417	272	175	59	4	0	0	0	0	28	201	420	1,576
Cooling Degree Days (base 65°F)	0	4	29	150	377	618	797	771	562	242	19	0	3,569
Mean Precipitation (in.)	0.91	0.95	1.21	0.34	0.21	0.10	0.99	1.37	0.81	0.85	0.73	1.15	9.62
Days With ≥ 0.1" Precipitation	2	2	3	1	1	0	3	3	2	2	1	2	22
Days With ≥ 1.0" Precipitation	0	0	0	0	0	0	0	0	0	0	0	0	0
Mean Snowfall (in.)	0.0	0.0	0.0	0.0	0.0	0.0	0.0	0.0	0.0	0.0	0.0	0.0	0.0
Days With ≥ 1.0" Snow Depth	0	0	0	0	0	0	0	0	0	0	0	0	0

Cascabel *Cochise County*   Elevation: 3,143 ft.   Latitude: 32° 19' N   Longitude: 110° 25' W

	JAN	FEB	MAR	APR	MAY	JUN	JUL	AUG	SEP	OCT	NOV	DEC	YEAR
Mean Maximum Temp. (°F)	64.5	68.7	73.4	81.5	89.9	99.6	99.2	96.6	93.0	83.8	72.9	64.6	82.3
Mean Temp. (°F)	47.4	50.8	54.6	60.5	68.3	77.6	82.2	80.6	75.5	65.3	54.1	47.5	63.7
Mean Minimum Temp. (°F)	30.3	32.9	35.7	39.5	46.6	55.5	65.2	64.6	57.9	46.6	35.2	30.4	45.1
Extreme Maximum Temp. (°F)	87	88	96	103	109	116	115	109	108	101	90	84	116
Extreme Minimum Temp. (°F)	6	9	13	20	25	38	48	52	41	20	12	6	6
Days Maximum Temp. ≥ 90°F	0	0	1	4	17	28	29	28	23	8	0	0	138
Days Maximum Temp. ≤ 32°F	0	0	0	0	0	0	0	0	0	0	0	0	0
Days Minimum Temp. ≤ 32°F	20	14	10	5	0	0	0	0	0	1	10	20	80
Days Minimum Temp. ≤ 0°F	0	0	0	0	0	0	0	0	0	0	0	0	0
Heating Degree Days (base 65°F)	538	394	319	157	30	1	0	0	1	73	322	534	2,369
Cooling Degree Days (base 65°F)	0	0	2	36	154	394	542	500	333	87	1	0	2,049
Mean Precipitation (in.)	1.26	1.24	0.96	0.32	0.35	0.39	2.34	2.75	1.49	1.18	0.67	1.22	14.17
Days With ≥ 0.1" Precipitation	3	3	3	1	1	1	6	6	3	3	2	3	35
Days With ≥ 1.0" Precipitation	0	0	0	0	0	0	0	0	1	0	0	0	1
Mean Snowfall (in.)	0.9	0.7	0.4	trace	0.0	0.0	0.0	0.0	0.0	trace	trace	0.4	2.4
Days With ≥ 1.0" Snow Depth	0	0	0	0	0	0	0	0	0	0	0	0	0

Castle Hot Springs *Yavapai County*   Elevation: 1,988 ft.   Latitude: 33° 59' N   Longitude: 112° 22' W

	JAN	FEB	MAR	APR	MAY	JUN	JUL	AUG	SEP	OCT	NOV	DEC	YEAR
Mean Maximum Temp. (°F)	65.6	69.1	72.7	80.1	89.1	99.6	102.5	100.5	95.4	85.3	73.9	65.9	83.3
Mean Temp. (°F)	52.9	56.2	59.4	65.5	73.9	83.7	88.6	86.9	81.8	71.6	60.4	53.3	69.5
Mean Minimum Temp. (°F)	40.2	43.3	46.1	50.7	58.5	67.8	74.6	73.3	68.1	57.8	46.8	40.7	55.7
Extreme Maximum Temp. (°F)	86	91	94	99	109	117	120	113	111	104	93	85	120
Extreme Minimum Temp. (°F)	17	24	24	32	40	47	60	58	48	32	25	23	17
Days Maximum Temp. ≥ 90°F	0	0	0	4	16	28	31	29	26	10	0	0	144
Days Maximum Temp. ≤ 32°F	0	0	0	0	0	0	0	0	0	0	0	0	0
Days Minimum Temp. ≤ 32°F	3	1	0	0	0	0	0	0	0	0	1	3	8
Days Minimum Temp. ≤ 0°F	0	0	0	0	0	0	0	0	0	0	0	0	0
Heating Degree Days (base 65°F)	368	248	193	75	8	0	0	0	0	21	162	354	1,429
Cooling Degree Days (base 65°F)	0	8	27	119	292	546	715	682	506	238	35	0	3,168
Mean Precipitation (in.)	1.93	2.08	2.20	0.65	0.30	0.12	1.37	2.01	1.28	0.90	1.22	1.46	15.52
Days With ≥ 0.1" Precipitation	3	3	4	1	1	0	3	3	2	2	2	2	26
Days With ≥ 1.0" Precipitation	1	1	0	0	0	0	0	0	0	0	0	1	3
Mean Snowfall (in.)	trace	0.2	0.0	0.0	0.0	0.0	0.0	0.0	0.0	0.0	trace	trace	0.2
Days With ≥ 1.0" Snow Depth	0	0	0	0	0	0	0	0	0	0	0	0	0

Chandler Heights *Maricopa County*   Elevation: 1,423 ft.   Latitude: 33° 12' N   Longitude: 111° 41' W

	JAN	FEB	MAR	APR	MAY	JUN	JUL	AUG	SEP	OCT	NOV	DEC	YEAR
Mean Maximum Temp. (°F)	65.0	69.9	75.3	83.9	93.1	102.4	104.4	101.9	97.3	86.7	73.6	64.6	84.8
Mean Temp. (°F)	51.9	56.0	60.4	67.4	76.5	85.6	90.0	88.1	82.9	71.8	59.3	51.8	70.1
Mean Minimum Temp. (°F)	38.7	42.1	45.5	50.9	59.8	68.8	75.6	74.2	68.3	56.9	44.9	38.9	55.4
Extreme Maximum Temp. (°F)	86	87	97	102	112	117	116	115	110	107	91	83	117
Extreme Minimum Temp. (°F)	14	20	23	32	38	51	59	54	47	29	24	19	14
Days Maximum Temp. ≥ 90°F	0	0	1	8	23	29	31	30	27	13	0	0	162
Days Maximum Temp. ≤ 32°F	0	0	0	0	0	0	0	0	0	0	0	0	0
Days Minimum Temp. ≤ 32°F	5	2	1	0	0	0	0	0	0	0	1	5	14
Days Minimum Temp. ≤ 0°F	0	0	0	0	0	0	0	0	0	0	0	0	0
Heating Degree Days (base 65°F)	400	252	166	56	4	0	0	0	0	26	189	404	1,497
Cooling Degree Days (base 65°F)	0	5	29	157	389	638	789	753	563	254	29	1	3,607
Mean Precipitation (in.)	0.95	1.11	1.24	0.39	0.19	0.04	0.91	1.31	0.84	0.70	0.94	1.09	9.71
Days With ≥ 0.1" Precipitation	2	2	3	1	1	0	2	3	2	2	2	2	22
Days With ≥ 1.0" Precipitation	0	0	0	0	0	0	0	0	0	0	0	0	0
Mean Snowfall (in.)	0.0	0.0	0.0	0.0	0.0	0.0	0.0	0.0	0.0	0.0	0.0	0.0	0.0
Days With ≥ 1.0" Snow Depth	0	0	0	0	0	0	0	0	0	0	0	0	0

Childs *Yavapai County*   Elevation: 2,647 ft.   Latitude: 34° 21' N   Longitude: 111° 42' W

	JAN	FEB	MAR	APR	MAY	JUN	JUL	AUG	SEP	OCT	NOV	DEC	YEAR
Mean Maximum Temp. (°F)	60.6	65.9	70.2	78.4	87.7	98.9	102.0	99.5	93.7	83.4	70.7	60.5	81.0
Mean Temp. (°F)	46.3	50.4	54.4	60.6	69.2	78.6	84.7	83.1	76.7	65.8	54.1	46.4	64.2
Mean Minimum Temp. (°F)	32.0	34.8	38.5	42.7	50.5	58.3	67.5	66.5	59.6	48.0	37.3	32.2	47.3
Extreme Maximum Temp. (°F)	83	88	93	100	109	116	117	114	109	106	96	83	117
Extreme Minimum Temp. (°F)	14	12	22	22	31	20	47	46	40	20	20	16	12
Days Maximum Temp. ≥ 90°F	0	0	0	3	14	26	30	29	23	9	0	0	134
Days Maximum Temp. ≤ 32°F	0	0	0	0	0	0	0	0	0	0	0	0	0
Days Minimum Temp. ≤ 32°F	17	10	4	1	0	0	0	0	0	1	6	17	56
Days Minimum Temp. ≤ 0°F	0	0	0	0	0	0	0	0	0	0	0	0	0
Heating Degree Days (base 65°F)	573	407	327	159	34	2	0	0	3	77	325	570	2,477
Cooling Degree Days (base 65°F)	0	0	4	43	174	413	611	575	358	106	4	0	2,288
Mean Precipitation (in.)	2.14	2.21	2.30	0.87	0.45	0.22	1.90	2.59	2.03	1.41	1.46	1.90	19.48
Days With ≥ 0.1" Precipitation	4	4	5	2	1	1	5	6	4	2	3	4	41
Days With ≥ 1.0" Precipitation	0	1	0	0	0	0	0	0	1	0	0	0	2
Mean Snowfall (in.)	0.1	0.6	trace	0.0	0.0	0.0	0.0	0.0	0.0	0.0	0.2	0.2	1.1
Days With ≥ 1.0" Snow Depth	0	0	0	0	0	0	0	0	0	0	0	0	0

Chino Valley *Yavapai County*   Elevation: 4,747 ft.   Latitude: 34° 45' N   Longitude: 112° 27' W

	JAN	FEB	MAR	APR	MAY	JUN	JUL	AUG	SEP	OCT	NOV	DEC	YEAR
Mean Maximum Temp. (°F)	na	na	na	*69.4*	na	*88.5*	*91.8*	*89.5*	na	na	na	na	na
Mean Temp. (°F)	na	na	na	*52.1*	na	*69.7*	*75.6*	*73.7*	na	na	na	na	na
Mean Minimum Temp. (°F)	na	na	na	34.6	*42.4*	50.9	59.5	57.8	na	na	na	na	na
Extreme Maximum Temp. (°F)	76	80	82	90	98	104	105	105	100	97	83	76	105
Extreme Minimum Temp. (°F)	-4	5	10	15	21	33	39	40	33	5	8	-9	-9
Days Maximum Temp. ≥ 90°F	0	0	0	0	1	12	18	15	5	1	0	0	52
Days Maximum Temp. ≤ 32°F	0	0	0	0	0	0	0	0	0	0	0	0	0
Days Minimum Temp. ≤ 32°F	23	20	18	10	2	0	0	0	0	5	18	23	119
Days Minimum Temp. ≤ 0°F	0	0	0	0	0	0	0	0	0	0	0	0	0
Heating Degree Days (base 65°F)	na	na	na	*380*	na	*22*	*0*	*1*	na	na	na	na	na
Cooling Degree Days (base 65°F)	na	na	na	*2*	na	na	na	na	na	na	na	na	na
Mean Precipitation (in.)	1.07	1.30	1.26	0.54	0.48	0.35	1.81	2.04	1.63	0.84	0.75	0.93	13.00
Days With ≥ 0.1" Precipitation	2	2	3	1	1	1	4	4	2	2	1	2	25
Days With ≥ 1.0" Precipitation	0	0	0	0	0	0	0	0	0	0	0	0	0
Mean Snowfall (in.)	1.1	1.0	0.8	0.2	0.0	0.0	0.0	0.0	0.0	0.0	0.2	1.3	4.6
Days With ≥ 1.0" Snow Depth	*0*	*0*	0	0	0	0	0	0	0	0	0	0	*0*

Chiricahua Nat'l Monument *Cochise County*   Elevation: 5,298 ft.   Latitude: 32° 00' N   Longitude: 109° 21' W

	JAN	FEB	MAR	APR	MAY	JUN	JUL	AUG	SEP	OCT	NOV	DEC	YEAR
Mean Maximum Temp. (°F)	56.9	59.9	65.3	72.4	80.6	89.7	88.7	85.9	83.2	75.0	64.9	57.5	73.3
Mean Temp. (°F)	43.7	46.0	50.2	56.1	63.8	73.1	74.7	72.8	69.5	60.8	50.6	44.2	58.8
Mean Minimum Temp. (°F)	30.4	32.0	35.1	39.7	46.9	56.4	60.6	59.7	55.7	46.4	36.3	30.8	44.2
Extreme Maximum Temp. (°F)	80	79	86	93	97	106	105	103	97	93	85	82	106
Extreme Minimum Temp. (°F)	4	10	10	20	23	35	51	45	37	21	11	-1	-1
Days Maximum Temp. ≥ 90°F	0	0	0	0	2	16	14	7	3	0	0	0	42
Days Maximum Temp. ≤ 32°F	0	0	0	0	0	0	0	0	0	0	0	0	0
Days Minimum Temp. ≤ 32°F	20	15	12	5	1	0	0	0	0	2	9	19	83
Days Minimum Temp. ≤ 0°F	0	0	0	0	0	0	0	0	0	0	0	0	0
Heating Degree Days (base 65°F)	654	531	451	267	88	5	0	0	15	157	425	638	3,231
Cooling Degree Days (base 65°F)	0	0	0	8	64	261	306	253	163	33	0	0	1,088
Mean Precipitation (in.)	1.56	1.34	1.35	0.51	0.44	0.79	4.11	3.75	1.94	1.54	1.23	1.99	20.55
Days With ≥ 0.1" Precipitation	4	3	3	1	1	2	8	8	4	3	3	3	43
Days With ≥ 1.0" Precipitation	0	0	0	0	0	0	1	1	0	0	0	0	0
Mean Snowfall (in.)	1.6	1.5	1.8	0.3	trace	0.0	0.0	0.0	0.0	trace	0.6	2.3	8.1
Days With ≥ 1.0" Snow Depth	0	0	0	0	0	0	0	0	0	0	0	1	1

Clifton *Greenlee County*   Elevation: 3,517 ft.   Latitude: 33° 03' N   Longitude: 109° 18' W

	JAN	FEB	MAR	APR	MAY	JUN	JUL	AUG	SEP	OCT	NOV	DEC	YEAR
Mean Maximum Temp. (°F)	60.6	66.1	71.8	79.9	88.5	98.6	99.5	96.9	91.7	81.3	69.1	60.3	80.4
Mean Temp. (°F)	46.4	51.4	56.6	63.8	72.2	82.0	84.8	83.2	77.6	66.9	54.3	46.4	65.5
Mean Minimum Temp. (°F)	32.1	36.7	41.4	47.5	56.0	65.3	70.1	69.3	63.4	52.4	39.6	32.5	50.5
Extreme Maximum Temp. (°F)	83	86	92	98	106	116	115	109	105	97	85	77	116
Extreme Minimum Temp. (°F)	16	19	22	30	34	30	55	58	47	32	4	12	4
Days Maximum Temp. ≥ 90°F	0	0	1	2	14	29	30	29	21	5	0	0	131
Days Maximum Temp. ≤ 32°F	0	0	0	0	0	0	0	0	0	0	0	0	0
Days Minimum Temp. ≤ 32°F	17	8	2	0	0	0	0	0	0	0	4	17	48
Days Minimum Temp. ≤ 0°F	0	0	0	0	0	0	0	0	0	0	0	0	0
Heating Degree Days (base 65°F)	571	378	262	91	12	0	0	0	0	57	316	569	2,256
Cooling Degree Days (base 65°F)	0	0	6	72	258	521	617	574	394	125	3	0	2,570
Mean Precipitation (in.)	1.11	1.03	0.90	0.33	0.43	0.34	2.00	2.37	1.54	1.15	0.81	1.32	13.33
Days With ≥ 0.1" Precipitation	3	3	3	1	2	1	5	6	3	3	2	3	35
Days With ≥ 1.0" Precipitation	0	0	0	0	0	0	0	0	0	0	0	0	0
Mean Snowfall (in.)	0.0	0.0	0.0	0.0	0.0	0.0	0.0	0.0	0.0	0.0	0.0	trace	trace
Days With ≥ 1.0" Snow Depth	0	0	0	0	0	0	0	0	0	0	0	0	0

Colorado City *Mohave County*   Elevation: 5,009 ft.   Latitude: 37° 00' N   Longitude: 112° 58' W

	JAN	FEB	MAR	APR	MAY	JUN	JUL	AUG	SEP	OCT	NOV	DEC	YEAR
Mean Maximum Temp. (°F)	47.7	52.9	58.4	66.4	76.3	87.5	92.6	90.0	82.8	71.6	57.8	49.2	69.4
Mean Temp. (°F)	35.7	40.6	45.5	52.1	60.8	70.9	76.6	74.9	67.8	56.6	44.4	36.6	55.2
Mean Minimum Temp. (°F)	23.7	28.3	32.4	37.6	45.3	54.1	60.6	59.8	52.8	41.6	31.0	23.9	40.9
Extreme Maximum Temp. (°F)	70	78	81	90	97	105	108	105	98	92	80	69	108
Extreme Minimum Temp. (°F)	-9	-4	6	13	22	28	43	46	31	6	1	-9	-9
Days Maximum Temp. ≥ 90°F	0	0	0	0	1	14	23	18	5	0	0	0	61
Days Maximum Temp. ≤ 32°F	1	0	0	0	0	0	0	0	0	0	0	1	2
Days Minimum Temp. ≤ 32°F	27	20	16	7	1	0	0	0	0	4	17	26	118
Days Minimum Temp. ≤ 0°F	0	0	0	0	0	0	0	0	0	0	0	0	0
Heating Degree Days (base 65°F)	901	682	599	384	156	22	0	1	37	265	611	874	4,532
Cooling Degree Days (base 65°F)	0	0	0	4	39	209	366	329	132	12	0	0	1,091
Mean Precipitation (in.)	1.39	1.36	1.69	0.92	0.67	0.40	1.33	1.66	1.15	0.90	1.16	0.77	13.40
Days With ≥ 0.1" Precipitation	4	4	5	2	2	1	3	4	3	3	3	3	37
Days With ≥ 1.0" Precipitation	0	0	0	0	0	0	0	0	0	0	0	0	0
Mean Snowfall (in.)	5.7	4.8	3.7	1.4	trace	0.0	0.0	0.0	0.0	0.4	2.6	3.6	22.2
Days With ≥ 1.0" Snow Depth	7	3	1	0	0	0	0	0	0	0	0	2	4	17

Cordes *Yavapai County*   Elevation: 3,769 ft.   Latitude: 34° 18' N   Longitude: 112° 10' W

	JAN	FEB	MAR	APR	MAY	JUN	JUL	AUG	SEP	OCT	NOV	DEC	YEAR
Mean Maximum Temp. (°F)	57.8	61.1	64.9	72.6	81.5	92.4	95.7	93.5	87.9	77.5	65.9	58.2	75.7
Mean Temp. (°F)	45.3	48.0	51.1	57.0	65.0	74.7	80.3	78.9	73.0	62.9	52.1	45.6	61.2
Mean Minimum Temp. (°F)	32.7	34.9	37.3	41.4	48.4	57.2	64.9	64.3	58.0	48.3	38.3	32.9	46.5
Extreme Maximum Temp. (°F)	81	85	87	93	102	111	115	107	103	100	88	80	115
Extreme Minimum Temp. (°F)	10	12	20	23	29	37	50	44	38	23	19	8	8
Days Maximum Temp. ≥ 90°F	0	0	0	0	5	20	27	25	13	3	0	0	93
Days Maximum Temp. ≤ 32°F	0	0	0	0	0	0	0	0	0	0	0	0	0
Days Minimum Temp. ≤ 32°F	15	10	7	3	0	0	0	0	0	0	6	15	56
Days Minimum Temp. ≤ 0°F	0	0	0	0	0	0	0	0	0	0	0	0	0
Heating Degree Days (base 65°F)	606	474	424	247	78	5	0	0	7	121	381	595	2,938
Cooling Degree Days (base 65°F)	0	0	1	18	89	303	480	453	260	64	2	0	1,670
Mean Precipitation (in.)	1.71	1.87	1.68	0.63	0.46	0.20	1.82	2.24	2.09	1.06	1.18	1.36	16.30
Days With ≥ 0.1" Precipitation	3	3	4	2	1	1	4	5	3	2	2	3	33
Days With ≥ 1.0" Precipitation	0	0	0	0	0	0	0	0	1	0	0	0	1
Mean Snowfall (in.)	trace	0.4	0.3	0.3	0.0	0.0	0.0	0.0	0.0	0.0	0.3	0.3	1.6
Days With ≥ 1.0" Snow Depth	0	0	0	0	0	0	0	0	0	0	0	0	0

Coronado Nat'l Monument HQ *Cochise County*   Elevation: 5,239 ft.   Latitude: 31° 21' N   Longitude: 110° 15' W

	JAN	FEB	MAR	APR	MAY	JUN	JUL	AUG	SEP	OCT	NOV	DEC	YEAR
Mean Maximum Temp. (°F)	58.2	62.2	67.3	74.4	82.0	91.6	89.8	87.1	84.5	76.1	66.2	58.8	74.9
Mean Temp. (°F)	45.3	48.4	52.4	58.8	66.4	75.4	76.0	73.8	70.8	62.2	52.5	46.0	60.7
Mean Minimum Temp. (°F)	32.4	34.5	37.5	43.2	50.8	59.2	62.1	60.5	57.1	48.3	38.6	33.1	46.4
Extreme Maximum Temp. (°F)	80	80	86	93	100	105	104	99	98	94	85	78	105
Extreme Minimum Temp. (°F)	6	12	11	13	29	37	48	48	42	22	17	1	1
Days Maximum Temp. ≥ 90°F	0	0	0	0	4	19	17	9	5	1	0	0	55
Days Maximum Temp. ≤ 32°F	0	0	0	0	0	0	0	0	0	0	0	0	0
Days Minimum Temp. ≤ 32°F	16	11	8	3	0	0	0	0	0	1	7	15	61
Days Minimum Temp. ≤ 0°F	0	0	0	0	0	0	0	0	0	0	0	0	0
Heating Degree Days (base 65°F)	603	462	384	194	46	2	0	0	6	120	370	583	2,770
Cooling Degree Days (base 65°F)	0	0	1	18	104	317	342	273	184	37	0	0	1,276
Mean Precipitation (in.)	1.86	1.64	1.25	0.47	0.32	0.55	4.45	3.74	1.89	1.53	1.05	2.01	20.76
Days With ≥ 0.1" Precipitation	4	3	3	1	1	2	9	8	4	3	2	3	43
Days With ≥ 1.0" Precipitation	0	0	0	0	0	0	1	1	0	0	0	0	2
Mean Snowfall (in.)	0.9	1.6	1.5	0.2	0.0	0.0	0.0	0.0	0.0	0.0	0.3	2.3	6.8
Days With ≥ 1.0" Snow Depth	1	0	0	0	0	0	0	0	0	0	0	0	1

Douglas *Cochise County* Elevation: 4,038 ft. Latitude: 31° 21' N Longitude: 109° 32' W

	JAN	FEB	MAR	APR	MAY	JUN	JUL	AUG	SEP	OCT	NOV	DEC	YEAR
Mean Maximum Temp. (°F)	62.0	66.9	71.9	79.3	86.4	95.7	94.0	91.4	88.8	80.3	69.7	62.8	79.1
Mean Temp. (°F)	45.4	49.3	54.0	60.4	67.9	76.9	79.1	77.1	72.9	63.0	51.8	45.7	62.0
Mean Minimum Temp. (°F)	28.8	31.7	36.1	41.4	49.4	58.1	64.2	62.8	56.9	45.7	33.9	28.6	44.8
Extreme Maximum Temp. (°F)	82	86	91	97	102	109	107	104	101	95	87	79	109
Extreme Minimum Temp. (°F)	7	12	19	24	30	38	44	45	42	20	9	2	2
Days Maximum Temp. ≥ 90°F	0	0	0	1	9	26	25	21	14	3	0	0	99
Days Maximum Temp. ≤ 32°F	0	0	0	0	0	0	0	0	0	0	0	0	0
Days Minimum Temp. ≤ 32°F	22	16	10	3	0	0	0	0	0	2	14	21	88
Days Minimum Temp. ≤ 0°F	0	0	0	0	0	0	0	0	0	0	0	0	0
Heating Degree Days (base 65°F)	600	436	335	151	27	0	0	0	2	99	389	592	2,631
Cooling Degree Days (base 65°F)	0	0	na	25	134	366	441	380	251	43	1	na	na
Mean Precipitation (in.)	0.90	0.68	0.58	0.30	0.37	0.59	3.58	3.19	1.62	1.29	0.72	1.11	14.93
Days With ≥ 0.1" Precipitation	3	2	2	1	1	2	8	6	3	3	2	3	36
Days With ≥ 1.0" Precipitation	0	0	0	0	0	0	1	1	0	0	0	0	2
Mean Snowfall (in.)	trace	trace	0.0	0.0	0.0	0.0	0.0	0.0	0.0	0.0	0.0	0.0	trace
Days With ≥ 1.0" Snow Depth	0	0	0	0	0	0	0	0	0	0	0	0	0

Douglas Bisbee-Douglas Int'l *Cochise County* Elevation: 4,097 ft. Latitude: 31° 28' N Longitude: 109° 36' W

	JAN	FEB	MAR	APR	MAY	JUN	JUL	AUG	SEP	OCT	NOV	DEC	YEAR
Mean Maximum Temp. (°F)	61.5	65.6	70.7	77.9	85.7	94.7	93.1	91.0	87.9	79.7	69.6	62.0	78.3
Mean Temp. (°F)	45.5	49.1	53.8	60.0	68.2	77.3	79.1	77.5	73.4	63.4	52.6	45.9	62.2
Mean Minimum Temp. (°F)	29.5	32.4	36.9	42.2	50.7	59.8	65.1	63.9	58.9	47.1	35.5	29.7	46.0
Extreme Maximum Temp. (°F)	81	85	92	99	101	110	109	103	101	95	87	80	110
Extreme Minimum Temp. (°F)	7	10	18	21	30	40	55	52	43	19	15	-4	-4
Days Maximum Temp. ≥ 90°F	0	0	0	1	9	25	24	21	13	3	0	0	96
Days Maximum Temp. ≤ 32°F	0	0	0	0	0	0	0	0	0	0	0	0	0
Days Minimum Temp. ≤ 32°F	21	14	8	3	0	0	0	0	0	1	11	21	79
Days Minimum Temp. ≤ 0°F	0	0	0	0	0	0	0	0	0	0	0	0	0
Heating Degree Days (base 65°F)	597	444	340	163	27	1	0	0	2	96	367	587	2,624
Cooling Degree Days (base 65°F)	0	0	1	26	149	380	450	402	271	57	0	0	1,736
Mean Precipitation (in.)	0.75	0.65	0.48	0.21	0.33	0.56	3.11	2.91	1.65	1.16	0.70	1.07	13.58
Days With ≥ 0.1" Precipitation	2	2	2	1	1	1	7	7	3	2	2	3	33
Days With ≥ 1.0" Precipitation	0	0	0	0	0	0	1	1	0	0	0	0	2
Mean Snowfall (in.)	0.2	0.1	0.1	trace	trace	trace	trace	trace	trace	trace	0.1	0.3	0.8
Days With ≥ 1.0" Snow Depth	0	0	0	0	0	0	0	0	0	0	0	0	0

Duncan *Greenlee County* Elevation: 3,658 ft. Latitude: 32° 45' N Longitude: 109° 07' W

	JAN	FEB	MAR	APR	MAY	JUN	JUL	AUG	SEP	OCT	NOV	DEC	YEAR
Mean Maximum Temp. (°F)	59.6	64.8	70.8	78.9	87.4	96.8	96.9	94.2	89.8	80.2	68.5	59.6	79.0
Mean Temp. (°F)	41.8	45.8	51.0	57.2	65.9	75.2	80.1	78.2	72.2	60.5	48.5	41.3	59.8
Mean Minimum Temp. (°F)	23.9	26.7	31.1	35.4	44.4	53.5	63.2	62.2	54.2	40.7	28.5	23.0	40.5
Extreme Maximum Temp. (°F)	78	85	95	99	103	111	110	106	103	98	86	78	111
Extreme Minimum Temp. (°F)	4	5	10	13	22	34	42	41	35	19	7	0	0
Days Maximum Temp. ≥ 90°F	0	0	0	2	12	27	29	26	17	4	0	0	117
Days Maximum Temp. ≤ 32°F	0	0	0	0	0	0	0	0	0	0	0	0	0
Days Minimum Temp. ≤ 32°F	25	21	18	11	1	0	0	0	0	6	21	26	129
Days Minimum Temp. ≤ 0°F	0	0	0	0	0	0	0	0	0	0	0	0	0
Heating Degree Days (base 65°F)	713	537	428	236	51	1	0	0	6	161	489	729	3,351
Cooling Degree Days (base 65°F)	0	0	0	12	97	330	482	434	238	27	0	0	1,620
Mean Precipitation (in.)	0.95	0.97	0.64	0.24	0.38	0.34	2.30	2.10	1.12	1.21	0.70	1.20	12.15
Days With ≥ 0.1" Precipitation	3	3	2	1	1	1	5	5	3	3	2	3	32
Days With ≥ 1.0" Precipitation	0	0	0	0	0	0	0	0	0	0	0	0	0
Mean Snowfall (in.)	0.1	trace	trace	0.0	0.0	0.0	0.0	0.0	0.0	0.0	trace	0.3	0.4
Days With ≥ 1.0" Snow Depth	0	0	0	0	0	0	0	0	0	0	0	0	0

Eloy 4 NE *Pinal County* Elevation: 1,541 ft. Latitude: 32° 47' N Longitude: 111° 31' W

	JAN	FEB	MAR	APR	MAY	JUN	JUL	AUG	SEP	OCT	NOV	DEC	YEAR
Mean Maximum Temp. (°F)	67.5	72.0	76.7	85.1	94.1	103.6	104.8	102.6	98.4	88.8	76.3	67.3	86.4
Mean Temp. (°F)	52.0	56.1	60.6	67.6	76.4	85.4	89.3	88.0	82.5	71.8	59.6	51.9	70.1
Mean Minimum Temp. (°F)	36.5	40.2	44.4	50.1	58.5	67.1	73.8	73.2	66.5	54.6	42.9	36.4	53.7
Extreme Maximum Temp. (°F)	87	90	98	103	110	119	117	116	111	107	93	85	119
Extreme Minimum Temp. (°F)	13	20	23	27	29	46	60	54	38	30	22	15	13
Days Maximum Temp. ≥ 90°F	0	0	2	10	24	29	31	31	28	15	0	0	170
Days Maximum Temp. ≤ 32°F	0	0	0	0	0	0	0	0	0	0	0	0	0
Days Minimum Temp. ≤ 32°F	9	3	1	0	0	0	0	0	0	0	3	9	25
Days Minimum Temp. ≤ 0°F	0	0	0	0	0	0	0	0	0	0	0	0	0
Heating Degree Days (base 65°F)	395	248	159	51	3	0	0	0	0	23	182	400	1,461
Cooling Degree Days (base 65°F)	0	5	27	137	361	610	756	721	529	225	15	0	3,386
Mean Precipitation (in.)	0.94	1.08	1.14	0.28	0.26	0.12	1.13	1.60	1.02	0.97	0.79	1.28	10.61
Days With ≥ 0.1" Precipitation	2	2	3	1	1	0	2	3	2	2	2	2	22
Days With ≥ 1.0" Precipitation	0	0	0	0	0	0	0	0	0	0	0	0	0
Mean Snowfall (in.)	trace	0.0	0.0	0.0	0.0	0.0	0.0	0.0	0.0	0.0	0.0	trace	trace
Days With ≥ 1.0" Snow Depth	0	0	0	0	0	0	0	0	0	0	0	0	0

Florence *Pinal County*   Elevation: 1,502 ft.   Latitude: 33° 02' N   Longitude: 111° 24' W

	JAN	FEB	MAR	APR	MAY	JUN	JUL	AUG	SEP	OCT	NOV	DEC	YEAR
Mean Maximum Temp. (°F)	66.9	71.4	76.1	84.7	93.6	103.4	104.9	103.1	98.5	88.2	75.3	66.7	86.1
Mean Temp. (°F)	52.8	56.5	60.5	67.2	75.9	85.3	90.2	88.9	83.4	72.5	59.9	52.8	70.5
Mean Minimum Temp. (°F)	38.6	41.4	44.9	49.7	58.2	67.1	75.5	74.6	68.3	56.7	44.4	38.8	54.8
Extreme Maximum Temp. (°F)	87	91	99	104	114	118	119	118	115	112	96	86	119
Extreme Minimum Temp. (°F)	14	20	20	31	37	49	61	59	48	32	25	16	14
Days Maximum Temp. ≥ 90°F	0	0	2	10	23	29	31	30	28	15	1	0	169
Days Maximum Temp. ≤ 32°F	0	0	0	0	0	0	0	0	0	0	0	0	0
Days Minimum Temp. ≤ 32°F	6	3	1	0	0	0	0	0	0	0	2	6	18
Days Minimum Temp. ≤ 0°F	0	0	0	0	0	0	0	0	0	0	0	0	0
Heating Degree Days (base 65°F)	372	240	166	55	4	0	0	0	0	22	172	373	1,404
Cooling Degree Days (base 65°F)	1	7	35	149	361	608	769	744	555	263	26	1	3,519
Mean Precipitation (in.)	1.07	1.05	1.22	0.39	0.26	0.16	0.97	1.24	0.94	0.85	1.00	1.25	10.40
Days With ≥ 0.1" Precipitation	3	3	3	1	1	0	2	2	2	2	2	2	23
Days With ≥ 1.0" Precipitation	0	0	0	0	0	0	0	0	0	0	0	0	0
Mean Snowfall (in.)	0.0	0.0	trace	0.0	0.0	0.0	0.0	0.0	0.0	0.0	0.0	trace	trace
Days With ≥ 1.0" Snow Depth	0	0	0	0	0	0	0	0	0	0	0	0	0

Fort Thomas 2 SW *Graham County*   Elevation: 2,798 ft.   Latitude: 33° 01' N   Longitude: 110° 00' W

	JAN	FEB	MAR	APR	MAY	JUN	JUL	AUG	SEP	OCT	NOV	DEC	YEAR
Mean Maximum Temp. (°F)	60.1	65.8	72.0	80.2	88.6	98.0	98.3	96.2	91.8	81.4	68.8	59.6	80.1
Mean Temp. (°F)	44.5	49.5	54.3	60.9	69.8	79.2	83.4	81.6	75.8	64.1	51.7	44.3	63.3
Mean Minimum Temp. (°F)	28.8	33.1	36.6	41.6	50.9	60.2	68.4	67.0	59.8	46.7	34.5	28.9	46.4
Extreme Maximum Temp. (°F)	81	84	93	100	105	113	111	109	105	99	93	80	113
Extreme Minimum Temp. (°F)	3	7	15	23	30	40	53	50	*26*	24	7	8	*3*
Days Maximum Temp. ≥ 90°F	0	0	0	3	15	28	29	27	21	5	0	0	128
Days Maximum Temp. ≤ 32°F	0	0	0	0	0	0	0	0	0	0	0	0	0
Days Minimum Temp. ≤ 32°F	22	14	9	3	0	0	0	0	0	1	12	22	83
Days Minimum Temp. ≤ 0°F	0	0	0	0	0	0	0	0	0	0	0	0	0
Heating Degree Days (base 65°F)	630	431	327	149	21	0	0	0	2	90	394	636	2,680
Cooling Degree Days (base 65°F)	0	0	2	40	188	423	572	527	336	70	1	0	2,159
Mean Precipitation (in.)	1.01	1.03	0.86	0.27	0.34	0.22	1.29	1.22	1.10	0.99	0.64	1.11	10.08
Days With ≥ 0.1" Precipitation	3	3	2	1	1	1	3	3	3	2	2	3	27
Days With ≥ 1.0" Precipitation	0	0	0	0	0	0	0	0	0	0	0	0	0
Mean Snowfall (in.)	trace	trace	trace	0.0	0.0	0.0	0.0	0.0	0.0	0.0	trace	0.2	0.2
Days With ≥ 1.0" Snow Depth	0	0	0	0	0	0	0	0	0	0	0	0	0

Fort Valley *Coconino County*   Elevation: 7,345 ft.   Latitude: 35° 16' N   Longitude: 111° 44' W

	JAN	FEB	MAR	APR	MAY	JUN	JUL	AUG	SEP	OCT	NOV	DEC	YEAR
Mean Maximum Temp. (°F)	42.8	45.5	49.8	57.6	67.4	78.6	81.3	78.8	73.2	63.4	51.7	43.6	61.1
Mean Temp. (°F)	26.9	29.8	34.0	40.0	47.6	56.4	62.4	61.1	54.6	44.7	34.7	27.5	43.3
Mean Minimum Temp. (°F)	10.9	14.0	18.2	22.3	27.8	34.1	43.4	43.3	36.0	25.9	17.6	11.3	25.4
Extreme Maximum Temp. (°F)	65	69	72	80	90	96	98	93	90	85	74	64	98
Extreme Minimum Temp. (°F)	-33	-32	-17	-6	10	20	26	24	13	-3	-15	-30	-33
Days Maximum Temp. ≥ 90°F	0	0	0	0	0	2	3	1	0	0	0	0	6
Days Maximum Temp. ≤ 32°F	3	2	1	0	0	0	0	0	0	0	1	3	10
Days Minimum Temp. ≤ 32°F	31	28	31	29	25	13	2	2	10	26	29	31	257
Days Minimum Temp. ≤ 0°F	6	3	1	0	0	0	0	0	0	0	1	5	16
Heating Degree Days (base 65°F)	1,176	986	954	744	532	259	97	124	306	624	903	1,158	7,863
Cooling Degree Days (base 65°F)	0	0	0	0	0	7	19	12	1	0	0	0	39
Mean Precipitation (in.)	2.28	2.27	2.65	1.26	0.87	0.40	2.78	2.90	2.13	1.60	1.67	1.53	22.34
Days With ≥ 0.1" Precipitation	5	4	5	3	3	1	6	6	4	3	3	3	46
Days With ≥ 1.0" Precipitation	0	0	0	0	0	0	0	0	1	0	0	0	1
Mean Snowfall (in.)	18.6	14.7	18.4	5.9	0.3	trace	0.0	0.0	0.0	1.6	8.7	11.1	79.3
Days With ≥ 1.0" Snow Depth	*18*	*15*	*15*	3	0	0	0	0	0	1	*5*	*14*	*71*

Gila Bend *Maricopa County*   Elevation: 734 ft.   Latitude: 32° 57' N   Longitude: 112° 43' W

	JAN	FEB	MAR	APR	MAY	JUN	JUL	AUG	SEP	OCT	NOV	DEC	YEAR
Mean Maximum Temp. (°F)	69.2	74.2	79.5	87.7	96.5	106.3	109.0	107.1	102.3	91.3	78.4	69.2	89.2
Mean Temp. (°F)	54.9	59.1	63.8	70.7	79.3	88.5	94.2	92.9	87.2	75.2	62.7	54.9	73.6
Mean Minimum Temp. (°F)	40.5	44.0	48.1	53.6	62.0	70.7	79.3	78.7	72.0	59.1	47.0	40.5	58.0
Extreme Maximum Temp. (°F)	87	92	100	110	116	122	122	120	118	114	96	87	122
Extreme Minimum Temp. (°F)	17	24	25	36	43	54	63	62	50	32	27	19	17
Days Maximum Temp. ≥ 90°F	0	0	4	14	26	30	31	31	29	20	2	0	187
Days Maximum Temp. ≤ 32°F	0	0	0	0	0	0	0	0	0	0	0	0	0
Days Minimum Temp. ≤ 32°F	4	1	0	0	0	0	0	0	0	0	1	3	9
Days Minimum Temp. ≤ 0°F	0	0	0	0	0	0	0	0	0	0	0	0	0
Heating Degree Days (base 65°F)	310	173	94	26	1	0	0	0	0	12	114	309	1,039
Cooling Degree Days (base 65°F)	2	17	68	228	466	709	902	889	681	344	56	1	4,363
Mean Precipitation (in.)	0.62	0.87	0.74	0.20	0.15	0.03	0.78	1.18	0.59	0.45	0.60	0.82	7.03
Days With ≥ 0.1" Precipitation	2	2	2	1	0	0	2	3	1	1	1	2	17
Days With ≥ 1.0" Precipitation	0	0	0	0	0	0	0	0	0	0	0	0	0
Mean Snowfall (in.)	0.0	0.0	0.0	0.0	0.0	0.0	0.0	0.0	0.0	0.0	0.0	0.0	0.0
Days With ≥ 1.0" Snow Depth	0	0	0	0	0	0	0	0	0	0	0	0	0

Greer *Apache County* Elevation: 8,487 ft. Latitude: 34° 00' N Longitude: 109° 28' W

	JAN	FEB	MAR	APR	MAY	JUN	JUL	AUG	SEP	OCT	NOV	DEC	YEAR
Mean Maximum Temp. (°F)	41.2	43.7	48.1	56.0	64.8	74.6	75.4	72.5	68.0	59.4	49.5	42.4	58.0
Mean Temp. (°F)	28.5	31.1	34.9	41.3	49.1	58.0	61.5	59.6	54.6	45.5	36.2	29.7	44.1
Mean Minimum Temp. (°F)	15.7	18.4	21.6	26.5	33.4	41.2	47.4	46.5	41.1	31.6	22.7	16.9	30.3
Extreme Maximum Temp. (°F)	65	65	70	74	83	89	90	87	80	77	74	63	90
Extreme Minimum Temp. (°F)	-24	-13	-4	-4	14	25	37	34	24	8	-12	-20	-24
Days Maximum Temp. ≥ 90°F	0	0	0	0	0	0	0	0	0	0	0	0	0
Days Maximum Temp. ≤ 32°F	4	3	1	0	0	0	0	0	0	0	1	4	13
Days Minimum Temp. ≤ 32°F	31	28	30	25	13	2	0	0	2	16	28	31	206
Days Minimum Temp. ≤ 0°F	2	1	0	0	0	0	0	0	0	0	0	1	4
Heating Degree Days (base 65°F)	1,126	951	927	704	487	211	110	164	306	597	859	1,089	7,531
Cooling Degree Days (base 65°F)	0	0	0	0	0	6	7	2	0	0	0	0	15
Mean Precipitation (in.)	1.49	1.38	1.65	0.85	0.93	0.93	3.84	4.38	2.56	2.00	1.50	1.48	22.99
Days With ≥ 0.1" Precipitation	4	4	5	3	3	3	10	11	6	4	3	4	60
Days With ≥ 1.0" Precipitation	0	0	0	0	0	0	1	1	0	0	0	0	2
Mean Snowfall (in.)	na	20.8	20.2	8.0	0.8	0.1	trace	0.0	trace	1.6	11.1	19.8	na
Days With ≥ 1.0" Snow Depth	25	20	15	3	0	0	0	0	0	1	7	19	90

Heber Ranger Station *Navajo County* Elevation: 6,587 ft. Latitude: 34° 24' N Longitude: 110° 33' W

	JAN	FEB	MAR	APR	MAY	JUN	JUL	AUG	SEP	OCT	NOV	DEC	YEAR
Mean Maximum Temp. (°F)	na	51.1	55.6	63.2	71.7	82.7	84.6	81.7	76.8	66.6	54.6	47.1	na
Mean Temp. (°F)	na	35.9	40.3	45.9	53.8	63.2	68.6	66.7	60.8	50.1	39.2	32.5	na
Mean Minimum Temp. (°F)	na	20.5	24.9	28.6	36.0	43.7	52.5	51.7	44.8	33.5	23.9	18.0	na
Extreme Maximum Temp. (°F)	68	71	76	81	91	100	100	95	94	87	78	68	100
Extreme Minimum Temp. (°F)	-24	-14	-2	2	15	26	33	36	23	9	-11	-21	-24
Days Maximum Temp. ≥ 90°F	0	0	0	0	0	4	6	1	0	0	0	0	11
Days Maximum Temp. ≤ 32°F	2	0	0	0	0	0	0	0	0	0	0	2	4
Days Minimum Temp. ≤ 32°F	24	22	24	20	10	2	0	0	1	13	25	28	169
Days Minimum Temp. ≤ 0°F	1	1	0	0	0	0	0	0	0	0	0	1	3
Heating Degree Days (base 65°F)	na	814	761	565	342	98	8	20	135	454	769	999	na
Cooling Degree Days (base 65°F)	na	0	0	0	1	47	122	82	15	0	0	0	na
Mean Precipitation (in.)	1.50	1.52	1.62	0.62	0.75	0.39	2.73	3.22	2.14	1.54	1.42	1.55	19.00
Days With ≥ 0.1" Precipitation	3	3	3	2	1	1	6	7	4	3	2	3	38
Days With ≥ 1.0" Precipitation	0	0	0	0	0	0	1	1	0	1	0	0	3
Mean Snowfall (in.)	9.5	8.8	4.8	3.1	trace	0.0	0.0	0.0	0.0	trace	3.3	7.4	36.9
Days With ≥ 1.0" Snow Depth	7	3	2	0	0	0	0	0	0	0	1	6	19

Hillside 4 NNE *Yavapai County* Elevation: 3,316 ft. Latitude: 34° 28' N Longitude: 112° 53' W

	JAN	FEB	MAR	APR	MAY	JUN	JUL	AUG	SEP	OCT	NOV	DEC	YEAR
Mean Maximum Temp. (°F)	59.0	63.0	66.4	74.5	83.3	94.0	97.3	94.8	89.8	78.9	67.2	59.9	77.3
Mean Temp. (°F)	42.4	45.6	48.9	54.5	62.5	71.3	78.6	77.5	70.7	59.3	48.2	42.6	58.5
Mean Minimum Temp. (°F)	25.7	28.2	31.3	34.6	41.7	48.6	59.9	60.0	51.7	39.6	29.1	25.3	39.6
Extreme Maximum Temp. (°F)	82	84	87	97	104	112	113	110	111	101	88	80	113
Extreme Minimum Temp. (°F)	3	5	13	19	20	31	34	40	30	18	8	0	0
Days Maximum Temp. ≥ 90°F	0	0	0	1	6	22	28	25	15	4	0	0	101
Days Maximum Temp. ≤ 32°F	0	0	0	0	0	0	0	0	0	0	0	0	0
Days Minimum Temp. ≤ 32°F	25	21	19	12	2	0	0	0	0	6	21	26	132
Days Minimum Temp. ≤ 0°F	0	0	0	0	0	0	0	0	0	0	0	0	0
Heating Degree Days (base 65°F)	694	540	493	310	113	13	0	0	16	189	497	687	3,552
Cooling Degree Days (base 65°F)	0	0	0	4	44	191	403	394	188	19	0	0	1,243
Mean Precipitation (in.)	1.95	1.91	2.17	0.72	0.44	0.17	1.25	2.49	1.35	1.02	1.31	1.35	16.13
Days With ≥ 0.1" Precipitation	4	4	5	2	1	1	3	5	3	2	2	3	35
Days With ≥ 1.0" Precipitation	1	1	0	0	0	0	0	1	0	0	0	0	3
Mean Snowfall (in.)	0.3	0.6	0.5	trace	0.0	0.0	0.0	0.0	0.0	0.0	0.0	0.3	1.7
Days With ≥ 1.0" Snow Depth	0	0	0	0	0	0	0	0	0	0	0	0	0

Jerome *Yavapai County* Elevation: 4,947 ft. Latitude: 34° 45' N Longitude: 112° 07' W

	JAN	FEB	MAR	APR	MAY	JUN	JUL	AUG	SEP	OCT	NOV	DEC	YEAR
Mean Maximum Temp. (°F)	49.6	54.1	59.1	67.0	76.3	86.9	90.5	87.6	81.6	70.7	58.5	50.2	69.4
Mean Temp. (°F)	41.6	44.9	49.2	56.0	64.7	75.1	78.9	76.7	71.1	60.9	49.5	42.1	59.2
Mean Minimum Temp. (°F)	33.6	36.0	39.2	44.9	53.0	63.2	67.1	65.7	60.6	50.9	40.6	33.9	49.1
Extreme Maximum Temp. (°F)	74	78	80	88	95	104	104	102	99	93	80	73	104
Extreme Minimum Temp. (°F)	9	10	17	25	32	39	44	49	40	21	16	5	5
Days Maximum Temp. ≥ 90°F	0	0	0	0	1	11	18	11	3	0	0	0	44
Days Maximum Temp. ≤ 32°F	0	0	0	0	0	0	0	0	0	0	0	0	0
Days Minimum Temp. ≤ 32°F	13	8	7	3	0	0	0	0	0	0	4	12	47
Days Minimum Temp. ≤ 0°F	0	0	0	0	0	0	0	0	0	0	0	0	0
Heating Degree Days (base 65°F)	718	560	485	280	90	7	0	1	14	169	460	703	3,487
Cooling Degree Days (base 65°F)	0	0	1	22	97	325	447	381	205	48	0	0	1,526
Mean Precipitation (in.)	1.80	2.07	2.29	1.07	0.70	0.37	2.58	3.12	1.83	1.32	1.46	1.22	19.83
Days With ≥ 0.1" Precipitation	4	4	5	3	2	1	5	6	3	3	3	3	42
Days With ≥ 1.0" Precipitation	0	1	1	0	0	0	1	1	0	0	0	0	4
Mean Snowfall (in.)	2.7	2.0	2.2	1.3	trace	0.0	0.0	0.0	0.0	trace	0.5	1.2	9.9
Days With ≥ 1.0" Snow Depth	1	0	0	0	0	0	0	0	0	0	0	0	1

Kingman 2 *Mohave County*   Elevation: 3,536 ft.   Latitude: 35° 12' N   Longitude: 114° 01' W

	JAN	FEB	MAR	APR	MAY	JUN	JUL	AUG	SEP	OCT	NOV	DEC	YEAR
Mean Maximum Temp. (°F)	53.9	59.2	62.9	71.2	80.7	91.8	95.9	93.8	88.0	77.1	63.4	55.1	74.4
Mean Temp. (°F)	42.6	47.0	50.6	57.8	66.9	77.3	82.7	80.6	74.4	63.5	50.9	43.6	61.5
Mean Minimum Temp. (°F)	31.2	34.8	38.2	44.4	53.0	62.8	69.4	67.3	60.7	49.8	38.5	32.0	48.5
Extreme Maximum Temp. (°F)	77	82	84	93	102	109	110	108	103	100	85	75	110
Extreme Minimum Temp. (°F)	4	12	11	22	30	42	51	54	36	23	18	6	4
Days Maximum Temp. ≥ 90°F	0	0	0	0	4	19	28	25	14	3	0	0	93
Days Maximum Temp. ≤ 32°F	0	0	0	0	0	0	0	0	0	0	0	0	0
Days Minimum Temp. ≤ 32°F	17	10	7	2	0	0	0	0	0	0	6	16	58
Days Minimum Temp. ≤ 0°F	0	0	0	0	0	0	0	0	0	0	0	0	0
Heating Degree Days (base 65°F)	688	502	441	234	70	4	0	0	10	120	415	656	3,140
Cooling Degree Days (base 65°F)	0	0	2	35	143	374	540	487	na	na	na	na	na
Mean Precipitation (in.)	1.30	1.05	1.42	0.49	0.34	0.23	1.03	1.50	0.72	0.82	0.76	0.97	10.63
Days With ≥ 0.1" Precipitation	3	3	3	1	1	1	2	3	2	2	2	2	25
Days With ≥ 1.0" Precipitation	0	0	0	0	0	0	0	0	0	0	0	0	0
Mean Snowfall (in.)	0.2	0.7	0.3	trace	0.0	0.0	0.0	0.0	0.0	0.0	0.2	na	na
Days With ≥ 1.0" Snow Depth	na	0	0	0	0	0	0	0	0	0	0	na	na

Kitt Peak *Pima County*   Elevation: 6,788 ft.   Latitude: 31° 58' N   Longitude: 111° 36' W

	JAN	FEB	MAR	APR	MAY	JUN	JUL	AUG	SEP	OCT	NOV	DEC	YEAR
Mean Maximum Temp. (°F)	49.3	51.4	54.8	62.2	70.4	80.8	81.0	78.4	75.1	66.9	57.1	50.2	64.8
Mean Temp. (°F)	41.1	42.6	45.3	51.5	59.3	69.6	70.8	68.9	65.6	57.3	48.0	41.8	55.1
Mean Minimum Temp. (°F)	32.8	33.7	35.7	40.7	48.3	58.5	60.5	59.3	56.1	47.7	38.8	33.4	45.5
Extreme Maximum Temp. (°F)	71	74	78	88	90	98	98	94	91	88	87	72	98
Extreme Minimum Temp. (°F)	2	5	9	15	27	37	49	42	35	20	14	6	2
Days Maximum Temp. ≥ 90°F	0	0	0	0	0	3	2	1	0	0	0	0	6
Days Maximum Temp. ≤ 32°F	1	1	1	0	0	0	0	0	0	0	0	1	4
Days Minimum Temp. ≤ 32°F	14	12	12	6	1	0	0	0	0	1	7	13	66
Days Minimum Temp. ≤ 0°F	0	0	0	0	0	0	0	0	0	0	0	0	0
Heating Degree Days (base 65°F)	735	626	605	402	193	26	5	11	48	249	504	713	4,117
Cooling Degree Days (base 65°F)	0	0	0	5	29	174	195	145	77	20	0	0	645
Mean Precipitation (in.)	1.87	1.62	1.98	0.47	0.51	0.34	4.62	4.74	2.51	1.78	1.19	2.44	24.07
Days With ≥ 0.1" Precipitation	3	3	3	1	1	1	8	8	4	3	2	4	41
Days With ≥ 1.0" Precipitation	0	0	0	0	0	0	1	1	1	0	0	1	4
Mean Snowfall (in.)	3.4	4.5	4.2	1.4	trace	0.0	0.0	0.0	0.0	0.4	1.2	2.2	17.3
Days With ≥ 1.0" Snow Depth	2	2	3	1	0	0	0	0	0	0	0	2	10

Kofa Mine *Yuma County*   Elevation: 1,774 ft.   Latitude: 33° 16' N   Longitude: 113° 58' W

	JAN	FEB	MAR	APR	MAY	JUN	JUL	AUG	SEP	OCT	NOV	DEC	YEAR
Mean Maximum Temp. (°F)	66.1	70.0	74.7	82.1	90.1	100.2	103.5	102.0	96.5	85.8	74.0	65.4	84.2
Mean Temp. (°F)	56.3	59.7	63.4	69.8	77.4	87.1	91.5	90.3	85.0	74.9	63.7	55.8	72.9
Mean Minimum Temp. (°F)	46.3	49.2	52.1	57.4	64.7	73.9	79.5	78.6	73.5	64.0	53.5	46.2	61.6
Extreme Maximum Temp. (°F)	86	93	95	104	112	117	119	116	111	109	93	81	119
Extreme Minimum Temp. (°F)	25	28	34	38	46	49	66	60	50	36	34	28	25
Days Maximum Temp. ≥ 90°F	0	0	1	7	18	28	31	30	26	11	1	0	153
Days Maximum Temp. ≤ 32°F	0	0	0	0	0	0	0	0	0	0	0	0	0
Days Minimum Temp. ≤ 32°F	1	0	0	0	0	0	0	0	0	0	0	0	1
Days Minimum Temp. ≤ 0°F	0	0	0	0	0	0	0	0	0	0	0	0	0
Heating Degree Days (base 65°F)	270	170	119	46	5	0	0	0	0	15	103	281	1,009
Cooling Degree Days (base 65°F)	5	27	73	214	407	663	827	804	617	346	76	4	4,063
Mean Precipitation (in.)	0.85	0.81	0.79	0.23	0.15	0.03	0.67	1.08	1.13	0.53	0.40	0.63	7.30
Days With ≥ 0.1" Precipitation	2	2	2	1	0	0	1	2	2	1	1	1	15
Days With ≥ 1.0" Precipitation	0	0	0	0	0	0	0	0	0	0	0	0	0
Mean Snowfall (in.)	0.0	trace	0.0	0.0	0.0	0.0	0.0	0.0	0.0	0.0	0.0	0.0	trace
Days With ≥ 1.0" Snow Depth	0	0	0	0	0	0	0	0	0	0	0	0	0

Laveen 3 SSE *Maricopa County*   Elevation: 1,112 ft.   Latitude: 33° 20' N   Longitude: 112° 09' W

	JAN	FEB	MAR	APR	MAY	JUN	JUL	AUG	SEP	OCT	NOV	DEC	YEAR
Mean Maximum Temp. (°F)	66.6	71.7	76.6	85.0	94.0	103.7	105.4	103.6	98.5	88.2	75.4	66.6	86.3
Mean Temp. (°F)	52.8	57.2	61.5	68.4	77.4	86.8	91.3	89.8	83.7	72.5	60.2	52.8	71.2
Mean Minimum Temp. (°F)	38.9	42.6	46.2	51.8	60.8	69.9	77.2	76.0	68.9	56.7	45.0	38.9	56.1
Extreme Maximum Temp. (°F)	89	90	97	106	113	122	125	118	113	107	94	85	125
Extreme Minimum Temp. (°F)	16	23	25	34	43	52	59	61	50	28	28	20	16
Days Maximum Temp. ≥ 90°F	0	0	2	10	24	29	31	31	28	15	1	0	171
Days Maximum Temp. ≤ 32°F	0	0	0	0	0	0	0	0	0	0	0	0	0
Days Minimum Temp. ≤ 32°F	6	2	0	0	0	0	0	0	0	0	1	5	14
Days Minimum Temp. ≤ 0°F	0	0	0	0	0	0	0	0	0	0	0	0	0
Heating Degree Days (base 65°F)	372	222	143	44	2	0	0	0	0	21	162	372	1,338
Cooling Degree Days (base 65°F)	0	8	45	178	413	661	818	790	578	271	29	1	3,792
Mean Precipitation (in.)	0.78	0.90	1.07	0.25	0.17	0.05	1.20	0.93	0.86	0.75	0.70	0.90	8.56
Days With ≥ 0.1" Precipitation	2	2	3	1	1	0	2	2	2	2	2	2	21
Days With ≥ 1.0" Precipitation	0	0	0	0	0	0	0	0	0	0	0	0	0
Mean Snowfall (in.)	0.0	0.0	0.0	0.0	0.0	0.0	0.0	0.0	0.0	0.0	0.0	0.0	0.0
Days With ≥ 1.0" Snow Depth	0	0	0	0	0	0	0	0	0	0	0	0	0

Litchfield Park *Maricopa County*   Elevation: 1,026 ft.   Latitude: 33° 30' N   Longitude: 112° 22' W

	JAN	FEB	MAR	APR	MAY	JUN	JUL	AUG	SEP	OCT	NOV	DEC	YEAR
Mean Maximum Temp. (°F)	67.5	72.8	78.0	86.9	96.0	105.8	108.0	106.3	101.0	90.4	76.5	67.4	88.1
Mean Temp. (°F)	52.6	57.0	61.7	68.8	77.6	86.8	91.7	90.5	84.1	72.6	59.8	52.4	71.3
Mean Minimum Temp. (°F)	37.6	41.2	45.4	50.8	59.2	67.8	75.5	74.6	67.3	54.7	43.1	37.2	54.5
Extreme Maximum Temp. (°F)	89	92	100	105	115	120	125	120	116	109	95	87	125
Extreme Minimum Temp. (°F)	18	25	22	32	36	50	58	57	46	31	22	20	18
Days Maximum Temp. ≥ 90°F	0	0	3	12	24	29	30	31	29	18	1	0	177
Days Maximum Temp. ≤ 32°F	0	0	0	0	0	0	0	0	0	0	0	0	0
Days Minimum Temp. ≤ 32°F	7	2	0	0	0	0	0	0	0	0	1	7	17
Days Minimum Temp. ≤ 0°F	0	0	0	0	0	0	0	0	0	0	0	0	0
Heating Degree Days (base 65°F)	379	224	133	39	2	0	0	0	0	19	166	385	1,347
Cooling Degree Days (base 65°F)	0	7	40	*193*	429	667	832	815	593	275	18	0	*3,869*
Mean Precipitation (in.)	0.95	1.13	1.11	0.33	0.12	0.05	0.71	0.95	1.05	0.64	0.68	1.04	8.76
Days With ≥ 0.1" Precipitation	2	2	2	1	0	0	2	2	2	1	1	2	17
Days With ≥ 1.0" Precipitation	0	0	0	0	0	0	0	0	0	0	0	0	0
Mean Snowfall (in.)	0.0	0.0	0.0	0.0	0.0	0.0	0.0	0.0	0.0	0.0	0.0	0.0	0.0
Days With ≥ 1.0" Snow Depth	0	0	0	0	0	0	0	0	0	0	0	0	0

Maricopa 4 N *Pinal County*   Elevation: 1,158 ft.   Latitude: 33° 07' N   Longitude: 112° 02' W

	JAN	FEB	MAR	APR	MAY	JUN	JUL	AUG	SEP	OCT	NOV	DEC	YEAR
Mean Maximum Temp. (°F)	66.2	71.3	77.0	85.7	94.8	105.1	107.0	104.8	99.6	88.4	75.2	66.1	86.8
Mean Temp. (°F)	50.6	55.0	60.1	67.1	76.2	86.1	91.5	89.8	83.2	70.8	57.8	50.2	69.9
Mean Minimum Temp. (°F)	34.9	38.7	43.3	48.4	57.6	66.9	75.9	74.7	66.7	53.1	40.3	34.4	52.9
Extreme Maximum Temp. (°F)	86	90	99	106	113	122	124	117	112	107	94	84	124
Extreme Minimum Temp. (°F)	14	17	21	30	35	48	58	56	46	26	24	17	14
Days Maximum Temp. ≥ 90°F	0	0	2	11	25	30	31	31	28	15	1	0	174
Days Maximum Temp. ≤ 32°F	0	0	0	0	0	0	0	0	0	0	0	0	0
Days Minimum Temp. ≤ 32°F	12	6	2	0	0	0	0	0	0	0	4	13	37
Days Minimum Temp. ≤ 0°F	0	0	0	0	0	0	0	0	0	0	0	0	0
Heating Degree Days (base 65°F)	441	277	171	54	4	0	0	0	0	30	220	450	1,647
Cooling Degree Days (base 65°F)	0	2	25	144	382	644	822	794	563	223	11	0	3,610
Mean Precipitation (in.)	0.75	0.81	0.99	0.26	0.14	0.07	0.99	0.86	0.79	0.60	0.61	0.99	7.86
Days With ≥ 0.1" Precipitation	2	2	3	1	0	0	2	2	2	1	2	2	19
Days With ≥ 1.0" Precipitation	0	0	0	0	0	0	0	0	0	0	0	0	0
Mean Snowfall (in.)	0.0	0.0	trace	0.0	0.0	0.0	0.0	0.0	0.0	0.0	0.0	0.0	trace
Days With ≥ 1.0" Snow Depth	0	0	0	0	0	0	0	0	0	0	0	0	0

McNary 2 N *Apache County*   Elevation: 7,339 ft.   Latitude: 34° 07' N   Longitude: 109° 51' W

	JAN	FEB	MAR	APR	MAY	JUN	JUL	AUG	SEP	OCT	NOV	DEC	YEAR
Mean Maximum Temp. (°F)	44.6	47.3	51.7	59.7	69.0	79.5	81.0	78.1	73.9	65.2	53.7	46.1	62.5
Mean Temp. (°F)	31.5	34.0	37.9	44.2	52.4	61.5	65.5	63.6	58.7	49.5	39.4	32.6	47.6
Mean Minimum Temp. (°F)	18.2	20.6	24.1	28.7	35.7	43.4	49.9	49.0	43.4	33.8	25.1	19.0	32.6
Extreme Maximum Temp. (°F)	68	72	74	80	88	98	98	90	88	88	79	73	98
Extreme Minimum Temp. (°F)	-19	-8	0	5	13	26	36	33	27	6	-5	-15	-19
Days Maximum Temp. ≥ 90°F	0	0	0	0	0	2	2	0	0	0	0	0	4
Days Maximum Temp. ≤ 32°F	3	2	1	0	0	0	0	0	0	0	1	3	10
Days Minimum Temp. ≤ 32°F	30	27	29	21	9	1	0	0	1	12	26	29	185
Days Minimum Temp. ≤ 0°F	1	0	0	0	0	0	0	0	0	0	0	1	2
Heating Degree Days (base 65°F)	1,033	868	834	617	386	127	34	60	187	473	762	999	6,380
Cooling Degree Days (base 65°F)	0	0	0	0	0	27	54	25	3	0	0	0	109
Mean Precipitation (in.)	2.78	2.45	3.12	1.27	0.89	0.74	3.32	3.96	2.62	2.49	2.26	2.44	28.34
Days With ≥ 0.1" Precipitation	5	5	6	4	2	2	8	10	5	4	4	5	60
Days With ≥ 1.0" Precipitation	1	1	1	0	0	0	0	0	0	1	1	1	6
Mean Snowfall (in.)	19.0	16.9	18.2	*8.2*	0.6	trace	trace	0.0	0.0	3.1	8.1	*13.5*	*87.6*
Days With ≥ 1.0" Snow Depth	22	18	13	*5*	0	0	0	0	0	1	*6*	14	*79*

Miami *Gila County*   Elevation: 3,559 ft.   Latitude: 33° 24' N   Longitude: 110° 52' W

	JAN	FEB	MAR	APR	MAY	JUN	JUL	AUG	SEP	OCT	NOV	DEC	YEAR
Mean Maximum Temp. (°F)	57.1	61.2	66.0	74.0	83.1	93.6	96.3	94.3	89.2	78.7	66.2	57.4	76.4
Mean Temp. (°F)	45.3	48.8	53.4	60.5	69.3	79.1	83.3	81.5	75.9	65.1	53.2	45.6	63.4
Mean Minimum Temp. (°F)	33.4	36.3	40.7	46.8	55.4	64.4	70.3	68.6	62.7	51.5	40.2	33.7	50.3
Extreme Maximum Temp. (°F)	80	84	89	95	102	111	112	108	104	100	87	78	112
Extreme Minimum Temp. (°F)	14	19	19	30	32	47	48	56	43	26	20	17	14
Days Maximum Temp. ≥ 90°F	0	0	0	1	6	23	28	26	16	3	0	0	103
Days Maximum Temp. ≤ 32°F	0	0	0	0	0	0	0	0	0	0	0	0	0
Days Minimum Temp. ≤ 32°F	14	7	2	1	0	0	0	0	0	0	4	13	41
Days Minimum Temp. ≤ 0°F	0	0	0	0	0	0	0	0	0	0	0	0	0
Heating Degree Days (base 65°F)	604	451	357	168	34	1	0	0	3	89	349	594	2,650
Cooling Degree Days (base 65°F)	0	0	4	50	190	439	574	529	352	107	4	0	2,249
Mean Precipitation (in.)	2.12	2.08	2.20	0.58	0.47	0.26	2.20	2.61	1.68	1.55	1.50	2.04	19.29
Days With ≥ 0.1" Precipitation	4	4	4	2	1	1	5	6	3	3	3	3	39
Days With ≥ 1.0" Precipitation	0	0	0	0	0	0	0	1	0	1	0	0	2
Mean Snowfall (in.)	trace	0.5	trace	trace	0.0	0.0	0.0	0.0	0.0	trace	0.1	0.2	0.8
Days With ≥ 1.0" Snow Depth	0	0	0	0	0	0	0	0	0	0	0	0	0

Montezuma Castle Nat'l Mon. *Yavapai County* Elevation: 3,179 ft. Latitude: 34° 37' N Longitude: 111° 50' W

	JAN	FEB	MAR	APR	MAY	JUN	JUL	AUG	SEP	OCT	NOV	DEC	YEAR
Mean Maximum Temp. (°F)	60.3	65.6	70.5	78.3	87.2	97.8	100.8	98.3	92.3	81.9	69.2	59.6	80.1
Mean Temp. (°F)	43.3	47.7	52.7	58.8	67.0	76.0	82.2	80.5	73.7	62.4	50.5	42.8	61.5
Mean Minimum Temp. (°F)	26.3	29.9	34.9	39.2	46.7	54.2	63.5	62.7	54.9	42.8	31.8	26.0	42.7
Extreme Maximum Temp. (°F)	80	89	94	99	107	117	115	112	109	104	88	78	117
Extreme Minimum Temp. (°F)	2	8	12	19	25	37	45	48	31	20	11	4	2
Days Maximum Temp. ≥ 90°F	0	0	0	3	13	26	30	29	21	6	0	0	128
Days Maximum Temp. ≤ 32°F	0	0	0	0	0	0	0	0	0	0	0	0	0
Days Minimum Temp. ≤ 32°F	25	19	11	5	0	0	0	0	0	3	17	26	106
Days Minimum Temp. ≤ 0°F	0	0	0	0	0	0	0	0	0	0	0	0	0
Heating Degree Days (base 65°F)	666	481	375	200	45	2	0	0	4	122	428	682	3,005
Cooling Degree Days (base 65°F)	0	0	1	26	120	335	531	496	273	48	0	0	1,830
Mean Precipitation (in.)	1.26	1.39	1.46	0.70	0.42	0.28	1.62	2.04	1.92	1.14	1.03	1.12	14.38
Days With ≥ 0.1" Precipitation	3	3	4	2	1	1	4	4	3	3	2	3	33
Days With ≥ 1.0" Precipitation	0	0	0	0	0	0	0	0	1	0	0	0	1
Mean Snowfall (in.)	0.2	0.5	0.1	0.0	0.0	0.0	0.0	0.0	0.0	0.0	0.0	0.6	1.4
Days With ≥ 1.0" Snow Depth	0	0	0	0	0	0	0	0	0	0	0	0	0

Nogales 6 N *Santa Cruz County* Elevation: 3,559 ft. Latitude: 31° 27' N Longitude: 110° 58' W

	JAN	FEB	MAR	APR	MAY	JUN	JUL	AUG	SEP	OCT	NOV	DEC	YEAR
Mean Maximum Temp. (°F)	63.8	67.1	71.3	78.2	86.2	95.8	94.3	92.3	90.1	82.3	72.0	64.5	79.8
Mean Temp. (°F)	45.6	48.6	52.7	58.2	65.8	75.0	79.0	77.6	73.0	63.0	52.4	46.1	61.4
Mean Minimum Temp. (°F)	27.2	30.1	34.1	38.2	45.2	54.1	63.6	63.1	55.7	43.8	32.7	27.6	42.9
Extreme Maximum Temp. (°F)	85	85	93	99	103	112	109	107	103	101	90	84	112
Extreme Minimum Temp. (°F)	8	11	13	7	25	35	44	45	37	19	12	-4	-4
Days Maximum Temp. ≥ 90°F	0	0	0	2	9	26	25	23	18	6	0	0	109
Days Maximum Temp. ≤ 32°F	0	0	0	0	0	0	0	0	0	0	0	0	0
Days Minimum Temp. ≤ 32°F	24	19	14	7	1	0	0	0	0	2	15	24	106
Days Minimum Temp. ≤ 0°F	0	0	0	0	0	0	0	0	0	0	0	0	0
Heating Degree Days (base 65°F)	596	456	376	210	57	2	0	0	2	106	372	578	2,755
Cooling Degree Days (base 65°F)	0	0	0	14	91	303	447	413	252	47	0	0	1,567
Mean Precipitation (in.)	1.31	1.09	1.02	0.49	0.32	0.36	4.32	4.13	1.73	1.55	0.73	1.47	18.52
Days With ≥ 0.1" Precipitation	3	3	3	1	1	1	9	9	4	2	2	3	41
Days With ≥ 1.0" Precipitation	0	0	0	0	0	0	1	1	0	0	0	0	2
Mean Snowfall (in.)	0.2	trace	trace	trace	0.0	0.0	0.0	0.0	0.0	0.0	trace	0.3	0.5
Days With ≥ 1.0" Snow Depth	0	0	0	0	0	0	0	0	0	0	0	0	0

Oracle 2 SE *Pinal County* Elevation: 4,507 ft. Latitude: 32° 36' N Longitude: 110° 44' W

	JAN	FEB	MAR	APR	MAY	JUN	JUL	AUG	SEP	OCT	NOV	DEC	YEAR
Mean Maximum Temp. (°F)	56.2	59.9	64.4	72.0	81.7	91.8	92.0	89.4	85.6	76.3	64.8	56.4	74.2
Mean Temp. (°F)	45.6	48.4	52.1	58.6	67.9	77.8	79.4	77.5	73.4	63.7	52.9	45.7	61.9
Mean Minimum Temp. (°F)	34.9	36.9	39.8	45.2	53.9	63.7	66.7	65.6	61.2	51.1	40.9	35.1	49.6
Extreme Maximum Temp. (°F)	78	79	86	90	99	107	109	101	98	94	85	77	109
Extreme Minimum Temp. (°F)	5	12	18	22	32	44	46	52	42	25	19	6	5
Days Maximum Temp. ≥ 90°F	0	0	0	0	3	20	22	17	7	1	0	0	70
Days Maximum Temp. ≤ 32°F	0	0	0	0	0	0	0	0	0	0	0	0	0
Days Minimum Temp. ≤ 32°F	11	8	6	2	0	0	0	0	0	1	4	11	43
Days Minimum Temp. ≤ 0°F	0	0	0	0	0	0	0	0	0	0	0	0	0
Heating Degree Days (base 65°F)	596	462	396	207	44	2	0	0	4	105	359	591	2,766
Cooling Degree Days (base 65°F)	0	0	1	26	141	392	452	392	262	70	1	0	1,737
Mean Precipitation (in.)	2.46	2.59	2.62	0.94	0.62	0.32	3.25	4.06	2.04	1.85	1.74	2.30	24.79
Days With ≥ 0.1" Precipitation	4	5	5	2	2	1	6	7	4	3	3	4	46
Days With ≥ 1.0" Precipitation	1	1	1	0	0	0	1	1	0	1	1	1	8
Mean Snowfall (in.)	2.8	3.1	2.3	1.0	0.0	0.0	0.0	0.0	0.0	0.0	0.6	2.6	12.4
Days With ≥ 1.0" Snow Depth	0	0	0	0	0	0	0	0	0	0	0	0	0

Organ Pipe Cactus Nat'l Mon. *Pima County* Elevation: 1,676 ft. Latitude: 31° 57' N Longitude: 112° 48' W

	JAN	FEB	MAR	APR	MAY	JUN	JUL	AUG	SEP	OCT	NOV	DEC	YEAR
Mean Maximum Temp. (°F)	68.9	73.0	77.2	84.5	92.0	101.3	103.6	102.1	98.1	88.6	77.1	68.6	86.3
Mean Temp. (°F)	54.1	57.3	61.0	66.9	74.3	83.2	88.7	87.5	82.6	72.4	61.1	54.0	70.3
Mean Minimum Temp. (°F)	39.1	41.6	44.7	49.3	56.5	65.1	73.8	72.8	67.1	56.1	45.0	39.3	54.2
Extreme Maximum Temp. (°F)	89	94	99	104	111	118	118	116	111	107	97	87	118
Extreme Minimum Temp. (°F)	21	19	25	31	30	47	52	50	48	32	26	21	19
Days Maximum Temp. ≥ 90°F	0	0	3	9	20	29	31	31	28	15	1	0	167
Days Maximum Temp. ≤ 32°F	0	0	0	0	0	0	0	0	0	0	0	0	0
Days Minimum Temp. ≤ 32°F	5	2	1	0	0	0	0	0	0	0	1	4	13
Days Minimum Temp. ≤ 0°F	0	0	0	0	0	0	0	0	0	0	0	0	0
Heating Degree Days (base 65°F)	333	218	153	57	6	0	0	0	0	18	139	336	1,260
Cooling Degree Days (base 65°F)	1	9	38	145	320	559	745	719	547	267	31	0	3,381
Mean Precipitation (in.)	0.84	0.82	0.97	0.20	0.08	0.02	1.41	2.20	0.97	0.74	0.60	1.16	10.01
Days With ≥ 0.1" Precipitation	2	2	2	1	0	0	3	4	2	1	1	2	20
Days With ≥ 1.0" Precipitation	0	0	0	0	0	0	0	1	0	0	0	0	1
Mean Snowfall (in.)	0.0	trace	0.0	0.0	0.0	0.0	0.0	0.0	0.0	0.0	0.0	trace	trace
Days With ≥ 1.0" Snow Depth	0	0	0	0	0	0	0	0	0	0	0	0	0

Page *Coconino County*   Elevation: 4,268 ft.   Latitude: 36° 55' N   Longitude: 111° 27' W

	JAN	FEB	MAR	APR	MAY	JUN	JUL	AUG	SEP	OCT	NOV	DEC	YEAR
Mean Maximum Temp. (°F)	43.3	50.7	60.1	69.0	79.1	91.2	95.9	92.9	84.2	70.7	54.7	44.1	69.7
Mean Temp. (°F)	35.0	41.1	49.2	56.9	66.4	77.5	82.7	80.3	71.7	59.0	45.2	35.8	58.4
Mean Minimum Temp. (°F)	26.7	31.4	38.2	44.8	53.7	63.7	69.4	67.6	59.2	47.3	35.6	27.4	47.1
Extreme Maximum Temp. (°F)	64	72	82	91	98	107	107	103	100	92	77	66	107
Extreme Minimum Temp. (°F)	1	6	20	25	32	44	56	56	40	24	16	1	1
Days Maximum Temp. ≥ 90°F	0	0	0	0	3	19	28	24	7	0	0	0	81
Days Maximum Temp. ≤ 32°F	2	1	0	0	0	0	0	0	0	0	0	2	5
Days Minimum Temp. ≤ 32°F	26	16	5	1	0	0	0	0	0	1	9	25	83
Days Minimum Temp. ≤ 0°F	0	0	0	0	0	0	0	0	0	0	0	0	0
Heating Degree Days (base 65°F)	922	669	483	254	66	3	0	0	16	206	588	899	4,106
Cooling Degree Days (base 65°F)	0	0	0	21	115	384	549	478	225	26	0	0	1,798
Mean Precipitation (in.)	0.63	0.50	0.68	0.51	0.41	0.14	0.60	0.68	0.68	0.89	0.57	0.46	6.75
Days With ≥ 0.1" Precipitation	2	2	2	1	1	1	2	2	2	2	2	1	20
Days With ≥ 1.0" Precipitation	0	0	0	0	0	0	0	0	0	0	0	0	0
Mean Snowfall (in.)	*1.9*	0.9	0.1	trace	0.0	0.0	0.0	0.0	0.0	trace	0.6	*1.3*	*4.8*
Days With ≥ 1.0" Snow Depth	*0*	0	0	0	0	0	0	0	0	0	0	*0*	*0*

Parker *La Paz County*   Elevation: 410 ft.   Latitude: 34° 09' N   Longitude: 114° 18' W

	JAN	FEB	MAR	APR	MAY	JUN	JUL	AUG	SEP	OCT	NOV	DEC	YEAR
Mean Maximum Temp. (°F)	67.1	72.8	78.6	86.6	95.1	104.5	108.3	106.7	101.1	89.9	76.3	67.0	87.9
Mean Temp. (°F)	53.7	58.6	63.7	70.5	79.2	87.8	93.5	92.6	86.3	74.6	61.8	53.6	73.0
Mean Minimum Temp. (°F)	40.3	44.4	48.8	54.4	63.2	71.1	78.7	78.5	71.4	59.2	47.1	40.2	58.1
Extreme Maximum Temp. (°F)	87	93	98	105	115	121	124	118	116	110	95	85	124
Extreme Minimum Temp. (°F)	17	24	27	38	45	56	63	61	51	32	28	24	17
Days Maximum Temp. ≥ 90°F	0	0	3	12	25	28	31	31	29	17	1	0	177
Days Maximum Temp. ≤ 32°F	0	0	0	0	0	0	0	0	0	0	0	0	0
Days Minimum Temp. ≤ 32°F	3	1	0	0	0	0	0	0	0	0	0	3	7
Days Minimum Temp. ≤ 0°F	0	0	0	0	0	0	0	0	0	0	0	0	0
Heating Degree Days (base 65°F)	343	183	90	22	0	0	0	0	0	10	127	345	1,120
Cooling Degree Days (base 65°F)	1	13	59	217	461	671	873	871	647	319	43	0	4,175
Mean Precipitation (in.)	0.87	0.71	0.71	0.17	0.09	0.02	0.27	0.61	0.58	0.31	0.34	0.57	5.25
Days With ≥ 0.1" Precipitation	2	2	2	1	0	0	1	1	1	1	1	1	13
Days With ≥ 1.0" Precipitation	0	0	0	0	0	0	0	0	0	0	0	0	0
Mean Snowfall (in.)	0.0	0.0	0.0	0.0	0.0	0.0	0.0	0.0	0.0	0.0	0.0	0.0	0.0
Days With ≥ 1.0" Snow Depth	0	0	0	0	0	0	0	0	0	0	0	0	0

Payson *Gila County*   Elevation: 4,911 ft.   Latitude: 34° 14' N   Longitude: 111° 20' W

	JAN	FEB	MAR	APR	MAY	JUN	JUL	AUG	SEP	OCT	NOV	DEC	YEAR
Mean Maximum Temp. (°F)	53.7	57.8	62.2	70.1	78.8	89.5	92.4	90.2	84.6	74.5	62.3	54.2	72.5
Mean Temp. (°F)	39.1	42.3	46.2	52.2	60.1	69.4	75.1	73.9	67.4	57.2	46.0	39.4	55.7
Mean Minimum Temp. (°F)	24.5	26.8	30.1	34.4	41.4	49.3	57.8	57.5	50.2	39.9	29.6	24.6	38.8
Extreme Maximum Temp. (°F)	77	80	89	91	99	106	107	104	98	94	83	75	107
Extreme Minimum Temp. (°F)	-8	2	5	17	22	31	40	40	33	16	6	-2	-8
Days Maximum Temp. ≥ 90°F	0	0	0	0	2	15	23	19	7	1	0	0	67
Days Maximum Temp. ≤ 32°F	0	0	0	0	0	0	0	0	0	0	0	0	0
Days Minimum Temp. ≤ 32°F	28	23	21	13	2	0	0	0	0	4	21	27	139
Days Minimum Temp. ≤ 0°F	0	0	0	0	0	0	0	0	0	0	0	0	0
Heating Degree Days (base 65°F)	795	632	575	377	162	20	0	0	33	243	564	786	4,187
Cooling Degree Days (base 65°F)	0	0	0	1	22	159	319	296	123	10	0	0	930
Mean Precipitation (in.)	2.34	2.33	2.69	1.18	0.66	0.34	2.55	2.95	2.03	1.70	1.66	1.79	22.22
Days With ≥ 0.1" Precipitation	4	4	5	2	2	1	6	6	4	3	3	4	44
Days With ≥ 1.0" Precipitation	1	1	0	0	0	0	0	1	0	0	0	0	3
Mean Snowfall (in.)	5.3	5.3	4.8	2.9	trace	0.0	0.0	0.0	0.0	trace	2.4	4.1	24.8
Days With ≥ 1.0" Snow Depth	2	2	1	0	0	0	0	0	0	0	0	2	7

Petrified Forest Nat'l Park *Navajo County*   Elevation: 5,442 ft.   Latitude: 34° 48' N   Longitude: 109° 53' W

	JAN	FEB	MAR	APR	MAY	JUN	JUL	AUG	SEP	OCT	NOV	DEC	YEAR
Mean Maximum Temp. (°F)	48.0	55.0	61.9	70.0	78.8	89.5	92.2	89.5	83.1	71.6	58.9	48.7	70.6
Mean Temp. (°F)	34.6	39.9	45.6	52.5	60.9	70.7	75.9	74.2	67.5	55.6	43.6	34.9	54.7
Mean Minimum Temp. (°F)	21.1	24.8	29.3	34.9	42.9	51.9	59.6	58.9	51.8	39.6	28.3	21.1	38.7
Extreme Maximum Temp. (°F)	73	74	83	92	97	107	105	101	97	90	81	70	107
Extreme Minimum Temp. (°F)	-27	-4	7	12	24	31	42	42	33	16	-13	-18	-27
Days Maximum Temp. ≥ 90°F	0	0	0	0	2	16	22	17	3	0	0	0	60
Days Maximum Temp. ≤ 32°F	2	0	0	0	0	0	0	0	0	0	0	2	4
Days Minimum Temp. ≤ 32°F	28	24	21	11	2	0	0	0	0	5	22	27	140
Days Minimum Temp. ≤ 0°F	1	0	0	0	0	0	0	0	0	0	0	1	2
Heating Degree Days (base 65°F)	936	702	594	371	146	12	0	0	30	287	634	926	4,638
Cooling Degree Days (base 65°F)	0	0	0	2	31	196	344	301	114	3	0	0	991
Mean Precipitation (in.)	0.66	0.58	0.76	0.43	0.53	0.29	1.48	1.60	1.41	1.12	0.76	0.80	10.42
Days With ≥ 0.1" Precipitation	2	2	3	1	1	1	4	4	3	3	2	3	29
Days With ≥ 1.0" Precipitation	0	0	0	0	0	0	0	0	0	0	0	0	0
Mean Snowfall (in.)	2.3	1.0	0.6	0.6	trace	0.0	0.0	0.0	0.0	trace	0.8	2.1	7.4
Days With ≥ 1.0" Snow Depth	na	0	0	0	0	0	0	0	0	0	0	*2*	na

Phantom Ranch *Coconino County*   Elevation: 2,568 ft.   Latitude: 36° 06' N   Longitude: 112° 06' W

	JAN	FEB	MAR	APR	MAY	JUN	JUL	AUG	SEP	OCT	NOV	DEC	YEAR
Mean Maximum Temp. (°F)	55.9	63.6	72.3	*81.4*	91.2	102.5	105.8	102.7	95.1	82.7	67.4	56.5	*81.4*
Mean Temp. (°F)	46.5	52.6	59.8	*67.6*	76.7	87.0	91.1	88.5	81.5	69.8	56.5	47.4	*68.8*
Mean Minimum Temp. (°F)	36.9	41.6	47.3	53.8	62.2	71.4	76.4	74.3	67.8	56.9	45.6	38.1	56.0
Extreme Maximum Temp. (°F)	73	83	93	106	109	119	120	120	110	102	87	77	120
Extreme Minimum Temp. (°F)	-9	21	*29*	28	32	50	64	59	48	40	31	20	*-9*
Days Maximum Temp. ≥ 90°F	0	0	0	6	*19*	*29*	31	30	25	7	0	0	*147*
Days Maximum Temp. ≤ 32°F	0	0	0	0	0	0	0	0	0	0	0	0	0
Days Minimum Temp. ≤ 32°F	6	1	0	0	0	0	0	0	0	0	0	4	11
Days Minimum Temp. ≤ 0°F	0	0	0	0	0	0	0	0	0	0	0	0	0
Heating Degree Days (base 65°F)	569	343	180	*62*	6	0	0	0	0	33	256	541	*1,990*
Cooling Degree Days (base 65°F)	0	1	30	160	383	660	801	719	480	168	6	0	3,408
Mean Precipitation (in.)	1.10	1.05	1.15	0.55	0.39	0.21	0.95	1.29	0.99	0.82	0.88	0.71	10.09
Days With ≥ 0.1" Precipitation	3	3	4	2	1	1	3	3	3	2	2	2	29
Days With ≥ 1.0" Precipitation	0	0	0	0	0	0	0	0	0	0	0	0	0
Mean Snowfall (in.)	0.2	trace	0.0	0.0	0.0	0.0	0.0	0.0	0.0	0.0	trace	trace	0.2
Days With ≥ 1.0" Snow Depth	0	0	0	0	0	0	0	0	0	0	0	0	0

Pipe Springs Nat'l Monument *Mohave County*   Elevation: 4,917 ft.   Latitude: 36° 52' N   Longitude: 112° 44' W

	JAN	FEB	MAR	APR	MAY	JUN	JUL	AUG	SEP	OCT	NOV	DEC	YEAR
Mean Maximum Temp. (°F)	47.8	54.0	61.0	68.9	78.7	89.8	94.4	91.8	84.6	72.8	58.3	48.8	70.9
Mean Temp. (°F)	34.7	40.0	45.5	51.9	60.8	70.5	76.5	74.7	67.2	55.6	43.4	35.5	54.7
Mean Minimum Temp. (°F)	21.6	25.8	29.9	34.8	42.9	51.0	58.7	57.5	49.7	38.4	28.4	22.2	38.4
Extreme Maximum Temp. (°F)	79	78	82	89	97	110	108	105	100	93	79	68	110
Extreme Minimum Temp. (°F)	-12	-8	4	8	22	34	41	42	28	10	0	-13	-13
Days Maximum Temp. ≥ 90°F	0	0	0	0	2	17	26	22	7	0	0	0	74
Days Maximum Temp. ≤ 32°F	1	0	0	0	0	0	0	0	0	0	0	1	2
Days Minimum Temp. ≤ 32°F	28	23	20	11	2	0	0	0	0	6	22	28	140
Days Minimum Temp. ≤ 0°F	1	0	0	0	0	0	0	0	0	0	0	0	1
Heating Degree Days (base 65°F)	932	701	598	389	151	18	0	1	38	290	641	907	4,666
Cooling Degree Days (base 65°F)	0	0	0	2	32	190	364	321	108	5	0	0	1,022
Mean Precipitation (in.)	1.33	1.25	1.23	0.69	0.57	0.32	0.99	1.44	0.93	0.87	0.93	0.67	11.22
Days With ≥ 0.1" Precipitation	4	3	4	2	2	1	2	4	2	2	2	2	30
Days With ≥ 1.0" Precipitation	0	0	0	0	0	0	0	0	0	0	0	0	0
Mean Snowfall (in.)	3.3	1.6	1.2	0.2	trace	0.0	0.0	0.0	0.0	trace	1.5	1.1	8.9
Days With ≥ 1.0" Snow Depth	2	1	0	0	0	0	0	0	0	0	0	*1*	*4*

Pleasant Valley Ranger Station *Gila County*   Elevation: 5,049 ft.   Latitude: 34° 06' N   Longitude: 110° 56' W

	JAN	FEB	MAR	APR	MAY	JUN	JUL	AUG	SEP	OCT	NOV	DEC	YEAR
Mean Maximum Temp. (°F)	54.6	58.2	61.9	69.0	77.3	87.5	90.3	87.8	83.3	74.2	63.1	55.2	71.9
Mean Temp. (°F)	37.9	41.0	44.5	49.6	57.0	65.9	72.4	71.2	65.1	54.8	44.4	38.4	53.5
Mean Minimum Temp. (°F)	21.2	23.8	27.0	30.3	36.8	44.3	54.5	54.4	46.8	35.4	25.8	21.6	35.2
Extreme Maximum Temp. (°F)	78	84	84	88	98	103	105	100	97	94	81	76	105
Extreme Minimum Temp. (°F)	-21	-8	-6	11	17	25	35	36	25	10	-6	-22	-22
Days Maximum Temp. ≥ 90°F	0	0	0	0	1	12	18	11	4	0	0	0	46
Days Maximum Temp. ≤ 32°F	0	0	0	0	0	0	0	0	0	0	0	0	0
Days Minimum Temp. ≤ 32°F	28	25	26	20	8	1	0	0	1	10	26	27	172
Days Minimum Temp. ≤ 0°F	1	0	0	0	0	0	0	0	0	0	0	0	1
Heating Degree Days (base 65°F)	832	672	630	455	245	53	2	3	57	310	611	818	4,688
Cooling Degree Days (base 65°F)	0	0	0	0	5	86	234	217	70	2	0	0	614
Mean Precipitation (in.)	2.32	2.10	2.64	0.86	0.69	0.36	2.64	3.18	2.13	1.56	1.65	1.92	22.05
Days With ≥ 0.1" Precipitation	4	4	6	3	2	1	7	7	4	3	3	4	48
Days With ≥ 1.0" Precipitation	1	0	0	0	0	0	0	1	1	0	0	0	3
Mean Snowfall (in.)	na	*1.9*	*trace*	0.4	trace	0.0	0.0	0.0	0.0	trace	1.2	*0.1*	na
Days With ≥ 1.0" Snow Depth	na	*0*	*0*	0	0	0	0	0	0	0	0	*0*	na

Portal 4 SW *Cochise County*   Elevation: 5,387 ft.   Latitude: 31° 53' N   Longitude: 109° 12' W

	JAN	FEB	MAR	APR	MAY	JUN	JUL	AUG	SEP	OCT	NOV	DEC	YEAR
Mean Maximum Temp. (°F)	53.4	58.1	63.8	71.0	78.7	87.5	86.2	83.2	79.5	71.7	61.5	53.8	70.7
Mean Temp. (°F)	38.3	41.7	46.6	52.3	59.7	68.0	70.9	68.8	63.9	54.8	45.0	38.7	54.1
Mean Minimum Temp. (°F)	23.2	25.2	29.4	33.7	40.7	48.5	55.6	54.4	48.3	38.0	28.4	23.6	37.4
Extreme Maximum Temp. (°F)	76	76	84	87	94	101	101	95	93	89	80	73	101
Extreme Minimum Temp. (°F)	-1	2	8	16	24	32	44	42	31	16	10	-5	-5
Days Maximum Temp. ≥ 90°F	0	0	0	0	1	11	9	2	0	0	0	0	23
Days Maximum Temp. ≤ 32°F	0	0	0	0	0	0	0	0	0	0	0	0	0
Days Minimum Temp. ≤ 32°F	27	24	22	15	3	0	0	0	0	7	23	26	147
Days Minimum Temp. ≤ 0°F	0	0	0	0	0	0	0	0	0	0	0	0	0
Heating Degree Days (base 65°F)	820	652	564	374	168	21	0	4	61	309	595	807	4,375
Cooling Degree Days (base 65°F)	0	0	0	1	11	120	186	136	34	1	0	0	489
Mean Precipitation (in.)	1.44	1.26	1.00	0.55	0.54	0.94	4.46	3.73	2.38	1.77	1.39	1.91	21.37
Days With ≥ 0.1" Precipitation	4	4	3	1	1	2	9	8	5	4	3	4	48
Days With ≥ 1.0" Precipitation	0	0	0	0	0	0	1	1	0	0	0	0	2
Mean Snowfall (in.)	1.8	0.7	0.9	0.2	0.0	0.0	0.0	0.0	0.0	0.0	0.5	1.0	5.1
Days With ≥ 1.0" Snow Depth	*1*	1	0	0	0	0	0	0	0	0	0	1	*3*

Prescott *Yavapai County*   Elevation: 5,203 ft.   Latitude: 34° 34' N   Longitude: 112° 26' W

	JAN	FEB	MAR	APR	MAY	JUN	JUL	AUG	SEP	OCT	NOV	DEC	YEAR
Mean Maximum Temp. (°F)	51.1	54.7	58.6	65.6	74.0	84.8	88.3	85.5	80.5	71.3	60.2	51.6	68.8
Mean Temp. (°F)	37.1	40.3	44.3	50.6	58.5	68.0	73.4	71.5	65.4	55.3	44.5	37.5	53.8
Mean Minimum Temp. (°F)	23.0	25.7	30.0	35.5	42.9	51.1	58.6	57.3	50.2	39.1	28.9	23.3	38.8
Extreme Maximum Temp. (°F)	73	77	80	87	94	103	102	99	94	92	78	72	103
Extreme Minimum Temp. (°F)	-5	-5	9	15	23	33	42	42	27	14	5	-8	-8
Days Maximum Temp. ≥ 90°F	0	0	0	0	0	8	14	7	2	0	0	0	31
Days Maximum Temp. ≤ 32°F	1	0	0	0	0	0	0	0	0	0	0	1	2
Days Minimum Temp. ≤ 32°F	29	24	20	10	2	0	0	0	0	6	21	28	140
Days Minimum Temp. ≤ 0°F	0	0	0	0	0	0	0	0	0	0	0	0	0
Heating Degree Days (base 65°F)	859	692	636	427	214	40	1	4	57	300	607	846	4,683
Cooling Degree Days (base 65°F)	0	0	0	1	24	144	278	232	80	6	0	0	765
Mean Precipitation (in.)	1.60	1.83	1.92	0.77	0.65	0.35	3.06	3.31	2.13	1.12	1.26	1.31	19.31
Days With ≥ 0.1" Precipitation	4	3	4	2	2	1	6	6	4	2	2	3	39
Days With ≥ 1.0" Precipitation	0	0	0	0	0	0	1	1	0	0	0	0	2
Mean Snowfall (in.)	3.5	4.7	5.7	1.6	trace	0.0	0.0	0.0	0.0	0.2	1.4	2.9	20.0
Days With ≥ 1.0" Snow Depth	3	2	2	1	0	0	0	0	0	0	1	3	12

Roosevelt 1 WNW *Gila County*   Elevation: 2,204 ft.   Latitude: 33° 40' N   Longitude: 111° 09' W

	JAN	FEB	MAR	APR	MAY	JUN	JUL	AUG	SEP	OCT	NOV	DEC	YEAR
Mean Maximum Temp. (°F)	59.1	64.8	70.6	79.4	88.6	99.4	102.1	99.8	94.3	82.8	69.0	59.4	80.8
Mean Temp. (°F)	48.4	52.6	57.6	65.2	74.1	84.1	88.1	86.5	80.9	69.7	57.1	48.9	67.8
Mean Minimum Temp. (°F)	37.7	40.5	44.7	50.9	59.6	68.9	74.1	73.1	67.5	56.7	45.1	38.2	54.7
Extreme Maximum Temp. (°F)	77	82	91	99	107	117	116	114	109	101	86	77	117
Extreme Minimum Temp. (°F)	21	21	27	29	35	43	49	50	50	34	24	24	21
Days Maximum Temp. ≥ 90°F	0	0	0	3	15	28	30	29	24	7	0	0	136
Days Maximum Temp. ≤ 32°F	0	0	0	0	0	0	0	0	0	0	0	0	0
Days Minimum Temp. ≤ 32°F	4	1	1	0	0	0	0	0	0	0	0	4	10
Days Minimum Temp. ≤ 0°F	0	0	0	0	0	0	0	0	0	0	0	0	0
Heating Degree Days (base 65°F)	507	344	235	80	10	0	0	0	0	33	236	493	1,938
Cooling Degree Days (base 65°F)	0	0	11	112	318	594	730	693	501	196	6	0	3,161
Mean Precipitation (in.)	2.21	1.96	2.33	0.59	0.47	0.14	1.32	1.74	1.42	1.35	1.48	1.79	16.80
Days With ≥ 0.1" Precipitation	4	4	4	2	1	0	3	4	3	2	2	3	32
Days With ≥ 1.0" Precipitation	1	0	1	0	0	0	0	0	0	0	0	0	2
Mean Snowfall (in.)	trace	trace	0.0	0.0	0.0	0.0	0.0	0.0	0.0	0.0	0.0	0.0	trace
Days With ≥ 1.0" Snow Depth	0	0	0	0	0	0	0	0	0	0	0	0	0

Safford Agricultural Center *Graham County*   Elevation: 2,952 ft.   Latitude: 32° 49' N   Longitude: 109° 41' W

	JAN	FEB	MAR	APR	MAY	JUN	JUL	AUG	SEP	OCT	NOV	DEC	YEAR
Mean Maximum Temp. (°F)	59.8	65.0	70.8	79.1	88.3	98.1	98.2	95.9	91.6	81.8	69.3	60.0	79.8
Mean Temp. (°F)	44.5	48.9	54.3	61.0	69.9	79.4	83.1	81.3	75.6	64.6	52.4	44.5	63.3
Mean Minimum Temp. (°F)	29.2	32.8	37.8	42.9	51.5	60.6	67.9	66.6	59.5	47.4	35.4	29.0	46.7
Extreme Maximum Temp. (°F)	79	84	92	99	106	114	113	108	105	99	87	78	114
Extreme Minimum Temp. (°F)	10	10	20	26	31	42	52	49	43	23	15	7	7
Days Maximum Temp. ≥ 90°F	0	0	0	3	15	28	29	28	21	6	0	0	130
Days Maximum Temp. ≤ 32°F	0	0	0	0	0	0	0	0	0	0	0	0	0
Days Minimum Temp. ≤ 32°F	22	14	6	2	0	0	0	0	0	1	10	23	78
Days Minimum Temp. ≤ 0°F	0	0	0	0	0	0	0	0	0	0	0	0	0
Heating Degree Days (base 65°F)	629	448	327	152	25	0	0	0	2	88	374	629	2,674
Cooling Degree Days (base 65°F)	0	0	3	50	204	445	562	515	335	84	1	0	2,199
Mean Precipitation (in.)	0.74	0.80	0.64	0.23	0.27	0.28	1.46	1.65	1.17	1.00	0.52	0.92	9.68
Days With ≥ 0.1" Precipitation	2	2	2	1	1	1	4	4	3	2	1	2	25
Days With ≥ 1.0" Precipitation	0	0	0	0	0	0	0	0	0	0	0	0	0
Mean Snowfall (in.)	0.3	0.3	trace	trace	0.0	0.0	0.0	0.0	0.0	0.0	trace	0.2	0.8
Days With ≥ 1.0" Snow Depth	0	0	0	0	0	0	0	0	0	0	0	0	0

Saint Johns *Apache County*   Elevation: 5,787 ft.   Latitude: 34° 31' N   Longitude: 109° 24' W

	JAN	FEB	MAR	APR	MAY	JUN	JUL	AUG	SEP	OCT	NOV	DEC	YEAR
Mean Maximum Temp. (°F)	48.3	55.0	61.3	69.3	78.1	88.0	89.7	87.0	81.6	71.3	58.9	49.0	69.8
Mean Temp. (°F)	33.9	39.2	45.1	51.6	60.4	69.5	73.9	71.8	65.5	54.3	42.6	34.0	53.5
Mean Minimum Temp. (°F)	19.4	23.3	28.9	33.9	42.6	51.0	58.0	56.5	49.3	37.3	26.2	19.0	37.1
Extreme Maximum Temp. (°F)	71	75	84	88	96	102	103	101	95	88	81	73	103
Extreme Minimum Temp. (°F)	-29	-10	7	17	24	35	42	40	28	14	-9	-25	-29
Days Maximum Temp. ≥ 90°F	0	0	0	0	1	13	17	10	2	0	0	0	43
Days Maximum Temp. ≤ 32°F	2	0	0	0	0	0	0	0	0	0	0	2	4
Days Minimum Temp. ≤ 32°F	28	25	22	13	2	0	0	0	0	8	24	29	151
Days Minimum Temp. ≤ 0°F	1	0	0	0	0	0	0	0	0	0	0	1	2
Heating Degree Days (base 65°F)	958	722	610	395	156	15	0	1	47	325	666	954	4,849
Cooling Degree Days (base 65°F)	0	0	0	1	21	156	274	216	65	1	0	0	734
Mean Precipitation (in.)	0.76	0.56	0.76	0.47	0.47	0.46	1.76	2.33	1.46	1.07	0.63	0.71	11.44
Days With ≥ 0.1" Precipitation	2	2	2	2	1	1	5	5	3	3	2	2	30
Days With ≥ 1.0" Precipitation	0	0	0	0	0	0	0	0	0	0	0	0	0
Mean Snowfall (in.)	3.4	1.8	2.7	1.1	trace	0.0	0.0	0.0	0.0	0.3	1.4	3.0	13.7
Days With ≥ 1.0" Snow Depth	1	0	0	0	0	0	0	0	0	0	0	1	2

San Carlos Reservoir *Gila County*   Elevation: 2,529 ft.   Latitude: 33° 11' N   Longitude: 110° 32' W

	JAN	FEB	MAR	APR	MAY	JUN	JUL	AUG	SEP	OCT	NOV	DEC	YEAR
Mean Maximum Temp. (°F)	59.0	64.5	70.0	78.7	88.1	98.5	100.3	97.9	93.0	82.1	68.8	59.1	80.0
Mean Temp. (°F)	46.2	50.9	55.8	63.2	72.5	82.2	86.6	84.5	78.7	67.6	54.6	46.5	65.8
Mean Minimum Temp. (°F)	33.5	37.3	41.5	47.7	56.8	65.8	73.0	71.1	64.4	53.0	40.3	33.9	51.5
Extreme Maximum Temp. (°F)	83	86	91	102	108	116	116	116	108	101	88	76	116
Extreme Minimum Temp. (°F)	11	22	25	32	19	42	50	45	43	30	22	12	11
Days Maximum Temp. ≥ 90°F	0	0	0	3	14	27	30	29	22	6	0	0	131
Days Maximum Temp. ≤ 32°F	0	0	0	0	0	0	0	0	0	0	0	0	0
Days Minimum Temp. ≤ 32°F	13	5	2	0	0	0	0	0	0	0	3	13	36
Days Minimum Temp. ≤ 0°F	0	0	0	0	0	0	0	0	0	0	0	0	0
Heating Degree Days (base 65°F)	574	392	286	113	16	1	0	0	1	56	308	567	2,314
Cooling Degree Days (base 65°F)	0	0	7	79	274	538	682	627	437	148	3	0	2,795
Mean Precipitation (in.)	1.80	1.76	1.84	0.46	0.42	0.21	1.42	2.17	1.49	1.38	1.22	1.77	15.94
Days With ≥ 0.1" Precipitation	4	4	4	1	1	1	4	5	3	2	3	3	35
Days With ≥ 1.0" Precipitation	0	0	0	0	0	0	0	1	0	0	0	0	1
Mean Snowfall (in.)	0.0	0.3	0.0	0.0	0.0	0.0	0.0	0.0	0.0	0.0	0.0	0.0	0.3
Days With ≥ 1.0" Snow Depth	0	0	0	0	0	0	0	0	0	0	0	0	0

Sanders *Apache County*   Elevation: 5,853 ft.   Latitude: 35° 13' N   Longitude: 109° 19' W

	JAN	FEB	MAR	APR	MAY	JUN	JUL	AUG	SEP	OCT	NOV	DEC	YEAR
Mean Maximum Temp. (°F)	46.7	52.6	59.2	67.1	76.1	87.4	91.0	88.3	81.6	70.1	57.7	47.8	68.8
Mean Temp. (°F)	32.6	37.7	42.6	48.9	57.3	67.2	73.3	72.1	64.9	53.5	41.9	33.5	52.1
Mean Minimum Temp. (°F)	18.4	22.8	26.1	30.7	38.5	47.0	55.5	55.8	48.1	36.9	26.1	19.2	35.4
Extreme Maximum Temp. (°F)	70	74	80	86	94	102	107	101	100	90	79	69	107
Extreme Minimum Temp. (°F)	-23	-17	0	8	14	29	36	32	28	12	-18	-20	-23
Days Maximum Temp. ≥ 90°F	0	0	0	0	1	12	20	14	3	0	0	0	50
Days Maximum Temp. ≤ 32°F	2	1	0	0	0	0	0	0	0	0	0	2	5
Days Minimum Temp. ≤ 32°F	30	26	26	19	5	0	0	0	0	8	23	29	166
Days Minimum Temp. ≤ 0°F	2	0	0	0	0	0	0	0	0	0	0	1	3
Heating Degree Days (base 65°F)	998	764	687	477	236	39	1	2	63	351	685	970	5,273
Cooling Degree Days (base 65°F)	0	0	0	0	7	113	267	249	68	1	0	0	705
Mean Precipitation (in.)	0.99	1.10	1.08	0.57	0.70	0.31	1.37	1.95	1.18	1.18	1.08	0.86	12.37
Days With ≥ 0.1" Precipitation	2	2	3	2	2	1	3	4	3	3	2	2	29
Days With ≥ 1.0" Precipitation	0	0	0	0	0	0	0	0	0	0	0	0	0
Mean Snowfall (in.)	na	na	na	*trace*	trace	0.0	0.0	0.0	0.0	trace	1.2	*1.1*	na
Days With ≥ 1.0" Snow Depth	na	na	*0*	*0*	0	0	0	0	0	0	0	*1*	na

Santa Rita Exp. Range *Pima County*   Elevation: 4,297 ft.   Latitude: 31° 46' N   Longitude: 110° 51' W

	JAN	FEB	MAR	APR	MAY	JUN	JUL	AUG	SEP	OCT	NOV	DEC	YEAR
Mean Maximum Temp. (°F)	60.1	64.1	68.2	75.5	83.6	93.3	92.0	89.0	86.1	78.6	67.8	60.4	76.6
Mean Temp. (°F)	48.5	51.7	55.4	61.6	69.6	79.0	79.4	77.2	74.0	66.5	55.3	*48.7*	*63.9*
Mean Minimum Temp. (°F)	36.9	39.2	42.6	47.8	55.6	64.5	66.8	65.2	62.1	54.4	42.8	*37.2*	*51.3*
Extreme Maximum Temp. (°F)	81	82	89	95	100	107	106	104	100	94	87	80	107
Extreme Minimum Temp. (°F)	13	11	17	24	33	40	38	44	45	23	9	*11*	*9*
Days Maximum Temp. ≥ 90°F	0	0	0	0	6	22	20	15	8	2	0	0	73
Days Maximum Temp. ≤ 32°F	0	0	0	0	0	0	0	0	0	0	0	0	0
Days Minimum Temp. ≤ 32°F	8	5	3	1	0	0	0	0	0	0	4	*7*	*28*
Days Minimum Temp. ≤ 0°F	0	0	0	0	0	0	0	0	0	0	0	0	0
Heating Degree Days (base 65°F)	504	369	301	143	27	1	0	0	2	67	291	*496*	*2,201*
Cooling Degree Days (base 65°F)	0	2	10	59	191	435	458	387	293	129	9	0	1,973
Mean Precipitation (in.)	1.73	1.64	1.79	0.69	0.30	0.57	4.90	4.25	2.47	1.81	1.19	1.87	23.21
Days With ≥ 0.1" Precipitation	4	3	3	2	1	1	9	8	5	3	2	3	44
Days With ≥ 1.0" Precipitation	0	0	0	0	0	0	1	1	1	0	0	0	3
Mean Snowfall (in.)	0.7	0.9	0.8	trace	0.0	0.0	0.0	0.0	0.0	0.0	0.1	1.3	3.8
Days With ≥ 1.0" Snow Depth	0	0	0	0	0	0	0	0	0	0	0	0	0

Sasabe *Pima County*   Elevation: 3,589 ft.   Latitude: 31° 29' N   Longitude: 111° 33' W

	JAN	FEB	MAR	APR	MAY	JUN	JUL	AUG	SEP	OCT	NOV	DEC	YEAR
Mean Maximum Temp. (°F)	63.2	66.3	69.6	77.1	84.7	94.6	94.6	92.0	89.3	81.3	70.8	63.1	78.9
Mean Temp. (°F)	49.4	52.2	55.0	61.0	67.8	77.8	80.7	78.8	75.0	66.1	56.0	49.5	64.1
Mean Minimum Temp. (°F)	35.6	38.0	40.5	44.8	50.9	60.9	66.7	65.5	60.6	51.0	41.1	35.8	49.3
Extreme Maximum Temp. (°F)	85	85	90	97	103	111	109	105	105	100	90	84	111
Extreme Minimum Temp. (°F)	14	14	13	25	34	42	51	49	45	27	24	15	13
Days Maximum Temp. ≥ 90°F	0	0	0	1	8	24	25	22	16	5	0	0	101
Days Maximum Temp. ≤ 32°F	0	0	0	0	0	0	0	0	0	0	0	0	0
Days Minimum Temp. ≤ 32°F	9	6	3	1	0	0	0	0	0	0	3	8	30
Days Minimum Temp. ≤ 0°F	0	0	0	0	0	0	0	0	0	0	0	0	0
Heating Degree Days (base 65°F)	477	357	308	148	39	1	0	0	1	63	270	474	2,138
Cooling Degree Days (base 65°F)	0	1	3	40	143	381	489	432	308	103	5	0	1,905
Mean Precipitation (in.)	1.32	1.54	1.31	0.43	0.19	0.26	3.53	3.40	1.98	1.34	0.87	1.72	17.89
Days With ≥ 0.1" Precipitation	3	3	3	1	1	1	7	7	4	2	2	3	37
Days With ≥ 1.0" Precipitation	0	0	0	0	0	0	1	1	0	0	0	0	2
Mean Snowfall (in.)	0.1	0.3	trace	0.0	0.0	0.0	0.0	0.0	0.0	0.0	trace	0.6	1.0
Days With ≥ 1.0" Snow Depth	0	0	0	0	0	0	0	0	0	0	0	0	0

Sedona Ranger Station *Coconino County*   Elevation: 4,219 ft.   Latitude: 34° 52' N   Longitude: 111° 46' W

	JAN	FEB	MAR	APR	MAY	JUN	JUL	AUG	SEP	OCT	NOV	DEC	YEAR
Mean Maximum Temp. (°F)	56.3	60.5	65.0	72.9	82.1	93.2	96.6	94.2	87.9	77.5	64.7	56.5	75.6
Mean Temp. (°F)	43.4	47.0	50.8	57.3	65.6	75.5	80.3	78.8	72.7	62.6	50.6	43.6	60.7
Mean Minimum Temp. (°F)	30.5	33.3	36.8	41.5	49.0	57.7	64.0	63.3	57.4	47.7	36.5	30.7	45.7
Extreme Maximum Temp. (°F)	77	82	86	93	101	110	110	110	103	100	85	74	110
Extreme Minimum Temp. (°F)	2	10	9	18	24	36	50	48	37	23	11	4	2
Days Maximum Temp. ≥ 90°F	0	0	0	1	5	21	28	26	13	2	0	0	96
Days Maximum Temp. ≤ 32°F	0	0	0	0	0	0	0	0	0	0	0	0	0
Days Minimum Temp. ≤ 32°F	19	12	8	3	0	0	0	0	0	1	9	19	71
Days Minimum Temp. ≤ 0°F	0	0	0	0	0	0	0	0	0	0	0	0	0
Heating Degree Days (base 65°F)	662	501	434	244	70	5	0	0	8	124	425	656	3,129
Cooling Degree Days (base 65°F)	0	0	1	27	115	347	495	455	261	66	1	0	1,768
Mean Precipitation (in.)	2.12	2.13	2.49	1.19	0.71	0.34	1.67	1.89	2.15	1.49	1.41	1.57	19.16
Days With ≥ 0.1" Precipitation	4	4	5	2	2	1	3	4	4	3	2	3	37
Days With ≥ 1.0" Precipitation	1	1	0	0	0	0	0	0	0	0	0	0	2
Mean Snowfall (in.)	*0.3*	0.6	0.3	0.3	0.0	0.0	0.0	0.0	0.0	trace	0.2	0.2	*1.9*
Days With ≥ 1.0" Snow Depth	*0*	0	0	0	0	0	0	0	0	0	0	0	*0*

Seligman *Yavapai County*   Elevation: 5,249 ft.   Latitude: 35° 20' N   Longitude: 112° 53' W

	JAN	FEB	MAR	APR	MAY	JUN	JUL	AUG	SEP	OCT	NOV	DEC	YEAR
Mean Maximum Temp. (°F)	51.0	55.4	60.4	67.5	76.6	87.2	90.9	88.6	83.0	73.0	60.8	52.1	70.5
Mean Temp. (°F)	36.6	39.9	44.0	49.6	57.7	67.0	72.9	71.4	65.2	54.7	44.1	37.1	53.3
Mean Minimum Temp. (°F)	22.3	24.5	27.6	31.6	38.8	46.7	54.9	54.2	47.2	36.3	27.3	22.0	36.1
Extreme Maximum Temp. (°F)	73	77	84	89	98	105	106	106	97	93	81	73	106
Extreme Minimum Temp. (°F)	-11	-3	-5	11	14	27	33	37	29	12	4	-12	-12
Days Maximum Temp. ≥ 90°F	0	0	0	0	1	12	19	14	4	0	0	0	50
Days Maximum Temp. ≤ 32°F	1	0	0	0	0	0	0	0	0	0	0	1	2
Days Minimum Temp. ≤ 32°F	29	25	24	16	5	0	0	0	0	8	24	28	159
Days Minimum Temp. ≤ 0°F	0	0	0	0	0	0	0	0	0	0	0	0	0
Heating Degree Days (base 65°F)	873	702	644	456	229	43	1	3	57	315	621	858	4,802
Cooling Degree Days (base 65°F)	0	0	0	1	14	115	265	231	71	2	0	0	699
Mean Precipitation (in.)	1.20	1.13	1.37	0.55	0.57	0.30	2.07	1.96	1.30	0.81	0.91	0.82	12.99
Days With ≥ 0.1" Precipitation	3	3	4	2	2	1	5	5	3	2	2	3	35
Days With ≥ 1.0" Precipitation	0	0	0	0	0	0	0	0	0	0	0	0	0
Mean Snowfall (in.)	2.7	1.9	0.8	0.3	0.0	0.0	0.0	0.0	0.0	trace	0.7	1.6	8.0
Days With ≥ 1.0" Snow Depth	3	1	*0*	0	0	0	0	0	0	0	0	1	*5*

Show Low Municipal Airport *Navajo County*   Elevation: 6,410 ft.   Latitude: 34° 16' N   Longitude: 110° 00' W

	JAN	FEB	MAR	APR	MAY	JUN	JUL	AUG	SEP	OCT	NOV	DEC	YEAR
Mean Maximum Temp. (°F)	45.4	50.6	56.0	63.9	72.8	83.7	85.8	82.9	77.8	67.4	55.4	46.3	65.7
Mean Temp. (°F)	33.0	37.4	42.5	48.9	57.5	67.2	71.7	69.5	63.8	52.9	41.7	33.7	51.7
Mean Minimum Temp. (°F)	20.5	24.2	29.0	33.9	42.0	50.7	57.4	56.1	49.8	38.4	28.0	21.0	37.6
Extreme Maximum Temp. (°F)	67	71	77	83	91	98	98	95	93	86	77	68	98
Extreme Minimum Temp. (°F)	-25	-3	-6	4	22	30	38	42	28	12	-14	-22	-25
Days Maximum Temp. ≥ 90°F	0	0	0	0	0	6	8	2	0	0	0	0	16
Days Maximum Temp. ≤ 32°F	3	1	0	0	0	0	0	0	0	0	0	3	7
Days Minimum Temp. ≤ 32°F	28	24	21	13	3	0	0	0	0	7	21	27	144
Days Minimum Temp. ≤ 0°F	1	0	0	0	0	0	0	0	0	0	0	1	2
Heating Degree Days (base 65°F)	986	772	690	476	235	40	2	5	74	369	691	963	5,303
Cooling Degree Days (base 65°F)	0	0	0	1	13	122	221	164	48	1	0	0	570
Mean Precipitation (in.)	1.31	1.39	1.43	0.71	0.72	0.43	2.25	3.22	1.88	1.73	1.48	1.61	18.16
Days With ≥ 0.1" Precipitation	3	3	4	2	2	1	6	7	4	3	3	3	41
Days With ≥ 1.0" Precipitation	0	0	0	0	0	0	0	0	0	0	0	0	0
Mean Snowfall (in.)	6.3	5.5	5.9	2.0	trace	0.0	0.0	0.0	0.0	0.6	2.4	5.6	28.3
Days With ≥ 1.0" Snow Depth	*4*	*1*	*1*	0	0	0	0	0	0	0	1	*4*	*11*

Snowflake *Navajo County*   Elevation: 5,639 ft.   Latitude: 34° 30' N   Longitude: 110° 05' W

	JAN	FEB	MAR	APR	MAY	JUN	JUL	AUG	SEP	OCT	NOV	DEC	YEAR
Mean Maximum Temp. (°F)	48.8	55.0	60.5	68.0	76.8	87.2	89.9	87.3	81.6	71.4	58.8	49.3	69.6
Mean Temp. (°F)	34.3	39.0	44.2	50.3	58.5	67.5	73.3	71.5	64.8	53.7	42.6	34.8	52.9
Mean Minimum Temp. (°F)	19.7	23.0	27.8	32.5	40.1	47.8	56.7	55.6	48.0	36.0	26.4	20.2	36.1
Extreme Maximum Temp. (°F)	72	77	82	87	96	102	102	99	95	90	80	72	102
Extreme Minimum Temp. (°F)	-29	-4	7	12	21	27	39	39	29	12	-15	-21	-29
Days Maximum Temp. ≥ 90°F	0	0	0	0	1	11	17	11	3	0	0	0	43
Days Maximum Temp. ≤ 32°F	2	0	0	0	0	0	0	0	0	0	0	2	4
Days Minimum Temp. ≤ 32°F	28	24	24	15	4	0	0	0	0	10	24	28	157
Days Minimum Temp. ≤ 0°F	1	0	0	0	0	0	0	0	0	0	0	1	2
Heating Degree Days (base 65°F)	946	727	639	436	205	33	0	1	60	343	666	931	4,987
Cooling Degree Days (base 65°F)	0	0	0	0	13	119	266	220	67	1	0	0	686
Mean Precipitation (in.)	0.74	0.72	0.98	0.44	0.59	0.32	1.81	2.41	1.69	1.21	0.90	0.88	12.69
Days With ≥ 0.1" Precipitation	2	2	3	2	2	1	5	6	4	3	2	3	35
Days With ≥ 1.0" Precipitation	0	0	0	0	0	0	0	1	0	0	0	0	1
Mean Snowfall (in.)	3.6	2.9	2.0	1.1	0.3	0.0	0.0	0.0	0.0	0.4	1.9	3.9	16.1
Days With ≥ 1.0" Snow Depth	3	1	0	0	0	0	0	0	0	0	1	3	8

Snowflake 15 W *Navajo County*   Elevation: 6,079 ft.   Latitude: 34° 30' N   Longitude: 110° 20' W

	JAN	FEB	MAR	APR	MAY	JUN	JUL	AUG	SEP	OCT	NOV	DEC	YEAR
Mean Maximum Temp. (°F)	45.3	50.9	56.7	64.7	73.5	84.4	87.5	84.8	78.9	68.2	55.5	46.3	66.4
Mean Temp. (°F)	32.6	37.2	42.5	49.1	57.3	67.4	72.6	70.7	64.2	53.4	41.6	33.4	51.8
Mean Minimum Temp. (°F)	19.8	23.4	28.3	33.5	41.1	50.4	57.7	56.6	49.4	38.5	27.6	20.5	37.2
Extreme Maximum Temp. (°F)	70	75	79	85	95	100	101	99	94	86	77	71	101
Extreme Minimum Temp. (°F)	-25	-3	7	11	18	28	39	38	30	14	-10	-14	-25
Days Maximum Temp. ≥ 90°F	0	0	0	0	0	8	12	6	1	0	0	0	27
Days Maximum Temp. ≤ 32°F	3	1	0	0	0	0	0	0	0	0	0	3	7
Days Minimum Temp. ≤ 32°F	29	26	22	13	4	0	0	0	0	7	22	28	151
Days Minimum Temp. ≤ 0°F	1	0	0	0	0	0	0	0	0	0	0	1	2
Heating Degree Days (base 65°F)	998	779	690	471	245	45	1	5	77	358	696	972	5,337
Cooling Degree Days (base 65°F)	0	0	0	1	17	117	241	195	62	3	0	0	636
Mean Precipitation (in.)	0.73	0.62	0.88	0.39	0.58	0.40	1.67	2.57	1.61	1.12	0.91	0.83	12.31
Days With ≥ 0.1" Precipitation	3	2	3	1	2	1	4	6	3	3	2	3	33
Days With ≥ 1.0" Precipitation	0	0	0	0	0	0	0	1	0	0	0	0	1
Mean Snowfall (in.)	4.6	2.8	2.5	0.5	trace	0.0	0.0	0.0	0.0	0.2	1.9	4.0	16.5
Days With ≥ 1.0" Snow Depth	5	2	1	0	0	0	0	0	0	0	1	5	14

South Phoenix *Maricopa County*   Elevation: 1,154 ft.   Latitude: 33° 23' N   Longitude: 112° 04' W

	JAN	FEB	MAR	APR	MAY	JUN	JUL	AUG	SEP	OCT	NOV	DEC	YEAR
Mean Maximum Temp. (°F)	66.4	71.7	77.0	84.6	92.1	100.6	102.4	101.1	96.6	86.7	74.4	66.1	85.0
Mean Temp. (°F)	52.7	57.0	61.4	67.4	74.9	83.2	88.2	87.3	81.7	71.3	59.5	52.5	69.8
Mean Minimum Temp. (°F)	39.0	42.3	45.7	50.1	57.7	65.6	74.0	73.5	66.8	55.8	44.6	38.8	54.5
Extreme Maximum Temp. (°F)	87	90	98	101	110	114	113	113	109	106	90	83	114
Extreme Minimum Temp. (°F)	16	24	26	35	36	50	58	56	47	29	28	20	16
Days Maximum Temp. ≥ 90°F	0	0	2	9	22	29	31	31	27	12	0	0	163
Days Maximum Temp. ≤ 32°F	0	0	0	0	0	0	0	0	0	0	0	0	0
Days Minimum Temp. ≤ 32°F	5	2	0	0	0	0	0	0	0	0	1	5	13
Days Minimum Temp. ≤ 0°F	0	0	0	0	0	0	0	0	0	0	0	0	0
Heating Degree Days (base 65°F)	374	224	138	45	4	0	0	0	0	23	174	382	1,364
Cooling Degree Days (base 65°F)	0	5	32	145	339	554	727	720	523	231	17	0	3,293
Mean Precipitation (in.)	0.92	0.95	1.23	0.28	0.20	0.08	0.94	1.11	0.91	0.74	0.73	0.93	9.02
Days With ≥ 0.1" Precipitation	2	2	3	1	1	0	2	3	2	2	1	2	21
Days With ≥ 1.0" Precipitation	0	0	0	0	0	0	0	0	0	0	0	0	0
Mean Snowfall (in.)	0.0	0.0	0.0	0.0	0.0	0.0	0.0	0.0	0.0	0.0	0.0	0.0	0.0
Days With ≥ 1.0" Snow Depth	0	0	0	0	0	0	0	0	0	0	0	0	0

Springerville *Apache County*   Elevation: 7,034 ft.   Latitude: 34° 08' N   Longitude: 109° 18' W

	JAN	FEB	MAR	APR	MAY	JUN	JUL	AUG	SEP	OCT	NOV	DEC	YEAR
Mean Maximum Temp. (°F)	48.1	51.7	57.0	64.0	71.6	80.6	82.2	79.9	75.6	67.0	56.9	49.0	65.3
Mean Temp. (°F)	32.0	35.2	39.8	45.5	53.4	61.6	66.4	64.6	58.9	48.6	39.0	32.3	48.1
Mean Minimum Temp. (°F)	15.9	18.8	22.6	27.0	35.1	42.6	50.5	49.3	42.1	30.2	21.0	15.5	30.9
Extreme Maximum Temp. (°F)	68	71	77	87	87	97	97	93	92	83	76	68	97
Extreme Minimum Temp. (°F)	-21	-10	-11	7	15	24	30	34	22	3	-17	-25	-25
Days Maximum Temp. ≥ 90°F	0	0	0	0	0	2	3	1	0	0	0	0	6
Days Maximum Temp. ≤ 32°F	1	1	0	0	0	0	0	0	0	0	0	1	3
Days Minimum Temp. ≤ 32°F	30	26	27	22	11	2	0	0	3	20	27	29	197
Days Minimum Temp. ≤ 0°F	2	1	0	0	0	0	0	0	0	0	0	2	5
Heating Degree Days (base 65°F)	1,016	834	774	580	354	123	18	42	182	501	773	1,008	6,205
Cooling Degree Days (base 65°F)	0	0	0	0	1	28	70	41	5	0	0	0	145
Mean Precipitation (in.)	0.51	0.50	0.48	0.29	0.45	0.54	2.54	3.07	1.53	1.00	0.53	0.48	11.92
Days With ≥ 0.1" Precipitation	1	2	1	1	2	2	6	8	4	3	2	2	34
Days With ≥ 1.0" Precipitation	0	0	0	0	0	0	0	0	0	0	0	0	0
Mean Snowfall (in.)	1.8	0.8	1.2	0.1	trace	0.0	0.0	0.0	0.0	1.0	0.8	0.9	6.6
Days With ≥ 1.0" Snow Depth	1	0	0	0	0	0	0	0	0	0	0	1	2

Stewart Mountain *Maricopa County*   Elevation: 1,420 ft.   Latitude: 33° 33' N   Longitude: 111° 32' W

	JAN	FEB	MAR	APR	MAY	JUN	JUL	AUG	SEP	OCT	NOV	DEC	YEAR
Mean Maximum Temp. (°F)	65.7	69.5	74.5	82.4	91.2	101.3	103.6	102.2	97.4	87.1	74.6	66.1	84.6
Mean Temp. (°F)	51.6	54.7	59.1	65.9	74.5	83.9	88.8	87.6	82.0	70.8	58.2	51.6	69.1
Mean Minimum Temp. (°F)	37.6	39.9	43.7	49.4	57.7	66.4	74.0	72.9	66.5	54.3	42.2	37.0	53.5
Extreme Maximum Temp. (°F)	87	88	98	103	109	120	119	114	112	106	94	85	120
Extreme Minimum Temp. (°F)	17	23	22	32	36	43	59	59	47	30	24	18	17
Days Maximum Temp. ≥ 90°F	0	0	1	7	19	28	30	30	27	13	1	0	156
Days Maximum Temp. ≤ 32°F	0	0	0	0	0	0	0	0	0	0	0	0	0
Days Minimum Temp. ≤ 32°F	7	3	1	0	0	0	0	0	0	0	2	8	21
Days Minimum Temp. ≤ 0°F	0	0	0	0	0	0	0	0	0	0	0	0	0
Heating Degree Days (base 65°F)	410	286	197	72	8	0	0	0	0	31	212	409	1,625
Cooling Degree Days (base 65°F)	0	3	21	123	318	563	728	704	509	215	17	1	3,202
Mean Precipitation (in.)	1.69	1.59	1.86	0.49	0.30	0.12	1.11	1.55	1.26	1.12	1.22	1.36	13.67
Days With ≥ 0.1" Precipitation	4	3	3	1	1	0	3	4	2	2	2	3	28
Days With ≥ 1.0" Precipitation	0	0	0	0	0	0	0	0	0	0	0	0	0
Mean Snowfall (in.)	0.0	0.0	0.0	0.0	0.0	0.0	0.0	0.0	0.0	0.0	trace	0.0	trace
Days With ≥ 1.0" Snow Depth	0	0	0	0	0	0	0	0	0	0	0	0	0

Sunset Crater Nat'l Monument *Coconino County*   Elevation: 6,978 ft.   Latitude: 35° 22' N   Longitude: 111° 33' W

	JAN	FEB	MAR	APR	MAY	JUN	JUL	AUG	SEP	OCT	NOV	DEC	YEAR
Mean Maximum Temp. (°F)	43.8	47.2	53.0	61.0	70.3	81.5	84.3	81.4	75.4	64.4	52.4	44.4	63.3
Mean Temp. (°F)	28.2	31.6	36.9	43.3	51.7	60.9	65.9	63.8	57.1	46.0	35.5	28.5	45.8
Mean Minimum Temp. (°F)	12.5	16.0	20.7	25.6	33.0	40.2	47.4	46.1	38.9	27.6	18.6	12.4	28.2
Extreme Maximum Temp. (°F)	68	70	74	82	90	99	98	97	91	85	74	68	99
Extreme Minimum Temp. (°F)	-26	-28	-9	-1	12	21	27	27	12	2	-12	-25	-28
Days Maximum Temp. ≥ 90°F	0	0	0	0	0	4	6	2	0	0	0	0	12
Days Maximum Temp. ≤ 32°F	3	2	0	0	0	0	0	0	0	0	0	3	8
Days Minimum Temp. ≤ 32°F	31	28	28	24	16	6	0	1	6	24	28	30	222
Days Minimum Temp. ≤ 0°F	4	2	0	0	0	0	0	0	0	0	1	4	11
Heating Degree Days (base 65°F)	1,135	936	866	643	410	152	36	65	234	581	878	1,126	7,062
Cooling Degree Days (base 65°F)	0	0	0	0	0	3	33	68	38	4	0	0	146
Mean Precipitation (in.)	1.23	1.28	1.41	0.80	0.72	0.48	2.51	2.80	1.96	1.30	1.25	1.39	17.13
Days With ≥ 0.1" Precipitation	3	3	4	2	2	1	6	7	5	3	3	3	42
Days With ≥ 1.0" Precipitation	0	0	0	0	0	0	0	0	0	0	0	0	0
Mean Snowfall (in.)	14.2	11.8	11.3	4.8	0.1	0.0	0.0	0.0	trace	1.8	6.4	14.6	65.0
Days With ≥ 1.0" Snow Depth	20	15	7	2	0	0	0	0	0	0	4	15	63

Superior *Pinal County*   Elevation: 2,798 ft.   Latitude: 33° 18' N   Longitude: 111° 07' W

	JAN	FEB	MAR	APR	MAY	JUN	JUL	AUG	SEP	OCT	NOV	DEC	YEAR
Mean Maximum Temp. (°F)	60.8	64.3	68.7	76.2	85.6	95.9	97.8	95.9	92.2	82.2	69.8	61.3	79.2
Mean Temp. (°F)	51.6	54.9	58.3	64.9	73.8	83.9	86.5	85.0	81.4	71.8	60.2	52.4	68.7
Mean Minimum Temp. (°F)	42.4	45.4	47.9	53.7	61.9	72.0	75.3	74.1	70.6	61.4	50.5	43.4	58.2
Extreme Maximum Temp. (°F)	81	85	91	96	104	111	112	110	105	102	89	83	112
Extreme Minimum Temp. (°F)	20	20	24	29	38	51	59	61	50	33	29	19	19
Days Maximum Temp. ≥ 90°F	0	0	0	1	10	25	29	27	20	7	0	0	119
Days Maximum Temp. ≤ 32°F	0	0	0	0	0	0	0	0	0	0	0	0	0
Days Minimum Temp. ≤ 32°F	2	1	1	0	0	0	0	0	0	0	0	2	6
Days Minimum Temp. ≤ 0°F	0	0	0	0	0	0	0	0	0	0	0	0	0
Heating Degree Days (base 65°F)	409	285	231	93	13	0	0	0	0	34	174	387	1,626
Cooling Degree Days (base 65°F)	1	8	30	117	313	570	659	624	500	257	42	1	3,122
Mean Precipitation (in.)	2.25	2.32	2.49	0.76	0.49	0.28	1.94	2.92	1.92	1.30	1.68	2.01	20.36
Days With ≥ 0.1" Precipitation	4	4	5	2	1	1	4	5	3	2	3	3	37
Days With ≥ 1.0" Precipitation	0	1	1	0	0	0	0	1	1	0	0	1	5
Mean Snowfall (in.)	trace	trace	0.3	trace	0.0	0.0	0.0	0.0	0.0	0.0	trace	trace	0.3
Days With ≥ 1.0" Snow Depth	0	0	0	0	0	0	0	0	0	0	0	0	0

Tacna 3 NE *Yuma County*   Elevation: 321 ft.   Latitude: 32° 43' N   Longitude: 113° 55' W

	JAN	FEB	MAR	APR	MAY	JUN	JUL	AUG	SEP	OCT	NOV	DEC	YEAR
Mean Maximum Temp. (°F)	68.5	73.8	79.3	86.4	94.0	103.1	106.1	105.1	100.2	89.9	77.4	68.1	87.6
Mean Temp. (°F)	52.0	56.6	61.5	67.7	75.4	84.0	90.4	90.0	84.0	72.1	59.2	51.4	70.4
Mean Minimum Temp. (°F)	35.4	39.3	43.7	48.9	56.8	64.8	74.6	74.8	67.7	54.3	41.0	34.8	53.0
Extreme Maximum Temp. (°F)	89	92	100	108	115	121	126	118	115	110	96	83	126
Extreme Minimum Temp. (°F)	14	23	25	31	37	42	52	51	43	27	24	13	13
Days Maximum Temp. ≥ 90°F	0	0	3	12	23	29	31	31	28	18	1	0	176
Days Maximum Temp. ≤ 32°F	0	0	0	0	0	0	0	0	0	0	0	0	0
Days Minimum Temp. ≤ 32°F	11	5	1	0	0	0	0	0	0	0	4	13	34
Days Minimum Temp. ≤ 0°F	0	0	0	0	0	0	0	0	0	0	0	0	0
Heating Degree Days (base 65°F)	398	235	137	44	4	0	0	0	0	21	182	414	1,435
Cooling Degree Days (base 65°F)	0	6	39	156	359	590	808	815	599	265	19	0	3,656
Mean Precipitation (in.)	0.50	0.42	0.48	0.19	0.10	trace	0.38	0.77	0.45	0.26	0.27	0.48	4.30
Days With ≥ 0.1" Precipitation	1	1	1	1	0	0	1	2	1	1	1	1	11
Days With ≥ 1.0" Precipitation	0	0	0	0	0	0	0	0	0	0	0	0	0
Mean Snowfall (in.)	trace	0.0	0.0	0.0	0.0	0.0	0.0	0.0	0.0	0.0	0.0	0.0	trace
Days With ≥ 1.0" Snow Depth	0	0	0	0	0	0	0	0	0	0	0	0	0

Teec Nos Pos *Apache County*   Elevation: 5,288 ft.   Latitude: 36° 55' N   Longitude: 109° 05' W

	JAN	FEB	MAR	APR	MAY	JUN	JUL	AUG	SEP	OCT	NOV	DEC	YEAR
Mean Maximum Temp. (°F)	41.6	49.2	58.0	67.5	77.4	88.6	92.4	90.0	81.6	69.3	54.1	43.4	67.8
Mean Temp. (°F)	31.3	37.7	45.3	53.3	63.0	73.1	78.2	76.1	67.6	55.0	42.4	32.6	54.6
Mean Minimum Temp. (°F)	21.0	26.2	32.6	39.1	48.4	57.7	63.9	62.1	53.4	40.6	30.6	21.6	41.4
Extreme Maximum Temp. (°F)	69	73	82	102	98	105	104	103	97	88	77	79	105
Extreme Minimum Temp. (°F)	-18	-11	12	17	27	38	44	40	32	21	5	-12	-18
Days Maximum Temp. ≥ 90°F	0	0	0	0	1	15	23	18	3	0	0	0	60
Days Maximum Temp. ≤ 32°F	5	1	0	0	0	0	0	0	0	0	0	3	9
Days Minimum Temp. ≤ 32°F	28	23	16	6	0	0	0	0	0	5	19	28	125
Days Minimum Temp. ≤ 0°F	1	0	0	0	0	0	0	0	0	0	0	1	2
Heating Degree Days (base 65°F)	1,037	762	605	349	114	11	0	1	41	307	672	1,000	4,899
Cooling Degree Days (base 65°F)	0	0	0	7	58	266	425	358	134	4	0	0	1,252
Mean Precipitation (in.)	0.71	0.44	0.67	0.47	0.63	0.23	0.94	1.15	0.84	0.92	0.61	0.55	8.16
Days With ≥ 0.1" Precipitation	2	1	2	2	2	1	3	3	2	2	2	2	24
Days With ≥ 1.0" Precipitation	0	0	0	0	0	0	0	0	0	0	0	0	0
Mean Snowfall (in.)	3.2	0.9	0.3	0.1	trace	0.0	0.0	0.0	0.0	trace	0.7	1.6	6.8
Days With ≥ 1.0" Snow Depth	2	0	0	0	0	0	0	0	0	0	0	0	2

Tempe A S U *Maricopa County*   Elevation: 1,167 ft.   Latitude: 33° 25' N   Longitude: 111° 56' W

	JAN	FEB	MAR	APR	MAY	JUN	JUL	AUG	SEP	OCT	NOV	DEC	YEAR
Mean Maximum Temp. (°F)	67.7	72.5	77.4	85.5	93.9	103.3	105.5	103.8	99.1	88.9	76.4	67.7	86.8
Mean Temp. (°F)	53.5	57.4	61.9	68.6	76.8	85.5	90.7	89.4	83.8	73.0	60.8	53.4	71.2
Mean Minimum Temp. (°F)	39.2	42.2	46.3	51.6	59.8	67.5	76.0	74.9	68.4	57.0	45.2	39.0	55.6
Extreme Maximum Temp. (°F)	87	91	99	105	112	119	118	119	113	108	95	85	119
Extreme Minimum Temp. (°F)	21	23	24	30	35	45	58	54	47	26	26	22	21
Days Maximum Temp. ≥ 90°F	0	0	2	11	24	29	31	30	28	16	1	0	172
Days Maximum Temp. ≤ 32°F	0	0	0	0	0	0	0	0	0	0	0	0	0
Days Minimum Temp. ≤ 32°F	5	3	1	0	0	0	0	0	0	0	1	6	16
Days Minimum Temp. ≤ 0°F	0	0	0	0	0	0	0	0	0	0	0	0	0
Heating Degree Days (base 65°F)	351	217	135	43	4	0	0	0	0	20	152	354	1,276
Cooling Degree Days (base 65°F)	1	12	54	197	417	644	814	794	601	307	45	1	3,887
Mean Precipitation (in.)	1.00	1.07	1.19	0.25	0.21	0.06	0.90	1.24	0.92	0.80	0.77	1.07	9.48
Days With ≥ 0.1" Precipitation	2	2	3	1	1	0	2	3	2	1	2	2	21
Days With ≥ 1.0" Precipitation	0	0	0	0	0	0	0	0	0	0	0	0	0
Mean Snowfall (in.)	trace	0.0	trace	0.0	0.0	0.0	0.0	0.0	0.0	0.0	0.0	trace	trace
Days With ≥ 1.0" Snow Depth	0	0	0	0	0	0	0	0	0	0	0	0	0

Tombstone *Cochise County*   Elevation: 4,609 ft.   Latitude: 31° 42' N   Longitude: 110° 03' W

	JAN	FEB	MAR	APR	MAY	JUN	JUL	AUG	SEP	OCT	NOV	DEC	YEAR
Mean Maximum Temp. (°F)	59.2	63.4	68.6	76.3	84.7	94.5	93.3	90.5	87.4	78.4	67.9	59.7	77.0
Mean Temp. (°F)	47.6	50.9	55.2	61.7	69.8	78.9	79.9	77.9	74.4	65.3	55.4	48.3	63.8
Mean Minimum Temp. (°F)	35.9	38.4	41.8	47.0	54.7	63.1	66.5	65.2	61.4	52.3	42.9	36.8	50.5
Extreme Maximum Temp. (°F)	82	85	92	99	104	110	112	106	101	98	87	79	112
Extreme Minimum Temp. (°F)	15	19	18	23	35	46	57	54	45	27	22	3	3
Days Maximum Temp. ≥ 90°F	0	0	0	1	8	24	23	19	11	2	0	0	88
Days Maximum Temp. ≤ 32°F	0	0	0	0	0	0	0	0	0	0	0	0	0
Days Minimum Temp. ≤ 32°F	9	5	2	1	0	0	0	0	0	0	3	8	28
Days Minimum Temp. ≤ 0°F	0	0	0	0	0	0	0	0	0	0	0	0	0
Heating Degree Days (base 65°F)	534	390	302	135	23	0	0	0	2	73	285	512	2,256
Cooling Degree Days (base 65°F)	0	0	6	49	191	423	465	401	295	92	4	0	1,926
Mean Precipitation (in.)	1.03	0.73	0.74	0.25	0.27	0.52	2.82	3.05	1.59	1.09	0.62	1.07	13.78
Days With ≥ 0.1" Precipitation	3	2	2	1	1	1	7	7	4	2	2	3	35
Days With ≥ 1.0" Precipitation	0	0	0	0	0	0	0	1	0	0	0	0	1
Mean Snowfall (in.)	0.3	trace	trace	trace	0.0	0.0	0.0	0.0	0.0	0.0	0.0	0.3	0.6
Days With ≥ 1.0" Snow Depth	0	0	0	0	0	0	0	0	0	0	0	0	0

Tucson Camp Ave. Exp. Farm *Pima County*   Elevation: 2,329 ft.   Latitude: 32° 17' N   Longitude: 110° 57' W

	JAN	FEB	MAR	APR	MAY	JUN	JUL	AUG	SEP	OCT	NOV	DEC	YEAR
Mean Maximum Temp. (°F)	66.2	70.0	74.8	82.3	91.0	100.5	100.6	98.8	95.4	86.0	74.8	66.5	83.9
Mean Temp. (°F)	50.3	53.7	58.1	64.2	72.8	82.3	86.2	84.8	80.1	69.1	57.3	50.5	67.5
Mean Minimum Temp. (°F)	34.4	37.3	41.3	46.0	54.7	64.0	71.7	70.8	64.7	52.2	39.8	34.5	51.0
Extreme Maximum Temp. (°F)	88	89	96	99	107	115	114	110	108	103	94	85	115
Extreme Minimum Temp. (°F)	11	15	21	30	34	43	54	56	45	25	20	12	11
Days Maximum Temp. ≥ 90°F	0	0	1	5	19	29	30	30	26	11	1	0	152
Days Maximum Temp. ≤ 32°F	0	0	0	0	0	0	0	0	0	0	0	0	0
Days Minimum Temp. ≤ 32°F	13	7	3	1	0	0	0	0	0	0	5	13	42
Days Minimum Temp. ≤ 0°F	0	0	0	0	0	0	0	0	0	0	0	0	0
Heating Degree Days (base 65°F)	448	314	219	88	8	0	0	0	0	37	232	442	1,788
Cooling Degree Days (base 65°F)	0	1	10	84	279	533	661	633	473	178	10	0	2,862
Mean Precipitation (in.)	1.07	1.08	1.04	0.37	0.21	0.18	1.89	2.08	1.27	1.13	0.78	1.26	12.36
Days With ≥ 0.1" Precipitation	2	3	3	1	1	0	4	5	3	2	2	3	29
Days With ≥ 1.0" Precipitation	0	0	0	0	0	0	0	0	0	0	0	0	0
Mean Snowfall (in.)	0.2	trace	trace	0.0	0.0	0.0	0.0	0.0	0.0	0.0	0.0	0.2	0.4
Days With ≥ 1.0" Snow Depth	0	0	0	0	0	0	0	0	0	0	0	0	0

Tucson Magnetic Observatory *Pima County*   Elevation: 2,522 ft.   Latitude: 32° 15' N   Longitude: 110° 50' W

	JAN	FEB	MAR	APR	MAY	JUN	JUL	AUG	SEP	OCT	NOV	DEC	YEAR
Mean Maximum Temp. (°F)	65.1	68.9	72.9	81.8	90.6	101.0	101.0	98.6	95.3	85.4	73.7	65.9	83.4
Mean Temp. (°F)	50.1	53.4	57.1	63.9	72.5	82.5	86.4	84.5	79.9	69.3	57.1	50.6	67.3
Mean Minimum Temp. (°F)	35.1	37.9	41.3	45.9	54.3	63.9	71.8	70.4	64.5	53.0	40.5	35.3	51.1
Extreme Maximum Temp. (°F)	87	88	97	103	108	118	114	112	108	104	92	85	118
Extreme Minimum Temp. (°F)	15	19	21	31	36	46	57	57	43	27	22	15	15
Days Maximum Temp. ≥ 90°F	0	0	1	6	19	29	30	29	25	10	0	0	149
Days Maximum Temp. ≤ 32°F	0	0	0	0	0	0	0	0	0	0	0	0	0
Days Minimum Temp. ≤ 32°F	13	6	3	1	0	0	0	0	0	0	4	12	39
Days Minimum Temp. ≤ 0°F	0	0	0	0	0	0	0	0	0	0	0	0	0
Heating Degree Days (base 65°F)	455	321	251	101	15	0	0	0	0	40	240	440	1,863
Cooling Degree Days (base 65°F)	0	1	14	94	274	538	665	611	454	179	12	0	2,842
Mean Precipitation (in.)	1.41	1.15	1.42	0.32	0.33	0.31	2.02	2.44	1.40	1.34	0.86	1.40	14.40
Days With ≥ 0.1" Precipitation	4	3	3	1	1	1	5	6	3	2	2	3	34
Days With ≥ 1.0" Precipitation	0	0	0	0	0	0	0	1	0	0	0	0	1
Mean Snowfall (in.)	trace	trace	trace	trace	0.0	0.0	0.0	0.0	0.0	0.0	0.0	0.3	0.3
Days With ≥ 1.0" Snow Depth	0	0	0	0	0	0	0	0	0	0	0	0	0

Tucson NWSO *Pima County*   Elevation: 2,477 ft.   Latitude: 32° 14' N   Longitude: 110° 57' W

	JAN	FEB	MAR	APR	MAY	JUN	JUL	AUG	SEP	OCT	NOV	DEC	YEAR
Mean Maximum Temp. (°F)	66.0	70.2	74.7	82.4	90.9	100.6	100.5	98.8	95.0	85.5	74.4	66.5	83.8
Mean Temp. (°F)	53.9	57.5	61.7	68.2	76.8	86.2	88.5	87.1	82.9	72.6	61.2	54.3	70.9
Mean Minimum Temp. (°F)	41.7	44.8	48.6	53.9	62.7	71.8	76.5	75.3	70.7	59.5	48.5	42.1	58.0
Extreme Maximum Temp. (°F)	90	90	98	104	110	115	115	112	108	103	92	88	115
Extreme Minimum Temp. (°F)	19	27	27	33	45	53	66	64	52	32	28	22	19
Days Maximum Temp. ≥ 90°F	0	0	1	7	19	29	30	30	26	11	0	0	153
Days Maximum Temp. ≤ 32°F	0	0	0	0	0	0	0	0	0	0	0	0	0
Days Minimum Temp. ≤ 32°F	3	1	0	0	0	0	0	0	0	0	0	2	6
Days Minimum Temp. ≤ 0°F	0	0	0	0	0	0	0	0	0	0	0	0	0
Heating Degree Days (base 65°F)	339	211	144	51	3	0	0	0	0	20	143	327	1,238
Cooling Degree Days (base 65°F)	1	9	49	174	400	656	738	695	553	271	39	2	3,587
Mean Precipitation (in.)	1.03	0.97	0.90	0.33	0.20	0.23	2.05	2.26	1.28	1.08	0.67	1.00	12.00
Days With ≥ 0.1" Precipitation	2	3	3	1	1	0	5	5	3	2	2	3	30
Days With ≥ 1.0" Precipitation	0	0	0	0	0	0	0	0	0	0	0	0	0
Mean Snowfall (in.)	0.2	trace	0.2	trace	0.0	0.0	0.0	0.0	0.0	0.0	0.0	0.1	0.5
Days With ≥ 1.0" Snow Depth	0	0	0	0	0	0	0	0	0	0	0	0	0

Tumacacori Nat'l Monument *Santa Cruz County*   Elevation: 3,264 ft.   Latitude: 31° 34' N   Longitude: 111° 03' W

	JAN	FEB	MAR	APR	MAY	JUN	JUL	AUG	SEP	OCT	NOV	DEC	YEAR
Mean Maximum Temp. (°F)	65.5	69.2	73.3	80.4	88.5	98.4	96.8	94.0	91.3	83.2	73.0	65.8	81.6
Mean Temp. (°F)	48.8	51.6	55.7	61.0	68.4	78.2	81.4	79.4	75.0	65.4	55.2	49.2	64.1
Mean Minimum Temp. (°F)	32.0	34.0	37.8	41.4	48.3	57.8	65.9	64.7	58.6	47.5	37.3	32.5	46.5
Extreme Maximum Temp. (°F)	89	88	95	100	108	113	113	107	105	104	93	88	113
Extreme Minimum Temp. (°F)	8	15	18	26	30	38	42	50	42	21	16	5	5
Days Maximum Temp. ≥ 90°F	0	0	1	3	14	28	27	26	20	6	0	0	125
Days Maximum Temp. ≤ 32°F	0	0	0	0	0	0	0	0	0	0	0	0	0
Days Minimum Temp. ≤ 32°F	17	12	6	2	0	0	0	0	0	1	7	16	61
Days Minimum Temp. ≤ 0°F	0	0	0	0	0	0	0	0	0	0	0	0	0
Heating Degree Days (base 65°F)	497	372	288	145	28	1	0	0	1	67	290	482	2,171
Cooling Degree Days (base 65°F)	0	0	4	38	147	395	510	450	299	83	3	0	1,929
Mean Precipitation (in.)	1.23	1.12	1.01	0.35	0.22	0.37	3.84	3.95	1.74	1.18	0.69	1.35	17.05
Days With ≥ 0.1" Precipitation	3	2	2	1	1	1	8	8	4	2	1	2	35
Days With ≥ 1.0" Precipitation	0	0	0	0	0	0	1	1	0	0	0	0	2
Mean Snowfall (in.)	0.1	0.2	trace	trace	0.0	0.0	0.0	0.0	0.0	0.0	trace	0.5	0.8
Days With ≥ 1.0" Snow Depth	0	0	0	0	0	0	0	0	0	0	0	0	0

Wahweap *Coconino County*   Elevation: 3,727 ft.   Latitude: 36° 59' N   Longitude: 111° 29' W

	JAN	FEB	MAR	APR	MAY	JUN	JUL	AUG	SEP	OCT	NOV	DEC	YEAR
Mean Maximum Temp. (°F)	47.2	54.0	63.4	72.5	83.0	94.0	98.0	95.5	87.4	73.2	58.2	48.2	72.9
Mean Temp. (°F)	37.2	43.0	50.9	58.5	68.7	78.7	84.1	82.2	73.8	60.9	47.3	38.1	60.3
Mean Minimum Temp. (°F)	27.0	31.9	38.2	44.4	54.2	63.5	70.1	68.7	60.1	48.5	36.3	27.9	47.6
Extreme Maximum Temp. (°F)	64	75	85	94	101	110	120	115	105	93	80	73	120
Extreme Minimum Temp. (°F)	-2	4	21	16	32	40	48	51	39	24	15	4	-2
Days Maximum Temp. ≥ 90°F	0	0	0	0	6	22	27	27	12	0	0	0	94
Days Maximum Temp. ≤ 32°F	1	0	0	0	0	0	0	0	0	0	0	1	2
Days Minimum Temp. ≤ 32°F	25	15	5	1	0	0	0	0	0	1	8	25	80
Days Minimum Temp. ≤ 0°F	0	0	0	0	0	0	0	0	0	0	0	0	0
Heating Degree Days (base 65°F)	855	614	433	211	42	1	0	0	6	161	526	829	3,678
Cooling Degree Days (base 65°F)	0	0	1	25	162	409	589	531	273	36	0	0	2,026
Mean Precipitation (in.)	0.60	0.58	0.68	0.42	0.43	0.23	0.66	0.71	0.64	0.77	0.68	0.38	6.78
Days With ≥ 0.1" Precipitation	2	2	2	1	1	1	2	2	2	2	2	1	20
Days With ≥ 1.0" Precipitation	0	0	0	0	0	0	0	0	0	0	0	0	0
Mean Snowfall (in.)	0.2	*0.3*	trace	trace	0.0	0.0	0.0	0.0	0.0	trace	trace	*trace*	*0.5*
Days With ≥ 1.0" Snow Depth	0	0	0	0	0	0	0	0	0	0	0	0	0

Walnut Creek *Yavapai County*   Elevation: 5,088 ft.   Latitude: 34° 56' N   Longitude: 112° 49' W

	JAN	FEB	MAR	APR	MAY	JUN	JUL	AUG	SEP	OCT	NOV	DEC	YEAR
Mean Maximum Temp. (°F)	51.1	56.1	61.6	69.4	77.5	87.6	90.5	87.9	82.9	72.9	60.6	51.3	70.8
Mean Temp. (°F)	36.2	39.9	44.3	50.0	57.5	65.9	72.1	70.4	64.0	53.5	42.9	36.0	52.7
Mean Minimum Temp. (°F)	21.3	23.7	26.9	30.5	37.5	44.3	53.6	52.8	45.2	34.0	25.2	20.6	34.6
Extreme Maximum Temp. (°F)	74	79	85	92	97	104	106	102	97	92	86	71	106
Extreme Minimum Temp. (°F)	-15	-4	5	10	14	26	31	30	22	8	5	-11	-15
Days Maximum Temp. ≥ 90°F	0	0	0	0	1	13	19	12	4	0	0	0	49
Days Maximum Temp. ≤ 32°F	0	0	0	0	0	0	0	0	0	0	0	0	0
Days Minimum Temp. ≤ 32°F	29	25	26	19	8	1	0	0	1	13	26	28	176
Days Minimum Temp. ≤ 0°F	0	0	0	0	0	0	0	0	0	0	0	0	0
Heating Degree Days (base 65°F)	885	701	636	444	233	55	3	5	76	351	656	894	4,939
Cooling Degree Days (base 65°F)	0	0	0	1	9	85	225	196	57	0	0	0	573
Mean Precipitation (in.)	1.50	1.94	1.73	0.57	0.56	0.24	2.05	2.59	1.41	0.98	1.16	1.15	15.88
Days With ≥ 0.1" Precipitation	4	4	4	2	2	1	5	5	3	2	2	3	37
Days With ≥ 1.0" Precipitation	0	1	0	0	0	0	0	1	0	0	0	0	2
Mean Snowfall (in.)	0.5	0.7	0.0	0.5	0.0	0.0	0.0	0.0	0.0	0.0	trace	0.3	2.0
Days With ≥ 1.0" Snow Depth	0	0	0	0	0	0	0	0	0	0	0	0	0

Whiteriver 1 SW *Navajo County*   Elevation: 5,118 ft.   Latitude: 33° 49' N   Longitude: 109° 59' W

	JAN	FEB	MAR	APR	MAY	JUN	JUL	AUG	SEP	OCT	NOV	DEC	YEAR
Mean Maximum Temp. (°F)	na	na	na	67.9	76.4	87.1	89.3	86.8	82.6	72.6	62.5	na	na
Mean Temp. (°F)	na	na	na	51.4	59.4	69.2	73.7	71.9	66.9	56.4	46.2	na	na
Mean Minimum Temp. (°F)	na	na	na	34.9	42.3	51.2	58.0	56.9	51.2	40.1	29.7	na	na
Extreme Maximum Temp. (°F)	74	78	83	89	93	102	102	98	96	90	82	73	102
Extreme Minimum Temp. (°F)	-11	4	11	20	26	33	42	46	31	17	6	-2	-11
Days Maximum Temp. ≥ 90°F	0	0	0	0	1	11	16	8	3	0	0	0	39
Days Maximum Temp. ≤ 32°F	0	0	0	0	0	0	0	0	0	0	0	0	0
Days Minimum Temp. ≤ 32°F	23	20	18	10	1	0	0	0	0	5	19	23	119
Days Minimum Temp. ≤ 0°F	0	0	0	0	0	0	0	0	0	0	0	0	0
Heating Degree Days (base 65°F)	na	na	na	400	181	22	0	1	34	265	557	na	na
Cooling Degree Days (base 65°F)	na	na	na	0	16	147	266	222	98	na	0	na	na
Mean Precipitation (in.)	1.73	1.58	2.06	0.85	0.64	0.52	2.42	3.50	1.84	1.71	1.41	1.43	19.69
Days With ≥ 0.1" Precipitation	3	3	4	2	2	1	6	7	4	3	3	2	40
Days With ≥ 1.0" Precipitation	0	0	0	0	0	0	0	1	0	1	0	0	2
Mean Snowfall (in.)	3.5	1.9	3.6	1.6	trace	0.0	0.0	0.0	0.0	0.1	1.3	1.3	13.3
Days With ≥ 1.0" Snow Depth	2	1	1	0	0	0	0	0	0	0	1	1	6

Wickenburg *Maricopa County*   Elevation: 2,093 ft.   Latitude: 33° 59' N   Longitude: 112° 44' W

	JAN	FEB	MAR	APR	MAY	JUN	JUL	AUG	SEP	OCT	NOV	DEC	YEAR
Mean Maximum Temp. (°F)	65.2	69.6	74.2	82.5	90.8	101.3	104.4	102.1	96.5	86.1	74.1	65.9	84.4
Mean Temp. (°F)	48.7	52.6	56.7	63.0	70.7	80.0	86.5	85.2	78.4	67.1	55.6	48.9	66.1
Mean Minimum Temp. (°F)	32.1	35.5	39.2	43.3	50.5	58.8	68.6	68.2	60.2	48.1	37.1	31.7	47.8
Extreme Maximum Temp. (°F)	88	89	97	102	109	118	121	117	111	106	93	84	121
Extreme Minimum Temp. (°F)	12	16	23	27	33	41	50	48	42	23	19	15	12
Days Maximum Temp. ≥ 90°F	0	0	1	6	19	29	31	31	27	11	1	0	156
Days Maximum Temp. ≤ 32°F	0	0	0	0	0	0	0	0	0	0	0	0	0
Days Minimum Temp. ≤ 32°F	17	9	4	1	0	0	0	0	0	0	7	18	56
Days Minimum Temp. ≤ 0°F	0	0	0	0	0	0	0	0	0	0	0	0	0
Heating Degree Days (base 65°F)	499	345	260	108	20	0	0	0	1	56	278	491	2,058
Cooling Degree Days (base 65°F)	0	0	7	60	200	434	660	647	420	132	4	0	2,564
Mean Precipitation (in.)	1.43	1.48	1.65	0.44	0.27	0.13	1.24	1.83	1.44	0.56	0.87	1.01	12.35
Days With ≥ 0.1" Precipitation	3	3	3	1	1	0	3	4	2	1	1	2	24
Days With ≥ 1.0" Precipitation	0	0	0	0	0	0	0	0	0	0	0	0	0
Mean Snowfall (in.)	0.0	0.2	trace	trace	0.0	0.0	0.0	0.0	0.0	0.0	0.0	trace	0.2
Days With ≥ 1.0" Snow Depth	0	0	0	0	0	0	0	0	0	0	0	0	0

Wikieup *Mohave County*   Elevation: 2,007 ft.   Latitude: 34° 42' N   Longitude: 113° 37' W

	JAN	FEB	MAR	APR	MAY	JUN	JUL	AUG	SEP	OCT	NOV	DEC	YEAR
Mean Maximum Temp. (°F)	64.3	69.0	73.2	81.6	90.5	100.5	105.0	103.1	96.9	86.8	73.5	65.3	84.1
Mean Temp. (°F)	48.8	52.4	55.8	62.4	70.8	79.5	86.6	85.3	78.6	67.6	55.8	48.8	66.1
Mean Minimum Temp. (°F)	33.3	35.9	38.4	43.1	51.1	58.8	68.2	67.4	60.2	48.4	38.1	32.3	47.9
Extreme Maximum Temp. (°F)	82	93	94	103	110	117	119	116	111	109	94	84	119
Extreme Minimum Temp. (°F)	17	15	24	24	30	43	50	49	41	25	21	14	14
Days Maximum Temp. ≥ 90°F	0	0	1	7	19	28	31	30	26	12	1	0	155
Days Maximum Temp. ≤ 32°F	0	0	0	0	0	0	0	0	0	0	0	0	0
Days Minimum Temp. ≤ 32°F	14	8	4	1	0	0	0	0	0	0	6	16	49
Days Minimum Temp. ≤ 0°F	0	0	0	0	0	0	0	0	0	0	0	0	0
Heating Degree Days (base 65°F)	494	348	282	126	26	1	0	0	2	53	274	495	2,101
Cooling Degree Days (base 65°F)	0	1	5	60	221	439	671	645	411	132	5	0	2,590
Mean Precipitation (in.)	1.78	1.68	1.57	0.43	0.28	0.07	0.72	1.20	0.97	0.51	0.77	0.87	10.85
Days With ≥ 0.1" Precipitation	3	3	3	1	1	0	2	3	2	1	2	2	23
Days With ≥ 1.0" Precipitation	1	0	0	0	0	0	0	0	0	0	0	0	1
Mean Snowfall (in.)	0.1	0.0	0.0	0.0	0.0	0.0	0.0	0.0	0.0	0.0	0.0	0.0	0.1
Days With ≥ 1.0" Snow Depth	0	0	0	0	0	0	0	0	0	0	0	0	0

Willcox *Cochise County*   Elevation: 4,173 ft.   Latitude: 32° 15' N   Longitude: 109° 50' W

	JAN	FEB	MAR	APR	MAY	JUN	JUL	AUG	SEP	OCT	NOV	DEC	YEAR
Mean Maximum Temp. (°F)	60.1	65.0	70.6	78.2	86.2	95.4	95.0	92.7	88.7	79.3	68.4	60.2	78.3
Mean Temp. (°F)	43.8	47.4	52.1	58.1	66.2	75.3	79.3	77.7	72.1	61.3	50.2	43.7	60.6
Mean Minimum Temp. (°F)	27.5	29.8	33.6	37.9	46.2	55.1	63.6	62.6	55.4	43.2	32.0	27.1	42.8
Extreme Maximum Temp. (°F)	80	86	91	97	103	110	108	105	101	96	87	78	110
Extreme Minimum Temp. (°F)	3	2	11	17	11	27	48	45	33	15	12	-7	-7
Days Maximum Temp. ≥ 90°F	0	0	0	1	9	26	27	24	15	3	0	0	105
Days Maximum Temp. ≤ 32°F	0	0	0	0	0	0	0	0	0	0	0	0	0
Days Minimum Temp. ≤ 32°F	23	19	13	6	1	0	0	0	0	3	16	24	105
Days Minimum Temp. ≤ 0°F	0	0	0	0	0	0	0	0	0	0	0	0	0
Heating Degree Days (base 65°F)	650	490	392	213	47	2	0	0	5	139	436	653	3,027
Cooling Degree Days (base 65°F)	0	0	0	15	106	322	452	407	234	29	0	0	1,565
Mean Precipitation (in.)	1.11	0.96	0.70	0.26	0.36	0.35	2.42	2.65	1.30	1.15	0.67	1.30	13.23
Days With ≥ 0.1" Precipitation	3	2	2	1	1	1	6	5	3	3	2	3	32
Days With ≥ 1.0" Precipitation	0	0	0	0	0	0	0	0	0	0	0	0	0
Mean Snowfall (in.)	0.8	0.9	0.5	0.1	trace	0.0	0.0	trace	trace	trace	0.1	0.8	3.2
Days With ≥ 1.0" Snow Depth	0	0	0	0	0	0	0	0	0	0	0	0	0

Williams *Coconino County*   Elevation: 6,748 ft.   Latitude: 35° 14' N   Longitude: 112° 11' W

	JAN	FEB	MAR	APR	MAY	JUN	JUL	AUG	SEP	OCT	NOV	DEC	YEAR
Mean Maximum Temp. (°F)	45.8	48.6	52.5	60.0	68.8	79.8	82.9	80.4	74.8	65.0	53.8	46.8	63.3
Mean Temp. (°F)	34.1	36.5	39.9	46.0	54.3	64.1	68.6	66.8	61.1	51.2	41.0	34.9	49.9
Mean Minimum Temp. (°F)	22.3	24.4	27.2	31.9	39.8	48.4	54.3	53.2	47.4	37.4	28.2	23.0	36.4
Extreme Maximum Temp. (°F)	74	74	72	80	88	100	99	94	89	84	77	74	100
Extreme Minimum Temp. (°F)	-13	-12	0	9	19	24	37	32	22	10	4	-12	-13
Days Maximum Temp. ≥ 90°F	0	0	0	0	0	2	3	1	0	0	0	0	6
Days Maximum Temp. ≤ 32°F	2	1	0	0	0	0	0	0	0	0	1	2	6
Days Minimum Temp. ≤ 32°F	29	24	24	16	5	0	0	0	0	8	21	28	155
Days Minimum Temp. ≤ 0°F	0	0	0	0	0	0	0	0	0	0	0	0	0
Heating Degree Days (base 65°F)	952	797	772	565	328	84	9	21	129	421	713	926	5,717
Cooling Degree Days (base 65°F)	0	0	0	0	4	63	125	87	17	0	0	0	296
Mean Precipitation (in.)	2.06	2.29	2.38	1.01	0.80	0.46	2.68	3.03	1.76	1.60	1.77	1.57	21.41
Days With ≥ 0.1" Precipitation	4	4	6	3	3	1	6	7	4	3	3	4	48
Days With ≥ 1.0" Precipitation	0	1	0	0	0	0	1	0	0	0	0	0	2
Mean Snowfall (in.)	17.5	13.9	16.8	7.5	0.3	0.0	0.0	0.0	0.0	0.5	6.9	9.4	72.8
Days With ≥ 1.0" Snow Depth	9	6	na	3	0	0	0	0	0	0	2	6	na

Willow Beach *Mohave County*   Elevation: 738 ft.   Latitude: 35° 52' N   Longitude: 114° 40' W

	JAN	FEB	MAR	APR	MAY	JUN	JUL	AUG	SEP	OCT	NOV	DEC	YEAR
Mean Maximum Temp. (°F)	63.2	69.3	76.0	84.6	94.5	105.5	110.4	108.3	101.1	88.2	73.3	63.6	86.5
Mean Temp. (°F)	51.2	56.5	62.5	70.3	79.7	89.1	94.7	93.0	85.6	73.5	60.1	51.6	72.3
Mean Minimum Temp. (°F)	39.1	43.7	48.9	55.9	64.8	72.7	79.0	77.6	70.1	58.6	46.9	39.5	58.1
Extreme Maximum Temp. (°F)	82	91	97	106	115	123	125	121	117	108	93	81	125
Extreme Minimum Temp. (°F)	22	25	35	41	48	51	65	64	52	34	31	21	21
Days Maximum Temp. ≥ 90°F	0	0	2	9	23	29	31	31	28	15	0	0	168
Days Maximum Temp. ≤ 32°F	0	0	0	0	0	0	0	0	0	0	0	0	0
Days Minimum Temp. ≤ 32°F	3	1	0	0	0	0	0	0	0	0	0	3	7
Days Minimum Temp. ≤ 0°F	0	0	0	0	0	0	0	0	0	0	0	0	0
Heating Degree Days (base 65°F)	422	238	122	28	2	0	0	0	0	14	166	410	1,402
Cooling Degree Days (base 65°F)	0	6	50	211	467	711	904	877	632	293	34	0	4,185
Mean Precipitation (in.)	0.70	0.75	0.87	0.21	0.24	0.10	0.38	0.62	0.59	0.38	0.36	0.45	5.65
Days With ≥ 0.1" Precipitation	2	2	2	1	1	0	1	1	1	1	1	1	14
Days With ≥ 1.0" Precipitation	0	0	0	0	0	0	0	0	0	0	0	0	0
Mean Snowfall (in.)	trace	0.0	0.0	0.0	0.0	0.0	0.0	0.0	0.0	0.0	0.0	0.0	trace
Days With ≥ 1.0" Snow Depth	0	0	0	0	0	0	0	0	0	0	0	0	0

Wupatki Nat'l Monument *Coconino County*   Elevation: 4,908 ft.   Latitude: 35° 31' N   Longitude: 111° 22' W

	JAN	FEB	MAR	APR	MAY	JUN	JUL	AUG	SEP	OCT	NOV	DEC	YEAR
Mean Maximum Temp. (°F)	47.6	55.6	63.2	71.1	80.6	91.6	95.1	92.0	85.0	72.8	58.4	47.1	71.7
Mean Temp. (°F)	36.5	42.8	49.4	56.3	65.4	75.8	80.5	77.9	70.7	58.9	45.9	36.1	58.0
Mean Minimum Temp. (°F)	25.3	30.0	35.6	41.4	50.2	59.9	65.8	63.8	56.4	44.9	33.4	25.0	44.3
Extreme Maximum Temp. (°F)	74	77	84	91	99	107	108	105	100	92	80	71	108
Extreme Minimum Temp. (°F)	-4	-2	15	20	30	41	46	48	36	23	7	-5	-5
Days Maximum Temp. ≥ 90°F	0	0	0	0	4	19	26	22	8	0	0	0	79
Days Maximum Temp. ≤ 32°F	2	0	0	0	0	0	0	0	0	0	0	2	4
Days Minimum Temp. ≤ 32°F	27	18	10	3	0	0	0	0	0	2	13	27	100
Days Minimum Temp. ≤ 0°F	0	0	0	0	0	0	0	0	0	0	0	0	0
Heating Degree Days (base 65°F)	877	620	476	269	76	5	0	0	17	209	565	889	4,003
Cooling Degree Days (base 65°F)	0	0	0	18	99	328	475	402	189	25	0	0	1,536
Mean Precipitation (in.)	0.53	0.53	0.74	0.44	0.38	0.27	1.44	1.61	1.05	0.78	0.67	0.54	8.98
Days With ≥ 0.1" Precipitation	2	2	2	1	1	1	3	4	3	2	2	2	25
Days With ≥ 1.0" Precipitation	0	0	0	0	0	0	0	0	0	0	0	0	0
Mean Snowfall (in.)	1.3	1.3	1.1	0.4	trace	0.0	0.0	0.0	0.0	trace	0.3	1.7	6.1
Days With ≥ 1.0" Snow Depth	na	0	0	0	0	0	0	0	0	0	0	1	na

Youngtown *Maricopa County*   Elevation: 1,131 ft.   Latitude: 33° 36' N   Longitude: 112° 18' W

	JAN	FEB	MAR	APR	MAY	JUN	JUL	AUG	SEP	OCT	NOV	DEC	YEAR
Mean Maximum Temp. (°F)	66.9	71.9	77.1	85.4	94.1	103.5	105.9	104.3	99.0	88.4	75.4	66.8	86.6
Mean Temp. (°F)	53.4	57.7	62.3	69.2	77.9	87.0	91.9	90.6	84.5	73.2	60.7	53.3	71.8
Mean Minimum Temp. (°F)	39.9	43.4	47.5	52.9	61.7	70.4	77.9	76.9	69.9	57.9	45.9	39.7	57.0
Extreme Maximum Temp. (°F)	87	89	98	103	112	122	122	116	112	108	95	84	122
Extreme Minimum Temp. (°F)	20	24	24	32	41	52	62	58	51	35	28	21	20
Days Maximum Temp. ≥ 90°F	0	0	2	10	24	29	31	31	28	15	1	0	171
Days Maximum Temp. ≤ 32°F	0	0	0	0	0	0	0	0	0	0	0	0	0
Days Minimum Temp. ≤ 32°F	4	1	0	0	0	0	0	0	0	0	0	4	9
Days Minimum Temp. ≤ 0°F	0	0	0	0	0	0	0	0	0	0	0	0	0
Heating Degree Days (base 65°F)	352	208	123	36	2	0	0	0	0	16	149	357	1,243
Cooling Degree Days (base 65°F)	1	10	50	197	434	676	850	832	612	296	33	1	3,992
Mean Precipitation (in.)	1.03	1.16	1.17	0.29	0.14	0.04	0.82	1.08	0.90	0.66	0.68	1.11	9.08
Days With ≥ 0.1" Precipitation	2	2	3	1	1	0	2	2	2	1	2	2	20
Days With ≥ 1.0" Precipitation	0	0	0	0	0	0	0	0	0	0	0	0	0
Mean Snowfall (in.)	0.0	0.0	0.0	0.0	0.0	0.0	0.0	0.0	0.0	0.0	0.0	trace	trace
Days With ≥ 1.0" Snow Depth	0	0	0	0	0	0	0	0	0	0	0	0	0

Yucca 1 NNE *Mohave County*   Elevation: 1,948 ft.   Latitude: 34° 53' N   Longitude: 114° 08' W

	JAN	FEB	MAR	APR	MAY	JUN	JUL	AUG	SEP	OCT	NOV	DEC	YEAR
Mean Maximum Temp. (°F)	59.7	64.8	69.7	77.8	87.0	98.1	102.4	100.6	94.5	82.6	68.9	59.7	80.5
Mean Temp. (°F)	48.5	52.7	56.8	63.5	72.6	82.9	89.2	87.6	80.5	68.6	56.2	48.5	67.3
Mean Minimum Temp. (°F)	37.2	40.4	43.8	49.1	58.2	67.6	76.0	74.5	66.4	54.5	43.4	37.2	54.0
Extreme Maximum Temp. (°F)	82	87	93	102	108	117	120	119	111	105	89	79	120
Extreme Minimum Temp. (°F)	4	18	27	31	35	46	48	48	40	28	23	19	4
Days Maximum Temp. ≥ 90°F	0	0	0	3	13	26	30	30	23	8	0	0	133
Days Maximum Temp. ≤ 32°F	0	0	0	0	0	0	0	0	0	0	0	0	0
Days Minimum Temp. ≤ 32°F	7	3	1	0	0	0	0	0	0	0	2	7	20
Days Minimum Temp. ≤ 0°F	0	0	0	0	0	0	0	0	0	0	0	0	0
Heating Degree Days (base 65°F)	505	344	263	111	18	0	0	0	1	50	267	506	2,065
Cooling Degree Days (base 65°F)	0	2	16	93	277	560	771	742	494	176	11	0	3,142
Mean Precipitation (in.)	1.12	1.06	1.31	0.35	0.20	0.07	0.73	0.93	0.74	0.46	0.53	0.64	8.14
Days With ≥ 0.1" Precipitation	3	2	3	1	1	0	1	2	1	1	1	2	18
Days With ≥ 1.0" Precipitation	0	0	0	0	0	0	0	0	0	0	0	0	0
Mean Snowfall (in.)	trace	0.1	trace	0.0	0.0	0.0	0.0	0.0	0.0	0.0	0.0	0.0	0.1
Days With ≥ 1.0" Snow Depth	0	0	0	0	0	0	0	0	0	0	0	0	0

Yuma Citrus Station *Yuma County*   Elevation: 190 ft.   Latitude: 32° 37' N   Longitude: 114° 39' W

	JAN	FEB	MAR	APR	MAY	JUN	JUL	AUG	SEP	OCT	NOV	DEC	YEAR
Mean Maximum Temp. (°F)	67.9	73.2	78.7	85.6	93.2	102.7	105.8	105.0	100.3	89.5	76.6	67.6	87.2
Mean Temp. (°F)	54.1	57.8	62.7	68.5	75.9	84.5	90.5	90.3	84.8	73.3	61.1	53.9	71.5
Mean Minimum Temp. (°F)	40.2	42.3	46.7	51.3	58.6	66.3	75.2	75.5	69.4	57.1	45.5	40.1	55.7
Extreme Maximum Temp. (°F)	88	93	97	106	115	122	124	119	115	110	95	81	124
Extreme Minimum Temp. (°F)	26	25	30	36	35	50	56	58	43	33	26	25	25
Days Maximum Temp. ≥ 90°F	0	0	3	10	22	28	30	30	28	16	1	0	168
Days Maximum Temp. ≤ 32°F	0	0	0	0	0	0	0	0	0	0	0	0	0
Days Minimum Temp. ≤ 32°F	3	1	0	0	0	0	0	0	0	0	0	0	0
Days Minimum Temp. ≤ 0°F	0	0	0	0	0	0	0	0	0	0	0	3	7
Heating Degree Days (base 65°F)	333	204	113	38	4	0	0	0	0	15	140	339	1,186
Cooling Degree Days (base 65°F)	0	9	51	171	369	590	803	817	617	291	34	0	3,752
Mean Precipitation (in.)	0.47	0.38	0.40	0.12	0.05	0.03	0.31	0.67	0.51	0.30	0.17	0.51	3.92
Days With ≥ 0.1" Precipitation	1	1	1	0	0	0	0	1	1	1	0	1	7
Days With ≥ 1.0" Precipitation	0	0	0	0	0	0	0	0	0	0	0	0	0
Mean Snowfall (in.)	0.0	0.0	0.0	0.0	0.0	0.0	0.0	0.0	0.0	0.0	0.0	0.0	0.0
Days With ≥ 1.0" Snow Depth	0	0	0	0	0	0	0	0	0	0	0	0	0

Yuma Proving Ground *Yuma County*   Elevation: 321 ft.   Latitude: 32° 50' N   Longitude: 114° 24' W

	JAN	FEB	MAR	APR	MAY	JUN	JUL	AUG	SEP	OCT	NOV	DEC	YEAR
Mean Maximum Temp. (°F)	68.4	73.6	78.5	85.5	93.4	103.3	106.5	105.4	100.3	89.7	76.9	68.0	87.5
Mean Temp. (°F)	56.0	60.5	65.0	71.3	78.9	88.0	93.4	92.9	87.2	75.9	63.2	55.5	74.0
Mean Minimum Temp. (°F)	43.5	47.3	51.6	57.0	64.3	72.7	80.3	80.4	73.9	62.0	49.5	42.9	60.4
Extreme Maximum Temp. (°F)	89	94	100	106	117	121	124	118	115	112	95	85	124
Extreme Minimum Temp. (°F)	23	26	35	37	48	55	65	67	52	36	29	25	23
Days Maximum Temp. ≥ 90°F	0	0	3	11	22	29	31	31	28	17	1	0	173
Days Maximum Temp. ≤ 32°F	0	0	0	0	0	0	0	0	0	0	0	0	0
Days Minimum Temp. ≤ 32°F	1	0	0	0	0	0	0	0	0	0	0	1	2
Days Minimum Temp. ≤ 0°F	0	0	0	0	0	0	0	0	0	0	0	0	0
Heating Degree Days (base 65°F)	275	140	72	22	1	0	0	0	0	7	99	289	905
Cooling Degree Days (base 65°F)	1	24	83	245	454	694	887	891	684	362	58	1	4,384
Mean Precipitation (in.)	0.46	0.44	0.40	0.16	0.04	0.05	0.25	0.65	0.45	0.30	0.23	0.44	3.87
Days With ≥ 0.1" Precipitation	1	1	1	0	0	0	1	1	1	0	0	1	7
Days With ≥ 1.0" Precipitation	0	0	0	0	0	0	0	0	0	0	0	0	0
Mean Snowfall (in.)	0.0	0.0	trace	0.0	0.0	0.0	0.0	0.0	0.0	0.0	0.0	0.0	trace
Days With ≥ 1.0" Snow Depth	0	0	0	0	0	0	0	0	0	0	0	0	0

Yuma Valley *Yuma County*   Elevation: 118 ft.   Latitude: 32° 43' N   Longitude: 114° 43' W

	JAN	FEB	MAR	APR	MAY	JUN	JUL	AUG	SEP	OCT	NOV	DEC	YEAR
Mean Maximum Temp. (°F)	69.0	74.4	78.5	85.5	92.7	na	105.0	na	na	na	na	na	na
Mean Temp. (°F)	54.6	58.4	62.5	68.4	75.6	na	89.8	na	na	na	na	na	na
Mean Minimum Temp. (°F)	40.2	42.5	46.5	51.4	58.4	na	74.5	na	na	na	na	na	na
Extreme Maximum Temp. (°F)	88	95	101	107	118	119	115	118	113	108	96	85	119
Extreme Minimum Temp. (°F)	22	25	29	36	45	51	60	61	51	29	27	23	22
Days Maximum Temp. ≥ 90°F	0	0	3	10	22	28	30	30	27	na	1	0	na
Days Maximum Temp. ≤ 32°F	0	0	0	0	0	0	0	0	0	0	0	0	0
Days Minimum Temp. ≤ 32°F	3	1	0	0	0	0	0	0	0	0	0	3	7
Days Minimum Temp. ≤ 0°F	0	0	0	0	0	0	0	0	0	0	0	0	0
Heating Degree Days (base 65°F)	316	187	114	34	2	na	0	na	na	na	na	na	na
Cooling Degree Days (base 65°F)	na	na	na	na	na	na	na	na	na	na	na	na	na
Mean Precipitation (in.)	0.43	0.28	0.40	0.13	0.03	0.01	0.19	0.66	0.17	0.28	0.15	0.42	3.15
Days With ≥ 0.1" Precipitation	1	1	1	0	0	0	1	1	0	1	0	1	6
Days With ≥ 1.0" Precipitation	0	0	0	0	0	0	0	0	0	0	0	0	0
Mean Snowfall (in.)	0.0	0.0	0.0	0.0	0.0	0.0	0.0	0.0	0.0	0.0	0.0	0.0	0.0
Days With ≥ 1.0" Snow Depth	0	0	0	0	0	0	0	0	0	0	0	0	0

Note: See Appendix D for explanation of data.

ARKANSAS

PHYSICAL FEATURES. Arkansas is divided geographically into two principal divisions on the basis of topography, and to a lesser extent, climate. The dividing line between these two sections cuts diagonally across the State from the northeast to the southwest. West and north of this line are the interior highlands; to the east and south are the lowlands.

Much of western and northern Arkansas is hilly and mountainous. In the southern part, or that portion south of the Arkansas River, are the Ouachita Mountains made up of a number of narrow east-west ridges separated by rather narrow valleys. Some of these ridges reach elevations of 2,500 feet or more. The Arkansas valley, between the Ozark and Ouachita highlands, is an area of fairly low relief with a few isolated ridges and mountains. One of these mountains in the Arkansas valley, Mt. Magazine, with an elevation of 2,823 feet above sea level, is the highest point in the State.

The Ozark Mountains and particularly that portion known as the Boston Mountains are the largest and most massive in Arkansas. It is this topographical feature of the State that has the most noticeable effect upon Arkansas weather.

GENERAL CLIMATE. Climatic differences between the two areas are not as great as the local differences between mountain and valley weather stations in the highlands. Generally, the climate of western and northern Arkansas is a little cooler and there are greater temperature extremes; humidities are lower and there is less cloudiness.

Average maximum or minimum temperatures show little variation over the State. Winter temperatures vary more noticeably from northwest to southeast than is the case in the summer. Maximum temperatures exceed 100°F. at times during July and August, particularly in the valley weather stations in the highlands. The winters are short, but cold periods of brief duration do occur. In the northern part of the State, zero temperatures are of occasional occurrence in January and February and zero has been recorded to the southern border.

PRECIPITATION. Precipitation in Arkansas is predominantly of the shower type except for occasional periods of general rain during the late fall, winter, and early spring. The average number of days with measurable precipitation averages around 100 per year.

Rainfall is normally abundant and well distributed throughout the year. However, extended rain-free periods, as well as flooding local storms, are by no means unusual.

Annual precipitation amounts display both local orographic influence and geographic location with the State. Just by virtue of being closer to the Gulf of Mexico moisture source, the southeast counties receive, on the average, five to six inches more rainfall per year than the northwest counties. However, noticeable exceptions to this are a number of Ozark and Ouachita Mountain weather stations where the year's totals average 55 to nearly 56 inches.

Winter and spring are the wettest times of the year. December and January are the wet months on the average in the southern counties and March through May is the wet period in the north. The fall of the year is uniformly the dry time of the year when monthly precipitation totals average two to three inches.

The State is subject to heavy local rains which frequently give storm totals of from five to 10 inches. Floods are frequent along the White, Black, and Ouachita Rivers. Disastrous floods are of rare occurrence.

Most of the State's precipitation falls as rain. Snow does occur, principally in the northwest. The average annual totals range from a little over a foot on the ground in the higher Ozark elevations in the northwest to one to two inches in the delta flat lands of the extreme southeast counties. Snowfall in these southern and eastern lowlands is generally light and remains on the ground only briefly.

Despite the generally abundant rainfall, short periods of dry weather are frequent over small areas of the State. Occasionally severe droughts of longer duration and involving large areas do occur. Severe droughts covering the greater part of the State occur infrequently.

OTHER CLIMATIC ELEMENTS. The long growing season, averaging from 180 days in the northwest up to more than 230 days in the principal cotton producing areas, favors agricultural activity. In addition to adequate moisture conditions, the eastern and southern Arkansas areas have dry, sunny weather during the early fall. Extended warm and humid summer periods are common.

An average of 17 tornadoes per year have been observed in Arkansas. The severe thunderstorms and tornadoes occur most frequently in the period March through May. With the advent of summer heat in June, the tornado occurrence falls off sharply.

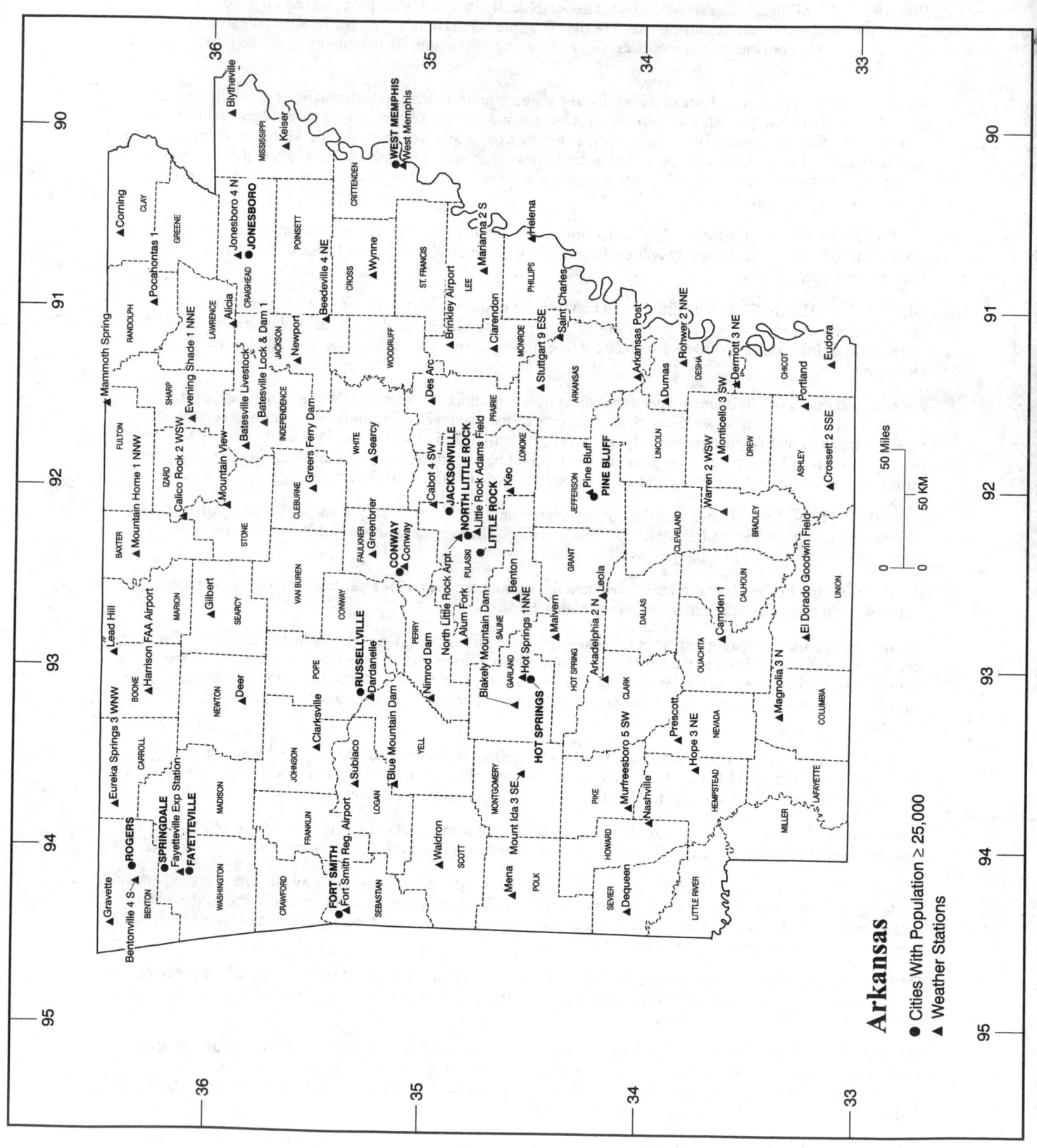

Arkansas

● Cities With Population ≥ 25,000
▲ Weather Stations

Arkansas Weather Stations by County

County	Station Name
Arkansas	Arkansas Post Saint Charles Stuttgart 9 ESE
Ashley	Crossett 2 SSE Portland
Baxter	Mountain Home 1 NNW
Benton	Bentonville 4 S Gravette
Boone	Harrison FAA Airport Lead Hill
Bradley	Warren 2 WSW
Carroll	Eureka Springs 3 WNW
Chicot	Dermott 3 NE Eudora
Clark	Arkadelphia 2 N
Clay	Corning
Cleburne	Greers Ferry Dam
Columbia	Magnolia 3 N
Craighead	Jonesboro 4 N
Crittenden	West Memphis
Cross	Wynne
Desha	Dumas Rohwer 2 NNE
Drew	Monticello 3 SW
Faulkner	Conway Greenbrier
Fulton	Mammoth Spring
Garland	Blakely Mountain Dam Hot Springs 1 NNE
Grant	Leola
Hempstead	Hope 3 NE
Hot Spring	Malvern
Howard	Nashville
Independence	Batesville Livestock Batesville Lock & Dam 1
Izard	Calico Rock 2 WSW
Jackson	Beedeville 4 NE Newport
Jefferson	Pine Bluff

County	Station Name
Johnson	Clarksville
Lawrence	Alicia
Lee	Marianna 2 S
Logan	Subiaco
Lonoke	Keo
Mississippi	Blytheville Keiser
Monroe	Brinkley Airport Clarendon
Montgomery	Mount Ida 3 SE
Nevada	Prescott
Newton	Deer
Ouachita	Camden 1
Perry	Nimrod Dam
Phillips	Helena
Pike	Murfreesboro 5 SW
Polk	Mena
Prairie	Des Arc
Pulaski	Cabot 4 SW Little Rock Adams Field North Little Rock Airport
Randolph	Pocahontas 1
Saline	Alum Fork Benton
Scott	Waldron
Searcy	Gilbert
Sebastian	Fort Smith Regional Airport
Sevier	Dequeen
Sharp	Evening Shade 1 NNE
Stone	Mountain View
Union	El Dorado Goodwin Field
Washington	Fayetteville Exp. Station
White	Searcy
Yell	Blue Mountain Dam Dardanelle

Arkansas Weather Stations by City

City	Station Name	Miles
Conway	Conway	1
	Greenbrier	11
Fayetteville	Bentonville 4 S	17
	Fayetteville Exp. Station	2
Fort Smith	Fort Smith Regional Airport	3
Hot Springs	Blakely Mountain Dam	10
	Hot Springs 1 NNE	2
	Malvern	16
Jacksonville	Cabot 4 SW	6
	Little Rock Adams Field	11
	North Little Rock Airport	9
Jonesboro	Jonesboro 4 N	4
Little Rock	Benton	18
	Little Rock Adams Field	7
	North Little Rock Airport	8
North Little Rock	Cabot 4 SW	15
	Keo	19
	Little Rock Adams Field	3
	North Little Rock Airport	3
Pine Bluff	Pine Bluff	2
Rogers	Bentonville 4 S	5
	Fayetteville Exp. Station	16
	Gravette	19
Russellville	Dardanelle	4
Springdale	Bentonville 4 S	10
	Fayetteville Exp. Station	6
West Memphis	West Memphis	2
	Memphis Int'l Airport, TN	12

Note: Miles is the distance between the geographic center of the city and the weather station.

Arkansas Weather Stations by Elevation

Feet	Station Name
2,372	Deer
1,417	Eureka Springs 3 WNW
1,371	Harrison FAA Airport
1,269	Fayetteville Exp. Station
1,259	Gravette
1,217	Bentonville 4 S
1,128	Mena
797	Mountain Home 1 NNW
777	Mountain View
711	Lead Hill
695	Alum Fork
695	Mount Ida 3 SE
679	Hot Springs 1 NNE
672	Waldron
649	Mammoth Spring
620	Gilbert
570	Batesville Livestock
561	North Little Rock Airport
524	Greers Ferry Dam
498	Evening Shade 1 NNE
498	Subiaco
479	Nimrod Dam
459	Murfreesboro 5 SW
452	Clarksville
446	Fort Smith Regional Airport
423	Blakely Mountain Dam
423	Blue Mountain Dam
419	Dequeen
396	Nashville
387	Jonesboro 4 N
374	Hope 3 NE
367	Dardanelle
347	Calico Rock 2 WSW
328	Greenbrier
318	Magnolia 3 N
314	Conway
314	Pocahontas 1
308	Benton
308	Malvern
305	Prescott
298	Corning
288	Monticello 3 SW
278	Cabot 4 SW
259	Batesville Lock & Dam 1
259	Wynne
255	Alicia
255	Little Rock Adams Field
252	El Dorado Goodwin Field
252	Leola
249	Blytheville
242	Searcy
239	Beedeville 4 NE
232	Marianna 2 S
229	Keiser
229	Keo

Feet	Station Name
226	Newport
213	Pine Bluff
213	West Memphis
209	Warren 2 WSW
200	Des Arc
200	Saint Charles
196	Stuttgart 9 ESE
193	Arkadelphia 2 N
193	Arkansas Post
193	Brinkley Airport
193	Helena
177	Clarendon
177	Crossett 2 SSE
160	Dumas
147	Rohwer 2 NNE
141	Dermott 3 NE
134	Eudora
118	Portland
114	Camden 1

Fort Smith Regional Airport

The weather station at Fort Smith, Arkansas, was established on June 1, 1882 by the U. S. Army Signal Service. For the first 63 years, offices were located at several places within a few blocks of each other in downtown Fort Smith. Since 1945 the station has been at the Fort Smith Municipal Airport, about five miles southeast of its original location.

Fort Smith is located on the Arkansas River at its confluence with the Poteau River and at the point where it enters the state from Oklahoma. The river valley is broad and fairly flat, although elevations in the city of Fort Smith range from 390 feet at the river to about 700 feet. Within 20 miles to the north are the Boston Mountains with elevations to about 2,100 feet and about the same distance south are the Ouachita Mountains with a maximum elevation of about 2,600 feet. The general terrain in the area consists of low broken hills separated by creek and river bottom land.

The surrounding terrain has a definite influence on the weather of Fort Smith. Under conditions of light wind, the direction is prevailing northeast throughout the year. When there is a fairly strong inversion these winds may remain northeasterly even though a strong gradient is present. Although infrequent, dense fog will move in from the river to the east and persist longer than would be expected. In the summer this will result in uncomfortably high humidities and in the winter in cooler temperatures than reported at surrounding stations. Summertime temperatures in the mountains to the north are generally several degrees cooler than in the river valley.

Temperature extremes do occur. In summer there is an average of 10 days when the temperature rises to 100 degrees or higher. On the other hand, in about one year in five, the temperature does not reach 100 degrees. Wintertime temperatures rarely fall to zero or below.

Rainfall is well distributed throughout the growing season. January is the driest month, May the wettest. The difference is almost three inches, but rainfall is generally adequate for agricultural pursuits. Summer precipitation comes in the form of convective showers. Dry spells occur, but true droughts are infrequent.

Snowfall varies widely from season to season. Although snowfall averages a little over six inches, some years go by with no measurable amount being recorded. Ice storms are much more frequent, causing many problems with traffic movement.

Based on the 1951-1980 period, the average first occurrence of 32 degrees Fahrenheit in the fall is October 30 and the average last occurrence in the spring is April 3.

Fort Smith Regional Airport *Sebastian County*   Elevation: 446 ft.   Latitude: 35° 20' N   Longitude: 94° 22' W

	JAN	FEB	MAR	APR	MAY	JUN	JUL	AUG	SEP	OCT	NOV	DEC	YEAR
Mean Maximum Temp. (°F)	47.9	54.6	63.9	73.3	80.0	87.8	92.9	92.4	84.8	74.8	61.6	51.5	72.1
Mean Temp. (°F)	37.4	43.1	51.9	60.8	69.0	77.1	81.8	81.0	73.6	62.2	50.2	41.1	60.8
Mean Minimum Temp. (°F)	26.8	31.6	39.9	48.3	58.0	66.5	70.6	69.5	62.2	49.5	38.8	30.7	49.4
Extreme Maximum Temp. (°F)	79	82	94	95	97	103	109	108	109	94	86	80	109
Extreme Minimum Temp. (°F)	-10	-5	10	22	37	47	50	51	36	24	8	-5	-10
Days Maximum Temp. ≥ 90°F	0	0	0	1	2	13	23	22	10	1	0	0	72
Days Maximum Temp. ≤ 32°F	3	2	0	0	0	0	0	0	0	0	0	2	7
Days Minimum Temp. ≤ 32°F	23	15	7	1	0	0	0	0	0	1	8	18	73
Days Minimum Temp. ≤ 0°F	0	0	0	0	0	0	0	0	0	0	0	0	0
Heating Degree Days (base 65°F)	850	612	407	165	32	1	0	0	22	142	443	734	3,408
Cooling Degree Days (base 65°F)	0	1	10	46	170	389	543	518	288	64	6	1	2,036
Mean Precipitation (in.)	2.33	2.62	3.95	4.15	5.20	4.09	3.12	2.67	3.75	4.10	4.62	3.32	43.92
Maximum Precipitation (in.)	11.3	7.9	8.5	10.3	13.4	10.4	10.4	6.6	9.0	12.0	13.9	10.1	61.2
Minimum Precipitation (in.)	0.2	0.5	0.8	0.6	0.8	0.4	0.2	0.4	0.1	trace	0.6	0.3	26.4
Maximum 24-hr. Precipitation (in.)	4.8	3.2	3.6	5.1	4.3	3.3	5.7	5.1	2.9	5.3	6.8	3.6	6.8
Days With ≥ 0.1" Precipitation	5	4	6	6	7	6	5	4	6	5	6	5	65
Days With ≥ 1.0" Precipitation	1	1	1	1	2	1	1	1	1	1	2	1	14
Mean Snowfall (in.)	3.0	1.6	0.6	trace	trace	trace	0.0	0.0	0.0	trace	0.5	0.9	6.6
Maximum Snowfall (in.)	13	12	5	trace	0	0	0	0	0	trace	5	7	22
Maximum 24-hr. Snowfall (in.)	11	6	4	trace	0	0	0	0	0	trace	4	7	11
Days With ≥ 1.0" Snow Depth	3	2	0	0	0	0	0	0	0	0	0	1	6
Thunderstorm Days	1	2	5	7	8	8	8	7	5	3	3	2	59
Foggy Days	11	9	8	6	8	7	6	9	9	9	9	10	101
Predominant Sky Cover	OVR	OVR	OVR	OVR	OVR	CLR	CLR	CLR	CLR	CLR	OVR	OVR	OVR
Mean Relative Humidity 6am (%)	81	81	79	82	88	89	89	89	89	87	83	82	85
Mean Relative Humidity 3pm (%)	55	50	46	46	52	52	49	47	48	45	48	53	49
Mean Dewpoint (°F)	28	31	37	47	58	66	69	67	61	50	38	31	49
Prevailing Wind Direction	ENE	ENE	ENE	E	ENE	ENE	ENE	ENE	ENE	ENE	ENE	ENE	ENE
Prevailing Wind Speed (mph)	8	8	8	9	7	6	7	7	7	7	7	8	7
Maximum Wind Gust (mph)	54	58	56	76	71	71	85	63	55	60	60	59	85

Little Rock Adams Field

Little Rock is located on the Arkansas River near the geographical center of the state. It is situated on the dividing line between the Ouachita Mountains to the west and the flat lowlands comprising the Mississippi River Valley to the east. Elevations range from 222 feet at the river level to 257 feet over much of the flat land, including the airport in the southeast, to near 600 feet in the hilly residential area of the western portions of the city. Two minor temperature variations are observed due to the terrain; somewhat lower minimum temperatures are observed in the airport vicinity and a slight downslope adiabatic heating effect accompanies airflow from the ridges and hills in the west and northwest.

The modified continental climate of Little Rock includes exposure to all of the North American air mass types. However, with its proximity to the Gulf of Mexico, the summer season is marked by prolonged periods of warm and humid weather. The growing season averages 233 days in which 62 percent of the normal precipitation occurs. Winters are mild, but polar and Arctic outbreaks are not uncommon.

Precipitation is fairly well distributed throughout the year. Summer rainfall is almost completely of the convective type. The driest period usually occurs in the late summer and early fall. Snow is almost negligible. Glaze and ice storms, although infrequent, are at times severe. Warm front weather in the winter and early spring, characterized by shallow surface cold air flow from the north under warm moist Gulf air, results in excellent conditions for the production of freezing precipitation.

Little Rock Adams Field *Pulaski County*   Elevation: 255 ft.   Latitude: 34° 45' N   Longitude: 92° 14' W

	JAN	FEB	MAR	APR	MAY	JUN	JUL	AUG	SEP	OCT	NOV	DEC	YEAR
Mean Maximum Temp. (°F)	49.3	55.3	63.9	73.0	81.1	89.1	92.7	91.8	85.2	74.9	62.2	53.0	72.6
Mean Temp. (°F)	39.9	45.0	53.4	61.8	70.4	78.6	82.4	81.2	74.6	63.3	51.9	43.7	62.2
Mean Minimum Temp. (°F)	30.5	34.6	42.8	50.6	59.6	68.1	72.1	70.5	63.9	51.7	41.7	34.4	51.7
Extreme Maximum Temp. (°F)	80	85	91	95	98	105	112	108	104	93	85	79	112
Extreme Minimum Temp. (°F)	-2	5	17	28	40	49	54	52	42	29	17	-1	-2
Days Maximum Temp. ≥ 90°F	0	0	0	0	3	16	23	21	10	1	0	0	74
Days Maximum Temp. ≤ 32°F	3	1	0	0	0	0	0	0	0	0	0	1	5
Days Minimum Temp. ≤ 32°F	19	11	4	1	0	0	0	0	0	0	5	14	54
Days Minimum Temp. ≤ 0°F	0	0	0	0	0	0	0	0	0	0	0	0	0
Heating Degree Days (base 65°F)	772	559	367	144	22	0	0	0	12	120	394	655	3,045
Cooling Degree Days (base 65°F)	0	1	14	54	200	425	566	528	311	75	9	3	2,186
Mean Precipitation (in.)	3.61	3.35	4.91	5.64	4.88	3.84	3.38	3.00	3.73	4.48	5.43	4.72	50.97
Maximum Precipitation (in.)	12.5	11.0	10.4	14.2	12.7	7.8	7.9	14.5	10.2	15.3	13.1	16.5	74.4
Minimum Precipitation (in.)	0.5	0.9	0.7	0.5	0.7	trace	0.1	trace	0.3	0.1	0.3	1.3	28.3
Maximum 24-hr. Precipitation (in.)	3.6	4.0	2.9	7.6	7.7	3.8	3.6	6.8	8.1	5.1	6.2	5.8	8.1
Days With ≥ 0.1" Precipitation	6	5	7	7	7	6	6	5	6	5	6	7	73
Days With ≥ 1.0" Precipitation	1	1	2	2	1	1	1	1	1	2	2	1	16
Mean Snowfall (in.)	2.1	1.3	0.6	trace	trace	trace	0.0	0.0	0.0	trace	0.3	0.1	4.4
Maximum Snowfall (in.)	14	10	7	trace	0	0	0	0	0	trace	5	10	33
Maximum 24-hr. Snowfall (in.)	11	9	5	trace	0	0	0	0	0	trace	4	10	11
Days With ≥ 1.0" Snow Depth	2	1	0	0	0	0	0	0	0	0	0	0	3
Thunderstorm Days	2	2	5	6	7	8	9	7	4	3	3	2	58
Foggy Days	14	12	11	10	13	11	12	14	15	13	12	13	150
Predominant Sky Cover	OVR	OVR	OVR	OVR	OVR	SCT	SCT	SCT	CLR	CLR	OVR	OVR	OVR
Mean Relative Humidity 6am (%)	80	80	78	82	87	87	88	88	88	86	82	81	84
Mean Relative Humidity 3pm (%)	58	53	50	51	54	53	54	52	52	48	52	57	53
Mean Dewpoint (°F)	30	33	40	49	59	67	70	69	62	51	41	33	51
Prevailing Wind Direction	WSW	N	S	S	S	SW	SW	SW	NE	WSW	S	WSW	SW
Prevailing Wind Speed (mph)	8	10	9	9	9	8	8	8	8	7	9	8	8
Maximum Wind Gust (mph)	62	63	46	52	58	60	56	47	47	45	59	60	63

Alicia *Lawrence County*   Elevation: 255 ft.   Latitude: 35° 54' N   Longitude: 91° 05' W

	JAN	FEB	MAR	APR	MAY	JUN	JUL	AUG	SEP	OCT	NOV	DEC	YEAR
Mean Maximum Temp. (°F)	46.4	52.8	62.2	73.1	81.3	89.7	93.6	92.1	84.9	75.1	60.8	50.4	71.9
Mean Temp. (°F)	37.1	42.4	51.3	61.1	69.6	78.2	81.9	80.2	72.7	61.9	50.2	41.2	60.6
Mean Minimum Temp. (°F)	27.8	32.0	40.3	49.0	57.9	66.7	70.2	68.1	60.5	48.6	39.4	31.9	49.4
Extreme Maximum Temp. (°F)	75	80	87	96	97	103	113	107	104	95	84	77	113
Extreme Minimum Temp. (°F)	-10	-1	13	26	34	44	46	48	35	25	12	-6	-10
Days Maximum Temp. ≥ 90°F	0	0	0	0	3	16	24	21	9	1	0	0	74
Days Maximum Temp. ≤ 32°F	4	1	0	0	0	0	0	0	0	0	0	2	7
Days Minimum Temp. ≤ 32°F	21	15	7	1	0	0	0	0	0	1	7	16	68
Days Minimum Temp. ≤ 0°F	0	0	0	0	0	0	0	0	0	0	0	0	0
Heating Degree Days (base 65°F)	859	631	426	162	28	0	0	0	21	149	444	734	3,454
Cooling Degree Days (base 65°F)	0	0	7	47	185	408	552	493	269	60	4	0	2,025
Mean Precipitation (in.)	3.22	3.30	4.53	4.65	4.43	3.20	2.85	3.05	3.57	3.74	4.68	4.52	45.74
Days With ≥ 0.1" Precipitation	5	5	7	6	7	5	5	5	5	5	6	6	67
Days With ≥ 1.0" Precipitation	1	1	1	2	1	1	1	1	1	1	2	1	14
Mean Snowfall (in.)	2.1	1.4	0.6	0.0	0.0	0.0	0.0	0.0	0.0	0.0	trace	0.5	4.6
Days With ≥ 1.0" Snow Depth	na	0	0	0	0	0	0	0	0	0	0	0	na

Alum Fork *Saline County*   Elevation: 695 ft.   Latitude: 34° 48' N   Longitude: 92° 51' W

	JAN	FEB	MAR	APR	MAY	JUN	JUL	AUG	SEP	OCT	NOV	DEC	YEAR
Mean Maximum Temp. (°F)	50.8	57.1	65.5	74.5	80.6	87.5	92.4	91.4	84.8	75.6	62.7	53.9	73.1
Mean Temp. (°F)	40.4	45.2	53.4	61.9	69.2	76.5	80.9	79.8	73.5	63.3	52.0	43.8	61.7
Mean Minimum Temp. (°F)	29.9	33.3	41.2	49.2	57.8	65.4	69.4	68.0	62.1	51.1	41.2	33.6	50.2
Extreme Maximum Temp. (°F)	77	85	91	95	96	99	110	106	104	94	85	78	110
Extreme Minimum Temp. (°F)	-3	0	12	27	37	47	52	50	37	28	13	-3	-3
Days Maximum Temp. ≥ 90°F	0	0	0	0	1	11	22	21	9	1	0	0	65
Days Maximum Temp. ≤ 32°F	2	1	0	0	0	0	0	0	0	0	0	1	4
Days Minimum Temp. ≤ 32°F	19	13	6	1	0	0	0	0	0	0	6	15	60
Days Minimum Temp. ≤ 0°F	0	0	0	0	0	0	0	0	0	0	0	0	0
Heating Degree Days (base 65°F)	757	553	365	140	25	1	0	0	15	117	390	653	3,016
Cooling Degree Days (base 65°F)	1	1	12	52	162	359	505	475	277	68	6	1	1,919
Mean Precipitation (in.)	3.60	3.97	5.43	5.60	5.53	4.41	3.77	3.04	3.86	5.15	5.78	5.27	55.41
Days With ≥ 0.1" Precipitation	6	6	7	7	8	6	6	5	6	5	7	7	76
Days With ≥ 1.0" Precipitation	1	1	2	2	2	1	1	1	1	2	2	2	18
Mean Snowfall (in.)	1.3	0.6	0.1	trace	0.0	0.0	0.0	0.0	0.0	0.0	0.1	0.2	2.3
Days With ≥ 1.0" Snow Depth	0	1	0	0	0	0	0	0	0	0	0	0	1

Arkadelphia 2 N *Clark County*   Elevation: 193 ft.   Latitude: 34° 09' N   Longitude: 93° 03' W

	JAN	FEB	MAR	APR	MAY	JUN	JUL	AUG	SEP	OCT	NOV	DEC	YEAR
Mean Maximum Temp. (°F)	52.0	58.6	67.3	75.9	82.2	89.0	92.9	92.2	85.9	75.9	63.6	55.0	74.2
Mean Minimum Temp. (°F)	41.3	46.6	54.7	62.7	70.2	77.5	81.3	80.4	74.0	62.8	52.3	44.3	62.3
Mean Minimum Temp. (°F)	30.5	34.4	41.9	49.4	58.2	65.9	69.7	68.5	61.9	49.6	40.9	33.6	50.4
Extreme Maximum Temp. (°F)	79	87	92	95	94	100	106	105	104	93	84	79	106
Extreme Minimum Temp. (°F)	1	5	14	25	38	46	53	48	34	26	13	0	0
Days Maximum Temp. ≥ 90°F	0	0	0	0	2	16	25	22	10	1	0	0	76
Days Maximum Temp. ≤ 32°F	1	1	0	0	0	0	0	0	0	0	0	1	3
Days Minimum Temp. ≤ 32°F	19	13	6	1	0	0	0	0	0	1	7	15	62
Days Minimum Temp. ≤ 0°F	0	0	0	0	0	0	0	0	0	0	0	0	0
Heating Degree Days (base 65°F)	729	516	330	122	19	0	0	0	14	127	383	636	2,876
Cooling Degree Days (base 65°F)	0	2	16	59	187	386	520	494	287	66	9	3	2,029
Mean Precipitation (in.)	3.94	3.67	5.07	4.72	5.75	4.21	4.14	2.91	3.61	4.76	5.70	4.93	53.41
Days With ≥ 0.1" Precipitation	6	6	7	5	7	6	6	4	5	5	6	6	69
Days With ≥ 1.0" Precipitation	1	1	2	2	2	1	1	1	1	2	2	1	17
Mean Snowfall (in.)	0.9	0.7	trace	0.0	0.0	0.0	0.0	0.0	0.0	0.0	trace	0.4	2.0
Days With ≥ 1.0" Snow Depth	1	1	0	0	0	0	0	0	0	0	0	1	3

Arkansas Post *Arkansas County*   Elevation: 193 ft.   Latitude: 34° 01' N   Longitude: 91° 21' W

	JAN	FEB	MAR	APR	MAY	JUN	JUL	AUG	SEP	OCT	NOV	DEC	YEAR
Mean Maximum Temp. (°F)	50.7	57.1	66.0	74.6	82.1	89.1	92.3	91.0	85.8	76.1	63.0	54.1	73.5
Mean Temp. (°F)	41.6	47.0	55.3	63.8	71.7	78.9	82.2	80.7	75.1	64.6	53.4	45.3	63.3
Mean Minimum Temp. (°F)	32.5	36.9	44.7	53.0	61.1	68.7	71.9	70.3	64.3	53.0	43.8	36.5	53.0
Extreme Maximum Temp. (°F)	83	82	87	93	98	102	106	103	103	94	83	81	106
Extreme Minimum Temp. (°F)	2	9	18	29	41	51	54	51	42	30	11	1	1
Days Maximum Temp. ≥ 90°F	0	0	0	0	3	15	23	21	9	1	0	0	72
Days Maximum Temp. ≤ 32°F	2	1	0	0	0	0	0	0	0	0	0	1	4
Days Minimum Temp. ≤ 32°F	16	10	3	0	0	0	0	0	0	0	4	11	44
Days Minimum Temp. ≤ 0°F	0	0	0	0	0	0	0	0	0	0	0	0	0
Heating Degree Days (base 65°F)	721	502	311	109	13	0	0	0	9	100	353	605	2,723
Cooling Degree Days (base 65°F)	0	3	15	76	227	429	548	505	320	87	11	3	2,224
Mean Precipitation (in.)	4.69	4.50	5.79	4.86	4.89	3.84	3.46	2.76	3.16	3.97	4.87	5.11	51.90
Days With ≥ 0.1" Precipitation	7	6	7	6	7	5	5	4	4	4	6	6	67
Days With ≥ 1.0" Precipitation	2	2	2	2	2	1	1	1	1	1	2	2	19
Mean Snowfall (in.)	1.5	0.7	0.2	trace	0.0	0.0	0.0	0.0	0.0	0.0	trace	0.3	2.7
Days With ≥ 1.0" Snow Depth	1	1	0	0	0	0	0	0	0	0	0	0	2

Batesville Livestock *Independence County*   Elevation: 570 ft.   Latitude: 35° 50' N   Longitude: 91° 46' W

	JAN	FEB	MAR	APR	MAY	JUN	JUL	AUG	SEP	OCT	NOV	DEC	YEAR
Mean Maximum Temp. (°F)	48.1	54.8	63.4	73.5	80.2	87.7	92.8	91.8	84.9	75.1	61.5	51.5	72.1
Mean Temp. (°F)	37.7	43.3	51.6	60.9	68.1	76.0	80.8	79.3	72.5	62.0	50.8	41.5	60.4
Mean Minimum Temp. (°F)	27.3	31.7	39.7	48.1	56.0	64.2	68.7	66.7	60.0	48.8	40.1	31.4	48.6
Extreme Maximum Temp. (°F)	78	83	87	94	96	105	111	107	105	93	86	77	111
Extreme Minimum Temp. (°F)	-11	-3	10	24	32	44	51	44	34	22	10	-9	-11
Days Maximum Temp. ≥ 90°F	0	0	0	0	2	12	23	20	9	1	0	0	67
Days Maximum Temp. ≤ 32°F	4	1	0	0	0	0	0	0	0	0	0	1	6
Days Minimum Temp. ≤ 32°F	21	15	8	2	0	0	0	0	0	1	7	17	71
Days Minimum Temp. ≤ 0°F	0	0	0	0	0	0	0	0	0	0	0	0	0
Heating Degree Days (base 65°F)	839	607	419	167	40	2	0	0	22	147	425	722	3,390
Cooling Degree Days (base 65°F)	0	1	10	51	154	354	518	474	265	63	7	1	1,898
Mean Precipitation (in.)	2.85	3.26	4.64	4.54	4.68	3.41	3.26	3.29	3.97	4.02	5.22	4.07	47.21
Days With ≥ 0.1" Precipitation	5	5	6	6	8	5	5	5	5	5	6	6	67
Days With ≥ 1.0" Precipitation	1	1	1	1	1	1	1	1	1	1	2	1	13
Mean Snowfall (in.)	2.8	2.4	0.7	trace	0.0	0.0	0.0	0.0	0.0	trace	1.0	0.7	7.6
Days With ≥ 1.0" Snow Depth	3	3	0	0	0	0	0	0	0	0	0	1	7

Batesville Lock & Dam 1 *Independence County*   Elevation: 259 ft.   Latitude: 35° 45' N   Longitude: 91° 38' W

	JAN	FEB	MAR	APR	MAY	JUN	JUL	AUG	SEP	OCT	NOV	DEC	YEAR
Mean Maximum Temp. (°F)	46.6	53.2	61.9	71.9	80.2	88.1	93.0	91.3	83.8	73.0	60.4	50.8	71.2
Mean Temp. (°F)	36.5	41.9	50.5	59.8	68.4	76.4	81.0	79.2	72.1	60.7	49.7	40.9	59.8
Mean Minimum Temp. (°F)	26.4	30.6	39.1	47.5	56.5	64.6	69.0	67.1	60.3	48.3	39.0	31.0	48.3
Extreme Maximum Temp. (°F)	77	82	87	93	98	104	112	110	103	95	84	77	112
Extreme Minimum Temp. (°F)	-11	-5	13	23	33	43	48	46	36	24	9	-6	-11
Days Maximum Temp. ≥ 90°F	0	0	0	0	2	13	24	20	8	0	0	0	67
Days Maximum Temp. ≤ 32°F	4	2	0	0	0	0	0	0	0	0	0	2	8
Days Minimum Temp. ≤ 32°F	23	16	9	2	0	0	0	0	0	1	9	18	78
Days Minimum Temp. ≤ 0°F	1	0	0	0	0	0	0	0	0	0	0	0	1
Heating Degree Days (base 65°F)	875	647	449	193	41	1	0	0	26	177	457	740	3,606
Cooling Degree Days (base 65°F)	0	0	7	37	153	355	515	458	241	45	5	1	1,817
Mean Precipitation (in.)	3.16	3.20	4.58	4.79	4.80	3.48	3.20	3.27	3.75	4.23	5.28	4.57	48.31
Days With ≥ 0.1" Precipitation	6	5	7	7	7	6	5	6	5	5	6	7	72
Days With ≥ 1.0" Precipitation	1	1	1	2	2	1	1	1	1	2	2	1	16
Mean Snowfall (in.)	2.6	2.7	0.4	trace	0.0	0.0	0.0	0.0	0.0	0.0	0.6	0.9	7.2
Days With ≥ 1.0" Snow Depth	3	2	0	0	0	0	0	0	0	0	0	1	6

Beedeville 4 NE *Jackson County*   Elevation: 239 ft.   Latitude: 35° 28' N   Longitude: 91° 03' W

	JAN	FEB	MAR	APR	MAY	JUN	JUL	AUG	SEP	OCT	NOV	DEC	YEAR
Mean Maximum Temp. (°F)	45.9	52.6	61.9	72.5	80.8	88.6	92.9	91.2	84.5	74.4	60.6	50.7	71.4
Mean Temp. (°F)	37.4	42.9	51.6	61.2	69.9	77.9	81.9	79.5	72.6	61.8	50.6	41.8	60.8
Mean Minimum Temp. (°F)	28.8	33.2	41.2	49.9	59.0	67.1	71.0	67.8	60.6	49.2	40.5	32.9	50.1
Extreme Maximum Temp. (°F)	75	78	84	94	96	104	112	106	104	93	85	78	112
Extreme Minimum Temp. (°F)	-6	2	13	27	34	49	56	51	36	25	12	-5	-6
Days Maximum Temp. ≥ 90°F	0	0	0	0	3	14	23	21	8	1	0	0	70
Days Maximum Temp. ≤ 32°F	4	2	0	0	0	0	0	0	0	0	0	1	7
Days Minimum Temp. ≤ 32°F	20	13	6	1	0	0	0	0	0	1	6	16	63
Days Minimum Temp. ≤ 0°F	0	0	0	0	0	0	0	0	0	0	0	0	0
Heating Degree Days (base 65°F)	850	617	415	159	27	0	0	0	22	149	433	713	3,385
Cooling Degree Days (base 65°F)	0	0	8	47	188	398	540	458	248	55	5	1	1,948
Mean Precipitation (in.)	3.83	3.41	4.97	5.18	4.93	3.88	2.66	2.43	3.74	3.77	5.19	4.85	48.84
Days With ≥ 0.1" Precipitation	5	4	6	6	6	5	4	4	4	5	6	5	60
Days With ≥ 1.0" Precipitation	1	1	2	2	2	1	1	1	1	1	2	2	17
Mean Snowfall (in.)	1.7	1.1	0.2	trace	0.0	0.0	0.0	0.0	0.0	trace	0.3	0.1	3.4
Days With ≥ 1.0" Snow Depth	na	0	0	0	0	0	0	0	0	0	0	0	na

Benton *Saline County*   Elevation: 308 ft.   Latitude: 34° 34' N   Longitude: 92° 36' W

	JAN	FEB	MAR	APR	MAY	JUN	JUL	AUG	SEP	OCT	NOV	DEC	YEAR
Mean Maximum Temp. (°F)	52.2	59.0	66.9	75.4	81.9	88.5	93.0	92.2	85.8	76.3	63.8	55.3	74.2
Mean Temp. (°F)	40.7	46.3	54.2	62.2	69.7	76.9	81.1	79.7	73.4	62.7	51.9	44.0	61.9
Mean Minimum Temp. (°F)	29.1	33.5	41.5	48.9	57.4	65.2	69.0	67.1	61.0	49.0	39.9	32.8	49.5
Extreme Maximum Temp. (°F)	79	87	91	95	97	103	112	108	104	94	84	78	112
Extreme Minimum Temp. (°F)	-3	1	14	23	36	49	50	46	36	20	7	-2	-3
Days Maximum Temp. ≥ 90°F	0	0	0	0	2	13	24	22	10	1	0	0	72
Days Maximum Temp. ≤ 32°F	2	1	0	0	0	0	0	0	0	0	0	1	4
Days Minimum Temp. ≤ 32°F	20	13	6	2	0	0	0	0	0	1	8	16	66
Days Minimum Temp. ≤ 0°F	0	0	0	0	0	0	0	0	0	0	0	0	0
Heating Degree Days (base 65°F)	747	524	343	135	24	0	0	0	17	131	394	646	2,961
Cooling Degree Days (base 65°F)	0	2	15	58	183	378	524	481	282	67	7	2	1,999
Mean Precipitation (in.)	3.66	3.40	5.03	5.39	4.94	4.16	4.16	3.02	4.47	4.63	5.80	5.00	53.66
Days With ≥ 0.1" Precipitation	6	5	7	6	7	6	5	4	6	5	7	6	70
Days With ≥ 1.0" Precipitation	1	1	2	2	2	2	1	1	1	2	2	2	19
Mean Snowfall (in.)	1.5	1.5	0.1	trace	0.0	0.0	0.0	0.0	0.0	0.0	0.3	0.1	3.5
Days With ≥ 1.0" Snow Depth	1	0	0	0	0	0	0	0	0	0	0	0	1

Bentonville 4 S *Benton County*   Elevation: 1,217 ft.   Latitude: 36° 19' N   Longitude: 94° 13' W

	JAN	FEB	MAR	APR	MAY	JUN	JUL	AUG	SEP	OCT	NOV	DEC	YEAR
Mean Maximum Temp. (°F)	43.6	49.7	58.5	68.6	75.7	83.5	88.9	88.6	80.8	70.7	57.4	48.0	67.8
Mean Temp. (°F)	32.8	38.1	46.7	56.2	64.3	72.6	77.6	76.5	69.0	57.9	46.2	37.3	56.3
Mean Minimum Temp. (°F)	22.0	26.4	34.9	43.7	52.9	61.7	66.2	64.3	57.1	45.1	35.0	26.6	44.7
Extreme Maximum Temp. (°F)	74	86	87	90	93	98	105	104	104	90	82	76	105
Extreme Minimum Temp. (°F)	-15	-16	2	20	32	40	45	47	30	18	5	-15	-16
Days Maximum Temp. ≥ 90°F	0	0	0	0	0	4	15	14	5	0	0	0	38
Days Maximum Temp. ≤ 32°F	6	3	1	0	0	0	0	0	0	0	1	3	14
Days Minimum Temp. ≤ 32°F	26	21	13	4	0	0	0	0	0	3	13	23	103
Days Minimum Temp. ≤ 0°F	2	1	0	0	0	0	0	0	0	0	0	1	4
Heating Degree Days (base 65°F)	992	753	563	278	94	9	1	2	55	238	558	851	4,394
Cooling Degree Days (base 65°F)	0	0	3	18	80	251	407	377	180	25	2	0	1,343
Mean Precipitation (in.)	2.18	2.49	4.46	4.30	5.35	4.95	3.04	3.38	4.95	3.78	4.74	3.45	47.07
Days With ≥ 0.1" Precipitation	4	5	7	7	8	7	5	5	7	6	6	5	72
Days With ≥ 1.0" Precipitation	0	1	1	1	2	2	1	1	2	1	2	1	15
Mean Snowfall (in.)	*3.6*	2.5	2.3	trace	0.0	0.0	0.0	0.0	0.0	trace	0.8	1.2	*10.4*
Days With ≥ 1.0" Snow Depth	4	3	1	0	0	0	0	0	0	0	0	1	9

Blakely Mountain Dam *Garland County*   Elevation: 423 ft.   Latitude: 34° 34' N   Longitude: 93° 12' W

	JAN	FEB	MAR	APR	MAY	JUN	JUL	AUG	SEP	OCT	NOV	DEC	YEAR
Mean Maximum Temp. (°F)	*49.3*	55.1	63.5	73.1	*79.5*	87.5	92.6	91.5	84.6	74.3	61.8	53.7	72.2
Mean Temp. (°F)	*37.9*	42.3	50.4	58.9	*66.6*	74.7	*79.5*	78.1	71.8	60.5	*49.5*	42.2	*59.4*
Mean Minimum Temp. (°F)	26.5	29.5	37.2	44.6	*53.6*	62.2	*66.4*	64.8	58.9	46.7	*37.4*	30.6	*46.5*
Extreme Maximum Temp. (°F)	77	84	87	95	93	102	109	111	104	94	85	77	111
Extreme Minimum Temp. (°F)	2	1	12	24	34	45	49	45	35	25	12	0	0
Days Maximum Temp. ≥ 90°F	0	0	0	0	1	12	21	20	8	1	0	0	63
Days Maximum Temp. ≤ 32°F	2	1	0	0	0	0	0	0	0	0	0	1	4
Days Minimum Temp. ≤ 32°F	22	18	10	3	0	0	0	0	0	1	10	19	83
Days Minimum Temp. ≤ 0°F	0	0	0	0	0	0	0	0	0	0	0	0	0
Heating Degree Days (base 65°F)	*834*	635	452	203	*54*	2	*0*	0	24	173	*462*	700	*3,539*
Cooling Degree Days (base 65°F)	*0*	0	5	25	*110*	307	*465*	423	231	*42*	*3*	1	*1,612*
Mean Precipitation (in.)	3.50	3.96	5.33	5.60	5.70	4.65	4.44	2.97	3.91	5.31	6.29	5.19	56.85
Days With ≥ 0.1" Precipitation	6	5	7	6	7	6	5	5	5	5	6	6	69
Days With ≥ 1.0" Precipitation	1	1	2	2	2	2	1	1	1	2	2	1	18
Mean Snowfall (in.)	*0.6*	1.0	0.1	0.0	0.0	0.0	0.0	0.0	0.0	0.0	0.1	trace	*1.8*
Days With ≥ 1.0" Snow Depth	na	*0*	0	0	0	0	0	0	0	0	0	0	na

Blue Mountain Dam *Yell County*   Elevation: 423 ft.   Latitude: 35° 07' N   Longitude: 93° 39' W

	JAN	FEB	MAR	APR	MAY	JUN	JUL	AUG	SEP	OCT	NOV	DEC	YEAR
Mean Maximum Temp. (°F)	47.6	54.4	63.1	72.9	79.7	87.8	93.2	92.7	84.6	73.7	60.7	51.3	71.8
Mean Temp. (°F)	37.5	42.8	51.4	60.4	68.2	76.2	81.0	80.0	72.8	61.3	49.8	41.1	60.2
Mean Minimum Temp. (°F)	27.2	31.2	39.6	47.8	56.8	64.6	68.8	67.4	60.9	48.8	38.8	30.8	48.6
Extreme Maximum Temp. (°F)	77	82	90	95	95	104	111	112	107	96	84	80	112
Extreme Minimum Temp. (°F)	-3	3	11	26	37	46	50	49	36	22	12	-3	-3
Days Maximum Temp. ≥ 90°F	0	0	0	0	2	13	23	22	10	1	0	0	71
Days Maximum Temp. ≤ 32°F	3	1	0	0	0	0	0	0	0	0	0	1	5
Days Minimum Temp. ≤ 32°F	23	16	7	1	0	0	0	0	0	1	8	19	75
Days Minimum Temp. ≤ 0°F	0	0	0	0	0	0	0	0	0	0	0	0	0
Heating Degree Days (base 65°F)	847	621	424	177	41	1	0	0	24	165	457	736	3,493
Cooling Degree Days (base 65°F)	0	1	10	44	149	353	513	485	266	55	6	1	1,883
Mean Precipitation (in.)	2.91	3.07	4.61	4.33	5.51	3.73	3.39	2.62	3.76	4.04	4.84	4.30	47.11
Days With ≥ 0.1" Precipitation	6	5	7	6	7	6	5	5	6	5	6	6	70
Days With ≥ 1.0" Precipitation	1	1	1	1	2	1	1	1	1	1	2	1	14
Mean Snowfall (in.)	2.4	1.4	0.2	trace	0.0	0.0	0.0	0.0	0.0	0.0	0.3	0.6	4.9
Days With ≥ 1.0" Snow Depth	2	1	0	0	0	0	0	0	0	0	0	0	3

Blytheville *Mississippi County*   Elevation: 249 ft.   Latitude: 35° 55' N   Longitude: 89° 54' W

	JAN	FEB	MAR	APR	MAY	JUN	JUL	AUG	SEP	OCT	NOV	DEC	YEAR
Mean Maximum Temp. (°F)	44.8	50.5	60.1	71.1	80.9	89.0	92.5	90.1	84.2	73.4	60.3	49.7	70.5
Mean Temp. (°F)	36.6	41.5	50.6	60.9	70.6	78.7	82.4	80.0	73.6	62.3	51.1	41.5	60.8
Mean Minimum Temp. (°F)	28.4	32.5	41.3	50.8	60.3	68.3	72.2	69.7	62.9	51.2	42.0	33.3	51.1
Extreme Maximum Temp. (°F)	79	78	85	94	98	103	108	105	100	92	85	79	108
Extreme Minimum Temp. (°F)	-14	-1	11	29	40	50	53	51	41	28	16	-7	-14
Days Maximum Temp. ≥ 90°F	0	0	0	0	*3*	15	23	18	8	0	0	0	*67*
Days Maximum Temp. ≤ 32°F	5	3	0	0	0	0	0	0	0	0	0	2	10
Days Minimum Temp. ≤ 32°F	20	14	5	0	0	0	0	0	0	0	5	15	59
Days Minimum Temp. ≤ 0°F	0	0	0	0	0	0	0	0	0	0	0	0	0
Heating Degree Days (base 65°F)	872	657	447	174	28	0	0	0	16	146	420	721	3,481
Cooling Degree Days (base 65°F)	0	0	10	55	202	423	551	482	273	68	7	1	2,072
Mean Precipitation (in.)	3.37	3.89	4.90	5.41	4.87	4.56	4.03	3.00	3.37	3.80	4.72	4.85	50.77
Days With ≥ 0.1" Precipitation	6	6	8	7	7	7	6	4	5	5	6	7	74
Days With ≥ 1.0" Precipitation	1	1	1	2	2	1	1	1	1	1	1	1	14
Mean Snowfall (in.)	na	*0.5*	0.4	0.0	0.0	0.0	0.0	0.0	0.0	0.0	trace	0.2	na
Days With ≥ 1.0" Snow Depth	na	*0*	0	0	0	0	0	0	0	0	0	0	na

Brinkley Airport *Monroe County*   Elevation: 193 ft.   Latitude: 34° 53' N   Longitude: 91° 11' W

	JAN	FEB	MAR	APR	MAY	JUN	JUL	AUG	SEP	OCT	NOV	DEC	YEAR
Mean Maximum Temp. (°F)	47.0	53.0	61.6	71.5	80.0	87.9	91.4	90.1	84.1	74.2	61.0	51.1	71.1
Mean Temp. (°F)	38.1	43.1	51.3	60.7	69.6	77.6	81.2	79.4	72.8	61.7	50.8	42.1	60.7
Mean Minimum Temp. (°F)	29.1	33.1	41.0	49.7	59.1	67.3	71.0	68.5	61.5	49.0	40.0	33.1	50.2
Extreme Maximum Temp. (°F)	80	80	83	92	98	105	105	104	101	95	87	78	105
Extreme Minimum Temp. (°F)	-4	3	16	28	40	50	53	50	40	28	14	-3	-4
Days Maximum Temp. ≥ 90°F	0	0	0	0	2	13	21	18	9	1	0	0	64
Days Maximum Temp. ≤ 32°F	4	2	0	0	0	0	0	0	0	0	0	2	8
Days Minimum Temp. ≤ 32°F	20	13	6	1	0	0	0	0	0	0	6	16	62
Days Minimum Temp. ≤ 0°F	0	0	0	0	0	0	0	0	0	0	0	0	0
Heating Degree Days (base 65°F)	828	612	426	174	32	0	0	0	22	155	425	704	3,378
Cooling Degree Days (base 65°F)	0	1	9	48	184	396	520	465	265	61	7	1	1,957
Mean Precipitation (in.)	3.78	3.87	4.90	5.32	5.57	4.00	3.36	2.85	3.05	3.71	4.56	4.53	49.50
Days With ≥ 0.1" Precipitation	6	6	8	7	7	6	5	4	5	5	6	6	71
Days With ≥ 1.0" Precipitation	1	1	1	2	2	1	1	1	1	1	2	2	16
Mean Snowfall (in.)	1.9	1.3	0.4	trace	0.0	0.0	0.0	0.0	0.0	0.0	0.2	0.2	4.0
Days With ≥ 1.0" Snow Depth	2	1	0	0	0	0	0	0	0	0	0	0	3

Cabot 4 SW *Pulaski County*   Elevation: 278 ft.   Latitude: 34° 57' N   Longitude: 92° 05' W

	JAN	FEB	MAR	APR	MAY	JUN	JUL	AUG	SEP	OCT	NOV	DEC	YEAR
Mean Maximum Temp. (°F)	48.8	55.1	63.6	72.6	79.5	87.1	91.0	90.0	84.0	74.1	61.4	52.2	71.6
Mean Temp. (°F)	38.9	44.1	52.6	60.9	68.6	76.4	80.1	78.7	72.7	61.6	50.7	42.5	60.6
Mean Minimum Temp. (°F)	28.8	33.2	41.5	49.0	57.6	65.6	69.1	67.3	61.2	49.0	39.9	32.7	49.6
Extreme Maximum Temp. (°F)	80	83	91	93	98	103	112	106	104	92	84	78	112
Extreme Minimum Temp. (°F)	-5	-1	11	24	36	46	51	49	36	24	11	-7	-7
Days Maximum Temp. ≥ 90°F	0	0	0	0	1	11	19	17	7	1	0	0	56
Days Maximum Temp. ≤ 32°F	3	1	0	0	0	0	0	0	0	0	0	1	5
Days Minimum Temp. ≤ 32°F	20	14	6	1	0	0	0	0	0	1	8	16	66
Days Minimum Temp. ≤ 0°F	0	0	0	0	0	0	0	0	0	0	0	0	0
Heating Degree Days (base 65°F)	804	584	390	165	34	1	0	0	20	155	430	693	3,276
Cooling Degree Days (base 65°F)	0	1	11	43	151	349	470	431	250	52	5	2	1,765
Mean Precipitation (in.)	3.50	3.42	5.08	5.06	5.14	3.80	3.31	3.00	3.31	4.27	5.81	4.72	50.42
Days With ≥ 0.1" Precipitation	6	6	8	7	7	6	5	5	5	5	7	6	73
Days With ≥ 1.0" Precipitation	1	1	2	2	2	1	1	1	1	2	2	1	17
Mean Snowfall (in.)	2.0	1.5	0.4	trace	0.0	0.0	0.0	0.0	0.0	trace	0.4	0.4	4.7
Days With ≥ 1.0" Snow Depth	2	1	0	0	0	0	0	0	0	0	0	0	3

Calico Rock 2 WSW *Izard County*   Elevation: 347 ft.   Latitude: 36° 07' N   Longitude: 92° 10' W

	JAN	FEB	MAR	APR	MAY	JUN	JUL	AUG	SEP	OCT	NOV	DEC	YEAR
Mean Maximum Temp. (°F)	47.3	53.6	62.9	73.1	79.9	87.4	92.7	91.4	83.8	73.8	60.5	51.0	71.4
Mean Temp. (°F)	35.6	40.5	49.0	58.3	66.1	73.8	78.5	77.1	70.1	59.2	48.2	39.6	58.0
Mean Minimum Temp. (°F)	23.9	27.4	35.3	43.5	52.2	60.2	64.2	62.8	56.3	44.5	35.8	28.1	44.5
Extreme Maximum Temp. (°F)	77	85	90	95	96	103	111	110	103	95	87	80	111
Extreme Minimum Temp. (°F)	-15	-7	6	19	30	40	45	40	31	19	4	-8	-15
Days Maximum Temp. ≥ 90°F	0	0	0	0	2	12	23	20	8	1	0	0	66
Days Maximum Temp. ≤ 32°F	4	2	0	0	0	0	0	0	0	0	0	2	8
Days Minimum Temp. ≤ 32°F	24	20	14	5	0	0	0	0	0	4	13	21	101
Days Minimum Temp. ≤ 0°F	1	0	0	0	0	0	0	0	0	0	0	0	1
Heating Degree Days (base 65°F)	904	686	494	226	65	4	0	1	37	206	501	781	3,905
Cooling Degree Days (base 65°F)	1	0	6	28	105	276	429	388	190	34	3	1	1,461
Mean Precipitation (in.)	2.68	3.02	4.70	4.45	4.61	3.77	3.05	3.08	4.25	3.70	4.84	4.16	46.31
Days With ≥ 0.1" Precipitation	6	5	7	7	8	6	5	5	6	5	6	6	72
Days With ≥ 1.0" Precipitation	1	1	1	2	2	1	1	1	2	1	2	1	16
Mean Snowfall (in.)	*2.4*	*1.6*	0.9	trace	0.0	0.0	0.0	0.0	0.0	0.0	0.6	0.2	*5.7*
Days With ≥ 1.0" Snow Depth	*1*	*0*	0	0	0	0	0	0	0	0	0	0	*1*

Camden 1 *Ouachita County*   Elevation: 114 ft.   Latitude: 33° 36' N   Longitude: 92° 49' W

	JAN	FEB	MAR	APR	MAY	JUN	JUL	AUG	SEP	OCT	NOV	DEC	YEAR
Mean Maximum Temp. (°F)	52.7	58.7	67.1	75.6	81.8	88.9	92.5	92.1	85.9	76.2	64.9	56.3	74.4
Mean Temp. (°F)	41.4	46.3	54.4	62.5	70.1	77.7	81.4	80.4	73.9	62.9	52.4	45.0	62.4
Mean Minimum Temp. (°F)	30.2	33.8	41.7	49.4	58.4	66.5	70.3	68.6	62.0	49.5	39.9	33.6	50.3
Extreme Maximum Temp. (°F)	82	89	91	94	97	101	105	105	102	95	87	81	105
Extreme Minimum Temp. (°F)	2	2	16	26	40	47	55	49	38	27	15	1	1
Days Maximum Temp. ≥ 90°F	0	0	0	0	3	16	23	22	11	1	0	0	76
Days Maximum Temp. ≤ 32°F	2	1	0	0	0	0	0	0	0	0	0	1	4
Days Minimum Temp. ≤ 32°F	20	13	6	1	0	0	0	0	0	1	8	16	65
Days Minimum Temp. ≤ 0°F	0	0	0	0	0	0	0	0	0	0	0	0	0
Heating Degree Days (base 65°F)	725	525	337	130	24	0	0	0	16	133	382	616	2,888
Cooling Degree Days (base 65°F)	1	2	15	60	190	391	523	492	288	70	10	3	2,045
Mean Precipitation (in.)	4.52	4.23	5.14	4.69	4.57	4.58	4.03	3.01	3.58	4.53	5.01	4.99	52.88
Days With ≥ 0.1" Precipitation	7	6	7	6	7	6	6	5	5	5	7	7	74
Days With ≥ 1.0" Precipitation	2	2	2	2	1	1	1	1	1	1	2	2	18
Mean Snowfall (in.)	0.7	0.6	trace	0.0	0.0	trace	0.0	0.0	0.0	0.0	trace	0.3	1.6
Days With ≥ 1.0" Snow Depth	0	0	0	0	0	0	0	0	0	0	0	0	0

Clarendon *Monroe County*   Elevation: 177 ft.   Latitude: 34° 41' N   Longitude: 91° 12' W

	JAN	FEB	MAR	APR	MAY	JUN	JUL	AUG	SEP	OCT	NOV	DEC	YEAR
Mean Maximum Temp. (°F)	49.3	55.8	63.4	72.7	81.1	88.3	91.6	90.4	84.4	75.8	62.4	52.7	72.3
Mean Temp. (°F)	40.2	45.6	53.1	61.6	70.2	77.8	81.1	79.3	72.6	62.6	51.8	43.5	61.6
Mean Minimum Temp. (°F)	31.1	35.2	42.9	50.5	59.1	67.1	70.6	68.3	60.8	49.4	41.1	34.3	50.9
Extreme Maximum Temp. (°F)	78	85	86	93	95	102	106	101	101	94	85	79	106
Extreme Minimum Temp. (°F)	-4	3	15	28	39	50	53	49	36	28	16	-2	-4
Days Maximum Temp. ≥ 90°F	0	0	0	0	2	14	21	18	8	1	0	0	64
Days Maximum Temp. ≤ 32°F	3	1	0	0	0	0	0	0	0	0	0	1	5
Days Minimum Temp. ≤ 32°F	18	11	4	1	0	0	0	0	0	1	6	14	55
Days Minimum Temp. ≤ 0°F	0	0	0	0	0	0	0	0	0	0	0	0	0
Heating Degree Days (base 65°F)	761	544	374	154	23	0	0	0	22	139	398	662	3,077
Cooling Degree Days (base 65°F)	0	1	11	52	187	396	520	462	250	61	7	1	1,948
Mean Precipitation (in.)	3.83	3.96	5.43	5.42	4.89	4.08	3.80	2.63	3.16	4.22	5.03	5.31	51.76
Days With ≥ 0.1" Precipitation	6	5	8	6	7	6	5	4	5	5	7	7	71
Days With ≥ 1.0" Precipitation	1	1	1	2	2	1	1	1	1	2	2	2	17
Mean Snowfall (in.)	1.0	trace	0.0	0.0	0.0	0.0	0.0	0.0	0.0	0.0	trace	0.0	1.0
Days With ≥ 1.0" Snow Depth	na	0	0	0	0	0	0	0	0	0	0	0	na

Clarksville *Johnson County*   Elevation: 452 ft.   Latitude: 35° 29' N   Longitude: 93° 27' W

	JAN	FEB	MAR	APR	MAY	JUN	JUL	AUG	SEP	OCT	NOV	DEC	YEAR
Mean Maximum Temp. (°F)	47.8	54.4	63.4	72.7	79.6	87.2	92.7	92.0	84.9	73.9	61.4	51.5	71.8
Mean Temp. (°F)	36.0	41.3	50.2	59.1	67.3	75.4	80.3	79.3	72.3	60.1	48.9	39.9	59.2
Mean Minimum Temp. (°F)	24.1	28.2	37.0	45.5	54.9	63.5	67.9	66.4	59.6	46.3	36.5	28.1	46.5
Extreme Maximum Temp. (°F)	77	83	92	94	94	103	109	107	104	93	85	79	109
Extreme Minimum Temp. (°F)	-11	-1	9	23	34	44	50	46	35	20	6	-9	-11
Days Maximum Temp. ≥ 90°F	0	0	0	0	1	11	23	21	9	1	0	0	66
Days Maximum Temp. ≤ 32°F	3	1	0	0	0	0	0	0	0	0	0	1	5
Days Minimum Temp. ≤ 32°F	25	19	11	3	0	0	0	0	0	3	12	21	94
Days Minimum Temp. ≤ 0°F	1	0	0	0	0	0	0	0	0	0	0	0	1
Heating Degree Days (base 65°F)	893	662	456	204	52	2	0	0	28	188	479	774	3,738
Cooling Degree Days (base 65°F)	0	na	5	30	124	326	488	457	250	40	na	na	na
Mean Precipitation (in.)	2.56	3.15	4.57	4.61	5.31	4.16	2.81	2.74	4.34	4.42	4.95	4.56	48.18
Days With ≥ 0.1" Precipitation	5	5	7	7	8	7	5	5	6	6	6	6	73
Days With ≥ 1.0" Precipitation	1	1	1	2	2	1	1	1	1	1	2	1	15
Mean Snowfall (in.)	na	na	trace	trace	0.0	0.0	0.0	0.0	0.0	0.0	0.3	trace	na
Days With ≥ 1.0" Snow Depth	na	na	0	0	0	0	0	0	0	0	0	0	na

Conway *Faulkner County*   Elevation: 314 ft.   Latitude: 35° 05' N   Longitude: 92° 26' W

	JAN	FEB	MAR	APR	MAY	JUN	JUL	AUG	SEP	OCT	NOV	DEC	YEAR
Mean Maximum Temp. (°F)	49.6	56.8	65.6	74.7	81.2	88.7	93.2	92.6	85.8	75.6	62.5	53.3	73.3
Mean Temp. (°F)	39.5	45.0	53.7	62.4	69.8	77.6	81.9	80.7	74.1	62.8	51.5	43.2	61.9
Mean Minimum Temp. (°F)	29.2	33.2	41.8	50.0	58.4	66.5	70.5	68.9	62.5	49.9	40.5	33.1	50.4
Extreme Maximum Temp. (°F)	79	84	92	92	97	101	111	108	105	95	84	78	111
Extreme Minimum Temp. (°F)	-5	3	14	27	37	48	51	50	37	27	12	-2	-5
Days Maximum Temp. ≥ 90°F	0	0	0	0	2	14	24	22	10	1	0	0	73
Days Maximum Temp. ≤ 32°F	3	1	0	0	0	0	0	0	0	0	0	1	5
Days Minimum Temp. ≤ 32°F	20	14	6	1	0	0	0	0	0	1	7	15	64
Days Minimum Temp. ≤ 0°F	0	0	0	0	0	0	0	0	0	0	0	0	0
Heating Degree Days (base 65°F)	786	558	362	136	23	0	0	0	16	130	405	669	3,085
Cooling Degree Days (base 65°F)	1	0	17	62	185	398	545	511	299	65	7	2	2,092
Mean Precipitation (in.)	3.24	3.18	4.69	5.18	4.61	4.48	3.05	2.80	3.72	4.20	5.00	4.98	49.13
Days With ≥ 0.1" Precipitation	6	5	7	7	7	6	5	5	6	5	6	6	71
Days With ≥ 1.0" Precipitation	1	1	1	2	2	1	1	1	1	2	2	2	17
Mean Snowfall (in.)	2.1	1.5	0.4	trace	0.0	0.0	0.0	0.0	0.0	trace	0.3	0.3	4.6
Days With ≥ 1.0" Snow Depth	3	1	0	0	0	0	0	0	0	0	0	0	4

Corning *Clay County*   Elevation: 298 ft.   Latitude: 36° 26' N   Longitude: 90° 35' W

	JAN	FEB	MAR	APR	MAY	JUN	JUL	AUG	SEP	OCT	NOV	DEC	YEAR
Mean Maximum Temp. (°F)	44.5	51.4	60.9	71.9	80.3	88.1	92.2	90.2	83.8	73.3	59.6	48.7	70.4
Mean Temp. (°F)	35.5	41.3	50.5	60.4	69.2	77.2	81.2	78.9	71.9	60.8	49.7	40.0	59.7
Mean Minimum Temp. (°F)	26.5	31.2	40.0	48.9	58.0	66.3	70.2	67.5	60.1	48.3	39.8	31.1	49.0
Extreme Maximum Temp. (°F)	75	78	86	95	95	103	109	106	103	93	84	76	109
Extreme Minimum Temp. (°F)	-13	-1	9	26	36	45	48	48	35	24	10	-8	-13
Days Maximum Temp. ≥ 90°F	0	0	0	0	3	14	22	18	8	0	0	0	65
Days Maximum Temp. ≤ 32°F	5	2	0	0	0	0	0	0	0	0	0	2	9
Days Minimum Temp. ≤ 32°F	23	15	8	1	0	0	0	0	0	1	7	17	72
Days Minimum Temp. ≤ 0°F	1	0	0	0	0	0	0	0	0	0	0	0	1
Heating Degree Days (base 65°F)	908	663	452	180	34	1	0	0	26	173	457	770	3,664
Cooling Degree Days (base 65°F)	0	0	9	47	174	385	524	453	244	49	4	1	1,890
Mean Precipitation (in.)	3.14	3.58	4.98	4.48	4.79	3.52	3.53	3.30	3.66	3.57	4.95	4.48	47.98
Days With ≥ 0.1" Precipitation	5	6	8	7	7	6	6	5	5	5	7	6	73
Days With ≥ 1.0" Precipitation	1	1	1	1	1	1	1	1	1	1	2	1	13
Mean Snowfall (in.)	4.0	3.1	1.1	trace	0.0	0.0	0.0	0.0	0.0	trace	0.6	1.1	9.9
Days With ≥ 1.0" Snow Depth	3	1	0	0	0	0	0	0	0	0	0	1	5

Crossett 2 SSE *Ashley County*   Elevation: 177 ft.   Latitude: 33° 07' N   Longitude: 91° 57' W

	JAN	FEB	MAR	APR	MAY	JUN	JUL	AUG	SEP	OCT	NOV	DEC	YEAR
Mean Maximum Temp. (°F)	53.0	58.9	67.0	75.6	82.1	88.8	92.0	91.7	86.4	76.8	65.1	56.5	74.5
Mean Temp. (°F)	41.5	46.2	53.9	62.0	69.3	76.7	80.1	79.1	73.2	62.1	52.2	44.8	61.8
Mean Minimum Temp. (°F)	29.8	33.4	40.6	48.4	56.6	64.4	68.1	66.5	60.0	47.4	39.5	33.0	49.0
Extreme Maximum Temp. (°F)	81	87	92	95	97	102	105	104	101	95	85	85	105
Extreme Minimum Temp. (°F)	1	5	11	26	35	43	52	51	34	22	15	0	0
Days Maximum Temp. ≥ 90°F	0	0	0	0	3	15	23	21	12	1	0	0	75
Days Maximum Temp. ≤ 32°F	1	1	0	0	0	0	0	0	0	0	0	1	3
Days Minimum Temp. ≤ 32°F	20	15	8	2	0	0	0	0	0	2	9	17	73
Days Minimum Temp. ≤ 0°F	0	0	0	0	0	0	0	0	0	0	0	0	0
Heating Degree Days (base 65°F)	725	527	353	143	29	1	0	0	18	148	386	623	2,953
Cooling Degree Days (base 65°F)	1	2	12	*54*	160	358	476	445	259	63	9	3	*1,842*
Mean Precipitation (in.)	5.76	5.35	5.89	5.49	5.70	4.54	4.17	3.33	3.28	4.40	4.78	5.25	57.94
Days With ≥ 0.1" Precipitation	8	6	8	6	7	6	6	5	5	5	6	7	75
Days With ≥ 1.0" Precipitation	2	2	2	2	2	2	1	1	1	2	2	2	21
Mean Snowfall (in.)	0.5	0.2	trace	0.0	0.0	0.0	0.0	0.0	0.0	0.0	trace	0.1	0.8
Days With ≥ 1.0" Snow Depth	0	0	0	0	0	0	0	0	0	0	0	0	0

Dardanelle *Yell County*   Elevation: 367 ft.   Latitude: 35° 14' N   Longitude: 93° 10' W

	JAN	FEB	MAR	APR	MAY	JUN	JUL	AUG	SEP	OCT	NOV	DEC	YEAR
Mean Maximum Temp. (°F)	49.3	56.6	65.2	74.8	81.4	88.7	93.2	92.4	85.4	75.6	61.8	52.3	73.1
Mean Temp. (°F)	38.8	44.8	53.0	61.8	69.5	77.1	81.4	80.2	73.6	62.8	50.9	42.2	61.3
Mean Minimum Temp. (°F)	28.4	32.8	40.8	48.7	57.6	65.5	69.6	68.0	61.8	49.8	39.9	32.1	49.6
Extreme Maximum Temp. (°F)	78	82	92	94	96	102	110	109	105	94	85	80	110
Extreme Minimum Temp. (°F)	-7	-1	13	24	36	47	53	47	36	26	14	-3	-7
Days Maximum Temp. ≥ 90°F	0	0	0	0	2	14	24	22	10	1	0	0	73
Days Maximum Temp. ≤ 32°F	3	1	0	0	0	0	0	0	0	0	0	1	5
Days Minimum Temp. ≤ 32°F	20	14	7	1	0	0	0	0	0	1	8	17	68
Days Minimum Temp. ≤ 0°F	0	0	0	0	0	0	0	0	0	0	0	0	0
Heating Degree Days (base 65°F)	804	565	374	142	25	0	0	0	16	126	423	702	3,177
Cooling Degree Days (base 65°F)	*0*	1	11	50	174	376	522	496	279	61	5	1	*1,976*
Mean Precipitation (in.)	3.14	3.27	4.76	4.52	5.51	4.08	3.59	2.71	3.82	4.44	5.25	4.31	49.40
Days With ≥ 0.1" Precipitation	6	5	7	6	7	7	5	5	6	5	6	6	71
Days With ≥ 1.0" Precipitation	1	1	1	2	2	1	1	1	1	1	2	1	15
Mean Snowfall (in.)	2.2	1.1	0.4	trace	0.0	0.0	0.0	0.0	0.0	trace	0.4	0.4	4.5
Days With ≥ 1.0" Snow Depth	3	1	0	0	0	0	0	0	0	0	0	1	5

Deer *Newton County*   Elevation: 2,372 ft.   Latitude: 35° 50' N   Longitude: 93° 12' W

	JAN	FEB	MAR	APR	MAY	JUN	JUL	AUG	SEP	OCT	NOV	DEC	YEAR
Mean Maximum Temp. (°F)	*40.8*	*47.3*	*55.3*	*64.2*	*70.9*	*78.6*	*83.8*	*83.3*	*75.8*	*65.7*	*54.1*	*44.8*	*63.7*
Mean Temp. (°F)	*31.4*	*37.1*	*44.8*	*53.9*	*61.9*	*70.1*	*75.3*	*74.4*	*66.9*	*56.3*	*44.9*	*35.8*	*54.4*
Mean Minimum Temp. (°F)	*22.0*	*26.9*	*34.2*	*43.5*	*52.8*	*61.6*	*66.7*	*65.4*	*58.0*	*46.8*	*35.7*	*26.7*	*45.0*
Extreme Maximum Temp. (°F)	*69*	*78*	*83*	*86*	*85*	*92*	*102*	*102*	*97*	*86*	*79*	*70*	*102*
Extreme Minimum Temp. (°F)	*-20*	*-10*	*2*	*16*	*31*	*44*	*52*	*45*	*32*	*15*	*4*	*-13*	*-20*
Days Maximum Temp. ≥ 90°F	*0*	*0*	*0*	*0*	*0*	*0*	*4*	*5*	*1*	*0*	*0*	*0*	*10*
Days Maximum Temp. ≤ 32°F	*8*	*5*	*2*	*0*	*0*	*0*	*0*	*0*	*0*	*0*	*1*	*4*	*20*
Days Minimum Temp. ≤ 32°F	*25*	*18*	*13*	*4*	*0*	*0*	*0*	*0*	*0*	*1*	*12*	*22*	*95*
Days Minimum Temp. ≤ 0°F	*2*	*1*	*0*	*0*	*0*	*0*	*0*	*0*	*0*	*0*	*0*	*1*	*4*
Heating Degree Days (base 65°F)	*1,034*	*782*	*620*	*335*	*131*	*17*	*1*	*4*	*66*	*281*	*595*	*899*	*4,765*
Cooling Degree Days (base 65°F)	*0*	*0*	*1*	*10*	*41*	*182*	*329*	*314*	*134*	*16*	*0*	*0*	*1,027*
Mean Precipitation (in.)	*3.26*	*3.47*	*5.38*	*5.01*	*6.55*	*4.64*	*3.44*	*3.47*	*4.25*	*4.34*	*6.20*	*4.48*	*54.49*
Days With ≥ 0.1" Precipitation	*6*	*5*	*8*	*7*	*9*	*7*	*5*	*5*	*6*	*6*	*6*	*6*	*76*
Days With ≥ 1.0" Precipitation	*1*	*1*	*2*	*2*	*2*	*1*	*1*	*1*	*1*	*1*	*2*	*1*	*16*
Mean Snowfall (in.)	*5.2*	*4.1*	*1.9*	*0.4*	*0.0*	*0.0*	*0.0*	*0.0*	*0.0*	*trace*	*0.8*	*1.5*	*13.9*
Days With ≥ 1.0" Snow Depth	*8*	*6*	*1*	*0*	*0*	*0*	*0*	*0*	*0*	*0*	*1*	*2*	*18*

Dequeen *Sevier County*   Elevation: 419 ft.   Latitude: 34° 02' N   Longitude: 94° 21' W

	JAN	FEB	MAR	APR	MAY	JUN	JUL	AUG	SEP	OCT	NOV	DEC	YEAR
Mean Maximum Temp. (°F)	52.7	58.8	67.0	75.2	81.8	88.9	93.2	93.3	86.7	76.8	64.3	55.8	74.5
Mean Temp. (°F)	40.8	45.9	53.7	61.7	69.8	77.3	81.3	80.8	74.3	63.2	51.9	44.2	62.1
Mean Minimum Temp. (°F)	29.0	32.9	40.4	48.2	57.8	65.6	69.3	68.3	61.8	49.6	39.4	32.6	49.6
Extreme Maximum Temp. (°F)	78	88	94	94	95	102	107	108	106	94	88	80	108
Extreme Minimum Temp. (°F)	0	4	11	25	36	46	52	52	37	21	8	-3	-3
Days Maximum Temp. ≥ 90°F	0	0	0	0	2	15	25	24	12	1	0	0	79
Days Maximum Temp. ≤ 32°F	1	1	0	0	0	0	0	0	0	0	0	1	3
Days Minimum Temp. ≤ 32°F	21	15	7	1	0	0	0	0	0	1	9	18	72
Days Minimum Temp. ≤ 0°F	0	0	0	0	0	0	0	0	0	0	0	0	0
Heating Degree Days (base 65°F)	742	534	356	144	24	1	0	0	16	124	397	640	2,978
Cooling Degree Days (base 65°F)	0	1	12	43	171	373	516	512	305	77	10	2	2,022
Mean Precipitation (in.)	3.55	3.80	5.24	4.91	5.98	4.41	4.11	2.60	4.42	5.36	5.35	5.20	54.93
Days With ≥ 0.1" Precipitation	6	6	7	6	8	6	5	4	6	6	6	6	72
Days With ≥ 1.0" Precipitation	1	1	2	2	2	2	1	1	1	2	2	2	19
Mean Snowfall (in.)	*0.9*	*0.3*	trace	0.0	0.0	0.0	0.0	0.0	0.0	0.0	trace	trace	*1.2*
Days With ≥ 1.0" Snow Depth	na	*0*	0	0	0	0	0	0	0	0	0	0	na

Dermott 3 NE *Chicot County*   Elevation: 141 ft.   Latitude: 33° 33' N   Longitude: 91° 23' W

	JAN	FEB	MAR	APR	MAY	JUN	JUL	AUG	SEP	OCT	NOV	DEC	YEAR
Mean Maximum Temp. (°F)	50.8	56.9	65.5	74.8	83.1	90.4	93.5	92.3	87.2	77.4	64.7	55.1	74.3
Mean Temp. (°F)	41.4	46.5	54.8	63.2	71.8	79.3	82.4	80.7	74.8	63.8	53.5	45.3	63.1
Mean Minimum Temp. (°F)	31.9	36.0	44.0	51.5	60.4	68.2	71.3	69.1	62.4	50.2	42.3	35.5	51.9
Extreme Maximum Temp. (°F)	81	85	89	95	99	106	107	106	106	98	88	83	107
Extreme Minimum Temp. (°F)	1	9	15	27	36	49	54	51	39	25	17	1	1
Days Maximum Temp. ≥ 90°F	0	0	0	1	6	19	25	22	13	2	0	0	88
Days Maximum Temp. ≤ 32°F	3	1	0	0	0	0	0	0	0	0	0	1	5
Days Minimum Temp. ≤ 32°F	17	11	4	0	0	0	0	0	0	1	6	13	52
Days Minimum Temp. ≤ 0°F	0	0	0	0	0	0	0	0	0	0	0	0	0
Heating Degree Days (base 65°F)	726	519	330	129	20	0	0	0	14	123	354	607	2,822
Cooling Degree Days (base 65°F)	1	3	20	83	247	449	564	513	324	97	17	4	2,322
Mean Precipitation (in.)	5.26	5.01	5.55	5.06	4.89	4.17	3.99	2.70	2.91	4.06	4.94	5.57	54.11
Days With ≥ 0.1" Precipitation	8	6	8	6	7	6	6	5	5	5	7	7	76
Days With ≥ 1.0" Precipitation	1	2	2	2	2	1	1	1	1	2	2		18
Mean Snowfall (in.)	1.1	0.5	trace	trace	0.0	0.0	0.0	0.0	0.0	0.0	trace	0.1	1.7
Days With ≥ 1.0" Snow Depth	1	0	0	0	0	0	0	0	0	0	0	0	1

Des Arc *Prairie County*   Elevation: 200 ft.   Latitude: 34° 58' N   Longitude: 91° 30' W

	JAN	FEB	MAR	APR	MAY	JUN	JUL	AUG	SEP	OCT	NOV	DEC	YEAR
Mean Maximum Temp. (°F)	48.1	54.5	63.3	73.5	81.2	89.0	92.9	91.3	84.7	75.3	61.9	52.5	72.3
Mean Temp. (°F)	39.3	44.5	53.1	62.6	71.0	78.7	82.3	80.3	73.3	63.2	52.1	43.5	62.0
Mean Minimum Temp. (°F)	30.4	34.5	42.8	51.8	60.5	68.3	71.7	69.2	62.0	50.9	42.2	34.4	51.6
Extreme Maximum Temp. (°F)	79	80	87	93	97	105	108	109	102	95	87	77	109
Extreme Minimum Temp. (°F)	-5	4	15	29	38	52	56	50	40	28	15	-2	-5
Days Maximum Temp. ≥ 90°F	0	0	0	0	3	16	24	21	9	1	0	0	74
Days Maximum Temp. ≤ 32°F	4	2	0	0	0	0	0	0	0	0	0	1	7
Days Minimum Temp. ≤ 32°F	19	11	4	0	0	0	0	0	0	0	5	13	52
Days Minimum Temp. ≤ 0°F	0	0	0	0	0	0	0	0	0	0	0	0	0
Heating Degree Days (base 65°F)	792	572	376	131	21	0	0	0	17	126	392	662	3,089
Cooling Degree Days (base 65°F)	0	0	13	63	214	430	560	499	272	69	9	1	2,130
Mean Precipitation (in.)	3.69	3.87	5.25	5.66	4.70	3.97	3.46	2.67	3.31	3.92	5.04	4.21	49.75
Days With ≥ 0.1" Precipitation	6	5	8	6	7	6	5	4	5	5	6	6	69
Days With ≥ 1.0" Precipitation	1	1	2	2	1	1	1	1	1	1	2	1	15
Mean Snowfall (in.)	1.0	0.7	0.3	0.0	0.0	0.0	0.0	0.0	0.0	0.0	0.1	trace	2.1
Days With ≥ 1.0" Snow Depth	na	0	0	0	0	0	0	0	0	0	0	0	na

Dumas *Desha County*   Elevation: 160 ft.   Latitude: 33° 53' N   Longitude: 91° 29' W

	JAN	FEB	MAR	APR	MAY	JUN	JUL	AUG	SEP	OCT	NOV	DEC	YEAR
Mean Maximum Temp. (°F)	51.8	58.4	66.9	76.0	83.2	90.0	92.7	91.5	85.9	76.3	64.1	55.4	74.4
Mean Temp. (°F)	42.5	47.8	55.8	64.3	72.3	79.4	82.2	80.7	74.8	64.4	53.9	46.0	63.7
Mean Minimum Temp. (°F)	33.0	37.2	44.6	52.7	61.4	68.8	71.7	69.9	63.6	52.4	43.6	36.6	53.0
Extreme Maximum Temp. (°F)	82	83	88	95	98	102	107	104	105	95	85	81	107
Extreme Minimum Temp. (°F)	2	8	17	30	41	52	57	51	41	32	17	1	1
Days Maximum Temp. ≥ 90°F	0	0	0	1	5	18	24	22	10	1	0	0	81
Days Maximum Temp. ≤ 32°F	2	1	0	0	0	0	0	0	0	0	0	1	4
Days Minimum Temp. ≤ 32°F	16	10	3	0	0	0	0	0	0	0	4	12	45
Days Minimum Temp. ≤ 0°F	0	0	0	0	0	0	0	0	0	0	0	0	0
Heating Degree Days (base 65°F)	693	481	300	101	10	0	0	0	11	102	340	585	2,623
Cooling Degree Days (base 65°F)	1	3	19	88	247	444	547	503	307	86	12	4	2,261
Mean Precipitation (in.)	4.83	4.40	5.64	5.10	4.50	3.61	3.91	3.01	3.38	4.31	4.82	4.88	52.39
Days With ≥ 0.1" Precipitation	7	5	7	6	6	5	6	4	4	5	6	6	67
Days With ≥ 1.0" Precipitation	2	2	2	2	1	1	1	1	1	2	2	2	19
Mean Snowfall (in.)	1.3	0.5	trace	0.0	0.0	0.0	0.0	0.0	0.0	0.0	trace	0.2	2.0
Days With ≥ 1.0" Snow Depth	1	0	0	0	0	0	0	0	0	0	0	0	1

El Dorado Goodwin Field *Union County*   Elevation: 252 ft.   Latitude: 33° 13' N   Longitude: 92° 48' W

	JAN	FEB	MAR	APR	MAY	JUN	JUL	AUG	SEP	OCT	NOV	DEC	YEAR
Mean Maximum Temp. (°F)	53.9	59.7	68.1	76.2	82.5	89.2	92.4	92.1	86.6	76.8	65.3	57.3	75.0
Mean Temp. (°F)	43.3	48.0	55.9	63.6	71.2	78.3	81.8	81.0	75.1	64.2	53.7	46.5	63.6
Mean Minimum Temp. (°F)	32.7	36.2	43.7	51.0	59.9	67.3	71.2	69.8	63.6	51.6	42.1	35.7	52.1
Extreme Maximum Temp. (°F)	82	88	91	96	97	102	106	108	104	94	88	82	108
Extreme Minimum Temp. (°F)	1	7	14	26	39	48	55	51	39	26	15	3	1
Days Maximum Temp. ≥ 90°F	0	0	0	0	3	16	24	23	13	1	0	0	80
Days Maximum Temp. ≤ 32°F	1	1	0	0	0	0	0	0	0	0	0	1	3
Days Minimum Temp. ≤ 32°F	17	12	5	1	0	0	0	0	0	0	6	14	55
Days Minimum Temp. ≤ 0°F	0	0	0	0	0	0	0	0	0	0	0	0	0
Heating Degree Days (base 65°F)	669	478	298	112	17	0	0	0	11	108	348	570	2,611
Cooling Degree Days (base 65°F)	2	5	22	78	223	416	544	518	323	90	17	6	2,244
Mean Precipitation (in.)	4.89	4.35	5.20	4.60	5.35	5.08	4.22	3.33	3.25	4.47	4.65	4.70	54.09
Days With ≥ 0.1" Precipitation	7	6	7	6	8	6	6	5	4	5	5	6	71
Days With ≥ 1.0" Precipitation	1	2	2	2	2	2	1	1	1	1	2		18
Mean Snowfall (in.)	0.7	0.4	trace	trace	0.0	0.0	trace	0.0	0.0	0.0	trace	trace	1.1
Days With ≥ 1.0" Snow Depth	1	1	0	0	0	0	0	0	0	0	0	0	2

Eudora *Chicot County*   Elevation: 134 ft.   Latitude: 33° 07' N   Longitude: 91° 16' W

	JAN	FEB	MAR	APR	MAY	JUN	JUL	AUG	SEP	OCT	NOV	DEC	YEAR
Mean Maximum Temp. (°F)	51.9	57.6	65.9	74.6	82.6	89.7	92.5	91.9	87.0	77.4	65.4	56.1	74.4
Mean Temp. (°F)	42.4	47.2	55.3	63.5	72.1	79.4	82.2	81.1	75.5	64.8	54.2	46.2	63.7
Mean Minimum Temp. (°F)	32.9	36.8	44.6	52.2	61.6	69.1	71.8	70.2	64.0	52.1	43.0	36.3	52.9
Extreme Maximum Temp. (°F)	80	83	89	96	98	103	105	105	105	98	88	83	105
Extreme Minimum Temp. (°F)	3	10	16	29	37	52	57	54	42	27	16	3	3
Days Maximum Temp. ≥ 90°F	0	0	0	0	4	18	24	23	14	2	0	0	85
Days Maximum Temp. ≤ 32°F	2	1	0	0	0	0	0	0	0	0	0	1	4
Days Minimum Temp. ≤ 32°F	16	10	3	0	0	0	0	0	0	0	4	12	45
Days Minimum Temp. ≤ 0°F	0	0	0	0	0	0	0	0	0	0	0	0	0
Heating Degree Days (base 65°F)	694	498	312	119	15	0	0	0	11	104	334	580	2,667
Cooling Degree Days (base 65°F)	1	4	18	78	249	449	550	516	330	105	18	5	2,323
Mean Precipitation (in.)	5.60	5.12	5.86	6.11	5.39	4.11	3.75	2.98	2.64	4.13	5.12	5.77	56.58
Days With ≥ 0.1" Precipitation	7	6	7	6	7	6	6	5	4	5	6	7	72
Days With ≥ 1.0" Precipitation	2	2	2	2	2	1	1	1	1	1	2	2	19
Mean Snowfall (in.)	trace	trace	0.0	0.0	0.0	0.0	0.0	0.0	0.0	0.0	0.0	trace	trace
Days With ≥ 1.0" Snow Depth	0	0	0	0	0	0	0	0	0	0	0	0	0

Eureka Springs 3 WNW *Carroll County*   Elevation: 1,417 ft.   Latitude: 36° 25' N   Longitude: 93° 47' W

	JAN	FEB	MAR	APR	MAY	JUN	JUL	AUG	SEP	OCT	NOV	DEC	YEAR
Mean Maximum Temp. (°F)	45.1	51.7	61.4	71.8	77.7	84.9	90.5	89.9	81.2	na	58.3	49.0	na
Mean Temp. (°F)	35.6	41.3	50.2	59.9	66.7	74.3	79.4	78.2	70.5	na	48.8	39.6	na
Mean Minimum Temp. (°F)	25.9	30.8	38.9	47.9	55.6	63.6	68.3	66.5	59.8	na	39.3	30.1	na
Extreme Maximum Temp. (°F)	78	81	88	96	94	101	110	108	105	94	85	76	110
Extreme Minimum Temp. (°F)	-14	-8	2	25	34	46	47	47	34	19	6	-15	-15
Days Maximum Temp. ≥ 90°F	0	0	0	0	1	7	18	17	5	0	0	0	48
Days Maximum Temp. ≤ 32°F	5	3	0	0	0	0	0	0	0	0	0	3	11
Days Minimum Temp. ≤ 32°F	21	15	9	2	0	0	0	0	0	1	8	18	74
Days Minimum Temp. ≤ 0°F	1	0	0	0	0	0	0	0	0	0	0	0	1
Heating Degree Days (base 65°F)	906	664	463	197	57	4	0	1	40	na	483	781	na
Cooling Degree Days (base 65°F)	0	1	12	51	118	295	467	435	215	na	5	0	na
Mean Precipitation (in.)	2.33	2.73	4.47	4.42	4.81	4.43	3.37	3.40	4.63	3.71	4.60	3.38	46.28
Days With ≥ 0.1" Precipitation	5	5	7	7	8	7	5	5	6	5	6	5	71
Days With ≥ 1.0" Precipitation	0	1	1	1	1	1	1	1	2	1	2	1	13
Mean Snowfall (in.)	4.8	3.5	3.1	0.4	0.0	0.0	0.0	0.0	0.0	trace	1.2	1.9	14.9
Days With ≥ 1.0" Snow Depth	7	4	1	0	0	0	0	0	0	0	1	2	15

Evening Shade 1 NNE *Sharp County*   Elevation: 498 ft.   Latitude: 36° 05' N   Longitude: 91° 37' W

	JAN	FEB	MAR	APR	MAY	JUN	JUL	AUG	SEP	OCT	NOV	DEC	YEAR
Mean Maximum Temp. (°F)	48.2	54.3	62.9	73.4	80.2	88.1	93.3	92.1	84.9	74.9	61.7	51.4	72.1
Mean Temp. (°F)	36.1	41.3	49.7	59.1	66.8	75.0	79.8	78.1	71.2	59.8	49.0	39.8	58.8
Mean Minimum Temp. (°F)	24.1	28.2	36.4	44.9	53.3	61.8	66.2	64.1	57.6	44.6	36.2	28.1	45.5
Extreme Maximum Temp. (°F)	77	86	89	96	95	104	109	107	104	94	88	80	109
Extreme Minimum Temp. (°F)	-15	-13	9	20	30	40	47	44	30	19	5	-13	-15
Days Maximum Temp. ≥ 90°F	0	0	0	0	2	14	24	22	9	1	0	0	72
Days Maximum Temp. ≤ 32°F	3	1	0	0	0	0	0	0	0	0	0	1	5
Days Minimum Temp. ≤ 32°F	24	18	12	4	0	0	0	0	0	4	12	20	94
Days Minimum Temp. ≤ 0°F	1	0	0	0	0	0	0	0	0	0	0	0	1
Heating Degree Days (base 65°F)	888	662	474	204	54	2	0	0	30	190	475	775	3,754
Cooling Degree Days (base 65°F)	0	0	6	34	122	321	480	430	221	37	3	1	1,655
Mean Precipitation (in.)	3.19	3.41	4.63	4.77	4.52	3.48	3.47	3.51	3.94	3.91	5.45	4.50	48.78
Days With ≥ 0.1" Precipitation	6	6	7	7	8	6	5	5	6	5	7	7	75
Days With ≥ 1.0" Precipitation	1	1	1	2	1	1	1	1	1	1	2	1	14
Mean Snowfall (in.)	*3.4*	3.1	1.5	trace	0.0	0.0	0.0	0.0	0.0	trace	0.5	1.1	*9.6*
Days With ≥ 1.0" Snow Depth	na	*0*	0	0	0	0	0	0	0	0	0	*0*	na

Fayetteville Exp. Station *Washington County*   Elevation: 1,269 ft.   Latitude: 36° 06' N   Longitude: 94° 10' W

	JAN	FEB	MAR	APR	MAY	JUN	JUL	AUG	SEP	OCT	NOV	DEC	YEAR
Mean Maximum Temp. (°F)	44.9	51.0	59.2	69.1	76.1	83.9	89.4	89.2	81.1	70.9	58.2	49.3	68.5
Mean Temp. (°F)	34.7	40.1	48.5	57.9	65.6	73.9	79.0	78.0	70.3	59.1	48.0	39.1	57.8
Mean Minimum Temp. (°F)	24.4	29.1	37.7	46.6	55.0	63.8	68.6	66.9	59.4	47.3	37.7	28.9	47.1
Extreme Maximum Temp. (°F)	75	86	88	89	90	100	107	105	103	90	82	75	107
Extreme Minimum Temp. (°F)	-13	-8	-4	21	33	44	48	47	29	19	6	-12	-13
Days Maximum Temp. ≥ 90°F	0	0	0	0	0	5	16	15	5	0	0	0	41
Days Maximum Temp. ≤ 32°F	6	3	1	0	0	0	0	0	0	0	0	3	13
Days Minimum Temp. ≤ 32°F	23	17	10	2	0	0	0	0	0	2	10	20	84
Days Minimum Temp. ≤ 0°F	1	1	0	0	0	0	0	0	0	0	0	1	3
Heating Degree Days (base 65°F)	932	700	513	240	77	7	0	1	44	211	507	795	4,027
Cooling Degree Days (base 65°F)	0	0	6	30	99	284	450	422	207	33	3	0	1,534
Mean Precipitation (in.)	2.12	2.40	4.21	4.55	4.92	4.88	3.08	2.99	4.98	3.87	4.60	3.19	45.79
Days With ≥ 0.1" Precipitation	4	4	7	7	8	7	5	5	6	5	6	5	69
Days With ≥ 1.0" Precipitation	1	1	1	1	1	1	1	1	2	1	2	1	14
Mean Snowfall (in.)	2.0	2.1	0.5	trace	0.0	0.0	0.0	0.0	0.0	trace	0.7	1.0	6.3
Days With ≥ 1.0" Snow Depth	3	1	0	0	0	0	0	0	0	0	0	1	5

Gilbert *Searcy County*   Elevation: 620 ft.   Latitude: 35° 59' N   Longitude: 92° 43' W

	JAN	FEB	MAR	APR	MAY	JUN	JUL	AUG	SEP	OCT	NOV	DEC	YEAR
Mean Maximum Temp. (°F)	49.6	55.4	64.1	73.6	80.1	87.2	92.6	92.0	84.8	75.2	62.3	52.9	72.5
Mean Temp. (°F)	36.4	41.4	49.9	58.8	66.4	74.0	78.6	77.3	70.6	59.5	48.5	39.9	58.4
Mean Minimum Temp. (°F)	23.2	27.3	35.6	43.8	52.6	60.7	64.5	62.7	56.3	43.7	34.6	26.9	44.3
Extreme Maximum Temp. (°F)	78	84	92	94	95	102	111	107	106	95	87	80	111
Extreme Minimum Temp. (°F)	-18	-11	5	18	27	41	47	41	28	15	0	-14	-18
Days Maximum Temp. ≥ 90°F	0	0	0	0	2	12	23	21	9	1	0	0	68
Days Maximum Temp. ≤ 32°F	3	1	0	0	0	0	0	0	0	0	0	1	5
Days Minimum Temp. ≤ 32°F	25	19	14	5	0	0	0	0	0	5	14	21	103
Days Minimum Temp. ≤ 0°F	1	0	0	0	0	0	0	0	0	0	0	0	1
Heating Degree Days (base 65°F)	880	661	470	216	61	4	0	1	34	200	494	772	3,793
Cooling Degree Days (base 65°F)	0	1	9	31	111	286	436	400	203	36	4	2	1,519
Mean Precipitation (in.)	2.63	2.96	4.16	4.32	4.98	4.16	2.58	2.92	4.08	3.53	5.05	3.87	45.24
Days With ≥ 0.1" Precipitation	5	5	7	7	8	7	5	5	6	5	6	6	72
Days With ≥ 1.0" Precipitation	1	1	1	1	2	1	1	1	1	1	2	1	14
Mean Snowfall (in.)	2.2	1.4	1.0	trace	0.0	0.0	0.0	0.0	0.0	0.0	0.9	1.0	6.5
Days With ≥ 1.0" Snow Depth	3	1	0	0	0	0	0	0	0	0	0	1	5

Gravette *Benton County*   Elevation: 1,259 ft.   Latitude: 36° 26' N   Longitude: 94° 27' W

	JAN	FEB	MAR	APR	MAY	JUN	JUL	AUG	SEP	OCT	NOV	DEC	YEAR
Mean Maximum Temp. (°F)	45.6	52.1	61.4	71.0	77.8	85.5	91.2	90.7	82.4	72.1	58.9	49.6	69.9
Mean Temp. (°F)	35.1	40.8	49.6	58.8	66.2	74.1	78.9	78.0	70.3	59.9	48.2	39.2	58.3
Mean Minimum Temp. (°F)	24.4	29.4	37.8	46.5	54.6	62.6	66.5	65.2	58.2	47.6	37.5	28.8	46.6
Extreme Maximum Temp. (°F)	76	88	90	92	92	100	108	106	104	92	84	77	108
Extreme Minimum Temp. (°F)	-15	-14	2	19	29	42	44	44	28	15	4	-16	-16
Days Maximum Temp. ≥ 90°F	0	0	0	0	0	7	20	19	7	0	0	0	53
Days Maximum Temp. ≤ 32°F	5	2	0	0	0	0	0	0	0	0	0	2	9
Days Minimum Temp. ≤ 32°F	23	17	10	3	0	0	0	0	0	2	10	20	85
Days Minimum Temp. ≤ 0°F	1	1	0	0	0	0	0	0	0	0	0	1	3
Heating Degree Days (base 65°F)	922	679	477	215	65	5	0	1	44	192	500	791	3,891
Cooling Degree Days (base 65°F)	0	1	7	35	114	291	446	418	210	38	3	0	1,563
Mean Precipitation (in.)	2.22	2.44	4.26	4.64	5.28	5.00	3.03	3.26	5.05	3.97	4.72	3.43	47.30
Days With ≥ 0.1" Precipitation	4	4	7	7	8	7	4	5	6	5	6	5	68
Days With ≥ 1.0" Precipitation	1	1	1	2	2	2	1	1	2	1	2	1	17
Mean Snowfall (in.)	5.5	4.0	3.3	trace	0.0	0.0	0.0	0.0	0.0	trace	0.8	2.6	16.2
Days With ≥ 1.0" Snow Depth	7	3	1	0	0	0	0	0	0	0	0	2	13

Greenbrier *Faulkner County*   Elevation: 328 ft.   Latitude: 35° 14' N   Longitude: 92° 22' W

	JAN	FEB	MAR	APR	MAY	JUN	JUL	AUG	SEP	OCT	NOV	DEC	YEAR
Mean Maximum Temp. (°F)	*49.4*	*56.0*	*63.7*	72.8	*79.9*	87.3	91.9	91.4	84.4	74.3	61.1	*51.5*	72.0
Mean Temp. (°F)	*38.4*	*43.9*	*51.5*	59.9	*67.9*	75.5	79.8	78.7	71.8	60.8	49.3	*41.1*	59.9
Mean Minimum Temp. (°F)	*27.4*	*31.6*	*39.2*	46.9	*55.9*	63.6	67.6	65.9	59.2	47.1	37.5	*30.5*	47.7
Extreme Maximum Temp. (°F)	*77*	*84*	*92*	91	*96*	*100*	111	*105*	103	93	84	79	*111*
Extreme Minimum Temp. (°F)	*-7*	*-7*	*10*	22	*33*	*45*	49	*44*	32	23	8	-6	*-7*
Days Maximum Temp. ≥ 90°F	*0*	*0*	*0*	0	*1*	*11*	22	20	8	0	0	0	*62*
Days Maximum Temp. ≤ 32°F	*3*	*1*	*0*	0	*0*	*0*	0	*0*	0	0	0	1	*5*
Days Minimum Temp. ≤ 32°F	*22*	*16*	*9*	2	*0*	*0*	0	*0*	0	2	11	18	*80*
Days Minimum Temp. ≤ 0°F	*0*	*0*	*0*	0	*0*	*0*	0	*0*	0	0	0	0	*0*
Heating Degree Days (base 65°F)	*817*	*591*	*421*	184	*39*	*1*	0	*1*	27	173	469	*736*	*3,459*
Cooling Degree Days (base 65°F)	*0*	*0*	*9*	33	140	326	470	436	235	44	5	1	1,699
Mean Precipitation (in.)	*3.08*	*3.44*	*4.78*	5.13	*4.79*	*4.40*	3.13	*2.56*	*3.81*	4.53	5.19	4.61	*49.45*
Days With ≥ 0.1" Precipitation	*5*	*5*	*7*	7	*7*	*6*	4	*5*	5	6	6	6	*69*
Days With ≥ 1.0" Precipitation	*1*	*1*	*2*	2	*2*	*1*	1	*1*	1	2	2	2	*18*
Mean Snowfall (in.)	*1.9*	*0.7*	*0.6*	trace	*0.0*	*0.0*	0.0	*0.0*	0.0	trace	0.4	0.5	*4.1*
Days With ≥ 1.0" Snow Depth	*2*	*1*	*0*	0	*0*	*0*	0	*0*	0	0	0	1	*4*

Greers Ferry Dam *Cleburne County*   Elevation: 524 ft.   Latitude: 35° 31' N   Longitude: 92° 00' W

	JAN	FEB	MAR	APR	MAY	JUN	JUL	AUG	SEP	OCT	NOV	DEC	YEAR
Mean Maximum Temp. (°F)	46.8	52.9	61.4	71.5	78.8	86.7	91.7	90.9	83.8	73.4	60.4	50.8	70.8
Mean Temp. (°F)	36.0	40.7	49.4	58.7	66.9	75.4	80.1	78.7	71.7	60.5	49.2	40.4	59.0
Mean Minimum Temp. (°F)	25.2	28.8	37.3	45.9	54.9	64.0	68.4	66.4	59.6	47.4	37.9	29.9	47.1
Extreme Maximum Temp. (°F)	78	82	86	94	97	103	110	111	102	94	84	77	111
Extreme Minimum Temp. (°F)	-7	2	12	26	35	46	50	49	38	24	8	-5	-7
Days Maximum Temp. ≥ 90°F	0	0	0	0	1	10	21	19	7	0	0	0	58
Days Maximum Temp. ≤ 32°F	4	2	0	0	0	0	0	0	0	0	0	2	8
Days Minimum Temp. ≤ 32°F	24	18	11	2	0	0	0	0	0	1	9	19	84
Days Minimum Temp. ≤ 0°F	0	0	0	0	0	0	0	0	0	0	0	0	0
Heating Degree Days (base 65°F)	891	679	484	212	57	2	0	0	26	177	471	758	3,757
Cooling Degree Days (base 65°F)	0	0	6	29	126	330	492	452	243	46	4	1	1,729
Mean Precipitation (in.)	3.22	3.57	5.13	5.12	4.93	3.87	3.54	3.06	4.14	4.39	5.75	4.74	51.46
Days With ≥ 0.1" Precipitation	6	5	7	7	7	6	5	5	6	5	6	6	71
Days With ≥ 1.0" Precipitation	1	1	1	2	2	1	1	1	1	2	2	1	16
Mean Snowfall (in.)	na	1.3	trace	trace	0.0	0.0	0.0	0.0	0.0	0.0	trace	trace	na
Days With ≥ 1.0" Snow Depth	na	0	0	0	0	0	0	0	0	0	0	0	na

Harrison FAA Airport *Boone County*   Elevation: 1,371 ft.   Latitude: 36° 16' N   Longitude: 93° 09' W

	JAN	FEB	MAR	APR	MAY	JUN	JUL	AUG	SEP	OCT	NOV	DEC	YEAR
Mean Maximum Temp. (°F)	44.4	50.4	59.4	69.2	76.1	83.7	89.0	88.1	80.1	70.4	57.3	48.3	68.0
Mean Temp. (°F)	34.9	40.1	48.7	58.2	65.9	73.6	78.7	77.3	69.7	59.5	47.8	39.0	57.8
Mean Minimum Temp. (°F)	25.3	29.8	38.0	47.2	55.6	63.5	68.3	66.5	59.3	48.5	38.3	29.6	47.5
Extreme Maximum Temp. (°F)	74	80	86	92	94	99	107	105	102	92	82	76	107
Extreme Minimum Temp. (°F)	-13	-6	4	24	33	46	50	48	33	21	8	-11	-13
Days Maximum Temp. ≥ 90°F	0	0	0	0	0	5	16	13	4	0	0	0	38
Days Maximum Temp. ≤ 32°F	6	3	1	0	0	0	0	0	0	0	1	3	14
Days Minimum Temp. ≤ 32°F	23	16	10	2	0	0	0	0	0	1	9	19	80
Days Minimum Temp. ≤ 0°F	1	0	0	0	0	0	0	0	0	0	0	0	1
Heating Degree Days (base 65°F)	927	696	503	232	70	4	0	1	44	201	512	800	3,990
Cooling Degree Days (base 65°F)	0	0	7	36	109	277	444	406	195	37	3	0	1,514
Mean Precipitation (in.)	2.43	2.74	4.33	4.28	4.93	4.32	2.54	3.55	4.31	3.69	4.73	3.60	45.45
Days With ≥ 0.1" Precipitation	5	4	7	7	8	7	5	5	6	6	6	5	71
Days With ≥ 1.0" Precipitation	1	1	1	1	2	1	1	1	1	1	2	1	14
Mean Snowfall (in.)	4.4	3.5	2.5	0.7	trace	trace	trace	trace	trace	trace	0.8	1.6	13.5
Days With ≥ 1.0" Snow Depth	6	4	1	0	0	0	0	0	0	0	1	2	14

Helena *Phillips County*   Elevation: 193 ft.   Latitude: 34° 31' N   Longitude: 90° 35' W

	JAN	FEB	MAR	APR	MAY	JUN	JUL	AUG	SEP	OCT	NOV	DEC	YEAR
Mean Maximum Temp. (°F)	47.6	53.7	62.7	72.9	80.8	88.4	91.7	90.4	84.5	74.6	61.8	52.3	71.8
Mean Temp. (°F)	38.4	43.7	52.4	61.8	70.4	78.0	81.7	80.2	73.7	62.6	51.4	43.0	61.4
Mean Minimum Temp. (°F)	29.1	33.6	42.0	50.6	59.9	67.7	71.7	69.9	62.8	50.6	41.0	33.6	51.1
Extreme Maximum Temp. (°F)	79	80	84	95	98	102	107	103	100	96	88	80	107
Extreme Minimum Temp. (°F)	-3	5	15	28	39	51	52	50	38	26	13	-4	-4
Days Maximum Temp. ≥ 90°F	0	0	0	0	3	14	22	19	9	1	0	0	68
Days Maximum Temp. ≤ 32°F	4	2	0	0	0	0	0	0	0	0	0	1	7
Days Minimum Temp. ≤ 32°F	20	13	5	1	0	0	0	0	0	0	6	14	59
Days Minimum Temp. ≤ 0°F	0	0	0	0	0	0	0	0	0	0	0	0	0
Heating Degree Days (base 65°F)	818	595	395	152	28	0	0	0	17	135	409	677	3,226
Cooling Degree Days (base 65°F)	0	1	12	66	219	429	553	504	299	74	9	1	2,167
Mean Precipitation (in.)	4.60	4.27	5.03	5.23	5.58	4.88	3.79	2.88	3.24	3.92	5.29	5.51	54.22
Days With ≥ 0.1" Precipitation	7	6	7	6	7	6	5	4	4	5	6	7	70
Days With ≥ 1.0" Precipitation	1	1	2	2	2	2	1	1	1	1	2	2	18
Mean Snowfall (in.)	*0.9*	*0.2*	trace	0.0	0.0	0.0	0.0	0.0	0.0	trace	trace	trace	*1.1*
Days With ≥ 1.0" Snow Depth	*0*	0	0	0	0	0	0	0	0	0	0	0	*0*

Hope 3 NE *Hempstead County*   Elevation: 374 ft.   Latitude: 33° 43' N   Longitude: 93° 33' W

	JAN	FEB	MAR	APR	MAY	JUN	JUL	AUG	SEP	OCT	NOV	DEC	YEAR
Mean Maximum Temp. (°F)	51.0	57.3	65.4	74.0	80.7	88.0	92.2	92.0	85.4	75.7	63.6	55.0	73.4
Mean Temp. (°F)	40.2	45.2	53.0	61.2	69.2	76.8	80.8	79.9	73.4	62.5	51.7	44.0	61.5
Mean Minimum Temp. (°F)	29.4	33.1	40.5	48.4	57.7	65.6	69.3	67.8	61.4	49.4	39.7	32.9	49.6
Extreme Maximum Temp. (°F)	81	87	87	92	95	100	108	108	104	93	85	79	108
Extreme Minimum Temp. (°F)	1	6	13	26	40	46	54	50	39	25	13	2	1
Days Maximum Temp. ≥ 90°F	0	0	0	0	2	13	23	22	10	1	0	0	71
Days Maximum Temp. ≤ 32°F	2	1	0	0	0	0	0	0	0	0	0	1	4
Days Minimum Temp. ≤ 32°F	21	15	7	1	0	0	0	0	0	1	8	17	70
Days Minimum Temp. ≤ 0°F	0	0	0	0	0	0	0	0	0	0	0	0	0
Heating Degree Days (base 65°F)	763	554	378	155	31	1	0	0	19	139	404	648	3,092
Cooling Degree Days (base 65°F)	0	2	11	46	167	363	506	483	281	69	10	3	1,941
Mean Precipitation (in.)	4.03	4.06	5.05	5.03	4.91	4.49	3.90	3.79	4.04	4.66	5.54	5.06	54.56
Days With ≥ 0.1" Precipitation	7	6	7	6	7	6	5	5	5	5	6	6	71
Days With ≥ 1.0" Precipitation	1	1	2	2	2	2	1	1	1	2	2	2	19
Mean Snowfall (in.)	*0.9*	0.8	0.1	0.0	0.0	0.0	0.0	0.0	0.0	0.0	trace	0.3	*2.1*
Days With ≥ 1.0" Snow Depth	na	0	0	0	0	0	0	0	0	0	0	0	na

Hot Springs 1 NNE *Garland County*   Elevation: 679 ft.   Latitude: 34° 31' N   Longitude: 93° 03' W

	JAN	FEB	MAR	APR	MAY	JUN	JUL	AUG	SEP	OCT	NOV	DEC	YEAR
Mean Maximum Temp. (°F)	50.5	56.8	65.2	74.4	81.3	89.0	94.3	93.6	86.5	75.8	62.7	53.6	73.6
Mean Temp. (°F)	40.0	45.0	53.1	61.8	69.6	77.4	82.2	81.0	74.1	63.1	51.6	43.3	61.8
Mean Minimum Temp. (°F)	29.4	33.2	41.0	49.1	57.9	65.8	70.1	68.3	61.6	50.3	40.4	32.9	50.0
Extreme Maximum Temp. (°F)	78	87	89	97	96	106	114	115	107	96	86	78	115
Extreme Minimum Temp. (°F)	0	4	12	26	39	49	52	50	37	25	14	-5	-5
Days Maximum Temp. ≥ 90°F	0	0	0	1	4	16	25	24	12	2	0	0	84
Days Maximum Temp. ≤ 32°F	2	1	0	0	0	0	0	0	0	0	0	1	4
Days Minimum Temp. ≤ 32°F	20	14	6	1	0	0	0	0	0	0	7	16	64
Days Minimum Temp. ≤ 0°F	0	0	0	0	0	0	0	0	0	0	0	0	0
Heating Degree Days (base 65°F)	769	559	375	148	28	1	0	0	16	129	404	668	3,097
Cooling Degree Days (base 65°F)	0	2	14	56	182	389	552	520	299	71	6	1	2,092
Mean Precipitation (in.)	3.71	4.00	5.39	5.50	6.22	4.84	4.19	3.12	4.04	5.40	5.99	5.18	57.58
Days With ≥ 0.1" Precipitation	6	6	7	7	8	7	6	5	6	6	7	7	78
Days With ≥ 1.0" Precipitation	1	1	2	2	2	2	1	1	1	2	2	2	19
Mean Snowfall (in.)	*1.1*	0.4	0.2	trace	0.0	0.0	0.0	0.0	0.0	trace	0.2	trace	*1.9*
Days With ≥ 1.0" Snow Depth	*0*	*0*	0	0	0	0	0	0	0	0	0	0	*0*

Jonesboro 4 N *Craighead County*　Elevation: 387 ft.　Latitude: 35° 53' N　Longitude: 90° 42' W

	JAN	FEB	MAR	APR	MAY	JUN	JUL	AUG	SEP	OCT	NOV	DEC	YEAR
Mean Maximum Temp. (°F)	45.0	51.1	60.8	71.5	80.0	87.9	91.8	90.0	83.4	73.3	59.4	49.2	70.3
Mean Temp. (°F)	36.3	41.7	50.8	60.7	69.3	77.5	81.5	79.4	72.4	61.5	49.8	40.7	60.1
Mean Minimum Temp. (°F)	27.7	32.3	40.8	49.8	58.6	67.0	71.1	68.8	61.4	49.6	40.2	32.2	50.0
Extreme Maximum Temp. (°F)	74	78	84	93	97	105	107	105	99	93	84	77	107
Extreme Minimum Temp. (°F)	-11	-2	9	28	37	48	54	50	40	23	13	-7	-11
Days Maximum Temp. ≥ 90°F	0	0	0	0	2	13	22	17	7	0	0	0	61
Days Maximum Temp. ≤ 32°F	5	3	0	0	0	0	0	0	0	0	0	2	10
Days Minimum Temp. ≤ 32°F	21	14	7	1	0	0	0	0	0	0	7	16	66
Days Minimum Temp. ≤ 0°F	0	0	0	0	0	0	0	0	0	0	0	0	0
Heating Degree Days (base 65°F)	882	652	439	173	33	0	0	0	21	160	454	746	3,560
Cooling Degree Days (base 65°F)	0	0	8	44	173	390	526	469	253	56	4	1	1,924
Mean Precipitation (in.)	3.32	3.59	4.46	5.17	4.80	3.27	2.76	2.78	3.35	4.14	4.85	4.24	46.73
Days With ≥ 0.1" Precipitation	6	5	7	7	7	5	5	4	5	5	7	7	70
Days With ≥ 1.0" Precipitation	1	1	1	2	2	1	1	1	1	1	2	1	15
Mean Snowfall (in.)	2.6	1.1	0.7	trace	0.0	0.0	0.0	0.0	0.0	trace	0.2	0.5	5.1
Days With ≥ 1.0" Snow Depth	1	0	0	0	0	0	0	0	0	0	0	0	1

Keiser *Mississippi County*　Elevation: 229 ft.　Latitude: 35° 40' N　Longitude: 90° 05' W

	JAN	FEB	MAR	APR	MAY	JUN	JUL	AUG	SEP	OCT	NOV	DEC	YEAR
Mean Maximum Temp. (°F)	44.6	50.2	59.8	70.5	79.9	88.3	91.5	89.3	83.3	73.3	59.8	49.5	70.0
Mean Temp. (°F)	36.0	40.8	49.9	59.8	69.2	77.6	81.0	78.5	71.7	60.5	49.7	40.5	59.6
Mean Minimum Temp. (°F)	27.4	31.4	40.0	49.0	58.4	66.9	70.4	67.6	60.0	47.7	39.6	31.6	49.2
Extreme Maximum Temp. (°F)	75	77	84	90	98	101	106	105	100	94	82	78	106
Extreme Minimum Temp. (°F)	-9	-3	10	28	36	48	54	47	36	25	12	-6	-9
Days Maximum Temp. ≥ 90°F	0	0	0	0	3	15	21	16	7	0	0	0	62
Days Maximum Temp. ≤ 32°F	5	3	0	0	0	0	0	0	0	0	0	2	10
Days Minimum Temp. ≤ 32°F	22	15	7	1	0	0	0	0	0	1	8	17	71
Days Minimum Temp. ≤ 0°F	0	0	0	0	0	0	0	0	0	0	0	0	0
Heating Degree Days (base 65°F)	891	677	467	197	39	1	0	0	29	183	457	751	3,692
Cooling Degree Days (base 65°F)	0	0	8	44	178	396	514	440	237	52	5	1	1,875
Mean Precipitation (in.)	3.72	3.71	4.91	5.08	5.43	4.12	3.59	2.73	3.80	3.56	4.67	4.64	49.96
Days With ≥ 0.1" Precipitation	7	6	8	7	7	6	6	5	5	5	6	7	75
Days With ≥ 1.0" Precipitation	1	1	1	2	2	1	1	1	1	1	1	2	15
Mean Snowfall (in.)	0.6	0.3	0.3	trace	0.0	0.0	0.0	0.0	0.0	0.0	trace	trace	1.2
Days With ≥ 1.0" Snow Depth	na	0	0	0	0	0	0	0	0	0	0	0	na

Keo *Lonoke County*　Elevation: 229 ft.　Latitude: 34° 36' N　Longitude: 92° 00' W

	JAN	FEB	MAR	APR	MAY	JUN	JUL	AUG	SEP	OCT	NOV	DEC	YEAR
Mean Maximum Temp. (°F)	48.4	54.9	63.8	73.3	80.7	87.8	91.0	89.6	83.7	74.3	61.4	52.4	71.8
Mean Temp. (°F)	39.9	45.4	53.7	62.6	70.7	78.1	81.3	79.6	73.4	63.1	52.0	43.9	62.0
Mean Minimum Temp. (°F)	31.3	35.8	43.5	51.8	60.7	68.3	71.5	69.6	63.0	51.7	42.6	35.2	52.1
Extreme Maximum Temp. (°F)	79	83	91	92	96	100	105	102	101	93	83	78	105
Extreme Minimum Temp. (°F)	-2	2	15	29	39	52	54	51	41	30	15	0	-2
Days Maximum Temp. ≥ 90°F	0	0	0	0	2	12	21	17	7	0	0	0	59
Days Maximum Temp. ≤ 32°F	4	1	0	0	0	0	0	0	0	0	0	1	6
Days Minimum Temp. ≤ 32°F	18	11	4	0	0	0	0	0	0	0	5	13	51
Days Minimum Temp. ≤ 0°F	0	0	0	0	0	0	0	0	0	0	0	0	0
Heating Degree Days (base 65°F)	771	550	359	132	18	0	0	0	16	123	391	650	3,010
Cooling Degree Days (base 65°F)	1	2	14	65	207	410	527	477	277	70	9	2	2,061
Mean Precipitation (in.)	3.53	3.49	4.73	5.23	4.71	3.77	3.61	2.01	3.12	4.12	4.71	4.66	47.69
Days With ≥ 0.1" Precipitation	6	6	7	6	7	5	5	4	5	5	6	7	69
Days With ≥ 1.0" Precipitation	1	1	1	2	1	1	1	1	1	1	2	1	14
Mean Snowfall (in.)	2.3	1.2	0.2	0.0	0.0	0.0	0.0	0.0	0.0	0.0	0.2	0.2	4.1
Days With ≥ 1.0" Snow Depth	3	1	0	0	0	0	0	0	0	0	0	1	5

Lead Hill *Boone County*　Elevation: 711 ft.　Latitude: 36° 26' N　Longitude: 92° 56' W

	JAN	FEB	MAR	APR	MAY	JUN	JUL	AUG	SEP	OCT	NOV	DEC	YEAR
Mean Maximum Temp. (°F)	47.5	53.5	62.9	72.2	78.7	86.4	92.3	91.1	83.1	73.5	60.7	50.8	71.1
Mean Temp. (°F)	35.8	40.8	49.6	58.2	66.4	74.3	79.7	78.0	70.4	59.9	48.6	39.6	58.4
Mean Minimum Temp. (°F)	24.0	28.1	35.9	44.3	54.0	62.2	67.0	64.9	57.6	46.1	36.3	28.0	45.7
Extreme Maximum Temp. (°F)	76	85	90	94	94	102	108	110	105	95	87	80	110
Extreme Minimum Temp. (°F)	-14	-15	5	18	30	40	49	42	28	18	7	-12	-15
Days Maximum Temp. ≥ 90°F	0	0	0	0	1	10	22	19	7	0	0	0	59
Days Maximum Temp. ≤ 32°F	4	2	0	0	0	0	0	0	0	0	0	2	8
Days Minimum Temp. ≤ 32°F	24	18	13	4	0	0	0	0	0	3	11	20	93
Days Minimum Temp. ≤ 0°F	1	0	0	0	0	0	0	0	0	0	0	0	1
Heating Degree Days (base 65°F)	900	679	480	228	62	5	0	1	38	191	490	783	3,857
Cooling Degree Days (base 65°F)	0	0	6	25	104	283	454	406	192	36	3	1	1,510
Mean Precipitation (in.)	2.45	2.84	4.38	4.26	4.73	4.38	2.85	3.03	4.15	3.37	4.65	3.53	44.62
Days With ≥ 0.1" Precipitation	5	5	7	7	8	7	5	5	6	5	6	6	72
Days With ≥ 1.0" Precipitation	1	1	1	1	1	1	1	1	1	1	2	1	13
Mean Snowfall (in.)	na	2.4	1.9	0.0	0.0	trace	0.0	0.0	0.0	trace	0.2	1.0	na
Days With ≥ 1.0" Snow Depth	na	0	0	0	0	0	0	0	0	0	0	0	na

Leola *Grant County*   Elevation: 252 ft.   Latitude: 34° 10' N   Longitude: 92° 35' W

	JAN	FEB	MAR	APR	MAY	JUN	JUL	AUG	SEP	OCT	NOV	DEC	YEAR
Mean Maximum Temp. (°F)	51.7	58.4	66.8	75.2	81.3	88.2	92.0	*91.4*	na	*75.3*	63.0	55.2	na
Mean Temp. (°F)	41.0	46.4	54.3	62.3	69.6	76.9	80.8	*79.6*	na	*62.0*	51.6	44.4	na
Mean Minimum Temp. (°F)	30.2	34.3	41.9	49.4	57.8	65.5	69.5	*67.9*	na	*48.6*	40.1	33.7	na
Extreme Maximum Temp. (°F)	80	86	93	95	97	102	108	*105*	*104*	*93*	85	80	*108*
Extreme Minimum Temp. (°F)	-1	-2	12	24	34	47	52	44	*37*	*26*	10	0	*-2*
Days Maximum Temp. ≥ 90°F	0	0	0	0	2	13	22	20	*9*	*1*	0	0	*67*
Days Maximum Temp. ≤ 32°F	2	1	0	0	0	0	0	0	*0*	*0*	0	1	*4*
Days Minimum Temp. ≤ 32°F	19	13	6	1	0	0	0	0	*0*	*2*	9	15	*65*
Days Minimum Temp. ≤ 0°F	0	0	0	0	0	0	0	0	*0*	*0*	0	0	*0*
Heating Degree Days (base 65°F)	739	521	341	137	28	0	0	*0*	na	*151*	405	633	na
Cooling Degree Days (base 65°F)	1	2	18	60	174	364	501	*477*	na	*59*	9	4	na
Mean Precipitation (in.)	4.34	3.98	5.08	4.85	5.37	4.12	4.15	*3.34*	*3.80*	*4.64*	5.01	5.33	*54.01*
Days With ≥ 0.1" Precipitation	6	5	7	6	7	6	5	5	*5*	*5*	6	7	*70*
Days With ≥ 1.0" Precipitation	1	1	2	2	1	1	1	1	*1*	*2*	2	2	*17*
Mean Snowfall (in.)	1.3	1.2	0.1	trace	0.0	0.0	0.0	0.0	0.0	*0.0*	0.2	0.3	*3.1*
Days With ≥ 1.0" Snow Depth	2	1	0	0	0	0	0	0	0	*0*	0	1	*4*

Magnolia 3 N *Columbia County*   Elevation: 318 ft.   Latitude: 33° 20' N   Longitude: 93° 15' W

	JAN	FEB	MAR	APR	MAY	JUN	JUL	AUG	SEP	OCT	NOV	DEC	YEAR
Mean Maximum Temp. (°F)	53.7	60.3	68.5	75.9	82.1	88.6	92.1	92.3	86.0	76.5	65.1	57.2	74.9
Mean Temp. (°F)	43.2	48.4	56.2	63.3	70.7	77.6	81.0	80.4	74.4	63.9	53.6	46.5	63.3
Mean Minimum Temp. (°F)	32.7	36.4	43.7	50.7	59.3	66.5	69.7	68.4	62.6	51.3	42.2	35.7	51.6
Extreme Maximum Temp. (°F)	82	88	91	96	96	101	105	109	105	93	85	79	109
Extreme Minimum Temp. (°F)	1	8	14	25	38	47	52	47	39	24	13	-3	-3
Days Maximum Temp. ≥ 90°F	0	0	0	0	2	14	23	22	10	1	0	0	72
Days Maximum Temp. ≤ 32°F	1	0	0	0	0	0	0	0	0	0	0	1	2
Days Minimum Temp. ≤ 32°F	17	11	5	1	0	0	0	0	0	1	7	14	56
Days Minimum Temp. ≤ 0°F	0	0	0	0	0	0	0	0	0	0	0	0	0
Heating Degree Days (base 65°F)	670	467	290	117	19	0	0	0	14	113	351	573	2,614
Cooling Degree Days (base 65°F)	2	5	23	71	210	401	518	506	311	89	17	5	2,158
Mean Precipitation (in.)	4.09	4.11	5.15	4.71	4.73	4.97	3.51	3.33	3.30	4.23	5.10	4.68	51.91
Days With ≥ 0.1" Precipitation	7	6	7	6	6	6	5	5	5	5	6	7	71
Days With ≥ 1.0" Precipitation	1	1	2	1	2	2	1	1	1	1	2	1	16
Mean Snowfall (in.)	1.0	0.7	trace	0.0	0.0	0.0	0.0	0.0	0.0	0.0	trace	0.3	2.0
Days With ≥ 1.0" Snow Depth	*0*	0	0	0	0	0	0	0	0	0	0	0	*0*

Malvern *Hot Spring County*   Elevation: 308 ft.   Latitude: 34° 23' N   Longitude: 92° 49' W

	JAN	FEB	MAR	APR	MAY	JUN	JUL	AUG	SEP	OCT	NOV	DEC	YEAR
Mean Maximum Temp. (°F)	51.9	58.8	67.4	76.2	82.1	89.0	93.1	91.7	85.0	75.0	63.2	54.8	74.0
Mean Temp. (°F)	40.7	46.0	54.0	62.2	69.6	76.8	80.6	79.3	73.1	62.2	51.7	43.9	61.7
Mean Minimum Temp. (°F)	29.3	33.1	40.7	48.2	57.0	64.6	68.1	66.9	61.1	49.3	40.1	33.0	49.3
Extreme Maximum Temp. (°F)	80	85	91	96	97	103	110	107	102	91	89	79	110
Extreme Minimum Temp. (°F)	0	4	13	24	35	47	52	49	34	25	9	-2	-2
Days Maximum Temp. ≥ 90°F	0	0	0	0	3	15	24	21	8	0	0	0	71
Days Maximum Temp. ≤ 32°F	2	1	0	0	0	0	0	0	0	0	0	1	4
Days Minimum Temp. ≤ 32°F	20	15	8	2	0	0	0	0	0	1	8	17	71
Days Minimum Temp. ≤ 0°F	0	0	0	0	0	0	0	0	0	0	0	0	0
Heating Degree Days (base 65°F)	749	533	346	134	25	0	0	0	18	139	401	649	2,994
Cooling Degree Days (base 65°F)	1	2	14	55	177	373	504	467	273	62	8	3	1,939
Mean Precipitation (in.)	4.00	3.91	5.50	5.56	5.55	4.51	4.23	3.05	4.03	4.94	5.71	5.43	56.42
Days With ≥ 0.1" Precipitation	6	6	7	6	8	6	6	5	5	6	6	7	74
Days With ≥ 1.0" Precipitation	1	1	2	2	2	1	2	1	1	2	2	2	19
Mean Snowfall (in.)	1.4	1.1	0.3	trace	0.0	0.0	0.0	0.0	0.0	0.0	0.2	0.2	3.2
Days With ≥ 1.0" Snow Depth	1	1	0	0	0	0	0	0	0	0	0	0	2

Mammoth Spring *Fulton County*   Elevation: 649 ft.   Latitude: 36° 29' N   Longitude: 91° 32' W

	JAN	FEB	MAR	APR	MAY	JUN	JUL	AUG	SEP	OCT	NOV	DEC	YEAR
Mean Maximum Temp. (°F)	45.5	52.3	62.0	72.2	79.2	86.2	91.6	90.1	82.9	73.4	60.0	49.8	70.4
Mean Temp. (°F)	34.0	39.7	48.9	58.4	66.2	73.9	78.6	77.0	69.8	58.9	47.6	38.4	57.6
Mean Minimum Temp. (°F)	22.4	27.0	35.7	44.6	53.2	61.6	65.6	63.9	56.7	44.4	35.2	26.9	44.8
Extreme Maximum Temp. (°F)	76	85	88	95	94	102	110	106	100	95	87	79	110
Extreme Minimum Temp. (°F)	-17	-7	8	19	30	42	45	40	31	18	3	-9	-17
Days Maximum Temp. ≥ 90°F	0	0	0	1	1	10	21	18	6	0	0	0	57
Days Maximum Temp. ≤ 32°F	5	2	0	0	0	0	0	0	0	0	0	2	9
Days Minimum Temp. ≤ 32°F	25	20	13	4	0	0	0	0	0	4	13	21	100
Days Minimum Temp. ≤ 0°F	1	0	0	0	0	0	0	0	0	0	0	0	1
Heating Degree Days (base 65°F)	956	708	499	225	66	4	0	1	42	214	517	819	4,051
Cooling Degree Days (base 65°F)	0	0	5	28	108	279	437	390	183	31	3	1	1,465
Mean Precipitation (in.)	2.77	2.65	4.16	4.65	3.80	3.76	3.23	3.32	3.78	3.66	5.05	4.09	44.92
Days With ≥ 0.1" Precipitation	5	4	7	7	7	6	5	5	5	5	6	6	68
Days With ≥ 1.0" Precipitation	1	1	1	1	1	1	1	1	1	1	2	1	13
Mean Snowfall (in.)	*2.1*	*1.5*	0.4	trace	0.0	0.0	0.0	0.0	0.0	0.0	0.9	0.5	*5.4*
Days With ≥ 1.0" Snow Depth	*4*	*1*	*0*	0	0	0	0	0	0	0	0	1	*6*

Marianna 2 S *Lee County*   Elevation: 232 ft.   Latitude: 34° 44' N   Longitude: 90° 46' W

	JAN	FEB	MAR	APR	MAY	JUN	JUL	AUG	SEP	OCT	NOV	DEC	YEAR
Mean Maximum Temp. (°F)	47.7	54.0	62.7	72.6	81.0	88.6	91.8	90.4	84.8	74.9	61.6	52.1	71.9
Mean Temp. (°F)	38.7	44.0	52.5	61.6	70.4	78.2	81.3	79.4	73.3	62.6	51.5	42.9	61.4
Mean Minimum Temp. (°F)	29.6	34.1	42.2	50.6	59.8	67.7	70.7	68.3	61.8	50.2	41.3	33.7	50.8
Extreme Maximum Temp. (°F)	78	79	84	92	98	104	106	106	101	95	83	79	106
Extreme Minimum Temp. (°F)	-5	1	16	25	39	49	53	48	40	27	15	-4	-5
Days Maximum Temp. ≥ 90°F	0	0	0	0	3	14	22	20	9	1	0	0	69
Days Maximum Temp. ≤ 32°F	4	2	0	0	0	0	0	0	0	0	0	2	8
Days Minimum Temp. ≤ 32°F	20	13	5	1	0	0	0	0	0	0	6	15	60
Days Minimum Temp. ≤ 0°F	0	0	0	0	0	0	0	0	0	0	0	0	0
Heating Degree Days (base 65°F)	809	586	392	154	25	0	0	0	18	141	407	679	3,211
Cooling Degree Days (base 65°F)	0	0	10	51	195	404	518	460	267	68	7	2	1,982
Mean Precipitation (in.)	4.13	3.98	5.58	5.42	5.31	4.35	3.96	2.97	3.18	4.04	5.03	5.28	53.23
Days With ≥ 0.1" Precipitation	7	6	8	7	7	6	5	5	5	5	6	7	74
Days With ≥ 1.0" Precipitation	1	1	2	2	2	1	1	1	1	1	2	2	17
Mean Snowfall (in.)	1.3	0.5	0.1	trace	trace	0.0	0.0	0.0	0.0	trace	trace	trace	1.9
Days With ≥ 1.0" Snow Depth	1	1	0	0	0	0	0	0	0	0	0	0	2

Mena *Polk County*   Elevation: 1,128 ft.   Latitude: 34° 34' N   Longitude: 94° 16' W

	JAN	FEB	MAR	APR	MAY	JUN	JUL	AUG	SEP	OCT	NOV	DEC	YEAR
Mean Maximum Temp. (°F)	48.9	54.9	62.7	71.3	77.8	85.1	90.0	89.6	82.7	72.6	60.6	51.7	70.7
Mean Temp. (°F)	38.2	43.2	51.0	59.1	66.9	74.5	78.8	77.9	71.3	60.6	49.7	41.4	59.4
Mean Minimum Temp. (°F)	27.4	31.4	39.1	46.9	56.0	63.8	67.5	66.1	59.8	48.6	38.8	31.0	48.0
Extreme Maximum Temp. (°F)	75	84	90	92	92	100	107	105	101	91	84	76	107
Extreme Minimum Temp. (°F)	-3	-4	12	22	35	44	50	48	35	20	13	-7	-7
Days Maximum Temp. ≥ 90°F	0	0	0	0	0	6	17	17	5	0	0	0	45
Days Maximum Temp. ≤ 32°F	3	2	0	0	0	0	0	0	0	0	0	2	7
Days Minimum Temp. ≤ 32°F	22	16	9	2	0	0	0	0	0	1	9	18	77
Days Minimum Temp. ≤ 0°F	0	0	0	0	0	0	0	0	0	0	0	0	0
Heating Degree Days (base 65°F)	825	610	435	200	53	3	0	1	29	173	456	726	3,511
Cooling Degree Days (base 65°F)	0	0	5	25	108	289	428	403	214	42	4	1	1,519
Mean Precipitation (in.)	3.25	3.75	5.31	5.45	6.41	4.96	5.05	2.59	5.14	5.93	5.62	5.05	58.51
Days With ≥ 0.1" Precipitation	5	6	7	7	9	7	6	5	6	6	6	6	76
Days With ≥ 1.0" Precipitation	1	1	2	2	2	1	2	0	2	2	2	1	18
Mean Snowfall (in.)	1.5	1.4	0.1	trace	0.0	0.0	0.0	0.0	0.0	trace	0.2	0.1	3.3
Days With ≥ 1.0" Snow Depth	2	1	0	0	0	0	0	0	0	0	0	0	3

Monticello 3 SW *Drew County*   Elevation: 288 ft.   Latitude: 33° 36' N   Longitude: 91° 48' W

	JAN	FEB	MAR	APR	MAY	JUN	JUL	AUG	SEP	OCT	NOV	DEC	YEAR
Mean Maximum Temp. (°F)	51.2	57.1	65.2	73.7	81.2	88.1	91.7	91.1	85.9	75.9	63.9	55.4	73.4
Mean Temp. (°F)	40.7	45.6	53.9	61.7	69.8	77.2	80.6	79.5	73.9	62.9	53.0	44.8	62.0
Mean Minimum Temp. (°F)	30.1	34.1	42.5	49.6	58.5	66.3	69.4	67.9	61.9	49.9	41.7	34.1	50.5
Extreme Maximum Temp. (°F)	83	84	89	95	97	100	107	105	103	96	85	82	107
Extreme Minimum Temp. (°F)	-6	4	11	22	37	47	52	50	35	24	11	0	-6
Days Maximum Temp. ≥ 90°F	0	0	0	0	2	13	22	20	11	1	0	0	69
Days Maximum Temp. ≤ 32°F	2	1	0	0	0	0	0	0	0	0	0	1	4
Days Minimum Temp. ≤ 32°F	19	13	5	1	0	0	0	0	0	1	6	15	60
Days Minimum Temp. ≤ 0°F	0	0	0	0	0	0	0	0	0	0	0	0	0
Heating Degree Days (base 65°F)	748	543	354	154	30	0	0	0	17	136	368	623	2,973
Cooling Degree Days (base 65°F)	1	3	16	61	192	384	501	469	296	81	12	3	2,019
Mean Precipitation (in.)	5.13	4.68	5.91	5.29	4.65	4.32	4.15	3.36	3.17	4.58	4.91	5.11	55.26
Days With ≥ 0.1" Precipitation	7	6	8	6	7	6	6	5	5	5	6	7	74
Days With ≥ 1.0" Precipitation	2	2	2	2	1	1	1	1	1	1	2	2	18
Mean Snowfall (in.)	0.5	0.2	trace	trace	0.0	0.0	0.0	0.0	0.0	0.0	trace	trace	0.7
Days With ≥ 1.0" Snow Depth	0	0	0	0	0	0	0	0	0	0	0	0	0

Mount Ida 3 SE *Montgomery County*   Elevation: 695 ft.   Latitude: 34° 32' N   Longitude: 93° 35' W

	JAN	FEB	MAR	APR	MAY	JUN	JUL	AUG	SEP	OCT	NOV	DEC	YEAR
Mean Maximum Temp. (°F)	49.4	55.2	63.2	72.4	78.9	86.5	91.7	91.2	83.7	73.3	61.7	52.7	71.7
Mean Temp. (°F)	37.3	41.9	50.0	58.4	66.4	74.4	79.2	78.0	70.9	59.2	48.9	40.8	58.8
Mean Minimum Temp. (°F)	25.3	28.6	36.8	44.4	53.8	62.2	66.6	64.7	58.0	45.0	36.0	28.8	45.8
Extreme Maximum Temp. (°F)	77	86	86	93	96	101	108	109	104	93	84	78	109
Extreme Minimum Temp. (°F)	-2	-3	6	20	30	41	48	43	31	21	6	-6	-6
Days Maximum Temp. ≥ 90°F	0	0	0	0	1	10	21	20	8	0	0	0	60
Days Maximum Temp. ≤ 32°F	3	1	0	0	0	0	0	0	0	0	0	1	5
Days Minimum Temp. ≤ 32°F	24	20	12	4	0	0	0	0	0	4	13	21	98
Days Minimum Temp. ≤ 0°F	0	0	0	0	0	0	0	0	0	0	0	0	0
Heating Degree Days (base 65°F)	852	645	466	223	65	4	0	1	36	212	482	746	3,732
Cooling Degree Days (base 65°F)	0	0	8	30	115	300	455	419	216	37	5	1	1,586
Mean Precipitation (in.)	3.66	3.93	5.48	5.44	6.10	4.86	4.05	2.74	4.84	5.65	5.89	5.43	58.07
Days With ≥ 0.1" Precipitation	6	6	7	7	8	6	6	5	6	6	6	7	76
Days With ≥ 1.0" Precipitation	1	1	2	2	2	2	1	1	1	2	2	2	19
Mean Snowfall (in.)	2.0	1.9	0.3	0.1	0.0	0.0	0.0	0.0	0.0	0.0	0.2	0.4	4.9
Days With ≥ 1.0" Snow Depth	3	2	0	0	0	0	0	0	0	0	0	1	6

Mountain Home 1 NNW *Baxter County*   Elevation: 797 ft.   Latitude: 36° 20' N   Longitude: 92° 23' W

	JAN	FEB	MAR	APR	MAY	JUN	JUL	AUG	SEP	OCT	NOV	DEC	YEAR
Mean Maximum Temp. (°F)	45.0	51.6	60.6	70.7	77.7	85.3	90.8	89.9	82.2	72.5	58.7	48.8	69.5
Mean Temp. (°F)	34.5	40.1	48.6	58.3	66.2	74.1	79.2	77.9	70.4	59.8	48.0	38.6	58.0
Mean Minimum Temp. (°F)	24.0	28.5	36.7	45.9	54.7	62.9	67.5	65.8	58.6	46.9	37.2	28.3	46.4
Extreme Maximum Temp. (°F)	78	83	88	93	93	103	107	107	101	92	84	80	107
Extreme Minimum Temp. (°F)	-14	-8	6	23	35	44	46	47	35	23	9	-10	-14
Days Maximum Temp. ≥ 90°F	0	0	0	0	0	7	20	17	6	0	0	0	50
Days Maximum Temp. ≤ 32°F	6	2	0	0	0	0	0	0	0	0	0	3	11
Days Minimum Temp. ≤ 32°F	24	18	12	2	0	0	0	0	0	2	10	21	89
Days Minimum Temp. ≤ 0°F	1	0	0	0	0	0	0	0	0	0	0	0	1
Heating Degree Days (base 65°F)	937	698	507	229	62	4	0	1	35	193	505	813	3,984
Cooling Degree Days (base 65°F)	0	0	5	31	104	290	455	420	200	34	2	0	1,541
Mean Precipitation (in.)	2.67	2.99	4.55	4.26	4.75	4.00	2.62	2.70	4.41	3.27	5.21	3.92	45.35
Days With ≥ 0.1" Precipitation	5	5	7	7	8	6	4	5	6	5	6	6	70
Days With ≥ 1.0" Precipitation	1	1	1	1	1	1	1	1	1	1	2	1	13
Mean Snowfall (in.)	4.3	3.2	1.9	trace	0.0	0.0	0.0	0.0	0.0	trace	0.7	1.3	11.4
Days With ≥ 1.0" Snow Depth	na	1	0	0	0	0	0	0	0	0	0	0	na

Mountain View *Stone County*   Elevation: 777 ft.   Latitude: 35° 55' N   Longitude: 92° 06' W

	JAN	FEB	MAR	APR	MAY	JUN	JUL	AUG	SEP	OCT	NOV	DEC	YEAR
Mean Maximum Temp. (°F)	46.1	52.4	61.0	71.4	78.7	86.5	91.7	90.7	83.5	73.5	60.4	50.2	70.5
Mean Temp. (°F)	35.2	40.6	49.0	58.7	66.6	74.9	79.8	78.1	70.9	59.8	48.9	39.6	58.5
Mean Minimum Temp. (°F)	24.3	28.7	36.9	45.9	54.5	63.2	67.8	65.5	58.2	46.1	37.4	28.9	46.5
Extreme Maximum Temp. (°F)	76	83	87	94	95	102	108	110	104	93	86	76	110
Extreme Minimum Temp. (°F)	-12	-7	7	21	32	44	49	42	32	21	8	-9	-12
Days Maximum Temp. ≥ 90°F	0	0	0	0	1	11	22	19	8	1	0	0	62
Days Maximum Temp. ≤ 32°F	5	2	0	0	0	0	0	0	0	0	0	2	9
Days Minimum Temp. ≤ 32°F	25	18	12	3	0	0	0	0	0	3	11	20	92
Days Minimum Temp. ≤ 0°F	1	0	0	0	0	0	0	0	0	0	0	0	1
Heating Degree Days (base 65°F)	916	683	496	222	66	4	0	1	38	203	482	782	3,893
Cooling Degree Days (base 65°F)	0	0	8	38	128	318	482	431	224	46	6	1	1,682
Mean Precipitation (in.)	3.06	3.15	4.94	5.05	4.88	3.76	3.33	3.46	4.36	4.16	5.28	4.53	49.96
Days With ≥ 0.1" Precipitation	6	5	7	7	7	6	5	5	6	5	7	6	72
Days With ≥ 1.0" Precipitation	1	1	1	2	1	1	1	1	1	1	2	1	14
Mean Snowfall (in.)	1.4	1.4	1.0	trace	0.0	0.0	0.0	0.0	0.0	0.0	1.0	0.5	5.3
Days With ≥ 1.0" Snow Depth	5	3	1	0	0	0	0	0	0	0	0	1	10

Murfreesboro 5 SW *Pike County*   Elevation: 459 ft.   Latitude: 34° 02' N   Longitude: 93° 46' W

	JAN	FEB	MAR	APR	MAY	JUN	JUL	AUG	SEP	OCT	NOV	DEC	YEAR
Mean Maximum Temp. (°F)	50.5	56.6	65.0	73.0	79.5	86.8	91.2	91.1	84.4	74.5	62.5	54.0	72.4
Mean Temp. (°F)	39.3	44.1	52.1	59.9	68.0	75.5	79.6	79.0	72.4	61.7	50.5	42.8	60.4
Mean Minimum Temp. (°F)	28.1	31.6	39.2	46.7	56.5	64.2	68.1	66.8	60.4	48.9	38.6	31.5	48.4
Extreme Maximum Temp. (°F)	78	86	86	93	94	101	108	108	105	91	82	78	108
Extreme Minimum Temp. (°F)	-1	4	13	22	37	46	52	51	33	22	9	-2	-2
Days Maximum Temp. ≥ 90°F	0	0	0	0	1	9	20	19	7	0	0	0	56
Days Maximum Temp. ≤ 32°F	2	1	0	0	0	0	0	0	0	0	0	1	4
Days Minimum Temp. ≤ 32°F	22	16	8	2	0	0	0	0	0	1	9	18	76
Days Minimum Temp. ≤ 0°F	0	0	0	0	0	0	0	0	0	0	0	0	0
Heating Degree Days (base 65°F)	791	584	400	179	39	1	0	0	21	149	433	682	3,279
Cooling Degree Days (base 65°F)	0	0	6	29	135	326	463	446	249	52	5	1	1,712
Mean Precipitation (in.)	3.73	4.00	5.51	5.11	5.25	4.57	4.86	3.47	4.27	5.07	5.67	5.08	56.59
Days With ≥ 0.1" Precipitation	7	6	7	7	7	7	5	5	6	5	6	6	74
Days With ≥ 1.0" Precipitation	1	1	2	2	1	1	2	1	1	2	2	2	18
Mean Snowfall (in.)	1.0	0.8	trace	0.0	0.0	0.0	0.0	0.0	0.0	0.0	0.0	0.3	2.1
Days With ≥ 1.0" Snow Depth	0	0	0	0	0	0	0	0	0	0	0	0	0

Nashville *Howard County*   Elevation: 396 ft.   Latitude: 33° 56' N   Longitude: 93° 51' W

	JAN	FEB	MAR	APR	MAY	JUN	JUL	AUG	SEP	OCT	NOV	DEC	YEAR
Mean Maximum Temp. (°F)	50.8	56.6	64.5	73.2	80.1	87.5	91.8	91.8	85.1	75.2	63.2	54.4	72.9
Mean Temp. (°F)	40.5	45.3	53.0	61.1	69.2	76.8	80.9	80.4	74.1	63.3	52.2	44.1	61.7
Mean Minimum Temp. (°F)	30.1	33.8	41.5	49.0	58.3	66.1	69.8	68.9	63.0	51.3	41.1	33.8	50.6
Extreme Maximum Temp. (°F)	78	85	87	92	95	99	106	107	105	94	84	80	107
Extreme Minimum Temp. (°F)	-1	6	12	23	36	47	56	52	41	24	12	-5	-5
Days Maximum Temp. ≥ 90°F	0	0	0	0	1	11	22	21	9	1	0	0	65
Days Maximum Temp. ≤ 32°F	2	1	0	0	0	0	0	0	0	0	0	1	4
Days Minimum Temp. ≤ 32°F	19	13	6	1	0	0	0	0	0	0	7	15	61
Days Minimum Temp. ≤ 0°F	0	0	0	0	0	0	0	0	0	0	0	0	0
Heating Degree Days (base 65°F)	752	552	375	156	29	1	0	0	15	124	388	642	3,034
Cooling Degree Days (base 65°F)	0	1	12	46	170	370	508	496	296	79	11	2	1,991
Mean Precipitation (in.)	3.42	3.89	5.18	4.85	5.13	4.66	4.10	3.33	3.97	5.22	5.33	5.09	54.17
Days With ≥ 0.1" Precipitation	6	6	7	6	7	6	5	5	5	5	6	7	71
Days With ≥ 1.0" Precipitation	1	1	2	2	1	2	2	1	1	2	2	2	19
Mean Snowfall (in.)	1.0	1.2	trace	trace	0.0	0.0	0.0	0.0	0.0	0.0	trace	0.4	2.6
Days With ≥ 1.0" Snow Depth	1	1	0	0	0	0	0	0	0	0	0	0	2

Newport *Jackson County*   Elevation: 226 ft.   Latitude: 35° 36' N   Longitude: 91° 17' W

	JAN	FEB	MAR	APR	MAY	JUN	JUL	AUG	SEP	OCT	NOV	DEC	YEAR
Mean Maximum Temp. (°F)	44.8	51.4	60.6	71.0	79.5	87.7	91.8	90.2	83.5	73.2	59.7	49.3	70.2
Mean Temp. (°F)	36.1	41.8	51.0	60.7	69.6	77.7	81.7	79.7	72.5	61.2	50.1	40.7	60.2
Mean Minimum Temp. (°F)	27.3	32.1	41.4	50.4	59.6	67.8	71.6	69.0	61.4	49.1	40.4	32.1	50.2
Extreme Maximum Temp. (°F)	74	80	85	97	97	102	108	109	102	94	85	77	109
Extreme Minimum Temp. (°F)	-7	-3	13	30	38	51	56	48	40	26	12	-17	-17
Days Maximum Temp. ≥ 90°F	0	0	0	0	2	13	22	17	7	0	0	0	61
Days Maximum Temp. ≤ 32°F	5	2	0	0	0	0	0	0	0	0	0	2	9
Days Minimum Temp. ≤ 32°F	21	13	6	0	0	0	0	0	0	0	6	16	62
Days Minimum Temp. ≤ 0°F	0	0	0	0	0	0	0	0	0	0	0	0	0
Heating Degree Days (base 65°F)	890	650	435	171	32	0	0	0	23	166	447	747	3,561
Cooling Degree Days (base 65°F)	0	0	8	47	183	400	543	489	265	54	5	1	1,995
Mean Precipitation (in.)	3.42	3.30	4.87	5.05	4.67	3.78	3.42	3.17	3.58	3.78	5.33	4.89	49.26
Days With ≥ 0.1" Precipitation	6	5	8	7	7	6	5	5	5	5	7	7	73
Days With ≥ 1.0" Precipitation	1	1	1	2	1	1	1	1	1	1	2	1	14
Mean Snowfall (in.)	2.7	1.6	0.3	trace	0.0	0.0	0.0	0.0	0.0	0.0	0.3	0.3	5.2
Days With ≥ 1.0" Snow Depth	na	na	0	0	0	0	0	0	0	0	0	0	na

Nimrod Dam *Perry County*   Elevation: 479 ft.   Latitude: 34° 57' N   Longitude: 93° 10' W

	JAN	FEB	MAR	APR	MAY	JUN	JUL	AUG	SEP	OCT	NOV	DEC	YEAR
Mean Maximum Temp. (°F)	47.8	54.2	62.7	72.3	79.1	86.6	91.9	91.1	83.5	73.6	61.1	51.5	71.3
Mean Temp. (°F)	36.9	42.0	50.5	59.4	67.4	75.1	79.9	78.6	71.6	60.7	49.3	40.8	59.3
Mean Minimum Temp. (°F)	25.9	29.7	38.2	46.4	55.4	63.5	67.8	66.0	59.7	47.7	37.5	29.9	47.3
Extreme Maximum Temp. (°F)	76	82	88	94	95	103	110	109	105	93	83	79	110
Extreme Minimum Temp. (°F)	-2	-1	11	25	35	45	50	43	37	25	11	-3	-3
Days Maximum Temp. ≥ 90°F	0	0	0	0	1	10	21	19	8	0	0	0	59
Days Maximum Temp. ≤ 32°F	4	2	0	0	0	0	0	0	0	0	0	2	8
Days Minimum Temp. ≤ 32°F	24	17	10	1	0	0	0	0	0	2	10	20	84
Days Minimum Temp. ≤ 0°F	0	0	0	0	0	0	0	0	0	0	0	0	0
Heating Degree Days (base 65°F)	865	643	453	197	49	2	0	1	27	174	469	746	3,626
Cooling Degree Days (base 65°F)	0	0	9	35	136	324	481	447	240	48	5	2	1,727
Mean Precipitation (in.)	3.06	3.52	4.98	4.80	5.04	4.10	3.36	2.82	3.88	4.62	4.70	4.91	49.79
Days With ≥ 0.1" Precipitation	6	5	7	6	8	6	5	5	6	5	5	6	70
Days With ≥ 1.0" Precipitation	1	1	2	2	2	1	1	1	1	1	1	2	16
Mean Snowfall (in.)	1.0	1.2	0.3	0.0	0.0	0.0	0.0	0.0	0.0	0.0	0.2	0.5	3.2
Days With ≥ 1.0" Snow Depth	1	0	0	0	0	0	0	0	0	0	0	0	1

North Little Rock Airport *Pulaski County*   Elevation: 561 ft.   Latitude: 34° 50' N   Longitude: 92° 16' W

	JAN	FEB	MAR	APR	MAY	JUN	JUL	AUG	SEP	OCT	NOV	DEC	YEAR
Mean Maximum Temp. (°F)	47.2	53.4	62.8	72.3	79.8	87.8	92.4	91.2	84.0	73.2	60.7	51.2	71.3
Mean Temp. (°F)	38.9	44.4	53.1	62.3	70.3	78.3	82.6	81.3	74.2	63.3	51.9	42.9	62.0
Mean Minimum Temp. (°F)	30.5	35.3	43.5	52.2	60.9	68.7	72.8	71.3	64.3	53.4	42.9	34.6	52.5
Extreme Maximum Temp. (°F)	78	83	87	94	98	102	110	105	102	92	83	78	110
Extreme Minimum Temp. (°F)	-6	4	14	30	40	52	60	53	41	27	14	-2	-6
Days Maximum Temp. ≥ 90°F	0	0	0	0	2	13	22	20	8	0	0	0	65
Days Maximum Temp. ≤ 32°F	4	2	0	0	0	0	0	0	0	0	0	2	8
Days Minimum Temp. ≤ 32°F	18	11	4	0	0	0	0	0	0	0	4	12	49
Days Minimum Temp. ≤ 0°F	0	0	0	0	0	0	0	0	0	0	0	0	0
Heating Degree Days (base 65°F)	803	576	376	141	26	0	0	0	15	120	396	679	3,132
Cooling Degree Days (base 65°F)	0	1	16	64	197	407	555	516	299	77	9	2	2,143
Mean Precipitation (in.)	3.52	3.42	4.81	5.21	5.34	3.33	3.28	3.06	3.41	4.10	5.42	4.59	49.49
Days With ≥ 0.1" Precipitation	6	5	7	7	8	6	5	4	5	5	6	6	70
Days With ≥ 1.0" Precipitation	1	1	1	2	2	1	1	1	1	1	2	2	16
Mean Snowfall (in.)	2.6	2.0	0.4	trace	trace	trace	trace	0.0	0.0	trace	0.4	0.5	5.9
Days With ≥ 1.0" Snow Depth	3	2	0	0	0	0	0	0	0	0	0	1	6

Pine Bluff *Jefferson County*   Elevation: 213 ft.   Latitude: 34° 14' N   Longitude: 92° 01' W

	JAN	FEB	MAR	APR	MAY	JUN	JUL	AUG	SEP	OCT	NOV	DEC	YEAR
Mean Maximum Temp. (°F)	50.2	56.6	65.0	74.5	81.7	88.7	92.5	91.4	85.5	75.9	63.6	54.5	73.3
Mean Temp. (°F)	40.7	45.9	54.0	62.9	71.0	78.5	82.1	80.8	74.4	63.8	52.7	44.6	62.6
Mean Minimum Temp. (°F)	31.1	35.1	43.0	51.2	60.2	68.2	71.8	70.2	63.3	51.6	41.7	34.6	51.8
Extreme Maximum Temp. (°F)	83	84	93	92	97	102	108	105	103	94	84	80	108
Extreme Minimum Temp. (°F)	1	8	16	29	40	49	56	55	39	28	14	1	1
Days Maximum Temp. ≥ 90°F	0	0	0	0	3	15	23	21	10	1	0	0	73
Days Maximum Temp. ≤ 32°F	2	1	0	0	0	0	0	0	0	0	0	1	4
Days Minimum Temp. ≤ 32°F	18	12	4	0	0	0	0	0	0	0	6	14	54
Days Minimum Temp. ≤ 0°F	0	0	0	0	0	0	0	0	0	0	0	0	0
Heating Degree Days (base 65°F)	751	534	352	132	21	0	0	0	13	117	377	630	2,927
Cooling Degree Days (base 65°F)	1	2	15	65	210	411	542	504	297	84	12	3	2,146
Mean Precipitation (in.)	4.34	4.17	5.21	5.41	4.85	3.79	4.19	3.55	3.28	4.72	4.48	5.34	53.33
Days With ≥ 0.1" Precipitation	7	6	7	7	7	6	6	5	5	6	6	7	75
Days With ≥ 1.0" Precipitation	1	1	2	2	2	1	1	1	1	2	1	2	17
Mean Snowfall (in.)	1.1	0.6	trace	trace	0.0	0.0	0.0	0.0	0.0	0.0	trace	0.2	1.9
Days With ≥ 1.0" Snow Depth	0	0	0	0	0	0	0	0	0	0	0	0	0

Pocahontas 1 *Randolph County* Elevation: 314 ft. Latitude: 36° 16' N Longitude: 90° 58' W

	JAN	FEB	MAR	APR	MAY	JUN	JUL	AUG	SEP	OCT	NOV	DEC	YEAR
Mean Maximum Temp. (°F)	44.8	51.7	61.3	72.2	80.2	87.9	92.2	89.9	83.0	72.8	59.2	48.9	70.3
Mean Temp. (°F)	35.4	41.1	50.2	60.0	68.4	76.7	80.9	78.6	71.6	60.5	49.0	39.7	59.4
Mean Minimum Temp. (°F)	26.0	30.4	39.1	47.8	56.6	65.3	69.6	67.3	60.2	48.2	38.8	30.4	48.3
Extreme Maximum Temp. (°F)	77	81	88	95	94	106	110	109	101	91	86	76	110
Extreme Minimum Temp. (°F)	-15	-2	9	20	31	48	53	47	36	23	9	-9	-15
Days Maximum Temp. ≥ 90°F	0	0	0	0	2	13	22	17	6	0	0	0	60
Days Maximum Temp. ≤ 32°F	5	2	0	0	0	0	0	0	0	0	0	2	9
Days Minimum Temp. ≤ 32°F	23	16	9	1	0	0	0	0	0	1	9	18	77
Days Minimum Temp. ≤ 0°F	0	0	0	0	0	0	0	0	0	0	0	0	0
Heating Degree Days (base 65°F)	910	669	455	183	37	1	0	0	24	175	477	778	3,709
Cooling Degree Days (base 65°F)	0	0	6	39	151	359	508	443	223	39	3	0	1,771
Mean Precipitation (in.)	3.52	3.70	5.20	4.62	4.60	3.15	3.33	3.40	3.65	3.75	5.39	4.66	48.97
Days With ≥ 0.1" Precipitation	6	5	8	7	7	5	5	5	5	5	7	7	72
Days With ≥ 1.0" Precipitation	1	1	1	2	1	1	1	1	1	2	2	1	15
Mean Snowfall (in.)	4.1	3.2	1.0	trace	0.0	0.0	0.0	0.0	0.0	trace	0.7	1.1	10.1
Days With ≥ 1.0" Snow Depth	3	1	0	0	0	0	0	0	0	0	0	0	4

Portland *Ashley County* Elevation: 118 ft. Latitude: 33° 14' N Longitude: 91° 30' W

	JAN	FEB	MAR	APR	MAY	JUN	JUL	AUG	SEP	OCT	NOV	DEC	YEAR
Mean Maximum Temp. (°F)	53.4	60.3	68.4	76.2	83.9	90.4	93.1	92.5	87.3	78.3	66.4	57.0	75.6
Mean Temp. (°F)	42.8	48.6	56.6	64.1	72.4	79.5	82.4	81.1	75.2	64.9	54.7	46.3	64.1
Mean Minimum Temp. (°F)	32.1	37.0	44.8	51.9	60.9	68.6	71.6	69.6	63.0	51.4	43.0	35.6	52.4
Extreme Maximum Temp. (°F)	79	86	88	95	99	103	106	106	102	96	87	80	106
Extreme Minimum Temp. (°F)	4	6	18	28	41	49	54	52	41	25	17	0	0
Days Maximum Temp. ≥ 90°F	0	0	0	0	6	18	25	23	13	2	0	0	87
Days Maximum Temp. ≤ 32°F	2	1	0	0	0	0	0	0	0	0	0	1	4
Days Minimum Temp. ≤ 32°F	17	9	3	0	0	0	0	0	0	0	5	13	47
Days Minimum Temp. ≤ 0°F	0	0	0	0	0	0	0	0	0	0	0	0	0
Heating Degree Days (base 65°F)	683	458	275	103	10	0	0	0	10	94	320	575	2,528
Cooling Degree Days (base 65°F)	1	3	23	92	260	457	561	526	333	105	18	3	2,382
Mean Precipitation (in.)	5.76	5.62	5.66	5.66	5.36	4.51	4.04	2.97	2.87	4.10	5.20	5.69	57.44
Days With ≥ 0.1" Precipitation	7	6	7	6	7	6	5	5	4	5	6	6	70
Days With ≥ 1.0" Precipitation	2	2	2	2	2	1	1	1	1	1	2	2	19
Mean Snowfall (in.)	na	0.2	trace	trace	0.0	0.0	0.0	0.0	0.0	0.0	trace	trace	na
Days With ≥ 1.0" Snow Depth	na	0	0	0	0	0	0	0	0	0	0	0	na

Prescott *Nevada County* Elevation: 305 ft. Latitude: 33° 48' N Longitude: 93° 23' W

	JAN	FEB	MAR	APR	MAY	JUN	JUL	AUG	SEP	OCT	NOV	DEC	YEAR
Mean Maximum Temp. (°F)	52.3	59.5	68.0	76.3	82.5	89.1	92.8	92.6	86.2	76.2	63.5	55.2	74.5
Mean Temp. (°F)	42.2	47.8	55.7	63.7	71.1	78.1	81.8	81.1	74.9	64.2	52.9	45.3	63.2
Mean Minimum Temp. (°F)	32.1	36.1	43.4	51.0	59.5	67.1	70.6	69.6	63.5	52.1	42.3	35.3	51.9
Extreme Maximum Temp. (°F)	81	88	93	94	95	102	107	108	108	94	83	78	108
Extreme Minimum Temp. (°F)	1	7	15	28	41	51	56	52	39	27	13	0	0
Days Maximum Temp. ≥ 90°F	0	0	0	0	3	16	24	23	11	1	0	0	78
Days Maximum Temp. ≤ 32°F	1	0	0	0	0	0	0	0	0	0	0	1	2
Days Minimum Temp. ≤ 32°F	17	11	4	1	0	0	0	0	0	0	5	14	52
Days Minimum Temp. ≤ 0°F	0	0	0	0	0	0	0	0	0	0	0	0	0
Heating Degree Days (base 65°F)	701	482	299	104	14	0	0	0	11	106	367	607	2,691
Cooling Degree Days (base 65°F)	1	3	16	68	202	399	526	513	310	84	10	3	2,135
Mean Precipitation (in.)	4.19	4.15	5.09	5.08	5.04	4.41	4.42	3.30	4.30	5.08	5.60	5.45	56.11
Days With ≥ 0.1" Precipitation	7	6	7	6	7	7	6	5	5	6	6	7	75
Days With ≥ 1.0" Precipitation	1	1	2	2	2	1	2	1	1	2	2	2	19
Mean Snowfall (in.)	1.9	1.4	0.1	trace	0.0	0.0	0.0	0.0	0.0	0.0	trace	0.5	3.9
Days With ≥ 1.0" Snow Depth	2	1	0	0	0	0	0	0	0	0	0	1	4

Rohwer 2 NNE *Desha County* Elevation: 147 ft. Latitude: 33° 48' N Longitude: 91° 16' W

	JAN	FEB	MAR	APR	MAY	JUN	JUL	AUG	SEP	OCT	NOV	DEC	YEAR
Mean Maximum Temp. (°F)	50.0	55.8	64.2	73.4	81.7	89.2	92.1	91.0	85.8	75.9	63.7	54.5	73.1
Mean Temp. (°F)	40.6	45.6	53.4	62.3	71.0	78.7	81.6	79.9	73.9	62.9	52.7	44.6	62.3
Mean Minimum Temp. (°F)	31.3	35.2	42.8	51.2	60.3	68.1	71.1	68.7	61.9	49.9	41.6	34.7	51.4
Extreme Maximum Temp. (°F)	78	83	88	95	98	103	105	103	102	97	86	82	105
Extreme Minimum Temp. (°F)	0	7	16	28	39	49	51	50	40	26	17	0	0
Days Maximum Temp. ≥ 90°F	0	0	0	0	4	16	23	21	11	1	0	0	76
Days Maximum Temp. ≤ 32°F	3	1	0	0	0	0	0	0	0	0	0	1	5
Days Minimum Temp. ≤ 32°F	18	11	4	0	0	0	0	0	0	1	6	15	55
Days Minimum Temp. ≤ 0°F	0	0	0	0	0	0	0	0	0	0	0	0	0
Heating Degree Days (base 65°F)	748	544	366	141	21	0	0	0	16	136	374	628	2,974
Cooling Degree Days (base 65°F)	0	2	12	68	225	429	535	482	291	81	11	2	2,138
Mean Precipitation (in.)	5.06	4.35	5.44	5.08	4.69	3.81	3.88	2.62	2.95	3.50	5.07	5.44	51.89
Days With ≥ 0.1" Precipitation	7	6	7	6	7	6	6	4	4	4	6	7	70
Days With ≥ 1.0" Precipitation	2	2	2	2	2	1	1	1	1	1	2	2	19
Mean Snowfall (in.)	trace	trace	0.0	0.0	0.0	0.0	0.0	0.0	0.0	0.0	trace	trace	trace
Days With ≥ 1.0" Snow Depth	0	0	0	0	0	0	0	0	0	0	0	0	0

Saint Charles *Arkansas County*   Elevation: 200 ft.   Latitude: 34° 23' N   Longitude: 91° 08' W

	JAN	FEB	MAR	APR	MAY	JUN	JUL	AUG	SEP	OCT	NOV	DEC	YEAR
Mean Maximum Temp. (°F)	48.9	54.6	63.5	73.1	80.8	88.5	92.5	91.6	85.6	75.7	63.3	53.4	72.6
Mean Temp. (°F)	39.4	44.2	53.0	61.8	70.0	78.0	81.9	80.4	74.1	63.1	52.1	43.7	61.8
Mean Minimum Temp. (°F)	29.9	33.8	42.4	50.4	59.2	67.2	71.0	69.1	62.5	50.5	41.0	34.0	50.9
Extreme Maximum Temp. (°F)	81	82	85	94	99	102	108	106	101	96	86	82	108
Extreme Minimum Temp. (°F)	0	0	12	29	40	51	54	55	41	29	15	-2	-2
Days Maximum Temp. ≥ 90°F	0	0	0	0	2	14	21	19	10	1	0	0	67
Days Maximum Temp. ≤ 32°F	3	1	0	0	0	0	0	0	0	0	0	1	5
Days Minimum Temp. ≤ 32°F	18	12	4	0	0	0	0	0	0	0	5	13	52
Days Minimum Temp. ≤ 0°F	0	0	0	0	0	0	0	0	0	0	0	0	0
Heating Degree Days (base 65°F)	788	586	377	149	26	0	0	0	16	130	390	654	3,116
Cooling Degree Days (base 65°F)	0	1	13	59	190	409	548	512	304	79	9	2	2,126
Mean Precipitation (in.)	4.14	4.01	5.66	5.51	4.90	3.90	3.75	2.49	3.10	4.07	5.24	4.93	51.70
Days With ≥ 0.1" Precipitation	6	5	7	6	6	5	4	4	4	4	6	6	63
Days With ≥ 1.0" Precipitation	1	1	2	2	1	1	1	1	1	1	2	1	15
Mean Snowfall (in.)	1.2	0.4	0.1	0.0	0.0	0.0	0.0	0.0	0.0	0.0	0.0	0.2	1.9
Days With ≥ 1.0" Snow Depth	0	0	0	0	0	0	0	0	0	0	0	0	0

Searcy *White County*   Elevation: 242 ft.   Latitude: 35° 14' N   Longitude: 91° 50' W

	JAN	FEB	MAR	APR	MAY	JUN	JUL	AUG	SEP	OCT	NOV	DEC	YEAR
Mean Maximum Temp. (°F)	49.5	55.8	64.8	74.6	82.0	89.6	93.7	92.4	85.9	75.4	62.1	52.6	73.2
Mean Temp. (°F)	39.2	44.3	52.9	62.0	70.1	78.0	82.0	80.3	73.8	62.2	51.1	42.6	61.6
Mean Minimum Temp. (°F)	28.9	32.8	41.0	49.3	58.1	66.4	70.3	68.3	61.6	48.9	40.1	32.5	49.8
Extreme Maximum Temp. (°F)	79	83	90	95	98	104	110	109	104	98	85	79	110
Extreme Minimum Temp. (°F)	-7	0	14	28	36	48	52	48	36	24	11	-4	-7
Days Maximum Temp. ≥ 90°F	0	0	0	0	3	17	25	22	10	1	0	0	78
Days Maximum Temp. ≤ 32°F	3	1	0	0	0	0	0	0	0	0	0	1	5
Days Minimum Temp. ≤ 32°F	21	14	7	1	0	0	0	0	0	1	8	16	68
Days Minimum Temp. ≤ 0°F	0	0	0	0	0	0	0	0	0	0	0	0	0
Heating Degree Days (base 65°F)	793	578	381	144	24	0	0	0	15	144	417	690	3,186
Cooling Degree Days (base 65°F)	1	1	13	59	196	411	550	501	290	62	7	2	2,093
Mean Precipitation (in.)	3.71	3.44	5.29	5.16	5.23	3.59	3.62	3.23	3.42	4.06	5.55	4.99	51.29
Days With ≥ 0.1" Precipitation	6	6	8	7	7	6	5	5	5	5	6	6	72
Days With ≥ 1.0" Precipitation	1	1	2	2	2	1	1	1	1	1	2	2	17
Mean Snowfall (in.)	1.6	1.3	0.3	trace	0.0	0.0	0.0	0.0	0.0	trace	0.2	0.2	3.6
Days With ≥ 1.0" Snow Depth	na	0	0	0	0	0	0	0	0	0	0	0	na

Stuttgart 9 ESE *Arkansas County*   Elevation: 196 ft.   Latitude: 34° 28' N   Longitude: 91° 25' W

	JAN	FEB	MAR	APR	MAY	JUN	JUL	AUG	SEP	OCT	NOV	DEC	YEAR
Mean Maximum Temp. (°F)	47.7	53.6	62.4	72.1	80.3	87.8	91.4	90.3	84.7	74.8	61.8	52.4	71.6
Mean Temp. (°F)	39.0	44.1	52.6	61.7	70.6	78.4	81.8	80.0	73.7	62.7	51.8	43.4	61.6
Mean Minimum Temp. (°F)	30.3	34.5	42.7	51.3	60.9	68.8	72.1	69.7	62.6	50.6	41.8	34.3	51.6
Extreme Maximum Temp. (°F)	80	80	89	94	97	101	105	103	101	95	84	79	105
Extreme Minimum Temp. (°F)	-3	6	16	28	42	53	55	50	39	27	16	-2	-3
Days Maximum Temp. ≥ 90°F	0	0	0	0	2	13	22	18	9	0	0	0	64
Days Maximum Temp. ≤ 32°F	4	2	0	0	0	0	0	0	0	0	0	2	8
Days Minimum Temp. ≤ 32°F	19	12	4	0	0	0	0	0	0	0	5	14	54
Days Minimum Temp. ≤ 0°F	0	0	0	0	0	0	0	0	0	0	0	0	0
Heating Degree Days (base 65°F)	799	586	386	152	24	0	0	0	18	138	396	665	3,164
Cooling Degree Days (base 65°F)	0	1	10	57	206	419	541	488	289	74	7	2	2,094
Mean Precipitation (in.)	3.85	3.61	4.95	5.38	4.90	3.91	3.37	2.51	2.87	3.96	4.87	4.97	49.15
Days With ≥ 0.1" Precipitation	6	5	7	6	7	6	5	4	4	5	6	7	68
Days With ≥ 1.0" Precipitation	1	1	1	2	1	1	1	1	1	1	1	2	14
Mean Snowfall (in.)	0.8	0.3	0.2	0.0	0.0	0.0	0.0	0.0	0.0	0.0	trace	trace	1.3
Days With ≥ 1.0" Snow Depth	1	0	0	0	0	0	0	0	0	0	0	0	1

Subiaco *Logan County*   Elevation: 498 ft.   Latitude: 35° 18' N   Longitude: 93° 39' W

	JAN	FEB	MAR	APR	MAY	JUN	JUL	AUG	SEP	OCT	NOV	DEC	YEAR
Mean Maximum Temp. (°F)	48.7	55.7	64.7	74.0	80.6	88.3	93.2	92.1	84.5	74.3	61.6	52.1	72.5
Mean Temp. (°F)	38.9	44.7	53.2	62.0	69.5	77.2	81.7	80.3	73.4	62.7	51.3	42.5	61.4
Mean Minimum Temp. (°F)	29.1	33.6	41.7	49.9	58.4	66.0	70.1	68.5	62.3	51.0	40.8	32.9	50.4
Extreme Maximum Temp. (°F)	78	83	93	95	97	104	109	107	105	94	85	79	109
Extreme Minimum Temp. (°F)	-6	1	13	26	41	45	53	47	37	24	14	-4	-6
Days Maximum Temp. ≥ 90°F	0	0	0	0	3	14	24	22	9	1	0	0	73
Days Maximum Temp. ≤ 32°F	3	1	0	0	0	0	0	0	0	0	0	1	5
Days Minimum Temp. ≤ 32°F	20	13	6	1	0	0	0	0	0	1	6	15	62
Days Minimum Temp. ≤ 0°F	0	0	0	0	0	0	0	0	0	0	0	0	0
Heating Degree Days (base 65°F)	801	568	372	143	25	1	0	0	18	130	413	692	3,163
Cooling Degree Days (base 65°F)	0	1	13	53	163	368	523	486	271	61	6	2	1,947
Mean Precipitation (in.)	2.85	2.99	4.03	4.33	4.96	4.13	3.39	3.15	3.89	3.94	4.98	4.01	46.65
Days With ≥ 0.1" Precipitation	5	5	7	6	8	6	5	5	6	6	6	5	70
Days With ≥ 1.0" Precipitation	1	1	1	2	1	1	1	1	1	1	2	1	14
Mean Snowfall (in.)	2.1	1.1	0.1	trace	0.0	0.0	0.0	0.0	0.0	trace	0.3	0.5	4.1
Days With ≥ 1.0" Snow Depth	3	2	0	0	0	0	0	0	0	0	0	1	6

Waldron *Scott County* Elevation: 672 ft. Latitude: 34° 54' N Longitude: 94° 06' W

	JAN	FEB	MAR	APR	MAY	JUN	JUL	AUG	SEP	OCT	NOV	DEC	YEAR
Mean Maximum Temp. (°F)	51.5	58.1	66.7	75.6	81.7	88.9	93.7	93.3	85.8	76.3	63.7	54.9	74.2
Mean Temp. (°F)	39.1	44.8	53.3	61.7	69.2	76.6	80.7	79.7	72.5	62.0	50.9	42.8	61.1
Mean Minimum Temp. (°F)	26.6	31.3	39.9	47.7	56.6	64.2	67.6	66.0	59.3	47.7	38.1	30.7	48.0
Extreme Maximum Temp. (°F)	78	89	95	94	96	105	111	107	105	95	87	78	111
Extreme Minimum Temp. (°F)	-9	-2	9	22	35	44	49	48	30	22	6	-3	-9
Days Maximum Temp. ≥ 90°F	0	0	0	0	2	15	25	23	10	1	0	0	76
Days Maximum Temp. ≤ 32°F	2	1	0	0	0	0	0	0	0	0	0	1	4
Days Minimum Temp. ≤ 32°F	22	16	8	2	0	0	0	0	0	2	10	18	78
Days Minimum Temp. ≤ 0°F	0	0	0	0	0	0	0	0	0	0	0	0	0
Heating Degree Days (base 65°F)	797	567	367	151	32	1	0	0	27	144	423	682	3,191
Cooling Degree Days (base 65°F)	0	1	11	52	*165*	355	491	462	247	55	8	1	*1,848*
Mean Precipitation (in.)	2.79	2.92	4.21	4.93	5.76	5.05	3.57	2.86	4.11	4.19	4.84	4.39	49.62
Days With ≥ 0.1" Precipitation	5	5	7	7	8	6	5	5	6	5	6	6	71
Days With ≥ 1.0" Precipitation	1	1	1	2	2	2	1	1	1	1	2	1	16
Mean Snowfall (in.)	3.8	2.3	0.2	trace	0.0	0.0	0.0	0.0	0.0	0.0	0.4	0.9	7.6
Days With ≥ 1.0" Snow Depth	*2*	1	0	0	0	0	0	0	0	0	0	0	*3*

Warren 2 WSW *Bradley County* Elevation: 209 ft. Latitude: 33° 36' N Longitude: 92° 06' W

	JAN	FEB	MAR	APR	MAY	JUN	JUL	AUG	SEP	OCT	NOV	DEC	YEAR
Mean Maximum Temp. (°F)	51.7	57.4	65.5	74.1	80.8	88.2	91.9	91.7	86.0	75.5	64.0	55.6	73.5
Mean Temp. (°F)	41.0	45.8	53.5	61.9	69.4	77.3	80.8	79.8	74.0	62.6	52.4	44.9	62.0
Mean Minimum Temp. (°F)	30.3	34.2	41.5	49.6	58.0	66.3	69.7	67.9	61.9	49.5	40.7	34.2	50.3
Extreme Maximum Temp. (°F)	83	84	88	91	96	102	106	104	102	93	86	83	106
Extreme Minimum Temp. (°F)	0	5	12	26	40	46	53	48	38	25	13	3	0
Days Maximum Temp. ≥ 90°F	0	0	0	0	2	13	22	22	11	1	0	0	71
Days Maximum Temp. ≤ 32°F	2	1	0	0	0	0	0	0	0	0	0	1	4
Days Minimum Temp. ≤ 32°F	19	13	6	1	0	0	0	0	0	0	7	15	61
Days Minimum Temp. ≤ 0°F	0	0	0	0	0	0	0	0	0	0	0	0	0
Heating Degree Days (base 65°F)	738	538	361	143	30	0	0	0	16	139	383	618	2,966
Cooling Degree Days (base 65°F)	1	2	14	55	176	375	507	473	282	72	11	4	1,972
Mean Precipitation (in.)	4.89	4.57	6.28	5.34	4.43	4.13	4.09	3.04	3.63	4.71	4.79	5.32	55.22
Days With ≥ 0.1" Precipitation	7	6	8	6	7	6	6	4	5	5	6	7	73
Days With ≥ 1.0" Precipitation	2	2	2	2	1	1	1	1	1	2	2	2	19
Mean Snowfall (in.)	1.0	*0.1*	trace	trace	0.0	0.0	0.0	0.0	0.0	0.0	trace	0.2	*1.3*
Days With ≥ 1.0" Snow Depth	0	*0*	0	0	0	0	0	0	0	0	0	0	*0*

West Memphis *Crittenden County* Elevation: 213 ft. Latitude: 35° 07' N Longitude: 90° 11' W

	JAN	FEB	MAR	APR	MAY	JUN	JUL	AUG	SEP	OCT	NOV	DEC	YEAR
Mean Maximum Temp. (°F)	47.4	53.9	62.6	72.4	80.7	88.1	91.4	89.8	84.4	74.9	61.5	52.2	71.6
Mean Temp. (°F)	38.5	43.9	52.4	61.5	70.2	78.1	81.6	79.7	73.8	62.8	51.8	43.4	61.5
Mean Minimum Temp. (°F)	29.6	33.9	42.2	50.4	59.6	68.1	71.7	69.5	63.0	50.9	42.1	34.6	51.3
Extreme Maximum Temp. (°F)	76	78	85	94	106	101	105	103	99	95	83	79	106
Extreme Minimum Temp. (°F)	-9	-8	10	26	37	51	54	48	36	29	11	-5	-9
Days Maximum Temp. ≥ 90°F	0	0	0	0	2	14	21	17	7	0	0	0	61
Days Maximum Temp. ≤ 32°F	4	1	0	0	0	0	0	0	0	0	0	1	6
Days Minimum Temp. ≤ 32°F	19	13	5	1	0	0	0	0	0	0	6	13	57
Days Minimum Temp. ≤ 0°F	0	0	0	0	0	0	0	0	0	0	0	0	0
Heating Degree Days (base 65°F)	814	588	392	157	26	0	0	0	18	136	399	662	3,192
Cooling Degree Days (base 65°F)	0	0	9	51	192	404	528	471	286	71	10	2	2,024
Mean Precipitation (in.)	4.04	4.00	5.60	5.74	4.92	4.47	3.46	3.08	3.31	3.60	5.45	5.52	53.19
Days With ≥ 0.1" Precipitation	7	6	8	8	7	6	5	5	6	5	7	7	77
Days With ≥ 1.0" Precipitation	1	1	2	2	2	1	1	1	1	1	2	2	17
Mean Snowfall (in.)	*1.4*	*0.4*	trace	0.0	0.0	0.0	0.0	0.0	0.0	0.0	trace	trace	*1.8*
Days With ≥ 1.0" Snow Depth	*0*	*0*	0	0	0	0	0	0	0	0	0	0	*0*

Wynne *Cross County* Elevation: 259 ft. Latitude: 35° 15' N Longitude: 90° 48' W

	JAN	FEB	MAR	APR	MAY	JUN	JUL	AUG	SEP	OCT	NOV	DEC	YEAR
Mean Maximum Temp. (°F)	47.0	53.6	62.8	72.9	81.3	89.1	91.9	90.1	84.3	75.2	61.2	51.6	71.7
Mean Temp. (°F)	38.2	43.7	52.3	61.6	70.2	78.2	81.3	79.0	72.7	62.7	51.3	42.6	61.1
Mean Minimum Temp. (°F)	29.4	33.6	41.9	50.2	59.1	67.2	70.8	67.8	61.1	50.0	41.3	33.7	50.5
Extreme Maximum Temp. (°F)	75	78	83	91	97	100	106	103	99	96	85	80	106
Extreme Minimum Temp. (°F)	-8	-5	12	25	38	47	51	48	34	25	15	-4	-8
Days Maximum Temp. ≥ 90°F	0	0	0	0	2	15	22	18	8	1	0	0	66
Days Maximum Temp. ≤ 32°F	4	2	0	0	0	0	0	0	0	0	0	1	7
Days Minimum Temp. ≤ 32°F	20	13	6	1	0	0	0	0	0	1	6	15	62
Days Minimum Temp. ≤ 0°F	0	0	0	0	0	0	0	0	0	0	0	0	0
Heating Degree Days (base 65°F)	824	597	397	155	27	0	0	0	22	140	414	687	3,263
Cooling Degree Days (base 65°F)	0	1	12	51	191	415	514	444	253	69	8	2	1,960
Mean Precipitation (in.)	3.50	3.37	4.89	5.95	4.73	3.67	2.97	2.33	3.54	3.95	4.88	4.89	48.67
Days With ≥ 0.1" Precipitation	6	6	7	7	7	5	5	4	5	5	7	7	71
Days With ≥ 1.0" Precipitation	1	1	1	2	2	1	1	1	1	1	2	2	16
Mean Snowfall (in.)	2.7	1.5	0.1	trace	0.0	0.0	0.0	0.0	0.0	trace	trace	trace	4.3
Days With ≥ 1.0" Snow Depth	*2*	1	0	0	0	0	0	0	0	0	0	0	*3*

Note: See Appendix D for explanation of data.

CALIFORNIA

PHYSICAL FEATURES. The State of California extends along the shore of the Pacific Ocean between latitudes 32.5° N. and 42° N. Its more than 1,340 miles of coastline constitute nearly three-fourths of the Pacific coastline of the conterminous United States. The total land area amounts to 158,693 square miles. With its major axis oriented in a northwest-southeast direction, the State is 800 miles in length. Its greatest east-west dimension at a given latitude is about 360 miles though its average width is only 250 miles. However, it spreads over more than 10° of longitude, a distance of 550 miles.

The topography of the State is varied. Included are Death Valley, the lowest point in the U.S., with an elevation of 276 feet below sea level, and less than 85 miles away, Mt. Whitney, the highest peak in the conterminous states, reaching to 14,495 feet above sea level. These wide ranges of altitude and latitude are responsible in part for the variety of climates and vegetation found in various areas of the State. Another significant factor is the continuous interaction of maritime air masses with those of continental origin. The combination of these influences results in pronounced climatic changes with short distances.

The Coast Range parallels the coastline from the Oregon border to just north of the Los Angeles Basin. It is generally no more than 50 miles from the coast to the crest of the range. The principal break in the Coast Range is at San Francisco Bay where a sea level opening permits an abundant inflow of marine air to the interior of the State under certain circulation patterns. In the northern end of the State, the Coast Range merges with the Cascade Range, farther inland, to create an extensive area of rugged terrain more than 200 miles in width. The Cascades, in turn, extend southeastward until they merge into the Sierra Nevada. The Sierra Nevada, like the Coast Range, lies parallel to the coast, but the crest over most of its length is about 150 miles inland. Thus, between the two ranges there is a broad, flat valley averaging 45 miles or more in width. In length the valley extends nearly 500 miles.

Both the extreme northeastern portion of California and the desert area of southern California east of the mountains lie within the Great Basin. The Great Basin extends from Utah to the Sierra Nevada and has no surface drainage to the ocean. It is an area of climatological extremes.

GENERAL CLIMATE. Along the western side of the Coast Range the climate is dominated by the Pacific Ocean. Warm winters, cool summers, small daily and seasonal temperature ranges, and high relative humidities are characteristic of this area. With increasing distance from the ocean the maritime influence decreases. Areas that are well protected from the ocean experience a more continental type of climate with warmer summers, colder winters, greater daily and seasonal temperature ranges, and generally lower relative humidities. Many parts of the State lie within a transitional zone, where conditions range between these two climatic extremes. Summer is a dry period over most of the State. With the northward migration of the semi-permanent Pacific high during summer, most storm tracks are deflected far to the north. In winter, the Pacific high decreases in intensity and drops further south, permitting storms to move into and across the State, producing widespread rain at low elevations and snow at high elevations.

The easternmost mountain chains form a barrier that protects much of California from the extremely cold air of the Great Basin in winter. The ranges of mountains to the west offer some protection to the interior from the strong flow of air off the Pacific Ocean. As a result, precipitation is heavy on the coastward or western side of both the Coast Range and the Sierra Nevada, and lighter on the eastern slopes. Temperature tends toward uniformity from day to day and from season to season on the ocean side of the Coast Range and in coastal valleys. East of the Sierra Nevada temperature patterns are continental in character with wide excursions from high readings to low. Between the two mountain chains and over much of the desert area the temperature regime is intermediate between the maritime and the continental models. Hot summers are the rule while winters are moderate to cold. In the basins and valleys adjoining the coast, climate is subject to wide variations within short distances as a result of the influence of topography on the circulation of marine air. The Los Angeles Basin and the San Francisco Bay area offer many varieties of climate within a few miles.

A dominating factor in the weather of California is the semi-permanent high pressure area of the north Pacific Ocean. This pressure center moves northward in summer, holding storm tracks well to the north, and as a result California receives little or no precipitation from this source during that period. In winter, the Pacific high retreats southward permitting storm centers to swing into and across California. These are the storms that bring widespread, moderate precipitation to the State. When changes in the circulation pattern permit storm centers to approach the California coast from a southwesterly direction, copious amounts of moisture are carried by the northeastward streaming air. This results in heavy rains and often produces widespread flooding.

There is another California weather characteristic that results from the location of the Pacific high. The steady flow of air from the northwest during the summer helps to drive the California Current of the Pacific Ocean as it sweeps southward almost parallel to the California coastline. However, since the mean drift is slightly offshore there is a band of upwelling immediately off the coast as water from deeper layers is drawn into the surface circulation. The water from below the surface is colder than the surface water, and as a result there is a semi-permanent band of cold water just offshore. The temperature of water reaching the surface from deeper levels ranges from about 49°F. in winter to 55°F. in late summer along the northern California coast, and from 57°F. to 65°F. on the southern California coast. Comparatively warm, moist Pacific air masses drifting over this band of cold water form a bank of fog which is swept inland by the prevailing northwest winds out of the high pressure center. In general, heat is added to the air as it moves inland during these summer months, and the fog quickly lifts to form a deck of low clouds that extend inland only a short distance before evaporating completely. Characteristically this deck of clouds extends inland further during the night and then recedes to the vicinity of the coast during the day.

PRECIPITATION. In the northern part of the State the months of heaviest precipitation are October through April. The rainy season becomes shorter in the southern part of the State, November through March marking the wet period here. During the rest of the year precipitation is infrequent and usually light. In the north and over the central and northern mountains there are usually from 60 to 100 days of precipitation per year, while in the southern desert there may be as few as 10 days. It is apparent, therefore, that the rainy season is made up of periods of stormy weather alternating with longer periods of pleasant weather. A typical winter storm situation brings intermittent rain over a period of from two to five days, followed by seven to 14 days of dry weather.

SNOWFALL. Snow has been reported at one time or another in nearly every part of California but it is very infrequent west of the Sierra Nevada except at high elevations of the Coast Range and the Cascades. In the Sierra Nevada, snow in moderate amounts is reported nearly every winter at elevations as low as 2,000 feet. Amounts and intensities increase with elevation to around 7,000 or 8,000 feet. Above 4,000 feet elevation snow remains on the ground for appreciable lengths of time each winter.

RELATIVE HUMIDITY. In general, relative humidities are moderate to high along the coast throughout the year. Inland humidities are high during the winter and low during the summer. Since the ocean is the source of the cool, humid, maritime air of summer, it follows that with increasing distance from the ocean, relative humidity tends to decrease. Where mountain barriers prevent the free flow of marine air inland, humidities decrease rapidly. Where openings in these barriers permit a significant influx of cool, moist air it mixes with the drier inland air, resulting in a more gradual decrease of moisture. This pattern is characteristic of most coastal valleys.

STORMS. Thunderstorms may occur in California at any time of the year. Near the coast and over the Central Valley there appears to be no prevailing season. The storms are usually light and infrequent. Over the interior mountain areas storms are more intense, and they may become unusually strong on occasion at intermediate and high elevations of the Sierra Nevada. Many California thunderstorms produce so little precipitation that range and forest fires often result from the lightning strikes. Heavy precipitation occasionally results. Some flash flooding has been reported as a result of thundershowers. Hail diameters from one quarter of an inch to one half inch are sometimes reported. Serious hail damage is infrequent. Tornadoes have been reported in California but with a frequency of only one or two per year. They are generally not severe, in many cases amounting to little more than a local whirlwind.

DROUGHT. Drought must be evaluated on a different basis than in other parts of the country. Typically there are extended periods every summer with little or no precipitation. This is the normal and expected condition. A deficiency of precipitation becomes significant in the State when the normal winter water supply fails to materialize.

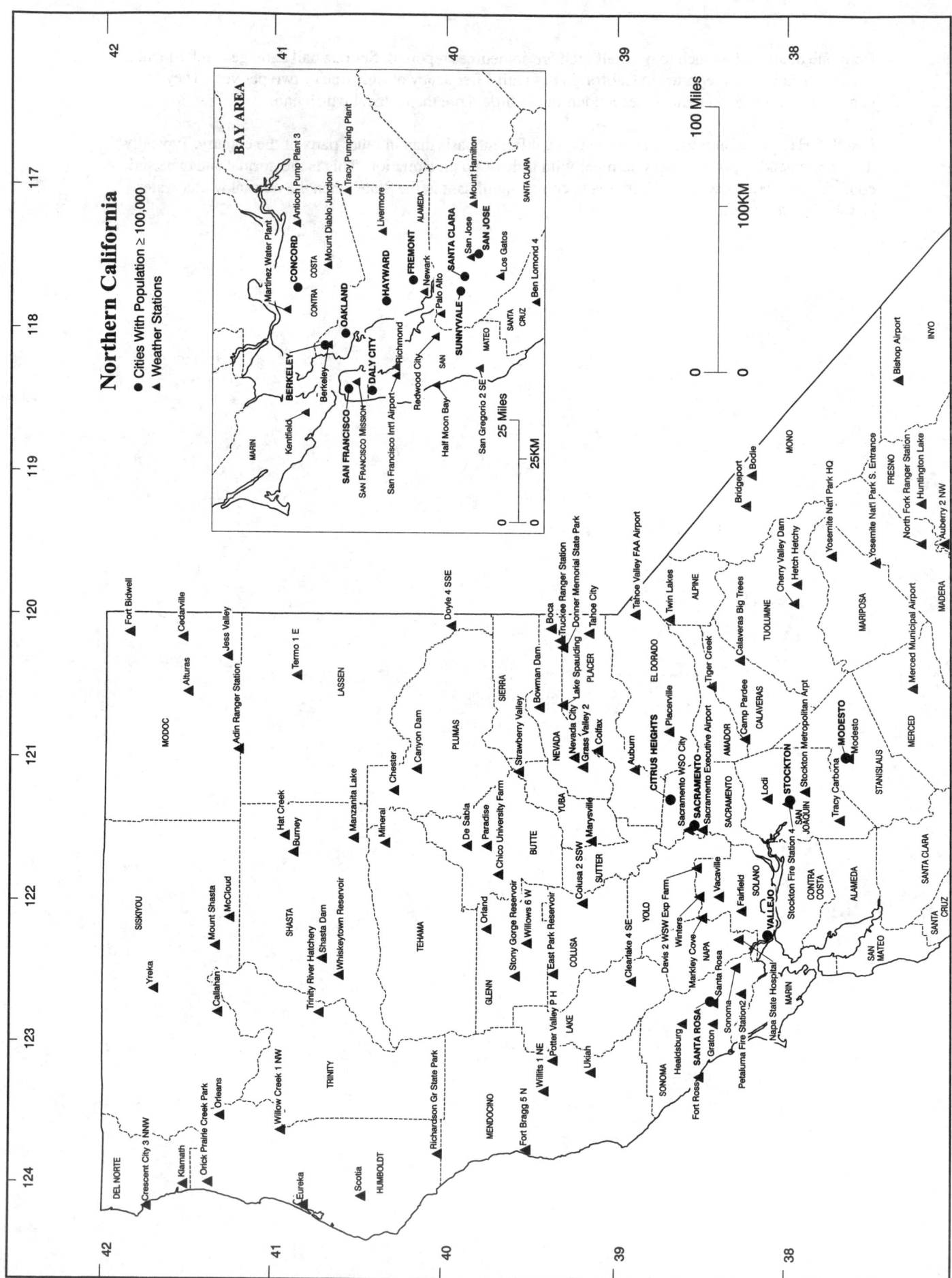

Northern California

● Cities With Population ≥ 100,000
▲ Weather Stations

BAY AREA

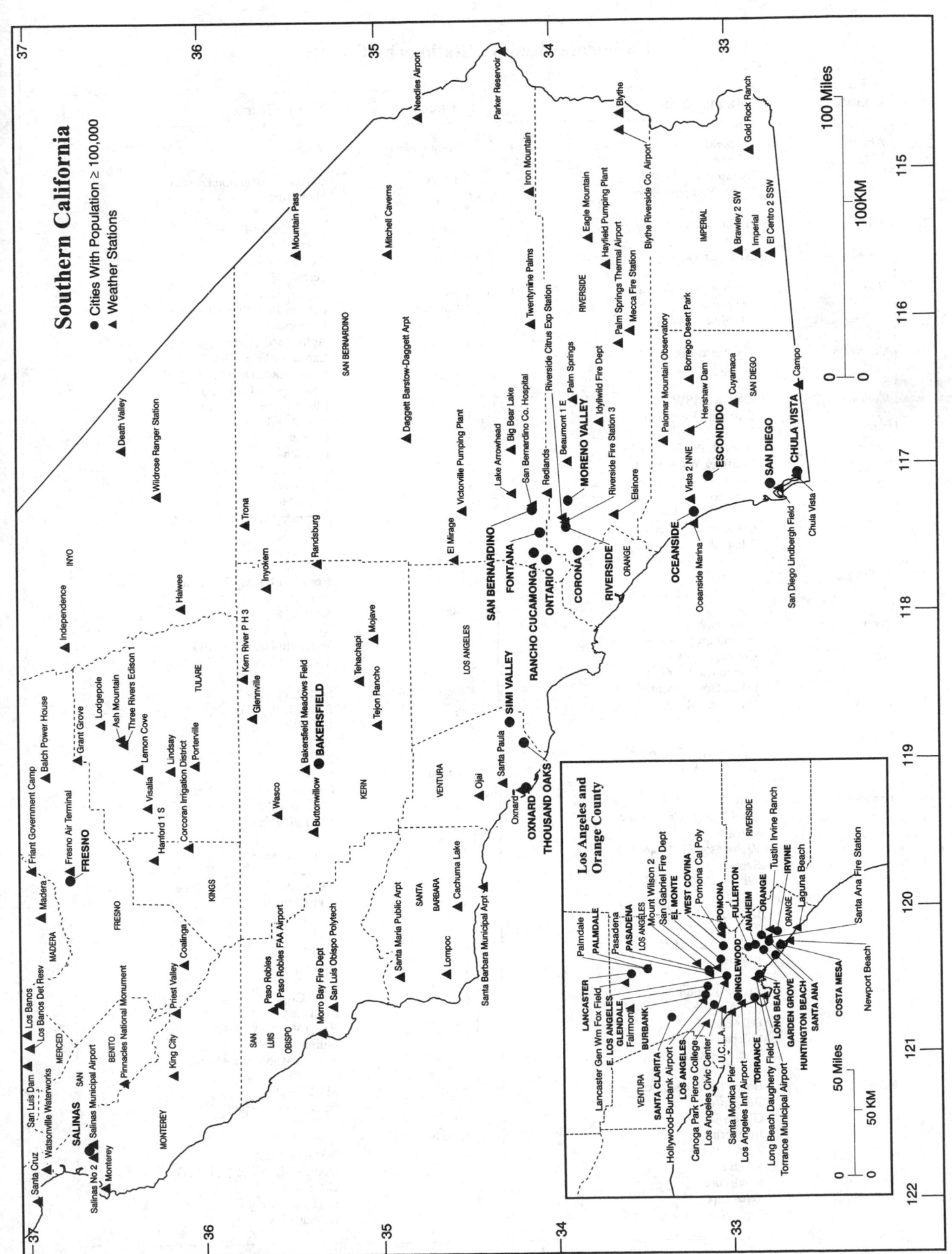

Southern California

- Cities With Population ≥ 100,000
- ▲ Weather Stations

Los Angeles and Orange County

California Weather Stations by County

County	Station Name
Alameda	Berkeley
	Livermore
	Newark
	Tracy Pumping Plant
Alpine	Twin Lakes
Amador	Tiger Creek
Butte	Chico University Farm
	De Sabla
	Paradise
Calaveras	Calaveras Big Trees
	Camp Pardee
Colusa	Colusa 2 SSW
	East Park Reservoir
Contra Costa	Antioch Pump Plant 3
	Martinez Water Plant
	Mount Diablo Junction
	Richmond
Del Norte	Crescent City 3 NNW
	Klamath
El Dorado	Placerville
	Tahoe Valley FAA Airport
Fresno	Auberry 2 NW
	Balch Power House
	Coalinga
	Fresno Air Terminal
	Friant Government Camp
	Huntington Lake
Glenn	Orland
	Stony Gorge Reservoir
	Willows 6 W
Humboldt	Eureka
	Orick Prairie Creek Park
	Orleans
	Richardson Gr. State Park
	Scotia
	Willow Creek 1 NW
Imperial	Brawley 2 SW
	El Centro 2 SSW
	Gold Rock Ranch
	Imperial
Inyo	Bishop Airport
	Death Valley
	Haiwee
	Independence
	Wildrose Ranger Station
Kern	Bakersfield Meadows Field
	Buttonwillow
	Glennville
	Inyokern
	Kern River P H 3
	Mojave
	Randsburg
	Tehachapi
	Tejon Rancho

County	Station Name
Kern (cont.)	Wasco
Kings	Corcoran Irrigation District
	Hanford 1 S
Lake	Clearlake 4 SE
Lassen	Doyle 4 SSE
	Termo 1 E
Los Angeles	Canoga Park Pierce College
	Fairmont
	Hollywood-Burbank Airport
	Lancaster Gen. Wm. Fox Field
	Long Beach Daugherty Field
	Los Angeles Civic Center
	Los Angeles Int'l Airport
	Mount Wilson 2
	Palmdale
	Pasadena
	Pomona Cal Poly
	San Gabriel Fire Dept.
	Santa Monica Pier
	Torrance Municipal Airport
	U.C.L.A.
Madera	Madera
	North Fork Ranger Station
Marin	Kentfield
Mariposa	Yosemite Nat'l Park HQ
	Yosemite Nat'l Park S. Entrance
Mendocino	Fort Bragg 5 N
	Potter Valley P H
	Ukiah
	Willits 1 NE
Merced	Los Banos
	Los Banos Det. Reservation
	Merced Municipal Airport
	San Luis Dam
Modoc	Adin Ranger Station
	Alturas
	Cedarville
	Fort Bidwell
	Jess Valley
Mono	Bodie
	Bridgeport
Monterey	King City
	Monterey
	Priest Valley
	Salinas 2
	Salinas Municipal Airport
Napa	Markley Cove
	Napa State Hospital
Nevada	Boca
	Bowman Dam
	Donner Memorial State Park
	Grass Valley 2
	Lake Spaulding
	Nevada City

County	Station Name
Nevada *(cont.)*	Truckee Ranger Station
Orange	Laguna Beach
	Newport Beach
	Santa Ana Fire Station
	Tustin Irvine Ranch
Placer	Auburn
	Colfax
	Tahoe City
Plumas	Canyon Dam
	Chester
Riverside	Beaumont 1 E
	Blythe
	Blythe Riverside Co. Airport
	Eagle Mountain
	Elsinore
	Hayfield Pumping Plant
	Idyllwild Fire Dept.
	Mecca Fire Station
	Palm Springs
	Palm Springs Thermal Airport
	Riverside Citrus Exp. Station
	Riverside Fire Station 3
Sacramento	Sacramento Executive Airport
	Sacramento WSO City
San Benito	Pinnacles National Monument
San Bernardino	Big Bear Lake
	Daggett Barstow-Daggett Airport
	El Mirage
	Iron Mountain
	Lake Arrowhead
	Mitchell Caverns
	Mountain Pass
	Needles Airport
	Parker Reservoir
	Redlands
	San Bernardino Co. Hospital
	Trona
	Twentynine Palms
	Victorville Pumping Plant
San Diego	Borrego Desert Park
	Campo
	Chula Vista
	Cuyamaca
	Henshaw Dam
	Oceanside Marina
	Palomar Mountain Observatory
	San Diego Lindbergh Field
	Vista 2 NNE
San Francisco	San Francisco Mission
San Joaquin	Lodi
	Stockton Fire Station 4
	Stockton Metropolitan Airport
	Tracy Carbona
San Luis Obispo	Morro Bay Fire Dept.
	Paso Robles
	Paso Robles FAA Airport
	San Luis Obispo Polytech

County	Station Name
San Mateo	Half Moon Bay
	Redwood City
	San Francisco Int'l Airport
	San Gregorio 2 SE
Santa Barbara	Cachuma Lake
	Lompoc
	Santa Barbara Municipal Airport
	Santa Maria Public Airport
Santa Clara	Los Gatos
	Mount Hamilton
	Palo Alto
	San Jose
Santa Cruz	Ben Lomond 4
	Santa Cruz
	Watsonville Waterworks
Shasta	Burney
	Hat Creek
	Manzanita Lake
	Shasta Dam
	Whiskeytown Reservoir
Siskiyou	Callahan
	McCloud
	Mount Shasta
	Yreka
Solano	Fairfield
	Vacaville
Sonoma	Fort Ross
	Graton
	Healdsburg
	Petaluma Fire Station 2
	Santa Rosa
	Sonoma
Stanislaus	Modesto
Tehama	Mineral
Trinity	Trinity River Hatchery
Tulare	Ash Mountain
	Grant Grove
	Lemon Cove
	Lindsay
	Lodgepole
	Porterville
	Three Rivers Edison 1
	Visalia
Tuolumne	Cherry Valley Dam
	Hetch Hetchy
Ventura	Ojai
	Oxnard
	Santa Paula
Yolo	Davis 2 WSW Exp. Farm
	Winters
Yuba	Marysville
	Strawberry Valley

California Weather Stations by City

City	Station Name	Miles
Anaheim	Long Beach Daugherty Field	15
	Newport Beach	16
	Pomona Cal Poly	17
	Santa Ana Fire Station	6
	Tustin Irvine Ranch	10
Bakersfield	Bakersfield Meadows Field	5
Berkeley	Berkeley	0
	Kentfield	17
	Martinez Water Plant	13
	Mount Diablo Junction	18
	Richmond	18
	San Francisco Int'l Airport	19
	San Francisco Mission	11
Burbank	Canoga Park Pierce College	14
	Hollywood-Burbank Airport	3
	Los Angeles Civic Center	10
	Los Angeles Int'l Airport	18
	Mount Wilson 2	15
	Pasadena	10
	San Gabriel Fire Dept.	14
	Santa Monica Pier	16
	U.C.L.A.	11
Chula Vista	Chula Vista	2
	San Diego Lindbergh Field	10
Citrus Heights	Auburn	18
	Sacramento Executive Airport	17
	Sacramento WSO City	14
Concord	Antioch Pump Plant 3	15
	Berkeley	16
	Martinez Water Plant	7
	Mount Diablo Junction	8
Corona	Elsinore	20
	Pomona Cal Poly	19
	Riverside Citrus Exp. Station	14
	Riverside Fire Station 3	12
	Santa Ana Fire Station	19
	Tustin Irvine Ranch	15
Costa Mesa	Laguna Beach	11
	Long Beach Daugherty Field	19
	Newport Beach	5
	Santa Ana Fire Station	7
	Tustin Irvine Ranch	9
Daly City	Berkeley	16
	Half Moon Bay	16
	Kentfield	18
	Richmond	8
	San Francisco Int'l Airport	7
	San Francisco Mission	5
East Los Angeles	Hollywood-Burbank Airport	16
	Long Beach Daugherty Field	14
	Los Angeles Civic Center	4
	Los Angeles Int'l Airport	15
	Mount Wilson 2	15
	Pasadena	8

City	Station Name	Miles
East Los Angeles (cont.)	San Gabriel Fire Dept.	6
	Santa Monica Pier	19
	Torrance Municipal Airport	19
	U.C.L.A.	16
El Monte	Long Beach Daugherty Field	18
	Los Angeles Civic Center	12
	Mount Wilson 2	11
	Pasadena	9
	Pomona Cal Poly	12
	San Gabriel Fire Dept.	5
Escondido	Henshaw Dam	19
	Oceanside Marina	20
	Vista 2 NNE	12
Fontana	Lake Arrowhead	19
	Redlands	16
	Riverside Citrus Exp. Station	10
	Riverside Fire Station 3	10
	San Bernardino Co. Hospital	11
Fremont	Livermore	15
	Newark	3
	Palo Alto	10
	Redwood City	15
	San Jose	16
Fresno	Fresno Air Terminal	4
	Friant Government Camp	16
	Madera	18
Fullerton	Long Beach Daugherty Field	14
	Newport Beach	19
	Pomona Cal Poly	14
	San Gabriel Fire Dept.	18
	Santa Ana Fire Station	10
	Tustin Irvine Ranch	13
Garden Grove	Laguna Beach	18
	Long Beach Daugherty Field	13
	Newport Beach	13
	Santa Ana Fire Station	5
	Tustin Irvine Ranch	10
Glendale	Canoga Park Pierce College	18
	Hollywood-Burbank Airport	7
	Los Angeles Civic Center	8
	Los Angeles Int'l Airport	18
	Mount Wilson 2	12
	Pasadena	6
	San Gabriel Fire Dept.	10
	Santa Monica Pier	18
	U.C.L.A.	13
Hayward	Berkeley	18
	Livermore	17
	Mount Diablo Junction	17
	Newark	9
	Palo Alto	14
	Redwood City	15
	Richmond	16
	San Francisco Int'l Airport	18

City	Station Name	Miles
Huntington Beach (cont.)	Laguna Beach	16
	Long Beach Daugherty Field	14
	Newport Beach	9
	Santa Ana Fire Station	9
	Tustin Irvine Ranch	13
Inglewood	Hollywood-Burbank Airport	17
	Long Beach Daugherty Field	13
	Los Angeles Civic Center	9
	Los Angeles Int'l Airport	3
	Pasadena	17
	San Gabriel Fire Dept.	17
	Santa Monica Pier	9
	Torrance Municipal Airport	11
	U.C.L.A.	10
Irvine	Laguna Beach	9
	Newport Beach	7
	Santa Ana Fire Station	6
	Tustin Irvine Ranch	4
Lancaster	Fairmont	17
	Lancaster Gen. Wm. Fox Field	5
	Palmdale	8
Long Beach	Long Beach Daugherty Field	2
	Los Angeles Civic Center	17
	Los Angeles Int'l Airport	16
	Santa Ana Fire Station	17
	Torrance Municipal Airport	10
Los Angeles	Canoga Park Pierce College	10
	Hollywood-Burbank Airport	6
	Los Angeles Civic Center	11
	Los Angeles Int'l Airport	13
	Pasadena	15
	San Gabriel Fire Dept.	18
	Santa Monica Pier	10
	U.C.L.A.	4
Modesto	Modesto	1
Moreno Valley	Beaumont 1 E	15
	Elsinore	19
	Redlands	9
	Riverside Citrus Exp. Station	7
	Riverside Fire Station 3	9
	San Bernardino Co. Hospital	14
Oakland	Berkeley	6
	Martinez Water Plant	16
	Mount Diablo Junction	16
	Richmond	15
	San Francisco Int'l Airport	16
	San Francisco Mission	12
Oceanside	Oceanside Marina	5
	Vista 2 NNE	5
Ontario	Pomona Cal Poly	10
	Riverside Citrus Exp. Station	18
	Riverside Fire Station 3	16
Orange	Laguna Beach	18
	Long Beach Daugherty Field	19

City	Station Name	Miles
Orange (cont.)	Newport Beach	14
	Pomona Cal Poly	18
	Santa Ana Fire Station	4
	Tustin Irvine Ranch	6
Oxnard	Ojai	18
	Oxnard	1
	Santa Paula	9
Palmdale	Lancaster Gen. Wm. Fox Field	13
	Palmdale	1
Pasadena	Hollywood-Burbank Airport	14
	Los Angeles Civic Center	9
	Mount Wilson 2	7
	Pasadena	1
	Pomona Cal Poly	19
	San Gabriel Fire Dept.	4
	U.C.L.A.	19
Pomona	Pomona Cal Poly	4
	San Gabriel Fire Dept.	20
Rancho Cucamonga	Pomona Cal Poly	14
	Riverside Citrus Exp. Station	17
	Riverside Fire Station 3	17
	San Bernardino Co. Hospital	18
Riverside	Elsinore	20
	Redlands	15
	Riverside Citrus Exp. Station	4
	Riverside Fire Station 3	2
	San Bernardino Co. Hospital	16
Sacramento	Davis 2 WSW Exp. Farm	16
	Sacramento Executive Airport	4
	Sacramento WSO City	3
Salinas	Monterey	16
	Salinas 2	2
	Salinas Municipal Airport	3
	Watsonville Waterworks	18
San Bernardino	Lake Arrowhead	10
	Redlands	9
	Riverside Citrus Exp. Station	12
	Riverside Fire Station 3	14
	San Bernardino Co. Hospital	2
San Diego	Chula Vista	10
	San Diego Lindbergh Field	4
San Francisco	Berkeley	12
	Kentfield	15
	Richmond	11
	San Francisco Int'l Airport	10
	San Francisco Mission	1
San Jose	Ben Lomond 4	19
	Los Gatos	7
	Mount Hamilton	12
	Newark	17
	Palo Alto	18
	San Jose	2

City	Station Name	Miles
Santa Ana	Laguna Beach	14
	Long Beach Daugherty Field	17
	Newport Beach	10
	Santa Ana Fire Station	1
	Tustin Irvine Ranch	6
Santa Clara	Ben Lomond 4	20
	Los Gatos	8
	Mount Hamilton	18
	Newark	12
	Palo Alto	11
	Redwood City	16
	San Jose	5
Santa Clarita	Canoga Park Pierce College	16
	Hollywood-Burbank Airport	17
Santa Rosa	Graton	9
	Healdsburg	14
	Petaluma Fire Station 2	13
	Santa Rosa	1
	Sonoma	17
Simi Valley	Canoga Park Pierce College	11
Stockton	Lodi	9
	Stockton Fire Station 4	1
	Stockton Metropolitan Airport	7
	Tracy Pumping Plant	20
Sunnyvale	Ben Lomond 4	20
	Los Gatos	10
	Newark	10
	Palo Alto	8
	Redwood City	13
	San Gregorio 2 SE	19
	San Jose	8
Thousand Oaks	Canoga Park Pierce College	18
	Oxnard	18
	Santa Paula	18
Torrance	Long Beach Daugherty Field	10
	Los Angeles Civic Center	16
	Los Angeles Int'l Airport	7
	Santa Monica Pier	14
	Torrance Municipal Airport	3
	U.C.L.A.	17
Vallejo	Berkeley	17
	Fairfield	14
	Martinez Water Plant	9
	Napa State Hospital	12
	Sonoma	18
West Covina	Los Angeles Civic Center	18
	Mount Wilson 2	15
	Pasadena	15
	Pomona Cal Poly	6
	San Gabriel Fire Dept.	11

Note: Miles is the distance between the geographic center of the city and the weather station.

California Weather Stations by Elevation

Feet	Station Name
8,369	Bodie
7,998	Twin Lakes
7,017	Huntington Lake
6,788	Big Bear Lake
6,732	Lodgepole
6,597	Grant Grove
6,469	Bridgeport
6,253	Tahoe Valley FAA Airport
6,227	Tahoe City
6,017	Truckee Ranger Station
5,935	Donner Memorial State Park
5,748	Manzanita Lake
5,708	Mount Wilson 2
5,574	Boca
5,547	Palomar Mountain Observatory
5,396	Jess Valley
5,380	Bowman Dam
5,377	Idyllwild Fire Dept.
5,298	Termo 1 E
5,203	Lake Arrowhead
5,154	Lake Spaulding
5,118	Yosemite Nat'l Park S. Entrance
4,872	Mineral
4,763	Cherry Valley Dam
4,727	Mountain Pass
4,691	Calaveras Big Trees
4,668	Cedarville
4,639	Cuyamaca
4,557	Canyon Dam
4,524	Chester
4,498	Fort Bidwell
4,399	Alturas
4,389	Doyle 4 SSE
4,347	Mitchell Caverns
4,202	Mount Hamilton
4,192	Adin Ranger Station
4,101	Bishop Airport
4,097	Wildrose Ranger Station
4,015	Tehachapi
3,963	Yosemite Nat'l Park HQ
3,943	Independence
3,868	Hetch Hetchy
3,822	Haiwee
3,805	Strawberry Valley
3,569	Randsburg
3,533	Mount Shasta
3,277	McCloud
3,182	Callahan
3,156	Burney
3,139	Glennville
3,057	Fairmont
3,015	Hat Creek
2,949	El Mirage
2,857	Victorville Pumping Plant
2,778	Nevada City

Feet	Station Name
2,732	Mojave
2,709	De Sabla
2,700	Henshaw Dam
2,700	Kern River P H 3
2,627	Campo
2,627	North Fork Ranger Station
2,624	Yreka
2,598	Beaumont 1 E
2,595	Palmdale
2,437	Inyokern
2,398	Colfax
2,398	Grass Valley 2
2,352	Tiger Creek
2,335	Lancaster Gen. Wm. Fox Field
2,299	Priest Valley
2,168	Mount Diablo Junction
2,089	Auberry 2 NW
1,975	Twentynine Palms
1,919	Daggett Barstow-Daggett Airport
1,856	Trinity River Hatchery
1,847	Placerville
1,748	Paradise
1,719	Balch Power House
1,706	Ash Mountain
1,692	Trona
1,423	Tejon Rancho
1,368	Hayfield Pumping Plant
1,348	Clearlake 4 SE
1,348	Willits 1 NE
1,315	Redlands
1,305	Pinnacles National Monument
1,292	Whiskeytown Reservoir
1,289	Auburn
1,282	Elsinore
1,204	East Park Reservoir
1,138	Three Rivers Edison 1
1,122	San Bernardino Co. Hospital
1,072	Shasta Dam
1,013	Potter Valley P H
984	Riverside Citrus Exp. Station
971	Eagle Mountain
921	Iron Mountain
912	Needles Airport
862	Pasadena
839	Riverside Fire Station 3
813	Paso Robles FAA Airport
803	Borrego Desert Park
797	Stony Gorge Reservoir
787	Canoga Park Pierce College
780	Cachuma Lake
748	Ojai
738	Pomona Cal Poly
734	Parker Reservoir
725	Hollywood-Burbank Airport
698	Paso Robles

Feet	Station Name
669	Coalinga
656	Camp Pardee
629	Ukiah
511	Lemon Cove
508	Vista 2 NNE
498	Richardson Gr. State Park
488	Bakersfield Meadows Field
482	Gold Rock Ranch
479	Livermore
479	Markley Cove
459	Willow Creek 1 NW
449	San Gabriel Fire Dept.
429	U.C.L.A.
419	Ben Lomond 4
419	Lindsay
419	Palm Springs
410	Friant Government Camp
406	Los Banos Det. Reservation
396	Orleans
390	Porterville
387	Blythe Riverside Co. Airport
383	Monterey
364	Los Gatos
344	Wasco
331	Fresno Air Terminal
324	Visalia
318	King City
314	San Luis Obispo Polytech
308	Berkeley
275	San Luis Dam
272	San Gregorio 2 SE
269	Buttonwillow
269	Los Angeles Civic Center
269	Madera
265	Blythe
252	Orland
252	Santa Maria Public Airport
242	Hanford 1 S
236	Santa Paula
232	Willows 6 W
200	Corcoran Irrigation District
200	Graton
183	Chico University Farm
173	San Francisco Mission
164	Santa Rosa
157	Orick Prairie Creek Park
150	Merced Municipal Airport
137	Scotia
137	Tracy Carbona
134	Santa Ana Fire Station
134	Winters
127	Kentfield
127	Santa Cruz
118	Fort Bragg 5 N
118	Los Banos

Feet	Station Name
118	Tustin Irvine Ranch
114	Morro Bay Fire Dept.
111	Fort Ross
108	Torrance Municipal Airport
108	Vacaville
104	Healdsburg
98	Los Angeles Int'l Airport
95	Lompoc
95	San Jose
95	Sonoma
95	Watsonville Waterworks
88	Modesto
68	Crescent City 3 NNW
68	Salinas Municipal Airport
59	Antioch Pump Plant 3
59	Davis 2 WSW Exp. Farm
59	Tracy Pumping Plant
55	Chula Vista
55	Marysville
49	Colusa 2 SSW
45	Oxnard
42	Salinas 2
39	Fairfield
39	Lodi
39	Martinez Water Plant
32	Laguna Beach
32	Napa State Hospital
29	Petaluma Fire Station 2
29	Redwood City
22	Klamath
22	Long Beach Daugherty Field
22	Palo Alto
22	Sacramento WSO City
19	Eureka
19	Richmond
19	Stockton Metropolitan Airport
13	Half Moon Bay
13	Sacramento Executive Airport
13	San Diego Lindbergh Field
13	Santa Monica Pier
9	Newark
9	Newport Beach
9	Oceanside Marina
9	Stockton Fire Station 4
6	San Francisco Int'l Airport
6	Santa Barbara Municipal Airport
-29	El Centro 2 SSW
-62	Imperial
-98	Brawley 2 SW
-111	Palm Springs Thermal Airport
-177	Mecca Fire Station
-193	Death Valley

Bakersfield Meadows Field

Bakersfield, situated in the extreme south end of the great San Joaquin Valley, is partially surrounded by a horseshoe-shaped rim of mountains with an open side to the northwest and the crest at an average distance of 40 miles.

The Sierra Nevada mountains to the northeast shut out most of the cold air that flows southward over the continent during winter. They also catch and store snow, which provides irrigation water for use during the dry months. The Tehachapi Mountains, forming the southern boundary, act as an obstruction to northwest wind, causing heavier precipitation on the windward slopes, high wind velocity over the ridges and, at times, continuing cloudiness in the south end of the valley after skies have cleared elsewhere.

Because of the nature of the surrounding topography, there are large climatic variations within relatively short distances. These zones of variation may be classified as valley, mountain, and desert areas. The overall climate, however, is warm and semi-arid. There is only one wet season during the year, as 90 percent of all precipitation falls from October through April, inclusive. Snow in the valley is infrequent, with only a trace occurring in about one year out of seven. Thunderstorms seldom occur in the valley.

Summers are cloudless, hot and dry. Cotton, potatoes, grapes, and cattle are the principal agricultural products. Severe freezes seldom occur and there are occasional years with no frost at all in certain warm areas.

Winters are mild and semi-arid, yet fairly humid. December and January are characterized by frequent fog, mostly nocturnal, which prevails when marine air is trapped in the valley by a high pressure system. In extreme cases this fog may last continuously for two or three weeks. Another local characteristic is the occasionally warm, dry, southeast chinook wind that spills through the Tehachapi Pass during winter. This wind usually attains velocities of 30 to 40 miles an hour, sometimes reaching as high as 60 miles an hour.

During summer months northwest sea breezes frequent the Bakersfield area about twice weekly. When above normal temperatures prevail for several days, the gradient builds up sufficiently to draw in cooler air from the coastal section. During prolonged periods of drought this late afternoon breeze may carry varying amounts of dust, and thermal instability sometimes causes the dust to rise as high as 7,000 feet.

Based on the 1951-1980 period, the average first occurrence of 32 degrees Fahrenheit in the fall is December 11 and the average last occurrence in the spring is January 31.

Bakersfield Meadows Field *Kern County*   Elevation: 488 ft.   Latitude: 35° 26' N   Longitude: 119° 03' W

	JAN	FEB	MAR	APR	MAY	JUN	JUL	AUG	SEP	OCT	NOV	DEC	YEAR
Mean Maximum Temp. (°F)	57.4	64.3	69.0	76.1	84.5	92.4	98.2	96.6	90.9	81.1	66.9	57.3	77.9
Mean Temp. (°F)	48.4	53.7	57.7	62.8	70.7	78.1	83.9	82.6	77.4	68.0	55.7	47.9	65.6
Mean Minimum Temp. (°F)	39.4	43.0	46.3	49.5	56.9	63.7	69.5	68.5	63.9	54.9	44.4	38.4	53.2
Extreme Maximum Temp. (°F)	82	87	91	101	107	114	113	112	110	103	88	83	114
Extreme Minimum Temp. (°F)	23	25	32	33	37	45	52	55	47	29	28	19	19
Days Maximum Temp. ≥ 90°F	0	0	0	2	10	19	28	26	18	6	0	0	109
Days Maximum Temp. ≤ 32°F	0	0	0	0	0	0	0	0	0	0	0	0	0
Days Minimum Temp. ≤ 32°F	5	1	0	0	0	0	0	0	0	0	0	5	11
Days Minimum Temp. ≤ 0°F	0	0	0	0	0	0	0	0	0	0	0	0	0
Heating Degree Days (base 65°F)	507	314	228	115	29	2	0	0	2	48	278	525	2,048
Cooling Degree Days (base 65°F)	0	0	5	63	186	361	563	535	361	133	3	0	2,210
Mean Precipitation (in.)	1.17	1.20	1.38	0.44	0.24	0.11	trace	0.08	0.15	0.29	0.67	0.78	6.51
Maximum Precipitation (in.)	2.6	4.7	4.3	2.6	2.4	1.1	0.3	1.2	1.1	1.8	3.0	2.0	10.9
Minimum Precipitation (in.)	trace	trace	trace	0	0	0	0	0	0	0	0	0	1.9
Maximum 24-hr. Precipitation (in.)	1.4	2.3	1.0	0.9	0.8	1.1	0.3	1.0	0.6	1.2	1.4	1.0	2.3
Days With ≥ 0.1" Precipitation	3	3	4	1	1	0	0	0	1	1	2	2	18
Days With ≥ 1.0" Precipitation	0	0	0	0	0	0	0	0	0	0	0	0	0
Mean Snowfall (in.)	0.1	trace	trace	trace	0.0	0.0	0.0	0.0	0.0	0.0	0.0	trace	0.1
Maximum Snowfall (in.)	trace	trace	2	0	0	0	0	0	0	0	0	trace	2
Maximum 24-hr. Snowfall (in.)	trace	trace	2	0	0	0	0	0	0	0	0	trace	2
Days With ≥ 1.0" Snow Depth	0	0	0	0	0	0	0	0	0	0	0	0	0
Thunderstorm Days	< 1	< 1	1	< 1	< 1	< 1	< 1	< 1	1	< 1	< 1	< 1	2
Foggy Days	18	10	4	1	< 1	< 1	< 1	< 1	1	2	10	18	64
Predominant Sky Cover	OVR	OVR	CLR	CLR	CLR	CLR	CLR	CLR	CLR	CLR	CLR	OVR	CLR
Mean Relative Humidity 7am (%)	86	82	75	63	53	46	44	50	56	63	77	86	65
Mean Relative Humidity 4pm (%)	61	50	42	33	27	23	21	24	28	33	48	61	38
Mean Dewpoint (°F)	39	41	41	42	44	48	51	53	51	46	42	39	45
Prevailing Wind Direction	E	E	NNW	NW	NW	NW	NW	NW	NW	NW	E	E	NW
Prevailing Wind Speed (mph)	6	6	9	10	10	10	10	9	9	8	6	6	8
Maximum Wind Gust (mph)	48	58	51	48	45	58	36	49	48	48	49	63	63

Bishop Airport

The station at Bishop is located at the Municipal Airport two and a half miles east of the town, one mile west of the Owens River, on the floor of the Owens Valley, which is orientated northwest to southeast and at this point is 12 miles wide, level, and semi-arid. Peaks of the 12,000 to 14,000 feet Sierra Nevadas are 25 miles west, and the 12,000 to 14,000 feet White Mountains are 10 miles east. The northern end of the valley is partly cut off by 6,000 to 8,000 feet mountains about 45 miles distant. The southern end of the valley makes a gradual descent to the Mojave Desert about 150 miles distant.

During the summer and autumn, the Mojave Desert causes an early morning and late evening northerly wind. Conversely, in the heat of the afternoon, it causes a southerly wind that is occasionally strong. Summer skies are mostly clear with thunderstorms from May through August. The days are hot and dry, the nights cool.

Winter and spring, although seasons of adverse weather, are quite mild. The skies are partly cloudy with the years greatest amounts of precipitation falling during the months of November through April. At times, strong northerly winds blow, especially in the spring during the months of February, March, and April. East and west winds frequently give pronounced warm mountain wind effects and turbulence.

During the winter and spring, strong westerly winds aloft, flowing over the Sierra Nevadas, create the Sierra Wave, known to sailplane pilots the world over.

Based on the 1951-1980 period, the average first occurrence of 32 degrees Fahrenheit in the fall is October 13 and the average last occurrence in the spring is May 7.

Bishop Airport *Inyo County*   Elevation: 4,101 ft.   Latitude: 37° 22' N   Longitude: 118° 21' W

	JAN	FEB	MAR	APR	MAY	JUN	JUL	AUG	SEP	OCT	NOV	DEC	YEAR
Mean Maximum Temp. (°F)	53.2	58.2	63.9	71.2	80.5	90.7	97.2	95.3	87.0	75.6	62.2	53.6	74.0
Mean Temp. (°F)	37.8	42.3	47.4	53.5	62.1	70.7	76.6	74.6	66.9	56.3	44.8	37.7	55.9
Mean Minimum Temp. (°F)	22.4	26.5	30.9	35.8	43.7	50.7	55.8	53.8	46.8	37.0	27.3	21.7	37.7
Extreme Maximum Temp. (°F)	76	81	85	93	100	108	109	107	112	97	84	73	112
Extreme Minimum Temp. (°F)	-7	3	9	17	26	29	34	40	26	16	9	-8	-8
Days Maximum Temp. ≥ 90°F	0	0	0	0	5	19	29	27	12	1	0	0	93
Days Maximum Temp. ≤ 32°F	1	0	0	0	0	0	0	0	0	0	0	0	1
Days Minimum Temp. ≤ 32°F	29	24	18	9	1	0	0	0	0	8	24	29	142
Days Minimum Temp. ≤ 0°F	0	0	0	0	0	0	0	0	0	0	0	0	0
Heating Degree Days (base 65°F)	836	633	537	340	132	20	1	1	44	270	601	841	4,256
Cooling Degree Days (base 65°F)	0	0	0	4	47	192	357	305	108	9	0	0	1,022
Mean Precipitation (in.)	0.90	0.95	0.61	0.24	0.26	0.21	0.17	0.12	0.28	0.19	0.49	0.63	5.05
Maximum Precipitation (in.)	8.9	6.0	2.9	2.3	1.3	1.3	1.5	0.6	1.3	1.6	2.6	5.8	17.1
Minimum Precipitation (in.)	0	0	0	0	0	0	0	0	0	0	0	0	1.8
Maximum 24-hr. Precipitation (in.)	3.3	3.5	1.8	1.6	0.9	0.7	0.8	0.4	1.3	0.9	1.3	2.7	3.5
Days With ≥ 0.1" Precipitation	2	2	2	1	1	1	1	0	1	1	1	1	14
Days With ≥ 1.0" Precipitation	0	0	0	0	0	0	0	0	0	0	0	0	0
Mean Snowfall (in.)	3.4	1.4	0.6	trace	trace	0.0	*0.0*	*0.0*	*0.0*	*trace*	0.3	1.2	*6.9*
Maximum Snowfall (in.)	23	32	15	9	2	0	0	0	0	2	4	13	57
Maximum 24-hr. Snowfall (in.)	13	12	8	7	2	0	0	0	0	2	2	6	13
Days With ≥ 1.0" Snow Depth	3	1	0	0	*0*	0	*0*	0	*0*	0	0	1	*5*
Thunderstorm Days	0	0	< 1	< 1	1	2	5	2	1	1	0	0	12
Foggy Days	1	1	1	1	0	1	0	0	0	0	< 1	2	6
Predominant Sky Cover	CLR	CLR	CLR	CLR	CLR	CLR	CLR	CLR	CLR	CLR	CLR	CLR	CLR
Mean Relative Humidity 7am (%)	71	68	58	44	39	34	35	39	43	52	63	68	51
Mean Relative Humidity 4pm (%)	35	27	21	17	16	13	14	14	15	18	27	35	21
Mean Dewpoint (°F)	19	20	19	20	27	31	36	35	31	25	21	19	25
Prevailing Wind Direction	NW	N	N	N	N	S	S	S	S	S	N	N	N
Prevailing Wind Speed (mph)	7	13	14	13	13	13	13	13	12	12	12	12	12
Maximum Wind Gust (mph)	60	63	59	62	66	60	60	75	53	56	93	68	93

Eureka

Humboldt Bay is one-quarter mile north and one mile west of the station. There are no hills in Eureka of any consequence. The land slopes upward gently from the Bay toward the Coast Range, which begins about 3 miles east of the station and reaches the top of its first ridge approximately 10 miles to the east. The elevation of the ridge is 2,000 feet and extends in a semicircle from a point 20 miles north of Eureka to a point 25 miles south.

The climate of Eureka is completely maritime with high humidity prevailing the entire year. The rainy season begins in October and continues through April, accounting for about 90 percent of the annual precipitation. The dry season from May through September is marked by considerable fog or low cloudiness that usually clears in the late morning.

Temperatures are moderate the entire year. Although record highs have reached the mid 80s and record lows near 20 degrees, the usual yearly range is from lows in the mid 30s to highs in the mid 70s.

The principal industries are lumbering, fishing, tourism, and dairy farming. There is very little truck farming due to the low temperatures and lack of sunshine, however, the climate is nearly ideal for berries and flowers.

Based on the 1951-1980 period, the average first occurrence of 32 degrees Fahrenheit in the fall is December 10 and the average last occurrence in the spring is February 6.

Eureka *Humboldt County*   Elevation: 19 ft.   Latitude: 40° 49' N   Longitude: 124° 10' W

	JAN	FEB	MAR	APR	MAY	JUN	JUL	AUG	SEP	OCT	NOV	DEC	YEAR
Mean Maximum Temp. (°F)	55.4	56.3	56.4	57.2	59.2	61.2	62.8	63.7	63.5	61.3	58.2	55.2	59.2
Mean Temp. (°F)	48.7	49.7	50.1	51.1	53.6	56.0	57.7	58.6	57.6	54.9	51.6	48.3	53.2
Mean Minimum Temp. (°F)	42.0	43.1	43.7	44.9	47.9	50.7	52.6	53.4	51.6	48.4	44.8	41.5	47.1
Extreme Maximum Temp. (°F)	78	80	76	80	82	81	76	82	86	87	78	75	87
Extreme Minimum Temp. (°F)	4	27	31	32	37	40	46	45	42	32	29	21	4
Days Maximum Temp. ≥ 90°F	0	0	0	0	0	0	0	0	0	0	0	0	0
Days Maximum Temp. ≤ 32°F	0	0	0	0	0	0	0	0	0	0	0	0	0
Days Minimum Temp. ≤ 32°F	2	1	0	0	0	0	0	0	0	0	1	2	6
Days Minimum Temp. ≤ 0°F	0	0	0	0	0	0	0	0	0	0	0	0	0
Heating Degree Days (base 65°F)	498	424	456	411	346	265	219	192	217	309	397	510	4,244
Cooling Degree Days (base 65°F)	0	0	0	0	1	0	0	1	1	2	0	0	5
Mean Precipitation (in.)	6.06	5.38	5.54	2.89	1.61	0.64	0.16	0.38	0.86	2.33	6.10	6.63	38.58
Maximum Precipitation (in.)	13.9	10.8	11.2	10.7	6.0	2.6	1.2	3.4	3.3	13.0	16.6	14.1	67.2
Minimum Precipitation (in.)	0.7	0.1	1.2	0.3	trace	trace	0	trace	trace	trace	0.3	0.5	21.1
Maximum 24-hr. Precipitation (in.)	3.7	4.8	2.9	2.3	2.1	1.2	1.0	1.6	1.4	5.0	2.8	3.4	5.0
Days With ≥ 0.1" Precipitation	11	10	11	7	4	2	0	1	2	5	10	11	74
Days With ≥ 1.0" Precipitation	1	1	1	0	0	0	0	0	0	0	2	2	7
Mean Snowfall (in.)	trace	0.2	trace	trace	0.0	0.0	0.0	0.0	0.0	0.0	trace	trace	0.2
Maximum Snowfall (in.)	3	4	1	trace	0	0	0	0	0	0	trace	2	4
Maximum 24-hr. Snowfall (in.)	2	2	1	trace	0	0	0	0	0	0	trace	2	2
Days With ≥ 1.0" Snow Depth	0	0	0	0	0	0	0	0	0	0	0	0	0
Thunderstorm Days	1	1	< 1	< 1	< 1	< 1	< 1	< 1	< 1	< 1	1	1	4
Foggy Days	13	11	10	12	13	16	22	22	21	21	15	15	191
Predominant Sky Cover	na	na	na	na	na	na	na	na	na	na	na	na	na
Mean Relative Humidity 7am (%)	na	na	na	na	na	na	na	na	na	na	na	na	na
Mean Relative Humidity 4pm (%)	na	na	na	na	na	na	na	na	na	na	na	na	na
Mean Dewpoint (°F)	na	na	na	na	na	na	na	na	na	na	na	na	na
Prevailing Wind Direction	na	na	na	na	na	na	na	na	na	na	na	na	na
Prevailing Wind Speed (mph)	na	na	na	na	na	na	na	na	na	na	na	na	na
Maximum Wind Gust (mph)	69	60	58	53	60	51	47	38	49	49	69	62	69

Fresno Air Terminal

Fresno is located about midway and toward the eastern edge of the San Joaquin Valley, which is oriented northwest to southeast and has a length of about 225 miles and an average width of 50 miles. The San Joaquin Valley is generally flat. About 15 miles east of Fresno the terrain slopes upward with the foothills of the Sierra Nevada. The Sierra Nevada attain an elevation of more than 14,000 feet 50 miles east of Fresno. West of the city 45 miles lie the foothills of the Coastal Range.

The climate of Fresno is dry and mild in winter and hot in summer. Nearly nine-tenths of the annual precipitation falls in the six months from November to April.

Due to clear skies during the summer and the protection of the San Joaquin Valley from marine effects, the normal daily maximum temperature reaches the high 90s during the latter part of July. The daily maximum temperature during the warmest month has ranged from 76 to 115 degrees. Low relative humidities and some wind movement substantially lower the sensible temperature during periods of high readings. Humidity readings of 15 percent are common on summer afternoons, and readings as low as eight percent have been recorded. In contrast to this, humidity readings average 90 percent during the morning hours of December and January.

Winds flow with the major axis of the San Joaquin Valley, generally from the northwest. This feature is especially beneficial since, during the warmest months, the northwest winds increase during the evenings. These refreshing breezes and the normally large temperature variation of about 35 degrees between the highest and lowest readings of the day, generally result in comfortable evening and night temperatures.

Winter temperatures are usually mild with infrequent cold spells dropping the readings below freezing. Heavy frost occurs almost every year, and the first frost usually occurs during the last week of November. The last frost in spring is usually in early March. The growing season is 291 days.

Although the heaviest rains recorded at Fresno for short periods have occurred in June, usually any rainfall during the summer is very light. Snow is a rare occurrence in Fresno.

Fresno enjoys a very high percentage of sunshine, receiving more than 80 percent of the possible amounts during all but the four months of November, December, January, and February.

During foggy periods, sunshine is reduced to a minimum and fog frequently lifts to a few hundred feet above the surface of the valley, appearing as a heavy, solid cloud layer.

Fresno Air Terminal *Fresno County*   Elevation: 331 ft.   Latitude: 36° 47' N   Longitude: 119° 43' W

	JAN	FEB	MAR	APR	MAY	JUN	JUL	AUG	SEP	OCT	NOV	DEC	YEAR
Mean Maximum Temp. (°F)	54.5	62.1	67.1	74.9	84.0	92.1	98.1	96.3	90.5	79.9	64.9	54.5	76.6
Mean Temp. (°F)	46.5	51.7	55.9	61.5	69.4	76.6	82.2	80.6	75.4	65.8	53.7	45.8	63.8
Mean Minimum Temp. (°F)	38.4	41.3	44.8	48.1	54.7	61.1	66.2	64.8	60.2	51.7	42.4	37.0	50.9
Extreme Maximum Temp. (°F)	78	80	90	100	107	109	112	112	107	102	84	75	112
Extreme Minimum Temp. (°F)	20	24	27	32	36	45	52	51	43	27	26	18	18
Days Maximum Temp. ≥ 90°F	0	0	0	2	9	20	28	27	17	4	0	0	107
Days Maximum Temp. ≤ 32°F	0	0	0	0	0	0	0	0	0	0	0	0	0
Days Minimum Temp. ≤ 32°F	7	2	0	0	0	0	0	0	0	0	1	8	18
Days Minimum Temp. ≤ 0°F	0	0	0	0	0	0	0	0	0	0	0	0	0
Heating Degree Days (base 65°F)	567	369	276	138	34	3	0	0	2	68	334	589	2,380
Cooling Degree Days (base 65°F)	0	0	3	52	179	358	553	517	338	105	1	0	2,106
Mean Precipitation (in.)	2.18	1.96	2.21	0.73	0.39	0.22	0.01	0.01	0.25	0.57	1.17	1.43	11.13
Maximum Precipitation (in.)	8.6	6.0	7.2	4.4	1.6	1.6	0.2	0.3	1.2	2.2	3.5	6.7	21.6
Minimum Precipitation (in.)	trace	trace	0	trace	0	0	0	0	0	0	0	0	6.1
Maximum 24-hr. Precipitation (in.)	2.2	1.8	2.4	1.4	1.1	1.3	0.2	0.3	0.9	1.5	1.3	1.7	2.4
Days With ≥ 0.1" Precipitation	5	5	5	2	1	0	0	0	1	1	3	4	27
Days With ≥ 1.0" Precipitation	0	0	0	0	0	0	0	0	0	0	0	0	0
Mean Snowfall (in.)	trace	trace	trace	0.0	0.0	trace	0.0	0.0	0.0	trace	0.0	trace	trace
Maximum Snowfall (in.)	2	trace	trace	0	0	0	0	0	0	0	trace	1	2
Maximum 24-hr. Snowfall (in.)	2	trace	trace	0	0	0	0	0	0	0	trace	1	2
Days With ≥ 1.0" Snow Depth	0	0	0	0	0	0	0	0	0	0	0	0	0
Thunderstorm Days	< 1	< 1	1	1	1	< 1	< 1	< 1	1	1	< 1	< 1	5
Foggy Days	23	15	8	3	1	< 1	< 1	< 1	1	5	17	23	96
Predominant Sky Cover	OVR	OVR	CLR	CLR	CLR	CLR	CLR	CLR	CLR	CLR	CLR	OVR	CLR
Mean Relative Humidity 7am (%)	92	91	86	75	63	56	54	61	69	77	88	92	75
Mean Relative Humidity 4pm (%)	67	56	46	35	27	23	21	24	27	34	53	68	40
Mean Dewpoint (°F)	40	42	43	44	46	49	53	54	52	47	43	40	46
Prevailing Wind Direction	SE	NW	NW	NW	NW	NW	WNW	WNW	WNW	NW	NW	ESE	NW
Prevailing Wind Speed (mph)	7	8	9	9	10	9	9	8	8	8	8	7	8
Maximum Wind Gust (mph)	55	49	48	48	44	39	30	36	39	51	46	48	55

Long Beach Daugherty Field

The climate of the Long Beach Airport is considerably influenced by local topography, which plays a greater role in the climatic conditions at this station than the more general movements of pressure systems which dominate other sections of the country.

The Pacific Ocean, four miles south and 12 miles west, has a moderating effect on temperatures. The annual range of temperatures at the airport is much less than is experienced at stations further inland in the Los Angeles basin. Low coastal hills lie immediately between the station and the sea, the highest being Signal Hill, one and five eithths miles southwest and 498 feet above sea level. The Palos Verdes Hills, 11 miles west-southwest of the station, slope upward to 1,480 feet above sea level. These natural barriers between the ocean and the station cause slightly greater ranges of high and low temperatures locally than at stations on the coast. During the winter months high temperatures are usually in the upper 60s, and lows in the 40s. In the summer highs are in the 70s and low 80s, and lows in the high 50s.

Precipitation is sparse during the summer months, with an average of only about 0.60 inch for the months of May through October. The greatest rainfall occurs during the winter months. The coastal hills influence the local precipitation with greater amounts of rainfall occurring just one or two miles south and southwest of the station. Snow is an extremely rare phenomenon locally, although the San Gabriel Mountains are blanketed in the higher elevations much of the winter, and occasionally have snow down to the 2,500-foot level. Thunderstorms occur only sporadically at Long Beach.

The coastal hills to the southwest combine with the lowest mountain passes leading to the interior desert valleys east of the Los Angeles basin to produce a sea breeze from a westerly component in the afternoon and early evening hours. Occasionally, strong dry northeasterly winds descend the mountain slopes in the fall, winter, and early spring months, but ordinarily by-pass the station. Actually, the highest winds at Long Beach are recorded in association with the winter and spring storms which invade southern California from the Pacific.

During the summer months low clouds are quite common in the late night and morning hours at this station due to its proximity to the ocean. By late morning or early afternoon the clouds have disappeared and the balance of the day is sunny and comfortable. Here again is a moderating influence on summertime temperatures locally which is not so prominent at stations further inland where the coastal cloudiness arrives later, burns off earlier, and penetrates less frequently.

Long Beach Daugherty Field *Los Angeles County*   Elevation: 22 ft.   Latitude: 33° 50' N   Longitude: 118° 10' W

	JAN	FEB	MAR	APR	MAY	JUN	JUL	AUG	SEP	OCT	NOV	DEC	YEAR
Mean Maximum Temp. (°F)	66.9	67.9	68.5	72.3	73.7	77.9	82.6	84.3	82.6	78.2	72.5	67.6	74.6
Mean Temp. (°F)	56.5	58.0	59.4	62.6	65.6	69.4	73.4	74.8	73.1	68.3	61.4	56.5	64.9
Mean Minimum Temp. (°F)	45.9	48.0	50.2	52.8	57.3	60.8	64.2	65.2	63.5	58.3	50.3	45.3	55.2
Extreme Maximum Temp. (°F)	91	91	98	105	102	109	107	103	108	109	98	89	109
Extreme Minimum Temp. (°F)	30	34	35	38	47	50	57	55	51	39	35	28	28
Days Maximum Temp. ≥ 90°F	0	0	0	1	1	2	4	6	6	3	1	0	24
Days Maximum Temp. ≤ 32°F	0	0	0	0	0	0	0	0	0	0	0	0	0
Days Minimum Temp. ≤ 32°F	0	0	0	0	0	0	0	0	0	0	0	0	0
Days Minimum Temp. ≤ 0°F	0	0	0	0	0	0	0	0	0	0	0	0	0
Heating Degree Days (base 65°F)	261	197	178	95	35	4	0	0	1	14	121	260	1,166
Cooling Degree Days (base 65°F)	2	7	10	39	59	134	268	315	251	124	18	2	1,229
Mean Precipitation (in.)	2.99	2.98	2.41	0.56	0.23	0.07	0.02	0.10	0.24	0.32	1.23	1.88	13.03
Maximum Precipitation (in.)	12.8	9.4	8.8	4.4	2.3	0.9	0.2	2.0	1.4	1.6	6.0	5.3	27.7
Minimum Precipitation (in.)	0	0	0	0	0	0	0	0	0	0	0	trace	2.8
Maximum 24-hr. Precipitation (in.)	5.0	2.4	3.5	1.2	2.0	0.9	0.2	1.8	1.4	1.2	2.0	3.2	5.0
Days With ≥ 0.1" Precipitation	5	4	5	1	0	0	0	0	0	1	2	3	21
Days With ≥ 1.0" Precipitation	1	1	0	0	0	0	0	0	0	0	0	0	2
Mean Snowfall (in.)	trace	trace	0.0	0.0	trace	0.0	0.0	0.0	0.0	0.0	0.	0.0	trace
Maximum Snowfall (in.)	trace	0	0	0	0	0	0	0	0	0	0	0	trace
Maximum 24-hr. Snowfall (in.)	trace	0	0	0	0	0	0	0	0	0	0	0	trace
Days With ≥ 1.0" Snow Depth	0	0	0	0	0	0	0	0	0	0	0	0	0
Thunderstorm Days	< 1	1	1	< 1	< 1	< 1	< 1	< 1	< 1	< 1	< 1	< 1	2
Foggy Days	14	12	11	8	7	8	8	9	12	14	12	15	133
Predominant Sky Cover	CLR	OVR	CLR	CLR	OVR	CLR	CLR	CLR	CLR	CLR	CLR	CLR	CLR
Mean Relative Humidity 7am (%)	77	79	80	77	76	78	79	80	81	80	76	75	78
Mean Relative Humidity 4pm (%)	54	54	55	52	55	56	54	54	55	55	52	53	54
Mean Dewpoint (°F)	42	44	46	48	52	56	60	61	59	54	46	42	51
Prevailing Wind Direction	WNW	WNW	W	S	S	S	S	WNW	WNW	WNW	NW	WNW	WNW
Prevailing Wind Speed (mph)	7	8	10	9	9	8	8	8	8	8	7	7	8
Maximum Wind Gust (mph)	49	49	49	47	43	40	28	29	51	49	78	45	78

Los Angeles Civic Center

The climate of Los Angeles is normally pleasant and mild through the year. The Pacific Ocean is the primary moderating influence. The coastal mountain ranges lying along the north and east sides of the Los Angeles coastal basin act as a buffer against extremes of summer heat and winter cold occurring in desert and plateau regions in the interior. A variable balance between mild sea breezes, and either hot or cold winds from the interior, results in some variety in weather conditions, but temperature and humidity are usually well within the comfort level. The climate of the Los Angeles metropolitan area is marked by a difference in temperature, humidity, cloudiness, fog, rain, and sunshine over fairly short distances.

These differences are closely related to the distance from, and elevation above, the Pacific Ocean. Both high and low temperatures become more extreme and the average relative humidity becomes lower inland and up slopes. Relative humidity is frequently high near the coast, but may be quite low along the foothills. During periods of high temperatures, the relative humidity is usually below normal. Like other Pacific Coast areas, most rainfall comes during the winter with nearly 85 percent of the annual total occurring from November through March, while summers are practically rainless. Precipitation generally increases with distance from the ocean, from a yearly total of around 12 inches in coastal sections to the south of the city to over 20 inches in foothill areas. Destructive flash floods occasionally develop in and below some mountain canyons. Snow is often visible on nearby mountains in the winter, but is extremely rare in the coastal basin.

Prevailing winds are from the west during the spring, summer, and early autumn, with northeasterly wind predominating the remainder of the year. At times, the lack of air movement, combined with a frequent and persistent temperature inversion, is associated with concentrations of air pollution in the Los Angeles coastal basin and some adjacent areas. In fall, winter, and early spring months, occasional foehn-like descending Santa Ana winds come from the northeast over ridges and through passes in the coastal mountains. Sunshine, fog, and clouds depend a great deal on topography and distance from the ocean. Low clouds are common at night and in the morning along the coast during spring and summer, but form later and clear earlier near the foothills so that annual cloudiness and fog frequencies are greatest near the ocean, and sunshine totals are highest on the inland side of the city. The sun shines about 75 percent of daytime hours at the Civic Center. Light fog may accompany the usual night and morning low clouds, but dense fog is more likely to occur during the night and early morning hours of the winter months.

Los Angeles Civic Center *Los Angeles County*   Elevation: 269 ft.   Latitude: 34° 03' N   Longitude: 118° 14' W

	JAN	FEB	MAR	APR	MAY	JUN	JUL	AUG	SEP	OCT	NOV	DEC	YEAR
Mean Maximum Temp. (°F)	68.1	69.5	69.8	73.0	74.6	79.4	83.9	84.8	83.4	79.1	73.3	68.5	75.6
Mean Temp. (°F)	58.8	60.4	61.2	64.1	66.6	70.8	74.6	75.5	74.4	69.9	63.5	58.9	66.6
Mean Minimum Temp. (°F)	49.5	51.3	52.6	55.1	58.7	62.1	65.2	66.2	65.3	60.6	53.6	49.3	57.5
Extreme Maximum Temp. (°F)	95	95	98	106	101	112	107	105	110	108	99	91	112
Extreme Minimum Temp. (°F)	32	34	35	39	50	52	57	56	54	41	38	30	30
Days Maximum Temp. ≥ 90°F	0	0	0	1	1	3	5	6	7	3	1	0	27
Days Maximum Temp. ≤ 32°F	0	0	0	0	0	0	0	0	0	0	0	0	0
Days Minimum Temp. ≤ 32°F	0	0	0	0	0	0	0	0	0	0	0	0	0
Days Minimum Temp. ≤ 0°F	0	0	0	0	0	0	0	0	0	0	0	0	0
Heating Degree Days (base 65°F)	200	146	137	80	33	4	0	0	0	10	86	196	892
Cooling Degree Days (base 65°F)	16	30	33	77	103	190	314	351	300	186	48	14	1,662
Mean Precipitation (in.)	3.35	3.63	3.12	0.78	0.32	0.06	0.01	0.13	0.32	0.34	1.22	2.07	15.35
Maximum Precipitation (in.)	10.0	12.4	8.1	9.9	3.6	1.1	trace	0.4	5.7	2.3	6.0	8.5	31.3
Minimum Precipitation (in.)	trace	0	0	trace	0	0	0	0	0	0	0	0	4.1
Maximum 24-hr. Precipitation (in.)	5.7	3.6	5.9	2.7	1.0	0.5	trace	0.4	4.0	1.7	2.0	4.9	5.9
Days With ≥ 0.1" Precipitation	5	5	5	2	1	0	0	0	1	1	2	3	25
Days With ≥ 1.0" Precipitation	1	1	1	0	0	0	0	0	0	0	0	1	4
Mean Snowfall (in.)	na	na	na	na	na	na	na	na	na	na	na	na	na
Maximum Snowfall (in.)	trace	0	0	0	0	0	0	0	0	0	0	0	trace
Maximum 24-hr. Snowfall (in.)	trace	0	0	0	0	0	0	0	0	0	0	0	trace
Days With ≥ 1.0" Snow Depth	na	na	na	na	na	na	na	na	na	na	na	na	na
Thunderstorm Days	< 1	1	< 1	1	< 1	< 1	< 1	< 1	< 1	< 1	< 1	< 1	2
Foggy Days	3	4	3	4	4	6	5	5	8	6	5	3	56
Predominant Sky Cover	na	na	na	na	na	na	na	na	na	na	na	na	na
Mean Relative Humidity 7am (%)	na	na	na	na	na	na	na	na	na	na	na	na	na
Mean Relative Humidity 4pm (%)	na	na	na	na	na	na	na	na	na	na	na	na	na
Mean Dewpoint (°F)	na	na	na	na	na	na	na	na	na	na	na	na	na
Prevailing Wind Direction	na	na	na	na	na	na	na	na	na	na	na	na	na
Prevailing Wind Speed (mph)	na	na	na	na	na	na	na	na	na	na	na	na	na
Maximum Wind Gust (mph)	na	na	na	na	na	na	na	na	na	na	na	na	na

Los Angeles Int'l Airport

Predominating influences on the climate of the Los Angeles International Airport are the Pacific Ocean, three miles to the west, the southern California coastal mountain ranges which line the inland side of the coastal plain surrounding the airport, and the large scale weather patterns associated with Pacific storm paths. Marine air covers the coastal plain most of the year but air from the interior reaches the coast at times, especially during the fall and winter months. The coast ranges act as a buffer to the more extreme conditions of the interior. Pronounced differences in temperature, humidity, cloudiness, fog, sunshine, and rain occur over fairly short distances on the coastal plains and the adjoining foothills due to the local topography and the decreased marine effect further inland. In general, temperature ranges are least and humidity highest close to the coast, while precipitation increases with elevation.

The most characteristic feature of the climate of the coastal plain around the station is the night and morning low cloudiness and sunny afternoons which prevail during the spring and summer months and occur often during the remainder of the year. The coastal low cloudiness, combined with the westerly sea breeze, produces mild temperatures throughout the year. Daily temperature range is usually less than 15 degrees in spring and summer and about 20 degrees in fall and winter. Hot weather is not frequent at any season along the coast. When high temperatures do occur, the humidity is almost always low. Nighttime temperatures are generally cool but minimum temperatures below 40 degrees are rare and periods of over 10 years have passed with no readings below freezing at the airport. Prevailing daytime winds are from the west, but night and early morning breezes are usually light and from the east and northeast. Strongest winds observed at the station have been from the west and north following winter storms. During the fall, winter, and spring, gusty dry northeasterly Santa Ana winds blow over southern California mountains and through passes to the coast, but rarely reach L.A. International Airport.

Precipitation occurs mainly in the winter. Measurable rain may fall on about one day in four from late October into early April, but in three years out of four, traces or less are reported for the entire months of July and August. Thunderstorms do not occur often near the coast, but showers and thunderstorms are observed over the coastal ranges during the summer. Traces of snow have fallen at Los Angeles International Airport only a few times, melting as they fell.

Visibility at Los Angeles International Airport is frequently restricted by haze, fog, or smoke. Low visibilities are favored by a layer of moist marine air with warm dry air above and light winds. Light fog occurs at some time nearly every month, but heavy fog is observed least during the summer.

Los Angeles Int'l Airport *Los Angeles County*   Elevation: 98 ft.   Latitude: 33° 56' N   Longitude: 118° 24' W

	JAN	FEB	MAR	APR	MAY	JUN	JUL	AUG	SEP	OCT	NOV	DEC	YEAR
Mean Maximum Temp. (°F)	65.5	66.0	65.4	68.0	69.3	72.5	75.3	76.8	76.5	74.4	70.5	66.6	70.6
Mean Temp. (°F)	57.1	58.1	58.4	60.8	63.1	66.3	69.4	70.6	70.1	66.9	61.7	57.5	63.3
Mean Minimum Temp. (°F)	48.6	50.1	51.4	53.5	56.9	60.1	63.3	64.5	63.6	59.4	52.9	48.5	56.1
Extreme Maximum Temp. (°F)	88	90	95	102	97	104	97	97	106	103	96	90	106
Extreme Minimum Temp. (°F)	33	35	39	42	49	50	53	56	54	43	39	33	33
Days Maximum Temp. ≥ 90°F	0	0	0	0	0	1	0	0	2	1	1	0	5
Days Maximum Temp. ≤ 32°F	0	0	0	0	0	0	0	0	0	0	0	0	0
Days Minimum Temp. ≤ 32°F	0	0	0	0	0	0	0	0	0	0	0	0	0
Days Minimum Temp. ≤ 0°F	0	0	0	0	0	0	0	0	0	0	0	0	0
Heating Degree Days (base 65°F)	244	196	204	136	72	16	0	0	1	19	115	228	1,231
Cooling Degree Days (base 65°F)	5	9	7	22	21	60	146	185	157	89	22	4	727
Mean Precipitation (in.)	3.00	3.00	2.36	0.56	0.24	0.08	0.02	0.14	0.25	0.38	1.25	1.93	13.21
Maximum Precipitation (in.)	12.7	11.1	6.4	4.5	2.5	0.7	0.3	2.5	1.9	1.8	7.5	5.7	29.5
Minimum Precipitation (in.)	0	0	0	0	0	0	0	0	0	0	0	0	3.1
Maximum 24-hr. Precipitation (in.)	4.6	3.9	3.1	1.3	1.7	0.7	0.3	2.1	1.7	1.8	5.6	2.8	5.6
Days With ≥ 0.1" Precipitation	5	5	5	2	0	0	0	0	0	1	2	3	23
Days With ≥ 1.0" Precipitation	1	1	0	0	0	0	0	0	0	0	0	1	3
Mean Snowfall (in.)	trace	0.0	trace	0.0	0.0	0.0	0.0	0.0	0.0	0.0	0.0	trace	trace
Maximum Snowfall (in.)	trace	0	0	0	0	0	0	0	0	0	0	0	trace
Maximum 24-hr. Snowfall (in.)	trace	0	0	0	0	0	0	0	0	0	0	0	trace
Days With ≥ 1.0" Snow Depth	0	0	0	0	0	0	0	0	0	0	0	0	0
Thunderstorm Days	< 1	1	1	< 1	< 1	< 1	< 1	< 1	< 1	< 1	< 1	< 1	2
Foggy Days	11	10	8	7	6	6	7	8	9	11	11	11	105
Predominant Sky Cover	CLR	CLR	CLR	CLR	OVR	OVR	CLR	CLR	CLR	CLR	CLR	CLR	CLR
Mean Relative Humidity 7am (%)	70	72	76	76	77	80	80	82	81	76	69	68	76
Mean Relative Humidity 4pm (%)	61	62	64	64	66	67	67	68	67	66	61	61	64
Mean Dewpoint (°F)	42	44	46	49	53	56	60	61	59	54	46	42	51
Prevailing Wind Direction	WSW	WSW	WSW	WSW	WSW	WSW	WSW	WSW	WSW	WSW	WSW	WSW	WSW
Prevailing Wind Speed (mph)	9	9	10	10	10	10	9	9	9	9	9	8	9
Maximum Wind Gust (mph)	51	56	62	59	49	40	31	33	39	46	60	49	62

Sacramento Executive Airport

Sacramento, and the lower Sacramento Valley, has a mild climate with abundant sunshine most of the year. A nearly cloud-free sky prevails throughout the summer months, and in much of the spring and fall. The summers are usually dry with warm to hot afternoons and mostly mild nights. The rainy season generally is November through March. About 75 percent of the annual precipitation occurs then, but measurable rain falls only on an average of nine days per month during that period. The shielding effect of mountains to the north, east, and west usually modifies winter storms. The Sierra Nevada snow fields, only 70 miles east of Sacramento, usually provide an adequate water supply during the dry season, and an important recreational area in winter. Heavy snowfall and torrential rains frequently fall on the western Sierra slopes, and may produce flood conditions along the Sacramento River and its tributaries. In the valley, however, excessive rainfall as well as damaging winds are rare.

The prevailing wind at Sacramento is southerly every month but November, when it is northerly. Topographic effects, the north-south alignment of the valley, the coast range, and the Sierra Nevada strongly influence the wind flow in the valley. A sea level gap in the coast range permits cool, oceanic air to flow, occasionally, into the valley during the summer season with a marked lowering of temperature through the Sacramento-San Joaquin River Delta to the capital. In the spring and fall, a large north-to-south pressure gradient develops over the northern part of the state.

Extreme hot spells, with temperatures exceeding 100 degrees, are usually caused by air flow from a sub-tropical high pressure area that brings light to nearly calm winds and humidities below 20 percent.

Thunderstorms are few in number, usually mild in character, and occur mainly in the spring. An occasional thunderstorm may drift over the valley from the Sierra Nevada in the summer. Snow falls so rarely, and in such small amounts, that its occurrence may be disregarded as a climatic feature. Heavy fog occurs mostly in midwinter, never in summer, and seldom in spring or autumn. An occasional winter fog, under stagnant atmospheric conditions, may continue for several days. Light and moderate fogs are more frequent, and may come anytime during the wet, cold season. The fog is the radiational cooling type, and is usually confined to the early morning hours.

Based on the 1951-1980 period, the average first occurrence of 32 degrees Fahrenheit in the fall is December 1 and the average last occurrence in the spring is February 14.

Sacramento Executive Airport *Sacramento County*   Elevation: 13 ft.   Latitude: 38° 30' N   Longitude: 121° 30' W

	JAN	FEB	MAR	APR	MAY	JUN	JUL	AUG	SEP	OCT	NOV	DEC	YEAR
Mean Maximum Temp. (°F)	53.5	60.4	64.6	71.5	80.2	87.4	92.7	91.6	87.6	78.4	63.7	53.6	73.8
Mean Temp. (°F)	46.2	51.2	54.4	58.8	65.6	71.5	75.5	74.8	71.8	64.5	53.5	45.7	61.1
Mean Minimum Temp. (°F)	38.9	41.8	44.1	46.1	50.9	55.5	58.3	58.1	55.9	50.6	43.2	37.8	48.4
Extreme Maximum Temp. (°F)	70	76	88	95	105	108	114	110	108	101	85	72	114
Extreme Minimum Temp. (°F)	23	23	26	31	36	41	48	49	43	36	26	18	18
Days Maximum Temp. ≥ 90°F	0	0	0	0	6	12	21	19	13	3	0	0	74
Days Maximum Temp. ≤ 32°F	0	0	0	0	0	0	0	0	0	0	0	0	0
Days Minimum Temp. ≤ 32°F	5	2	0	0	0	0	0	0	0	0	1	7	15
Days Minimum Temp. ≤ 0°F	0	0	0	0	0	0	0	0	0	0	0	0	0
Heating Degree Days (base 65°F)	574	384	322	192	70	10	1	0	7	75	340	591	2,566
Cooling Degree Days (base 65°F)	0	0	0	19	88	203	329	313	215	68	1	0	1,237
Mean Precipitation (in.)	3.89	3.31	2.79	0.99	0.49	0.20	0.05	0.06	0.37	0.86	2.41	2.54	17.96
Maximum Precipitation (in.)	9.7	8.8	8.1	4.2	3.1	1.3	0.8	0.6	2.8	7.5	7.4	12.6	33.4
Minimum Precipitation (in.)	0.2	0.1	0	0	0	0	0	0	0	0	trace	0	5.6
Maximum 24-hr. Precipitation (in.)	3.0	2.6	1.8	2.2	1.5	1.1	0.8	0.6	1.8	3.8	2.4	2.9	3.8
Days With ≥ 0.1" Precipitation	7	6	6	3	1	1	0	0	1	2	5	5	37
Days With ≥ 1.0" Precipitation	1	1	0	0	0	0	0	0	0	0	1	0	3
Mean Snowfall (in.)	trace	trace	trace	0.0	trace	0.0	0.0	0.0	0.0	0.0	0.0	trace	trace
Maximum Snowfall (in.)	trace	2	trace	trace	0	0	0	0	0	0	0	trace	2
Maximum 24-hr. Snowfall (in.)	trace	2	trace	trace	0	0	0	0	0	0	0	trace	2
Days With ≥ 1.0" Snow Depth	0	0	0	0	0	0	0	0	0	0	0	0	0
Thunderstorm Days	< 1	1	1	1	< 1	< 1	< 1	< 1	< 1	< 1	< 1	< 1	3
Foggy Days	22	14	8	3	1	< 1	< 1	1	2	7	16	22	96
Predominant Sky Cover	OVR	OVR	CLR	CLR	CLR	CLR	CLR	CLR	CLR	CLR	CLR	OVR	CLR
Mean Relative Humidity 7am (%)	91	89	85	78	72	67	69	74	75	81	87	91	80
Mean Relative Humidity 4pm (%)	70	59	52	43	36	31	29	29	31	38	56	70	45
Mean Dewpoint (°F)	39	42	43	44	47	50	53	53	51	47	43	39	46
Prevailing Wind Direction	SE	SE	SW	SW	SW	SW	SSW	SSW	SSW	NNW	NNW	SE	SW
Prevailing Wind Speed (mph)	9	9	10	10	12	13	10	10	10	10	9	9	10
Maximum Wind Gust (mph)	53	46	47	45	51	45	37	33	38	40	56	51	56

San Diego Lindbergh Field

The city of San Diego is located on San Diego Bay in the southwest corner of southern California. The prevailing winds and weather are tempered by the Pacific Ocean. Temperatures of freezing or below have rarely occurred at the station since the record began in 1871, but hot weather, 90 degrees or above, is more frequent.

Dry easterly winds sometimes blow in the vicinity for several days at a time, bringing temperatures in the 90s and at times even in the 100s in the eastern sections of the city and outlying suburbs. As these hot winds are predominant in the fall, highest temperatures occur in the months of September and October. Records show that over 60 percent of the days with 90 degrees or higher have occurred in these two months. High temperatures are almost invariably accompanied by very low relative humidities, which often drop below 20 percent and occasionally below 10 percent.

A marked feature of the climate is the wide variation in temperature within short distances. In nearby valleys daytimes are much warmer in summer and nights noticeably cooler in winter, and freezing occurs much more frequently than in the city. Although records show unusually small daily temperature ranges, only about 15 degrees between the highest and lowest readings, a few miles inland these ranges increase to 30 degrees or more.

Strong winds and gales associated with Pacific, or tropical storms, are infrequent due to the latitude.

The seasonal rainfall is about 10 inches in the city, but increases with elevation and distance from the coast. In the mountains to the north and east the average is between 20 and 40 inches, depending on slope and elevation. Most of the precipitation falls in winter, except in the mountains where there is an occasional thunderstorm. Eighty-five percent of the rainfall occurs from November through March, but wide variations take place in monthly and seasonal totals. In each occurrence of snowfall only a trace was recorded officially.

As on the rest of the Pacific Coast, a dominant characteristic of spring and summer is the nighttime and early morning cloudiness. Low clouds form regularly and frequently extend inland over the coastal valleys and foothills, but they usually dissipate during the morning and the afternoons are generally clear.

Considerable fog occurs along the coast, but the amount decreases with distance inland. The fall and winter months are usually the foggiest. Thunderstorms are rare, averaging about three a year in the city.

San Diego Lindbergh Field *San Diego County*   Elevation: 13 ft.   Latitude: 32° 44' N   Longitude: 117° 10' W

	JAN	FEB	MAR	APR	MAY	JUN	JUL	AUG	SEP	OCT	NOV	DEC	YEAR
Mean Maximum Temp. (°F)	65.8	66.4	66.4	68.7	69.3	72.2	75.9	77.5	77.0	74.1	70.0	66.1	70.8
Mean Temp. (°F)	57.7	59.0	60.0	62.5	64.5	67.3	70.9	72.5	71.6	67.7	61.9	57.5	64.4
Mean Minimum Temp. (°F)	49.7	51.5	53.6	56.3	59.7	62.5	65.9	67.4	66.1	61.2	53.8	48.9	58.0
Extreme Maximum Temp. (°F)	86	90	93	98	94	101	95	94	107	104	97	87	107
Extreme Minimum Temp. (°F)	33	38	39	45	50	54	59	58	53	43	39	34	33
Days Maximum Temp. ≥ 90°F	0	0	0	0	0	1	0	0	1	1	0	0	3
Days Maximum Temp. ≤ 32°F	0	0	0	0	0	0	0	0	0	0	0	0	0
Days Minimum Temp. ≤ 32°F	0	0	0	0	0	0	0	0	0	0	0	0	0
Days Minimum Temp. ≤ 0°F	0	0	0	0	0	0	0	0	0	0	0	0	0
Heating Degree Days (base 65°F)	220	169	152	86	43	8	0	0	0	11	103	226	1,018
Cooling Degree Days (base 65°F)	2	6	6	24	38	84	192	242	202	99	14	1	910
Mean Precipitation (in.)	2.30	2.00	2.28	0.73	0.20	0.09	0.03	0.09	0.21	0.40	1.13	1.38	10.84
Maximum Precipitation (in.)	9.1	5.4	7.0	3.7	1.8	0.9	0.2	2.1	1.9	1.8	5.8	6.6	19.4
Minimum Precipitation (in.)	trace	0	trace	0	0	0	0	0	0	0	0	trace	3.4
Maximum 24-hr. Precipitation (in.)	2.6	1.7	2.1	1.4	1.5	0.5	0.2	1.4	0.9	1.0	2.0	2.1	2.6
Days With ≥ 0.1" Precipitation	4	4	4	2	0	0	0	0	0	1	2	3	20
Days With ≥ 1.0" Precipitation	1	1	0	0	0	0	0	0	0	0	0	0	2
Mean Snowfall (in.)	0.0	0.0	trace	trace	0.0	0.0	0.0	0.0	0.0	0.0	trace	0.0	trace
Maximum Snowfall (in.)	trace	0	0	0	0	0	0	0	0	0	0	trace	trace
Maximum 24-hr. Snowfall (in.)	trace	0	0	0	0	0	0	0	0	0	0	trace	trace
Days With ≥ 1.0" Snow Depth	0	0	0	0	0	0	0	0	0	0	0	0	0
Thunderstorm Days	< 1	< 1	< 1	< 1	< 1	< 1	< 1	< 1	< 1	< 1	< 1	< 1	6
Foggy Days	11	9	8	6	6	7	6	7	9	11	11	11	102
Predominant Sky Cover	CLR	CLR	OVR	OVR	OVR	OVR	OVR	OVR	CLR	CLR	CLR	CLR	OVR
Mean Relative Humidity 7am (%)	70	72	73	72	74	78	80	79	78	75	69	68	74
Mean Relative Humidity 4pm (%)	58	58	59	60	64	66	66	66	65	64	60	58	62
Mean Dewpoint (°F)	43	45	47	50	53	57	61	62	61	56	48	43	52
Prevailing Wind Direction	NW	WNW	WNW	WNW	WNW	WNW	WNW	WNW	WNW	WNW	WNW	NW	WNW
Prevailing Wind Speed (mph)	8	9	10	10	9	9	9	9	9	9	9	8	9
Maximum Wind Gust (mph)	64	52	53	43	40	37	30	33	44	35	48	44	64

San Francisco Int'l Airport

The station is located in the central Terminal Building of the San Francisco International Airport, which is on flat filled tideland on the west shore of San Francisco Bay. The bay borders the airport from the north to the south-southeast. San Bruno Mountain, five miles to the north-northwest, rises to 1,300 feet. A north-south trending ridge of coastal mountains, four miles to the west, varies in elevation from 700 to 1,900 feet, being highest southward along the peninsula. The Pacific Ocean west of the ridge is six miles from the airport. A broad gap to the northwest of the station, between San Bruno Mountain and the coastal mountains, allows a strong flow of marine air over the station and dominate the local climate.

San Francisco Airport enjoys a marine-type climate characterized by mild and moderately wet winters and by dry, cool summers. Winter rains, occurring from November through March, account for over 80 percent of the annual rainfall, and measurable precipitation occurs on an average of 10 days per month during this period. However, there are frequent dry periods lasting well over a week. Severe winter storms with gale winds and heavy rains occur only occasionally. Thunderstorms average two a year and may occur in any month.

The daily and annual range in temperature is small. A few frosty mornings occur during the winter but the temperature seldom drops below freezing. Winter temperatures generally rise to the high 50s in the early afternoon.

The summer weather is dominated by a cool sea breeze resulting in an average summer wind speed of nearly 15 mph. Winds are light in the early morning but normally reach 20 to 25 mph in the afternoon.

A sea fog, arriving over the station during the late evening or night as a low cloud, is another persistent feature of the summer weather. This high fog, occasionally producing drizzle or mist, usually disappears during the late forenoon. Despite the morning overcast, summer days are sunny. On the average a total of only 14 days during the four months from June through September are classified as cloudy.

Daytime temperatures are held down both by the morning low overcast and the afternoon strengthening sea breeze, resulting in daily maximum readings averaging about 70 degrees from May through August. However, during these months occasional hot spells, lasting a few days, are experienced without the usual high fog and sea breeze. September, when the sea breeze becomes less pronounced, is the warmest month with highs in the 70s. Low temperatures during the summer are in the mid-50s.

San Francisco Int'l Airport *San Mateo County*   Elevation: 6 ft.   Latitude: 37° 37' N   Longitude: 122° 24' W

	JAN	FEB	MAR	APR	MAY	JUN	JUL	AUG	SEP	OCT	NOV	DEC	YEAR
Mean Maximum Temp. (°F)	56.1	59.6	61.5	64.4	67.3	70.5	72.0	72.5	73.5	70.4	62.7	56.3	65.6
Mean Temp. (°F)	49.6	52.6	54.2	56.2	58.9	61.7	63.3	64.0	64.3	61.3	55.1	49.6	57.6
Mean Minimum Temp. (°F)	42.9	45.4	46.8	48.0	50.5	52.9	54.5	55.4	55.0	52.3	47.6	42.9	49.5
Extreme Maximum Temp. (°F)	71	77	79	92	97	98	105	100	103	99	79	71	105
Extreme Minimum Temp. (°F)	30	31	35	37	42	46	48	49	45	39	35	24	24
Days Maximum Temp. ≥ 90°F	0	0	0	0	0	1	1	0	1	0	0	0	3
Days Maximum Temp. ≤ 32°F	0	0	0	0	0	0	0	0	0	0	0	0	0
Days Minimum Temp. ≤ 32°F	0	0	0	0	0	0	0	0	0	0	0	1	1
Days Minimum Temp. ≤ 0°F	0	0	0	0	0	0	0	0	0	0	0	0	0
Heating Degree Days (base 65°F)	471	345	329	261	193	114	72	53	57	128	290	469	2,782
Cooling Degree Days (base 65°F)	0	0	0	6	11	21	27	31	40	24	1	0	161
Mean Precipitation (in.)	4.54	3.80	3.24	1.14	0.36	0.11	0.03	0.07	0.20	0.99	2.67	3.08	20.23
Maximum Precipitation (in.)	11.3	9.5	9.0	6.4	3.8	0.9	0.3	0.7	2.3	7.3	7.9	12.3	38.3
Minimum Precipitation (in.)	0.2	trace	0	trace	trace	trace	0	trace	trace	trace	trace	trace	8.7
Maximum 24-hr. Precipitation (in.)	5.6	2.2	2.0	2.3	1.5	0.8	0.3	0.3	2.3	2.6	2.4	3.2	5.6
Days With ≥ 0.1" Precipitation	8	7	7	3	1	0	0	0	1	2	5	6	40
Days With ≥ 1.0" Precipitation	1	1	1	0	0	0	0	0	0	0	1	1	5
Mean Snowfall (in.)	trace	trace	trace	0.0	0.0	0.0	0.0	0.0	0.0	0.0	0.0	trace	trace
Maximum Snowfall (in.)	2	trace	trace	0	0	0	0	0	0	0	0	trace	2
Maximum 24-hr. Snowfall (in.)	2	trace	trace	0	0	0	0	0	0	0	0	trace	2
Days With ≥ 1.0" Snow Depth	0	0	0	0	0	0	0	0	0	0	0	0	0
Thunderstorm Days	< 1	< 1	< 1	< 1	< 1	< 1	< 1	< 1	< 1	< 1	< 1	< 1	5
Foggy Days	17	12	7	4	4	3	4	4	6	9	12	17	99
Predominant Sky Cover	OVR	OVR	OVR	CLR	CLR	CLR	CLR	CLR	CLR	CLR	CLR	OVR	CLR
Mean Relative Humidity 7am (%)	87	86	82	79	78	77	81	83	82	83	85	86	82
Mean Relative Humidity 4pm (%)	68	66	64	62	61	60	61	62	60	60	63	68	63
Mean Dewpoint (°F)	42	44	44	45	47	50	52	53	52	50	46	42	47
Prevailing Wind Direction	SE	WNW	WNW	WNW	WNW	WNW	WNW	WNW	WNW	WNW	WNW	WNW	WNW
Prevailing Wind Speed (mph)	9	13	14	15	16	16	15	14	13	13	12	10	14
Maximum Wind Gust (mph)	78	69	64	61	62	58	52	49	56	64	68	74	78

San Francisco Mission

San Francisco is located at the northern end of a narrow peninsula which separates San Francisco Bay from the Pacific Ocean. It is known as the air conditioned city with cool pleasant summers and mild winters.

Precipitation averages about 20 inches a year with pronounced wet and dry seasons, characteristic of its Mediterranean climate. Little or no rain falls from June through September while about 80 percent of the annual total falls from November through March. Snow and freezing temperatures are extremely rare. On average, thunderstorms occur on only two days each year. The average annual wind speed is about nine mph.

Sea fogs, and the low stratus clouds associated with them are most common in the summertime, but may occur at any time of the year. In the summer the temperature of the Pacific Ocean is much lower than the temperature inland, particularly in the Central Valley of California. This condition tends to enhance the sea breeze effect common to coastal areas. Brisk westerly winds blow throughout the afternoon and evening hours. The fog is carried inland by these westerly winds in the late afternoon and evening and then evaporates during the subsequent forenoon.

The complex topography of San Francisco causes complex patterns of fog and sun as well as temperature. A range of hills with elevations of nearly 1000 feet above sea level, bisects the city from north to south. This range partially blocks the inland movement of the fog, but gaps in the hills permit small masses of fog to pass through, further complicating the pattern.

Sunshine varies greatly from one part of the city to another, especially in the summer. Spring and fall are the sunniest seasons. The percent of possible summer sunshine varies from an estimated 25 to 35 percent at the ocean to 70 to 80 percent in the sunniest area.

The extent and behavior of the summertime fog on a particular day depends on several factors. A typical day would find the fog covering the entire city at sunrise and little wind. During the forenoon the skies become sunny in the eastern part of the city with some partial clearing reaching the ocean for a couple of hours in the early afternoon. By early afternoon the winds pick up and by late afternoon the fog is rolling inland again.

Temperature patterns in the city are the same as those of sunshine. In the winter there is little variation, with average maximums from 55 to 60 degrees and average minimums in the mid to upper 40s. Average temperatures rise until June and remain nearly constant through August with average maximums in the lower 60s near the ocean and upper 60s in the sunny eastern half of the city. Summer minimums range from 50 to 55. The warmest time of the year is September and October when the fog diminishes greatly.

San Francisco Mission *San Francisco County*   Elevation: 173 ft.   Latitude: 37° 46' N   Longitude: 122° 26' W

	JAN	FEB	MAR	APR	MAY	JUN	JUL	AUG	SEP	OCT	NOV	DEC	YEAR
Mean Maximum Temp. (°F)	57.5	61.0	62.1	63.9	64.9	67.1	67.6	68.5	71.0	70.1	63.7	57.8	64.6
Mean Temp. (°F)	52.0	54.8	55.7	57.0	58.2	60.1	61.0	62.0	63.5	62.3	57.4	52.3	58.0
Mean Minimum Temp. (°F)	46.4	48.6	49.3	50.0	51.4	53.2	54.4	55.5	56.0	54.5	51.0	46.7	51.4
Extreme Maximum Temp. (°F)	73	81	83	94	96	99	103	98	101	102	83	73	103
Extreme Minimum Temp. (°F)	36	31	40	23	44	47	48	50	49	46	40	28	23
Days Maximum Temp. ≥ 90°F	0	0	0	0	0	1	0	0	1	1	0	0	3
Days Maximum Temp. ≤ 32°F	0	0	0	0	0	0	0	0	0	0	0	0	0
Days Minimum Temp. ≤ 32°F	0	0	0	0	0	0	0	0	0	0	0	0	0
Days Minimum Temp. ≤ 0°F	0	0	0	0	0	0	0	0	0	0	0	0	0
Heating Degree Days (base 65°F)	397	282	282	241	216	159	134	104	78	111	227	388	2,619
Cooling Degree Days (base 65°F)	0	1	2	12	12	22	23	25	40	40	4	0	181
Mean Precipitation (in.)	4.57	3.75	3.24	1.17	0.50	0.14	0.03	0.09	0.27	1.10	3.38	3.20	21.44
Maximum Precipitation (in.)	10.7	10.1	9.0	5.5	4.0	1.4	0.2	0.5	2.1	5.5	8.2	11.5	43.8
Minimum Precipitation (in.)	0.5	trace	trace	trace	0	0	0	0	0	trace	0	0	10.0
Maximum 24-hr. Precipitation (in.)	3.2	2.1	2.5	2.0	1.4	1.3	0.1	0.5	2.0	2.3	2.5	3.1	3.2
Days With ≥ 0.1" Precipitation	8	7	7	3	1	0	0	0	1	2	6	7	42
Days With ≥ 1.0" Precipitation	1	1	1	0	0	0	0	0	0	0	1	1	5
Mean Snowfall (in.)	na	na	na	na	na	na	na	na	na	na	na	na	na
Maximum Snowfall (in.)	trace	trace	trace	0	0	0	0	0	0	0	0	1	1
Maximum 24-hr. Snowfall (in.)	trace	trace	trace	0	0	0	0	0	0	0	0	1	1
Days With ≥ 1.0" Snow Depth	na	na	na	na	na	na	na	na	na	na	na	na	na
Thunderstorm Days	< 1	1	< 1	1	0	< 1	1	1	< 1	1	< 1	0	5
Foggy Days	< 1	1	0	0	0	0	0	0	0	0	0	0	1
Predominant Sky Cover	na	na	na	na	na	na	na	na	na	na	na	na	na
Mean Relative Humidity 7am (%)	na	na	na	na	na	na	na	na	na	na	na	na	na
Mean Relative Humidity 4pm (%)	na	na	na	na	na	na	na	na	na	na	na	na	na
Mean Dewpoint (°F)	na	na	na	na	na	na	na	na	na	na	na	na	na
Prevailing Wind Direction	na	na	na	na	na	na	na	na	na	na	na	na	na
Prevailing Wind Speed (mph)	na	na	na	na	na	na	na	na	na	na	na	na	na
Maximum Wind Gust (mph)	na	na	na	na	na	na	na	na	na	na	na	na	na

Santa Maria Public Airport

Santa Maria Valley is a flat, fertile valley opening on the Pacific Ocean where it is widest and tapering inland for a distance approximately 30 miles. The valley is 10 miles wide at the site of the station, which is located 13 miles inland at an elevation of 236 feet. It is bounded by the foothills of the San Rafael Mountains, the Solomon Hills, and the Casmalia Hills ranging from 1,300 to 4,000 feet.

Located 150 miles west-northwest of Los Angeles and 250 miles south of San Francisco, Santa Maria has a maritime climate, displaying characteristics of those of both neighbors. Year-round mild temperatures moving through gradual transitions characterize the climate more than do clearly defined seasons. The annual range of temperatures is about 13 degrees, while the daily temperature range is about 20 degrees for May through September and a few degrees higher from October through April.

Based on the 1951-1980 period, the average first occurrence of 32 degrees Fahrenheit in the fall is December 5 and the average last occurrence in the spring is March 15.

The rainfall season, typical of the mid-California coast, is in the winter. About three-fourths of the total annual rainfall occurs from December through March in connection with Pacific cold fronts and storm centers passing inland. During the remainder of the year, and particularly from June to October, the northward displacement and intensification of the semipermanent Pacific anticyclone produces a circulation resulting in little or no precipitation here. Thunderstorms are rare.

During most days, clear, sunny afternoons prevail. But under the influence of the Pacific high, considerable advective and radiative cooling frequently produces nightly low stratus clouds, known as California stratus, and early-morning fog. Both clouds and fog, however, are generally dissipated before noon.

The unequal daytime solar heating over land and ocean, in conjunction with the Pacific high, gives rise to a consistent and prevailing westerly sea breeze during most afternoons. The winds generally decrease to a calm by sundown. Thus the two factors of nighttime stratus and daytime sea breezes effectively combine to maintain relatively cool days and warm nights with little diurnal change.

Santa Maria Public Airport *Santa Barbara County*   Elevation: 252 ft.   Latitude: 34° 55' N   Longitude: 120° 28' W

	JAN	FEB	MAR	APR	MAY	JUN	JUL	AUG	SEP	OCT	NOV	DEC	YEAR
Mean Maximum Temp. (°F)	63.9	64.9	64.9	67.6	68.7	71.3	73.5	74.0	74.7	73.8	69.0	64.5	69.2
Mean Temp. (°F)	51.6	53.2	53.8	55.4	57.8	60.8	63.5	64.1	63.7	60.9	55.5	51.3	57.6
Mean Minimum Temp. (°F)	39.3	41.3	42.6	43.1	46.9	50.3	53.5	54.2	52.7	48.1	42.0	38.1	46.0
Extreme Maximum Temp. (°F)	86	89	95	103	100	102	104	96	103	108	93	85	108
Extreme Minimum Temp. (°F)	20	22	24	31	32	38	44	43	39	26	26	20	20
Days Maximum Temp. ≥ 90°F	0	0	0	0	0	1	0	0	1	1	0	0	3
Days Maximum Temp. ≤ 32°F	0	0	0	0	0	0	0	0	0	0	0	0	0
Days Minimum Temp. ≤ 32°F	5	2	1	1	0	0	0	0	0	0	2	6	17
Days Minimum Temp. ≤ 0°F	0	0	0	0	0	0	0	0	0	0	0	0	0
Heating Degree Days (base 65°F)	409	329	342	286	222	129	63	48	67	138	281	416	2,730
Cooling Degree Days (base 65°F)	0	1	1	6	5	8	31	32	37	23	4	0	148
Mean Precipitation (in.)	2.66	3.07	2.96	0.81	0.32	0.05	0.03	0.05	0.31	0.43	1.33	1.95	13.97
Maximum Precipitation (in.)	11.8	9.7	9.4	4.2	2.4	0.9	0.4	0.9	3.0	2.1	4.7	4.8	26.8
Minimum Precipitation (in.)	trace	0	trace	trace	0	trace	0	0	0	0	0	trace	3.3
Maximum 24-hr. Precipitation (in.)	2.3	2.3	3.1	1.3	1.3	0.7	0.3	0.8	1.7	1.9	1.9	3.0	3.1
Days With ≥ 0.1" Precipitation	5	5	5	2	1	0	0	0	1	1	3	4	27
Days With ≥ 1.0" Precipitation	1	1	1	0	0	0	0	0	0	0	0	0	3
Mean Snowfall (in.)	0.0	trace	trace	0.0	0.0	0.0	0.0	0.0	0.0	0.0	trace	trace	trace
Maximum Snowfall (in.)	trace	trace	0	0	0	0	0	0	0	0	trace	trace	trace
Maximum 24-hr. Snowfall (in.)	trace	trace	0	0	0	0	0	0	0	0	trace	trace	trace
Days With ≥ 1.0" Snow Depth	0	0	0	0	0	0	0	0	0	0	0	0	0
Thunderstorm Days	< 1	< 1	1	< 1	< 1	< 1	< 1	< 1	1	< 1	< 1	< 1	2
Foggy Days	14	14	15	18	21	25	28	28	26	22	15	14	240
Predominant Sky Cover	CLR	OVR	CLR	CLR	CLR	CLR	CLR	CLR	CLR	CLR	CLR	CLR	CLR
Mean Relative Humidity 7am (%)	81	84	86	83	84	84	88	90	88	84	80	79	84
Mean Relative Humidity 4pm (%)	59	62	63	61	61	60	61	62	63	61	60	58	61
Mean Dewpoint (°F)	40	43	44	46	48	51	53	54	54	49	43	40	47
Prevailing Wind Direction	WNW	WNW	WNW	WNW	WNW	WNW	WNW	WNW	WNW	WNW	WNW	WNW	WNW
Prevailing Wind Speed (mph)	9	12	13	14	14	13	12	10	10	12	10	9	12
Maximum Wind Gust (mph)	54	58	53	47	47	45	41	35	38	37	40	52	58

Stockton Metropolitan Airport

Stockton, the county seat of San Joaquin County, is located near the center of the Great Central Valley of California. It is on the southeast corner of the broad delta formed by the confluence of the San Joaquin and Sacramento Rivers. The surrounding terrain is flat, irrigated farm and orchard land, near sea level, with the rivers and canals of the delta controlled by a system of levees.

Approximately 25 miles east and northeast of Stockton lie the foothills of the Sierra Nevada, rising gradually to an elevation of about 1,000 feet. Beyond the foothills, the mountains rise abruptly to the crest of the Sierra, at a distance of about 75 miles, with some peaks here exceeding 9,000 feet in elevation. On a few days during the year, when atmospheric conditions are favorable, the downslope effect of a north or northeast wind can bring unseasonably dry weather to the delta area, but on the whole the Sierra Nevada has little or no effect on the weather of San Joaquin County. The Sierra Nevada does affect the area, however, to the extent that the entire economy of the Great Valley depends upon the water supplied by the melting snows in the mountains.

To the west and southwest, the Coast Range, with peaks above 2,000 feet, form a barrier separating the Great Valley from the marine air which dominates the climate of the coastal communities. Several gaps in the Coast Range in the San Francisco Bay Area, however, permit the passage inland of a sea breeze which fans out into the delta and has a moderating effect on summer heat, with the result that Stockton enjoys slightly cooler summer days than communities in the upper San Joaquin and Sacramento Valleys.

The summer climate in Stockton is characterized by warm, dry days and relatively cool nights with clear skies and no rainfall. Winter brings mild temperatures and relatively light rains with frequent heavy fogs.

The annual rainfall averages about 14 inches, with 90 percent of the precipitation falling from November through April. Thunderstorms are infrequent, occurring on three or four days a year. Snow is practically unknown in the Stockton area.

In summer, temperatures exceeding 100 degrees can be expected on about 15 days. During these hot afternoons the air is extremely dry, with relative humidities running generally less than 20 percent. Even on these hot days, however, temperatures will fall into the low 60s at night. In winter the nighttime temperature on clear nights will fall to or slightly below freezing, and will rise in the afternoon into the low 50s.

In late autumn and early winter, clear still nights give rise to the formation of dense fogs, which normally settle in during the night and burn off sometime during the day. In December and January, the so-called fog season, under stagnant atmospheric conditions the fog may last for as long as four or five weeks, with only brief and temporary periods of clearing.

Stockton Metropolitan Airport *San Joaquin County*   Elevation: 19 ft.   Latitude: 37° 54' N   Longitude: 121° 14' W

	JAN	FEB	MAR	APR	MAY	JUN	JUL	AUG	SEP	OCT	NOV	DEC	YEAR
Mean Maximum Temp. (°F)	53.7	61.2	66.1	73.1	81.4	88.8	94.0	92.6	88.3	78.7	64.2	53.7	74.6
Mean Temp. (°F)	46.0	51.2	54.9	59.9	66.9	73.3	77.6	76.7	73.1	64.9	53.5	45.4	62.0
Mean Minimum Temp. (°F)	38.3	41.1	43.7	46.6	52.4	57.8	61.3	60.8	57.9	51.0	42.8	37.1	49.2
Extreme Maximum Temp. (°F)	71	78	87	100	107	110	114	109	108	101	84	72	114
Extreme Minimum Temp. (°F)	21	22	27	32	39	45	49	50	43	33	25	17	17
Days Maximum Temp. ≥ 90°F	0	0	0	1	7	14	23	21	14	3	0	0	83
Days Maximum Temp. ≤ 32°F	0	0	0	0	0	0	0	0	0	0	0	0	0
Days Minimum Temp. ≤ 32°F	7	2	0	0	0	0	0	0	0	0	1	8	18
Days Minimum Temp. ≤ 0°F	0	0	0	0	0	0	0	0	0	0	0	0	0
Heating Degree Days (base 65°F)	581	384	307	166	51	6	0	0	4	73	339	599	2,510
Cooling Degree Days (base 65°F)	0	0	0	23	111	248	393	368	250	73	1	0	1,467
Mean Precipitation (in.)	2.83	2.34	2.34	0.95	0.47	0.09	0.05	0.05	0.33	0.76	1.97	1.93	14.11
Maximum Precipitation (in.)	7.1	6.0	6.5	3.5	2.3	0.7	0.6	0.8	3.0	2.2	6.2	8.0	26.6
Minimum Precipitation (in.)	0.1	0	trace	0	0	0	0	0	0	0	0	trace	5.4
Maximum 24-hr. Precipitation (in.)	3.0	1.6	1.5	1.5	1.7	0.3	0.5	0.8	2.6	1.4	2.2	2.4	3.0
Days With ≥ 0.1" Precipitation	6	5	6	3	1	0	0	0	1	2	4	5	33
Days With ≥ 1.0" Precipitation	0	0	0	0	0	0	0	0	0	0	0	0	0
Mean Snowfall (in.)	0.0	trace	trace	trace	trace	0.0	0.0	0.0	0.0	0.0	0.0	trace	trace
Maximum Snowfall (in.)	trace	trace	trace	trace	0	0	0	0	0	0	0	trace	trace
Maximum 24-hr. Snowfall (in.)	trace	trace	trace	trace	0	0	0	0	0	0	0	trace	trace
Days With ≥ 1.0" Snow Depth	0	0	0	0	0	0	0	0	0	0	0	0	0
Thunderstorm Days	< 1	< 1	1	1	< 1	< 1	< 1	< 1	< 1	< 1	< 1	< 1	2
Foggy Days	24	17	11	5	2	< 1	< 1	< 1	2	8	18	24	111
Predominant Sky Cover	OVR	OVR	OVR	CLR	CLR	CLR	CLR	CLR	CLR	CLR	OVR	OVR	CLR
Mean Relative Humidity 7am (%)	90	90	85	76	65	60	61	65	70	77	87	91	76
Mean Relative Humidity 4pm (%)	70	60	51	41	33	29	26	28	31	37	59	71	45
Mean Dewpoint (°F)	39	42	42	43	46	49	52	52	51	47	44	40	46
Prevailing Wind Direction	SE	SE	WNW	WNW	W	W	WNW	WNW	WNW	NW	SE	SE	WNW
Prevailing Wind Speed (mph)	9	9	9	9	10	12	10	9	9	9	9	9	9
Maximum Wind Gust (mph)	60	53	52	45	49	43	32	37	39	54	49	54	60

Adin Ranger Station *Modoc County*   Elevation: 4,192 ft.   Latitude: 41° 12' N   Longitude: 120° 57' W

	JAN	FEB	MAR	APR	MAY	JUN	JUL	AUG	SEP	OCT	NOV	DEC	YEAR
Mean Maximum Temp. (°F)	na	*47.6*	*52.8*	58.9	*67.6*	76.0	*85.2*	83.9	*77.8*	*65.9*	na	na	na
Mean Temp. (°F)	na	*36.4*	*40.4*	45.0	*52.3*	59.4	*67.0*	65.5	*59.6*	*49.6*	na	na	na
Mean Minimum Temp. (°F)	na	24.2	27.9	31.0	*37.0*	42.9	*48.4*	47.0	*41.1*	*33.2*	na	na	na
Extreme Maximum Temp. (°F)	62	71	74	85	93	98	110	104	96	90	80	65	110
Extreme Minimum Temp. (°F)	-16	-14	-1	7	12	12	26	32	15	7	-10	-26	-26
Days Maximum Temp. ≥ 90°F	0	0	0	0	0	2	8	7	2	0	0	0	19
Days Maximum Temp. ≤ 32°F	2	1	0	0	0	0	0	0	0	0	1	3	7
Days Minimum Temp. ≤ 32°F	23	22	22	*16*	*6*	1	0	0	3	*12*	20	*24*	*149*
Days Minimum Temp. ≤ 0°F	1	1	0	0	0	0	0	0	0	0	0	1	3
Heating Degree Days (base 65°F)	na	*801*	*759*	595	*389*	187	*41*	59	*178*	*471*	na	na	na
Cooling Degree Days (base 65°F)	na	*0*	*0*	0	na	20	na	78	*24*	na	na	na	na
Mean Precipitation (in.)	2.09	1.79	1.91	1.21	1.59	1.06	0.36	0.43	0.85	1.16	1.94	1.81	16.20
Days With ≥ 0.1" Precipitation	5	4	4	3	3	3	1	1	2	3	4	5	38
Days With ≥ 1.0" Precipitation	0	0	0	0	0	0	0	0	0	0	0	0	0
Mean Snowfall (in.)	*8.7*	*9.3*	*7.9*	2.4	1.0	0.1	0.0	0.0	0.1	0.5	5.0	10.1	*45.1*
Days With ≥ 1.0" Snow Depth	na	na	na	*0*	0	0	0	0	0	0	0	*1*	na

Alturas *Modoc County*   Elevation: 4,399 ft.   Latitude: 41° 30' N   Longitude: 120° 33' W

	JAN	FEB	MAR	APR	MAY	JUN	JUL	AUG	SEP	OCT	NOV	DEC	YEAR
Mean Maximum Temp. (°F)	42.0	46.5	51.5	58.1	67.3	77.1	87.0	86.5	78.1	66.3	50.0	41.8	62.7
Mean Temp. (°F)	29.6	33.5	38.3	43.0	50.7	58.6	65.4	64.2	56.8	47.0	36.4	29.1	46.0
Mean Minimum Temp. (°F)	17.1	20.4	24.9	27.9	34.0	40.0	43.8	41.9	35.5	27.7	22.8	16.5	29.4
Extreme Maximum Temp. (°F)	67	72	78	85	95	100	104	104	100	90	78	63	104
Extreme Minimum Temp. (°F)	-25	-33	-7	7	17	21	28	26	17	8	-17	-34	-34
Days Maximum Temp. ≥ 90°F	0	0	0	0	0	3	13	12	3	0	0	0	31
Days Maximum Temp. ≤ 32°F	4	1	0	0	0	0	0	0	0	0	1	4	10
Days Minimum Temp. ≤ 32°F	28	26	26	22	13	4	1	1	10	24	26	29	210
Days Minimum Temp. ≤ 0°F	3	1	0	0	0	0	0	0	0	0	0	3	7
Heating Degree Days (base 65°F)	1,091	884	822	654	440	210	67	80	247	550	851	1,105	7,001
Cooling Degree Days (base 65°F)	0	0	0	0	2	25	86	62	11	0	0	0	186
Mean Precipitation (in.)	1.37	1.27	1.55	1.11	1.29	0.88	0.29	0.36	0.66	0.70	1.55	1.34	12.37
Days With ≥ 0.1" Precipitation	4	3	4	4	4	2	1	1	2	2	5	4	36
Days With ≥ 1.0" Precipitation	0	0	0	0	0	0	0	0	0	0	0	0	0
Mean Snowfall (in.)	5.9	5.1	4.3	2.0	0.7	trace	trace	0.0	0.0	0.2	3.6	5.7	27.5
Days With ≥ 1.0" Snow Depth	*5*	*5*	*2*	1	0	0	0	0	0	0	*3*	*5*	*21*

Antioch Pump Plant 3 *Contra Costa County*   Elevation: 59 ft.   Latitude: 37° 59' N   Longitude: 121° 44' W

	JAN	FEB	MAR	APR	MAY	JUN	JUL	AUG	SEP	OCT	NOV	DEC	YEAR
Mean Maximum Temp. (°F)	53.5	60.3	65.1	71.4	78.9	85.9	90.8	89.8	86.0	77.5	64.0	54.5	73.2
Mean Temp. (°F)	45.5	50.7	54.7	59.2	65.5	71.1	74.5	73.6	70.9	64.3	53.8	45.9	60.8
Mean Minimum Temp. (°F)	37.4	41.1	44.3	47.0	51.9	56.4	58.1	57.3	55.8	50.9	43.6	37.1	48.4
Extreme Maximum Temp. (°F)	72	76	88	94	103	109	110	109	107	101	82	75	110
Extreme Minimum Temp. (°F)	19	25	28	29	35	35	42	46	41	28	27	18	18
Days Maximum Temp. ≥ 90°F	0	0	0	0	4	9	18	15	10	2	0	0	58
Days Maximum Temp. ≤ 32°F	0	0	0	0	0	0	0	0	0	0	0	0	0
Days Minimum Temp. ≤ 32°F	7	2	0	0	0	0	0	0	0	0	1	7	17
Days Minimum Temp. ≤ 0°F	0	0	0	0	0	0	0	0	0	0	0	0	0
Heating Degree Days (base 65°F)	597	397	313	184	71	14	2	0	8	83	329	584	2,582
Cooling Degree Days (base 65°F)	0	0	1	22	99	218	319	292	209	74	2	0	1,236
Mean Precipitation (in.)	2.72	2.38	2.17	0.70	0.45	0.09	0.03	0.03	0.24	0.73	1.86	1.91	13.31
Days With ≥ 0.1" Precipitation	6	5	6	2	1	0	0	0	1	2	4	5	32
Days With ≥ 1.0" Precipitation	0	0	0	0	0	0	0	0	0	0	0	0	0
Mean Snowfall (in.)	0.0	trace	0.0	0.0	0.0	0.0	0.0	0.0	0.0	0.0	0.0	trace	trace
Days With ≥ 1.0" Snow Depth	0	0	0	0	0	0	0	0	0	0	0	0	0

Ash Mountain *Tulare County*   Elevation: 1,706 ft.   Latitude: 36° 29' N   Longitude: 118° 50' W

	JAN	FEB	MAR	APR	MAY	JUN	JUL	AUG	SEP	OCT	NOV	DEC	YEAR
Mean Maximum Temp. (°F)	58.1	61.7	64.5	70.2	79.8	89.8	97.3	96.5	90.5	80.4	66.2	58.5	76.1
Mean Temp. (°F)	47.6	50.8	53.5	58.0	66.4	75.5	82.4	81.7	75.7	66.4	54.5	47.7	63.3
Mean Minimum Temp. (°F)	37.0	39.9	42.4	45.8	52.9	61.1	67.4	66.8	60.8	52.5	42.8	36.9	50.5
Extreme Maximum Temp. (°F)	84	85	86	94	105	109	112	114	109	103	89	80	114
Extreme Minimum Temp. (°F)	24	22	29	28	34	42	50	46	37	30	25	17	17
Days Maximum Temp. ≥ 90°F	0	0	0	0	6	16	28	26	18	6	0	0	100
Days Maximum Temp. ≤ 32°F	0	0	0	0	0	0	0	0	0	0	0	0	0
Days Minimum Temp. ≤ 32°F	8	3	1	1	0	0	0	0	0	0	1	7	21
Days Minimum Temp. ≤ 0°F	0	0	0	0	0	0	0	0	0	0	0	0	0
Heating Degree Days (base 65°F)	534	394	353	227	86	11	0	0	8	77	316	529	2,535
Cooling Degree Days (base 65°F)	0	0	2	30	135	324	546	539	346	137	8	0	2,067
Mean Precipitation (in.)	5.10	4.40	4.96	2.09	1.02	0.41	0.10	0.11	0.66	1.30	2.98	3.32	26.45
Days With ≥ 0.1" Precipitation	7	7	7	4	2	1	0	0	1	2	5	5	41
Days With ≥ 1.0" Precipitation	2	2	2	0	0	0	0	0	0	0	1	1	8
Mean Snowfall (in.)	0.4	0.1	0.2	trace	0.0	0.0	0.0	0.0	0.0	0.0	0.6	0.2	1.5
Days With ≥ 1.0" Snow Depth	0	0	0	0	0	0	0	0	0	0	0	0	0

Auberry 2 NW *Fresno County*   Elevation: 2,089 ft.   Latitude: 37° 05' N   Longitude: 119° 30' W

	JAN	FEB	MAR	APR	MAY	JUN	JUL	AUG	SEP	OCT	NOV	DEC	YEAR
Mean Maximum Temp. (°F)	55.4	58.2	60.9	67.7	77.5	87.0	93.7	92.5	86.4	76.1	62.3	55.2	72.7
Mean Temp. (°F)	46.1	48.7	51.2	56.4	64.8	73.5	80.5	79.5	74.0	64.4	52.2	45.9	61.4
Mean Minimum Temp. (°F)	36.7	39.2	41.4	45.0	52.0	60.0	67.3	66.4	61.5	52.6	41.9	36.6	50.0
Extreme Maximum Temp. (°F)	79	78	81	90	101	105	107	109	103	96	86	77	109
Extreme Minimum Temp. (°F)	21	17	24	27	28	36	44	46	41	27	25	10	10
Days Maximum Temp. ≥ 90°F	0	0	0	0	3	13	24	22	13	2	0	0	77
Days Maximum Temp. ≤ 32°F	0	0	0	0	0	0	0	0	0	0	0	0	0
Days Minimum Temp. ≤ 32°F	8	4	3	1	0	0	0	0	0	0	2	8	26
Days Minimum Temp. ≤ 0°F	0	0	0	0	0	0	0	0	0	0	0	0	0
Heating Degree Days (base 65°F)	580	453	424	270	108	19	0	0	14	109	382	585	2,944
Cooling Degree Days (base 65°F)	0	0	1	22	102	267	483	468	294	97	3	0	1,737
Mean Precipitation (in.)	5.21	4.51	4.81	1.76	0.81	0.30	0.08	0.05	0.49	1.33	2.89	3.64	25.88
Days With ≥ 0.1" Precipitation	7	6	7	3	2	1	0	0	1	2	4	6	39
Days With ≥ 1.0" Precipitation	2	1	1	0	0	0	0	0	0	0	1	1	6
Mean Snowfall (in.)	0.2	0.1	1.0	0.1	0.0	0.0	0.0	0.0	0.0	0.0	trace	0.4	1.8
Days With ≥ 1.0" Snow Depth	0	0	0	0	0	0	0	0	0	0	0	0	0

Auburn *Placer County*   Elevation: 1,289 ft.   Latitude: 38° 54' N   Longitude: 121° 05' W

	JAN	FEB	MAR	APR	MAY	JUN	JUL	AUG	SEP	OCT	NOV	DEC	YEAR
Mean Maximum Temp. (°F)	54.2	58.4	61.7	67.5	76.0	84.5	91.5	90.7	85.3	75.7	61.6	54.3	71.8
Mean Temp. (°F)	45.6	49.1	51.8	56.3	63.4	70.8	77.1	76.2	71.8	63.6	52.1	45.6	60.3
Mean Minimum Temp. (°F)	36.9	40.0	42.0	45.0	50.6	57.0	62.6	61.6	58.2	51.5	42.6	36.9	48.7
Extreme Maximum Temp. (°F)	72	78	82	89	101	105	113	111	105	98	83	74	113
Extreme Minimum Temp. (°F)	23	22	25	30	35	39	48	49	44	31	25	16	16
Days Maximum Temp. ≥ 90°F	0	0	0	0	3	9	20	18	10	2	0	0	62
Days Maximum Temp. ≤ 32°F	0	0	0	0	0	0	0	0	0	0	0	0	0
Days Minimum Temp. ≤ 32°F	8	2	1	0	0	0	0	0	0	0	1	8	20
Days Minimum Temp. ≤ 0°F	0	0	0	0	0	0	0	0	0	0	0	0	0
Heating Degree Days (base 65°F)	596	441	401	266	124	27	2	2	18	114	381	594	2,966
Cooling Degree Days (base 65°F)	0	0	1	15	78	197	382	360	229	79	1	0	1,342
Mean Precipitation (in.)	6.76	5.87	6.20	2.45	1.23	0.38	0.14	0.14	0.74	1.87	5.27	5.68	36.73
Days With ≥ 0.1" Precipitation	8	8	9	5	3	1	0	0	1	3	7	8	53
Days With ≥ 1.0" Precipitation	2	2	2	1	0	0	0	0	0	1	2	2	12
Mean Snowfall (in.)	0.4	0.2	0.3	0.2	0.0	0.0	0.0	0.0	0.0	0.0	0.2	0.2	1.5
Days With ≥ 1.0" Snow Depth	0	0	0	0	0	0	0	0	0	0	0	0	0

Balch Power House *Fresno County*   Elevation: 1,719 ft.   Latitude: 36° 55' N   Longitude: 119° 05' W

	JAN	FEB	MAR	APR	MAY	JUN	JUL	AUG	SEP	OCT	NOV	DEC	YEAR
Mean Maximum Temp. (°F)	52.5	58.2	63.2	69.6	77.6	85.8	93.4	93.3	88.0	77.2	60.2	52.1	72.6
Mean Temp. (°F)	45.0	49.0	52.7	57.5	65.0	72.6	80.0	80.0	74.7	65.2	51.8	44.9	61.5
Mean Minimum Temp. (°F)	37.4	39.7	42.1	45.4	52.3	59.3	66.6	66.7	61.4	53.1	43.4	37.7	50.4
Extreme Maximum Temp. (°F)	69	79	82	91	100	105	106	110	109	101	82	68	110
Extreme Minimum Temp. (°F)	24	22	27	28	22	35	39	50	31	32	23	18	18
Days Maximum Temp. ≥ 90°F	0	0	0	0	3	11	24	23	15	3	0	0	79
Days Maximum Temp. ≤ 32°F	0	0	0	0	0	0	0	0	0	0	0	0	0
Days Minimum Temp. ≤ 32°F	6	2	1	1	0	0	0	0	0	0	1	5	16
Days Minimum Temp. ≤ 0°F	0	0	0	0	0	0	0	0	0	0	0	0	0
Heating Degree Days (base 65°F)	613	446	375	236	90	17	0	0	9	88	389	615	2,878
Cooling Degree Days (base 65°F)	0	0	1	21	91	236	465	487	320	103	2	0	1,726
Mean Precipitation (in.)	6.18	5.37	5.41	2.34	1.11	0.47	0.17	0.05	0.92	1.45	3.45	3.93	30.85
Days With ≥ 0.1" Precipitation	7	7	8	4	2	1	0	0	1	2	5	5	42
Days With ≥ 1.0" Precipitation	2	2	2	0	0	0	0	0	0	0	1	1	8
Mean Snowfall (in.)	trace	trace	trace	0.0	0.0	0.0	0.0	0.0	0.0	0.0	0.0	0.1	0.1
Days With ≥ 1.0" Snow Depth	0	1	0	0	0	0	0	0	0	0	0	0	1

Beaumont 1 E *Riverside County*   Elevation: 2,598 ft.   Latitude: 33° 56' N   Longitude: 116° 58' W

	JAN	FEB	MAR	APR	MAY	JUN	JUL	AUG	SEP	OCT	NOV	DEC	YEAR
Mean Maximum Temp. (°F)	61.8	65.0	67.3	73.4	80.1	89.2	96.0	95.9	90.3	81.0	69.9	62.3	77.7
Mean Temp. (°F)	50.8	52.6	54.2	58.5	64.5	71.5	77.6	77.8	73.5	65.5	56.5	50.8	62.8
Mean Minimum Temp. (°F)	39.7	40.2	41.1	43.5	48.8	53.7	59.1	59.7	56.7	49.9	43.1	39.3	47.9
Extreme Maximum Temp. (°F)	83	88	95	100	105	108	114	113	112	106	92	86	114
Extreme Minimum Temp. (°F)	21	19	25	29	32	38	45	46	39	29	21	21	19
Days Maximum Temp. ≥ 90°F	0	0	0	1	5	15	27	26	18	6	0	0	98
Days Maximum Temp. ≤ 32°F	0	0	0	0	0	0	0	0	0	0	0	0	0
Days Minimum Temp. ≤ 32°F	4	3	2	1	0	0	0	0	0	0	1	5	16
Days Minimum Temp. ≤ 0°F	0	0	0	0	0	0	0	0	0	0	0	0	0
Heating Degree Days (base 65°F)	435	345	331	209	88	16	0	0	8	72	257	434	2,195
Cooling Degree Days (base 65°F)	0	2	4	27	79	213	395	426	282	98	11	1	1,538
Mean Precipitation (in.)	4.20	3.96	3.79	1.06	0.72	0.21	0.27	0.32	0.63	0.69	1.55	2.12	19.52
Days With ≥ 0.1" Precipitation	5	5	6	3	2	0	1	1	1	2	3	4	33
Days With ≥ 1.0" Precipitation	1	1	1	0	0	0	0	0	0	1	1	1	5
Mean Snowfall (in.)	0.5	0.5	trace	trace	0.0	0.0	0.0	0.0	0.0	0.0	0.1	0.4	1.5
Days With ≥ 1.0" Snow Depth	0	0	0	0	0	0	0	0	0	0	0	0	0

Ben Lomond 4 *Santa Cruz County*   Elevation: 419 ft.   Latitude: 37° 05' N   Longitude: 122° 05' W

	JAN	FEB	MAR	APR	MAY	JUN	JUL	AUG	SEP	OCT	NOV	DEC	YEAR
Mean Maximum Temp. (°F)	61.6	63.9	66.0	72.0	76.3	81.8	85.2	85.4	83.9	78.4	67.5	61.7	73.6
Mean Temp. (°F)	49.4	51.5	53.4	56.9	60.9	65.2	67.9	68.0	66.6	61.6	53.6	48.9	58.6
Mean Minimum Temp. (°F)	37.1	39.0	40.7	41.8	45.4	48.4	50.5	50.6	49.2	44.7	39.7	36.0	43.6
Extreme Maximum Temp. (°F)	83	87	92	100	104	109	108	110	105	112	95	81	112
Extreme Minimum Temp. (°F)	21	20	27	29	33	35	40	38	38	31	25	15	15
Days Maximum Temp. ≥ 90°F	0	0	0	1	3	6	8	8	8	4	0	0	38
Days Maximum Temp. ≤ 32°F	0	0	0	0	0	0	0	0	0	0	0	0	0
Days Minimum Temp. ≤ 32°F	10	5	3	1	0	0	0	0	0	0	4	11	34
Days Minimum Temp. ≤ 0°F	0	0	0	0	0	0	0	0	0	0	0	0	0
Heating Degree Days (base 65°F)	478	375	354	241	147	50	13	11	29	128	336	494	2,656
Cooling Degree Days (base 65°F)	0	0	0	8	23	56	107	117	81	29	1	0	422
Mean Precipitation (in.)	10.40	9.89	8.03	2.75	1.10	0.23	0.12	0.16	0.48	2.05	6.28	7.21	48.70
Days With ≥ 0.1" Precipitation	8	8	9	4	2	1	0	0	1	2	6	7	48
Days With ≥ 1.0" Precipitation	3	3	2	1	0	0	0	0	0	1	2	2	14
Mean Snowfall (in.)	trace	trace	trace	0.0	0.0	0.0	0.0	0.0	0.0	0.0	trace	trace	trace
Days With ≥ 1.0" Snow Depth	0	0	0	0	0	0	0	0	0	0	0	0	0

Berkeley *Alameda County*   Elevation: 308 ft.   Latitude: 37° 52' N   Longitude: 122° 16' W

	JAN	FEB	MAR	APR	MAY	JUN	JUL	AUG	SEP	OCT	NOV	DEC	YEAR
Mean Maximum Temp. (°F)	56.7	59.6	61.3	63.9	66.6	69.8	70.6	70.5	71.7	69.7	62.3	56.6	64.9
Mean Temp. (°F)	50.5	53.1	54.3	56.1	58.9	61.7	62.7	63.0	63.9	61.5	55.5	50.4	57.6
Mean Minimum Temp. (°F)	44.3	46.5	47.2	48.4	51.0	53.5	54.7	55.5	55.9	53.2	48.6	44.1	50.2
Extreme Maximum Temp. (°F)	72	77	81	91	98	103	97	94	103	99	82	73	103
Extreme Minimum Temp. (°F)	31	31	33	36	41	45	48	50	48	41	35	24	24
Days Maximum Temp. ≥ 90°F	0	0	0	0	0	1	0	0	1	0	0	0	2
Days Maximum Temp. ≤ 32°F	0	0	0	0	0	0	0	0	0	0	0	0	0
Days Minimum Temp. ≤ 32°F	0	0	0	0	0	0	0	0	0	0	0	1	1
Days Minimum Temp. ≤ 0°F	0	0	0	0	0	0	0	0	0	0	0	0	0
Heating Degree Days (base 65°F)	442	331	327	265	197	120	89	75	71	129	281	447	2,774
Cooling Degree Days (base 65°F)	0	0	0	9	10	23	26	21	36	27	2	0	154
Mean Precipitation (in.)	5.57	4.49	3.87	1.66	0.61	0.14	0.08	0.12	0.40	1.28	4.00	3.70	25.92
Days With ≥ 0.1" Precipitation	8	7	6	4	1	0	0	0	1	2	6	6	41
Days With ≥ 1.0" Precipitation	2	2	1	0	0	0	0	0	0	0	1	1	7
Mean Snowfall (in.)	trace	trace	trace	0.0	0.0	0.0	0.0	0.0	0.0	0.0	0.0	trace	trace
Days With ≥ 1.0" Snow Depth	0	0	0	0	0	0	0	0	0	0	0	0	0

Big Bear Lake *San Bernardino County*   Elevation: 6,788 ft.   Latitude: 34° 15' N   Longitude: 116° 53' W

	JAN	FEB	MAR	APR	MAY	JUN	JUL	AUG	SEP	OCT	NOV	DEC	YEAR
Mean Maximum Temp. (°F)	47.1	48.3	51.0	57.6	65.9	75.5	80.6	79.1	73.5	64.6	54.5	47.1	62.1
Mean Temp. (°F)	33.9	35.3	37.9	43.0	50.2	58.5	64.1	63.0	57.3	48.6	40.1	33.9	47.2
Mean Minimum Temp. (°F)	20.7	22.3	24.7	28.4	34.5	41.3	47.5	46.9	41.1	32.5	25.6	20.6	32.2
Extreme Maximum Temp. (°F)	71	72	80	82	84	90	94	92	87	85	74	69	94
Extreme Minimum Temp. (°F)	-25	-3	2	7	20	25	32	31	22	10	3	-8	-25
Days Maximum Temp. ≥ 90°F	0	0	0	0	0	0	1	0	0	0	0	0	1
Days Maximum Temp. ≤ 32°F	2	1	1	0	0	0	0	0	0	0	0	2	6
Days Minimum Temp. ≤ 32°F	29	26	28	23	12	2	0	0	3	15	26	30	194
Days Minimum Temp. ≤ 0°F	0	0	0	0	0	0	0	0	0	0	0	0	0
Heating Degree Days (base 65°F)	956	833	834	654	450	198	59	82	226	502	740	958	6,492
Cooling Degree Days (base 65°F)	0	0	0	0	0	7	34	28	2	0	0	0	71
Mean Precipitation (in.)	4.23	4.10	3.64	0.97	0.50	0.18	0.76	1.00	0.53	0.76	1.71	2.90	21.28
Days With ≥ 0.1" Precipitation	6	4	5	2	1	1	2	2	1	2	3	4	33
Days With ≥ 1.0" Precipitation	1	1	1	0	0	0	0	0	0	0	1	1	5
Mean Snowfall (in.)	15.1	13.0	16.4	3.3	0.6	trace	0.0	0.0	trace	0.3	5.9	10.7	65.3
Days With ≥ 1.0" Snow Depth	na	na	na	1	0	0	0	0	0	0	2	na	na

Blythe *Riverside County*   Elevation: 265 ft.   Latitude: 33° 37' N   Longitude: 114° 36' W

	JAN	FEB	MAR	APR	MAY	JUN	JUL	AUG	SEP	OCT	NOV	DEC	YEAR
Mean Maximum Temp. (°F)	67.1	72.8	78.9	86.8	95.5	104.6	108.4	106.9	101.1	89.6	75.4	66.2	87.8
Mean Temp. (°F)	53.2	58.1	63.4	70.1	78.5	86.7	92.6	91.5	84.9	73.1	60.1	52.5	72.1
Mean Minimum Temp. (°F)	39.3	43.4	47.8	53.4	61.4	68.7	76.8	75.9	68.8	56.5	44.8	38.8	56.3
Extreme Maximum Temp. (°F)	87	93	100	115	113	122	122	118	116	111	95	85	122
Extreme Minimum Temp. (°F)	0	26	28	34	42	50	61	58	50	29	28	22	0
Days Maximum Temp. ≥ 90°F	0	0	3	12	24	29	31	30	28	16	0	0	173
Days Maximum Temp. ≤ 32°F	0	0	0	0	0	0	0	0	0	0	0	0	0
Days Minimum Temp. ≤ 32°F	5	1	0	0	0	0	0	0	0	0	0	4	10
Days Minimum Temp. ≤ 0°F	0	0	0	0	0	0	0	0	0	0	0	0	0
Heating Degree Days (base 65°F)	359	194	97	24	1	0	0	0	0	13	159	380	1,227
Cooling Degree Days (base 65°F)	0	8	58	213	449	651	857	846	611	277	22	0	3,992
Mean Precipitation (in.)	0.51	0.57	0.35	0.11	0.07	0.03	0.18	0.70	0.55	0.26	0.23	0.50	4.06
Days With ≥ 0.1" Precipitation	1	2	1	0	0	0	0	1	1	0	1	1	8
Days With ≥ 1.0" Precipitation	0	0	0	0	0	0	0	0	0	0	0	0	0
Mean Snowfall (in.)	0.0	0.0	0.0	0.0	0.0	0.0	0.0	0.0	0.0	0.0	0.0	0.0	0.0
Days With ≥ 1.0" Snow Depth	0	0	0	0	0	0	0	0	0	0	0	0	0

Blythe Riverside Co. Airport *Riverside County*   Elevation: 387 ft.   Latitude: 33° 37' N   Longitude: 114° 43' W

	JAN	FEB	MAR	APR	MAY	JUN	JUL	AUG	SEP	OCT	NOV	DEC	YEAR
Mean Maximum Temp. (°F)	66.8	72.4	78.6	86.3	95.0	105.1	108.4	106.7	100.7	89.2	75.3	66.3	87.6
Mean Temp. (°F)	54.4	59.1	64.6	71.2	79.6	88.9	94.5	93.3	86.6	74.7	61.6	53.9	73.5
Mean Minimum Temp. (°F)	41.9	45.8	50.5	56.1	64.1	72.6	80.5	79.7	72.5	60.2	47.8	41.3	59.4
Extreme Maximum Temp. (°F)	85	93	100	107	114	123	123	120	116	111	95	87	123
Extreme Minimum Temp. (°F)	20	22	31	38	43	46	62	62	53	27	27	24	20
Days Maximum Temp. ≥ 90°F	0	0	3	11	24	29	31	31	28	16	1	0	174
Days Maximum Temp. ≤ 32°F	0	0	0	0	0	0	0	0	0	0	0	0	0
Days Minimum Temp. ≤ 32°F	3	1	0	0	0	0	0	0	0	0	0	2	6
Days Minimum Temp. ≤ 0°F	0	0	0	0	0	0	0	0	0	0	0	0	0
Heating Degree Days (base 65°F)	323	173	78	23	1	0	0	0	0	11	130	339	1,078
Cooling Degree Days (base 65°F)	1	17	76	245	474	708	909	899	665	334	39	1	4,368
Mean Precipitation (in.)	0.47	0.58	0.46	0.15	0.03	trace	0.32	0.65	0.50	0.23	0.19	0.50	4.08
Days With ≥ 0.1" Precipitation	1	1	1	0	0	0	1	1	1	0	0	1	7
Days With ≥ 1.0" Precipitation	0	0	0	0	0	0	0	0	0	0	0	0	0
Mean Snowfall (in.)	0.0	trace	trace	0.0	0.0	0.0	0.0	0.0	0.0	0.0	0.0	0.0	trace
Days With ≥ 1.0" Snow Depth	0	0	0	0	0	0	0	0	0	0	0	0	0

Boca *Nevada County*   Elevation: 5,574 ft.   Latitude: 39° 23' N   Longitude: 120° 06' W

	JAN	FEB	MAR	APR	MAY	JUN	JUL	AUG	SEP	OCT	NOV	DEC	YEAR
Mean Maximum Temp. (°F)	42.0	45.9	50.1	57.1	66.0	75.1	83.5	82.9	76.1	65.9	51.5	42.8	61.6
Mean Temp. (°F)	26.4	29.9	35.0	40.3	47.8	54.6	60.5	59.4	53.3	45.5	35.7	28.1	43.0
Mean Minimum Temp. (°F)	10.8	13.9	19.8	23.4	29.5	34.0	37.6	35.9	30.4	25.0	19.9	13.3	24.4
Extreme Maximum Temp. (°F)	64	68	75	81	90	96	98	99	95	89	79	68	99
Extreme Minimum Temp. (°F)	-30	-43	-14	0	13	16	21	21	14	8	-4	-28	-43
Days Maximum Temp. ≥ 90°F	0	0	0	0	0	1	6	5	1	0	0	0	13
Days Maximum Temp. ≤ 32°F	4	2	1	0	0	0	0	0	0	0	1	4	12
Days Minimum Temp. ≤ 32°F	30	28	30	28	22	13	7	9	20	28	28	30	273
Days Minimum Temp. ≤ 0°F	7	3	1	0	0	0	0	0	0	0	0	3	14
Heating Degree Days (base 65°F)	1,190	985	924	735	528	310	151	177	346	599	872	1,138	7,955
Cooling Degree Days (base 65°F)	0	0	0	0	0	3	18	9	0	0	0	0	30
Mean Precipitation (in.)	3.78	3.33	3.06	1.10	1.03	0.61	0.61	0.51	0.88	1.40	2.85	3.35	22.51
Days With ≥ 0.1" Precipitation	6	5	6	4	3	2	1	2	2	3	5	6	45
Days With ≥ 1.0" Precipitation	1	1	1	0	0	0	0	0	0	0	1	1	5
Mean Snowfall (in.)	18.1	19.6	15.5	4.5	1.6	0.1	0.0	0.0	0.2	1.2	8.8	18.6	88.2
Days With ≥ 1.0" Snow Depth	23	21	14	3	1	0	0	0	0	1	6	18	87

Bodie *Mono County*   Elevation: 8,369 ft.   Latitude: 38° 13' N   Longitude: 119° 01' W

	JAN	FEB	MAR	APR	MAY	JUN	JUL	AUG	SEP	OCT	NOV	DEC	YEAR
Mean Maximum Temp. (°F)	40.0	41.6	44.0	50.0	59.7	69.2	76.6	76.2	69.4	59.6	48.3	40.5	56.3
Mean Temp. (°F)	22.9	24.6	28.1	33.9	42.2	50.0	55.8	54.9	48.2	39.6	30.5	23.2	37.8
Mean Minimum Temp. (°F)	5.9	7.5	12.2	17.7	24.6	30.8	35.0	33.7	27.0	19.5	12.7	5.8	19.4
Extreme Maximum Temp. (°F)	60	63	65	75	81	90	91	88	88	83	71	62	91
Extreme Minimum Temp. (°F)	-27	-33	-17	-16	-13	6	12	14	1	-10	-20	-31	-33
Days Maximum Temp. ≥ 90°F	0	0	0	0	0	0	0	0	0	0	0	0	0
Days Maximum Temp. ≤ 32°F	6	5	4	1	0	0	0	0	0	0	2	6	24
Days Minimum Temp. ≤ 32°F	31	28	31	30	27	19	11	14	24	29	29	31	304
Days Minimum Temp. ≤ 0°F	10	7	4	1	0	0	0	0	0	0	3	10	35
Heating Degree Days (base 65°F)	1,298	1,134	1,136	927	700	443	280	306	498	782	1,027	1,290	9,821
Cooling Degree Days (base 65°F)	0	0	0	0	0	0	1	1	0	0	0	0	2
Mean Precipitation (in.)	1.73	1.90	1.69	0.90	0.80	0.79	0.91	0.50	0.61	0.66	1.32	1.37	13.18
Days With ≥ 0.1" Precipitation	5	4	5	3	2	2	2	2	2	2	3	4	36
Days With ≥ 1.0" Precipitation	0	0	0	0	0	0	0	0	0	0	0	0	0
Mean Snowfall (in.)	15.4	18.7	18.2	6.0	4.1	0.5	trace	trace	0.5	3.2	10.6	na	na
Days With ≥ 1.0" Snow Depth	26	25	25	13	3	0	0	0	0	1	10	24	127

Borrego Desert Park *San Diego County*   Elevation: 803 ft.   Latitude: 33° 14' N   Longitude: 116° 25' W

	JAN	FEB	MAR	APR	MAY	JUN	JUL	AUG	SEP	OCT	NOV	DEC	YEAR
Mean Maximum Temp. (°F)	69.0	72.9	77.5	84.6	92.5	102.7	107.2	105.9	100.4	90.0	77.8	69.2	87.5
Mean Temp. (°F)	56.3	59.9	63.6	69.1	76.3	85.4	91.2	90.5	85.0	75.2	63.9	56.3	72.7
Mean Minimum Temp. (°F)	43.6	46.7	49.6	53.6	60.0	68.1	75.0	75.1	69.5	60.5	49.9	43.4	57.9
Extreme Maximum Temp. (°F)	90	95	101	111	114	122	121	120	117	113	98	87	122
Extreme Minimum Temp. (°F)	20	24	23	28	34	45	56	55	49	33	32	23	20
Days Maximum Temp. ≥ 90°F	0	1	3	10	21	28	31	31	28	17	2	0	172
Days Maximum Temp. ≤ 32°F	0	0	0	0	0	0	0	0	0	0	0	0	0
Days Minimum Temp. ≤ 32°F	1	0	0	0	0	0	0	0	0	0	0	1	2
Days Minimum Temp. ≤ 0°F	0	0	0	0	0	0	0	0	0	0	0	0	0
Heating Degree Days (base 65°F)	267	162	108	47	10	0	0	0	0	10	97	266	967
Cooling Degree Days (base 65°F)	3	26	69	203	371	605	810	813	612	343	73	5	3,933
Mean Precipitation (in.)	1.43	1.41	0.97	0.21	0.10	0.02	0.34	0.59	0.50	0.21	0.46	0.80	7.04
Days With ≥ 0.1" Precipitation	3	3	3	1	0	0	1	1	1	1	1	2	17
Days With ≥ 1.0" Precipitation	0	0	0	0	0	0	0	0	0	0	0	0	0
Mean Snowfall (in.)	0.0	trace	0.0	0.0	0.0	0.0	0.0	0.0	0.0	0.0	0.0	0.0	trace
Days With ≥ 1.0" Snow Depth	0	0	0	0	0	0	0	0	0	0	0	0	0

Bowman Dam *Nevada County*   Elevation: 5,380 ft.   Latitude: 39° 27' N   Longitude: 120° 39' W

	JAN	FEB	MAR	APR	MAY	JUN	JUL	AUG	SEP	OCT	NOV	DEC	YEAR
Mean Maximum Temp. (°F)	45.5	46.2	48.3	53.7	63.1	72.0	*79.3*	79.5	74.2	64.2	51.2	*45.2*	60.2
Mean Temp. (°F)	36.3	36.4	38.4	42.6	50.9	59.0	*65.7*	65.9	61.2	52.5	41.6	*36.1*	48.9
Mean Minimum Temp. (°F)	27.0	26.6	28.4	31.4	38.6	46.0	*52.1*	*52.1*	48.1	40.8	31.8	27.0	*37.5*
Extreme Maximum Temp. (°F)	68	70	73	79	89	92	98	98	97	90	78	72	98
Extreme Minimum Temp. (°F)	5	1	8	9	17	25	32	30	28	18	11	1	1
Days Maximum Temp. ≥ 90°F	0	0	0	0	0	0	1	2	0	0	0	0	3
Days Maximum Temp. ≤ 32°F	2	2	1	0	0	0	0	0	0	0	1	2	8
Days Minimum Temp. ≤ 32°F	23	22	23	15	6	1	0	0	0	4	15	23	132
Days Minimum Temp. ≤ 0°F	0	0	0	0	0	0	0	0	0	0	0	0	0
Heating Degree Days (base 65°F)	883	800	819	666	431	200	*62*	*61*	146	387	697	*887*	6,039
Cooling Degree Days (base 65°F)	0	0	0	*0*	*1*	22	*80*	*96*	38	8	0	*0*	245
Mean Precipitation (in.)	12.62	10.48	10.14	4.49	3.33	1.25	0.37	0.58	1.46	4.11	9.66	10.13	68.62
Days With ≥ 0.1" Precipitation	8	8	10	6	5	3	0	1	2	4	8	8	63
Days With ≥ 1.0" Precipitation	3	3	3	1	1	0	0	0	1	1	3	4	20
Mean Snowfall (in.)	40.4	49.8	46.8	21.0	5.9	0.3	0.0	0.0	0.3	2.1	21.9	39.7	228.2
Days With ≥ 1.0" Snow Depth	24	25	27	15	4	0	0	0	0	1	9	20	125

Brawley 2 SW *Imperial County*   Elevation: -98 ft.   Latitude: 32° 57' N   Longitude: 115° 33' W

	JAN	FEB	MAR	APR	MAY	JUN	JUL	AUG	SEP	OCT	NOV	DEC	YEAR
Mean Maximum Temp. (°F)	69.8	74.2	78.9	85.3	93.2	102.9	106.8	105.8	101.4	91.1	78.7	69.6	88.1
Mean Temp. (°F)	54.8	58.8	63.2	68.8	76.0	84.5	90.5	90.6	85.4	74.6	62.4	54.5	72.0
Mean Minimum Temp. (°F)	39.7	43.4	47.4	52.2	58.8	66.1	74.2	75.2	69.3	58.0	46.0	39.3	55.8
Extreme Maximum Temp. (°F)	89	97	99	108	114	121	121	119	116	111	98	86	121
Extreme Minimum Temp. (°F)	20	25	28	37	41	50	60	59	50	30	11	22	11
Days Maximum Temp. ≥ 90°F	0	0	3	10	22	29	31	31	28	19	2	0	175
Days Maximum Temp. ≤ 32°F	0	0	0	0	0	0	0	0	0	0	0	0	0
Days Minimum Temp. ≤ 32°F	4	1	0	0	0	0	0	0	0	0	0	3	8
Days Minimum Temp. ≤ 0°F	0	0	0	0	0	0	0	0	0	0	0	0	0
Heating Degree Days (base 65°F)	311	178	101	32	3	0	0	0	0	9	114	319	1,067
Cooling Degree Days (base 65°F)	1	13	55	178	368	586	799	821	634	327	48	1	3,831
Mean Precipitation (in.)	0.51	0.46	0.42	0.09	0.05	trace	0.07	0.42	0.27	0.26	0.19	0.43	3.17
Days With ≥ 0.1" Precipitation	1	1	1	0	0	0	0	1	1	1	0	1	7
Days With ≥ 1.0" Precipitation	0	0	0	0	0	0	0	0	0	0	0	0	0
Mean Snowfall (in.)	0.0	0.0	0.0	0.0	0.0	0.0	0.0	0.0	0.0	0.0	0.0	0.0	0.0
Days With ≥ 1.0" Snow Depth	0	0	0	0	0	0	0	0	0	0	0	0	0

Bridgeport *Mono County*   Elevation: 6,469 ft.   Latitude: 38° 15' N   Longitude: 119° 14' W

	JAN	FEB	MAR	APR	MAY	JUN	JUL	AUG	SEP	OCT	NOV	DEC	YEAR
Mean Maximum Temp. (°F)	42.5	46.2	52.0	59.4	67.2	76.0	83.5	82.4	75.8	66.8	53.7	44.0	62.5
Mean Temp. (°F)	25.9	29.4	35.6	41.2	48.5	56.2	62.0	60.6	53.7	44.8	35.5	27.1	43.4
Mean Minimum Temp. (°F)	9.1	12.4	19.2	22.9	29.7	36.3	40.4	38.8	31.5	22.8	17.1	10.1	24.2
Extreme Maximum Temp. (°F)	68	71	73	84	88	94	98	96	91	89	80	70	98
Extreme Minimum Temp. (°F)	-31	-27	-10	-2	6	17	21	19	11	-5	-14	-28	-31
Days Maximum Temp. ≥ 90°F	0	0	0	0	0	0	4	2	0	0	0	0	6
Days Maximum Temp. ≤ 32°F	5	2	0	0	0	0	0	0	0	0	1	5	13
Days Minimum Temp. ≤ 32°F	30	27	29	27	20	8	3	5	17	28	28	29	251
Days Minimum Temp. ≤ 0°F	7	4	1	0	0	0	0	0	0	0	1	6	19
Heating Degree Days (base 65°F)	1,208	1,000	905	708	504	262	107	140	334	618	879	1,169	7,834
Cooling Degree Days (base 65°F)	0	0	0	0	0	5	27	15	0	0	0	0	47
Mean Precipitation (in.)	1.30	1.43	1.02	0.39	0.53	0.60	0.47	0.46	0.50	0.33	0.96	1.03	9.02
Days With ≥ 0.1" Precipitation	3	3	2	1	2	1	1	1	1	1	2	2	20
Days With ≥ 1.0" Precipitation	0	0	0	0	0	0	0	0	0	0	0	0	0
Mean Snowfall (in.)	8.5	10.5	5.9	2.0	1.2	trace	0.0	0.0	0.3	0.6	3.3	*6.3*	*38.6*
Days With ≥ 1.0" Snow Depth	*14*	11	6	0	0	0	0	0	0	0	2	*8*	*41*

Burney *Shasta County*   Elevation: 3,156 ft.   Latitude: 40° 53' N   Longitude: 121° 40' W

	JAN	FEB	MAR	APR	MAY	JUN	JUL	AUG	SEP	OCT	NOV	DEC	YEAR
Mean Maximum Temp. (°F)	*44.1*	*49.9*	54.8	61.5	70.9	79.4	*87.6*	*87.0*	80.4	*69.1*	52.1	*43.6*	*65.0*
Mean Temp. (°F)	*31.2*	*36.2*	40.1	44.9	52.4	*59.7*	65.2	*63.6*	57.4	48.2	37.8	*31.1*	*47.3*
Mean Minimum Temp. (°F)	*18.2*	*22.4*	25.3	28.1	33.8	*39.9*	42.8	40.1	*34.3*	27.2	23.5	*18.4*	*29.5*
Extreme Maximum Temp. (°F)	*68*	*74*	*77*	*87*	*96*	*102*	*107*	*108*	*105*	*94*	*78*	*64*	*108*
Extreme Minimum Temp. (°F)	*-18*	*-18*	*1*	*12*	*17*	*21*	*25*	*24*	*18*	*10*	*-3*	*-26*	*-26*
Days Maximum Temp. ≥ 90°F	*0*	*0*	0	0	1	4	*14*	*13*	5	*1*	*0*	*0*	*38*
Days Maximum Temp. ≤ 32°F	*1*	*0*	0	0	0	0	*0*	*0*	*0*	*0*	*0*	*2*	*3*
Days Minimum Temp. ≤ 32°F	*28*	*26*	27	23	14	5	*2*	*4*	*13*	*25*	*26*	*29*	*222*
Days Minimum Temp. ≤ 0°F	*2*	*0*	0	0	0	0	*0*	*0*	*0*	*0*	*0*	*2*	*4*
Heating Degree Days (base 65°F)	*1,041*	*808*	765	598	387	*177*	*67*	*90*	232	514	808	*1,046*	6,533
Cooling Degree Days (base 65°F)	*0*	*0*	*0*	*0*	4	24	*83*	*50*	*16*	na	*0*	*0*	na
Mean Precipitation (in.)	*4.13*	*4.08*	3.85	1.70	1.47	0.81	0.22	*0.42*	*1.03*	1.78	3.88	3.66	27.03
Days With ≥ 0.1" Precipitation	*8*	*8*	8	5	4	2	1	*1*	*2*	4	8	8	59
Days With ≥ 1.0" Precipitation	*1*	*1*	1	0	0	0	0	*0*	*0*	0	1	1	5
Mean Snowfall (in.)	na	na	na	*1.0*	*trace*	0.0	0.0	*0.0*	*0.1*	0.1	na	na	na
Days With ≥ 1.0" Snow Depth	*11*	5	3	*1*	*0*	0	*0*	*0*	*0*	*0*	na	na	na

Buttonwillow *Kern County*   Elevation: 269 ft.   Latitude: 35° 24' N   Longitude: 119° 28' W

	JAN	FEB	MAR	APR	MAY	JUN	JUL	AUG	SEP	OCT	NOV	DEC	YEAR
Mean Maximum Temp. (°F)	55.9	63.5	68.8	75.8	84.7	92.1	97.1	95.7	90.8	81.8	67.2	56.6	77.5
Mean Temp. (°F)	45.8	51.6	56.4	61.3	69.2	76.1	81.1	79.6	74.5	65.4	53.4	45.2	63.3
Mean Minimum Temp. (°F)	35.7	39.7	43.9	46.7	53.7	60.0	65.1	63.4	58.2	48.9	39.5	33.8	49.1
Extreme Maximum Temp. (°F)	77	83	92	98	107	109	114	109	108	102	87	80	114
Extreme Minimum Temp. (°F)	16	22	26	31	38	42	49	51	41	25	23	12	12
Days Maximum Temp. ≥ 90°F	0	0	0	2	10	19	28	26	18	6	0	0	109
Days Maximum Temp. ≤ 32°F	0	0	0	0	0	0	0	0	0	0	0	0	0
Days Minimum Temp. ≤ 32°F	11	4	1	0	0	0	0	0	0	0	5	13	34
Days Minimum Temp. ≤ 0°F	0	0	0	0	0	0	0	0	0	0	0	0	0
Heating Degree Days (base 65°F)	587	372	264	140	33	2	0	0	3	76	344	606	2,427
Cooling Degree Days (base 65°F)	0	0	5	47	172	333	504	468	301	96	4	0	1,930
Mean Precipitation (in.)	1.22	1.17	1.38	0.47	0.23	0.07	trace	0.04	0.20	0.28	0.59	0.71	6.36
Days With ≥ 0.1" Precipitation	4	3	4	1	1	0	0	0	0	1	2	2	18
Days With ≥ 1.0" Precipitation	0	0	0	0	0	0	0	0	0	0	0	0	0
Mean Snowfall (in.)	0.0	0.0	0.0	0.0	0.0	0.0	0.0	0.0	0.0	0.0	0.0	0.0	0.0
Days With ≥ 1.0" Snow Depth	0	0	0	0	0	0	0	0	0	0	0	0	0

Cachuma Lake *Santa Barbara County*   Elevation: 780 ft.   Latitude: 34° 35' N   Longitude: 119° 59' W

	JAN	FEB	MAR	APR	MAY	JUN	JUL	AUG	SEP	OCT	NOV	DEC	YEAR
Mean Maximum Temp. (°F)	65.6	67.4	68.6	73.4	77.7	84.3	89.9	90.9	87.6	82.2	73.2	66.4	77.2
Mean Temp. (°F)	52.5	54.1	55.5	58.5	62.6	67.1	71.2	72.0	69.8	65.2	58.0	52.5	61.6
Mean Minimum Temp. (°F)	39.4	40.9	42.4	43.6	47.4	49.8	52.5	53.1	51.9	48.2	42.8	38.6	45.9
Extreme Maximum Temp. (°F)	88	92	95	105	104	107	110	112	115	110	100	90	115
Extreme Minimum Temp. (°F)	21	22	27	30	34	39	42	44	40	28	29	16	16
Days Maximum Temp. ≥ 90°F	0	0	0	2	4	8	16	17	12	7	1	0	67
Days Maximum Temp. ≤ 32°F	0	0	0	0	0	0	0	0	0	0	0	0	0
Days Minimum Temp. ≤ 32°F	4	2	1	0	0	0	0	0	0	0	1	5	13
Days Minimum Temp. ≤ 0°F	0	0	0	0	0	0	0	0	0	0	0	0	0
Heating Degree Days (base 65°F)	381	303	290	205	112	29	3	2	11	67	219	381	2,003
Cooling Degree Days (base 65°F)	0	3	4	23	46	103	214	243	163	88	16	1	904
Mean Precipitation (in.)	4.42	5.06	4.90	1.12	0.40	0.04	0.01	0.03	0.30	0.67	1.77	3.21	21.93
Days With ≥ 0.1" Precipitation	5	5	6	2	1	0	0	0	1	1	3	4	28
Days With ≥ 1.0" Precipitation	2	2	2	0	0	0	0	0	0	0	1	1	8
Mean Snowfall (in.)	0.0	0.0	0.0	0.0	0.0	0.0	0.0	0.0	0.0	0.0	0.0	0.0	0.0
Days With ≥ 1.0" Snow Depth	0	0	0	0	0	0	0	0	0	0	0	0	0

Calaveras Big Trees *Calaveras County*   Elevation: 4,691 ft.   Latitude: 38° 17' N   Longitude: 120° 19' W

	JAN	FEB	MAR	APR	MAY	JUN	JUL	AUG	SEP	OCT	NOV	DEC	YEAR
Mean Maximum Temp. (°F)	44.4	46.2	48.8	55.1	64.3	74.1	81.4	81.1	74.3	64.0	50.9	44.3	60.7
Mean Temp. (°F)	36.2	37.3	39.4	44.0	51.8	60.3	66.8	66.3	60.7	52.1	41.6	36.2	49.4
Mean Minimum Temp. (°F)	28.0	28.4	30.0	32.9	39.3	46.5	52.1	51.5	47.1	40.1	32.2	28.0	38.0
Extreme Maximum Temp. (°F)	66	70	72	85	93	95	100	98	94	88	79	65	100
Extreme Minimum Temp. (°F)	5	5	10	15	22	28	32	35	28	20	14	0	0
Days Maximum Temp. ≥ 90°F	0	0	0	0	0	1	3	3	1	0	0	0	8
Days Maximum Temp. ≤ 32°F	2	1	1	0	0	0	0	0	0	0	0	3	7
Days Minimum Temp. ≤ 32°F	24	22	22	15	5	1	0	0	1	5	17	24	136
Days Minimum Temp. ≤ 0°F	0	0	0	0	0	0	0	0	0	0	0	0	0
Heating Degree Days (base 65°F)	886	774	786	622	405	168	43	47	155	398	696	887	5,867
Cooling Degree Days (base 65°F)	0	0	0	0	4	29	100	97	30	6	0	0	266
Mean Precipitation (in.)	10.85	9.45	9.06	4.17	2.01	0.79	0.28	0.22	1.00	3.02	6.88	7.93	55.66
Days With ≥ 0.1" Precipitation	9	9	10	6	4	2	0	0	2	4	7	8	61
Days With ≥ 1.0" Precipitation	4	3	3	1	1	0	0	0	0	1	2	3	18
Mean Snowfall (in.)	25.1	23.3	25.0	12.9	1.8	trace	0.0	0.0	trace	0.8	6.7	19.2	114.8
Days With ≥ 1.0" Snow Depth	10	11	12	na	0	0	0	0	0	0	2	6	na

Callahan *Siskiyou County*   Elevation: 3,182 ft.   Latitude: 41° 19' N   Longitude: 122° 48' W

	JAN	FEB	MAR	APR	MAY	JUN	JUL	AUG	SEP	OCT	NOV	DEC	YEAR
Mean Maximum Temp. (°F)	44.7	50.7	56.0	62.0	70.5	78.4	86.1	85.5	78.6	67.2	51.2	43.8	64.6
Mean Temp. (°F)	35.5	39.7	43.5	47.8	54.6	61.3	67.8	66.9	60.6	51.6	40.9	35.0	50.4
Mean Minimum Temp. (°F)	26.2	28.7	30.9	33.5	38.7	44.2	49.4	48.2	42.6	36.1	30.5	26.2	36.3
Extreme Maximum Temp. (°F)	65	72	76	84	94	100	105	102	98	89	75	65	105
Extreme Minimum Temp. (°F)	-1	-1	4	19	24	23	30	34	23	15	11	-9	-9
Days Maximum Temp. ≥ 90°F	0	0	0	0	0	3	10	9	2	0	0	0	24
Days Maximum Temp. ≤ 32°F	2	0	0	0	0	0	0	0	0	0	0	1	3
Days Minimum Temp. ≤ 32°F	25	20	19	15	6	1	0	0	1	9	20	25	141
Days Minimum Temp. ≤ 0°F	0	0	0	0	0	0	0	0	0	0	0	0	0
Heating Degree Days (base 65°F)	910	707	661	510	320	140	33	38	148	408	718	923	5,516
Cooling Degree Days (base 65°F)	0	0	0	0	0	6	33	119	101	24	1	0	284
Mean Precipitation (in.)	3.82	2.89	2.41	1.29	1.13	0.86	0.43	0.35	0.64	1.38	3.18	3.38	21.76
Days With ≥ 0.1" Precipitation	7	6	6	4	3	3	1	1	2	3	6	7	49
Days With ≥ 1.0" Precipitation	1	1	0	0	0	0	0	0	0	0	0	1	3
Mean Snowfall (in.)	1.6	0.5	1.4	0.3	0.1	0.0	0.0	0.0	0.0	0.1	0.8	1.3	6.1
Days With ≥ 1.0" Snow Depth	na	0	0	0	0	0	0	0	0	0	0	0	na

Camp Pardee *Calaveras County*   Elevation: 656 ft.   Latitude: 38° 15' N   Longitude: 120° 52' W

	JAN	FEB	MAR	APR	MAY	JUN	JUL	AUG	SEP	OCT	NOV	DEC	YEAR
Mean Maximum Temp. (°F)	53.8	59.7	63.8	70.4	79.8	88.5	94.9	93.5	88.4	78.2	63.5	54.2	74.1
Mean Temp. (°F)	46.4	50.8	54.0	58.4	65.6	72.8	78.3	77.3	73.5	65.5	54.3	46.5	62.0
Mean Minimum Temp. (°F)	38.8	41.9	44.2	46.4	51.5	56.9	61.7	61.1	58.5	52.7	45.0	38.8	49.8
Extreme Maximum Temp. (°F)	71	76	85	99	108	109	114	111	107	102	83	72	114
Extreme Minimum Temp. (°F)	25	23	28	33	36	42	49	45	42	33	25	17	17
Days Maximum Temp. ≥ 90°F	0	0	0	0	5	14	24	22	14	3	0	0	82
Days Maximum Temp. ≤ 32°F	0	0	0	0	0	0	0	0	0	0	0	0	0
Days Minimum Temp. ≤ 32°F	5	1	0	0	0	0	0	0	0	0	0	5	11
Days Minimum Temp. ≤ 0°F	0	0	0	0	0	0	0	0	0	0	0	0	0
Heating Degree Days (base 65°F)	573	395	336	209	80	12	0	1	8	79	319	568	2,580
Cooling Degree Days (base 65°F)	0	0	1	23	103	243	417	397	273	103	3	0	1,563
Mean Precipitation (in.)	4.21	3.64	4.08	1.76	0.89	0.27	0.10	0.10	0.51	1.21	3.07	3.18	23.02
Days With ≥ 0.1" Precipitation	8	7	7	4	2	1	0	0	1	2	6	7	45
Days With ≥ 1.0" Precipitation	1	1	1	0	0	0	0	0	0	0	1	1	5
Mean Snowfall (in.)	0.0	trace	trace	0.0	0.0	0.0	0.0	0.0	0.0	0.0	0.0	0.0	trace
Days With ≥ 1.0" Snow Depth	0	0	0	0	0	0	0	0	0	0	0	0	0

Campo *San Diego County*   Elevation: 2,627 ft.   Latitude: 32° 37' N   Longitude: 116° 28' W

	JAN	FEB	MAR	APR	MAY	JUN	JUL	AUG	SEP	OCT	NOV	DEC	YEAR
Mean Maximum Temp. (°F)	62.2	64.3	66.1	71.8	77.9	87.4	93.7	93.7	88.7	79.5	69.5	62.7	76.5
Mean Temp. (°F)	48.1	49.3	50.9	54.5	59.6	66.2	72.5	73.1	68.7	60.7	52.6	47.6	58.6
Mean Minimum Temp. (°F)	33.9	34.3	35.7	37.2	41.2	44.9	51.3	52.5	48.6	41.8	35.6	32.5	40.8
Extreme Maximum Temp. (°F)	84	86	92	99	102	107	108	107	107	103	92	86	108
Extreme Minimum Temp. (°F)	10	13	15	21	25	29	34	30	29	22	16	12	10
Days Maximum Temp. ≥ 90°F	0	0	0	1	4	14	24	25	16	5	0	0	89
Days Maximum Temp. ≤ 32°F	0	0	0	0	0	0	0	0	0	0	0	0	0
Days Minimum Temp. ≤ 32°F	14	12	10	6	2	0	0	0	0	2	11	17	74
Days Minimum Temp. ≤ 0°F	0	0	0	0	0	0	0	0	0	0	0	0	0
Heating Degree Days (base 65°F)	517	436	430	311	182	56	6	8	35	158	367	532	3,038
Cooling Degree Days (base 65°F)	0	0	0	4	24	95	236	281	159	30	1	0	830
Mean Precipitation (in.)	3.37	2.93	2.90	0.96	0.26	0.09	0.29	0.63	0.40	0.63	1.27	1.89	15.62
Days With ≥ 0.1" Precipitation	5	5	5	3	1	0	1	1	1	1	3	4	30
Days With ≥ 1.0" Precipitation	1	1	1	0	0	0	0	0	0	0	0	0	3
Mean Snowfall (in.)	trace	trace	trace	0.0	0.0	0.0	0.0	0.0	0.0	0.0	trace	trace	trace
Days With ≥ 1.0" Snow Depth	0	0	0	0	0	0	0	0	0	0	0	0	0

Canoga Park Pierce College *Los Angeles County*   Elevation: 787 ft.   Latitude: 34° 11' N   Longitude: 118° 34' W

	JAN	FEB	MAR	APR	MAY	JUN	JUL	AUG	SEP	OCT	NOV	DEC	YEAR
Mean Maximum Temp. (°F)	68.6	70.8	72.6	77.8	81.5	89.0	95.4	96.3	91.8	84.6	75.2	69.1	81.1
Mean Temp. (°F)	54.2	56.1	57.6	61.3	65.5	71.3	76.4	77.1	73.6	67.1	58.8	53.8	64.4
Mean Minimum Temp. (°F)	39.8	41.3	42.5	44.7	49.4	53.5	57.3	57.8	55.3	49.5	42.3	38.5	47.7
Extreme Maximum Temp. (°F)	93	94	101	105	113	113	115	116	115	110	99	93	116
Extreme Minimum Temp. (°F)	22	18	28	30	37	40	46	45	42	27	26	20	18
Days Maximum Temp. ≥ 90°F	0	0	1	4	7	15	24	25	18	9	2	0	105
Days Maximum Temp. ≤ 32°F	0	0	0	0	0	0	0	0	0	0	0	0	0
Days Minimum Temp. ≤ 32°F	4	2	1	0	0	0	0	0	0	0	1	5	13
Days Minimum Temp. ≤ 0°F	0	0	0	0	0	0	0	0	0	0	0	0	0
Heating Degree Days (base 65°F)	330	250	233	140	68	13	0	0	5	42	194	342	1,617
Cooling Degree Days (base 65°F)	2	4	9	48	93	201	356	396	272	116	13	1	1,511
Mean Precipitation (in.)	3.85	4.30	3.67	0.79	0.32	0.07	0.01	0.14	0.24	0.61	1.57	2.59	18.16
Days With ≥ 0.1" Precipitation	5	4	5	1	1	0	0	0	1	1	2	3	23
Days With ≥ 1.0" Precipitation	1	1	1	0	0	0	0	0	0	0	0	1	4
Mean Snowfall (in.)	0.0	trace	0.0	0.0	0.0	0.0	0.0	0.0	0.0	0.0	0.0	trace	trace
Days With ≥ 1.0" Snow Depth	0	0	0	0	0	0	0	0	0	0	0	0	0

Canyon Dam *Plumas County*   Elevation: 4,557 ft.   Latitude: 40° 10' N   Longitude: 121° 05' W

	JAN	FEB	MAR	APR	MAY	JUN	JUL	AUG	SEP	OCT	NOV	DEC	YEAR
Mean Maximum Temp. (°F)	39.9	44.0	49.5	57.3	67.6	75.9	84.2	83.5	76.2	64.1	48.2	40.2	60.9
Mean Temp. (°F)	31.5	34.4	38.5	43.9	52.2	59.4	66.1	65.0	58.9	49.4	38.5	31.8	47.5
Mean Minimum Temp. (°F)	23.0	24.7	27.5	30.4	36.7	42.8	47.9	46.5	41.6	34.7	28.7	23.4	34.0
Extreme Maximum Temp. (°F)	57	63	71	81	92	96	101	102	97	85	69	60	102
Extreme Minimum Temp. (°F)	-5	-10	5	14	23	27	34	31	26	13	8	-14	-14
Days Maximum Temp. ≥ 90°F	0	0	0	0	0	1	7	6	1	0	0	0	15
Days Maximum Temp. ≤ 32°F	3	1	0	0	0	0	0	0	0	0	0	3	7
Days Minimum Temp. ≤ 32°F	29	26	27	21	8	1	0	0	1	11	23	29	176
Days Minimum Temp. ≤ 0°F	0	0	0	0	0	0	0	0	0	0	0	0	0
Heating Degree Days (base 65°F)	1,033	858	814	627	393	184	52	63	190	477	789	1,021	6,501
Cooling Degree Days (base 65°F)	0	0	0	0	2	19	86	66	16	0	0	0	189
Mean Precipitation (in.)	6.94	6.46	5.77	2.39	1.54	0.81	0.25	0.35	0.92	2.15	5.00	5.66	38.24
Days With ≥ 0.1" Precipitation	8	8	9	5	4	2	1	1	2	3	8	7	58
Days With ≥ 1.0" Precipitation	2	2	2	1	0	0	0	0	0	1	2	2	12
Mean Snowfall (in.)	25.3	23.5	17.4	6.2	0.7	trace	0.0	0.0	trace	0.6	9.5	23.1	106.3
Days With ≥ 1.0" Snow Depth	28	26	20	6	0	0	0	0	0	0	7	21	108

Cedarville *Modoc County*   Elevation: 4,668 ft.   Latitude: 41° 32' N   Longitude: 120° 10' W

	JAN	FEB	MAR	APR	MAY	JUN	JUL	AUG	SEP	OCT	NOV	DEC	YEAR
Mean Maximum Temp. (°F)	39.4	44.2	50.1	56.6	65.9	76.0	85.8	85.1	76.8	64.7	48.4	40.0	61.1
Mean Temp. (°F)	29.8	34.1	39.5	44.9	52.9	61.7	69.9	68.6	60.1	49.5	37.5	30.0	48.2
Mean Minimum Temp. (°F)	20.1	23.9	28.8	33.1	39.9	47.3	53.9	52.1	43.4	34.2	26.5	20.0	35.3
Extreme Maximum Temp. (°F)	64	69	74	82	93	99	100	102	98	90	75	64	102
Extreme Minimum Temp. (°F)	-15	-17	-2	14	22	29	35	33	24	7	-5	-28	-28
Days Maximum Temp. ≥ 90°F	0	0	0	0	0	2	11	10	2	0	0	0	25
Days Maximum Temp. ≤ 32°F	7	2	1	0	0	0	0	0	0	0	1	6	17
Days Minimum Temp. ≤ 32°F	27	24	22	14	5	0	0	0	2	12	23	28	157
Days Minimum Temp. ≤ 0°F	1	1	0	0	0	0	0	0	0	0	0	2	4
Heating Degree Days (base 65°F)	1,085	867	785	597	375	152	29	38	174	475	820	1,078	6,475
Cooling Degree Days (base 65°F)	0	0	0	0	10	54	178	152	36	1	0	0	431
Mean Precipitation (in.)	1.88	1.40	1.59	1.19	1.16	0.74	0.29	0.38	0.62	0.88	1.78	1.61	13.52
Days With ≥ 0.1" Precipitation	5	4	5	4	4	2	1	1	2	3	6	5	42
Days With ≥ 1.0" Precipitation	0	0	0	0	0	0	0	0	0	0	0	0	0
Mean Snowfall (in.)	5.6	3.8	3.3	1.6	0.4	trace	0.0	0.0	trace	0.4	2.1	4.9	22.1
Days With ≥ 1.0" Snow Depth	8	3	2	1	0	0	0	0	0	0	1	4	19

Cherry Valley Dam *Tuolumne County*   Elevation: 4,763 ft.   Latitude: 37° 58' N   Longitude: 119° 55' W

	JAN	FEB	MAR	APR	MAY	JUN	JUL	AUG	SEP	OCT	NOV	DEC	YEAR
Mean Maximum Temp. (°F)	48.4	50.9	53.6	60.2	68.8	78.3	86.6	86.3	79.0	68.3	55.2	48.3	65.3
Mean Temp. (°F)	38.7	40.0	42.1	47.5	55.5	63.8	71.2	70.7	64.5	55.2	44.5	38.6	52.7
Mean Minimum Temp. (°F)	28.8	29.1	30.6	34.7	42.1	49.3	55.7	55.2	50.0	42.1	33.9	28.9	40.0
Extreme Maximum Temp. (°F)	70	74	76	84	91	97	105	103	98	93	79	70	105
Extreme Minimum Temp. (°F)	8	0	7	14	22	29	39	40	30	17	12	-3	-3
Days Maximum Temp. ≥ 90°F	0	0	0	0	0	3	11	10	3	0	0	0	27
Days Maximum Temp. ≤ 32°F	1	1	0	0	0	0	0	0	0	0	0	1	3
Days Minimum Temp. ≤ 32°F	21	20	19	12	3	0	0	0	0	3	14	21	113
Days Minimum Temp. ≤ 0°F	0	0	0	0	0	0	0	0	0	0	0	0	0
Heating Degree Days (base 65°F)	810	699	701	519	303	103	13	15	91	310	608	810	4,982
Cooling Degree Days (base 65°F)	0	0	0	1	15	75	211	211	87	16	0	0	616
Mean Precipitation (in.)	9.33	7.97	7.38	3.44	1.65	0.84	0.18	0.20	1.03	2.61	6.29	6.07	46.99
Days With ≥ 0.1" Precipitation	8	7	8	5	3	2	0	0	2	3	6	6	50
Days With ≥ 1.0" Precipitation	4	2	3	1	0	0	0	0	0	1	2	2	15
Mean Snowfall (in.)	25.2	22.5	24.5	9.6	0.7	trace	0.0	0.0	trace	0.4	7.4	18.4	108.7
Days With ≥ 1.0" Snow Depth	18	18	11	4	0	0	0	0	0	0	5	13	69

Chester *Plumas County*   Elevation: 4,524 ft.   Latitude: 40° 18' N   Longitude: 121° 14' W

	JAN	FEB	MAR	APR	MAY	JUN	JUL	AUG	SEP	OCT	NOV	DEC	YEAR
Mean Maximum Temp. (°F)	41.8	46.0	51.1	58.3	67.6	76.3	84.5	83.8	77.5	66.1	49.9	41.8	62.0
Mean Temp. (°F)	30.9	34.2	38.4	43.5	51.0	58.5	64.7	63.5	57.8	48.8	37.9	31.1	46.7
Mean Minimum Temp. (°F)	19.9	22.4	25.7	28.6	34.4	40.6	44.8	43.1	38.0	31.4	25.9	20.4	31.3
Extreme Maximum Temp. (°F)	60	70	74	84	93	96	100	103	98	89	75	62	103
Extreme Minimum Temp. (°F)	-10	-10	3	5	20	24	29	27	20	12	3	-16	-16
Days Maximum Temp. ≥ 90°F	0	0	0	0	0	2	7	6	2	0	0	0	17
Days Maximum Temp. ≤ 32°F	2	1	0	0	0	0	0	0	0	0	0	3	6
Days Minimum Temp. ≤ 32°F	30	27	28	23	13	2	0	0	5	19	26	29	202
Days Minimum Temp. ≤ 0°F	1	0	0	0	0	0	0	0	0	0	0	1	2
Heating Degree Days (base 65°F)	1,051	863	817	639	428	205	65	84	216	496	806	1,045	6,715
Cooling Degree Days (base 65°F)	0	0	0	0	1	17	64	44	8	0	0	0	134
Mean Precipitation (in.)	6.14	5.36	4.94	1.99	1.54	0.85	0.36	0.39	0.87	1.98	4.20	4.83	33.45
Days With ≥ 0.1" Precipitation	9	8	8	5	4	2	1	1	2	3	7	8	58
Days With ≥ 1.0" Precipitation	2	2	1	0	0	0	0	0	0	0	1	1	7
Mean Snowfall (in.)	32.6	26.9	19.0	6.5	0.6	0.1	0.0	0.0	trace	0.5	12.1	27.7	126.0
Days With ≥ 1.0" Snow Depth	25	23	16	4	0	0	0	0	0	0	5	19	92

Chico University Farm *Butte County*   Elevation: 183 ft.   Latitude: 39° 41' N   Longitude: 121° 49' W

	JAN	FEB	MAR	APR	MAY	JUN	JUL	AUG	SEP	OCT	NOV	DEC	YEAR
Mean Maximum Temp. (°F)	54.6	60.8	65.3	72.1	80.8	88.7	94.2	93.2	89.1	78.8	63.9	55.1	74.7
Mean Temp. (°F)	45.0	49.8	53.3	58.3	66.1	72.9	77.7	75.9	71.9	62.8	52.0	45.1	60.9
Mean Minimum Temp. (°F)	35.4	38.8	41.4	44.6	51.3	57.1	60.9	58.6	54.6	47.0	40.1	35.1	47.1
Extreme Maximum Temp. (°F)	76	81	87	95	104	108	117	114	114	103	85	76	117
Extreme Minimum Temp. (°F)	18	16	23	29	30	38	40	38	35	23	21	13	13
Days Maximum Temp. ≥ 90°F	0	0	0	0	6	14	24	22	17	4	0	0	87
Days Maximum Temp. ≤ 32°F	0	0	0	0	0	0	0	0	0	0	0	0	0
Days Minimum Temp. ≤ 32°F	13	6	3	0	0	0	0	0	0	0	4	12	38
Days Minimum Temp. ≤ 0°F	0	0	0	0	0	0	0	0	0	0	0	0	0
Heating Degree Days (base 65°F)	613	423	355	208	69	10	0	1	12	113	383	611	2,798
Cooling Degree Days (base 65°F)	0	0	0	20	107	245	403	345	232	49	0	0	1,401
Mean Precipitation (in.)	5.38	4.38	4.26	1.52	0.88	0.50	0.05	0.16	0.58	1.28	3.43	3.80	26.22
Days With ≥ 0.1" Precipitation	7	6	7	3	2	1	0	0	1	2	5	6	40
Days With ≥ 1.0" Precipitation	2	1	1	0	0	0	0	0	0	0	1	1	6
Mean Snowfall (in.)	trace	0.0	trace	0.0	0.0	0.0	0.0	0.0	0.0	0.0	0.0	0.1	0.1
Days With ≥ 1.0" Snow Depth	0	0	0	0	0	0	0	0	0	0	0	0	0

Chula Vista *San Diego County*   Elevation: 55 ft.   Latitude: 32° 38' N   Longitude: 117° 05' W

	JAN	FEB	MAR	APR	MAY	JUN	JUL	AUG	SEP	OCT	NOV	DEC	YEAR
Mean Maximum Temp. (°F)	66.0	66.5	66.2	68.0	68.4	70.6	74.2	76.3	76.5	74.3	69.8	66.3	70.3
Mean Temp. (°F)	55.9	57.0	58.1	60.3	62.7	65.4	69.1	70.8	70.0	65.8	59.8	55.8	62.6
Mean Minimum Temp. (°F)	45.7	47.4	49.9	52.6	57.0	60.2	63.9	65.3	63.4	57.6	49.8	45.2	54.8
Extreme Maximum Temp. (°F)	88	90	95	102	89	96	97	96	108	106	96	84	108
Extreme Minimum Temp. (°F)	29	29	32	40	43	49	54	42	43	36	35	28	28
Days Maximum Temp. ≥ 90°F	0	0	0	0	0	0	0	0	1	1	0	0	2
Days Maximum Temp. ≤ 32°F	0	0	0	0	0	0	0	0	0	0	0	0	0
Days Minimum Temp. ≤ 32°F	0	0	0	0	0	0	0	0	0	0	0	0	0
Days Minimum Temp. ≤ 0°F	0	0	0	0	0	0	0	0	0	0	0	0	0
Heating Degree Days (base 65°F)	278	223	214	145	84	28	2	1	4	36	158	280	1,453
Cooling Degree Days (base 65°F)	2	4	6	17	27	62	166	221	188	85	11	1	790
Mean Precipitation (in.)	2.02	1.92	2.12	0.70	0.13	0.08	0.03	0.08	0.20	0.39	1.22	1.26	10.15
Days With ≥ 0.1" Precipitation	4	4	4	2	0	0	0	0	0	1	2	3	20
Days With ≥ 1.0" Precipitation	0	0	0	0	0	0	0	0	0	0	0	0	0
Mean Snowfall (in.)	trace	0.0	0.0	0.0	0.0	0.0	0.0	0.0	trace	0.0	0.0	0.2	0.2
Days With ≥ 1.0" Snow Depth	0	0	0	0	0	0	0	0	0	0	0	0	0

Clearlake 4 SE *Lake County*   Elevation: 1,348 ft.   Latitude: 38° 55' N   Longitude: 122° 34' W

	JAN	FEB	MAR	APR	MAY	JUN	JUL	AUG	SEP	OCT	NOV	DEC	YEAR
Mean Maximum Temp. (°F)	55.1	58.3	61.6	67.9	76.2	85.1	92.6	91.7	85.8	75.7	61.9	54.8	72.2
Mean Temp. (°F)	43.1	45.9	48.8	53.3	60.4	68.0	73.7	72.4	67.1	58.6	48.6	42.8	56.9
Mean Minimum Temp. (°F)	31.0	33.3	35.9	38.6	44.6	50.8	54.7	53.0	48.3	41.6	35.2	30.8	41.5
Extreme Maximum Temp. (°F)	76	81	84	94	101	114	113	112	107	99	84	78	114
Extreme Minimum Temp. (°F)	8	16	20	24	28	34	40	41	34	21	20	6	6
Days Maximum Temp. ≥ 90°F	0	0	0	0	3	10	21	20	12	3	0	0	69
Days Maximum Temp. ≤ 32°F	0	0	0	0	0	0	0	0	0	0	0	0	0
Days Minimum Temp. ≤ 32°F	20	14	9	4	0	0	0	0	0	2	12	20	81
Days Minimum Temp. ≤ 0°F	0	0	0	0	0	0	0	0	0	0	0	0	0
Heating Degree Days (base 65°F)	673	534	496	348	171	41	5	5	44	208	487	681	3,693
Cooling Degree Days (base 65°F)	0	0	0	2	32	122	267	231	117	21	0	0	792
Mean Precipitation (in.)	6.26	4.88	4.32	1.33	0.89	0.21	0.06	0.08	0.51	1.41	3.63	4.51	28.09
Days With ≥ 0.1" Precipitation	8	7	7	4	2	1	0	0	1	3	6	7	46
Days With ≥ 1.0" Precipitation	2	2	1	0	0	0	0	0	0	0	1	1	7
Mean Snowfall (in.)	1.8	0.2	0.3	trace	0.0	0.0	0.0	0.0	0.0	trace	trace	0.1	2.4
Days With ≥ 1.0" Snow Depth	1	0	0	0	0	0	0	0	0	0	0	*0*	*1*

Coalinga *Fresno County*   Elevation: 669 ft.   Latitude: 36° 08' N   Longitude: 120° 22' W

	JAN	FEB	MAR	APR	MAY	JUN	JUL	AUG	SEP	OCT	NOV	DEC	YEAR
Mean Maximum Temp. (°F)	58.1	64.8	69.9	77.2	86.1	93.8	99.1	97.5	92.4	82.8	67.8	58.6	79.0
Mean Temp. (°F)	47.5	52.4	56.4	61.7	69.5	76.7	82.1	80.6	75.7	66.4	54.4	47.1	64.2
Mean Minimum Temp. (°F)	36.8	40.0	42.8	46.1	52.7	59.5	65.1	63.7	58.9	49.9	40.8	35.3	49.3
Extreme Maximum Temp. (°F)	77	83	91	99	109	109	114	113	110	103	88	79	114
Extreme Minimum Temp. (°F)	20	21	26	30	36	35	44	48	42	30	25	11	11
Days Maximum Temp. ≥ 90°F	0	0	0	3	11	22	29	28	20	7	0	0	120
Days Maximum Temp. ≤ 32°F	0	0	0	0	0	0	0	0	0	0	0	0	0
Days Minimum Temp. ≤ 32°F	9	4	1	0	0	0	0	0	0	0	4	12	30
Days Minimum Temp. ≤ 0°F	0	0	0	0	0	0	0	0	0	0	0	0	0
Heating Degree Days (base 65°F)	537	348	265	138	35	3	0	0	4	62	314	550	2,256
Cooling Degree Days (base 65°F)	0	0	6	59	190	366	555	512	350	120	2	0	2,160
Mean Precipitation (in.)	1.78	1.75	1.57	0.44	0.24	0.06	trace	0.03	0.33	0.35	0.71	1.13	8.39
Days With ≥ 0.1" Precipitation	4	4	4	1	1	0	0	0	1	1	2	3	21
Days With ≥ 1.0" Precipitation	0	0	0	0	0	0	0	0	0	0	0	0	0
Mean Snowfall (in.)	trace	trace	0.0	0.0	0.0	0.0	0.0	0.0	0.0	0.0	0.0	trace	trace
Days With ≥ 1.0" Snow Depth	0	0	0	0	0	0	0	0	0	0	0	0	0

Colfax *Placer County*   Elevation: 2,398 ft.   Latitude: 39° 07' N   Longitude: 120° 57' W

	JAN	FEB	MAR	APR	MAY	JUN	JUL	AUG	SEP	OCT	NOV	DEC	YEAR
Mean Maximum Temp. (°F)	55.5	58.0	60.3	66.2	74.1	83.3	90.3	89.8	84.8	74.9	60.4	54.9	71.0
Mean Temp. (°F)	45.3	47.5	49.5	54.0	61.0	69.3	75.6	74.5	69.8	61.1	49.6	44.6	58.5
Mean Minimum Temp. (°F)	35.2	36.8	38.7	41.7	47.8	55.2	60.8	59.2	54.8	47.2	38.8	34.2	45.9
Extreme Maximum Temp. (°F)	77	81	87	89	99	104	113	107	105	97	85	79	113
Extreme Minimum Temp. (°F)	20	15	21	27	30	38	44	43	32	24	20	9	9
Days Maximum Temp. ≥ 90°F	0	0	0	0	1	8	18	17	10	2	0	0	56
Days Maximum Temp. ≤ 32°F	0	0	0	0	0	0	0	0	0	0	0	0	0
Days Minimum Temp. ≤ 32°F	11	7	5	2	0	0	0	0	0	0	5	12	42
Days Minimum Temp. ≤ 0°F	0	0	0	0	0	0	0	0	0	0	0	0	0
Heating Degree Days (base 65°F)	603	489	475	329	169	43	3	4	36	164	454	626	3,395
Cooling Degree Days (base 65°F)	0	0	0	8	50	158	317	302	177	45	0	0	1,057
Mean Precipitation (in.)	8.79	7.79	7.77	3.23	1.56	0.63	0.20	0.24	1.04	2.56	7.13	7.46	48.40
Days With ≥ 0.1" Precipitation	8	8	9	5	3	1	0	0	2	3	8	8	55
Days With ≥ 1.0" Precipitation	3	3	3	1	0	0	0	0	0	1	2	3	16
Mean Snowfall (in.)	2.8	2.8	1.8	0.9	trace	0.0	0.0	0.0	0.0	0.0	0.4	1.9	10.6
Days With ≥ 1.0" Snow Depth	1	*0*	*0*	0	0	0	0	0	0	0	0	0	*1*

Colusa 2 SSW *Colusa County*   Elevation: 49 ft.   Latitude: 39° 12' N   Longitude: 122° 01' W

	JAN	FEB	MAR	APR	MAY	JUN	JUL	AUG	SEP	OCT	NOV	DEC	YEAR
Mean Maximum Temp. (°F)	54.2	60.7	66.0	73.5	81.9	89.4	94.4	93.1	89.1	79.3	63.5	54.3	75.0
Mean Temp. (°F)	46.0	50.8	54.7	59.5	67.3	73.3	76.8	75.2	71.6	63.7	52.3	45.5	61.4
Mean Minimum Temp. (°F)	37.7	40.8	43.3	45.4	52.6	57.1	59.2	57.2	54.0	47.9	41.2	36.6	47.8
Extreme Maximum Temp. (°F)	77	80	88	95	106	108	112	113	108	100	85	74	113
Extreme Minimum Temp. (°F)	21	21	25	29	34	38	40	43	35	32	23	15	15
Days Maximum Temp. ≥ 90°F	0	0	0	1	7	15	24	21	15	4	0	0	87
Days Maximum Temp. ≤ 32°F	0	0	0	0	0	0	0	0	0	0	0	0	0
Days Minimum Temp. ≤ 32°F	8	3	1	0	0	0	0	0	0	0	3	8	23
Days Minimum Temp. ≤ 0°F	0	0	0	0	0	0	0	0	0	0	0	0	0
Heating Degree Days (base 65°F)	584	395	314	192	53	6	0	0	9	96	373	598	2,620
Cooling Degree Days (base 65°F)	0	0	1	24	127	253	365	315	212	62	1	0	1,360
Mean Precipitation (in.)	3.72	3.01	2.69	0.74	0.60	0.19	0.04	0.04	0.33	0.88	2.41	2.41	17.06
Days With ≥ 0.1" Precipitation	7	6	6	2	1	1	0	0	1	2	5	5	36
Days With ≥ 1.0" Precipitation	1	1	0	0	0	0	0	0	0	0	0	0	2
Mean Snowfall (in.)	0.0	0.0	0.0	0.0	0.0	0.0	0.0	0.0	0.0	0.0	0.0	trace	trace
Days With ≥ 1.0" Snow Depth	0	0	0	0	0	0	0	0	0	0	0	0	0

Corcoran Irrigation District *Kings County*   Elevation: 200 ft.   Latitude: 36° 06' N   Longitude: 119° 34' W

	JAN	FEB	MAR	APR	MAY	JUN	JUL	AUG	SEP	OCT	NOV	DEC	YEAR
Mean Maximum Temp. (°F)	54.7	62.6	68.3	76.3	85.5	93.2	98.1	96.3	91.0	81.4	65.9	54.8	77.4
Mean Temp. (°F)	46.1	51.5	55.9	61.3	69.0	75.8	80.4	79.0	74.2	65.5	53.2	45.3	63.1
Mean Minimum Temp. (°F)	37.4	40.2	43.5	46.2	52.4	58.3	62.6	61.6	57.3	49.5	40.5	35.6	48.8
Extreme Maximum Temp. (°F)	75	81	88	100	107	111	112	110	106	105	85	78	112
Extreme Minimum Temp. (°F)	19	24	26	29	36	44	49	49	39	27	25	17	17
Days Maximum Temp. ≥ 90°F	0	0	0	2	11	21	29	27	19	5	0	0	114
Days Maximum Temp. ≤ 32°F	0	0	0	0	0	0	0	0	0	0	0	0	0
Days Minimum Temp. ≤ 32°F	8	3	1	0	0	0	0	0	0	0	4	11	27
Days Minimum Temp. ≤ 0°F	0	0	0	0	0	0	0	0	0	0	0	0	0
Heating Degree Days (base 65°F)	580	376	276	140	34	2	0	0	3	70	348	605	2,434
Cooling Degree Days (base 65°F)	0	0	3	47	166	326	482	444	290	95	1	0	1,854
Mean Precipitation (in.)	1.57	1.48	1.44	0.50	0.23	0.05	trace	trace	0.24	0.35	0.81	1.00	7.67
Days With ≥ 0.1" Precipitation	4	4	4	2	1	0	0	0	1	1	2	3	22
Days With ≥ 1.0" Precipitation	0	0	0	0	0	0	0	0	0	0	0	0	0
Mean Snowfall (in.)	0.1	0.0	0.0	0.0	0.0	0.0	0.0	0.0	0.0	0.0	0.0	0.0	0.1
Days With ≥ 1.0" Snow Depth	0	0	0	0	0	0	0	0	0	0	0	0	0

Crescent City 3 NNW *Del Norte County*   Elevation: 68 ft.   Latitude: 41° 44' N   Longitude: 124° 12' W

	JAN	FEB	MAR	APR	MAY	JUN	JUL	AUG	SEP	OCT	NOV	DEC	YEAR
Mean Maximum Temp. (°F)	55.4	56.3	56.9	58.1	60.8	63.3	65.5	66.1	66.3	63.7	57.9	55.2	60.5
Mean Temp. (°F)	48.2	49.2	49.9	50.8	53.6	56.3	58.5	59.1	58.3	55.4	50.9	47.8	53.2
Mean Minimum Temp. (°F)	41.0	42.0	42.8	43.5	46.4	49.2	51.4	52.1	50.2	47.1	44.0	40.3	45.8
Extreme Maximum Temp. (°F)	75	78	76	84	92	93	83	84	92	93	76	80	93
Extreme Minimum Temp. (°F)	24	24	28	30	34	37	40	41	38	33	28	19	19
Days Maximum Temp. ≥ 90°F	0	0	0	0	0	0	0	0	0	0	0	0	0
Days Maximum Temp. ≤ 32°F	0	0	0	0	0	0	0	0	0	0	0	0	0
Days Minimum Temp. ≤ 32°F	2	2	1	0	0	0	0	0	0	0	1	3	9
Days Minimum Temp. ≤ 0°F	0	0	0	0	0	0	0	0	0	0	0	0	0
Heating Degree Days (base 65°F)	510	440	463	419	345	257	197	177	198	292	416	527	4,241
Cooling Degree Days (base 65°F)	0	0	0	0	1	0	1	1	2	3	0	0	8
Mean Precipitation (in.)	10.27	8.88	9.21	5.09	3.06	1.52	0.40	0.74	1.66	4.50	10.14	11.53	67.00
Days With ≥ 0.1" Precipitation	na	na	na	7	5	2	1	1	2	5	na	na	na
Days With ≥ 1.0" Precipitation	3	na	2	1	1	0	0	0	0	1	na	na	na
Mean Snowfall (in.)	0.2	0.0	0.0	trace	0.0	0.0	0.0	0.0	0.0	0.0	0.0	trace	0.2
Days With ≥ 1.0" Snow Depth	0	0	0	0	0	0	0	0	0	0	0	0	0

Cuyamaca *San Diego County*   Elevation: 4,639 ft.   Latitude: 32° 59' N   Longitude: 116° 35' W

	JAN	FEB	MAR	APR	MAY	JUN	JUL	AUG	SEP	OCT	NOV	DEC	YEAR
Mean Maximum Temp. (°F)	51.0	53.1	54.9	60.1	66.9	76.5	83.5	83.6	78.8	69.1	58.9	51.8	65.7
Mean Temp. (°F)	40.7	42.2	44.2	48.3	54.2	62.7	69.4	69.3	64.0	54.6	46.4	40.6	53.1
Mean Minimum Temp. (°F)	30.4	31.2	33.5	36.4	41.5	49.0	55.3	54.8	49.2	40.1	33.9	29.4	40.4
Extreme Maximum Temp. (°F)	74	74	80	85	90	98	101	99	95	91	80	75	101
Extreme Minimum Temp. (°F)	3	4	10	20	22	29	36	36	25	18	12	5	3
Days Maximum Temp. ≥ 90°F	0	0	0	0	0	1	4	5	1	0	0	0	11
Days Maximum Temp. ≤ 32°F	1	0	0	0	0	0	0	0	0	0	0	1	2
Days Minimum Temp. ≤ 32°F	20	17	13	8	2	0	0	0	0	4	13	21	98
Days Minimum Temp. ≤ 0°F	0	0	0	0	0	0	0	0	0	0	0	0	0
Heating Degree Days (base 65°F)	745	638	637	496	333	120	19	23	90	319	551	749	4,720
Cooling Degree Days (base 65°F)	0	0	0	0	5	49	149	170	68	6	0	0	447
Mean Precipitation (in.)	6.33	6.32	7.21	2.58	1.12	0.27	0.45	0.91	1.03	1.60	3.57	4.65	36.04
Days With ≥ 0.1" Precipitation	7	6	7	4	2	1	1	2	1	2	4	5	42
Days With ≥ 1.0" Precipitation	2	2	3	1	0	0	0	0	0	1	1	2	12
Mean Snowfall (in.)	5.9	6.2	10.1	3.8	0.1	0.0	0.0	0.0	0.0	0.2	1.5	4.0	31.8
Days With ≥ 1.0" Snow Depth	4	2	4	1	0	0	0	0	0	0	0	3	14

Daggett Barstow-Daggett Arpt. *San Bernardino Co.*   Elevation: 1,919 ft.   Latitude: 34° 51' N   Longitude: 116° 48' W

	JAN	FEB	MAR	APR	MAY	JUN	JUL	AUG	SEP	OCT	NOV	DEC	YEAR
Mean Maximum Temp. (°F)	60.8	66.2	71.2	78.7	87.9	98.5	104.4	102.5	94.7	83.2	69.8	60.7	81.6
Mean Temp. (°F)	49.1	54.0	58.7	65.2	73.8	83.1	89.1	87.6	80.4	69.3	56.7	48.6	68.0
Mean Minimum Temp. (°F)	37.2	41.7	46.3	51.6	59.6	67.6	73.8	72.7	66.1	55.3	43.6	36.4	54.3
Extreme Maximum Temp. (°F)	83	87	94	100	106	118	117	117	111	105	90	80	118
Extreme Minimum Temp. (°F)	17	19	26	34	40	45	50	59	49	25	23	5	5
Days Maximum Temp. ≥ 90°F	0	0	0	4	15	26	31	30	23	8	0	0	137
Days Maximum Temp. ≤ 32°F	0	0	0	0	0	0	0	0	0	0	0	0	0
Days Minimum Temp. ≤ 32°F	7	3	0	0	0	0	0	0	0	0	2	9	21
Days Minimum Temp. ≤ 0°F	0	0	0	0	0	0	0	0	0	0	0	0	0
Heating Degree Days (base 65°F)	488	308	209	83	15	1	0	0	1	40	252	503	1,900
Cooling Degree Days (base 65°F)	0	3	19	106	289	533	737	712	473	183	12	0	3,067
Mean Precipitation (in.)	0.70	0.58	0.56	0.18	0.08	0.10	0.47	0.38	0.33	0.17	0.18	0.49	4.22
Days With ≥ 0.1" Precipitation	2	2	2	1	0	0	1	1	1	1	1	1	13
Days With ≥ 1.0" Precipitation	0	0	0	0	0	0	0	0	0	0	0	0	0
Mean Snowfall (in.)	trace	trace	trace	trace	0.0	0.0	0.0	0.0	trace	0.0	trace	trace	trace
Days With ≥ 1.0" Snow Depth	0	0	0	0	0	0	0	0	0	0	0	0	0

Davis 2 WSW Exp. Farm *Yolo County*   Elevation: 59 ft.   Latitude: 38° 32' N   Longitude: 121° 46' W

	JAN	FEB	MAR	APR	MAY	JUN	JUL	AUG	SEP	OCT	NOV	DEC	YEAR
Mean Maximum Temp. (°F)	53.3	59.9	64.7	71.8	80.3	88.2	92.9	91.7	88.0	79.0	63.8	53.7	74.0
Mean Temp. (°F)	45.3	50.0	53.6	58.4	65.2	71.3	74.5	73.4	70.7	63.5	52.5	45.1	60.3
Mean Minimum Temp. (°F)	37.3	39.9	42.5	44.9	50.0	54.4	55.9	54.9	53.3	48.0	41.2	36.4	46.6
Extreme Maximum Temp. (°F)	71	78	89	94	106	106	113	110	107	101	86	74	113
Extreme Minimum Temp. (°F)	21	4	27	28	37	42	46	45	41	34	25	16	4
Days Maximum Temp. ≥ 90°F	0	0	0	0	6	13	22	19	14	4	0	0	78
Days Maximum Temp. ≤ 32°F	0	0	0	0	0	0	0	0	0	0	0	0	0
Days Minimum Temp. ≤ 32°F	8	3	1	0	0	0	0	0	0	0	2	9	23
Days Minimum Temp. ≤ 0°F	0	0	0	0	0	0	0	0	0	0	0	0	0
Heating Degree Days (base 65°F)	604	418	346	206	79	14	1	1	12	96	368	611	2,756
Cooling Degree Days (base 65°F)	0	0	1	19	89	207	309	279	198	60	1	0	1,163
Mean Precipitation (in.)	4.11	3.55	3.03	0.93	0.52	0.19	0.03	0.04	0.29	0.85	2.62	2.95	19.11
Days With ≥ 0.1" Precipitation	7	6	6	2	1	1	0	0	1	2	5	5	36
Days With ≥ 1.0" Precipitation	1	1	1	0	0	0	0	0	0	0	1	1	5
Mean Snowfall (in.)	trace	trace	0.0	0.0	0.0	0.0	0.0	0.0	0.0	0.0	0.0	trace	trace
Days With ≥ 1.0" Snow Depth	0	0	0	0	0	0	0	0	0	0	0	0	0

De Sabla *Butte County*   Elevation: 2,709 ft.   Latitude: 39° 52' N   Longitude: 121° 37' W

	JAN	FEB	MAR	APR	MAY	JUN	JUL	AUG	SEP	OCT	NOV	DEC	YEAR
Mean Maximum Temp. (°F)	52.0	54.9	58.1	64.4	73.1	82.0	89.2	88.8	83.2	72.7	57.6	51.3	68.9
Mean Temp. (°F)	41.9	44.2	46.6	51.2	58.6	66.2	71.9	71.1	66.4	58.0	46.6	41.4	55.3
Mean Minimum Temp. (°F)	31.8	33.5	35.0	38.0	44.1	50.3	54.6	53.4	49.5	43.2	35.6	31.5	41.7
Extreme Maximum Temp. (°F)	74	77	80	88	97	103	106	109	105	96	82	74	109
Extreme Minimum Temp. (°F)	12	11	18	22	26	31	39	36	30	19	15	5	5
Days Maximum Temp. ≥ 90°F	0	0	0	0	1	7	17	16	8	2	0	0	51
Days Maximum Temp. ≤ 32°F	0	0	0	0	0	0	0	0	0	0	0	0	0
Days Minimum Temp. ≤ 32°F	17	13	12	7	1	0	0	0	0	2	9	18	79
Days Minimum Temp. ≤ 0°F	0	0	0	0	0	0	0	0	0	0	0	0	0
Heating Degree Days (base 65°F)	708	580	565	410	220	69	11	13	64	239	544	724	4,147
Cooling Degree Days (base 65°F)	0	0	0	3	26	104	227	209	110	27	0	0	706
Mean Precipitation (in.)	12.77	10.81	10.39	4.53	2.43	0.95	0.16	0.32	1.47	3.58	9.11	11.10	67.62
Days With ≥ 0.1" Precipitation	10	9	10	6	4	2	0	1	2	4	8	9	65
Days With ≥ 1.0" Precipitation	5	4	4	1	1	0	0	0	0	1	3	4	23
Mean Snowfall (in.)	5.0	1.4	4.1	1.0	trace	0.0	0.0	0.0	0.0	0.0	0.5	2.7	14.7
Days With ≥ 1.0" Snow Depth	1	0	0	0	0	0	0	0	0	0	0	0	1

Death Valley *Inyo County*   Elevation: -193 ft.   Latitude: 36° 28' N   Longitude: 116° 52' W

	JAN	FEB	MAR	APR	MAY	JUN	JUL	AUG	SEP	OCT	NOV	DEC	YEAR
Mean Maximum Temp. (°F)	65.8	73.6	81.1	89.7	99.2	109.1	115.2	113.5	105.6	92.5	76.2	65.3	90.6
Mean Temp. (°F)	52.5	59.8	67.5	75.5	85.1	94.6	100.9	99.1	90.3	76.7	61.7	51.7	76.3
Mean Minimum Temp. (°F)	39.1	45.9	53.9	61.3	71.0	80.1	86.5	84.7	74.9	60.9	47.2	38.1	62.0
Extreme Maximum Temp. (°F)	84	97	102	111	118	128	129	127	123	113	98	88	129
Extreme Minimum Temp. (°F)	0	26	26	39	46	54	67	65	55	37	30	22	0
Days Maximum Temp. ≥ 90°F	0	0	5	16	27	30	31	31	29	20	1	0	190
Days Maximum Temp. ≤ 32°F	0	0	0	0	0	0	0	0	0	0	0	0	0
Days Minimum Temp. ≤ 32°F	4	1	0	0	0	0	0	0	0	0	0	6	11
Days Minimum Temp. ≤ 0°F	0	0	0	0	0	0	0	0	0	0	0	0	0
Heating Degree Days (base 65°F)	383	160	47	7	1	0	0	0	0	6	135	406	1,145
Cooling Degree Days (base 65°F)	1	23	130	343	626	874	1,100	1,066	761	366	46	2	5,338
Mean Precipitation (in.)	0.35	0.45	0.41	0.12	0.10	0.04	0.11	0.14	0.19	0.13	0.15	0.19	2.38
Days With ≥ 0.1" Precipitation	1	1	1	0	0	0	0	0	1	0	0	1	5
Days With ≥ 1.0" Precipitation	0	0	0	0	0	0	0	0	0	0	0	0	0
Mean Snowfall (in.)	trace	0.0	0.0	0.0	0.0	0.0	0.0	0.0	0.0	0.0	0.0	0.0	trace
Days With ≥ 1.0" Snow Depth	0	0	0	0	0	0	0	0	0	0	0	0	0

Donner Memorial State Park *Nevada County* Elevation: 5,935 ft. Latitude: 39° 19' N Longitude: 120° 14' W

	JAN	FEB	MAR	APR	MAY	JUN	JUL	AUG	SEP	OCT	NOV	DEC	YEAR
Mean Maximum Temp. (°F)	40.3	43.3	46.6	53.2	62.6	72.3	80.5	80.3	73.4	62.7	48.2	40.1	58.6
Mean Temp. (°F)	27.4	29.8	33.9	39.2	46.9	54.6	60.8	60.2	53.9	45.1	35.0	27.7	42.9
Mean Minimum Temp. (°F)	14.4	16.3	21.1	25.1	31.2	36.8	41.1	40.1	34.4	27.6	21.7	15.2	27.1
Extreme Maximum Temp. (°F)	61	65	69	79	87	95	98	99	92	90	75	60	99
Extreme Minimum Temp. (°F)	-16	-27	-6	0	10	22	23	20	16	6	0	-20	-27
Days Maximum Temp. ≥ 90°F	0	0	0	0	0	0	2	2	0	0	0	0	4
Days Maximum Temp. ≤ 32°F	5	3	2	0	0	0	0	0	0	0	1	6	17
Days Minimum Temp. ≤ 32°F	31	28	30	27	20	7	2	2	11	26	29	30	243
Days Minimum Temp. ≤ 0°F	3	2	0	0	0	0	0	0	0	0	0	2	7
Heating Degree Days (base 65°F)	1,160	986	958	768	554	310	143	157	326	609	893	1,150	8,014
Cooling Degree Days (base 65°F)	0	0	0	0	0	4	20	16	2	0	0	0	42
Mean Precipitation (in.)	7.04	6.38	5.91	2.51	1.48	0.85	0.47	0.59	1.09	2.13	5.37	5.80	39.62
Days With ≥ 0.1" Precipitation	8	8	8	5	4	3	1	1	2	4	7	7	58
Days With ≥ 1.0" Precipitation	3	2	2	0	0	0	0	0	0	1	2	2	12
Mean Snowfall (in.)	39.1	43.1	35.1	16.3	4.2	0.5	0.0	0.0	0.3	2.0	15.9	32.3	188.8
Days With ≥ 1.0" Snow Depth	30	28	29	14	4	0	0	0	0	1	11	23	140

Doyle 4 SSE *Lassen County* Elevation: 4,389 ft. Latitude: 39° 58' N Longitude: 120° 05' W

	JAN	FEB	MAR	APR	MAY	JUN	JUL	AUG	SEP	OCT	NOV	DEC	YEAR
Mean Maximum Temp. (°F)	42.5	48.3	54.7	61.4	70.6	80.0	88.6	87.5	79.4	67.3	51.9	42.4	64.6
Mean Temp. (°F)	32.7	37.4	42.4	47.1	54.7	62.3	69.0	67.8	60.8	50.9	39.8	32.2	49.8
Mean Minimum Temp. (°F)	22.9	26.5	30.0	32.7	38.8	44.4	49.4	47.9	42.2	34.4	27.7	22.0	34.9
Extreme Maximum Temp. (°F)	66	70	77	85	95	101	102	105	99	89	75	69	105
Extreme Minimum Temp. (°F)	-9	-17	5	16	21	27	30	33	22	14	-2	-25	-25
Days Maximum Temp. ≥ 90°F	0	0	0	0	0	5	15	13	4	0	0	0	37
Days Maximum Temp. ≤ 32°F	4	1	0	0	0	0	0	0	0	0	1	4	10
Days Minimum Temp. ≤ 32°F	26	22	21	16	6	1	0	0	2	12	21	27	154
Days Minimum Temp. ≤ 0°F	1	0	0	0	0	0	0	0	0	0	0	1	2
Heating Degree Days (base 65°F)	993	772	695	532	319	125	23	31	149	432	747	1,009	5,827
Cooling Degree Days (base 65°F)	0	0	0	0	6	41	139	117	31	0	0	0	334
Mean Precipitation (in.)	2.70	2.51	2.22	0.87	1.12	0.81	0.48	0.39	0.77	1.05	2.49	2.32	17.73
Days With ≥ 0.1" Precipitation	5	4	4	2	3	2	1	1	2	2	4	4	34
Days With ≥ 1.0" Precipitation	1	1	1	0	0	0	0	0	0	0	1	1	5
Mean Snowfall (in.)	8.8	5.2	5.0	1.9	1.1	trace	0.0	0.0	0.1	0.3	2.5	6.8	31.7
Days With ≥ 1.0" Snow Depth	9	4	1	0	0	0	0	0	0	0	2	6	22

Eagle Mountain *Riverside County* Elevation: 971 ft. Latitude: 33° 48' N Longitude: 115° 27' W

	JAN	FEB	MAR	APR	MAY	JUN	JUL	AUG	SEP	OCT	NOV	DEC	YEAR
Mean Maximum Temp. (°F)	64.9	69.7	75.1	82.4	90.5	100.5	104.6	103.3	97.5	86.4	73.7	65.1	84.5
Mean Temp. (°F)	55.2	59.5	64.4	71.3	79.3	88.9	93.8	92.4	86.4	75.4	63.4	55.4	73.8
Mean Minimum Temp. (°F)	45.4	49.3	53.6	60.1	68.1	77.2	82.9	81.4	75.3	64.3	53.0	45.5	63.0
Extreme Maximum Temp. (°F)	85	91	102	105	111	120	118	117	114	109	92	83	120
Extreme Minimum Temp. (°F)	26	29	34	43	45	57	66	66	56	37	36	25	25
Days Maximum Temp. ≥ 90°F	0	0	1	7	19	27	31	31	27	11	0	0	154
Days Maximum Temp. ≤ 32°F	0	0	0	0	0	0	0	0	0	0	0	0	0
Days Minimum Temp. ≤ 32°F	1	0	0	0	0	0	0	0	0	0	0	1	2
Days Minimum Temp. ≤ 0°F	0	0	0	0	0	0	0	0	0	0	0	0	0
Heating Degree Days (base 65°F)	300	167	90	26	2	0	0	0	0	10	102	295	992
Cooling Degree Days (base 65°F)	1	21	79	247	462	709	881	863	649	341	60	2	4,315
Mean Precipitation (in.)	0.59	0.53	0.50	0.08	0.08	0.06	0.44	0.78	0.47	0.23	0.18	0.45	4.39
Days With ≥ 0.1" Precipitation	1	1	1	0	0	0	1	1	1	1	1	1	9
Days With ≥ 1.0" Precipitation	0	0	0	0	0	0	0	0	0	0	0	0	0
Mean Snowfall (in.)	trace	0.0	0.0	0.0	0.0	0.0	0.0	0.0	0.0	0.0	0.0	0.0	trace
Days With ≥ 1.0" Snow Depth	0	0	0	0	0	0	0	0	0	0	0	0	0

East Park Reservoir *Colusa County* Elevation: 1,204 ft. Latitude: 39° 22' N Longitude: 122° 31' W

	JAN	FEB	MAR	APR	MAY	JUN	JUL	AUG	SEP	OCT	NOV	DEC	YEAR
Mean Maximum Temp. (°F)	55.8	59.0	62.2	68.5	77.5	86.4	93.3	92.3	87.2	77.4	63.6	56.3	73.3
Mean Temp. (°F)	43.9	46.9	49.8	54.3	62.1	69.9	76.2	74.6	69.7	60.8	50.2	43.8	58.5
Mean Minimum Temp. (°F)	31.9	34.7	37.3	40.1	46.6	53.4	59.0	57.0	52.2	44.3	36.8	31.3	43.7
Extreme Maximum Temp. (°F)	75	80	86	90	102	107	115	114	110	101	85	79	115
Extreme Minimum Temp. (°F)	10	16	20	26	30	35	43	41	36	25	17	12	10
Days Maximum Temp. ≥ 90°F	0	0	0	0	4	12	22	21	13	4	0	0	76
Days Maximum Temp. ≤ 32°F	0	0	0	0	0	0	0	0	0	0	0	0	0
Days Minimum Temp. ≤ 32°F	19	11	7	3	0	0	0	0	0	1	8	19	68
Days Minimum Temp. ≤ 0°F	0	0	0	0	0	0	0	0	0	0	0	0	0
Heating Degree Days (base 65°F)	649	506	465	317	140	31	2	3	26	162	437	650	3,388
Cooling Degree Days (base 65°F)	0	0	0	4	51	171	350	313	180	43	0	0	1,112
Mean Precipitation (in.)	5.04	4.15	3.20	0.95	0.61	0.27	0.06	0.10	0.27	1.02	2.79	3.40	21.86
Days With ≥ 0.1" Precipitation	8	6	7	3	2	1	0	0	1	2	5	6	41
Days With ≥ 1.0" Precipitation	2	1	1	0	0	0	0	0	0	0	1	1	6
Mean Snowfall (in.)	2.2	0.6	0.3	0.0	0.0	0.0	0.0	0.0	0.0	0.0	0.4	0.4	3.9
Days With ≥ 1.0" Snow Depth	1	0	0	0	0	0	0	0	0	0	0	0	1

El Centro 2 SSW *Imperial County*   Elevation: -29 ft.   Latitude: 32° 46' N   Longitude: 115° 34' W

	JAN	FEB	MAR	APR	MAY	JUN	JUL	AUG	SEP	OCT	NOV	DEC	YEAR
Mean Maximum Temp. (°F)	70.1	74.6	79.2	85.8	93.9	103.4	107.1	105.8	101.1	91.0	78.3	69.6	88.3
Mean Temp. (°F)	55.6	59.7	63.9	69.5	77.1	85.8	91.5	91.2	85.8	75.0	62.9	55.0	72.7
Mean Minimum Temp. (°F)	41.0	44.7	48.5	53.2	60.3	68.1	75.7	76.6	70.4	59.0	47.4	40.4	57.1
Extreme Maximum Temp. (°F)	90	93	97	106	116	120	122	120	119	112	98	85	122
Extreme Minimum Temp. (°F)	16	26	29	36	42	50	60	56	48	35	28	22	16
Days Maximum Temp. ≥ 90°F	0	0	3	11	23	29	31	31	28	19	1	0	176
Days Maximum Temp. ≤ 32°F	0	0	0	0	0	0	0	0	0	0	0	0	0
Days Minimum Temp. ≤ 32°F	3	1	0	0	0	0	0	0	0	0	0	2	6
Days Minimum Temp. ≤ 0°F	0	0	0	0	0	0	0	0	0	0	0	0	0
Heating Degree Days (base 65°F)	287	157	89	29	1	0	0	0	0	8	104	303	978
Cooling Degree Days (base 65°F)	1	17	69	201	401	625	829	833	646	342	56	1	4,021
Mean Precipitation (in.)	0.51	0.39	0.30	0.05	0.03	trace	0.06	0.33	0.36	0.33	0.17	0.43	2.96
Days With ≥ 0.1" Precipitation	1	1	1	0	0	0	0	1	1	1	0	1	7
Days With ≥ 1.0" Precipitation	0	0	0	0	0	0	0	0	0	0	0	0	0
Mean Snowfall (in.)	0.0	0.0	0.0	0.0	0.0	0.0	0.0	0.0	0.0	0.0	0.0	0.0	0.0
Days With ≥ 1.0" Snow Depth	0	0	0	0	0	0	0	0	0	0	0	0	0

El Mirage *San Bernardino County*   Elevation: 2,949 ft.   Latitude: 34° 35' N   Longitude: 117° 38' W

	JAN	FEB	MAR	APR	MAY	JUN	JUL	AUG	SEP	OCT	NOV	DEC	YEAR
Mean Maximum Temp. (°F)	56.9	61.2	65.1	72.6	80.6	91.1	97.3	96.1	89.0	78.0	65.3	57.1	75.8
Mean Temp. (°F)	42.8	46.6	50.3	56.1	63.6	72.4	78.1	77.1	70.9	60.6	49.2	42.2	59.2
Mean Minimum Temp. (°F)	28.7	32.0	35.6	39.6	46.5	53.8	58.7	58.0	52.8	43.1	33.2	27.2	42.4
Extreme Maximum Temp. (°F)	76	82	88	96	105	110	112	108	106	98	84	80	112
Extreme Minimum Temp. (°F)	3	5	18	23	29	32	41	41	33	14	14	1	1
Days Maximum Temp. ≥ 90°F	0	0	0	1	6	19	29	27	16	3	0	0	101
Days Maximum Temp. ≤ 32°F	0	0	0	0	0	0	0	0	0	0	0	0	0
Days Minimum Temp. ≤ 32°F	22	15	10	4	0	0	0	0	0	2	13	24	90
Days Minimum Temp. ≤ 0°F	0	0	0	0	0	0	0	0	0	0	0	0	0
Heating Degree Days (base 65°F)	681	513	449	273	113	18	0	1	22	165	467	700	3,402
Cooling Degree Days (base 65°F)	0	0	0	17	87	257	431	410	218	39	0	0	1,459
Mean Precipitation (in.)	1.25	1.06	1.11	0.24	0.27	0.08	0.14	0.38	0.33	0.18	0.29	0.70	6.03
Days With ≥ 0.1" Precipitation	3	2	3	1	1	0	0	1	1	1	1	2	16
Days With ≥ 1.0" Precipitation	0	0	0	0	0	0	0	0	0	0	0	0	0
Mean Snowfall (in.)	0.8	0.4	0.2	trace	0.0	0.0	0.0	0.0	0.0	0.0	trace	0.4	1.8
Days With ≥ 1.0" Snow Depth	0	0	0	0	0	0	0	0	0	0	0	0	0

Elsinore *Riverside County*   Elevation: 1,282 ft.   Latitude: 33° 40' N   Longitude: 117° 20' W

	JAN	FEB	MAR	APR	MAY	JUN	JUL	AUG	SEP	OCT	NOV	DEC	YEAR
Mean Maximum Temp. (°F)	*65.6*	68.3	71.1	77.1	*82.2*	91.2	98.2	*98.3*	*92.8*	83.7	73.2	66.2	*80.7*
Mean Temp. (°F)	*51.8*	54.2	56.9	61.3	*66.7*	73.9	79.8	*80.3*	*75.8*	67.2	57.8	51.7	*64.8*
Mean Minimum Temp. (°F)	*37.9*	40.1	42.6	45.4	51.2	56.3	61.3	*62.2*	*58.5*	50.8	42.3	37.1	*48.8*
Extreme Maximum Temp. (°F)	91	93	95	103	104	112	114	*115*	114	106	96	89	*115*
Extreme Minimum Temp. (°F)	18	23	24	30	35	40	48	*44*	38	25	*27*	10	*10*
Days Maximum Temp. ≥ 90°F	0	0	1	3	*8*	18	28	*28*	*20*	9	1	0	*116*
Days Maximum Temp. ≤ 32°F	0	0	0	0	0	0	0	0	0	0	0	0	0
Days Minimum Temp. ≤ 32°F	6	3	1	0	0	0	0	0	0	0	2	7	19
Days Minimum Temp. ≤ 0°F	0	0	0	0	0	0	0	0	0	0	0	0	0
Heating Degree Days (base 65°F)	*404*	299	250	140	*47*	4	0	*0*	*2*	44	218	408	*1,816*
Cooling Degree Days (base 65°F)	0	2	5	45	123	267	465	499	340	126	8	1	1,881
Mean Precipitation (in.)	2.85	2.91	2.32	0.58	0.22	0.02	0.10	0.13	0.31	0.34	0.90	1.77	12.45
Days With ≥ 0.1" Precipitation	4	4	4	2	1	0	0	0	1	1	2	3	22
Days With ≥ 1.0" Precipitation	1	1	0	0	0	0	0	0	0	0	0	0	2
Mean Snowfall (in.)	0.0	0.0	0.0	0.0	0.0	0.0	0.0	0.0	0.0	0.0	trace	0.0	trace
Days With ≥ 1.0" Snow Depth	0	0	0	0	0	0	0	0	0	0	0	0	0

Fairfield *Solano County*   Elevation: 39 ft.   Latitude: 38° 16' N   Longitude: 122° 04' W

	JAN	FEB	MAR	APR	MAY	JUN	JUL	AUG	SEP	OCT	NOV	DEC	YEAR
Mean Maximum Temp. (°F)	54.9	61.5	65.8	71.4	78.2	84.8	89.2	88.6	86.4	78.3	65.0	55.5	73.3
Mean Temp. (°F)	46.3	51.3	54.9	58.8	64.3	69.5	72.8	72.3	70.5	64.1	54.0	46.3	60.4
Mean Minimum Temp. (°F)	37.6	41.0	44.0	46.2	50.4	54.0	56.1	56.1	54.5	49.8	42.9	37.0	47.5
Extreme Maximum Temp. (°F)	73	78	87	95	111	111	113	111	109	102	84	78	113
Extreme Minimum Temp. (°F)	18	24	29	30	35	37	42	40	39	33	21	17	17
Days Maximum Temp. ≥ 90°F	0	0	0	0	4	9	15	13	11	3	0	0	55
Days Maximum Temp. ≤ 32°F	0	0	0	0	0	0	0	0	0	0	0	0	0
Days Minimum Temp. ≤ 32°F	7	2	1	0	0	0	0	0	0	0	2	8	20
Days Minimum Temp. ≤ 0°F	0	0	0	0	0	0	0	0	0	0	0	0	0
Heating Degree Days (base 65°F)	574	381	306	194	87	19	2	2	10	85	326	574	2,560
Cooling Degree Days (base 65°F)	0	1	1	20	77	171	273	258	192	71	2	0	1,066
Mean Precipitation (in.)	5.23	4.24	3.55	1.08	0.60	0.17	0.03	0.05	0.29	1.18	3.24	3.81	23.47
Days With ≥ 0.1" Precipitation	8	7	7	3	1	0	0	0	1	2	5	6	40
Days With ≥ 1.0" Precipitation	2	1	1	0	0	0	0	0	0	0	1	1	6
Mean Snowfall (in.)	0.0	0.0	0.0	0.0	0.0	0.0	0.0	0.0	0.0	0.0	0.0	trace	trace
Days With ≥ 1.0" Snow Depth	0	0	0	0	0	0	0	0	0	0	0	0	0

Fairmont *Los Angeles County*   Elevation: 3,057 ft.   Latitude: 34° 42' N   Longitude: 118° 26' W

	JAN	FEB	MAR	APR	MAY	JUN	JUL	AUG	SEP	OCT	NOV	DEC	YEAR
Mean Maximum Temp. (°F)	53.6	56.8	60.4	66.0	73.9	83.3	90.0	90.2	85.1	74.6	62.1	53.8	70.8
Mean Temp. (°F)	44.9	47.7	50.8	55.3	62.5	71.4	78.0	78.0	72.8	63.1	52.3	45.0	60.2
Mean Minimum Temp. (°F)	36.2	38.5	41.1	44.6	51.2	59.5	66.0	65.7	60.6	51.6	42.5	36.2	49.5
Extreme Maximum Temp. (°F)	75	78	84	93	100	108	110	107	107	96	83	77	110
Extreme Minimum Temp. (°F)	17	12	20	19	25	32	48	47	34	28	22	11	11
Days Maximum Temp. ≥ 90°F	0	0	0	0	2	9	17	18	11	2	0	0	59
Days Maximum Temp. ≤ 32°F	0	0	0	0	0	0	0	0	0	0	0	0	0
Days Minimum Temp. ≤ 32°F	9	5	3	1	0	0	0	0	0	0	2	8	28
Days Minimum Temp. ≤ 0°F	0	0	0	0	0	0	0	0	0	0	0	0	0
Heating Degree Days (base 65°F)	617	482	436	303	156	39	2	3	24	133	377	613	3,185
Cooling Degree Days (base 65°F)	0	0	2	23	86	227	400	423	268	80	4	0	1,513
Mean Precipitation (in.)	3.42	3.82	2.95	0.83	0.43	0.08	0.07	0.14	0.33	0.47	1.47	2.49	16.50
Days With ≥ 0.1" Precipitation	5	4	4	2	1	0	0	0	1	1	2	4	24
Days With ≥ 1.0" Precipitation	1	1	1	0	0	0	0	0	0	0	0	1	4
Mean Snowfall (in.)	2.1	1.0	0.2	trace	0.0	0.0	0.0	0.0	0.0	0.0	trace	3.5	6.8
Days With ≥ 1.0" Snow Depth	1	0	0	0	0	0	0	0	0	0	0	1	2

Fort Bidwell *Modoc County*   Elevation: 4,498 ft.   Latitude: 41° 51' N   Longitude: 120° 08' W

	JAN	FEB	MAR	APR	MAY	JUN	JUL	AUG	SEP	OCT	NOV	DEC	YEAR
Mean Maximum Temp. (°F)	39.7	45.3	51.9	59.1	68.0	76.3	85.1	84.5	77.0	65.5	48.9	39.7	61.7
Mean Temp. (°F)	30.0	34.6	40.2	45.7	53.2	60.3	67.4	66.4	59.3	49.7	38.0	30.1	47.9
Mean Minimum Temp. (°F)	20.3	23.9	28.5	32.1	38.3	44.3	49.7	48.3	41.4	33.9	27.0	20.5	34.0
Extreme Maximum Temp. (°F)	65	69	76	83	97	97	99	100	97	88	77	63	100
Extreme Minimum Temp. (°F)	-22	-19	-5	13	21	28	32	30	17	5	-4	-26	-26
Days Maximum Temp. ≥ 90°F	0	0	0	0	0	2	9	8	2	0	0	0	21
Days Maximum Temp. ≤ 32°F	6	2	0	0	0	0	0	0	0	0	1	6	15
Days Minimum Temp. ≤ 32°F	27	24	22	16	7	1	0	0	3	13	22	27	162
Days Minimum Temp. ≤ 0°F	2	1	0	0	0	0	0	0	0	0	0	2	5
Heating Degree Days (base 65°F)	1,078	852	761	574	365	163	37	46	185	468	805	1,074	6,408
Cooling Degree Days (base 65°F)	0	0	0	0	7	28	120	103	24	0	0	0	282
Mean Precipitation (in.)	2.59	2.19	2.11	1.47	1.36	0.92	0.40	0.46	0.69	1.07	2.55	2.65	18.46
Days With ≥ 0.1" Precipitation	8	7	7	5	4	3	1	1	2	3	8	8	57
Days With ≥ 1.0" Precipitation	0	0	0	0	0	0	0	0	0	0	0	0	0
Mean Snowfall (in.)	11.9	10.4	6.8	3.4	0.7	trace	0.0	0.0	trace	0.6	7.1	12.3	53.2
Days With ≥ 1.0" Snow Depth	13	7	2	0	0	0	0	0	0	0	4	11	37

Fort Bragg 5 N *Mendocino County*   Elevation: 118 ft.   Latitude: 39° 31' N   Longitude: 123° 46' W

	JAN	FEB	MAR	APR	MAY	JUN	JUL	AUG	SEP	OCT	NOV	DEC	YEAR
Mean Maximum Temp. (°F)	55.4	56.6	57.9	59.7	61.9	64.3	66.1	66.2	66.3	63.7	58.8	55.0	61.0
Mean Temp. (°F)	47.8	48.8	50.0	51.3	53.7	56.2	57.8	58.1	57.8	55.0	50.8	47.3	52.9
Mean Minimum Temp. (°F)	40.2	41.0	42.0	42.8	45.4	47.9	49.5	49.9	49.1	46.2	42.9	39.6	44.7
Extreme Maximum Temp. (°F)	76	79	75	80	85	86	83	83	87	94	76	69	94
Extreme Minimum Temp. (°F)	26	24	30	30	35	37	42	37	38	31	29	18	18
Days Maximum Temp. ≥ 90°F	0	0	0	0	0	0	0	0	0	0	0	0	0
Days Maximum Temp. ≤ 32°F	0	0	0	0	0	0	0	0	0	0	0	0	0
Days Minimum Temp. ≤ 32°F	4	2	1	0	0	0	0	0	0	0	1	4	12
Days Minimum Temp. ≤ 0°F	0	0	0	0	0	0	0	0	0	0	0	0	0
Heating Degree Days (base 65°F)	527	451	459	403	345	260	216	208	213	305	419	542	4,348
Cooling Degree Days (base 65°F)	0	0	0	0	1	1	1	1	1	2	0	0	7
Mean Precipitation (in.)	7.45	6.72	6.38	2.77	1.52	0.41	0.14	0.35	0.75	2.52	5.64	6.73	41.38
Days With ≥ 0.1" Precipitation	10	11	10	6	3	1	0	1	1	4	9	11	67
Days With ≥ 1.0" Precipitation	2	2	2	1	0	0	0	0	0	1	1	2	11
Mean Snowfall (in.)	0.0	trace	trace	0.0	0.0	0.0	0.0	0.0	0.0	0.0	0.0	0.0	trace
Days With ≥ 1.0" Snow Depth	0	0	0	0	0	0	0	0	0	0	0	0	0

Fort Ross *Sonoma County*   Elevation: 111 ft.   Latitude: 38° 31' N   Longitude: 123° 15' W

	JAN	FEB	MAR	APR	MAY	JUN	JUL	AUG	SEP	OCT	NOV	DEC	YEAR
Mean Maximum Temp. (°F)	57.3	58.8	59.5	61.3	63.1	65.6	66.4	67.4	68.3	66.1	61.6	57.4	62.7
Mean Temp. (°F)	49.3	50.5	50.9	51.6	53.4	56.0	57.0	58.0	58.2	56.1	52.4	48.9	53.5
Mean Minimum Temp. (°F)	41.0	42.2	42.4	41.9	43.7	46.3	47.6	48.5	48.0	46.1	43.2	40.3	44.3
Extreme Maximum Temp. (°F)	75	79	77	80	92	88	88	81	93	87	77	74	93
Extreme Minimum Temp. (°F)	22	25	26	26	30	36	35	30	35	35	27	20	20
Days Maximum Temp. ≥ 90°F	0	0	0	0	0	0	0	0	0	0	0	0	0
Days Maximum Temp. ≤ 32°F	0	0	0	0	0	0	0	0	0	0	0	0	0
Days Minimum Temp. ≤ 32°F	2	1	0	1	0	0	0	0	0	0	1	3	8
Days Minimum Temp. ≤ 0°F	0	0	0	0	0	0	0	0	0	0	0	0	0
Heating Degree Days (base 65°F)	482	403	429	395	352	265	241	212	202	272	371	494	4,118
Cooling Degree Days (base 65°F)	0	0	0	0	0	2	*0*	2	3	3	0	0	*10*
Mean Precipitation (in.)	7.87	5.99	5.70	2.33	1.03	0.36	0.15	0.28	0.65	2.30	5.63	5.98	38.27
Days With ≥ 0.1" Precipitation	10	9	8	5	2	1	0	1	1	4	7	8	56
Days With ≥ 1.0" Precipitation	2	2	1	0	0	0	0	0	0	1	2	2	10
Mean Snowfall (in.)	trace	trace	0.0	0.0	0.0	0.0	0.0	0.0	0.0	0.0	trace	trace	trace
Days With ≥ 1.0" Snow Depth	0	0	0	0	0	0	0	0	0	0	0	0	0

Friant Government Camp *Fresno County*   Elevation: 410 ft.   Latitude: 37° 00' N   Longitude: 119° 43' W

	JAN	FEB	MAR	APR	MAY	JUN	JUL	AUG	SEP	OCT	NOV	DEC	YEAR
Mean Maximum Temp. (°F)	55.3	61.6	65.9	73.5	83.9	92.7	99.2	97.9	91.8	81.4	66.0	55.6	77.1
Mean Temp. (°F)	46.3	50.9	53.8	58.2	66.3	73.9	79.8	78.7	74.0	65.4	53.7	45.8	62.2
Mean Minimum Temp. (°F)	37.3	40.1	41.7	42.8	48.6	55.1	60.5	59.4	56.2	49.4	41.4	36.1	47.4
Extreme Maximum Temp. (°F)	77	79	87	98	107	110	114	114	108	102	87	74	114
Extreme Minimum Temp. (°F)	22	21	27	28	32	37	45	38	40	29	24	16	16
Days Maximum Temp. ≥ 90°F	0	0	0	1	9	20	29	27	19	6	0	0	111
Days Maximum Temp. ≤ 32°F	0	0	0	0	0	0	0	0	0	0	0	0	0
Days Minimum Temp. ≤ 32°F	8	3	2	1	0	0	0	0	0	0	2	9	25
Days Minimum Temp. ≤ 0°F	0	0	0	0	0	0	0	0	0	0	0	0	0
Heating Degree Days (base 65°F)	573	393	341	217	71	9	0	0	7	80	335	587	2,613
Cooling Degree Days (base 65°F)	0	0	1	26	118	275	465	439	289	102	2	0	1,717
Mean Precipitation (in.)	2.77	2.50	2.89	0.96	0.42	0.20	0.02	0.02	0.26	0.74	1.71	2.04	14.53
Days With ≥ 0.1" Precipitation	6	5	6	2	1	0	0	0	1	1	4	4	30
Days With ≥ 1.0" Precipitation	0	0	1	0	0	0	0	0	0	0	0	0	1
Mean Snowfall (in.)	0.0	0.0	0.0	0.0	0.0	0.0	0.0	0.0	0.0	0.0	0.0	0.0	0.0
Days With ≥ 1.0" Snow Depth	0	0	0	0	0	0	0	0	0	0	0	0	0

Glennville *Kern County*   Elevation: 3,139 ft.   Latitude: 35° 44' N   Longitude: 118° 42' W

	JAN	FEB	MAR	APR	MAY	JUN	JUL	AUG	SEP	OCT	NOV	DEC	YEAR
Mean Maximum Temp. (°F)	56.8	58.4	59.6	65.4	73.8	83.3	89.9	88.9	83.3	73.6	62.2	56.5	71.0
Mean Temp. (°F)	43.1	44.9	46.5	50.3	57.0	64.4	70.5	69.6	64.7	56.1	47.2	42.4	54.7
Mean Minimum Temp. (°F)	29.4	31.4	33.4	35.2	40.0	45.4	51.0	50.2	46.1	38.6	32.1	28.2	38.4
Extreme Maximum Temp. (°F)	80	81	83	89	99	103	103	102	101	97	86	80	103
Extreme Minimum Temp. (°F)	9	1	17	19	26	30	37	36	29	15	10	3	1
Days Maximum Temp. ≥ 90°F	0	0	0	0	1	8	17	15	7	1	0	0	49
Days Maximum Temp. ≤ 32°F	0	0	0	0	0	0	0	0	0	0	0	0	0
Days Minimum Temp. ≤ 32°F	22	17	15	9	3	0	0	0	0	5	17	24	112
Days Minimum Temp. ≤ 0°F	0	0	0	0	0	0	0	0	0	0	0	0	0
Heating Degree Days (base 65°F)	671	561	567	434	253	81	10	15	73	276	529	694	4,164
Cooling Degree Days (base 65°F)	0	0	0	0	10	63	178	170	73	9	0	0	503
Mean Precipitation (in.)	4.00	3.31	3.76	1.55	0.72	0.14	0.05	0.16	0.52	0.85	2.36	2.67	20.09
Days With ≥ 0.1" Precipitation	6	6	7	3	2	0	0	0	1	2	4	5	36
Days With ≥ 1.0" Precipitation	1	1	1	0	0	0	0	0	0	0	1	1	5
Mean Snowfall (in.)	2.7	1.2	2.5	1.0	trace	0.0	0.0	0.0	0.0	0.0	0.9	1.4	9.7
Days With ≥ 1.0" Snow Depth	0	0	0	0	0	0	0	0	0	0	0	0	0

Gold Rock Ranch *Imperial County*   Elevation: 482 ft.   Latitude: 32° 53' N   Longitude: 114° 52' W

	JAN	FEB	MAR	APR	MAY	JUN	JUL	AUG	SEP	OCT	NOV	DEC	YEAR
Mean Maximum Temp. (°F)	67.8	74.0	78.2	86.4	94.0	104.2	107.3	105.7	100.6	89.5	76.5	67.7	87.6
Mean Temp. (°F)	57.0	61.5	64.7	71.5	78.5	88.6	93.5	92.5	87.2	76.3	64.2	56.8	74.4
Mean Minimum Temp. (°F)	46.1	48.8	51.4	56.5	63.0	72.9	79.6	79.3	73.7	63.1	51.9	45.9	61.0
Extreme Maximum Temp. (°F)	87	96	99	107	116	122	127	119	118	112	95	84	127
Extreme Minimum Temp. (°F)	27	30	26	38	23	50	64	62	54	38	32	22	22
Days Maximum Temp. ≥ 90°F	0	1	3	11	23	29	30	31	28	16	1	0	173
Days Maximum Temp. ≤ 32°F	0	0	0	0	0	0	0	0	0	0	0	0	0
Days Minimum Temp. ≤ 32°F	0	0	0	0	0	0	0	0	0	0	0	1	1
Days Minimum Temp. ≤ 0°F	0	0	0	0	0	0	0	0	0	0	0	0	0
Heating Degree Days (base 65°F)	249	129	81	20	3	0	0	0	0	6	87	251	826
Cooling Degree Days (base 65°F)	5	47	91	259	449	719	894	884	684	373	72	4	4,481
Mean Precipitation (in.)	0.63	0.48	0.42	0.10	0.08	trace	0.32	0.62	0.31	0.39	0.20	0.55	4.10
Days With ≥ 0.1" Precipitation	1	1	1	0	0	0	1	1	0	1	1	1	8
Days With ≥ 1.0" Precipitation	0	0	0	0	0	0	0	0	0	0	0	0	0
Mean Snowfall (in.)	trace	0.0	0.0	0.0	0.0	0.0	0.0	0.0	0.0	0.0	0.0	0.0	trace
Days With ≥ 1.0" Snow Depth	0	0	0	0	0	0	0	0	0	0	0	0	0

Grant Grove *Tulare County*   Elevation: 6,597 ft.   Latitude: 36° 44' N   Longitude: 118° 58' W

	JAN	FEB	MAR	APR	MAY	JUN	JUL	AUG	SEP	OCT	NOV	DEC	YEAR
Mean Maximum Temp. (°F)	43.6	44.2	44.6	48.9	56.7	67.2	74.9	74.3	68.4	59.0	49.2	44.1	56.3
Mean Temp. (°F)	35.1	35.4	35.9	39.7	47.0	56.5	63.4	62.8	57.6	49.2	40.5	35.7	46.6
Mean Minimum Temp. (°F)	26.6	26.3	27.2	30.5	37.3	45.6	51.9	51.4	46.8	39.4	31.8	27.2	36.8
Extreme Maximum Temp. (°F)	65	67	68	73	82	87	90	89	86	82	71	66	90
Extreme Minimum Temp. (°F)	4	1	6	9	14	25	32	33	21	11	8	-4	-4
Days Maximum Temp. ≥ 90°F	0	0	0	0	0	0	0	0	0	0	0	0	0
Days Maximum Temp. ≤ 32°F	4	3	3	2	0	0	0	0	0	0	2	4	18
Days Minimum Temp. ≤ 32°F	24	22	23	18	8	1	0	0	1	6	16	22	141
Days Minimum Temp. ≤ 0°F	0	0	0	0	0	0	0	0	0	0	0	0	0
Heating Degree Days (base 65°F)	920	830	895	752	552	260	90	105	229	483	728	902	6,746
Cooling Degree Days (base 65°F)	0	0	0	0	1	10	46	44	11	2	0	0	114
Mean Precipitation (in.)	8.01	7.03	7.50	3.04	1.44	0.54	0.25	0.11	1.24	2.06	4.58	5.86	41.66
Days With ≥ 0.1" Precipitation	7	7	9	5	3	1	1	1	2	3	5	6	50
Days With ≥ 1.0" Precipitation	3	2	3	1	0	0	0	0	0	1	2	2	14
Mean Snowfall (in.)	36.2	33.8	44.7	18.0	5.2	0.4	0.0	0.0	0.2	3.0	16.8	28.6	186.9
Days With ≥ 1.0" Snow Depth	27	26	29	20	7	1	0	0	0	2	12	23	147

Grass Valley 2 *Nevada County*   Elevation: 2,398 ft.   Latitude: 39° 12' N   Longitude: 121° 04' W

	JAN	FEB	MAR	APR	MAY	JUN	JUL	AUG	SEP	OCT	NOV	DEC	YEAR
Mean Maximum Temp. (°F)	53.9	55.9	57.6	62.9	70.7	79.3	86.9	86.7	81.7	72.5	59.3	53.7	68.4
Mean Temp. (°F)	42.9	44.8	46.8	50.8	57.8	65.1	71.1	70.5	65.7	57.7	47.6	42.5	55.3
Mean Minimum Temp. (°F)	31.8	33.6	36.0	38.8	44.9	50.8	55.3	54.2	49.7	42.8	35.9	31.2	42.1
Extreme Maximum Temp. (°F)	77	81	81	88	99	99	108	108	104	95	82	80	108
Extreme Minimum Temp. (°F)	15	9	19	26	27	36	40	41	35	28	19	3	3
Days Maximum Temp. ≥ 90°F	0	0	0	0	0	4	12	12	6	1	0	0	35
Days Maximum Temp. ≤ 32°F	0	0	0	0	0	0	0	0	0	0	0	0	0
Days Minimum Temp. ≤ 32°F	18	13	9	4	0	0	0	0	0	1	9	20	74
Days Minimum Temp. ≤ 0°F	0	0	0	0	0	0	0	0	0	0	0	0	0
Heating Degree Days (base 65°F)	679	564	557	419	237	80	15	15	66	239	515	692	4,078
Cooling Degree Days (base 65°F)	0	0	0	1	20	80	202	186	89	17	0	0	595
Mean Precipitation (in.)	10.11	8.64	8.54	3.63	1.86	0.64	0.17	0.23	1.04	2.65	7.43	8.37	53.31
Days With ≥ 0.1" Precipitation	10	9	10	5	3	1	0	0	2	3	8	9	60
Days With ≥ 1.0" Precipitation	4	3	3	1	0	0	0	0	0	1	2	3	17
Mean Snowfall (in.)	1.9	1.7	1.9	0.7	trace	0.0	0.0	0.0	0.0	0.0	0.4	2.1	8.7
Days With ≥ 1.0" Snow Depth	1	1	0	0	0	0	0	0	0	0	0	1	3

Graton *Sonoma County*   Elevation: 200 ft.   Latitude: 38° 26' N   Longitude: 122° 52' W

	JAN	FEB	MAR	APR	MAY	JUN	JUL	AUG	SEP	OCT	NOV	DEC	YEAR
Mean Maximum Temp. (°F)	57.0	62.0	65.0	70.3	76.1	81.4	83.9	83.9	82.7	77.0	65.6	57.3	71.8
Mean Temp. (°F)	46.3	49.8	52.2	55.3	59.9	64.1	66.3	66.2	64.8	59.9	52.0	45.9	56.9
Mean Minimum Temp. (°F)	35.5	37.6	39.3	40.2	43.7	46.7	48.6	48.4	47.0	42.8	38.3	34.4	41.9
Extreme Maximum Temp. (°F)	80	82	90	98	100	108	113	107	112	106	87	77	113
Extreme Minimum Temp. (°F)	20	17	26	27	31	33	39	36	33	22	22	14	14
Days Maximum Temp. ≥ 90°F	0	0	0	0	2	5	7	7	7	3	0	0	31
Days Maximum Temp. ≤ 32°F	0	0	0	0	0	0	0	0	0	0	0	0	0
Days Minimum Temp. ≤ 32°F	13	7	4	2	0	0	0	0	0	1	7	15	49
Days Minimum Temp. ≤ 0°F	0	0	0	0	0	0	0	0	0	0	0	0	0
Heating Degree Days (base 65°F)	573	423	391	288	171	72	28	28	53	169	384	586	3,166
Cooling Degree Days (base 65°F)	0	0	0	4	19	51	74	73	52	20	0	0	293
Mean Precipitation (in.)	9.12	7.29	6.14	2.16	0.97	0.25	0.08	0.11	0.50	2.01	6.18	6.74	41.55
Days With ≥ 0.1" Precipitation	9	8	8	4	2	1	0	0	1	3	7	8	51
Days With ≥ 1.0" Precipitation	3	3	2	0	0	0	0	0	0	1	2	2	13
Mean Snowfall (in.)	trace	0.0	0.0	trace	0.0	0.0	0.0	0.0	0.0	0.0	0.0	trace	trace
Days With ≥ 1.0" Snow Depth	0	0	0	0	0	0	0	0	0	0	0	0	0

Haiwee *Inyo County*   Elevation: 3,822 ft.   Latitude: 36° 08' N   Longitude: 117° 57' W

	JAN	FEB	MAR	APR	MAY	JUN	JUL	AUG	SEP	OCT	NOV	DEC	YEAR
Mean Maximum Temp. (°F)	52.3	57.5	63.2	70.1	79.5	89.7	95.8	94.2	86.9	76.1	62.4	52.8	73.4
Mean Temp. (°F)	40.6	44.9	50.0	56.1	64.8	74.1	80.0	78.6	71.6	61.1	48.9	40.8	59.3
Mean Minimum Temp. (°F)	28.9	32.3	36.7	41.9	50.0	58.3	64.2	63.0	56.2	46.0	35.3	28.8	45.1
Extreme Maximum Temp. (°F)	75	79	83	94	99	107	113	113	105	97	83	75	113
Extreme Minimum Temp. (°F)	9	11	18	22	32	38	44	49	41	26	16	1	1
Days Maximum Temp. ≥ 90°F	0	0	0	0	4	16	27	25	12	2	0	0	86
Days Maximum Temp. ≤ 32°F	0	0	0	0	0	0	0	0	0	0	0	1	1
Days Minimum Temp. ≤ 32°F	23	14	7	2	0	0	0	0	0	1	10	23	80
Days Minimum Temp. ≤ 0°F	0	0	0	0	0	0	0	0	0	0	0	0	0
Heating Degree Days (base 65°F)	749	560	460	274	95	12	0	0	16	157	477	743	3,543
Cooling Degree Days (base 65°F)	0	0	0	18	98	287	467	441	224	45	0	0	1,580
Mean Precipitation (in.)	1.23	1.50	1.33	0.31	0.33	0.08	0.35	0.36	0.39	0.15	0.56	0.90	7.49
Days With ≥ 0.1" Precipitation	3	3	3	1	1	0	1	1	1	0	1	2	17
Days With ≥ 1.0" Precipitation	0	0	0	0	0	0	0	0	0	0	0	0	0
Mean Snowfall (in.)	1.0	1.0	trace	trace	0.0	0.0	0.0	0.0	0.0	0.0	0.1	0.5	2.6
Days With ≥ 1.0" Snow Depth	1	1	0	0	0	0	0	0	0	0	0	1	3

Half Moon Bay *San Mateo County*   Elevation: 13 ft.   Latitude: 37° 28' N   Longitude: 122° 27' W

	JAN	FEB	MAR	APR	MAY	JUN	JUL	AUG	SEP	OCT	NOV	DEC	YEAR
Mean Maximum Temp. (°F)	58.8	59.9	59.9	60.9	61.3	63.0	64.4	65.8	67.0	65.6	62.5	58.7	62.3
Mean Temp. (°F)	51.0	52.0	52.2	52.7	54.4	56.4	58.1	59.4	59.4	57.1	54.1	50.9	54.8
Mean Minimum Temp. (°F)	43.3	44.1	44.5	44.4	47.5	49.7	51.7	52.9	51.5	48.6	45.7	43.2	47.3
Extreme Maximum Temp. (°F)	72	78	78	87	90	86	81	91	94	94	85	74	94
Extreme Minimum Temp. (°F)	28	28	30	32	35	37	40	41	40	35	33	18	18
Days Maximum Temp. ≥ 90°F	0	0	0	0	0	0	0	0	0	0	0	0	0
Days Maximum Temp. ≤ 32°F	0	0	0	0	0	0	0	0	0	0	0	0	0
Days Minimum Temp. ≤ 32°F	0	0	0	0	0	0	0	0	0	0	0	1	1
Days Minimum Temp. ≤ 0°F	0	0	0	0	0	0	0	0	0	0	0	0	0
Heating Degree Days (base 65°F)	426	361	390	363	322	252	208	169	166	241	320	429	3,647
Cooling Degree Days (base 65°F)	0	0	0	0	1	1	0	0	2	4	5	1	14
Mean Precipitation (in.)	5.58	4.62	4.34	1.67	0.74	0.26	0.15	0.26	0.43	1.73	3.73	4.33	27.84
Days With ≥ 0.1" Precipitation	8	7	8	4	2	1	0	1	1	3	6	7	48
Days With ≥ 1.0" Precipitation	2	1	1	0	0	0	0	0	0	0	1	1	6
Mean Snowfall (in.)	0.0	trace	0.0	0.0	0.0	0.0	0.0	0.0	0.0	0.0	trace	trace	trace
Days With ≥ 1.0" Snow Depth	0	0	0	0	0	0	0	0	0	0	0	0	0

Hanford 1 S *Kings County*   Elevation: 242 ft.   Latitude: 36° 18' N   Longitude: 119° 39' W

	JAN	FEB	MAR	APR	MAY	JUN	JUL	AUG	SEP	OCT	NOV	DEC	YEAR
Mean Maximum Temp. (°F)	53.6	61.3	66.9	74.7	83.4	90.8	95.8	94.3	89.2	80.3	65.2	53.8	75.8
Mean Temp. (°F)	44.9	50.3	55.2	60.7	68.3	74.8	79.2	77.8	73.0	64.5	52.8	44.2	62.2
Mean Minimum Temp. (°F)	36.1	39.3	43.5	46.7	53.2	58.8	62.7	61.3	56.8	48.7	40.0	34.4	48.5
Extreme Maximum Temp. (°F)	76	79	87	96	107	109	110	109	105	101	85	77	110
Extreme Minimum Temp. (°F)	20	23	26	31	36	42	47	50	42	28	23	15	15
Days Maximum Temp. ≥ 90°F	0	0	0	1	8	17	27	25	16	4	0	0	98
Days Maximum Temp. ≤ 32°F	0	0	0	0	0	0	0	0	0	0	0	0	0
Days Minimum Temp. ≤ 32°F	10	4	1	0	0	0	0	0	0	0	4	12	31
Days Minimum Temp. ≤ 0°F	0	0	0	0	0	0	0	0	0	0	0	0	0
Heating Degree Days (base 65°F)	616	408	299	155	39	3	0	0	5	81	366	639	2,611
Cooling Degree Days (base 65°F)	0	0	3	43	155	307	464	428	267	78	1	0	1,746
Mean Precipitation (in.)	1.66	1.56	1.75	0.61	0.24	0.07	trace	trace	0.25	0.40	0.86	1.10	8.50
Days With ≥ 0.1" Precipitation	4	4	4	2	1	0	0	0	0	1	3	3	22
Days With ≥ 1.0" Precipitation	0	0	0	0	0	0	0	0	0	0	0	0	0
Mean Snowfall (in.)	0.0	trace	0.0	0.0	0.0	0.0	0.0	0.0	0.0	0.0	0.0	0.0	trace
Days With ≥ 1.0" Snow Depth	0	0	0	0	0	0	0	0	0	0	0	0	0

Hat Creek *Shasta County*   Elevation: 3,015 ft.   Latitude: 40° 56' N   Longitude: 121° 33' W

	JAN	FEB	MAR	APR	MAY	JUN	JUL	AUG	SEP	OCT	NOV	DEC	YEAR
Mean Maximum Temp. (°F)	47.9	53.0	57.4	64.5	73.7	81.8	90.0	89.7	83.2	71.6	55.1	46.8	67.9
Mean Temp. (°F)	35.2	39.5	43.5	48.7	56.3	63.2	68.9	67.6	61.4	52.1	41.3	34.6	51.0
Mean Minimum Temp. (°F)	22.6	26.0	29.6	32.8	38.9	44.5	47.8	45.4	39.6	32.5	27.8	22.3	34.2
Extreme Maximum Temp. (°F)	66	78	78	90	*101*	103	108	110	107	98	80	68	*110*
Extreme Minimum Temp. (°F)	-8	-5	10	18	*18*	29	31	30	22	14	7	-20	*-20*
Days Maximum Temp. ≥ 90°F	0	0	0	0	2	7	17	18	9	1	0	0	54
Days Maximum Temp. ≤ 32°F	0	0	0	0	0	0	0	0	0	0	0	1	1
Days Minimum Temp. ≤ 32°F	26	23	21	15	5	1	0	0	3	17	23	27	161
Days Minimum Temp. ≤ 0°F	0	0	0	0	0	0	0	0	0	0	0	0	0
Heating Degree Days (base 65°F)	915	713	659	484	276	108	27	36	134	395	706	937	5,390
Cooling Degree Days (base 65°F)	0	0	0	0	15	60	155	123	39	2	0	0	394
Mean Precipitation (in.)	2.92	2.85	2.87	1.34	1.29	0.83	0.18	0.36	0.76	1.29	2.50	2.54	19.73
Days With ≥ 0.1" Precipitation	7	7	7	4	3	2	1	1	2	3	6	6	49
Days With ≥ 1.0" Precipitation	0	0	0	0	0	0	0	0	0	0	0	0	0
Mean Snowfall (in.)	5.9	3.2	2.3	0.8	0.0	0.0	0.0	0.0	0.1	trace	0.9	5.8	19.0
Days With ≥ 1.0" Snow Depth	8	4	2	0	0	0	0	0	0	0	1	6	21

Hayfield Pumping Plant *Riverside County*   Elevation: 1,368 ft.   Latitude: 33° 42' N   Longitude: 115° 38' W

	JAN	FEB	MAR	APR	MAY	JUN	JUL	AUG	SEP	OCT	NOV	DEC	YEAR
Mean Maximum Temp. (°F)	65.4	69.8	74.5	81.5	89.6	99.6	104.1	102.8	97.4	86.7	74.3	65.9	84.3
Mean Temp. (°F)	52.6	56.4	60.5	66.6	74.4	83.2	89.4	88.3	82.1	71.1	59.8	52.6	69.8
Mean Minimum Temp. (°F)	39.7	43.0	46.5	51.7	59.2	66.8	74.7	73.8	66.8	55.5	45.2	39.3	55.2
Extreme Maximum Temp. (°F)	86	91	95	105	111	119	119	116	112	108	91	84	119
Extreme Minimum Temp. (°F)	17	21	18	31	31	49	56	56	46	29	27	18	17
Days Maximum Temp. ≥ 90°F	0	0	1	6	18	27	31	30	26	13	1	0	153
Days Maximum Temp. ≤ 32°F	0	0	0	0	0	0	0	0	0	0	0	0	0
Days Minimum Temp. ≤ 32°F	5	2	1	0	0	0	0	0	0	0	1	6	15
Days Minimum Temp. ≤ 0°F	0	0	0	0	0	0	0	0	0	0	0	0	0
Heating Degree Days (base 65°F)	381	243	166	63	11	0	0	0	0	26	172	378	1,440
Cooling Degree Days (base 65°F)	0	8	33	135	320	540	753	746	525	223	24	1	3,308
Mean Precipitation (in.)	0.74	0.66	0.61	0.11	0.11	trace	0.23	0.76	0.35	0.29	0.25	0.45	4.56
Days With ≥ 0.1" Precipitation	2	1	2	0	0	0	0	2	1	1	1	1	11
Days With ≥ 1.0" Precipitation	0	0	0	0	0	0	0	0	0	0	0	0	0
Mean Snowfall (in.)	trace	0.0	0.0	0.0	0.0	0.0	0.0	0.0	0.0	0.0	0.0	0.0	trace
Days With ≥ 1.0" Snow Depth	0	0	0	0	0	0	0	0	0	0	0	0	0

Healdsburg *Sonoma County*   Elevation: 104 ft.   Latitude: 38° 37' N   Longitude: 122° 52' W

	JAN	FEB	MAR	APR	MAY	JUN	JUL	AUG	SEP	OCT	NOV	DEC	YEAR
Mean Maximum Temp. (°F)	58.0	63.1	66.5	72.3	78.9	85.1	89.0	88.2	85.2	77.8	65.4	58.0	73.9
Mean Temp. (°F)	48.7	52.6	55.2	59.0	64.3	69.2	71.7	71.0	69.1	63.3	54.5	48.3	60.6
Mean Minimum Temp. (°F)	39.4	42.0	43.8	45.7	49.7	53.2	54.3	53.7	52.9	48.7	43.5	38.6	47.1
Extreme Maximum Temp. (°F)	83	84	90	96	105	110	116	109	114	108	89	78	116
Extreme Minimum Temp. (°F)	25	21	29	33	37	39	45	38	40	30	26	14	14
Days Maximum Temp. ≥ 90°F	0	0	0	1	4	9	14	13	9	4	0	0	54
Days Maximum Temp. ≤ 32°F	0	0	0	0	0	0	0	0	0	0	0	0	0
Days Minimum Temp. ≤ 32°F	5	2	0	0	0	0	0	0	0	0	1	6	14
Days Minimum Temp. ≤ 0°F	0	0	0	0	0	0	0	0	0	0	0	0	0
Heating Degree Days (base 65°F)	497	345	300	187	80	17	2	2	14	94	311	510	2,359
Cooling Degree Days (base 65°F)	0	0	2	16	60	143	211	189	128	44	2	0	795
Mean Precipitation (in.)	9.33	7.77	6.52	2.14	1.00	0.17	0.07	0.13	0.55	2.11	6.38	6.87	43.04
Days With ≥ 0.1" Precipitation	9	8	8	4	2	1	0	0	1	4	7	8	52
Days With ≥ 1.0" Precipitation	3	3	2	1	0	0	0	0	0	1	2	2	14
Mean Snowfall (in.)	trace	trace	trace	0.0	0.0	0.0	0.0	0.0	0.0	0.0	0.0	trace	trace
Days With ≥ 1.0" Snow Depth	0	0	0	0	0	0	0	0	0	0	0	0	0

Henshaw Dam *San Diego County*   Elevation: 2,700 ft.   Latitude: 33° 14' N   Longitude: 116° 46' W

	JAN	FEB	MAR	APR	MAY	JUN	JUL	AUG	SEP	OCT	NOV	DEC	YEAR
Mean Maximum Temp. (°F)	60.1	62.6	64.1	68.7	74.7	84.9	92.3	92.9	87.8	78.8	68.0	60.7	74.6
Mean Temp. (°F)	45.0	47.2	49.4	53.1	58.5	65.7	72.2	72.9	67.8	*59.1*	50.1	44.5	*57.1*
Mean Minimum Temp. (°F)	29.9	31.8	34.7	37.3	42.2	46.4	52.1	52.8	47.8	39.2	32.0	28.2	39.5
Extreme Maximum Temp. (°F)	89	84	90	93	104	107	120	113	109	113	92	83	120
Extreme Minimum Temp. (°F)	12	14	15	21	28	29	36	34	32	20	11	8	8
Days Maximum Temp. ≥ 90°F	0	0	0	0	2	11	22	23	16	5	0	0	79
Days Maximum Temp. ≤ 32°F	0	0	0	0	0	0	0	0	0	0	0	0	0
Days Minimum Temp. ≤ 32°F	22	17	11	5	1	0	0	0	0	4	17	24	101
Days Minimum Temp. ≤ 0°F	0	0	0	0	0	0	0	0	0	0	0	0	0
Heating Degree Days (base 65°F)	612	496	476	352	210	64	7	7	44	*196*	442	628	*3,534*
Cooling Degree Days (base 65°F)	0	0	0	1	14	82	223	269	136	19	0	0	744
Mean Precipitation (in.)	5.73	5.30	6.04	1.74	0.65	0.17	0.40	0.65	0.65	0.89	2.47	3.41	28.10
Days With ≥ 0.1" Precipitation	6	5	7	3	2	0	1	1	1	2	3	5	36
Days With ≥ 1.0" Precipitation	2	2	2	0	0	0	0	0	0	0	1	1	8
Mean Snowfall (in.)	trace	0.6	trace	0.0	0.0	0.0	0.0	0.0	0.0	0.0	trace	0.1	0.7
Days With ≥ 1.0" Snow Depth	0	0	0	0	0	0	0	0	0	0	0	0	0

Hetch Hetchy *Tuolumne County*   Elevation: 3,868 ft.   Latitude: 37° 57' N   Longitude: 119° 47' W

	JAN	FEB	MAR	APR	MAY	JUN	JUL	AUG	SEP	OCT	NOV	DEC	YEAR
Mean Maximum Temp. (°F)	48.0	52.7	56.1	61.8	69.2	77.6	84.7	84.6	79.4	70.1	56.1	47.7	65.7
Mean Temp. (°F)	39.2	42.0	44.9	49.6	56.6	64.1	70.5	70.3	65.3	56.5	45.4	39.0	53.6
Mean Minimum Temp. (°F)	30.3	31.3	33.6	37.4	43.9	50.5	56.2	55.9	51.1	42.9	34.7	30.1	41.5
Extreme Maximum Temp. (°F)	72	78	78	86	95	95	101	102	99	93	81	69	102
Extreme Minimum Temp. (°F)	14	6	15	19	26	31	41	31	34	23	16	2	2
Days Maximum Temp. ≥ 90°F	0	0	0	0	0	2	6	7	2	0	0	0	17
Days Maximum Temp. ≤ 32°F	0	0	0	0	0	0	0	0	0	0	0	1	1
Days Minimum Temp. ≤ 32°F	20	17	14	7	1	0	0	0	0	2	10	21	92
Days Minimum Temp. ≤ 0°F	0	0	0	0	0	0	0	0	0	0	0	0	0
Heating Degree Days (base 65°F)	794	642	617	455	272	93	12	15	72	273	580	800	4,625
Cooling Degree Days (base 65°F)	0	0	0	2	16	67	187	189	90	20	0	0	571
Mean Precipitation (in.)	6.50	5.79	5.85	2.95	1.71	0.83	0.29	0.20	0.92	2.10	4.71	4.84	36.69
Days With ≥ 0.1" Precipitation	8	*7*	9	6	4	2	0	0	2	3	6	*6*	*53*
Days With ≥ 1.0" Precipitation	2	2	2	1	0	0	0	0	0	1	1	*1*	*10*
Mean Snowfall (in.)	9.6	9.1	9.4	4.1	trace	trace	0.0	0.0	0.0	trace	*2.8*	9.6	*44.6*
Days With ≥ 1.0" Snow Depth	11	7	4	1	0	0	0	0	0	0	3	7	33

Hollywood-Burbank Airport *Los Angeles County*   Elevation: 725 ft.   Latitude: 34° 12' N   Longitude: 118° 22' W

	JAN	FEB	MAR	APR	MAY	JUN	JUL	AUG	SEP	OCT	NOV	DEC	YEAR
Mean Maximum Temp. (°F)	67.9	70.3	71.3	75.6	78.2	83.9	89.6	90.5	88.0	82.2	73.9	68.1	78.3
Mean Temp. (°F)	54.8	57.1	58.5	62.2	66.0	70.9	75.6	76.1	73.9	67.8	59.6	54.5	64.7
Mean Minimum Temp. (°F)	41.5	43.9	45.7	48.8	53.7	57.8	61.4	61.7	59.7	53.4	45.3	40.8	51.2
Extreme Maximum Temp. (°F)	92	92	98	105	107	111	108	110	113	108	98	90	113
Extreme Minimum Temp. (°F)	22	27	22	32	39	43	45	46	45	33	29	22	22
Days Maximum Temp. ≥ 90°F	0	0	1	2	3	7	16	17	13	7	1	0	67
Days Maximum Temp. ≤ 32°F	0	0	0	0	0	0	0	0	0	0	0	0	0
Days Minimum Temp. ≤ 32°F	2	1	1	0	0	0	0	0	0	0	0	2	6
Days Minimum Temp. ≤ 0°F	0	0	0	0	0	0	0	0	0	0	0	0	0
Heating Degree Days (base 65°F)	313	222	205	118	49	9	0	0	2	31	171	320	1,440
Cooling Degree Days (base 65°F)	1	9	14	57	89	182	331	365	284	133	16	2	1,483
Mean Precipitation (in.)	3.55	4.16	3.87	0.93	0.37	0.12	0.02	0.18	0.30	0.54	1.27	2.34	17.65
Days With ≥ 0.1" Precipitation	5	5	5	2	1	0	0	0	0	1	2	3	25
Days With ≥ 1.0" Precipitation	1	1	1	0	0	0	0	0	0	0	0	1	4
Mean Snowfall (in.)	0.0	trace	0.0	0.0	0.0	0.0	0.0	0.0	0.0	0.0	0.0	trace	trace
Days With ≥ 1.0" Snow Depth	0	0	0	0	0	0	0	0	0	0	0	0	0

Huntington Lake *Fresno County*   Elevation: 7,017 ft.   Latitude: 37° 14' N   Longitude: 119° 13' W

	JAN	FEB	MAR	APR	MAY	JUN	JUL	AUG	SEP	OCT	NOV	DEC	YEAR
Mean Maximum Temp. (°F)	45.9	46.2	47.0	50.9	57.0	66.3	73.8	73.3	67.4	59.2	49.9	45.3	56.8
Mean Temp. (°F)	35.9	35.8	36.7	40.0	45.9	54.0	60.9	60.6	55.5	48.2	40.1	35.9	45.8
Mean Minimum Temp. (°F)	25.9	25.2	26.3	29.0	34.7	41.7	47.9	47.8	43.5	37.0	30.1	26.3	34.6
Extreme Maximum Temp. (°F)	67	66	67	76	82	82	88	88	87	80	76	65	88
Extreme Minimum Temp. (°F)	0	3	5	6	15	26	31	33	26	16	10	-9	-9
Days Maximum Temp. ≥ 90°F	0	0	0	0	0	0	0	0	0	0	0	0	0
Days Maximum Temp. ≤ 32°F	2	1	2	1	0	0	0	0	0	0	1	3	10
Days Minimum Temp. ≤ 32°F	25	23	25	21	10	2	0	0	1	7	18	25	157
Days Minimum Temp. ≤ 0°F	0	0	0	0	0	0	0	0	0	0	0	0	0
Heating Degree Days (base 65°F)	894	819	871	745	585	325	137	148	282	514	743	896	6,959
Cooling Degree Days (base 65°F)	0	0	0	0	0	0	2	19	19	3	0	0	43
Mean Precipitation (in.)	*8.58*	*8.37*	*8.07*	*3.47*	*2.03*	*0.73*	*0.37*	*0.26*	*1.37*	*2.31*	na	*5.65*	na
Days With ≥ 0.1" Precipitation	*8*	*9*	*11*	*7*	*5*	*2*	*1*	*1*	*3*	*4*	7	7	*65*
Days With ≥ 1.0" Precipitation	*3*	*3*	*3*	*1*	*0*	*0*	*0*	*0*	*0*	*1*	2	2	*15*
Mean Snowfall (in.)	na	na	na	na	na	*0.0*	na	*0.0*	*trace*	*1.4*	na	na	na
Days With ≥ 1.0" Snow Depth	na	na	na	na	na	na	na	*0*	na	*0*	na	na	na

Idyllwild Fire Dept. *Riverside County*   Elevation: 5,377 ft.   Latitude: 33° 45' N   Longitude: 116° 42' W

	JAN	FEB	MAR	APR	MAY	JUN	JUL	AUG	SEP	OCT	NOV	DEC	YEAR
Mean Maximum Temp. (°F)	53.2	54.6	56.3	61.9	69.7	78.9	84.3	83.4	78.7	70.0	60.5	54.1	67.1
Mean Temp. (°F)	40.9	42.0	43.2	47.7	54.3	62.2	68.3	67.9	63.3	55.0	46.5	41.3	52.7
Mean Minimum Temp. (°F)	28.6	29.2	30.1	33.5	38.8	45.5	52.3	52.4	47.9	40.0	32.4	28.5	38.3
Extreme Maximum Temp. (°F)	74	76	77	83	93	99	100	98	99	93	80	76	100
Extreme Minimum Temp. (°F)	1	9	9	16	24	26	34	35	28	11	14	6	1
Days Maximum Temp. ≥ 90°F	0	0	0	0	0	2	5	3	1	0	0	0	11
Days Maximum Temp. ≤ 32°F	0	0	0	0	0	0	0	0	0	0	0	0	0
Days Minimum Temp. ≤ 32°F	23	21	21	14	6	1	0	0	0	5	16	23	130
Days Minimum Temp. ≤ 0°F	0	0	0	0	0	0	0	0	0	0	0	0	0
Heating Degree Days (base 65°F)	741	644	669	511	329	122	22	27	97	308	551	727	4,748
Cooling Degree Days (base 65°F)	0	0	0	1	3	39	116	129	50	6	0	0	344
Mean Precipitation (in.)	5.53	5.12	5.12	1.71	0.72	0.23	0.80	1.01	0.98	1.05	2.40	3.37	28.04
Days With ≥ 0.1" Precipitation	6	5	7	4	1	1	1	2	2	2	3	5	39
Days With ≥ 1.0" Precipitation	2	2	2	0	0	0	0	0	0	0	1	1	8
Mean Snowfall (in.)	10.0	5.4	9.8	3.4	0.6	trace	0.0	0.0	0.0	0.2	2.0	5.7	37.1
Days With ≥ 1.0" Snow Depth	6	3	3	1	0	0	0	0	0	0	1	3	17

Imperial *Imperial County*   Elevation: -62 ft.   Latitude: 32° 51' N   Longitude: 115° 34' W

	JAN	FEB	MAR	APR	MAY	JUN	JUL	AUG	SEP	OCT	NOV	DEC	YEAR
Mean Maximum Temp. (°F)	69.7	74.3	78.8	85.4	93.2	102.6	106.2	105.1	100.2	89.7	77.7	69.2	87.7
Mean Temp. (°F)	56.3	60.5	64.9	70.7	77.7	86.3	91.7	91.4	86.2	75.4	63.5	55.8	73.4
Mean Minimum Temp. (°F)	42.8	46.7	50.9	55.8	62.3	69.9	77.1	77.8	72.2	61.1	49.4	42.4	59.0
Extreme Maximum Temp. (°F)	90	96	99	105	114	119	121	118	116	110	96	85	121
Extreme Minimum Temp. (°F)	23	28	32	41	48	50	61	64	56	36	33	21	21
Days Maximum Temp. ≥ 90°F	0	0	3	10	22	29	31	31	28	17	1	0	172
Days Maximum Temp. ≤ 32°F	0	0	0	0	0	0	0	0	0	0	0	0	0
Days Minimum Temp. ≤ 32°F	1	0	0	0	0	0	0	0	0	0	0	1	2
Days Minimum Temp. ≤ 0°F	0	0	0	0	0	0	0	0	0	0	0	0	0
Heating Degree Days (base 65°F)	265	138	66	20	1	0	0	0	0	7	90	279	866
Cooling Degree Days (base 65°F)	1	19	70	216	407	630	823	835	650	340	55	1	4,047
Mean Precipitation (in.)	0.48	0.41	0.37	0.08	0.04	trace	0.13	0.32	0.36	0.26	0.19	0.42	3.06
Days With ≥ 0.1" Precipitation	1	1	1	0	0	0	0	1	1	1	0	1	7
Days With ≥ 1.0" Precipitation	0	0	0	0	0	0	0	0	0	0	0	0	0
Mean Snowfall (in.)	0.0	0.0	0.0	0.0	0.0	0.0	0.0	0.0	0.0	0.0	0.0	0.0	0.0
Days With ≥ 1.0" Snow Depth	0	0	0	0	0	0	0	0	0	0	0	0	0

Independence *Inyo County*   Elevation: 3,943 ft.   Latitude: 36° 48' N   Longitude: 118° 12' W

	JAN	FEB	MAR	APR	MAY	JUN	JUL	AUG	SEP	OCT	NOV	DEC	YEAR
Mean Maximum Temp. (°F)	54.6	59.8	65.6	73.0	82.2	92.2	98.2	96.4	89.2	77.5	64.0	55.1	75.7
Mean Temp. (°F)	41.4	46.0	51.3	57.8	66.6	75.8	81.5	79.5	72.7	61.5	49.3	41.6	60.4
Mean Minimum Temp. (°F)	28.1	32.3	36.9	42.6	51.0	59.4	64.8	62.6	56.1	45.3	34.5	28.0	45.1
Extreme Maximum Temp. (°F)	80	86	90	102	104	109	114	109	108	99	91	77	114
Extreme Minimum Temp. (°F)	3	12	15	21	30	38	43	47	38	22	16	-2	-2
Days Maximum Temp. ≥ 90°F	0	0	0	1	6	20	29	27	16	3	0	0	102
Days Maximum Temp. ≤ 32°F	0	0	0	0	0	0	0	0	0	0	0	0	0
Days Minimum Temp. ≤ 32°F	24	15	7	2	0	0	0	0	0	1	11	24	84
Days Minimum Temp. ≤ 0°F	0	0	0	0	0	0	0	0	0	0	0	0	0
Heating Degree Days (base 65°F)	725	529	420	232	75	10	0	1	12	153	467	720	3,344
Cooling Degree Days (base 65°F)	0	1	3	34	143	350	530	480	266	57	1	0	1,865
Mean Precipitation (in.)	1.02	1.14	0.76	0.21	0.19	0.18	0.13	0.12	0.26	0.17	0.58	0.63	5.39
Days With ≥ 0.1" Precipitation	2	2	2	1	1	0	0	1	1	1	1	1	12
Days With ≥ 1.0" Precipitation	0	0	0	0	0	0	0	0	0	0	0	0	0
Mean Snowfall (in.)	1.3	0.2	trace	trace	0.0	0.0	0.0	0.0	0.0	0.0	trace	0.4	1.9
Days With ≥ 1.0" Snow Depth	0	na	0	0	0	0	0	0	0	0	0	0	na

Inyokern *Kern County*   Elevation: 2,437 ft.   Latitude: 35° 39' N   Longitude: 117° 49' W

	JAN	FEB	MAR	APR	MAY	JUN	JUL	AUG	SEP	OCT	NOV	DEC	YEAR
Mean Maximum Temp. (°F)	60.1	65.8	71.3	78.2	87.0	96.9	102.8	101.2	93.9	83.2	69.2	60.1	80.8
Mean Temp. (°F)	45.5	50.5	55.3	61.2	69.9	78.6	84.5	83.1	76.0	65.6	53.2	45.2	64.1
Mean Minimum Temp. (°F)	30.9	35.1	39.3	44.1	52.8	60.1	66.1	64.9	58.2	48.1	37.1	30.3	47.3
Extreme Maximum Temp. (°F)	80	86	90	100	105	113	119	114	110	105	87	79	119
Extreme Minimum Temp. (°F)	8	11	15	0	26	40	48	45	35	20	14	5	0
Days Maximum Temp. ≥ 90°F	0	0	0	3	13	26	31	30	23	7	0	0	133
Days Maximum Temp. ≤ 32°F	0	0	0	0	0	0	0	0	0	0	0	0	0
Days Minimum Temp. ≤ 32°F	19	10	4	2	0	0	0	0	0	1	8	21	65
Days Minimum Temp. ≤ 0°F	0	0	0	0	0	0	0	0	0	0	0	0	0
Heating Degree Days (base 65°F)	597	404	298	150	35	2	0	0	4	77	351	607	2,525
Cooling Degree Days (base 65°F)	0	1	7	56	198	411	604	583	357	109	4	0	2,330
Mean Precipitation (in.)	0.90	1.16	0.81	0.18	0.10	0.02	0.12	0.33	0.26	0.07	0.34	0.57	4.86
Days With ≥ 0.1" Precipitation	2	2	2	1	0	0	0	1	1	0	1	1	10
Days With ≥ 1.0" Precipitation	0	0	0	0	0	0	0	0	0	0	0	0	0
Mean Snowfall (in.)	0.5	trace	trace	0.0	0.0	0.0	0.0	0.0	0.0	0.0	0.0	0.4	0.9
Days With ≥ 1.0" Snow Depth	0	0	0	0	0	0	0	0	0	0	0	0	0

Iron Mountain *San Bernardino County*   Elevation: 921 ft.   Latitude: 34° 08' N   Longitude: 115° 08' W

	JAN	FEB	MAR	APR	MAY	JUN	JUL	AUG	SEP	OCT	NOV	DEC	YEAR
Mean Maximum Temp. (°F)	65.0	70.9	76.8	84.5	93.5	103.6	108.3	106.6	100.2	88.6	74.8	65.2	86.5
Mean Temp. (°F)	54.1	59.1	64.3	71.2	79.9	89.6	94.7	93.0	86.6	74.9	62.5	54.1	73.7
Mean Minimum Temp. (°F)	43.3	47.3	51.6	57.8	66.3	75.5	81.0	79.4	72.9	61.1	50.1	43.0	60.8
Extreme Maximum Temp. (°F)	84	92	98	105	113	121	122	121	117	112	94	82	122
Extreme Minimum Temp. (°F)	22	27	33	36	42	55	64	60	55	33	22	22	22
Days Maximum Temp. ≥ 90°F	0	0	3	9	22	29	31	31	27	15	1	0	168
Days Maximum Temp. ≤ 32°F	0	0	0	0	0	0	0	0	0	0	0	0	0
Days Minimum Temp. ≤ 32°F	1	0	0	0	0	0	0	0	0	0	0	1	2
Days Minimum Temp. ≤ 0°F	0	0	0	0	0	0	0	0	0	0	0	0	0
Heating Degree Days (base 65°F)	332	177	94	27	2	0	0	0	0	12	121	332	1,097
Cooling Degree Days (base 65°F)	1	21	80	246	487	732	919	891	662	334	59	2	4,434
Mean Precipitation (in.)	0.61	0.48	0.52	0.11	0.10	0.05	0.29	0.38	0.29	0.29	0.22	0.47	3.81
Days With ≥ 0.1" Precipitation	2	1	2	0	0	0	1	1	1	1	1	1	11
Days With ≥ 1.0" Precipitation	0	0	0	0	0	0	0	0	0	0	0	0	0
Mean Snowfall (in.)	0.0	0.0	0.0	0.0	0.0	0.0	0.0	0.0	0.0	0.0	0.0	0.0	0.0
Days With ≥ 1.0" Snow Depth	0	0	0	0	0	0	0	0	0	0	0	0	0

Jess Valley *Modoc County*   Elevation: 5,396 ft.   Latitude: 41° 16' N   Longitude: 120° 18' W

	JAN	FEB	MAR	APR	MAY	JUN	JUL	AUG	SEP	OCT	NOV	DEC	YEAR
Mean Maximum Temp. (°F)	41.9	44.6	48.1	54.7	64.1	73.3	83.0	81.9	74.9	63.4	48.5	41.4	60.0
Mean Temp. (°F)	30.6	33.2	36.5	41.4	49.3	57.0	64.7	63.6	57.2	47.8	36.9	30.1	45.7
Mean Minimum Temp. (°F)	19.4	21.9	24.9	27.9	34.2	40.7	46.3	45.3	39.2	32.1	25.1	19.2	31.4
Extreme Maximum Temp. (°F)	64	67	71	81	89	95	98	105	95	88	78	64	105
Extreme Minimum Temp. (°F)	-14	-28	-7	5	18	21	29	30	19	3	-5	-28	-28
Days Maximum Temp. ≥ 90°F	0	0	0	0	0	1	5	5	1	0	0	0	12
Days Maximum Temp. ≤ 32°F	4	2	1	0	0	0	0	0	0	0	2	5	14
Days Minimum Temp. ≤ 32°F	29	25	26	23	13	3	0	0	5	16	25	29	194
Days Minimum Temp. ≤ 0°F	1	1	0	0	0	0	0	0	0	0	0	2	4
Heating Degree Days (base 65°F)	1,062	892	878	702	481	244	71	91	239	530	838	1,076	7,104
Cooling Degree Days (base 65°F)	0	0	0	0	1	11	62	52	12	1	0	0	139
Mean Precipitation (in.)	1.95	1.66	2.18	1.94	2.31	1.53	0.52	0.62	0.94	1.26	2.17	2.03	19.11
Days With ≥ 0.1" Precipitation	6	5	7	6	6	4	2	2	2	4	7	7	58
Days With ≥ 1.0" Precipitation	0	0	0	0	0	0	0	0	0	0	0	0	0
Mean Snowfall (in.)	11.2	10.6	11.8	8.4	4.7	0.4	trace	0.0	0.6	2.0	10.2	12.4	72.3
Days With ≥ 1.0" Snow Depth	15	10	6	1	0	0	0	0	0	1	5	12	50

Kentfield *Marin County*   Elevation: 127 ft.   Latitude: 37° 57' N   Longitude: 122° 34' W

	JAN	FEB	MAR	APR	MAY	JUN	JUL	AUG	SEP	OCT	NOV	DEC	YEAR
Mean Maximum Temp. (°F)	56.1	61.5	65.3	70.4	76.1	81.7	85.1	84.2	82.2	75.3	63.3	56.1	71.4
Mean Temp. (°F)	48.3	52.2	54.6	57.8	62.0	66.3	68.7	68.3	66.9	62.1	54.0	48.2	59.1
Mean Minimum Temp. (°F)	40.5	42.8	43.8	45.1	47.9	50.8	52.2	52.4	51.6	48.9	44.8	40.2	46.7
Extreme Maximum Temp. (°F)	71	79	85	96	101	107	111	106	106	101	83	77	111
Extreme Minimum Temp. (°F)	27	24	29	33	23	39	42	41	41	34	30	18	18
Days Maximum Temp. ≥ 90°F	0	0	0	0	2	5	7	6	6	2	0	0	28
Days Maximum Temp. ≤ 32°F	0	0	0	0	0	0	0	0	0	0	0	0	0
Days Minimum Temp. ≤ 32°F	2	1	0	0	0	0	0	0	0	0	0	3	6
Days Minimum Temp. ≤ 0°F	0	0	0	0	0	0	0	0	0	0	0	0	0
Heating Degree Days (base 65°F)	510	356	316	217	118	37	8	10	26	115	323	515	2,551
Cooling Degree Days (base 65°F)	0	0	1	10	31	83	135	129	93	38	1	0	521
Mean Precipitation (in.)	10.14	8.68	7.05	2.48	1.14	0.26	0.12	0.12	0.50	2.33	7.96	7.94	48.72
Days With ≥ 0.1" Precipitation	9	8	9	4	2	1	0	0	1	2	7	8	51
Days With ≥ 1.0" Precipitation	4	3	2	1	0	0	0	0	0	1	3	3	17
Mean Snowfall (in.)	trace	0.0	0.0	0.0	0.0	0.0	0.0	0.0	0.0	0.0	0.0	trace	trace
Days With ≥ 1.0" Snow Depth	0	0	0	0	0	0	0	0	0	0	0	0	0

Kern River P H 3 *Kern County*   Elevation: 2,700 ft.   Latitude: 35° 47' N   Longitude: 118° 26' W

	JAN	FEB	MAR	APR	MAY	JUN	JUL	AUG	SEP	OCT	NOV	DEC	YEAR
Mean Maximum Temp. (°F)	59.8	63.4	66.5	72.6	81.0	90.3	97.3	96.6	90.4	80.0	67.0	59.9	77.1
Mean Temp. (°F)	46.6	49.7	52.7	58.0	66.1	74.5	81.0	80.2	74.4	64.2	52.5	46.2	62.2
Mean Minimum Temp. (°F)	33.4	36.0	38.8	43.4	51.1	58.6	64.6	63.7	58.3	48.4	37.9	32.5	47.2
Extreme Maximum Temp. (°F)	80	86	88	97	102	109	112	109	106	102	89	84	112
Extreme Minimum Temp. (°F)	15	14	24	26	30	39	42	50	38	23	22	10	10
Days Maximum Temp. ≥ 90°F	0	0	0	1	6	17	29	27	19	5	0	0	104
Days Maximum Temp. ≤ 32°F	0	0	0	0	0	0	0	0	0	0	0	0	0
Days Minimum Temp. ≤ 32°F	15	10	6	1	0	0	0	0	0	0	8	16	56
Days Minimum Temp. ≤ 0°F	0	0	0	0	0	0	0	0	0	0	0	0	0
Heating Degree Days (base 65°F)	566	426	378	229	79	10	0	0	8	103	373	576	2,748
Cooling Degree Days (base 65°F)	0	0	2	33	117	289	495	488	298	89	2	0	1,813
Mean Precipitation (in.)	2.92	2.67	2.35	0.66	0.27	0.13	0.13	0.19	0.42	0.47	1.34	1.82	13.37
Days With ≥ 0.1" Precipitation	5	5	5	2	1	0	0	1	1	1	3	4	28
Days With ≥ 1.0" Precipitation	1	1	1	0	0	0	0	0	0	0	0	0	3
Mean Snowfall (in.)	0.2	trace	0.0	0.0	0.0	0.0	0.0	0.0	0.0	0.0	0.0	trace	0.2
Days With ≥ 1.0" Snow Depth	0	0	0	0	0	0	0	0	0	0	0	0	0

King City *Monterey County*   Elevation: 318 ft.   Latitude: 36° 12' N   Longitude: 121° 08' W

	JAN	FEB	MAR	APR	MAY	JUN	JUL	AUG	SEP	OCT	NOV	DEC	YEAR
Mean Maximum Temp. (°F)	62.8	66.0	68.6	74.0	78.1	82.5	84.8	84.9	84.7	79.6	68.8	62.6	74.8
Mean Temp. (°F)	49.3	52.4	55.0	57.9	61.9	65.8	68.3	68.4	67.2	62.3	53.9	48.6	59.2
Mean Minimum Temp. (°F)	35.7	38.7	41.0	41.7	45.8	49.0	51.6	51.8	49.7	45.0	39.0	34.7	43.6
Extreme Maximum Temp. (°F)	86	90	90	102	108	112	109	109	111	109	93	84	112
Extreme Minimum Temp. (°F)	15	20	22	27	31	35	38	37	35	26	24	14	14
Days Maximum Temp. ≥ 90°F	0	0	0	2	4	5	6	6	8	5	0	0	36
Days Maximum Temp. ≤ 32°F	0	0	0	0	0	0	0	0	0	0	0	0	0
Days Minimum Temp. ≤ 32°F	11	5	3	1	0	0	0	0	0	1	6	14	41
Days Minimum Temp. ≤ 0°F	0	0	0	0	0	0	0	0	0	0	0	0	0
Heating Degree Days (base 65°F)	475	345	305	219	122	40	9	7	23	116	328	501	2,490
Cooling Degree Days (base 65°F)	0	0	1	14	32	67	118	128	96	40	1	0	497
Mean Precipitation (in.)	2.36	2.53	2.52	0.70	0.24	0.05	0.01	0.05	0.27	0.52	1.40	1.76	12.41
Days With ≥ 0.1" Precipitation	4	5	5	2	1	0	0	0	0	1	3	4	25
Days With ≥ 1.0" Precipitation	1	1	1	0	0	0	0	0	0	0	0	0	3
Mean Snowfall (in.)	0.0	0.0	0.0	0.0	0.0	0.0	0.0	0.0	0.0	0.0	0.0	trace	trace
Days With ≥ 1.0" Snow Depth	0	0	0	0	0	0	0	0	0	0	0	0	0

Klamath *Del Norte County*   Elevation: 22 ft.   Latitude: 41° 31' N   Longitude: 124° 02' W

	JAN	FEB	MAR	APR	MAY	JUN	JUL	AUG	SEP	OCT	NOV	DEC	YEAR
Mean Maximum Temp. (°F)	55.1	56.3	57.2	58.8	62.0	64.7	66.7	66.7	67.0	64.2	58.2	54.6	61.0
Mean Temp. (°F)	47.0	48.1	49.0	50.5	53.9	57.1	59.5	59.7	58.5	55.1	50.2	46.4	52.9
Mean Minimum Temp. (°F)	38.7	39.9	40.7	42.0	45.8	49.5	52.2	52.7	50.0	45.9	42.2	38.3	44.8
Extreme Maximum Temp. (°F)	75	80	81	85	91	93	87	86	94	90	77	72	94
Extreme Minimum Temp. (°F)	22	19	27	28	32	37	41	43	38	28	25	16	16
Days Maximum Temp. ≥ 90°F	0	0	0	0	0	0	0	0	0	0	0	0	0
Days Maximum Temp. ≤ 32°F	0	0	0	0	0	0	0	0	0	0	0	0	0
Days Minimum Temp. ≤ 32°F	6	4	2	1	0	0	0	0	0	0	2	6	21
Days Minimum Temp. ≤ 0°F	0	0	0	0	0	0	0	0	0	0	0	0	0
Heating Degree Days (base 65°F)	552	469	489	430	338	232	166	159	190	302	437	568	4,332
Cooling Degree Days (base 65°F)	0	0	0	0	1	1	1	1	2	2	0	0	8
Mean Precipitation (in.)	12.51	10.93	11.01	5.93	3.67	1.67	0.37	0.74	1.97	5.16	12.42	13.88	80.26
Days With ≥ 0.1" Precipitation	14	13	14	10	6	3	1	1	3	6	14	14	99
Days With ≥ 1.0" Precipitation	5	4	4	2	1	0	0	1	1	2	4	5	28
Mean Snowfall (in.)	0.3	0.7	trace	0.0	0.0	0.0	0.0	0.0	0.0	0.0	trace	0.3	1.3
Days With ≥ 1.0" Snow Depth	0	0	0	0	0	0	0	0	0	0	0	0	0

Laguna Beach *Orange County*   Elevation: 32 ft.   Latitude: 33° 33' N   Longitude: 117° 47' W

	JAN	FEB	MAR	APR	MAY	JUN	JUL	AUG	SEP	OCT	NOV	DEC	YEAR
Mean Maximum Temp. (°F)	66.5	67.5	67.7	70.3	71.2	74.0	77.2	78.6	78.6	76.0	71.2	67.0	72.1
Mean Temp. (°F)	54.5	55.5	56.4	58.7	*61.7*	64.8	67.9	68.8	68.3	64.6	58.6	54.4	*61.2*
Mean Minimum Temp. (°F)	42.4	43.4	45.0	47.1	*52.3*	55.6	58.6	58.6	57.9	53.1	45.9	42.0	*50.2*
Extreme Maximum Temp. (°F)	89	90	92	97	96	100	104	97	102	98	96	87	104
Extreme Minimum Temp. (°F)	27	30	28	34	36	39	30	38	40	33	28	28	27
Days Maximum Temp. ≥ 90°F	0	0	0	0	0	0	0	1	2	1	0	0	4
Days Maximum Temp. ≤ 32°F	0	0	0	0	0	0	0	0	0	0	0	0	0
Days Minimum Temp. ≤ 32°F	1	1	0	0	0	0	0	0	0	0	0	1	3
Days Minimum Temp. ≤ 0°F	0	0	0	0	0	0	0	0	0	0	0	0	0
Heating Degree Days (base 65°F)	321	264	262	189	*112*	43	11	8	16	58	193	322	*1,799*
Cooling Degree Days (base 65°F)	1	3	2	11	21	51	130	152	132	*59*	6	0	*568*
Mean Precipitation (in.)	2.82	2.88	2.65	0.80	0.25	0.14	0.04	0.11	0.35	0.40	1.36	2.00	13.80
Days With ≥ 0.1" Precipitation	5	4	4	2	1	0	0	0	1	1	2	3	23
Days With ≥ 1.0" Precipitation	1	1	1	0	0	0	0	0	0	0	0	0	3
Mean Snowfall (in.)	0.0	0.0	0.0	0.0	0.0	0.0	0.0	0.0	0.0	0.0	0.0	0.0	0.0
Days With ≥ 1.0" Snow Depth	0	0	0	0	0	0	0	0	0	0	0	0	0

Lake Arrowhead *San Bernardino County*   Elevation: 5,203 ft.   Latitude: 34° 15' N   Longitude: 117° 11' W

	JAN	FEB	MAR	APR	MAY	JUN	JUL	AUG	SEP	OCT	NOV	DEC	YEAR
Mean Maximum Temp. (°F)	45.4	48.2	53.0	59.9	67.1	76.6	82.0	81.6	76.1	64.7	52.7	45.7	62.8
Mean Temp. (°F)	37.4	39.3	42.5	47.4	54.0	62.9	69.1	69.0	63.4	53.4	43.5	37.6	51.6
Mean Minimum Temp. (°F)	29.4	30.4	31.9	34.9	41.0	49.1	56.3	56.2	50.7	42.0	34.1	29.5	40.4
Extreme Maximum Temp. (°F)	68	68	77	94	90	106	100	96	93	93	72	68	106
Extreme Minimum Temp. (°F)	10	10	13	17	25	30	40	37	33	18	10	6	6
Days Maximum Temp. ≥ 90°F	0	0	0	0	0	1	3	3	0	0	0	0	7
Days Maximum Temp. ≤ 32°F	1	1	0	0	0	0	0	0	0	0	0	2	4
Days Minimum Temp. ≤ 32°F	22	19	17	11	3	0	0	0	0	3	12	21	108
Days Minimum Temp. ≤ 0°F	0	0	0	0	0	0	0	0	0	0	0	0	0
Heating Degree Days (base 65°F)	848	719	692	523	337	116	18	22	98	358	640	843	5,214
Cooling Degree Days (base 65°F)	0	0	0	0	0	54	145	163	62	5	0	0	433
Mean Precipitation (in.)	8.40	8.74	8.11	2.57	1.36	0.29	0.10	0.37	1.08	1.95	3.75	5.44	42.16
Days With ≥ 0.1" Precipitation	6	5	6	4	2	0	0	1	1	2	3	5	35
Days With ≥ 1.0" Precipitation	3	3	3	1	0	0	0	0	1	1	1	2	14
Mean Snowfall (in.)	8.3	*5.3*	*9.3*	*2.5*	0.7	0.0	0.0	0.0	0.0	0.4	1.8	5.0	*33.3*
Days With ≥ 1.0" Snow Depth	*5*	na	*3*	0	0	0	0	0	0	0	1	2	na

Lake Spaulding *Nevada County*   Elevation: 5,154 ft.   Latitude: 39° 19' N   Longitude: 120° 38' W

	JAN	FEB	MAR	APR	MAY	JUN	JUL	AUG	SEP	OCT	NOV	DEC	YEAR
Mean Maximum Temp. (°F)	45.4	47.8	50.6	56.6	65.5	74.9	82.2	81.7	75.8	65.0	50.7	44.6	61.7
Mean Temp. (°F)	34.9	36.4	38.7	43.0	50.6	58.5	64.3	63.7	59.0	50.3	39.6	34.3	47.8
Mean Minimum Temp. (°F)	24.4	24.9	26.8	29.3	35.6	42.1	46.2	45.6	42.1	35.7	28.5	23.9	33.8
Extreme Maximum Temp. (°F)	69	71	72	82	94	100	98	104	97	94	77	70	104
Extreme Minimum Temp. (°F)	-4	-1	-1	6	13	24	31	30	23	13	4	-14	-14
Days Maximum Temp. ≥ 90°F	0	0	0	0	0	1	4	3	1	0	0	0	9
Days Maximum Temp. ≤ 32°F	2	1	1	0	0	0	0	0	0	0	0	3	7
Days Minimum Temp. ≤ 32°F	28	26	28	22	10	2	0	0	2	10	23	28	179
Days Minimum Temp. ≤ 0°F	0	0	0	0	0	0	0	0	0	0	0	0	0
Heating Degree Days (base 65°F)	927	801	808	654	442	204	71	82	188	451	755	947	6,330
Cooling Degree Days (base 65°F)	0	0	0	0	2	14	53	48	14	3	0	0	134
Mean Precipitation (in.)	13.38	11.58	11.45	5.49	3.34	1.21	0.39	0.53	1.74	4.04	9.97	11.40	74.52
Days With ≥ 0.1" Precipitation	11	10	11	8	5	2	1	1	2	5	9	9	74
Days With ≥ 1.0" Precipitation	5	5	4	2	1	0	0	0	1	1	3	4	26
Mean Snowfall (in.)	48.8	52.1	47.3	24.8	5.4	0.3	0.0	0.0	trace	2.3	21.6	44.4	247.0
Days With ≥ 1.0" Snow Depth	28	27	29	18	4	0	0	0	0	1	10	23	140

Lancaster Gen. Wm. Fox Field *Los Angeles County*   Elevation: 2,335 ft.   Latitude: 34° 44' N   Longitude: 118° 13' W

	JAN	FEB	MAR	APR	MAY	JUN	JUL	AUG	SEP	OCT	NOV	DEC	YEAR
Mean Maximum Temp. (°F)	57.3	60.7	64.4	71.3	79.1	88.8	95.3	94.7	88.6	78.4	65.7	57.1	75.1
Mean Temp. (°F)	44.4	47.9	52.0	58.2	66.1	74.6	80.7	79.5	73.1	62.4	50.6	43.1	61.0
Mean Minimum Temp. (°F)	31.4	35.1	39.5	44.9	53.0	60.4	66.1	64.2	57.5	46.3	35.4	28.9	46.9
Extreme Maximum Temp. (°F)	77	83	86	96	104	109	110	110	105	100	85	79	110
Extreme Minimum Temp. (°F)	10	11	20	25	33	40	47	46	38	24	15	2	2
Days Maximum Temp. ≥ 90°F	0	0	0	1	5	15	25	24	16	4	0	0	90
Days Maximum Temp. ≤ 32°F	0	0	0	0	0	0	0	0	0	0	0	0	0
Days Minimum Temp. ≤ 32°F	18	11	5	1	0	0	0	0	0	1	11	21	68
Days Minimum Temp. ≤ 0°F	0	0	0	0	0	0	0	0	0	0	0	0	0
Heating Degree Days (base 65°F)	632	475	397	221	80	12	0	0	12	126	427	673	3,055
Cooling Degree Days (base 65°F)	0	0	1	26	125	301	495	471	256	49	1	0	1,725
Mean Precipitation (in.)	1.69	1.75	1.54	0.29	0.13	0.06	0.12	0.17	0.22	0.31	0.49	1.13	7.90
Days With ≥ 0.1" Precipitation	4	3	3	1	0	0	0	0	1	1	1	2	16
Days With ≥ 1.0" Precipitation	0	0	0	0	0	0	0	0	0	0	0	0	0
Mean Snowfall (in.)	1.1	0.6	trace	trace	trace	0.0	0.0	0.0	0.0	0.0	trace	1.0	2.7
Days With ≥ 1.0" Snow Depth	0	1	0	0	0	0	0	0	0	0	0	1	2

Lemon Cove *Tulare County*   Elevation: 511 ft.   Latitude: 36° 23' N   Longitude: 119° 02' W

	JAN	FEB	MAR	APR	MAY	JUN	JUL	AUG	SEP	OCT	NOV	DEC	YEAR
Mean Maximum Temp. (°F)	56.3	63.3	68.2	75.0	83.9	92.0	97.4	96.0	90.7	80.9	66.4	56.5	77.2
Mean Temp. (°F)	46.9	52.2	56.5	61.0	68.3	75.2	80.3	78.9	74.3	65.7	54.1	46.5	63.3
Mean Minimum Temp. (°F)	37.4	41.2	44.5	46.9	52.7	58.3	63.1	61.8	57.8	50.5	41.7	36.4	49.4
Extreme Maximum Temp. (°F)	79	82	88	96	104	110	110	112	106	101	87	78	112
Extreme Minimum Temp. (°F)	23	25	28	32	35	42	47	50	42	29	27	19	19
Days Maximum Temp. ≥ 90°F	0	0	0	2	9	20	29	27	18	5	0	0	110
Days Maximum Temp. ≤ 32°F	0	0	0	0	0	0	0	0	0	0	0	0	0
Days Minimum Temp. ≤ 32°F	8	1	1	0	0	0	0	0	0	0	2	9	21
Days Minimum Temp. ≤ 0°F	0	0	0	0	0	0	0	0	0	0	0	0	0
Heating Degree Days (base 65°F)	554	355	262	152	46	5	0	0	5	71	323	566	2,339
Cooling Degree Days (base 65°F)	0	0	5	50	155	312	481	453	297	103	2	0	1,858
Mean Precipitation (in.)	2.84	2.40	2.96	1.06	0.51	0.14	0.01	0.04	0.33	0.71	1.70	1.83	14.53
Days With ≥ 0.1" Precipitation	6	5	6	2	1	0	0	0	1	1	3	4	29
Days With ≥ 1.0" Precipitation	1	0	1	0	0	0	0	0	0	0	0	0	2
Mean Snowfall (in.)	0.0	0.0	0.0	0.0	0.0	0.0	0.0	0.0	0.0	0.0	0.0	0.0	0.0
Days With ≥ 1.0" Snow Depth	0	0	0	0	0	0	0	0	0	0	0	0	0

Lindsay *Tulare County*   Elevation: 419 ft.   Latitude: 36° 12' N   Longitude: 119° 03' W

	JAN	FEB	MAR	APR	MAY	JUN	JUL	AUG	SEP	OCT	NOV	DEC	YEAR
Mean Maximum Temp. (°F)	57.6	64.6	69.5	76.7	85.0	92.4	97.5	96.1	90.9	81.0	66.8	57.4	78.0
Mean Temp. (°F)	47.0	51.7	55.8	60.8	67.9	74.5	79.6	78.0	73.0	64.0	53.0	46.0	62.6
Mean Minimum Temp. (°F)	36.3	38.8	42.0	44.7	50.8	56.6	61.5	59.8	55.0	47.0	39.2	34.5	47.2
Extreme Maximum Temp. (°F)	78	84	88	100	104	111	110	110	109	102	88	82	111
Extreme Minimum Temp. (°F)	22	22	25	30	34	40	48	45	39	30	24	17	17
Days Maximum Temp. ≥ 90°F	0	0	0	2	10	20	29	27	19	5	0	0	112
Days Maximum Temp. ≤ 32°F	0	0	0	0	0	0	0	0	0	0	0	0	0
Days Minimum Temp. ≤ 32°F	10	5	2	0	0	0	0	0	0	0	4	12	33
Days Minimum Temp. ≤ 0°F	0	0	0	0	0	0	0	0	0	0	0	0	0
Heating Degree Days (base 65°F)	552	369	281	150	45	4	0	0	7	88	353	582	2,431
Cooling Degree Days (base 65°F)	0	0	3	38	134	284	453	420	257	62	1	0	1,652
Mean Precipitation (in.)	2.48	2.13	2.56	0.89	0.40	0.12	trace	0.02	0.34	0.61	1.45	1.54	12.54
Days With ≥ 0.1" Precipitation	5	5	6	2	1	0	0	0	1	2	3	4	29
Days With ≥ 1.0" Precipitation	0	0	0	0	0	0	0	0	0	0	0	0	0
Mean Snowfall (in.)	0.1	0.0	0.0	0.0	0.0	0.0	0.0	0.0	0.0	0.0	0.0	trace	0.1
Days With ≥ 1.0" Snow Depth	0	0	0	0	0	0	0	0	0	0	0	0	0

Livermore *Alameda County*   Elevation: 479 ft.   Latitude: 37° 40' N   Longitude: 121° 46' W

	JAN	FEB	MAR	APR	MAY	JUN	JUL	AUG	SEP	OCT	NOV	DEC	YEAR
Mean Maximum Temp. (°F)	57.0	62.0	65.6	71.2	77.3	84.0	89.4	88.9	86.2	78.2	65.3	57.0	73.5
Mean Temp. (°F)	47.2	51.1	53.9	57.6	62.9	68.2	72.2	71.8	69.6	63.2	53.6	47.0	59.8
Mean Minimum Temp. (°F)	37.3	40.1	42.1	43.9	48.4	52.4	54.9	54.7	53.0	48.2	41.8	36.9	46.1
Extreme Maximum Temp. (°F)	75	80	88	96	103	112	115	110	110	106	86	74	115
Extreme Minimum Temp. (°F)	20	24	22	29	35	40	36	40	37	29	25	18	18
Days Maximum Temp. ≥ 90°F	0	0	0	0	4	9	16	15	11	4	0	0	59
Days Maximum Temp. ≤ 32°F	0	0	0	0	0	0	0	0	0	0	0	0	0
Days Minimum Temp. ≤ 32°F	9	4	1	1	0	0	0	0	0	0	3	9	27
Days Minimum Temp. ≤ 0°F	0	0	0	0	0	0	0	0	0	0	0	0	0
Heating Degree Days (base 65°F)	546	386	339	226	112	30	5	3	13	98	337	553	2,648
Cooling Degree Days (base 65°F)	0	0	0	13	48	129	240	234	165	52	1	0	882
Mean Precipitation (in.)	3.02	2.65	2.47	0.95	0.41	0.10	0.03	0.08	0.23	0.81	2.01	2.20	14.96
Days With ≥ 0.1" Precipitation	6	6	6	3	1	0	0	0	1	2	4	5	34
Days With ≥ 1.0" Precipitation	1	0	0	0	0	0	0	0	0	0	0	0	1
Mean Snowfall (in.)	0.0	0.0	trace	0.0	0.0	0.0	0.0	0.0	0.0	0.0	0.0	trace	trace
Days With ≥ 1.0" Snow Depth	0	0	0	0	0	0	0	0	0	0	0	0	0

Lodgepole *Tulare County*   Elevation: 6,732 ft.   Latitude: 36° 36' N   Longitude: 118° 44' W

	JAN	FEB	MAR	APR	MAY	JUN	JUL	AUG	SEP	OCT	NOV	DEC	YEAR
Mean Maximum Temp. (°F)	38.5	41.6	43.9	49.0	57.3	67.6	75.1	74.7	68.1	58.1	45.5	37.9	54.8
Mean Temp. (°F)	27.1	29.4	32.5	36.9	44.5	53.0	59.5	58.8	52.8	44.0	34.0	26.9	41.6
Mean Minimum Temp. (°F)	15.7	17.1	20.9	24.7	31.6	38.4	44.0	42.9	37.5	29.9	22.4	15.9	28.4
Extreme Maximum Temp. (°F)	65	62	65	72	85	86	91	89	86	81	67	57	91
Extreme Minimum Temp. (°F)	-10	-12	-2	-1	9	23	28	28	19	1	-3	-16	-16
Days Maximum Temp. ≥ 90°F	0	0	0	0	0	0	0	0	0	0	0	0	0
Days Maximum Temp. ≤ 32°F	7	4	3	2	0	0	0	0	0	0	2	7	25
Days Minimum Temp. ≤ 32°F	31	28	31	28	18	5	1	1	6	21	29	31	230
Days Minimum Temp. ≤ 0°F	1	1	0	0	0	0	0	0	0	0	0	1	3
Heating Degree Days (base 65°F)	1,168	998	1,001	837	629	355	173	192	360	644	925	1,174	8,456
Cooling Degree Days (base 65°F)	0	0	0	0	0	1	10	9	0	0	0	0	20
Mean Precipitation (in.)	8.72	8.23	7.73	3.06	1.27	0.66	0.47	0.33	1.54	1.81	4.74	6.31	44.87
Days With ≥ 0.1" Precipitation	8	7	8	6	3	1	1	1	2	3	5	6	51
Days With ≥ 1.0" Precipitation	3	3	3	1	0	0	0	0	0	1	1	2	14
Mean Snowfall (in.)	51.6	48.4	51.0	19.9	5.7	0.6	0.0	0.0	0.2	2.8	21.4	35.9	237.5
Days With ≥ 1.0" Snow Depth	31	28	31	23	9	2	0	0	0	2	14	27	167

Lodi *San Joaquin County*   Elevation: 39 ft.   Latitude: 38° 07' N   Longitude: 121° 17' W

	JAN	FEB	MAR	APR	MAY	JUN	JUL	AUG	SEP	OCT	NOV	DEC	YEAR
Mean Maximum Temp. (°F)	54.6	61.9	66.7	73.4	81.1	87.3	91.2	90.2	87.2	78.6	64.3	54.7	74.3
Mean Temp. (°F)	46.1	*51.3*	54.6	59.2	65.5	70.6	73.8	73.0	70.3	63.0	52.6	45.5	*60.4*
Mean Minimum Temp. (°F)	37.6	40.1	42.5	44.9	49.8	53.9	56.5	55.7	53.3	47.3	40.9	36.1	46.5
Extreme Maximum Temp. (°F)	72	78	86	95	102	108	110	110	103	99	87	70	110
Extreme Minimum Temp. (°F)	21	18	22	32	32	39	43	41	39	30	25	13	13
Days Maximum Temp. ≥ 90°F	0	0	0	1	6	12	20	16	12	3	0	0	70
Days Maximum Temp. ≤ 32°F	0	0	0	0	0	0	0	0	0	0	0	0	0
Days Minimum Temp. ≤ 32°F	9	4	1	0	0	0	0	0	0	0	3	11	28
Days Minimum Temp. ≤ 0°F	0	0	0	0	0	0	0	0	0	0	0	0	0
Heating Degree Days (base 65°F)	579	*382*	315	183	68	10	1	1	11	101	366	599	*2,616*
Cooling Degree Days (base 65°F)	0	*0*	0	17	82	168	269	253	168	44	0	0	*1,001*
Mean Precipitation (in.)	3.62	3.24	3.12	1.12	0.54	0.13	0.07	0.06	0.35	1.01	2.52	2.72	18.50
Days With ≥ 0.1" Precipitation	7	7	7	3	1	1	0	0	1	2	5	6	40
Days With ≥ 1.0" Precipitation	1	1	0	0	0	0	0	0	0	0	1	1	4
Mean Snowfall (in.)	0.0	0.0	0.0	0.0	0.0	0.0	0.0	0.0	0.0	0.0	0.0	trace	trace
Days With ≥ 1.0" Snow Depth	0	0	0	0	0	0	0	0	0	0	0	0	0

Lompoc *Santa Barbara County*   Elevation: 95 ft.   Latitude: 34° 39' N   Longitude: 120° 27' W

	JAN	FEB	MAR	APR	MAY	JUN	JUL	AUG	SEP	OCT	NOV	DEC	YEAR
Mean Maximum Temp. (°F)	65.7	67.0	67.6	70.1	70.4	72.6	74.4	75.4	76.6	75.5	70.4	66.0	71.0
Mean Temp. (°F)	53.5	55.1	56.0	57.7	59.5	62.0	63.9	64.9	65.0	62.6	57.2	53.0	59.2
Mean Minimum Temp. (°F)	41.3	43.1	44.4	45.4	48.6	51.3	53.4	54.3	53.3	49.4	43.9	39.9	47.4
Extreme Maximum Temp. (°F)	86	89	96	105	98	100	101	96	106	110	98	85	110
Extreme Minimum Temp. (°F)	24	26	28	30	34	34	42	44	41	29	27	20	20
Days Maximum Temp. ≥ 90°F	0	0	0	1	0	1	0	0	1	1	0	0	4
Days Maximum Temp. ≤ 32°F	0	0	0	0	0	0	0	0	0	0	0	0	0
Days Minimum Temp. ≤ 32°F	2	1	1	0	0	0	0	0	0	0	1	3	8
Days Minimum Temp. ≤ 0°F	0	0	0	0	0	0	0	0	0	0	0	0	0
Heating Degree Days (base 65°F)	348	275	273	219	171	99	56	36	43	99	234	366	2,219
Cooling Degree Days (base 65°F)	0	2	2	11	10	16	39	53	55	37	7	1	233
Mean Precipitation (in.)	3.26	3.46	3.39	0.82	0.31	0.04	trace	0.05	0.24	0.41	1.43	2.33	15.74
Days With ≥ 0.1" Precipitation	6	5	6	2	1	0	0	0	0	1	3	4	28
Days With ≥ 1.0" Precipitation	1	1	1	0	0	0	0	0	0	0	0	1	4
Mean Snowfall (in.)	0.0	0.0	trace	0.0	0.0	0.0	0.0	0.0	0.0	0.0	0.0	0.0	trace
Days With ≥ 1.0" Snow Depth	0	0	0	0	0	0	0	0	0	0	0	0	0

Los Banos *Merced County*   Elevation: 118 ft.   Latitude: 37° 03' N   Longitude: 120° 52' W

	JAN	FEB	MAR	APR	MAY	JUN	JUL	AUG	SEP	OCT	NOV	DEC	YEAR
Mean Maximum Temp. (°F)	55.1	62.6	67.8	74.3	81.9	89.1	94.9	93.6	89.2	79.9	65.6	55.1	75.8
Mean Temp. (°F)	46.1	51.6	55.9	60.5	67.3	73.3	78.1	76.9	73.2	65.3	53.8	45.5	62.3
Mean Minimum Temp. (°F)	37.0	40.6	43.9	46.8	52.6	57.4	61.2	60.2	57.2	50.6	41.9	35.7	48.8
Extreme Maximum Temp. (°F)	75	79	86	97	105	106	110	110	106	99	83	71	110
Extreme Minimum Temp. (°F)	20	20	24	32	38	41	45	48	42	28	27	14	14
Days Maximum Temp. ≥ 90°F	0	0	0	1	7	15	25	23	15	4	0	0	90
Days Maximum Temp. ≤ 32°F	0	0	0	0	0	0	0	0	0	0	0	0	0
Days Minimum Temp. ≤ 32°F	9	3	1	0	0	0	0	0	0	0	2	10	25
Days Minimum Temp. ≤ 0°F	0	0	0	0	0	0	0	0	0	0	0	0	0
Heating Degree Days (base 65°F)	580	371	278	154	48	6	0	0	5	69	331	599	2,441
Cooling Degree Days (base 65°F)	0	0	2	36	128	257	417	388	266	89	1	0	1,584
Mean Precipitation (in.)	1.93	1.90	1.67	0.59	0.43	0.06	0.03	0.05	0.28	0.48	1.18	1.29	9.89
Days With ≥ 0.1" Precipitation	5	5	4	2	1	0	0	0	1	1	3	4	26
Days With ≥ 1.0" Precipitation	0	0	0	0	0	0	0	0	0	0	0	0	0
Mean Snowfall (in.)	0.0	trace	0.0	0.0	0.0	0.0	0.0	0.0	0.0	0.0	0.0	0.0	trace
Days With ≥ 1.0" Snow Depth	0	0	0	0	0	0	0	0	0	0	0	0	0

Los Banos Det. Reservation *Merced County*   Elevation: 406 ft.   Latitude: 37° 01' N   Longitude: 120° 56' W

	JAN	FEB	MAR	APR	MAY	JUN	JUL	AUG	SEP	OCT	NOV	DEC	YEAR
Mean Maximum Temp. (°F)	53.4	60.1	65.2	72.0	79.7	87.6	94.1	92.8	87.4	77.8	63.9	53.9	74.0
Mean Temp. (°F)	46.2	51.5	55.7	60.7	67.2	74.0	79.2	78.1	74.1	66.2	54.9	46.2	62.8
Mean Minimum Temp. (°F)	38.9	42.9	46.1	49.3	54.7	60.2	64.2	63.3	60.7	54.5	45.8	38.4	51.6
Extreme Maximum Temp. (°F)	73	76	86	95	105	109	110	109	107	98	81	70	110
Extreme Minimum Temp. (°F)	25	21	31	30	36	34	50	48	40	34	28	16	16
Days Maximum Temp. ≥ 90°F	0	0	0	0	5	13	23	21	13	3	0	0	78
Days Maximum Temp. ≤ 32°F	0	0	0	0	0	0	0	0	0	0	0	0	0
Days Minimum Temp. ≤ 32°F	4	1	0	0	0	0	0	0	0	0	0	5	10
Days Minimum Temp. ≤ 0°F	0	0	0	0	0	0	0	0	0	0	0	0	0
Heating Degree Days (base 65°F)	577	374	284	154	58	10	0	0	5	59	299	576	2,396
Cooling Degree Days (base 65°F)	0	0	2	39	132	275	446	420	285	103	2	0	1,704
Mean Precipitation (in.)	1.68	1.63	1.40	0.46	0.32	0.05	0.03	0.03	0.28	0.36	1.00	1.13	8.37
Days With ≥ 0.1" Precipitation	5	4	4	2	1	0	0	0	1	1	3	3	24
Days With ≥ 1.0" Precipitation	0	0	0	0	0	0	0	0	0	0	0	0	0
Mean Snowfall (in.)	0.0	0.0	0.0	0.0	0.0	0.0	0.0	0.0	0.0	0.0	0.0	0.0	0.0
Days With ≥ 1.0" Snow Depth	0	0	0	0	0	0	0	0	0	0	0	0	0

Los Gatos *Santa Clara County*   Elevation: 364 ft.   Latitude: 37° 14' N   Longitude: 121° 58' W

	JAN	FEB	MAR	APR	MAY	JUN	JUL	AUG	SEP	OCT	NOV	DEC	YEAR
Mean Maximum Temp. (°F)	58.6	62.6	65.5	70.6	76.1	81.7	85.6	84.9	82.7	75.7	64.8	57.9	72.2
Mean Temp. (°F)	48.6	51.7	54.1	57.2	61.8	66.5	70.0	69.6	67.8	62.0	53.6	47.9	59.2
Mean Minimum Temp. (°F)	38.5	40.7	42.5	43.6	47.4	51.2	54.4	54.3	52.9	48.4	42.4	37.9	46.2
Extreme Maximum Temp. (°F)	76	80	87	96	101	106	113	106	107	103	85	78	113
Extreme Minimum Temp. (°F)	23	22	28	31	35	37	37	39	38	31	29	16	16
Days Maximum Temp. ≥ 90°F	0	0	0	0	2	6	8	7	6	1	0	0	30
Days Maximum Temp. ≤ 32°F	0	0	0	0	0	0	0	0	0	0	0	0	0
Days Minimum Temp. ≤ 32°F	7	3	1	0	0	0	0	0	0	0	1	7	19
Days Minimum Temp. ≤ 0°F	0	0	0	0	0	0	0	0	0	0	0	0	0
Heating Degree Days (base 65°F)	501	369	333	235	129	40	7	4	18	117	336	522	2,611
Cooling Degree Days (base 65°F)	0	0	0	10	34	92	174	159	107	33	0	0	609
Mean Precipitation (in.)	5.16	4.62	3.98	1.16	0.45	0.10	0.04	0.08	0.24	0.97	2.72	3.58	23.10
Days With ≥ 0.1" Precipitation	7	6	7	3	1	0	0	0	1	2	5	6	38
Days With ≥ 1.0" Precipitation	2	2	1	0	0	0	0	0	0	0	1	1	7
Mean Snowfall (in.)	0.0	trace	0.0	0.0	0.0	0.0	0.0	0.0	0.0	0.0	0.0	trace	trace
Days With ≥ 1.0" Snow Depth	0	0	0	0	0	0	0	0	0	0	0	0	0

Madera *Madera County*   Elevation: 269 ft.   Latitude: 36° 57' N   Longitude: 120° 02' W

	JAN	FEB	MAR	APR	MAY	JUN	JUL	AUG	SEP	OCT	NOV	DEC	YEAR
Mean Maximum Temp. (°F)	54.2	61.5	66.6	74.1	83.3	91.0	96.8	95.3	89.9	80.1	65.2	54.3	76.0
Mean Temp. (°F)	45.4	50.2	54.7	60.0	67.7	74.3	79.4	78.1	73.1	64.1	52.5	44.5	62.0
Mean Minimum Temp. (°F)	36.6	38.8	42.8	45.7	52.0	57.7	62.0	60.8	56.2	48.0	39.8	34.8	47.9
Extreme Maximum Temp. (°F)	79	79	88	98	105	109	112	112	105	99	85	74	112
Extreme Minimum Temp. (°F)	17	21	27	31	35	38	45	39	40	28	23	18	17
Days Maximum Temp. ≥ 90°F	0	0	0	1	8	18	27	25	16	4	0	0	99
Days Maximum Temp. ≤ 32°F	0	0	0	0	0	0	0	0	0	0	0	0	0
Days Minimum Temp. ≤ 32°F	9	4	1	0	0	0	0	0	0	0	4	12	30
Days Minimum Temp. ≤ 0°F	0	0	0	0	0	0	0	0	0	0	0	0	0
Heating Degree Days (base 65°F)	600	412	314	170	47	7	0	0	7	93	368	627	2,645
Cooling Degree Days (base 65°F)	0	0	1	33	136	283	453	427	262	68	1	0	1,664
Mean Precipitation (in.)	2.18	1.93	2.31	0.96	0.43	0.10	trace	0.02	0.22	0.64	1.30	1.55	11.64
Days With ≥ 0.1" Precipitation	6	5	6	2	1	0	0	0	1	1	3	4	29
Days With ≥ 1.0" Precipitation	0	0	0	0	0	0	0	0	0	0	0	0	0
Mean Snowfall (in.)	0.0	trace	0.0	0.0	0.0	0.0	0.0	0.0	0.0	0.0	0.0	0.0	trace
Days With ≥ 1.0" Snow Depth	0	0	0	0	0	0	0	0	0	0	0	0	0

Manzanita Lake *Shasta County*   Elevation: 5,748 ft.   Latitude: 40° 32' N   Longitude: 121° 34' W

	JAN	FEB	MAR	APR	MAY	JUN	JUL	AUG	SEP	OCT	NOV	DEC	YEAR
Mean Maximum Temp. (°F)	42.5	43.6	46.0	51.5	60.9	69.7	78.0	77.3	71.4	60.8	47.0	42.1	57.6
Mean Temp. (°F)	31.9	32.5	35.0	39.5	47.5	55.1	61.5	60.5	55.6	47.1	36.6	31.8	44.5
Mean Minimum Temp. (°F)	21.2	21.4	23.9	27.4	34.1	40.4	44.9	43.6	39.7	33.4	26.1	21.4	31.5
Extreme Maximum Temp. (°F)	66	68	69	78	87	91	96	96	96	88	75	68	96
Extreme Minimum Temp. (°F)	-4	-7	-3	4	11	20	30	28	19	10	2	-13	-13
Days Maximum Temp. ≥ 90°F	0	0	0	0	0	0	1	1	0	0	0	0	2
Days Maximum Temp. ≤ 32°F	4	3	2	0	0	0	0	0	0	0	2	5	16
Days Minimum Temp. ≤ 32°F	29	27	28	24	14	4	1	1	4	14	25	29	200
Days Minimum Temp. ≤ 0°F	1	0	0	0	0	0	0	0	0	0	0	1	2
Heating Degree Days (base 65°F)	1,020	911	924	759	537	299	136	159	281	549	846	1,023	7,444
Cooling Degree Days (base 65°F)	0	0	0	0	1	6	31	27	7	1	0	0	73
Mean Precipitation (in.)	6.18	5.40	5.94	3.22	2.83	1.68	0.47	0.68	1.53	3.05	5.53	5.35	41.86
Days With ≥ 0.1" Precipitation	10	9	11	7	6	4	1	1	2	5	9	9	74
Days With ≥ 1.0" Precipitation	2	1	1	1	1	0	0	0	0	1	1	1	9
Mean Snowfall (in.)	32.4	33.6	33.2	18.9	7.2	1.3	trace	0.0	0.5	3.7	18.2	31.2	180.2
Days With ≥ 1.0" Snow Depth	29	26	27	16	4	0	0	0	0	2	13	26	143

Markley Cove *Napa County*   Elevation: 479 ft.   Latitude: 38° 30' N   Longitude: 122° 07' W

	JAN	FEB	MAR	APR	MAY	JUN	JUL	AUG	SEP	OCT	NOV	DEC	YEAR
Mean Maximum Temp. (°F)	55.1	59.9	64.0	70.1	78.3	86.5	93.1	92.1	87.7	77.9	63.8	55.6	73.7
Mean Temp. (°F)	45.5	49.1	52.3	56.7	63.5	70.3	75.2	74.1	70.6	62.8	52.4	45.7	59.9
Mean Minimum Temp. (°F)	35.8	38.2	40.7	43.2	48.6	54.0	57.3	56.1	53.5	47.6	41.0	35.7	46.0
Extreme Maximum Temp. (°F)	74	81	86	92	104	105	113	111	110	100	85	76	113
Extreme Minimum Temp. (°F)	20	19	27	30	34	39	45	47	42	35	26	13	13
Days Maximum Temp. ≥ 90°F	0	0	0	0	5	12	22	20	14	4	0	0	77
Days Maximum Temp. ≤ 32°F	0	0	0	0	0	0	0	0	0	0	0	0	0
Days Minimum Temp. ≤ 32°F	11	5	2	0	0	0	0	0	0	0	2	10	30
Days Minimum Temp. ≤ 0°F	0	0	0	0	0	0	0	0	0	0	0	0	0
Heating Degree Days (base 65°F)	597	442	386	250	108	21	2	2	15	110	371	592	2,896
Cooling Degree Days (base 65°F)	0	0	0	10	69	186	332	296	198	52	0	0	1,143
Mean Precipitation (in.)	5.86	5.54	4.66	1.36	0.74	0.12	0.03	0.07	0.34	1.26	3.48	4.53	27.99
Days With ≥ 0.1" Precipitation	8	7	7	3	2	0	0	0	1	2	5	6	41
Days With ≥ 1.0" Precipitation	2	2	1	0	0	0	0	0	0	0	1	1	7
Mean Snowfall (in.)	trace	0.0	trace	0.0	0.0	0.0	0.0	0.0	0.0	0.0	0.0	0.0	trace
Days With ≥ 1.0" Snow Depth	0	0	0	0	0	0	0	0	0	0	0	0	0

Martinez Water Plant *Contra Costa County*   Elevation: 39 ft.   Latitude: 38° 01' N   Longitude: 122° 07' W

	JAN	FEB	MAR	APR	MAY	JUN	JUL	AUG	SEP	OCT	NOV	DEC	YEAR
Mean Maximum Temp. (°F)	55.0	61.2	66.0	72.3	79.0	85.2	89.3	88.4	85.1	76.9	64.1	55.4	73.1
Mean Temp. (°F)	47.1	51.6	55.2	59.2	64.4	69.4	72.1	71.7	69.5	63.2	54.0	47.1	60.4
Mean Minimum Temp. (°F)	39.1	42.0	44.4	46.1	49.8	53.6	54.9	54.9	53.8	49.5	43.8	38.7	47.5
Extreme Maximum Temp. (°F)	71	80	88	98	104	110	115	107	108	103	82	74	115
Extreme Minimum Temp. (°F)	25	26	29	29	34	31	41	42	41	34	25	19	19
Days Maximum Temp. ≥ 90°F	0	0	0	1	4	9	15	13	9	2	0	0	53
Days Maximum Temp. ≤ 32°F	0	0	0	0	0	0	0	0	0	0	0	0	0
Days Minimum Temp. ≤ 32°F	4	1	0	0	0	0	0	0	0	0	1	5	11
Days Minimum Temp. ≤ 0°F	0	0	0	0	0	0	0	0	0	0	0	0	0
Heating Degree Days (base 65°F)	549	373	297	181	78	17	2	1	10	91	325	550	2,474
Cooling Degree Days (base 65°F)	0	0	1	19	65	156	227	214	147	42	1	0	872
Mean Precipitation (in.)	4.33	3.59	3.23	1.02	0.43	0.12	0.02	0.08	0.24	0.90	2.75	2.97	19.68
Days With ≥ 0.1" Precipitation	8	7	7	3	1	0	0	0	1	2	5	6	40
Days With ≥ 1.0" Precipitation	1	1	1	0	0	0	0	0	0	0	1	1	5
Mean Snowfall (in.)	trace	0.0	0.0	0.0	0.0	0.0	0.0	0.0	0.0	0.0	0.0	trace	trace
Days With ≥ 1.0" Snow Depth	0	0	0	0	0	0	0	0	0	0	0	0	0

Marysville *Yuba County*   Elevation: 55 ft.   Latitude: 39° 09' N   Longitude: 121° 35' W

	JAN	FEB	MAR	APR	MAY	JUN	JUL	AUG	SEP	OCT	NOV	DEC	YEAR
Mean Maximum Temp. (°F)	54.6	61.8	66.9	73.6	82.4	90.1	95.8	94.2	89.2	79.7	64.3	54.9	75.6
Mean Temp. (°F)	46.6	52.1	56.1	60.9	68.5	74.8	79.2	77.5	73.5	65.7	54.1	46.6	63.0
Mean Minimum Temp. (°F)	38.6	42.3	45.3	48.2	54.5	59.5	62.5	60.9	57.7	51.6	43.8	38.3	50.3
Extreme Maximum Temp. (°F)	73	83	89	95	105	107	111	111	107	101	84	73	111
Extreme Minimum Temp. (°F)	26	23	26	34	38	47	50	47	43	34	27	17	17
Days Maximum Temp. ≥ 90°F	0	0	0	1	7	16	25	23	16	4	0	0	92
Days Maximum Temp. ≤ 32°F	0	0	0	0	0	0	0	0	0	0	0	0	0
Days Minimum Temp. ≤ 32°F	5	1	0	0	0	0	0	0	0	0	1	5	12
Days Minimum Temp. ≤ 0°F	0	0	0	0	0	0	0	0	0	0	0	0	0
Heating Degree Days (base 65°F)	564	359	271	147	40	5	0	0	5	65	321	563	2,340
Cooling Degree Days (base 65°F)	0	0	3	39	153	305	455	413	279	97	1	0	1,745
Mean Precipitation (in.)	4.41	3.64	3.56	1.42	0.72	0.26	0.07	0.08	0.39	1.20	2.99	3.52	22.26
Days With ≥ 0.1" Precipitation	8	6	7	3	2	1	0	0	1	2	6	6	42
Days With ≥ 1.0" Precipitation	1	1	1	0	0	0	0	0	0	0	1	1	5
Mean Snowfall (in.)	trace	trace	trace	0.0	0.0	0.0	0.0	0.0	0.0	0.0	0.0	trace	trace
Days With ≥ 1.0" Snow Depth	0	0	0	0	0	0	0	0	0	0	0	0	0

McCloud *Siskiyou County*   Elevation: 3,277 ft.   Latitude: 41° 15' N   Longitude: 122° 08' W

	JAN	FEB	MAR	APR	MAY	JUN	JUL	AUG	SEP	OCT	NOV	DEC	YEAR
Mean Maximum Temp. (°F)	47.1	49.9	53.8	60.6	70.5	79.1	87.5	87.1	80.8	69.4	53.5	47.1	65.5
Mean Temp. (°F)	35.8	38.2	41.3	46.4	54.3	61.9	68.3	67.0	61.1	52.0	41.1	35.8	50.3
Mean Minimum Temp. (°F)	24.5	26.5	28.7	32.1	38.2	44.7	49.0	46.8	41.4	34.4	28.6	24.5	35.0
Extreme Maximum Temp. (°F)	69	79	84	90	100	102	106	107	105	96	82	71	107
Extreme Minimum Temp. (°F)	-1	-12	4	15	18	29	34	33	24	15	9	-9	-12
Days Maximum Temp. ≥ 90°F	0	0	0	0	1	5	14	13	6	1	0	0	40
Days Maximum Temp. ≤ 32°F	1	0	0	0	0	0	0	0	0	0	0	1	2
Days Minimum Temp. ≤ 32°F	27	24	24	17	6	1	0	0	1	12	23	28	163
Days Minimum Temp. ≤ 0°F	0	0	0	0	0	0	0	0	0	0	0	0	0
Heating Degree Days (base 65°F)	897	751	728	552	335	137	36	45	147	401	712	897	5,638
Cooling Degree Days (base 65°F)	0	0	0	0	14	52	144	116	40	5	0	0	371
Mean Precipitation (in.)	9.06	7.86	7.68	3.09	2.31	0.98	0.26	0.42	1.10	2.80	6.64	7.30	49.50
Days With ≥ 0.1" Precipitation	10	9	10	6	5	2	1	1	2	4	8	9	67
Days With ≥ 1.0" Precipitation	3	3	3	1	0	0	0	0	0	1	2	3	16
Mean Snowfall (in.)	15.0	14.3	10.2	1.8	trace	trace	0.0	0.0	0.0	0.2	5.5	17.5	64.5
Days With ≥ 1.0" Snow Depth	15	11	6	1	0	0	0	0	0	0	3	10	46

Mecca Fire Station *Riverside County*   Elevation: -177 ft.   Latitude: 33° 34' N   Longitude: 116° 05' W

	JAN	FEB	MAR	APR	MAY	JUN	JUL	AUG	SEP	OCT	NOV	DEC	YEAR
Mean Maximum Temp. (°F)	70.8	76.2	81.3	88.8	96.0	104.8	108.5	107.4	102.6	92.3	79.5	70.5	89.9
Mean Temp. (°F)	54.7	59.6	64.9	71.2	78.5	86.1	91.2	90.7	85.1	74.4	61.7	53.8	72.7
Mean Minimum Temp. (°F)	38.5	43.0	48.5	53.7	60.9	67.4	73.9	74.0	67.6	56.4	43.9	37.1	55.4
Extreme Maximum Temp. (°F)	89	100	103	110	115	126	125	123	121	117	100	90	126
Extreme Minimum Temp. (°F)	18	20	23	35	38	48	58	51	45	28	25	18	18
Days Maximum Temp. ≥ 90°F	0	1	5	14	25	29	31	31	29	20	2	0	187
Days Maximum Temp. ≤ 32°F	0	0	0	0	0	0	0	0	0	0	0	0	0
Days Minimum Temp. ≤ 32°F	6	2	0	0	0	0	0	0	0	0	1	7	16
Days Minimum Temp. ≤ 0°F	0	0	0	0	0	0	0	0	0	0	0	0	0
Heating Degree Days (base 65°F)	315	161	70	17	1	0	0	0	0	9	128	341	1,042
Cooling Degree Days (base 65°F)	1	20	75	238	443	637	824	823	625	325	40	1	4,052
Mean Precipitation (in.)	0.69	0.60	0.42	0.09	0.02	trace	0.13	0.24	0.42	0.24	0.21	0.32	3.38
Days With ≥ 0.1" Precipitation	2	1	1	0	0	0	0	0	1	1	0	1	7
Days With ≥ 1.0" Precipitation	0	0	0	0	0	0	0	0	0	0	0	0	0
Mean Snowfall (in.)	0.0	0.0	0.0	0.0	0.0	0.0	0.0	0.0	0.0	0.0	0.0	0.0	0.0
Days With ≥ 1.0" Snow Depth	0	0	0	0	0	0	0	0	0	0	0	0	0

Merced Municipal Airport *Merced County*   Elevation: 150 ft.   Latitude: 37° 17' N   Longitude: 120° 31' W

	JAN	FEB	MAR	APR	MAY	JUN	JUL	AUG	SEP	OCT	NOV	DEC	YEAR
Mean Maximum Temp. (°F)	55.1	62.7	67.8	75.3	83.7	91.3	96.8	95.1	90.6	81.2	65.8	55.1	76.7
Mean Temp. (°F)	46.0	51.0	55.0	60.0	67.3	73.8	78.8	77.2	73.0	64.5	53.1	45.3	62.1
Mean Minimum Temp. (°F)	36.9	39.3	42.1	44.6	50.9	56.3	60.8	59.1	55.3	47.7	40.4	35.4	47.4
Extreme Maximum Temp. (°F)	75	79	88	98	105	109	109	110	108	100	85	72	110
Extreme Minimum Temp. (°F)	18	20	26	22	30	37	42	35	35	28	25	15	15
Days Maximum Temp. ≥ 90°F	0	0	0	1	8	18	27	26	18	5	0	0	103
Days Maximum Temp. ≤ 32°F	0	0	0	0	0	0	0	0	0	0	0	0	0
Days Minimum Temp. ≤ 32°F	8	4	1	1	0	0	0	0	0	0	3	11	28
Days Minimum Temp. ≤ 0°F	0	0	0	0	0	0	0	0	0	0	0	0	0
Heating Degree Days (base 65°F)	581	389	305	167	49	5	0	0	5	80	350	604	2,535
Cooling Degree Days (base 65°F)	0	0	1	30	120	267	437	402	258	73	1	0	1,589
Mean Precipitation (in.)	2.44	2.31	2.28	0.83	0.47	0.10	0.03	0.02	0.19	0.62	1.51	1.70	12.50
Days With ≥ 0.1" Precipitation	6	6	5	3	1	0	0	0	1	2	4	4	32
Days With ≥ 1.0" Precipitation	0	0	0	0	0	0	0	0	0	0	0	0	0
Mean Snowfall (in.)	0.0	trace	0.0	0.0	0.0	0.0	0.0	0.0	0.0	0.0	0.0	0.0	trace
Days With ≥ 1.0" Snow Depth	0	0	0	0	0	0	0	0	0	0	0	0	0

Mineral *Tehama County*   Elevation: 4,872 ft.   Latitude: 40° 21' N   Longitude: 121° 36' W

	JAN	FEB	MAR	APR	MAY	JUN	JUL	AUG	SEP	OCT	NOV	DEC	YEAR
Mean Maximum Temp. (°F)	41.6	43.6	46.6	52.9	62.2	71.3	80.2	80.1	73.2	62.0	47.3	41.4	58.5
Mean Temp. (°F)	31.8	33.3	36.1	40.5	47.8	55.1	61.4	60.5	55.2	46.7	36.9	31.9	44.8
Mean Minimum Temp. (°F)	21.8	23.0	25.5	28.1	33.3	39.0	42.5	40.9	37.0	31.3	26.4	22.2	30.9
Extreme Maximum Temp. (°F)	61	65	70	77	85	92	99	100	98	87	72	61	100
Extreme Minimum Temp. (°F)	-5	-5	5	5	16	25	27	28	23	15	3	-9	-9
Days Maximum Temp. ≥ 90°F	0	0	0	0	0	0	3	3	1	0	0	0	7
Days Maximum Temp. ≤ 32°F	3	2	1	0	0	0	0	0	0	0	1	4	11
Days Minimum Temp. ≤ 32°F	29	27	28	24	15	4	1	1	6	19	26	29	209
Days Minimum Temp. ≤ 0°F	0	0	0	0	0	0	0	0	0	0	0	0	0
Heating Degree Days (base 65°F)	1,024	888	890	728	528	295	134	155	293	559	836	1,021	7,351
Cooling Degree Days (base 65°F)	0	0	0	0	0	4	27	20	5	0	0	0	56
Mean Precipitation (in.)	9.93	8.33	8.48	4.06	2.93	1.56	0.34	0.48	1.42	3.80	7.66	8.12	57.11
Days With ≥ 0.1" Precipitation	10	10	11	7	5	3	1	1	2	5	8	10	73
Days With ≥ 1.0" Precipitation	3	3	3	1	1	0	0	0	0	1	2	2	16
Mean Snowfall (in.)	29.8	29.3	29.4	11.8	2.5	0.2	0.0	0.0	0.1	1.6	10.6	26.6	141.9
Days With ≥ 1.0" Snow Depth	25	24	22	*11*	1	0	0	0	0	1	7	19	*110*

Mitchell Caverns *San Bernardino County*   Elevation: 4,347 ft.   Latitude: 34° 57' N   Longitude: 115° 33' W

	JAN	FEB	MAR	APR	MAY	JUN	JUL	AUG	SEP	OCT	NOV	DEC	YEAR
Mean Maximum Temp. (°F)	54.1	57.3	61.3	69.4	78.4	88.7	93.6	91.4	85.0	74.4	62.3	54.6	72.5
Mean Temp. (°F)	45.9	48.6	51.7	58.7	67.1	77.0	82.0	80.2	74.2	64.3	53.2	46.3	62.4
Mean Minimum Temp. (°F)	37.6	39.9	42.4	47.9	55.8	65.3	70.5	69.0	63.3	54.1	44.0	38.0	52.3
Extreme Maximum Temp. (°F)	77	81	83	89	98	106	110	106	100	97	83	75	110
Extreme Minimum Temp. (°F)	16	12	21	26	32	34	48	44	38	24	22	11	11
Days Maximum Temp. ≥ 90°F	0	0	0	0	2	15	24	20	8	1	0	0	70
Days Maximum Temp. ≤ 32°F	0	0	0	0	0	0	0	0	0	0	0	0	0
Days Minimum Temp. ≤ 32°F	6	4	2	1	0	0	0	0	0	0	3	7	23
Days Minimum Temp. ≤ 0°F	0	0	0	0	0	0	0	0	0	0	0	0	0
Heating Degree Days (base 65°F)	585	458	408	222	68	8	0	0	11	112	353	574	2,799
Cooling Degree Days (base 65°F)	0	1	4	43	137	363	512	482	284	91	5	0	1,922
Mean Precipitation (in.)	1.56	1.71	1.73	0.54	0.27	0.14	0.90	1.80	0.90	0.67	0.63	1.00	11.85
Days With ≥ 0.1" Precipitation	3	3	3	1	1	0	1	2	1	1	1	2	19
Days With ≥ 1.0" Precipitation	0	0	0	0	0	0	0	1	0	0	0	0	1
Mean Snowfall (in.)	*0.5*	0.3	0.7	0.2	trace	0.0	0.0	0.0	0.0	trace	0.1	0.7	*2.5*
Days With ≥ 1.0" Snow Depth	1	0	0	0	0	0	0	0	0	0	0	0	1

Modesto *Stanislaus County*   Elevation: 88 ft.   Latitude: 37° 39' N   Longitude: 121° 00' W

	JAN	FEB	MAR	APR	MAY	JUN	JUL	AUG	SEP	OCT	NOV	DEC	YEAR
Mean Maximum Temp. (°F)	54.3	62.4	67.7	74.1	81.7	88.6	93.9	92.2	88.0	78.4	64.3	54.2	75.0
Mean Temp. (°F)	46.8	52.5	56.5	61.1	67.4	73.3	77.6	76.5	72.9	65.0	54.0	46.2	62.5
Mean Minimum Temp. (°F)	39.3	42.6	45.3	48.1	53.1	58.0	61.4	60.6	57.8	51.5	43.7	38.1	49.9
Extreme Maximum Temp. (°F)	75	80	87	100	105	109	111	108	105	101	88	75	111
Extreme Minimum Temp. (°F)	25	24	27	35	39	43	51	49	44	33	28	19	19
Days Maximum Temp. ≥ 90°F	0	0	0	1	7	14	23	20	13	3	0	0	81
Days Maximum Temp. ≤ 32°F	0	0	0	0	0	0	0	0	0	0	0	0	0
Days Minimum Temp. ≤ 32°F	5	1	0	0	0	0	0	0	0	0	1	6	13
Days Minimum Temp. ≤ 0°F	0	0	0	0	0	0	0	0	0	0	0	0	0
Heating Degree Days (base 65°F)	557	346	259	139	47	6	0	0	4	73	325	576	2,332
Cooling Degree Days (base 65°F)	0	0	4	40	130	261	406	378	257	85	2	0	1,563
Mean Precipitation (in.)	2.57	2.21	2.36	0.85	0.52	0.09	0.05	0.06	0.27	0.74	1.65	1.75	13.12
Days With ≥ 0.1" Precipitation	6	6	6	3	1	0	0	0	1	2	4	4	33
Days With ≥ 1.0" Precipitation	0	0	0	0	0	0	0	0	0	0	0	0	0
Mean Snowfall (in.)	0.0	trace	trace	0.0	0.0	0.0	0.0	0.0	0.0	0.0	0.0	trace	trace
Days With ≥ 1.0" Snow Depth	0	0	0	0	0	0	0	0	0	0	0	0	0

Mojave *Kern County*   Elevation: 2,732 ft.   Latitude: 35° 03' N   Longitude: 118° 10' W

	JAN	FEB	MAR	APR	MAY	JUN	JUL	AUG	SEP	OCT	NOV	DEC	YEAR
Mean Maximum Temp. (°F)	57.4	61.7	65.3	71.6	80.0	89.9	97.0	96.0	89.2	78.4	65.1	57.3	75.7
Mean Temp. (°F)	45.5	49.2	53.2	58.9	67.1	76.5	82.8	81.5	74.7	64.0	52.3	45.0	62.6
Mean Minimum Temp. (°F)	33.3	36.8	40.9	46.0	54.2	63.0	68.6	67.0	60.2	49.6	39.4	32.6	49.3
Extreme Maximum Temp. (°F)	78	90	87	94	101	112	111	110	107	100	83	79	112
Extreme Minimum Temp. (°F)	11	16	5	27	34	40	43	42	38	22	13	8	5
Days Maximum Temp. ≥ 90°F	0	0	0	1	5	17	28	27	16	3	0	0	97
Days Maximum Temp. ≤ 32°F	0	0	0	0	0	0	0	0	0	0	0	0	0
Days Minimum Temp. ≤ 32°F	14	8	3	1	0	0	0	0	0	0	5	16	47
Days Minimum Temp. ≤ 0°F	0	0	0	0	0	0	0	0	0	0	0	0	0
Heating Degree Days (base 65°F)	598	440	363	207	73	9	0	0	9	104	376	614	2,793
Cooling Degree Days (base 65°F)	0	0	3	44	148	357	550	535	320	89	2	0	2,048
Mean Precipitation (in.)	1.34	1.47	1.14	0.22	0.14	0.05	0.18	0.27	0.28	0.27	0.52	0.86	6.74
Days With ≥ 0.1" Precipitation	3	3	3	1	0	0	0	0	1	1	1	2	15
Days With ≥ 1.0" Precipitation	0	0	0	0	0	0	0	0	0	0	0	0	0
Mean Snowfall (in.)	0.5	0.1	0.1	trace	0.0	0.0	0.0	0.0	0.0	0.0	0.0	0.3	1.0
Days With ≥ 1.0" Snow Depth	0	0	0	0	0	0	0	0	0	0	0	0	0

Monterey *Monterey County*   Elevation: 383 ft.   Latitude: 36° 36' N   Longitude: 121° 54' W

	JAN	FEB	MAR	APR	MAY	JUN	JUL	AUG	SEP	OCT	NOV	DEC	YEAR
Mean Maximum Temp. (°F)	60.1	61.7	62.2	64.1	64.9	67.1	68.6	69.8	71.8	70.3	64.7	59.9	65.4
Mean Temp. (°F)	52.1	53.4	54.0	55.2	56.6	58.7	60.5	61.6	62.6	60.7	55.9	51.7	56.9
Mean Minimum Temp. (°F)	43.9	45.0	45.7	46.1	48.2	50.4	52.4	53.4	53.3	51.1	47.2	43.6	48.4
Extreme Maximum Temp. (°F)	80	86	84	93	95	100	97	96	101	104	91	85	104
Extreme Minimum Temp. (°F)	29	26	32	35	40	43	46	48	44	37	35	20	20
Days Maximum Temp. ≥ 90°F	0	0	0	0	0	0	0	0	1	1	0	0	2
Days Maximum Temp. ≤ 32°F	0	0	0	0	0	0	0	0	0	0	0	0	0
Days Minimum Temp. ≤ 32°F	0	0	0	0	0	0	0	0	0	0	0	1	1
Days Minimum Temp. ≤ 0°F	0	0	0	0	0	0	0	0	0	0	0	0	0
Heating Degree Days (base 65°F)	394	322	336	294	260	189	141	108	93	148	269	404	2,958
Cooling Degree Days (base 65°F)	0	1	1	7	5	8	12	11	21	27	5	0	98
Mean Precipitation (in.)	4.16	3.55	3.56	1.46	0.47	0.21	0.09	0.11	0.27	0.93	2.61	2.89	20.31
Days With ≥ 0.1" Precipitation	7	7	7	3	1	1	0	0	1	2	5	6	40
Days With ≥ 1.0" Precipitation	1	1	1	0	0	0	0	0	0	0	0	0	3
Mean Snowfall (in.)	trace	trace	trace	0.0	0.0	0.0	0.0	0.0	0.0	0.0	0.0	trace	trace
Days With ≥ 1.0" Snow Depth	0	0	0	0	0	0	0	0	0	0	0	0	0

Morro Bay Fire Dept. *San Luis Obispo County*   Elevation: 114 ft.   Latitude: 35° 22' N   Longitude: 120° 51' W

	JAN	FEB	MAR	APR	MAY	JUN	JUL	AUG	SEP	OCT	NOV	DEC	YEAR
Mean Maximum Temp. (°F)	62.3	63.1	63.0	63.8	63.2	64.4	65.5	66.4	68.3	69.0	66.6	62.6	64.9
Mean Temp. (°F)	52.3	53.5	53.8	54.4	55.3	57.2	58.8	59.7	60.3	59.5	56.3	52.2	56.1
Mean Minimum Temp. (°F)	42.2	43.8	44.4	44.8	47.5	50.1	52.1	53.0	52.3	50.0	45.9	41.7	47.3
Extreme Maximum Temp. (°F)	89	87	92	100	98	101	89	87	102	98	90	81	102
Extreme Minimum Temp. (°F)	23	25	30	33	33	39	35	40	41	37	31	22	22
Days Maximum Temp. ≥ 90°F	0	0	0	0	0	0	0	0	1	0	0	0	1
Days Maximum Temp. ≤ 32°F	0	0	0	0	0	0	0	0	0	0	0	0	0
Days Minimum Temp. ≤ 32°F	2	1	0	0	0	0	0	0	0	0	0	2	5
Days Minimum Temp. ≤ 0°F	0	0	0	0	0	0	0	0	0	0	0	0	0
Heating Degree Days (base 65°F)	388	320	343	315	296	232	187	160	153	179	260	391	3,224
Cooling Degree Days (base 65°F)	0	1	2	5	3	3	2	5	16	17	5	0	59
Mean Precipitation (in.)	3.50	3.39	3.70	1.04	0.33	0.06	0.03	0.09	0.37	0.65	1.69	2.67	17.52
Days With ≥ 0.1" Precipitation	6	6	6	3	1	0	0	0	1	2	4	5	34
Days With ≥ 1.0" Precipitation	1	1	1	0	0	0	0	0	0	0	0	1	4
Mean Snowfall (in.)	0.0	0.0	0.0	0.0	0.0	0.0	0.0	0.0	0.0	0.0	0.0	trace	trace
Days With ≥ 1.0" Snow Depth	0	0	0	0	0	0	0	0	0	0	0	0	0

Mount Diablo Junction *Contra Costa County*   Elevation: 2,168 ft.   Latitude: 37° 52' N   Longitude: 121° 56' W

	JAN	FEB	MAR	APR	MAY	JUN	JUL	AUG	SEP	OCT	NOV	DEC	YEAR
Mean Maximum Temp. (°F)	55.6	57.4	59.1	64.6	70.9	78.6	85.6	85.4	82.4	74.4	61.9	55.9	69.3
Mean Temp. (°F)	47.5	49.0	50.0	53.8	59.2	65.8	72.7	72.6	70.0	63.1	52.9	47.8	58.7
Mean Minimum Temp. (°F)	39.3	40.6	40.7	43.0	47.4	53.1	59.8	59.7	57.5	51.8	43.9	39.6	48.0
Extreme Maximum Temp. (°F)	77	80	84	89	102	101	111	107	107	100	89	77	111
Extreme Minimum Temp. (°F)	23	14	25	28	31	37	42	42	40	31	26	14	14
Days Maximum Temp. ≥ 90°F	0	0	0	0	1	5	11	11	7	2	0	0	37
Days Maximum Temp. ≤ 32°F	0	0	0	0	0	0	0	0	0	0	0	0	0
Days Minimum Temp. ≤ 32°F	4	3	3	1	0	0	0	0	0	0	1	4	16
Days Minimum Temp. ≤ 0°F	0	0	0	0	0	0	0	0	0	0	0	0	0
Heating Degree Days (base 65°F)	536	446	460	336	223	95	24	20	40	135	362	528	3,205
Cooling Degree Days (base 65°F)	0	0	0	10	42	109	247	250	186	75	5	0	924
Mean Precipitation (in.)	4.82	4.25	3.93	1.40	0.79	0.16	0.05	0.09	0.35	1.24	3.65	3.56	24.29
Days With ≥ 0.1" Precipitation	8	7	8	4	2	0	0	0	1	2	6	6	44
Days With ≥ 1.0" Precipitation	1	1	1	0	0	0	0	0	0	0	1	1	5
Mean Snowfall (in.)	0.4	trace	0.4	0.6	0.0	0.0	0.0	0.0	0.0	0.0	trace	0.1	1.5
Days With ≥ 1.0" Snow Depth	0	0	0	0	0	0	0	0	0	0	0	0	0

Mount Hamilton *Santa Clara County*   Elevation: 4,202 ft.   Latitude: 37° 20' N   Longitude: 121° 39' W

	JAN	FEB	MAR	APR	MAY	JUN	JUL	AUG	SEP	OCT	NOV	DEC	YEAR
Mean Maximum Temp. (°F)	49.4	49.8	50.5	55.6	63.6	72.0	78.4	77.9	73.8	65.5	54.2	49.4	61.7
Mean Temp. (°F)	43.5	43.5	43.8	47.7	55.2	63.5	70.9	70.3	66.0	58.2	47.7	43.3	54.5
Mean Minimum Temp. (°F)	37.5	37.2	37.0	39.7	46.7	55.0	63.3	62.7	58.2	50.8	41.2	37.2	47.2
Extreme Maximum Temp. (°F)	73	72	74	84	91	94	100	103	98	93	81	76	103
Extreme Minimum Temp. (°F)	18	17	18	21	26	31	38	40	35	20	21	7	7
Days Maximum Temp. ≥ 90°F	0	0	0	0	0	0	2	2	1	0	0	0	5
Days Maximum Temp. ≤ 32°F	1	1	0	0	0	0	0	0	0	0	0	1	3
Days Minimum Temp. ≤ 32°F	9	8	10	7	2	0	0	0	0	1	4	9	50
Days Minimum Temp. ≤ 0°F	0	0	0	0	0	0	0	0	0	0	0	0	0
Heating Degree Days (base 65°F)	661	599	651	516	325	133	30	36	93	249	513	665	4,471
Cooling Degree Days (base 65°F)	0	0	0	4	22	85	212	210	130	44	1	0	708
Mean Precipitation (in.)	4.41	3.80	3.85	1.75	0.91	0.23	0.05	0.09	0.42	1.41	3.32	3.27	23.51
Days With ≥ 0.1" Precipitation	8	7	8	5	2	1	0	0	1	2	6	7	47
Days With ≥ 1.0" Precipitation	1	1	1	0	0	0	0	0	0	0	1	1	5
Mean Snowfall (in.)	*3.8*	3.5	4.1	1.4	trace	trace	0.0	0.0	0.0	trace	0.2	*1.4*	*14.4*
Days With ≥ 1.0" Snow Depth	1	1	2	1	0	0	0	0	0	0	0	2	7

Mount Shasta *Siskiyou County*   Elevation: 3,533 ft.   Latitude: 41° 20' N   Longitude: 122° 20' W

	JAN	FEB	MAR	APR	MAY	JUN	JUL	AUG	SEP	OCT	NOV	DEC	YEAR
Mean Maximum Temp. (°F)	43.7	47.8	52.1	58.8	67.7	75.9	84.4	83.3	76.3	65.0	50.2	43.4	62.4
Mean Temp. (°F)	35.0	38.1	41.2	46.1	53.6	60.8	67.3	65.9	59.9	50.9	40.3	34.6	49.5
Mean Minimum Temp. (°F)	26.2	28.3	30.2	33.3	39.5	45.8	50.1	48.4	43.4	36.8	30.4	25.8	36.5
Extreme Maximum Temp. (°F)	64	70	76	86	94	96	100	105	97	93	77	66	105
Extreme Minimum Temp. (°F)	0	-3	13	19	23	28	32	34	28	20	6	-13	-13
Days Maximum Temp. ≥ 90°F	0	0	0	0	0	2	8	7	2	0	0	0	19
Days Maximum Temp. ≤ 32°F	2	0	0	0	0	0	0	0	0	0	0	2	4
Days Minimum Temp. ≤ 32°F	24	21	21	15	4	0	0	0	1	8	19	25	138
Days Minimum Temp. ≤ 0°F	0	0	0	0	0	0	0	0	0	0	0	0	0
Heating Degree Days (base 65°F)	925	755	733	561	353	157	40	56	172	431	735	935	5,853
Cooling Degree Days (base 65°F)	0	0	0	0	5	32	105	80	23	2	*0*	*0*	*247*
Mean Precipitation (in.)	7.32	5.80	5.86	2.56	1.88	1.02	0.34	0.43	0.88	2.20	5.40	5.69	39.38
Days With ≥ 0.1" Precipitation	9	8	9	5	4	3	1	1	2	4	8	8	62
Days With ≥ 1.0" Precipitation	2	2	2	1	0	0	0	0	0	1	2	2	11
Mean Snowfall (in.)	17.9	17.8	12.3	4.7	0.5	trace	0.0	0.0	0.0	0.5	9.4	21.7	84.8
Days With ≥ 1.0" Snow Depth	13	10	5	1	0	0	0	0	0	0	3	11	43

Mount Wilson 2 *Los Angeles County* Elevation: 5,708 ft. Latitude: 34° 14' N Longitude: 118° 04' W

	JAN	FEB	MAR	APR	MAY	JUN	JUL	AUG	SEP	OCT	NOV	DEC	YEAR
Mean Maximum Temp. (°F)	52.6	53.4	54.8	59.9	67.2	76.6	82.0	81.3	77.0	68.5	59.4	53.1	65.5
Mean Temp. (°F)	45.0	45.4	46.3	50.7	57.6	67.0	72.7	72.2	67.9	59.9	51.3	45.5	56.8
Mean Minimum Temp. (°F)	37.4	37.4	37.8	41.1	47.9	57.3	63.4	62.9	58.7	51.4	43.2	37.8	48.0
Extreme Maximum Temp. (°F)	74	80	79	86	91	97	99	97	94	93	82	76	99
Extreme Minimum Temp. (°F)	11	13	14	18	23	31	38	42	35	18	15	10	10
Days Maximum Temp. ≥ 90°F	0	0	0	0	0	1	3	3	1	0	0	0	8
Days Maximum Temp. ≤ 32°F	1	0	0	0	0	0	0	0	0	0	0	1	2
Days Minimum Temp. ≤ 32°F	9	9	10	7	2	0	0	0	0	1	4	9	51
Days Minimum Temp. ≤ 0°F	0	0	0	0	0	0	0	0	0	0	0	0	0
Heating Degree Days (base 65°F)	612	547	573	430	258	74	8	13	54	204	411	598	3,782
Cooling Degree Days (base 65°F)	0	0	1	9	33	131	255	256	155	54	6	0	900
Mean Precipitation (in.)	8.12	9.46	8.49	2.21	0.96	0.27	0.08	0.29	1.00	1.51	3.66	5.22	41.27
Days With ≥ 0.1" Precipitation	6	5	6	3	2	1	0	1	1	2	3	5	35
Days With ≥ 1.0" Precipitation	2	3	3	1	0	0	0	0	0	1	1	2	13
Mean Snowfall (in.)	na	na	na	na	0.3	0.0	0.0	0.0	0.0	trace	*0.8*	na	na
Days With ≥ 1.0" Snow Depth	*8*	5	6	3	0	0	0	0	0	0	1	*4*	*27*

Mountain Pass *San Bernardino County* Elevation: 4,727 ft. Latitude: 35° 28' N Longitude: 115° 33' W

	JAN	FEB	MAR	APR	MAY	JUN	JUL	AUG	SEP	OCT	NOV	DEC	YEAR
Mean Maximum Temp. (°F)	na	na	59.4	66.8	na	na	na	na	na	na	na	na	na
Mean Temp. (°F)	na	na	47.5	*53.6*	na	na	na	na	na	na	na	na	na
Mean Minimum Temp. (°F)	na	*31.7*	35.5	*40.4*	na	na	na	na	na	na	na	na	na
Extreme Maximum Temp. (°F)	71	79	88	90	98	104	108	107	*102*	96	80	70	*108*
Extreme Minimum Temp. (°F)	3	4	12	19	20	32	46	44	35	20	8	-2	-2
Days Maximum Temp. ≥ 90°F	0	0	0	0	1	*11*	19	17	6	1	0	0	*55*
Days Maximum Temp. ≤ 32°F	1	0	0	0	0	0	0	0	0	0	0	1	2
Days Minimum Temp. ≤ 32°F	17	12	10	4	1	0	0	0	0	1	7	18	70
Days Minimum Temp. ≤ 0°F	0	0	0	0	0	0	0	0	0	0	0	0	0
Heating Degree Days (base 65°F)	na	na	537	*345*	na	na	na	na	na	na	na	na	na
Cooling Degree Days (base 65°F)	na	na	1	*17*	na	na	na	na	na	na	na	na	na
Mean Precipitation (in.)	1.03	1.07	1.12	0.40	0.34	0.27	1.07	1.12	0.71	0.41	0.67	0.72	8.93
Days With ≥ 0.1" Precipitation	2	2	3	1	1	0	2	2	*1*	1	1	1	*17*
Days With ≥ 1.0" Precipitation	0	0	0	0	0	0	0	0	0	0	0	0	0
Mean Snowfall (in.)	2.4	2.7	1.9	0.7	trace	0.0	0.0	0.0	0.0	0.1	*0.4*	1.8	*10.0*
Days With ≥ 1.0" Snow Depth	2	1	1	0	0	0	0	0	0	0	1	1	6

Napa State Hospital *Napa County* Elevation: 32 ft. Latitude: 38° 17' N Longitude: 122° 16' W

	JAN	FEB	MAR	APR	MAY	JUN	JUL	AUG	SEP	OCT	NOV	DEC	YEAR
Mean Maximum Temp. (°F)	57.6	62.6	65.9	71.0	75.8	80.6	82.9	82.6	82.4	77.1	65.2	57.6	71.8
Mean Temp. (°F)	48.4	52.2	54.5	57.7	62.3	66.6	68.7	68.5	67.7	63.0	54.2	48.1	59.3
Mean Minimum Temp. (°F)	39.2	41.6	43.1	44.4	48.6	52.5	54.5	54.4	53.0	48.8	43.2	38.5	46.8
Extreme Maximum Temp. (°F)	79	80	87	95	103	109	112	106	108	106	87	76	112
Extreme Minimum Temp. (°F)	24	25	28	31	30	38	43	41	40	32	27	14	14
Days Maximum Temp. ≥ 90°F	0	0	0	0	3	5	5	5	7	3	0	0	28
Days Maximum Temp. ≤ 32°F	0	0	0	0	0	0	0	0	0	0	0	0	0
Days Minimum Temp. ≤ 32°F	7	2	1	0	0	0	0	0	0	0	1	7	18
Days Minimum Temp. ≤ 0°F	0	0	0	0	0	0	0	0	0	0	0	0	0
Heating Degree Days (base 65°F)	508	357	319	221	120	38	8	8	19	98	319	518	2,533
Cooling Degree Days (base 65°F)	0	1	0	12	38	93	133	134	105	45	3	0	563
Mean Precipitation (in.)	5.63	4.76	4.06	1.40	0.73	0.17	0.05	0.11	0.41	1.41	3.91	4.13	26.77
Days With ≥ 0.1" Precipitation	8	7	8	3	1	1	0	0	1	2	6	7	43
Days With ≥ 1.0" Precipitation	2	1	1	0	0	0	0	0	0	0	1	1	6
Mean Snowfall (in.)	trace	0.0	trace	0.0	0.0	0.0	0.0	0.0	0.0	0.0	trace	trace
Days With ≥ 1.0" Snow Depth	0	0	0	0	0	0	0	0	0	0	0	0	0

Needles Airport *San Bernardino County* Elevation: 912 ft. Latitude: 34° 46' N Longitude: 114° 37' W

	JAN	FEB	MAR	APR	MAY	JUN	JUL	AUG	SEP	OCT	NOV	DEC	YEAR
Mean Maximum Temp. (°F)	64.4	70.6	76.9	84.6	93.8	104.2	108.7	106.6	100.2	87.9	73.7	64.3	86.3
Mean Temp. (°F)	53.3	58.5	63.9	70.9	80.2	90.1	96.1	94.1	87.1	74.5	61.6	53.3	73.6
Mean Minimum Temp. (°F)	42.3	46.3	50.8	57.1	66.6	76.1	83.4	81.5	73.9	61.1	49.4	42.2	60.9
Extreme Maximum Temp. (°F)	85	92	97	104	113	121	121	121	115	109	92	83	121
Extreme Minimum Temp. (°F)	23	24	32	40	46	53	57	66	52	34	31	13	13
Days Maximum Temp. ≥ 90°F	0	0	2	10	23	29	31	30	27	14	0	0	166
Days Maximum Temp. ≤ 32°F	0	0	0	0	0	0	0	0	0	0	0	0	0
Days Minimum Temp. ≤ 32°F	2	0	0	0	0	0	0	0	0	0	0	2	4
Days Minimum Temp. ≤ 0°F	0	0	0	0	0	0	0	0	0	0	0	0	0
Heating Degree Days (base 65°F)	355	190	99	28	1	0	0	0	0	14	135	357	1,179
Cooling Degree Days (base 65°F)	0	15	78	238	490	756	965	929	682	328	46	1	4,528
Mean Precipitation (in.)	0.74	0.65	0.65	0.23	0.11	0.03	0.34	0.76	0.60	0.29	0.35	0.46	5.21
Days With ≥ 0.1" Precipitation	2	2	2	1	0	0	1	1	1	1	1	1	13
Days With ≥ 1.0" Precipitation	0	0	0	0	0	0	0	0	0	0	0	0	0
Mean Snowfall (in.)	trace	trace	trace	0.0	0.0	0.0	0.0	0.0	trace	trace	0.0	0.0	trace
Days With ≥ 1.0" Snow Depth	0	0	0	0	0	0	0	0	0	0	0	0	0

Nevada City *Nevada County*   Elevation: 2,778 ft.   Latitude: 39° 15' N   Longitude: 121° 00' W

	JAN	FEB	MAR	APR	MAY	JUN	JUL	AUG	SEP	OCT	NOV	DEC	YEAR
Mean Maximum Temp. (°F)	50.7	53.5	56.1	62.4	70.6	79.5	86.8	86.1	80.2	70.2	56.4	49.9	66.9
Mean Temp. (°F)	41.4	43.5	45.7	50.2	57.5	65.2	71.4	70.5	65.2	57.2	46.4	41.0	54.6
Mean Minimum Temp. (°F)	32.1	33.4	35.3	38.1	44.3	50.8	56.0	54.8	50.3	44.0	36.5	32.1	42.3
Extreme Maximum Temp. (°F)	72	77	78	89	97	99	106	104	100	95	83	76	106
Extreme Minimum Temp. (°F)	11	13	18	23	28	32	37	37	31	20	19	-1	-1
Days Maximum Temp. ≥ 90°F	0	0	0	0	0	4	12	11	3	1	0	0	31
Days Maximum Temp. ≤ 32°F	0	0	0	0	0	0	0	0	0	0	0	0	0
Days Minimum Temp. ≤ 32°F	17	13	11	7	1	0	0	0	0	2	9	16	76
Days Minimum Temp. ≤ 0°F	0	0	0	0	0	0	0	0	0	0	0	0	0
Heating Degree Days (base 65°F)	724	601	590	438	249	81	12	17	81	261	550	736	4,340
Cooling Degree Days (base 65°F)	0	0	0	3	27	95	228	220	116	33	0	0	722
Mean Precipitation (in.)	11.40	9.97	9.45	4.04	2.14	0.70	0.19	0.28	1.14	2.77	8.15	9.16	59.39
Days With ≥ 0.1" Precipitation	10	9	10	6	4	2	0	1	2	4	8	9	65
Days With ≥ 1.0" Precipitation	4	4	3	1	1	0	0	0	0	1	3	3	20
Mean Snowfall (in.)	3.8	3.8	3.4	0.8	trace	0.0	0.0	0.0	0.0	trace	0.9	4.1	16.8
Days With ≥ 1.0" Snow Depth	*4*	3	2	1	0	0	0	0	0	0	0	3	*13*

Newark *Alameda County*   Elevation: 9 ft.   Latitude: 37° 31' N   Longitude: 122° 02' W

	JAN	FEB	MAR	APR	MAY	JUN	JUL	AUG	SEP	OCT	NOV	DEC	YEAR
Mean Maximum Temp. (°F)	57.6	61.2	63.8	67.1	70.4	74.3	76.8	77.0	76.9	72.8	64.3	57.5	68.3
Mean Temp. (°F)	49.8	53.1	55.6	58.3	61.7	65.2	67.2	67.6	67.2	63.3	55.8	49.6	59.5
Mean Minimum Temp. (°F)	42.0	45.0	47.3	49.6	52.9	55.9	57.6	58.2	57.4	53.7	47.2	41.6	50.7
Extreme Maximum Temp. (°F)	71	78	82	92	98	102	105	102	103	96	80	72	105
Extreme Minimum Temp. (°F)	28	27	34	33	42	46	49	48	41	38	30	21	21
Days Maximum Temp. ≥ 90°F	0	0	0	0	1	2	2	2	2	1	0	0	10
Days Maximum Temp. ≤ 32°F	0	0	0	0	0	0	0	0	0	0	0	0	0
Days Minimum Temp. ≤ 32°F	1	0	0	0	0	0	0	0	0	0	0	2	3
Days Minimum Temp. ≤ 0°F	0	0	0	0	0	0	0	0	0	0	0	0	0
Heating Degree Days (base 65°F)	465	330	286	204	129	52	17	10	21	86	272	471	2,343
Cooling Degree Days (base 65°F)	0	0	1	16	31	67	101	107	93	44	1	0	461
Mean Precipitation (in.)	2.99	2.72	2.38	0.92	0.40	0.12	0.03	0.06	0.20	0.85	2.02	2.22	14.91
Days With ≥ 0.1" Precipitation	7	6	6	3	1	0	0	0	1	2	5	5	36
Days With ≥ 1.0" Precipitation	0	0	0	0	0	0	0	0	0	0	0	0	0
Mean Snowfall (in.)	0.0	0.0	0.0	0.0	0.0	0.0	0.0	0.0	0.0	0.0	0.0	trace	trace
Days With ≥ 1.0" Snow Depth	0	0	0	0	0	0	0	0	0	0	0	0	0

Newport Beach *Orange County*   Elevation: 9 ft.   Latitude: 33° 36' N   Longitude: 117° 53' W

	JAN	FEB	MAR	APR	MAY	JUN	JUL	AUG	SEP	OCT	NOV	DEC	YEAR
Mean Maximum Temp. (°F)	63.6	63.7	63.5	65.4	66.5	68.9	71.7	73.0	73.0	71.3	67.8	64.5	67.7
Mean Temp. (°F)	55.9	56.7	57.3	59.3	61.8	64.5	67.3	68.6	68.0	65.0	60.0	56.2	61.7
Mean Minimum Temp. (°F)	48.1	49.5	51.0	53.2	57.0	60.0	63.0	64.2	63.0	58.7	52.2	47.8	55.6
Extreme Maximum Temp. (°F)	87	86	86	98	86	102	88	94	98	95	89	94	102
Extreme Minimum Temp. (°F)	30	31	37	38	40	51	56	55	52	32	38	32	30
Days Maximum Temp. ≥ 90°F	0	0	0	0	0	0	0	0	1	0	0	0	1
Days Maximum Temp. ≤ 32°F	0	0	0	0	0	0	0	0	0	0	0	0	0
Days Minimum Temp. ≤ 32°F	0	0	0	0	0	0	0	0	0	0	0	0	0
Days Minimum Temp. ≤ 0°F	0	0	0	0	0	0	0	0	0	0	0	0	0
Heating Degree Days (base 65°F)	279	232	233	169	103	39	5	2	7	40	152	269	1,530
Cooling Degree Days (base 65°F)	3	3	1	8	11	30	92	126	104	53	10	3	444
Mean Precipitation (in.)	2.65	2.53	2.29	0.68	0.18	0.08	0.02	0.08	0.31	0.24	1.11	1.70	11.87
Days With ≥ 0.1" Precipitation	5	4	4	2	0	0	0	0	1	1	2	3	22
Days With ≥ 1.0" Precipitation	1	1	1	0	0	0	0	0	0	0	0	0	3
Mean Snowfall (in.)	0.0	0.0	0.0	0.0	0.0	0.0	0.0	0.0	0.0	0.0	0.0	0.0	0.0
Days With ≥ 1.0" Snow Depth	0	0	0	0	0	0	0	0	0	0	0	0	0

North Fork Ranger Station *Madera County*   Elevation: 2,627 ft.   Latitude: 37° 14' N   Longitude: 119° 30' W

	JAN	FEB	MAR	APR	MAY	JUN	JUL	AUG	SEP	OCT	NOV	DEC	YEAR
Mean Maximum Temp. (°F)	na	na	na	*66.5*	76.3	85.3	93.2	93.1	86.8	76.4	63.9	na	na
Mean Temp. (°F)	na	na	na	*52.0*	60.3	68.1	75.2	74.9	69.3	60.0	49.6	na	na
Mean Minimum Temp. (°F)	na	na	na	*37.5*	44.2	50.8	57.1	56.6	51.7	43.6	35.4	na	na
Extreme Maximum Temp. (°F)	76	82	84	91	102	104	108	109	104	100	88	78	109
Extreme Minimum Temp. (°F)	10	10	15	22	26	32	38	42	36	19	16	6	6
Days Maximum Temp. ≥ 90°F	0	0	0	0	2	10	23	23	13	3	0	0	74
Days Maximum Temp. ≤ 32°F	0	0	0	0	0	0	0	0	0	0	0	0	0
Days Minimum Temp. ≤ 32°F	*15*	*11*	*9*	*5*	1	0	0	0	0	1	*9*	*16*	*67*
Days Minimum Temp. ≤ 0°F	0	0	0	0	0	0	0	0	0	0	0	0	0
Heating Degree Days (base 65°F)	na	na	na	*386*	184	47	3	3	36	187	*466*	na	na
Cooling Degree Days (base 65°F)	na	na	na	*2*	41	140	326	325	173	39	*1*	na	na
Mean Precipitation (in.)	6.78	5.98	6.20	2.39	1.27	0.48	0.10	0.08	0.70	1.56	3.84	4.59	33.97
Days With ≥ 0.1" Precipitation	5	4	6	3	2	1	0	0	1	3	4	4	33
Days With ≥ 1.0" Precipitation	2	1	2	0	0	0	0	0	0	0	1	1	7
Mean Snowfall (in.)	*0.1*	*0.0*	0.3	0.3	0.0	0.0	0.0	0.0	0.0	0.0	0.2	*0.1*	*1.0*
Days With ≥ 1.0" Snow Depth	*0*	0	0	0	0	0	0	0	0	0	0	*0*	*0*

Oceanside Marina *San Diego County*   Elevation: 9 ft.   Latitude: 33° 13' N   Longitude: 117° 24' W

	JAN	FEB	MAR	APR	MAY	JUN	JUL	AUG	SEP	OCT	NOV	DEC	YEAR
Mean Maximum Temp. (°F)	64.1	64.1	64.1	65.5	66.7	69.0	72.3	73.8	73.8	71.7	68.3	64.9	68.2
Mean Temp. (°F)	54.5	55.0	56.0	57.9	60.8	63.8	67.2	68.6	67.5	63.9	58.5	54.7	60.7
Mean Minimum Temp. (°F)	44.8	45.9	47.9	50.3	54.9	58.5	62.1	63.3	61.2	56.0	48.7	44.4	53.2
Extreme Maximum Temp. (°F)	85	90	90	93	89	90	103	94	104	100	100	89	104
Extreme Minimum Temp. (°F)	29	28	34	33	38	43	44	47	43	36	34	27	27
Days Maximum Temp. ≥ 90°F	0	0	0	0	0	0	0	0	0	0	0	0	0
Days Maximum Temp. ≤ 32°F	0	0	0	0	0	0	0	0	0	0	0	0	0
Days Minimum Temp. ≤ 32°F	0	0	0	0	0	0	0	0	0	0	0	0	0
Days Minimum Temp. ≤ 0°F	0	0	0	0	0	0	0	0	0	0	0	0	0
Heating Degree Days (base 65°F)	321	276	274	207	127	56	9	5	13	63	198	314	1,863
Cooling Degree Days (base 65°F)	1	1	0	3	4	18	78	108	82	29	5	0	329
Mean Precipitation (in.)	2.43	2.19	2.15	0.90	0.23	0.10	0.02	0.13	0.31	0.36	1.00	1.46	11.28
Days With ≥ 0.1" Precipitation	5	4	4	2	1	0	0	0	1	1	2	3	23
Days With ≥ 1.0" Precipitation	1	0	0	0	0	0	0	0	0	0	0	0	1
Mean Snowfall (in.)	trace	0.0	0.0	0.0	0.0	0.0	0.0	0.0	0.0	0.0	0.0	0.0	trace
Days With ≥ 1.0" Snow Depth	0	0	0	0	0	0	0	0	0	0	0	0	0

Ojai *Ventura County*   Elevation: 748 ft.   Latitude: 34° 27' N   Longitude: 119° 14' W

	JAN	FEB	MAR	APR	MAY	JUN	JUL	AUG	SEP	OCT	NOV	DEC	YEAR
Mean Maximum Temp. (°F)	67.2	68.7	69.6	74.4	77.0	83.1	88.8	89.9	87.0	81.5	73.7	68.2	77.4
Mean Temp. (°F)	52.1	54.0	55.5	59.0	62.5	67.4	72.1	72.8	70.3	64.6	57.2	52.2	61.7
Mean Minimum Temp. (°F)	37.0	39.3	41.4	43.5	48.0	51.8	55.4	55.6	53.5	47.6	40.6	36.3	45.8
Extreme Maximum Temp. (°F)	90	90	96	103	105	110	111	111	111	107	100	88	111
Extreme Minimum Temp. (°F)	24	22	28	29	36	39	44	42	39	30	27	16	16
Days Maximum Temp. ≥ 90°F	0	0	0	2	3	7	14	16	13	6	1	0	62
Days Maximum Temp. ≤ 32°F	0	0	0	0	0	0	0	0	0	0	0	0	0
Days Minimum Temp. ≤ 32°F	8	3	1	0	0	0	0	0	0	0	2	8	22
Days Minimum Temp. ≤ 0°F	0	0	0	0	0	0	0	0	0	0	0	0	0
Heating Degree Days (base 65°F)	393	304	289	189	111	34	1	1	14	76	236	389	2,037
Cooling Degree Days (base 65°F)	0	2	2	22	40	102	221	253	183	67	7	0	899
Mean Precipitation (in.)	4.86	5.51	4.45	0.92	0.48	0.08	0.03	0.08	0.41	0.57	1.71	3.04	22.14
Days With ≥ 0.1" Precipitation	5	5	5	2	1	0	0	0	1	1	2	3	25
Days With ≥ 1.0" Precipitation	2	2	2	0	0	0	0	0	0	0	0	1	7
Mean Snowfall (in.)	0.0	0.0	0.0	0.0	0.0	0.0	0.0	0.0	0.0	0.0	0.0	0.0	0.0
Days With ≥ 1.0" Snow Depth	0	0	0	0	0	0	0	0	0	0	0	0	0

Orick Prairie Creek Park *Humboldt County*   Elevation: 157 ft.   Latitude: 41° 22' N   Longitude: 124° 01' W

	JAN	FEB	MAR	APR	MAY	JUN	JUL	AUG	SEP	OCT	NOV	DEC	YEAR
Mean Maximum Temp. (°F)	53.4	56.0	57.9	59.9	63.2	65.9	68.9	69.9	71.2	66.1	57.5	52.1	61.8
Mean Temp. (°F)	45.3	47.3	48.4	49.5	52.8	55.9	58.7	59.3	58.5	54.1	48.7	44.5	51.9
Mean Minimum Temp. (°F)	37.1	38.5	38.7	39.1	42.3	45.9	48.5	48.8	45.8	42.0	39.9	36.9	42.0
Extreme Maximum Temp. (°F)	69	75	80	84	93	95	88	94	97	98	73	68	98
Extreme Minimum Temp. (°F)	19	21	26	27	29	31	37	31	31	25	23	17	17
Days Maximum Temp. ≥ 90°F	0	0	0	0	0	0	0	0	0	0	0	0	0
Days Maximum Temp. ≤ 32°F	0	0	0	0	0	0	0	0	0	0	0	0	0
Days Minimum Temp. ≤ 32°F	8	6	6	5	1	0	0	0	0	1	5	10	42
Days Minimum Temp. ≤ 0°F	0	0	0	0	0	0	0	0	0	0	0	0	0
Heating Degree Days (base 65°F)	604	494	508	457	373	267	189	170	191	333	481	628	4,695
Cooling Degree Days (base 65°F)	0	0	0	0	1	1	2	1	3	2	0	0	10
Mean Precipitation (in.)	9.98	9.46	9.22	5.32	3.13	1.27	0.31	0.48	1.62	4.26	10.84	10.96	66.85
Days With ≥ 0.1" Precipitation	12	12	13	9	6	3	1	1	3	5	11	12	88
Days With ≥ 1.0" Precipitation	3	3	3	2	1	0	0	0	0	1	3	4	20
Mean Snowfall (in.)	0.2	0.0	trace	0.0	0.0	0.0	0.0	0.0	0.0	0.0	trace	0.2	0.4
Days With ≥ 1.0" Snow Depth	0	0	0	0	0	0	0	0	0	0	0	0	0

Orland *Glenn County*   Elevation: 252 ft.   Latitude: 39° 45' N   Longitude: 122° 12' W

	JAN	FEB	MAR	APR	MAY	JUN	JUL	AUG	SEP	OCT	NOV	DEC	YEAR
Mean Maximum Temp. (°F)	55.1	61.0	65.4	72.4	81.1	89.0	94.6	93.3	89.1	79.2	63.9	55.1	74.9
Mean Temp. (°F)	45.9	50.4	54.2	59.2	67.1	74.2	78.5	76.7	73.0	64.4	52.8	45.5	61.8
Mean Minimum Temp. (°F)	36.6	39.8	42.9	45.9	53.1	59.2	62.4	60.1	56.8	49.6	41.6	36.0	48.7
Extreme Maximum Temp. (°F)	78	82	88	95	104	112	115	117	114	103	87	81	117
Extreme Minimum Temp. (°F)	20	23	26	30	34	31	49	48	39	33	21	15	15
Days Maximum Temp. ≥ 90°F	0	0	0	1	7	14	24	22	16	5	0	0	89
Days Maximum Temp. ≤ 32°F	0	0	0	0	0	0	0	0	0	0	0	0	0
Days Minimum Temp. ≤ 32°F	10	3	1	0	0	0	0	0	0	0	2	9	25
Days Minimum Temp. ≤ 0°F	0	0	0	0	0	0	0	0	0	0	0	0	0
Heating Degree Days (base 65°F)	586	405	330	189	60	8	0	0	8	90	361	596	2,633
Cooling Degree Days (base 65°F)	0	0	2	26	128	279	423	373	257	78	2	0	1,568
Mean Precipitation (in.)	4.49	3.70	3.52	1.08	0.92	0.42	0.08	0.15	0.39	1.13	2.97	3.17	22.02
Days With ≥ 0.1" Precipitation	7	6	7	3	2	1	0	0	1	2	5	6	40
Days With ≥ 1.0" Precipitation	2	1	1	0	0	0	0	0	0	0	1	1	6
Mean Snowfall (in.)	0.2	0.0	0.1	0.0	0.0	0.0	0.0	0.0	0.0	0.0	0.0	trace	0.3
Days With ≥ 1.0" Snow Depth	0	0	0	0	0	0	0	0	0	0	0	0	0

Orleans *Humboldt County*   Elevation: 396 ft.   Latitude: 41° 18' N   Longitude: 123° 32' W

	JAN	FEB	MAR	APR	MAY	JUN	JUL	AUG	SEP	OCT	NOV	DEC	YEAR
Mean Maximum Temp. (°F)	52.1	57.5	63.6	70.0	77.2	84.7	92.2	91.8	86.9	74.2	57.6	50.6	71.5
Mean Temp. (°F)	43.8	47.7	51.8	55.7	61.5	67.5	73.3	72.6	68.2	59.2	49.2	43.0	57.8
Mean Minimum Temp. (°F)	35.4	37.8	39.9	41.4	45.7	50.4	54.3	53.4	49.4	44.2	40.8	35.4	44.0
Extreme Maximum Temp. (°F)	70	78	86	97	103	107	112	112	107	98	77	68	112
Extreme Minimum Temp. (°F)	12	16	26	29	31	38	43	39	35	24	22	5	5
Days Maximum Temp. ≥ 90°F	0	0	0	1	4	10	19	20	13	2	0	0	69
Days Maximum Temp. ≤ 32°F	0	0	0	0	0	0	0	0	0	0	0	0	0
Days Minimum Temp. ≤ 32°F	11	5	3	1	0	0	0	0	0	1	3	10	34
Days Minimum Temp. ≤ 0°F	0	0	0	0	0	0	0	0	0	0	0	0	0
Heating Degree Days (base 65°F)	651	482	403	276	142	38	4	4	28	189	466	674	3,357
Cooling Degree Days (base 65°F)	0	0	0	7	40	112	262	246	126	16	0	0	809
Mean Precipitation (in.)	9.03	7.82	7.14	3.34	2.07	0.76	0.18	0.47	1.22	3.77	8.64	9.44	53.88
Days With ≥ 0.1" Precipitation	11	10	11	7	4	2	0	1	2	5	11	12	76
Days With ≥ 1.0" Precipitation	3	3	2	1	0	0	0	0	0	1	3	3	16
Mean Snowfall (in.)	0.7	0.3	0.3	trace	trace	0.0	0.0	0.0	0.0	0.0	0.2	1.8	3.3
Days With ≥ 1.0" Snow Depth	0	0	0	0	0	0	0	0	0	0	0	1	1

Oxnard *Ventura County*   Elevation: 45 ft.   Latitude: 34° 12' N   Longitude: 119° 11' W

	JAN	FEB	MAR	APR	MAY	JUN	JUL	AUG	SEP	OCT	NOV	DEC	YEAR
Mean Maximum Temp. (°F)	65.9	66.4	66.4	68.5	69.0	71.6	74.3	75.5	75.2	74.0	70.4	66.6	70.3
Mean Temp. (°F)	55.7	56.5	57.2	59.0	61.1	63.9	66.7	67.6	66.9	64.3	59.7	55.9	61.2
Mean Minimum Temp. (°F)	45.4	46.5	47.9	49.4	53.1	56.2	59.1	59.8	58.5	54.4	49.0	45.2	52.0
Extreme Maximum Temp. (°F)	88	90	94	100	98	102	89	97	103	102	98	88	103
Extreme Minimum Temp. (°F)	30	32	32	36	41	43	50	50	47	37	36	30	30
Days Maximum Temp. ≥ 90°F	0	0	0	0	0	0	0	0	1	1	0	0	2
Days Maximum Temp. ≤ 32°F	0	0	0	0	0	0	0	0	0	0	0	0	0
Days Minimum Temp. ≤ 32°F	0	0	0	0	0	0	0	0	0	0	0	0	0
Days Minimum Temp. ≤ 0°F	0	0	0	0	0	0	0	0	0	0	0	0	0
Heating Degree Days (base 65°F)	288	240	241	183	125	51	11	8	18	60	169	278	1,672
Cooling Degree Days (base 65°F)	6	8	6	13	7	24	71	92	72	46	16	5	366
Mean Precipitation (in.)	3.49	3.82	3.03	0.65	0.21	0.05	0.02	0.07	0.35	0.34	1.54	2.26	15.83
Days With ≥ 0.1" Precipitation	5	4	5	1	1	0	0	0	1	1	2	3	23
Days With ≥ 1.0" Precipitation	1	1	1	0	0	0	0	0	0	0	0	1	4
Mean Snowfall (in.)	trace	0.0	0.0	0.0	0.0	0.0	0.0	0.0	0.0	0.0	0.0	0.0	trace
Days With ≥ 1.0" Snow Depth	0	0	0	0	0	0	0	0	0	0	0	0	0

Palm Springs *Riverside County*   Elevation: 419 ft.   Latitude: 33° 54' N   Longitude: 116° 33' W

	JAN	FEB	MAR	APR	MAY	JUN	JUL	AUG	SEP	OCT	NOV	DEC	YEAR
Mean Maximum Temp. (°F)	70.3	75.0	79.7	87.1	94.4	103.9	108.3	106.9	101.2	91.0	78.4	69.9	88.9
Mean Temp. (°F)	57.1	61.1	65.1	71.4	78.5	86.7	92.2	91.4	85.7	76.0	64.2	56.6	73.8
Mean Minimum Temp. (°F)	43.9	47.2	50.5	55.6	62.6	69.4	76.0	75.9	70.1	60.9	49.8	43.2	58.8
Extreme Maximum Temp. (°F)	95	99	103	112	116	121	123	123	120	116	100	90	123
Extreme Minimum Temp. (°F)	23	28	32	35	43	44	54	52	51	35	31	24	23
Days Maximum Temp. ≥ 90°F	0	1	4	13	23	29	31	31	28	18	2	0	180
Days Maximum Temp. ≤ 32°F	0	0	0	0	0	0	0	0	0	0	0	0	0
Days Minimum Temp. ≤ 32°F	1	0	0	0	0	0	0	0	0	0	0	1	2
Days Minimum Temp. ≤ 0°F	0	0	0	0	0	0	0	0	0	0	0	0	0
Heating Degree Days (base 65°F)	248	134	77	25	1	0	0	0	0	6	86	259	836
Cooling Degree Days (base 65°F)	8	35	91	257	445	658	848	848	639	371	76	6	4,282
Mean Precipitation (in.)	1.27	1.14	0.67	0.07	0.06	0.05	0.18	0.38	0.40	0.10	0.29	0.59	5.20
Days With ≥ 0.1" Precipitation	2	2	2	0	0	0	0	1	1	0	1	1	10
Days With ≥ 1.0" Precipitation	0	0	0	0	0	0	0	0	0	0	0	0	0
Mean Snowfall (in.)	trace	0.0	0.0	0.0	0.0	0.0	0.0	0.0	0.0	0.0	0.0	0.0	trace
Days With ≥ 1.0" Snow Depth	0	0	0	0	0	0	0	0	0	0	0	0	0

Palm Springs Thermal Airport *Riverside County*   Elevation: -111 ft.   Latitude: 33° 38' N   Longitude: 116° 10' W

	JAN	FEB	MAR	APR	MAY	JUN	JUL	AUG	SEP	OCT	NOV	DEC	YEAR
Mean Maximum Temp. (°F)	70.7	75.0	80.0	86.7	93.7	102.9	106.5	105.1	100.4	90.5	78.6	70.3	88.4
Mean Temp. (°F)	54.8	59.1	64.3	70.6	78.1	86.0	90.8	90.0	84.3	73.6	61.3	53.9	72.2
Mean Minimum Temp. (°F)	38.8	43.2	48.6	54.5	62.4	69.0	75.2	74.7	68.2	56.5	43.9	37.4	56.0
Extreme Maximum Temp. (°F)	92	100	102	110	116	122	126	121	121	114	98	91	126
Extreme Minimum Temp. (°F)	17	20	26	32	42	51	57	52	48	28	24	17	17
Days Maximum Temp. ≥ 90°F	0	1	4	12	23	29	31	31	28	18	2	0	179
Days Maximum Temp. ≤ 32°F	0	0	0	0	0	0	0	0	0	0	0	0	0
Days Minimum Temp. ≤ 32°F	6	2	0	0	0	0	0	0	0	0	2	7	17
Days Minimum Temp. ≤ 0°F	0	0	0	0	0	0	0	0	0	0	0	0	0
Heating Degree Days (base 65°F)	313	175	84	23	1	0	0	0	0	12	137	340	1,085
Cooling Degree Days (base 65°F)	2	20	72	223	429	630	801	789	590	289	36	2	3,883
Mean Precipitation (in.)	0.74	0.65	0.44	0.06	0.06	0.02	0.21	0.39	0.41	0.15	0.21	0.31	3.65
Days With ≥ 0.1" Precipitation	2	1	1	0	0	0	0	1	1	0	1	1	8
Days With ≥ 1.0" Precipitation	0	0	0	0	0	0	0	0	0	0	0	0	0
Mean Snowfall (in.)	trace	0.0	0.0	0.0	0.0	0.0	0.0	0.0	0.0	0.0	0.0	0.0	trace
Days With ≥ 1.0" Snow Depth	0	0	0	0	0	0	0	0	0	0	0	0	0

Palmdale *Los Angeles County*   Elevation: 2,595 ft.   Latitude: 34° 35' N   Longitude: 118° 06' W

	JAN	FEB	MAR	APR	MAY	JUN	JUL	AUG	SEP	OCT	NOV	DEC	YEAR
Mean Maximum Temp. (°F)	58.6	63.2	67.6	74.4	82.4	91.4	97.6	97.0	91.0	80.3	67.2	58.3	77.4
Mean Temp. (°F)	45.9	49.7	53.5	58.9	66.6	74.7	80.9	80.3	74.3	64.1	52.6	45.1	62.2
Mean Minimum Temp. (°F)	32.9	36.2	39.3	43.4	50.9	58.0	64.3	63.5	57.5	47.8	37.9	31.8	47.0
Extreme Maximum Temp. (°F)	79	84	91	98	103	112	113	112	109	105	93	81	113
Extreme Minimum Temp. (°F)	8	15	14	20	28	38	44	41	34	23	16	9	8
Days Maximum Temp. ≥ 90°F	0	0	0	2	8	19	28	28	19	5	0	0	109
Days Maximum Temp. ≤ 32°F	0	0	0	0	0	0	0	0	0	0	0	0	0
Days Minimum Temp. ≤ 32°F	15	9	5	1	0	0	0	0	0	1	8	17	56
Days Minimum Temp. ≤ 0°F	0	0	0	0	0	0	0	0	0	0	0	0	0
Heating Degree Days (base 65°F)	586	424	353	202	68	9	0	0	8	102	367	610	2,729
Cooling Degree Days (base 65°F)	0	0	2	38	132	309	506	499	307	85	2	0	1,880
Mean Precipitation (in.)	1.56	1.66	1.39	0.30	0.16	0.06	0.06	0.12	0.22	0.23	0.53	1.15	7.44
Days With ≥ 0.1" Precipitation	3	3	3	1	1	0	0	0	0	1	1	2	15
Days With ≥ 1.0" Precipitation	0	1	0	0	0	0	0	0	0	0	0	0	1
Mean Snowfall (in.)	0.7	0.0	trace	0.0	0.0	0.0	0.0	0.0	0.0	0.0	0.0	trace	0.7
Days With ≥ 1.0" Snow Depth	0	0	0	0	0	0	0	0	0	0	0	0	0

Palo Alto *Santa Clara County*   Elevation: 22 ft.   Latitude: 37° 27' N   Longitude: 122° 08' W

	JAN	FEB	MAR	APR	MAY	JUN	JUL	AUG	SEP	OCT	NOV	DEC	YEAR
Mean Maximum Temp. (°F)	57.7	61.3	64.3	68.9	73.2	77.3	78.7	78.6	77.8	72.7	64.2	57.9	69.4
Mean Temp. (°F)	48.2	51.3	54.1	56.9	60.9	64.8	66.8	66.7	65.4	60.5	53.3	47.7	58.0
Mean Minimum Temp. (°F)	38.6	41.3	43.7	44.8	48.6	52.3	54.8	54.8	52.9	48.1	42.3	37.5	46.6
Extreme Maximum Temp. (°F)	75	84	85	94	100	106	105	100	105	100	83	73	106
Extreme Minimum Temp. (°F)	24	26	30	31	33	40	41	44	41	34	26	20	20
Days Maximum Temp. ≥ 90°F	0	0	0	0	2	2	2	2	2	1	0	0	11
Days Maximum Temp. ≤ 32°F	0	0	0	0	0	0	0	0	0	0	0	0	0
Days Minimum Temp. ≤ 32°F	6	2	0	0	0	0	0	0	0	0	1	7	16
Days Minimum Temp. ≤ 0°F	0	0	0	0	0	0	0	0	0	0	0	0	0
Heating Degree Days (base 65°F)	514	380	333	243	146	59	21	16	42	152	345	530	2,781
Cooling Degree Days (base 65°F)	0	0	0	9	24	59	82	75	54	19	0	0	322
Mean Precipitation (in.)	3.30	3.11	2.62	0.87	0.34	0.10	0.03	0.08	0.19	0.83	2.05	2.55	16.07
Days With ≥ 0.1" Precipitation	7	6	6	3	1	0	0	0	1	2	4	6	36
Days With ≥ 1.0" Precipitation	1	1	0	0	0	0	0	0	0	0	0	0	2
Mean Snowfall (in.)	0.0	0.0	0.0	0.0	0.0	0.0	0.0	0.0	0.0	0.0	0.0	0.0	0.0
Days With ≥ 1.0" Snow Depth	0	0	0	0	0	0	0	0	0	0	0	0	0

Palomar Mountain Observatory *San Diego County*   Elevation: 5,547 ft.   Latitude: 33° 23' N   Longitude: 116° 50' W

	JAN	FEB	MAR	APR	MAY	JUN	JUL	AUG	SEP	OCT	NOV	DEC	YEAR
Mean Maximum Temp. (°F)	50.7	52.0	55.2	61.2	68.5	78.8	84.7	83.6	78.5	68.0	57.8	50.9	65.8
Mean Temp. (°F)	42.4	43.4	45.4	50.3	57.0	66.9	73.0	72.8	67.4	58.0	48.7	42.6	55.7
Mean Minimum Temp. (°F)	34.0	34.6	35.7	39.4	45.4	55.0	61.1	61.8	56.3	47.9	39.6	34.3	45.4
Extreme Maximum Temp. (°F)	80	77	78	81	91	99	100	100	100	97	79	76	100
Extreme Minimum Temp. (°F)	11	12	18	19	20	30	39	41	34	18	17	11	11
Days Maximum Temp. ≥ 90°F	0	0	0	0	0	2	6	4	2	0	0	0	14
Days Maximum Temp. ≤ 32°F	1	1	0	0	0	0	0	0	0	0	0	1	3
Days Minimum Temp. ≤ 32°F	14	12	12	8	3	0	0	0	0	1	6	12	68
Days Minimum Temp. ≤ 0°F	0	0	0	0	0	0	0	0	0	0	0	0	0
Heating Degree Days (base 65°F)	694	605	599	438	263	71	6	7	52	240	482	687	4,144
Cooling Degree Days (base 65°F)	0	0	0	5	23	122	250	264	134	32	1	0	831
Mean Precipitation (in.)	5.77	6.01	6.33	1.73	0.70	0.18	0.42	1.01	0.70	0.95	2.74	3.73	30.27
Days With ≥ 0.1" Precipitation	5	4	5	3	1	0	1	1	1	2	3	4	30
Days With ≥ 1.0" Precipitation	2	2	2	0	0	0	0	0	0	0	1	1	8
Mean Snowfall (in.)	4.8	3.3	11.2	3.7	0.2	trace	0.0	0.0	0.0	0.1	2.0	4.9	30.2
Days With ≥ 1.0" Snow Depth	2	1	3	2	0	0	0	0	0	0	1	3	12

Paradise *Butte County*   Elevation: 1,748 ft.   Latitude: 39° 45' N   Longitude: 121° 37' W

	JAN	FEB	MAR	APR	MAY	JUN	JUL	AUG	SEP	OCT	NOV	DEC	YEAR
Mean Maximum Temp. (°F)	53.8	56.6	59.9	66.3	75.3	84.3	91.3	90.2	84.7	73.9	59.8	53.5	70.8
Mean Temp. (°F)	46.1	48.6	51.2	56.2	63.8	71.6	78.0	76.8	72.3	63.3	51.7	45.8	60.4
Mean Minimum Temp. (°F)	38.4	40.6	42.5	46.1	52.2	59.0	64.6	63.3	59.9	52.6	43.5	38.1	50.1
Extreme Maximum Temp. (°F)	77	81	83	90	101	105	108	113	108	98	84	78	113
Extreme Minimum Temp. (°F)	20	22	26	29	35	41	47	41	38	29	26	14	14
Days Maximum Temp. ≥ 90°F	0	0	0	0	2	9	20	17	10	2	0	0	60
Days Maximum Temp. ≤ 32°F	0	0	0	0	0	0	0	0	0	0	0	0	0
Days Minimum Temp. ≤ 32°F	5	3	2	0	0	0	0	0	0	0	1	5	16
Days Minimum Temp. ≤ 0°F	0	0	0	0	0	0	0	0	0	0	0	0	0
Heating Degree Days (base 65°F)	580	456	421	274	125	29	2	3	22	127	396	588	3,023
Cooling Degree Days (base 65°F)	0	0	1	25	93	232	420	398	265	86	2	0	1,522
Mean Precipitation (in.)	11.08	8.96	9.28	3.78	1.87	0.74	0.12	0.26	1.11	2.78	7.82	8.71	56.51
Days With ≥ 0.1" Precipitation	9	9	9	6	3	2	0	1	2	3	8	9	61
Days With ≥ 1.0" Precipitation	4	3	3	1	1	0	0	0	0	1	3	3	19
Mean Snowfall (in.)	1.2	0.5	0.5	trace	trace	0.0	0.0	0.0	trace	0.0	0.0	0.8	3.0
Days With ≥ 1.0" Snow Depth	0	0	0	0	0	0	0	0	0	0	0	0	0

Parker Reservoir *San Bernardino County*   Elevation: 734 ft.   Latitude: 34° 17' N   Longitude: 114° 10' W

	JAN	FEB	MAR	APR	MAY	JUN	JUL	AUG	SEP	OCT	NOV	DEC	YEAR
Mean Maximum Temp. (°F)	64.4	70.4	76.3	84.1	93.0	103.3	107.5	106.0	100.0	88.3	74.2	64.8	86.0
Mean Temp. (°F)	53.7	58.9	64.4	71.6	80.4	90.2	95.3	93.9	87.7	75.9	62.5	53.9	74.0
Mean Minimum Temp. (°F)	43.0	47.3	52.5	59.0	67.7	77.0	83.1	81.6	75.3	63.5	50.8	43.0	62.0
Extreme Maximum Temp. (°F)	86	92	97	105	115	122	123	119	116	110	94	82	123
Extreme Minimum Temp. (°F)	27	27	36	35	47	56	64	67	53	38	28	25	25
Days Maximum Temp. ≥ 90°F	0	0	2	9	22	29	31	31	27	15	1	0	167
Days Maximum Temp. ≤ 32°F	0	0	0	0	0	0	0	0	0	0	0	0	0
Days Minimum Temp. ≤ 32°F	1	0	0	0	0	0	0	0	0	0	0	1	2
Days Minimum Temp. ≤ 0°F	0	0	0	0	0	0	0	0	0	0	0	0	0
Heating Degree Days (base 65°F)	343	182	94	26	1	0	0	0	0	10	121	337	1,114
Cooling Degree Days (base 65°F)	0	18	84	254	495	754	936	911	681	355	57	0	4,545
Mean Precipitation (in.)	1.09	0.91	0.91	0.21	0.12	0.05	0.41	0.66	0.56	0.43	0.40	0.59	6.34
Days With ≥ 0.1" Precipitation	2	2	2	1	0	0	1	1	1	1	1	1	13
Days With ≥ 1.0" Precipitation	0	0	0	0	0	0	0	0	0	0	0	0	0
Mean Snowfall (in.)	0.0	0.0	trace	0.0	0.0	0.0	0.0	0.0	0.0	0.0	0.0	0.0	trace
Days With ≥ 1.0" Snow Depth	0	0	0	0	0	0	0	0	0	0	0	0	0

Pasadena *Los Angeles County*   Elevation: 862 ft.   Latitude: 34° 09' N   Longitude: 118° 09' W

	JAN	FEB	MAR	APR	MAY	JUN	JUL	AUG	SEP	OCT	NOV	DEC	YEAR
Mean Maximum Temp. (°F)	67.7	70.4	71.3	75.8	78.1	83.8	89.4	90.6	88.4	82.6	73.8	67.8	78.3
Mean Temp. (°F)	56.0	58.2	59.2	62.8	65.8	70.6	75.3	76.3	74.5	68.9	61.0	55.9	65.4
Mean Minimum Temp. (°F)	44.1	45.9	47.1	49.7	53.4	57.3	61.2	61.9	60.5	55.1	48.2	44.0	52.4
Extreme Maximum Temp. (°F)	93	92	96	105	101	110	107	107	110	108	98	88	110
Extreme Minimum Temp. (°F)	29	27	23	35	39	41	47	50	48	37	31	26	23
Days Maximum Temp. ≥ 90°F	0	0	1	2	3	7	15	17	14	6	1	0	66
Days Maximum Temp. ≤ 32°F	0	0	0	0	0	0	0	0	0	0	0	0	0
Days Minimum Temp. ≤ 32°F	0	0	0	0	0	0	0	0	0	0	0	0	0
Days Minimum Temp. ≤ 0°F	0	0	0	0	0	0	0	0	0	0	0	0	0
Heating Degree Days (base 65°F)	279	198	187	108	52	11	0	0	1	23	139	279	1,277
Cooling Degree Days (base 65°F)	4	15	18	66	88	185	334	377	305	160	27	2	1,581
Mean Precipitation (in.)	4.51	4.82	4.38	1.13	0.45	0.22	0.05	0.21	0.47	0.61	1.72	2.63	21.20
Days With ≥ 0.1" Precipitation	5	5	5	2	1	0	0	0	1	1	2	3	25
Days With ≥ 1.0" Precipitation	2	2	1	0	0	0	0	0	0	0	1	1	7
Mean Snowfall (in.)	trace	0.0	0.0	0.0	0.0	0.0	0.0	0.0	0.0	0.0	0.0	0.0	trace
Days With ≥ 1.0" Snow Depth	0	0	0	0	0	0	0	0	0	0	0	0	0

Paso Robles *San Luis Obispo County*   Elevation: 698 ft.   Latitude: 35° 38' N   Longitude: 120° 41' W

	JAN	FEB	MAR	APR	MAY	JUN	JUL	AUG	SEP	OCT	NOV	DEC	YEAR
Mean Maximum Temp. (°F)	62.0	65.3	68.1	74.0	80.5	87.2	92.2	92.5	88.9	81.3	68.8	61.8	76.9
Mean Temp. (°F)	48.0	51.2	53.9	57.2	62.5	67.7	71.9	71.9	68.6	61.8	52.6	46.6	59.5
Mean Minimum Temp. (°F)	33.9	37.1	39.7	40.3	44.4	48.3	51.5	51.1	48.3	42.3	36.3	31.5	42.1
Extreme Maximum Temp. (°F)	82	85	91	98	103	107	110	111	110	108	94	87	111
Extreme Minimum Temp. (°F)	11	17	20	24	31	31	38	39	33	19	17	7	7
Days Maximum Temp. ≥ 90°F	0	0	0	1	6	13	19	21	15	6	0	0	81
Days Maximum Temp. ≤ 32°F	0	0	0	0	0	0	0	0	0	0	0	0	0
Days Minimum Temp. ≤ 32°F	15	8	4	2	0	0	0	0	0	2	10	19	60
Days Minimum Temp. ≤ 0°F	0	0	0	0	0	0	0	0	0	0	0	0	0
Heating Degree Days (base 65°F)	521	382	338	235	117	34	6	4	25	128	367	562	2,719
Cooling Degree Days (base 65°F)	0	0	0	10	50	121	222	232	143	39	0	0	817
Mean Precipitation (in.)	3.25	3.15	2.89	0.76	0.24	0.03	0.01	0.06	0.34	0.55	1.40	2.09	14.77
Days With ≥ 0.1" Precipitation	6	5	5	2	1	0	0	0	1	1	3	4	28
Days With ≥ 1.0" Precipitation	1	1	1	0	0	0	0	0	0	0	0	1	4
Mean Snowfall (in.)	trace	trace	trace	trace	0.0	0.0	0.0	0.0	0.0	trace	0.0	0.1	0.1
Days With ≥ 1.0" Snow Depth	0	0	0	0	0	0	0	0	0	0	0	0	0

Paso Robles FAA Airport *San Luis Obispo County*   Elevation: 813 ft.   Latitude: 35° 36' N   Longitude: 120° 39' W

	JAN	FEB	MAR	APR	MAY	JUN	JUL	AUG	SEP	OCT	NOV	DEC	YEAR
Mean Maximum Temp. (°F)	59.9	63.2	66.0	72.8	80.3	88.0	93.4	93.0	88.4	79.7	67.2	59.9	76.0
Mean Temp. (°F)	47.4	50.5	53.0	56.7	63.0	69.2	73.6	73.4	69.6	62.1	52.4	46.4	59.8
Mean Minimum Temp. (°F)	34.8	37.8	40.0	40.6	45.6	50.2	53.8	53.7	50.8	44.4	37.6	32.9	43.5
Extreme Maximum Temp. (°F)	83	83	89	99	105	111	113	114	111	106	94	78	114
Extreme Minimum Temp. (°F)	13	18	20	27	30	36	43	43	37	20	19	8	8
Days Maximum Temp. ≥ 90°F	0	0	0	1	6	14	22	21	15	5	0	0	84
Days Maximum Temp. ≤ 32°F	0	0	0	0	0	0	0	0	0	0	0	0	0
Days Minimum Temp. ≤ 32°F	14	7	4	2	0	0	0	0	0	1	8	17	53
Days Minimum Temp. ≤ 0°F	0	0	0	0	0	0	0	0	0	0	0	0	0
Heating Degree Days (base 65°F)	539	403	364	249	113	22	3	4	22	127	372	570	2,788
Cooling Degree Days (base 65°F)	0	0	0	11	59	150	276	278	171	48	1	0	994
Mean Precipitation (in.)	2.84	2.76	2.67	0.64	0.23	0.02	trace	0.06	0.36	0.48	1.20	1.88	13.14
Days With ≥ 0.1" Precipitation	6	5	5	2	1	0	0	0	1	1	3	3	27
Days With ≥ 1.0" Precipitation	1	1	1	0	0	0	0	0	0	0	0	0	3
Mean Snowfall (in.)	trace	trace	trace	trace	0.0	trace	0.0	0.0	0.0	0.0	0.0	0.1	0.1
Days With ≥ 1.0" Snow Depth	0	0	0	0	0	0	0	0	0	0	0	0	0

Petaluma Fire Station 2 *Sonoma County*   Elevation: 29 ft.   Latitude: 38° 16' N   Longitude: 122° 39' W

	JAN	FEB	MAR	APR	MAY	JUN	JUL	AUG	SEP	OCT	NOV	DEC	YEAR
Mean Maximum Temp. (°F)	57.2	62.1	64.6	68.8	73.2	78.6	82.2	82.3	81.5	76.2	65.1	57.4	70.8
Mean Temp. (°F)	47.8	51.4	53.5	56.1	60.2	64.5	67.2	67.3	66.4	61.7	53.6	47.5	58.1
Mean Minimum Temp. (°F)	38.3	40.5	42.2	43.4	46.9	50.5	52.2	52.3	51.2	47.1	41.9	37.5	45.3
Extreme Maximum Temp. (°F)	79	81	87	97	101	107	110	104	109	106	87	79	110
Extreme Minimum Temp. (°F)	22	18	28	24	27	33	40	36	37	29	23	19	18
Days Maximum Temp. ≥ 90°F	0	0	0	0	1	3	5	5	6	2	0	0	22
Days Maximum Temp. ≤ 32°F	0	0	0	0	0	0	0	0	0	0	0	0	0
Days Minimum Temp. ≤ 32°F	7	3	1	0	0	0	0	0	0	0	2	8	21
Days Minimum Temp. ≤ 0°F	0	0	0	0	0	0	0	0	0	0	0	0	0
Heating Degree Days (base 65°F)	527	379	352	264	161	61	16	13	28	122	337	537	2,797
Cooling Degree Days (base 65°F)	0	0	0	5	19	50	91	90	68	26	1	0	350
Mean Precipitation (in.)	5.62	5.05	3.87	1.35	0.58	0.17	0.05	0.08	0.29	1.38	3.74	4.12	26.30
Days With ≥ 0.1" Precipitation	8	8	7	3	1	1	0	0	1	2	6	7	43
Days With ≥ 1.0" Precipitation	2	1	1	0	0	0	0	0	0	0	1	1	6
Mean Snowfall (in.)	trace	trace	0.0	trace	0.0	0.0	0.0	0.0	0.0	0.0	0.0	trace	trace
Days With ≥ 1.0" Snow Depth	0	0	0	0	0	0	0	0	0	0	0	0	0

Pinnacles National Monument *San Benito County*   Elevation: 1,305 ft.   Latitude: 36° 29' N   Longitude: 121° 11' W

	JAN	FEB	MAR	APR	MAY	JUN	JUL	AUG	SEP	OCT	NOV	DEC	YEAR
Mean Maximum Temp. (°F)	61.7	64.0	65.5	71.2	79.0	87.5	94.4	94.1	89.8	81.2	69.0	61.8	76.6
Mean Temp. (°F)	47.4	49.7	51.5	55.1	60.9	67.2	72.6	72.2	68.9	61.7	52.8	47.0	58.9
Mean Minimum Temp. (°F)	33.0	35.3	37.4	38.9	42.8	46.8	50.7	50.2	48.0	42.3	36.6	32.1	41.2
Extreme Maximum Temp. (°F)	86	86	90	100	103	108	116	111	112	116	93	83	116
Extreme Minimum Temp. (°F)	17	17	21	26	26	34	36	37	32	25	15	10	10
Days Maximum Temp. ≥ 90°F	0	0	0	1	5	14	23	23	16	7	0	0	89
Days Maximum Temp. ≤ 32°F	0	0	0	0	0	0	0	0	0	0	0	0	0
Days Minimum Temp. ≤ 32°F	16	9	7	3	1	0	0	0	0	1	8	18	63
Days Minimum Temp. ≤ 0°F	0	0	0	0	0	0	0	0	0	0	0	0	0
Heating Degree Days (base 65°F)	539	425	413	298	164	48	7	5	31	145	362	553	2,990
Cooling Degree Days (base 65°F)	0	0	0	10	39	111	242	238	149	51	2	0	842
Mean Precipitation (in.)	3.26	3.30	3.48	1.07	0.47	0.07	0.04	0.09	0.32	0.84	1.92	2.53	17.39
Days With ≥ 0.1" Precipitation	6	5	6	3	1	0	0	0	1	2	4	5	33
Days With ≥ 1.0" Precipitation	1	1	1	0	0	0	0	0	0	0	0	1	4
Mean Snowfall (in.)	0.2	trace	trace	trace	0.0	0.0	0.0	0.0	0.0	0.0	0.0	trace	0.2
Days With ≥ 1.0" Snow Depth	0	0	0	0	0	0	0	0	0	0	0	0	0

Placerville *El Dorado County*   Elevation: 1,847 ft.   Latitude: 38° 42' N   Longitude: 120° 49' W

	JAN	FEB	MAR	APR	MAY	JUN	JUL	AUG	SEP	OCT	NOV	DEC	YEAR
Mean Maximum Temp. (°F)	54.7	58.2	60.7	66.6	74.9	83.5	91.5	91.1	86.1	75.3	61.6	54.8	71.6
Mean Temp. (°F)	43.9	46.9	49.5	53.8	60.6	67.9	74.6	74.1	69.7	60.5	49.7	44.0	57.9
Mean Minimum Temp. (°F)	33.0	35.7	38.2	40.9	46.4	52.2	57.7	57.0	53.3	45.8	37.7	33.1	44.2
Extreme Maximum Temp. (°F)	75	78	83	92	104	105	110	109	108	100	83	73	110
Extreme Minimum Temp. (°F)	16	15	22	25	29	36	39	37	34	23	21	8	8
Days Maximum Temp. ≥ 90°F	0	0	0	0	2	8	20	19	11	2	0	0	62
Days Maximum Temp. ≤ 32°F	0	0	0	0	0	0	0	0	0	0	0	0	0
Days Minimum Temp. ≤ 32°F	16	9	6	3	0	0	0	0	0	1	6	16	57
Days Minimum Temp. ≤ 0°F	0	0	0	0	0	0	0	0	0	0	0	0	0
Heating Degree Days (base 65°F)	649	504	474	336	174	50	8	5	33	179	454	645	3,511
Cooling Degree Days (base 65°F)	0	0	0	9	52	150	333	318	201	58	1	0	1,122
Mean Precipitation (in.)	7.60	6.23	6.10	2.80	1.44	0.46	0.19	0.15	0.90	1.98	5.22	5.83	38.90
Days With ≥ 0.1" Precipitation	8	8	9	4	3	1	0	0	1	3	7	7	51
Days With ≥ 1.0" Precipitation	2	2	2	1	0	0	0	0	0	1	2	2	12
Mean Snowfall (in.)	*0.2*	0.0	0.1	trace	0.0	0.0	0.0	0.0	0.0	0.0	0.0	trace	*0.3*
Days With ≥ 1.0" Snow Depth	*0*	0	0	0	0	0	0	0	0	0	0	0	*0*

Pomona Cal Poly *Los Angeles County*   Elevation: 738 ft.   Latitude: 34° 04' N   Longitude: 117° 49' W

	JAN	FEB	MAR	APR	MAY	JUN	JUL	AUG	SEP	OCT	NOV	DEC	YEAR
Mean Maximum Temp. (°F)	67.7	69.8	69.5	74.4	77.0	*82.9*	*89.0*	*88.9*	*87.3*	*80.8*	*73.4*	*68.4*	*77.4*
Mean Temp. (°F)	54.7	56.7	57.2	60.8	64.2	*68.9*	*74.0*	*74.2*	*72.7*	*67.0*	*59.6*	*54.8*	*63.7*
Mean Minimum Temp. (°F)	41.5	43.5	44.9	47.1	51.4	*54.8*	*58.9*	*59.4*	*58.1*	*53.1*	*45.7*	*41.1*	*50.0*
Extreme Maximum Temp. (°F)	90	94	100	104	*106*	*105*	*105*	*106*	*110*	*105*	*97*	*93*	*110*
Extreme Minimum Temp. (°F)	25	23	28	*34*	39	*40*	*47*	*47*	*46*	*35*	*29*	*22*	*22*
Days Maximum Temp. ≥ 90°F	0	0	0	1	2	*7*	*15*	*14*	*13*	*6*	*1*	*0*	*59*
Days Maximum Temp. ≤ 32°F	0	0	0	0	0	*0*	*0*	*0*	*0*	*0*	*0*	*0*	*0*
Days Minimum Temp. ≤ 32°F	2	1	0	0	0	*0*	*0*	*0*	*0*	*0*	*0*	*2*	*5*
Days Minimum Temp. ≤ 0°F	0	0	0	0	0	*0*	*0*	*0*	*0*	*0*	*0*	*0*	*0*
Heating Degree Days (base 65°F)	318	235	243	144	77	*19*	*0*	*0*	*4*	*42*	*174*	*312*	*1,568*
Cooling Degree Days (base 65°F)	*3*	*11*	*10*	*36*	*61*	*129*	na	*296*	*252*	*115*	*15*	*1*	na
Mean Precipitation (in.)	*4.16*	3.83	3.79	0.76	0.25	*0.06*	*trace*	0.15	0.34	0.67	1.46	2.28	17.75
Days With ≥ 0.1" Precipitation	*5*	4	5	2	1	*0*	*0*	*0*	*1*	*1*	*2*	*3*	*24*
Days With ≥ 1.0" Precipitation	*2*	1	1	0	0	*0*	*0*	*0*	*0*	*0*	*0*	*1*	*5*
Mean Snowfall (in.)	0.0	trace	0.0	0.0	0.0	*0.0*	*0.0*	*0.0*	*0.0*	*0.0*	*0.0*	*0.0*	*trace*
Days With ≥ 1.0" Snow Depth	0	0	0	0	0	*0*	*0*	*0*	*0*	*0*	*0*	*0*	*0*

Porterville *Tulare County* Elevation: 390 ft. Latitude: 36° 04' N Longitude: 119° 01' W

	JAN	FEB	MAR	APR	MAY	JUN	JUL	AUG	SEP	OCT	NOV	DEC	YEAR
Mean Maximum Temp. (°F)	57.6	64.7	69.6	76.5	85.1	93.0	98.2	96.8	91.8	82.4	67.9	57.8	78.5
Mean Temp. (°F)	47.6	53.0	57.2	62.2	69.8	76.8	82.1	80.7	75.7	66.9	55.0	47.1	64.5
Mean Minimum Temp. (°F)	37.5	41.2	44.7	48.0	54.3	60.6	65.9	64.5	59.5	51.2	42.0	36.4	50.5
Extreme Maximum Temp. (°F)	79	85	90	99	109	112	113	112	108	103	88	80	113
Extreme Minimum Temp. (°F)	23	23	28	32	37	30	51	50	44	35	27	16	16
Days Maximum Temp. ≥ 90°F	0	0	0	2	10	21	29	27	20	6	0	0	115
Days Maximum Temp. ≤ 32°F	0	0	0	0	0	0	0	0	0	0	0	0	0
Days Minimum Temp. ≤ 32°F	7	2	0	0	0	0	0	0	0	0	2	9	20
Days Minimum Temp. ≤ 0°F	0	0	0	0	0	0	0	0	0	0	0	0	0
Heating Degree Days (base 65°F)	534	334	242	126	33	3	0	0	3	53	297	547	2,172
Cooling Degree Days (base 65°F)	0	1	8	64	186	355	538	508	342	123	4	0	2,129
Mean Precipitation (in.)	2.20	1.88	2.32	0.85	0.41	0.10	0.01	0.02	0.35	0.61	1.25	1.50	11.50
Days With ≥ 0.1" Precipitation	5	5	5	2	1	0	0	0	1	1	3	4	27
Days With ≥ 1.0" Precipitation	0	0	0	0	0	0	0	0	0	0	0	0	0
Mean Snowfall (in.)	0.0	0.0	0.0	0.0	0.0	0.0	0.0	0.0	0.0	0.0	0.0	trace	trace
Days With ≥ 1.0" Snow Depth	0	0	0	0	0	0	0	0	0	0	0	0	0

Potter Valley P H *Mendocino County* Elevation: 1,013 ft. Latitude: 39° 22' N Longitude: 123° 08' W

	JAN	FEB	MAR	APR	MAY	JUN	JUL	AUG	SEP	OCT	NOV	DEC	YEAR
Mean Maximum Temp. (°F)	56.5	60.1	63.2	68.5	76.5	84.5	92.3	91.4	87.2	77.0	62.1	55.7	72.9
Mean Temp. (°F)	45.6	48.6	50.9	54.2	60.4	66.9	72.8	71.9	68.1	60.1	50.1	44.8	57.9
Mean Minimum Temp. (°F)	34.6	37.0	38.6	39.8	44.2	49.3	53.3	52.2	48.8	43.2	37.9	33.9	42.8
Extreme Maximum Temp. (°F)	82	87	90	94	102	108	113	116	110	103	90	83	116
Extreme Minimum Temp. (°F)	17	21	24	22	29	32	40	41	35	21	20	12	12
Days Maximum Temp. ≥ 90°F	0	0	0	0	4	9	20	19	14	4	0	0	70
Days Maximum Temp. ≤ 32°F	0	0	0	0	0	0	0	0	0	0	0	0	0
Days Minimum Temp. ≤ 32°F	14	8	5	2	0	0	0	0	0	1	7	15	52
Days Minimum Temp. ≤ 0°F	0	0	0	0	0	0	0	0	0	0	0	0	0
Heating Degree Days (base 65°F)	595	457	430	320	172	52	7	6	34	174	442	619	3,308
Cooling Degree Days (base 65°F)	0	0	0	3	30	101	242	211	122	27	0	0	736
Mean Precipitation (in.)	9.36	7.72	6.87	2.79	1.57	0.37	0.08	0.18	0.87	2.59	6.61	7.28	46.29
Days With ≥ 0.1" Precipitation	10	9	9	5	3	1	0	1	2	4	8	9	61
Days With ≥ 1.0" Precipitation	3	3	2	1	0	0	0	0	0	1	2	2	14
Mean Snowfall (in.)	0.0	0.0	0.0	0.0	0.0	0.0	0.0	0.0	0.0	0.0	0.0	trace	trace
Days With ≥ 1.0" Snow Depth	0	0	0	0	0	0	0	0	0	0	0	0	0

Priest Valley *Monterey County* Elevation: 2,299 ft. Latitude: 36° 11' N Longitude: 120° 42' W

	JAN	FEB	MAR	APR	MAY	JUN	JUL	AUG	SEP	OCT	NOV	DEC	YEAR
Mean Maximum Temp. (°F)	57.7	60.0	62.5	69.0	77.6	87.0	93.9	93.1	87.6	77.7	64.3	57.8	74.0
Mean Temp. (°F)	43.8	46.0	48.2	51.8	58.7	65.9	71.9	71.2	66.5	58.1	48.1	43.0	56.1
Mean Minimum Temp. (°F)	29.9	32.1	33.8	34.5	39.7	44.8	49.8	49.3	45.4	38.5	31.9	28.2	38.2
Extreme Maximum Temp. (°F)	79	81	85	98	103	110	113	111	108	103	90	82	113
Extreme Minimum Temp. (°F)	8	12	13	17	25	29	33	36	27	17	15	2	2
Days Maximum Temp. ≥ 90°F	0	0	0	0	4	12	23	22	14	4	0	0	79
Days Maximum Temp. ≤ 32°F	0	0	0	0	0	0	0	0	0	0	0	0	0
Days Minimum Temp. ≤ 32°F	21	16	14	12	4	0	0	0	0	5	18	23	113
Days Minimum Temp. ≤ 0°F	0	0	0	0	0	0	0	0	0	0	0	0	0
Heating Degree Days (base 65°F)	650	530	515	390	211	59	7	8	50	225	500	676	3,821
Cooling Degree Days (base 65°F)	0	0	0	1	21	89	227	215	105	19	0	0	677
Mean Precipitation (in.)	4.44	3.87	4.07	1.28	0.48	0.09	0.06	0.08	0.46	1.01	2.19	3.13	21.16
Days With ≥ 0.1" Precipitation	7	6	6	3	1	0	0	0	1	2	4	5	35
Days With ≥ 1.0" Precipitation	1	1	1	0	0	0	0	0	0	0	0	1	4
Mean Snowfall (in.)	0.8	0.2	0.3	trace	0.0	0.0	0.0	0.0	0.0	0.0	trace	0.3	1.6
Days With ≥ 1.0" Snow Depth	0	0	0	0	0	0	0	0	0	0	0	0	0

Randsburg *Kern County* Elevation: 3,569 ft. Latitude: 35° 22' N Longitude: 117° 39' W

	JAN	FEB	MAR	APR	MAY	JUN	JUL	AUG	SEP	OCT	NOV	DEC	YEAR
Mean Maximum Temp. (°F)	54.0	58.6	63.6	71.5	81.2	91.3	97.8	96.1	88.3	76.1	62.6	53.9	74.6
Mean Temp. (°F)	45.1	48.8	52.4	58.7	67.5	76.8	83.0	81.4	74.9	64.2	52.5	45.0	62.5
Mean Minimum Temp. (°F)	36.2	39.0	41.1	46.0	53.7	62.3	68.0	66.7	61.5	52.3	42.4	36.1	50.5
Extreme Maximum Temp. (°F)	89	80	84	94	102	111	111	110	104	98	83	74	111
Extreme Minimum Temp. (°F)	17	17	16	25	35	39	49	49	41	27	12	9	9
Days Maximum Temp. ≥ 90°F	0	0	0	0	6	19	29	27	14	2	0	0	97
Days Maximum Temp. ≤ 32°F	0	0	0	0	0	0	0	0	0	0	0	0	0
Days Minimum Temp. ≤ 32°F	8	4	3	1	0	0	0	0	0	0	2	8	26
Days Minimum Temp. ≤ 0°F	0	0	0	0	0	0	0	0	0	0	0	0	0
Heating Degree Days (base 65°F)	609	450	385	213	68	9	0	0	8	108	372	614	2,836
Cooling Degree Days (base 65°F)	0	0	2	42	148	355	554	524	314	92	3	0	2,034
Mean Precipitation (in.)	1.34	1.51	1.25	0.31	0.14	0.04	0.13	0.23	0.28	0.32	0.50	0.83	6.88
Days With ≥ 0.1" Precipitation	2	2	3	1	0	0	0	1	1	1	1	2	14
Days With ≥ 1.0" Precipitation	0	0	0	0	0	0	0	0	0	0	0	0	0
Mean Snowfall (in.)	1.2	0.3	0.4	0.0	0.0	0.0	0.0	0.0	0.0	0.0	0.1	1.3	3.3
Days With ≥ 1.0" Snow Depth	0	0	0	0	0	0	0	0	0	0	0	0	0

Redlands *San Bernardino County*   Elevation: 1,315 ft.   Latitude: 34° 03' N   Longitude: 117° 11' W

	JAN	FEB	MAR	APR	MAY	JUN	JUL	AUG	SEP	OCT	NOV	DEC	YEAR
Mean Maximum Temp. (°F)	66.2	68.4	69.5	75.3	79.6	88.1	95.0	95.3	90.4	82.2	73.1	66.8	79.2
Mean Temp. (°F)	53.3	55.4	57.0	61.3	66.0	72.4	78.3	78.8	74.7	67.3	58.5	53.3	64.7
Mean Minimum Temp. (°F)	40.2	42.5	44.4	47.2	52.3	56.6	61.5	62.1	59.0	52.5	43.9	39.7	50.2
Extreme Maximum Temp. (°F)	93	92	97	106	109	110	111	112	115	110	97	89	115
Extreme Minimum Temp. (°F)	25	25	30	33	38	41	50	49	43	28	28	23	23
Days Maximum Temp. ≥ 90°F	0	0	1	3	6	14	26	26	17	7	1	0	101
Days Maximum Temp. ≤ 32°F	0	0	0	0	0	0	0	0	0	0	0	0	0
Days Minimum Temp. ≤ 32°F	3	1	0	0	0	0	0	0	0	0	1	3	8
Days Minimum Temp. ≤ 0°F	0	0	0	0	0	0	0	0	0	0	0	0	0
Heating Degree Days (base 65°F)	358	271	251	144	62	11	0	0	3	46	200	356	1,702
Cooling Degree Days (base 65°F)	1	5	11	55	107	237	419	450	317	129	16	1	1,748
Mean Precipitation (in.)	2.98	3.03	2.63	0.80	0.42	0.13	0.10	0.24	0.42	0.48	0.98	1.62	13.83
Days With ≥ 0.1" Precipitation	5	4	5	2	1	0	0	0	1	1	2	3	24
Days With ≥ 1.0" Precipitation	1	1	1	0	0	0	0	0	0	0	0	0	3
Mean Snowfall (in.)	0.0	0.0	0.0	0.0	0.0	0.0	0.0	0.0	0.0	0.0	0.0	trace	trace
Days With ≥ 1.0" Snow Depth	0	0	0	0	0	0	0	0	0	0	0	0	0

Redwood City *San Mateo County*   Elevation: 29 ft.   Latitude: 37° 28' N   Longitude: 122° 14' W

	JAN	FEB	MAR	APR	MAY	JUN	JUL	AUG	SEP	OCT	NOV	DEC	YEAR
Mean Maximum Temp. (°F)	58.6	62.5	65.3	70.4	75.1	80.2	82.9	82.5	80.7	74.9	65.0	58.5	71.4
Mean Temp. (°F)	49.3	52.4	54.8	58.0	62.1	66.4	69.0	68.8	67.0	62.1	54.4	48.9	59.4
Mean Minimum Temp. (°F)	39.9	42.4	44.3	45.5	49.0	52.5	55.0	54.9	53.4	49.2	43.8	39.3	47.4
Extreme Maximum Temp. (°F)	73	80	84	96	101	104	110	105	106	104	83	74	110
Extreme Minimum Temp. (°F)	24	25	30	33	38	39	40	43	38	33	29	19	19
Days Maximum Temp. ≥ 90°F	0	0	0	0	2	5	5	4	5	1	0	0	22
Days Maximum Temp. ≤ 32°F	0	0	0	0	0	0	0	0	0	0	0	0	0
Days Minimum Temp. ≤ 32°F	4	1	0	0	0	0	0	0	0	0	0	5	10
Days Minimum Temp. ≤ 0°F	0	0	0	0	0	0	0	0	0	0	0	0	0
Heating Degree Days (base 65°F)	481	349	308	211	121	42	9	5	21	111	311	492	2,461
Cooling Degree Days (base 65°F)	0	0	0	10	34	90	143	133	87	32	1	0	530
Mean Precipitation (in.)	4.35	3.82	3.26	1.05	0.41	0.10	0.03	0.10	0.21	1.00	2.82	3.17	20.32
Days With ≥ 0.1" Precipitation	7	7	7	3	1	0	0	0	1	2	5	6	39
Days With ≥ 1.0" Precipitation	1	1	1	0	0	0	0	0	0	0	1	1	5
Mean Snowfall (in.)	0.0	0.0	trace	0.0	0.0	0.0	0.0	0.0	0.0	0.0	0.0	0.0	trace
Days With ≥ 1.0" Snow Depth	0	0	0	0	0	0	0	0	0	0	0	0	0

Richardson Gr. State Park *Humboldt County*   Elevation: 498 ft.   Latitude: 40° 02' N   Longitude: 123° 48' W

	JAN	FEB	MAR	APR	MAY	JUN	JUL	AUG	SEP	OCT	NOV	DEC	YEAR
Mean Maximum Temp. (°F)	50.1	54.4	59.1	64.5	71.2	78.2	85.9	86.7	82.9	70.3	55.6	49.1	67.3
Mean Temp. (°F)	43.7	46.4	49.5	52.8	58.4	64.1	69.5	69.8	66.2	57.5	48.1	43.1	55.8
Mean Minimum Temp. (°F)	37.4	38.3	39.8	41.1	45.5	50.0	53.1	52.9	49.4	44.6	40.5	36.9	44.1
Extreme Maximum Temp. (°F)	66	77	81	90	101	105	112	112	106	100	73	74	112
Extreme Minimum Temp. (°F)	22	20	29	30	32	38	41	43	38	28	26	15	15
Days Maximum Temp. ≥ 90°F	0	0	0	0	1	3	11	11	7	1	0	0	34
Days Maximum Temp. ≤ 32°F	0	0	0	0	0	0	0	0	0	0	0	0	0
Days Minimum Temp. ≤ 32°F	8	5	2	0	0	0	0	0	0	0	3	8	26
Days Minimum Temp. ≤ 0°F	0	0	0	0	0	0	0	0	0	0	0	0	0
Heating Degree Days (base 65°F)	653	519	474	360	215	80	15	11	48	237	501	673	3,786
Cooling Degree Days (base 65°F)	0	0	0	1	17	52	152	162	86	11	0	0	481
Mean Precipitation (in.)	13.37	11.00	10.33	4.43	2.01	0.65	0.09	0.36	1.30	3.91	10.38	11.73	69.56
Days With ≥ 0.1" Precipitation	12	11	11	7	4	1	0	1	2	5	11	12	77
Days With ≥ 1.0" Precipitation	5	4	3	1	0	0	0	0	0	1	4	4	22
Mean Snowfall (in.)	0.1	trace	trace	0.0	0.0	0.0	0.0	0.0	0.0	0.0	trace	0.2	0.3
Days With ≥ 1.0" Snow Depth	0	0	0	0	0	0	0	0	0	0	0	0	0

Richmond *Contra Costa County*   Elevation: 19 ft.   Latitude: 37° 37' N   Longitude: 122° 22' W

	JAN	FEB	MAR	APR	MAY	JUN	JUL	AUG	SEP	OCT	NOV	DEC	YEAR
Mean Maximum Temp. (°F)	57.8	61.8	64.1	67.3	69.4	71.5	71.6	71.7	74.2	72.4	64.5	58.0	67.0
Mean Temp. (°F)	50.3	53.7	55.6	58.1	60.6	63.0	63.7	64.0	65.3	62.8	56.2	50.5	58.7
Mean Minimum Temp. (°F)	42.7	45.6	47.1	48.8	51.7	54.5	55.8	56.4	56.4	53.2	48.0	43.0	50.3
Extreme Maximum Temp. (°F)	72	88	84	93	100	102	98	98	107	100	82	83	107
Extreme Minimum Temp. (°F)	27	29	35	31	38	43	44	44	46	41	34	24	24
Days Maximum Temp. ≥ 90°F	0	0	0	0	0	1	0	0	2	1	0	0	4
Days Maximum Temp. ≤ 32°F	0	0	0	0	0	0	0	0	0	0	0	0	0
Days Minimum Temp. ≤ 32°F	1	0	0	0	0	0	0	0	0	0	0	1	2
Days Minimum Temp. ≤ 0°F	0	0	0	0	0	0	0	0	0	0	0	0	0
Heating Degree Days (base 65°F)	450	312	285	209	147	84	64	52	42	92	258	443	2,438
Cooling Degree Days (base 65°F)	0	0	0	1	11	15	34	35	51	35	2	0	213
Mean Precipitation (in.)	5.06	4.16	3.54	1.30	0.50	0.18	0.07	0.09	0.27	1.22	3.67	3.48	23.54
Days With ≥ 0.1" Precipitation	7	7	7	3	1	0	0	0	1	2	6	6	40
Days With ≥ 1.0" Precipitation	2	1	1	0	0	0	0	0	0	0	1	1	6
Mean Snowfall (in.)	0.0	trace	0.0	0.0	0.0	0.0	0.0	0.0	0.0	0.0	0.0	0.0	trace
Days With ≥ 1.0" Snow Depth	0	0	0	0	0	0	0	0	0	0	0	0	0

Riverside Citrus Exp. Station *Riverside County*   Elevation: 984 ft.   Latitude: 33° 58' N   Longitude: 117° 21' W

	JAN	FEB	MAR	APR	MAY	JUN	JUL	AUG	SEP	OCT	NOV	DEC	YEAR
Mean Maximum Temp. (°F)	65.8	68.1	69.3	75.1	79.3	86.9	93.3	93.9	89.7	82.0	72.9	66.7	78.6
Mean Temp. (°F)	54.1	56.1	57.6	61.7	66.2	71.9	77.2	77.8	74.5	67.5	59.2	54.1	64.8
Mean Minimum Temp. (°F)	42.3	43.9	45.8	48.3	53.1	56.8	61.1	61.8	59.3	52.9	45.4	41.4	51.0
Extreme Maximum Temp. (°F)	89	91	98	104	108	110	111	112	113	108	97	89	113
Extreme Minimum Temp. (°F)	27	29	31	34	40	44	50	49	42	32	31	22	22
Days Maximum Temp. ≥ 90°F	0	0	1	2	4	12	23	24	16	7	1	0	90
Days Maximum Temp. ≤ 32°F	0	0	0	0	0	0	0	0	0	0	0	0	0
Days Minimum Temp. ≤ 32°F	2	0	0	0	0	0	0	0	0	0	0	1	3
Days Minimum Temp. ≤ 0°F	0	0	0	0	0	0	0	0	0	0	0	0	0
Heating Degree Days (base 65°F)	333	252	231	128	50	9	0	0	3	40	185	331	1,562
Cooling Degree Days (base 65°F)	0	6	9	48	96	215	385	420	301	124	16	1	1,621
Mean Precipitation (in.)	2.46	2.33	2.21	0.58	0.25	0.10	0.03	0.18	0.25	0.24	0.84	1.26	10.73
Days With ≥ 0.1" Precipitation	5	4	5	2	1	0	0	0	1	1	2	3	24
Days With ≥ 1.0" Precipitation	1	1	0	0	0	0	0	0	0	0	0	0	2
Mean Snowfall (in.)	0.0	0.0	0.0	trace	0.0	0.0	0.0	0.0	0.0	0.0	0.0	trace	trace
Days With ≥ 1.0" Snow Depth	0	0	0	0	0	0	0	0	0	0	0	0	0

Riverside Fire Station 3 *Riverside County*   Elevation: 839 ft.   Latitude: 33° 57' N   Longitude: 117° 23' W

	JAN	FEB	MAR	APR	MAY	JUN	JUL	AUG	SEP	OCT	NOV	DEC	YEAR
Mean Maximum Temp. (°F)	67.6	70.1	71.7	77.1	81.3	88.6	94.5	95.1	90.6	83.1	74.1	68.1	80.2
Mean Temp. (°F)	54.7	56.9	58.6	62.8	67.5	73.2	78.5	79.1	75.4	68.1	59.5	54.3	65.7
Mean Minimum Temp. (°F)	41.7	43.5	45.5	48.4	53.6	57.8	62.4	63.0	60.0	53.1	44.9	40.4	51.2
Extreme Maximum Temp. (°F)	90	91	99	105	110	111	112	113	113	109	96	89	113
Extreme Minimum Temp. (°F)	25	28	30	29	40	46	51	50	45	30	28	22	22
Days Maximum Temp. ≥ 90°F	0	0	1	3	5	14	25	25	17	8	1	0	99
Days Maximum Temp. ≤ 32°F	0	0	0	0	0	0	0	0	0	0	0	0	0
Days Minimum Temp. ≤ 32°F	2	1	0	0	0	0	0	0	0	0	0	2	5
Days Minimum Temp. ≤ 0°F	0	0	0	0	0	0	0	0	0	0	0	0	0
Heating Degree Days (base 65°F)	315	228	201	105	31	4	0	0	2	31	172	325	1,414
Cooling Degree Days (base 65°F)	2	5	12	61	126	258	433	471	340	149	17	1	1,875
Mean Precipitation (in.)	2.33	2.30	2.12	0.56	0.20	0.09	0.03	0.18	0.24	0.29	0.79	1.19	10.32
Days With ≥ 0.1" Precipitation	5	4	4	1	1	0	0	0	0	1	2	3	21
Days With ≥ 1.0" Precipitation	0	1	1	0	0	0	0	0	0	0	0	0	2
Mean Snowfall (in.)	0.0	0.0	0.0	0.0	0.0	0.0	0.0	0.0	0.0	0.0	0.0	0.0	0.0
Days With ≥ 1.0" Snow Depth	0	0	0	0	0	0	0	0	0	0	0	0	0

Sacramento WSO City *Sacramento County*   Elevation: 22 ft.   Latitude: 38° 35' N   Longitude: 121° 30' W

	JAN	FEB	MAR	APR	MAY	JUN	JUL	AUG	SEP	OCT	NOV	DEC	YEAR
Mean Maximum Temp. (°F)	55.0	62.3	67.0	73.7	81.7	88.6	93.9	92.5	88.7	79.3	64.4	54.8	75.1
Mean Temp. (°F)	48.1	53.5	57.1	61.6	68.0	73.5	77.4	76.6	73.8	66.5	55.3	47.7	63.3
Mean Minimum Temp. (°F)	41.2	44.7	47.1	49.4	54.1	58.3	61.0	60.7	59.0	53.6	46.2	40.5	51.3
Extreme Maximum Temp. (°F)	75	80	90	97	107	108	113	111	108	102	86	72	113
Extreme Minimum Temp. (°F)	28	23	32	35	41	46	50	51	46	38	30	18	18
Days Maximum Temp. ≥ 90°F	0	0	0	1	7	13	23	20	15	4	0	0	83
Days Maximum Temp. ≤ 32°F	0	0	0	0	0	0	0	0	0	0	0	0	0
Days Minimum Temp. ≤ 32°F	1	0	0	0	0	0	0	0	0	0	0	3	4
Days Minimum Temp. ≤ 0°F	0	0	0	0	0	0	0	0	0	0	0	0	0
Heating Degree Days (base 65°F)	515	318	243	131	43	6	0	0	4	55	286	530	2,131
Cooling Degree Days (base 65°F)	0	0	4	44	139	265	398	379	281	109	2	0	1,621
Mean Precipitation (in.)	3.92	3.52	3.13	1.10	0.55	0.18	0.05	0.05	0.36	0.94	2.81	2.87	19.48
Days With ≥ 0.1" Precipitation	7	6	7	3	1	1	0	0	1	2	5	5	38
Days With ≥ 1.0" Precipitation	1	1	1	0	0	0	0	0	0	0	1	0	4
Mean Snowfall (in.)	na	na	na	na	na	na	na	na	na	na	na	na	na
Days With ≥ 1.0" Snow Depth	na	na	na	na	na	na	na	na	na	na	na	na	na

Salinas 2 *Monterey County*   Elevation: 42 ft.   Latitude: 36° 40' N   Longitude: 121° 40' W

	JAN	FEB	MAR	APR	MAY	JUN	JUL	AUG	SEP	OCT	NOV	DEC	YEAR
Mean Maximum Temp. (°F)	62.5	64.6	65.3	67.3	68.4	70.4	71.4	72.9	74.6	73.4	67.4	62.6	68.4
Mean Temp. (°F)	51.9	53.9	55.0	56.5	58.9	61.2	63.0	64.0	64.2	61.5	56.1	51.7	58.1
Mean Minimum Temp. (°F)	41.3	43.1	44.6	45.7	49.3	51.8	54.4	55.1	53.7	49.7	44.6	40.7	47.8
Extreme Maximum Temp. (°F)	85	86	88	98	99	103	97	97	106	105	94	83	106
Extreme Minimum Temp. (°F)	26	26	25	32	39	42	43	44	41	34	29	24	24
Days Maximum Temp. ≥ 90°F	0	0	0	0	1	1	1	0	1	1	0	0	5
Days Maximum Temp. ≤ 32°F	0	0	0	0	0	0	0	0	0	0	0	0	0
Days Minimum Temp. ≤ 32°F	3	1	0	0	0	0	0	0	0	0	0	3	7
Days Minimum Temp. ≤ 0°F	0	0	0	0	0	0	0	0	0	0	0	0	0
Heating Degree Days (base 65°F)	398	308	305	253	191	122	73	48	56	126	266	406	2,552
Cooling Degree Days (base 65°F)	0	1	1	7	9	11	19	29	36	29	4	0	146
Mean Precipitation (in.)	2.98	2.79	2.76	1.01	0.34	0.11	0.04	0.06	0.17	0.68	1.99	2.15	15.08
Days With ≥ 0.1" Precipitation	5	5	5	2	1	0	0	0	0	1	4	4	27
Days With ≥ 1.0" Precipitation	1	0	0	0	0	0	0	0	0	0	0	0	1
Mean Snowfall (in.)	0.0	0.0	0.0	0.0	0.0	0.0	0.0	0.0	0.0	0.0	0.0	0.0	0.0
Days With ≥ 1.0" Snow Depth	0	0	0	0	0	0	0	0	0	0	0	0	0

Salinas Municipal Airport *Monterey County*   Elevation: 68 ft.   Latitude: 36° 40' N   Longitude: 121° 36' W

	JAN	FEB	MAR	APR	MAY	JUN	JUL	AUG	SEP	OCT	NOV	DEC	YEAR
Mean Maximum Temp. (°F)	61.0	62.8	63.5	66.7	67.8	70.2	71.2	72.2	74.5	72.8	66.3	61.1	67.5
Mean Temp. (°F)	51.1	52.9	54.0	56.2	58.8	61.4	62.9	63.7	64.3	61.5	55.2	50.4	57.7
Mean Minimum Temp. (°F)	41.1	42.9	44.5	45.7	49.8	52.6	54.5	55.3	54.2	50.2	44.0	39.7	47.9
Extreme Maximum Temp. (°F)	81	85	87	98	99	104	99	97	105	105	91	84	105
Extreme Minimum Temp. (°F)	24	26	29	33	38	42	46	44	40	31	30	24	24
Days Maximum Temp. ≥ 90°F	0	0	0	0	0	1	0	0	2	1	0	0	4
Days Maximum Temp. ≤ 32°F	0	0	0	0	0	0	0	0	0	0	0	0	0
Days Minimum Temp. ≤ 32°F	3	1	0	0	0	0	0	0	0	0	0	3	7
Days Minimum Temp. ≤ 0°F	0	0	0	0	0	0	0	0	0	0	0	0	0
Heating Degree Days (base 65°F)	426	335	334	261	193	115	79	54	54	128	289	445	2,713
Cooling Degree Days (base 65°F)	0	1	1	7	6	14	25	23	35	30	2	0	144
Mean Precipitation (in.)	2.53	2.41	2.45	0.89	0.22	0.09	0.04	0.05	0.22	0.58	1.63	1.73	12.84
Days With ≥ 0.1" Precipitation	6	6	6	3	1	0	0	0	0	1	2	4	33
Days With ≥ 1.0" Precipitation	0	0	0	0	0	0	0	0	0	0	0	0	0
Mean Snowfall (in.)	trace	trace	trace	trace	0.0	0.0	0.0	0.0	0.0	0.0	trace	trace	trace
Days With ≥ 1.0" Snow Depth	0	0	0	0	0	0	0	0	0	0	0	0	0

San Bernardino Co. Hospital *San Bernardino County*   Elevation: 1,122 ft.   Latitude: 34° 08' N   Longitude: 117° 16' W

	JAN	FEB	MAR	APR	MAY	JUN	JUL	AUG	SEP	OCT	NOV	DEC	YEAR
Mean Maximum Temp. (°F)	66.2	68.6	70.1	76.1	80.8	89.5	95.8	95.8	91.2	82.6	73.1	66.9	79.7
Mean Temp. (°F)	54.0	56.2	57.9	62.5	67.2	73.7	79.4	79.7	75.9	68.2	59.3	54.0	65.7
Mean Minimum Temp. (°F)	41.8	43.8	45.6	48.8	53.6	57.9	62.9	63.5	60.6	53.7	45.5	41.1	51.6
Extreme Maximum Temp. (°F)	94	92	96	100	112	111	111	111	117	111	98	89	117
Extreme Minimum Temp. (°F)	21	27	28	32	39	45	50	50	43	30	31	22	21
Days Maximum Temp. ≥ 90°F	0	0	0	2	6	15	26	26	18	8	1	0	102
Days Maximum Temp. ≤ 32°F	0	0	0	0	0	0	0	0	0	0	0	0	0
Days Minimum Temp. ≤ 32°F	2	1	0	0	0	0	0	0	0	0	0	2	5
Days Minimum Temp. ≤ 0°F	0	0	0	0	0	0	0	0	0	0	0	0	0
Heating Degree Days (base 65°F)	334	246	222	112	44	6	0	0	2	33	183	336	1,518
Cooling Degree Days (base 65°F)	1	5	9	58	124	267	445	471	343	140	15	1	1,879
Mean Precipitation (in.)	3.55	3.63	3.31	0.89	0.41	0.09	0.04	0.23	0.42	0.68	1.30	2.04	16.59
Days With ≥ 0.1" Precipitation	5	5	5	2	1	0	0	0	1	1	2	3	25
Days With ≥ 1.0" Precipitation	1	1	1	0	0	0	0	0	0	0	0	1	4
Mean Snowfall (in.)	0.0	0.0	0.0	0.0	0.0	0.0	0.0	0.0	0.0	0.0	0.0	0.0	0.0
Days With ≥ 1.0" Snow Depth	0	0	0	0	0	0	0	0	0	0	0	0	0

San Gabriel Fire Dept. *Los Angeles County*   Elevation: 449 ft.   Latitude: 34° 06' N   Longitude: 118° 06' W

	JAN	FEB	MAR	APR	MAY	JUN	JUL	AUG	SEP	OCT	NOV	DEC	YEAR
Mean Maximum Temp. (°F)	69.8	71.8	72.4	76.5	78.5	84.2	89.2	90.6	88.5	83.2	75.5	70.4	79.2
Mean Temp. (°F)	56.2	58.2	59.7	63.1	66.5	71.2	75.6	76.5	74.6	68.9	61.0	56.1	65.6
Mean Minimum Temp. (°F)	42.4	44.6	47.0	49.5	54.3	58.3	62.0	62.5	60.6	54.4	46.3	41.6	52.0
Extreme Maximum Temp. (°F)	94	94	101	106	103	111	108	112	112	108	101	92	112
Extreme Minimum Temp. (°F)	27	25	31	34	42	43	51	51	47	33	31	24	24
Days Maximum Temp. ≥ 90°F	0	1	1	3	3	6	14	17	13	7	1	0	66
Days Maximum Temp. ≤ 32°F	0	0	0	0	0	0	0	0	0	0	0	0	0
Days Minimum Temp. ≤ 32°F	1	0	0	0	0	0	0	0	0	0	0	2	3
Days Minimum Temp. ≤ 0°F	0	0	0	0	0	0	0	0	0	0	0	0	0
Heating Degree Days (base 65°F)	270	192	172	97	40	6	0	0	1	19	135	272	1,204
Cooling Degree Days (base 65°F)	2	11	18	62	101	204	346	382	309	162	21	2	1,620
Mean Precipitation (in.)	4.09	4.54	3.85	0.93	0.41	0.16	0.03	0.10	0.44	0.53	1.47	2.22	18.77
Days With ≥ 0.1" Precipitation	5	4	5	2	1	0	0	0	1	1	2	3	24
Days With ≥ 1.0" Precipitation	2	1	1	0	0	0	0	0	0	0	1	1	5
Mean Snowfall (in.)	0.0	0.0	0.0	0.0	0.0	0.0	0.0	0.0	0.0	0.0	0.0	0.0	0.0
Days With ≥ 1.0" Snow Depth	0	0	0	0	0	0	0	0	0	0	0	0	0

San Gregorio 2 SE *San Mateo County*   Elevation: 272 ft.   Latitude: 37° 18' N   Longitude: 122° 22' W

	JAN	FEB	MAR	APR	MAY	JUN	JUL	AUG	SEP	OCT	NOV	DEC	YEAR
Mean Maximum Temp. (°F)	58.8	59.9	60.4	62.6	64.4	67.4	69.6	70.1	71.1	68.1	62.5	58.4	64.4
Mean Temp. (°F)	49.6	50.7	51.3	52.6	55.2	57.8	60.1	60.6	60.2	56.8	52.2	48.8	54.7
Mean Minimum Temp. (°F)	40.5	41.6	42.3	42.6	45.9	48.2	50.5	51.0	49.2	45.4	41.8	39.2	44.8
Extreme Maximum Temp. (°F)	76	82	81	91	95	97	92	94	98	99	85	77	99
Extreme Minimum Temp. (°F)	25	26	27	29	32	36	38	38	35	29	27	20	20
Days Maximum Temp. ≥ 90°F	0	0	0	0	0	0	0	0	1	0	0	0	1
Days Maximum Temp. ≤ 32°F	0	0	0	0	0	0	0	0	0	0	0	0	0
Days Minimum Temp. ≤ 32°F	4	2	1	1	0	0	0	0	0	0	1	4	13
Days Minimum Temp. ≤ 0°F	0	0	0	0	0	0	0	0	0	0	0	0	0
Heating Degree Days (base 65°F)	469	396	417	367	298	211	149	133	146	254	378	494	3,712
Cooling Degree Days (base 65°F)	0	0	0	2	1	2	6	4	6	6	0	0	27
Mean Precipitation (in.)	5.74	5.03	4.60	1.89	0.84	0.29	0.13	0.21	0.41	1.62	4.17	4.66	29.59
Days With ≥ 0.1" Precipitation	8	8	9	5	2	1	0	0	1	3	6	8	51
Days With ≥ 1.0" Precipitation	2	1	1	0	0	0	0	0	0	0	1	1	6
Mean Snowfall (in.)	trace	trace	0.0	0.0	0.0	0.0	0.0	0.0	0.0	0.0	0.0	trace	trace
Days With ≥ 1.0" Snow Depth	0	0	0	0	0	0	0	0	0	0	0	0	0

San Jose *Santa Clara County* Elevation: 95 ft. Latitude: 37° 20' N Longitude: 121° 53' W

	JAN	FEB	MAR	APR	MAY	JUN	JUL	AUG	SEP	OCT	NOV	DEC	YEAR
Mean Maximum Temp. (°F)	58.4	62.5	65.8	70.4	75.2	80.0	82.8	82.3	80.9	74.7	64.5	57.6	71.3
Mean Temp. (°F)	50.1	53.5	56.2	59.2	63.5	67.6	70.2	70.0	68.7	63.5	55.1	49.3	60.6
Mean Minimum Temp. (°F)	41.7	44.5	46.4	48.0	51.8	55.3	57.5	57.6	56.4	52.2	45.8	41.0	49.9
Extreme Maximum Temp. (°F)	76	81	84	95	101	105	108	105	104	101	83	72	108
Extreme Minimum Temp. (°F)	27	26	31	36	39	43	48	47	45	36	21	19	19
Days Maximum Temp. ≥ 90°F	0	0	0	1	2	4	5	4	4	1	0	0	21
Days Maximum Temp. ≤ 32°F	0	0	0	0	0	0	0	0	0	0	0	0	0
Days Minimum Temp. ≤ 32°F	2	0	0	0	0	0	0	0	0	0	0	3	5
Days Minimum Temp. ≤ 0°F	0	0	0	0	0	0	0	0	0	0	0	0	0
Heating Degree Days (base 65°F)	457	317	268	181	91	24	3	2	9	85	290	478	2,205
Cooling Degree Days (base 65°F)	0	0	2	21	50	115	185	182	134	52	1	0	742
Mean Precipitation (in.)	3.05	2.74	2.61	1.00	0.43	0.09	0.06	0.07	0.23	0.82	1.92	2.12	15.14
Days With ≥ 0.1" Precipitation	7	6	6	3	1	0	0	0	1	2	4	5	35
Days With ≥ 1.0" Precipitation	1	0	0	0	0	0	0	0	0	0	0	0	1
Mean Snowfall (in.)	trace	trace	trace	trace	0.0	0.0	0.0	0.0	0.0	0.0	0.0	trace	trace
Days With ≥ 1.0" Snow Depth	0	0	0	0	0	0	0	0	0	0	0	0	0

San Luis Dam *Merced County* Elevation: 275 ft. Latitude: 37° 03' N Longitude: 121° 03' W

	JAN	FEB	MAR	APR	MAY	JUN	JUL	AUG	SEP	OCT	NOV	DEC	YEAR
Mean Maximum Temp. (°F)	54.1	60.5	65.3	71.4	78.4	85.4	91.4	90.5	86.6	77.9	64.6	54.7	73.4
Mean Temp. (°F)	46.1	51.2	55.8	60.4	66.4	72.3	77.6	77.0	73.6	65.8	54.8	46.1	62.3
Mean Minimum Temp. (°F)	38.0	42.0	46.2	49.5	54.4	59.1	63.8	63.5	60.5	53.7	45.0	37.5	51.1
Extreme Maximum Temp. (°F)	73	75	84	94	104	106	108	107	105	99	81	72	108
Extreme Minimum Temp. (°F)	22	22	28	32	36	40	44	45	45	33	28	14	14
Days Maximum Temp. ≥ 90°F	0	0	0	0	5	10	19	18	12	3	0	0	67
Days Maximum Temp. ≤ 32°F	0	0	0	0	0	0	0	0	0	0	0	0	0
Days Minimum Temp. ≤ 32°F	6	1	0	0	0	0	0	0	0	0	1	6	14
Days Minimum Temp. ≤ 0°F	0	0	0	0	0	0	0	0	0	0	0	0	0
Heating Degree Days (base 65°F)	580	382	281	158	65	13	1	1	4	61	301	579	2,426
Cooling Degree Days (base 65°F)	0	0	2	36	115	231	399	392	273	97	3	0	1,548
Mean Precipitation (in.)	2.12	2.01	1.76	0.53	0.49	0.05	0.03	0.10	0.23	0.47	1.34	1.41	10.54
Days With ≥ 0.1" Precipitation	6	5	4	2	1	0	0	0	1	1	3	4	27
Days With ≥ 1.0" Precipitation	0	0	0	0	0	0	0	0	0	0	0	0	0
Mean Snowfall (in.)	trace	0.0	0.0	0.0	0.0	0.0	0.0	0.0	0.0	0.0	0.0	0.0	trace
Days With ≥ 1.0" Snow Depth	0	0	0	0	0	0	0	0	0	0	0	0	0

San Luis Obispo Polytech *San Luis Obispo County* Elevation: 314 ft. Latitude: 35° 18' N Longitude: 120° 40' W

	JAN	FEB	MAR	APR	MAY	JUN	JUL	AUG	SEP	OCT	NOV	DEC	YEAR
Mean Maximum Temp. (°F)	63.8	65.4	65.8	69.0	71.2	75.6	79.0	80.1	79.9	76.5	70.3	64.7	71.8
Mean Temp. (°F)	52.9	54.5	55.1	57.0	59.3	63.0	65.9	66.7	66.5	63.1	57.9	53.0	59.6
Mean Minimum Temp. (°F)	41.9	43.6	44.4	45.0	47.4	50.4	52.7	53.2	52.8	49.6	45.4	41.3	47.3
Extreme Maximum Temp. (°F)	88	89	89	104	99	106	106	102	112	109	98	86	112
Extreme Minimum Temp. (°F)	26	28	31	29	34	37	41	40	41	30	30	12	12
Days Maximum Temp. ≥ 90°F	0	0	0	1	1	2	2	3	4	3	0	0	16
Days Maximum Temp. ≤ 32°F	0	0	0	0	0	0	0	0	0	0	0	0	0
Days Minimum Temp. ≤ 32°F	1	1	0	0	0	0	0	0	0	0	0	2	4
Days Minimum Temp. ≤ 0°F	0	0	0	0	0	0	0	0	0	0	0	0	0
Heating Degree Days (base 65°F)	370	292	302	244	191	91	31	20	35	99	218	366	2,259
Cooling Degree Days (base 65°F)	0	3	2	18	19	39	72	89	87	56	13	1	399
Mean Precipitation (in.)	5.46	5.13	4.55	1.25	0.48	0.08	0.03	0.09	0.47	0.92	2.27	3.89	24.62
Days With ≥ 0.1" Precipitation	7	6	6	3	1	0	0	0	1	2	4	5	35
Days With ≥ 1.0" Precipitation	2	2	2	0	0	0	0	0	0	0	1	1	8
Mean Snowfall (in.)	0.0	0.0	0.0	0.0	0.0	0.0	0.0	0.0	0.0	0.0	0.0	0.0	0.0
Days With ≥ 1.0" Snow Depth	0	0	0	0	0	0	0	0	0	0	0	0	0

Santa Ana Fire Station *Orange County* Elevation: 134 ft. Latitude: 33° 45' N Longitude: 117° 52' W

	JAN	FEB	MAR	APR	MAY	JUN	JUL	AUG	SEP	OCT	NOV	DEC	YEAR
Mean Maximum Temp. (°F)	69.0	70.1	70.5	73.2	74.4	78.1	82.5	84.0	83.3	79.3	73.5	68.9	75.6
Mean Temp. (°F)	57.8	59.0	60.1	62.8	65.4	69.0	72.8	74.2	73.1	68.7	62.1	57.4	65.2
Mean Minimum Temp. (°F)	46.6	48.0	49.7	52.2	56.4	59.9	63.1	64.3	62.8	57.9	50.5	45.9	54.8
Extreme Maximum Temp. (°F)	92	95	98	104	100	109	110	101	108	104	98	92	110
Extreme Minimum Temp. (°F)	32	30	36	34	39	49	51	52	51	37	36	32	30
Days Maximum Temp. ≥ 90°F	0	0	0	1	1	2	3	5	5	3	1	0	21
Days Maximum Temp. ≤ 32°F	0	0	0	0	0	0	0	0	0	0	0	0	0
Days Minimum Temp. ≤ 32°F	0	0	0	0	0	0	0	0	0	0	0	0	0
Days Minimum Temp. ≤ 0°F	0	0	0	0	0	0	0	0	0	0	0	0	0
Heating Degree Days (base 65°F)	221	171	157	92	41	6	0	0	0	13	102	233	1,036
Cooling Degree Days (base 65°F)	6	13	14	44	65	130	253	302	249	142	24	5	1,247
Mean Precipitation (in.)	3.23	2.96	2.88	0.64	0.25	0.11	0.02	0.12	0.33	0.31	1.25	1.89	13.99
Days With ≥ 0.1" Precipitation	5	4	5	1	1	0	0	0	1	1	2	4	24
Days With ≥ 1.0" Precipitation	1	1	1	0	0	0	0	0	0	0	0	1	4
Mean Snowfall (in.)	0.0	0.0	0.0	0.0	0.0	0.0	0.0	0.0	0.0	0.0	0.0	0.0	0.0
Days With ≥ 1.0" Snow Depth	0	0	0	0	0	0	0	0	0	0	0	0	0

Santa Barbara Municipal Airport *Santa Barbara County*   Elevation: 6 ft.   Latitude: 34° 26' N   Longitude: 119° 51' W

	JAN	FEB	MAR	APR	MAY	JUN	JUL	AUG	SEP	OCT	NOV	DEC	YEAR
Mean Maximum Temp. (°F)	64.1	65.0	65.7	68.3	69.2	72.3	74.5	75.7	75.5	73.0	69.2	64.8	69.8
Mean Temp. (°F)	52.4	54.4	55.8	57.8	59.8	63.1	65.8	66.9	65.9	62.3	56.6	52.4	59.4
Mean Minimum Temp. (°F)	40.6	43.7	46.0	47.3	50.4	53.8	57.1	58.1	56.3	51.6	43.9	39.8	49.0
Extreme Maximum Temp. (°F)	86	86	94	96	92	109	109	105	104	103	97	83	109
Extreme Minimum Temp. (°F)	25	25	32	37	38	42	49	47	45	31	30	20	20
Days Maximum Temp. ≥ 90°F	0	0	0	0	0	1	0	0	1	1	0	0	3
Days Maximum Temp. ≤ 32°F	0	0	0	0	0	0	0	0	0	0	0	0	0
Days Minimum Temp. ≤ 32°F	3	1	0	0	0	0	0	0	0	0	0	2	6
Days Minimum Temp. ≤ 0°F	0	0	0	0	0	0	0	0	0	0	0	0	0
Heating Degree Days (base 65°F)	385	294	279	213	162	75	22	13	32	97	249	384	2,205
Cooling Degree Days (base 65°F)	1	1	3	7	7	23	62	76	61	21	2	0	264
Mean Precipitation (in.)	3.63	3.85	3.75	0.67	0.21	0.06	0.04	0.12	0.48	0.50	1.55	2.43	17.29
Days With ≥ 0.1" Precipitation	5	5	5	1	0	0	0	0	1	1	3	3	24
Days With ≥ 1.0" Precipitation	1	1	1	0	0	0	0	0	0	0	0	1	4
Mean Snowfall (in.)	0.0	0.0	0.0	0.0	0.0	0.0	0.0	0.0	0.0	0.0	0.0	0.0	0.0
Days With ≥ 1.0" Snow Depth	0	0	0	0	0	0	0	0	0	0	0	0	0

Santa Cruz *Santa Cruz County*   Elevation: 127 ft.   Latitude: 36° 59' N   Longitude: 121° 59' W

	JAN	FEB	MAR	APR	MAY	JUN	JUL	AUG	SEP	OCT	NOV	DEC	YEAR
Mean Maximum Temp. (°F)	60.8	62.9	64.4	68.2	70.7	73.9	74.6	75.4	75.5	72.4	65.2	60.4	68.7
Mean Temp. (°F)	50.4	52.4	53.8	56.1	58.9	62.1	63.6	64.2	63.7	60.2	54.3	49.8	57.5
Mean Minimum Temp. (°F)	39.9	41.8	43.1	43.9	47.1	50.3	52.5	52.9	51.8	48.0	43.3	39.3	46.2
Extreme Maximum Temp. (°F)	81	84	88	94	98	106	102	98	107	103	90	80	107
Extreme Minimum Temp. (°F)	23	24	28	32	34	36	40	38	38	30	28	19	19
Days Maximum Temp. ≥ 90°F	0	0	0	0	1	1	1	1	2	1	0	0	7
Days Maximum Temp. ≤ 32°F	0	0	0	0	0	0	0	0	0	0	0	0	0
Days Minimum Temp. ≤ 32°F	4	2	1	0	0	0	0	0	0	0	1	4	12
Days Minimum Temp. ≤ 0°F	0	0	0	0	0	0	0	0	0	0	0	0	0
Heating Degree Days (base 65°F)	447	349	341	264	191	99	61	47	66	157	316	463	2,801
Cooling Degree Days (base 65°F)	0	0	0	5	9	18	26	30	30	18	1	0	137
Mean Precipitation (in.)	6.53	5.79	4.81	1.93	0.66	0.19	0.14	0.10	0.40	1.32	4.36	4.46	30.69
Days With ≥ 0.1" Precipitation	8	7	8	4	1	1	0	0	1	2	6	7	45
Days With ≥ 1.0" Precipitation	2	2	1	0	0	0	0	0	0	0	1	1	7
Mean Snowfall (in.)	0.0	0.0	0.0	0.0	trace	0.0	0.0	0.0	0.0	0.0	0.0	0.0	trace
Days With ≥ 1.0" Snow Depth	0	0	0	0	0	0	0	0	0	0	0	0	0

Santa Monica Pier *Los Angeles County*   Elevation: 13 ft.   Latitude: 34° 00' N   Longitude: 118° 30' W

	JAN	FEB	MAR	APR	MAY	JUN	JUL	AUG	SEP	OCT	NOV	DEC	YEAR
Mean Maximum Temp. (°F)	64.3	64.1	63.0	64.0	64.3	66.8	69.5	70.7	71.1	70.2	67.9	64.9	66.7
Mean Temp. (°F)	57.3	57.7	57.5	58.9	60.4	63.1	65.8	66.9	66.8	65.0	61.2	57.8	61.5
Mean Minimum Temp. (°F)	50.3	51.3	52.0	53.7	56.3	59.4	62.1	63.1	62.5	59.7	54.5	50.6	56.3
Extreme Maximum Temp. (°F)	85	89	90	99	86	90	84	95	94	99	93	89	99
Extreme Minimum Temp. (°F)	37	38	41	42	43	50	53	54	55	42	37	34	34
Days Maximum Temp. ≥ 90°F	0	0	0	0	0	0	0	0	0	0	0	0	0
Days Maximum Temp. ≤ 32°F	0	0	0	0	0	0	0	0	0	0	0	0	0
Days Minimum Temp. ≤ 32°F	0	0	0	0	0	0	0	0	0	0	0	0	0
Days Minimum Temp. ≤ 0°F	0	0	0	0	0	0	0	0	0	0	0	0	0
Heating Degree Days (base 65°F)	235	206	229	183	144	68	18	12	18	42	127	223	1,505
Cooling Degree Days (base 65°F)	6	8	4	10	7	20	57	84	79	49	17	5	346
Mean Precipitation (in.)	3.02	3.19	2.29	0.50	0.25	0.04	trace	0.13	0.17	0.30	1.19	2.01	13.09
Days With ≥ 0.1" Precipitation	4	4	3	1	0	0	0	0	0	1	2	3	18
Days With ≥ 1.0" Precipitation	1	1	1	0	0	0	0	0	0	0	0	1	4
Mean Snowfall (in.)	0.0	0.0	0.0	0.0	0.0	0.0	0.0	0.0	0.0	0.0	0.0	0.0	0.0
Days With ≥ 1.0" Snow Depth	0	0	0	0	0	0	0	0	0	0	0	0	0

Santa Paula *Ventura County*   Elevation: 236 ft.   Latitude: 34° 19' N   Longitude: 119° 09' W

	JAN	FEB	MAR	APR	MAY	JUN	JUL	AUG	SEP	OCT	NOV	DEC	YEAR
Mean Maximum Temp. (°F)	68.0	69.1	70.0	73.6	74.4	77.6	80.9	81.6	81.0	78.3	73.0	68.4	74.6
Mean Temp. (°F)	54.8	56.0	57.0	59.7	62.0	65.3	68.4	68.7	67.9	64.1	58.4	54.6	61.4
Mean Minimum Temp. (°F)	41.8	42.9	44.0	45.8	49.7	52.9	55.7	55.7	54.6	49.9	43.9	40.7	48.1
Extreme Maximum Temp. (°F)	91	92	96	105	102	106	105	105	108	103	99	90	108
Extreme Minimum Temp. (°F)	25	26	30	31	35	40	44	40	43	32	28	25	25
Days Maximum Temp. ≥ 90°F	0	0	0	1	1	1	2	3	4	3	1	0	16
Days Maximum Temp. ≤ 32°F	0	0	0	0	0	0	0	0	0	0	0	0	0
Days Minimum Temp. ≤ 32°F	2	1	0	0	0	0	0	0	0	0	1	3	7
Days Minimum Temp. ≤ 0°F	0	0	0	0	0	0	0	0	0	0	0	0	0
Heating Degree Days (base 65°F)	315	255	245	167	109	37	6	9	18	70	204	318	1,753
Cooling Degree Days (base 65°F)	5	9	5	21	22	44	130	137	108	54	13	2	550
Mean Precipitation (in.)	4.17	4.60	3.60	0.67	0.32	0.05	0.01	0.08	0.33	0.47	1.66	2.80	18.76
Days With ≥ 0.1" Precipitation	5	5	5	1	1	0	0	0	0	1	2	3	23
Days With ≥ 1.0" Precipitation	1	2	1	0	0	0	0	0	0	0	0	1	5
Mean Snowfall (in.)	0.0	0.0	0.0	0.0	0.0	0.0	0.0	0.0	0.0	0.0	0.0	0.0	0.0
Days With ≥ 1.0" Snow Depth	0	0	0	0	0	0	0	0	0	0	0	0	0

Santa Rosa *Sonoma County*   Elevation: 164 ft.   Latitude: 38° 27' N   Longitude: 122° 43' W

	JAN	FEB	MAR	APR	MAY	JUN	JUL	AUG	SEP	OCT	NOV	DEC	YEAR
Mean Maximum Temp. (°F)	57.6	62.2	64.7	69.4	74.1	79.6	82.3	82.3	81.9	76.9	65.2	57.8	71.2
Mean Temp. (°F)	48.1	51.8	53.8	56.8	60.9	65.5	67.3	67.4	66.8	62.5	54.1	48.0	58.6
Mean Minimum Temp. (°F)	38.6	41.3	42.9	44.1	47.7	51.3	52.3	52.5	51.7	48.0	42.8	38.2	46.0
Extreme Maximum Temp. (°F)	77	79	87	98	100	108	110	106	110	105	88	78	110
Extreme Minimum Temp. (°F)	22	23	28	30	32	39	43	42	38	30	27	16	16
Days Maximum Temp. ≥ 90°F	0	0	0	0	2	4	6	6	6	3	0	0	27
Days Maximum Temp. ≤ 32°F	0	0	0	0	0	0	0	0	0	0	0	0	0
Days Minimum Temp. ≤ 32°F	6	2	1	0	0	0	0	0	0	0	1	7	17
Days Minimum Temp. ≤ 0°F	0	0	0	0	0	0	0	0	0	0	0	0	0
Heating Degree Days (base 65°F)	515	366	341	246	148	57	23	20	31	111	323	519	2,700
Cooling Degree Days (base 65°F)	0	0	1	9	25	73	94	97	84	44	2	0	429
Mean Precipitation (in.)	6.49	5.73	4.77	1.61	0.83	0.20	0.06	0.10	0.48	1.77	4.45	4.83	31.32
Days With ≥ 0.1" Precipitation	9	8	8	4	2	1	0	0	1	3	7	7	50
Days With ≥ 1.0" Precipitation	2	2	1	0	0	0	0	0	0	1	2	2	10
Mean Snowfall (in.)	trace	0.0	0.0	0.0	0.0	0.0	0.0	0.0	0.0	0.0	0.0	0.0	trace
Days With ≥ 1.0" Snow Depth	0	0	0	0	0	0	0	0	0	0	0	0	0

Scotia *Humboldt County*   Elevation: 137 ft.   Latitude: 40° 29' N   Longitude: 124° 06' W

	JAN	FEB	MAR	APR	MAY	JUN	JUL	AUG	SEP	OCT	NOV	DEC	YEAR
Mean Maximum Temp. (°F)	55.7	57.5	58.3	60.1	62.9	65.9	69.0	70.2	70.6	66.9	59.7	55.1	62.7
Mean Temp. (°F)	47.7	49.1	50.1	51.7	54.9	58.1	60.6	61.5	60.4	56.8	51.3	47.2	54.1
Mean Minimum Temp. (°F)	39.6	40.8	41.9	43.3	46.8	50.2	52.1	52.7	50.2	46.7	42.9	39.2	45.5
Extreme Maximum Temp. (°F)	76	79	82	90	89	98	87	92	95	97	79	72	98
Extreme Minimum Temp. (°F)	26	23	29	32	36	40	40	45	38	28	27	18	18
Days Maximum Temp. ≥ 90°F	0	0	0	0	0	0	0	0	0	0	0	0	0
Days Maximum Temp. ≤ 32°F	0	0	0	0	0	0	0	0	0	0	0	0	0
Days Minimum Temp. ≤ 32°F	4	2	1	0	0	0	0	0	0	0	1	5	13
Days Minimum Temp. ≤ 0°F	0	0	0	0	0	0	0	0	0	0	0	0	0
Heating Degree Days (base 65°F)	530	441	455	393	310	205	133	109	138	250	403	546	3,913
Cooling Degree Days (base 65°F)	0	0	0	1	3	2	4	7	6	6	0	0	29
Mean Precipitation (in.)	8.69	7.46	7.43	3.34	1.70	0.54	0.11	0.34	0.81	2.77	7.20	8.65	49.04
Days With ≥ 0.1" Precipitation	11	11	12	7	4	1	0	1	2	5	11	12	77
Days With ≥ 1.0" Precipitation	3	2	2	0	0	0	0	0	0	1	2	3	13
Mean Snowfall (in.)	trace	0.3	trace	trace	0.0	0.0	0.0	0.0	0.0	0.0	trace	0.3	0.6
Days With ≥ 1.0" Snow Depth	0	0	0	0	0	0	0	0	0	0	0	0	0

Shasta Dam *Shasta County*   Elevation: 1,072 ft.   Latitude: 40° 43' N   Longitude: 122° 25' W

	JAN	FEB	MAR	APR	MAY	JUN	JUL	AUG	SEP	OCT	NOV	DEC	YEAR
Mean Maximum Temp. (°F)	53.1	57.2	61.3	68.1	77.5	86.3	94.6	93.5	87.2	75.6	60.1	53.0	72.3
Mean Temp. (°F)	46.4	49.3	52.4	57.7	66.1	74.3	81.3	80.0	74.6	65.1	52.7	46.3	62.2
Mean Minimum Temp. (°F)	39.5	41.3	43.3	47.3	54.8	62.1	68.0	66.3	61.9	54.5	45.3	39.6	52.0
Extreme Maximum Temp. (°F)	74	81	83	95	107	108	115	115	112	103	81	74	115
Extreme Minimum Temp. (°F)	7	21	29	29	37	41	50	44	43	34	30	14	7
Days Maximum Temp. ≥ 90°F	0	0	0	0	4	12	24	22	14	3	0	0	79
Days Maximum Temp. ≤ 32°F	0	0	0	0	0	0	0	0	0	0	0	0	0
Days Minimum Temp. ≤ 32°F	3	1	1	0	0	0	0	0	0	0	0	3	8
Days Minimum Temp. ≤ 0°F	0	0	0	0	0	0	0	0	0	0	0	0	0
Heating Degree Days (base 65°F)	572	437	386	234	86	15	1	1	14	97	363	573	2,779
Cooling Degree Days (base 65°F)	0	0	1	29	125	286	509	479	318	109	2	0	1,858
Mean Precipitation (in.)	12.05	10.02	10.69	3.98	2.75	1.28	0.26	0.44	1.51	2.96	8.74	9.44	64.12
Days With ≥ 0.1" Precipitation	10	9	10	6	4	2	0	1	2	3	9	9	65
Days With ≥ 1.0" Precipitation	4	4	4	1	1	0	0	0	0	1	3	3	21
Mean Snowfall (in.)	trace	0.0	0.4	0.0	0.0	0.0	0.0	0.0	0.0	0.0	0.3	0.7	1.4
Days With ≥ 1.0" Snow Depth	0	0	0	0	0	0	0	0	0	0	0	0	0

Sonoma *Sonoma County*   Elevation: 95 ft.   Latitude: 38° 18' N   Longitude: 122° 28' W

	JAN	FEB	MAR	APR	MAY	JUN	JUL	AUG	SEP	OCT	NOV	DEC	YEAR
Mean Maximum Temp. (°F)	58.2	63.7	67.0	71.8	78.1	85.1	89.8	89.3	87.2	80.0	66.4	58.3	74.6
Mean Temp. (°F)	47.8	51.8	54.3	57.2	62.2	67.8	70.8	70.4	68.6	63.0	53.7	47.4	59.6
Mean Minimum Temp. (°F)	37.3	39.8	41.5	42.6	46.2	50.2	51.8	51.5	49.9	46.0	40.9	36.5	44.5
Extreme Maximum Temp. (°F)	78	84	87	100	105	111	116	108	110	107	91	79	116
Extreme Minimum Temp. (°F)	21	20	25	27	31	34	40	36	35	30	22	13	13
Days Maximum Temp. ≥ 90°F	0	0	0	0	4	9	15	14	12	5	0	0	59
Days Maximum Temp. ≤ 32°F	0	0	0	0	0	0	0	0	0	0	0	0	0
Days Minimum Temp. ≤ 32°F	10	5	2	1	0	0	0	0	0	0	3	10	31
Days Minimum Temp. ≤ 0°F	0	0	0	0	0	0	0	0	0	0	0	0	0
Heating Degree Days (base 65°F)	528	368	327	234	123	29	6	4	16	98	335	537	2,605
Cooling Degree Days (base 65°F)	0	0	0	9	36	112	188	178	122	42	1	0	688
Mean Precipitation (in.)	6.87	5.84	4.63	1.51	0.78	0.19	0.05	0.12	0.32	1.64	4.54	4.69	31.18
Days With ≥ 0.1" Precipitation	8	8	7	4	2	1	0	0	1	2	6	7	46
Days With ≥ 1.0" Precipitation	2	2	1	0	0	0	0	0	0	1	1	1	8
Mean Snowfall (in.)	0.0	trace	0.0	0.0	0.0	0.0	0.0	0.0	0.0	0.0	0.0	0.0	trace
Days With ≥ 1.0" Snow Depth	0	0	0	0	0	0	0	0	0	0	0	0	0

Stockton Fire Station 4 *San Joaquin County* Elevation: 9 ft. Latitude: 38° 00' N Longitude: 121° 19' W

	JAN	FEB	MAR	APR	MAY	JUN	JUL	AUG	SEP	OCT	NOV	DEC	YEAR
Mean Maximum Temp. (°F)	54.7	62.2	67.0	73.5	81.0	87.8	92.4	91.7	88.3	79.6	65.4	55.3	74.9
Mean Temp. (°F)	45.6	50.8	54.8	59.3	65.6	71.3	74.7	73.8	70.8	63.6	53.1	45.3	60.7
Mean Minimum Temp. (°F)	36.6	39.6	42.7	45.2	50.2	54.7	56.9	55.9	53.1	47.5	40.7	35.4	46.5
Extreme Maximum Temp. (°F)	72	78	87	95	103	108	112	110	106	101	85	73	112
Extreme Minimum Temp. (°F)	17	13	25	29	34	31	40	37	29	30	23	15	13
Days Maximum Temp. ≥ 90°F	0	0	0	1	6	12	21	19	14	4	0	0	77
Days Maximum Temp. ≤ 32°F	0	0	0	0	0	0	0	0	0	0	0	0	0
Days Minimum Temp. ≤ 32°F	10	3	1	0	0	0	0	0	0	0	3	10	27
Days Minimum Temp. ≤ 0°F	0	0	0	0	0	0	0	0	0	0	0	0	0
Heating Degree Days (base 65°F)	595	393	309	180	72	14	1	2	15	98	351	605	2,635
Cooling Degree Days (base 65°F)	0	0	1	23	97	205	304	279	192	60	1	0	1,162
Mean Precipitation (in.)	3.35	2.88	2.67	1.12	0.52	0.11	0.04	0.05	0.34	0.91	2.19	2.38	16.56
Days With ≥ 0.1" Precipitation	7	6	6	3	1	0	0	0	1	2	4	6	36
Days With ≥ 1.0" Precipitation	1	1	0	0	0	0	0	0	0	0	0	0	2
Mean Snowfall (in.)	0.0	trace	0.0	0.0	0.0	0.0	0.0	0.0	0.0	0.0	0.0	0.0	trace
Days With ≥ 1.0" Snow Depth	0	0	0	0	0	0	0	0	0	0	0	0	0

Stony Gorge Reservoir *Glenn County* Elevation: 797 ft. Latitude: 39° 35' N Longitude: 122° 32' W

	JAN	FEB	MAR	APR	MAY	JUN	JUL	AUG	SEP	OCT	NOV	DEC	YEAR
Mean Maximum Temp. (°F)	55.6	59.5	63.1	69.8	79.7	88.6	95.4	94.2	89.3	78.8	63.5	55.7	74.4
Mean Temp. (°F)	44.6	47.9	51.0	55.7	64.0	72.1	78.0	76.6	71.7	62.5	50.6	44.1	59.9
Mean Minimum Temp. (°F)	33.6	36.1	38.6	41.4	48.3	55.5	60.6	58.9	54.0	46.2	37.6	32.5	45.3
Extreme Maximum Temp. (°F)	79	81	86	94	105	109	116	115	114	104	87	80	116
Extreme Minimum Temp. (°F)	18	14	21	27	32	39	47	46	38	26	22	9	9
Days Maximum Temp. ≥ 90°F	0	0	0	0	5	14	25	23	16	5	0	0	88
Days Maximum Temp. ≤ 32°F	0	0	0	0	0	0	0	0	0	0	0	0	0
Days Minimum Temp. ≤ 32°F	15	8	5	2	0	0	0	0	0	0	7	17	54
Days Minimum Temp. ≤ 0°F	0	0	0	0	0	0	0	0	0	0	0	0	0
Heating Degree Days (base 65°F)	625	477	428	280	110	18	1	1	16	130	426	640	3,152
Cooling Degree Days (base 65°F)	0	0	0	8	82	221	404	369	227	62	0	0	1,373
Mean Precipitation (in.)	4.84	3.83	3.33	1.07	0.82	0.46	0.11	0.23	0.29	1.09	2.52	3.25	21.84
Days With ≥ 0.1" Precipitation	8	6	6	3	2	1	0	0	1	2	5	6	40
Days With ≥ 1.0" Precipitation	1	1	1	0	0	0	0	0	0	0	0	1	4
Mean Snowfall (in.)	0.6	0.2	trace	0.0	0.0	0.0	0.0	0.0	0.0	0.0	trace	0.1	0.9
Days With ≥ 1.0" Snow Depth	0	0	0	0	0	0	0	0	0	0	0	0	0

Strawberry Valley *Yuba County* Elevation: 3,805 ft. Latitude: 39° 34' N Longitude: 121° 06' W

	JAN	FEB	MAR	APR	MAY	JUN	JUL	AUG	SEP	OCT	NOV	DEC	YEAR
Mean Maximum Temp. (°F)	49.4	50.7	53.3	59.3	67.6	75.6	82.9	82.7	78.0	68.4	54.7	49.4	64.3
Mean Temp. (°F)	39.5	40.4	42.5	46.8	54.0	61.0	66.9	66.4	62.3	54.5	44.1	39.5	51.5
Mean Minimum Temp. (°F)	29.6	30.2	31.7	34.3	40.2	46.5	50.9	50.0	46.6	40.5	33.5	29.5	38.6
Extreme Maximum Temp. (°F)	73	77	77	86	94	96	101	102	98	94	81	75	102
Extreme Minimum Temp. (°F)	9	7	12	17	22	29	34	36	31	21	15	4	4
Days Maximum Temp. ≥ 90°F	0	0	0	0	0	2	5	5	2	0	0	0	14
Days Maximum Temp. ≤ 32°F	1	1	0	0	0	0	0	0	0	0	0	1	3
Days Minimum Temp. ≤ 32°F	22	20	18	13	3	0	0	0	0	3	13	22	114
Days Minimum Temp. ≤ 0°F	0	0	0	0	0	0	0	0	0	0	0	0	0
Heating Degree Days (base 65°F)	783	687	690	540	343	151	40	46	121	330	620	785	5,136
Cooling Degree Days (base 65°F)	0	0	0	1	6	35	103	97	48	14	0	0	304
Mean Precipitation (in.)	15.63	13.07	12.60	5.65	3.19	1.07	0.28	0.32	1.60	4.30	11.25	12.76	81.72
Days With ≥ 0.1" Precipitation	11	10	11	7	5	2	0	1	2	4	9	10	72
Days With ≥ 1.0" Precipitation	5	5	5	2	1	0	0	0	1	2	4	4	29
Mean Snowfall (in.)	20.1	20.6	23.3	9.8	0.7	trace	0.0	0.0	0.0	0.2	5.6	19.5	99.8
Days With ≥ 1.0" Snow Depth	13	12	9	4	0	0	0	0	0	0	3	10	51

Tahoe City *Placer County* Elevation: 6,227 ft. Latitude: 39° 10' N Longitude: 120° 08' W

	JAN	FEB	MAR	APR	MAY	JUN	JUL	AUG	SEP	OCT	NOV	DEC	YEAR
Mean Maximum Temp. (°F)	40.5	42.1	45.0	50.9	60.0	69.0	77.6	77.1	70.0	59.9	48.0	41.1	56.8
Mean Temp. (°F)	30.1	31.5	34.4	39.0	46.6	54.2	61.0	60.8	54.7	46.1	36.9	30.7	43.8
Mean Minimum Temp. (°F)	19.8	20.8	23.7	27.0	33.1	39.2	44.5	44.5	39.3	32.2	25.8	20.2	30.8
Extreme Maximum Temp. (°F)	59	60	67	74	81	88	91	91	86	79	70	60	91
Extreme Minimum Temp. (°F)	-6	-15	-2	5	9	24	22	31	25	9	4	-16	-16
Days Maximum Temp. ≥ 90°F	0	0	0	0	0	0	0	0	0	0	0	0	0
Days Maximum Temp. ≤ 32°F	3	2	2	0	0	0	0	0	0	0	1	3	11
Days Minimum Temp. ≤ 32°F	30	27	29	26	15	3	0	0	3	16	26	30	205
Days Minimum Temp. ≤ 0°F	0	0	0	0	0	0	0	0	0	0	0	0	0
Heating Degree Days (base 65°F)	1,074	940	942	774	564	321	131	134	303	579	837	1,058	7,657
Cooling Degree Days (base 65°F)	0	0	0	0	0	2	16	13	1	0	0	0	32
Mean Precipitation (in.)	6.12	5.49	4.62	1.82	1.14	0.84	0.33	0.46	0.88	1.92	4.44	4.90	32.96
Days With ≥ 0.1" Precipitation	8	8	7	5	3	3	1	1	2	4	7	7	56
Days With ≥ 1.0" Precipitation	2	2	1	0	0	0	0	0	0	0	1	1	7
Mean Snowfall (in.)	36.4	38.2	31.2	13.1	3.0	0.3	0.0	0.0	0.4	2.3	17.4	30.0	172.3
Days With ≥ 1.0" Snow Depth	29	26	27	12	2	0	0	0	0	1	11	23	131

Tahoe Valley FAA Airport *El Dorado County*   Elevation: 6,253 ft.   Latitude: 38° 54' N   Longitude: 120° 00' W

	JAN	FEB	MAR	APR	MAY	JUN	JUL	AUG	SEP	OCT	NOV	DEC	YEAR
Mean Maximum Temp. (°F)	41.2	42.5	45.8	52.7	61.4	70.4	79.1	78.8	72.3	62.0	49.0	41.8	58.1
Mean Temp. (°F)	28.7	30.0	34.1	39.4	46.7	53.8	60.1	59.5	53.6	45.1	35.6	28.5	42.9
Mean Minimum Temp. (°F)	16.2	17.6	22.5	26.1	32.0	37.1	41.0	40.1	34.9	28.1	22.3	15.2	27.7
Extreme Maximum Temp. (°F)	60	62	70	76	84	90	99	96	94	84	70	63	99
Extreme Minimum Temp. (°F)	-21	-29	-10	-1	7	21	25	24	19	11	-6	-29	-29
Days Maximum Temp. ≥ 90°F	0	0	0	0	0	0	1	1	0	0	0	0	2
Days Maximum Temp. ≤ 32°F	4	3	2	1	0	0	0	0	0	0	1	5	16
Days Minimum Temp. ≤ 32°F	29	27	28	26	18	7	2	3	11	25	27	29	232
Days Minimum Temp. ≤ 0°F	3	2	0	0	0	0	0	0	0	0	0	3	8
Heating Degree Days (base 65°F)	1,117	980	949	762	561	331	159	178	335	611	874	1,124	7,981
Cooling Degree Days (base 65°F)	0	0	0	0	0	2	15	14	2	0	0	0	33
Mean Precipitation (in.)	na	na	na	na	na	na	na	na	na	na	na	na	na
Days With ≥ 0.1" Precipitation	na	na	na	na	na	na	na	na	na	na	na	na	na
Days With ≥ 1.0" Precipitation	na	na	na	na	na	na	na	na	na	na	na	na	na
Mean Snowfall (in.)	na	na	na	na	na	na	na	na	na	na	na	na	na
Days With ≥ 1.0" Snow Depth	na	na	na	na	na	na	na	na	na	na	na	na	na

Tehachapi *Kern County*   Elevation: 4,015 ft.   Latitude: 35° 08' N   Longitude: 118° 27' W

	JAN	FEB	MAR	APR	MAY	JUN	JUL	AUG	SEP	OCT	NOV	DEC	YEAR
Mean Maximum Temp. (°F)	51.8	54.8	56.4	62.5	71.0	79.8	86.5	85.7	80.3	70.7	58.5	51.6	67.5
Mean Temp. (°F)	41.6	43.7	45.7	50.3	57.9	66.1	72.5	71.1	65.5	56.5	46.8	41.2	54.9
Mean Minimum Temp. (°F)	31.3	32.6	34.9	38.0	44.9	52.4	58.5	56.6	50.6	42.2	35.1	30.8	42.3
Extreme Maximum Temp. (°F)	74	76	81	89	95	100	103	100	101	96	80	72	103
Extreme Minimum Temp. (°F)	8	9	19	17	26	35	41	38	28	19	8	7	7
Days Maximum Temp. ≥ 90°F	0	0	0	0	1	4	10	9	4	0	0	0	28
Days Maximum Temp. ≤ 32°F	0	0	0	0	0	0	0	0	0	0	0	1	1
Days Minimum Temp. ≤ 32°F	17	14	11	6	1	0	0	0	0	3	11	18	81
Days Minimum Temp. ≤ 0°F	0	0	0	0	0	0	0	0	0	0	0	0	0
Heating Degree Days (base 65°F)	717	594	592	436	233	65	6	10	66	268	539	730	4,256
Cooling Degree Days (base 65°F)	0	0	0	1	20	96	239	212	85	15	0	0	668
Mean Precipitation (in.)	2.15	1.81	2.36	0.70	0.45	0.13	0.09	0.31	0.23	0.55	1.38	1.63	11.79
Days With ≥ 0.1" Precipitation	5	4	5	2	1	0	0	1	1	1	3	4	27
Days With ≥ 1.0" Precipitation	0	0	0	0	0	0	0	0	0	0	0	0	0
Mean Snowfall (in.)	2.7	2.0	4.3	0.8	trace	0.0	0.0	0.0	0.0	trace	1.0	2.8	13.6
Days With ≥ 1.0" Snow Depth	1	0	0	0	0	0	0	0	0	0	0	1	2

Tejon Rancho *Kern County*   Elevation: 1,423 ft.   Latitude: 35° 02' N   Longitude: 118° 45' W

	JAN	FEB	MAR	APR	MAY	JUN	JUL	AUG	SEP	OCT	NOV	DEC	YEAR
Mean Maximum Temp. (°F)	58.4	62.8	67.0	73.9	82.6	91.0	96.7	95.2	89.9	80.6	66.6	58.0	76.9
Mean Temp. (°F)	46.8	51.0	54.7	60.0	68.0	75.8	81.5	79.7	74.8	66.1	53.8	46.3	63.2
Mean Minimum Temp. (°F)	35.1	39.1	42.3	46.1	53.4	60.4	66.2	64.1	59.7	51.7	41.0	34.6	49.5
Extreme Maximum Temp. (°F)	82	84	89	100	109	110	111	109	108	101	90	81	111
Extreme Minimum Temp. (°F)	17	14	23	26	35	39	46	43	41	31	23	14	14
Days Maximum Temp. ≥ 90°F	0	0	0	1	7	18	28	26	17	5	0	0	102
Days Maximum Temp. ≤ 32°F	0	0	0	0	0	0	0	0	0	0	0	0	0
Days Minimum Temp. ≤ 32°F	12	4	1	0	0	0	0	0	0	0	2	11	30
Days Minimum Temp. ≤ 0°F	0	0	0	0	0	0	0	0	0	0	0	0	0
Heating Degree Days (base 65°F)	558	389	316	177	56	6	0	0	6	74	332	573	2,487
Cooling Degree Days (base 65°F)	0	0	2	43	148	321	518	480	317	120	2	0	1,951
Mean Precipitation (in.)	2.08	1.76	2.62	1.12	0.50	0.14	0.05	0.11	0.31	0.57	1.56	1.31	12.13
Days With ≥ 0.1" Precipitation	5	4	5	2	2	0	0	0	1	1	3	4	27
Days With ≥ 1.0" Precipitation	0	0	0	0	0	0	0	0	0	0	0	0	0
Mean Snowfall (in.)	trace	trace	0.0	0.0	0.0	0.0	0.0	0.0	0.0	0.0	0.0	trace	trace
Days With ≥ 1.0" Snow Depth	0	0	0	0	0	0	0	0	0	0	0	0	0

Termo 1 E *Lassen County*   Elevation: 5,298 ft.   Latitude: 40° 52' N   Longitude: 120° 26' W

	JAN	FEB	MAR	APR	MAY	JUN	JUL	AUG	SEP	OCT	NOV	DEC	YEAR
Mean Maximum Temp. (°F)	38.8	43.2	48.8	56.3	65.4	75.0	84.8	83.9	75.4	63.3	47.7	39.0	60.1
Mean Temp. (°F)	26.9	31.5	36.7	41.5	49.2	56.8	64.1	62.5	55.1	45.2	34.3	26.9	44.2
Mean Minimum Temp. (°F)	14.9	19.8	24.6	26.6	32.8	38.5	43.3	40.9	34.7	27.0	20.8	14.8	28.2
Extreme Maximum Temp. (°F)	60	65	71	84	91	98	99	101	96	87	73	60	101
Extreme Minimum Temp. (°F)	-24	-35	-10	7	12	19	19	22	14	-3	-18	-40	-40
Days Maximum Temp. ≥ 90°F	0	0	0	0	0	1	9	7	1	0	0	0	18
Days Maximum Temp. ≤ 32°F	6	3	1	0	0	0	0	0	0	0	2	7	19
Days Minimum Temp. ≤ 32°F	29	26	26	24	15	6	2	3	11	24	26	29	221
Days Minimum Temp. ≤ 0°F	5	2	0	0	0	0	0	0	0	0	1	5	13
Heating Degree Days (base 65°F)	1,176	938	871	699	485	250	84	114	295	608	914	1,174	7,608
Cooling Degree Days (base 65°F)	0	0	0	0	1	9	55	39	4	0	0	0	108
Mean Precipitation (in.)	1.08	1.03	1.17	0.77	1.21	0.99	0.40	0.28	0.60	0.79	1.20	1.24	10.76
Days With ≥ 0.1" Precipitation	4	4	4	2	4	2	1	1	2	2	4	4	34
Days With ≥ 1.0" Precipitation	0	0	0	0	0	0	0	0	0	0	0	0	0
Mean Snowfall (in.)	na	na	5.4	3.3	2.0	0.4	0.1	0.0	0.4	1.5	5.3	na	na
Days With ≥ 1.0" Snow Depth	20	12	3	0	0	0	0	0	0	0	5	16	56

Three Rivers Edison 1 *Tulare County*　Elevation: 1,138 ft.　Latitude: 36° 28' N　Longitude: 118° 52' W

	JAN	FEB	MAR	APR	MAY	JUN	JUL	AUG	SEP	OCT	NOV	DEC	YEAR
Mean Maximum Temp. (°F)	59.1	64.2	68.0	75.2	84.5	93.4	99.5	98.3	92.5	82.1	67.2	59.1	78.6
Mean Temp. (°F)	47.2	51.2	54.6	59.9	67.8	75.8	82.1	81.0	75.3	65.6	53.5	46.9	63.4
Mean Minimum Temp. (°F)	35.2	38.2	41.2	44.5	51.0	58.1	64.6	63.7	58.1	49.0	39.8	34.6	48.2
Extreme Maximum Temp. (°F)	79	85	86	100	106	112	112	114	109	102	88	78	114
Extreme Minimum Temp. (°F)	23	19	27	22	33	40	48	46	41	28	25	16	16
Days Maximum Temp. ≥ 90°F	0	0	0	2	10	21	30	29	20	7	0	0	119
Days Maximum Temp. ≤ 32°F	0	0	0	0	0	0	0	0	0	0	0	0	0
Days Minimum Temp. ≤ 32°F	12	5	2	1	0	0	0	0	0	0	3	12	35
Days Minimum Temp. ≤ 0°F	0	0	0	0	0	0	0	0	0	0	0	0	0
Heating Degree Days (base 65°F)	546	382	317	175	53	6	0	0	5	73	340	556	2,453
Cooling Degree Days (base 65°F)	0	0	1	34	138	325	533	511	322	95	1	0	1,960
Mean Precipitation (in.)	4.83	4.22	4.90	1.82	0.82	0.32	0.10	0.06	0.68	1.07	2.74	3.09	24.65
Days With ≥ 0.1" Precipitation	6	6	7	4	2	1	0	0	1	2	4	5	38
Days With ≥ 1.0" Precipitation	2	1	1	0	0	0	0	0	0	0	1	1	6
Mean Snowfall (in.)	*0.0*	0.0	0.0	0.0	0.0	0.0	0.0	0.0	0.0	0.0	0.0	0.0	*0.0*
Days With ≥ 1.0" Snow Depth	*0*	0	0	0	0	0	0	0	0	0	0	0	*0*

Tiger Creek *Amador County*　Elevation: 2,352 ft.　Latitude: 38° 27' N　Longitude: 120° 30' W

	JAN	FEB	MAR	APR	MAY	JUN	JUL	AUG	SEP	OCT	NOV	DEC	YEAR
Mean Maximum Temp. (°F)	51.3	57.8	60.8	66.7	74.7	83.5	90.6	90.2	85.1	75.0	59.2	49.2	70.3
Mean Temp. (°F)	42.2	46.2	48.6	52.9	59.8	67.0	73.2	72.9	68.4	59.9	48.1	41.0	56.7
Mean Minimum Temp. (°F)	33.1	34.5	36.4	39.0	44.8	50.5	55.7	55.5	51.7	44.7	37.0	32.7	43.0
Extreme Maximum Temp. (°F)	70	79	85	90	100	103	110	106	103	98	85	66	110
Extreme Minimum Temp. (°F)	17	14	20	25	29	36	40	42	35	24	23	10	10
Days Maximum Temp. ≥ 90°F	0	0	0	0	1	8	19	18	10	2	0	0	58
Days Maximum Temp. ≤ 32°F	0	0	0	0	0	0	0	0	0	0	0	0	0
Days Minimum Temp. ≤ 32°F	15	11	8	4	0	0	0	0	0	1	7	15	61
Days Minimum Temp. ≤ 0°F	0	0	0	0	0	0	0	0	0	0	0	0	0
Heating Degree Days (base 65°F)	700	525	500	359	187	51	6	5	37	185	500	738	3,793
Cooling Degree Days (base 65°F)	0	0	0	3	28	107	249	256	145	32	0	0	820
Mean Precipitation (in.)	9.16	7.33	7.84	3.45	1.82	0.61	0.21	0.20	1.00	2.54	6.31	6.77	47.24
Days With ≥ 0.1" Precipitation	9	9	9	6	3	1	0	0	1	3	8	8	57
Days With ≥ 1.0" Precipitation	3	3	3	1	0	0	0	0	0	1	2	2	15
Mean Snowfall (in.)	3.0	2.9	3.1	2.1	0.0	0.0	0.0	0.0	0.0	0.0	0.3	4.4	15.8
Days With ≥ 1.0" Snow Depth	1	1	1	0	0	0	0	0	0	0	0	2	5

Torrance Municipal Airport *Los Angeles County*　Elevation: 108 ft.　Latitude: 33° 48' N　Longitude: 118° 20' W

	JAN	FEB	MAR	APR	MAY	JUN	JUL	AUG	SEP	OCT	NOV	DEC	YEAR
Mean Maximum Temp. (°F)	66.6	67.6	67.9	70.8	72.2	75.3	78.6	79.7	79.0	76.3	71.2	67.1	72.7
Mean Temp. (°F)	56.4	57.6	58.4	60.9	63.4	66.5	69.9	70.9	70.0	66.5	60.7	56.5	63.1
Mean Minimum Temp. (°F)	46.2	47.5	48.8	51.0	54.6	57.7	61.1	62.0	61.0	56.7	50.2	45.9	53.6
Extreme Maximum Temp. (°F)	89	88	96	104	100	104	102	101	108	102	96	90	108
Extreme Minimum Temp. (°F)	30	33	32	39	44	42	50	51	51	37	36	27	27
Days Maximum Temp. ≥ 90°F	0	0	0	0	0	1	1	1	2	2	0	0	7
Days Maximum Temp. ≤ 32°F	0	0	0	0	0	0	0	0	0	0	0	0	0
Days Minimum Temp. ≤ 32°F	0	0	0	0	0	0	0	0	0	0	0	0	0
Days Minimum Temp. ≤ 0°F	0	0	0	0	0	0	0	0	0	0	0	0	0
Heating Degree Days (base 65°F)	263	210	205	134	71	20	0	0	2	27	140	258	1,330
Cooling Degree Days (base 65°F)	3	7	7	25	29	71	162	195	158	86	17	2	762
Mean Precipitation (in.)	3.64	3.15	2.75	0.69	0.25	0.08	0.04	0.13	0.22	0.40	1.44	2.13	14.92
Days With ≥ 0.1" Precipitation	5	4	4	2	1	0	0	0	0	1	2	3	22
Days With ≥ 1.0" Precipitation	1	1	1	0	0	0	0	0	0	0	0	1	4
Mean Snowfall (in.)	trace	0.0	0.0	0.0	0.0	0.0	0.0	0.0	0.0	0.0	0.0	0.0	trace
Days With ≥ 1.0" Snow Depth	0	0	0	0	0	0	0	0	0	0	0	0	0

Tracy Carbona *San Joaquin County*　Elevation: 137 ft.　Latitude: 37° 42' N　Longitude: 121° 26' W

	JAN	FEB	MAR	APR	MAY	JUN	JUL	AUG	SEP	OCT	NOV	DEC	YEAR
Mean Maximum Temp. (°F)	*54.7*	61.7	66.8	73.1	80.9	88.0	93.4	92.0	87.9	79.0	na	na	na
Mean Temp. (°F)	*45.9*	50.7	54.9	59.2	65.5	71.4	75.2	73.8	70.9	63.8	na	na	na
Mean Minimum Temp. (°F)	*36.9*	39.7	42.9	45.3	50.1	54.6	56.9	55.5	53.9	48.7	na	*36.0*	na
Extreme Maximum Temp. (°F)	74	81	87	94	105	107	111	109	104	99	83	73	111
Extreme Minimum Temp. (°F)	21	23	26	32	35	37	38	38	40	32	28	17	17
Days Maximum Temp. ≥ 90°F	0	0	0	1	6	13	23	20	13	3	0	0	79
Days Maximum Temp. ≤ 32°F	0	0	0	0	0	0	0	0	0	0	0	0	0
Days Minimum Temp. ≤ 32°F	8	2	0	0	0	0	0	0	0	0	1	8	19
Days Minimum Temp. ≤ 0°F	0	0	0	0	0	0	0	0	0	0	0	0	0
Heating Degree Days (base 65°F)	*588*	396	309	183	73	14	1	1	8	92	na	na	na
Cooling Degree Days (base 65°F)	na	0	*1*	22	97	199	321	276	187	57	na	na	na
Mean Precipitation (in.)	2.11	1.82	1.72	0.70	0.60	0.08	0.04	0.06	0.26	0.59	1.37	1.51	10.86
Days With ≥ 0.1" Precipitation	5	5	5	2	1	0	0	0	1	2	3	4	28
Days With ≥ 1.0" Precipitation	0	0	0	0	0	0	0	0	0	0	0	0	0
Mean Snowfall (in.)	0.0	trace	0.0	0.0	0.0	0.0	0.0	0.0	0.0	0.0	0.0	0.0	trace
Days With ≥ 1.0" Snow Depth	0	0	0	0	0	0	0	0	0	0	0	0	0

Tracy Pumping Plant *Alameda County*   Elevation: 59 ft.   Latitude: 37° 48' N   Longitude: 121° 35' W

	JAN	FEB	MAR	APR	MAY	JUN	JUL	AUG	SEP	OCT	NOV	DEC	YEAR
Mean Maximum Temp. (°F)	*54.7*	61.6	66.3	72.6	80.1	87.2	92.3	91.8	87.5	78.6	*64.9*	*55.1*	*74.4*
Mean Temp. (°F)	*46.7*	51.6	55.7	60.3	66.8	72.3	76.4	76.1	73.0	65.4	*54.6*	*46.6*	*62.1*
Mean Minimum Temp. (°F)	*38.6*	41.6	44.9	47.8	53.4	57.3	60.5	60.2	58.3	52.1	*44.2*	38.0	*49.7*
Extreme Maximum Temp. (°F)	70	77	88	97	105	109	112	111	109	102	84	74	112
Extreme Minimum Temp. (°F)	21	23	25	35	37	37	47	48	44	30	24	17	17
Days Maximum Temp. ≥ 90°F	0	0	0	1	6	12	21	18	13	3	0	0	74
Days Maximum Temp. ≤ 32°F	0	0	0	0	0	0	0	0	0	0	0	0	0
Days Minimum Temp. ≤ 32°F	7	2	0	0	0	0	0	0	0	0	1	7	17
Days Minimum Temp. ≤ 0°F	0	0	0	0	0	0	0	0	0	0	0	0	0
Heating Degree Days (base 65°F)	*561*	371	284	158	59	11	1	0	4	61	*308*	563	2,381
Cooling Degree Days (base 65°F)	*0*	0	1	29	118	233	364	361	*250*	84	*3*	*0*	1,443
Mean Precipitation (in.)	2.65	2.22	1.98	0.73	0.43	0.10	0.04	0.06	0.25	0.61	1.73	1.77	12.57
Days With ≥ 0.1" Precipitation	6	5	5	2	1	0	0	0	0	1	4	5	29
Days With ≥ 1.0" Precipitation	0	0	0	0	0	0	0	0	0	0	0	0	0
Mean Snowfall (in.)	0.0	0.0	0.0	0.0	0.0	0.0	0.0	0.0	0.0	0.0	0.0	0.0	0.0
Days With ≥ 1.0" Snow Depth	0	0	0	0	0	0	0	0	0	0	0	0	0

Trinity River Hatchery *Trinity County*   Elevation: 1,856 ft.   Latitude: 40° 44' N   Longitude: 122° 48' W

	JAN	FEB	MAR	APR	MAY	JUN	JUL	AUG	SEP	OCT	NOV	DEC	YEAR
Mean Maximum Temp. (°F)	47.8	53.6	58.9	*65.7*	74.8	83.8	91.8	*91.0*	85.4	73.8	55.2	47.3	*69.1*
Mean Temp. (°F)	39.7	43.0	46.8	*51.4*	58.4	65.8	71.9	*70.9*	65.3	56.4	45.2	39.4	*54.5*
Mean Minimum Temp. (°F)	31.6	32.5	34.7	*37.0*	42.1	47.7	52.0	*50.7*	45.2	39.0	35.2	31.4	*39.9*
Extreme Maximum Temp. (°F)	63	75	84	*94*	100	106	109	*113*	108	99	77	67	*113*
Extreme Minimum Temp. (°F)	14	10	20	*23*	27	33	37	*38*	32	25	15	4	*4*
Days Maximum Temp. ≥ 90°F	0	0	0	*0*	3	9	20	*19*	12	2	0	0	*65*
Days Maximum Temp. ≤ 32°F	0	0	0	*0*	0	0	0	*0*	0	0	0	0	*0*
Days Minimum Temp. ≤ 32°F	17	14	12	*7*	1	0	0	*0*	0	4	10	18	*83*
Days Minimum Temp. ≤ 0°F	0	0	0	*0*	0	0	0	*0*	0	0	0	0	*0*
Heating Degree Days (base 65°F)	776	613	558	*403*	222	70	12	*13*	65	268	587	787	4,374
Cooling Degree Days (base 65°F)	0	0	0	*2*	28	96	232	204	79	10	0	0	651
Mean Precipitation (in.)	5.89	5.33	5.03	*2.00*	1.51	0.68	0.23	*0.30*	0.87	1.85	4.30	5.00	32.99
Days With ≥ 0.1" Precipitation	9	9	9	*5*	3	2	1	*1*	2	3	8	9	*61*
Days With ≥ 1.0" Precipitation	2	1	1	*0*	0	0	0	*0*	0	0	1	1	*6*
Mean Snowfall (in.)	*1.1*	*0.9*	1.3	*trace*	0.0	0.0	0.0	*0.0*	0.0	0.0	0.2	*0.9*	*4.4*
Days With ≥ 1.0" Snow Depth	*0*	*0*	0	*0*	0	0	0	*0*	0	0	*0*	*0*	*0*

Trona *San Bernardino County*   Elevation: 1,692 ft.   Latitude: 35° 46' N   Longitude: 117° 23' W

	JAN	FEB	MAR	APR	MAY	JUN	JUL	AUG	SEP	OCT	NOV	DEC	YEAR
Mean Maximum Temp. (°F)	58.6	65.6	70.8	78.6	87.8	98.5	104.8	102.8	95.1	83.5	69.1	58.3	81.1
Mean Temp. (°F)	46.9	53.2	58.4	65.2	73.9	83.7	90.3	88.7	81.3	69.5	56.2	46.4	67.8
Mean Minimum Temp. (°F)	35.2	40.2	45.9	51.8	60.1	68.9	75.7	74.5	67.6	55.4	43.2	34.6	54.4
Extreme Maximum Temp. (°F)	83	88	92	102	109	118	118	118	112	105	88	76	118
Extreme Minimum Temp. (°F)	12	10	23	33	40	45	50	50	45	23	23	8	8
Days Maximum Temp. ≥ 90°F	0	0	0	4	15	26	31	30	23	8	0	0	137
Days Maximum Temp. ≤ 32°F	0	0	0	0	0	0	0	0	0	0	0	0	0
Days Minimum Temp. ≤ 32°F	12	5	1	0	0	0	0	0	0	0	3	13	34
Days Minimum Temp. ≤ 0°F	0	0	0	0	0	0	0	0	0	0	0	0	0
Heating Degree Days (base 65°F)	553	333	215	83	13	1	0	0	1	37	268	*571*	2,075
Cooling Degree Days (base 65°F)	1	8	25	125	322	588	810	772	528	201	15	0	3,395
Mean Precipitation (in.)	0.89	0.90	0.62	0.13	0.13	0.10	0.10	0.34	0.25	0.12	0.28	0.44	4.30
Days With ≥ 0.1" Precipitation	2	2	2	1	0	0	0	1	0	0	1	1	10
Days With ≥ 1.0" Precipitation	0	0	0	0	0	0	0	0	0	0	0	0	0
Mean Snowfall (in.)	0.3	trace	trace	0.0	0.0	0.0	0.0	0.0	0.0	0.0	0.0	trace	0.3
Days With ≥ 1.0" Snow Depth	0	0	0	0	0	0	0	0	0	0	0	0	0

Truckee Ranger Station *Nevada County*   Elevation: 6,017 ft.   Latitude: 39° 20' N   Longitude: 120° 11' W

	JAN	FEB	MAR	APR	MAY	JUN	JUL	AUG	SEP	OCT	NOV	DEC	YEAR
Mean Maximum Temp. (°F)	40.0	43.7	47.6	53.9	63.4	73.2	82.1	81.2	74.3	63.5	48.6	40.4	59.3
Mean Temp. (°F)	27.9	30.8	35.1	40.0	47.7	55.4	62.1	61.3	55.2	46.2	35.6	28.3	43.8
Mean Minimum Temp. (°F)	15.8	17.8	22.5	26.0	31.9	37.6	42.2	41.4	36.0	28.9	22.6	16.2	28.2
Extreme Maximum Temp. (°F)	60	68	71	80	88	93	99	97	95	87	77	62	99
Extreme Minimum Temp. (°F)	-13	-22	-10	3	10	20	15	24	21	7	-3	-22	-22
Days Maximum Temp. ≥ 90°F	0	0	0	0	0	0	4	3	1	0	0	0	8
Days Maximum Temp. ≤ 32°F	5	3	1	0	0	0	0	0	0	0	1	5	15
Days Minimum Temp. ≤ 32°F	30	27	29	26	18	6	1	2	9	23	28	30	229
Days Minimum Temp. ≤ 0°F	3	1	0	0	0	0	0	0	0	0	0	2	6
Heating Degree Days (base 65°F)	1,143	959	920	743	531	286	114	133	291	576	875	1,130	7,701
Cooling Degree Days (base 65°F)	0	0	0	0	0	6	35	31	4	0	0	0	76
Mean Precipitation (in.)	5.61	5.05	4.53	1.91	1.28	0.68	0.42	0.56	0.98	1.71	3.99	4.60	31.32
Days With ≥ 0.1" Precipitation	8	7	8	5	4	2	1	1	2	3	7	7	55
Days With ≥ 1.0" Precipitation	2	2	1	0	0	0	0	0	0	0	1	2	8
Mean Snowfall (in.)	43.1	44.0	35.3	15.3	4.5	0.7	0.0	0.0	0.6	3.2	20.3	36.4	203.4
Days With ≥ 1.0" Snow Depth	29	27	27	13	3	0	0	0	0	2	12	26	139

Tustin Irvine Ranch *Orange County*   Elevation: 118 ft.   Latitude: 33° 44' N   Longitude: 117° 47' W

	JAN	FEB	MAR	APR	MAY	JUN	JUL	AUG	SEP	OCT	NOV	DEC	YEAR
Mean Maximum Temp. (°F)	67.7	69.2	69.6	73.7	75.2	79.5	84.1	85.8	84.3	79.7	73.4	68.2	75.9
Mean Temp. (°F)	54.8	56.4	57.6	61.0	64.3	68.2	72.4	73.4	71.7	66.5	59.4	54.6	63.4
Mean Minimum Temp. (°F)	41.8	43.6	45.6	48.3	53.3	56.9	60.5	60.7	58.9	53.2	45.2	40.7	50.7
Extreme Maximum Temp. (°F)	90	92	98	106	102	109	102	110	108	108	105	97	110
Extreme Minimum Temp. (°F)	27	26	31	34	34	42	48	43	42	29	28	26	26
Days Maximum Temp. ≥ 90°F	0	0	0	1	1	2	5	8	7	4	1	0	29
Days Maximum Temp. ≤ 32°F	0	0	0	0	0	0	0	0	0	0	0	0	0
Days Minimum Temp. ≤ 32°F	2	0	0	0	0	0	0	0	0	0	0	2	4
Days Minimum Temp. ≤ 0°F	0	0	0	0	0	0	0	0	0	0	0	0	0
Heating Degree Days (base 65°F)	312	239	228	135	65	15	0	1	4	37	173	318	1,527
Cooling Degree Days (base 65°F)	3	4	8	30	57	121	259	301	221	105	13	2	1,124
Mean Precipitation (in.)	2.99	3.05	2.79	0.72	0.27	0.10	0.01	0.14	0.34	0.36	1.34	1.90	14.01
Days With ≥ 0.1" Precipitation	5	4	5	2	1	0	0	0	1	1	2	4	25
Days With ≥ 1.0" Precipitation	1	1	1	0	0	0	0	0	0	0	0	0	3
Mean Snowfall (in.)	0.0	trace	0.0	0.0	0.0	0.0	0.0	0.0	0.0	0.0	0.0	0.0	trace
Days With ≥ 1.0" Snow Depth	0	0	0	0	0	0	0	0	0	0	0	0	0

Twentynine Palms *San Bernardino County*   Elevation: 1,975 ft.   Latitude: 34° 08' N   Longitude: 116° 02' W

	JAN	FEB	MAR	APR	MAY	JUN	JUL	AUG	SEP	OCT	NOV	DEC	YEAR
Mean Maximum Temp. (°F)	63.4	68.6	74.4	82.2	91.2	101.3	105.8	103.6	97.0	85.6	71.8	63.0	84.0
Mean Temp. (°F)	49.7	54.0	58.9	65.6	74.0	83.1	88.4	86.8	80.2	68.8	56.4	49.0	67.9
Mean Minimum Temp. (°F)	35.9	39.3	43.4	48.9	56.8	64.8	70.9	70.1	63.3	52.0	40.9	35.0	51.8
Extreme Maximum Temp. (°F)	85	90	92	101	110	116	117	115	111	106	92	92	117
Extreme Minimum Temp. (°F)	13	18	23	24	33	43	53	54	38	24	25	10	10
Days Maximum Temp. ≥ 90°F	0	0	1	7	19	28	31	31	26	10	0	0	153
Days Maximum Temp. ≤ 32°F	0	0	0	0	0	0	0	0	0	0	0	0	0
Days Minimum Temp. ≤ 32°F	9	4	1	0	0	0	0	0	0	0	3	10	27
Days Minimum Temp. ≤ 0°F	0	0	0	0	0	0	0	0	0	0	0	0	0
Heating Degree Days (base 65°F)	469	307	201	76	11	0	0	0	1	43	258	488	1,854
Cooling Degree Days (base 65°F)	0	2	21	118	308	547	724	699	472	171	7	0	3,069
Mean Precipitation (in.)	0.57	0.53	0.50	0.14	0.12	trace	0.68	0.73	0.55	0.15	0.21	0.41	4.59
Days With ≥ 0.1" Precipitation	2	2	1	0	0	0	1	1	1	0	1	1	10
Days With ≥ 1.0" Precipitation	0	0	0	0	0	0	0	0	0	0	0	0	0
Mean Snowfall (in.)	0.0	trace	0.0	0.0	0.0	0.0	0.0	0.0	0.0	trace	0.0	0.0	trace
Days With ≥ 1.0" Snow Depth	0	0	0	0	0	0	0	0	0	0	0	0	0

Twin Lakes *Alpine County*   Elevation: 7,998 ft.   Latitude: 38° 42' N   Longitude: 120° 02' W

	JAN	FEB	MAR	APR	MAY	JUN	JUL	AUG	SEP	OCT	NOV	DEC	YEAR
Mean Maximum Temp. (°F)	38.6	39.5	42.0	46.6	54.6	63.5	71.9	71.0	64.8	55.7	44.1	39.1	52.6
Mean Temp. (°F)	28.4	28.7	31.0	34.9	42.4	50.6	57.6	57.2	51.8	43.6	33.7	28.6	40.7
Mean Minimum Temp. (°F)	18.1	17.9	19.9	23.3	30.2	37.7	43.5	43.4	38.8	31.4	23.2	18.4	28.8
Extreme Maximum Temp. (°F)	68	76	66	72	79	83	95	85	82	78	70	70	95
Extreme Minimum Temp. (°F)	-17	-11	-9	-10	2	17	19	23	18	8	-4	-15	-17
Days Maximum Temp. ≥ 90°F	0	0	0	0	0	0	0	0	0	0	0	0	0
Days Maximum Temp. ≤ 32°F	9	7	4	2	1	0	0	0	0	1	4	8	36
Days Minimum Temp. ≤ 32°F	30	28	30	26	19	7	2	2	4	16	25	30	219
Days Minimum Temp. ≤ 0°F	1	1	1	0	0	0	0	0	0	0	0	1	4
Heating Degree Days (base 65°F)	1,130	1,020	1,048	903	693	426	226	240	389	655	933	1,121	8,784
Cooling Degree Days (base 65°F)	0	0	0	0	0	1	5	3	0	0	0	0	9
Mean Precipitation (in.)	8.07	7.46	6.66	3.38	2.19	1.36	0.65	0.63	1.42	2.76	6.31	7.00	47.89
Days With ≥ 0.1" Precipitation	10	9	9	6	5	3	1	1	3	4	7	8	66
Days With ≥ 1.0" Precipitation	3	3	2	1	0	0	0	0	0	1	2	2	14
Mean Snowfall (in.)	75.0	78.4	77.5	31.2	10.5	2.1	trace	0.1	1.4	11.6	43.7	63.3	394.8
Days With ≥ 1.0" Snow Depth	na	na	na	na	na	1	0	0	0	2	na	na	na

U.C.L.A. *Los Angeles County*   Elevation: 429 ft.   Latitude: 34° 04' N   Longitude: 118° 27' W

	JAN	FEB	MAR	APR	MAY	JUN	JUL	AUG	SEP	OCT	NOV	DEC	YEAR
Mean Maximum Temp. (°F)	66.2	67.1	66.8	69.2	69.6	73.2	77.0	78.2	78.0	75.3	70.7	66.8	71.5
Mean Temp. (°F)	58.2	58.9	58.7	60.9	62.3	65.6	69.0	70.2	69.8	66.9	62.4	58.7	63.5
Mean Minimum Temp. (°F)	50.2	50.5	50.6	52.5	55.0	58.0	61.0	62.1	61.5	58.5	54.0	50.6	55.4
Extreme Maximum Temp. (°F)	91	91	94	103	97	108	100	98	106	102	97	92	108
Extreme Minimum Temp. (°F)	37	36	38	40	45	47	54	54	49	40	41	33	33
Days Maximum Temp. ≥ 90°F	0	0	0	0	0	1	1	1	3	2	0	0	8
Days Maximum Temp. ≤ 32°F	0	0	0	0	0	0	0	0	0	0	0	0	0
Days Minimum Temp. ≤ 32°F	0	0	0	0	0	0	0	0	0	0	0	0	0
Days Minimum Temp. ≤ 0°F	0	0	0	0	0	0	0	0	0	0	0	0	0
Heating Degree Days (base 65°F)	223	187	203	147	104	36	2	2	8	29	114	207	1,262
Cooling Degree Days (base 65°F)	19	22	16	41	23	57	139	182	160	103	41	17	820
Mean Precipitation (in.)	4.12	4.78	3.50	0.79	0.34	0.11	0.02	0.16	0.31	0.51	1.56	2.57	18.77
Days With ≥ 0.1" Precipitation	5	5	5	2	1	0	0	0	1	1	2	3	25
Days With ≥ 1.0" Precipitation	2	2	1	0	0	0	0	0	0	0	1	1	6
Mean Snowfall (in.)	0.0	trace	trace	0.0	0.0	0.0	0.0	0.0	0.0	0.0	trace	0.0	trace
Days With ≥ 1.0" Snow Depth	0	0	0	0	0	0	0	0	0	0	0	0	0

Ukiah *Mendocino County*   Elevation: 629 ft.   Latitude: 39° 09' N   Longitude: 123° 13' W

	JAN	FEB	MAR	APR	MAY	JUN	JUL	AUG	SEP	OCT	NOV	DEC	YEAR
Mean Maximum Temp. (°F)	57.4	60.9	64.5	69.6	76.7	83.9	91.5	91.1	86.8	77.1	63.0	56.4	73.3
Mean Temp. (°F)	47.2	50.1	52.6	55.9	62.0	68.2	73.7	73.0	69.2	61.5	51.8	46.3	59.3
Mean Minimum Temp. (°F)	37.0	39.3	40.7	42.3	47.1	52.4	55.9	54.9	51.5	45.8	40.6	36.2	45.3
Extreme Maximum Temp. (°F)	82	85	88	97	105	107	114	113	110	105	88	75	114
Extreme Minimum Temp. (°F)	21	18	25	28	31	37	43	41	38	24	24	13	13
Days Maximum Temp. ≥ 90°F	0	0	0	0	4	9	19	18	13	4	0	0	67
Days Maximum Temp. ≤ 32°F	0	0	0	0	0	0	0	0	0	0	0	0	0
Days Minimum Temp. ≤ 32°F	10	5	2	1	0	0	0	0	0	0	4	12	34
Days Minimum Temp. ≤ 0°F	0	0	0	0	0	0	0	0	0	0	0	0	0
Heating Degree Days (base 65°F)	544	414	378	272	137	35	4	3	21	141	389	572	2,910
Cooling Degree Days (base 65°F)	0	0	0	9	45	129	276	256	154	41	0	0	910
Mean Precipitation (in.)	8.47	6.90	5.91	2.20	1.12	0.25	0.05	0.15	0.68	2.05	5.57	6.30	39.65
Days With ≥ 0.1" Precipitation	10	9	9	5	2	1	0	0	1	4	8	9	58
Days With ≥ 1.0" Precipitation	3	3	2	0	0	0	0	0	0	0	2	2	12
Mean Snowfall (in)	trace	0.0	trace	0.0	0.0	0.0	0.0	0.0	0.0	0.0	0.0	trace	trace
Days With ≥ 1.0" Snow Depth	0	0	0	0	0	0	0	0	0	0	0	0	0

Vacaville *Solano County*   Elevation: 108 ft.   Latitude: 38° 24' N   Longitude: 121° 58' W

	JAN	FEB	MAR	APR	MAY	JUN	JUL	AUG	SEP	OCT	NOV	DEC	YEAR
Mean Maximum Temp. (°F)	55.0	61.8	66.4	73.2	81.4	88.9	94.4	93.1	89.3	79.6	64.8	55.5	75.3
Mean Temp. (°F)	46.2	51.0	54.6	59.0	65.6	71.6	75.7	74.6	71.7	64.4	53.5	46.3	61.2
Mean Minimum Temp. (°F)	37.4	40.1	42.7	44.8	49.8	54.3	57.0	55.9	54.0	49.2	42.2	37.0	47.0
Extreme Maximum Temp. (°F)	77	78	90	97	104	109	111	111	109	102	87	76	111
Extreme Minimum Temp. (°F)	20	16	26	29	32	39	40	41	40	32	27	17	16
Days Maximum Temp. ≥ 90°F	0	0	0	1	7	14	23	21	16	4	0	0	86
Days Maximum Temp. ≤ 32°F	0	0	0	0	0	0	0	0	0	0	0	0	0
Days Minimum Temp. ≤ 32°F	9	4	1	0	0	0	0	0	0	0	2	8	24
Days Minimum Temp. ≤ 0°F	0	0	0	0	0	0	0	0	0	0	0	0	0
Heating Degree Days (base 65°F)	575	391	316	191	68	10	1	0	8	80	339	573	2,552
Cooling Degree Days (base 65°F)	0	0	1	25	97	218	358	319	229	80	2	0	1,329
Mean Precipitation (in.)	5.70	4.74	3.80	1.13	0.60	0.09	0.05	0.03	0.34	1.11	3.47	4.04	25.10
Days With ≥ 0.1" Precipitation	7	6	7	2	1	0	0	0	1	2	5	6	37
Days With ≥ 1.0" Precipitation	2	2	1	0	0	0	0	0	0	0	1	1	7
Mean Snowfall (in.)	trace	trace	0.0	0.0	0.0	0.0	0.0	0.0	0.0	0.0	0.0	trace	trace
Days With ≥ 1.0" Snow Depth	0	0	0	0	0	0	0	0	0	0	0	0	0

Victorville Pumping Plant *San Bernardino County*   Elevation: 2,857 ft.   Latitude: 34° 32' N   Longitude: 117° 18' W

	JAN	FEB	MAR	APR	MAY	JUN	JUL	AUG	SEP	OCT	NOV	DEC	YEAR
Mean Maximum Temp. (°F)	58.5	62.5	66.4	73.2	81.7	91.6	97.5	96.9	90.5	79.9	67.6	58.9	77.1
Mean Temp. (°F)	44.9	48.6	52.1	57.5	65.1	73.3	79.2	78.9	72.9	62.5	51.7	44.5	60.9
Mean Minimum Temp. (°F)	31.2	34.5	37.7	41.8	48.5	55.0	60.9	60.8	55.2	45.0	35.6	30.1	44.7
Extreme Maximum Temp. (°F)	80	86	91	98	104	111	113	112	108	101	88	81	113
Extreme Minimum Temp. (°F)	11	15	17	25	32	36	36	44	34	21	16	6	6
Days Maximum Temp. ≥ 90°F	0	0	0	2	7	19	28	27	19	5	0	0	107
Days Maximum Temp. ≤ 32°F	0	0	0	0	0	0	0	0	0	0	0	0	0
Days Minimum Temp. ≤ 32°F	19	11	6	2	0	0	0	0	0	1	10	21	70
Days Minimum Temp. ≤ 0°F	0	0	0	0	0	0	0	0	0	0	0	0	0
Heating Degree Days (base 65°F)	617	457	396	239	88	14	1	0	15	131	395	629	2,982
Cooling Degree Days (base 65°F)	0	0	2	28	106	267	445	454	268	63	1	0	1,634
Mean Precipitation (in.)	1.11	1.16	1.18	0.28	0.23	0.06	0.16	0.26	0.32	0.25	0.42	0.87	6.30
Days With ≥ 0.1" Precipitation	3	2	3	1	0	0	0	1	1	1	1	2	15
Days With ≥ 1.0" Precipitation	0	0	0	0	0	0	0	0	0	0	0	0	0
Mean Snowfall (in.)	0.6	0.0	0.0	0.0	0.0	0.0	0.0	0.0	0.0	0.0	0.0	trace	0.6
Days With ≥ 1.0" Snow Depth	0	0	0	0	0	0	0	0	0	0	0	0	0

Visalia *Tulare County*   Elevation: 324 ft.   Latitude: 36° 20' N   Longitude: 119° 18' W

	JAN	FEB	MAR	APR	MAY	JUN	JUL	AUG	SEP	OCT	NOV	DEC	YEAR
Mean Maximum Temp. (°F)	54.3	61.8	67.0	73.7	82.2	90.0	94.8	93.3	88.0	79.0	64.7	54.4	75.3
Mean Temp. (°F)	46.3	51.8	56.3	61.2	68.5	75.4	80.2	78.6	73.8	65.6	53.9	45.7	63.1
Mean Minimum Temp. (°F)	38.2	41.8	45.6	48.6	54.8	60.7	65.5	64.0	59.6	52.1	43.0	37.0	50.9
Extreme Maximum Temp. (°F)	79	81	87	97	105	109	109	106	104	98	86	78	109
Extreme Minimum Temp. (°F)	23	24	29	34	37	42	52	51	41	32	28	21	21
Days Maximum Temp. ≥ 90°F	0	0	0	1	7	16	26	24	13	3	0	0	90
Days Maximum Temp. ≤ 32°F	0	0	0	0	0	0	0	0	0	0	0	0	0
Days Minimum Temp. ≤ 32°F	5	1	0	0	0	0	0	0	0	0	1	6	13
Days Minimum Temp. ≤ 0°F	0	0	0	0	0	0	0	0	0	0	0	0	0
Heating Degree Days (base 65°F)	574	367	267	142	39	3	0	0	4	66	328	590	2,380
Cooling Degree Days (base 65°F)	0	0	3	44	150	310	472	436	275	87	1	0	1,778
Mean Precipitation (in.)	2.06	1.85	2.17	0.77	0.36	0.11	trace	0.01	0.25	0.58	1.26	1.55	10.97
Days With ≥ 0.1" Precipitation	5	5	5	2	1	0	0	0	0	1	3	4	27
Days With ≥ 1.0" Precipitation	0	0	0	0	0	0	0	0	0	0	0	0	0
Mean Snowfall (in.)	trace	0.0	0.0	0.0	0.0	0.0	0.0	0.0	0.0	0.0	0.0	0.0	trace
Days With ≥ 1.0" Snow Depth	0	0	0	0	0	0	0	0	0	0	0	0	0

Vista 2 NNE *San Diego County*   Elevation: 508 ft.   Latitude: 33° 14' N   Longitude: 117° 14' W

	JAN	FEB	MAR	APR	MAY	JUN	JUL	AUG	SEP	OCT	NOV	DEC	YEAR
Mean Maximum Temp. (°F)	67.4	68.3	68.3	71.7	73.2	77.5	82.1	83.5	82.5	78.5	73.0	67.9	74.5
Mean Temp. (°F)	55.9	56.8	57.5	60.5	63.5	67.3	71.4	72.7	71.4	66.7	60.6	56.0	63.4
Mean Minimum Temp. (°F)	44.3	45.3	46.6	49.2	53.6	57.0	60.6	61.8	60.2	54.9	48.1	44.1	52.1
Extreme Maximum Temp. (°F)	88	90	96	101	99	108	107	106	107	104	97	90	108
Extreme Minimum Temp. (°F)	20	31	29	35	42	45	50	46	47	36	33	27	20
Days Maximum Temp. ≥ 90°F	0	0	0	1	1	2	3	5	5	3	1	0	21
Days Maximum Temp. ≤ 32°F	0	0	0	0	0	0	0	0	0	0	0	0	0
Days Minimum Temp. ≤ 32°F	1	0	0	0	0	0	0	0	0	0	0	1	2
Days Minimum Temp. ≤ 0°F	0	0	0	0	0	0	0	0	0	0	0	0	0
Heating Degree Days (base 65°F)	280	231	232	148	77	18	0	0	3	30	144	275	1,438
Cooling Degree Days (base 65°F)	4	9	8	27	44	105	228	277	220	107	20	4	1,053
Mean Precipitation (in.)	3.15	2.38	2.86	0.88	0.26	0.14	0.05	0.11	0.31	0.43	1.35	1.62	13.54
Days With ≥ 0.1" Precipitation	5	4	5	2	1	0	0	0	1	1	3	4	26
Days With ≥ 1.0" Precipitation	1	1	1	0	0	0	0	0	0	0	0	0	3
Mean Snowfall (in.)	trace	0.0	0.0	trace	0.0	0.0	0.0	0.0	0.0	0.0	0.0	0.0	trace
Days With ≥ 1.0" Snow Depth	0	0	0	0	0	0	0	0	0	0	0	0	0

Wasco *Kern County*   Elevation: 344 ft.   Latitude: 35° 36' N   Longitude: 119° 21' W

	JAN	FEB	MAR	APR	MAY	JUN	JUL	AUG	SEP	OCT	NOV	DEC	YEAR
Mean Maximum Temp. (°F)	56.5	64.2	69.9	77.7	86.2	93.8	98.9	97.3	91.7	82.0	67.0	56.3	78.5
Mean Temp. (°F)	46.6	52.3	57.2	62.7	70.3	77.1	82.0	80.4	75.3	65.9	53.8	45.6	64.1
Mean Minimum Temp. (°F)	36.8	40.3	44.4	47.7	54.3	60.4	65.1	63.5	58.8	49.9	40.5	34.9	49.7
Extreme Maximum Temp. (°F)	81	83	90	101	107	111	114	113	111	105	87	78	114
Extreme Minimum Temp. (°F)	21	24	30	31	39	43	50	46	43	29	23	14	14
Days Maximum Temp. ≥ 90°F	0	0	0	3	11	22	29	28	19	6	0	0	118
Days Maximum Temp. ≤ 32°F	0	0	0	0	0	0	0	0	0	0	0	0	0
Days Minimum Temp. ≤ 32°F	8	3	0	0	0	0	0	0	0	0	3	12	26
Days Minimum Temp. ≤ 0°F	0	0	0	0	0	0	0	0	0	0	0	0	0
Heating Degree Days (base 65°F)	562	353	240	113	25	2	0	0	2	64	332	594	2,287
Cooling Degree Days (base 65°F)	0	0	6	65	195	354	526	488	321	99	1	0	2,055
Mean Precipitation (in.)	1.34	1.35	1.59	0.56	0.24	0.12	trace	0.03	0.18	0.33	0.71	0.92	7.37
Days With ≥ 0.1" Precipitation	4	4	4	2	1	0	0	0	1	1	2	3	22
Days With ≥ 1.0" Precipitation	0	0	0	0	0	0	0	0	0	0	0	0	0
Mean Snowfall (in.)	0.1	0.0	0.0	0.0	0.0	0.0	0.0	0.0	0.0	0.0	0.0	0.0	0.1
Days With ≥ 1.0" Snow Depth	0	0	0	0	0	0	0	0	0	0	0	0	0

Watsonville Waterworks *Santa Cruz County*   Elevation: 95 ft.   Latitude: 36° 56' N   Longitude: 121° 46' W

	JAN	FEB	MAR	APR	MAY	JUN	JUL	AUG	SEP	OCT	NOV	DEC	YEAR
Mean Maximum Temp. (°F)	60.6	62.7	64.0	67.3	68.8	71.0	71.7	72.4	73.6	71.7	65.9	60.7	67.5
Mean Temp. (°F)	50.0	52.3	53.8	56.1	58.5	61.0	62.4	63.0	63.0	59.9	54.3	49.6	57.0
Mean Minimum Temp. (°F)	39.4	41.8	43.7	44.9	48.2	51.0	53.1	53.6	52.2	48.0	42.7	38.5	46.4
Extreme Maximum Temp. (°F)	79	85	84	96	98	103	100	98	105	106	92	78	106
Extreme Minimum Temp. (°F)	26	24	29	32	31	40	44	43	40	31	25	12	12
Days Maximum Temp. ≥ 90°F	0	0	0	0	0	1	1	0	2	1	0	0	5
Days Maximum Temp. ≤ 32°F	0	0	0	0	0	0	0	0	0	0	0	0	0
Days Minimum Temp. ≤ 32°F	4	1	0	0	0	0	0	0	0	0	1	4	10
Days Minimum Temp. ≤ 0°F	0	0	0	0	0	0	0	0	0	0	0	0	0
Heating Degree Days (base 65°F)	457	353	340	264	204	129	92	73	87	171	316	470	2,956
Cooling Degree Days (base 65°F)	0	0	0	8	10	18	24	24	31	20	2	0	137
Mean Precipitation (in.)	4.64	4.17	3.94	1.59	0.50	0.12	0.08	0.06	0.29	0.98	3.23	3.56	23.16
Days With ≥ 0.1" Precipitation	7	6	7	3	1	0	0	0	1	2	5	6	38
Days With ≥ 1.0" Precipitation	1	1	1	0	0	0	0	0	0	0	1	1	5
Mean Snowfall (in.)	0.0	0.0	0.0	0.0	0.0	0.0	0.0	0.0	0.0	0.0	0.0	0.0	0.0
Days With ≥ 1.0" Snow Depth	0	0	0	0	0	0	0	0	0	0	0	0	0

Whiskeytown Reservoir *Shasta County*   Elevation: 1,292 ft.   Latitude: 40° 37' N   Longitude: 122° 32' W

	JAN	FEB	MAR	APR	MAY	JUN	JUL	AUG	SEP	OCT	NOV	DEC	YEAR
Mean Maximum Temp. (°F)	53.6	57.3	61.5	68.0	77.2	86.4	95.3	95.0	88.4	76.6	60.4	53.4	72.8
Mean Temp. (°F)	44.9	47.7	51.1	56.2	64.5	72.4	79.3	78.4	72.9	63.2	50.8	44.7	60.5
Mean Minimum Temp. (°F)	36.2	38.1	40.7	44.3	51.7	58.3	63.4	61.7	57.3	49.8	41.3	36.0	48.2
Extreme Maximum Temp. (°F)	78	82	85	93	101	106	112	115	114	104	87	80	115
Extreme Minimum Temp. (°F)	21	18	26	28	33	41	49	49	40	28	25	11	11
Days Maximum Temp. ≥ 90°F	0	0	0	0	4	13	25	24	16	4	0	0	86
Days Maximum Temp. ≤ 32°F	0	0	0	0	0	0	0	0	0	0	0	0	0
Days Minimum Temp. ≤ 32°F	8	5	2	1	0	0	0	0	0	0	2	8	26
Days Minimum Temp. ≤ 0°F	0	0	0	0	0	0	0	0	0	0	0	0	0
Heating Degree Days (base 65°F)	615	481	424	270	106	22	1	2	21	131	419	623	3,115
Cooling Degree Days (base 65°F)	0	0	1	16	97	241	448	429	268	83	1	0	1,584
Mean Precipitation (in.)	11.91	9.93	11.07	3.96	2.69	1.11	0.41	0.24	1.46	2.92	8.78	9.30	63.78
Days With ≥ 0.1" Precipitation	10	9	10	6	4	2	1	1	2	3	8	9	65
Days With ≥ 1.0" Precipitation	4	4	4	1	1	0	0	0	0	1	3	3	21
Mean Snowfall (in.)	1.6	0.4	0.0	trace	0.0	0.0	0.0	0.0	0.0	0.0	0.6	0.8	3.4
Days With ≥ 1.0" Snow Depth	1	0	0	0	0	0	0	0	0	0	0	0	1

Wildrose Ranger Station *Inyo County* Elevation: 4,097 ft. Latitude: 36° 16' N Longitude: 117° 11' W

	JAN	FEB	MAR	APR	MAY	JUN	JUL	AUG	SEP	OCT	NOV	DEC	YEAR
Mean Maximum Temp. (°F)	51.0	55.5	61.9	69.9	79.3	89.5	95.2	93.1	85.9	73.4	59.8	51.8	72.2
Mean Temp. (°F)	40.5	44.3	49.1	55.4	64.4	73.5	79.6	77.9	71.4	60.3	47.9	40.8	58.8
Mean Minimum Temp. (°F)	29.9	32.9	36.2	40.8	49.4	57.5	63.9	62.6	57.0	47.0	36.0	29.7	45.2
Extreme Maximum Temp. (°F)	73	75	87	91	102	105	110	107	100	94	80	79	110
Extreme Minimum Temp. (°F)	5	11	16	18	25	34	46	44	36	22	8	4	4
Days Maximum Temp. ≥ 90°F	0	0	0	0	3	16	27	24	10	1	0	0	81
Days Maximum Temp. ≤ 32°F	0	0	0	0	0	0	0	0	0	0	0	1	1
Days Minimum Temp. ≤ 32°F	19	13	9	4	0	0	0	0	0	1	10	20	76
Days Minimum Temp. ≤ 0°F	0	0	0	0	0	0	0	0	0	0	0	0	0
Heating Degree Days (base 65°F)	753	579	487	294	104	12	0	1	17	180	506	745	3,678
Cooling Degree Days (base 65°F)	0	0	0	15	95	273	454	430	233	46	0	0	1,546
Mean Precipitation (in.)	1.01	1.06	1.12	0.33	0.44	0.13	0.33	0.65	0.49	0.29	0.43	0.56	6.84
Days With ≥ 0.1" Precipitation	2	2	2	1	1	1	1	1	1	1	1	1	15
Days With ≥ 1.0" Precipitation	0	0	0	0	0	0	0	0	0	0	0	0	0
Mean Snowfall (in.)	1.0	trace	0.5	trace	0.0	0.0	0.0	0.0	0.0	0.0	trace	*0.1*	*1.6*
Days With ≥ 1.0" Snow Depth	0	0	0	0	0	0	0	0	0	0	0	*0*	*0*

Willits 1 NE *Mendocino County* Elevation: 1,348 ft. Latitude: 39° 25' N Longitude: 123° 21' W

	JAN	FEB	MAR	APR	MAY	JUN	JUL	AUG	SEP	OCT	NOV	DEC	YEAR
Mean Maximum Temp. (°F)	55.5	58.5	60.9	64.9	72.0	78.4	85.4	85.2	82.9	74.5	61.0	54.6	69.5
Mean Temp. (°F)	44.5	46.9	48.8	51.0	56.3	61.5	66.5	65.6	62.9	56.5	48.3	43.5	54.4
Mean Minimum Temp. (°F)	33.4	35.2	36.7	37.0	40.6	44.5	47.6	46.0	42.8	38.5	35.6	32.3	39.2
Extreme Maximum Temp. (°F)	76	80	83	92	98	103	108	107	105	102	83	72	108
Extreme Minimum Temp. (°F)	12	13	10	21	27	31	32	35	28	17	13	5	5
Days Maximum Temp. ≥ 90°F	0	0	0	0	1	5	11	10	8	2	0	0	37
Days Maximum Temp. ≤ 32°F	0	0	0	0	0	0	0	0	0	0	0	0	0
Days Minimum Temp. ≤ 32°F	15	11	9	6	2	0	0	0	1	5	11	17	77
Days Minimum Temp. ≤ 0°F	0	0	0	0	0	0	0	0	0	0	0	0	0
Heating Degree Days (base 65°F)	629	506	495	414	271	134	46	51	95	261	494	661	4,057
Cooling Degree Days (base 65°F)	0	0	0	1	7	30	91	69	35	6	0	0	239
Mean Precipitation (in.)	10.63	8.27	7.62	3.11	1.56	0.32	0.10	0.21	0.89	2.74	7.07	8.23	50.75
Days With ≥ 0.1" Precipitation	11	*10*	10	6	3	1	0	1	2	4	9	10	*67*
Days With ≥ 1.0" Precipitation	4	3	3	1	0	0	0	0	0	1	3	3	18
Mean Snowfall (in.)	1.2	0.6	0.4	trace	0.0	0.0	0.0	0.0	0.0	0.0	trace	0.4	2.6
Days With ≥ 1.0" Snow Depth	0	0	0	0	0	0	0	0	0	0	0	0	0

Willow Creek 1 NW *Humboldt County* Elevation: 459 ft. Latitude: 40° 57' N Longitude: 123° 38' W

	JAN	FEB	MAR	APR	MAY	JUN	JUL	AUG	SEP	OCT	NOV	DEC	YEAR
Mean Maximum Temp. (°F)	na	57.0	62.5	69.4	77.5	86.2	94.6	94.4	87.7	74.6	*58.3*	*50.2*	na
Mean Temp. (°F)	na	46.5	50.4	54.5	60.6	67.5	73.7	73.1	67.5	58.3	*48.9*	*42.7*	na
Mean Minimum Temp. (°F)	na	35.9	38.1	39.6	43.7	48.7	52.7	51.6	47.3	42.1	*39.4*	*35.2*	na
Extreme Maximum Temp. (°F)	70	76	85	96	105	112	119	115	108	99	80	65	119
Extreme Minimum Temp. (°F)	17	13	22	24	29	29	35	39	32	22	19	5	5
Days Maximum Temp. ≥ 90°F	0	0	0	0	4	12	22	23	14	2	0	0	77
Days Maximum Temp. ≤ 32°F	0	0	0	0	0	0	0	0	0	0	0	0	0
Days Minimum Temp. ≤ 32°F	9	6	4	3	0	0	0	0	0	1	3	9	35
Days Minimum Temp. ≤ 0°F	0	0	0	0	0	0	0	0	0	0	0	0	0
Heating Degree Days (base 65°F)	na	*511*	*449*	310	167	50	8	6	37	215	478	na	na
Cooling Degree Days (base 65°F)	na	0	*0*	5	37	126	286	268	123	16	0	na	na
Mean Precipitation (in.)	9.59	8.62	7.86	3.40	2.01	0.63	0.15	0.42	1.13	3.20	8.62	9.77	55.40
Days With ≥ 0.1" Precipitation	na	na	na	*5*	4	2	0	1	2	4	na	na	na
Days With ≥ 1.0" Precipitation	na	na	*2*	1	0	0	0	0	0	1	*2*	*2*	na
Mean Snowfall (in.)	0.4	0.4	trace	0.0	0.0	0.0	0.0	0.0	0.0	0.0	trace	0.5	1.3
Days With ≥ 1.0" Snow Depth	0	0	0	0	0	0	0	0	0	0	0	0	0

Willows 6 W *Glenn County* Elevation: 232 ft. Latitude: 39° 31' N Longitude: 122° 18' W

	JAN	FEB	MAR	APR	MAY	JUN	JUL	AUG	SEP	OCT	NOV	DEC	YEAR
Mean Maximum Temp. (°F)	55.8	61.4	65.9	73.0	81.3	88.6	93.7	92.3	89.1	79.7	64.3	55.8	75.1
Mean Temp. (°F)	46.0	50.2	53.8	58.7	66.3	73.0	77.2	75.5	72.5	64.6	52.6	45.6	61.3
Mean Minimum Temp. (°F)	36.1	39.0	41.6	44.3	51.2	57.4	60.5	58.6	56.0	49.4	40.8	35.3	47.5
Extreme Maximum Temp. (°F)	79	80	88	93	102	112	117	115	113	103	88	81	117
Extreme Minimum Temp. (°F)	20	21	22	23	33	39	45	45	37	33	22	11	11
Days Maximum Temp. ≥ 90°F	0	0	0	1	6	14	23	21	16	5	0	0	86
Days Maximum Temp. ≤ 32°F	0	0	0	0	0	0	0	0	0	0	0	0	0
Days Minimum Temp. ≤ 32°F	10	4	2	0	0	0	0	0	0	0	2	10	28
Days Minimum Temp. ≤ 0°F	0	0	0	0	0	0	0	0	0	0	0	0	0
Heating Degree Days (base 65°F)	583	410	343	200	70	12	0	1	9	88	368	595	2,679
Cooling Degree Days (base 65°F)	0	0	1	22	108	246	375	330	246	88	2	*0*	*1,418*
Mean Precipitation (in.)	3.99	3.45	2.92	0.92	0.73	0.29	0.06	0.09	0.33	0.94	2.60	2.75	19.07
Days With ≥ 0.1" Precipitation	6	5	6	2	2	1	0	0	1	2	5	5	35
Days With ≥ 1.0" Precipitation	1	1	0	0	0	0	0	0	0	0	1	1	4
Mean Snowfall (in.)	0.2	0.0	0.0	0.0	0.0	0.0	0.0	0.0	0.0	0.0	trace	0.3	0.5
Days With ≥ 1.0" Snow Depth	0	0	0	0	0	0	0	0	0	0	0	0	0

Winters *Yolo County*　Elevation: 134 ft.　Latitude: 38° 31' N　Longitude: 121° 58' W

	JAN	FEB	MAR	APR	MAY	JUN	JUL	AUG	SEP	OCT	NOV	DEC	YEAR
Mean Maximum Temp. (°F)	55.5	62.2	67.2	74.6	83.3	91.2	96.4	95.0	90.5	81.0	65.9	56.0	76.6
Mean Temp. (°F)	46.7	51.8	55.8	61.2	68.4	74.7	78.4	77.1	73.8	66.0	54.5	46.7	62.9
Mean Minimum Temp. (°F)	37.9	41.3	44.4	47.8	53.5	58.2	60.2	59.2	57.1	50.9	43.1	37.3	49.2
Extreme Maximum Temp. (°F)	77	80	92	96	107	109	115	113	111	102	88	77	115
Extreme Minimum Temp. (°F)	22	22	29	33	30	44	50	51	43	33	26	15	15
Days Maximum Temp. ≥ 90°F	0	0	0	1	9	18	27	25	18	5	0	0	103
Days Maximum Temp. ≤ 32°F	0	0	0	0	0	0	0	0	0	0	0	0	0
Days Minimum Temp. ≤ 32°F	7	2	0	0	0	0	0	0	0	0	1	7	17
Days Minimum Temp. ≤ 0°F	0	0	0	0	0	0	0	0	0	0	0	0	0
Heating Degree Days (base 65°F)	560	368	281	142	42	5	0	0	5	60	309	560	2,332
Cooling Degree Days (base 65°F)	0	1	4	46	156	302	424	391	284	103	4	0	1,715
Mean Precipitation (in.)	5.33	4.42	3.58	0.97	0.60	0.12	0.03	0.05	0.26	0.92	3.10	3.64	23.02
Days With ≥ 0.1" Precipitation	7	6	6	3	1	0	0	0	1	2	5	6	37
Days With ≥ 1.0" Precipitation	2	1	1	0	0	0	0	0	0	0	1	1	6
Mean Snowfall (in.)	0.1	trace	trace	0.0	0.0	0.0	0.0	0.0	0.0	0.0	0.0	trace	0.1
Days With ≥ 1.0" Snow Depth	0	0	0	0	0	0	0	0	0	0	0	0	0

Yosemite Nat'l Park HQ *Mariposa County*　Elevation: 3,963 ft.　Latitude: 37° 45' N　Longitude: 119° 35' W

	JAN	FEB	MAR	APR	MAY	JUN	JUL	AUG	SEP	OCT	NOV	DEC	YEAR
Mean Maximum Temp. (°F)	48.4	54.1	58.4	64.9	72.4	81.2	89.5	89.8	83.6	73.2	57.4	48.0	68.4
Mean Temp. (°F)	37.9	41.7	45.3	50.7	57.5	65.1	72.3	72.0	66.3	56.7	44.5	37.4	54.0
Mean Minimum Temp. (°F)	27.4	29.3	32.2	36.4	42.6	49.0	55.1	54.2	48.9	40.3	31.7	26.9	39.5
Extreme Maximum Temp. (°F)	72	82	83	87	94	103	105	109	108	96	86	73	109
Extreme Minimum Temp. (°F)	9	6	13	15	27	30	40	38	28	21	13	-1	-1
Days Maximum Temp. ≥ 90°F	0	0	0	0	0	5	17	17	8	2	0	0	49
Days Maximum Temp. ≤ 32°F	0	0	0	0	0	0	0	0	0	0	0	1	1
Days Minimum Temp. ≤ 32°F	26	21	17	9	2	0	0	0	0	5	18	27	125
Days Minimum Temp. ≤ 0°F	0	0	0	0	0	0	0	0	0	0	0	0	0
Heating Degree Days (base 65°F)	831	650	603	423	239	76	7	7	62	270	607	848	4,623
Cooling Degree Days (base 65°F)	0	0	0	0	14	87	247	247	110	22	0	0	727
Mean Precipitation (in.)	6.82	6.64	5.89	2.52	1.49	0.78	0.51	0.21	0.90	2.21	4.94	5.08	37.99
Days With ≥ 0.1" Precipitation	8	7	8	5	3	2	1	1	2	3	6	6	52
Days With ≥ 1.0" Precipitation	3	3	2	1	0	0	0	0	1	2	2	14
Mean Snowfall (in.)	17.1	8.3	6.9	2.4	trace	0.0	0.0	0.0	0.0	trace	3.6	6.7	45.0
Days With ≥ 1.0" Snow Depth	7	7	4	1	0	0	0	0	0	0	1	5	25

Yosemite Nat'l Park S. Entrance *Mariposa County*　Elevation: 5,118 ft.　Latitude: 37° 30' N　Longitude: 119° 38' W

	JAN	FEB	MAR	APR	MAY	JUN	JUL	AUG	SEP	OCT	NOV	DEC	YEAR
Mean Maximum Temp. (°F)	45.6	47.3	49.0	55.0	63.7	72.4	79.7	79.1	73.2	64.1	52.4	46.7	60.7
Mean Temp. (°F)	36.0	37.0	38.6	43.1	50.6	58.3	64.7	64.3	59.1	50.8	41.3	36.5	48.4
Mean Minimum Temp. (°F)	26.5	26.7	28.2	31.2	37.5	44.2	49.7	49.3	45.1	37.4	30.2	26.2	36.0
Extreme Maximum Temp. (°F)	68	71	73	82	86	98	101	99	95	90	78	68	101
Extreme Minimum Temp. (°F)	4	2	13	12	22	29	33	35	28	21	7	-1	-1
Days Maximum Temp. ≥ 90°F	0	0	0	0	0	0	2	1	0	0	0	0	3
Days Maximum Temp. ≤ 32°F	2	1	1	0	0	0	0	0	0	0	1	2	7
Days Minimum Temp. ≤ 32°F	27	25	26	18	7	1	0	0	1	8	20	27	160
Days Minimum Temp. ≤ 0°F	0	0	0	0	0	0	0	0	0	0	0	0	0
Heating Degree Days (base 65°F)	891	783	810	650	440	212	71	76	187	436	704	879	6,139
Cooling Degree Days (base 65°F)	0	0	0	0	1	12	51	51	11	2	0	0	128
Mean Precipitation (in.)	8.56	7.81	7.60	3.08	1.57	0.74	0.17	0.09	0.84	2.16	4.71	5.43	42.76
Days With ≥ 0.1" Precipitation	8	7	8	5	3	1	0	0	2	3	6	6	49
Days With ≥ 1.0" Precipitation	3	2	2	1	0	0	0	0	1	1	2	12
Mean Snowfall (in.)	na	na	na	7.2	0.6	trace	0.0	0.0	trace	0.7	5.6	15.9	na
Days With ≥ 1.0" Snow Depth	17	13	na	5	0	0	0	0	0	0	3	na	na

Yreka *Siskiyou County*　Elevation: 2,624 ft.　Latitude: 41° 42' N　Longitude: 122° 38' W

	JAN	FEB	MAR	APR	MAY	JUN	JUL	AUG	SEP	OCT	NOV	DEC	YEAR
Mean Maximum Temp. (°F)	45.1	51.3	56.9	62.8	72.7	81.1	90.5	90.1	81.9	69.9	52.7	44.3	66.6
Mean Temp. (°F)	34.9	39.2	43.7	48.4	56.5	63.9	71.3	70.7	63.3	52.9	41.1	34.5	51.7
Mean Minimum Temp. (°F)	24.6	27.2	30.6	34.0	40.3	46.7	52.0	51.1	44.6	35.9	29.5	24.6	36.8
Extreme Maximum Temp. (°F)	64	73	79	90	103	106	107	110	106	93	76	65	110
Extreme Minimum Temp. (°F)	1	-2	12	20	24	31	34	33	30	18	10	-11	-11
Days Maximum Temp. ≥ 90°F	0	0	0	0	2	7	18	19	7	1	0	0	54
Days Maximum Temp. ≤ 32°F	1	0	0	0	0	0	0	0	0	0	0	2	3
Days Minimum Temp. ≤ 32°F	26	23	21	13	4	0	0	0	0	9	21	26	143
Days Minimum Temp. ≤ 0°F	0	0	0	0	0	0	0	0	0	0	0	0	0
Heating Degree Days (base 65°F)	927	721	653	492	277	109	21	20	108	371	710	940	5,349
Cooling Degree Days (base 65°F)	0	0	0	0	21	69	207	194	64	4	0	0	560
Mean Precipitation (in.)	3.37	2.11	2.06	1.08	1.14	1.01	0.56	0.55	0.80	1.12	3.01	3.31	20.12
Days With ≥ 0.1" Precipitation	7	5	5	3	3	2	1	2	2	3	6	7	46
Days With ≥ 1.0" Precipitation	1	0	0	0	0	0	0	0	0	0	1	1	3
Mean Snowfall (in.)	4.4	2.2	2.2	0.3	trace	0.0	0.0	0.0	0.0	trace	1.5	4.0	14.6
Days With ≥ 1.0" Snow Depth	5	1	1	0	0	0	0	0	0	0	1	3	11

Note: See Appendix D for explanation of data.

COLORADO

PHYSICAL FEATURES. Colorado lies astride the highest mountains of the Continental Divide. Nearly rectangular, its north and south boundaries are the 41° and 37° N. parallels, and the east and west boundaries are the 102° and 109° W. meridians. It is eighth in size among the 50 states, with an area of 104,247 square miles. Although primarily a mountain state, nearly 40 percent of its area is taken up by the eastern high plains.

The principal features of Colorado geography are its inland continental location in the middle latitudes, and the mountains and ranges extending north and south approximately through the middle of the State. With an average altitude about 6,800 feet above sea level, Colorado is the highest state in the Union. Roughly three-quarters of the Nation's land above 10,000 feet altitude lies within its borders. The State has 54 mountains 14,000 feet or higher, and about 830 mountains between 11,000 and 14,000 feet in elevation.

Emerging gradually from the plains of Kansas and Nebraska, the high plains of Colorado slope gently upward for a distance of some 200 miles from the eastern border to the base of the foothills of the Rocky Mountains. The eastern portion of the State is generally level to rolling prairie broken by occasional hills and bluffs. The northern part of the plains area slopes to the northeast and the southern part to the southeast, divided by higher country and hills extending eastward from the mountains near the center of the State. Elevations along the eastern border range from about 3,350 feet at the lowest point in the State (where the Arkansas River crosses the border) to near 4,000 feet.

At elevations between 5,000 and 6,000 feet the plains give way abruptly to foothills with elevations of 7,000 to 9,000 feet. Backing the foothills are the mountain ranges above 9,000 feet with the higher peaks over 14,000 feet. West of these "front ranges" are additional ranges, generally extending north and south, but with many spurs and extensions in other directions. These ranges enclose numerous high mountain peaks and valleys. Farther westward the mountains give way to rugged plateau country in the form of high mesas (some more than 10,000 feet in elevation) which extends to the western border of the State. This land is often cut by rugged canyons, the work of the many streams fed by accumulations of winter snow.

All rivers in Colorado rise within its borders and flow outward, with the exception of the Green River which flows diagonally across the extreme northwestern corner of the State. Four of the Nation's major rivers have their source in Colorado: the Colorado, the Rio Grande, the Arkansas, and the Platte.

GENERAL CLIMATE. Most of Colorado has a cool and invigorating climate that could be termed a highland or mountain climate of a continental location. During summer there are hot days in the plains, but these are often relieved by afternoon thundershowers. Mountain regions are nearly always cool. Humidity is generally quite low; this favors rapid evaporation and a relatively comfortable feeling even on hot days. The thin atmosphere allows greater penetration of solar radiation and results in pleasant daytime conditions even during the winter. This is why skiers at high elevations are often pictured in very light clothing, although surrounded by heavy snow.

The climates of local areas are profoundly affected by differences in elevation, and to a lesser degree, by the orientation of mountain ranges and valleys with respect to general air movements. While temperature decreases, and precipitation generally increases with altitude, these patterns are modified by the orientation of mountain slopes with respect to the prevailing winds and by the effect of topographical features in creating local air movements.

As a result of the State's distance from major sources of moisture (the Pacific Ocean and the Gulf of Mexico), precipitation is generally light in the lower elevations. Prevailing air currents reach Colorado from westerly directions. Eastward-moving storms originating in the Pacific Ocean lose much of their moisture in passage over mountain ranges to the west; a large part of the remaining moisture falls as rain or snow on the mountaintops and westward-facing slopes. Eastern slope areas receive relatively small amounts of precipitation from these storms.

Storms moving from the north usually carry little moisture. The frequency of such storms increases during the fall and winter months, and decreases rapidly in the spring. The accompanying outbreaks of polar air are responsible for the sudden drops in temperature often experienced in the plains section. Occasionally these outbreaks are attended by strong northerly winds which come in contact with moist air from the south; the interaction of these air masses causes a heavy fall of snow and the most severe of all weather conditions of the high plains, the blizzard. This cold air is frequently too shallow to cross the mountains to the western portion of the State so while the plains are in the grip of a very severe storm, the weather in the mountains and western valleys may be mild.

Occasionally, when the plains are covered with a shallow layer of cold air, strong westerly winds aloft work their way to the surface. Warmed by rapid descent from higher levels, these winds bring large and sudden temperature rises. This phenomenon is called the "chinook" of the high plains and temperature rises of 25 to 35°F. within a short time are not uncommon. Chinook winds greatly moderate average winter temperatures in areas near enough to the mountains to experience them frequently.

Warm, moist air from the south moves into Colorado most frequently in the spring. As this air is carried northward and westward to higher elevations, the heaviest and most general rainfalls of the year occur over the eastern portions of the State. Frequent showers and thunderstorms continue well into the summer.

CLIMATE OF THE EASTERN PLAINS. The climate of the plains is comparatively uniform from place to place, with characteristic features of low relative humidity, abundant sunshine, light rainfall, moderate to high wind movement, and a large daily range in temperature. Because of the very low relative humidity, hot days cause less discomfort than in more humid areas. Summer precipitation in the plains is largely from thunderstorm activity and is sometimes extremely heavy. Strong winds occur frequently in winter and spring. These winds tend to dry out soils, which are not well supplied with moisture because of the low annual precipitation. During periods of drought such winds give rise to the duststorms which are especially characteristic of the southeastern plains.

At the western edge of the plains and near the foothills of the mountains, there are a number of significant changes in climate as compared to the plains proper. Average wind movement is less. Temperature changes from day to day are not as great; summer temperatures are lower, and winter temperatures are higher. Precipitation, which decreases gradually from the eastern border to a minimum near the mountains, increases rapidly with the increasing elevation of the foothills and proximity to higher ranges.

CLIMATE OF WESTERN COLORADO. The rugged topography of western Colorado causes large variations in climate within short distances, and few climatic generalizations apply to the whole area. Snow-covered mountain peaks and valleys often have very cold nighttime temperatures in winter, when skies are clear and the air is still — occasionally to 50°F below zero. Summer in the mountains is a cool and refreshing season. At typical mountain weather stations the average July temperature is in the neighborhood of 60°F. The highest temperatures are usually in the 70s and 80s, but may reach 95°F. Above 7,000 feet, the nights are quite cool throughout the summer, while bright sunshine makes the days comfortably warm.

Precipitation west of the Continental Divide is more evenly distributed throughout the year than in the eastern plains. For most of western Colorado, the greatest monthly precipitation occurs in the winter months, while June is the driest month. In contrast, June is one of the wetter months in most of the eastern portion of the State.

STORMS. Thunderstorms are quite prevalent in the eastern plains and along the eastern slopes of the mountains during the spring and summer. These often become quite severe, and the frequency of hail damage to crops in northeastern Colorado is quite high. Tornadoes almost never occur in the mountains, and are relatively infrequent over the eastern plains. A spring flood potential results from the melting of snow. In years when snow cover is heavy, or when there is a sudden warming in the spring at high elevations, there may be extensive flooding. Heavy thunderstorms in the eastern foothills and plains occasionally cause damaging flash floods. Similar flash floods occur on the western slopes but with somewhat lower frequency.

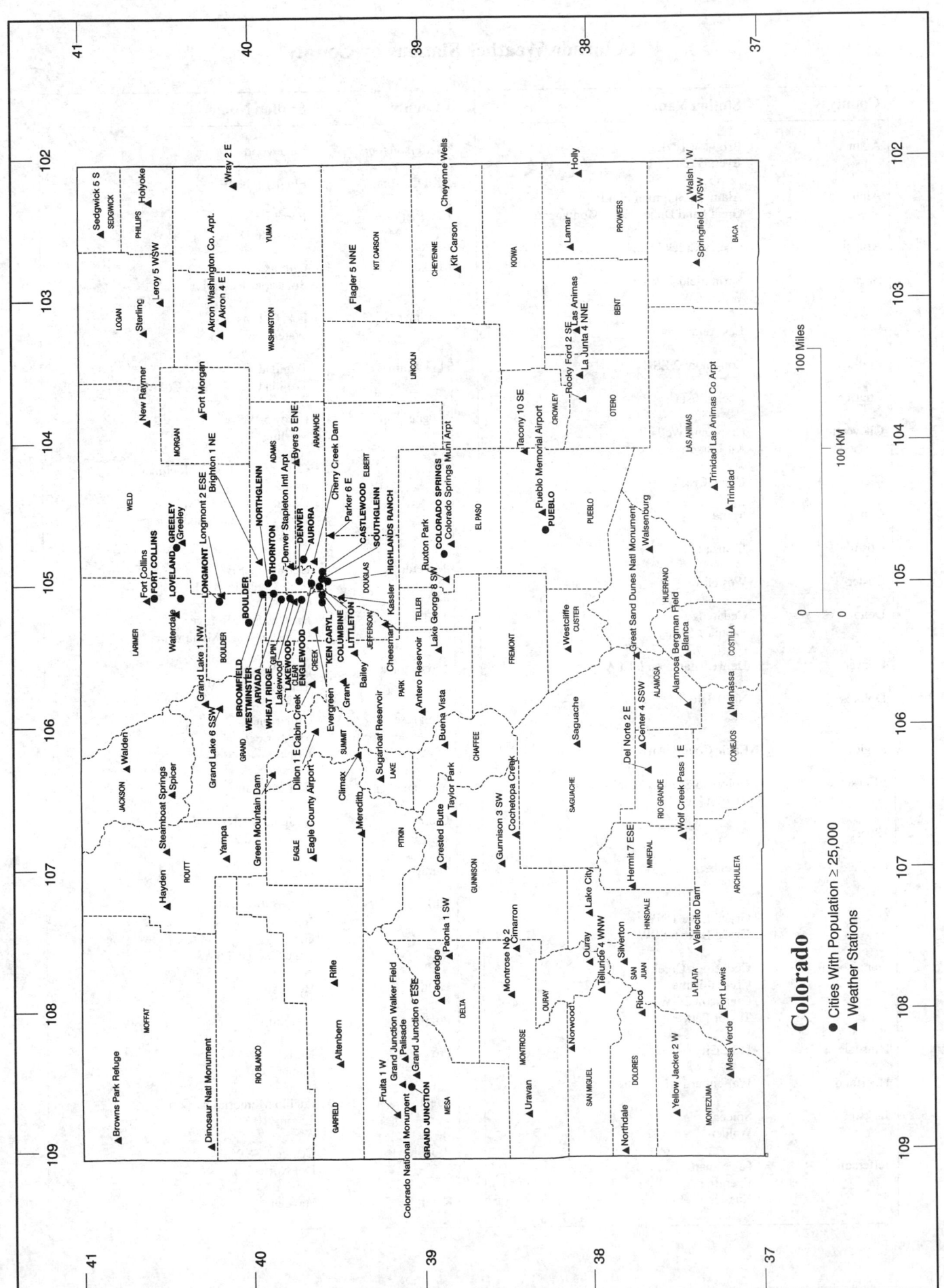

Colorado

● Cities With Population ≥ 25,000
▲ Weather Stations

Colorado Weather Stations by County

County	Station Name
Adams	Brighton 1 NE
	Byers 5 ENE
Alamosa	Alamosa Bergman Field
	Great Sand Dunes Nat'l Monument
Arapahoe	Cherry Creek Dam
Baca	Springfield 7 WSW
	Walsh 1 W
Bent	Las Animas
Boulder	Longmont 2 ESE
Chaffee	Buena Vista
Cheyenne	Cheyenne Wells
	Kit Carson
Clear Creek	Cabin Creek
Conejos	Manassa
Costilla	Blanca
Custer	Westcliffe
Delta	Cedaredge
	Paonia 1 SW
Denver	Denver Stapleton Int'l Airport
Dolores	Northdale
	Rico
Eagle	Eagle County Airport
El Paso	Colorado Springs Muni Airport
	Ruxton Park
Elbert	Parker 6 E
Garfield	Altenbern
	Rifle
Grand	Grand Lake 1 NW
	Grand Lake 6 SSW
Gunnison	Cochetopa Creek
	Crested Butte
	Gunnison 3 SW
	Taylor Park
Hinsdale	Lake City
Huerfano	Walsenburg
Jackson	Spicer
	Walden
Jefferson	Cheesman
	Evergreen
	Kassler

County	Station Name
Jefferson (cont.)	Lakewood
Kit Carson	Flagler 5 NNE
La Plata	Fort Lewis
	Vallecito Dam
Lake	Climax
	Sugarloaf Reservoir
Larimer	Fort Collins
	Waterdale
Las Animas	Trinidad
	Trinidad Las Animas Co. Airport
Logan	Leroy 5 WSW
	Sterling
Mesa	Colorado National Monument
	Fruita 1 W
	Grand Junction 6 ESE
	Grand Junction Walker Field
	Palisade
Mineral	Hermit 7 ESE
	Wolf Creek Pass 1 E
Moffat	Browns Park Refuge
	Dinosaur Nat'l Monument
Montezuma	Mesa Verde
	Yellow Jacket 2 W
Montrose	Cimarron
	Montrose 2
	Uravan
Morgan	Fort Morgan
Otero	La Junta 4 NNE
	Rocky Ford 2 SE
Ouray	Ouray
Park	Antero Reservoir
	Bailey
	Grant
	Lake George 8 SW
Phillips	Holyoke
Pitkin	Meredith
Prowers	Holly
	Lamar
Pueblo	Pueblo Memorial Airport
	Tacony 10 SE
Rio Grande	Center 4 SSW
	Del Norte 2 E
Routt	Hayden

County	Station Name
Routt *(cont.)*	Steamboat Springs
	Yampa
Saguache	Saguache
San Juan	Silverton
San Miguel	Norwood
	Telluride 4 WNW
Sedgwick	Sedgwick 5 S
Summit	Dillon 1 E
	Green Mountain Dam
Washington	Akron 4 E
	Akron Washington Co. Airport
Weld	Greeley
	New Raymer
Yuma	Wray 2 E

Colorado Weather Stations by City

City	Station Name	Miles
Arvada	Brighton 1 NE	17
	Cherry Creek Dam	19
	Denver Stapleton Int'l Airport	13
	Evergreen	18
	Lakewood	5
Aurora	Brighton 1 NE	18
	Cherry Creek Dam	4
	Denver Stapleton Int'l Airport	6
	Lakewood	16
	Parker 6 E	14
Boulder	Lakewood	19
	Longmont 2 ESE	15
Broomfield	Brighton 1 NE	12
	Denver Stapleton Int'l Airport	15
	Lakewood	13
	Longmont 2 ESE	16
Castlewood	Cherry Creek Dam	5
	Denver Stapleton Int'l Airport	13
	Kassler	12
	Lakewood	16
	Parker 6 E	14
Colorado Springs	Colorado Springs Muni Airport	5
	Ruxton Park	10
Columbine	Cherry Creek Dam	13
	Denver Stapleton Int'l Airport	17
	Evergreen	13
	Kassler	7
	Lakewood	12
Denver	Brighton 1 NE	18
	Cherry Creek Dam	9
	Denver Stapleton Int'l Airport	6
	Evergreen	19
	Kassler	18
	Lakewood	8
Englewood	Cherry Creek Dam	8
	Denver Stapleton Int'l Airport	10
	Evergreen	17
	Kassler	13
	Lakewood	10
	Parker 6 E	20
Fort Collins	Fort Collins	2
	Waterdale	11
Grand Junction	Colorado National Monument	10
	Fruita 1 W	12
	Grand Junction Walker Field	4
	Grand Junction 6 ESE	5
	Palisade	11
Greeley	Greeley	1
Highlands Ranch	Cherry Creek Dam	9
	Denver Stapleton Int'l Airport	16
	Evergreen	19
	Kassler	8

City	Station Name	Miles
Highlands Ranch (cont.)	Lakewood	16
	Parker 6 E	17
Ken Caryl	Cherry Creek Dam	15
	Denver Stapleton Int'l Airport	18
	Evergreen	12
	Kassler	7
	Lakewood	12
Lakewood	Cherry Creek Dam	15
	Denver Stapleton Int'l Airport	13
	Evergreen	12
	Kassler	15
	Lakewood	3
Littleton	Cherry Creek Dam	10
	Denver Stapleton Int'l Airport	14
	Evergreen	16
	Kassler	9
	Lakewood	12
	Parker 6 E	20
Longmont	Longmont 2 ESE	2
	Waterdale	18
Loveland	Fort Collins	12
	Longmont 2 ESE	17
	Waterdale	6
Northglenn	Brighton 1 NE	9
	Cherry Creek Dam	20
	Denver Stapleton Int'l Airport	11
	Lakewood	12
	Longmont 2 ESE	19
Pueblo	Pueblo Memorial Airport	7
Southglenn	Cherry Creek Dam	7
	Denver Stapleton Int'l Airport	13
	Evergreen	20
	Kassler	11
	Lakewood	14
	Parker 6 E	17
Thornton	Brighton 1 NE	8
	Cherry Creek Dam	18
	Denver Stapleton Int'l Airport	9
	Lakewood	12
Westminster	Brighton 1 NE	13
	Denver Stapleton Int'l Airport	12
	Lakewood	9
Wheat Ridge	Brighton 1 NE	18
	Cherry Creek Dam	17
	Denver Stapleton Int'l Airport	12
	Evergreen	15
	Kassler	20
	Lakewood	2

Note: Miles is the distance between the geographic center of the city and the weather station.

Colorado Weather Stations by Elevation

Feet	Station Name	Feet	Station Name
11,318	Climax	5,777	Colorado National Monument
10,639	Wolf Creek Pass 1 E	5,744	Trinidad Las Animas Co. Airport
10,019	Cabin Creek	5,675	Altenbern
9,737	Sugarloaf Reservoir	5,646	Cherry Creek Dam
9,317	Silverton	5,639	Lakewood
9,206	Taylor Park	5,577	Paonia 1 SW
9,064	Dillon 1 E	5,498	Kassler
9,048	Ruxton Park	5,351	Browns Park Refuge
8,999	Hermit 7 ESE	5,318	Rifle
8,917	Antero Reservoir	5,285	Denver Stapleton Int'l Airport
8,858	Crested Butte	5,229	Waterdale
8,799	Rico	5,098	Byers 5 ENE
8,717	Grand Lake 1 NW	5,013	Brighton 1 NE
8,674	Grant	5,009	Uravan
8,671	Telluride 4 WNW	5,003	Fort Collins
8,667	Lake City	4,957	Tacony 10 SE
8,517	Lake George 8 SW	4,947	Longmont 2 ESE
8,333	Spicer	4,872	Flagler 5 NNE
8,287	Grand Lake 6 SSW	4,839	Grand Junction Walker Field
8,120	Great Sand Dunes Nat'l Monument	4,809	Palisade
8,120	Walden	4,780	New Raymer
7,998	Cochetopa Creek	4,757	Grand Junction 6 ESE
7,929	Buena Vista	4,714	Greeley
7,887	Yampa	4,681	Pueblo Memorial Airport
7,867	Del Norte 2 E	4,662	Akron Washington Co. Airport
7,857	Westcliffe	4,619	Springfield 7 WSW
7,837	Ouray	4,537	Akron 4 E
7,824	Meredith	4,478	Fruita 1 W
7,749	Blanca	4,468	Leroy 5 WSW
7,739	Green Mountain Dam	4,330	Fort Morgan
7,729	Bailey	4,278	Kit Carson
7,690	Saguache	4,248	Cheyenne Wells
7,687	Manassa	4,202	La Junta 4 NNE
7,670	Center 4 SSW	4,169	Rocky Ford 2 SE
7,647	Vallecito Dam	3,989	Sedgwick 5 S
7,637	Gunnison 3 SW	3,976	Walsh 1 W
7,598	Fort Lewis	3,937	Sterling
7,532	Alamosa Bergman Field	3,887	Las Animas
7,112	Mesa Verde	3,727	Holyoke
7,017	Norwood	3,625	Lamar
6,998	Evergreen	3,526	Wray 2 E
6,893	Cimarron	3,389	Holly
6,879	Cheesman		
6,856	Yellow Jacket 2 W		
6,679	Northdale		
6,633	Steamboat Springs		
6,496	Eagle County Airport		
6,437	Hayden		
6,309	Parker 6 E		
6,243	Cedaredge		
6,148	Walsenburg		
6,138	Colorado Springs Muni Airport		
6,026	Trinidad		
5,918	Dinosaur Nat'l Monument		
5,784	Montrose 2		

Alamosa Bergman Field

Alamosa is located in the south-central part of Colorado, near the center of the San Luis Valley which lies in a broad depression between mountain ranges converging to the north. The valley is the first of a series of basins along the Rio Grande River. The mountain ranges to the east reach altitudes over 14,000 feet and those to the west are between 13,000 and 14,000 feet. The length of the valley from north to south is over 80 miles, and its greatest width is about 50 miles. The valley floor ranges in altitude from 7,500 to near 8,000 feet and has a remarkably flat surface, except for a range of low hills across the southern portion. From the lowest areas which lie along an axis near the eastern border, the valley floor rises to the foothills, steeply to the east and more gently to the west.

The climate of the San Luis Valley is marked by cold winters and moderate summers, light precipitation, and much sunshine. At Alamosa about 80 percent of the annual precipitation occurs from April to October, most of it in the form of scattered light showers and thunderstorms that develop over the mountains and move into the valley during the afternoon. More than half of these thunderstorms occur during July and August; hail frequently falls in some parts of the valley during these storms. Winter snows occur mainly in frequent light falls, with occasional falls as early as September or as late as May. A good snow cover will remain on the ground for several weeks during the coldest months.

All agriculture in the valley is dependent on irrigation, using water supplied by the more abundant precipitation in the surrounding mountains. Summer grazing of cattle and sheep on nearby mountain ranges and smaller valleys is extensive. A wide variety of vegetables, grains and feed crops are grown locally, with potatoes being the main commercial crop.

Summer is characterized by frequent days with maximum temperatures in the middle 80s and minimum temperatures in the low 40s. Relative humidity ranges from about 76 percent in the early mornings to around 40 percent during the afternoons. Winds are light during the coldest weather, but are strong with occasional blowing dust during the spring and early summer months.

Based on the 1951-1980 period, the average first occurrence of 32 degrees Fahrenheit in the fall is September 8 and the average last occurrence in the spring is June 8.

Alamosa Bergman Field *Alamosa County*   Elevation: 7,532 ft.   Latitude: 37° 26' N   Longitude: 105° 52' W

	JAN	FEB	MAR	APR	MAY	JUN	JUL	AUG	SEP	OCT	NOV	DEC	YEAR
Mean Maximum Temp. (°F)	33.4	40.7	49.7	58.4	68.1	78.2	81.9	79.4	72.9	61.9	46.4	35.6	58.9
Mean Temp. (°F)	15.1	23.1	33.2	40.9	50.5	59.5	64.4	62.5	54.8	43.0	29.0	17.8	41.2
Mean Minimum Temp. (°F)	-3.3	5.5	16.6	23.3	32.9	40.8	46.9	45.5	36.8	24.1	11.7	-0.1	23.4
Extreme Maximum Temp. (°F)	62	66	73	80	85	95	96	90	87	81	71	60	96
Extreme Minimum Temp. (°F)	-40	-30	-12	-6	13	24	30	31	15	-9	-26	-42	-42
Days Maximum Temp. ≥ 90°F	0	0	0	0	0	0	1	0	0	0	0	0	1
Days Maximum Temp. ≤ 32°F	14	6	1	0	0	0	0	0	0	0	4	11	36
Days Minimum Temp. ≤ 32°F	31	28	31	27	14	2	0	0	7	27	29	31	227
Days Minimum Temp. ≤ 0°F	19	9	1	0	0	0	0	0	0	0	4	16	49
Heating Degree Days (base 65°F)	1,542	1,176	980	717	442	166	42	84	299	675	1,072	1,459	8,654
Cooling Degree Days (base 65°F)	0	0	0	0	0	9	31	14	1	0	0	0	55
Mean Precipitation (in.)	0.24	0.21	0.47	0.53	0.72	0.59	0.98	1.20	0.94	0.68	0.48	0.33	7.37
Maximum Precipitation (in.)	0.8	1.4	1.6	1.7	1.8	2.6	3.5	5.4	1.9	2.4	1.2	1.5	11.5
Minimum Precipitation (in.)	trace	trace	trace	trace	trace	trace	trace	0.2	trace	0	trace	trace	3.4
Maximum 24-hr. Precipitation (in.)	0.4	0.9	1.1	1.2	0.9	1.0	1.6	1.3	1.8	1.1	0.7	0.9	1.8
Days With ≥ 0.1" Precipitation	1	1	2	2	2	2	3	4	3	2	2	1	25
Days With ≥ 1.0" Precipitation	0	0	0	0	0	0	0	0	0	0	0	0	0
Mean Snowfall (in.)	4.3	2.9	6.2	4.0	2.1	trace	trace	0.0	0.2	3.5	4.5	5.1	32.8
Maximum Snowfall (in.)	14	16	29	14	14	1	0	0	4	20	20	28	69
Maximum 24-hr. Snowfall (in.)	7	10	14	9	8	1	0	0	4	13	8	16	16
Days With ≥ 1.0" Snow Depth	17	9	4	1	0	0	0	0	0	1	6	12	50
Thunderstorm Days	0	< 1	< 1	2	7	9	9	8	6	1	0	0	42
Foggy Days	14	10	7	6	4	2	2	6	6	5	9	13	84
Predominant Sky Cover	CLR	CLR	CLR	SCT	SCT	SCT	SCT	SCT	CLR	CLR	CLR	CLR	CLR
Mean Relative Humidity 5am (%)	78	78	75	71	74	76	84	86	82	77	78	77	78
Mean Relative Humidity 5pm (%)	58	49	38	29	29	26	36	39	34	34	49	59	40
Mean Dewpoint (°F)	7	12	16	19	27	34	44	45	36	25	16	8	24
Prevailing Wind Direction	SW	SW	SW	SW	SW	SW	S	S	S	S	S	SW	SW
Prevailing Wind Speed (mph)	9	10	14	15	15	14	9	8	9	9	10	8	12
Maximum Wind Gust (mph)	69	66	71	67	70	68	58	48	56	62	54	54	71

Colorado Springs Muni Airport

At an elevation near 6,200 feet above sea level, Colorado Springs is located in relatively flat semi-arid country on the eastern slope of the Rocky Mountains. Immediately to the west the mountains rise abruptly to heights ranging from 10,000 to 14,000 feet but generally averaging near 11,000 feet. To the east lie gently undulating prairie lands. The land slopes upward to the north, reaching an average height of about 8,000 feet in 20 miles at the top of Palmer Lake Divide.

Colorado Springs is in the Arkansas River drainage basin. The principal tributary feeding the Arkansas from this area is Fountain Creek which rises in the high mountains west of the city and is fed by Monument Creek originating to the north in the Palmer Lake Divide area.

Other topographical features of the area, and particularly its wide range of elevations, help to give Colorado Springs the various and altogether delightful plains and mountain mixture of climate that has established the locality as a highly desirable place to live. The higher elevations immediately to the west and north of the city produce significant differences in temperature and precipitation. Precipitation amounts at these higher elevations are approximately twice those at nearby lower elevations and the number of rainy days is almost triple.

In Colorado Springs itself, precipitation is relatively sparse. Over 80 percent of it falls between April 1 and September 30, mostly as heavy downpours accompanying summer thunderstorms. Temperatures, in view of the station latitude and elevation, are mild. Uncomfortable extremes, in either summer or winter, are comparatively rare and of short duration. Relative humidity is normally low and wind movement moderately high. This is notably true of the west-to-east movement of the chinook winds, that cause rapid rises in winter temperatures and remind us that the Indian meaning of chinook is snow eater.

Colorado Springs is best known as a resort city, but is also important to the high-tech industry and military community. Several military installations, including the United States Air Force Academy and the Space Command are located within or near the city. The surrounding prairie is also important for cattle raising and a considerable amount of grazing land is used for sheep in the summer months. The growing season varies considerably in length but averages from the first week in May to the first week of October.

Colorado Springs Muni Airport *El Paso County*   Elevation: 6,138 ft.   Latitude: 38° 49' N   Longitude: 104° 43' W

	JAN	FEB	MAR	APR	MAY	JUN	JUL	AUG	SEP	OCT	NOV	DEC	YEAR
Mean Maximum Temp. (°F)	41.5	45.5	51.3	59.0	68.4	79.2	84.4	81.6	73.9	63.2	50.1	42.7	61.7
Mean Temp. (°F)	29.1	32.8	38.5	46.0	55.4	65.4	70.6	68.7	60.6	49.7	37.5	30.3	48.7
Mean Minimum Temp. (°F)	16.5	20.0	25.6	32.9	42.4	51.5	56.9	55.7	47.3	36.1	24.8	17.9	35.6
Extreme Maximum Temp. (°F)	73	72	81	87	93	99	98	97	94	86	78	75	99
Extreme Minimum Temp. (°F)	-20	-19	-3	4	22	33	46	39	22	7	-8	-24	-24
Days Maximum Temp. ≥ 90°F	0	0	0	0	0	4	8	3	1	0	0	0	16
Days Maximum Temp. ≤ 32°F	7	5	3	1	0	0	0	0	0	0	3	6	25
Days Minimum Temp. ≤ 32°F	30	27	25	14	2	0	0	0	1	10	25	29	163
Days Minimum Temp. ≤ 0°F	3	1	0	0	0	0	0	0	0	0	0	2	6
Heating Degree Days (base 65°F)	1,108	903	815	564	296	73	10	18	161	469	819	1,068	6,304
Cooling Degree Days (base 65°F)	0	0	0	1	7	86	188	137	36	0	0	0	455
Mean Precipitation (in.)	0.26	0.35	1.03	1.63	2.36	2.40	2.89	3.43	1.25	0.86	0.53	0.41	17.40
Maximum Precipitation (in.)	1.2	2.4	2.4	3.6	5.0	7.8	5.1	6.1	3.0	5.0	2.0	1.0	21.9
Minimum Precipitation (in.)	trace	trace	0.3	0.1	0.7	0.1	0.7	1.4	0	trace	trace	trace	12.6
Maximum 24-hr. Precipitation (in.)	0.8	1.5	1.4	1.3	1.9	2.5	2.0	2.7	1.3	1.1	0.8	0.7	2.7
Days With ≥ 0.1" Precipitation	1	1	3	4	5	5	6	7	4	2	2	1	41
Days With ≥ 1.0" Precipitation	0	0	0	0	1	0	1	1	0	0	0	0	3
Mean Snowfall (in.)	5.2	5.3	9.6	6.6	1.3	trace	trace	trace	0.5	3.9	6.1	6.6	45.1
Maximum Snowfall (in.)	29	23	23	20	19	0	0	0	2	26	26	18	88
Maximum 24-hr. Snowfall (in.)	22	15	12	7	15	0	0	0	1	9	9	9	22
Days With ≥ 1.0" Snow Depth	7	4	5	2	0	0	0	0	0	1	4	8	31
Thunderstorm Days	0	< 1	1	2	8	10	12	13	4	1	0	0	51
Foggy Days	6	7	7	6	5	4	3	4	4	4	6	7	63
Predominant Sky Cover	CLR	CLR	OVR	OVR	OVR	CLR	SCT	CLR	CLR	CLR	CLR	CLR	CLR
Mean Relative Humidity 5am (%)	57	59	62	63	67	66	68	70	65	58	59	56	63
Mean Relative Humidity 5pm (%)	46	41	39	36	38	35	39	41	36	36	45	47	40
Mean Dewpoint (°F)	10	13	16	23	33	41	47	47	38	26	17	11	27
Prevailing Wind Direction	NNE	N	N	N	N	SSE	N	N	N	N	NNE	NNE	N
Prevailing Wind Speed (mph)	9	12	14	14	13	12	10	10	10	12	9	9	12
Maximum Wind Gust (mph)	63	61	71	64	70	64	58	56	54	58	62	68	71

Denver Stapleton Int'l Airport

Denver enjoys the invigorating climate that prevails over much of the central Rocky Mountain region, without the extremely cold mornings of the high elevations during winter, or the hot afternoons of summer at lower altitudes. Extremely warm or cold weather in Denver is usually of short duration.

Situated a long distance from any moisture source, and separated from the Pacific Ocean by several high mountain barriers, Denver enjoys low relative humidity, light precipitation, and abundant sunshine.

Air masses from four different sources influence Denver weather. These include arctic air from Canada and Alaska, warm, moist air from the Gulf of Mexico, warm, dry air from Mexico and the southwestern deserts, and Pacific air modified by its passage over mountains to the west.

In winter, the high altitude and mountains to the west combine to moderate temperatures in Denver. Invasions of cold air from the north, intensified by the high altitude, can be abrupt and severe. However, many of the cold air masses that spread southward out of Canada never reach the altitude of Denver, but move off over the lower plains to the east. Surges of air from the west are moderated in their descent down the east face of the Rockies, and reach Denver in the form of chinook winds that often raise temperatures into the 60s, even in midwinter.

In spring, polar air often collides with warm, moist air from the Gulf of Mexico and these collisions result in frequent, rapid and drastic weather changes. Spring is the cloudiest, windiest, and wettest season in the city. Much of the precipitation falls as snow, especially in March and early April. Stormy periods are interspersed with stretches of mild, sunny weather that quickly melt previous snow cover.

Summer precipitation falls mainly from scattered thunderstorms during the afternoon and evening. Mornings are usually clear and sunny, with clouds forming during early afternoon to cut off the sunshine at what would otherwise be the hottest part of the day. Severe thunderstorms, with large hail and heavy rain occasionally occur in the city, but these conditions are more common on the plains to the east.

Autumn is the most pleasant season. Few thunderstorms occur and invasions of cold air are infrequent. As a result, there is more sunshine and less severe weather than at any other time of the year.

Based on the 1951-1980 period, the average first occurrence of 32 degrees Fahrenheit in the fall is October 8 and the average last occurrence in the spring is May 3.

Denver Stapleton Int'l Airport *Denver County*   Elevation: 5,285 ft.   Latitude: 39° 46' N   Longitude: 104° 52' W

	JAN	FEB	MAR	APR	MAY	JUN	JUL	AUG	SEP	OCT	NOV	DEC	YEAR
Mean Maximum Temp. (°F)	43.5	47.6	54.0	61.1	70.9	82.4	88.0	85.9	77.2	65.8	51.9	44.6	64.4
Mean Temp. (°F)	30.3	34.6	40.7	48.0	57.6	67.9	73.4	71.7	62.8	51.2	38.7	31.5	50.7
Mean Minimum Temp. (°F)	17.1	21.4	27.3	34.9	44.2	53.3	58.9	57.5	48.2	36.6	25.5	18.2	36.9
Extreme Maximum Temp. (°F)	74	74	84	90	95	104	103	100	97	89	79	75	104
Extreme Minimum Temp. (°F)	-19	-24	-5	-2	23	36	43	44	17	7	-8	-25	-25
Days Maximum Temp. ≥ 90°F	0	0	0	0	0	7	15	10	3	0	0	0	35
Days Maximum Temp. ≤ 32°F	6	4	2	0	0	0	0	0	0	0	3	5	20
Days Minimum Temp. ≤ 32°F	30	26	23	11	1	0	0	0	1	9	24	29	154
Days Minimum Temp. ≤ 0°F	3	2	0	0	0	0	0	0	0	0	0	2	7
Heating Degree Days (base 65°F)	1,070	853	747	504	240	48	5	7	129	422	782	1,033	5,840
Cooling Degree Days (base 65°F)	0	0	0	3	20	145	280	233	75	2	0	0	758
Mean Precipitation (in.)	0.49	0.48	1.28	1.93	2.29	1.61	2.17	1.72	1.17	1.00	1.00	0.63	15.77
Maximum Precipitation (in.)	1.4	1.6	4.6	4.1	7.3	4.7	6.4	5.8	4.7	4.2	2.7	2.8	23.3
Minimum Precipitation (in.)	trace	trace	0.2	trace	0.1	0.1	0.5	0.1	trace	0	trace	trace	7.5
Maximum 24-hr. Precipitation (in.)	0.9	1.0	2.7	3.3	3.3	3.2	2.0	2.0	1.4	1.6	0.9	2.0	3.3
Days With ≥ 0.1" Precipitation	1	2	4	5	5	4	4	4	3	3	3	2	40
Days With ≥ 1.0" Precipitation	0	0	0	0	0	0	1	0	0	0	0	0	1
Mean Snowfall (in.)	7.5	6.3	12.1	9.1	1.3	trace	trace	trace	2.1	4.1	10.7	8.8	62.0
Maximum Snowfall (in.)	24	18	31	26	14	trace	0	0	17	31	30	31	112
Maximum 24-hr. Snowfall (in.)	14	10	18	17	9	trace	0	0	12	10	14	24	24
Days With ≥ 1.0" Snow Depth	14	7	5	3	0	0	0	0	0	1	8	11	49
Thunderstorm Days	< 1	< 1	< 1	2	6	10	10	8	3	1	< 1	0	40
Foggy Days	5	6	7	5	5	3	2	3	4	4	6	5	55
Predominant Sky Cover	CLR	OVR	OVR	OVR	OVR	SCT	SCT	SCT	CLR	CLR	CLR	CLR	CLR
Mean Relative Humidity 5am (%)	62	66	67	66	70	68	68	68	66	63	66	63	66
Mean Relative Humidity 5pm (%)	49	44	39	35	38	34	33	34	32	35	47	50	39
Mean Dewpoint (°F)	13	16	19	26	36	43	48	47	39	28	20	14	29
Prevailing Wind Direction	S	S	S	S	S	S	S	S	S	SSW	S	S	S
Prevailing Wind Speed (mph)	9	9	9	10	10	9	9	9	8	8	8	9	9
Maximum Wind Gust (mph)	62	66	62	70	63	64	70	59	59	60	56	67	70

Grand Junction Walker Field

Grand Junction is located at the junction of the Colorado and Gunnison Rivers. It is on the west slope of the Rockies, in a large mountain valley. The area has a climate marked by the wide seasonal range usual to interior localities at this latitude. Thanks, however, to the protective topography of the vicinity, sudden and severe weather changes are very infrequent. The valley floor slopes from 4,800 feet near Palisade to 4,400 feet at the west end near Fruita. Mountains are on all sides at distances of from 10 to 60 miles and reach heights of 9,000 to over 12,000 feet.

This mountain valley location, with attendant valley breezes, provides protection from spring and fall frosts. This results in a growing season averaging 191 days in the city. This varies considerably in the outlying districts. It is about the same in the upper valley around Palisade, and three to four weeks shorter near the river west of Grand Junction. The growing season is sufficiently long to permit commercial growth of almost all fruits except citrus varieties. Summer grazing of cattle and sheep on nearby mountain ranges is extensive.

The interior, continental location, ringed by mountains on all sides, results in quite low precipitation in all seasons. Consequently, agriculture is dependent on irrigation. Adequate supplies of water are available from mountain snows and rains. Summer rains occur chiefly as scattered light showers and thunderstorms which develop over nearby mountains. Winter snows are fairly frequent, but are mostly light and quick to melt. Even the infrequent snows of from four to eight inches seldom remain on the ground for prolonged periods. Blizzard conditions in the valley are extremely rare.

Temperatures above 100 degrees are infrequent, and about one-third of the winters have no readings below zero. Summer days with maximum temperatures in the middle 90s and minimums in the low 60s are common. Relative humidity is very low during the summer, with values similar to other dry locations such as the southern parts of New Mexico and Arizona. Spells of cold winter weather are sometimes prolonged due to cold air becoming trapped in the valley. Winds are usually very light during the coldest weather. Changes in winter are normally gradual, and abrupt changes are much less frequent than in eastern Colorado. Cold waves are rare. Sunny days predominate in all seasons.

The prevailing wind is from the east-southeast due to the valley breeze effect. The strongest winds are associated with thunderstorms or with pre-frontal weather. They usually are from the south or southwest.

Grand Junction Walker Field *Mesa County*   Elevation: 4,839 ft.   Latitude: 39° 08' N   Longitude: 108° 32' W

	JAN	FEB	MAR	APR	MAY	JUN	JUL	AUG	SEP	OCT	NOV	DEC	YEAR
Mean Maximum Temp. (°F)	36.7	46.0	56.3	65.0	75.7	88.0	93.1	90.4	80.9	67.1	50.6	39.1	65.7
Mean Temp. (°F)	26.6	34.8	44.1	51.7	61.7	72.5	78.4	76.4	66.9	54.0	39.5	29.1	53.0
Mean Minimum Temp. (°F)	16.5	23.5	31.9	38.4	47.6	57.0	63.6	62.2	52.9	40.8	28.4	18.9	40.2
Extreme Maximum Temp. (°F)	60	68	81	89	94	105	105	103	100	86	75	64	105
Extreme Minimum Temp. (°F)	-15	-18	6	11	26	34	44	45	29	18	-2	-17	-18
Days Maximum Temp. ≥ 90°F	0	0	0	0	1	15	24	20	4	0	0	0	64
Days Maximum Temp. ≤ 32°F	10	2	0	0	0	0	0	0	0	0	1	6	19
Days Minimum Temp. ≤ 32°F	30	24	16	7	0	0	0	0	0	4	22	30	133
Days Minimum Temp. ≤ 0°F	3	1	0	0	0	0	0	0	0	0	0	1	5
Heating Degree Days (base 65°F)	1,183	846	639	396	145	20	0	1	57	340	757	1,107	5,491
Cooling Degree Days (base 65°F)	0	0	0	4	49	248	411	357	121	4	0	0	1,194
Mean Precipitation (in.)	0.57	0.48	1.02	0.87	0.96	0.43	0.67	0.83	0.91	1.01	0.72	0.52	8.99
Maximum Precipitation (in.)	2.5	1.5	2.0	1.9	2.0	2.1	1.9	3.5	2.8	3.4	2.0	1.9	15.7
Minimum Precipitation (in.)	trace	trace	trace	0.1	trace	trace	trace	trace	trace	0	trace	trace	4.4
Maximum 24-hr. Precipitation (in.)	0.6	0.5	1.0	0.9	1.0	1.1	1.4	1.2	1.0	0.9	0.8	1.2	1.4
Days With ≥ 0.1" Precipitation	2	1	3	3	3	1	2	3	3	3	2	2	28
Days With ≥ 1.0" Precipitation	0	0	0	0	0	0	0	0	0	0	0	0	0
Mean Snowfall (in.)	6.1	3.2	3.0	1.5	0.2	trace	0.0	trace	trace	0.8	2.2	4.9	21.9
Maximum Snowfall (in.)	34	18	15	14	5	0	0	0	3	6	12	19	56
Maximum 24-hr. Snowfall (in.)	8	9	6	6	5	0	0	0	3	3	8	5	9
Days With ≥ 1.0" Snow Depth	13	7	1	0	0	0	0	0	0	0	1	7	29
Thunderstorm Days	< 1	< 1	1	2	5	5	8	8	5	2	< 1	< 1	36
Foggy Days	8	5	3	1	< 1	< 1	< 1	< 1	< 1	1	3	5	26
Predominant Sky Cover	OVR	OVR	OVR	OVR	SCT	CLR	SCT	SCT	CLR	CLR	CLR	OVR	CLR
Mean Relative Humidity 5am (%)	77	73	64	56	52	43	47	51	51	57	69	76	60
Mean Relative Humidity 5pm (%)	62	50	36	27	24	18	21	24	25	32	47	60	35
Mean Dewpoint (°F)	16	20	22	25	31	34	43	44	36	29	24	18	28
Prevailing Wind Direction	ESE	ESE	ESE	ESE	ESE	SE	SE	SE	ESE	ESE	ESE	ESE	ESE
Prevailing Wind Speed (mph)	7	8	9	9	10	10	10	9	10	9	8	8	9
Maximum Wind Gust (mph)	59	59	59	78	62	69	64	74	64	54	53	45	78

Pueblo Memorial Airport

The city of Pueblo is located about 40 miles east-southeast of the Royal Gorge, at the junction of the Arkansas and Fountain Rivers. The mountains west of the city extend from within 25 miles to the southwest to about 35 miles to the northwest. Lake Pueblo, the largest body of water in southern Colorado, is located 7 miles west of the city and provides a variety of water sports, fishing, picnicing, and a wildlife preserve. The countryside surrounding Pueblo consists of rolling plains, broken by normally dry arroyos, and is generally treeless, covered mainly with sparse bunchgrass and occasional cacti. The business section of the city is 4,663 feet above sea level. The National Weather Service Office is located at Pueblo Memorial Airport, six miles east of the Pueblo Post Office, and about one and a half miles north of the Arkansas River. Terrain at the airport is relatively flat, and from 50 to 100 feet above the river. The air quality in Pueblo is rated the best of large Colorado cities along the front range.

The climate is semi-arid and marked by large daily temperature variations. The temperature reaches 90 degrees or more about half the time during the summer, but thanks to the low relative humidity, the heat is not oppressive. Summer nights are invariably cool since mountain breezes prevail from shortly after sunset to about noon the following day. The sun shines about 76 percent of the time. Winter is comparatively mild due to the abundant sunshine and the protection afforded by the nearby mountains. Temperatures reach 50 degrees or higher in the winter. The temperature drops to zero or below about eight times during the winter. Cold spells are generally broken after a few days by chinook winds, a very dry, warm, downslope westerly wind.

The probability of measurable precipitation in summer is one day out of four and in winter one out of eight. Summer rains usually occur in the form of afternoon thunderstorms. Blowing dust frequently develops during the spring months of abnormally dry years, especially in areas where dry farming has been attempted.

Agriculture consists chiefly of cattle grazing on the dry plains and irrigated farming near streams. Sugar beets, corn, chili peppers, and melons are the most important crops. In addition, a variety of vegetables, from asparagus to zucchini, are grown. Some dry farming is attempted, but the extent of such operations is limited by the annual precipitation of less than 12 inches.

Pueblo Memorial Airport *Pueblo County*   Elevation: 4,681 ft.   Latitude: 38° 17' N   Longitude: 104° 30' W

	JAN	FEB	MAR	APR	MAY	JUN	JUL	AUG	SEP	OCT	NOV	DEC	YEAR
Mean Maximum Temp. (°F)	45.7	51.8	58.8	66.9	76.3	87.8	92.8	89.8	81.6	70.0	55.6	47.0	68.7
Mean Temp. (°F)	29.9	35.4	42.5	50.7	60.7	70.7	76.2	74.0	65.2	52.6	39.3	31.2	52.4
Mean Minimum Temp. (°F)	14.0	18.9	26.2	34.6	45.0	53.6	59.6	58.2	48.7	35.2	23.0	15.4	36.0
Extreme Maximum Temp. (°F)	81	81	86	93	99	108	106	104	101	94	84	82	108
Extreme Minimum Temp. (°F)	-21	-26	-8	2	26	36	44	42	21	4	-17	-25	-26
Days Maximum Temp. ≥ 90°F	0	0	0	0	2	15	22	19	7	0	0	0	65
Days Maximum Temp. ≤ 32°F	6	3	1	0	0	0	0	0	0	0	2	5	17
Days Minimum Temp. ≤ 32°F	30	27	24	11	1	0	0	0	1	12	27	30	163
Days Minimum Temp. ≤ 0°F	4	1	0	0	0	0	0	0	0	0	0	3	8
Heating Degree Days (base 65°F)	1,082	830	690	424	163	22	1	3	85	380	765	1,040	5,485
Cooling Degree Days (base 65°F)	0	0	0	3	34	185	343	284	95	3	0	0	947
Mean Precipitation (in.)	0.32	0.26	0.90	1.25	1.48	1.33	1.96	2.30	0.87	0.65	0.59	0.38	12.29
Maximum Precipitation (in.)	0.9	1.4	2.3	4.0	5.4	4.3	5.1	5.8	2.7	4.9	2.5	1.0	23.1
Minimum Precipitation (in.)	trace	trace	0	trace	0.3	trace	0.1	0.1	trace	trace	trace	trace	6.3
Maximum 24-hr. Precipitation (in.)	0.5	0.6	0.9	2.0	2.7	2.2	2.0	2.9	1.6	2.8	0.8	0.6	2.9
Days With ≥ 0.1" Precipitation	1	1	3	3	4	3	5	5	2	2	2	1	32
Days With ≥ 1.0" Precipitation	0	0	0	0	0	0	0	0	0	0	0	0	0
Mean Snowfall (in.)	5.7	3.6	6.6	4.9	0.6	trace	trace	trace	0.5	2.1	4.7	5.4	34.1
Maximum Snowfall (in.)	18	14	16	21	11	0	0	0	14	16	26	15	72
Maximum 24-hr. Snowfall (in.)	12	8	9	13	6	0	0	0	10	13	16	7	16
Days With ≥ 1.0" Snow Depth	7	3	2	1	0	0	0	0	0	0	3	5	21
Thunderstorm Days	0	0	< 1	2	6	8	11	9	3	1	< 1	0	40
Foggy Days	5	5	5	3	3	2	1	2	4	3	5	5	43
Predominant Sky Cover	CLR	CLR	OVR	CLR	OVR	CLR	SCT	SCT	CLR	CLR	CLR	CLR	CLR
Mean Relative Humidity 5am (%)	70	69	68	66	70	71	72	75	71	67	73	69	70
Mean Relative Humidity 5pm (%)	49	40	35	30	32	29	32	34	32	32	45	49	37
Mean Dewpoint (°F)	15	17	21	27	37	45	51	52	42	30	23	16	31
Prevailing Wind Direction	W	W	W	SE	SE	SE	SE	SE	SE	W	W	W	SE
Prevailing Wind Speed (mph)	9	9	12	10	12	12	10	10	9	8	8	9	10
Maximum Wind Gust (mph)	68	71	86	73	76	69	70	63	59	67	68	63	86

Akron 4 E *Washington County*   Elevation: 4,537 ft.   Latitude: 40° 09' N   Longitude: 103° 09' W

	JAN	FEB	MAR	APR	MAY	JUN	JUL	AUG	SEP	OCT	NOV	DEC	YEAR
Mean Maximum Temp. (°F)	38.5	44.0	51.7	*60.0*	69.8	*81.3*	88.5	86.7	78.0	65.5	49.4	40.2	*62.8*
Mean Temp. (°F)	25.9	31.0	38.2	*46.0*	56.1	*66.4*	73.0	71.3	62.3	50.0	36.2	27.5	*48.7*
Mean Minimum Temp. (°F)	13.2	18.0	24.6	*32.0*	42.3	*51.6*	57.4	55.8	46.7	34.4	22.9	14.8	*34.5*
Extreme Maximum Temp. (°F)	75	75	82	*90*	97	*105*	107	105	102	92	81	75	*107*
Extreme Minimum Temp. (°F)	-22	-26	-13	*-1*	19	*31*	41	36	14	1	-12	-32	*-32*
Days Maximum Temp. ≥ 90°F	0	0	0	0	1	7	16	14	5	0	0	0	*43*
Days Maximum Temp. ≤ 32°F	10	5	4	1	0	*0*	0	0	0	0	5	8	*33*
Days Minimum Temp. ≤ 32°F	31	27	26	*16*	3	*0*	0	0	2	12	26	30	*173*
Days Minimum Temp. ≤ 0°F	5	2	1	0	0	*0*	0	0	0	0	0	4	*12*
Heating Degree Days (base 65°F)	1,206	953	824	*563*	283	*69*	10	16	146	462	858	1,157	*6,547*
Cooling Degree Days (base 65°F)	0	0	0	1	16	120	260	221	73	3	0	0	*694*
Mean Precipitation (in.)	0.38	0.37	1.02	1.36	3.02	*2.39*	2.86	2.33	0.98	0.85	0.72	0.37	*16.65*
Days With ≥ 0.1" Precipitation	1	1	*3*	*4*	6	*5*	6	5	2	2	2	1	*38*
Days With ≥ 1.0" Precipitation	0	0	0	0	1	*0*	0	1	0	0	0	0	*2*
Mean Snowfall (in.)	na	na	na	na	0.1	*0.0*	0.0	0.0	0.4	1.4	na	na	na
Days With ≥ 1.0" Snow Depth	na	na	na	na	0	*0*	0	0	0	1	na	na	na

Akron Washington Co. Airport *Washington County*   Elevation: 4,662 ft.   Latitude: 40° 10' N   Longitude: 103° 14' W

	JAN	FEB	MAR	APR	MAY	JUN	JUL	AUG	SEP	OCT	NOV	DEC	YEAR
Mean Maximum Temp. (°F)	37.7	43.1	51.1	60.0	69.6	81.5	87.3	*85.9*	76.5	64.2	48.2	*40.1*	*62.1*
Mean Temp. (°F)	26.1	31.0	38.2	46.7	56.5	67.4	73.0	*71.7*	62.4	50.3	36.2	*28.4*	*49.0*
Mean Minimum Temp. (°F)	14.4	18.8	25.2	33.3	43.4	53.2	58.7	*57.5*	48.2	36.4	24.0	*16.6*	*35.8*
Extreme Maximum Temp. (°F)	74	73	81	91	96	103	104	101	98	88	77	*73*	*104*
Extreme Minimum Temp. (°F)	-18	-21	-10	-3	21	37	42	42	17	4	-9	*-25*	*-25*
Days Maximum Temp. ≥ 90°F	0	0	0	0	0	7	14	12	3	0	0	*0*	*36*
Days Maximum Temp. ≤ 32°F	10	6	3	1	0	0	0	0	0	0	5	*8*	*33*
Days Minimum Temp. ≤ 32°F	30	26	25	14	2	0	0	0	1	10	24	*29*	*161*
Days Minimum Temp. ≤ 0°F	5	2	0	0	0	0	0	0	0	0	0	*3*	*10*
Heating Degree Days (base 65°F)	1,201	955	826	545	272	58	9	*15*	147	451	859	*1,129*	*6,467*
Cooling Degree Days (base 65°F)	0	*0*	0	3	17	137	263	*236*	79	3	0	*0*	*738*
Mean Precipitation (in.)	0.35	0.37	1.08	1.59	3.24	2.40	2.85	*1.91*	0.90	0.84	0.70	*0.42*	*16.65*
Days With ≥ 0.1" Precipitation	1	1	3	4	6	6	6	4	3	2	2	*1*	*39*
Days With ≥ 1.0" Precipitation	0	0	0	0	1	0	1	0	0	0	0	*0*	*2*
Mean Snowfall (in.)	5.7	4.2	10.2	5.1	0.7	trace	trace	trace	0.7	3.0	7.5	*6.0*	*43.1*
Days With ≥ 1.0" Snow Depth	16	10	8	3	0	0	0	0	0	*1*	7	*12*	*57*

Altenbern *Garfield County*   Elevation: 5,675 ft.   Latitude: 39° 30' N   Longitude: 108° 23' W

	JAN	FEB	MAR	APR	MAY	JUN	JUL	AUG	SEP	OCT	NOV	DEC	YEAR
Mean Maximum Temp. (°F)	36.0	43.2	52.9	61.6	71.5	82.9	88.3	85.4	77.0	64.6	48.7	37.8	62.5
Mean Temp. (°F)	23.1	30.0	38.6	45.7	54.6	63.5	69.2	67.3	59.3	48.0	34.9	24.8	46.6
Mean Minimum Temp. (°F)	10.1	16.7	24.2	29.7	37.7	43.9	50.1	49.1	41.5	31.4	21.1	11.8	30.6
Extreme Maximum Temp. (°F)	57	67	75	84	88	102	104	98	97	85	72	61	104
Extreme Minimum Temp. (°F)	-25	-28	0	1	19	22	30	26	20	8	-7	-23	-28
Days Maximum Temp. ≥ 90°F	0	0	0	0	0	6	14	8	1	0	0	0	29
Days Maximum Temp. ≤ 32°F	10	2	0	0	0	0	0	0	0	0	1	8	21
Days Minimum Temp. ≤ 32°F	31	27	28	21	6	1	0	0	3	18	28	31	194
Days Minimum Temp. ≤ 0°F	6	2	0	0	0	0	0	0	0	0	0	4	12
Heating Degree Days (base 65°F)	1,293	983	812	574	316	89	8	19	179	520	895	1,239	6,927
Cooling Degree Days (base 65°F)	0	0	0	0	1	43	136	98	15	0	0	0	293
Mean Precipitation (in.)	1.12	1.24	1.66	1.53	1.77	0.97	1.38	1.33	1.64	1.81	1.44	1.06	16.95
Days With ≥ 0.1" Precipitation	4	4	5	5	5	3	4	4	5	5	5	4	53
Days With ≥ 1.0" Precipitation	0	0	0	0	0	0	0	0	0	0	0	0	0
Mean Snowfall (in.)	14.7	10.1	7.3	3.6	0.6	0.1	0.0	0.0	0.0	1.7	7.5	13.8	59.4
Days With ≥ 1.0" Snow Depth	23	14	4	0	0	0	0	0	0	0	4	16	61

Antero Reservoir *Park County*   Elevation: 8,917 ft.   Latitude: 39° 00' N   Longitude: 105° 54' W

	JAN	FEB	MAR	APR	MAY	JUN	JUL	AUG	SEP	OCT	NOV	DEC	YEAR
Mean Maximum Temp. (°F)	32.4	35.8	41.5	47.9	59.1	70.2	75.6	73.2	66.7	55.9	41.4	32.9	52.7
Mean Temp. (°F)	14.3	17.6	25.9	33.0	43.4	52.4	57.9	56.2	48.9	37.7	25.0	15.3	35.6
Mean Minimum Temp. (°F)	-3.7	-0.7	10.2	18.0	27.7	34.5	40.1	39.1	31.1	19.4	8.5	-2.3	18.5
Extreme Maximum Temp. (°F)	59	58	62	72	75	85	88	85	83	78	68	57	88
Extreme Minimum Temp. (°F)	-47	-51	-35	-29	1	15	27	25	3	-14	-33	-49	-51
Days Maximum Temp. ≥ 90°F	0	0	0	0	0	0	0	0	0	0	0	0	0
Days Maximum Temp. ≤ 32°F	14	10	5	2	0	0	0	0	0	1	6	14	52
Days Minimum Temp. ≤ 32°F	31	28	31	29	24	11	1	3	17	30	30	31	266
Days Minimum Temp. ≤ 0°F	18	14	6	2	0	0	0	0	0	1	7	18	66
Heating Degree Days (base 65°F)	1,566	1,333	1,205	955	662	373	216	267	475	839	1,193	1,535	10,619
Cooling Degree Days (base 65°F)	0	0	0	0	0	0	0	1	0	0	0	0	1
Mean Precipitation (in.)	0.20	0.26	0.52	0.72	1.01	1.17	1.85	2.12	0.99	0.64	0.37	0.26	10.11
Days With ≥ 0.1" Precipitation	1	1	2	3	3	3	5	5	3	2	1	1	30
Days With ≥ 1.0" Precipitation	0	0	0	0	0	0	0	0	0	0	0	0	0
Mean Snowfall (in.)	4.3	5.2	8.1	8.7	2.2	0.5	0.0	0.0	1.4	4.5	6.2	5.9	47.0
Days With ≥ 1.0" Snow Depth	20	19	14	8	1	0	0	0	0	3	12	19	96

Bailey *Park County*   Elevation: 7,729 ft.   Latitude: 39° 24' N   Longitude: 105° 29' W

	JAN	FEB	MAR	APR	MAY	JUN	JUL	AUG	SEP	OCT	NOV	DEC	YEAR
Mean Maximum Temp. (°F)	38.3	41.8	46.9	53.0	62.6	73.7	78.2	76.1	69.5	59.1	45.8	38.4	56.9
Mean Temp. (°F)	23.3	26.2	31.9	37.8	46.7	55.6	60.8	59.2	51.7	41.5	31.0	23.7	40.8
Mean Minimum Temp. (°F)	8.2	10.5	16.9	22.5	30.7	37.5	43.3	42.2	34.0	23.9	16.2	8.9	24.6
Extreme Maximum Temp. (°F)	63	63	72	75	83	92	95	93	87	81	70	65	95
Extreme Minimum Temp. (°F)	-32	-32	-19	-15	7	22	31	26	7	-9	-24	-33	-33
Days Maximum Temp. ≥ 90°F	0	0	0	0	0	0	1	0	0	0	0	0	1
Days Maximum Temp. ≤ 32°F	8	5	3	1	0	0	0	0	0	1	4	9	31
Days Minimum Temp. ≤ 32°F	31	28	30	28	19	5	0	1	11	28	29	31	241
Days Minimum Temp. ≤ 0°F	8	5	2	0	0	0	0	0	0	0	2	7	24
Heating Degree Days (base 65°F)	1,286	1,088	1,019	810	560	278	131	176	391	720	1,014	1,275	8,748
Cooling Degree Days (base 65°F)	0	0	0	0	0	2	7	2	0	0	0	0	11
Mean Precipitation (in.)	0.40	0.54	1.31	1.88	2.11	1.80	2.48	2.64	1.32	1.19	0.91	0.56	17.14
Days With ≥ 0.1" Precipitation	2	2	4	5	5	5	7	7	4	3	3	2	49
Days With ≥ 1.0" Precipitation	0	0	0	0	0	0	0	0	0	0	0	0	0
Mean Snowfall (in.)	7.0	9.2	*18.2*	17.0	3.3	0.3	0.0	0.0	1.7	7.4	12.8	9.8	*86.7*
Days With ≥ 1.0" Snow Depth	na	*25*	na	*11*	2	0	0	0	1	na	*18*	na	na

Blanca *Costilla County*   Elevation: 7,749 ft.   Latitude: 37° 26' N   Longitude: 105° 31' W

	JAN	FEB	MAR	APR	MAY	JUN	JUL	AUG	SEP	OCT	NOV	DEC	YEAR
Mean Maximum Temp. (°F)	34.4	40.7	49.0	57.3	67.0	77.4	81.5	79.0	72.6	61.6	46.9	36.3	58.6
Mean Temp. (°F)	17.8	24.9	33.8	41.1	50.5	59.8	64.6	62.5	55.1	44.0	30.8	19.9	42.1
Mean Minimum Temp. (°F)	1.2	8.9	18.5	24.9	34.0	42.0	47.7	46.0	37.6	26.0	14.4	3.4	25.4
Extreme Maximum Temp. (°F)	61	64	72	80	83	92	93	90	88	80	71	59	93
Extreme Minimum Temp. (°F)	-38	-24	-14	1	10	22	34	31	16	-4	-16	-32	-38
Days Maximum Temp. ≥ 90°F	0	0	0	0	0	0	1	0	0	0	0	0	1
Days Maximum Temp. ≤ 32°F	12	6	1	0	0	0	0	0	0	0	3	10	32
Days Minimum Temp. ≤ 32°F	31	28	31	25	12	2	0	0	7	25	29	31	221
Days Minimum Temp. ≤ 0°F	14	6	0	0	0	0	0	0	0	0	3	12	35
Heating Degree Days (base 65°F)	1,458	1,128	962	709	443	162	45	87	289	645	1,019	1,393	8,340
Cooling Degree Days (base 65°F)	0	0	0	0	0	13	45	21	2	0	0	0	81
Mean Precipitation (in.)	0.31	0.31	0.56	0.66	0.99	0.75	1.42	1.50	1.08	0.75	0.57	0.33	9.23
Days With ≥ 0.1" Precipitation	1	1	2	2	3	2	4	4	3	3	2	1	28
Days With ≥ 1.0" Precipitation	0	0	0	0	0	0	0	0	0	0	0	0	0
Mean Snowfall (in.)	4.7	3.9	5.6	4.6	0.9	0.0	0.0	0.0	trace	2.0	4.8	4.8	31.3
Days With ≥ 1.0" Snow Depth	*11*	*9*	5	*2*	0	0	0	0	0	1	*5*	*8*	*41*

Brighton 1 NE *Adams County*   Elevation: 5,013 ft.   Latitude: 39° 57' N   Longitude: 104° 50' W

	JAN	FEB	MAR	APR	MAY	JUN	JUL	AUG	SEP	OCT	NOV	DEC	YEAR
Mean Maximum Temp. (°F)	42.3	47.6	55.5	63.1	*72.4*	*83.3*	88.5	86.2	78.7	67.5	51.7	44.0	*65.1*
Mean Temp. (°F)	28.2	33.3	40.6	48.2	*57.6*	*67.5*	72.6	70.6	62.4	51.0	37.5	30.0	*49.9*
Mean Minimum Temp. (°F)	14.1	18.9	25.6	33.2	*42.8*	*51.7*	56.7	54.9	46.1	34.3	23.2	15.9	*34.8*
Extreme Maximum Temp. (°F)	74	77	82	90	*94*	*102*	103	101	97	90	81	74	*103*
Extreme Minimum Temp. (°F)	-22	-24	-8	-8	*22*	*34*	44	41	19	0	-14	-26	*-26*
Days Maximum Temp. ≥ 90°F	0	0	0	0	*1*	*8*	15	10	3	0	0	0	*37*
Days Maximum Temp. ≤ 32°F	7	4	2	0	*0*	*0*	0	0	0	0	3	6	*22*
Days Minimum Temp. ≤ 32°F	30	27	26	14	*2*	*0*	0	0	1	12	26	30	*168*
Days Minimum Temp. ≤ 0°F	4	2	0	0	*0*	*0*	0	0	0	0	1	3	*10*
Heating Degree Days (base 65°F)	1,133	889	749	499	*236*	*45*	3	7	126	429	819	1,079	*6,014*
Cooling Degree Days (base 65°F)	0	0	0	1	*16*	*129*	250	203	55	1	0	0	*655*
Mean Precipitation (in.)	0.48	0.39	1.22	1.73	*2.54*	*1.79*	1.68	1.55	1.04	0.87	0.88	0.53	*14.70*
Days With ≥ 0.1" Precipitation	2	1	3	4	*5*	*4*	3	3	3	2	3	2	*35*
Days With ≥ 1.0" Precipitation	0	0	0	0	*1*	*0*	0	0	0	0	0	0	*1*
Mean Snowfall (in.)	6.1	4.4	7.6	5.7	*1.3*	*0.0*	0.0	0.0	0.6	2.3	*8.1*	6.4	*42.5*
Days With ≥ 1.0" Snow Depth	13	7	*4*	2	*0*	*0*	*0*	0	0	1	7	10	*44*

Browns Park Refuge *Moffat County*   Elevation: 5,351 ft.   Latitude: 40° 48' N   Longitude: 108° 55' W

	JAN	FEB	MAR	APR	MAY	JUN	JUL	AUG	SEP	OCT	NOV	DEC	YEAR
Mean Maximum Temp. (°F)	38.3	44.2	52.5	62.0	71.7	83.2	89.2	87.9	78.4	66.0	48.9	39.9	63.5
Mean Temp. (°F)	22.8	28.4	37.1	44.9	53.8	62.5	68.0	66.3	57.2	46.3	33.4	24.6	45.4
Mean Minimum Temp. (°F)	7.2	12.7	21.6	27.8	35.8	41.9	46.7	44.6	35.9	26.5	17.8	9.2	27.3
Extreme Maximum Temp. (°F)	59	71	74	84	89	101	104	101	96	88	74	65	104
Extreme Minimum Temp. (°F)	-34	-39	-5	5	9	27	27	24	11	-9	-22	-41	-41
Days Maximum Temp. ≥ 90°F	0	0	0	0	0	6	*16*	*12*	2	0	0	0	*36*
Days Maximum Temp. ≤ 32°F	8	3	0	0	0	0	0	0	0	0	2	6	19
Days Minimum Temp. ≤ 32°F	31	28	29	22	9	2	0	1	*10*	25	29	31	*217*
Days Minimum Temp. ≤ 0°F	10	5	0	0	0	0	0	0	0	0	1	6	22
Heating Degree Days (base 65°F)	1,302	1,026	859	596	343	105	17	32	236	574	941	1,247	7,278
Cooling Degree Days (base 65°F)	0	0	0	0	2	39	121	86	11	0	0	0	259
Mean Precipitation (in.)	0.36	0.44	0.74	0.80	1.15	0.67	0.71	0.61	0.96	1.20	0.61	0.39	8.64
Days With ≥ 0.1" Precipitation	1	1	2	3	4	2	2	2	3	3	2	2	27
Days With ≥ 1.0" Precipitation	0	0	0	0	0	0	0	0	0	0	0	0	0
Mean Snowfall (in.)	na	na	na	*0.8*	0.4	trace	0.0	0.0	0.0	*1.1*	na	na	na
Days With ≥ 1.0" Snow Depth	na	na	na	*0*	0	0	0	0	0	*0*	na	na	na

Buena Vista *Chaffee County*   Elevation: 7,929 ft.   Latitude: 38° 52' N   Longitude: 106° 08' W

	JAN	FEB	MAR	APR	MAY	JUN	JUL	AUG	SEP	OCT	NOV	DEC	YEAR
Mean Maximum Temp. (°F)	39.8	42.9	48.5	54.8	64.9	76.4	80.9	78.1	71.6	61.1	47.4	39.8	58.8
Mean Temp. (°F)	25.2	28.4	34.6	40.2	49.5	59.1	64.1	62.0	54.7	44.2	33.0	25.1	43.3
Mean Minimum Temp. (°F)	10.4	13.7	20.5	25.6	34.1	42.0	47.1	46.0	37.8	27.3	18.5	10.4	27.8
Extreme Maximum Temp. (°F)	61	64	71	76	81	93	95	90	88	79	71	61	95
Extreme Minimum Temp. (°F)	-25	-23	-4	-9	6	25	34	29	17	0	-14	-25	-25
Days Maximum Temp. ≥ 90°F	0	0	0	0	0	0	1	0	0	0	0	0	1
Days Maximum Temp. ≤ 32°F	6	3	2	1	0	0	0	0	0	0	2	7	21
Days Minimum Temp. ≤ 32°F	31	28	30	25	11	1	0	0	5	24	28	31	214
Days Minimum Temp. ≤ 0°F	4	2	0	0	0	0	0	0	0	0	1	5	12
Heating Degree Days (base 65°F)	1,227	1,026	937	736	473	178	56	101	305	638	954	1,230	7,861
Cooling Degree Days (base 65°F)	0	0	0	0	0	9	32	13	1	0	0	0	55
Mean Precipitation (in.)	0.27	0.39	0.72	0.97	1.11	0.83	1.44	1.74	1.03	0.81	0.55	0.36	10.22
Days With ≥ 0.1" Precipitation	1	1	3	3	3	3	4	5	3	2	2	1	31
Days With ≥ 1.0" Precipitation	0	0	0	0	0	0	0	0	0	0	0	0	0
Mean Snowfall (in.)	4.2	3.8	6.9	5.8	1.4	0.3	0.0	0.0	0.4	1.4	4.0	4.3	32.5
Days With ≥ 1.0" Snow Depth	na	na	na	2	0	0	0	0	0	1	na	na	na

Byers 5 ENE *Adams County*   Elevation: 5,098 ft.   Latitude: 39° 44' N   Longitude: 104° 08' W

	JAN	FEB	MAR	APR	MAY	JUN	JUL	AUG	SEP	OCT	NOV	DEC	YEAR
Mean Maximum Temp. (°F)	41.1	46.3	54.0	62.4	72.0	83.4	89.7	87.5	79.1	67.1	51.4	42.8	64.7
Mean Temp. (°F)	26.3	31.6	38.9	46.8	56.6	66.8	72.7	71.1	62.2	50.0	36.2	28.0	48.9
Mean Minimum Temp. (°F)	11.5	16.8	23.7	31.2	41.2	50.2	55.7	54.6	45.3	32.9	21.0	13.2	33.1
Extreme Maximum Temp. (°F)	74	75	85	92	98	105	106	102	101	91	81	76	106
Extreme Minimum Temp. (°F)	-32	-27	-15	-9	20	32	38	37	10	-3	-16	-33	-33
Days Maximum Temp. ≥ 90°F	0	0	0	0	1	9	17	13	5	0	0	0	45
Days Maximum Temp. ≤ 32°F	7	4	2	0	0	0	0	0	0	0	3	6	22
Days Minimum Temp. ≤ 32°F	31	28	27	18	3	0	0	0	2	15	27	30	181
Days Minimum Temp. ≤ 0°F	6	2	1	0	0	0	0	0	0	0	1	4	14
Heating Degree Days (base 65°F)	1,192	937	803	539	266	59	6	8	138	459	857	1,140	6,404
Cooling Degree Days (base 65°F)	0	0	0	1	16	124	258	214	67	1	0	0	681
Mean Precipitation (in.)	0.42	0.34	1.01	1.55	2.72	1.90	2.31	1.80	1.13	0.81	0.81	0.42	15.22
Days With ≥ 0.1" Precipitation	2	1	3	4	6	4	5	4	3	2	2	1	37
Days With ≥ 1.0" Precipitation	0	0	0	0	1	0	0	0	0	0	0	0	1
Mean Snowfall (in.)	6.3	4.2	9.6	5.4	0.4	0.0	0.0	0.0	1.3	2.6	7.5	5.8	43.1
Days With ≥ 1.0" Snow Depth	16	12	6	2	0	0	0	0	0	1	8	14	59

Cabin Creek *Clear Creek County*   Elevation: 10,019 ft.   Latitude: 39° 39' N   Longitude: 105° 42' W

	JAN	FEB	MAR	APR	MAY	JUN	JUL	AUG	SEP	OCT	NOV	DEC	YEAR
Mean Maximum Temp. (°F)	31.3	33.4	37.4	42.8	52.7	63.8	68.6	67.0	60.5	50.4	38.2	32.9	48.2
Mean Temp. (°F)	20.0	21.8	25.6	31.1	40.9	50.5	55.2	53.9	47.5	38.2	27.0	21.8	36.1
Mean Minimum Temp. (°F)	8.7	10.2	13.8	19.6	29.2	37.3	41.9	40.8	34.5	26.2	15.6	10.6	24.0
Extreme Maximum Temp. (°F)	56	55	62	64	73	84	83	78	78	72	63	57	84
Extreme Minimum Temp. (°F)	-28	-26	-20	-14	8	8	27	24	9	-5	-21	-23	-28
Days Maximum Temp. ≥ 90°F	0	0	0	0	0	0	0	0	0	0	0	0	0
Days Maximum Temp. ≤ 32°F	17	11	9	4	1	0	0	0	0	2	9	14	67
Days Minimum Temp. ≤ 32°F	31	28	31	28	21	7	1	1	10	24	29	31	242
Days Minimum Temp. ≤ 0°F	7	5	3	1	0	0	0	0	0	0	3	5	24
Heating Degree Days (base 65°F)	1,388	1,213	1,215	1,010	739	429	298	338	519	824	1,135	1,334	10,442
Cooling Degree Days (base 65°F)	0	0	0	0	0	0	0	0	0	0	0	0	0
Mean Precipitation (in.)	0.68	0.83	1.62	2.47	2.10	1.79	2.54	2.65	1.68	1.21	1.13	0.76	19.46
Days With ≥ 0.1" Precipitation	3	3	5	7	5	5	7	8	5	4	4	3	59
Days With ≥ 1.0" Precipitation	0	0	0	0	0	0	0	0	0	0	0	0	0
Mean Snowfall (in.)	11.6	14.0	24.6	25.8	8.6	2.1	0.0	trace	3.9	9.0	17.3	12.8	129.7
Days With ≥ 1.0" Snow Depth	17	15	17	11	3	0	0	0	1	3	11	18	96

Cedaredge *Delta County*   Elevation: 6,243 ft.   Latitude: 38° 54' N   Longitude: 107° 56' W

	JAN	FEB	MAR	APR	MAY	JUN	JUL	AUG	SEP	OCT	NOV	DEC	YEAR
Mean Maximum Temp. (°F)	38.6	44.6	53.3	62.2	72.2	83.5	88.4	86.0	77.7	65.3	49.1	39.7	63.4
Mean Temp. (°F)	26.6	32.4	40.3	47.7	56.4	66.6	71.9	70.0	61.8	50.5	37.1	28.3	49.1
Mean Minimum Temp. (°F)	14.5	20.2	27.0	33.1	40.6	49.6	55.3	53.9	45.8	35.7	25.0	16.7	34.8
Extreme Maximum Temp. (°F)	63	68	75	88	90	102	103	97	95	85	74	66	103
Extreme Minimum Temp. (°F)	-16	-20	4	12	22	28	38	35	25	8	-6	-15	-20
Days Maximum Temp. ≥ 90°F	0	0	0	0	0	7	14	9	1	0	0	0	31
Days Maximum Temp. ≤ 32°F	7	2	0	0	0	0	0	0	0	0	1	6	16
Days Minimum Temp. ≤ 32°F	31	27	25	14	4	0	0	0	1	9	24	30	165
Days Minimum Temp. ≤ 0°F	3	1	0	0	0	0	0	0	0	0	0	1	5
Heating Degree Days (base 65°F)	1,184	913	760	514	263	57	2	9	124	443	832	1,132	6,233
Cooling Degree Days (base 65°F)	0	0	0	0	0	7	116	na	176	35	0	0	na
Mean Precipitation (in.)	1.07	0.86	1.41	0.96	1.18	0.67	0.91	1.14	1.24	1.64	1.27	1.02	13.37
Days With ≥ 0.1" Precipitation	4	3	5	3	4	2	3	4	3	4	4	4	43
Days With ≥ 1.0" Precipitation	0	0	0	0	0	0	0	0	0	0	0	0	0
Mean Snowfall (in.)	14.2	8.6	9.4	1.6	0.4	trace	0.0	0.0	trace	2.0	5.9	10.6	52.7
Days With ≥ 1.0" Snow Depth	17	10	2	0	0	0	0	0	0	0	3	na	na

Center 4 SSW *Rio Grande County*   Elevation: 7,670 ft.   Latitude: 37° 42' N   Longitude: 106° 09' W

	JAN	FEB	MAR	APR	MAY	JUN	JUL	AUG	SEP	OCT	NOV	DEC	YEAR
Mean Maximum Temp. (°F)	31.9	39.4	48.6	57.5	66.3	75.4	78.9	77.3	72.0	61.1	45.2	34.1	57.3
Mean Temp. (°F)	14.6	22.2	33.0	41.1	50.0	57.6	61.9	60.4	54.2	43.5	29.2	17.6	40.4
Mean Minimum Temp. (°F)	-2.8	4.9	17.4	24.5	33.6	39.8	44.9	43.5	36.4	25.8	13.2	1.0	23.5
Extreme Maximum Temp. (°F)	59	65	72	79	83	90	91	89	87	79	68	60	91
Extreme Minimum Temp. (°F)	-38	-32	-12	-4	15	25	31	28	16	-4	-25	-41	-41
Days Maximum Temp. ≥ 90°F	0	0	0	0	0	0	0	0	0	0	0	0	0
Days Maximum Temp. ≤ 32°F	16	8	1	0	0	0	0	0	0	0	4	13	42
Days Minimum Temp. ≤ 32°F	31	28	31	26	12	2	0	0	7	26	30	31	224
Days Minimum Temp. ≤ 0°F	18	10	1	0	0	0	0	0	0	0	3	13	45
Heating Degree Days (base 65°F)	1,558	1,204	985	711	460	217	97	139	318	660	1,067	1,465	8,881
Cooling Degree Days (base 65°F)	0	0	0	0	0	3	9	4	0	0	0	0	16
Mean Precipitation (in.)	0.15	0.17	0.35	0.36	0.61	0.69	1.13	1.28	0.95	0.55	0.46	0.25	6.95
Days With ≥ 0.1" Precipitation	0	1	1	1	2	2	3	4	3	2	1	1	21
Days With ≥ 1.0" Precipitation	0	0	0	0	0	0	0	0	0	0	0	0	0
Mean Snowfall (in.)	*3.0*	na	*5.1*	1.2	0.4	0.0	0.0	0.0	trace	1.4	na	*4.1*	na
Days With ≥ 1.0" Snow Depth	na	na	na	*0*	0	0	0	0	0	0	na	na	na

Cheesman *Jefferson County*   Elevation: 6,879 ft.   Latitude: 39° 13' N   Longitude: 105° 17' W

	JAN	FEB	MAR	APR	MAY	JUN	JUL	AUG	SEP	OCT	NOV	DEC	YEAR
Mean Maximum Temp. (°F)	45.0	47.9	51.5	57.3	67.0	78.3	83.4	81.4	74.6	64.8	51.7	45.2	62.4
Mean Temp. (°F)	25.9	28.6	34.3	40.5	49.5	59.3	64.2	62.5	55.2	45.1	34.1	27.1	43.9
Mean Minimum Temp. (°F)	6.7	9.2	16.9	23.6	32.0	40.2	44.9	43.5	35.8	25.3	16.5	8.9	25.3
Extreme Maximum Temp. (°F)	69	72	75	82	89	99	98	97	96	90	77	69	99
Extreme Minimum Temp. (°F)	-28	-31	-17	-11	13	18	25	26	11	-3	-21	-32	-32
Days Maximum Temp. ≥ 90°F	0	0	0	0	0	2	5	2	0	0	0	0	9
Days Maximum Temp. ≤ 32°F	4	3	1	1	0	0	0	0	0	0	2	4	15
Days Minimum Temp. ≤ 32°F	31	28	30	26	16	3	1	1	9	27	29	31	232
Days Minimum Temp. ≤ 0°F	9	6	2	0	0	0	0	0	0	0	2	7	26
Heating Degree Days (base 65°F)	1,206	1,023	946	728	473	180	60	95	289	610	919	1,168	7,697
Cooling Degree Days (base 65°F)	0	0	0	0	1	15	43	23	2	0	0	0	84
Mean Precipitation (in.)	0.39	0.57	1.44	1.76	2.05	1.96	2.60	2.73	1.19	1.10	0.90	0.65	17.34
Days With ≥ 0.1" Precipitation	1	2	4	5	5	5	7	7	3	3	3	2	47
Days With ≥ 1.0" Precipitation	0	0	0	0	0	0	0	0	0	0	0	0	0
Mean Snowfall (in.)	5.8	7.8	13.8	10.7	1.6	0.0	0.0	0.0	1.1	4.9	10.5	9.3	65.5
Days With ≥ 1.0" Snow Depth	12	7	7	4	1	0	0	0	0	2	8	12	53

Cherry Creek Dam *Arapahoe County*   Elevation: 5,646 ft.   Latitude: 39° 38' N   Longitude: 104° 50' W

	JAN	FEB	MAR	APR	MAY	JUN	JUL	AUG	SEP	OCT	NOV	DEC	YEAR
Mean Maximum Temp. (°F)	44.9	48.8	54.8	61.1	71.6	83.2	89.7	87.2	78.6	67.2	*53.6*	46.5	*65.6*
Mean Temp. (°F)	29.6	33.6	39.5	46.1	55.9	66.1	72.2	70.3	61.6	50.4	*38.4*	31.5	*49.6*
Mean Minimum Temp. (°F)	14.2	18.3	24.1	31.0	40.1	49.0	54.7	53.3	44.6	33.4	*23.2*	16.3	*33.5*
Extreme Maximum Temp. (°F)	76	75	83	89	97	105	108	104	100	96	81	73	108
Extreme Minimum Temp. (°F)	-22	-24	-7	-7	17	31	41	40	15	0	-12	-27	-27
Days Maximum Temp. ≥ 90°F	0	0	0	0	1	9	17	12	5	0	0	0	44
Days Maximum Temp. ≤ 32°F	5	3	2	0	0	0	0	0	0	0	2	4	16
Days Minimum Temp. ≤ 32°F	30	26	25	18	4	0	0	0	2	13	25	29	172
Days Minimum Temp. ≤ 0°F	4	2	0	0	0	0	0	0	0	0	1	3	10
Heating Degree Days (base 65°F)	1,091	880	784	561	287	70	8	13	150	448	*792*	1,033	*6,117*
Cooling Degree Days (base 65°F)	0	0	0	1	11	110	243	193	62	2	0	0	622
Mean Precipitation (in.)	0.47	0.46	1.41	2.09	2.71	2.11	2.46	1.99	1.50	1.06	1.26	0.60	18.12
Days With ≥ 0.1" Precipitation	2	2	*4*	5	6	4	4	4	3	3	3	2	*42*
Days With ≥ 1.0" Precipitation	0	0	0	0	1	0	0	0	0	0	0	0	1
Mean Snowfall (in.)	*6.8*	*6.6*	*10.4*	7.7	0.5	0.0	0.0	0.0	1.4	2.3	*9.5*	*8.0*	*53.2*
Days With ≥ 1.0" Snow Depth	15	8	*5*	4	0	0	0	0	0	2	*7*	*14*	*55*

Cheyenne Wells *Cheyenne County*   Elevation: 4,248 ft.   Latitude: 38° 49' N   Longitude: 102° 22' W

	JAN	FEB	MAR	APR	MAY	JUN	JUL	AUG	SEP	OCT	NOV	DEC	YEAR
Mean Maximum Temp. (°F)	42.7	48.4	56.3	65.0	74.0	85.2	90.8	88.7	80.6	69.1	53.0	44.4	66.5
Mean Temp. (°F)	29.5	34.3	41.4	49.8	59.4	69.6	75.1	73.6	65.1	53.4	39.3	31.2	51.8
Mean Minimum Temp. (°F)	16.0	20.2	26.5	34.5	44.8	54.0	59.3	58.5	49.4	37.6	25.5	18.0	37.0
Extreme Maximum Temp. (°F)	78	77	86	95	98	107	105	104	100	94	83	77	107
Extreme Minimum Temp. (°F)	-22	-18	-5	7	27	31	41	41	18	6	-10	-26	-26
Days Maximum Temp. ≥ 90°F	0	0	0	0	1	11	20	16	7	1	0	0	56
Days Maximum Temp. ≤ 32°F	7	4	2	0	0	0	0	0	0	0	2	5	20
Days Minimum Temp. ≤ 32°F	30	26	24	12	1	0	0	0	1	8	24	30	156
Days Minimum Temp. ≤ 0°F	3	2	0	0	0	0	0	0	0	0	0	2	7
Heating Degree Days (base 65°F)	1,092	861	724	455	197	33	3	4	98	362	764	1,040	5,633
Cooling Degree Days (base 65°F)	0	0	0	5	30	171	324	287	112	9	0	0	938
Mean Precipitation (in.)	0.24	0.33	0.79	1.26	2.87	2.44	2.67	2.47	1.33	0.82	0.60	0.25	16.07
Days With ≥ 0.1" Precipitation	1	1	3	3	6	5	5	4	3	2	2	1	36
Days With ≥ 1.0" Precipitation	0	0	0	0	1	1	1	1	0	0	0	0	4
Mean Snowfall (in.)	3.4	3.5	4.5	3.9	0.9	0.0	0.0	0.0	0.2	2.1	3.4	3.1	25.0
Days With ≥ 1.0" Snow Depth	7	4	2	1	0	0	0	0	0	1	3	6	24

Cimarron *Montrose County* Elevation: 6,893 ft.   Latitude: 38° 27' N   Longitude: 107° 34' W

	JAN	FEB	MAR	APR	MAY	JUN	JUL	AUG	SEP	OCT	NOV	DEC	YEAR
Mean Maximum Temp. (°F)	33.2	38.2	47.7	56.7	67.8	79.6	84.3	82.3	74.6	63.1	46.5	35.0	59.1
Mean Temp. (°F)	17.2	22.6	33.0	40.7	49.5	58.2	64.0	62.8	54.6	43.7	31.1	19.5	41.4
Mean Minimum Temp. (°F)	1.1	6.9	18.2	24.6	31.3	36.7	43.7	43.3	34.6	24.2	15.7	3.9	23.7
Extreme Maximum Temp. (°F)	56	65	70	79	84	94	97	94	94	83	69	57	97
Extreme Minimum Temp. (°F)	-36	-35	-13	-9	4	19	29	27	13	5	-17	-33	-36
Days Maximum Temp. ≥ 90°F	0	0	0	0	0	1	4	2	0	0	0	0	7
Days Maximum Temp. ≤ 32°F	14	7	1	0	0	0	0	0	0	0	2	12	36
Days Minimum Temp. ≤ 32°F	31	28	30	26	19	7	1	1	12	27	28	31	241
Days Minimum Temp. ≤ 0°F	16	9	2	0	0	0	0	0	0	0	2	13	42
Heating Degree Days (base 65°F)	1,477	1,193	985	726	473	203	52	80	306	654	1,009	1,404	8,562
Cooling Degree Days (base 65°F)	0	0	0	0	0	5	31	22	2	0	0	0	60
Mean Precipitation (in.)	0.90	0.74	1.08	1.12	1.12	0.86	1.30	1.42	1.46	1.41	1.12	0.73	13.26
Days With ≥ 0.1" Precipitation	3	3	3	4	4	3	4	4	4	4	4	3	43
Days With ≥ 1.0" Precipitation	0	0	0	0	0	0	0	0	0	0	0	0	0
Mean Snowfall (in.)	12.3	*11.3*	*10.9*	*5.5*	0.5	trace	0.0	0.0	trace	*1.6*	*9.3*	*13.7*	*65.1*
Days With ≥ 1.0" Snow Depth	na	na	na	na	0	0	0	0	0	*0*	na	na	na

Climax *Lake County* Elevation: 11,318 ft.   Latitude: 39° 23' N   Longitude: 106° 12' W

	JAN	FEB	MAR	APR	MAY	JUN	JUL	AUG	SEP	OCT	NOV	DEC	YEAR
Mean Maximum Temp. (°F)	24.7	28.5	33.1	38.3	47.3	58.4	64.7	62.8	56.4	45.4	32.7	26.1	43.2
Mean Temp. (°F)	12.7	15.4	20.0	25.4	35.3	45.7	51.6	50.2	43.6	32.9	20.9	14.4	30.7
Mean Minimum Temp. (°F)	0.6	2.3	6.7	12.5	23.3	32.9	38.5	37.6	30.7	20.5	9.0	2.6	18.1
Extreme Maximum Temp. (°F)	50	53	57	59	65	78	85	84	82	73	60	52	85
Extreme Minimum Temp. (°F)	-30	-28	-21	-20	2	10	12	18	6	-9	-27	-33	-33
Days Maximum Temp. ≥ 90°F	0	0	0	0	0	0	0	0	0	0	0	0	0
Days Maximum Temp. ≤ 32°F	24	18	14	8	1	0	0	0	0	4	15	22	106
Days Minimum Temp. ≤ 32°F	31	28	31	30	29	14	2	3	17	30	30	31	276
Days Minimum Temp. ≤ 0°F	15	11	7	3	0	0	0	0	0	1	6	13	56
Heating Degree Days (base 65°F)	1,617	1,394	1,390	1,181	915	572	408	452	637	987	1,318	1,565	12,436
Cooling Degree Days (base 65°F)	0	0	0	0	0	0	0	0	0	0	0	0	0
Mean Precipitation (in.)	2.02	1.74	2.34	2.39	2.08	1.19	2.22	2.11	1.50	1.45	1.99	1.82	22.85
Days With ≥ 0.1" Precipitation	7	6	8	9	6	4	7	7	5	5	7	6	77
Days With ≥ 1.0" Precipitation	0	0	0	0	0	0	0	0	0	0	0	0	0
Mean Snowfall (in.)	38.9	33.0	41.0	38.9	21.5	4.8	0.2	0.1	4.4	18.3	35.1	34.8	271.0
Days With ≥ 1.0" Snow Depth	31	28	31	30	26	3	0	0	1	10	26	31	217

Cochetopa Creek *Gunnison County* Elevation: 7,998 ft.   Latitude: 38° 27' N   Longitude: 106° 46' W

	JAN	FEB	MAR	APR	MAY	JUN	JUL	AUG	SEP	OCT	NOV	DEC	YEAR
Mean Maximum Temp. (°F)	28.5	34.3	44.4	54.0	65.1	75.8	80.7	79.0	72.2	60.6	44.5	31.9	55.9
Mean Temp. (°F)	11.9	17.4	28.9	37.6	46.9	55.7	61.4	60.3	52.4	41.0	28.1	15.5	38.1
Mean Minimum Temp. (°F)	-4.7	0.5	13.4	21.2	28.7	35.5	42.1	41.5	32.7	21.5	11.7	-0.9	20.3
Extreme Maximum Temp. (°F)	50	58	67	78	82	93	93	92	90	80	66	55	93
Extreme Minimum Temp. (°F)	-40	-36	-18	-10	8	18	30	24	9	-7	-25	-36	-40
Days Maximum Temp. ≥ 90°F	0	0	0	0	0	0	1	0	0	0	0	0	1
Days Maximum Temp. ≤ 32°F	19	11	3	0	0	0	0	0	0	0	4	16	53
Days Minimum Temp. ≤ 32°F	31	28	31	29	23	9	1	2	15	29	30	31	259
Days Minimum Temp. ≤ 0°F	21	14	4	0	0	0	0	0	0	0	4	18	61
Heating Degree Days (base 65°F)	1,640	1,339	1,112	814	553	275	114	147	371	736	1,101	1,528	9,730
Cooling Degree Days (base 65°F)	0	0	0	0	0	2	14	8	1	0	0	0	25
Mean Precipitation (in.)	0.72	0.66	0.82	0.92	0.98	0.71	1.52	1.80	1.16	0.84	0.74	0.79	11.66
Days With ≥ 0.1" Precipitation	3	3	4	4	4	2	5	6	4	3	3	3	44
Days With ≥ 1.0" Precipitation	0	0	0	0	0	0	0	0	0	0	0	0	0
Mean Snowfall (in.)	10.7	8.7	7.8	4.6	0.7	trace	0.0	0.0	trace	1.7	7.2	10.7	52.1
Days With ≥ 1.0" Snow Depth	*15*	15	*14*	*4*	1	0	0	0	0	1	7	13	*70*

Colorado National Monument *Mesa County* Elevation: 5,777 ft.   Latitude: 39° 06' N   Longitude: 108° 44' W

	JAN	FEB	MAR	APR	MAY	JUN	JUL	AUG	SEP	OCT	NOV	DEC	YEAR
Mean Maximum Temp. (°F)	36.7	44.6	53.8	*63.1*	73.4	85.8	91.3	88.9	79.7	65.6	48.8	38.5	*64.2*
Mean Temp. (°F)	27.4	34.1	42.1	*50.0*	59.8	71.0	76.7	74.4	65.6	52.9	38.6	29.3	*51.8*
Mean Minimum Temp. (°F)	18.1	23.7	30.4	*36.7*	46.2	56.2	62.0	59.9	51.5	40.3	28.4	20.0	*39.4*
Extreme Maximum Temp. (°F)	54	66	76	87	92	104	105	102	98	85	70	62	105
Extreme Minimum Temp. (°F)	-9	-12	7	11	25	31	42	40	27	9	2	-11	-12
Days Maximum Temp. ≥ 90°F	0	0	0	0	0	11	21	16	3	0	0	0	51
Days Maximum Temp. ≤ 32°F	8	2	0	0	0	0	0	0	0	0	1	6	17
Days Minimum Temp. ≤ 32°F	29	24	19	9	2	0	0	0	0	6	21	29	139
Days Minimum Temp. ≤ 0°F	1	0	0	0	0	0	0	0	0	0	0	0	1
Heating Degree Days (base 65°F)	1,159	866	703	*446*	189	28	1	3	72	370	786	1,101	*5,724*
Cooling Degree Days (base 65°F)	0	0	0	*5*	31	208	357	291	94	2	0	0	*988*
Mean Precipitation (in.)	0.69	0.65	1.15	0.95	1.22	0.69	0.92	1.02	0.93	1.30	0.97	0.78	11.27
Days With ≥ 0.1" Precipitation	3	2	4	3	4	2	3	3	3	3	3	3	36
Days With ≥ 1.0" Precipitation	0	0	0	0	0	0	0	0	0	0	0	0	0
Mean Snowfall (in.)	6.4	*4.8*	3.6	1.5	0.2	trace	0.0	0.0	trace	1.1	2.8	7.0	*27.4*
Days With ≥ 1.0" Snow Depth	15	*9*	2	*0*	0	0	0	0	0	1	2	10	*39*

Crested Butte *Gunnison County*   Elevation: 8,858 ft.   Latitude: 38° 53' N   Longitude: 106° 59' W

	JAN	FEB	MAR	APR	MAY	JUN	JUL	AUG	SEP	OCT	NOV	DEC	YEAR
Mean Maximum Temp. (°F)	26.7	31.5	38.8	46.0	57.5	69.1	74.2	73.0	65.4	54.2	38.8	28.5	50.3
Mean Temp. (°F)	10.2	14.4	23.1	31.6	42.6	51.1	56.3	55.4	47.9	37.8	24.0	12.2	33.9
Mean Minimum Temp. (°F)	-6.3	-2.7	7.4	17.3	27.7	33.1	38.3	37.6	30.5	21.3	9.3	-4.0	17.5
Extreme Maximum Temp. (°F)	47	50	56	69	75	86	88	85	83	76	65	51	88
Extreme Minimum Temp. (°F)	-42	-47	-30	-17	8	17	23	23	10	-11	-28	-38	-47
Days Maximum Temp. ≥ 90°F	0	0	0	0	0	0	0	0	0	0	0	0	0
Days Maximum Temp. ≤ 32°F	24	15	6	2	0	0	0	0	0	1	9	21	78
Days Minimum Temp. ≤ 32°F	31	28	31	30	25	14	3	5	19	29	30	31	276
Days Minimum Temp. ≤ 0°F	21	17	9	2	0	0	0	0	0	0	7	20	76
Heating Degree Days (base 65°F)	1,694	1,423	1,292	996	686	410	264	292	506	836	1,223	1,630	11,252
Cooling Degree Days (base 65°F)	0	0	0	0	0	0	0	0	0	0	0	0	0
Mean Precipitation (in.)	2.52	2.36	2.37	1.88	1.60	1.19	1.93	1.93	2.05	1.81	2.14	2.17	23.95
Days With ≥ 0.1" Precipitation	7	7	8	6	5	4	6	6	6	5	6	7	73
Days With ≥ 1.0" Precipitation	0	0	0	0	0	0	0	0	0	0	0	0	0
Mean Snowfall (in.)	41.9	39.2	34.4	19.7	8.0	0.8	0.0	0.0	1.0	9.9	31.7	37.3	223.9
Days With ≥ 1.0" Snow Depth	31	28	30	20	3	0	0	0	0	5	21	29	167

Del Norte 2 E *Rio Grande County*   Elevation: 7,867 ft.   Latitude: 37° 40' N   Longitude: 106° 19' W

	JAN	FEB	MAR	APR	MAY	JUN	JUL	AUG	SEP	OCT	NOV	DEC	YEAR
Mean Maximum Temp. (°F)	34.6	40.9	49.9	58.4	67.1	75.6	78.3	76.3	70.7	61.6	46.9	36.8	58.1
Mean Temp. (°F)	20.7	26.8	35.5	42.8	51.3	59.2	63.4	61.9	55.4	46.0	32.8	22.8	43.2
Mean Minimum Temp. (°F)	6.6	12.7	21.1	27.2	35.4	42.8	48.4	47.4	40.1	30.4	18.7	8.8	28.3
Extreme Maximum Temp. (°F)	61	68	73	80	87	91	89	89	87	81	70	60	91
Extreme Minimum Temp. (°F)	-27	-20	-5	-4	18	26	33	34	15	5	-14	-23	-27
Days Maximum Temp. ≥ 90°F	0	0	0	0	0	0	0	0	0	0	0	0	0
Days Maximum Temp. ≤ 32°F	13	6	1	0	0	0	0	0	0	0	3	10	33
Days Minimum Temp. ≤ 32°F	31	28	30	23	9	1	0	0	2	19	29	31	203
Days Minimum Temp. ≤ 0°F	8	3	0	0	0	0	0	0	0	0	1	6	18
Heating Degree Days (base 65°F)	1,368	1,071	907	659	418	174	64	99	281	581	958	1,301	7,881
Cooling Degree Days (base 65°F)	0	0	0	0	0	9	25	12	0	0	0	0	46
Mean Precipitation (in.)	0.32	0.33	0.77	0.69	0.89	0.77	1.59	1.93	1.18	0.83	0.65	0.47	10.42
Days With ≥ 0.1" Precipitation	1	1	2	2	2	3	5	6	4	3	2	2	33
Days With ≥ 1.0" Precipitation	0	0	0	0	0	0	0	0	0	0	0	0	0
Mean Snowfall (in.)	5.3	5.7	9.1	4.7	1.6	trace	trace	0.0	trace	3.7	7.0	7.8	44.9
Days With ≥ 1.0" Snow Depth	na	na	na	na	0	0	0	0	0	1	na	na	na

Dillon 1 E *Summit County*   Elevation: 9,064 ft.   Latitude: 39° 38' N   Longitude: 106° 02' W

	JAN	FEB	MAR	APR	MAY	JUN	JUL	AUG	SEP	OCT	NOV	DEC	YEAR
Mean Maximum Temp. (°F)	31.0	34.5	39.1	46.2	56.7	67.7	73.2	71.8	64.6	53.9	40.0	32.4	50.9
Mean Temp. (°F)	16.2	19.3	25.4	32.3	41.9	50.6	55.9	54.8	47.7	37.8	26.4	18.3	35.5
Mean Minimum Temp. (°F)	1.3	4.0	11.6	18.3	27.1	33.5	38.6	37.8	30.8	21.7	12.7	4.1	20.1
Extreme Maximum Temp. (°F)	55	53	62	68	72	82	85	84	83	73	64	58	85
Extreme Minimum Temp. (°F)	-30	-36	-22	-12	3	20	26	23	9	-4	-29	-30	-36
Days Maximum Temp. ≥ 90°F	0	0	0	0	0	0	0	0	0	0	0	0	0
Days Maximum Temp. ≤ 32°F	17	11	7	3	0	0	0	0	0	1	8	14	61
Days Minimum Temp. ≤ 32°F	31	28	31	30	27	12	2	4	18	30	30	31	274
Days Minimum Temp. ≤ 0°F	15	11	4	1	0	0	0	0	0	0	3	12	46
Heating Degree Days (base 65°F)	1,507	1,286	1,222	974	709	425	275	310	512	836	1,153	1,441	10,650
Cooling Degree Days (base 65°F)	0	0	0	0	0	0	0	0	0	0	0	0	0
Mean Precipitation (in.)	0.85	0.93	1.13	1.20	1.43	1.20	1.81	1.61	1.35	0.79	0.88	0.81	13.99
Days With ≥ 0.1" Precipitation	3	3	4	5	4	4	6	6	5	3	3	3	49
Days With ≥ 1.0" Precipitation	0	0	0	0	0	0	0	0	0	0	0	0	0
Mean Snowfall (in.)	16.4	16.2	19.2	16.6	7.2	1.4	trace	trace	1.6	6.2	15.4	15.3	115.5
Days With ≥ 1.0" Snow Depth	29	25	22	12	3	0	0	0	1	4	15	25	136

Dinosaur Nat'l Monument *Moffat County*   Elevation: 5,918 ft.   Latitude: 40° 15' N   Longitude: 108° 58' W

	JAN	FEB	MAR	APR	MAY	JUN	JUL	AUG	SEP	OCT	NOV	DEC	YEAR
Mean Maximum Temp. (°F)	32.5	39.0	50.4	60.7	71.6	84.0	90.5	88.4	78.2	63.6	45.6	34.5	61.6
Mean Temp. (°F)	21.2	26.9	37.6	46.0	55.9	66.7	73.4	71.6	61.8	49.1	34.3	23.6	47.3
Mean Minimum Temp. (°F)	9.8	14.7	24.8	31.4	40.1	49.3	56.2	54.7	45.4	34.6	22.9	12.7	33.0
Extreme Maximum Temp. (°F)	57	64	73	87	92	100	103	102	96	84	69	58	103
Extreme Minimum Temp. (°F)	-23	-24	0	3	16	24	37	34	21	0	-9	-29	-29
Days Maximum Temp. ≥ 90°F	0	0	0	0	0	9	18	14	2	0	0	0	43
Days Maximum Temp. ≤ 32°F	15	6	1	0	0	0	0	0	0	0	3	12	37
Days Minimum Temp. ≤ 32°F	31	28	27	17	5	0	0	0	1	12	27	31	179
Days Minimum Temp. ≤ 0°F	6	3	0	0	0	0	0	0	0	0	0	4	13
Heating Degree Days (base 65°F)	1,352	1,069	842	562	283	60	2	5	132	485	916	1,275	6,983
Cooling Degree Days (base 65°F)	0	0	0	0	8	115	264	217	46	0	0	0	650
Mean Precipitation (in.)	0.67	0.59	1.01	1.21	1.40	0.95	1.04	0.83	1.17	1.55	0.82	0.58	11.82
Days With ≥ 0.1" Precipitation	2	2	3	4	4	3	3	3	3	4	3	2	36
Days With ≥ 1.0" Precipitation	0	0	0	0	0	0	0	0	0	0	0	0	0
Mean Snowfall (in.)	10.5	6.8	7.2	4.1	0.8	0.3	0.0	0.0	trace	2.1	5.7	8.5	46.0
Days With ≥ 1.0" Snow Depth	24	18	7	1	0	0	0	0	0	1	6	17	74

Eagle County Airport *Eagle County*   Elevation: 6,496 ft.   Latitude: 39° 39' N   Longitude: 106° 55' W

	JAN	FEB	MAR	APR	MAY	JUN	JUL	AUG	SEP	OCT	NOV	DEC	YEAR
Mean Maximum Temp. (°F)	34.2	41.1	49.4	58.6	69.0	80.5	85.4	83.4	75.3	63.1	45.9	35.2	60.1
Mean Temp. (°F)	19.6	26.2	35.4	42.5	51.6	60.6	66.1	64.4	56.2	45.0	31.6	20.8	43.3
Mean Minimum Temp. (°F)	4.7	11.1	21.3	26.4	34.2	40.7	46.8	45.3	37.1	26.9	17.3	6.3	26.5
Extreme Maximum Temp. (°F)	58	65	73	82	87	100	99	96	93	84	69	61	100
Extreme Minimum Temp. (°F)	-36	-35	-10	-8	12	24	32	27	16	2	-24	-29	-36
Days Maximum Temp. ≥ 90°F	0	0	0	0	0	3	8	4	1	0	0	0	16
Days Maximum Temp. ≤ 32°F	12	4	1	0	0	0	0	0	0	0	3	11	31
Days Minimum Temp. ≤ 32°F	30	28	30	24	12	2	0	0	7	25	29	30	217
Days Minimum Temp. ≤ 0°F	11	6	0	0	0	0	0	0	0	0	1	9	27
Heating Degree Days (base 65°F)	1,401	1,091	912	668	408	143	24	52	261	613	994	1,365	7,932
Cooling Degree Days (base 65°F)	0	0	0	0	0	20	67	44	4	0	0	na	na
Mean Precipitation (in.)	0.74	0.59	0.83	0.80	0.87	0.83	1.42	0.94	1.11	1.14	0.71	0.88	10.86
Days With ≥ 0.1" Precipitation	2	2	3	3	3	3	4	3	3	3	3	3	35
Days With ≥ 1.0" Precipitation	0	0	0	0	0	0	0	0	0	0	0	0	0
Mean Snowfall (in.)	8.9	5.8	6.2	3.7	1.8	0.2	0.0	0.0	0.4	2.9	5.9	10.7	46.5
Days With ≥ 1.0" Snow Depth	22	18	7	1	0	0	0	0	0	1	5	16	70

Evergreen *Jefferson County*   Elevation: 6,998 ft.   Latitude: 39° 38' N   Longitude: 105° 19' W

	JAN	FEB	MAR	APR	MAY	JUN	JUL	AUG	SEP	OCT	NOV	DEC	YEAR
Mean Maximum Temp. (°F)	43.8	45.8	49.9	55.7	64.4	75.5	80.7	79.2	71.9	61.7	50.2	44.7	60.3
Mean Temp. (°F)	26.9	29.2	34.4	40.5	49.1	58.4	63.6	62.3	54.6	44.3	34.1	27.8	43.8
Mean Minimum Temp. (°F)	10.0	12.6	18.8	25.3	33.8	41.2	46.4	45.3	37.2	26.8	18.0	10.8	27.2
Extreme Maximum Temp. (°F)	74	71	78	81	89	96	96	94	92	85	77	69	96
Extreme Minimum Temp. (°F)	-28	-28	-12	-9	12	27	33	30	8	-5	-15	-29	-29
Days Maximum Temp. ≥ 90°F	0	0	0	0	0	1	2	1	0	0	0	0	4
Days Maximum Temp. ≤ 32°F	5	4	3	1	0	0	0	0	0	1	3	5	22
Days Minimum Temp. ≤ 32°F	31	28	30	26	12	1	0	0	7	26	29	31	221
Days Minimum Temp. ≤ 0°F	6	4	1	0	0	0	0	0	0	0	1	5	17
Heating Degree Days (base 65°F)	1,174	1,002	942	728	486	199	69	95	308	634	920	1,147	7,704
Cooling Degree Days (base 65°F)	0	0	0	0	0	9	35	20	3	0	0	0	67
Mean Precipitation (in.)	0.52	0.66	1.72	2.45	2.66	2.12	2.38	2.35	1.49	1.29	1.09	0.75	19.48
Days With ≥ 0.1" Precipitation	2	2	4	5	6	5	6	6	4	3	3	2	48
Days With ≥ 1.0" Precipitation	0	0	0	0	1	0	0	0	0	0	0	0	1
Mean Snowfall (in.)	7.9	8.5	19.6	16.4	2.6	0.2	0.0	0.0	2.2	6.7	14.4	9.0	87.5
Days With ≥ 1.0" Snow Depth	na	na	na	na	0	0	0	0	0	na	na	na	na

Flagler 5 NNE *Kit Carson County*   Elevation: 4,872 ft.   Latitude: 39° 22' N   Longitude: 103° 03' W

	JAN	FEB	MAR	APR	MAY	JUN	JUL	AUG	SEP	OCT	NOV	DEC	YEAR
Mean Maximum Temp. (°F)	41.7	46.0	53.9	61.9	70.8	82.3	88.3	86.0	78.4	66.9	50.5	43.4	64.2
Mean Temp. (°F)	27.4	31.7	38.7	46.4	56.1	66.5	72.6	70.8	62.5	50.4	36.2	29.3	49.1
Mean Minimum Temp. (°F)	13.0	17.3	23.6	30.9	41.4	50.7	56.8	55.5	46.4	33.9	21.9	15.2	33.9
Extreme Maximum Temp. (°F)	78	77	82	90	94	102	103	102	99	91	81	76	103
Extreme Minimum Temp. (°F)	-29	-25	-10	1	20	31	37	33	21	-6	-15	-29	-29
Days Maximum Temp. ≥ 90°F	0	0	0	0	0	6	15	11	4	0	0	0	36
Days Maximum Temp. ≤ 32°F	7	5	2	0	0	0	0	0	0	0	3	6	23
Days Minimum Temp. ≤ 32°F	31	28	27	18	3	0	0	0	2	13	26	30	178
Days Minimum Temp. ≤ 0°F	4	2	1	0	0	0	0	0	0	0	1	3	11
Heating Degree Days (base 65°F)	1,160	935	807	551	278	60	8	14	135	447	856	1,099	6,350
Cooling Degree Days (base 65°F)	0	0	0	1	10	103	238	196	65	2	0	0	615
Mean Precipitation (in.)	0.35	0.35	0.93	1.45	2.78	2.63	2.73	2.32	1.07	0.77	0.70	0.34	16.42
Days With ≥ 0.1" Precipitation	1	1	2	4	6	5	5	4	2	2	2	1	35
Days With ≥ 1.0" Precipitation	0	0	0	0	1	1	1	1	0	0	0	0	4
Mean Snowfall (in.)	4.5	4.1	6.6	5.2	1.0	0.0	0.0	0.0	0.6	2.4	7.1	5.1	36.6
Days With ≥ 1.0" Snow Depth	6	4	4	2	0	0	0	0	0	1	4	4	25

Fort Collins *Larimer County*   Elevation: 5,003 ft.   Latitude: 40° 35' N   Longitude: 105° 05' W

	JAN	FEB	MAR	APR	MAY	JUN	JUL	AUG	SEP	OCT	NOV	DEC	YEAR
Mean Maximum Temp. (°F)	41.9	46.5	53.3	60.9	70.0	80.4	85.2	83.3	75.2	64.0	50.3	42.9	62.8
Mean Temp. (°F)	28.7	33.3	40.0	47.5	56.8	66.2	71.3	69.5	60.9	49.8	37.5	29.9	49.3
Mean Minimum Temp. (°F)	15.4	20.1	26.7	34.1	43.5	51.9	57.3	55.6	46.6	35.5	24.6	17.0	35.7
Extreme Maximum Temp. (°F)	73	76	80	89	92	100	101	99	97	88	77	73	101
Extreme Minimum Temp. (°F)	-28	-19	-1	-5	27	34	43	39	18	4	-7	-24	-28
Days Maximum Temp. ≥ 90°F	0	0	0	0	0	4	9	5	1	0	0	0	19
Days Maximum Temp. ≤ 32°F	7	4	2	0	0	0	0	0	0	0	2	5	20
Days Minimum Temp. ≤ 32°F	30	26	25	12	1	0	0	0	1	10	25	30	160
Days Minimum Temp. ≤ 0°F	3	1	0	0	0	0	0	0	0	0	0	3	7
Heating Degree Days (base 65°F)	1,120	889	768	518	255	57	6	11	150	465	819	1,080	6,138
Cooling Degree Days (base 65°F)	0	0	0	0	9	95	209	164	36	0	0	0	513
Mean Precipitation (in.)	0.42	0.36	1.46	2.10	2.59	2.04	1.93	1.38	1.35	0.99	0.83	0.48	15.93
Days With ≥ 0.1" Precipitation	2	1	4	4	5	4	4	3	3	3	3	1	37
Days With ≥ 1.0" Precipitation	0	0	0	0	1	0	0	0	0	0	0	0	1
Mean Snowfall (in.)	8.2	6.2	12.4	7.2	1.5	trace	0.0	0.0	1.2	4.0	10.0	8.4	59.1
Days With ≥ 1.0" Snow Depth	15	7	5	2	0	0	0	0	0	1	6	11	47

Fort Lewis *La Plata County* Elevation: 7,598 ft. Latitude: 37° 14' N Longitude: 108° 03' W

	JAN	FEB	MAR	APR	MAY	JUN	JUL	AUG	SEP	OCT	NOV	DEC	YEAR
Mean Maximum Temp. (°F)	36.5	41.1	47.2	56.0	65.7	76.9	81.1	78.7	71.7	60.9	46.5	38.3	58.4
Mean Temp. (°F)	22.9	27.4	33.9	41.1	49.6	58.9	64.9	63.3	56.0	45.4	32.9	24.9	43.5
Mean Minimum Temp. (°F)	9.3	13.6	20.5	26.1	33.5	40.9	48.7	47.9	40.0	29.8	19.4	11.6	28.4
Extreme Maximum Temp. (°F)	55	60	68	76	83	99	102	91	88	80	70	59	102
Extreme Minimum Temp. (°F)	-26	-20	-6	0	11	22	29	33	17	3	-10	-24	-26
Days Maximum Temp. ≥ 90°F	0	0	0	0	0	1	1	0	0	0	0	0	2
Days Maximum Temp. ≤ 32°F	9	3	1	0	0	0	0	0	0	0	2	7	22
Days Minimum Temp. ≤ 32°F	31	28	30	24	13	3	0	0	4	19	28	30	210
Days Minimum Temp. ≤ 0°F	6	2	0	0	0	0	0	0	0	0	1	4	13
Heating Degree Days (base 65°F)	1,297	1,057	959	711	469	188	42	70	266	601	956	1,235	7,851
Cooling Degree Days (base 65°F)	0	0	0	0	0	11	50	30	3	0	0	0	94
Mean Precipitation (in.)	1.61	1.37	1.73	1.06	1.22	0.65	2.20	2.39	2.05	1.90	1.74	1.24	19.16
Days With ≥ 0.1" Precipitation	4	4	5	3	3	2	6	6	4	4	4	3	48
Days With ≥ 1.0" Precipitation	0	0	0	0	0	0	0	0	0	0	0	0	0
Mean Snowfall (in.)	*19.9*	*15.4*	*10.6*	4.5	0.4	0.0	0.0	0.0	0.0	1.7	11.1	*17.3*	*80.9*
Days With ≥ 1.0" Snow Depth	*26*	22	*18*	*4*	0	0	0	0	0	1	*7*	*21*	*99*

Fort Morgan *Morgan County* Elevation: 4,330 ft. Latitude: 40° 16' N Longitude: 103° 48' W

	JAN	FEB	MAR	APR	MAY	JUN	JUL	AUG	SEP	OCT	NOV	DEC	YEAR
Mean Maximum Temp. (°F)	38.6	45.5	53.8	62.2	72.3	83.6	90.2	87.9	79.2	67.2	50.9	41.3	64.4
Mean Temp. (°F)	24.6	31.3	39.5	48.2	58.7	69.2	75.3	73.0	63.5	50.9	36.8	27.1	49.8
Mean Minimum Temp. (°F)	10.6	17.1	25.1	34.1	45.2	54.8	60.1	58.0	47.6	34.5	22.8	12.9	35.2
Extreme Maximum Temp. (°F)	75	75	84	90	97	105	107	104	103	92	80	74	107
Extreme Minimum Temp. (°F)	-32	-25	-10	-1	23	37	42	40	11	5	-9	-26	-32
Days Maximum Temp. ≥ 90°F	0	0	0	0	1	10	18	15	6	0	0	0	50
Days Maximum Temp. ≤ 32°F	9	5	2	1	0	0	0	0	0	0	3	7	27
Days Minimum Temp. ≤ 32°F	31	28	26	13	1	0	0	0	1	12	27	31	170
Days Minimum Temp. ≤ 0°F	6	3	0	0	0	0	0	0	0	0	1	4	14
Heating Degree Days (base 65°F)	1,246	945	785	499	217	42	5	8	124	434	838	1,168	6,311
Cooling Degree Days (base 65°F)	0	0	0	2	32	171	331	269	91	4	0	0	900
Mean Precipitation (in.)	0.21	0.17	0.72	1.32	2.39	2.04	1.90	1.56	1.19	0.81	0.50	0.26	13.07
Days With ≥ 0.1" Precipitation	1	1	2	3	5	5	4	4	3	2	2	1	33
Days With ≥ 1.0" Precipitation	0	0	0	0	0	0	0	0	0	0	0	0	0
Mean Snowfall (in.)	4.6	2.2	5.3	2.7	0.4	0.0	0.0	0.0	0.3	0.9	3.9	4.4	24.7
Days With ≥ 1.0" Snow Depth	na	na	na	*0*	0	0	0	0	0	0	na	na	na

Fruita 1 W *Mesa County* Elevation: 4,478 ft. Latitude: 39° 10' N Longitude: 108° 45' W

	JAN	FEB	MAR	APR	MAY	JUN	JUL	AUG	SEP	OCT	NOV	DEC	YEAR
Mean Maximum Temp. (°F)	37.3	46.3	57.1	65.8	75.9	87.6	92.6	90.1	81.8	68.5	52.3	40.6	66.3
Mean Temp. (°F)	24.8	32.4	42.0	49.6	59.3	68.7	74.6	72.7	63.5	50.9	37.9	27.8	50.3
Mean Minimum Temp. (°F)	12.2	18.5	27.0	33.3	42.7	49.8	56.5	55.2	45.0	33.2	23.4	14.9	34.3
Extreme Maximum Temp. (°F)	61	70	79	89	94	105	106	102	98	89	75	64	106
Extreme Minimum Temp. (°F)	-21	-36	4	14	23	28	41	37	24	14	-5	-19	-36
Days Maximum Temp. ≥ 90°F	0	0	0	0	1	13	23	18	4	0	0	0	59
Days Maximum Temp. ≤ 32°F	9	2	0	0	0	0	0	0	0	0	0	5	16
Days Minimum Temp. ≤ 32°F	30	26	23	14	2	0	0	0	2	16	26	30	169
Days Minimum Temp. ≤ 0°F	5	1	0	0	0	0	0	0	0	0	0	2	8
Heating Degree Days (base 65°F)	1,239	914	705	457	187	35	1	2	95	432	807	1,149	6,023
Cooling Degree Days (base 65°F)	0	0	0	1	21	*148*	299	246	59	0	0	0	*774*
Mean Precipitation (in.)	0.64	0.56	0.97	0.76	1.06	0.53	0.80	0.73	0.77	1.05	0.79	0.62	9.28
Days With ≥ 0.1" Precipitation	2	2	3	2	3	1	2	2	2	3	2	2	26
Days With ≥ 1.0" Precipitation	0	0	0	0	0	0	0	0	0	0	0	0	0
Mean Snowfall (in.)	4.5	*1.6*	1.1	0.4	trace	0.0	0.0	0.0	0.0	0.3	na	3.4	na
Days With ≥ 1.0" Snow Depth	*8*	*3*	1	0	0	0	0	0	0	0	na	5	na

Grand Junction 6 ESE *Mesa County* Elevation: 4,757 ft. Latitude: 39° 03' N Longitude: 108° 28' W

	JAN	FEB	MAR	APR	MAY	JUN	JUL	AUG	SEP	OCT	NOV	DEC	YEAR
Mean Maximum Temp. (°F)	37.8	46.3	56.4	64.7	75.0	86.6	92.1	89.7	80.7	67.4	51.5	40.5	65.7
Mean Temp. (°F)	27.4	35.0	44.4	51.8	61.4	71.9	77.5	75.6	66.5	53.9	40.2	30.0	53.0
Mean Minimum Temp. (°F)	16.8	23.6	32.4	38.9	47.8	57.1	62.9	61.4	52.2	40.3	28.7	19.5	40.1
Extreme Maximum Temp. (°F)	59	68	79	88	93	104	104	102	99	87	74	67	104
Extreme Minimum Temp. (°F)	-12	-21	9	11	28	33	42	43	27	15	-2	-13	-21
Days Maximum Temp. ≥ 90°F	0	0	0	0	1	13	22	18	4	0	0	0	58
Days Maximum Temp. ≤ 32°F	9	2	0	0	0	0	0	0	0	0	1	5	17
Days Minimum Temp. ≤ 32°F	31	25	16	7	1	0	0	0	0	5	21	30	136
Days Minimum Temp. ≤ 0°F	2	1	0	0	0	0	0	0	0	0	0	1	4
Heating Degree Days (base 65°F)	1,160	842	631	394	154	26	0	1	64	342	739	1,078	5,431
Cooling Degree Days (base 65°F)	0	0	0	7	54	241	400	344	121	4	0	0	1,171
Mean Precipitation (in.)	0.52	0.45	0.96	0.86	1.07	0.50	0.80	0.72	0.84	0.98	0.80	0.55	9.05
Days With ≥ 0.1" Precipitation	2	2	3	3	3	1	2	3	3	3	3	2	30
Days With ≥ 1.0" Precipitation	0	0	0	0	0	0	0	0	0	0	0	0	0
Mean Snowfall (in.)	*3.7*	1.8	1.6	0.4	0.1	0.0	0.0	0.0	0.0	0.4	*1.3*	3.7	*13.0*
Days With ≥ 1.0" Snow Depth	na	*2*	*0*	0	0	0	0	0	0	0	*0*	na	na

Grand Lake 1 NW *Grand County*   Elevation: 8,717 ft.   Latitude: 40° 16' N   Longitude: 105° 50' W

	JAN	FEB	MAR	APR	MAY	JUN	JUL	AUG	SEP	OCT	NOV	DEC	YEAR
Mean Maximum Temp. (°F)	31.4	36.1	42.2	49.1	59.4	70.7	75.7	74.0	67.4	56.2	40.1	32.2	52.9
Mean Temp. (°F)	17.3	20.7	27.3	34.1	43.5	52.3	57.3	55.7	49.2	39.4	26.6	18.4	36.8
Mean Minimum Temp. (°F)	3.3	5.3	12.4	19.0	27.5	33.8	38.8	37.4	30.9	22.5	13.0	4.6	20.7
Extreme Maximum Temp. (°F)	53	56	67	74	81	89	92	92	89	75	68	54	92
Extreme Minimum Temp. (°F)	-37	-35	-27	-19	4	16	27	18	12	-8	-28	-35	-37
Days Maximum Temp. ≥ 90°F	0	0	0	0	0	0	0	0	0	0	0	0	0
Days Maximum Temp. ≤ 32°F	17	8	4	2	0	0	0	0	0	1	7	15	54
Days Minimum Temp. ≤ 32°F	31	28	31	30	27	12	2	4	18	29	30	31	273
Days Minimum Temp. ≤ 0°F	12	10	4	1	0	0	0	0	0	0	3	12	42
Heating Degree Days (base 65°F)	1,472	1,245	1,161	922	660	376	234	281	469	787	1,146	1,437	10,190
Cooling Degree Days (base 65°F)	0	0	0	0	0	0	2	1	0	0	0	0	3
Mean Precipitation (in.)	1.81	1.45	1.52	2.00	2.02	1.49	2.14	2.15	1.69	1.56	1.37	1.53	20.73
Days With ≥ 0.1" Precipitation	6	5	5	6	6	5	7	6	5	5	5	6	67
Days With ≥ 1.0" Precipitation	0	0	0	0	0	0	0	0	0	0	0	0	0
Mean Snowfall (in.)	30.2	21.0	16.7	15.7	4.3	0.8	0.0	trace	0.6	7.6	20.8	24.8	142.5
Days With ≥ 1.0" Snow Depth	30	28	30	21	3	0	0	0	0	4	18	30	164

Grand Lake 6 SSW *Grand County*   Elevation: 8,287 ft.   Latitude: 40° 11' N   Longitude: 105° 52' W

	JAN	FEB	MAR	APR	MAY	JUN	JUL	AUG	SEP	OCT	NOV	DEC	YEAR
Mean Maximum Temp. (°F)	26.8	31.5	39.0	47.0	58.6	69.1	74.1	72.8	65.8	54.5	39.1	29.3	50.6
Mean Temp. (°F)	13.8	17.0	25.2	33.4	44.0	52.7	58.0	56.9	49.9	39.8	27.7	17.6	36.3
Mean Minimum Temp. (°F)	0.8	2.4	11.4	19.8	29.5	36.3	41.8	40.9	34.1	25.0	16.2	5.9	22.0
Extreme Maximum Temp. (°F)	48	52	58	73	75	86	87	85	83	74	65	58	87
Extreme Minimum Temp. (°F)	-38	-42	-25	-17	12	21	27	25	15	-3	-22	-35	-42
Days Maximum Temp. ≥ 90°F	0	0	0	0	0	0	0	0	0	0	0	0	0
Days Maximum Temp. ≤ 32°F	23	14	7	2	0	0	0	0	0	1	7	20	74
Days Minimum Temp. ≤ 32°F	31	28	31	29	23	6	0	1	12	27	29	31	248
Days Minimum Temp. ≤ 0°F	15	13	5	1	0	0	0	0	0	0	2	10	46
Heating Degree Days (base 65°F)	1,582	1,350	1,227	940	643	362	211	246	446	775	1,113	1,462	10,357
Cooling Degree Days (base 65°F)	0	0	0	0	0	0	0	0	0	0	0	0	0
Mean Precipitation (in.)	0.98	0.83	0.91	1.27	1.52	1.21	1.67	1.56	1.20	1.08	0.92	0.80	13.95
Days With ≥ 0.1" Precipitation	3	3	3	4	5	4	5	5	4	4	3	3	46
Days With ≥ 1.0" Precipitation	0	0	0	0	0	0	0	0	0	0	0	0	0
Mean Snowfall (in.)	na	na	na	8.6	1.9	0.7	0.0	0.0	0.6	*1.8*	na	na	na
Days With ≥ 1.0" Snow Depth	na	na	na	12	1	0	0	0	0	*1*	na	na	na

Grant *Park County*   Elevation: 8,674 ft.   Latitude: 39° 28' N   Longitude: 105° 41' W

	JAN	FEB	MAR	APR	MAY	JUN	JUL	AUG	SEP	OCT	NOV	DEC	YEAR
Mean Maximum Temp. (°F)	33.3	37.7	43.4	50.3	60.7	71.1	75.4	73.0	66.1	55.9	40.9	33.4	53.4
Mean Temp. (°F)	20.9	24.1	29.8	36.2	45.4	54.1	58.8	57.2	50.1	40.8	28.6	21.6	39.0
Mean Minimum Temp. (°F)	8.5	10.5	16.2	22.0	30.1	37.0	42.2	41.3	34.0	25.6	16.2	9.9	24.5
Extreme Maximum Temp. (°F)	58	58	65	76	79	90	89	85	82	77	67	57	90
Extreme Minimum Temp. (°F)	-23	30	-15	-10	3	20	28	26	7	-5	-18	-27	-30
Days Maximum Temp. ≥ 90°F	0	0	0	0	0	0	0	0	0	0	0	0	0
Days Maximum Temp. ≤ 32°F	13	7	5	2	0	0	0	0	0	1	6	14	48
Days Minimum Temp. ≤ 32°F	31	28	31	29	21	5	0	1	11	28	30	31	246
Days Minimum Temp. ≤ 0°F	7	5	2	1	0	0	0	0	0	0	2	6	23
Heating Degree Days (base 65°F)	1,360	1,148	1,084	857	600	322	186	237	441	745	1,087	1,338	9,405
Cooling Degree Days (base 65°F)	0	0	0	0	0	0	2	0	0	0	0	0	2
Mean Precipitation (in.)	0.49	0.57	1.16	1.49	1.72	1.59	2.41	2.47	1.42	1.11	0.89	0.67	15.99
Days With ≥ 0.1" Precipitation	2	2	4	5	5	5	7	7	4	3	3	2	49
Days With ≥ 1.0" Precipitation	0	0	0	0	0	0	0	0	0	0	0	0	0
Mean Snowfall (in.)	8.8	10.5	18.1	16.7	6.3	1.2	0.0	0.0	2.6	8.7	13.6	12.2	98.7
Days With ≥ 1.0" Snow Depth	28	26	27	15	3	0	0	0	1	5	21	27	153

Great Sand Dunes Nat'l Mon. *Alamosa County*   Elevation: 8,120 ft.   Latitude: 37° 44' N   Longitude: 105° 31' W

	JAN	FEB	MAR	APR	MAY	JUN	JUL	AUG	SEP	OCT	NOV	DEC	YEAR
Mean Maximum Temp. (°F)	34.4	39.5	47.5	55.8	65.7	76.5	80.4	77.8	71.1	60.0	45.5	36.2	57.5
Mean Temp. (°F)	21.6	26.8	34.7	41.7	51.1	60.9	65.5	63.2	56.5	45.7	32.7	23.5	43.7
Mean Minimum Temp. (°F)	8.7	14.1	21.9	27.5	36.4	45.2	50.5	48.6	41.9	31.4	20.0	10.5	29.7
Extreme Maximum Temp. (°F)	67	63	72	78	85	96	94	88	87	78	67	60	96
Extreme Minimum Temp. (°F)	-24	-22	-3	-6	16	26	36	35	22	2	-11	-18	-24
Days Maximum Temp. ≥ 90°F	0	0	0	0	0	0	1	0	0	0	0	0	1
Days Maximum Temp. ≤ 32°F	12	6	1	0	0	0	0	0	0	0	4	11	34
Days Minimum Temp. ≤ 32°F	31	28	29	22	8	1	0	0	2	16	29	31	197
Days Minimum Temp. ≤ 0°F	6	2	0	0	0	0	0	0	0	0	1	4	13
Heating Degree Days (base 65°F)	1,338	1,070	933	693	426	139	39	72	252	590	964	1,280	7,796
Cooling Degree Days (base 65°F)	0	0	0	0	1	24	64	26	5	0	0	0	120
Mean Precipitation (in.)	0.45	0.38	0.88	0.91	1.12	0.90	1.72	2.01	1.30	0.92	0.62	0.43	11.64
Days With ≥ 0.1" Precipitation	1	1	3	3	4	3	5	6	4	3	2	1	36
Days With ≥ 1.0" Precipitation	0	0	0	0	0	0	0	0	0	0	0	0	0
Mean Snowfall (in.)	*7.6*	5.1	8.5	*5.6*	*1.9*	trace	0.0	0.0	trace	2.6	*5.9*	*7.1*	*44.3*
Days With ≥ 1.0" Snow Depth	*15*	*11*	na	*3*	0	0	0	0	0	1	*7*	na	na

Greeley *Weld County*   Elevation: 4,714 ft.   Latitude: 40° 24' N   Longitude: 104° 42' W

	JAN	FEB	MAR	APR	MAY	JUN	JUL	AUG	SEP	OCT	NOV	DEC	YEAR
Mean Maximum Temp. (°F)	40.4	46.7	55.1	63.1	72.6	83.4	88.9	86.9	78.5	66.3	50.4	41.8	64.5
Mean Temp. (°F)	27.5	33.3	41.0	48.8	58.4	68.2	73.4	71.5	62.6	50.9	37.5	29.1	50.2
Mean Minimum Temp. (°F)	14.6	19.9	26.8	34.6	44.2	53.0	57.9	56.0	46.7	35.4	24.5	16.4	35.8
Extreme Maximum Temp. (°F)	74	76	82	91	95	103	106	102	99	91	80	75	106
Extreme Minimum Temp. (°F)	-25	-20	-4	-3	25	35	42	41	17	5	-7	-24	-25
Days Maximum Temp. ≥ 90°F	0	0	0	0	1	8	15	12	3	0	0	0	39
Days Maximum Temp. ≤ 32°F	8	4	2	0	0	0	0	0	0	0	3	6	23
Days Minimum Temp. ≤ 32°F	30	27	24	12	1	0	0	0	1	11	25	30	161
Days Minimum Temp. ≤ 0°F	4	1	0	0	0	0	0	0	0	0	0	3	8
Heating Degree Days (base 65°F)	1,155	889	737	479	215	41	4	6	122	432	819	1,107	6,006
Cooling Degree Days (base 65°F)	0	0	0	1	20	139	271	222	62	1	0	0	716
Mean Precipitation (in.)	0.53	0.38	1.18	1.84	2.53	1.89	1.46	1.18	1.20	0.91	0.83	0.47	14.40
Days With ≥ 0.1" Precipitation	2	1	3	4	6	4	3	3	3	2	2	2	35
Days With ≥ 1.0" Precipitation	0	0	0	0	0	0	0	0	0	0	0	0	0
Mean Snowfall (in.)	6.5	4.3	7.7	6.3	0.8	0.0	0.0	0.0	0.9	2.8	8.5	5.7	43.5
Days With ≥ 1.0" Snow Depth	15	8	4	2	0	0	0	0	0	1	6	12	48

Green Mountain Dam *Summit County*   Elevation: 7,739 ft.   Latitude: 39° 53' N   Longitude: 106° 20' W

	JAN	FEB	MAR	APR	MAY	JUN	JUL	AUG	SEP	OCT	NOV	DEC	YEAR
Mean Maximum Temp. (°F)	28.6	33.8	42.6	51.3	62.4	73.4	78.1	76.5	68.7	56.7	41.0	30.5	53.6
Mean Temp. (°F)	16.4	19.9	29.0	37.7	47.6	56.4	61.1	59.8	52.3	41.7	29.3	19.0	39.2
Mean Minimum Temp. (°F)	4.1	5.9	15.4	24.0	32.7	39.3	44.0	43.1	36.0	26.6	17.5	7.5	24.7
Extreme Maximum Temp. (°F)	52	58	63	73	80	87	91	91	86	78	67	57	91
Extreme Minimum Temp. (°F)	-31	-46	-26	-8	12	23	24	24	14	1	-17	-25	-46
Days Maximum Temp. ≥ 90°F	0	0	0	0	0	0	0	0	0	0	0	0	0
Days Maximum Temp. ≤ 32°F	19	11	4	1	0	0	0	0	0	1	6	18	60
Days Minimum Temp. ≤ 32°F	31	28	31	27	15	3	1	1	9	25	29	31	231
Days Minimum Temp. ≤ 0°F	13	10	3	0	0	0	0	0	0	0	2	9	37
Heating Degree Days (base 65°F)	1,501	1,269	1,108	812	534	253	123	158	374	716	1,066	1,419	9,333
Cooling Degree Days (base 65°F)	0	0	0	0	0	1	7	5	0	0	0	0	13
Mean Precipitation (in.)	0.94	0.94	1.38	1.39	1.62	1.14	1.60	1.33	1.31	1.17	1.16	0.99	14.97
Days With ≥ 0.1" Precipitation	4	3	5	5	5	4	5	4	4	4	4	4	51
Days With ≥ 1.0" Precipitation	0	0	0	0	0	0	0	0	0	0	0	0	0
Mean Snowfall (in.)	13.1	12.4	13.7	7.7	2.6	0.3	0.0	0.0	0.4	3.3	10.8	11.8	76.1
Days With ≥ 1.0" Snow Depth	28	25	22	6	1	0	0	0	0	2	10	23	117

Gunnison 3 SW *Gunnison County*   Elevation: 7,637 ft.   Latitude: 38° 32' N   Longitude: 106° 58' W

	JAN	FEB	MAR	APR	MAY	JUN	JUL	AUG	SEP	OCT	NOV	DEC	YEAR
Mean Maximum Temp. (°F)	26.3	31.9	43.6	55.1	65.6	75.8	80.3	78.5	71.5	60.5	43.7	30.0	55.2
Mean Temp. (°F)	10.2	16.0	28.9	38.4	47.6	55.9	61.4	59.8	52.2	41.1	27.7	14.2	37.8
Mean Minimum Temp. (°F)	-6.0	0.1	14.1	21.7	29.5	36.0	42.5	40.9	32.6	21.7	11.7	-1.7	20.3
Extreme Maximum Temp. (°F)	55	57	67	78	82	91	92	91	89	79	66	57	92
Extreme Minimum Temp. (°F)	-40	-38	-23	-14	12	22	28	24	9	-6	-26	-37	-40
Days Maximum Temp. ≥ 90°F	0	0	0	0	0	0	1	0	0	0	0	0	1
Days Maximum Temp. ≤ 32°F	21	13	3	0	0	0	0	0	0	0	4	19	60
Days Minimum Temp. ≤ 32°F	30	28	30	29	21	8	0	3	15	28	29	31	252
Days Minimum Temp. ≤ 0°F	21	14	3	0	0	0	0	0	0	0	3	18	59
Heating Degree Days (base 65°F)	1,695	1,377	1,112	790	532	266	111	159	379	733	1,112	1,569	9,835
Cooling Degree Days (base 65°F)	0	0	0	0	*0*	1	11	*5*	0	0	0	0	*17*
Mean Precipitation (in.)	0.73	0.59	0.53	0.65	0.80	0.61	1.29	1.64	1.10	0.77	0.58	0.76	10.05
Days With ≥ 0.1" Precipitation	3	2	2	2	3	2	4	5	3	3	2	2	33
Days With ≥ 1.0" Precipitation	0	0	0	0	0	0	0	0	0	0	0	0	0
Mean Snowfall (in.)	11.2	7.2	6.4	3.6	*0.6*	trace	0.0	0.0	trace	1.6	5.6	9.7	*45.9*
Days With ≥ 1.0" Snow Depth	*25*	*22*	*8*	*1*	0	0	0	0	0	*1*	*6*	*16*	*79*

Hayden *Routt County*   Elevation: 6,437 ft.   Latitude: 40° 30' N   Longitude: 107° 15' W

	JAN	FEB	MAR	APR	MAY	JUN	JUL	AUG	SEP	OCT	NOV	DEC	YEAR
Mean Maximum Temp. (°F)	29.6	34.5	44.8	56.9	67.9	78.8	84.8	83.1	74.2	61.4	44.1	31.9	57.7
Mean Temp. (°F)	18.2	22.4	32.6	42.6	52.2	61.0	66.9	65.5	56.9	45.4	32.0	20.5	43.0
Mean Minimum Temp. (°F)	6.9	10.3	20.3	28.3	36.4	43.2	48.9	47.9	39.5	29.3	19.7	9.0	28.3
Extreme Maximum Temp. (°F)	60	61	72	80	88	95	98	98	94	83	74	61	98
Extreme Minimum Temp. (°F)	-34	-44	-16	-3	15	25	32	28	14	-1	-17	-33	-44
Days Maximum Temp. ≥ 90°F	0	0	0	0	0	2	5	3	0	0	0	0	10
Days Maximum Temp. ≤ 32°F	18	10	3	0	0	0	0	0	0	0	5	16	52
Days Minimum Temp. ≤ 32°F	31	28	30	22	7	1	0	0	5	21	28	31	204
Days Minimum Temp. ≤ 0°F	9	6	1	0	0	0	0	0	0	0	1	7	24
Heating Degree Days (base 65°F)	1,444	1,197	999	665	390	138	22	37	244	601	985	1,374	8,096
Cooling Degree Days (base 65°F)	0	0	0	0	0	23	88	65	8	0	0	0	184
Mean Precipitation (in.)	1.63	1.17	1.25	1.59	1.62	1.17	1.45	1.30	1.42	1.73	1.50	1.49	17.32
Days With ≥ 0.1" Precipitation	6	4	5	5	5	3	4	4	5	5	5	5	55
Days With ≥ 1.0" Precipitation	0	0	0	0	0	0	0	0	0	0	0	0	0
Mean Snowfall (in.)	29.2	18.5	14.6	8.8	1.5	0.3	0.0	0.0	0.2	6.3	17.7	24.3	121.4
Days With ≥ 1.0" Snow Depth	30	27	18	*2*	0	0	0	0	0	2	12	26	*117*

Hermit 7 ESE *Mineral County*   Elevation: 8,999 ft.   Latitude: 37° 46' N   Longitude: 107° 08' W

	JAN	FEB	MAR	APR	MAY	JUN	JUL	AUG	SEP	OCT	NOV	DEC	YEAR
Mean Maximum Temp. (°F)	28.0	32.6	37.7	45.4	58.8	70.6	74.8	72.6	67.3	57.8	42.7	30.6	51.6
Mean Temp. (°F)	10.5	14.9	21.6	29.9	41.8	50.6	56.2	55.0	48.3	38.7	24.9	13.0	33.8
Mean Minimum Temp. (°F)	-7.1	-2.8	5.5	14.4	24.7	30.5	37.5	37.3	29.4	19.5	7.0	-4.7	15.9
Extreme Maximum Temp. (°F)	56	59	62	73	78	88	90	87	83	78	69	60	90
Extreme Minimum Temp. (°F)	-45	-40	-30	-25	2	15	23	23	9	-8	-28	-44	-45
Days Maximum Temp. ≥ 90°F	0	0	0	0	0	0	0	0	0	0	0	0	0
Days Maximum Temp. ≤ 32°F	21	15	10	2	0	0	0	0	0	0	6	20	74
Days Minimum Temp. ≤ 32°F	31	28	31	30	28	20	6	6	20	29	30	31	290
Days Minimum Temp. ≤ 0°F	23	18	10	2	0	0	0	0	0	0	8	21	82
Heating Degree Days (base 65°F)	1,686	1,408	1,339	1,047	714	426	268	303	493	809	1,198	1,608	11,299
Cooling Degree Days (base 65°F)	0	0	0	0	0	0	0	0	0	0	0	0	0
Mean Precipitation (in.)	0.68	0.68	1.13	1.05	1.04	0.82	2.30	2.45	1.54	1.42	1.16	0.80	15.07
Days With ≥ 0.1" Precipitation	2	2	3	3	3	3	7	8	4	3	3	2	43
Days With ≥ 1.0" Precipitation	0	0	0	0	0	0	0	0	0	0	0	0	0
Mean Snowfall (in.)	*8.9*	9.0	13.4	*7.6*	1.3	0.0	0.0	0.0	0.2	4.2	*10.6*	10.8	*66.0*
Days With ≥ 1.0" Snow Depth	na	na	na	na	0	0	0	0	0	*0*	na	na	na

Holly *Prowers County*   Elevation: 3,389 ft.   Latitude: 38° 03' N   Longitude: 102° 07' W

	JAN	FEB	MAR	APR	MAY	JUN	JUL	AUG	SEP	OCT	NOV	DEC	YEAR
Mean Maximum Temp. (°F)	43.6	50.2	58.9	68.8	77.7	89.2	93.9	91.4	82.5	71.5	55.4	45.9	69.1
Mean Temp. (°F)	28.5	34.2	42.5	52.3	62.1	72.8	77.9	75.6	66.2	53.9	39.6	30.9	53.0
Mean Minimum Temp. (°F)	13.4	18.2	26.0	35.7	46.4	56.3	61.9	59.8	49.8	36.2	23.7	15.8	36.9
Extreme Maximum Temp. (°F)	79	84	92	99	102	109	109	107	104	95	86	76	109
Extreme Minimum Temp. (°F)	-28	-22	-9	10	25	38	40	40	19	13	-9	-22	-28
Days Maximum Temp. ≥ 90°F	0	0	0	1	4	16	23	20	9	1	0	0	74
Days Maximum Temp. ≤ 32°F	7	4	1	0	0	0	0	0	0	0	2	5	19
Days Minimum Temp. ≤ 32°F	31	27	25	11	1	0	0	0	1	9	26	30	161
Days Minimum Temp. ≤ 0°F	3	2	0	0	0	0	0	0	0	0	0	2	7
Heating Degree Days (base 65°F)	1,125	864	691	385	142	16	2	3	85	347	756	1,053	5,469
Cooling Degree Days (base 65°F)	0	0	0	10	54	250	407	342	132	9	0	0	1,204
Mean Precipitation (in.)	0.34	0.38	1.00	1.27	2.59	2.43	2.61	2.91	1.36	0.97	0.66	0.32	16.84
Days With ≥ 0.1" Precipitation	1	1	3	3	5	5	5	4	4	2	2	1	36
Days With ≥ 1.0" Precipitation	0	0	0	0	1	1	0	1	0	0	0	0	3
Mean Snowfall (in.)	5.4	4.5	5.8	1.9	trace	0.0	0.0	0.0	trace	0.8	3.7	4.5	26.6
Days With ≥ 1.0" Snow Depth	*9*	*6*	*2*	0	0	0	0	0	0	0	2	5	*24*

Holyoke *Phillips County*   Elevation: 3,727 ft.   Latitude: 40° 35' N   Longitude: 102° 18' W

	JAN	FEB	MAR	APR	MAY	JUN	JUL	AUG	SEP	OCT	NOV	DEC	YEAR
Mean Maximum Temp. (°F)	39.9	46.3	53.3	62.8	72.2	82.8	88.2	86.4	77.6	65.8	51.0	43.0	64.1
Mean Temp. (°F)	26.8	32.4	39.2	48.4	58.5	68.6	73.8	72.1	62.8	50.7	37.5	29.5	50.0
Mean Minimum Temp. (°F)	13.6	18.4	25.0	34.0	44.8	54.3	59.4	57.7	47.8	35.6	23.8	16.0	35.9
Extreme Maximum Temp. (°F)	75	78	84	92	97	105	109	105	99	90	83	73	109
Extreme Minimum Temp. (°F)	-19	-24	-8	2	22	34	41	41	18	3	-11	-33	-33
Days Maximum Temp. ≥ 90°F	0	0	0	0	1	8	15	12	4	0	0	0	40
Days Maximum Temp. ≤ 32°F	8	5	3	0	0	0	0	0	0	0	3	6	25
Days Minimum Temp. ≤ 32°F	30	27	26	13	2	0	0	0	1	10	26	30	165
Days Minimum Temp. ≤ 0°F	5	2	0	0	0	0	0	0	0	0	0	3	10
Heating Degree Days (base 65°F)	1,179	915	794	493	222	41	6	10	133	439	820	1,093	6,145
Cooling Degree Days (base 65°F)	0	0	0	3	29	147	277	237	75	3	0	0	771
Mean Precipitation (in.)	0.50	0.47	1.27	1.77	3.45	2.95	2.65	2.13	1.07	0.83	0.73	0.37	18.19
Days With ≥ 0.1" Precipitation	2	1	3	4	7	6	5	4	3	2	2	1	40
Days With ≥ 1.0" Precipitation	0	0	0	0	1	1	1	1	0	0	0	0	4
Mean Snowfall (in.)	6.2	4.0	*8.1*	3.0	0.2	0.0	0.0	0.0	0.3	1.4	5.6	4.8	*33.6*
Days With ≥ 1.0" Snow Depth	10	7	4	2	0	0	0	0	0	0	4	6	33

Kassler *Jefferson County*   Elevation: 5,498 ft.   Latitude: 39° 29' N   Longitude: 105° 06' W

	JAN	FEB	MAR	APR	MAY	JUN	JUL	AUG	SEP	OCT	NOV	DEC	YEAR
Mean Maximum Temp. (°F)	45.6	49.0	54.3	61.2	70.4	81.6	87.2	85.3	77.4	66.4	53.6	46.4	64.9
Mean Temp. (°F)	30.2	34.0	39.8	46.9	56.3	66.7	72.5	70.9	62.4	50.9	38.9	31.3	50.1
Mean Minimum Temp. (°F)	15.0	19.2	25.3	32.5	42.1	51.7	57.7	56.5	47.4	35.5	24.2	16.1	35.3
Extreme Maximum Temp. (°F)	76	76	83	88	94	105	105	100	98	90	82	75	105
Extreme Minimum Temp. (°F)	-26	-25	-10	-10	22	32	37	40	18	-8	-14	-31	-31
Days Maximum Temp. ≥ 90°F	0	0	0	0	0	6	12	9	3	0	0	0	30
Days Maximum Temp. ≤ 32°F	5	3	2	0	0	0	0	0	0	0	2	5	17
Days Minimum Temp. ≤ 32°F	29	25	24	15	3	0	0	0	2	11	23	29	161
Days Minimum Temp. ≤ 0°F	4	2	0	0	0	0	0	0	0	0	1	4	11
Heating Degree Days (base 65°F)	1,073	868	773	537	276	65	8	13	139	433	777	1,039	6,001
Cooling Degree Days (base 65°F)	0	0	0	1	13	113	242	202	70	2	0	0	643
Mean Precipitation (in.)	0.55	0.58	1.72	2.23	2.80	1.72	1.62	1.71	1.53	1.31	1.38	0.78	17.93
Days With ≥ 0.1" Precipitation	2	2	5	5	6	4	4	4	4	3	3	2	44
Days With ≥ 1.0" Precipitation	0	0	0	0	1	0	0	0	0	0	0	0	1
Mean Snowfall (in.)	10.8	8.2	15.6	10.7	0.1	0.0	0.0	0.0	1.4	3.8	13.1	13.6	77.3
Days With ≥ 1.0" Snow Depth	12	8	7	4	0	0	0	0	0	0	2	8	13	54

Kit Carson *Cheyenne County*   Elevation: 4,278 ft.   Latitude: 38° 46' N   Longitude: 102° 47' W

	JAN	FEB	MAR	APR	MAY	JUN	JUL	AUG	SEP	OCT	NOV	DEC	YEAR
Mean Maximum Temp. (°F)	41.9	47.5	56.1	65.0	74.4	85.6	91.1	89.2	80.3	68.4	52.9	43.9	66.4
Mean Temp. (°F)	26.3	31.7	40.0	48.6	*59.1*	*69.6*	75.1	73.4	64.2	51.1	37.3	28.4	*50.4*
Mean Minimum Temp. (°F)	10.7	15.9	24.0	32.2	43.6	53.6	58.9	57.4	47.8	33.7	21.5	12.9	34.3
Extreme Maximum Temp. (°F)	77	78	86	92	*98*	108	107	105	102	91	83	76	*108*
Extreme Minimum Temp. (°F)	-30	-24	-8	5	23	*31*	36	39	17	9	-20	-29	*-30*
Days Maximum Temp. ≥ 90°F	0	0	0	0	2	11	20	17	7	0	0	0	*57*
Days Maximum Temp. ≤ 32°F	7	4	2	0	0	0	0	0	0	0	2	6	21
Days Minimum Temp. ≤ 32°F	31	28	27	15	2	0	0	0	1	14	27	31	176
Days Minimum Temp. ≤ 0°F	5	2	0	0	0	0	0	0	0	0	0	3	10
Heating Degree Days (base 65°F)	1,193	934	768	486	*208*	*34*	3	5	112	425	823	1,128	*6,119*
Cooling Degree Days (base 65°F)	0	0	0	2	*29*	*169*	319	269	94	1	0	0	*883*
Mean Precipitation (in.)	0.28	0.30	0.81	1.05	2.78	2.40	2.57	2.25	1.07	0.81	0.54	0.26	15.12
Days With ≥ 0.1" Precipitation	1	1	2	3	5	4	5	5	3	2	*2*	1	*34*
Days With ≥ 1.0" Precipitation	0	0	0	0	1	1	1	1	0	0	0	0	4
Mean Snowfall (in.)	*2.9*	*1.9*	*2.4*	2.3	0.4	0.0	0.0	0.0	0.3	0.7	na	2.5	na
Days With ≥ 1.0" Snow Depth	na	*1*	na	*0*	0	0	0	0	0	0	na	na	na

La Junta 4 NNE *Otero County*   Elevation: 4,202 ft.   Latitude: 38° 03' N   Longitude: 103° 32' W

	JAN	FEB	MAR	APR	MAY	JUN	JUL	AUG	SEP	OCT	NOV	DEC	YEAR
Mean Maximum Temp. (°F)	43.4	*50.1*	59.6	68.6	77.5	89.9	94.6	92.2	83.1	71.0	55.2	45.5	*69.2*
Mean Temp. (°F)	29.6	*35.6*	44.3	53.1	62.7	73.9	79.0	76.9	67.5	54.8	40.3	31.5	*54.1*
Mean Minimum Temp. (°F)	15.7	*21.0*	28.9	37.6	47.9	57.9	63.3	61.5	51.8	38.6	25.3	17.4	*38.9*
Extreme Maximum Temp. (°F)	78	*81*	90	95	100	110	108	107	104	95	85	81	*110*
Extreme Minimum Temp. (°F)	-16	*-20*	0	13	26	40	50	43	22	9	-11	-21	*-21*
Days Maximum Temp. ≥ 90°F	0	*0*	0	1	4	17	25	22	10	1	0	0	*80*
Days Maximum Temp. ≤ 32°F	8	*4*	1	0	0	0	0	0	0	0	2	6	21
Days Minimum Temp. ≤ 32°F	30	*26*	21	7	0	0	0	0	1	6	24	30	*145*
Days Minimum Temp. ≤ 0°F	3	*2*	0	0	0	0	0	0	0	0	0	2	7
Heating Degree Days (base 65°F)	1,088	*824*	636	361	131	14	1	2	70	318	735	1,033	*5,213*
Cooling Degree Days (base 65°F)	0	*0*	1	*11*	64	274	431	381	155	9	0	0	*1,326*
Mean Precipitation (in.)	0.31	*0.35*	0.87	1.31	1.83	1.41	2.01	1.51	0.82	0.60	0.51	0.27	*11.80*
Days With ≥ 0.1" Precipitation	1	*1*	2	4	4	3	4	3	2	2	2	1	29
Days With ≥ 1.0" Precipitation	0	*0*	0	0	0	0	0	0	0	0	0	0	*0*
Mean Snowfall (in.)	4.4	*4.4*	7.0	3.5	0.6	trace	trace	trace	0.2	1.5	4.3	4.0	*29.9*
Days With ≥ 1.0" Snow Depth	10	*6*	2	1	0	0	0	0	0	0	3	7	29

Lake City *Hinsdale County*   Elevation: 8,667 ft.   Latitude: 38° 01' N   Longitude: 107° 19' W

	JAN	FEB	MAR	APR	MAY	JUN	JUL	AUG	SEP	OCT	NOV	DEC	YEAR
Mean Maximum Temp. (°F)	34.6	39.2	45.3	53.0	62.4	73.3	76.6	74.0	69.2	60.1	45.1	35.4	55.7
Mean Temp. (°F)	16.3	21.2	29.5	37.4	46.6	55.7	60.3	58.5	52.3	42.7	28.8	18.2	38.9
Mean Minimum Temp. (°F)	-2.1	3.0	13.7	21.8	30.6	38.1	44.0	42.9	35.3	25.1	12.4	0.9	22.2
Extreme Maximum Temp. (°F)	56	62	68	78	82	88	98	90	88	83	70	59	98
Extreme Minimum Temp. (°F)	-38	-30	-18	-10	7	16	25	27	12	-2	-20	-32	-38
Days Maximum Temp. ≥ 90°F	0	0	0	0	0	0	0	0	0	0	0	0	0
Days Maximum Temp. ≤ 32°F	12	5	2	0	0	0	0	0	0	0	3	11	33
Days Minimum Temp. ≤ 32°F	31	28	31	28	19	5	0	1	10	26	29	31	239
Days Minimum Temp. ≤ 0°F	19	12	3	0	0	0	0	0	0	0	4	15	53
Heating Degree Days (base 65°F)	1,504	1,233	1,093	823	564	274	143	196	377	685	1,080	1,444	9,416
Cooling Degree Days (base 65°F)	0	0	0	0	0	2	6	1	0	0	0	0	9
Mean Precipitation (in.)	0.78	0.69	0.96	1.08	1.07	0.79	2.04	2.24	1.38	1.21	1.08	0.86	14.18
Days With ≥ 0.1" Precipitation	3	2	4	3	3	3	6	7	4	4	4	3	46
Days With ≥ 1.0" Precipitation	0	0	0	0	0	0	0	0	0	0	0	0	0
Mean Snowfall (in.)	12.4	9.7	15.0	9.9	4.0	0.2	0.0	0.0	0.2	4.0	14.4	14.0	83.8
Days With ≥ 1.0" Snow Depth	na	*10*	na	na	*1*	0	0	0	0	*1*	*8*	12	na

Lake George 8 SW *Park County*   Elevation: 8,517 ft.   Latitude: 38° 54' N   Longitude: 105° 28' W

	JAN	FEB	MAR	APR	MAY	JUN	JUL	AUG	SEP	OCT	NOV	DEC	YEAR
Mean Maximum Temp. (°F)	31.5	35.8	42.3	49.5	59.7	70.7	75.6	73.3	67.0	56.8	42.1	33.0	53.1
Mean Temp. (°F)	14.9	19.0	27.9	35.7	45.8	55.2	60.7	59.1	51.8	41.3	28.2	17.7	38.1
Mean Minimum Temp. (°F)	-1.7	2.1	13.4	21.8	31.9	39.7	45.7	44.7	36.5	25.7	14.3	2.3	23.0
Extreme Maximum Temp. (°F)	61	60	68	73	78	87	88	85	83	79	65	58	88
Extreme Minimum Temp. (°F)	-43	-42	-22	-14	10	24	32	30	9	-2	-33	-40	-43
Days Maximum Temp. ≥ 90°F	0	0	0	0	0	0	0	0	0	0	0	0	0
Days Maximum Temp. ≤ 32°F	15	10	6	2	0	0	0	0	0	1	6	14	54
Days Minimum Temp. ≤ 32°F	31	28	31	28	16	3	0	0	7	28	30	31	233
Days Minimum Temp. ≤ 0°F	17	12	4	1	0	0	0	0	0	0	3	13	50
Heating Degree Days (base 65°F)	1,547	1,293	1,145	874	587	287	131	179	390	729	1,096	1,462	9,720
Cooling Degree Days (base 65°F)	0	0	0	0	0	0	1	5	1	0	0	0	7
Mean Precipitation (in.)	0.30	0.29	0.82	0.95	1.40	1.38	2.28	2.55	1.11	0.76	0.50	0.38	12.72
Days With ≥ 0.1" Precipitation	1	1	3	3	3	4	6	7	3	2	2	1	36
Days With ≥ 1.0" Precipitation	0	0	0	0	0	0	0	0	0	0	0	0	0
Mean Snowfall (in.)	5.3	5.0	13.7	13.1	3.2	0.3	0.0	0.0	1.1	5.6	*7.5*	7.4	*62.2*
Days With ≥ 1.0" Snow Depth	21	16	14	8	1	0	0	0	0	3	11	19	93

Lakewood *Jefferson County*   Elevation: 5,639 ft.   Latitude: 39° 45' N   Longitude: 105° 07' W

	JAN	FEB	MAR	APR	MAY	JUN	JUL	AUG	SEP	OCT	NOV	DEC	YEAR
Mean Maximum Temp. (°F)	43.7	46.9	52.4	58.9	68.7	79.7	85.8	83.9	75.6	64.7	51.5	45.1	63.1
Mean Temp. (°F)	30.7	34.0	39.6	46.1	55.6	65.8	71.7	70.1	61.4	50.4	38.6	32.1	49.7
Mean Minimum Temp. (°F)	17.6	21.2	26.8	33.2	42.4	51.9	57.6	56.1	47.1	36.1	25.7	19.0	36.2
Extreme Maximum Temp. (°F)	72	76	81	85	93	104	101	100	96	88	88	74	104
Extreme Minimum Temp. (°F)	-18	-23	-3	-1	12	27	37	43	16	5	-5	-25	-25
Days Maximum Temp. ≥ 90°F	0	0	0	0	0	4	10	6	2	0	0	0	22
Days Maximum Temp. ≤ 32°F	6	4	2	0	0	0	0	0	0	0	3	5	20
Days Minimum Temp. ≤ 32°F	28	24	24	14	2	0	0	0	1	10	23	28	154
Days Minimum Temp. ≤ 0°F	3	2	0	0	0	0	0	0	0	0	0	2	7
Heating Degree Days (base 65°F)	1,059	867	780	560	296	78	10	15	156	447	784	1,014	6,066
Cooling Degree Days (base 65°F)	0	0	0	1	11	103	223	177	54	2	0	0	571
Mean Precipitation (in.)	0.46	0.45	1.43	2.07	2.58	2.19	1.82	1.78	1.47	1.04	1.16	0.59	17.04
Days With ≥ 0.1" Precipitation	2	2	4	5	6	4	4	4	4	3	3	2	43
Days With ≥ 1.0" Precipitation	0	0	0	0	1	1	0	0	0	0	0	0	2
Mean Snowfall (in.)	7.7	6.7	10.7	9.0	1.2	0.0	0.0	0.0	1.1	3.4	10.6	7.9	58.3
Days With ≥ 1.0" Snow Depth	12	8	7	4	1	0	0	0	0	2	9	12	55

Lamar *Prowers County*   Elevation: 3,625 ft.   Latitude: 38° 06' N   Longitude: 102° 38' W

	JAN	FEB	MAR	APR	MAY	JUN	JUL	AUG	SEP	OCT	NOV	DEC	YEAR
Mean Maximum Temp. (°F)	43.8	50.8	59.6	69.0	77.6	88.3	93.1	90.7	82.4	70.6	55.0	45.7	68.9
Mean Temp. (°F)	29.1	35.4	43.6	52.9	62.5	72.6	77.8	75.8	66.8	53.8	39.6	31.0	53.4
Mean Minimum Temp. (°F)	14.4	19.9	27.5	36.6	47.4	57.0	62.4	60.8	51.2	36.9	24.2	16.2	37.9
Extreme Maximum Temp. (°F)	80	84	92	98	101	107	106	106	103	95	84	76	107
Extreme Minimum Temp. (°F)	-22	-19	-5	8	28	36	45	40	23	8	-18	-23	-23
Days Maximum Temp. ≥ 90°F	0	0	0	1	4	15	22	19	9	1	0	0	71
Days Maximum Temp. ≤ 32°F	7	3	1	0	0	0	0	0	0	0	2	5	18
Days Minimum Temp. ≤ 32°F	31	27	22	9	1	0	0	0	0	9	26	31	156
Days Minimum Temp. ≤ 0°F	3	1	0	0	0	0	0	0	0	0	0	2	6
Heating Degree Days (base 65°F)	1,105	831	658	369	136	16	1	3	77	348	755	1,049	5,348
Cooling Degree Days (base 65°F)	0	0	0	10	62	240	395	341	137	7	0	0	1,192
Mean Precipitation (in.)	0.42	0.45	1.03	1.32	2.45	2.29	2.33	2.37	1.31	0.83	0.72	0.35	15.87
Days With ≥ 0.1" Precipitation	2	1	3	3	5	4	5	4	3	2	2	1	35
Days With ≥ 1.0" Precipitation	0	0	0	0	0	0	0	0	0	0	0	0	0
Mean Snowfall (in.)	5.4	4.4	6.2	2.1	trace	0.0	0.0	0.0	0.1	2.3	5.0	4.3	29.8
Days With ≥ 1.0" Snow Depth	8	4	2	1	0	0	0	0	0	0	4	6	25

Las Animas *Bent County*   Elevation: 3,887 ft.   Latitude: 38° 04' N   Longitude: 103° 13' W

	JAN	FEB	MAR	APR	MAY	JUN	JUL	AUG	SEP	OCT	NOV	DEC	YEAR
Mean Maximum Temp. (°F)	45.8	52.7	61.9	70.4	79.5	90.5	95.2	92.7	84.1	72.6	57.0	47.3	70.8
Mean Temp. (°F)	30.0	36.3	44.8	53.4	63.4	73.6	78.7	76.5	67.5	55.0	40.7	31.6	54.3
Mean Minimum Temp. (°F)	14.3	19.8	27.6	36.4	47.3	56.7	62.1	60.3	50.9	37.2	24.3	16.1	37.7
Extreme Maximum Temp. (°F)	81	83	91	100	104	109	112	109	104	97	87	78	112
Extreme Minimum Temp. (°F)	-29	-20	-4	11	26	29	42	41	22	6	-13	-21	-29
Days Maximum Temp. ≥ 90°F	0	0	0	1	5	18	25	22	10	1	0	0	82
Days Maximum Temp. ≤ 32°F	6	3	1	0	0	0	0	0	0	0	1	4	15
Days Minimum Temp. ≤ 32°F	31	27	22	9	1	0	0	0	1	9	25	30	155
Days Minimum Temp. ≤ 0°F	3	2	0	0	0	0	0	0	0	0	1	2	8
Heating Degree Days (base 65°F)	1,078	803	621	350	114	12	0	1	64	314	722	1,028	5,107
Cooling Degree Days (base 65°F)	0	0	1	11	77	273	428	374	150	10	0	0	1,324
Mean Precipitation (in.)	0.34	0.41	0.82	1.23	2.13	1.66	2.32	1.56	1.08	0.77	0.54	0.27	13.13
Days With ≥ 0.1" Precipitation	1	1	3	3	5	4	4	3	3	2	1	1	31
Days With ≥ 1.0" Precipitation	0	0	0	0	0	0	1	0	0	0	0	0	1
Mean Snowfall (in.)	3.8	3.5	4.3	1.2	trace	0.0	0.0	0.0	0.2	1.8	4.0	3.2	22.0
Days With ≥ 1.0" Snow Depth	7	3	1	0	0	0	0	0	0	0	3	5	19

Leroy 5 WSW *Logan County*   Elevation: 4,468 ft.   Latitude: 40° 31' N   Longitude: 103° 00' W

	JAN	FEB	MAR	APR	MAY	JUN	JUL	AUG	SEP	OCT	NOV	DEC	YEAR
Mean Maximum Temp. (°F)	38.0	43.6	51.2	60.5	69.6	80.9	88.4	86.1	78.3	65.4	49.6	40.8	62.7
Mean Temp. (°F)	25.8	30.9	37.9	46.6	56.2	66.7	73.3	71.4	62.9	50.3	36.8	28.5	48.9
Mean Minimum Temp. (°F)	13.6	18.2	24.5	32.6	42.7	52.3	58.2	56.5	47.4	35.0	24.0	16.2	35.1
Extreme Maximum Temp. (°F)	75	74	84	91	97	107	108	102	102	92	80	72	108
Extreme Minimum Temp. (°F)	-23	-25	-9	-3	24	35	35	41	14	3	-10	-25	-25
Days Maximum Temp. ≥ 90°F	0	0	0	0	0	6	15	12	5	0	0	0	38
Days Maximum Temp. ≤ 32°F	10	6	4	1	0	0	0	0	0	0	5	8	34
Days Minimum Temp. ≤ 32°F	31	26	25	15	2	0	0	0	1	11	24	29	164
Days Minimum Temp. ≤ 0°F	5	3	1	0	0	0	0	0	0	0	1	3	13
Heating Degree Days (base 65°F)	1,206	956	834	547	283	63	7	16	136	455	839	1,124	6,466
Cooling Degree Days (base 65°F)	0	0	0	1	16	121	266	225	78	5	0	0	712
Mean Precipitation (in.)	0.33	0.33	1.00	1.55	3.11	2.93	3.37	2.00	1.19	0.84	0.57	0.35	17.57
Days With ≥ 0.1" Precipitation	1	1	3	4	7	6	6	5	3	2	2	1	41
Days With ≥ 1.0" Precipitation	0	0	0	0	1	0	1	0	0	0	0	0	2
Mean Snowfall (in.)	6.5	5.2	9.3	7.4	0.9	trace	0.0	0.0	1.0	2.9	7.0	6.3	46.5
Days With ≥ 1.0" Snow Depth	15	9	6	3	0	0	0	0	0	1	5	11	50

Longmont 2 ESE *Boulder County*   Elevation: 4,947 ft.   Latitude: 40° 10' N   Longitude: 105° 04' W

	JAN	FEB	MAR	APR	MAY	JUN	JUL	AUG	SEP	OCT	NOV	DEC	YEAR
Mean Maximum Temp. (°F)	41.9	46.5	54.0	61.9	71.9	82.9	88.7	86.8	78.1	66.6	51.6	43.8	64.6
Mean Temp. (°F)	27.0	31.8	39.1	46.9	57.0	66.8	72.0	70.2	61.0	49.6	36.8	28.8	48.9
Mean Minimum Temp. (°F)	12.0	17.0	24.2	31.8	42.1	50.6	55.3	53.5	44.1	32.5	21.9	13.8	33.2
Extreme Maximum Temp. (°F)	75	77	85	88	96	106	106	104	100	90	80	73	106
Extreme Minimum Temp. (°F)	-30	-28	-10	-7	18	29	40	37	18	1	-16	-31	-31
Days Maximum Temp. ≥ 90°F	0	0	0	0	1	8	15	13	5	0	0	0	42
Days Maximum Temp. ≤ 32°F	8	5	2	0	0	0	0	0	0	0	3	5	23
Days Minimum Temp. ≤ 32°F	30	27	27	16	2	0	0	0	2	15	27	30	176
Days Minimum Temp. ≤ 0°F	5	2	0	0	0	0	0	0	0	0	1	4	12
Heating Degree Days (base 65°F)	1,173	930	795	538	255	58	8	13	160	471	841	1,115	6,357
Cooling Degree Days (base 65°F)	0	0	0	1	15	112	231	185	50	1	0	0	595
Mean Precipitation (in.)	0.42	0.36	1.23	2.02	2.36	1.73	1.12	1.38	1.46	0.81	0.81	0.56	14.26
Days With ≥ 0.1" Precipitation	2	1	3	5	5	4	3	4	2	2	2		37
Days With ≥ 1.0" Precipitation	0	0	0	0	1	0	0	0	0	0	0	0	1
Mean Snowfall (in.)	5.2	3.5	5.5	4.7	0.5	0.0	0.0	0.0	0.6	1.3	5.5	6.6	33.4
Days With ≥ 1.0" Snow Depth	9	na	3	1	0	0	0	0	0	0	1	3	na	na

Manassa *Conejos County*   Elevation: 7,687 ft.   Latitude: 37° 10' N   Longitude: 105° 56' W

	JAN	FEB	MAR	APR	MAY	JUN	JUL	AUG	SEP	OCT	NOV	DEC	YEAR
Mean Maximum Temp. (°F)	34.8	41.6	50.8	59.2	68.2	77.6	80.8	78.7	73.0	63.0	47.8	37.2	59.4
Mean Temp. (°F)	18.2	25.3	34.8	41.8	50.8	59.5	63.7	62.0	55.4	44.8	31.2	20.7	42.4
Mean Minimum Temp. (°F)	1.6	9.0	18.7	24.4	33.4	41.4	46.6	45.3	37.6	26.6	14.7	4.2	25.3
Extreme Maximum Temp. (°F)	63	64	73	80	88	93	94	90	87	82	74	62	94
Extreme Minimum Temp. (°F)	-34	-28	-9	-2	12	23	32	29	15	-4	-20	-28	-34
Days Maximum Temp. ≥ 90°F	0	0	0	0	0	0	1	0	0	0	0	0	1
Days Maximum Temp. ≤ 32°F	12	5	0	0	0	0	0	0	0	0	3	9	29
Days Minimum Temp. ≤ 32°F	31	28	30	25	13	2	0	0	6	24	28	31	218
Days Minimum Temp. ≤ 0°F	14	6	1	0	0	0	0	0	0	0	3	11	35
Heating Degree Days (base 65°F)	1,444	1,116	929	690	434	166	58	97	283	619	1,007	1,368	8,211
Cooling Degree Days (base 65°F)	0	0	0	0	0	9	26	10	1	0	0	0	46
Mean Precipitation (in.)	0.26	0.26	0.42	0.47	0.80	0.47	1.12	1.50	1.07	0.68	0.57	0.34	7.96
Days With ≥ 0.1" Precipitation	1	1	1	2	3	2	4	4	3	2	2	1	26
Days With ≥ 1.0" Precipitation	0	0	0	0	0	0	0	0	0	0	0	0	0
Mean Snowfall (in.)	4.4	4.9	4.6	2.6	0.9	0.0	0.0	0.0	0.0	2.4	4.6	5.8	30.2
Days With ≥ 1.0" Snow Depth	na	na	na	0	0	0	0	0	0	1	3	na	na

Meredith *Pitkin County*   Elevation: 7,824 ft.   Latitude: 39° 22' N   Longitude: 106° 45' W

	JAN	FEB	MAR	APR	MAY	JUN	JUL	AUG	SEP	OCT	NOV	DEC	YEAR
Mean Maximum Temp. (°F)	33.4	37.3	42.0	49.8	62.3	73.4	79.6	78.1	70.8	58.5	42.8	34.6	55.2
Mean Temp. (°F)	17.7	21.2	27.4	35.1	45.7	53.8	59.7	58.5	51.5	40.7	28.4	19.7	38.3
Mean Minimum Temp. (°F)	1.9	5.1	12.9	20.4	28.9	34.2	39.8	38.8	32.1	22.9	14.0	4.8	21.3
Extreme Maximum Temp. (°F)	52	59	65	75	80	90	98	93	90	80	68	59	98
Extreme Minimum Temp. (°F)	-29	-38	-16	-5	11	17	24	23	12	-5	-21	-32	-38
Days Maximum Temp. ≥ 90°F	0	0	0	0	0	0	1	0	0	0	0	0	1
Days Maximum Temp. ≤ 32°F	14	7	4	1	0	0	0	0	0	0	6	12	44
Days Minimum Temp. ≤ 32°F	30	27	30	29	23	12	2	3	15	28	29	30	258
Days Minimum Temp. ≤ 0°F	14	9	3	0	0	0	0	0	0	0	2	10	38
Heating Degree Days (base 65°F)	1,461	1,230	1,163	882	593	330	162	197	399	748	1,089	1,397	9,651
Cooling Degree Days (base 65°F)	0	0	0	0	0	1	6	3	0	0	0	0	10
Mean Precipitation (in.)	1.17	1.12	1.27	1.22	1.51	1.35	1.67	1.66	1.65	1.43	1.17	1.20	16.42
Days With ≥ 0.1" Precipitation	4	4	4	4	4	3	5	5	4	4	4	3	48
Days With ≥ 1.0" Precipitation	0	0	0	0	0	0	0	0	0	0	0	0	0
Mean Snowfall (in.)	17.4	18.3	15.2	7.9	1.5	0.2	0.0	0.0	0.0	1.5	9.3	16.5	87.8
Days With ≥ 1.0" Snow Depth	27	23	24	11	1	0	0	0	0	1	8	na	na

Mesa Verde *Montezuma County*   Elevation: 7,112 ft.   Latitude: 37° 12' N   Longitude: 108° 29' W

	JAN	FEB	MAR	APR	MAY	JUN	JUL	AUG	SEP	OCT	NOV	DEC	YEAR
Mean Maximum Temp. (°F)	39.0	43.7	49.9	58.3	68.7	80.2	85.4	83.0	75.2	63.2	48.8	40.3	61.3
Mean Temp. (°F)	28.4	32.8	38.5	45.2	54.7	65.0	70.7	68.8	61.3	50.1	37.7	29.7	48.6
Mean Minimum Temp. (°F)	17.7	21.9	27.0	32.2	40.6	49.7	56.0	54.5	47.3	36.9	26.4	19.0	35.8
Extreme Maximum Temp. (°F)	59	66	73	79	88	99	100	96	91	82	72	63	100
Extreme Minimum Temp. (°F)	-13	-15	3	4	21	27	38	38	26	10	-2	-15	-15
Days Maximum Temp. ≥ 90°F	0	0	0	0	0	3	7	3	0	0	0	0	13
Days Maximum Temp. ≤ 32°F	7	3	1	0	0	0	0	0	0	0	2	5	18
Days Minimum Temp. ≤ 32°F	30	26	25	16	4	0	0	0	1	8	24	30	164
Days Minimum Temp. ≤ 0°F	1	0	0	0	0	0	0	0	0	0	0	1	2
Heating Degree Days (base 65°F)	1,129	901	816	586	317	80	6	14	137	457	813	1,089	6,345
Cooling Degree Days (base 65°F)	0	0	0	0	4	71	167	123	26	0	0	0	391
Mean Precipitation (in.)	1.83	1.50	1.90	1.25	1.25	0.57	1.75	2.02	1.74	1.81	1.70	1.36	18.68
Days With ≥ 0.1" Precipitation	5	4	5	4	4	2	5	5	5	4	4	4	50
Days With ≥ 1.0" Precipitation	0	0	0	0	0	0	0	0	0	0	0	0	0
Mean Snowfall (in.)	21.0	14.9	14.7	6.3	0.9	trace	0.0	0.0	0.0	2.0	9.8	14.0	83.6
Days With ≥ 1.0" Snow Depth	25	23	14	3	0	0	0	0	0	1	9	21	96

Montrose 2 *Montrose County*　Elevation: 5,784 ft.　Latitude: 38° 29' N　Longitude: 107° 53' W

	JAN	FEB	MAR	APR	MAY	JUN	JUL	AUG	SEP	OCT	NOV	DEC	YEAR
Mean Maximum Temp. (°F)	37.5	44.7	53.9	61.7	71.8	82.8	87.7	85.6	77.4	65.1	49.4	39.0	63.1
Mean Temp. (°F)	25.8	32.4	40.9	47.8	57.2	66.9	72.2	70.4	61.9	50.3	37.3	27.6	49.2
Mean Minimum Temp. (°F)	14.1	20.0	27.9	33.9	42.5	51.1	56.6	55.1	46.4	35.4	25.1	16.1	35.4
Extreme Maximum Temp. (°F)	62	70	79	84	89	98	99	98	93	84	73	64	99
Extreme Minimum Temp. (°F)	-21	-14	7	9	25	30	41	39	26	14	-3	-16	-21
Days Maximum Temp. ≥ 90°F	0	0	0	0	0	6	13	7	1	0	0	0	27
Days Maximum Temp. ≤ 32°F	9	2	0	0	0	0	0	0	0	0	2	7	20
Days Minimum Temp. ≤ 32°F	31	27	23	13	2	0	0	0	1	10	25	30	162
Days Minimum Temp. ≤ 0°F	3	1	0	0	0	0	0	0	0	0	0	1	5
Heating Degree Days (base 65°F)	1,207	914	739	509	246	55	3	8	124	449	825	1,153	6,232
Cooling Degree Days (base 65°F)	0	0	0	0	12	118	228	184	38	0	0	0	580
Mean Precipitation (in.)	0.54	0.36	0.73	0.81	0.97	0.61	1.00	1.10	1.11	1.09	0.89	0.60	9.81
Days With ≥ 0.1" Precipitation	2	2	2	3	3	2	3	3	3	3	3	2	31
Days With ≥ 1.0" Precipitation	0	0	0	0	0	0	0	0	0	0	0	0	0
Mean Snowfall (in.)	na	na	na	*0.2*	0.0	0.0	0.0	0.0	0.0	0.5	na	na	na
Days With ≥ 1.0" Snow Depth	na	na	na	*0*	0	0	0	0	0	0	na	na	na

New Raymer *Weld County*　Elevation: 4,780 ft.　Latitude: 40° 36' N　Longitude: 103° 51' W

	JAN	FEB	MAR	APR	MAY	JUN	JUL	AUG	SEP	OCT	NOV	DEC	YEAR
Mean Maximum Temp. (°F)	39.6	45.9	53.7	61.8	71.8	82.4	89.3	87.3	78.7	66.4	49.5	41.4	64.0
Mean Temp. (°F)	25.7	31.1	38.2	46.0	56.3	66.2	72.6	70.8	61.7	49.6	35.2	27.5	48.4
Mean Minimum Temp. (°F)	11.6	16.3	22.7	30.0	40.7	49.9	55.8	54.3	44.7	32.7	20.8	13.4	32.7
Extreme Maximum Temp. (°F)	73	77	80	88	95	103	105	104	100	88	81	72	105
Extreme Minimum Temp. (°F)	-30	-29	-10	-7	19	29	39	38	10	4	-14	-32	-32
Days Maximum Temp. ≥ 90°F	0	0	0	0	0	7	17	13	4	0	0	0	41
Days Maximum Temp. ≤ 32°F	8	4	2	0	0	0	0	0	0	0	4	7	25
Days Minimum Temp. ≤ 32°F	31	27	27	18	4	0	0	0	2	15	27	30	181
Days Minimum Temp. ≤ 0°F	6	2	1	0	0	0	0	0	0	0	1	4	14
Heating Degree Days (base 65°F)	1,211	951	824	565	273	65	7	10	146	471	887	1,155	6,565
Cooling Degree Days (base 65°F)	0	0	0	1	12	104	240	193	53	1	0	0	604
Mean Precipitation (in.)	0.28	0.18	0.85	1.35	2.52	2.66	2.54	1.98	1.38	0.83	0.47	0.23	15.27
Days With ≥ 0.1" Precipitation	1	0	2	3	6	5	5	4	3	2	2	1	34
Days With ≥ 1.0" Precipitation	0	0	0	0	0	1	1	0	0	0	0	0	2
Mean Snowfall (in.)	5.5	3.1	7.0	5.2	0.4	0.0	0.0	0.0	0.8	2.4	5.9	5.0	35.3
Days With ≥ 1.0" Snow Depth	14	7	4	2	0	0	0	0	0	1	6	11	45

Northdale *Dolores County*　Elevation: 6,679 ft.　Latitude: 37° 49' N　Longitude: 109° 01' W

	JAN	FEB	MAR	APR	MAY	JUN	JUL	AUG	SEP	OCT	NOV	DEC	YEAR
Mean Maximum Temp. (°F)	36.8	41.8	50.3	59.0	69.4	80.9	86.1	83.7	75.8	63.5	48.2	38.5	61.2
Mean Temp. (°F)	23.2	28.4	36.9	43.5	52.5	62.0	68.4	66.9	58.7	47.2	34.6	25.3	45.6
Mean Minimum Temp. (°F)	9.6	15.0	23.5	28.0	35.6	43.0	50.6	50.0	41.6	30.8	20.9	12.1	30.0
Extreme Maximum Temp. (°F)	57	67	72	80	88	97	99	97	98	86	70	64	99
Extreme Minimum Temp. (°F)	-33	-26	-4	-5	16	24	32	32	18	8	-18	-28	-33
Days Maximum Temp. ≥ 90°F	0	0	0	0	0	3	9	4	0	0	0	0	16
Days Maximum Temp. ≤ 32°F	9	3	0	0	0	0	0	0	0	0	2	7	21
Days Minimum Temp. ≤ 32°F	31	28	28	23	10	1	0	0	3	20	28	30	202
Days Minimum Temp. ≤ 0°F	8	3	0	0	0	0	0	0	0	0	1	4	16
Heating Degree Days (base 65°F)	1,289	1,025	864	638	380	120	11	24	194	546	907	1,224	7,222
Cooling Degree Days (base 65°F)	0	0	0	0	1	39	126	95	12	0	0	0	273
Mean Precipitation (in.)	0.76	0.74	0.97	0.79	0.96	0.46	1.35	1.32	1.38	1.80	1.10	0.78	12.41
Days With ≥ 0.1" Precipitation	3	2	4	3	3	1	4	4	4	4	3	2	37
Days With ≥ 1.0" Precipitation	0	0	0	0	0	0	0	0	0	0	0	0	0
Mean Snowfall (in.)	na	na	*7.1*	*1.5*	trace	0.0	0.0	0.0	0.0	0.7	*2.4*	na	na
Days With ≥ 1.0" Snow Depth	na	na	na	*2*	0	0	0	0	0	1	na	*7*	na

Norwood *San Miguel County*　Elevation: 7,017 ft.　Latitude: 38° 08' N　Longitude: 108° 17' W

	JAN	FEB	MAR	APR	MAY	JUN	JUL	AUG	SEP	OCT	NOV	DEC	YEAR
Mean Maximum Temp. (°F)	37.9	42.6	49.6	57.4	67.3	78.6	83.2	81.0	73.2	61.4	47.7	38.9	59.9
Mean Temp. (°F)	23.9	29.2	36.2	42.6	51.6	61.1	66.5	65.0	57.5	46.3	34.2	25.3	45.0
Mean Minimum Temp. (°F)	9.9	15.6	22.9	27.8	35.9	43.6	49.8	48.9	41.8	31.4	20.6	11.6	30.0
Extreme Maximum Temp. (°F)	58	65	71	80	87	97	96	95	89	81	71	60	97
Extreme Minimum Temp. (°F)	-30	-27	-13	-3	8	22	29	30	15	1	-10	-27	-30
Days Maximum Temp. ≥ 90°F	0	0	0	0	0	1	3	1	0	0	0	0	5
Days Maximum Temp. ≤ 32°F	8	3	1	0	0	0	0	0	0	0	2	6	20
Days Minimum Temp. ≤ 32°F	31	27	27	21	9	2	0	0	3	16	28	31	195
Days Minimum Temp. ≤ 0°F	6	3	1	0	0	0	0	0	0	0	1	4	15
Heating Degree Days (base 65°F)	1,267	1,006	885	665	409	136	23	41	225	572	918	1,225	7,372
Cooling Degree Days (base 65°F)	0	0	0	0	1	27	82	52	7	0	0	0	169
Mean Precipitation (in.)	1.04	0.69	1.24	1.21	1.26	0.91	1.91	1.86	1.78	1.72	1.40	0.84	15.86
Days With ≥ 0.1" Precipitation	4	3	4	4	4	3	5	5	4	4	4	3	47
Days With ≥ 1.0" Precipitation	0	0	0	0	0	0	0	0	0	0	0	0	0
Mean Snowfall (in.)	13.7	9.5	*11.0*	6.7	0.9	trace	0.0	0.0	0.1	3.4	*8.5*	*11.6*	*65.4*
Days With ≥ 1.0" Snow Depth	na	na	na	na	0	0	0	0	0	0	*0*	na	na

Ouray *Ouray County*   Elevation: 7,837 ft.   Latitude: 38° 01' N   Longitude: 107° 40' W

	JAN	FEB	MAR	APR	MAY	JUN	JUL	AUG	SEP	OCT	NOV	DEC	YEAR
Mean Maximum Temp. (°F)	36.1	39.1	44.7	52.7	62.8	73.5	77.7	75.8	69.4	58.5	44.1	36.4	55.9
Mean Temp. (°F)	25.2	28.2	33.8	40.9	50.2	59.3	64.3	63.0	56.3	46.0	33.5	26.0	43.9
Mean Minimum Temp. (°F)	14.3	17.3	22.8	29.0	37.5	45.1	50.9	50.2	43.2	33.4	22.9	15.5	31.8
Extreme Maximum Temp. (°F)	59	61	68	75	81	89	91	90	86	84	75	59	91
Extreme Minimum Temp. (°F)	-16	-19	-4	2	18	27	36	34	16	8	-3	-17	-19
Days Maximum Temp. ≥ 90°F	0	0	0	0	0	0	0	0	0	0	0	0	0
Days Maximum Temp. ≤ 32°F	10	6	3	1	0	0	0	0	0	1	5	10	36
Days Minimum Temp. ≤ 32°F	31	28	28	20	7	1	0	0	2	13	26	30	186
Days Minimum Temp. ≤ 0°F	2	1	0	0	0	0	0	0	0	0	0	2	5
Heating Degree Days (base 65°F)	1,227	1,032	961	717	454	178	54	76	258	583	938	1,204	7,682
Cooling Degree Days (base 65°F)	0	0	0	0	0	15	41	22	3	0	0	0	81
Mean Precipitation (in.)	1.78	1.73	2.61	2.29	2.00	1.30	2.07	2.26	2.09	2.29	2.41	1.73	24.56
Days With ≥ 0.1" Precipitation	6	5	8	7	5	4	6	7	6	6	7	6	73
Days With ≥ 1.0" Precipitation	0	0	0	0	0	0	0	0	0	0	0	0	0
Mean Snowfall (in.)	24.3	20.8	27.1	15.5	5.1	0.4	0.0	0.0	0.3	7.4	22.5	21.9	145.3
Days With ≥ 1.0" Snow Depth	30	27	27	12	2	0	0	0	0	4	17	29	148

Palisade *Mesa County*   Elevation: 4,809 ft.   Latitude: 39° 07' N   Longitude: 108° 21' W

	JAN	FEB	MAR	APR	MAY	JUN	JUL	AUG	SEP	OCT	NOV	DEC	YEAR
Mean Maximum Temp. (°F)	39.7	48.1	57.7	66.1	76.5	88.4	94.3	91.7	82.6	69.4	52.9	41.7	67.4
Mean Temp. (°F)	29.4	36.9	45.7	53.1	62.7	73.2	79.2	77.0	68.0	55.5	41.6	31.5	54.5
Mean Minimum Temp. (°F)	19.1	25.6	33.6	40.1	48.9	58.0	64.1	62.3	53.3	41.7	30.3	21.2	41.5
Extreme Maximum Temp. (°F)	61	74	82	89	96	106	108	106	101	90	76	69	108
Extreme Minimum Temp. (°F)	-8	-12	9	16	25	34	46	45	33	20	5	-10	-12
Days Maximum Temp. ≥ 90°F	0	0	0	0	2	15	25	20	6	0	0	0	68
Days Maximum Temp. ≤ 32°F	7	1	0	1	0	0	0	0	0	0	0	4	13
Days Minimum Temp. ≤ 32°F	30	23	13	5	0	0	0	0	0	3	19	30	123
Days Minimum Temp. ≤ 0°F	1	0	0	0	0	0	0	0	0	0	0	0	1
Heating Degree Days (base 65°F)	1,096	787	592	356	129	18	0	0	47	297	695	1,032	5,049
Cooling Degree Days (base 65°F)	0	0	0	9	66	270	444	378	140	9	0	0	1,316
Mean Precipitation (in.)	0.57	0.55	1.21	1.14	1.17	0.73	0.78	0.83	1.06	1.24	0.95	0.61	10.84
Days With ≥ 0.1" Precipitation	2	2	4	4	4	2	2	3	3	3	3	2	34
Days With ≥ 1.0" Precipitation	0	0	0	0	0	0	0	0	0	0	0	0	0
Mean Snowfall (in.)	*4.4*	*1.7*	*1.4*	0.4	trace	trace	0.0	0.0	0.0	trace	1.7	*3.3*	*12.9*
Days With ≥ 1.0" Snow Depth	na	*5*	*1*	0	0	0	0	0	0	0	*1*	*4*	na

Paonia 1 SW *Delta County*   Elevation: 5,577 ft.   Latitude: 38° 51' N   Longitude: 107° 37' W

	JAN	FEB	MAR	APR	MAY	JUN	JUL	AUG	SEP	OCT	NOV	DEC	YEAR
Mean Maximum Temp. (°F)	39.1	45.8	54.5	62.8	73.2	84.4	90.2	88.0	79.0	67.3	51.6	41.4	64.8
Mean Temp. (°F)	26.5	33.0	41.2	48.2	57.5	67.2	73.2	71.5	63.1	52.1	39.0	29.1	50.1
Mean Minimum Temp. (°F)	13.8	20.1	27.9	33.7	41.7	49.9	56.2	55.1	47.1	36.9	26.3	16.4	35.4
Extreme Maximum Temp. (°F)	63	70	77	85	93	101	105	104	97	85	77	67	105
Extreme Minimum Temp. (°F)	-26	-17	-4	7	15	31	43	41	24	13	-4	-16	-26
Days Maximum Temp. ≥ 90°F	0	0	0	0	0	9	18	13	2	0	0	0	42
Days Maximum Temp. ≤ 32°F	7	2	0	0	0	0	0	0	0	0	1	4	14
Days Minimum Temp. ≤ 32°F	30	27	22	12	3	0	0	0	1	7	23	30	155
Days Minimum Temp. ≤ 0°F	4	1	0	0	0	0	0	0	0	0	0	2	7
Heating Degree Days (base 65°F)	1,188	897	731	497	236	50	2	5	105	394	774	1,105	5,984
Cooling Degree Days (base 65°F)	0	0	0	0	13	131	280	235	60	1	0	0	720
Mean Precipitation (in.)	1.17	1.06	1.51	1.25	1.45	0.81	1.16	1.09	1.42	1.69	1.41	1.20	15.22
Days With ≥ 0.1" Precipitation	4	4	5	4	4	3	3	4	4	5	5	4	49
Days With ≥ 1.0" Precipitation	0	0	0	0	0	0	0	0	0	0	0	0	0
Mean Snowfall (in.)	13.3	7.9	*5.9*	2.2	0.3	0.0	0.0	0.0	trace	1.1	5.4	11.1	*47.2*
Days With ≥ 1.0" Snow Depth	19	12	3	1	0	0	0	0	0	0	3	12	50

Parker 6 E *Elbert County*   Elevation: 6,309 ft.   Latitude: 39° 32' N   Longitude: 104° 39' W

	JAN	FEB	MAR	APR	MAY	JUN	JUL	AUG	SEP	OCT	NOV	DEC	YEAR
Mean Maximum Temp. (°F)	42.3	45.7	51.6	59.6	68.5	79.7	85.2	83.5	75.9	65.4	50.1	43.4	62.6
Mean Temp. (°F)	29.7	32.9	38.5	45.8	54.8	65.2	70.9	69.5	61.7	51.1	37.7	31.1	49.1
Mean Minimum Temp. (°F)	17.0	20.1	25.4	32.0	41.0	50.6	56.6	55.4	47.4	36.7	25.2	18.8	35.5
Extreme Maximum Temp. (°F)	73	71	80	85	92	98	99	97	95	88	78	74	99
Extreme Minimum Temp. (°F)	-22	-28	-7	-1	17	30	40	35	11	0	-10	-32	-32
Days Maximum Temp. ≥ 90°F	0	0	0	0	0	3	8	4	1	0	0	0	16
Days Maximum Temp. ≤ 32°F	6	4	2	1	0	0	0	0	0	0	3	6	22
Days Minimum Temp. ≤ 32°F	28	25	24	16	4	0	0	0	2	10	22	27	158
Days Minimum Temp. ≤ 0°F	3	2	1	0	0	0	0	0	0	0	1	2	9
Heating Degree Days (base 65°F)	1,087	900	805	569	316	79	10	13	145	428	814	1,043	6,209
Cooling Degree Days (base 65°F)	0	0	0	1	8	95	206	170	55	4	0	0	539
Mean Precipitation (in.)	0.27	0.30	1.04	1.45	2.59	2.08	2.41	2.10	1.20	0.73	0.85	0.34	15.36
Days With ≥ 0.1" Precipitation	1	1	3	4	6	5	5	5	3	2	2	1	38
Days With ≥ 1.0" Precipitation	0	0	0	0	0	0	0	0	0	0	0	0	0
Mean Snowfall (in.)	4.7	4.3	8.3	9.7	2.2	0.2	0.0	0.0	1.5	4.0	9.0	*5.3*	*49.2*
Days With ≥ 1.0" Snow Depth	14	*9*	6	*3*	0	0	0	0	0	*2*	*8*	*11*	*53*

Rico *Dolores County* Elevation: 8,799 ft. Latitude: 37° 43' N Longitude: 108° 02' W

	JAN	FEB	MAR	APR	MAY	JUN	JUL	AUG	SEP	OCT	NOV	DEC	YEAR
Mean Maximum Temp. (°F)	38.0	40.4	43.7	50.1	60.0	70.5	74.7	72.9	66.3	57.3	45.1	39.2	54.9
Mean Temp. (°F)	21.8	24.3	28.9	35.4	44.0	52.3	57.4	56.2	49.4	40.9	29.9	23.1	38.6
Mean Minimum Temp. (°F)	5.5	8.2	14.0	20.6	28.0	33.9	40.0	39.4	32.4	24.5	14.6	6.9	22.3
Extreme Maximum Temp. (°F)	64	62	65	75	80	87	88	89	83	80	72	61	89
Extreme Minimum Temp. (°F)	-33	-29	-15	-11	4	18	22	22	10	-2	-15	-27	-33
Days Maximum Temp. ≥ 90°F	0	0	0	0	0	0	0	0	0	0	0	0	0
Days Maximum Temp. ≤ 32°F	10	6	2	1	0	0	0	0	0	0	4	8	31
Days Minimum Temp. ≤ 32°F	31	28	31	29	26	12	2	3	15	29	30	31	267
Days Minimum Temp. ≤ 0°F	10	7	3	1	0	0	0	0	0	0	2	9	32
Heating Degree Days (base 65°F)	1,334	1,142	1,112	883	644	376	230	270	463	739	1,047	1,293	9,533
Cooling Degree Days (base 65°F)	0	0	0	0	0	0	0	0	0	0	0	0	0
Mean Precipitation (in.)	2.30	2.32	2.72	1.73	1.76	1.54	2.87	2.97	2.46	2.26	2.11	2.02	27.06
Days With ≥ 0.1" Precipitation	6	6	8	6	5	4	8	8	6	6	5	6	74
Days With ≥ 1.0" Precipitation	0	0	0	0	0	0	0	0	0	0	0	0	0
Mean Snowfall (in.)	29.3	28.8	34.1	17.0	6.2	0.2	0.0	trace	0.3	7.3	21.3	23.2	167.7
Days With ≥ 1.0" Snow Depth	26	24	26	17	3	0	0	0	0	4	15	22	137

Rifle *Garfield County* Elevation: 5,318 ft. Latitude: 39° 32' N Longitude: 107° 48' W

	JAN	FEB	MAR	APR	MAY	JUN	JUL	AUG	SEP	OCT	NOV	DEC	YEAR
Mean Maximum Temp. (°F)	37.3	45.6	55.2	63.7	73.0	84.0	*89.4*	87.8	79.1	67.2	50.6	39.4	*64.4*
Mean Temp. (°F)	23.7	31.4	40.2	47.3	55.8	64.8	*70.9*	69.4	60.6	49.2	36.5	25.7	*47.9*
Mean Minimum Temp. (°F)	10.0	17.0	25.1	30.9	38.6	45.4	*52.4*	50.9	42.1	31.2	22.2	11.9	*31.5*
Extreme Maximum Temp. (°F)	62	69	79	90	91	99	*103*	99	98	*88*	77	65	*103*
Extreme Minimum Temp. (°F)	-27	-32	2	8	17	27	*38*	34	22	*7*	*-9*	-24	*-32*
Days Maximum Temp. ≥ 90°F	0	0	0	0	0	8	*17*	13	2	0	0	0	*40*
Days Maximum Temp. ≤ 32°F	9	2	0	0	0	0	*0*	0	0	0	1	7	*19*
Days Minimum Temp. ≤ 32°F	31	28	26	18	5	0	0	0	3	19	27	30	187
Days Minimum Temp. ≤ 0°F	7	2	0	0	0	0	0	0	0	0	0	4	13
Heating Degree Days (base 65°F)	1,274	943	764	525	281	69	*4*	8	149	483	849	1,212	*6,561*
Cooling Degree Days (base 65°F)	0	0	0	0	3	73	*206*	169	30	0	0	0	*481*
Mean Precipitation (in.)	0.86	0.84	1.07	1.11	1.15	0.92	1.13	1.02	1.19	1.33	1.05	1.06	12.73
Days With ≥ 0.1" Precipitation	3	3	4	4	4	3	3	3	4	4	4	4	43
Days With ≥ 1.0" Precipitation	0	0	0	0	0	0	0	0	0	0	0	0	0
Mean Snowfall (in.)	14.1	9.0	3.9	0.6	trace	trace	0.0	0.0	0.0	1.0	5.1	14.7	48.4
Days With ≥ 1.0" Snow Depth	21	12	2	0	0	0	0	0	0	0	2	13	50

Rocky Ford 2 SE *Otero County* Elevation: 4,169 ft. Latitude: 38° 02' N Longitude: 103° 42' W

	JAN	FEB	MAR	APR	MAY	JUN	JUL	AUG	SEP	OCT	NOV	DEC	YEAR
Mean Maximum Temp. (°F)	46.0	53.1	61.7	70.0	78.8	89.5	93.4	91.1	83.9	73.0	56.6	47.5	70.4
Mean Temp. (°F)	29.9	36.0	44.2	52.6	62.4	72.2	76.6	74.4	66.3	54.2	40.0	31.5	53.4
Mean Minimum Temp. (°F)	13.7	19.0	26.6	35.2	46.0	54.9	59.7	57.7	48.7	35.3	23.3	15.4	36.3
Extreme Maximum Temp. (°F)	78	80	90	95	103	106	106	104	103	94	82	80	106
Extreme Minimum Temp. (°F)	-22	-25	-7	10	21	36	47	39	25	8	-16	-22	-25
Days Maximum Temp. ≥ 90°F	0	0	0	0	3	17	24	20	9	1	0	0	74
Days Maximum Temp. ≤ 32°F	5	3	1	0	0	0	0	0	0	0	1	4	14
Days Minimum Temp. ≤ 32°F	30	27	24	11	1	0	0	0	1	11	26	30	161
Days Minimum Temp. ≤ 0°F	4	2	0	0	0	0	0	0	0	0	1	3	10
Heating Degree Days (base 65°F)	1,083	812	640	370	128	12	1	1	67	334	744	1,032	5,224
Cooling Degree Days (base 65°F)	0	0	0	5	58	234	367	311	119	5	0	0	1,099
Mean Precipitation (in.)	0.26	0.30	0.83	1.21	1.76	1.32	2.08	1.61	0.90	0.72	0.53	0.30	11.82
Days With ≥ 0.1" Precipitation	1	1	2	3	4	3	4	4	2	2	2	1	29
Days With ≥ 1.0" Precipitation	0	0	0	0	0	0	0	0	0	0	0	0	0
Mean Snowfall (in.)	3.8	3.3	5.3	2.5	0.5	0.0	0.0	0.0	0.2	1.7	3.8	4.6	25.7
Days With ≥ 1.0" Snow Depth	7	3	1	1	0	0	0	0	0	0	3	6	21

Ruxton Park *El Paso County* Elevation: 9,048 ft. Latitude: 38° 51' N Longitude: 104° 58' W

	JAN	FEB	MAR	APR	MAY	JUN	JUL	AUG	SEP	OCT	NOV	DEC	YEAR
Mean Maximum Temp. (°F)	32.5	34.7	38.6	44.9	55.1	65.9	70.8	68.6	62.3	52.4	39.6	33.8	49.9
Mean Temp. (°F)	19.4	20.9	25.5	31.9	41.5	50.8	55.4	53.6	47.1	37.7	26.8	20.6	35.9
Mean Minimum Temp. (°F)	6.2	7.1	12.5	18.7	27.9	35.6	39.9	38.6	31.9	23.1	14.0	7.4	21.9
Extreme Maximum Temp. (°F)	57	60	65	71	77	86	86	86	81	76	66	63	86
Extreme Minimum Temp. (°F)	-30	-33	-20	-18	3	14	28	24	4	-9	-25	-30	-33
Days Maximum Temp. ≥ 90°F	0	0	0	0	0	0	0	0	0	0	0	0	0
Days Maximum Temp. ≤ 32°F	14	11	8	4	1	0	0	0	0	2	8	14	62
Days Minimum Temp. ≤ 32°F	31	28	31	29	24	10	1	2	15	28	30	31	260
Days Minimum Temp. ≤ 0°F	9	7	4	1	0	0	0	0	0	0	4	8	33
Heating Degree Days (base 65°F)	1,408	1,239	1,218	988	722	421	292	347	529	839	1,140	1,370	10,513
Cooling Degree Days (base 65°F)	0	0	0	0	0	0	0	1	0	0	0	0	1
Mean Precipitation (in.)	0.55	0.73	2.02	3.21	2.71	2.48	3.82	3.99	1.71	1.30	1.02	0.93	24.47
Days With ≥ 0.1" Precipitation	2	2	6	6	6	6	9	10	5	3	3	3	61
Days With ≥ 1.0" Precipitation	0	0	0	1	0	0	1	1	0	0	0	0	3
Mean Snowfall (in.)	10.1	13.5	30.9	34.9	12.8	1.9	trace	0.0	1.5	13.5	16.4	16.5	152.0
Days With ≥ 1.0" Snow Depth	*21*	*20*	*24*	na	*6*	0	0	0	1	*4*	*17*	na	na

Saguache *Saguache County*   Elevation: 7,690 ft.   Latitude: 38° 05' N   Longitude: 106° 08' W

	JAN	FEB	MAR	APR	MAY	JUN	JUL	AUG	SEP	OCT	NOV	DEC	YEAR
Mean Maximum Temp. (°F)	34.1	40.1	49.1	57.9	66.8	76.5	80.1	77.8	71.9	61.6	46.6	36.0	58.2
Mean Temp. (°F)	18.2	24.3	33.9	41.1	49.8	58.8	63.4	61.6	54.3	44.2	30.8	20.2	41.7
Mean Minimum Temp. (°F)	2.3	8.5	18.6	24.4	32.8	41.0	46.6	45.3	36.8	26.8	14.9	4.4	25.2
Extreme Maximum Temp. (°F)	62	63	75	81	83	97	93	90	88	80	68	60	97
Extreme Minimum Temp. (°F)	-34	-25	-4	-3	8	22	31	26	13	0	-22	-26	-34
Days Maximum Temp. ≥ 90°F	0	0	0	0	0	0	1	0	0	0	0	0	1
Days Maximum Temp. ≤ 32°F	13	6	1	0	0	0	0	0	0	0	3	11	34
Days Minimum Temp. ≤ 32°F	31	28	31	27	14	2	0	1	7	24	30	31	226
Days Minimum Temp. ≤ 0°F	13	6	0	0	0	0	0	0	0	0	2	10	31
Heating Degree Days (base 65°F)	1,444	1,143	957	710	463	187	68	113	314	637	1,020	1,382	8,438
Cooling Degree Days (base 65°F)	0	0	0	0	0	8	28	15	1	0	0	0	52
Mean Precipitation (in.)	0.28	0.19	0.42	0.61	0.73	0.58	1.38	1.61	1.06	0.65	0.52	0.25	8.28
Days With ≥ 0.1" Precipitation	1	1	2	2	2	2	4	5	3	2	2	1	27
Days With ≥ 1.0" Precipitation	0	0	0	0	0	0	0	0	0	0	0	0	0
Mean Snowfall (in.)	4.7	2.8	4.8	3.1	0.4	0.0	0.0	0.0	trace	0.9	3.3	3.6	23.6
Days With ≥ 1.0" Snow Depth	na	na	na	2	0	0	0	0	0	1	3	na	na

Sedgwick 5 S *Sedgwick County*   Elevation: 3,989 ft.   Latitude: 40° 52' N   Longitude: 102° 31' W

	JAN	FEB	MAR	APR	MAY	JUN	JUL	AUG	SEP	OCT	NOV	DEC	YEAR
Mean Maximum Temp. (°F)	38.3	45.2	52.9	62.5	72.1	83.2	89.5	88.3	79.7	66.8	49.9	40.8	64.1
Mean Temp. (°F)	26.3	32.4	39.4	48.3	58.4	68.6	74.5	73.3	64.3	51.8	37.4	28.7	50.3
Mean Minimum Temp. (°F)	14.3	19.6	25.7	34.0	44.6	53.9	59.5	58.1	48.8	36.8	24.8	16.5	36.4
Extreme Maximum Temp. (°F)	73	77	84	94	98	109	108	104	102	93	80	72	109
Extreme Minimum Temp. (°F)	-26	-26	-9	6	21	36	45	42	17	3	-7	-30	-30
Days Maximum Temp. ≥ 90°F	0	0	0	0	1	7	16	14	6	0	0	0	44
Days Maximum Temp. ≤ 32°F	9	5	3	0	0	0	0	0	0	0	3	7	27
Days Minimum Temp. ≤ 32°F	30	26	24	13	1	0	0	0	1	9	24	30	158
Days Minimum Temp. ≤ 0°F	5	2	1	0	0	0	0	0	0	0	0	3	11
Heating Degree Days (base 65°F)	1,193	913	788	497	222	38	4	6	112	407	823	1,121	6,124
Cooling Degree Days (base 65°F)	0	0	0	4	24	154	305	268	99	5	0	0	859
Mean Precipitation (in.)	0.45	0.52	1.27	1.78	3.30	2.92	2.59	1.94	1.20	0.89	0.77	0.44	18.07
Days With ≥ 0.1" Precipitation	1	2	4	4	7	6	5	4	3	3	2	2	43
Days With ≥ 1.0" Precipitation	0	0	0	0	1	1	1	0	0	0	0	0	3
Mean Snowfall (in.)	7.3	6.1	10.2	4.9	0.2	0.0	0.0	0.0	0.4	1.1	6.9	6.0	43.1
Days With ≥ 1.0" Snow Depth	15	9	6	2	0	0	0	0	0	1	5	11	49

Silverton *San Juan County*   Elevation: 9,317 ft.   Latitude: 37° 49' N   Longitude: 107° 40' W

	JAN	FEB	MAR	APR	MAY	JUN	JUL	AUG	SEP	OCT	NOV	DEC	YEAR
Mean Maximum Temp. (°F)	33.9	37.9	42.1	47.4	58.0	68.5	73.3	70.9	64.1	54.7	42.6	34.5	52.3
Mean Temp. (°F)	14.6	18.6	24.9	32.2	42.3	50.2	55.4	54.0	47.1	37.8	25.6	16.2	34.9
Mean Minimum Temp. (°F)	-4.7	-0.6	7.7	16.9	26.5	31.8	37.4	37.1	30.1	20.9	8.5	-2.2	17.4
Extreme Maximum Temp. (°F)	52	55	63	71	75	85	88	83	88	73	68	56	88
Extreme Minimum Temp. (°F)	-38	-39	-24	-18	7	15	21	23	11	-6	-20	-35	-39
Days Maximum Temp. ≥ 90°F	0	0	0	0	0	0	0	0	0	0	0	0	0
Days Maximum Temp. ≤ 32°F	13	7	4	2	0	0	0	0	0	1	4	12	43
Days Minimum Temp. ≤ 32°F	31	28	31	30	27	17	5	6	20	29	30	31	285
Days Minimum Temp. ≤ 0°F	22	15	8	1	0	0	0	0	0	0	7	20	73
Heating Degree Days (base 65°F)	1,556	1,303	1,236	979	697	438	291	334	529	834	1,177	1,506	10,880
Cooling Degree Days (base 65°F)	0	0	0	0	0	0	0	0	0	0	0	0	0
Mean Precipitation (in.)	1.57	1.70	2.26	1.70	1.78	1.27	2.86	3.13	2.86	2.30	1.86	1.76	25.05
Days With ≥ 0.1" Precipitation	5	4	7	6	6	4	8	10	8	6	6	5	75
Days With ≥ 1.0" Precipitation	0	0	0	0	0	0	0	0	0	0	0	0	0
Mean Snowfall (in.)	25.3	24.5	27.8	15.9	5.9	0.2	0.0	0.0	1.0	8.0	26.8	24.0	159.4
Days With ≥ 1.0" Snow Depth	30	26	28	17	2	0	0	0	0	4	19	27	153

Spicer *Jackson County*   Elevation: 8,333 ft.   Latitude: 40° 28' N   Longitude: 106° 28' W

	JAN	FEB	MAR	APR	MAY	JUN	JUL	AUG	SEP	OCT	NOV	DEC	YEAR
Mean Maximum Temp. (°F)	28.7	32.4	39.2	47.4	58.9	69.3	74.9	73.7	66.3	54.2	37.9	29.7	51.1
Mean Temp. (°F)	17.5	20.0	26.4	33.9	43.7	52.0	57.3	56.1	48.8	38.6	25.9	18.4	36.6
Mean Minimum Temp. (°F)	6.3	7.6	13.6	20.4	28.5	34.7	39.7	38.5	31.4	22.9	13.9	7.1	22.0
Extreme Maximum Temp. (°F)	49	52	59	71	77	86	90	88	83	76	65	56	90
Extreme Minimum Temp. (°F)	-37	-50	-31	-17	1	17	22	22	4	-13	-32	-43	-50
Days Maximum Temp. ≥ 90°F	0	0	0	0	0	0	0	0	0	0	0	0	0
Days Maximum Temp. ≤ 32°F	19	12	6	2	0	0	0	0	0	1	9	18	67
Days Minimum Temp. ≤ 32°F	31	28	30	28	24	11	3	5	15	28	30	31	264
Days Minimum Temp. ≤ 0°F	9	7	4	1	0	0	0	0	0	0	4	8	33
Heating Degree Days (base 65°F)	1,468	1,263	1,189	926	653	383	233	268	478	811	1,167	1,437	10,276
Cooling Degree Days (base 65°F)	0	0	0	0	0	0	0	0	0	0	0	0	0
Mean Precipitation (in.)	1.06	0.82	0.93	1.21	1.57	1.27	1.78	1.35	1.37	1.19	1.08	0.99	14.62
Days With ≥ 0.1" Precipitation	4	3	3	4	5	4	6	4	5	4	4	4	50
Days With ≥ 1.0" Precipitation	0	0	0	0	0	0	0	0	0	0	0	0	0
Mean Snowfall (in.)	24.0	20.1	23.2	18.5	5.4	0.7	0.0	0.0	0.7	6.5	21.5	25.0	145.6
Days With ≥ 1.0" Snow Depth	na	na	na	11	1	0	0	0	0	2	11	na	na

Springfield 7 WSW *Baca County*   Elevation: 4,619 ft.   Latitude: 37° 22' N   Longitude: 102° 45' W

	JAN	FEB	MAR	APR	MAY	JUN	JUL	AUG	SEP	OCT	NOV	DEC	YEAR
Mean Maximum Temp. (°F)	46.4	51.9	59.7	68.1	76.2	87.0	91.6	89.0	81.3	70.8	56.3	47.9	68.9
Mean Temp. (°F)	32.2	36.8	43.6	51.7	60.7	71.1	75.8	74.0	66.0	54.9	41.7	34.0	53.6
Mean Minimum Temp. (°F)	17.9	21.6	27.5	35.3	45.3	55.1	60.0	58.9	50.9	38.9	27.1	20.1	38.2
Extreme Maximum Temp. (°F)	79	83	90	97	103	111	109	104	101	92	86	78	111
Extreme Minimum Temp. (°F)	-23	-22	-4	5	23	37	44	44	21	6	-11	-18	-23
Days Maximum Temp. ≥ 90°F	0	0	0	0	2	12	21	15	7	0	0	0	57
Days Maximum Temp. ≤ 32°F	5	3	1	0	0	0	0	0	0	0	2	4	15
Days Minimum Temp. ≤ 32°F	30	26	22	11	2	0	0	0	1	6	21	28	147
Days Minimum Temp. ≤ 0°F	2	1	0	0	0	0	0	0	0	0	0	2	5
Heating Degree Days (base 65°F)	1,011	789	657	398	166	21	1	3	80	317	692	954	5,089
Cooling Degree Days (base 65°F)	0	0	1	7	48	221	358	308	124	11	0	0	1,078
Mean Precipitation (in.)	0.45	0.48	1.06	1.66	2.85	1.97	2.47	2.36	1.44	0.93	0.78	0.41	16.86
Days With ≥ 0.1" Precipitation	1	1	3	4	5	4	5	5	3	2	2	1	36
Days With ≥ 1.0" Precipitation	0	0	0	0	1	0	0	0	0	0	0	0	1
Mean Snowfall (in.)	5.1	4.3	7.1	3.7	1.1	0.0	0.0	0.0	0.4	2.1	5.0	4.9	33.7
Days With ≥ 1.0" Snow Depth	7	3	2	1	0	0	0	0	0	0	0	3	6	22

Steamboat Springs *Routt County*   Elevation: 6,633 ft.   Latitude: 40° 30' N   Longitude: 106° 52' W

	JAN	FEB	MAR	APR	MAY	JUN	JUL	AUG	SEP	OCT	NOV	DEC	YEAR
Mean Maximum Temp. (°F)	28.5	33.9	43.1	53.4	64.4	75.4	82.0	80.7	72.3	59.6	41.9	29.4	55.4
Mean Temp. (°F)	15.5	19.6	29.9	38.9	48.2	55.9	62.1	60.9	52.9	42.0	28.8	16.6	39.3
Mean Minimum Temp. (°F)	2.6	5.2	16.7	24.3	31.8	36.4	42.1	40.9	33.5	24.3	15.6	3.8	23.1
Extreme Maximum Temp. (°F)	55	55	67	77	84	96	95	95	91	81	68	56	96
Extreme Minimum Temp. (°F)	-39	-44	-21	-10	12	22	29	22	12	-4	-28	-37	-44
Days Maximum Temp. ≥ 90°F	0	0	0	0	0	0	2	1	0	0	0	0	3
Days Maximum Temp. ≤ 32°F	21	12	3	0	0	0	0	0	0	0	6	20	62
Days Minimum Temp. ≤ 32°F	31	28	31	27	17	7	1	2	13	27	29	31	244
Days Minimum Temp. ≤ 0°F	14	11	2	0	0	0	0	0	0	0	2	13	42
Heating Degree Days (base 65°F)	1,527	1,276	1,081	777	515	267	99	129	356	706	1,079	1,493	9,305
Cooling Degree Days (base 65°F)	0	0	0	0	0	4	20	9	1	0	0	0	34
Mean Precipitation (in.)	2.64	2.08	2.04	2.34	2.28	1.51	1.48	1.44	1.67	1.93	2.32	2.40	24.13
Days With ≥ 0.1" Precipitation	9	7	7	7	7	4	4	5	5	5	7	8	75
Days With ≥ 1.0" Precipitation	0	0	0	0	0	0	0	0	0	0	0	0	0
Mean Snowfall (in.)	40.5	27.8	20.6	13.0	2.5	0.3	0.0	0.0	0.3	8.1	25.0	35.2	173.3
Days With ≥ 1.0" Snow Depth	30	28	24	6	0	0	0	0	0	3	17	30	138

Sterling *Logan County*   Elevation: 3,937 ft.   Latitude: 40° 37' N   Longitude: 103° 13' W

	JAN	FEB	MAR	APR	MAY	JUN	JUL	AUG	SEP	OCT	NOV	DEC	YEAR
Mean Maximum Temp. (°F)	38.3	45.6	53.5	62.4	72.3	83.9	90.1	88.4	79.2	66.8	50.5	40.6	64.3
Mean Temp. (°F)	24.9	31.6	39.1	48.0	58.4	69.1	74.8	73.1	63.0	50.2	36.3	26.9	49.6
Mean Minimum Temp. (°F)	11.4	17.4	24.7	33.5	44.5	54.2	59.5	57.7	46.7	33.7	22.1	13.3	34.9
Extreme Maximum Temp. (°F)	71	76	85	92	98	110	108	105	103	93	83	74	110
Extreme Minimum Temp. (°F)	-26	-30	-11	-3	23	30	44	39	14	3	-8	-35	-35
Days Maximum Temp. ≥ 90°F	0	0	0	0	1	10	17	15	6	0	0	0	49
Days Maximum Temp. ≤ 32°F	9	5	3	1	0	0	0	0	0	0	3	7	28
Days Minimum Temp. ≤ 32°F	31	28	26	13	2	0	0	0	1	13	27	31	172
Days Minimum Temp. ≤ 0°F	6	3	0	0	0	0	0	0	0	0	1	4	14
Heating Degree Days (base 65°F)	1,236	937	795	506	227	44	5	9	133	452	853	1,174	6,371
Cooling Degree Days (base 65°F)	0	0	0	1	31	169	317	275	86	2	0	0	881
Mean Precipitation (in.)	0.40	0.30	1.05	1.33	2.81	2.95	2.58	1.86	1.18	0.86	0.64	0.32	16.28
Days With ≥ 0.1" Precipitation	1	1	3	3	6	5	5	4	3	2	2	1	36
Days With ≥ 1.0" Precipitation	0	0	0	0	1	1	1	0	0	0	0	0	3
Mean Snowfall (in.)	5.2	*3.6*	*4.8*	2.3	0.1	0.0	0.0	0.0	0.3	*0.4*	*4.5*	*4.3*	*25.5*
Days With ≥ 1.0" Snow Depth	na	na	na	1	0	0	0	0	0	*0*	na	na	na

Sugarloaf Reservoir *Lake County*   Elevation: 9,737 ft.   Latitude: 39° 15' N   Longitude: 106° 22' W

	JAN	FEB	MAR	APR	MAY	JUN	JUL	AUG	SEP	OCT	NOV	DEC	YEAR
Mean Maximum Temp. (°F)	*30.1*	33.2	37.7	43.3	54.0	65.8	71.2	69.0	62.1	50.9	37.7	*31.5*	*48.9*
Mean Temp. (°F)	*16.4*	18.2	23.5	30.1	40.5	49.9	55.1	53.5	46.8	37.1	25.5	*18.9*	*34.6*
Mean Minimum Temp. (°F)	*2.6*	3.1	9.2	16.8	26.9	33.9	38.9	38.0	31.5	23.2	13.5	*6.3*	*20.3*
Extreme Maximum Temp. (°F)	55	54	59	66	70	82	85	82	80	71	63	56	85
Extreme Minimum Temp. (°F)	-37	-37	-26	-11	4	17	26	24	4	-9	-18	-32	-37
Days Maximum Temp. ≥ 90°F	0	0	0	0	0	0	0	0	0	0	0	0	0
Days Maximum Temp. ≤ 32°F	*18*	12	8	4	0	0	0	0	0	2	10	16	*70*
Days Minimum Temp. ≤ 32°F	30	28	31	30	27	12	2	4	16	29	30	30	269
Days Minimum Temp. ≤ 0°F	*11*	10	6	1	0	0	0	0	0	0	3	8	*39*
Heating Degree Days (base 65°F)	*1,502*	1,317	1,281	1,040	753	447	301	349	539	859	1,170	*1,422*	*10,980*
Cooling Degree Days (base 65°F)	0	0	0	0	0	0	0	0	0	0	0	0	0
Mean Precipitation (in.)	1.35	1.21	1.41	1.36	1.40	1.10	1.89	1.91	1.33	1.11	1.35	1.16	16.58
Days With ≥ 0.1" Precipitation	4	3	*4*	4	4	4	*5*	*5*	4	4	4	3	*48*
Days With ≥ 1.0" Precipitation	0	0	0	0	0	0	0	0	0	0	0	0	0
Mean Snowfall (in.)	20.0	18.7	20.9	18.1	9.5	1.4	0.0	trace	1.9	7.3	19.6	*15.0*	*132.4*
Days With ≥ 1.0" Snow Depth	26	23	25	21	5	0	0	0	1	3	*15*	25	*144*

Tacony 10 SE *Pueblo County*   Elevation: 4,957 ft.   Latitude: 38° 23' N   Longitude: 104° 04' W

	JAN	FEB	MAR	APR	MAY	JUN	JUL	AUG	SEP	OCT	NOV	DEC	YEAR
Mean Maximum Temp. (°F)	44.2	50.0	58.3	67.2	75.7	87.6	91.6	88.8	81.4	69.5	53.8	46.0	67.8
Mean Temp. (°F)	29.1	34.5	41.8	50.4	59.8	70.2	74.9	72.8	64.6	52.6	38.6	31.2	51.7
Mean Minimum Temp. (°F)	14.0	18.9	25.4	33.4	43.9	52.8	58.1	56.7	47.9	35.7	23.3	16.3	35.5
Extreme Maximum Temp. (°F)	76	78	85	93	100	107	106	105	102	91	82	77	107
Extreme Minimum Temp. (°F)	-25	-23	-3	1	26	35	43	40	24	5	-12	-28	-28
Days Maximum Temp. ≥ 90°F	0	0	0	0	2	13	21	16	6	0	0	0	58
Days Maximum Temp. ≤ 32°F	6	3	1	0	0	0	0	0	0	0	2	4	16
Days Minimum Temp. ≤ 32°F	31	27	25	13	2	0	0	0	1	10	26	30	165
Days Minimum Temp. ≤ 0°F	4	2	0	0	0	0	0	0	0	0	0	3	9
Heating Degree Days (base 65°F)	1,106	856	712	434	182	25	2	3	89	378	786	1,043	5,616
Cooling Degree Days (base 65°F)	0	0	0	2	30	186	312	254	85	2	0	0	871
Mean Precipitation (in.)	0.21	0.18	0.53	0.99	1.60	1.44	1.90	2.21	0.96	0.63	0.37	0.25	11.27
Days With ≥ 0.1" Precipitation	1	1	1	2	4	3	4	5	2	2	1	1	27
Days With ≥ 1.0" Precipitation	0	0	0	0	0	0	0	1	0	0	0	0	1
Mean Snowfall (in.)	4.5	3.1	5.7	3.7	0.8	trace	0.0	0.0	0.3	1.4	4.6	4.9	29.0
Days With ≥ 1.0" Snow Depth	8	3	1	1	0	0	0	0	0	0	3	7	23

Taylor Park *Gunnison County*   Elevation: 9,206 ft.   Latitude: 38° 49' N   Longitude: 106° 37' W

	JAN	FEB	MAR	APR	MAY	JUN	JUL	AUG	SEP	OCT	NOV	DEC	YEAR
Mean Maximum Temp. (°F)	26.3	32.4	38.1	44.7	55.3	67.0	71.1	69.1	62.7	52.4	37.9	27.4	48.7
Mean Temp. (°F)	7.0	11.3	18.9	28.3	40.3	50.1	55.4	54.0	47.1	37.3	23.6	10.2	32.0
Mean Minimum Temp. (°F)	-12.2	-9.9	-0.5	11.9	25.2	33.1	39.6	38.8	31.4	22.1	9.3	-7.0	15.2
Extreme Maximum Temp. (°F)	49	51	55	66	72	83	83	82	79	73	61	51	83
Extreme Minimum Temp. (°F)	-56	-60	-42	-27	-5	15	20	17	4	-5	-30	-53	-60
Days Maximum Temp. ≥ 90°F	0	0	0	0	0	0	0	0	0	0	0	0	0
Days Maximum Temp. ≤ 32°F	24	14	6	2	0	0	0	0	0	1	9	22	78
Days Minimum Temp. ≤ 32°F	31	28	31	30	28	13	2	3	17	29	30	31	273
Days Minimum Temp. ≤ 0°F	24	21	16	5	0	0	0	0	0	0	7	22	95
Heating Degree Days (base 65°F)	1,793	1,513	1,424	1,094	759	439	292	335	532	853	1,234	1,694	11,962
Cooling Degree Days (base 65°F)	0	0	0	0	0	0	0	0	0	0	0	0	0
Mean Precipitation (in.)	1.27	1.35	1.52	1.44	1.37	0.99	1.77	1.68	1.50	1.28	1.40	1.28	16.85
Days With ≥ 0.1" Precipitation	6	5	7	6	5	4	6	7	5	5	6	6	68
Days With ≥ 1.0" Precipitation	0	0	0	0	0	0	0	0	0	0	0	0	0
Mean Snowfall (in.)	na	na	na	na	0.6	trace	0.0	0.0	0.5	1.6	na	na	na
Days With ≥ 1.0" Snow Depth	na	na	na	na	1	0	0	0	0	1	na	na	na

Telluride 4 WNW *San Miguel County*   Elevation: 8,671 ft.   Latitude: 37° 57' N   Longitude: 107° 52' W

	JAN	FEB	MAR	APR	MAY	JUN	JUL	AUG	SEP	OCT	NOV	DEC	YEAR
Mean Maximum Temp. (°F)	37.5	40.7	44.8	52.1	62.1	73.2	77.6	75.3	69.1	59.3	45.7	38.3	56.3
Mean Temp. (°F)	21.9	25.3	30.5	37.6	46.4	54.9	59.9	58.7	52.2	42.6	30.7	23.0	40.3
Mean Minimum Temp. (°F)	6.2	9.9	16.2	23.0	30.7	36.6	42.2	42.0	35.3	25.7	15.7	7.6	24.3
Extreme Maximum Temp. (°F)	58	65	73	78	83	90	93	91	88	83	72	66	93
Extreme Minimum Temp. (°F)	-31	-24	-17	-10	8	20	27	26	15	1	-18	-23	-31
Days Maximum Temp. ≥ 90°F	0	0	0	0	0	0	0	0	0	0	0	0	0
Days Maximum Temp. ≤ 32°F	9	5	2	1	0	0	0	0	0	0	3	8	28
Days Minimum Temp. ≤ 32°F	31	28	30	27	19	7	1	1	9	26	29	31	239
Days Minimum Temp. ≤ 0°F	9	5	2	0	0	0	0	0	0	0	2	8	26
Heating Degree Days (base 65°F)	1,329	1,114	1,061	816	570	297	152	191	378	689	1,021	1,297	8,915
Cooling Degree Days (base 65°F)	0	0	0	0	0	1	3	2	0	0	0	0	6
Mean Precipitation (in.)	1.67	1.44	2.13	2.00	2.00	1.34	2.47	2.62	2.36	2.09	1.95	1.49	23.56
Days With ≥ 0.1" Precipitation	6	5	7	6	6	4	8	8	7	5	6	5	73
Days With ≥ 1.0" Precipitation	0	0	0	0	0	0	0	0	0	0	0	0	0
Mean Snowfall (in.)	33.7	27.6	39.3	25.2	9.6	0.8	0.0	0.0	0.9	10.5	28.4	29.8	205.8
Days With ≥ 1.0" Snow Depth	na	27	na	14	2	0	0	0	0	3	na	na	na

Trinidad *Las Animas County*   Elevation: 6,026 ft.   Latitude: 37° 11' N   Longitude: 104° 29' W

	JAN	FEB	MAR	APR	MAY	JUN	JUL	AUG	SEP	OCT	NOV	DEC	YEAR
Mean Maximum Temp. (°F)	48.2	51.8	57.9	65.1	73.7	83.3	86.5	84.2	78.6	69.3	56.1	48.5	66.9
Mean Temp. (°F)	33.7	37.1	43.1	49.9	58.7	68.0	71.9	70.0	63.6	53.3	41.5	34.3	52.1
Mean Minimum Temp. (°F)	19.1	22.3	28.3	34.6	43.7	52.6	57.3	55.7	48.5	37.3	26.9	20.1	37.2
Extreme Maximum Temp. (°F)	78	76	84	86	93	101	99	95	94	89	80	78	101
Extreme Minimum Temp. (°F)	-20	-20	0	2	22	32	43	37	23	2	-15	-16	-20
Days Maximum Temp. ≥ 90°F	0	0	0	0	0	6	9	4	1	0	0	0	20
Days Maximum Temp. ≤ 32°F	4	2	1	0	0	0	0	0	0	0	1	3	11
Days Minimum Temp. ≤ 32°F	29	25	22	12	2	0	0	0	1	8	22	28	149
Days Minimum Temp. ≤ 0°F	2	1	0	0	0	0	0	0	0	0	0	1	4
Heating Degree Days (base 65°F)	964	782	672	449	207	37	2	6	95	357	698	944	5,213
Cooling Degree Days (base 65°F)	0	0	0	1	24	133	226	171	60	1	0	0	616
Mean Precipitation (in.)	0.46	0.50	1.08	1.22	1.96	1.56	2.74	2.72	1.36	1.02	1.00	0.47	16.09
Days With ≥ 0.1" Precipitation	2	2	3	3	5	4	6	6	3	2	3	2	41
Days With ≥ 1.0" Precipitation	0	0	0	0	0	0	0	0	0	0	0	0	0
Mean Snowfall (in.)	7.0	7.2	9.0	5.8	1.1	0.0	trace	0.0	0.1	2.1	7.2	6.9	46.4
Days With ≥ 1.0" Snow Depth	5	4	3	1	0	0	0	0	0	1	4	7	25

Trinidad Las Animas Co. Arpt. *Las Animas County*   Elevation: 5,744 ft.   Latitude: 37° 16' N   Longitude: 104° 20' W

	JAN	FEB	MAR	APR	MAY	JUN	JUL	AUG	SEP	OCT	NOV	DEC	YEAR
Mean Maximum Temp. (°F)	46.6	51.4	57.8	65.0	74.0	84.6	88.7	86.3	79.2	69.0	55.6	47.3	67.1
Mean Temp. (°F)	31.8	35.9	42.2	49.5	58.8	68.8	73.6	71.7	64.1	53.0	40.5	32.5	51.9
Mean Minimum Temp. (°F)	16.9	20.4	26.4	34.0	43.6	52.9	58.3	57.1	48.9	37.0	25.4	17.7	36.5
Extreme Maximum Temp. (°F)	80	82	85	91	97	103	103	100	100	89	81	81	103
Extreme Minimum Temp. (°F)	-17	-24	-4	3	22	35	43	43	23	1	-17	-19	-24
Days Maximum Temp. ≥ 90°F	0	0	0	0	1	10	15	10	3	0	0	0	39
Days Maximum Temp. ≤ 32°F	5	3	1	0	0	0	0	0	0	0	2	4	15
Days Minimum Temp. ≤ 32°F	30	26	24	13	2	0	0	0	1	9	24	29	158
Days Minimum Temp. ≤ 0°F	2	2	0	0	0	0	0	0	0	0	0	2	6
Heating Degree Days (base 65°F)	1,022	815	702	460	208	36	2	6	100	368	728	1,001	5,448
Cooling Degree Days (base 65°F)	0	0	0	2	24	151	272	222	80	3	0	0	754
Mean Precipitation (in.)	0.41	0.45	0.92	1.05	1.83	1.35	2.31	2.24	1.31	0.87	0.85	0.52	14.11
Days With ≥ 0.1" Precipitation	1	2	3	3	5	4	5	5	3	2	3	2	38
Days With ≥ 1.0" Precipitation	0	0	0	0	0	0	0	0	0	0	0	0	0
Mean Snowfall (in.)	4.8	4.9	7.7	4.8	2.0	tracc	trace	trace	0.7	4.4	7.7	5.8	42.8
Days With ≥ 1.0" Snow Depth	9	5	4	2	0	0	0	0	0	1	5	10	36

Uravan *Montrose County*   Elevation: 5,009 ft.   Latitude: 38° 23' N   Longitude: 108° 45' W

	JAN	FEB	MAR	APR	MAY	JUN	JUL	AUG	SEP	OCT	NOV	DEC	YEAR
Mean Maximum Temp. (°F)	42.1	50.0	58.9	67.0	77.8	89.4	94.8	92.2	83.8	71.1	54.8	43.7	68.8
Mean Temp. (°F)	28.8	36.1	44.2	51.2	61.1	70.9	76.8	75.2	66.1	53.9	40.7	30.8	53.0
Mean Minimum Temp. (°F)	15.4	22.1	29.5	35.3	44.3	52.3	58.8	58.1	48.5	36.6	26.5	17.8	37.1
Extreme Maximum Temp. (°F)	66	73	81	90	99	107	110	105	104	90	77	65	110
Extreme Minimum Temp. (°F)	-14	-10	11	15	28	30	44	25	30	16	2	-15	-15
Days Maximum Temp. ≥ 90°F	0	0	0	0	2	17	26	22	7	0	0	0	74
Days Maximum Temp. ≤ 32°F	4	1	0	0	0	0	0	0	0	0	0	2	7
Days Minimum Temp. ≤ 32°F	30	26	22	11	1	0	0	0	0	8	25	30	153
Days Minimum Temp. ≤ 0°F	3	0	0	0	0	0	0	0	0	0	0	1	4
Heating Degree Days (base 65°F)	1,115	807	638	409	150	22	0	1	57	339	723	1,053	5,314
Cooling Degree Days (base 65°F)	0	0	0	1	36	212	370	331	101	1	0	0	1,052
Mean Precipitation (in.)	0.84	0.72	1.09	1.02	1.00	0.53	1.23	1.34	1.47	1.56	1.09	0.76	12.65
Days With ≥ 0.1" Precipitation	3	3	4	4	3	1	4	4	4	4	3	3	40
Days With ≥ 1.0" Precipitation	0	0	0	0	0	0	0	0	0	0	0	0	0
Mean Snowfall (in.)	na	na	*0.2*	0.3	0.0	0.0	0.0	0.0	0.0	0.2	na	na	na
Days With ≥ 1.0" Snow Depth	na	na	*0*	0	0	0	0	0	0	0	na	na	na

Vallecito Dam *La Plata County*   Elevation: 7,647 ft.   Latitude: 37° 23' N   Longitude: 107° 35' W

	JAN	FEB	MAR	APR	MAY	JUN	JUL	AUG	SEP	OCT	NOV	DEC	YEAR
Mean Maximum Temp. (°F)	36.5	40.7	46.9	54.8	64.0	74.9	79.4	77.2	70.7	60.1	46.4	38.5	57.5
Mean Temp. (°F)	21.2	25.5	32.6	39.7	48.1	57.2	63.0	61.4	54.6	44.5	32.9	24.8	42.1
Mean Minimum Temp. (°F)	5.7	10.2	18.2	24.4	32.2	39.5	46.5	45.7	38.5	28.9	19.4	10.9	26.7
Extreme Maximum Temp. (°F)	57	63	68	79	84	92	92	90	88	82	70	61	92
Extreme Minimum Temp. (°F)	-30	-25	-9	-4	15	23	32	28	22	7	-6	-22	-30
Days Maximum Temp. ≥ 90°F	0	0	0	0	0	0	0	0	0	0	0	0	0
Days Maximum Temp. ≤ 32°F	10	5	1	0	0	0	0	0	0	0	3	7	26
Days Minimum Temp. ≤ 32°F	31	28	31	27	16	3	0	0	5	23	29	31	224
Days Minimum Temp. ≤ 0°F	10	5	1	0	0	0	0	0	0	0	1	4	21
Heating Degree Days (base 65°F)	1,353	1,109	999	753	517	232	80	114	305	628	956	1,241	8,287
Cooling Degree Days (base 65°F)	0	0	0	0	0	4	24	12	1	0	0	0	41
Mean Precipitation (in.)	2.28	2.18	2.44	1.62	1.61	1.04	2.71	3.69	2.91	2.78	2.47	2.03	27.76
Days With ≥ 0.1" Precipitation	5	5	6	4	5	3	7	9	6	6	5	4	65
Days With ≥ 1.0" Precipitation	0	0	0	0	0	0	0	1	1	1	1	0	4
Mean Snowfall (in.)	26.5	22.2	21.4	8.6	1.4	0.0	0.0	0.0	trace	2.9	13.6	21.0	117.6
Days With ≥ 1.0" Snow Depth	na	na	na	na	0	0	0	0	0	0	*4*	na	na

Walden *Jackson County*   Elevation: 8,120 ft.   Latitude: 40° 44' N   Longitude: 106° 17' W

	JAN	FEB	MAR	APR	MAY	JUN	JUL	AUG	SEP	OCT	NOV	DEC	YEAR
Mean Maximum Temp. (°F)	29.7	33.4	40.7	49.5	60.5	71.7	77.9	76.5	67.7	55.5	39.1	31.2	52.8
Mean Temp. (°F)	17.3	20.2	27.7	35.2	44.5	54.0	59.0	57.2	49.3	38.9	26.4	18.8	37.4
Mean Minimum Temp. (°F)	4.9	6.9	14.7	20.8	28.4	36.2	39.9	37.9	30.9	22.2	13.6	6.3	21.9
Extreme Maximum Temp. (°F)	56	53	70	74	80	91	94	96	89	78	64	57	96
Extreme Minimum Temp. (°F)	-39	-47	-22	-16	7	20	27	19	8	-12	-28	-36	-47
Days Maximum Temp. ≥ 90°F	0	0	0	0	0	0	0	0	0	0	0	0	0
Days Maximum Temp. ≤ 32°F	18	11	6	2	0	0	0	0	0	1	8	17	63
Days Minimum Temp. ≤ 32°F	31	28	31	28	24	7	2	5	17	28	29	31	261
Days Minimum Temp. ≤ 0°F	11	8	3	1	0	0	0	0	0	0	4	10	37
Heating Degree Days (base 65°F)	1,473	1,260	1,149	889	629	325	182	234	463	802	1,151	1,427	9,984
Cooling Degree Days (base 65°F)	0	0	0	0	0	0	2	0	0	0	0	0	0
Mean Precipitation (in.)	0.63	0.59	0.81	1.04	1.51	1.09	1.29	1.00	1.19	0.96	0.87	0.60	11.58
Days With ≥ 0.1" Precipitation	2	2	3	3	5	3	4	4	4	3	3	2	38
Days With ≥ 1.0" Precipitation	0	0	0	0	0	0	0	0	0	0	0	0	0
Mean Snowfall (in.)	9.3	7.6	9.6	8.6	4.1	0.8	trace	trace	1.3	5.0	11.1	8.8	66.2
Days With ≥ 1.0" Snow Depth	26	23	11	2	0	0	0	0	0	2	12	22	98

Walsenburg *Huerfano County*   Elevation: 6,148 ft.   Latitude: 37° 39' N   Longitude: 104° 46' W

	JAN	FEB	MAR	APR	MAY	JUN	JUL	AUG	SEP	OCT	NOV	DEC	YEAR
Mean Maximum Temp. (°F)	47.0	50.7	56.9	64.4	73.4	83.5	87.4	84.7	78.6	69.0	55.2	47.5	66.5
Mean Temp. (°F)	33.8	36.8	42.3	48.9	57.8	67.2	72.0	70.1	63.2	53.1	41.6	34.6	51.8
Mean Minimum Temp. (°F)	20.6	22.8	27.7	33.3	42.2	50.7	56.5	55.4	47.7	37.0	27.9	21.8	37.0
Extreme Maximum Temp. (°F)	73	75	80	87	93	101	100	98	95	87	83	76	101
Extreme Minimum Temp. (°F)	-23	-24	-3	3	19	32	44	41	21	-1	-19	-27	-27
Days Maximum Temp. ≥ 90°F	0	0	0	0	0	7	12	5	1	0	0	0	25
Days Maximum Temp. ≤ 32°F	3	2	1	0	0	0	0	0	0	0	1	3	10
Days Minimum Temp. ≤ 32°F	26	23	22	14	2	0	0	0	1	8	20	25	141
Days Minimum Temp. ≤ 0°F	2	1	0	0	0	0	0	0	0	0	0	2	5
Heating Degree Days (base 65°F)	960	790	696	477	228	43	3	8	106	365	696	934	5,306
Cooling Degree Days (base 65°F)	0	0	0	1	15	115	230	181	59	2	0	0	603
Mean Precipitation (in.)	0.69	0.80	1.73	1.88	1.95	1.38	2.15	2.29	1.09	1.08	1.46	0.94	17.44
Days With ≥ 0.1" Precipitation	2	2	4	4	4	3	5	5	3	3	3	3	41
Days With ≥ 1.0" Precipitation	0	0	0	0	0	0	0	0	0	0	0	0	0
Mean Snowfall (in.)	11.9	12.2	18.5	13.9	3.5	trace	0.0	0.0	0.9	6.7	16.7	15.9	100.2
Days With ≥ 1.0" Snow Depth	7	5	4	2	0	0	0	0	0	1	na	10	na

Walsh 1 W *Baca County*   Elevation: 3,976 ft.   Latitude: 37° 23' N   Longitude: 102° 18' W

	JAN	FEB	MAR	APR	MAY	JUN	JUL	AUG	SEP	OCT	NOV	DEC	YEAR
Mean Maximum Temp. (°F)	44.8	50.3	58.2	67.1	76.2	86.9	91.6	88.8	81.1	69.8	55.6	46.9	68.1
Mean Temp. (°F)	31.0	35.8	43.2	51.7	61.6	71.9	76.8	74.7	66.4	54.3	41.3	33.0	53.5
Mean Minimum Temp. (°F)	17.1	21.1	28.1	36.3	47.1	56.9	61.9	60.5	51.7	38.6	26.9	19.3	38.8
Extreme Maximum Temp. (°F)	79	82	88	96	102	108	106	103	102	93	88	78	108
Extreme Minimum Temp. (°F)	-25	-19	-6	8	28	38	45	41	20	8	-9	-20	-25
Days Maximum Temp. ≥ 90°F	0	0	0	1	3	13	20	16	7	0	0	0	60
Days Maximum Temp. ≤ 32°F	6	4	2	0	0	0	0	0	0	0	2	5	19
Days Minimum Temp. ≤ 32°F	30	26	21	10	1	0	0	0	0	7	23	29	147
Days Minimum Temp. ≤ 0°F	2	1	0	0	0	0	0	0	0	0	0	2	5
Heating Degree Days (base 65°F)	1,048	819	669	400	150	21	2	4	83	338	705	987	5,226
Cooling Degree Days (base 65°F)	0	0	0	9	54	231	375	323	137	11	0	0	1,140
Mean Precipitation (in.)	0.41	0.42	0.94	1.41	2.76	2.29	3.32	2.66	1.52	1.07	0.68	0.39	17.87
Days With ≥ 0.1" Precipitation	1	1	3	4	5	5	5	4	3	2	2	1	36
Days With ≥ 1.0" Precipitation	0	0	0	0	1	1	1	1	0	0	0	0	4
Mean Snowfall (in.)	4.9	3.7	4.6	2.0	0.4	0.0	0.0	0.0	0.2	1.1	3.2	4.2	24.3
Days With ≥ 1.0" Snow Depth	6	3	2	1	0	0	0	0	0	1	3	5	21

Waterdale *Larimer County*   Elevation: 5,229 ft.   Latitude: 40° 26' N   Longitude: 105° 12' W

	JAN	FEB	MAR	APR	MAY	JUN	JUL	AUG	SEP	OCT	NOV	DEC	YEAR
Mean Maximum Temp. (°F)	42.4	46.1	52.5	59.8	69.4	80.3	86.2	84.3	75.5	64.0	50.6	44.0	62.9
Mean Temp. (°F)	28.0	31.9	38.4	45.8	55.2	64.6	70.3	68.8	60.2	49.1	37.2	29.9	48.3
Mean Minimum Temp. (°F)	13.6	17.7	24.3	31.8	41.0	48.9	54.3	53.2	44.8	34.0	23.7	15.7	33.6
Extreme Maximum Temp. (°F)	71	76	80	89	94	102	102	101	98	88	78	70	102
Extreme Minimum Temp. (°F)	-29	-25	-14	-6	17	33	42	38	18	2	-11	-30	-30
Days Maximum Temp. ≥ 90°F	0	0	0	0	0	5	11	7	2	0	0	0	25
Days Maximum Temp. ≤ 32°F	7	4	2	1	0	0	0	0	0	0	3	5	22
Days Minimum Temp. ≤ 32°F	30	27	27	16	3	0	0	0	2	12	25	30	172
Days Minimum Temp. ≤ 0°F	5	2	0	0	0	0	0	0	0	0	1	3	11
Heating Degree Days (base 65°F)	1,140	929	817	569	303	83	12	19	173	487	828	1,082	6,442
Cooling Degree Days (base 65°F)	0	0	0	1	8	75	181	149	39	1	0	0	454
Mean Precipitation (in.)	0.44	0.45	1.36	2.03	3.12	1.99	1.85	1.65	1.67	1.06	0.84	0.51	16.97
Days With ≥ 0.1" Precipitation	2	2	3	4	6	4	4	4	4	3	2	2	40
Days With ≥ 1.0" Precipitation	0	0	0	0	1	1	0	0	0	0	0	0	2
Mean Snowfall (in.)	6.6	5.5	9.3	6.3	0.1	0.0	0.0	0.0	0.9	2.9	7.3	8.3	47.2
Days With ≥ 1.0" Snow Depth	6	4	4	2	0	0	0	0	0	1	3	4	24

Westcliffe *Custer County*   Elevation: 7,857 ft.   Latitude: 38° 08' N   Longitude: 105° 28' W

	JAN	FEB	MAR	APR	MAY	JUN	JUL	AUG	SEP	OCT	NOV	DEC	YEAR
Mean Maximum Temp. (°F)	39.2	42.6	48.0	55.3	65.2	76.2	80.5	77.8	71.5	61.2	47.6	40.1	58.8
Mean Temp. (°F)	22.8	26.5	33.1	40.1	49.3	58.2	62.6	60.7	53.9	43.4	31.7	23.9	42.2
Mean Minimum Temp. (°F)	6.4	10.3	18.2	24.9	33.3	40.1	44.6	43.5	36.1	25.5	15.8	7.6	25.5
Extreme Maximum Temp. (°F)	64	72	72	77	83	91	94	90	86	79	71	69	94
Extreme Minimum Temp. (°F)	-41	-33	-20	-12	12	20	32	28	4	-12	-24	-39	-41
Days Maximum Temp. ≥ 90°F	0	0	0	0	0	0	0	0	0	0	0	0	0
Days Maximum Temp. ≤ 32°F	7	4	2	1	0	0	0	0	0	0	4	7	25
Days Minimum Temp. ≤ 32°F	31	28	29	24	14	3	0	0	9	25	28	30	221
Days Minimum Temp. ≤ 0°F	9	7	2	1	0	0	0	0	0	0	3	9	31
Heating Degree Days (base 65°F)	1,301	1,081	981	739	482	206	84	132	327	663	989	1,268	8,253
Cooling Degree Days (base 65°F)	0	0	0	0	0	7	15	5	1	0	0	0	28
Mean Precipitation (in.)	0.43	0.50	1.24	1.35	1.48	1.00	2.18	2.45	1.15	1.11	0.98	0.58	14.45
Days With ≥ 0.1" Precipitation	1	2	4	4	4	3	6	7	3	3	2	2	41
Days With ≥ 1.0" Precipitation	0	0	0	0	0	0	0	0	0	0	0	0	0
Mean Snowfall (in.)	8.8	10.9	21.4	15.7	5.1	0.2	0.0	0.0	1.6	9.6	15.5	11.4	100.2
Days With ≥ 1.0" Snow Depth	8	7	6	3	1	0	0	0	0	2	8	10	45

Wolf Creek Pass 1 E *Mineral County*   Elevation: 10,639 ft.   Latitude: 37° 28' N   Longitude: 106° 47' W

	JAN	FEB	MAR	APR	MAY	JUN	JUL	AUG	SEP	OCT	NOV	DEC	YEAR
Mean Maximum Temp. (°F)	30.9	32.2	35.3	*41.1*	*50.7*	*60.9*	65.9	64.3	57.1	47.8	*36.9*	*30.7*	*46.1*
Mean Temp. (°F)	17.2	19.1	23.0	*29.0*	*39.0*	*47.7*	*52.9*	51.3	45.0	35.5	*24.5*	*17.8*	*33.5*
Mean Minimum Temp. (°F)	3.4	5.9	10.7	16.8	*27.2*	*34.4*	*40.0*	38.6	33.1	23.5	12.0	*4.8*	*20.9*
Extreme Maximum Temp. (°F)	57	58	61	69	68	80	80	78	81	68	65	56	81
Extreme Minimum Temp. (°F)	-28	-40	-20	-12	1	15	18	15	13	-10	-28	-27	-40
Days Maximum Temp. ≥ 90°F	0	0	0	0	0	0	0	0	0	0	0	0	0
Days Maximum Temp. ≤ 32°F	16	14	12	6	1	0	0	0	0	2	10	16	77
Days Minimum Temp. ≤ 32°F	30	28	31	28	*24*	10	0	1	13	29	30	*31*	255
Days Minimum Temp. ≤ 0°F	11	8	4	1	0	0	0	0	0	0	3	9	36
Heating Degree Days (base 65°F)	1,476	1,290	1,294	*1,074*	*800*	*513*	*367*	417	592	908	*1,209*	*1,457*	*11,397*
Cooling Degree Days (base 65°F)	0	0	0	*0*	*0*	*0*	0	0	0	0	*0*	*0*	*0*
Mean Precipitation (in.)	3.95	4.11	5.28	3.34	2.42	1.76	3.85	4.72	4.63	4.91	4.62	3.87	47.46
Days With ≥ 0.1" Precipitation	7	8	9	7	*6*	5	9	11	8	7	8	7	*92*
Days With ≥ 1.0" Precipitation	1	1	1	0	0	0	1	1	1	2	1	1	10
Mean Snowfall (in.)	*76.3*	*64.9*	*75.1*	*42.0*	*14.8*	1.5	trace	trace	2.3	*27.3*	*59.6*	*71.8*	435.6
Days With ≥ 1.0" Snow Depth	na	na	na	na	na	1	0	0	*1*	na	na	na	na

Wray 2 E *Yuma County*   Elevation: 3,526 ft.   Latitude: 40° 05' N   Longitude: 102° 11' W

	JAN	FEB	MAR	APR	MAY	JUN	JUL	AUG	SEP	OCT	NOV	DEC	YEAR
Mean Maximum Temp. (°F)	43.9	50.5	57.3	66.1	75.3	86.1	91.6	90.5	82.4	*70.7*	53.8	*45.2*	67.8
Mean Temp. (°F)	28.3	34.0	41.0	49.9	60.0	70.5	76.1	74.3	65.1	*52.5*	*38.4*	*30.0*	*51.7*
Mean Minimum Temp. (°F)	12.7	17.8	24.6	33.5	44.7	54.7	60.5	58.3	47.8	34.2	22.8	15.4	35.6
Extreme Maximum Temp. (°F)	76	80	86	93	101	107	109	109	104	95	84	*74*	*109*
Extreme Minimum Temp. (°F)	-25	-22	-12	7	21	32	42	40	18	7	-15	*-33*	*-33*
Days Maximum Temp. ≥ 90°F	0	0	0	1	2	11	20	19	10	1	*0*	*0*	*64*
Days Maximum Temp. ≤ 32°F	7	3	2	0	0	0	0	0	0	0	*2*	*6*	*20*
Days Minimum Temp. ≤ 32°F	31	*27*	25	14	2	0	0	0	1	13	26	30	*169*
Days Minimum Temp. ≤ 0°F	5	2	0	0	0	0	0	0	0	0	0	3	10
Heating Degree Days (base 65°F)	1,129	866	738	452	189	28	4	5	105	*387*	793	*1,080*	*5,776*
Cooling Degree Days (base 65°F)	0	0	0	4	*36*	190	*337*	298	114	*5*	*0*	*0*	*984*
Mean Precipitation (in.)	0.54	0.41	1.12	1.79	3.05	2.54	3.01	2.01	1.10	0.90	0.77	0.38	17.62
Days With ≥ 0.1" Precipitation	2	2	3	4	6	5	5	4	3	2	2	1	39
Days With ≥ 1.0" Precipitation	0	0	0	0	1	1	1	0	0	0	0	0	3
Mean Snowfall (in.)	6.2	3.8	6.3	3.2	0.1	trace	0.0	trace	0.2	1.6	*4.9*	4.0	*30.3*
Days With ≥ 1.0" Snow Depth	*6*	4	3	1	0	0	0	0	0	1	3	5	23

Yampa *Routt County*   Elevation: 7,887 ft.   Latitude: 40° 09' N   Longitude: 106° 55' W

	JAN	FEB	MAR	APR	MAY	JUN	JUL	AUG	SEP	OCT	NOV	DEC	YEAR
Mean Maximum Temp. (°F)	31.2	35.2	41.4	50.5	61.8	71.5	76.4	75.7	68.1	56.8	41.2	32.4	53.5
Mean Temp. (°F)	18.8	22.0	28.8	36.9	46.9	55.3	60.8	60.0	52.3	41.8	28.9	20.3	39.4
Mean Minimum Temp. (°F)	6.2	8.7	16.1	23.3	32.0	39.0	45.2	44.3	36.4	26.6	16.5	8.2	25.2
Extreme Maximum Temp. (°F)	55	57	68	73	85	90	90	89	86	76	69	61	90
Extreme Minimum Temp. (°F)	-31	-35	-24	-14	7	18	29	24	12	-5	-25	-36	-36
Days Maximum Temp. ≥ 90°F	0	0	0	0	0	0	0	0	0	0	0	0	0
Days Maximum Temp. ≤ 32°F	17	10	5	1	0	0	0	0	0	1	7	15	56
Days Minimum Temp. ≤ 32°F	31	28	30	26	16	4	0	1	8	24	29	31	228
Days Minimum Temp. ≤ 0°F	9	6	2	1	0	0	0	0	0	0	2	7	27
Heating Degree Days (base 65°F)	1,426	1,210	1,117	837	554	287	131	150	377	712	1,076	1,378	9,255
Cooling Degree Days (base 65°F)	0	0	0	0	0	2	9	3	0	0	0	0	14
Mean Precipitation (in.)	1.25	0.97	1.27	1.39	1.59	1.38	2.11	1.65	1.41	1.33	1.26	1.14	16.75
Days With ≥ 0.1" Precipitation	5	3	4	5	5	4	6	6	5	4	4	4	55
Days With ≥ 1.0" Precipitation	0	0	0	0	0	0	0	0	0	0	0	0	0
Mean Snowfall (in.)	21.8	15.4	17.7	12.6	2.7	0.2	0.0	trace	0.6	8.0	19.0	19.6	117.6
Days With ≥ 1.0" Snow Depth	29	28	26	8	1	0	0	0	0	3	16	29	140

Yellow Jacket 2 W *Montezuma County*   Elevation: 6,856 ft.   Latitude: 37° 31' N   Longitude: 108° 45' W

	JAN	FEB	MAR	APR	MAY	JUN	JUL	AUG	SEP	OCT	NOV	DEC	YEAR
Mean Maximum Temp. (°F)	38.0	43.1	49.9	59.1	69.2	81.4	86.7	84.3	76.0	63.3	48.5	39.8	61.6
Mean Temp. (°F)	26.6	31.3	37.7	45.2	54.5	64.8	70.6	69.0	61.3	50.0	37.0	28.7	48.1
Mean Minimum Temp. (°F)	15.2	19.5	25.5	31.2	39.7	48.2	54.5	53.6	46.5	36.6	25.4	17.6	34.4
Extreme Maximum Temp. (°F)	60	65	73	80	86	98	99	98	94	86	75	62	99
Extreme Minimum Temp. (°F)	-19	-21	-5	8	22	24	40	36	22	9	-10	-20	-21
Days Maximum Temp. ≥ 90°F	0	0	0	0	0	3	9	5	1	0	0	0	18
Days Maximum Temp. ≤ 32°F	7	3	1	0	0	0	0	0	0	0	2	6	19
Days Minimum Temp. ≤ 32°F	31	27	26	17	5	0	0	0	0	8	24	30	168
Days Minimum Temp. ≤ 0°F	2	1	0	0	0	0	0	0	0	0	0	1	4
Heating Degree Days (base 65°F)	1,183	945	840	590	321	74	4	10	135	460	835	1,119	6,516
Cooling Degree Days (base 65°F)	0	0	0	0	0	2	75	184	148	30	0	0	439
Mean Precipitation (in.)	1.17	1.27	1.40	0.92	1.32	0.59	1.55	1.59	1.63	1.93	1.54	1.06	15.97
Days With ≥ 0.1" Precipitation	4	3	4	3	4	2	4	5	4	5	4	3	45
Days With ≥ 1.0" Precipitation	0	0	0	0	0	0	0	0	0	0	0	0	0
Mean Snowfall (in.)	17.2	14.0	11.1	2.7	1.2	0.0	0.0	0.0	0.0	1.5	8.2	13.5	69.4
Days With ≥ 1.0" Snow Depth	*16*	*13*	*5*	*1*	0	0	0	0	0	0	2	na	na

Note: See Appendix D for explanation of data.

CONNECTICUT

PHYSICAL FEATURES. Connecticut occupies the southwestern portion of the region known as New England. The State extends for 90 miles in an east-west direction and 75 miles from north to south. The total area of 5,009 square miles makes Connecticut the third smallest state in the Nation.

The topography of Connecticut is predominantly hilly. The highest terrain is found in the northwest portion of the State, with elevations of 1,000 to 2,000 feet. The southwestern quarter and most of the eastern half have elevations of 300 to 1,000 feet. The State of Connecticut is bisected by the Connecticut River which rises in Canada. Smaller river basins in the State with their headwaters in the southern half of Massachusetts include the Housatonic in the west and the Shetucket, Quinebaug, and Thames in the east. The narrow river valleys and steep hillsides in much of the western highlands make for destructive flash floods during periods of unusually heavy or intense rainfall.

The entire southern border of Connecticut is washed by the waters of Long Island Sound. The coastline of approximately 100 miles is indented by small coves and the mouths of numerous rivers and streams. Beaches are found along the greater length.

GENERAL CLIMATE. The chief characteristics of Connecticut's climate are: (1) equable distribution of precipitation among the four seasons, (2) large ranges of temperature both daily and annually, (3) great differences in the same season or month of different years, and (4) considerable diversity of the weather over short periods of time.

Connecticut lies in the "prevailing westerlies," the belt of generally eastward air movement which encircles the globe in middle latitudes. Embedded in this circulation are extensive masses of air originating in higher and lower latitudes and interacting to produce low-pressure storm systems. A large number of storm centers and air-mass fronts pass near or over Connecticut during a year. Three types of air affect this State: (1) cold, dry air pouring down from subarctic North America, (2) warm, moist air streaming up on a long overland journey from the Gulf of Mexico and subtropical waters of the Atlantic, and (3) cool, damp air moving in from the North Atlantic. Because the flow of air is usually from continental areas, Connecticut is more influenced by the first two types than it is by the third. The procession of contrasting air masses and the relatively frequent passage of storms bring about a roughly twice weekly alternation from fair to cloudy or storm conditions, usually attended by abrupt changes in temperature, moisture, sunshine, and wind direction and speed. There is no regular or persistent rhythm to this sequence; it is sometimes interrupted by periods during which the weather pattern continues much the same for several days, and infrequently for a few weeks.

TEMPERATURE. Despite the small size of Connecticut, there is a difference of about 6°F. in mean annual temperature from north to south. The greater contrast of temperature over the State occurs during the winter season. The number of days with minimum temperatures of zero or below average about 10 per year at the higher elevations, about five in the lower uplands and central valley, and two or less along the shore of Long Island Sound. Summer temperatures are comparatively uniform over the State. The central valley experiences the greatest number of hot days. Temperatures of 90°F. or higher occur on an average on about 10 days per year. At the higher elevations and near the coast, the average number is approximately three days per year. In much of the western and eastern highlands, the occurrence of 90°F. temperatures is a little less frequent than in the central valley.

During the warmest month of the summer the average minimum temperature ranges from about 56°F. in the cool northwestern corner of the State to about 63°F. in the warmer coastal sections. Over most of the State the average July minimum temperature is within a degree or two of 60°F.

The period free from temperatures of 32°F. or lower has an average length of 155 to 170 days over the greater portion of Connecticut. In the northwest as well as in local areas of the western and eastern highlands, the freeze-free season lasts about 125 to 135 days. Along the immediate coast approximately 190 days will elapse between the last spring and first fall freeze.

PRECIPITATION. Precipitation tends to become evenly distributed throughout the year in all parts of Connecticut. Low-pressure centers and their accompanying air mass fronts are the principal year-round producers of precipitation. Storms moving up the Atlantic coast generally yield the heaviest amounts of rain and snow. In the summer bands and patches of thunderstorms and convective showers add considerable precipitation and make up the difference resulting from decreased activity of low-pressure storm centers. Thunderstorms are of brief duration and often scattered in comparison with the general storms, but they yield the heaviest local rainfall.

Variations in precipitation from month to month are sometimes extreme. A month yielding five inches or more may be preceded or followed by one with less than two inches of precipitation, in any season. Months with less than one inch are known to occur, as well as those with precipitation in excess of 10 inches. Such large fluctuations, however, are not characteristic of the precipitation supply in Connecticut. Consequently, prolonged droughts and widespread floods are infrequent.

While there are no pronounced wet and dry months as in other climates, February and October are relatively dry. The average total precipitation for each of these months is three inches or slightly less in comparison with 3.5 to four inches in the other 10 months. Measurable precipitation falls on an average of one day in three, with the yearly total approximating 120 days. Periods of five days or more of successive daily precipitation occur a few times during most years.

The average annual snowfall increases from the coast to the northwestern corner of the State. Most of the snow falls in January and February, but in the majority of winters substantial amounts fall in December or March storms as well. Except for the northwestern highlands, snowfalls of more than one inch are quite rare before mid-November and after April 15. The average number of days per year with snow on the ground similarly shows an increase from the shore to the northwest. During an average winter a measurable snow cover is present most of the time from late December through the early half of March in the greater portion of the State. In the immediate coastal areas a snow cover does not last more than a few days unless a heavy snowstorm is followed by prolonged cold temperatures.

OTHER CLIMATIC ELEMENTS. During the colder months the prevailing wind is northwest to north over Connecticut, while from April through September southwest or south winds predominate. The mean hourly speed ranges from about seven m.p.h. in the summer and early fall to about 10 m.p.h. in the winter and spring seasons. An important feature of the climate is the sea breeze along the coast. During the summer and late spring this onshore wind blows from the cool ocean during the afternoon and penetrates inland from five to 10 miles. It occurs often enough to give lower mean summer maximum temperatures in a narrow coastal belt than prevail over interior lowlands.

Thunderstorms occur on an average of 20 to 30 days per year, with the greatest frequency during the summer months and in the afternoon or evening hours. Often these storms are accompanied by destructive hail and/or wind. Aside from infrequent tornadoes and hurricanes, coastal storms or "northeasters" are the most serious weather hazard in Connecticut. They generate very strong winds and heavy rain and produce the greatest snowstorms in the winter. If these storms occur at the time of high tide, heavy water damage results along the shore. In occasional years a tornado or storm with tornadic characteristics strikes some part of the State. The central valley appears to be the most likely to be struck, and the summer months the most likely season. Storms of tropical origin occasionally affect Connecticut during the summer or fall months, as they move on a path well out over the ocean.

The Connecticut River shows an annual rise in early spring as the result of the melting of high elevation snow in northern and central New England. A secondary period of flooding (occasionally of major proportions) is caused by heavy rains which may be associated with hurricanes or storms of tropical origin in late summer or fall, normally the low water season.

The percentage of possible sunshine averages 55 to 60 percent, ranging from 45 percent in the interior during the months of November through January to near 65 percent along the coast in the summer. The average number of clear days per year is between 100 and 125, with the greatest number per month usually occurring in September and October. An average of about 140 cloudy days occur per year. Heavy or dense fog is observed on an average of about 25 days per year in both coastal and inland sections. In the former section, heavy fog is most common during the late winter and spring seasons, while inland the late summer and fall is the period of maximum occurrence. The humidity tends to be lowest in the spring and highest in the late summer and early fall.

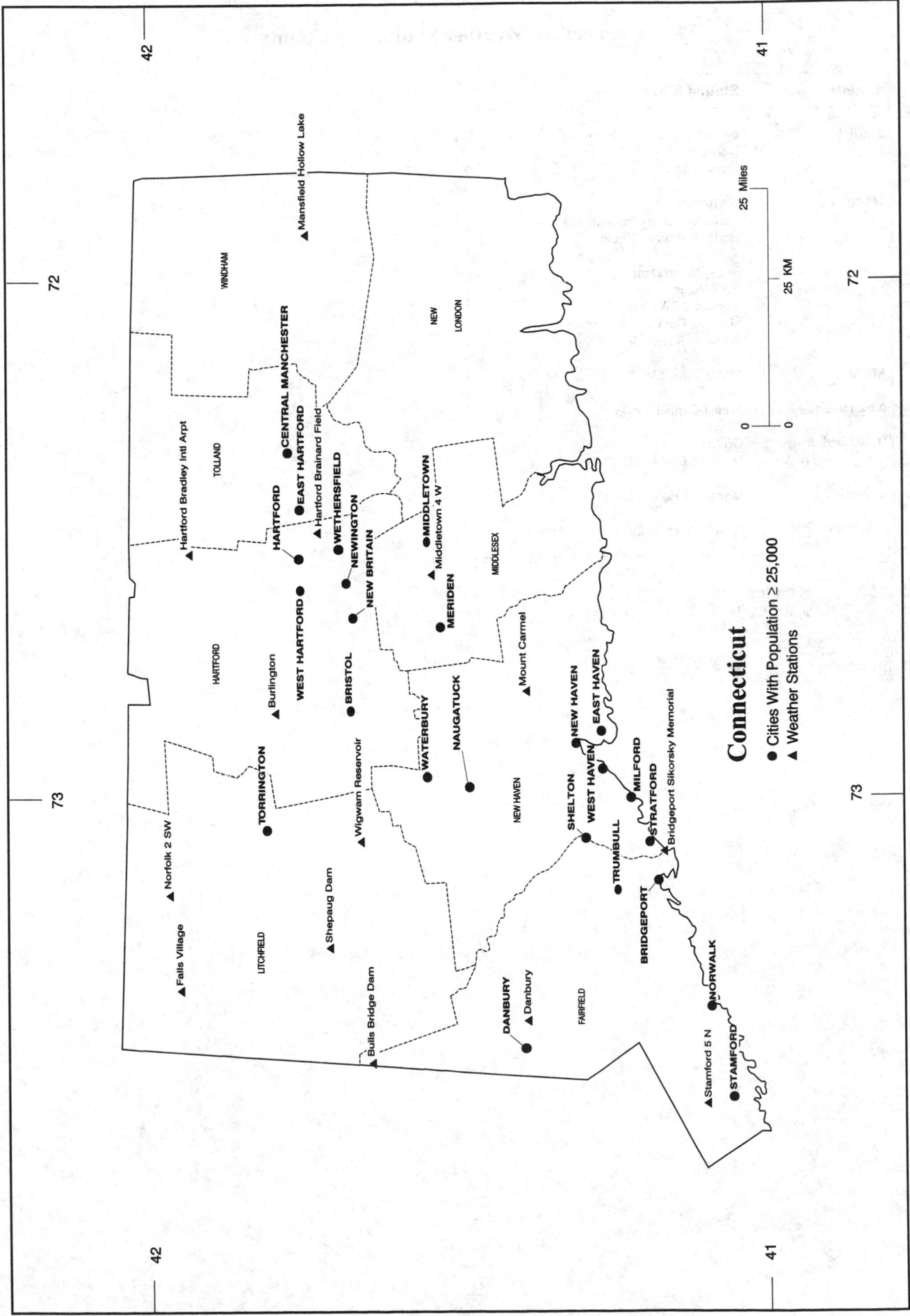

Connecticut

● Cities With Population ≥ 25,000
▲ Weather Stations

Connecticut Weather Stations by County

County	Station Name
Fairfield	Bridgeport Sikorsky Memorial Danbury Stamford 5 N
Hartford	Burlington Hartford Bradley Int'l Airport Hartford Brainard Field
Litchfield	Bulls Bridge Dam Falls Village Norfolk 2 SW Shepaug Dam Wigwam Reservoir
Middlesex	Middletown 4 W
New Haven	Mount Carmel
New London	Groton Norwich Public Util. Plant
Tolland	Mansfield Hollow Lake
Windham	West Thompson Lake

Connecticut Weather Stations by City

City	Station Name	Miles
Bridgeport	Bridgeport Sikorsky Memorial	2
	Danbury	18
	Stamford 5 N	19
	Setauket Strong, NY	16
Bristol	Burlington	8
	Hartford Brainard Field	15
	Middletown 4 W	14
	Mount Carmel	20
	Shepaug Dam	19
	Wigwam Reservoir	11
Central Manchester	Hartford Brainard Field	7
	Hartford Bradley Int'l Airport	14
	Mansfield Hollow Lake	18
	Middletown 4 W	19
Danbury	Bulls Bridge Dam	17
	Danbury	2
East Hartford	Burlington	17
	Hartford Brainard Field	3
	Hartford Bradley Int'l Airport	12
	Middletown 4 W	16
East Haven	Bridgeport Sikorsky Memorial	17
	Middletown 4 W	19
	Mount Carmel	8
Hartford	Burlington	13
	Hartford Brainard Field	3
	Hartford Bradley Int'l Airport	12
	Middletown 4 W	15
Meriden	Burlington	20
	Hartford Brainard Field	16
	Middletown 4 W	4
	Mount Carmel	11
	Wigwam Reservoir	20
Middletown	Hartford Brainard Field	12
	Middletown 4 W	3
	Mount Carmel	16
Milford	Bridgeport Sikorsky Memorial	5
	Mount Carmel	15
	Setauket Strong, NY	17
Naugatuck	Middletown 4 W	18
	Mount Carmel	10
	Wigwam Reservoir	13
New Britain	Burlington	12
	Hartford Brainard Field	8
	Hartford Bradley Int'l Airport	19
	Middletown 4 W	9
	Mount Carmel	20
	Wigwam Reservoir	18
New Haven	Bridgeport Sikorsky Memorial	15
	Middletown 4 W	20
	Mount Carmel	6
Newington	Burlington	13

City	Station Name	Miles
Newington (cont.)	Hartford Brainard Field	5
	Hartford Bradley Int'l Airport	17
	Middletown 4 W	9
Norwalk	Bridgeport Sikorsky Memorial	15
	Danbury	20
	Stamford 5 N	7
	Setauket Strong, NY	19
	White Plains Westchester Co. Arpt., NY	16
Norwich	Groton	13
	Mansfield Hollow Lake	16
	Norwich Public Util. Plant	1
Shelton	Bridgeport Sikorsky Memorial	8
	Danbury	16
	Mount Carmel	14
Stamford	Stamford 5 N	3
	Dobbs Ferry Ardsley, NY	16
	White Plains Westchester Co. Arpt., NY	9
	Yorktown Heights 1 W, NY	19
Stratford	Bridgeport Sikorsky Memorial	2
	Danbury	20
	Mount Carmel	18
	Setauket Strong, NY	17
Torrington	Burlington	9
	Falls Village	16
	Norfolk 2 SW	12
	Shepaug Dam	12
	Wigwam Reservoir	10
Trumbull	Bridgeport Sikorsky Memorial	6
	Danbury	15
	Mount Carmel	19
Waterbury	Burlington	18
	Middletown 4 W	16
	Mount Carmel	13
	Shepaug Dam	18
	Wigwam Reservoir	9
West Hartford	Burlington	10
	Hartford Brainard Field	5
	Hartford Bradley Int'l Airport	12
	Middletown 4 W	15
West Haven	Bridgeport Sikorsky Memorial	11
	Mount Carmel	10
Wethersfield	Burlington	15
	Hartford Brainard Field	3
	Hartford Bradley Int'l Airport	16
	Middletown 4 W	11

Note: Miles is the distance between the geographic center of the city and the weather station.

Connecticut Weather Stations by Elevation

Feet	Station Name
1,338	Norfolk 2 SW
839	Shepaug Dam
567	Wigwam Reservoir
547	Falls Village
508	Burlington
403	Danbury
367	Middletown 4 W
357	West Thompson Lake
259	Bulls Bridge Dam
249	Mansfield Hollow Lake
187	Stamford 5 N
177	Mount Carmel
157	Hartford Bradley Int'l Airport
39	Groton
19	Hartford Brainard Field
19	Norwich Public Util. Plant
9	Bridgeport Sikorsky Memorial

Bridgeport Sikorsky Memorial

The airport is located on Stratford Point, a peninsula jutting out into Long Island Sound. Station instrumentation is located approximately 1 mile from the sound. Land around the airport is flat, with marshes to the south. The terrain is of glacial origin, rising in a rolling, mostly wooded manner, to the foothills of the Berkshires, 30 miles to the north and northwest.

Cities in close proximity to the station are Bridgeport, Fairfield, and Milford, while Danbury, New Haven, Norwalk and Stamford are located within a 35-mile radius.

The most pronounced topographical effect is the land-sea breeze, an occurrence generally associated with the spring through early autumn months.

Mean monthly temperatures during the summer months average three to five degrees lower than nearby inland stations because of the sea-breeze effect. Temperatures during the fall and winter months are moderated because of the proximity of Long Island Sound.

Winter snowfall is generally around 10 inches less than areas a few miles inland, also due to the proximity of the station to Long Island Sound.

One of the hazards along the coastal areas is the flooding of low-lying areas (usually during periods of high tide) with the approach of slow-moving deepening low pressure systems, resulting in 3 to 5 feet higher tides than normal.

Bridgeport Sikorsky Memorial *Fairfield County*   Elevation: 9 ft.   Latitude: 41° 11' N   Longitude: 73° 09' W

	JAN	FEB	MAR	APR	MAY	JUN	JUL	AUG	SEP	OCT	NOV	DEC	YEAR
Mean Maximum Temp. (°F)	36.7	38.8	46.7	57.1	67.4	76.4	82.1	80.9	73.9	63.4	52.9	42.2	59.9
Mean Temp. (°F)	29.7	31.6	39.1	48.8	59.0	68.1	74.2	73.2	65.8	55.0	45.4	35.3	52.1
Mean Minimum Temp. (°F)	22.7	24.3	31.3	40.4	50.6	59.7	66.2	65.5	57.8	46.6	38.0	28.4	44.3
Extreme Maximum Temp. (°F)	65	67	84	91	97	96	100	96	93	86	78	76	100
Extreme Minimum Temp. (°F)	-7	0	6	18	35	44	49	44	38	26	16	-4	-7
Days Maximum Temp. ≥ 90°F	0	0	0	0	0	1	3	2	0	0	0	0	6
Days Maximum Temp. ≤ 32°F	10	7	1	0	0	0	0	0	0	0	0	4	22
Days Minimum Temp. ≤ 32°F	26	22	16	3	0	0	0	0	0	1	8	21	97
Days Minimum Temp. ≤ 0°F	0	0	0	0	0	0	0	0	0	0	0	0	0
Heating Degree Days (base 65°F)	1,087	937	798	481	199	30	2	4	64	310	580	913	5,405
Cooling Degree Days (base 65°F)	0	0	0	1	25	134	298	257	91	8	0	0	814
Mean Precipitation (in.)	3.67	3.01	4.15	3.95	3.96	3.52	3.61	3.64	3.49	3.58	3.71	3.47	43.76
Maximum Precipitation (in.)	11.2	6.6	9.4	10.7	9.5	17.7	12.8	13.3	7.4	10.7	10.2	7.9	73.9
Minimum Precipitation (in.)	0.4	0.4	0.7	0.7	0.4	0.1	0.5	0.7	0.4	0.3	0.4	0.3	23.0
Maximum 24-hr. Precipitation (in.)	4.3	2.3	4.2	3.1	3.2	6.2	5.9	4.7	4.5	4.8	3.1	3.7	6.2
Days With ≥ 0.1" Precipitation	7	6	8	6	7	6	6	6	6	6	6	7	77
Days With ≥ 1.0" Precipitation	1	1	1	1	1	1	1	1	1	1	1	1	12
Mean Snowfall (in.)	8.0	7.2	4.4	0.9	trace	0.0	*trace*	*trace*	*0.0*	trace	0.7	3.6	*24.8*
Maximum Snowfall (in.)	26	28	22	6	trace	0	0	0	0	1	7	21	60
Maximum 24-hr. Snowfall (in.)	16	16	11	6	trace	0	0	0	0	1	6	15	16
Days With ≥ 1.0" Snow Depth	11	8	3	0	0	0	0	0	0	0	0	4	26
Thunderstorm Days	< 1	< 1	1	2	3	4	5	4	2	1	< 1	< 1	22
Foggy Days	12	12	14	14	16	16	16	17	15	14	13	13	172
Predominant Sky Cover	OVR	OVR	OVR	OVR	OVR	OVR	OVR	OVR	OVR	OVR	OVR	OVR	OVR
Mean Relative Humidity 7am (%)	73	72	72	72	75	77	79	80	81	79	77	74	76
Mean Relative Humidity 4pm (%)	61	59	56	55	58	60	60	61	61	60	62	63	60
Mean Dewpoint (°F)	20	20	26	36	47	57	63	63	56	46	35	25	41
Prevailing Wind Direction	WNW	NW	NW	SW	SW	SW	SW	SW	SW	NE	WNW	WNW	WSW
Prevailing Wind Speed (mph)	15	16	16	13	12	10	10	10	13	12	14	15	13
Maximum Wind Gust (mph)	69	66	71	63	59	55	62	77	69	76	61	66	77

Hartford Bradley Int'l Airport

Bradley International Airport is located about 3 miles west of the Connecticut River on a slight rise of ground in a broad portion of the Connecticut River Valley between north-south mountain ranges whose heights do not exceed 1,200 feet.

The station is in the northern temperate climate zone. The prevailing west to east movement of air brings the majority of weather systems into Connecticut from the west. The average wintertime position of the Polar Front boundary between cold, dry polar air and warm, moist tropical air is just south of New England, which helps to explain the extensive winter storm activity and day to day variability of local weather. In summer, the Polar Front has an average position along the New England-Canada border with this station in a warm and pleasant atmosphere.

Relative to continent and ocean, is also significant. Rapid weather changes result when storms move northward along the mid-Atlantic coast, frequently producing strong and persistent northeast winds associated with storms known locally as coastals or northeasters. Seasonally, weather characteristics vary from the cold and dry continental-polar air of winter to the warm and humid maritime air of summer.

Summer thunderstorms develop in the Berkshire Mountains to the west and northwest, move over the Connecticut Valley, and when accompanied by wind and hail, sometimes cause considerable damage to crops, particularly tobacco. During the winter, rain often falls through cold air trapped in the valley, creating extremely hazardous ice conditions. On clear nights in the late summer or early autumn, cool air drainage into the valley, and moisture from the Connecticut River, produce steam and/or ground fog which becomes quite dense throughout the valley, hampering ground and air transportation.

The mean date of the last springtime temperature of 32 degrees or lower is April 22, and the mean date of the first autumn temperature of 32 degrees is October 15.

Hartford Bradley Int'l Airport *Hartford County*   Elevation: 157 ft.   Latitude: 41° 56' N   Longitude: 72° 41' W

	JAN	FEB	MAR	APR	MAY	JUN	JUL	AUG	SEP	OCT	NOV	DEC	YEAR
Mean Maximum Temp. (°F)	33.9	37.7	47.3	60.0	71.8	80.0	85.1	82.8	74.4	63.2	51.0	39.0	60.5
Mean Temp. (°F)	25.4	28.7	37.7	49.0	60.0	68.5	73.9	71.8	63.3	52.0	41.9	30.9	50.3
Mean Minimum Temp. (°F)	16.9	19.8	28.1	37.9	48.2	57.0	62.6	60.8	52.2	40.7	32.7	22.7	40.0
Extreme Maximum Temp. (°F)	64	73	89	96	99	98	101	101	99	86	81	76	101
Extreme Minimum Temp. (°F)	-21	-13	1	9	28	37	46	39	30	17	1	-14	-21
Days Maximum Temp. ≥ 90°F	0	0	0	0	1	3	8	5	1	0	0	0	18
Days Maximum Temp. ≤ 32°F	14	9	2	0	0	0	0	0	0	0	0	8	33
Days Minimum Temp. ≤ 32°F	28	25	21	8	0	0	0	0	0	6	16	26	130
Days Minimum Temp. ≤ 0°F	3	1	0	0	0	0	0	0	0	0	0	1	5
Heating Degree Days (base 65°F)	1,219	1,017	839	479	188	36	3	11	115	403	687	1,051	6,048
Cooling Degree Days (base 65°F)	0	0	1	3	36	142	282	222	71	6	0	0	763
Mean Precipitation (in.)	3.76	3.06	3.89	3.86	4.36	3.70	3.54	3.98	4.11	3.98	4.09	3.63	45.96
Maximum Precipitation (in.)	9.6	7.3	9.5	9.9	12.0	13.6	8.4	21.9	9.0	11.6	8.5	8.4	64.5
Minimum Precipitation (in.)	0.4	0.4	0.3	1.4	0.7	0.3	1.1	0.5	0.8	0.3	0.5	0.8	29.0
Maximum 24-hr. Precipitation (in.)	2.2	2.2	2.5	3.0	4.8	5.9	3.0	7.7	5.1	4.3	3.3	3.0	7.7
Days With ≥ 0.1" Precipitation	7	6	8	7	8	7	6	6	6	6	7	7	81
Days With ≥ 1.0" Precipitation	1	1	1	1	1	1	1	1	1	1	1	1	12
Mean Snowfall (in.)	13.8	10.9	7.9	1.5	trace	trace	0.0	0.0	0.0	trace	2.3	8.5	44.9
Maximum Snowfall (in.)	37	32	43	14	1	0	0	0	0	2	9	35	88
Maximum 24-hr. Snowfall (in.)	14	14	14	14	1	0	0	0	0	2	8	14	14
Days With ≥ 1.0" Snow Depth	17	15	6	1	0	0	0	0	0	0	2	9	50
Thunderstorm Days	< 1	< 1	1	1	2	4	5	4	2	1	< 1	< 1	20
Foggy Days	12	10	12	12	13	15	16	17	16	14	13	12	162
Predominant Sky Cover	OVR	OVR	OVR	OVR	OVR	OVR	OVR	OVR	OVR	OVR	OVR	OVR	OVR
Mean Relative Humidity 7am (%)	73	73	72	70	73	77	79	83	86	84	79	76	77
Mean Relative Humidity 4pm (%)	58	54	51	46	48	51	52	54	55	53	58	61	53
Mean Dewpoint (°F)	15	17	24	33	45	56	61	60	53	42	32	20	38
Prevailing Wind Direction	NW	NW	NW	S	S	S	S	S	S	S	N	NW	S
Prevailing Wind Speed (mph)	12	13	13	10	9	9	8	8	8	8	8	12	10
Maximum Wind Gust (mph)	66	53	62	60	48	59	89	58	66	86	64	58	89

Bulls Bridge Dam *Litchfield County*   Elevation: 259 ft.   Latitude: 41° 39' N   Longitude: 73° 29' W

	JAN	FEB	MAR	APR	MAY	JUN	JUL	AUG	SEP	OCT	NOV	DEC	YEAR
Mean Maximum Temp. (°F)	34.6	38.1	47.5	59.9	71.4	79.1	83.8	81.7	73.5	62.7	50.4	39.3	60.2
Mean Temp. (°F)	24.8	27.8	36.6	47.5	58.6	66.7	71.8	70.0	62.0	50.7	40.4	30.4	48.9
Mean Minimum Temp. (°F)	14.9	17.4	25.7	35.2	45.7	54.3	59.7	58.4	50.5	38.4	30.2	21.3	37.6
Extreme Maximum Temp. (°F)	63	72	88	93	94	98	101	96	97	87	84	73	101
Extreme Minimum Temp. (°F)	-24	-14	-5	12	25	35	38	34	30	16	11	-15	-24
Days Maximum Temp. ≥ 90°F	0	0	0	0	1	2	5	3	1	0	0	0	12
Days Maximum Temp. ≤ 32°F	13	8	2	0	0	0	0	0	0	0	0	6	29
Days Minimum Temp. ≤ 32°F	29	26	25	12	1	0	0	0	0	9	19	28	149
Days Minimum Temp. ≤ 0°F	4	2	0	0	0	0	0	0	0	0	0	1	7
Heating Degree Days (base 65°F)	1,241	1,044	873	519	217	52	8	16	134	439	733	1,068	6,344
Cooling Degree Days (base 65°F)	0	0	0	2	26	112	231	175	50	3	0	0	599
Mean Precipitation (in.)	3.61	2.96	3.91	4.15	4.22	3.80	4.69	4.29	4.21	3.97	4.10	3.62	47.53
Days With ≥ 0.1" Precipitation	7	6	7	7	8	7	8	7	7	6	7	7	84
Days With ≥ 1.0" Precipitation	1	1	1	1	1	1	1	1	1	1	1	1	12
Mean Snowfall (in.)	na	na	na	na	0.0	0.0	0.0	0.0	0.0	0.0	na	na	na
Days With ≥ 1.0" Snow Depth	na	na	na	na	0	0	0	0	0	0	na	na	na

Burlington *Hartford County*   Elevation: 508 ft.   Latitude: 41° 48' N   Longitude: 72° 56' W

	JAN	FEB	MAR	APR	MAY	JUN	JUL	AUG	SEP	OCT	NOV	DEC	YEAR
Mean Maximum Temp. (°F)	34.6	37.1	45.9	58.0	69.4	77.5	82.6	80.6	72.8	61.9	51.2	39.7	59.3
Mean Temp. (°F)	24.5	26.8	35.6	46.8	57.6	66.0	71.2	69.5	61.5	50.2	41.1	30.5	48.4
Mean Minimum Temp. (°F)	14.3	16.4	25.2	35.4	45.8	54.6	59.8	58.3	50.2	38.5	31.0	21.3	37.6
Extreme Maximum Temp. (°F)	64	70	83	93	95	95	100	98	95	86	80	75	100
Extreme Minimum Temp. (°F)	-18	-13	-1	14	28	27	40	37	24	19	1	-13	-18
Days Maximum Temp. ≥ 90°F	0	0	0	0	0	2	4	2	1	0	0	0	9
Days Maximum Temp. ≤ 32°F	13	9	3	0	0	0	0	0	0	0	1	7	33
Days Minimum Temp. ≤ 32°F	30	26	25	12	1	0	0	0	0	8	19	28	149
Days Minimum Temp. ≤ 0°F	4	2	0	0	0	0	0	0	0	0	0	1	7
Heating Degree Days (base 65°F)	1,250	1,072	906	543	246	63	9	22	147	454	711	1,062	6,485
Cooling Degree Days (base 65°F)	0	0	0	1	24	104	213	164	52	2	0	0	560
Mean Precipitation (in.)	4.21	3.39	4.59	4.41	4.60	4.04	4.11	4.59	4.80	4.46	4.59	4.04	51.83
Days With ≥ 0.1" Precipitation	6	6	7	7	8	6	7	7	7	6	6	6	79
Days With ≥ 1.0" Precipitation	1	1	1	1	1	1	1	1	1	1	1	1	12
Mean Snowfall (in.)	*6.6*	na	na	*1.2*	trace	0.0	0.0	0.0	0.0	0.1	*1.3*	na	na
Days With ≥ 1.0" Snow Depth	na	na	na	na	0	0	0	0	0	0	na	na	na

Danbury *Fairfield County*   Elevation: 403 ft.   Latitude: 41° 24' N   Longitude: 73° 25' W

	JAN	FEB	MAR	APR	MAY	JUN	JUL	AUG	SEP	OCT	NOV	DEC	YEAR
Mean Maximum Temp. (°F)	*34.8*	38.5	47.5	*59.9*	71.4	79.3	84.2	81.8	*73.5*	*62.3*	50.8	*40.1*	*60.4*
Mean Temp. (°F)	*26.2*	29.2	37.5	*48.4*	*59.2*	67.7	*72.8*	71.0	*62.7*	*51.5*	41.9	*32.0*	*50.0*
Mean Minimum Temp. (°F)	*17.4*	19.7	27.6	*36.8*	*47.1*	56.1	*61.4*	60.1	*51.9*	40.6	32.8	23.8	39.6
Extreme Maximum Temp. (°F)	*63*	*73*	92	*94*	97	98	*106*	*99*	98	86	*80*	76	*106*
Extreme Minimum Temp. (°F)	*-18*	*-10*	-3	14	26	36	40	38	31	19	10	*-11*	*-18*
Days Maximum Temp. ≥ 90°F	*0*	0	0	0	1	3	6	3	*1*	0	*0*	*0*	*14*
Days Maximum Temp. ≤ 32°F	*13*	8	2	0	0	0	0	0	*0*	*0*	*1*	*6*	*30*
Days Minimum Temp. ≤ 32°F	*28*	25	22	9	*1*	*0*	*0*	0	*0*	7	16	26	*134*
Days Minimum Temp. ≤ 0°F	*2*	1	0	0	*0*	*0*	*0*	0	*0*	*0*	*0*	*0*	*3*
Heating Degree Days (base 65°F)	*1,198*	1,006	846	*496*	*205*	*44*	*5*	12	*128*	*416*	688	*1,018*	*6,062*
Cooling Degree Days (base 65°F)	*0*	*0*	*1*	*3*	34	*144*	275	*210*	68	3	*0*	*0*	*738*
Mean Precipitation (in.)	*4.26*	3.32	4.65	*4.30*	4.45	4.31	4.52	4.33	*5.10*	*4.17*	4.43	*4.15*	*51.99*
Days With ≥ 0.1" Precipitation	7	6	8	7	*8*	8	6	6	*6*	6	7	7	*82*
Days With ≥ 1.0" Precipitation	*1*	1	1	1	1	1	1	*1*	*1*	*1*	2	*1*	*13*
Mean Snowfall (in.)	*11.3*	11.0	8.0	*1.6*	trace	0.0	0.0	0.0	*0.0*	0.2	1.1	6.4	*39.6*
Days With ≥ 1.0" Snow Depth	*16*	13	6	1	0	0	0	0	*0*	*0*	1	8	*45*

Falls Village *Litchfield County*   Elevation: 547 ft.   Latitude: 41° 57' N   Longitude: 73° 22' W

	JAN	FEB	MAR	APR	MAY	JUN	JUL	AUG	SEP	OCT	NOV	DEC	YEAR
Mean Maximum Temp. (°F)	34.4	37.6	46.8	59.7	72.2	79.4	84.0	81.7	73.4	62.3	50.2	39.0	60.1
Mean Temp. (°F)	23.7	26.5	35.4	46.6	58.2	66.1	70.9	69.1	61.2	49.7	39.7	29.2	48.0
Mean Minimum Temp. (°F)	13.0	15.4	24.0	33.4	44.2	52.8	57.8	56.5	48.8	37.1	29.1	19.4	36.0
Extreme Maximum Temp. (°F)	63	70	88	93	92	95	100	95	94	84	81	72	100
Extreme Minimum Temp. (°F)	-27	-22	-8	10	20	32	37	32	27	14	5	-16	-27
Days Maximum Temp. ≥ 90°F	0	0	0	0	0	2	5	2	0	0	0	0	9
Days Maximum Temp. ≤ 32°F	13	9	2	0	0	0	0	0	0	0	1	7	32
Days Minimum Temp. ≤ 32°F	30	26	26	15	3	0	0	0	1	11	20	29	161
Days Minimum Temp. ≤ 0°F	5	4	0	0	0	0	0	0	0	0	0	2	11
Heating Degree Days (base 65°F)	1,274	1,079	910	549	228	57	9	24	155	469	753	1,103	6,610
Cooling Degree Days (base 65°F)	0	0	0	2	24	103	212	164	50	2	0	0	557
Mean Precipitation (in.)	3.45	2.69	3.57	3.78	4.20	3.91	4.14	4.42	3.97	3.80	3.79	3.44	45.16
Days With ≥ 0.1" Precipitation	7	6	7	7	8	7	7	7	7	7	8	7	85
Days With ≥ 1.0" Precipitation	1	1	1	1	1	1	1	1	1	1	1	1	12
Mean Snowfall (in.)	na	na	*6.0*	2.0	0.0	0.0	0.0	0.0	0.0	0.1	1.3	na	na
Days With ≥ 1.0" Snow Depth	*8*	na	na	1	0	0	0	0	0	0	0	na	na

Groton *New London County*   Elevation: 39 ft.   Latitude: 41° 21' N   Longitude: 72° 03' W

	JAN	FEB	MAR	APR	MAY	JUN	JUL	AUG	SEP	OCT	NOV	DEC	YEAR
Mean Maximum Temp. (°F)	37.6	39.4	46.8	56.4	66.3	74.9	80.7	79.8	72.7	62.5	52.8	42.7	59.4
Mean Temp. (°F)	28.6	30.4	37.9	47.2	56.9	65.6	71.8	70.9	63.5	52.9	43.9	34.2	50.3
Mean Minimum Temp. (°F)	19.6	21.5	28.9	37.9	47.4	56.4	62.8	61.9	54.2	43.2	35.0	25.6	41.2
Extreme Maximum Temp. (°F)	62	67	78	84	91	95	101	99	93	80	75	69	101
Extreme Minimum Temp. (°F)	-13	-11	5	14	32	39	47	43	34	23	8	-10	-13
Days Maximum Temp. ≥ 90°F	0	0	0	0	0	1	2	1	0	0	0	0	4
Days Maximum Temp. ≤ 32°F	9	6	1	0	0	0	0	0	0	0	0	4	20
Days Minimum Temp. ≤ 32°F	28	24	21	6	0	0	0	0	0	3	13	24	119
Days Minimum Temp. ≤ 0°F	1	1	0	0	0	0	0	0	0	0	0	0	2
Heating Degree Days (base 65°F)	1,121	969	834	529	256	53	4	9	102	373	626	948	5,824
Cooling Degree Days (base 65°F)	0	0	0	0	12	85	228	194	64	5	0	0	588
Mean Precipitation (in.)	4.31	3.61	4.51	4.17	3.65	3.54	3.27	4.44	3.86	4.08	4.61	4.38	48.43
Days With ≥ 0.1" Precipitation	7	6	8	7	7	6	5	6	6	6	7	8	79
Days With ≥ 1.0" Precipitation	1	1	1	1	1	1	1	1	1	1	1	1	12
Mean Snowfall (in.)	7.1	6.4	3.2	0.6	trace	0.0	0.0	0.0	0.0	trace	0.6	3.2	21.1
Days With ≥ 1.0" Snow Depth	9	6	2	0	0	0	0	0	0	0	0	3	20

Hartford Brainard Field *Hartford County*   Elevation: 19 ft.   Latitude: 41° 44' N   Longitude: 72° 39' W

	JAN	FEB	MAR	APR	MAY	JUN	JUL	AUG	SEP	OCT	NOV	DEC	YEAR
Mean Maximum Temp. (°F)	35.3	38.3	46.7	58.6	70.3	78.6	83.7	81.9	74.2	62.6	51.4	40.2	60.2
Mean Temp. (°F)	26.0	28.8	37.1	48.4	59.4	67.9	73.5	71.7	63.2	51.4	42.0	31.5	50.1
Mean Minimum Temp. (°F)	16.7	19.5	27.4	38.0	48.3	57.3	63.1	61.4	52.3	40.1	32.5	22.7	39.9
Extreme Maximum Temp. (°F)	65	74	82	93	99	98	101	102	98	88	79	75	102
Extreme Minimum Temp. (°F)	-15	-10	1	13	25	39	47	38	30	19	5	-10	-15
Days Maximum Temp. ≥ 90°F	0	0	0	0	1	3	5	4	1	0	0	0	14
Days Maximum Temp. ≤ 32°F	12	8	2	0	0	0	0	0	0	0	1	7	30
Days Minimum Temp. ≤ 32°F	29	25	22	7	0	0	0	0	0	6	16	27	132
Days Minimum Temp. ≤ 0°F	2	1	0	0	0	0	0	0	0	0	0	0	3
Heating Degree Days (base 65°F)	1,203	1,015	859	497	201	42	4	10	115	420	686	1,032	6,084
Cooling Degree Days (base 65°F)	0	0	0	3	36	139	275	224	69	5	0	0	751
Mean Precipitation (in.)	3.57	2.77	3.66	3.85	3.98	3.77	3.84	3.81	3.70	4.05	3.85	3.54	44.39
Days With ≥ 0.1" Precipitation	6	5	6	6	7	6	6	5	6	6	6	7	72
Days With ≥ 1.0" Precipitation	1	1	1	1	1	1	1	1	1	1	1	1	12
Mean Snowfall (in.)	na	5.3	*3.8*	0.7	trace	0.0	0.0	0.0	0.0	trace	0.4	na	na
Days With ≥ 1.0" Snow Depth	10	7	*3*	0	0	0	0	0	0	0	1	*4*	25

Mansfield Hollow Lake *Tolland County*   Elevation: 249 ft.   Latitude: 41° 45' N   Longitude: 72° 11' W

	JAN	FEB	MAR	APR	MAY	JUN	JUL	AUG	SEP	OCT	NOV	DEC	YEAR
Mean Maximum Temp. (°F)	35.5	38.0	46.9	57.8	69.3	77.6	82.7	*81.2*	73.3	63.0	51.6	40.3	*59.8*
Mean Temp. (°F)	24.5	27.1	36.2	46.2	56.9	65.4	71.0	*69.4*	60.9	49.9	40.8	30.3	*48.2*
Mean Minimum Temp. (°F)	13.6	16.1	25.5	34.6	44.5	53.2	59.3	*57.5*	48.5	36.8	30.0	20.2	*36.6*
Extreme Maximum Temp. (°F)	64	69	82	91	92	95	100	100	98	86	80	75	100
Extreme Minimum Temp. (°F)	-23	-19	-6	9	25	34	40	36	30	16	1	-18	-23
Days Maximum Temp. ≥ 90°F	0	0	0	0	0	1	4	2	1	0	0	0	8
Days Maximum Temp. ≤ 32°F	11	8	2	0	0	0	0	0	0	0	1	6	28
Days Minimum Temp. ≤ 32°F	28	25	24	13	2	0	0	0	1	11	19	26	149
Days Minimum Temp. ≤ 0°F	4	3	0	0	0	0	0	0	0	0	0	1	8
Heating Degree Days (base 65°F)	1,248	1,064	884	558	261	70	11	*24*	158	462	719	1,070	*6,529*
Cooling Degree Days (base 65°F)	0	0	0	0	15	88	211	*165*	*43*	*3*	*0*	*0*	*525*
Mean Precipitation (in.)	4.58	3.51	4.60	4.32	4.10	3.76	4.20	4.18	4.25	4.48	4.78	4.32	51.08
Days With ≥ 0.1" Precipitation	8	7	8	7	8	6	7	6	6	6	7	8	84
Days With ≥ 1.0" Precipitation	1	1	1	1	1	1	1	1	1	2	1	1	13
Mean Snowfall (in.)	9.6	7.8	5.6	1.9	trace	0.0	0.0	0.0	0.0	trace	1.3	5.8	32.0
Days With ≥ 1.0" Snow Depth	14	13	6	1	0	0	0	0	0	0	1	7	42

Middletown 4 W *Middlesex County*   Elevation: 367 ft.   Latitude: 41° 33' N   Longitude: 72° 43' W

	JAN	FEB	MAR	APR	MAY	JUN	JUL	AUG	SEP	OCT	NOV	DEC	YEAR
Mean Maximum Temp. (°F)	35.6	38.2	47.0	58.7	70.6	79.3	84.0	81.3	72.5	61.5	51.1	40.2	60.0
Mean Temp. (°F)	27.6	29.8	38.2	48.6	59.5	68.3	73.3	71.3	63.0	52.3	43.0	32.9	50.6
Mean Minimum Temp. (°F)	19.6	21.3	29.3	38.5	48.3	57.2	62.5	61.2	53.4	43.0	35.0	25.5	41.2
Extreme Maximum Temp. (°F)	62	65	78	90	92	98	102	96	95	87	74	68	102
Extreme Minimum Temp. (°F)	-14	-10	4	17	30	38	46	40	30	21	12	-8	-14
Days Maximum Temp. ≥ 90°F	0	0	0	0	0	2	6	3	0	0	0	0	11
Days Maximum Temp. ≤ 32°F	12	8	2	0	0	0	0	0	0	0	0	6	28
Days Minimum Temp. ≤ 32°F	27	24	20	7	0	0	0	0	0	4	13	24	119
Days Minimum Temp. ≤ 0°F	2	1	0	0	0	0	0	0	0	0	0	0	3
Heating Degree Days (base 65°F)	1,153	989	825	487	198	36	4	15	123	394	653	989	5,866
Cooling Degree Days (base 65°F)	0	0	0	2	37	151	288	*226*	71	6	0	0	*781*
Mean Precipitation (in.)	4.26	3.40	4.39	4.47	4.35	4.47	4.23	4.38	4.49	4.88	4.65	4.32	52.29
Days With ≥ 0.1" Precipitation	7	7	7	7	8	7	7	6	6	6	7	7	82
Days With ≥ 1.0" Precipitation	1	1	1	1	1	1	1	1	1	2	1	1	13
Mean Snowfall (in.)	10.7	8.9	5.6	1.3	0.0	0.0	0.0	0.0	0.0	0.1	1.4	6.1	34.1
Days With ≥ 1.0" Snow Depth	*15*	14	7	1	0	0	0	0	0	0	1	*7*	*45*

Mount Carmel *New Haven County*   Elevation: 177 ft.   Latitude: 41° 24' N   Longitude: 72° 54' W

	JAN	FEB	MAR	APR	MAY	JUN	JUL	AUG	SEP	OCT	NOV	DEC	YEAR
Mean Maximum Temp. (°F)	36.8	39.7	48.2	59.7	70.6	*78.8*	84.0	82.4	74.6	64.0	52.5	41.0	*61.0*
Mean Temp. (°F)	28.0	30.5	38.5	48.8	59.2	*67.7*	73.2	71.8	64.0	53.2	43.4	32.9	*50.9*
Mean Minimum Temp. (°F)	19.1	21.2	28.8	37.8	47.7	*56.5*	62.4	61.3	53.3	42.4	34.2	24.7	*40.8*
Extreme Maximum Temp. (°F)	65	69	83	93	94	*96*	*103*	98	95	85	78	71	*103*
Extreme Minimum Temp. (°F)	-15	-13	2	14	28	*36*	*42*	*39*	31	20	6	-13	*-15*
Days Maximum Temp. ≥ 90°F	0	0	0	0	1	*2*	5	3	1	0	0	0	*12*
Days Maximum Temp. ≤ 32°F	10	6	1	0	0	*0*	0	0	0	0	0	6	*23*
Days Minimum Temp. ≤ 32°F	28	24	20	7	1	*0*	0	0	0	5	14	25	*124*
Days Minimum Temp. ≤ 0°F	2	1	0	0	0	*0*	0	0	0	0	0	0	*3*
Heating Degree Days (base 65°F)	1,141	969	814	483	204	*37*	3	9	103	364	642	988	*5,757*
Cooling Degree Days (base 65°F)	0	0	0	2	34	*133*	278	232	83	6	0	0	*768*
Mean Precipitation (in.)	4.14	3.32	4.55	4.78	4.65	*4.60*	4.44	4.38	4.63	4.52	4.62	4.12	*52.75*
Days With ≥ 0.1" Precipitation	7	6	7	7	8	*7*	6	6	7	6	7	7	*81*
Days With ≥ 1.0" Precipitation	1	1	1	1	1	*1*	1	1	2	1	2	1	*14*
Mean Snowfall (in.)	8.5	8.2	5.2	0.9	trace	*0.0*	0.0	0.0	0.0	trace	1.1	5.1	*29.0*
Days With ≥ 1.0" Snow Depth	15	12	5	0	0	*0*	0	0	0	0	1	6	*39*

Norfolk 2 SW *Litchfield County*   Elevation: 1,338 ft.   Latitude: 41° 58' N   Longitude: 73° 13' W

	JAN	FEB	MAR	APR	MAY	JUN	JUL	AUG	SEP	OCT	NOV	DEC	YEAR
Mean Maximum Temp. (°F)	28.5	30.8	40.2	52.8	65.2	73.1	77.7	75.8	67.6	56.2	44.5	33.4	53.8
Mean Temp. (°F)	20.1	22.1	31.0	42.8	54.8	63.0	67.9	66.2	58.2	46.9	37.0	26.1	44.7
Mean Minimum Temp. (°F)	11.7	13.3	21.7	32.7	44.3	53.0	58.1	56.5	48.7	37.6	29.4	18.7	35.5
Extreme Maximum Temp. (°F)	58	63	79	88	88	91	92	90	89	81	75	67	92
Extreme Minimum Temp. (°F)	-21	-17	-8	7	25	32	43	37	29	17	4	-20	-21
Days Maximum Temp. ≥ 90°F	0	0	0	0	0	0	0	0	0	0	0	0	0
Days Maximum Temp. ≤ 32°F	20	16	7	0	0	0	0	0	0	0	3	15	61
Days Minimum Temp. ≤ 32°F	30	27	28	16	2	0	0	0	1	9	21	29	163
Days Minimum Temp. ≤ 0°F	6	4	1	0	0	0	0	0	0	0	0	2	13
Heating Degree Days (base 65°F)	1,386	1,206	1,048	661	323	109	29	53	223	555	835	1,200	7,628
Cooling Degree Days (base 65°F)	0	0	0	1	12	59	130	96	25	1	0	0	324
Mean Precipitation (in.)	4.37	3.58	4.55	4.55	4.76	4.36	4.66	4.74	4.52	4.42	4.68	4.30	53.49
Days With ≥ 0.1" Precipitation	8	7	8	8	9	7	8	7	7	7	8	8	92
Days With ≥ 1.0" Precipitation	1	1	1	1	1	1	1	1	1	1	1	1	12
Mean Snowfall (in.)	20.8	17.9	16.1	7.7	0.7	trace	0.0	0.0	0.0	0.8	5.6	18.1	87.7
Days With ≥ 1.0" Snow Depth	27	26	22	5	0	0	0	0	0	0	5	20	105

Norwich Public Util. Plant *New London County*   Elevation: 19 ft.   Latitude: 41° 32' N   Longitude: 72° 04' W

	JAN	FEB	MAR	APR	MAY	JUN	JUL	AUG	SEP	OCT	NOV	DEC	YEAR
Mean Maximum Temp. (°F)	38.3	40.6	48.8	59.3	70.2	78.3	83.4	81.6	74.4	64.0	53.3	42.9	61.2
Mean Temp. (°F)	*28.5*	*30.7*	*38.8*	48.4	58.6	67.0	72.9	71.2	63.6	52.2	43.0	33.4	*50.7*
Mean Minimum Temp. (°F)	18.3	20.8	28.5	37.4	47.1	55.9	62.4	60.6	52.4	40.5	32.7	24.0	40.1
Extreme Maximum Temp. (°F)	65	72	85	91	98	98	101	99	97	87	79	77	101
Extreme Minimum Temp. (°F)	-13	17	4	17	27	33	43	40	30	18	6	-13	-17
Days Maximum Temp. ≥ 90°F	0	0	0	0	1	2	5	3	1	0	0	0	12
Days Maximum Temp. ≤ 32°F	8	6	1	0	0	0	0	0	0	0	0	4	19
Days Minimum Temp. ≤ 32°F	28	24	20	8	0	0	0	0	0	6	16	26	128
Days Minimum Temp. ≤ 0°F	2	1	0	0	0	0	0	0	0	0	0	0	3
Heating Degree Days (base 65°F)	*1,125*	*959*	*808*	490	212	45	4	11	107	394	654	973	*5,782*
Cooling Degree Days (base 65°F)	0	0	0	1	24	118	268	217	69	5	0	0	702
Mean Precipitation (in.)	4.62	3.89	4.91	4.52	4.15	3.58	3.62	4.78	4.20	4.61	4.99	4.67	52.54
Days With ≥ 0.1" Precipitation	7	6	8	7	8	6	5	6	6	6	7	8	80
Days With ≥ 1.0" Precipitation	1	1	1	1	1	1	1	1	1	1	2	1	13
Mean Snowfall (in.)	na	na	na	*0.9*	trace	0.0	0.0	trace	0.0	trace	*0.3*	na	na
Days With ≥ 1.0" Snow Depth	na	na	na	*0*	0	0	0	0	0	0	*0*	na	na

Shepaug Dam *Litchfield County*   Elevation: 839 ft.   Latitude: 41° 43' N   Longitude: 73° 18' W

	JAN	FEB	MAR	APR	MAY	JUN	JUL	AUG	SEP	OCT	NOV	DEC	YEAR
Mean Maximum Temp. (°F)	33.4	36.1	45.1	56.9	*68.4*	75.3	79.9	78.4	70.6	60.8	*49.9*	38.1	*57.8*
Mean Temp. (°F)	23.5	25.9	34.7	45.5	*56.9*	64.6	69.5	68.1	60.4	50.1	*40.6*	29.2	*47.4*
Mean Minimum Temp. (°F)	13.6	15.6	24.3	34.1	*45.3*	53.8	59.1	57.7	50.2	39.4	*31.3*	20.3	*37.0*
Extreme Maximum Temp. (°F)	62	70	85	91	90	92	95	95	92	85	79	68	95
Extreme Minimum Temp. (°F)	-24	-20	-10	8	25	33	42	37	30	20	5	-17	-24
Days Maximum Temp. ≥ 90°F	0	0	0	0	0	1	2	1	0	0	0	0	4
Days Maximum Temp. ≤ 32°F	14	10	3	0	0	0	0	0	0	0	1	8	36
Days Minimum Temp. ≤ 32°F	29	25	25	13	1	0	0	0	0	7	17	27	144
Days Minimum Temp. ≤ 0°F	5	3	1	0	0	0	0	0	0	0	0	1	10
Heating Degree Days (base 65°F)	1,280	1,098	932	580	*262*	79	16	30	168	457	*723*	1,103	*6,728*
Cooling Degree Days (base 65°F)	0	0	0	1	*15*	71	161	126	34	2	*0*	0	*410*
Mean Precipitation (in.)	3.83	3.15	4.41	4.22	4.48	4.04	4.66	4.45	4.61	4.22	4.21	3.86	50.14
Days With ≥ 0.1" Precipitation	7	7	8	8	9	8	8	6	7	6	7	7	88
Days With ≥ 1.0" Precipitation	1	1	1	1	1	1	1	1	1	1	1	1	12
Mean Snowfall (in.)	14.7	11.0	9.3	3.1	trace	0.0	0.0	0.0	0.0	0.3	2.6	8.9	49.9
Days With ≥ 1.0" Snow Depth	na	na	na	na	0	0	0	0	0	0	na	na	na

Stamford 5 N *Fairfield County*   Elevation: 187 ft.   Latitude: 41° 07' N   Longitude: 73° 33' W

	JAN	FEB	MAR	APR	MAY	JUN	JUL	AUG	SEP	OCT	NOV	DEC	YEAR
Mean Maximum Temp. (°F)	37.9	41.2	50.0	61.9	72.6	80.4	85.4	83.3	75.7	65.0	53.7	42.6	62.5
Mean Temp. (°F)	28.5	31.0	39.3	49.7	60.0	68.3	73.6	72.0	64.5	53.4	43.7	33.7	51.5
Mean Minimum Temp. (°F)	18.9	20.7	28.6	37.4	47.4	56.2	61.8	60.6	53.3	41.7	33.6	24.8	40.4
Extreme Maximum Temp. (°F)	68	74	85	93	97	97	102	98	97	86	80	76	102
Extreme Minimum Temp. (°F)	-18	-14	1	16	28	35	43	39	30	16	13	-13	-18
Days Maximum Temp. ≥ 90°F	0	0	0	0	1	3	7	4	1	0	0	0	16
Days Maximum Temp. ≤ 32°F	9	5	1	0	0	0	0	0	0	0	0	4	19
Days Minimum Temp. ≤ 32°F	28	25	21	9	1	0	0	0	0	5	15	25	129
Days Minimum Temp. ≤ 0°F	2	1	0	0	0	0	0	0	0	0	0	0	3
Heating Degree Days (base 65°F)	1,126	956	789	455	180	32	2	7	88	358	634	963	5,590
Cooling Degree Days (base 65°F)	0	0	0	2	35	149	291	234	83	5	0	0	799
Mean Precipitation (in.)	4.60	3.49	4.74	4.52	4.89	4.26	3.92	4.18	4.76	4.49	4.59	4.21	52.65
Days With ≥ 0.1" Precipitation	7	6	8	7	8	7	6	6	6	6	6	7	80
Days With ≥ 1.0" Precipitation	1	1	1	1	1	1	1	1	1	1	2	1	13
Mean Snowfall (in.)	9.7	8.7	5.3	0.8	trace	0.0	0.0	0.0	0.0	trace	0.7	4.2	29.4
Days With ≥ 1.0" Snow Depth	na	na	2	0	0	0	0	0	0	0	0	3	na

West Thompson Lake *Windham County*   Elevation: 357 ft.   Latitude: 41° 57' N   Longitude: 71° 54' W

	JAN	FEB	MAR	APR	MAY	JUN	JUL	AUG	SEP	OCT	NOV	DEC	YEAR
Mean Maximum Temp. (°F)	34.4	37.3	46.4	57.8	69.4	77.3	82.6	80.5	72.6	61.9	51.3	39.3	59.2
Mean Temp. (°F)	23.2	26.1	35.7	45.9	56.9	65.3	70.7	69.0	60.6	49.3	na	29.2	na
Mean Minimum Temp. (°F)	11.9	14.8	24.7	34.1	44.3	53.3	58.8	57.4	48.5	36.4	na	19.3	na
Extreme Maximum Temp. (°F)	65	70	84	94	96	96	100	100	97	85	80	74	100
Extreme Minimum Temp. (°F)	-23	-21	-6	2	26	32	40	35	29	16	-2	-20	-23
Days Maximum Temp. ≥ 90°F	0	0	0	0	1	2	4	2	1	0	0	0	10
Days Maximum Temp. ≤ 32°F	11	8	2	0	0	0	0	0	0	0	1	7	29
Days Minimum Temp. ≤ 32°F	27	24	24	13	2	0	0	0	1	11	18	25	145
Days Minimum Temp. ≤ 0°F	5	3	0	0	0	0	0	0	0	0	0	1	9
Heating Degree Days (base 65°F)	1,290	1,091	903	567	263	73	13	28	166	484	na	1,104	na
Cooling Degree Days (base 65°F)	na	na	0	1	18	89	195	152	38	3	na	na	na
Mean Precipitation (in.)	4.56	3.41	4.40	4.32	3.98	3.92	4.45	4.56	3.99	4.49	4.73	4.25	51.06
Days With ≥ 0.1" Precipitation	7	6	7	7	8	6	6	7	6	6	7	7	80
Days With ≥ 1.0" Precipitation	1	1	1	1	1	1	1	2	1	1	1	1	13
Mean Snowfall (in.)	10.8	9.1	5.9	2.2	0.0	0.0	0.0	0.0	0.0	trace	1.8	7.0	36.8
Days With ≥ 1.0" Snow Depth	14	11	6	1	0	0	0	0	0	0	1	8	41

Wigwam Reservoir *Litchfield County*   Elevation: 567 ft.   Latitude: 41° 40' N   Longitude: 73° 08' W

	JAN	FEB	MAR	APR	MAY	JUN	JUL	AUG	SEP	OCT	NOV	DEC	YEAR
Mean Maximum Temp. (°F)	34.6	37.3	47.0	59.0	70.6	78.2	83.3	81.3	73.4	62.8	51.5	39.3	59.9
Mean Temp. (°F)	24.1	26.1	35.6	46.0	57.1	65.4	70.6	68.9	60.9	50.1	40.5	29.9	47.9
Mean Minimum Temp. (°F)	13.7	14.9	24.1	33.0	43.6	52.5	57.8	56.5	48.4	37.4	29.5	19.8	35.9
Extreme Maximum Temp. (°F)	63	67	81	93	96	96	100	98	94	88	78	68	100
Extreme Minimum Temp. (°F)	-21	-18	-9	0	23	32	38	35	23	14	5	-14	-21
Days Maximum Temp. ≥ 90°F	0	0	0	0	0	2	4	3	1	0	0	0	10
Days Maximum Temp. ≤ 32°F	12	9	2	0	0	0	0	0	0	0	0	7	30
Days Minimum Temp. ≤ 32°F	30	27	25	15	3	0	0	0	1	11	20	28	160
Days Minimum Temp. ≤ 0°F	4	4	0	0	0	0	0	0	0	0	0	2	10
Heating Degree Days (base 65°F)	1,260	1,091	906	566	255	70	11	25	160	457	727	1,083	6,611
Cooling Degree Days (base 65°F)	0	0	0	1	18	91	211	161	44	2	0	0	528
Mean Precipitation (in.)	3.79	3.21	4.37	4.31	4.45	4.09	4.36	4.53	4.46	4.52	4.44	4.23	50.76
Days With ≥ 0.1" Precipitation	6	6	7	8	8	7	7	6	6	6	7	7	81
Days With ≥ 1.0" Precipitation	1	1	1	1	1	1	1	1	1	1	1	1	12
Mean Snowfall (in.)	na	na	na	0.7	0.0	0.0	0.0	0.0	0.0	trace	na	na	na
Days With ≥ 1.0" Snow Depth	na	na	na	na	0	0	0	0	0	0	na	na	na

Note: See Appendix D for explanation of data.

DELAWARE

PHYSICAL FEATURES. The State of Delaware is located on the east coast of the United States midway between the north and the south. Delaware lies in a north-south position, spanning a distance of 96 miles. The width increases from nine miles in the northern portion to 35 miles in the extreme southern portion. The State occupies the eastern and northern portion of the Delmarva Peninsula which is bounded by the Chesapeake Bay on the west and the Delaware Bay and Atlantic Ocean on the east. The total area of Delaware is 2,057 square miles.

Over 95 percent of the land area of the State is more or less flat and without topographic features; however, the extreme northern portion, about 120 square miles, which lies on the Piedmont, is undulating and hilly with elevations rising to 438 feet above mean sea level. This increase in elevation no doubt contributes to a slight decrease in local temperatures under certain circumstances.

GENERAL CLIMATE. Since the flow of the atmosphere in temperate latitudes is from west to east, the distribution of land and water masses, i.e., the expansive North American continent situated immediately to the west, predisposes the Delaware area to a continental type of climate. This type of climate in middle latitudes is marked by well-defined seasons. Winter is the dormant season for plant growth and is one of low temperature rather than drought. In spring and fall the changeability of the weather is a striking characteristic. It is occasioned by a rapid succession of warm and cold periods associated with storms, which generally move from a westerly direction over the eastern portion of the United States. Summers are warm to hot. The higher atmospheric humidity along the sea coast causes the summer heat to be more oppressive or sultry and the winter cold more raw and penetrating than in drier climates of the interior.

The topography of the eastern United States is characterized by the Appalachian Mountains, which extend along a northeast-southwest axis about 150 miles to the northwest of Delaware. To the west and northwest of Delaware, these mountains range in height from 2,000 to 3,000 feet above mean sea level and contribute to some slight tempering of the cold air masses which move rapidly out of the interior of the continent over the Delaware region in the winter.

A semipermanent high pressure area with a clockwise circulation virtually overspreads the entire Atlantic Ocean at middle latitudes and exerts a pronounced effect on the weather regimes of the east coast. During the winter season the Atlantic High (or Azores High) maintains an average position between latitude 30 N. and 33 N. and longitudes 25 W. and 35 W. and overspreads the eastern portion of the south Atlantic Ocean. As the summer season approaches, the Atlantic High moves westward and slightly northward to a mean position between latitudes 32 N. and 35 N. and longitudes 40 W. and 45 W. During this period it becomes more intense and widespread as the semipermanent low of the north Atlantic Ocean becomes smaller and weaker. In the summer location the Atlantic High dominates the flow of air over the eastern United States much of the time. A persistence of the Atlantic High in a westerly position in the vicinity of Bermuda results in a prolonged flow of moist, warm tropical air over the entire eastern United States. Weather in this type of air mass consists of scattered thunderstorms, considerable daytime cloudiness, and hot, sultry conditions. In the westerly position the High exerts blocking action on Lows which are forced to travel across more northerly latitudes. Persistence of this High over the eastern United States frequently results in drought conditions over the Delaware region, as the dry, subsiding air of the High prevents the formation of precipitation.

WINDS. Prevailing surface winds in northern Delaware blow from the northwesterly quadrant in all months except June, when southerly winds prevail. However, during the periods of May and July through September, winds come from the southwesterly quadrant a high proportion of the time. In southern Delaware surface winds prevail from the southwesterly quadrant from May through September and from the northwesterly quadrant from October through April.

Average wind speeds are higher during the period January through April, largely due to the rapid succession of well-developed storm systems which migrate from a westerly to easterly direction. During this period average wind speeds of about 10 miles per hour prevail. From July through October winds are somewhat lighter, averaging from seven to nine miles per hour.

During the fall, winter, and spring seasons, it is not unusual to experience brief windstorms associated with violent, fast-moving cold fronts with gusts from 50 to 60 m.p.h. In the summer, rare occurrences of violent windstorms are associated with severe thunderstorms. From June through October, it is estimated that wind speeds of more than 75 m.p.h. could occur anywhere in Delaware during the rare event of a hurricane traversing or passing very near the State.

Delaware lies in the mean zone of the westerlies in the winter and slightly south of the tracks followed by most of the migrating cyclones in their movement from some point in the United States to the region of semipermanent low pressure in the Iceland or North Atlantic area. Cyclones which have their origin in the south Pacific coastal region, Texas, or the Gulf or South Atlantic States have a greater tendency to follow a track through the Delaware region. Storms of the south Pacific coast, Texas, east Gulf, and sometimes of the south Atlantic bring the heaviest widespread rains to the Delaware area.

TEMPERATURE. The difference in latitude of northern Delaware and southern Delaware contributes in some part to the difference in mean temperature between these two regions of the State. The mean temperature difference of 3 to 4°F. between northern and southern portions in winter and 1 to 2°F. in summer is largely but not entirely due to the variation in solar radiational heating. In the extreme northern portion where elevations range from 300 to 400 feet on the higher hills, altitude is a controlling factor, although a small one, and reduces temperatures by approximately 1 on the average as compared to the nearby lower terrain.

In order for ocean currents to have a direct temperature control, the winds must be prevailing onshore. The relatively frequent occurrence of easterly winds associated with cyclonic storms to the southeast brings about advection of air off the mild waters and consequently tends to raise the normal winter temperatures and lower the summer temperatures. Therefore, mean winter temperatures of Delaware are roughly 5°F. higher than for regions of the continental interior at the same latitude.

The climate of Delaware is humid, temperate, with hot summers and mild winters. The winter climate is intermediate between the cold of the northeast and the mild weather of the south. The average frost penetration ranges from about five inches in southern Delaware to about 10 inches in northern Delaware. Summer weather is characterized by considerable warm weather, including at least several hot, humid periods. However, nights are usually quite comfortable. The average length of the growing (frost-free) season ranges from about 175 to 195 days.

PRECIPITATION. The average annual precipitation ranges from 44 inches in northern Delaware to 47 inches in southern Delaware. The monthly distribution is fairly uniform throughout the year, with July and August the months with heaviest amounts. Precipitation in the summer season is less dependable and more variable than in winter. The seasonal increase in evapotranspiration during the summer results in a rapid loss of soil moisture and contributes to the development of drought conditions. Flooding occurs infrequently, and results largely from tides pushed by strong easterly winds. The passage through the area of storms of tropical origin, usually during the late summer or fall, with their high winds and intense rains constitute the most serious flood threat.

The mean snowfall is 18 inches in northern Delaware and 14 inches in southern Delaware. The snow season runs from December through March, with a few light flurries in some years as early as November or late October and as late as early April. Heaviest snowfalls in Delaware generally occur in February and March.

STORMS. Thunderstorms occur at a given station on the average of 30 to 33 days per year. The Atlantic coastal region has fewer thunderstorms than interior portions, on the average. They have been observed in every month of the year; however, July is the month with the greatest frequency of thunderstorms, on the average. Hail is uncommon in Delaware. The frequency of occurrence of tornadoes in Delaware is estimated at about one in two or three years, on the average.

Average relative humidity in Delaware is lowest in winter and early spring, and highest in the late summer and early fall. February and March have average relative humidities of about 60 to 65 percent, whereas August, September, and October have average relative humidities of about 75 to 80 percent.

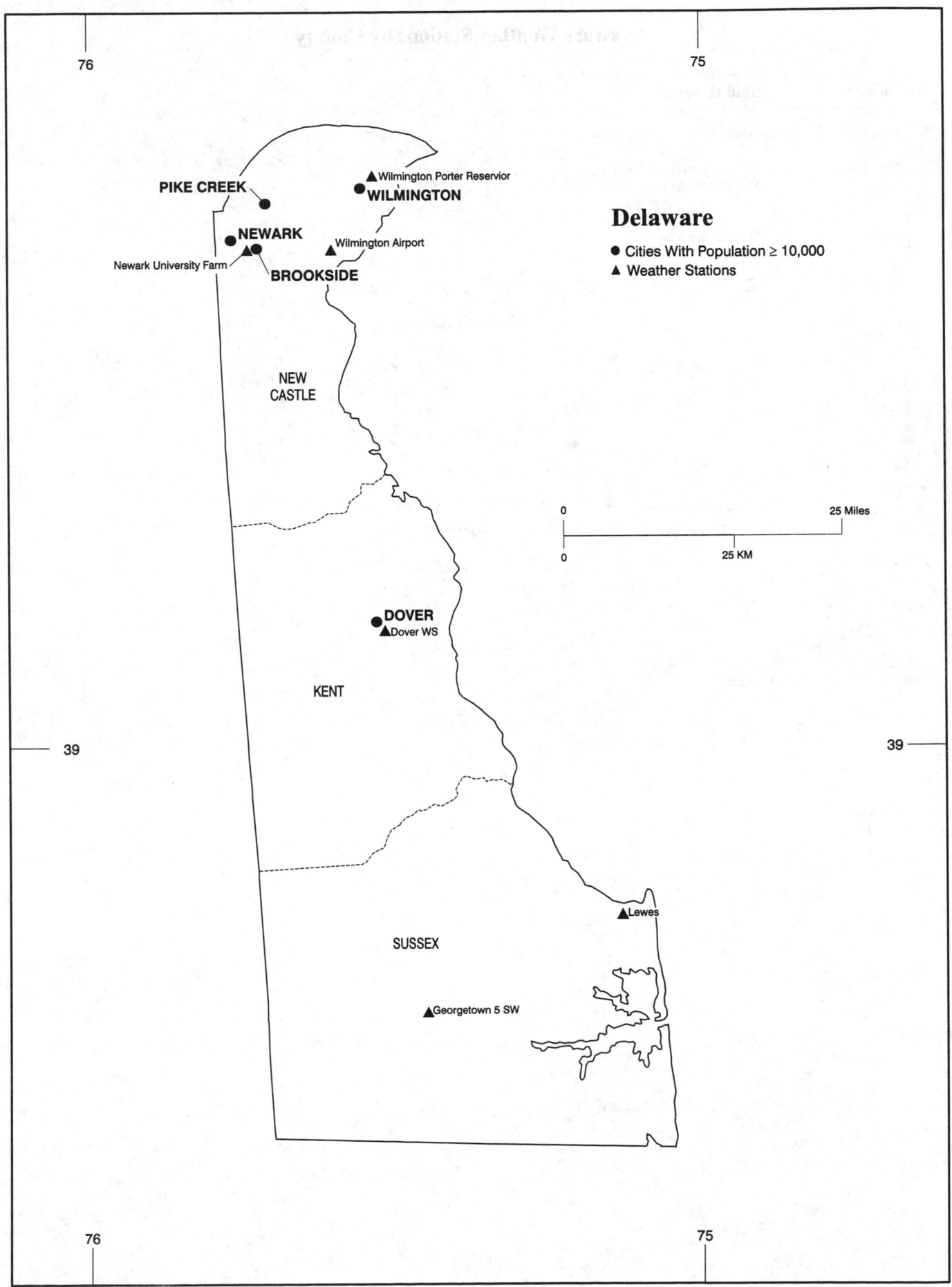

PIKE CREEK

▲ Wilmington Porter Reservior

● **WILMINGTON**

● **NEWARK**

▲ Wilmington Airport

Newark University Farm

● **BROOKSIDE**

Delaware

● Cities With Population ≥ 10,000
▲ Weather Stations

NEW
CASTLE

| 0 | | 25 Miles |
| 0 | 25 KM | |

● **DOVER**
▲Dover WS

KENT

▲Lewes

SUSSEX

▲Georgetown 5 SW

Delaware Weather Stations by County

County	Station Name
Kent	Dover
New Castle	Newark University Farm Wilmington Airport Wilmington Porter Reservior
Sussex	Georgetown 5 SW Lewes

Delaware Weather Stations by City

City	Station Name	Miles
Brookside	Newark University Farm	1
	Wilmington Airport	6
	Wilmington Porter Reservior	12
	Marcus Hook, PA	19
Dover	Dover	1
Newark	Newark University Farm	2
	Wilmington Airport	8
	Wilmington Porter Reservior	13
Pike Creek	Newark University Farm	5
	Wilmington Airport	7
	Wilmington Porter Reservior	9
	Marcus Hook, PA	16
Wilmington	Newark University Farm	11
	Wilmington Airport	6
	Wilmington Porter Reservior	2
	Woodstown, NJ	14
	Marcus Hook, PA	9
	Philadelphia Int'l Airport, PA	19

Note: Miles is the distance between the geographic center of the city and the weather station.

Delaware Weather Stations by Elevation

Feet	Station Name
269	Wilmington Porter Reservior
88	Newark University Farm
72	Wilmington Airport
42	Georgetown 5 SW
29	Dover
13	Lewes

Wilmington Airport

Delaware is part of the Atlantic Coastal Plain consisting mainly of flat low land with many marshes. Small streams and tidal estuaries comprise the drainage of the State. Wilmington, at the northern end of the State, marks the beginning of low rolling hills extending northward and northwestward into Pennsylvania. The Delaware River, the Delaware Bay, and the Atlantic Ocean are along the eastern boundary of the State. The broad Chesapeake Bay lies 35 miles, or less, to the west of the western boundary of nearly the entire State. These large water areas considerably influence the climate of the Wilmington, Delaware region.

Summers are warm and humid, winters are usually mild. During the summer maximum temperatures are usually in the 80s. The temperature reaches 100 degrees on the average once in six years. During January, the coldest month of the year, the daily average temperature is 32 degrees. Temperatures of zero may be expected once in four years. Most of the winter precipitation falls as rain. Seasonal snowfall has been as little as one inch, and as much as 50 inches. Snow is frequently mixed with rain and sleet, and seldom remains on the ground more than a few days.

The proximity of large water areas and the inflow of southerly winds cause the relative humidity to be quite high all year. During the summer months the relative humidity is approximately 75 percent. Fog is relatively frequent and may occur in any month. Light southeast winds blowing up the Delaware Bay favor the formation of fog. Light north-northeast winds bring in smoke from Philadelphia and from the heavy industry area located along the Delaware River north of Wilmington.

Rainfall distribution throughout the year is fairly uniform, however, the greatest amounts normally come during the summer months. Mostly, the summer rainfall comes in the form of thunderstorms. Moisture deficiencies for crops occur occasionally, but severe droughts are rare. During the fall, winter, and spring seasons, much of the rainfall comes from storms forming over the southern states or the South Atlantic and moving northward along the coast. During the late summer and early fall, hurricanes occasionally cause heavy rainfall, but winds seldom reach hurricane force in Wilmington. Heavy rains occasionally cause minor flooding. Strong easterly and southeasterly winds sometimes cause high tides in the Delaware Bay and the Delaware River.

Based on the 1951-1980 period, the average first occurrence of 32 degrees Fahrenheit in the fall is October 29 and the average last occurrence in the spring is April 13.

Wilmington Airport *New Castle County*   Elevation: 72 ft.   Latitude: 39° 40' N   Longitude: 75° 36' W

	JAN	FEB	MAR	APR	MAY	JUN	JUL	AUG	SEP	OCT	NOV	DEC	YEAR
Mean Maximum Temp. (°F)	39.6	43.0	52.2	63.3	73.1	81.4	86.2	84.4	77.6	66.3	55.5	45.0	64.0
Mean Temp. (°F)	31.6	34.4	42.8	52.8	62.8	71.7	76.9	75.2	68.1	56.1	46.3	36.9	54.6
Mean Minimum Temp. (°F)	23.5	25.8	33.4	42.2	52.5	61.9	67.5	66.0	58.4	45.9	37.2	28.7	45.3
Extreme Maximum Temp. (°F)	68	78	86	94	96	100	100	100	100	88	80	75	100
Extreme Minimum Temp. (°F)	-14	-6	2	18	30	41	48	43	36	24	15	-7	-14
Days Maximum Temp. ≥ 90°F	0	0	0	0	1	3	9	6	2	0	0	0	21
Days Maximum Temp. ≤ 32°F	8	5	1	0	0	0	0	0	0	0	0	3	17
Days Minimum Temp. ≤ 32°F	25	21	14	3	0	0	0	0	0	1	10	21	95
Days Minimum Temp. ≤ 0°F	1	0	0	0	0	0	0	0	0	0	0	0	1
Heating Degree Days (base 65°F)	1,029	857	684	370	127	14	1	2	45	286	554	864	4,833
Cooling Degree Days (base 65°F)	0	0	2	9	70	228	391	317	139	18	0	0	1,174
Mean Precipitation (in.)	3.38	2.81	3.78	3.47	4.08	3.63	4.32	3.51	3.79	3.17	3.24	3.41	42.59
Maximum Precipitation (in.)	8.4	7.0	7.5	6.8	7.4	7.5	12.6	12.1	9.5	8.0	7.8	7.9	54.7
Minimum Precipitation (in.)	0.5	0.8	0.8	0.3	0.2	0.2	0.2	0.3	0.8	0.2	0.5	0.2	24.9
Maximum 24-hr. Precipitation (in.)	2.0	2.3	2.6	2.3	2.7	4.1	6.6	3.8	4.6	3.7	2.8	2.0	6.6
Days With ≥ 0.1" Precipitation	6	5	7	6	7	7	6	5	6	5	6	6	72
Days With ≥ 1.0" Precipitation	1	1	1	1	1	1	1	1	1	1	1	1	12
Mean Snowfall (in.)	7.5	6.1	2.2	0.3	trace	trace	trace	0.0	0.0	trace	0.6	2.0	18.7
Maximum Snowfall (in.)	21	28	20	3	trace	0	0	0	0	3	12	22	49
Maximum 24-hr. Snowfall (in.)	12	15	13	2	trace	0	0	0	0	3	7	12	15
Days With ≥ 1.0" Snow Depth	8	5	1	0	0	0	0	0	0	0	0	2	16
Thunderstorm Days	< 1	< 1	1	2	4	6	6	6	2	1	1	< 1	29
Foggy Days	12	11	13	12	15	15	16	17	16	15	13	13	168
Predominant Sky Cover	OVR	OVR	OVR	OVR	OVR	OVR	OVR	OVR	OVR	OVR	OVR	OVR	OVR
Mean Relative Humidity 7am (%)	75	74	74	73	76	78	80	83	85	84	80	76	78
Mean Relative Humidity 4pm (%)	60	56	52	50	53	54	55	57	56	55	58	61	55
Mean Dewpoint (°F)	22	23	29	39	50	60	65	64	58	46	36	26	43
Prevailing Wind Direction	WNW	NW	NW	WNW	S	S	S	S	NW	NW	NW	NW	NW
Prevailing Wind Speed (mph)	13	13	14	12	10	9	9	9	8	9	12	12	10
Maximum Wind Gust (mph)	67	58	71	62	71	61	66	60	64	58	59	69	71

Dover *Kent County*   Elevation: 29 ft.   Latitude: 39° 09' N   Longitude: 75° 31' W

	JAN	FEB	MAR	APR	MAY	JUN	JUL	AUG	SEP	OCT	NOV	DEC	YEAR
Mean Maximum Temp. (°F)	43.5	46.6	54.9	65.5	74.8	82.9	87.6	85.8	79.8	69.0	58.8	48.6	66.5
Mean Temp. (°F)	35.0	37.3	45.0	54.5	64.1	72.6	77.6	76.0	69.7	58.4	49.1	39.9	56.6
Mean Minimum Temp. (°F)	26.4	28.0	35.1	43.5	53.4	62.3	67.6	66.2	59.5	47.9	39.3	31.2	46.7
Extreme Maximum Temp. (°F)	74	77	86	97	97	100	101	102	98	90	82	75	102
Extreme Minimum Temp. (°F)	-5	-1	9	17	34	43	51	45	38	27	16	1	-5
Days Maximum Temp. ≥ 90°F	0	0	0	0	1	5	12	8	3	0	0	0	29
Days Maximum Temp. ≤ 32°F	5	3	0	0	0	0	0	0	0	0	0	2	10
Days Minimum Temp. ≤ 32°F	23	19	12	2	0	0	0	0	0	1	8	18	83
Days Minimum Temp. ≤ 0°F	0	0	0	0	0	0	0	0	0	0	0	0	0
Heating Degree Days (base 65°F)	924	775	618	323	104	11	0	1	29	225	476	771	4,257
Cooling Degree Days (base 65°F)	0	0	4	14	88	254	416	344	175	31	3	0	1,329
Mean Precipitation (in.)	3.86	3.00	4.26	3.51	4.26	3.80	4.14	4.51	4.39	3.35	3.17	3.50	45.75
Days With ≥ 0.1" Precipitation	7	6	7	7	8	6	7	6	6	5	6	7	78
Days With ≥ 1.0" Precipitation	1	1	1	1	1	1	1	1	1	1	1	1	12
Mean Snowfall (in.)	5.0	6.2	1.1	trace	0.0	0.0	0.0	0.0	0.0	trace	0.3	1.4	14.0
Days With ≥ 1.0" Snow Depth	4	3	1	0	0	0	0	0	0	0	0	2	10

Georgetown 5 SW *Sussex County*   Elevation: 42 ft.   Latitude: 38° 38' N   Longitude: 75° 27' W

	JAN	FEB	MAR	APR	MAY	JUN	JUL	AUG	SEP	OCT	NOV	DEC	YEAR
Mean Maximum Temp. (°F)	42.8	45.3	53.8	64.0	73.0	81.9	86.6	84.8	79.0	68.2	58.2	48.2	65.5
Mean Temp. (°F)	33.6	35.8	43.6	52.7	62.3	71.3	76.0	74.4	68.0	56.8	47.6	38.6	55.1
Mean Minimum Temp. (°F)	24.3	26.2	33.4	41.4	51.5	60.7	65.4	64.0	57.0	45.3	37.1	29.1	44.6
Extreme Maximum Temp. (°F)	71	76	87	92	96	100	101	98	97	89	82	77	101
Extreme Minimum Temp. (°F)	-13	-8	10	21	30	41	44	42	35	23	15	2	-13
Days Maximum Temp. ≥ 90°F	0	0	0	0	1	4	10	6	2	0	0	0	23
Days Maximum Temp. ≤ 32°F	6	4	1	0	0	0	0	0	0	0	0	2	13
Days Minimum Temp. ≤ 32°F	24	21	15	5	0	0	0	0	0	3	11	20	99
Days Minimum Temp. ≤ 0°F	1	0	0	0	0	0	0	0	0	0	0	0	1
Heating Degree Days (base 65°F)	968	819	658	373	140	19	1	4	49	272	517	810	4,630
Cooling Degree Days (base 65°F)	0	0	2	10	65	227	367	299	141	25	3	0	1,139
Mean Precipitation (in.)	3.71	3.08	4.15	3.53	3.96	3.48	3.61	5.45	3.70	3.58	3.33	3.41	44.99
Days With ≥ 0.1" Precipitation	7	7	7	7	7	6	6	6	5	6	6	6	76
Days With ≥ 1.0" Precipitation	1	1	1	1	1	1	1	2	1	1	1	1	13
Mean Snowfall (in.)	4.4	5.0	1.2	0.1	0.0	0.0	0.0	0.0	0.0	trace	0.1	1.4	12.2
Days With ≥ 1.0" Snow Depth	3	3	1	0	0	0	0	0	0	0	0	1	8

Lewes *Sussex County*   Elevation: 13 ft.   Latitude: 38° 46' N   Longitude: 75° 08' W

	JAN	FEB	MAR	APR	MAY	JUN	JUL	AUG	SEP	OCT	NOV	DEC	YEAR
Mean Maximum Temp. (°F)	44.2	46.5	54.1	64.4	73.5	81.7	85.9	84.4	78.7	68.4	58.9	49.6	65.9
Mean Temp. (°F)	36.1	38.0	45.1	54.3	63.6	72.4	77.1	75.7	70.1	59.2	50.1	41.3	56.9
Mean Minimum Temp. (°F)	27.9	29.4	36.0	44.1	53.8	63.0	68.3	67.1	61.3	49.9	41.2	33.0	47.9
Extreme Maximum Temp. (°F)	72	86	89	92	97	102	101	101	98	88	83	77	102
Extreme Minimum Temp. (°F)	-11	0	11	18	34	41	51	47	38	27	17	3	-11
Days Maximum Temp. ≥ 90°F	0	0	0	0	1	5	9	6	2	0	0	0	23
Days Maximum Temp. ≤ 32°F	4	3	0	0	0	0	0	0	0	0	0	2	9
Days Minimum Temp. ≤ 32°F	21	17	11	2	0	0	0	0	0	1	6	15	73
Days Minimum Temp. ≤ 0°F	0	0	0	0	0	0	0	0	0	0	0	0	0
Heating Degree Days (base 65°F)	891	757	617	329	113	13	1	1	22	206	445	728	4,123
Cooling Degree Days (base 65°F)	0	0	6	17	90	269	421	355	193	38	5	1	1,395
Mean Precipitation (in.)	3.96	3.28	4.32	3.50	3.87	3.21	4.08	5.37	3.62	3.49	3.34	3.83	45.87
Days With ≥ 0.1" Precipitation	7	6	7	6	7	6	7	6	5	5	6	7	75
Days With ≥ 1.0" Precipitation	1	1	1	1	1	1	1	2	1	1	1	1	13
Mean Snowfall (in.)	3.6	4.3	1.1	trace	0.0	0.0	0.0	0.0	0.0	0.0	0.3	1.1	10.4
Days With ≥ 1.0" Snow Depth	2	2	1	0	0	0	0	0	0	0	0	1	6

Newark University Farm *New Castle County*   Elevation: 88 ft.   Latitude: 39° 40' N   Longitude: 75° 44' W

	JAN	FEB	MAR	APR	MAY	JUN	JUL	AUG	SEP	OCT	NOV	DEC	YEAR
Mean Maximum Temp. (°F)	41.1	44.9	54.1	65.3	75.5	83.3	87.6	85.9	79.4	68.0	56.9	46.2	65.7
Mean Temp. (°F)	32.3	35.1	43.2	53.2	63.4	71.8	76.6	74.9	68.2	56.4	46.6	37.4	54.9
Mean Minimum Temp. (°F)	23.5	25.2	32.2	40.9	51.2	60.2	65.6	63.9	56.9	44.8	36.4	28.5	44.1
Extreme Maximum Temp. (°F)	72	79	89	93	96	99	105	100	100	89	81	74	105
Extreme Minimum Temp. (°F)	-10	-8	4	14	28	38	41	42	35	24	15	-6	-10
Days Maximum Temp. ≥ 90°F	0	0	0	0	1	5	11	7	2	0	0	0	26
Days Maximum Temp. ≤ 32°F	6	4	0	0	0	0	0	0	0	0	0	2	12
Days Minimum Temp. ≤ 32°F	26	22	17	5	0	0	0	0	0	2	10	21	103
Days Minimum Temp. ≤ 0°F	1	0	0	0	0	0	0	0	0	0	0	0	1
Heating Degree Days (base 65°F)	1,006	839	671	358	114	13	1	2	44	277	546	850	4,721
Cooling Degree Days (base 65°F)	0	0	2	9	73	233	389	316	147	19	1	0	1,189
Mean Precipitation (in.)	3.42	2.71	3.87	3.57	4.34	4.11	4.56	3.98	4.09	3.43	3.44	3.56	45.08
Days With ≥ 0.1" Precipitation	6	5	7	7	8	7	7	6	6	5	6	6	76
Days With ≥ 1.0" Precipitation	1	1	1	1	1	1	1	1	1	1	1	1	12
Mean Snowfall (in.)	5.5	3.6	1.5	trace	0.0	0.0	0.0	0.0	0.0	trace	0.1	0.9	11.6
Days With ≥ 1.0" Snow Depth	6	4	1	0	0	0	0	0	0	0	0	1	12

Wilmington Porter Reservior *New Castle County* Elevation: 269 ft. Latitude: 39° 46' N Longitude: 75° 32' W

	JAN	FEB	MAR	APR	MAY	JUN	JUL	AUG	SEP	OCT	NOV	DEC	YEAR
Mean Maximum Temp. (°F)	38.7	42.1	50.9	62.0	72.1	80.5	85.1	83.4	76.3	65.0	54.3	44.1	62.9
Mean Temp. (°F)	31.2	34.0	42.0	52.2	62.5	71.2	76.0	74.3	67.2	55.7	45.9	36.5	54.1
Mean Minimum Temp. (°F)	23.6	25.9	33.1	42.3	52.7	61.9	67.0	65.2	58.0	46.3	37.5	28.9	45.2
Extreme Maximum Temp. (°F)	68	74	87	94	94	97	100	99	97	86	80	73	100
Extreme Minimum Temp. (°F)	-9	-5	5	19	29	45	51	43	35	24	14	-1	-9
Days Maximum Temp. ≥ 90°F	0	0	0	0	1	3	7	4	1	0	0	0	16
Days Maximum Temp. ≤ 32°F	8	5	1	0	0	0	0	0	0	0	0	3	17
Days Minimum Temp. ≤ 32°F	25	21	14	3	0	0	0	0	0	1	9	21	94
Days Minimum Temp. ≤ 0°F	1	0	0	0	0	0	0	0	0	0	0	0	1
Heating Degree Days (base 65°F)	1,041	869	707	386	134	15	1	3	54	296	567	876	4,949
Cooling Degree Days (base 65°F)	0	0	3	8	69	225	379	308	132	17	1	0	1,142
Mean Precipitation (in.)	4.04	3.09	4.36	4.18	4.71	4.11	4.68	3.95	4.54	3.67	3.78	3.91	49.02
Days With ≥ 0.1" Precipitation	7	6	7	7	8	7	7	6	6	6	6	6	79
Days With ≥ 1.0" Precipitation	1	1	1	1	1	1	2	1	1	1	1	1	13
Mean Snowfall (in.)	6.0	5.5	1.8	trace	0.0	0.0	0.0	0.0	0.0	trace	0.5	1.1	14.9
Days With ≥ 1.0" Snow Depth	5	5	1	0	0	0	0	0	0	0	0	1	12

Note: See Appendix D for explanation of data.

FLORIDA

PHYSICAL FEATURES. Florida, situated between latitudes 24° 30' and 31° N., and longitudes 80° and 87° 30' W., is largely a lowland peninsula comprising about 54,100 square miles of land area and is surrounded on three sides by the waters of the Atlantic Ocean and the Gulf of Mexico. Countless shallow lakes, which exist particularly on the peninsula and range in size from small cypress ponds to that of Lake Okeechobee, account for approximately 4,400 square miles of additional water area.

No point in the State is more than 70 miles from salt water, and the highest natural land in the Northwest Division is only 345 feet above sea level. Coastal areas are low and flat and are indented by many small bays or inlets. Many small islands dot the shorelines. The elevation of most of the interior ranges from 50 to 100 feet above sea level, though gentle hills in the interior of the peninsula and across the northern and western portions of the State rise above 200 feet.

A large portion of the southern one-third of the peninsula is the swampland known as the Everglades. An ill-defined divide of low, rolling hills, extending north-to-south near the middle of the peninsula and terminating north of Lake Okeechobee, gives rise to most peninsula streams, chains of lakes, and many springs. Stream gradients are slight and often insufficient to handle the runoff following heavy rainfall. Consequently, there are sizable areas of swamp and marshland near these streams.

GENERAL CLIMATE. Climate is probably Florida's greatest natural resource. General climatic conditions range from a zone of transition between temperate and subtropical conditions in the extreme northern interior portion of the State to the tropical conditions found on the Florida Keys. The chief factors of climatic control are: latitude, proximity to the Atlantic Ocean and Gulf of Mexico, and numerous inland lakes.

Summers throughout the State are long, warm, and relatively humid; winters, although punctuated with periodic invasions of cool to occasionally cold air from the north, are mild because of the southern latitude and relatively warm adjacent ocean waters. The Gulf Stream, which flows around the western tip of Cuba, through the Straits of Florida, and northward along the lower east coast, exerts a warming influence to the southern east coast largely because the predominate wind direction is from the east. Coastal weather stations throughout the State average slightly warmer in winter and cooler in summer than do inland weather stations at the same latitude.

Florida enjoys abundant rainfall. Except for the northwestern portion of the State, the average year can be divided into two seasons—the so-called "rainy season" and the long, relatively dry season. On the peninsula, generally more than one-half of the precipitation for an average year can be expected to fall during the four-month period, June through September. In northwest Florida, there is a secondary rainfall maximum in late winter and in early spring.

The summer heat is tempered by sea breezes along the coast and by frequent afternoon or early evening thunderstorms in all areas. During the warm season, sea breezes are felt almost daily within several miles of the coast and occasionally 20 to 30 miles inland. Thundershowers, which on the average occur about one-half of the days in summer, frequently are accompanied by as much as a rapid 10 to 20°F. drop in temperature, resulting in comfortable weather for the remainder of the day. Gentle breezes occur almost daily in all areas and serve to mitigate further the oppressiveness that otherwise would accompany the prevailing summer temperature and humidity conditions. Because most of the large-scale wind patterns affecting Florida have passed over water surfaces, hot drying winds seldom occur.

Most of the summer rainfall is derived from "local" showers or thundershowers. Many weather stations average more than 80 thundershowers per year, and some average more than 100. Showers are often heavy, usually lasting only one or two hours, and generally occur near the hottest part of the day. The more severe thundershowers are occasionally attended by hail or locally strong winds which may inflict serious local damage to crops and property. Day-long summer rains are usually associated with tropical disturbances and are infrequent. Even in the wet season, the rainfall duration is generally less than 10 percent of the time.

DROUGHTS. Florida is not immune from drought, even though annual rainfall amounts are relatively large. Prolonged periods of deficient rainfall are occasionally experienced even during the time of the expected rainy season. Several such dry periods, in the course of one or two years, can lead to significantly lowered water tables and lake levels which, in turn, may cause serious water shortages for those communities that depend upon lakes and shallow wells for their water supply. Statewide droughts during summer are rare, but it is not unusual during a drought in one portion of the State for other portions to receive generous rainfall. In a few instances, individual weather stations have experienced periods of a month or more without rainfall.

SNOW. Snowfall in Florida is unusual, although measurable amounts have fallen in the northern portions at irregular intervals, and a trace of snow has been recorded as far south as Fort Myers.

WIND. Prevailing winds over the southern peninsula are southeast and east. Over the remainder of the State, wind directions are influenced locally by convectional forces inland and by the land-and-sea-breeze-effect near the coast. Consequently, prevailing directions are somewhat erratic, but, in general, follow a pattern from the north in winter and from the south in summer. The windiest months are March and April. High local winds of short duration occur occasionally in connection with thunderstorms in summer and with cold fronts moving across the State in other seasons. Tornadoes, funnel clouds, and waterspouts also occur, averaging 10 to 15 in a year. Tornadoes have occurred in all seasons, but are most frequent in spring; they also occur in connection with tropical storms. Generally, tornado paths in Florida are short. Occasionally, waterspouts come inland, but they usually dissipate soon after reaching land and affect only very small areas.

TROPICAL STORMS. Storms that produce high winds and are often destructive are usually tropical in origin. Florida, jutting out into the ocean between the subtropical Atlantic and the Gulf of Mexico, is the most exposed of all States to these storms. In particular, hurricanes can approach from the Atlantic Ocean to the east, from the Caribbean Sea to the south, and from the Gulf of Mexico to the west.

The vulnerability of the State to tropical storms varies with the progress of the hurricane season. In August and early September, tropical storms normally approach the State from the east or southeast, but as the season progresses into late September and October, the region of maximum hurricane activity (insofar as Florida is concerned) shifts to the western Caribbean. Most of those storms that move into Florida approach the State from the south or southwest, entering the Keys, the Miami area, or along the west coast. Some of the world's heaviest rainfalls have occurred within tropical cyclones. Rainfall over 20 inches in 24 hours is not uncommon. The intensity of the rainfall, however, does not seem to bear any relation to the intensity of the wind circulation.

OTHER CLIMATIC ELEMENTS. The climate of Florida is humid. Inland areas with greater temperature extremes enjoy slightly lower relative humidity, especially during times of hot weather. On the average, variations in relative humidity from one place to another are small; humidities range from about 50 to 65 percent during the afternoon hours to about 85 to 95 percent during the night and early morning hours.

Heavy fogs are usually confined to the night and early morning hours in the late fall, winter, and early spring months. On the average, they occur about 35 to 40 days in a year over the extreme northern portion; about 25 to 30 days in a year over the central portion; and less than 10 days in a year over the extreme southern portion of the State. These fogs usually dissipate or thin soon after sunrise; heavy daytime fog is seldom observed in Florida.

Florida has been nicknamed the Sunshine State. Sunshine measurements made at widely separated stations in the State indicate the sun shines about two-thirds of the possible sunlight hours during the year, ranging from slightly more than 60 percent of possible in December and January to more than 70 percent of possible in April and May. In general, southern Florida enjoys a higher percentage of possible sunshine hours than does northern Florida. The length of day operates to Florida's advantage. In winter, when sunshine is highly valued, the sun can shine longer in Florida than in the more northern latitudes. In summer, the situation reverses itself with longer days returning to the north.

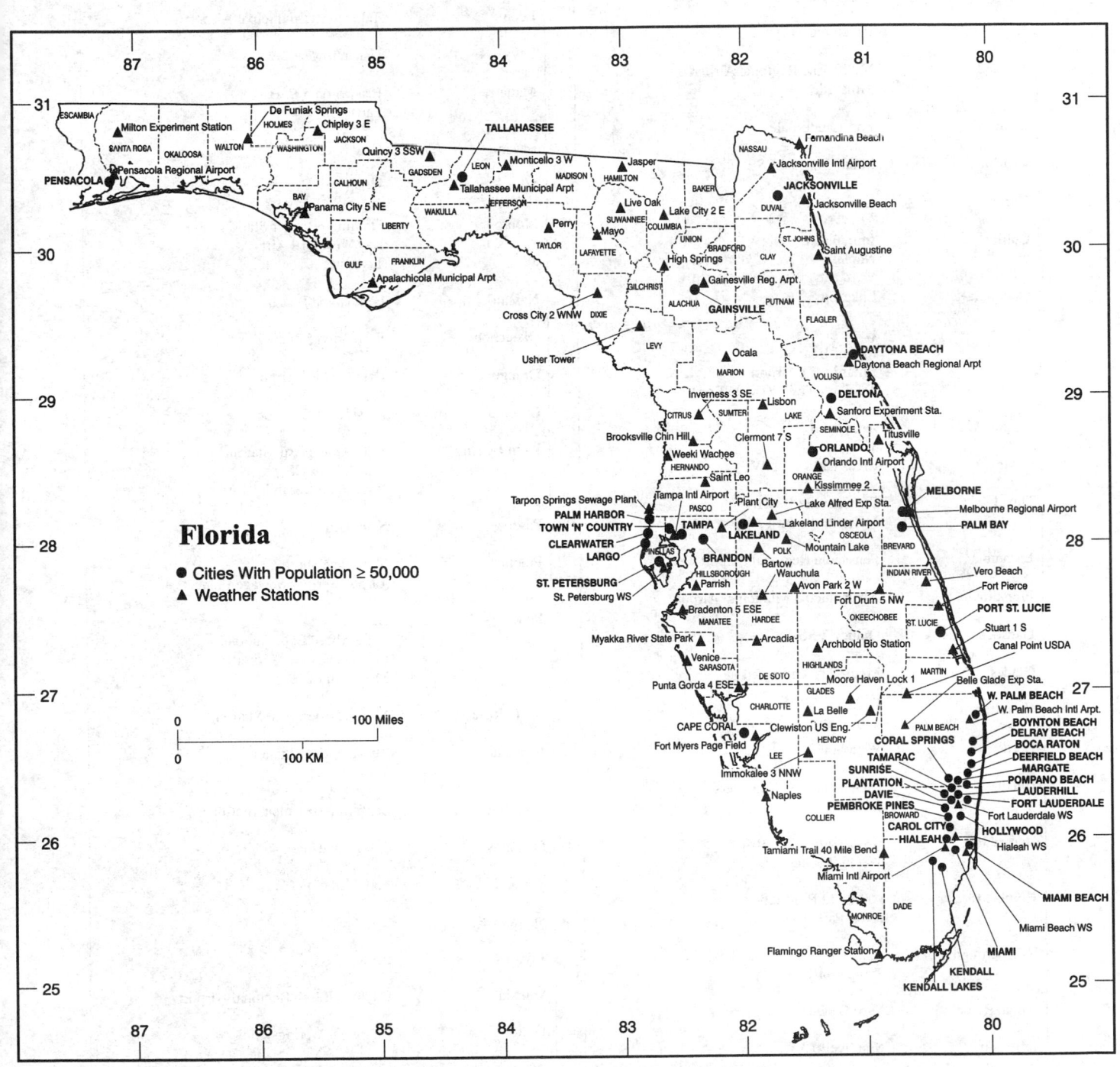

Florida

- ● Cities With Population ≥ 50,000
- ▲ Weather Stations

PENSACOLA

Milton Experiment Station
De Funiak Springs
Chipley 3 E
Quincy 3 SSW
Pensacola Regional Airport
Panama City 5 NE
Apalachicola Municipal Arpt

TALLAHASSEE
Monticello 3 W
Tallahassee Municipal Arpt
Jasper
Live Oak
Lake City 2 E
Perry
Mayo
High Springs
Cross City 2 WNW
Usher Tower
Gainesville Reg. Arpt.
GAINESVILLE

Fernandina Beach
Jacksonville Intl Airport
JACKSONVILLE
Jacksonville Beach
Saint Augustine

Ocala
DAYTONA BEACH
Daytona Beach Regional Arpt

Inverness 3 SE
Lisbon
Brooksville Chin Hill
Clermont 7 S
DELTONA
Sanford Experiment Sta.
Titusville
Weeki Wachee
ORLANDO
Saint Leo
Orlando Intl Airport
Tampa Intl Airport
Kissimmee 2
Plant City
Lake Alfred Exp Sta.
MELBORNE
Tarpon Springs Sewage Plant
PALM HARBOR
Melbourne Regional Airport
TOWN 'N' COUNTRY
TAMPA
LAKELAND
Lakeland Linder Airport
PALM BAY
CLEARWATER
BRANDON
Mountain Lake
LARGO
Bartow
ST. PETERSBURG
Parrish
Wauchula
Vero Beach
St. Petersburg WS
Avon Park 2 W
Fort Pierce
Bradenton 5 ESE
PORT ST. LUCIE
Myakka River State Park
Fort Drum 5 NW
Stuart 1 S
Arcadia
Venice
Archbold Bio Station
Canal Point USDA
Punta Gorda 4 ESE
Moore Haven Lock 1
Belle Glade Exp Sta.
La Belle
W. PALM BEACH
CAPE CORAL
W. Palm Beach Intl Arpt.
Clewiston US Eng.
BOYNTON BEACH
Fort Myers Page Field
CORAL SPRINGS
DELRAY BEACH
TAMARAC
BOCA RATON
Immokalee 3 NNW
SUNRISE
DEERFIELD BEACH
PLANTATION
MARGATE
Naples
DAVIE
POMPANO BEACH
PEMBROKE PINES
LAUDERHILL
CAROL CITY
FORT LAUDERDALE
HIALEAH
Fort Lauderdale WS
Tamiami Trail 40 Mile Bend
HOLLYWOOD
Hialeah WS
Miami Intl Airport
MIAMI BEACH
Miami Beach WS
Flamingo Ranger Station
MIAMI
KENDALL
KENDALL LAKES

0 —— 100 Miles
0 —— 100 KM

Florida Weather Stations by County

County	Station Name
Alachua	Gainesville Regional Airport High Springs
Bay	Panama City 5 NE
Brevard	Melbourne Regional Airport Titusville
Broward	Fort Lauderdale
Charlotte	Punta Gorda 4 ESE
Citrus	Inverness 3 SE
Collier	Immokalee 3 NNW Naples
Columbia	Lake City 2 E
Dade	Hialeah Miami Beach Miami Int'l Airport Tamiami Trail 40 Mile Bend
Desoto	Arcadia
Dixie	Cross City 2 WNW
Duval	Jacksonville Beach Jacksonville Int'l Airport
Escambia	Pensacola Regional Airport
Franklin	Apalachicola Municipal Airport
Gadsden	Quincy 3 SSW
Glades	Moore Haven Lock 1
Hamilton	Jasper
Hardee	Wauchula
Hendry	Clewiston U.S. Engineers La Belle
Hernando	Brooksville Chin Hill Weeki Wachee
Highlands	Archbold Bio Station Avon Park 2 W
Hillsborough	Plant City Tampa Int'l Airport
Indian River	Vero Beach
Jefferson	Monticello 3 W
Lafayette	Mayo
Lake	Clermont 7 S Lisbon

County	Station Name
Lee	Fort Myers Page Field
Leon	Tallahassee Municipal Airport
Levy	Usher Tower
Manatee	Bradenton 5 ESE Parrish
Marion	Ocala
Martin	Stuart 1 S
Monroe	Flamingo Ranger Station Key West Int'l Airport Tavernier
Nassau	Fernandina Beach
Okeechobee	Fort Drum 5 NW
Orange	Orlando Int'l Airport
Osceola	Kissimmee 2
Palm Beach	Belle Glade Exp. Station Canal Point USDA West Palm Beach Int'l Airport
Pasco	Saint Leo
Pinellas	Saint Petersburg Tarpon Springs Sewage Plant
Polk	Bartow Lake Alfred Exp. Station Lakeland Linder Airport Mountain Lake
Santa Rosa	Milton Experiment Station
Sarasota	Myakka River State Park Venice
Seminole	Sanford Experiment Station
St. Johns	Saint Augustine
St. Lucie	Fort Pierce
Suwannee	Live Oak
Taylor	Perry
Volusia	Daytona Beach Regional Airport
Walton	De Funiak Springs
Washington	Chipley 3 E

Florida Weather Stations by City

City	Station Name	Miles
Boca Raton	Fort Lauderdale	19
Boynton Beach	West Palm Beach Int'l Airport	11
Brandon	Plant City	11
	Tampa Int'l Airport	15
Cape Coral	Fort Myers Page Field	6
Carol City	Fort Lauderdale	12
	Hialeah	8
	Miami Beach	14
	Miami Int'l Airport	9
Clearwater	Saint Petersburg	17
	Tampa Int'l Airport	14
	Tarpon Springs Sewage Plant	12
Coral Springs	Fort Lauderdale	12
Davie	Fort Lauderdale	5
	Hialeah	17
	Miami Int'l Airport	18
Daytona Beach	Daytona Beach Regional Airport	2
Deerfield Beach	Fort Lauderdale	15
Delray Beach	West Palm Beach Int'l Airport	16
Deltona	Sanford Experiment Station	7
Fort Lauderdale	Fort Lauderdale	5
Gainesville	High Springs	19
	Gainesville Regional Airport	4
Hialeah	Fort Lauderdale	18
	Hialeah	2
	Miami Beach	12
	Miami Int'l Airport	3
Hollywood	Fort Lauderdale	6
	Hialeah	14
	Miami Beach	17
	Miami Int'l Airport	16
Jacksonville	Jacksonville Int'l Airport	14
	Jacksonville Beach	15
Kendale Lakes	Hialeah	12
	Miami Beach	18
	Miami Int'l Airport	10
Kendall	Hialeah	12
	Miami Beach	15
	Miami Int'l Airport	10
Lakeland	Bartow	11
	Lake Alfred Exp. Station	15
	Lakeland Linder Airport	0
	Plant City	11
Largo	Saint Petersburg	13

City	Station Name	Miles
Largo (cont.)	Tampa Int'l Airport	16
	Tarpon Springs Sewage Plant	17
Lauderhill	Fort Lauderdale	5
Margate	Fort Lauderdale	10
Melbourne	Melbourne Regional Airport	1
Miami	Hialeah	5
	Miami Beach	6
	Miami Int'l Airport	5
Miami Beach	Hialeah	9
	Miami Beach	2
	Miami Int'l Airport	10
Orlando	Kissimmee 2	18
	Orlando Int'l Airport	7
Palm Bay	Melbourne Regional Airport	7
Palm Harbor	Tampa Int'l Airport	15
	Tarpon Springs Sewage Plant	5
Pembroke Pines	Fort Lauderdale	8
	Hialeah	12
	Miami Beach	18
	Miami Int'l Airport	14
Pensacola	Pensacola Regional Airport	2
Plantation	Fort Lauderdale	4
Pompano Beach	Fort Lauderdale	10
Port St. Lucie	Fort Pierce	13
	Stuart 1 S	10
St. Petersburg	Saint Petersburg	2
	Tampa Int'l Airport	15
Sunrise	Fort Lauderdale	6
Tallahassee	Quincy 3 SSW	19
	Tallahassee Municipal Airport	6
Tamarac	Fort Lauderdale	8
Tampa	Saint Petersburg	17
	Tampa Int'l Airport	4
Town 'n' Country	Saint Petersburg	17
	Tampa Int'l Airport	4
	Tarpon Springs Sewage Plant	14
West Palm Beach	West Palm Beach Int'l Airport	3

Note: Miles is the distance between the geographic center of the city and the weather station.

Florida Weather Stations by Elevation

Feet	Station Name
242	Quincy 3 SSW
239	Brooksville Chin Hill
229	De Funiak Springs
216	Milton Experiment Station
209	Lakeland Linder Airport
193	Lake City 2 E
187	Saint Leo
150	Avon Park 2 W
144	Jasper
144	Monticello 3 W
137	Archbold Bio Station
137	Lake Alfred Exp. Station
131	Gainesville Regional Airport
127	Chipley 3 E
124	Bartow
124	Mountain Lake
118	Live Oak
118	Plant City
111	Pensacola Regional Airport
108	Clermont 7 S
95	Orlando Int'l Airport
72	Ocala
68	Fort Drum 5 NW
65	Lisbon
62	Arcadia
62	High Springs
62	Mayo
59	Kissimmee 2
59	Parrish
59	Wauchula
52	Tallahassee Municipal Airport
42	Perry
39	Cross City 2 WNW
39	Inverness 3 SE
32	Immokalee 3 NNW
32	Melbourne Regional Airport
32	Miami Int'l Airport
32	Moore Haven Lock 1
32	Usher Tower
29	Canal Point USDA
29	Panama City 5 NE
29	Titusville
26	Daytona Beach Regional Airport
22	Fort Pierce
22	Jacksonville Int'l Airport
19	Apalachicola Municipal Airport
19	Bradenton 5 ESE
19	Clewiston U.S. Engineers
19	Myakka River State Park
19	Punta Gorda 4 ESE
19	Vero Beach
19	Weeki Wachee
16	Tampa Int'l Airport
16	West Palm Beach Int'l Airport
13	Belle Glade Exp. Station

Feet	Station Name
13	Fernandina Beach
13	Fort Lauderdale
13	Fort Myers Page Field
13	La Belle
13	Sanford Experiment Station
13	Tamiami Trail 40 Mile Bend
9	Hialeah
9	Jacksonville Beach
9	Stuart 1 S
6	Saint Augustine
6	Saint Petersburg
6	Tarpon Springs Sewage Plant
6	Tavernier
6	Venice
3	Key West Int'l Airport
3	Miami Beach
3	Naples
0	Flamingo Ranger Station

Apalachicola Municipal Airport

Apalachicola is located in a coastal area that is low and flat and bordered by the Gulf of Mexico from the east-northeast through the south to the west-southwest. There are many rivers, creeks, lakes, and bays to the north. Apalachicola is situated at the mouth of the Apalachicola River and on the Apalachicola Bay. Several islands to the east and south offer very good protection from the occasionally rough seas of the Gulf. The land area is generally sandy, and is heavily covered with pine and cypress forests and scattered palmetto palms.

The climate of this locality is typical of that experienced on the northern Gulf of Mexico. Because of the moderating effect of the surrounding Gulf, temperatures are usually mild and subtropical in nature, but are subject to occasional wide winter variations.

Average annual rainfall is about 57 inches, but actual monthly and yearly totals vary widely. Sandy soil and generally adequate drainage allow rapid absorption and runoff during occasional tropical downpours. Thunderstorms occur in all months. About three-fourths of the average annual number occur during the summer months. Very few tropical storms affect Apalachicola.

Hail has fallen on occasions, but averages less than one occurrence a year. There is no record of sleet or glaze. Snow has fallen on rare occasions, but generally melted as it fell. A measurable amount of snow is rare.

Apalachicola Municipal Airport *Franklin County*   Elevation: 19 ft.   Latitude: 29° 44' N   Longitude: 85° 02' W

	JAN	FEB	MAR	APR	MAY	JUN	JUL	AUG	SEP	OCT	NOV	DEC	YEAR
Mean Maximum Temp. (°F)	62.1	64.6	69.9	76.1	83.1	88.2	89.7	89.3	86.9	79.9	71.9	65.1	77.2
Mean Temp. (°F)	53.1	55.6	61.1	67.1	74.3	80.1	81.9	81.8	79.2	70.6	62.4	55.9	68.6
Mean Minimum Temp. (°F)	44.1	46.6	52.4	58.0	65.5	71.9	74.2	74.1	71.3	61.3	52.8	46.6	59.9
Extreme Maximum Temp. (°F)	80	80	85	90	98	100	101	103	97	92	85	83	103
Extreme Minimum Temp. (°F)	9	19	22	36	47	48	63	62	52	33	27	14	9
Days Maximum Temp. ≥ 90°F	0	0	0	0	2	10	16	14	7	1	0	0	50
Days Maximum Temp. ≤ 32°F	0	0	0	0	0	0	0	0	0	0	0	0	0
Days Minimum Temp. ≤ 32°F	5	2	0	0	0	0	0	0	0	0	0	3	10
Days Minimum Temp. ≤ 0°F	0	0	0	0	0	0	0	0	0	0	0	0	0
Heating Degree Days (base 65°F)	368	268	151	40	1	0	0	0	0	20	135	294	1,277
Cooling Degree Days (base 65°F)	6	11	39	105	300	462	542	534	427	208	67	20	2,721
Mean Precipitation (in.)	4.92	3.82	5.00	3.05	2.86	4.26	7.10	7.89	6.59	4.39	3.45	3.58	56.91
Maximum Precipitation (in.)	20.8	8.9	13.5	12.1	12.1	18.3	18.1	21.1	18.3	11.2	6.7	9.7	88.2
Minimum Precipitation (in.)	0.8	0.5	0.7	0.1	0.3	0.3	0.8	2.3	0.6	0.1	0.5	0.9	38.1
Maximum 24-hr. Precipitation (in.)	4.0	4.4	8.2	6.2	6.8	4.2	6.3	5.4	7.7	6.2	4.2	3.6	8.2
Days With ≥ 0.1" Precipitation	7	5	6	4	3	6	9	9	8	4	5	6	72
Days With ≥ 1.0" Precipitation	2	1	2	1	1	1	2	2	2	1	1	1	17
Mean Snowfall (in.)	trace	trace	trace	0.0	0.0	0.0	0.0	0.0	0.0	0.0	0.0	trace	trace
Maximum Snowfall (in.)	trace	trace	trace	0	0	0	0	0	0	0	0	trace	trace
Maximum 24-hr. Snowfall (in.)	trace	trace	trace	0	0	0	0	0	0	0	0	trace	trace
Days With ≥ 1.0" Snow Depth	0	0	0	0	0	0	0	0	0	0	0	0	0
Thunderstorm Days	2	3	4	3	5	11	17	17	10	2	2	2	78
Foggy Days	17	15	17	14	12	8	7	8	9	11	13	16	147
Predominant Sky Cover	OVR	OVR	OVR	CLR	SCT	SCT	SCT	SCT	SCT	CLR	CLR	OVR	OVR
Mean Relative Humidity 7am (%)	83	86	88	87	87	87	89	91	89	86	86	85	87
Mean Relative Humidity 4pm (%)	62	64	66	62	65	67	70	69	67	60	64	65	65
Mean Dewpoint (°F)	42	47	53	58	66	71	74	74	70	60	54	47	60
Prevailing Wind Direction	N	SE	SE	SE	S	SW	SW	SE	NE	NE	NE	N	SE
Prevailing Wind Speed (mph)	10	9	10	10	8	8	7	9	8	8	8	10	9
Maximum Wind Gust (mph)	41	49	41	43	61	38	41	68	68	44	85	47	85

Daytona Beach Regional Airport

Daytona Beach is located on the Atlantic Ocean. The Halifax River, part of the Florida Inland Waterway, runs through the city. The terrain in the area is flat and the soil is mostly sandy. Elevations in the area range from three to 15 feet above mean sea level near the ocean to about 31 feet at the airport and on a ridge running along the western city limits.

Nearness to the ocean results in a climate tempered by the effect of land and sea breezes. In the summer, while maximum temperatures reach 90 degrees or above during the late morning or early afternoon, the number of hours of 90 degrees or above is relatively small due to the beginning of the sea breeze near midday and the occurrence of local afternoon convective thunderstorms which lower the temperature to the comfortable 80s. Winters, although subject to invasions of cold air, are relatively mild due to the nearness of the ocean and latitudinal location.

The rainy season from June through mid-October produces 60 percent of the annual rainfall. The major portion of the summer rainfall occurs in the form of local convective thunderstorms which are occasionally heavy and produce as much as two or three inches of rain. The more severe thunderstorms may be attended by strong gusty winds. Almost all rainfall during the winter months is associated with frontal passages.

Long periods of cloudiness and rain are infrequent, usually not lasting over two or three days. These periods are usually associated with a stationary front, a so-called northeaster, or a tropical disturbance.

Tropical disturbances or hurricanes are not considered a great threat to this area of the state. Generally hurricanes in this latitude tend to pass well offshore or lose much of their intensity while crossing the state before reaching this area. Only in gusts have hurricane-force winds been recorded at this station.

Heavy fog occurs mostly during the winter and early spring. These fogs usually form by radiational cooling at night and dissipate soon after sunrise. On rare occasions sea fog moves in from the ocean and persists for two or three days. There is no significant source in the area for air pollution.

Daytona Beach Regional Airport *Volusia County*   Elevation: 26 ft.   Latitude: 29° 11' N   Longitude: 81° 04' W

	JAN	FEB	MAR	APR	MAY	JUN	JUL	AUG	SEP	OCT	NOV	DEC	YEAR
Mean Maximum Temp. (°F)	68.7	70.4	75.2	79.7	84.7	88.5	90.5	89.6	87.3	82.0	76.0	70.9	80.3
Mean Temp. (°F)	58.2	59.9	64.6	69.2	74.9	79.8	81.6	81.3	79.7	73.9	66.6	60.8	70.9
Mean Minimum Temp. (°F)	47.5	49.2	54.1	58.7	65.0	71.0	72.7	73.0	72.0	65.7	57.2	50.6	61.4
Extreme Maximum Temp. (°F)	87	89	92	94	97	101	102	100	96	93	88	88	102
Extreme Minimum Temp. (°F)	15	26	26	36	44	52	60	65	53	41	30	19	15
Days Maximum Temp. ≥ 90°F	0	0	0	2	5	11	19	15	7	1	0	0	60
Days Maximum Temp. ≤ 32°F	0	0	0	0	0	0	0	0	0	0	0	0	0
Days Minimum Temp. ≤ 32°F	2	1	0	0	0	0	0	0	0	0	0	1	4
Days Minimum Temp. ≤ 0°F	0	0	0	0	0	0	0	0	0	0	0	0	0
Heating Degree Days (base 65°F)	242	181	95	26	1	0	0	0	0	6	67	179	797
Cooling Degree Days (base 65°F)	31	45	83	149	308	450	525	517	439	288	127	53	3,015
Mean Precipitation (in.)	3.20	2.84	3.68	2.57	3.18	5.67	5.12	6.10	6.28	4.58	3.00	2.70	48.92
Maximum Precipitation (in.)	7.2	9.1	8.1	7.1	12.3	15.2	14.4	19.9	15.2	13.0	12.9	12.0	79.3
Minimum Precipitation (in.)	0.1	0.6	0.3	trace	0.1	1.0	0.2	2.0	0.4	0.2	trace	0.1	31.4
Maximum 24-hr. Precipitation (in.)	5.7	3.6	5.0	4.0	4.0	6.1	3.3	4.4	6.2	9.1	9.0	3.6	9.1
Days With ≥ 0.1" Precipitation	5	5	5	3	5	8	8	10	8	6	4	5	72
Days With ≥ 1.0" Precipitation	1	1	1	1	1	2	1	2	2	1	1	1	15
Mean Snowfall (in.)	trace	0.0	trace	0.0	0.0	trace	0.0	trace	0.0	0.0	0.0	trace	trace
Maximum Snowfall (in.)	trace	trace	0	0	0	0	0	0	0	0	0	trace	trace
Maximum 24-hr. Snowfall (in.)	trace	trace	0	0	0	0	0	0	0	0	0	trace	trace
Days With ≥ 1.0" Snow Depth	0	0	0	0	0	0	0	0	0	0	0	0	0
Thunderstorm Days	1	2	3	4	8	14	17	15	9	3	1	1	78
Foggy Days	15	12	12	10	10	10	8	9	8	9	12	14	129
Predominant Sky Cover	OVR	OVR	CLR	CLR	SCT	SCT	SCT	SCT	SCT	SCT	CLR	OVR	SCT
Mean Relative Humidity 7am (%)	87	86	86	85	85	87	89	91	90	87	87	87	87
Mean Relative Humidity 4pm (%)	61	59	57	56	61	68	69	71	71	66	64	63	64
Mean Dewpoint (°F)	49	50	54	58	65	70	72	73	71	65	57	52	61
Prevailing Wind Direction	NW	N	WSW	ESE	ESE	E	SW	E	ENE	ENE	NW	NW	E
Prevailing Wind Speed (mph)	9	12	12	12	12	10	7	10	12	12	8	8	10
Maximum Wind Gust (mph)	62	58	77	58	69	74	67	68	55	56	55	60	77

Fort Myers Page Field

Located on the south bank of the Caloosahatchee River, about 15 miles from the Gulf of Mexico, Fort Myers has a climate characterized as subtropical, with temperature extremes of both summer and winter tempered by the marine influence of the Gulf.

Temperatures generally range from the low 60s in winter to the low 80s in summer. Winters are mild, with many bright, warm days and moderately cool nights. Occasional cold snaps bring temperatures in the 30s, but only rarely do temperatures drop into the 20s. Frost occurs in the farming areas on only a few occasions each year, and usually is light and scattered. In the summer, temperatures have reached 100 degrees, but these occurrences are very rare.

About two-thirds of annual precipitation occurs during June through September. There are frequent long periods during the winter when only very light, or no rain falls. Most rain during the summer occurs as late afternoon or early evening thunderstorms, which bring welcome cooling on hot summer days. These showers seldom last long, even though they yield large amounts of rain. Exceptions are during the late summer or fall when tropical storms or hurricanes may pass near the Fort Myers area. These may result in heavy downpours that may reach torrential proportions. 24 hour amounts of from six to over 10 inches may occur.

The prevailing wind direction is east and, except during the passage of tropical storms, high velocities are not experienced. During winter and spring there are usually a few days with 20 to 30 mph winds and thunderstorms are sometimes accompanied by strong gusts for brief periods. Winds approximating 100 mph have been experienced with the passage of hurricanes during the fall months.

Thunderstorms have occurred during every month, but are infrequent from November to April. From June through September they occur on 2 out of every 3 days on an average, and as a general rule, in the late afternoons or early evenings. Heavy fog is rather infrequent, occurring mostly in winter during the early mornings. There is seldom a day without sunshine at some time.

Relative humidity is high during the night, dropping off in the middle of the day.

Fort Myers Page Field *Lee County*   Elevation: 13 ft.   Latitude: 26° 35' N   Longitude: 81° 52' W

	JAN	FEB	MAR	APR	MAY	JUN	JUL	AUG	SEP	OCT	NOV	DEC	YEAR
Mean Maximum Temp. (°F)	74.8	76.1	80.2	84.6	88.8	91.1	91.7	91.7	90.3	86.4	81.4	76.7	84.5
Mean Temp. (°F)	64.5	65.5	69.5	73.6	78.5	82.1	83.1	83.3	82.2	77.6	71.8	66.4	74.9
Mean Minimum Temp. (°F)	54.1	54.9	58.9	62.7	68.0	73.2	74.5	74.8	74.2	68.8	62.2	56.2	65.2
Extreme Maximum Temp. (°F)	88	91	93	96	99	103	98	98	96	95	95	90	103
Extreme Minimum Temp. (°F)	28	32	33	42	52	60	67	69	64	48	34	27	27
Days Maximum Temp. ≥ 90°F	0	0	1	4	14	21	25	25	20	7	1	0	118
Days Maximum Temp. ≤ 32°F	0	0	0	0	0	0	0	0	0	0	0	0	0
Days Minimum Temp. ≤ 32°F	0	0	0	0	0	0	0	0	0	0	0	0	0
Days Minimum Temp. ≤ 0°F	0	0	0	0	0	0	0	0	0	0	0	0	0
Heating Degree Days (base 65°F)	107	76	26	3	0	0	0	0	0	1	17	73	303
Cooling Degree Days (base 65°F)	93	112	176	275	434	539	578	582	532	410	239	128	4,098
Mean Precipitation (in.)	2.36	2.12	3.27	1.62	3.56	9.68	9.00	9.58	7.80	2.49	1.79	1.59	54.86
Maximum Precipitation (in.)	7.9	10.8	18.6	5.7	10.3	20.1	16.7	16.7	16.6	11.9	8.1	5.2	74.8
Minimum Precipitation (in.)	0	0.1	trace	trace	0.3	2.0	2.3	4.0	1.9	0	trace	trace	32.8
Maximum 24-hr. Precipitation (in.)	2.6	2.6	5.6	3.8	7.8	5.7	7.3	5.1	5.5	6.2	3.6	3.0	7.8
Days With ≥ 0.1" Precipitation	3	3	4	3	5	11	13	13	11	4	3	3	76
Days With ≥ 1.0" Precipitation	1	1	1	0	1	3	3	3	2	1	0	0	16
Mean Snowfall (in.)	0.0	0.0	0.0	0.0	0.0	0.0	0.0	0.0	0.0	0.0	0.0	0.0	0.0
Maximum Snowfall (in.)	0	0	0	0	0	0	0	0	0	0	0	0	0
Maximum 24-hr. Snowfall (in.)	0	0	0	0	0	0	0	0	0	0	0	0	0
Days With ≥ 1.0" Snow Depth	0	0	0	0	0	0	0	0	0	0	0	0	0
Thunderstorm Days	1	1	2	3	6	16	22	21	14	4	1	1	92
Foggy Days	15	12	13	10	9	6	3	3	4	8	11	13	107
Predominant Sky Cover	CLR	CLR	CLR	CLR	SCT	SCT	BRK	BRK	SCT	SCT	SCT	CLR	SCT
Mean Relative Humidity 7am (%)	90	89	89	88	87	89	90	91	92	90	90	90	90
Mean Relative Humidity 4pm (%)	56	54	52	50	53	64	68	67	66	59	58	57	59
Mean Dewpoint (°F)	55	55	58	61	66	72	73	74	73	67	61	57	64
Prevailing Wind Direction	NE	NE	ENE	E	E	E	E	E	ENE	NE	NE	NE	ENE
Prevailing Wind Speed (mph)	8	9	9	9	8	7	7	7	7	9	8	8	8
Maximum Wind Gust (mph)	45	46	39	38	45	71	45	48	41	40	37	47	71

Gainesville Regional Airport

Gainsville lies in the north central part of the Florida peninsula, almost midway between the coasts of the Atlantic Ocean and the Gulf of Mexico. The terrain is fairly level with several nearby lakes to the east and south. Due to its centralized location, maritime influences are somewhat less than they would be along coastlines at the same latitude.

Maximum temperatures in summer average slightly more than 90 degrees. From June to September, the number of days when temperatures exceed 89 degrees is 84 on average. Record high temperatures are in excess of 100 degrees. Minimum temperatures in winter average a little more than 44 degrees. The average number of days per year when temperatures are freezing or below is 18. Record lows occur in the teens. Low temperatures are a consequence of cold winds from the north or nighttime radiational cooling of the ground in contact with rather calm air.

Rainfall is appreciable in every month but is most abundant from showers and thunderstorms in summer. The average number of thunderstorm hours yearly is approximately 160. In winter, large-scale cyclone and frontal activity is responsible for some of the precipitation. Monthly average values range from about two inches in November to about eight inches in August. Snowfall is practically unknown.

Because of its inland location, Gainesville does not have serious problems with hurricanes. An occasional hurricane will cross the Gulf or Atlantic coast and head toward Gainesville, but before it arrives it is weakened by surface friction and a depletion of water vapor.

Gainesville Regional Airport *Alachua County*   Elevation: 131 ft.   Latitude: 29° 42' N   Longitude: 82° 17' W

	JAN	FEB	MAR	APR	MAY	JUN	JUL	AUG	SEP	OCT	NOV	DEC	YEAR
Mean Maximum Temp. (°F)	na	na	na	na	na	na	na	na	na	na	na	na	na
Mean Temp. (°F)	na	na	na	na	na	na	na	na	na	na	na	na	na
Mean Minimum Temp. (°F)	na	na	na	na	na	na	na	na	na	na	na	na	na
Extreme Maximum Temp. (°F)	na	na	na	na	na	na	na	na	na	na	na	na	na
Extreme Minimum Temp. (°F)	na	na	na	na	na	na	na	na	na	na	na	na	na
Days Maximum Temp. ≥ 90°F	na	na	na	na	na	na	na	na	na	na	na	na	na
Days Maximum Temp. ≤ 32°F	na	na	na	na	na	na	na	na	na	na	na	na	na
Days Minimum Temp. ≤ 32°F	na	na	na	na	na	na	na	na	na	na	na	na	na
Days Minimum Temp. ≤ 0°F	na	na	na	na	na	na	na	na	na	na	na	na	na
Heating Degree Days (base 65°F)	na	na	na	na	na	na	na	na	na	na	na	na	na
Cooling Degree Days (base 65°F)	*17*	*29*	*63*	*130*	*312*	*443*	*511*	*497*	*405*	*214*	*83*	*25*	*2,729*
Mean Precipitation (in.)	na	na	na	na	na	na	na	na	na	na	na	na	na
Maximum Precipitation (in.)	9.0	6.9	9.8	6.0	7.2	14.8	12.2	15.8	12.0	8.0	4.5	6.4	70.8
Minimum Precipitation (in.)	0.5	0.3	0.7	0.4	0.2	2.2	1.5	2.5	1.9	trace	0.3	0.2	40.5
Maximum 24-hr. Precipitation (in.)	2.2	2.6	3.3	2.8	3.5	4.3	3.2	3.8	6.2	5.1	2.0	2.3	6.2
Days With ≥ 0.1" Precipitation	na	na	na	na	na	na	na	na	na	na	na	na	na
Days With ≥ 1.0" Precipitation	na	na	na	na	na	na	na	na	na	na	na	na	na
Mean Snowfall (in.)	na	na	na	na	na	na	na	na	na	na	na	na	na
Maximum Snowfall (in.)	0	trace	0	0	0	0	0	0	0	0	0	trace	trace
Maximum 24-hr. Snowfall (in.)	0	trace	0	0	0	0	0	0	0	0	0	trace	trace
Days With ≥ 1.0" Snow Depth	na	na	na	na	na	na	na	na	na	na	na	na	na
Thunderstorm Days	1	2	3	3	6	13	20	17	8	3	1	1	78
Foggy Days	19	17	20	21	22	23	21	24	23	21	21	19	251
Predominant Sky Cover	OVR	OVR	CLR	CLR	SCT	BRK	SCT	BRK	SCT	CLR	CLR	OVR	SCT
Mean Relative Humidity 7am (%)	90	90	92	92	91	93	94	96	96	94	94	92	93
Mean Relative Humidity 4pm (%)	60	55	52	50	51	61	67	67	67	63	63	61	60
Mean Dewpoint (°F)	47	49	53	56	63	70	73	73	70	63	57	49	60
Prevailing Wind Direction	WNW	W	W	W	ESE	WSW	WSW	E	E	NE	NE	NW	E
Prevailing Wind Speed (mph)	9	10	10	9	9	9	9	7	8	9	9	8	9
Maximum Wind Gust (mph)	na	na	na	na	na	na	na	na	na	na	na	na	na

Jacksonville Int'l Airport

Jacksonville, a very large metropolitan area covering 840 square miles, extends from the Atlantic Ocean to about 40 miles inland. Downtown Jacksonville is located some 16 miles inland on the St. Johns River. The surrounding terrain is level. Easterly winds blowing about 40 percent of the time produce a maritime influence that modifies to some extent the heat of summer and the cold of winter. Summers are long, warm and relatively humid. Winters, although punctuated with periodic invasions of cool to occasionally cold air from the north, are mild because of the southern latitude and the proximity to the warm Atlantic Ocean waters. Because of the nearness to the ocean, climatic features across the city vary. For example, during the summer months temperatures at Jacksonville International Airport, located 17 miles inland, usually reach into the low and mid-90s before being tempered by sea breezes. Temperatures along the beaches rarely exceed 90 degrees. Summer thunderstorms usually occur before the noon hour along the beaches, while afternoon thunderstorms are the rule inland.

The annual temperature for Jacksonville is between 68 and 69 degrees. June, July, and August are the hottest months, with temperatures averaging near 80 degrees. December, January, and February are the coolest months, with temperatures near the middle 50s. Temperatures exceed 95 degrees only about ten times a year. Night temperatures in summer are usually comfortable, rarely failing to drop below 80 degrees.

The greatest rainfall, mostly in the form of local thundershowers, occurs during the summer months when a measurable amount can be expected one day in two. Rainfall of one inch or more in 24 hours normally occurs about fourteen times a year, and very infrequently heavy rains, associated with tropical storms, reach amounts of several inches with durations of more than 24 hours.

The atmosphere is moist, with an average relative humidity of about 75 percent, ranging from about 90 percent in early morning hours to about 55 percent during the afternoon.

Prevailing winds are northeasterly in the fall and winter months, and southwesterly in spring and summer. Wind movement, which averages slightly less than nine mph, is two to three mph higher in the early afternoon than the early morning hours, and slightly higher in spring than in other seasons of the year. Although this area is in the Hurricane Belt, this section of the coast has been very fortunate in escaping hurricane-force winds. Most hurricanes reaching this latitude have tended to move parallel to the coastline, keeping well out to sea.

Jacksonville Int'l Airport *Duval County*   Elevation: 22 ft.   Latitude: 30° 30' N   Longitude: 81° 42' W

	JAN	FEB	MAR	APR	MAY	JUN	JUL	AUG	SEP	OCT	NOV	DEC	YEAR
Mean Maximum Temp. (°F)	64.6	67.7	73.9	79.5	85.1	89.7	92.1	90.6	87.4	80.2	73.4	66.9	79.3
Mean Temp. (°F)	53.2	56.0	61.9	67.2	73.8	79.6	82.3	81.5	78.5	70.1	62.1	55.7	68.5
Mean Minimum Temp. (°F)	41.8	44.3	49.9	55.0	62.5	69.4	72.5	72.3	69.4	59.9	50.8	44.4	57.7
Extreme Maximum Temp. (°F)	84	86	91	94	98	103	103	102	98	94	88	84	103
Extreme Minimum Temp. (°F)	7	19	23	34	45	47	61	63	48	36	21	11	7
Days Maximum Temp. ≥ 90°F	0	0	0	1	6	16	24	20	10	1	0	0	78
Days Maximum Temp. ≤ 32°F	0	0	0	0	0	0	0	0	0	0	0	0	0
Days Minimum Temp. ≤ 32°F	7	4	1	0	0	0	0	0	0	0	1	5	18
Days Minimum Temp. ≤ 0°F	0	0	0	0	0	0	0	0	0	0	0	0	0
Heating Degree Days (base 65°F)	373	269	150	51	4	0	0	0	0	27	146	305	1,325
Cooling Degree Days (base 65°F)	12	25	60	125	289	459	557	528	405	198	70	22	2,750
Mean Precipitation (in.)	3.73	3.40	4.21	3.11	3.51	5.37	6.04	6.99	7.62	3.98	2.28	2.64	52.88
Maximum Precipitation (in.)	10.2	8.8	10.2	11.6	10.4	14.0	16.2	16.2	19.4	13.4	5.0	7.1	79.6
Minimum Precipitation (in.)	0.1	0.5	0.7	0.1	0.2	1.6	2.0	2.2	1.0	0.3	trace	trace	31.2
Maximum 24-hr. Precipitation (in.)	2.9	4.9	7.1	7.3	5.4	5.9	7.3	7.8	10.+	7.8	2.8	2.9	10.+
Days With ≥ 0.1" Precipitation	6	5	6	4	5	9	10	10	9	5	4	5	78
Days With ≥ 1.0" Precipitation	1	1	1	1	1	1	2	2	2	1	1	1	15
Mean Snowfall (in.)	trace	trace	trace	trace	0.0	trace	trace	0.0	0.0	0.0	0.0	trace	trace
Maximum Snowfall (in.)	trace	2	1	0	0	0	0	0	0	0	0	1	2
Maximum 24-hr. Snowfall (in.)	trace	2	1	0	0	0	0	0	0	0	0	1	2
Days With ≥ 1.0" Snow Depth	0	0	0	0	0	0	0	0	0	0	0	0	0
Thunderstorm Days	1	2	3	4	6	11	16	13	7	2	1	1	67
Foggy Days	18	14	15	13	14	13	11	15	16	17	16	17	179
Predominant Sky Cover	OVR	OVR	OVR	CLR	SCT	BRK	BRK	SCT	SCT	CLR	CLR	OVR	OVR
Mean Relative Humidity 7am (%)	87	86	87	87	87	88	89	92	92	91	90	88	89
Mean Relative Humidity 4pm (%)	57	53	50	49	54	61	64	66	67	62	59	59	58
Mean Dewpoint (°F)	44	46	50	56	63	70	72	73	70	62	53	47	59
Prevailing Wind Direction	NW	NW	WSW	SE	SE	SW	SW	SW	NE	NE	NW	NW	SW
Prevailing Wind Speed (mph)	9	10	10	10	10	8	7	7	10	12	8	9	9
Maximum Wind Gust (mph)	64	62	66	67	71	67	69	66	59	43	49	61	71

Key West Int'l Airport

Key West is located at the end of the Overseas Highway and near the western end of the Florida Keys, which are a chain of islands swinging in a southwesterly arc from the southeast coast of the Florida peninsula. The nearest point of the mainland is about 60 statute miles to the northeast, while Cuba at its closest point is 98 miles south. The city occupies the island of the same name which is three and a half miles long and one mile wide. Its mean elevation is around eight feet. The maximum elevation of 18 feet covers only about one acre in the western portion. Soil is a thin layer of sand, or marlfill, overlying a stratum of Oolitic limestone. Vegetation on the eastern end of the island is scanty, chiefly of low growth. The western end, where settlement and landscaping are older, has a little heavier growth. The airport and Weather Service Office are located on the southeast shore on partially filled mangrove swamp.

The waters surrounding the key are quite shallow up to the mainland on the northeast and for six miles to the reef on the south. There is little wave action because the reef disrupts any established wave pattern.

Because of the nearness of the Gulf Stream in the Straits of Florida, about 12 miles south and southeast, and the tempering effects of the Gulf of Mexico to the west and north, Key West has a notably mild, tropical-maritime climate in which the average temperatures during the winter are about 14 degrees lower than in summer. Cold fronts are strongly modified by the warm water as they move in from northerly quadrants in winter. There is no known record of frost, ice, sleet, or snow in Key West. Prevailing easterly tradewinds and sea breezes suppress the usual summertime heating. Diurnal variations throughout the year average only about 10 degrees.

Precipitation is characterized by dry and wet seasons. The period of December through April receives abundant sunshine and slightly less than 25 percent of the annual rainfall. This rainfall usually occurs in advance of cold fronts in a few heavy showers, or occasionally five to eight light showers per month. June through October is normally the wet season, receiving approximately 53 percent of the yearly total in numerous showers and thunderstorms. Early morning is the favored time for diurnal showers. Easterly waves during this season occasionally bring excessive rainfall, while infrequent hurricanes may be accompanied by unusually heavy amounts. Humidity remains relatively high during the entire year.

Key West Int'l Airport *Monroe County*   Elevation: 3 ft.   Latitude: 24° 33' N   Longitude: 81° 45' W

	JAN	FEB	MAR	APR	MAY	JUN	JUL	AUG	SEP	OCT	NOV	DEC	YEAR
Mean Maximum Temp. (°F)	75.2	75.8	78.7	81.9	85.3	88.0	89.3	89.4	88.1	84.7	80.5	76.8	82.8
Mean Temp. (°F)	70.2	70.7	73.7	77.1	80.6	83.4	84.5	84.3	83.3	80.3	76.2	72.1	78.0
Mean Minimum Temp. (°F)	65.1	65.6	68.8	72.3	75.9	78.7	79.6	79.2	78.4	75.7	71.9	67.3	73.2
Extreme Maximum Temp. (°F)	86	85	88	90	91	93	94	98	93	91	89	86	98
Extreme Minimum Temp. (°F)	41	45	47	48	64	70	71	71	69	65	50	44	41
Days Maximum Temp. ≥ 90°F	0	0	0	0	1	7	15	16	7	0	0	0	46
Days Maximum Temp. ≤ 32°F	0	0	0	0	0	0	0	0	0	0	0	0	0
Days Minimum Temp. ≤ 32°F	0	0	0	0	0	0	0	0	0	0	0	0	0
Days Minimum Temp. ≤ 0°F	0	0	0	0	0	0	0	0	0	0	0	0	0
Heating Degree Days (base 65°F)	25	17	6	0	0	0	0	0	0	0	0	13	61
Cooling Degree Days (base 65°F)	186	199	272	363	491	566	616	612	557	482	348	234	4,926
Mean Precipitation (in.)	2.47	1.56	1.88	1.99	3.52	4.52	3.53	5.24	5.50	4.40	2.63	2.08	39.32
Maximum Precipitation (in.)	17.6	4.5	9.7	10.6	12.9	14.4	11.7	10.4	18.4	21.6	27.7	11.2	62.9
Minimum Precipitation (in.)	trace	trace	trace	0	0.3	0.3	0.4	2.2	1.7	0.7	trace	0.1	20.0
Maximum 24-hr. Precipitation (in.)	6.4	2.5	5.3	6.2	7.2	5.1	3.0	3.3	6.1	6.5	23.+	6.7	23.+
Days With ≥ 0.1" Precipitation	4	3	3	3	4	7	7	9	10	6	3	3	62
Days With ≥ 1.0" Precipitation	1	0	0	1	1	1	1	2	1	1	1	1	11
Mean Snowfall (in.)	0.0	0.0	0.0	0.0	0.0	0.0	0.0	0.0	0.0	0.0	0.0	0.0	0.0
Maximum Snowfall (in.)	0	0	0	0	0	0	0	0	0	0	0	0	0
Maximum 24-hr. Snowfall (in.)	0	0	0	0	0	0	0	0	0	0	0	0	0
Days With ≥ 1.0" Snow Depth	0	0	0	0	0	0	0	0	0	0	0	0	0
Thunderstorm Days	1	1	2	2	4	10	13	15	12	4	1	1	66
Foggy Days	3	1	1	< 1	< 1	< 1	< 1	< 1	< 1	< 1	1	1	7
Predominant Sky Cover	SCT	SCT	SCT	SCT	SCT	SCT	SCT	SCT	SCT	SCT	SCT	SCT	SCT
Mean Relative Humidity 7am (%)	82	81	79	76	76	78	76	78	81	82	83	82	79
Mean Relative Humidity 4pm (%)	69	67	66	63	65	68	66	67	69	69	70	70	68
Mean Dewpoint (°F)	62	62	64	66	70	74	74	75	74	71	67	63	69
Prevailing Wind Direction	NE	NE	SE	ESE	ESE	SE	ESE	ESE	ESE	ENE	NE	NE	ESE
Prevailing Wind Speed (mph)	12	12	13	14	13	10	12	12	12	13	13	12	12
Maximum Wind Gust (mph)	58	55	75	78	53	70	67	56	87	90	69	54	90

Miami Int'l Airport

Miami is located on the lower east coast of Florida. To the east of the city lies Biscayne Bay, an arm of the ocean, about 15 miles long and three miles wide. East of the bay is the island of Miami Beach, a mile or less wide and about 10 miles long, and beyond Miami Beach is the Atlantic Ocean. The surrounding countryside is level and sparsely wooded.

The climate of Miami is essentially subtropical marine, featured by a long and warm summer, with abundant rainfall, followed by a mild, dry winter. The marine influence is evidenced by the low daily range of temperature and the rapid warming of cold air masses which pass to the east of the state. The Miami area is subject to winds from the east or southeast about half the time, and in several specific respects has a climate whose features differ from those farther inland.

One of these features is the annual precipitation for the area. During the early morning hours more rainfall occurs at Miami Beach than at the airport, while during the afternoon the reverse is true. The airport office is about nine miles inland.

An even more striking difference appears in the annual number of days with temperatures reaching 90 degrees or higher, with inland stations having about four times more than the beach. Minimum temperature contrasts also are particularly marked under proper conditions, with the difference between inland locations and the Miami Beach station frequently reaching to 15 degrees or more, especially in winter.

Freezing temperatures occur occasionally in the suburbs and farming districts southwest, west, and northwest of the city, but rarely near the ocean.

Hurricanes occasionally affect the area. The months of greatest frequency are September and October. Destructive tornadoes are very rare. Funnel clouds are occasionally sighted and a few touch the ground briefly but significant damage is seldom reported. Waterspouts are often visible from the beaches during the summer months, however, significant damage is seldom reported. June, July, and August have the highest frequency of dangerous lightning events.

Miami Int'l Airport *Dade County* Elevation: 32 ft. Latitude: 25° 49' N Longitude: 80° 18' W

	JAN	FEB	MAR	APR	MAY	JUN	JUL	AUG	SEP	OCT	NOV	DEC	YEAR
Mean Maximum Temp. (°F)	75.9	76.8	79.6	82.8	86.0	88.4	89.7	89.7	88.3	85.1	80.9	77.4	83.4
Mean Temp. (°F)	68.0	69.0	72.1	75.6	79.3	82.0	83.3	83.4	82.3	79.0	74.4	70.1	76.6
Mean Minimum Temp. (°F)	60.1	61.1	64.7	68.4	72.5	75.6	76.9	77.0	76.2	72.8	67.9	62.8	69.7
Extreme Maximum Temp. (°F)	88	89	92	96	96	98	98	98	97	95	89	87	98
Extreme Minimum Temp. (°F)	30	37	32	46	56	60	69	69	68	53	40	30	30
Days Maximum Temp. ≥ 90°F	0	0	0	2	5	11	17	17	11	3	0	0	66
Days Maximum Temp. ≤ 32°F	0	0	0	0	0	0	0	0	0	0	0	0	0
Days Minimum Temp. ≤ 32°F	0	0	0	0	0	0	0	0	0	0	0	0	0
Days Minimum Temp. ≤ 0°F	0	0	0	0	0	0	0	0	0	0	0	0	0
Heating Degree Days (base 65°F)	58	37	14	1	0	0	0	0	0	0	5	36	151
Cooling Degree Days (base 65°F)	157	170	237	321	454	530	590	589	533	455	306	201	4,543
Mean Precipitation (in.)	1.95	2.09	2.64	3.28	5.82	8.55	5.77	8.51	8.32	5.67	3.42	1.98	58.00
Maximum Precipitation (in.)	6.7	8.1	10.6	10.2	18.5	22.4	11.2	16.6	24.4	21.6	13.8	6.4	89.3
Minimum Precipitation (in.)	trace	0.1	trace	0	0.4	2.0	1.8	1.6	2.6	1.3	0.1	0.1	37.0
Maximum 24-hr. Precipitation (in.)	2.4	4.5	7.1	7.3	12.+	6.6	4.5	6.6	6.1	9.9	7.6	4.4	12.+
Days With ≥ 0.1" Precipitation	4	4	4	4	8	11	11	12	12	8	5	3	86
Days With ≥ 1.0" Precipitation	0	0	1	1	2	3	2	2	3	2	1	0	17
Mean Snowfall (in.)	0.0	0.0	0.0	0.0	trace	0.0	0.0	0.0	0.0	0.0	0.0	0.0	trace
Maximum Snowfall (in.)	0	0	0	0	0	0	0	0	0	0	0	0	0
Maximum 24-hr. Snowfall (in.)	0	0	0	0	0	0	0	0	0	0	0	0	0
Days With ≥ 1.0" Snow Depth	0	0	0	0	0	0	0	0	0	0	0	0	0
Thunderstorm Days	1	1	2	3	6	12	15	16	12	5	1	1	75
Foggy Days	7	5	4	3	3	1	1	1	1	3	5	6	40
Predominant Sky Cover	SCT	SCT	SCT	SCT	SCT	SCT	SCT	SCT	SCT	SCT	SCT	SCT	SCT
Mean Relative Humidity 7am (%)	85	84	82	80	81	84	84	86	88	87	85	84	84
Mean Relative Humidity 4pm (%)	60	58	57	57	61	68	66	67	69	65	63	60	63
Mean Dewpoint (°F)	58	58	60	63	68	72	73	74	73	69	64	59	66
Prevailing Wind Direction	NNW	ESE	SE	ESE	ESE	ESE	ESE	ESE	E	ENE	ENE	NNW	ESE
Prevailing Wind Speed (mph)	9	12	12	12	10	10	9	9	9	12	13	9	10
Maximum Wind Gust (mph)	58	61	60	78	62	68	56	115	94	125	53	46	125

Orlando Int'l Airport

Orlando is located in the central section of the Florida peninsula, surrounded by many lakes. Relative humidities remain high the year-round, with values near 90 percent at night and 40 to 50 percent in the afternoon. On some winter days, the humidity may drop to 20 percent.

The rainy season extends from June through September, sometimes through October when tropical storms are near. During this period, scattered afternoon thunderstorms are an almost daily occurrence, and these bring a drop in temperature to make the climate bearable. Summer temperatures above 95 degrees are rather rare. There is usually a breeze which contributes to the general comfort.

During the winter months rainfall is light. While temperatures, on infrequent occasion, may drop at night to near freezing, they rise rapidly during the day and, in brilliant sunshine, afternoons are pleasant.

Frozen precipitation in the form of snowflakes, snow pellets, or sleet is rare. However, hail is occasionally reported during thunderstorms.

Hurricanes are usually not considered a great threat to Orlando, since, to reach this area, they must pass over a substantial stretch of land and, in so doing, lose much of their punch. Sustained hurricane winds of 75 mph or higher rarely occur. Orlando, being inland, is relatively safe from high water, although heavy rains sometimes briefly flood sections of the city.

Orlando Int'l Airport *Orange County*   Elevation: 95 ft.   Latitude: 28° 26' N   Longitude: 81° 20' W

	JAN	FEB	MAR	APR	MAY	JUN	JUL	AUG	SEP	OCT	NOV	DEC	YEAR
Mean Maximum Temp. (°F)	70.9	73.8	78.3	82.8	87.9	90.8	91.9	91.6	89.8	84.5	78.6	72.9	82.8
Mean Temp. (°F)	59.9	62.6	67.0	71.4	77.1	81.3	82.6	82.7	81.2	75.2	68.7	62.5	72.7
Mean Minimum Temp. (°F)	48.9	51.3	55.7	59.9	66.2	71.8	73.3	73.8	72.5	65.8	58.6	52.2	62.5
Extreme Maximum Temp. (°F)	87	89	92	95	97	100	101	100	98	95	89	90	101
Extreme Minimum Temp. (°F)	19	26	25	38	48	53	64	65	57	44	35	20	19
Days Maximum Temp. ≥ 90°F	0	0	0	3	12	20	25	25	19	4	0	0	108
Days Maximum Temp. ≤ 32°F	0	0	0	0	0	0	0	0	0	0	0	0	0
Days Minimum Temp. ≤ 32°F	2	1	0	0	0	0	0	0	0	0	0	1	4
Days Minimum Temp. ≤ 0°F	0	0	0	0	0	0	0	0	0	0	0	0	0
Heating Degree Days (base 65°F)	197	126	59	9	1	0	0	0	0	3	42	141	578
Cooling Degree Days (base 65°F)	50	67	124	203	382	498	559	562	491	336	160	75	3,507
Mean Precipitation (in.)	2.51	2.43	3.70	2.51	3.85	7.42	7.36	6.38	5.89	2.87	2.44	2.34	49.70
Maximum Precipitation (in.)	7.2	8.3	11.4	9.1	10.4	15.3	13.3	11.6	10.3	5.6	10.3	5.3	67.8
Minimum Precipitation (in.)	0.2	0.1	1.1	0.1	0.5	3.5	2.6	2.9	2.5	0.4	0.2	0.2	31.7
Maximum 24-hr. Precipitation (in.)	4.2	2.4	4.1	5.1	3.1	4.4	4.1	3.0	3.6	2.4	3.8	2.8	5.1
Days With ≥ 0.1" Precipitation	4	4	5	3	6	10	11	11	9	5	4	4	76
Days With ≥ 1.0" Precipitation	1	1	1	1	1	2	2	2	2	1	1	1	16
Mean Snowfall (in.)	trace	0.0	trace	trace	trace	0.0	trace	trace	0.0	0.0	0.0	0.0	trace
Maximum Snowfall (in.)	trace	0	0	0	0	0	0	0	0	0	0	0	trace
Maximum 24-hr. Snowfall (in.)	trace	0	0	0	0	0	0	0	0	0	0	0	trace
Days With ≥ 1.0" Snow Depth	0	0	0	0	0	0	0	0	0	0	0	0	0
Thunderstorm Days	1	2	3	3	8	16	19	19	11	3	1	1	87
Foggy Days	16	14	15	13	13	12	10	9	11	14	16	17	160
Predominant Sky Cover	OVR	OVR	OVR	CLR	SCT	BRK	BRK	BRK	BRK	SCT	OVR	OVR	BRK
Mean Relative Humidity 7am (%)	88	89	90	88	89	91	91	93	93	91	91	90	90
Mean Relative Humidity 4pm (%)	54	50	48	47	51	61	64	66	65	59	58	58	57
Mean Dewpoint (°F)	50	51	55	58	65	71	72	73	72	65	59	53	62
Prevailing Wind Direction	N	N	S	E	E	S	S	E	NE	N	N	N	N
Prevailing Wind Speed (mph)	9	9	10	9	9	8	8	8	8	8	9	9	9
Maximum Wind Gust (mph)	48	51	62	56	68	62	74	62	56	40	49	44	74

Pensacola Regional Airport

Pensacola is situated on a somewhat hilly, sandy slope which borders Pensacola Bay, an expanse of deep water several miles in width. The bay is separated from the Gulf of Mexico by a long, narrow island that forms a natural breakwater for the harbor. Elevations in the city range from a few feet above sea level to more than 100 feet in portions of the residential sections, and most of the city is well above storm tides.

The Gulf of Mexico, about six miles distant, moderates the climate of Pensacola by tempering the cold Northers of winter and causing cool and refreshing sea breezes during the daytime in summer.

The average temperature for the summer months is around 80 degrees with an average daily range of 12.5 degrees. Temperatures of 90 degrees or higher occur on the average of 39 times yearly. A temperature of 100 degrees or higher occurs occasionally. The average winter temperature is in the low to mid 50s with an average daily range of 15.7 degrees. On the average, the temperature falls to freezing or below on only ninc days of the year. The average occurrence of the last temperature as low as 32 degrees in spring is mid-February, and the average earliest occurrence in autumn is early December, making the average growing season 292 days. Severe cold waves are rather infrequent.

Rainfall is usually well distributed through the year with the greatest frequency normally being in July and August. The greatest monthly rainfall occurs, on average, in July and least in October. Much of the rainfall in summer occurs during the daylight hours and comes in the form of thunderstorms, often producing excessive amounts. Winter rains are frequently lighter, but extend over longer periods. Snow has occurred in about 30 percent of the winters but measurable amounts are less frequent.

A moderate sea breeze usually blows off the Gulf of Mexico during most of the day in summer. Seriously destructive hurricanes are occasionally experienced in this vicinity but loss of life is rare. Hurricanes have occurred from early July to mid-October.

Pensacola Regional Airport *Escambia County*   Elevation: 111 ft.   Latitude: 30° 29' N   Longitude: 87° 11' W

	JAN	FEB	MAR	APR	MAY	JUN	JUL	AUG	SEP	OCT	NOV	DEC	YEAR
Mean Maximum Temp. (°F)	60.8	64.1	70.0	76.3	83.4	89.0	90.5	90.0	87.1	79.3	70.3	63.6	77.0
Mean Temp. (°F)	51.7	54.6	60.9	67.1	74.6	80.6	82.5	82.1	78.9	69.6	60.7	54.3	68.1
Mean Minimum Temp. (°F)	42.6	45.1	51.7	57.9	65.8	72.1	74.5	74.2	70.6	59.8	51.0	45.0	59.2
Extreme Maximum Temp. (°F)	80	82	86	96	98	101	106	104	98	92	85	81	106
Extreme Minimum Temp. (°F)	5	15	22	33	48	56	66	62	49	32	25	11	5
Days Maximum Temp. ≥ 90°F	0	0	0	0	3	13	19	18	10	0	0	0	63
Days Maximum Temp. ≤ 32°F	0	0	0	0	0	0	0	0	0	0	0	0	0
Days Minimum Temp. ≤ 32°F	6	3	1	0	0	0	0	0	0	0	1	4	15
Days Minimum Temp. ≤ 0°F	0	0	0	0	0	0	0	0	0	0	0	0	0
Heating Degree Days (base 65°F)	415	297	166	44	1	0	0	0	1	32	172	344	1,472
Cooling Degree Days (base 65°F)	6	11	41	106	302	473	552	541	413	179	48	18	2,690
Mean Precipitation (in.)	5.44	4.90	6.53	3.90	4.65	6.59	8.03	7.01	5.57	4.35	4.23	3.98	65.18
Maximum Precipitation (in.)	18.8	11.7	13.0	15.5	10.3	21.1	20.4	14.1	15.7	14.8	12.0	15.3	92.7
Minimum Precipitation (in.)	0.6	0.5	0.8	0.4	0.1	0.3	1.7	0.9	0.4	0	0.3	0.6	28.5
Maximum 24-hr. Precipitation (in.)	5.4	4.7	11.+	5.9	4.9	6.4	5.1	6.3	9.3	5.0	3.3	3.5	11.+
Days With ≥ 0.1" Precipitation	7	6	7	5	5	7	10	9	6	4	5	6	77
Days With ≥ 1.0" Precipitation	2	1	2	1	2	2	2	2	2	1	1	1	19
Mean Snowfall (in.)	trace	trace	trace	0.0	0.0	0.0	trace	0.0	0.0	0.0	0.0	trace	trace
Maximum Snowfall (in.)	3	2	2	0	0	0	0	0	0	0	0	trace	3
Maximum 24-hr. Snowfall (in.)	2	2	2	0	0	0	0	0	0	0	0	trace	2
Days With ≥ 1.0" Snow Depth	0	0	0	0	0	0	0	0	0	0	0	0	0
Thunderstorm Days	2	3	4	4	5	10	15	14	7	2	2	1	69
Foggy Days	18	15	18	16	15	13	12	15	14	14	14	17	181
Predominant Sky Cover	OVR	OVR	OVR	CLR	SCT	SCT	SCT	SCT	SCT	CLR	CLR	OVR	SCT
Mean Relative Humidity 7am (%)	84	84	82	80	78	79	81	83	83	81	83	85	82
Mean Relative Humidity 4pm (%)	64	62	60	59	61	63	67	67	64	59	63	67	63
Mean Dewpoint (°F)	44	47	50	56	65	71	73	73	68	59	51	46	58
Prevailing Wind Direction	NNW	N	NNW	SE	SSE	SSW	SW	NE	N	N	NNW	N	N
Prevailing Wind Speed (mph)	10	10	12	12	10	9	8	7	8	8	10	9	9
Maximum Wind Gust (mph)	na	na	na	na	na	na	na	na	na	na	na	na	na

Tallahassee Municipal Airport

Located about 20 miles from the Gulf of Mexico, Tallahassee has a mild, moist climate of the Gulf States. In contrast to the southern part of the Florida Peninsula, there is a definite march of the four seasons with considerable winter rainfall and quite a bit less winter sunshine. The annual average temperature is about 68 degrees.

During the winter, topographic effects and cold air drainage into lower elevations produce a wide variation of low temperatures on cold, clear and calm nights. Freezing temperatures at the airport and surrounding suburban areas average about thirty-six occurrences each winter, but freezing temperatures in the city are about half that number. Temperatures of 25 degrees or lower in the suburban areas average about twelve times per winter, with temperatures dropping into the teens on occasions. Below zero temperatures are rarely recorded. Snow in Tallahassee is infrequent. The date for the last occurrence of 32 degrees is February 28, but has been as late as April 8. The date of the first occurrence of 32 degrees in the fall is November 25, but has been as early as October 18. This gives an average growing season of some 270 days.

Summer is the least pleasant time of the year. Thunderstorms occur every other day. Rather high temperatures and very high humidities cause considerable discomfort. Occurrences of temperatures of 90 degrees or higher average about 90 days per year, but only about 22 of these days have readings as high as 95 degrees. Temperatures reach 100 degrees once or twice in less than half the years. In general, summertime cloudiness holds the high temperatures about 90 degrees.

July is the wettest month followed by August, September, and June. The driest months are October, November, and April.

Extended droughts are infrequent, shorter droughts are rather common, but both are significant. Droughts, or rainfall deficiencies, when extended over months or years, cause the disappearance of large lakes and cypress ponds. Droughts of shorter duration create fire danger in the nearby forests.

High winds are infrequent and of short duration, usually associated with strong cold fronts in the late winter and early spring months. The likelihood of a hurricane occurrence in our coastal area is about once every 17 years with fringe effects felt about once every five years.

Tallahassee Municipal Airport *Leon County*   Elevation: 52 ft.   Latitude: 30° 24' N   Longitude: 84° 21' W

	JAN	FEB	MAR	APR	MAY	JUN	JUL	AUG	SEP	OCT	NOV	DEC	YEAR
Mean Maximum Temp. (°F)	63.5	67.2	73.8	80.1	86.3	90.8	91.8	91.3	88.7	81.2	72.9	66.1	79.5
Mean Temp. (°F)	51.3	54.2	60.5	66.0	73.6	79.6	81.6	81.4	78.4	68.7	60.0	53.6	67.4
Mean Minimum Temp. (°F)	39.1	41.1	47.1	51.8	60.9	68.4	71.3	71.4	68.1	56.3	47.0	41.2	55.3
Extreme Maximum Temp. (°F)	82	85	89	95	99	103	103	103	99	94	87	84	103
Extreme Minimum Temp. (°F)	6	14	20	29	34	46	59	57	45	30	13	13	6
Days Maximum Temp. ≥ 90°F	0	0	0	1	8	19	24	23	16	2	0	0	93
Days Maximum Temp. ≤ 32°F	0	0	0	0	0	0	0	0	0	0	0	0	0
Days Minimum Temp. ≤ 32°F	11	7	3	0	0	0	0	0	0	0	4	9	34
Days Minimum Temp. ≤ 0°F	0	0	0	0	0	0	0	0	0	0	0	0	0
Heating Degree Days (base 65°F)	427	312	180	67	5	0	0	0	1	45	193	362	1,592
Cooling Degree Days (base 65°F)	6	15	46	101	288	457	533	526	406	181	53	15	2,627
Mean Precipitation (in.)	5.49	4.74	6.74	3.67	5.09	6.99	8.41	7.06	4.78	3.38	3.84	4.12	64.31
Maximum Precipitation (in.)	18.9	11.5	16.5	13.1	11.7	17.4	20.1	15.7	20.3	12.3	10.4	12.6	104.
Minimum Precipitation (in.)	0.2	0.8	1.0	0.3	trace	2.1	2.3	2.4	0.1	trace	0.4	0.9	31.0
Maximum 24-hr. Precipitation (in.)	4.9	5.6	7.1	4.9	5.1	6.7	8.2	7.1	8.9	6.6	4.9	5.0	8.9
Days With ≥ 0.1" Precipitation	7	6	6	4	6	9	11	10	7	4	4	6	80
Days With ≥ 1.0" Precipitation	2	2	2	1	2	2	2	2	1	1	1	1	19
Mean Snowfall (in.)	trace	trace	trace	0.0	*0.0*	trace	trace	0.0	trace	0.0	0.0	trace	*trace*
Maximum Snowfall (in.)	trace	3	trace	0	0	0	0	0	0	0	0	1	3
Maximum 24-hr. Snowfall (in.)	trace	2	trace	0	0	0	0	0	0	0	0	1	2
Days With ≥ 1.0" Snow Depth	0	0	0	0	0	0	0	0	0	0	0	0	0
Thunderstorm Days	2	2	4	4	8	14	19	16	8	2	2	2	83
Foggy Days	17	16	18	17	19	18	17	19	18	16	16	17	208
Predominant Sky Cover	OVR	OVR	OVR	CLR	SCT	SCT	BRK	SCT	SCT	CLR	CLR	OVR	OVR
Mean Relative Humidity 7am (%)	87	87	88	89	89	91	93	94	92	90	89	87	90
Mean Relative Humidity 4pm (%)	54	51	49	46	50	58	66	64	60	51	52	55	55
Mean Dewpoint (°F)	42	44	49	55	62	69	72	72	69	58	49	44	57
Prevailing Wind Direction	N	N	S	S	S	S	S	E	ENE	N	N	N	N
Prevailing Wind Speed (mph)	8	9	10	10	9	8	7	6	8	7	8	8	8
Maximum Wind Gust (mph)	53	51	53	54	81	76	67	64	83	58	68	43	83

Tampa Int'l Airport

Tampa is on west central coast of the Florida Peninsula. Very near the Gulf of Mexico at the upper end of Tampa Bay, land and sea breezes modify the subtropical climate. Major rivers flowing into the area are the Hillsborough, the Alafia, and the Little Manatee.

Winters are mild. Summers are long, rather warm, and humid. Low temperatures are about 50 degrees in the winter and 70 degrees during the summer. Afternoon highs range from the low 70s in the winter to around 90 degrees from June through September. Invasions of cold northern air produce an occasional cool winter morning. Freezing temperatures occur on one or two mornings per year during December, January, and February. In some years no freezing temperatures occur. Temperatures rarely fail to recover to the 60s on the cooler winter days. Temperatures above the low 90s are uncommon because of the afternoon sea breezes and thunderstorms. An outstanding feature of the Tampa climate is the summer thunderstorm season. Most of the thunderstorms occur in the late afternoon hours from June through September. The resulting sudden drop in temperature from about 90 degrees to around 70 degrees makes for a pleasant change. Between a dry spring and a dry fall, some 30 inches of rain, about 60 percent of the annual total, falls during the summer months. Snowfall is very rare.

A large part of the generally flat sandy land near the coast has an elevation of under 15 feet above sea level. This does make the area vulnerable to tidal surges. Tropical storms threaten the area on a few occasions most years. The greatest risk of hurricanes has been during the months of June and October. Many hurricanes, by replenishing the soil moisture and raising the water table, do far more good than harm. The heaviest rains in a 24-hour period, around 12 inches, have been associated with hurricanes.

Fittingly named the Suncoast, the sun shines more than 65 percent of the possible, with the sunniest months being April and May. Afternoon humidities are usually 60 percent or higher in the summer months, but range from 50 to 60 percent the remainder of the year.

Night ground fogs occur frequently during the cooler winter months. Prevailing winds are easterly, but westerly afternoon and early evening sea breezes occur most months of the year. Winds in excess of 25 mph are not common and usually occur only with thunderstorms or tropical disturbances.

Based on the 1951-1980 period, the average first occurrence of 32 degrees Fahrenheit in the fall is December 26 and the average last occurrence in the spring is February 3.

Tampa Int'l Airport *Hillsborough County*   Elevation: 16 ft.   Latitude: 27° 58' N   Longitude: 82° 32' W

	JAN	FEB	MAR	APR	MAY	JUN	JUL	AUG	SEP	OCT	NOV	DEC	YEAR
Mean Maximum Temp. (°F)	70.5	72.2	76.9	81.5	87.2	89.9	90.7	90.6	89.3	84.4	78.2	72.6	82.0
Mean Temp. (°F)	60.6	62.2	67.0	71.5	77.6	81.7	82.8	82.8	81.3	75.4	68.5	62.8	72.8
Mean Minimum Temp. (°F)	50.6	52.1	56.9	61.4	68.0	73.5	74.8	74.8	73.3	66.3	58.8	53.0	63.6
Extreme Maximum Temp. (°F)	86	88	89	93	98	99	97	98	96	94	90	86	99
Extreme Minimum Temp. (°F)	21	25	29	40	49	53	63	67	57	44	23	19	19
Days Maximum Temp. ≥ 90°F	0	0	0	1	8	17	22	22	17	3	0	0	90
Days Maximum Temp. ≤ 32°F	0	0	0	0	0	0	0	0	0	0	0	0	0
Days Minimum Temp. ≤ 32°F	1	1	0	0	0	0	0	0	0	0	0	1	3
Days Minimum Temp. ≤ 0°F	0	0	0	0	0	0	0	0	0	0	0	0	0
Heating Degree Days (base 65°F)	187	134	61	11	0	0	0	0	0	3	47	139	582
Cooling Degree Days (base 65°F)	54	70	124	209	405	513	561	562	494	337	166	80	3,575
Mean Precipitation (in.)	2.31	2.80	3.03	1.81	2.99	5.42	6.31	7.70	6.50	2.32	1.59	2.29	45.07
Maximum Precipitation (in.)	8.0	7.9	12.6	6.6	17.6	13.8	20.6	18.6	14.0	7.4	6.1	6.7	76.6
Minimum Precipitation (in.)	trace	0.2	0.1	trace	0.1	1.9	1.6	2.3	1.3	0.1	trace	0.1	28.9
Maximum 24-hr. Precipitation (in.)	3.3	3.1	4.3	3.3	11.+	5.5	9.1	4.9	4.4	2.7	3.8	2.7	11.+
Days With ≥ 0.1" Precipitation	4	4	4	3	4	8	10	11	8	4	3	4	67
Days With ≥ 1.0" Precipitation	1	1	1	0	1	2	2	3	2	1	0	1	15
Mean Snowfall (in.)	trace	0.0	trace	trace	0.0	0.0	trace	0.0	0.0	0.0	0.0	trace	trace
Maximum Snowfall (in.)	trace	trace	trace	0	0	0	0	0	0	0	0	trace	trace
Maximum 24-hr. Snowfall (in.)	trace	trace	trace	0	0	0	0	0	0	0	0	trace	trace
Days With ≥ 1.0" Snow Depth	0	0	0	0	0	0	0	0	0	0	0	0	0
Thunderstorm Days	1	2	3	3	5	14	21	20	12	3	1	1	86
Foggy Days	15	13	13	10	10	8	6	8	9	9	12	14	127
Predominant Sky Cover	OVR	OVR	SCT	CLR	SCT	SCT	BRK	BRK	SCT	SCT	CLR	CLR	SCT
Mean Relative Humidity 7am (%)	87	87	87	86	85	86	88	90	91	89	88	87	88
Mean Relative Humidity 4pm (%)	57	55	54	51	52	60	65	66	64	57	56	58	58
Mean Dewpoint (°F)	51	52	56	60	65	71	73	73	72	65	58	53	62
Prevailing Wind Direction	NE	E	E	E	E	W	E	E	ENE	NE	NE	NE	ENE
Prevailing Wind Speed (mph)	8	8	8	9	9	10	7	7	8	9	8	8	8
Maximum Wind Gust (mph)	55	73	58	56	99	78	67	59	75	53	54	60	99

Vero Beach

Vero Beach is located on the southeast coast of Florida, separated from the Atlantic Ocean by the Inland Waterway and a narrow island offshore. Its climate is strongly influenced by this maritime location. Temperatures in summer rarely reach 100 degrees. The average maximum temperature in July and August is about 90 degrees. In winter the average minimum temperature is slightly above 50 degrees with record lows near 20 degrees. On average, only one day a year experiences freezing temperatures, usually in January.

Rainfall occurs in all seasons but most abundantly in summer when showers are common. Thunderstorms are present approximately 70 to 80 days a year. Monthly precipitation amounts in winter are about half those in summer, and are due in part to cold frontal systems traversing the region. Throughout the year, relative humidity at 7 A.M. tends to range from 80 to 90 percent. The 1 P.M. humidity ranges from 60 to 70 percent with lower values occurring in midafternoon when temperatures are the highest.

Vero Beach lies at the northern boundary of a tropical rainy region. Within that region during summer and fall there may be hurricane activity. Of those hurricanes that pass close to Vero Beach, many move northward offshore, some cross the peninsula of Florida moving generally eastward but being weakened by their passage over land, and some enter the coastal area from the Atlantic Ocean. The frequency of the latter group has been small, about five in 114 years.

Vero Beach *Indian River County*   Elevation: 19 ft.   Latitude: 27° 38' N   Longitude: 80° 27' W

	JAN	FEB	MAR	APR	MAY	JUN	JUL	AUG	SEP	OCT	NOV	DEC	YEAR
Mean Maximum Temp. (°F)	73.1	74.1	77.9	81.5	85.6	88.6	90.4	90.3	88.6	84.5	79.5	74.8	82.4
Mean Temp. (°F)	61.9	63.0	67.1	70.8	75.6	79.5	81.1	81.2	80.1	75.5	69.7	64.1	72.5
Mean Minimum Temp. (°F)	50.6	51.8	56.2	60.1	65.5	70.4	71.7	72.1	71.5	66.5	59.9	53.5	62.5
Extreme Maximum Temp. (°F)	86	89	92	95	97	98	99	97	96	93	90	87	99
Extreme Minimum Temp. (°F)	23	29	26	37	46	56	62	63	63	44	31	24	23
Days Maximum Temp. ≥ 90°F	0	0	0	2	5	13	21	21	13	2	0	0	77
Days Maximum Temp. ≤ 32°F	0	0	0	0	0	0	0	0	0	0	0	0	0
Days Minimum Temp. ≤ 32°F	1	1	0	0	0	0	0	0	0	0	0	0	2
Days Minimum Temp. ≤ 0°F	0	0	0	0	0	0	0	0	0	0	0	0	0
Heating Degree Days (base 65°F)	152	117	55	13	1	0	0	0	0	2	32	107	479
Cooling Degree Days (base 65°F)	61	73	123	188	334	448	515	516	459	342	185	89	3,333
Mean Precipitation (in.)	2.79	2.98	3.96	2.49	4.46	6.94	6.18	6.95	7.24	5.61	3.83	2.28	55.71
Maximum Precipitation (in.)	8.9	6.8	12.8	8.8	5.8	10.8	11.1	11.7	15.4	12.4	11.8	5.9	66.7
Minimum Precipitation (in.)	0.3	0.3	0.2	trace	0.3	1.5	2.9	2.0	1.7	0.8	0.3	0.2	35.2
Maximum 24-hr. Precipitation (in.)	2.8	2.5	6.8	4.1	2.7	2.6	3.4	6.4	7.2	4.5	4.8	2.6	7.2
Days With ≥ 0.1" Precipitation	5	5	5	5	7	9	10	10	11	8	5	4	84
Days With ≥ 1.0" Precipitation	1	1	1	1	1	2	2	2	2	1	1	0	15
Mean Snowfall (in.)	trace	0.0	0.0	0.0	0.0	0.0	0.0	0.0	0.0	0.0	0.0	0.0	trace
Maximum Snowfall (in.)	0	0	0	0	0	0	0	0	0	0	0	0	0
Maximum 24-hr. Snowfall (in.)	0	0	0	0	0	0	0	0	0	0	0	0	0
Days With ≥ 1.0" Snow Depth	0	0	0	0	0	0	0	0	0	0	0	0	0
Thunderstorm Days	1	1	3	4	6	12	16	15	10	4	1	< 1	73
Foggy Days	12	12	12	10	10	8	7	9	7	9	11	12	119
Predominant Sky Cover	SCT	SCT	SCT	SCT	SCT	SCT	SCT	SCT	SCT	SCT	SCT	SCT	SCT
Mean Relative Humidity 7am (%)	89	88	86	84	83	86	88	90	90	87	87	88	87
Mean Relative Humidity 4pm (%)	63	60	59	58	62	69	69	70	70	68	66	64	65
Mean Dewpoint (°F)	56	56	58	61	67	72	73	74	73	68	62	56	65
Prevailing Wind Direction	NW	ESE	SE	ESE	ESE	ESE	ESE	ESE	ENE	NE	NW	NW	ESE
Prevailing Wind Speed (mph)	10	12	14	12	12	12	10	10	10	12	9	9	12
Maximum Wind Gust (mph)	na	na	na	na	na	na	na	na	na	na	na	na	na

West Palm Beach Int'l Airport

West Palm Beach and Palm Beach, both located on the coastal sand ridge of southeastern Florida, are separated by Lake Worth, a portion of the Inland Waterway. The entire coastal ridge is only about five miles wide and in early times the Everglades reached to its western edge. Now most of the swampland has been drained and is devoted to agriculture, the peat-like muck soil being very fertile when fortified with certain lacking minerals. The Atlantic Ocean forms the eastern edge of Palm Beach, and the Gulf Stream flows northward about two miles offshore, its nearest approach to the Florida coast.

Because of its southerly location and marine influences, the Palm Beach area has a notably equable climate. Cold continental air must either travel over water or flow down the Florida Peninsula to reach the area, and in either case its cold is appreciably modified. Actually, the coldest weather, with infrequent frosts, is experienced the second or third night after the arrival of the cold air, due to the loss of heat through radiation cooling. The frequency of temperatures as low as the freezing mark is about one per three years at the National Weather Service Office, but in the farmlands farther from the coast the frequency of light freezes is much higher.

Summer temperatures are tempered by the ocean breeze, and by the frequent formation of cumulus clouds, which shade the land somewhat without completely obscuring the sun. Temperatures of 89 degrees or higher have occurred in all months of the year, but the 100 degree mark has rarely occurred. August is the warmest month and has an average maximum temperature of about 90 degrees. The occurrence of 90 degree temperatures in August is so common that such can be expected on more than two-thirds of the days. However, temperatures as high as 100 degrees rarely occur.

The moist, unstable air in this area results in frequent showers, usually of short duration. Thunderstorms are frequent during the summer, occurring every other day. Rainfall is heaviest during the summer and fall, the fall rainfall occurring from occasional heavy rains accompanying tropical disturbances. High winds, associated with hurricanes, have been estimated at about 140 mph in the city.

Flying weather is usually very good in this area, with instrument weather occurring only rarely. Heavy fog occurs on an average of only one morning a month in the winter and spring, and almost never in the summer and fall.

West Palm Beach Int'l Airport *Palm Beach County*   Elevation: 16 ft.   Latitude: 26° 41' N   Longitude: 80° 06' W

	JAN	FEB	MAR	APR	MAY	JUN	JUL	AUG	SEP	OCT	NOV	DEC	YEAR
Mean Maximum Temp. (°F)	75.0	76.1	79.0	82.2	85.8	88.6	90.1	90.1	88.6	85.1	80.4	76.6	83.1
Mean Temp. (°F)	66.1	67.1	70.4	73.8	78.2	81.1	82.6	82.8	81.6	78.2	73.0	68.3	75.3
Mean Minimum Temp. (°F)	57.1	58.0	61.8	65.5	70.5	73.7	75.0	75.4	74.7	71.3	65.6	60.0	67.4
Extreme Maximum Temp. (°F)	87	89	94	99	96	98	99	97	95	95	91	88	99
Extreme Minimum Temp. (°F)	27	32	30	43	51	61	68	69	67	48	37	28	27
Days Maximum Temp. ≥ 90°F	0	0	0	2	4	11	19	20	11	2	0	0	69
Days Maximum Temp. ≤ 32°F	0	0	0	0	0	0	0	0	0	0	0	0	0
Days Minimum Temp. ≤ 32°F	0	0	0	0	0	0	0	0	0	0	0	0	0
Days Minimum Temp. ≤ 0°F	0	0	0	0	0	0	0	0	0	0	0	0	0
Heating Degree Days (base 65°F)	84	59	26	3	0	0	0	0	0	0	11	55	238
Cooling Degree Days (base 65°F)	122	137	196	274	416	501	561	564	512	426	266	164	4,139
Mean Precipitation (in.)	3.86	2.63	4.01	3.47	5.57	7.75	5.86	6.73	8.12	5.37	5.38	3.06	61.81
Maximum Precipitation (in.)	11.0	8.7	16.8	12.6	15.2	17.9	13.3	20.1	24.9	18.7	14.6	11.7	85.9
Minimum Precipitation (in.)	0.2	0.3	0.3	trace	0.4	1.1	1.2	1.7	1.8	1.2	0.2	0.1	37.3
Maximum 24-hr. Precipitation (in.)	6.8	2.9	5.6	6.5	7.0	4.9	5.3	8.0	5.7	7.1	7.4	6.4	8.0
Days With ≥ 0.1" Precipitation	5	5	5	4	7	11	10	11	12	8	6	5	89
Days With ≥ 1.0" Precipitation	1	1	1	1	2	3	1	2	3	1	2	1	19
Mean Snowfall (in.)	trace	0.0	trace	0.0	0.0	0.0	0.0	trace	0.0	0.0	0.0	0.0	trace
Maximum Snowfall (in.)	trace	0	0	0	0	0	0	0	0	0	0	0	trace
Maximum 24-hr. Snowfall (in.)	trace	0	0	0	0	0	0	0	0	0	0	0	trace
Days With ≥ 1.0" Snow Depth	0	0	0	0	0	0	0	0	0	0	0	0	0
Thunderstorm Days	1	1	3	4	7	13	16	16	11	4	2	1	79
Foggy Days	7	6	6	4	3	3	2	2	2	4	5	6	50
Predominant Sky Cover	SCT	SCT	SCT	SCT	SCT	SCT	SCT	SCT	SCT	SCT	SCT	SCT	SCT
Mean Relative Humidity 7am (%)	84	84	83	79	80	84	85	86	87	85	84	84	84
Mean Relative Humidity 4pm (%)	61	59	58	58	63	69	68	68	70	66	64	62	64
Mean Dewpoint (°F)	56	57	59	62	67	72	73	73	73	68	63	58	65
Prevailing Wind Direction	NW	NW	SE	SE	ESE	ESE	ESE	ESE	E	ENE	E	NW	E
Prevailing Wind Speed (mph)	10	10	13	13	12	10	10	10	12	14	14	10	12
Maximum Wind Gust (mph)	62	52	74	63	74	92	59	66	75	49	47	53	92

Arcadia *Desoto County*   Elevation: 62 ft.   Latitude: 27° 14' N   Longitude: 81° 51' W

	JAN	FEB	MAR	APR	MAY	JUN	JUL	AUG	SEP	OCT	NOV	DEC	YEAR
Mean Maximum Temp. (°F)	73.8	75.4	80.1	84.3	89.2	91.1	91.8	91.5	89.8	85.5	79.8	75.1	83.9
Mean Temp. (°F)	61.4	62.6	67.2	70.9	76.4	79.9	81.3	81.3	80.0	74.9	68.5	63.4	72.3
Mean Minimum Temp. (°F)	49.0	49.6	54.2	57.4	63.3	68.7	70.7	71.1	70.2	64.4	57.0	51.7	60.6
Extreme Maximum Temp. (°F)	88	92	94	98	100	104	100	98	97	98	92	89	104
Extreme Minimum Temp. (°F)	18	24	26	32	43	52	61	62	56	41	23	22	18
Days Maximum Temp. ≥ 90°F	0	0	1	5	16	22	26	26	19	5	0	0	120
Days Maximum Temp. ≤ 32°F	0	0	0	0	0	0	0	0	0	0	0	0	0
Days Minimum Temp. ≤ 32°F	3	2	0	0	0	0	0	0	0	0	0	2	7
Days Minimum Temp. ≤ 0°F	0	0	0	0	0	0	0	0	0	0	0	0	0
Heating Degree Days (base 65°F)	164	124	56	14	0	0	0	0	0	3	40	122	523
Cooling Degree Days (base 65°F)	51	64	121	189	364	460	519	515	457	326	154	79	3,299
Mean Precipitation (in.)	2.20	2.55	3.28	1.74	4.15	8.04	7.39	6.96	6.75	2.85	2.11	1.80	49.82
Days With ≥ 0.1" Precipitation	3	3	4	3	5	9	10	10	9	4	3	3	66
Days With ≥ 1.0" Precipitation	1	1	1	1	1	3	2	2	2	1	1	1	17
Mean Snowfall (in.)	0.0	0.0	0.0	0.0	0.0	0.0	0.0	0.0	0.0	0.0	0.0	0.0	0.0
Days With ≥ 1.0" Snow Depth	0	0	0	0	0	0	0	0	0	0	0	0	0

Archbold Bio Station *Highlands County*   Elevation: 137 ft.   Latitude: 27° 11' N   Longitude: 81° 21' W

	JAN	FEB	MAR	APR	MAY	JUN	JUL	AUG	SEP	OCT	NOV	DEC	YEAR
Mean Maximum Temp. (°F)	74.3	76.3	80.8	85.3	89.8	91.9	93.0	92.8	91.0	86.6	81.0	75.8	84.9
Mean Temp. (°F)	61.0	62.3	66.8	70.5	75.7	79.6	80.7	81.1	79.9	74.8	68.9	63.2	72.0
Mean Minimum Temp. (°F)	47.6	48.3	52.7	55.6	61.6	67.2	68.4	69.2	68.7	63.0	56.8	50.5	59.1
Extreme Maximum Temp. (°F)	87	91	94	98	100	102	103	99	98	96	96	90	103
Extreme Minimum Temp. (°F)	13	21	24	27	36	50	58	60	56	38	28	18	13
Days Maximum Temp. ≥ 90°F	0	0	2	7	17	23	28	28	23	8	1	0	137
Days Maximum Temp. ≤ 32°F	0	0	0	0	0	0	0	0	0	0	0	0	0
Days Minimum Temp. ≤ 32°F	4	3	1	0	0	0	0	0	0	0	0	2	10
Days Minimum Temp. ≤ 0°F	0	0	0	0	0	0	0	0	0	0	0	0	0
Heating Degree Days (base 65°F)	177	136	67	23	1	0	0	0	0	4	40	129	577
Cooling Degree Days (base 65°F)	58	72	125	189	337	451	501	511	451	319	163	79	3,256
Mean Precipitation (in.)	2.44	2.48	3.48	2.28	4.11	7.90	7.79	7.50	6.40	3.06	2.06	1.94	51.44
Days With ≥ 0.1" Precipitation	4	4	4	4	6	11	11	11	10	5	3	3	76
Days With ≥ 1.0" Precipitation	1	1	1	1	2	3	3	2	2	1	1	1	19
Mean Snowfall (in.)	trace	0.0	0.0	0.0	0.0	0.0	0.0	0.0	0.0	0.0	0.0	0.0	trace
Days With ≥ 1.0" Snow Depth	0	0	0	0	0	0	0	0	0	0	0	0	0

Avon Park 2 W *Highlands County*   Elevation: 150 ft.   Latitude: 27° 36' N   Longitude: 81° 32' W

	JAN	FEB	MAR	APR	MAY	JUN	JUL	AUG	SEP	OCT	NOV	DEC	YEAR
Mean Maximum Temp. (°F)	72.3	75.1	79.2	83.8	88.5	90.8	91.8	91.6	89.9	85.2	79.4	74.5	83.5
Mean Temp. (°F)	60.0	62.7	67.0	71.5	76.7	80.4	81.7	81.7	80.3	74.9	68.3	62.9	72.3
Mean Minimum Temp. (°F)	47.7	50.3	54.7	59.1	64.9	70.0	71.5	71.8	70.7	64.5	57.3	51.3	61.1
Extreme Maximum Temp. (°F)	88	92	93	95	98	101	100	99	99	96	92	88	101
Extreme Minimum Temp. (°F)	18	26	23	34	44	50	62	59	58	43	29	23	18
Days Maximum Temp. ≥ 90°F	0	0	0	4	13	21	26	25	19	5	0	0	113
Days Maximum Temp. ≤ 32°F	0	0	0	0	0	0	0	0	0	0	0	0	0
Days Minimum Temp. ≤ 32°F	3	1	0	0	0	0	0	0	0	0	0	1	5
Days Minimum Temp. ≤ 0°F	0	0	0	0	0	0	0	0	0	0	0	0	0
Heating Degree Days (base 65°F)	201	126	62	14	1	0	0	0	0	4	45	137	590
Cooling Degree Days (base 65°F)	49	74	122	203	366	470	526	526	462	319	149	75	3,341
Mean Precipitation (in.)	2.57	2.47	3.16	2.16	3.75	8.23	7.10	7.21	5.99	3.10	2.28	1.84	49.86
Days With ≥ 0.1" Precipitation	4	4	4	3	6	10	11	11	9	5	3	3	73
Days With ≥ 1.0" Precipitation	1	1	1	1	1	3	2	2	2	1	1	1	17
Mean Snowfall (in.)	trace	0.0	0.0	0.0	0.0	0.0	0.0	0.0	0.0	0.0	0.0	0.0	trace
Days With ≥ 1.0" Snow Depth	0	0	0	0	0	0	0	0	0	0	0	0	0

Bartow *Polk County*   Elevation: 124 ft.   Latitude: 27° 54' N   Longitude: 81° 51' W

	JAN	FEB	MAR	APR	MAY	JUN	JUL	AUG	SEP	OCT	NOV	DEC	YEAR
Mean Maximum Temp. (°F)	73.4	75.2	80.0	84.3	88.9	91.4	92.3	92.3	90.4	85.4	79.7	74.7	84.0
Mean Temp. (°F)	61.8	63.4	67.9	72.2	77.5	81.3	82.4	82.5	81.0	75.2	69.2	63.5	73.2
Mean Minimum Temp. (°F)	50.1	51.6	55.8	60.1	66.0	71.2	72.4	72.7	71.5	64.9	58.6	52.2	62.3
Extreme Maximum Temp. (°F)	86	89	93	96	98	103	101	99	96	94	93	90	103
Extreme Minimum Temp. (°F)	20	23	23	39	49	59	63	63	56	42	32	22	20
Days Maximum Temp. ≥ 90°F	0	0	1	4	14	23	27	27	21	4	0	0	121
Days Maximum Temp. ≤ 32°F	0	0	0	0	0	0	0	0	0	0	0	0	0
Days Minimum Temp. ≤ 32°F	2	1	0	0	0	0	0	0	0	0	0	1	4
Days Minimum Temp. ≤ 0°F	0	0	0	0	0	0	0	0	0	0	0	0	0
Heating Degree Days (base 65°F)	158	112	47	7	0	0	0	0	0	2	36	121	483
Cooling Degree Days (base 65°F)	62	85	143	232	402	510	563	568	496	339	176	83	3,659
Mean Precipitation (in.)	2.58	2.89	3.31	2.54	3.95	6.76	8.44	6.56	6.62	2.74	2.17	2.38	50.94
Days With ≥ 0.1" Precipitation	4	4	5	4	5	9	12	11	9	5	4	4	76
Days With ≥ 1.0" Precipitation	1	1	1	1	1	2	3	2	2	1	1	1	17
Mean Snowfall (in.)	0.0	0.0	0.0	0.0	0.0	0.0	0.0	0.0	0.0	0.0	0.0	0.0	0.0
Days With ≥ 1.0" Snow Depth	0	0	0	0	0	0	0	0	0	0	0	0	0

Belle Glade Exp. Station *Palm Beach County*   Elevation: 13 ft.   Latitude: 26° 39' N   Longitude: 80° 38' W

	JAN	FEB	MAR	APR	MAY	JUN	JUL	AUG	SEP	OCT	NOV	DEC	YEAR
Mean Maximum Temp. (°F)	75.0	76.4	79.9	83.6	87.3	89.8	91.2	91.2	89.7	85.9	80.9	76.5	84.0
Mean Temp. (°F)	63.5	64.5	68.2	71.5	76.1	79.9	81.2	81.3	80.1	75.8	70.4	65.5	73.2
Mean Minimum Temp. (°F)	51.9	52.5	56.6	59.4	64.9	70.0	71.1	71.3	70.5	65.6	60.0	54.4	62.3
Extreme Maximum Temp. (°F)	88	90	92	95	97	98	97	98	97	96	91	89	98
Extreme Minimum Temp. (°F)	21	29	29	34	45	55	64	65	60	39	36	24	21
Days Maximum Temp. ≥ 90°F	0	0	1	3	8	17	24	25	18	5	0	0	101
Days Maximum Temp. ≤ 32°F	0	0	0	0	0	0	0	0	0	0	0	0	0
Days Minimum Temp. ≤ 32°F	1	0	0	0	0	0	0	0	0	0	0	1	2
Days Minimum Temp. ≤ 0°F	0	0	0	0	0	0	0	0	0	0	0	0	0
Heating Degree Days (base 65°F)	124	93	41	11	0	0	0	0	0	2	22	87	380
Cooling Degree Days (base 65°F)	80	93	144	210	350	464	516	519	460	351	196	107	3,490
Mean Precipitation (in.)	2.58	1.93	3.07	2.17	5.16	7.40	7.44	7.44	7.13	3.50	2.78	1.81	52.41
Days With ≥ 0.1" Precipitation	4	4	4	4	7	10	11	11	11	6	4	3	79
Days With ≥ 1.0" Precipitation	1	0	1	1	2	2	2	2	2	1	1	0	15
Mean Snowfall (in.)	trace	0.0	0.0	0.0	0.0	0.0	0.0	0.0	0.0	0.0	0.0	0.0	trace
Days With ≥ 1.0" Snow Depth	0	0	0	0	0	0	0	0	0	0	0	0	0

Bradenton 5 ESE *Manatee County*   Elevation: 19 ft.   Latitude: 27° 27' N   Longitude: 82° 28' W

	JAN	FEB	MAR	APR	MAY	JUN	JUL	AUG	SEP	OCT	NOV	DEC	YEAR
Mean Maximum Temp. (°F)	72.5	74.0	78.1	82.3	87.4	90.3	91.5	91.5	90.0	85.3	79.5	74.3	83.1
Mean Temp. (°F)	61.3	62.8	67.0	70.9	76.3	80.5	82.0	82.2	80.9	75.2	68.9	63.3	72.6
Mean Minimum Temp. (°F)	50.0	51.5	55.9	59.4	65.1	70.6	72.3	72.9	71.8	65.1	58.2	52.3	62.1
Extreme Maximum Temp. (°F)	89	88	90	94	95	100	100	99	97	95	90	89	100
Extreme Minimum Temp. (°F)	23	24	30	38	46	52	62	60	59	44	29	20	20
Days Maximum Temp. ≥ 90°F	0	0	0	1	10	20	25	25	19	5	0	0	105
Days Maximum Temp. ≤ 32°F	0	0	0	0	0	0	0	0	0	0	0	0	0
Days Minimum Temp. ≤ 32°F	1	1	0	0	0	0	0	0	0	0	0	1	3
Days Minimum Temp. ≤ 0°F	0	0	0	0	0	0	0	0	0	0	0	0	0
Heating Degree Days (base 65°F)	173	125	59	14	0	0	0	0	0	3	42	128	544
Cooling Degree Days (base 65°F)	62	78	129	202	368	486	548	554	489	341	175	86	3,518
Mean Precipitation (in.)	2.99	2.72	3.52	1.79	2.96	7.42	8.50	9.43	7.17	2.99	2.34	2.44	54.27
Days With ≥ 0.1" Precipitation	4	4	4	3	4	9	12	13	10	4	3	4	74
Days With ≥ 1.0" Precipitation	1	1	1	0	1	3	3	3	2	1	1	1	18
Mean Snowfall (in.)	0.0	0.0	0.0	0.0	0.0	0.0	0.0	0.0	0.0	0.0	0.0	0.0	0.0
Days With ≥ 1.0" Snow Depth	0	0	0	0	0	0	0	0	0	0	0	0	0

Brooksville Chin Hill *Hernando County*   Elevation: 239 ft.   Latitude: 28° 37' N   Longitude: 82° 22' W

	JAN	FEB	MAR	APR	MAY	JUN	JUL	AUG	SEP	OCT	NOV	DEC	YEAR
Mean Maximum Temp. (°F)	70.8	72.7	78.2	82.3	*87.6*	89.9	90.7	90.2	89.1	83.9	77.9	72.5	*82.1*
Mean Temp. (°F)	59.7	61.2	66.5	70.7	*76.3*	80.0	81.2	81.1	79.8	73.9	67.1	61.7	*71.6*
Mean Minimum Temp. (°F)	48.5	49.6	54.8	59.2	*64.8*	70.1	71.7	71.8	70.4	63.9	56.3	50.8	*61.0*
Extreme Maximum Temp. (°F)	89	89	90	96	100	104	100	99	96	94	89	86	104
Extreme Minimum Temp. (°F)	13	21	20	36	48	55	61	62	55	40	22	15	13
Days Maximum Temp. ≥ 90°F	0	0	0	2	9	*17*	21	21	15	2	0	0	*87*
Days Maximum Temp. ≤ 32°F	0	0	0	0	0	0	0	0	0	0	0	0	0
Days Minimum Temp. ≤ 32°F	2	1	0	0	0	0	0	0	0	0	0	1	4
Days Minimum Temp. ≤ 0°F	0	0	0	0	0	0	0	0	0	0	0	0	0
Heating Degree Days (base 65°F)	209	150	62	15	*1*	0	0	0	0	4	57	157	*655*
Cooling Degree Days (base 65°F)	45	53	109	187	*361*	458	513	*511*	449	290	131	60	*3,167*
Mean Precipitation (in.)	3.36	3.36	4.36	2.65	3.44	7.04	6.86	8.47	6.13	2.44	2.36	2.47	52.94
Days With ≥ 0.1" Precipitation	5	4	5	3	5	9	10	11	8	4	3	4	71
Days With ≥ 1.0" Precipitation	1	1	1	1	1	2	2	3	2	1	1	1	17
Mean Snowfall (in.)	0.0	0.0	0.0	0.0	0.0	0.0	0.0	0.0	0.0	0.0	0.0	0.0	0.0
Days With ≥ 1.0" Snow Depth	0	0	0	0	0	0	0	0	0	0	0	0	0

Canal Point USDA *Palm Beach County*   Elevation: 29 ft.   Latitude: 26° 52' N   Longitude: 80° 37' W

	JAN	FEB	MAR	APR	MAY	JUN	JUL	AUG	SEP	OCT	NOV	DEC	YEAR
Mean Maximum Temp. (°F)	74.4	75.7	79.8	84.1	87.9	90.3	91.8	91.6	90.3	86.4	81.0	76.1	84.1
Mean Temp. (°F)	63.7	64.9	68.8	72.5	76.8	80.3	81.4	81.5	80.6	76.9	71.3	65.9	73.7
Mean Minimum Temp. (°F)	52.9	54.1	57.8	60.9	65.6	70.2	71.0	71.4	70.8	67.2	61.4	55.8	63.3
Extreme Maximum Temp. (°F)	89	90	92	95	97	98	100	98	98	96	91	89	100
Extreme Minimum Temp. (°F)	25	29	31	41	48	54	62	61	60	42	39	25	25
Days Maximum Temp. ≥ 90°F	0	0	1	3	11	20	26	26	21	7	0	0	115
Days Maximum Temp. ≤ 32°F	0	0	0	0	0	0	0	0	0	0	0	0	0
Days Minimum Temp. ≤ 32°F	0	0	0	0	0	0	0	0	0	0	0	0	0
Days Minimum Temp. ≤ 0°F	0	0	0	0	0	0	0	0	0	0	0	0	0
Heating Degree Days (base 65°F)	108	79	30	4	0	0	0	0	0	1	14	72	308
Cooling Degree Days (base 65°F)	73	96	158	238	376	473	524	527	478	385	218	111	3,657
Mean Precipitation (in.)	2.68	2.34	3.83	2.18	4.80	7.46	6.27	7.00	7.04	3.94	2.94	2.05	52.53
Days With ≥ 0.1" Precipitation	4	4	5	3	6	10	10	11	10	6	4	4	77
Days With ≥ 1.0" Precipitation	1	1	1	1	2	2	2	2	2	1	1	1	17
Mean Snowfall (in.)	0.0	0.0	0.0	0.0	0.0	0.0	0.0	0.0	0.0	0.0	0.0	0.0	0.0
Days With ≥ 1.0" Snow Depth	0	0	0	0	0	0	0	0	0	0	0	0	0

Chipley 3 E *Washington County*   Elevation: 127 ft.   Latitude: 30° 47' N   Longitude: 85° 29' W

	JAN	FEB	MAR	APR	MAY	JUN	JUL	AUG	SEP	OCT	NOV	DEC	YEAR
Mean Maximum Temp. (°F)	60.2	64.5	71.7	78.4	85.1	89.7	91.4	90.8	87.6	79.7	70.7	63.5	77.8
Mean Temp. (°F)	48.9	52.5	59.4	65.6	72.9	78.7	81.1	80.5	76.7	66.8	58.1	51.7	66.1
Mean Minimum Temp. (°F)	37.6	40.4	47.0	52.7	60.6	67.8	70.7	70.1	65.8	53.9	45.5	39.9	54.3
Extreme Maximum Temp. (°F)	81	83	88	94	100	104	104	102	98	94	88	85	104
Extreme Minimum Temp. (°F)	2	13	20	31	39	47	61	55	43	29	17	10	2
Days Maximum Temp. ≥ 90°F	0	0	0	1	6	16	22	21	13	1	0	0	80
Days Maximum Temp. ≤ 32°F	0	0	0	0	0	0	0	0	0	0	0	0	0
Days Minimum Temp. ≤ 32°F	11	7	2	0	0	0	0	0	0	0	3	10	33
Days Minimum Temp. ≤ 0°F	0	0	0	0	0	0	0	0	0	0	0	0	0
Heating Degree Days (base 65°F)	499	358	206	75	6	0	0	0	2	66	234	421	1,867
Cooling Degree Days (base 65°F)	5	12	35	92	260	421	509	488	344	133	33	13	2,345
Mean Precipitation (in.)	6.11	5.04	6.18	3.80	4.31	5.32	6.88	5.47	4.62	3.11	3.93	3.84	58.61
Days With ≥ 0.1" Precipitation	8	6	7	5	6	8	10	8	6	4	5	6	79
Days With ≥ 1.0" Precipitation	2	2	2	1	1	2	2	2	1	1	1	1	18
Mean Snowfall (in.)	trace	0.0	0.0	0.0	0.0	0.0	0.0	0.0	0.0	0.0	0.0	0.0	trace
Days With ≥ 1.0" Snow Depth	0	0	0	0	0	0	0	0	0	0	0	0	0

Clermont 7 S *Lake County*   Elevation: 108 ft.   Latitude: 28° 27' N   Longitude: 81° 45' W

	JAN	FEB	MAR	APR	MAY	JUN	JUL	AUG	SEP	OCT	NOV	DEC	YEAR
Mean Maximum Temp. (°F)	70.3	72.9	78.2	83.0	87.6	90.1	91.6	91.0	88.9	83.3	77.1	71.8	82.2
Mean Temp. (°F)	59.9	61.8	66.8	71.1	76.3	80.3	81.8	81.8	80.2	74.3	67.5	61.8	71.9
Mean Minimum Temp. (°F)	49.3	50.6	55.4	59.1	65.0	70.4	71.9	72.5	71.4	65.2	57.8	51.7	61.7
Extreme Maximum Temp. (°F)	86	89	91	94	99	101	101	98	96	94	88	87	101
Extreme Minimum Temp. (°F)	18	27	25	39	49	51	62	64	55	41	28	19	18
Days Maximum Temp. ≥ 90°F	0	0	0	3	10	17	24	21	15	2	0	0	92
Days Maximum Temp. ≤ 32°F	0	0	0	0	0	0	0	0	0	0	0	0	0
Days Minimum Temp. ≤ 32°F	2	1	0	0	0	0	0	0	0	0	0	1	4
Days Minimum Temp. ≤ 0°F	0	0	0	0	0	0	0	0	0	0	0	0	0
Heating Degree Days (base 65°F)	199	139	61	13	0	0	0	0	0	4	51	150	617
Cooling Degree Days (base 65°F)	43	60	115	189	351	463	531	528	453	301	139	59	3,232
Mean Precipitation (in.)	3.15	2.73	3.96	2.17	3.76	7.91	6.76	6.85	5.75	2.48	2.37	2.43	50.32
Days With ≥ 0.1" Precipitation	5	5	5	3	5	10	11	11	8	4	3	4	74
Days With ≥ 1.0" Precipitation	1	1	1	1	1	2	2	2	1	1	1	1	15
Mean Snowfall (in.)	trace	trace	0.0	0.0	0.0	0.0	0.0	0.0	0.0	0.0	0.0	0.0	trace
Days With ≥ 1.0" Snow Depth	0	0	0	0	0	0	0	0	0	0	0	0	0

Clewiston U.S. Engineers *Hendry County*   Elevation: 19 ft.   Latitude: 26° 45' N   Longitude: 80° 55' W

	JAN	FEB	MAR	APR	MAY	JUN	JUL	AUG	SEP	OCT	NOV	DEC	YEAR
Mean Maximum Temp. (°F)	73.4	75.3	79.8	83.7	87.6	90.1	91.8	91.3	89.8	*85.2*	*80.0*	*74.9*	*83.6*
Mean Temp. (°F)	63.8	65.4	69.6	73.3	77.7	81.0	82.2	82.3	81.5	*77.3*	*71.9*	*66.1*	*74.3*
Mean Minimum Temp. (°F)	54.2	55.6	59.2	62.9	67.8	71.9	72.5	73.1	73.1	*69.4*	*63.7*	57.4	*65.1*
Extreme Maximum Temp. (°F)	90	92	95	98	98	101	101	101	98	97	93	90	101
Extreme Minimum Temp. (°F)	26	32	29	40	51	62	66	67	65	49	35	26	26
Days Maximum Temp. ≥ 90°F	0	0	2	4	9	17	24	23	17	4	1	0	101
Days Maximum Temp. ≤ 32°F	0	0	0	0	0	0	0	0	0	0	0	0	0
Days Minimum Temp. ≤ 32°F	1	0	0	0	0	0	0	0	0	0	0	0	1
Days Minimum Temp. ≤ 0°F	0	0	0	0	0	0	0	0	0	0	0	0	0
Heating Degree Days (base 65°F)	120	81	31	6	0	0	0	0	0	*1*	*17*	*79*	*335*
Cooling Degree Days (base 65°F)	*84*	114	*176*	*260*	410	*500*	*548*	*551*	*501*	*397*	*245*	*119*	*3,905*
Mean Precipitation (in.)	2.18	2.07	3.02	2.13	4.65	7.19	6.53	6.36	4.93	2.97	2.25	1.51	45.79
Days With ≥ 0.1" Precipitation	4	4	4	3	5	9	9	10	8	4	3	3	66
Days With ≥ 1.0" Precipitation	1	1	1	1	1	2	2	2	1	1	1	0	14
Mean Snowfall (in.)	0.0	0.0	0.0	0.0	0.0	0.0	0.0	0.0	0.0	0.0	0.0	0.0	0.0
Days With ≥ 1.0" Snow Depth	0	0	0	0	0	0	0	0	0	0	0	0	0

Cross City 2 WNW *Dixie County*   Elevation: 39 ft.   Latitude: 29° 39' N   Longitude: 83° 10' W

	JAN	FEB	MAR	APR	MAY	JUN	JUL	AUG	SEP	OCT	NOV	DEC	YEAR
Mean Maximum Temp. (°F)	65.1	67.9	73.9	79.2	85.5	89.5	*90.4*	*90.1*	88.0	81.8	*74.3*	67.7	*79.4*
Mean Temp. (°F)	52.6	55.4	61.3	66.3	73.0	78.5	*80.4*	*80.2*	77.8	*69.8*	*62.0*	55.3	*67.7*
Mean Minimum Temp. (°F)	39.8	42.9	48.7	53.4	60.5	67.4	*70.3*	70.4	67.7	57.4	49.2	42.4	*55.8*
Extreme Maximum Temp. (°F)	84	84	90	92	100	100	101	100	96	96	89	85	101
Extreme Minimum Temp. (°F)	10	16	20	31	38	50	57	55	49	31	15	13	10
Days Maximum Temp. ≥ 90°F	0	0	0	0	5	16	*20*	*19*	13	2	0	0	75
Days Maximum Temp. ≤ 32°F	0	0	0	0	0	0	0	0	0	0	0	0	0
Days Minimum Temp. ≤ 32°F	9	5	1	0	0	0	0	0	0	0	2	7	24
Days Minimum Temp. ≤ 0°F	0	0	0	0	0	0	0	0	0	0	0	0	0
Heating Degree Days (base 65°F)	389	278	158	59	5	0	*0*	*0*	0	*33*	*150*	319	*1,391*
Cooling Degree Days (base 65°F)	9	18	49	96	264	416	*486*	*487*	385	198	70	21	*2,499*
Mean Precipitation (in.)	4.49	3.59	4.70	3.51	3.20	6.27	8.91	9.79	5.78	3.02	2.40	3.37	59.03
Days With ≥ 0.1" Precipitation	7	5	5	4	5	8	11	12	8	4	4	5	78
Days With ≥ 1.0" Precipitation	1	1	2	1	1	2	3	3	2	1	1	1	19
Mean Snowfall (in.)	0.0	0.0	0.0	0.0	0.0	0.0	0.0	0.0	0.0	0.0	0.0	0.0	0.0
Days With ≥ 1.0" Snow Depth	0	0	0	0	0	0	0	0	0	0	0	0	0

De Funiak Springs *Walton County*   Elevation: 229 ft.   Latitude: 30° 44' N   Longitude: 86° 04' W

	JAN	FEB	MAR	APR	MAY	JUN	JUL	AUG	SEP	OCT	NOV	DEC	YEAR
Mean Maximum Temp. (°F)	62.5	66.0	72.7	79.2	85.6	90.4	91.8	91.2	88.1	80.5	71.3	64.5	78.6
Mean Temp. (°F)	50.4	53.5	59.9	65.7	73.0	78.7	81.0	80.4	76.8	67.2	58.2	52.6	66.4
Mean Minimum Temp. (°F)	38.2	40.9	47.1	52.2	60.3	67.0	70.1	69.5	65.4	53.9	45.1	40.6	54.2
Extreme Maximum Temp. (°F)	81	82	90	95	*99*	*104*	*105*	*101*	*99*	93	88	*83*	*105*
Extreme Minimum Temp. (°F)	3	12	19	28	*35*	*44*	*55*	*58*	*40*	28	16	7	3
Days Maximum Temp. ≥ 90°F	0	0	0	1	6	17	23	22	14	1	0	0	84
Days Maximum Temp. ≤ 32°F	0	0	0	0	0	0	0	0	0	0	0	0	0
Days Minimum Temp. ≤ 32°F	12	7	3	0	0	0	0	0	0	0	4	9	35
Days Minimum Temp. ≤ 0°F	0	0	0	0	0	0	0	0	0	0	0	0	0
Heating Degree Days (base 65°F)	455	330	191	69	5	0	0	0	2	55	228	395	1,730
Cooling Degree Days (base 65°F)	4	12	36	90	262	*425*	510	490	*353*	139	*29*	15	*2,365*
Mean Precipitation (in.)	5.39	5.75	6.40	3.96	5.03	6.93	7.95	7.04	5.91	3.60	4.68	4.42	67.06
Days With ≥ 0.1" Precipitation	7	7	7	5	6	10	12	10	7	3	5	6	85
Days With ≥ 1.0" Precipitation	2	2	3	1	1	2	2	2	2	1	2	1	21
Mean Snowfall (in.)	trace	trace	trace	0.0	0.0	0.0	0.0	0.0	0.0	0.0	0.0	0.0	trace
Days With ≥ 1.0" Snow Depth	0	0	0	0	0	0	0	0	0	0	0	0	0

Fernandina Beach *Nassau County*   Elevation: 13 ft.   Latitude: 30° 40' N   Longitude: 81° 28' W

	JAN	FEB	MAR	APR	MAY	JUN	JUL	AUG	SEP	OCT	NOV	DEC	YEAR
Mean Maximum Temp. (°F)	62.2	65.1	70.9	76.6	82.5	87.4	89.9	88.5	85.5	78.5	71.4	65.1	77.0
Mean Temp. (°F)	52.7	55.5	61.2	67.1	73.7	79.3	81.9	81.1	78.6	71.1	62.9	56.1	68.4
Mean Minimum Temp. (°F)	43.2	45.9	51.4	57.6	65.0	71.2	73.7	73.7	71.6	63.7	54.4	47.1	59.9
Extreme Maximum Temp. (°F)	88	85	88	94	96	102	102	101	99	94	87	85	102
Extreme Minimum Temp. (°F)	4	20	22	37	40	51	63	61	52	41	24	12	4
Days Maximum Temp. ≥ 90°F	0	0	0	1	3	10	16	11	4	1	0	0	46
Days Maximum Temp. ≤ 32°F	0	0	0	0	0	0	0	0	0	0	0	0	0
Days Minimum Temp. ≤ 32°F	4	2	0	0	0	0	0	0	0	0	0	2	8
Days Minimum Temp. ≤ 0°F	0	0	0	0	0	0	0	0	0	0	0	0	0
Heating Degree Days (base 65°F)	383	276	156	49	3	0	0	0	0	17	125	288	1,297
Cooling Degree Days (base 65°F)	8	16	43	111	282	445	539	515	411	217	71	19	2,677
Mean Precipitation (in.)	3.85	3.32	4.17	2.78	2.98	5.31	5.92	5.46	7.37	4.45	2.52	2.74	50.87
Days With ≥ 0.1" Precipitation	7	6	6	4	5	8	9	8	9	5	4	5	76
Days With ≥ 1.0" Precipitation	1	1	1	1	1	1	2	2	2	1	1	1	15
Mean Snowfall (in.)	trace	trace	trace	0.0	0.0	0.0	0.0	0.0	0.0	0.0	0.0	0.0	trace
Days With ≥ 1.0" Snow Depth	0	0	0	0	0	0	0	0	0	0	0	0	0

Flamingo Ranger Station *Monroe County*   Elevation: 0 ft.   Latitude: 25° 09' N   Longitude: 80° 55' W

	JAN	FEB	MAR	APR	MAY	JUN	JUL	AUG	SEP	OCT	NOV	DEC	YEAR
Mean Maximum Temp. (°F)	76.6	77.2	79.5	82.9	86.0	88.2	89.3	89.8	88.9	86.1	82.3	78.4	83.8
Mean Temp. (°F)	66.3	67.1	69.9	73.5	77.3	80.8	81.7	81.9	81.1	77.6	73.2	68.5	74.9
Mean Minimum Temp. (°F)	56.0	56.9	60.2	64.1	68.7	73.3	74.1	74.0	73.3	69.1	63.9	58.5	66.0
Extreme Maximum Temp. (°F)	88	92	88	94	96	104	100	97	101	99	91	89	104
Extreme Minimum Temp. (°F)	27	24	33	44	48	58	62	28	60	41	36	25	24
Days Maximum Temp. ≥ 90°F	0	0	0	0	3	9	16	19	13	2	0	0	62
Days Maximum Temp. ≤ 32°F	0	0	0	0	0	0	0	0	0	0	0	0	0
Days Minimum Temp. ≤ 32°F	0	0	0	0	0	0	0	0	0	0	0	0	0
Days Minimum Temp. ≤ 0°F	0	0	0	0	0	0	0	0	0	0	0	0	0
Heating Degree Days (base 65°F)	71	53	21	2	0	0	0	0	0	0	6	38	191
Cooling Degree Days (base 65°F)	117	132	180	268	396	489	535	535	490	410	265	160	3,977
Mean Precipitation (in.)	2.02	1.61	1.87	2.06	5.01	7.29	4.93	7.53	7.25	4.27	2.46	1.51	47.81
Days With ≥ 0.1" Precipitation	4	3	3	3	6	9	9	10	11	6	4	3	71
Days With ≥ 1.0" Precipitation	0	0	0	0	2	2	1	2	2	1	1	0	11
Mean Snowfall (in.)	0.0	0.0	0.0	0.0	0.0	0.0	0.0	0.0	0.0	0.0	0.0	0.0	0.0
Days With ≥ 1.0" Snow Depth	0	0	0	0	0	0	0	0	0	0	0	0	0

Fort Drum 5 NW *Okeechobee County*   Elevation: 68 ft.   Latitude: 27° 35' N   Longitude: 80° 50' W

	JAN	FEB	MAR	APR	MAY	JUN	JUL	AUG	SEP	OCT	NOV	DEC	YEAR
Mean Maximum Temp. (°F)	74.7	75.9	79.7	83.7	87.8	90.4	*91.5*	91.5	89.8	*85.5*	80.4	75.6	*83.9*
Mean Temp. (°F)	62.4	63.4	67.2	70.9	75.7	79.9	*81.1*	81.5	80.1	*75.4*	69.4	64.0	*72.6*
Mean Minimum Temp. (°F)	50.1	51.0	54.7	58.0	63.5	69.3	*70.8*	71.5	70.4	*65.2*	58.5	52.3	*61.3*
Extreme Maximum Temp. (°F)	89	88	92	97	98	102	101	99	97	98	93	87	102
Extreme Minimum Temp. (°F)	17	20	27	32	42	55	60	62	60	41	24	22	17
Days Maximum Temp. ≥ 90°F	0	0	0	3	9	17	22	23	18	4	0	0	96
Days Maximum Temp. ≤ 32°F	0	0	0	0	0	0	0	0	0	0	0	0	0
Days Minimum Temp. ≤ 32°F	2	1	0	0	0	0	0	0	0	0	0	1	4
Days Minimum Temp. ≤ 0°F	0	0	0	0	0	0	0	0	0	0	0	0	0
Heating Degree Days (base 65°F)	139	108	48	10	0	0	0	*0*	0	2	30	109	*446*
Cooling Degree Days (base 65°F)	67	78	123	194	341	464	*522*	530	463	*345*	181	82	*3,390*
Mean Precipitation (in.)	2.35	2.51	3.89	2.38	4.53	8.06	7.78	7.16	6.71	3.65	2.31	1.89	53.22
Days With ≥ 0.1" Precipitation	2	4	3	3	5	9	8	8	8	4	3	3	60
Days With ≥ 1.0" Precipitation	0	1	1	1	1	3	3	2	2	1	1	0	16
Mean Snowfall (in.)	trace	0.0	0.0	0.0	0.0	0.0	0.0	0.0	0.0	0.0	0.0	0.0	trace
Days With ≥ 1.0" Snow Depth	0	0	0	0	0	0	0	0	0	0	0	0	0

Fort Lauderdale *Broward County*   Elevation: 13 ft.   Latitude: 26° 06' N   Longitude: 80° 12' W

	JAN	FEB	MAR	APR	MAY	JUN	JUL	AUG	SEP	OCT	NOV	DEC	YEAR
Mean Maximum Temp. (°F)	76.2	76.8	79.4	82.5	85.6	88.3	89.5	89.8	88.6	85.5	81.1	77.6	83.4
Mean Temp. (°F)	67.4	67.9	71.1	74.4	78.2	81.2	82.4	82.8	81.7	78.5	73.8	69.4	75.7
Mean Minimum Temp. (°F)	58.6	59.0	62.7	66.3	70.7	74.1	75.3	75.6	74.8	71.6	66.4	61.3	68.0
Extreme Maximum Temp. (°F)	88	89	92	94	97	97	99	97	98	95	89	88	99
Extreme Minimum Temp. (°F)	28	34	32	42	54	63	64	66	65	47	36	30	28
Days Maximum Temp. ≥ 90°F	0	0	0	1	4	10	15	18	9	2	0	0	59
Days Maximum Temp. ≤ 32°F	0	0	0	0	0	0	0	0	0	0	0	0	0
Days Minimum Temp. ≤ 32°F	0	0	0	0	0	0	0	0	0	0	0	0	0
Days Minimum Temp. ≤ 0°F	0	0	0	0	0	0	0	0	0	0	0	0	0
Heating Degree Days (base 65°F)	62	45	17	2	0	0	0	0	0	0	7	39	172
Cooling Degree Days (base 65°F)	149	154	213	295	423	500	557	567	514	442	291	190	4,295
Mean Precipitation (in.)	3.03	2.79	3.02	3.77	6.43	9.92	6.59	6.95	8.34	6.21	4.55	2.53	64.13
Days With ≥ 0.1" Precipitation	5	4	4	4	8	11	10	11	12	9	6	4	88
Days With ≥ 1.0" Precipitation	1	1	1	1	2	3	2	2	2	2	1	1	19
Mean Snowfall (in.)	0.0	0.0	0.0	0.0	0.0	0.0	0.0	0.0	0.0	0.0	0.0	0.0	0.0
Days With ≥ 1.0" Snow Depth	0	0	0	0	0	0	0	0	0	0	0	0	0

Fort Pierce *St. Lucie County*   Elevation: 22 ft.   Latitude: 27° 28' N   Longitude: 80° 21' W

	JAN	FEB	MAR	APR	MAY	JUN	JUL	AUG	SEP	OCT	NOV	DEC	YEAR
Mean Maximum Temp. (°F)	74.3	75.3	78.9	82.3	86.3	89.4	91.2	90.9	89.4	85.4	80.4	76.0	83.3
Mean Temp. (°F)	63.0	64.1	68.0	71.8	76.7	80.3	81.7	81.7	80.6	76.5	70.5	65.2	73.3
Mean Minimum Temp. (°F)	51.7	52.8	57.2	61.4	67.0	71.0	72.2	72.4	71.8	67.5	60.7	54.4	63.3
Extreme Maximum Temp. (°F)	89	89	92	97	98	100	101	98	99	96	92	88	101
Extreme Minimum Temp. (°F)	19	25	26	33	45	56	64	61	63	42	31	19	19
Days Maximum Temp. ≥ 90°F	0	0	1	2	6	14	24	24	16	4	0	0	91
Days Maximum Temp. ≤ 32°F	0	0	0	0	0	0	0	0	0	0	0	0	0
Days Minimum Temp. ≤ 32°F	1	0	0	0	0	0	0	0	0	0	0	1	2
Days Minimum Temp. ≤ 0°F	0	0	0	0	0	0	0	0	0	0	0	0	0
Heating Degree Days (base 65°F)	134	101	48	9	0	0	0	0	0	2	25	95	414
Cooling Degree Days (base 65°F)	73	87	140	213	371	471	533	528	474	365	199	105	3,559
Mean Precipitation (in.)	2.75	3.03	3.43	2.66	4.62	5.75	5.65	6.38	8.07	5.92	3.53	2.29	54.08
Days With ≥ 0.1" Precipitation	5	5	5	4	7	9	8	10	11	8	5	4	81
Days With ≥ 1.0" Precipitation	1	1	1	1	1	2	2	2	2	2	1	0	16
Mean Snowfall (in.)	trace	0.0	0.0	0.0	0.0	0.0	0.0	0.0	0.0	0.0	0.0	0.0	trace
Days With ≥ 1.0" Snow Depth	0	0	0	0	0	0	0	0	0	0	0	0	0

Hialeah *Dade County*   Elevation: 9 ft.   Latitude: 25° 50' N   Longitude: 80° 17' W

	JAN	FEB	MAR	APR	MAY	JUN	JUL	AUG	SEP	OCT	NOV	DEC	YEAR
Mean Maximum Temp. (°F)	77.2	77.5	80.5	83.3	86.8	89.1	90.8	90.8	89.5	86.2	82.0	78.3	84.3
Mean Temp. (°F)	68.1	68.5	72.4	75.1	79.1	81.8	83.4	83.5	82.4	78.8	74.3	69.8	76.4
Mean Minimum Temp. (°F)	58.5	59.5	63.9	66.9	71.3	74.5	75.9	76.0	75.2	71.3	66.6	61.2	68.4
Extreme Maximum Temp. (°F)	89	90	92	95	97	99	100	99	97	95	91	90	100
Extreme Minimum Temp. (°F)	28	36	32	40	55	60	62	60	62	51	38	30	28
Days Maximum Temp. ≥ 90°F	0	0	0	2	7	14	22	23	16	5	0	0	89
Days Maximum Temp. ≤ 32°F	0	0	0	0	0	0	0	0	0	0	0	0	0
Days Minimum Temp. ≤ 32°F	0	0	0	0	0	0	0	0	0	0	0	0	0
Days Minimum Temp. ≤ 0°F	0	0	0	0	0	0	0	0	0	0	0	0	0
Heating Degree Days (base 65°F)	55	42	14	2	0	0	0	0	0	0	6	36	155
Cooling Degree Days (base 65°F)	166	169	255	320	458	527	595	597	539	448	307	205	4,586
Mean Precipitation (in.)	2.47	2.25	3.20	3.82	6.32	10.37	6.95	9.00	8.89	6.43	3.81	2.41	65.92
Days With ≥ 0.1" Precipitation	5	4	4	4	8	12	11	12	13	9	6	4	92
Days With ≥ 1.0" Precipitation	1	1	1	1	2	3	2	3	3	2	1	1	21
Mean Snowfall (in.)	0.0	0.0	0.0	0.0	0.0	0.0	0.0	0.0	0.0	0.0	0.0	0.0	0.0
Days With ≥ 1.0" Snow Depth	0	0	0	0	0	0	0	0	0	0	0	0	0

High Springs *Alachua County*   Elevation: 62 ft.   Latitude: 29° 50' N   Longitude: 82° 36' W

	JAN	FEB	MAR	APR	MAY	JUN	JUL	AUG	SEP	OCT	NOV	DEC	YEAR
Mean Maximum Temp. (°F)	68.0	71.9	77.9	83.3	88.6	91.6	92.5	92.0	89.8	83.4	76.8	70.5	82.2
Mean Temp. (°F)	54.1	57.6	63.5	68.4	75.1	80.1	81.5	81.3	78.7	70.5	63.2	56.9	69.2
Mean Minimum Temp. (°F)	40.2	43.1	48.9	53.4	61.6	68.5	70.6	70.6	67.6	57.8	49.4	43.2	56.2
Extreme Maximum Temp. (°F)	87	88	92	96	101	104	107	104	99	99	90	89	107
Extreme Minimum Temp. (°F)	9	17	20	30	*41*	45	55	59	49	29	26	8	*8*
Days Maximum Temp. ≥ 90°F	0	0	0	4	*15*	*22*	25	24	18	3	0	0	*111*
Days Maximum Temp. ≤ 32°F	0	0	0	0	0	0	0	0	0	0	0	0	0
Days Minimum Temp. ≤ 32°F	9	5	1	0	0	0	0	0	0	0	2	6	23
Days Minimum Temp. ≤ 0°F	0	0	0	0	0	0	0	0	0	0	0	0	0
Heating Degree Days (base 65°F)	*344*	225	114	38	*1*	0	0	0	0	23	125	269	*1,139*
Cooling Degree Days (base 65°F)	13	27	68	135	327	461	528	523	413	203	79	24	2,801
Mean Precipitation (in.)	4.42	3.80	4.52	3.36	3.81	6.81	7.34	8.19	4.37	3.05	2.19	2.72	54.58
Days With ≥ 0.1" Precipitation	6	5	6	4	6	9	11	11	7	4	4	4	77
Days With ≥ 1.0" Precipitation	2	1	2	1	1	2	2	3	1	1	1	1	18
Mean Snowfall (in.)	trace	0.0	0.0	0.0	0.0	0.0	0.0	0.0	0.0	0.0	0.0	0.0	trace
Days With ≥ 1.0" Snow Depth	0	0	0	0	0	0	0	0	0	0	0	0	0

Immokalee 3 NNW *Collier County*   Elevation: 32 ft.   Latitude: 26° 28' N   Longitude: 81° 26' W

	JAN	FEB	MAR	APR	MAY	JUN	JUL	AUG	SEP	OCT	NOV	DEC	YEAR
Mean Maximum Temp. (°F)	76.5	78.0	81.6	84.9	89.0	90.8	91.6	91.4	89.9	86.4	81.5	77.6	84.9
Mean Temp. (°F)	64.3	65.3	69.0	72.0	76.9	80.4	81.7	82.0	80.9	76.4	70.8	66.0	73.8
Mean Minimum Temp. (°F)	52.0	52.6	56.4	59.1	64.7	69.9	71.7	72.5	71.8	66.3	60.1	54.3	62.6
Extreme Maximum Temp. (°F)	88	90	99	96	99	101	98	100	96	94	91	89	101
Extreme Minimum Temp. (°F)	20	25	30	38	49	54	63	64	64	45	27	24	20
Days Maximum Temp. ≥ 90°F	0	0	1	5	14	20	26	25	19	6	0	0	116
Days Maximum Temp. ≤ 32°F	0	0	0	0	0	0	0	0	0	0	0	0	0
Days Minimum Temp. ≤ 32°F	1	1	0	0	0	0	0	0	0	0	0	1	3
Days Minimum Temp. ≤ 0°F	0	0	0	0	0	0	0	0	0	0	0	0	0
Heating Degree Days (base 65°F)	106	81	32	7	0	0	0	0	0	1	21	75	323
Cooling Degree Days (base 65°F)	86	104	162	226	374	479	529	539	483	366	210	113	3,671
Mean Precipitation (in.)	2.34	2.30	2.98	2.42	4.23	7.92	7.04	7.53	6.43	2.82	2.31	1.76	50.08
Days With ≥ 0.1" Precipitation	4	4	4	3	6	10	12	13	10	5	3	3	77
Days With ≥ 1.0" Precipitation	1	1	1	1	1	3	2	2	2	1	1	1	17
Mean Snowfall (in.)	0.0	0.0	0.0	0.0	0.0	0.0	0.0	0.0	0.0	0.0	0.0	0.0	0.0
Days With ≥ 1.0" Snow Depth	0	0	0	0	0	0	0	0	0	0	0	0	0

Inverness 3 SE *Citrus County*   Elevation: 39 ft.   Latitude: 28° 48' N   Longitude: 82° 19' W

	JAN	FEB	MAR	APR	MAY	JUN	JUL	AUG	SEP	OCT	NOV	DEC	YEAR
Mean Maximum Temp. (°F)	69.6	71.7	77.2	82.1	87.6	90.5	91.7	91.1	89.6	83.7	77.3	72.1	82.0
Mean Temp. (°F)	56.9	58.7	64.2	69.2	75.4	80.2	81.6	81.4	79.6	72.7	65.2	59.4	70.4
Mean Minimum Temp. (°F)	44.1	45.6	51.2	56.3	63.1	69.7	71.4	71.6	69.6	61.6	53.1	46.6	58.7
Extreme Maximum Temp. (°F)	85	89	92	94	100	101	100	99	101	94	92	89	101
Extreme Minimum Temp. (°F)	15	21	24	32	42	52	61	61	51	33	24	15	15
Days Maximum Temp. ≥ 90°F	0	0	0	3	10	19	24	23	18	4	0	0	101
Days Maximum Temp. ≤ 32°F	0	0	0	0	0	0	0	0	0	0	0	0	0
Days Minimum Temp. ≤ 32°F	5	4	1	0	0	0	0	0	0	0	1	3	14
Days Minimum Temp. ≤ 0°F	0	0	0	0	0	0	0	0	0	0	0	0	0
Heating Degree Days (base 65°F)	277	207	106	29	1	0	0	0	0	11	89	209	929
Cooling Degree Days (base 65°F)	24	36	76	145	320	456	514	513	431	258	104	39	2,916
Mean Precipitation (in.)	3.61	3.08	4.26	2.41	3.48	7.30	6.90	7.76	5.89	2.73	2.26	2.56	52.24
Days With ≥ 0.1" Precipitation	5	4	5	3	5	9	11	12	9	4	4	4	75
Days With ≥ 1.0" Precipitation	1	1	1	1	1	2	2	2	2	1	1	1	16
Mean Snowfall (in.)	0.0	0.0	0.0	0.0	0.0	0.0	0.0	0.0	0.0	0.0	0.0	0.0	0.0
Days With ≥ 1.0" Snow Depth	0	0	0	0	0	0	0	0	0	0	0	0	0

Jacksonville Beach *Duval County*   Elevation: 9 ft.   Latitude: 30° 17' N   Longitude: 81° 24' W

	JAN	FEB	MAR	APR	MAY	JUN	JUL	AUG	SEP	OCT	NOV	DEC	YEAR
Mean Maximum Temp. (°F)	63.8	65.9	71.4	76.9	82.7	87.1	89.8	88.5	86.0	79.8	*72.3*	66.5	*77.6*
Mean Temp. (°F)	54.9	57.0	62.5	68.1	74.5	79.5	81.7	81.3	79.4	72.7	*64.1*	58.1	*69.5*
Mean Minimum Temp. (°F)	46.0	48.0	53.6	59.3	66.2	71.7	73.7	74.1	72.9	65.5	*55.8*	49.6	*61.4*
Extreme Maximum Temp. (°F)	85	85	89	94	97	99	103	102	98	93	88	85	103
Extreme Minimum Temp. (°F)	14	21	24	37	50	55	63	64	53	40	25	15	14
Days Maximum Temp. ≥ 90°F	0	0	0	1	2	8	14	9	3	1	0	0	38
Days Maximum Temp. ≤ 32°F	0	0	0	0	0	0	0	0	0	0	0	0	0
Days Minimum Temp. ≤ 32°F	3	2	0	0	0	0	0	0	0	0	0	1	6
Days Minimum Temp. ≤ 0°F	0	0	0	0	0	0	0	0	0	0	0	0	0
Heating Degree Days (base 65°F)	320	238	123	31	1	0	0	0	0	9	*102*	235	*1,059*
Cooling Degree Days (base 65°F)	9	18	50	128	305	445	533	522	437	259	*76*	28	*2,810*
Mean Precipitation (in.)	3.66	3.04	4.11	2.84	3.09	5.69	5.18	6.10	7.06	5.17	2.30	2.77	51.01
Days With ≥ 0.1" Precipitation	6	5	6	4	5	8	8	8	9	6	4	5	74
Days With ≥ 1.0" Precipitation	1	1	1	1	1	2	2	2	2	1	1	1	16
Mean Snowfall (in.)	trace	trace	0.0	0.0	0.0	0.0	0.0	0.0	0.0	0.0	0.0	trace	trace
Days With ≥ 1.0" Snow Depth	0	0	0	0	0	0	0	0	0	0	0	0	0

Jasper *Hamilton County*   Elevation: 144 ft.   Latitude: 30° 31' N   Longitude: 82° 57' W

	JAN	FEB	MAR	APR	MAY	JUN	JUL	AUG	SEP	OCT	NOV	DEC	YEAR
Mean Maximum Temp. (°F)	64.0	66.9	73.8	79.4	85.5	90.0	91.6	91.2	88.8	81.2	73.7	66.3	79.4
Mean Temp. (°F)	51.2	54.0	60.6	66.1	72.9	78.6	80.9	80.4	77.4	68.3	60.4	53.5	67.0
Mean Minimum Temp. (°F)	38.4	41.3	47.4	52.7	60.2	67.2	70.1	69.6	66.0	55.3	47.1	40.5	54.6
Extreme Maximum Temp. (°F)	83	84	90	93	97	103	102	103	102	94	89	86	103
Extreme Minimum Temp. (°F)	4	14	19	33	39	47	59	59	45	31	15	12	4
Days Maximum Temp. ≥ 90°F	0	0	0	1	6	18	24	22	15	2	0	0	88
Days Maximum Temp. ≤ 32°F	0	0	0	0	0	0	0	0	0	0	0	0	0
Days Minimum Temp. ≤ 32°F	11	6	2	0	0	0	0	0	0	0	3	9	31
Days Minimum Temp. ≤ 0°F	0	0	0	0	0	0	0	0	0	0	0	0	0
Heating Degree Days (base 65°F)	432	316	175	66	6	0	0	0	0	47	182	367	1,591
Cooling Degree Days (base 65°F)	6	14	45	101	260	421	506	489	368	160	54	16	2,440
Mean Precipitation (in.)	4.96	4.14	5.28	3.46	3.42	5.99	5.74	6.47	3.88	2.92	2.78	3.45	52.49
Days With ≥ 0.1" Precipitation	7	6	6	4	5	9	10	10	6	3	4	5	75
Days With ≥ 1.0" Precipitation	2	1	2	1	1	2	2	2	1	1	1	1	17
Mean Snowfall (in.)	trace	trace	trace	0.0	0.0	0.0	0.0	0.0	0.0	0.0	0.0	trace	trace
Days With ≥ 1.0" Snow Depth	0	0	0	0	0	0	0	0	0	0	0	0	0

Kissimmee 2 *Osceola County*   Elevation: 59 ft.   Latitude: 28° 17' N   Longitude: 81° 25' W

	JAN	FEB	MAR	APR	MAY	JUN	JUL	AUG	SEP	OCT	NOV	DEC	YEAR
Mean Maximum Temp. (°F)	73.4	75.2	79.3	83.2	87.5	90.7	91.8	91.6	89.8	85.0	79.8	74.7	83.5
Mean Temp. (°F)	61.6	63.1	67.5	71.3	76.3	80.7	82.1	82.2	80.7	75.2	68.9	63.2	72.8
Mean Minimum Temp. (°F)	49.8	51.0	55.6	59.3	65.1	70.8	72.4	72.8	71.6	65.3	58.0	51.7	62.0
Extreme Maximum Temp. (°F)	85	89	91	98	97	101	101	100	97	95	89	88	101
Extreme Minimum Temp. (°F)	19	27	25	38	46	53	63	65	56	42	29	20	19
Days Maximum Temp. ≥ 90°F	0	0	0	2	9	20	26	25	18	4	0	0	104
Days Maximum Temp. ≤ 32°F	0	0	0	0	0	0	0	0	0	0	0	0	0
Days Minimum Temp. ≤ 32°F	2	1	0	0	0	0	0	0	0	0	0	1	4
Days Minimum Temp. ≤ 0°F	0	0	0	0	0	0	0	0	0	0	0	0	0
Heating Degree Days (base 65°F)	159	113	52	10	0	0	0	0	0	3	37	123	497
Cooling Degree Days (base 65°F)	57	72	130	201	360	484	550	551	478	335	168	77	3,463
Mean Precipitation (in.)	2.42	2.80	3.58	2.04	3.91	6.03	6.59	7.23	5.91	3.20	2.41	2.22	48.34
Days With ≥ 0.1" Precipitation	4	4	5	3	6	9	11	11	9	5	3	4	74
Days With ≥ 1.0" Precipitation	1	1	1	0	1	2	2	2	2	1	1	1	15
Mean Snowfall (in.)	0.0	0.0	0.0	0.0	0.0	0.0	0.0	0.0	0.0	0.0	0.0	0.0	0.0
Days With ≥ 1.0" Snow Depth	0	0	0	0	0	0	0	0	0	0	0	0	0

La Belle *Hendry County*   Elevation: 13 ft.   Latitude: 26° 45' N   Longitude: 81° 26' W

	JAN	FEB	MAR	APR	MAY	JUN	JUL	AUG	SEP	OCT	NOV	DEC	YEAR
Mean Maximum Temp. (°F)	na	77.9	*81.8*	85.9	na	92.0	na	na	na	*87.0*	na	na	na
Mean Temp. (°F)	na	64.9	*68.5*	72.2	na	80.6	na	na	na	*76.1*	na	na	na
Mean Minimum Temp. (°F)	na	51.8	*55.0*	58.6	*63.8*	69.1	na	na	na	*65.2*	na	na	na
Extreme Maximum Temp. (°F)	90	92	95	98	104	102	101	*99*	97	96	94	90	*104*
Extreme Minimum Temp. (°F)	19	24	28	37	47	55	61	*62*	60	42	27	*24*	*19*
Days Maximum Temp. ≥ 90°F	0	1	3	7	14	22	23	*24*	19	8	1	0	*122*
Days Maximum Temp. ≤ 32°F	0	0	0	0	0	0	0	0	0	0	0	0	0
Days Minimum Temp. ≤ 32°F	1	1	0	0	0	0	0	0	0	0	0	1	3
Days Minimum Temp. ≤ 0°F	0	0	0	0	0	0	0	0	0	0	0	0	0
Heating Degree Days (base 65°F)	na	91	*45*	9	na	0	na	na	na	*1*	na	na	na
Cooling Degree Days (base 65°F)	na	103	na	229	na	485	na	na	*488*	357	na	na	na
Mean Precipitation (in.)	2.44	2.23	3.30	2.27	4.10	8.86	7.73	7.79	6.26	3.36	2.30	1.68	52.32
Days With ≥ 0.1" Precipitation	3	3	4	3	5	9	10	9	8	4	2	2	62
Days With ≥ 1.0" Precipitation	1	1	1	1	1	2	2	2	2	1	1	0	15
Mean Snowfall (in.)	trace	0.0	0.0	0.0	0.0	0.0	0.0	0.0	0.0	0.0	0.0	0.0	trace
Days With ≥ 1.0" Snow Depth	0	0	0	0	0	0	0	0	0	0	0	0	0

Lake Alfred Exp. Station *Polk County*   Elevation: 137 ft.   Latitude: 28° 06' N   Longitude: 81° 43' W

	JAN	FEB	MAR	APR	MAY	JUN	JUL	AUG	SEP	OCT	NOV	DEC	YEAR
Mean Maximum Temp. (°F)	72.1	74.2	78.7	83.5	88.6	91.4	92.8	92.8	90.8	85.8	79.8	74.0	83.7
Mean Temp. (°F)	59.6	61.6	66.5	70.9	76.4	80.8	82.3	82.3	80.4	74.5	68.1	62.0	72.1
Mean Minimum Temp. (°F)	47.1	49.0	54.1	58.2	64.3	70.1	71.8	71.7	70.0	63.2	56.5	50.0	60.5
Extreme Maximum Temp. (°F)	88	89	93	96	99	104	103	101	98	95	90	88	104
Extreme Minimum Temp. (°F)	19	25	24	35	45	50	61	60	54	38	26	19	19
Days Maximum Temp. ≥ 90°F	0	0	1	4	14	22	27	27	21	6	0	0	122
Days Maximum Temp. ≤ 32°F	0	0	0	0	0	0	0	0	0	0	0	0	0
Days Minimum Temp. ≤ 32°F	3	1	0	0	0	0	0	0	0	0	0	2	6
Days Minimum Temp. ≤ 0°F	0	0	0	0	0	0	0	0	0	0	0	0	0
Heating Degree Days (base 65°F)	211	150	72	18	0	0	0	0	0	5	51	155	662
Cooling Degree Days (base 65°F)	46	66	119	196	366	484	551	548	466	317	157	72	3,388
Mean Precipitation (in.)	2.57	2.81	3.66	1.99	4.20	6.89	7.23	7.27	6.47	2.99	2.28	2.24	50.60
Days With ≥ 0.1" Precipitation	4	5	5	3	6	9	11	11	9	4	3	3	73
Days With ≥ 1.0" Precipitation	1	1	1	1	1	2	2	2	2	1	1	1	16
Mean Snowfall (in.)	trace	0.0	0.0	0.0	0.0	0.0	0.0	0.0	0.0	0.0	0.0	0.0	trace
Days With ≥ 1.0" Snow Depth	0	0	0	0	0	0	0	0	0	0	0	0	0

Lake City 2 E *Columbia County*   Elevation: 193 ft.   Latitude: 30° 11' N   Longitude: 82° 36' W

	JAN	FEB	MAR	APR	MAY	JUN	JUL	AUG	SEP	OCT	NOV	DEC	YEAR
Mean Maximum Temp. (°F)	64.4	67.7	74.1	79.6	85.8	89.8	91.4	90.7	87.9	80.8	73.6	67.0	79.4
Mean Temp. (°F)	53.1	56.0	62.0	67.1	73.8	79.2	81.2	80.7	77.9	69.8	62.3	55.8	68.2
Mean Minimum Temp. (°F)	41.8	44.3	49.8	54.8	61.8	68.5	71.0	70.7	68.0	58.7	50.9	44.5	57.1
Extreme Maximum Temp. (°F)	84	88	89	96	96	104	102	104	97	93	87	91	104
Extreme Minimum Temp. (°F)	7	16	19	34	41	49	57	62	47	34	18	9	7
Days Maximum Temp. ≥ 90°F	0	0	0	1	7	17	23	22	13	1	0	0	84
Days Maximum Temp. ≤ 32°F	0	0	0	0	0	0	0	0	0	0	0	0	0
Days Minimum Temp. ≤ 32°F	8	4	1	0	0	0	0	0	0	0	2	5	20
Days Minimum Temp. ≤ 0°F	0	0	0	0	0	0	0	0	0	0	0	0	0
Heating Degree Days (base 65°F)	377	269	150	53	4	0	0	0	0	30	146	304	1,333
Cooling Degree Days (base 65°F)	13	23	62	125	295	448	522	507	390	190	76	26	2,677
Mean Precipitation (in.)	4.53	3.79	5.06	3.25	3.84	6.76	6.70	7.36	4.59	2.88	2.39	3.00	54.15
Days With ≥ 0.1" Precipitation	7	5	6	4	6	9	10	11	7	4	3	5	77
Days With ≥ 1.0" Precipitation	2	1	2	1	1	2	2	2	1	1	1	1	17
Mean Snowfall (in.)	trace	0.0	0.0	0.0	0.0	0.0	0.0	0.0	0.0	0.0	0.0	0.0	trace
Days With ≥ 1.0" Snow Depth	0	0	0	0	0	0	0	0	0	0	0	0	0

Lakeland Linder Airport *Polk County*   Elevation: 209 ft.   Latitude: 28° 02' N   Longitude: 81° 57' W

	JAN	FEB	MAR	APR	MAY	JUN	JUL	AUG	SEP	OCT	NOV	DEC	YEAR
Mean Maximum Temp. (°F)	72.0	74.5	79.7	84.0	88.9	91.7	92.9	92.5	90.8	85.2	78.9	73.7	83.7
Mean Temp. (°F)	61.3	63.2	68.2	72.3	77.7	81.5	82.7	82.8	81.3	75.4	68.9	63.2	73.2
Mean Minimum Temp. (°F)	50.4	51.9	56.7	60.6	66.4	71.4	72.6	73.0	71.8	65.5	58.8	52.7	62.6
Extreme Maximum Temp. (°F)	87	90	92	95	103	105	100	100	98	96	93	87	105
Extreme Minimum Temp. (°F)	20	27	25	35	47	52	64	66	57	42	28	21	20
Days Maximum Temp. ≥ 90°F	0	0	1	4	14	22	26	26	20	5	0	0	118
Days Maximum Temp. ≤ 32°F	0	0	0	0	0	0	0	0	0	0	0	0	0
Days Minimum Temp. ≤ 32°F	1	1	0	0	0	0	0	0	0	0	0	1	3
Days Minimum Temp. ≤ 0°F	0	0	0	0	0	0	0	0	0	0	0	0	0
Heating Degree Days (base 65°F)	173	117	44	7	0	0	0	0	0	2	44	127	514
Cooling Degree Days (base 65°F)	62	86	154	237	419	523	578	579	508	351	184	81	3,762
Mean Precipitation (in.)	2.54	2.77	3.59	1.95	4.24	7.08	7.80	7.41	6.10	2.26	2.25	2.12	50.11
Days With ≥ 0.1" Precipitation	4	4	5	4	5	10	12	11	9	3	3	4	74
Days With ≥ 1.0" Precipitation	1	1	1	1	1	2	3	2	2	1	1	0	16
Mean Snowfall (in.)	trace	0.0	0.0	0.0	0.0	0.0	0.0	0.0	0.0	0.0	0.0	0.0	trace
Days With ≥ 1.0" Snow Depth	0	0	0	0	0	0	0	0	0	0	0	0	0

Lisbon *Lake County*   Elevation: 65 ft.   Latitude: 28° 52' N   Longitude: 81° 47' W

	JAN	FEB	MAR	APR	MAY	JUN	JUL	AUG	SEP	OCT	NOV	DEC	YEAR
Mean Maximum Temp. (°F)	68.7	71.2	76.6	81.3	86.5	89.8	91.3	91.1	89.0	83.0	76.2	70.2	81.3
Mean Temp. (°F)	57.7	60.0	65.1	69.7	75.7	80.2	81.9	81.7	79.9	73.2	65.6	59.6	70.9
Mean Minimum Temp. (°F)	46.7	48.6	53.5	58.3	64.9	70.5	72.3	72.3	70.7	63.4	55.0	49.0	60.4
Extreme Maximum Temp. (°F)	86	89	91	95	98	100	100	101	100	97	89	86	101
Extreme Minimum Temp. (°F)	16	24	25	39	46	53	62	61	52	39	24	18	16
Days Maximum Temp. ≥ 90°F	0	0	0	1	8	17	23	23	15	2	0	0	89
Days Maximum Temp. ≤ 32°F	0	0	0	0	0	0	0	0	0	0	0	0	0
Days Minimum Temp. ≤ 32°F	3	2	0	0	0	0	0	0	0	0	0	2	7
Days Minimum Temp. ≤ 0°F	0	0	0	0	0	0	0	0	0	0	0	0	0
Heating Degree Days (base 65°F)	254	175	89	22	1	0	0	0	0	8	79	202	830
Cooling Degree Days (base 65°F)	26	41	84	159	336	468	539	536	446	265	100	36	3,036
Mean Precipitation (in.)	3.41	3.03	4.16	2.83	4.18	6.12	5.51	6.25	5.61	2.63	2.51	2.64	48.88
Days With ≥ 0.1" Precipitation	5	4	5	4	6	9	10	11	8	5	4	5	76
Days With ≥ 1.0" Precipitation	1	1	2	1	1	2	1	2	2	1	1	1	16
Mean Snowfall (in.)	trace	trace	0.0	0.0	0.0	0.0	0.0	0.0	0.0	0.0	0.0	0.0	trace
Days With ≥ 1.0" Snow Depth	0	0	0	0	0	0	0	0	0	0	0	0	0

Live Oak *Suwannee County*   Elevation: 118 ft.   Latitude: 30° 14' N   Longitude: 82° 58' W

	JAN	FEB	MAR	APR	MAY	JUN	JUL	AUG	SEP	OCT	NOV	DEC	YEAR
Mean Maximum Temp. (°F)	67.1	70.5	76.7	82.2	88.3	91.9	93.1	92.4	89.9	83.1	75.8	69.0	81.7
Mean Temp. (°F)	54.7	57.4	63.2	68.5	75.2	80.2	82.2	81.7	79.0	70.8	63.2	56.6	69.4
Mean Minimum Temp. (°F)	42.1	44.1	49.7	54.7	62.0	68.5	71.1	70.9	68.0	58.5	50.5	44.2	57.0
Extreme Maximum Temp. (°F)	86	88	91	96	100	106	104	103	99	95	88	86	106
Extreme Minimum Temp. (°F)	6	16	19	31	40	47	60	60	46	29	15	13	6
Days Maximum Temp. ≥ 90°F	0	0	0	2	12	22	27	26	19	4	0	0	112
Days Maximum Temp. ≤ 32°F	0	0	0	0	0	0	0	0	0	0	0	0	0
Days Minimum Temp. ≤ 32°F	8	5	2	0	0	0	0	0	0	0	2	6	23
Days Minimum Temp. ≤ 0°F	0	0	0	0	0	0	0	0	0	0	0	0	0
Heating Degree Days (base 65°F)	335	237	123	39	2	0	0	0	0	25	131	281	1,173
Cooling Degree Days (base 65°F)	16	32	74	151	333	473	550	533	420	220	87	30	2,919
Mean Precipitation (in.)	5.00	3.98	5.42	3.47	3.33	6.08	6.54	6.63	4.33	3.32	2.43	3.09	53.62
Days With ≥ 0.1" Precipitation	7	5	6	4	5	9	9	9	6	3	4	5	72
Days With ≥ 1.0" Precipitation	2	1	2	1	1	2	2	2	1	1	1	1	17
Mean Snowfall (in.)	trace	trace	trace	0.0	0.0	0.0	0.0	0.0	0.0	0.0	0.0	0.1	0.1
Days With ≥ 1.0" Snow Depth	0	0	0	0	0	0	0	0	0	0	0	0	0

Mayo *Lafayette County*   Elevation: 62 ft.   Latitude: 30° 03' N   Longitude: 83° 10' W

	JAN	FEB	MAR	APR	MAY	JUN	JUL	AUG	SEP	OCT	NOV	DEC	YEAR
Mean Maximum Temp. (°F)	65.1	68.6	75.2	80.8	87.0	90.8	92.2	91.7	89.3	82.3	74.7	67.4	80.4
Mean Temp. (°F)	52.7	55.7	62.2	67.4	74.4	79.7	81.8	81.3	78.5	69.5	61.9	54.9	68.3
Mean Minimum Temp. (°F)	40.2	42.7	49.1	54.0	61.7	68.6	71.3	70.8	67.6	56.7	49.2	42.4	56.2
Extreme Maximum Temp. (°F)	86	86	91	96	98	104	103	103	99	96	90	86	104
Extreme Minimum Temp. (°F)	7	12	19	32	41	47	60	60	46	32	25	12	7
Days Maximum Temp. ≥ 90°F	0	0	0	2	10	20	25	24	18	3	0	0	102
Days Maximum Temp. ≤ 32°F	0	0	0	0	0	0	0	0	0	0	0	0	0
Days Minimum Temp. ≤ 32°F	9	6	1	0	0	0	0	0	0	0	2	7	25
Days Minimum Temp. ≤ 0°F	0	0	0	0	0	0	0	0	0	0	0	0	0
Heating Degree Days (base 65°F)	390	277	148	52	4	0	0	0	0	38	156	329	1,394
Cooling Degree Days (base 65°F)	12	23	63	128	307	456	535	520	405	195	74	26	2,744
Mean Precipitation (in.)	5.01	3.74	5.14	3.16	3.23	5.86	7.67	8.12	4.73	3.05	2.57	3.31	55.59
Days With ≥ 0.1" Precipitation	6	6	6	4	5	9	11	11	7	3	4	5	77
Days With ≥ 1.0" Precipitation	2	1	2	1	1	2	3	2	1	1	1	1	18
Mean Snowfall (in.)	trace	0.0	0.0	0.0	0.0	0.0	0.0	0.0	0.0	0.0	0.0	0.0	trace
Days With ≥ 1.0" Snow Depth	0	0	0	0	0	0	0	0	0	0	0	0	0

Melbourne Regional Airport *Brevard County*   Elevation: 32 ft.   Latitude: 28° 07' N   Longitude: 80° 39' W

	JAN	FEB	MAR	APR	MAY	JUN	JUL	AUG	SEP	OCT	NOV	DEC	YEAR
Mean Maximum Temp. (°F)	71.7	72.9	77.2	80.6	85.1	88.7	90.5	89.9	88.1	83.3	78.1	73.4	81.6
Mean Temp. (°F)	61.5	62.5	66.8	70.8	76.0	80.0	81.4	81.4	80.1	75.5	69.4	63.6	72.4
Mean Minimum Temp. (°F)	51.2	52.0	56.5	60.9	66.8	71.2	72.3	72.9	72.2	67.6	60.5	53.7	63.2
Extreme Maximum Temp. (°F)	88	88	93	97	97	101	102	101	98	93	91	89	102
Extreme Minimum Temp. (°F)	17	28	25	25	47	55	60	60	58	41	31	21	17
Days Maximum Temp. ≥ 90°F	0	0	1	2	5	12	19	17	9	2	0	0	67
Days Maximum Temp. ≤ 32°F	0	0	0	0	0	0	0	0	0	0	0	0	0
Days Minimum Temp. ≤ 32°F	1	1	0	0	0	0	0	0	0	0	0	1	3
Days Minimum Temp. ≤ 0°F	0	0	0	0	0	0	0	0	0	0	0	0	0
Heating Degree Days (base 65°F)	164	127	61	16	0	0	0	0	0	3	36	122	529
Cooling Degree Days (base 65°F)	56	70	115	187	346	464	521	520	461	347	178	83	3,348
Mean Precipitation (in.)	2.54	2.52	3.01	2.05	4.05	5.67	5.35	5.70	7.15	4.72	3.11	2.29	48.16
Days With ≥ 0.1" Precipitation	4	5	4	3	6	9	8	9	9	7	4	4	72
Days With ≥ 1.0" Precipitation	1	1	1	0	1	2	2	2	2	1	1	1	15
Mean Snowfall (in.)	0.0	0.0	0.0	0.0	0.0	0.0	0.0	0.0	0.0	0.0	0.0	0.0	0.0
Days With ≥ 1.0" Snow Depth	0	0	0	0	0	0	0	0	0	0	0	0	0

Miami Beach *Dade County*   Elevation: 3 ft.   Latitude: 25° 47' N   Longitude: 80° 08' W

	JAN	FEB	MAR	APR	MAY	JUN	JUL	AUG	SEP	OCT	NOV	DEC	YEAR
Mean Maximum Temp. (°F)	74.2	74.8	76.7	79.4	82.7	85.8	87.4	87.6	86.3	83.2	79.1	75.7	81.1
Mean Temp. (°F)	68.6	69.2	71.8	74.9	78.4	81.3	82.9	83.1	82.0	79.0	74.8	70.7	76.4
Mean Minimum Temp. (°F)	63.0	63.5	66.8	70.2	74.0	76.7	78.4	78.5	77.7	74.8	70.5	65.6	71.6
Extreme Maximum Temp. (°F)	84	88	92	94	95	97	98	98	96	95	89	85	98
Extreme Minimum Temp. (°F)	32	37	32	46	58	66	66	67	67	54	39	32	32
Days Maximum Temp. ≥ 90°F	0	0	0	0	1	3	5	5	2	1	0	0	17
Days Maximum Temp. ≤ 32°F	0	0	0	0	0	0	0	0	0	0	0	0	0
Days Minimum Temp. ≤ 32°F	0	0	0	0	0	0	0	0	0	0	0	0	0
Days Minimum Temp. ≤ 0°F	0	0	0	0	0	0	0	0	0	0	0	0	0
Heating Degree Days (base 65°F)	48	32	14	2	0	0	0	0	0	0	4	30	130
Cooling Degree Days (base 65°F)	169	173	226	303	425	503	574	579	524	452	316	218	4,462
Mean Precipitation (in.)	2.49	2.18	2.20	2.66	5.04	6.91	3.31	5.24	6.85	4.57	3.35	1.95	46.75
Days With ≥ 0.1" Precipitation	4	4	4	4	6	9	7	9	9	7	5	3	71
Days With ≥ 1.0" Precipitation	1	1	1	1	2	2	1	1	2	1	1	1	15
Mean Snowfall (in.)	0.0	0.0	0.0	0.0	0.0	0.0	0.0	0.0	0.0	0.0	0.0	0.0	0.0
Days With ≥ 1.0" Snow Depth	0	0	0	0	0	0	0	0	0	0	0	0	0

Milton Experiment Station *Santa Rosa County*   Elevation: 216 ft.   Latitude: 30° 47' N   Longitude: 87° 08' W

	JAN	FEB	MAR	APR	MAY	JUN	JUL	AUG	SEP	OCT	NOV	DEC	YEAR
Mean Maximum Temp. (°F)	61.0	64.9	71.6	78.2	85.0	90.1	91.5	91.4	88.3	80.4	71.1	63.9	78.1
Mean Temp. (°F)	50.1	53.3	60.1	66.1	73.5	79.4	81.4	81.0	77.4	67.8	59.2	52.8	66.8
Mean Minimum Temp. (°F)	39.1	41.6	48.6	54.0	61.9	68.7	71.2	70.6	66.5	55.1	47.2	41.7	55.5
Extreme Maximum Temp. (°F)	79	83	88	94	99	102	103	101	102	93	88	82	103
Extreme Minimum Temp. (°F)	3	12	20	30	39	50	61	57	45	31	19	8	3
Days Maximum Temp. ≥ 90°F	0	0	0	0	6	18	22	23	15	2	0	0	86
Days Maximum Temp. ≤ 32°F	0	0	0	0	0	0	0	0	0	0	0	0	0
Days Minimum Temp. ≤ 32°F	10	6	2	0	0	0	0	0	0	0	3	8	29
Days Minimum Temp. ≤ 0°F	0	0	0	0	0	0	0	0	0	0	0	0	0
Heating Degree Days (base 65°F)	465	335	186	65	4	0	0	0	2	56	208	389	1,710
Cooling Degree Days (base 65°F)	5	12	38	98	274	441	519	510	374	149	40	15	2,475
Mean Precipitation (in.)	6.40	5.14	7.37	4.31	5.08	7.39	8.12	6.70	6.08	4.02	5.22	4.37	70.20
Days With ≥ 0.1" Precipitation	8	6	7	5	6	8	11	10	7	4	6	6	84
Days With ≥ 1.0" Precipitation	2	2	2	1	1	2	2	2	2	1	2	1	20
Mean Snowfall (in.)	0.1	0.1	trace	0.0	0.0	0.0	0.0	0.0	0.0	0.0	0.0	0.0	0.2
Days With ≥ 1.0" Snow Depth	0	0	0	0	0	0	0	0	0	0	0	0	0

Monticello 3 W *Jefferson County*   Elevation: 144 ft.   Latitude: 30° 32' N   Longitude: 83° 55' W

	JAN	FEB	MAR	APR	MAY	JUN	JUL	AUG	SEP	OCT	NOV	DEC	YEAR
Mean Maximum Temp. (°F)	61.7	65.9	72.3	78.2	84.5	89.3	90.6	89.9	87.2	79.7	71.8	64.8	78.0
Mean Temp. (°F)	49.8	53.2	59.9	65.3	72.3	78.2	80.2	79.7	76.4	66.8	59.0	52.4	66.1
Mean Minimum Temp. (°F)	37.8	40.5	47.4	52.4	60.1	67.1	69.9	69.4	65.6	53.9	46.1	39.9	54.2
Extreme Maximum Temp. (°F)	83	85	90	93	96	103	102	100	97	93	87	84	103
Extreme Minimum Temp. (°F)	4	14	18	31	38	44	58	58	43	31	13	11	4
Days Maximum Temp. ≥ 90°F	0	0	0	0	4	15	20	18	10	1	0	0	68
Days Maximum Temp. ≤ 32°F	0	0	0	0	0	0	0	0	0	0	0	0	0
Days Minimum Temp. ≤ 32°F	12	7	2	0	0	0	0	0	0	0	4	10	35
Days Minimum Temp. ≤ 0°F	0	0	0	0	0	0	0	0	0	0	0	0	0
Heating Degree Days (base 65°F)	471	338	193	77	8	0	0	0	2	64	216	398	1,767
Cooling Degree Days (base 65°F)	4	13	39	90	249	414	492	472	344	137	46	14	2,314
Mean Precipitation (in.)	5.63	4.62	6.02	3.63	4.06	5.71	6.65	6.75	4.47	3.41	3.57	3.89	58.41
Days With ≥ 0.1" Precipitation	7	5	6	4	6	8	10	10	6	4	4	5	75
Days With ≥ 1.0" Precipitation	2	1	2	1	1	2	2	2	1	1	1	1	17
Mean Snowfall (in.)	trace	trace	trace	0.0	0.0	0.0	0.0	0.0	0.0	0.0	0.0	trace	trace
Days With ≥ 1.0" Snow Depth	0	0	0	0	0	0	0	0	0	0	0	0	0

Moore Haven Lock 1 *Glades County* Elevation: 32 ft. Latitude: 26° 50' N Longitude: 81° 05' W

	JAN	FEB	MAR	APR	MAY	JUN	JUL	AUG	SEP	OCT	NOV	DEC	YEAR
Mean Maximum Temp. (°F)	74.0	75.6	79.5	83.4	87.7	90.4	91.7	91.3	89.5	85.2	79.9	75.4	83.6
Mean Temp. (°F)	62.8	63.9	68.1	72.0	76.8	80.6	81.9	82.0	80.9	76.2	70.2	64.8	73.4
Mean Minimum Temp. (°F)	51.6	52.3	56.5	60.6	65.8	70.7	72.1	72.6	72.3	67.2	60.5	54.2	63.0
Extreme Maximum Temp. (°F)	88	90	93	97	98	101	100	98	99	95	91	89	101
Extreme Minimum Temp. (°F)	23	29	26	39	44	57	62	63	62	45	32	23	23
Days Maximum Temp. ≥ 90°F	0	0	1	4	11	18	25	24	17	5	0	0	105
Days Maximum Temp. ≤ 32°F	0	0	0	0	0	0	0	0	0	0	0	0	0
Days Minimum Temp. ≤ 32°F	1	0	0	0	0	0	0	0	0	0	0	1	2
Days Minimum Temp. ≤ 0°F	0	0	0	0	0	0	0	0	0	0	0	0	0
Heating Degree Days (base 65°F)	138	104	46	9	0	0	0	0	0	1	27	99	424
Cooling Degree Days (base 65°F)	76	90	149	223	378	483	540	544	487	364	194	101	3,629
Mean Precipitation (in.)	2.13	2.12	3.29	2.21	3.78	7.15	6.71	6.94	6.13	3.06	1.90	1.63	47.05
Days With ≥ 0.1" Precipitation	4	3	4	4	6	11	10	11	8	5	3	3	72
Days With ≥ 1.0" Precipitation	1	1	1	1	1	2	2	2	2	1	0	0	14
Mean Snowfall (in.)	0.0	0.0	0.0	0.0	0.0	0.0	0.0	0.0	0.0	0.0	0.0	0.0	0.0
Days With ≥ 1.0" Snow Depth	0	0	0	0	0	0	0	0	0	0	0	0	0

Mountain Lake *Polk County* Elevation: 124 ft. Latitude: 27° 56' N Longitude: 81° 36' W

	JAN	FEB	MAR	APR	MAY	JUN	JUL	AUG	SEP	OCT	NOV	DEC	YEAR
Mean Maximum Temp. (°F)	73.8	76.0	80.6	84.9	89.5	92.0	92.8	92.5	90.5	85.7	79.7	75.1	84.4
Mean Temp. (°F)	61.4	63.1	67.7	71.8	76.9	80.8	81.8	82.0	80.5	74.8	68.3	63.1	72.7
Mean Minimum Temp. (°F)	49.0	50.1	54.7	58.6	64.2	69.6	70.8	71.5	70.4	63.9	56.9	51.2	60.9
Extreme Maximum Temp. (°F)	89	91	95	96	99	101	105	100	98	96	91	89	105
Extreme Minimum Temp. (°F)	16	24	25	34	44	50	53	62	57	40	24	19	16
Days Maximum Temp. ≥ 90°F	0	0	3	7	16	22	27	27	20	6	0	0	128
Days Maximum Temp. ≤ 32°F	0	0	0	0	0	0	0	0	0	0	0	0	0
Days Minimum Temp. ≤ 32°F	3	1	0	0	0	0	0	0	0	0	0	2	6
Days Minimum Temp. ≤ 0°F	0	0	0	0	0	0	0	0	0	0	0	0	0
Heating Degree Days (base 65°F)	169	120	53	10	0	0	0	0	0	3	44	127	526
Cooling Degree Days (base 65°F)	57	74	128	212	371	481	526	535	464	314	149	71	3,382
Mean Precipitation (in.)	2.44	2.49	3.27	2.02	4.02	7.47	7.52	6.61	5.81	2.51	2.22	2.14	48.52
Days With ≥ 0.1" Precipitation	4	4	5	3	6	10	12	10	8	5	4	4	75
Days With ≥ 1.0" Precipitation	1	1	1	1	1	2	2	2	2	1	1	1	16
Mean Snowfall (in.)	trace	0.0	0.0	0.0	0.0	0.0	0.0	0.0	0.0	0.0	0.0	0.0	trace
Days With ≥ 1.0" Snow Depth	0	0	0	0	0	0	0	0	0	0	0	0	0

Myakka River State Park *Sarasota County* Elevation: 19 ft. Latitude: 27° 14' N Longitude: 82° 19' W

	JAN	FEB	MAR	APR	MAY	JUN	JUL	AUG	SEP	OCT	NOV	DEC	YEAR
Mean Maximum Temp. (°F)	74.7	76.8	81.4	85.7	90.9	92.4	93.0	92.9	91.4	87.1	81.3	76.3	85.3
Mean Temp. (°F)	62.1	63.7	68.2	71.9	77.1	80.8	82.0	82.6	81.4	76.0	69.5	64.2	73.3
Mean Minimum Temp. (°F)	49.4	50.6	54.9	58.0	63.2	69.1	71.0	72.2	71.3	64.8	57.6	52.0	61.2
Extreme Maximum Temp. (°F)	89	91	93	98	104	105	101	104	103	97	95	90	105
Extreme Minimum Temp. (°F)	18	22	28	34	43	50	63	63	58	42	24	22	18
Days Maximum Temp. ≥ 90°F	0	0	2	8	21	25	28	28	23	11	1	0	147
Days Maximum Temp. ≤ 32°F	0	0	0	0	0	0	0	0	0	0	0	0	0
Days Minimum Temp. ≤ 32°F	2	1	0	0	0	0	0	0	0	0	0	1	4
Days Minimum Temp. ≤ 0°F	0	0	0	0	0	0	0	0	0	0	0	0	0
Heating Degree Days (base 65°F)	148	107	43	9	0	0	0	0	0	2	33	108	450
Cooling Degree Days (base 65°F)	66	90	148	223	388	493	542	562	501	360	183	96	3,652
Mean Precipitation (in.)	3.16	2.91	3.61	2.11	3.37	8.92	9.63	9.61	8.05	3.21	2.23	2.30	59.11
Days With ≥ 0.1" Precipitation	4	4	4	3	5	10	13	13	10	5	4	3	78
Days With ≥ 1.0" Precipitation	1	1	1	1	1	3	3	3	3	1	1	1	20
Mean Snowfall (in.)	0.0	0.0	0.0	0.0	0.0	0.0	0.0	0.0	0.0	0.0	0.0	trace	trace
Days With ≥ 1.0" Snow Depth	0	0	0	0	0	0	0	0	0	0	0	0	0

Naples *Collier County* Elevation: 3 ft. Latitude: 26° 10' N Longitude: 81° 47' W

	JAN	FEB	MAR	APR	MAY	JUN	JUL	AUG	SEP	OCT	NOV	DEC	YEAR
Mean Maximum Temp. (°F)	76.6	77.6	80.9	84.4	88.0	90.4	91.7	91.9	90.9	87.6	82.9	78.3	85.1
Mean Temp. (°F)	65.3	66.2	69.7	73.2	77.5	81.1	82.1	82.5	81.8	77.9	72.4	67.3	74.8
Mean Minimum Temp. (°F)	54.0	54.7	58.4	62.0	67.0	71.7	72.5	73.1	72.7	68.0	61.8	56.2	64.4
Extreme Maximum Temp. (°F)	88	89	91	93	95	98	98	97	99	95	91	89	99
Extreme Minimum Temp. (°F)	26	28	33	39	52	59	62	63	59	48	31	27	26
Days Maximum Temp. ≥ 90°F	0	0	0	2	9	20	27	28	24	9	1	0	120
Days Maximum Temp. ≤ 32°F	0	0	0	0	0	0	0	0	0	0	0	0	0
Days Minimum Temp. ≤ 32°F	1	0	0	0	0	0	0	0	0	0	0	0	1
Days Minimum Temp. ≤ 0°F	0	0	0	0	0	0	0	0	0	0	0	0	0
Heating Degree Days (base 65°F)	88	64	24	4	0	0	0	0	0	0	11	58	249
Cooling Degree Days (base 65°F)	100	114	175	257	399	497	546	557	512	416	243	137	3,953
Mean Precipitation (in.)	2.06	2.21	2.49	1.95	4.33	8.20	7.98	7.68	8.22	3.69	2.00	1.52	52.33
Days With ≥ 0.1" Precipitation	3	4	3	3	5	10	12	12	11	5	3	3	74
Days With ≥ 1.0" Precipitation	1	1	1	0	2	3	3	2	2	1	1	0	17
Mean Snowfall (in.)	0.0	0.0	0.0	0.0	0.0	0.0	0.0	0.0	0.0	0.0	0.0	0.0	0.0
Days With ≥ 1.0" Snow Depth	0	0	0	0	0	0	0	0	0	0	0	0	0

Ocala *Marion County*   Elevation: 72 ft.   Latitude: 29° 12' N   Longitude: 82° 05' W

	JAN	FEB	MAR	APR	MAY	JUN	JUL	AUG	SEP	OCT	NOV	DEC	YEAR
Mean Maximum Temp. (°F)	70.3	72.8	78.3	83.0	88.3	91.1	92.3	91.7	89.9	84.2	77.5	72.0	82.6
Mean Temp. (°F)	57.9	59.9	65.3	69.6	75.7	80.2	81.7	81.3	79.4	72.8	65.7	59.7	70.8
Mean Minimum Temp. (°F)	45.6	46.9	52.3	56.2	63.0	69.2	71.1	70.8	68.7	61.3	53.6	47.4	58.8
Extreme Maximum Temp. (°F)	86	89	91	97	101	105	100	100	97	95	89	88	105
Extreme Minimum Temp. (°F)	11	20	23	33	45	48	58	60	45	32	23	15	11
Days Maximum Temp. ≥ 90°F	0	0	0	3	12	21	26	24	19	4	0	0	109
Days Maximum Temp. ≤ 32°F	0	0	0	0	0	0	0	0	0	0	0	0	0
Days Minimum Temp. ≤ 32°F	5	3	1	0	0	0	0	0	0	0	1	3	13
Days Minimum Temp. ≤ 0°F	0	0	0	0	0	0	0	0	0	0	0	0	0
Heating Degree Days (base 65°F)	250	181	90	25	1	0	0	0	0	11	81	202	841
Cooling Degree Days (base 65°F)	32	47	98	168	339	465	531	518	430	258	111	44	3,041
Mean Precipitation (in.)	3.64	3.28	4.18	2.87	3.81	7.11	6.39	6.05	5.46	2.77	2.43	2.69	50.68
Days With ≥ 0.1" Precipitation	6	5	6	4	5	9	11	12	8	4	4	4	78
Days With ≥ 1.0" Precipitation	1	1	1	1	1	2	2	1	2	1	1	1	15
Mean Snowfall (in.)	trace	trace	0.0	0.0	0.0	0.0	0.0	0.0	0.0	0.0	0.0	0.0	trace
Days With ≥ 1.0" Snow Depth	0	0	0	0	0	0	0	0	0	0	0	0	0

Panama City 5 NE *Bay County*   Elevation: 29 ft.   Latitude: 30° 13' N   Longitude: 85° 36' W

	JAN	FEB	MAR	APR	MAY	JUN	JUL	AUG	SEP	OCT	NOV	DEC	YEAR
Mean Maximum Temp. (°F)	62.7	65.4	71.1	77.2	83.6	88.5	89.9	90.0	87.8	80.4	72.5	64.9	77.8
Mean Temp. (°F)	51.2	53.7	59.8	65.5	72.7	78.7	80.9	80.7	77.8	68.3	60.5	53.2	66.9
Mean Minimum Temp. (°F)	39.7	42.1	48.3	53.9	61.7	68.9	71.8	71.4	67.8	56.3	48.4	41.4	56.0
Extreme Maximum Temp. (°F)	80	82	87	93	100	100	101	100	98	93	91	82	101
Extreme Minimum Temp. (°F)	6	15	23	34	40	46	60	59	45	33	26	11	6
Days Maximum Temp. ≥ 90°F	0	0	0	0	3	13	18	19	12	1	0	0	66
Days Maximum Temp. ≤ 32°F	0	0	0	0	0	0	0	0	0	0	0	0	0
Days Minimum Temp. ≤ 32°F	10	6	2	0	0	0	0	0	0	0	2	8	28
Days Minimum Temp. ≤ 0°F	0	0	0	0	0	0	0	0	0	0	0	0	0
Heating Degree Days (base 65°F)	428	322	190	65	5	0	0	0	1	43	179	375	1,608
Cooling Degree Days (base 65°F)	5	12	32	82	249	416	498	497	384	162	47	15	2,399
Mean Precipitation (in.)	5.95	4.90	6.23	3.93	4.03	6.12	8.86	7.52	6.19	3.67	4.57	4.10	66.07
Days With ≥ 0.1" Precipitation	7	6	7	4	5	8	11	11	7	4	5	6	81
Days With ≥ 1.0" Precipitation	2	2	2	1	1	2	3	2	2	1	1	1	20
Mean Snowfall (in.)	trace	trace	0.0	0.0	0.0	0.0	0.0	0.0	0.0	0.0	0.0	0.0	trace
Days With ≥ 1.0" Snow Depth	0	0	0	0	0	0	0	0	0	0	0	0	0

Parrish *Manatee County*   Elevation: 59 ft.   Latitude: 27° 37' N   Longitude: 82° 21' W

	JAN	FEB	MAR	APR	MAY	JUN	JUL	AUG	SEP	OCT	NOV	DEC	YEAR
Mean Maximum Temp. (°F)	72.9	74.4	78.4	82.7	87.6	90.2	91.2	91.1	89.9	85.4	79.6	74.5	83.2
Mean Temp. (°F)	61.5	62.6	66.8	70.7	75.9	80.2	81.6	81.8	80.6	75.1	68.8	63.3	72.4
Mean Minimum Temp. (°F)	50.0	50.8	55.1	58.7	64.2	70.2	72.0	72.4	71.3	64.8	57.9	52.0	61.6
Extreme Maximum Temp. (°F)	86	88	91	93	97	101	98	101	99	93	91	87	101
Extreme Minimum Temp. (°F)	18	24	29	36	41	51	62	64	57	44	25	23	18
Days Maximum Temp. ≥ 90°F	0	0	0	1	9	20	25	24	20	5	0	0	104
Days Maximum Temp. ≤ 32°F	0	0	0	0	0	0	0	0	0	0	0	0	0
Days Minimum Temp. ≤ 32°F	2	1	0	0	0	0	0	0	0	0	0	1	4
Days Minimum Temp. ≤ 0°F	0	0	0	0	0	0	0	0	0	0	0	0	0
Heating Degree Days (base 65°F)	167	125	61	16	1	0	0	0	0	4	40	129	543
Cooling Degree Days (base 65°F)	55	67	111	182	336	466	522	526	470	326	158	79	3,298
Mean Precipitation (in.)	2.85	3.19	3.23	2.03	3.18	7.15	7.45	8.68	7.39	2.86	2.31	2.26	52.58
Days With ≥ 0.1" Precipitation	4	4	4	3	4	9	11	12	9	4	3	3	70
Days With ≥ 1.0" Precipitation	1	1	1	1	1	3	2	3	2	1	1	1	18
Mean Snowfall (in.)	trace	0.0	0.0	0.0	0.0	0.0	0.0	0.0	0.0	0.0	0.0	0.0	trace
Days With ≥ 1.0" Snow Depth	0	0	0	0	0	0	0	0	0	0	0	0	0

Perry *Taylor County*   Elevation: 42 ft.   Latitude: 30° 06' N   Longitude: 83° 34' W

	JAN	FEB	MAR	APR	MAY	JUN	JUL	AUG	SEP	OCT	NOV	DEC	YEAR
Mean Maximum Temp. (°F)	67.0	70.3	76.2	81.8	87.8	91.4	92.7	92.2	90.3	83.6	76.4	69.7	81.6
Mean Temp. (°F)	54.2	56.9	62.5	67.7	74.7	79.7	81.7	81.4	78.9	70.5	62.8	56.5	69.0
Mean Minimum Temp. (°F)	41.4	43.4	48.8	53.6	61.5	67.9	70.7	70.4	67.5	57.2	49.1	43.2	56.2
Extreme Maximum Temp. (°F)	85	87	90	94	99	103	104	102	99	94	90	86	104
Extreme Minimum Temp. (°F)	7	14	19	29	40	46	59	59	45	28	14	12	7
Days Maximum Temp. ≥ 90°F	0	0	0	2	11	22	26	25	20	4	0	0	110
Days Maximum Temp. ≤ 32°F	0	0	0	0	0	0	0	0	0	0	0	0	0
Days Minimum Temp. ≤ 32°F	8	5	2	0	0	0	0	0	0	0	3	7	25
Days Minimum Temp. ≤ 0°F	0	0	0	0	0	0	0	0	0	0	0	0	0
Heating Degree Days (base 65°F)	343	244	132	45	2	0	0	0	0	26	136	282	1,210
Cooling Degree Days (base 65°F)	12	25	60	126	309	446	526	518	414	208	80	27	2,751
Mean Precipitation (in.)	4.91	4.00	5.59	3.35	3.52	6.02	8.48	8.86	5.01	3.15	2.70	3.38	58.97
Days With ≥ 0.1" Precipitation	7	6	6	4	6	8	12	11	7	4	4	6	81
Days With ≥ 1.0" Precipitation	2	1	2	1	1	2	2	3	2	1	1	1	19
Mean Snowfall (in.)	trace	0.0	0.0	0.0	0.0	0.0	0.0	0.0	0.0	0.0	0.0	0.0	trace
Days With ≥ 1.0" Snow Depth	0	0	0	0	0	0	0	0	0	0	0	0	0

Plant City *Hillsborough County*   Elevation: 118 ft.   Latitude: 28° 01' N   Longitude: 82° 08' W

	JAN	FEB	MAR	APR	MAY	JUN	JUL	AUG	SEP	OCT	NOV	DEC	YEAR
Mean Maximum Temp. (°F)	73.0	74.7	79.4	83.6	88.5	90.8	91.8	91.4	90.2	85.5	79.5	74.6	83.6
Mean Temp. (°F)	61.2	62.6	67.2	71.2	76.6	80.6	81.8	81.9	80.5	75.0	68.3	63.0	72.5
Mean Minimum Temp. (°F)	49.3	50.5	54.9	58.9	64.6	70.4	71.8	72.2	70.8	64.6	57.1	51.3	61.4
Extreme Maximum Temp. (°F)	87	89	91	96	99	102	102	99	98	94	92	89	102
Extreme Minimum Temp. (°F)	17	25	24	35	43	49	62	63	55	39	21	20	17
Days Maximum Temp. ≥ 90°F	0	0	1	3	12	21	26	25	20	5	0	0	113
Days Maximum Temp. ≤ 32°F	0	0	0	0	0	0	0	0	0	0	0	0	0
Days Minimum Temp. ≤ 32°F	2	1	0	0	0	0	0	0	0	0	0	1	4
Days Minimum Temp. ≤ 0°F	0	0	0	0	0	0	0	0	0	0	0	0	0
Heating Degree Days (base 65°F)	176	127	60	15	0	0	0	0	0	4	47	133	562
Cooling Degree Days (base 65°F)	56	76	126	203	370	483	535	536	468	321	155	75	3,404
Mean Precipitation (in.)	2.74	3.17	3.56	2.13	3.81	7.01	7.35	7.83	6.56	2.41	2.11	2.55	51.23
Days With ≥ 0.1" Precipitation	4	4	5	4	5	9	11	12	9	4	3	4	74
Days With ≥ 1.0" Precipitation	1	1	1	1	1	2	2	2	2	1	1	1	16
Mean Snowfall (in.)	0.0	0.0	0.0	0.0	0.0	0.0	0.0	0.0	0.0	0.0	0.0	0.0	0.0
Days With ≥ 1.0" Snow Depth	0	0	0	0	0	0	0	0	0	0	0	0	0

Punta Gorda 4 ESE *Charlotte County*   Elevation: 19 ft.   Latitude: 26° 55' N   Longitude: 82° 00' W

	JAN	FEB	MAR	APR	MAY	JUN	JUL	AUG	SEP	OCT	NOV	DEC	YEAR
Mean Maximum Temp. (°F)	74.3	75.9	80.2	84.4	89.1	91.5	92.2	92.2	90.7	86.3	80.8	76.2	84.5
Mean Temp. (°F)	63.0	64.4	68.6	72.4	77.5	81.4	82.6	82.8	81.6	76.4	70.2	65.1	73.8
Mean Minimum Temp. (°F)	51.7	52.9	56.9	60.4	65.9	71.2	72.9	73.3	72.4	66.4	59.5	54.0	63.1
Extreme Maximum Temp. (°F)	89	92	91	94	98	101	99	97	95	94	93	89	101
Extreme Minimum Temp. (°F)	23	27	29	38	49	57	63	65	61	46	28	25	23
Days Maximum Temp. ≥ 90°F	0	0	1	3	14	23	27	27	22	6	0	0	123
Days Maximum Temp. ≤ 32°F	0	0	0	0	0	0	0	0	0	0	0	0	0
Days Minimum Temp. ≤ 32°F	1	0	0	0	0	0	0	0	0	0	0	1	2
Days Minimum Temp. ≤ 0°F	0	0	0	0	0	0	0	0	0	0	0	0	0
Heating Degree Days (base 65°F)	130	91	35	4	0	0	0	0	0	1	25	88	374
Cooling Degree Days (base 65°F)	79	94	154	241	401	512	566	571	510	375	197	105	3,805
Mean Precipitation (in.)	2.33	2.35	3.01	1.69	3.35	8.46	7.72	7.76	6.58	3.12	1.86	1.78	50.01
Days With ≥ 0.1" Precipitation	4	4	4	3	5	10	13	11	10	5	3	3	75
Days With ≥ 1.0" Precipitation	1	1	1	0	1	3	2	2	2	1	0	1	15
Mean Snowfall (in.)	0.0	0.0	0.0	0.0	0.0	0.0	0.0	0.0	0.0	0.0	0.0	0.0	0.0
Days With ≥ 1.0" Snow Depth	0	0	0	0	0	0	0	0	0	0	0	0	0

Quincy 3 SSW *Gadsden County*   Elevation: 242 ft.   Latitude: 30° 36' N   Longitude: 84° 33' W

	JAN	FEB	MAR	APR	MAY	JUN	JUL	AUG	SEP	OCT	NOV	DEC	YEAR
Mean Maximum Temp. (°F)	61.7	65.7	72.1	78.4	84.9	89.4	90.7	90.0	87.4	79.8	71.7	65.0	78.1
Mean Temp. (°F)	50.8	53.9	60.3	66.1	73.3	79.1	80.8	80.4	77.3	68.3	60.3	53.9	67.0
Mean Minimum Temp. (°F)	39.8	42.0	48.6	53.7	61.6	68.5	70.9	70.7	67.1	56.7	48.8	42.7	55.9
Extreme Maximum Temp. (°F)	83	85	90	92	99	102	102	101	98	93	86	84	102
Extreme Minimum Temp. (°F)	4	0	19	33	36	49	62	59	48	33	20	12	0
Days Maximum Temp. ≥ 90°F	0	0	0	0	5	15	21	18	11	1	0	0	71
Days Maximum Temp. ≤ 32°F	0	0	0	0	0	0	0	0	0	0	0	0	0
Days Minimum Temp. ≤ 32°F	9	6	1	0	0	0	0	0	0	0	2	6	24
Days Minimum Temp. ≤ 0°F	0	0	0	0	0	0	0	0	0	0	0	0	0
Heating Degree Days (base 65°F)	442	320	183	67	6	0	0	0	1	44	183	356	1,602
Cooling Degree Days (base 65°F)	6	14	41	101	272	440	510	496	370	159	49	16	2,474
Mean Precipitation (in.)	5.68	4.49	6.21	3.64	4.81	5.59	6.85	5.64	3.74	3.43	3.53	3.59	57.20
Days With ≥ 0.1" Precipitation	7	6	7	4	6	8	10	9	6	4	4	6	77
Days With ≥ 1.0" Precipitation	2	1	2	1	2	2	2	1	1	1	1	1	17
Mean Snowfall (in.)	trace	trace	trace	0.0	0.0	0.0	0.0	0.0	0.0	0.0	0.0	0.0	trace
Days With ≥ 1.0" Snow Depth	0	0	0	0	0	0	0	0	0	0	0	0	0

Saint Augustine *St. Johns County*   Elevation: 6 ft.   Latitude: 29° 54' N   Longitude: 81° 19' W

	JAN	FEB	MAR	APR	MAY	JUN	JUL	AUG	SEP	OCT	NOV	DEC	YEAR
Mean Maximum Temp. (°F)	*66.8*	69.2	73.6	78.7	83.9	88.1	90.6	89.2	86.5	80.7	74.6	68.3	*79.2*
Mean Temp. (°F)	*56.4*	58.5	63.3	68.4	74.4	79.4	81.5	80.8	78.9	72.4	65.4	58.6	*60.4*
Mean Minimum Temp. (°F)	*46.0*	47.8	52.9	58.0	64.9	70.5	72.4	72.4	71.2	64.0	56.1	48.8	*60.4*
Extreme Maximum Temp. (°F)	*86*	87	93	95	97	101	103	101	98	94	88	86	*103*
Extreme Minimum Temp. (°F)	*10*	21	23	34	45	52	59	61	51	36	31	16	*10*
Days Maximum Temp. ≥ 90°F	*0*	0	0	1	4	11	18	13	6	1	0	0	*54*
Days Maximum Temp. ≤ 32°F	*0*	0	0	0	0	0	0	0	0	0	0	0	*0*
Days Minimum Temp. ≤ 32°F	*3*	2	0	0	0	0	0	0	0	0	0	2	*7*
Days Minimum Temp. ≤ 0°F	*0*	0	0	0	0	0	0	0	0	0	0	0	*0*
Heating Degree Days (base 65°F)	*278*	202	109	29	1	0	0	0	0	9	81	224	*933*
Cooling Degree Days (base 65°F)	16	25	55	134	296	439	521	501	413	251	98	32	*2,781*
Mean Precipitation (in.)	3.21	2.96	*3.73*	2.69	3.17	5.24	4.57	5.92	6.57	4.58	2.27	2.90	*47.81*
Days With ≥ 0.1" Precipitation	*5*	5	*5*	4	5	8	7	9	9	6	4	5	*72*
Days With ≥ 1.0" Precipitation	*1*	1	*1*	1	1	1	1	2	2	1	0	1	*13*
Mean Snowfall (in.)	trace	0.0	trace	0.0	0.0	0.0	0.0	0.0	0.0	0.0	0.0	0.0	trace
Days With ≥ 1.0" Snow Depth	0	0	0	0	0	0	0	0	0	0	0	0	0

Saint Leo *Pasco County*   Elevation: 187 ft.   Latitude: 28° 20' N   Longitude: 82° 16' W

	JAN	FEB	MAR	APR	MAY	JUN	JUL	AUG	SEP	OCT	NOV	DEC	YEAR
Mean Maximum Temp. (°F)	71.7	74.3	79.2	83.8	89.1	91.5	92.4	92.1	90.7	85.4	79.2	74.0	83.6
Mean Temp. (°F)	60.2	62.5	67.2	71.6	77.1	81.0	82.2	82.1	80.6	74.7	68.1	62.7	72.5
Mean Minimum Temp. (°F)	48.7	50.6	55.2	59.4	65.1	70.5	71.9	72.0	70.5	63.9	57.1	51.4	61.4
Extreme Maximum Temp. (°F)	87	90	92	95	99	103	100	99	98	96	92	88	103
Extreme Minimum Temp. (°F)	18	22	24	38	46	54	64	63	53	39	27	20	18
Days Maximum Temp. ≥ 90°F	0	0	1	4	16	22	27	26	21	6	0	0	123
Days Maximum Temp. ≤ 32°F	0	0	0	0	0	0	0	0	0	0	0	0	0
Days Minimum Temp. ≤ 32°F	2	1	0	0	0	0	0	0	0	0	0	1	4
Days Minimum Temp. ≤ 0°F	0	0	0	0	0	0	0	0	0	0	0	0	0
Heating Degree Days (base 65°F)	193	130	58	10	0	0	0	0	0	3	48	138	580
Cooling Degree Days (base 65°F)	53	75	130	215	395	497	551	547	476	316	157	75	3,487
Mean Precipitation (in.)	3.48	3.55	4.25	2.37	4.10	6.94	7.66	7.40	6.52	2.86	2.49	2.67	54.29
Days With ≥ 0.1" Precipitation	5	5	5	3	5	9	12	12	9	4	4	4	77
Days With ≥ 1.0" Precipitation	1	1	2	1	1	2	3	2	1	1	1	1	18
Mean Snowfall (in.)	trace	0.0	0.0	0.0	0.0	0.0	0.0	0.0	0.0	0.0	0.0	0.0	trace
Days With ≥ 1.0" Snow Depth	0	0	0	0	0	0	0	0	0	0	0	0	0

Saint Petersburg *Pinellas County*   Elevation: 6 ft.   Latitude: 27° 46' N   Longitude: 82° 38' W

	JAN	FEB	MAR	APR	MAY	JUN	JUL	AUG	SEP	OCT	NOV	DEC	YEAR
Mean Maximum Temp. (°F)	70.0	71.6	76.0	80.8	86.2	89.5	90.6	90.2	88.7	83.7	77.3	72.0	81.4
Mean Temp. (°F)	62.2	63.6	68.2	73.0	78.6	82.4	83.7	83.4	82.1	76.9	70.1	64.4	74.1
Mean Minimum Temp. (°F)	54.3	55.6	60.3	65.2	71.0	75.4	76.7	76.6	75.6	70.1	62.9	56.8	66.7
Extreme Maximum Temp. (°F)	88	90	88	93	96	99	100	99	97	92	89	88	100
Extreme Minimum Temp. (°F)	27	28	34	46	55	61	69	67	61	51	35	24	24
Days Maximum Temp. ≥ 90°F	0	0	0	0	5	16	22	21	13	2	0	0	79
Days Maximum Temp. ≤ 32°F	0	0	0	0	0	0	0	0	0	0	0	0	0
Days Minimum Temp. ≤ 32°F	0	0	0	0	0	0	0	0	0	0	0	0	0
Days Minimum Temp. ≤ 0°F	0	0	0	0	0	0	0	0	0	0	0	0	0
Heating Degree Days (base 65°F)	140	97	38	4	0	0	0	0	0	1	26	97	403
Cooling Degree Days (base 65°F)	50	68	133	237	428	529	586	582	515	375	184	83	3,770
Mean Precipitation (in.)	2.78	2.99	3.52	1.92	2.90	5.99	6.25	8.09	7.51	2.69	2.03	2.62	49.29
Days With ≥ 0.1" Precipitation	5	4	5	3	4	7	10	11	9	4	3	4	69
Days With ≥ 1.0" Precipitation	1	1	1	0	1	2	2	3	2	1	1	1	16
Mean Snowfall (in.)	trace	0.0	0.0	0.0	0.0	0.0	0.0	0.0	0.0	0.0	0.0	0.0	trace
Days With ≥ 1.0" Snow Depth	0	0	0	0	0	0	0	0	0	0	0	0	0

Sanford Experiment Station *Seminole County*   Elevation: 13 ft.   Latitude: 28° 48' N   Longitude: 81° 14' W

	JAN	FEB	MAR	APR	MAY	JUN	JUL	AUG	SEP	OCT	NOV	DEC	YEAR
Mean Maximum Temp. (°F)	70.4	72.2	77.1	81.6	87.0	90.5	92.0	91.6	89.2	83.6	77.6	72.0	82.1
Mean Temp. (°F)	59.1	60.7	65.6	69.7	75.3	80.1	81.8	81.8	80.0	74.0	67.4	61.5	71.4
Mean Minimum Temp. (°F)	47.7	49.1	54.0	57.8	63.6	69.6	71.6	72.0	70.7	64.3	57.2	50.8	60.7
Extreme Maximum Temp. (°F)	89	89	92	96	100	102	103	100	98	95	92	87	103
Extreme Minimum Temp. (°F)	19	26	27	36	45	52	60	65	52	39	30	19	19
Days Maximum Temp. ≥ 90°F	0	0	0	2	10	18	25	24	16	3	0	0	98
Days Maximum Temp. ≤ 32°F	0	0	0	0	0	0	0	0	0	0	0	0	0
Days Minimum Temp. ≤ 32°F	2	1	0	0	0	0	0	0	0	0	0	1	4
Days Minimum Temp. ≤ 0°F	0	0	0	0	0	0	0	0	0	0	0	0	0
Heating Degree Days (base 65°F)	220	161	79	22	1	0	0	0	0	5	54	162	704
Cooling Degree Days (base 65°F)	36	48	97	164	327	461	536	533	450	296	139	58	3,145
Mean Precipitation (in.)	3.01	3.07	3.92	2.57	3.64	6.46	6.80	7.35	5.72	3.65	2.96	2.58	51.73
Days With ≥ 0.1" Precipitation	4	4	5	3	5	9	9	10	7	6	3	4	69
Days With ≥ 1.0" Precipitation	1	1	1	1	1	2	2	2	1	1	1	1	16
Mean Snowfall (in.)	0.0	0.0	0.0	0.0	0.0	0.0	0.0	0.0	0.0	0.0	0.0	0.0	0.0
Days With ≥ 1.0" Snow Depth	0	0	0	0	0	0	0	0	0	0	0	0	0

Stuart 1 S *Martin County*   Elevation: 9 ft.   Latitude: 27° 10' N   Longitude: 80° 14' W

	JAN	FEB	MAR	APR	MAY	JUN	JUL	AUG	SEP	OCT	NOV	DEC	YEAR
Mean Maximum Temp. (°F)	75.3	76.2	79.0	82.2	85.5	88.6	90.0	90.1	89.0	85.5	80.5	76.8	83.2
Mean Temp. (°F)	65.2	65.8	69.5	73.0	77.1	80.6	82.0	82.3	81.5	77.5	72.0	67.5	74.5
Mean Minimum Temp. (°F)	55.1	55.5	59.8	63.7	68.7	72.7	73.9	74.4	73.9	69.5	63.5	58.2	65.7
Extreme Maximum Temp. (°F)	89	89	93	95	96	98	101	99	97	96	89	89	101
Extreme Minimum Temp. (°F)	23	28	26	37	45	55	63	61	65	44	33	27	23
Days Maximum Temp. ≥ 90°F	0	0	0	2	5	11	17	18	13	3	0	0	69
Days Maximum Temp. ≤ 32°F	0	0	0	0	0	0	0	0	0	0	0	0	0
Days Minimum Temp. ≤ 32°F	1	0	0	0	0	0	0	0	0	0	0	0	1
Days Minimum Temp. ≤ 0°F	0	0	0	0	0	0	0	0	0	0	0	0	0
Heating Degree Days (base 65°F)	87	67	28	5	0	0	0	0	0	1	12	55	255
Cooling Degree Days (base 65°F)	105	109	170	252	395	489	550	558	511	411	246	148	3,944
Mean Precipitation (in.)	3.12	3.35	4.57	2.78	5.43	6.93	6.25	6.43	8.16	6.42	4.18	2.72	60.34
Days With ≥ 0.1" Precipitation	5	5	6	6	8	11	11	11	11	9	6	5	94
Days With ≥ 1.0" Precipitation	1	1	1	1	2	2	2	2	2	2	1	1	18
Mean Snowfall (in.)	0.0	0.0	0.0	0.0	0.0	0.0	0.0	0.0	0.0	0.0	0.0	0.0	0.0
Days With ≥ 1.0" Snow Depth	0	0	0	0	0	0	0	0	0	0	0	0	0

Tamiami Trail 40 Mile Bend *Dade County*   Elevation: 13 ft.   Latitude: 25° 46' N   Longitude: 80° 49' W

	JAN	FEB	MAR	APR	MAY	JUN	JUL	AUG	SEP	OCT	NOV	DEC	YEAR
Mean Maximum Temp. (°F)	77.6	78.7	*82.0*	85.6	89.1	91.0	92.2	92.4	90.9	*87.1*	82.6	78.7	*85.7*
Mean Temp. (°F)	67.4	68.0	*70.9*	74.2	78.2	81.5	83.2	83.7	82.8	*79.1*	74.1	69.1	*76.0*
Mean Minimum Temp. (°F)	57.0	57.3	*59.8*	62.7	67.2	71.9	74.2	75.0	74.6	*71.1*	65.5	59.4	*66.3*
Extreme Maximum Temp. (°F)	89	90	92	98	98	102	99	101	97	97	93	95	102
Extreme Minimum Temp. (°F)	28	33	34	42	45	59	63	64	65	52	36	28	28
Days Maximum Temp. ≥ 90°F	0	0	1	6	14	22	27	27	*22*	9	1	0	*129*
Days Maximum Temp. ≤ 32°F	0	0	0	0	0	0	0	0	0	0	0	0	0
Days Minimum Temp. ≤ 32°F	0	0	0	0	0	0	0	0	0	0	0	0	0
Days Minimum Temp. ≤ 0°F	0	0	0	0	0	0	0	0	0	0	0	0	0
Heating Degree Days (base 65°F)	61	43	*16*	3	0	0	0	0	0	0	6	39	*168*
Cooling Degree Days (base 65°F)	140	153	216	298	427	513	588	603	545	*457*	295	177	*4,412*
Mean Precipitation (in.)	1.90	2.00	2.30	2.38	4.96	8.54	7.60	6.91	6.56	4.46	2.28	1.63	51.52
Days With ≥ 0.1" Precipitation	3	3	3	4	7	11	11	11	10	6	3	3	75
Days With ≥ 1.0" Precipitation	0	0	0	1	1	3	2	2	2	1	1	0	13
Mean Snowfall (in.)	0.0	0.0	0.0	0.0	0.0	0.0	0.0	0.0	0.0	0.0	0.0	0.0	0.0
Days With ≥ 1.0" Snow Depth	0	0	0	0	0	0	0	0	0	0	0	0	0

Tarpon Springs Sewage Plant *Pinellas County*   Elevation: 6 ft.   Latitude: 28° 09' N   Longitude: 82° 45' W

	JAN	FEB	MAR	APR	MAY	JUN	JUL	AUG	SEP	OCT	NOV	DEC	YEAR
Mean Maximum Temp. (°F)	71.1	72.8	77.4	81.6	86.9	90.0	91.4	91.5	90.2	85.2	79.0	73.5	82.5
Mean Temp. (°F)	60.6	62.2	66.9	71.2	76.8	81.0	82.5	82.5	81.0	75.2	68.6	62.8	72.6
Mean Minimum Temp. (°F)	50.1	51.6	56.3	60.8	66.6	71.9	73.5	73.5	71.9	65.1	58.2	52.1	62.6
Extreme Maximum Temp. (°F)	87	88	89	92	97	100	102	99	97	93	90	87	102
Extreme Minimum Temp. (°F)	19	23	31	37	45	51	64	64	55	42	28	21	19
Days Maximum Temp. ≥ 90°F	0	0	0	1	8	18	24	24	19	5	0	0	99
Days Maximum Temp. ≤ 32°F	0	0	0	0	0	0	0	0	0	0	0	0	0
Days Minimum Temp. ≤ 32°F	2	1	0	0	0	0	0	0	0	0	0	1	4
Days Minimum Temp. ≤ 0°F	0	0	0	0	0	0	0	0	0	0	0	0	0
Heating Degree Days (base 65°F)	183	132	58	10	0	0	0	0	0	3	43	137	566
Cooling Degree Days (base 65°F)	56	69	123	208	388	501	562	566	497	338	173	82	3,563
Mean Precipitation (in.)	3.26	3.31	4.05	1.95	3.15	5.67	6.72	8.31	7.04	3.41	2.36	3.01	52.24
Days With ≥ 0.1" Precipitation	5	4	5	3	4	8	10	11	9	5	4	4	72
Days With ≥ 1.0" Precipitation	1	1	2	1	1	2	2	3	2	1	1	1	18
Mean Snowfall (in.)	0.0	0.0	0.0	0.0	0.0	0.0	0.0	0.0	0.0	0.0	0.0	0.0	0.0
Days With ≥ 1.0" Snow Depth	0	0	0	0	0	0	0	0	0	0	0	0	0

Tavernier *Monroe County*   Elevation: 6 ft.   Latitude: 25° 00' N   Longitude: 80° 31' W

	JAN	FEB	MAR	APR	MAY	JUN	JUL	AUG	SEP	OCT	NOV	DEC	YEAR
Mean Maximum Temp. (°F)	76.6	77.5	80.5	83.6	86.7	88.8	*90.9*	90.4	89.0	85.7	81.5	77.9	*84.1*
Mean Temp. (°F)	70.0	70.7	73.8	77.0	80.3	*82.8*	*84.6*	84.2	83.0	79.9	75.9	71.8	*77.8*
Mean Minimum Temp. (°F)	63.3	63.8	67.0	70.3	73.9	*76.7*	*78.2*	77.9	77.0	74.1	70.2	65.7	*71.5*
Extreme Maximum Temp. (°F)	86	87	90	94	93	*96*	*97*	97	95	94	90	89	*97*
Extreme Minimum Temp. (°F)	35	39	40	51	62	*68*	*69*	69	66	57	42	35	*35*
Days Maximum Temp. ≥ 90°F	0	0	0	1	4	12	20	20	13	3	0	0	73
Days Maximum Temp. ≤ 32°F	0	0	0	0	0	0	0	0	0	0	0	0	0
Days Minimum Temp. ≤ 32°F	0	0	0	0	0	0	0	0	0	0	0	0	0
Days Minimum Temp. ≤ 0°F	0	0	0	0	0	0	0	0	0	0	0	0	0
Heating Degree Days (base 65°F)	33	19	7	0	0	0	*0*	0	0	0	2	20	*81*
Cooling Degree Days (base 65°F)	*191*	201	276	362	487	*552*	*622*	606	551	473	341	237	*4,899*
Mean Precipitation (in.)	2.50	1.97	2.26	1.94	3.91	6.80	3.25	5.11	6.74	5.36	2.99	1.99	44.82
Days With ≥ 0.1" Precipitation	3	3	3	3	5	*8*	5	8	9	7	4	3	*61*
Days With ≥ 1.0" Precipitation	1	1	1	1	1	2	1	1	2	1	1	1	14
Mean Snowfall (in.)	0.0	0.0	0.0	0.0	0.0	0.0	0.0	0.0	0.0	0.0	0.0	0.0	0.0
Days With ≥ 1.0" Snow Depth	0	0	0	0	0	0	0	0	0	0	0	0	0

Titusville *Brevard County*   Elevation: 29 ft.   Latitude: 28° 37' N   Longitude: 80° 50' W

	JAN	FEB	MAR	APR	MAY	JUN	JUL	AUG	SEP	OCT	NOV	DEC	YEAR
Mean Maximum Temp. (°F)	70.4	72.3	77.3	81.2	86.3	89.6	91.5	91.1	88.7	83.4	77.5	72.5	81.8
Mean Temp. (°F)	59.4	61.1	66.3	70.2	75.8	79.9	81.7	81.5	79.9	74.3	67.7	62.0	71.6
Mean Minimum Temp. (°F)	48.3	49.8	55.1	59.1	65.2	70.2	71.7	71.9	71.0	65.2	57.8	51.4	61.4
Extreme Maximum Temp. (°F)	88	88	92	96	101	103	101	100	98	98	93	88	103
Extreme Minimum Temp. (°F)	19	23	26	35	45	56	62	62	57	40	30	19	19
Days Maximum Temp. ≥ 90°F	0	0	1	2	8	16	23	22	13	3	0	0	88
Days Maximum Temp. ≤ 32°F	0	0	0	0	0	0	0	0	0	0	0	0	0
Days Minimum Temp. ≤ 32°F	2	1	0	0	0	0	0	0	0	0	0	1	4
Days Minimum Temp. ≤ 0°F	0	0	0	0	0	0	0	0	0	0	0	0	0
Heating Degree Days (base 65°F)	212	153	71	18	0	0	0	0	0	4	52	153	663
Cooling Degree Days (base 65°F)	34	50	111	171	339	456	531	521	446	303	143	65	3,170
Mean Precipitation (in.)	2.54	2.81	3.80	2.81	3.66	6.17	7.27	7.52	6.80	4.40	3.47	2.54	53.79
Days With ≥ 0.1" Precipitation	4	5	5	4	6	10	10	11	10	7	5	5	82
Days With ≥ 1.0" Precipitation	1	1	1	1	1	2	3	2	2	1	1	1	17
Mean Snowfall (in.)	trace	0.0	0.0	0.0	0.0	0.0	0.0	0.0	0.0	0.0	0.0	0.0	trace
Days With ≥ 1.0" Snow Depth	0	0	0	0	0	0	0	0	0	0	0	0	0

Usher Tower Levy County   Elevation: 32 ft.   Latitude: 29° 25' N   Longitude: 82° 49' W

	JAN	FEB	MAR	APR	MAY	JUN	JUL	AUG	SEP	OCT	NOV	DEC	YEAR
Mean Maximum Temp. (°F)	68.2	71.0	77.0	82.3	87.8	91.0	91.9	91.3	89.7	83.8	76.2	70.2	81.7
Mean Temp. (°F)	55.8	58.3	63.8	68.7	74.7	79.5	81.1	81.1	79.1	71.5	63.6	57.7	69.6
Mean Minimum Temp. (°F)	43.4	45.6	50.6	55.1	61.5	67.9	70.2	70.8	68.5	59.3	51.1	45.2	57.4
Extreme Maximum Temp. (°F)	87	86	92	96	102	105	102	100	99	96	92	86	105
Extreme Minimum Temp. (°F)	9	17	22	32	42	44	59	61	48	32	17	12	9
Days Maximum Temp. ≥ 90°F	0	0	0	2	11	21	25	23	18	3	0	0	103
Days Maximum Temp. ≤ 32°F	0	0	0	0	0	0	0	0	0	0	0	0	0
Days Minimum Temp. ≤ 32°F	6	4	1	0	0	0	0	0	0	0	1	5	17
Days Minimum Temp. ≤ 0°F	0	0	0	0	0	0	0	0	0	0	0	0	0
Heating Degree Days (base 65°F)	299	210	107	29	1	0	0	0	0	16	118	249	1,029
Cooling Degree Days (base 65°F)	17	30	75	149	313	445	515	511	424	233	90	32	2,834
Mean Precipitation (in.)	4.57	3.52	4.81	3.66	3.09	6.72	8.49	10.22	6.38	2.99	2.54	3.32	60.31
Days With ≥ 0.1" Precipitation	7	5	6	4	5	9	12	14	9	4	4	5	84
Days With ≥ 1.0" Precipitation	2	1	2	1	1	2	2	3	2	1	1	1	19
Mean Snowfall (in.)	0.0	trace	0.0	0.0	0.0	0.0	0.0	0.0	0.0	0.0	0.0	0.0	trace
Days With ≥ 1.0" Snow Depth	0	0	0	0	0	0	0	0	0	0	0	0	0

Venice Sarasota County   Elevation: 6 ft.   Latitude: 27° 06' N   Longitude: 82° 26' W

	JAN	FEB	MAR	APR	MAY	JUN	JUL	AUG	SEP	OCT	NOV	DEC	YEAR
Mean Maximum Temp. (°F)	71.8	73.6	77.4	81.5	86.4	89.5	91.0	91.2	90.0	85.6	79.8	74.4	82.7
Mean Temp. (°F)	61.4	63.0	67.3	71.4	76.7	80.9	82.2	82.5	81.4	75.9	69.5	64.4	73.1
Mean Minimum Temp. (°F)	51.0	52.3	57.2	61.1	66.9	72.2	73.4	73.8	72.8	66.3	59.1	54.1	63.4
Extreme Maximum Temp. (°F)	89	89	90	95	98	100	99	99	99	95	91	89	100
Extreme Minimum Temp. (°F)	23	26	33	41	51	56	62	65	61	45	29	24	23
Days Maximum Temp. ≥ 90°F	0	0	0	1	7	14	22	23	18	4	0	0	89
Days Maximum Temp. ≤ 32°F	0	0	0	0	0	0	0	0	0	0	0	0	0
Days Minimum Temp. ≤ 32°F	1	0	0	0	0	0	0	0	0	0	0	1	2
Days Minimum Temp. ≤ 0°F	0	0	0	0	0	0	0	0	0	0	0	0	0
Heating Degree Days (base 65°F)	166	117	50	9	0	0	0	0	0	2	31	115	490
Cooling Degree Days (base 65°F)	59	79	133	205	374	498	559	568	513	364	176	109	3,637
Mean Precipitation (in.)	2.73	2.15	3.60	1.85	2.28	6.74	6.64	8.30	7.39	3.12	2.09	2.34	49.23
Days With ≥ 0.1" Precipitation	4	4	4	3	4	8	10	12	10	4	3	3	69
Days With ≥ 1.0" Precipitation	1	1	1	1	1	2	2	2	2	1	1	1	16
Mean Snowfall (in.)	trace	0.0	0.0	0.0	0.0	0.0	0.0	0.0	0.0	0.0	0.0	0.0	trace
Days With ≥ 1.0" Snow Depth	0	0	0	0	0	0	0	0	0	0	0	0	0

Wauchula Hardee County   Elevation: 59 ft.   Latitude: 27° 33' N   Longitude: 81° 48' W

	JAN	FEB	MAR	APR	MAY	JUN	JUL	AUG	SEP	OCT	NOV	DEC	YEAR
Mean Maximum Temp. (°F)	74.1	75.9	80.3	84.4	89.1	91.3	92.4	92.3	90.7	85.9	80.2	75.4	84.3
Mean Temp. (°F)	61.9	63.3	67.4	71.2	76.6	80.6	81.9	82.2	80.8	75.3	68.8	63.6	72.8
Mean Minimum Temp. (°F)	49.7	50.6	54.5	57.9	64.1	69.8	71.4	72.0	70.7	64.5	57.3	51.7	61.2
Extreme Maximum Temp. (°F)	87	90	94	96	99	102	100	98	96	95	90	92	102
Extreme Minimum Temp. (°F)	20	25	23	35	44	51	62	64	58	39	26	22	20
Days Maximum Temp. ≥ 90°F	0	0	1	5	15	22	27	27	22	6	0	0	125
Days Maximum Temp. ≤ 32°F	0	0	0	0	0	0	0	0	0	0	0	0	0
Days Minimum Temp. ≤ 32°F	2	1	0	0	0	0	0	0	0	0	0	1	4
Days Minimum Temp. ≤ 0°F	0	0	0	0	0	0	0	0	0	0	0	0	0
Heating Degree Days (base 65°F)	157	117	55	12	0	0	0	0	0	3	40	121	505
Cooling Degree Days (base 65°F)	63	81	127	196	364	479	538	545	477	331	161	80	3,442
Mean Precipitation (in.)	2.41	2.71	3.47	2.33	4.00	8.01	8.07	7.32	6.03	2.73	2.08	1.98	51.14
Days With ≥ 0.1" Precipitation	4	4	5	3	5	10	11	12	9	4	3	3	73
Days With ≥ 1.0" Precipitation	1	1	1	1	1	2	3	2	2	1	0	1	16
Mean Snowfall (in.)	trace	0.0	0.0	0.0	0.0	0.0	0.0	0.0	0.0	0.0	0.0	0.0	trace
Days With ≥ 1.0" Snow Depth	0	0	0	0	0	0	0	0	0	0	0	0	0

Weeki Wachee Hernando County   Elevation: 19 ft.   Latitude: 28° 31' N   Longitude: 82° 35' W

	JAN	FEB	MAR	APR	MAY	JUN	JUL	AUG	SEP	OCT	NOV	DEC	YEAR
Mean Maximum Temp. (°F)	70.3	72.2	77.2	82.2	87.1	90.2	91.6	91.5	90.3	85.0	78.7	72.8	82.4
Mean Temp. (°F)	57.4	59.2	64.3	69.1	74.8	79.8	81.2	81.1	79.6	73.1	66.1	59.6	70.4
Mean Minimum Temp. (°F)	44.5	46.1	51.4	55.9	62.4	69.2	70.8	70.7	68.8	61.0	53.3	46.4	58.4
Extreme Maximum Temp. (°F)	88	91	92	96	100	100	100	98	98	97	91	90	100
Extreme Minimum Temp. (°F)	13	22	21	34	44	47	60	63	48	36	23	19	13
Days Maximum Temp. ≥ 90°F	0	0	0	2	9	19	25	25	19	5	0	0	104
Days Maximum Temp. ≤ 32°F	0	0	0	0	0	0	0	0	0	0	0	0	0
Days Minimum Temp. ≤ 32°F	5	3	1	0	0	0	0	0	0	0	0	3	12
Days Minimum Temp. ≤ 0°F	0	0	0	0	0	0	0	0	0	0	0	0	0
Heating Degree Days (base 65°F)	264	197	106	30	1	0	0	0	0	9	76	208	891
Cooling Degree Days (base 65°F)	34	45	89	161	321	464	525	519	444	276	127	52	3,057
Mean Precipitation (in.)	3.84	3.20	4.24	2.51	2.95	5.92	8.31	7.60	6.46	2.29	2.12	2.50	51.94
Days With ≥ 0.1" Precipitation	5	4	4	3	4	7	11	10	7	3	3	4	65
Days With ≥ 1.0" Precipitation	1	1	1	1	1	2	3	2	1	1	1	1	17
Mean Snowfall (in.)	0.0	0.0	0.0	0.0	0.0	0.0	0.0	0.0	0.0	0.0	0.0	0.0	0.0
Days With ≥ 1.0" Snow Depth	0	0	0	0	0	0	0	0	0	0	0	0	0

Note: See Appendix D for explanation of data.

GEORGIA

PHYSICAL FEATURES. Georgia is located roughly between latitudes 30° and 35° N. and longitudes 81° and 86° W. From north to south its length is 320 miles, and its maximum width is about 250 miles. With an area of almost 59,000 square miles, it is the largest State east of the Mississippi River. Its elevation ranges from near sea level along the southeast coast to almost 5,000 feet at its highest point in the northeast.

Georgia's land area is made up of four principal physiographic provinces: the Blue Ridge or Mountain Province, the Valley and Ridge Province, the Piedmont Province, and the Coastal Plain Province.

The Blue Ridge or Mountain Province is located in the northeastern part of the State. The terrain in this area is characterized by forest-covered mountains and narrow valleys with rapidly flowing streams. The average elevation of the area is less than 2,000 feet, but the higher mountains reach altitudes between 4,000 and 5,000 feet above sea level. The Valley and Ridge Province, located in northwest Georgia, is composed of wide, flat valleys separated by narrow, steep, wooded ridges than run more or less northeast-southwest. The elevation of the valleys ranges mostly between 500 and 800 feet above sea level, with the ridges rising to heights of 600 to 2,000 feet.

The Piedmont Plateau Province is a wide area extending from the foothills of the Appalachian Mountains to the Coastal Plain and comprising nearly one-third of the area of the State. The terrain is mostly hilly in the north to rolling in the south, where it merges with the Coastal Plain. Elevations range from near 1,200 feet in the north to less than 500 feet in the south. The boundary between the Piedmont Province and the Coastal Plain is called the Fall Line, because of the steep fall of rivers as they cross this boundary. The Fall Line extends across the State from west-southwest to east-northeast. The Coastal Plain Province includes all of Georgia south of the Fall Line and comprises about three-fifths of the total area of the State. The terrain is slightly rolling to level and ranges in altitude from near sea level along the coast to a maximum of 600 feet. The low-lying coastal sections are rather marshy and the large slow-moving streams are bordered by wide, swampy, densely wooded areas.

Georgia streams are divided into two main groups — those flowing southeastward into the Atlantic and those flowing southward directly into the Gulf of Mexico, or indirectly into the Gulf through the Alabama-Mobile and Tennessee River systems. The Chattahoochee Ridge marks the dividing line between the parts of the State that are drained into the Atlantic and into the Gulf. The main streams in the Atlantic drainage system are the Savannah and Altamaha Rivers. The Savannah and its headwater streams form the boundary between Georgia and South Carolina throughout its entire length. The Altamaha drains a large area of central Georgia. The Chattahoochee and Flint River systems constitute the major streams of west Georgia, which drain directly into the Gulf of Mexico.

GENERAL CLIMATE. Georgia's climate is determined primarily by its latitude, the proximity of the Gulf of Mexico and the Atlantic Ocean, and by the altitude.

Average annual rainfall in Georgia ranges from more than 75 inches in the extreme northeast corner to about 40 inches in a small area of the East Central Division. Total rainfall varies greatly from year to year in all parts of the State, and most stations with several years of record show more than twice as much rain in their wettest year as in their driest. The distribution of rainfall throughout the year is also highly variable in all parts of the State, but the extremes occur at different seasons in different areas.

Most of the State shows two maxima and two minima in the annual rainfall curve. One maximum occurs in winter and early spring and the other in midsummer. The driest season for all the State is autumn, with most areas showing a secondary minimum about May. In the northern third of the State, the cool season rainfall maximum predominates, with either January or March normally the wettest month. This is due to the greater influence in that area of the cyclonic storms that move across the country with regularity during winter and early spring. The mountains of north Georgia add enough lift to the moist air that is drawn into the forward side of these storms from the Gulf to add materially to the total annual rainfall of the area. Most sections of central and south Georgia have their greatest rainfall in midsummer, with a secondary maximum about March. The lower east coastal area has its highest normal rainfall in September, due to the occasional extremely heavy rains that occur with late summer and autumn tropical storms. October is normally the driest month in most of the State. Snowfall is light in Georgia and of no significance at all in most of the State.

Due to its latitude and proximity to the warm waters of the Gulf of Mexico and Atlantic Ocean, most of Georgia has warm, humid summers and short, mild winters. However, in the northern part of the State, altitude becomes the more predominant influence with resulting cool summers and colder, but not severe, winters. All four seasons are apparent, but spring is usually short and blustery with rather frequent periods of storminess of varying intensity. In autumn long periods of mild, sunny weather are the rule for all of Georgia.

TEMPERATURE. Average summer temperatures range from about 73°F. in the extreme north to nearly 82°F. in parts of south Georgia. There is little difference in summer averages over the southern two-thirds of the State, where they range between 80 and 82°F. Summer days are characteristically warm and humid in this area, with high temperatures exceeding 90°F. on most days and reaching 100°F. during most years. Temperatures usually drop to the middle or low 70s, or even below 70°F. by early morning, giving some relief from the daytime warmth. The flow of moist air from the Gulf over the warm land surface results in frequent afternoon thundershowers in south and central Georgia during summer. These showers not only provide most of the summer rainfall, but oftentimes bring welcome relief from the afternoon heat. All parts of the State have experienced 100°F. weather at one time or another during the period of official records, but such occurrences are highly unusual in the mountain section of the north.

Winter temperatures show more variation from north to south than do those of summer. There is also a much greater variation in winter from day to day in all sections of the State. The average temperature for the three winter months ranges from 41°F. in the north to about 56°F. on the lower east coast, with the increase being almost uniform from north to south. All of Georgia experiences freezing temperatures almost every year, but the frequency of such occurrences varies greatly from the mountains to the coast. The average annual number of days with a temperature of 32°F. or less ranges from 110 in the north to about 10 in the lower coastal region.

Georgia winters are characterized by frequent and sometimes large fluctuations in temperature. The cold snaps, which usually occur with regularity from mid-November to mid-March, alternate with longer periods of mild weather. Daytime temperatures almost always rise to above freezing in the southern three-fourths of the State, even during the coldest weather. There is approximately four months difference in the average length of the freeze-free growing season from north to south, ranging from about 170 days in the northernmost areas to near 300 days on the lower coast.

Relative humidity averages are moderately high in most of Georgia, as would be expected from its location in relation to the Gulf of Mexico and the Atlantic Ocean and from the high frequency of wind flow from the direction of these warm waters. Year-round averages at about 7:00 a.m. are approximately 85 percent, or slightly higher in the south. By 1:00 p.m. the average drops to about 55 percent. Monthly averages for both morning and afternoon are higher in summer than in other seasons in all sections of the State.

STORMS. Several tornadoes may be expected in Georgia each year. These storms have occurred during every month of the year, but have their highest frequency in spring. Approximately 50 percent of Georgia's tornadoes have occurred in March and April. Local windstorms, other than tornadoes, occur frequently in spring and early summer. These storms usually occur in connection with thunderstorms, the more severe of which may also produce hail. The southeast Georgia coast has been battered by hurricane winds on a few occasions but, since most of these storms do not reach the State or move into the State after having traveled over land areas, they usually produce only moderate winds and heavy to copious rains. Tropical storm rainfall contributes materially to the precipitation normals for the late summer and fall months in southeast Georgia and to a lesser extent in other areas of the State.

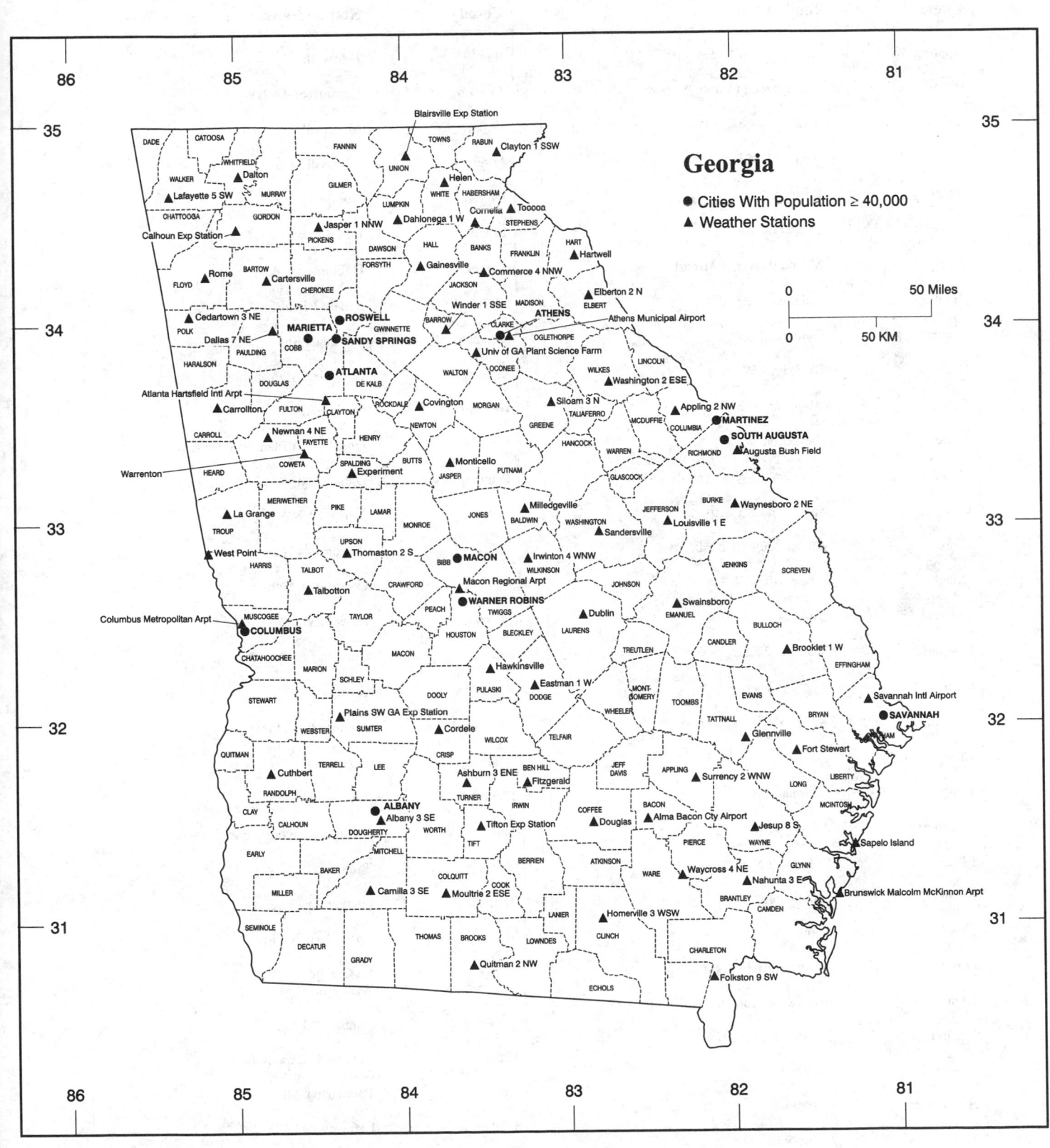

Georgia

● Cities With Population ≥ 40,000
▲ Weather Stations

Blairsville Exp Station
Clayton 1 SSW
DADE CATOOSA FANNIN TOWNS RABUN
WHITFIELD Dalton UNION
WALKER MURRAY GILMER Helen
Lafayette 5 SW WHITE HABERSHAM
CHATTOOGA GORDON Jasper 1 NNW Dahlonega 1 W Cornelia Toccoa
Calhoun Exp Station PICKENS DAWSON LUMPKIN STEPHENS
BARTOW FORSYTH HALL BANKS FRANKLIN HART
FLOYD Rome Cartersville Gainesville Commerce 4 NNW Hartwell
Cedartown 3 NE CHEROKEE JACKSON Elberton 2 N
POLK Dallas 7 NE MARIETTA ROSWELL Winder 1 SSE MADISON ELBERT
HARALSON PAULDING COBB SANDY SPRINGS GWINNETTE BARROW CLARKE ATHENS
DOUGLAS ATLANTA DE KALB Univ of GA Plant Science Farm Athens Municipal Airport
Atlanta Hartsfield Intl Arpt FULTON WALTON OCONEE OGLETHORPE LINCOLN
CARROLL Carrollton CLAYTON ROCKDALE Covington MORGAN Washington 2 ESE WILKES
Newnan 4 NE HENRY NEWTON Siloam 3 N TALIAFERRO MCDUFFIE COLUMBIA MARTINEZ
HEARD COWETA FAYETTE SPALDING Experiment BUTTS GREENE HANCOCK WARREN RICHMOND SOUTH AUGUSTA
Warrenton MERIWETHER PIKE LAMAR Monticello JASPER PUTNAM GLASCOCK Augusta Bush Field
La Grange MONROE JONES Milledgeville BALDWIN WASHINGTON Sandersville JEFFERSON BURKE Waynesboro 2 NE
TROUP UPSON Louisville 1 E
West Point HARRIS TALBOT Thomaston 2 S LAMAR CRAWFORD BIBB MACON WILKINSON Irwinton 4 WNW JOHNSON JENKINS SCREVEN
Talbotton TAYLOR Macon Regional Arpt PEACH WARNER ROBINS TWIGGS Dublin LAURENS Swainsboro EMANUEL BULLOCH
Columbus Metropolitan Arpt MUSCOGEE MACON HOUSTON TREUTLEN CANDLER Brooklet 1 W
COLUMBUS MARION SCHLEY Hawkinsville PULASKI DOOLY BLECKLEY MONT-GOMERY EVANS EFFINGHAM
CHATAHOOCHEE STEWART Eastman 1 W DODGE WHEELER TOOMBS Savannah Intl Airport
Plains SW GA Exp Station WEBSTER SUMTER Cordele TELFAIR TATTNALL BRYAN SAVANNAH
QUITMAN Cuthbert TERRELL LEE Ashburn 3 ENE WILCOX CRISP JEFF DAVIS APPLING Glennville Fort Stewart
CLAY RANDOLPH CALHOUN ALBANY Albany 3 SE TURNER IRWIN Fitzgerald BEN HILL COFFEE BACON Surrency 2 WNW LONG LIBERTY
EARLY DOUGHERTY WORTH Tifton Exp Station Douglas Alma Bacon Cty Airport Jesup 8 S MCINTOSH
BAKER MITCHELL TIFT BERRIEN ATKINSON PIERCE WAYNE Sapelo Island
MILLER Camilla 3 SE Moultrie 2 ESE COLQUITT COOK WARE Waycross 4 NE Nahunta 3 E GLYNN
SEMINOLE DECATUR GRADY THOMAS BROOKS LANIER Homerville 3 WSW CLINCH BRANTLEY CAMDEN Brunswick Malcolm McKinnon Arpt
Quitman 2 NW LOWNDES CHARLTON
ECHOLS Folkston 9 SW

0   50 Miles
0   50 KM

Georgia Weather Stations by County

County	Station Name	County	Station Name
Appling	Surrency 2 WNW	Hart	Hartwell
Bacon	Alma Bacon County Airport	Jackson	Commerce 4 NNW
Baldwin	Milledgeville	Jasper	Monticello
Barrow	Winder 1 SSE	Jefferson	Louisville 1 E
Bartow	Cartersville	Laurens	Dublin
Ben Hill	Fitzgerald	Liberty	Fort Stewart
Bibb	Macon Regional Airport	Lumpkin	Dahlonega 1 W
Brantley	Nahunta 3 E	McIntosh	Sapelo Island
Brooks	Quitman 2 NW	Mitchell	Camilla 3 SE
Bulloch	Brooklet 1 W	Muscogee	Columbus Metropolitan Airport
Burke	Waynesboro 2 NE	Newton	Covington
Carroll	Carrollton	Oconee	Univ. of GA Plant Science Farm
Charlton	Folkston 9 SW	Paulding	Dallas 7 NE
Chatham	Savannah Int'l Airport	Pickens	Jasper 1 NNW
Clarke	Athens Municipal Airport	Pierce	Waycross 4 NE
Clinch	Homerville 3 WSW	Polk	Cedartown 3 NE
Coffee	Douglas	Pulaski	Hawkinsville
Colquitt	Moultrie 2 ESE	Rabun	Clayton 1 SSW
Columbia	Appling 2 NW	Randolph	Cuthbert
Coweta	Newnan 4 NE	Richmond	Augusta Bush Field
Crisp	Cordele	Spalding	Experiment
Dodge	Eastman 1 W	Stephens	Toccoa
Dougherty	Albany 3 SE	Sumter	Plains SW Georgia Exp. Station
Elbert	Elberton 2 N	Talbot	Talbotton
Emanuel	Swainsboro	Tattnall	Glennville
Floyd	Rome	Tift	Tifton Exp. Station
Fulton	Atlanta Hartsfield Int'l Arpt.	Troup	La Grange
Glynn	Brunswick Malcolm McKinnon Arpt.		West Point
Gordon	Calhoun Exp. Station	Turner	Ashburn 3 ENE
Greene	Siloam 3 N	Union	Blairsville Exp. Station
Habersham	Cornelia	Upson	Thomaston 2 S
Hall	Gainesville	Walker	Lafayette 5 SW
		Warren	Warrenton

County	Station Name
Washington	Sandersville
Wayne	Jesup 8 S
White	Helen
Whitfield	Dalton
Wilkes	Washington 2 ESE
Wilkinson	Irwinton 4 WNW

Georgia Weather Stations by City

City	Station Name	Miles
Albany	Albany 3 SE	4
Athens	Athens Municipal Airport	3
	Univ. of GA Plant Science Farm	10
	Winder 1 SSE	19
Atlanta	Atlanta Hartsfield Int'l Arpt.	9
Columbus	Columbus Metropolitan Airport	3
Macon	Macon Regional Airport	10
Marietta	Dallas 7 NE	12
Martinez	Appling 2 NW	15
	Augusta Bush Field	12
	Clark Hill 1 W, SC	12
Savannah	Savannah Int'l Airport	8
South Augusta	Appling 2 NW	20
	Augusta Bush Field	6
	Clark Hill 1 W, SC	19
Warner Robins	Macon Regional Airport	5

Note: Miles is the distance between the geographic center of the city and the weather station.

Georgia Weather Stations by Elevation

Feet	Station Name
1,916	Blairsville Exp. Station
1,879	Clayton 1 SSW
1,469	Cornelia
1,463	Jasper 1 NNW
1,437	Helen
1,259	Dahlonega 1 W
1,167	Gainesville
1,099	Dallas 7 NE
1,017	Toccoa
1,007	Atlanta Hartsfield Int'l Arpt.
994	Carrollton
958	Winder 1 SSE
921	Experiment
918	Newnan 4 NE
839	Univ. of GA Plant Science Farm
797	Athens Municipal Airport
797	Lafayette 5 SW
784	Cedartown 3 NE
767	Covington
748	Commerce 4 NNW
728	Talbotton
718	Cartersville
711	La Grange
698	Dalton
688	Hartwell
688	Siloam 3 N
662	Thomaston 2 S
652	Calhoun Exp. Station
620	Rome
620	Washington 2 ESE
574	West Point
538	Elberton 2 N
528	Monticello
515	Irwinton 4 WNW
508	Warrenton
498	Plains SW Georgia Exp. Station
459	Cuthbert
433	Ashburn 3 ENE
433	Sandersville
396	Eastman 1 W
396	Milledgeville
390	Columbus Metropolitan Airport
377	Tifton Exp. Station
367	Appling 2 NW
367	Fitzgerald
351	Macon Regional Airport
337	Moultrie 2 ESE
324	Swainsboro
321	Louisville 1 E
305	Cordele
269	Hawkinsville
269	Waynesboro 2 NE
229	Dublin
223	Douglas
200	Surrency 2 WNW

Feet	Station Name
196	Alma Bacon County Airport
187	Brooklet 1 W
187	Homerville 3 WSW
183	Quitman 2 NW
177	Albany 3 SE
173	Camilla 3 SE
167	Glennville
144	Waycross 4 NE
131	Augusta Bush Field
118	Folkston 9 SW
98	Jesup 8 S
91	Fort Stewart
75	Nahunta 3 E
45	Savannah Int'l Airport
13	Brunswick Malcolm McKinnon Arpt.
9	Sapelo Island

Athens Municipal Airport

Athens is located in northeast Georgia, in the Piedmont Plateau section of the state. The terrain is rolling to hilly with the elevation within the city averaging about 700 feet above sea level, and that of the county ranging mostly between 600 and 850 feet. The Atlantic Ocean 200 miles to the southeast, the Gulf of Mexico 275 miles to the south, and the southern Appalachian Mountains to the north and northwest, all exert some influence on the climate of Athens, with the total effect being a moderation of both summer and winter weather.

Summers are warm and somewhat humid in Athens, but there is a noticeable absence of prolonged periods of extreme heat. The maximum temperature reaches 90 degrees or higher on about one-half the days during the three months, June through August, but a temperature of 100 degrees or higher occurs during fewer than one-half the years.

With the mountains to the north serving as a partial barrier to the flow of extremely cold air into the area, winters in Athens are not severe. Cold spells are usually short-lived, interspersed with periods of warm southerly air flow, making normal outside activities possible throughout most years.

Average annual precipitation in Athens is fairly evenly distributed throughout the year, with slight maxima in winter, early spring, and in midsummer. In spite of what appears to be an abundant supply of moisture, dry spells occur during most years. Fortunately, they are more frequent in autumn when long periods of clear, mild, weather but offer ideal conditions for harvesting operations.

Snowfall is not of much importance in the area. Measurable amounts occur rather infrequently, but occasionally there is sufficient fall to cause some accumulation on the ground.

The average length of the freeze-free growing season in Athens is 220 days, from early April, the average occurrence of the last spring freeze, to early November, the average occurrence of the first fall freeze.

Thunderstorms occur in all months of the year but are most frequent in June and July. Severe thunderstorms are infrequent, but may occur as isolated summer storms, or in squall lines of winter and spring. A few tornadoes have crossed the city and county since 1930, causing several deaths.

Athens Municipal Airport *Clarke County*   Elevation: 797 ft.   Latitude: 33° 57' N   Longitude: 83° 20' W

	JAN	FEB	MAR	APR	MAY	JUN	JUL	AUG	SEP	OCT	NOV	DEC	YEAR
Mean Maximum Temp. (°F)	52.3	57.3	65.2	73.6	80.6	87.2	90.4	88.5	83.3	73.6	64.2	55.6	72.6
Mean Temp. (°F)	42.7	46.5	54.0	61.6	69.4	76.7	80.2	78.9	73.4	62.5	53.4	45.9	62.1
Mean Minimum Temp. (°F)	33.0	35.7	42.7	49.5	58.2	66.1	70.0	69.2	63.4	51.4	42.6	36.0	51.5
Extreme Maximum Temp. (°F)	80	81	88	93	94	103	104	107	97	92	85	79	107
Extreme Minimum Temp. (°F)	-4	7	11	26	37	45	57	56	44	28	15	3	-4
Days Maximum Temp. ≥ 90°F	0	0	0	0	2	11	18	14	5	0	0	0	50
Days Maximum Temp. ≤ 32°F	1	0	0	0	0	0	0	0	0	0	0	0	1
Days Minimum Temp. ≤ 32°F	15	11	4	0	0	0	0	0	0	0	5	12	47
Days Minimum Temp. ≤ 0°F	0	0	0	0	0	0	0	0	0	0	0	0	0
Heating Degree Days (base 65°F)	686	517	343	147	26	1	0	0	8	127	349	588	2,792
Cooling Degree Days (base 65°F)	0	1	9	50	180	375	501	450	265	61	7	2	1,901
Mean Precipitation (in.)	4.61	4.39	5.08	3.35	3.92	3.92	4.43	3.76	3.60	3.64	3.62	3.69	48.01
Maximum Precipitation (in.)	9.5	9.2	10.9	9.5	11.3	13.3	10.5	7.4	10.3	7.7	9.2	8.4	71.4
Minimum Precipitation (in.)	0.6	0.8	1.1	0.7	0.4	0.9	1.4	0.5	0.6	trace	1.0	0.8	32.4
Maximum 24-hr. Precipitation (in.)	3.0	2.7	3.8	3.4	5.5	9.9	4.1	4.3	5.3	5.4	2.9	2.8	9.9
Days With ≥ 0.1" Precipitation	8	7	7	5	6	6	7	6	5	5	6	6	74
Days With ≥ 1.0" Precipitation	1	1	2	1	1	1	1	1	1	1	1	1	13
Mean Snowfall (in.)	1.1	0.7	0.6	0.0	trace	0.0	0.0	0.0	0.0	0.0	trace	0.3	2.7
Maximum Snowfall (in.)	7	5	9	0	0	0	0	0	0	0	2	3	11
Maximum 24-hr. Snowfall (in.)	7	5	9	0	0	0	0	0	0	0	2	3	9
Days With ≥ 1.0" Snow Depth	1	0	0	0	0	0	0	0	0	0	0	0	1
Thunderstorm Days	1	1	3	4	6	9	12	8	3	1	1	1	50
Foggy Days	15	12	13	11	16	16	19	22	20	16	13	14	187
Predominant Sky Cover	OVR	OVR	OVR	CLR	OVR	OVR	OVR	SCT	OVR	CLR	CLR	OVR	OVR
Mean Relative Humidity 7am (%)	80	79	80	82	86	87	90	92	92	89	85	81	85
Mean Relative Humidity 4pm (%)	54	50	48	45	51	53	57	57	57	52	51	54	52
Mean Dewpoint (°F)	31	32	39	47	57	65	69	69	63	51	41	34	50
Prevailing Wind Direction	WNW	WNW	WNW	WNW	WNW	WSW	WSW	NE	NE	NE	WNW	WNW	WNW
Prevailing Wind Speed (mph)	10	10	10	10	8	7	7	7	8	8	9	10	9
Maximum Wind Gust (mph)	55	56	83	60	52	58	78	49	55	47	59	45	83

Atlanta Hartsfield Int'l Arpt.

Atlanta is located in the foothills of the southern Appalachians in north-central Georgia. The terrain is rolling to hilly and slopes downward toward the east, west, and south so that drainage of the major river systems is generally into the Gulf of Mexico from the western and southern sections of the city and to the Atlantic from the eastern portions of the city.

The Gulf of Mexico and the Atlantic Ocean are approximately 250 miles south and southeast of the city, respectively. Both the Appalachian chain of mountains and the two nearby maritime bodies exert an important influence on the Atlanta climate. Temperatures are moderated throughout the year while abundant precipitation fosters natural vegetation and growth of crops. Summer temperatures in Atlanta are moderated somewhat by elevation but are still rather warm. However, prolonged periods of hot weather are unusual and 100 degree heat is rarely experienced.

With the mountains to the north blocking the southward movement of Polar air masses, Atlanta winters are rather mild. Cold spells are not unusual but they are rather short-lived and seldom disrupt outdoor activities for an extended period of time. Late March is the average date of the last temperature of 32 degrees in the spring and mid-November is the average date of the first temperature of 32 degrees in the fall, which gives an average growing season of about 234 days.

Minimum dry precipitation periods occur mainly during the late summer and early autumn. Maximum thunderstorm activity occurs during July, but severe local thunderstorms occur most frequently in March, April, and May, some spawning highly damaging tornadoes.

The average annual snowfall varies widely from year to year. A fall of four inches or more occurs about once every five years. Most snows melt in a short period of time due to the rapid warming which often follows the storm. Ice storms, freezing rain or glaze, occur about two out of every three years, causing hazardous travel and disruption of utilities. Severe ice storms occur about once in ten years, causing major disruption of utilities and significant property damage.

The Bermuda High pressure area has a dominant effect on Atlanta weather, particularly in the summer months. East or northeast winds produce the most unpleasant weather although southerly winds are quite humid during the summer. The generally light wind conditions contribute to the formation of an occasional early morning fog.

Atlanta Hartsfield Int'l Arpt. *Fulton County*   Elevation: 1,007 ft.   Latitude: 33° 38' N   Longitude: 84° 26' W

	JAN	FEB	MAR	APR	MAY	JUN	JUL	AUG	SEP	OCT	NOV	DEC	YEAR
Mean Maximum Temp. (°F)	51.7	56.6	64.9	73.1	80.0	86.4	89.3	87.8	82.5	72.9	63.4	55.0	72.0
Mean Temp. (°F)	42.5	46.5	54.2	61.9	69.7	76.7	79.9	78.9	73.5	62.9	53.4	45.8	62.2
Mean Minimum Temp. (°F)	33.2	36.3	43.4	50.6	59.4	67.0	70.6	69.9	64.5	52.9	43.4	36.5	52.3
Extreme Maximum Temp. (°F)	77	80	89	93	95	99	105	102	97	89	83	79	105
Extreme Minimum Temp. (°F)	-8	6	11	26	37	48	58	55	43	28	14	0	-8
Days Maximum Temp. ≥ 90°F	0	0	0	0	1	9	15	11	4	0	0	0	40
Days Maximum Temp. ≤ 32°F	1	0	0	0	0	0	0	0	0	0	0	0	1
Days Minimum Temp. ≤ 32°F	15	11	4	0	0	0	0	0	0	0	4	11	45
Days Minimum Temp. ≤ 0°F	0	0	0	0	0	0	0	0	0	0	0	0	0
Heating Degree Days (base 65°F)	691	518	340	143	24	1	0	0	10	120	349	590	2,786
Cooling Degree Days (base 65°F)	0	2	14	62	195	384	503	455	276	66	8	2	1,967
Mean Precipitation (in.)	4.96	4.74	5.49	3.64	3.99	3.68	5.15	3.65	3.98	3.29	4.00	3.85	50.42
Maximum Precipitation (in.)	10.2	12.8	11.7	11.9	8.4	10.0	17.7	8.7	11.6	11.0	15.7	9.9	71.2
Minimum Precipitation (in.)	0.8	0.8	1.9	0.5	0.4	0.2	0.6	0.5	trace	trace	0.8	0.7	31.8
Maximum 24-hr. Precipitation (in.)	3.5	3.7	4.6	4.4	4.4	3.8	5.3	3.0	5.3	6.7	3.5	3.1	6.7
Days With ≥ 0.1" Precipitation	8	7	7	6	6	6	8	6	5	4	6	6	75
Days With ≥ 1.0" Precipitation	1	1	2	1	1	1	2	1	1	1	1	1	14
Mean Snowfall (in.)	1.1	0.5	0.6	trace	0.0	0.0	0.0	0.0	0.0	trace	trace	0.2	2.4
Maximum Snowfall (in.)	7	4	8	trace	0	0	0	0	0	trace	1	3	10
Maximum 24-hr. Snowfall (in.)	5	4	8	trace	0	0	0	0	0	trace	1	2	8
Days With ≥ 1.0" Snow Depth	0	0	0	0	0	0	0	0	0	0	0	0	0
Thunderstorm Days	1	2	3	4	6	8	10	7	3	1	1	1	47
Foggy Days	14	11	11	9	11	11	14	16	14	12	12	13	148
Predominant Sky Cover	OVR	OVR	OVR	OVR	OVR	SCT	SCT	SCT	OVR	CLR	OVR	OVR	OVR
Mean Relative Humidity 7am (%)	79	77	78	78	82	84	88	89	88	84	81	80	82
Mean Relative Humidity 4pm (%)	56	50	48	45	49	53	57	56	56	51	52	56	52
Mean Dewpoint (°F)	32	33	39	47	56	64	68	68	62	51	41	34	49
Prevailing Wind Direction	NW	NW	NW	NW	NW	NW	W	E	ENE	ENE	NW	NW	NW
Prevailing Wind Speed (mph)	13	13	13	12	10	9	8	8	10	9	12	12	10
Maximum Wind Gust (mph)	62	71	70	61	73	60	77	61	58	48	56	67	77

Augusta Bush Field

The boundary between the Piedmont Plateau and the Coastal Plain, known as the Fall Line, crosses the Savannah River basin in a general northeast-southwest direction near Augusta, Georgia. The Weather Service Office at Bush Field is located in the Savannah River Valley approximately two miles west of the river and 203 miles above the mouth of the Savannah. Hills some 200 feet higher than the station are found slightly more than one mile to the west and approximately four miles to the southwest, and some five miles to the south and southeast. Swampland is found immediately to the north, east, and south of the station.

The length of the growing season averages 241 days. The average last occurrence in the spring of temperatures of 32 degrees is mid-March, and the first in the fall is mid-November.

Measurable snow is a rarity and then remains on the ground only a short time. Ice storms, damaging winds, and very low temperatures are also of rare occurrence.

Augusta has been protected, to a great extent, from flooding of the Savannah River by the construction of two multipurpose dams. The Clark Hill Dam is located 21.7 miles above the city and Hartwell Dam has been constructed 89 miles above Augusta.

Augusta Bush Field *Richmond County*   Elevation: 131 ft.   Latitude: 33° 22' N   Longitude: 81° 58' W

	JAN	FEB	MAR	APR	MAY	JUN	JUL	AUG	SEP	OCT	NOV	DEC	YEAR
Mean Maximum Temp. (°F)	56.6	61.2	69.0	76.6	83.6	89.7	92.5	90.8	86.0	76.9	68.1	59.8	75.9
Mean Temp. (°F)	44.9	48.4	55.8	62.5	70.5	77.8	81.5	80.1	74.8	63.9	55.0	47.7	63.6
Mean Minimum Temp. (°F)	33.2	35.6	42.5	48.4	57.4	65.8	70.3	69.3	63.5	51.0	41.8	35.6	51.2
Extreme Maximum Temp. (°F)	80	85	89	96	98	104	107	108	101	95	87	82	108
Extreme Minimum Temp. (°F)	-1	9	12	26	35	47	56	55	41	26	15	5	-1
Days Maximum Temp. ≥ 90°F	0	0	0	1	6	16	23	19	10	1	0	0	76
Days Maximum Temp. ≤ 32°F	0	0	0	0	0	0	0	0	0	0	0	0	0
Days Minimum Temp. ≤ 32°F	15	12	5	1	0	0	0	0	0	1	7	13	54
Days Minimum Temp. ≤ 0°F	0	0	0	0	0	0	0	0	0	0	0	0	0
Heating Degree Days (base 65°F)	617	465	295	124	19	0	0	0	5	106	310	532	2,473
Cooling Degree Days (base 65°F)	1	3	16	58	206	410	538	485	299	88	16	3	2,123
Mean Precipitation (in.)	4.37	4.16	4.72	2.93	3.19	4.06	4.17	4.44	3.41	3.33	2.58	3.26	44.62
Maximum Precipitation (in.)	8.9	7.7	11.9	8.4	9.6	8.8	12.2	11.3	9.5	14.8	7.8	8.6	66.0
Minimum Precipitation (in.)	0.8	0.3	0.9	0.6	0.5	0.7	1.0	0.6	0.3	trace	0.1	0.3	31.5
Maximum 24-hr. Precipitation (in.)	2.8	3.5	5.3	3.2	4.4	2.9	3.7	5.9	4.5	5.3	3.4	2.9	5.9
Days With ≥ 0.1" Precipitation	8	6	7	5	6	6	7	7	5	4	4	6	71
Days With ≥ 1.0" Precipitation	1	1	1	1	1	1	1	1	1	1	1	1	12
Mean Snowfall (in.)	0.3	1.0	trace	trace	0.0	trace	0.0	0.0	0.0	0.0	0.0	trace	1.3
Maximum Snowfall (in.)	3	14	1	0	0	0	0	0	0	0	trace	1	14
Maximum 24-hr. Snowfall (in.)	3	8	1	0	0	0	0	0	0	0	trace	1	8
Days With ≥ 1.0" Snow Depth	0	0	0	0	0	0	0	0	0	0	0	0	0
Thunderstorm Days	1	2	3	4	6	10	13	10	4	1	1	1	56
Foggy Days	15	12	13	13	16	17	18	22	20	17	16	15	194
Predominant Sky Cover	OVR	OVR	OVR	CLR	OVR	SCT	SCT	SCT	OVR	CLR	CLR	OVR	OVR
Mean Relative Humidity 7am (%)	84	82	84	85	86	86	88	91	92	91	88	85	87
Mean Relative Humidity 4pm (%)	51	47	45	43	47	51	56	56	55	49	47	51	50
Mean Dewpoint (°F)	34	36	41	49	59	66	70	70	64	53	43	36	52
Prevailing Wind Direction	W	WNW	WNW	SE	SE	SE	SE	SE	NE	NE	WNW	W	SE
Prevailing Wind Speed (mph)	10	12	12	8	7	7	7	6	8	8	9	9	8
Maximum Wind Gust (mph)	55	55	66	54	58	60	69	62	47	63	48	49	69

Columbus Metropolitan Airport

Columbus is located on the Chattahoochee River at the western boundary of Georgia, about 225 miles west of the Atlantic Ocean and 170 miles north of the Gulf of Mexico. Elevation of the ground above sea level ranges from 200 to 500 feet and effects of terrain on the weather are negligible. The climate is that of the humid southeast, with pronounced maritime effects at some periods, and equally pronounced continental effects at others.

Annual rainfall is variable, the months of highest rainfall are generally March and July, and the driest are usually October and November. Heavy midsummer rainfall is commonly the result of frequent local thunderstorms. Heavy rains which occasionally come in autumn are likely to be due to Gulf or Caribbean hurricanes moving inland near the Columbus area.

Snow is rare, but almost every winter sees a few snowflakes falling in the area and occasionally a moderate to heavy snowfall is experienced.

The coldest month is usually January and the warmest is usually July.

Most days in summer will have a high temperature of 90 degrees or more, but few will reach 100 degrees. During many winters the minimum temperature does not drop below 20 degrees, but about one year in ten it will drop to 10 degrees or lower.

Based on the 1951-1980 period, the average first occurrence of 32 degrees Fahrenheit in the fall is November 9 and the average last occurrence in the spring is March 21.

Columbus Metropolitan Airport *Muscogee County*   Elevation: 390 ft.   Latitude: 32° 31' N   Longitude: 84° 57' W

	JAN	FEB	MAR	APR	MAY	JUN	JUL	AUG	SEP	OCT	NOV	DEC	YEAR
Mean Maximum Temp. (°F)	57.0	61.6	69.4	76.9	83.4	89.6	91.8	91.0	86.4	77.2	68.0	60.1	76.0
Mean Temp. (°F)	46.8	50.3	57.6	64.6	72.4	79.3	82.2	81.5	76.7	66.0	56.8	49.8	65.3
Mean Minimum Temp. (°F)	36.5	39.0	45.8	52.1	61.3	68.9	72.5	71.9	66.8	54.8	45.6	39.4	54.6
Extreme Maximum Temp. (°F)	82	83	89	93	97	104	104	103	100	93	85	82	104
Extreme Minimum Temp. (°F)	-2	10	16	30	40	48	61	58	45	29	19	8	-2
Days Maximum Temp. ≥ 90°F	0	0	0	1	5	17	23	21	11	1	0	0	79
Days Maximum Temp. ≤ 32°F	0	0	0	0	0	0	0	0	0	0	0	0	0
Days Minimum Temp. ≤ 32°F	13	8	2	0	0	0	0	0	0	0	3	9	35
Days Minimum Temp. ≤ 0°F	0	0	0	0	0	0	0	0	0	0	0	0	0
Heating Degree Days (base 65°F)	559	412	248	90	7	0	0	0	3	73	261	471	2,124
Cooling Degree Days (base 65°F)	1	5	26	80	250	448	557	529	357	116	22	5	2,396
Mean Precipitation (in.)	4.74	4.58	5.74	3.90	3.73	3.67	5.17	3.76	3.00	2.45	3.87	4.50	49.11
Maximum Precipitation (in.)	8.3	9.4	12.5	11.7	8.4	10.8	13.2	10.1	6.9	8.4	12.4	9.4	73.2
Minimum Precipitation (in.)	0.7	1.0	1.4	0.1	0.2	0.7	1.7	0.8	0.2	0	0.3	0.4	30.2
Maximum 24-hr. Precipitation (in.)	3.2	5.5	5.4	5.7	4.3	3.9	5.4	5.3	4.1	5.0	4.1	4.3	5.7
Days With ≥ 0.1" Precipitation	8	7	7	5	6	6	8	6	5	4	5	6	73
Days With ≥ 1.0" Precipitation	1	2	2	1	1	1	1	1	1	1	1	2	15
Mean Snowfall (in.)	0.2	0.5	0.1	trace	trace	0.0	0.0	0.0	0.0	0.0	trace	trace	0.8
Maximum Snowfall (in.)	2	14	3	trace	0	0	0	0	0	0	trace	2	14
Maximum 24-hr. Snowfall (in.)	1	11	3	trace	0	0	0	0	0	0	trace	1	11
Days With ≥ 1.0" Snow Depth	0	0	0	0	0	0	0	0	0	0	0	0	0
Thunderstorm Days	1	2	4	4	6	8	13	9	4	1	1	1	54
Foggy Days	15	13	14	12	15	15	19	19	16	14	14	15	181
Predominant Sky Cover	OVR	OVR	OVR	CLR	OVR	SCT	SCT	SCT	OVR	CLR	CLR	OVR	OVR
Mean Relative Humidity 7am (%)	84	83	85	86	86	86	90	91	90	89	87	85	87
Mean Relative Humidity 4pm (%)	54	50	46	43	48	51	57	55	54	49	50	54	51
Mean Dewpoint (°F)	36	38	43	51	60	66	71	70	65	54	45	39	53
Prevailing Wind Direction	NW	NW	NW	NW	ENE	ENE	SW	ENE	ENE	ENE	ENE	ENE	ENE
Prevailing Wind Speed (mph)	10	10	10	10	8	8	8	7	9	9	8	9	9
Maximum Wind Gust (mph)	58	61	99	67	82	54	64	71	61	52	52	56	99

Macon Regional Airport

Located very near the geographical center of Georgia, Macon is well situated to escape rigorous climatic extremes. The climate is a blend of the maritime and continental types. Rarely does either dominate for long unbroken periods. The prevailing northwesterly winds of winter and early spring are frequently superseded by southerly flows of warm, moist tropical air. The southern extremity of the Appalachians presents an effective barrier to the rapid flow of cold air in winter. In summertime the prevailing southerlies frequently give way to the drier westerly and northerly winds. In short, the climate is truly equable.

Severe storms occur occasionally in this locality. Tornadoes occur, about twice each year within the area covered by Bibb and adjacent counties. Thunderstorms occur on approximately two days out of five from June through August. Occasionally, thunderstorms are accompanied by severe squalls, but property damage from this cause has been heavy in only a few instances. As Macon is some 200 miles from both the Atlantic and the Gulf of Mexico, hurricanes offer no direct threat, and secondary effects are generally milder than those produced by the heavier thunderstorms. Property damage of a minor nature occurs occasionally due to gale force winds and heavy rainfall.

Snow occurs at some time during most winters, but amounts of snow are usually quite small. However, on rare occasions heavy snow does occur in this area.

Based on the 1951-1980 period, the average first occurrence of 32 degrees Fahrenheit in the fall is November 8 and the average last occurrence in the spring is March 17.

The National Weather Service Office is surrounded by predominantly flat terrain. Flanking the station on the west, a range of wooded hills about 300 feet in height runs in a general northwest-southeast direction. The nearest point of these hills is about two and a half miles to the southwest. Most of the countryside is well wooded, except for a few farms. Much of the outlying area is swampy, especially in the river and creek bottoms. Besides the swamps, the only bodies of water in the vicinity are the Ocmulgee River, Echeconnee Creek, and Tobesofkee Creek. These have little influence on the climate, except that when other conditions are favorable, they contribute to the formation of fog.

Macon Regional Airport *Bibb County*   Elevation: 351 ft.   Latitude: 32° 41' N   Longitude: 83° 39' W

	JAN	FEB	MAR	APR	MAY	JUN	JUL	AUG	SEP	OCT	NOV	DEC	YEAR
Mean Maximum Temp. (°F)	57.5	61.9	69.6	77.2	84.3	90.1	92.6	91.4	86.8	77.9	68.7	60.6	76.6
Mean Temp. (°F)	46.5	50.0	57.3	64.1	72.0	78.9	82.1	81.0	75.9	65.3	56.3	49.4	64.9
Mean Minimum Temp. (°F)	35.5	38.0	44.9	51.0	59.7	67.6	71.5	70.6	65.0	52.7	43.8	38.1	53.2
Extreme Maximum Temp. (°F)	80	85	90	96	96	105	108	105	102	94	85	82	108
Extreme Minimum Temp. (°F)	-6	9	14	29	40	46	58	57	44	28	16	7	-6
Days Maximum Temp. ≥ 90°F	0	0	0	1	6	17	23	22	12	1	0	0	82
Days Maximum Temp. ≤ 32°F	0	0	0	0	0	0	0	0	0	0	0	0	0
Days Minimum Temp. ≤ 32°F	13	9	3	0	0	0	0	0	0	0	5	11	41
Days Minimum Temp. ≤ 0°F	0	0	0	0	0	0	0	0	0	0	0	0	0
Heating Degree Days (base 65°F)	568	421	256	99	10	0	0	0	4	85	274	483	2,200
Cooling Degree Days (base 65°F)	1	4	23	75	239	432	547	507	323	102	20	5	2,278
Mean Precipitation (in.)	4.93	4.63	5.03	3.17	3.09	3.52	4.38	3.75	2.92	2.57	3.11	4.06	45.16
Maximum Precipitation (in.)	10.9	9.3	11.9	8.4	11.8	9.1	18.2	8.6	8.8	9.4	10.3	10.4	60.7
Minimum Precipitation (in.)	0.7	0.6	1.2	0.1	0.3	0.9	0.4	1.1	0.3	0	0.4	0.6	26.0
Maximum 24-hr. Precipitation (in.)	4.7	4.0	4.3	3.5	3.6	4.1	10.+	3.0	4.1	5.3	3.1	2.8	10.+
Days With ≥ 0.1" Precipitation	8	6	7	5	5	6	8	7	5	4	5	6	72
Days With ≥ 1.0" Precipitation	1	2	1	1	1	1	1	1	1	1	1	1	13
Mean Snowfall (in.)	0.3	0.8	0.1	0.0	trace	0.0	trace	0.0	0.0	0.0	trace	trace	1.2
Maximum Snowfall (in.)	4	17	3	0	0	0	0	0	0	0	trace	2	17
Maximum 24-hr. Snowfall (in.)	4	11	3	0	0	0	0	0	0	0	trace	1	11
Days With ≥ 1.0" Snow Depth	0	0	0	0	0	0	0	0	0	0	0	0	0
Thunderstorm Days	1	2	3	4	6	9	13	9	3	1	1	1	53
Foggy Days	14	12	14	11	15	15	17	21	21	16	14	15	185
Predominant Sky Cover	OVR	OVR	OVR	CLR	OVR	SCT	BRK	SCT	OVR	CLR	CLR	OVR	OVR
Mean Relative Humidity 7am (%)	83	83	84	85	86	86	89	91	92	89	87	84	87
Mean Relative Humidity 4pm (%)	52	48	46	42	46	51	55	54	54	48	47	52	50
Mean Dewpoint (°F)	36	37	43	50	59	66	70	70	65	53	44	38	53
Prevailing Wind Direction	NW	NW	WNW	WNW	WNW	WNW	WSW	NE	NE	NE	NW	NW	WNW
Prevailing Wind Speed (mph)	10	10	10	9	8	8	7	8	9	9	9	10	9
Maximum Wind Gust (mph)	59	87	74	64	71	59	63	54	44	45	58	59	87

Savannah Int'l Airport

Savannah is surrounded by flat terrain, low and marshy to the north and east, and rising to several feet above sea level to the west and south. About half the land to the west and south is cleared and the other half is wooded and swampy.

The area has a temperate climate, with a seasonal low temperature of 51 degrees in winter, 66 degrees in spring, 80 degrees in summer, and 66 degrees in autumn. The lowest temperatures are below 10 degrees and the highest temperatures are about 100 degrees.

The normal annual rainfall is about 49 inches. About half falls in the thunderstorm season of June 15 through September 15. The remainder, produced principally by squall-line and frontal showers, is spread over the other nine months with a minor peak in March. Considerable periods of fair, mild weather are experienced in October, November, April, and to a less extent, in May. Snow is a rarity and even a trace does not occur on an average of once a year. The heaviest snowfalls are under five inches. Severe tropical storms affect this area about once in ten years. Rainfall from these storms constitute the heaviest sustained precipitation. Accumulations exceeding 22 inches have occurred.

The present exposure of the thermometers gives readings more nearly commensurate with those of suburban street levels of Savannah than was the case of previous locations atop various buildings. During that time, especially on still, clear nights, temperatures near the ground and in lower inland areas were as much as 15 degrees lower than the official low temperature. Present differences on comparable nights range from three to eight degrees.

Sunshine is adequate at all seasons and seldom are there two or more days in succession without it. Sea and land-breeze effect is usually not felt in Savannah, though it is a daily feature on the nearby islands. Dry, continental air masses reach this area in summer mostly by sliding down the Atlantic coast and giving cooler northeast winds. Such masses reaching this area from the northwest or west in summer bring mostly clear skies and high temperatures.

Based on the 1951-1980 period, the average first occurrence of 32 degrees Fahrenheit in the fall is November 15 and the average last occurrence in the spring is March 10.

Savannah Int'l Airport *Chatham County*   Elevation: 45 ft.   Latitude: 32° 07' N   Longitude: 81° 12' W

	JAN	FEB	MAR	APR	MAY	JUN	JUL	AUG	SEP	OCT	NOV	DEC	YEAR
Mean Maximum Temp. (°F)	60.2	64.0	70.9	77.8	84.2	89.4	92.2	90.2	86.2	78.2	70.5	63.0	77.2
Mean Temp. (°F)	49.7	52.9	59.7	66.1	73.4	79.5	82.6	81.4	77.3	67.9	59.4	52.4	66.9
Mean Minimum Temp. (°F)	39.1	41.9	48.5	54.3	62.5	69.5	73.1	72.5	68.3	57.5	48.2	41.8	56.4
Extreme Maximum Temp. (°F)	83	86	91	95	98	104	105	102	98	97	86	83	105
Extreme Minimum Temp. (°F)	3	17	20	32	40	51	61	57	48	30	15	9	3
Days Maximum Temp. ≥ 90°F	0	0	0	1	5	15	23	19	8	1	0	0	72
Days Maximum Temp. ≤ 32°F	0	0	0	0	0	0	0	0	0	0	0	0	0
Days Minimum Temp. ≤ 32°F	9	6	1	0	0	0	0	0	0	0	2	6	24
Days Minimum Temp. ≤ 0°F	0	0	0	0	0	0	0	0	0	0	0	0	0
Heating Degree Days (base 65°F)	473	346	198	68	6	0	0	0	1	52	203	395	1,742
Cooling Degree Days (base 65°F)	4	13	38	107	277	456	575	524	372	153	42	11	2,572
Mean Precipitation (in.)	3.96	2.94	3.78	3.25	3.75	5.51	6.12	7.41	5.03	3.19	2.29	2.83	50.06
Maximum Precipitation (in.)	9.0	7.9	9.6	10.6	10.1	14.4	20.1	17.0	13.5	19.8	5.3	5.8	73.2
Minimum Precipitation (in.)	0.4	0.3	0.2	0.4	0.5	0.8	1.3	1.0	0.3	trace	0.1	0.1	32.8
Maximum 24-hr. Precipitation (in.)	3.3	3.5	3.6	5.6	4.2	3.8	3.8	7.0	6.8	7.1	3.6	3.3	7.1
Days With ≥ 0.1" Precipitation	7	5	6	4	5	8	8	9	7	4	4	5	72
Days With ≥ 1.0" Precipitation	1	1	1	1	1	2	2	2	1	1	1	1	15
Mean Snowfall (in.)	trace	0.2	trace	0.0	0.0	trace	0.0	0.0	0.0	0.0	0.0	0.1	0.3
Maximum Snowfall (in.)	2	4	1	0	0	0	0	0	0	0	trace	4	5
Maximum 24-hr. Snowfall (in.)	1	4	1	0	0	0	0	0	0	0	trace	3	4
Days With ≥ 1.0" Snow Depth	0	0	0	0	0	0	0	0	0	0	0	0	0
Thunderstorm Days	1	1	3	4	7	10	15	12	6	2	1	1	63
Foggy Days	14	12	14	12	15	15	15	18	18	15	14	13	173
Predominant Sky Cover	OVR	OVR	OVR	CLR	OVR	SCT	SCT	SCT	OVR	CLR	CLR	OVR	OVR
Mean Relative Humidity 7am (%)	83	82	83	84	85	87	88	91	91	88	86	83	86
Mean Relative Humidity 4pm (%)	53	50	49	48	52	58	61	63	62	55	53	54	55
Mean Dewpoint (°F)	38	40	46	53	61	68	72	72	68	57	48	41	55
Prevailing Wind Direction	WNW	WNW	WNW	WSW	SSE	SW	SW	SW	NE	NE	NE	WNW	NE
Prevailing Wind Speed (mph)	12	12	12	9	9	8	7	7	9	9	9	10	9
Maximum Wind Gust (mph)	60	59	68	74	68	81	64	58	68	61	62	54	81

Albany 3 SE *Dougherty County*   Elevation: 177 ft.   Latitude: 31° 32' N   Longitude: 84° 08' W

	JAN	FEB	MAR	APR	MAY	JUN	JUL	AUG	SEP	OCT	NOV	DEC	YEAR
Mean Maximum Temp. (°F)	59.6	64.1	71.6	78.5	85.2	90.1	92.5	91.8	88.4	80.1	71.0	63.3	78.0
Mean Temp. (°F)	47.2	50.8	58.1	64.3	72.1	78.4	81.4	80.9	76.7	66.4	57.4	50.6	65.4
Mean Minimum Temp. (°F)	34.8	37.6	44.5	50.1	58.9	66.6	70.2	69.9	65.1	52.7	43.7	37.8	52.7
Extreme Maximum Temp. (°F)	82	86	91	97	98	104	107	104	102	98	90	85	107
Extreme Minimum Temp. (°F)	1	14	10	27	39	46	58	56	44	28	14	8	1
Days Maximum Temp. ≥ 90°F	0	0	0	1	7	18	23	23	15	2	0	0	89
Days Maximum Temp. ≤ 32°F	0	0	0	0	0	0	0	0	0	0	0	0	0
Days Minimum Temp. ≤ 32°F	15	10	4	1	0	0	0	0	0	0	5	11	46
Days Minimum Temp. ≤ 0°F	0	0	0	0	0	0	0	0	0	0	0	0	0
Heating Degree Days (base 65°F)	548	402	238	96	9	0	0	0	3	72	251	453	2,072
Cooling Degree Days (base 65°F)	2	11	31	78	237	418	531	510	361	130	29	10	2,348
Mean Precipitation (in.)	6.08	4.86	5.84	3.48	4.05	4.94	6.22	4.55	3.54	2.57	3.66	3.82	53.61
Days With ≥ 0.1" Precipitation	8	6	7	5	6	8	9	7	5	4	5	6	76
Days With ≥ 1.0" Precipitation	2	2	2	1	1	2	2	1	1	1	1	1	17
Mean Snowfall (in.)	trace	0.1	0.0	0.0	0.0	0.0	0.0	0.0	0.0	0.0	0.0	0.0	0.1
Days With ≥ 1.0" Snow Depth	0	0	0	0	0	0	0	0	0	0	0	0	0

Alma Bacon County Airport *Bacon County*   Elevation: 196 ft.   Latitude: 31° 32' N   Longitude: 82° 31' W

	JAN	FEB	MAR	APR	MAY	JUN	JUL	AUG	SEP	OCT	NOV	DEC	YEAR
Mean Maximum Temp. (°F)	61.3	65.2	72.1	78.8	85.0	89.7	91.9	90.9	86.9	79.1	71.3	64.0	78.0
Mean Temp. (°F)	51.0	54.1	60.4	66.4	73.3	79.0	81.7	80.9	77.1	68.1	60.0	53.4	67.1
Mean Minimum Temp. (°F)	40.6	42.9	48.6	53.9	61.5	68.3	71.4	70.9	67.3	57.1	48.8	42.8	56.2
Extreme Maximum Temp. (°F)	83	86	88	96	97	104	103	105	101	95	87	83	105
Extreme Minimum Temp. (°F)	-1	13	18	31	40	47	60	58	42	34	16	9	-1
Days Maximum Temp. ≥ 90°F	0	0	0	1	6	16	23	21	11	1	0	0	79
Days Maximum Temp. ≤ 32°F	0	0	0	0	0	0	0	0	0	0	0	0	0
Days Minimum Temp. ≤ 32°F	9	5	2	0	0	0	0	0	0	0	2	6	24
Days Minimum Temp. ≤ 0°F	0	0	0	0	0	0	0	0	0	0	0	0	0
Heating Degree Days (base 65°F)	437	317	179	61	4	0	0	0	1	47	187	366	1,599
Cooling Degree Days (base 65°F)	7	17	41	109	273	439	538	509	366	157	45	14	2,515
Mean Precipitation (in.)	4.80	4.02	4.85	3.09	3.21	5.41	5.93	5.75	3.19	2.84	2.51	3.71	49.31
Days With ≥ 0.1" Precipitation	8	6	6	4	5	8	9	8	6	4	4	6	74
Days With ≥ 1.0" Precipitation	2	1	2	1	1	2	2	1	1	1	1	1	16
Mean Snowfall (in.)	trace	0.2	0.0	trace	0.0	0.0	0.0	0.0	0.0	0.0	0.0	trace	0.2
Days With ≥ 1.0" Snow Depth	0	0	0	0	0	0	0	0	0	0	0	0	0

Appling 2 NW *Columbia County*   Elevation: 367 ft.   Latitude: 33° 34' N   Longitude: 82° 20' W

	JAN	FEB	MAR	APR	MAY	JUN	JUL	AUG	SEP	OCT	NOV	DEC	YEAR
Mean Maximum Temp. (°F)	54.3	59.3	67.1	75.1	82.2	88.4	91.5	89.9	85.2	75.7	66.5	57.6	74.4
Mean Temp. (°F)	42.5	46.1	53.5	60.7	68.6	76.0	79.5	78.2	72.8	61.7	52.9	45.4	61.5
Mean Minimum Temp. (°F)	30.7	32.8	39.8	46.3	54.9	63.5	67.5	66.6	60.5	47.6	39.2	33.0	48.5
Extreme Maximum Temp. (°F)	81	83	88	93	94	103	106	105	102	93	88	80	106
Extreme Minimum Temp. (°F)	-4	6	6	22	32	40	52	53	38	25	13	1	-4
Days Maximum Temp. ≥ 90°F	0	0	0	1	3	13	21	17	9	1	0	0	65
Days Maximum Temp. ≤ 32°F	1	0	0	0	0	0	0	0	0	0	0	0	1
Days Minimum Temp. ≤ 32°F	19	15	8	2	0	0	0	0	0	2	9	16	71
Days Minimum Temp. ≤ 0°F	0	0	0	0	0	0	0	0	0	0	0	0	0
Heating Degree Days (base 65°F)	691	528	360	166	35	2	0	0	12	144	366	603	2,907
Cooling Degree Days (base 65°F)	0	1	10	41	152	342	472	419	244	46	7	1	1,735
Mean Precipitation (in.)	4.80	4.28	5.03	3.36	3.56	4.03	4.17	3.97	3.62	3.66	3.17	3.86	47.51
Days With ≥ 0.1" Precipitation	8	6	7	5	6	6	7	6	5	4	5	7	72
Days With ≥ 1.0" Precipitation	2	1	2	1	1	1	1	1	1	1	1	1	14
Mean Snowfall (in.)	0.1	0.4	0.2	0.0	0.0	0.0	0.0	0.0	0.0	0.0	0.0	trace	0.7
Days With ≥ 1.0" Snow Depth	0	0	0	0	0	0	0	0	0	0	0	0	0

Ashburn 3 ENE *Turner County*   Elevation: 433 ft.   Latitude: 31° 43' N   Longitude: 83° 37' W

	JAN	FEB	MAR	APR	MAY	JUN	JUL	AUG	SEP	OCT	NOV	DEC	YEAR
Mean Maximum Temp. (°F)	57.6	*61.4*	69.5	76.6	83.3	88.6	90.6	90.0	86.5	78.1	69.0	61.4	*76.0*
Mean Temp. (°F)	47.2	*50.5*	58.1	65.0	72.3	78.2	80.7	79.9	76.0	66.2	57.4	50.6	*65.2*
Mean Minimum Temp. (°F)	36.8	*39.6*	46.8	53.4	61.3	67.7	70.8	69.8	65.4	54.2	45.7	39.8	*54.3*
Extreme Maximum Temp. (°F)	79	87	87	94	96	102	102	101	99	97	86	81	102
Extreme Minimum Temp. (°F)	1	12	16	31	44	51	60	57	45	31	17	8	1
Days Maximum Temp. ≥ 90°F	0	0	0	1	4	14	20	18	9	1	0	0	67
Days Maximum Temp. ≤ 32°F	0	0	0	0	0	0	0	0	0	0	0	0	0
Days Minimum Temp. ≤ 32°F	11	6	2	0	0	0	0	0	0	0	2	7	28
Days Minimum Temp. ≤ 0°F	0	0	0	0	0	0	0	0	0	0	0	0	0
Heating Degree Days (base 65°F)	545	*408*	233	85	8	0	0	0	3	69	245	446	*2,042*
Cooling Degree Days (base 65°F)	1	*5*	26	90	249	415	511	480	335	119	21	6	*2,258*
Mean Precipitation (in.)	5.36	4.56	5.15	3.28	3.62	4.78	4.66	4.44	3.45	2.53	3.38	3.55	48.76
Days With ≥ 0.1" Precipitation	7	6	7	5	5	7	8	7	5	4	5	5	71
Days With ≥ 1.0" Precipitation	2	1	2	1	1	2	1	1	1	1	1	1	15
Mean Snowfall (in.)	trace	0.1	trace	0.0	0.0	0.0	0.0	0.0	0.0	0.0	0.0	0.0	0.1
Days With ≥ 1.0" Snow Depth	0	0	0	0	0	0	0	0	0	0	0	0	0

Blairsville Exp. Station *Union County*   Elevation: 1,916 ft.   Latitude: 34° 51' N   Longitude: 83° 57' W

	JAN	FEB	MAR	APR	MAY	JUN	JUL	AUG	SEP	OCT	NOV	DEC	YEAR
Mean Maximum Temp. (°F)	47.5	51.6	59.2	68.0	74.9	81.1	84.6	83.5	78.5	69.4	60.0	51.8	67.5
Mean Temp. (°F)	36.0	39.1	46.5	54.1	62.0	69.2	73.2	72.2	66.7	55.7	47.1	39.9	55.2
Mean Minimum Temp. (°F)	24.4	26.6	33.8	40.2	49.1	57.3	61.7	60.7	54.8	42.0	34.2	27.9	42.7
Extreme Maximum Temp. (°F)	74	76	82	88	88	95	97	97	94	85	79	73	97
Extreme Minimum Temp. (°F)	-16	-8	-5	16	26	35	47	45	32	20	5	-8	-16
Days Maximum Temp. ≥ 90°F	0	0	0	0	0	1	5	2	0	0	0	0	8
Days Maximum Temp. ≤ 32°F	3	2	0	0	0	0	0	0	0	0	0	1	6
Days Minimum Temp. ≤ 32°F	23	20	15	7	1	0	0	0	0	7	15	21	109
Days Minimum Temp. ≤ 0°F	1	0	0	0	0	0	0	0	0	0	0	0	1
Heating Degree Days (base 65°F)	892	724	566	326	126	18	1	1	48	289	530	772	4,293
Cooling Degree Days (base 65°F)	0	0	1	5	45	166	280	235	102	10	0	0	844
Mean Precipitation (in.)	5.82	5.15	6.40	4.55	4.80	4.67	4.56	4.51	4.29	4.00	4.82	4.76	58.33
Days With ≥ 0.1" Precipitation	9	8	9	8	8	8	8	8	7	6	7	8	94
Days With ≥ 1.0" Precipitation	2	2	2	1	1	1	1	1	1	1	2	1	16
Mean Snowfall (in.)	*1.5*	*0.7*	1.5	0.4	0.0	0.0	0.0	0.0	0.0	trace	trace	0.4	*4.5*
Days With ≥ 1.0" Snow Depth	*0*	0	*0*	0	0	0	0	0	0	0	0	0	*0*

Brooklet 1 W *Bulloch County*   Elevation: 187 ft.   Latitude: 32° 22' N   Longitude: 81° 41' W

	JAN	FEB	MAR	APR	MAY	JUN	JUL	AUG	SEP	OCT	NOV	DEC	YEAR
Mean Maximum Temp. (°F)	59.3	63.6	70.6	78.0	84.4	89.5	92.2	90.1	85.8	77.9	70.0	62.4	77.0
Mean Temp. (°F)	48.8	52.2	58.8	65.6	72.7	78.5	81.5	80.0	75.8	66.7	58.5	51.6	65.9
Mean Minimum Temp. (°F)	38.3	40.8	47.0	53.2	61.0	67.5	70.8	69.8	65.7	55.4	46.8	40.8	54.7
Extreme Maximum Temp. (°F)	82	85	90	95	98	104	109	104	100	93	88	82	109
Extreme Minimum Temp. (°F)	1	15	15	31	43	49	58	56	43	29	15	7	1
Days Maximum Temp. ≥ 90°F	0	0	0	1	6	15	23	18	9	1	0	0	73
Days Maximum Temp. ≤ 32°F	0	0	0	0	0	0	0	0	0	0	0	0	0
Days Minimum Temp. ≤ 32°F	10	6	2	0	0	0	0	0	0	0	3	7	28
Days Minimum Temp. ≤ 0°F	0	0	0	0	0	0	0	0	0	0	0	0	0
Heating Degree Days (base 65°F)	499	364	217	73	5	0	0	0	2	63	222	418	1,863
Cooling Degree Days (base 65°F)	3	11	29	96	259	433	542	484	328	128	32	9	2,354
Mean Precipitation (in.)	4.51	3.75	4.09	2.91	3.73	4.88	4.80	6.28	3.86	2.70	2.74	3.32	47.57
Days With ≥ 0.1" Precipitation	8	6	7	5	7	8	8	8	6	4	4	5	76
Days With ≥ 1.0" Precipitation	1	1	1	1	1	2	1	2	1	1	1	1	14
Mean Snowfall (in.)	0.2	0.2	0.0	0.0	0.0	0.0	0.0	0.0	0.0	0.0	0.0	0.1	0.5
Days With ≥ 1.0" Snow Depth	0	0	0	0	0	0	0	0	0	0	0	0	0

Brunswick Malcolm McKinnon Arpt. *Glynn County*   Elevation: 13 ft.   Latitude: 31° 09' N   Longitude: 81° 23' W

	JAN	FEB	MAR	APR	MAY	JUN	JUL	AUG	SEP	OCT	NOV	DEC	YEAR
Mean Maximum Temp. (°F)	60.0	62.5	68.8	75.1	81.4	86.9	90.1	88.3	84.8	77.2	69.8	62.9	75.7
Mean Temp. (°F)	51.4	53.9	60.3	66.6	73.9	79.7	82.6	81.5	78.3	69.7	61.5	54.4	67.8
Mean Minimum Temp. (°F)	42.6	45.2	51.8	58.1	66.3	72.5	75.1	74.6	71.7	62.2	53.1	45.9	59.9
Extreme Maximum Temp. (°F)	83	83	88	94	96	103	104	100	97	95	85	84	104
Extreme Minimum Temp. (°F)	6	16	22	37	47	52	66	64	52	40	24	12	6
Days Maximum Temp. ≥ 90°F	0	0	0	0	2	9	17	10	4	0	0	0	42
Days Maximum Temp. ≤ 32°F	0	0	0	0	0	0	0	0	0	0	0	0	0
Days Minimum Temp. ≤ 32°F	6	3	0	0	0	0	0	0	0	0	0	3	12
Days Minimum Temp. ≤ 0°F	0	0	0	0	0	0	0	0	0	0	0	0	0
Heating Degree Days (base 65°F)	422	315	175	55	3	0	0	0	0	30	155	335	1,490
Cooling Degree Days (base 65°F)	3	8	32	105	286	456	564	524	397	188	56	14	2,633
Mean Precipitation (in.)	3.82	3.61	3.95	2.75	2.82	5.05	4.85	6.28	5.89	4.08	2.50	2.85	48.45
Days With ≥ 0.1" Precipitation	6	5	5	4	5	7	8	9	8	4	4	5	70
Days With ≥ 1.0" Precipitation	1	1	1	1	1	2	1	2	2	1	1	1	15
Mean Snowfall (in.)	trace	trace	trace	0.0	0.0	0.0	0.0	0.0	0.0	0.0	0.0	0.1	0.1
Days With ≥ 1.0" Snow Depth	0	0	0	0	0	0	0	0	0	0	0	0	0

Calhoun Exp. Station *Gordon County*   Elevation: 652 ft.   Latitude: 34° 29' N   Longitude: 84° 58' W

	JAN	FEB	MAR	APR	MAY	JUN	JUL	AUG	SEP	OCT	NOV	DEC	YEAR
Mean Maximum Temp. (°F)	49.8	55.4	63.8	72.8	79.7	86.9	90.1	88.8	83.1	73.1	62.7	53.8	71.7
Mean Temp. (°F)	39.1	43.3	51.5	59.1	67.0	74.6	78.4	77.3	71.3	59.6	50.4	42.8	59.5
Mean Minimum Temp. (°F)	28.4	31.0	39.1	45.4	54.4	62.3	66.6	65.8	59.4	46.1	38.0	31.7	47.4
Extreme Maximum Temp. (°F)	76	80	86	91	96	103	105	104	100	90	85	77	105
Extreme Minimum Temp. (°F)	-10	2	4	22	33	40	54	51	37	23	12	-2	-10
Days Maximum Temp. ≥ 90°F	0	0	0	0	1	9	17	14	5	0	0	0	46
Days Maximum Temp. ≤ 32°F	2	1	0	0	0	0	0	0	0	0	0	1	4
Days Minimum Temp. ≤ 32°F	20	16	9	3	0	0	0	0	0	3	10	18	79
Days Minimum Temp. ≤ 0°F	0	0	0	0	0	0	0	0	0	0	0	0	0
Heating Degree Days (base 65°F)	795	608	418	199	50	2	0	0	20	192	435	682	3,401
Cooling Degree Days (base 65°F)	0	0	5	24	119	303	435	390	198	31	3	1	1,509
Mean Precipitation (in.)	5.43	4.87	6.42	4.26	4.37	4.06	4.07	3.61	4.17	3.48	4.54	4.68	53.96
Days With ≥ 0.1" Precipitation	8	6	9	6	7	7	7	6	6	5	7	7	81
Days With ≥ 1.0" Precipitation	1	1	2	1	1	1	1	1	1	1	2	1	14
Mean Snowfall (in.)	0.6	*0.2*	0.7	0.2	0.0	0.0	0.0	0.0	*0.0*	0.0	0.0	trace	*1.7*
Days With ≥ 1.0" Snow Depth	1	0	0	0	0	0	0	*0*	0	0	0	0	*1*

Camilla 3 SE *Mitchell County*   Elevation: 173 ft.   Latitude: 31° 11' N   Longitude: 84° 12' W

	JAN	FEB	MAR	APR	MAY	JUN	JUL	AUG	SEP	OCT	NOV	DEC	YEAR
Mean Maximum Temp. (°F)	61.3	65.7	72.9	79.7	86.2	90.7	92.4	91.7	88.4	80.4	71.5	64.1	78.7
Mean Temp. (°F)	50.3	53.9	60.5	66.6	73.8	79.4	81.8	81.2	77.6	67.9	59.4	52.9	67.1
Mean Minimum Temp. (°F)	39.3	42.1	48.2	53.5	61.4	68.2	71.1	70.6	66.7	55.5	47.4	41.7	55.5
Extreme Maximum Temp. (°F)	83	87	90	95	100	103	107	103	100	98	90	85	107
Extreme Minimum Temp. (°F)	2	12	17	33	40	49	58	60	46	31	15	10	2
Days Maximum Temp. ≥ 90°F	0	0	0	2	8	18	24	23	14	2	0	0	91
Days Maximum Temp. ≤ 32°F	0	0	0	0	0	0	0	0	0	0	0	0	0
Days Minimum Temp. ≤ 32°F	9	6	2	0	0	0	0	0	0	0	3	8	28
Days Minimum Temp. ≤ 0°F	0	0	0	0	0	0	0	0	0	0	0	0	0
Heating Degree Days (base 65°F)	453	319	177	59	4	0	0	0	1	50	200	381	1,644
Cooling Degree Days (base 65°F)	4	15	44	110	291	450	538	514	375	155	43	12	2,551
Mean Precipitation (in.)	5.86	4.94	6.19	3.86	3.77	5.16	5.73	4.59	3.39	2.50	3.24	3.92	53.15
Days With ≥ 0.1" Precipitation	8	6	7	5	5	7	9	7	5	4	5	6	74
Days With ≥ 1.0" Precipitation	2	2	2	1	1	2	2	1	1	1	1	1	17
Mean Snowfall (in.)	trace	0.1	0.0	0.0	0.0	0.0	0.0	0.0	0.0	0.0	0.0	0.0	0.1
Days With ≥ 1.0" Snow Depth	0	0	0	0	0	0	0	0	0	0	0	0	0

Carrollton *Carroll County*   Elevation: 994 ft.   Latitude: 33° 36' N   Longitude: 85° 05' W

	JAN	FEB	MAR	APR	MAY	JUN	JUL	AUG	SEP	OCT	NOV	DEC	YEAR
Mean Maximum Temp. (°F)	53.1	57.9	66.4	74.3	80.5	86.2	88.9	87.8	82.8	73.8	64.9	56.1	72.7
Mean Temp. (°F)	42.0	45.8	53.2	60.3	67.7	74.3	77.9	76.8	71.4	60.7	52.5	44.8	60.6
Mean Minimum Temp. (°F)	30.9	33.5	40.0	46.2	54.8	62.3	66.7	65.7	59.9	47.6	40.0	33.5	48.4
Extreme Maximum Temp. (°F)	78	79	86	90	94	100	103	102	96	88	86	81	103
Extreme Minimum Temp. (°F)	-9	4	9	24	30	36	47	53	38	26	11	3	-9
Days Maximum Temp. ≥ 90°F	0	0	0	0	1	7	14	11	4	0	0	0	37
Days Maximum Temp. ≤ 32°F	1	0	0	0	0	0	0	0	0	0	0	1	1
Days Minimum Temp. ≤ 32°F	17	14	7	2	0	0	0	0	0	1	7	15	63
Days Minimum Temp. ≤ 0°F	0	0	0	0	0	0	0	0	0	0	0	0	0
Heating Degree Days (base 65°F)	695	537	365	164	33	2	0	0	15	162	371	621	2,965
Cooling Degree Days (base 65°F)	0	0	6	29	129	299	416	377	206	37	3	2	1,504
Mean Precipitation (in.)	5.46	5.08	6.22	4.39	4.34	4.04	4.74	3.75	3.14	3.59	4.36	4.50	53.61
Days With ≥ 0.1" Precipitation	8	7	8	6	6	7	7	6	5	4	6	7	77
Days With ≥ 1.0" Precipitation	2	2	2	1	1	1	1	1	1	1	1	1	15
Mean Snowfall (in.)	0.2	trace	0.0	0.0	0.0	0.0	0.0	0.0	0.0	0.0	0.0	trace	0.2
Days With ≥ 1.0" Snow Depth	0	0	0	0	0	0	0	0	0	0	0	0	0

Cartersville *Bartow County*   Elevation: 718 ft.   Latitude: 34° 14' N   Longitude: 84° 47' W

	JAN	FEB	MAR	APR	MAY	JUN	JUL	AUG	SEP	OCT	NOV	DEC	YEAR
Mean Maximum Temp. (°F)	51.2	56.9	65.8	74.0	80.1	86.4	89.4	88.1	83.0	73.5	63.2	54.5	72.2
Mean Temp. (°F)	41.5	45.5	53.4	60.5	68.0	74.9	78.4	77.4	72.2	61.3	52.0	44.7	60.8
Mean Minimum Temp. (°F)	31.8	34.1	40.8	47.0	55.8	63.4	67.3	66.7	61.3	49.0	40.7	34.7	49.4
Extreme Maximum Temp. (°F)	77	83	86	93	96	100	104	103	100	91	83	78	104
Extreme Minimum Temp. (°F)	-9	1	10	22	33	40	51	52	34	24	10	-3	-9
Days Maximum Temp. ≥ 90°F	0	0	0	0	1	8	16	12	4	0	0	0	41
Days Maximum Temp. ≤ 32°F	1	0	0	0	0	0	0	0	0	0	0	0	1
Days Minimum Temp. ≤ 32°F	17	13	7	3	0	0	0	0	0	2	9	14	65
Days Minimum Temp. ≤ 0°F	0	0	0	0	0	0	0	0	0	0	0	0	0
Heating Degree Days (base 65°F)	722	545	363	169	40	1	0	0	15	155	390	625	3,025
Cooling Degree Days (base 65°F)	0	1	11	41	147	321	438	399	232	52	6	2	1,650
Mean Precipitation (in.)	3.81	4.06	5.31	4.02	3.25	3.11	3.65	3.04	3.19	2.57	3.26	3.72	42.99
Days With ≥ 0.1" Precipitation	6	5	6	5	5	5	6	5	4	3	5	5	60
Days With ≥ 1.0" Precipitation	1	2	2	1	1	1	1	1	1	1	1	1	14
Mean Snowfall (in.)	0.5	0.4	trace	trace	0.0	0.0	0.0	0.0	0.0	0.0	trace	0.2	1.1
Days With ≥ 1.0" Snow Depth	0	0	0	0	0	0	0	0	0	0	0	0	0

Cedartown 3 NE *Polk County*   Elevation: 784 ft.   Latitude: 34° 03' N   Longitude: 85° 15' W

	JAN	FEB	MAR	APR	MAY	JUN	JUL	AUG	SEP	OCT	NOV	DEC	YEAR
Mean Maximum Temp. (°F)	52.5	57.5	66.3	74.6	80.7	87.0	90.0	89.1	83.7	74.2	64.1	55.8	73.0
Mean Temp. (°F)	42.0	45.4	53.2	60.7	68.0	75.2	79.0	78.0	72.2	61.1	51.9	44.8	61.0
Mean Minimum Temp. (°F)	31.4	33.3	40.2	46.8	55.2	63.4	68.0	66.8	60.6	47.8	39.6	33.8	48.9
Extreme Maximum Temp. (°F)	78	83	88	92	95	99	104	104	99	91	86	79	104
Extreme Minimum Temp. (°F)	-9	3	5	24	33	41	52	45	30	18	12	0	-9
Days Maximum Temp. ≥ 90°F	0	0	0	0	2	10	18	14	6	0	0	0	50
Days Maximum Temp. ≤ 32°F	1	0	0	0	0	0	0	0	0	0	0	0	1
Days Minimum Temp. ≤ 32°F	17	14	8	2	0	0	0	0	0	2	9	15	67
Days Minimum Temp. ≤ 0°F	0	0	0	0	0	0	0	0	0	0	0	0	0
Heating Degree Days (base 65°F)	707	548	368	163	36	1	0	0	15	159	392	621	3,010
Cooling Degree Days (base 65°F)	0	1	11	41	141	324	455	413	228	46	4	2	1,666
Mean Precipitation (in.)	5.36	4.71	6.21	4.74	4.24	4.64	4.51	3.73	3.82	3.42	4.06	4.16	53.60
Days With ≥ 0.1" Precipitation	8	6	8	7	6	7	7	6	5	5	6	7	79
Days With ≥ 1.0" Precipitation	2	1	2	1	1	2	1	1	1	1	1	1	15
Mean Snowfall (in.)	0.9	0.6	0.7	0.2	0.0	0.0	0.0	0.0	0.0	0.0	0.0	0.2	2.6
Days With ≥ 1.0" Snow Depth	1	0	0	0	0	0	0	0	0	0	0	0	1

Clayton 1 SSW *Rabun County*   Elevation: 1,879 ft.   Latitude: 34° 52' N   Longitude: 83° 24' W

	JAN	FEB	MAR	APR	MAY	JUN	JUL	AUG	SEP	OCT	NOV	DEC	YEAR
Mean Maximum Temp. (°F)	50.4	54.8	62.4	70.7	76.6	82.4	85.3	84.2	79.6	71.2	62.0	53.7	69.4
Mean Temp. (°F)	39.1	42.2	49.0	56.2	63.3	70.1	73.8	72.9	67.9	57.8	49.0	41.9	56.9
Mean Minimum Temp. (°F)	27.7	29.5	35.6	41.6	50.0	57.8	62.3	61.6	56.0	44.3	36.1	30.1	44.4
Extreme Maximum Temp. (°F)	79	78	84	89	92	97	97	98	93	86	80	75	98
Extreme Minimum Temp. (°F)	-11	3	6	12	28	36	47	47	32	19	8	-4	-11
Days Maximum Temp. ≥ 90°F	0	0	0	0	0	2	6	3	1	0	0	0	12
Days Maximum Temp. ≤ 32°F	1	0	0	0	0	0	0	0	0	0	0	0	1
Days Minimum Temp. ≤ 32°F	21	18	12	5	1	0	0	0	0	3	12	19	91
Days Minimum Temp. ≤ 0°F	0	0	0	0	0	0	0	0	0	0	0	0	0
Heating Degree Days (base 65°F)	798	639	489	266	94	11	1	1	34	230	473	710	3,746
Cooling Degree Days (base 65°F)	0	0	0	8	51	177	296	260	125	14	0	0	931
Mean Precipitation (in.)	7.29	6.36	7.39	5.05	6.79	5.77	5.43	6.17	5.53	5.35	6.21	6.44	73.78
Days With ≥ 0.1" Precipitation	9	8	9	7	9	8	8	8	7	6	8	8	95
Days With ≥ 1.0" Precipitation	2	2	3	2	2	2	2	2	2	2	2	2	25
Mean Snowfall (in.)	1.2	1.1	1.0	trace	0.0	0.0	0.0	0.0	0.0	0.0	trace	0.3	3.6
Days With ≥ 1.0" Snow Depth	1	0	0	0	0	0	0	0	0	0	0	0	1

Commerce 4 NNW *Jackson County*   Elevation: 748 ft.   Latitude: 34° 16' N   Longitude: 83° 29' W

	JAN	FEB	MAR	APR	MAY	JUN	JUL	AUG	SEP	OCT	NOV	DEC	YEAR
Mean Maximum Temp. (°F)	51.7	56.6	64.8	73.8	80.0	86.7	90.0	88.5	83.1	73.3	63.6	55.7	72.3
Mean Temp. (°F)	41.1	44.7	52.3	60.2	67.4	75.2	78.8	77.5	72.0	60.7	51.6	44.5	60.5
Mean Minimum Temp. (°F)	30.4	32.9	39.8	46.7	54.7	63.4	67.4	66.3	60.7	47.9	39.4	33.1	48.6
Extreme Maximum Temp. (°F)	78	80	88	92	95	102	105	105	97	90	84	79	105
Extreme Minimum Temp. (°F)	-5	6	11	25	34	43	55	52	34	26	11	0	-5
Days Maximum Temp. ≥ 90°F	0	0	0	0	2	9	18	13	5	0	0	0	47
Days Maximum Temp. ≤ 32°F	1	0	0	0	0	0	0	0	0	0	0	0	1
Days Minimum Temp. ≤ 32°F	18	14	8	2	0	0	0	0	0	1	9	16	68
Days Minimum Temp. ≤ 0°F	0	0	0	0	0	0	0	0	0	0	0	0	0
Heating Degree Days (base 65°F)	734	568	389	172	43	2	0	0	14	164	400	629	3,115
Cooling Degree Days (base 65°F)	0	0	5	35	129	323	454	403	219	41	3	1	1,613
Mean Precipitation (in.)	5.41	4.86	5.71	3.62	4.30	4.16	4.06	3.88	3.79	4.15	4.17	4.18	52.29
Days With ≥ 0.1" Precipitation	8	7	9	6	6	7	7	6	6	5	6	7	80
Days With ≥ 1.0" Precipitation	2	2	2	1	1	1	1	1	1	1	1	1	15
Mean Snowfall (in.)	0.7	0.2	0.2	0.0	0.0	0.0	0.0	0.0	0.0	0.0	trace	0.1	1.2
Days With ≥ 1.0" Snow Depth	0	0	0	0	0	0	0	0	0	0	0	0	0

Cordele *Crisp County*   Elevation: 305 ft.   Latitude: 31° 59' N   Longitude: 83° 47' W

	JAN	FEB	MAR	APR	MAY	JUN	JUL	AUG	SEP	OCT	NOV	DEC	YEAR
Mean Maximum Temp. (°F)	59.6	64.3	72.4	80.0	86.8	91.8	94.2	92.7	88.5	79.8	70.5	62.5	78.6
Mean Temp. (°F)	48.8	52.5	59.8	66.6	74.1	80.1	82.9	81.7	77.2	67.1	58.6	51.5	66.7
Mean Minimum Temp. (°F)	37.9	40.5	46.9	53.1	61.4	68.3	71.5	70.6	66.0	54.4	46.7	40.5	54.8
Extreme Maximum Temp. (°F)	80	84	90	96	98	106	104	104	101	96	87	82	106
Extreme Minimum Temp. (°F)	-3	13	15	30	40	47	59	56	45	29	23	8	-3
Days Maximum Temp. ≥ 90°F	0	0	0	2	9	21	27	25	15	1	0	0	100
Days Maximum Temp. ≤ 32°F	0	0	0	0	0	0	0	0	0	0	0	0	0
Days Minimum Temp. ≤ 32°F	11	7	2	0	0	0	0	0	0	0	3	8	31
Days Minimum Temp. ≤ 0°F	0	0	0	0	0	0	0	0	0	0	0	0	0
Heating Degree Days (base 65°F)	499	357	197	63	3	0	0	0	2	59	218	422	1,820
Cooling Degree Days (base 65°F)	4	11	40	120	306	481	586	537	378	145	35	10	2,653
Mean Precipitation (in.)	5.04	4.41	5.10	3.26	3.33	4.14	4.77	3.56	3.49	2.19	3.29	3.79	46.37
Days With ≥ 0.1" Precipitation	7	6	7	5	6	7	8	7	5	3	5	5	71
Days With ≥ 1.0" Precipitation	2	1	2	1	1	1	1	1	1	1	1	1	14
Mean Snowfall (in.)	0.0	0.1	0.0	0.0	0.0	0.0	0.0	0.0	0.0	0.0	0.0	0.0	0.1
Days With ≥ 1.0" Snow Depth	0	0	0	0	0	0	0	0	0	0	0	0	0

Cornelia *Habersham County*   Elevation: 1,469 ft.   Latitude: 34° 31' N   Longitude: 83° 32' W

	JAN	FEB	MAR	APR	MAY	JUN	JUL	AUG	SEP	OCT	NOV	DEC	YEAR
Mean Maximum Temp. (°F)	49.0	53.8	62.1	70.4	76.4	82.7	85.9	84.3	79.1	69.9	60.3	52.1	68.8
Mean Temp. (°F)	39.1	42.8	50.2	57.6	64.7	71.8	75.6	74.2	68.8	58.3	49.4	42.2	57.9
Mean Minimum Temp. (°F)	29.1	31.8	38.3	44.8	53.0	60.9	65.2	64.2	58.5	46.7	38.5	32.3	46.9
Extreme Maximum Temp. (°F)	77	77	85	90	91	100	101	99	93	87	83	76	101
Extreme Minimum Temp. (°F)	-10	3	5	18	29	39	51	51	35	24	7	-1	-10
Days Maximum Temp. ≥ 90°F	0	0	0	0	0	3	9	5	1	0	0	0	18
Days Maximum Temp. ≤ 32°F	1	1	0	0	0	0	0	0	0	0	0	1	3
Days Minimum Temp. ≤ 32°F	20	15	10	3	0	0	0	0	0	2	10	17	77
Days Minimum Temp. ≤ 0°F	0	0	0	0	0	0	0	0	0	0	0	0	0
Heating Degree Days (base 65°F)	798	620	453	232	75	7	1	1	29	218	462	699	3,595
Cooling Degree Days (base 65°F)	0	0	2	19	82	238	358	305	152	20	1	0	1,177
Mean Precipitation (in.)	6.17	5.54	6.48	4.31	4.99	4.48	4.93	5.12	4.12	4.77	4.57	4.88	60.36
Days With ≥ 0.1" Precipitation	8	7	8	6	8	7	7	7	6	5	6	8	83
Days With ≥ 1.0" Precipitation	2	2	2	1	1	1	1	1	1	2	2	1	17
Mean Snowfall (in.)	0.4	trace	0.3	0.0	0.0	0.0	0.0	0.0	0.0	0.0	0.0	trace	0.7
Days With ≥ 1.0" Snow Depth	0	0	0	0	0	0	0	0	0	0	0	0	0

Covington *Newton County*   Elevation: 767 ft.   Latitude: 33° 36' N   Longitude: 83° 53' W

	JAN	FEB	MAR	APR	MAY	JUN	JUL	AUG	SEP	OCT	NOV	DEC	YEAR
Mean Maximum Temp. (°F)	52.4	58.0	66.7	74.4	81.2	87.2	90.0	88.3	83.4	73.4	63.8	55.4	72.8
Mean Temp. (°F)	42.4	46.4	54.5	61.4	69.2	76.0	79.3	78.1	73.0	62.0	52.8	45.4	61.7
Mean Minimum Temp. (°F)	32.5	34.8	42.3	48.3	57.2	64.9	68.6	67.9	62.6	50.6	41.7	35.3	50.5
Extreme Maximum Temp. (°F)	80	81	87	95	94	102	104	105	99	91	87	79	105
Extreme Minimum Temp. (°F)	-7	9	12	26	35	44	55	55	41	26	14	1	-7
Days Maximum Temp. ≥ 90°F	0	0	0	0	2	10	17	13	6	0	0	0	48
Days Maximum Temp. ≤ 32°F	1	0	0	0	0	0	0	0	0	0	0	0	1
Days Minimum Temp. ≤ 32°F	16	12	5	1	0	0	0	0	0	0	7	13	54
Days Minimum Temp. ≤ 0°F	0	0	0	0	0	0	0	0	0	0	0	0	0
Heating Degree Days (base 65°F)	693	520	329	149	26	1	0	0	11	137	368	603	2,837
Cooling Degree Days (base 65°F)	0	1	11	44	169	353	471	421	250	54	7	1	1,782
Mean Precipitation (in.)	5.11	4.67	5.42	3.56	3.85	3.81	4.74	3.97	3.45	3.38	3.71	4.02	49.69
Days With ≥ 0.1" Precipitation	8	7	7	5	6	6	7	7	6	4	6	7	76
Days With ≥ 1.0" Precipitation	1	2	2	1	1	1	1	1	1	1	1	1	14
Mean Snowfall (in.)	0.6	0.3	0.3	0.0	0.0	0.0	0.0	0.0	0.0	0.0	0.0	trace	1.2
Days With ≥ 1.0" Snow Depth	1	0	0	0	0	0	0	0	0	0	0	0	1

Cuthbert *Randolph County*   Elevation: 459 ft.   Latitude: 31° 46' N   Longitude: 84° 47' W

	JAN	FEB	MAR	APR	MAY	JUN	JUL	AUG	SEP	OCT	NOV	DEC	YEAR
Mean Maximum Temp. (°F)	59.5	64.0	71.9	79.1	85.5	90.5	92.3	91.4	87.7	78.9	69.9	62.4	77.8
Mean Temp. (°F)	48.9	52.4	59.4	66.1	73.4	79.3	81.8	81.0	77.0	67.2	58.6	51.9	66.4
Mean Minimum Temp. (°F)	38.3	40.7	46.9	53.1	61.3	68.2	71.1	70.5	66.3	55.6	47.0	41.1	55.0
Extreme Maximum Temp. (°F)	81	82	89	95	98	105	105	102	100	93	88	82	105
Extreme Minimum Temp. (°F)	-2	9	15	32	43	50	58	58	45	30	18	5	-2
Days Maximum Temp. ≥ 90°F	0	0	0	1	7	19	24	22	13	1	0	0	87
Days Maximum Temp. ≤ 32°F	0	0	0	0	0	0	0	0	0	0	0	0	0
Days Minimum Temp. ≤ 32°F	10	7	2	0	0	0	0	0	0	0	3	8	30
Days Minimum Temp. ≤ 0°F	0	0	0	0	0	0	0	0	0	0	0	0	0
Heating Degree Days (base 65°F)	496	357	201	65	3	0	0	0	2	57	216	411	1,808
Cooling Degree Days (base 65°F)	2	9	35	100	275	445	539	506	362	135	28	8	2,444
Mean Precipitation (in.)	5.59	5.15	5.74	3.85	3.84	4.68	6.48	3.60	3.45	2.74	3.78	4.11	53.01
Days With ≥ 0.1" Precipitation	8	6	8	5	6	7	8	7	5	4	5	6	75
Days With ≥ 1.0" Precipitation	2	2	2	1	1	1	2	1	1	1	1	1	16
Mean Snowfall (in.)	trace	0.3	trace	0.0	0.0	0.0	0.0	0.0	0.0	0.0	trace	trace	0.3
Days With ≥ 1.0" Snow Depth	0	0	0	0	0	0	0	0	0	0	0	0	0

Dahlonega 1 W *Lumpkin County*   Elevation: 1,259 ft.   Latitude: 34° 32' N   Longitude: 84° 00' W

	JAN	FEB	MAR	APR	MAY	JUN	JUL	AUG	SEP	OCT	NOV	DEC	YEAR
Mean Maximum Temp. (°F)	48.9	53.4	61.3	70.4	76.8	82.9	86.3	84.8	79.3	70.3	61.0	52.6	69.0
Mean Temp. (°F)	38.4	41.7	48.8	56.7	63.9	71.4	75.2	74.3	68.5	57.9	49.0	41.7	57.3
Mean Minimum Temp. (°F)	27.9	30.0	36.4	42.8	51.0	59.8	64.1	63.7	57.6	45.5	36.9	30.8	45.6
Extreme Maximum Temp. (°F)	76	78	85	92	90	98	101	99	94	88	82	74	101
Extreme Minimum Temp. (°F)	-12	2	5	24	30	41	51	49	34	25	12	-2	-12
Days Maximum Temp. ≥ 90°F	0	0	0	0	0	3	9	5	1	0	0	0	18
Days Maximum Temp. ≤ 32°F	2	1	0	0	0	0	0	0	0	0	0	1	4
Days Minimum Temp. ≤ 32°F	21	18	11	3	0	0	0	0	0	3	11	19	86
Days Minimum Temp. ≤ 0°F	0	0	0	0	0	0	0	0	0	0	0	0	0
Heating Degree Days (base 65°F)	817	652	495	258	88	8	1	0	32	229	475	715	3,770
Cooling Degree Days (base 65°F)	0	0	1	12	59	211	334	293	131	19	1	0	1,061
Mean Precipitation (in.)	6.92	5.85	6.94	4.86	5.55	4.45	5.24	4.89	4.51	4.74	5.23	5.66	64.84
Days With ≥ 0.1" Precipitation	9	8	8	7	8	7	8	7	6	5	7	8	88
Days With ≥ 1.0" Precipitation	2	2	2	1	2	1	1	1	2	2	2	2	20
Mean Snowfall (in.)	0.8	0.3	0.1	trace	0.0	0.0	0.0	0.0	0.0	0.0	trace	0.1	1.3
Days With ≥ 1.0" Snow Depth	*0*	0	0	0	0	0	0	0	0	0	0	0	*0*

Dallas 7 NE *Paulding County*   Elevation: 1,099 ft.   Latitude: 33° 59' N   Longitude: 84° 45' W

	JAN	FEB	MAR	APR	MAY	JUN	JUL	AUG	SEP	OCT	NOV	DEC	YEAR
Mean Maximum Temp. (°F)	49.9	55.1	63.5	72.4	79.2	85.7	89.2	88.0	82.9	72.9	63.0	53.9	71.3
Mean Temp. (°F)	39.2	43.1	50.7	58.9	66.5	73.9	77.8	76.7	70.9	59.8	50.7	42.8	59.2
Mean Minimum Temp. (°F)	28.4	30.8	38.1	45.2	53.8	62.1	66.4	65.4	59.0	46.6	38.3	31.6	47.1
Extreme Maximum Temp. (°F)	78	80	86	93	96	101	104	103	99	92	83	79	104
Extreme Minimum Temp. (°F)	-12	-2	8	21	34	40	52	53	34	25	9	-2	-12
Days Maximum Temp. ≥ 90°F	0	0	0	0	1	8	16	13	5	0	0	0	43
Days Maximum Temp. ≤ 32°F	2	1	0	0	0	0	0	0	0	0	0	1	4
Days Minimum Temp. ≤ 32°F	21	17	10	3	0	0	0	0	0	2	10	19	82
Days Minimum Temp. ≤ 0°F	0	0	0	0	0	0	0	0	0	0	0	0	0
Heating Degree Days (base 65°F)	794	614	442	211	59	4	0	0	23	190	426	684	3,447
Cooling Degree Days (base 65°F)	0	0	7	34	118	293	422	375	203	36	4	1	1,493
Mean Precipitation (in.)	5.74	5.08	6.03	4.48	4.35	4.35	4.65	4.33	3.41	3.63	4.05	4.39	54.49
Days With ≥ 0.1" Precipitation	9	7	8	7	7	7	7	7	5	5	6	8	83
Days With ≥ 1.0" Precipitation	2	2	2	1	1	1	2	1	1	1	1	1	16
Mean Snowfall (in.)	1.3	0.7	1.0	0.2	0.0	0.0	0.0	0.0	0.0	0.0	trace	0.2	3.4
Days With ≥ 1.0" Snow Depth	1	1	0	0	0	0	0	0	0	0	0	0	2

Dalton *Whitfield County*   Elevation: 698 ft.   Latitude: 34° 45' N   Longitude: 84° 57' W

	JAN	FEB	MAR	APR	MAY	JUN	JUL	AUG	SEP	OCT	NOV	DEC	YEAR
Mean Maximum Temp. (°F)	49.1	53.6	62.4	72.0	79.3	86.0	89.2	88.3	83.4	72.9	62.3	53.1	71.0
Mean Temp. (°F)	39.0	42.8	50.5	59.3	67.4	74.8	78.7	77.8	72.4	60.3	50.9	43.0	59.7
Mean Minimum Temp. (°F)	29.1	31.9	38.8	46.3	55.3	63.7	68.1	67.2	61.3	47.7	39.4	32.9	48.5
Extreme Maximum Temp. (°F)	75	79	87	91	94	103	102	103	99	90	83	76	103
Extreme Minimum Temp. (°F)	-10	3	7	25	33	42	55	53	38	24	14	-4	-10
Days Maximum Temp. ≥ 90°F	0	0	0	0	1	8	15	13	6	0	0	0	43
Days Maximum Temp. ≤ 32°F	2	1	0	0	0	0	0	0	0	0	0	1	4
Days Minimum Temp. ≤ 32°F	20	15	8	1	0	0	0	0	0	1	8	17	70
Days Minimum Temp. ≤ 0°F	0	0	0	0	0	0	0	0	0	0	0	0	0
Heating Degree Days (base 65°F)	800	622	447	198	49	2	0	0	15	177	419	673	3,402
Cooling Degree Days (base 65°F)	0	0	6	31	134	321	456	414	245	42	3	1	1,653
Mean Precipitation (in.)	5.73	4.93	6.31	4.43	4.33	4.42	4.83	3.69	4.92	3.54	4.66	4.83	56.62
Days With ≥ 0.1" Precipitation	9	7	9	7	7	7	8	6	6	5	7	7	85
Days With ≥ 1.0" Precipitation	2	2	2	1	1	1	2	1	2	1	1	2	18
Mean Snowfall (in.)	0.7	0.8	0.8	trace	0.0	0.0	0.0	0.0	0.0	trace	trace	trace	2.3
Days With ≥ 1.0" Snow Depth	*0*	0	0	0	0	0	0	0	0	0	0	0	*0*

Douglas *Coffee County*   Elevation: 223 ft.   Latitude: 31° 31' N   Longitude: 82° 51' W

	JAN	FEB	MAR	APR	MAY	JUN	JUL	AUG	SEP	OCT	NOV	DEC	YEAR
Mean Maximum Temp. (°F)	60.3	64.5	72.5	79.5	86.1	91.2	93.2	92.0	88.4	79.6	71.0	63.0	78.4
Mean Temp. (°F)	48.2	51.4	58.8	65.4	72.7	78.8	81.5	80.4	76.5	66.5	57.8	50.4	65.7
Mean Minimum Temp. (°F)	36.0	38.2	45.1	51.2	59.3	66.4	69.7	68.8	64.6	53.4	44.6	37.7	52.9
Extreme Maximum Temp. (°F)	83	87	90	97	99	104	106	105	103	96	87	83	106
Extreme Minimum Temp. (°F)	1	13	18	29	43	51	60	56	44	32	17	9	1
Days Maximum Temp. ≥ 90°F	0	0	0	2	10	21	26	24	15	2	0	0	100
Days Maximum Temp. ≤ 32°F	0	0	0	0	0	0	0	0	0	0	0	0	0
Days Minimum Temp. ≤ 32°F	13	9	2	0	0	0	0	0	0	0	4	11	39
Days Minimum Temp. ≤ 0°F	0	0	0	0	0	0	0	0	0	0	0	0	0
Heating Degree Days (base 65°F)	520	387	218	78	7	0	0	0	2	71	240	454	1,977
Cooling Degree Days (base 65°F)	3	10	31	95	268	433	533	491	345	128	29	7	2,373
Mean Precipitation (in.)	5.17	4.26	4.94	3.41	3.44	4.74	6.12	6.13	3.97	3.09	2.71	3.90	51.88
Days With ≥ 0.1" Precipitation	8	6	7	5	6	8	10	9	6	4	4	6	79
Days With ≥ 1.0" Precipitation	2	2	1	1	1	1	2	2	1	1	1	1	16
Mean Snowfall (in.)	trace	0.1	trace	0.0	0.0	0.0	0.0	0.0	0.0	0.0	0.0	0.1	0.2
Days With ≥ 1.0" Snow Depth	0	0	0	0	0	0	0	0	0	0	0	0	0

Dublin *Laurens County*   Elevation: 229 ft.   Latitude: 32° 33' N   Longitude: 82° 54' W

	JAN	FEB	MAR	APR	MAY	JUN	JUL	AUG	SEP	OCT	NOV	DEC	YEAR
Mean Maximum Temp. (°F)	57.4	62.0	70.2	78.1	85.4	91.2	94.0	92.3	87.7	78.5	69.3	60.8	77.2
Mean Temp. (°F)	45.6	48.9	56.5	63.5	71.5	78.3	81.6	80.3	75.2	64.7	55.6	48.4	64.2
Mean Minimum Temp. (°F)	33.8	35.8	42.8	48.9	57.6	65.4	69.2	68.1	62.8	50.9	42.0	35.9	51.1
Extreme Maximum Temp. (°F)	82	85	92	98	99	106	109	107	103	95	90	83	109
Extreme Minimum Temp. (°F)	0	11	14	28	38	45	56	56	40	28	15	5	0
Days Maximum Temp. ≥ 90°F	0	0	0	2	9	20	26	23	14	2	0	0	96
Days Maximum Temp. ≤ 32°F	0	0	0	0	0	0	0	0	0	0	0	0	0
Days Minimum Temp. ≤ 32°F	15	11	5	0	0	0	0	0	0	0	7	13	51
Days Minimum Temp. ≤ 0°F	0	0	0	0	0	0	0	0	0	0	0	0	0
Heating Degree Days (base 65°F)	596	451	277	111	13	0	0	0	5	95	293	514	2,355
Cooling Degree Days (base 65°F)	2	5	21	69	230	424	547	492	315	99	19	5	2,228
Mean Precipitation (in.)	5.10	4.39	4.86	3.18	2.91	4.25	4.64	4.90	3.32	2.82	3.39	3.79	47.55
Days With ≥ 0.1" Precipitation	8	6	7	5	5	7	8	7	5	4	5	6	73
Days With ≥ 1.0" Precipitation	1	1	2	1	1	1	1	1	1	1	1	1	13
Mean Snowfall (in.)	0.1	0.5	trace	0.0	0.0	0.0	0.0	0.0	0.0	0.0	trace	0.0	0.6
Days With ≥ 1.0" Snow Depth	*0*	0	0	0	0	0	0	0	0	0	0	0	*0*

Eastman 1 W *Dodge County*   Elevation: 396 ft.   Latitude: 32° 12' N   Longitude: 83° 12' W

	JAN	FEB	MAR	APR	MAY	JUN	JUL	AUG	SEP	OCT	NOV	DEC	YEAR
Mean Maximum Temp. (°F)	57.5	62.2	70.0	77.4	84.4	89.9	91.9	91.2	87.4	78.7	69.5	61.2	76.8
Mean Temp. (°F)	46.8	50.4	57.9	64.5	72.2	78.6	81.3	80.4	76.1	66.1	57.2	50.1	65.1
Mean Minimum Temp. (°F)	36.1	38.5	45.7	51.7	59.9	67.3	70.5	69.6	64.7	53.4	44.8	38.9	53.4
Extreme Maximum Temp. (°F)	81	82	89	95	97	105	107	103	101	95	86	81	107
Extreme Minimum Temp. (°F)	-2	10	15	29	39	45	56	56	45	28	15	7	-2
Days Maximum Temp. ≥ 90°F	0	0	0	1	6	17	22	22	12	1	0	0	81
Days Maximum Temp. ≤ 32°F	0	0	0	0	0	0	0	0	0	0	0	0	0
Days Minimum Temp. ≤ 32°F	12	8	3	0	0	0	0	0	0	0	3	9	35
Days Minimum Temp. ≤ 0°F	0	0	0	0	0	0	0	0	0	0	0	0	0
Heating Degree Days (base 65°F)	559	413	244	94	9	0	0	0	3	72	250	463	2,107
Cooling Degree Days (base 65°F)	2	6	27	83	244	428	529	493	332	113	19	6	2,282
Mean Precipitation (in.)	4.98	4.31	4.96	3.62	3.17	4.50	5.33	3.94	3.18	2.84	3.06	3.69	47.58
Days With ≥ 0.1" Precipitation	7	6	7	5	5	7	9	7	5	4	5	6	73
Days With ≥ 1.0" Precipitation	2	1	2	1	1	1	2	1	1	1	1	1	15
Mean Snowfall (in.)	0.1	0.0	0.0	0.0	0.0	0.0	0.0	0.0	0.0	0.0	0.0	0.0	0.1
Days With ≥ 1.0" Snow Depth	0	0	0	0	0	0	0	0	0	0	0	0	0

Elberton 2 N *Elbert County*   Elevation: 538 ft.   Latitude: 34° 09' N   Longitude: 82° 51' W

	JAN	FEB	MAR	APR	MAY	JUN	JUL	AUG	SEP	OCT	NOV	DEC	YEAR
Mean Maximum Temp. (°F)	52.6	58.0	66.7	74.8	80.8	86.8	89.8	88.3	83.2	73.5	63.6	55.2	72.8
Mean Temp. (°F)	41.3	44.9	52.6	59.8	67.3	74.5	78.1	76.9	71.2	60.0	50.7	43.5	60.1
Mean Minimum Temp. (°F)	30.0	31.7	38.5	44.8	53.7	62.1	66.3	65.4	59.1	46.4	37.8	31.9	47.3
Extreme Maximum Temp. (°F)	78	80	89	92	93	101	105	106	97	92	83	78	106
Extreme Minimum Temp. (°F)	-5	6	10	21	30	38	50	51	35	21	11	2	-5
Days Maximum Temp. ≥ 90°F	0	0	0	0	1	9	17	13	4	0	0	0	44
Days Maximum Temp. ≤ 32°F	1	0	0	0	0	0	0	0	0	0	0	0	1
Days Minimum Temp. ≤ 32°F	19	16	10	3	0	0	0	0	0	3	12	17	80
Days Minimum Temp. ≤ 0°F	0	0	0	0	0	0	0	0	0	0	0	0	0
Heating Degree Days (base 65°F)	728	564	383	181	44	3	0	0	18	183	426	659	3,189
Cooling Degree Days (base 65°F)	0	0	5	30	121	303	427	377	200	36	2	1	1,502
Mean Precipitation (in.)	5.21	4.63	5.28	3.43	4.10	3.83	4.49	3.89	3.20	3.55	3.56	3.85	49.02
Days With ≥ 0.1" Precipitation	8	7	8	6	7	6	7	6	5	5	6	7	78
Days With ≥ 1.0" Precipitation	2	1	2	1	1	1	1	1	1	1	1	1	14
Mean Snowfall (in.)	trace	0.0	0.1	0.0	0.0	0.0	0.0	0.0	0.0	0.0	0.0	0.0	0.1
Days With ≥ 1.0" Snow Depth	0	0	0	0	0	0	0	0	0	0	0	0	0

Experiment *Spalding County*   Elevation: 921 ft.   Latitude: 33° 16' N   Longitude: 84° 17' W

	JAN	FEB	MAR	APR	MAY	JUN	JUL	AUG	SEP	OCT	NOV	DEC	YEAR
Mean Maximum Temp. (°F)	52.3	57.0	64.8	72.7	79.5	86.0	89.0	87.6	82.9	73.5	64.5	56.0	72.2
Mean Temp. (°F)	42.3	46.0	53.5	60.9	68.4	75.4	78.6	77.3	72.2	61.5	53.2	45.6	61.2
Mean Minimum Temp. (°F)	32.2	34.9	42.2	48.9	57.2	64.6	68.1	67.0	61.5	49.6	41.8	35.2	50.3
Extreme Maximum Temp. (°F)	78	80	87	91	95	100	102	101	97	90	84	79	102
Extreme Minimum Temp. (°F)	-8	7	11	25	37	44	54	51	40	26	13	0	-8
Days Maximum Temp. ≥ 90°F	0	0	0	0	1	8	15	11	4	0	0	0	39
Days Maximum Temp. ≤ 32°F	1	0	0	0	0	0	0	0	0	0	0	0	1
Days Minimum Temp. ≤ 32°F	16	12	5	1	0	0	0	0	0	1	6	14	55
Days Minimum Temp. ≤ 0°F	0	0	0	0	0	0	0	0	0	0	0	0	0
Heating Degree Days (base 65°F)	697	531	358	162	33	2	0	1	13	148	355	595	2,895
Cooling Degree Days (base 65°F)	0	1	9	40	146	328	437	388	224	47	6	1	1,627
Mean Precipitation (in.)	5.19	4.69	5.61	4.12	3.95	3.94	5.11	4.15	3.26	3.06	3.82	4.42	51.32
Days With ≥ 0.1" Precipitation	8	7	7	6	6	7	8	7	5	5	6	7	79
Days With ≥ 1.0" Precipitation	2	1	2	1	1	1	1	1	1	1	1	1	14
Mean Snowfall (in.)	0.2	0.2	0.3	trace	0.0	0.0	0.0	0.0	0.0	0.0	0.0	trace	0.7
Days With ≥ 1.0" Snow Depth	0	0	0	0	0	0	0	0	0	0	0	0	0

Fitzgerald *Ben Hill County*   Elevation: 367 ft.   Latitude: 31° 43' N   Longitude: 83° 15' W

	JAN	FEB	MAR	APR	MAY	JUN	JUL	AUG	SEP	OCT	NOV	DEC	YEAR
Mean Maximum Temp. (°F)	59.3	63.3	70.8	77.7	84.3	89.4	92.0	90.8	87.0	78.6	69.9	62.3	77.1
Mean Temp. (°F)	49.1	52.3	59.2	65.9	73.2	79.1	82.0	81.0	76.8	67.3	58.6	51.8	66.4
Mean Minimum Temp. (°F)	38.9	41.2	47.7	54.0	62.0	68.8	72.0	71.2	66.5	56.0	47.3	41.3	55.6
Extreme Maximum Temp. (°F)	82	84	89	94	97	101	104	102	99	94	86	83	104
Extreme Minimum Temp. (°F)	9	13	17	33	44	48	59	57	41	32	19	8	8
Days Maximum Temp. ≥ 90°F	0	0	0	1	5	16	24	21	12	1	0	0	80
Days Maximum Temp. ≤ 32°F	0	0	0	0	0	0	0	0	0	0	0	0	0
Days Minimum Temp. ≤ 32°F	9	6	1	0	0	0	0	0	0	0	2	6	24
Days Minimum Temp. ≤ 0°F	0	0	0	0	0	0	0	0	0	0	0	0	0
Heating Degree Days (base 65°F)	489	362	210	73	6	0	0	0	2	57	217	411	1,827
Cooling Degree Days (base 65°F)	2	10	30	92	256	430	539	498	342	129	29	8	2,365
Mean Precipitation (in.)	5.02	3.98	4.91	3.00	3.31	4.33	4.34	4.95	3.18	2.53	3.04	3.43	46.02
Days With ≥ 0.1" Precipitation	7	6	7	4	5	7	7	8	5	4	4	5	69
Days With ≥ 1.0" Precipitation	2	1	1	1	1	1	1	1	1	1	1	1	13
Mean Snowfall (in.)	trace	trace	trace	0.0	0.0	0.0	0.0	0.0	0.0	0.0	0.0	trace	trace
Days With ≥ 1.0" Snow Depth	0	0	0	0	0	0	0	0	0	0	0	0	0

Folkston 9 SW *Charlton County*   Elevation: 118 ft.   Latitude: 30° 44' N   Longitude: 82° 08' W

	JAN	FEB	MAR	APR	MAY	JUN	JUL	AUG	SEP	OCT	NOV	DEC	YEAR
Mean Maximum Temp. (°F)	65.4	69.4	76.2	82.5	87.9	92.1	94.2	92.8	89.3	82.0	74.5	67.6	81.2
Mean Temp. (°F)	53.0	56.3	62.5	68.0	74.3	79.6	82.1	81.4	78.1	69.8	62.1	55.4	68.5
Mean Minimum Temp. (°F)	40.6	43.0	48.6	53.3	60.5	66.9	69.9	69.8	66.9	57.5	49.7	43.1	55.8
Extreme Maximum Temp. (°F)	84	86	92	97	100	104	106	104	98	96	93	86	106
Extreme Minimum Temp. (°F)	5	13	21	33	38	46	58	60	44	34	19	11	5
Days Maximum Temp. ≥ 90°F	0	0	0	4	12	22	27	25	16	3	0	0	109
Days Maximum Temp. ≤ 32°F	0	0	0	0	0	0	0	0	0	0	0	0	0
Days Minimum Temp. ≤ 32°F	8	5	2	0	0	0	0	0	0	0	2	6	23
Days Minimum Temp. ≤ 0°F	0	0	0	0	0	0	0	0	0	0	0	0	0
Heating Degree Days (base 65°F)	376	259	139	43	3	0	0	0	0	29	144	313	1,306
Cooling Degree Days (base 65°F)	10	24	69	146	308	461	555	525	399	194	71	21	2,783
Mean Precipitation (in.)	4.19	3.58	4.61	3.14	3.65	5.93	7.20	7.38	4.71	3.26	2.50	2.77	52.92
Days With ≥ 0.1" Precipitation	7	5	6	4	5	8	10	10	7	4	4	5	75
Days With ≥ 1.0" Precipitation	1	1	1	1	1	2	2	2	1	1	1	1	15
Mean Snowfall (in.)	0.0	trace	trace	0.0	0.0	0.0	0.0	0.0	0.0	0.0	0.0	trace	trace
Days With ≥ 1.0" Snow Depth	0	0	0	0	0	0	0	0	0	0	0	0	0

Fort Stewart *Liberty County*   Elevation: 91 ft.   Latitude: 31° 52' N   Longitude: 81° 38' W

	JAN	FEB	MAR	APR	MAY	JUN	JUL	AUG	SEP	OCT	NOV	DEC	YEAR
Mean Maximum Temp. (°F)	62.5	66.3	73.1	79.6	85.8	90.5	93.3	91.3	87.5	79.7	72.0	64.7	78.9
Mean Temp. (°F)	51.5	54.5	60.9	67.0	73.9	79.6	82.6	81.4	77.7	68.8	60.8	53.8	67.7
Mean Minimum Temp. (°F)	40.4	42.7	48.6	54.3	62.1	68.7	71.8	71.5	67.8	57.9	49.4	42.9	56.5
Extreme Maximum Temp. (°F)	85	85	91	97	98	104	110	106	100	95	88	83	110
Extreme Minimum Temp. (°F)	0	16	19	32	42	53	62	56	48	32	19	10	0
Days Maximum Temp. ≥ 90°F	0	0	0	2	7	18	25	22	11	1	0	0	86
Days Maximum Temp. ≤ 32°F	0	0	0	0	0	0	0	0	0	0	0	0	0
Days Minimum Temp. ≤ 32°F	8	5	1	0	0	0	0	0	0	0	2	6	22
Days Minimum Temp. ≤ 0°F	0	0	0	0	0	0	0	0	0	0	0	0	0
Heating Degree Days (base 65°F)	420	304	168	54	3	0	0	0	0	39	171	355	1,514
Cooling Degree Days (base 65°F)	6	17	45	120	294	462	569	524	384	170	52	14	2,657
Mean Precipitation (in.)	4.29	3.36	3.88	2.90	3.80	5.09	5.80	6.00	4.73	3.27	2.63	3.05	48.80
Days With ≥ 0.1" Precipitation	8	5	6	5	6	8	9	9	7	4	4	5	76
Days With ≥ 1.0" Precipitation	1	1	1	1	1	2	2	2	2	1	1	1	16
Mean Snowfall (in.)	trace	0.0	trace	0.0	0.0	0.0	0.0	0.0	0.0	0.0	0.0	0.1	0.1
Days With ≥ 1.0" Snow Depth	0	0	0	0	0	0	0	0	0	0	0	0	0

Gainesville *Hall County*   Elevation: 1,167 ft.   Latitude: 34° 18' N   Longitude: 83° 52' W

	JAN	FEB	MAR	APR	MAY	JUN	JUL	AUG	SEP	OCT	NOV	DEC	YEAR
Mean Maximum Temp. (°F)	49.9	54.8	63.2	71.8	77.5	83.8	87.3	85.9	80.5	71.2	62.2	53.7	70.1
Mean Temp. (°F)	40.5	44.0	51.7	59.5	66.6	73.7	77.7	76.5	70.9	60.5	51.8	44.1	59.8
Mean Minimum Temp. (°F)	31.1	33.2	40.1	47.2	55.6	63.6	68.1	67.2	61.3	49.8	41.4	34.6	49.4
Extreme Maximum Temp. (°F)	77	78	85	93	93	98	103	100	96	88	84	78	103
Extreme Minimum Temp. (°F)	-8	4	10	26	34	43	56	55	41	28	11	-1	-8
Days Maximum Temp. ≥ 90°F	0	0	0	0	0	5	11	8	2	0	0	0	26
Days Maximum Temp. ≤ 32°F	2	1	0	0	0	0	0	0	0	0	0	0	3
Days Minimum Temp. ≤ 32°F	18	14	6	1	0	0	0	0	0	0	6	14	59
Days Minimum Temp. ≤ 0°F	0	0	0	0	0	0	0	0	0	0	0	0	0
Heating Degree Days (base 65°F)	754	586	410	190	51	3	0	0	17	166	392	640	3,209
Cooling Degree Days (base 65°F)	0	0	5	35	124	300	439	389	209	41	3	1	1,546
Mean Precipitation (in.)	5.95	5.05	6.15	4.12	4.37	3.90	4.27	3.93	4.22	4.20	4.28	4.53	54.97
Days With ≥ 0.1" Precipitation	9	7	9	7	7	6	7	6	6	5	7	8	84
Days With ≥ 1.0" Precipitation	2	2	2	1	1	1	1	1	1	1	1	1	15
Mean Snowfall (in.)	1.3	0.4	0.3	0.0	0.0	0.0	0.0	0.0	0.0	0.0	trace	0.1	2.1
Days With ≥ 1.0" Snow Depth	0	0	0	0	0	0	0	0	0	0	0	0	0

Glennville *Tattnall County*   Elevation: 167 ft.   Latitude: 31° 56' N   Longitude: 81° 56' W

	JAN	FEB	MAR	APR	MAY	JUN	JUL	AUG	SEP	OCT	NOV	DEC	YEAR
Mean Maximum Temp. (°F)	60.9	64.9	72.2	78.8	85.3	90.1	92.6	90.8	87.0	78.9	70.7	63.6	78.0
Mean Temp. (°F)	50.0	53.2	60.0	66.1	73.5	79.3	82.1	81.0	77.2	67.9	59.5	52.7	66.9
Mean Minimum Temp. (°F)	39.1	41.4	47.7	53.5	61.6	68.4	71.7	71.1	67.2	56.8	48.1	41.7	55.7
Extreme Maximum Temp. (°F)	83	85	91	97	98	102	106	103	100	95	89	83	106
Extreme Minimum Temp. (°F)	1	14	17	31	40	52	60	52	48	33	19	9	1
Days Maximum Temp. ≥ 90°F	0	0	0	1	7	18	24	21	10	1	0	0	82
Days Maximum Temp. ≤ 32°F	0	0	0	0	0	0	0	0	0	0	0	0	0
Days Minimum Temp. ≤ 32°F	9	6	2	0	0	0	0	0	0	0	2	7	26
Days Minimum Temp. ≤ 0°F	0	0	0	0	0	0	0	0	0	0	0	0	0
Heating Degree Days (base 65°F)	463	339	191	66	4	0	0	0	1	48	199	387	1,698
Cooling Degree Days (base 65°F)	4	13	36	103	274	448	552	505	360	143	40	10	2,488
Mean Precipitation (in.)	4.42	3.75	4.11	3.02	3.48	4.77	4.99	5.91	4.17	3.08	2.69	3.51	47.90
Days With ≥ 0.1" Precipitation	7	5	6	5	6	7	9	9	6	4	4	5	73
Days With ≥ 1.0" Precipitation	1	1	1	1	1	1	1	2	1	1	1	1	13
Mean Snowfall (in.)	trace	0.1	0.0	0.0	0.0	0.0	0.0	0.0	0.0	0.0	trace	trace	0.1
Days With ≥ 1.0" Snow Depth	0	0	0	0	0	0	0	0	0	0	0	0	0

Hartwell *Hart County*   Elevation: 688 ft.   Latitude: 34° 21' N   Longitude: 82° 56' W

	JAN	FEB	MAR	APR	MAY	JUN	JUL	AUG	SEP	OCT	NOV	DEC	YEAR
Mean Maximum Temp. (°F)	52.3	57.5	66.1	74.5	80.8	87.0	90.3	88.2	83.1	73.4	64.6	56.4	72.8
Mean Temp. (°F)	42.6	46.4	54.3	61.8	69.2	76.2	80.0	78.5	73.0	62.4	53.5	46.1	62.0
Mean Minimum Temp. (°F)	32.9	35.2	42.4	49.1	57.8	65.6	69.7	68.7	62.9	51.5	42.3	36.0	51.2
Extreme Maximum Temp. (°F)	80	82	91	94	98	104	105	108	100	95	85	82	108
Extreme Minimum Temp. (°F)	-5	7	11	27	35	45	56	55	44	28	13	3	-5
Days Maximum Temp. ≥ 90°F	0	0	0	0	2	11	18	13	5	0	0	0	49
Days Maximum Temp. ≤ 32°F	1	0	0	0	0	0	0	0	0	0	0	0	1
Days Minimum Temp. ≤ 32°F	15	11	5	0	0	0	0	0	0	0	5	11	47
Days Minimum Temp. ≤ 0°F	0	0	0	0	0	0	0	0	0	0	0	0	0
Heating Degree Days (base 65°F)	689	518	336	140	24	1	0	0	9	124	348	575	2,764
Cooling Degree Days (base 65°F)	0	0	8	46	160	348	485	423	238	52	6	2	1,768
Mean Precipitation (in.)	5.34	4.60	5.93	3.54	4.50	4.05	4.20	3.99	3.78	4.04	3.76	4.53	52.26
Days With ≥ 0.1" Precipitation	7	7	8	5	6	6	7	6	5	5	5	7	74
Days With ≥ 1.0" Precipitation	2	2	2	1	2	1	1	1	1	1	1	2	17
Mean Snowfall (in.)	0.8	0.3	0.2	0.0	0.0	0.0	0.0	0.0	0.0	0.0	0.0	0.1	1.4
Days With ≥ 1.0" Snow Depth	1	0	0	0	0	0	0	0	0	0	0	0	1

Hawkinsville *Pulaski County*   Elevation: 269 ft.   Latitude: 32° 17' N   Longitude: 83° 28' W

	JAN	FEB	MAR	APR	MAY	JUN	JUL	AUG	SEP	OCT	NOV	DEC	YEAR
Mean Maximum Temp. (°F)	58.5	62.6	70.6	78.0	84.9	90.8	93.2	*91.9*	88.1	79.4	70.1	61.9	*77.5*
Mean Temp. (°F)	46.4	49.5	57.0	64.1	71.8	78.7	81.3	*80.4*	75.7	65.5	56.4	49.4	*64.7*
Mean Minimum Temp. (°F)	34.3	36.4	43.4	50.1	58.6	66.5	69.4	*68.8*	63.3	51.5	42.8	36.8	*51.8*
Extreme Maximum Temp. (°F)	83	84	92	96	97	104	105	105	104	98	87	85	105
Extreme Minimum Temp. (°F)	-2	11	15	28	38	45	56	52	37	23	14	8	-2
Days Maximum Temp. ≥ 90°F	0	0	0	1	8	19	23	23	14	2	0	0	*90*
Days Maximum Temp. ≤ 32°F	0	0	0	0	0	0	0	0	0	0	0	0	0
Days Minimum Temp. ≤ 32°F	15	11	4	0	0	0	0	0	0	0	5	12	47
Days Minimum Temp. ≤ 0°F	0	0	0	0	0	0	0	0	0	0	0	0	0
Heating Degree Days (base 65°F)	571	434	261	101	11	0	0	*0*	5	84	274	484	*2,225*
Cooling Degree Days (base 65°F)	2	5	22	79	239	424	534	496	323	107	22	5	2,258
Mean Precipitation (in.)	5.34	4.54	4.73	3.47	3.28	4.13	4.35	3.50	3.50	2.74	3.27	3.92	46.77
Days With ≥ 0.1" Precipitation	7	6	7	5	5	7	7	6	5	4	5	6	70
Days With ≥ 1.0" Precipitation	2	1	2	1	1	1	1	1	1	1	1	1	14
Mean Snowfall (in.)	*0.1*	0.5	trace	0.0	0.0	0.0	0.0	0.0	0.0	0.0	trace	trace	*0.6*
Days With ≥ 1.0" Snow Depth	*0*	0	0	0	0	0	0	0	0	0	0	0	*0*

Helen *White County*   Elevation: 1,437 ft.   Latitude: 34° 43' N   Longitude: 83° 43' W

	JAN	FEB	MAR	APR	MAY	JUN	JUL	AUG	SEP	OCT	NOV	DEC	YEAR
Mean Maximum Temp. (°F)	*50.9*	*55.9*	*63.6*	*72.7*	*78.3*	*83.7*	*86.8*	*85.1*	*80.5*	*71.8*	*61.6*	*53.9*	*70.4*
Mean Temp. (°F)	*40.5*	*43.8*	*50.7*	*58.2*	*65.3*	*71.9*	*75.5*	*74.4*	*69.3*	*59.2*	*49.9*	*43.4*	*58.5*
Mean Minimum Temp. (°F)	*30.0*	*31.6*	*37.9*	*43.7*	*52.1*	*59.9*	*64.3*	*63.7*	*58.0*	*46.6*	*38.1*	*32.9*	*46.6*
Extreme Maximum Temp. (°F)	*84*	*80*	*85*	*91*	*94*	*98*	*100*	*99*	*95*	*89*	*83*	*76*	*100*
Extreme Minimum Temp. (°F)	*-12*	*0*	*6*	*23*	*29*	*39*	*51*	*51*	*37*	*22*	*10*	*4*	*-12*
Days Maximum Temp. ≥ 90°F	*0*	*0*	*0*	*0*	*1*	*4*	*10*	*5*	*2*	*0*	*0*	*0*	*22*
Days Maximum Temp. ≤ 32°F	*1*	*0*	*0*	*0*	*0*	*0*	*0*	*0*	*0*	*0*	*0*	*0*	*1*
Days Minimum Temp. ≤ 32°F	*19*	*16*	*10*	*4*	*0*	*0*	*0*	*0*	*0*	*2*	*10*	*16*	*77*
Days Minimum Temp. ≤ 0°F	*0*	*0*	*0*	*0*	*0*	*0*	*0*	*0*	*0*	*0*	*0*	*0*	*0*
Heating Degree Days (base 65°F)	*753*	*591*	*436*	*213*	*61*	*7*	*0*	*0*	*23*	*197*	*448*	*664*	*3,393*
Cooling Degree Days (base 65°F)	*0*	*0*	*2*	*19*	*89*	*243*	*362*	*319*	*160*	*28*	*1*	*0*	*1,223*
Mean Precipitation (in.)	*7.33*	*5.94*	*7.56*	*4.78*	*6.59*	*5.36*	*5.85*	*5.73*	*5.46*	*4.87*	*5.80*	*6.09*	*71.36*
Days With ≥ 0.1" Precipitation	*9*	*7*	*9*	*7*	*8*	*8*	*9*	*8*	*7*	*6*	*7*	*8*	*93*
Days With ≥ 1.0" Precipitation	*3*	*2*	*2*	*2*	*2*	*2*	*2*	*2*	*2*	*2*	*2*	*2*	*25*
Mean Snowfall (in.)	na	*0.6*	*0.4*	*0.0*	*0.0*	*0.0*	*0.0*	*0.0*	*0.0*	*trace*	*trace*	*0.3*	na
Days With ≥ 1.0" Snow Depth	na	na	*0*	*0*	*0*	*0*	*0*	*0*	*0*	*0*	*0*	*0*	na

Homerville 3 WSW *Clinch County*   Elevation: 187 ft.   Latitude: 31° 02' N   Longitude: 82° 48' W

	JAN	FEB	MAR	APR	MAY	JUN	JUL	AUG	SEP	OCT	NOV	DEC	YEAR
Mean Maximum Temp. (°F)	62.0	65.9	73.1	79.7	85.9	90.5	92.6	91.2	87.6	79.6	71.5	64.6	78.7
Mean Temp. (°F)	50.2	53.2	59.7	65.6	72.4	78.1	80.7	79.9	76.5	67.2	58.9	52.4	66.2
Mean Minimum Temp. (°F)	38.4	40.5	46.3	51.4	58.9	65.7	68.7	68.5	65.3	54.8	46.3	40.2	53.7
Extreme Maximum Temp. (°F)	82	85	89	94	97	104	103	101	99	93	87	84	104
Extreme Minimum Temp. (°F)	3	14	19	31	38	45	57	57	44	27	17	11	3
Days Maximum Temp. ≥ 90°F	0	0	0	1	7	19	26	23	13	1	0	0	90
Days Maximum Temp. ≤ 32°F	0	0	0	0	0	0	0	0	0	0	0	0	0
Days Minimum Temp. ≤ 32°F	11	7	3	0	0	0	0	0	0	0	4	9	34
Days Minimum Temp. ≤ 0°F	0	0	0	0	0	0	0	0	0	0	0	0	0
Heating Degree Days (base 65°F)	458	337	194	71	7	0	0	0	1	60	213	394	1,735
Cooling Degree Days (base 65°F)	4	10	30	89	242	404	499	465	332	130	36	9	2,250
Mean Precipitation (in.)	5.28	4.12	4.93	3.56	3.38	5.43	6.52	6.36	4.10	2.88	2.88	3.70	53.14
Days With ≥ 0.1" Precipitation	7	6	6	4	6	9	10	9	6	4	4	5	76
Days With ≥ 1.0" Precipitation	2	1	1	1	1	2	2	2	1	1	1	1	16
Mean Snowfall (in.)	trace	trace	trace	0.0	0.0	0.0	0.0	0.0	0.0	0.0	0.0	trace	trace
Days With ≥ 1.0" Snow Depth	0	0	0	0	0	0	0	0	0	0	0	0	0

Irwinton 4 WNW *Wilkinson County*   Elevation: 515 ft.   Latitude: 32° 50' N   Longitude: 83° 14' W

	JAN	FEB	MAR	APR	MAY	JUN	JUL	AUG	SEP	OCT	NOV	DEC	YEAR
Mean Maximum Temp. (°F)	*58.3*	63.1	71.3	78.9	84.7	90.1	92.8	91.5	87.3	78.1	70.0	61.5	*77.3*
Mean Temp. (°F)	*47.1*	51.1	58.0	65.0	71.9	78.2	81.3	80.4	75.8	65.8	57.1	50.2	*65.1*
Mean Minimum Temp. (°F)	35.9	39.0	44.7	51.0	59.0	66.1	69.8	69.2	64.2	53.4	44.1	38.8	52.9
Extreme Maximum Temp. (°F)	85	85	90	96	96	106	107	105	102	93	87	83	107
Extreme Minimum Temp. (°F)	-4	8	10	28	33	44	57	56	40	31	16	5	-4
Days Maximum Temp. ≥ 90°F	0	0	0	1	6	18	24	21	12	1	0	0	83
Days Maximum Temp. ≤ 32°F	0	0	0	0	0	0	0	0	0	0	0	0	0
Days Minimum Temp. ≤ 32°F	12	8	3	0	0	0	0	0	0	0	3	8	34
Days Minimum Temp. ≤ 0°F	0	0	0	0	0	0	0	0	0	0	0	0	0
Heating Degree Days (base 65°F)	*549*	391	234	81	9	0	0	0	3	74	246	454	*2,041*
Cooling Degree Days (base 65°F)	2	5	25	85	235	418	530	491	332	111	17	4	*2,255*
Mean Precipitation (in.)	5.04	4.42	4.89	2.93	3.03	3.52	4.67	4.05	3.64	2.86	3.08	4.18	46.31
Days With ≥ 0.1" Precipitation	7	6	6	5	5	6	7	7	5	4	5	5	*68*
Days With ≥ 1.0" Precipitation	2	1	2	1	1	1	1	1	1	1	1	1	*14*
Mean Snowfall (in.)	0.2	0.5	trace	0.0	0.0	0.0	0.0	0.0	0.0	0.0	0.0	trace	0.7
Days With ≥ 1.0" Snow Depth	0	0	0	0	0	0	0	0	0	0	0	0	0

Jasper 1 NNW *Pickens County*   Elevation: 1,463 ft.   Latitude: 34° 30' N   Longitude: 84° 28' W

	JAN	FEB	MAR	APR	MAY	JUN	JUL	AUG	SEP	OCT	NOV	DEC	YEAR
Mean Maximum Temp. (°F)	47.7	52.8	61.2	69.7	76.7	83.0	86.5	85.2	80.0	69.7	59.8	51.4	68.6
Mean Temp. (°F)	38.7	42.7	50.6	58.0	65.5	72.4	76.1	75.1	69.6	58.8	50.1	42.6	58.4
Mean Minimum Temp. (°F)	29.8	32.5	39.9	46.3	54.3	61.8	65.7	64.9	59.2	47.9	40.3	33.7	48.0
Extreme Maximum Temp. (°F)	74	78	83	90	90	97	103	100	96	87	81	75	103
Extreme Minimum Temp. (°F)	-14	-1	5	21	30	37	50	53	36	23	8	-5	-14
Days Maximum Temp. ≥ 90°F	0	0	0	0	0	3	8	5	2	0	0	0	18
Days Maximum Temp. ≤ 32°F	3	1	0	0	0	0	0	0	0	0	0	1	5
Days Minimum Temp. ≤ 32°F	18	14	7	2	0	0	0	0	0	1	8	15	65
Days Minimum Temp. ≤ 0°F	0	0	0	0	0	0	0	0	0	0	0	0	0
Heating Degree Days (base 65°F)	808	625	443	225	65	5	0	0	25	206	442	689	3,533
Cooling Degree Days (base 65°F)	0	0	3	20	89	246	370	325	167	24	1	0	1,245
Mean Precipitation (in.)	6.11	5.23	6.67	5.08	4.72	4.68	5.28	4.71	3.71	4.28	4.91	5.05	60.43
Days With ≥ 0.1" Precipitation	9	7	9	7	7	8	8	7	6	5	7	8	88
Days With ≥ 1.0" Precipitation	2	2	2	1	1	1	2	1	1	1	2	2	18
Mean Snowfall (in.)	0.6	0.5	0.5	trace	0.0	0.0	0.0	0.0	0.0	trace	trace	0.3	1.9
Days With ≥ 1.0" Snow Depth	*0*	0	0	0	0	0	0	0	0	0	0	0	*0*

Jesup 8 S *Wayne County*   Elevation: 98 ft.   Latitude: 31° 29' N   Longitude: 81° 53' W

	JAN	FEB	MAR	APR	MAY	JUN	JUL	AUG	SEP	OCT	NOV	DEC	YEAR
Mean Maximum Temp. (°F)	62.3	66.5	73.4	80.4	86.0	90.6	93.3	91.0	87.4	80.0	72.3	64.9	79.0
Mean Temp. (°F)	50.3	53.4	59.7	65.9	72.6	78.7	81.6	80.1	76.6	67.4	59.6	52.8	66.6
Mean Minimum Temp. (°F)	38.2	40.2	46.0	51.4	59.0	66.7	69.9	69.1	65.6	54.8	46.9	40.5	54.0
Extreme Maximum Temp. (°F)	83	86	91	98	100	103	107	102	99	97	90	84	107
Extreme Minimum Temp. (°F)	3	13	18	28	38	44	55	54	44	27	16	11	3
Days Maximum Temp. ≥ 90°F	0	0	0	3	8	18	24	20	11	1	0	0	85
Days Maximum Temp. ≤ 32°F	0	0	0	0	0	0	0	0	0	0	0	0	0
Days Minimum Temp. ≤ 32°F	11	7	3	0	0	0	0	0	0	0	4	9	34
Days Minimum Temp. ≤ 0°F	0	0	0	0	0	0	0	0	0	0	0	0	0
Heating Degree Days (base 65°F)	454	334	196	67	6	0	0	0	1	60	195	386	1,699
Cooling Degree Days (base 65°F)	2	13	33	100	247	429	533	471	339	141	41	12	2,361
Mean Precipitation (in.)	4.51	3.63	4.43	2.81	3.64	5.34	5.80	6.56	3.97	3.07	2.38	2.98	49.12
Days With ≥ 0.1" Precipitation	7	5	6	4	6	7	8	8	6	4	4	5	70
Days With ≥ 1.0" Precipitation	1	1	1	1	1	2	2	2	1	1	1	1	15
Mean Snowfall (in.)	trace	0.2	0.0	0.0	0.0	0.0	0.0	0.0	0.0	0.0	0.0	0.0	0.2
Days With ≥ 1.0" Snow Depth	0	0	0	0	0	0	0	0	0	0	0	0	0

La Grange *Troup County*   Elevation: 711 ft.   Latitude: 33° 04' N   Longitude: 85° 02' W

	JAN	FEB	MAR	APR	MAY	JUN	JUL	AUG	SEP	OCT	NOV	DEC	YEAR
Mean Maximum Temp. (°F)	55.2	60.3	69.0	76.4	82.5	88.3	90.4	88.8	84.0	75.1	66.1	58.1	74.5
Mean Temp. (°F)	44.3	48.1	55.6	62.4	69.7	76.4	79.5	78.4	73.2	62.5	53.9	47.0	62.6
Mean Minimum Temp. (°F)	33.3	35.9	42.2	48.3	56.9	64.5	68.6	67.8	62.2	49.8	41.6	36.0	50.6
Extreme Maximum Temp. (°F)	79	81	88	93	97	102	102	101	98	89	83	80	102
Extreme Minimum Temp. (°F)	-5	6	13	26	34	41	54	55	39	25	12	2	-5
Days Maximum Temp. ≥ 90°F	0	0	0	0	3	13	18	14	5	0	0	0	53
Days Maximum Temp. ≤ 32°F	0	0	0	0	0	0	0	0	0	0	0	0	0
Days Minimum Temp. ≤ 32°F	16	12	6	1	0	0	0	0	0	1	7	13	56
Days Minimum Temp. ≤ 0°F	0	0	0	0	0	0	0	0	0	0	0	0	0
Heating Degree Days (base 65°F)	636	471	301	127	21	1	0	0	9	128	335	552	2,581
Cooling Degree Days (base 65°F)	0	2	18	52	174	365	473	430	251	60	8	3	1,836
Mean Precipitation (in.)	5.28	4.99	6.27	4.52	3.60	4.08	5.60	3.89	3.43	3.20	4.16	4.85	53.87
Days With ≥ 0.1" Precipitation	8	7	7	6	6	7	8	7	5	4	6	7	78
Days With ≥ 1.0" Precipitation	2	2	2	2	1	1	2	1	1	1	1	1	17
Mean Snowfall (in.)	0.4	trace	0.2	0.0	0.0	0.0	0.0	0.0	0.0	0.0	0.0	trace	0.6
Days With ≥ 1.0" Snow Depth	0	0	0	0	0	0	0	0	0	0	0	0	0

Lafayette 5 SW *Walker County*   Elevation: 797 ft.   Latitude: 34° 39' N   Longitude: 85° 22' W

	JAN	FEB	MAR	APR	MAY	JUN	JUL	AUG	SEP	OCT	NOV	DEC	YEAR
Mean Maximum Temp. (°F)	48.5	53.9	62.9	71.7	78.6	84.9	88.9	88.0	82.2	72.0	61.5	52.4	70.4
Mean Temp. (°F)	38.1	42.1	50.1	57.9	65.7	73.1	77.4	76.4	70.4	58.9	49.5	41.6	58.4
Mean Minimum Temp. (°F)	27.8	30.2	37.2	44.0	52.6	61.3	65.9	64.8	58.6	45.8	37.4	30.8	46.4
Extreme Maximum Temp. (°F)	78	82	87	90	93	98	106	103	98	90	82	78	106
Extreme Minimum Temp. (°F)	-13	-3	7	22	30	39	47	50	36	24	11	-2	-13
Days Maximum Temp. ≥ 90°F	0	0	0	0	1	7	15	12	4	0	0	0	39
Days Maximum Temp. ≤ 32°F	3	1	0	0	0	0	0	0	0	0	0	1	5
Days Minimum Temp. ≤ 32°F	21	17	10	3	0	0	0	0	0	2	11	19	83
Days Minimum Temp. ≤ 0°F	0	0	0	0	0	0	0	0	0	0	0	0	0
Heating Degree Days (base 65°F)	826	642	458	229	68	5	0	0	24	205	460	720	3,637
Cooling Degree Days (base 65°F)	0	0	3	18	95	257	400	359	183	27	2	1	1,345
Mean Precipitation (in.)	5.84	5.28	6.61	4.46	4.60	4.61	4.85	3.50	4.72	3.57	4.97	5.49	58.50
Days With ≥ 0.1" Precipitation	9	7	8	6	7	8	7	6	6	5	7	8	84
Days With ≥ 1.0" Precipitation	2	2	2	1	1	1	2	1	1	1	2	2	18
Mean Snowfall (in.)	*0.7*	0.4	0.7	0.1	0.0	0.0	0.0	0.0	0.0	trace	trace	0.1	*2.0*
Days With ≥ 1.0" Snow Depth	*0*	0	0	0	0	0	0	0	0	0	0	0	*0*

Louisville 1 E *Jefferson County*   Elevation: 321 ft.   Latitude: 33° 01' N   Longitude: 82° 23' W

	JAN	FEB	MAR	APR	MAY	JUN	JUL	AUG	SEP	OCT	NOV	DEC	YEAR
Mean Maximum Temp. (°F)	58.4	63.2	70.9	78.2	84.9	90.1	92.6	90.9	86.9	78.0	69.4	61.1	77.0
Mean Temp. (°F)	47.2	50.8	57.7	64.5	71.9	78.5	81.5	80.1	75.5	65.4	56.8	49.5	64.9
Mean Minimum Temp. (°F)	36.0	38.3	44.5	50.7	58.9	66.8	70.3	69.2	64.2	52.7	44.1	37.9	52.8
Extreme Maximum Temp. (°F)	82	85	90	96	98	105	105	105	102	94	90	82	105
Extreme Minimum Temp. (°F)	-2	12	14	28	38	46	57	56	42	25	15	6	-2
Days Maximum Temp. ≥ 90°F	0	0	0	1	6	17	23	19	10	1	0	0	77
Days Maximum Temp. ≤ 32°F	0	0	0	0	0	0	0	0	0	0	0	0	0
Days Minimum Temp. ≤ 32°F	13	9	3	0	0	0	0	0	0	0	5	11	41
Days Minimum Temp. ≤ 0°F	0	0	0	0	0	0	0	0	0	0	0	0	0
Heating Degree Days (base 65°F)	547	400	245	90	11	0	0	0	3	82	260	478	2,116
Cooling Degree Days (base 65°F)	2	6	24	79	236	420	540	485	323	105	22	4	2,246
Mean Precipitation (in.)	4.84	4.22	4.99	2.98	3.04	4.06	4.41	4.85	3.51	3.20	2.77	3.64	46.51
Days With ≥ 0.1" Precipitation	8	6	7	5	5	6	7	7	5	4	5	6	71
Days With ≥ 1.0" Precipitation	1	1	2	1	1	1	1	1	1	1	1	1	13
Mean Snowfall (in.)	trace	0.7	trace	0.0	0.0	0.0	0.0	0.0	0.0	0.0	trace	trace	0.7
Days With ≥ 1.0" Snow Depth	0	0	0	0	0	0	0	0	0	0	0	0	0

Milledgeville *Baldwin County*   Elevation: 396 ft.   Latitude: 33° 05' N   Longitude: 83° 15' W

	JAN	FEB	MAR	APR	MAY	JUN	JUL	AUG	SEP	OCT	NOV	DEC	YEAR
Mean Maximum Temp. (°F)	56.3	61.2	69.2	77.0	83.2	89.6	92.7	90.9	86.5	77.2	68.2	59.7	76.0
Mean Temp. (°F)	44.0	47.3	54.7	61.9	69.5	77.0	80.6	79.4	74.4	63.3	54.2	46.9	62.8
Mean Minimum Temp. (°F)	31.7	33.4	40.1	46.7	55.7	64.4	68.4	67.7	62.3	49.4	40.2	34.1	49.5
Extreme Maximum Temp. (°F)	81	85	90	97	99	106	109	107	103	94	88	83	109
Extreme Minimum Temp. (°F)	-3	8	13	25	37	45	54	56	38	26	16	0	-3
Days Maximum Temp. ≥ 90°F	0	0	0	1	5	15	23	19	11	1	0	0	75
Days Maximum Temp. ≤ 32°F	0	0	0	0	0	0	0	0	0	0	0	0	0
Days Minimum Temp. ≤ 32°F	18	14	8	1	0	0	0	0	0	1	9	15	66
Days Minimum Temp. ≤ 0°F	0	0	0	0	0	0	0	0	0	0	0	0	0
Heating Degree Days (base 65°F)	645	495	327	139	27	1	0	0	7	115	329	555	2,640
Cooling Degree Days (base 65°F)	1	2	14	55	184	387	512	464	292	75	12	3	2,001
Mean Precipitation (in.)	4.83	4.48	5.27	3.32	3.07	3.71	3.93	4.39	3.44	3.17	3.44	3.79	46.84
Days With ≥ 0.1" Precipitation	7	6	7	5	5	6	7	7	5	4	5	6	70
Days With ≥ 1.0" Precipitation	1	1	1	1	1	1	1	1	1	1	1	1	12
Mean Snowfall (in.)	0.1	0.7	trace	0.0	0.0	0.0	0.0	0.0	0.0	0.0	0.0	trace	0.8
Days With ≥ 1.0" Snow Depth	0	0	0	0	0	0	0	0	0	0	0	0	0

Monticello *Jasper County*   Elevation: 528 ft.   Latitude: 33° 19' N   Longitude: 83° 42' W

	JAN	FEB	MAR	APR	MAY	JUN	JUL	AUG	SEP	OCT	NOV	DEC	YEAR
Mean Maximum Temp. (°F)	54.8	59.6	67.9	75.5	81.8	87.8	90.7	89.4	84.9	75.6	66.5	57.9	74.3
Mean Temp. (°F)	44.2	47.8	55.2	62.7	69.8	76.9	80.2	79.1	74.1	63.6	54.6	46.9	62.9
Mean Minimum Temp. (°F)	33.7	35.9	42.6	49.7	57.9	65.9	69.6	68.7	63.3	51.7	42.7	35.9	51.4
Extreme Maximum Temp. (°F)	81	82	89	93	94	103	103	103	99	92	83	79	103
Extreme Minimum Temp. (°F)	-7	7	12	28	37	47	56	54	42	30	15	2	-7
Days Maximum Temp. ≥ 90°F	0	0	0	0	3	12	19	16	7	0	0	0	57
Days Maximum Temp. ≤ 32°F	1	0	0	0	0	0	0	0	0	0	0	0	1
Days Minimum Temp. ≤ 32°F	14	11	5	1	0	0	0	0	0	0	6	12	49
Days Minimum Temp. ≤ 0°F	0	0	0	0	0	0	0	0	0	0	0	0	0
Heating Degree Days (base 65°F)	638	482	311	125	21	1	0	0	6	105	316	555	2,560
Cooling Degree Days (base 65°F)	0	2	15	58	182	364	487	443	274	74	9	1	1,909
Mean Precipitation (in.)	4.64	4.63	5.56	3.64	3.54	3.55	4.65	4.17	2.97	3.00	3.41	3.88	47.64
Days With ≥ 0.1" Precipitation	8	6	7	5	6	6	7	6	5	4	5	6	71
Days With ≥ 1.0" Precipitation	2	1	2	1	1	1	1	1	1	1	1	1	14
Mean Snowfall (in.)	0.3	0.6	0.1	0.0	0.0	0.0	0.0	0.0	0.0	trace	0.0	trace	1.0
Days With ≥ 1.0" Snow Depth	0	0	0	0	0	0	0	0	0	0	0	0	0

Moultrie 2 ESE *Colquitt County*   Elevation: 337 ft.   Latitude: 31° 10' N   Longitude: 83° 45' W

	JAN	FEB	MAR	APR	MAY	JUN	JUL	AUG	SEP	OCT	NOV	DEC	YEAR
Mean Maximum Temp. (°F)	61.3	65.4	72.7	79.2	85.4	90.2	92.3	91.3	87.7	79.7	71.5	64.3	78.4
Mean Temp. (°F)	50.5	53.8	60.5	66.4	73.5	79.0	81.6	80.8	77.1	68.0	59.9	53.3	67.0
Mean Minimum Temp. (°F)	39.7	42.1	48.3	53.7	61.5	67.7	70.9	70.2	66.4	56.2	48.2	42.1	55.6
Extreme Maximum Temp. (°F)	84	85	89	94	96	102	104	102	100	94	87	84	104
Extreme Minimum Temp. (°F)	0	13	17	32	41	50	59	55	46	34	15	9	0
Days Maximum Temp. ≥ 90°F	0	0	0	1	6	18	24	22	13	2	0	0	86
Days Maximum Temp. ≤ 32°F	0	0	0	0	0	0	0	0	0	0	0	0	0
Days Minimum Temp. ≤ 32°F	9	5	1	0	0	0	0	0	0	0	2	6	23
Days Minimum Temp. ≤ 0°F	0	0	0	0	0	0	0	0	0	0	0	0	0
Heating Degree Days (base 65°F)	450	322	175	59	3	0	0	0	1	48	190	371	1,619
Cooling Degree Days (base 65°F)	5	13	43	106	274	441	540	508	366	157	46	14	2,513
Mean Precipitation (in.)	5.70	4.66	5.65	3.37	3.54	5.15	5.52	4.80	3.42	2.43	3.18	3.63	51.05
Days With ≥ 0.1" Precipitation	8	6	7	5	5	8	9	8	5	4	5	6	76
Days With ≥ 1.0" Precipitation	2	2	2	1	1	2	2	1	1	1	1	1	17
Mean Snowfall (in.)	trace	trace	trace	0.0	0.0	0.0	0.0	0.0	0.0	0.0	0.0	trace	trace
Days With ≥ 1.0" Snow Depth	0	0	0	0	0	0	0	0	0	0	0	0	0

Nahunta 3 E *Brantley County* Elevation: 75 ft. Latitude: 31° 13' N Longitude: 81° 56' W

	JAN	FEB	MAR	APR	MAY	JUN	JUL	AUG	SEP	OCT	NOV	DEC	YEAR
Mean Maximum Temp. (°F)	63.6	67.2	73.7	79.8	85.2	89.4	91.5	90.1	86.9	80.0	na	66.2	na
Mean Temp. (°F)	51.5	54.3	60.4	66.0	72.4	78.3	81.1	80.2	77.0	68.3	na	54.2	na
Mean Minimum Temp. (°F)	39.0	41.4	47.2	52.0	59.7	67.2	70.6	70.2	67.1	56.6	47.9	41.8	55.1
Extreme Maximum Temp. (°F)	83	85	89	96	96	101	104	102	101	96	89	85	104
Extreme Minimum Temp. (°F)	3	15	21	31	38	40	57	59	44	30	16	9	3
Days Maximum Temp. ≥ 90°F	0	0	0	1	5	15	20	18	8	1	0	0	68
Days Maximum Temp. ≤ 32°F	0	0	0	0	0	0	0	0	0	0	0	0	0
Days Minimum Temp. ≤ 32°F	10	6	2	0	0	0	0	0	0	0	3	7	28
Days Minimum Temp. ≤ 0°F	0	0	0	0	0	0	0	0	0	0	0	0	0
Heating Degree Days (base 65°F)	421	308	176	63	5	0	0	0	0	43	na	343	na
Cooling Degree Days (base 65°F)	na	12	37	93	238	417	521	485	na	na	na	na	na
Mean Precipitation (in.)	4.26	3.94	4.60	2.72	3.42	6.05	6.29	8.00	4.29	3.02	2.48	2.96	52.03
Days With ≥ 0.1" Precipitation	5	5	6	4	5	8	8	9	6	3	4	4	67
Days With ≥ 1.0" Precipitation	1	1	1	1	1	2	2	2	1	1	1	1	15
Mean Snowfall (in.)	0.0	trace	0.0	0.0	0.0	0.0	0.0	0.0	0.0	0.0	0.0	0.0	trace
Days With ≥ 1.0" Snow Depth	0	0	0	0	0	0	0	0	0	0	0	0	0

Newnan 4 NE *Coweta County* Elevation: 918 ft. Latitude: 33° 27' N Longitude: 84° 47' W

	JAN	FEB	MAR	APR	MAY	JUN	JUL	AUG	SEP	OCT	NOV	DEC	YEAR
Mean Maximum Temp. (°F)	53.6	58.8	67.4	75.1	81.1	86.9	89.6	88.4	83.7	74.2	65.0	56.6	73.4
Mean Temp. (°F)	43.0	46.9	54.7	61.6	68.7	75.3	78.6	77.5	72.5	62.0	53.2	45.9	61.7
Mean Minimum Temp. (°F)	32.4	35.0	41.9	48.0	56.3	63.7	67.5	66.5	61.2	49.7	41.4	35.2	49.9
Extreme Maximum Temp. (°F)	77	81	87	92	95	99	103	101	97	91	84	79	103
Extreme Minimum Temp. (°F)	-8	4	11	24	35	41	54	52	37	25	13	1	-8
Days Maximum Temp. ≥ 90°F	0	0	0	0	1	9	16	13	5	0	0	0	44
Days Maximum Temp. ≤ 32°F	1	0	0	0	0	0	0	0	0	0	0	0	1
Days Minimum Temp. ≤ 32°F	16	12	6	2	0	0	0	0	0	1	7	14	58
Days Minimum Temp. ≤ 0°F	0	0	0	0	0	0	0	0	0	0	0	0	0
Heating Degree Days (base 65°F)	675	506	324	144	27	1	0	0	12	139	352	585	2,765
Cooling Degree Days (base 65°F)	0	1	11	43	146	320	437	395	232	53	5	2	1,645
Mean Precipitation (in.)	5.46	5.20	6.17	4.20	4.45	3.99	4.86	3.89	3.20	3.04	4.08	4.26	52.80
Days With ≥ 0.1" Precipitation	9	7	8	6	6	7	8	6	5	4	6	7	79
Days With ≥ 1.0" Precipitation	2	2	2	1	1	1	1	1	1	1	1	1	15
Mean Snowfall (in.)	0.7	0.3	0.5	trace	0.0	0.0	0.0	0.0	0.0	0.0	0.0	0.2	1.7
Days With ≥ 1.0" Snow Depth	1	0	0	0	0	0	0	0	0	0	0	0	1

Plains SW Georgia Exp. Station *Sumter County* Elevation: 498 ft. Latitude: 32° 03' N Longitude: 84° 22' W

	JAN	FEB	MAR	APR	MAY	JUN	JUL	AUG	SEP	OCT	NOV	DEC	YEAR
Mean Maximum Temp. (°F)	56.9	61.4	68.7	76.4	83.3	88.8	91.1	90.2	86.3	77.7	68.6	60.6	75.8
Mean Temp. (°F)	45.9	49.5	56.9	63.9	71.6	77.8	80.5	79.5	75.2	65.1	56.5	49.3	64.3
Mean Minimum Temp. (°F)	34.8	37.5	45.0	51.4	59.9	66.8	69.8	68.8	64.1	52.5	44.3	37.9	52.7
Extreme Maximum Temp. (°F)	80	83	89	93	98	101	102	103	100	93	86	82	103
Extreme Minimum Temp. (°F)	-2	8	14	30	41	47	60	55	44	30	16	6	-2
Days Maximum Temp. ≥ 90°F	0	0	0	0	4	15	21	18	10	1	0	0	69
Days Maximum Temp. ≤ 32°F	0	0	0	0	0	0	0	0	0	0	0	0	0
Days Minimum Temp. ≤ 32°F	14	10	3	0	0	0	0	0	0	0	4	11	42
Days Minimum Temp. ≤ 0°F	0	0	0	0	0	0	0	0	0	0	0	0	0
Heating Degree Days (base 65°F)	588	436	267	103	11	0	0	0	5	87	270	487	2,254
Cooling Degree Days (base 65°F)	1	5	22	74	230	401	502	465	308	101	20	6	2,135
Mean Precipitation (in.)	5.53	4.79	5.39	3.47	3.55	4.47	5.59	3.70	3.02	2.43	3.69	3.88	49.51
Days With ≥ 0.1" Precipitation	8	7	7	5	6	7	9	7	5	4	5	6	76
Days With ≥ 1.0" Precipitation	2	2	2	1	1	1	1	1	1	1	1	1	15
Mean Snowfall (in.)	trace	0.3	trace	0.0	0.0	0.0	0.0	0.0	0.0	0.0	0.0	trace	0.3
Days With ≥ 1.0" Snow Depth	0	0	0	0	0	0	0	0	0	0	0	0	0

Quitman 2 NW *Brooks County* Elevation: 183 ft. Latitude: 30° 48' N Longitude: 83° 35' W

	JAN	FEB	MAR	APR	MAY	JUN	JUL	AUG	SEP	OCT	NOV	DEC	YEAR
Mean Maximum Temp. (°F)	61.7	66.2	72.9	79.2	85.8	90.6	92.0	91.4	88.5	80.2	72.4	64.4	78.8
Mean Temp. (°F)	49.6	53.5	60.0	65.9	73.0	78.9	80.9	80.3	76.8	67.0	59.3	52.3	66.5
Mean Minimum Temp. (°F)	37.7	40.7	47.1	52.3	60.3	67.1	69.8	69.2	65.1	53.8	46.2	40.0	54.1
Extreme Maximum Temp. (°F)	82	85	90	92	98	105	103	102	103	97	87	85	105
Extreme Minimum Temp. (°F)	3	14	18	32	40	51	58	54	42	33	16	6	3
Days Maximum Temp. ≥ 90°F	0	0	0	1	6	19	25	24	15	2	0	0	92
Days Maximum Temp. ≤ 32°F	0	0	0	0	0	0	0	0	0	0	0	0	0
Days Minimum Temp. ≤ 32°F	11	6	2	0	0	0	0	0	0	0	3	8	30
Days Minimum Temp. ≤ 0°F	0	0	0	0	0	0	0	0	0	0	0	0	0
Heating Degree Days (base 65°F)	476	328	187	67	5	0	0	0	0	2	58	203	400	1,726
Cooling Degree Days (base 65°F)	4	11	37	95	266	432	506	481	345	135	40	11	2,363
Mean Precipitation (in.)	5.74	4.52	5.42	3.47	3.33	5.14	6.29	5.52	3.90	3.24	3.14	3.78	53.49
Days With ≥ 0.1" Precipitation	6	5	5	3	4	6	8	5	4	3	3	4	56
Days With ≥ 1.0" Precipitation	2	1	2	1	1	2	2	2	1	1	1	1	17
Mean Snowfall (in.)	trace	trace	trace	0.0	0.0	0.0	0.0	0.0	0.0	0.0	0.0	0.2	0.2
Days With ≥ 1.0" Snow Depth	0	0	0	0	0	0	0	0	0	0	0	0	0

Rome *Floyd County*   Elevation: 620 ft.   Latitude: 34° 15' N   Longitude: 85° 09' W

	JAN	FEB	MAR	APR	MAY	JUN	JUL	AUG	SEP	OCT	NOV	DEC	YEAR
Mean Maximum Temp. (°F)	50.3	55.9	64.6	72.8	78.7	84.5	87.8	86.9	81.8	72.2	62.6	53.8	71.0
Mean Temp. (°F)	39.7	43.7	51.8	59.2	66.6	73.7	77.6	76.6	71.0	59.7	50.6	42.9	59.4
Mean Minimum Temp. (°F)	29.2	31.5	38.8	45.6	54.4	62.7	67.4	66.3	60.2	47.1	38.5	32.0	47.8
Extreme Maximum Temp. (°F)	77	81	87	90	93	100	104	103	98	88	85	78	104
Extreme Minimum Temp. (°F)	-9	5	8	23	35	42	52	53	39	23	12	-2	-9
Days Maximum Temp. ≥ 90°F	0	0	0	0	0	5	12	9	3	0	0	0	29
Days Maximum Temp. ≤ 32°F	2	0	0	0	0	0	0	0	0	0	0	1	3
Days Minimum Temp. ≤ 32°F	20	16	9	2	0	0	0	0	0	2	10	18	77
Days Minimum Temp. ≤ 0°F	0	0	0	0	0	0	0	0	0	0	0	0	0
Heating Degree Days (base 65°F)	776	595	408	196	52	3	0	0	20	190	429	678	3,347
Cooling Degree Days (base 65°F)	0	0	4	25	109	278	412	368	191	29	2	1	1,419
Mean Precipitation (in.)	5.33	4.88	6.72	4.79	4.28	4.68	4.86	4.45	3.80	3.62	4.38	4.42	56.21
Days With ≥ 0.1" Precipitation	9	7	9	7	7	7	7	6	6	5	7	7	84
Days With ≥ 1.0" Precipitation	1	1	2	2	1	1	1	1	1	1	1	1	14
Mean Snowfall (in.)	0.6	trace	0.5	0.2	0.0	0.0	0.0	0.0	0.0	0.0	trace	trace	1.3
Days With ≥ 1.0" Snow Depth	0	0	0	0	0	0	0	0	0	0	0	0	0

Sandersville *Washington County*   Elevation: 433 ft.   Latitude: 32° 58' N   Longitude: 82° 48' W

	JAN	FEB	MAR	APR	MAY	JUN	JUL	AUG	SEP	OCT	NOV	DEC	YEAR
Mean Maximum Temp. (°F)	55.6	60.4	68.1	75.5	82.3	88.1	90.8	89.0	84.6	75.4	66.5	58.8	74.6
Mean Temp. (°F)	44.9	48.4	55.6	62.5	70.1	76.9	80.3	78.9	74.0	63.6	54.6	47.8	63.1
Mean Minimum Temp. (°F)	34.2	36.2	43.1	49.4	57.8	65.6	69.7	68.7	63.4	51.8	42.7	36.8	51.6
Extreme Maximum Temp. (°F)	80	84	90	94	95	102	107	102	99	92	84	80	107
Extreme Minimum Temp. (°F)	-3	7	14	26	36	45	54	56	43	24	18	5	-3
Days Maximum Temp. ≥ 90°F	0	0	0	0	3	12	19	15	7	0	0	0	56
Days Maximum Temp. ≤ 32°F	1	0	0	0	0	0	0	0	0	0	0	0	1
Days Minimum Temp. ≤ 32°F	15	11	5	1	0	0	0	0	0	0	6	12	50
Days Minimum Temp. ≤ 0°F	0	0	0	0	0	0	0	0	0	0	0	0	0
Heating Degree Days (base 65°F)	617	466	301	126	22	1	0	0	8	112	317	529	2,499
Cooling Degree Days (base 65°F)	1	3	14	53	183	369	497	444	272	77	11	3	1,927
Mean Precipitation (in.)	4.95	4.48	5.13	3.20	2.84	3.62	4.41	4.66	3.70	3.02	3.11	3.76	46.88
Days With ≥ 0.1" Precipitation	8	6	7	5	5	7	7	7	5	4	5	6	72
Days With ≥ 1.0" Precipitation	2	1	2	1	1	1	1	1	1	1	1	1	14
Mean Snowfall (in.)	0.3	0.6	trace	0.0	0.0	0.0	0.0	0.0	0.0	0.0	0.0	trace	0.9
Days With ≥ 1.0" Snow Depth	0	0	0	0	0	0	0	0	0	0	0	0	0

Sapelo Island *McIntosh County*   Elevation: 9 ft.   Latitude: 31° 24' N   Longitude: 81° 17' W

	JAN	FEB	MAR	APR	MAY	JUN	JUL	AUG	SEP	OCT	NOV	DEC	YEAR
Mean Maximum Temp. (°F)	60.8	63.3	69.4	75.8	81.7	87.0	90.3	88.7	85.3	77.9	70.4	63.2	76.1
Mean Temp. (°F)	51.0	53.1	59.5	65.8	72.7	78.6	81.7	80.8	77.6	69.3	60.9	53.8	67.1
Mean Minimum Temp. (°F)	41.2	42.9	49.5	55.7	63.7	70.1	73.1	72.7	69.9	60.6	51.4	44.3	57.9
Extreme Maximum Temp. (°F)	82	83	87	95	95	101	105	102	97	94	87	84	105
Extreme Minimum Temp. (°F)	3	18	20	33	44	51	60	58	51	37	23	9	3
Days Maximum Temp. ≥ 90°F	0	0	0	0	2	9	17	12	4	0	0	0	44
Days Maximum Temp. ≤ 32°F	0	0	0	0	0	0	0	0	0	0	0	0	0
Days Minimum Temp. ≤ 32°F	7	4	1	0	0	0	0	0	0	0	1	4	17
Days Minimum Temp. ≤ 0°F	0	0	0	0	0	0	0	0	0	0	0	0	0
Heating Degree Days (base 65°F)	432	334	192	62	4	0	0	0	0	30	159	350	1,563
Cooling Degree Days (base 65°F)	2	5	25	85	249	422	539	502	377	170	47	10	2,433
Mean Precipitation (in.)	4.46	3.62	4.03	2.95	2.91	4.93	5.09	7.61	7.15	4.04	2.81	2.99	52.59
Days With ≥ 0.1" Precipitation	7	6	6	4	5	7	8	9	8	5	4	5	74
Days With ≥ 1.0" Precipitation	1	1	1	1	1	1	1	3	2	1	1	1	15
Mean Snowfall (in.)	trace	trace	trace	0.0	0.0	0.0	0.0	0.0	0.0	0.0	0.0	0.2	0.2
Days With ≥ 1.0" Snow Depth	0	0	0	0	0	0	0	0	0	0	0	0	0

Siloam 3 N *Greene County*   Elevation: 688 ft.   Latitude: 33° 37' N   Longitude: 83° 05' W

	JAN	FEB	MAR	APR	MAY	JUN	JUL	AUG	SEP	OCT	NOV	DEC	YEAR
Mean Maximum Temp. (°F)	54.0	59.0	67.0	74.8	81.7	88.4	91.1	89.4	84.7	75.2	65.9	57.2	74.1
Mean Temp. (°F)	43.7	47.3	54.8	61.9	69.4	76.6	80.0	78.7	73.6	63.1	54.2	46.7	62.5
Mean Minimum Temp. (°F)	33.2	35.6	42.5	48.9	57.0	64.6	68.8	68.0	62.4	50.9	42.5	36.1	50.9
Extreme Maximum Temp. (°F)	81	82	89	93	95	103	106	107	100	94	88	80	107
Extreme Minimum Temp. (°F)	-7	7	9	24	35	43	56	53	41	27	14	2	-7
Days Maximum Temp. ≥ 90°F	0	0	0	0	3	12	19	16	8	0	0	0	58
Days Maximum Temp. ≤ 32°F	1	0	0	0	0	0	0	0	0	0	0	0	1
Days Minimum Temp. ≤ 32°F	15	11	6	1	0	0	0	0	0	0	6	13	52
Days Minimum Temp. ≤ 0°F	0	0	0	0	0	0	0	0	0	0	0	0	0
Heating Degree Days (base 65°F)	656	493	323	142	27	1	0	0	10	120	329	562	2,663
Cooling Degree Days (base 65°F)	0	1	11	49	168	361	489	433	259	65	10	2	1,848
Mean Precipitation (in.)	5.08	4.82	5.16	3.57	3.69	3.22	4.75	3.91	3.33	3.02	3.35	3.69	47.59
Days With ≥ 0.1" Precipitation	8	7	7	5	6	6	7	7	6	4	5	6	74
Days With ≥ 1.0" Precipitation	1	2	1	1	1	1	1	1	1	1	1	1	13
Mean Snowfall (in.)	0.7	0.8	0.2	0.0	0.0	0.0	0.0	0.0	0.0	0.0	0.0	trace	1.7
Days With ≥ 1.0" Snow Depth	0	0	0	0	0	0	0	0	0	0	0	0	0

Surrency 2 WNW *Appling County*   Elevation: 200 ft.   Latitude: 31° 44' N   Longitude: 82° 14' W

	JAN	FEB	MAR	APR	MAY	JUN	JUL	AUG	SEP	OCT	NOV	DEC	YEAR
Mean Maximum Temp. (°F)	61.7	65.9	73.0	79.7	85.6	90.2	92.4	90.9	87.4	79.7	71.4	64.0	78.5
Mean Temp. (°F)	49.9	53.1	59.6	65.4	72.2	78.0	80.9	79.8	76.1	67.0	58.7	52.0	66.0
Mean Minimum Temp. (°F)	38.0	40.1	46.0	51.0	58.6	65.8	69.4	68.6	64.8	54.2	45.9	40.0	53.5
Extreme Maximum Temp. (°F)	81	88	90	96	97	103	104	102	100	94	86	83	104
Extreme Minimum Temp. (°F)	1	12	17	29	39	48	57	56	41	29	15	9	1
Days Maximum Temp. ≥ 90°F	0	0	0	1	6	17	24	21	11	1	0	0	81
Days Maximum Temp. ≤ 32°F	0	0	0	0	0	0	0	0	0	0	0	0	0
Days Minimum Temp. ≤ 32°F	11	7	3	0	0	0	0	0	0	0	5	9	35
Days Minimum Temp. ≤ 0°F	0	0	0	0	0	0	0	0	0	0	0	0	0
Heating Degree Days (base 65°F)	467	342	199	74	7	0	0	0	1	59	218	405	1,772
Cooling Degree Days (base 65°F)	4	11	33	90	237	406	514	466	331	130	36	9	2,267
Mean Precipitation (in.)	4.42	3.76	4.37	2.74	3.22	4.75	5.52	6.34	3.40	2.85	2.34	3.62	47.33
Days With ≥ 0.1" Precipitation	7	6	6	5	5	8	8	8	6	4	4	5	72
Days With ≥ 1.0" Precipitation	1	1	1	1	1	1	2	2	1	1	1	1	14
Mean Snowfall (in.)	trace	0.2	trace	0.0	0.0	0.0	0.0	0.0	0.0	0.0	0.0	trace	0.2
Days With ≥ 1.0" Snow Depth	0	0	0	0	0	0	0	0	0	0	0	0	0

Swainsboro *Emanuel County*   Elevation: 324 ft.   Latitude: 32° 36' N   Longitude: 82° 20' W

	JAN	FEB	MAR	APR	MAY	JUN	JUL	AUG	SEP	OCT	NOV	DEC	YEAR
Mean Maximum Temp. (°F)	59.0	63.7	71.5	78.6	85.3	90.9	92.9	91.3	87.0	78.1	69.8	62.6	77.6
Mean Temp. (°F)	48.1	51.5	58.6	64.8	72.5	78.8	81.5	80.5	76.1	66.2	57.6	50.8	65.6
Mean Minimum Temp. (°F)	37.1	39.2	45.6	51.0	59.6	66.7	70.1	69.6	65.1	54.1	45.2	39.3	53.5
Extreme Maximum Temp. (°F)	83	84	90	96	98	107	107	106	103	93	87	84	107
Extreme Minimum Temp. (°F)	-3	10	18	26	36	47	57	56	42	29	12	7	-3
Days Maximum Temp. ≥ 90°F	0	0	0	1	6	18	24	21	10	1	0	0	81
Days Maximum Temp. ≤ 32°F	0	0	0	0	0	0	0	0	0	0	0	0	0
Days Minimum Temp. ≤ 32°F	11	8	3	0	0	0	0	0	0	0	5	10	37
Days Minimum Temp. ≤ 0°F	0	0	0	0	0	0	0	0	0	0	0	0	0
Heating Degree Days (base 65°F)	520	384	224	88	8	0	0	0	2	69	245	441	1,981
Cooling Degree Days (base 65°F)	3	10	30	84	259	441	537	494	335	119	30	7	2,349
Mean Precipitation (in.)	4.54	3.98	4.88	3.11	2.76	4.04	4.63	5.04	3.46	2.81	2.78	3.37	45.40
Days With ≥ 0.1" Precipitation	7	5	6	5	5	6	7	7	5	3	4	5	65
Days With ≥ 1.0" Precipitation	2	1	2	1	1	1	1	2	1	1	1	1	15
Mean Snowfall (in.)	trace	0.3	trace	0.0	0.0	0.0	0.0	0.0	0.0	0.0	0.0	trace	0.3
Days With ≥ 1.0" Snow Depth	0	0	0	0	0	0	0	0	0	0	0	0	0

Talbotton *Talbot County*   Elevation: 728 ft.   Latitude: 32° 41' N   Longitude: 84° 33' W

	JAN	FEB	MAR	APR	MAY	JUN	JUL	AUG	SEP	OCT	NOV	DEC	YEAR
Mean Maximum Temp. (°F)	57.0	62.2	70.1	77.3	83.2	88.5	90.6	90.2	86.4	76.9	68.5	60.2	75.9
Mean Temp. (°F)	45.2	49.0	56.4	63.0	69.9	76.4	79.5	78.8	74.3	63.5	55.1	48.3	63.3
Mean Minimum Temp. (°F)	33.3	35.8	42.6	48.7	56.5	64.2	68.2	67.4	62.2	50.2	41.7	36.3	50.6
Extreme Maximum Temp. (°F)	80	83	92	93	98	102	104	104	100	94	85	81	104
Extreme Minimum Temp. (°F)	-5	6	12	25	33	42	48	51	40	24	14	4	-5
Days Maximum Temp. ≥ 90°F	0	0	0	1	4	13	19	18	10	0	0	0	65
Days Maximum Temp. ≤ 32°F	0	0	0	0	0	0	0	0	0	0	0	0	0
Days Minimum Temp. ≤ 32°F	16	12	6	1	0	0	0	0	0	1	7	13	56
Days Minimum Temp. ≤ 0°F	0	0	0	0	0	0	0	0	0	0	0	0	0
Heating Degree Days (base 65°F)	608	448	279	116	20	1	1	0	6	110	303	515	2,407
Cooling Degree Days (base 65°F)	0	3	17	55	170	347	457	434	*275*	73	11	2	*1,844*
Mean Precipitation (in.)	5.00	4.84	6.05	4.01	3.38	4.06	4.93	4.08	3.28	3.04	3.74	4.64	51.05
Days With ≥ 0.1" Precipitation	7	6	7	5	6	6	7	6	5	4	5	6	70
Days With ≥ 1.0" Precipitation	2	2	2	2	1	1	1	1	1	1	1	2	17
Mean Snowfall (in.)	0.2	0.5	0.1	0.0	0.0	0.0	0.0	0.0	0.0	0.0	0.0	trace	0.8
Days With ≥ 1.0" Snow Depth	0	0	0	0	0	0	0	0	0	0	0	0	0

Thomaston 2 S *Upson County*   Elevation: 662 ft.   Latitude: 32° 52' N   Longitude: 84° 19' W

	JAN	FEB	MAR	APR	MAY	JUN	JUL	AUG	SEP	OCT	NOV	DEC	YEAR
Mean Maximum Temp. (°F)	57.8	63.0	71.3	78.2	83.7	89.4	91.4	90.3	86.5	78.3	69.4	61.1	76.7
Mean Temp. (°F)	45.7	49.3	56.9	63.2	70.4	76.9	80.0	79.3	74.8	65.0	56.1	48.8	63.9
Mean Minimum Temp. (°F)	33.5	35.6	42.4	48.2	57.0	64.3	68.5	68.2	63.0	51.6	42.7	36.4	51.0
Extreme Maximum Temp. (°F)	80	85	91	95	98	109	107	107	102	95	88	82	109
Extreme Minimum Temp. (°F)	-5	5	13	25	35	45	56	56	43	26	15	3	-5
Days Maximum Temp. ≥ 90°F	0	0	0	1	4	14	20	18	10	1	0	0	68
Days Maximum Temp. ≤ 32°F	0	0	0	0	0	0	0	0	0	0	0	0	0
Days Minimum Temp. ≤ 32°F	15	12	5	1	0	0	0	0	0	0	6	12	51
Days Minimum Temp. ≤ 0°F	0	0	0	0	0	0	0	0	0	0	0	0	0
Heating Degree Days (base 65°F)	592	439	263	106	13	0	0	0	4	81	276	499	2,273
Cooling Degree Days (base 65°F)	0	2	18	55	186	365	482	452	292	89	14	3	1,958
Mean Precipitation (in.)	4.91	4.86	6.16	3.88	3.62	3.50	5.64	4.02	3.14	2.73	3.57	4.46	50.49
Days With ≥ 0.1" Precipitation	8	6	7	5	6	6	8	6	5	4	5	6	72
Days With ≥ 1.0" Precipitation	1	2	2	1	1	1	2	1	1	1	1	1	15
Mean Snowfall (in.)	0.4	0.7	trace	0.0	0.0	0.0	0.0	0.0	0.0	0.0	0.0	0.0	1.1
Days With ≥ 1.0" Snow Depth	*0*	0	0	0	0	0	0	0	0	0	0	0	*0*

Tifton Exp. Station *Tift County*   Elevation: 377 ft.   Latitude: 31° 30' N   Longitude: 83° 32' W

	JAN	FEB	MAR	APR	MAY	JUN	JUL	AUG	SEP	OCT	NOV	DEC	YEAR
Mean Maximum Temp. (°F)	58.9	62.8	69.9	76.9	83.6	88.8	91.0	90.3	87.0	78.7	69.9	62.3	76.7
Mean Temp. (°F)	48.5	51.7	58.8	65.3	72.7	78.6	81.1	80.4	76.7	67.1	58.6	51.5	65.9
Mean Minimum Temp. (°F)	37.9	40.5	47.5	53.6	61.7	68.3	71.1	70.5	66.4	55.4	47.3	40.7	55.1
Extreme Maximum Temp. (°F)	81	85	89	93	96	104	102	101	100	95	88	84	104
Extreme Minimum Temp. (°F)	0	12	16	32	41	50	60	57	47	34	19	9	0
Days Maximum Temp. ≥ 90°F	0	0	0	0	4	13	22	20	11	1	0	0	71
Days Maximum Temp. ≤ 32°F	0	0	0	0	0	0	0	0	0	0	0	0	0
Days Minimum Temp. ≤ 32°F	11	6	2	0	0	0	0	0	0	0	2	7	28
Days Minimum Temp. ≤ 0°F	0	0	0	0	0	0	0	0	0	0	0	0	0
Heating Degree Days (base 65°F)	510	377	220	80	7	0	0	0	2	62	218	421	1,897
Cooling Degree Days (base 65°F)	3	10	31	89	256	419	516	486	347	136	34	9	2,336
Mean Precipitation (in.)	5.29	4.43	5.17	3.49	3.42	4.04	4.57	4.38	3.13	2.69	3.05	3.66	47.32
Days With ≥ 0.1" Precipitation	8	6	7	5	5	7	8	7	5	4	5	5	72
Days With ≥ 1.0" Precipitation	2	1	2	1	1	1	1	1	1	1	1	1	14
Mean Snowfall (in.)	0.0	trace	0.0	0.0	0.0	0.0	0.0	0.0	0.0	0.0	0.0	0.0	trace
Days With ≥ 1.0" Snow Depth	0	0	0	0	0	0	0	0	0	0	0	0	0

Toccoa *Stephens County*   Elevation: 1,017 ft.   Latitude: 34° 35' N   Longitude: 83° 19' W

	JAN	FEB	MAR	APR	MAY	JUN	JUL	AUG	SEP	OCT	NOV	DEC	YEAR
Mean Maximum Temp. (°F)	52.0	56.5	64.9	73.5	79.8	85.7	89.0	87.3	82.4	73.1	63.3	54.9	71.9
Mean Temp. (°F)	42.0	45.5	52.9	60.5	67.7	74.6	78.4	77.0	71.7	61.6	52.5	45.1	60.8
Mean Minimum Temp. (°F)	32.0	34.4	40.9	47.5	55.6	63.3	67.7	66.7	61.0	50.1	41.5	35.2	49.7
Extreme Maximum Temp. (°F)	79	79	88	92	95	98	104	104	98	93	88	80	104
Extreme Minimum Temp. (°F)	-4	4	11	25	33	39	54	50	42	29	11	4	-4
Days Maximum Temp. ≥ 90°F	0	0	0	0	1	8	15	10	4	0	0	0	38
Days Maximum Temp. ≤ 32°F	1	0	0	0	0	0	0	0	0	0	0	0	1
Days Minimum Temp. ≤ 32°F	16	12	6	2	0	0	0	0	0	1	6	13	56
Days Minimum Temp. ≤ 0°F	0	0	0	0	0	0	0	0	0	0	0	0	0
Heating Degree Days (base 65°F)	705	545	372	168	38	2	0	0	13	143	374	612	2,972
Cooling Degree Days (base 65°F)	0	0	6	39	132	308	439	389	221	48	4	1	1,587
Mean Precipitation (in.)	6.21	5.36	6.23	4.42	5.12	4.70	5.18	5.14	4.25	4.70	4.63	5.13	61.07
Days With ≥ 0.1" Precipitation	9	7	8	7	7	7	7	7	6	5	7	8	85
Days With ≥ 1.0" Precipitation	2	2	2	1	2	1	2	2	1	2	1	1	19
Mean Snowfall (in.)	1.3	0.7	0.6	trace	0.0	0.0	0.0	0.0	0.0	0.0	trace	trace	2.6
Days With ≥ 1.0" Snow Depth	0	0	0	0	0	0	0	0	0	0	0	0	0

Univ. of GA Plant Science Farm *Oconee County*   Elevation: 839 ft.   Latitude: 33° 52' N   Longitude: 83° 32' W

	JAN	FEB	MAR	APR	MAY	JUN	JUL	AUG	SEP	OCT	NOV	DEC	YEAR
Mean Maximum Temp. (°F)	52.4	57.4	65.8	73.7	81.1	87.5	90.5	89.0	83.6	74.2	64.5	55.9	73.0
Mean Temp. (°F)	42.4	46.1	53.8	61.0	69.2	76.1	79.6	78.3	72.6	62.2	53.2	45.7	61.7
Mean Minimum Temp. (°F)	32.3	34.7	41.7	48.1	57.2	64.7	68.7	67.5	61.5	50.1	41.9	35.4	50.3
Extreme Maximum Temp. (°F)	78	79	87	94	95	102	105	104	98	90	84	78	105
Extreme Minimum Temp. (°F)	-1	6	9	26	38	38	56	55	41	27	18	0	-1
Days Maximum Temp. ≥ 90°F	0	0	0	0	2	11	19	14	5	0	0	0	51
Days Maximum Temp. ≤ 32°F	1	0	0	0	0	0	0	0	0	0	0	0	1
Days Minimum Temp. ≤ 32°F	16	12	6	1	0	0	0	0	0	0	6	13	54
Days Minimum Temp. ≤ 0°F	0	0	0	0	0	0	0	0	0	0	0	0	0
Heating Degree Days (base 65°F)	695	527	350	161	28	1	0	0	11	132	353	593	2,851
Cooling Degree Days (base 65°F)	0	0	7	44	165	352	477	424	239	54	6	1	1,769
Mean Precipitation (in.)	5.10	4.55	5.17	3.72	4.10	3.96	4.14	4.03	4.08	3.28	4.07	4.02	50.22
Days With ≥ 0.1" Precipitation	8	7	8	6	7	6	7	6	6	4	6	6	77
Days With ≥ 1.0" Precipitation	1	1	2	1	1	1	1	1	1	1	1	1	13
Mean Snowfall (in.)	0.4	0.1	0.3	0.0	0.0	0.0	0.0	0.0	0.0	0.0	0.0	0.0	0.8
Days With ≥ 1.0" Snow Depth	0	0	0	0	0	0	0	0	0	0	0	0	0

Warrenton *Warren County*   Elevation: 508 ft.   Latitude: 33° 22' N   Longitude: 84° 34' W

	JAN	FEB	MAR	APR	MAY	JUN	JUL	AUG	SEP	OCT	NOV	DEC	YEAR
Mean Maximum Temp. (°F)	54.0	59.1	67.3	75.3	82.4	88.8	91.5	89.7	84.6	74.7	66.0	57.4	74.2
Mean Temp. (°F)	43.2	46.6	54.1	61.6	69.6	76.7	80.1	78.9	73.5	62.6	53.7	46.0	62.2
Mean Minimum Temp. (°F)	32.2	34.1	40.9	47.7	56.7	64.5	68.7	67.9	62.4	50.4	41.3	34.5	50.1
Extreme Maximum Temp. (°F)	81	82	89	93	97	104	108	105	99	90	83	80	108
Extreme Minimum Temp. (°F)	-3	8	11	26	37	40	50	54	43	28	16	5	-3
Days Maximum Temp. ≥ 90°F	0	0	0	1	4	13	20	17	8	0	0	0	63
Days Maximum Temp. ≤ 32°F	1	0	0	0	0	0	0	0	0	0	0	0	1
Days Minimum Temp. ≤ 32°F	17	13	6	1	0	0	0	0	0	0	6	14	57
Days Minimum Temp. ≤ 0°F	0	0	0	0	0	0	0	0	0	0	0	0	0
Heating Degree Days (base 65°F)	669	514	340	146	25	1	0	0	9	131	343	585	2,763
Cooling Degree Days (base 65°F)	0	1	8	41	165	355	479	429	257	65	10	2	1,812
Mean Precipitation (in.)	5.18	4.67	5.45	3.59	3.72	3.76	4.21	4.64	3.65	3.60	3.43	4.01	49.91
Days With ≥ 0.1" Precipitation	8	6	7	5	6	6	6	7	5	4	4	6	70
Days With ≥ 1.0" Precipitation	2	1	2	1	1	1	1	2	1	1	1	1	15
Mean Snowfall (in.)	trace	0.6	0.1	0.0	0.0	0.0	0.0	0.0	0.0	0.0	0.0	0.0	0.7
Days With ≥ 1.0" Snow Depth	0	0	0	0	0	0	0	0	0	0	0	0	0

Washington 2 ESE *Wilkes County*　Elevation: 620 ft.　Latitude: 33° 43' N　Longitude: 82° 44' W

	JAN	FEB	MAR	APR	MAY	JUN	JUL	AUG	SEP	OCT	NOV	DEC	YEAR
Mean Maximum Temp. (°F)	52.9	57.9	65.8	74.0	80.7	87.1	90.3	88.8	84.2	74.3	65.2	56.2	73.1
Mean Temp. (°F)	42.0	45.6	53.0	60.7	68.4	75.7	79.4	78.2	72.9	62.0	53.0	45.1	61.3
Mean Minimum Temp. (°F)	31.2	33.2	40.1	47.4	56.1	64.2	68.4	67.5	61.5	49.5	40.7	34.0	49.5
Extreme Maximum Temp. (°F)	81	81	87	93	95	102	105	106	98	92	85	79	106
Extreme Minimum Temp. (°F)	-5	6	9	27	33	44	56	55	42	25	12	3	-5
Days Maximum Temp. ≥ 90°F	0	0	0	0	2	10	18	15	7	0	0	0	52
Days Maximum Temp. ≤ 32°F	1	0	0	0	0	0	0	0	0	0	0	0	1
Days Minimum Temp. ≤ 32°F	17	14	7	1	0	0	0	0	0	1	7	14	61
Days Minimum Temp. ≤ 0°F	0	0	0	0	0	0	0	0	0	0	0	0	0
Heating Degree Days (base 65°F)	705	543	374	166	36	2	0	0	11	141	361	611	2,950
Cooling Degree Days (base 65°F)	0	1	8	46	160	345	473	427	252	61	7	1	1,781
Mean Precipitation (in.)	4.92	4.43	4.90	3.35	3.93	3.60	4.33	3.69	3.33	3.45	3.30	3.71	46.94
Days With ≥ 0.1" Precipitation	8	7	7	6	6	6	7	6	5	5	5	6	74
Days With ≥ 1.0" Precipitation	2	2	2	1	1	1	1	1	1	1	1	1	15
Mean Snowfall (in.)	0.1	trace	trace	0.0	0.0	0.0	0.0	0.0	0.0	0.0	0.0	0.0	0.1
Days With ≥ 1.0" Snow Depth	0	0	0	0	0	0	0	0	0	0	0	0	0

Waycross 4 NE *Pierce County*　Elevation: 144 ft.　Latitude: 31° 15' N　Longitude: 82° 19' W

	JAN	FEB	MAR	APR	MAY	JUN	JUL	AUG	SEP	OCT	NOV	DEC	YEAR
Mean Maximum Temp. (°F)	62.8	66.5	73.9	80.7	87.2	91.7	94.2	92.7	89.3	81.2	73.6	65.5	79.9
Mean Temp. (°F)	49.1	52.1	59.1	65.2	72.7	78.9	82.0	81.1	77.0	67.0	59.0	51.5	66.2
Mean Minimum Temp. (°F)	35.7	37.8	44.4	49.7	58.1	66.1	69.7	69.5	64.8	52.8	44.5	37.5	52.5
Extreme Maximum Temp. (°F)	88	88	91	98	101	106	108	104	102	97	90	86	108
Extreme Minimum Temp. (°F)	2	10	15	22	38	43	54	*59*	41	29	18	8	*2*
Days Maximum Temp. ≥ 90°F	0	0	0	3	12	21	27	25	17	4	0	0	109
Days Maximum Temp. ≤ 32°F	0	0	0	0	0	0	0	0	0	0	0	0	0
Days Minimum Temp. ≤ 32°F	14	10	4	1	0	0	0	0	0	1	6	12	48
Days Minimum Temp. ≤ 0°F	0	0	0	0	0	0	0	0	0	0	0	0	0
Heating Degree Days (base 65°F)	494	369	212	85	9	0	0	0	1	67	217	422	1,876
Cooling Degree Days (base 65°F)	6	13	34	98	263	440	548	511	355	141	46	10	2,465
Mean Precipitation (in.)	4.95	3.68	4.54	2.93	3.56	5.70	6.18	6.45	3.63	2.99	2.73	3.18	50.52
Days With ≥ 0.1" Precipitation	7	5	6	4	6	8	10	8	6	4	4	5	73
Days With ≥ 1.0" Precipitation	2	1	1	1	1	2	2	2	1	1	1	1	16
Mean Snowfall (in.)	0.0	trace	0.0	0.0	0.0	0.0	0.0	0.0	0.0	0.0	0.0	0.0	trace
Days With ≥ 1.0" Snow Depth	0	0	0	0	0	0	0	0	0	0	0	0	0

Waynesboro 2 NE *Burke County*　Elevation: 269 ft.　Latitude: 33° 06' N　Longitude: 81° 59' W

	JAN	FEB	MAR	APR	MAY	JUN	JUL	AUG	SEP	OCT	NOV	DEC	YEAR
Mean Maximum Temp. (°F)	56.4	60.8	68.6	76.2	83.2	89.0	91.6	89.9	85.5	76.7	68.5	59.4	75.5
Mean Temp. (°F)	44.3	47.6	55.0	61.9	69.8	76.6	80.1	78.6	73.8	63.1	54.5	47.0	62.7
Mean Minimum Temp. (°F)	32.2	34.4	41.4	47.6	56.3	64.3	68.6	67.3	62.1	49.3	40.5	34.5	49.9
Extreme Maximum Temp. (°F)	83	85	91	98	96	105	108	106	103	93	87	82	108
Extreme Minimum Temp. (°F)	-1	9	16	27	36	44	54	52	40	23	15	6	-1
Days Maximum Temp. ≥ 90°F	0	0	0	1	5	14	21	17	8	0	0	0	66
Days Maximum Temp. ≤ 32°F	1	0	0	0	0	0	0	0	0	0	0	0	1
Days Minimum Temp. ≤ 32°F	17	12	6	1	0	0	0	0	0	1	8	15	60
Days Minimum Temp. ≤ 0°F	0	0	0	0	0	0	0	0	0	0	0	0	0
Heating Degree Days (base 65°F)	636	487	317	142	23	1	0	0	6	122	322	556	2,612
Cooling Degree Days (base 65°F)	1	2	11	51	179	370	490	435	271	69	12	3	1,894
Mean Precipitation (in.)	4.54	4.25	4.81	3.19	3.19	4.47	4.79	4.98	3.53	3.32	2.69	3.72	47.48
Days With ≥ 0.1" Precipitation	7	5	6	5	5	6	7	7	4	4	4	6	66
Days With ≥ 1.0" Precipitation	1	1	1	1	1	1	2	1	1	1	1	1	13
Mean Snowfall (in.)	trace	0.9	0.0	0.0	0.0	0.0	0.0	0.0	0.0	0.0	0.0	0.0	0.9
Days With ≥ 1.0" Snow Depth	0	*0*	0	0	0	0	0	0	0	0	0	0	*0*

West Point *Troup County*　Elevation: 574 ft.　Latitude: 32° 52' N　Longitude: 85° 11' W

	JAN	FEB	MAR	APR	MAY	JUN	JUL	AUG	SEP	OCT	NOV	DEC	YEAR
Mean Maximum Temp. (°F)	55.0	59.4	67.3	75.1	81.8	88.1	91.1	90.0	85.5	76.0	66.5	58.2	74.5
Mean Temp. (°F)	43.4	46.8	54.3	61.6	69.2	76.4	80.1	79.2	74.0	63.0	53.8	46.5	62.4
Mean Minimum Temp. (°F)	31.9	34.2	41.3	48.0	56.5	64.7	69.1	68.4	62.5	49.9	40.9	34.8	50.2
Extreme Maximum Temp. (°F)	80	81	88	91	96	102	106	103	99	92	85	80	106
Extreme Minimum Temp. (°F)	-8	7	13	28	35	44	53	50	41	27	14	2	-8
Days Maximum Temp. ≥ 90°F	0	0	0	0	3	13	21	18	9	1	0	0	65
Days Maximum Temp. ≤ 32°F	1	0	0	0	0	0	0	0	0	0	0	0	1
Days Minimum Temp. ≤ 32°F	18	14	5	0	0	0	0	0	0	0	7	14	58
Days Minimum Temp. ≤ 0°F	0	0	0	0	0	0	0	0	0	0	0	0	0
Heating Degree Days (base 65°F)	662	509	334	143	25	1	0	0	8	121	340	567	2,710
Cooling Degree Days (base 65°F)	0	1	10	43	168	357	488	454	281	68	9	2	1,881
Mean Precipitation (in.)	4.93	5.02	5.65	4.59	3.52	3.72	5.68	3.53	3.40	3.08	3.83	4.79	51.74
Days With ≥ 0.1" Precipitation	8	6	7	5	6	6	8	6	5	4	5	7	73
Days With ≥ 1.0" Precipitation	1	2	2	1	1	1	2	1	1	1	1	2	16
Mean Snowfall (in.)	0.1	0.0	trace	0.0	0.0	0.0	0.0	0.0	0.0	0.0	0.0	0.0	0.1
Days With ≥ 1.0" Snow Depth	0	0	0	0	0	0	0	0	0	0	0	0	0

Winder 1 SSE *Barrow County*   Elevation: 958 ft.   Latitude: 33° 59' N   Longitude: 83° 43' W

	JAN	FEB	MAR	APR	MAY	JUN	JUL	AUG	SEP	OCT	NOV	DEC	YEAR
Mean Maximum Temp. (°F)	52.4	57.7	65.8	74.2	80.6	86.7	89.6	88.1	82.7	73.3	64.1	55.3	72.6
Mean Temp. (°F)	42.1	45.8	53.0	60.4	67.8	74.6	78.2	77.1	71.8	61.4	52.7	44.9	60.8
Mean Minimum Temp. (°F)	31.8	33.9	40.3	46.5	54.9	62.4	66.7	66.0	60.8	49.5	41.3	34.5	49.1
Extreme Maximum Temp. (°F)	78	79	87	94	93	100	104	103	97	89	84	76	104
Extreme Minimum Temp. (°F)	-8	2	5	24	34	40	51	53	37	27	13	0	-8
Days Maximum Temp. ≥ 90°F	0	0	0	0	1	9	16	11	4	0	0	0	41
Days Maximum Temp. ≤ 32°F	1	0	0	0	0	0	0	0	0	0	0	0	1
Days Minimum Temp. ≤ 32°F	17	13	7	1	0	0	0	0	0	1	7	14	60
Days Minimum Temp. ≤ 0°F	0	0	0	0	0	0	0	0	0	0	0	0	0
Heating Degree Days (base 65°F)	702	536	369	167	35	1	0	0	14	147	366	615	2,952
Cooling Degree Days (base 65°F)	0	0	6	37	130	309	428	387	216	45	4	1	1,563
Mean Precipitation (in.)	5.24	4.39	5.55	3.89	3.95	3.66	4.21	3.72	3.72	3.79	3.55	3.83	49.50
Days With ≥ 0.1" Precipitation	7	6	8	5	6	6	7	6	5	5	5	6	72
Days With ≥ 1.0" Precipitation	2	1	2	1	1	1	1	1	1	1	1	1	14
Mean Snowfall (in.)	0.3	trace	trace	0.0	0.0	0.0	0.0	0.0	0.0	0.0	0.0	trace	0.3
Days With ≥ 1.0" Snow Depth	0	0	0	0	0	0	0	0	0	0	0	0	0

Note: See Appendix D for explanation of data.

HAWAII

PHYSICAL FEATURES. West and south of California, 2,100 miles away, lies Hawaii. Among the 50 states it is the only one surrounded by the ocean. It is the only state within the tropics. Both of these facts contribute significantly to its climate, as do also its division into separate, widely-spaced islands and its topographic diversity.

The islands of the State are the easternmost members of the Hawaiian Island Chain. This Chain extends for a distance of 2,000 miles from the Kure and Midway Islands at the northwest to the Island of Hawaii at the extreme southeast end. In longitude, the Hawaiian Chain reaches from 178° to 154° W.; in latitude, from 28° to 19° N. The islands of the State of Hawaii cover a far lesser range: from 160° to 154° W. and from 22° to 19° N. They occupy a narrow zone 430 miles long. There are six major islands in the State. From west to east these are Kauai, Oahu, Molokai, Lanai, Maui, and Hawaii. Taken together with the much smaller islands of Niihau and Kahoolawe, their total area is 6,424 square miles. The islands are terrestrial, summit portions of the long range of volcanic mountains that comprise the Hawaiian Chain. The mountainous nature of Hawaii is indicated by the fact that 50 percent of the State lies above an elevation of 2,000 feet and 10 percent lies above 7,000 feet. Almost half of the area of Hawaii lies within five miles of the coast. Because of this extreme insularity the marine influence upon the climate is very great, yet the mountains, especially the massive ones on Hawaii and Maui, strongly modify the marine effect and result in conditions that are semi-continental in some localities.

GENERAL CLIMATE. The most prominent feature of the circulation of air across the tropical Pacific is the trade-wind flow in a general east-to-west direction. In the central North Pacific the trade winds blow from the northeast quadrant, and represent the outflow of air from the great region of high pressure, the Pacific Anticyclone, whose typical location is well north and east of the Hawaiian Island Chain. The Pacific High, and with it the trade-wind zone, moves north and south with the sun, so that it reaches its northernmost position in the summer half-year. This brings the heart of the trade winds across Hawaii during the period May through September, when the trades are prevalent 80 to 95 percent of the time. From October through April, Hawaii is located to the north of the heart of the trade winds. Nevertheless, the trades still blow across the islands much of the time.

The dominance of the trades and the influence of terrain give special character to the climate of the Islands. Completely cloudless skies are extremely rare, even though much of the time the dense cloud cover is confined to the mountain areas and windward slopes, while the leeward lowlands have only a few scattered clouds. Showers are very common; while some of these are very heavy, the vast majority are light and brief — a sudden sprinkle of rain. Even the heavy showers are of a special character, in that they are seldom accompanied by thunder and lightning. Finally, the trade winds provide a system of natural ventilation much of the time throughout most of the State and bring to the land, at least in the lower lying regions, the mildly warm temperatures that are characteristic of air that has moved great distances across the tropical seas.

The relatively slight variations in the length of the daylight period in Hawaii, together with the smaller annual variations in the altitude of the sun above the horizon, result in relatively small variations in the amount of incoming solar energy from one time of the year to another. This small variation partly explains why seasonal changes in temperature are so slight throughout much of Hawaii. The other principal reason for the slightness of the variation is the virtually constant flow of fresh ocean air across the islands. Just as the temperature of the ocean surface varies comparatively little from season to season, so does the temperature of air that has moved great distances across the ocean.

The rugged configuration of the islands produces marked variations in conditions from one locality to another. Air swept inland on the trade winds or as part of storm circulations is shunted one way and another by the mountains and valleys and great open slopes. This complex three-dimensional flow of air results in striking differences from place to place in windspeed, cloudiness, and rainfall. Together with variations in the elevation of the land, it results in differences in air temperature.

The native Hawaiians recognize only two seasons. KAU is the fruitful season, the season when the sun was directly or almost directly overhead, when the weather was warmer, and when the trade winds were most reliable. HOO-ILO is the season when the sun was in the south, when the weather was cooler, and when the trade winds were most often interrupted by other winds. Modern analysis of the climatic records shows the soundness of the Hawaiian seasons.

In terms of variations in climatic conditions from one part of the State to another, the most striking contrasts are those in rainfall. At one extreme the annual rainfall averages 20 inches and less in leeward coastal areas and near the summits of the very high mountains, Mauna Loa and Mauna Kea. At the other extreme the annual average exceeds 300 inches along the lower windward slopes of these high mountains and of Haleakala and at or near the summit of the lower mountains.

In general the Hawaiian climate is characterized by a two-season year, by mild and fairly uniform temperature conditions everywhere but at high elevations, by strikingly marked geographic differences in rainfall, by generally humid conditions and high cloudiness except on the driest coasts and at high elevations, and by a general dominance of trade-wind flow especially at elevations below a few thousand feet.

The surface waters of the open ocean around Hawaii have an average temperature that ranges from a minimum of 73 or 74°F. between late February and early April to a maximum of 79 or 80°F. in late September or early October. With temperatures as mild as these — and with temperatures almost as mild for hundreds of miles around, even to the north — the air that reaches Hawaii is neither very hot nor cold. The mild, equable temperatures of the ocean give rise to mild, equable temperatures in the air that moves across the oceans and onto the islands of Hawaii.

PRECIPITATION. If the islands of the State of Hawaii did not exist, the average annual rainfall upon the water where the islands actually lie would be about 25 inches. Instead, the actual average is about 70 inches. Thus the islands extract from the air that passes across them about 45 inches of rainfall that otherwise would not fall. The mountains are dominantly responsible for this added water bonus. The driest areas are on the upper slopes of the high mountains, on leeward coasts, or in leeward locations in the interior of the islands. In the driest of these areas the average annual rainfall is less than 10 inches. The contrast in rainfall between the rainier winter season and the drier summer season is generally most pronounced at low elevations in the areas with low annual rainfall. In the lowlands at all times of the year, rainfall is most likely to occur during the nighttime or in the morning hours, and least likely to occur during midafternoon.

In most parts of the tropics the rainfall is highly variable from one year to another. Hawaii is no exception. Even in areas where the rainfall is very high and the monthly averages are all above 10 inches, the rainfall of particular months may vary by 200 to 300% from one year to another and there may be very occasional months with only one or two inches of rain. With such wide swings in rainfall it is inevitable that there are occasional droughts.

STORMS. Intense local rainstorms other than those that occur under trade-wind conditions are small features that seldom cover more than a few square miles and sometimes less than a single square mile. They occur most typically in the late afternoon or early evening. In some areas in which there are well developed sea breezes, they are common occurrences, especially in summer. In most areas, however, they are apt to occur on only a few days per year when the overall winds are light and variable or when there is a gentle flow of air from a southerly direction.

Intense local storms are sometimes accompanied by lightning and thunder. Lightning and thunder also occasionally accompany very intense rainfall along a cold front moving across the islands. Thunderstorms are reported from somewhere in the State on 20 to 30 days a year, and more often in winter than in summer. Waterspouts and other funnel clouds are not uncommon in the Hawaiian area, about 20 of them being sighted in the average year. Often they are accompanied by towering cumulus clouds and rain, although they have also been observed under trade wind conditions. Hail falls somewhere in Hawaii between five and 10 times in the average year. Almost always it is quite small — 1/4 inch or less in diameter — but on several occasions hail the size of marbles, and discs about 5/8 of an inch in diameter, have been reported.

Kona storms, like cold front storms, are features of the winter season. They are so-called because they often bring winds from "kona" or leeward directions. Kona rains last from several hours to several days.

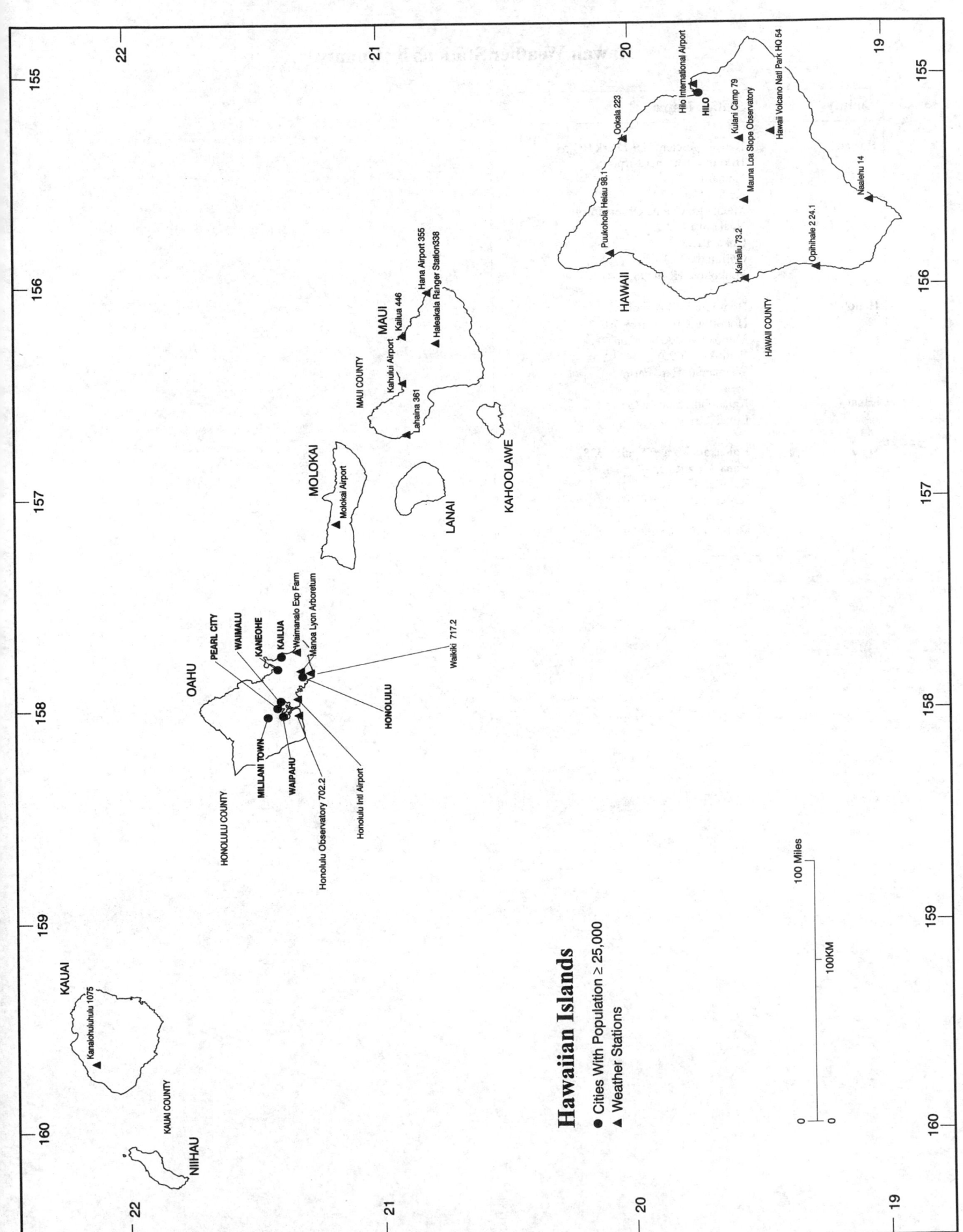

Hawaiian Islands

- ● Cities With Population ≥ 25,000
- ▲ Weather Stations

KAUAI

Kanalohuluhulu 1075

KAUAI COUNTY

NIIHAU

OAHU

PEARL CITY

WAIMALU

KANEOHE

KAILUA

Waimanalo Exp Farm

Manoa Lyon Arboretum

HONOLULU

MILILANI TOWN

WAIPAHU

HONOLULU COUNTY

Honolulu Observatory 702.2

Honolulu Intl Airport

Waikiki 717.2

MOLOKAI

Molokai Airport

LANAI

KAHOOLAWE

MAUI COUNTY

MAUI

Kahului Airport

Kailua 446

Hana Airport 355

Haleakala Ranger Station 338

Lahaina 361

HAWAII

Puukohola Heiau 98.1

Ookala 223

Hilo International Airport

HILO

Kulani Camp 79

Hawaii Volcano Natl Park HO 54

Mauna Loa Slope Observatory

Kainaliu 73.2

Opihihale 2 24.1

Naalehu 14

HAWAII COUNTY

100 Miles

100KM

Hawaii Weather Stations by County

County	Station Name
Hawaii	Hawaii Volcano Nat'l Park HQ 54
	Hilo International Airport
	Kainaliu 73.2
	Kulani Camp 79
	Mauna Loa Slope Observatory
	Naalehu 14
	Ookala 223
	Opihihale 2 24.1
	Puukohola Heiau 98.1
Honolulu	Honolulu Int'l Airport
	Honolulu Observatory 702.2
	Manoa Lyon Arboretum
	Waikiki 717.2
	Waimanalo Exp. Farm
Kauai	Kanalohuluhulu 1075
	Lihue Airport
Maui	Haleakala Ranger Station 338
	Hana Airport 355
	Kahului Airport
	Kailua 446
	Lahaina 361
	Molokai Airport

Hawaii Weather Stations by City

City	Station Name	Miles
Hilo	Hilo International Airport	3
	Kulani Camp 79	17
Honolulu	Honolulu Observatory 702.2	11
	Honolulu Int'l Airport	7
	Manoa Lyon Arboretum	1
	Waikiki 717.2	3
	Waimanalo Exp. Farm	7
Kailua	Honolulu Observatory 702.2	18
	Honolulu Int'l Airport	14
	Manoa Lyon Arboretum	7
	Waikiki 717.2	10
	Waimanalo Exp. Farm	4
Kaneohe	Honolulu Observatory 702.2	14
	Honolulu Int'l Airport	11
	Manoa Lyon Arboretum	6
	Waikiki 717.2	10
	Waimanalo Exp. Farm	7
Mililani Town	Honolulu Observatory 702.2	9
	Honolulu Int'l Airport	10
	Manoa Lyon Arboretum	16
	Waikiki 717.2	18
Pearl City	Honolulu Observatory 702.2	7
	Honolulu Int'l Airport	7
	Manoa Lyon Arboretum	11
	Waikiki 717.2	14
	Waimanalo Exp. Farm	17
Waimalu	Honolulu Observatory 702.2	7
	Honolulu Int'l Airport	5
	Manoa Lyon Arboretum	10
	Waikiki 717.2	12
	Waimanalo Exp. Farm	15
Waipahu	Honolulu Observatory 702.2	5
	Honolulu Int'l Airport	7
	Manoa Lyon Arboretum	13
	Waikiki 717.2	15
	Waimanalo Exp. Farm	19

Note: Miles is the distance between the geographic center of the city and the weather station.

Hawaii Weather Stations by Elevation

Feet	Station Name
11,148	Mauna Loa Slope Observatory
6,958	Haleakala Ranger Station 338
5,167	Kulani Camp 79
3,969	Hawaii Volcano Nat'l Park HQ 54
3,599	Kanalohuluhulu 1075
1,499	Kainaliu 73.2
1,358	Opihihale 2 24.1
797	Naalehu 14
698	Kailua 446
498	Manoa Lyon Arboretum
449	Molokai Airport
429	Ookala 223
137	Puukohola Heiau 98.1
101	Lihue Airport
72	Hana Airport 355
59	Waimanalo Exp. Farm
49	Kahului Airport
42	Lahaina 361
29	Hilo International Airport
9	Waikiki 717.2
6	Honolulu Int'l Airport
3	Honolulu Observatory 702.2

Hilo International Airport

The city of Hilo is located near the midpoint of the eastern shore of the Island of Hawaii. This island is by far the largest of the Hawaiian group, with an area of 4,038 square miles, more than twice that of all the other islands combined. Its topography is dominated by the great volcanic masses of Mauna Loa (13,653 feet), Mauna Kea (13,796 feet), and of Haulalai, the Kohala Mountains, and Kilauea. In fact, the island consists entirely of the slopes of these mountains and of the broad saddles between them. Mauna Loa and Kilauea, which occupy the southern half of the island, are still active volcanoes.

Hawaii lies well within the belt of northeasterly trade winds generated by the semi-permanent Pacific high pressure cell to the north and east. The climate provides equable temperatures from day to day and season to season. In Hilo, July and August are the warmest months, with average daily highs and lows of 83 and 68 degrees. January and February, the coolest months, have highs of 80 degrees and lows of 63 degrees. Greater variations occur in localities with less rain and cloud, but temperatures in the mid-90s and low 50s are uncommon anywhere on the island near sea level.

Over the windward slopes of Hawaii , rainfall occurs principally as orographic showers within the ascending moist trade winds. Mean annual rainfall, except for the semi-sheltered Hamakua district, increases from 100 inches or more along the coasts to a maximum of over 300 inches at elevations of 2,000 to 3,000 feet, and then declines to about 15 inches at the summits of Mauna Kea and Mauna Loa. Leeward areas are topographically sheltered from the trades and are therefore drier, although sea breezes can cause afternoon and evening cloudiness and showers. The driest locality on the island, and in the State, with an annual rainfall of less than 10 inches, is the coastal strip just leeward of the southern portion of the Kohala Mountains and of the saddle between the Kohalas and Mauna Kea.

Within the city of Hilo, average rainfall varies from about 130 inches a year near the shore to as much as 200 upslope. The wettest part of the island, with a mean annual rainfall exceeding 300 inches, lies about six miles upslope from the city limits. Relative humidity at Hilo is in the moderate range, however.

The trade winds prevail throughout the year and profoundly influence the climate. The islands entire western coast is sheltered from the trades by high mountains, except that unusually strong trade winds may sweep through the saddle between the Kohala Mountains and Mauna Kea. Except for heavy rain, really severe weather seldom occurs. During the winter, cold fronts or the cyclonic storms of subtropical origin may bring blizzards to the upper slopes of Mauna Loa and Mauna Kea, with snow extending at times to 9,000 feet or below and icing nearer the summit.

Hilo International Airport *Hawaii County*   Elevation: 29 ft.   Latitude: 19° 43' N   Longitude: 155° 03' W

	JAN	FEB	MAR	APR	MAY	JUN	JUL	AUG	SEP	OCT	NOV	DEC	YEAR
Mean Maximum Temp. (°F)	79.8	79.8	79.6	79.8	81.0	82.6	83.0	83.7	84.0	83.3	81.3	80.0	81.5
Mean Temp. (°F)	71.8	71.7	72.1	72.7	73.9	75.3	76.1	76.5	76.5	75.9	74.3	72.5	74.1
Mean Minimum Temp. (°F)	63.6	63.5	64.5	65.6	66.7	68.0	69.1	69.3	68.9	68.4	67.1	64.9	66.6
Extreme Maximum Temp. (°F)	92	91	93	89	89	88	89	91	91	91	92	93	93
Extreme Minimum Temp. (°F)	54	54	54	59	59	62	62	64	61	62	58	55	54
Days Maximum Temp. ≥ 90°F	0	0	0	0	0	0	0	0	0	0	0	0	0
Days Maximum Temp. ≤ 32°F	0	0	0	0	0	0	0	0	0	0	0	0	0
Days Minimum Temp. ≤ 32°F	0	0	0	0	0	0	0	0	0	0	0	0	0
Days Minimum Temp. ≤ 0°F	0	0	0	0	0	0	0	0	0	0	0	0	0
Heating Degree Days (base 65°F)	na	na	na	na	na	na	na	na	na	na	na	na	na
Cooling Degree Days (base 65°F)	215	193	227	238	287	322	357	366	352	344	288	241	3,430
Mean Precipitation (in.)	9.24	8.93	14.32	13.25	8.63	7.28	10.68	10.12	9.02	9.33	14.29	11.12	126.21
Maximum Precipitation (in.)	32.2	45.5	49.9	43.2	25.0	13.3	28.6	26.9	21.8	26.1	45.8	50.8	211.
Minimum Precipitation (in.)	0.4	0.6	0.9	2.9	2.7	1.8	3.8	2.7	1.6	2.4	1.0	0.3	68.1
Maximum 24-hr. Precipitation (in.)	9.5	17.+	16.+	9.7	7.9	2.8	5.9	9.6	8.7	8.6	15.+	9.3	17.+
Days With ≥ 0.1" Precipitation	11	11	17	19	17	16	20	18	16	17	17	15	194
Days With ≥ 1.0" Precipitation	3	2	4	3	2	1	2	2	2	2	4	3	30
Mean Snowfall (in.)	0.0	0.0	0.0	0.0	0.0	0.0	0.0	0.0	0.0	0.0	0.0	0.0	0.0
Maximum Snowfall (in.)	0	0	0	0	0	0	0	0	0	0	0	0	0
Maximum 24-hr. Snowfall (in.)	0	0	0	0	0	0	0	0	0	0	0	0	0
Days With ≥ 1.0" Snow Depth	0	0	0	0	0	0	0	0	0	0	0	0	0
Thunderstorm Days	1	1	2	1	1	< 1	< 1	< 1	1	1	1	1	10
Foggy Days	< 1	< 1	< 1	< 1	0	< 1	< 1	< 1	< 1	< 1	< 1	< 1	1
Predominant Sky Cover	OVR	OVR	OVR	OVR	OVR	OVR	OVR	OVR	OVR	OVR	OVR	OVR	OVR
Mean Relative Humidity 5am (%)	82	82	85	88	88	87	88	88	86	86	86	84	86
Mean Relative Humidity 5pm (%)	73	72	73	75	73	71	73	74	74	76	78	76	74
Mean Dewpoint (°F)	63	63	63	65	66	67	68	69	68	68	67	64	66
Prevailing Wind Direction	SW	SW	SW	SW	SW	SW	SW	SW	SW	SW	SW	SW	SW
Prevailing Wind Speed (mph)	6	7	6	6	6	6	6	6	6	6	6	6	6
Maximum Wind Gust (mph)	47	55	40	40	41	33	36	38	37	43	36	48	55

Honolulu Int'l Airport

Oahu, on which Honolulu is located, is the third largest of the Hawaiian Islands. The Koolau Range, at an average elevation of 2,000 feet parallels the northeastern coast. The Waianae Mountains, somewhat higher in elevation, parallel the west coast. Honolulu Airport, the business and Waikiki districts, and a number of the residential areas of Honolulu lie along the southern coastal plain.

The climate of Hawaii is unusually pleasant for the tropics. Its outstanding features are the persistence of the trade winds, the remarkable variability in rainfall over short distances, the sunniness of the leeward lowlands in contrast to the persistent cloudiness over nearby mountain crests, the equable temperature, and the general infrequency of severe storms.

The prevailing wind throughout the year is the northeasterly trade wind, although its average frequency varies from more than 90 percent during the summer to only 50 percent in January.

Heavy mountain rainfall sustains extensive irrigation of cane fields and the water supply for Honolulu. Oahu is driest along the coast west of the Waianaes where rainfall drops to about 20 inches a year. Daytime showers, usually light, often occur while the sun continues to shine, a phenomenon referred to locally as liquid sunshine.

The moderate temperature range is associated with the small seasonal variation in the energy received from the sun and the tempering effect of the surrounding ocean. Honolulu Airport has recorded as high as the lower 90s and as low as the lower 50s.

Because of the trade winds, even the warmest months are usually comfortable. But when the trades diminish or give way to southerly winds, a situation known locally as kona weather, or kona storms when stormy, the humidity may become oppressively high.

Intense rains of the October to April winter season sometimes cause serious, flash flooding. Thunderstorms are infrequent and usually mild and hail seldom occurs. Infrequently, a small tornado or a waterspout may do some damage. Only a few tropical cyclones have struck Hawaii, although others have come near enough for their outlying winds, waves, clouds, and rain to affect the Islands.

Honolulu Int'l Airport *Honolulu County* Elevation: 6 ft. Latitude: 21° 19' N Longitude: 157° 56' W

	JAN	FEB	MAR	APR	MAY	JUN	JUL	AUG	SEP	OCT	NOV	DEC	YEAR
Mean Maximum Temp. (°F)	80.5	80.7	81.8	83.2	85.0	86.9	87.9	89.0	88.8	87.2	84.3	81.6	84.7
Mean Temp. (°F)	73.0	73.1	74.6	76.1	77.7	79.7	80.8	81.7	81.3	79.9	77.4	74.5	77.5
Mean Minimum Temp. (°F)	65.4	65.4	67.3	68.9	70.3	72.5	73.7	74.4	73.7	72.6	70.5	67.4	70.2
Extreme Maximum Temp. (°F)	88	88	88	91	93	92	94	93	95	94	93	89	95
Extreme Minimum Temp. (°F)	53	53	55	57	60	65	66	67	66	61	57	55	53
Days Maximum Temp. ≥ 90°F	0	0	0	0	0	2	6	13	10	5	0	0	36
Days Maximum Temp. ≤ 32°F	0	0	0	0	0	0	0	0	0	0	0	0	0
Days Minimum Temp. ≤ 32°F	0	0	0	0	0	0	0	0	0	0	0	0	0
Days Minimum Temp. ≤ 0°F	0	0	0	0	0	0	0	0	0	0	0	0	0
Heating Degree Days (base 65°F)	na	na	na	na	na	na	na	na	na	na	na	na	na
Cooling Degree Days (base 65°F)	258	234	305	342	400	460	508	536	511	480	394	310	4,738
Mean Precipitation (in.)	2.75	2.37	1.88	1.12	0.78	0.44	0.55	0.43	0.72	2.23	2.39	2.88	18.54
Maximum Precipitation (in.)	13.3	13.7	20.8	8.9	7.2	2.5	2.3	3.1	2.1	11.1	14.7	17.3	42.8
Minimum Precipitation (in.)	0.2	0.1	trace	trace	0.1	trace	trace	trace	0	0.1	trace	0.1	5.0
Maximum 24-hr. Precipitation (in.)	6.4	5.5	15.+	3.9	3.4	2.0	2.2	2.1	1.3	7.5	5.4	7.9	15.+
Days With ≥ 0.1" Precipitation	4	4	3	3	2	1	1	1	2	3	3	4	31
Days With ≥ 1.0" Precipitation	1	1	1	0	0	0	0	0	0	1	1	1	6
Mean Snowfall (in.)	0.0	0.0	0.0	0.0	0.0	0.0	0.0	0.0	0.0	0.0	0.0	0.0	0.0
Maximum Snowfall (in.)	0	0	0	0	0	0	0	0	0	0	0	0	0
Maximum 24-hr. Snowfall (in.)	0	0	0	0	0	0	0	0	0	0	0	0	0
Days With ≥ 1.0" Snow Depth	0	0	0	0	0	0	0	0	0	0	0	0	0
Thunderstorm Days	1	1	1	< 1	< 1	< 1	< 1	< 1	< 1	1	1	1	6
Foggy Days	0	0	< 1	< 1	< 1	< 1	0	0	0	< 1	< 1	< 1	< 1
Predominant Sky Cover	SCT	SCT	SCT	SCT	SCT	SCT	SCT	SCT	SCT	SCT	SCT	SCT	SCT
Mean Relative Humidity 5am (%)	82	80	78	77	76	75	75	75	77	78	79	80	78
Mean Relative Humidity 5pm (%)	66	64	62	61	60	58	58	58	60	63	66	66	62
Mean Dewpoint (°F)	63	62	62	63	64	65	66	67	67	67	66	64	64
Prevailing Wind Direction	ENE	ENE	ENE	ENE	ENE	ENE	ENE	ENE	ENE	ENE	ENE	ENE	ENE
Prevailing Wind Speed (mph)	13	13	14	14	13	14	14	14	13	13	13	13	13
Maximum Wind Gust (mph)	61	53	51	47	46	43	51	43	49	43	81	51	81

Kahului Airport

Kahului Airport is located in the relatively broad central valley of Maui near the northern coast of the island. Five miles to the west, the mountains of west Maui rise abruptly, reaching an elevation of 5,788 feet above sea level at the crest of Puu Kukui 10 miles west of the station. To the southeast the terrain rises gradually to the summit of Haleakala at 10,023 feet, located 17 miles from the airport.

The outstanding features of climate are the equable temperature marked seasonal variation in rainfall, persistent surface winds, and the rarity of severe storms.

The extremely equable temperatures at Kahului are associated with the tempering effect of the Pacific Ocean and the small seasonal variation in the amount of energy received from the sun. The range in normal temperature between the warmest month, August, and the coldest month, February, is 7.2 degrees.

Rainfall is relatively light. The contrast between the dry season, which extends from May through October, and the wet season, November through April, is quite pronounced. Major widespread rainstorms, which account for the bulk of the precipitation in the area, usually occur several times during each wet season, but are infrequent in the dry season. Approximately 50 percent of the normal annual rainfall occurs in the three months of December through February, and over 80 percent in the six months of the wet season.

Showers constitute the greatest number of rainfall occurrences and although most of these are light and short-lived, very heavy showers do occur at times. Thunderstorms, which are reported rather infrequently, are usually associated with major storms in the wet season.

Tropical storms, may produce heavy rain and strong wind at Kahului once every several years. The large Pacific semipermanent high pressure cell, produces a rather persistent flow of air from the northeast known as the Northeast Trades. Thus, surface wind at Kahului is predominantly from the northeast quadrant. The and flow is most prevalent during the dry season. Wind is more variable during the wet season although, on the average, the trades still blow more than 50 percent of the time during this period.

The normal trade winds, often attain a speed of 40 to 45 mph at the airport, but make living conditions in the nearby Kahului-Wailuku community pleasant and comfortable.

Humidity at Kahului is usually moderate to high, with wet season humidities averaging slightly higher than those in the dry season. However, due to the system of natural ventilation provided by the prevailing winds, the weather is seldom oppressive even during the warmer months of the year.

Kahului Airport *Maui County*   Elevation: 49 ft.   Latitude: 20° 54' N   Longitude: 156° 26' W

	JAN	FEB	MAR	APR	MAY	JUN	JUL	AUG	SEP	OCT	NOV	DEC	YEAR
Mean Maximum Temp. (°F)	80.3	80.7	81.5	82.6	84.3	86.0	86.9	88.0	88.2	86.9	84.1	81.6	84.3
Mean Temp. (°F)	71.9	72.0	73.2	74.4	75.8	77.7	79.0	79.7	79.3	78.3	76.2	73.6	75.9
Mean Minimum Temp. (°F)	63.5	63.2	64.8	66.2	67.2	69.5	70.9	71.3	70.3	69.7	68.1	65.5	67.5
Extreme Maximum Temp. (°F)	89	89	90	91	92	94	95	97	96	96	93	90	97
Extreme Minimum Temp. (°F)	50	50	52	54	57	58	59	61	60	59	55	52	50
Days Maximum Temp. ≥ 90°F	0	0	0	0	1	2	3	6	8	5	1	0	26
Days Maximum Temp. ≤ 32°F	0	0	0	0	0	0	0	0	0	0	0	0	0
Days Minimum Temp. ≤ 32°F	0	0	0	0	0	0	0	0	0	0	0	0	0
Days Minimum Temp. ≤ 0°F	0	0	0	0	0	0	0	0	0	0	0	0	0
Heating Degree Days (base 65°F)	na	na	na	na	na	na	na	na	na	na	na	na	na
Cooling Degree Days (base 65°F)	231	209	261	287	347	402	452	467	443	422	351	274	4,146
Mean Precipitation (in.)	3.82	2.41	2.35	1.75	0.65	0.23	0.46	0.50	0.39	1.04	2.35	3.13	19.08
Maximum Precipitation (in.)	14.5	8.3	10.9	14.3	4.4	2.5	1.6	1.5	1.4	5.7	9.3	10.2	40.6
Minimum Precipitation (in.)	0.1	0.1	0.1	0.1	trace	trace	trace	trace	trace	trace	0.1	trace	8.6
Maximum 24-hr. Precipitation (in.)	4.7	4.4	4.9	3.9	2.4	2.2	1.0	1.1	1.2	2.9	5.5	4.6	5.5
Days With ≥ 0.1" Precipitation	5	4	4	4	2	1	1	1	1	2	4	5	34
Days With ≥ 1.0" Precipitation	1	1	1	0	0	0	0	0	0	0	1	1	5
Mean Snowfall (in.)	0.0	0.0	0.0	0.0	0.0	0.0	0.0	0.0	0.0	0.0	0.0	0.0	0.0
Maximum Snowfall (in.)	0	0	0	0	0	0	0	0	0	0	0	0	0
Maximum 24-hr. Snowfall (in.)	0	0	0	0	0	0	0	0	0	0	0	0	0
Days With ≥ 1.0" Snow Depth	0	0	0	0	0	0	0	0	0	0	0	0	0
Thunderstorm Days	1	1	< 1	< 1	< 1	< 1	< 1	< 1	< 1	< 1	< 1	< 1	2
Foggy Days	< 1	0	< 1	0	0	0	0	0	0	0	0	0	< 1
Predominant Sky Cover	SCT	SCT	SCT	SCT	SCT	SCT	SCT	SCT	SCT	SCT	SCT	SCT	SCT
Mean Relative Humidity 5am (%)	84	83	82	82	82	81	80	81	81	82	82	83	82
Mean Relative Humidity 5pm (%)	66	65	64	63	61	59	60	61	61	63	67	67	63
Mean Dewpoint (°F)	63	62	63	64	65	66	67	68	67	67	66	64	65
Prevailing Wind Direction	NE	NE	NE	NE	NE	NE	NE	NE	NE	NE	NE	NE	NE
Prevailing Wind Speed (mph)	14	15	16	16	16	17	17	17	16	15	16	15	16
Maximum Wind Gust (mph)	58	53	52	49	47	47	47	47	44	46	59	54	59

Lihue Airport

Lihue Airport, a little more than 100 feet above sea level, is located near the eastern shore of the island of Kauai. The island is 33 miles long and 25 miles wide and has an area of 555 square miles. The eastern one third of Kauai consists of broadly eroded valley lands, the western two thirds is mostly mountainous. Kawaikini, the highest elevation on the island, 5,170 feet above sea level, lies near the center of Kauai and is 20 miles northwest of the airport.

The outstanding features of the climate are the equable temperatures from day to day and season to season, the persistent northeasterly trade winds and the marked variation in rainfall from the wet to the dry season and place to place.

The equable temperatures are associated with the mid-ocean location of the island and to the small seasonal variation in the amount of energy received from the sun. The range in normal temperature from February to August is less than eight degrees.

The trade winds blow across the island during most of each year and the dominance of these winds has a marked influence on the climate of the area. Completely cloudless skies are quite rare. On the average, six tenths to seven tenths of the sky is covered by clouds during the daylight hours.

Trade-wind showers are relatively common. Although heavy at times, most of the showers are light and of short duration. The frequency and intensity of the showers increase toward the mountains to the west. Mt. Waialeale receives 486 inches annually, the highest recorded annual average in the world. Mt. Waialeale has recorded annual rainfalls over 620 inches.

Normal annual rainfall is over 40 inches. Three-fourths of this total, on the average, falls during the seven-month wet season which extends from October through April. Widespread rainstorms, which account for much of the precipitation, occur most frequently during this period. Normal precipitation in January, the wettest month, is over six inches.

The dry season includes the months of May through September. June, the driest month, receives only about one and a half inches of rain, on the average.

Hurricanes and other severe windstorms are quite rare. Strong winds do occur at times in connection with storm systems moving through the area, but seldom cause extensive damage.

Relative humidity, moderate to high in all seasons, is slightly higher in the wet season than in the dry. However, even during periods when the temperature and humidity are both high, the weather is seldom oppressive. This is due to the trade winds which provide a system of natural ventilation during most of each year.

Lihue Airport *Kauai County*   Elevation: 101 ft.   Latitude: 21° 59' N   Longitude: 159° 20' W

	JAN	FEB	MAR	APR	MAY	JUN	JUL	AUG	SEP	OCT	NOV	DEC	YEAR
Mean Maximum Temp. (°F)	78.0	78.2	78.6	79.4	81.0	82.9	83.9	84.8	84.8	83.3	80.8	78.8	81.2
Mean Temp. (°F)	71.7	71.8	73.0	74.2	75.7	77.8	79.0	79.7	79.4	78.1	75.8	73.3	75.8
Mean Minimum Temp. (°F)	65.4	65.5	67.3	69.0	70.3	72.8	74.0	74.5	74.0	72.8	70.7	67.7	70.3
Extreme Maximum Temp. (°F)	85	86	88	88	88	88	89	90	90	89	89	86	90
Extreme Minimum Temp. (°F)	53	54	56	59	58	61	62	66	65	61	58	55	53
Days Maximum Temp. ≥ 90°F	0	0	0	0	0	0	0	0	0	0	0	0	0
Days Maximum Temp. ≤ 32°F	0	0	0	0	0	0	0	0	0	0	0	0	0
Days Minimum Temp. ≤ 32°F	0	0	0	0	0	0	0	0	0	0	0	0	0
Days Minimum Temp. ≤ 0°F	0	0	0	0	0	0	0	0	0	0	0	0	0
Heating Degree Days (base 65°F)	na	na	na	na	na	na	na	na	na	na	na	na	na
Cooling Degree Days (base 65°F)	207	192	247	277	328	394	442	463	440	409	331	258	3,988
Mean Precipitation (in.)	4.75	3.28	3.58	2.99	3.06	1.81	2.13	1.94	2.59	4.31	5.03	4.82	40.29
Maximum Precipitation (in.)	17.6	11.3	14.5	10.6	12.6	4.8	8.8	8.1	10.9	18.0	18.4	22.9	74.4
Minimum Precipitation (in.)	0.3	trace	0.3	0.3	0.4	0.4	0.8	0.7	0.4	1.0	0.6	0.5	16.4
Maximum 24-hr. Precipitation (in.)	11.+	5.4	5.1	5.3	5.0	2.1	5.0	5.3	7.1	7.8	9.8	11.+	11.+
Days With ≥ 0.1" Precipitation	6	5	6	7	6	5	6	6	5	8	8	7	75
Days With ≥ 1.0" Precipitation	1	1	1	1	1	0	0	0	0	1	1	1	8
Mean Snowfall (in.)	0.0	0.0	0.0	0.0	0.0	0.0	0.0	0.0	0.0	0.0	0.0	0.0	0.0
Maximum Snowfall (in.)	0	0	0	0	0	0	0	0	0	0	0	0	0
Maximum 24-hr. Snowfall (in.)	0	0	0	0	0	0	0	0	0	0	0	0	0
Days With ≥ 1.0" Snow Depth	0	0	0	0	0	0	0	0	0	0	0	0	0
Thunderstorm Days	1	1	1	< 1	1	< 1	< 1	< 1	< 1	1	1	1	7
Foggy Days	< 1	< 1	< 1	< 1	< 1	< 1	< 1	0	0	< 1	< 1	< 1	1
Predominant Sky Cover	SCT	SCT	BRK	BRK	BRK	BRK	BRK	BRK	SCT	SCT	BRK	BRK	BRK
Mean Relative Humidity 5am (%)	82	82	81	81	81	80	80	81	82	83	82	81	81
Mean Relative Humidity 5pm (%)	70	70	70	71	71	69	70	70	70	73	74	73	71
Mean Dewpoint (°F)	63	62	63	65	66	68	69	70	69	69	67	64	66
Prevailing Wind Direction	ENE	NE	ENE	NE	NE	ENE	ENE	ENE	ENE	ENE	ENE	NE	ENE
Prevailing Wind Speed (mph)	14	15	15	15	14	14	15	14	13	14	14	15	14
Maximum Wind Gust (mph)	84	60	54	47	43	39	41	38	115	41	85	55	115

Haleakala Ranger Station 338 *Maui County*   Elevation: 6,958 ft.   Latitude: 20° 46' N   Longitude: 156° 15' W

	JAN	FEB	MAR	APR	MAY	JUN	JUL	AUG	SEP	OCT	NOV	DEC	YEAR
Mean Maximum Temp. (°F)	59.9	59.1	59.7	60.2	62.2	65.3	65.5	66.1	64.8	64.3	63.1	60.9	62.6
Mean Temp. (°F)	51.0	50.2	50.9	51.4	53.0	56.0	56.6	56.9	55.7	55.3	54.5	52.2	53.6
Mean Minimum Temp. (°F)	42.1	41.2	42.1	42.5	43.8	46.6	47.6	47.8	46.7	46.3	45.8	43.4	44.7
Extreme Maximum Temp. (°F)	78	74	75	73	75	78	76	76	76	80	75	73	80
Extreme Minimum Temp. (°F)	31	28	32	32	32	33	32	33	36	31	29	30	28
Days Maximum Temp. ≥ 90°F	0	0	0	0	0	0	0	0	0	0	0	0	0
Days Maximum Temp. ≤ 32°F	0	0	0	0	0	0	0	0	0	0	0	0	0
Days Minimum Temp. ≤ 32°F	0	0	0	0	0	0	0	0	0	0	0	0	0
Days Minimum Temp. ≤ 0°F	0	0	0	0	0	0	0	0	0	0	0	0	0
Heating Degree Days (base 65°F)	na	na	na	na	na	na	na	na	na	na	na	na	na
Cooling Degree Days (base 65°F)	0	0	0	0	0	0	0	0	0	0	0	0	0
Mean Precipitation (in.)	9.44	6.27	8.53	5.33	1.85	1.38	2.42	2.06	2.17	2.71	5.42	6.72	54.30
Days With ≥ 0.1" Precipitation	7	7	8	8	5	3	6	4	6	5	7	7	73
Days With ≥ 1.0" Precipitation	2	2	2	1	0	0	0	0	0	1	1	2	11
Mean Snowfall (in.)	0.0	0.0	0.0	0.0	0.0	0.0	0.0	0.0	0.0	0.0	0.0	0.0	0.0
Days With ≥ 1.0" Snow Depth	0	0	0	0	0	0	0	0	0	0	0	0	0

Hana Airport 355 *Maui County*   Elevation: 72 ft.   Latitude: 20° 48' N   Longitude: 156° 01' W

	JAN	FEB	MAR	APR	MAY	JUN	JUL	AUG	SEP	OCT	NOV	DEC	YEAR
Mean Maximum Temp. (°F)	78.1	78.2	78.3	79.0	80.4	81.9	82.4	83.4	83.7	82.6	80.4	78.5	80.6
Mean Temp. (°F)	71.2	71.3	71.9	73.1	74.1	75.7	76.4	77.2	77.0	76.3	74.6	72.6	74.3
Mean Minimum Temp. (°F)	64.3	64.3	65.4	67.1	67.9	69.4	70.3	70.9	70.2	70.0	68.8	66.5	67.9
Extreme Maximum Temp. (°F)	89	87	88	88	88	88	90	89	90	91	94	89	94
Extreme Minimum Temp. (°F)	51	54	52	57	56	59	58	59	59	58	54	56	51
Days Maximum Temp. ≥ 90°F	0	0	0	0	0	0	0	0	0	0	0	0	0
Days Maximum Temp. ≤ 32°F	0	0	0	0	0	0	0	0	0	0	0	0	0
Days Minimum Temp. ≤ 32°F	0	0	0	0	0	0	0	0	0	0	0	0	0
Days Minimum Temp. ≤ 0°F	0	0	0	0	0	0	0	0	0	0	0	0	0
Heating Degree Days (base 65°F)	na	na	na	na	na	na	na	na	na	na	na	na	na
Cooling Degree Days (base 65°F)	202	182	217	245	283	329	364	386	366	361	304	240	3,479
Mean Precipitation (in.)	8.54	5.80	9.10	7.71	5.94	4.08	5.88	5.62	5.77	6.86	7.93	6.18	79.41
Days With ≥ 0.1" Precipitation	*11*	9	13	14	13	13	16	15	13	14	14	*13*	*158*
Days With ≥ 1.0" Precipitation	2	2	2	1	1	0	1	1	1	1	2	1	15
Mean Snowfall (in.)	0.0	0.0	0.0	0.0	0.0	0.0	0.0	0.0	0.0	0.0	0.0	0.0	0.0
Days With ≥ 1.0" Snow Depth	0	0	0	0	0	0	0	0	0	0	0	0	0

Hawaii Volcano Nat'l Park HQ 54 *Hawaii County*   Elevation: 3,969 ft.   Latitude: 19° 26' N   Longitude: 155° 16' W

	JAN	FEB	MAR	APR	MAY	JUN	JUL	AUG	SEP	OCT	NOV	DEC	YEAR
Mean Maximum Temp. (°F)	67.6	67.3	67.0	67.3	68.9	70.3	71.4	72.9	72.9	71.9	69.5	67.3	69.5
Mean Temp. (°F)	58.6	58.3	58.6	59.4	60.7	62.1	63.3	64.2	64.0	63.3	61.5	59.2	61.1
Mean Minimum Temp. (°F)	49.5	49.3	50.2	51.5	52.5	53.9	55.1	55.4	55.1	54.7	53.5	51.0	52.6
Extreme Maximum Temp. (°F)	79	81	78	79	81	93	87	81	82	80	79	78	93
Extreme Minimum Temp. (°F)	34	35	38	42	42	45	45	44	45	45	42	31	31
Days Maximum Temp. ≥ 90°F	0	0	0	0	0	0	0	0	0	0	0	0	0
Days Maximum Temp. ≤ 32°F	0	0	0	0	0	0	0	0	0	0	0	0	0
Days Minimum Temp. ≤ 32°F	0	0	0	0	0	0	0	0	0	0	0	0	0
Days Minimum Temp. ≤ 0°F	0	0	0	0	0	0	0	0	0	0	0	0	0
Heating Degree Days (base 65°F)	na	na	na	na	na	na	na	na	na	na	na	na	na
Cooling Degree Days (base 65°F)	0	0	0	0	3	5	14	23	20	15	5	1	86
Mean Precipitation (in.)	10.55	9.13	13.98	10.75	6.73	5.23	7.08	6.54	5.96	6.58	13.33	12.08	107.94
Days With ≥ 0.1" Precipitation	11	10	16	18	16	13	14	12	*12*	14	14	15	*165*
Days With ≥ 1.0" Precipitation	2	2	4	3	1	1	1	1	1	1	3	3	23
Mean Snowfall (in.)	0.0	0.0	0.0	0.0	0.0	0.0	0.0	0.0	0.0	0.0	0.0	0.0	0.0
Days With ≥ 1.0" Snow Depth	0	0	0	0	0	0	0	0	0	0	0	0	0

Honolulu Observatory 702.2 *Honolulu County*   Elevation: 3 ft.   Latitude: 21° 19' N   Longitude: 158° 00' W

	JAN	FEB	MAR	APR	MAY	JUN	JUL	AUG	SEP	OCT	NOV	DEC	YEAR
Mean Maximum Temp. (°F)	na	na	*81.7*	*83.3*	*84.6*	*86.7*	*87.8*	*88.6*	*88.7*	*87.1*	*84.5*	*81.8*	na
Mean Temp. (°F)	na	na	*72.9*	*74.6*	*75.8*	*78.1*	*79.3*	*79.9*	*79.5*	*78.2*	*76.1*	*73.4*	na
Mean Minimum Temp. (°F)	na	na	*64.0*	65.7	66.9	69.5	70.8	71.1	70.3	69.3	67.6	*64.9*	na
Extreme Maximum Temp. (°F)	na	na	89	89	90	93	94	94	93	94	91	89	na
Extreme Minimum Temp. (°F)	na	na	53	56	58	61	61	63	59	60	58	53	na
Days Maximum Temp. ≥ 90°F	na	na	*0*	*0*	*1*	*2*	*8*	*12*	*11*	*4*	*0*	*0*	na
Days Maximum Temp. ≤ 32°F	*0*	*0*	*0*	*0*	*0*	*0*	*0*	*0*	*0*	*0*	*0*	*0*	*0*
Days Minimum Temp. ≤ 32°F	*0*	*0*	*0*	*0*	*0*	*0*	*0*	*0*	*0*	*0*	*0*	*0*	*0*
Days Minimum Temp. ≤ 0°F	*0*	*0*	*0*	*0*	*0*	*0*	*0*	*0*	*0*	*0*	*0*	*0*	*0*
Heating Degree Days (base 65°F)	na	na	na	na	na	na	na	na	na	na	na	na	na
Cooling Degree Days (base 65°F)	212	191	254	295	340	400	451	470	442	416	343	267	4,081
Mean Precipitation (in.)	2.85	2.61	1.64	1.06	0.79	0.44	0.53	0.38	0.67	2.20	2.35	2.70	18.22
Days With ≥ 0.1" Precipitation	5	3	3	3	2	1	1	1	2	2	3	4	30
Days With ≥ 1.0" Precipitation	1	1	1	0	0	0	0	0	0	1	1	1	6
Mean Snowfall (in.)	0.0	0.0	0.0	0.0	0.0	0.0	0.0	0.0	0.0	0.0	0.0	0.0	0.0
Days With ≥ 1.0" Snow Depth	0	0	0	0	0	0	0	0	0	0	0	0	0

Kailua 446 *Maui County*   Elevation: 698 ft.   Latitude: 20° 54' N   Longitude: 156° 13' W

	JAN	FEB	MAR	APR	MAY	JUN	JUL	AUG	SEP	OCT	NOV	DEC	YEAR
Mean Maximum Temp. (°F)	na	75.1	74.8	75.2	76.3	77.6	na	79.1	79.9	78.8	na	na	na
Mean Temp. (°F)	na	68.3	68.7	69.6	70.6	71.9	na	73.4	73.8	72.8	na	na	na
Mean Minimum Temp. (°F)	na	61.4	62.6	63.9	64.9	66.2	na	67.6	67.5	66.8	na	na	na
Extreme Maximum Temp. (°F)	85	84	86	83	86	86	83	87	87	86	85	84	87
Extreme Minimum Temp. (°F)	53	51	53	57	56	58	59	60	58	60	56	55	51
Days Maximum Temp. ≥ 90°F	0	0	0	0	0	0	0	0	0	0	0	0	0
Days Maximum Temp. ≤ 32°F	0	0	0	0	0	0	0	0	0	0	0	0	0
Days Minimum Temp. ≤ 32°F	0	0	0	0	0	0	0	0	0	0	0	0	0
Days Minimum Temp. ≤ 0°F	0	0	0	0	0	0	0	0	0	0	0	0	0
Heating Degree Days (base 65°F)	na	na	na	na	na	na	na	na	na	na	na	na	na
Cooling Degree Days (base 65°F)	na	100	123	150	179	221	na	270	269	249	na	na	na
Mean Precipitation (in.)	11.24	9.04	14.96	13.42	9.09	7.62	10.63	9.03	7.84	9.07	12.43	9.76	124.13
Days With ≥ 0.1" Precipitation	9	7	11	13	11	11	14	12	na	na	na	na	na
Days With ≥ 1.0" Precipitation	3	2	2	2	1	1	2	1	1	1	2	2	20
Mean Snowfall (in.)	0.0	0.0	0.0	0.0	0.0	0.0	0.0	0.0	0.0	0.0	0.0	0.0	0.0
Days With ≥ 1.0" Snow Depth	0	0	0	0	0	0	0	0	0	0	0	0	0

Kainaliu 73.2 *Hawaii County*   Elevation: 1,499 ft.   Latitude: 19° 32' N   Longitude: 155° 56' W

	JAN	FEB	MAR	APR	MAY	JUN	JUL	AUG	SEP	OCT	NOV	DEC	YEAR
Mean Maximum Temp. (°F)	na	76.5	na	76.3	na	76.8	na	na	79.6	79.8	na	na	na
Mean Temp. (°F)	na	67.7	na	68.5	na	69.8	na	na	71.7	71.7	na	na	na
Mean Minimum Temp. (°F)	na	58.8	na	60.7	na	62.9	na	na	63.8	63.6	na	na	na
Extreme Maximum Temp. (°F)	86	83	84	83	84	83	85	86	86	88	87	86	88
Extreme Minimum Temp. (°F)	52	48	51	54	57	57	58	59	57	56	57	52	48
Days Maximum Temp. ≥ 90°F	0	0	0	0	0	0	0	0	0	0	0	0	0
Days Maximum Temp. ≤ 32°F	0	0	0	0	0	0	0	0	0	0	0	0	0
Days Minimum Temp. ≤ 32°F	0	0	0	0	0	0	0	0	0	0	0	0	0
Days Minimum Temp. ≤ 0°F	0	0	0	0	0	0	0	0	0	0	0	0	0
Heating Degree Days (base 65°F)	na	na	na	na	na	na	na	na	na	na	na	na	na
Cooling Degree Days (base 65°F)	na	90	na	na	na	na	na	na	na	223	na	na	na
Mean Precipitation (in.)	4.12	2.73	3.70	4.10	4.45	6.27	6.67	5.80	6.85	4.70	2.72	2.68	54.79
Days With ≥ 0.1" Precipitation	4	3	4	5	7	8	8	8	8	5	3	3	66
Days With ≥ 1.0" Precipitation	1	0	0	1	1	1	1	1	1	1	0	0	8
Mean Snowfall (in.)	0.0	0.0	0.0	0.0	0.0	0.0	0.0	0.0	0.0	0.0	0.0	0.0	0.0
Days With ≥ 1.0" Snow Depth	0	0	0	0	0	0	0	0	0	0	0	0	0

Kanalohuluhulu 1075 *Kauai County*   Elevation: 3,599 ft.   Latitude: 22° 08' N   Longitude: 159° 40' W

	JAN	FEB	MAR	APR	MAY	JUN	JUL	AUG	SEP	OCT	NOV	DEC	YEAR
Mean Maximum Temp. (°F)	62.9	63.5	64.4	65.6	67.4	69.7	70.5	71.7	71.6	69.8	66.5	63.4	67.2
Mean Temp. (°F)	54.7	55.0	56.4	57.8	59.1	61.5	62.7	63.3	62.5	61.3	58.8	56.0	59.1
Mean Minimum Temp. (°F)	46.4	46.3	48.2	49.9	50.8	53.4	54.9	54.9	53.4	52.8	51.0	48.5	50.9
Extreme Maximum Temp. (°F)	79	74	78	83	80	90	79	80	86	80	78	75	90
Extreme Minimum Temp. (°F)	31	32	29	32	35	40	41	39	39	35	33	31	29
Days Maximum Temp. ≥ 90°F	0	0	0	0	0	0	0	0	0	0	0	0	0
Days Maximum Temp. ≤ 32°F	0	0	0	0	0	0	0	0	0	0	0	0	0
Days Minimum Temp. ≤ 32°F	0	0	0	0	0	0	0	0	0	0	0	0	0
Days Minimum Temp. ≤ 0°F	0	0	0	0	0	0	0	0	0	0	0	0	0
Heating Degree Days (base 65°F)	na	na	na	na	na	na	na	na	na	na	na	na	na
Cooling Degree Days (base 65°F)	0	0	0	1	0	2	6	9	6	2	0	0	26
Mean Precipitation (in.)	10.76	7.92	6.88	4.27	3.05	1.90	2.07	2.24	2.22	4.53	7.72	9.43	62.99
Days With ≥ 0.1" Precipitation	11	9	10	9	7	5	6	5	5	6	9	10	92
Days With ≥ 1.0" Precipitation	3	3	2	1	1	0	0	0	0	1	2	2	15
Mean Snowfall (in.)	0.0	0.0	0.0	0.0	0.0	0.0	0.0	0.0	0.0	0.0	0.0	0.0	0.0
Days With ≥ 1.0" Snow Depth	0	0	0	0	0	0	0	0	0	0	0	0	0

Kulani Camp 79 *Hawaii County*   Elevation: 5,167 ft.   Latitude: 19° 33' N   Longitude: 155° 18' W

	JAN	FEB	MAR	APR	MAY	JUN	JUL	AUG	SEP	OCT	NOV	DEC	YEAR
Mean Maximum Temp. (°F)	63.0	62.2	61.0	61.2	62.3	63.9	65.1	65.9	66.1	65.8	64.0	62.6	63.6
Mean Temp. (°F)	52.9	52.7	52.8	53.7	54.8	56.4	57.7	58.2	58.2	57.8	56.0	53.9	55.4
Mean Minimum Temp. (°F)	43.0	43.1	44.5	46.2	47.1	48.8	50.3	50.4	50.4	49.8	48.0	45.1	47.2
Extreme Maximum Temp. (°F)	79	77	76	76	82	81	78	83	78	89	78	83	89
Extreme Minimum Temp. (°F)	31	31	28	32	37	36	35	30	40	39	35	30	28
Days Maximum Temp. ≥ 90°F	0	0	0	0	0	0	0	0	0	0	0	0	0
Days Maximum Temp. ≤ 32°F	0	0	0	0	0	0	0	0	0	0	0	0	0
Days Minimum Temp. ≤ 32°F	0	0	0	0	0	0	0	0	0	0	0	0	0
Days Minimum Temp. ≤ 0°F	0	0	0	0	0	0	0	0	0	0	0	0	0
Heating Degree Days (base 65°F)	na	na	na	na	na	na	na	na	na	na	na	na	na
Cooling Degree Days (base 65°F)	0	0	0	0	0	0	0	0	0	1	0	3	5
Mean Precipitation (in.)	9.62	7.32	15.02	11.02	6.58	4.75	8.44	7.58	6.97	6.20	13.17	12.40	109.07
Days With ≥ 0.1" Precipitation	9	9	15	18	15	11	13	11	12	13	13	13	152
Days With ≥ 1.0" Precipitation	2	2	4	3	1	1	2	2	1	1	3	3	25
Mean Snowfall (in.)	0.0	0.0	0.0	0.0	0.0	0.0	0.0	0.0	0.0	0.0	0.0	0.0	0.0
Days With ≥ 1.0" Snow Depth	0	0	0	0	0	0	0	0	0	0	0	0	0

Lahaina 361 *Maui County*   Elevation: 42 ft.   Latitude: 20° 53' N   Longitude: 156° 41' W

	JAN	FEB	MAR	APR	MAY	JUN	JUL	AUG	SEP	OCT	NOV	DEC	YEAR
Mean Maximum Temp. (°F)	81.8	81.8	82.9	83.9	85.0	86.6	87.6	88.5	88.7	87.8	85.6	na	na
Mean Temp. (°F)	73.0	72.7	73.8	74.9	76.2	77.6	78.7	79.5	79.5	78.7	76.7	na	na
Mean Minimum Temp. (°F)	64.1	63.6	64.6	65.9	67.3	68.7	69.8	70.6	70.4	69.6	67.7	na	na
Extreme Maximum Temp. (°F)	88	89	91	89	91	93	93	97	94	94	92	91	97
Extreme Minimum Temp. (°F)	54	56	55	56	60	60	63	63	64	58	57	52	52
Days Maximum Temp. ≥ 90°F	0	0	0	0	0	1	3	6	8	4	1	0	23
Days Maximum Temp. ≤ 32°F	0	0	0	0	0	0	0	0	0	0	0	0	0
Days Minimum Temp. ≤ 32°F	0	0	0	0	0	0	0	0	0	0	0	0	0
Days Minimum Temp. ≤ 0°F	0	0	0	0	0	0	0	0	0	0	0	0	0
Heating Degree Days (base 65°F)	na	na	na	na	na	na	na	na	na	na	na	na	na
Cooling Degree Days (base 65°F)	259	229	284	312	363	404	454	474	458	441	377	na	na
Mean Precipitation (in.)	3.11	2.27	1.51	0.83	0.42	0.09	0.09	0.14	0.30	0.98	1.48	2.55	13.77
Days With ≥ 0.1" Precipitation	3	2	2	1	1	0	0	0	0	1	1	2	13
Days With ≥ 1.0" Precipitation	1	1	0	0	0	0	0	0	0	0	0	0	2
Mean Snowfall (in.)	0.0	0.0	0.0	0.0	0.0	0.0	0.0	0.0	0.0	0.0	0.0	0.0	0.0
Days With ≥ 1.0" Snow Depth	0	0	0	0	0	0	0	0	0	0	0	0	0

Manoa Lyon Arboretum *Honolulu County*   Elevation: 498 ft.   Latitude: 21° 19' N   Longitude: 157° 49' W

	JAN	FEB	MAR	APR	MAY	JUN	JUL	AUG	SEP	OCT	NOV	DEC	YEAR
Mean Maximum Temp. (°F)	77.4	77.6	76.9	76.9	78.3	78.8	79.9	81.5	82.4	81.7	79.5	78.2	79.1
Mean Temp. (°F)	70.0	69.9	70.2	70.8	72.1	73.2	74.4	75.6	76.0	75.3	73.4	71.4	72.7
Mean Minimum Temp. (°F)	62.5	62.1	63.5	64.6	65.9	67.6	69.0	69.7	69.7	68.8	67.2	64.5	66.3
Extreme Maximum Temp. (°F)	88	87	90	86	88	87	96	90	92	91	90	92	96
Extreme Minimum Temp. (°F)	52	50	52	58	56	59	55	61	63	59	57	49	49
Days Maximum Temp. ≥ 90°F	0	0	0	0	0	0	0	0	0	0	0	0	0
Days Maximum Temp. ≤ 32°F	0	0	0	0	0	0	0	0	0	0	0	0	0
Days Minimum Temp. ≤ 32°F	0	0	0	0	0	0	0	0	0	0	0	0	0
Days Minimum Temp. ≤ 0°F	0	0	0	0	0	0	0	0	0	0	0	0	0
Heating Degree Days (base 65°F)	na	na	na	na	na	na	na	na	na	na	na	na	na
Cooling Degree Days (base 65°F)	164	149	177	187	233	263	313	344	348	331	263	204	2,976
Mean Precipitation (in.)	10.78	9.65	14.33	15.68	12.33	13.04	15.57	12.64	10.88	11.65	13.98	12.96	153.49
Days With ≥ 0.1" Precipitation	12	12	16	19	18	20	22	20	17	18	18	15	207
Days With ≥ 1.0" Precipitation	3	3	4	5	4	3	5	3	3	3	4	4	44
Mean Snowfall (in.)	0.0	0.0	0.0	0.0	0.0	0.0	0.0	0.0	0.0	0.0	0.0	0.0	0.0
Days With ≥ 1.0" Snow Depth	0	0	0	0	0	0	0	0	0	0	0	0	0

Mauna Loa Slope Observatory *Hawaii County*   Elevation: 11,148 ft.   Latitude: 19° 32' N   Longitude: 155° 35' W

	JAN	FEB	MAR	APR	MAY	JUN	JUL	AUG	SEP	OCT	NOV	DEC	YEAR
Mean Maximum Temp. (°F)	49.9	50.1	50.9	52.1	54.1	57.4	56.4	56.5	55.4	54.8	na	50.7	na
Mean Temp. (°F)	42.0	41.9	42.5	43.6	45.7	48.8	47.9	48.1	47.2	46.7	na	42.9	na
Mean Minimum Temp. (°F)	34.1	33.7	34.0	35.1	37.3	40.2	39.3	39.6	38.9	38.5	na	35.0	na
Extreme Maximum Temp. (°F)	67	64	65	64	64	71	68	68	67	66	64	64	71
Extreme Minimum Temp. (°F)	19	23	23	25	27	29	30	29	30	30	28	23	19
Days Maximum Temp. ≥ 90°F	0	0	0	0	0	0	0	0	0	0	0	0	0
Days Maximum Temp. ≤ 32°F	0	0	0	0	0	0	0	0	0	0	0	0	0
Days Minimum Temp. ≤ 32°F	9	10	10	7	3	0	0	0	0	1	2	7	49
Days Minimum Temp. ≤ 0°F	0	0	0	0	0	0	0	0	0	0	0	0	0
Heating Degree Days (base 65°F)	na	na	na	na	na	na	na	na	na	na	na	na	na
Cooling Degree Days (base 65°F)	na	0	0	0	0	0	0	0	0	0	na	0	na
Mean Precipitation (in.)	3.02	1.70	2.29	1.27	0.79	0.52	1.33	1.38	1.21	1.07	2.31	1.95	18.84
Days With ≥ 0.1" Precipitation	2	2	2	2	2	1	2	2	2	2	2	1	22
Days With ≥ 1.0" Precipitation	0	0	0	0	0	0	0	0	0	0	0	0	0
Mean Snowfall (in.)	na	na	na	na	na	na	na	na	na	na	na	na	na
Days With ≥ 1.0" Snow Depth	na	na	na	na	na	na	na	na	na	na	na	na	na

Molokai Airport *Maui County*   Elevation: 449 ft.   Latitude: 21° 10' N   Longitude: 157° 06' W

	JAN	FEB	MAR	APR	MAY	JUN	JUL	AUG	SEP	OCT	NOV	DEC	YEAR
Mean Maximum Temp. (°F)	77.9	78.0	79.1	80.2	81.9	83.6	84.7	85.8	86.1	84.8	82.1	79.4	82.0
Mean Temp. (°F)	70.7	70.4	71.6	72.9	74.4	76.5	77.6	78.4	78.5	77.5	75.1	72.3	74.7
Mean Minimum Temp. (°F)	63.5	62.8	64.0	65.6	66.9	69.3	70.5	71.0	70.9	70.0	68.0	65.2	67.3
Extreme Maximum Temp. (°F)	88	89	89	96	89	92	91	93	93	92	90	88	96
Extreme Minimum Temp. (°F)	52	48	46	48	52	57	52	56	60	60	57	50	46
Days Maximum Temp. ≥ 90°F	0	0	0	0	0	0	0	1	2	1	0	0	4
Days Maximum Temp. ≤ 32°F	0	0	0	0	0	0	0	0	0	0	0	0	0
Days Minimum Temp. ≤ 32°F	0	0	0	0	0	0	0	0	0	0	0	0	0
Days Minimum Temp. ≤ 0°F	0	0	0	0	0	0	0	0	0	0	0	0	0
Heating Degree Days (base 65°F)	na	na	na	na	na	na	na	na	na	na	na	na	na
Cooling Degree Days (base 65°F)	181	159	203	241	293	354	401	425	414	392	313	231	3,607
Mean Precipitation (in.)	3.77	3.56	2.44	1.99	1.44	0.69	0.61	0.56	0.73	1.86	3.12	3.96	24.73
Days With ≥ 0.1" Precipitation	7	6	5	4	3	2	2	2	2	3	5	6	47
Days With ≥ 1.0" Precipitation	1	1	0	0	0	0	0	0	0	0	1	1	4
Mean Snowfall (in.)	0.0	0.0	0.0	0.0	0.0	0.0	0.0	0.0	0.0	0.0	0.0	0.0	0.0
Days With ≥ 1.0" Snow Depth	0	0	0	0	0	0	0	0	0	0	0	0	0

Naalehu 14 *Hawaii County*   Elevation: 797 ft.   Latitude: 19° 04' N   Longitude: 155° 35' W

	JAN	FEB	MAR	APR	MAY	JUN	JUL	AUG	SEP	OCT	NOV	DEC	YEAR
Mean Maximum Temp. (°F)	77.3	77.9	77.8	77.8	78.4	79.4	na	81.5	81.9	81.1	79.3	77.6	na
Mean Temp. (°F)	69.9	70.2	70.5	70.9	71.7	72.8	na	74.6	74.8	74.3	72.9	70.9	na
Mean Minimum Temp. (°F)	62.3	62.4	63.1	64.0	65.0	66.1	na	67.7	67.6	67.5	66.4	64.3	na
Extreme Maximum Temp. (°F)	89	90	93	89	93	87	91	92	90	90	90	89	93
Extreme Minimum Temp. (°F)	50	54	50	50	51	54	58	60	56	59	55	54	50
Days Maximum Temp. ≥ 90°F	0	0	0	0	0	0	0	0	0	0	0	0	0
Days Maximum Temp. ≤ 32°F	0	0	0	0	0	0	0	0	0	0	0	0	0
Days Minimum Temp. ≤ 32°F	0	0	0	0	0	0	0	0	0	0	0	0	0
Days Minimum Temp. ≤ 0°F	0	0	0	0	0	0	0	0	0	0	0	0	0
Heating Degree Days (base 65°F)	na	na	na	na	na	na	na	na	na	na	na	na	na
Cooling Degree Days (base 65°F)	160	163	182	192	221	252	293	309	299	300	250	200	2,821
Mean Precipitation (in.)	6.00	3.72	5.37	3.34	2.06	1.51	3.23	3.29	3.51	4.03	6.41	5.97	48.44
Days With ≥ 0.1" Precipitation	6	4	6	5	5	4	4	5	6	7	7	6	65
Days With ≥ 1.0" Precipitation	1	1	1	0	0	0	1	1	1	1	2	2	11
Mean Snowfall (in.)	0.0	0.0	0.0	0.0	0.0	0.0	0.0	0.0	0.0	0.0	0.0	0.0	0.0
Days With ≥ 1.0" Snow Depth	0	0	0	0	0	0	0	0	0	0	0	0	0

Ookala 223 *Hawaii County*   Elevation: 429 ft.   Latitude: 20° 01' N   Longitude: 155° 17' W

	JAN	FEB	MAR	APR	MAY	JUN	JUL	AUG	SEP	OCT	NOV	DEC	YEAR
Mean Maximum Temp. (°F)	76.7	76.5	76.3	76.8	78.2	80.0	80.3	81.1	81.8	80.9	79.1	77.2	78.7
Mean Temp. (°F)	70.4	70.1	70.3	70.9	72.1	73.8	74.4	75.2	75.6	74.9	73.4	71.3	72.7
Mean Minimum Temp. (°F)	64.1	63.7	64.3	64.9	66.0	67.6	68.4	69.3	69.4	68.8	67.5	65.4	66.6
Extreme Maximum Temp. (°F)	85	88	84	89	83	87	87	86	87	89	85	86	89
Extreme Minimum Temp. (°F)	54	52	57	56	58	59	57	60	62	51	56	54	51
Days Maximum Temp. ≥ 90°F	0	0	0	0	0	0	0	0	0	0	0	0	0
Days Maximum Temp. ≤ 32°F	0	0	0	0	0	0	0	0	0	0	0	0	0
Days Minimum Temp. ≤ 32°F	0	0	0	0	0	0	0	0	0	0	0	0	0
Days Minimum Temp. ≤ 0°F	0	0	0	0	0	0	0	0	0	0	0	0	0
Heating Degree Days (base 65°F)	na	na	na	na	na	na	na	na	na	na	na	na	na
Cooling Degree Days (base 65°F)	189	163	180	na	na	na	na	340	338	na	na	na	na
Mean Precipitation (in.)	12.29	8.66	15.80	16.65	8.32	5.21	9.40	9.36	5.79	7.37	13.33	11.45	123.63
Days With ≥ 0.1" Precipitation	11	9	16	17	13	10	15	13	10	12	12	12	150
Days With ≥ 1.0" Precipitation	3	3	5	4	2	1	2	2	1	2	4	3	32
Mean Snowfall (in.)	0.0	0.0	0.0	0.0	0.0	0.0	0.0	0.0	0.0	0.0	0.0	0.0	0.0
Days With ≥ 1.0" Snow Depth	0	0	0	0	0	0	0	0	0	0	0	0	0

Opihihale 2 24.1 *Hawaii County*   Elevation: 1,358 ft.   Latitude: 19° 16' N   Longitude: 155° 53' W

	JAN	FEB	MAR	APR	MAY	JUN	JUL	AUG	SEP	OCT	NOV	DEC	YEAR
Mean Maximum Temp. (°F)	76.7	76.9	77.1	77.6	78.3	79.0	80.2	81.1	81.1	80.9	79.3	77.8	78.8
Mean Temp. (°F)	67.1	67.2	67.8	68.7	69.8	70.9	71.8	72.5	72.2	71.6	70.2	68.1	69.8
Mean Minimum Temp. (°F)	57.5	57.4	58.5	59.7	61.2	62.6	63.4	63.8	63.2	62.4	60.9	58.4	60.8
Extreme Maximum Temp. (°F)	91	87	87	87	86	87	87	90	91	90	90	89	91
Extreme Minimum Temp. (°F)	50	50	51	51	50	50	57	57	56	53	49	50	49
Days Maximum Temp. ≥ 90°F	0	0	0	0	0	0	0	0	0	0	0	0	0
Days Maximum Temp. ≤ 32°F	0	0	0	0	0	0	0	0	0	0	0	0	0
Days Minimum Temp. ≤ 32°F	0	0	0	0	0	0	0	0	0	0	0	0	0
Days Minimum Temp. ≤ 0°F	0	0	0	0	0	0	0	0	0	0	0	0	0
Heating Degree Days (base 65°F)	na	na	na	na	na	na	na	na	na	na	na	na	na
Cooling Degree Days (base 65°F)	89	84	107	128	171	197	235	251	238	228	178	120	2,026
Mean Precipitation (in.)	3.15	2.58	3.38	2.91	3.09	3.04	3.65	3.64	4.16	3.61	2.93	2.57	38.71
Days With ≥ 0.1" Precipitation	5	4	6	7	8	8	8	8	9	7	5	4	79
Days With ≥ 1.0" Precipitation	1	1	1	1	0	0	0	0	1	1	1	1	8
Mean Snowfall (in.)	0.0	0.0	0.0	0.0	0.0	0.0	0.0	0.0	0.0	0.0	0.0	0.0	0.0
Days With ≥ 1.0" Snow Depth	0	0	0	0	0	0	0	0	0	0	0	0	0

Puukohola Heiau 98.1 *Hawaii County*   Elevation: 137 ft.   Latitude: 20° 02' N   Longitude: 155° 49' W

	JAN	FEB	MAR	APR	MAY	JUN	JUL	AUG	SEP	OCT	NOV	DEC	YEAR
Mean Maximum Temp. (°F)	81.4	81.4	82.8	84.2	84.9	86.2	87.1	87.6	87.4	86.6	84.4	82.4	84.7
Mean Temp. (°F)	na	72.8	74.1	75.5	76.4	77.8	78.9	79.3	79.1	78.5	76.6	74.2	na
Mean Minimum Temp. (°F)	na	64.2	65.5	66.9	67.9	69.4	70.6	70.9	70.8	70.4	68.7	66.1	na
Extreme Maximum Temp. (°F)	91	90	93	95	98	95	97	96	96	96	96	91	98
Extreme Minimum Temp. (°F)	41	55	55	54	57	54	43	60	56	51	60	59	41
Days Maximum Temp. ≥ 90°F	0	0	0	1	3	5	9	na	10	7	3	0	na
Days Maximum Temp. ≤ 32°F	0	0	0	0	0	0	0	0	0	0	0	0	0
Days Minimum Temp. ≤ 32°F	0	0	0	0	0	0	0	0	0	0	0	0	0
Days Minimum Temp. ≤ 0°F	0	0	0	0	0	0	0	0	0	0	0	0	0
Heating Degree Days (base 65°F)	na	na	na	na	na	na	na	na	na	na	na	na	na
Cooling Degree Days (base 65°F)	243	223	287	319	353	388	429	445	425	416	353	286	4,167
Mean Precipitation (in.)	1.75	1.19	1.02	0.90	0.44	0.49	0.42	0.56	0.84	0.68	0.92	2.12	11.33
Days With ≥ 0.1" Precipitation	2	2	2	1	1	1	na	1	1	1	2	2	na
Days With ≥ 1.0" Precipitation	1	0	0	0	0	0	0	0	0	0	0	1	2
Mean Snowfall (in.)	0.0	0.0	0.0	0.0	0.0	0.0	0.0	0.0	0.0	0.0	0.0	0.0	0.0
Days With ≥ 1.0" Snow Depth	0	0	0	0	0	0	0	0	0	0	0	0	0

Waikiki 717.2 *Honolulu County*   Elevation: 9 ft.   Latitude: 21° 16' N   Longitude: 157° 49' W

	JAN	FEB	MAR	APR	MAY	JUN	JUL	AUG	SEP	OCT	NOV	DEC	YEAR
Mean Maximum Temp. (°F)	81.0	81.1	82.0	83.1	84.6	86.2	87.2	88.2	88.1	86.9	84.2	81.9	84.5
Mean Temp. (°F)	72.8	72.8	74.2	75.5	76.7	78.6	79.7	80.4	80.1	79.0	76.9	74.3	76.7
Mean Minimum Temp. (°F)	64.5	64.5	66.3	67.7	68.7	70.9	72.2	72.6	72.0	71.1	69.5	66.6	68.9
Extreme Maximum Temp. (°F)	89	90	92	89	93	93	95	92	95	95	92	90	95
Extreme Minimum Temp. (°F)	52	51	53	55	59	52	63	62	62	62	56	46	46
Days Maximum Temp. ≥ 90°F	0	0	0	0	0	1	4	6	6	3	0	0	20
Days Maximum Temp. ≤ 32°F	0	0	0	0	0	0	0	0	0	0	0	0	0
Days Minimum Temp. ≤ 32°F	0	0	0	0	0	0	0	0	0	0	0	0	0
Days Minimum Temp. ≤ 0°F	0	0	0	0	0	0	0	0	0	0	0	0	0
Heating Degree Days (base 65°F)	na	na	na	na	na	na	na	na	na	na	na	na	na
Cooling Degree Days (base 65°F)	250	232	297	330	379	432	477	496	473	448	375	301	4,490
Mean Precipitation (in.)	3.45	2.42	2.27	1.38	1.20	0.72	0.90	0.59	0.94	2.13	3.08	3.51	22.59
Days With ≥ 0.1" Precipitation	5	4	4	4	2	1	2	1	2	3	5	5	38
Days With ≥ 1.0" Precipitation	1	1	1	0	0	0	0	0	0	1	1	1	6
Mean Snowfall (in.)	0.0	0.0	0.0	0.0	0.0	0.0	0.0	0.0	0.0	0.0	0.0	0.0	0.0
Days With ≥ 1.0" Snow Depth	0	0	0	0	0	0	0	0	0	0	0	0	0

Waimanalo Exp. Farm *Honolulu County*   Elevation: 59 ft.   Latitude: 21° 20' N   Longitude: 157° 43' W

	JAN	FEB	MAR	APR	MAY	JUN	JUL	AUG	SEP	OCT	NOV	DEC	YEAR
Mean Maximum Temp. (°F)	77.8	78.0	78.3	79.2	80.7	82.4	83.4	84.4	84.8	83.5	80.8	78.8	81.0
Mean Temp. (°F)	71.2	71.2	72.2	73.7	75.1	77.0	78.1	79.0	79.3	77.7	75.4	72.9	75.2
Mean Minimum Temp. (°F)	64.6	64.4	66.1	68.1	69.4	71.6	72.7	73.4	73.7	71.9	69.9	66.9	69.4
Extreme Maximum Temp. (°F)	85	85	84	87	86	89	90	89	92	95	89	86	95
Extreme Minimum Temp. (°F)	52	52	54	57	49	62	65	65	59	59	57	54	49
Days Maximum Temp. ≥ 90°F	0	0	0	0	0	0	0	0	0	0	0	0	0
Days Maximum Temp. ≤ 32°F	0	0	0	0	0	0	0	0	0	0	0	0	0
Days Minimum Temp. ≤ 32°F	0	0	0	0	0	0	0	0	0	0	0	0	0
Days Minimum Temp. ≤ 0°F	0	0	0	0	0	0	0	0	0	0	0	0	0
Heating Degree Days (base 65°F)	na	na	na	na	na	na	na	na	na	na	na	na	na
Cooling Degree Days (base 65°F)	196	177	227	270	316	372	417	440	425	399	322	246	3,807
Mean Precipitation (in.)	6.94	4.69	3.37	3.30	3.18	1.44	1.64	1.44	1.97	3.79	6.16	5.44	43.36
Days With ≥ 0.1" Precipitation	9	7	6	6	5	3	5	4	5	6	8	8	72
Days With ≥ 1.0" Precipitation	2	1	1	1	1	0	0	0	0	1	2	2	11
Mean Snowfall (in.)	0.0	0.0	0.0	0.0	0.0	0.0	0.0	0.0	0.0	0.0	0.0	0.0	0.0
Days With ≥ 1.0" Snow Depth	0	0	0	0	0	0	0	0	0	0	0	0	0

Note: See Appendix D for explanation of data.

IDAHO

PHYSICAL FEATURES. Idaho lies entirely west of the Continental Divide, which forms its boundary for some distance westward from Yellowstone National Park. With a maximum north-south extent of 7° of latitude, its east-west extent is 6° of longitude at latitude 42° N., but only 1° of longitude at 49° N. The northern part of the State averages lower in elevation than the much larger central and southern portions, where numerous mountain ranges form barriers to the free flow of air from all points of the compass. In the north the main barrier is the rugged chain of Bitterroot Mountains forming much of the boundary between Idaho and Montana. The extreme range of elevation in the State is from 738 feet at the confluence of the Clearwater and Snake Rivers to 12,655 feet at Mt. Borah in Custer County.

GENERAL CLIMATE. Comprising rugged mountain ranges, canyons, high grassy valleys, arid plains, and fertile lowlands, the State reflects in its topography and vegetation a wide range of climates. Located some 300 miles from the Pacific Ocean, Idaho is, nevertheless, influenced by maritime air borne eastward on the prevailing westerly winds. Particularly in winter, the maritime influence is noticeable in the greater average cloudiness, greater frequency of precipitation, and mean temperatures, which are above those at the same latitude and altitude in midcontinent. This maritime influence is most marked in the northern part of the State, where the air arrives via the Columbia River Gorge with a greater burden of moisture than at lower latitudes. Eastern Idaho's climate has a more continental character than the west and north, a fact quite evident not only in the somewhat greater range between winter and summer temperatures, but also in the reversal of the wet winter-dry summer patterns.

The pattern of average annual temperatures for the State indicates the effect both of latitude and altitude. The highest annual averages are found in the lower elevations of the Clearwater and Little Salmon River Basins, and in the stretch of the Snake River Valley from the vicinity of Bliss downstream to Lewiston, including the open valleys of the Boise, Payette, and Weiser Rivers. The diurnal range of temperature is, of course, most extreme in high valleys and in the semiarid plains of the Snake River Valley. The magnitude of diurnal range varies with the season, being lowest in winter when cloudiness is much more prevalent, and greatest in the warmer part of the year. In summer, periods of extreme heat extending beyond a week are quite rare, and the same can be said of periods of extremely low temperatures in winter. In both cases the normal progress of weather systems across the State usually results in a change at rather frequent intervals.

PRECIPITATION. To a large extent the source of moisture for precipitation in Idaho is the Pacific Ocean. In summer there are some exceptions to this when moisture-laden air is brought in from the south at high levels to produce thundershower activity, particularly in the eastern part of Idaho. The source of this moisture from the south is apparently the Gulf of Mexico and Caribbean region. The average precipitation map for Idaho is as complex as the physiography of the State. Partly because of the greater moisture supply in the west winds over the northern part of the State (less formidable barriers to the west) and partly because of greater frequency of cyclonic activity in the north, the average valley precipitation is considerably greater than in southern sections. Peaks on the average annual precipitation map are found, however, in nearly all parts of the State at higher elevations. Sizable areas in the Clearwater, Payette, and Boise River Basins receive an average of 40 to 50 inches per year, with a few points or small areas receiving in excess of 60 inches. Large areas including the northeastern valleys, much of the Upper Snake River Plains, Central Plains, and the lower elevations of the Southwestern Valleys receive less than 10 inches annually.

Seasonal distribution of precipitation shows a very marked pattern of winter maximum and midsummer minimum in the northern and western portions of the State. In the eastern part of the State, however, many reporting weather stations show maximum monthly amounts in summer and minimum amounts in winter. In the divisions called Northeastern Valleys and Eastern Highlands, more than 50 percent of the annual rainfall occurs during the period April through September. Over nearly all of the northern part of the State, however, less than 40 percent of the annual rainfall occurs in this same period, and in portions of the Boise, Payette, and Weiser River drainages less than 30 percent of the annual amount comes in that 6-month period.

SNOW. Snowfall distribution is affected both by availability of moisture and by elevation. The major mountain ranges of the State accumulate a deep snow cover during the winter months, and the release of water from a melting snowpack in late spring furnishes irrigation water for more than two million acres, mainly within the Snake River Basin above Weiser.

FLOODS. Floods in Idaho occur most often during the period of seasonal snowmelt in spring, particularly in April and May. A few areas in the State are actually flooded or threatened by flood waters nearly every year.

So-called "out-of-season" floods do occur occasionally at a number of points in the State. Flash floods on small streams, or occasionally in ravines or dry gulches, occur a few times each year as the result of heavy rains associated with thunderstorms.

HUMIDITY. The diurnal range of relative humidity generally follows a pattern which is the reverse of the diurnal temperature curve. Precipitation or fog interferes with such a pattern, but the averages show maximum humidity at the time of minimum temperature and vice versa. In winter, average relative humidities are considerably higher than during hot weather. Comfort during the summer months is greatly affected by the moisture content of the air. In Idaho, where maximum temperatures above 90°F. are not uncommon in July and August, humidity at the time of maximum temperature is usually below 25 percent, and often down to 15 percent or lower. With any kind of air movement the higher temperatures are quite within the range of adjustment of the human system.

FOG. Fogs in Idaho are extremely variable. At Boise, heavy fog (visibility 1/4 mile or less) is experienced on an average of 17 days per year, with a maximum of six occurrences in December. The year-to-year variation is considerable, however.

STORMS. Windstorms are not uncommon in Idaho, but the State has no such destructive storms as hurricanes, and an extremely small incidence of tornadoes. Windstorms associated with cyclonic systems, and their cold fronts, do some damage each year. Storms of this type may occur at any time from October into June, while during the remaining 3 months of the year strong winds almost invariably come with thunderstorms. Hail damage in Idaho is very small in comparison with such damage in other areas of the central part of the United States. Often the hail that occurs does not grow to a size larger than 1/2 inch in diameter, and the areas affected are usually limited in size. Quite often hail comes in springtime storms, when it is mostly of the small, soft variety with a limited damaging effect. The incidence of summer thunderstorms is greatest in mountainous areas, with an important influence on the economy of the State, resulting from the lightning-caused forest and range fires.

SUNSHINE. The annual average percentage of possible sunshine ranges from about 50 in the north to about 70 in the south. Winter, with its frequent periods of cloudy weather, has about 40 percent of possible sunshine in the large open valleys of the south and less than 30 percent in the north, but in July and August the average percentage rises to the upper 80s in the southwest and to near 80 percent in the east and north.

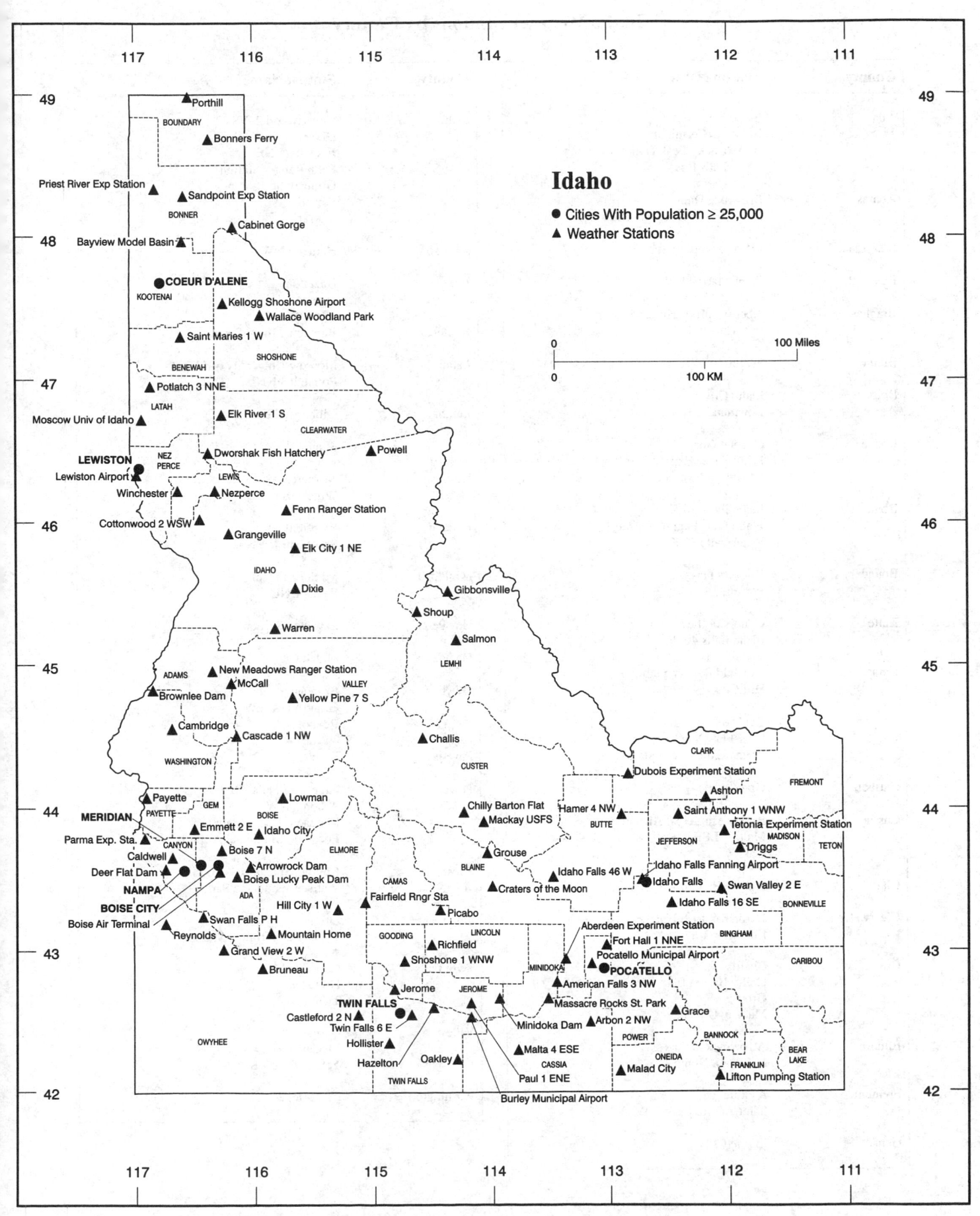

Idaho

● Cities With Population ≥ 25,000
▲ Weather Stations

▲ Porthill

BOUNDARY

▲ Bonners Ferry

Priest River Exp Station ▲

▲ Sandpoint Exp Station

BONNER

▲ Cabinet Gorge

Bayview Model Basin ▲

● COEUR D'ALENE

KOOTENAI

▲ Kellogg Shoshone Airport

▲ Wallace Woodland Park

▲ Saint Maries 1 W

SHOSHONE

BENEWAH

▲ Potlatch 3 NNE

LATAH

▲ Elk River 1 S

Moscow Univ of Idaho ▲

CLEARWATER

NEZ PERCE

▲ Dworshak Fish Hatchery   ▲ Powell

LEWISTON

Lewiston Airport ▲✕

LEWIS

Winchester ▲   ▲ Nezperce

Cottonwood 2 WSW ▲

▲ Fenn Ranger Station

▲ Grangeville

▲ Elk City 1 NE

IDAHO

▲ Dixie

▲ Gibbonsville

▲ Shoup

▲ Warren

▲ Salmon

LEMHI

New Meadows Ranger Station ▲

ADAMS

▲ McCall

VALLEY

▲ Brownlee Dam

▲ Yellow Pine 7 S

▲ Cambridge

▲ Cascade 1 NW

▲ Challis

WASHINGTON

CUSTER

CLARK

▲ Dubois Experiment Station

FREMONT

▲ Ashton

▲ Payette   ▲ Lowman   Chilly Barton Flat ▲   Hamer 4 NW ▲   ▲ Saint Anthony 1 WNW

MERIDIAN ●   GEM   BOISE   ▲ Mackay USFS   BUTTE

PAYETTE   ▲ Emmett 2 E   ▲ Idaho City   ▲ Tetonia Experiment Station

Parma Exp. Sta. ▲   JEFFERSON   MADISON

CANYON   ▲ Boise 7 N   ▲ Driggs   TETON

Caldwell ●   ELMORE   ▲ Grouse   Idaho Falls Fanning Airport ▲

Deer Flat Dam ●   ● ▲ Arrowrock Dam   BLAINE   Idaho Falls 46 W ▲

NAMPA ●   ● Boise Lucky Peak Dam   Craters of the Moon ▲   ● Idaho Falls   ▲ Swan Valley 2 E

BOISE CITY ●   ADA   BONNEVILLE

Boise Air Terminal ▲   ▲ Swan Falls P H   Hill City 1 W ▲   Fairfield Rngr Sta ▲   ▲ Idaho Falls 16 SE

Reynolds ▲   Mountain Home ▲   CAMAS   ▲ Picabo   Aberdeen Experiment Station ▲   BINGHAM

▲ Grand View 2 W   LINCOLN   Fort Hall 1 NNE ▲

GOODING   ▲ Richfield   Pocatello Municipal Airport ▲   CARIBOU

▲ Bruneau   ▲ Shoshone 1 WNW   MINIDOKA   ● POCATELLO

Jerome ▲   ▲ American Falls 3 NW   ▲ Grace

TWIN FALLS   JEROME   Massacre Rocks St. Park ▲

Castleford 2 N ▲   ● ▲   ▲ Minidoka Dam   ▲ Arbon 2 NW

Twin Falls 6 E ▲   POWER   BANNOCK

Hollister ▲   ▲   ▲ Malta 4 ESE   ONEIDA   FRANKLIN   BEAR LAKE

Hazelton   ▲ Oakley ▲   ▲ Paul 1 ENE   ▲ Malad City   ▲ Lifton Pumping Station

OWYHEE   CASSIA

TWIN FALLS   Burley Municipal Airport

Idaho Weather Stations by County

County	Station Name
Ada	Boise 7 N
	Boise Air Terminal
	Boise Lucky Peak Dam
	Swan Falls P H
Adams	Brownlee Dam
	New Meadows Ranger Station
Bear Lake	Lifton Pumping Station
Benewah	Saint Maries 1 W
Bingham	Aberdeen Experiment Station
	Fort Hall 1 NNE
Blaine	Picabo
Boise	Idaho City
	Lowman
Bonner	Cabinet Gorge
	Priest River Exp. Station
	Sandpoint Exp. Station
Bonneville	Idaho Falls 16 SE
	Idaho Falls Fanning Airport
	Swan Valley 2 E
Boundary	Bonners Ferry
	Porthill
Butte	Craters of the Moon
	Idaho Falls 46 W
Camas	Fairfield Ranger Station
	Hill City 1 W
Canyon	Caldwell
	Deer Flat Dam
	Parma Experiment Station
Caribou	Grace
Cassia	Burley Municipal Airport
	Malta 4 ESE
	Oakley
Clark	Dubois Experiment Station
Clearwater	Dworshak Fish Hatchery
	Elk River 1 S
Custer	Challis
	Chilly Barton Flat
	Grouse
	Mackay USFS
Elmore	Arrowrock Dam
	Mountain Home
Fremont	Ashton
	Saint Anthony 1 WNW
Gem	Emmett 2 E

County	Station Name
Idaho	Cottonwood 2 WSW
	Dixie
	Elk City 1 NE
	Fenn Ranger Station
	Grangeville
	Powell
	Warren
Jefferson	Hamer 4 NW
Jerome	Hazelton
	Jerome
Kootenai	Bayview Model Basin
Latah	Moscow University of Idaho
	Potlatch 3 NNE
Lemhi	Gibbonsville
	Salmon
	Shoup
Lewis	Nezperce
	Winchester
Lincoln	Richfield
	Shoshone 1 WNW
Minidoka	Minidoka Dam
	Paul 1 ENE
Nez Perce	Lewiston Airport
Oneida	Malad City
Owyhee	Bruneau
	Grand View 2 W
	Reynolds
Payette	Payette
Power	American Falls 3 NW
	Arbon 2 NW
	Massacre Rocks State Park
	Pocatello Municipal Airport
Shoshone	Kellogg Shoshone Airport
	Wallace Woodland Park
Teton	Driggs
	Tetonia Experiment Station
Twin Falls	Castleford 2 N
	Hollister
	Twin Falls 6 E
Valley	Cascade 1 NW
	McCall
	Yellow Pine 7 S
Washington	Cambridge

Idaho Weather Stations by City

City	Station Name	Miles
Boise City	Arrowrock Dam	16
	Boise 7 N	7
	Boise Lucky Peak Dam	11
	Boise Air Terminal	3
Idaho Falls	Idaho Falls 16 SE	16
	Idaho Falls Fanning Airport	3
Lewiston	Lewiston Airport	2
Meridian	Boise 7 N	12
	Boise Lucky Peak Dam	19
	Boise Air Terminal	10
	Caldwell	14
	Deer Flat Dam	17
	Emmett 2 E	18
Nampa	Boise Air Terminal	18
	Caldwell	9
	Deer Flat Dam	9
Pocatello	Fort Hall 1 NNE	12
	Pocatello Municipal Airport	7
Twin Falls	Hazelton	17
	Hollister	16
	Jerome	12
	Twin Falls 6 E	6

Note: Miles is the distance between the geographic center of the city and the weather station.

Idaho Weather Stations by Elevation

Feet	Station Name
6,259	Chilly Barton Flat
6,167	Tetonia Experiment Station
6,135	Grouse
6,115	Driggs
5,925	Lifton Pumping Station
5,905	Warren
5,895	Craters of the Moon
5,895	Mackay USFS
5,849	Idaho Falls 16 SE
5,620	Dixie
5,547	Grace
5,449	Dubois Experiment Station
5,357	Swan Valley 2 E
5,209	Arbon 2 NW
5,209	Ashton
5,173	Challis
5,098	Hill City 1 W
5,098	Yellow Pine 7 S
5,062	Fairfield Ranger Station
5,022	McCall
4,947	Saint Anthony 1 WNW
4,937	Idaho Falls 46 W
4,895	Cascade 1 NW
4,829	Picabo
4,790	Hamer 4 NW
4,727	Idaho Falls Fanning Airport
4,589	Malta 4 ESE
4,557	Oakley
4,524	Hollister
4,478	Gibbonsville
4,468	Malad City
4,461	Fort Hall 1 NNE
4,438	Pocatello Municipal Airport
4,402	Aberdeen Experiment Station
4,402	American Falls 3 NW
4,281	Richfield
4,209	Minidoka Dam
4,192	Massacre Rocks State Park
4,156	Burley Municipal Airport
4,146	Paul 1 ENE
4,058	Hazelton
4,055	Elk City 1 NE
3,963	Idaho City
3,959	Twin Falls 6 E
3,950	Shoshone 1 WNW
3,950	Winchester
3,943	Cottonwood 2 WSW
3,930	Salmon
3,927	Reynolds
3,917	Lowman
3,884	Boise 7 N
3,868	New Meadows Ranger Station
3,822	Castleford 2 N
3,740	Jerome
3,526	Powell

Feet	Station Name
3,398	Shoup
3,359	Grangeville
3,274	Arrowrock Dam
3,238	Nezperce
3,139	Mountain Home
2,939	Wallace Woodland Park
2,916	Elk River 1 S
2,837	Boise Lucky Peak Dam
2,837	Boise Air Terminal
2,657	Moscow University of Idaho
2,647	Cambridge
2,598	Potlatch 3 NNE
2,529	Bruneau
2,509	Deer Flat Dam
2,398	Grand View 2 W
2,388	Emmett 2 E
2,378	Priest River Exp. Station
2,368	Caldwell
2,322	Swan Falls P H
2,319	Saint Maries 1 W
2,290	Parma Experiment Station
2,257	Cabinet Gorge
2,230	Kellogg Shoshone Airport
2,148	Payette
2,099	Sandpoint Exp. Station
2,073	Bayview Model Basin
1,847	Bonners Ferry
1,843	Brownlee Dam
1,774	Porthill
1,587	Fenn Ranger Station
1,433	Lewiston Airport
994	Dworshak Fish Hatchery

Boise Air Terminal

Boise is situated in the Boise River Valley about eight miles below the mouth of a mountain canyon where the valley proper begins. Sheltered by large shade trees and averaging 2,710 feet in elevation, the denser part of the city covers a gentle alluvial slope about two miles wide, stretching southwest from the foothills of the Boise Mountains to the river. The Boise Mountains immediately north of the city rise 5,000 to 6,000 feet above sea level in about eight miles, the slopes partly mantled with sagebrush and then chaparral giving way near the summit to ridges of fir, spruce, and pine.

Although air masses from the Pacific are considerably modified by the time they reach Boise, their influence, particularly in winter, alternates with that of atmospheric developments from other directions. The result is almost a typical upland continental type of climate in summer, while winters are usually tempered by periods of cloudy or stormy and mild weather. Autumns have prolonged periods of near ideal weather, while springtime is noted by changeable weather and varied temperatures.

Summer hot periods rarely last longer than a few days. Temperatures of 100 degrees or higher occur nearly every year.

Winter cold spells with temperatures of 10 degrees or lower generally last longer than the summer hot spells, but rarely include windy conditions.

The normal precipitation pattern in the Boise area shows a winter high and a very pronounced summer low. Total amounts and intensity are generally greatest near the foothills, dwindling to westward and southward.

Destructive force winds are rare. Northwesterly winds, drying and rather raw are common from March through May. Diurnal southeasterly winds, descending from nearby foothills at night, frequently have a moderating effect on winter temperatures. There is an occasional, but moderate, duststorm during the warmer months.

Relative humidity is low but widespread irrigation maintains humidity several percent above the general dryness of western arid conditions in summer. Thunderstorms occur primarily during spring and summer, with less frequency during fall and occasionally during winter. December and January are the months of heavy fog or low stratus cloud conditions. Winter has a moderate amount of sunshine but periods of clear, sunny weather are the rule in summer.

Based on the 1951-1980 period, the average first occurrence of 32 degrees Fahrenheit in the fall is October 9 and the average last occurrence in the spring is May 8.

Boise Air Terminal *Ada County*   Elevation: 2,837 ft.   Latitude: 43° 34' N   Longitude: 116° 13' W

	JAN	FEB	MAR	APR	MAY	JUN	JUL	AUG	SEP	OCT	NOV	DEC	YEAR
Mean Maximum Temp. (°F)	37.0	44.8	53.7	61.6	71.1	80.8	89.9	88.8	77.7	64.8	48.3	37.7	63.0
Mean Temp. (°F)	29.7	36.2	43.2	49.6	57.8	66.3	73.8	73.0	63.1	51.9	39.5	30.1	51.2
Mean Minimum Temp. (°F)	22.4	27.6	32.6	37.5	44.4	51.8	57.7	57.1	48.5	38.9	30.7	22.4	39.3
Extreme Maximum Temp. (°F)	61	71	81	92	98	105	108	109	101	94	78	63	109
Extreme Minimum Temp. (°F)	-14	-15	6	20	22	31	35	34	23	11	-3	-25	-25
Days Maximum Temp. ≥ 90°F	0	0	0	0	1	6	18	17	4	0	0	0	46
Days Maximum Temp. ≤ 32°F	9	3	0	0	0	0	0	0	0	0	1	8	21
Days Minimum Temp. ≤ 32°F	25	20	15	8	2	0	0	0	1	6	17	26	120
Days Minimum Temp. ≤ 0°F	2	1	0	0	0	0	0	0	0	0	0	2	5
Heating Degree Days (base 65°F)	1,087	806	669	459	248	77	10	14	126	405	758	1,076	5,735
Cooling Degree Days (base 65°F)	0	0	0	3	34	118	281	275	84	5	0	0	800
Mean Precipitation (in.)	1.47	1.08	1.39	1.26	1.27	0.80	0.39	0.30	0.77	0.70	1.43	1.40	12.26
Maximum Precipitation (in.)	3.9	3.7	3.5	3.0	4.1	2.9	1.6	2.4	2.9	2.3	3.4	4.2	18.8
Minimum Precipitation (in.)	0.1	0.2	0.2	0.1	trace	trace	trace	trace	0	0	0.1	0.1	6.6
Maximum 24-hr. Precipitation (in.)	1.1	0.9	1.6	1.3	1.8	1.9	0.9	1.6	1.7	0.7	0.8	1.0	1.9
Days With ≥ 0.1" Precipitation	5	4	5	4	4	2	1	1	2	3	5	5	41
Days With ≥ 1.0" Precipitation	0	0	0	0	0	0	0	0	0	0	0	0	0
Mean Snowfall (in.)	4.8	3.2	1.5	0.4	trace	trace	trace	trace	trace	0.1	2.7	6.6	19.3
Maximum Snowfall (in.)	21	25	12	8	4	trace	0	0	0	3	19	26	47
Maximum 24-hr. Snowfall (in.)	7	7	6	7	4	trace	0	0	0	1	5	7	7
Days With ≥ 1.0" Snow Depth	11	5	1	0	0	0	0	0	0	0	2	8	27
Thunderstorm Days	< 1	< 1	1	1	3	3	2	3	1	< 1	< 1	< 1	14
Foggy Days	14	8	3	2	1	1	< 1	< 1	1	2	7	13	52
Predominant Sky Cover	OVR	OVR	OVR	OVR	OVR	CLR	CLR	CLR	CLR	CLR	OVR	OVR	OVR
Mean Relative Humidity 7am (%)	81	80	75	69	65	59	48	50	58	67	77	81	68
Mean Relative Humidity 4pm (%)	68	58	45	35	34	29	22	23	28	36	55	67	42
Mean Dewpoint (°F)	21	26	28	31	38	42	44	42	38	33	28	24	33
Prevailing Wind Direction	SE	SE	SE	NW	NW	NW	NW	NW	SE	SE	SE	SE	SE
Prevailing Wind Speed (mph)	10	10	10	13	12	12	10	10	8	9	10	10	10
Maximum Wind Gust (mph)	59	64	58	59	55	63	71	60	49	47	55	56	71

Lewiston Airport

Lewiston is located at the confluence of the Snake and Clearwater Rivers at an elevation of 738 feet above mean sea level. Lower Granite Lake extends from the confluence of the two rivers, 32 miles downstream in the Snake River channel, to Lower Granite Dam. The valley is rather narrow with a range of hills to the north sloping abruptly to about 2,000 feet above the valley floor. To the south the terrain rises more gradually to a more or less flat bench about 700 feet above the valley. The Weather Office is located on the bench at an elevation of 1,413 feet above sea level and about two miles south of Lewiston.

Considerable variations in the climate are to be found within relatively short distances from the valley itself. On the prairies surrounding the valley, winter temperatures are much lower and the precipitation is normally almost double that recorded in the valley and at the airport location.

Precipitation normally amounts to about 13 inches annually, which is rather evenly distributed through the year except for the months of July and August, which are characterized by infrequent thunderstorms that usually drop only small amounts of rain. Records show that several times during these two months not more than a trace of rain has been recorded. The thunderstorms on the prairie are, at times, accompanied by heavy hail and windstorms. Snowfall in the valley averages about 18 inches during the year, concentrated mostly in the three months of December, January, and February.

Temperatures show a wide range from more than 115 degrees to less than -20 degrees. Many winters have gone by without a temperature of zero being recorded in the valley, but the prairie sections usually experience lower temperatures. The summers experience hot and dry periods with as many as 10 consecutive days with afternoon temperatures reaching 100 degrees or more. Considerable cooling after sunset makes the nights very comfortable. Cold waves occur when arctic air, originating in the Yukon Territory, moves southward.

Winds are light, usually prevailing from the east, with occasional stronger winds accompanying the well-developed frontal systems from the west.

Relative humidity averages about 70 percent during the winter months and gradually lowers to about 40 percent during July and August.

The growing season of approximately 200 days in this part of the country, makes conditions favorable for the growing of many types of fruits, vegetables, and berries.

Lewiston Airport *Nez Perce County*   Elevation: 1,433 ft.   Latitude: 46° 22' N   Longitude: 117° 01' W

	JAN	FEB	MAR	APR	MAY	JUN	JUL	AUG	SEP	OCT	NOV	DEC	YEAR
Mean Maximum Temp. (°F)	40.1	46.5	54.6	62.1	70.8	78.9	88.5	88.6	77.6	63.0	48.0	40.1	63.2
Mean Temp. (°F)	34.0	38.9	45.1	51.3	58.9	66.3	73.9	74.0	64.2	52.1	41.1	34.3	52.8
Mean Minimum Temp. (°F)	27.9	31.2	35.5	40.4	47.0	53.7	59.3	59.3	50.8	41.2	34.3	28.5	42.4
Extreme Maximum Temp. (°F)	63	72	76	97	100	107	109	108	102	89	77	62	109
Extreme Minimum Temp. (°F)	-8	-10	15	26	31	38	43	41	31	16	-1	-16	-16
Days Maximum Temp. ≥ 90°F	0	0	0	0	1	5	15	16	4	0	0	0	41
Days Maximum Temp. ≤ 32°F	7	2	0	0	0	0	0	0	0	0	1	5	15
Days Minimum Temp. ≤ 32°F	19	14	9	3	0	0	0	0	0	3	11	21	80
Days Minimum Temp. ≤ 0°F	1	0	0	0	0	0	0	0	0	0	0	1	2
Heating Degree Days (base 65°F)	954	732	611	409	211	67	9	9	102	396	709	944	5,153
Cooling Degree Days (base 65°F)	0	0	0	3	34	101	276	291	91	4	0	0	800
Mean Precipitation (in.)	1.23	0.90	1.12	1.31	1.55	1.20	0.76	0.75	0.77	0.95	1.24	1.03	12.81
Maximum Precipitation (in.)	3.5	2.0	2.7	3.3	4.8	4.7	2.6	3.0	2.2	2.8	2.8	3.3	18.6
Minimum Precipitation (in.)	0.1	0.2	0.3	0	0.3	0.2	trace	trace	trace	trace	0.2	0.1	8.4
Maximum 24-hr. Precipitation (in.)	1.1	0.7	0.8	0.9	1.6	1.6	1.1	1.4	1.7	1.1	0.9	0.9	1.7
Days With ≥ 0.1" Precipitation	4	3	4	4	5	4	2	2	3	3	4	4	42
Days With ≥ 1.0" Precipitation	0	0	0	0	0	0	0	0	0	0	0	0	0
Mean Snowfall (in.)	4.1	2.4	0.9	trace	trace	0.0	trace	0.0	0.0	0.1	1.8	3.3	12.6
Maximum Snowfall (in.)	26	15	10	1	trace	0	0	0	0	3	3	19	34
Maximum 24-hr. Snowfall (in.)	9	7	5	1	trace	0	0	0	0	1	1	8	9
Days With ≥ 1.0" Snow Depth	6	3	0	0	0	0	0	0	0	0	1	4	14
Thunderstorm Days	0	< 1	< 1	2	3	6	7	5	2	< 1	0	< 1	25
Foggy Days	10	9	4	1	1	1	< 1	1	1	6	8	13	55
Predominant Sky Cover	OVR	OVR	OVR	OVR	OVR	OVR	CLR	CLR	CLR	OVR	OVR	OVR	OVR
Mean Relative Humidity 7am (%)	81	80	77	71	68	64	55	55	66	80	83	82	72
Mean Relative Humidity 4pm (%)	71	62	49	42	39	35	25	25	32	49	69	74	48
Mean Dewpoint (°F)	25	29	31	34	41	46	46	44	42	38	33	28	36
Prevailing Wind Direction	E	E	E	E	WNW	NW	NW	NW	E	E	E	E	E
Prevailing Wind Speed (mph)	7	8	8	7	10	9	9	9	6	7	7	8	8
Maximum Wind Gust (mph)	73	64	60	58	54	54	51	51	59	59	59	63	73

Pocatello Municipal Airport

Pocatello is located in the Snake River Valley at the mouth of Portneuf Canyon at an elevation of about 4,500 feet above sea level. A desert composed of sand, lava rock, and craters, extends to the west, while to the east the ground level rises steadily towards the crests of the Continental Divide.

Except in autumn, which is the season of the finest weather in Pocatello, the main feature of the climate is its variety. In winter there are frequent periods of persistent southwest wind, with a resulting mildness that matches the winters of the north Pacific Coast. There are also periods of several days when the temperature stays below freezing and approaches or falls below zero.

During cold periods, precipitation falling as snow occasionally accumulates to a depth of a foot or more. Cloudy and unsettled weather prevails throughout the winter, with measurable amounts of precipitation on about one-third of the days.

In the spring there is a gradual warming. Normally, spring months are the wettest and windiest. Winds of 20 to 30 mph for days at a time are common.

The summer season begins with a relatively sudden break in the disagreeable spring weather. Home heating, usually discontinued about the first of June, is sometimes needed intermittently until the first part of July. Suitable weather for outside evening activities is very uncertain during June, even though the afternoons may be mild. As night falls, the temperature often drops rapidly into the 40s, accompanied by a chilling wind from snows remaining on the nearby mountains. During the summer, precipitation usually falls as local showers, often accompanied by light to moderate thunderstorms and occasionally by hail. Damage by excessive precipitation, lightning, high winds, or hail is uncommon and quite localized. Long periods of extremely hot weather in July and August are also uncommon. Although afternoon temperatures may run into the 90s, nights are usually cool.

Exceptionally fine weather predominates during the autumn season. The sudden summer showers are gradually replaced by short periods of cloudy and unsettled weather with more general rains. Continuous home heating is not needed until mid-October. Evenings during September are ideal for outdoor activities, and pleasant afternoons are the rule until toward the end of November. The first cold wave may appear during late November but usually not until late December.

The average first occurrence of 32 degrees Fahrenheit in the fall is September 20 and the average last occurrence in the spring is May 20.

Pocatello Municipal Airport *Power County*   Elevation: 4,438 ft.   Latitude: 42° 55' N   Longitude: 112° 34' W

	JAN	FEB	MAR	APR	MAY	JUN	JUL	AUG	SEP	OCT	NOV	DEC	YEAR
Mean Maximum Temp. (°F)	32.5	39.1	48.4	57.9	67.5	78.0	87.3	86.9	75.6	61.9	44.8	33.8	59.5
Mean Temp. (°F)	24.1	29.8	37.8	45.4	53.8	62.5	69.8	68.9	59.0	47.6	34.9	25.0	46.5
Mean Minimum Temp. (°F)	15.7	20.4	27.2	32.8	40.0	46.8	52.2	50.9	42.2	33.2	25.0	16.2	33.6
Extreme Maximum Temp. (°F)	57	65	75	86	90	103	102	104	98	91	75	64	104
Extreme Minimum Temp. (°F)	-28	-33	-12	13	20	28	34	30	19	10	-14	-29	-33
Days Maximum Temp. ≥ 90°F	0	0	0	0	0	4	14	13	2	0	0	0	33
Days Maximum Temp. ≤ 32°F	14	7	1	0	0	0	0	0	0	0	4	12	38
Days Minimum Temp. ≤ 32°F	28	25	24	15	4	0	0	0	3	14	24	28	165
Days Minimum Temp. ≤ 0°F	5	2	0	0	0	0	0	0	0	0	1	3	11
Heating Degree Days (base 65°F)	1,260	989	836	583	345	125	19	24	199	533	897	1,233	7,043
Cooling Degree Days (base 65°F)	0	0	0	0	5	49	161	154	25	0	0	0	394
Mean Precipitation (in.)	1.16	0.96	1.39	1.20	1.55	0.94	0.73	0.66	0.88	0.95	1.17	1.12	12.71
Maximum Precipitation (in.)	3.2	2.6	2.9	3.3	3.3	3.3	2.3	4.0	3.4	2.6	2.8	3.4	20.3
Minimum Precipitation (in.)	0.2	0.1	0.1	0.1	0.2	trace	trace	trace	0	0	trace	0.1	5.3
Maximum 24-hr. Precipitation (in.)	0.9	0.7	1.0	0.9	1.3	1.0	1.0	1.0	1.1	1.7	0.8	0.9	1.7
Days With ≥ 0.1" Precipitation	4	3	5	4	5	3	2	2	3	3	4	4	42
Days With ≥ 1.0" Precipitation	0	0	0	0	0	0	0	0	0	0	0	0	0
Mean Snowfall (in.)	9.1	6.7	6.0	4.0	0.9	trace	trace	trace	trace	2.3	6.0	9.7	44.7
Maximum Snowfall (in.)	30	21	17	16	6	trace	0	0	2	13	28	34	80
Maximum 24-hr. Snowfall (in.)	8	6	8	9	5	trace	0	0	2	8	7	11	11
Days With ≥ 1.0" Snow Depth	16	10	4	1	0	0	0	0	0	1	5	14	51
Thunderstorm Days	< 1	< 1	< 1	1	4	5	6	5	3	1	< 1	< 1	25
Foggy Days	12	8	5	2	1	1	< 1	< 1	1	2	6	11	49
Predominant Sky Cover	OVR	OVR	OVR	OVR	OVR	CLR	CLR	CLR	CLR	CLR	OVR	OVR	OVR
Mean Relative Humidity 5am (%)	80	80	77	70	71	70	62	60	64	70	77	81	72
Mean Relative Humidity 5pm (%)	71	63	51	38	35	31	23	22	27	37	60	72	44
Mean Dewpoint (°F)	17	21	24	27	34	40	43	40	35	29	24	19	29
Prevailing Wind Direction	SW	SW	SW	WSW	SW	SW	SW	SW	SW	SW	SW	SW	SW
Prevailing Wind Speed (mph)	13	13	13	16	13	12	10	10	12	12	13	13	13
Maximum Wind Gust (mph)	68	60	64	61	61	62	82	68	74	53	60	77	82

Aberdeen Experiment Station *Bingham County* Elevation: 4,402 ft. Latitude: 42° 57' N Longitude: 112° 50' W

	JAN	FEB	MAR	APR	MAY	JUN	JUL	AUG	SEP	OCT	NOV	DEC	YEAR
Mean Maximum Temp. (°F)	31.4	37.6	47.4	57.6	67.0	76.5	85.2	85.3	74.6	61.8	44.4	32.9	58.5
Mean Temp. (°F)	21.8	27.2	35.8	43.8	52.5	60.7	67.2	66.1	56.1	45.1	32.8	22.4	44.3
Mean Minimum Temp. (°F)	12.1	16.8	24.2	29.9	38.1	44.9	49.2	46.8	37.7	28.4	21.2	12.2	30.1
Extreme Maximum Temp. (°F)	54	63	76	86	89	100	99	103	98	89	73	62	103
Extreme Minimum Temp. (°F)	-33	-38	-17	10	15	29	31	29	19	8	-15	-32	-38
Days Maximum Temp. ≥ 90°F	0	0	0	0	0	2	10	9	1	0	0	0	22
Days Maximum Temp. ≤ 32°F	15	7	2	0	0	0	0	0	0	0	4	13	41
Days Minimum Temp. ≤ 32°F	30	27	28	20	6	0	0	0	7	22	28	30	198
Days Minimum Temp. ≤ 0°F	7	3	1	0	0	0	0	0	0	0	1	5	17
Heating Degree Days (base 65°F)	1,334	1,060	899	631	382	159	39	51	270	610	960	1,314	7,709
Cooling Degree Days (base 65°F)	0	0	0	0	3	35	110	96	12	0	0	0	256
Mean Precipitation (in.)	0.78	0.70	0.87	0.77	1.16	0.95	0.58	0.53	0.77	0.81	0.78	0.72	9.42
Days With ≥ 0.1" Precipitation	3	3	3	3	4	3	2	2	3	3	3	2	34
Days With ≥ 1.0" Precipitation	0	0	0	0	0	0	0	0	0	0	0	0	0
Mean Snowfall (in.)	na	na	2.0	1.1	0.3	trace	0.0	0.0	trace	0.5	2.2	na	na
Days With ≥ 1.0" Snow Depth	16	9	4	1	0	0	0	0	0	0	4	14	48

American Falls 3 NW *Power County* Elevation: 4,402 ft. Latitude: 42° 47' N Longitude: 112° 55' W

	JAN	FEB	MAR	APR	MAY	JUN	JUL	AUG	SEP	OCT	NOV	DEC	YEAR
Mean Maximum Temp. (°F)	33.0	39.1	49.5	59.2	68.6	78.6	87.1	86.7	76.0	62.4	45.4	34.5	60.0
Mean Temp. (°F)	25.1	30.0	38.9	46.8	55.2	63.7	70.8	70.0	60.4	49.1	36.4	26.5	47.8
Mean Minimum Temp. (°F)	17.0	21.0	28.3	34.4	41.8	48.8	54.4	53.3	44.8	35.8	27.4	18.5	35.4
Extreme Maximum Temp. (°F)	55	65	78	87	92	103	102	103	95	87	71	72	103
Extreme Minimum Temp. (°F)	-28	-30	-11	15	21	32	36	33	22	10	-12	-23	-30
Days Maximum Temp. ≥ 90°F	0	0	0	0	0	4	13	12	2	0	0	0	31
Days Maximum Temp. ≤ 32°F	14	6	1	0	0	0	0	0	0	0	3	12	36
Days Minimum Temp. ≤ 32°F	28	24	22	12	2	0	0	0	2	10	21	28	149
Days Minimum Temp. ≤ 0°F	4	2	0	0	0	0	0	0	0	0	0	2	8
Heating Degree Days (base 65°F)	1,232	981	802	540	305	103	15	17	168	487	851	1,188	6,689
Cooling Degree Days (base 65°F)	0	0	0	1	11	68	200	192	40	1	0	0	513
Mean Precipitation (in.)	1.12	0.92	1.35	1.20	1.63	0.98	0.67	0.63	0.85	0.89	1.22	1.08	12.54
Days With ≥ 0.1" Precipitation	4	3	4	4	5	3	2	2	3	2	4	4	40
Days With ≥ 1.0" Precipitation	0	0	0	0	0	0	0	0	0	0	0	0	0
Mean Snowfall (in.)	7.6	4.6	2.6	0.8	0.6	0.0	0.0	0.0	trace	1.0	3.4	7.0	27.6
Days With ≥ 1.0" Snow Depth	17	10	3	0	0	0	0	0	0	0	3	12	45

Arbon 2 NW *Power County* Elevation: 5,209 ft. Latitude: 42° 30' N Longitude: 112° 35' W

	JAN	FEB	MAR	APR	MAY	JUN	JUL	AUG	SEP	OCT	NOV	DEC	YEAR
Mean Maximum Temp. (°F)	30.3	35.7	45.7	56.8	66.6	76.9	85.9	85.5	75.1	61.5	43.5	32.4	58.0
Mean Temp. (°F)	22.4	26.7	35.3	43.6	51.6	60.2	67.6	66.9	57.5	46.5	33.5	23.6	44.6
Mean Minimum Temp. (°F)	14.1	17.6	24.9	30.3	36.7	43.5	49.2	48.3	39.9	31.5	23.5	14.7	31.2
Extreme Maximum Temp. (°F)	55	60	74	83	88	99	100	100	93	88	69	56	100
Extreme Minimum Temp. (°F)	-28	-32	-8	9	15	23	31	23	17	3	-15	-37	-37
Days Maximum Temp. ≥ 90°F	0	0	0	0	0	3	10	9	1	0	0	0	23
Days Maximum Temp. ≤ 32°F	18	9	1	0	0	0	0	0	0	0	5	14	47
Days Minimum Temp. ≤ 32°F	30	26	25	18	8	1	0	0	5	17	25	30	185
Days Minimum Temp. ≤ 0°F	4	3	0	0	0	0	0	0	0	0	1	3	11
Heating Degree Days (base 65°F)	1,315	1,076	915	636	408	169	31	38	232	567	938	1,278	7,603
Cooling Degree Days (base 65°F)	0	0	0	0	1	26	114	108	18	0	0	0	267
Mean Precipitation (in.)	1.70	1.40	1.66	1.46	1.94	1.27	0.99	0.88	1.02	1.11	1.51	1.37	16.31
Days With ≥ 0.1" Precipitation	6	5	6	5	6	4	3	3	3	4	6	5	56
Days With ≥ 1.0" Precipitation	0	0	0	0	0	0	0	0	0	0	0	0	0
Mean Snowfall (in.)	na	na	na	na	0.5	trace	0.0	0.0	0.1	0.9	7.6	na	na
Days With ≥ 1.0" Snow Depth	na	na	na	0	0	0	0	0	0	0	na	na	na

Arrowrock Dam *Elmore County* Elevation: 3,274 ft. Latitude: 43° 36' N Longitude: 115° 55' W

	JAN	FEB	MAR	APR	MAY	JUN	JUL	AUG	SEP	OCT	NOV	DEC	YEAR
Mean Maximum Temp. (°F)	34.3	41.3	50.4	59.6	69.2	79.1	88.8	89.2	77.4	63.3	45.2	35.0	61.1
Mean Temp. (°F)	27.2	32.3	40.0	47.5	55.7	64.1	72.0	72.2	61.4	49.9	37.1	28.2	49.0
Mean Minimum Temp. (°F)	20.1	23.2	29.5	35.4	42.2	49.1	55.3	55.0	45.3	36.5	29.0	21.3	36.8
Extreme Maximum Temp. (°F)	55	67	77	92	95	103	106	108	103	94	73	59	108
Extreme Minimum Temp. (°F)	-12	-16	-1	21	21	33	37	39	26	16	-3	-18	-18
Days Maximum Temp. ≥ 90°F	0	0	0	0	1	5	16	16	4	0	0	0	42
Days Maximum Temp. ≤ 32°F	11	4	0	0	0	0	0	0	0	0	2	9	26
Days Minimum Temp. ≤ 32°F	27	24	21	11	1	0	0	0	1	8	20	26	139
Days Minimum Temp. ≤ 0°F	2	1	0	0	0	0	0	0	0	0	0	1	4
Heating Degree Days (base 65°F)	1,165	918	769	518	297	106	17	16	152	463	831	1,136	6,388
Cooling Degree Days (base 65°F)	0	0	0	2	22	86	236	252	59	2	0	0	659
Mean Precipitation (in.)	3.04	2.33	1.98	1.51	1.42	1.02	0.42	0.33	0.86	1.05	2.81	3.01	19.78
Days With ≥ 0.1" Precipitation	6	6	6	5	4	3	1	1	3	3	7	7	52
Days With ≥ 1.0" Precipitation	0	0	0	0	0	0	0	0	0	0	0	0	0
Mean Snowfall (in.)	11.0	6.5	2.0	trace	trace	0.0	0.0	0.0	0.0	0.1	5.6	12.0	37.2
Days With ≥ 1.0" Snow Depth	20	17	5	0	0	0	0	0	0	0	4	16	62

Ashton *Fremont County*   Elevation: 5,209 ft.   Latitude: 44° 05' N   Longitude: 111° 27' W

	JAN	FEB	MAR	APR	MAY	JUN	JUL	AUG	SEP	OCT	NOV	DEC	YEAR
Mean Maximum Temp. (°F)	28.2	33.4	41.5	52.8	63.8	73.2	81.1	80.8	70.8	58.0	39.5	29.0	54.3
Mean Temp. (°F)	19.4	23.9	31.4	40.7	50.2	58.0	64.4	63.6	54.6	44.0	30.1	20.0	41.7
Mean Minimum Temp. (°F)	10.5	14.2	21.3	28.6	36.5	42.9	47.7	46.3	38.2	29.9	20.7	11.0	29.0
Extreme Maximum Temp. (°F)	54	54	69	81	89	96	93	94	89	83	69	59	96
Extreme Minimum Temp. (°F)	-32	-28	-13	-1	19	26	28	27	12	0	-16	-32	-32
Days Maximum Temp. ≥ 90°F	0	0	0	0	0	1	2	1	0	0	0	0	4
Days Maximum Temp. ≤ 32°F	20	12	3	0	0	0	0	0	0	0	7	20	62
Days Minimum Temp. ≤ 32°F	30	28	29	21	9	1	0	0	6	20	26	31	201
Days Minimum Temp. ≤ 0°F	7	4	1	0	0	0	0	0	0	0	2	6	20
Heating Degree Days (base 65°F)	1,408	1,156	1,034	721	454	218	66	78	311	645	1,040	1,388	8,519
Cooling Degree Days (base 65°F)	0	0	0	0	1	14	57	49	5	0	0	0	126
Mean Precipitation (in.)	2.32	1.66	1.66	1.52	2.38	1.67	1.05	1.06	1.27	1.43	2.11	2.28	20.41
Days With ≥ 0.1" Precipitation	8	5	5	5	6	5	3	3	3	4	6	7	60
Days With ≥ 1.0" Precipitation	0	0	0	0	0	0	0	0	0	0	0	0	0
Mean Snowfall (in.)	24.4	15.5	10.7	4.6	1.8	trace	0.0	trace	0.3	2.4	16.7	24.6	101.0
Days With ≥ 1.0" Snow Depth	30	28	27	8	0	0	0	0	0	2	14	29	138

Bayview Model Basin *Kootenai County*   Elevation: 2,073 ft.   Latitude: 47° 59' N   Longitude: 116° 34' W

	JAN	FEB	MAR	APR	MAY	JUN	JUL	AUG	SEP	OCT	NOV	DEC	YEAR
Mean Maximum Temp. (°F)	35.0	38.5	45.9	54.7	63.8	71.2	78.4	78.5	67.9	55.4	42.7	35.6	55.6
Mean Temp. (°F)	28.3	31.4	36.8	43.6	51.3	58.2	63.8	63.4	54.2	44.1	35.7	29.1	45.0
Mean Minimum Temp. (°F)	21.6	24.2	27.6	32.5	38.8	45.3	49.3	48.3	40.4	32.6	28.7	22.6	34.3
Extreme Maximum Temp. (°F)	55	62	69	81	92	98	98	101	95	78	69	58	101
Extreme Minimum Temp. (°F)	-15	-11	-5	16	24	29	32	31	20	11	-6	-15	-15
Days Maximum Temp. ≥ 90°F	0	0	0	0	0	0	3	2	0	0	0	0	5
Days Maximum Temp. ≤ 32°F	10	5	1	0	0	0	0	0	0	0	2	9	27
Days Minimum Temp. ≤ 32°F	28	24	25	17	5	0	0	0	4	15	21	27	166
Days Minimum Temp. ≤ 0°F	1	1	0	0	0	0	0	0	0	0	0	1	3
Heating Degree Days (base 65°F)	1,130	942	868	635	419	215	90	93	321	643	872	1,106	7,334
Cooling Degree Days (base 65°F)	0	0	0	0	3	14	55	49	3	0	0	0	124
Mean Precipitation (in.)	2.79	2.41	2.18	1.93	2.26	1.96	1.26	1.20	1.27	1.80	3.08	3.32	25.46
Days With ≥ 0.1" Precipitation	8	7	7	6	7	5	4	3	4	5	9	9	74
Days With ≥ 1.0" Precipitation	0	0	0	0	0	0	0	0	0	0	0	1	1
Mean Snowfall (in.)	13.1	7.0	2.7	0.3	0.0	0.0	0.0	0.0	0.0	trace	3.4	11.4	37.9
Days With ≥ 1.0" Snow Depth	17	11	4	0	0	0	0	0	0	0	3	na	na

Boise 7 N *Ada County*   Elevation: 3,884 ft.   Latitude: 43° 43' N   Longitude: 116° 12' W

	JAN	FEB	MAR	APR	MAY	JUN	JUL	AUG	SEP	OCT	NOV	DEC	YEAR
Mean Maximum Temp. (°F)	35.8	41.9	50.4	58.5	67.6	77.9	87.7	86.6	75.9	62.1	45.9	36.7	60.6
Mean Temp. (°F)	28.8	34.0	41.0	47.3	54.8	63.5	71.9	71.5	62.5	50.9	37.9	29.5	49.5
Mean Minimum Temp. (°F)	21.7	26.0	31.5	36.0	41.9	49.1	56.1	56.4	49.1	39.7	29.9	22.2	38.3
Extreme Maximum Temp. (°F)	57	67	75	88	95	101	105	106	100	92	72	62	106
Extreme Minimum Temp. (°F)	-10	-16	9	18	20	28	36	34	27	17	-4	-23	-23
Days Maximum Temp. ≥ 90°F	0	0	0	0	1	4	14	13	2	0	0	0	34
Days Maximum Temp. ≤ 32°F	10	3	0	0	0	0	0	0	0	0	2	9	24
Days Minimum Temp. ≤ 32°F	27	21	18	11	4	0	0	0	1	6	18	27	133
Days Minimum Temp. ≤ 0°F	1	1	0	0	0	0	0	0	0	0	0	1	3
Heating Degree Days (base 65°F)	1,118	870	738	527	328	124	22	23	139	434	807	1,095	6,225
Cooling Degree Days (base 65°F)	0	0	0	2	21	81	233	245	72	5	0	0	659
Mean Precipitation (in.)	2.12	1.97	2.22	2.03	2.08	1.14	0.53	0.48	1.08	1.17	2.24	2.23	19.29
Days With ≥ 0.1" Precipitation	6	6	7	6	5	3	1	1	3	3	7	7	55
Days With ≥ 1.0" Precipitation	0	0	0	0	0	0	0	0	0	0	0	0	0
Mean Snowfall (in.)	12.6	10.6	6.8	3.1	0.5	trace	0.0	trace	trace	0.4	8.4	13.1	55.5
Days With ≥ 1.0" Snow Depth	19	14	4	0	0	0	0	0	0	0	6	14	57

Boise Lucky Peak Dam *Ada County*   Elevation: 2,837 ft.   Latitude: 43° 32' N   Longitude: 116° 03' W

	JAN	FEB	MAR	APR	MAY	JUN	JUL	AUG	SEP	OCT	NOV	DEC	YEAR
Mean Maximum Temp. (°F)	na	na	na	na	71.9	81.0	89.6	89.4	78.5	na	na	na	na
Mean Temp. (°F)	na	na	na	na	58.0	65.8	73.1	73.1	63.4	na	na	na	na
Mean Minimum Temp. (°F)	na	na	na	na	44.1	50.6	56.5	56.8	48.3	na	na	na	na
Extreme Maximum Temp. (°F)	61	72	80	93	97	104	109	109	104	95	80	65	109
Extreme Minimum Temp. (°F)	-10	-17	7	17	23	33	40	36	27	10	-3	-17	-17
Days Maximum Temp. ≥ 90°F	0	0	0	0	2	7	18	18	5	0	0	0	50
Days Maximum Temp. ≤ 32°F	8	2	0	0	0	0	0	0	0	0	1	6	17
Days Minimum Temp. ≤ 32°F	22	17	14	8	1	0	0	0	1	4	14	21	102
Days Minimum Temp. ≤ 0°F	1	1	0	0	0	0	0	0	0	0	0	1	3
Heating Degree Days (base 65°F)	na	na	na	na	245	86	15	15	123	na	na	na	na
Cooling Degree Days (base 65°F)	na	na	na	na	43	113	255	271	88	na	na	na	na
Mean Precipitation (in.)	1.85	1.41	1.68	1.50	1.50	1.02	0.41	0.33	0.83	0.86	1.89	1.81	15.09
Days With ≥ 0.1" Precipitation	4	3	4	4	4	3	1	1	2	2	4	na	na
Days With ≥ 1.0" Precipitation	0	0	0	0	0	0	0	0	0	0	0	0	0
Mean Snowfall (in.)	na	na	na	trace	0.0	0.0	0.0	0.0	0.0	trace	na	na	na
Days With ≥ 1.0" Snow Depth	na	na	0	0	0	0	0	0	0	0	na	na	na

Bonners Ferry *Boundary County*   Elevation: 1,847 ft.   Latitude: 48° 42' N   Longitude: 116° 18' W

	JAN	FEB	MAR	APR	MAY	JUN	JUL	AUG	SEP	OCT	NOV	DEC	YEAR
Mean Maximum Temp. (°F)	33.0	39.3	49.3	60.0	69.4	76.1	83.2	83.5	72.3	57.1	41.3	33.5	58.2
Mean Temp. (°F)	26.6	31.8	39.0	47.1	55.3	61.8	66.9	66.6	56.9	45.4	34.8	27.7	46.7
Mean Minimum Temp. (°F)	20.1	24.3	28.6	34.2	41.3	47.5	50.5	49.7	41.6	33.7	28.2	21.8	35.1
Extreme Maximum Temp. (°F)	55	61	70	89	95	98	103	101	96	84	67	56	103
Extreme Minimum Temp. (°F)	-22	-15	-2	12	24	31	32	32	21	12	-8	-17	-22
Days Maximum Temp. ≥ 90°F	0	0	0	0	0	2	8	8	1	0	0	0	19
Days Maximum Temp. ≤ 32°F	12	5	1	0	0	0	0	0	0	0	3	12	33
Days Minimum Temp. ≤ 32°F	27	23	22	13	3	0	0	0	3	*14*	20	28	*153*
Days Minimum Temp. ≤ 0°F	2	1	0	0	0	0	0	0	0	0	0	1	4
Heating Degree Days (base 65°F)	1,184	931	800	530	299	130	44	45	242	601	899	1,150	6,855
Cooling Degree Days (base 65°F)	0	0	0	0	8	37	106	101	9	0	0	0	261
Mean Precipitation (in.)	2.72	1.83	1.52	1.45	1.77	1.62	1.05	1.09	1.17	1.61	3.06	3.11	22.00
Days With ≥ 0.1" Precipitation	7	6	5	5	5	5	3	3	4	5	8	8	64
Days With ≥ 1.0" Precipitation	0	0	0	0	0	0	0	0	0	0	0	0	0
Mean Snowfall (in.)	18.4	9.8	4.4	0.3	trace	trace	0.0	0.0	0.0	0.5	8.4	20.9	62.7
Days With ≥ 1.0" Snow Depth	22	12	*4*	0	0	0	0	0	0	0	5	18	*61*

Brownlee Dam *Adams County*   Elevation: 1,843 ft.   Latitude: 44° 50' N   Longitude: 116° 52' W

	JAN	FEB	MAR	APR	MAY	JUN	JUL	AUG	SEP	OCT	NOV	DEC	YEAR
Mean Maximum Temp. (°F)	38.1	45.3	55.5	64.8	74.4	83.6	94.0	93.9	82.2	67.7	49.6	39.5	65.7
Mean Temp. (°F)	30.9	36.4	44.8	52.6	61.1	69.5	77.9	77.8	67.4	55.0	41.5	32.5	54.0
Mean Minimum Temp. (°F)	23.6	27.5	34.1	40.4	47.8	55.4	61.8	61.6	52.5	42.3	33.3	25.4	42.1
Extreme Maximum Temp. (°F)	65	69	84	95	103	107	113	112	103	95	74	65	113
Extreme Minimum Temp. (°F)	-13	-13	11	24	31	38	41	42	35	23	2	-7	-13
Days Maximum Temp. ≥ 90°F	0	0	0	0	3	10	22	22	9	0	0	0	66
Days Maximum Temp. ≤ 32°F	7	2	0	0	0	0	0	0	0	0	1	5	15
Days Minimum Temp. ≤ 32°F	26	20	12	3	0	0	0	0	0	2	12	25	100
Days Minimum Temp. ≤ 0°F	1	0	0	0	0	0	0	0	0	0	0	0	1
Heating Degree Days (base 65°F)	1,050	801	619	371	169	44	4	6	65	314	699	1,001	5,143
Cooling Degree Days (base 65°F)	0	0	0	9	66	185	404	417	156	13	0	0	1,250
Mean Precipitation (in.)	2.22	1.64	1.80	1.56	1.89	1.36	0.61	0.59	0.84	1.05	1.96	2.19	17.71
Days With ≥ 0.1" Precipitation	7	5	6	5	5	4	·2	2	2	3	6	6	53
Days With ≥ 1.0" Precipitation	0	0	0	0	0	0	0	0	0	0	0	0	0
Mean Snowfall (in.)	*8.8*	2.2	0.3	trace	trace	0.0	0.0	0.0	0.0	0.0	*1.1*	*4.3*	*16.7*
Days With ≥ 1.0" Snow Depth	11	5	1	0	0	0	0	0	0	0	1	5	23

Bruneau *Owyhee County*   Elevation: 2,529 ft.   Latitude: 42° 53' N   Longitude: 115° 48' W

	JAN	FEB	MAR	APR	MAY	JUN	JUL	AUG	SEP	OCT	NOV	DEC	YEAR
Mean Maximum Temp. (°F)	40.1	48.7	58.3	66.4	75.3	84.8	93.0	92.0	81.3	68.4	51.3	40.1	66.6
Mean Temp. (°F)	31.4	37.6	45.1	51.5	59.9	68.2	75.0	73.7	63.5	52.6	40.4	31.1	52.5
Mean Minimum Temp. (°F)	22.6	26.7	31.8	36.7	44.3	51.7	57.0	55.3	45.8	36.7	29.5	22.2	38.3
Extreme Maximum Temp. (°F)	67	74	84	94	99	107	111	108	103	95	81	68	111
Extreme Minimum Temp. (°F)	-16	-16	0	20	24	33	39	37	26	12	-4	-32	-32
Days Maximum Temp. ≥ 90°F	0	0	0	0	3	10	22	21	6	0	0	0	62
Days Maximum Temp. ≤ 32°F	7	2	0	0	0	0	0	0	0	0	1	6	16
Days Minimum Temp. ≤ 32°F	25	21	17	*7*	2	0	0	0	1	9	19	25	*126*
Days Minimum Temp. ≤ 0°F	1	1	0	0	0	0	0	0	0	0	0	1	3
Heating Degree Days (base 65°F)	1,034	769	611	403	190	47	4	6	107	380	731	1,043	5,325
Cooling Degree Days (base 65°F)	0	0	0	5	42	140	300	285	75	3	0	0	850
Mean Precipitation (in.)	0.87	0.57	0.84	0.69	0.82	0.80	0.20	0.19	0.55	0.53	0.98	0.77	7.81
Days With ≥ 0.1" Precipitation	3	2	3	3	3	2	1	1	1	2	3	*2*	*26*
Days With ≥ 1.0" Precipitation	0	0	0	0	0	0	0	0	0	0	0	0	0
Mean Snowfall (in.)	na	*0.4*	*0.1*	trace	0.0	0.0	0.0	0.0	trace	trace	0.7	na	na
Days With ≥ 1.0" Snow Depth	na	na	*0*	0	0	0	0	0	0	0	0	na	na

Burley Municipal Airport *Cassia County*   Elevation: 4,156 ft.   Latitude: 42° 32' N   Longitude: 113° 46' W

	JAN	FEB	MAR	APR	MAY	JUN	JUL	AUG	SEP	OCT	NOV	DEC	YEAR
Mean Maximum Temp. (°F)	36.0	43.0	51.6	60.0	68.7	78.5	86.5	86.2	75.7	63.4	47.3	37.3	61.2
Mean Temp. (°F)	27.6	33.2	40.3	47.1	55.3	63.7	70.4	69.4	59.9	49.2	37.0	28.3	48.5
Mean Minimum Temp. (°F)	19.1	23.3	28.9	34.2	41.9	49.0	54.3	52.5	44.0	34.8	26.7	19.3	35.7
Extreme Maximum Temp. (°F)	60	72	78	89	92	102	104	105	97	91	77	65	105
Extreme Minimum Temp. (°F)	-23	-26	-3	12	22	32	33	34	23	9	-6	-23	-26
Days Maximum Temp. ≥ 90°F	0	0	0	0	0	4	12	11	2	0	0	0	29
Days Maximum Temp. ≤ 32°F	10	4	1	0	0	0	0	0	0	0	3	9	27
Days Minimum Temp. ≤ 32°F	27	24	22	12	2	0	0	0	2	12	23	28	152
Days Minimum Temp. ≤ 0°F	3	1	0	0	0	0	0	0	0	0	0	2	6
Heating Degree Days (base 65°F)	1,151	892	759	530	304	104	17	23	181	485	833	1,130	6,409
Cooling Degree Days (base 65°F)	0	0	0	1	13	76	201	185	41	2	0	0	519
Mean Precipitation (in.)	1.22	0.79	1.08	0.98	1.30	0.94	0.35	0.41	0.65	0.62	1.05	1.03	10.42
Days With ≥ 0.1" Precipitation	4	3	3	3	4	3	1	1	2	2	4	4	34
Days With ≥ 1.0" Precipitation	0	0	0	0	0	0	0	0	0	0	0	0	0
Mean Snowfall (in.)	5.8	4.0	2.1	1.0	0.2	trace	0.0	trace	trace	0.2	3.3	6.1	22.7
Days With ≥ 1.0" Snow Depth	14	7	2	0	0	0	0	0	0	0	3	10	36

Cabinet Gorge *Bonner County*   Elevation: 2,257 ft.   Latitude: 48° 05' N   Longitude: 116° 04' W

	JAN	FEB	MAR	APR	MAY	JUN	JUL	AUG	SEP	OCT	NOV	DEC	YEAR
Mean Maximum Temp. (°F)	32.9	39.0	47.4	57.2	66.9	73.7	82.0	82.1	71.2	57.1	40.7	33.2	57.0
Mean Temp. (°F)	27.2	31.5	37.7	45.3	53.5	60.0	66.0	65.9	57.0	46.3	35.1	28.2	46.2
Mean Minimum Temp. (°F)	21.4	24.1	28.0	33.4	40.1	46.2	50.0	49.6	42.8	35.3	29.5	23.0	35.3
Extreme Maximum Temp. (°F)	55	60	71	88	95	98	101	98	98	81	68	54	101
Extreme Minimum Temp. (°F)	-23	-14	-3	15	23	31	35	34	25	12	-3	-25	-25
Days Maximum Temp. ≥ 90°F	0	0	0	0	0	1	7	6	1	0	0	0	15
Days Maximum Temp. ≤ 32°F	12	5	1	0	0	0	0	0	0	0	4	12	34
Days Minimum Temp. ≤ 32°F	29	25	24	14	3	0	0	0	2	10	20	28	155
Days Minimum Temp. ≤ 0°F	2	1	0	0	0	0	0	0	0	0	0	1	4
Heating Degree Days (base 65°F)	1,165	939	838	584	352	169	53	54	240	574	889	1,136	6,993
Cooling Degree Days (base 65°F)	0	0	0	0	4	24	86	88	9	0	0	0	211
Mean Precipitation (in.)	4.18	3.14	2.67	2.20	2.41	2.37	1.29	1.34	1.50	2.31	4.46	4.51	32.38
Days With ≥ 0.1" Precipitation	10	8	8	7	7	6	4	4	5	6	11	11	87
Days With ≥ 1.0" Precipitation	0	0	0	0	0	0	0	0	0	0	1	0	1
Mean Snowfall (in.)	23.6	12.4	4.1	0.5	trace	0.0	0.0	0.0	0.0	0.4	6.3	20.5	67.8
Days With ≥ 1.0" Snow Depth	24	21	9	0	0	0	0	0	0	0	0	4	17	75

Caldwell *Canyon County*   Elevation: 2,368 ft.   Latitude: 43° 40' N   Longitude: 116° 41' W

	JAN	FEB	MAR	APR	MAY	JUN	JUL	AUG	SEP	OCT	NOV	DEC	YEAR
Mean Maximum Temp. (°F)	36.8	46.1	57.2	65.9	75.2	84.1	92.5	91.4	80.2	66.6	49.1	38.0	65.3
Mean Temp. (°F)	29.2	36.3	45.0	52.0	60.5	68.5	75.5	73.8	63.2	51.9	39.2	30.2	52.1
Mean Minimum Temp. (°F)	21.5	26.5	32.7	38.1	45.8	52.8	58.4	56.2	46.0	37.2	29.3	22.3	38.9
Extreme Maximum Temp. (°F)	63	70	84	94	102	105	108	109	101	94	73	67	109
Extreme Minimum Temp. (°F)	-17	-20	9	22	28	35	38	38	25	15	-4	-24	-24
Days Maximum Temp. ≥ 90°F	0	0	0	0	3	9	21	20	6	0	0	0	59
Days Maximum Temp. ≤ 32°F	10	3	0	0	0	0	0	0	0	0	1	8	22
Days Minimum Temp. ≤ 32°F	27	21	16	7	0	0	0	0	0	8	20	26	125
Days Minimum Temp. ≤ 0°F	1	1	0	0	0	0	0	0	0	0	0	2	4
Heating Degree Days (base 65°F)	1,103	804	614	387	180	48	5	8	114	401	768	1,074	5,506
Cooling Degree Days (base 65°F)	0	0	0	6	52	151	319	288	69	3	0	0	888
Mean Precipitation (in.)	1.55	1.04	1.32	1.10	0.93	0.72	0.31	0.37	0.65	0.73	1.31	1.46	11.49
Days With ≥ 0.1" Precipitation	5	3	4	4	3	3	1	1	2	3	5	5	39
Days With ≥ 1.0" Precipitation	0	0	0	0	0	0	0	0	0	0	0	0	0
Mean Snowfall (in.)	*4.6*	*2.0*	0.3	trace	0.0	0.0	0.0	0.0	0.0	trace	*2.3*	*5.3*	*14.5*
Days With ≥ 1.0" Snow Depth	na	*1*	0	0	0	0	0	0	0	0	*0*	*3*	na

Cambridge *Washington County*   Elevation: 2,647 ft.   Latitude: 44° 34' N   Longitude: 116° 41' W

	JAN	FEB	MAR	APR	MAY	JUN	JUL	AUG	SEP	OCT	NOV	DEC	YEAR
Mean Maximum Temp. (°F)	30.8	38.4	51.6	62.5	71.9	81.0	90.5	89.9	79.4	65.0	45.4	32.6	61.6
Mean Temp. (°F)	22.9	28.9	40.2	48.6	56.7	64.8	72.1	70.9	60.9	49.1	35.9	24.6	48.0
Mean Minimum Temp. (°F)	14.9	19.4	28.7	34.7	41.5	48.6	53.7	51.9	42.4	33.2	26.5	16.5	34.3
Extreme Maximum Temp. (°F)	50	65	78	90	98	102	107	107	103	95	69	60	107
Extreme Minimum Temp. (°F)	-28	-31	-11	17	22	28	32	32	21	13	-16	-26	-31
Days Maximum Temp. ≥ 90°F	0	0	0	0	1	6	19	18	5	0	0	0	49
Days Maximum Temp. ≤ 32°F	15	6	0	0	0	0	0	0	0	0	2	13	36
Days Minimum Temp. ≤ 32°F	30	26	22	12	4	0	0	0	3	15	22	30	164
Days Minimum Temp. ≤ 0°F	5	2	0	0	0	0	0	0	0	0	1	3	11
Heating Degree Days (base 65°F)	1,298	1,014	762	486	264	87	14	20	156	488	866	1,247	6,702
Cooling Degree Days (base 65°F)	0	0	0	1	18	87	239	224	49	1	0	0	619
Mean Precipitation (in.)	3.11	2.53	2.17	1.36	1.53	1.10	0.45	0.45	0.86	1.14	2.84	3.33	20.87
Days With ≥ 0.1" Precipitation	8	7	6	5	4	3	1	1	2	3	8	8	56
Days With ≥ 1.0" Precipitation	0	0	0	0	0	0	0	0	0	0	0	0	0
Mean Snowfall (in.)	na	na	2.1	0.1	0.0	0.0	0.0	0.0	0.0	trace	7.7	na	na
Days With ≥ 1.0" Snow Depth	na	na	na	0	0	0	0	0	0	0	na	na	na

Cascade 1 NW *Valley County*   Elevation: 4,895 ft.   Latitude: 44° 31' N   Longitude: 116° 03' W

	JAN	FEB	MAR	APR	MAY	JUN	JUL	AUG	SEP	OCT	NOV	DEC	YEAR
Mean Maximum Temp. (°F)	29.7	35.6	43.1	52.1	62.4	71.4	80.7	80.8	70.3	57.5	39.5	29.9	54.4
Mean Temp. (°F)	20.0	24.3	31.3	38.9	47.6	55.3	62.1	61.4	52.0	42.0	30.2	20.8	40.5
Mean Minimum Temp. (°F)	10.3	13.0	19.5	25.7	32.8	39.1	43.6	41.9	33.6	26.5	20.7	11.7	26.6
Extreme Maximum Temp. (°F)	50	58	68	83	88	93	97	97	90	84	67	52	97
Extreme Minimum Temp. (°F)	-32	-28	-12	2	15	21	27	24	14	5	-21	-36	-36
Days Maximum Temp. ≥ 90°F	0	0	0	0	0	1	3	3	0	0	0	0	7
Days Maximum Temp. ≤ 32°F	18	9	2	0	0	0	0	0	0	0	6	18	53
Days Minimum Temp. ≤ 32°F	31	28	30	26	15	5	1	2	13	26	28	30	235
Days Minimum Temp. ≤ 0°F	9	5	1	0	0	0	0	0	0	0	1	6	22
Heating Degree Days (base 65°F)	1,388	1,142	1,037	776	532	294	121	131	384	706	1,038	1,363	8,912
Cooling Degree Days (base 65°F)	0	0	0	0	1	5	29	23	0	0	0	0	58
Mean Precipitation (in.)	2.83	2.40	2.21	1.86	1.89	1.74	0.69	0.71	1.08	1.49	2.92	3.15	22.97
Days With ≥ 0.1" Precipitation	8	7	7	6	5	5	2	2	3	4	8	8	65
Days With ≥ 1.0" Precipitation	0	0	0	0	0	0	0	0	0	0	0	0	0
Mean Snowfall (in.)	21.8	17.3	9.0	3.7	0.5	trace	0.0	trace	0.1	1.5	13.2	22.1	89.2
Days With ≥ 1.0" Snow Depth	30	27	23	4	0	0	0	0	0	1	12	26	123

Castleford 2 N *Twin Falls County*   Elevation: 3,822 ft.   Latitude: 42° 33' N   Longitude: 114° 52' W

	JAN	FEB	MAR	APR	MAY	JUN	JUL	AUG	SEP	OCT	NOV	DEC	YEAR
Mean Maximum Temp. (°F)	36.5	44.0	53.5	62.3	71.1	80.3	87.6	86.2	76.4	64.3	47.7	37.0	62.2
Mean Temp. (°F)	28.1	34.0	41.3	48.3	56.0	64.1	70.6	69.1	60.2	49.8	37.4	28.2	48.9
Mean Minimum Temp. (°F)	19.6	24.0	29.1	34.2	41.0	48.0	53.5	52.1	43.9	35.3	27.1	19.4	35.6
Extreme Maximum Temp. (°F)	62	69	80	89	92	103	105	102	96	89	79	64	105
Extreme Minimum Temp. (°F)	-23	-14	0	14	22	30	34	35	15	11	-5	-26	-26
Days Maximum Temp. ≥ 90°F	0	0	0	0	0	5	14	10	1	0	0	0	30
Days Maximum Temp. ≤ 32°F	10	3	0	0	0	0	0	0	0	0	2	9	24
Days Minimum Temp. ≤ 32°F	28	24	21	12	4	0	0	0	2	11	22	28	152
Days Minimum Temp. ≤ 0°F	2	1	0	0	0	0	0	0	0	0	0	2	5
Heating Degree Days (base 65°F)	1,138	868	727	497	284	96	17	23	168	464	821	1,133	6,236
Cooling Degree Days (base 65°F)	0	0	0	1	16	72	195	161	34	2	0	0	481
Mean Precipitation (in.)	1.43	0.81	1.10	0.97	1.37	0.87	0.24	0.37	0.61	0.65	1.14	1.04	10.60
Days With ≥ 0.1" Precipitation	5	3	4	3	4	3	1	1	2	2	4	3	35
Days With ≥ 1.0" Precipitation	0	0	0	0	0	0	0	0	0	0	0	0	0
Mean Snowfall (in.)	*4.9*	2.6	1.1	0.4	0.3	0.0	0.0	0.0	0.0	trace	1.9	4.3	*15.5*
Days With ≥ 1.0" Snow Depth	na	5	1	0	0	0	0	0	0	0	1	*5*	na

Challis *Custer County*   Elevation: 5,173 ft.   Latitude: 44° 30' N   Longitude: 114° 14' W

	JAN	FEB	MAR	APR	MAY	JUN	JUL	AUG	SEP	OCT	NOV	DEC	YEAR
Mean Maximum Temp. (°F)	30.4	38.4	47.8	57.2	66.4	76.6	84.7	83.4	73.4	60.2	41.6	30.8	57.6
Mean Temp. (°F)	20.5	27.2	36.2	44.3	52.8	61.5	68.2	66.6	57.1	45.9	*31.4*	21.1	*44.4*
Mean Minimum Temp. (°F)	10.5	16.1	24.6	31.4	39.2	46.3	51.7	49.7	40.8	31.6	*21.1*	11.2	*31.2*
Extreme Maximum Temp. (°F)	59	60	74	85	90	100	99	99	93	82	68	*59*	*100*
Extreme Minimum Temp. (°F)	-27	-24	-4	11	20	27	33	31	21	1	-17	-34	-34
Days Maximum Temp. ≥ 90°F	0	0	0	0	0	3	9	7	1	0	0	0	20
Days Maximum Temp. ≤ 32°F	16	8	1	0	0	0	0	0	0	0	5	*17*	*47*
Days Minimum Temp. ≤ 32°F	30	27	28	17	5	1	0	0	4	17	27	30	186
Days Minimum Temp. ≤ 0°F	7	2	0	0	0	0	0	0	0	0	1	5	15
Heating Degree Days (base 65°F)	1,374	1,062	885	614	375	147	36	49	242	584	*1,002*	*1,361*	*7,731*
Cooling Degree Days (base 65°F)	0	0	0	0	5	46	*137*	*109*	*13*	*0*	*0*	*0*	*310*
Mean Precipitation (in.)	0.42	0.33	0.61	0.59	1.12	1.00	0.81	0.69	0.66	0.43	0.59	0.52	7.77
Days With ≥ 0.1" Precipitation	2	1	2	2	4	3	3	2	2	*1*	2	2	*26*
Days With ≥ 1.0" Precipitation	0	0	0	0	0	0	0	0	0	0	0	0	0
Mean Snowfall (in.)	*4.1*	*2.2*	*2.2*	0.8	trace	0.0	0.0	0.0	trace	*trace*	*3.2*	*4.4*	*16.9*
Days With ≥ 1.0" Snow Depth	na	na	na	0	0	0	0	0	0	*0*	na	na	na

Chilly Barton Flat *Custer County*   Elevation: 6,259 ft.   Latitude: 43° 59' N   Longitude: 113° 50' W

	JAN	FEB	MAR	APR	MAY	JUN	JUL	AUG	SEP	OCT	NOV	DEC	YEAR
Mean Maximum Temp. (°F)	30.1	35.4	42.8	53.1	62.8	72.2	81.2	80.2	70.8	58.3	39.9	30.3	54.7
Mean Temp. (°F)	17.5	21.9	30.6	39.3	47.8	55.8	63.0	61.5	52.7	42.3	27.8	17.9	39.8
Mean Minimum Temp. (°F)	4.8	8.4	18.4	25.5	32.8	39.5	44.8	42.9	34.5	26.2	15.9	5.4	24.9
Extreme Maximum Temp. (°F)	50	55	67	78	87	94	94	95	91	80	64	53	95
Extreme Minimum Temp. (°F)	-32	-32	-16	3	15	21	25	24	13	-3	-21	-37	-37
Days Maximum Temp. ≥ 90°F	0	0	0	0	0	0	2	1	0	0	0	0	3
Days Maximum Temp. ≤ 32°F	18	10	3	0	0	0	0	0	0	0	6	18	55
Days Minimum Temp. ≤ 32°F	31	28	30	26	15	4	0	1	11	25	29	31	231
Days Minimum Temp. ≤ 0°F	11	7	1	0	0	0	0	0	0	0	2	11	32
Heating Degree Days (base 65°F)	1,467	1,210	1,059	763	527	276	91	122	366	696	1,110	1,455	9,142
Cooling Degree Days (base 65°F)	0	0	0	0	0	7	38	19	1	0	0	0	65
Mean Precipitation (in.)	0.31	0.26	0.48	0.60	1.27	1.32	0.95	0.84	0.76	0.52	0.45	0.34	8.10
Days With ≥ 0.1" Precipitation	1	1	2	2	4	4	3	3	2	2	2	1	27
Days With ≥ 1.0" Precipitation	0	0	0	0	0	0	0	0	0	0	0	0	0
Mean Snowfall (in.)	na	na	na	*0.7*	0.2	0.2	0.0	0.0	0.2	0.4	*1.1*	na	na
Days With ≥ 1.0" Snow Depth	na	na	na	0	0	0	0	0	0	0	*1*	na	na

Cottonwood 2 WSW *Idaho County*   Elevation: 3,943 ft.   Latitude: 46° 02' N   Longitude: 116° 24' W

	JAN	FEB	MAR	APR	MAY	JUN	JUL	AUG	SEP	OCT	NOV	DEC	YEAR
Mean Maximum Temp. (°F)	*35.1*	*39.9*	*46.8*	*54.4*	*61.3*	*69.2*	*77.5*	79.3	70.1	57.5	*41.9*	35.0	55.7
Mean Temp. (°F)	*29.0*	*33.0*	*38.5*	*44.8*	*51.4*	*58.5*	*65.6*	na	na	47.9	35.5	28.9	na
Mean Minimum Temp. (°F)	*22.9*	*25.9*	*30.2*	*35.2*	*41.3*	*47.8*	*53.8*	na	na	38.2	29.0	22.8	na
Extreme Maximum Temp. (°F)	*53*	*64*	*72*	*83*	*85*	*92*	*95*	98	94	87	68	58	98
Extreme Minimum Temp. (°F)	*-9*	*-20*	*4*	*18*	*24*	*32*	*31*	na	27	15	-5	*-18*	na
Days Maximum Temp. ≥ 90°F	*0*	*0*	*0*	*0*	*0*	*0*	*2*	3	1	0	0	0	6
Days Maximum Temp. ≤ 32°F	*10*	*5*	*0*	*0*	*0*	*0*	*0*	0	0	0	4	11	30
Days Minimum Temp. ≤ 32°F	*27*	*21*	*20*	*12*	*3*	*0*	*0*	0	1	na	20	28	na
Days Minimum Temp. ≤ 0°F	*1*	*1*	*0*	*0*	*0*	*0*	*0*	0	0	0	0	1	3
Heating Degree Days (base 65°F)	*1,109*	*898*	*813*	*600*	*424*	*216*	*82*	na	na	526	875	*1,113*	na
Cooling Degree Days (base 65°F)	*0*	*0*	*0*	*0*	*8*	*27*	*108*	127	36	2	0	0	308
Mean Precipitation (in.)	*1.77*	*1.49*	*1.75*	*2.46*	*3.27*	*2.47*	*1.64*	1.27	*1.24*	*1.44*	*2.21*	*1.87*	22.88
Days With ≥ 0.1" Precipitation	na	na	*6*	*8*	*9*	*7*	*4*	3	*4*	*5*	*8*	6	na
Days With ≥ 1.0" Precipitation	*0*	*0*	*0*	*0*	*1*	*0*	*0*	*0*	*0*	*0*	*0*	*0*	*1*
Mean Snowfall (in.)	na	na	na	na	na	*0.0*	*0.0*	*0.0*	*trace*	na	na	na	na
Days With ≥ 1.0" Snow Depth	na	na	na	na	*0*	*0*	*0*	*0*	*0*	*0*	na	na	na

Craters of the Moon *Butte County*   Elevation: 5,895 ft.   Latitude: 43° 28' N   Longitude: 113° 33' W

	JAN	FEB	MAR	APR	MAY	JUN	JUL	AUG	SEP	OCT	NOV	DEC	YEAR
Mean Maximum Temp. (°F)	29.1	34.4	42.3	54.3	64.8	75.2	84.3	83.3	71.9	*59.3*	40.3	29.6	*55.7*
Mean Temp. (°F)	19.9	24.3	31.8	41.2	50.9	59.9	68.1	66.9	56.4	*45.3*	30.2	20.2	*42.9*
Mean Minimum Temp. (°F)	10.5	14.4	21.3	28.5	37.0	44.6	51.8	50.5	40.8	*31.3*	20.1	10.8	*30.1*
Extreme Maximum Temp. (°F)	58	60	67	83	88	98	100	97	92	85	66	51	100
Extreme Minimum Temp. (°F)	-23	-19	-18	7	16	25	30	31	16	2	-11	-37	-37
Days Maximum Temp. ≥ 90°F	0	0	0	0	0	1	6	5	0	0	0	0	12
Days Maximum Temp. ≤ 32°F	18	10	3	0	0	0	0	0	0	0	6	19	56
Days Minimum Temp. ≤ 32°F	30	27	29	21	9	2	0	0	5	15	27	30	195
Days Minimum Temp. ≤ 0°F	5	3	0	0	0	0	0	0	0	0	1	5	14
Heating Degree Days (base 65°F)	1,394	1,141	1,023	708	432	183	35	47	269	*603*	1,038	1,383	*8,256*
Cooling Degree Days (base 65°F)	0	0	0	0	4	40	152	129	20	na	*0*	0	na
Mean Precipitation (in.)	1.83	1.58	1.39	1.13	1.82	1.16	0.82	0.78	0.85	0.91	1.52	1.63	15.42
Days With ≥ 0.1" Precipitation	4	4	4	3	5	3	2	2	2	2	4	4	39
Days With ≥ 1.0" Precipitation	0	0	0	0	0	0	0	0	0	0	0	0	0
Mean Snowfall (in.)	21.4	19.4	10.1	*3.7*	2.4	trace	0.0	0.0	0.1	1.6	12.5	*20.7*	*91.9*
Days With ≥ 1.0" Snow Depth	27	23	20	5	1	0	0	0	0	1	10	25	112

Deer Flat Dam *Canyon County*   Elevation: 2,509 ft.   Latitude: 43° 35' N   Longitude: 116° 45' W

	JAN	FEB	MAR	APR	MAY	JUN	JUL	AUG	SEP	OCT	NOV	DEC	YEAR
Mean Maximum Temp. (°F)	37.6	45.8	56.5	64.0	72.6	80.6	88.0	87.5	78.5	66.1	49.3	38.4	63.7
Mean Temp. (°F)	29.9	36.5	44.8	51.4	59.3	66.5	72.7	71.9	63.3	52.2	39.9	30.5	51.6
Mean Minimum Temp. (°F)	22.3	27.0	33.1	38.6	46.0	52.4	57.4	56.1	48.0	38.2	30.3	22.5	39.3
Extreme Maximum Temp. (°F)	63	68	79	87	97	98	104	101	99	94	73	64	104
Extreme Minimum Temp. (°F)	-18	-20	6	22	28	34	31	37	26	17	-5	-22	-22
Days Maximum Temp. ≥ 90°F	0	0	0	0	1	5	14	13	2	0	0	0	35
Days Maximum Temp. ≤ 32°F	9	2	0	0	0	0	0	0	0	0	1	7	19
Days Minimum Temp. ≤ 32°F	25	21	14	6	1	0	0	0	1	7	17	26	118
Days Minimum Temp. ≤ 0°F	2	1	0	0	0	0	0	0	0	0	0	2	5
Heating Degree Days (base 65°F)	1,080	800	619	405	200	61	10	11	108	393	748	1,064	5,499
Cooling Degree Days (base 65°F)	0	0	0	2	36	110	255	238	73	3	0	0	717
Mean Precipitation (in.)	1.20	0.88	1.19	1.07	1.03	0.78	0.36	0.35	0.57	0.58	1.11	1.14	10.26
Days With ≥ 0.1" Precipitation	4	3	4	3	3	2	1	1	2	2	4	4	33
Days With ≥ 1.0" Precipitation	0	0	0	0	0	0	0	0	0	0	0	0	0
Mean Snowfall (in.)	na	na	0.3	trace	0.0	0.0	0.0	0.0	0.0	trace	0.5	na	na
Days With ≥ 1.0" Snow Depth	na	*3*	0	0	0	0	0	0	0	0	0	na	na

Dixie *Idaho County*   Elevation: 5,620 ft.   Latitude: 45° 33' N   Longitude: 115° 28' W

	JAN	FEB	MAR	APR	MAY	JUN	JUL	AUG	SEP	OCT	NOV	DEC	YEAR
Mean Maximum Temp. (°F)	30.4	35.3	40.1	46.4	55.9	65.6	74.3	*75.2*	66.0	52.9	37.0	30.1	*50.8*
Mean Temp. (°F)	17.3	20.9	27.0	33.8	42.4	50.4	56.0	*55.5*	47.4	37.7	25.5	17.3	*35.9*
Mean Minimum Temp. (°F)	4.2	6.5	13.9	21.1	28.9	35.2	37.6	*35.8*	28.8	22.4	14.0	4.5	*21.1*
Extreme Maximum Temp. (°F)	51	59	64	78	86	88	92	*94*	90	80	64	52	*94*
Extreme Minimum Temp. (°F)	-42	-40	-23	-9	4	19	23	*19*	11	-13	-33	-49	*-49*
Days Maximum Temp. ≥ 90°F	0	0	0	0	0	0	0	*0*	0	0	0	0	*0*
Days Maximum Temp. ≤ 32°F	18	10	5	1	0	0	0	0	0	1	10	18	63
Days Minimum Temp. ≤ 32°F	30	28	31	29	24	11	5	*9*	23	30	29	31	*280*
Days Minimum Temp. ≤ 0°F	12	9	3	0	0	0	0	0	0	0	4	12	40
Heating Degree Days (base 65°F)	1,472	1,238	1,171	929	693	432	278	*290*	521	841	1,178	1,471	*10,514*
Cooling Degree Days (base 65°F)	0	0	0	0	0	1	3	*3*	0	0	0	0	*7*
Mean Precipitation (in.)	3.46	2.62	2.49	2.10	2.13	2.24	1.29	1.25	1.35	1.42	3.28	3.58	27.21
Days With ≥ 0.1" Precipitation	10	8	8	7	7	6	4	*3*	4	5	10	11	*83*
Days With ≥ 1.0" Precipitation	0	0	0	0	0	0	0	0	0	0	0	0	0
Mean Snowfall (in.)	41.4	28.6	25.4	16.7	5.8	0.8	0.0	trace	1.0	5.6	31.7	40.1	197.1
Days With ≥ 1.0" Snow Depth	30	28	31	28	11	1	0	*0*	0	4	24	31	*188*

Driggs *Teton County*   Elevation: 6,115 ft.   Latitude: 43° 44' N   Longitude: 111° 07' W

	JAN	FEB	MAR	APR	MAY	JUN	JUL	AUG	SEP	OCT	NOV	DEC	YEAR
Mean Maximum Temp. (°F)	29.2	34.7	41.8	52.0	62.8	72.2	79.9	79.3	69.7	57.5	40.4	30.5	54.2
Mean Temp. (°F)	18.5	22.8	30.3	39.1	48.3	56.6	63.0	62.0	53.1	42.5	29.6	19.7	40.5
Mean Minimum Temp. (°F)	7.7	10.9	18.8	26.1	33.7	40.9	46.1	44.6	36.4	27.4	18.7	8.7	26.7
Extreme Maximum Temp. (°F)	60	58	69	79	84	92	92	92	89	81	71	55	92
Extreme Minimum Temp. (°F)	-36	-33	-17	0	12	23	29	24	9	-7	-20	-40	-40
Days Maximum Temp. ≥ 90°F	0	0	0	0	0	0	1	1	0	0	0	0	2
Days Maximum Temp. ≤ 32°F	19	10	3	0	0	0	0	0	0	1	7	17	57
Days Minimum Temp. ≤ 32°F	30	28	29	24	13	3	0	1	9	23	27	30	217
Days Minimum Temp. ≤ 0°F	10	7	2	0	0	0	0	0	0	0	2	9	30
Heating Degree Days (base 65°F)	1,436	1,186	1,069	771	514	253	90	107	353	692	1,056	1,400	8,927
Cooling Degree Days (base 65°F)	0	0	0	0	0	8	29	20	2	0	0	0	59
Mean Precipitation (in.)	1.37	0.99	1.25	1.37	2.05	1.29	1.33	1.08	1.20	1.16	1.18	1.44	15.71
Days With ≥ 0.1" Precipitation	5	4	5	5	6	4	4	4	4	4	5	5	55
Days With ≥ 1.0" Precipitation	0	0	0	0	0	0	0	0	0	0	0	0	0
Mean Snowfall (in.)	18.4	*11.6*	11.5	*6.1*	2.9	0.5	0.0	0.0	0.4	*3.2*	11.8	17.7	*84.1*
Days With ≥ 1.0" Snow Depth	*21*	na	na	na	0	0	0	0	0	*1*	8	na	na

Dubois Experiment Station *Clark County*   Elevation: 5,449 ft.   Latitude: 44° 15' N   Longitude: 112° 12' W

	JAN	FEB	MAR	APR	MAY	JUN	JUL	AUG	SEP	OCT	NOV	DEC	YEAR
Mean Maximum Temp. (°F)	27.8	33.1	41.7	54.2	64.8	74.8	84.1	83.6	72.6	58.0	39.0	28.7	55.2
Mean Temp. (°F)	19.6	24.0	32.0	42.1	51.5	60.1	68.0	67.3	57.3	45.3	30.3	20.4	43.2
Mean Minimum Temp. (°F)	11.3	15.0	22.3	29.9	38.1	45.4	51.8	50.9	42.0	32.5	21.6	12.1	31.1
Extreme Maximum Temp. (°F)	53	52	71	81	87	98	97	98	92	83	66	53	98
Extreme Minimum Temp. (°F)	-25	-22	-8	3	20	27	32	33	15	5	-11	-31	-31
Days Maximum Temp. ≥ 90°F	0	0	0	0	0	1	7	6	0	0	0	0	14
Days Maximum Temp. ≤ 32°F	21	13	3	0	0	0	0	0	0	1	8	20	66
Days Minimum Temp. ≤ 32°F	31	28	29	19	7	1	0	0	3	15	28	31	192
Days Minimum Temp. ≤ 0°F	6	3	0	0	0	0	0	0	0	0	1	4	14
Heating Degree Days (base 65°F)	1,402	1,151	1,016	681	414	173	34	41	241	605	1,034	1,377	8,169
Cooling Degree Days (base 65°F)	0	0	0	0	2	30	128	123	21	0	0	0	304
Mean Precipitation (in.)	0.77	0.67	0.95	1.11	1.99	1.74	1.09	1.02	1.01	0.83	1.07	0.93	13.18
Days With ≥ 0.1" Precipitation	3	2	3	4	6	5	3	3	3	3	4	3	42
Days With ≥ 1.0" Precipitation	0	0	0	0	0	0	0	0	0	0	0	0	0
Mean Snowfall (in.)	9.5	7.4	5.8	3.1	1.3	0.1	0.0	0.0	0.2	1.8	8.5	11.6	49.3
Days With ≥ 1.0" Snow Depth	30	28	20	3	0	0	0	0	0	1	10	27	119

Dworshak Fish Hatchery *Clearwater County*   Elevation: 994 ft.   Latitude: 46° 30' N   Longitude: 116° 19' W

	JAN	FEB	MAR	APR	MAY	JUN	JUL	AUG	SEP	OCT	NOV	DEC	YEAR
Mean Maximum Temp. (°F)	39.2	46.3	55.4	63.6	72.3	79.7	88.8	89.9	79.5	64.6	47.6	39.2	63.8
Mean Temp. (°F)	32.9	37.8	44.6	51.2	58.8	65.6	72.4	72.6	63.4	51.7	40.3	33.3	52.0
Mean Minimum Temp. (°F)	26.4	29.1	33.7	38.7	45.2	51.4	55.9	55.2	47.3	38.7	33.0	27.4	40.2
Extreme Maximum Temp. (°F)	61	66	82	95	104	105	110	108	105	90	69	61	110
Extreme Minimum Temp. (°F)	-11	-9	12	27	30	35	41	39	28	15	1	-10	-11
Days Maximum Temp. ≥ 90°F	0	0	0	0	2	6	16	18	6	0	0	0	48
Days Maximum Temp. ≤ 32°F	5	1	0	0	0	0	0	0	0	0	1	4	11
Days Minimum Temp. ≤ 32°F	23	19	13	4	0	0	0	0	0	5	12	23	99
Days Minimum Temp. ≤ 0°F	1	0	0	0	0	0	0	0	0	0	0	1	2
Heating Degree Days (base 65°F)	989	763	627	409	216	76	11	12	113	408	733	976	5,333
Cooling Degree Days (base 65°F)	0	0	0	3	36	99	243	256	82	2	0	0	721
Mean Precipitation (in.)	2.97	2.35	2.44	2.37	2.50	1.75	1.24	0.90	1.35	1.63	3.29	3.03	25.82
Days With ≥ 0.1" Precipitation	9	7	9	7	7	5	4	3	4	5	10	9	79
Days With ≥ 1.0" Precipitation	0	0	0	0	0	0	0	0	0	0	0	0	0
Mean Snowfall (in.)	na	na	*0.8*	trace	0.0	0.0	0.0	0.0	0.0	trace	*0.4*	na	na
Days With ≥ 1.0" Snow Depth	na	na	0	0	0	0	0	0	0	0	*0*	na	na

Elk City 1 NE *Idaho County*   Elevation: 4,055 ft.   Latitude: 45° 50' N   Longitude: 115° 28' W

	JAN	FEB	MAR	APR	MAY	JUN	JUL	AUG	SEP	OCT	NOV	DEC	YEAR
Mean Maximum Temp. (°F)	34.3	41.2	46.6	53.5	62.3	70.8	79.8	81.3	71.5	59.2	42.1	33.4	56.3
Mean Temp. (°F)	22.9	27.6	33.4	39.9	47.6	55.0	60.6	60.1	51.9	42.6	31.4	22.3	41.3
Mean Minimum Temp. (°F)	11.4	14.0	20.1	26.3	32.8	39.1	41.3	38.8	32.2	26.0	20.8	11.2	26.2
Extreme Maximum Temp. (°F)	60	68	74	87	94	100	98	101	98	88	72	61	101
Extreme Minimum Temp. (°F)	-41	-36	-23	6	11	23	23	22	12	-11	-28	-48	-48
Days Maximum Temp. ≥ 90°F	0	0	0	0	0	1	4	6	1	0	0	0	12
Days Maximum Temp. ≤ 32°F	11	4	1	0	0	0	0	0	0	0	4	12	32
Days Minimum Temp. ≤ 32°F	31	28	30	26	16	5	2	5	15	26	29	30	243
Days Minimum Temp. ≤ 0°F	7	4	1	0	0	0	0	0	0	0	1	6	19
Heating Degree Days (base 65°F)	1,299	1,049	974	747	534	302	154	163	390	686	1,000	1,317	8,615
Cooling Degree Days (base 65°F)	0	0	0	0	1	6	22	18	2	0	0	0	49
Mean Precipitation (in.)	3.42	2.53	2.67	2.77	3.18	3.22	1.92	1.44	1.79	1.94	3.27	3.17	31.32
Days With ≥ 0.1" Precipitation	9	7	9	9	9	8	5	4	5	6	9	9	89
Days With ≥ 1.0" Precipitation	0	0	0	0	0	0	0	0	0	0	0	0	0
Mean Snowfall (in.)	30.3	19.2	17.1	10.1	1.7	trace	0.0	0.0	trace	3.0	19.2	28.0	128.6
Days With ≥ 1.0" Snow Depth	30	27	27	12	1	0	0	0	0	2	15	29	143

Elk River 1 S *Clearwater County*   Elevation: 2,916 ft.   Latitude: 46° 46' N   Longitude: 116° 11' W

	JAN	FEB	MAR	APR	MAY	JUN	JUL	AUG	SEP	OCT	NOV	DEC	YEAR
Mean Maximum Temp. (°F)	34.1	39.8	46.4	54.1	63.6	71.3	79.8	81.1	70.9	58.2	41.3	33.6	56.2
Mean Temp. (°F)	26.0	30.0	35.8	42.6	50.4	57.4	63.1	63.0	54.0	44.0	33.5	26.0	43.8
Mean Minimum Temp. (°F)	17.8	20.2	25.1	31.0	37.2	43.4	46.3	44.8	37.1	29.8	25.7	18.4	31.4
Extreme Maximum Temp. (°F)	50	63	72	87	95	95	104	101	100	86	66	58	104
Extreme Minimum Temp. (°F)	-31	-21	-8	11	20	27	26	27	20	4	-24	-27	-31
Days Maximum Temp. ≥ 90°F	0	0	0	0	0	1	4	5	1	0	0	0	11
Days Maximum Temp. ≤ 32°F	10	4	1	0	0	0	0	0	0	0	3	11	29
Days Minimum Temp. ≤ 32°F	30	28	28	19	7	1	0	1	6	20	25	30	195
Days Minimum Temp. ≤ 0°F	4	2	0	0	0	0	0	0	0	0	0	2	8
Heating Degree Days (base 65°F)	1,203	983	899	667	448	241	109	107	326	643	938	1,200	7,764
Cooling Degree Days (base 65°F)	0	0	0	*0*	*4*	17	51	54	*5*	*0*	0	0	*131*
Mean Precipitation (in.)	4.93	4.11	3.18	2.55	2.95	2.41	1.49	1.10	1.81	2.41	4.68	4.91	36.53
Days With ≥ 0.1" Precipitation	12	10	9	7	7	7	4	3	5	6	11	11	92
Days With ≥ 1.0" Precipitation	1	1	0	0	0	0	0	0	0	0	1	1	3
Mean Snowfall (in.)	29.3	17.5	10.0	2.2	0.1	0.0	0.0	0.0	trace	0.2	13.4	27.5	100.2
Days With ≥ 1.0" Snow Depth	30	28	26	9	0	0	0	0	0	0	12	28	133

Emmett 2 E *Gem County*   Elevation: 2,388 ft.   Latitude: 43° 52' N   Longitude: 116° 28' W

	JAN	FEB	MAR	APR	MAY	JUN	JUL	AUG	SEP	OCT	NOV	DEC	YEAR
Mean Maximum Temp. (°F)	37.6	45.6	55.6	63.8	72.9	82.1	90.6	89.7	79.1	66.3	49.4	38.4	64.3
Mean Temp. (°F)	29.8	36.1	43.7	50.1	58.1	66.2	73.1	72.1	62.6	51.8	39.5	30.4	51.1
Mean Minimum Temp. (°F)	21.7	26.5	31.8	36.4	43.2	50.3	55.6	54.5	46.0	37.2	29.5	22.3	37.9
Extreme Maximum Temp. (°F)	63	70	82	94	98	106	109	106	101	95	74	64	109
Extreme Minimum Temp. (°F)	-18	-16	9	19	23	32	37	36	27	14	-10	-22	-22
Days Maximum Temp. ≥ 90°F	0	0	0	0	2	7	19	18	4	0	0	0	50
Days Maximum Temp. ≤ 32°F	9	3	0	0	0	0	0	0	0	0	1	6	19
Days Minimum Temp. ≤ 32°F	26	22	18	10	2	0	0	0	1	8	19	27	133
Days Minimum Temp. ≤ 0°F	2	1	0	0	0	0	0	0	0	0	0	2	5
Heating Degree Days (base 65°F)	1,085	811	652	442	236	74	12	14	127	405	760	1,066	5,684
Cooling Degree Days (base 65°F)	0	0	0	2	29	106	255	241	65	3	0	0	701
Mean Precipitation (in.)	1.81	1.52	1.56	1.19	1.28	0.88	0.30	0.33	0.73	0.83	1.79	1.68	13.90
Days With ≥ 0.1" Precipitation	6	5	5	4	4	3	1	1	2	3	6	5	45
Days With ≥ 1.0" Precipitation	0	0	0	0	0	0	0	0	0	0	0	0	0
Mean Snowfall (in.)	na	na	0.1	trace	0.0	0.0	0.0	0.0	0.0	0.0	1.0	na	na
Days With ≥ 1.0" Snow Depth	na	na	0	0	0	0	0	0	0	0	1	na	na

Fairfield Ranger Station *Camas County*   Elevation: 5,062 ft.   Latitude: 43° 21' N   Longitude: 114° 48' W

	JAN	FEB	MAR	APR	MAY	JUN	JUL	AUG	SEP	OCT	NOV	DEC	YEAR
Mean Maximum Temp. (°F)	30.0	35.2	43.4	55.7	66.8	75.8	85.1	84.6	74.8	63.2	43.2	31.4	57.4
Mean Temp. (°F)	18.0	21.9	30.8	41.6	50.8	58.2	65.6	64.4	54.6	45.0	30.5	19.4	41.8
Mean Minimum Temp. (°F)	6.0	8.6	18.0	27.5	34.8	40.5	46.2	44.2	34.7	26.8	17.9	7.4	26.0
Extreme Maximum Temp. (°F)	48	63	70	83	89	98	99	98	93	87	69	55	99
Extreme Minimum Temp. (°F)	-42	-36	-21	3	15	20	26	23	11	2	-20	-40	-42
Days Maximum Temp. ≥ 90°F	0	0	0	0	0	2	8	8	1	0	0	0	19
Days Maximum Temp. ≤ 32°F	17	9	1	0	0	0	0	0	0	0	4	14	45
Days Minimum Temp. ≤ 32°F	30	27	29	22	11	4	0	2	10	23	27	29	214
Days Minimum Temp. ≤ 0°F	10	8	2	0	0	0	0	0	0	0	2	9	31
Heating Degree Days (base 65°F)	1,451	1,210	1,054	695	434	217	57	75	308	617	1,026	1,404	8,548
Cooling Degree Days (base 65°F)	0	0	0	0	2	17	80	63	5	0	0	0	167
Mean Precipitation (in.)	2.21	1.69	1.51	1.06	1.40	0.94	0.64	0.42	0.67	0.81	1.89	2.07	15.31
Days With ≥ 0.1" Precipitation	5	4	4	3	4	3	2	1	2	2	5	5	40
Days With ≥ 1.0" Precipitation	0	0	0	0	0	0	0	0	0	0	0	0	0
Mean Snowfall (in.)	18.8	11.8	4.8	2.2	0.5	trace	0.0	0.0	0.1	0.6	9.1	18.4	66.3
Days With ≥ 1.0" Snow Depth	24	23	19	2	0	0	0	0	0	0	7	21	96

Fenn Ranger Station *Idaho County*   Elevation: 1,587 ft.   Latitude: 46° 06' N   Longitude: 115° 33' W

	JAN	FEB	MAR	APR	MAY	JUN	JUL	AUG	SEP	OCT	NOV	DEC	YEAR
Mean Maximum Temp. (°F)	36.1	42.8	52.1	61.3	70.5	78.0	87.0	87.8	75.5	60.5	44.3	36.0	61.0
Mean Temp. (°F)	30.1	34.7	41.6	48.5	56.2	63.1	69.4	69.3	59.8	48.5	37.7	30.8	49.2
Mean Minimum Temp. (°F)	24.1	26.6	31.2	35.8	41.9	48.1	51.8	50.8	44.1	36.6	31.1	25.6	37.3
Extreme Maximum Temp. (°F)	57	67	77	94	100	103	107	104	98	87	68	60	107
Extreme Minimum Temp. (°F)	-12	-13	9	19	27	35	37	36	27	9	-1	-12	-13
Days Maximum Temp. ≥ 90°F	0	0	0	0	2	5	14	15	2	0	0	0	38
Days Maximum Temp. ≤ 32°F	7	2	0	0	0	0	0	0	0	0	1	5	15
Days Minimum Temp. ≤ 32°F	28	24	18	8	1	0	0	0	1	7	16	26	129
Days Minimum Temp. ≤ 0°F	1	1	0	0	0	0	0	0	0	0	0	1	3
Heating Degree Days (base 65°F)	1,074	849	717	488	278	112	24	23	174	503	812	1,053	6,107
Cooling Degree Days (base 65°F)	0	0	0	1	16	60	166	167	29	0	0	0	439
Mean Precipitation (in.)	4.82	3.50	3.76	3.70	3.47	3.14	1.42	1.27	2.16	2.70	4.91	4.28	39.13
Days With ≥ 0.1" Precipitation	11	9	10	10	9	7	4	3	5	7	12	10	97
Days With ≥ 1.0" Precipitation	1	0	0	0	0	0	0	0	0	0	1	0	2
Mean Snowfall (in.)	18.4	7.8	2.1	0.2	trace	0.0	0.0	0.0	0.0	0.3	6.5	17.2	52.5
Days With ≥ 1.0" Snow Depth	25	18	5	0	0	0	0	0	0	0	4	16	68

Fort Hall 1 NNE *Bingham County*   Elevation: 4,461 ft.   Latitude: 43° 03' N   Longitude: 112° 25' W

	JAN	FEB	MAR	APR	MAY	JUN	JUL	AUG	SEP	OCT	NOV	DEC	YEAR
Mean Maximum Temp. (°F)	32.7	39.3	49.1	58.6	67.7	77.2	85.3	85.2	74.9	62.1	44.8	33.5	59.2
Mean Temp. (°F)	23.3	28.8	37.4	45.1	53.6	61.9	68.2	67.4	58.0	46.9	34.1	23.9	45.7
Mean Minimum Temp. (°F)	14.0	18.3	25.8	31.6	39.5	46.5	51.1	49.7	41.0	31.8	23.4	14.3	32.2
Extreme Maximum Temp. (°F)	58	66	76	85	93	100	99	101	98	90	74	63	101
Extreme Minimum Temp. (°F)	-29	-33	-11	11	17	25	35	29	14	8	-20	-30	-33
Days Maximum Temp. ≥ 90°F	0	0	0	0	0	3	9	9	1	0	0	0	22
Days Maximum Temp. ≤ 32°F	14	7	1	0	0	0	0	0	0	0	4	13	39
Days Minimum Temp. ≤ 32°F	29	26	25	17	5	1	0	0	4	16	25	29	177
Days Minimum Temp. ≤ 0°F	6	2	0	0	0	0	0	0	0	0	1	4	13
Heating Degree Days (base 65°F)	1,284	1,017	847	591	351	133	25	33	222	554	919	1,267	7,243
Cooling Degree Days (base 65°F)	0	0	0	1	4	38	119	116	17	0	0	0	295
Mean Precipitation (in.)	0.95	0.88	1.20	1.12	1.66	1.02	0.73	0.77	0.85	1.06	1.02	0.97	12.23
Days With ≥ 0.1" Precipitation	3	3	4	3	4	3	2	2	2	3	3	3	35
Days With ≥ 1.0" Precipitation	0	0	0	0	0	0	0	0	0	0	0	0	0
Mean Snowfall (in.)	6.4	3.9	2.4	0.9	0.3	trace	0.0	0.0	trace	1.1	3.0	6.7	24.7
Days With ≥ 1.0" Snow Depth	18	9	3	0	0	0	0	0	0	1	4	13	48

Gibbonsville *Lemhi County*   Elevation: 4,478 ft.   Latitude: 45° 34' N   Longitude: 113° 56' W

	JAN	FEB	MAR	APR	MAY	JUN	JUL	AUG	SEP	OCT	NOV	DEC	YEAR
Mean Maximum Temp. (°F)	28.4	36.0	46.3	56.6	66.0	74.6	84.4	83.5	73.2	59.3	40.0	27.8	56.3
Mean Temp. (°F)	18.6	24.4	34.1	42.4	50.3	57.7	64.8	63.7	54.8	43.7	30.3	18.3	41.9
Mean Minimum Temp. (°F)	8.7	12.9	21.8	28.2	34.5	40.8	45.3	43.9	36.2	28.0	20.7	8.8	27.5
Extreme Maximum Temp. (°F)	48	55	73	85	94	100	100	99	98	85	67	52	100
Extreme Minimum Temp. (°F)	-33	-26	-9	8	16	25	29	21	16	0	-20	-36	-36
Days Maximum Temp. ≥ 90°F	0	0	0	0	0	2	10	7	1	0	0	0	20
Days Maximum Temp. ≤ 32°F	19	8	1	0	0	0	0	0	0	0	5	20	53
Days Minimum Temp. ≤ 32°F	31	28	30	23	11	3	0	0	9	24	28	31	218
Days Minimum Temp. ≤ 0°F	9	4	0	0	0	0	0	0	0	0	1	7	21
Heating Degree Days (base 65°F)	1,435	1,140	952	671	451	228	67	80	304	655	1,032	1,441	8,456
Cooling Degree Days (base 65°F)	0	0	0	0	2	15	66	45	6	0	0	0	134
Mean Precipitation (in.)	2.03	1.18	1.12	1.13	1.61	1.69	0.90	0.96	0.85	0.74	1.63	1.81	15.65
Days With ≥ 0.1" Precipitation	7	4	5	4	6	5	3	3	3	2	5	7	54
Days With ≥ 1.0" Precipitation	0	0	0	0	0	0	0	0	0	0	0	0	0
Mean Snowfall (in.)	25.7	12.2	7.3	2.8	0.3	trace	0.0	trace	trace	0.9	13.8	23.2	86.2
Days With ≥ 1.0" Snow Depth	31	28	26	4	0	0	0	0	0	1	12	30	132

Grace *Caribou County*   Elevation: 5,547 ft.   Latitude: 42° 35' N   Longitude: 111° 45' W

	JAN	FEB	MAR	APR	MAY	JUN	JUL	AUG	SEP	OCT	NOV	DEC	YEAR
Mean Maximum Temp. (°F)	31.0	36.4	45.3	55.8	65.9	75.6	83.8	83.8	74.0	61.3	43.1	32.7	57.4
Mean Temp. (°F)	21.1	25.1	33.7	42.2	51.0	59.1	65.7	65.0	56.0	45.5	32.3	22.7	43.3
Mean Minimum Temp. (°F)	11.2	13.7	22.1	28.6	36.2	42.4	47.4	46.2	38.0	29.6	21.3	12.6	29.1
Extreme Maximum Temp. (°F)	55	60	72	80	88	99	100	99	95	86	70	60	100
Extreme Minimum Temp. (°F)	-34	-36	-15	1	11	27	28	26	15	8	-20	-40	-40
Days Maximum Temp. ≥ 90°F	0	0	0	0	0	1	5	5	0	0	0	0	11
Days Maximum Temp. ≤ 32°F	17	8	2	0	0	0	0	0	0	0	5	14	46
Days Minimum Temp. ≤ 32°F	30	27	28	21	8	1	0	1	7	20	27	30	200
Days Minimum Temp. ≤ 0°F	7	6	1	0	0	0	0	0	0	0	1	6	21
Heating Degree Days (base 65°F)	1,355	1,122	962	677	426	188	45	56	270	600	976	1,304	7,981
Cooling Degree Days (base 65°F)	0	0	0	0	0	15	74	70	9	0	0	0	168
Mean Precipitation (in.)	1.29	1.08	1.41	1.42	2.20	1.36	1.12	1.18	1.37	1.35	1.19	1.20	16.17
Days With ≥ 0.1" Precipitation	4	4	5	5	6	4	3	3	4	4	5	4	51
Days With ≥ 1.0" Precipitation	0	0	0	0	0	0	0	0	0	0	0	0	0
Mean Snowfall (in.)	na	na	na	1.6	0.0	0.0	0.0	0.0	0.0	0.5	na	na	na
Days With ≥ 1.0" Snow Depth	na	na	na	1	0	0	0	0	0	0	na	na	na

Grand View 2 W *Owyhee County*   Elevation: 2,398 ft.   Latitude: 43° 01' N   Longitude: 116° 11' W

	JAN	FEB	MAR	APR	MAY	JUN	JUL	AUG	SEP	OCT	NOV	DEC	YEAR
Mean Maximum Temp. (°F)	39.8	48.5	58.7	66.9	75.7	84.3	92.0	91.2	80.6	67.7	51.2	39.5	66.3
Mean Temp. (°F)	30.7	36.9	44.8	51.8	60.2	68.1	74.1	72.6	62.8	51.4	39.6	30.2	51.9
Mean Minimum Temp. (°F)	21.6	25.3	30.7	36.8	44.7	51.8	56.2	53.9	44.6	35.1	28.1	20.7	37.5
Extreme Maximum Temp. (°F)	67	76	83	92	100	107	107	108	101	93	80	68	108
Extreme Minimum Temp. (°F)	-21	-20	1	16	25	31	39	37	25	14	-5	-26	-26
Days Maximum Temp. ≥ 90°F	0	0	0	0	2	9	20	20	5	0	0	0	56
Days Maximum Temp. ≤ 32°F	7	2	0	0	0	0	0	0	0	0	1	6	16
Days Minimum Temp. ≤ 32°F	26	23	18	9	1	0	0	0	2	12	20	27	138
Days Minimum Temp. ≤ 0°F	2	0	0	0	0	0	0	0	0	0	0	2	4
Heating Degree Days (base 65°F)	1,055	784	621	393	179	45	5	10	114	416	754	1,074	5,450
Cooling Degree Days (base 65°F)	0	0	0	5	44	134	286	265	60	2	0	0	796
Mean Precipitation (in.)	0.67	0.52	0.77	0.68	0.85	0.71	0.26	0.22	0.60	0.48	0.81	0.60	7.17
Days With ≥ 0.1" Precipitation	3	2	3	2	3	2	1	1	2	2	3	2	26
Days With ≥ 1.0" Precipitation	0	0	0	0	0	0	0	0	0	0	0	0	0
Mean Snowfall (in.)	na	1.6	trace	0.0	0.0	0.0	0.0	0.0	0.0	0.0	0.8	na	na
Days With ≥ 1.0" Snow Depth	na	0	0	0	0	0	0	0	0	0	0	1	na

Grangeville *Idaho County*   Elevation: 3,359 ft.   Latitude: 45° 56' N   Longitude: 116° 07' W

	JAN	FEB	MAR	APR	MAY	JUN	JUL	AUG	SEP	OCT	NOV	DEC	YEAR
Mean Maximum Temp. (°F)	37.3	43.0	49.5	56.3	64.1	71.6	80.9	82.0	71.4	59.0	44.5	37.4	58.1
Mean Temp. (°F)	29.9	34.0	39.1	44.7	51.9	58.8	65.6	65.9	56.6	46.7	36.5	30.0	46.6
Mean Minimum Temp. (°F)	22.4	24.9	28.7	33.0	39.6	45.9	50.2	49.7	41.6	34.3	28.5	22.4	35.1
Extreme Maximum Temp. (°F)	62	69	78	88	91	96	99	103	97	87	72	61	103
Extreme Minimum Temp. (°F)	-16	-23	1	18	21	28	33	29	19	0	-12	-22	-23
Days Maximum Temp. ≥ 90°F	0	0	0	0	0	1	6	7	1	0	0	0	15
Days Maximum Temp. ≤ 32°F	9	3	0	0	0	0	0	0	0	0	2	8	22
Days Minimum Temp. ≤ 32°F	26	23	23	16	5	0	0	0	3	13	21	26	156
Days Minimum Temp. ≤ 0°F	2	1	0	0	0	0	0	0	0	0	0	1	4
Heating Degree Days (base 65°F)	1,082	870	796	603	404	206	69	65	260	563	848	1,079	6,845
Cooling Degree Days (base 65°F)	0	0	0	0	5	24	91	102	18	0	0	0	240
Mean Precipitation (in.)	1.54	1.28	2.39	2.85	3.58	2.87	1.69	1.15	1.72	1.75	1.85	1.52	24.19
Days With ≥ 0.1" Precipitation	5	4	7	8	9	7	4	3	4	5	6	5	67
Days With ≥ 1.0" Precipitation	0	0	0	0	0	0	0	0	0	0	0	0	0
Mean Snowfall (in.)	8.9	7.3	8.1	3.1	0.2	0.0	0.0	0.0	0.0	1.4	6.1	10.0	45.1
Days With ≥ 1.0" Snow Depth	15	9	4	1	0	0	0	0	0	0	4	12	45

Grouse *Custer County*   Elevation: 6,135 ft.   Latitude: 43° 42' N   Longitude: 113° 36' W

	JAN	FEB	MAR	APR	MAY	JUN	JUL	AUG	SEP	OCT	NOV	DEC	YEAR
Mean Maximum Temp. (°F)	28.1	33.9	41.8	52.1	*62.1*	*71.0*	*79.4*	78.9	69.7	57.1	38.9	28.8	*53.5*
Mean Temp. (°F)	14.0	18.7	28.0	38.0	*46.9*	*54.1*	*60.1*	59.3	*50.6*	40.0	25.6	14.9	*37.5*
Mean Minimum Temp. (°F)	-0.2	3.4	14.1	23.8	*31.6*	*37.1*	*40.7*	39.7	*31.4*	22.9	12.2	0.9	*21.5*
Extreme Maximum Temp. (°F)	50	55	64	78	84	88	94	*94*	88	78	63	52	*94*
Extreme Minimum Temp. (°F)	-40	-35	-26	-10	10	22	21	*21*	9	-11	-26	-42	*-42*
Days Maximum Temp. ≥ 90°F	0	0	0	0	0	0	1	1	0	0	0	0	2
Days Maximum Temp. ≤ 32°F	19	11	3	0	0	0	0	0	0	0	7	19	59
Days Minimum Temp. ≤ 32°F	30	28	30	26	17	6	2	*3*	16	27	28	30	*243*
Days Minimum Temp. ≤ 0°F	16	11	3	0	0	0	0	*0*	0	0	5	15	*50*
Heating Degree Days (base 65°F)	1,575	1,302	1,141	803	*554*	*321*	*157*	*177*	*426*	767	1,177	1,546	*9,946*
Cooling Degree Days (base 65°F)	0	0	0	0	*0*	*1*	*12*	*10*	*0*	0	*0*	*0*	*23*
Mean Precipitation (in.)	1.07	1.16	1.30	0.98	1.62	1.64	1.11	*0.95*	0.79	0.74	1.10	1.20	*13.66*
Days With ≥ 0.1" Precipitation	4	4	4	3	5	5	3	3	3	3	4	4	45
Days With ≥ 1.0" Precipitation	0	0	0	0	0	0	0	0	0	0	0	0	0
Mean Snowfall (in.)	12.7	14.2	*10.4*	3.7	1.5	trace	0.0	*0.0*	0.6	1.4	na	*14.4*	na
Days With ≥ 1.0" Snow Depth	na	na	na	9	1	0	0	0	0	0	na	na	na

Hamer 4 NW *Jefferson County*   Elevation: 4,790 ft.   Latitude: 43° 58' N   Longitude: 112° 16' W

	JAN	FEB	MAR	APR	MAY	JUN	JUL	AUG	SEP	OCT	NOV	DEC	YEAR
Mean Maximum Temp. (°F)	28.2	35.2	46.8	59.4	69.3	78.7	86.9	86.1	75.3	61.7	42.4	29.7	58.3
Mean Temp. (°F)	15.8	22.1	33.0	43.0	52.5	60.6	66.8	65.5	*55.5*	43.7	29.0	17.2	*42.1*
Mean Minimum Temp. (°F)	3.2	9.1	19.1	26.4	35.6	42.4	46.6	44.8	*35.4*	25.6	15.7	4.7	*25.7*
Extreme Maximum Temp. (°F)	55	58	74	86	89	102	99	101	94	88	69	60	102
Extreme Minimum Temp. (°F)	-48	-46	-22	6	14	27	28	20	10	2	-26	-40	-48
Days Maximum Temp. ≥ 90°F	0	0	0	0	0	3	*11*	10	1	0	0	0	25
Days Maximum Temp. ≤ 32°F	20	10	2	0	0	0	0	0	0	0	5	19	56
Days Minimum Temp. ≤ 32°F	30	28	30	23	10	2	0	1	10	*25*	28	30	*217*
Days Minimum Temp. ≤ 0°F	13	7	1	0	0	0	0	0	0	0	3	12	36
Heating Degree Days (base 65°F)	1,522	1,204	985	653	383	157	37	51	*285*	653	1,068	1,476	*8,474*
Cooling Degree Days (base 65°F)	0	0	0	0	1	25	92	74	*11*	0	0	0	*203*
Mean Precipitation (in.)	0.65	0.48	0.69	0.87	1.53	1.24	0.92	0.77	0.61	0.65	0.77	0.70	9.88
Days With ≥ 0.1" Precipitation	2	2	2	3	5	4	2	2	2	2	3	3	32
Days With ≥ 1.0" Precipitation	0	0	0	0	0	0	0	0	0	0	0	0	0
Mean Snowfall (in.)	7.5	5.7	3.3	1.3	0.2	trace	0.0	0.0	0.1	0.7	4.8	9.7	33.3
Days With ≥ 1.0" Snow Depth	26	19	9	1	0	0	0	0	0	0	6	20	81

Hazelton *Jerome County*   Elevation: 4,058 ft.   Latitude: 42° 36' N   Longitude: 114° 08' W

	JAN	FEB	MAR	APR	MAY	JUN	JUL	AUG	SEP	OCT	NOV	DEC	YEAR
Mean Maximum Temp. (°F)	35.3	42.2	51.5	60.7	69.7	79.9	88.4	87.9	77.7	64.6	47.1	36.8	61.8
Mean Temp. (°F)	26.8	32.2	39.8	46.8	55.2	64.1	71.2	70.0	60.2	49.0	36.4	27.5	48.3
Mean Minimum Temp. (°F)	18.2	22.1	28.1	32.9	40.7	48.2	53.9	52.1	42.7	33.3	25.8	18.3	34.7
Extreme Maximum Temp. (°F)	59	71	78	91	95	102	103	106	100	91	77	71	106
Extreme Minimum Temp. (°F)	-18	-17	-2	9	22	32	33	34	24	10	-6	-23	-23
Days Maximum Temp. ≥ 90°F	0	0	0	0	1	5	15	14	3	0	0	0	38
Days Maximum Temp. ≤ 32°F	11	4	1	0	0	0	0	0	0	0	3	10	29
Days Minimum Temp. ≤ 32°F	29	26	24	14	3	0	0	0	2	14	24	29	165
Days Minimum Temp. ≤ 0°F	2	1	0	0	0	0	0	0	0	0	0	2	5
Heating Degree Days (base 65°F)	1,178	921	773	541	309	103	15	20	172	492	850	1,155	6,529
Cooling Degree Days (base 65°F)	0	0	0	2	16	83	214	190	39	0	0	0	544
Mean Precipitation (in.)	1.46	0.95	1.10	0.82	1.15	0.71	0.23	0.29	0.65	0.69	1.35	1.27	10.67
Days With ≥ 0.1" Precipitation	5	3	4	3	4	3	1	1	2	2	4	4	36
Days With ≥ 1.0" Precipitation	0	0	0	0	0	0	0	0	0	0	0	0	0
Mean Snowfall (in.)	*4.7*	*2.4*	*1.1*	0.5	0.3	0.0	0.0	0.0	trace	trace	*2.8*	*4.2*	*16.0*
Days With ≥ 1.0" Snow Depth	na	*3*	*1*	0	0	0	0	0	0	0	*1*	*4*	na

Hill City 1 W *Camas County*   Elevation: 5,098 ft.   Latitude: 43° 18' N   Longitude: 115° 04' W

	JAN	FEB	MAR	APR	MAY	JUN	JUL	AUG	SEP	OCT	NOV	DEC	YEAR
Mean Maximum Temp. (°F)	29.4	33.9	41.8	54.0	65.2	74.6	84.3	84.4	74.5	61.5	42.1	30.7	56.4
Mean Temp. (°F)	18.4	21.8	30.5	40.9	50.1	57.2	64.6	64.0	54.9	44.3	30.6	19.5	41.4
Mean Minimum Temp. (°F)	7.3	9.8	19.2	27.8	34.8	39.7	44.8	43.6	35.2	27.0	19.2	8.3	26.4
Extreme Maximum Temp. (°F)	49	59	70	83	90	97	100	100	94	85	73	53	100
Extreme Minimum Temp. (°F)	-42	-37	-25	-1	17	20	21	21	12	0	-22	-40	-42
Days Maximum Temp. ≥ 90°F	0	0	0	0	0	2	8	8	1	0	0	0	19
Days Maximum Temp. ≤ 32°F	18	11	3	0	0	0	0	0	0	0	5	17	54
Days Minimum Temp. ≤ 32°F	31	28	29	22	12	4	1	2	10	23	27	30	219
Days Minimum Temp. ≤ 0°F	10	7	2	0	0	0	0	0	0	0	2	9	30
Heating Degree Days (base 65°F)	1,441	1,213	1,063	716	457	241	73	83	302	635	1,024	1,403	8,651
Cooling Degree Days (base 65°F)	0	0	0	0	1	11	63	57	6	0	0	0	138
Mean Precipitation (in.)	2.33	1.40	1.26	1.02	1.16	0.99	0.53	0.32	0.75	0.89	1.73	2.06	14.44
Days With ≥ 0.1" Precipitation	6	5	4	3	4	3	1	1	2	3	5	6	43
Days With ≥ 1.0" Precipitation	0	0	0	0	0	0	0	0	0	0	0	0	0
Mean Snowfall (in.)	na	na	5.9	1.0	0.2	0.0	0.0	0.0	0.0	0.4	*6.8*	na	na
Days With ≥ 1.0" Snow Depth	21	*22*	na	5	0	0	0	0	0	0	*8*	*16*	na

Hollister *Twin Falls County*   Elevation: 4,524 ft.   Latitude: 42° 21' N   Longitude: 114° 34' W

	JAN	FEB	MAR	APR	MAY	JUN	JUL	AUG	SEP	OCT	NOV	DEC	YEAR
Mean Maximum Temp. (°F)	na	42.7	50.9	59.4	67.2	77.5	86.0	84.4	na	na	na	na	na
Mean Temp. (°F)	na	32.8	39.6	46.1	53.2	62.3	70.3	68.8	na	na	na	na	na
Mean Minimum Temp. (°F)	na	22.9	28.2	32.8	39.1	47.1	54.5	53.2	na	na	na	na	na
Extreme Maximum Temp. (°F)	60	72	75	85	89	97	103	101	96	88	77	64	103
Extreme Minimum Temp. (°F)	-23	-19	-3	12	20	27	30	32	20	6	-1	-27	-27
Days Maximum Temp. ≥ 90°F	0	0	0	0	0	3	9	6	1	0	0	0	19
Days Maximum Temp. ≤ 32°F	7	3	1	0	0	0	0	0	0	0	2	6	19
Days Minimum Temp. ≤ 32°F	23	20	20	15	5	1	0	0	2	9	17	23	135
Days Minimum Temp. ≤ 0°F	2	1	0	0	0	0	0	0	0	0	0	1	4
Heating Degree Days (base 65°F)	na	902	780	561	368	139	22	31	na	na	na	na	na
Cooling Degree Days (base 65°F)	na	0	0	1	10	62	190	164	na	na	na	na	na
Mean Precipitation (in.)	0.94	0.54	0.88	0.97	1.53	1.18	0.51	0.50	0.80	0.80	1.02	0.85	10.52
Days With ≥ 0.1" Precipitation	2	2	2	3	4	3	2	2	2	2	2	2	28
Days With ≥ 1.0" Precipitation	0	0	0	0	0	0	0	0	0	0	0	0	0
Mean Snowfall (in.)	na	na	na	1.4	1.1	trace	0.0	0.0	0.0	0.2	na	na	na
Days With ≥ 1.0" Snow Depth	na	na	na	0	0	0	0	0	0	0	na	na	na

Idaho City *Boise County*   Elevation: 3,963 ft.   Latitude: 43° 50' N   Longitude: 115° 50' W

	JAN	FEB	MAR	APR	MAY	JUN	JUL	AUG	SEP	OCT	NOV	DEC	YEAR
Mean Maximum Temp. (°F)	35.5	41.6	48.6	57.7	67.4	76.7	86.2	86.4	75.7	63.2	44.4	35.1	59.9
Mean Temp. (°F)	24.7	28.9	35.6	42.8	51.2	58.8	65.7	65.3	55.9	45.7	33.5	24.5	44.4
Mean Minimum Temp. (°F)	13.9	16.2	22.7	27.8	34.8	40.7	45.2	44.1	36.0	28.1	22.6	13.9	28.8
Extreme Maximum Temp. (°F)	54	65	75	88	94	98	103	104	100	90	74	55	104
Extreme Minimum Temp. (°F)	-24	-24	-6	9	18	26	27	25	17	2	-18	-32	-32
Days Maximum Temp. ≥ 90°F	0	0	0	0	0	3	12	12	2	0	0	0	29
Days Maximum Temp. ≤ 32°F	9	3	0	0	0	0	0	0	0	0	2	9	23
Days Minimum Temp. ≤ 32°F	31	28	29	24	12	3	0	1	9	23	27	30	217
Days Minimum Temp. ≤ 0°F	6	3	0	0	0	0	0	0	0	0	1	4	14
Heating Degree Days (base 65°F)	1,243	1,013	903	661	425	205	63	67	277	592	938	1,248	7,635
Cooling Degree Days (base 65°F)	0	0	0	0	3	24	88	87	11	0	0	0	213
Mean Precipitation (in.)	3.65	2.71	2.44	1.86	1.87	1.41	0.68	0.52	1.16	1.40	3.21	3.63	24.54
Days With ≥ 0.1" Precipitation	8	8	7	5	5	4	2	1	3	4	8	9	64
Days With ≥ 1.0" Precipitation	0	0	0	0	0	0	0	0	0	0	0	0	0
Mean Snowfall (in.)	20.8	12.4	4.7	1.0	trace	0.0	0.0	0.0	trace	1.1	10.3	23.8	74.1
Days With ≥ 1.0" Snow Depth	31	27	21	3	0	0	0	0	0	0	10	28	120

Idaho Falls 16 SE *Bonneville County*   Elevation: 5,849 ft.   Latitude: 43° 21' N   Longitude: 111° 47' W

	JAN	FEB	MAR	APR	MAY	JUN	JUL	AUG	SEP	OCT	NOV	DEC	YEAR
Mean Maximum Temp. (°F)	30.8	35.6	42.1	51.9	61.8	71.3	79.6	78.8	69.2	57.0	41.0	31.6	54.2
Mean Temp. (°F)	21.0	24.9	31.8	39.8	48.3	56.0	62.8	61.7	52.8	42.5	30.4	21.6	41.1
Mean Minimum Temp. (°F)	11.1	14.1	21.4	27.7	34.7	40.8	45.9	44.4	36.5	27.9	19.9	11.5	28.0
Extreme Maximum Temp. (°F)	52	56	68	78	85	95	94	96	89	80	70	56	96
Extreme Minimum Temp. (°F)	-40	-40	-23	-6	11	21	28	19	7	-8	-25	-42	-42
Days Maximum Temp. ≥ 90°F	0	0	0	0	0	0	1	1	0	0	0	0	2
Days Maximum Temp. ≤ 32°F	17	9	3	0	0	0	0	0	0	0	6	16	51
Days Minimum Temp. ≤ 32°F	30	27	28	23	12	3	0	1	9	22	27	30	212
Days Minimum Temp. ≤ 0°F	7	4	1	0	0	0	0	0	0	0	2	6	20
Heating Degree Days (base 65°F)	1,358	1,128	1,024	749	512	270	95	118	362	691	1,028	1,340	8,675
Cooling Degree Days (base 65°F)	0	0	0	0	0	6	30	22	2	0	0	0	60
Mean Precipitation (in.)	1.45	1.11	1.50	1.47	2.05	1.29	1.11	0.91	1.16	1.13	1.64	1.39	16.21
Days With ≥ 0.1" Precipitation	5	4	5	5	7	5	3	3	4	4	5	5	55
Days With ≥ 1.0" Precipitation	0	0	0	0	0	0	0	0	0	0	0	0	0
Mean Snowfall (in.)	17.1	12.5	10.6	6.2	1.9	0.2	0.0	0.0	0.1	2.4	10.3	17.4	78.7
Days With ≥ 1.0" Snow Depth	30	26	18	4	0	0	0	0	0	1	10	24	113

Idaho Falls 46 W *Butte County*   Elevation: 4,937 ft.   Latitude: 43° 32' N   Longitude: 112° 57' W

	JAN	FEB	MAR	APR	MAY	JUN	JUL	AUG	SEP	OCT	NOV	DEC	YEAR
Mean Maximum Temp. (°F)	28.0	34.3	44.7	56.6	66.3	76.8	86.6	85.6	74.3	60.7	41.7	29.3	57.1
Mean Temp. (°F)	16.6	22.3	32.8	42.2	51.2	60.2	67.7	66.5	55.9	43.8	29.5	17.6	42.2
Mean Minimum Temp. (°F)	5.2	10.3	20.9	27.8	36.2	43.5	48.9	47.2	37.4	26.7	17.3	5.7	27.3
Extreme Maximum Temp. (°F)	51	60	73	86	90	100	101	101	95	87	67	57	101
Extreme Minimum Temp. (°F)	-35	-36	-14	6	13	23	28	24	12	1	-24	-47	-47
Days Maximum Temp. ≥ 90°F	0	0	0	0	0	3	12	11	1	0	0	0	27
Days Maximum Temp. ≤ 32°F	20	11	3	0	0	0	0	0	0	0	6	18	58
Days Minimum Temp. ≤ 32°F	31	28	29	22	9	2	0	1	8	23	28	31	212
Days Minimum Temp. ≤ 0°F	11	7	1	0	0	0	0	0	0	0	2	11	32
Heating Degree Days (base 65°F)	1,495	1,199	991	677	421	174	36	46	277	652	1,058	1,466	8,492
Cooling Degree Days (base 65°F)	0	0	0	0	2	33	129	106	12	0	0	0	282
Mean Precipitation (in.)	0.63	0.59	0.70	0.81	1.24	1.11	0.66	0.45	0.73	0.55	0.73	0.70	8.90
Days With ≥ 0.1" Precipitation	2	2	2	3	4	3	2	1	2	2	3	3	29
Days With ≥ 1.0" Precipitation	0	0	0	0	0	0	0	0	0	0	0	0	0
Mean Snowfall (in.)	5.9	5.1	2.3	1.0	0.5	0.0	0.0	0.0	trace	0.7	4.1	6.6	26.2
Days With ≥ 1.0" Snow Depth	26	19	8	1	0	0	0	0	0	0	6	20	80

Idaho Falls Fanning Airport *Bonneville County*   Elevation: 4,727 ft.   Latitude: 43° 31' N   Longitude: 112° 04' W

	JAN	FEB	MAR	APR	MAY	JUN	JUL	AUG	SEP	OCT	NOV	DEC	YEAR
Mean Maximum Temp. (°F)	26.5	33.3	44.6	56.7	66.3	76.9	85.1	84.3	73.0	59.5	40.9	29.0	56.4
Mean Temp. (°F)	18.4	24.3	34.7	44.1	52.6	61.5	68.0	66.6	56.6	45.2	31.5	20.3	43.7
Mean Minimum Temp. (°F)	10.2	15.1	24.8	31.5	38.9	46.0	50.9	49.0	40.2	30.9	22.1	11.5	30.9
Extreme Maximum Temp. (°F)	53	61	73	85	89	102	100	100	94	87	66	56	102
Extreme Minimum Temp. (°F)	-33	-38	-10	14	17	29	33	28	18	8	-19	-31	-38
Days Maximum Temp. ≥ 90°F	0	0	0	0	0	3	10	9	1	0	0	0	23
Days Maximum Temp. ≤ 32°F	21	12	2	0	0	0	0	0	0	0	6	18	59
Days Minimum Temp. ≤ 32°F	30	27	27	17	5	0	0	0	4	18	27	30	185
Days Minimum Temp. ≤ 0°F	8	4	1	0	0	0	0	0	0	0	1	6	20
Heating Degree Days (base 65°F)	1,439	1,144	932	620	380	140	26	41	255	606	997	1,381	7,961
Cooling Degree Days (base 65°F)	0	0	0	0	3	39	120	107	11	0	0	0	280
Mean Precipitation (in.)	0.77	0.77	0.97	1.02	1.55	1.08	0.69	0.73	0.79	0.90	1.00	0.85	11.12
Days With ≥ 0.1" Precipitation	3	3	3	3	5	3	2	2	2	3	3	3	35
Days With ≥ 1.0" Precipitation	0	0	0	0	0	0	0	0	0	0	0	0	0
Mean Snowfall (in.)	8.9	6.3	3.9	2.5	0.4	trace	trace	trace	trace	0.8	6.0	9.6	38.4
Days With ≥ 1.0" Snow Depth	26	19	9	2	0	0	0	0	0	1	6	19	82

Jerome *Jerome County*   Elevation: 3,740 ft.   Latitude: 42° 44' N   Longitude: 114° 31' W

	JAN	FEB	MAR	APR	MAY	JUN	JUL	AUG	SEP	OCT	NOV	DEC	YEAR
Mean Maximum Temp. (°F)	35.9	42.8	52.4	61.2	70.9	81.2	90.3	89.6	78.2	65.2	48.0	37.1	62.7
Mean Temp. (°F)	27.4	32.7	40.4	47.3	56.1	65.1	72.7	71.8	61.6	50.4	37.3	28.1	49.2
Mean Minimum Temp. (°F)	18.9	22.5	28.3	33.4	41.2	48.9	55.1	54.0	44.9	35.5	26.6	19.0	35.7
Extreme Maximum Temp. (°F)	57	69	79	90	94	103	108	106	100	94	78	65	108
Extreme Minimum Temp. (°F)	-17	-13	-1	18	26	29	38	37	26	12	-4	-24	-24
Days Maximum Temp. ≥ 90°F	0	0	0	0	1	7	18	18	4	0	0	0	48
Days Maximum Temp. ≤ 32°F	10	4	0	0	0	0	0	0	0	0	2	8	24
Days Minimum Temp. ≤ 32°F	29	25	23	15	3	0	0	0	1	11	23	29	159
Days Minimum Temp. ≤ 0°F	2	1	0	0	0	0	0	0	0	0	0	2	5
Heating Degree Days (base 65°F)	1,158	906	756	525	287	96	14	16	150	450	825	1,138	6,321
Cooling Degree Days (base 65°F)	0	0	0	1	21	94	249	238	58	3	0	0	664
Mean Precipitation (in.)	1.47	1.02	1.28	0.91	1.15	0.80	0.23	0.29	0.50	0.73	1.36	1.25	10.99
Days With ≥ 0.1" Precipitation	5	3	4	3	4	3	1	1	2	2	4	4	36
Days With ≥ 1.0" Precipitation	0	0	0	0	0	0	0	0	0	0	0	0	0
Mean Snowfall (in.)	na	na	1.0	0.3	0.1	0.0	0.0	0.0	0.0	0.1	na	na	na
Days With ≥ 1.0" Snow Depth	na	na	1	0	0	0	0	0	0	0	1	na	na

Kellogg Shoshone Airport *Shoshone County*   Elevation: 2,230 ft.   Latitude: 47° 33' N   Longitude: 116° 10' W

	JAN	FEB	MAR	APR	MAY	JUN	JUL	AUG	SEP	OCT	NOV	DEC	YEAR
Mean Maximum Temp. (°F)	35.6	41.8	49.7	58.6	68.5	75.7	84.3	84.6	74.0	59.5	43.3	34.9	59.2
Mean Temp. (°F)	28.7	33.3	39.6	46.5	54.9	61.5	67.7	67.3	58.1	46.7	36.1	28.6	47.4
Mean Minimum Temp. (°F)	21.8	24.7	29.4	34.4	41.3	47.3	51.1	50.0	42.2	34.0	28.9	22.3	35.6
Extreme Maximum Temp. (°F)	56	65	78	93	101	103	106	104	100	87	69	61	106
Extreme Minimum Temp. (°F)	-19	-13	1	21	25	30	36	32	23	8	-8	-20	-20
Days Maximum Temp. ≥ 90°F	0	0	0	0	1	3	11	11	2	0	0	0	28
Days Maximum Temp. ≤ 32°F	9	3	0	0	0	0	0	0	0	0	2	10	24
Days Minimum Temp. ≤ 32°F	27	23	22	12	2	0	0	0	2	12	20	27	147
Days Minimum Temp. ≤ 0°F	1	1	0	0	0	0	0	0	0	0	0	1	3
Heating Degree Days (base 65°F)	1,117	889	782	548	319	149	49	51	218	559	860	1,122	6,663
Cooling Degree Days (base 65°F)	0	0	0	1	15	49	131	124	20	0	0	0	340
Mean Precipitation (in.)	3.81	2.85	2.97	2.59	2.75	2.29	1.46	1.41	1.66	2.36	4.15	4.26	32.56
Days With ≥ 0.1" Precipitation	11	9	9	8	8	6	4	4	5	7	11	11	93
Days With ≥ 1.0" Precipitation	0	0	0	0	0	0	0	0	0	0	0	0	0
Mean Snowfall (in.)	14.1	7.6	3.9	1.0	trace	0.0	0.0	0.0	0.0	0.1	5.9	15.3	47.9
Days With ≥ 1.0" Snow Depth	na	na	na	0	0	0	0	0	0	0	3	na	na

Lifton Pumping Station *Bear Lake County*   Elevation: 5,925 ft.   Latitude: 42° 07' N   Longitude: 111° 19' W

	JAN	FEB	MAR	APR	MAY	JUN	JUL	AUG	SEP	OCT	NOV	DEC	YEAR
Mean Maximum Temp. (°F)	29.9	33.1	40.9	51.1	61.6	72.3	80.8	79.9	69.6	57.2	41.4	31.6	54.1
Mean Temp. (°F)	18.2	19.8	29.4	40.2	50.4	59.4	66.0	63.8	54.1	43.2	30.7	20.8	41.3
Mean Minimum Temp. (°F)	6.5	6.5	17.8	29.3	39.1	46.5	51.1	47.6	38.5	29.1	20.0	9.9	28.5
Extreme Maximum Temp. (°F)	52	55	69	76	83	94	94	93	89	81	65	58	94
Extreme Minimum Temp. (°F)	-37	-41	-20	-1	20	30	29	30	19	3	-12	-33	-41
Days Maximum Temp. ≥ 90°F	0	0	0	0	0	0	1	1	0	0	0	0	2
Days Maximum Temp. ≤ 32°F	18	12	4	0	0	0	0	0	0	0	5	16	55
Days Minimum Temp. ≤ 32°F	31	28	30	20	5	0	0	0	6	21	29	31	201
Days Minimum Temp. ≤ 0°F	10	9	2	0	0	0	0	0	0	0	1	6	28
Heating Degree Days (base 65°F)	1,445	1,270	1,098	738	447	181	38	72	323	670	1,022	1,364	8,668
Cooling Degree Days (base 65°F)	0	0	0	0	0	0	19	74	44	2	0	0	139
Mean Precipitation (in.)	0.81	0.77	0.82	1.08	1.61	1.00	0.93	0.85	1.19	1.16	0.89	0.59	11.70
Days With ≥ 0.1" Precipitation	3	2	3	4	5	3	3	3	3	3	3	2	37
Days With ≥ 1.0" Precipitation	0	0	0	0	0	0	0	0	0	0	0	0	0
Mean Snowfall (in.)	8.9	7.8	4.6	2.2	0.4	0.0	trace	0.0	trace	1.4	5.9	6.7	37.9
Days With ≥ 1.0" Snow Depth	29	25	15	2	0	0	0	0	0	1	9	20	101

Lowman *Boise County*   Elevation: 3,917 ft.   Latitude: 44° 05' N   Longitude: 115° 36' W

	JAN	FEB	MAR	APR	MAY	JUN	JUL	AUG	SEP	OCT	NOV	DEC	YEAR
Mean Maximum Temp. (°F)	34.3	40.8	50.2	59.9	68.3	76.9	86.6	85.9	76.4	62.7	42.0	32.6	59.7
Mean Temp. (°F)	24.4	29.1	37.1	44.6	51.6	58.5	64.6	63.6	55.7	45.2	32.6	23.1	44.2
Mean Minimum Temp. (°F)	14.4	17.4	23.9	29.3	34.8	40.0	42.8	41.1	34.9	27.6	23.0	13.7	28.6
Extreme Maximum Temp. (°F)	50	63	75	86	95	100	103	104	101	89	70	60	104
Extreme Minimum Temp. (°F)	-24	-21	-4	12	18	25	28	20	15	10	-16	-32	-32
Days Maximum Temp. ≥ 90°F	0	0	0	0	0	2	12	11	2	0	0	0	27
Days Maximum Temp. ≤ 32°F	10	3	0	0	0	0	0	0	0	0	3	13	29
Days Minimum Temp. ≤ 32°F	31	27	28	21	11	4	1	3	12	24	26	30	218
Days Minimum Temp. ≤ 0°F	6	3	0	0	0	0	0	0	0	0	1	4	14
Heating Degree Days (base 65°F)	1,253	1,006	858	604	412	204	66	85	277	607	966	1,291	7,629
Cooling Degree Days (base 65°F)	0	0	0	0	1	15	48	45	4	0	0	0	113
Mean Precipitation (in.)	3.42	3.09	2.47	2.32	2.06	1.52	0.76	0.74	1.26	1.52	3.43	3.62	26.21
Days With ≥ 0.1" Precipitation	8	8	7	6	6	4	2	2	3	4	9	8	67
Days With ≥ 1.0" Precipitation	1	0	0	0	0	0	0	0	0	0	0	0	1
Mean Snowfall (in.)	na	17.6	na	1.6	trace	trace	0.0	0.0	trace	0.5	na	23.8	na
Days With ≥ 1.0" Snow Depth	30	27	20	1	0	0	0	0	0	0	na	25	na

Mackay USFS *Custer County*   Elevation: 5,895 ft.   Latitude: 43° 55' N   Longitude: 113° 38' W

	JAN	FEB	MAR	APR	MAY	JUN	JUL	AUG	SEP	OCT	NOV	DEC	YEAR
Mean Maximum Temp. (°F)	30.0	35.7	43.7	55.0	65.0	74.8	83.1	82.3	72.8	59.7	41.2	30.2	56.1
Mean Temp. (°F)	18.1	23.1	31.6	41.3	50.3	58.5	65.2	64.0	54.9	44.0	29.6	18.9	41.6
Mean Minimum Temp. (°F)	6.2	10.4	19.5	27.5	35.4	42.2	47.2	45.6	37.0	28.7	18.1	7.5	27.1
Extreme Maximum Temp. (°F)	51	56	68	85	86	98	99	96	92	84	65	56	99
Extreme Minimum Temp. (°F)	-25	-33	-8	5	16	19	31	27	10	-1	-17	-32	-33
Days Maximum Temp. ≥ 90°F	0	0	0	0	0	1	5	4	0	0	0	0	10
Days Maximum Temp. ≤ 32°F	18	9	2	0	0	0	0	0	0	0	6	18	53
Days Minimum Temp. ≤ 32°F	30	28	30	23	9	2	0	1	7	20	28	30	208
Days Minimum Temp. ≤ 0°F	9	5	1	0	0	0	0	0	0	0	1	7	23
Heating Degree Days (base 65°F)	1,448	1,178	1,026	705	452	204	59	77	299	644	1,055	1,421	8,568
Cooling Degree Days (base 65°F)	0	0	0	0	1	14	65	48	3	0	0	0	131
Mean Precipitation (in.)	0.65	0.54	0.80	0.66	1.22	1.33	1.11	0.90	0.72	0.52	0.67	0.73	9.85
Days With ≥ 0.1" Precipitation	2	1	2	2	3	4	3	3	2	2	2	2	28
Days With ≥ 1.0" Precipitation	0	0	0	0	0	0	0	0	0	0	0	0	0
Mean Snowfall (in.)	na	na	na	trace	trace	trace	0.0	0.0	trace	0.2	na	na	na
Days With ≥ 1.0" Snow Depth	na	na	na	0	0	0	0	0	0	0	na	na	na

Malad City *Oneida County*   Elevation: 4,468 ft.   Latitude: 42° 09' N   Longitude: 112° 17' W

	JAN	FEB	MAR	APR	MAY	JUN	JUL	AUG	SEP	OCT	NOV	DEC	YEAR
Mean Maximum Temp. (°F)	32.5	39.2	50.1	59.9	69.3	80.1	89.0	88.1	77.8	64.3	46.3	34.3	60.9
Mean Temp. (°F)	22.5	27.5	37.3	45.0	53.3	61.9	68.9	68.0	58.3	46.9	34.2	23.7	45.6
Mean Minimum Temp. (°F)	12.4	15.7	24.4	30.1	37.4	43.7	48.8	47.8	38.7	29.5	22.0	13.0	30.3
Extreme Maximum Temp. (°F)	50	63	75	85	89	102	102	102	96	89	73	63	102
Extreme Minimum Temp. (°F)	-33	-35	-10	7	17	27	32	26	18	11	-18	-32	-35
Days Maximum Temp. ≥ 90°F	0	0	0	0	0	4	16	15	2	0	0	0	37
Days Maximum Temp. ≤ 32°F	14	6	1	0	0	0	0	0	0	0	2	12	35
Days Minimum Temp. ≤ 32°F	30	27	27	19	7	1	0	0	6	21	27	30	195
Days Minimum Temp. ≤ 0°F	7	4	0	0	0	0	0	0	0	0	1	5	17
Heating Degree Days (base 65°F)	1,312	1,054	853	593	356	127	18	24	210	554	917	1,273	7,291
Cooling Degree Days (base 65°F)	0	0	0	0	1	39	143	132	19	0	0	0	334
Mean Precipitation (in.)	1.34	1.01	1.20	1.25	2.03	1.18	1.11	0.97	1.11	1.19	1.08	1.08	14.55
Days With ≥ 0.1" Precipitation	4	3	4	4	6	3	2	3	3	3	4	4	43
Days With ≥ 1.0" Precipitation	0	0	0	0	0	0	0	0	0	0	0	0	0
Mean Snowfall (in.)	10.5	7.8	3.7	1.5	0.2	trace	trace	trace	trace	0.6	5.6	9.7	39.6
Days With ≥ 1.0" Snow Depth	24	18	8	0	0	0	0	0	0	0	5	17	72

Malta 4 ESE *Cassia County*   Elevation: 4,589 ft.   Latitude: 42° 18' N   Longitude: 113° 18' W

	JAN	FEB	MAR	APR	MAY	JUN	JUL	AUG	SEP	OCT	NOV	DEC	YEAR
Mean Maximum Temp. (°F)	36.9	43.0	52.2	61.3	69.7	80.0	88.9	88.5	77.7	64.8	48.0	38.1	62.4
Mean Temp. (°F)	26.8	32.2	39.7	46.6	54.2	62.2	69.5	68.6	58.9	48.4	36.2	27.4	47.6
Mean Minimum Temp. (°F)	16.7	21.4	27.1	31.9	38.6	44.3	50.0	48.6	40.0	31.9	24.3	16.7	32.6
Extreme Maximum Temp. (°F)	60	71	80	86	93	102	111	105	99	90	73	68	111
Extreme Minimum Temp. (°F)	-25	-26	-4	13	16	26	32	28	14	8	-13	-29	-29
Days Maximum Temp. ≥ 90°F	0	0	0	0	0	4	17	16	3	0	0	0	40
Days Maximum Temp. ≤ 32°F	9	4	0	0	0	0	0	0	0	0	2	7	22
Days Minimum Temp. ≤ 32°F	29	25	23	16	6	1	0	0	5	15	24	29	173
Days Minimum Temp. ≤ 0°F	3	2	0	0	0	0	0	0	0	0	1	3	9
Heating Degree Days (base 65°F)	1,177	920	779	545	332	129	21	27	201	508	858	1,159	6,656
Cooling Degree Days (base 65°F)	0	0	0	0	5	45	155	149	27	1	0	0	382
Mean Precipitation (in.)	0.80	0.63	1.00	1.12	1.73	1.22	0.91	0.87	0.90	0.76	0.76	0.68	11.38
Days With ≥ 0.1" Precipitation	3	3	3	4	6	4	3	3	3	3	3	3	41
Days With ≥ 1.0" Precipitation	0	0	0	0	0	0	0	0	0	0	0	0	0
Mean Snowfall (in.)	na	2.1	2.0	0.5	0.4	0.0	0.0	0.0	trace	trace	1.9	na	na
Days With ≥ 1.0" Snow Depth	14	8	2	0	0	0	0	0	0	0	4	11	39

Massacre Rocks State Park *Power County*   Elevation: 4,192 ft.   Latitude: 42° 40' N   Longitude: 113° 00' W

	JAN	FEB	MAR	APR	MAY	JUN	JUL	AUG	SEP	OCT	NOV	DEC	YEAR
Mean Maximum Temp. (°F)	36.0	42.6	52.6	62.1	70.7	81.8	90.9	90.5	80.5	66.2	47.7	37.8	63.3
Mean Temp. (°F)	26.7	32.1	40.5	47.9	55.7	64.9	72.4	71.6	62.1	50.2	36.8	28.1	49.1
Mean Minimum Temp. (°F)	17.2	21.6	28.3	33.7	40.7	47.9	53.8	52.6	43.7	34.2	26.0	18.4	34.8
Extreme Maximum Temp. (°F)	58	71	79	90	94	105	106	108	101	90	77	67	108
Extreme Minimum Temp. (°F)	-30	-24	-10	15	15	29	35	31	21	12	-8	-26	-30
Days Maximum Temp. ≥ 90°F	0	0	0	0	1	7	19	19	6	0	0	0	52
Days Maximum Temp. ≤ 32°F	11	4	0	0	0	0	0	0	0	0	3	8	26
Days Minimum Temp. ≤ 32°F	29	24	22	13	3	0	0	0	2	12	22	28	155
Days Minimum Temp. ≤ 0°F	4	1	0	0	0	0	0	0	0	0	1	2	8
Heating Degree Days (base 65°F)	1,182	922	753	507	292	88	11	13	134	453	831	1,137	6,323
Cooling Degree Days (base 65°F)	0	0	0	2	13	93	246	247	60	1	0	0	662
Mean Precipitation (in.)	1.11	1.03	1.35	1.33	1.66	0.93	0.69	0.50	0.78	0.93	1.21	1.06	12.58
Days With ≥ 0.1" Precipitation	4	3	4	4	4	3	1	1	2	3	3	3	35
Days With ≥ 1.0" Precipitation	0	0	0	0	0	0	0	0	0	0	0	0	0
Mean Snowfall (in.)	na	3.4	2.2	0.9	0.5	0.0	0.0	0.0	trace	0.3	na	5.1	na
Days With ≥ 1.0" Snow Depth	14	7	3	0	0	0	0	0	0	0	4	11	39

McCall *Valley County*   Elevation: 5,022 ft.   Latitude: 44° 53' N   Longitude: 116° 06' W

	JAN	FEB	MAR	APR	MAY	JUN	JUL	AUG	SEP	OCT	NOV	DEC	YEAR
Mean Maximum Temp. (°F)	32.0	37.6	43.8	51.9	62.2	70.7	80.2	80.7	70.5	58.3	40.4	31.8	55.0
Mean Temp. (°F)	22.4	26.2	32.2	39.4	48.1	55.1	61.6	60.8	51.8	42.4	31.4	23.0	41.2
Mean Minimum Temp. (°F)	12.7	14.7	20.6	26.8	33.9	39.4	42.9	40.9	33.1	26.5	22.3	14.1	27.3
Extreme Maximum Temp. (°F)	49	59	66	84	88	93	99	98	94	85	68	49	99
Extreme Minimum Temp. (°F)	-26	-23	-13	-2	15	22	22	20	15	4	-14	-31	-31
Days Maximum Temp. ≥ 90°F	0	0	0	0	0	0	2	3	0	0	0	0	5
Days Maximum Temp. ≤ 32°F	15	6	1	0	0	0	0	0	0	0	5	15	42
Days Minimum Temp. ≤ 32°F	30	28	30	25	14	5	1	3	14	25	27	30	232
Days Minimum Temp. ≤ 0°F	6	4	1	0	0	0	0	0	0	0	1	4	16
Heating Degree Days (base 65°F)	1,315	1,090	1,009	762	520	298	130	147	390	694	1,002	1,296	8,653
Cooling Degree Days (base 65°F)	0	0	0	0	1	5	26	24	2	0	0	0	58
Mean Precipitation (in.)	3.42	2.86	2.55	2.08	2.31	2.18	1.03	1.05	1.50	1.73	3.31	3.58	27.60
Days With ≥ 0.1" Precipitation	10	8	8	6	7	6	3	3	4	4	10	10	79
Days With ≥ 1.0" Precipitation	0	0	0	0	0	0	0	0	0	0	0	0	0
Mean Snowfall (in.)	34.7	25.9	16.0	5.7	0.8	trace	0.0	0.0	trace	2.2	21.1	32.5	138.9
Days With ≥ 1.0" Snow Depth	31	28	30	12	0	0	0	0	0	1	15	30	147

Minidoka Dam *Minidoka County*   Elevation: 4,209 ft.   Latitude: 42° 40' N   Longitude: 113° 29' W

	JAN	FEB	MAR	APR	MAY	JUN	JUL	AUG	SEP	OCT	NOV	DEC	YEAR
Mean Maximum Temp. (°F)	34.6	41.0	50.8	59.3	68.6	79.0	87.4	87.3	76.8	63.6	46.4	35.7	60.9
Mean Temp. (°F)	25.8	31.0	39.3	46.2	54.8	63.8	70.9	70.3	60.7	49.4	36.3	26.8	47.9
Mean Minimum Temp. (°F)	16.9	20.9	27.7	33.1	41.1	48.6	54.4	53.2	44.5	35.1	26.2	17.8	35.0
Extreme Maximum Temp. (°F)	58	69	77	87	90	100	106	105	99	88	75	67	106
Extreme Minimum Temp. (°F)	-26	-29	-7	16	18	30	36	33	23	6	-6	-26	-29
Days Maximum Temp. ≥ 90°F	0	0	0	0	0	4	13	13	2	0	0	0	32
Days Maximum Temp. ≤ 32°F	11	5	1	0	0	0	0	0	0	0	2	10	29
Days Minimum Temp. ≤ 32°F	29	26	23	14	3	0	0	0	2	10	23	29	159
Days Minimum Temp. ≤ 0°F	3	1	0	0	0	0	0	0	0	0	0	3	7
Heating Degree Days (base 65°F)	1,209	955	792	557	316	105	16	19	165	477	855	1,178	6,644
Cooling Degree Days (base 65°F)	0	0	0	1	11	74	202	199	50	1	0	0	538
Mean Precipitation (in.)	1.06	0.80	1.05	0.97	1.17	0.91	0.35	0.38	0.69	0.67	1.09	0.96	10.10
Days With ≥ 0.1" Precipitation	3	3	4	3	4	3	1	1	2	2	4	3	33
Days With ≥ 1.0" Precipitation	0	0	0	0	0	0	0	0	0	0	0	0	0
Mean Snowfall (in.)	6.2	4.1	2.4	0.8	0.2	trace	0.0	0.0	0.0	0.3	3.4	5.5	22.9
Days With ≥ 1.0" Snow Depth	15	10	3	0	0	0	0	0	0	0	3	11	42

Moscow University of Idaho *Latah County*   Elevation: 2,657 ft.   Latitude: 46° 44' N   Longitude: 116° 58' W

	JAN	FEB	MAR	APR	MAY	JUN	JUL	AUG	SEP	OCT	NOV	DEC	YEAR
Mean Maximum Temp. (°F)	35.5	41.4	48.8	57.1	65.9	73.3	82.7	84.1	74.3	60.4	43.4	35.5	58.5
Mean Temp. (°F)	29.4	34.2	40.0	46.2	53.3	59.3	65.6	66.5	58.6	48.2	36.8	29.6	47.3
Mean Minimum Temp. (°F)	23.2	26.8	31.1	35.2	40.6	45.3	48.6	48.8	42.8	36.0	30.2	23.5	36.0
Extreme Maximum Temp. (°F)	58	66	73	88	92	97	103	102	100	88	73	59	103
Extreme Minimum Temp. (°F)	-22	-26	0	18	24	28	31	30	21	14	-11	-29	-29
Days Maximum Temp. ≥ 90°F	0	0	0	0	0	1	7	9	2	0	0	0	19
Days Maximum Temp. ≤ 32°F	9	3	0	0	0	0	0	0	0	0	3	10	25
Days Minimum Temp. ≤ 32°F	25	21	19	11	4	1	0	0	3	10	18	26	138
Days Minimum Temp. ≤ 0°F	2	1	0	0	0	0	0	0	0	0	0	1	4
Heating Degree Days (base 65°F)	1,097	865	769	559	363	189	66	59	211	514	839	1,093	6,624
Cooling Degree Days (base 65°F)	0	0	0	0	8	21	87	112	29	2	0	0	259
Mean Precipitation (in.)	3.18	2.50	2.55	2.50	2.57	1.91	1.18	1.19	1.26	2.04	3.59	3.16	27.63
Days With ≥ 0.1" Precipitation	9	7	8	7	6	6	3	3	4	5	10	8	76
Days With ≥ 1.0" Precipitation	0	0	0	0	0	0	0	0	0	0	0	0	0
Mean Snowfall (in.)	15.1	8.2	4.3	1.1	trace	0.0	trace	0.0	trace	0.2	6.5	14.8	50.2
Days With ≥ 1.0" Snow Depth	17	9	3	0	0	0	0	0	0	0	4	14	47

Mountain Home *Elmore County*   Elevation: 3,139 ft.   Latitude: 43° 08' N   Longitude: 115° 43' W

	JAN	FEB	MAR	APR	MAY	JUN	JUL	AUG	SEP	OCT	NOV	DEC	YEAR
Mean Maximum Temp. (°F)	37.8	45.0	53.8	62.3	71.8	82.5	91.7	91.4	79.7	66.3	48.8	38.0	64.1
Mean Temp. (°F)	29.3	34.8	41.8	48.6	57.3	66.5	74.2	73.4	62.7	50.8	38.2	29.2	50.6
Mean Minimum Temp. (°F)	20.8	24.6	29.7	34.9	42.7	50.4	56.6	55.4	45.6	35.3	27.5	20.4	37.0
Extreme Maximum Temp. (°F)	60	70	80	94	98	107	112	109	102	94	80	60	112
Extreme Minimum Temp. (°F)	-16	-13	4	16	21	29	36	35	22	12	-3	-25	-25
Days Maximum Temp. ≥ 90°F	0	0	0	0	2	9	21	20	6	0	0	0	58
Days Maximum Temp. ≤ 32°F	8	2	0	0	0	0	0	0	0	0	2	7	19
Days Minimum Temp. ≤ 32°F	27	23	21	12	2	0	0	0	1	11	21	27	145
Days Minimum Temp. ≤ 0°F	1	1	0	0	0	0	0	0	0	0	0	1	3
Heating Degree Days (base 65°F)	1,099	844	713	489	262	81	11	12	133	438	797	1,104	5,983
Cooling Degree Days (base 65°F)	0	0	0	4	40	133	307	296	84	4	0	0	868
Mean Precipitation (in.)	1.41	0.92	1.19	0.93	0.89	0.70	0.40	0.21	0.68	0.73	1.40	1.42	10.88
Days With ≥ 0.1" Precipitation	4	3	4	3	3	2	1	1	2	2	5	5	35
Days With ≥ 1.0" Precipitation	0	0	0	0	0	0	0	0	0	0	0	0	0
Mean Snowfall (in.)	na	1.6	0.3	0.0	trace	0.0	0.0	0.0	0.0	trace	1.5	na	na
Days With ≥ 1.0" Snow Depth	na	4	0	0	0	0	0	0	0	0	1	na	na

New Meadows Ranger Station *Adams County*   Elevation: 3,868 ft.   Latitude: 44° 58' N   Longitude: 116° 17' W

	JAN	FEB	MAR	APR	MAY	JUN	JUL	AUG	SEP	OCT	NOV	DEC	YEAR
Mean Maximum Temp. (°F)	30.4	37.4	46.0	55.1	64.6	73.2	83.1	83.6	73.2	60.7	41.9	30.6	56.6
Mean Temp. (°F)	19.4	24.3	32.9	40.8	48.7	56.2	62.7	62.2	52.9	42.6	30.8	19.7	41.1
Mean Minimum Temp. (°F)	8.2	11.1	19.7	26.5	32.8	39.2	42.2	40.5	32.5	24.4	19.9	8.9	25.5
Extreme Maximum Temp. (°F)	47	62	73	86	90	99	103	100	96	89	72	54	103
Extreme Minimum Temp. (°F)	-41	-40	-17	7	12	20	29	18	11	8	-19	-45	-45
Days Maximum Temp. ≥ 90°F	0	0	0	0	0	2	7	7	1	0	0	0	17
Days Maximum Temp. ≤ 32°F	15	6	1	0	0	0	0	0	0	0	4	15	41
Days Minimum Temp. ≤ 32°F	28	26	29	23	14	5	2	3	15	26	26	27	224
Days Minimum Temp. ≤ 0°F	9	6	1	0	0	0	0	0	0	0	2	7	25
Heating Degree Days (base 65°F)	1,409	1,144	989	719	499	271	111	116	359	689	1,020	1,399	8,725
Cooling Degree Days (base 65°F)	na	0	0	0	1	8	33	33	3	0	0	na	na
Mean Precipitation (in.)	3.10	2.56	2.42	2.08	2.26	1.96	0.91	0.81	1.30	1.52	2.80	3.42	25.14
Days With ≥ 0.1" Precipitation	6	6	5	4	5	4	2	2	3	3	6	6	52
Days With ≥ 1.0" Precipitation	0	0	0	0	0	0	0	0	0	0	0	0	0
Mean Snowfall (in.)	21.4	13.9	5.7	1.7	0.3	0.0	0.0	0.0	trace	0.3	9.3	20.0	72.6
Days With ≥ 1.0" Snow Depth	24	22	15	2	0	0	0	0	0	0	7	20	90

Nezperce *Lewis County*   Elevation: 3,238 ft.   Latitude: 46° 14' N   Longitude: 116° 15' W

	JAN	FEB	MAR	APR	MAY	JUN	JUL	AUG	SEP	OCT	NOV	DEC	YEAR
Mean Maximum Temp. (°F)	34.9	41.2	47.6	55.1	63.1	70.6	79.7	80.8	70.9	58.0	42.4	34.8	56.6
Mean Temp. (°F)	28.3	33.1	38.4	44.3	51.2	57.8	64.3	64.7	56.3	46.3	35.2	28.4	45.7
Mean Minimum Temp. (°F)	21.7	25.1	29.1	33.5	39.3	44.9	48.8	48.6	41.6	34.5	28.0	22.0	34.7
Extreme Maximum Temp. (°F)	61	67	75	87	90	94	98	102	97	85	71	59	102
Extreme Minimum Temp. (°F)	-19	-19	-1	19	23	29	32	25	21	0	-13	-27	-27
Days Maximum Temp. ≥ 90°F	0	0	0	0	0	1	4	5	1	0	0	0	11
Days Maximum Temp. ≤ 32°F	10	4	1	0	0	0	0	0	0	0	3	11	29
Days Minimum Temp. ≤ 32°F	27	23	22	15	5	0	0	0	3	12	21	27	155
Days Minimum Temp. ≤ 0°F	2	1	0	0	0	0	0	0	0	0	0	1	4
Heating Degree Days (base 65°F)	1,130	893	818	614	424	228	86	80	266	574	887	1,127	7,127
Cooling Degree Days (base 65°F)	0	0	0	0	5	16	62	78	15	0	0	0	176
Mean Precipitation (in.)	1.52	1.30	1.85	2.14	2.97	2.03	1.27	1.12	1.28	1.43	1.95	1.41	20.27
Days With ≥ 0.1" Precipitation	5	5	7	7	8	6	4	3	4	4	7	5	65
Days With ≥ 1.0" Precipitation	0	0	0	0	0	0	0	0	0	0	0	0	0
Mean Snowfall (in.)	12.3	7.3	6.1	2.7	0.3	trace	trace	0.0	trace	1.3	7.5	9.5	47.0
Days With ≥ 1.0" Snow Depth	19	11	4	1	0	0	0	0	0	1	7	16	59

Oakley *Cassia County*   Elevation: 4,557 ft.   Latitude: 42° 14' N   Longitude: 113° 54' W

	JAN	FEB	MAR	APR	MAY	JUN	JUL	AUG	SEP	OCT	NOV	DEC	YEAR
Mean Maximum Temp. (°F)	38.0	43.9	51.2	58.7	67.0	76.4	83.8	84.0	74.7	63.4	47.6	38.8	60.6
Mean Temp. (°F)	29.1	33.9	40.1	46.0	53.8	62.1	69.1	68.9	59.8	49.8	37.7	29.6	48.3
Mean Minimum Temp. (°F)	20.0	23.9	28.9	33.3	40.5	47.9	54.3	53.8	45.0	36.2	27.7	20.4	36.0
Extreme Maximum Temp. (°F)	61	70	75	86	88	96	101	100	92	90	73	65	101
Extreme Minimum Temp. (°F)	-16	-18	4	12	20	28	33	34	20	9	-8	-24	-24
Days Maximum Temp. ≥ 90°F	0	0	0	0	0	2	5	6	1	0	0	0	14
Days Maximum Temp. ≤ 32°F	8	3	0	0	0	0	0	0	0	0	2	7	20
Days Minimum Temp. ≤ 32°F	27	23	21	14	4	0	0	0	2	9	20	28	148
Days Minimum Temp. ≤ 0°F	2	1	0	0	0	0	0	0	0	0	0	1	4
Heating Degree Days (base 65°F)	1,107	872	767	563	346	133	24	28	181	466	813	1,091	6,391
Cooling Degree Days (base 65°F)	0	0	0	0	7	49	155	164	38	0	0	0	414
Mean Precipitation (in.)	0.87	0.59	1.11	1.10	1.75	1.30	0.84	0.76	0.99	0.75	0.81	0.71	11.58
Days With ≥ 0.1" Precipitation	3	2	3	4	5	4	3	2	3	2	3	3	37
Days With ≥ 1.0" Precipitation	0	0	0	0	0	0	0	0	0	0	0	0	0
Mean Snowfall (in.)	7.2	4.5	3.4	1.6	0.8	0.0	0.0	0.0	trace	0.1	3.8	5.7	27.1
Days With ≥ 1.0" Snow Depth	7	3	1	0	0	0	0	0	0	0	2	6	19

Parma Experiment Station *Canyon County* Elevation: 2,290 ft. Latitude: 43° 48' N Longitude: 116° 57' W

	JAN	FEB	MAR	APR	MAY	JUN	JUL	AUG	SEP	OCT	NOV	DEC	YEAR
Mean Maximum Temp. (°F)	35.6	44.0	55.6	64.2	72.8	81.6	90.7	90.5	79.6	66.5	48.7	37.2	63.9
Mean Temp. (°F)	27.3	34.2	42.9	49.8	58.1	65.8	72.4	71.2	61.3	49.9	37.6	28.6	49.9
Mean Minimum Temp. (°F)	18.8	24.3	30.0	35.4	43.4	49.9	54.2	51.9	42.8	33.3	26.4	19.9	35.9
Extreme Maximum Temp. (°F)	61	67	84	93	100	106	106	106	102	95	70	64	106
Extreme Minimum Temp. (°F)	-25	-25	2	19	22	31	37	34	24	14	-2	-27	-27
Days Maximum Temp. ≥ 90°F	0	0	0	0	2	7	19	19	5	0	0	0	52
Days Maximum Temp. ≤ 32°F	11	3	0	0	0	0	0	0	0	0	1	8	23
Days Minimum Temp. ≤ 32°F	28	24	20	11	2	0	0	0	2	14	23	28	152
Days Minimum Temp. ≤ 0°F	3	1	0	0	0	0	0	0	0	0	0	2	6
Heating Degree Days (base 65°F)	1,164	863	680	451	236	79	15	19	151	461	816	1,123	6,058
Cooling Degree Days (base 65°F)	0	0	0	2	32	102	242	218	51	1	0	0	648
Mean Precipitation (in.)	1.49	0.96	1.25	0.95	1.14	0.89	0.35	0.41	0.69	0.65	1.28	1.35	11.41
Days With ≥ 0.1" Precipitation	5	3	4	4	4	3	1	1	2	2	4	5	38
Days With ≥ 1.0" Precipitation	0	0	0	0	0	0	0	0	0	0	0	0	0
Mean Snowfall (in.)	5.9	1.9	0.7	trace	0.0	0.0	0.0	0.0	0.0	trace	2.5	4.9	15.9
Days With ≥ 1.0" Snow Depth	14	6	1	0	0	0	0	0	0	0	2	8	31

Paul 1 ENE *Minidoka County* Elevation: 4,146 ft. Latitude: 42° 38' N Longitude: 113° 46' W

	JAN	FEB	MAR	APR	MAY	JUN	JUL	AUG	SEP	OCT	NOV	DEC	YEAR
Mean Maximum Temp. (°F)	35.0	41.8	50.6	59.2	68.1	78.1	86.9	86.9	76.0	63.5	46.9	36.6	60.8
Mean Temp. (°F)	26.3	31.7	38.9	45.8	54.3	62.9	70.0	68.9	58.9	48.2	36.1	27.2	47.4
Mean Minimum Temp. (°F)	17.5	21.5	27.1	32.4	40.4	47.7	53.0	50.8	41.7	32.9	25.3	17.8	34.0
Extreme Maximum Temp. (°F)	60	68	78	88	92	102	104	104	100	89	74	65	104
Extreme Minimum Temp. (°F)	-20	-16	-3	18	21	30	35	32	24	8	-3	-25	-25
Days Maximum Temp. ≥ 90°F	0	0	0	0	0	4	13	12	2	0	0	0	31
Days Maximum Temp. ≤ 32°F	11	5	1	0	0	0	0	0	0	0	3	10	30
Days Minimum Temp. ≤ 32°F	29	26	25	16	3	0	0	0	3	15	25	29	171
Days Minimum Temp. ≤ 0°F	3	1	0	0	0	0	0	0	0	0	0	2	6
Heating Degree Days (base 65°F)	1,193	935	802	569	334	124	23	31	204	513	860	1,165	6,753
Cooling Degree Days (base 65°F)	0	0	0	1	12	70	191	175	34	1	0	0	484
Mean Precipitation (in.)	1.03	0.67	0.96	0.88	1.34	0.93	0.42	0.39	0.67	0.66	1.04	0.93	9.92
Days With ≥ 0.1" Precipitation	3	2	3	3	4	3	1	1	2	2	3	3	30
Days With ≥ 1.0" Precipitation	0	0	0	0	0	0	0	0	0	0	0	0	0
Mean Snowfall (in.)	4.5	2.4	1.7	0.6	0.4	0.0	0.0	0.0	0.0	trace	2.4	4.7	16.7
Days With ≥ 1.0" Snow Depth	8	2	1	0	0	0	0	0	0	0	2	6	19

Payette *Payette County* Elevation: 2,148 ft. Latitude: 44° 05' N Longitude: 116° 56' W

	JAN	FEB	MAR	APR	MAY	JUN	JUL	AUG	SEP	OCT	NOV	DEC	YEAR
Mean Maximum Temp. (°F)	36.8	46.1	58.0	66.5	75.1	83.5	91.7	91.0	80.9	68.0	51.0	38.9	65.6
Mean Temp. (°F)	28.2	35.5	44.8	51.5	59.9	67.7	74.3	73.0	63.3	51.8	39.7	30.1	51.6
Mean Minimum Temp. (°F)	19.6	24.9	31.6	36.5	44.5	51.8	57.0	55.0	45.7	35.4	28.3	21.2	37.6
Extreme Maximum Temp. (°F)	59	70	81	92	97	104	106	109	100	96	71	63	109
Extreme Minimum Temp. (°F)	-21	-23	8	19	24	31	38	37	25	17	-2	-21	-23
Days Maximum Temp. ≥ 90°F	0	0	0	0	2	8	21	20	5	0	0	0	56
Days Maximum Temp. ≤ 32°F	10	3	0	0	0	0	0	0	0	0	1	6	20
Days Minimum Temp. ≤ 32°F	27	23	17	9	2	0	0	0	2	11	21	27	139
Days Minimum Temp. ≤ 0°F	3	1	0	0	0	0	0	0	0	0	0	1	5
Heating Degree Days (base 65°F)	1,134	827	619	401	188	51	6	10	113	406	753	1,076	5,584
Cooling Degree Days (base 65°F)	0	0	0	3	41	136	303	278	80	3	0	0	844
Mean Precipitation (in.)	1.55	1.10	1.09	0.78	0.98	0.80	0.32	0.32	0.49	0.63	1.49	1.67	11.22
Days With ≥ 0.1" Precipitation	5	4	4	3	3	2	1	1	1	2	5	5	36
Days With ≥ 1.0" Precipitation	0	0	0	0	0	0	0	0	0	0	0	0	0
Mean Snowfall (in.)	na	na	0.2	trace	0.0	0.0	0.0	0.0	0.0	trace	1.2	na	na
Days With ≥ 1.0" Snow Depth	na	na	3	0	0	0	0	0	0	0	0	na	na

Picabo *Blaine County* Elevation: 4,829 ft. Latitude: 43° 18' N Longitude: 114° 04' W

	JAN	FEB	MAR	APR	MAY	JUN	JUL	AUG	SEP	OCT	NOV	DEC	YEAR
Mean Maximum Temp. (°F)	30.8	36.2	45.1	56.6	66.6	76.5	86.0	85.4	74.0	61.5	43.1	32.0	57.8
Mean Temp. (°F)	18.9	23.6	32.6	41.8	50.6	58.8	66.2	65.5	55.6	44.9	31.0	20.5	42.5
Mean Minimum Temp. (°F)	7.1	10.9	20.1	27.1	34.5	41.1	46.3	45.5	37.1	28.2	18.8	9.0	27.1
Extreme Maximum Temp. (°F)	53	63	72	86	91	98	102	100	99	90	67	62	102
Extreme Minimum Temp. (°F)	-28	-30	-11	9	14	24	29	27	17	3	-15	-37	-37
Days Maximum Temp. ≥ 90°F	0	0	0	0	0	3	11	9	1	0	0	0	24
Days Maximum Temp. ≤ 32°F	16	8	2	0	0	0	0	0	0	0	4	15	45
Days Minimum Temp. ≤ 32°F	31	28	30	24	12	3	0	0	8	22	29	31	218
Days Minimum Temp. ≤ 0°F	10	6	1	0	0	0	0	0	0	0	1	7	25
Heating Degree Days (base 65°F)	1,422	1,163	998	688	441	203	53	60	286	618	1,014	1,372	8,318
Cooling Degree Days (base 65°F)	0	0	0	0	2	24	91	84	10	0	0	0	211
Mean Precipitation (in.)	1.66	1.37	1.33	0.92	1.26	1.00	0.47	0.38	0.71	0.86	1.56	1.62	13.14
Days With ≥ 0.1" Precipitation	5	4	5	4	4	3	2	2	2	3	5	5	44
Days With ≥ 1.0" Precipitation	0	0	0	0	0	0	0	0	0	0	0	0	0
Mean Snowfall (in.)	11.8	9.7	3.4	1.2	0.5	trace	0.0	0.0	trace	0.4	6.7	10.8	44.5
Days With ≥ 1.0" Snow Depth	27	24	13	2	0	0	0	0	0	0	8	20	94

Porthill *Boundary County*   Elevation: 1,774 ft.   Latitude: 49° 00' N   Longitude: 116° 30' W

	JAN	FEB	MAR	APR	MAY	JUN	JUL	AUG	SEP	OCT	NOV	DEC	YEAR
Mean Maximum Temp. (°F)	33.0	38.5	48.1	58.9	67.9	74.3	81.3	81.5	70.8	56.3	41.5	33.5	57.1
Mean Temp. (°F)	25.5	30.2	37.7	46.4	54.5	60.9	66.2	65.3	55.6	44.2	34.1	26.5	45.6
Mean Minimum Temp. (°F)	18.1	21.8	27.2	33.9	41.1	47.5	51.1	48.9	40.4	32.1	26.6	19.5	34.0
Extreme Maximum Temp. (°F)	53	57	68	84	94	97	100	101	97	79	67	59	101
Extreme Minimum Temp. (°F)	-24	-15	-8	15	23	28	37	33	24	11	-11	-20	-24
Days Maximum Temp. ≥ 90°F	0	0	0	0	0	2	6	6	0	0	0	0	14
Days Maximum Temp. ≤ 32°F	13	5	1	0	0	0	0	0	0	0	4	13	36
Days Minimum Temp. ≤ 32°F	29	26	25	13	2	0	0	0	3	17	22	29	166
Days Minimum Temp. ≤ 0°F	3	2	0	0	0	0	0	0	0	0	0	2	7
Heating Degree Days (base 65°F)	1,217	977	839	552	323	152	58	69	280	637	922	1,187	7,213
Cooling Degree Days (base 65°F)	0	0	0	0	8	35	102	82	6	0	0	0	233
Mean Precipitation (in.)	2.16	1.70	1.50	1.42	1.89	1.85	1.29	1.24	1.28	1.41	2.79	2.50	21.03
Days With ≥ 0.1" Precipitation	7	6	5	5	6	6	4	4	4	5	9	7	68
Days With ≥ 1.0" Precipitation	0	0	0	0	0	0	0	0	0	0	0	0	0
Mean Snowfall (in.)	na	5.8	2.7	0.1	0.0	0.0	0.0	0.0	0.0	0.2	*6.3*	na	na
Days With ≥ 1.0" Snow Depth	20	13	4	0	0	0	0	0	0	0	5	16	58

Potlatch 3 NNE *Latah County*   Elevation: 2,598 ft.   Latitude: 46° 58' N   Longitude: 116° 53' W

	JAN	FEB	MAR	APR	MAY	JUN	JUL	AUG	SEP	OCT	NOV	DEC	YEAR
Mean Maximum Temp. (°F)	35.7	41.7	48.3	56.2	64.7	71.5	80.3	81.7	72.3	59.4	43.2	35.8	57.6
Mean Temp. (°F)	28.8	33.5	38.7	44.6	51.3	57.2	62.6	62.7	54.6	45.2	35.9	29.0	45.3
Mean Minimum Temp. (°F)	21.8	25.3	29.0	32.9	37.9	42.8	44.9	43.7	37.0	31.0	28.5	22.1	33.1
Extreme Maximum Temp. (°F)	58	65	75	89	95	95	102	102	101	90	70	57	102
Extreme Minimum Temp. (°F)	-30	-32	-5	17	20	25	27	25	16	9	-20	-29	-32
Days Maximum Temp. ≥ 90°F	0	0	0	0	0	1	5	6	1	0	0	0	13
Days Maximum Temp. ≤ 32°F	10	4	0	0	0	0	0	0	0	0	2	9	25
Days Minimum Temp. ≤ 32°F	26	22	23	15	7	2	1	1	8	18	21	26	170
Days Minimum Temp. ≤ 0°F	2	1	0	0	0	0	0	0	0	0	0	2	5
Heating Degree Days (base 65°F)	1,115	883	809	607	419	238	108	111	309	607	866	1,111	7,183
Cooling Degree Days (base 65°F)	0	0	0	0	3	7	40	49	7	1	0	0	107
Mean Precipitation (in.)	2.98	2.65	2.44	2.28	2.59	1.79	1.27	1.12	1.23	1.81	3.30	3.18	26.64
Days With ≥ 0.1" Precipitation	8	8	8	7	7	5	3	3	4	5	9	8	75
Days With ≥ 1.0" Precipitation	0	0	0	0	0	0	0	0	0	0	0	0	0
Mean Snowfall (in.)	14.2	7.6	3.8	1.0	0.2	0.0	0.0	0.0	0.0	0.4	4.5	*11.1*	*42.8*
Days With ≥ 1.0" Snow Depth	na	na	na	0	0	0	0	0	0	0	*1*	na	na

Powell *Idaho County*   Elevation: 3,526 ft.   Latitude: 46° 31' N   Longitude: 114° 43' W

	JAN	FEB	MAR	APR	MAY	JUN	JUL	AUG	SEP	OCT	NOV	DEC	YEAR
Mean Maximum Temp. (°F)	32.5	38.8	46.0	54.3	64.4	73.0	82.2	82.5	71.5	58.1	39.7	31.5	56.2
Mean Temp. (°F)	24.1	28.3	34.6	41.3	49.3	57.1	63.3	62.7	53.5	43.5	31.5	23.7	42.7
Mean Minimum Temp. (°F)	15.7	17.7	23.2	28.2	34.1	41.1	44.4	42.8	35.4	28.8	23.3	16.0	29.2
Extreme Maximum Temp. (°F)	50	64	74	87	96	99	102	101	102	88	67	47	102
Extreme Minimum Temp. (°F)	-28	-25	-8	8	20	24	28	21	18	2	-12	-31	-31
Days Maximum Temp. ≥ 90°F	0	0	0	0	0	2	8	8	1	0	0	0	19
Days Maximum Temp. ≤ 32°F	12	5	1	0	0	0	0	0	0	0	4	14	36
Days Minimum Temp. ≤ 32°F	31	27	30	25	13	2	0	1	10	24	28	30	221
Days Minimum Temp. ≤ 0°F	4	2	0	0	0	0	0	0	0	0	1	2	9
Heating Degree Days (base 65°F)	1,261	1,032	935	705	481	249	100	109	344	661	997	1,272	8,146
Cooling Degree Days (base 65°F)	0	0	0	0	2	15	52	44	6	0	0	0	119
Mean Precipitation (in.)	5.25	3.79	3.26	2.75	2.94	2.90	1.61	1.57	2.15	2.65	4.94	5.42	39.23
Days With ≥ 0.1" Precipitation	13	10	10	8	9	8	5	4	6	7	12	12	104
Days With ≥ 1.0" Precipitation	1	0	0	0	0	0	0	0	0	0	1	1	3
Mean Snowfall (in.)	*45.2*	*27.5*	17.3	7.4	0.8	0.0	0.0	0.0	trace	2.1	*21.7*	*44.0*	*166.0*
Days With ≥ 1.0" Snow Depth	*30*	*27*	25	12	1	0	0	0	0	1	*15*	29	*140*

Priest River Exp. Station *Bonner County*   Elevation: 2,378 ft.   Latitude: 48° 21' N   Longitude: 116° 50' W

	JAN	FEB	MAR	APR	MAY	JUN	JUL	AUG	SEP	OCT	NOV	DEC	YEAR
Mean Maximum Temp. (°F)	30.0	36.2	45.5	56.4	66.7	73.6	81.3	81.5	70.9	55.2	37.4	30.2	55.4
Mean Temp. (°F)	25.0	29.5	36.0	43.9	52.8	59.2	64.6	64.2	55.1	43.8	32.4	25.8	44.3
Mean Minimum Temp. (°F)	19.9	22.6	26.3	31.3	38.8	44.8	47.8	46.8	39.2	32.3	27.3	21.5	33.2
Extreme Maximum Temp. (°F)	49	56	70	85	92	96	100	99	97	81	63	54	100
Extreme Minimum Temp. (°F)	-27	-17	-10	13	21	30	31	30	19	3	-12	-28	-28
Days Maximum Temp. ≥ 90°F	0	0	0	0	0	1	6	6	0	0	0	0	13
Days Maximum Temp. ≤ 32°F	17	6	1	0	0	0	0	0	0	0	7	18	49
Days Minimum Temp. ≤ 32°F	30	26	26	19	5	0	0	0	6	16	23	29	180
Days Minimum Temp. ≤ 0°F	3	2	0	0	0	0	0	0	0	0	0	1	6
Heating Degree Days (base 65°F)	1,235	998	893	627	375	187	75	81	295	651	971	1,208	7,596
Cooling Degree Days (base 65°F)	0	0	0	0	3	16	60	55	4	0	0	0	138
Mean Precipitation (in.)	3.81	3.15	2.69	2.21	2.57	2.19	1.38	1.32	1.45	1.96	4.29	4.52	31.54
Days With ≥ 0.1" Precipitation	10	8	8	6	7	6	4	3	4	6	10	11	83
Days With ≥ 1.0" Precipitation	1	0	0	0	0	0	0	0	0	0	1	1	3
Mean Snowfall (in.)	21.3	13.8	5.2	0.2	trace	0.0	0.0	0.0	trace	0.3	10.9	22.8	74.5
Days With ≥ 1.0" Snow Depth	30	27	20	2	0	0	0	0	0	0	10	27	116

Reynolds *Owyhee County*   Elevation: 3,927 ft.   Latitude: 43° 12' N   Longitude: 116° 45' W

	JAN	FEB	MAR	APR	MAY	JUN	JUL	AUG	SEP	OCT	NOV	DEC	YEAR
Mean Maximum Temp. (°F)	38.7	43.7	50.8	58.4	67.2	76.8	85.7	85.6	74.9	63.3	48.3	39.4	61.1
Mean Temp. (°F)	29.4	33.5	39.5	45.5	53.4	61.5	69.0	68.5	58.5	48.1	37.0	29.3	47.8
Mean Minimum Temp. (°F)	20.0	23.2	28.1	32.6	39.6	46.1	52.2	51.4	42.0	32.8	25.7	19.1	34.4
Extreme Maximum Temp. (°F)	62	70	78	87	94	102	103	105	98	93	75	65	105
Extreme Minimum Temp. (°F)	-20	-13	-2	14	20	27	32	33	19	12	-7	-22	-22
Days Maximum Temp. ≥ 90°F	0	0	0	0	0	4	11	11	1	0	0	0	27
Days Maximum Temp. ≤ 32°F	8	3	1	0	0	0	0	0	0	0	1	6	19
Days Minimum Temp. ≤ 32°F	27	25	23	15	5	1	0	0	4	15	24	28	167
Days Minimum Temp. ≤ 0°F	2	1	0	0	0	0	0	0	0	0	0	2	5
Heating Degree Days (base 65°F)	1,098	884	784	578	362	157	39	41	217	518	832	1,100	6,610
Cooling Degree Days (base 65°F)	0	0	0	1	12	56	168	162	34	1	0	0	434
Mean Precipitation (in.)	1.23	0.85	1.10	1.04	1.28	1.02	0.38	0.43	0.62	0.74	1.14	1.16	10.99
Days With ≥ 0.1" Precipitation	4	3	4	3	4	3	1	1	2	2	4	3	34
Days With ≥ 1.0" Precipitation	0	0	0	0	0	0	0	0	0	0	0	0	0
Mean Snowfall (in.)	na	2.5	1.0	0.7	trace	0.0	0.0	0.0	0.0	0.4	1.1	na	na
Days With ≥ 1.0" Snow Depth	na	na	1	0	0	0	0	0	0	0	0	1	na

Richfield *Lincoln County*   Elevation: 4,281 ft.   Latitude: 43° 03' N   Longitude: 114° 09' W

	JAN	FEB	MAR	APR	MAY	JUN	JUL	AUG	SEP	OCT	NOV	DEC	YEAR
Mean Maximum Temp. (°F)	31.2	37.7	48.3	59.5	68.3	78.1	86.6	86.3	75.9	62.7	43.9	32.6	59.3
Mean Temp. (°F)	22.5	27.7	36.7	45.0	53.4	61.9	69.1	68.5	58.9	47.3	33.6	23.7	45.7
Mean Minimum Temp. (°F)	13.7	17.6	25.0	30.5	38.5	45.6	51.5	50.7	41.8	32.0	23.4	14.7	32.1
Extreme Maximum Temp. (°F)	53	65	76	90	91	101	105	105	99	90	71	60	105
Extreme Minimum Temp. (°F)	-24	-28	-8	10	17	27	29	31	22	7	-15	-36	-36
Days Maximum Temp. ≥ 90°F	0	0	0	0	0	4	11	11	2	0	0	0	28
Days Maximum Temp. ≤ 32°F	15	8	1	0	0	0	0	0	0	0	4	14	42
Days Minimum Temp. ≤ 32°F	31	27	26	18	7	1	0	0	3	16	26	30	185
Days Minimum Temp. ≤ 0°F	5	2	0	0	0	0	0	0	0	0	1	3	11
Heating Degree Days (base 65°F)	1,312	1,047	870	593	361	141	28	34	207	541	934	1,275	7,343
Cooling Degree Days (base 65°F)	0	0	0	1	10	56	165	167	37	1	0	0	437
Mean Precipitation (in.)	1.64	1.25	1.18	0.76	1.07	0.68	0.38	0.34	0.59	0.70	1.40	1.34	11.33
Days With ≥ 0.1" Precipitation	5	4	4	3	3	2	1	1	2	2	4	4	35
Days With ≥ 1.0" Precipitation	0	0	0	0	0	0	0	0	0	0	0	0	0
Mean Snowfall (in.)	na	5.5	2.2	trace	0.5	0.0	0.0	0.0	0.0	0.2	5.4	7.1	na
Days With ≥ 1.0" Snow Depth	23	17	8	0	0	0	0	0	0	0	4	14	66

Saint Anthony 1 WNW *Fremont County*   Elevation: 4,947 ft.   Latitude: 43° 58' N   Longitude: 111° 43' W

	JAN	FEB	MAR	APR	MAY	JUN	JUL	AUG	SEP	OCT	NOV	DEC	YEAR
Mean Maximum Temp. (°F)	28.7	33.7	43.2	55.0	65.3	74.0	82.0	82.1	72.0	59.5	41.3	30.1	55.6
Mean Temp. (°F)	18.5	22.2	31.1	40.9	50.1	57.9	64.1	63.3	54.2	43.6	30.1	19.2	41.3
Mean Minimum Temp. (°F)	7.9	10.6	19.1	26.7	34.9	41.8	46.2	44.5	36.2	27.6	18.8	8.1	26.9
Extreme Maximum Temp. (°F)	52	58	74	85	89	100	98	98	92	86	71	59	100
Extreme Minimum Temp. (°F)	-32	-34	-21	1	14	25	30	22	15	2	-21	-40	-40
Days Maximum Temp. ≥ 90°F	0	0	0	0	0	1	4	3	0	0	0	0	8
Days Maximum Temp. ≤ 32°F	19	10	2	0	0	0	0	0	0	0	5	18	54
Days Minimum Temp. ≤ 32°F	31	28	30	24	11	2	0	1	9	23	28	30	217
Days Minimum Temp. ≤ 0°F	10	6	1	0	0	0	0	0	0	0	2	8	27
Heating Degree Days (base 65°F)	1,435	1,203	1,043	718	456	220	73	85	321	654	1,041	1,433	8,682
Cooling Degree Days (base 65°F)	0	0	0	0	1	12	50	39	4	0	0	0	106
Mean Precipitation (in.)	1.27	0.87	1.11	1.17	1.99	1.58	0.98	0.76	0.98	0.99	1.33	1.33	14.36
Days With ≥ 0.1" Precipitation	4	3	4	4	6	4	3	2	3	3	5	5	46
Days With ≥ 1.0" Precipitation	0	0	0	0	0	0	0	0	0	0	0	0	0
Mean Snowfall (in.)	na	na	1.9	1.0	trace	0.0	0.0	0.0	0.0	0.7	5.5	na	na
Days With ≥ 1.0" Snow Depth	na	na	na	1	0	0	0	0	0	1	2	na	na

Saint Maries 1 W *Benewah County*   Elevation: 2,319 ft.   Latitude: 47° 19' N   Longitude: 116° 35' W

	JAN	FEB	MAR	APR	MAY	JUN	JUL	AUG	SEP	OCT	NOV	DEC	YEAR
Mean Maximum Temp. (°F)	34.6	41.4	49.8	58.5	67.3	74.8	83.5	84.3	73.6	58.5	41.6	34.1	58.5
Mean Temp. (°F)	29.0	33.9	40.0	46.6	54.1	60.9	67.0	67.1	58.0	46.5	35.8	29.0	47.3
Mean Minimum Temp. (°F)	23.3	26.2	30.2	34.6	40.9	46.9	50.4	49.8	42.2	34.5	29.9	23.8	36.1
Extreme Maximum Temp. (°F)	56	66	79	95	95	100	105	106	104	87	69	54	106
Extreme Minimum Temp. (°F)	-20	-14	-2	16	25	30	33	30	21	9	-5	-24	-24
Days Maximum Temp. ≥ 90°F	0	0	0	0	1	2	10	10	2	0	0	0	25
Days Maximum Temp. ≤ 32°F	10	4	0	0	0	0	0	0	0	0	3	11	28
Days Minimum Temp. ≤ 32°F	26	22	20	12	3	0	0	0	3	12	19	26	143
Days Minimum Temp. ≤ 0°F	2	1	0	0	0	0	0	0	0	0	0	1	4
Heating Degree Days (base 65°F)	1,111	873	767	547	339	157	50	49	223	566	871	1,110	6,663
Cooling Degree Days (base 65°F)	0	0	0	1	8	34	111	119	20	0	0	0	293
Mean Precipitation (in.)	4.07	3.07	2.61	2.30	2.37	1.99	1.32	1.15	1.34	2.01	4.16	4.20	30.59
Days With ≥ 0.1" Precipitation	9	7	8	6	6	5	3	3	3	5	9	9	73
Days With ≥ 1.0" Precipitation	0	0	0	0	0	0	0	0	0	0	1	0	1
Mean Snowfall (in.)	16.1	8.2	3.4	0.3	trace	trace	0.0	0.0	trace	0.4	6.5	17.1	52.0
Days With ≥ 1.0" Snow Depth	19	11	5	0	0	0	0	0	0	0	5	15	55

Salmon *Lemhi County*   Elevation: 3,930 ft.   Latitude: 45° 11' N   Longitude: 113° 54' W

	JAN	FEB	MAR	APR	MAY	JUN	JUL	AUG	SEP	OCT	NOV	DEC	YEAR
Mean Maximum Temp. (°F)	30.2	38.9	51.0	61.2	70.1	78.8	87.9	86.7	75.8	61.3	42.8	30.7	59.6
Mean Temp. (°F)	21.0	28.2	38.6	46.8	54.8	62.6	69.4	67.9	58.2	46.4	33.2	21.9	45.8
Mean Minimum Temp. (°F)	11.8	17.5	26.3	32.3	39.5	46.2	50.9	49.0	40.6	31.4	23.5	13.2	31.8
Extreme Maximum Temp. (°F)	57	62	76	89	95	103	105	102	97	87	69	59	105
Extreme Minimum Temp. (°F)	-34	-26	-3	14	19	28	34	29	20	3	-12	-31	-34
Days Maximum Temp. ≥ 90°F	0	0	0	0	1	4	15	13	2	0	0	0	35
Days Maximum Temp. ≤ 32°F	16	6	0	0	0	0	0	0	0	0	4	17	43
Days Minimum Temp. ≤ 32°F	30	27	25	16	4	1	0	0	4	17	26	30	180
Days Minimum Temp. ≤ 0°F	6	3	0	0	0	0	0	0	0	0	1	4	14
Heating Degree Days (base 65°F)	1,357	1,034	810	540	313	119	23	31	211	571	948	1,328	7,285
Cooling Degree Days (base 65°F)	0	0	0	0	8	49	163	131	15	0	0	0	366
Mean Precipitation (in.)	0.68	0.47	0.57	0.78	1.45	1.47	1.04	0.82	0.78	0.59	0.79	0.78	10.22
Days With ≥ 0.1" Precipitation	2	2	2	2	5	5	3	3	2	2	3	3	34
Days With ≥ 1.0" Precipitation	0	0	0	0	0	0	0	0	0	0	0	0	0
Mean Snowfall (in.)	8.4	4.3	2.4	1.3	0.1	trace	trace	trace	trace	trace	4.3	8.1	28.9
Days With ≥ 1.0" Snow Depth	27	17	3	0	0	0	0	0	0	0	0	4	20	71

Sandpoint Exp. Station *Bonner County*   Elevation: 2,099 ft.   Latitude: 48° 18' N   Longitude: 116° 33' W

	JAN	FEB	MAR	APR	MAY	JUN	JUL	AUG	SEP	OCT	NOV	DEC	YEAR
Mean Maximum Temp. (°F)	33.0	38.5	47.1	56.8	66.1	72.9	80.6	80.8	70.2	56.6	41.0	33.4	56.4
Mean Temp. (°F)	27.2	31.3	37.8	45.5	53.4	59.7	65.0	64.5	55.7	44.9	34.8	27.9	45.6
Mean Minimum Temp. (°F)	21.4	24.1	28.4	34.1	40.6	46.5	49.3	48.2	41.0	33.2	28.6	22.4	34.8
Extreme Maximum Temp. (°F)	52	61	68	87	92	96	104	98	95	81	66	55	104
Extreme Minimum Temp. (°F)	-22	-14	-5	19	22	30	33	30	21	12	-2	-20	-22
Days Maximum Temp. ≥ 90°F	0	0	0	0	0	1	5	5	0	0	0	0	11
Days Maximum Temp. ≤ 32°F	12	5	1	0	0	0	0	0	0	0	3	12	33
Days Minimum Temp. ≤ 32°F	27	24	22	13	4	0	0	0	3	15	20	28	156
Days Minimum Temp. ≤ 0°F	2	1	0	0	0	0	0	0	0	0	0	1	4
Heating Degree Days (base 65°F)	1,163	945	837	579	358	179	69	75	279	616	899	1,142	7,141
Cooling Degree Days (base 65°F)	0	0	0	0	6	26	79	71	6	0	0	0	188
Mean Precipitation (in.)	4.04	3.48	2.79	2.23	2.71	2.45	1.65	1.42	1.63	2.34	4.77	4.86	34.37
Days With ≥ 0.1" Precipitation	10	8	8	6	7	7	4	4	4	6	10	11	85
Days With ≥ 1.0" Precipitation	1	1	0	0	0	0	0	0	0	0	1	1	4
Mean Snowfall (in.)	19.3	11.9	3.6	0.3	0.0	0.0	0.0	0.0	0.0	0.1	7.0	19.9	62.1
Days With ≥ 1.0" Snow Depth	25	19	8	0	0	0	0	0	0	0	4	19	75

Shoshone 1 WNW *Lincoln County*   Elevation: 3,950 ft.   Latitude: 42° 56' N   Longitude: 114° 25' W

	JAN	FEB	MAR	APR	MAY	JUN	JUL	AUG	SEP	OCT	NOV	DEC	YEAR
Mean Maximum Temp. (°F)	34.1	40.8	51.5	62.1	72.3	83.2	91.5	90.7	78.7	64.7	46.0	35.3	62.6
Mean Temp. (°F)	25.7	30.9	39.5	47.8	57.0	66.1	73.7	72.9	62.1	50.0	36.1	26.6	49.0
Mean Minimum Temp. (°F)	17.2	20.9	27.4	33.3	41.5	49.0	55.9	55.0	45.2	35.2	26.1	17.9	35.4
Extreme Maximum Temp. (°F)	55	65	77	90	97	105	109	105	99	92	72	59	109
Extreme Minimum Temp. (°F)	-17	-20	-2	15	15	28	35	37	25	9	-2	-27	-27
Days Maximum Temp. ≥ 90°F	0	0	0	0	1	8	21	20	4	0	0	0	54
Days Maximum Temp. ≤ 32°F	11	5	0	0	0	0	0	0	0	0	3	10	29
Days Minimum Temp. ≤ 32°F	29	25	24	14	*4*	0	0	0	2	11	22	29	*160*
Days Minimum Temp. ≤ 0°F	2	1	0	0	0	0	0	0	0	0	0	2	5
Heating Degree Days (base 65°F)	1,210	957	785	512	266	80	10	13	143	461	859	1,184	6,480
Cooling Degree Days (base 65°F)	0	0	0	3	29	118	274	270	65	2	0	0	761
Mean Precipitation (in.)	1.47	1.06	1.27	0.71	0.95	0.66	0.27	0.33	0.58	0.63	1.36	1.24	10.53
Days With ≥ 0.1" Precipitation	5	3	4	2	3	2	1	1	2	2	5	4	34
Days With ≥ 1.0" Precipitation	0	0	0	0	0	0	0	0	0	0	0	0	0
Mean Snowfall (in.)	na	na	*1.3*	trace	trace	0.0	0.0	0.0	0.0	trace	*2.8*	na	na
Days With ≥ 1.0" Snow Depth	na	na	*0*	0	0	0	0	0	0	0	0	*0*	na	na

Shoup *Lemhi County*   Elevation: 3,398 ft.   Latitude: 45° 23' N   Longitude: 114° 17' W

	JAN	FEB	MAR	APR	MAY	JUN	JUL	AUG	SEP	OCT	NOV	DEC	YEAR
Mean Maximum Temp. (°F)	30.9	39.4	51.6	62.1	71.4	80.1	89.2	88.3	77.4	61.3	42.4	30.6	60.4
Mean Temp. (°F)	22.9	29.5	39.5	47.6	55.4	62.9	69.9	68.9	59.5	47.2	34.0	23.3	46.7
Mean Minimum Temp. (°F)	14.9	19.5	27.5	33.0	39.4	45.6	50.7	49.5	41.6	33.0	25.5	16.0	33.0
Extreme Maximum Temp. (°F)	55	61	76	88	96	100	109	106	104	87	64	53	109
Extreme Minimum Temp. (°F)	-23	-21	2	11	11	22	29	28	22	6	-8	-25	-25
Days Maximum Temp. ≥ 90°F	0	0	0	0	1	5	17	15	4	0	0	0	42
Days Maximum Temp. ≤ 32°F	15	5	0	0	0	0	0	0	0	0	3	16	39
Days Minimum Temp. ≤ 32°F	30	27	25	15	3	0	0	0	2	15	25	29	171
Days Minimum Temp. ≤ 0°F	4	1	0	0	0	0	0	0	0	0	0	2	7
Heating Degree Days (base 65°F)	1,298	997	782	516	298	109	20	25	184	547	923	1,287	6,986
Cooling Degree Days (base 65°F)	0	0	0	0	9	52	183	171	32	0	0	0	447
Mean Precipitation (in.)	*1.37*	1.30	0.90	1.17	1.65	1.77	1.01	0.92	1.02	0.87	1.46	*1.50*	*14.94*
Days With ≥ 0.1" Precipitation	*5*	4	3	4	5	5	3	3	3	3	5	*5*	*48*
Days With ≥ 1.0" Precipitation	*0*	0	0	0	0	0	0	0	0	0	0	*0*	*0*
Mean Snowfall (in.)	*11.4*	4.8	*1.3*	0.1	0.0	0.0	0.0	0.0	0.0	trace	*3.4*	na	na
Days With ≥ 1.0" Snow Depth	*29*	*19*	*6*	0	0	0	0	0	0	0	*2*	na	na

Swan Falls P H *Ada County*   Elevation: 2,322 ft.   Latitude: 43° 15' N   Longitude: 116° 23' W

	JAN	FEB	MAR	APR	MAY	JUN	JUL	AUG	SEP	OCT	NOV	DEC	YEAR
Mean Maximum Temp. (°F)	40.7	49.2	59.1	67.2	77.0	87.0	95.3	94.7	83.7	69.9	52.1	40.7	68.1
Mean Temp. (°F)	32.8	39.2	47.2	54.0	62.7	71.5	78.9	77.8	67.5	55.8	42.4	32.6	55.2
Mean Minimum Temp. (°F)	24.8	29.1	35.3	40.6	48.4	56.0	62.5	60.8	51.2	41.5	32.6	24.6	42.3
Extreme Maximum Temp. (°F)	66	74	84	96	103	109	111	115	103	98	78	66	115
Extreme Minimum Temp. (°F)	-7	-13	13	22	28	29	42	43	32	22	4	-21	-21
Days Maximum Temp. ≥ 90°F	0	0	0	0	4	13	25	24	10	0	0	0	76
Days Maximum Temp. ≤ 32°F	6	2	0	0	0	0	0	0	0	0	1	5	14
Days Minimum Temp. ≤ 32°F	24	19	10	3	0	0	0	0	0	3	15	25	99
Days Minimum Temp. ≤ 0°F	1	0	0	0	0	0	0	0	0	0	0	1	2
Heating Degree Days (base 65°F)	992	723	545	333	135	28	1	2	57	293	673	999	4,781
Cooling Degree Days (base 65°F)	0	0	0	10	75	223	422	405	145	15	0	0	1,295
Mean Precipitation (in.)	0.89	0.55	0.93	1.06	1.07	0.74	0.29	0.22	0.54	0.51	0.88	0.81	8.49
Days With ≥ 0.1" Precipitation	3	2	3	4	4	2	1	1	2	2	3	3	30
Days With ≥ 1.0" Precipitation	0	0	0	0	0	0	0	0	0	0	0	0	0
Mean Snowfall (in.)	*1.6*	*0.5*	0.1	trace	0.0	0.0	0.0	0.0	0.0	0.0	0.4	1.4	*4.0*
Days With ≥ 1.0" Snow Depth	2	0	0	0	0	0	0	0	0	0	1	2	5

Swan Valley 2 E *Bonneville County*   Elevation: 5,357 ft.   Latitude: 43° 27' N   Longitude: 111° 18' W

	JAN	FEB	MAR	APR	MAY	JUN	JUL	AUG	SEP	OCT	NOV	DEC	YEAR
Mean Maximum Temp. (°F)	29.9	35.6	44.2	54.6	64.5	74.8	83.6	83.1	73.1	59.8	41.6	30.9	56.3
Mean Temp. (°F)	20.3	24.4	32.8	41.1	49.6	57.7	64.2	63.5	54.6	43.8	31.3	21.3	42.0
Mean Minimum Temp. (°F)	10.6	13.1	21.4	27.5	34.7	40.5	44.8	43.9	36.0	27.7	20.9	11.6	27.7
Extreme Maximum Temp. (°F)	55	59	71	83	88	101	101	101	96	83	69	58	101
Extreme Minimum Temp. (°F)	-40	-36	-25	-3	12	20	26	24	8	0	-21	-43	-43
Days Maximum Temp. ≥ 90°F	0	0	0	0	0	1	6	4	1	0	0	0	12
Days Maximum Temp. ≤ 32°F	17	9	2	0	0	0	0	0	0	0	6	17	51
Days Minimum Temp. ≤ 32°F	30	27	28	23	12	3	1	1	10	23	26	29	213
Days Minimum Temp. ≤ 0°F	8	6	1	0	0	0	0	0	0	0	2	6	23
Heating Degree Days (base 65°F)	1,381	1,141	992	711	470	225	71	81	313	652	1,006	1,349	8,392
Cooling Degree Days (base 65°F)	0	0	0	0	1	14	59	49	8	0	0	0	131
Mean Precipitation (in.)	1.60	0.93	1.35	1.63	2.75	1.55	1.47	1.33	1.43	1.34	1.58	1.31	18.27
Days With ≥ 0.1" Precipitation	6	3	5	6	8	5	4	4	4	4	5	5	59
Days With ≥ 1.0" Precipitation	0	0	0	0	0	0	0	0	0	0	0	0	0
Mean Snowfall (in.)	*15.9*	8.7	7.2	4.4	1.3	trace	0.0	0.0	0.2	1.2	*9.1*	*12.7*	*60.7*
Days With ≥ 1.0" Snow Depth	*24*	*21*	15	2	0	0	0	0	0	0	7	*20*	*89*

Tetonia Experiment Station *Teton County*   Elevation: 6,167 ft.   Latitude: 43° 51' N   Longitude: 111° 16' W

	JAN	FEB	MAR	APR	MAY	JUN	JUL	AUG	SEP	OCT	NOV	DEC	YEAR
Mean Maximum Temp. (°F)	na	*34.5*	40.4	50.0	na	71.4	na	na	na	*56.2*	na	na	na
Mean Temp. (°F)	na	*22.1*	28.4	37.5	na	55.4	na	na	na	*41.1*	na	na	na
Mean Minimum Temp. (°F)	na	*9.4*	16.5	25.0	*32.4*	39.6	na	na	na	*25.9*	na	na	na
Extreme Maximum Temp. (°F)	59	53	65	79	82	95	94	94	90	81	67	57	95
Extreme Minimum Temp. (°F)	-38	-37	-16	-7	10	21	29	22	6	-8	-21	-45	-45
Days Maximum Temp. ≥ 90°F	0	0	0	0	0	0	0	1	0	0	0	0	1
Days Maximum Temp. ≤ 32°F	17	10	4	0	0	0	0	0	0	0	7	15	53
Days Minimum Temp. ≤ 32°F	27	25	27	24	13	3	1	1	10	21	25	25	202
Days Minimum Temp. ≤ 0°F	10	7	2	0	0	0	0	0	0	0	2	8	29
Heating Degree Days (base 65°F)	na	*1,207*	1,124	819	na	289	na	na	na	*726*	na	na	na
Cooling Degree Days (base 65°F)	na	na	*0*	*0*	na	*6*	na	na	na	na	na	na	na
Mean Precipitation (in.)	1.95	1.14	1.29	1.40	2.58	1.71	1.35	1.27	1.44	1.41	1.46	1.64	18.64
Days With ≥ 0.1" Precipitation	*5*	3	3	4	6	4	3	4	3	4	3	4	*46*
Days With ≥ 1.0" Precipitation	0	0	0	0	0	0	0	0	0	0	0	0	0
Mean Snowfall (in.)	na	na	na	na	0.3	trace	0.0	0.0	0.1	*trace*	na	na	na
Days With ≥ 1.0" Snow Depth	na	na	na	na	0	0	0	0	0	0	na	na	na

Twin Falls 6 E *Twin Falls County*   Elevation: 3,959 ft.   Latitude: 42° 33' N   Longitude: 114° 21' W

	JAN	FEB	MAR	APR	MAY	JUN	JUL	AUG	SEP	OCT	NOV	DEC	YEAR
Mean Maximum Temp. (°F)	35.3	41.8	50.6	58.4	67.1	76.4	84.4	84.0	74.1	62.6	46.9	36.8	59.9
Mean Temp. (°F)	27.3	32.5	39.7	45.9	54.1	62.2	68.7	67.6	58.4	48.4	36.8	28.0	47.5
Mean Minimum Temp. (°F)	19.2	23.2	28.8	33.4	41.1	48.0	52.9	51.2	42.6	34.0	26.7	19.2	35.0
Extreme Maximum Temp. (°F)	58	68	79	87	92	100	101	99	95	89	76	65	101
Extreme Minimum Temp. (°F)	-14	-17	3	17	22	28	33	32	25	9	-4	-23	-23
Days Maximum Temp. ≥ 90°F	0	0	0	0	0	3	8	7	1	0	0	0	19
Days Maximum Temp. ≤ 32°F	11	5	1	0	0	0	0	0	0	0	2	9	28
Days Minimum Temp. ≤ 32°F	28	25	23	14	3	0	0	0	3	12	23	28	159
Days Minimum Temp. ≤ 0°F	2	1	0	0	0	0	0	0	0	0	0	2	5
Heating Degree Days (base 65°F)	1,162	911	778	567	339	136	31	38	214	510	839	1,140	6,665
Cooling Degree Days (base 65°F)	0	0	0	0	10	57	148	132	25	1	0	0	373
Mean Precipitation (in.)	1.34	0.88	1.20	0.99	1.40	0.89	0.31	0.38	0.66	0.76	1.23	1.13	11.17
Days With ≥ 0.1" Precipitation	4	3	4	3	4	3	1	1	2	2	4	4	35
Days With ≥ 1.0" Precipitation	0	0	0	0	0	0	0	0	0	0	0	0	0
Mean Snowfall (in.)	7.1	5.3	3.4	1.5	0.6	trace	0.0	0.0	0.1	0.3	3.9	6.6	28.8
Days With ≥ 1.0" Snow Depth	13	7	2	1	0	0	0	0	0	0	3	10	36

Wallace Woodland Park *Shoshone County*   Elevation: 2,939 ft.   Latitude: 47° 28' N   Longitude: 115° 48' W

	JAN	FEB	MAR	APR	MAY	JUN	JUL	AUG	SEP	OCT	NOV	DEC	YEAR
Mean Maximum Temp. (°F)	33.5	39.1	46.0	54.3	63.4	70.8	79.3	80.4	70.3	57.5	40.9	33.2	55.7
Mean Temp. (°F)	26.6	30.9	36.4	43.4	51.1	58.0	64.1	64.3	55.4	45.3	34.3	27.0	44.7
Mean Minimum Temp. (°F)	19.7	22.6	26.8	32.4	38.8	45.1	48.8	48.3	40.6	33.1	27.6	20.8	33.7
Extreme Maximum Temp. (°F)	57	66	77	91	95	97	102	99	98	87	68	56	102
Extreme Minimum Temp. (°F)	-23	-19	-3	17	23	31	33	33	23	9	-8	-26	-26
Days Maximum Temp. ≥ 90°F	0	0	0	0	0	1	5	5	1	0	0	0	12
Days Maximum Temp. ≤ 32°F	12	5	1	0	0	0	0	0	0	0	3	12	33
Days Minimum Temp. ≤ 32°F	29	25	25	15	4	0	0	0	3	15	22	28	166
Days Minimum Temp. ≤ 0°F	3	1	0	0	0	0	0	0	0	0	0	2	6
Heating Degree Days (base 65°F)	1,183	958	878	642	426	228	96	88	290	603	915	1,171	7,478
Cooling Degree Days (base 65°F)	0	0	0	0	6	21	70	73	13	0	0	0	183
Mean Precipitation (in.)	5.27	4.10	3.68	3.01	2.97	2.67	1.49	1.40	1.75	2.74	5.40	5.37	39.85
Days With ≥ 0.1" Precipitation	12	10	11	9	9	7	4	4	5	7	12	12	102
Days With ≥ 1.0" Precipitation	1	1	0	0	0	0	0	0	0	0	1	1	4
Mean Snowfall (in.)	20.0	14.8	9.4	2.6	0.2	0.0	0.0	0.0	trace	0.7	9.9	21.2	78.8
Days With ≥ 1.0" Snow Depth	27	22	18	3	0	0	0	0	0	1	9	23	103

Warren *Idaho County*   Elevation: 5,905 ft.   Latitude: 45° 16' N   Longitude: 115° 40' W

	JAN	FEB	MAR	APR	MAY	JUN	JUL	AUG	SEP	OCT	NOV	DEC	YEAR
Mean Maximum Temp. (°F)	33.5	38.9	43.2	49.1	58.0	67.4	76.3	76.3	66.9	55.8	39.7	32.2	53.1
Mean Temp. (°F)	20.6	24.4	29.1	35.1	43.0	50.4	56.4	55.7	47.9	39.6	27.9	20.1	37.5
Mean Minimum Temp. (°F)	7.5	9.9	14.9	21.0	27.9	33.4	36.5	35.1	28.9	23.2	16.1	8.1	21.9
Extreme Maximum Temp. (°F)	54	62	64	79	84	87	97	92	90	79	66	55	97
Extreme Minimum Temp. (°F)	-44	-41	-24	-9	9	17	21	16	11	-12	-24	-45	-45
Days Maximum Temp. ≥ 90°F	0	0	0	0	0	0	0	0	0	0	0	0	0
Days Maximum Temp. ≤ 32°F	12	6	2	0	0	0	0	0	0	0	6	15	41
Days Minimum Temp. ≤ 32°F	30	28	31	28	24	14	7	10	22	29	29	30	282
Days Minimum Temp. ≤ 0°F	9	6	3	0	0	0	0	0	0	0	2	8	28
Heating Degree Days (base 65°F)	1,370	1,140	1,107	891	676	431	262	282	506	782	1,106	1,386	9,939
Cooling Degree Days (base 65°F)	0	0	0	0	0	0	4	3	0	0	0	0	7
Mean Precipitation (in.)	2.75	2.00	2.45	2.26	2.46	2.59	1.43	1.30	1.49	1.80	2.68	2.77	25.98
Days With ≥ 0.1" Precipitation	7	6	6	6	7	7	3	3	4	4	7	7	67
Days With ≥ 1.0" Precipitation	0	0	0	0	0	0	0	0	0	0	0	0	0
Mean Snowfall (in.)	32.0	23.3	25.1	13.5	4.8	0.9	0.0	trace	0.5	4.9	23.4	31.7	160.1
Days With ≥ 1.0" Snow Depth	30	27	29	23	6	0	0	0	0	3	19	30	167

Winchester *Lewis County*   Elevation: 3,950 ft.   Latitude: 46° 14' N   Longitude: 116° 37' W

	JAN	FEB	MAR	APR	MAY	JUN	JUL	AUG	SEP	OCT	NOV	DEC	YEAR
Mean Maximum Temp. (°F)	35.1	39.6	44.4	51.4	59.4	67.1	76.0	77.5	68.2	56.6	41.6	34.8	54.3
Mean Temp. (°F)	27.1	30.8	35.1	41.1	48.0	54.7	60.9	61.5	53.5	44.4	33.6	27.1	43.2
Mean Minimum Temp. (°F)	19.2	22.0	25.6	30.6	36.5	42.2	45.8	45.5	38.8	32.1	25.7	19.4	32.0
Extreme Maximum Temp. (°F)	58	67	70	84	86	90	94	96	95	88	67	60	96
Extreme Minimum Temp. (°F)	-26	-28	-10	11	19	23	28	25	17	-10	-21	-33	-33
Days Maximum Temp. ≥ 90°F	0	0	0	0	0	0	1	2	0	0	0	0	3
Days Maximum Temp. ≤ 32°F	11	5	2	0	0	0	0	0	0	0	4	11	33
Days Minimum Temp. ≤ 32°F	28	25	25	19	9	2	1	0	6	16	24	28	183
Days Minimum Temp. ≤ 0°F	3	1	0	0	0	0	0	0	0	0	1	2	7
Heating Degree Days (base 65°F)	1,167	959	922	711	523	310	151	142	344	632	934	1,168	7,963
Cooling Degree Days (base 65°F)	0	0	0	0	2	5	28	43	8	1	0	0	87
Mean Precipitation (in.)	2.02	1.66	2.51	2.80	3.12	2.18	1.54	1.23	1.41	1.86	2.58	2.00	24.91
Days With ≥ 0.1" Precipitation	6	6	9	8	8	7	4	3	4	5	8	6	74
Days With ≥ 1.0" Precipitation	0	0	0	0	0	0	0	0	0	0	0	0	0
Mean Snowfall (in.)	17.9	13.1	16.0	9.1	2.1	trace	0.0	0.0	0.1	2.2	15.5	18.4	94.4
Days With ≥ 1.0" Snow Depth	24	17	14	4	0	0	0	0	0	0	9	21	90

Yellow Pine 7 S *Valley County*   Elevation: 5,098 ft.   Latitude: 44° 47' N   Longitude: 115° 30' W

	JAN	FEB	MAR	APR	MAY	JUN	JUL	AUG	SEP	OCT	NOV	DEC	YEAR
Mean Maximum Temp. (°F)	33.1	38.5	45.0	*51.7*	*61.0*	69.7	79.6	79.8	69.8	57.6	40.2	32.4	*54.9*
Mean Temp. (°F)	21.1	24.8	31.4	*37.8*	*45.6*	52.7	59.3	58.7	50.1	41.1	29.3	20.9	*39.4*
Mean Minimum Temp. (°F)	9.0	11.1	17.9	*23.8*	*30.2*	35.6	38.9	37.5	30.4	24.6	18.2	9.4	*23.9*
Extreme Maximum Temp. (°F)	52	63	75	85	89	92	96	96	93	83	69	51	96
Extreme Minimum Temp. (°F)	-35	-33	-20	-4	16	22	26	21	13	-1	-20	-33	-35
Days Maximum Temp. ≥ 90°F	0	0	0	0	0	0	2	3	0	0	0	0	5
Days Maximum Temp. ≤ 32°F	13	5	1	0	0	0	0	0	0	0	4	13	36
Days Minimum Temp. ≤ 32°F	30	28	30	26	*20*	9	3	5	21	28	28	29	*257*
Days Minimum Temp. ≤ 0°F	9	7	2	0	0	0	0	0	0	0	2	8	28
Heating Degree Days (base 65°F)	1,356	1,128	1,034	*811*	*594*	365	179	197	441	733	1,066	1,361	*9,265*
Cooling Degree Days (base 65°F)	0	0	0	*0*	*0*	1	9	8	0	0	0	*0*	*18*
Mean Precipitation (in.)	3.21	2.91	2.42	2.02	2.10	2.05	1.12	1.13	1.65	1.85	3.46	3.62	27.54
Days With ≥ 0.1" Precipitation	8	8	7	6	*6*	6	3	3	4	5	8	9	*73*
Days With ≥ 1.0" Precipitation	0	0	0	0	0	0	0	0	0	0	0	0	0
Mean Snowfall (in.)	24.7	20.1	11.8	6.5	1.1	trace	trace	0.0	trace	2.5	16.3	25.8	108.8
Days With ≥ 1.0" Snow Depth	31	28	28	13	1	0	0	0	0	2	15	29	147

Note: See Appendix D for explanation of data.

ILLINOIS

PHYSICAL FEATURES. Illinois lies midway between the Continental Divide and the Atlantic Ocean and some 500 miles north of the Gulf of Mexico. Its climate is typically continental with cold winters, warm summers, and frequent short period fluctuations in temperature, humidity, cloudiness, and wind direction.

The irregular shape of the State has a width of less than 200 miles at most points, but extends for 385 miles in the north-south direction. Except for a few low hills in the extreme south and a small unglaciated area in the extreme northwest, the terrain is flat. Differences in elevation have no significant influence on the climate. River drainage is mainly toward the Mississippi River, which forms the entire western boundary of the State. From north to south the principal rivers entering the Mississippi are the Rock, Illinois, Kaskaskia, and the Big Muddy. Approximately one-seventh of the State area drains southeastward into the Wabash and Ohio Rivers. Only a small area drains into Lake Michigan.

GENERAL CLIMATE. Without the protection of natural barriers, such as mountain ranges, Illinois experiences the full sweep of the winds which are constantly bringing in the climates of other areas. Southeast and easterly winds bring mild and wet weather; southerly winds are warm and showery; westerly winds are dry with moderate temperatures; and winds from the northwest and north are cool and dry. Winds are controlled by the storm systems and weather fronts which move eastward and northeastward through this area.

Storm systems move through the State most frequently during the winter and spring months and cause a maximum of cloudiness during those seasons. Summer-season storm systems tend to be weaker and to stay farther north, leaving Illinois with much sunshine interspersed with thunderstorm situations of comparatively short duration. The retreat of the sun in autumn is associated with variable periods of pleasant dry weather of the Indian summer variety. This season ends rather abruptly with the returning storminess which usually begins in November.

TEMPERATURE. Because Illinois extends so far in a north-south direction, the contrasts in winter temperature conditions are rather strong. The extreme north has frequent snow and temperatures drop to below zero several times each winter. The soil freezes to a depth of about three feet and occasionally remains snow-covered for weeks at a time. In the extreme south snow falls only occasionally and leaves after a few days, while temperatures drop to zero on an average of only about one day each winter. The soil freezes, but only to a depth of eight to 12 inches, with great variation in the duration of soil-frost periods. The north-south range in winter mean temperatures is approximately 14°F.

During the summer season the sun heats the entire State quite strongly and uniformly. The north-south range of mean temperatures in July is only about 6°F. The annual average of days with temperatures of 90°F. or higher is near 20 in the north and near 50 in the south and west-central. Summer also brings periods of uncomfortably hot and humid weather, which are most persistent in the south. In the north the heat is usually broken after a few days by the arrival of cool air from Canada, but this cooling does not always penetrate to the southern portions of the State.

PRECIPITATION. Latitude is the principal control for both temperature and precipitation, with the northern counties averaging cooler and drier than the south. Distance from the Gulf of Mexico and lower airmass temperatures both tend to reduce the amounts of precipitation in the northern portion. Annual precipitation is approximately one and one-half times as great in the extreme south as in the extreme north, but most of the excess in the southern portion falls during winter and early spring. Mean total precipitation for the four-month period of December through March ranges from near seven inches in the extreme northwest to more than 14 inches in the extreme southeast. Precipitation during the warm season is more uniform. Totals for the six-month period of April through September range from 21 to 24 inches throughout the State. The driest month is February. The wettest months are May and June.

Precipitation during fall, winter, and spring tends to fall uniformly over large areas. In contrast, summer rainfall occurs principally as brief showers affecting relatively small areas. The erratic occurrence of summer showers results in uneven distribution. The high rates of summer rainfall also cause runoff and soil erosion. Summer showers are usually accompanied by thunder and, sometimes, by hail or destructive windstorms.

Floods occur nearly every year in at least some part of the State. The spring and early summer flood season results from a tendency for heavy general rainfall at that time of the year. The extreme north frequently has late winter or early spring flooding with the breakup of river ice, especially if there is an appreciable snow cover which is taken off by rain. River stages tend to decline during late summer, but local flash floods in minor streams, due to heavy thunderstorm rains, are common throughout the warm season. The interior rivers in the central and south have flat beds and sluggish currents so that they rise slowly and remain in flood conditions for relatively long periods.

SNOWFALL. The annual average of snowfall ranges from near 30 inches in the extreme north to only 10 inches in the extreme south. In the extreme north the most likely form of winter precipitation is snow. In contrast, more than 90% of Cairo's winter precipitation falls as rain. In a large number of winter storm situations, only a slight change in the temperature pattern would suffice to change rain to snow or vice versa. For this reason, Illinois snowfall records show great variability. Snowfalls of one inch or more occur on an average of 10 to 12 days per year in the extreme north and decrease to three or four in the far south. The two northern divisions average about 50 days annually when the ground is covered with one inch or more of snow, and this average decreases to about 15 days in the two southern divisions.

STORMS. Heavy snows of four to six inches or more average one or two per year in the north and less frequently in the south. Strong winds will drift snow and make driving hazardous. Moderate to heavy ice storms average about once every four or five years and can be quite damaging. Thunderstorms average about 35 to 50 annually, but most are quite harmless. On occasion they provide the source for hail, damaging winds, and tornadoes. Hail falls on an average of two or three days annually in the same locality, but usually causes little damage.

More than 65 percent of Illinois tornadoes occur during the months of March, April, May, and June. This "tornado season" is marked by a rapid increase in activity during March, a peak in April and May, and a decline during June. Tornadoes have occurred during each of the twelve months of the year.

INFLUENCE OF LAKE MICHIGAN. Because prevailing winds are westerly and storm systems move from the same direction, the influence of the lake on Illinois weather is not large. When the wind blows from the lake toward the shore, which it does for approximately one-fourth of the time during spring and summer and for about one-eighth of the time during fall and winter, the result is a moderation of temperature. In addition to the general occurrence of onshore winds, there is the local "sea breeze" effect on summer afternoons which is usually observable in a narrow strip near the lake shore.

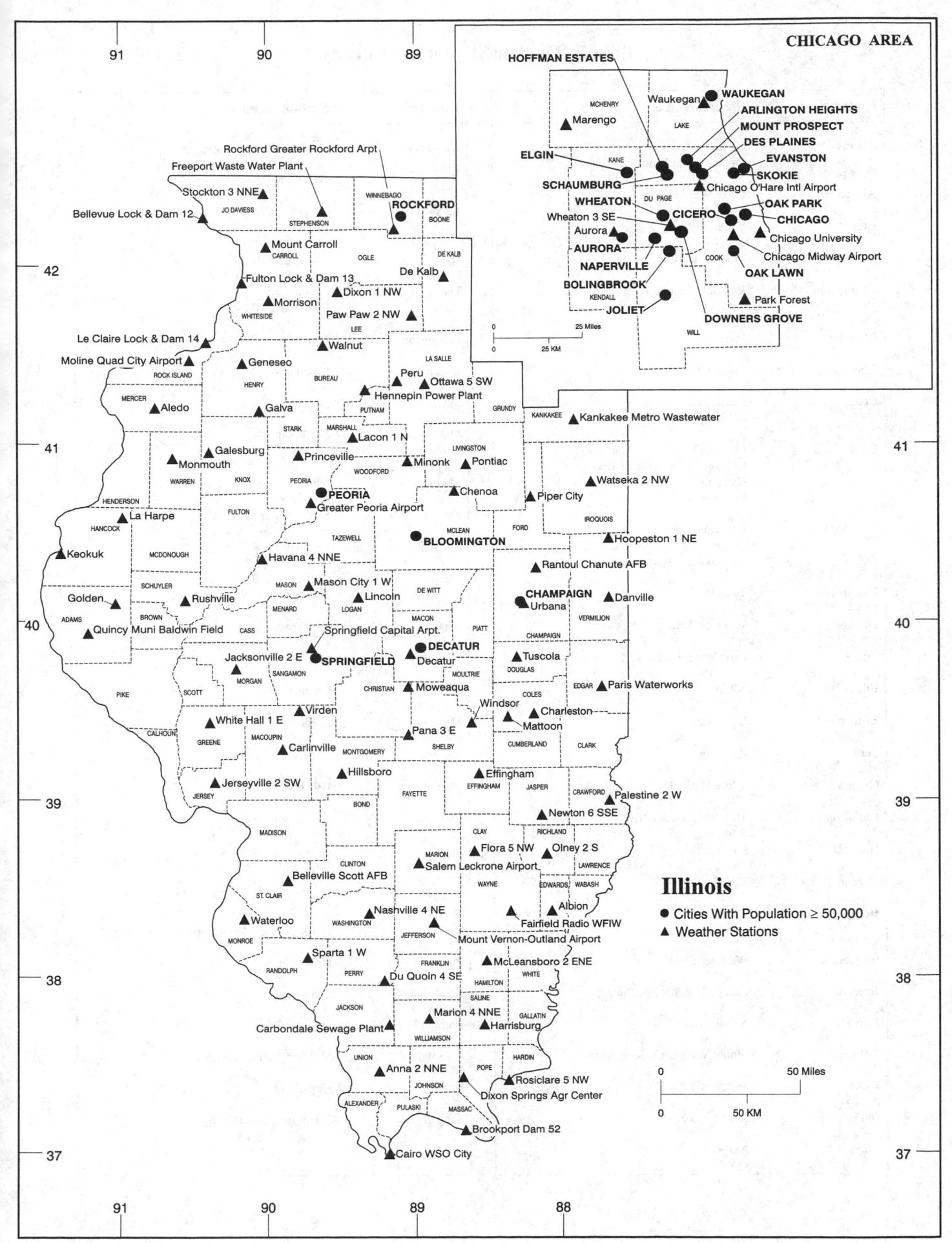

CHICAGO AREA

HOFFMAN ESTATES

Waukegan ● **WAUKEGAN**
ARLINGTON HEIGHTS
MOUNT PROSPECT
DES PLAINES
▲ Marengo
ELGIN
EVANSTON
SKOKIE
Chicago O'Hare Intl Airport
SCHAUMBURG
WHEATON
OAK PARK
CHICAGO
Wheaton 3 SE
CICERO
Chicago University
Aurora
Chicago Midway Airport
AURORA
NAPERVILLE
OAK LAWN
BOLINGBROOK
▲ Park Forest
JOLIET
DOWNERS GROVE

0   25 Miles
0   25 KM

Rockford Greater Rockford Arpt
Freeport Waste Water Plant
Stockton 3 NNE ▲
Bellevue Lock & Dam 12 ▲
WINNEBAGO
BOONE
JO DAVIESS
STEPHENSON
ROCKFORD ●
▲ Mount Carroll
CARROLL
OGLE
DE KALB
De Kalb
42
▲ Fulton Lock & Dam 13
▲ Morrison
▲ Dixon 1 NW
WHITESIDE
LEE
Paw Paw 2 NW ▲
Le Claire Lock & Dam 14 ▲
Moline Quad City Airport ▲
▲ Walnut
ROCK ISLAND
▲ Geneseo
BUREAU
LA SALLE
MERCER
Peru
Ottawa 5 SW ▲
▲ Aledo
HENRY
Hennepin Power Plant ▲
PUTNAM
GRUNDY
41
STARK
MARSHALL
▲ Galva
KANKAKEE
▲ Galesburg
Lacon 1 N ▲
▲ Kankakee Metro Wastewater
▲ Monmouth
▲ Princeville
LIVINGSTON
WARREN
KNOX
WOODFORD
▲ Minonk
▲ Pontiac
PEORIA
FORD
▲ Watseka 2 NW
▲ La Harpe
● **PEORIA**
▲ Chenoa
Greater Peoria Airport
HANCOCK
▲ Piper City
IROQUOIS
▲ Keokuk
MCLEAN
● **BLOOMINGTON**
▲ Hoopeston 1 NE
MCDONOUGH
TAZEWELL
▲ Havana 4 NNE
SCHUYLER
MASON
▲ Rantoul Chanute AFB
Golden ▲
▲ Rushville
▲ Mason City 1 W
DE WITT
MENARD
▲ Lincoln
CHAMPAIGN
40
LOGAN
MACON
● Urbana
▲ Danville
ADAMS
BROWN
CASS
PIATT
CHAMPAIGN
VERMILION
▲ Quincy Muni Baldwin Field
Springfield Capital Arpt.
● **DECATUR**
PIKE
Jacksonville 2 E ▲
● **SPRINGFIELD**
Decatur
▲ Tuscola
DOUGLAS
SANGAMON
MORGAN
SCOTT
MOULTRIE
EDGAR
▲ Paris Waterworks
CHRISTIAN
MACON
▲ Moweaqua
CALHOUN
▲ Virden
Windsor
COLES
▲ Charleston
GREENE
▲ White Hall 1 E
Pana 3 E ▲
Mattoon
CLARK
MACOUPIN
CUMBERLAND
▲ Carlinville
SHELBY
39
MONTGOMERY
▲ Jerseyville 2 SW
▲ Hillsboro
▲ Effingham
CRAWFORD
▲ Palestine 2 W
JERSEY
FAYETTE
EFFINGHAM
JASPER
BOND
Newton 6 SSE ▲
MADISON
CLAY
RICHLAND
LAWRENCE
CLINTON
▲ Flora 5 NW
Olney 2 S ▲
MARION
▲ Belleville Scott AFB
Salem Leckrone Airport ▲
WAYNE
EDWARDS WABASH
ST. CLAIR
▲ Nashville 4 NE
▲ Albion
▲ Waterloo
Fairfield Radio WFIW ▲
WASHINGTON
JEFFERSON
MONROE
Mount Vernon-Outland Airport
38
▲ Sparta 1 W
FRANKLIN
▲ McLeansboro 2 ENE
PERRY
▲ Du Quoin 4 SE
HAMILTON
WHITE
RANDOLPH
SALINE
JACKSON
GALLATIN
▲ Marion 4 NNE
▲ Harrisburg
WILLIAMSON
Carbondale Sewage Plant ▲
UNION
HARDIN
▲ Anna 2 NNE
POPE
▲ Rosiclare 5 NW
JOHNSON
Dixon Springs Agr Center
ALEXANDER
PULASKI
MASSAC
▲ Brookport Dam 52
37
▲ Cairo WSO City

Illinois

● Cities With Population ≥ 50,000
▲ Weather Stations

0   50 Miles
0   50 KM

91   90   89   88

Illinois Weather Stations by County

County	Station Name
Adams	Golden Quincy Muni Baldwin Field
Alexander	Cairo WSO City
Bureau	Walnut
Carroll	Mount Carroll
Champaign	Rantoul Chanute AFB Urbana
Christian	Pana 3 E
Clay	Flora 5 NW
Coles	Charleston Mattoon
Cook	Chicago Midway Airport Chicago O'Hare Int'l Airport Chicago University Park Forest
Crawford	Palestine 2 W
Dekalb	De Kalb
Douglas	Tuscola
Dupage	Wheaton 3 SE
Edgar	Paris Waterworks
Edwards	Albion
Effingham	Effingham
Ford	Piper City
Greene	White Hall 1 E
Hamilton	McLeansboro 2 ENE
Hancock	La Harpe
Hardin	Rosiclare 5 NW
Henry	Galva Geneseo
Iroquois	Watseka 2 NW
Jackson	Carbondale Sewage Plant
Jasper	Newton 6 SSE
Jefferson	Mount Vernon-Outland Airport
Jersey	Jerseyville 2 SW
Jo Daviess	Stockton 3 NNE
Kane	Aurora

County	Station Name
Kankakee	Kankakee Metro Wastewater
Knox	Galesburg
La Salle	Ottawa 5 SW Peru
Lake	Waukegan
Lee	Dixon 1 NW Paw Paw 2 NW
Livingston	Pontiac
Logan	Lincoln
Macon	Decatur
Macoupin	Carlinville Virden
Madison	Alton Melvin Price Lock & Dam
Marion	Salem Leckrone Airport
Marshall	Lacon 1 N
Mason	Havana 4 NNE Mason City 1 W
Massac	Brookport Dam 52
McHenry	Marengo
McLean	Chenoa
Mercer	Aledo
Monroe	Waterloo
Montgomery	Hillsboro
Morgan	Jacksonville 2 E
Peoria	Greater Peoria Airport Princeville
Perry	Du Quoin 4 SE
Pope	Dixon Springs Agr. Center
Putnam	Hennepin Power Plant
Randolph	Sparta 1 W
Richland	Olney 2 S
Rock Island	Moline Quad City Airport
Saline	Harrisburg
Sangamon	Springfield Capital Airport

County	Station Name
Schuyler	Rushville
Shelby	Moweaqua Windsor
St. Clair	Belleville Scott AFB
Stephenson	Freeport Waste Water Plant
Union	Anna 2 NNE
Vermilion	Danville Hoopeston 1 NE
Warren	Monmouth
Washington	Nashville 4 NE
Wayne	Fairfield Radio WFIW
Whiteside	Fulton Lock & Dam 13 Morrison
Williamson	Marion 4 NNE
Winnebago	Rockford Greater Rockford Arpt.
Woodford	Minonk

Illinois Weather Stations by City

City	Station Name	Miles
Arlington Heights	Chicago O'Hare Int'l Airport	8
	Waukegan	18
	Wheaton 3 SE	20
Aurora	Aurora	1
	Wheaton 3 SE	13
Bolingbrook	Aurora	13
	Chicago Midway Airport	17
	Wheaton 3 SE	8
Champaign	Rantoul Chanute AFB	14
	Urbana	1
Chicago	Chicago O'Hare Int'l Airport	15
	Chicago University	7
	Chicago Midway Airport	6
Cicero	Chicago O'Hare Int'l Airport	12
	Chicago University	9
	Chicago Midway Airport	4
	Wheaton 3 SE	16
Decatur	Decatur	4
	Moweaqua	16
Des Plaines	Chicago O'Hare Int'l Airport	4
	Chicago Midway Airport	19
	Wheaton 3 SE	17
Downers Grove	Aurora	16
	Chicago O'Hare Int'l Airport	14
	Chicago Midway Airport	14
	Wheaton 3 SE	3
Elgin	Aurora	19
	Chicago O'Hare Int'l Airport	19
	Wheaton 3 SE	19
Evanston	Chicago O'Hare Int'l Airport	12
	Chicago University	19
	Chicago Midway Airport	18
Hoffman Estates	Chicago O'Hare Int'l Airport	11
	Wheaton 3 SE	17
Joliet	Aurora	20
	Wheaton 3 SE	20
Mount Prospect	Chicago O'Hare Int'l Airport	6
	Wheaton 3 SE	18
Naperville	Aurora	9
	Chicago O'Hare Int'l Airport	20
	Wheaton 3 SE	6
Oak Lawn	Chicago University	9
	Chicago Midway Airport	5
	Park Forest	15
	Wheaton 3 SE	18
Oak Park	Chicago O'Hare Int'l Airport	9
	Chicago University	12
	Chicago Midway Airport	7

City	Station Name	Miles
Oak Park (cont.)	Wheaton 3 SE	15
Peoria	Greater Peoria Airport	5
	Princeville	17
Rockford	Rockford Greater Rockford Arpt.	6
	Beloit, WI	16
Schaumburg	Chicago O'Hare Int'l Airport	9
	Wheaton 3 SE	15
Skokie	Chicago O'Hare Int'l Airport	10
	Chicago University	19
	Chicago Midway Airport	17
Springfield	Springfield Capital Airport	4
Waukegan	Waukegan	2
	Kenosha, WI	14
Wheaton	Aurora	13
	Chicago O'Hare Int'l Airport	13
	Chicago Midway Airport	19
	Wheaton 3 SE	3

Note: Miles is the distance between the geographic center of the city and the weather station.

Illinois Weather Stations by Elevation

Feet	Station Name
967	Stockton 3 NNE
948	Paw Paw 2 NW
872	De Kalb
816	Marengo
807	Galva
770	Galesburg
761	Quincy Muni Baldwin Field
754	Rantoul Chanute AFB
748	Freeport Waste Water Plant
748	Minonk
744	Monmouth
741	Urbana
734	Princeville
725	Golden
718	Aledo
715	Mattoon
711	Chenoa
708	Hoopeston 1 NE
708	Park Forest
698	Dixon 1 NW
698	La Harpe
698	Pana 3 E
698	Waukegan
688	Walnut
688	Windsor
679	Charleston
679	Paris Waterworks
679	Rockford Greater Rockford Arpt.
679	Wheaton 3 SE
672	Virden
669	Piper City
659	Rushville
656	Chicago O'Hare Int'l Airport
652	Tuscola
649	Greater Peoria Airport
649	Pontiac
649	Waterloo
639	Aurora
639	Kankakee Metro Wastewater
639	Mount Carroll
636	Geneseo
629	Carlinville
629	Hillsboro
629	Jerseyville 2 SW
620	Decatur
620	Peru
620	Watseka 2 NW
613	Moweaqua
610	Chicago Midway Airport
606	Effingham
606	Jacksonville 2 E
600	Morrison
597	Anna 2 NNE
593	Chicago University
590	Fulton Lock & Dam 13

Feet	Station Name
590	Moline Quad City Airport
583	Mason City 1 W
583	Springfield Capital Airport
580	Lincoln
577	White Hall 1 E
567	Salem Leckrone Airport
557	Danville
538	Dixon Springs Agr. Center
534	Sparta 1 W
528	Albion
524	Ottawa 5 SW
515	Nashville 4 NE
508	Newton 6 SSE
498	Flora 5 NW
479	McLeansboro 2 ENE
479	Olney 2 S
475	Marion 4 NNE
469	Palestine 2 W
465	Mount Vernon-Outland Airport
459	Havana 4 NNE
459	Hennepin Power Plant
459	Lacon 1 N
442	Belleville Scott AFB
429	Alton Melvin Price Lock & Dam
429	Fairfield Radio WFIW
419	Du Quoin 4 SE
396	Rosiclare 5 NW
387	Carbondale Sewage Plant
364	Harrisburg
328	Brookport Dam 52
311	Cairo WSO City

Chicago O'Hare Int'l Airport

Chicago is located along the southwest shore of Lake Michigan and occupies a plain which, for the most part, is only some tens of feet above the lake. Lake Michigan averages 579 feet above sea level. Natural water drainage over most of the city would be into Lake Michigan, and from areas west of the city is into the Mississippi River System. But actual drainage over most of the city is artificially channeled also into the Mississippi system.

Chicago is in a region of frequently changeable weather. The climate is predominately continental, ranging from relatively warm in summer to relatively cold in winter. In late autumn and winter however, air masses that are initially very cold often reach the city only after being tempered by passage over one or more of the lakes. Similarly, in late spring and summer, air masses reaching the city from the north, northeast, or east are cooler because of movement over the Great Lakes. Very low winter temperatures most often occur in air that flows southward to the west of Lake Superior before reaching the Chicago area. In summer the higher temperatures are with south or southwest flow and are therefore not influenced by the lakes, the only modifying effect being a local lake breeze.

During the warm season, when the lake is cold relative to land, there is frequently a lake breeze that reduces daytime temperature near the shore. When the breeze off the lake is light this effect usually reaches inland only a mile or two, but with stronger on-shore winds the whole city is cooled. On the other hand, temperatures at night are warmer near the lake.

At the O'Hare International Airport temperatures of 96 degrees or higher occur in about half the summers, while about half the winters have a minimum as low as -15 degrees. The average occurrence of the first temperature as low as 32 degrees in the fall is mid-October and the average occurrence of the last temperature as low as 32 degrees in the spring is late April.

Precipitation falls mostly from air that has passed over the Gulf of Mexico. But in winter there is sometimes snowfall, light inland but locally heavy near the lakeshore, with Lake Michigan as the principal moisture source. The effect of Lake Michigan, both on winter temperatures and lake-produced snowfall, is enhanced by non-freezing of much of the lake during the winter, even though areas and harbors are often ice-choked.

Summer thunderstorms are often locally heavy and variable, parts of the city may receive substantial rainfall and other parts none. Longer periods of continuous precipitation are mostly in autumn, winter, and spring.

Chicago O'Hare Int'l Airport *Cook County*   Elevation: 656 ft.   Latitude: 41° 59' N   Longitude: 87° 55' W

	JAN	FEB	MAR	APR	MAY	JUN	JUL	AUG	SEP	OCT	NOV	DEC	YEAR
Mean Maximum Temp. (°F)	29.6	34.6	45.8	58.3	70.2	79.8	84.3	82.0	74.6	62.7	47.8	35.3	58.7
Mean Temp. (°F)	21.8	26.9	37.3	48.4	59.2	68.7	74.0	72.3	64.3	52.5	39.8	28.1	49.5
Mean Minimum Temp. (°F)	14.1	19.2	28.7	38.4	48.1	57.7	63.7	62.5	54.0	42.3	31.8	20.8	40.1
Extreme Maximum Temp. (°F)	65	71	88	91	93	104	104	101	99	90	78	71	104
Extreme Minimum Temp. (°F)	-27	-19	-3	7	27	36	43	42	28	17	1	-25	-27
Days Maximum Temp. ≥ 90°F	0	0	0	0	1	4	8	4	2	0	0	0	19
Days Maximum Temp. ≤ 32°F	17	12	4	0	0	0	0	0	0	0	2	10	45
Days Minimum Temp. ≤ 32°F	29	24	21	7	1	0	0	0	0	4	16	26	128
Days Minimum Temp. ≤ 0°F	6	3	0	0	0	0	0	0	0	0	0	2	11
Heating Degree Days (base 65°F)	1,332	1,069	853	503	225	46	5	8	107	391	751	1,137	6,427
Cooling Degree Days (base 65°F)	0	0	2	9	47	163	292	238	91	8	0	0	850
Mean Precipitation (in.)	1.73	1.58	2.68	3.65	3.49	3.72	3.53	4.59	3.44	2.75	3.01	2.42	36.59
Maximum Precipitation (in.)	4.1	3.5	5.9	7.7	7.1	10.0	8.3	17.1	11.4	7.4	8.2	8.6	49.3
Minimum Precipitation (in.)	0.1	0.1	0.6	1.0	0.3	0.9	1.2	0.5	trace	0.2	0.6	0.2	21.8
Maximum 24-hr. Precipitation (in.)	2.0	1.4	1.8	2.4	3.4	3.1	2.9	6.5	2.9	4.3	2.9	4.5	6.5
Days With ≥ 0.1" Precipitation	5	4	6	7	7	6	6	7	6	5	6	5	70
Days With ≥ 1.0" Precipitation	0	0	0	1	1	1	1	1	1	1	1	1	9
Mean Snowfall (in.)	11.1	8.1	6.4	1.8	trace	trace	trace	trace	0.0	0.3	1.8	7.8	37.3
Maximum Snowfall (in.)	34	26	25	11	2	0	0	0	0	7	10	35	75
Maximum 24-hr. Snowfall (in.)	15	10	9	11	2	0	0	0	0	4	5	10	15
Days With ≥ 1.0" Snow Depth	18	12	4	1	0	0	0	0	0	0	1	8	44
Thunderstorm Days	< 1	< 1	2	4	5	6	6	6	4	2	1	1	37
Foggy Days	12	11	12	10	10	8	9	12	11	11	12	13	131
Predominant Sky Cover	OVR	OVR	OVR	OVR	OVR	OVR	SCT	SCT	OVR	OVR	OVR	OVR	OVR
Mean Relative Humidity 6am (%)	77	78	79	77	77	78	82	85	85	82	81	80	80
Mean Relative Humidity 3pm (%)	66	63	59	53	51	52	54	55	55	53	62	68	58
Mean Dewpoint (°F)	14	18	27	36	46	56	62	61	54	42	31	21	39
Prevailing Wind Direction	W	W	W	NNE	NNE	SSW	SW	SSW	S	S	SSW	WNW	SSW
Prevailing Wind Speed (mph)	12	10	12	13	12	10	9	9	9	10	13	12	10
Maximum Wind Gust (mph)	58	54	84	69	58	63	76	64	58	58	62	62	84

Greater Peoria Airport

The airport station is situated on a rather level tableland surrounded by well-drained and gently rolling terrain. It is set back a mile from the rim of the Illinois River Valley and is almost 200 feet above the river bed. Exposures of all instruments are good. The climate of this area is typically continental as shown by its changeable weather and the wide range of temperature extremes.

June and September are usually the most pleasant months of the year. Then during October or the first of November, Indian Summer is often experienced with an extended period of warm, dry weather.

Precipitation is normally heaviest during the growing season and lowest during midwinter.

The earliest snowfalls have occurred in September and the latest in the spring have occurred as late as May. Heavy snowfalls have rarely exceeded 20 inches.

Based on the 1951-1980 period, the average first occurrence of 32 degrees Fahrenheit in the fall is October 20 and the average last occurrence in the spring is April 24.

Greater Peoria Airport *Peoria County*   Elevation: 649 ft.   Latitude: 40° 40' N   Longitude: 89° 41' W

	JAN	FEB	MAR	APR	MAY	JUN	JUL	AUG	SEP	OCT	NOV	DEC	YEAR
Mean Maximum Temp. (°F)	30.4	36.3	48.9	62.0	73.0	82.2	85.8	83.4	76.6	64.3	48.9	36.0	60.7
Mean Temp. (°F)	22.3	28.0	39.5	51.3	62.1	71.3	75.4	73.3	65.7	53.5	40.4	28.4	50.9
Mean Minimum Temp. (°F)	14.2	19.5	30.1	40.6	51.0	60.4	65.0	63.1	54.6	42.8	31.8	20.8	41.2
Extreme Maximum Temp. (°F)	70	72	86	92	93	105	102	103	97	87	78	71	105
Extreme Minimum Temp. (°F)	-25	-19	-6	14	29	39	47	41	29	19	-2	-23	-25
Days Maximum Temp. ≥ 90°F	0	0	0	0	1	5	9	6	2	0	0	0	23
Days Maximum Temp. ≤ 32°F	17	11	3	0	0	0	0	0	0	0	2	11	44
Days Minimum Temp. ≤ 32°F	29	24	19	5	0	0	0	0	0	4	17	27	125
Days Minimum Temp. ≤ 0°F	6	3	0	0	0	0	0	0	0	0	0	2	11
Heating Degree Days (base 65°F)	1,318	1,040	785	416	153	18	2	6	90	360	733	1,127	6,048
Cooling Degree Days (base 65°F)	0	0	2	12	68	222	342	280	117	11	0	0	1,054
Mean Precipitation (in.)	1.49	1.63	2.83	3.71	4.17	3.84	4.14	3.24	3.42	2.85	2.92	2.41	36.65
Maximum Precipitation (in.)	8.1	4.9	6.9	8.7	11.5	11.7	10.1	8.6	13.1	10.5	7.6	6.3	55.3
Minimum Precipitation (in.)	0.1	0.1	0.4	0.7	0.5	0.4	0.3	0.3	trace	trace	0.1	0.3	22.2
Maximum 24-hr. Precipitation (in.)	4.4	2.8	2.9	5.1	5.5	4.7	3.6	4.3	4.1	3.6	4.3	2.5	5.5
Days With ≥ 0.1" Precipitation	4	4	6	7	8	6	6	6	6	6	6	5	70
Days With ≥ 1.0" Precipitation	0	0	0	1	1	1	1	1	1	1	1	1	9
Mean Snowfall (in.)	8.0	5.8	3.5	1.1	trace	0.0	trace	0.0	trace	trace	2.1	6.3	26.8
Maximum Snowfall (in.)	25	15	18	13	trace	0	0	0	1	3	11	22	52
Maximum 24-hr. Snowfall (in.)	12	9	9	6	trace	0	0	0	1	3	8	7	12
Days With ≥ 1.0" Snow Depth	16	11	3	1	0	0	0	0	0	0	1	8	40
Thunderstorm Days	< 1	1	3	5	7	9	8	7	5	2	1	1	49
Foggy Days	11	10	9	7	7	6	7	9	9	10	10	12	107
Predominant Sky Cover	OVR	OVR	OVR	OVR	OVR	OVR	SCT	CLR	CLR	OVR	OVR	OVR	OVR
Mean Relative Humidity 6am (%)	80	81	81	78	80	82	86	89	87	84	83	83	83
Mean Relative Humidity 3pm (%)	67	64	58	52	52	52	55	56	52	52	61	69	57
Mean Dewpoint (°F)	16	20	29	38	49	59	64	63	54	43	32	22	41
Prevailing Wind Direction	S	S	S	S	S	S	S	S	S	S	S	S	S
Prevailing Wind Speed (mph)	12	12	13	12	10	10	9	8	9	10	12	12	10
Maximum Wind Gust (mph)	54	53	68	69	61	75	85	54	75	48	62	59	85

Moline Quad City Airport

The locality is in the heart of the Corn Belt. Agricultural crops include many important staple products in addition to corn. Cattle, hogs, horses, and poultry produced in Iowa and Illinois rank high in the nation. Close to the Mississippi River there is large scale truck gardening and considerable dairying. Field production of grains and livestock attains greater development farther away from the large streams, where the countryside is rolling prairie. Damaging droughts are not common. This, together with the variety of agricultural products, has led to designating the section as the Bread Basket of America.

The climate is favorable for many industries as evidenced by the large number and variety of manufacturing and other enterprises which have located and developed in the community. Among these are some of the largest producers of agricultural machinery in the world.

This area has a temperate continental climate, with a wide temperature range throughout the year. There are some intensely hot, unusually humid, periods in summer and severely cold periods in winter. Maxima of 90 degrees or more have occurred in summer as frequently as 55 days and zero or lower readings have occurred during every winter.

Freezing temperatures have occurred as late in spring as late May and as early in autumn as late September. Precipitation is usually well distributed throughout the year with the greatest amounts falling during the 177-day average crop growing season. Substantial weather changes frequently occur at three or four day intervals, as a direct result of proximity to some of the most important storm tracks.

Moline Quad City Airport *Rock Island County*   Elevation: 590 ft.   Latitude: 41° 28' N   Longitude: 90° 31' W

	JAN	FEB	MAR	APR	MAY	JUN	JUL	AUG	SEP	OCT	NOV	DEC	YEAR
Mean Maximum Temp. (°F)	28.9	34.9	47.5	61.5	73.1	82.6	86.1	83.6	76.1	63.9	47.7	34.5	60.0
Mean Temp. (°F)	20.5	26.4	38.1	50.5	61.6	71.2	75.3	73.0	64.8	52.7	39.0	26.7	50.0
Mean Minimum Temp. (°F)	12.0	17.8	28.6	39.4	50.1	59.8	64.5	62.3	53.4	41.5	30.2	18.8	39.9
Extreme Maximum Temp. (°F)	69	71	88	93	95	104	103	103	98	93	79	71	104
Extreme Minimum Temp. (°F)	-27	-28	-7	7	29	39	46	40	30	16	-9	-24	-28
Days Maximum Temp. ≥ 90°F	0	0	0	0	1	5	9	6	2	0	0	0	23
Days Maximum Temp. ≤ 32°F	18	11	3	0	0	0	0	0	0	0	3	12	47
Days Minimum Temp. ≤ 32°F	29	24	20	7	1	0	0	0	0	6	18	28	133
Days Minimum Temp. ≤ 0°F	7	4	0	0	0	0	0	0	0	0	0	3	14
Heating Degree Days (base 65°F)	1,376	1,085	828	443	166	17	2	7	104	386	774	1,181	6,369
Cooling Degree Days (base 65°F)	0	0	2	13	61	213	334	265	103	11	0	0	1,002
Mean Precipitation (in.)	1.55	1.42	2.98	3.83	4.47	4.52	4.08	4.48	3.46	2.81	2.71	2.19	38.50
Maximum Precipitation (in.)	4.4	2.8	7.4	11.3	11.4	13.2	11.8	15.2	14.2	8.5	6.8	5.0	56.4
Minimum Precipitation (in.)	0.3	0.2	0.3	0.7	0.3	1.0	0.4	0.3	trace	trace	0.5	0.3	20.2
Maximum 24-hr. Precipitation (in.)	1.7	1.8	2.2	4.3	3.2	4.6	5.1	4.6	6.2	4.8	2.0	3.1	6.2
Days With ≥ 0.1" Precipitation	4	4	6	7	7	7	6	7	6	5	5	5	69
Days With ≥ 1.0" Precipitation	0	0	1	1	1	1	1	2	1	1	0	0	9
Mean Snowfall (in.)	9.8	6.7	5.2	1.6	trace	trace	trace	0.0	trace	0.2	3.0	7.3	33.8
Maximum Snowfall (in.)	27	21	20	13	trace	0	0	0	0	7	16	22	63
Maximum 24-hr. Snowfall (in.)	16	9	10	8	trace	0	0	0	0	7	8	9	16
Days With ≥ 1.0" Snow Depth	19	14	5	1	0	0	0	0	0	0	2	10	51
Thunderstorm Days	< 1	< 1	2	5	7	8	8	7	5	2	1	< 1	45
Foggy Days	12	11	13	10	11	9	12	15	14	13	12	13	145
Predominant Sky Cover	OVR	OVR	OVR	OVR	OVR	OVR	CLR	CLR	CLR	CLR	OVR	OVR	OVR
Mean Relative Humidity 6am (%)	76	78	79	78	79	81	85	89	87	82	80	79	81
Mean Relative Humidity 3pm (%)	66	63	57	50	49	50	54	55	52	49	59	67	56
Mean Dewpoint (°F)	13	18	27	37	48	59	64	63	54	42	30	19	40
Prevailing Wind Direction	WNW	WNW	WNW	WNW	S	S	S	S	S	S	WNW	WNW	WNW
Prevailing Wind Speed (mph)	14	14	14	15	12	10	9	9	10	12	14	14	13
Maximum Wind Gust (mph)	59	54	69	81	66	79	66	81	59	61	60	69	81

Rockford Greater Rockford Arpt.

The climate of Rockford is characterized by hot summers and cold winters.

When winter northeasterly winds blow across Lake Michigan, cloudiness often is increased in the Rockford area, and temperatures are somewhat higher than those westward around the Mississippi River. Conversely, in summer, the cooling effect of Lake Michigan sometimes is felt as far westward as Rockford.

While 34 percent of the precipitation occurs in the three summer months of June to August, and 64 percent in the six months, April to September, no month averages less than four percent of the annual total.

Though summers may be described as hot, seldom does oppressive heat prevail for extended periods. In general, the summers are pleasant.

Winters are cold. Snow cover is adequate for diversified winter sports, and usually is continuous from late December through February.

Based on the 1951-1980 period, the average first occurrence of 32 degrees Fahrenheit in the fall is October 11 and the average last occurrence in the spring is April 29.

Rockford Greater Rockford Arpt. *Winnebago County*   Elevation: 679 ft.   Latitude: 42° 12' N   Longitude: 89° 07' W

	JAN	FEB	MAR	APR	MAY	JUN	JUL	AUG	SEP	OCT	NOV	DEC	YEAR
Mean Maximum Temp. (°F)	26.9	32.5	44.6	58.7	71.4	80.6	83.9	81.5	74.2	61.9	45.7	32.5	57.9
Mean Temp. (°F)	18.7	24.3	35.5	47.9	59.7	69.2	73.4	71.2	63.0	51.0	37.3	25.0	48.0
Mean Minimum Temp. (°F)	10.5	16.0	26.5	37.0	48.0	57.8	62.7	60.8	51.7	40.0	28.9	17.3	38.1
Extreme Maximum Temp. (°F)	63	68	85	91	95	101	102	104	95	90	75	66	104
Extreme Minimum Temp. (°F)	-27	-24	-9	5	27	37	45	41	27	17	-10	-24	-27
Days Maximum Temp. ≥ 90°F	0	0	0	0	1	3	6	3	1	0	0	0	14
Days Maximum Temp. ≤ 32°F	20	13	5	0	0	0	0	0	0	0	3	14	55
Days Minimum Temp. ≤ 32°F	30	26	23	9	1	0	0	0	1	7	20	28	145
Days Minimum Temp. ≤ 0°F	9	5	0	0	0	0	0	0	0	0	0	4	18
Heating Degree Days (base 65°F)	1,430	1,145	907	514	209	34	4	13	131	435	824	1,235	6,881
Cooling Degree Days (base 65°F)	0	0	1	8	48	171	275	215	76	6	0	0	800
Mean Precipitation (in.)	1.38	1.29	2.42	3.62	3.99	4.67	4.09	4.11	3.56	2.67	2.61	2.04	36.45
Maximum Precipitation (in.)	4.7	3.0	5.6	9.9	7.0	11.8	11.8	13.5	10.7	8.3	5.5	5.0	56.5
Minimum Precipitation (in.)	0.2	trace	0.6	1.0	0.5	0.5	0.8	0.7	0	trace	0.4	0.4	23.3
Maximum 24-hr. Precipitation (in.)	2.5	1.6	2.5	3.4	3.6	3.9	5.0	5.7	5.6	4.8	2.1	2.0	5.7
Days With ≥ 0.1" Precipitation	4	3	5	7	7	7	7	7	6	5	5	5	68
Days With ≥ 1.0" Precipitation	0	0	0	1	1	1	1	1	1	1	1	0	8
Mean Snowfall (in.)	10.1	7.6	5.7	1.6	trace	trace	trace	trace	0.0	trace	2.6	9.8	37.4
Maximum Snowfall (in.)	26	30	23	8	1	0	0	0	0	2	15	25	59
Maximum 24-hr. Snowfall (in.)	10	8	10	6	1	0	0	0	0	2	7	11	11
Days With ≥ 1.0" Snow Depth	22	17	7	1	0	0	0	0	0	0	2	14	63
Thunderstorm Days	< 1	< 1	2	4	5	8	8	6	5	2	1	< 1	41
Foggy Days	12	11	12	11	11	8	12	16	14	12	13	14	146
Predominant Sky Cover	OVR	OVR	OVR	OVR	OVR	OVR	OVR	OVR	OVR	OVR	OVR	OVR	OVR
Mean Relative Humidity 6am (%)	80	81	82	80	80	81	86	90	90	86	83	83	84
Mean Relative Humidity 3pm (%)	69	64	60	51	50	51	53	56	54	53	63	70	58
Mean Dewpoint (°F)	13	17	26	36	47	57	62	62	53	41	30	19	39
Prevailing Wind Direction	WNW	WNW	WNW	ENE	S	S	S	S	S	S	S	WNW	S
Prevailing Wind Speed (mph)	13	13	13	13	10	9	8	8	8	9	10	13	10
Maximum Wind Gust (mph)	56	54	54	64	81	67	79	67	58	59	59	62	81

Springfield Capital Airport

The location of Springfield near the center of North America gives it a typical continental climate with warm summers and fairly cold winters. The surrounding country is nearly level. There are no large hills in the vicinity, but rolling terrain is found near the Sangamon River and Spring Creek.

Monthly temperatures range from the upper 20s for January to the upper 70s for July. Considerable variation may take place within the seasons. Temperatures of 70 degrees or higher may occur in winter and temperatures near 50 degrees are sometimes recorded during the summer months.

There are no wet and dry seasons. Monthly precipitation ranges from a little over four inches in May and June to about two inches in January. There is some variation in rainfall totals from year to year. Thunderstorms are common during hot weather, and these are sometimes locally severe with brief but heavy showers. The average year has about fifty thunderstorms of which two-thirds occur during the months of May through August. Damaging hail accompanies only a few of the thunderstorms and the areas affected are usually small.

Sunshine is particularly abundant during the summer months when days are long and not very cloudy. January is the cloudiest month, with only about a third as much sunshine as July or August. March is the windiest month, and August the month with the least wind. Velocities of more than 40 mph are not unusual for brief periods in most months of the year. The prevailing wind direction is southerly during most of the year with northwesterly winds during the late fall and early spring months.

An overall description of the climate of Springfield would be one indicating pleasant conditions with sharp seasonal changes, but no extended periods of severely cold weather. Summer weather is often uncomfortably warm and humid.

Based on the 1951-1980 period, the average first occurrence of 32 degrees Fahrenheit in the fall is October 19 and the average last occurrence in the spring is April 17.

Springfield Capital Airport *Sangamon County*   Elevation: 583 ft.   Latitude: 39° 51' N   Longitude: 89° 41' W

	JAN	FEB	MAR	APR	MAY	JUN	JUL	AUG	SEP	OCT	NOV	DEC	YEAR
Mean Maximum Temp. (°F)	32.8	38.7	50.9	63.8	74.8	83.6	87.0	84.7	78.6	66.7	51.2	38.6	62.6
Mean Temp. (°F)	24.8	30.3	41.6	53.1	63.8	72.8	76.5	74.3	67.1	55.5	42.6	30.9	52.8
Mean Minimum Temp. (°F)	16.8	21.8	32.2	42.4	52.7	61.9	66.0	63.9	55.5	44.3	33.8	23.2	42.9
Extreme Maximum Temp. (°F)	69	74	87	90	94	101	102	102	101	90	82	74	102
Extreme Minimum Temp. (°F)	-21	-20	-6	19	29	42	48	43	32	19	1	-21	-21
Days Maximum Temp. ≥ 90°F	0	0	0	0	1	7	11	7	3	0	0	0	29
Days Maximum Temp. ≤ 32°F	14	9	2	0	0	0	0	0	0	0	1	8	34
Days Minimum Temp. ≤ 32°F	28	22	16	4	0	0	0	0	0	4	14	25	113
Days Minimum Temp. ≤ 0°F	4	3	0	0	0	0	0	0	0	0	0	2	9
Heating Degree Days (base 65°F)	1,239	975	722	368	121	13	1	3	74	311	668	1,050	5,545
Cooling Degree Days (base 65°F)	0	0	3	16	86	254	369	307	140	22	1	0	1,198
Mean Precipitation (in.)	1.62	1.78	3.13	3.60	4.09	3.68	3.51	3.44	3.03	2.62	2.79	2.56	35.85
Maximum Precipitation (in.)	6.2	4.9	7.9	9.9	10.6	10.8	10.8	8.4	15.2	13.4	6.9	8.9	54.5
Minimum Precipitation (in.)	trace	0.3	0.2	0.7	0.3	0.2	0.3	0.1	trace	0.1	trace	0.1	22.8
Maximum 24-hr. Precipitation (in.)	2.4	2.4	3.3	4.4	3.6	5.1	4.3	4.4	5.4	4.7	2.4	4.7	5.4
Days With ≥ 0.1" Precipitation	4	4	7	7	7	6	6	5	5	5	6	5	67
Days With ≥ 1.0" Precipitation	0	0	1	1	1	1	1	1	1	1	0	1	9
Mean Snowfall (in.)	7.4	5.9	3.4	0.8	trace	0.0	trace	0.0	0.0	trace	1.6	5.0	24.1
Maximum Snowfall (in.)	21	18	23	8	1	0	0	0	0	3	9	23	48
Maximum 24-hr. Snowfall (in.)	8	10	9	6	1	0	0	0	0	3	8	11	11
Days With ≥ 1.0" Snow Depth	13	9	3	0	0	0	0	0	0	0	1	6	32
Thunderstorm Days	< 1	1	3	5	7	9	8	7	5	2	2	< 1	49
Foggy Days	9	8	8	6	6	5	6	9	8	8	8	10	91
Predominant Sky Cover	OVR	OVR	OVR	OVR	OVR	OVR	SCT	CLR	CLR	CLR	OVR	OVR	OVR
Mean Relative Humidity 6am (%)	80	81	81	79	81	82	85	89	87	83	82	82	83
Mean Relative Humidity 3pm (%)	67	65	59	52	51	51	54	56	50	50	60	69	57
Mean Dewpoint (°F)	18	22	31	41	51	61	65	64	56	44	33	24	43
Prevailing Wind Direction	S	S	S	S	S	S	S	S	S	S	S	S	S
Prevailing Wind Speed (mph)	15	14	15	15	13	12	9	9	10	13	14	15	13
Maximum Wind Gust (mph)	55	53	71	63	67	59	60	69	61	53	76	73	76

Albion *Edwards County*   Elevation: 528 ft.   Latitude: 38° 23' N   Longitude: 88° 03' W

	JAN	FEB	MAR	APR	MAY	JUN	JUL	AUG	SEP	OCT	NOV	DEC	YEAR
Mean Maximum Temp. (°F)	39.5	45.5	56.0	67.3	77.0	85.9	90.0	88.3	81.8	70.7	55.4	43.9	66.8
Mean Temp. (°F)	31.3	36.2	46.0	56.3	66.2	75.2	79.1	77.3	70.3	59.0	46.3	35.7	56.6
Mean Minimum Temp. (°F)	23.0	26.9	35.9	45.3	55.4	64.5	68.1	66.3	58.7	47.3	37.1	27.5	46.3
Extreme Maximum Temp. (°F)	70	78	85	89	95	101	105	104	100	92	80	75	105
Extreme Minimum Temp. (°F)	-20	-11	2	22	34	42	50	47	36	24	9	-18	-20
Days Maximum Temp. ≥ 90°F	0	0	0	0	2	10	18	14	6	0	0	0	50
Days Maximum Temp. ≤ 32°F	9	5	1	0	0	0	0	0	0	0	1	5	21
Days Minimum Temp. ≤ 32°F	24	19	13	3	0	0	0	0	0	1	10	21	91
Days Minimum Temp. ≤ 0°F	1	1	0	0	0	0	0	0	0	0	0	1	3
Heating Degree Days (base 65°F)	1,040	807	587	282	76	5	0	1	37	217	557	902	4,511
Cooling Degree Days (base 65°F)	0	0	5	28	124	325	454	398	205	38	2	0	1,579
Mean Precipitation (in.)	2.55	2.82	4.19	5.34	4.73	4.19	3.80	3.14	2.95	3.48	4.33	3.34	44.86
Days With ≥ 0.1" Precipitation	5	5	7	8	7	6	5	5	5	5	6	6	70
Days With ≥ 1.0" Precipitation	1	1	1	2	1	1	1	1	1	1	1	1	13
Mean Snowfall (in.)	2.7	2.7	2.0	0.1	0.0	0.0	0.0	0.0	0.0	0.1	0.2	2.5	10.3
Days With ≥ 1.0" Snow Depth	4	3	1	0	0	0	0	0	0	0	0	1	9

Aledo *Mercer County*   Elevation: 718 ft.   Latitude: 41° 12' N   Longitude: 90° 45' W

	JAN	FEB	MAR	APR	MAY	JUN	JUL	AUG	SEP	OCT	NOV	DEC	YEAR
Mean Maximum Temp. (°F)	30.0	35.7	48.4	62.4	73.5	82.4	85.9	83.7	76.4	64.5	47.9	34.8	60.5
Mean Temp. (°F)	21.7	27.2	38.8	51.2	62.0	71.2	74.6	72.8	64.7	53.4	39.2	27.1	50.3
Mean Minimum Temp. (°F)	13.4	18.6	29.0	39.7	50.7	60.0	63.5	61.8	53.1	42.2	30.5	19.3	40.1
Extreme Maximum Temp. (°F)	69	70	87	91	93	103	103	102	97	91	77	70	103
Extreme Minimum Temp. (°F)	-25	-28	-7	10	30	36	44	43	30	17	-6	-20	-28
Days Maximum Temp. ≥ 90°F	0	0	0	0	1	4	9	6	2	0	0	0	22
Days Maximum Temp. ≤ 32°F	17	11	3	0	0	0	0	0	0	0	3	11	45
Days Minimum Temp. ≤ 32°F	29	25	20	6	0	0	0	0	0	5	18	28	131
Days Minimum Temp. ≤ 0°F	6	3	0	0	0	0	0	0	0	0	0	3	12
Heating Degree Days (base 65°F)	1,333	1,062	806	424	151	18	3	7	103	364	766	1,170	6,207
Cooling Degree Days (base 65°F)	0	0	2	13	60	207	303	264	99	10	0	0	958
Mean Precipitation (in.)	1.28	1.25	2.46	3.63	3.97	4.37	4.10	4.40	3.44	2.76	2.51	1.95	36.12
Days With ≥ 0.1" Precipitation	3	3	6	7	8	7	6	7	6	5	5	4	67
Days With ≥ 1.0" Precipitation	0	0	1	1	1	1	1	1	1	1	0	0	8
Mean Snowfall (in.)	8.7	6.1	4.0	1.1	trace	0.0	0.0	0.0	0.0	0.2	2.2	5.8	28.1
Days With ≥ 1.0" Snow Depth	na	na	2	0	0	0	0	0	0	0	1	na	na

Alton Melvin Price Lock & Dam *Madison County*   Elevation: 429 ft.   Latitude: 38° 49' N   Longitude: 90° 09' W

	JAN	FEB	MAR	APR	MAY	JUN	JUL	AUG	SEP	OCT	NOV	DEC	YEAR
Mean Maximum Temp. (°F)	35.3	41.3	52.2	64.1	74.6	83.8	88.1	86.3	79.4	67.3	52.9	41.5	63.9
Mean Temp. (°F)	27.0	32.3	42.8	54.4	64.8	74.0	78.3	76.3	68.8	56.7	44.0	33.4	54.4
Mean Minimum Temp. (°F)	18.7	23.3	33.4	44.6	54.9	64.2	68.5	66.3	58.2	46.1	35.1	25.4	44.9
Extreme Maximum Temp. (°F)	71	74	85	90	93	98	106	103	98	90	81	73	106
Extreme Minimum Temp. (°F)	-16	-15	2	20	36	44	50	46	37	25	6	-16	-16
Days Maximum Temp. ≥ 90°F	0	0	0	0	1	6	14	9	3	0	0	0	33
Days Maximum Temp. ≤ 32°F	12	7	1	0	0	0	0	0	0	0	1	6	27
Days Minimum Temp. ≤ 32°F	28	22	15	3	0	0	0	0	0	1	12	23	104
Days Minimum Temp. ≤ 0°F	2	1	0	0	0	0	0	0	0	0	0	1	4
Heating Degree Days (base 65°F)	1,172	916	684	328	96	8	1	1	50	271	622	972	5,121
Cooling Degree Days (base 65°F)	0	0	3	15	94	292	432	372	174	22	1	0	1,405
Mean Precipitation (in.)	2.00	2.14	3.49	4.40	4.29	3.23	3.49	3.13	3.08	2.73	3.83	2.95	38.76
Days With ≥ 0.1" Precipitation	5	4	7	7	7	5	6	5	5	6	7	6	70
Days With ≥ 1.0" Precipitation	0	0	1	1	1	1	1	1	1	1	1	1	10
Mean Snowfall (in.)	na	na	2.1	0.4	0.0	0.0	0.0	0.0	0.0	trace	0.3	0.4	na
Days With ≥ 1.0" Snow Depth	7	4	1	0	0	0	0	0	0	0	0	2	14

Anna 2 NNE *Union County*   Elevation: 597 ft.   Latitude: 37° 28' N   Longitude: 89° 14' W

	JAN	FEB	MAR	APR	MAY	JUN	JUL	AUG	SEP	OCT	NOV	DEC	YEAR
Mean Maximum Temp. (°F)	40.9	47.3	57.5	68.4	77.1	85.2	88.9	87.7	80.8	70.2	56.8	45.6	67.2
Mean Temp. (°F)	32.1	37.4	47.0	57.2	66.0	74.3	78.3	76.6	69.6	58.4	47.1	37.0	56.8
Mean Minimum Temp. (°F)	23.3	27.5	36.4	46.0	54.9	63.4	67.6	65.5	58.3	46.5	37.4	28.4	46.3
Extreme Maximum Temp. (°F)	70	77	84	90	93	100	104	103	101	90	83	76	104
Extreme Minimum Temp. (°F)	-17	-10	1	21	31	45	49	46	32	20	9	-14	-17
Days Maximum Temp. ≥ 90°F	0	0	0	0	1	7	16	12	4	0	0	0	40
Days Maximum Temp. ≤ 32°F	8	4	1	0	0	0	0	0	0	0	0	4	17
Days Minimum Temp. ≤ 32°F	24	18	12	3	0	0	0	0	0	2	11	20	90
Days Minimum Temp. ≤ 0°F	1	0	0	0	0	0	0	0	0	0	0	1	2
Heating Degree Days (base 65°F)	1,012	773	557	254	71	4	0	0	40	226	531	860	4,328
Cooling Degree Days (base 65°F)	0	0	4	27	111	295	431	380	181	29	2	0	1,460
Mean Precipitation (in.)	3.48	3.34	4.82	4.89	5.19	4.25	3.21	3.59	3.12	3.51	4.62	4.26	48.28
Days With ≥ 0.1" Precipitation	6	6	8	8	8	6	5	5	5	6	7	7	77
Days With ≥ 1.0" Precipitation	1	1	1	1	2	1	1	1	1	1	1	1	13
Mean Snowfall (in.)	4.9	4.5	2.3	0.1	0.0	0.0	0.0	0.0	0.0	0.1	0.5	2.3	14.7
Days With ≥ 1.0" Snow Depth	6	5	1	0	0	0	0	0	0	0	0	3	15

Aurora *Kane County*   Elevation: 639 ft.   Latitude: 41° 46' N   Longitude: 88° 19' W

	JAN	FEB	MAR	APR	MAY	JUN	JUL	AUG	SEP	OCT	NOV	DEC	YEAR
Mean Maximum Temp. (°F)	29.5	35.1	46.6	59.8	72.1	81.3	84.8	82.6	75.4	63.4	47.8	34.6	59.4
Mean Temp. (°F)	20.3	26.0	37.0	48.8	60.1	69.4	73.6	71.5	63.7	51.7	38.8	26.3	48.9
Mean Minimum Temp. (°F)	11.4	16.6	27.2	37.7	48.0	57.5	62.4	60.5	51.9	40.2	29.7	18.3	38.5
Extreme Maximum Temp. (°F)	66	70	83	91	95	103	102	101	95	90	77	68	103
Extreme Minimum Temp. (°F)	-26	-20	-1	8	26	35	42	43	28	15	-2	-22	-26
Days Maximum Temp. ≥ 90°F	0	0	0	0	1	5	7	4	1	0	0	0	18
Days Maximum Temp. ≤ 32°F	17	11	3	0	0	0	0	0	0	0	2	11	44
Days Minimum Temp. ≤ 32°F	30	26	23	8	1	0	0	0	0	6	19	28	141
Days Minimum Temp. ≤ 0°F	8	4	0	0	0	0	0	0	0	0	0	3	15
Heating Degree Days (base 65°F)	1,381	1,092	863	487	200	35	4	10	117	413	779	1,194	6,575
Cooling Degree Days (base 65°F)	0	0	1	6	50	176	283	224	81	6	0	0	827
Mean Precipitation (in.)	1.62	1.50	2.58	3.95	3.99	4.35	4.32	4.42	3.63	2.73	3.15	2.44	38.68
Days With ≥ 0.1" Precipitation	5	4	6	8	7	7	6	7	6	5	6	5	72
Days With ≥ 1.0" Precipitation	0	0	0	1	1	1	1	1	1	1	1	1	9
Mean Snowfall (in.)	9.9	6.9	3.8	0.9	0.0	0.0	0.0	0.0	0.0	trace	1.5	6.7	29.7
Days With ≥ 1.0" Snow Depth	20	14	5	0	0	0	0	0	0	0	1	11	51

Belleville Scott AFB *St. Clair County*   Elevation: 442 ft.   Latitude: 38° 33' N   Longitude: 89° 51' W

	JAN	FEB	MAR	APR	MAY	JUN	JUL	AUG	SEP	OCT	NOV	DEC	YEAR
Mean Maximum Temp. (°F)	39.2	45.8	56.8	68.0	77.2	85.6	89.6	87.7	81.7	70.8	56.1	44.2	66.9
Mean Temp. (°F)	30.5	36.0	46.1	56.3	65.5	74.1	78.0	75.6	68.9	57.9	46.1	35.6	55.9
Mean Minimum Temp. (°F)	21.7	26.2	35.3	44.6	53.7	62.4	66.3	63.5	56.1	44.9	36.1	27.0	44.8
Extreme Maximum Temp. (°F)	72	80	89	90	94	101	105	100	101	92	82	76	105
Extreme Minimum Temp. (°F)	-27	-21	-8	19	28	38	43	39	26	20	2	-19	-27
Days Maximum Temp. ≥ 90°F	0	0	0	0	1	9	16	12	5	0	0	0	43
Days Maximum Temp. ≤ 32°F	10	5	1	0	0	0	0	0	0	0	0	4	20
Days Minimum Temp. ≤ 32°F	25	20	14	4	0	0	0	0	0	4	12	22	101
Days Minimum Temp. ≤ 0°F	2	1	0	0	0	0	0	0	0	0	0	1	4
Heating Degree Days (base 65°F)	1,064	812	586	281	85	6	1	2	50	245	563	904	4,599
Cooling Degree Days (base 65°F)	0	0	6	28	111	292	424	351	171	32	2	0	1,417
Mean Precipitation (in.)	1.98	2.15	3.55	3.96	4.15	3.82	3.31	3.34	3.06	2.92	3.80	2.99	39.03
Days With ≥ 0.1" Precipitation	4	4	7	7	7	7	5	5	5	5	6	5	67
Days With ≥ 1.0" Precipitation	0	0	1	1	1	1	1	1	1	1	1	1	10
Mean Snowfall (in.)	6.5	3.2	2.1	0.8	0.0	0.0	0.0	0.0	0.0	0.0	0.9	2.6	16.1
Days With ≥ 1.0" Snow Depth	9	5	1	0	0	0	0	0	0	0	1	4	20

Brookport Dam 52 *Massac County*   Elevation: 328 ft.   Latitude: 37° 08' N   Longitude: 88° 39' W

	JAN	FEB	MAR	APR	MAY	JUN	JUL	AUG	SEP	OCT	NOV	DEC	YEAR
Mean Maximum Temp. (°F)	42.2	48.0	58.1	68.9	77.6	85.7	89.5	88.3	81.6	70.8	57.8	47.0	68.0
Mean Temp. (°F)	33.4	38.4	47.8	57.8	66.8	74.9	78.9	77.2	70.3	58.9	48.1	38.2	57.6
Mean Minimum Temp. (°F)	24.5	28.8	37.4	46.7	55.9	64.1	68.3	66.1	58.9	46.8	38.3	29.4	47.1
Extreme Maximum Temp. (°F)	72	74	83	89	94	100	105	101	99	92	82	74	105
Extreme Minimum Temp. (°F)	-21	-9	0	21	32	42	48	42	29	18	9	-13	-21
Days Maximum Temp. ≥ 90°F	0	0	0	0	1	8	17	13	5	0	0	0	44
Days Maximum Temp. ≤ 32°F	6	3	0	0	0	0	0	0	0	0	0	3	12
Days Minimum Temp. ≤ 32°F	23	17	11	2	0	0	0	0	0	2	9	19	83
Days Minimum Temp. ≤ 0°F	1	0	0	0	0	0	0	0	0	0	0	0	1
Heating Degree Days (base 65°F)	973	744	531	235	60	3	0	0	37	218	504	824	4,129
Cooling Degree Days (base 65°F)	0	0	4	24	120	306	448	393	195	35	2	0	1,527
Mean Precipitation (in.)	3.40	3.83	4.54	4.85	4.66	4.12	4.18	3.03	3.22	3.36	4.38	4.47	48.04
Days With ≥ 0.1" Precipitation	6	6	8	7	8	7	6	5	5	6	7	7	78
Days With ≥ 1.0" Precipitation	1	1	1	1	1	1	2	1	1	1	1	1	13
Mean Snowfall (in.)	3.3	3.0	1.3	trace	0.0	0.0	0.0	0.0	0.0	0.0	trace	1.0	8.6
Days With ≥ 1.0" Snow Depth	5	5	1	0	0	0	0	0	0	0	0	1	12

Cairo WSO City *Alexander County*   Elevation: 311 ft.   Latitude: 37° 00' N   Longitude: 89° 10' W

	JAN	FEB	MAR	APR	MAY	JUN	JUL	AUG	SEP	OCT	NOV	DEC	YEAR
Mean Maximum Temp. (°F)	40.6	47.3	57.1	68.6	78.0	86.4	89.7	87.4	81.1	70.4	56.9	46.2	67.5
Mean Temp. (°F)	33.3	39.0	48.5	59.2	68.5	76.8	80.5	78.1	71.3	60.1	48.4	38.6	58.5
Mean Minimum Temp. (°F)	25.9	30.7	39.9	49.7	59.0	67.2	71.2	68.7	61.5	49.7	39.8	31.0	49.5
Extreme Maximum Temp. (°F)	71	77	85	91	96	*100*	104	102	*99*	*89*	*82*	*79*	*104*
Extreme Minimum Temp. (°F)	-12	-5	10	27	38	*49*	57	50	*39*	*27*	*13*	*-9*	*-12*
Days Maximum Temp. ≥ 90°F	0	0	0	0	2	10	17	11	4	0	0	0	44
Days Maximum Temp. ≤ 32°F	8	4	1	0	0	0	0	0	0	0	0	4	17
Days Minimum Temp. ≤ 32°F	23	16	7	1	0	0	0	0	0	1	6	17	71
Days Minimum Temp. ≤ 0°F	1	0	0	0	0	0	0	0	0	0	0	0	1
Heating Degree Days (base 65°F)	977	727	510	212	44	2	0	0	28	191	495	811	3,997
Cooling Degree Days (base 65°F)	0	0	8	42	152	357	487	413	212	42	2	1	1,716
Mean Precipitation (in.)	3.02	3.50	4.55	4.98	4.82	4.29	4.29	3.77	3.10	3.52	4.26	4.06	48.16
Days With ≥ 0.1" Precipitation	5	5	8	7	8	6	6	5	5	5	7	6	73
Days With ≥ 1.0" Precipitation	1	1	1	2	2	1	1	1	1	1	1	1	14
Mean Snowfall (in.)	4.0	2.7	1.7	trace	0.0	0.0	0.0	0.0	0.0	0.1	0.2	0.9	9.6
Days With ≥ 1.0" Snow Depth	6	4	1	0	0	0	0	0	0	0	0	1	12

Carbondale Sewage Plant *Jackson County* Elevation: 387 ft. Latitude: 37° 44' N Longitude: 89° 10' W

	JAN	FEB	MAR	APR	MAY	JUN	JUL	AUG	SEP	OCT	NOV	DEC	YEAR
Mean Maximum Temp. (°F)	39.5	45.7	55.4	67.1	76.4	84.8	88.6	87.6	80.8	69.5	56.0	44.9	66.4
Mean Temp. (°F)	30.2	35.1	44.7	55.3	64.6	73.5	77.5	75.4	68.0	55.9	45.4	35.4	55.1
Mean Minimum Temp. (°F)	20.8	24.4	34.0	43.5	52.8	62.2	66.4	63.3	55.2	42.3	34.8	25.9	43.8
Extreme Maximum Temp. (°F)	70	79	83	90	95	102	103	102	99	92	83	77	103
Extreme Minimum Temp. (°F)	-25	-11	-11	21	30	41	42	43	30	18	9	-14	-25
Days Maximum Temp. ≥ 90°F	0	0	0	0	1	7	14	12	4	0	0	0	38
Days Maximum Temp. ≤ 32°F	9	5	1	0	0	0	0	0	0	0	1	4	20
Days Minimum Temp. ≤ 32°F	26	21	15	4	0	0	0	0	0	6	14	23	109
Days Minimum Temp. ≤ 0°F	2	1	0	0	0	0	0	0	0	0	0	0	3
Heating Degree Days (base 65°F)	1,074	839	624	306	98	7	1	1	60	295	582	910	4,797
Cooling Degree Days (base 65°F)	0	0	4	20	87	268	401	334	146	19	1	0	1,280
Mean Precipitation (in.)	2.96	2.84	4.39	4.62	4.74	4.49	3.28	3.97	3.08	2.83	4.45	3.68	45.33
Days With ≥ 0.1" Precipitation	6	5	8	8	8	7	6	6	5	5	7	7	78
Days With ≥ 1.0" Precipitation	1	1	1	1	1	1	1	1	1	1	1	1	12
Mean Snowfall (in.)	4.9	3.8	2.0	0.3	0.0	0.0	0.0	0.0	0.0	0.1	0.5	2.2	13.8
Days With ≥ 1.0" Snow Depth	6	5	1	0	0	0	0	0	0	0	0	2	14

Carlinville *Macoupin County* Elevation: 629 ft. Latitude: 39° 17' N Longitude: 89° 53' W

	JAN	FEB	MAR	APR	MAY	JUN	JUL	AUG	SEP	OCT	NOV	DEC	YEAR
Mean Maximum Temp. (°F)	35.0	41.8	53.4	66.1	75.9	84.2	88.0	85.9	79.7	68.0	52.8	40.7	64.3
Mean Temp. (°F)	26.7	32.8	43.3	54.8	64.5	73.2	77.1	74.9	68.0	56.5	43.8	32.8	54.0
Mean Minimum Temp. (°F)	18.4	23.7	33.1	43.4	53.0	62.1	66.1	63.9	56.2	44.9	34.8	24.8	43.7
Extreme Maximum Temp. (°F)	71	78	86	90	92	99	103	105	99	92	81	74	105
Extreme Minimum Temp. (°F)	-19	-17	-9	18	30	39	45	41	31	20	1	-15	-19
Days Maximum Temp. ≥ 90°F	0	0	0	0	1	6	13	9	3	0	0	0	32
Days Maximum Temp. ≤ 32°F	13	7	1	0	0	0	0	0	0	0	1	7	29
Days Minimum Temp. ≤ 32°F	27	21	16	4	0	0	0	0	0	3	13	24	108
Days Minimum Temp. ≤ 0°F	3	2	0	0	0	0	0	0	0	0	0	1	6
Heating Degree Days (base 65°F)	1,181	903	670	323	104	10	1	2	61	280	630	992	5,157
Cooling Degree Days (base 65°F)	0	0	4	21	94	267	388	323	152	22	1	0	1,272
Mean Precipitation (in.)	1.95	1.93	3.54	4.16	4.25	3.83	3.60	3.36	3.08	2.66	3.56	2.87	38.79
Days With ≥ 0.1" Precipitation	5	4	7	8	7	6	5	5	5	6	7	5	70
Days With ≥ 1.0" Precipitation	0	0	1	1	1	1	1	1	1	0	1	1	9
Mean Snowfall (in.)	6.8	4.4	3.3	0.7	trace	0.0	0.0	0.0	0.0	trace	1.4	3.6	20.2
Days With ≥ 1.0" Snow Depth	11	6	2	0	0	0	0	0	0	0	1	4	24

Charleston *Coles County* Elevation: 679 ft. Latitude: 39° 29' N Longitude: 88° 10' W

	JAN	FEB	MAR	APR	MAY	JUN	JUL	AUG	SEP	OCT	NOV	DEC	YEAR
Mean Maximum Temp. (°F)	34.8	40.7	52.3	64.7	74.6	83.1	86.4	84.3	78.4	66.8	52.2	40.2	63.2
Mean Temp. (°F)	26.8	32.1	42.8	54.0	64.1	72.7	76.4	74.3	67.6	56.2	43.6	32.5	53.6
Mean Minimum Temp. (°F)	18.7	23.4	33.2	43.3	53.4	62.2	66.3	64.3	56.6	45.5	35.0	24.8	43.9
Extreme Maximum Temp. (°F)	69	74	84	88	92	102	101	102	97	89	79	71	102
Extreme Minimum Temp. (°F)	-27	-18	-5	17	30	41	49	42	32	20	3	-20	-27
Days Maximum Temp. ≥ 90°F	0	0	0	0	0	5	9	6	2	0	0	0	22
Days Maximum Temp. ≤ 32°F	13	8	2	0	0	0	0	0	0	0	1	7	31
Days Minimum Temp. ≤ 32°F	27	21	16	5	0	0	0	0	0	3	13	24	109
Days Minimum Temp. ≤ 0°F	4	2	0	0	0	0	0	0	0	0	0	1	7
Heating Degree Days (base 65°F)	1,179	925	685	340	110	12	1	2	63	290	635	1,001	5,243
Cooling Degree Days (base 65°F)	0	0	3	16	85	256	370	304	146	23	1	0	1,204
Mean Precipitation (in.)	2.16	2.35	3.36	4.10	4.18	3.74	4.53	3.27	3.13	3.21	3.77	3.21	41.01
Days With ≥ 0.1" Precipitation	5	5	8	9	7	6	6	5	5	5	7	6	74
Days With ≥ 1.0" Precipitation	0	0	1	1	1	1	1	1	1	1	1	1	10
Mean Snowfall (in.)	9.3	4.1	2.7	0.2	trace	0.0	0.0	0.0	0.0	trace	1.6	4.2	22.1
Days With ≥ 1.0" Snow Depth	13	9	3	0	0	0	0	0	0	0	1	6	32

Chenoa *McLean County* Elevation: 711 ft. Latitude: 40° 44' N Longitude: 88° 43' W

	JAN	FEB	MAR	APR	MAY	JUN	JUL	AUG	SEP	OCT	NOV	DEC	YEAR
Mean Maximum Temp. (°F)	31.1	37.0	49.1	62.9	74.3	83.3	85.7	83.6	77.7	65.4	49.5	36.6	61.4
Mean Temp. (°F)	23.1	28.3	39.5	51.4	62.4	71.7	74.7	72.5	65.7	54.0	40.8	29.1	51.1
Mean Minimum Temp. (°F)	14.8	19.6	29.9	39.8	50.5	59.9	63.5	61.3	53.7	42.5	31.9	21.4	40.7
Extreme Maximum Temp. (°F)	66	73	85	91	95	102	101	103	97	90	78	70	103
Extreme Minimum Temp. (°F)	-23	-19	-2	7	26	36	45	40	24	17	-2	-26	-26
Days Maximum Temp. ≥ 90°F	0	0	0	0	2	6	8	5	2	0	0	0	23
Days Maximum Temp. ≤ 32°F	16	10	2	0	0	0	0	0	0	0	2	10	40
Days Minimum Temp. ≤ 32°F	29	24	20	7	0	0	0	0	0	5	17	27	129
Days Minimum Temp. ≤ 0°F	5	3	0	0	0	0	0	0	0	0	0	2	10
Heating Degree Days (base 65°F)	1,293	1,030	783	413	147	17	3	8	87	350	721	1,106	5,958
Cooling Degree Days (base 65°F)	0	0	2	11	72	229	319	254	114	13	0	0	1,014
Mean Precipitation (in.)	1.55	1.42	3.00	3.42	3.88	4.11	3.40	3.29	3.13	2.69	2.64	2.46	34.99
Days With ≥ 0.1" Precipitation	4	4	6	7	8	7	6	5	6	6	6	5	70
Days With ≥ 1.0" Precipitation	0	0	0	1	1	1	1	1	1	0	1	1	8
Mean Snowfall (in.)	7.0	5.4	2.8	1.1	trace	0.0	0.0	0.0	0.0	trace	1.6	4.8	22.7
Days With ≥ 1.0" Snow Depth	14	10	3	0	0	0	0	0	0	0	1	6	34

Chicago Midway Airport *Cook County*   Elevation: 610 ft.   Latitude: 41° 47' N   Longitude: 87° 45' W

	JAN	FEB	MAR	APR	MAY	JUN	JUL	AUG	SEP	OCT	NOV	DEC	YEAR
Mean Maximum Temp. (°F)	30.4	35.6	46.7	59.0	71.1	80.7	84.9	82.6	75.4	63.3	48.3	36.2	59.5
Mean Temp. (°F)	23.1	28.3	38.6	49.7	60.9	70.8	75.7	73.8	66.1	54.1	41.0	29.4	51.0
Mean Minimum Temp. (°F)	15.9	20.9	30.4	40.4	50.8	60.7	66.3	65.0	56.7	44.8	33.6	22.6	42.3
Extreme Maximum Temp. (°F)	67	75	86	91	95	104	106	102	98	92	79	71	106
Extreme Minimum Temp. (°F)	-25	-17	0	10	28	40	46	46	34	20	0	-20	-25
Days Maximum Temp. ≥ 90°F	0	0	0	0	1	5	9	5	2	0	0	0	22
Days Maximum Temp. ≤ 32°F	16	11	3	0	0	0	0	0	0	0	2	10	42
Days Minimum Temp. ≤ 32°F	28	23	19	6	0	0	0	0	0	2	14	25	117
Days Minimum Temp. ≤ 0°F	5	2	0	0	0	0	0	0	0	0	0	2	9
Heating Degree Days (base 65°F)	1,291	1,031	814	465	190	31	2	4	82	347	715	1,098	6,070
Cooling Degree Days (base 65°F)	0	0	2	12	69	213	349	290	122	13	0	0	1,070
Mean Precipitation (in.)	1.93	1.76	2.88	3.89	3.79	4.23	3.77	3.91	3.46	2.89	3.25	2.72	38.48
Days With ≥ 0.1" Precipitation	5	5	7	7	7	6	6	6	6	6	7	5	73
Days With ≥ 1.0" Precipitation	0	0	0	1	1	1	1	1	1	1	1	1	9
Mean Snowfall (in.)	13.0	10.2	6.6	1.8	trace	0.0	trace	0.0	trace	0.1	2.4	8.7	42.8
Days With ≥ 1.0" Snow Depth	20	13	5	1	0	0	0	0	0	0	1	10	50

Chicago University *Cook County*   Elevation: 593 ft.   Latitude: 41° 47' N   Longitude: 87° 36' W

	JAN	FEB	MAR	APR	MAY	JUN	JUL	AUG	SEP	OCT	NOV	DEC	YEAR
Mean Maximum Temp. (°F)	31.4	36.3	46.9	58.9	70.4	80.4	84.5	82.8	76.1	64.1	49.4	36.9	59.8
Mean Temp. (°F)	24.7	29.4	39.4	50.2	60.8	70.6	75.7	74.3	67.3	55.6	42.8	30.5	51.8
Mean Minimum Temp. (°F)	18.0	22.5	31.8	41.5	51.2	60.7	66.8	65.6	58.4	47.1	36.1	24.0	43.6
Extreme Maximum Temp. (°F)	62	71	84	91	94	104	102	101	97	92	77	69	104
Extreme Minimum Temp. (°F)	-24	-9	4	13	33	41	51	49	37	24	2	-20	-24
Days Maximum Temp. ≥ 90°F	0	0	0	0	1	4	8	5	2	0	0	0	20
Days Maximum Temp. ≤ 32°F	16	11	3	0	0	0	0	0	0	0	1	9	40
Days Minimum Temp. ≤ 32°F	27	22	16	4	0	0	0	0	0	1	11	24	105
Days Minimum Temp. ≤ 0°F	4	1	0	0	0	0	0	0	0	0	0	1	6
Heating Degree Days (base 65°F)	1,242	998	788	452	191	32	2	3	63	302	660	1,064	5,797
Cooling Degree Days (base 65°F)	0	0	2	16	72	211	350	309	140	15	0	0	1,115
Mean Precipitation (in.)	1.90	1.69	3.05	3.67	3.52	4.20	3.54	4.13	3.39	2.77	3.47	2.85	38.18
Days With ≥ 0.1" Precipitation	5	5	7	7	7	7	6	7	6	5	7	6	75
Days With ≥ 1.0" Precipitation	0	0	0	1	1	1	1	1	1	1	1	0	8
Mean Snowfall (in.)	na	na	na	na	na	na	na	na	na	na	na	na	na
Days With ≥ 1.0" Snow Depth	na	na	na	na	na	na	na	na	na	na	na	na	na

Danville *Vermilion County*   Elevation: 557 ft.   Latitude: 40° 08' N   Longitude: 87° 39' W

	JAN	FEB	MAR	APR	MAY	JUN	JUL	AUG	SEP	OCT	NOV	DEC	YEAR
Mean Maximum Temp. (°F)	34.0	39.8	51.5	64.5	75.2	83.6	86.3	84.1	78.5	66.5	51.7	39.3	62.9
Mean Temp. (°F)	25.5	30.7	41.4	52.8	63.0	71.8	75.4	73.4	66.7	54.9	42.8	31.5	52.5
Mean Minimum Temp. (°F)	17.0	21.6	31.3	41.1	50.7	60.0	64.3	62.5	54.9	43.2	33.8	23.5	42.0
Extreme Maximum Temp. (°F)	68	71	84	90	94	102	102	102	96	89	79	72	102
Extreme Minimum Temp. (°F)	-26	-22	-8	12	28	38	45	41	29	18	5	-25	-26
Days Maximum Temp. ≥ 90°F	0	0	0	0	1	6	9	5	2	0	0	0	23
Days Maximum Temp. ≤ 32°F	14	8	2	0	0	0	0	0	0	0	1	7	32
Days Minimum Temp. ≤ 32°F	27	23	17	6	0	0	0	0	0	5	15	24	117
Days Minimum Temp. ≤ 0°F	4	3	0	0	0	0	0	0	0	0	0	2	9
Heating Degree Days (base 65°F)	1,217	962	726	374	132	16	2	4	73	323	659	1,034	5,522
Cooling Degree Days (base 65°F)	0	0	2	14	75	230	338	276	127	17	1	0	1,080
Mean Precipitation (in.)	2.00	1.93	3.18	4.10	4.51	4.53	4.54	3.95	3.03	3.13	3.46	2.75	41.11
Days With ≥ 0.1" Precipitation	5	5	7	8	8	7	7	6	5	6	7	6	77
Days With ≥ 1.0" Precipitation	0	0	1	1	1	1	1	1	1	1	1	0	9
Mean Snowfall (in.)	6.2	4.1	3.1	0.3	trace	0.0	0.0	0.0	0.0	0.2	1.2	4.7	19.8
Days With ≥ 1.0" Snow Depth	10	6	2	0	0	0	0	0	0	0	1	5	24

De Kalb *Dekalb County*   Elevation: 872 ft.   Latitude: 41° 56' N   Longitude: 88° 47' W

	JAN	FEB	MAR	APR	MAY	JUN	JUL	AUG	SEP	OCT	NOV	DEC	YEAR
Mean Maximum Temp. (°F)	26.8	33.3	45.1	59.3	71.7	81.3	84.5	82.0	75.6	63.1	46.4	33.6	58.5
Mean Temp. (°F)	18.9	25.2	36.1	48.5	60.1	70.0	73.7	71.4	64.2	52.0	38.1	26.3	48.7
Mean Minimum Temp. (°F)	10.9	17.1	27.2	37.6	48.4	58.6	62.8	60.7	52.7	40.8	29.8	18.9	38.8
Extreme Maximum Temp. (°F)	60	68	81	91	95	101	102	103	94	89	76	66	103
Extreme Minimum Temp. (°F)	-27	-23	-6	8	24	34	45	42	27	13	-8	-22	-27
Days Maximum Temp. ≥ 90°F	0	0	0	0	1	4	6	4	1	0	0	0	16
Days Maximum Temp. ≤ 32°F	21	13	4	0	0	0	0	0	0	0	3	12	53
Days Minimum Temp. ≤ 32°F	30	26	23	9	1	0	0	0	1	6	18	28	142
Days Minimum Temp. ≤ 0°F	8	4	0	0	0	0	0	0	0	0	0	3	15
Heating Degree Days (base 65°F)	1,425	1,118	888	499	200	31	5	14	112	406	800	1,194	6,692
Cooling Degree Days (base 65°F)	0	0	1	9	46	185	279	220	92	8	0	0	840
Mean Precipitation (in.)	1.54	1.35	2.49	3.49	4.25	4.46	4.35	4.48	3.68	2.65	2.79	2.16	37.69
Days With ≥ 0.1" Precipitation	4	3	6	7	8	7	6	7	6	6	6	5	71
Days With ≥ 1.0" Precipitation	0	0	0	1	1	1	1	1	1	0	1	0	7
Mean Snowfall (in.)	9.7	7.1	5.1	1.3	trace	0.0	0.0	0.0	0.0	0.1	2.1	8.6	34.0
Days With ≥ 1.0" Snow Depth	23	16	6	1	0	0	0	0	0	0	2	12	60

Decatur *Macon County* Elevation: 620 ft. Latitude: 39° 49' N Longitude: 89° 01' W

	JAN	FEB	MAR	APR	MAY	JUN	JUL	AUG	SEP	OCT	NOV	DEC	YEAR
Mean Maximum Temp. (°F)	34.0	40.5	52.0	65.1	75.9	84.5	87.8	85.8	79.9	67.6	52.0	40.0	63.8
Mean Temp. (°F)	25.4	31.2	41.8	53.5	63.6	72.5	76.1	74.3	67.4	55.7	42.7	31.8	53.0
Mean Minimum Temp. (°F)	16.7	21.8	31.5	41.8	51.3	60.4	64.4	62.7	54.9	43.7	33.4	23.4	42.2
Extreme Maximum Temp. (°F)	67	76	86	93	95	103	104	106	100	91	80	72	106
Extreme Minimum Temp. (°F)	-23	-20	-10	15	27	39	46	42	29	18	0	-22	-23
Days Maximum Temp. ≥ 90°F	0	0	0	0	2	7	13	8	4	0	0	0	34
Days Maximum Temp. ≤ 32°F	13	7	2	0	0	0	0	0	0	0	1	7	30
Days Minimum Temp. ≤ 32°F	28	23	17	5	0	0	0	0	0	4	15	25	117
Days Minimum Temp. ≤ 0°F	5	3	0	0	0	0	0	0	0	0	0	1	9
Heating Degree Days (base 65°F)	1,222	950	714	356	120	13	1	4	67	303	664	1,025	5,439
Cooling Degree Days (base 65°F)	0	0	2	17	78	245	360	309	144	21	1	0	1,177
Mean Precipitation (in.)	2.10	1.91	3.28	3.83	4.58	3.94	4.41	4.04	3.01	2.78	3.09	2.84	39.81
Days With ≥ 0.1" Precipitation	5	4	7	7	7	6	6	5	5	5	6	6	69
Days With ≥ 1.0" Precipitation	0	0	1	1	1	1	1	1	1	1	1	0	9
Mean Snowfall (in.)	7.8	5.1	2.7	0.4	trace	0.0	0.0	0.0	0.0	trace	1.1	5.4	22.5
Days With ≥ 1.0" Snow Depth	13	9	3	0	0	0	0	0	0	0	.1	6	32

Dixon 1 NW *Lee County* Elevation: 698 ft. Latitude: 41° 51' N Longitude: 89° 30' W

	JAN	FEB	MAR	APR	MAY	JUN	JUL	AUG	SEP	OCT	NOV	DEC	YEAR
Mean Maximum Temp. (°F)	27.5	33.4	45.5	59.8	71.6	80.6	83.9	81.9	74.7	62.9	46.7	33.3	58.5
Mean Temp. (°F)	18.7	24.4	36.2	48.8	60.2	69.4	73.2	71.0	63.1	51.3	37.8	25.3	48.3
Mean Minimum Temp. (°F)	9.7	15.4	26.9	37.7	48.7	58.0	62.5	60.1	51.4	39.6	28.8	17.3	38.0
Extreme Maximum Temp. (°F)	59	69	87	93	95	100	101	103	99	91	77	68	103
Extreme Minimum Temp. (°F)	-27	-26	-6	8	27	36	45	40	28	17	-8	-25	-27
Days Maximum Temp. ≥ 90°F	0	0	0	0	1	3	7	5	2	0	0	0	18
Days Maximum Temp. ≤ 32°F	19	12	4	0	0	0	0	0	0	0	3	13	51
Days Minimum Temp. ≤ 32°F	30	26	22	9	1	0	0	0	1	7	20	29	145
Days Minimum Temp. ≤ 0°F	9	5	0	0	0	0	0	0	0	0	0	4	18
Heating Degree Days (base 65°F)	1,432	1,140	886	490	198	32	6	15	131	428	811	1,224	6,793
Cooling Degree Days (base 65°F)	0	0	1	7	47	160	258	202	70	8	0	0	753
Mean Precipitation (in.)	1.56	1.36	2.56	3.57	4.43	4.79	3.36	4.41	3.47	2.78	2.80	2.12	37.21
Days With ≥ 0.1" Precipitation	4	4	6	7	7	7	6	7	5	6	6	5	70
Days With ≥ 1.0" Precipitation	0	0	1	1	1	1	1	1	1	1	0	0	8
Mean Snowfall (in.)	11.1	6.8	4.6	1.2	0.0	0.0	0.0	0.0	0.0	trace	2.1	8.4	34.2
Days With ≥ 1.0" Snow Depth	20	15	5	0	0	0	0	0	0	0	1	12	53

Dixon Springs Agr. Center *Pope County* Elevation: 538 ft. Latitude: 37° 26' N Longitude: 88° 40' W

	JAN	FEB	MAR	APR	MAY	JUN	JUL	AUG	SEP	OCT	NOV	DEC	YEAR
Mean Maximum Temp. (°F)	41.8	48.3	58.8	69.4	77.6	85.4	89.0	88.1	82.0	71.5	57.9	47.0	68.1
Mean Temp. (°F)	33.0	38.4	48.2	58.0	66.2	74.2	78.0	76.6	70.1	59.1	48.3	38.4	57.4
Mean Minimum Temp. (°F)	24.2	28.5	37.5	46.5	54.8	63.1	67.0	65.0	58.1	46.7	38.6	29.6	46.6
Extreme Maximum Temp. (°F)	70	78	83	89	92	100	101	102	100	91	83	77	102
Extreme Minimum Temp. (°F)	-20	-10	-3	21	29	39	46	46	32	17	6	-9	-20
Days Maximum Temp. ≥ 90°F	0	0	0	0	1	8	15	13	5	0	0	0	42
Days Maximum Temp. ≤ 32°F	7	4	0	0	0	0	0	0	0	0	0	3	14
Days Minimum Temp. ≤ 32°F	23	17	11	3	0	0	0	0	0	3	10	18	85
Days Minimum Temp. ≤ 0°F	1	1	0	0	0	0	0	0	0	0	0	0	2
Heating Degree Days (base 65°F)	984	745	521	239	74	5	0	1	39	216	500	820	4,144
Cooling Degree Days (base 65°F)	0	0	8	36	125	304	433	388	200	43	4	1	1,542
Mean Precipitation (in.)	3.18	3.30	4.68	4.90	5.22	4.07	3.74	3.61	3.23	3.31	4.64	4.34	48.22
Days With ≥ 0.1" Precipitation	6	6	8	8	8	7	6	5	5	5	7	7	78
Days With ≥ 1.0" Precipitation	1	1	1	1	2	1	1	1	1	1	1	1	13
Mean Snowfall (in.)	3.8	3.3	1.5	0.1	0.0	0.0	0.0	0.0	0.0	0.2	trace	0.8	9.7
Days With ≥ 1.0" Snow Depth	6	5	1	0	0	0	0	0	0	0	0	1	13

Du Quoin 4 SE *Perry County* Elevation: 419 ft. Latitude: 37° 59' N Longitude: 89° 12' W

	JAN	FEB	MAR	APR	MAY	JUN	JUL	AUG	SEP	OCT	NOV	DEC	YEAR
Mean Maximum Temp. (°F)	38.9	45.6	56.3	67.6	77.0	85.5	89.7	87.8	81.1	70.0	55.6	43.7	66.6
Mean Temp. (°F)	30.2	35.9	45.9	56.4	65.8	74.4	78.5	76.1	69.0	57.5	45.7	35.0	55.9
Mean Minimum Temp. (°F)	21.5	26.1	35.4	45.1	54.5	63.2	67.3	64.3	56.7	45.0	35.7	26.6	45.1
Extreme Maximum Temp. (°F)	70	77	85	92	94	106	106	106	100	92	84	75	106
Extreme Minimum Temp. (°F)	-20	-16	-10	22	30	41	49	43	31	20	8	-14	-20
Days Maximum Temp. ≥ 90°F	0	0	0	0	2	9	16	12	5	0	0	0	44
Days Maximum Temp. ≤ 32°F	9	5	1	0	0	0	0	0	0	0	0	5	20
Days Minimum Temp. ≤ 32°F	26	19	13	3	0	0	0	0	0	3	12	22	98
Days Minimum Temp. ≤ 0°F	2	1	0	0	0	0	0	0	0	0	0	1	4
Heating Degree Days (base 65°F)	1,072	816	588	279	81	5	0	1	48	254	576	923	4,643
Cooling Degree Days (base 65°F)	0	0	4	25	110	301	429	358	164	29	2	0	1,422
Mean Precipitation (in.)	2.73	2.57	4.31	4.27	4.83	4.09	3.52	3.18	3.31	3.28	4.36	3.41	43.86
Days With ≥ 0.1" Precipitation	5	5	7	8	7	7	5	5	5	5	6	6	71
Days With ≥ 1.0" Precipitation	1	1	1	1	2	1	1	1	1	1	1	1	13
Mean Snowfall (in.)	5.1	3.4	1.2	0.5	0.0	0.0	0.0	0.0	0.0	0.2	0.8	2.5	13.7
Days With ≥ 1.0" Snow Depth	8	5	1	0	0	0	0	0	0	0	0	3	17

Effingham *Effingham County*   Elevation: 606 ft.   Latitude: 39° 09' N   Longitude: 88° 33' W

	JAN	FEB	MAR	APR	MAY	JUN	JUL	AUG	SEP	OCT	NOV	DEC	YEAR
Mean Maximum Temp. (°F)	34.2	39.8	51.7	64.0	74.2	83.5	87.4	85.2	78.6	66.5	52.7	40.3	63.2
Mean Temp. (°F)	25.8	30.3	42.0	53.3	63.1	72.5	76.6	74.3	66.9	55.0	43.4	31.9	52.9
Mean Minimum Temp. (°F)	17.4	20.9	32.2	42.4	52.0	61.4	65.8	63.3	55.2	43.3	34.1	23.3	42.6
Extreme Maximum Temp. (°F)	69	78	84	89	94	102	102	103	100	92	81	71	103
Extreme Minimum Temp. (°F)	-24	-19	-11	21	29	40	48	44	34	20	5	-16	-24
Days Maximum Temp. ≥ 90°F	0	0	0	0	1	6	12	9	3	0	0	0	31
Days Maximum Temp. ≤ 32°F	14	8	2	0	0	0	0	0	0	0	0	7	32
Days Minimum Temp. ≤ 32°F	28	23	17	5	0	0	0	0	0	5	14	24	116
Days Minimum Temp. ≤ 0°F	4	3	0	0	0	0	0	0	0	0	0	2	9
Heating Degree Days (base 65°F)	1,209	972	709	363	128	14	1	4	76	324	642	1,021	5,463
Cooling Degree Days (base 65°F)	0	0	3	17	74	254	381	307	135	17	1	0	1,189
Mean Precipitation (in.)	2.11	2.37	3.67	4.00	4.22	4.21	4.32	2.88	3.17	3.04	4.01	3.36	41.36
Days With ≥ 0.1" Precipitation	5	5	7	8	7	7	7	5	5	5	7	6	74
Days With ≥ 1.0" Precipitation	0	1	1	1	1	1	1	1	1	1	1	1	11
Mean Snowfall (in.)	7.3	5.2	2.9	0.2	0.0	0.0	0.0	0.0	0.0	trace	1.3	3.8	20.7
Days With ≥ 1.0" Snow Depth	10	na	2	0	0	0	0	0	0	0	1	4	na

Fairfield Radio WFIW *Wayne County*   Elevation: 429 ft.   Latitude: 38° 23' N   Longitude: 88° 20' W

	JAN	FEB	MAR	APR	MAY	JUN	JUL	AUG	SEP	OCT	NOV	DEC	YEAR
Mean Maximum Temp. (°F)	37.6	43.8	54.9	66.5	76.1	84.8	88.2	86.6	80.3	68.6	54.3	42.8	65.4
Mean Temp. (°F)	29.3	34.5	44.7	55.2	64.6	73.2	77.0	75.0	68.2	56.7	45.0	34.5	54.8
Mean Minimum Temp. (°F)	21.0	25.2	34.4	43.8	53.1	61.6	65.7	63.4	56.1	44.7	35.6	26.2	44.2
Extreme Maximum Temp. (°F)	72	78	84	89	94	102	102	104	100	91	81	74	104
Extreme Minimum Temp. (°F)	-23	-16	-8	17	30	39	46	43	32	19	7	-18	-23
Days Maximum Temp. ≥ 90°F	0	0	0	0	1	8	14	10	4	0	0	0	37
Days Maximum Temp. ≤ 32°F	11	6	1	0	0	0	0	0	0	0	0	5	24
Days Minimum Temp. ≤ 32°F	26	21	14	4	0	0	0	0	0	1	13	22	104
Days Minimum Temp. ≤ 0°F	2	1	0	0	0	0	0	0	0	0	0	1	4
Heating Degree Days (base 65°F)	1,100	855	626	310	99	8	1	2	58	277	595	937	4,868
Cooling Degree Days (base 65°F)	0	0	3	20	95	263	384	323	150	25	1	0	1,264
Mean Precipitation (in.)	2.75	2.62	4.63	4.90	4.71	4.01	3.80	3.22	2.89	3.43	4.28	3.45	44.69
Days With ≥ 0.1" Precipitation	6	5	8	9	8	7	6	5	5	5	7	7	78
Days With ≥ 1.0" Precipitation	1	1	1	1	1	1	1	1	1	1	1	1	12
Mean Snowfall (in.)	5.2	3.7	2.4	0.3	0.0	0.0	0.0	0.0	0.0	trace	0.7	2.9	15.2
Days With ≥ 1.0" Snow Depth	7	5	1	0	0	0	0	0	0	0	0	2	15

Flora 5 NW *Clay County*   Elevation: 498 ft.   Latitude: 38° 43' N   Longitude: 88° 35' W

	JAN	FEB	MAR	APR	MAY	JUN	JUL	AUG	SEP	OCT	NOV	DEC	YEAR
Mean Maximum Temp. (°F)	38.1	43.9	55.3	67.2	76.9	85.5	89.2	87.5	81.1	69.6	55.1	43.1	66.0
Mean Temp. (°F)	29.4	34.4	44.7	55.4	64.8	73.5	77.3	75.3	68.5	57.2	45.3	34.5	55.0
Mean Minimum Temp. (°F)	20.6	24.7	34.2	43.5	52.7	61.5	65.4	63.1	55.8	44.8	35.4	25.8	44.0
Extreme Maximum Temp. (°F)	70	79	85	97	94	104	104	105	100	93	82	73	105
Extreme Minimum Temp. (°F)	-24	-25	-14	18	29	38	44	39	29	17	5	-21	-25
Days Maximum Temp. ≥ 90°F	0	0	0	0	1	8	15	11	5	0	0	0	40
Days Maximum Temp. ≤ 32°F	10	6	1	0	0	0	0	0	0	0	0	5	22
Days Minimum Temp. ≤ 32°F	26	20	15	4	0	0	0	0	0	0	12	22	103
Days Minimum Temp. ≤ 0°F	3	2	0	0	0	0	0	0	0	0	0	1	6
Heating Degree Days (base 65°F)	1,097	859	626	306	97	8	1	2	55	263	588	939	4,841
Cooling Degree Days (base 65°F)	0	0	5	24	100	282	404	339	162	32	2	0	1,350
Mean Precipitation (in.)	2.55	2.38	4.04	4.29	4.23	4.24	3.77	3.17	3.15	3.02	4.01	3.31	42.16
Days With ≥ 0.1" Precipitation	5	5	8	8	8	7	6	5	5	5	7	6	75
Days With ≥ 1.0" Precipitation	0	1	1	1	1	1	1	1	1	1	1	1	11
Mean Snowfall (in.)	2.5	2.1	1.2	0.2	trace	0.0	0.0	0.0	0.0	trace	0.8	1.5	8.3
Days With ≥ 1.0" Snow Depth	8	6	1	0	0	0	0	0	0	0	1	3	19

Freeport Waste Water Plant *Stephenson County*   Elevation: 748 ft.   Latitude: 42° 18' N   Longitude: 89° 36' W

	JAN	FEB	MAR	APR	MAY	JUN	JUL	AUG	SEP	OCT	NOV	DEC	YEAR
Mean Maximum Temp. (°F)	26.4	32.2	43.9	58.1	70.5	79.9	83.8	81.0	73.5	61.6	45.6	31.9	57.4
Mean Temp. (°F)	17.7	23.2	34.5	47.3	59.1	68.6	72.8	70.0	61.7	50.0	36.7	23.9	47.1
Mean Minimum Temp. (°F)	9.0	14.1	25.1	36.4	47.6	57.2	61.8	59.0	49.8	38.2	27.8	15.9	36.8
Extreme Maximum Temp. (°F)	59	65	85	92	95	100	101	101	96	90	75	66	101
Extreme Minimum Temp. (°F)	-27	-27	-6	9	27	38	46	40	28	15	-5	-22	-27
Days Maximum Temp. ≥ 90°F	0	0	0	0	1	3	6	4	1	0	0	0	15
Days Maximum Temp. ≤ 32°F	21	14	5	0	0	0	0	0	0	0	3	14	57
Days Minimum Temp. ≤ 32°F	30	26	25	10	1	0	0	0	1	9	22	29	153
Days Minimum Temp. ≤ 0°F	9	6	1	0	0	0	0	0	0	0	0	5	21
Heating Degree Days (base 65°F)	1,460	1,176	938	533	225	41	7	21	155	465	841	1,267	7,129
Cooling Degree Days (base 65°F)	0	0	0	7	43	156	250	186	63	5	0	0	710
Mean Precipitation (in.)	1.29	1.26	2.18	3.23	3.95	4.30	3.55	4.05	3.72	2.62	2.68	1.69	34.52
Days With ≥ 0.1" Precipitation	4	4	5	6	7	7	6	6	6	5	5	4	65
Days With ≥ 1.0" Precipitation	0	0	0	1	1	1	1	1	1	1	1	0	8
Mean Snowfall (in.)	9.6	6.5	4.4	1.7	trace	0.0	0.0	0.0	0.0	trace	2.5	7.3	32.0
Days With ≥ 1.0" Snow Depth	19	15	6	1	0	0	0	0	0	0	2	13	56

Fulton Lock & Dam 13 *Whiteside County*   Elevation: 590 ft.   Latitude: 41° 54' N   Longitude: 90° 09' W

	JAN	FEB	MAR	APR	MAY	JUN	JUL	AUG	SEP	OCT	NOV	DEC	YEAR
Mean Maximum Temp. (°F)	27.9	32.8	44.6	58.7	70.7	80.1	83.9	81.8	74.5	62.8	46.6	33.2	58.1
Mean Temp. (°F)	19.4	24.3	35.8	49.0	60.7	70.0	74.2	72.2	64.1	52.5	38.5	25.7	48.9
Mean Minimum Temp. (°F)	10.8	15.8	27.0	39.2	50.6	59.9	64.5	62.4	53.7	42.2	30.4	18.1	39.5
Extreme Maximum Temp. (°F)	62	68	82	91	92	98	99	102	96	90	74	66	102
Extreme Minimum Temp. (°F)	-23	-26	-7	13	30	40	47	42	30	16	-5	-21	-26
Days Maximum Temp. ≥ 90°F	0	0	0	0	0	3	5	4	1	0	0	0	13
Days Maximum Temp. ≤ 32°F	19	13	4	0	0	0	0	0	0	0	3	13	52
Days Minimum Temp. ≤ 32°F	30	26	22	6	0	0	0	0	0	4	18	28	134
Days Minimum Temp. ≤ 0°F	8	5	0	0	0	0	0	0	0	0	0	3	16
Heating Degree Days (base 65°F)	1,410	1,143	897	484	180	24	2	6	109	390	789	1,212	6,646
Cooling Degree Days (base 65°F)	0	0	0	9	45	178	292	240	87	8	0	0	859
Mean Precipitation (in.)	1.28	1.20	2.39	3.41	3.90	4.18	3.41	4.50	3.26	2.72	2.65	1.80	34.70
Days With ≥ 0.1" Precipitation	3	3	5	6	7	7	6	7	5	5	5	4	63
Days With ≥ 1.0" Precipitation	0	0	0	1	1	1	1	1	1	1	1	0	8
Mean Snowfall (in.)	*6.4*	*3.8*	2.0	0.8	0.0	0.0	0.0	0.0	0.0	trace	0.9	*3.8*	*17.7*
Days With ≥ 1.0" Snow Depth	14	14	5	0	0	0	0	0	0	0	1	9	43

Galesburg *Knox County*   Elevation: 770 ft.   Latitude: 40° 57' N   Longitude: 90° 23' W

	JAN	FEB	MAR	APR	MAY	JUN	JUL	AUG	SEP	OCT	NOV	DEC	YEAR
Mean Maximum Temp. (°F)	29.2	35.3	47.6	61.1	72.3	81.5	84.9	82.4	75.4	63.5	47.6	34.6	59.6
Mean Temp. (°F)	21.2	27.1	38.3	50.7	61.9	71.2	75.1	72.8	65.1	53.2	39.3	27.2	50.3
Mean Minimum Temp. (°F)	13.1	18.8	29.1	40.2	51.4	60.9	65.3	63.1	54.7	42.9	30.8	19.7	40.8
Extreme Maximum Temp. (°F)	66	71	86	91	92	101	102	101	96	91	76	69	102
Extreme Minimum Temp. (°F)	-25	-24	-5	9	29	41	46	42	29	19	-5	-21	-25
Days Maximum Temp. ≥ 90°F	0	0	0	0	0	4	8	4	1	0	0	0	17
Days Maximum Temp. ≤ 32°F	17	11	4	0	0	0	0	0	0	0	3	12	47
Days Minimum Temp. ≤ 32°F	29	25	20	6	0	0	0	0	0	4	18	27	129
Days Minimum Temp. ≤ 0°F	7	3	0	0	0	0	0	0	0	0	0	3	13
Heating Degree Days (base 65°F)	1,352	1,064	821	434	156	18	3	7	99	371	765	1,166	6,256
Cooling Degree Days (base 65°F)	0	0	2	11	64	216	331	263	106	11	0	0	1,004
Mean Precipitation (in.)	1.40	1.51	2.84	3.90	4.03	4.15	4.44	4.21	3.72	2.52	2.70	2.28	37.70
Days With ≥ 0.1" Precipitation	4	4	6	7	8	7	7	7	6	5	6	5	72
Days With ≥ 1.0" Precipitation	0	0	1	1	1	1	1	1	1	0	1	1	9
Mean Snowfall (in.)	8.2	5.4	3.0	1.8	trace	0.0	0.0	0.0	0.0	trace	1.8	5.1	25.3
Days With ≥ 1.0" Snow Depth	18	11	4	1	0	0	0	0	0	0	1	8	43

Galva *Henry County*   Elevation: 807 ft.   Latitude: 41° 11' N   Longitude: 90° 02' W

	JAN	FEB	MAR	APR	MAY	JUN	JUL	AUG	SEP	OCT	NOV	DEC	YEAR
Mean Maximum Temp. (°F)	28.1	33.9	46.3	60.2	71.9	81.5	85.0	82.7	75.8	63.3	47.0	33.8	59.1
Mean Temp. (°F)	20.0	25.5	36.9	49.5	61.2	70.5	74.5	72.2	64.5	52.3	38.6	26.0	49.3
Mean Minimum Temp. (°F)	11.8	17.1	27.4	38.7	50.4	59.5	64.0	61.6	53.1	41.3	30.1	18.2	39.4
Extreme Maximum Temp. (°F)	64	69	85	90	92	100	103	101	99	91	78	69	103
Extreme Minimum Temp. (°F)	-23	-21	-6	11	28	39	45	42	29	19	-7	-22	-23
Days Maximum Temp. ≥ 90°F	0	0	0	0	0	4	8	5	2	0	0	0	19
Days Maximum Temp. ≤ 32°F	19	12	4	0	0	0	0	0	0	0	3	13	51
Days Minimum Temp. ≤ 32°F	30	25	22	8	0	0	0	0	0	5	18	28	136
Days Minimum Temp. ≤ 0°F	8	4	0	0	0	0	0	0	0	0	0	4	16
Heating Degree Days (base 65°F)	1,389	1,109	868	469	176	23	5	9	108	396	786	1,202	6,540
Cooling Degree Days (base 65°F)	0	0	2	9	61	201	314	250	97	10	0	0	944
Mean Precipitation (in.)	1.48	1.48	2.80	3.90	4.20	4.46	4.03	4.36	3.71	2.76	2.92	2.32	38.42
Days With ≥ 0.1" Precipitation	4	4	6	7	8	7	7	6	6	5	6	4	70
Days With ≥ 1.0" Precipitation	0	0	1	1	1	1	1	2	1	1	1	1	11
Mean Snowfall (in.)	8.2	6.2	4.2	1.7	0.0	0.0	0.0	0.0	0.0	0.4	2.2	5.7	28.6
Days With ≥ 1.0" Snow Depth	19	14	6	1	0	0	0	0	0	0	2	11	53

Geneseo *Henry County*   Elevation: 636 ft.   Latitude: 41° 27' N   Longitude: 90° 09' W

	JAN	FEB	MAR	APR	MAY	JUN	JUL	AUG	SEP	OCT	NOV	DEC	YEAR
Mean Maximum Temp. (°F)	28.4	34.2	47.0	61.1	73.1	82.5	85.9	83.2	75.6	63.2	47.0	33.8	59.6
Mean Temp. (°F)	20.4	26.3	37.9	50.4	62.1	71.6	75.5	72.9	64.8	52.8	38.8	26.4	50.0
Mean Minimum Temp. (°F)	12.3	18.3	28.7	39.7	51.1	60.8	65.0	62.5	53.9	42.3	30.5	18.9	40.3
Extreme Maximum Temp. (°F)	66	70	87	92	95	101	103	103	99	92	77	70	103
Extreme Minimum Temp. (°F)	-23	-24	-5	12	29	39	47	40	31	19	-7	-20	-24
Days Maximum Temp. ≥ 90°F	0	0	0	0	1	5	9	6	2	0	0	0	23
Days Maximum Temp. ≤ 32°F	18	12	4	0	0	0	0	0	0	0	3	12	49
Days Minimum Temp. ≤ 32°F	30	25	21	6	0	0	0	0	0	4	18	28	132
Days Minimum Temp. ≤ 0°F	7	3	0	0	0	0	0	0	0	0	0	3	13
Heating Degree Days (base 65°F)	1,377	1,087	836	443	155	16	2	7	103	385	781	1,191	6,383
Cooling Degree Days (base 65°F)	0	0	1	12	68	225	339	263	100	11	0	0	1,019
Mean Precipitation (in.)	1.50	1.52	2.70	3.76	4.36	4.18	4.00	4.32	3.23	3.04	2.85	2.15	37.61
Days With ≥ 0.1" Precipitation	4	4	6	7	7	7	6	6	5	5	6	5	68
Days With ≥ 1.0" Precipitation	0	0	1	1	1	1	1	1	1	1	1	0	9
Mean Snowfall (in.)	7.8	5.1	3.7	1.7	0.0	0.0	0.0	0.0	0.0	trace	2.2	6.6	27.1
Days With ≥ 1.0" Snow Depth	*19*	*14*	5	1	0	0	0	0	0	0	2	10	*51*

Golden *Adams County*   Elevation: 725 ft.   Latitude: 40° 06' N   Longitude: 91° 01' W

	JAN	FEB	MAR	APR	MAY	JUN	JUL	AUG	SEP	OCT	NOV	DEC	YEAR
Mean Maximum Temp. (°F)	31.9	38.2	50.6	63.3	73.9	83.3	87.1	85.0	78.1	66.6	50.2	37.5	62.1
Mean Temp. (°F)	23.6	29.2	40.7	52.3	63.0	72.5	76.2	74.0	66.4	55.1	41.2	29.5	52.0
Mean Minimum Temp. (°F)	15.2	20.2	30.8	41.3	52.1	61.5	65.3	63.0	54.7	43.5	32.1	21.3	41.8
Extreme Maximum Temp. (°F)	67	76	84	93	92	101	102	103	98	93	79	71	103
Extreme Minimum Temp. (°F)	-23	-20	-14	13	31	41	46	43	30	19	-2	-22	-23
Days Maximum Temp. ≥ 90°F	0	0	0	0	1	6	11	8	3	0	0	0	29
Days Maximum Temp. ≤ 32°F	15	9	3	0	0	0	0	0	0	0	2	9	38
Days Minimum Temp. ≤ 32°F	29	24	19	5	0	0	0	0	0	4	16	27	124
Days Minimum Temp. ≤ 0°F	5	3	0	0	0	0	0	0	0	0	0	2	10
Heating Degree Days (base 65°F)	1,278	1,004	747	390	130	14	2	5	82	320	709	1,095	5,776
Cooling Degree Days (base 65°F)	0	0	2	14	70	244	357	299	125	17	0	0	1,128
Mean Precipitation (in.)	1.15	1.52	2.69	3.61	5.01	3.71	4.31	3.69	3.86	3.05	2.96	2.14	37.70
Days With ≥ 0.1" Precipitation	4	4	6	7	8	7	6	6	6	6	6	4	70
Days With ≥ 1.0" Precipitation	0	0	1	1	1	1	1	1	1	1	1	1	10
Mean Snowfall (in.)	6.0	4.9	2.0	0.6	0.0	0.0	0.0	0.0	0.0	trace	1.6	*3.9*	*19.0*
Days With ≥ 1.0" Snow Depth	*9*	*6*	*2*	0	0	0	0	0	0	0	*1*	*4*	*22*

Harrisburg *Saline County*   Elevation: 364 ft.   Latitude: 37° 44' N   Longitude: 88° 31' W

	JAN	FEB	MAR	APR	MAY	JUN	JUL	AUG	SEP	OCT	NOV	DEC	YEAR
Mean Maximum Temp. (°F)	39.8	46.9	57.3	69.0	78.4	86.3	90.2	88.5	82.1	70.8	57.2	46.3	67.7
Mean Temp. (°F)	31.2	36.9	46.7	57.3	66.6	75.0	78.9	77.0	69.9	58.1	47.2	37.5	56.9
Mean Minimum Temp. (°F)	22.6	27.0	36.1	45.5	54.7	63.6	67.5	65.3	57.6	45.3	37.2	28.6	45.9
Extreme Maximum Temp. (°F)	71	79	85	90	95	101	105	104	100	90	83	78	105
Extreme Minimum Temp. (°F)	-22	-8	-7	22	32	41	45	43	32	18	9	-10	-22
Days Maximum Temp. ≥ 90°F	0	0	0	0	2	10	18	14	6	0	0	0	50
Days Maximum Temp. ≤ 32°F	9	4	1	0	0	0	0	0	0	0	0	3	17
Days Minimum Temp. ≤ 32°F	25	19	13	3	0	0	0	0	0	3	11	20	94
Days Minimum Temp. ≤ 0°F	2	1	0	0	0	0	0	0	0	0	0	0	3
Heating Degree Days (base 65°F)	1,040	786	565	258	69	4	0	1	43	239	530	846	4,381
Cooling Degree Days (base 65°F)	0	0	5	26	117	302	434	378	185	29	2	0	1,478
Mean Precipitation (in.)	2.99	2.73	4.45	4.76	4.82	4.43	4.02	3.22	3.09	3.14	4.09	3.96	45.70
Days With ≥ 0.1" Precipitation	6	6	8	8	7	6	6	5	5	5	7	7	76
Days With ≥ 1.0" Precipitation	1	1	1	1	1	1	1	1	1	1	1	1	12
Mean Snowfall (in.)	*4.8*	*3.8*	2.3	0.4	0.0	0.0	0.0	0.0	0.0	trace	0.6	1.7	*13.6*
Days With ≥ 1.0" Snow Depth	*7*	*5*	*1*	0	0	0	0	0	0	0	0	*1*	*14*

Havana 4 NNE *Mason County*   Elevation: 459 ft.   Latitude: 40° 21' N   Longitude: 90° 01' W

	JAN	FEB	MAR	APR	MAY	JUN	JUL	AUG	SEP	OCT	NOV	DEC	YEAR
Mean Maximum Temp. (°F)	32.2	38.5	50.9	63.8	74.3	84.1	88.3	85.8	79.4	67.2	51.0	38.1	62.8
Mean Temp. (°F)	23.4	29.1	40.6	52.3	62.7	72.6	76.6	74.1	66.5	54.5	41.3	29.5	51.9
Mean Minimum Temp. (°F)	14.5	19.7	30.3	40.8	51.2	61.1	64.8	62.3	53.6	41.9	31.6	20.8	41.0
Extreme Maximum Temp. (°F)	67	75	88	95	96	104	106	106	100	92	81	72	106
Extreme Minimum Temp. (°F)	-30	-25	-13	16	31	42	46	38	28	19	1	-23	-30
Days Maximum Temp. ≥ 90°F	0	0	0	0	1	8	13	9	4	0	0	0	35
Days Maximum Temp. ≤ 32°F	15	9	2	0	0	0	0	0	0	0	2	9	37
Days Minimum Temp. ≤ 32°F	29	24	19	5	0	0	0	0	0	6	17	27	127
Days Minimum Temp. ≤ 0°F	6	4	0	0	0	0	0	0	0	0	0	2	12
Heating Degree Days (base 65°F)	1,285	1,008	752	391	138	15	1	5	80	336	705	1,092	5,808
Cooling Degree Days (base 65°F)	0	0	2	12	72	246	366	295	123	15	0	0	1,131
Mean Precipitation (in.)	1.82	1.91	2.97	3.52	4.53	3.73	3.81	3.62	3.49	2.94	3.21	2.63	38.18
Days With ≥ 0.1" Precipitation	5	4	6	7	8	6	7	6	6	5	6	5	71
Days With ≥ 1.0" Precipitation	0	0	1	1	1	1	1	1	1	1	1	1	10
Mean Snowfall (in.)	9.9	7.7	3.8	1.1	0.0	0.0	0.0	0.0	0.0	trace	1.5	6.1	30.1
Days With ≥ 1.0" Snow Depth	15	9	*2*	0	0	0	0	0	0	0	1	6	*33*

Hennepin Power Plant *Putnam County*   Elevation: 459 ft.   Latitude: 41° 18' N   Longitude: 89° 19' W

	JAN	FEB	MAR	APR	MAY	JUN	JUL	AUG	SEP	OCT	NOV	DEC	YEAR
Mean Maximum Temp. (°F)	30.2	36.0	48.0	61.9	73.7	82.8	86.2	84.2	77.6	65.1	49.3	36.1	60.9
Mean Temp. (°F)	20.3	26.3	37.9	50.0	61.1	70.3	74.0	72.1	64.7	52.3	39.2	27.1	49.6
Mean Minimum Temp. (°F)	10.6	16.4	27.8	38.1	48.4	57.7	61.7	59.9	51.6	39.5	29.2	17.9	38.2
Extreme Maximum Temp. (°F)	63	72	86	93	95	104	104	104	97	89	80	70	104
Extreme Minimum Temp. (°F)	-30	-21	-8	9	27	34	43	40	28	15	-4	-25	-30
Days Maximum Temp. ≥ 90°F	0	0	0	0	2	5	10	7	2	0	0	0	26
Days Maximum Temp. ≤ 32°F	16	11	3	0	0	0	0	0	0	0	2	10	42
Days Minimum Temp. ≤ 32°F	30	26	22	9	1	0	0	0	1	8	20	28	145
Days Minimum Temp. ≤ 0°F	8	4	0	0	0	0	0	0	0	0	0	3	15
Heating Degree Days (base 65°F)	1,379	1,087	834	456	174	24	5	11	104	398	767	1,170	6,409
Cooling Degree Days (base 65°F)	0	0	2	10	56	188	291	244	95	8	0	0	894
Mean Precipitation (in.)	*1.10*	1.09	*2.16*	3.25	3.75	4.26	3.90	4.47	3.88	2.73	2.49	*2.18*	35.26
Days With ≥ 0.1" Precipitation	na	3	4	6	7	7	6	6	6	5	5	*3*	na
Days With ≥ 1.0" Precipitation	na	0	1	1	1	1	1	1	1	1	1	*1*	na
Mean Snowfall (in.)	na	na	na	*0.4*	0.0	0.0	0.0	0.0	0.0	trace	*0.8*	na	na
Days With ≥ 1.0" Snow Depth	na	na	na	0	0	0	0	0	0	0	*1*	na	na

Hillsboro *Montgomery County*   Elevation: 629 ft.   Latitude: 39° 09' N   Longitude: 89° 29' W

	JAN	FEB	MAR	APR	MAY	JUN	JUL	AUG	SEP	OCT	NOV	DEC	YEAR
Mean Maximum Temp. (°F)	36.5	43.0	54.6	67.1	77.0	85.6	89.5	87.4	81.0	69.3	54.0	41.8	65.6
Mean Temp. (°F)	27.6	33.4	44.0	55.4	65.2	74.1	77.9	75.5	68.5	57.1	44.5	33.3	54.7
Mean Minimum Temp. (°F)	18.8	23.6	33.3	43.7	53.4	62.5	66.3	63.6	55.8	44.8	35.0	24.7	43.8
Extreme Maximum Temp. (°F)	70	78	88	92	95	103	104	105	101	90	81	74	105
Extreme Minimum Temp. (°F)	-21	-17	-3	20	30	43	46	39	29	20	2	-20	-21
Days Maximum Temp. ≥ 90°F	0	0	0	0	1	10	16	11	4	0	0	0	42
Days Maximum Temp. ≤ 32°F	11	6	1	0	0	0	0	0	0	0	1	6	25
Days Minimum Temp. ≤ 32°F	27	21	15	4	0	0	0	0	0	3	13	24	107
Days Minimum Temp. ≤ 0°F	3	1	0	0	0	0	0	0	0	0	0	2	6
Heating Degree Days (base 65°F)	1,153	887	648	305	91	8	1	1	54	263	610	978	4,999
Cooling Degree Days (base 65°F)	0	0	4	23	113	311	441	364	167	27	2	0	1,452
Mean Precipitation (in.)	2.08	1.96	3.54	4.36	4.31	4.04	3.49	3.38	3.24	2.88	3.73	2.97	39.98
Days With ≥ 0.1" Precipitation	4	4	7	7	7	7	6	6	5	5	7	5	70
Days With ≥ 1.0" Precipitation	0	0	1	1	1	1	1	1	1	1	1	1	10
Mean Snowfall (in.)	5.8	4.2	3.2	0.5	trace	0.0	0.0	0.0	0.0	trace	1.0	3.9	18.6
Days With ≥ 1.0" Snow Depth	na	na	na	0	0	0	0	0	0	0	0	na	na

Hoopeston 1 NE *Vermilion County*   Elevation: 708 ft.   Latitude: 40° 28' N   Longitude: 87° 39' W

	JAN	FEB	MAR	APR	MAY	JUN	JUL	AUG	SEP	OCT	NOV	DEC	YEAR
Mean Maximum Temp. (°F)	31.6	37.4	49.4	62.4	73.9	82.6	85.4	83.1	77.3	64.8	49.8	37.2	61.2
Mean Temp. (°F)	24.1	29.3	40.2	51.5	62.7	71.8	75.0	72.7	66.1	54.4	41.8	30.1	51.7
Mean Minimum Temp. (°F)	16.5	21.2	31.0	40.7	51.5	61.0	64.6	62.3	54.9	43.9	33.7	23.0	42.0
Extreme Maximum Temp. (°F)	64	71	84	88	94	104	102	104	96	89	77	70	104
Extreme Minimum Temp. (°F)	-24	-17	-1	9	28	38	43	42	30	20	3	-21	-24
Days Maximum Temp. ≥ 90°F	0	0	0	0	1	5	8	4	2	0	0	0	20
Days Maximum Temp. ≤ 32°F	16	10	2	0	0	0	0	0	0	0	1	9	38
Days Minimum Temp. ≤ 32°F	28	23	18	6	1	0	0	0	0	3	14	26	119
Days Minimum Temp. ≤ 0°F	5	3	0	0	0	0	0	0	0	0	0	2	10
Heating Degree Days (base 65°F)	1,262	1,001	763	408	144	19	3	7	81	337	690	1,075	5,790
Cooling Degree Days (base 65°F)	0	0	2	11	79	239	332	263	122	15	0	0	1,063
Mean Precipitation (in.)	1.54	1.57	2.95	3.66	4.17	4.01	4.08	3.80	2.91	3.05	2.93	2.35	37.02
Days With ≥ 0.1" Precipitation	4	4	7	8	8	7	6	6	5	5	6	6	72
Days With ≥ 1.0" Precipitation	0	0	1	1	1	1	1	1	1	1	1	0	9
Mean Snowfall (in.)	5.4	4.1	2.2	0.6	trace	0.0	0.0	0.0	0.0	0.1	1.2	4.2	17.8
Days With ≥ 1.0" Snow Depth	14	11	4	0	0	0	0	0	0	0	1	7	37

Jacksonville 2 E *Morgan County*   Elevation: 606 ft.   Latitude: 39° 44' N   Longitude: 90° 12' W

	JAN	FEB	MAR	APR	MAY	JUN	JUL	AUG	SEP	OCT	NOV	DEC	YEAR
Mean Maximum Temp. (°F)	33.1	39.1	50.8	63.4	73.7	82.7	86.5	84.3	78.6	66.8	51.7	39.1	62.5
Mean Temp. (°F)	24.3	29.3	40.0	51.6	62.0	71.2	75.0	72.6	65.7	54.2	41.6	30.3	51.5
Mean Minimum Temp. (°F)	15.3	19.5	29.2	39.8	50.2	59.6	63.6	60.9	52.8	41.5	31.5	21.4	40.4
Extreme Maximum Temp. (°F)	71	74	87	90	93	101	101	103	99	90	80	74	103
Extreme Minimum Temp. (°F)	-21	-21	-9	18	30	36	45	39	29	20	0	-20	-21
Days Maximum Temp. ≥ 90°F	0	0	0	0	1	5	10	6	3	0	0	0	25
Days Maximum Temp. ≤ 32°F	15	9	3	0	0	0	0	0	0	0	1	8	36
Days Minimum Temp. ≤ 32°F	29	24	20	6	0	0	0	0	0	6	17	27	129
Days Minimum Temp. ≤ 0°F	5	3	0	0	0	0	0	0	0	0	0	2	10
Heating Degree Days (base 65°F)	1,257	1,001	769	407	153	20	3	9	91	345	694	1,070	5,819
Cooling Degree Days (base 65°F)	0	0	3	11	62	212	325	260	117	16	0	0	1,006
Mean Precipitation (in.)	1.35	1.66	3.15	3.91	5.04	4.29	3.75	3.39	3.61	2.69	3.42	2.56	38.82
Days With ≥ 0.1" Precipitation	4	3	6	7	8	6	6	6	6	6	6	5	69
Days With ≥ 1.0" Precipitation	0	0	1	1	1	2	1	1	1	1	1	1	11
Mean Snowfall (in.)	7.3	5.6	3.1	0.5	0.0	0.0	0.0	0.0	0.0	trace	1.4	5.0	22.9
Days With ≥ 1.0" Snow Depth	13	10	3	0	0	0	0	0	0	0	1	6	33

Jerseyville 2 SW *Jersey County*   Elevation: 629 ft.   Latitude: 39° 06' N   Longitude: 90° 21' W

	JAN	FEB	MAR	APR	MAY	JUN	JUL	AUG	SEP	OCT	NOV	DEC	YEAR
Mean Maximum Temp. (°F)	35.3	41.5	52.6	64.6	74.6	83.3	87.8	86.0	79.1	67.6	52.8	40.8	63.8
Mean Temp. (°F)	26.3	31.7	42.5	53.5	63.4	72.3	76.7	74.4	66.8	55.3	43.2	32.0	53.2
Mean Minimum Temp. (°F)	17.2	22.0	32.2	42.4	52.2	61.4	65.4	62.7	54.5	42.9	33.5	23.2	42.5
Extreme Maximum Temp. (°F)	71	80	86	91	92	100	104	104	101	90	80	73	104
Extreme Minimum Temp. (°F)	-25	-22	-10	20	28	37	44	38	27	17	-2	-19	-25
Days Maximum Temp. ≥ 90°F	0	0	0	0	1	6	13	9	3	0	0	0	32
Days Maximum Temp. ≤ 32°F	13	7	2	0	0	0	0	0	0	0	1	7	30
Days Minimum Temp. ≤ 32°F	28	22	17	5	0	0	0	0	0	5	15	25	117
Days Minimum Temp. ≤ 0°F	4	2	0	0	0	0	0	0	0	0	0	1	7
Heating Degree Days (base 65°F)	1,194	935	695	356	123	14	2	4	78	314	648	1,016	5,379
Cooling Degree Days (base 65°F)	0	0	4	17	81	249	379	306	135	16	1	0	1,188
Mean Precipitation (in.)	1.89	1.96	3.47	4.28	3.92	3.65	3.39	2.92	3.39	2.86	3.73	2.82	38.28
Days With ≥ 0.1" Precipitation	4	4	7	7	7	6	6	5	5	6	6	5	68
Days With ≥ 1.0" Precipitation	0	0	1	1	1	1	1	1	1	1	1	1	10
Mean Snowfall (in.)	5.1	3.7	2.8	0.5	0.0	0.0	0.0	0.0	0.0	trace	1.2	3.5	16.8
Days With ≥ 1.0" Snow Depth	11	7	2	0	0	0	0	0	0	0	1	5	26

Kankakee Metro Wastewater *Kankakee County* Elevation: 639 ft. Latitude: 41° 08' N Longitude: 87° 53' W

	JAN	FEB	MAR	APR	MAY	JUN	JUL	AUG	SEP	OCT	NOV	DEC	YEAR
Mean Maximum Temp. (°F)	30.6	36.1	47.6	60.4	72.5	82.4	85.8	83.4	77.3	64.7	49.8	36.4	60.6
Mean Temp. (°F)	21.8	26.8	37.8	49.4	60.7	70.6	74.6	72.2	64.8	52.4	40.4	28.2	50.0
Mean Minimum Temp. (°F)	12.9	17.6	27.9	38.4	48.9	58.8	63.3	60.9	52.2	40.0	30.9	20.1	39.3
Extreme Maximum Temp. (°F)	65	71	84	91	94	103	103	107	99	89	78	70	107
Extreme Minimum Temp. (°F)	-29	-21	-6	8	27	39	47	39	30	18	1	-26	-29
Days Maximum Temp. ≥ 90°F	0	0	0	0	1	6	9	5	2	0	0	0	23
Days Maximum Temp. ≤ 32°F	16	11	3	0	0	0	0	0	0	0	1	9	40
Days Minimum Temp. ≤ 32°F	29	25	21	7	0	0	0	0	0	5	17	28	132
Days Minimum Temp. ≤ 0°F	6	4	0	0	0	0	0	0	0	0	0	3	13
Heating Degree Days (base 65°F)	1,333	1,069	838	470	186	26	3	9	100	393	733	1,134	6,294
Cooling Degree Days (base 65°F)	0	0	1	7	55	202	306	237	99	7	0	0	914
Mean Precipitation (in.)	1.86	1.68	2.80	3.81	4.61	4.43	4.27	3.20	3.29	2.72	3.41	2.50	38.58
Days With ≥ 0.1" Precipitation	5	4	6	8	8	7	6	6	6	6	6	5	73
Days With ≥ 1.0" Precipitation	0	0	0	1	1	1	1	1	1	1	1	0	8
Mean Snowfall (in.)	8.9	6.4	2.9	1.0	trace	0.0	0.0	0.0	0.0	trace	1.0	5.6	25.8
Days With ≥ 1.0" Snow Depth	17	12	4	0	0	0	0	0	0	0	1	8	42

La Harpe *Hancock County* Elevation: 698 ft. Latitude: 40° 35' N Longitude: 90° 58' W

	JAN	FEB	MAR	APR	MAY	JUN	JUL	AUG	SEP	OCT	NOV	DEC	YEAR
Mean Maximum Temp. (°F)	31.8	38.3	50.1	63.1	73.9	83.2	87.4	84.8	77.6	66.0	50.0	37.3	62.0
Mean Temp. (°F)	22.3	28.3	39.3	51.1	62.0	71.3	75.4	72.9	65.0	53.5	39.9	28.1	50.8
Mean Minimum Temp. (°F)	12.7	18.3	28.5	39.1	50.2	59.4	63.3	60.9	52.5	41.0	29.9	18.9	39.6
Extreme Maximum Temp. (°F)	66	74	87	92	93	105	104	105	98	92	79	72	105
Extreme Minimum Temp. (°F)	-23	-22	-8	9	28	39	42	40	29	18	-1	-23	-23
Days Maximum Temp. ≥ 90°F	0	0	0	0	1	6	12	7	2	0	0	0	28
Days Maximum Temp. ≤ 32°F	15	9	2	0	0	0	0	0	0	0	2	9	37
Days Minimum Temp. ≤ 32°F	30	25	21	7	0	0	0	0	0	7	19	28	137
Days Minimum Temp. ≤ 0°F	7	3	0	0	0	0	0	0	0	0	0	3	13
Heating Degree Days (base 65°F)	1,318	1,032	790	421	151	17	3	6	99	361	746	1,137	6,081
Cooling Degree Days (base 65°F)	0	0	2	10	60	217	334	265	104	10	0	0	1,002
Mean Precipitation (in.)	1.43	1.59	2.87	3.92	4.62	4.19	4.47	3.89	4.30	2.85	3.13	2.25	39.51
Days With ≥ 0.1" Precipitation	4	4	6	7	8	7	6	6	6	5	6	5	70
Days With ≥ 1.0" Precipitation	0	0	1	1	1	1	1	1	1	1	1	1	10
Mean Snowfall (in.)	7.8	5.1	3.7	1.1	0.0	0.0	0.0	0.0	0.0	trace	1.9	5.5	25.1
Days With ≥ 1.0" Snow Depth	17	11	4	0	0	0	0	0	0	0	1	9	42

Lacon 1 N *Marshall County* Elevation: 459 ft. Latitude: 41° 02' N Longitude: 89° 24' W

	JAN	FEB	MAR	APR	MAY	JUN	JUL	AUG	SEP	OCT	NOV	DEC	YEAR
Mean Maximum Temp. (°F)	31.4	37.7	49.8	63.7	74.8	83.7	87.1	85.3	78.4	66.5	50.5	37.5	62.2
Mean Temp. (°F)	23.3	28.9	39.9	52.2	62.8	71.7	75.7	73.8	66.3	54.8	41.5	29.6	51.7
Mean Minimum Temp. (°F)	14.9	20.1	30.0	40.6	50.7	59.8	64.1	62.3	54.2	43.1	32.4	21.6	41.2
Extreme Maximum Temp. (°F)	70	73	81	91	92	102	103	102	99	90	78	71	103
Extreme Minimum Temp. (°F)	-27	-21	-5	11	26	36	44	45	28	18	-3	-24	-27
Days Maximum Temp. ≥ 90°F	0	0	0	0	1	6	11	7	2	0	0	0	27
Days Maximum Temp. ≤ 32°F	15	10	2	0	0	0	0	0	0	0	1	9	37
Days Minimum Temp. ≤ 32°F	28	24	19	7	0	0	0	0	0	4	16	27	125
Days Minimum Temp. ≤ 0°F	6	3	0	0	0	0	0	0	0	0	0	2	11
Heating Degree Days (base 65°F)	1,286	1,013	772	394	137	16	2	5	80	325	699	1,091	5,820
Cooling Degree Days (base 65°F)	0	0	2	14	70	231	351	298	125	16	0	0	1,107
Mean Precipitation (in.)	1.57	1.61	3.18	4.05	4.38	4.33	4.18	3.66	3.72	3.13	3.02	2.33	39.16
Days With ≥ 0.1" Precipitation	4	4	7	7	8	7	6	6	5	6	6	5	71
Days With ≥ 1.0" Precipitation	0	0	1	1	1	1	1	1	1	1	1	1	10
Mean Snowfall (in.)	7.3	4.6	2.8	0.8	trace	0.0	0.0	0.0	0.0	trace	1.7	5.4	22.6
Days With ≥ 1.0" Snow Depth	16	11	4	1	0	0	0	0	0	0	1	8	41

Lincoln *Logan County* Elevation: 580 ft. Latitude: 40° 08' N Longitude: 89° 22' W

	JAN	FEB	MAR	APR	MAY	JUN	JUL	AUG	SEP	OCT	NOV	DEC	YEAR
Mean Maximum Temp. (°F)	32.2	38.6	50.6	63.8	74.7	83.4	86.5	84.2	78.5	66.5	51.0	39.0	62.4
Mean Temp. (°F)	23.8	29.6	40.6	52.3	63.2	72.3	75.7	73.4	66.4	54.5	41.8	30.7	52.0
Mean Minimum Temp. (°F)	15.4	20.6	30.6	40.7	51.6	61.1	64.8	62.6	54.3	42.4	32.4	22.3	41.6
Extreme Maximum Temp. (°F)	68	75	86	91	95	102	103	104	97	89	80	72	104
Extreme Minimum Temp. (°F)	-25	-20	-4	15	25	41	47	39	28	21	2	-19	-25
Days Maximum Temp. ≥ 90°F	0	0	0	0	1	6	9	6	2	0	0	0	24
Days Maximum Temp. ≤ 32°F	15	9	2	0	0	0	0	0	0	0	1	8	35
Days Minimum Temp. ≤ 32°F	29	24	19	6	0	0	0	0	0	5	16	26	125
Days Minimum Temp. ≤ 0°F	5	3	0	0	0	0	0	0	0	0	0	2	10
Heating Degree Days (base 65°F)	1,271	992	751	389	129	16	1	5	77	334	690	1,057	5,712
Cooling Degree Days (base 65°F)	0	0	2	12	76	245	345	281	123	14	0	0	1,098
Mean Precipitation (in.)	1.69	1.47	3.09	3.79	4.56	3.97	4.24	4.01	3.21	2.93	2.96	2.61	38.53
Days With ≥ 0.1" Precipitation	4	4	7	7	7	6	6	6	6	5	6	6	69
Days With ≥ 1.0" Precipitation	0	0	0	1	1	1	1	1	1	1	1	0	8
Mean Snowfall (in.)	6.6	4.8	2.1	0.6	0.0	0.0	0.0	0.0	0.0	trace	1.2	4.6	19.9
Days With ≥ 1.0" Snow Depth	13	8	2	0	0	0	0	0	0	0	1	5	29

Marengo *McHenry County*   Elevation: 816 ft.   Latitude: 42° 15' N   Longitude: 88° 36' W

	JAN	FEB	MAR	APR	MAY	JUN	JUL	AUG	SEP	OCT	NOV	DEC	YEAR
Mean Maximum Temp. (°F)	27.8	32.8	44.9	59.0	71.8	81.6	85.0	82.4	75.3	62.9	46.7	32.9	58.6
Mean Temp. (°F)	18.8	23.4	35.1	47.3	58.9	69.0	73.1	70.7	62.8	50.8	37.4	24.6	47.7
Mean Minimum Temp. (°F)	9.7	14.0	25.2	35.6	46.0	56.4	61.1	58.9	50.2	38.5	28.2	16.3	36.7
Extreme Maximum Temp. (°F)	61	68	84	91	95	105	105	103	98	90	76	64	105
Extreme Minimum Temp. (°F)	-29	-23	-10	6	26	29	39	39	25	14	-8	-23	-29
Days Maximum Temp. ≥ 90°F	0	0	0	0	1	5	8	4	1	0	0	0	19
Days Maximum Temp. ≤ 32°F	19	13	4	0	0	0	0	0	0	0	2	13	51
Days Minimum Temp. ≤ 32°F	30	27	24	12	2	0	0	0	1	8	20	29	153
Days Minimum Temp. ≤ 0°F	9	6	1	0	0	0	0	0	0	0	0	4	20
Heating Degree Days (base 65°F)	1,429	1,169	921	533	232	40	7	18	136	441	820	1,245	6,991
Cooling Degree Days (base 65°F)	0	0	0	9	44	167	267	202	71	6	0	0	766
Mean Precipitation (in.)	1.40	1.21	2.36	3.57	3.94	4.36	3.89	4.40	3.55	2.67	2.68	1.97	36.00
Days With ≥ 0.1" Precipitation	4	4	6	7	7	7	6	7	6	5	6	5	70
Days With ≥ 1.0" Precipitation	0	0	0	1	1	1	1	1	1	1	1	0	8
Mean Snowfall (in.)	11.7	7.7	4.8	1.7	0.1	0.0	0.0	0.0	0.0	trace	2.5	8.4	36.9
Days With ≥ 1.0" Snow Depth	20	16	7	1	0	0	0	0	0	0	2	11	57

Marion 4 NNE *Williamson County*   Elevation: 475 ft.   Latitude: 37° 46' N   Longitude: 88° 54' W

	JAN	FEB	MAR	APR	MAY	JUN	JUL	AUG	SEP	OCT	NOV	DEC	YEAR
Mean Maximum Temp. (°F)	38.0	43.9	54.7	65.9	74.9	83.2	87.3	85.9	79.2	68.0	54.7	43.3	64.9
Mean Temp. (°F)	29.0	33.8	44.1	54.5	63.7	72.4	76.7	74.8	67.6	55.9	44.8	34.3	54.3
Mean Minimum Temp. (°F)	20.0	23.7	33.5	43.1	52.5	61.6	66.0	63.7	56.0	43.6	34.9	25.4	43.7
Extreme Maximum Temp. (°F)	70	79	85	89	93	100	103	104	100	90	82	77	104
Extreme Minimum Temp. (°F)	-22	-11	-8	19	31	40	49	43	33	19	7	-17	-22
Days Maximum Temp. ≥ 90°F	0	0	0	0	0	5	11	9	3	0	0	0	28
Days Maximum Temp. ≤ 32°F	10	6	1	0	0	0	0	0	0	0	1	5	23
Days Minimum Temp. ≤ 32°F	27	22	15	5	0	0	0	0	0	5	14	23	111
Days Minimum Temp. ≤ 0°F	2	1	0	0	0	0	0	0	0	0	0	1	4
Heating Degree Days (base 65°F)	1,109	876	643	327	115	11	1	3	67	298	602	944	4,996
Cooling Degree Days (base 65°F)	0	0	4	18	83	248	381	323	142	23	2	0	1,224
Mean Precipitation (in.)	2.98	3.03	4.62	4.67	5.03	4.08	3.80	3.81	3.26	3.14	4.91	3.68	47.01
Days With ≥ 0.1" Precipitation	6	6	8	8	8	7	6	6	6	5	7	7	80
Days With ≥ 1.0" Precipitation	0	1	1	1	2	1	1	1	1	1	1	1	12
Mean Snowfall (in.)	5.9	5.4	2.5	0.5	0.0	0.0	0.0	0.0	0.0	0.2	0.8	2.9	18.2
Days With ≥ 1.0" Snow Depth	7	6	2	0	0	0	0	0	0	0	0	3	18

Mason City 1 W *Mason County*   Elevation: 583 ft.   Latitude: 40° 12' N   Longitude: 89° 42' W

	JAN	FEB	MAR	APR	MAY	JUN	JUL	AUG	SEP	OCT	NOV	DEC	YEAR
Mean Maximum Temp. (°F)	32.6	38.8	51.2	64.6	75.0	83.7	86.8	84.6	78.9	66.9	51.0	38.1	62.7
Mean Temp. (°F)	24.5	30.0	41.3	53.2	63.7	72.6	75.9	73.7	66.9	55.3	42.0	30.3	52.4
Mean Minimum Temp. (°F)	16.2	21.2	31.4	41.6	52.2	61.4	65.0	62.8	54.9	43.7	32.9	22.4	42.2
Extreme Maximum Temp. (°F)	70	75	87	91	94	103	102	103	99	90	80	73	103
Extreme Minimum Temp. (°F)	-24	-21	-8	15	29	39	48	40	28	19	-1	-23	-24
Days Maximum Temp. ≥ 90°F	0	0	0	0	1	6	10	6	3	0	0	0	26
Days Maximum Temp. ≤ 32°F	14	9	2	0	0	0	0	0	0	0	1	9	35
Days Minimum Temp. ≤ 32°F	28	23	17	5	0	0	0	0	0	4	15	25	117
Days Minimum Temp. ≤ 0°F	5	3	0	0	0	0	0	0	0	0	0	2	10
Heating Degree Days (base 65°F)	1,251	982	730	364	120	12	2	4	71	312	684	1,069	5,601
Cooling Degree Days (base 65°F)	0	0	4	16	86	254	357	294	135	19	0	0	1,165
Mean Precipitation (in.)	1.54	1.49	2.76	3.52	4.33	3.63	3.89	3.49	3.15	2.79	2.88	2.42	35.89
Days With ≥ 0.1" Precipitation	4	4	6	7	7	7	6	6	6	5	6	5	69
Days With ≥ 1.0" Precipitation	0	0	1	1	1	1	1	1	1	1	0	1	9
Mean Snowfall (in.)	6.0	4.9	2.4	0.6	trace	0.0	0.0	0.0	0.0	trace	1.3	4.6	19.8
Days With ≥ 1.0" Snow Depth	13	10	2	0	0	0	0	0	0	0	1	7	33

Mattoon *Coles County*   Elevation: 715 ft.   Latitude: 39° 28' N   Longitude: 88° 21' W

	JAN	FEB	MAR	APR	MAY	JUN	JUL	AUG	SEP	OCT	NOV	DEC	YEAR
Mean Maximum Temp. (°F)	33.4	39.1	50.7	63.3	74.3	83.4	86.6	84.7	78.7	66.1	51.0	38.8	62.5
Mean Temp. (°F)	25.4	30.7	41.3	52.6	63.4	72.7	76.2	74.1	67.3	55.2	42.4	31.0	52.7
Mean Minimum Temp. (°F)	17.4	22.2	31.8	41.9	52.5	61.9	65.7	63.5	55.8	44.3	33.8	23.1	42.8
Extreme Maximum Temp. (°F)	67	73	85	89	95	103	102	104	98	90	79	71	104
Extreme Minimum Temp. (°F)	-23	-17	-3	17	30	41	49	40	33	20	4	-20	-23
Days Maximum Temp. ≥ 90°F	0	0	0	0	1	6	10	7	3	0	0	0	27
Days Maximum Temp. ≤ 32°F	14	9	2	0	0	0	0	0	0	0	1	8	34
Days Minimum Temp. ≤ 32°F	28	23	18	5	0	0	0	0	0	3	14	25	116
Days Minimum Temp. ≤ 0°F	4	2	0	0	0	0	0	0	0	0	0	2	8
Heating Degree Days (base 65°F)	1,221	963	731	378	125	13	1	3	67	314	671	1,048	5,535
Cooling Degree Days (base 65°F)	0	0	2	12	83	260	367	303	142	18	0	0	1,187
Mean Precipitation (in.)	2.01	2.03	3.07	4.01	3.91	4.13	4.07	3.12	3.09	3.03	3.65	2.72	38.84
Days With ≥ 0.1" Precipitation	5	5	7	8	7	7	7	5	5	6	6	5	73
Days With ≥ 1.0" Precipitation	0	0	1	1	1	1	1	1	1	1	1	1	10
Mean Snowfall (in.)	6.9	3.4	1.9	0.1	trace	0.0	0.0	0.0	0.0	trace	1.0	4.4	17.7
Days With ≥ 1.0" Snow Depth	11	7	2	0	0	0	0	0	0	0	1	5	26

McLeansboro 2 ENE *Hamilton County*   Elevation: 479 ft.   Latitude: 38° 06' N   Longitude: 88° 30' W

	JAN	FEB	MAR	APR	MAY	JUN	JUL	AUG	SEP	OCT	NOV	DEC	YEAR
Mean Maximum Temp. (°F)	38.0	44.0	54.4	65.8	75.7	84.7	88.9	87.6	81.3	69.4	55.3	43.7	65.7
Mean Temp. (°F)	29.2	34.1	44.1	54.8	64.4	73.4	77.4	75.3	68.4	56.4	45.2	34.6	54.8
Mean Minimum Temp. (°F)	20.3	24.2	33.7	43.7	53.1	62.1	65.9	63.1	55.4	43.5	35.0	25.4	43.8
Extreme Maximum Temp. (°F)	69	79	84	90	92	102	103	103	103	92	83	75	103
Extreme Minimum Temp. (°F)	-21	-11	-5	20	31	40	45	44	32	19	9	-20	-21
Days Maximum Temp. ≥ 90°F	0	0	0	0	1	8	15	12	6	0	0	0	42
Days Maximum Temp. ≤ 32°F	10	6	1	0	0	0	0	0	0	0	0	5	22
Days Minimum Temp. ≤ 32°F	27	21	15	4	0	0	0	0	0	4	13	23	107
Days Minimum Temp. ≤ 0°F	2	1	0	0	0	0	0	0	0	0	0	1	4
Heating Degree Days (base 65°F)	1,103	866	645	321	103	9	1	2	57	283	589	937	4,916
Cooling Degree Days (base 65°F)	0	0	4	19	90	271	399	337	161	25	2	0	1,308
Mean Precipitation (in.)	3.09	2.68	4.50	4.72	4.63	3.80	3.46	3.02	2.91	3.08	4.51	3.55	43.95
Days With ≥ 0.1" Precipitation	6	6	8	8	8	6	6	6	5	5	7	7	78
Days With ≥ 1.0" Precipitation	1	0	1	1	1	1	1	1	1	1	1	1	11
Mean Snowfall (in.)	5.0	4.4	2.5	0.4	0.0	0.0	0.0	0.0	0.0	0.2	0.7	3.1	16.3
Days With ≥ 1.0" Snow Depth	8	6	2	0	0	0	0	0	0	0	0	3	19

Minonk *Woodford County*   Elevation: 748 ft.   Latitude: 40° 54' N   Longitude: 89° 02' W

	JAN	FEB	MAR	APR	MAY	JUN	JUL	AUG	SEP	OCT	NOV	DEC	YEAR
Mean Maximum Temp. (°F)	29.9	35.9	47.8	61.9	73.5	83.5	86.4	84.2	78.3	65.6	49.0	35.9	61.0
Mean Temp. (°F)	21.3	27.0	38.1	50.2	61.3	71.2	74.5	72.2	65.3	53.3	39.7	27.6	50.1
Mean Minimum Temp. (°F)	12.7	18.2	28.3	38.4	49.0	58.8	62.6	60.1	52.2	40.9	30.4	19.4	39.3
Extreme Maximum Temp. (°F)	65	74	88	93	96	103	103	102	99	90	81	70	103
Extreme Minimum Temp. (°F)	-25	-22	-6	7	27	36	44	38	25	16	-3	-22	-25
Days Maximum Temp. ≥ 90°F	0	0	0	0	1	7	10	6	3	0	0	0	27
Days Maximum Temp. ≤ 32°F	17	10	4	0	0	0	0	0	0	0	2	10	43
Days Minimum Temp. ≤ 32°F	30	25	21	8	1	0	0	0	0	6	18	28	137
Days Minimum Temp. ≤ 0°F	7	4	0	0	0	0	0	0	0	0	0	3	14
Heating Degree Days (base 65°F)	1,349	1,066	829	449	176	24	5	10	97	372	752	1,152	6,281
Cooling Degree Days (base 65°F)	0	0	2	11	64	211	308	240	104	12	0	0	952
Mean Precipitation (in.)	1.76	1.89	3.22	3.67	4.35	3.70	3.83	3.42	3.29	2.88	3.33	2.39	37.73
Days With ≥ 0.1" Precipitation	5	4	7	8	7	7	6	6	5	6	7	6	74
Days With ≥ 1.0" Precipitation	0	0	1	1	1	1	1	1	1	0	1	1	9
Mean Snowfall (in.)	9.0	6.8	3.6	0.9	trace	0.0	0.0	0.0	0.0	trace	1.6	6.2	28.1
Days With ≥ 1.0" Snow Depth	15	10	5	0	0	0	0	0	0	0	1	8	39

Monmouth *Warren County*   Elevation: 744 ft.   Latitude: 40° 55' N   Longitude: 90° 38' W

	JAN	FEB	MAR	APR	MAY	JUN	JUL	AUG	SEP	OCT	NOV	DEC	YEAR
Mean Maximum Temp. (°F)	31.0	37.6	50.0	63.9	74.6	83.2	86.8	84.4	77.6	65.5	49.3	36.2	61.7
Mean Temp. (°F)	22.7	28.8	40.0	52.2	62.8	71.7	75.5	73.0	65.7	54.3	40.4	28.4	51.3
Mean Minimum Temp. (°F)	14.4	20.1	30.0	40.5	50.9	60.1	64.1	61.6	53.7	43.0	31.5	20.6	40.9
Extreme Maximum Temp. (°F)	69	72	87	93	93	103	104	104	98	91	80	69	104
Extreme Minimum Temp. (°F)	-25	-24	-6	12	29	37	45	41	27	17	-3	-21	-25
Days Maximum Temp. ≥ 90°F	0	0	0	0	1	5	10	6	2	0	0	0	24
Days Maximum Temp. ≤ 32°F	16	10	2	0	0	0	0	0	0	0	2	10	40
Days Minimum Temp. ≤ 32°F	29	24	19	6	0	0	0	0	0	4	17	27	126
Days Minimum Temp. ≤ 0°F	6	3	0	0	0	0	0	0	0	0	0	3	12
Heating Degree Days (base 65°F)	1,304	1,015	769	391	136	15	2	6	87	339	731	1,127	5,922
Cooling Degree Days (base 65°F)	0	0	2	14	71	228	340	269	112	14	0	0	1,050
Mean Precipitation (in.)	1.61	1.66	2.87	3.83	4.34	4.08	4.36	4.17	3.70	2.99	2.72	2.31	38.64
Days With ≥ 0.1" Precipitation	4	4	7	7	8	7	6	6	6	6	6	5	72
Days With ≥ 1.0" Precipitation	0	0	1	1	1	1	1	1	1	1	0	1	8
Mean Snowfall (in.)	8.6	5.8	3.5	1.6	0.0	0.0	0.0	0.0	0.0	trace	2.3	6.4	28.2
Days With ≥ 1.0" Snow Depth	19	13	4	1	0	0	0	0	0	0	2	9	48

Morrison *Whiteside County*   Elevation: 600 ft.   Latitude: 41° 48' N   Longitude: 89° 58' W

	JAN	FEB	MAR	APR	MAY	JUN	JUL	AUG	SEP	OCT	NOV	DEC	YEAR
Mean Maximum Temp. (°F)	28.7	34.5	46.6	60.5	72.6	82.0	85.3	83.0	76.0	64.1	47.6	34.4	59.6
Mean Temp. (°F)	19.4	25.0	36.8	49.0	60.8	70.0	73.9	71.4	63.5	51.7	38.2	25.8	48.8
Mean Minimum Temp. (°F)	10.1	15.5	27.0	37.5	48.9	58.1	62.4	59.7	50.9	39.3	28.7	17.1	37.9
Extreme Maximum Temp. (°F)	62	69	86	92	95	102	103	105	96	92	79	70	105
Extreme Minimum Temp. (°F)	-28	-25	-9	8	27	35	45	40	27	16	-7	-23	-28
Days Maximum Temp. ≥ 90°F	0	0	0	0	1	5	8	5	2	0	0	0	21
Days Maximum Temp. ≤ 32°F	18	12	3	0	0	0	0	0	0	0	2	11	46
Days Minimum Temp. ≤ 32°F	30	26	23	9	1	0	0	0	1	8	20	29	147
Days Minimum Temp. ≤ 0°F	9	5	0	0	0	0	0	0	0	0	0	4	18
Heating Degree Days (base 65°F)	1,408	1,123	867	481	183	27	4	12	121	414	799	1,209	6,648
Cooling Degree Days (base 65°F)	0	0	1	8	52	187	288	223	77	6	0	0	842
Mean Precipitation (in.)	1.49	1.44	2.79	3.68	4.68	4.19	3.76	4.78	3.09	2.86	2.90	2.13	37.79
Days With ≥ 0.1" Precipitation	4	4	6	7	8	7	6	7	5	5	6	5	70
Days With ≥ 1.0" Precipitation	0	0	0	1	1	1	1	1	1	1	1	0	8
Mean Snowfall (in.)	10.7	6.8	4.6	1.4	0.0	0.0	0.0	0.0	0.0	trace	2.2	8.3	34.0
Days With ≥ 1.0" Snow Depth	22	17	6	1	0	0	0	0	0	0	2	14	62

Mount Carroll *Carroll County*   Elevation: 639 ft.   Latitude: 42° 06' N   Longitude: 89° 59' W

	JAN	FEB	MAR	APR	MAY	JUN	JUL	AUG	SEP	OCT	NOV	DEC	YEAR
Mean Maximum Temp. (°F)	27.8	33.7	45.6	59.6	71.7	81.0	84.7	82.4	75.0	62.9	46.6	33.5	58.7
Mean Temp. (°F)	17.6	23.2	35.0	47.2	58.9	67.8	71.6	69.5	61.2	49.5	36.6	24.0	46.8
Mean Minimum Temp. (°F)	7.5	12.7	24.4	34.7	45.9	54.4	58.7	56.5	47.3	35.9	26.5	14.5	34.9
Extreme Maximum Temp. (°F)	60	65	85	91	93	100	101	102	95	91	77	69	102
Extreme Minimum Temp. (°F)	-29	-30	-13	-2	24	31	39	32	23	5	-15	-24	-30
Days Maximum Temp. ≥ 90°F	0	0	0	0	1	4	7	4	1	0	0	0	17
Days Maximum Temp. ≤ 32°F	18	12	4	0	0	0	0	0	0	0	2	12	48
Days Minimum Temp. ≤ 32°F	30	27	25	13	2	0	0	0	2	13	22	30	164
Days Minimum Temp. ≤ 0°F	11	7	1	0	0	0	0	0	0	0	0	5	24
Heating Degree Days (base 65°F)	1,464	1,173	922	535	227	48	11	26	169	482	844	1,264	7,165
Cooling Degree Days (base 65°F)	0	0	1	7	38	133	217	167	58	4	0	0	625
Mean Precipitation (in.)	1.41	1.44	2.66	3.65	4.50	4.56	3.71	4.51	3.65	2.77	2.82	2.01	37.69
Days With ≥ 0.1" Precipitation	4	4	6	7	7	7	6	7	6	6	6	5	71
Days With ≥ 1.0" Precipitation	0	0	0	1	1	1	1	1	1	1	1	0	8
Mean Snowfall (in.)	10.5	6.7	4.3	1.6	trace	0.0	0.0	0.0	trace	0.2	2.6	7.0	32.9
Days With ≥ 1.0" Snow Depth	22	17	7	1	0	0	0	0	0	0	0	2	14	63

Mount Vernon-Outland Airport *Jefferson County*   Elevation: 465 ft.   Latitude: 38° 19' N   Longitude: 88° 52' W

	JAN	FEB	MAR	APR	MAY	JUN	JUL	AUG	SEP	OCT	NOV	DEC	YEAR
Mean Maximum Temp. (°F)	37.3	43.2	53.9	65.4	75.2	84.2	88.3	86.6	79.8	68.4	54.3	42.7	65.0
Mean Temp. (°F)	28.4	33.5	43.8	54.6	64.0	73.2	77.4	75.3	68.0	56.1	44.7	33.9	54.4
Mean Minimum Temp. (°F)	19.6	23.8	33.6	43.7	52.9	62.1	66.5	64.0	56.1	43.7	35.1	25.0	43.8
Extreme Maximum Temp. (°F)	69	79	83	90	94	101	103	102	98	93	81	78	103
Extreme Minimum Temp. (°F)	-21	-12	-10	19	31	41	49	42	29	18	8	-19	-21
Days Maximum Temp. ≥ 90°F	0	0	0	0	1	7	14	10	4	0	0	0	36
Days Maximum Temp. ≤ 32°F	11	6	1	0	0	0	0	0	0	0	1	5	24
Days Minimum Temp. ≤ 32°F	27	21	15	4	0	0	0	0	0	5	13	24	109
Days Minimum Temp. ≤ 0°F	3	1	0	0	0	0	0	0	0	0	0	1	5
Heating Degree Days (base 65°F)	1,127	884	653	326	110	9	0	2	62	292	603	959	5,027
Cooling Degree Days (base 65°F)	0	0	3	18	78	257	384	319	144	21	1	0	1,225
Mean Precipitation (in.)	2.45	2.59	4.01	4.44	4.52	3.53	3.50	3.24	3.18	2.98	4.27	3.18	41.89
Days With ≥ 0.1" Precipitation	5	5	8	8	7	7	6	5	5	5	7	6	74
Days With ≥ 1.0" Precipitation	1	1	1	1	1	1	1	1	1	1	1	1	12
Mean Snowfall (in.)	6.4	4.8	1.9	0.4	0.0	0.0	0.0	0.0	0.0	0.2	0.7	*2.9*	*17.3*
Days With ≥ 1.0" Snow Depth	*9*	*5*	1	0	0	0	0	0	0	0	0	*3*	*18*

Moweaqua *Shelby County*   Elevation: 613 ft.   Latitude: 39° 38' N   Longitude: 89° 02' W

	JAN	FEB	MAR	APR	MAY	JUN	JUL	AUG	SEP	OCT	NOV	DEC	YEAR
Mean Maximum Temp. (°F)	34.0	40.2	52.2	64.7	75.4	84.0	87.4	85.5	79.9	67.9	52.1	39.7	63.6
Mean Temp. (°F)	25.4	30.8	41.8	53.0	63.5	72.4	75.9	73.7	67.1	55.5	42.6	31.3	52.8
Mean Minimum Temp. (°F)	16.8	21.3	31.3	41.2	51.6	60.8	64.4	61.9	54.2	43.1	33.1	22.8	41.9
Extreme Maximum Temp. (°F)	68	76	86	89	93	104	103	104	99	91	80	72	104
Extreme Minimum Temp. (°F)	-26	-21	-9	17	29	41	46	40	29	19	3	-21	-26
Days Maximum Temp. ≥ 90°F	0	0	0	0	1	7	12	8	4	0	0	0	32
Days Maximum Temp. ≤ 32°F	13	8	2	0	0	0	0	0	0	0	1	7	31
Days Minimum Temp. ≤ 32°F	28	23	18	5	0	0	0	0	0	5	16	26	121
Days Minimum Temp. ≤ 0°F	4	2	0	0	0	0	0	0	0	0	0	2	8
Heating Degree Days (base 65°F)	1,219	960	715	369	120	14	1	4	72	308	667	1,035	5,484
Cooling Degree Days (base 65°F)	0	0	2	13	74	245	348	285	135	18	0	0	1,120
Mean Precipitation (in.)	1.70	1.94	2.87	3.93	4.22	4.21	4.02	3.33	2.99	2.83	3.55	2.24	37.83
Days With ≥ 0.1" Precipitation	*4*	4	6	8	7	7	6	5	5	5	6	4	*67*
Days With ≥ 1.0" Precipitation	0	0	1	1	1	1	1	1	1	1	1	0	9
Mean Snowfall (in.)	na	na	*0.9*	0.2	trace	0.0	0.0	0.0	0.0	trace	0.5	na	na
Days With ≥ 1.0" Snow Depth	na	na	*1*	0	0	0	0	0	0	0	0	*3*	na

Nashville 4 NE *Washington County*   Elevation: 515 ft.   Latitude: 38° 22' N   Longitude: 89° 18' W

	JAN	FEB	MAR	APR	MAY	JUN	JUL	AUG	SEP	OCT	NOV	DEC	YEAR
Mean Maximum Temp. (°F)	37.6	43.7	55.1	66.5	76.0	84.7	88.4	86.5	80.1	68.8	54.4	42.8	65.4
Mean Temp. (°F)	29.5	34.9	45.2	55.9	65.5	74.3	78.1	75.9	69.1	58.0	45.5	34.9	55.6
Mean Minimum Temp. (°F)	21.4	26.0	35.2	45.3	55.0	63.8	67.7	65.2	58.1	47.1	36.6	27.0	45.7
Extreme Maximum Temp. (°F)	69	76	84	90	93	101	106	105	100	91	82	73	106
Extreme Minimum Temp. (°F)	-18	-13	2	22	32	43	52	46	33	25	6	-21	-21
Days Maximum Temp. ≥ 90°F	0	0	0	0	1	7	13	9	4	0	0	0	34
Days Maximum Temp. ≤ 32°F	10	6	1	0	0	0	0	0	0	0	1	5	23
Days Minimum Temp. ≤ 32°F	26	20	13	3	0	0	0	0	0	2	11	21	96
Days Minimum Temp. ≤ 0°F	2	1	0	0	0	0	0	0	0	0	0	1	4
Heating Degree Days (base 65°F)	1,093	844	610	290	85	5	1	1	47	242	579	926	4,723
Cooling Degree Days (base 65°F)	0	0	3	22	108	297	418	355	170	31	1	0	1,405
Mean Precipitation (in.)	2.15	2.30	3.54	3.92	4.09	3.59	3.41	2.73	3.22	3.07	3.74	2.98	38.74
Days With ≥ 0.1" Precipitation	5	5	7	7	7	6	6	5	5	5	6	6	70
Days With ≥ 1.0" Precipitation	0	0	1	1	1	1	1	1	1	1	1	1	10
Mean Snowfall (in.)	5.8	4.3	1.5	0.6	0.0	0.0	0.0	0.0	0.0	trace	0.9	3.2	16.3
Days With ≥ 1.0" Snow Depth	10	6	2	0	0	0	0	0	0	0	1	3	22

Newton 6 SSE *Jasper County*   Elevation: 508 ft.   Latitude: 38° 55' N   Longitude: 88° 07' W

	JAN	FEB	MAR	APR	MAY	JUN	JUL	AUG	SEP	OCT	NOV	DEC	YEAR
Mean Maximum Temp. (°F)	34.9	40.8	51.7	63.4	74.0	83.2	87.1	85.2	79.4	67.5	53.0	40.7	63.4
Mean Temp. (°F)	26.6	31.7	42.2	52.8	63.0	72.5	76.2	73.8	67.0	55.2	43.5	32.5	53.1
Mean Minimum Temp. (°F)	18.3	22.4	32.6	42.2	52.0	61.7	65.3	62.3	54.5	42.9	34.1	24.3	42.7
Extreme Maximum Temp. (°F)	68	77	83	88	94	103	102	104	98	91	81	73	104
Extreme Minimum Temp. (°F)	-28	-21	-12	21	30	41	47	39	31	20	6	-19	-28
Days Maximum Temp. ≥ 90°F	0	0	0	0	1	6	10	8	3	0	0	0	28
Days Maximum Temp. ≤ 32°F	13	8	2	0	0	0	0	0	0	0	1	7	31
Days Minimum Temp. ≤ 32°F	27	22	16	5	0	0	0	0	0	5	14	24	113
Days Minimum Temp. ≤ 0°F	3	2	0	0	0	0	0	0	0	0	0	1	6
Heating Degree Days (base 65°F)	1,184	935	703	372	127	14	1	3	71	317	638	1,001	5,366
Cooling Degree Days (base 65°F)	0	0	2	12	74	248	361	282	130	20	1	0	1,130
Mean Precipitation (in.)	2.38	2.26	3.81	3.94	4.38	3.65	4.19	3.29	3.22	2.82	3.92	2.88	40.74
Days With ≥ 0.1" Precipitation	5	5	7	8	8	7	6	5	5	5	6	6	73
Days With ≥ 1.0" Precipitation	0	0	1	1	1	1	1	1	1	1	1	1	10
Mean Snowfall (in.)	4.9	3.2	2.2	0.1	trace	0.0	0.0	0.0	0.0	0.1	0.9	3.4	14.8
Days With ≥ 1.0" Snow Depth	9	7	2	0	0	0	0	0	0	0	1	5	24

Olney 2 S *Richland County*   Elevation: 479 ft.   Latitude: 38° 42' N   Longitude: 88° 05' W

	JAN	FEB	MAR	APR	MAY	JUN	JUL	AUG	SEP	OCT	NOV	DEC	YEAR
Mean Maximum Temp. (°F)	37.2	43.2	54.5	66.3	76.4	84.9	88.4	86.7	80.8	69.2	54.7	42.6	65.4
Mean Temp. (°F)	28.9	34.1	44.5	55.3	64.9	73.7	77.4	75.4	68.8	57.2	45.4	34.5	55.0
Mean Minimum Temp. (°F)	20.6	24.9	34.5	44.2	53.4	62.4	66.3	64.1	56.8	45.2	36.0	26.3	44.6
Extreme Maximum Temp. (°F)	70	78	85	89	93	103	101	103	98	92	81	74	103
Extreme Minimum Temp. (°F)	-24	-21	-15	21	29	38	46	46	32	18	6	-19	-24
Days Maximum Temp. ≥ 90°F	0	0	0	0	1	7	13	9	4	0	0	0	34
Days Maximum Temp. ≤ 32°F	11	6	1	0	0	0	0	0	0	0	1	5	24
Days Minimum Temp. ≤ 32°F	25	20	14	4	0	0	0	0	0	4	12	22	101
Days Minimum Temp. ≤ 0°F	3	2	0	0	0	0	0	0	0	0	0	1	6
Heating Degree Days (base 65°F)	1,113	866	631	306	95	7	0	0	50	264	584	940	4,856
Cooling Degree Days (base 65°F)	0	0	4	19	100	280	400	338	166	28	1	0	1,336
Mean Precipitation (in.)	2.84	2.60	4.31	4.64	4.56	3.97	3.89	3.25	3.05	3.33	4.41	3.60	44.45
Days With ≥ 0.1" Precipitation	6	5	8	8	7	7	6	5	5	5	7	6	75
Days With ≥ 1.0" Precipitation	1	1	1	1	1	1	1	1	1	1	1	1	12
Mean Snowfall (in.)	4.2	3.3	*1.9*	0.2	0.0	0.0	0.0	0.0	0.0	trace	0.8	2.9	*13.3*
Days With ≥ 1.0" Snow Depth	na	na	*0*	0	0	0	0	0	0	0	0	*1*	na

Ottawa 5 SW *La Salle County*   Elevation: 524 ft.   Latitude: 41° 20' N   Longitude: 88° 55' W

	JAN	FEB	MAR	APR	MAY	JUN	JUL	AUG	SEP	OCT	NOV	DEC	YEAR
Mean Maximum Temp. (°F)	30.6	36.9	48.7	62.5	74.0	82.4	85.4	83.6	77.4	65.6	49.6	36.5	61.1
Mean Temp. (°F)	22.3	28.1	39.2	51.3	62.4	71.5	75.0	73.1	65.9	54.0	40.8	28.6	51.0
Mean Minimum Temp. (°F)	13.8	19.2	29.7	40.0	50.7	60.5	64.6	62.5	54.3	42.5	32.0	20.6	40.9
Extreme Maximum Temp. (°F)	64	72	82	92	96	100	104	102	99	93	80	70	104
Extreme Minimum Temp. (°F)	-25	-21	-2	12	29	39	47	46	30	19	-2	-20	-25
Days Maximum Temp. ≥ 90°F	0	0	0	0	2	5	8	6	2	0	0	0	23
Days Maximum Temp. ≤ 32°F	16	9	3	0	0	0	0	0	0	0	2	9	39
Days Minimum Temp. ≤ 32°F	29	24	19	6	0	0	0	0	0	4	16	27	125
Days Minimum Temp. ≤ 0°F	6	3	0	0	0	0	0	0	0	0	0	3	12
Heating Degree Days (base 65°F)	1,319	1,037	794	419	148	19	3	6	85	347	719	1,122	6,018
Cooling Degree Days (base 65°F)	0	0	2	12	68	207	312	256	107	12	0	0	976
Mean Precipitation (in.)	1.48	1.33	2.62	3.51	4.13	4.22	3.66	3.78	3.70	2.62	2.90	2.25	36.20
Days With ≥ 0.1" Precipitation	4	3	6	7	7	7	6	6	6	5	6	5	68
Days With ≥ 1.0" Precipitation	0	0	0	1	1	1	1	1	1	0	1	1	8
Mean Snowfall (in.)	8.6	5.0	3.2	0.8	0.0	0.0	0.0	0.0	0.0	trace	1.0	5.4	24.0
Days With ≥ 1.0" Snow Depth	19	12	4	0	0	0	0	0	0	0	1	8	44

Palestine 2 W *Crawford County*   Elevation: 469 ft.   Latitude: 39° 00' N   Longitude: 87° 39' W

	JAN	FEB	MAR	APR	MAY	JUN	JUL	AUG	SEP	OCT	NOV	DEC	YEAR
Mean Maximum Temp. (°F)	36.8	42.6	54.1	65.9	76.2	84.8	88.1	86.2	80.1	68.3	54.1	42.3	64.9
Mean Temp. (°F)	28.6	34.0	44.5	55.1	65.1	73.5	77.2	75.6	67.8	56.6	45.1	34.4	54.8
Mean Minimum Temp. (°F)	20.4	25.2	34.9	44.4	54.0	62.3	66.4	64.9	55.5	44.9	36.2	26.5	44.6
Extreme Maximum Temp. (°F)	70	77	86	94	98	102	104	107	98	92	82	74	107
Extreme Minimum Temp. (°F)	-21	-18	-9	21	32	34	44	44	30	20	7	-23	-23
Days Maximum Temp. ≥ 90°F	0	0	0	0	1	8	13	9	4	0	0	0	35
Days Maximum Temp. ≤ 32°F	11	6	1	0	0	0	0	0	0	0	0	5	23
Days Minimum Temp. ≤ 32°F	26	20	13	3	0	0	0	0	0	3	12	22	99
Days Minimum Temp. ≤ 0°F	3	1	0	0	0	0	0	0	0	0	0	1	5
Heating Degree Days (base 65°F)	1,121	870	633	312	94	11	1	0	60	276	590	942	4,910
Cooling Degree Days (base 65°F)	0	0	3	20	107	282	400	354	142	22	1	0	1,331
Mean Precipitation (in.)	2.53	2.49	3.79	4.10	4.63	3.82	3.94	3.66	3.26	2.92	3.87	3.11	42.12
Days With ≥ 0.1" Precipitation	5	5	7	8	8	7	6	6	6	5	6	6	74
Days With ≥ 1.0" Precipitation	0	0	1	1	1	1	1	1	1	1	1	1	10
Mean Snowfall (in.)	6.4	4.5	2.6	0.2	0.0	0.0	0.0	0.0	0.0	trace	1.0	3.8	18.5
Days With ≥ 1.0" Snow Depth	10	7	2	0	0	0	0	0	0	0	1	3	23

Pana 3 E *Christian County*   Elevation: 698 ft.   Latitude: 39° 22' N   Longitude: 89° 02' W

	JAN	FEB	MAR	APR	MAY	JUN	JUL	AUG	SEP	OCT	NOV	DEC	YEAR
Mean Maximum Temp. (°F)	34.7	40.7	52.6	65.4	75.0	83.6	87.2	84.9	78.9	67.0	52.7	40.3	63.6
Mean Temp. (°F)	26.6	32.0	42.8	54.1	63.9	72.7	76.5	74.2	67.4	55.9	43.8	32.4	53.5
Mean Minimum Temp. (°F)	18.5	23.2	32.9	42.8	52.8	61.8	65.7	63.4	55.8	44.7	34.8	24.5	43.4
Extreme Maximum Temp. (°F)	70	75	87	90	98	103	103	104	102	90	80	72	104
Extreme Minimum Temp. (°F)	-21	-13	-5	20	31	42	48	41	28	23	4	-20	-21
Days Maximum Temp. ≥ 90°F	0	0	0	0	1	6	11	7	3	0	0	0	28
Days Maximum Temp. ≤ 32°F	13	7	1	0	0	0	0	0	0	0	1	7	29
Days Minimum Temp. ≤ 32°F	28	22	16	4	0	0	0	0	0	3	13	24	110
Days Minimum Temp. ≤ 0°F	3	1	0	0	0	0	0	0	0	0	0	1	5
Heating Degree Days (base 65°F)	1,184	925	684	337	110	11	1	2	64	296	631	1,004	5,249
Cooling Degree Days (base 65°F)	0	0	3	17	84	263	382	308	142	20	1	0	1,220
Mean Precipitation (in.)	2.23	2.23	3.54	4.00	3.98	4.46	3.94	2.98	3.06	2.94	3.77	3.22	40.35
Days With ≥ 0.1" Precipitation	5	5	8	8	7	7	6	5	5	6	7	6	75
Days With ≥ 1.0" Precipitation	0	0	1	1	1	2	1	1	1	1	1	1	11
Mean Snowfall (in.)	7.4	5.0	4.2	0.9	trace	0.0	0.0	0.0	0.0	0.1	1.8	5.4	24.8
Days With ≥ 1.0" Snow Depth	13	10	3	0	0	0	0	0	0	0	1	6	33

Paris Waterworks *Edgar County*   Elevation: 679 ft.   Latitude: 39° 38' N   Longitude: 87° 42' W

	JAN	FEB	MAR	APR	MAY	JUN	JUL	AUG	SEP	OCT	NOV	DEC	YEAR
Mean Maximum Temp. (°F)	34.0	40.0	51.5	63.8	74.7	83.2	86.5	84.3	78.5	66.3	51.8	39.6	62.9
Mean Temp. (°F)	26.0	31.3	42.1	53.2	63.9	72.7	76.2	74.0	67.5	55.6	43.2	32.0	53.2
Mean Minimum Temp. (°F)	17.9	22.6	32.6	42.6	53.1	62.2	65.9	63.7	56.5	44.9	34.6	24.2	43.4
Extreme Maximum Temp. (°F)	66	74	85	88	94	104	104	101	97	91	80	73	104
Extreme Minimum Temp. (°F)	-22	-17	-4	17	28	40	48	42	31	22	2	-22	-22
Days Maximum Temp. ≥ 90°F	0	0	0	0	1	6	10	6	2	0	0	0	25
Days Maximum Temp. ≤ 32°F	14	8	2	0	0	0	0	0	0	0	1	7	32
Days Minimum Temp. ≤ 32°F	27	22	16	5	0	0	0	0	0	3	14	24	111
Days Minimum Temp. ≤ 0°F	4	2	0	0	0	0	0	0	0	0	0	1	7
Heating Degree Days (base 65°F)	1,204	945	707	362	116	13	1	3	66	304	647	1,018	5,386
Cooling Degree Days (base 65°F)	0	0	3	14	89	255	359	293	145	20	1	0	1,179
Mean Precipitation (in.)	2.21	2.16	3.28	4.08	4.23	4.07	4.43	4.36	2.96	2.81	3.63	3.09	41.31
Days With ≥ 0.1" Precipitation	6	5	8	8	8	7	7	6	5	5	7	6	78
Days With ≥ 1.0" Precipitation	0	0	0	1	1	1	1	1	1	1	1	1	9
Mean Snowfall (in.)	10.4	6.6	3.6	0.3	0.0	0.0	0.0	0.0	0.0	0.1	1.3	5.9	28.2
Days With ≥ 1.0" Snow Depth	13	9	2	0	0	0	0	0	0	0	1	6	31

Park Forest *Cook County*   Elevation: 708 ft.   Latitude: 41° 30' N   Longitude: 87° 41' W

	JAN	FEB	MAR	APR	MAY	JUN	JUL	AUG	SEP	OCT	NOV	DEC	YEAR
Mean Maximum Temp. (°F)	29.0	34.5	45.4	58.4	70.1	80.1	83.8	81.5	74.6	62.9	47.9	35.2	58.6
Mean Temp. (°F)	21.1	26.4	36.8	48.5	59.6	69.4	73.9	71.9	64.4	52.4	39.9	27.8	49.3
Mean Minimum Temp. (°F)	13.2	18.1	28.1	38.4	49.0	58.7	63.9	62.1	54.0	41.9	31.8	20.3	40.0
Extreme Maximum Temp. (°F)	64	70	83	89	94	102	102	103	95	89	77	70	103
Extreme Minimum Temp. (°F)	-27	-18	-2	9	28	36	45	41	29	18	1	-21	-27
Days Maximum Temp. ≥ 90°F	0	0	0	0	1	4	6	3	1	0	0	0	15
Days Maximum Temp. ≤ 32°F	18	12	4	0	0	0	0	0	0	0	2	11	47
Days Minimum Temp. ≤ 32°F	30	25	22	8	1	0	0	0	0	4	17	27	134
Days Minimum Temp. ≤ 0°F	6	3	0	0	0	0	0	0	0	0	0	2	11
Heating Degree Days (base 65°F)	1,355	1,085	869	499	218	41	7	11	110	393	747	1,148	6,483
Cooling Degree Days (base 65°F)	0	0	1	9	56	184	295	238	95	10	0	0	888
Mean Precipitation (in.)	1.76	1.62	2.75	3.85	4.19	4.55	4.15	3.86	3.31	2.82	3.40	2.54	38.80
Days With ≥ 0.1" Precipitation	4	4	6	8	7	7	6	6	6	6	6	5	71
Days With ≥ 1.0" Precipitation	0	0	0	1	1	1	1	1	1	1	1	0	8
Mean Snowfall (in.)	10.6	7.6	4.7	1.0	trace	0.0	0.0	0.0	0.0	0.2	1.0	5.7	30.8
Days With ≥ 1.0" Snow Depth	20	14	6	0	0	0	0	0	0	0	1	9	50

Paw Paw 2 NW *Lee County*   Elevation: 948 ft.   Latitude: 41° 43' N   Longitude: 89° 00' W

	JAN	FEB	MAR	APR	MAY	JUN	JUL	AUG	SEP	OCT	NOV	DEC	YEAR
Mean Maximum Temp. (°F)	26.1	31.4	43.1	57.6	70.1	79.7	82.9	80.1	73.7	61.6	45.3	32.0	57.0
Mean Temp. (°F)	18.1	23.4	34.3	46.9	58.9	68.6	72.3	69.8	62.6	50.5	36.8	24.4	47.2
Mean Minimum Temp. (°F)	10.2	15.3	25.4	36.1	47.5	57.4	61.7	59.4	51.4	39.3	28.3	16.7	37.4
Extreme Maximum Temp. (°F)	61	68	83	90	94	101	100	99	93	88	75	65	101
Extreme Minimum Temp. (°F)	-25	-33	-9	9	26	36	43	37	29	17	-7	-23	-33
Days Maximum Temp. ≥ 90°F	0	0	0	0	0	3	4	2	1	0	0	0	10
Days Maximum Temp. ≤ 32°F	21	14	6	0	0	0	0	0	0	0	4	15	60
Days Minimum Temp. ≤ 32°F	30	27	25	10	1	0	0	0	0	7	20	29	149
Days Minimum Temp. ≤ 0°F	8	5	0	0	0	0	0	0	0	0	0	4	17
Heating Degree Days (base 65°F)	1,447	1,168	945	543	230	40	9	19	135	450	839	1,252	7,077
Cooling Degree Days (base 65°F)	0	0	0	4	41	158	243	174	65	5	0	0	690
Mean Precipitation (in.)	1.40	1.21	2.32	3.54	4.33	4.54	3.60	4.17	4.15	2.72	2.98	2.15	37.11
Days With ≥ 0.1" Precipitation	4	3	6	8	8	7	6	6	6	5	6	5	70
Days With ≥ 1.0" Precipitation	0	0	0	1	1	1	1	1	1	1	1	0	8
Mean Snowfall (in.)	9.0	5.8	4.2	1.0	trace	0.0	0.0	0.0	0.0	0.2	2.6	7.4	30.2
Days With ≥ 1.0" Snow Depth	20	13	5	0	0	0	0	0	0	0	2	11	51

Peru *La Salle County*   Elevation: 620 ft.   Latitude: 41° 21' N   Longitude: 89° 06' W

	JAN	FEB	MAR	APR	MAY	JUN	JUL	AUG	SEP	OCT	NOV	DEC	YEAR
Mean Maximum Temp. (°F)	29.3	35.3	47.4	61.5	73.4	82.6	85.9	83.7	77.1	65.1	48.7	35.8	60.5
Mean Temp. (°F)	20.7	26.5	37.7	49.9	61.4	70.6	74.6	72.4	64.7	53.1	39.7	27.7	49.9
Mean Minimum Temp. (°F)	12.2	17.7	28.1	38.4	49.3	58.7	63.2	61.0	52.2	41.0	30.8	19.6	39.3
Extreme Maximum Temp. (°F)	64	72	82	91	93	101	104	103	96	90	78	69	104
Extreme Minimum Temp. (°F)	-26	-21	-4	13	25	38	42	40	27	16	-5	-21	-26
Days Maximum Temp. ≥ 90°F	0	0	0	0	2	5	10	6	2	0	0	0	25
Days Maximum Temp. ≤ 32°F	17	11	4	0	0	0	0	0	0	0	2	10	44
Days Minimum Temp. ≤ 32°F	30	26	21	8	1	0	0	0	0	6	18	28	138
Days Minimum Temp. ≤ 0°F	8	4	0	0	0	0	0	0	0	0	0	3	15
Heating Degree Days (base 65°F)	1,366	1,080	839	456	173	24	4	10	103	373	751	1,149	6,328
Cooling Degree Days (base 65°F)	0	0	1	8	63	202	308	249	94	9	0	0	934
Mean Precipitation (in.)	1.38	1.40	2.76	3.82	4.82	4.24	4.12	4.25	3.82	3.06	2.78	2.27	38.72
Days With ≥ 0.1" Precipitation	4	4	6	7	8	7	6	6	6	6	6	5	71
Days With ≥ 1.0" Precipitation	0	0	0	1	1	1	1	1	1	1	1	1	9
Mean Snowfall (in.)	8.0	4.5	3.6	0.6	trace	0.0	0.0	0.0	0.0	0.1	1.3	5.6	23.7
Days With ≥ 1.0" Snow Depth	20	10	3	0	0	0	0	0	0	0	0	1	8	42

Piper City *Ford County*   Elevation: 669 ft.   Latitude: 40° 42' N   Longitude: 88° 11' W

	JAN	FEB	MAR	APR	MAY	JUN	JUL	AUG	SEP	OCT	NOV	DEC	YEAR
Mean Maximum Temp. (°F)	30.7	36.7	48.9	62.7	74.9	83.9	86.4	83.9	78.2	65.5	49.4	36.7	61.5
Mean Temp. (°F)	22.3	27.9	38.9	50.6	62.3	71.6	74.7	72.0	65.3	53.5	40.4	28.7	50.7
Mean Minimum Temp. (°F)	13.8	19.0	29.0	38.4	49.5	59.2	63.0	60.1	52.4	41.3	31.3	20.6	39.8
Extreme Maximum Temp. (°F)	66	72	86	93	97	106	105	108	98	90	80	70	108
Extreme Minimum Temp. (°F)	-25	-20	-4	7	25	37	42	37	26	17	0	-23	-25
Days Maximum Temp. ≥ 90°F	0	0	0	0	3	8	10	6	2	0	0	0	29
Days Maximum Temp. ≤ 32°F	16	10	3	0	0	0	0	0	0	0	2	10	41
Days Minimum Temp. ≤ 32°F	29	25	22	8	1	0	0	0	0	6	18	27	136
Days Minimum Temp. ≤ 0°F	6	3	0	0	0	0	0	0	0	0	0	2	11
Heating Degree Days (base 65°F)	1,318	1,042	803	436	154	21	4	10	92	365	733	1,118	6,096
Cooling Degree Days (base 65°F)	0	0	2	9	70	225	322	239	102	13	0	0	982
Mean Precipitation (in.)	1.84	1.73	2.75	3.44	4.24	3.74	4.18	3.88	3.03	2.60	2.87	2.50	36.80
Days With ≥ 0.1" Precipitation	5	4	6	7	8	7	6	6	5	5	6	5	70
Days With ≥ 1.0" Precipitation	0	0	1	1	1	1	1	1	1	1	1	0	9
Mean Snowfall (in.)	9.4	6.2	3.4	1.1	trace	0.0	0.0	0.0	0.0	0.2	2.0	5.8	28.1
Days With ≥ 1.0" Snow Depth	14	10	5	0	0	0	0	0	0	0	1	6	36

Pontiac *Livingston County*   Elevation: 649 ft.   Latitude: 40° 53' N   Longitude: 88° 38' W

	JAN	FEB	MAR	APR	MAY	JUN	JUL	AUG	SEP	OCT	NOV	DEC	YEAR
Mean Maximum Temp. (°F)	29.9	36.3	48.2	61.9	73.5	82.3	85.1	82.9	77.3	64.9	48.9	36.0	60.6
Mean Temp. (°F)	22.1	27.9	38.8	50.8	62.1	71.4	74.8	72.6	65.8	53.7	40.5	28.6	50.8
Mean Minimum Temp. (°F)	14.2	19.4	29.5	39.7	50.7	60.5	64.5	62.3	54.4	42.5	31.9	21.1	40.9
Extreme Maximum Temp. (°F)	65	72	81	89	95	103	101	104	96	91	77	71	104
Extreme Minimum Temp. (°F)	-23	-18	-8	11	25	39	45	47	31	19	1	-20	-23
Days Maximum Temp. ≥ 90°F	0	0	0	0	1	5	8	5	2	0	0	0	21
Days Maximum Temp. ≤ 32°F	17	10	3	0	0	0	0	0	0	0	2	10	42
Days Minimum Temp. ≤ 32°F	29	25	20	7	0	0	0	0	0	4	17	27	129
Days Minimum Temp. ≤ 0°F	6	3	0	0	0	0	0	0	0	0	0	2	11
Heating Degree Days (base 65°F)	1,325	1,041	806	432	155	21	3	7	85	358	729	1,122	6,084
Cooling Degree Days (base 65°F)	0	0	2	11	64	211	311	247	109	11	0	0	966
Mean Precipitation (in.)	1.64	1.38	2.81	3.49	3.99	4.13	4.07	3.60	3.23	2.68	2.94	2.48	36.44
Days With ≥ 0.1" Precipitation	4	4	6	7	8	7	6	6	5	5	6	5	69
Days With ≥ 1.0" Precipitation	0	0	0	1	1	1	1	1	1	0	0	0	6
Mean Snowfall (in.)	8.9	5.7	3.3	1.0	0.0	0.0	0.0	0.0	0.0	trace	1.7	5.2	25.8
Days With ≥ 1.0" Snow Depth	11	7	2	0	0	0	0	0	0	0	1	4	25

Princeville *Peoria County*   Elevation: 734 ft.   Latitude: 40° 56' N   Longitude: 89° 46' W

	JAN	FEB	MAR	APR	MAY	JUN	JUL	AUG	SEP	OCT	NOV	DEC	YEAR
Mean Maximum Temp. (°F)	29.9	36.3	48.7	62.4	73.0	81.4	85.0	82.7	76.3	64.5	49.0	35.6	60.4
Mean Temp. (°F)	20.5	26.5	37.8	50.0	60.7	69.5	73.1	70.8	63.5	52.1	39.0	26.7	49.2
Mean Minimum Temp. (°F)	11.1	16.7	26.9	37.4	48.2	57.4	61.1	58.9	50.7	39.7	28.9	17.8	37.9
Extreme Maximum Temp. (°F)	65	72	87	93	94	101	104	105	99	90	82	70	105
Extreme Minimum Temp. (°F)	-26	-26	-7	5	22	35	44	36	26	12	-3	-26	-26
Days Maximum Temp. ≥ 90°F	0	0	0	0	1	4	8	5	2	0	0	0	20
Days Maximum Temp. ≤ 32°F	17	11	3	0	0	0	0	0	0	0	2	10	43
Days Minimum Temp. ≤ 32°F	30	25	23	10	1	0	0	0	1	8	19	28	145
Days Minimum Temp. ≤ 0°F	8	5	0	0	0	0	0	0	0	0	0	4	17
Heating Degree Days (base 65°F)	1,373	1,080	837	455	182	31	7	16	125	402	774	1,179	6,461
Cooling Degree Days (base 65°F)	0	0	1	8	45	158	250	191	73	7	0	0	733
Mean Precipitation (in.)	1.74	1.65	3.07	3.86	4.66	3.94	3.97	3.74	3.72	2.86	2.96	2.48	38.65
Days With ≥ 0.1" Precipitation	4	3	6	7	8	7	7	7	6	6	6	5	72
Days With ≥ 1.0" Precipitation	0	0	1	1	1	1	1	1	1	1	1	1	10
Mean Snowfall (in.)	6.4	5.6	2.9	0.7	trace	0.0	0.0	0.0	0.0	0.1	2.1	5.5	23.3
Days With ≥ 1.0" Snow Depth	10	6	1	0	0	0	0	0	0	0	1	3	21

Quincy Muni Baldwin Field *Adams County* Elevation: 761 ft. Latitude: 39° 56' N Longitude: 91° 12' W

	JAN	FEB	MAR	APR	MAY	JUN	JUL	AUG	SEP	OCT	NOV	DEC	YEAR
Mean Maximum Temp. (°F)	31.9	38.0	50.1	62.8	72.8	82.1	86.5	84.2	77.1	65.3	50.1	37.5	61.5
Mean Temp. (°F)	24.2	29.9	41.1	52.8	63.0	72.2	76.6	74.2	66.6	55.0	41.7	30.0	52.3
Mean Minimum Temp. (°F)	16.4	21.7	32.1	42.9	53.1	62.3	66.6	64.3	56.0	44.6	33.3	22.6	43.0
Extreme Maximum Temp. (°F)	72	76	85	92	91	101	105	103	100	92	78	71	105
Extreme Minimum Temp. (°F)	-21	-18	-8	17	32	42	48	42	32	20	0	-22	-22
Days Maximum Temp. ≥ 90°F	0	0	0	0	0	5	10	7	2	0	0	0	24
Days Maximum Temp. ≤ 32°F	15	9	2	0	0	0	0	0	0	0	2	10	38
Days Minimum Temp. ≤ 32°F	28	22	16	4	0	0	0	0	0	3	14	26	113
Days Minimum Temp. ≤ 0°F	5	3	0	0	0	0	0	0	0	0	0	2	10
Heating Degree Days (base 65°F)	1,258	986	736	373	129	14	1	4	81	322	692	1,077	5,673
Cooling Degree Days (base 65°F)	0	0	3	15	68	236	367	303	132	17	1	0	1,142
Mean Precipitation (in.)	1.35	1.72	3.14	3.85	5.02	3.55	3.87	3.63	4.13	3.25	3.23	2.41	39.15
Days With ≥ 0.1" Precipitation	3	4	6	7	8	6	6	6	6	6	6	5	69
Days With ≥ 1.0" Precipitation	0	0	1	1	2	1	1	1	1	1	1	1	11
Mean Snowfall (in.)	7.6	6.0	2.9	0.9	trace	trace	trace	trace	trace	trace	2.2	4.8	24.4
Days With ≥ 1.0" Snow Depth	15	11	3	0	0	0	0	0	0	0	1	6	36

Rantoul Chanute AFB *Champaign County* Elevation: 754 ft. Latitude: 40° 18' N Longitude: 88° 09' W

	JAN	FEB	MAR	APR	MAY	JUN	JUL	AUG	SEP	OCT	NOV	DEC	YEAR
Mean Maximum Temp. (°F)	32.2	37.3	48.6	62.2	73.9	83.3	86.6	84.3	78.5	66.0	50.3	37.9	61.7
Mean Temp. (°F)	23.2	27.9	38.8	50.6	62.1	71.7	75.2	72.8	65.9	53.7	40.7	29.5	51.0
Mean Minimum Temp. (°F)	14.2	18.6	29.0	39.0	50.2	60.1	63.7	61.2	53.3	41.4	31.1	21.0	40.2
Extreme Maximum Temp. (°F)	65	72	85	90	97	104	105	102	98	90	78	70	105
Extreme Minimum Temp. (°F)	-27	-19	-13	10	27	38	46	38	31	21	3	-22	-27
Days Maximum Temp. ≥ 90°F	0	0	0	0	2	7	10	6	3	0	0	0	28
Days Maximum Temp. ≤ 32°F	15	10	2	0	0	0	0	0	0	0	1	8	36
Days Minimum Temp. ≤ 32°F	29	25	21	7	0	0	0	0	0	6	18	27	133
Days Minimum Temp. ≤ 0°F	6	3	0	0	0	0	0	0	0	0	0	2	11
Heating Degree Days (base 65°F)	1,290	1,041	808	434	155	21	3	7	87	356	723	1,095	6,020
Cooling Degree Days (base 65°F)	0	0	2	9	64	231	330	256	113	12	0	0	1,017
Mean Precipitation (in.)	1.72	1.79	3.13	3.88	4.16	3.92	4.52	4.33	3.17	2.94	3.10	2.64	39.30
Days With ≥ 0.1" Precipitation	5	4	6	8	7	7	6	6	5	6	6	6	72
Days With ≥ 1.0" Precipitation	0	0	1	1	1	1	2	1	1	1	1	1	11
Mean Snowfall (in.)	na	na	1.9	0.4	trace	0.0	0.0	0.0	0.0	trace	0.5	na	na
Days With ≥ 1.0" Snow Depth	na	9	1	0	0	0	0	0	0	0	0	4	na

Rosiclare 5 NW *Hardin County* Elevation: 396 ft. Latitude: 37° 25' N Longitude: 88° 21' W

	JAN	FEB	MAR	APR	MAY	JUN	JUL	AUG	SEP	OCT	NOV	DEC	YEAR
Mean Maximum Temp. (°F)	41.5	47.9	58.1	68.9	76.8	84.2	88.0	87.1	80.8	70.4	57.5	46.7	67.3
Mean Temp. (°F)	31.9	37.0	46.6	56.2	64.7	72.9	77.0	75.5	68.5	57.3	46.8	36.9	55.9
Mean Minimum Temp. (°F)	22.3	26.0	35.2	43.5	52.9	61.4	66.0	64.0	56.2	44.2	36.1	27.1	44.6
Extreme Maximum Temp. (°F)	72	77	84	90	92	100	102	101	100	90	83	76	102
Extreme Minimum Temp. (°F)	-22	-12	3	16	31	39	47	36	32	18	3	-17	-22
Days Maximum Temp. ≥ 90°F	0	0	0	0	0	5	13	10	4	0	0	0	32
Days Maximum Temp. ≤ 32°F	7	3	1	0	0	0	0	0	0	0	0	3	14
Days Minimum Temp. ≤ 32°F	25	20	14	5	0	0	0	0	0	4	12	21	101
Days Minimum Temp. ≤ 0°F	2	1	0	0	0	0	0	0	0	0	0	0	3
Heating Degree Days (base 65°F)	1,019	785	569	281	92	7	0	1	51	257	540	864	4,466
Cooling Degree Days (base 65°F)	0	0	6	20	87	247	385	337	152	22	2	0	1,258
Mean Precipitation (in.)	3.34	3.56	4.81	4.96	5.04	4.27	4.22	3.48	3.18	3.37	4.34	4.25	48.82
Days With ≥ 0.1" Precipitation	6	6	8	8	8	7	6	5	5	5	6	7	77
Days With ≥ 1.0" Precipitation	1	1	1	1	1	1	1	1	1	1	1	1	12
Mean Snowfall (in.)	4.3	3.3	1.4	0.1	0.0	0.0	0.0	0.0	0.0	0.2	0.1	1.3	10.7
Days With ≥ 1.0" Snow Depth	7	5	1	0	0	0	0	0	0	0	0	1	14

Rushville *Schuyler County* Elevation: 659 ft. Latitude: 40° 07' N Longitude: 90° 33' W

	JAN	FEB	MAR	APR	MAY	JUN	JUL	AUG	SEP	OCT	NOV	DEC	YEAR
Mean Maximum Temp. (°F)	32.6	39.0	50.6	63.7	74.1	82.7	87.2	85.2	78.2	66.5	50.7	38.0	62.4
Mean Temp. (°F)	24.0	29.9	40.7	52.7	62.9	71.9	76.3	74.0	66.5	54.9	41.4	29.9	52.1
Mean Minimum Temp. (°F)	15.4	20.7	30.8	41.7	51.7	61.0	65.3	62.8	54.7	43.3	32.1	21.6	41.8
Extreme Maximum Temp. (°F)	69	78	86	91	93	101	102	103	98	91	79	76	103
Extreme Minimum Temp. (°F)	-21	-20	-7	15	30	41	46	42	30	17	-1	-19	-21
Days Maximum Temp. ≥ 90°F	0	0	0	0	0	5	11	7	2	0	0	0	25
Days Maximum Temp. ≤ 32°F	15	9	2	0	0	0	0	0	0	0	2	8	36
Days Minimum Temp. ≤ 32°F	29	24	18	4	0	0	0	0	0	4	16	26	121
Days Minimum Temp. ≤ 0°F	5	3	0	0	0	0	0	0	0	0	0	2	10
Heating Degree Days (base 65°F)	1,265	985	749	378	130	16	1	3	79	321	702	1,083	5,712
Cooling Degree Days (base 65°F)	0	0	3	15	68	228	364	294	128	17	0	0	1,117
Mean Precipitation (in.)	1.54	1.84	3.06	4.04	5.19	4.04	3.79	3.69	3.96	3.27	3.14	2.45	40.01
Days With ≥ 0.1" Precipitation	3	3	6	7	7	6	6	5	5	5	5	5	63
Days With ≥ 1.0" Precipitation	0	0	1	1	2	1	1	1	1	1	1	1	11
Mean Snowfall (in.)	5.6	4.6	2.3	0.7	0.0	0.0	0.0	0.0	0.0	trace	1.0	3.7	17.9
Days With ≥ 1.0" Snow Depth	10	8	2	0	0	0	0	0	0	0	1	5	26

Salem Leckrone Airport *Marion County*   Elevation: 567 ft.   Latitude: 38° 39' N   Longitude: 88° 58' W

	JAN	FEB	MAR	APR	MAY	JUN	JUL	AUG	SEP	OCT	NOV	DEC	YEAR
Mean Maximum Temp. (°F)	37.6	43.9	55.1	67.0	76.7	85.3	89.1	87.3	80.7	69.2	54.7	42.9	65.8
Mean Temp. (°F)	29.1	34.5	44.8	55.6	65.2	74.0	78.0	76.0	68.9	57.3	45.2	34.5	55.3
Mean Minimum Temp. (°F)	20.5	25.0	34.4	44.3	53.7	62.7	66.9	64.6	57.1	45.4	35.7	26.1	44.7
Extreme Maximum Temp. (°F)	70	78	85	91	94	101	104	105	99	90	82	74	105
Extreme Minimum Temp. (°F)	-23	-23	-8	20	31	42	49	45	33	21	6	-20	-23
Days Maximum Temp. ≥ 90°F	0	0	0	0	1	8	15	11	4	0	0	0	39
Days Maximum Temp. ≤ 32°F	10	6	1	0	0	0	0	0	0	0	0	5	22
Days Minimum Temp. ≤ 32°F	27	20	14	4	0	0	0	0	0	3	12	23	103
Days Minimum Temp. ≤ 0°F	2	1	0	0	0	0	0	0	0	0	0	1	4
Heating Degree Days (base 65°F)	1,107	856	625	299	89	6	1	1	48	259	589	938	4,818
Cooling Degree Days (base 65°F)	0	0	4	22	103	293	425	358	167	28	1	0	1,401
Mean Precipitation (in.)	2.42	2.45	3.95	4.16	4.25	4.21	3.79	3.31	3.23	3.11	3.98	3.23	42.09
Days With ≥ 0.1" Precipitation	5	5	7	8	8	7	5	6	5	5	7	6	74
Days With ≥ 1.0" Precipitation	0	0	1	1	1	1	1	1	1	1	1	1	10
Mean Snowfall (in.)	5.4	3.5	1.1	0.3	0.0	0.0	0.0	0.0	0.0	trace	0.7	2.7	13.7
Days With ≥ 1.0" Snow Depth	9	5	1	0	0	0	0	0	0	0	0	4	19

Sparta 1 W *Randolph County*   Elevation: 534 ft.   Latitude: 38° 07' N   Longitude: 89° 43' W

	JAN	FEB	MAR	APR	MAY	JUN	JUL	AUG	SEP	OCT	NOV	DEC	YEAR
Mean Maximum Temp. (°F)	38.8	46.0	56.7	67.9	77.2	85.8	89.6	87.9	81.2	70.2	55.6	44.0	66.8
Mean Temp. (°F)	30.4	36.4	46.1	56.6	65.7	74.8	78.5	76.5	69.5	58.3	46.2	35.7	56.2
Mean Minimum Temp. (°F)	21.9	26.7	35.5	45.1	54.2	63.6	67.4	65.1	57.6	46.4	36.7	27.2	45.6
Extreme Maximum Temp. (°F)	72	81	86	92	94	103	108	105	99	92	85	76	108
Extreme Minimum Temp. (°F)	-16	-11	0	23	29	43	48	41	31	23	8	-16	-16
Days Maximum Temp. ≥ 90°F	0	0	0	0	2	9	17	12	4	0	0	0	44
Days Maximum Temp. ≤ 32°F	10	5	1	0	0	0	0	0	0	0	1	4	21
Days Minimum Temp. ≤ 32°F	26	19	13	3	0	0	0	0	0	3	11	21	96
Days Minimum Temp. ≤ 0°F	2	0	0	0	0	0	0	0	0	0	0	1	3
Heating Degree Days (base 65°F)	1,067	802	583	277	83	6	0	1	48	235	560	903	4,565
Cooling Degree Days (base 65°F)	0	0	6	28	110	310	426	368	180	33	2	0	1,463
Mean Precipitation (in.)	2.37	2.49	4.16	4.14	4.47	3.74	3.88	3.25	2.93	3.35	4.13	3.27	42.18
Days With ≥ 0.1" Precipitation	4	5	7	7	7	6	6	5	5	5	6	6	69
Days With ≥ 1.0" Precipitation	0	0	1	1	1	1	1	1	1	1	1	1	10
Mean Snowfall (in.)	5.1	3.5	2.0	0.5	0.0	0.0	0.0	0.0	0.0	trace	1.0	2.7	14.8
Days With ≥ 1.0" Snow Depth	8	5	1	0	0	0	0	0	0	0	1	3	18

Stockton 3 NNE *Jo Daviess County*   Elevation: 967 ft.   Latitude: 42° 24' N   Longitude: 90° 00' W

	JAN	FEB	MAR	APR	MAY	JUN	JUL	AUG	SEP	OCT	NOV	DEC	YEAR
Mean Maximum Temp. (°F)	25.7	31.5	43.0	57.7	70.0	78.8	82.0	79.8	72.3	60.7	44.2	31.1	56.4
Mean Temp. (°F)	17.4	23.2	34.2	47.1	59.0	68.2	71.8	69.7	61.6	50.1	36.0	23.4	46.8
Mean Minimum Temp. (°F)	8.8	14.8	25.4	36.5	47.9	57.4	61.6	59.5	50.8	39.5	27.9	15.7	37.2
Extreme Maximum Temp. (°F)	57	62	84	91	93	99	99	99	95	87	75	66	99
Extreme Minimum Temp. (°F)	-28	-30	-8	7	24	37	40	39	27	13	-8	-24	-30
Days Maximum Temp. ≥ 90°F	0	0	0	0	0	2	4	2	0	0	0	0	8
Days Maximum Temp. ≤ 32°F	21	14	5	0	0	0	0	0	0	0	4	16	60
Days Minimum Temp. ≤ 32°F	31	26	24	10	1	0	0	0	1	8	21	29	151
Days Minimum Temp. ≤ 0°F	9	5	1	0	0	0	0	0	0	0	0	5	20
Heating Degree Days (base 65°F)	1,471	1,175	947	537	226	41	10	22	156	460	863	1,282	7,190
Cooling Degree Days (base 65°F)	0	0	1	6	41	143	223	173	56	5	0	0	648
Mean Precipitation (in.)	1.16	1.31	2.38	3.52	3.82	4.58	3.16	4.30	3.85	2.77	2.70	1.60	35.15
Days With ≥ 0.1" Precipitation	3	4	5	7	8	7	6	7	6	6	5	4	68
Days With ≥ 1.0" Precipitation	0	0	0	1	1	2	1	1	1	1	1	0	9
Mean Snowfall (in.)	*8.8*	6.5	*4.8*	2.0	trace	0.0	0.0	0.0	0.0	0.3	2.6	7.4	*32.4*
Days With ≥ 1.0" Snow Depth	na	*13*	*5*	1	0	0	0	0	0	0	2	*11*	na

Tuscola *Douglas County*   Elevation: 652 ft.   Latitude: 39° 48' N   Longitude: 88° 17' W

	JAN	FEB	MAR	APR	MAY	JUN	JUL	AUG	SEP	OCT	NOV	DEC	YEAR
Mean Maximum Temp. (°F)	34.2	40.2	52.3	65.5	76.5	85.4	88.2	86.1	80.5	68.2	52.1	40.3	64.1
Mean Temp. (°F)	25.7	31.1	42.2	53.7	64.5	73.5	76.5	74.3	67.9	56.1	42.8	32.3	53.4
Mean Minimum Temp. (°F)	17.3	22.0	31.9	41.7	52.5	61.6	64.9	62.5	55.2	43.9	33.4	24.2	42.6
Extreme Maximum Temp. (°F)	67	73	86	90	95	104	104	104	99	91	79	70	104
Extreme Minimum Temp. (°F)	-24	-18	-5	15	30	40	46	43	31	20	1	-26	-26
Days Maximum Temp. ≥ 90°F	0	0	0	0	2	9	13	9	4	0	0	0	37
Days Maximum Temp. ≤ 32°F	13	8	1	0	0	0	0	0	0	0	1	6	29
Days Minimum Temp. ≤ 32°F	28	23	17	5	0	0	0	0	0	4	15	24	116
Days Minimum Temp. ≤ 0°F	4	2	0	0	0	0	0	0	0	0	0	1	7
Heating Degree Days (base 65°F)	1,211	950	703	349	106	10	1	2	59	292	661	1,009	5,353
Cooling Degree Days (base 65°F)	0	0	2	14	99	280	379	310	153	22	0	0	1,259
Mean Precipitation (in.)	2.12	2.08	3.18	4.03	3.96	4.05	4.72	3.74	3.23	2.92	3.76	3.00	40.79
Days With ≥ 0.1" Precipitation	5	5	7	8	8	7	6	5	5	6	7	6	75
Days With ≥ 1.0" Precipitation	0	1	0	1	1	1	1	1	1	1	1	1	10
Mean Snowfall (in.)	8.0	4.8	2.5	0.3	trace	0.0	0.0	0.0	0.0	trace	1.7	*4.8*	*22.1*
Days With ≥ 1.0" Snow Depth	*10*	7	2	0	0	0	0	0	0	0	*0*	5	24

Urbana *Champaign County*   Elevation: 741 ft.   Latitude: 40° 06' N   Longitude: 88° 14' W

	JAN	FEB	MAR	APR	MAY	JUN	JUL	AUG	SEP	OCT	NOV	DEC	YEAR
Mean Maximum Temp. (°F)	31.7	37.4	49.2	62.3	73.7	82.7	85.3	83.2	77.7	65.0	49.7	37.4	61.3
Mean Temp. (°F)	24.1	29.4	40.2	51.8	62.8	71.8	75.1	73.0	66.2	54.2	41.4	30.1	51.7
Mean Minimum Temp. (°F)	16.5	21.5	31.1	41.0	51.9	61.0	64.8	62.8	54.7	43.3	33.1	22.8	42.0
Extreme Maximum Temp. (°F)	66	71	84	91	94	103	101	102	97	90	78	71	103
Extreme Minimum Temp. (°F)	-25	-17	-1	16	29	41	47	40	30	19	4	-20	-25
Days Maximum Temp. ≥ 90°F	0	0	0	0	1	6	7	5	2	0	0	0	21
Days Maximum Temp. ≤ 32°F	16	10	2	0	0	0	0	0	0	0	2	9	39
Days Minimum Temp. ≤ 32°F	29	24	18	5	0	0	0	0	0	4	15	26	121
Days Minimum Temp. ≤ 0°F	4	2	0	0	0	0	0	0	0	0	0	2	8
Heating Degree Days (base 65°F)	1,261	998	763	405	138	17	2	4	78	343	701	1,074	5,784
Cooling Degree Days (base 65°F)	0	0	1	9	72	232	329	269	120	13	0	0	1,045
Mean Precipitation (in.)	1.86	1.96	3.23	3.81	4.65	4.16	4.74	4.35	3.31	2.82	3.37	2.73	40.99
Days With ≥ 0.1" Precipitation	5	5	7	8	8	6	7	7	5	6	6	6	76
Days With ≥ 1.0" Precipitation	0	0	1	1	1	1	1	1	1	1	1	0	9
Mean Snowfall (in.)	8.5	5.7	3.3	0.6	trace	0.0	0.0	0.0	0.0	0.1	2.1	5.6	25.9
Days With ≥ 1.0" Snow Depth	14	9	3	0	0	0	0	0	0	0	1	6	33

Virden *Macoupin County*   Elevation: 672 ft.   Latitude: 39° 30' N   Longitude: 89° 46' W

	JAN	FEB	MAR	APR	MAY	JUN	JUL	AUG	SEP	OCT	NOV	DEC	YEAR
Mean Maximum Temp. (°F)	34.5	40.2	52.5	65.6	75.8	84.2	88.0	86.2	80.2	68.1	52.4	40.0	64.0
Mean Temp. (°F)	26.3	31.7	42.7	54.6	64.7	73.3	76.9	74.8	68.1	56.6	43.4	32.1	53.8
Mean Minimum Temp. (°F)	18.0	23.0	32.9	43.6	53.5	62.4	65.7	63.3	55.9	45.1	34.4	24.1	43.5
Extreme Maximum Temp. (°F)	70	75	85	90	93	100	102	105	99	90	80	74	105
Extreme Minimum Temp. (°F)	-22	-19	-7	19	30	40	44	39	30	18	-1	-20	-22
Days Maximum Temp. ≥ 90°F	0	0	0	0	1	7	13	9	4	0	0	0	34
Days Maximum Temp. ≤ 32°F	13	8	2	0	0	0	0	0	0	0	1	7	31
Days Minimum Temp. ≤ 32°F	27	21	16	4	0	0	0	0	0	3	14	24	109
Days Minimum Temp. ≤ 0°F	4	2	0	0	0	0	0	0	0	0	0	1	7
Heating Degree Days (base 65°F)	1,195	936	687	327	101	10	1	2	61	278	641	1,015	5,254
Cooling Degree Days (base 65°F)	0	0	3	21	100	276	392	330	162	25	1	0	1,310
Mean Precipitation (in.)	1.84	2.03	3.27	3.80	4.41	3.90	3.53	3.06	3.02	2.54	3.26	2.47	37.13
Days With ≥ 0.1" Precipitation	4	4	7	7	7	6	5	5	5	5	6	4	65
Days With ≥ 1.0" Precipitation	0	0	1	1	1	1	1	1	1	1	1	1	10
Mean Snowfall (in.)	6.5	6.5	3.9	0.7	0.0	0.0	0.0	0.0	0.0	trace	1.5	4.7	23.8
Days With ≥ 1.0" Snow Depth	12	8	3	0	0	0	0	0	0	0	1	6	30

Walnut *Bureau County*   Elevation: 688 ft.   Latitude: 41° 33' N   Longitude: 89° 36' W

	JAN	FEB	MAR	APR	MAY	JUN	JUL	AUG	SEP	OCT	NOV	DEC	YEAR
Mean Maximum Temp. (°F)	28.3	34.0	46.4	60.5	72.8	81.8	85.1	82.9	75.9	64.0	47.0	34.0	59.4
Mean Temp. (°F)	19.5	25.4	37.0	49.4	61.4	70.5	74.1	71.8	64.2	52.4	38.3	25.9	49.2
Mean Minimum Temp. (°F)	10.6	16.7	27.5	38.2	50.0	59.1	63.1	60.7	52.4	40.7	29.6	17.8	38.9
Extreme Maximum Temp. (°F)	63	69	87	93	95	101	103	104	97	90	77	68	104
Extreme Minimum Temp. (°F)	-27	-23	-6	6	25	38	46	39	29	15	-8	-22	-27
Days Maximum Temp. ≥ 90°F	0	0	0	0	1	4	8	4	1	0	0	0	18
Days Maximum Temp. ≤ 32°F	18	12	4	0	0	0	0	0	0	0	3	12	49
Days Minimum Temp. ≤ 32°F	30	26	23	8	1	0	0	0	1	7	19	29	144
Days Minimum Temp. ≤ 0°F	8	5	0	0	0	0	0	0	0	0	0	4	17
Heating Degree Days (base 65°F)	1,406	1,112	863	472	173	23	4	11	111	395	793	1,204	6,567
Cooling Degree Days (base 65°F)	0	0	1	9	63	192	293	229	84	9	0	0	880
Mean Precipitation (in.)	1.31	1.34	2.67	3.50	4.43	4.62	3.60	4.44	3.64	2.93	2.61	2.04	37.13
Days With ≥ 0.1" Precipitation	4	4	6	7	8	7	6	7	6	6	6	5	72
Days With ≥ 1.0" Precipitation	0	0	0	1	1	1	1	1	1	1	0	0	7
Mean Snowfall (in.)	10.8	6.7	4.3	1.3	trace	0.0	0.0	0.0	0.0	0.1	1.9	7.8	32.9
Days With ≥ 1.0" Snow Depth	19	13	4	0	0	0	0	0	0	0	1	10	47

Waterloo *Monroe County*   Elevation: 649 ft.   Latitude: 38° 20' N   Longitude: 90° 09' W

	JAN	FEB	MAR	APR	MAY	JUN	JUL	AUG	SEP	OCT	NOV	DEC	YEAR
Mean Maximum Temp. (°F)	37.9	44.2	54.9	66.5	76.0	84.7	88.9	87.0	80.5	68.8	54.7	42.9	65.6
Mean Temp. (°F)	29.4	34.9	45.0	55.7	65.4	74.1	78.3	76.3	69.4	57.7	45.7	34.5	55.5
Mean Minimum Temp. (°F)	20.9	25.6	35.0	44.9	54.7	63.5	67.6	65.6	58.2	46.7	36.6	26.2	45.4
Extreme Maximum Temp. (°F)	75	81	88	93	95	103	105	105	102	92	89	75	105
Extreme Minimum Temp. (°F)	-16	-12	0	21	30	42	47	46	34	22	6	-18	-18
Days Maximum Temp. ≥ 90°F	0	0	0	0	1	8	15	12	5	0	0	0	41
Days Maximum Temp. ≤ 32°F	11	6	1	0	0	0	0	0	0	0	1	6	25
Days Minimum Temp. ≤ 32°F	26	20	13	3	0	0	0	0	0	2	11	23	98
Days Minimum Temp. ≤ 0°F	2	1	0	0	0	0	0	0	0	0	0	1	4
Heating Degree Days (base 65°F)	1,096	843	620	301	90	8	1	2	51	251	576	939	4,778
Cooling Degree Days (base 65°F)	0	0	6	29	109	296	427	367	185	32	4	0	1,455
Mean Precipitation (in.)	2.27	2.35	3.75	4.22	4.04	3.79	3.96	3.12	3.30	3.08	4.03	3.41	41.32
Days With ≥ 0.1" Precipitation	4	4	7	7	7	6	6	5	5	5	7	6	69
Days With ≥ 1.0" Precipitation	1	0	1	1	1	1	1	1	1	1	1	1	11
Mean Snowfall (in.)	4.5	3.2	2.0	0.7	0.0	0.0	0.0	0.0	0.0	0.0	1.2	3.0	14.6
Days With ≥ 1.0" Snow Depth	8	5	2	0	0	0	0	0	0	0	1	3	19

Watseka 2 NW *Iroquois County*   Elevation: 620 ft.   Latitude: 40° 47' N   Longitude: 87° 46' W

	JAN	FEB	MAR	APR	MAY	JUN	JUL	AUG	SEP	OCT	NOV	DEC	YEAR
Mean Maximum Temp. (°F)	30.2	36.1	47.6	60.3	72.4	82.0	84.8	82.7	77.1	64.4	49.2	36.3	60.3
Mean Temp. (°F)	22.1	27.2	38.2	49.2	60.7	70.3	73.7	71.3	64.6	52.4	40.3	28.6	49.9
Mean Minimum Temp. (°F)	14.0	18.2	28.8	38.2	49.0	58.6	62.5	59.8	51.9	40.3	31.4	20.8	39.5
Extreme Maximum Temp. (°F)	65	71	78	88	93	104	102	*105*	97	89	79	70	*105*
Extreme Minimum Temp. (°F)	-28	-27	-13	3	26	36	43	43	27	18	0	-26	-28
Days Maximum Temp. ≥ 90°F	0	0	0	0	1	5	7	4	1	0	0	0	18
Days Maximum Temp. ≤ 32°F	17	10	3	0	0	0	0	0	0	0	2	10	42
Days Minimum Temp. ≤ 32°F	29	25	21	8	1	0	0	0	0	7	18	27	136
Days Minimum Temp. ≤ 0°F	6	4	0	0	0	0	0	0	0	0	0	2	12
Heating Degree Days (base 65°F)	1,323	1,063	824	473	187	28	5	12	104	397	734	1,123	6,273
Cooling Degree Days (base 65°F)	0	0	1	5	60	203	290	221	95	12	0	0	887
Mean Precipitation (in.)	1.67	1.64	3.48	4.05	4.20	4.67	4.18	3.75	3.58	2.81	3.32	2.57	39.92
Days With ≥ 0.1" Precipitation	4	4	7	8	7	7	7	6	6	5	6	5	72
Days With ≥ 1.0" Precipitation	0	0	1	1	1	1	1	1	1	1	1	1	10
Mean Snowfall (in.)	*6.9*	4.6	2.5	0.9	0.0	0.0	0.0	0.0	0.0	trace	1.3	5.2	*21.4*
Days With ≥ 1.0" Snow Depth	14	9	3	0	0	0	0	0	0	0	1	7	34

Waukegan *Lake County*   Elevation: 698 ft.   Latitude: 42° 21' N   Longitude: 87° 53' W

	JAN	FEB	MAR	APR	MAY	JUN	JUL	AUG	SEP	OCT	NOV	DEC	YEAR
Mean Maximum Temp. (°F)	28.5	32.7	42.5	54.3	66.5	76.6	81.4	79.6	72.4	60.9	46.8	34.1	56.4
Mean Temp. (°F)	20.3	24.5	34.1	45.0	56.2	66.0	71.4	70.0	62.4	50.9	38.5	26.6	47.2
Mean Minimum Temp. (°F)	12.2	16.3	25.6	35.7	45.8	55.2	61.4	60.4	52.3	40.9	30.1	19.0	37.9
Extreme Maximum Temp. (°F)	64	69	81	90	93	101	102	102	96	89	76	66	102
Extreme Minimum Temp. (°F)	-27	-22	-5	8	28	34	45	40	29	18	-3	-23	-27
Days Maximum Temp. ≥ 90°F	0	0	0	0	0	2	4	3	1	0	0	0	10
Days Maximum Temp. ≤ 32°F	19	13	5	0	0	0	0	0	0	0	2	13	52
Days Minimum Temp. ≤ 32°F	29	26	24	10	1	0	0	0	0	5	18	28	141
Days Minimum Temp. ≤ 0°F	7	4	0	0	0	0	0	0	0	0	0	3	14
Heating Degree Days (base 65°F)	1,379	1,138	952	598	299	79	16	21	138	437	789	1,186	7,032
Cooling Degree Days (base 65°F)	0	0	1	5	33	116	228	192	65	6	0	0	646
Mean Precipitation (in.)	1.58	1.34	2.18	3.65	3.44	3.62	3.40	4.18	3.53	2.46	2.67	2.05	34.10
Days With ≥ 0.1" Precipitation	4	4	5	7	7	6	6	6	6	5	6	5	67
Days With ≥ 1.0" Precipitation	0	0	1	1	1	1	1	1	1	0	0	0	7
Mean Snowfall (in.)	12.0	9.2	5.7	1.7	trace	0.0	0.0	0.0	0.0	0.1	1.9	7.3	37.9
Days With ≥ 1.0" Snow Depth	na	na	5	1	0	0	0	0	0	0	*1*	na	na

Wheaton 3 SE *Dupage County*   Elevation: 679 ft.   Latitude: 41° 49' N   Longitude: 88° 04' W

	JAN	FEB	MAR	APR	MAY	JUN	JUL	AUG	SEP	OCT	NOV	DEC	YEAR
Mean Maximum Temp. (°F)	31.0	37.0	48.9	62.1	74.2	83.4	86.7	84.7	77.8	65.8	49.4	36.9	61.5
Mean Temp. (°F)	22.3	27.6	38.5	49.8	60.8	70.3	74.7	73.0	65.4	53.7	40.4	28.8	50.4
Mean Minimum Temp. (°F)	13.5	18.2	27.9	37.4	47.3	57.2	62.6	61.2	53.0	41.5	31.4	20.6	39.3
Extreme Maximum Temp. (°F)	65	70	85	90	94	103	105	100	97	90	78	68	105
Extreme Minimum Temp. (°F)	-26	-21	-3	4	26	32	42	42	27	14	-3	-21	-26
Days Maximum Temp. ≥ 90°F	0	0	0	0	1	7	10	7	2	0	0	0	27
Days Maximum Temp. ≤ 32°F	16	10	2	0	0	0	0	0	0	0	1	9	38
Days Minimum Temp. ≤ 32°F	29	25	21	9	2	0	0	0	0	6	17	26	135
Days Minimum Temp. ≤ 0°F	6	4	0	0	0	0	0	0	0	0	0	2	12
Heating Degree Days (base 65°F)	1,318	1,050	817	461	184	28	3	6	92	359	731	1,116	6,165
Cooling Degree Days (base 65°F)	0	0	2	11	61	203	326	278	113	13	0	0	1,007
Mean Precipitation (in.)	1.83	1.58	2.65	3.81	3.99	3.86	3.93	4.68	3.46	2.65	3.15	2.42	38.01
Days With ≥ 0.1" Precipitation	5	4	6	7	7	7	6	7	6	5	6	5	71
Days With ≥ 1.0" Precipitation	0	0	0	1	1	1	1	1	1	1	1	1	9
Mean Snowfall (in.)	11.1	7.8	4.8	0.8	trace	0.0	0.0	0.0	0.0	trace	1.9	6.1	32.5
Days With ≥ 1.0" Snow Depth	*18*	*12*	4	0	0	0	0	0	0	0	1	8	*43*

White Hall 1 E *Greene County*   Elevation: 577 ft.   Latitude: 39° 26' N   Longitude: 90° 23' W

	JAN	FEB	MAR	APR	MAY	JUN	JUL	AUG	SEP	OCT	NOV	DEC	YEAR
Mean Maximum Temp. (°F)	34.7	41.0	52.4	64.7	74.7	83.4	87.4	85.2	78.8	67.7	52.6	40.3	63.6
Mean Temp. (°F)	25.7	31.2	41.9	53.5	63.5	72.5	76.5	74.3	67.0	55.8	42.9	31.6	53.0
Mean Minimum Temp. (°F)	16.7	21.3	31.4	42.1	52.3	61.5	65.5	63.3	55.1	43.8	33.2	22.8	42.4
Extreme Maximum Temp. (°F)	71	79	85	92	92	100	104	101	99	90	80	73	104
Extreme Minimum Temp. (°F)	-20	-19	-13	21	27	39	44	42	33	19	0	-20	-20
Days Maximum Temp. ≥ 90°F	0	0	0	0	1	6	12	8	3	0	0	0	30
Days Maximum Temp. ≤ 32°F	13	7	2	0	0	0	0	0	0	0	1	7	30
Days Minimum Temp. ≤ 32°F	28	23	18	5	0	0	0	0	0	4	15	26	119
Days Minimum Temp. ≤ 0°F	4	3	0	0	0	0	0	0	0	0	0	2	9
Heating Degree Days (base 65°F)	1,212	949	711	358	118	13	1	4	72	301	657	1,029	5,425
Cooling Degree Days (base 65°F)	0	0	3	15	72	243	362	299	131	18	1	0	1,144
Mean Precipitation (in.)	1.61	1.72	3.26	3.78	4.53	3.56	3.28	2.99	3.10	2.61	3.21	2.54	36.19
Days With ≥ 0.1" Precipitation	4	4	7	7	7	6	5	6	5	5	5	5	67
Days With ≥ 1.0" Precipitation	0	0	1	1	1	1	1	1	1	0	1	1	9
Mean Snowfall (in.)	na	na	*2.0*	0.5	0.0	0.0	0.0	0.0	0.0	trace	*0.7*	*2.9*	na
Days With ≥ 1.0" Snow Depth	na	na	*1*	0	0	0	0	0	0	0	0	*3*	na

Windsor *Shelby County*   Elevation: 688 ft.   Latitude: 39° 26' N   Longitude: 88° 36' W

	JAN	FEB	MAR	APR	MAY	JUN	JUL	AUG	SEP	OCT	NOV	DEC	YEAR
Mean Maximum Temp. (°F)	34.5	40.7	52.3	65.1	75.4	83.8	87.3	85.5	80.0	67.8	52.3	40.1	63.7
Mean Temp. (°F)	26.6	32.0	42.6	54.1	64.4	72.9	76.5	74.5	68.2	56.5	43.6	32.5	53.7
Mean Minimum Temp. (°F)	18.6	23.3	32.9	42.9	53.2	61.9	65.6	63.4	56.4	45.2	34.8	24.8	43.6
Extreme Maximum Temp. (°F)	67	75	84	87	92	102	102	102	99	89	79	71	102
Extreme Minimum Temp. (°F)	-22	-18	-3	19	30	38	48	38	32	20	3	-20	-22
Days Maximum Temp. ≥ 90°F	0	0	0	0	1	6	11	7	3	0	0	0	28
Days Maximum Temp. ≤ 32°F	13	8	2	0	0	0	0	0	0	0	1	7	31
Days Minimum Temp. ≤ 32°F	27	21	16	4	0	0	0	0	0	3	13	24	108
Days Minimum Temp. ≤ 0°F	3	2	0	0	0	0	0	0	0	0	0	1	6
Heating Degree Days (base 65°F)	1,185	926	690	338	106	10	1	2	55	279	636	1,002	5,230
Cooling Degree Days (base 65°F)	0	0	3	16	93	263	375	312	153	24	0	0	1,239
Mean Precipitation (in.)	1.97	1.87	3.31	3.93	3.96	3.94	3.96	3.10	3.02	2.99	3.73	2.95	38.73
Days With ≥ 0.1" Precipitation	5	4	7	8	7	7	6	5	5	5	6	6	71
Days With ≥ 1.0" Precipitation	0	0	1	1	1	1	1	1	1	1	1	1	10
Mean Snowfall (in.)	7.9	4.3	3.0	0.3	0.0	0.0	0.0	0.0	0.0	trace	1.3	5.0	21.8
Days With ≥ 1.0" Snow Depth	12	8	2	0	0	0	0	0	0	0	1	5	28

Note: See Appendix D for explanation of data.

INDIANA

PHYSICAL FEATURES AND GENERAL CLIMATE. Indiana has an invigorating climate of warm summers and cool winters, because of its location in the middle latitudes in the interior of a large continent. Imposed on the well-known daily and seasonal changes of temperature are changes occurring every few days as surges of polar air move southeastward or air of tropical origin moves northeastward. These outbreaks are more frequent and pronounced in the winter than in the summer. A winter may be unusually cold or a summer cool if the influence of polar air is rather continuous. Likewise, a summer may be unusually warm or a winter mild if air of tropical origin predominates. The action between these two air masses with a contrast in temperature and density fosters the development of low pressure centers which in moving generally eastward frequently pass through or near Indiana, resulting in normally abundant rain. The cyclones are least active and frequently pass north of Indiana in midsummer. Thunderstorms, often local in areal coverage, are important at such times when evaporation and loss of moisture from the soil and vegetation exceeds rainfall. Major climatological variations within the State are caused by differences of latitude, elevation, terrain, soil, and lakes.

The effect of the Great Lakes and more specifically, Lake Michigan, on the climate of northern Indiana is most pronounced just inland from the Lake Michigan shore and diminishes to insignificance in central Indiana. The result of cold air passing over the warmer lake water of Lake Michigan induces precipitation in the lee of Lake Michigan in fall and winter. Average daily minimum temperatures in the fall are higher and daily maximum temperatures in the spring are lower in northwestern Indiana than farther south. Winter precipitation, especially snowfall, is several times greater in the counties of Lake, Porter, and LaPorte as the result of this phenomena. Lake related snowfall and cloudiness often extends to central Indiana in the winter. Very local severe snowstorms have occurred just inland from Lake Michigan.

Another important variable in the composition of Indiana weather is the topography of the State. Elevations range from a little more than 300 feet at the mouth of the Wabash in the southwest corner of the State, to a little over 1,200 feet in the east-central portion (Randolph County) and northeastern section (Steuben County). Differences of terrain affect the climate considerably. South-central Indiana is unglaciated and has the most rugged relief. The Kankakee Valley in the northwest has but little slope to the west and drains what was formerly marshlands. Many small lakes abound in northeastern Indiana among numerous glacial moraines and hills. Most of the north, central, and southwest is rolling country.

TEMPERATURE. Variations of temperature and precipitation occur in short distances where terrain is hilly. On calm, clear nights the valley bottoms have lower temperatures than the slopes and tops of the surrounding hills. Mean maximum as well as mean minimum temperatures decrease from south to north with latitude and decrease from west to east with elevation. Near Lake Michigan temperatures average higher than expected for the latitude in the fall and winter, and lower than expected for the latitude in the spring and summer.

The average date of the last freezing temperature in the spring ranges from the first week of April in the Ohio River Valley of the southwest to the second week of May in the extreme northeast. The usual trend of a later date toward the north is reversed in extreme northwestern Indiana, where the average date is about April 30 near Lake Michigan. In the fall the average date of the first temperature of 32°F. or colder is from October 7 in the extreme northeast to October 26 along the Ohio River in the southwest.

Spring freezes are later in valleys and hollows and fall freezes are earlier. Longer freeze-free periods occur on ridges and hills. Southern Indiana has much of this type of terrain. The gradual slope upward from southwestern Indiana to northeastern Indiana results in lower minimum temperatures and shorter growing seasons in the east compared to the west at the same latitude. In the Kankakee Valley, peat or muck lands experience late spring and early fall frosts because of the radiative characteristic of the soil.

PRECIPITATION. Average annual rainfall ranges from 36 inches in northern Indiana to 43 inches in southern Indiana. July rainfall averages about the same in all areas. The greater precipitation in the south compared with the north comes in the winter months. Southern Indiana has the greatest rainfall in March and the least in October. The wettest month in northern and central Indiana is June and the driest is February. A drought occasionally occurs in the summer when evaporation is highest and dependence on rainfall is greatest.

Most of the state is drained by the Wabash River system. Other river basins are the Maumee in the extreme northeast, the St. Joseph (Lake Michigan) and Kankakee (Illinois River) in the north-central and northwest, and some Ohio River drainage in the extreme south and southeast. Floods occur in some part of the State nearly every year and have occurred in every month of the year. The season of greatest flood frequency is during the winter and spring months. The primary cause of floods is prolonged periods of heavy rains, although occasionally the rains falling on a snow cover and the formation of ice jams are an added factor. The most common type of flood-producing storm in the area is that having a quasi-stationary front oriented from west-southwest to east-northeast with a series of waves or perturbations moving to the east along the front.

Average annual snowfall increases from about 10 inches in southern Indiana to 40 inches in the northern portion of the State and higher in the three county areas along Lake Michigan. From year to year snowfall varies greatly, depending both on temperatures and the frequency of winter storms. At a given latitude in central and southern Indiana snowfall is greatest toward the east because of higher elevation.

OTHER CLIMATIC ELEMENTS. Cloudiness is least in the fall and greatest in the winter. The north is cloudier than the south, particularly in the winter when the Great Lakes have the greatest effect upon the weather.

Average relative humidity differs very little at night over Indiana. During the day relative humidity is usually lower in the south than in the north. This is true for all seasons. However, the simultaneous occurrence of high temperatures and high relative humidity is most frequent in the south.

Prevailing winds are from the southwest quadrant throughout most of the year. Winds from the northern quadrant occur in the winter and persist for a longer time in the north. Along the shore of Lake Michigan the sea-breeze effect is observed in the summer when winds in central United States are light or calm. Vertical currents from the heating of land during the day cause wind near the ground to flow from over water to land reducing the maximum temperature of the day. At night the breezes are in the opposite direction or from the land to water because of land cooling. These breezes are important in limiting extremely high temperatures of a summer day and account for rapid changes in short distances within a mile or so of the lake shore. Winds meet less friction passing over water so off-lake winds have a considerably higher speed than those off or over land.

Severe storms are most frequent in the spring. About one-half of the tornadoes occur between 2 p.m. and 6 p.m. and nearly three-fourths between 10 a.m. and 10 p.m. Hail falls occasionally in very local areas.

88   87   86   85

HAMMOND
GARY   Hobart 2 WNW
South Bend Michiana Regional
LA PORTE
La Porte
MISHAWAKA   ELKHART
SOUTH BEND
LA GRANGE   Lagrange Sewage Plant   Angola
STEUBEN
Valparaiso Waterworks
Wanatah 2 WNW
ST JOSEPH
Goshen College
ELKHART
KOSCIUSKO
NOBLE
DE KALB

LAKE   PORTER   STARKE
Lowell   MARSHALL

NEWTON   JASPER   PULASKI   FULTON
Rensselaer
Winamac 2 SSE   Rochester
Warsaw
WHITLEY   Columbia City   ALLEN   FORT WAYNE
Fort Wayne Baer Field

41   WHITE   CASS   MIAMI   WABASH   HUNTINGTON   41

Kentland
BENTON   CARROLL
Delphi 3 S
GRANT   Marion 2 N   WELLS   Bluffton 1 N   ADAMS
Berne

Kokomo 3 WSW
KOKOMO   BLACKFORD   JAY   Hartford City 4 ESE
Portland 1 SW

West Lafayette 6 NW   HOWARD
West Lafayette Purdue Univ Arpt   LAFAYETTE
TIPPECANOE   Lafayette 8 S   TIPTON
Frankfort Disposal Plant   Elwood Wastewater Plant
Muncie   Farmland 5 NNW
MUNCIE   Winchester Airport 3E
WARREN   CLINTON   HAMILTON   MADISON   DELAWARE   RANDOLPH

40   FOUNTAIN   MONTGOMERY   BOONE   Anderson Sewage Plant   ANDERSON   40
Whitestown
CARMEL   HENRY   New Castle 4 N   WAYNE   Richmond Water Works
Oaklandon Geist Reservoir   Cambridge City 3 N
VERMILLION   HENDRICKS   MARION   HANCOCK
Rockville   INDIANAPOLIS   Greenfield   UNION
Indianapolis SE Side   FAYETTE
Greencastle 1 SE   Indianapolis Intl Airport   Rushville Sewage Plant
PARKE   PUTNAM   New Whiteland   RUSH
Terre Haute Indiana State   TERRE HAUTE   MORGAN   JOHNSON   Brookville
VIGO   CLAY   Martinsville 2 SW   SHELBY   FRANKLIN
Greensburg
OWEN   Spencer   BARTHOLOMEW   DECATUR
BLOOMINGTON   Columbus   RIPLEY
SULLIVAN   GREENE   Bloomington Indiana Univ   DEARBORN

39   MONROE   BROWN   North Vernon 1 NW   OHIO   39
Crane Naval Depot   Seymour 2 N
JACKSON   JENNINGS   SWITZERLAND
MARTIN   Oolitic Purdue Exp Farm   JEFFERSON   Vevay
LAWRENCE   Scottsburg
DAVIESS   Shoals Hiway 50 Bridge   Salem   SCOTT
KNOX   Washington   WASHINGTON   CLARK
Paoli
PIKE   ORANGE
Dubois S Ind Forage Farm
DUBOIS   CRAWFORD   FLOYD
Princeton 1 W   English 4 S
GIBSON
WARRICK   Saint Meinrad   HARRISON
VANDERBURGH   PERRY

POSEY   Mount Vernon   **Indiana**
Evansville Regional Airport
38   EVANSVILLE   SPENCER   Tell City   ● Cities With Population ≥ 40,000   38
Evansville Museum   ▲ Weather Stations

0   50 Miles

0   50 KM

88   87   86   85

Indiana Weather Stations by County

County	Station Name
Adams	Berne
Allen	Fort Wayne Baer Field
Bartholomew	Columbus
Blackford	Hartford City 4 ESE
Boone	Whitestown
Carroll	Delphi 3 S
Clinton	Frankfort Disposal Plant
Crawford	English 4 S
Daviess	Washington
Decatur	Greensburg
Delaware	Muncie
Dubois	Dubois S Ind. Forage Farm
Elkhart	Goshen College
Franklin	Brookville
Fulton	Rochester
Gibson	Princeton 1 W
Grant	Marion 2 N
Hancock	Greenfield
Henry	New Castle 4 N
Howard	Kokomo 3 WSW
Jackson	Seymour 2 N
Jasper	Rensselaer
Jay	Portland 1 SW
Jefferson	Madison Sewage Plant
Jennings	North Vernon 1 NW
Johnson	New Whiteland
Kosciusko	Warsaw
La Porte	La Porte
Lagrange	Lagrange Sewage Plant
Lake	Hobart 2 WNW Lowell
Lawrence	Oolitic Purdue Exp. Farm
Madison	Anderson Sewage Plant

County	Station Name
Madison (*cont.*)	Elwood Wastewater Plant
Marion	Indianapolis Int'l Airport Indianapolis SE Side Oaklandon Geist Reservoir
Martin	Crane Naval Depot Shoals Hiway 50 Bridge
Monroe	Bloomington Indiana Univ.
Morgan	Martinsville 2 SW
Newton	Kentland
Orange	Paoli
Owen	Spencer
Parke	Rockville
Perry	Tell City
Porter	Valparaiso Waterworks Wanatah 2 WNW
Posey	Mount Vernon
Pulaski	Winamac 2 SSE
Putnam	Greencastle 1 SE
Randolph	Farmland 5 NNW Winchester Airport 3E
Rush	Rushville Sewage Plant
Scott	Scottsburg
Spencer	Saint Meinrad
St. Joseph	South Bend Michiana Regional
Steuben	Angola
Switzerland	Vevay
Tippecanoe	Lafayette 8 S West Lafayette 6 NW West Lafayette Purdue Univ. Arpt.
Vanderburgh	Evansville Museum Evansville Regional Airport
Vigo	Terre Haute Indiana State
Washington	Salem
Wayne	Cambridge City 3 N Richmond Water Works
Wells	Bluffton 1 N
Whitley	Columbia City

Indiana Weather Stations by City

City	Station Name	Miles
Anderson	Anderson Sewage Plant	2
	Elwood Wastewater Plant	15
	Muncie	18
	New Castle 4 N	19
Bloomington	Bloomington Indiana Univ.	0
	Martinsville 2 SW	17
	Oolitic Purdue Exp. Farm	20
	Spencer	15
Carmel	Indianapolis Int'l Airport	19
	Indianapolis SE Side	18
	Oaklandon Geist Reservoir	8
	Whitestown	13
Elkhart	Goshen College	10
	South Bend Michiana Regional	19
Evansville	Evansville Museum	1
	Evansville Regional Airport	5
	Mount Vernon	19
	Henderson 7 SSW, KY	16
Fort Wayne	Columbia City	19
	Fort Wayne Baer Field	6
Gary	Chicago University, IL	19
	Park Forest, IL	18
	Hobart 2 WNW	4
	Valparaiso Waterworks	17
Hammond	Chicago University, IL	13
	Chicago Midway Airport, IL	18
	Park Forest, IL	12
	Hobart 2 WNW	11
Indianapolis	Indianapolis Int'l Airport	9
	Indianapolis SE Side	7
	New Whiteland	17
	Oaklandon Geist Reservoir	11
	Whitestown	18
Kokomo	Kokomo 3 WSW	2
Lafayette	Delphi 3 S	14
	Lafayette 8 S	8
	West Lafayette Purdue Univ. Arpt.	3
	West Lafayette 6 NW	8
Mishawaka	Goshen College	17
	South Bend Michiana Regional	9
Muncie	Anderson Sewage Plant	18
	Farmland 5 NNW	13
	Hartford City 4 ESE	18
	Muncie	3
	New Castle 4 N	15
South Bend	South Bend Michiana Regional	5
Terre Haute	Paris Waterworks, IL	20
	Terre Haute Indiana State	1

Note: Miles is the distance between the geographic center of the city and the weather station.

Indiana Weather Stations by Elevation

Feet	Station Name
1,108	Winchester Airport 3E
1,062	New Castle 4 N
1,013	Richmond Water Works
1,007	Angola
997	Cambridge City 3 N
977	Muncie
964	Farmland 5 NNW
958	Rushville Sewage Plant
941	Hartford City 4 ESE
935	Greensburg
935	Whitestown
908	Portland 1 SW
892	Lagrange Sewage Plant
872	Goshen College
862	Greenfield
859	Berne
859	Greencastle 1 SE
849	Columbia City
843	Anderson Sewage Plant
843	Indianapolis SE Side
839	Elwood Wastewater Plant
833	Frankfort Disposal Plant
830	Bloomington Indiana Univ.
823	Bluffton 1 N
816	Kokomo 3 WSW
807	La Porte
807	Warsaw
797	Salem
797	Valparaiso Waterworks
793	Oaklandon Geist Reservoir
790	Fort Wayne Baer Field
790	Indianapolis Int'l Airport
787	Marion 2 N
784	New Whiteland
770	South Bend Michiana Regional
767	Rochester
744	North Vernon 1 NW
734	Wanatah 2 WNW
731	Lafayette 8 S
728	Crane Naval Depot
702	West Lafayette 6 NW
692	Kentland
688	Dubois S Ind. Forage Farm
688	Rockville
688	Winamac 2 SSE
669	Delphi 3 S
662	Lowell
649	Oolitic Purdue Exp. Farm
649	Rensselaer
639	Hobart 2 WNW
629	Brookville
620	Columbus
606	Martinsville 2 SW
597	West Lafayette Purdue Univ. Arpt.
567	Seymour 2 N

Feet	Station Name
557	Paoli
547	Scottsburg
547	Shoals Hiway 50 Bridge
547	Spencer
524	Washington
508	English 4 S
508	Saint Meinrad
505	Terre Haute Indiana State
479	Princeton 1 W
469	Vevay
459	Madison Sewage Plant
419	Mount Vernon
396	Tell City
380	Evansville Regional Airport
377	Evansville Museum

Evansville Regional Airport

Evansville, Indiana, is located on the Ohio River. The country around Evansville ranges from level to areas of rolling terrain near the river. Dress Regional Airport, where weather observations are taken, is located in a shallow valley with low hills to the east and west which parallel the valley, but slope down to the south. There are hills five miles to the north which are about 100 feet higher than the field. The open end of the valley slopes down and south toward the city of Evansville and the Ohio River.

Prevailing wind direction is from the south-southwest. The strongest winds occur during a deep winter storm passage through the Lower Ohio Valley. Strong and cold north to northwest winds occur from late autumn to early spring, most often, in January and February, as large domes of arctic high pressure moves into the midwest.

Geographically, Evansville lies in the path of moisture-bearing low pressure formations that move from the western Gulf region, northeastward over the Mississippi and Ohio Valleys to the Great Lakes and northern Atlantic Coast. Much of the precipitation results from these storm systems, especially in the cooler part of the year.

Both temperature and precipitation are closely related to the movement of the polar front and the storms which move along the front. This is especially true in the winter and spring months. In summer and early autumn changes are less severe and periods of polar air invasions are less prolonged. There is considerable variation in seasonal and monthly temperature and precipitation from year to year as these factors depend greatly on the frequency of storm and frontal passages.

Convective thunderstorms, developing in the maritime tropical air from the Gulf of Mexico and squall line activity, combine to supply the summer rainfall. The greatest precipitation intensities for short periods of time come in the months of greatest thunderstorm frequency. The greatest intensities for 24 hours or more are confined to the winter months.

Severe storms are rather infrequent but thunderstorms cause some wind damage each year. Hail often occurs with the stronger thunderstorms. Evansville is in tornado alley with the most frequent occurrence in early spring and late fall.

Snowfall varies greatly from season to season, as do rainfall and temperature. Snowfalls of two or more inches are very infrequent, and these amounts are usually melted within a day or two.

The growing season averages 199 days, but has been as long as 250 days and as short as 169 days.

Evansville Regional Airport *Vanderburgh County*   Elevation: 380 ft.   Latitude: 38° 03' N   Longitude: 87° 32' W

	JAN	FEB	MAR	APR	MAY	JUN	JUL	AUG	SEP	OCT	NOV	DEC	YEAR
Mean Maximum Temp. (°F)	39.1	44.9	55.9	67.2	76.8	85.6	88.9	87.2	80.9	69.4	55.5	44.5	66.3
Mean Temp. (°F)	31.0	35.7	46.0	56.1	65.8	74.9	78.6	76.4	69.4	57.4	46.2	36.3	56.2
Mean Minimum Temp. (°F)	22.9	26.5	35.9	44.9	54.8	64.1	68.3	65.6	57.9	45.4	36.9	28.1	45.9
Extreme Maximum Temp. (°F)	71	77	84	91	95	102	102	102	100	91	82	77	102
Extreme Minimum Temp. (°F)	-21	-9	-6	23	32	42	51	43	34	23	10	-15	-21
Days Maximum Temp. ≥ 90°F	0	0	0	0	2	9	16	11	5	0	0	0	43
Days Maximum Temp. ≤ 32°F	9	5	1	0	0	0	0	0	0	0	0	5	20
Days Minimum Temp. ≤ 32°F	25	19	13	3	0	0	0	0	0	2	11	21	94
Days Minimum Temp. ≤ 0°F	2	1	0	0	0	0	0	0	0	0	0	1	4
Heating Degree Days (base 65°F)	1,047	820	588	287	81	5	0	1	42	255	559	883	4,568
Cooling Degree Days (base 65°F)	0	0	4	22	114	312	442	374	178	29	1	1	1,477
Mean Precipitation (in.)	2.80	2.94	4.39	4.66	5.03	4.10	3.73	3.05	2.94	2.95	4.14	3.50	44.23
Maximum Precipitation (in.)	13.5	7.3	12.8	10.3	13.5	6.9	9.7	8.4	7.0	7.9	8.5	8.2	63.1
Minimum Precipitation (in.)	0.5	0.6	1.3	1.1	0.9	0.6	0.2	0.2	0.5	trace	0.9	0.6	27.9
Maximum 24-hr. Precipitation (in.)	3.7	2.7	4.3	3.9	4.9	3.3	4.1	3.5	3.1	2.4	3.5	2.3	4.9
Days With ≥ 0.1" Precipitation	5	5	8	8	8	7	6	5	5	5	7	7	76
Days With ≥ 1.0" Precipitation	0	1	1	1	1	1	1	1	1	1	1	1	11
Mean Snowfall (in.)	4.7	4.1	2.5	0.4	trace	trace	0.0	0.0	trace	0.2	0.4	2.5	14.8
Maximum Snowfall (in.)	21	18	20	9	0	0	0	0	0	5	7	10	36
Maximum 24-hr. Snowfall (in.)	8	11	8	9	0	0	0	0	0	4	7	7	11
Days With ≥ 1.0" Snow Depth	6	6	1	0	0	0	0	0	0	0	0	2	15
Thunderstorm Days	1	1	4	5	6	7	7	5	3	2	2	1	44
Foggy Days	12	12	12	9	11	11	13	16	15	12	11	13	147
Predominant Sky Cover	OVR	OVR	OVR	OVR	OVR	OVR	SCT	CLR	CLR	CLR	OVR	OVR	OVR
Mean Relative Humidity 7am (%)	80	80	78	73	75	75	78	82	83	83	80	81	79
Mean Relative Humidity 4pm (%)	66	61	56	50	52	52	54	54	52	50	59	67	56
Mean Dewpoint (°F)	24	27	35	44	54	63	67	66	58	46	36	28	46
Prevailing Wind Direction	NW	NW	NW	SSW	S	SW	SW	SW	S	NW	S	NW	NW
Prevailing Wind Speed (mph)	12	12	12	13	9	9	8	8	8	7	10	10	10
Maximum Wind Gust (mph)	55	53	52	63	71	76	56	46	59	52	70	56	76

Fort Wayne Baer Field

Fort Wayne is located at the junction of the St. Marys, St. Joseph, and Maumee Rivers in northeastern Indiana. The surrounding area is generally level south and east of the city. Southwest and west, the terrain is somewhat rolling, while to the northwest and a few miles north from the city, it becomes quite hilly. The highest point in the general area is about 40 miles due north of Fort Wayne, near Angola, Indiana. At this point, the elevation rises to 1,060 feet above sea level.

The climate is representative of northeastern Indiana and is influenced to some extent by the Great Lakes. It does not differ greatly from the climates of other midwestern cities of the same general latitude. Temperature differences between daily highs and lows are invigorating and average about 20 degrees. The average occurrence of the last freeze in the spring is late April, and the first freeze in the fall is mid-October, making the average freeze-free period 173 days. The length of the growing season is favorable for the maturing of all crops and vegetables normally grown in the midwest.

Annual precipitation is well distributed, with somewhat larger monthly amounts falling in late spring and early summer. Damaging hailstorms occur at an average of about twice a year. One of the most notable storms caused severe damage to property, many thousands of trees, and power and telephone lines in the area. Severe flooding has also occurred in the area. Snow usually covers the ground for about 30 days during the winter months, but heavy snowstorms are not frequent.

Except for the considerable cloudiness that occurs during the winter months, Fort Wayne enjoys a good midwestern average sunshine. Heavy fog occurrence is infrequent.

Fort Wayne Baer Field *Allen County*   Elevation: 790 ft.   Latitude: 41° 00' N   Longitude: 85° 12' W

	JAN	FEB	MAR	APR	MAY	JUN	JUL	AUG	SEP	OCT	NOV	DEC	YEAR
Mean Maximum Temp. (°F)	31.0	35.3	47.0	60.0	71.8	80.9	84.6	82.1	75.7	63.1	48.8	36.6	59.7
Mean Temp. (°F)	23.6	27.4	38.0	49.3	60.7	70.2	73.9	71.6	64.6	52.7	40.9	29.8	50.2
Mean Minimum Temp. (°F)	16.2	19.4	28.9	38.7	49.6	59.4	63.2	61.0	53.4	42.1	33.0	23.0	40.6
Extreme Maximum Temp. (°F)	63	71	82	88	94	106	102	99	97	87	78	71	106
Extreme Minimum Temp. (°F)	-22	-18	-7	7	28	38	46	40	29	19	7	-18	-22
Days Maximum Temp. ≥ 90°F	0	0	0	0	1	4	7	3	1	0	0	0	16
Days Maximum Temp. ≤ 32°F	16	11	3	0	0	0	0	0	0	0	2	10	42
Days Minimum Temp. ≤ 32°F	28	24	20	8	1	0	0	0	0	5	16	26	128
Days Minimum Temp. ≤ 0°F	5	3	0	0	0	0	0	0	0	0	0	2	10
Heating Degree Days (base 65°F)	1,277	1,056	831	471	182	28	3	9	100	385	715	1,084	6,141
Cooling Degree Days (base 65°F)	0	0	1	7	55	194	295	226	90	9	0	0	877
Mean Precipitation (in.)	2.04	1.92	2.87	3.68	3.72	3.84	3.68	3.52	2.84	2.67	3.01	2.73	36.52
Maximum Precipitation (in.)	9.7	6.8	5.3	7.1	8.8	8.3	11.0	7.7	6.8	9.3	8.0	7.6	54.6
Minimum Precipitation (in.)	0.4	0.3	0.7	1.3	1.0	0.8	0.4	0.4	0.3	0.1	0.6	0.4	24.4
Maximum 24-hr. Precipitation (in.)	2.4	3.0	2.1	2.6	4.3	4.4	2.6	3.9	3.5	2.7	2.4	2.1	4.4
Days With ≥ 0.1" Precipitation	5	5	7	8	7	7	6	6	5	6	7	6	75
Days With ≥ 1.0" Precipitation	0	0	0	1	1	1	1	1	1	1	0	0	7
Mean Snowfall (in.)	9.9	7.7	4.6	1.2	trace	trace	0.0	trace	0.0	0.5	3.0	7.9	34.8
Maximum Snowfall (in.)	30	17	20	12	trace	0	0	0	0	8	14	20	62
Maximum 24-hr. Snowfall (in.)	11	8	13	6	trace	0	0	0	0	6	6	11	13
Days With ≥ 1.0" Snow Depth	16	13	4	0	0	0	0	0	0	0	2	8	43
Thunderstorm Days	< 1	1	2	4	5	7	7	6	4	2	1	< 1	39
Foggy Days	14	13	13	11	12	10	14	17	14	14	13	15	160
Predominant Sky Cover	OVR	OVR	OVR	OVR	OVR	OVR	SCT	SCT	OVR	OVR	OVR	OVR	OVR
Mean Relative Humidity 7am (%)	81	81	80	78	77	78	82	86	87	85	83	83	82
Mean Relative Humidity 4pm (%)	72	67	62	54	52	52	53	55	53	54	67	74	60
Mean Dewpoint (°F)	18	20	28	38	48	57	62	61	54	43	33	23	41
Prevailing Wind Direction	W	W	W	SW	SW	SW	SW	SW	SW	SW	SW	W	SW
Prevailing Wind Speed (mph)	14	14	14	14	12	12	9	9	10	12	13	13	12
Maximum Wind Gust (mph)	69	54	59	61	59	64	67	59	53	63	58	58	69

Indianapolis Int'l Airport

Indianapolis is located in the central part of the state and is situated on level or slightly rolling terrain. The greater part of the city lies east of the White River which flows in a general north to south direction.

The National Weather Service Forecast Office is located approximately seven miles southwest of the central part of the city at the Indianapolis International Airport. From a field elevation of 797 feet above sea level at the Indianapolis International Airport the terrain slopes gradually downward to a little below 645 feet at the White River, then upward to just over 910 feet in the northwest corner and eastern sections of the county. The street elevation at the former city office located in the Old Federal Building is 718 feet.

Indianapolis has a temperate climate, with very warm summers and without a dry season. Very cold temperatures may be produced by the invasion of continental polar air in the winter from northern latitudes. The polar air can be quite frigid with very low humidity. The arrival of maritime tropical air from the Gulf in the summer brings warm temperatures and moderate humidity. One of the longest and most severe heat waves brought temperatures of 100 degrees or more for nine consecutive days.

Precipitation is distributed fairly evenly throughout the year, and therefore there is no pronounced wet or dry season. Rainfall in the spring and summer is produced mostly by showers and thunderstorms. A rainfall of about two and a half inches in a 24-hour period can be expected about once a year. Snowfalls of three inches or more occur on an average of two or three times in the winter.

Local levees and/or channel improvements now protect some formerly flood-prone areas.

Based on the 1951-1980 period, the average first occurrence of 32 degrees Fahrenheit in the fall is October 20 and the average last occurrence in the spring is April 22.

Indianapolis Int'l Airport *Marion County*   Elevation: 790 ft.   Latitude: 39° 43' N   Longitude: 86° 16' W

	JAN	FEB	MAR	APR	MAY	JUN	JUL	AUG	SEP	OCT	NOV	DEC	YEAR
Mean Maximum Temp. (°F)	34.2	39.6	51.0	63.1	73.6	82.2	85.7	83.8	77.6	65.5	51.7	39.8	62.3
Mean Temp. (°F)	26.3	31.1	41.6	52.3	62.8	71.9	75.7	73.7	66.6	54.7	43.0	32.2	52.7
Mean Minimum Temp. (°F)	18.4	22.5	32.1	41.6	52.1	61.5	65.6	63.6	55.6	43.8	34.3	24.7	43.0
Extreme Maximum Temp. (°F)	66	75	85	89	93	102	103	102	96	88	79	74	103
Extreme Minimum Temp. (°F)	-27	-21	-7	18	30	37	48	42	32	20	7	-23	-27
Days Maximum Temp. ≥ 90°F	0	0	0	0	0	3	8	5	2	0	0	0	18
Days Maximum Temp. ≤ 32°F	13	8	2	0	0	0	0	0	0	0	1	7	31
Days Minimum Temp. ≤ 32°F	27	22	17	5	0	0	0	0	0	4	14	24	113
Days Minimum Temp. ≤ 0°F	4	2	0	0	0	0	0	0	0	0	0	1	7
Heating Degree Days (base 65°F)	1,193	952	720	385	135	14	1	3	73	328	654	1,009	5,467
Cooling Degree Days (base 65°F)	0	0	2	10	69	232	349	285	127	15	0	0	1,089
Mean Precipitation (in.)	2.45	2.38	3.46	3.70	4.27	4.04	4.47	3.73	2.80	2.78	3.60	3.01	40.69
Maximum Precipitation (in.)	12.7	5.3	10.7	8.1	9.3	7.4	11.8	8.3	8.1	7.8	8.5	7.7	55.8
Minimum Precipitation (in.)	0.4	0.4	0.9	1.0	1.1	0.4	1.2	0.7	0.2	0.2	0.8	0.4	27.9
Maximum 24-hr. Precipitation (in.)	2.8	2.5	3.0	2.6	3.1	3.8	5.1	4.5	2.9	3.9	4.1	2.1	5.1
Days With ≥ 0.1" Precipitation	6	5	7	8	8	7	7	6	5	5	7	6	77
Days With ≥ 1.0" Precipitation	0	0	1	1	1	1	1	1	1	1	1	0	9
Mean Snowfall (in.)	9.2	6.3	3.0	0.4	trace	trace	0.0	trace	0.0	0.4	1.3	5.8	26.4
Maximum Snowfall (in.)	31	18	11	4	trace	0	0	0	0	9	8	28	45
Maximum 24-hr. Snowfall (in.)	10	8	6	3	trace	0	0	0	0	8	8	10	10
Days With ≥ 1.0" Snow Depth	12	8	3	0	0	0	0	0	0	0	1	5	29
Thunderstorm Days	1	1	3	5	6	7	8	6	3	2	1	< 1	43
Foggy Days	15	13	13	11	13	12	16	18	15	13	14	15	168
Predominant Sky Cover	OVR	OVR	OVR	OVR	OVR	OVR	SCT	SCT	CLR	OVR	OVR	OVR	OVR
Mean Relative Humidity 7am (%)	81	81	79	77	80	80	84	88	87	85	83	83	82
Mean Relative Humidity 4pm (%)	69	64	59	54	53	53	56	56	53	53	63	70	59
Mean Dewpoint (°F)	20	23	31	40	51	60	65	64	56	44	34	25	43
Prevailing Wind Direction	WSW	WNW	WNW	SW	SW	SW	SW	SW	SW	SW	SW	SW	SW
Prevailing Wind Speed (mph)	12	13	14	13	10	9	8	8	9	10	12	12	10
Maximum Wind Gust (mph)	60	62	75	75	69	70	81	70	74	64	79	64	81

South Bend Michiana Regional

South Bend is located on the Saint Joseph River in the northern portion of Saint Joseph County, situated on mostly level to gently rolling terrain and some former marshland. Drainage for the area is through the Saint Joseph River and Kankakee River.

South Bend is under the climatic influence of Lake Michigan with its nearest shore 20 miles to the northwest. The lake has a moderating effect on the temperature. Temperatures of 100 degrees or higher are rare and cold waves are less severe than at many locations at the same latitude. This results in favorable conditions for orchard and vegetable growth.

Based on the 1951-1980 period, the average first occurrence of 32 degrees Fahrenheit in the fall is October 18 and the average last occurrence in the spring is May 1.

Precipitation is fairly evenly distributed throughout the year with the greatest amounts during the growing season. The predominant snow season is from November through March, although there are also generally lighter amounts in October and April.

Winter is marked by considerable cloudiness and rather high humidity along with frequent periods of snow. Heavy snowfalls, resulting from a cold northwest wind passing over Lake Michigan are not uncommon.

South Bend Michiana Regional *St. Joseph County*   Elevation: 770 ft.   Latitude: 41° 42' N   Longitude: 86° 20' W

	JAN	FEB	MAR	APR	MAY	JUN	JUL	AUG	SEP	OCT	NOV	DEC	YEAR
Mean Maximum Temp. (°F)	30.9	35.2	46.3	58.8	70.6	79.8	83.4	81.0	74.0	62.2	48.2	36.3	58.9
Mean Temp. (°F)	23.8	27.6	37.7	48.8	59.9	69.3	73.4	71.5	64.1	52.8	40.9	29.9	50.0
Mean Minimum Temp. (°F)	16.7	20.0	29.0	38.7	49.1	58.9	63.4	61.8	54.2	43.2	33.6	23.4	41.0
Extreme Maximum Temp. (°F)	64	72	85	89	92	104	102	103	95	86	78	70	104
Extreme Minimum Temp. (°F)	-21	-14	-2	11	28	35	44	42	32	20	5	-15	-21
Days Maximum Temp. ≥ 90°F	0	0	0	0	1	3	6	3	1	0	0	0	14
Days Maximum Temp. ≤ 32°F	17	12	4	0	0	0	0	0	0	0	2	9	44
Days Minimum Temp. ≤ 32°F	28	24	20	8	0	0	0	0	0	3	14	25	122
Days Minimum Temp. ≤ 0°F	4	3	0	0	0	0	0	0	0	0	0	1	8
Heating Degree Days (base 65°F)	1,270	1,049	842	491	207	39	5	12	109	382	715	1,082	6,203
Cooling Degree Days (base 65°F)	0	0	1	9	54	178	284	227	89	8	0	0	850
Mean Precipitation (in.)	2.23	1.95	2.92	3.67	3.46	4.07	3.77	4.04	3.86	3.32	3.41	3.08	39.78
Maximum Precipitation (in.)	5.3	4.5	8.0	6.0	6.9	10.9	7.5	8.3	9.0	9.8	6.7	5.5	55.6
Minimum Precipitation (in.)	0.7	0.5	0.5	0.5	0.8	0.5	1.2	0.3	trace	0.4	1.4	0.7	25.1
Maximum 24-hr. Precipitation (in.)	2.8	1.9	2.1	1.9	2.9	4.7	3.6	4.0	3.0	3.5	3.9	3.0	4.7
Days With ≥ 0.1" Precipitation	6	6	7	8	7	7	7	7	6	6	8	8	83
Days With ≥ 1.0" Precipitation	0	0	0	1	0	1	1	1	1	1	1	1	8
Mean Snowfall (in.)	22.9	15.5	9.2	2.0	trace	trace	trace	trace	trace	0.5	7.7	18.8	76.6
Maximum Snowfall (in.)	86	35	34	14	1	0	0	0	0	9	30	42	142
Maximum 24-hr. Snowfall (in.)	16	12	9	8	1	0	0	0	0	7	15	11	16
Days With ≥ 1.0" Snow Depth	22	16	7	1	0	0	0	0	0	0	4	14	64
Thunderstorm Days	< 1	< 1	2	4	5	8	7	6	4	2	1	< 1	39
Foggy Days	15	14	15	13	13	12	14	18	16	16	15	17	178
Predominant Sky Cover	OVR	OVR	OVR	OVR	OVR	OVR	OVR	OVR	OVR	OVR	OVR	OVR	OVR
Mean Relative Humidity 7am (%)	82	82	80	77	76	78	82	86	86	84	83	83	82
Mean Relative Humidity 4pm (%)	73	69	62	55	53	52	55	57	55	57	68	75	61
Mean Dewpoint (°F)	18	20	28	37	47	57	62	62	54	43	33	23	41
Prevailing Wind Direction	SW	SW	SW	NNW	SSW	SSW	SW	SW	SSW	SSW	SW	SW	SW
Prevailing Wind Speed (mph)	13	13	13	13	12	10	9	9	10	12	12	13	12
Maximum Wind Gust (mph)	67	58	55	66	86	71	66	59	63	59	74	69	86

Anderson Sewage Plant *Madison County*   Elevation: 843 ft.   Latitude: 40° 06' N   Longitude: 85° 43' W

	JAN	FEB	MAR	APR	MAY	JUN	JUL	AUG	SEP	OCT	NOV	DEC	YEAR
Mean Maximum Temp. (°F)	33.4	38.3	48.5	60.6	71.5	80.3	83.7	81.8	75.5	63.9	50.1	38.1	60.5
Mean Temp. (°F)	26.0	30.4	39.9	50.5	61.2	70.4	74.0	72.0	65.0	53.7	42.4	31.3	51.4
Mean Minimum Temp. (°F)	18.7	22.5	31.3	40.5	50.8	60.4	64.2	62.0	54.4	43.4	34.6	24.3	42.3
Extreme Maximum Temp. (°F)	65	73	81	87	93	101	103	101	95	88	78	75	103
Extreme Minimum Temp. (°F)	-24	-14	-7	17	27	37	47	40	31	20	10	-22	-24
Days Maximum Temp. ≥ 90°F	0	0	0	0	0	3	5	3	1	0	0	0	12
Days Maximum Temp. ≤ 32°F	14	10	3	0	0	0	0	0	0	0	1	9	37
Days Minimum Temp. ≤ 32°F	27	22	18	7	1	0	0	0	0	4	14	24	117
Days Minimum Temp. ≤ 0°F	3	2	0	0	0	0	0	0	0	0	0	1	6
Heating Degree Days (base 65°F)	1,201	971	771	435	174	25	4	9	97	358	673	1,040	5,758
Cooling Degree Days (base 65°F)	0	0	2	10	67	202	306	242	106	14	0	0	949
Mean Precipitation (in.)	2.10	2.31	3.24	3.84	4.11	4.15	4.34	3.25	2.95	2.79	3.73	2.84	39.65
Days With ≥ 0.1" Precipitation	6	5	7	9	8	7	7	6	5	6	7	7	80
Days With ≥ 1.0" Precipitation	0	0	0	1	1	1	1	1	1	0	1	0	7
Mean Snowfall (in.)	6.6	4.6	2.1	0.2	0.0	0.0	0.0	0.0	0.0	trace	0.7	3.6	17.8
Days With ≥ 1.0" Snow Depth	9	5	2	0	0	0	0	0	0	0	1	3	20

Angola *Steuben County*   Elevation: 1,007 ft.   Latitude: 41° 38' N   Longitude: 84° 59' W

	JAN	FEB	MAR	APR	MAY	JUN	JUL	AUG	SEP	OCT	NOV	DEC	YEAR
Mean Maximum Temp. (°F)	29.3	32.9	43.1	56.6	69.2	78.3	82.1	80.0	73.5	60.9	46.8	34.9	57.3
Mean Temp. (°F)	21.5	23.9	33.4	45.9	58.1	67.3	71.4	69.3	62.1	50.0	38.4	27.6	47.4
Mean Minimum Temp. (°F)	13.5	14.8	23.7	35.2	46.9	56.2	60.8	58.5	50.7	39.1	29.9	20.4	37.5
Extreme Maximum Temp. (°F)	60	70	78	85	90	101	98	97	93	89	75	69	101
Extreme Minimum Temp. (°F)	-27	-18	-13	4	25	32	40	37	27	16	8	-19	-27
Days Maximum Temp. ≥ 90°F	0	0	0	0	0	2	4	2	0	0	0	0	8
Days Maximum Temp. ≤ 32°F	19	14	6	0	0	0	0	0	0	0	3	12	54
Days Minimum Temp. ≤ 32°F	30	27	26	12	1	0	0	0	0	8	19	28	151
Days Minimum Temp. ≤ 0°F	5	5	1	0	0	0	0	0	0	0	0	2	13
Heating Degree Days (base 65°F)	1,344	1,154	973	568	246	59	14	25	143	463	792	1,152	6,933
Cooling Degree Days (base 65°F)	0	0	1	4	37	136	227	167	56	3	0	0	631
Mean Precipitation (in.)	1.96	1.75	2.68	3.46	3.98	3.71	3.91	3.89	3.39	2.74	3.15	2.67	37.29
Days With ≥ 0.1" Precipitation	5	5	6	8	7	6	7	7	6	6	7	7	77
Days With ≥ 1.0" Precipitation	0	0	0	1	1	1	1	1	1	1	1	0	8
Mean Snowfall (in.)	10.4	7.8	4.2	0.7	trace	0.0	0.0	0.0	0.0	0.3	2.2	8.0	33.6
Days With ≥ 1.0" Snow Depth	18	15	7	0	0	0	0	0	0	0	2	9	51

Berne *Adams County*   Elevation: 859 ft.   Latitude: 40° 40' N   Longitude: 84° 57' W

	JAN	FEB	MAR	APR	MAY	JUN	JUL	AUG	SEP	OCT	NOV	DEC	YEAR
Mean Maximum Temp. (°F)	32.2	37.0	48.3	60.8	72.3	81.1	84.8	82.7	76.4	63.8	49.8	37.8	60.6
Mean Temp. (°F)	24.8	28.8	39.1	50.2	61.4	70.6	74.5	72.4	65.6	53.7	41.9	30.9	51.2
Mean Minimum Temp. (°F)	17.3	20.6	29.8	39.6	50.5	60.1	64.1	62.0	54.7	43.4	34.0	23.9	41.7
Extreme Maximum Temp. (°F)	65	72	82	88	94	104	101	99	96	90	77	72	104
Extreme Minimum Temp. (°F)	-24	-14	-4	10	27	39	46	42	31	20	5	-19	-24
Days Maximum Temp. ≥ 90°F	0	0	0	0	1	4	7	4	2	0	0	0	18
Days Maximum Temp. ≤ 32°F	15	10	3	0	0	0	0	0	0	0	1	9	38
Days Minimum Temp. ≤ 32°F	28	23	20	7	0	0	0	0	0	3	14	25	120
Days Minimum Temp. ≤ 0°F	4	2	0	0	0	0	0	0	0	0	0	1	7
Heating Degree Days (base 65°F)	1,242	1,017	800	448	172	25	2	7	87	360	688	1,053	5,901
Cooling Degree Days (base 65°F)	0	0	2	9	64	205	315	250	110	14	0	0	969
Mean Precipitation (in.)	2.14	2.13	2.88	3.79	3.78	4.41	4.12	3.63	3.02	2.58	3.22	2.71	38.41
Days With ≥ 0.1" Precipitation	6	5	7	8	8	8	7	6	6	6	7	6	80
Days With ≥ 1.0" Precipitation	0	0	0	1	1	1	1	1	1	0	1	0	7
Mean Snowfall (in.)	9.4	7.2	4.4	1.1	0.0	0.0	0.0	0.0	0.0	0.4	2.1	6.1	30.7
Days With ≥ 1.0" Snow Depth	16	11	4	0	0	0	0	0	0	0	1	7	39

Bloomington Indiana Univ. *Monroe County*   Elevation: 830 ft.   Latitude: 39° 10' N   Longitude: 86° 31' W

	JAN	FEB	MAR	APR	MAY	JUN	JUL	AUG	SEP	OCT	NOV	DEC	YEAR
Mean Maximum Temp. (°F)	36.2	41.7	52.0	63.9	74.0	81.9	86.1	84.6	78.3	66.7	53.7	41.9	63.4
Mean Temp. (°F)	27.8	32.3	41.9	53.1	63.2	71.9	76.1	74.2	67.2	55.6	44.7	33.5	53.5
Mean Minimum Temp. (°F)	19.3	22.8	31.8	42.2	52.5	61.8	66.1	63.8	56.1	44.4	35.5	25.1	43.5
Extreme Maximum Temp. (°F)	69	74	82	88	93	101	104	100	97	90	80	74	104
Extreme Minimum Temp. (°F)	-21	-13	-2	18	31	41	49	44	33	23	6	-20	-21
Days Maximum Temp. ≥ 90°F	0	0	0	0	0	4	9	6	2	0	0	0	21
Days Maximum Temp. ≤ 32°F	12	7	2	0	0	0	0	0	0	0	1	6	28
Days Minimum Temp. ≤ 32°F	27	22	17	5	0	0	0	0	0	3	13	23	110
Days Minimum Temp. ≤ 0°F	3	2	0	0	0	0	0	0	0	0	0	1	6
Heating Degree Days (base 65°F)	1,146	917	712	370	129	16	1	3	67	304	605	968	5,238
Cooling Degree Days (base 65°F)	0	0	3	16	77	237	362	302	136	20	1	0	1,154
Mean Precipitation (in.)	2.60	2.62	3.70	4.46	5.07	4.08	4.32	3.94	3.52	3.12	3.95	3.34	44.72
Days With ≥ 0.1" Precipitation	6	5	7	8	8	7	7	6	6	5	7	7	79
Days With ≥ 1.0" Precipitation	0	1	1	1	2	1	1	1	1	1	1	1	12
Mean Snowfall (in.)	na	na	na	trace	0.0	0.0	0.0	0.0	0.0	0.2	trace	1.6	na
Days With ≥ 1.0" Snow Depth	na	na	1	0	0	0	0	0	0	0	0	2	na

Bluffton 1 N *Wells County*   Elevation: 823 ft.   Latitude: 40° 45' N   Longitude: 85° 10' W

	JAN	FEB	MAR	APR	MAY	JUN	JUL	AUG	SEP	OCT	NOV	DEC	YEAR
Mean Maximum Temp. (°F)	30.5	34.6	46.4	59.0	70.8	80.0	83.7	81.4	75.2	62.9	48.5	36.7	59.1
Mean Temp. (°F)	22.8	26.0	37.0	48.6	60.0	69.5	73.1	70.7	63.8	51.8	40.0	29.3	49.4
Mean Minimum Temp. (°F)	15.1	17.3	27.5	38.1	49.2	58.9	62.4	59.9	52.4	40.6	31.5	21.8	39.6
Extreme Maximum Temp. (°F)	64	72	80	87	91	100	104	99	97	88	77	70	104
Extreme Minimum Temp. (°F)	-24	-18	-7	8	22	37	41	40	27	10	5	-18	-24
Days Maximum Temp. ≥ 90°F	0	0	0	0	0	3	6	2	1	0	0	0	12
Days Maximum Temp. ≤ 32°F	17	13	4	0	0	0	0	0	0	0	2	10	46
Days Minimum Temp. ≤ 32°F	29	25	22	8	1	0	0	0	0	6	18	26	135
Days Minimum Temp. ≤ 0°F	5	4	0	0	0	0	0	0	0	0	0	2	11
Heating Degree Days (base 65°F)	1,303	1,097	863	493	202	37	6	17	117	412	742	1,100	6,389
Cooling Degree Days (base 65°F)	0	0	1	7	54	183	274	208	90	11	0	0	828
Mean Precipitation (in.)	2.06	1.81	2.64	3.33	4.07	3.82	3.98	3.62	3.02	2.53	3.07	2.65	36.60
Days With ≥ 0.1" Precipitation	6	5	7	7	8	7	6	6	6	6	7	7	78
Days With ≥ 1.0" Precipitation	0	0	0	1	1	1	1	1	1	0	1	0	7
Mean Snowfall (in.)	8.4	7.1	3.7	1.1	0.0	0.0	trace	0.0	0.0	0.2	1.8	5.6	27.9
Days With ≥ 1.0" Snow Depth	15	12	4	1	0	0	0	0	0	0	1	7	40

Brookville *Franklin County*   Elevation: 629 ft.   Latitude: 39° 25' N   Longitude: 85° 01' W

	JAN	FEB	MAR	APR	MAY	JUN	JUL	AUG	SEP	OCT	NOV	DEC	YEAR
Mean Maximum Temp. (°F)	36.3	41.2	52.2	64.2	74.6	83.0	86.9	85.2	79.1	66.5	53.7	41.8	63.7
Mean Temp. (°F)	26.8	30.4	40.5	51.2	61.5	70.4	74.6	72.8	65.7	53.2	42.9	32.7	51.9
Mean Minimum Temp. (°F)	17.2	19.7	28.6	38.2	48.4	57.7	62.3	60.4	52.4	39.8	32.1	23.5	40.0
Extreme Maximum Temp. (°F)	66	75	84	89	94	102	102	103	97	91	82	76	103
Extreme Minimum Temp. (°F)	-31	-15	-9	16	26	36	44	41	30	17	2	-20	-31
Days Maximum Temp. ≥ 90°F	0	0	0	0	1	5	10	7	3	0	0	0	26
Days Maximum Temp. ≤ 32°F	12	7	1	0	0	0	0	0	0	0	1	6	27
Days Minimum Temp. ≤ 32°F	28	24	21	9	1	0	0	0	0	8	17	24	132
Days Minimum Temp. ≤ 0°F	4	3	0	0	0	0	0	0	0	0	0	1	8
Heating Degree Days (base 65°F)	1,177	968	755	414	162	24	3	6	85	372	655	995	5,616
Cooling Degree Days (base 65°F)	0	0	2	8	60	198	320	261	109	14	0	0	972
Mean Precipitation (in.)	2.83	2.64	3.65	4.03	4.55	3.96	4.28	3.92	2.56	3.01	3.70	3.28	42.41
Days With ≥ 0.1" Precipitation	6	6	8	8	8	7	7	6	5	6	7	7	81
Days With ≥ 1.0" Precipitation	0	0	1	1	1	1	1	1	1	1	1	1	10
Mean Snowfall (in.)	na	*3.8*	2.3	0.3	trace	0.0	0.0	0.0	0.0	trace	1.1	*2.8*	na
Days With ≥ 1.0" Snow Depth	*11*	*8*	2	0	0	0	0	0	0	0	1	3	*25*

Cambridge City 3 N *Wayne County*   Elevation: 997 ft.   Latitude: 39° 52' N   Longitude: 85° 11' W

	JAN	FEB	MAR	APR	MAY	JUN	JUL	AUG	SEP	OCT	NOV	DEC	YEAR
Mean Maximum Temp. (°F)	32.8	37.7	48.6	60.8	71.3	79.8	83.5	81.9	76.1	64.2	50.6	38.8	60.5
Mean Temp. (°F)	24.1	27.9	38.1	48.9	59.7	68.6	72.3	70.4	63.5	51.5	40.8	30.3	49.7
Mean Minimum Temp. (°F)	15.3	18.1	27.5	37.0	48.1	57.5	61.2	58.8	50.8	38.8	30.9	21.8	38.8
Extreme Maximum Temp. (°F)	64	71	82	86	90	100	99	97	94	88	79	73	100
Extreme Minimum Temp. (°F)	-31	-19	-14	13	26	35	44	38	26	16	6	-22	-31
Days Maximum Temp. ≥ 90°F	0	0	0	0	0	2	5	2	1	0	0	0	10
Days Maximum Temp. ≤ 32°F	15	10	3	0	0	0	0	0	0	0	1	9	38
Days Minimum Temp. ≤ 32°F	29	25	22	10	1	0	0	0	0	9	18	26	140
Days Minimum Temp. ≤ 0°F	5	4	0	0	0	0	0	0	0	0	0	2	11
Heating Degree Days (base 65°F)	1,263	1,042	829	480	202	39	7	16	119	417	721	1,069	6,204
Cooling Degree Days (base 65°F)	0	0	1	4	40	153	240	186	72	7	0	0	703
Mean Precipitation (in.)	2.39	2.30	3.36	4.21	4.78	4.35	4.19	3.46	2.76	2.84	3.52	2.96	41.12
Days With ≥ 0.1" Precipitation	6	6	7	9	9	7	7	6	5	6	7	7	82
Days With ≥ 1.0" Precipitation	0	0	1	1	1	1	1	1	1	1	1	1	10
Mean Snowfall (in.)	7.2	5.4	3.5	0.5	trace	0.0	0.0	0.0	0.0	0.1	1.1	4.0	21.8
Days With ≥ 1.0" Snow Depth	12	9	4	0	0	0	0	0	0	0	1	5	31

Columbia City *Whitley County*   Elevation: 849 ft.   Latitude: 41° 09' N   Longitude: 85° 29' W

	JAN	FEB	MAR	APR	MAY	JUN	JUL	AUG	SEP	OCT	NOV	DEC	YEAR
Mean Maximum Temp. (°F)	30.5	34.9	45.9	58.6	70.6	79.5	83.3	81.2	74.9	62.3	48.4	36.2	58.9
Mean Temp. (°F)	22.4	26.1	36.2	47.7	59.1	68.4	72.2	70.1	63.1	51.1	39.9	28.7	48.7
Mean Minimum Temp. (°F)	14.3	17.1	26.5	36.7	47.6	57.2	61.1	58.9	51.3	39.8	31.3	21.1	38.6
Extreme Maximum Temp. (°F)	66	72	80	88	91	103	101	98	95	88	77	70	103
Extreme Minimum Temp. (°F)	-24	-16	-6	7	27	36	44	36	27	17	5	-22	-24
Days Maximum Temp. ≥ 90°F	0	0	0	0	0	2	5	2	1	0	0	0	10
Days Maximum Temp. ≤ 32°F	17	12	4	0	0	0	0	0	0	0	2	10	45
Days Minimum Temp. ≤ 32°F	29	25	23	10	1	0	0	0	0	7	18	27	140
Days Minimum Temp. ≤ 0°F	6	4	0	0	0	0	0	0	0	0	0	2	12
Heating Degree Days (base 65°F)	1,314	1,093	886	518	219	44	8	18	126	432	747	1,119	6,524
Cooling Degree Days (base 65°F)	0	0	1	5	40	156	246	188	73	6	0	0	715
Mean Precipitation (in.)	2.09	1.75	2.92	3.75	3.63	4.25	3.86	3.51	3.63	2.86	3.32	2.78	38.35
Days With ≥ 0.1" Precipitation	6	5	7	8	8	7	7	7	6	6	7	7	81
Days With ≥ 1.0" Precipitation	0	0	0	1	1	1	1	1	1	0	1	0	8
Mean Snowfall (in.)	9.4	7.4	4.1	1.0	trace	0.0	0.0	0.0	0.0	0.3	2.1	7.2	31.5
Days With ≥ 1.0" Snow Depth	18	13	5	1	0	0	0	0	0	0	2	9	48

Columbus *Bartholomew County*   Elevation: 620 ft.   Latitude: 39° 12' N   Longitude: 85° 55' W

	JAN	FEB	MAR	APR	MAY	JUN	JUL	AUG	SEP	OCT	NOV	DEC	YEAR
Mean Maximum Temp. (°F)	36.2	41.3	52.0	63.8	73.8	82.1	86.0	84.5	78.5	66.6	53.3	41.8	63.3
Mean Temp. (°F)	27.4	31.6	41.4	52.3	62.6	71.5	75.4	73.5	66.5	54.3	43.5	33.3	52.8
Mean Minimum Temp. (°F)	18.6	21.8	30.8	40.8	51.4	60.9	64.9	62.4	54.5	41.9	33.7	24.7	42.2
Extreme Maximum Temp. (°F)	67	73	83	88	94	100	103	103	95	90	80	73	103
Extreme Minimum Temp. (°F)	-26	-11	-6	18	30	41	48	43	34	17	4	-20	-26
Days Maximum Temp. ≥ 90°F	0	0	0	0	0	4	8	6	2	0	0	0	20
Days Maximum Temp. ≤ 32°F	12	7	1	0	0	0	0	0	0	0	1	6	27
Days Minimum Temp. ≤ 32°F	27	23	19	6	0	0	0	0	0	5	15	24	119
Days Minimum Temp. ≤ 0°F	3	2	0	0	0	0	0	0	0	0	0	1	6
Heating Degree Days (base 65°F)	1,158	936	726	385	137	17	1	3	73	340	637	976	5,389
Cooling Degree Days (base 65°F)	0	0	2	11	70	231	348	284	122	15	0	0	1,083
Mean Precipitation (in.)	2.59	2.54	3.67	4.50	4.54	3.35	3.99	3.75	2.99	2.79	3.72	3.12	41.55
Days With ≥ 0.1" Precipitation	6	5	8	8	8	6	7	6	5	5	7	6	77
Days With ≥ 1.0" Precipitation	0	0	1	1	1	1	1	1	1	1	1	1	10
Mean Snowfall (in.)	*5.1*	*3.5*	*1.9*	trace	trace	0.0	0.0	0.0	0.0	trace	0.5	2.1	*13.1*
Days With ≥ 1.0" Snow Depth	na	na	*1*	0	0	0	0	0	0	0	*0*	*3*	na

Crane Naval Depot *Martin County*   Elevation: 728 ft.   Latitude: 38° 52' N   Longitude: 86° 50' W

	JAN	FEB	MAR	APR	MAY	JUN	JUL	AUG	SEP	OCT	NOV	DEC	YEAR
Mean Maximum Temp. (°F)	38.8	44.8	55.7	67.3	76.5	84.0	87.8	86.3	80.5	69.2	55.9	*44.8*	*66.0*
Mean Temp. (°F)	30.2	35.2	45.1	55.8	65.1	73.1	77.2	75.5	69.2	57.7	46.4	*36.0*	*55.5*
Mean Minimum Temp. (°F)	21.5	25.6	34.3	44.1	53.5	62.1	66.6	64.6	57.8	46.2	36.9	*27.2*	*45.0*
Extreme Maximum Temp. (°F)	68	76	83	88	92	100	104	101	99	90	80	74	104
Extreme Minimum Temp. (°F)	-23	-12	-2	17	32	35	49	47	32	20	8	-20	-23
Days Maximum Temp. ≥ 90°F	0	0	0	0	1	5	11	8	3	0	0	0	28
Days Maximum Temp. ≤ 32°F	9	5	1	0	0	0	0	0	0	0	0	4	19
Days Minimum Temp. ≤ 32°F	25	20	14	4	0	0	0	0	0	2	11	19	95
Days Minimum Temp. ≤ 0°F	2	1	0	0	0	0	0	0	0	0	0	1	4
Heating Degree Days (base 65°F)	1,073	833	606	294	94	9	1	1	44	248	553	*890*	*4,646*
Cooling Degree Days (base 65°F)	0	0	5	22	100	262	397	336	169	30	2	*0*	*1,323*
Mean Precipitation (in.)	3.01	2.72	4.14	4.97	5.48	3.92	4.94	3.96	3.31	3.44	4.24	3.42	47.55
Days With ≥ 0.1" Precipitation	6	4	7	8	8	6	6	5	5	5	6	5	71
Days With ≥ 1.0" Precipitation	1	1	1	1	2	1	2	1	1	1	1	1	14
Mean Snowfall (in.)	na	na	*1.8*	trace	0.0	0.0	0.0	0.0	0.0	trace	trace	na	na
Days With ≥ 1.0" Snow Depth	na	na	*0*	0	0	0	0	0	0	0	0	na	na

Delphi 3 S *Carroll County*   Elevation: 669 ft.   Latitude: 40° 33' N   Longitude: 86° 41' W

	JAN	FEB	MAR	APR	MAY	JUN	JUL	AUG	SEP	OCT	NOV	DEC	YEAR
Mean Maximum Temp. (°F)	33.0	38.4	50.5	63.5	74.4	82.9	85.8	83.5	77.9	65.5	51.3	38.7	62.1
Mean Temp. (°F)	25.0	29.7	40.7	51.7	62.3	71.2	74.5	72.3	65.9	54.1	42.7	31.3	51.8
Mean Minimum Temp. (°F)	17.0	20.9	30.8	39.8	50.2	59.6	63.2	61.1	53.8	42.6	34.1	23.7	41.4
Extreme Maximum Temp. (°F)	66	73	84	89	96	105	103	100	96	89	78	71	105
Extreme Minimum Temp. (°F)	-24	-20	0	10	26	36	42	38	27	18	6	-21	-24
Days Maximum Temp. ≥ 90°F	0	0	0	0	1	5	9	4	2	0	0	0	21
Days Maximum Temp. ≤ 32°F	14	9	2	0	0	0	0	0	0	0	1	7	33
Days Minimum Temp. ≤ 32°F	28	23	18	7	1	0	0	0	0	5	15	25	122
Days Minimum Temp. ≤ 0°F	5	3	0	0	0	0	0	0	0	0	0	1	9
Heating Degree Days (base 65°F)	1,234	991	749	405	146	19	3	6	81	345	662	1,039	5,680
Cooling Degree Days (base 65°F)	0	0	2	10	71	221	318	252	115	15	1	0	1,005
Mean Precipitation (in.)	1.94	1.90	2.99	3.64	3.92	3.90	4.23	4.05	3.01	2.69	3.12	2.67	38.06
Days With ≥ 0.1" Precipitation	5	4	6	8	7	6	6	6	5	6	6	6	71
Days With ≥ 1.0" Precipitation	0	0	1	0	1	1	1	1	1	1	1	0	8
Mean Snowfall (in.)	6.2	4.6	2.5	0.8	trace	0.0	0.0	0.0	0.0	0.2	0.9	5.3	20.5
Days With ≥ 1.0" Snow Depth	13	10	3	0	0	0	0	0	0	0	1	6	33

Dubois S Ind. Forage Farm *Dubois County*   Elevation: 688 ft.   Latitude: 38° 27' N   Longitude: 86° 42' W

	JAN	FEB	MAR	APR	MAY	JUN	JUL	AUG	SEP	OCT	NOV	DEC	YEAR
Mean Maximum Temp. (°F)	37.3	43.0	53.4	64.6	73.9	82.1	86.0	84.9	78.7	67.2	54.4	43.2	64.1
Mean Temp. (°F)	28.6	33.0	43.1	53.9	63.1	71.7	75.7	74.2	67.6	55.6	44.8	34.3	53.8
Mean Minimum Temp. (°F)	19.8	23.0	32.7	43.1	52.3	61.3	65.5	63.5	56.4	44.0	35.2	25.4	43.5
Extreme Maximum Temp. (°F)	68	75	82	88	91	101	102	100	99	89	81	75	102
Extreme Minimum Temp. (°F)	-25	-11	-6	17	27	39	46	42	33	18	8	-20	-25
Days Maximum Temp. ≥ 90°F	0	0	0	0	0	3	8	7	2	0	0	0	20
Days Maximum Temp. ≤ 32°F	11	6	2	0	0	0	0	0	0	0	1	6	26
Days Minimum Temp. ≤ 32°F	27	22	16	5	0	0	0	0	0	4	14	22	110
Days Minimum Temp. ≤ 0°F	3	2	0	0	0	0	0	0	0	0	0	1	6
Heating Degree Days (base 65°F)	1,122	896	677	348	131	17	2	3	66	307	600	944	5,113
Cooling Degree Days (base 65°F)	0	0	5	20	82	236	362	309	148	25	1	0	1,188
Mean Precipitation (in.)	2.89	2.63	4.19	4.73	5.28	4.73	4.36	4.01	3.47	3.33	4.24	3.49	47.35
Days With ≥ 0.1" Precipitation	6	5	7	8	9	8	7	6	6	6	7	6	81
Days With ≥ 1.0" Precipitation	1	1	1	1	1	1	1	1	1	1	1	1	12
Mean Snowfall (in.)	na	na	na	trace	0.0	0.0	0.0	0.0	0.0	0.2	trace	na	na
Days With ≥ 1.0" Snow Depth	na	na	*1*	0	0	0	0	0	0	0	0	na	na

Elwood Wastewater Plant *Madison County*   Elevation: 839 ft.   Latitude: 40° 16' N   Longitude: 85° 51' W

	JAN	FEB	MAR	APR	MAY	JUN	JUL	AUG	SEP	OCT	NOV	DEC	YEAR
Mean Maximum Temp. (°F)	32.2	37.3	48.0	60.9	72.1	81.1	84.9	82.9	77.1	64.9	50.6	38.2	60.8
Mean Temp. (°F)	23.7	28.1	38.0	49.3	60.3	69.5	73.4	71.1	64.5	52.5	41.2	30.0	50.1
Mean Minimum Temp. (°F)	15.2	18.8	27.9	37.6	48.5	58.0	61.7	59.2	51.8	40.0	31.7	21.8	39.4
Extreme Maximum Temp. (°F)	64	74	81	88	92	102	101	99	96	89	79	72	102
Extreme Minimum Temp. (°F)	-24	-23	-8	12	27	38	46	38	29	18	5	-20	-24
Days Maximum Temp. ≥ 90°F	0	0	0	0	0	3	7	4	2	0	0	0	16
Days Maximum Temp. ≤ 32°F	15	10	3	0	0	0	0	0	0	0	1	9	38
Days Minimum Temp. ≤ 32°F	28	25	22	10	1	0	0	0	0	8	18	26	138
Days Minimum Temp. ≤ 0°F	5	3	0	0	0	0	0	0	0	0	0	2	10
Heating Degree Days (base 65°F)	1,277	1,035	832	472	192	32	4	14	105	392	709	1,078	6,142
Cooling Degree Days (base 65°F)	0	0	1	7	53	184	282	217	95	10	0	0	849
Mean Precipitation (in.)	2.28	1.91	2.99	3.77	4.05	4.32	4.49	3.91	3.22	2.68	3.61	2.95	40.18
Days With ≥ 0.1" Precipitation	6	4	7	8	8	7	7	6	6	5	7	7	78
Days With ≥ 1.0" Precipitation	0	0	0	1	1	1	1	1	1	0	1	0	7
Mean Snowfall (in.)	na	na	na	trace	0.0	0.0	0.0	0.0	0.0	trace	*trace*	na	na
Days With ≥ 1.0" Snow Depth	na	na	na	0	0	0	0	0	0	0	0	*0*	na

English 4 S *Crawford County*   Elevation: 508 ft.   Latitude: 38° 17' N   Longitude: 86° 28' W

	JAN	FEB	MAR	APR	MAY	JUN	JUL	AUG	SEP	OCT	NOV	DEC	YEAR
Mean Maximum Temp. (°F)	40.9	47.5	58.0	68.1	76.9	84.2	88.1	86.9	80.5	69.8	56.9	45.6	66.9
Mean Temp. (°F)	30.9	35.7	45.2	54.4	63.2	71.3	75.7	74.0	66.9	55.2	45.4	35.5	54.5
Mean Minimum Temp. (°F)	20.8	23.9	32.5	40.6	49.5	58.4	63.2	61.1	53.2	40.7	33.9	25.3	41.9
Extreme Maximum Temp. (°F)	72	79	85	91	97	102	104	102	98	90	84	76	104
Extreme Minimum Temp. (°F)	-31	-15	-10	15	25	36	41	35	28	14	1	-21	-31
Days Maximum Temp. ≥ 90°F	0	0	0	0	1	5	13	10	3	0	0	0	32
Days Maximum Temp. ≤ 32°F	7	4	0	0	0	0	0	0	0	0	0	4	15
Days Minimum Temp. ≤ 32°F	25	21	17	8	1	0	0	0	0	8	14	22	116
Days Minimum Temp. ≤ 0°F	3	2	0	0	0	0	0	0	0	0	0	1	6
Heating Degree Days (base 65°F)	1,052	820	606	328	120	15	1	3	66	312	581	909	4,813
Cooling Degree Days (base 65°F)	0	0	3	14	68	217	345	290	126	17	1	1	1,082
Mean Precipitation (in.)	3.49	3.22	4.90	4.95	5.11	4.85	4.15	3.82	3.48	3.31	4.28	3.99	49.55
Days With ≥ 0.1" Precipitation	7	6	9	8	8	8	6	6	6	5	8	7	84
Days With ≥ 1.0" Precipitation	1	1	1	1	1	1	1	1	1	1	1	1	12
Mean Snowfall (in.)	*2.4*	na	*0.5*	trace	0.0	0.0	0.0	0.0	0.0	trace	0.3	0.5	na
Days With ≥ 1.0" Snow Depth	7	4	1	0	0	0	0	0	0	0	0	2	14

Evansville Museum *Vanderburgh County*   Elevation: 377 ft.   Latitude: 37° 58' N   Longitude: 87° 34' W

	JAN	FEB	MAR	APR	MAY	JUN	JUL	AUG	SEP	OCT	NOV	DEC	YEAR
Mean Maximum Temp. (°F)	40.3	46.6	58.2	69.5	78.2	*86.7*	*89.7*	88.4	81.8	70.4	57.1	45.7	*67.7*
Mean Temp. (°F)	32.4	37.4	48.0	58.2	67.1	*75.7*	*79.4*	78.0	71.0	59.2	48.2	37.8	*57.7*
Mean Minimum Temp. (°F)	24.4	28.2	37.7	46.8	55.9	*64.7*	*69.0*	67.4	60.2	47.8	39.3	29.9	*47.6*
Extreme Maximum Temp. (°F)	71	78	86	91	94	*101*	*102*	*102*	98	*91*	83	78	*102*
Extreme Minimum Temp. (°F)	-17	-8	4	24	34	*45*	*50*	*46*	37	22	*11*	-15	*-17*
Days Maximum Temp. ≥ 90°F	0	0	0	0	2	*10*	*17*	14	6	0	0	0	*49*
Days Maximum Temp. ≤ 32°F	8	4	0	0	0	*0*	*0*	0	0	0	0	4	*16*
Days Minimum Temp. ≤ 32°F	23	18	11	2	0	*0*	*0*	0	0	1	8	18	*81*
Days Minimum Temp. ≤ 0°F	1	0	0	0	0	*0*	*0*	0	0	0	0	0	*1*
Heating Degree Days (base 65°F)	1,004	773	526	237	65	*2*	*0*	0	32	213	500	836	*4,188*
Cooling Degree Days (base 65°F)	*0*	*0*	*6*	*37*	*140*	*343*	*472*	*429*	*216*	*40*	*3*	*1*	*1,687*
Mean Precipitation (in.)	2.83	3.27	4.70	4.65	4.89	*3.89*	*4.22*	3.30	3.17	3.14	4.49	3.69	*46.24*
Days With ≥ 0.1" Precipitation	6	6	9	8	8	*6*	*6*	5	5	5	7	7	*78*
Days With ≥ 1.0" Precipitation	1	1	1	1	1	*1*	*1*	1	1	1	1	1	*12*
Mean Snowfall (in.)	*4.9*	3.5	2.6	0.5	trace	*0.0*	*0.0*	0.0	0.0	trace	0.3	*2.0*	*13.8*
Days With ≥ 1.0" Snow Depth	*7*	6	1	0	0	*0*	*0*	0	0	0	0	2	*16*

Farmland 5 NNW *Randolph County*   Elevation: 964 ft.   Latitude: 40° 15' N   Longitude: 85° 09' W

	JAN	FEB	MAR	APR	MAY	JUN	JUL	AUG	SEP	OCT	NOV	DEC	YEAR
Mean Maximum Temp. (°F)	32.0	36.6	47.4	60.1	71.4	80.4	84.2	82.2	76.4	64.1	50.0	38.2	60.2
Mean Temp. (°F)	23.7	27.3	37.5	49.0	60.3	69.5	73.2	70.8	64.1	52.1	41.0	30.1	49.9
Mean Minimum Temp. (°F)	15.4	17.9	27.4	37.9	49.0	58.7	62.3	59.5	51.8	40.1	31.9	22.0	39.5
Extreme Maximum Temp. (°F)	66	72	81	85	94	102	100	98	95	88	79	72	102
Extreme Minimum Temp. (°F)	-25	-21	-16	10	24	36	44	38	27	16	5	-21	-25
Days Maximum Temp. ≥ 90°F	0	0	0	0	0	3	6	3	1	0	0	0	13
Days Maximum Temp. ≤ 32°F	15	11	4	0	0	0	0	0	0	0	2	9	41
Days Minimum Temp. ≤ 32°F	29	25	22	9	1	0	0	0	1	7	17	26	137
Days Minimum Temp. ≤ 0°F	5	4	0	0	0	0	0	0	0	0	0	2	11
Heating Degree Days (base 65°F)	1,274	1,059	848	480	195	36	6	17	115	403	714	1,075	6,222
Cooling Degree Days (base 65°F)	0	0	1	7	55	187	282	213	95	11	0	0	851
Mean Precipitation (in.)	1.87	1.80	2.70	3.50	3.96	4.39	4.35	3.61	2.92	2.65	3.21	2.55	37.51
Days With ≥ 0.1" Precipitation	5	5	7	8	8	7	7	6	5	6	6	6	76
Days With ≥ 1.0" Precipitation	0	0	0	1	1	1	1	1	1	1	1	0	8
Mean Snowfall (in.)	8.1	6.2	4.0	0.7	trace	0.0	0.0	0.0	0.0	0.2	1.3	5.2	25.7
Days With ≥ 1.0" Snow Depth	15	11	4	0	0	0	0	0	0	0	1	6	37

Frankfort Disposal Plant *Clinton County*   Elevation: 833 ft.   Latitude: 40° 19' N   Longitude: 86° 30' W

	JAN	FEB	MAR	APR	MAY	JUN	JUL	AUG	SEP	OCT	NOV	DEC	YEAR
Mean Maximum Temp. (°F)	32.4	37.3	48.6	61.2	72.4	81.2	84.4	82.3	76.5	64.2	49.9	37.7	60.7
Mean Temp. (°F)	24.5	28.7	39.1	50.2	61.1	70.2	73.8	71.6	65.1	53.3	41.4	30.2	50.8
Mean Minimum Temp. (°F)	16.6	20.1	29.6	39.2	49.8	59.2	63.1	60.9	53.6	42.3	32.9	22.7	40.8
Extreme Maximum Temp. (°F)	64	73	83	89	92	101	105	98	95	89	78	72	105
Extreme Minimum Temp. (°F)	-25	-22	-13	14	18	36	45	38	28	18	5	-26	-26
Days Maximum Temp. ≥ 90°F	0	0	0	0	0	4	7	3	1	0	0	0	15
Days Maximum Temp. ≤ 32°F	15	10	3	0	0	0	0	0	0	0	1	9	38
Days Minimum Temp. ≤ 32°F	28	24	20	8	1	0	0	0	0	5	16	26	128
Days Minimum Temp. ≤ 0°F	4	3	0	0	0	0	0	0	0	0	0	2	9
Heating Degree Days (base 65°F)	1,250	1,018	797	443	173	26	4	10	95	368	701	1,072	5,957
Cooling Degree Days (base 65°F)	0	0	1	7	57	196	293	229	100	12	0	0	895
Mean Precipitation (in.)	1.99	1.96	3.20	3.71	4.06	4.33	4.24	3.96	3.03	2.88	3.35	2.87	39.58
Days With ≥ 0.1" Precipitation	6	5	7	8	8	7	7	6	5	6	7	7	79
Days With ≥ 1.0" Precipitation	0	0	1	1	1	1	1	1	1	0	1	0	8
Mean Snowfall (in.)	8.0	5.8	3.5	0.6	trace	0.0	0.0	0.0	0.0	0.4	1.1	6.2	25.6
Days With ≥ 1.0" Snow Depth	13	9	3	0	0	0	0	0	0	0	0	1	7	33

Goshen College *Elkhart County*   Elevation: 872 ft.   Latitude: 41° 33' N   Longitude: 85° 53' W

	JAN	FEB	MAR	APR	MAY	JUN	JUL	AUG	SEP	OCT	NOV	DEC	YEAR
Mean Maximum Temp. (°F)	30.9	35.4	46.8	60.0	71.6	80.7	84.1	81.6	74.9	62.5	48.3	36.2	59.4
Mean Temp. (°F)	23.8	27.5	37.8	49.4	60.4	69.7	73.5	71.3	64.4	52.6	40.7	29.8	50.1
Mean Minimum Temp. (°F)	16.6	19.5	28.8	38.8	49.1	58.7	62.9	61.0	53.7	42.6	33.2	23.3	40.7
Extreme Maximum Temp. (°F)	62	73	81	88	92	102	101	99	96	88	76	69	102
Extreme Minimum Temp. (°F)	-24	-14	-6	1	27	37	42	37	29	18	6	-18	-24
Days Maximum Temp. ≥ 90°F	0	0	0	0	1	4	6	3	1	0	0	0	15
Days Maximum Temp. ≤ 32°F	17	11	3	0	0	0	0	0	0	0	2	10	43
Days Minimum Temp. ≤ 32°F	29	24	20	8	1	0	0	0	0	5	15	26	128
Days Minimum Temp. ≤ 0°F	4	3	0	0	0	0	0	0	0	0	0	1	8
Heating Degree Days (base 65°F)	1,272	1,053	837	470	192	31	4	11	104	387	722	1,085	6,168
Cooling Degree Days (base 65°F)	0	0	1	7	56	184	284	222	88	7	0	0	849
Mean Precipitation (in.)	1.79	1.72	2.74	3.44	3.40	4.00	3.52	3.99	3.70	2.96	2.81	2.58	36.65
Days With ≥ 0.1" Precipitation	5	5	6	8	7	7	6	6	7	6	6	6	75
Days With ≥ 1.0" Precipitation	0	0	0	1	1	1	1	1	1	1	1	0	8
Mean Snowfall (in.)	10.7	8.0	5.0	1.3	trace	0.0	0.0	0.0	0.0	0.4	3.9	8.9	38.2
Days With ≥ 1.0" Snow Depth	18	14	5	0	0	0	0	0	0	0	2	10	49

Greencastle 1 SE *Putnam County*   Elevation: 859 ft.   Latitude: 39° 38' N   Longitude: 86° 51' W

	JAN	FEB	MAR	APR	MAY	JUN	JUL	AUG	SEP	OCT	NOV	DEC	YEAR
Mean Maximum Temp. (°F)	33.7	39.7	50.6	63.1	73.9	82.5	86.2	84.2	78.3	65.9	51.6	39.4	62.4
Mean Temp. (°F)	25.6	30.7	40.9	52.4	63.0	71.9	75.5	73.6	67.1	55.1	43.0	31.5	52.5
Mean Minimum Temp. (°F)	17.4	21.6	31.2	41.7	52.0	61.3	64.8	63.0	55.9	44.3	34.2	23.5	42.6
Extreme Maximum Temp. (°F)	69	72	84	90	94	103	103	102	98	90	81	74	103
Extreme Minimum Temp. (°F)	-23	-15	-3	16	30	37	47	42	32	20	5	-21	-23
Days Maximum Temp. ≥ 90°F	0	0	0	0	1	5	10	6	3	0	0	0	25
Days Maximum Temp. ≤ 32°F	14	8	3	0	0	0	0	0	0	0	1	8	34
Days Minimum Temp. ≤ 32°F	28	23	18	5	0	0	0	0	0	3	14	25	116
Days Minimum Temp. ≤ 0°F	4	2	0	0	0	0	0	0	0	0	0	2	8
Heating Degree Days (base 65°F)	1,216	963	742	388	136	19	2	5	71	321	656	1,032	5,551
Cooling Degree Days (base 65°F)	0	0	3	15	76	232	341	275	134	20	1	0	1,097
Mean Precipitation (in.)	2.40	2.45	3.66	3.84	4.73	4.24	5.18	4.18	3.15	3.12	3.93	3.07	43.95
Days With ≥ 0.1" Precipitation	6	5	7	8	8	8	7	6	5	5	7	6	78
Days With ≥ 1.0" Precipitation	0	0	1	1	1	1	2	1	1	1	1	1	11
Mean Snowfall (in.)	9.3	6.5	3.6	0.5	trace	0.0	0.0	0.0	0.0	0.2	1.5	5.7	27.3
Days With ≥ 1.0" Snow Depth	11	9	2	0	0	0	0	0	0	0	0	1	5	28

Greenfield *Hancock County*   Elevation: 862 ft.   Latitude: 39° 47' N   Longitude: 85° 45' W

	JAN	FEB	MAR	APR	MAY	JUN	JUL	AUG	SEP	OCT	NOV	DEC	YEAR
Mean Maximum Temp. (°F)	33.4	38.4	49.6	61.9	72.9	81.9	85.6	83.7	77.8	65.4	51.0	39.1	61.7
Mean Temp. (°F)	25.1	29.1	39.8	51.2	62.2	71.2	75.0	73.0	66.3	54.0	42.1	31.1	51.7
Mean Minimum Temp. (°F)	16.7	19.9	30.0	40.5	51.3	60.4	64.3	62.2	54.8	42.6	33.1	22.9	41.6
Extreme Maximum Temp. (°F)	65	72	84	87	93	103	102	101	95	90	79	72	103
Extreme Minimum Temp. (°F)	-29	-19	-6	16	30	39	46	41	31	19	6	-19	-29
Days Maximum Temp. ≥ 90°F	0	0	0	0	1	5	8	5	2	0	0	0	21
Days Maximum Temp. ≤ 32°F	14	9	3	0	0	0	0	0	0	0	1	8	35
Days Minimum Temp. ≤ 32°F	28	24	19	6	0	0	0	0	0	4	16	24	121
Days Minimum Temp. ≤ 0°F	4	3	0	0	0	0	0	0	0	0	0	1	8
Heating Degree Days (base 65°F)	1,233	1,005	775	418	155	24	2	6	78	349	682	1,046	5,773
Cooling Degree Days (base 65°F)	0	0	2	11	71	223	327	267	121	15	0	0	1,037
Mean Precipitation (in.)	2.45	2.35	3.34	4.06	4.74	4.36	5.01	3.97	3.05	3.10	3.90	3.08	43.41
Days With ≥ 0.1" Precipitation	6	5	7	8	9	8	7	6	6	6	7	7	82
Days With ≥ 1.0" Precipitation	0	0	1	1	1	1	2	1	1	1	1	1	10
Mean Snowfall (in.)	na	na	*1.5*	0.2	0.0	0.0	0.0	0.0	0.0	trace	0.7	*3.0*	na
Days With ≥ 1.0" Snow Depth	*9*	*6*	2	0	0	0	0	0	0	0	0	1	4	*22*

Greensburg *Decatur County*   Elevation: 935 ft.   Latitude: 39° 21' N   Longitude: 85° 30' W

	JAN	FEB	MAR	APR	MAY	JUN	JUL	AUG	SEP	OCT	NOV	DEC	YEAR
Mean Maximum Temp. (°F)	34.9	40.4	50.9	62.7	73.0	81.4	85.1	83.4	77.3	65.1	51.8	40.4	62.2
Mean Temp. (°F)	27.0	31.5	41.6	52.4	62.5	71.2	74.8	72.9	66.5	54.4	43.2	32.7	52.6
Mean Minimum Temp. (°F)	19.1	22.7	32.1	41.9	52.1	60.9	64.5	62.4	55.6	43.7	34.6	25.0	42.9
Extreme Maximum Temp. (°F)	67	75	82	86	90	101	101	101	95	87	79	73	101
Extreme Minimum Temp. (°F)	-24	-14	-12	17	24	39	44	42	32	17	6	-21	-24
Days Maximum Temp. ≥ 90°F	0	0	0	0	0	3	7	5	1	0	0	0	16
Days Maximum Temp. ≤ 32°F	13	8	2	0	0	0	0	0	0	0	1	7	31
Days Minimum Temp. ≤ 32°F	27	22	17	6	0	0	0	0	0	4	14	24	114
Days Minimum Temp. ≤ 0°F	4	2	0	0	0	0	0	0	0	0	0	1	7
Heating Degree Days (base 65°F)	1,170	938	722	387	142	19	2	6	77	337	648	995	5,443
Cooling Degree Days (base 65°F)	0	0	3	14	75	223	334	272	128	17	1	0	1,067
Mean Precipitation (in.)	2.46	2.31	3.69	4.43	4.86	4.23	4.06	4.17	3.04	3.07	3.78	3.15	43.25
Days With ≥ 0.1" Precipitation	6	5	7	9	8	7	7	6	6	6	7	7	81
Days With ≥ 1.0" Precipitation	0	0	1	1	1	1	1	1	1	1	1	1	10
Mean Snowfall (in.)	6.4	4.0	2.8	0.5	trace	0.0	0.0	0.0	0.0	0.2	0.8	3.3	18.0
Days With ≥ 1.0" Snow Depth	9	7	2	0	0	0	0	0	0	0	0	3	21

Hartford City 4 ESE *Blackford County*   Elevation: 941 ft.   Latitude: 40° 27' N   Longitude: 85° 18' W

	JAN	FEB	MAR	APR	MAY	JUN	JUL	AUG	SEP	OCT	NOV	DEC	YEAR
Mean Maximum Temp. (°F)	30.6	35.7	46.9	59.7	71.0	79.7	83.4	81.3	75.5	63.1	49.3	36.9	59.4
Mean Temp. (°F)	22.7	27.2	37.8	49.3	60.4	69.4	73.1	70.9	64.3	52.4	41.0	29.6	49.8
Mean Minimum Temp. (°F)	14.8	18.6	28.7	38.8	49.7	59.1	62.8	60.5	53.2	41.6	32.6	22.2	40.2
Extreme Maximum Temp. (°F)	64	71	82	87	90	103	99	98	95	87	77	71	103
Extreme Minimum Temp. (°F)	-26	-17	-10	8	26	37	45	39	29	19	5	-18	-26
Days Maximum Temp. ≥ 90°F	0	0	0	0	0	2	5	2	1	0	0	0	10
Days Maximum Temp. ≤ 32°F	16	12	4	0	0	0	0	0	0	0	2	10	44
Days Minimum Temp. ≤ 32°F	29	24	21	8	1	0	0	0	0	6	17	25	131
Days Minimum Temp. ≤ 0°F	6	4	0	0	0	0	0	0	0	0	0	2	12
Heating Degree Days (base 65°F)	1,305	1,062	837	472	188	33	6	14	103	393	715	1,092	6,220
Cooling Degree Days (base 65°F)	0	0	2	7	52	186	286	223	92	11	0	0	859
Mean Precipitation (in.)	1.93	2.01	2.76	3.40	3.73	4.49	4.06	4.09	2.81	2.38	3.27	2.58	37.51
Days With ≥ 0.1" Precipitation	5	5	6	7	8	8	6	6	5	5	6	7	74
Days With ≥ 1.0" Precipitation	0	0	1	1	1	1	1	1	1	0	1	0	8
Mean Snowfall (in.)	7.6	6.0	3.5	1.0	trace	0.0	0.0	0.0	0.0	0.4	1.6	5.9	26.0
Days With ≥ 1.0" Snow Depth	18	13	5	1	0	0	0	0	0	0	2	9	48

Hobart 2 WNW *Lake County*   Elevation: 639 ft.   Latitude: 41° 33' N   Longitude: 87° 17' W

	JAN	FEB	MAR	APR	MAY	JUN	JUL	AUG	SEP	OCT	NOV	DEC	YEAR
Mean Maximum Temp. (°F)	31.7	37.0	47.9	60.2	71.5	81.4	85.3	82.7	76.9	65.2	49.8	37.0	60.6
Mean Temp. (°F)	23.6	28.4	38.3	49.2	59.5	69.5	74.1	71.8	65.3	53.9	41.2	29.5	50.4
Mean Minimum Temp. (°F)	15.5	19.7	28.6	38.2	47.4	57.6	63.1	61.0	53.7	42.6	32.5	22.0	40.2
Extreme Maximum Temp. (°F)	65	71	84	90	93	105	103	102	97	90	76	69	105
Extreme Minimum Temp. (°F)	-25	-16	-1	13	27	34	42	41	29	22	4	-29	-29
Days Maximum Temp. ≥ 90°F	0	0	0	0	1	5	9	5	2	0	0	0	22
Days Maximum Temp. ≤ 32°F	15	10	2	0	0	0	0	0	0	0	1	9	37
Days Minimum Temp. ≤ 32°F	29	24	21	9	1	0	0	0	0	4	16	26	130
Days Minimum Temp. ≤ 0°F	5	3	0	0	0	0	0	0	0	0	0	2	10
Heating Degree Days (base 65°F)	1,276	1,026	821	480	220	42	6	10	94	347	710	1,092	6,124
Cooling Degree Days (base 65°F)	0	0	2	11	50	182	301	224	103	9	0	0	882
Mean Precipitation (in.)	1.88	1.55	2.68	3.63	3.88	4.39	3.48	3.73	3.70	3.02	3.47	2.41	37.82
Days With ≥ 0.1" Precipitation	5	4	6	8	7	6	6	6	6	6	7	5	72
Days With ≥ 1.0" Precipitation	0	0	0	1	1	1	1	1	1	1	1	0	8
Mean Snowfall (in.)	9.1	7.4	3.2	0.8	trace	0.0	0.0	0.0	0.0	trace	1.1	5.8	27.4
Days With ≥ 1.0" Snow Depth	17	11	4	0	0	0	0	0	0	0	1	8	41

Indianapolis SE Side *Marion County*   Elevation: 843 ft.   Latitude: 39° 43' N   Longitude: 86° 04' W

	JAN	FEB	MAR	APR	MAY	JUN	JUL	AUG	SEP	OCT	NOV	DEC	YEAR
Mean Maximum Temp. (°F)	33.8	38.8	49.6	61.8	72.8	81.4	85.1	83.3	77.3	65.2	51.4	39.6	61.7
Mean Temp. (°F)	25.9	30.1	40.1	51.4	62.2	71.3	75.2	73.2	66.3	54.3	42.7	31.7	52.0
Mean Minimum Temp. (°F)	17.9	21.3	30.6	40.9	51.6	61.1	65.3	63.0	55.3	43.3	33.9	23.8	42.3
Extreme Maximum Temp. (°F)	65	73	83	87	92	104	103	100	94	89	82	73	104
Extreme Minimum Temp. (°F)	-22	-12	0	18	29	35	49	45	30	20	3	-20	-22
Days Maximum Temp. ≥ 90°F	0	0	0	0	0	3	7	4	2	0	0	0	16
Days Maximum Temp. ≤ 32°F	14	9	3	0	0	0	0	0	0	0	1	7	34
Days Minimum Temp. ≤ 32°F	28	24	19	6	0	0	0	0	0	4	15	25	121
Days Minimum Temp. ≤ 0°F	4	2	0	0	0	0	0	0	0	0	0	1	7
Heating Degree Days (base 65°F)	1,207	980	766	413	151	22	2	5	77	339	664	1,024	5,650
Cooling Degree Days (base 65°F)	0	0	2	11	67	221	330	268	120	16	0	0	1,035
Mean Precipitation (in.)	2.02	2.02	3.09	3.82	4.55	4.05	4.91	3.58	2.51	2.83	3.66	2.77	39.81
Days With ≥ 0.1" Precipitation	5	5	7	8	8	7	7	5	5	5	6	6	74
Days With ≥ 1.0" Precipitation	0	0	1	1	1	1	1	1	1	1	1	0	8
Mean Snowfall (in.)	na	na	0.9	0.1	trace	0.0	0.0	0.0	0.0	0.2	0.2	1.4	na
Days With ≥ 1.0" Snow Depth	10	7	2	0	0	0	0	0	0	0	1	4	24

Kentland *Newton County*   Elevation: 692 ft.   Latitude: 40° 46' N   Longitude: 87° 26' W

	JAN	FEB	MAR	APR	MAY	JUN	JUL	AUG	SEP	OCT	NOV	DEC	YEAR
Mean Maximum Temp. (°F)	31.4	36.6	48.9	62.3	74.2	83.4	85.9	83.9	*77.9*	65.9	*49.7*	*36.8*	*61.4*
Mean Temp. (°F)	23.3	27.9	39.5	50.9	62.3	71.6	74.7	72.4	*65.8*	54.0	*41.2*	*29.2*	*51.1*
Mean Minimum Temp. (°F)	15.1	19.1	30.0	39.4	50.4	59.8	63.4	60.9	*53.7*	42.1	*32.6*	*21.4*	*40.6*
Extreme Maximum Temp. (°F)	61	72	85	89	94	104	103	104	*98*	90	*78*	*70*	*104*
Extreme Minimum Temp. (°F)	-25	-18	-6	3	28	37	45	44	*27*	17	*1*	*-21*	*-25*
Days Maximum Temp. ≥ 90°F	0	0	0	0	2	6	9	5	*2*	0	*0*	*0*	*24*
Days Maximum Temp. ≤ 32°F	16	10	3	0	0	0	0	0	*0*	0	*2*	*9*	*40*
Days Minimum Temp. ≤ 32°F	29	24	19	8	1	0	0	0	*0*	5	*16*	*27*	*129*
Days Minimum Temp. ≤ 0°F	5	4	0	0	0	0	0	0	*0*	0	*0*	*2*	*11*
Heating Degree Days (base 65°F)	1,286	1,043	785	428	155	19	3	8	*88*	350	*708*	*1,105*	*5,978*
Cooling Degree Days (base 65°F)	0	0	1	11	76	*226*	316	*244*	*110*	13	*0*	*0*	*997*
Mean Precipitation (in.)	1.62	1.53	2.78	3.53	4.29	4.33	4.18	3.88	*3.60*	2.91	*3.36*	*2.57*	*38.58*
Days With ≥ 0.1" Precipitation	4	4	6	8	8	7	7	6	*6*	6	*7*	*6*	*75*
Days With ≥ 1.0" Precipitation	0	0	0	1	1	1	1	1	*1*	1	*1*	*1*	*9*
Mean Snowfall (in.)	7.5	6.8	3.2	0.8	0.0	0.0	0.0	0.0	*0.0*	0.1	*2.0*	*6.3*	*26.7*
Days With ≥ 1.0" Snow Depth	14	11	4	0	0	0	0	0	*0*	0	*2*	*8*	*39*

Kokomo 3 WSW *Howard County*   Elevation: 816 ft.   Latitude: 40° 28' N   Longitude: 86° 10' W

	JAN	FEB	MAR	APR	MAY	JUN	JUL	AUG	SEP	OCT	NOV	DEC	YEAR
Mean Maximum Temp. (°F)	30.3	35.1	46.7	59.8	71.1	80.5	84.0	81.8	76.0	63.7	48.9	36.4	59.5
Mean Temp. (°F)	22.3	26.4	37.0	48.6	59.7	69.4	72.9	70.5	63.8	51.9	40.1	28.8	49.3
Mean Minimum Temp. (°F)	14.2	17.6	27.3	37.4	48.4	58.2	61.8	59.2	51.5	40.0	31.3	21.1	39.0
Extreme Maximum Temp. (°F)	62	74	82	88	93	104	102	100	95	89	81	71	104
Extreme Minimum Temp. (°F)	-26	-20	-10	8	27	34	44	37	27	17	3	-24	-26
Days Maximum Temp. ≥ 90°F	0	0	0	0	0	4	7	3	1	0	0	0	15
Days Maximum Temp. ≤ 32°F	17	12	4	0	0	0	0	0	0	0	2	11	46
Days Minimum Temp. ≤ 32°F	29	26	22	10	1	0	0	0	1	7	18	27	141
Days Minimum Temp. ≤ 0°F	6	4	0	0	0	0	0	0	0	0	0	2	12
Heating Degree Days (base 65°F)	1,320	1,085	862	493	205	38	8	19	118	410	739	1,117	6,414
Cooling Degree Days (base 65°F)	0	0	1	7	45	179	269	207	88	10	0	0	806
Mean Precipitation (in.)	2.49	2.28	3.28	3.90	4.04	3.91	4.54	4.24	3.14	3.09	3.65	3.13	41.69
Days With ≥ 0.1" Precipitation	7	6	8	8	8	7	7	6	5	6	7	8	83
Days With ≥ 1.0" Precipitation	0	0	0	1	1	1	2	1	1	1	1	1	10
Mean Snowfall (in.)	13.2	10.3	6.1	1.4	trace	0.0	0.0	0.0	0.0	0.4	2.1	9.6	43.1
Days With ≥ 1.0" Snow Depth	17	12	6	1	0	0	0	0	0	0	1	9	46

La Porte *La Porte County*   Elevation: 807 ft.   Latitude: 41° 37' N   Longitude: 86° 44' W

	JAN	FEB	MAR	APR	MAY	JUN	JUL	AUG	SEP	OCT	NOV	DEC	YEAR
Mean Maximum Temp. (°F)	29.9	34.7	45.9	58.2	70.4	79.4	83.0	80.7	73.9	61.9	47.5	35.4	58.4
Mean Temp. (°F)	22.9	27.4	37.5	48.8	60.2	69.4	73.6	71.6	64.4	52.7	40.3	29.0	49.8
Mean Minimum Temp. (°F)	15.8	20.0	29.2	39.2	50.0	59.4	64.1	62.5	54.9	43.5	33.2	22.6	41.2
Extreme Maximum Temp. (°F)	63	71	82	90	95	101	101	100	95	88	75	72	101
Extreme Minimum Temp. (°F)	-23	-16	-2	16	29	36	44	44	35	24	3	-18	-23
Days Maximum Temp. ≥ 90°F	0	0	0	0	1	3	5	2	1	0	0	0	12
Days Maximum Temp. ≤ 32°F	18	12	4	0	0	0	0	0	0	0	2	11	47
Days Minimum Temp. ≤ 32°F	29	25	21	7	0	0	0	0	0	2	15	26	125
Days Minimum Temp. ≤ 0°F	4	2	0	0	0	0	0	0	0	0	0	2	8
Heating Degree Days (base 65°F)	1,299	1,055	845	490	201	36	4	9	100	382	733	1,109	6,263
Cooling Degree Days (base 65°F)	0	0	1	8	56	175	278	225	88	7	0	0	838
Mean Precipitation (in.)	2.26	1.88	3.08	3.58	3.46	4.36	3.81	4.14	3.94	3.25	3.77	3.14	40.67
Days With ≥ 0.1" Precipitation	7	6	7	8	7	7	7	7	6	7	8	7	84
Days With ≥ 1.0" Precipitation	0	0	1	1	1	1	1	1	1	1	1	1	10
Mean Snowfall (in.)	21.6	12.6	*7.1*	1.4	trace	0.0	0.0	0.0	0.0	0.3	4.8	13.7	*61.5*
Days With ≥ 1.0" Snow Depth	*20*	*14*	*6*	0	0	0	0	0	0	0	*2*	*12*	*54*

Lafayette 8 S *Tippecanoe County*   Elevation: 731 ft.   Latitude: 40° 18' N   Longitude: 86° 54' W

	JAN	FEB	MAR	APR	MAY	JUN	JUL	AUG	SEP	OCT	NOV	DEC	YEAR
Mean Maximum Temp. (°F)	31.4	36.7	48.1	60.6	72.3	81.4	84.6	82.5	76.9	64.6	50.1	37.4	60.5
Mean Temp. (°F)	23.1	27.7	38.6	49.9	61.2	70.4	73.8	71.7	65.1	53.2	41.2	29.5	50.5
Mean Minimum Temp. (°F)	14.8	18.6	29.0	39.1	50.0	59.4	63.1	60.9	53.2	41.6	32.3	21.6	40.3
Extreme Maximum Temp. (°F)	63	73	82	89	92	104	102	98	96	90	80	71	104
Extreme Minimum Temp. (°F)	-25	-20	-8	4	26	36	43	37	26	19	5	-25	-25
Days Maximum Temp. ≥ 90°F	0	0	0	0	1	4	6	3	2	0	0	0	16
Days Maximum Temp. ≤ 32°F	16	11	3	0	0	0	0	0	0	0	1	10	41
Days Minimum Temp. ≤ 32°F	28	25	21	8	1	0	0	0	0	6	16	26	131
Days Minimum Temp. ≤ 0°F	6	4	0	0	0	0	0	0	0	0	0	2	12
Heating Degree Days (base 65°F)	1,292	1,048	814	457	177	30	6	12	100	373	707	1,093	6,109
Cooling Degree Days (base 65°F)	0	0	2	10	67	210	302	239	111	12	0	0	953
Mean Precipitation (in.)	1.83	1.67	3.02	3.52	4.14	4.15	4.04	3.68	2.79	2.50	3.02	2.52	36.88
Days With ≥ 0.1" Precipitation	5	4	7	8	7	7	6	6	5	5	6	6	72
Days With ≥ 1.0" Precipitation	0	0	0	1	1	1	1	1	1	0	1	0	7
Mean Snowfall (in.)	7.5	4.6	2.6	0.7	trace	0.0	0.0	0.0	0.0	0.5	0.8	5.1	21.8
Days With ≥ 1.0" Snow Depth	13	9	3	0	0	0	0	0	0	0	1	6	32

Lagrange Sewage Plant *Lagrange County*   Elevation: 892 ft.   Latitude: 41° 39' N   Longitude: 85° 25' W

	JAN	FEB	MAR	APR	MAY	JUN	JUL	AUG	SEP	OCT	NOV	DEC	YEAR
Mean Maximum Temp. (°F)	29.4	33.5	44.5	57.8	69.7	79.3	82.9	80.8	73.8	61.4	47.1	35.2	57.9
Mean Temp. (°F)	21.9	25.1	35.2	47.1	58.5	68.1	72.0	69.9	62.7	50.9	39.1	28.1	48.2
Mean Minimum Temp. (°F)	14.2	16.6	25.8	36.4	47.4	56.9	61.1	59.0	51.6	40.3	31.2	21.0	38.5
Extreme Maximum Temp. (°F)	61	71	79	87	93	104	101	99	95	88	75	70	104
Extreme Minimum Temp. (°F)	-22	-19	-5	8	25	32	40	38	28	18	6	-19	-22
Days Maximum Temp. ≥ 90°F	0	0	0	0	0	3	5	2	1	0	0	0	11
Days Maximum Temp. ≤ 32°F	18	14	5	0	0	0	0	0	0	0	2	11	50
Days Minimum Temp. ≤ 32°F	29	26	24	11	1	0	0	0	0	7	18	27	143
Days Minimum Temp. ≤ 0°F	5	4	0	0	0	0	0	0	0	0	0	2	11
Heating Degree Days (base 65°F)	1,330	1,121	918	537	239	52	12	22	136	438	771	1,137	6,713
Cooling Degree Days (base 65°F)	0	0	1	6	45	154	246	187	71	6	0	0	716
Mean Precipitation (in.)	1.76	1.72	2.69	3.44	3.59	4.06	3.68	3.92	3.54	2.84	2.92	2.55	36.71
Days With ≥ 0.1" Precipitation	5	5	6	8	7	7	7	7	6	6	7	7	78
Days With ≥ 1.0" Precipitation	0	0	0	1	1	1	1	1	1	0	1	0	7
Mean Snowfall (in.)	10.7	8.1	5.0	1.5	trace	0.0	0.0	0.0	0.0	0.5	3.4	9.5	38.7
Days With ≥ 1.0" Snow Depth	17	14	6	1	0	0	0	0	0	0	3	12	53

Lowell *Lake County*   Elevation: 662 ft.   Latitude: 41° 16' N   Longitude: 87° 25' W

	JAN	FEB	MAR	APR	MAY	JUN	JUL	AUG	SEP	OCT	NOV	DEC	YEAR
Mean Maximum Temp. (°F)	29.6	35.0	46.6	59.7	71.8	81.0	84.4	81.9	75.8	63.8	48.4	35.5	59.5
Mean Temp. (°F)	21.3	26.1	37.1	48.5	59.9	69.4	73.1	70.8	63.8	51.9	39.5	27.4	49.1
Mean Minimum Temp. (°F)	12.9	17.2	27.6	37.4	47.9	57.7	61.8	59.7	51.7	39.9	30.6	19.6	38.7
Extreme Maximum Temp. (°F)	65	68	84	91	93	104	101	104	98	90	76	69	104
Extreme Minimum Temp. (°F)	-28	-21	-8	7	26	33	41	38	28	18	2	-21	-28
Days Maximum Temp. ≥ 90°F	0	0	0	0	1	5	7	3	1	0	0	0	17
Days Maximum Temp. ≤ 32°F	18	12	3	0	0	0	0	0	0	0	2	11	46
Days Minimum Temp. ≤ 32°F	29	25	23	10	1	0	0	0	0	7	18	27	140
Days Minimum Temp. ≤ 0°F	7	4	0	0	0	0	0	0	0	0	0	3	14
Heating Degree Days (base 65°F)	1,350	1,092	859	496	209	39	7	15	116	409	758	1,158	6,508
Cooling Degree Days (base 65°F)	0	0	1	7	55	183	271	210	87	8	0	0	822
Mean Precipitation (in.)	1.84	1.67	2.98	4.19	4.39	4.61	3.95	3.85	3.51	3.06	3.58	2.67	40.30
Days With ≥ 0.1" Precipitation	5	4	7	8	8	8	7	6	6	6	7	6	78
Days With ≥ 1.0" Precipitation	0	0	0	1	1	1	1	1	1	1	1	1	9
Mean Snowfall (in.)	10.7	9.2	4.0	0.5	trace	0.0	0.0	0.0	0.0	0.2	1.9	6.6	33.1
Days With ≥ 1.0" Snow Depth	na	na	na	0	0	0	0	0	0	0	0	1	na

Madison Sewage Plant *Jefferson County*   Elevation: 459 ft.   Latitude: 38° 44' N   Longitude: 85° 24' W

	JAN	FEB	MAR	APR	MAY	JUN	JUL	AUG	SEP	OCT	NOV	DEC	YEAR
Mean Maximum Temp. (°F)	40.1	45.5	56.2	67.1	75.6	83.6	87.2	85.9	79.8	68.7	56.1	45.1	65.9
Mean Temp. (°F)	31.7	35.8	45.5	55.3	64.3	72.9	77.0	75.5	69.0	57.5	46.6	36.6	55.6
Mean Minimum Temp. (°F)	23.3	26.0	34.6	43.4	53.0	62.1	66.6	65.1	58.2	46.2	37.1	28.1	45.3
Extreme Maximum Temp. (°F)	68	75	84	91	93	103	103	104	97	90	84	77	104
Extreme Minimum Temp. (°F)	-17	-8	-2	19	31	40	48	43	33	23	10	-18	-18
Days Maximum Temp. ≥ 90°F	0	0	0	0	0	5	11	8	3	0	0	0	27
Days Maximum Temp. ≤ 32°F	8	4	1	0	0	0	0	0	0	0	0	4	17
Days Minimum Temp. ≤ 32°F	24	20	14	4	0	0	0	0	0	2	10	20	94
Days Minimum Temp. ≤ 0°F	1	0	0	0	0	0	0	0	0	0	0	0	1
Heating Degree Days (base 65°F)	1,025	820	601	300	102	9	0	1	43	249	546	873	4,569
Cooling Degree Days (base 65°F)	0	0	2	13	84	246	382	333	158	21	1	1	1,241
Mean Precipitation (in.)	2.95	2.82	4.27	4.28	4.94	4.33	4.30	3.98	2.90	3.28	3.83	3.61	45.49
Days With ≥ 0.1" Precipitation	6	6	8	9	9	8	7	6	5	6	7	6	83
Days With ≥ 1.0" Precipitation	1	1	1	1	1	1	1	1	1	1	1	1	12
Mean Snowfall (in.)	*5.7*	*4.2*	*2.4*	trace	trace	0.0	0.0	0.0	0.0	0.1	trace	*2.9*	*15.3*
Days With ≥ 1.0" Snow Depth	*7*	*5*	*1*	0	0	0	0	0	0	0	0	*1*	*14*

Marion 2 N *Grant County*   Elevation: 787 ft.   Latitude: 40° 34' N   Longitude: 85° 40' W

	JAN	FEB	MAR	APR	MAY	JUN	JUL	AUG	SEP	OCT	NOV	DEC	YEAR
Mean Maximum Temp. (°F)	31.6	36.3	47.5	60.2	71.7	80.9	84.5	82.3	76.4	64.1	49.8	37.6	60.2
Mean Temp. (°F)	23.8	27.6	37.7	48.9	60.1	69.7	73.7	71.4	64.7	52.7	41.2	30.0	50.1
Mean Minimum Temp. (°F)	16.0	18.7	27.9	37.5	48.5	58.5	62.8	60.4	52.9	41.2	32.6	22.5	40.0
Extreme Maximum Temp. (°F)	68	73	82	88	93	103	101	98	95	88	78	71	103
Extreme Minimum Temp. (°F)	-23	-15	-11	5	26	38	46	39	30	19	7	-20	-23
Days Maximum Temp. ≥ 90°F	0	0	0	0	0	4	7	4	1	0	0	0	16
Days Maximum Temp. ≤ 32°F	16	11	3	0	0	0	0	0	0	0	1	9	40
Days Minimum Temp. ≤ 32°F	28	25	22	10	1	0	0	0	0	6	17	26	135
Days Minimum Temp. ≤ 0°F	5	3	0	0	0	0	0	0	0	0	0	2	10
Heating Degree Days (base 65°F)	1,271	1,051	841	484	198	34	4	12	101	387	707	1,077	6,167
Cooling Degree Days (base 65°F)	0	0	1	7	52	190	291	225	98	12	0	0	876
Mean Precipitation (in.)	2.12	1.98	3.00	3.69	4.20	3.91	4.67	3.67	2.80	2.62	3.35	2.79	38.80
Days With ≥ 0.1" Precipitation	6	5	7	8	7	7	7	6	5	6	6	7	77
Days With ≥ 1.0" Precipitation	0	0	0	1	1	1	2	1	1	0	1	0	8
Mean Snowfall (in.)	7.7	6.8	3.2	1.0	0.0	0.0	0.0	0.0	0.0	0.4	1.1	6.0	26.2
Days With ≥ 1.0" Snow Depth	16	11	4	0	0	0	0	0	0	0	1	7	39

Martinsville 2 SW *Morgan County*   Elevation: 606 ft.   Latitude: 39° 24' N   Longitude: 86° 27' W

	JAN	FEB	MAR	APR	MAY	JUN	JUL	AUG	SEP	OCT	NOV	DEC	YEAR
Mean Maximum Temp. (°F)	35.7	40.6	51.1	63.0	73.0	81.3	85.5	84.2	77.8	66.3	53.0	41.2	62.7
Mean Temp. (°F)	26.9	30.6	40.4	51.3	61.3	70.3	74.3	72.4	65.0	53.4	42.8	32.4	51.8
Mean Minimum Temp. (°F)	18.0	20.6	29.8	39.6	49.5	59.2	63.2	60.6	52.1	40.4	32.6	23.6	40.8
Extreme Maximum Temp. (°F)	67	74	83	88	92	101	101	100	94	88	81	75	101
Extreme Minimum Temp. (°F)	-35	-20	-15	12	27	35	45	38	28	19	9	-22	-35
Days Maximum Temp. ≥ 90°F	0	0	0	0	0	3	7	6	2	0	0	0	18
Days Maximum Temp. ≤ 32°F	12	7	2	0	0	0	0	0	0	0	1	7	29
Days Minimum Temp. ≤ 32°F	28	24	20	8	1	0	0	0	0	8	16	25	130
Days Minimum Temp. ≤ 0°F	4	3	0	0	0	0	0	0	0	0	0	2	9
Heating Degree Days (base 65°F)	1,175	965	757	414	163	26	3	8	99	366	659	1,004	5,639
Cooling Degree Days (base 65°F)	0	0	1	9	52	188	309	244	99	11	0	0	913
Mean Precipitation (in.)	2.48	2.36	3.46	4.29	4.76	3.92	4.15	3.97	3.14	2.95	3.85	3.04	42.37
Days With ≥ 0.1" Precipitation	6	5	7	8	8	7	7	6	5	5	7	7	78
Days With ≥ 1.0" Precipitation	0	0	1	1	1	1	1	1	1	1	1	1	10
Mean Snowfall (in.)	*6.7*	*4.8*	2.6	*trace*	0.0	0.0	0.0	0.0	*0.0*	*0.2*	*0.7*	*2.7*	*17.7*
Days With ≥ 1.0" Snow Depth	na	na	na	*1*	0	0	0	0	0	*0*	na	na	na

Mount Vernon *Posey County*   Elevation: 419 ft.   Latitude: 37° 57' N   Longitude: 87° 53' W

	JAN	FEB	MAR	APR	MAY	JUN	JUL	AUG	SEP	OCT	NOV	DEC	YEAR
Mean Maximum Temp. (°F)	38.5	44.0	54.6	66.3	76.0	84.5	88.4	86.8	80.9	69.4	55.7	44.2	65.8
Mean Temp. (°F)	30.4	35.0	44.9	55.7	65.4	74.2	78.1	76.0	69.4	57.6	46.4	36.0	55.8
Mean Minimum Temp. (°F)	22.3	25.9	35.2	45.1	54.6	63.8	67.7	65.2	57.8	45.7	37.1	27.7	45.7
Extreme Maximum Temp. (°F)	71	76	83	90	93	101	102	103	99	91	82	77	103
Extreme Minimum Temp. (°F)	-16	-7	-3	25	35	44	50	45	35	22	10	-16	-16
Days Maximum Temp. ≥ 90°F	0	0	0	0	1	8	14	11	5	0	0	0	39
Days Maximum Temp. ≤ 32°F	10	6	1	0	0	0	0	0	0	0	0	5	22
Days Minimum Temp. ≤ 32°F	25	20	13	2	0	0	0	0	0	2	11	20	93
Days Minimum Temp. ≤ 0°F	2	1	0	0	0	0	0	0	0	0	0	1	4
Heating Degree Days (base 65°F)	1,065	841	619	298	88	7	1	1	45	253	554	893	4,665
Cooling Degree Days (base 65°F)	0	0	4	23	104	292	419	356	178	29	2	0	1,407
Mean Precipitation (in.)	3.20	3.02	4.66	4.53	5.42	3.92	4.15	3.04	2.78	3.04	4.29	3.68	45.73
Days With ≥ 0.1" Precipitation	6	6	8	8	8	7	6	5	5	5	7	7	78
Days With ≥ 1.0" Precipitation	1	1	1	1	2	1	1	1	1	1	1	1	13
Mean Snowfall (in.)	4.5	3.8	2.3	0.4	0.0	0.0	0.0	0.0	0.0	0.1	0.4	2.2	13.7
Days With ≥ 1.0" Snow Depth	7	6	1	0	0	0	0	0	0	0	0	3	17

Muncie *Delaware County*   Elevation: 977 ft.   Latitude: 40° 14' N   Longitude: 85° 23' W

	JAN	FEB	MAR	APR	MAY	JUN	JUL	AUG	SEP	OCT	NOV	DEC	YEAR
Mean Maximum Temp. (°F)	32.4	37.3	48.1	61.1	72.1	81.1	85.1	82.9	76.8	64.4	50.1	38.4	60.8
Mean Temp. (°F)	24.6	28.9	38.9	50.5	61.6	70.8	74.7	72.5	65.5	53.4	41.7	30.8	51.2
Mean Minimum Temp. (°F)	16.8	20.4	29.6	39.9	51.2	60.5	64.2	62.0	54.2	42.4	33.2	23.1	41.5
Extreme Maximum Temp. (°F)	64	71	80	88	93	102	100	99	96	90	79	71	102
Extreme Minimum Temp. (°F)	29	-13	-8	10	25	36	40	39	27	18	3	-21	-29
Days Maximum Temp. ≥ 90°F	0	0	0	0	0	3	7	4	2	0	0	0	16
Days Maximum Temp. ≤ 32°F	15	10	3	0	0	0	0	0	0	0	2	9	39
Days Minimum Temp. ≤ 32°F	28	24	20	8	1	0	0	0	0	5	16	25	127
Days Minimum Temp. ≤ 0°F	4	3	0	0	0	0	0	0	0	0	0	2	9
Heating Degree Days (base 65°F)	1,245	1,012	804	441	167	26	3	8	91	369	694	1,054	5,914
Cooling Degree Days (base 65°F)	0	0	2	9	64	201	304	240	103	13	0	0	936
Mean Precipitation (in.)	2.05	2.19	3.15	3.60	4.07	4.21	3.87	3.39	2.85	2.65	3.32	2.99	38.34
Days With ≥ 0.1" Precipitation	6	5	7	8	8	7	6	6	5	6	7	7	78
Days With ≥ 1.0" Precipitation	0	0	0	1	1	1	1	1	1	0	1	0	7
Mean Snowfall (in.)	8.4	*6.0*	3.0	0.5	trace	0.0	0.0	0.0	0.0	0.2	1.2	6.3	*25.6*
Days With ≥ 1.0" Snow Depth	13	*9*	3	0	0	0	0	0	0	0	1	*6*	*32*

New Castle 4 N *Henry County*   Elevation: 1,062 ft.   Latitude: 39° 59' N   Longitude: 85° 22' W

	JAN	FEB	MAR	APR	MAY	JUN	JUL	AUG	SEP	OCT	NOV	DEC	YEAR
Mean Maximum Temp. (°F)	32.5	37.2	48.2	60.4	71.6	80.5	84.0	82.3	76.3	63.9	50.0	38.5	60.5
Mean Temp. (°F)	24.3	28.1	38.4	49.1	60.0	69.2	73.0	71.2	64.4	52.5	41.2	30.6	50.2
Mean Minimum Temp. (°F)	16.0	18.9	28.5	37.8	48.4	57.9	61.9	59.9	52.5	41.0	32.3	22.6	39.8
Extreme Maximum Temp. (°F)	64	71	82	87	91	103	101	100	96	88	78	72	103
Extreme Minimum Temp. (°F)	-26	-19	-9	15	26	38	45	39	29	18	8	-21	-26
Days Maximum Temp. ≥ 90°F	0	0	0	0	0	3	5	3	1	0	0	0	12
Days Maximum Temp. ≤ 32°F	15	10	3	0	0	0	0	0	0	0	2	9	39
Days Minimum Temp. ≤ 32°F	29	24	21	9	1	0	0	0	0	6	17	25	132
Days Minimum Temp. ≤ 0°F	5	3	0	0	0	0	0	0	0	0	0	2	10
Heating Degree Days (base 65°F)	1,256	1,036	819	475	198	34	5	11	106	391	709	1,061	6,101
Cooling Degree Days (base 65°F)	0	0	1	5	46	169	262	211	90	10	0	0	794
Mean Precipitation (in.)	2.22	2.22	2.98	3.97	4.62	4.57	4.65	3.54	2.81	2.99	3.63	2.78	40.98
Days With ≥ 0.1" Precipitation	5	5	7	8	8	8	7	6	5	6	7	6	78
Days With ≥ 1.0" Precipitation	0	0	0	1	1	1	1	1	1	1	1	0	8
Mean Snowfall (in.)	na	na	2.2	0.3	trace	0.0	0.0	0.0	0.0	trace	0.8	na	na
Days With ≥ 1.0" Snow Depth	na	na	*1*	0	0	0	0	0	0	0	*0*	na	na

New Whiteland *Johnson County*   Elevation: 784 ft.   Latitude: 39° 33' N   Longitude: 86° 06' W

	JAN	FEB	MAR	APR	MAY	JUN	JUL	AUG	SEP	OCT	NOV	DEC	YEAR
Mean Maximum Temp. (°F)	33.5	38.5	50.6	62.0	72.8	81.5	85.1	83.5	77.5	65.4	51.4	39.0	61.7
Mean Temp. (°F)	24.7	28.8	40.4	51.1	61.7	70.8	74.2	72.2	65.3	53.1	41.7	30.7	51.2
Mean Minimum Temp. (°F)	16.0	19.0	30.2	40.2	50.6	60.0	63.3	60.8	53.1	40.8	32.0	22.4	40.7
Extreme Maximum Temp. (°F)	65	72	82	87	95	101	100	100	97	89	80	73	101
Extreme Minimum Temp. (°F)	-36	-21	-12	18	28	37	44	38	28	17	1	-26	-36
Days Maximum Temp. ≥ 90°F	0	0	0	0	0	3	7	5	2	0	0	0	17
Days Maximum Temp. ≤ 32°F	14	9	2	0	0	0	0	0	0	0	1	8	34
Days Minimum Temp. ≤ 32°F	29	24	19	7	1	0	0	0	0	7	17	26	130
Days Minimum Temp. ≤ 0°F	5	3	0	0	0	0	0	0	0	0	0	2	10
Heating Degree Days (base 65°F)	1,241	1,017	757	420	160	22	3	10	92	373	693	1,056	5,844
Cooling Degree Days (base 65°F)	0	0	1	10	63	206	303	243	106	12	0	0	944
Mean Precipitation (in.)	2.23	2.12	3.62	4.20	4.51	4.04	4.28	3.64	2.86	2.89	4.01	3.06	41.46
Days With ≥ 0.1" Precipitation	6	na	8	9	8	7	7	6	5	5	7	6	na
Days With ≥ 1.0" Precipitation	0	0	1	1	1	1	1	1	1	1	1	0	9
Mean Snowfall (in.)	na	na	na	0.4	0.0	0.0	0.0	0.0	0.0	0.3	0.4	na	na
Days With ≥ 1.0" Snow Depth	na	na	na	0	0	0	0	0	0	0	na	na	na

North Vernon 1 NW *Jennings County*   Elevation: 744 ft.   Latitude: 39° 02' N   Longitude: 85° 38' W

	JAN	FEB	MAR	APR	MAY	JUN	JUL	AUG	SEP	OCT	NOV	DEC	YEAR
Mean Maximum Temp. (°F)	38.6	44.7	55.0	66.5	75.3	83.6	86.8	84.8	na	67.6	54.2	44.1	na
Mean Temp. (°F)	29.9	34.7	44.5	54.6	63.6	72.2	75.8	73.9	na	56.1	45.1	35.4	na
Mean Minimum Temp. (°F)	21.2	24.8	34.0	42.7	51.8	60.7	64.8	62.9	na	44.5	35.9	26.8	na
Extreme Maximum Temp. (°F)	67	76	85	87	93	101	102	103	94	90	80	74	103
Extreme Minimum Temp. (°F)	-24	-12	-6	19	29	38	45	40	33	18	3	-22	-24
Days Maximum Temp. ≥ 90°F	0	0	0	0	0	4	8	5	2	0	0	0	19
Days Maximum Temp. ≤ 32°F	9	5	1	0	0	0	0	0	0	0	0	4	19
Days Minimum Temp. ≤ 32°F	24	19	15	5	1	0	0	0	0	4	12	20	100
Days Minimum Temp. ≤ 0°F	2	1	0	0	0	0	0	0	0	0	0	1	4
Heating Degree Days (base 65°F)	1,080	847	632	322	117	12	1	2	na	290	592	911	na
Cooling Degree Days (base 65°F)	0	0	5	18	79	245	362	293	na	23	1	0	na
Mean Precipitation (in.)	2.30	2.59	3.71	4.45	4.50	3.65	4.41	4.42	2.89	3.18	3.97	3.33	43.40
Days With ≥ 0.1" Precipitation	6	5	7	8	7	6	6	6	5	6	7	6	75
Days With ≥ 1.0" Precipitation	0	1	1	1	1	1	1	1	1	1	1	1	11
Mean Snowfall (in.)	4.0	2.8	1.7	0.1	trace	0.0	0.0	0.0	0.0	0.0	0.2	na	na
Days With ≥ 1.0" Snow Depth	na	5	1	0	0	0	0	0	0	0	0	na	na

Oaklandon Geist Reservoir *Marion County*   Elevation: 793 ft.   Latitude: 39° 54' N   Longitude: 85° 59' W

	JAN	FEB	MAR	APR	MAY	JUN	JUL	AUG	SEP	OCT	NOV	DEC	YEAR
Mean Maximum Temp. (°F)	33.4	38.2	49.3	61.6	72.2	80.8	84.4	82.7	76.6	64.7	50.5	38.7	61.1
Mean Temp. (°F)	25.1	28.9	39.3	50.4	61.2	70.2	74.1	72.0	65.3	53.3	41.8	30.8	51.0
Mean Minimum Temp. (°F)	16.8	19.5	29.3	39.1	50.2	59.5	63.7	61.3	53.9	41.8	32.9	22.8	40.9
Extreme Maximum Temp. (°F)	65	72	83	86	91	102	100	99	94	89	78	72	102
Extreme Minimum Temp. (°F)	-23	-17	-8	15	27	38	46	41	32	16	6	-20	-23
Days Maximum Temp. ≥ 90°F	0	0	0	0	0	3	6	4	1	0	0	0	14
Days Maximum Temp. ≤ 32°F	15	9	3	0	0	0	0	0	0	0	1	8	36
Days Minimum Temp. ≤ 32°F	28	24	20	8	0	0	0	0	0	6	16	25	127
Days Minimum Temp. ≤ 0°F	5	3	0	0	0	0	0	0	0	0	0	2	10
Heating Degree Days (base 65°F)	1,229	1,013	788	442	169	27	3	9	91	369	691	1,055	5,886
Cooling Degree Days (base 65°F)	0	0	2	8	54	189	293	236	97	13	0	0	892
Mean Precipitation (in.)	2.28	2.32	3.36	3.97	4.84	4.10	4.72	4.02	3.35	3.08	3.90	3.15	43.09
Days With ≥ 0.1" Precipitation	5	5	7	9	9	7	7	6	6	6	7	7	81
Days With ≥ 1.0" Precipitation	0	0	0	1	1	1	1	1	1	1	1	1	9
Mean Snowfall (in.)	7.6	5.7	2.8	0.4	0.0	0.0	0.0	0.0	0.0	0.3	0.9	5.4	23.1
Days With ≥ 1.0" Snow Depth	10	8	2	0	0	0	0	0	0	0	0	5	25

Oolitic Purdue Exp. Farm *Lawrence County*   Elevation: 649 ft.   Latitude: 38° 53' N   Longitude: 86° 33' W

	JAN	FEB	MAR	APR	MAY	JUN	JUL	AUG	SEP	OCT	NOV	DEC	YEAR
Mean Maximum Temp. (°F)	36.5	42.0	52.5	63.9	73.6	81.7	85.8	84.5	78.4	66.6	53.7	42.3	63.5
Mean Temp. (°F)	27.2	31.5	41.4	52.0	61.8	70.6	74.7	73.1	65.9	53.7	43.3	32.9	52.3
Mean Minimum Temp. (°F)	17.8	20.9	30.3	40.0	50.0	59.4	63.6	61.6	53.4	40.7	32.9	23.5	41.2
Extreme Maximum Temp. (°F)	68	74	82	88	91	102	102	102	96	88	81	75	102
Extreme Minimum Temp. (°F)	-29	-14	-5	15	27	38	47	41	31	16	6	-23	-29
Days Maximum Temp. ≥ 90°F	0	0	0	0	0	3	8	6	2	0	0	0	19
Days Maximum Temp. ≤ 32°F	11	7	2	0	0	0	0	0	0	0	1	6	27
Days Minimum Temp. ≤ 32°F	28	24	19	8	1	0	0	0	0	7	16	24	127
Days Minimum Temp. ≤ 0°F	4	3	0	0	0	0	0	0	0	0	0	1	8
Heating Degree Days (base 65°F)	1,165	940	726	393	153	21	2	5	84	357	645	988	5,479
Cooling Degree Days (base 65°F)	0	0	3	10	61	205	326	271	117	13	0	0	1,006
Mean Precipitation (in.)	2.70	2.61	3.80	4.59	4.99	3.94	4.39	4.09	2.93	3.31	3.87	3.27	44.49
Days With ≥ 0.1" Precipitation	6	5	7	8	8	7	6	6	5	6	7	6	77
Days With ≥ 1.0" Precipitation	1	0	1	1	1	1	1	1	1	1	1	1	11
Mean Snowfall (in.)	5.8	3.8	2.7	trace	trace	0.0	0.0	0.0	0.0	trace	0.4	2.6	15.3
Days With ≥ 1.0" Snow Depth	9	7	2	0	0	0	0	0	0	0	0	4	22

Paoli *Orange County*   Elevation: 557 ft.   Latitude: 38° 33' N   Longitude: 86° 29' W

	JAN	FEB	MAR	APR	MAY	JUN	JUL	AUG	SEP	OCT	NOV	DEC	YEAR
Mean Maximum Temp. (°F)	39.2	45.1	55.5	66.3	76.3	83.7	87.9	86.1	79.9	68.9	55.4	44.1	65.7
Mean Temp. (°F)	29.2	33.7	43.5	53.6	63.4	71.8	76.0	74.0	66.9	55.3	44.4	34.1	53.8
Mean Minimum Temp. (°F)	19.2	22.3	31.4	40.9	50.5	59.8	64.1	61.9	54.0	41.7	33.3	24.1	41.9
Extreme Maximum Temp. (°F)	70	76	85	90	93	98	103	101	99	90	81	77	103
Extreme Minimum Temp. (°F)	-29	-15	-9	16	26	37	42	44	30	15	5	-19	-29
Days Maximum Temp. ≥ 90°F	0	0	0	0	1	6	12	9	3	0	0	0	31
Days Maximum Temp. ≤ 32°F	9	5	1	0	0	0	0	0	0	0	1	5	21
Days Minimum Temp. ≤ 32°F	27	22	17	7	1	0	0	0	0	7	15	23	119
Days Minimum Temp. ≤ 0°F	3	2	0	0	0	0	0	0	0	0	0	1	6
Heating Degree Days (base 65°F)	1,102	877	664	352	124	17	2	3	72	313	612	950	5,088
Cooling Degree Days (base 65°F)	0	0	4	16	84	236	373	301	131	22	1	0	1,168
Mean Precipitation (in.)	3.11	2.91	4.49	5.08	5.13	4.24	4.38	4.04	3.26	3.12	4.22	3.51	47.49
Days With ≥ 0.1" Precipitation	6	6	8	9	8	7	7	6	5	5	7	6	80
Days With ≥ 1.0" Precipitation	1	1	1	1	1	1	2	1	1	1	1	1	13
Mean Snowfall (in.)	na	na	1.3	0.1	0.0	0.0	0.0	0.0	0.0	0.0	0.2	2.4	na
Days With ≥ 1.0" Snow Depth	na	na	1	0	0	0	0	0	0	0	0	2	na

Portland 1 SW *Jay County*   Elevation: 908 ft.   Latitude: 40° 25' N   Longitude: 85° 00' W

	JAN	FEB	MAR	APR	MAY	JUN	JUL	AUG	SEP	OCT	NOV	DEC	YEAR
Mean Maximum Temp. (°F)	31.5	36.1	47.2	60.1	71.0	80.0	84.0	81.6	76.1	63.0	49.6	37.4	59.8
Mean Temp. (°F)	23.6	27.0	37.2	48.9	59.9	69.2	73.2	70.6	63.9	51.5	40.6	29.6	49.6
Mean Minimum Temp. (°F)	15.6	17.8	27.2	37.6	48.7	58.3	62.4	59.6	51.6	39.9	31.6	21.7	39.3
Extreme Maximum Temp. (°F)	64	72	81	87	91	102	101	100	96	86	78	72	102
Extreme Minimum Temp. (°F)	-29	-16	-13	10	27	38	45	39	28	17	4	-21	-29
Days Maximum Temp. ≥ 90°F	0	0	0	0	0	3	6	3	1	0	0	0	13
Days Maximum Temp. ≤ 32°F	16	12	4	0	0	0	0	0	0	0	2	10	44
Days Minimum Temp. ≤ 32°F	28	25	22	9	1	0	0	0	0	7	18	26	136
Days Minimum Temp. ≤ 0°F	5	4	0	0	0	0	0	0	0	0	0	2	11
Heating Degree Days (base 65°F)	1,279	1,067	856	484	204	39	6	18	115	422	726	1,092	6,308
Cooling Degree Days (base 65°F)	0	0	2	7	51	177	274	206	88	11	0	0	816
Mean Precipitation (in.)	1.88	1.90	2.63	3.64	3.87	4.09	4.45	3.90	2.66	2.60	3.06	2.45	37.13
Days With ≥ 0.1" Precipitation	5	5	6	8	8	7	7	6	5	6	6	6	75
Days With ≥ 1.0" Precipitation	0	0	0	1	1	1	2	1	1	1	1	0	9
Mean Snowfall (in.)	6.3	5.8	2.9	0.4	0.0	0.0	0.0	0.0	0.0	0.2	0.7	4.7	21.0
Days With ≥ 1.0" Snow Depth	10	7	2	0	0	0	0	0	0	0	1	5	25

Princeton 1 W *Gibson County*   Elevation: 479 ft.   Latitude: 38° 21' N   Longitude: 87° 35' W

	JAN	FEB	MAR	APR	MAY	JUN	JUL	AUG	SEP	OCT	NOV	DEC	YEAR
Mean Maximum Temp. (°F)	37.2	43.6	54.6	66.1	75.8	84.7	88.2	86.5	80.2	68.5	54.3	42.9	65.2
Mean Temp. (°F)	29.4	34.9	44.9	55.6	65.3	74.2	77.9	76.0	69.3	57.6	45.8	35.2	55.5
Mean Minimum Temp. (°F)	21.5	26.0	35.2	45.0	54.6	63.6	67.6	65.6	58.3	46.5	37.1	27.4	45.7
Extreme Maximum Temp. (°F)	69	77	83	88	95	101	102	101	98	89	81	75	102
Extreme Minimum Temp. (°F)	-19	-10	-2	21	32	44	48	47	34	20	9	-15	-19
Days Maximum Temp. ≥ 90°F	0	0	0	0	1	8	14	10	4	0	0	0	37
Days Maximum Temp. ≤ 32°F	11	6	1	0	0	0	0	0	0	0	0	6	24
Days Minimum Temp. ≤ 32°F	26	19	13	3	0	0	0	0	0	2	10	21	94
Days Minimum Temp. ≤ 0°F	2	1	0	0	0	0	0	0	0	0	0	1	4
Heating Degree Days (base 65°F)	1,098	845	619	300	93	7	0	1	47	253	573	918	4,754
Cooling Degree Days (base 65°F)	0	0	3	21	109	297	422	356	175	29	1	0	1,413
Mean Precipitation (in.)	2.71	2.79	4.33	4.71	5.14	4.00	3.98	3.81	3.10	3.41	4.44	3.59	46.01
Days With ≥ 0.1" Precipitation	6	5	8	8	8	6	6	5	5	5	7	7	76
Days With ≥ 1.0" Precipitation	0	1	1	1	2	1	1	1	1	1	1	1	12
Mean Snowfall (in.)	na	3.8	1.0	0.3	0.0	0.0	0.0	0.0	0.0	0.1	0.3	2.1	na
Days With ≥ 1.0" Snow Depth	na	na	1	0	0	0	0	0	0	0	0	1	na

Rensselaer *Jasper County*   Elevation: 649 ft.   Latitude: 40° 56' N   Longitude: 87° 09' W

	JAN	FEB	MAR	APR	MAY	JUN	JUL	AUG	SEP	OCT	NOV	DEC	YEAR
Mean Maximum Temp. (°F)	31.1	36.0	46.9	59.8	72.5	81.5	84.6	82.3	75.8	63.5	48.7	35.9	59.9
Mean Temp. (°F)	23.2	27.5	37.9	49.2	61.4	70.6	74.1	71.7	64.2	52.3	40.3	28.5	50.1
Mean Minimum Temp. (°F)	15.3	18.9	28.9	38.9	50.2	59.6	63.5	61.1	52.7	41.0	31.9	21.3	40.3
Extreme Maximum Temp. (°F)	64	78	83	90	94	103	101	104	96	90	77	67	104
Extreme Minimum Temp. (°F)	-25	-22	-5	2	28	37	42	41	30	21	2	-23	-25
Days Maximum Temp. ≥ 90°F	0	0	0	0	1	5	8	4	1	0	0	0	19
Days Maximum Temp. ≤ 32°F	16	11	4	0	0	0	0	0	0	0	2	10	43
Days Minimum Temp. ≤ 32°F	29	24	20	7	0	0	0	0	0	5	17	26	128
Days Minimum Temp. ≤ 0°F	5	3	0	0	0	0	0	0	0	0	0	2	10
Heating Degree Days (base 65°F)	1,289	1,054	835	475	175	30	6	11	110	397	733	1,125	6,240
Cooling Degree Days (base 65°F)	0	0	2	9	66	210	304	236	98	9	0	0	934
Mean Precipitation (in.)	1.99	1.67	3.16	3.53	4.27	4.36	3.84	3.51	3.45	3.10	3.24	2.68	38.80
Days With ≥ 0.1" Precipitation	5	5	7	7	7	7	6	6	6	6	6	6	74
Days With ≥ 1.0" Precipitation	0	0	0	1	1	1	1	1	1	1	1	0	8
Mean Snowfall (in.)	na	na	na	0.3	0.0	0.0	0.0	0.0	0.0	trace	0.5	na	na
Days With ≥ 1.0" Snow Depth	na	na	na	0	0	0	0	0	0	0	1	na	na

Richmond Water Works *Wayne County*   Elevation: 1,013 ft.   Latitude: 39° 53' N   Longitude: 84° 53' W

	JAN	FEB	MAR	APR	MAY	JUN	JUL	AUG	SEP	OCT	NOV	DEC	YEAR
Mean Maximum Temp. (°F)	34.1	39.0	50.2	62.0	72.6	81.0	84.7	82.9	76.6	64.3	50.9	39.6	61.5
Mean Temp. (°F)	25.6	29.7	40.0	50.5	61.0	69.6	73.5	71.6	64.7	52.8	41.9	31.6	51.0
Mean Minimum Temp. (°F)	17.1	20.3	29.7	38.9	49.3	58.1	62.3	60.3	52.8	41.2	32.8	23.5	40.5
Extreme Maximum Temp. (°F)	64	73	82	87	92	99	100	100	94	88	78	72	100
Extreme Minimum Temp. (°F)	-27	-20	-9	14	26	37	42	41	30	16	-22	-27
Days Maximum Temp. ≥ 90°F	0	0	0	0	0	3	6	4	1	0	0	0	14
Days Maximum Temp. ≤ 32°F	13	9	3	0	0	0	0	0	0	0	1	8	34
Days Minimum Temp. ≤ 32°F	28	24	20	8	1	0	0	0	0	6	16	25	128
Days Minimum Temp. ≤ 0°F	5	3	0	0	0	0	0	0	0	0	0	1	9
Heating Degree Days (base 65°F)	1,214	991	771	436	173	29	3	8	97	381	688	1,029	5,820
Cooling Degree Days (base 65°F)	0	0	2	6	55	181	287	227	92	11	0	0	861
Mean Precipitation (in.)	2.46	2.25	3.18	3.91	4.33	4.22	3.78	3.59	2.45	3.05	3.30	2.88	39.40
Days With ≥ 0.1" Precipitation	6	5	7	8	8	8	6	6	5	6	6	6	77
Days With ≥ 1.0" Precipitation	0	0	0	1	1	1	1	1	1	0	1	1	8
Mean Snowfall (in.)	6.7	4.7	2.4	0.7	trace	0.0	0.0	0.0	0.0	0.2	0.9	3.1	18.7
Days With ≥ 1.0" Snow Depth	10	8	2	0	0	0	0	0	0	0	0	4	24

Rochester *Fulton County*   Elevation: 767 ft.   Latitude: 41° 04' N   Longitude: 86° 13' W

	JAN	FEB	MAR	APR	MAY	JUN	JUL	AUG	SEP	OCT	NOV	DEC	YEAR
Mean Maximum Temp. (°F)	30.0	35.1	46.2	59.1	71.1	80.0	83.9	81.7	75.3	62.9	48.3	36.2	59.1
Mean Temp. (°F)	22.1	26.3	36.6	48.2	59.8	69.1	73.0	70.8	63.6	51.7	39.9	28.6	49.1
Mean Minimum Temp. (°F)	14.1	17.3	26.9	37.3	48.5	58.2	62.2	59.8	51.9	40.4	31.5	21.1	39.1
Extreme Maximum Temp. (°F)	66	72	80	89	93	102	103	101	96	90	77	70	103
Extreme Minimum Temp. (°F)	-25	-16	-7	8	27	36	42	37	29	16	-22	-25
Days Maximum Temp. ≥ 90°F	0	0	0	0	1	3	7	3	1	0	0	0	15
Days Maximum Temp. ≤ 32°F	17	12	4	0	0	0	0	0	0	0	2	10	45
Days Minimum Temp. ≤ 32°F	29	25	23	9	1	0	0	0	0	6	17	27	137
Days Minimum Temp. ≤ 0°F	6	4	0	0	0	0	0	0	0	0	0	2	12
Heating Degree Days (base 65°F)	1,324	1,087	875	504	208	40	7	16	123	415	748	1,120	6,467
Cooling Degree Days (base 65°F)	0	0	1	7	52	174	268	206	82	8	0	0	798
Mean Precipitation (in.)	1.99	1.71	2.71	3.90	4.12	4.01	3.87	3.63	3.54	2.92	3.42	2.66	38.48
Days With ≥ 0.1" Precipitation	5	5	6	8	8	7	7	6	6	6	7	7	78
Days With ≥ 1.0" Precipitation	0	0	0	1	1	1	1	1	1	1	1	0	8
Mean Snowfall (in.)	*9.5*	8.3	3.8	1.2	0.0	0.0	0.0	0.0	0.0	0.3	2.7	6.7	*32.5*
Days With ≥ 1.0" Snow Depth	na	na	na	0	0	0	0	0	0	0	*0*	na	na

Rockville *Parke County*   Elevation: 688 ft.   Latitude: 39° 46' N   Longitude: 87° 14' W

	JAN	FEB	MAR	APR	MAY	JUN	JUL	AUG	SEP	OCT	NOV	DEC	YEAR
Mean Maximum Temp. (°F)	35.5	41.7	53.1	65.7	75.8	84.3	87.4	85.1	79.2	67.6	53.2	40.8	64.1
Mean Temp. (°F)	26.8	32.1	42.6	53.8	63.7	72.5	76.1	73.8	67.4	55.9	44.0	32.7	53.4
Mean Minimum Temp. (°F)	17.9	22.5	32.0	41.9	51.6	60.7	64.8	62.4	55.5	44.1	34.9	24.5	42.7
Extreme Maximum Temp. (°F)	66	73	84	89	93	103	104	102	96	89	79	74	104
Extreme Minimum Temp. (°F)	-25	-18	-5	15	31	38	46	39	31	19	6	-21	-25
Days Maximum Temp. ≥ 90°F	0	0	0	0	1	7	11	6	3	0	0	0	28
Days Maximum Temp. ≤ 32°F	12	7	1	0	0	0	0	0	0	0	1	6	27
Days Minimum Temp. ≤ 32°F	27	22	17	6	0	0	0	0	0	4	14	24	114
Days Minimum Temp. ≤ 0°F	4	2	0	0	0	0	0	0	0	0	0	1	7
Heating Degree Days (base 65°F)	1,180	923	690	347	116	12	1	5	63	295	625	995	5,252
Cooling Degree Days (base 65°F)	0	0	3	17	84	255	364	297	138	20	1	0	1,179
Mean Precipitation (in.)	2.51	2.15	3.74	4.25	4.76	4.11	4.81	4.24	3.15	3.08	4.25	3.47	44.52
Days With ≥ 0.1" Precipitation	6	5	7	8	8	7	6	6	5	6	7	6	77
Days With ≥ 1.0" Precipitation	0	1	1	1	1	1	2	1	1	1	1	1	12
Mean Snowfall (in.)	5.0	3.3	2.2	0.2	trace	0.0	0.0	0.0	0.0	0.0	0.4	5.2	16.3
Days With ≥ 1.0" Snow Depth	11	*7*	2	0	0	0	0	0	0	0	0	5	*25*

Rushville Sewage Plant *Rush County*   Elevation: 958 ft.   Latitude: 39° 36' N   Longitude: 85° 27' W

	JAN	FEB	MAR	APR	MAY	JUN	JUL	AUG	SEP	OCT	NOV	DEC	YEAR
Mean Maximum Temp. (°F)	33.3	38.7	49.1	61.9	72.6	80.9	84.4	82.7	77.0	65.0	51.0	39.4	61.3
Mean Temp. (°F)	24.9	29.2	39.1	50.6	61.4	70.2	73.8	71.6	65.0	53.0	41.7	31.3	51.0
Mean Minimum Temp. (°F)	16.4	19.4	29.2	39.2	50.2	59.5	63.1	60.5	52.9	41.0	32.4	23.1	40.6
Extreme Maximum Temp. (°F)	64	72	83	87	92	100	100	103	93	88	78	72	103
Extreme Minimum Temp. (°F)	-28	-20	-16	16	28	38	40	41	32	17	6	-23	-28
Days Maximum Temp. ≥ 90°F	0	0	0	0	0	3	6	3	1	0	0	0	13
Days Maximum Temp. ≤ 32°F	14	10	3	0	0	0	0	0	0	0	1	8	36
Days Minimum Temp. ≤ 32°F	28	24	21	7	0	0	0	0	0	6	17	25	128
Days Minimum Temp. ≤ 0°F	5	3	0	0	0	0	0	0	0	0	0	2	10
Heating Degree Days (base 65°F)	1,240	1,006	798	435	164	26	3	9	94	376	692	1,038	5,881
Cooling Degree Days (base 65°F)	0	0	1	8	61	199	295	226	99	11	0	0	900
Mean Precipitation (in.)	2.55	2.51	3.20	4.24	4.94	4.20	4.47	3.54	2.85	2.85	3.55	3.06	41.96
Days With ≥ 0.1" Precipitation	6	5	7	8	8	7	7	6	5	5	7	6	77
Days With ≥ 1.0" Precipitation	0	0	1	1	2	1	1	1	1	1	1	1	11
Mean Snowfall (in.)	5.7	4.4	2.0	0.3	trace	0.0	0.0	0.0	0.0	0.3	0.6	2.8	16.1
Days With ≥ 1.0" Snow Depth	10	7	2	0	0	0	0	0	0	0	0	4	23

Saint Meinrad *Spencer County*   Elevation: 508 ft.   Latitude: 38° 10' N   Longitude: 86° 48' W

	JAN	FEB	MAR	APR	MAY	JUN	JUL	AUG	SEP	OCT	NOV	DEC	YEAR
Mean Maximum Temp. (°F)	40.4	46.8	57.2	68.0	76.6	84.1	87.3	86.3	80.6	69.8	56.8	45.5	66.6
Mean Temp. (°F)	31.8	36.9	46.4	56.3	65.0	73.2	76.8	75.5	69.3	57.8	47.1	36.9	56.1
Mean Minimum Temp. (°F)	23.2	27.0	35.7	44.5	53.3	62.3	66.3	64.6	57.9	45.7	37.4	28.3	45.5
Extreme Maximum Temp. (°F)	70	75	86	89	92	100	102	100	98	90	81	76	102
Extreme Minimum Temp. (°F)	-26	-10	-6	21	29	40	48	43	34	20	6	-18	-26
Days Maximum Temp. ≥ 90°F	0	0	0	0	0	5	11	9	3	0	0	0	28
Days Maximum Temp. ≤ 32°F	8	4	1	0	0	0	0	0	0	0	0	4	17
Days Minimum Temp. ≤ 32°F	24	19	14	4	0	0	0	0	0	3	11	20	95
Days Minimum Temp. ≤ 0°F	2	1	0	0	0	0	0	0	0	0	0	1	4
Heating Degree Days (base 65°F)	1,022	786	573	278	91	7	0	1	44	247	533	864	4,446
Cooling Degree Days (base 65°F)	0	0	6	22	96	262	382	336	170	31	2	1	1,308
Mean Precipitation (in.)	3.08	2.98	4.38	4.74	4.72	4.10	4.66	3.75	3.30	3.03	4.00	3.66	46.40
Days With ≥ 0.1" Precipitation	6	6	8	8	8	7	7	5	5	5	7	7	79
Days With ≥ 1.0" Precipitation	1	1	1	1	1	1	1	1	1	1	1	1	12
Mean Snowfall (in.)	3.8	*2.8*	*1.4*	trace	0.0	0.0	0.0	0.0	0.0	trace	0.1	1.6	*9.7*
Days With ≥ 1.0" Snow Depth	6	5	1	0	0	0	0	0	0	0	0	2	14

Salem *Washington County*   Elevation: 797 ft.   Latitude: 38° 37' N   Longitude: 86° 05' W

	JAN	FEB	MAR	APR	MAY	JUN	JUL	AUG	SEP	OCT	NOV	DEC	YEAR
Mean Maximum Temp. (°F)	39.4	45.1	55.4	66.6	75.6	83.8	87.0	85.8	80.0	68.6	55.4	44.5	65.6
Mean Temp. (°F)	30.7	34.8	44.4	54.6	63.7	72.3	76.0	74.3	68.0	56.5	45.7	35.9	54.7
Mean Minimum Temp. (°F)	22.0	24.5	33.4	42.5	51.8	60.8	64.9	62.8	56.0	44.3	35.9	27.2	43.8
Extreme Maximum Temp. (°F)	68	78	84	88	91	102	103	100	96	89	81	75	103
Extreme Minimum Temp. (°F)	-29	-15	-10	17	28	39	47	40	31	18	10	-13	-29
Days Maximum Temp. ≥ 90°F	0	0	0	0	0	4	10	8	2	0	0	0	24
Days Maximum Temp. ≤ 32°F	9	5	1	0	0	0	0	0	0	0	0	5	20
Days Minimum Temp. ≤ 32°F	25	21	16	6	0	0	0	0	0	5	12	20	105
Days Minimum Temp. ≤ 0°F	2	2	0	0	0	0	0	0	0	0	0	1	5
Heating Degree Days (base 65°F)	1,057	845	635	323	114	12	1	2	57	282	574	896	4,798
Cooling Degree Days (base 65°F)	0	0	4	17	83	234	357	301	140	23	1	0	1,160
Mean Precipitation (in.)	3.19	2.85	4.27	4.72	5.05	3.88	4.42	3.54	2.86	2.93	4.01	*3.86*	*45.58*
Days With ≥ 0.1" Precipitation	6	6	8	9	9	7	7	6	5	5	7	7	82
Days With ≥ 1.0" Precipitation	1	1	1	1	1	1	1	1	1	1	1	1	12
Mean Snowfall (in.)	5.7	5.6	3.4	0.2	0.0	0.0	0.0	0.0	0.0	0.2	0.5	2.4	18.0
Days With ≥ 1.0" Snow Depth	8	7	1	0	0	0	0	0	0	0	*0*	2	*18*

Scottsburg *Scott County*   Elevation: 547 ft.   Latitude: 38° 42' N   Longitude: 85° 46' W

	JAN	FEB	MAR	APR	MAY	JUN	JUL	AUG	SEP	OCT	NOV	DEC	YEAR
Mean Maximum Temp. (°F)	38.1	43.9	54.2	65.7	75.5	83.5	87.5	86.2	80.0	68.2	54.9	43.7	65.1
Mean Temp. (°F)	29.0	33.3	43.0	53.6	63.7	72.4	76.3	74.5	67.5	55.3	44.5	34.6	54.0
Mean Minimum Temp. (°F)	19.8	22.6	31.7	41.5	51.9	61.2	65.2	62.8	55.0	42.3	34.0	25.4	42.8
Extreme Maximum Temp. (°F)	69	75	83	89	92	101	103	103	97	91	82	76	103
Extreme Minimum Temp. (°F)	-32	-14	-9	19	29	39	47	41	31	19	6	-19	-32
Days Maximum Temp. ≥ 90°F	0	0	0	0	1	6	12	9	4	0	0	0	32
Days Maximum Temp. ≤ 32°F	10	6	1	0	0	0	0	0	0	0	0	5	22
Days Minimum Temp. ≤ 32°F	26	23	18	6	0	0	0	0	0	5	14	23	115
Days Minimum Temp. ≤ 0°F	3	2	0	0	0	0	0	0	0	0	0	1	6
Heating Degree Days (base 65°F)	1,111	890	678	352	122	14	1	3	65	315	611	937	5,099
Cooling Degree Days (base 65°F)	0	0	3	16	87	245	372	306	140	20	0	0	1,189
Mean Precipitation (in.)	2.97	2.67	4.15	4.43	4.71	4.16	4.27	4.32	3.02	3.01	3.64	3.33	44.68
Days With ≥ 0.1" Precipitation	6	6	8	8	9	7	6	7	5	6	7	7	82
Days With ≥ 1.0" Precipitation	1	1	1	1	1	1	1	1	1	1	1	1	12
Mean Snowfall (in.)	5.1	4.8	3.7	0.1	0.0	0.0	0.0	0.0	0.0	0.1	0.5	2.4	16.7
Days With ≥ 1.0" Snow Depth	7	6	2	0	0	0	0	0	0	0	0	3	18

Seymour 2 N *Jackson County*   Elevation: 567 ft.   Latitude: 38° 59' N   Longitude: 85° 54' W

	JAN	FEB	MAR	APR	MAY	JUN	JUL	AUG	SEP	OCT	NOV	DEC	YEAR
Mean Maximum Temp. (°F)	37.0	42.2	52.8	64.5	74.0	81.8	85.4	84.2	78.5	67.2	53.8	42.2	63.6
Mean Temp. (°F)	28.0	32.0	41.7	52.3	62.4	70.9	74.5	72.5	65.7	53.9	43.3	33.3	52.5
Mean Minimum Temp. (°F)	18.9	21.7	30.5	40.1	50.7	60.0	63.6	60.9	52.8	40.5	32.8	24.4	41.4
Extreme Maximum Temp. (°F)	67	74	84	88	91	101	104	102	95	92	82	75	104
Extreme Minimum Temp. (°F)	-23	-14	-10	9	29	41	47	42	29	15	8	-22	-23
Days Maximum Temp. ≥ 90°F	0	0	0	0	0	4	8	6	2	0	0	0	20
Days Maximum Temp. ≤ 32°F	11	6	1	0	0	0	0	0	0	0	1	6	25
Days Minimum Temp. ≤ 32°F	27	23	20	7	0	0	0	0	0	7	16	25	125
Days Minimum Temp. ≤ 0°F	3	2	0	0	0	0	0	0	0	0	0	1	6
Heating Degree Days (base 65°F)	1,142	925	719	386	144	20	2	6	86	353	645	975	5,403
Cooling Degree Days (base 65°F)	0	0	2	11	66	209	315	251	108	14	0	0	976
Mean Precipitation (in.)	3.05	2.70	3.79	4.73	4.94	4.04	4.41	4.33	3.00	3.30	4.00	3.35	45.64
Days With ≥ 0.1" Precipitation	7	6	8	9	9	7	7	7	6	6	7	7	86
Days With ≥ 1.0" Precipitation	1	0	1	1	1	1	1	1	1	1	1	1	11
Mean Snowfall (in.)	na	na	2.3	trace	0.0	0.0	0.0	0.0	0.0	0.2	0.6	*1.9*	na
Days With ≥ 1.0" Snow Depth	8	6	2	0	0	0	0	0	0	0	0	2	18

Shoals Hiway 50 Bridge *Martin County*   Elevation: 547 ft.   Latitude: 38° 40' N   Longitude: 86° 48' W

	JAN	FEB	MAR	APR	MAY	JUN	JUL	AUG	SEP	OCT	NOV	DEC	YEAR
Mean Maximum Temp. (°F)	37.5	43.4	53.9	65.6	75.3	83.2	86.8	85.4	79.4	68.0	54.6	43.1	64.7
Mean Temp. (°F)	28.2	32.7	42.5	52.9	62.5	71.2	75.2	73.6	66.8	54.9	44.2	33.9	53.2
Mean Minimum Temp. (°F)	18.9	21.9	30.9	40.2	49.7	59.3	63.6	61.7	54.2	41.8	33.9	24.6	41.7
Extreme Maximum Temp. (°F)	68	75	82	89	98	101	102	100	99	91	82	77	102
Extreme Minimum Temp. (°F)	-23	-12	-9	17	28	39	46	42	32	18	6	-20	-23
Days Maximum Temp. ≥ 90°F	0	0	0	0	1	6	10	7	3	0	0	0	27
Days Maximum Temp. ≤ 32°F	10	6	1	0	0	0	0	0	0	0	1	6	24
Days Minimum Temp. ≤ 32°F	27	22	18	8	1	0	0	0	0	7	15	23	121
Days Minimum Temp. ≤ 0°F	4	2	0	0	0	0	0	0	0	0	0	1	7
Heating Degree Days (base 65°F)	1,134	906	695	373	142	19	2	3	73	324	617	958	5,246
Cooling Degree Days (base 65°F)	0	0	4	15	70	219	338	279	128	19	1	0	1,073
Mean Precipitation (in.)	3.04	2.81	4.34	4.59	5.58	4.21	4.65	3.62	3.28	3.28	4.41	3.50	47.31
Days With ≥ 0.1" Precipitation	6	6	8	8	9	7	7	6	5	6	7	7	82
Days With ≥ 1.0" Precipitation	1	0	1	1	2	1	1	1	1	1	1	1	12
Mean Snowfall (in.)	5.7	4.0	2.8	trace	0.0	0.0	0.0	0.0	0.0	0.1	0.3	2.7	15.6
Days With ≥ 1.0" Snow Depth	10	7	2	0	0	0	0	0	0	0	0	4	23

Spencer *Owen County*   Elevation: 547 ft.   Latitude: 39° 17' N   Longitude: 86° 46' W

	JAN	FEB	MAR	APR	MAY	JUN	JUL	AUG	SEP	OCT	NOV	DEC	YEAR
Mean Maximum Temp. (°F)	35.1	40.5	51.3	63.0	73.1	81.4	85.2	83.6	77.5	65.9	52.5	40.9	62.5
Mean Temp. (°F)	25.7	30.0	40.0	50.6	60.8	69.9	73.8	72.0	64.8	52.6	42.0	31.7	51.2
Mean Minimum Temp. (°F)	16.4	19.4	28.7	38.1	48.4	58.4	62.5	60.4	52.0	39.3	31.5	22.4	39.8
Extreme Maximum Temp. (°F)	66	71	83	87	91	100	101	100	95	90	79	76	101
Extreme Minimum Temp. (°F)	-33	-19	-12	15	27	34	46	40	28	18	5	-24	-33
Days Maximum Temp. ≥ 90°F	0	0	0	0	0	3	7	4	2	0	0	0	16
Days Maximum Temp. ≤ 32°F	13	8	2	0	0	0	0	0	0	0	1	7	31
Days Minimum Temp. ≤ 32°F	28	24	21	10	1	0	0	0	0	9	18	25	136
Days Minimum Temp. ≤ 0°F	5	3	0	0	0	0	0	0	0	0	0	2	10
Heating Degree Days (base 65°F)	1,211	982	769	433	174	27	4	8	100	386	684	1,026	5,804
Cooling Degree Days (base 65°F)	0	0	1	6	43	178	283	225	90	8	0	0	834
Mean Precipitation (in.)	2.54	2.52	3.75	4.46	4.97	4.56	4.65	4.50	3.15	3.12	4.04	3.25	45.51
Days With ≥ 0.1" Precipitation	6	5	7	8	8	7	7	6	5	5	7	6	77
Days With ≥ 1.0" Precipitation	0	0	1	1	1	1	1	1	1	1	1	1	10
Mean Snowfall (in.)	*5.8*	5.0	2.3	0.3	0.0	0.0	0.0	0.0	0.0	trace	0.5	3.0	*16.9*
Days With ≥ 1.0" Snow Depth	10	7	2	0	0	0	0	0	0	0	0	4	23

Tell City *Perry County*   Elevation: 396 ft.   Latitude: 37° 57' N   Longitude: 86° 46' W

	JAN	FEB	MAR	APR	MAY	JUN	JUL	AUG	SEP	OCT	NOV	DEC	YEAR
Mean Maximum Temp. (°F)	39.5	45.0	55.3	66.6	75.9	84.0	87.8	86.8	80.8	69.1	56.1	45.1	66.0
Mean Temp. (°F)	31.4	35.6	45.1	55.3	64.8	73.6	77.7	76.3	69.7	57.5	46.7	36.9	55.9
Mean Minimum Temp. (°F)	23.3	26.3	34.9	44.0	53.6	63.1	67.6	65.7	58.6	45.9	37.3	28.5	45.7
Extreme Maximum Temp. (°F)	69	74	84	89	93	99	103	100	100	91	83	77	103
Extreme Minimum Temp. (°F)	-17	-5	-1	20	32	43	52	46	36	21	13	-14	-17
Days Maximum Temp. ≥ 90°F	0	0	0	0	1	6	13	11	4	0	0	0	35
Days Maximum Temp. ≤ 32°F	9	5	1	0	0	0	0	0	0	0	0	4	19
Days Minimum Temp. ≤ 32°F	24	20	14	3	0	0	0	0	0	2	10	20	93
Days Minimum Temp. ≤ 0°F	1	0	0	0	0	0	0	0	0	0	0	0	1
Heating Degree Days (base 65°F)	1,034	823	613	306	98	8	0	1	41	255	544	867	4,590
Cooling Degree Days (base 65°F)	0	0	4	21	97	279	418	366	185	31	1	0	1,402
Mean Precipitation (in.)	3.22	3.16	4.55	4.86	5.10	4.32	4.58	3.72	3.34	3.20	4.12	4.00	48.17
Days With ≥ 0.1" Precipitation	6	6	8	7	8	8	7	5	5	5	7	7	79
Days With ≥ 1.0" Precipitation	1	1	1	1	1	1	1	1	1	1	1	1	12
Mean Snowfall (in.)	*4.4*	*2.6*	0.7	0.1	0.0	0.0	0.0	0.0	0.0	0.0	0.4	*1.0*	9.2
Days With ≥ 1.0" Snow Depth	4	4	1	0	0	0	0	0	0	0	0	1	10

Terre Haute Indiana State *Vigo County*   Elevation: 505 ft.   Latitude: 39° 28' N   Longitude: 87° 25' W

	JAN	FEB	MAR	APR	MAY	JUN	JUL	AUG	SEP	OCT	NOV	DEC	YEAR
Mean Maximum Temp. (°F)	35.2	40.5	52.4	63.8	75.0	83.3	87.3	85.0	*79.4*	67.6	52.9	41.3	*63.6*
Mean Temp. (°F)	26.2	30.7	42.2	52.8	63.3	72.0	76.1	73.8	*67.3*	55.3	43.1	32.3	*52.9*
Mean Minimum Temp. (°F)	17.1	20.9	31.9	41.8	51.7	60.7	64.9	62.5	*55.1*	42.9	33.2	23.2	*42.1*
Extreme Maximum Temp. (°F)	67	*73*	*83*	*86*	*94*	*102*	*102*	98	*99*	*90*	*81*	*74*	*102*
Extreme Minimum Temp. (°F)	-24	*-20*	*-7*	*17*	*29*	*36*	*41*	42	*30*	*19*	*5*	*-22*	*-24*
Days Maximum Temp. ≥ 90°F	0	0	0	0	1	6	10	7	*3*	*0*	0	0	*27*
Days Maximum Temp. ≤ 32°F	13	7	1	0	0	0	0	0	0	*0*	1	6	*28*
Days Minimum Temp. ≤ 32°F	27	23	18	6	0	0	0	0	0	*5*	15	24	*118*
Days Minimum Temp. ≤ 0°F	*4*	2	0	0	0	0	0	0	0	0	0	1	*7*
Heating Degree Days (base 65°F)	1,197	962	702	373	125	15	1	3	*69*	*314*	652	1,007	*5,420*
Cooling Degree Days (base 65°F)	*0*	*0*	3	*13*	81	*239*	*365*	290	*144*	21	*0*	*0*	*1,156*
Mean Precipitation (in.)	2.15	2.52	3.68	4.19	4.40	4.02	4.36	3.80	3.02	*2.84*	3.72	3.05	*41.75*
Days With ≥ 0.1" Precipitation	6	5	7	9	8	7	7	6	5	*5*	7	6	*78*
Days With ≥ 1.0" Precipitation	0	1	1	1	1	1	1	1	*1*	*1*	1	1	*11*
Mean Snowfall (in.)	na	na	*1.6*	*trace*	0.0	0.0	0.0	0.0	0.0	*0.0*	*0.5*	*2.2*	na
Days With ≥ 1.0" Snow Depth	na	na	*1*	0	0	0	0	0	0	*0*	*0*	*3*	na

Valparaiso Waterworks *Porter County*   Elevation: 797 ft.   Latitude: 41° 31' N   Longitude: 87° 02' W

	JAN	FEB	MAR	APR	MAY	JUN	JUL	AUG	SEP	OCT	NOV	DEC	YEAR
Mean Maximum Temp. (°F)	30.5	35.8	47.0	59.8	71.4	80.1	83.3	80.9	74.6	63.3	48.6	36.1	59.3
Mean Temp. (°F)	22.9	27.7	38.0	49.2	60.1	69.1	73.1	70.9	64.3	53.2	40.8	29.3	49.9
Mean Minimum Temp. (°F)	15.3	19.5	28.9	38.5	48.7	58.1	62.8	61.0	53.9	43.0	33.0	22.5	40.4
Extreme Maximum Temp. (°F)	63	69	83	88	90	100	99	99	94	88	76	68	100
Extreme Minimum Temp. (°F)	-25	-18	-3	12	28	34	43	39	31	20	2	-20	-25
Days Maximum Temp. ≥ 90°F	0	0	0	0	0	2	4	2	1	0	0	0	9
Days Maximum Temp. ≤ 32°F	17	11	3	0	0	0	0	0	0	0	2	10	43
Days Minimum Temp. ≤ 32°F	29	24	21	8	1	0	0	0	0	4	16	26	129
Days Minimum Temp. ≤ 0°F	5	3	0	0	0	0	0	0	0	0	0	2	10
Heating Degree Days (base 65°F)	1,299	1,048	833	477	199	37	6	12	104	370	720	1,099	6,204
Cooling Degree Days (base 65°F)	0	0	2	8	53	169	271	206	90	10	0	0	809
Mean Precipitation (in.)	2.08	1.77	2.98	3.71	3.94	4.52	3.94	3.92	3.77	3.21	3.58	2.82	40.24
Days With ≥ 0.1" Precipitation	5	5	7	8	8	7	6	7	7	7	8	6	81
Days With ≥ 1.0" Precipitation	0	0	0	1	1	1	1	1	1	1	1	1	9
Mean Snowfall (in.)	11.8	9.2	5.7	1.1	trace	0.0	0.0	0.0	0.0	0.2	3.2	8.6	39.8
Days With ≥ 1.0" Snow Depth	20	13	5	0	0	0	0	0	0	0	2	11	51

Vevay *Switzerland County*   Elevation: 469 ft.   Latitude: 38° 45' N   Longitude: 85° 04' W

	JAN	FEB	MAR	APR	MAY	JUN	JUL	AUG	SEP	OCT	NOV	DEC	YEAR
Mean Maximum Temp. (°F)	40.0	45.8	56.7	68.0	77.3	85.0	88.5	86.9	80.4	68.6	55.7	45.1	66.5
Mean Temp. (°F)	31.4	35.6	45.3	55.2	64.7	73.0	77.1	75.5	68.8	56.8	46.0	36.5	55.5
Mean Minimum Temp. (°F)	22.7	25.5	33.8	42.3	52.1	61.0	65.6	64.1	57.2	44.9	36.2	27.8	44.4
Extreme Maximum Temp. (°F)	75	75	84	89	94	104	106	103	99	88	83	75	106
Extreme Minimum Temp. (°F)	-24	-11	-4	16	30	37	45	41	34	20	1	-18	-24
Days Maximum Temp. ≥ 90°F	0	0	0	0	1	7	14	10	3	0	0	0	35
Days Maximum Temp. ≤ 32°F	8	4	1	0	0	0	0	0	0	0	0	4	17
Days Minimum Temp. ≤ 32°F	24	20	15	5	0	0	0	0	0	2	11	20	97
Days Minimum Temp. ≤ 0°F	2	1	0	0	0	0	0	0	0	0	0	1	4
Heating Degree Days (base 65°F)	1,035	822	608	303	96	9	0	1	43	268	565	876	4,626
Cooling Degree Days (base 65°F)	0	0	3	16	95	264	401	347	162	23	1	0	1,312
Mean Precipitation (in.)	3.06	2.88	4.10	4.27	4.65	4.55	3.81	3.91	3.13	3.11	3.64	3.71	44.82
Days With ≥ 0.1" Precipitation	7	6	8	8	8	8	7	6	6	5	7	7	83
Days With ≥ 1.0" Precipitation	1	1	1	1	1	1	1	1	1	1	1	1	12
Mean Snowfall (in.)	6.5	5.1	3.3	0.1	trace	0.0	0.0	0.0	0.0	0.3	0.6	2.7	18.6
Days With ≥ 1.0" Snow Depth	8	6	1	0	0	0	0	0	0	0	0	3	18

Wanatah 2 WNW *Porter County*   Elevation: 734 ft.   Latitude: 41° 27' N   Longitude: 86° 56' W

	JAN	FEB	MAR	APR	MAY	JUN	JUL	AUG	SEP	OCT	NOV	DEC	YEAR
Mean Maximum Temp. (°F)	29.7	34.8	45.6	58.3	70.2	80.1	83.4	81.4	75.0	63.0	48.2	35.6	58.8
Mean Temp. (°F)	21.6	26.3	36.6	47.9	58.9	68.8	72.3	70.3	63.2	51.7	39.8	28.1	48.8
Mean Minimum Temp. (°F)	13.4	17.7	27.5	37.4	47.6	57.5	61.2	59.2	51.2	40.3	31.4	20.5	38.7
Extreme Maximum Temp. (°F)	63	71	82	90	93	105	101	101	96	89	77	70	105
Extreme Minimum Temp. (°F)	-26	-21	-6	10	26	33	42	38	27	18	2	-20	-26
Days Maximum Temp. ≥ 90°F	0	0	0	0	1	4	6	3	1	0	0	0	15
Days Maximum Temp. ≤ 32°F	18	12	4	0	0	0	0	0	0	0	2	11	47
Days Minimum Temp. ≤ 32°F	29	25	23	9	1	0	0	0	0	6	18	27	138
Days Minimum Temp. ≤ 0°F	6	4	0	0	0	0	0	0	0	0	0	3	13
Heating Degree Days (base 65°F)	1,340	1,088	876	516	235	48	13	21	129	414	751	1,138	6,569
Cooling Degree Days (base 65°F)	0	0	1	9	50	173	251	199	78	7	0	0	768
Mean Precipitation (in.)	1.63	1.56	2.78	3.63	3.74	4.27	4.15	3.68	3.77	2.91	3.41	2.48	38.01
Days With ≥ 0.1" Precipitation	4	4	6	8	7	7	6	6	7	6	7	6	74
Days With ≥ 1.0" Precipitation	0	0	0	1	1	1	1	1	1	1	1	0	8
Mean Snowfall (in.)	13.5	10.9	6.4	1.2	trace	0.0	0.0	0.0	0.0	0.3	3.3	8.9	44.5
Days With ≥ 1.0" Snow Depth	20	15	6	1	0	0	0	0	0	0	0	11	56

Warsaw *Kosciusko County*   Elevation: 807 ft.   Latitude: 41° 14' N   Longitude: 85° 52' W

	JAN	FEB	MAR	APR	MAY	JUN	JUL	AUG	SEP	OCT	NOV	DEC	YEAR
Mean Maximum Temp. (°F)	30.7	36.0	46.6	59.4	71.4	79.8	83.0	80.9	74.9	62.6	48.8	36.8	59.2
Mean Temp. (°F)	22.9	27.5	37.3	48.9	60.4	68.9	72.7	70.7	63.9	52.2	40.4	29.6	49.6
Mean Minimum Temp. (°F)	14.7	18.2	28.0	38.4	49.3	58.0	62.4	60.4	53.1	41.8	31.9	22.0	39.9
Extreme Maximum Temp. (°F)	63	73	82	87	91	102	103	98	95	86	76	69	103
Extreme Minimum Temp. (°F)	-25	-17	-9	8	28	34	42	37	29	19	3	-20	-25
Days Maximum Temp. ≥ 90°F	0	0	0	0	0	2	5	2	1	0	0	0	10
Days Maximum Temp. ≤ 32°F	17	11	3	0	0	0	0	0	0	0	2	10	43
Days Minimum Temp. ≤ 32°F	29	25	21	8	1	0	0	0	0	5	17	26	132
Days Minimum Temp. ≤ 0°F	5	3	0	0	0	0	0	0	0	0	0	2	10
Heating Degree Days (base 65°F)	1,302	1,057	854	486	193	38	8	16	112	398	733	1,092	6,289
Cooling Degree Days (base 65°F)	0	0	1	7	52	169	266	215	84	7	0	0	801
Mean Precipitation (in.)	1.81	1.39	2.08	3.46	3.75	4.43	3.99	3.96	3.21	3.25	2.93	2.51	36.77
Days With ≥ 0.1" Precipitation	5	4	5	8	7	7	7	7	6	6	6	6	74
Days With ≥ 1.0" Precipitation	0	0	0	1	1	1	1	1	1	1	1	0	8
Mean Snowfall (in.)	na	na	na	0.2	0.0	0.0	0.0	0.0	0.0	trace	na	na	na
Days With ≥ 1.0" Snow Depth	na	na	na	0	0	0	0	0	0	0	na	na	na

Washington *Daviess County*   Elevation: 524 ft.   Latitude: 38° 35' N   Longitude: 87° 12' W

	JAN	FEB	MAR	APR	MAY	JUN	JUL	AUG	SEP	OCT	NOV	DEC	YEAR
Mean Maximum Temp. (°F)	38.8	44.9	56.2	67.3	76.6	85.0	88.3	86.3	80.1	68.6	55.1	43.7	65.9
Mean Temp. (°F)	31.0	36.0	46.1	56.3	65.7	74.4	78.0	76.0	69.2	57.7	46.5	36.1	56.1
Mean Minimum Temp. (°F)	23.1	27.0	36.0	45.1	54.7	63.8	67.6	65.6	58.4	46.9	37.9	28.4	46.2
Extreme Maximum Temp. (°F)	68	76	84	88	94	101	104	101	97	89	80	75	104
Extreme Minimum Temp. (°F)	-18	-9	1	20	32	40	50	45	33	21	9	-19	-19
Days Maximum Temp. ≥ 90°F	0	0	0	0	1	7	13	9	3	0	0	0	33
Days Maximum Temp. ≤ 32°F	9	5	1	0	0	0	0	0	0	0	0	5	20
Days Minimum Temp. ≤ 32°F	24	18	13	3	0	0	0	0	0	2	10	20	90
Days Minimum Temp. ≤ 0°F	2	1	0	0	0	0	0	0	0	0	0	1	4
Heating Degree Days (base 65°F)	1,049	813	583	283	86	5	0	1	45	249	550	890	4,554
Cooling Degree Days (base 65°F)	0	0	4	25	110	297	421	356	173	31	1	0	1,418
Mean Precipitation (in.)	2.74	2.64	4.24	4.18	5.39	3.95	4.88	3.70	2.88	3.17	4.31	3.37	45.45
Days With ≥ 0.1" Precipitation	6	5	8	8	8	7	6	5	5	5	7	7	77
Days With ≥ 1.0" Precipitation	0	1	1	1	2	1	2	1	1	1	1	1	13
Mean Snowfall (in.)	4.2	3.0	1.8	trace	trace	0.0	0.0	0.0	0.0	trace	0.3	2.2	11.5
Days With ≥ 1.0" Snow Depth	6	5	1	0	0	0	0	0	0	0	0	2	14

West Lafayette 6 NW *Tippecanoe County*   Elevation: 702 ft.   Latitude: 40° 28' N   Longitude: 87° 00' W

	JAN	FEB	MAR	APR	MAY	JUN	JUL	AUG	SEP	OCT	NOV	DEC	YEAR
Mean Maximum Temp. (°F)	30.9	36.3	47.6	60.4	72.0	81.0	84.1	82.1	76.6	64.4	49.7	37.2	60.2
Mean Temp. (°F)	22.8	27.5	38.3	49.9	61.2	70.3	73.6	71.3	64.9	53.0	41.0	29.4	50.3
Mean Minimum Temp. (°F)	14.7	18.7	28.9	39.3	50.3	59.6	63.0	60.6	53.0	41.5	32.2	21.6	40.3
Extreme Maximum Temp. (°F)	64	72	82	88	93	103	100	98	96	90	78	71	103
Extreme Minimum Temp. (°F)	-24	-16	-4	7	28	35	42	38	25	19	5	-22	-24
Days Maximum Temp. ≥ 90°F	0	0	0	0	0	4	6	3	2	0	0	0	15
Days Maximum Temp. ≤ 32°F	16	11	3	0	0	0	0	0	0	0	2	10	42
Days Minimum Temp. ≤ 32°F	29	25	21	8	1	0	0	0	0	6	16	26	132
Days Minimum Temp. ≤ 0°F	6	4	0	0	0	0	0	0	0	0	0	2	12
Heating Degree Days (base 65°F)	1,301	1,053	822	457	177	30	6	13	103	380	713	1,096	6,151
Cooling Degree Days (base 65°F)	0	0	2	9	65	204	286	222	104	13	0	0	905
Mean Precipitation (in.)	1.75	1.51	2.88	3.77	4.17	4.10	3.98	3.66	3.11	2.77	3.06	2.37	37.13
Days With ≥ 0.1" Precipitation	4	3	6	8	8	7	7	6	5	5	6	6	71
Days With ≥ 1.0" Precipitation	0	0	0	1	1	1	1	1	1	1	1	0	8
Mean Snowfall (in.)	7.4	4.8	2.4	0.7	0.0	0.0	0.0	0.0	0.0	0.2	1.0	5.0	21.5
Days With ≥ 1.0" Snow Depth	14	9	4	0	0	0	0	0	0	0	1	7	35

W. Lafayette Purdue Univ. Arpt. *Tippecanoe County*   Elevation: 597 ft.   Latitude: 40° 25' N   Longitude: 86° 56' W

	JAN	FEB	MAR	APR	MAY	JUN	JUL	AUG	SEP	OCT	NOV	DEC	YEAR
Mean Maximum Temp. (°F)	31.7	37.0	49.4	62.1	73.5	82.8	86.2	83.9	77.4	65.1	49.9	38.3	61.4
Mean Temp. (°F)	23.9	28.7	40.2	50.9	61.7	71.2	75.3	73.3	66.1	54.1	41.7	31.0	51.5
Mean Minimum Temp. (°F)	16.0	20.4	30.8	39.7	49.9	59.7	64.3	62.6	54.6	43.0	33.5	23.8	41.5
Extreme Maximum Temp. (°F)	66	72	84	89	94	105	105	100	97	92	77	73	105
Extreme Minimum Temp. (°F)	-23	-20	-3	7	27	35	43	40	29	19	6	-16	-23
Days Maximum Temp. ≥ 90°F	0	0	0	0	1	6	10	6	2	0	0	0	25
Days Maximum Temp. ≤ 32°F	16	10	3	0	0	0	0	0	0	0	1	8	38
Days Minimum Temp. ≤ 32°F	28	23	18	7	1	0	0	0	0	5	15	24	121
Days Minimum Temp. ≤ 0°F	5	3	0	0	0	0	0	0	0	0	0	1	9
Heating Degree Days (base 65°F)	1,268	1,020	765	428	161	20	2	6	79	349	691	1,047	5,836
Cooling Degree Days (base 65°F)	0	0	1	11	59	218	334	281	116	17	0	0	1,037
Mean Precipitation (in.)	1.74	1.47	2.95	3.65	3.78	4.14	3.92	3.86	2.91	2.40	2.97	2.53	36.32
Days With ≥ 0.1" Precipitation	4	4	7	7	7	6	6	6	5	5	6	6	69
Days With ≥ 1.0" Precipitation	0	0	0	1	1	1	1	1	1	0	1	0	7
Mean Snowfall (in.)	7.2	4.8	2.1	0.6	trace	0.0	0.0	0.0	0.0	0.3	0.9	5.7	21.6
Days With ≥ 1.0" Snow Depth	13	9	3	0	0	0	0	0	0	0	1	6	32

Whitestown *Boone County*   Elevation: 935 ft.   Latitude: 40° 00' N   Longitude: 86° 21' W

	JAN	FEB	MAR	APR	MAY	JUN	JUL	AUG	SEP	OCT	NOV	DEC	YEAR
Mean Maximum Temp. (°F)	33.0	38.7	50.1	62.9	73.9	82.6	85.7	83.9	78.1	65.7	51.1	38.7	62.0
Mean Temp. (°F)	24.4	29.2	39.8	51.3	62.0	71.0	74.4	72.2	65.5	53.8	42.0	30.8	51.4
Mean Minimum Temp. (°F)	15.8	19.6	29.5	39.5	50.1	59.4	62.9	60.5	52.9	41.9	32.8	22.9	40.7
Extreme Maximum Temp. (°F)	64	73	82	88	94	104	103	100	96	90	78	73	104
Extreme Minimum Temp. (°F)	-27	-20	-10	15	27	35	44	37	28	19	5	-22	-27
Days Maximum Temp. ≥ 90°F	0	0	0	0	1	5	8	5	2	0	0	0	21
Days Maximum Temp. ≤ 32°F	14	9	2	0	0	0	0	0	0	0	1	8	34
Days Minimum Temp. ≤ 32°F	28	24	20	8	1	0	0	0	0	6	16	25	128
Days Minimum Temp. ≤ 0°F	6	4	0	0	0	0	0	0	0	0	0	2	12
Heating Degree Days (base 65°F)	1,251	1,006	777	416	156	22	3	9	89	353	684	1,052	5,818
Cooling Degree Days (base 65°F)	0	0	2	11	71	224	319	254	118	15	0	0	1,014
Mean Precipitation (in.)	2.41	2.29	3.40	3.94	4.45	4.05	4.64	3.50	2.99	2.95	3.67	3.01	41.30
Days With ≥ 0.1" Precipitation	6	5	7	9	9	7	7	6	6	5	7	7	81
Days With ≥ 1.0" Precipitation	0	0	0	1	1	1	1	1	1	1	1	0	8
Mean Snowfall (in.)	9.1	6.0	3.0	0.3	0.0	0.0	0.0	0.0	0.0	0.3	1.0	5.7	25.4
Days With ≥ 1.0" Snow Depth	13	9	3	0	0	0	0	0	0	0	1	6	32

Winamac 2 SSE *Pulaski County*   Elevation: 688 ft.   Latitude: 41° 02' N   Longitude: 86° 35' W

	JAN	FEB	MAR	APR	MAY	JUN	JUL	AUG	SEP	OCT	NOV	DEC	YEAR
Mean Maximum Temp. (°F)	31.2	36.4	47.9	61.3	72.4	80.5	83.6	81.2	74.9	63.4	49.2	36.7	59.9
Mean Temp. (°F)	22.8	27.4	38.1	50.0	61.1	69.7	73.3	71.1	64.2	52.7	40.5	29.0	50.0
Mean Minimum Temp. (°F)	14.4	18.4	28.2	38.6	49.8	58.9	62.9	60.9	53.4	41.9	31.8	21.2	40.0
Extreme Maximum Temp. (°F)	63	75	86	92	93	102	100	102	100	86	78	71	102
Extreme Minimum Temp. (°F)	-29	-20	-8	8	28	32	43	36	29	20	4	-23	-29
Days Maximum Temp. ≥ 90°F	0	0	0	0	1	3	5	2	1	0	0	0	12
Days Maximum Temp. ≤ 32°F	16	10	3	0	0	0	0	0	0	0	2	10	41
Days Minimum Temp. ≤ 32°F	29	24	22	8	1	0	0	0	0	5	17	27	133
Days Minimum Temp. ≤ 0°F	6	4	0	0	0	0	0	0	0	0	0	2	12
Heating Degree Days (base 65°F)	1,302	1,054	829	456	177	32	5	12	107	384	728	1,111	6,197
Cooling Degree Days (base 65°F)	0	0	1	10	60	186	280	218	91	9	0	0	855
Mean Precipitation (in.)	1.92	1.64	2.77	3.65	3.79	4.05	3.93	3.83	3.38	2.96	3.05	2.53	37.50
Days With ≥ 0.1" Precipitation	5	5	7	8	7	7	7	6	6	5	7	6	76
Days With ≥ 1.0" Precipitation	0	0	0	1	1	1	1	1	1	1	1	0	8
Mean Snowfall (in.)	8.5	5.3	3.2	1.2	trace	0.0	0.0	0.0	0.0	0.1	2.1	5.4	25.8
Days With ≥ 1.0" Snow Depth	16	12	4	0	0	0	0	0	0	0	1	8	41

Winchester Airport 3E *Randolph County*   Elevation: 1,108 ft.   Latitude: 40° 11' N   Longitude: 84° 55' W

	JAN	FEB	MAR	APR	MAY	JUN	JUL	AUG	SEP	OCT	NOV	DEC	YEAR
Mean Maximum Temp. (°F)	32.0	36.2	47.3	59.8	70.9	79.8	83.3	81.4	75.6	63.2	49.4	37.8	59.7
Mean Temp. (°F)	24.2	27.7	38.2	49.6	60.7	69.7	73.2	71.2	64.8	53.0	41.1	30.4	50.3
Mean Minimum Temp. (°F)	16.3	19.1	29.0	39.3	50.4	59.6	63.1	60.9	53.9	42.5	32.8	22.9	40.8
Extreme Maximum Temp. (°F)	63	72	80	85	91	101	100	97	93	88	78	71	101
Extreme Minimum Temp. (°F)	-26	-18	-11	12	27	40	48	39	29	19	6	-22	-26
Days Maximum Temp. ≥ 90°F	0	0	0	0	0	2	4	2	1	0	0	0	9
Days Maximum Temp. ≤ 32°F	16	11	4	0	0	0	0	0	0	0	2	9	42
Days Minimum Temp. ≤ 32°F	29	24	21	8	0	0	0	0	0	4	16	25	127
Days Minimum Temp. ≤ 0°F	5	3	0	0	0	0	0	0	0	0	0	2	10
Heating Degree Days (base 65°F)	1,259	1,047	826	464	182	32	5	13	100	379	710	1,066	6,083
Cooling Degree Days (base 65°F)	0	0	1	8	58	184	273	210	98	13	0	0	845
Mean Precipitation (in.)	1.79	1.60	2.87	3.69	4.05	4.33	4.29	3.53	2.69	2.66	3.23	2.75	37.48
Days With ≥ 0.1" Precipitation	*4*	4	6	8	8	7	7	6	5	6	7	*6*	*74*
Days With ≥ 1.0" Precipitation	1	0	0	1	1	1	1	1	1	1	1	0	9
Mean Snowfall (in.)	*5.1*	4.9	2.7	0.3	trace	0.0	trace	0.0	0.0	trace	0.6	2.7	*16.3*
Days With ≥ 1.0" Snow Depth	*12*	10	3	0	0	0	0	0	0	0	*1*	5	*31*

Note: See Appendix D for explanation of data.

IOWA

PHYSICAL FEATURES. The State of Iowa comprises 56,290 square miles, primarily of rolling prairie, located in the middle latitudes between the Upper Mississippi and the Missouri Rivers. The interior continental location is 800 to 1,000 miles distant from the Gulf of Mexico, North Atlantic, and Hudson Bay. The North Pacific Ocean is approximately 1,300 miles west and the Rocky Mountains shield is some 400 to 700 miles west of Iowa.

The extreme north-south distance across Iowa is 205 miles; the extreme east-west distance, 310 miles. Elevational changes are small across the State, varying from 1,675 feet on Ocheyedan Mound in the northwest to 477 feet at the mouth of the Des Moines River in the southeast. There is some rugged terrain, mostly of forest soils, in the northeast. Most of the State's lakes are located in the northwest.

GENERAL CLIMATE. Iowa's climate, because of latitude and interior continental location, is characterized by marked seasonal variations. During the six warm months of the year the prevailing moist, southerly flow from the Gulf of Mexico produces a summer rainfall maximum. The prevailing northwesterly flow of dry Canadian air in the winter causes this season to be cold and relatively dry. At intervals throughout the year, airmasses from the Pacific Ocean moving across the western United States reach Iowa, producing comparatively mild and dry weather. The autumnal "Indian Summers" are a result of the dominance of these modified Pacific airmasses. Hot, dry winds, originating in the desert southwest United States, occasionally sweep into Iowa during the summer, producing unusually high temperatures.

TEMPERATURE. The average annual temperatures range from 46°F. in the northern counties to 52°F. in the southeastern counties. In July, the hottest month, the average daily maximum is around 85°F. and the daily minima are mostly in the lower 60s. In January daily maxima range from 24 to 34°F., north to south, and the minima from 4 to 14°F.. In almost every year at some location in the State, a maximum exceeds 100°F. and a minimum of less than -20°F. occurs. In half the years the maximum exceeds 104°F. and the minimum -31°F. The average number of days with temperatures 90°F. or higher range from six to 47. The number of days with zero or lower temperatures range from about 10 per year in the south to 30 in the north.

PRECIPITATION. Precipitation averages around 31 inches per year for the State, ranging from 25 inches in the extreme northwest to about 34 inches in the East Central and Southeast Divisions. However, annual totals vary widely from year to year and locality to locality. Nearly two-thirds of the annual precipitation is measured during the six months of April through September. Measurable rain occurs on about 100 days per year; the frequency of a tenth of an inch or more increases southeastward across the State from 44 days per year to 69 days. Half an inch or more of rain per day varies from 15 days in the extreme northwest to near 25 in the southeast.

SNOWFALL. The average seasonal snowfall varies from near 20 inches at Keokuk to 35-45 inches over northern counties. The season normally extends from October or November to April but measurable snow has fallen as late in the season as May and as early as September. The average number of days with snow cover one inch or deeper per season varies from about 40 days along the southern border to around 90 in the northernmost counties. The average date of the first 1-inch snowfall varies from November 25 in the north to December 10 in the southeast. The first trace of snow occurs about one month earlier. In about half the years a daily snowfall of five inches or more occurs over southern Iowa, six or more over central counties, and seven or eight over northern counties. Late winter snowstorms have produced as much as 31 inches of snow in a single storm and 24-hour amounts have exceeded 20 inches.

STORMS. Around 80 percent of the 40 to 50 thunderstorms per year occur in the warm half of the state. Occasionally hail, high winds, heavy rains, and even tornadoes, are associated with the thunderstorms. The probability of occurrence is highest in late spring and early summer. Tornado frequency is highest in May and June in the afternoon and early evening. Tornado occurrences average about 15 per year on eight days. Damaging hailstorms, reaching a maximum in early summer, average 58 per year. Severe hailstorms are slightly more frequent over northwestern counties. In any locality hail usually occurs from two to six times a year.

Floods are most frequent in June at the normal maximum rainfall period, but also occur near the end of March, usually as a consequence of rain on frozen ground, or rain and rapid snowmelt. Ice jams often contribute to the spring flooding.

High winds at 15 feet above the ground (house-top level) reach 50 m.p.h. in about half the years. Winds to 75 m.p.h. at the 15-foot-level, excluding gusts, may be expected once in 50 years.

Drought occurs periodically in Iowa.

Sunshine increases from northeast to southwest. The percent of the possible sunshine varies from 40-52 in December, the cloudiest month, to 72-76 in July, the sunniest month. Available solar energy is four times as abundant in July as in December. The growing season for warm weather crops extends from mid-May to early October. The spring growing season, suitable for hardy crops, lasts approximately six weeks and the autumn season about seven weeks.

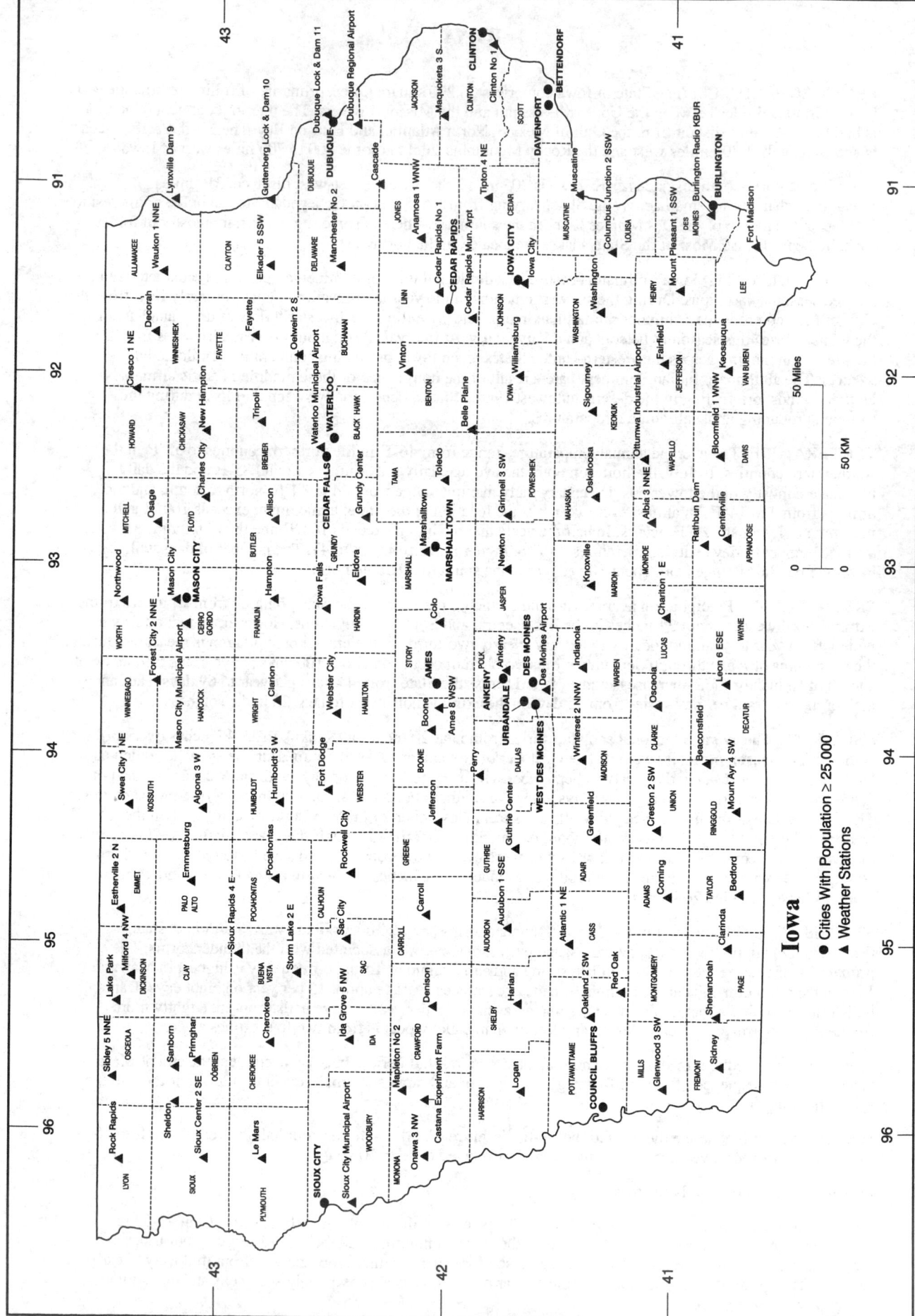

Iowa

● Cities With Population ≥ 25,000

▲ Weather Stations

Iowa Weather Stations by County

County	Station Name
Adair	Greenfield
Adams	Corning
Allamakee	Waukon 1 NNE
Appanoose	Centerville Rathbun Dam
Audubon	Audubon 1 SSE
Benton	Belle Plaine Vinton
Black Hawk	Waterloo Municipal Airport
Boone	Ames 8 WSW Boone
Bremer	Tripoli
Buena Vista	Sioux Rapids 4 E Storm Lake 2 E
Butler	Allison
Calhoun	Rockwell City
Carroll	Carroll
Cass	Atlantic 1 NE
Cedar	Tipton 4 NE
Cerro Gordo	Mason City Mason City Municipal Airport
Cherokee	Cherokee
Chickasaw	New Hampton
Clarke	Osceola
Clayton	Elkader 5 SSW Guttenberg Lock & Dam 10
Clinton	Clinton 1 Maquoketa 3 S
Crawford	Denison
Dallas	Perry
Davis	Bloomfield 1 WNW
Decatur	Leon 6 ESE
Delaware	Manchester 2
Des Moines	Burlington Radio KBUR
Dickinson	Lake Park Milford 4 NW

County	Station Name
Dubuque	Cascade Dubuque Lock & Dam 11 Dubuque Regional Airport
Emmet	Estherville 2 N
Fayette	Fayette Oelwein 2 S
Floyd	Charles City
Franklin	Hampton
Fremont	Sidney
Greene	Jefferson
Grundy	Grundy Center
Guthrie	Guthrie Center
Hamilton	Webster City
Hardin	Eldora Iowa Falls
Harrison	Logan
Henry	Mount Pleasant 1 SSW
Howard	Cresco 1 NE
Humboldt	Humboldt 3 W
Ida	Ida Grove 5 NW
Iowa	Williamsburg
Jackson	Bellevue Lock & Dam 12
Jasper	Newton
Jefferson	Fairfield
Johnson	Iowa City
Jones	Anamosa 1 WNW
Keokuk	Sigourney
Kossuth	Algona 3 W Swea City 1 NE
Lee	Fort Madison Keokuk
Linn	Cedar Rapids 1 Cedar Rapids Municipal Airport
Louisa	Columbus Junction 2 SSW
Lucas	Chariton 1 E
Lyon	Rock Rapids

County	Station Name
Madison	Winterset 2 NNW
Mahaska	Oskaloosa
Marion	Knoxville
Marshall	Marshalltown
Mills	Glenwood 3 SW
Mitchell	Osage
Monona	Castana Experiment Farm Mapleton 2 Onawa 3 NW
Monroe	Albia 3 NNE
Montgomery	Red Oak
Muscatine	Muscatine
O'brien	Primghar Sanborn Sheldon
Osceola	Sibley 5 NNE
Page	Clarinda Shenandoah
Palo Alto	Emmetsburg
Plymouth	Le Mars
Pocahontas	Pocahontas
Polk	Ankeny Des Moines Airport
Pottawattamie	Oakland 2 SW
Poweshiek	Grinnell 3 SW
Ringgold	Beaconsfield Mount Ayr 4 SW
Sac	Sac City
Scott	Le Claire Lock & Dam 14
Shelby	Harlan
Sioux	Hawarden Sioux Center 2 SE
Story	Colo
Tama	Toledo
Taylor	Bedford
Union	Creston 2 SW

County	Station Name
Van Buren	Keosauqua
Wapello	Ottumwa Industrial Airport
Warren	Indianola
Washington	Washington
Webster	Fort Dodge
Winnebago	Forest City 2 NNE
Winneshiek	Decorah
Woodbury	Sioux City Municipal Airport
Worth	Northwood
Wright	Clarion

Iowa Weather Stations by City

City	Station Name	Miles
Ames	Ames 8 WSW	7
	Boone	13
	Colo	17
Ankeny	Ankeny	2
	Des Moines Airport	14
Bettendorf	Geneseo, IL	19
	Moline Quad City Airport, IL	6
	Le Claire Lock & Dam 14	5
Burlington	La Harpe, IL	17
	Burlington Radio KBUR	3
	Fort Madison	17
Cedar Falls	Waterloo Municipal Airport	3
Cedar Rapids	Cedar Rapids Municipal Airport	8
	Cedar Rapids 1	5
Clinton	Fulton Lock & Dam 13, IL	4
	Morrison, IL	13
	Clinton 1	5
Council Bluffs	Glenwood 3 SW	19
	Omaha Eppley Airfield, NE	4
	Omaha WSFO, NE	11
Davenport	Moline Quad City Airport, IL	7
	Le Claire Lock & Dam 14	10
Des Moines	Ankeny	9
	Des Moines Airport	5
	Indianola	16
Dubuque	Dubuque Lock & Dam 11	3
	Dubuque Regional Airport	7
	Platteville, WI	20
Iowa City	Cedar Rapids Municipal Airport	18
	Iowa City	0
Marshalltown	Marshalltown	2
	Toledo	18
Mason City	Mason City	1
	Mason City Municipal Airport	7
	Northwood	20
Sioux City	Sioux City Municipal Airport	8
Urbandale	Ankeny	10
	Des Moines Airport	8
Waterloo	Waterloo Municipal Airport	5
West Des Moines	Ankeny	13
	Des Moines Airport	5
	Indianola	18

Note: Miles is the distance between the geographic center of the city and the weather station.

Iowa Weather Stations by Elevation

Feet	Station Name
1,669	Sibley 5 NNE
1,548	Sanborn
1,519	Primghar
1,463	Lake Park
1,450	Castana Experiment Farm
1,423	Storm Lake 2 E
1,417	Sheldon
1,417	Sioux Rapids 4 E
1,400	Denison
1,400	Milford 4 NW
1,358	Sioux Center 2 SE
1,348	Rock Rapids
1,338	Greenfield
1,318	Creston 2 SW
1,318	Ida Grove 5 NW
1,299	Estherville 2 N
1,299	Forest City 2 NNE
1,289	Audubon 1 SSE
1,269	Emmetsburg
1,253	Cresco 1 NE
1,243	Waukon 1 NNE
1,240	Carroll
1,240	Mount Ayr 4 SW
1,227	Algona 3 W
1,227	Hampton
1,227	Swea City 1 NE
1,213	Corning
1,210	Pocahontas
1,207	Harlan
1,197	Beaconsfield
1,197	Sac City
1,194	Le Mars
1,194	Rockwell City
1,190	Mason City Municipal Airport
1,187	Clarion
1,187	Hawarden
1,187	Mapleton 2
1,187	Northwood
1,177	Cherokee
1,167	Oakland 2 SW
1,167	Osage
1,167	Webster City
1,158	Atlantic 1 NE
1,158	New Hampton
1,141	Eldora
1,131	Bedford
1,128	Iowa Falls
1,128	Sidney
1,112	Fort Dodge
1,108	Humboldt 3 W
1,108	Osceola
1,099	Ames 8 WSW
1,092	Sioux City Municipal Airport
1,089	Mason City
1,072	Guthrie Center

Feet	Station Name
1,069	Winterset 2 NNW
1,059	Onawa 3 NW
1,053	Dubuque Regional Airport
1,049	Allison
1,049	Boone
1,049	Fayette
1,043	Jefferson
1,040	Red Oak
1,017	Charles City
1,017	Grundy Center
1,007	Oelwein 2 S
997	Colo
997	Leon 6 ESE
987	Logan
987	Manchester 2
977	Centerville
977	Clarinda
977	Glenwood 3 SW
974	Shenandoah
964	Perry
964	Rathbun Dam
958	Newton
958	Tripoli
954	Des Moines Airport
938	Ankeny
938	Chariton 1 E
938	Indianola
918	Knoxville
918	Toledo
902	Grinnell 3 SW
879	Albia 3 NNE
869	Marshalltown
862	Waterloo Municipal Airport
859	Decorah
849	Cascade
849	Cedar Rapids 1
849	Vinton
849	Williamsburg
839	Cedar Rapids Municipal Airport
839	Ottumwa Industrial Airport
830	Oskaloosa
810	Bloomfield 1 WNW
807	Belle Plaine
803	Anamosa 1 WNW
797	Sigourney
767	Elkader 5 SSW
767	Tipton 4 NE
754	Washington
738	Fairfield
728	Mount Pleasant 1 SSW
702	Burlington Radio KBUR
679	Maquoketa 3 S
669	Columbus Junction 2 SSW
639	Iowa City
623	Guttenberg Lock & Dam 10

Feet	Station Name
623	Keosauqua
620	Dubuque Lock & Dam 11
600	Bellevue Lock & Dam 12
583	Clinton 1
574	Keokuk
574	Le Claire Lock & Dam 14
547	Muscatine
528	Fort Madison

Des Moines Airport

Located in the heart of North America, Des Moines has a climate which is continental in character. This results in a marked seasonal contrast in both temperature and precipitation. There is a gently rolling terrain in and around the Des Moines metropolitan area. Drainage of the area is generally to the southeast to the Des Moines River and its tributaries.

Since agriculture and services for it are the mainstay of the area, it is convenient to separate the year into arbitrary seasons corresponding to the growing seasons of the principal crops of the section. The winter season, when most plant life is dormant, is from mid-November to late March. The summer season, when corn and soybeans can be grown, lasts from early May to early October. The spring growing season, including part of the growing season of oats and forage crops, and the fall harvest season, each runs about 6 weeks. There is a large variation in annual precipitation from a minimum of about 17 inches to a maximum of about 56 inches. The average annual snowfall is 32 inches. Annual variation of snowfall is also large, ranging from a minimum of about eight inches to as much as 72 inches.

The winter is a season of cold dry air, interrupted by occasional storms of short duration. At the beginning and the end of the season, the precipitation may occur as rain, but during the major portion of the season it falls as snow. Drifting snow may be extensive and impede transportation. The average precipitation for this season is approximately 20 percent of the annual amount. Although occasional cold waves follow the storms, bitterly cold days on which the temperatures fail to rise above zero occur on an average of only three days in four years.

The average growing season with temperatures above 32 degrees normally spans 160 to 165 days between late April and mid-October. The growing season is characterized by prevailing southerly winds and precipitation falling primarily as showers and thunderstorms, occasionally with damaging wind, erosive downpours or hail. Some 60 percent of the annual precipitation falls during the crop season with the maximum rate normally in late May and June. The autumn is characteristically sunny with diminishing precipitation, a condition favorable for drying and harvesting crops.

Des Moines Airport *Polk County*   Elevation: 954 ft.   Latitude: 41° 32' N   Longitude: 93° 40' W

	JAN	FEB	MAR	APR	MAY	JUN	JUL	AUG	SEP	OCT	NOV	DEC	YEAR
Mean Maximum Temp. (°F)	28.7	35.2	47.8	61.4	72.5	82.0	86.3	83.9	75.8	63.4	46.9	33.8	59.8
Mean Temp. (°F)	20.1	26.4	38.2	50.8	62.2	71.8	76.4	74.0	65.3	53.0	38.3	25.7	50.2
Mean Minimum Temp. (°F)	11.5	17.6	28.6	40.2	51.8	61.5	66.5	64.1	54.7	42.5	29.6	17.6	40.5
Extreme Maximum Temp. (°F)	65	73	91	93	93	103	104	108	98	92	81	69	108
Extreme Minimum Temp. (°F)	-24	-26	-9	9	31	41	47	41	28	14	-4	-22	-26
Days Maximum Temp. ≥ 90°F	0	0	0	0	0	5	10	7	2	0	0	0	24
Days Maximum Temp. ≤ 32°F	17	12	4	0	0	0	0	0	0	0	4	13	50
Days Minimum Temp. ≤ 32°F	30	25	20	6	0	0	0	0	0	5	19	29	134
Days Minimum Temp. ≤ 0°F	8	3	0	0	0	0	0	0	0	0	0	4	15
Heating Degree Days (base 65°F)	1,386	1,083	824	432	146	15	1	5	99	378	795	1,213	6,377
Cooling Degree Days (base 65°F)	0	0	2	14	59	219	356	292	113	10	0	0	1,065
Mean Precipitation (in.)	1.03	1.15	2.31	3.57	4.28	4.40	4.11	4.62	3.30	2.76	2.10	1.34	34.97
Maximum Precipitation (in.)	4.4	3.0	5.8	7.8	7.9	9.5	10.5	13.7	10.2	6.9	6.5	3.4	55.9
Minimum Precipitation (in.)	0.1	0.1	0.2	0.2	1.2	1.0	trace	0.3	0.4	trace	trace	0.1	17.1
Maximum 24-hr. Precipitation (in.)	2.1	1.8	2.1	3.8	2.8	4.2	3.2	6.2	4.4	2.3	2.5	1.5	6.2
Days With ≥ 0.1" Precipitation	3	3	5	7	8	7	6	7	6	5	4	3	64
Days With ≥ 1.0" Precipitation	0	0	1	1	1	1	1	2	1	1	0	0	9
Mean Snowfall (in.)	8.5	7.9	4.3	2.7	trace	trace	trace	0.0	trace	0.4	4.3	7.4	35.5
Maximum Snowfall (in.)	19	21	19	16	trace	0	0	0	trace	7	15	24	76
Maximum 24-hr. Snowfall (in.)	14	10	8	10	trace	0	0	0	trace	7	12	10	14
Days With ≥ 1.0" Snow Depth	19	14	5	1	0	0	0	0	0	0	3	12	54
Thunderstorm Days	< 1	< 1	2	4	7	9	8	7	5	3	1	< 1	46
Foggy Days	10	10	11	10	9	7	7	10	9	8	10	12	113
Predominant Sky Cover	OVR	OVR	OVR	OVR	OVR	OVR	CLR	CLR	CLR	CLR	OVR	OVR	OVR
Mean Relative Humidity 6am (%)	77	79	80	78	79	81	84	86	85	80	79	80	81
Mean Relative Humidity 3pm (%)	65	63	57	50	51	53	53	54	52	50	59	66	56
Mean Dewpoint (°F)	12	17	26	37	48	59	64	62	53	41	29	18	39
Prevailing Wind Direction	NW	NW	NW	NW	S	S	S	S	S	S	NW	NW	S
Prevailing Wind Speed (mph)	15	15	15	16	12	12	9	9	10	10	15	15	13
Maximum Wind Gust (mph)	59	62	58	67	59	76	83	73	54	61	62	56	83

Dubuque Regional Airport

The terrain around Dubuque varies from gently rolling, 10 to 15 miles to the south and west, to steep hills and bluffs around the city and along the Mississippi River.

The principal feature of the climate in Dubuque is its variety. The Dubuque area is subject to weather ranging from the cold, dry, arctic air masses in the winter, with readings as low as 32 degrees below zero, to the hot, dry weather of the desert southwest in the summer when the temperatures reach about 110. More often the area is covered by mild Pacific air that has lost considerable moisture in crossing the mountains far to the west, or by cool, dry Canadian air, or by warm, moist air from the Gulf regions. Most of the year the latter three types of air masses dominate Dubuque weather, with the invasions of Gulf air rarely occurring in the winter.

The seasons vary widely from year to year at Dubuque. For example, successive invasions of cold air from the north may bring a long, cold winter with snow-covered ground from mid November until March and many days of sub-zero temperatures. Another winter can be mild with bare ground most of the season and only a few sub-zero temperature readings. The summers, too, may vary from hot and humid with considerable thunderstorm activity when the Gulf air prevails, to relatively cool, dry weather when air of northerly origin dominates the season.

All seasons are marked by storms that accompany the changes from one type of air mass to another. In winter, rain changes to sleet and snow, and occasionally a peal of thunder is heard at the height of a snowstorm. In summer, thunderstorms are frequently heavy. They are occasionally accompanied by hail and on rare occasions by tornadoes. Thunderstorms have been sufficiently intense at times to raise the Mississippi River, which is about one-fourth mile wide at Debuque, nearly five feet overnight. Flash floods have drowned many people.

Most of the precipitation occurs during the spring and fall seasons. The last occurrence of snow and freezing rain can be in late May, and the first occurrence in late September.

While the climate of Dubuque does not lack for variety, there are times when a particular weather condition may persist for an extended period. Cold weather has lasted as long as 20 days in succession with sub-zero readings. Heat waves have persisted for 10 or more days with readings around 100 degrees each day. Hot, dry spells occasionally plague the crops and livestock in summer, but there are frequent periods of mild, dry weather in the spring and frequently in the autumn.

Dubuque Regional Airport *Dubuque County*   Elevation: 1,053 ft.   Latitude: 42° 24' N   Longitude: 90° 42' W

	JAN	FEB	MAR	APR	MAY	JUN	JUL	AUG	SEP	OCT	NOV	DEC	YEAR
Mean Maximum Temp. (°F)	24.7	30.6	43.0	57.5	69.3	78.9	82.2	79.8	71.9	60.2	43.5	30.2	56.0
Mean Temp. (°F)	16.9	22.8	34.4	47.6	58.9	68.5	72.3	70.0	61.8	50.3	35.6	22.9	46.8
Mean Minimum Temp. (°F)	9.0	15.0	25.8	37.5	48.4	58.1	62.2	60.1	51.7	40.4	27.6	15.5	37.6
Extreme Maximum Temp. (°F)	60	61	85	93	91	100	101	100	95	90	75	67	101
Extreme Minimum Temp. (°F)	-28	-27	-9	11	28	36	44	40	28	18	-17	-25	-28
Days Maximum Temp. ≥ 90°F	0	0	0	0	0	2	4	2	1	0	0	0	9
Days Maximum Temp. ≤ 32°F	22	15	6	0	0	0	0	0	0	0	5	17	65
Days Minimum Temp. ≤ 32°F	31	26	23	8	1	0	0	0	1	6	21	29	146
Days Minimum Temp. ≤ 0°F	9	5	1	0	0	0	0	0	0	0	0	5	20
Heating Degree Days (base 65°F)	1,487	1,185	941	524	223	35	7	18	154	454	875	1,300	7,203
Cooling Degree Days (base 65°F)	0	0	0	7	37	157	245	189	66	5	0	0	706
Mean Precipitation (in.)	1.23	1.43	2.59	3.47	4.00	4.06	3.74	4.67	3.74	2.51	2.51	1.70	35.65
Maximum Precipitation (in.)	6.0	3.6	6.5	7.7	9.4	10.5	12.2	9.9	15.5	8.6	10.6	4.1	63.3
Minimum Precipitation (in.)	0.3	0.1	0.4	0.8	0.7	0.7	0.9	0.1	0.1	trace	0.4	0.1	22.6
Maximum 24-hr. Precipitation (in.)	3.0	1.3	2.3	2.2	4.4	3.4	6.3	3.4	8.8	2.6	4.8	2.0	8.8
Days With ≥ 0.1" Precipitation	4	4	6	8	8	7	6	7	7	5	6	4	72
Days With ≥ 1.0" Precipitation	0	0	0	1	1	1	1	1	1	0	0	0	6
Mean Snowfall (in.)	10.2	8.6	7.6	3.2	trace	trace	0.0	0.0	0.0	0.2	4.5	9.5	43.8
Maximum Snowfall (in.)	29	25	30	20	3	0	0	0	0	2	14	26	74
Maximum 24-hr. Snowfall (in.)	11	10	15	9	3	0	0	0	0	2	10	14	15
Days With ≥ 1.0" Snow Depth	22	19	8	1	0	0	0	0	0	0	4	16	70
Thunderstorm Days	< 1	< 1	2	3	5	6	6	6	3	2	1	< 1	34
Foggy Days	12	11	11	9	9	8	11	13	11	9	11	13	128
Predominant Sky Cover	OVR	OVR	OVR	OVR	OVR	OVR	OVR	OVR	OVR	OVR	OVR	OVR	OVR
Mean Relative Humidity 6am (%)	78	79	80	77	78	82	86	88	87	82	82	82	82
Mean Relative Humidity 3pm (%)	68	64	59	52	52	55	57	58	56	53	62	70	59
Mean Dewpoint (°F)	10	15	24	35	46	57	62	61	52	40	27	17	37
Prevailing Wind Direction	WNW	S	NW	S	S	S	SSW	S	S	S	S	S	S
Prevailing Wind Speed (mph)	14	13	15	15	14	13	12	10	12	14	14	14	13
Maximum Wind Gust (mph)	58	53	62	68	74	55	74	67	58	54	55	59	74

Sioux City Municipal Airport

Sioux City is located along the Missouri River at a point where Iowa boarders both Nebraska and South Dakota. Except for the river valleys, the countryside is rolling. The Sioux City business section lies in the river valley and the residential sections, for the most part, are spread over the hills which range from 100 to 200 feet higher than the valley. The local topography causes minor variations in wind and temperature.

Located in the midland of a continent and in the northern half of the Great Plains, the climate of Sioux City is typically continental and is largely determined by the movement and interaction of the large-scale weather systems. Under normal conditions, winters are cold and summers warm, and most of the precipitation comes during the warmer months from April to September. There is considerable fluctuation in temperature and precipitation from season to season and from year to year, as elsewhere in the northern plains. Except for an occasional dry year, the climate is quite favorable for agriculture with corn, the small grains, and grasses producing abundantly.

The grass usually starts to grow about the middle of April. The growing season averages about 160 days. Summers are sunny and most summer rains are associated with showers or thunderstorms. Winds are lightest in the summer months, except for occasional strong gusts with thunderstorms. Winds gradually increase in autumn and winter and usually reach their highest average velocities in April.

Sioux City Municipal Airport *Woodbury County*   Elevation: 1,092 ft.   Latitude: 42° 23' N   Longitude: 96° 23' W

	JAN	FEB	MAR	APR	MAY	JUN	JUL	AUG	SEP	OCT	NOV	DEC	YEAR
Mean Maximum Temp. (°F)	27.9	34.4	46.5	61.4	72.8	82.2	85.9	83.5	75.7	63.4	45.1	31.8	59.2
Mean Temp. (°F)	18.3	25.1	36.3	49.6	61.3	70.8	75.0	72.7	63.7	51.2	35.5	22.8	48.5
Mean Minimum Temp. (°F)	8.7	15.7	26.0	37.7	49.8	59.5	64.0	61.9	51.6	39.0	25.8	13.7	37.8
Extreme Maximum Temp. (°F)	70	71	89	97	97	108	108	102	102	94	81	70	108
Extreme Minimum Temp. (°F)	-26	-24	-14	-2	25	39	42	39	25	12	-9	-24	-26
Days Maximum Temp. ≥ 90°F	0	0	0	1	1	6	10	7	2	0	0	0	27
Days Maximum Temp. ≤ 32°F	18	12	5	0	0	0	0	0	0	0	5	15	55
Days Minimum Temp. ≤ 32°F	31	27	23	9	1	0	0	0	1	8	23	30	153
Days Minimum Temp. ≤ 0°F	9	4	1	0	0	0	0	0	0	0	1	5	20
Heating Degree Days (base 65°F)	1,441	1,122	883	466	165	23	2	9	125	429	880	1,303	6,848
Cooling Degree Days (base 65°F)	0	0	0	13	56	201	311	249	92	8	0	0	930
Mean Precipitation (in.)	0.58	0.60	2.04	2.79	3.72	3.51	3.26	2.88	2.63	2.07	1.40	0.67	26.15
Maximum Precipitation (in.)	2.4	2.7	5.9	6.7	8.5	8.8	10.3	7.8	9.7	5.3	4.1	2.2	35.0
Minimum Precipitation (in.)	0.1	0.1	trace	0.5	0.6	0.5	0.4	0.1	0.1	trace	trace	0.1	14.3
Maximum 24-hr. Precipitation (in.)	1.1	2.1	1.7	2.0	2.2	3.9	5.5	4.3	2.9	4.4	3.2	1.1	5.5
Days With ≥ 0.1" Precipitation	2	2	5	5	7	6	6	5	5	4	3	2	52
Days With ≥ 1.0" Precipitation	0	0	1	1	1	1	1	1	1	0	0	0	7
Mean Snowfall (in.)	6.3	5.5	6.3	1.7	trace	trace	trace	0.0	trace	1.0	4.3	5.9	31.0
Maximum Snowfall (in.)	29	25	26	10	trace	0	0	0	trace	10	17	21	65
Maximum 24-hr. Snowfall (in.)	17	14	12	7	trace	0	0	0	trace	9	12	9	17
Days With ≥ 1.0" Snow Depth	20	13	7	1	0	0	0	0	0	0	4	15	60
Thunderstorm Days	< 1	< 1	1	3	7	8	8	7	5	2	< 1	< 1	41
Foggy Days	9	9	10	7	7	5	6	10	8	7	9	11	98
Predominant Sky Cover	OVR	OVR	OVR	OVR	OVR	OVR	CLR	CLR	CLR	CLR	OVR	OVR	OVR
Mean Relative Humidity 6am (%)	78	79	81	78	80	82	86	88	86	81	81	81	82
Mean Relative Humidity 3pm (%)	64	62	58	46	48	50	53	54	50	46	56	65	54
Mean Dewpoint (°F)	10	16	25	35	47	58	63	62	52	39	26	16	38
Prevailing Wind Direction	NW	NW	NW	NW	SE	SSE	SSE	SE	SE	SE	NW	NW	NW
Prevailing Wind Speed (mph)	15	15	15	16	12	13	12	9	9	10	16	15	13
Maximum Wind Gust (mph)	66	66	62	71	64	75	68	60	76	53	69	60	76

Waterloo Municipal Airport

Waterloo is situated on the banks of the Cedar River in northeast Iowa, and has a continental humid climate. A wide variation is experienced in both temperature and precipitation during the four distinct seasons.

The distribution of precipitation through the year is very favorable for agriculture with an average 72 percent of the annual total falling in the April to September crop season. The annual temperature range is large. January, the coldest month, averages near 14 degrees and July, the warmest month, averages about 73 degrees. Extreme temperatures range from about -35 to 112 degrees.

It is sometimes convenient to divide the year into periods corresponding to the growing season of the area. Winter extends from November through March, based on a mean daily temperature of 40 degrees. The winter period is a season of cold, dry weather occasionally broken by storms of short duration. Precipitation during the winter is mainly snow with rain dominant at the beginning and end of the season. Annual snowfall varies considerably from year to year. Temperatures of zero degrees or below occur on average about 29 days per year. Bitterly cold days with high temperatures of zero degrees or lower average about three days per year. During the winter, prevailing winds are from the northwest.

The spring growing season is marked by an increase in both frequency and intensity of rainfall and by a rapid increase in the mean daily temperature. Spring extends from the first of April to mid May, when daily mean temperatures range between 40 and 59 degrees.

The summer growing season extends from mid May to mid September, based on a mean daily temperature of 60 degrees. Precipitation increases during the spring and reaches a maximum monthly amount in July. In summer, precipitation falls mainly from thunderstorms, three-fourths of which occur during the summer growing season. The prevailing summer wind is southerly, supplying moisture from the Gulf of Mexico. Daily temperatures reach their highest level in July or early August.

The fall growing season extends from mid September to the first part of November, by which time the mean daily temperature has fallen to 40 degrees. Precipitation declines and frequent periods of warm days, cool nights, and cloudless, but hazy, skies persist.

Waterloo Municipal Airport *Black Hawk County*   Elevation: 862 ft.   Latitude: 42° 33' N   Longitude: 92° 24' W

	JAN	FEB	MAR	APR	MAY	JUN	JUL	AUG	SEP	OCT	NOV	DEC	YEAR
Mean Maximum Temp. (°F)	24.1	30.3	43.6	58.9	71.4	80.9	84.1	81.7	74.0	61.3	44.0	30.3	57.0
Mean Temp. (°F)	15.1	21.6	34.3	47.7	60.0	69.7	73.2	70.7	62.2	49.8	34.9	21.9	46.8
Mean Minimum Temp. (°F)	6.1	12.9	25.0	36.4	48.5	58.4	62.3	59.7	50.3	38.3	25.8	13.5	36.4
Extreme Maximum Temp. (°F)	58	66	87	100	93	103	105	105	97	95	80	67	105
Extreme Minimum Temp. (°F)	-33	-31	-12	-4	25	39	42	40	26	11	-17	-26	-33
Days Maximum Temp. ≥ 90°F	0	0	0	0	1	4	7	4	1	0	0	0	17
Days Maximum Temp. ≤ 32°F	22	14	6	0	0	0	0	0	0	0	5	16	63
Days Minimum Temp. ≤ 32°F	31	26	24	11	1	0	0	0	1	10	22	30	156
Days Minimum Temp. ≤ 0°F	12	7	1	0	0	0	0	0	0	0	1	6	27
Heating Degree Days (base 65°F)	1,543	1,220	946	521	198	27	6	18	151	471	896	1,330	7,327
Cooling Degree Days (base 65°F)	0	0	0	9	49	177	278	210	75	7	0	0	805
Mean Precipitation (in.)	0.82	1.04	2.18	3.18	4.08	4.65	4.22	4.06	3.07	2.57	2.06	1.15	33.08
Maximum Precipitation (in.)	1.8	3.5	5.4	8.5	7.7	10.1	12.6	9.6	11.4	5.4	5.6	3.8	53.1
Minimum Precipitation (in.)	0.1	trace	0.2	0.9	0.8	1.4	1.1	0.4	0.5	trace	0.1	0.2	19.0
Maximum 24-hr. Precipitation (in.)	1.5	1.3	1.7	2.6	3.4	4.3	5.3	4.9	3.0	2.6	2.1	1.7	5.3
Days With ≥ 0.1" Precipitation	2	3	5	7	7	7	7	6	5	5	4	3	61
Days With ≥ 1.0" Precipitation	0	0	0	0	1	1	1	1	1	1	0	0	6
Mean Snowfall (in.)	8.0	7.2	4.9	2.1	trace	trace	0.0	0.0	0.0	0.1	4.6	7.5	34.4
Maximum Snowfall (in.)	18	24	16	10	trace	0	0	0	0	1	16	20	56
Maximum 24-hr. Snowfall (in.)	13	8	8	6	trace	0	0	0	0	1	9	10	13
Days With ≥ 1.0" Snow Depth	23	19	8	1	0	0	0	0	0	0	4	17	72
Thunderstorm Days	< 1	< 1	2	4	6	8	8	7	5	2	< 1	< 1	42
Foggy Days	10	11	13	11	10	8	10	13	12	10	13	13	134
Predominant Sky Cover	OVR	OVR	OVR	OVR	OVR	OVR	SCT	CLR	OVR	OVR	OVR	OVR	OVR
Mean Relative Humidity 6am (%)	77	80	82	81	81	83	87	90	89	84	83	82	83
Mean Relative Humidity 3pm (%)	68	66	62	52	51	51	55	55	55	52	62	70	58
Mean Dewpoint (°F)	8	14	25	35	47	57	63	61	52	39	28	15	37
Prevailing Wind Direction	NW	NW	NW	NW	S	S	S	S	S	NW	NW	NW	NW
Prevailing Wind Speed (mph)	14	14	15	15	12	12	10	10	10	13	14	14	13
Maximum Wind Gust (mph)	58	52	59	76	68	86	105	51	53	49	59	53	105

Albia 3 NNE *Monroe County*   Elevation: 879 ft.   Latitude: 41° 04' N   Longitude: 92° 47' W

	JAN	FEB	MAR	APR	MAY	JUN	JUL	AUG	SEP	OCT	NOV	DEC	YEAR
Mean Maximum Temp. (°F)	31.7	38.0	49.9	63.2	73.2	82.2	86.8	84.6	77.1	65.2	48.8	35.7	61.4
Mean Temp. (°F)	22.8	28.6	39.7	51.9	62.1	71.3	76.0	73.8	65.8	54.1	39.8	27.4	51.1
Mean Minimum Temp. (°F)	13.9	19.2	29.5	40.5	51.0	60.3	65.2	63.0	54.5	42.9	30.7	19.0	40.8
Extreme Maximum Temp. (°F)	71	74	86	90	90	101	106	105	97	91	79	71	106
Extreme Minimum Temp. (°F)	-24	-31	-9	10	29	40	45	41	30	16	-7	-26	-31
Days Maximum Temp. ≥ 90°F	0	0	0	0	0	3	11	7	2	0	0	0	23
Days Maximum Temp. ≤ 32°F	15	10	3	0	0	0	0	0	0	0	3	11	42
Days Minimum Temp. ≤ 32°F	28	24	19	6	0	0	0	0	0	4	17	28	126
Days Minimum Temp. ≤ 0°F	6	3	0	0	0	0	0	0	0	0	0	3	12
Heating Degree Days (base 65°F)	1,302	1,022	779	401	143	17	2	6	91	346	750	1,159	6,018
Cooling Degree Days (base 65°F)	0	0	2	15	54	204	343	286	118	14	1	0	1,037
Mean Precipitation (in.)	1.10	1.25	2.38	3.70	4.81	4.34	5.00	3.93	4.47	2.75	2.67	1.41	37.81
Days With ≥ 0.1" Precipitation	3	4	6	8	9	7	6	6	6	5	5	3	68
Days With ≥ 1.0" Precipitation	0	0	0	1	1	1	2	1	1	1	1	0	9
Mean Snowfall (in.)	7.4	6.8	4.0	2.5	0.0	0.0	0.0	0.0	0.0	0.6	2.9	5.2	29.4
Days With ≥ 1.0" Snow Depth	15	12	5	1	0	0	0	0	0	0	3	10	46

Algona 3 W *Kossuth County*   Elevation: 1,227 ft.   Latitude: 43° 04' N   Longitude: 94° 18' W

	JAN	FEB	MAR	APR	MAY	JUN	JUL	AUG	SEP	OCT	NOV	DEC	YEAR
Mean Maximum Temp. (°F)	23.7	29.9	42.5	58.8	71.8	81.1	83.6	81.1	73.8	61.4	42.1	28.0	56.5
Mean Temp. (°F)	14.8	21.3	33.6	47.5	60.1	69.5	72.7	70.3	62.2	50.1	33.6	20.0	46.3
Mean Minimum Temp. (°F)	5.8	12.7	24.7	36.2	48.3	57.9	61.8	59.4	50.5	38.8	25.1	11.9	36.1
Extreme Maximum Temp. (°F)	61	65	83	93	94	105	101	101	97	94	81	68	105
Extreme Minimum Temp. (°F)	-29	-29	-10	6	27	39	43	43	24	13	-11	-30	-30
Days Maximum Temp. ≥ 90°F	0	0	0	0	1	4	6	3	1	0	0	0	15
Days Maximum Temp. ≤ 32°F	23	15	6	0	0	0	0	0	0	0	7	19	70
Days Minimum Temp. ≤ 32°F	31	27	25	11	1	0	0	0	1	8	24	30	158
Days Minimum Temp. ≤ 0°F	12	6	1	0	0	0	0	0	0	0	1	7	27
Heating Degree Days (base 65°F)	1,551	1,228	966	525	195	29	7	18	146	461	934	1,391	7,451
Cooling Degree Days (base 65°F)	0	0	0	6	46	168	246	186	68	6	0	0	726
Mean Precipitation (in.)	0.73	0.69	1.86	3.05	3.78	4.81	4.09	3.64	2.96	2.28	1.75	0.80	30.44
Days With ≥ 0.1" Precipitation	2	2	4	7	8	7	7	6	5	4	4	2	58
Days With ≥ 1.0" Precipitation	0	0	0	0	1	1	1	1	1	1	0	0	6
Mean Snowfall (in.)	9.0	6.3	6.2	2.1	0.0	0.0	0.0	0.0	0.0	0.2	4.6	7.4	35.8
Days With ≥ 1.0" Snow Depth	24	21	10	1	0	0	0	0	0	0	6	19	81

Allison *Butler County*   Elevation: 1,049 ft.   Latitude: 42° 45' N   Longitude: 92° 47' W

	JAN	FEB	MAR	APR	MAY	JUN	JUL	AUG	SEP	OCT	NOV	DEC	YEAR
Mean Maximum Temp. (°F)	24.9	31.0	43.6	60.0	72.4	81.7	84.6	82.2	74.7	62.4	43.8	29.7	57.6
Mean Temp. (°F)	16.3	22.5	34.4	48.6	60.8	70.2	73.5	71.1	63.1	51.3	35.4	21.9	47.4
Mean Minimum Temp. (°F)	7.5	13.9	25.2	37.2	49.1	58.7	62.3	60.0	51.5	40.1	26.9	14.1	37.2
Extreme Maximum Temp. (°F)	59	65	84	96	92	102	102	104	96	93	80	62	104
Extreme Minimum Temp. (°F)	-28	-31	-13	5	26	40	44	42	28	15	-16	-22	-31
Days Maximum Temp. ≥ 90°F	0	0	0	0	1	4	7	4	1	0	0	0	17
Days Maximum Temp. ≤ 32°F	21	14	6	0	0	0	0	0	0	0	5	17	63
Days Minimum Temp. ≤ 32°F	31	26	24	9	1	0	0	0	0	7	21	30	149
Days Minimum Temp. ≤ 0°F	10	6	1	0	0	0	0	0	0	0	1	5	23
Heating Degree Days (base 65°F)	1,506	1,195	940	493	177	23	5	13	128	426	882	1,330	7,118
Cooling Degree Days (base 65°F)	0	0	0	8	48	183	270	203	75	6	0	0	793
Mean Precipitation (in.)	0.83	0.89	1.81	3.22	4.37	4.84	4.36	4.27	3.53	2.58	2.12	0.99	33.81
Days With ≥ 0.1" Precipitation	3	3	4	6	8	7	7	6	6	5	5	3	63
Days With ≥ 1.0" Precipitation	0	0	0	1	1	1	1	1	1	1	0	0	6
Mean Snowfall (in.)	8.7	6.9	5.3	1.8	0.0	0.0	0.0	0.0	0.0	trace	4.8	6.4	33.9
Days With ≥ 1.0" Snow Depth	23	21	9	1	0	0	0	0	0	0	5	19	78

Ames 8 WSW *Boone County*   Elevation: 1,099 ft.   Latitude: 42° 01' N   Longitude: 93° 46' W

	JAN	FEB	MAR	APR	MAY	JUN	JUL	AUG	SEP	OCT	NOV	DEC	YEAR
Mean Maximum Temp. (°F)	27.1	33.6	46.4	61.7	73.0	82.0	84.8	82.4	76.2	63.8	45.4	31.9	59.0
Mean Temp. (°F)	18.2	24.6	36.7	49.9	61.4	70.6	74.0	71.6	64.2	52.1	36.5	23.6	48.6
Mean Minimum Temp. (°F)	9.2	15.6	26.9	38.1	49.8	59.2	63.2	60.7	52.2	40.4	27.5	15.4	38.2
Extreme Maximum Temp. (°F)	60	67	90	97	93	101	101	102	97	95	80	66	102
Extreme Minimum Temp. (°F)	-26	-28	-11	8	27	41	44	42	29	13	-7	-24	-28
Days Maximum Temp. ≥ 90°F	0	0	0	0	0	4	8	5	2	0	0	0	19
Days Maximum Temp. ≤ 32°F	20	13	5	0	0	0	0	0	0	0	4	14	56
Days Minimum Temp. ≤ 32°F	31	26	23	8	1	0	0	0	0	7	21	30	147
Days Minimum Temp. ≤ 0°F	9	5	1	0	0	0	0	0	0	0	0	4	19
Heating Degree Days (base 65°F)	1,446	1,134	870	457	161	19	4	10	113	403	849	1,276	6,742
Cooling Degree Days (base 65°F)	0	0	1	12	54	192	289	226	97	9	0	0	880
Mean Precipitation (in.)	0.73	0.80	2.12	3.53	4.44	4.97	4.46	4.48	3.23	2.72	1.95	1.04	34.47
Days With ≥ 0.1" Precipitation	2	2	5	7	8	7	7	6	6	5	4	3	62
Days With ≥ 1.0" Precipitation	0	0	0	1	1	2	1	2	1	1	0	0	9
Mean Snowfall (in.)	7.6	7.0	5.5	2.1	0.0	0.0	0.0	0.0	0.0	0.3	2.9	6.5	31.9
Days With ≥ 1.0" Snow Depth	19	14	6	1	0	0	0	0	0	0	3	14	57

Anamosa 1 WNW *Jones County*   Elevation: 803 ft.   Latitude: 42° 07' N   Longitude: 91° 18' W

	JAN	FEB	MAR	APR	MAY	JUN	JUL	AUG	SEP	OCT	NOV	DEC	YEAR
Mean Maximum Temp. (°F)	27.3	33.6	46.2	61.3	73.2	82.1	85.5	83.1	75.6	63.5	46.0	32.8	59.2
Mean Temp. (°F)	18.1	24.4	36.1	49.1	60.3	69.4	73.4	71.1	63.0	51.5	36.9	24.4	48.1
Mean Minimum Temp. (°F)	8.8	15.1	26.1	36.9	47.4	56.7	61.3	59.1	50.4	39.3	27.6	15.9	37.0
Extreme Maximum Temp. (°F)	66	67	87	95	93	100	102	102	97	93	78	71	102
Extreme Minimum Temp. (°F)	-30	-37	-15	0	26	33	39	37	23	11	-14	-27	-37
Days Maximum Temp. ≥ 90°F	0	0	0	0	1	4	7	5	1	0	0	0	18
Days Maximum Temp. ≤ 32°F	19	12	4	0	0	0	0	0	0	0	4	13	52
Days Minimum Temp. ≤ 32°F	30	26	23	11	2	0	0	0	1	9	21	29	152
Days Minimum Temp. ≤ 0°F	10	5	1	0	0	0	0	0	0	0	0	4	20
Heating Degree Days (base 65°F)	1,449	1,141	888	478	190	32	6	16	136	424	839	1,254	6,853
Cooling Degree Days (base 65°F)	0	0	1	10	46	173	276	214	82	8	0	0	810
Mean Precipitation (in.)	1.15	1.26	2.41	3.46	4.19	4.30	4.15	4.44	3.45	2.53	2.53	1.47	35.34
Days With ≥ 0.1" Precipitation	3	3	5	7	8	7	7	7	6	5	5	4	67
Days With ≥ 1.0" Precipitation	0	0	1	1	1	1	1	1	1	1	1	0	9
Mean Snowfall (in.)	*7.4*	4.7	3.4	1.3	0.0	0.0	0.0	0.0	0.0	0.1	*2.0*	*5.7*	*24.6*
Days With ≥ 1.0" Snow Depth	*21*	*13*	*4*	0	0	0	0	0	0	0	2	na	na

Ankeny *Polk County*   Elevation: 938 ft.   Latitude: 41° 43' N   Longitude: 93° 34' W

	JAN	FEB	MAR	APR	MAY	JUN	JUL	AUG	SEP	OCT	NOV	DEC	YEAR
Mean Maximum Temp. (°F)	27.8	34.2	46.6	60.9	72.2	81.4	85.7	82.9	75.7	63.1	46.1	32.8	59.1
Mean Temp. (°F)	18.5	24.7	36.6	49.5	61.1	70.5	74.8	71.9	63.9	51.3	36.6	24.1	48.6
Mean Minimum Temp. (°F)	9.2	15.0	26.5	38.2	49.9	59.5	63.8	60.8	52.0	39.4	27.5	15.3	38.1
Extreme Maximum Temp. (°F)	63	69	90	93	93	102	103	106	98	93	79	70	106
Extreme Minimum Temp. (°F)	-25	-34	-10	8	29	40	43	35	22	12	-7	-25	-34
Days Maximum Temp. ≥ 90°F	0	0	0	0	0	4	9	6	2	0	0	0	21
Days Maximum Temp. ≤ 32°F	19	13	5	0	0	0	0	0	0	0	4	14	55
Days Minimum Temp. ≤ 32°F	30	26	22	8	1	0	0	0	1	8	21	30	147
Days Minimum Temp. ≤ 0°F	9	4	1	0	0	0	0	0	0	0	0	4	18
Heating Degree Days (base 65°F)	1,436	1,133	877	470	171	22	5	11	122	427	845	1,263	6,782
Cooling Degree Days (base 65°F)	0	0	1	13	51	190	315	237	96	7	0	0	910
Mean Precipitation (in.)	0.68	0.93	2.14	3.22	4.46	4.89	4.13	4.45	3.15	2.59	1.94	1.00	33.58
Days With ≥ 0.1" Precipitation	2	3	5	6	8	7	6	6	6	5	4	3	61
Days With ≥ 1.0" Precipitation	0	0	0	1	1	1	1	1	1	1	0	0	7
Mean Snowfall (in.)	6.5	6.2	4.0	1.1	trace	0.0	0.0	0.0	trace	0.4	2.0	5.6	25.8
Days With ≥ 1.0" Snow Depth	20	15	5	0	0	0	0	0	0	0	2	11	53

Atlantic 1 NE *Cass County*   Elevation: 1,158 ft.   Latitude: 41° 25' N   Longitude: 95° 00' W

	JAN	FEB	MAR	APR	MAY	JUN	JUL	AUG	SEP	OCT	NOV	DEC	YEAR
Mean Maximum Temp. (°F)	29.2	35.2	47.8	62.2	73.1	82.8	85.9	83.2	76.3	63.9	46.4	33.4	59.9
Mean Temp. (°F)	19.2	25.1	36.9	49.8	61.1	70.9	74.5	71.9	63.7	51.4	36.6	24.2	48.8
Mean Minimum Temp. (°F)	9.1	14.9	26.0	37.4	49.1	58.9	63.0	60.5	51.2	39.0	26.8	15.0	37.6
Extreme Maximum Temp. (°F)	66	73	90	93	96	102	104	102	97	95	83	67	104
Extreme Minimum Temp. (°F)	-37	-36	-21	4	23	33	39	38	20	9	-12	-33	-37
Days Maximum Temp. ≥ 90°F	0	0	0	0	1	6	10	6	2	0	0	0	25
Days Maximum Temp. ≤ 32°F	17	12	4	0	0	0	0	0	0	0	4	14	51
Days Minimum Temp. ≤ 32°F	30	26	23	10	1	0	0	0	1	9	22	30	152
Days Minimum Temp. ≤ 0°F	9	5	1	0	0	0	0	0	0	0	0	5	20
Heating Degree Days (base 65°F)	1,416	1,121	863	460	169	22	4	15	127	424	846	1,258	6,725
Cooling Degree Days (base 65°F)	0	0	1	14	52	200	309	242	100	11	0	0	929
Mean Precipitation (in.)	0.86	0.90	2.40	3.50	4.36	4.83	4.59	3.76	3.89	2.84	1.81	1.09	34.83
Days With ≥ 0.1" Precipitation	3	3	5	7	8	6	7	6	6	5	4	3	63
Days With ≥ 1.0" Precipitation	0	0	1	1	1	1	1	1	1	1	0	0	8
Mean Snowfall (in.)	6.6	*5.7*	3.6	1.2	0.0	0.0	0.0	0.0	0.0	0.5	*2.5*	5.1	*25.2*
Days With ≥ 1.0" Snow Depth	na	na	na	0	0	0	0	0	0	0	*1*	na	na

Audubon 1 SSE *Audubon County*   Elevation: 1,289 ft.   Latitude: 41° 42' N   Longitude: 94° 55' W

	JAN	FEB	MAR	APR	MAY	JUN	JUL	AUG	SEP	OCT	NOV	DEC	YEAR
Mean Maximum Temp. (°F)	29.1	35.3	48.0	62.5	73.5	82.8	85.9	83.5	76.3	64.1	46.2	33.3	60.0
Mean Temp. (°F)	19.5	25.6	37.1	50.1	61.4	70.9	74.7	72.3	64.2	52.0	36.8	24.4	49.1
Mean Minimum Temp. (°F)	9.9	15.9	26.2	37.7	49.2	59.0	63.4	61.1	51.9	39.9	27.3	15.5	38.1
Extreme Maximum Temp. (°F)	67	69	90	93	93	101	106	101	96	93	78	66	106
Extreme Minimum Temp. (°F)	-25	-27	-16	5	26	40	43	39	27	12	-12	-29	-29
Days Maximum Temp. ≥ 90°F	0	0	0	0	0	5	9	6	2	0	0	0	22
Days Maximum Temp. ≤ 32°F	17	12	4	0	0	0	0	0	0	0	4	13	50
Days Minimum Temp. ≤ 32°F	30	26	23	9	1	0	0	0	1	7	21	29	147
Days Minimum Temp. ≤ 0°F	9	4	1	0	0	0	0	0	0	0	0	4	18
Heating Degree Days (base 65°F)	1,405	1,106	858	452	162	20	4	10	116	405	841	1,252	6,631
Cooling Degree Days (base 65°F)	0	0	1	13	52	197	301	238	94	8	0	0	904
Mean Precipitation (in.)	0.93	0.89	2.32	3.42	4.27	4.34	4.38	3.79	3.58	2.76	1.90	1.07	33.65
Days With ≥ 0.1" Precipitation	3	3	5	6	8	7	6	6	6	5	4	3	62
Days With ≥ 1.0" Precipitation	0	0	1	1	1	1	1	1	1	1	0	0	8
Mean Snowfall (in.)	6.9	5.8	5.0	1.9	0.0	0.0	0.0	0.0	trace	0.6	3.0	6.4	29.6
Days With ≥ 1.0" Snow Depth	na	na	na	0	0	0	0	0	0	0	na	na	na

Beaconsfield *Ringgold County* Elevation: 1,197 ft. Latitude: 40° 49' N Longitude: 94° 03' W

	JAN	FEB	MAR	APR	MAY	JUN	JUL	AUG	SEP	OCT	NOV	DEC	YEAR
Mean Maximum Temp. (°F)	29.6	37.0	48.7	61.6	71.6	81.2	85.6	83.7	76.0	64.3	47.5	34.9	60.1
Mean Temp. (°F)	20.7	27.5	38.3	50.3	60.9	70.3	74.9	72.8	64.5	52.7	38.3	26.3	49.8
Mean Minimum Temp. (°F)	11.7	17.9	27.9	39.1	50.3	59.3	64.2	61.8	52.9	41.2	28.9	17.7	39.4
Extreme Maximum Temp. (°F)	64	74	87	89	92	105	105	104	97	90	79	67	105
Extreme Minimum Temp. (°F)	-24	-25	-13	8	25	37	43	41	26	14	-13	-21	-25
Days Maximum Temp. ≥ 90°F	0	0	0	0	0	3	8	6	2	0	0	0	19
Days Maximum Temp. ≤ 32°F	17	11	4	0	0	0	0	0	0	0	3	12	47
Days Minimum Temp. ≤ 32°F	30	25	21	8	0	0	0	0	1	6	19	29	139
Days Minimum Temp. ≤ 0°F	7	4	0	0	0	0	0	0	0	0	0	3	14
Heating Degree Days (base 65°F)	1,369	1,054	821	443	165	22	3	8	112	383	796	1,192	6,368
Cooling Degree Days (base 65°F)	0	0	1	10	42	177	313	257	105	9	0	0	914
Mean Precipitation (in.)	0.79	0.99	2.40	3.49	4.63	4.15	4.53	3.87	4.35	2.96	2.28	1.14	35.58
Days With ≥ 0.1" Precipitation	2	3	5	7	8	7	6	6	6	5	5	3	63
Days With ≥ 1.0" Precipitation	0	0	1	1	1	1	2	1	1	1	1	0	10
Mean Snowfall (in.)	6.2	5.0	3,4	1.3	trace	0.0	0.0	0.0	0.0	0.5	2.4	5.3	24.1
Days With ≥ 1.0" Snow Depth	17	12	4	1	0	0	0	0	0	0	2	11	47

Bedford *Taylor County* Elevation: 1,131 ft. Latitude: 40° 40' N Longitude: 94° 44' W

	JAN	FEB	MAR	APR	MAY	JUN	JUL	AUG	SEP	OCT	NOV	DEC	YEAR
Mean Maximum Temp. (°F)	31.5	38.7	50.8	63.3	73.5	82.8	86.8	85.0	77.4	65.3	49.1	36.3	61.7
Mean Temp. (°F)	21.9	28.5	39.9	51.7	62.2	71.6	75.9	73.9	65.7	53.5	39.5	27.3	51.0
Mean Minimum Temp. (°F)	12.2	18.1	28.9	40.0	50.9	60.3	64.9	62.7	54.0	41.6	29.8	18.3	40.1
Extreme Maximum Temp. (°F)	68	76	85	93	92	101	105	103	99	94	81	68	105
Extreme Minimum Temp. (°F)	-32	-34	-24	5	28	40	40	44	26	11	-8	-26	-34
Days Maximum Temp. ≥ 90°F	0	0	0	0	0	5	11	8	2	0	0	0	26
Days Maximum Temp. ≤ 32°F	15	9	2	0	0	0	0	0	0	0	2	10	38
Days Minimum Temp. ≤ 32°F	30	25	19	7	0	0	0	0	0	6	18	29	134
Days Minimum Temp. ≤ 0°F	7	4	0	0	0	0	0	0	0	0	0	3	14
Heating Degree Days (base 65°F)	1,332	1,026	772	407	139	16	2	5	92	362	759	1,162	6,074
Cooling Degree Days (base 65°F)	0	0	2	16	57	222	352	292	125	10	0	0	1,076
Mean Precipitation (in.)	0.96	1.02	2.29	3.33	4.86	4.36	5.07	4.02	3.94	3.02	2.35	1.10	36.32
Days With ≥ 0.1" Precipitation	3	3	5	6	8	7	6	5	5	5	5	3	61
Days With ≥ 1.0" Precipitation	0	0	1	1	1	1	2	1	2	1	1	0	11
Mean Snowfall (in.)	6.4	5.7	3.9	1.7	0.0	0.0	0.0	0.0	0.0	0.2	2.2	*4.6*	*24.7*
Days With ≥ 1.0" Snow Depth	na	na	*2*	0	0	0	0	0	0	0	*1*	na	na

Belle Plaine *Benton County* Elevation: 807 ft. Latitude: 41° 53' N Longitude: 92° 18' W

	JAN	FEB	MAR	APR	MAY	JUN	JUL	AUG	SEP	OCT	NOV	DEC	YEAR
Mean Maximum Temp. (°F)	27.6	34.0	46.1	60.5	72.2	81.3	84.9	82.7	74.9	63.1	46.0	32.5	58.8
Mean Temp. (°F)	18.5	24.7	36.4	49.3	60.8	70.2	74.1	71.9	63.5	51.6	37.0	24.3	48.5
Mean Minimum Temp. (°F)	9.4	15.4	26.6	38.0	49.5	59.2	63.3	61.0	52.1	40.0	27.9	15.9	38.2
Extreme Maximum Temp. (°F)	65	68	88	95	92	102	103	105	98	92	80	69	105
Extreme Minimum Temp. (°F)	-28	-35	-10	8	28	38	43	41	26	11	-10	-30	-35
Days Maximum Temp. ≥ 90°F	0	0	0	0	0	3	8	5	1	0	0	0	17
Days Maximum Temp. ≤ 32°F	19	12	4	0	0	0	0	0	0	0	4	14	53
Days Minimum Temp. ≤ 32°F	30	26	22	9	1	0	0	0	1	8	21	29	147
Days Minimum Temp. ≤ 0°F	9	5	1	0	0	0	0	0	0	0	0	4	19
Heating Degree Days (base 65°F)	1,435	1,132	881	475	176	23	4	10	125	419	834	1,257	6,771
Cooling Degree Days (base 65°F)	0	0	1	11	49	185	293	232	85	7	0	0	863
Mean Precipitation (in.)	1.04	1.06	2.40	3.62	4.26	4.59	4.20	4.79	3.71	2.81	2.31	1.38	36.17
Days With ≥ 0.1" Precipitation	3	3	5	7	8	7	7	6	6	5	5	4	66
Days With ≥ 1.0" Precipitation	0	0	0	1	1	1	1	1	1	1	1	0	8
Mean Snowfall (in.)	8.1	6.5	4.4	2.3	trace	0.0	0.0	0.0	0.0	0.4	3.0	6.3	31.0
Days With ≥ 1.0" Snow Depth	20	16	6	1	0	0	0	0	0	0	3	13	59

Bellevue Lock & Dam 12 *Jackson County* Elevation: 600 ft. Latitude: 42° 16' N Longitude: 90° 25' W

	JAN	FEB	MAR	APR	MAY	JUN	JUL	AUG	SEP	OCT	NOV	DEC	YEAR
Mean Maximum Temp. (°F)	27.2	33.2	44.7	59.1	71.4	80.8	84.5	82.1	74.4	62.4	45.7	32.9	58.2
Mean Temp. (°F)	18.4	24.0	35.3	48.1	59.7	69.2	73.4	71.3	63.0	51.3	37.1	24.9	48.0
Mean Minimum Temp. (°F)	9.5	14.9	26.0	37.1	47.9	57.6	62.3	60.4	51.6	40.0	28.4	16.9	37.7
Extreme Maximum Temp. (°F)	61	65	87	94	94	100	102	103	99	95	77	66	103
Extreme Minimum Temp. (°F)	-28	-34	-9	5	27	35	41	40	27	14	-9	-22	-34
Days Maximum Temp. ≥ 90°F	0	0	0	0	1	3	7	4	1	0	0	0	16
Days Maximum Temp. ≤ 32°F	20	12	4	0	0	0	0	0	0	0	3	13	52
Days Minimum Temp. ≤ 32°F	30	26	23	10	1	0	0	0	1	7	20	29	147
Days Minimum Temp. ≤ 0°F	9	5	1	0	0	0	0	0	0	0	0	4	19
Heating Degree Days (base 65°F)	1,440	1,150	913	509	207	32	6	14	133	428	831	1,239	6,902
Cooling Degree Days (base 65°F)	0	0	0	8	40	162	268	212	74	6	0	0	770
Mean Precipitation (in.)	1.10	1.21	2.31	3.26	3.79	4.41	3.30	4.41	3.80	2.55	2.58	1.61	34.33
Days With ≥ 0.1" Precipitation	3	3	5	7	8	7	6	7	6	5	5	4	66
Days With ≥ 1.0" Precipitation	0	0	0	1	1	1	1	2	1	0	0	0	7
Mean Snowfall (in.)	10.4	5.9	4.1	1.4	0.1	0.0	0.0	0.0	0.0	trace	1.8	7.1	30.8
Days With ≥ 1.0" Snow Depth	22	19	7	1	0	0	0	0	0	0	3	16	68

Bloomfield 1 WNW *Davis County*   Elevation: 810 ft.   Latitude: 40° 46' N   Longitude: 92° 26' W

	JAN	FEB	MAR	APR	MAY	JUN	JUL	AUG	SEP	OCT	NOV	DEC	YEAR
Mean Maximum Temp. (°F)	32.3	38.8	50.7	63.8	73.6	82.7	87.3	85.1	77.4	66.1	50.2	37.2	62.1
Mean Temp. (°F)	23.1	29.1	40.3	52.5	62.5	71.8	76.2	74.0	66.0	54.7	40.8	28.6	51.6
Mean Minimum Temp. (°F)	13.8	19.3	29.8	41.1	51.5	60.8	65.1	62.9	54.5	43.3	31.3	20.0	41.1
Extreme Maximum Temp. (°F)	70	75	86	89	93	101	105	106	99	90	77	70	106
Extreme Minimum Temp. (°F)	-29	-26	-8	10	30	42	43	40	30	14	-6	-23	-29
Days Maximum Temp. ≥ 90°F	0	0	0	0	0	4	11	8	2	0	0	0	25
Days Maximum Temp. ≤ 32°F	14	10	2	0	0	0	0	0	0	0	2	9	37
Days Minimum Temp. ≤ 32°F	29	24	19	5	0	0	0	0	0	4	17	27	125
Days Minimum Temp. ≤ 0°F	7	3	0	0	0	0	0	0	0	0	0	3	13
Heating Degree Days (base 65°F)	1,293	1,008	761	384	134	14	2	5	88	327	721	1,122	5,859
Cooling Degree Days (base 65°F)	0	0	2	16	63	230	369	310	130	14	0	0	1,134
Mean Precipitation (in.)	1.14	1.17	2.48	3.61	4.96	4.34	4.78	4.85	4.30	2.88	2.59	1.54	38.64
Days With ≥ 0.1" Precipitation	3	4	5	7	9	7	7	7	7	5	5	3	69
Days With ≥ 1.0" Precipitation	0	0	0	1	1	1	2	2	1	1	0	0	9
Mean Snowfall (in.)	8.1	6.6	4.3	2.6	trace	0.0	0.0	0.0	0.0	0.2	2.4	5.7	29.9
Days With ≥ 1.0" Snow Depth	18	13	5	1	0	0	0	0	0	0	2	9	48

Boone *Boone County*   Elevation: 1,049 ft.   Latitude: 42° 03' N   Longitude: 93° 53' W

	JAN	FEB	MAR	APR	MAY	JUN	JUL	AUG	SEP	OCT	NOV	DEC	YEAR
Mean Maximum Temp. (°F)	27.6	34.1	46.1	59.9	72.1	81.3	85.5	82.9	76.0	63.9	45.8	32.3	59.0
Mean Temp. (°F)	16.7	23.0	35.4	48.1	59.8	69.1	73.4	70.9	62.7	50.4	35.5	22.5	47.3
Mean Minimum Temp. (°F)	5.7	11.8	24.6	36.2	47.5	56.7	61.3	58.8	49.4	37.0	25.2	12.7	35.6
Extreme Maximum Temp. (°F)	63	70	86	95	94	102	103	106	97	94	81	68	106
Extreme Minimum Temp. (°F)	-32	-35	-16	-1	27	35	41	37	23	14	-11	-25	-35
Days Maximum Temp. ≥ 90°F	0	0	0	0	1	4	9	6	2	0	0	0	22
Days Maximum Temp. ≤ 32°F	19	13	4	0	0	0	0	0	0	0	4	14	54
Days Minimum Temp. ≤ 32°F	31	28	25	10	1	0	0	0	1	11	23	30	160
Days Minimum Temp. ≤ 0°F	11	7	1	0	0	0	0	0	0	0	1	6	26
Heating Degree Days (base 65°F)	1,494	1,181	911	510	198	34	6	15	139	453	878	1,311	7,130
Cooling Degree Days (base 65°F)	0	0	1	10	41	160	270	210	79	8	0	0	779
Mean Precipitation (in.)	1.13	1.06	2.49	3.47	4.54	5.28	4.43	4.50	3.26	2.73	2.27	1.38	36.54
Days With ≥ 0.1" Precipitation	3	3	5	7	8	8	7	6	6	5	5	4	67
Days With ≥ 1.0" Precipitation	0	0	0	1	1	1	1	1	1	1	0	0	7
Mean Snowfall (in.)	8.1	6.7	5.0	1.5	trace	0.0	0.0	0.0	0.0	0.3	3.0	6.4	31.0
Days With ≥ 1.0" Snow Depth	21	16	7	1	0	0	0	0	0	0	4	15	64

Burlington Radio KBUR *Des Moines County*   Elevation: 702 ft.   Latitude: 40° 49' N   Longitude: 91° 10' W

	JAN	FEB	MAR	APR	MAY	JUN	JUL	AUG	SEP	OCT	NOV	DEC	YEAR
Mean Maximum Temp. (°F)	30.4	36.5	48.7	61.8	72.7	81.9	85.7	83.1	75.9	64.2	48.6	35.5	60.4
Mean Temp. (°F)	22.2	28.1	39.5	51.7	62.6	71.8	76.0	73.6	65.8	54.1	40.2	27.9	51.1
Mean Minimum Temp. (°F)	14.0	19.6	30.2	41.5	52.5	61.7	66.2	64.0	55.6	44.0	31.7	20.2	41.8
Extreme Maximum Temp. (°F)	70	72	88	92	94	104	103	105	97	91	78	71	105
Extreme Minimum Temp. (°F)	-23	-26	-6	11	29	40	46	42	30	18	-2	-20	-26
Days Maximum Temp. ≥ 90°F	0	0	0	0	0	4	9	5	2	0	0	0	20
Days Maximum Temp. ≤ 32°F	17	10	3	0	0	0	0	0	0	0	2	11	43
Days Minimum Temp. ≤ 32°F	29	24	18	5	0	0	0	0	0	3	16	27	122
Days Minimum Temp. ≤ 0°F	6	3	0	0	0	0	0	0	0	0	0	3	12
Heating Degree Days (base 65°F)	1,321	1,036	787	407	138	16	2	6	88	344	738	1,144	6,027
Cooling Degree Days (base 65°F)	0	0	2	14	71	241	363	296	123	14	0	0	1,124
Mean Precipitation (in.)	1.28	1.46	2.98	3.69	4.41	4.32	4.41	4.10	3.80	2.93	2.73	2.09	38.20
Days With ≥ 0.1" Precipitation	3	4	6	7	8	7	7	6	6	6	5	4	69
Days With ≥ 1.0" Precipitation	0	0	1	1	1	2	1	1	1	1	1	0	10
Mean Snowfall (in.)	7.8	5.6	3.4	1.4	0.0	0.0	0.0	0.0	0.0	trace	2.1	5.6	25.9
Days With ≥ 1.0" Snow Depth	16	10	3	1	0	0	0	0	0	0	1	7	38

Carroll *Carroll County*   Elevation: 1,240 ft.   Latitude: 42° 04' N   Longitude: 94° 51' W

	JAN	FEB	MAR	APR	MAY	JUN	JUL	AUG	SEP	OCT	NOV	DEC	YEAR
Mean Maximum Temp. (°F)	26.9	33.4	45.8	60.7	72.3	82.3	85.6	83.0	75.5	62.7	44.6	31.6	58.7
Mean Temp. (°F)	17.8	24.1	35.6	48.6	60.3	70.2	74.0	71.6	63.2	50.9	35.4	23.0	47.9
Mean Minimum Temp. (°F)	8.6	14.7	25.2	36.4	48.2	58.1	62.4	60.0	50.8	39.0	26.2	14.4	37.0
Extreme Maximum Temp. (°F)	63	69	88	94	96	102	103	103	97	92	78	67	103
Extreme Minimum Temp. (°F)	-32	-26	-15	4	25	39	39	35	25	10	-8	-24	-32
Days Maximum Temp. ≥ 90°F	0	0	0	0	1	6	9	6	2	0	0	0	24
Days Maximum Temp. ≤ 32°F	19	13	5	0	0	0	0	0	0	0	5	15	57
Days Minimum Temp. ≤ 32°F	30	27	24	10	1	0	0	0	1	8	23	30	154
Days Minimum Temp. ≤ 0°F	10	5	1	0	0	0	0	0	0	0	0	5	21
Heating Degree Days (base 65°F)	1,458	1,148	907	498	190	26	5	14	133	441	881	1,296	6,997
Cooling Degree Days (base 65°F)	0	0	0	11	47	181	285	218	82	8	0	0	832
Mean Precipitation (in.)	0.87	0.80	2.30	3.44	4.40	4.48	4.81	3.80	3.40	2.54	1.74	0.94	33.52
Days With ≥ 0.1" Precipitation	2	2	5	6	8	7	6	6	6	5	4	3	60
Days With ≥ 1.0" Precipitation	0	0	1	1	1	1	1	1	1	1	0	0	8
Mean Snowfall (in.)	7.2	5.9	5.9	2.0	trace	0.0	0.0	0.0	trace	0.5	3.2	6.5	31.2
Days With ≥ 1.0" Snow Depth	16	13	6	1	0	0	0	0	0	0	4	13	53

Cascade *Dubuque County*   Elevation: 849 ft.   Latitude: 42° 18' N   Longitude: 91° 01' W

	JAN	FEB	MAR	APR	MAY	JUN	JUL	AUG	SEP	OCT	NOV	DEC	YEAR
Mean Maximum Temp. (°F)	25.7	32.2	44.3	58.8	71.3	80.8	84.9	82.1	74.0	61.9	44.8	31.7	57.7
Mean Temp. (°F)	16.5	22.7	34.7	47.4	59.6	69.0	73.1	70.5	61.8	49.9	35.7	23.1	47.0
Mean Minimum Temp. (°F)	7.2	13.1	25.0	36.0	47.8	57.1	61.3	58.9	49.6	37.9	26.6	14.4	36.3
Extreme Maximum Temp. (°F)	59	63	87	95	93	101	101	103	97	92	77	69	103
Extreme Minimum Temp. (°F)	-35	-33	-14	-3	25	35	42	41	26	13	-14	-28	-35
Days Maximum Temp. ≥ 90°F	0	0	0	0	1	3	7	4	1	0	0	0	16
Days Maximum Temp. ≤ 32°F	21	14	5	0	0	0	0	0	0	0	4	14	58
Days Minimum Temp. ≤ 32°F	30	27	24	11	1	0	0	0	1	10	22	30	156
Days Minimum Temp. ≤ 0°F	11	6	1	0	0	0	0	0	0	0	0	6	24
Heating Degree Days (base 65°F)	1,501	1,190	933	528	207	33	6	18	154	467	872	1,293	7,202
Cooling Degree Days (base 65°F)	0	0	1	7	40	158	269	199	63	5	0	0	742
Mean Precipitation (in.)	1.17	1.17	2.25	2.98	3.66	4.46	3.35	4.72	3.52	2.37	2.42	1.47	33.54
Days With ≥ 0.1" Precipitation	4	3	5	6	8	7	6	6	6	5	5	4	65
Days With ≥ 1.0" Precipitation	0	0	0	1	1	1	1	2	1	1	0	0	8
Mean Snowfall (in.)	9.6	7.0	4.5	1.9	0.0	0.0	0.0	0.0	0.0	trace	2.9	7.0	32.9
Days With ≥ 1.0" Snow Depth	21	18	7	1	0	0	0	0	0	0	3	15	65

Castana Experiment Farm *Monona County*   Elevation: 1,450 ft.   Latitude: 42° 04' N   Longitude: 95° 50' W

	JAN	FEB	MAR	APR	MAY	JUN	JUL	AUG	SEP	OCT	NOV	DEC	YEAR
Mean Maximum Temp. (°F)	28.9	35.6	47.7	62.1	73.0	82.2	85.4	83.2	76.0	64.1	45.7	32.9	59.7
Mean Temp. (°F)	19.5	26.1	37.0	50.1	61.3	70.6	74.5	72.3	64.3	52.4	36.6	24.3	49.1
Mean Minimum Temp. (°F)	10.1	16.4	26.3	38.1	49.5	59.0	63.5	61.3	52.5	40.6	27.3	15.6	38.4
Extreme Maximum Temp. (°F)	65	71	87	94	93	104	101	102	97	91	79	68	104
Extreme Minimum Temp. (°F)	-27	-26	-12	4	24	39	44	38	24	12	-9	-26	-27
Days Maximum Temp. ≥ 90°F	0	0	0	0	1	4	8	5	2	0	0	0	20
Days Maximum Temp. ≤ 32°F	17	12	4	0	0	0	0	0	0	0	4	14	51
Days Minimum Temp. ≤ 32°F	30	26	23	9	1	0	0	0	1	7	21	30	148
Days Minimum Temp. ≤ 0°F	9	4	1	0	0	0	0	0	0	0	0	4	18
Heating Degree Days (base 65°F)	1,404	1,093	861	451	163	22	3	9	113	395	847	1,256	6,617
Cooling Degree Days (base 65°F)	0	0	1	14	53	200	304	242	102	12	0	0	928
Mean Precipitation (in.)	0.59	0.53	2.17	3.26	4.27	4.16	4.06	3.65	3.37	2.48	1.52	0.78	30.84
Days With ≥ 0.1" Precipitation	2	2	4	6	8	7	6	5	6	4	3	2	55
Days With ≥ 1.0" Precipitation	0	0	1	1	1	1	1	1	1	1	0	0	8
Mean Snowfall (in.)	7.0	5.7	6.3	2.1	trace	0.0	0.0	0.0	0.0	1.1	4.6	6.5	33.3
Days With ≥ 1.0" Snow Depth	19	14	7	1	0	0	0	0	0	0	5	15	61

Cedar Rapids Municipal Airport *Linn County*   Elevation: 839 ft.   Latitude: 41° 53' N   Longitude: 91° 43' W

	JAN	FEB	MAR	APR	MAY	JUN	JUL	AUG	SEP	OCT	NOV	DEC	YEAR
Mean Maximum Temp. (°F)	26.1	31.8	45.0	59.6	72.0	81.2	84.6	81.9	74.2	62.1	45.7	31.6	58.0
Mean Temp. (°F)	17.8	23.4	36.1	49.1	61.1	70.4	74.2	71.6	63.1	51.2	37.1	23.6	48.2
Mean Minimum Temp. (°F)	9.4	15.0	27.1	38.6	50.2	59.5	63.8	61.2	52.0	40.3	28.4	15.5	38.4
Extreme Maximum Temp. (°F)	65	66	88	95	96	100	104	102	97	90	78	67	104
Extreme Minimum Temp. (°F)	-28	-21	-9	1	30	39	47	40	27	18	-11	-22	-28
Days Maximum Temp. ≥ 90°F	0	0	0	0	1	4	7	5	2	0	0	0	19
Days Maximum Temp. ≤ 32°F	20	14	5	0	0	0	0	0	0	0	4	15	58
Days Minimum Temp. ≤ 32°F	30	26	21	7	0	0	0	0	0	7	20	29	140
Days Minimum Temp. ≤ 0°F	9	5	1	0	0	0	0	0	0	0	0	5	20
Heating Degree Days (base 65°F)	1,456	1,169	890	481	171	22	3	13	134	429	830	1,278	6,876
Cooling Degree Days (base 65°F)	0	0	1	11	52	192	303	234	83	7	0	0	883
Mean Precipitation (in.)	0.96	1.01	2.32	3.27	3.78	4.27	4.24	4.24	3.45	2.19	2.29	1.54	33.56
Days With ≥ 0.1" Precipitation	3	3	5	7	7	7	7	6	6	5	5	4	65
Days With ≥ 1.0" Precipitation	0	0	0	1	1	1	1	1	1	0	0	0	6
Mean Snowfall (in.)	7.3	6.5	3.6	1.8	trace	trace	0.0	0.0	0.0	trace	2.9	7.1	29.2
Days With ≥ 1.0" Snow Depth	20	15	5	1	0	0	0	0	0	0	2	11	54

Cedar Rapids 1 *Linn County*   Elevation: 849 ft.   Latitude: 42° 02' N   Longitude: 91° 35' W

	JAN	FEB	MAR	APR	MAY	JUN	JUL	AUG	SEP	OCT	NOV	DEC	YEAR
Mean Maximum Temp. (°F)	27.9	34.6	46.9	61.7	73.1	81.9	85.5	83.1	75.6	64.0	46.5	33.1	59.5
Mean Temp. (°F)	19.3	25.7	37.2	50.2	61.7	70.9	74.8	72.5	64.5	53.0	37.9	25.2	49.4
Mean Minimum Temp. (°F)	10.6	16.7	27.4	38.6	50.2	59.8	64.1	61.8	53.3	41.9	29.2	17.2	39.2
Extreme Maximum Temp. (°F)	68	66	88	94	93	101	105	102	98	94	80	69	105
Extreme Minimum Temp. (°F)	-25	-28	-8	3	28	38	45	41	26	15	-10	-21	-28
Days Maximum Temp. ≥ 90°F	0	0	0	0	0	3	8	5	1	0	0	0	17
Days Maximum Temp. ≤ 32°F	19	12	4	0	0	0	0	0	0	0	3	14	52
Days Minimum Temp. ≤ 32°F	30	26	22	9	0	0	0	0	0	6	20	29	142
Days Minimum Temp. ≤ 0°F	8	4	1	0	0	0	0	0	0	0	0	4	17
Heating Degree Days (base 65°F)	1,413	1,104	858	449	157	18	3	8	106	378	808	1,229	6,531
Cooling Degree Days (base 65°F)	0	0	1	12	57	201	316	253	98	11	0	0	949
Mean Precipitation (in.)	1.11	1.08	2.18	3.42	4.59	4.73	4.58	4.68	3.86	2.61	2.47	1.45	36.76
Days With ≥ 0.1" Precipitation	3	3	5	7	8	8	7	7	6	5	5	4	68
Days With ≥ 1.0" Precipitation	0	0	0	1	1	1	1	1	1	1	0	0	7
Mean Snowfall (in.)	8.1	6.1	4.3	2.4	trace	0.0	0.0	0.0	0.0	0.4	3.5	7.0	31.8
Days With ≥ 1.0" Snow Depth	21	16	5	1	0	0	0	0	0	0	2	13	58

Centerville *Appanoose County*   Elevation: 977 ft.   Latitude: 40° 44' N   Longitude: 92° 52' W

	JAN	FEB	MAR	APR	MAY	JUN	JUL	AUG	SEP	OCT	NOV	DEC	YEAR
Mean Maximum Temp. (°F)	31.4	37.9	49.8	62.6	72.8	81.8	*87.0*	*84.5*	76.1	64.5	48.8	36.0	*61.1*
Mean Temp. (°F)	22.8	28.7	39.8	51.7	62.2	71.5	na	*73.9*	65.5	54.0	40.0	27.9	na
Mean Minimum Temp. (°F)	14.1	19.5	29.8	40.9	51.5	61.0	*65.9*	*63.3*	54.9	43.5	31.0	19.7	*41.3*
Extreme Maximum Temp. (°F)	70	72	88	89	92	104	106	107	100	90	79	71	107
Extreme Minimum Temp. (°F)	-25	-24	-12	12	27	41	46	42	29	18	-8	-23	-25
Days Maximum Temp. ≥ 90°F	0	0	0	0	0	3	9	6	2	0	0	0	20
Days Maximum Temp. ≤ 32°F	15	10	3	0	0	0	0	0	0	0	2	11	41
Days Minimum Temp. ≤ 32°F	29	24	19	6	0	0	0	0	0	4	17	27	126
Days Minimum Temp. ≤ 0°F	6	3	0	0	0	0	0	0	0	0	0	3	12
Heating Degree Days (base 65°F)	1,303	1,019	775	406	140	16	na	5	96	347	746	1,144	na
Cooling Degree Days (base 65°F)	0	0	2	14	55	209	na	na	115	11	0	0	na
Mean Precipitation (in.)	0.89	0.94	2.27	3.54	4.69	4.33	*5.31*	4.41	4.13	3.00	2.36	1.31	*37.18*
Days With ≥ 0.1" Precipitation	2	3	5	6	8	7	6	5	6	5	5	3	61
Days With ≥ 1.0" Precipitation	0	0	0	1	1	1	1	1	1	1	1	0	8
Mean Snowfall (in.)	6.1	5.7	3.1	2.0	0.0	0.0	0.0	0.0	0.0	0.3	1.7	4.5	23.4
Days With ≥ 1.0" Snow Depth	*15*	*11*	*3*	1	0	0	0	0	0	0	1	*7*	*38*

Chariton 1 E *Lucas County*   Elevation: 938 ft.   Latitude: 41° 00' N   Longitude: 93° 17' W

	JAN	FEB	MAR	APR	MAY	JUN	JUL	AUG	SEP	OCT	NOV	DEC	YEAR
Mean Maximum Temp. (°F)	30.9	37.2	49.3	62.6	72.7	81.9	86.7	84.6	77.0	65.3	48.6	35.8	61.1
Mean Temp. (°F)	21.1	26.8	38.4	50.5	60.8	70.2	75.1	72.9	64.6	52.7	38.7	26.6	49.9
Mean Minimum Temp. (°F)	11.1	16.4	27.4	38.3	48.8	58.5	63.5	61.3	52.3	40.1	28.7	17.4	38.6
Extreme Maximum Temp. (°F)	62	73	87	90	91	102	103	103	98	91	79	69	103
Extreme Minimum Temp. (°F)	-28	-38	-17	8	26	36	39	38	23	11	-13	-31	-38
Days Maximum Temp. ≥ 90°F	0	0	0	0	0	4	11	8	2	0	0	0	25
Days Maximum Temp. ≤ 32°F	16	11	3	0	0	0	0	0	0	0	3	11	44
Days Minimum Temp. ≤ 32°F	30	26	21	9	1	0	0	0	1	8	20	29	145
Days Minimum Temp. ≤ 0°F	8	4	1	0	0	0	0	0	0	0	0	4	17
Heating Degree Days (base 65°F)	1,356	1,071	819	441	175	26	4	9	112	385	784	1,184	6,366
Cooling Degree Days (base 65°F)	0	0	1	14	44	182	320	263	105	9	0	0	938
Mean Precipitation (in.)	0.90	1.12	2.29	3.62	4.70	4.50	4.79	4.17	4.43	3.03	2.35	1.20	37.10
Days With ≥ 0.1" Precipitation	3	3	5	7	8	7	7	6	6	5	5	3	65
Days With ≥ 1.0" Precipitation	0	0	1	1	1	1	1	1	1	1	0	0	8
Mean Snowfall (in.)	7.3	6.1	4.0	2.0	trace	0.0	0.0	0.0	0.0	0.3	2.1	4.7	26.5
Days With ≥ 1.0" Snow Depth	17	11	5	1	0	0	0	0	0	0	2	9	45

Charles City *Floyd County*   Elevation: 1,017 ft.   Latitude: 43° 04' N   Longitude: 92° 40' W

	JAN	FEB	MAR	APR	MAY	JUN	JUL	AUG	SEP	OCT	NOV	DEC	YEAR
Mean Maximum Temp. (°F)	24.1	30.5	43.0	59.1	71.8	81.0	84.1	81.8	74.3	61.8	42.8	28.9	56.9
Mean Temp. (°F)	15.0	21.6	33.7	47.8	60.0	69.3	72.7	70.5	62.3	50.4	34.3	20.8	46.5
Mean Minimum Temp. (°F)	5.9	12.7	24.5	36.4	48.2	57.5	61.3	59.0	50.2	38.8	25.8	12.6	36.1
Extreme Maximum Temp. (°F)	59	65	85	94	93	102	102	104	97	93	78	62	104
Extreme Minimum Temp. (°F)	-29	-32	-13	3	24	36	45	39	25	10	-14	-24	-32
Days Maximum Temp. ≥ 90°F	0	0	0	0	1	3	6	3	1	0	0	0	14
Days Maximum Temp. ≤ 32°F	22	14	6	0	0	0	0	0	0	0	6	19	67
Days Minimum Temp. ≤ 32°F	31	27	25	10	1	0	0	0	1	9	23	30	157
Days Minimum Temp. ≤ 0°F	11	6	1	0	0	0	0	0	0	0	1	6	25
Heating Degree Days (base 65°F)	1,545	1,220	963	518	195	30	7	16	145	453	914	1,365	7,371
Cooling Degree Days (base 65°F)	0	0	0	8	43	162	245	186	67	4	0	0	715
Mean Precipitation (in.)	0.91	0.84	2.04	3.40	4.17	4.96	4.62	4.51	3.45	2.55	2.11	1.05	34.61
Days With ≥ 0.1" Precipitation	3	3	5	7	8	7	6	7	6	5	5	3	65
Days With ≥ 1.0" Precipitation	0	0	1	1	1	1	1	1	1	1	0	0	7
Mean Snowfall (in.)	9.8	6.4	6.2	2.9	trace	0.0	0.0	0.0	0.0	0.1	4.4	7.9	37.7
Days With ≥ 1.0" Snow Depth	25	23	13	2	0	0	0	0	0	0	5	22	90

Cherokee *Cherokee County*   Elevation: 1,177 ft.   Latitude: 42° 45' N   Longitude: 95° 32' W

	JAN	FEB	MAR	APR	MAY	JUN	JUL	AUG	SEP	OCT	NOV	DEC	YEAR
Mean Maximum Temp. (°F)	25.4	32.1	43.7	59.2	71.9	81.4	85.0	82.7	74.9	62.3	43.8	30.1	57.7
Mean Temp. (°F)	15.0	21.5	33.3	47.1	59.3	69.2	73.3	70.9	61.7	48.9	33.6	20.4	46.2
Mean Minimum Temp. (°F)	4.7	10.9	22.9	34.9	46.8	57.0	61.5	59.0	48.4	35.5	23.4	10.7	34.6
Extreme Maximum Temp. (°F)	67	68	86	94	95	103	104	102	101	91	80	68	104
Extreme Minimum Temp. (°F)	-35	-33	-18	-8	24	34	40	37	24	9	-17	-26	-35
Days Maximum Temp. ≥ 90°F	0	0	0	0	1	5	8	6	2	0	0	0	22
Days Maximum Temp. ≤ 32°F	21	14	6	1	0	0	0	0	0	0	6	16	64
Days Minimum Temp. ≤ 32°F	31	27	25	12	2	0	0	0	2	13	25	31	168
Days Minimum Temp. ≤ 0°F	12	7	2	0	0	0	0	0	0	0	1	7	29
Heating Degree Days (base 65°F)	1,545	1,223	976	540	217	39	7	19	164	497	935	1,376	7,538
Cooling Degree Days (base 65°F)	0	0	0	9	46	171	269	209	73	6	0	0	783
Mean Precipitation (in.)	0.58	0.56	1.98	2.81	3.73	4.51	3.87	3.47	3.21	2.11	1.64	0.76	29.23
Days With ≥ 0.1" Precipitation	2	2	4	6	7	7	6	6	5	4	4	2	55
Days With ≥ 1.0" Precipitation	0	0	0	1	1	1	1	1	1	1	0	0	7
Mean Snowfall (in.)	*6.4*	5.7	*5.7*	1.5	0.0	0.0	0.0	0.0	0.0	0.3	*4.8*	6.7	*31.1*
Days With ≥ 1.0" Snow Depth	na	na	*4*	1	0	0	0	0	0	0	na	na	na

Clarinda *Page County*   Elevation: 977 ft.   Latitude: 40° 43' N   Longitude: 95° 01' W

	JAN	FEB	MAR	APR	MAY	JUN	JUL	AUG	SEP	OCT	NOV	DEC	YEAR
Mean Maximum Temp. (°F)	31.3	38.3	50.1	63.1	73.5	83.3	87.0	84.8	77.1	65.1	48.3	35.8	61.5
Mean Temp. (°F)	21.7	28.0	39.0	51.2	61.9	71.7	75.8	73.4	65.0	53.0	38.4	26.7	50.5
Mean Minimum Temp. (°F)	12.0	17.6	27.9	39.2	50.3	60.1	64.5	62.0	52.8	40.9	28.5	17.6	39.4
Extreme Maximum Temp. (°F)	67	77	88	93	96	104	108	105	102	94	82	68	108
Extreme Minimum Temp. (°F)	-25	-24	-20	6	26	41	42	37	24	14	-5	-24	-25
Days Maximum Temp. ≥ 90°F	0	0	0	0	0	6	12	8	3	0	0	0	29
Days Maximum Temp. ≤ 32°F	16	10	3	0	0	0	0	0	0	0	3	11	43
Days Minimum Temp. ≤ 32°F	30	26	20	8	0	0	0	0	1	6	20	29	140
Days Minimum Temp. ≤ 0°F	7	3	1	0	0	0	0	0	0	0	0	3	14
Heating Degree Days (base 65°F)	1,337	1,039	800	423	147	16	2	7	105	376	791	1,180	6,223
Cooling Degree Days (base 65°F)	0	0	1	16	53	215	340	265	110	10	0	0	1,010
Mean Precipitation (in.)	0.93	0.98	2.45	3.35	4.82	4.50	4.94	4.40	3.98	2.72	2.38	1.15	36.60
Days With ≥ 0.1" Precipitation	3	3	5	6	8	7	7	6	6	5	5	3	64
Days With ≥ 1.0" Precipitation	0	0	0	1	1	1	2	1	1	1	1	0	9
Mean Snowfall (in.)	7.4	5.6	3.8	0.9	0.0	0.0	0.0	0.0	0.0	0.2	2.6	5.3	25.8
Days With ≥ 1.0" Snow Depth	16	11	4	0	0	0	0	0	0	0	2	10	43

Clarion *Wright County*   Elevation: 1,187 ft.   Latitude: 42° 44' N   Longitude: 93° 44' W

	JAN	FEB	MAR	APR	MAY	JUN	JUL	AUG	SEP	OCT	NOV	DEC	YEAR
Mean Maximum Temp. (°F)	23.1	29.6	41.6	57.6	71.0	80.5	83.5	80.8	73.8	61.4	42.7	28.3	56.2
Mean Temp. (°F)	13.7	20.4	32.5	46.5	59.4	69.1	72.5	69.8	61.5	49.2	33.6	19.6	45.6
Mean Minimum Temp. (°F)	4.4	11.2	23.4	35.4	47.7	57.6	61.5	58.7	49.2	37.0	24.4	10.7	35.1
Extreme Maximum Temp. (°F)	62	67	86	96	94	102	102	102	97	94	76	67	102
Extreme Minimum Temp. (°F)	-32	-30	-12	3	24	36	43	34	21	12	-18	-26	-32
Days Maximum Temp. ≥ 90°F	0	0	0	0	1	4	6	3	1	0	0	0	15
Days Maximum Temp. ≤ 32°F	23	16	7	1	0	0	0	0	0	0	6	19	72
Days Minimum Temp. ≤ 32°F	31	28	26	12	1	0	0	0	1	11	24	31	165
Days Minimum Temp. ≤ 0°F	12	8	1	0	0	0	0	0	0	0	1	7	29
Heating Degree Days (base 65°F)	1,586	1,254	999	556	215	38	9	23	165	490	936	1,403	7,674
Cooling Degree Days (base 65°F)	0	0	0	7	43	167	245	181	64	7	0	0	714
Mean Precipitation (in.)	0.71	0.71	2.00	3.28	4.19	5.07	4.22	4.08	3.23	2.47	1.91	1.01	32.88
Days With ≥ 0.1" Precipitation	2	2	5	7	8	8	7	7	6	5	4	3	64
Days With ≥ 1.0" Precipitation	0	0	0	1	1	2	1	1	1	1	0	0	8
Mean Snowfall (in.)	8.4	5.6	6.0	1.9	trace	0.0	0.0	0.0	trace	0.2	3.6	7.2	32.9
Days With ≥ 1.0" Snow Depth	23	19	8	1	0	0	0	0	0	0	4	17	72

Clinton 1 *Clinton County*   Elevation: 583 ft.   Latitude: 41° 48' N   Longitude: 90° 16' W

	JAN	FEB	MAR	APR	MAY	JUN	JUL	AUG	SEP	OCT	NOV	DEC	YEAR
Mean Maximum Temp. (°F)	28.6	34.8	47.5	62.1	73.6	82.2	85.6	83.3	76.1	64.2	47.6	34.2	60.0
Mean Temp. (°F)	20.3	26.2	38.0	50.8	62.2	71.2	75.0	72.8	64.9	53.3	39.1	26.6	50.0
Mean Minimum Temp. (°F)	11.9	17.6	28.5	39.5	50.7	60.2	64.5	62.3	53.7	42.3	30.5	19.0	40.0
Extreme Maximum Temp. (°F)	67	69	87	91	93	100	101	101	98	91	77	70	101
Extreme Minimum Temp. (°F)	-26	-29	-7	7	27	38	45	39	27	15	-8	-22	-29
Days Maximum Temp. ≥ 90°F	0	0	0	0	1	4	8	5	1	0	0	0	19
Days Maximum Temp. ≤ 32°F	18	11	3	0	0	0	0	0	0	0	2	12	46
Days Minimum Temp. ≤ 32°F	29	25	20	7	0	0	0	0	1	5	18	28	133
Days Minimum Temp. ≤ 0°F	8	4	0	0	0	0	0	0	0	0	0	3	15
Heating Degree Days (base 65°F)	1,381	1,089	830	432	152	17	2	6	101	369	772	1,185	6,336
Cooling Degree Days (base 65°F)	0	0	2	13	67	211	325	258	101	10	0	0	987
Mean Precipitation (in.)	1.46	1.36	2.53	3.29	4.08	4.54	3.53	4.53	3.33	2.74	2.36	2.01	35.76
Days With ≥ 0.1" Precipitation	4	4	6	7	7	7	6	7	6	5	6	4	69
Days With ≥ 1.0" Precipitation	0	0	0	1	1	1	1	1	1	0	0	0	6
Mean Snowfall (in.)	9.8	6.0	3.5	1.2	trace	0.0	0.0	0.0	0.0	0.2	2.2	7.0	29.9
Days With ≥ 1.0" Snow Depth	20	14	4	1	0	0	0	0	0	0	2	11	52

Colo *Story County*   Elevation: 997 ft.   Latitude: 42° 01' N   Longitude: 93° 19' W

	JAN	FEB	MAR	APR	MAY	JUN	JUL	AUG	SEP	OCT	NOV	DEC	YEAR
Mean Maximum Temp. (°F)	25.3	31.6	43.8	58.6	70.6	80.0	83.6	81.0	73.9	61.8	44.4	30.6	57.1
Mean Temp. (°F)	16.3	22.5	34.4	47.5	59.6	69.2	73.1	70.5	62.4	50.1	35.3	22.3	46.9
Mean Minimum Temp. (°F)	7.3	13.4	24.9	36.4	48.5	58.4	62.7	60.0	50.8	38.4	26.0	13.9	36.7
Extreme Maximum Temp. (°F)	59	66	89	96	92	101	103	104	97	93	80	68	104
Extreme Minimum Temp. (°F)	-28	-28	-10	4	24	40	44	40	26	11	-10	-23	-28
Days Maximum Temp. ≥ 90°F	0	0	0	0	0	3	6	4	1	0	0	0	14
Days Maximum Temp. ≤ 32°F	21	15	6	0	0	0	0	0	0	0	5	17	64
Days Minimum Temp. ≤ 32°F	31	27	24	10	1	0	0	0	1	9	23	30	156
Days Minimum Temp. ≤ 0°F	10	6	1	0	0	0	0	0	0	0	1	5	23
Heating Degree Days (base 65°F)	1,505	1,194	942	525	207	31	6	17	147	462	886	1,319	7,241
Cooling Degree Days (base 65°F)	0	0	1	8	42	167	266	205	76	8	0	0	773
Mean Precipitation (in.)	0.85	0.90	2.13	3.24	4.40	5.16	4.93	4.72	3.34	2.64	2.04	1.12	35.47
Days With ≥ 0.1" Precipitation	3	3	5	7	8	8	7	6	6	5	4	3	65
Days With ≥ 1.0" Precipitation	0	0	0	1	1	2	1	2	1	1	0	0	9
Mean Snowfall (in.)	6.7	5.4	4.7	1.6	0.0	0.0	0.0	0.0	0.0	0.4	2.8	6.3	27.9
Days With ≥ 1.0" Snow Depth	21	15	6	1	0	0	0	0	0	0	4	15	62

Columbus Junction 2 SSW *Louisa County*   Elevation: 669 ft.   Latitude: 41° 15' N   Longitude: 91° 22' W

	JAN	FEB	MAR	APR	MAY	JUN	JUL	AUG	SEP	OCT	NOV	DEC	YEAR
Mean Maximum Temp. (°F)	29.8	36.3	48.9	63.0	74.0	82.9	86.7	84.2	77.0	65.3	48.5	35.1	61.0
Mean Temp. (°F)	21.2	27.5	39.1	51.6	62.4	71.5	75.5	73.1	65.4	53.9	39.5	27.1	50.6
Mean Minimum Temp. (°F)	12.4	18.7	29.2	40.1	50.8	60.0	64.3	62.1	53.8	42.4	30.5	19.1	40.3
Extreme Maximum Temp. (°F)	68	70	88	91	94	102	106	105	99	92	78	72	106
Extreme Minimum Temp. (°F)	-25	-30	-10	8	30	38	43	39	27	15	-8	-24	-30
Days Maximum Temp. ≥ 90°F	0	0	0	0	1	5	11	7	2	0	0	0	26
Days Maximum Temp. ≤ 32°F	17	10	3	0	0	0	0	0	0	0	2	11	43
Days Minimum Temp. ≤ 32°F	29	24	19	7	0	0	0	0	0	5	18	28	130
Days Minimum Temp. ≤ 0°F	7	3	0	0	0	0	0	0	0	0	0	3	13
Heating Degree Days (base 65°F)	1,353	1,052	798	411	144	17	2	6	95	352	758	1,168	6,156
Cooling Degree Days (base 65°F)	0	0	2	14	65	219	338	272	113	11	0	0	1,034
Mean Precipitation (in.)	1.15	1.30	2.76	3.57	4.48	4.20	4.41	4.68	4.03	2.95	2.72	1.88	38.13
Days With ≥ 0.1" Precipitation	3	4	6	7	8	7	7	7	6	6	6	4	71
Days With ≥ 1.0" Precipitation	0	0	1	1	1	1	1	1	1	1	0	0	8
Mean Snowfall (in.)	10.0	7.9	6.0	2.6	0.0	0.0	0.0	0.0	0.0	0.4	3.6	8.4	38.9
Days With ≥ 1.0" Snow Depth	20	14	5	1	0	0	0	0	0	0	2	12	54

Corning *Adams County*   Elevation: 1,213 ft.   Latitude: 40° 59' N   Longitude: 94° 45' W

	JAN	FEB	MAR	APR	MAY	JUN	JUL	AUG	SEP	OCT	NOV	DEC	YEAR
Mean Maximum Temp. (°F)	30.2	36.5	48.3	61.4	72.0	81.7	86.2	84.1	76.4	64.5	47.7	35.0	60.3
Mean Temp. (°F)	19.7	25.6	36.8	49.2	60.1	69.9	74.4	72.1	63.6	51.6	37.1	25.2	48.8
Mean Minimum Temp. (°F)	9.1	14.6	25.5	37.0	48.1	58.1	62.6	60.2	50.9	38.7	26.5	15.4	37.2
Extreme Maximum Temp. (°F)	68	77	88	91	91	102	105	106	98	93	81	67	106
Extreme Minimum Temp. (°F)	-32	-29	-17	3	24	36	42	39	20	12	-7	-26	-32
Days Maximum Temp. ≥ 90°F	0	0	0	0	0	4	10	7	2	0	0	0	23
Days Maximum Temp. ≤ 32°F	16	11	4	0	0	0	0	0	0	0	4	12	47
Days Minimum Temp. ≤ 32°F	30	27	23	10	1	0	0	0	1	8	22	29	151
Days Minimum Temp. ≤ 0°F	9	5	1	0	0	0	0	0	0	0	0	4	19
Heating Degree Days (base 65°F)	1,399	1,107	867	476	188	29	4	13	129	419	830	1,227	6,688
Cooling Degree Days (base 65°F)	0	0	1	11	40	183	306	242	95	9	0	0	887
Mean Precipitation (in.)	0.91	0.95	2.39	3.52	4.63	4.40	4.44	4.37	4.54	2.70	2.22	1.19	36.26
Days With ≥ 0.1" Precipitation	2	3	5	6	9	7	6	6	6	5	4	3	62
Days With ≥ 1.0" Precipitation	0	0	0	1	1	1	2	1	1	1	1	0	9
Mean Snowfall (in.)	6.0	5.8	3.6	1.4	trace	0.0	0.0	0.0	0.0	0.2	2.3	5.3	24.6
Days With ≥ 1.0" Snow Depth	na	na	2	0	0	0	0	0	0	0	1	3	na

Cresco 1 NE *Howard County*   Elevation: 1,253 ft.   Latitude: 43° 23' N   Longitude: 92° 06' W

	JAN	FEB	MAR	APR	MAY	JUN	JUL	AUG	SEP	OCT	NOV	DEC	YEAR
Mean Maximum Temp. (°F)	20.9	27.3	39.5	55.5	68.6	78.1	81.6	79.3	71.0	58.5	40.9	26.8	54.0
Mean Temp. (°F)	11.8	18.2	30.5	44.7	57.2	66.9	70.6	68.3	59.4	47.3	32.2	18.3	43.8
Mean Minimum Temp. (°F)	2.7	9.1	21.5	33.9	45.7	55.6	59.6	57.3	47.8	36.1	23.5	9.8	33.5
Extreme Maximum Temp. (°F)	54	63	83	91	91	100	99	100	94	92	72	62	100
Extreme Minimum Temp. (°F)	-32	-36	-15	-1	23	34	40	39	25	10	-16	-30	-36
Days Maximum Temp. ≥ 90°F	0	0	0	0	0	2	3	2	0	0	0	0	7
Days Maximum Temp. ≤ 32°F	25	17	8	1	0	0	0	0	0	0	7	21	79
Days Minimum Temp. ≤ 32°F	31	28	27	14	2	0	0	0	1	13	25	30	171
Days Minimum Temp. ≤ 0°F	14	9	2	0	0	0	0	0	0	0	1	9	35
Heating Degree Days (base 65°F)	1,644	1,316	1,062	607	267	59	16	35	205	544	976	1,442	8,173
Cooling Degree Days (base 65°F)	0	0	0	5	27	118	192	143	44	3	0	0	532
Mean Precipitation (in.)	1.01	0.85	2.22	3.56	3.86	4.38	4.55	5.10	3.85	2.53	2.37	1.24	35.52
Days With ≥ 0.1" Precipitation	3	3	5	7	8	7	7	7	6	5	5	3	66
Days With ≥ 1.0" Precipitation	0	0	0	1	1	1	1	2	1	1	1	0	9
Mean Snowfall (in.)	10.9	7.1	6.9	2.5	trace	0.0	0.0	0.0	0.0	0.4	5.1	8.8	41.7
Days With ≥ 1.0" Snow Depth	na	na	na	0	0	0	0	0	0	0	1	na	na

Creston 2 SW *Union County*   Elevation: 1,318 ft.   Latitude: 41° 02' N   Longitude: 94° 24' W

	JAN	FEB	MAR	APR	MAY	JUN	JUL	AUG	SEP	OCT	NOV	DEC	YEAR
Mean Maximum Temp. (°F)	29.8	36.8	49.1	62.2	72.7	82.3	86.0	84.1	76.5	64.3	47.3	34.6	60.5
Mean Temp. (°F)	20.7	27.4	38.6	50.7	61.5	71.1	75.2	73.1	65.0	53.0	38.3	26.1	50.1
Mean Minimum Temp. (°F)	11.7	17.9	28.1	39.0	50.3	59.9	64.2	62.0	53.5	41.8	29.3	17.5	39.6
Extreme Maximum Temp. (°F)	65	74	86	91	90	101	104	103	96	92	78	66	104
Extreme Minimum Temp. (°F)	-23	-26	-10	7	27	40	40	40	24	13	-9	-26	-26
Days Maximum Temp. ≥ 90°F	0	0	0	0	0	4	10	7	2	0	0	0	23
Days Maximum Temp. ≤ 32°F	17	11	3	0	0	0	0	0	0	0	3	12	46
Days Minimum Temp. ≤ 32°F	30	25	20	8	0	0	0	0	0	5	19	29	136
Days Minimum Temp. ≤ 0°F	7	4	1	0	0	0	0	0	0	0	0	4	16
Heating Degree Days (base 65°F)	1,371	1,055	812	436	154	18	3	8	104	375	795	1,201	6,332
Cooling Degree Days (base 65°F)	0	0	1	13	51	203	330	267	111	11	0	0	987
Mean Precipitation (in.)	0.78	1.01	2.08	3.41	4.59	4.21	4.34	3.85	4.20	2.63	2.32	0.99	34.41
Days With ≥ 0.1" Precipitation	2	3	5	6	8	7	6	6	6	5	5	3	62
Days With ≥ 1.0" Precipitation	0	0	0	1	1	1	1	1	1	1	0	1	7
Mean Snowfall (in.)	6.6	na	3.3	1.1	0.0	0.0	0.0	0.0	0.0	0.4	2.6	na	na
Days With ≥ 1.0" Snow Depth	na	na	2	0	0	0	0	0	0	0	1	na	na

Decorah *Winneshiek County*   Elevation: 859 ft.   Latitude: 43° 18' N   Longitude: 91° 48' W

	JAN	FEB	MAR	APR	MAY	JUN	JUL	AUG	SEP	OCT	NOV	DEC	YEAR
Mean Maximum Temp. (°F)	23.7	30.3	42.6	58.4	70.9	79.8	83.3	81.0	73.1	60.9	42.9	29.1	56.3
Mean Temp. (°F)	14.9	21.4	33.3	47.3	59.3	68.4	72.4	70.3	62.0	50.2	34.7	21.1	46.3
Mean Minimum Temp. (°F)	5.9	12.4	24.0	36.1	47.6	56.9	61.5	59.5	50.8	39.5	26.5	13.1	36.2
Extreme Maximum Temp. (°F)	56	62	84	89	91	101	102	100	98	92	78	63	102
Extreme Minimum Temp. (°F)	-37	-41	-13	5	25	33	42	39	25	11	-16	-28	-41
Days Maximum Temp. ≥ 90°F	0	0	0	0	0	3	5	3	1	0	0	0	12
Days Maximum Temp. ≤ 32°F	22	15	6	0	0	0	0	0	0	0	5	18	66
Days Minimum Temp. ≤ 32°F	31	27	24	11	1	0	0	0	1	8	21	30	154
Days Minimum Temp. ≤ 0°F	11	7	2	0	0	0	0	0	0	0	1	6	27
Heating Degree Days (base 65°F)	1,551	1,226	974	532	213	38	8	19	153	458	901	1,355	7,428
Cooling Degree Days (base 65°F)	0	0	0	8	39	152	254	199	73	6	0	0	731
Mean Precipitation (in.)	0.92	0.84	1.85	3.70	3.84	4.38	4.23	4.43	3.62	2.40	2.15	1.05	33.41
Days With ≥ 0.1" Precipitation	3	3	5	8	8	7	7	6	7	5	5	3	67
Days With ≥ 1.0" Precipitation	0	0	0	1	1	1	1	1	1	1	0	0	7
Mean Snowfall (in.)	10.6	7.4	6.3	1.7	trace	0.0	0.0	0.0	0.0	0.2	4.6	8.6	39.4
Days With ≥ 1.0" Snow Depth	na	na	5	0	0	0	0	0	0	0	0	na	na	na

Denison *Crawford County*   Elevation: 1,400 ft.   Latitude: 42° 02' N   Longitude: 95° 20' W

	JAN	FEB	MAR	APR	MAY	JUN	JUL	AUG	SEP	OCT	NOV	DEC	YEAR
Mean Maximum Temp. (°F)	27.4	33.8	45.6	60.0	71.3	80.9	84.3	81.9	74.7	62.3	44.6	31.7	58.2
Mean Temp. (°F)	18.5	24.9	35.9	49.0	60.6	70.2	74.2	71.9	63.8	51.7	35.9	23.5	48.3
Mean Minimum Temp. (°F)	9.5	15.9	26.1	38.0	49.9	59.5	64.0	61.8	52.8	41.0	27.1	15.3	38.4
Extreme Maximum Temp. (°F)	65	69	88	94	92	101	105	100	96	91	79	67	105
Extreme Minimum Temp. (°F)	-27	-27	-10	6	27	39	44	43	28	14	-8	-26	-27
Days Maximum Temp. ≥ 90°F	0	0	0	0	0	4	7	4	1	0	0	0	16
Days Maximum Temp. ≤ 32°F	19	13	6	1	0	0	0	0	0	0	5	16	60
Days Minimum Temp. ≤ 32°F	30	26	23	9	0	0	0	0	0	6	21	30	145
Days Minimum Temp. ≤ 0°F	9	5	1	0	0	0	0	0	0	0	0	5	20
Heating Degree Days (base 65°F)	1,438	1,127	897	485	181	26	3	10	121	416	867	1,280	6,851
Cooling Degree Days (base 65°F)	0	0	1	13	50	185	293	229	93	9	0	0	873
Mean Precipitation (in.)	0.80	0.72	2.20	3.05	4.19	4.23	3.84	3.33	3.37	2.31	1.58	0.96	30.58
Days With ≥ 0.1" Precipitation	2	2	5	7	8	7	6	6	6	4	4	3	60
Days With ≥ 1.0" Precipitation	0	0	0	1	1	1	1	1	1	0	0		7
Mean Snowfall (in.)	8.1	6.5	6.8	2.3	trace	0.0	0.0	0.0	trace	0.8	4.0	7.6	36.1
Days With ≥ 1.0" Snow Depth	20	17	9	1	0	0	0	0	0	0	5	14	66

Dubuque Lock & Dam 11 *Dubuque County*   Elevation: 620 ft.   Latitude: 42° 32' N   Longitude: 90° 39' W

	JAN	FEB	MAR	APR	MAY	JUN	JUL	AUG	SEP	OCT	NOV	DEC	YEAR
Mean Maximum Temp. (°F)	27.0	33.0	44.7	59.2	72.0	81.1	84.7	82.3	74.2	62.3	45.4	32.4	58.2
Mean Temp. (°F)	18.7	24.6	36.2	49.6	61.9	71.1	75.2	73.1	64.7	53.1	38.2	25.3	49.3
Mean Minimum Temp. (°F)	10.4	16.1	27.6	39.9	51.7	61.1	65.7	63.8	55.3	43.9	30.9	18.1	40.4
Extreme Maximum Temp. (°F)	61	64	87	93	95	101	108	104	97	92	75	65	108
Extreme Minimum Temp. (°F)	-27	-32	-10	11	30	43	46	43	29	19	-8	-22	-32
Days Maximum Temp. ≥ 90°F	0	0	0	0	1	4	7	4	1	0	0	0	17
Days Maximum Temp. ≤ 32°F	20	12	4	0	0	0	0	0	0	0	3	13	52
Days Minimum Temp. ≤ 32°F	30	26	21	6	0	0	0	0	0	2	17	28	130
Days Minimum Temp. ≤ 0°F	8	5	1	0	0	0	0	0	0	0	0	4	18
Heating Degree Days (base 65°F)	1,430	1,136	888	465	156	17	1	5	100	373	798	1,225	6,594
Cooling Degree Days (base 65°F)	0	0	0	10	63	215	334	272	102	9	0	0	1,005
Mean Precipitation (in.)	1.13	1.06	2.19	3.27	3.85	4.16	4.29	4.23	3.80	2.42	2.32	1.41	34.13
Days With ≥ 0.1" Precipitation	3	3	5	7	8	7	6	6	6	5	5	4	65
Days With ≥ 1.0" Precipitation	0	0	0	1	1	1	1	1	1	0	0		7
Mean Snowfall (in.)	10.5	6.7	4.4	1.5	trace	0.0	0.0	0.0	0.0	trace	2.6	7.8	33.5
Days With ≥ 1.0" Snow Depth	25	20	8	1	0	0	0	0	0	0	3	17	74

Eldora *Hardin County*   Elevation: 1,141 ft.   Latitude: 42° 22' N   Longitude: 93° 06' W

	JAN	FEB	MAR	APR	MAY	JUN	JUL	AUG	SEP	OCT	NOV	DEC	YEAR
Mean Maximum Temp. (°F)	24.6	31.1	43.8	58.5	71.2	80.8	84.6	82.1	74.8	62.1	44.0	30.0	57.3
Mean Temp. (°F)	15.8	22.2	34.4	47.5	59.8	69.6	73.5	71.0	62.8	50.5	35.0	21.8	47.0
Mean Minimum Temp. (°F)	6.9	13.2	25.0	36.4	48.4	58.2	62.4	59.9	50.8	38.8	26.0	13.5	36.6
Extreme Maximum Temp. (°F)	61	66	87	98	93	104	103	108	98	94	80	65	108
Extreme Minimum Temp. (°F)	-27	-29	-6	6	28	40	45	41	28	17	-13	-23	-29
Days Maximum Temp. ≥ 90°F	0	0	0	0	1	4	8	5	2	0	0	0	20
Days Maximum Temp. ≤ 32°F	21	15	6	1	0	0	0	0	0	0	5	17	65
Days Minimum Temp. ≤ 32°F	31	27	24	10	1	0	0	0	1	9	23	30	156
Days Minimum Temp. ≤ 0°F	10	6	1	0	0	0	0	0	0	0	1	6	24
Heating Degree Days (base 65°F)	1,521	1,204	942	527	202	30	6	14	137	452	894	1,335	7,264
Cooling Degree Days (base 65°F)	0	0	0	9	46	178	280	216	81	8	0	0	818
Mean Precipitation (in.)	0.93	0.90	2.09	3.17	4.41	5.31	3.93	4.31	3.24	2.68	2.12	1.10	34.19
Days With ≥ 0.1" Precipitation	3	3	5	6	8	8	7	6	6	5	4	3	64
Days With ≥ 1.0" Precipitation	0	0	0	1	1	2	1	1	1	1	0	0	8
Mean Snowfall (in.)	8.6	6.8	5.3	1.8	0.0	0.0	0.0	0.0	0.0	trace	3.4	6.6	32.5
Days With ≥ 1.0" Snow Depth	25	20	9	1	0	0	0	0	0	0	4	18	77

Elkader 5 SSW *Clayton County* Elevation: 767 ft. Latitude: 42° 47' N Longitude: 91° 27' W

	JAN	FEB	MAR	APR	MAY	JUN	JUL	AUG	SEP	OCT	NOV	DEC	YEAR
Mean Maximum Temp. (°F)	26.6	33.0	45.1	60.3	72.2	81.0	84.7	82.4	74.6	62.8	45.0	31.5	58.3
Mean Temp. (°F)	16.5	22.6	34.3	47.6	58.9	67.8	72.1	70.0	61.7	50.2	35.3	22.5	46.6
Mean Minimum Temp. (°F)	6.4	12.2	23.5	34.9	45.6	54.5	59.5	57.7	48.8	37.6	25.6	13.4	35.0
Extreme Maximum Temp. (°F)	59	65	87	92	93	103	104	106	99	92	79	65	106
Extreme Minimum Temp. (°F)	-37	-47	-18	-1	23	33	35	37	20	9	-22	-29	-47
Days Maximum Temp. ≥ 90°F	0	0	0	0	1	3	7	5	1	0	0	0	17
Days Maximum Temp. ≤ 32°F	20	13	4	0	0	0	0	0	0	0	4	15	56
Days Minimum Temp. ≤ 32°F	31	27	25	13	3	0	0	0	2	11	22	30	164
Days Minimum Temp. ≤ 0°F	11	7	1	0	0	0	0	0	0	0	1	6	26
Heating Degree Days (base 65°F)	1,498	1,190	944	522	221	47	9	23	159	460	884	1,313	7,270
Cooling Degree Days (base 65°F)	0	0	1	8	37	137	241	191	67	6	0	0	688
Mean Precipitation (in.)	1.04	1.12	2.08	3.52	4.07	4.41	4.09	4.72	3.22	2.49	2.37	1.18	34.31
Days With ≥ 0.1" Precipitation	3	3	5	7	8	7	6	7	6	5	5	3	65
Days With ≥ 1.0" Precipitation	0	0	0	1	1	1	1	1	1	0	0	0	6
Mean Snowfall (in.)	9.6	7.0	5.2	2.0	0.0	0.0	0.0	0.0	0.0	0.2	4.0	8.2	36.2
Days With ≥ 1.0" Snow Depth	na	na	2	0	0	0	0	0	0	0	0	1	na	na

Emmetsburg *Palo Alto County* Elevation: 1,269 ft. Latitude: 43° 07' N Longitude: 94° 41' W

	JAN	FEB	MAR	APR	MAY	JUN	JUL	AUG	SEP	OCT	NOV	DEC	YEAR
Mean Maximum Temp. (°F)	24.3	30.9	42.7	59.0	72.5	81.6	84.1	81.8	74.5	61.9	42.5	29.3	57.1
Mean Temp. (°F)	15.1	22.0	33.5	47.7	60.5	70.0	73.2	70.9	62.7	50.2	33.6	20.8	46.7
Mean Minimum Temp. (°F)	5.9	13.0	24.3	36.4	48.5	58.3	62.3	59.9	50.8	38.3	24.7	12.2	36.2
Extreme Maximum Temp. (°F)	57	63	84	93	94	102	101	102	98	92	80	68	102
Extreme Minimum Temp. (°F)	-29	-29	-13	5	29	39	42	42	24	11	-11	-24	-29
Days Maximum Temp. ≥ 90°F	0	0	0	0	1	5	6	4	1	0	0	0	17
Days Maximum Temp. ≤ 32°F	21	14	6	0	0	0	0	0	0	0	7	18	66
Days Minimum Temp. ≤ 32°F	30	27	25	10	1	0	0	0	1	8	24	30	156
Days Minimum Temp. ≤ 0°F	12	6	1	0	0	0	0	0	0	0	1	6	26
Heating Degree Days (base 65°F)	1,543	1,210	968	520	182	28	5	15	137	459	935	1,365	7,367
Cooling Degree Days (base 65°F)	0	0	0	7	49	179	265	206	72	6	0	0	784
Mean Precipitation (in.)	0.83	0.63	2.14	3.15	3.67	4.55	4.12	4.22	2.80	2.32	1.87	0.88	31.18
Days With ≥ 0.1" Precipitation	2	2	5	6	8	7	7	6	5	4	4	2	58
Days With ≥ 1.0" Precipitation	0	0	0	1	1	1	1	1	1	1	0	0	7
Mean Snowfall (in.)	8.0	5.4	6.4	2.2	trace	0.0	0.0	0.0	0.0	0.2	4.8	7.1	34.1
Days With ≥ 1.0" Snow Depth	22	17	8	1	0	0	0	0	0	0	0	na	na	na

Estherville 2 N *Emmet County* Elevation: 1,299 ft. Latitude: 43° 26' N Longitude: 94° 50' W

	JAN	FEB	MAR	APR	MAY	JUN	JUL	AUG	SEP	OCT	NOV	DEC	YEAR
Mean Maximum Temp. (°F)	22.2	28.5	39.9	56.3	70.1	79.3	82.5	80.0	72.5	60.0	41.0	27.2	55.0
Mean Temp. (°F)	12.9	19.3	30.8	45.3	58.4	67.9	71.5	69.0	60.4	48.0	32.1	18.5	44.5
Mean Minimum Temp. (°F)	3.5	10.2	21.7	34.2	46.5	56.5	60.4	57.9	48.3	36.0	23.1	9.8	34.0
Extreme Maximum Temp. (°F)	64	65	85	90	93	102	101	102	99	93	80	67	102
Extreme Minimum Temp. (°F)	-30	-29	-13	7	27	37	41	41	24	13	-12	-25	-30
Days Maximum Temp. ≥ 90°F	0	0	0	0	1	3	5	3	1	0	0	0	13
Days Maximum Temp. ≤ 32°F	23	17	9	1	0	0	0	0	0	0	8	20	78
Days Minimum Temp. ≤ 32°F	31	28	27	13	1	0	0	0	1	12	25	31	169
Days Minimum Temp. ≤ 0°F	14	8	2	0	0	0	0	0	0	0	1	8	33
Heating Degree Days (base 65°F)	1,612	1,284	1,052	590	238	49	11	29	185	524	980	1,436	7,990
Cooling Degree Days (base 65°F)	0	0	0	6	36	137	218	158	53	4	0	0	612
Mean Precipitation (in.)	0.64	0.48	1.74	3.18	3.44	4.68	3.44	3.65	2.78	2.21	1.47	0.62	28.33
Days With ≥ 0.1" Precipitation	2	1	4	6	7	7	6	6	5	4	3	2	53
Days With ≥ 1.0" Precipitation	0	0	0	1	1	1	1	1	1	1	0	0	7
Mean Snowfall (in.)	7.4	5.6	6.8	2.5	0.0	0.0	0.0	0.0	trace	0.7	5.1	7.0	35.1
Days With ≥ 1.0" Snow Depth	na	na	na	1	0	0	0	0	0	0	2	na	na

Fairfield *Jefferson County* Elevation: 738 ft. Latitude: 41° 01' N Longitude: 91° 57' W

	JAN	FEB	MAR	APR	MAY	JUN	JUL	AUG	SEP	OCT	NOV	DEC	YEAR
Mean Maximum Temp. (°F)	30.3	36.7	49.3	63.1	74.0	83.2	87.4	84.8	76.8	64.8	48.3	35.5	61.2
Mean Temp. (°F)	21.5	27.7	39.3	51.8	62.7	72.0	76.4	73.8	65.7	54.0	39.6	27.4	51.0
Mean Minimum Temp. (°F)	12.7	18.7	29.3	40.5	51.3	60.8	65.3	62.8	54.5	43.1	30.9	19.2	40.8
Extreme Maximum Temp. (°F)	70	72	87	91	95	104	106	106	100	91	78	71	106
Extreme Minimum Temp. (°F)	-26	-31	-11	9	28	42	45	43	29	17	-4	-23	-31
Days Maximum Temp. ≥ 90°F	0	0	0	0	1	5	12	8	2	0	0	0	28
Days Maximum Temp. ≤ 32°F	16	11	3	0	0	0	0	0	0	0	3	11	44
Days Minimum Temp. ≤ 32°F	29	25	19	6	0	0	0	0	0	4	17	28	128
Days Minimum Temp. ≤ 0°F	7	4	0	0	0	0	0	0	0	0	0	3	14
Heating Degree Days (base 65°F)	1,342	1,046	790	404	138	14	2	5	93	348	754	1,160	6,096
Cooling Degree Days (base 65°F)	0	0	2	16	69	232	365	292	123	14	0	0	1,113
Mean Precipitation (in.)	1.24	1.19	2.45	3.51	4.72	3.77	4.42	4.38	4.15	2.97	2.46	1.75	37.01
Days With ≥ 0.1" Precipitation	3	3	5	7	8	7	7	7	6	6	6	4	69
Days With ≥ 1.0" Precipitation	0	0	0	1	1	1	1	1	1	1	1	0	8
Mean Snowfall (in.)	7.9	6.9	3.5	1.8	0.0	0.0	0.0	0.0	0.0	0.1	2.1	5.7	28.0
Days With ≥ 1.0" Snow Depth	17	11	4	1	0	0	0	0	0	0	2	6	41

Fayette *Fayette County*   Elevation: 1,049 ft.   Latitude: 42° 51' N   Longitude: 91° 49' W

	JAN	FEB	MAR	APR	MAY	JUN	JUL	AUG	SEP	OCT	NOV	DEC	YEAR
Mean Maximum Temp. (°F)	24.0	30.4	42.8	58.4	70.9	80.0	83.4	81.2	73.4	61.1	43.0	29.5	56.5
Mean Temp. (°F)	14.6	20.9	33.0	46.6	58.5	67.9	71.7	69.6	61.2	49.3	34.1	21.0	45.7
Mean Minimum Temp. (°F)	5.2	11.3	23.2	34.6	46.1	55.7	60.1	57.8	49.0	37.5	25.2	12.4	34.8
Extreme Maximum Temp. (°F)	58	64	85	96	92	100	103	104	96	91	77	63	104
Extreme Minimum Temp. (°F)	-33	-40	-17	-2	25	33	40	38	22	10	-20	-26	-40
Days Maximum Temp. ≥ 90°F	0	0	0	0	0	2	6	3	1	0	0	0	12
Days Maximum Temp. ≤ 32°F	23	14	6	0	0	0	0	0	0	0	5	17	65
Days Minimum Temp. ≤ 32°F	31	27	25	13	2	0	0	0	1	11	23	30	163
Days Minimum Temp. ≤ 0°F	12	7	2	0	0	0	0	0	0	0	0	6	28
Heating Degree Days (base 65°F)	1,557	1,241	985	553	231	45	11	25	169	484	920	1,360	7,581
Cooling Degree Days (base 65°F)	0	0	0	7	32	131	221	172	59	4	0	0	626
Mean Precipitation (in.)	1.11	1.10	2.16	3.56	4.36	4.58	4.37	4.90	3.53	2.62	2.32	1.33	35.94
Days With ≥ 0.1" Precipitation	4	3	5	8	8	7	7	7	6	5	5	4	69
Days With ≥ 1.0" Precipitation	0	0	0	1	1	1	1	1	1	1	1	0	8
Mean Snowfall (in.)	10.5	7.7	6.3	2.3	trace	0.0	0.0	0.0	0.0	0.2	4.4	9.0	40.4
Days With ≥ 1.0" Snow Depth	25	20	11	1	0	0	0	0	0	0	4	19	80

Forest City 2 NNE *Winnebago County*   Elevation: 1,299 ft.   Latitude: 43° 17' N   Longitude: 93° 38' W

	JAN	FEB	MAR	APR	MAY	JUN	JUL	AUG	SEP	OCT	NOV	DEC	YEAR
Mean Maximum Temp. (°F)	22.5	28.8	41.8	57.8	71.2	80.1	83.0	80.3	72.9	60.6	41.1	27.9	55.7
Mean Temp. (°F)	13.5	20.1	32.9	46.8	59.7	68.8	72.5	69.8	61.5	49.5	32.7	19.8	45.6
Mean Minimum Temp. (°F)	4.4	11.4	24.0	35.8	48.2	57.5	61.9	59.3	50.1	38.3	24.2	11.6	35.6
Extreme Maximum Temp. (°F)	58	65	83	91	93	100	101	99	96	92	79	69	101
Extreme Minimum Temp. (°F)	-30	-32	-10	6	25	38	45	40	26	14	-13	-25	-32
Days Maximum Temp. ≥ 90°F	0	0	0	0	1	3	5	2	1	0	0	0	12
Days Maximum Temp. ≤ 32°F	23	16	7	0	0	0	0	0	0	0	7	20	73
Days Minimum Temp. ≤ 32°F	31	27	25	11	1	0	0	0	1	9	24	30	159
Days Minimum Temp. ≤ 0°F	13	7	2	0	0	0	0	0	0	0	1	7	30
Heating Degree Days (base 65°F)	1,593	1,260	989	545	203	36	7	22	159	482	963	1,395	7,654
Cooling Degree Days (base 65°F)	0	0	0	6	44	158	236	170	59	5	0	0	678
Mean Precipitation (in.)	0.86	0.73	1.95	3.25	3.82	4.57	4.31	4.52	2.97	2.36	1.64	0.98	31.96
Days With ≥ 0.1" Precipitation	2	2	4	7	7	7	6	6	5	5	4	2	57
Days With ≥ 1.0" Precipitation	0	0	0	1	1	1	2	1	1	0	0	0	7
Mean Snowfall (in.)	10.6	6.3	6.0	2.2	trace	0.0	0.0	0.0	0.0	0.2	4.8	8.9	39.0
Days With ≥ 1.0" Snow Depth	20	17	9	1	0	0	0	0	0	0	5	16	68

Fort Dodge *Webster County*   Elevation: 1,112 ft.   Latitude: 42° 30' N   Longitude: 94° 12' W

	JAN	FEB	MAR	APR	MAY	JUN	JUL	AUG	SEP	OCT	NOV	DEC	YEAR
Mean Maximum Temp. (°F)	25.5	32.3	44.6	60.0	72.4	81.8	85.0	82.3	75.3	62.4	44.3	30.4	58.0
Mean Temp. (°F)	16.2	22.8	34.7	48.3	60.5	70.1	73.8	71.3	63.1	50.6	35.0	21.8	47.4
Mean Minimum Temp. (°F)	6.8	13.2	24.7	36.5	48.5	58.4	62.6	60.3	50.8	38.8	25.7	13.1	36.6
Extreme Maximum Temp. (°F)	64	67	88	100	96	103	103	106	98	95	77	67	106
Extreme Minimum Temp. (°F)	-27	-30	-10	6	27	38	43	40	26	14	-9	-26	-30
Days Maximum Temp. ≥ 90°F	0	0	0	0	1	5	8	5	2	0	0	0	21
Days Maximum Temp. ≤ 32°F	21	14	5	0	0	0	0	0	0	0	5	16	61
Days Minimum Temp. ≤ 32°F	31	27	24	11	1	0	0	0	1	8	23	30	156
Days Minimum Temp. ≤ 0°F	11	6	1	0	0	0	0	0	0	0	1	6	25
Heating Degree Days (base 65°F)	1,510	1,186	933	505	188	27	5	14	135	447	892	1,333	7,175
Cooling Degree Days (base 65°F)	0	0	0	10	53	189	289	220	86	8	0	0	855
Mean Precipitation (in.)	0.94	0.78	2.27	3.48	4.36	5.07	4.40	4.25	3.35	2.47	1.91	1.09	34.37
Days With ≥ 0.1" Precipitation	3	3	4	7	8	8	7	6	6	5	4	3	64
Days With ≥ 1.0" Precipitation	0	0	0	1	1	1	1	1	1	0	0	0	6
Mean Snowfall (in.)	8.6	7.1	6.2	2.0	0.0	0.0	0.0	0.0	0.0	0.2	4.5	7.6	36.2
Days With ≥ 1.0" Snow Depth	na	na	5	0	0	0	0	0	0	0	4	na	na

Fort Madison *Lee County*   Elevation: 528 ft.   Latitude: 40° 37' N   Longitude: 91° 20' W

	JAN	FEB	MAR	APR	MAY	JUN	JUL	AUG	SEP	OCT	NOV	DEC	YEAR
Mean Maximum Temp. (°F)	31.9	37.2	49.3	62.3	72.9	82.1	86.6	84.1	77.1	65.0	49.4	36.7	61.2
Mean Temp. (°F)	23.0	28.4	40.0	52.2	62.8	72.1	76.7	74.2	66.5	54.5	40.7	28.6	51.6
Mean Minimum Temp. (°F)	14.1	19.5	30.7	41.9	52.8	62.1	66.9	64.3	55.8	43.9	32.0	20.5	42.0
Extreme Maximum Temp. (°F)	62	71	78	89	90	104	103	104	98	90	79	70	104
Extreme Minimum Temp. (°F)	-23	-21	-1	11	29	42	47	42	31	15	-4	-19	-23
Days Maximum Temp. ≥ 90°F	0	0	0	0	0	4	10	6	2	0	0	0	22
Days Maximum Temp. ≤ 32°F	14	10	2	0	0	0	0	0	0	0	2	9	37
Days Minimum Temp. ≤ 32°F	29	24	18	5	0	0	0	0	0	3	16	26	121
Days Minimum Temp. ≤ 0°F	6	3	0	0	0	0	0	0	0	0	0	3	12
Heating Degree Days (base 65°F)	1,296	1,028	769	390	132	15	1	5	78	334	722	1,122	5,892
Cooling Degree Days (base 65°F)	0	0	1	11	67	251	378	318	133	12	0	0	1,171
Mean Precipitation (in.)	1.27	1.48	2.94	3.62	4.94	4.11	4.34	4.00	4.28	2.84	2.96	2.27	39.05
Days With ≥ 0.1" Precipitation	4	4	6	7	8	7	6	7	6	5	5	5	70
Days With ≥ 1.0" Precipitation	0	0	1	1	1	1	1	1	1	1	1	1	10
Mean Snowfall (in.)	6.4	4.3	1.6	0.6	0.0	0.0	0.0	0.0	0.0	trace	0.7	4.5	18.1
Days With ≥ 1.0" Snow Depth	na	na	1	0	0	0	0	0	0	0	0	na	na

Glenwood 3 SW *Mills County*   Elevation: 977 ft.   Latitude: 41° 00' N   Longitude: 95° 46' W

	JAN	FEB	MAR	APR	MAY	JUN	JUL	AUG	SEP	OCT	NOV	DEC	YEAR
Mean Maximum Temp. (°F)	32.1	38.8	51.1	64.4	74.8	84.3	87.6	85.5	78.7	66.9	49.3	36.4	62.5
Mean Temp. (°F)	21.6	28.0	39.5	51.8	62.7	72.2	76.2	74.0	65.8	53.5	38.8	26.7	50.9
Mean Minimum Temp. (°F)	11.2	17.1	27.9	39.1	50.5	60.1	64.7	62.4	52.9	40.1	28.2	17.0	39.2
Extreme Maximum Temp. (°F)	69	78	92	99	102	104	108	104	99	96	85	68	108
Extreme Minimum Temp. (°F)	-28	-24	-16	3	26	35	41	37	22	11	-7	-26	-28
Days Maximum Temp. ≥ 90°F	0	0	0	1	1	8	12	10	4	0	0	0	36
Days Maximum Temp. ≤ 32°F	15	10	3	0	0	0	0	0	0	0	3	11	42
Days Minimum Temp. ≤ 32°F	30	26	20	8	1	0	0	0	1	7	21	30	144
Days Minimum Temp. ≤ 0°F	7	4	1	0	0	0	0	0	0	0	0	3	15
Heating Degree Days (base 65°F)	1,339	1,040	785	408	137	16	2	7	98	364	780	1,180	6,156
Cooling Degree Days (base 65°F)	0	0	2	20	68	231	348	284	127	12	0	0	1,092
Mean Precipitation (in.)	0.71	0.78	2.15	3.40	4.89	4.62	4.47	3.80	3.45	2.34	1.80	0.99	33.40
Days With ≥ 0.1" Precipitation	2	2	5	6	8	7	6	6	5	4	4	2	57
Days With ≥ 1.0" Precipitation	0	0	0	1	1	1	1	1	1	0	0	0	7
Mean Snowfall (in.)	6.4	5.5	4.0	0.7	trace	0.0	0.0	0.0	0.0	0.4	2.2	4.6	23.8
Days With ≥ 1.0" Snow Depth	16	11	4	1	0	0	0	0	0	0	2	8	42

Greenfield *Adair County*   Elevation: 1,338 ft.   Latitude: 41° 18' N   Longitude: 94° 27' W

	JAN	FEB	MAR	APR	MAY	JUN	JUL	AUG	SEP	OCT	NOV	DEC	YEAR
Mean Maximum Temp. (°F)	30.1	36.9	49.5	63.3	73.6	82.9	86.6	84.3	77.4	65.4	47.7	34.9	61.1
Mean Temp. (°F)	20.9	27.3	38.7	51.4	62.2	71.5	75.6	73.2	65.7	53.8	38.5	26.3	50.4
Mean Minimum Temp. (°F)	11.6	17.6	27.9	39.5	50.6	60.0	64.8	62.4	53.9	42.0	29.3	17.7	39.8
Extreme Maximum Temp. (°F)	66	74	89	91	91	101	106	102	98	93	79	67	106
Extreme Minimum Temp. (°F)	-25	-26	-11	7	27	40	43	40	28	13	-4	-25	-26
Days Maximum Temp. ≥ 90°F	0	0	0	0	0	5	10	6	2	0	0	0	23
Days Maximum Temp. ≤ 32°F	16	11	3	0	0	0	0	0	0	0	3	12	45
Days Minimum Temp. ≤ 32°F	30	25	21	7	0	0	0	0	0	5	19	29	136
Days Minimum Temp. ≤ 0°F	8	4	1	0	0	0	0	0	0	0	0	4	17
Heating Degree Days (base 65°F)	1,361	1,059	810	414	143	16	2	6	93	356	788	1,194	6,242
Cooling Degree Days (base 65°F)	0	0	1	16	58	211	332	264	121	14	0	0	1,017
Mean Precipitation (in.)	0.98	0.99	2.30	3.74	4.36	4.17	4.56	3.80	4.03	2.61	2.22	1.29	35.05
Days With ≥ 0.1" Precipitation	3	3	5	7	8	7	6	6	6	5	5	3	64
Days With ≥ 1.0" Precipitation	0	0	1	1	1	1	1	1	1	1	0	0	8
Mean Snowfall (in.)	7.7	6.4	3.4	1.2	trace	0.0	trace	0.0	0.0	0.3	2.7	5.4	27.1
Days With ≥ 1.0" Snow Depth	19	15	5	1	0	0	0	0	0	0	3	12	55

Grinnell 3 SW *Poweshiek County*   Elevation: 902 ft.   Latitude: 41° 43' N   Longitude: 92° 45' W

	JAN	FEB	MAR	APR	MAY	JUN	JUL	AUG	SEP	OCT	NOV	DEC	YEAR
Mean Maximum Temp. (°F)	26.7	32.9	45.3	59.0	70.5	80.0	84.2	81.9	74.5	62.5	45.9	32.4	58.0
Mean Temp. (°F)	17.0	22.8	34.7	47.0	58.2	68.1	72.7	70.1	61.8	49.7	35.8	23.3	46.8
Mean Minimum Temp. (°F)	7.3	12.7	24.1	34.9	46.0	56.2	61.1	58.2	49.0	36.8	25.7	14.1	35.5
Extreme Maximum Temp. (°F)	59	68	88	92	91	100	102	103	96	91	79	69	103
Extreme Minimum Temp. (°F)	-34	-35	-14	1	24	35	40	37	21	10	-15	-32	-35
Days Maximum Temp. ≥ 90°F	0	0	0	0	0	2	7	5	1	0	0	0	15
Days Maximum Temp. ≤ 32°F	19	14	5	0	0	0	0	0	0	0	4	14	56
Days Minimum Temp. ≤ 32°F	31	27	24	12	2	0	0	0	2	12	23	30	163
Days Minimum Temp. ≤ 0°F	11	6	1	0	0	0	0	0	0	0	0	5	23
Heating Degree Days (base 65°F)	1,481	1,186	932	541	239	43	9	23	159	476	869	1,286	7,244
Cooling Degree Days (base 65°F)	0	0	0	7	34	145	256	197	70	7	0	0	716
Mean Precipitation (in.)	1.19	1.25	2.51	3.60	4.35	4.49	4.11	4.62	3.74	2.89	2.42	1.44	36.61
Days With ≥ 0.1" Precipitation	3	3	6	7	8	7	7	7	6	5	5	4	68
Days With ≥ 1.0" Precipitation	0	0	0	1	1	2	1	1	1	1	0	0	8
Mean Snowfall (in.)	8.3	6.7	4.1	1.6	trace	0.0	0.0	0.0	0.0	0.5	2.8	6.3	30.3
Days With ≥ 1.0" Snow Depth	*18*	13	5	1	0	0	0	0	0	0	2	11	*50*

Grundy Center *Grundy County*   Elevation: 1,017 ft.   Latitude: 42° 21' N   Longitude: 92° 46' W

	JAN	FEB	MAR	APR	MAY	JUN	JUL	AUG	SEP	OCT	NOV	DEC	YEAR
Mean Maximum Temp. (°F)	24.3	30.5	43.0	57.8	70.2	79.6	83.2	80.8	73.7	61.6	44.0	29.6	56.5
Mean Temp. (°F)	15.3	21.5	33.7	46.8	59.0	68.9	72.5	70.1	61.8	49.7	34.8	21.3	46.3
Mean Minimum Temp. (°F)	6.3	12.5	24.4	35.7	47.7	58.1	61.9	59.2	49.9	37.9	25.5	12.8	36.0
Extreme Maximum Temp. (°F)	60	67	87	96	92	101	99	102	96	94	80	64	102
Extreme Minimum Temp. (°F)	-27	-29	-11	-1	27	36	42	38	26	12	-14	-23	-29
Days Maximum Temp. ≥ 90°F	0	0	0	0	0	3	5	3	1	0	0	0	12
Days Maximum Temp. ≤ 32°F	22	15	6	1	0	0	0	0	0	0	5	17	66
Days Minimum Temp. ≤ 32°F	31	27	24	11	1	0	0	0	1	10	23	30	158
Days Minimum Temp. ≤ 0°F	11	7	1	0	0	0	0	0	0	0	1	6	26
Heating Degree Days (base 65°F)	1,535	1,222	964	547	221	36	8	22	157	474	901	1,350	7,437
Cooling Degree Days (base 65°F)	0	0	0	7	38	162	254	193	69	7	0	0	730
Mean Precipitation (in.)	0.87	0.96	2.31	3.25	4.37	5.00	4.05	3.93	3.13	2.65	2.21	1.20	33.93
Days With ≥ 0.1" Precipitation	3	3	5	7	8	7	7	6	6	5	5	3	65
Days With ≥ 1.0" Precipitation	0	0	1	1	1	2	1	1	1	1	0	0	9
Mean Snowfall (in.)	9.6	7.6	6.4	2.5	trace	0.0	trace	0.0	0.0	0.3	4.0	7.9	38.3
Days With ≥ 1.0" Snow Depth	24	20	10	1	0	0	0	0	0	0	4	18	77

Guthrie Center *Guthrie County*   Elevation: 1,072 ft.   Latitude: 41° 40' N   Longitude: 94° 30' W

	JAN	FEB	MAR	APR	MAY	JUN	JUL	AUG	SEP	OCT	NOV	DEC	YEAR
Mean Maximum Temp. (°F)	28.2	34.4	46.5	60.5	72.1	81.9	85.9	83.3	76.0	63.4	46.2	32.9	59.3
Mean Temp. (°F)	18.0	24.1	35.8	48.8	60.1	69.9	74.2	71.5	62.9	50.5	36.0	23.5	47.9
Mean Minimum Temp. (°F)	7.8	13.8	25.2	37.0	48.1	57.8	62.4	59.7	49.7	37.5	25.8	14.0	36.6
Extreme Maximum Temp. (°F)	68	71	89	93	93	101	105	103	99	94	80	67	105
Extreme Minimum Temp. (°F)	-27	-35	-15	8	26	38	41	37	26	9	-16	-31	-35
Days Maximum Temp. ≥ 90°F	0	0	0	0	1	5	10	6	2	0	0	0	24
Days Maximum Temp. ≤ 32°F	18	13	5	0	0	0	0	0	0	0	4	14	54
Days Minimum Temp. ≤ 32°F	31	27	24	10	1	0	0	0	1	10	23	30	157
Days Minimum Temp. ≤ 0°F	10	6	1	0	0	0	0	0	0	0	1	5	23
Heating Degree Days (base 65°F)	1,451	1,149	898	490	195	29	6	16	142	452	862	1,281	6,971
Cooling Degree Days (base 65°F)	0	0	1	11	47	179	296	221	85	8	0	0	848
Mean Precipitation (in.)	0.88	0.96	2.44	3.38	4.58	4.72	4.22	4.53	3.45	2.60	1.98	1.21	34.95
Days With ≥ 0.1" Precipitation	3	3	5	7	8	7	7	6	5	5	4	3	63
Days With ≥ 1.0" Precipitation	0	0	1	1	1	1	1	2	1	1	0	0	9
Mean Snowfall (in.)	8.0	7.1	4.8	1.7	trace	0.0	0.0	0.0	0.0	0.5	2.6	5.9	30.6
Days With ≥ 1.0" Snow Depth	na	na	2	0	0	0	0	0	0	0	0	2	na	na

Guttenberg Lock & Dam 10 *Clayton County*   Elevation: 623 ft.   Latitude: 42° 47' N   Longitude: 91° 06' W

	JAN	FEB	MAR	APR	MAY	JUN	JUL	AUG	SEP	OCT	NOV	DEC	YEAR
Mean Maximum Temp. (°F)	26.5	32.9	44.8	59.4	71.7	80.8	84.5	82.2	73.9	61.8	44.6	31.9	57.9
Mean Temp. (°F)	17.6	23.8	35.8	49.3	61.2	70.5	74.5	72.2	63.8	51.9	36.8	24.2	48.5
Mean Minimum Temp. (°F)	8.7	14.7	26.8	39.3	50.7	60.1	64.4	62.3	53.6	42.0	29.0	16.5	39.0
Extreme Maximum Temp. (°F)	59	64	87	97	95	101	102	102	96	94	78	65	102
Extreme Minimum Temp. (°F)	-33	-38	-11	7	28	40	46	40	27	14	-11	-23	-38
Days Maximum Temp. ≥ 90°F	0	0	0	0	0	3	6	4	1	0	0	0	14
Days Maximum Temp. ≤ 32°F	20	12	4	0	0	0	0	0	0	0	4	14	54
Days Minimum Temp. ≤ 32°F	30	26	22	7	0	0	0	0	0	4	19	29	137
Days Minimum Temp. ≤ 0°F	9	5	1	0	0	0	0	0	0	0	0	5	20
Heating Degree Days (base 65°F)	1,464	1,157	900	473	167	21	3	8	119	407	839	1,259	6,817
Cooling Degree Days (base 65°F)	0	0	0	10	54	195	311	248	91	8	0	0	917
Mean Precipitation (in.)	1.05	1.10	2.03	3.20	3.87	4.34	4.21	4.37	3.15	2.22	2.22	1.30	33.06
Days With ≥ 0.1" Precipitation	3	3	5	7	8	7	7	7	6	5	5	4	67
Days With ≥ 1.0" Precipitation	0	0	0	1	1	1	1	1	1	0	0	0	6
Mean Snowfall (in.)	10.7	5.6	4.0	1.2	0.0	0.0	0.0	0.0	0.0	0.1	2.3	7.0	30.9
Days With ≥ 1.0" Snow Depth	24	21	8	1	0	0	0	0	0	0	3	17	74

Hampton *Franklin County*   Elevation: 1,227 ft.   Latitude: 42° 45' N   Longitude: 93° 12' W

	JAN	FEB	MAR	APR	MAY	JUN	JUL	AUG	SEP	OCT	NOV	DEC	YEAR
Mean Maximum Temp. (°F)	23.7	30.1	42.4	57.8	71.0	80.4	83.3	80.9	73.8	61.4	42.7	29.2	56.4
Mean Temp. (°F)	15.4	21.5	33.5	46.9	59.6	69.3	72.6	70.2	62.1	50.2	34.1	21.1	46.4
Mean Minimum Temp. (°F)	6.8	12.8	24.5	36.0	48.2	58.1	61.9	59.4	50.4	38.9	25.5	13.2	36.3
Extreme Maximum Temp. (°F)	59	68	86	95	93	103	101	104	97	94	79	64	104
Extreme Minimum Temp. (°F)	-31	-31	-9	9	25	38	43	42	25	14	-14	-23	-31
Days Maximum Temp. ≥ 90°F	0	0	0	0	1	4	6	3	1	0	0	0	15
Days Maximum Temp. ≤ 32°F	22	15	7	1	0	0	0	0	0	0	6	19	70
Days Minimum Temp. ≤ 32°F	31	27	24	10	1	0	0	0	1	9	23	30	156
Days Minimum Temp. ≤ 0°F	11	6	1	0	0	0	0	0	0	0	1	6	25
Heating Degree Days (base 65°F)	1,532	1,224	970	543	205	34	8	19	148	461	919	1,355	7,418
Cooling Degree Days (base 65°F)	0	0	0	7	42	164	246	180	64	6	0	0	709
Mean Precipitation (in.)	0.94	0.84	2.18	3.20	4.45	4.88	4.69	4.32	3.23	2.56	1.97	1.18	34.44
Days With ≥ 0.1" Precipitation	2	2	5	7	9	7	7	6	6	5	5	3	64
Days With ≥ 1.0" Precipitation	0	0	0	1	1	1	1	1	1	0	0	0	6
Mean Snowfall (in.)	8.3	6.4	6.0	2.6	trace	0.0	trace	0.0	0.0	0.4	4.2	7.1	35.0
Days With ≥ 1.0" Snow Depth	24	20	9	1	0	0	0	0	0	0	5	19	78

Harlan *Shelby County*   Elevation: 1,207 ft.   Latitude: 41° 39' N   Longitude: 95° 19' W

	JAN	FEB	MAR	APR	MAY	JUN	JUL	AUG	SEP	OCT	NOV	DEC	YEAR
Mean Maximum Temp. (°F)	29.2	35.9	48.0	62.4	73.1	82.5	85.4	82.8	75.5	63.3	46.1	33.3	59.8
Mean Temp. (°F)	19.5	26.2	37.4	50.3	61.5	71.1	74.7	72.3	64.2	51.9	36.8	24.6	49.2
Mean Minimum Temp. (°F)	9.8	16.5	26.7	38.2	49.8	59.7	63.9	61.8	52.8	40.4	27.5	15.8	38.6
Extreme Maximum Temp. (°F)	66	71	89	93	94	102	104	100	98	92	79	67	104
Extreme Minimum Temp. (°F)	-29	-25	-13	2	26	40	40	40	27	12	-9	-26	-29
Days Maximum Temp. ≥ 90°F	0	0	0	0	1	5	8	5	2	0	0	0	21
Days Maximum Temp. ≤ 32°F	17	11	4	0	0	0	0	0	0	0	4	13	49
Days Minimum Temp. ≤ 32°F	31	26	22	8	1	0	0	0	0	7	22	30	147
Days Minimum Temp. ≤ 0°F	9	4	1	0	0	0	0	0	0	0	0	4	18
Heating Degree Days (base 65°F)	1,404	1,089	849	445	158	19	3	9	114	409	838	1,247	6,584
Cooling Degree Days (base 65°F)	0	0	0	13	56	211	310	249	101	9	0	0	949
Mean Precipitation (in.)	0.77	0.74	2.22	3.31	4.28	4.34	4.06	3.73	4.55	2.75	1.79	0.97	33.51
Days With ≥ 0.1" Precipitation	2	2	5	6	8	7	6	6	6	5	4	3	60
Days With ≥ 1.0" Precipitation	0	0	1	1	1	1	1	1	1	1	0	0	8
Mean Snowfall (in.)	7.6	6.5	5.3	1.6	trace	trace	trace	0.0	trace	0.9	3.1	6.2	31.2
Days With ≥ 1.0" Snow Depth	19	14	5	1	0	0	0	0	0	0	3	12	54

Hawarden *Sioux County*   Elevation: 1,187 ft.   Latitude: 43° 00' N   Longitude: 96° 30' W

	JAN	FEB	MAR	APR	MAY	JUN	JUL	AUG	SEP	OCT	NOV	DEC	YEAR
Mean Maximum Temp. (°F)	26.4	33.5	45.1	60.6	72.7	82.0	85.5	83.2	75.3	62.7	43.5	30.9	58.4
Mean Temp. (°F)	16.4	23.4	34.6	48.3	60.5	70.2	74.2	71.9	62.8	50.1	33.7	21.2	47.3
Mean Minimum Temp. (°F)	6.2	13.2	24.1	36.0	48.3	58.4	62.8	60.6	50.2	37.5	23.8	11.4	36.0
Extreme Maximum Temp. (°F)	66	68	85	93	97	107	104	103	100	91	80	66	107
Extreme Minimum Temp. (°F)	-30	-33	-18	-1	25	36	40	36	22	7	-19	-29	-33
Days Maximum Temp. ≥ 90°F	0	0	0	0	1	5	9	6	2	0	0	0	23
Days Maximum Temp. ≤ 32°F	19	12	5	0	0	0	0	0	0	0	6	16	58
Days Minimum Temp. ≤ 32°F	31	28	25	12	2	0	0	0	2	10	24	31	165
Days Minimum Temp. ≤ 0°F	11	5	1	0	0	0	0	0	0	0	1	6	24
Heating Degree Days (base 65°F)	1,503	1,171	936	503	187	28	5	13	143	462	934	1,353	7,238
Cooling Degree Days (base 65°F)	0	0	0	10	52	183	282	228	80	5	0	0	840
Mean Precipitation (in.)	0.52	0.57	1.98	2.86	3.56	3.71	3.55	3.06	2.83	2.02	1.57	0.69	26.92
Days With ≥ 0.1" Precipitation	2	2	4	6	7	6	5	5	5	4	3	2	51
Days With ≥ 1.0" Precipitation	0	0	0	1	1	1	1	1	1	0	0	0	6
Mean Snowfall (in.)	6.2	4.9	6.0	1.8	0.0	0.0	0.0	0.0	0.0	1.1	6.0	6.9	32.9
Days With ≥ 1.0" Snow Depth	18	13	6	1	0	0	0	0	0	0	5	13	56

Humboldt 3 W *Humboldt County*   Elevation: 1,108 ft.   Latitude: 42° 43' N   Longitude: 94° 16' W

	JAN	FEB	MAR	APR	MAY	JUN	JUL	AUG	SEP	OCT	NOV	DEC	YEAR
Mean Maximum Temp. (°F)	24.6	30.7	43.7	59.5	72.3	81.7	84.0	81.4	74.0	61.5	42.8	28.6	57.1
Mean Temp. (°F)	15.3	21.5	34.4	48.2	60.7	70.2	73.0	70.4	62.0	50.0	33.9	20.2	46.6
Mean Minimum Temp. (°F)	6.1	12.5	25.1	36.7	48.8	58.5	61.9	59.3	50.1	38.4	25.0	11.9	36.2
Extreme Maximum Temp. (°F)	63	67	87	95	95	104	102	100	98	91	79	65	104
Extreme Minimum Temp. (°F)	-33	-31	-13	6	26	39	41	37	26	14	-14	-26	-33
Days Maximum Temp. ≥ 90°F	0	0	0	0	1	4	7	4	1	0	0	0	17
Days Maximum Temp. ≤ 32°F	21	15	5	1	0	0	0	0	0	0	6	18	66
Days Minimum Temp. ≤ 32°F	31	27	24	10	1	0	0	0	1	9	23	31	157
Days Minimum Temp. ≤ 0°F	11	6	1	0	0	0	0	0	0	0	1	6	25
Heating Degree Days (base 65°F)	1,538	1,224	943	507	182	23	6	20	151	467	926	1,381	7,368
Cooling Degree Days (base 65°F)	0	0	0	10	53	184	255	196	71	5	0	0	774
Mean Precipitation (in.)	0.87	0.72	2.20	3.10	3.89	4.46	4.09	4.19	3.25	2.35	1.81	1.08	32.01
Days With ≥ 0.1" Precipitation	3	2	5	6	8	7	6	6	6	4	4	3	60
Days With ≥ 1.0" Precipitation	0	0	1	1	1	1	1	1	1	0	0	0	7
Mean Snowfall (in.)	6.9	5.2	5.1	1.5	0.0	0.0	0.0	0.0	0.0	0.2	3.3	6.9	29.1
Days With ≥ 1.0" Snow Depth	22	17	6	1	0	0	0	0	0	0	5	17	68

Ida Grove 5 NW *Ida County*   Elevation: 1,318 ft.   Latitude: 42° 24' N   Longitude: 95° 31' W

	JAN	FEB	MAR	APR	MAY	JUN	JUL	AUG	SEP	OCT	NOV	DEC	YEAR
Mean Maximum Temp. (°F)	26.6	33.3	45.7	60.7	72.2	82.1	85.2	82.7	75.5	63.2	44.6	31.1	58.6
Mean Temp. (°F)	16.8	23.2	35.0	48.5	60.1	70.1	73.9	71.4	63.3	50.9	34.9	22.1	47.5
Mean Minimum Temp. (°F)	7.3	13.4	24.4	36.1	47.8	58.3	62.6	60.2	51.1	38.5	25.2	13.3	36.5
Extreme Maximum Temp. (°F)	67	67	95	97	93	105	104	100	99	91	79	68	105
Extreme Minimum Temp. (°F)	-32	-28	-13	3	25	38	42	36	22	10	-8	-28	-32
Days Maximum Temp. ≥ 90°F	0	0	0	0	1	5	9	5	2	0	0	0	22
Days Maximum Temp. ≤ 32°F	20	14	5	0	0	0	0	0	0	0	5	15	59
Days Minimum Temp. ≤ 32°F	31	27	24	11	1	0	0	0	1	9	23	30	157
Days Minimum Temp. ≤ 0°F	11	6	1	0	0	0	0	0	0	0	1	5	24
Heating Degree Days (base 65°F)	1,490	1,172	925	499	193	29	5	12	133	439	895	1,325	7,117
Cooling Degree Days (base 65°F)	0	0	0	11	44	182	278	204	87	7	0	0	813
Mean Precipitation (in.)	0.79	0.63	1.99	3.17	3.99	4.67	3.84	3.79	2.92	2.27	1.41	0.79	30.26
Days With ≥ 0.1" Precipitation	2	2	4	6	8	7	6	6	5	4	3	2	55
Days With ≥ 1.0" Precipitation	0	0	0	1	1	2	1	1	1	1	0	0	8
Mean Snowfall (in.)	7.2	6.6	6.2	1.7	trace	0.0	0.0	0.0	0.0	0.4	4.1	6.7	32.9
Days With ≥ 1.0" Snow Depth	18	14	6	1	0	0	0	0	0	0	4	12	55

Indianola *Warren County*   Elevation: 938 ft.   Latitude: 41° 22' N   Longitude: 93° 33' W

	JAN	FEB	MAR	APR	MAY	JUN	JUL	AUG	SEP	OCT	NOV	DEC	YEAR
Mean Maximum Temp. (°F)	30.6	37.4	49.1	62.9	72.9	82.4	86.5	84.7	77.0	65.4	48.1	35.4	61.0
Mean Temp. (°F)	20.7	27.3	38.4	51.2	61.5	70.9	75.1	73.0	64.7	52.9	38.1	26.2	50.0
Mean Minimum Temp. (°F)	10.7	17.0	27.8	39.3	50.0	59.3	63.7	61.2	52.3	40.4	28.1	16.9	38.9
Extreme Maximum Temp. (°F)	69	73	88	91	92	101	104	105	98	92	82	69	105
Extreme Minimum Temp. (°F)	-28	-35	-14	-2	27	39	40	41	27	14	-9	-26	-35
Days Maximum Temp. ≥ 90°F	0	0	0	0	0	4	10	8	2	0	0	0	24
Days Maximum Temp. ≤ 32°F	15	11	3	0	0	0	0	0	0	0	3	11	43
Days Minimum Temp. ≤ 32°F	30	25	21	8	1	0	0	0	1	7	21	29	143
Days Minimum Temp. ≤ 0°F	8	4	1	0	0	0	0	0	0	0	0	4	17
Heating Degree Days (base 65°F)	1,368	1,058	819	424	159	20	3	7	112	379	799	1,197	6,345
Cooling Degree Days (base 65°F)	0	0	2	16	48	191	310	257	104	10	0	0	938
Mean Precipitation (in.)	0.99	1.11	2.22	3.70	4.72	4.44	4.20	3.66	3.82	2.97	2.12	1.24	35.19
Days With ≥ 0.1" Precipitation	3	3	5	7	8	7	7	6	6	5	5	3	65
Days With ≥ 1.0" Precipitation	0	0	1	1	1	1	1	1	1	1	0	0	8
Mean Snowfall (in.)	6.9	6.7	2.8	1.3	trace	0.0	0.0	0.0	0.0	0.4	2.6	4.5	25.2
Days With ≥ 1.0" Snow Depth	17	12	3	1	0	0	0	0	0	0	2	8	43

Iowa City *Johnson County*   Elevation: 639 ft.   Latitude: 41° 39' N   Longitude: 91° 32' W

	JAN	FEB	MAR	APR	MAY	JUN	JUL	AUG	SEP	OCT	NOV	DEC	YEAR
Mean Maximum Temp. (°F)	29.7	36.3	48.8	63.3	74.7	83.8	87.6	85.1	77.7	65.8	48.3	34.9	61.3
Mean Temp. (°F)	21.3	27.6	39.2	52.1	63.4	72.8	77.0	74.6	66.6	54.8	39.9	27.3	51.4
Mean Minimum Temp. (°F)	13.0	18.9	29.5	40.9	52.1	61.8	66.3	64.0	55.5	43.7	31.4	19.5	41.4
Extreme Maximum Temp. (°F)	68	68	88	93	95	102	104	103	99	92	77	71	104
Extreme Minimum Temp. (°F)	-23	-26	-5	10	32	41	47	44	29	20	-6	-20	-26
Days Maximum Temp. ≥ 90°F	0	0	0	0	1	6	12	7	2	0	0	0	28
Days Maximum Temp. ≤ 32°F	17	10	3	0	0	0	0	0	0	0	2	11	43
Days Minimum Temp. ≤ 32°F	29	24	18	5	0	0	0	0	0	4	16	28	124
Days Minimum Temp. ≤ 0°F	7	3	0	0	0	0	0	0	0	0	0	3	13
Heating Degree Days (base 65°F)	1,347	1,050	795	395	122	9	1	3	76	325	747	1,164	6,034
Cooling Degree Days (base 65°F)	0	0	2	15	78	255	388	319	133	14	0	0	1,204
Mean Precipitation (in.)	1.08	1.12	2.46	3.74	4.52	4.77	4.49	4.86	3.65	2.79	2.39	1.52	37.39
Days With ≥ 0.1" Precipitation	3	3	5	7	8	7	7	7	6	5	5	4	67
Days With ≥ 1.0" Precipitation	0	0	0	1	1	1	1	2	1	1	0	0	8
Mean Snowfall (in.)	8.0	5.3	3.7	1.9	trace	0.0	0.0	0.0	0.0	0.3	1.7	6.1	27.0
Days With ≥ 1.0" Snow Depth	20	14	5	1	0	0	0	0	0	0	2	12	54

Iowa Falls *Hardin County*   Elevation: 1,128 ft.   Latitude: 42° 31' N   Longitude: 93° 15' W

	JAN	FEB	MAR	APR	MAY	JUN	JUL	AUG	SEP	OCT	NOV	DEC	YEAR
Mean Maximum Temp. (°F)	25.3	31.5	44.4	59.6	72.7	81.6	84.8	81.9	75.0	62.5	43.8	30.1	57.8
Mean Temp. (°F)	16.3	22.5	35.0	48.2	60.7	70.0	73.5	70.8	62.9	50.8	35.0	21.9	47.3
Mean Minimum Temp. (°F)	7.3	13.5	25.6	36.8	48.7	58.3	62.2	59.6	50.9	39.1	26.2	13.5	36.8
Extreme Maximum Temp. (°F)	60	65	86	97	93	99	103	107	99	93	79	64	107
Extreme Minimum Temp. (°F)	-28	-30	-7	5	27	37	44	40	26	15	-13	-22	-30
Days Maximum Temp. ≥ 90°F	0	0	0	0	1	4	7	4	1	0	0	0	17
Days Maximum Temp. ≤ 32°F	21	14	5	0	0	0	0	0	0	0	5	16	61
Days Minimum Temp. ≤ 32°F	31	27	23	10	1	0	0	0	1	8	22	30	153
Days Minimum Temp. ≤ 0°F	10	6	1	0	0	0	0	0	0	0	1	5	23
Heating Degree Days (base 65°F)	1,504	1,193	923	506	179	24	6	15	134	440	894	1,331	7,149
Cooling Degree Days (base 65°F)	0	0	0	8	49	176	283	204	78	7	0	0	805
Mean Precipitation (in.)	1.10	0.96	2.18	3.35	4.33	5.37	3.96	4.42	3.28	2.75	2.15	1.22	35.07
Days With ≥ 0.1" Precipitation	3	3	5	7	8	7	6	7	6	5	5	3	65
Days With ≥ 1.0" Precipitation	0	0	0	1	1	1	1	2	1	1	0	0	8
Mean Snowfall (in.)	8.9	7.0	5.6	2.1	0.0	0.0	0.0	0.0	0.0	trace	4.1	7.5	35.2
Days With ≥ 1.0" Snow Depth	na	na	na	1	0	0	0	0	0	0	2	na	na

Jefferson *Greene County*   Elevation: 1,043 ft.   Latitude: 42° 01' N   Longitude: 94° 22' W

	JAN	FEB	MAR	APR	MAY	JUN	JUL	AUG	SEP	OCT	NOV	DEC	YEAR
Mean Maximum Temp. (°F)	28.7	35.6	48.0	63.3	74.5	83.6	87.1	84.4	77.6	65.1	46.6	33.3	60.7
Mean Temp. (°F)	19.4	25.9	37.5	50.9	62.2	71.7	75.7	73.1	65.2	52.9	37.3	24.6	49.7
Mean Minimum Temp. (°F)	10.0	16.2	27.0	38.4	49.9	59.7	64.2	61.7	52.7	40.6	27.9	15.9	38.7
Extreme Maximum Temp. (°F)	66	68	91	96	94	104	107	106	99	96	80	68	107
Extreme Minimum Temp. (°F)	-25	-27	-9	8	27	41	44	41	29	12	-9	-24	-27
Days Maximum Temp. ≥ 90°F	0	0	0	1	1	6	12	7	2	0	0	0	29
Days Maximum Temp. ≤ 32°F	18	11	4	0	0	0	0	0	0	0	4	13	50
Days Minimum Temp. ≤ 32°F	30	26	22	8	1	0	0	0	0	7	20	30	144
Days Minimum Temp. ≤ 0°F	9	4	1	0	0	0	0	0	0	0	0	4	18
Heating Degree Days (base 65°F)	1,408	1,098	845	432	145	15	2	7	100	381	825	1,246	6,504
Cooling Degree Days (base 65°F)	0	0	1	17	65	220	337	267	113	11	0	0	1,031
Mean Precipitation (in.)	0.95	0.90	2.22	3.21	4.25	4.57	4.03	3.95	3.02	2.50	1.91	1.13	32.64
Days With ≥ 0.1" Precipitation	3	3	5	6	8	7	6	6	5	5	4	3	61
Days With ≥ 1.0" Precipitation	0	0	0	1	1	1	1	1	1	1	0	0	7
Mean Snowfall (in.)	7.4	6.2	5.3	1.7	trace	0.0	0.0	0.0	0.0	0.2	2.9	6.3	30.0
Days With ≥ 1.0" Snow Depth	21	18	9	1	0	0	0	0	0	0	3	16	68

Keokuk *Lee County*   Elevation: 574 ft.   Latitude: 40° 23' N   Longitude: 91° 23' W

	JAN	FEB	MAR	APR	MAY	JUN	JUL	AUG	SEP	OCT	NOV	DEC	YEAR
Mean Maximum Temp. (°F)	32.8	39.1	50.7	63.7	73.9	83.3	87.6	85.3	77.9	66.6	50.7	38.2	62.5
Mean Temp. (°F)	24.5	30.2	41.1	53.3	63.6	73.0	77.5	75.2	67.4	56.0	42.1	30.2	52.8
Mean Minimum Temp. (°F)	16.1	21.3	31.4	42.8	53.3	62.8	67.4	65.2	56.7	45.3	33.4	22.1	43.2
Extreme Maximum Temp. (°F)	67	75	87	92	92	104	105	106	100	94	79	70	106
Extreme Minimum Temp. (°F)	-22	-19	-7	15	33	44	50	44	32	20	2	-20	-22
Days Maximum Temp. ≥ 90°F	0	0	0	0	1	6	12	9	3	0	0	0	31
Days Maximum Temp. ≤ 32°F	14	9	2	0	0	0	0	0	0	0	2	8	35
Days Minimum Temp. ≤ 32°F	28	23	17	4	0	0	0	0	0	2	13	26	113
Days Minimum Temp. ≤ 0°F	5	2	0	0	0	0	0	0	0	0	0	2	9
Heating Degree Days (base 65°F)	1,250	976	738	365	117	11	1	2	69	293	681	1,075	5,578
Cooling Degree Days (base 65°F)	0	0	3	18	74	255	398	329	141	18	1	0	1,237
Mean Precipitation (in.)	1.28	1.35	2.65	3.64	5.52	3.71	3.89	3.46	4.26	3.06	2.97	2.00	37.79
Days With ≥ 0.1" Precipitation	3	3	6	7	9	6	6	6	6	5	6	4	67
Days With ≥ 1.0" Precipitation	0	0	0	1	2	1	1	1	1	1	1	1	10
Mean Snowfall (in.)	7.3	5.0	2.5	1.0	0.0	0.0	0.0	0.0	0.0	trace	1.3	*4.0*	*21.1*
Days With ≥ 1.0" Snow Depth	14	10	3	1	0	0	0	0	0	0	1	6	35

Keosauqua *Van Buren County*   Elevation: 623 ft.   Latitude: 40° 44' N   Longitude: 91° 59' W

	JAN	FEB	MAR	APR	MAY	JUN	JUL	AUG	SEP	OCT	NOV	DEC	YEAR
Mean Maximum Temp. (°F)	32.7	39.4	51.6	64.9	75.3	84.1	88.4	86.3	78.5	66.8	50.5	37.4	63.0
Mean Temp. (°F)	23.2	29.3	40.7	52.6	62.9	71.9	76.5	74.3	66.2	54.6	40.8	28.6	51.8
Mean Minimum Temp. (°F)	13.7	19.2	29.6	40.2	50.5	59.7	64.5	62.3	53.9	42.5	31.0	19.8	40.6
Extreme Maximum Temp. (°F)	70	76	88	92	93	105	107	108	100	93	80	73	108
Extreme Minimum Temp. (°F)	-28	-29	-14	12	28	39	44	36	23	15	-6	-25	-29
Days Maximum Temp. ≥ 90°F	0	0	0	0	1	6	13	10	3	0	0	0	33
Days Maximum Temp. ≤ 32°F	14	9	2	0	0	0	0	0	0	0	2	9	36
Days Minimum Temp. ≤ 32°F	29	24	19	7	0	0	0	0	1	6	17	27	130
Days Minimum Temp. ≤ 0°F	6	3	0	0	0	0	0	0	0	0	0	3	12
Heating Degree Days (base 65°F)	1,289	1,002	751	382	131	14	1	5	85	332	719	1,121	5,832
Cooling Degree Days (base 65°F)	0	0	3	18	71	232	372	310	131	17	1	0	1,155
Mean Precipitation (in.)	1.36	1.32	2.69	3.66	4.92	4.37	4.94	4.03	4.06	2.93	2.89	1.97	39.14
Days With ≥ 0.1" Precipitation	4	4	6	7	8	7	6	7	6	6	6	5	72
Days With ≥ 1.0" Precipitation	0	0	1	1	1	1	2	1	1	1	1	0	10
Mean Snowfall (in.)	7.7	6.0	3.2	1.7	0.0	0.0	0.0	0.0	0.0	trace	2.0	6.0	26.6
Days With ≥ 1.0" Snow Depth	na	6	1	0	0	0	0	0	0	0	1	4	na

Knoxville *Marion County*   Elevation: 918 ft.   Latitude: 41° 20' N   Longitude: 93° 07' W

	JAN	FEB	MAR	APR	MAY	JUN	JUL	AUG	SEP	OCT	NOV	DEC	YEAR
Mean Maximum Temp. (°F)	30.3	36.9	48.9	62.3	73.5	82.7	87.2	84.5	76.9	64.7	48.1	35.1	60.9
Mean Temp. (°F)	21.4	27.6	38.9	51.5	62.9	72.0	76.6	74.0	65.9	53.9	39.3	26.8	50.9
Mean Minimum Temp. (°F)	12.5	18.3	28.9	40.6	52.2	61.3	66.0	63.5	54.8	43.0	30.4	18.4	40.8
Extreme Maximum Temp. (°F)	70	73	89	92	94	101	107	105	101	92	78	70	107
Extreme Minimum Temp. (°F)	-24	-29	-10	9	30	42	45	43	29	17	-5	-24	-29
Days Maximum Temp. ≥ 90°F	0	0	0	0	0	4	11	8	3	0	0	0	26
Days Maximum Temp. ≤ 32°F	16	11	3	0	0	0	0	0	0	0	3	11	44
Days Minimum Temp. ≤ 32°F	29	25	20	6	0	0	0	0	0	4	17	28	129
Days Minimum Temp. ≤ 0°F	7	3	0	0	0	0	0	0	0	0	0	4	14
Heating Degree Days (base 65°F)	1,345	1,049	803	413	132	14	2	5	92	352	767	1,179	6,153
Cooling Degree Days (base 65°F)	0	0	2	17	68	230	372	299	126	12	0	0	1,126
Mean Precipitation (in.)	0.85	1.12	2.00	3.94	4.48	4.17	4.17	4.31	3.79	2.82	2.17	1.15	34.97
Days With ≥ 0.1" Precipitation	2	3	5	7	8	7	6	6	6	5	4	3	62
Days With ≥ 1.0" Precipitation	0	0	0	1	1	1	1	1	1	1	0	0	7
Mean Snowfall (in.)	6.4	5.9	2.7	1.1	trace	0.0	0.0	0.0	0.0	0.4	2.0	5.6	24.1
Days With ≥ 1.0" Snow Depth	13	9	3	0	0	0	0	0	0	0	1	6	32

Lake Park *Dickinson County*   Elevation: 1,463 ft.   Latitude: 43° 27' N   Longitude: 95° 19' W

	JAN	FEB	MAR	APR	MAY	JUN	JUL	AUG	SEP	OCT	NOV	DEC	YEAR
Mean Maximum Temp. (°F)	21.9	28.1	39.4	55.7	69.3	79.0	82.7	80.1	72.1	59.1	40.4	27.0	54.6
Mean Temp. (°F)	12.5	18.9	30.4	45.1	58.1	68.1	72.0	69.4	60.6	47.8	31.7	18.4	44.4
Mean Minimum Temp. (°F)	2.9	9.6	21.4	34.6	46.9	57.1	61.3	58.7	49.0	36.6	23.1	9.7	34.2
Extreme Maximum Temp. (°F)	67	65	76	89	93	101	100	100	98	91	78	64	101
Extreme Minimum Temp. (°F)	-30	-30	-18	6	28	39	44	41	28	13	-11	-28	-30
Days Maximum Temp. ≥ 90°F	0	0	0	0	0	3	5	3	1	0	0	0	12
Days Maximum Temp. ≤ 32°F	24	17	9	1	0	0	0	0	0	0	8	20	79
Days Minimum Temp. ≤ 32°F	31	28	27	12	1	0	0	0	1	10	26	31	167
Days Minimum Temp. ≤ 0°F	14	8	2	0	0	0	0	0	0	0	1	8	33
Heating Degree Days (base 65°F)	1,625	1,298	1,065	594	242	46	9	25	180	529	991	1,439	8,043
Cooling Degree Days (base 65°F)	0	0	0	4	34	142	229	169	53	4	0	0	635
Mean Precipitation (in.)	0.66	0.55	1.98	2.82	3.47	4.54	3.73	3.79	2.77	1.99	1.62	0.68	28.60
Days With ≥ 0.1" Precipitation	2	2	4	6	8	7	6	5	5	4	3	2	54
Days With ≥ 1.0" Precipitation	0	0	0	1	1	1	1	1	1	1	0	0	7
Mean Snowfall (in.)	7.9	5.5	8.2	2.7	trace	0.0	0.0	0.0	trace	0.6	6.2	7.3	38.4
Days With ≥ 1.0" Snow Depth	na	na	na	1	0	0	0	0	0	0	3	na	na

Le Claire Lock & Dam 14 *Scott County*   Elevation: 574 ft.   Latitude: 41° 34' N   Longitude: 90° 24' W

	JAN	FEB	MAR	APR	MAY	JUN	JUL	AUG	SEP	OCT	NOV	DEC	YEAR
Mean Maximum Temp. (°F)	28.8	34.3	46.1	60.1	72.1	81.3	84.9	82.5	75.2	63.2	47.0	34.2	59.1
Mean Temp. (°F)	20.5	26.1	37.3	50.3	62.2	71.6	75.7	73.3	65.5	53.6	39.1	26.7	50.2
Mean Minimum Temp. (°F)	12.2	17.9	28.6	40.5	52.3	61.9	66.5	64.1	55.7	44.0	31.1	19.1	41.2
Extreme Maximum Temp. (°F)	63	68	83	88	93	100	102	103	97	90	78	69	103
Extreme Minimum Temp. (°F)	-23	-28	-5	11	30	42	48	43	32	20	-4	-21	-28
Days Maximum Temp. ≥ 90°F	0	0	0	0	0	4	8	4	1	0	0	0	17
Days Maximum Temp. ≤ 32°F	18	12	4	0	0	0	0	0	0	0	3	12	49
Days Minimum Temp. ≤ 32°F	30	25	21	6	0	0	0	0	0	3	16	28	129
Days Minimum Temp. ≤ 0°F	8	4	0	0	0	0	0	0	0	0	0	3	15
Heating Degree Days (base 65°F)	1,376	1,093	852	444	150	16	2	6	89	359	772	1,184	6,343
Cooling Degree Days (base 65°F)	0	0	0	9	65	225	347	279	107	10	0	0	1,042
Mean Precipitation (in.)	1.13	1.25	2.40	3.19	3.93	4.57	3.57	4.36	3.17	2.50	2.36	2.01	34.44
Days With ≥ 0.1" Precipitation	3	3	5	6	7	7	6	6	5	5	5	4	62
Days With ≥ 1.0" Precipitation	0	0	0	1	1	1	1	1	1	1	0	0	7
Mean Snowfall (in.)	na	3.3	1.9	0.7	0.0	0.0	0.0	0.0	0.0	trace	0.2	2.5	na
Days With ≥ 1.0" Snow Depth	na	12	4	0	0	0	0	0	0	0	1	6	na

Le Mars *Plymouth County*   Elevation: 1,194 ft.   Latitude: 42° 47' N   Longitude: 96° 09' W

	JAN	FEB	MAR	APR	MAY	JUN	JUL	AUG	SEP	OCT	NOV	DEC	YEAR
Mean Maximum Temp. (°F)	26.6	33.6	46.0	61.7	73.9	83.4	86.6	84.2	76.6	63.9	44.1	31.2	59.3
Mean Temp. (°F)	16.9	23.6	35.3	48.9	61.2	71.2	74.8	72.5	63.8	51.2	34.4	21.9	48.0
Mean Minimum Temp. (°F)	7.1	13.5	24.5	36.1	48.6	58.9	63.0	60.8	50.8	38.4	24.7	12.7	36.6
Extreme Maximum Temp. (°F)	67	70	86	96	98	105	106	103	103	92	80	68	106
Extreme Minimum Temp. (°F)	-35	-28	-16	-2	26	37	38	38	24	10	-14	-28	-35
Days Maximum Temp. ≥ 90°F	0	0	0	0	2	7	11	7	3	0	0	0	30
Days Maximum Temp. ≤ 32°F	20	13	5	0	0	0	0	0	0	0	6	16	60
Days Minimum Temp. ≤ 32°F	31	27	24	11	1	0	0	0	1	9	24	30	158
Days Minimum Temp. ≤ 0°F	11	6	1	0	0	0	0	0	0	0	1	6	25
Heating Degree Days (base 65°F)	1,486	1,164	914	488	172	24	4	10	127	431	910	1,330	7,060
Cooling Degree Days (base 65°F)	0	0	0	11	57	202	299	239	91	6	0	0	905
Mean Precipitation (in.)	0.63	0.52	1.97	2.73	3.42	3.93	3.33	3.33	2.66	1.95	1.38	0.71	26.56
Days With ≥ 0.1" Precipitation	2	2	4	6	7	7	5	5	5	4	3	2	52
Days With ≥ 1.0" Precipitation	0	0	0	0	1	1	1	1	1	0	0	0	5
Mean Snowfall (in.)	6.9	4.5	6.1	1.5	0.0	0.0	0.0	trace	0.0	0.7	3.8	6.1	29.6
Days With ≥ 1.0" Snow Depth	16	12	8	1	0	0	0	0	0	0	4	11	52

Leon 6 ESE *Decatur County*   Elevation: 997 ft.   Latitude: 40° 44' N   Longitude: 93° 38' W

	JAN	FEB	MAR	APR	MAY	JUN	JUL	AUG	SEP	OCT	NOV	DEC	YEAR
Mean Maximum Temp. (°F)	31.5	38.1	50.0	63.2	73.2	82.4	87.3	85.2	77.0	65.2	48.5	36.0	61.5
Mean Temp. (°F)	21.8	27.6	38.9	50.8	61.1	70.5	75.5	73.2	64.6	52.8	38.6	26.7	50.2
Mean Minimum Temp. (°F)	12.1	17.1	27.7	38.4	49.0	58.6	63.6	61.1	52.1	40.4	28.8	17.3	38.8
Extreme Maximum Temp. (°F)	63	75	87	92	93	107	105	107	100	91	80	68	107
Extreme Minimum Temp. (°F)	-28	-36	-21	7	26	35	44	35	22	13	-12	-33	-36
Days Maximum Temp. ≥ 90°F	0	0	0	0	0	4	11	8	2	0	0	0	25
Days Maximum Temp. ≤ 32°F	15	10	3	0	0	0	0	0	0	0	3	11	42
Days Minimum Temp. ≤ 32°F	30	25	21	9	1	0	0	0	1	7	20	29	143
Days Minimum Temp. ≤ 0°F	7	4	1	0	0	0	0	0	0	0	0	3	15
Heating Degree Days (base 65°F)	1,333	1,048	803	432	165	23	2	9	114	383	784	1,181	6,277
Cooling Degree Days (base 65°F)	0	0	1	13	42	178	317	258	99	9	0	0	917
Mean Precipitation (in.)	0.96	1.24	2.28	3.70	4.98	4.33	4.57	4.33	4.21	3.15	2.44	1.37	37.56
Days With ≥ 0.1" Precipitation	3	3	5	7	9	7	6	6	6	5	5	4	66
Days With ≥ 1.0" Precipitation	0	0	0	1	1	1	1	1	1	1	1	0	8
Mean Snowfall (in.)	6.8	5.5	3.6	1.7	0.0	0.0	0.0	0.0	0.0	0.1	2.5	6.1	26.3
Days With ≥ 1.0" Snow Depth	16	11	4	1	0	0	0	0	0	0	2	10	44

Logan *Harrison County*   Elevation: 987 ft.   Latitude: 41° 38' N   Longitude: 95° 47' W

	JAN	FEB	MAR	APR	MAY	JUN	JUL	AUG	SEP	OCT	NOV	DEC	YEAR
Mean Maximum Temp. (°F)	30.2	36.9	48.7	63.2	74.2	83.9	87.4	85.0	77.3	65.5	47.5	34.3	61.2
Mean Temp. (°F)	19.9	26.5	37.8	50.9	62.0	71.8	75.8	73.4	64.8	52.5	37.2	24.8	49.8
Mean Minimum Temp. (°F)	9.6	16.1	26.9	38.5	49.8	59.6	64.1	61.8	52.2	39.5	26.8	15.2	38.3
Extreme Maximum Temp. (°F)	69	74	88	99	95	103	106	105	99	94	83	72	106
Extreme Minimum Temp. (°F)	-30	-30	-17	5	26	39	40	37	26	12	-10	-30	-30
Days Maximum Temp. ≥ 90°F	0	0	0	1	1	7	12	8	3	0	0	0	32
Days Maximum Temp. ≤ 32°F	16	11	4	0	0	0	0	0	0	0	4	13	48
Days Minimum Temp. ≤ 32°F	30	26	22	8	1	0	0	0	1	8	22	30	148
Days Minimum Temp. ≤ 0°F	9	4	1	0	0	0	0	0	0	0	1	4	19
Heating Degree Days (base 65°F)	1,390	1,080	836	432	153	20	3	9	111	392	827	1,241	6,494
Cooling Degree Days (base 65°F)	0	0	1	17	62	222	336	266	110	8	0	0	1,022
Mean Precipitation (in.)	0.82	0.78	2.31	3.16	4.57	4.39	4.13	3.52	3.64	2.62	1.72	1.01	32.67
Days With ≥ 0.1" Precipitation	3	2	5	7	9	7	7	6	6	5	4	3	64
Days With ≥ 1.0" Precipitation	0	0	1	1	1	1	1	1	1	1	0	0	8
Mean Snowfall (in.)	7.7	6.8	6.1	1.9	0.0	0.0	0.0	0.0	trace	0.9	3.6	6.7	33.7
Days With ≥ 1.0" Snow Depth	19	14	6	1	0	0	0	0	0	0	4	12	56

Manchester 2 *Delaware County*   Elevation: 987 ft.   Latitude: 42° 28' N   Longitude: 91° 27' W

	JAN	FEB	MAR	APR	MAY	JUN	JUL	AUG	SEP	OCT	NOV	DEC	YEAR
Mean Maximum Temp. (°F)	24.6	31.0	43.6	58.4	70.8	80.1	83.4	81.3	73.8	61.2	44.1	30.8	56.9
Mean Temp. (°F)	15.4	21.9	33.9	46.7	58.9	68.4	72.2	69.7	61.3	49.0	34.6	22.0	46.1
Mean Minimum Temp. (°F)	6.1	12.5	24.3	35.2	47.1	56.6	61.0	58.0	48.7	36.8	25.1	13.1	35.4
Extreme Maximum Temp. (°F)	59	64	87	97	92	101	100	102	96	93	79	69	102
Extreme Minimum Temp. (°F)	-30	-32	-12	-9	26	35	42	39	23	11	-16	-26	-32
Days Maximum Temp. ≥ 90°F	0	0	0	0	0	3	5	3	1	0	0	0	12
Days Maximum Temp. ≤ 32°F	22	14	5	0	0	0	0	0	0	0	5	16	62
Days Minimum Temp. ≤ 32°F	30	25	25	11	1	0	0	0	1	11	23	30	157
Days Minimum Temp. ≤ 0°F	11	7	1	0	0	0	0	0	0	0	1	6	26
Heating Degree Days (base 65°F)	1,533	1,211	958	549	221	39	8	25	165	494	906	1,327	7,436
Cooling Degree Days (base 65°F)	0	0	0	6	35	145	237	177	57	5	0	0	662
Mean Precipitation (in.)	0.91	0.94	1.91	3.28	3.86	4.35	4.54	5.29	3.30	2.73	2.33	1.12	34.56
Days With ≥ 0.1" Precipitation	3	2	4	7	8	7	7	7	6	5	5	3	64
Days With ≥ 1.0" Precipitation	0	0	0	1	1	1	1	2	1	1	0	0	8
Mean Snowfall (in.)	9.3	6.0	3.8	1.5	trace	0.0	0.0	0.0	0.0	0.2	3.0	7.1	30.9
Days With ≥ 1.0" Snow Depth	24	20	9	1	0	0	0	0	0	0	3	16	73

Mapleton 2 *Monona County*   Elevation: 1,187 ft.   Latitude: 42° 10' N   Longitude: 95° 47' W

	JAN	FEB	MAR	APR	MAY	JUN	JUL	AUG	SEP	OCT	NOV	DEC	YEAR
Mean Maximum Temp. (°F)	28.7	35.5	47.5	62.8	73.7	82.3	85.2	83.3	76.1	64.3	45.6	32.5	59.8
Mean Temp. (°F)	19.1	25.7	36.9	50.4	61.6	70.8	74.4	72.5	64.2	52.1	36.2	23.6	49.0
Mean Minimum Temp. (°F)	9.6	15.9	26.4	37.9	49.5	59.2	63.5	61.6	52.1	39.9	26.8	14.7	38.1
Extreme Maximum Temp. (°F)	67	71	88	96	92	104	101	104	98	92	80	64	104
Extreme Minimum Temp. (°F)	-32	-27	-12	-1	26	37	42	37	24	10	-13	-28	-32
Days Maximum Temp. ≥ 90°F	0	0	0	0	1	4	8	6	2	0	0	0	21
Days Maximum Temp. ≤ 32°F	18	12	4	0	0	0	0	0	0	0	4	14	52
Days Minimum Temp. ≤ 32°F	30	26	22	9	1	0	0	0	1	8	22	30	149
Days Minimum Temp. ≤ 0°F	9	5	1	0	0	0	0	0	0	0	1	5	21
Heating Degree Days (base 65°F)	1,417	1,104	864	445	157	21	4	10	119	403	856	1,276	6,676
Cooling Degree Days (base 65°F)	0	0	0	16	58	203	305	254	102	11	0	0	949
Mean Precipitation (in.)	0.70	0.65	2.13	3.22	4.15	4.18	3.91	3.50	3.01	2.34	1.52	0.85	30.16
Days With ≥ 0.1" Precipitation	2	2	5	6	8	7	6	6	6	4	4	3	59
Days With ≥ 1.0" Precipitation	0	0	0	1	1	1	1	1	1	1	0	0	7
Mean Snowfall (in.)	7.2	6.5	5.7	1.5	trace	0.0	0.0	0.0	0.0	0.7	3.5	6.7	31.8
Days With ≥ 1.0" Snow Depth	20	14	7	1	0	0	0	0	0	0	4	16	62

Maquoketa 3 S *Clinton County*   Elevation: 679 ft.   Latitude: 42° 01' N   Longitude: 90° 39' W

	JAN	FEB	MAR	APR	MAY	JUN	JUL	AUG	SEP	OCT	NOV	DEC	YEAR
Mean Maximum Temp. (°F)	26.8	33.0	45.3	59.6	71.6	80.9	84.3	82.0	74.4	62.4	45.6	32.5	58.2
Mean Temp. (°F)	18.1	24.0	35.6	48.2	59.9	69.3	73.1	70.7	62.5	50.8	36.6	24.5	47.8
Mean Minimum Temp. (°F)	9.3	14.9	26.0	36.7	48.1	57.6	61.7	59.5	50.5	39.0	27.6	16.4	37.3
Extreme Maximum Temp. (°F)	59	69	85	93	94	101	103	103	97	94	77	68	103
Extreme Minimum Temp. (°F)	-27	-34	-12	5	28	38	41	37	24	12	-6	-23	-34
Days Maximum Temp. ≥ 90°F	0	0	0	0	1	3	7	4	1	0	0	0	16
Days Maximum Temp. ≤ 32°F	20	13	4	0	0	0	0	0	0	0	3	13	53
Days Minimum Temp. ≤ 32°F	30	26	23	10	1	0	0	0	1	8	21	29	149
Days Minimum Temp. ≤ 0°F	9	5	1	0	0	0	0	0	0	0	0	4	19
Heating Degree Days (base 65°F)	1,447	1,150	902	507	200	29	7	16	140	443	845	1,250	6,936
Cooling Degree Days (base 65°F)	0	0	0	8	42	155	253	192	65	5	0	0	720
Mean Precipitation (in.)	1.15	1.26	2.27	3.16	4.13	4.32	3.53	4.62	3.77	2.53	2.48	1.71	34.93
Days With ≥ 0.1" Precipitation	4	3	5	7	8	7	7	6	5	5	5	4	68
Days With ≥ 1.0" Precipitation	0	0	0	1	1	1	1	1	1	0	1	0	7
Mean Snowfall (in.)	8.8	5.3	3.6	1.8	trace	0.0	0.0	0.0	0.0	0.1	2.3	5.6	27.5
Days With ≥ 1.0" Snow Depth	17	13	3	0	0	0	0	0	0	0	2	10	45

Marshalltown *Marshall County*   Elevation: 869 ft.   Latitude: 42° 04' N   Longitude: 92° 56' W

	JAN	FEB	MAR	APR	MAY	JUN	JUL	AUG	SEP	OCT	NOV	DEC	YEAR
Mean Maximum Temp. (°F)	26.5	32.9	45.1	59.6	71.6	81.1	84.7	82.2	74.7	62.5	45.5	31.6	58.2
Mean Temp. (°F)	16.9	23.3	35.4	48.6	60.3	70.0	73.7	70.9	62.4	50.4	35.9	22.8	47.5
Mean Minimum Temp. (°F)	7.2	13.7	25.6	37.4	48.9	58.8	62.6	59.5	50.2	38.3	26.2	14.0	36.9
Extreme Maximum Temp. (°F)	62	65	90	94	96	101	103	102	97	92	80	71	103
Extreme Minimum Temp. (°F)	-28	-35	-10	4	27	39	43	39	26	13	-11	-28	-35
Days Maximum Temp. ≥ 90°F	0	0	0	0	1	4	8	5	1	0	0	0	19
Days Maximum Temp. ≤ 32°F	20	13	4	0	0	0	0	0	0	0	4	15	56
Days Minimum Temp. ≤ 32°F	31	27	24	9	1	0	0	0	1	10	22	30	155
Days Minimum Temp. ≤ 0°F	11	6	1	0	0	0	0	0	0	0	0	5	23
Heating Degree Days (base 65°F)	1,487	1,171	911	496	191	28	5	17	145	453	867	1,301	7,072
Cooling Degree Days (base 65°F)	0	0	1	10	46	181	282	215	78	8	0	0	821
Mean Precipitation (in.)	0.92	1.02	2.48	3.32	4.32	5.33	4.44	4.89	3.66	2.75	2.15	1.23	36.51
Days With ≥ 0.1" Precipitation	3	3	5	7	8	8	7	7	6	5	5	3	67
Days With ≥ 1.0" Precipitation	0	0	1	1	1	2	1	1	1	1	1	0	10
Mean Snowfall (in.)	7.6	6.4	4.9	1.2	trace	0.0	0.0	0.0	0.0	0.2	2.3	6.5	29.1
Days With ≥ 1.0" Snow Depth	18	15	6	1	0	0	0	0	0	0	2	12	54

Mason City *Cerro Gordo County*   Elevation: 1,089 ft.   Latitude: 43° 10' N   Longitude: 93° 12' W

	JAN	FEB	MAR	APR	MAY	JUN	JUL	AUG	SEP	OCT	NOV	DEC	YEAR
Mean Maximum Temp. (°F)	23.1	30.0	41.6	57.8	71.2	80.6	83.5	81.1	73.7	60.8	42.1	28.3	56.1
Mean Temp. (°F)	13.8	20.8	32.2	46.5	59.1	68.6	72.3	69.8	61.6	49.2	33.1	19.8	45.6
Mean Minimum Temp. (°F)	4.4	11.7	22.8	35.2	47.1	56.6	61.0	58.4	49.4	37.6	24.2	11.2	35.0
Extreme Maximum Temp. (°F)	59	67	84	95	93	102	103	102	99	93	78	65	103
Extreme Minimum Temp. (°F)	-33	-32	-12	5	25	36	41	35	22	13	-9	-26	-33
Days Maximum Temp. ≥ 90°F	0	0	0	0	1	4	6	4	1	0	0	0	16
Days Maximum Temp. ≤ 32°F	23	15	7	1	0	0	0	0	0	0	6	19	71
Days Minimum Temp. ≤ 32°F	31	27	26	12	2	0	0	0	1	10	24	30	163
Days Minimum Temp. ≤ 0°F	13	7	1	0	0	0	0	0	0	0	1	7	29
Heating Degree Days (base 65°F)	1,583	1,242	1,009	556	221	40	9	23	162	489	949	1,397	7,680
Cooling Degree Days (base 65°F)	0	0	0	7	36	144	234	173	62	4	0	0	660
Mean Precipitation (in.)	0.88	0.76	2.01	3.33	4.35	5.04	4.57	4.68	3.52	2.66	2.06	1.03	34.89
Days With ≥ 0.1" Precipitation	3	2	5	7	8	8	7	7	6	5	4	3	65
Days With ≥ 1.0" Precipitation	0	0	0	1	1	1	1	2	1	1	0	0	8
Mean Snowfall (in.)	8.3	5.3	5.6	0.9	0.0	0.0	0.0	0.0	0.0	0.2	3.0	na	na
Days With ≥ 1.0" Snow Depth	22	18	8	1	0	0	0	0	0	0	2	na	na

Mason City Municipal Airport *Cerro Gordo County*   Elevation: 1,190 ft.   Latitude: 43° 09' N   Longitude: 93° 20' W

	JAN	FEB	MAR	APR	MAY	JUN	JUL	AUG	SEP	OCT	NOV	DEC	YEAR
Mean Maximum Temp. (°F)	22.3	28.5	41.1	57.2	70.6	80.2	83.4	80.8	72.9	59.9	41.7	27.3	55.5
Mean Temp. (°F)	13.5	20.1	32.4	46.4	59.0	68.8	72.5	69.8	61.0	48.6	32.9	19.3	45.4
Mean Minimum Temp. (°F)	4.7	11.7	23.7	35.5	47.3	57.3	61.4	58.8	49.0	37.2	24.1	11.2	35.2
Extreme Maximum Temp. (°F)	59	66	84	93	94	103	104	101	97	95	78	67	104
Extreme Minimum Temp. (°F)	-29	-32	-17	6	25	36	44	39	25	12	-16	-26	-32
Days Maximum Temp. ≥ 90°F	0	0	0	0	1	4	6	3	1	0	0	0	15
Days Maximum Temp. ≤ 32°F	23	16	7	1	0	0	0	0	0	0	7	20	74
Days Minimum Temp. ≤ 32°F	30	27	25	11	1	0	0	0	1	10	24	30	159
Days Minimum Temp. ≤ 0°F	12	7	1	0	0	0	0	0	0	0	1	7	28
Heating Degree Days (base 65°F)	1,591	1,262	1,003	557	221	38	8	24	172	506	956	1,411	7,749
Cooling Degree Days (base 65°F)	0	0	0	7	37	155	241	179	56	5	0	0	680
Mean Precipitation (in.)	0.95	0.87	2.25	3.38	4.42	4.84	4.38	4.45	3.26	2.56	1.97	1.10	34.43
Days With ≥ 0.1" Precipitation	3	2	5	7	8	8	6	7	5	5	4	3	63
Days With ≥ 1.0" Precipitation	0	0	0	1	1	1	1	1	1	1	0	0	7
Mean Snowfall (in.)	10.9	6.6	6.7	2.4	trace	trace	trace	trace	trace	0.5	5.0	8.4	40.5
Days With ≥ 1.0" Snow Depth	24	20	10	1	0	0	0	0	0	0	5	18	78

Milford 4 NW *Dickinson County*   Elevation: 1,400 ft.   Latitude: 43° 23' N   Longitude: 95° 11' W

	JAN	FEB	MAR	APR	MAY	JUN	JUL	AUG	SEP	OCT	NOV	DEC	YEAR
Mean Maximum Temp. (°F)	22.4	29.3	41.2	57.5	71.0	80.1	83.4	80.7	72.6	60.1	40.9	27.2	55.5
Mean Temp. (°F)	13.3	20.4	32.0	46.3	59.2	68.7	72.4	70.0	61.3	49.2	32.4	19.0	45.4
Mean Minimum Temp. (°F)	4.2	11.4	22.9	35.1	47.5	57.1	61.3	59.1	50.1	38.2	23.9	10.7	35.1
Extreme Maximum Temp. (°F)	63	64	82	91	92	102	101	101	100	91	78	65	102
Extreme Minimum Temp. (°F)	-31	-28	-15	4	24	38	41	41	24	12	-12	-27	-31
Days Maximum Temp. ≥ 90°F	0	0	0	0	1	3	6	3	1	0	0	0	14
Days Maximum Temp. ≤ 32°F	23	16	7	1	0	0	0	0	0	0	8	20	75
Days Minimum Temp. ≤ 32°F	31	27	25	12	1	0	0	0	1	9	25	31	162
Days Minimum Temp. ≤ 0°F	13	7	2	0	0	0	0	0	0	0	1	8	31
Heating Degree Days (base 65°F)	1,598	1,255	1,016	559	214	38	8	20	164	490	971	1,422	7,755
Cooling Degree Days (base 65°F)	0	0	0	6	40	149	233	173	56	5	0	0	662
Mean Precipitation (in.)	0.60	0.58	1.95	3.07	3.76	4.56	3.61	3.84	2.96	2.16	1.77	0.76	29.62
Days With ≥ 0.1" Precipitation	2	2	4	6	7	7	6	5	5	4	4	2	54
Days With ≥ 1.0" Precipitation	0	0	0	1	1	1	1	1	1	1	0	0	7
Mean Snowfall (in.)	na	*5.4*	6.1	0.8	trace	0.0	0.0	0.0	trace	0.6	*3.1*	*6.5*	na
Days With ≥ 1.0" Snow Depth	na	na	na	1	0	0	0	0	0	0	*4*	na	na

Mount Ayr 4 SW *Ringgold County*   Elevation: 1,240 ft.   Latitude: 40° 41' N   Longitude: 94° 18' W

	JAN	FEB	MAR	APR	MAY	JUN	JUL	AUG	SEP	OCT	NOV	DEC	YEAR
Mean Maximum Temp. (°F)	30.9	37.3	49.4	62.2	71.5	81.0	85.4	*83.3*	76.2	64.9	48.3	36.3	*60.6*
Mean Temp. (°F)	21.5	27.4	38.6	50.8	61.0	70.6	75.0	*72.7*	65.0	53.3	38.8	27.4	*50.2*
Mean Minimum Temp. (°F)	12.0	17.3	27.8	39.3	50.4	60.1	64.6	62.2	53.7	41.7	29.3	18.6	39.8
Extreme Maximum Temp. (°F)	67	74	87	90	89	104	104	102	99	90	79	68	104
Extreme Minimum Temp. (°F)	-24	-29	-16	8	27	38	43	39	26	15	-9	-28	-29
Days Maximum Temp. ≥ 90°F	0	0	0	0	0	3	8	6	2	0	0	0	19
Days Maximum Temp. ≤ 32°F	16	10	3	0	0	0	0	0	0	0	3	11	43
Days Minimum Temp. ≤ 32°F	30	26	21	8	0	0	0	0	0	6	19	28	138
Days Minimum Temp. ≤ 0°F	7	4	1	0	0	0	0	0	0	0	0	3	15
Heating Degree Days (base 65°F)	1,343	1,057	812	433	165	20	3	*8*	107	366	778	1,157	*6,249*
Cooling Degree Days (base 65°F)	0	0	1	12	41	193	308	246	108	10	0	0	919
Mean Precipitation (in.)	0.80	1.05	2.26	3.13	4.54	4.29	4.76	4.32	3.89	2.92	2.29	1.25	35.50
Days With ≥ 0.1" Precipitation	2	3	5	6	7	6	6	6	5	5	4	3	58
Days With ≥ 1.0" Precipitation	0	0	1	1	1	1	2	1	1	1	0	0	9
Mean Snowfall (in.)	4.7	4.6	3.0	1.1	trace	0.0	0.0	0.0	0.0	0.4	*1.2*	*3.6*	*18.6*
Days With ≥ 1.0" Snow Depth	na	*6*	*1*	0	0	0	0	0	0	0	*1*	na	na

Mount Pleasant 1 SSW *Henry County*   Elevation: 728 ft.   Latitude: 40° 57' N   Longitude: 91° 34' W

	JAN	FEB	MAR	APR	MAY	JUN	JUL	AUG	SEP	OCT	NOV	DEC	YEAR
Mean Maximum Temp. (°F)	30.4	36.7	49.2	62.6	72.8	81.8	85.8	83.5	76.5	65.1	49.0	35.6	60.8
Mean Temp. (°F)	21.8	27.8	39.4	51.6	62.1	71.2	75.4	73.2	65.5	54.3	40.1	27.6	50.8
Mean Minimum Temp. (°F)	13.1	18.9	29.5	40.7	51.4	60.6	65.0	62.9	54.5	43.3	31.2	19.5	40.9
Extreme Maximum Temp. (°F)	68	72	87	89	91	102	106	105	98	92	79	72	106
Extreme Minimum Temp. (°F)	-26	-27	-8	9	29	40	47	42	29	17	-5	-25	-27
Days Maximum Temp. ≥ 90°F	0	0	0	0	0	3	9	6	2	0	0	0	20
Days Maximum Temp. ≤ 32°F	16	11	3	0	0	0	0	0	0	0	2	11	43
Days Minimum Temp. ≤ 32°F	29	24	19	6	0	0	0	0	0	5	17	28	128
Days Minimum Temp. ≤ 0°F	7	3	0	0	0	0	0	0	0	0	0	3	13
Heating Degree Days (base 65°F)	1,333	1,044	790	408	145	16	2	6	93	341	741	1,154	6,073
Cooling Degree Days (base 65°F)	0	0	2	13	57	205	331	272	112	13	0	0	1,005
Mean Precipitation (in.)	1.26	1.31	2.59	3.30	4.44	4.02	4.70	4.56	4.48	2.65	2.65	1.82	37.78
Days With ≥ 0.1" Precipitation	4	4	6	7	8	6	7	7	7	5	6	4	71
Days With ≥ 1.0" Precipitation	0	0	1	1	1	1	2	2	1	1	0	0	10
Mean Snowfall (in.)	8.1	5.7	3.0	1.4	0.0	0.0	0.0	0.0	0.0	trace	1.8	5.8	25.8
Days With ≥ 1.0" Snow Depth	*11*	*9*	3	1	0	0	0	0	0	0	1	5	*30*

Muscatine *Muscatine County*   Elevation: 547 ft.   Latitude: 41° 24' N   Longitude: 91° 04' W

	JAN	FEB	MAR	APR	MAY	JUN	JUL	AUG	SEP	OCT	NOV	DEC	YEAR
Mean Maximum Temp. (°F)	30.1	36.6	48.8	62.8	73.9	82.9	86.5	84.1	76.9	65.2	48.5	35.1	61.0
Mean Temp. (°F)	21.4	27.6	39.0	51.6	62.8	72.0	76.0	73.7	65.7	54.1	39.7	27.1	50.9
Mean Minimum Temp. (°F)	12.6	18.5	29.1	40.3	51.6	61.0	65.6	63.2	54.5	42.8	30.9	19.2	40.8
Extreme Maximum Temp. (°F)	69	69	89	91	94	104	105	105	98	96	80	72	105
Extreme Minimum Temp. (°F)	-28	-34	-7	10	28	39	45	39	26	17	-5	-23	-34
Days Maximum Temp. ≥ 90°F	0	0	0	0	1	5	10	6	2	0	0	0	24
Days Maximum Temp. ≤ 32°F	16	10	3	0	0	0	0	0	0	0	2	11	42
Days Minimum Temp. ≤ 32°F	29	25	20	6	0	0	0	0	0	5	17	28	130
Days Minimum Temp. ≤ 0°F	7	3	0	0	0	0	0	0	0	0	0	3	13
Heating Degree Days (base 65°F)	1,347	1,049	801	410	137	13	2	4	88	346	752	1,170	6,119
Cooling Degree Days (base 65°F)	0	0	2	14	74	236	362	292	114	12	0	0	1,106
Mean Precipitation (in.)	1.31	1.29	2.72	3.29	4.26	4.31	4.31	4.49	3.65	2.66	2.59	1.98	36.86
Days With ≥ 0.1" Precipitation	3	3	6	6	7	7	7	6	6	5	5	4	65
Days With ≥ 1.0" Precipitation	0	0	1	1	1	1	1	1	1	1	0	0	8
Mean Snowfall (in.)	8.4	5.7	2.9	1.1	trace	0.0	0.0	0.0	0.0	0.2	2.0	6.2	26.5
Days With ≥ 1.0" Snow Depth	18	13	4	0	0	0	0	0	0	0	1	10	46

New Hampton *Chickasaw County*   Elevation: 1,158 ft.   Latitude: 43° 04' N   Longitude: 92° 19' W

	JAN	FEB	MAR	APR	MAY	JUN	JUL	AUG	SEP	OCT	NOV	DEC	YEAR
Mean Maximum Temp. (°F)	23.4	30.0	42.1	58.0	70.6	79.7	82.8	80.5	72.9	60.7	42.5	28.5	56.0
Mean Temp. (°F)	14.8	21.7	33.4	47.4	59.6	68.8	72.5	70.3	62.1	50.2	34.3	20.7	46.3
Mean Minimum Temp. (°F)	6.4	13.3	24.5	36.7	48.5	57.9	62.1	59.9	51.3	39.7	26.2	13.0	36.6
Extreme Maximum Temp. (°F)	58	65	84	94	92	101	102	104	96	95	78	63	104
Extreme Minimum Temp. (°F)	-29	-32	-11	6	25	36	45	41	26	15	-14	-24	-32
Days Maximum Temp. ≥ 90°F	0	0	0	0	0	3	4	3	1	0	0	0	11
Days Maximum Temp. ≤ 32°F	23	15	6	0	0	0	0	0	0	0	6	19	69
Days Minimum Temp. ≤ 32°F	31	27	24	9	1	0	0	0	0	7	22	30	151
Days Minimum Temp. ≤ 0°F	11	6	1	0	0	0	0	0	0	0	1	6	25
Heating Degree Days (base 65°F)	1,551	1,217	975	528	205	34	8	17	148	458	913	1,368	7,422
Cooling Degree Days (base 65°F)	0	0	0	7	41	160	257	197	71	5	0	0	738
Mean Precipitation (in.)	1.08	0.96	2.29	3.76	4.34	4.70	4.59	4.79	3.41	2.73	2.43	1.29	36.37
Days With ≥ 0.1" Precipitation	3	3	5	7	8	7	7	7	6	5	5	4	67
Days With ≥ 1.0" Precipitation	0	0	0	1	1	1	1	1	1	1	1	0	8
Mean Snowfall (in.)	10.1	6.4	6.9	2.4	trace	0.0	0.0	0.0	trace	0.2	4.9	8.8	39.7
Days With ≥ 1.0" Snow Depth	25	23	11	2	0	0	0	0	0	0	5	21	87

Newton *Jasper County*   Elevation: 958 ft.   Latitude: 41° 43' N   Longitude: 93° 02' W

	JAN	FEB	MAR	APR	MAY	JUN	JUL	AUG	SEP	OCT	NOV	DEC	YEAR
Mean Maximum Temp. (°F)	28.0	34.7	47.4	61.9	73.0	82.4	86.1	83.5	76.2	63.6	46.2	33.0	59.7
Mean Temp. (°F)	19.3	25.7	37.5	50.6	61.8	71.3	75.2	72.9	64.8	52.6	37.4	24.9	49.5
Mean Minimum Temp. (°F)	10.5	16.7	27.5	39.3	50.4	60.1	64.4	62.2	53.4	41.6	28.5	16.7	39.3
Extreme Maximum Temp. (°F)	67	68	90	96	92	102	105	105	97	93	80	69	105
Extreme Minimum Temp. (°F)	-31	-26	-7	9	29	42	44	41	27	13	-5	-22	-31
Days Maximum Temp. ≥ 90°F	0	0	0	0	0	4	9	6	2	0	0	0	21
Days Maximum Temp. ≤ 32°F	18	12	4	0	0	0	0	0	0	0	4	14	52
Days Minimum Temp. ≤ 32°F	30	25	21	7	0	0	0	0	0	5	20	29	137
Days Minimum Temp. ≤ 0°F	8	4	1	0	0	0	0	0	0	0	0	4	17
Heating Degree Days (base 65°F)	1,412	1,102	846	436	153	18	2	7	105	390	822	1,236	6,529
Cooling Degree Days (base 65°F)	0	0	1	13	62	219	339	279	112	12	0	0	1,037
Mean Precipitation (in.)	0.95	1.07	2.25	3.31	4.60	4.28	3.99	4.21	3.78	2.92	2.25	1.12	34.73
Days With ≥ 0.1" Precipitation	3	3	5	6	9	7	6	6	6	5	5	3	64
Days With ≥ 1.0" Precipitation	0	0	0	1	1	1	1	1	1	1	0	0	7
Mean Snowfall (in.)	7.4	6.4	*4.4*	1.5	trace	0.0	0.0	0.0	0.0	0.4	*2.3*	5.8	*28.2*
Days With ≥ 1.0" Snow Depth	na	na	na	0	0	0	0	0	0	0	*1*	na	na

Northwood *Worth County*   Elevation: 1,187 ft.   Latitude: 43° 26' N   Longitude: 93° 13' W

	JAN	FEB	MAR	APR	MAY	JUN	JUL	AUG	SEP	OCT	NOV	DEC	YEAR
Mean Maximum Temp. (°F)	21.9	28.5	40.6	57.2	70.7	80.2	83.2	80.7	72.8	59.9	40.9	27.3	55.3
Mean Temp. (°F)	13.0	19.7	31.8	46.3	59.3	69.0	72.4	69.9	61.2	48.9	32.7	19.2	45.3
Mean Minimum Temp. (°F)	4.0	10.9	23.0	35.3	47.8	57.7	61.5	59.0	49.5	37.8	24.4	11.1	35.2
Extreme Maximum Temp. (°F)	57	65	83	93	94	102	102	101	97	90	79	66	102
Extreme Minimum Temp. (°F)	-30	-33	-11	6	25	37	44	40	26	15	-14	-27	-33
Days Maximum Temp. ≥ 90°F	0	0	0	0	1	3	6	3	1	0	0	0	14
Days Maximum Temp. ≤ 32°F	24	16	8	1	0	0	0	0	0	0	8	20	77
Days Minimum Temp. ≤ 32°F	31	27	26	12	1	0	0	0	1	9	24	30	161
Days Minimum Temp. ≤ 0°F	13	7	2	0	0	0	0	0	0	0	1	7	30
Heating Degree Days (base 65°F)	1,609	1,273	1,022	562	216	37	9	20	167	498	963	1,413	7,789
Cooling Degree Days (base 65°F)	0	0	0	7	40	155	232	168	55	3	0	0	660
Mean Precipitation (in.)	0.94	0.68	2.10	3.22	3.97	4.34	4.39	4.77	3.41	2.41	1.93	1.06	33.22
Days With ≥ 0.1" Precipitation	3	2	5	7	7	7	6	6	6	5	4	3	61
Days With ≥ 1.0" Precipitation	0	0	0	1	1	1	1	1	1	1	0	0	7
Mean Snowfall (in.)	9.8	6.2	5.8	2.1	0.0	0.0	0.0	0.0	0.0	0.3	4.9	9.5	38.6
Days With ≥ 1.0" Snow Depth	na	na	na	*0*	0	0	0	0	0	0	*4*	na	na

Oakland 2 SW *Pottawattamie County*   Elevation: 1,167 ft.   Latitude: 41° 19' N   Longitude: 95° 23' W

	JAN	FEB	MAR	APR	MAY	JUN	JUL	AUG	SEP	OCT	NOV	DEC	YEAR
Mean Maximum Temp. (°F)	30.1	36.3	48.6	62.7	73.2	83.0	85.9	83.3	77.0	64.8	47.0	34.2	60.5
Mean Temp. (°F)	20.0	26.2	37.4	50.2	61.3	71.1	74.5	72.2	64.6	52.1	37.0	25.0	49.3
Mean Minimum Temp. (°F)	9.8	16.0	26.2	37.6	49.3	59.3	63.3	61.0	52.0	39.4	26.9	15.7	38.0
Extreme Maximum Temp. (°F)	66	75	89	93	96	100	105	101	96	*91*	*83*	67	*105*
Extreme Minimum Temp. (°F)	-31	-29	-15	0	24	37	*36*	39	23	*12*	*-13*	-30	*-31*
Days Maximum Temp. ≥ 90°F	0	0	0	0	1	5	9	5	2	0	0	0	22
Days Maximum Temp. ≤ 32°F	16	11	4	0	0	0	0	0	0	0	4	12	47
Days Minimum Temp. ≤ 32°F	30	26	23	9	1	0	0	0	1	8	21	30	149
Days Minimum Temp. ≤ 0°F	9	4	1	0	0	0	0	0	0	0	0	4	18
Heating Degree Days (base 65°F)	1,391	1,091	848	450	164	19	4	10	108	402	834	1,235	6,556
Cooling Degree Days (base 65°F)	0	0	1	13	49	207	316	242	107	*6*	0	0	*941*
Mean Precipitation (in.)	0.77	0.82	2.27	3.42	4.59	4.60	4.22	4.09	3.65	2.56	1.76	0.94	33.69
Days With ≥ 0.1" Precipitation	2	2	5	6	8	6	6	6	6	4	4	2	57
Days With ≥ 1.0" Precipitation	0	0	0	1	1	1	1	1	1	1	0	0	7
Mean Snowfall (in.)	6.4	5.8	4.3	1.4	trace	0.0	0.0	0.0	trace	0.7	2.6	4.8	26.0
Days With ≥ 1.0" Snow Depth	*17*	12	5	0	0	0	0	0	0	0	2	10	*46*

Oelwein 2 S *Fayette County*   Elevation: 1,007 ft.   Latitude: 42° 39' N   Longitude: 91° 55' W

	JAN	FEB	MAR	APR	MAY	JUN	JUL	AUG	SEP	OCT	NOV	DEC	YEAR
Mean Maximum Temp. (°F)	24.0	30.4	42.9	58.2	70.7	79.8	82.7	80.5	72.9	61.0	43.2	29.7	56.3
Mean Temp. (°F)	14.9	21.7	33.8	47.4	59.6	68.8	72.3	70.1	61.9	50.1	34.5	21.5	46.4
Mean Minimum Temp. (°F)	6.0	12.9	24.7	36.5	48.3	57.8	61.8	59.6	50.8	39.2	25.9	13.4	36.4
Extreme Maximum Temp. (°F)	56	64	85	96	91	100	103	103	96	94	78	66	103
Extreme Minimum Temp. (°F)	-29	-32	-12	3	26	36	40	39	25	13	-18	-26	-32
Days Maximum Temp. ≥ 90°F	0	0	0	0	0	2	4	3	1	0	0	0	10
Days Maximum Temp. ≤ 32°F	22	15	6	0	0	0	0	0	0	0	5	17	65
Days Minimum Temp. ≤ 32°F	30	27	24	11	1	0	0	0	1	8	22	30	154
Days Minimum Temp. ≤ 0°F	12	7	1	0	0	0	0	0	0	0	1	6	27
Heating Degree Days (base 65°F)	1,549	1,217	960	529	207	33	8	20	154	462	907	1,343	7,389
Cooling Degree Days (base 65°F)	0	0	0	8	39	157	250	190	70	6	0	0	720
Mean Precipitation (in.)	1.14	1.09	1.97	3.30	3.96	4.45	4.17	4.91	3.65	2.57	2.08	1.35	34.64
Days With ≥ 0.1" Precipitation	4	3	5	7	8	7	7	7	6	5	5	4	68
Days With ≥ 1.0" Precipitation	0	0	0	1	1	1	1	2	1	1	0	0	8
Mean Snowfall (in.)	9.4	5.9	5.1	1.4	0.0	0.0	0.0	0.0	0.0	trace	4.0	7.4	33.2
Days With ≥ 1.0" Snow Depth	na	*14*	7	1	0	0	0	0	0	0	3	*13*	na

Onawa 3 NW *Monona County*   Elevation: 1,059 ft.   Latitude: 42° 04' N   Longitude: 96° 08' W

	JAN	FEB	MAR	APR	MAY	JUN	JUL	AUG	SEP	OCT	NOV	DEC	YEAR
Mean Maximum Temp. (°F)	29.9	36.5	49.0	63.6	74.3	83.6	86.9	84.5	77.1	65.1	46.7	33.7	60.9
Mean Temp. (°F)	20.0	26.5	38.0	51.1	62.3	71.8	75.6	73.4	65.0	52.9	37.0	24.7	49.8
Mean Minimum Temp. (°F)	10.1	16.4	26.9	38.6	50.2	60.0	64.3	62.2	52.8	40.6	27.3	15.5	38.7
Extreme Maximum Temp. (°F)	67	71	91	96	96	105	105	104	101	93	81	70	105
Extreme Minimum Temp. (°F)	-26	-24	-12	4	27	38	41	39	25	12	-10	-27	-27
Days Maximum Temp. ≥ 90°F	0	0	0	1	1	7	11	7	3	0	0	0	30
Days Maximum Temp. ≤ 32°F	16	11	3	0	0	0	0	0	0	0	3	13	46
Days Minimum Temp. ≤ 32°F	30	26	22	9	1	0	0	0	1	7	21	30	147
Days Minimum Temp. ≤ 0°F	8	4	1	0	0	0	0	0	0	0	0	4	17
Heating Degree Days (base 65°F)	1,389	1,082	831	425	146	18	2	7	104	381	833	1,244	6,462
Cooling Degree Days (base 65°F)	0	0	1	17	62	219	324	267	111	11	0	0	1,012
Mean Precipitation (in.)	0.64	0.63	2.15	3.08	4.19	4.24	3.97	3.43	3.06	2.42	1.58	0.83	30.22
Days With ≥ 0.1" Precipitation	2	2	5	7	8	7	6	5	5	4	4	2	57
Days With ≥ 1.0" Precipitation	0	0	0	1	1	1	1	1	1	1	0	0	7
Mean Snowfall (in.)	7.6	6.1	6.0	2.0	trace	0.0	0.0	0.0	0.0	0.7	3.7	6.2	32.3
Days With ≥ 1.0" Snow Depth	19	13	6	1	0	0	0	0	0	0	4	12	55

Osage *Mitchell County*   Elevation: 1,167 ft.   Latitude: 43° 17' N   Longitude: 92° 48' W

	JAN	FEB	MAR	APR	MAY	JUN	JUL	AUG	SEP	OCT	NOV	DEC	YEAR
Mean Maximum Temp. (°F)	23.2	29.7	41.9	57.8	70.7	79.9	82.9	80.5	72.7	60.6	42.2	28.2	55.9
Mean Temp. (°F)	14.7	21.2	33.3	47.3	59.8	69.2	72.7	70.4	62.0	50.1	34.1	20.4	46.3
Mean Minimum Temp. (°F)	6.0	12.7	24.7	36.7	48.8	58.4	62.6	60.1	51.1	39.6	25.9	12.5	36.6
Extreme Maximum Temp. (°F)	57	63	84	92	92	101	102	101	98	93	77	61	102
Extreme Minimum Temp. (°F)	-28	-32	-9	6	25	39	46	41	28	16	-15	-25	-32
Days Maximum Temp. ≥ 90°F	0	0	0	0	0	3	5	2	1	0	0	0	11
Days Maximum Temp. ≤ 32°F	23	15	7	0	0	0	0	0	0	0	6	19	70
Days Minimum Temp. ≤ 32°F	31	27	24	9	1	0	0	0	0	7	23	30	152
Days Minimum Temp. ≤ 0°F	11	6	1	0	0	0	0	0	0	0	1	6	25
Heating Degree Days (base 65°F)	1,556	1,231	975	533	202	33	6	16	149	460	920	1,379	7,460
Cooling Degree Days (base 65°F)	0	0	0	7	42	165	252	193	65	6	0	0	730
Mean Precipitation (in.)	1.00	0.73	1.95	3.49	4.18	4.57	4.26	4.74	3.75	2.52	2.05	1.20	34.44
Days With ≥ 0.1" Precipitation	3	2	4	6	8	7	6	7	6	4	4	3	60
Days With ≥ 1.0" Precipitation	0	0	0	1	1	1	1	2	1	1	0	0	8
Mean Snowfall (in.)	9.4	5.9	6.0	2.1	0.0	0.0	0.0	0.0	0.0	0.2	4.0	8.1	35.7
Days With ≥ 1.0" Snow Depth	24	21	8	1	0	0	0	0	0	0	4	17	75

Osceola *Clarke County*   Elevation: 1,108 ft.   Latitude: 41° 02' N   Longitude: 93° 45' W

	JAN	FEB	MAR	APR	MAY	JUN	JUL	AUG	SEP	OCT	NOV	DEC	YEAR
Mean Maximum Temp. (°F)	30.4	36.3	49.1	62.8	72.6	82.0	86.6	84.1	76.5	64.3	47.5	35.4	60.6
Mean Temp. (°F)	20.8	26.2	38.2	51.1	61.2	70.8	75.3	72.7	64.4	52.3	37.7	26.0	49.7
Mean Minimum Temp. (°F)	10.7	15.9	27.1	39.0	49.9	59.2	63.9	61.3	52.2	40.1	27.9	16.6	38.6
Extreme Maximum Temp. (°F)	64	75	87	90	92	102	106	103	96	92	80	68	106
Extreme Minimum Temp. (°F)	-28	-26	-16	7	27	37	42	42	28	9	-7	-25	-28
Days Maximum Temp. ≥ 90°F	0	0	0	0	0	4	10	7	2	0	0	0	23
Days Maximum Temp. ≤ 32°F	16	11	3	0	0	0	0	0	0	0	3	11	44
Days Minimum Temp. ≤ 32°F	30	26	21	8	0	0	0	0	0	7	21	29	142
Days Minimum Temp. ≤ 0°F	8	4	1	0	0	0	0	0	0	0	0	3	16
Heating Degree Days (base 65°F)	1,364	1,085	826	424	162	19	3	7	109	400	813	1,202	6,414
Cooling Degree Days (base 65°F)	0	0	1	9	42	190	333	250	92	8	0	0	925
Mean Precipitation (in.)	0.92	1.03	2.31	3.52	4.71	4.35	4.63	4.32	4.20	2.85	2.31	1.22	36.37
Days With ≥ 0.1" Precipitation	3	3	5	6	9	7	6	6	6	5	4	3	63
Days With ≥ 1.0" Precipitation	0	0	0	1	1	1	1	1	1	1	1	0	8
Mean Snowfall (in.)	6.7	6.0	3.9	1.9	0.0	0.0	0.0	0.0	0.0	0.6	2.1	4.2	25.4
Days With ≥ 1.0" Snow Depth	14	10	4	1	0	0	0	0	0	0	2	9	40

Oskaloosa *Mahaska County*   Elevation: 830 ft.   Latitude: 41° 19' N   Longitude: 92° 39' W

	JAN	FEB	MAR	APR	MAY	JUN	JUL	AUG	SEP	OCT	NOV	DEC	YEAR
Mean Maximum Temp. (°F)	29.9	36.2	48.6	62.2	72.9	82.1	86.2	83.8	76.5	64.2	47.8	34.8	60.4
Mean Temp. (°F)	20.5	26.9	38.3	50.8	61.8	71.2	75.4	72.8	64.8	52.9	38.3	26.5	50.0
Mean Minimum Temp. (°F)	11.3	17.5	27.9	39.3	50.5	60.2	64.5	61.8	53.0	41.5	28.9	18.0	39.6
Extreme Maximum Temp. (°F)	69	75	87	92	91	103	104	105	97	91	80	71	105
Extreme Minimum Temp. (°F)	-23	-29	-11	9	28	41	45	40	26	14	-5	-24	-29
Days Maximum Temp. ≥ 90°F	0	0	0	0	0	4	10	6	2	0	0	0	22
Days Maximum Temp. ≤ 32°F	17	12	3	0	0	0	0	0	0	0	3	12	47
Days Minimum Temp. ≤ 32°F	30	25	21	7	0	0	0	0	0	6	19	28	136
Days Minimum Temp. ≤ 0°F	8	4	0	0	0	0	0	0	0	0	0	4	16
Heating Degree Days (base 65°F)	1,374	1,069	824	432	152	17	2	8	106	381	794	1,188	6,347
Cooling Degree Days (base 65°F)	0	0	2	12	50	199	320	256	101	10	0	0	950
Mean Precipitation (in.)	1.09	1.20	2.24	3.51	4.62	4.30	4.29	4.55	4.04	3.05	2.83	1.43	37.15
Days With ≥ 0.1" Precipitation	3	3	5	7	8	7	6	6	6	6	6	4	67
Days With ≥ 1.0" Precipitation	0	0	0	1	1	1	1	1	1	1	1	0	8
Mean Snowfall (in.)	7.3	7.0	3.3	1.9	0.0	0.0	0.0	0.0	0.0	0.1	2.2	5.8	27.6
Days With ≥ 1.0" Snow Depth	14	na	3	1	0	0	0	0	0	0	1	6	na

Ottumwa Industrial Airport *Wapello County*   Elevation: 839 ft.   Latitude: 41° 06' N   Longitude: 92° 27' W

	JAN	FEB	MAR	APR	MAY	JUN	JUL	AUG	SEP	OCT	NOV	DEC	YEAR
Mean Maximum Temp. (°F)	29.7	35.8	48.2	61.4	72.6	82.3	86.4	83.9	75.8	63.8	47.8	34.7	60.2
Mean Temp. (°F)	21.3	27.3	38.9	51.2	62.6	72.2	76.5	74.0	65.5	53.6	39.4	27.0	50.8
Mean Minimum Temp. (°F)	12.8	18.7	29.5	40.9	52.5	62.2	66.6	64.1	55.1	43.5	31.0	19.3	41.4
Extreme Maximum Temp. (°F)	71	72	88	90	93	103	105	105	100	91	79	71	105
Extreme Minimum Temp. (°F)	-23	-27	-7	9	32	43	48	42	27	17	-5	-21	-27
Days Maximum Temp. ≥ 90°F	0	0	0	0	0	4	10	7	2	0	0	0	23
Days Maximum Temp. ≤ 32°F	17	12	3	0	0	0	0	0	0	0	3	12	47
Days Minimum Temp. ≤ 32°F	30	24	19	5	0	0	0	0	0	3	17	28	126
Days Minimum Temp. ≤ 0°F	7	3	0	0	0	0	0	0	0	0	0	3	13
Heating Degree Days (base 65°F)	1,349	1,058	805	422	138	13	1	5	96	358	760	1,171	6,176
Cooling Degree Days (base 65°F)	0	0	2	14	68	240	373	303	119	13	0	0	1,132
Mean Precipitation (in.)	0.97	1.11	2.39	3.27	4.49	4.25	4.40	4.23	3.98	2.78	2.43	1.38	35.68
Days With ≥ 0.1" Precipitation	3	3	5	7	8	7	7	6	6	5	5	4	66
Days With ≥ 1.0" Precipitation	0	0	0	1	1	1	1	1	1	1	0	0	7
Mean Snowfall (in.)	7.1	5.8	3.7	2.0	trace	trace	trace	trace	trace	0.4	1.9	5.7	26.6
Days With ≥ 1.0" Snow Depth	17	12	4	1	0	0	0	0	0	0	2	9	45

Perry *Dallas County*   Elevation: 964 ft.   Latitude: 41° 50' N   Longitude: 94° 07' W

	JAN	FEB	MAR	APR	MAY	JUN	JUL	AUG	SEP	OCT	NOV	DEC	YEAR
Mean Maximum Temp. (°F)	26.9	33.2	45.6	59.7	71.7	81.2	85.1	82.5	75.4	63.1	45.6	31.9	58.5
Mean Temp. (°F)	17.4	23.4	35.7	48.5	60.3	70.0	74.0	71.3	63.0	50.6	35.9	23.2	47.8
Mean Minimum Temp. (°F)	7.7	13.6	25.7	37.2	48.8	58.8	62.9	60.0	50.5	38.1	26.1	14.5	37.0
Extreme Maximum Temp. (°F)	62	68	89	95	94	101	104	106	97	94	81	69	106
Extreme Minimum Temp. (°F)	-32	-33	-11	6	27	40	42	37	26	14	-13	-28	-33
Days Maximum Temp. ≥ 90°F	0	0	0	0	1	4	8	5	2	0	0	0	20
Days Maximum Temp. ≤ 32°F	19	14	5	0	0	0	0	0	0	0	4	15	57
Days Minimum Temp. ≤ 32°F	31	27	23	9	1	0	0	0	1	9	22	30	153
Days Minimum Temp. ≤ 0°F	10	6	1	0	0	0	0	0	0	0	0	5	22
Heating Degree Days (base 65°F)	1,472	1,169	903	499	192	27	5	16	138	448	867	1,289	7,025
Cooling Degree Days (base 65°F)	0	0	1	11	48	183	291	224	86	9	0	0	853
Mean Precipitation (in.)	0.77	0.71	2.07	3.08	4.32	4.67	3.97	4.17	3.11	2.50	1.78	1.03	32.18
Days With ≥ 0.1" Precipitation	2	2	4	6	8	7	6	6	6	5	4	2	58
Days With ≥ 1.0" Precipitation	0	0	0	1	1	1	1	1	1	1	0	0	7
Mean Snowfall (in.)	5.9	4.8	4.6	0.6	0.0	0.0	0.0	0.0	0.0	0.1	2.4	4.6	23.0
Days With ≥ 1.0" Snow Depth	na	na	3	0	0	0	0	0	0	0	1	na	na

Pocahontas *Pocahontas County*　Elevation: 1,210 ft.　Latitude: 42° 44' N　Longitude: 94° 40' W

	JAN	FEB	MAR	APR	MAY	JUN	JUL	AUG	SEP	OCT	NOV	DEC	YEAR
Mean Maximum Temp. (°F)	24.2	30.2	42.5	58.7	72.1	81.7	84.2	81.4	74.6	61.9	43.0	28.8	57.0
Mean Temp. (°F)	14.6	20.8	32.8	47.1	59.8	69.8	72.7	70.0	61.9	49.2	33.4	19.9	46.0
Mean Minimum Temp. (°F)	5.0	11.3	23.1	35.4	47.5	57.9	61.1	58.4	49.1	36.5	23.7	10.9	35.0
Extreme Maximum Temp. (°F)	65	67	87	98	96	105	101	102	98	94	80	68	105
Extreme Minimum Temp. (°F)	-26	-27	-15	2	26	39	42	41	25	14	-13	-29	-29
Days Maximum Temp. ≥ 90°F	0	0	0	0	2	6	7	4	2	0	0	0	21
Days Maximum Temp. ≤ 32°F	22	15	7	1	0	0	0	0	0	0	6	18	69
Days Minimum Temp. ≤ 32°F	31	28	25	11	1	0	0	0	1	11	25	31	164
Days Minimum Temp. ≤ 0°F	12	7	2	0	0	0	0	0	0	0	1	7	29
Heating Degree Days (base 65°F)	1,556	1,244	990	541	206	32	6	20	159	489	942	1,393	7,578
Cooling Degree Days (base 65°F)	0	0	0	9	51	183	242	177	70	7	0	0	739
Mean Precipitation (in.)	0.87	0.68	2.19	3.17	3.88	4.45	4.22	4.56	3.29	2.19	1.83	0.93	32.26
Days With ≥ 0.1" Precipitation	2	2	5	7	8	7	7	6	6	4	4	2	60
Days With ≥ 1.0" Precipitation	0	0	0	1	1	1	1	1	1	0	0	0	6
Mean Snowfall (in.)	7.6	5.8	6.6	1.7	trace	0.0	0.0	0.0	0.0	0.3	4.8	7.5	34.3
Days With ≥ 1.0" Snow Depth	na	na	na	1	0	0	0	0	0	0	3	na	na

Primghar *O'brien County*　Elevation: 1,519 ft.　Latitude: 43° 05' N　Longitude: 95° 38' W

	JAN	FEB	MAR	APR	MAY	JUN	JUL	AUG	SEP	OCT	NOV	DEC	YEAR
Mean Maximum Temp. (°F)	24.6	31.6	44.0	60.0	72.8	82.1	84.9	82.5	75.2	62.7	42.6	28.9	57.7
Mean Temp. (°F)	15.4	22.5	34.1	48.1	60.7	70.2	73.7	71.5	63.1	50.8	33.8	20.4	47.0
Mean Minimum Temp. (°F)	6.2	13.2	24.1	36.2	48.5	58.3	62.4	60.3	50.9	38.9	24.9	11.8	36.3
Extreme Maximum Temp. (°F)	64	65	83	93	95	103	101	100	100	89	76	64	103
Extreme Minimum Temp. (°F)	-30	-29	-17	3	25	38	40	40	25	13	-12	-28	-30
Days Maximum Temp. ≥ 90°F	0	0	0	0	1	5	8	5	2	0	0	0	21
Days Maximum Temp. ≤ 32°F	21	14	6	1	0	0	0	0	0	0	6	19	67
Days Minimum Temp. ≤ 32°F	31	27	24	11	1	0	0	0	1	8	23	30	156
Days Minimum Temp. ≤ 0°F	11	6	2	0	0	0	0	0	0	0	1	7	27
Heating Degree Days (base 65°F)	1,533	1,195	953	509	183	26	5	12	132	441	929	1,376	7,294
Cooling Degree Days (base 65°F)	0	0	0	9	53	183	270	213	79	7	0	0	814
Mean Precipitation (in.)	0.66	0.53	1.92	2.99	3.64	4.94	4.38	4.22	2.74	2.14	1.51	0.72	30.39
Days With ≥ 0.1" Precipitation	2	2	4	6	8	7	6	6	6	4	3	2	56
Days With ≥ 1.0" Precipitation	0	0	0	1	1	1	1	1	1	1	0	0	7
Mean Snowfall (in.)	7.2	3.7	6.5	1.0	0.0	0.0	0.0	0.0	0.0	0.3	3.9	6.5	29.1
Days With ≥ 1.0" Snow Depth	na	na	5	0	0	0	0	0	0	0	1	na	na

Rathbun Dam *Appanoose County*　Elevation: 964 ft.　Latitude: 40° 50' N　Longitude: 92° 54' W

	JAN	FEB	MAR	APR	MAY	JUN	JUL	AUG	SEP	OCT	NOV	DEC	YEAR
Mean Maximum Temp. (°F)	29.7	35.7	47.8	60.7	71.2	80.8	85.8	83.5	75.9	64.1	47.9	35.0	59.9
Mean Temp. (°F)	20.3	25.6	37.7	50.2	60.8	70.5	75.3	72.8	64.4	52.4	38.5	26.1	49.5
Mean Minimum Temp. (°F)	10.9	15.7	27.4	39.5	50.3	60.1	64.7	62.0	52.9	40.7	29.1	17.1	39.2
Extreme Maximum Temp. (°F)	62	72	87	89	94	103	105	104	98	92	79	70	105
Extreme Minimum Temp. (°F)	-28	-26	-11	14	28	41	43	43	30	16	-8	-26	-28
Days Maximum Temp. ≥ 90°F	0	0	0	0	0	3	9	6	2	0	0	0	20
Days Maximum Temp. ≤ 32°F	16	12	4	0	0	0	0	0	0	0	3	12	47
Days Minimum Temp. ≤ 32°F	29	26	22	6	0	0	0	0	0	6	19	28	136
Days Minimum Temp. ≤ 0°F	7	5	1	0	0	0	0	0	0	0	0	3	16
Heating Degree Days (base 65°F)	1,378	1,108	842	451	171	22	3	8	113	394	787	1,200	6,477
Cooling Degree Days (base 65°F)	0	0	2	13	46	196	333	265	101	10	0	0	966
Mean Precipitation (in.)	0.91	1.07	2.24	3.44	4.74	4.43	5.07	4.29	4.15	3.01	2.35	1.35	37.05
Days With ≥ 0.1" Precipitation	3	3	5	7	8	7	6	7	6	5	5	3	65
Days With ≥ 1.0" Precipitation	0	0	0	1	1	1	2	1	1	1	0	0	8
Mean Snowfall (in.)	5.5	5.2	2.5	0.8	0.0	0.0	0.0	0.0	0.0	trace	0.7	4.0	18.7
Days With ≥ 1.0" Snow Depth	11	11	4	0	0	0	0	0	0	0	1	6	33

Red Oak *Montgomery County*　Elevation: 1,040 ft.　Latitude: 41° 11' N　Longitude: 95° 15' W

	JAN	FEB	MAR	APR	MAY	JUN	JUL	AUG	SEP	OCT	NOV	DEC	YEAR
Mean Maximum Temp. (°F)	31.8	38.6	50.8	64.6	75.2	84.7	88.2	86.3	78.7	66.4	48.8	36.6	62.5
Mean Temp. (°F)	21.8	28.1	39.5	52.0	62.8	72.2	76.3	74.1	65.8	53.5	38.6	27.2	51.0
Mean Minimum Temp. (°F)	11.8	17.5	28.1	39.4	50.4	59.7	64.3	61.9	52.8	40.6	28.4	17.7	39.4
Extreme Maximum Temp. (°F)	69	78	91	94	96	104	109	106	99	94	82	67	109
Extreme Minimum Temp. (°F)	-27	-28	-19	2	26	37	39	34	23	13	-6	-26	-28
Days Maximum Temp. ≥ 90°F	0	0	0	1	1	8	13	10	4	0	0	0	37
Days Maximum Temp. ≤ 32°F	15	10	3	0	0	0	0	0	0	0	3	10	41
Days Minimum Temp. ≤ 32°F	30	25	21	8	1	0	0	0	1	7	20	29	142
Days Minimum Temp. ≤ 0°F	7	4	1	0	0	0	0	0	0	0	0	3	15
Heating Degree Days (base 65°F)	1,333	1,036	785	400	133	14	2	7	95	364	785	1,165	6,119
Cooling Degree Days (base 65°F)	0	0	2	19	69	233	360	291	125	14	0	0	1,113
Mean Precipitation (in.)	0.97	1.11	2.35	3.73	4.75	4.79	4.52	4.14	4.17	2.70	2.14	1.22	36.59
Days With ≥ 0.1" Precipitation	3	3	5	7	8	7	6	6	5	5	5	3	62
Days With ≥ 1.0" Precipitation	0	0	1	1	1	2	2	1	1	1	1	0	11
Mean Snowfall (in.)	8.0	8.1	4.8	1.7	0.0	0.0	0.0	0.0	trace	0.6	3.1	6.1	32.4
Days With ≥ 1.0" Snow Depth	16	13	4	1	0	0	0	0	0	0	2	9	45

Rock Rapids *Lyon County*   Elevation: 1,348 ft.   Latitude: 43° 26' N   Longitude: 96° 10' W

	JAN	FEB	MAR	APR	MAY	JUN	JUL	AUG	SEP	OCT	NOV	DEC	YEAR
Mean Maximum Temp. (°F)	24.0	30.9	42.4	58.5	71.7	81.4	85.8	83.4	74.5	61.6	42.2	28.9	57.1
Mean Temp. (°F)	13.3	20.3	31.9	46.3	59.0	69.2	73.5	70.9	61.1	48.2	32.1	19.0	45.4
Mean Minimum Temp. (°F)	2.6	9.7	21.5	34.1	46.4	56.9	61.1	58.3	47.6	34.7	21.8	9.1	33.7
Extreme Maximum Temp. (°F)	66	68	84	95	93	107	108	104	104	91	80	70	108
Extreme Minimum Temp. (°F)	-32	-30	-18	7	25	36	41	35	23	12	-14	-26	-32
Days Maximum Temp. ≥ 90°F	0	0	0	0	1	5	10	7	2	0	0	0	25
Days Maximum Temp. ≤ 32°F	22	14	7	1	0	0	0	0	0	0	7	18	69
Days Minimum Temp. ≤ 32°F	31	28	26	13	2	0	0	2	13	27	31	173
Days Minimum Temp. ≤ 0°F	14	8	2	0	0	0	0	0	0	0	1	8	33
Heating Degree Days (base 65°F)	1,598	1,257	1,020	560	223	39	7	19	174	519	982	1,419	7,817
Cooling Degree Days (base 65°F)	0	0	0	7	40	168	265	201	61	4	0	0	746
Mean Precipitation (in.)	0.53	0.51	1.94	2.62	3.16	4.30	3.50	3.83	2.54	1.96	1.60	0.74	27.23
Days With ≥ 0.1" Precipitation	2	2	5	6	7	7	6	6	5	4	3	2	55
Days With ≥ 1.0" Precipitation	0	0	0	1	1	1	1	1	1	0	0	0	6
Mean Snowfall (in.)	5.7	*4.3*	6.4	1.6	trace	0.0	0.0	0.0	trace	0.6	4.6	5.3	*28.5*
Days With ≥ 1.0" Snow Depth	24	19	10	1	0	0	0	0	0	0	6	17	77

Rockwell City *Calhoun County*   Elevation: 1,194 ft.   Latitude: 42° 24' N   Longitude: 94° 38' W

	JAN	FEB	MAR	APR	MAY	JUN	JUL	AUG	SEP	OCT	NOV	DEC	YEAR
Mean Maximum Temp. (°F)	26.4	32.9	45.3	60.6	72.6	82.4	85.0	82.6	75.7	63.0	44.3	31.0	58.5
Mean Temp. (°F)	17.2	23.7	35.5	49.0	60.9	70.8	74.0	71.5	63.6	51.3	35.3	22.5	47.9
Mean Minimum Temp. (°F)	7.9	14.4	25.6	37.2	49.1	59.2	62.9	60.4	51.5	39.6	26.2	14.0	37.3
Extreme Maximum Temp. (°F)	65	66	87	97	92	101	103	102	98	93	80	68	103
Extreme Minimum Temp. (°F)	-26	-26	-12	6	27	40	43	39	27	14	-7	-25	-26
Days Maximum Temp. ≥ 90°F	0	0	0	0	1	5	8	5	2	0	0	0	21
Days Maximum Temp. ≤ 32°F	20	13	5	0	0	0	0	0	0	0	5	16	59
Days Minimum Temp. ≤ 32°F	31	27	24	9	1	0	0	0	1	7	23	31	154
Days Minimum Temp. ≤ 0°F	10	5	1	0	0	0	0	0	0	0	1	5	22
Heating Degree Days (base 65°F)	1,477	1,160	909	484	174	19	3	11	122	426	886	1,311	6,982
Cooling Degree Days (base 65°F)	0	0	0	11	50	195	282	218	87	8	0	0	851
Mean Precipitation (in.)	0.75	0.61	1.99	3.15	4.38	4.44	4.13	3.81	3.34	2.46	1.59	0.87	31.52
Days With ≥ 0.1" Precipitation	2	2	4	6	8	7	6	6	5	4	2	58
Days With ≥ 1.0" Precipitation	0	0	0	1	1	1	1	1	1	1	0	0	7
Mean Snowfall (in.)	7.8	6.0	6.3	2.5	trace	0.0	0.0	0.0	trace	0.7	4.2	6.9	34.4
Days With ≥ 1.0" Snow Depth	21	17	8	1	0	0	0	0	0	0	5	15	67

Sac City *Sac County*   Elevation: 1,197 ft.   Latitude: 42° 25' N   Longitude: 94° 59' W

	JAN	FEB	MAR	APR	MAY	JUN	JUL	AUG	SEP	OCT	NOV	DEC	YEAR
Mean Maximum Temp. (°F)	26.1	32.5	44.4	59.8	72.3	81.4	85.0	82.3	74.8	62.3	44.2	31.3	58.0
Mean Temp. (°F)	16.8	22.8	34.4	47.9	59.8	69.4	73.6	71.0	62.5	50.1	34.7	22.5	47.1
Mean Minimum Temp. (°F)	7.5	12.9	24.3	35.9	47.3	57.3	62.2	59.6	50.1	37.9	25.3	13.7	36.2
Extreme Maximum Temp. (°F)	63	66	88	96	93	102	100	102	96	91	78	67	102
Extreme Minimum Temp. (°F)	-29	-28	-12	4	25	38	44	39	27	9	-11	-27	-29
Days Maximum Temp. ≥ 90°F	0	0	0	0	1	4	8	5	1	0	0	0	19
Days Maximum Temp. ≤ 32°F	20	14	6	1	0	0	0	0	0	0	5	16	62
Days Minimum Temp. ≤ 32°F	31	28	25	10	1	0	0	0	1	9	24	30	159
Days Minimum Temp. ≤ 0°F	10	6	1	0	0	0	0	0	0	0	1	5	23
Heating Degree Days (base 65°F)	1,489	1,187	943	516	198	32	5	17	143	463	901	1,310	7,204
Cooling Degree Days (base 65°F)	0	0	0	9	39	159	267	200	68	5	0	0	747
Mean Precipitation (in.)	0.81	0.79	2.47	3.44	4.29	4.69	4.02	3.82	3.42	2.53	1.77	1.08	33.13
Days With ≥ 0.1" Precipitation	2	2	5	7	8	8	6	6	6	4	4	3	61
Days With ≥ 1.0" Precipitation	0	0	0	1	1	1	1	1	1	1	0	0	7
Mean Snowfall (in.)	6.8	6.0	5.9	1.7	trace	0.0	0.0	0.0	trace	0.4	2.9	7.0	30.7
Days With ≥ 1.0" Snow Depth	*20*	*16*	*6*	1	0	0	0	0	0	0	4	*14*	*61*

Sanborn *O'brien County*   Elevation: 1,548 ft.   Latitude: 43° 11' N   Longitude: 95° 40' W

	JAN	FEB	MAR	APR	MAY	JUN	JUL	AUG	SEP	OCT	NOV	DEC	YEAR
Mean Maximum Temp. (°F)	22.8	29.6	41.3	57.6	71.0	80.2	83.2	80.8	73.3	60.5	41.3	27.7	55.8
Mean Temp. (°F)	13.5	20.4	31.8	46.0	59.1	68.8	72.5	70.1	61.5	48.9	32.4	19.0	45.3
Mean Minimum Temp. (°F)	4.1	11.2	22.3	34.3	47.2	57.4	61.7	59.3	49.7	37.3	23.3	10.4	34.8
Extreme Maximum Temp. (°F)	64	64	83	92	94	102	101	99	101	90	77	62	102
Extreme Minimum Temp. (°F)	-33	-28	-16	3	23	38	38	40	25	11	-12	-29	-33
Days Maximum Temp. ≥ 90°F	0	0	0	0	1	3	6	3	1	0	0	0	14
Days Maximum Temp. ≤ 32°F	23	16	8	1	0	0	0	0	0	0	8	20	76
Days Minimum Temp. ≤ 32°F	31	28	26	14	1	0	0	0	1	10	25	31	167
Days Minimum Temp. ≤ 0°F	13	7	2	0	0	0	0	0	0	0	1	8	31
Heating Degree Days (base 65°F)	1,593	1,254	1,022	570	219	38	8	19	162	497	973	1,419	7,774
Cooling Degree Days (base 65°F)	0	0	0	5	40	155	238	178	63	4	0	0	683
Mean Precipitation (in.)	0.66	0.59	1.80	2.77	3.58	4.28	3.56	3.88	2.86	1.98	1.58	0.73	28.27
Days With ≥ 0.1" Precipitation	2	2	4	6	8	7	6	6	6	4	3	2	56
Days With ≥ 1.0" Precipitation	0	0	0	1	1	1	1	1	1	1	0	0	7
Mean Snowfall (in.)	8.6	6.3	8.1	2.5	trace	0.0	0.0	0.0	trace	0.6	5.9	8.0	40.0
Days With ≥ 1.0" Snow Depth	24	*17*	*10*	1	0	0	0	0	0	0	7	*19*	*78*

Sheldon *O'brien County*   Elevation: 1,417 ft.   Latitude: 43° 11' N   Longitude: 95° 51' W

	JAN	FEB	MAR	APR	MAY	JUN	JUL	AUG	SEP	OCT	NOV	DEC	YEAR
Mean Maximum Temp. (°F)	23.9	30.6	42.8	58.7	71.7	80.6	83.5	81.1	73.5	60.7	41.8	28.4	56.4
Mean Temp. (°F)	14.3	21.2	33.0	46.7	59.5	68.8	72.2	69.9	61.4	48.9	32.5	19.5	45.7
Mean Minimum Temp. (°F)	4.6	11.9	23.2	34.6	47.2	57.0	60.9	58.7	49.2	37.0	23.2	10.5	34.8
Extreme Maximum Temp. (°F)	66	66	82	93	95	102	101	98	100	90	77	66	102
Extreme Minimum Temp. (°F)	-32	-32	-16	3	22	33	41	39	23	10	-15	-24	-32
Days Maximum Temp. ≥ 90°F	0	0	0	0	1	4	6	4	1	0	0	0	16
Days Maximum Temp. ≤ 32°F	22	15	6	1	0	0	0	0	0	0	7	19	70
Days Minimum Temp. ≤ 32°F	31	27	26	13	2	0	0	0	1	11	25	31	167
Days Minimum Temp. ≤ 0°F	12	6	2	0	0	0	0	0	0	0	1	7	28
Heating Degree Days (base 65°F)	1,567	1,230	985	549	206	36	9	22	163	498	968	1,406	7,639
Cooling Degree Days (base 65°F)	0	0	0	7	39	150	234	178	59	5	0	0	672
Mean Precipitation (in.)	0.76	0.62	2.18	2.98	3.54	4.45	3.82	3.85	2.65	2.10	1.64	0.83	29.42
Days With ≥ 0.1" Precipitation	2	2	5	7	8	7	6	6	5	4	4	2	58
Days With ≥ 1.0" Precipitation	0	0	0	0	1	1	1	1	1	1	0	0	6
Mean Snowfall (in.)	7.9	5.2	8.2	2.5	trace	trace	0.0	trace	trace	0.8	5.5	7.2	37.3
Days With ≥ 1.0" Snow Depth	24	18	10	1	0	0	0	0	0	0	6	18	77

Shenandoah *Page County*   Elevation: 974 ft.   Latitude: 40° 46' N   Longitude: 95° 23' W

	JAN	FEB	MAR	APR	MAY	JUN	JUL	AUG	SEP	OCT	NOV	DEC	YEAR
Mean Maximum Temp. (°F)	31.8	38.8	51.1	64.3	74.6	84.3	87.8	86.0	78.8	67.1	49.4	36.7	62.6
Mean Temp. (°F)	22.2	28.7	40.2	52.4	63.0	72.6	76.6	74.5	66.4	54.5	39.4	27.6	51.5
Mean Minimum Temp. (°F)	12.6	18.5	29.3	40.4	51.3	61.0	65.4	63.0	54.0	41.9	29.4	18.5	40.4
Extreme Maximum Temp. (°F)	66	78	89	94	95	105	107	103	100	94	83	67	107
Extreme Minimum Temp. (°F)	-26	-24	-17	8	26	39	41	40	23	15	-5	-26	-26
Days Maximum Temp. ≥ 90°F	0	0	0	0	1	7	13	10	4	0	0	0	35
Days Maximum Temp. ≤ 32°F	15	10	3	0	0	0	0	0	0	0	3	10	41
Days Minimum Temp. ≤ 32°F	30	25	19	7	0	0	0	0	0	6	19	29	135
Days Minimum Temp. ≤ 0°F	7	3	0	0	0	0	0	0	0	0	0	3	13
Heating Degree Days (base 65°F)	1,321	1,018	764	392	130	12	2	4	91	335	761	1,152	5,982
Cooling Degree Days (base 65°F)	0	0	2	19	67	239	372	306	145	16	0	0	1,166
Mean Precipitation (in.)	0.82	0.93	2.32	3.37	4.49	4.54	4.46	3.69	3.59	2.62	2.12	1.11	34.06
Days With ≥ 0.1" Precipitation	3	3	5	7	8	6	6	6	5	5	4	3	61
Days With ≥ 1.0" Precipitation	0	0	1	1	1	1	2	1	1	1	1	0	10
Mean Snowfall (in.)	7.0	5.7	3.5	1.2	0.0	0.0	0.0	0.0	0.0	0.4	1.7	4.9	24.4
Days With ≥ 1.0" Snow Depth	*16*	*11*	*3*	0	0	0	0	0	0	0	1	*8*	*39*

Sibley 5 NNE *Osceola County*   Elevation: 1,669 ft.   Latitude: 43° 28' N   Longitude: 95° 43' W

	JAN	FEB	MAR	APR	MAY	JUN	JUL	AUG	SEP	OCT	NOV	DEC	YEAR
Mean Maximum Temp. (°F)	22.5	29.4	40.8	56.9	70.5	79.5	82.7	80.2	72.9	60.6	40.9	27.5	55.4
Mean Temp. (°F)	12.9	19.7	31.1	45.1	58.0	67.6	71.2	68.9	60.5	48.3	31.6	18.4	44.4
Mean Minimum Temp. (°F)	3.2	10.1	21.3	33.3	45.5	55.7	59.7	57.4	48.0	35.9	22.2	9.4	33.5
Extreme Maximum Temp. (°F)	63	65	80	93	94	102	101	104	102	92	77	64	104
Extreme Minimum Temp. (°F)	-30	-30	-20	3	22	34	40	39	23	12	-15	-29	-30
Days Maximum Temp. ≥ 90°F	0	0	0	0	1	4	6	3	1	0	0	0	15
Days Maximum Temp. ≤ 32°F	23	16	8	1	0	0	0	0	0	0	8	20	76
Days Minimum Temp. ≤ 32°F	31	28	27	15	2	0	0	0	2	12	26	30	173
Days Minimum Temp. ≤ 0°F	13	8	2	0	0	0	0	0	0	0	1	8	32
Heating Degree Days (base 65°F)	1,613	1,273	1,045	595	245	52	13	27	184	517	996	1,438	7,998
Cooling Degree Days (base 65°F)	0	0	0	5	30	127	194	138	48	3	0	0	545
Mean Precipitation (in.)	0.55	0.48	2.02	2.87	3.39	4.34	3.39	4.23	3.00	1.90	1.40	0.67	28.24
Days With ≥ 0.1" Precipitation	2	2	4	6	7	8	6	6	6	4	3	2	56
Days With ≥ 1.0" Precipitation	0	0	0	1	1	1	1	1	1	0	0	0	6
Mean Snowfall (in.)	7.6	4.6	8.1	3.2	trace	0.0	0.0	0.0	trace	1.0	5.8	6.9	37.2
Days With ≥ 1.0" Snow Depth	na	na	na	2	0	0	0	0	0	0	*6*	na	na

Sidney *Fremont County*   Elevation: 1,128 ft.   Latitude: 40° 45' N   Longitude: 95° 39' W

	JAN	FEB	MAR	APR	MAY	JUN	JUL	AUG	SEP	OCT	NOV	DEC	YEAR
Mean Maximum Temp. (°F)	32.5	39.6	51.6	64.7	74.7	84.3	87.9	86.1	78.8	67.2	49.3	36.9	62.8
Mean Temp. (°F)	23.0	29.5	40.6	52.8	63.5	73.1	77.0	75.0	67.0	55.2	39.8	28.0	52.1
Mean Minimum Temp. (°F)	13.5	19.4	29.5	40.9	52.3	61.8	66.1	63.8	55.0	43.2	30.2	19.1	41.2
Extreme Maximum Temp. (°F)	69	82	91	96	100	105	109	103	102	94	83	67	109
Extreme Minimum Temp. (°F)	-21	-23	-12	8	28	41	44	45	28	14	-3	-25	-25
Days Maximum Temp. ≥ 90°F	0	0	0	1	1	7	12	11	4	0	0	0	36
Days Maximum Temp. ≤ 32°F	15	9	3	0	0	0	0	0	0	0	3	11	41
Days Minimum Temp. ≤ 32°F	29	24	19	6	0	0	0	0	0	4	18	29	129
Days Minimum Temp. ≤ 0°F	6	3	0	0	0	0	0	0	0	0	0	3	12
Heating Degree Days (base 65°F)	1,295	995	752	381	119	11	1	3	81	314	750	1,139	5,841
Cooling Degree Days (base 65°F)	0	0	3	22	73	247	370	305	143	17	0	0	1,180
Mean Precipitation (in.)	0.82	0.93	2.45	3.39	4.53	4.17	4.98	3.87	3.70	2.72	2.06	1.07	34.69
Days With ≥ 0.1" Precipitation	2	3	5	7	8	6	6	6	5	5	4	3	60
Days With ≥ 1.0" Precipitation	0	0	1	1	1	1	2	1	1	1	1	0	10
Mean Snowfall (in.)	7.0	6.5	5.7	2.3	trace	0.0	0.0	0.0	0.0	0.7	3.3	6.1	31.6
Days With ≥ 1.0" Snow Depth	16	11	4	1	0	0	0	0	0	0	2	10	44

Sigourney *Keokuk County*   Elevation: 797 ft.   Latitude: 41° 20' N   Longitude: 92° 12' W

	JAN	FEB	MAR	APR	MAY	JUN	JUL	AUG	SEP	OCT	NOV	DEC	YEAR
Mean Maximum Temp. (°F)	29.4	36.1	48.0	61.5	72.7	82.0	86.4	84.0	76.1	64.2	47.8	34.7	60.2
Mean Temp. (°F)	20.5	26.7	38.1	50.4	61.9	71.3	75.8	73.3	65.0	53.2	38.9	26.4	50.1
Mean Minimum Temp. (°F)	11.6	17.3	28.2	39.3	51.0	60.6	65.1	62.6	54.0	42.1	29.9	18.1	40.0
Extreme Maximum Temp. (°F)	70	72	86	91	92	105	107	107	98	91	79	71	107
Extreme Minimum Temp. (°F)	-24	-27	-10	7	29	41	45	42	30	14	-5	-23	-27
Days Maximum Temp. ≥ 90°F	0	0	0	0	0	4	10	7	2	0	0	0	23
Days Maximum Temp. ≤ 32°F	17	11	4	0	0	0	0	0	0	0	0	3	12	47
Days Minimum Temp. ≤ 32°F	30	25	20	7	0	0	0	0	0	5	18	28	133
Days Minimum Temp. ≤ 0°F	8	4	0	0	0	0	0	0	0	0	0	3	15
Heating Degree Days (base 65°F)	1,373	1,076	827	444	155	18	3	7	103	371	778	1,189	6,344
Cooling Degree Days (base 65°F)	0	0	1	13	58	207	333	270	103	9	0	0	994
Mean Precipitation (in.)	1.06	0.97	2.37	3.62	4.30	4.01	4.10	4.43	3.89	2.83	2.57	1.32	35.47
Days With ≥ 0.1" Precipitation	3	3	5	7	8	7	6	7	6	6	5	3	66
Days With ≥ 1.0" Precipitation	0	0	1	1	1	1	1	1	1	1	1	0	9
Mean Snowfall (in.)	7.4	6.3	2.8	2.1	trace	0.0	0.0	0.0	0.0	0.4	2.3	5.4	26.7
Days With ≥ 1.0" Snow Depth	na	na	2	1	0	0	0	0	0	0	2	8	na

Sioux Center 2 SE *Sioux County*   Elevation: 1,358 ft.   Latitude: 43° 03' N   Longitude: 96° 09' W

	JAN	FEB	MAR	APR	MAY	JUN	JUL	AUG	SEP	OCT	NOV	DEC	YEAR
Mean Maximum Temp. (°F)	25.4	32.6	45.1	61.3	73.8	82.9	85.2	83.0	76.1	63.5	43.1	29.8	58.5
Mean Temp. (°F)	16.0	23.0	34.7	48.6	60.9	70.3	73.4	71.2	63.1	50.8	33.8	20.9	47.2
Mean Minimum Temp. (°F)	6.5	13.4	24.3	35.8	47.9	57.6	61.6	59.4	50.0	38.0	24.4	12.0	35.9
Extreme Maximum Temp. (°F)	65	68	83	93	98	105	103	101	102	91	79	66	105
Extreme Minimum Temp. (°F)	-30	-27	-15	-1	25	33	38	37	21	9	-14	-29	-30
Days Maximum Temp. ≥ 90°F	0	0	0	0	2	6	9	5	2	0	0	0	24
Days Maximum Temp. ≤ 32°F	20	13	5	0	0	0	0	0	0	0	6	17	61
Days Minimum Temp. ≤ 32°F	31	27	24	11	1	0	0	0	1	9	24	30	158
Days Minimum Temp. ≤ 0°F	11	6	1	0	0	0	0	0	0	0	1	6	25
Heating Degree Days (base 65°F)	1,516	1,179	931	495	179	26	5	16	135	442	929	1,360	7,213
Cooling Degree Days (base 65°F)	0	0	0	10	60	192	268	214	84	8	0	0	836
Mean Precipitation (in.)	0.73	0.66	2.09	2.85	3.54	4.53	3.78	3.29	2.75	2.16	1.58	0.81	28.77
Days With ≥ 0.1" Precipitation	2	2	4	6	7	7	6	5	5	4	4	3	55
Days With ≥ 1.0" Precipitation	0	0	0	0	1	1	1	1	1	0	0	0	5
Mean Snowfall (in.)	7.5	5.6	7.9	2.8	trace	0.0	0.0	0.0	trace	1.1	6.0	6.8	37.7
Days With ≥ 1.0" Snow Depth	25	19	10	1	0	0	0	0	0	0	6	20	81

Sioux Rapids 4 E *Buena Vista County*   Elevation: 1,417 ft.   Latitude: 42° 54' N   Longitude: 95° 04' W

	JAN	FEB	MAR	APR	MAY	JUN	JUL	AUG	SEP	OCT	NOV	DEC	YEAR
Mean Maximum Temp. (°F)	24.3	30.9	42.6	58.7	71.7	80.8	83.7	81.3	73.8	61.3	42.4	28.4	56.7
Mean Temp. (°F)	15.1	21.6	33.0	47.1	59.7	69.1	72.5	70.2	61.7	49.3	33.3	19.8	46.0
Mean Minimum Temp. (°F)	5.7	12.2	23.5	35.5	47.6	57.4	61.3	59.0	49.5	37.2	24.1	11.1	35.3
Extreme Maximum Temp. (°F)	66	67	83	94	93	101	101	102	101	92	80	68	102
Extreme Minimum Temp. (°F)	-32	-32	-14	3	24	37	41	42	26	11	-11	-26	-32
Days Maximum Temp. ≥ 90°F	0	0	0	0	1	4	6	4	1	0	0	0	16
Days Maximum Temp. ≤ 32°F	22	15	7	1	0	0	0	0	0	0	7	18	70
Days Minimum Temp. ≤ 32°F	31	27	25	11	1	0	0	0	1	10	24	30	160
Days Minimum Temp. ≤ 0°F	12	7	2	0	0	0	0	0	0	0	1	7	29
Heating Degree Days (base 65°F)	1,544	1,218	984	537	205	35	7	19	158	486	945	1,395	7,533
Cooling Degree Days (base 65°F)	0	0	0	8	47	161	235	182	60	6	0	0	699
Mean Precipitation (in.)	0.61	0.60	2.09	3.21	3.68	4.56	3.77	4.63	3.23	2.46	1.70	0.80	31.34
Days With ≥ 0.1" Precipitation	2	2	4	6	8	7	6	6	6	4	4	2	57
Days With ≥ 1.0" Precipitation	0	0	0	1	1	1	1	1	1	1	0	0	7
Mean Snowfall (in.)	7.5	4.9	5.9	1.9	trace	0.0	0.0	0.0	trace	0.3	na	6.1	na
Days With ≥ 1.0" Snow Depth	na	na	6	1	0	0	0	0	0	0	7	18	na

Storm Lake 2 E *Buena Vista County*   Elevation: 1,423 ft.   Latitude: 42° 38' N   Longitude: 95° 10' W

	JAN	FEB	MAR	APR	MAY	JUN	JUL	AUG	SEP	OCT	NOV	DEC	YEAR
Mean Maximum Temp. (°F)	24.1	30.5	42.3	57.6	70.0	79.5	82.9	80.5	73.4	61.1	42.2	28.9	56.1
Mean Temp. (°F)	14.8	21.0	32.5	46.2	58.5	68.2	72.1	69.7	61.6	49.4	33.2	20.3	45.6
Mean Minimum Temp. (°F)	5.4	11.5	22.7	34.7	46.9	56.8	61.2	58.8	49.7	37.6	24.1	11.5	35.1
Extreme Maximum Temp. (°F)	66	66	84	93	93	101	100	100	98	91	77	66	101
Extreme Minimum Temp. (°F)	-27	-27	-11	2	26	38	42	38	28	13	-7	-25	-27
Days Maximum Temp. ≥ 90°F	0	0	0	0	1	3	5	3	1	0	0	0	13
Days Maximum Temp. ≤ 32°F	21	15	8	1	0	0	0	0	0	0	7	18	70
Days Minimum Temp. ≤ 32°F	31	28	26	12	1	0	0	0	1	9	24	30	162
Days Minimum Temp. ≤ 0°F	12	7	2	0	0	0	0	0	0	0	1	6	28
Heating Degree Days (base 65°F)	1,554	1,236	1,000	563	235	43	8	24	161	483	948	1,380	7,635
Cooling Degree Days (base 65°F)	0	0	0	7	37	146	233	176	65	5	0	0	669
Mean Precipitation (in.)	0.58	0.56	2.03	3.70	4.15	5.10	4.61	4.59	3.57	2.60	1.64	0.85	33.98
Days With ≥ 0.1" Precipitation	1	2	4	6	8	7	7	6	6	5	3	2	57
Days With ≥ 1.0" Precipitation	0	0	0	1	1	2	1	1	1	1	0	0	8
Mean Snowfall (in.)	7.7	6.7	7.2	2.4	trace	0.0	0.0	0.0	trace	0.3	4.5	7.0	35.8
Days With ≥ 1.0" Snow Depth	22	17	9	2	0	0	0	0	0	0	5	18	73

Swea City 1 NE *Kossuth County*   Elevation: 1,227 ft.   Latitude: 43° 24' N   Longitude: 94° 17' W

	JAN	FEB	MAR	APR	MAY	JUN	JUL	AUG	SEP	OCT	NOV	DEC	YEAR
Mean Maximum Temp. (°F)	23.0	29.0	41.1	57.3	71.6	80.9	83.4	80.8	73.7	61.3	42.2	27.5	56.0
Mean Temp. (°F)	14.1	20.3	32.3	46.3	59.8	69.3	72.4	69.8	61.8	49.6	33.5	19.2	45.7
Mean Minimum Temp. (°F)	5.1	11.5	23.5	35.3	47.9	57.7	61.3	58.8	49.9	37.9	24.8	10.8	35.4
Extreme Maximum Temp. (°F)	55	66	83	93	94	102	102	101	98	92	80	69	102
Extreme Minimum Temp. (°F)	-32	-28	-10	0	26	38	37	39	25	12	-14	-28	-32
Days Maximum Temp. ≥ 90°F	0	0	0	0	1	4	6	2	1	0	0	0	14
Days Maximum Temp. ≤ 32°F	23	16	7	1	0	0	0	0	0	0	6	20	73
Days Minimum Temp. ≤ 32°F	31	27	26	12	1	0	0	0	1	9	24	30	161
Days Minimum Temp. ≤ 0°F	12	7	2	0	0	0	0	0	0	0	1	8	30
Heating Degree Days (base 65°F)	1,577	1,259	1,006	558	201	33	8	21	153	476	938	1,416	7,646
Cooling Degree Days (base 65°F)	0	0	0	5	49	181	256	185	69	6	0	0	751
Mean Precipitation (in.)	0.79	0.66	1.92	3.04	3.87	4.31	4.10	4.05	2.88	2.25	1.81	0.81	30.49
Days With ≥ 0.1" Precipitation	2	2	5	7	8	7	7	6	5	5	4	2	60
Days With ≥ 1.0" Precipitation	0	0	0	1	1	1	1	1	1	0	0	0	6
Mean Snowfall (in.)	*9.9*	6.1	6.5	1.6	trace	0.0	0.0	0.0	trace	0.4	5.3	8.0	*37.8*
Days With ≥ 1.0" Snow Depth	na	*21*	*11*	2	0	0	0	0	0	0	5	19	na

Tipton 4 NE *Cedar County*   Elevation: 767 ft.   Latitude: 41° 49' N   Longitude: 91° 05' W

	JAN	FEB	MAR	APR	MAY	JUN	JUL	AUG	SEP	OCT	NOV	DEC	YEAR
Mean Maximum Temp. (°F)	26.3	32.8	45.6	59.8	71.8	81.0	84.3	81.9	74.9	63.3	46.2	32.5	58.4
Mean Temp. (°F)	17.0	23.6	35.7	48.3	60.2	69.7	73.2	70.7	62.7	51.1	36.9	24.0	47.8
Mean Minimum Temp. (°F)	7.7	14.4	25.8	36.8	48.6	58.4	62.0	59.4	50.4	38.8	27.5	15.3	37.1
Extreme Maximum Temp. (°F)	66	66	87	93	95	100	103	103	98	92	78	70	103
Extreme Minimum Temp. (°F)	-25	-30	-12	9	29	37	44	41	26	15	-6	-25	-30
Days Maximum Temp. ≥ 90°F	0	0	0	0	1	3	7	4	1	0	0	0	16
Days Maximum Temp. ≤ 32°F	20	13	4	0	0	0	0	0	0	0	4	14	55
Days Minimum Temp. ≤ 32°F	30	26	24	9	1	0	0	0	1	8	22	29	150
Days Minimum Temp. ≤ 0°F	10	6	1	0	0	0	0	0	0	0	0	5	22
Heating Degree Days (base 65°F)	1,481	1,163	902	502	193	27	6	15	138	433	836	1,266	6,962
Cooling Degree Days (base 65°F)	0	0	1	9	46	175	266	204	75	6	0	0	782
Mean Precipitation (in.)	1.22	1.37	2.38	3.59	4.58	4.44	4.07	4.60	3.73	2.72	2.57	1.89	37.16
Days With ≥ 0.1" Precipitation	3	3	5	7	8	7	7	7	6	5	6	4	68
Days With ≥ 1.0" Precipitation	0	0	0	1	1	1	1	1	1	1	0	0	7
Mean Snowfall (in.)	6.5	5.8	2.9	1.3	trace	0.0	0.0	0.0	0.0	0.1	*2.0*	*5.6*	*24.2*
Days With ≥ 1.0" Snow Depth	*17*	na	*3*	1	0	0	0	0	0	0	*2*	na	na

Toledo *Tama County*   Elevation: 918 ft.   Latitude: 42° 00' N   Longitude: 92° 34' W

	JAN	FEB	MAR	APR	MAY	JUN	JUL	AUG	SEP	OCT	NOV	DEC	YEAR
Mean Maximum Temp. (°F)	26.4	33.1	45.0	59.2	71.1	80.8	85.0	82.6	75.3	63.0	46.0	31.9	58.3
Mean Temp. (°F)	17.0	23.4	35.2	47.8	59.6	69.4	73.6	71.3	62.8	50.8	36.4	23.1	47.5
Mean Minimum Temp. (°F)	7.5	13.8	25.3	36.5	48.0	58.0	62.1	59.9	50.3	38.5	26.7	14.2	36.7
Extreme Maximum Temp. (°F)	60	67	88	95	92	101	101	103	98	92	78	69	103
Extreme Minimum Temp. (°F)	-29	-34	-11	5	28	36	41	39	23	10	-10	-26	-34
Days Maximum Temp. ≥ 90°F	0	0	0	0	0	3	8	5	1	0	0	0	17
Days Maximum Temp. ≤ 32°F	20	13	5	0	0	0	0	0	0	0	4	14	56
Days Minimum Temp. ≤ 32°F	31	26	23	10	1	0	0	0	1	9	22	30	153
Days Minimum Temp. ≤ 0°F	11	6	1	0	0	0	0	0	0	0	0	5	23
Heating Degree Days (base 65°F)	1,484	1,167	918	516	208	31	6	15	138	444	852	1,295	7,074
Cooling Degree Days (base 65°F)	0	0	1	8	42	173	285	228	81	10	0	0	828
Mean Precipitation (in.)	1.02	1.03	2.38	3.42	4.70	4.96	4.27	4.59	3.57	2.68	2.24	1.22	36.08
Days With ≥ 0.1" Precipitation	3	3	5	7	9	7	7	6	6	5	5	3	66
Days With ≥ 1.0" Precipitation	0	0	0	1	1	1	1	1	1	1	1	0	8
Mean Snowfall (in.)	8.3	5.4	4.2	1.3	0.0	0.0	0.0	0.0	0.0	0.3	2.3	6.3	28.1
Days With ≥ 1.0" Snow Depth	18	13	5	1	0	0	0	0	0	0	2	12	51

Tripoli *Bremer County*   Elevation: 958 ft.   Latitude: 42° 49' N   Longitude: 92° 16' W

	JAN	FEB	MAR	APR	MAY	JUN	JUL	AUG	SEP	OCT	NOV	DEC	YEAR
Mean Maximum Temp. (°F)	23.3	29.6	42.9	58.3	71.1	80.2	83.3	80.9	73.5	61.0	42.9	29.4	56.4
Mean Temp. (°F)	14.2	20.7	33.6	47.3	59.5	68.9	72.4	69.8	61.8	49.7	34.3	21.0	46.1
Mean Minimum Temp. (°F)	5.1	11.8	24.4	36.1	47.9	57.4	61.3	58.8	50.0	38.3	25.7	12.7	35.8
Extreme Maximum Temp. (°F)	58	66	84	96	94	102	100	104	95	93	79	62	104
Extreme Minimum Temp. (°F)	-32	-32	-11	0	25	36	43	39	27	10	-15	-24	-32
Days Maximum Temp. ≥ 90°F	0	0	0	0	1	3	5	3	1	0	0	0	13
Days Maximum Temp. ≤ 32°F	22	15	6	0	0	0	0	0	0	0	5	18	66
Days Minimum Temp. ≤ 32°F	31	27	24	10	1	0	0	0	1	9	23	30	156
Days Minimum Temp. ≤ 0°F	12	7	1	0	0	0	0	0	0	0	1	6	27
Heating Degree Days (base 65°F)	1,569	1,244	966	532	207	36	8	21	156	474	914	1,356	7,483
Cooling Degree Days (base 65°F)	0	0	0	7	39	151	236	170	60	4	0	0	667
Mean Precipitation (in.)	1.01	0.96	2.14	3.55	4.40	4.81	4.59	5.28	3.36	2.71	2.34	1.14	36.29
Days With ≥ 0.1" Precipitation	4	3	5	8	8	8	7	7	6	5	5	4	70
Days With ≥ 1.0" Precipitation	0	0	0	1	1	1	1	2	1	1	1	0	9
Mean Snowfall (in.)	9.2	6.6	5.2	2.4	trace	0.0	0.0	0.0	0.0	0.1	4.6	7.9	36.0
Days With ≥ 1.0" Snow Depth	16	*15*	*6*	1	0	0	0	0	0	0	3	11	*52*

Vinton *Benton County*   Elevation: 849 ft.   Latitude: 42° 10' N   Longitude: 92° 00' W

	JAN	FEB	MAR	APR	MAY	JUN	JUL	AUG	SEP	OCT	NOV	DEC	YEAR
Mean Maximum Temp. (°F)	26.7	33.1	46.3	61.6	72.8	81.9	85.6	83.1	75.6	63.2	45.5	31.8	58.9
Mean Temp. (°F)	17.8	24.1	36.6	49.9	60.9	70.2	73.9	71.6	63.7	51.7	36.6	23.6	48.4
Mean Minimum Temp. (°F)	8.7	15.3	26.8	37.8	49.0	58.2	62.0	60.0	51.4	40.0	27.5	15.7	37.7
Extreme Maximum Temp. (°F)	62	66	88	90	93	101	105	104	97	92	79	68	105
Extreme Minimum Temp. (°F)	-29	-30	-11	4	28	36	44	39	23	14	-10	-27	-30
Days Maximum Temp. ≥ 90°F	0	0	0	0	1	4	8	5	1	0	0	0	19
Days Maximum Temp. ≤ 32°F	20	13	4	0	0	0	0	0	0	0	4	15	56
Days Minimum Temp. ≤ 32°F	30	26	22	9	1	0	0	0	1	8	21	29	147
Days Minimum Temp. ≤ 0°F	9	5	1	0	0	0	0	0	0	0	0	5	20
Heating Degree Days (base 65°F)	1,460	1,149	874	455	175	23	4	11	121	414	847	1,276	6,809
Cooling Degree Days (base 65°F)	0	0	1	10	49	185	290	227	87	7	0	0	856
Mean Precipitation (in.)	1.00	0.98	2.15	3.30	4.16	4.33	3.89	4.34	3.84	2.60	2.32	1.30	34.21
Days With ≥ 0.1" Precipitation	3	3	5	7	8	7	6	7	6	5	5	3	65
Days With ≥ 1.0" Precipitation	0	0	0	1	1	1	1	1	1	1	1	0	8
Mean Snowfall (in.)	8.1	6.3	4.8	1.9	trace	0.0	0.0	0.0	0.0	0.3	3.5	6.4	31.3
Days With ≥ 1.0" Snow Depth	22	18	6	1	0	0	0	0	0	0	3	13	63

Washington *Washington County*   Elevation: 754 ft.   Latitude: 41° 18' N   Longitude: 91° 41' W

	JAN	FEB	MAR	APR	MAY	JUN	JUL	AUG	SEP	OCT	NOV	DEC	YEAR
Mean Maximum Temp. (°F)	30.4	36.9	49.5	63.8	74.7	83.7	87.7	85.2	77.9	66.0	48.8	35.4	61.7
Mean Temp. (°F)	21.9	28.1	39.7	52.4	63.4	72.6	76.7	74.2	66.4	54.7	40.0	27.5	51.5
Mean Minimum Temp. (°F)	13.3	19.4	29.8	41.0	52.0	61.5	65.7	63.1	54.8	43.5	31.2	19.5	41.2
Extreme Maximum Temp. (°F)	70	71	89	91	94	103	105	106	100	92	78	71	106
Extreme Minimum Temp. (°F)	-23	-26	-6	10	31	40	48	42	28	19	-5	-24	-26
Days Maximum Temp. ≥ 90°F	0	0	0	0	1	5	12	8	3	0	0	0	29
Days Maximum Temp. ≤ 32°F	17	10	3	0	0	0	0	0	0	0	2	11	43
Days Minimum Temp. ≤ 32°F	29	24	18	5	0	0	0	0	0	4	17	28	125
Days Minimum Temp. ≤ 0°F	7	3	0	0	0	0	0	0	0	0	0	3	13
Heating Degree Days (base 65°F)	1,330	1,034	780	387	124	11	1	4	82	329	742	1,156	5,980
Cooling Degree Days (base 65°F)	0	0	2	16	75	244	371	301	127	15	0	0	1,151
Mean Precipitation (in.)	1.15	1.09	2.33	3.01	4.42	4.16	4.19	4.08	3.88	2.59	2.34	1.68	34.92
Days With ≥ 0.1" Precipitation	3	3	5	6	8	7	7	7	6	5	5	4	66
Days With ≥ 1.0" Precipitation	0	0	0	1	1	1	1	1	1	0	0	0	6
Mean Snowfall (in.)	7.4	4.9	2.5	1.3	trace	0.0	0.0	0.0	0.0	0.2	1.4	5.1	22.8
Days With ≥ 1.0" Snow Depth	18	13	4	1	0	0	0	0	0	0	2	10	48

Waukon 1 NNE *Allamakee County*   Elevation: 1,243 ft.   Latitude: 43° 16' N   Longitude: 91° 29' W

	JAN	FEB	MAR	APR	MAY	JUN	JUL	AUG	SEP	OCT	NOV	DEC	YEAR
Mean Maximum Temp. (°F)	23.1	29.3	41.7	57.0	68.8	77.7	81.5	78.9	71.5	60.0	42.0	28.3	55.0
Mean Temp. (°F)	14.7	20.8	32.8	46.6	58.2	67.4	71.6	69.4	61.2	49.7	33.9	20.7	45.6
Mean Minimum Temp. (°F)	6.4	12.3	23.8	35.9	47.6	57.1	61.7	59.6	50.9	39.3	25.7	12.9	36.1
Extreme Maximum Temp. (°F)	54	60	82	91	88	96	102	99	93	91	74	63	102
Extreme Minimum Temp. (°F)	-30	-34	-10	7	25	37	41	41	27	15	-13	-27	-34
Days Maximum Temp. ≥ 90°F	0	0	0	0	0	1	3	1	0	0	0	0	5
Days Maximum Temp. ≤ 32°F	23	15	6	0	0	0	0	0	0	0	6	19	69
Days Minimum Temp. ≤ 32°F	30	27	24	11	1	0	0	0	0	8	23	30	154
Days Minimum Temp. ≤ 0°F	11	7	1	0	0	0	0	0	0	0	1	6	26
Heating Degree Days (base 65°F)	1,554	1,243	992	552	236	43	9	21	162	474	926	1,369	7,581
Cooling Degree Days (base 65°F)	0	0	0	6	28	123	221	168	56	4	0	0	606
Mean Precipitation (in.)	0.61	0.44	1.55	3.39	3.59	4.55	4.52	4.41	3.42	2.22	1.97	0.77	31.44
Days With ≥ 0.1" Precipitation	2	1	4	7	7	7	7	7	6	5	4	3	60
Days With ≥ 1.0" Precipitation	0	0	0	1	1	1	1	1	1	0	0	0	6
Mean Snowfall (in.)	9.8	6.7	6.1	2.0	trace	0.0	0.0	0.0	0.0	trace	3.8	7.0	35.4
Days With ≥ 1.0" Snow Depth	na	na	na	1	0	0	0	0	0	0	na	na	na

Webster City *Hamilton County*   Elevation: 1,167 ft.   Latitude: 42° 28' N   Longitude: 93° 48' W

	JAN	FEB	MAR	APR	MAY	JUN	JUL	AUG	SEP	OCT	NOV	DEC	YEAR
Mean Maximum Temp. (°F)	25.9	32.5	44.9	60.5	72.6	81.4	84.7	82.0	75.0	62.7	44.5	30.8	58.1
Mean Temp. (°F)	16.7	23.3	35.2	48.6	60.5	69.8	73.4	70.9	62.8	50.8	35.4	22.1	47.5
Mean Minimum Temp. (°F)	7.4	14.1	25.5	36.7	48.3	58.1	62.1	59.8	50.7	38.9	26.2	13.5	36.7
Extreme Maximum Temp. (°F)	62	68	89	97	93	103	104	105	95	94	79	67	105
Extreme Minimum Temp. (°F)	-29	-32	-13	4	26	36	43	36	25	14	-16	-25	-32
Days Maximum Temp. ≥ 90°F	0	0	0	0	0	3	7	4	1	0	0	0	15
Days Maximum Temp. ≤ 32°F	20	13	5	0	0	0	0	0	0	0	5	16	59
Days Minimum Temp. ≤ 32°F	31	27	24	10	1	0	0	0	1	9	22	30	155
Days Minimum Temp. ≤ 0°F	10	6	1	0	0	0	0	0	0	0	1	5	23
Heating Degree Days (base 65°F)	1,494	1,172	917	494	183	26	5	16	135	441	882	1,323	7,088
Cooling Degree Days (base 65°F)	0	0	0	8	45	175	269	205	76	6	0	0	784
Mean Precipitation (in.)	0.82	0.81	1.92	3.08	4.15	5.15	4.29	4.59	3.14	2.55	1.82	1.16	33.48
Days With ≥ 0.1" Precipitation	3	3	4	7	8	8	7	6	6	5	4	3	64
Days With ≥ 1.0" Precipitation	0	0	0	0	1	1	1	2	1	1	0	0	7
Mean Snowfall (in.)	8.5	6.4	5.4	1.9	0.0	0.0	0.0	0.0	0.0	0.1	3.8	7.3	33.4
Days With ≥ 1.0" Snow Depth	23	18	7	1	0	0	0	0	0	0	5	17	71

Williamsburg *Iowa County*   Elevation: 849 ft.   Latitude: 41° 40' N   Longitude: 92° 01' W

	JAN	FEB	MAR	APR	MAY	JUN	JUL	AUG	SEP	OCT	NOV	DEC	YEAR
Mean Maximum Temp. (°F)	28.2	34.8	47.2	61.5	72.6	81.8	85.5	83.3	76.0	64.2	47.2	33.8	59.7
Mean Temp. (°F)	19.2	25.6	37.2	49.8	61.2	70.8	74.7	72.3	64.3	52.4	37.9	25.3	49.2
Mean Minimum Temp. (°F)	10.1	16.2	27.3	38.0	49.8	59.7	63.8	61.3	52.6	40.6	28.5	16.8	38.7
Extreme Maximum Temp. (°F)	67	68	88	92	92	101	104	105	98	93	80	71	105
Extreme Minimum Temp. (°F)	-28	-31	-8	5	28	37	45	40	28	15	-8	-27	-31
Days Maximum Temp. ≥ 90°F	0	0	0	0	1	4	9	6	2	0	0	0	22
Days Maximum Temp. ≤ 32°F	19	12	4	0	0	0	0	0	0	0	3	13	51
Days Minimum Temp. ≤ 32°F	30	26	22	9	1	0	0	0	0	7	20	29	144
Days Minimum Temp. ≤ 0°F	9	5	1	0	0	0	0	0	0	0	0	4	19
Heating Degree Days (base 65°F)	1,414	1,108	854	461	167	20	4	10	113	394	807	1,225	6,577
Cooling Degree Days (base 65°F)	0	0	1	11	51	194	307	243	94	8	0	0	909
Mean Precipitation (in.)	1.05	1.00	2.24	3.40	4.75	4.58	4.38	4.89	3.93	2.67	2.57	1.45	36.91
Days With ≥ 0.1" Precipitation	3	3	5	6	8	7	6	6	6	5	5	4	64
Days With ≥ 1.0" Precipitation	0	0	0	1	1	1	1	2	1	1	1	0	9
Mean Snowfall (in.)	8.9	6.3	4.0	2.1	trace	0.0	0.0	0.0	0.0	0.4	2.6	6.2	30.5
Days With ≥ 1.0" Snow Depth	21	14	6	1	0	0	0	0	0	0	2	11	55

Winterset 2 NNW *Madison County*   Elevation: 1,069 ft.   Latitude: 41° 22' N   Longitude: 94° 02' W

	JAN	FEB	MAR	APR	MAY	JUN	JUL	AUG	SEP	OCT	NOV	DEC	YEAR
Mean Maximum Temp. (°F)	29.8	36.1	48.5	62.4	72.6	81.8	85.9	83.6	76.0	64.3	47.3	34.9	60.3
Mean Temp. (°F)	20.2	26.2	37.8	50.4	61.1	70.1	74.6	72.4	64.1	52.5	37.7	25.9	49.4
Mean Minimum Temp. (°F)	10.5	16.1	27.0	38.3	49.5	58.4	63.3	61.1	52.2	40.6	28.1	17.0	38.5
Extreme Maximum Temp. (°F)	65	73	89	92	92	103	106	106	*98*	93	80	66	*106*
Extreme Minimum Temp. (°F)	-31	-31	-16	10	24	36	41	38	*26*	12	-8	-25	*-31*
Days Maximum Temp. ≥ 90°F	0	0	0	0	0	4	9	6	2	0	0	0	21
Days Maximum Temp. ≤ 32°F	16	12	4	0	0	0	0	0	0	0	3	12	47
Days Minimum Temp. ≤ 32°F	30	26	21	9	1	0	0	0	1	7	20	29	144
Days Minimum Temp. ≤ 0°F	9	4	1	0	0	0	0	0	0	0	0	4	18
Heating Degree Days (base 65°F)	1,384	1,091	839	443	167	24	4	10	118	392	810	1,204	6,486
Cooling Degree Days (base 65°F)	0	0	2	15	54	191	318	254	106	11	0	0	951
Mean Precipitation (in.)	0.96	1.00	2.24	3.56	4.31	4.48	4.14	4.30	3.85	2.56	2.19	1.08	34.67
Days With ≥ 0.1" Precipitation	3	3	5	6	8	7	7	6	6	5	5	3	64
Days With ≥ 1.0" Precipitation	0	0	0	1	1	1	1	1	1	1	1	0	8
Mean Snowfall (in.)	7.5	7.2	3.4	1.5	trace	0.0	0.0	0.0	0.0	0.4	3.0	5.8	28.8
Days With ≥ 1.0" Snow Depth	18	15	6	1	0	0	0	0	0	0	3	11	54

Note: See Appendix D for explanation of data.

KANSAS

PHYSICAL FEATURES AND GENERAL CLIMATE. Located at the geographical center of the contiguous 48 states, Kansas has a distinctly continental climate with characteristically changeable temperature and precipitation.

Kansas weather is affected largely by two physical features, both some distance from the State: the Rocky Mountains to the west and the Gulf of Mexico to the south. The mountains on the west prevent the importation of moisture from the Pacific Ocean, while the Gulf is the feeding source for much of the State's precipitation.

A third factor, differences in elevation, also influences the climate. Elevation changes are quite gradual rising from 800 or 1,000 feet above sea level in a number of extreme eastern and southeastern counties to approximately 1,500 feet about the center of the State, north to south, and to 3,500 feet at the Colorado line. Quite coincident with these gradations is a change in climate.

PRECIPITATION. Average annual precipitation totals range from slightly more than 40 inches in the southeastern counties to 30 to 35 inches in the northeast, decreasing gradually westward to the Colorado line where the average is from 16 to 18 inches. Distribution of rainfall through the year favors crop production, with an average of about 75 percent of the year's total falling in the crop growing season, April to September. January, the month of least precipitation, has an average of one to two inches at the more eastern stations, decreasing to less than an inch over the western three-fourths of the State and to near a quarter inch in the extreme west. May and June, in contrast, are the months of greatest rain with between four and five inches on the average in the eastern three-fifths of the State to between two and three inches in the western counties. In addition to the seasonal changes of precipitation amounts over the State, there is a secondary fluctuation in the average rainfall which is quite pronounced in the east. In this area a noticeable decrease in the average rainfall occurs during the latter part of July and the forepart of August, with an increase again in September.

Precipitation is most frequent in the extreme east where on the average measurable amounts are recorded on 90 to 100 days of the year. The average annual number of days with an inch or more of precipitation is 60 to 80 over two-thirds of the central portion and about 70 in the northwestern portion, but decreases to near 50 in the southwestern section.

All parts of Kansas may receive 24-hour rainfalls of five to 10 inches, with the more frequent occurrence of heavy rains in the eastern area during the month of September. Almost one-half of the total rain falls in daily amounts of 0.75 inch or less. Monthly precipitation totals of 20 inches or more have been recorded at some eastern stations. Protracted periods of successive days with rain are occasionally recorded. On the other hand, all parts of the State have experienced from 50 to 75 successive days without more than 0.25 inch of rain on any day during the period April to September.

Snowfall averages near 10 inches a year in the south-central counties and increases gradually in other parts of the State to the largest average of 24 inches in the northwest. Snow has been recorded in all months except July and August. The greatest average fall is in February with March snows only slightly less. Falls of 12 to 24 inches in 24 hours have been recorded in most sections. Ordinarily snow remains on the ground only a short time, but during the winter the ground may be snow-covered from 10 to 15 days in the south and from 30 to 35 days in the north. In rare instances snow has covered the ground continuously in western and northern sections from 40 to 60 days.

Wet and dry trends or periods are noted in the longer records. Dry periods may persist for several years with an occasional interim of a month or two of above average rainfall. There appears to be some indication of recurring patterns of years with similar trends.

The river drainage in Kansas is about equally divided between the Missouri and Arkansas Rivers, the northern half of the State draining into the Missouri, the southern half into the Arkansas. The Kansas River basin, occupying the north half, has a total drainage area of more than 60,000 square miles above its confluence with the Missouri River at Kansas City. The Arkansas River above the Oklahoma line drains an area of over 45,000 square miles.

Floods in Kansas are generally due to torrential and often prolonged rains. They are seldom caused by melting snow, except in the case of the Arkansas River, where melting snow and heavy rains near its source in the mountains of Colorado have caused flooding. Overflows in the Kansas River and tributaries are practically unknown during the winter season, November to February, but they do occur in the Marias des Cygnes River and in the Arkansas River basin in southeastern Kansas during that period.

For the State as a whole the period of greatest flood frequency is during the spring and summer, from general heavy and prolonged rains. Intense local convective storms also cause damaging flash floods in the smaller streams during the warmer season.

TEMPERATURE. The annual mean temperature ranges from about 58°F. along the south-central and southeastern border to 52°F. in the extreme northwest. Monthly mean temperatures in the northwest range from about 28°F. in July, and in the southeast and south-central from 34°F. in January to 80 or 81°F. in July. Daily temperature ranges, on the average, increase from 20°F. in the east to 30°F. in the higher and drier elevations of the northwest.

Temperatures of 100°F. or higher occur on an average of 10 days per year in the east and west and about 15 days in the central portion. In some of the hotter summers the number of days with 100°F. or higher has totalled 50 to 60 in the central and south-central counties. The number of days with zero or lower averages two to four days per year at the southeastern stations and eight to 10 days in the northwest. Freezing temperatures have been recorded somewhere in the State all months of the year.

During much of the year there is a progressive increase in mean temperature from the higher northwestern counties to the southeastern area. The exception is during the warm summer months when the higher mean temperatures are found in the central and south-central counties.

WINDS AND STORMS. The prevailing winds are from a southerly direction with the exception of the cold months of December through March, which have considerable wind from the north or northwest. Generally the extreme winds are from a northerly direction. In the western part of the State wind speeds are higher and average about 15 m.p.h., approximately five m.p.h. faster than in the eastern sections.

Although storms occasionally result in considerable damage, they are for the most part of short duration. In dry periods duststorms may occur frequently in the west, and at intervals a blizzard or severe snowstorm lasts for 36 to 48 hours. The damaging winds, hail, and tornadoes, however, are generally of short duration, although very severe, and seldom cover great areas.

Kansas

● Cities With Population ≥ 25,000
▲ Weather Stations

100 Miles

100 KM

0

Saint Francis, McDonald, Atwood 2 SW, Oberlin, Goodland Renner Field, Colby 1 SW, Hoxie, Oakley 4 W, Winona, Sharon Springs, Russell Springs 4 W, Tribune 1 W, Leoti 1 W, Scott City, Healy, Quinter, Wakeeney, Ness City, Hays 1 S, Bison, Larned, Garden City Exp Station, Garden City Municipal Arpt, GARDEN CITY, Lakin, Syracuse, Cimarron, Dodge City Municipal Arpt, Meade, Sublette, Ulysses, Hugoton, Liberal, Elkhart

Oberlin, Norton Dam, Norton 9 SSE, Phillipsburg, Kirwin Dam, Webster Dam, Plainville 4 WNW, Osborne, Alton 6 ESE, Smith Center, Mankato, Lovewell Lake, Belleville, Beloit, Glen Elder Lake, Concordia Blosser Muni Arpt, Clay Center, Washington, Marysville, Centralia

Minneapolis, Lincoln 1 ESE, Wilson Lake, Russell Municipal Airport, Great Bend, Sterling, Hudson, Pratt 4 W, Medicine Lodge, Coldwater, Ashland, Anthony, Kingman, Norwich, Wellington, Kinsley, Greensburg, Dodge City Municipal Arpt

SALINA, Salina Municipal Airport, Kanopolis Lake, Ellsworth, McPherson, Newton 2 SW, HUTCHINSON, Hutchinson 10 SW, WICHITA, Wichita Mid-Continent Arpt, Winfield No 1, El Dorado, Eureka, Cassoday, Florence, Marion Lake, Herington, Council Grove Lake, Cottonwood Falls, Abilene 1 W, MANHATTAN, Milford Lake, Tuttle Creek Lake, Wamego, Manhattan, Topeka Municipal Airport, TOPEKA, Eskridge

Washington, Concordia Blosser Muni Arpt, Holton 1 S, Horton, Troy 2 E, Atchison, LEAVENWORTH, Leavenworth, Oskaloosa, Perry Lake, Wyandotte, KANSAS CITY, SHAWNEE, LENEXA, OVERLAND PARK, LEAWOOD, OLATHE, Olathe 3 E, Lawrence, LAWRENCE, Pomona Lake, Ottawa, Garnett 1 E, Mound City, Paola, Miami, John Redmond Lake, Iola 1 W, Yates Center, Toronto Lake, Fall River Lake, Howard 5 NE, Chanute Martin Johnson Arpt, Parsons 2 NW, Girard, Fort Scott, Elk City Lake, Independence, Mound Valley 3 WSW, Columbus 1 SW, Cherokee, Sedan

County labels: CHEYENNE, RAWLINS, DECATUR, NORTON, PHILLIPS, SMITH, JEWELL, REPUBLIC, WASHINGTON, MARSHALL, NEMAHA, BROWN, DONIPHAN, ATCHISON, JACKSON, POTTAWATOMIE, RILEY, CLAY, CLOUD, MITCHELL, OSBORNE, ROOKS, GRAHAM, SHERIDAN, THOMAS, SHERMAN, WALLACE, LOGAN, GOVE, TREGO, ELLIS, RUSSELL, LINCOLN, OTTAWA, SALINE, DICKINSON, GEARY, MORRIS, WABAUNSEE, SHAWNEE, OSAGE, DOUGLAS, FRANKLIN, ANDERSON, COFFEY, LYON, CHASE, MARION, MCPHERSON, RICE, ELLSWORTH, BARTON, RUSH, NESS, LANE, SCOTT, WICHITA, GREELEY, HAMILTON, KEARNY, FINNEY, HODGEMAN, PAWNEE, STAFFORD, RENO, HARVEY, SEDGWICK, BUTLER, GREENWOOD, WOODSON, ALLEN, BOURBON, CRAWFORD, NEOSHO, WILSON, ELK, CHAUTAUQUA, COWLEY, SUMNER, HARPER, KINGMAN, PRATT, KIOWA, EDWARDS, FORD, GRAY, HASKELL, GRANT, STANTON, MORTON, STEVENS, SEWARD, MEADE, CLARK, COMANCHE, BARBER, LABETTE, MONTGOMERY, LINN, MIAMI, JOHNSON, WYANDOTTE, LEAVENWORTH, JEFFERSON

Kansas Weather Stations by County

County	Station Name
Allen	Iola 1 W
Anderson	Garnett 1 E
Atchison	Atchison
Barber	Medicine Lodge
Barton	Great Bend
Bourbon	Fort Scott
Brown	Horton
Butler	Cassoday El Dorado
Chase	Cottonwood Falls
Chautauqua	Sedan
Cherokee	Columbus 1 SW
Cheyenne	Saint Francis
Clark	Ashland
Clay	Clay Center
Cloud	Concordia Blosser Muni Airport
Coffey	John Redmond Lake
Comanche	Coldwater
Cowley	Winfield 1
Crawford	Girard
Decatur	Oberlin
Dickinson	Abilene 1 W Herington
Doniphan	Troy 2 E
Douglas	Lawrence
Edwards	Kinsley
Elk	Howard 5 NE
Ellis	Hays 1 S
Ellsworth	Ellsworth Kanopolis Lake
Finney	Garden City Exp. Station Garden City Municipal Airport
Ford	Dodge City Municipal Airport
Franklin	Ottawa

County	Station Name
Geary	Milford Lake
Gove	Quinter
Grant	Ulysses
Gray	Cimarron
Greeley	Tribune 1 W
Greenwood	Eureka Fall River Lake
Hamilton	Syracuse
Harper	Anthony
Harvey	Newton 2 SW
Haskell	Sublette
Jackson	Holton 1 S
Jefferson	Oskaloosa Perry Lake
Jewell	Lovewell Lake Mankato
Johnson	Olathe 3 E
Kearny	Lakin
Kingman	Kingman Norwich
Kiowa	Greensburg
Labette	Mound Valley 3 WSW Parsons 2 NW
Lane	Healy
Leavenworth	Leavenworth
Lincoln	Lincoln 1 ESE
Linn	Mound City
Logan	Oakley 4 W Russell Springs 4 W Winona
Marion	Florence Marion Lake
Marshall	Marysville
McPherson	McPherson
Meade	Meade
Miami	Paola

County	Station Name
Mitchell	Beloit Glen Elder Lake
Montgomery	Elk City Lake Independence
Morris	Council Grove Lake
Morton	Elkhart
Nemaha	Centralia
Neosho	Chanute Martin Johnson Airport
Ness	Ness City
Norton	Norton 9 SSE Norton Dam
Osage	Pomona Lake
Osborne	Alton 6 ESE
Ottawa	Minneapolis
Pawnee	Larned
Phillips	Kirwin Dam Phillipsburg
Pottawatomie	Wamego
Pratt	Pratt 4 W
Rawlins	Atwood 2 SW McDonald
Reno	Hutchinson 10 SW
Republic	Belleville
Rice	Sterling
Riley	Manhattan Tuttle Creek Lake
Rooks	Plainville 4 WNW Webster Dam
Rush	Bison
Russell	Russell Municipal Airport Wilson Lake
Saline	Salina Municipal Airport
Scott	Scott City
Sedgwick	Wichita Mid-Continent Airport
Seward	Liberal
Shawnee	Topeka Municipal Airport
Sheridan	Hoxie

County	Station Name
Sherman	Goodland Renner Field
Smith	Smith Center
Stafford	Hudson
Stevens	Hugoton
Sumner	Wellington
Thomas	Colby 1 SW
Trego	Wakeeney
Wabaunsee	Eskridge
Wallace	Sharon Springs
Washington	Washington
Wichita	Leoti 1 W
Woodson	Toronto Lake Yates Center

Kansas Weather Stations by City

City	Station Name	Miles
Garden City	Garden City Municipal Airport	9
	Garden City Exp. Station	3
Hutchinson	Hutchinson 10 SW	11
	Sterling	18
Kansas City	Leavenworth	17
	Olathe 3 E	16
	Kansas City Int'l Airport, MO	14
Lawrence	Lawrence	1
	Oskaloosa	18
	Perry Lake	14
Leavenworth	Atchison	20
	Leavenworth	4
	Kansas City Int'l Airport, MO	11
Leawood	Olathe 3 E	8
	Lees Summit Reed Wildlife Refuge, MO	16
Lenexa	Olathe 3 E	6
Manhattan	Manhattan	1
	Milford Lake	17
	Tuttle Creek Lake	4
	Wamego	15
Olathe	Olathe 3 E	2
Overland Park	Olathe 3 E	6
	Lees Summit Reed Wildlife Refuge, MO	19
Salina	Salina Municipal Airport	3
Shawnee	Leavenworth	20
	Olathe 3 E	9
	Kansas City Int'l Airport, MO	20
Topeka	Perry Lake	16
	Topeka Municipal Airport	4
Wichita	Wichita Mid-Continent Airport	6

Note: Miles is the distance between the geographic center of the city and the weather station.

Kansas Weather Stations by Elevation

Feet	Station Name
3,645	Goodland Renner Field
3,635	Tribune 1 W
3,599	Elkhart
3,448	Sharon Springs
3,362	McDonald
3,359	Saint Francis
3,320	Winona
3,307	Leoti 1 W
3,257	Syracuse
3,169	Colby 1 SW
3,106	Hugoton
3,097	Oakley 4 W
3,047	Ulysses
2,995	Lakin
2,969	Scott City
2,929	Russell Springs 4 W
2,919	Sublette
2,880	Garden City Municipal Airport
2,867	Garden City Exp. Station
2,860	Atwood 2 SW
2,847	Healy
2,831	Liberal
2,703	Hoxie
2,693	Cimarron
2,677	Quinter
2,604	Oberlin
2,575	Dodge City Municipal Airport
2,477	Meade
2,447	Wakeeney
2,358	Norton 9 SSE
2,339	Norton Dam
2,247	Ness City
2,227	Greensburg
2,165	Kinsley
2,080	Coldwater
2,080	Plainville 4 WNW
2,007	Bison
2,007	Hays 1 S
1,994	Larned
1,968	Ashland
1,938	Pratt 4 W
1,929	Phillipsburg
1,866	Hudson
1,860	Webster Dam
1,856	Great Bend
1,856	Russell Municipal Airport
1,778	Smith Center
1,751	Mankato
1,696	Kirwin Dam
1,633	Sterling
1,617	Alton 6 ESE
1,601	Lovewell Lake
1,568	Hutchinson 10 SW
1,558	Kingman
1,538	Belleville

Feet	Station Name
1,528	Ellsworth
1,509	Wilson Lake
1,499	Glen Elder Lake
1,499	Medicine Lodge
1,492	McPherson
1,489	Kanopolis Lake
1,489	Norwich
1,466	Concordia Blosser Muni Airport
1,459	Beloit
1,459	Cassoday
1,446	Newton 2 SW
1,414	Eskridge
1,377	Lincoln 1 ESE
1,368	Marion Lake
1,348	Herington
1,338	El Dorado
1,318	Anthony
1,318	Centralia
1,318	Council Grove Lake
1,318	Wichita Mid-Continent Airport
1,309	Minneapolis
1,302	Washington
1,292	Florence
1,263	Salina Municipal Airport
1,240	Cottonwood Falls
1,217	Clay Center
1,217	Wellington
1,207	Milford Lake
1,177	Marysville
1,177	Winfield 1
1,167	Abilene 1 W
1,118	Holton 1 S
1,112	Oskaloosa
1,099	Howard 5 NE
1,089	John Redmond Lake
1,062	Manhattan
1,062	Pomona Lake
1,059	Troy 2 E
1,056	Tuttle Creek Lake
1,053	Olathe 3 E
1,049	Yates Center
1,040	Eureka
1,026	Horton
1,017	Fall River Lake
1,007	Wamego
984	Girard
977	Chanute Martin Johnson Airport
977	Garnett 1 E
977	Lawrence
958	Perry Lake
951	Iola 1 W
948	Toronto Lake
944	Atchison
908	Parsons 2 NW
898	Columbus 1 SW

Feet	Station Name
898	Ottawa
882	Topeka Municipal Airport
879	Sedan
869	Leavenworth
859	Paola
846	Elk City Lake
843	Fort Scott
839	Mound City
803	Independence
797	Mound Valley 3 WSW

Concordia Blosser Muni Airport

A wide variety of weather occurs in the Concordia area which makes possible a great range in crop production. Wheat is ideally suited to the climate of north-central Kansas where a complete crop failure is unknown. Equally well suited to the climate are alfalfa, sweet clover, and sorghum. Corn is generally a successful crop although dry summers and hot winds occasionally prove disastrous. Adequate moisture throughout the year under normal conditions provides fine grazing conditions for a flourishing livestock industry.

Precipitation is light during the winter months, increasing in the spring until June and dropping off during the autumn months. Summer months with less than 1 inch of precipitation are common, even though monthly summer rainfall has exceeded 13 inches. Thunderstorms are frequent in May, June, July and August. Although heavy winter snowfalls are not uncommon, severe storms that paralyze industry and agriculture are very rare. Some periods have been distinguished by very dry

or very wet cycles. Sustained periods of hot, dry, and windy weather frequently occur in July and August with temperatures of 100 degrees or more recorded for a week or more at a time. The average last occurrence of temperatures as low as 32 degrees in the spring is mid April. The average first occurrence of 32 degrees in the autumn is late October.

Winds are southerly most of the year except for a short period of northerly winds during the winter. Velocities are nearly constant throughout the year except for a slight increase in the spring months.

The variety of weather in north-central Kansas is invigorating and healthful. Winters are usually mild, and summers are seldom oppressively hot. Spring and autumn, although very different in most respects, are very pleasant. A period of mild, dry Indian Summer weather usually occurs in October and early November before the winter snow and cold begin.

Concordia Blosser Muni Airport *Cloud County*   Elevation: 1,466 ft.   Latitude: 39° 33' N   Longitude: 97° 39' W

	JAN	FEB	MAR	APR	MAY	JUN	JUL	AUG	SEP	OCT	NOV	DEC	YEAR
Mean Maximum Temp. (°F)	36.0	42.9	53.7	64.5	74.0	85.0	90.8	88.3	79.6	67.6	51.2	40.2	64.5
Mean Temp. (°F)	26.4	32.3	42.3	52.8	63.0	73.4	79.0	76.9	67.8	55.7	40.9	30.7	53.4
Mean Minimum Temp. (°F)	16.7	21.6	30.8	41.2	51.9	61.8	67.3	65.5	56.0	43.8	30.7	21.1	42.4
Extreme Maximum Temp. (°F)	74	86	88	98	102	109	109	108	106	94	84	70	109
Extreme Minimum Temp. (°F)	-17	-15	-7	14	29	43	48	48	29	14	-4	-26	-26
Days Maximum Temp. ≥ 90°F	0	0	0	0	1	9	18	14	6	1	0	0	49
Days Maximum Temp. ≤ 32°F	12	8	2	0	0	0	0	0	0	0	2	8	32
Days Minimum Temp. ≤ 32°F	29	23	18	5	0	0	0	0	0	3	17	28	123
Days Minimum Temp. ≤ 0°F	4	2	0	0	0	0	0	0	0	0	0	2	8
Heating Degree Days (base 65°F)	1,191	917	700	374	124	13	1	2	75	304	716	1,057	5,474
Cooling Degree Days (base 65°F)	0	0	2	19	70	271	449	377	172	23	1	0	1,384
Mean Precipitation (in.)	0.66	0.68	2.27	2.48	4.46	3.96	4.24	3.28	2.62	1.84	1.43	0.85	28.77
Maximum Precipitation (in.)	1.8	2.6	8.3	6.0	9.7	14.1	16.8	10.7	8.5	4.9	4.9	3.6	44.8
Minimum Precipitation (in.)	0	trace	trace	0.4	0.3	1.3	0.1	0.4	0.2	trace	trace	trace	14.5
Maximum 24-hr. Precipitation (in.)	0.8	1.8	2.6	2.1	4.7	5.1	3.7	3.6	2.2	4.1	1.8	2.5	5.1
Days With ≥ 0.1" Precipitation	2	2	4	5	7	6	6	6	5	3	3	2	51
Days With ≥ 1.0" Precipitation	0	0	1	1	1	1	1	1	1	0	0	0	7
Mean Snowfall (in.)	6.1	*5.2*	*3.5*	0.8	trace	trace	trace	0.0	*trace*	*0.4*	*2.7*	*3.9*	*22.6*
Maximum Snowfall (in.)	16	21	17	6	trace	0	0	0	trace	5	10	17	56
Maximum 24-hr. Snowfall (in.)	9	13	9	3	trace	0	0	0	trace	5	7	12	13
Days With ≥ 1.0" Snow Depth	12	8	3	0	0	0	0	0	*0*	*0*	2	6	*31*
Thunderstorm Days	< 1	< 1	2	5	9	11	11	9	6	2	1	< 1	56
Foggy Days	8	8	10	9	10	7	5	8	8	7	9	10	99
Predominant Sky Cover	OVR	OVR	OVR	OVR	OVR	CLR	CLR	CLR	CLR	CLR	OVR	OVR	CLR
Mean Relative Humidity 6am (%)	79	79	79	81	85	85	82	83	84	79	81	80	81
Mean Relative Humidity 3pm (%)	59	56	50	49	53	49	45	47	48	45	54	59	51
Mean Dewpoint (°F)	17	21	29	40	51	60	63	62	54	42	31	21	41
Prevailing Wind Direction	N	N	N	S	S	S	S	S	S	S	S	N	S
Prevailing Wind Speed (mph)	14	15	15	16	15	15	14	14	15	15	14	14	15
Maximum Wind Gust (mph)	60	63	64	73	62	75	63	67	64	61	62	60	75

Dodge City Municipal Airport

The climate of Dodge City and southwestern Kansas is classified as semi-arid. Dodge City is nearly 300 miles east of the Rocky Mountains, but the weather reflects the influence of the mountains. The mountains form a barricade against all except high level moisture from the southwest, west, and northwest. Chinook winds occur occasionally but with less frequency and effect than at stations farther to the west. Relatively dry air predominating with an abundance of sunshine contribute to broad diurnal temperature ranges.

Thunderstorms during the growing season contribute most of the moisture. In general, the thunderstorms are widely scattered, occurring during the late afternoons and evenings. They are occasionally accompanied by hail and strong winds, but due to the local nature of the storms, damage to crops and buildings is spotty and variable. Winter is the dry season. However, the moisture accumulated during the winter months is important for the hard winter wheat. The duration of snow cover is generally brief due to mild temperatures and an abundance of sunshine. The exception results from the occasional blizzard that spreads across the flat treeless prairies of the high plains.

Afternoon temperatures in the 90s prevail during the summer months. Temperatures above 100 degrees are the exception. Due to low humidity and a continual breeze, these high temperatures are moderated. Temperatures normally drop sharply after sunset, allowing cool comfortable nights. During the winter months, large temperature changes are frequent, but the duration of extreme cold spells is brief.

The visibility at Dodge City is generally unrestricted as the terrain is favorable for unrestricted movement of air and air masses. Western Kansas is noted for clear skies and an abundance of sunshine.

Based on the 1951-1980 period, the average first occurrence of 32 degrees Fahrenheit in the fall is October 23 and the average last occurrence in the spring is April 21.

Dodge City Municipal Airport *Ford County*   Elevation: 2,575 ft.   Latitude: 37° 46' N   Longitude: 99° 58' W

	JAN	FEB	MAR	APR	MAY	JUN	JUL	AUG	SEP	OCT	NOV	DEC	YEAR
Mean Maximum Temp. (°F)	41.3	48.3	57.0	67.0	76.0	87.0	92.9	90.8	81.8	70.1	54.7	45.1	67.7
Mean Temp. (°F)	30.0	35.9	44.0	53.9	63.9	74.3	79.9	78.2	69.2	56.9	42.5	33.6	55.2
Mean Minimum Temp. (°F)	18.6	23.6	30.9	40.8	51.7	61.6	66.9	65.6	56.5	43.6	30.4	22.0	42.7
Extreme Maximum Temp. (°F)	80	85	93	100	105	110	109	107	104	95	91	76	110
Extreme Minimum Temp. (°F)	-13	-13	-5	14	30	42	46	48	29	14	1	-21	-21
Days Maximum Temp. ≥ 90°F	0	0	0	1	2	13	21	19	8	1	0	0	65
Days Maximum Temp. ≤ 32°F	9	5	2	0	0	0	0	0	0	0	2	5	23
Days Minimum Temp. ≤ 32°F	29	23	18	5	0	0	0	0	0	3	18	28	124
Days Minimum Temp. ≤ 0°F	2	1	0	0	0	0	0	0	0	0	0	1	4
Heating Degree Days (base 65°F)	1,079	814	647	346	114	12	1	2	65	276	668	968	4,992
Cooling Degree Days (base 65°F)	0	0	2	19	87	288	465	420	205	29	1	0	1,516
Mean Precipitation (in.)	0.58	0.66	1.76	2.24	2.96	3.09	3.09	2.68	1.78	1.37	1.00	0.75	21.96
Maximum Precipitation (in.)	2.0	2.9	8.8	6.3	8.7	7.9	9.1	7.4	6.8	4.9	3.8	2.4	32.8
Minimum Precipitation (in.)	0	trace	trace	0.1	0.4	0.1	0.2	0.7	trace	trace	trace	trace	10.0
Maximum 24-hr. Precipitation (in.)	1.3	1.8	2.5	1.7	2.7	3.0	3.5	3.2	2.5	4.1	1.5	1.4	4.1
Days With ≥ 0.1" Precipitation	2	2	4	4	6	5	5	5	3	3	2	2	43
Days With ≥ 1.0" Precipitation	0	0	0	1	1	1	1	1	0	0	0	0	5
Mean Snowfall (in.)	4.7	4.4	5.6	1.0	trace	trace	trace	trace	trace	0.5	1.9	3.5	21.6
Maximum Snowfall (in.)	16	20	24	9	1	0	0	0	1	5	17	10	45
Maximum 24-hr. Snowfall (in.)	11	12	9	6	1	0	0	0	1	4	12	7	12
Days With ≥ 1.0" Snow Depth	8	5	3	0	0	0	0	0	0	0	1	5	22
Thunderstorm Days	< 1	< 1	1	3	8	10	10	9	4	2	1	< 1	48
Foggy Days	8	9	9	7	8	5	4	6	7	6	7	8	84
Predominant Sky Cover	CLR	OVR	OVR	OVR	OVR	SCT	SCT	CLR	CLR	CLR	CLR	CLR	CLR
Mean Relative Humidity 6am (%)	77	78	76	76	82	80	77	79	78	74	76	76	77
Mean Relative Humidity 3pm (%)	51	49	44	40	46	42	38	39	40	38	45	50	43
Mean Dewpoint (°F)	18	22	27	36	49	57	60	59	51	39	28	21	39
Prevailing Wind Direction	N	N	S	S	S	S	S	S	S	S	S	N	S
Prevailing Wind Speed (mph)	16	16	16	17	17	17	15	14	16	15	15	16	16
Maximum Wind Gust (mph)	61	71	82	69	68	67	71	74	56	60	74	56	82

Goodland Renner Field

Goodland is situated on an intermediate plain with few native trees. The terrain rises from east to west with only minor variations from north to south. The rate of rise is about 1,600 feet per 150 miles east of Goodland and about 2,500 feet per 150 miles west. This gradual slope in terrain makes conditions favorable for upslope fog, low clouds, and drizzle with easterly winds.

This is a typical steppe climate with wide variations in precipitation from year to year. Evaporation generally exceeds precipitation during the summer months. The number of subnormal years of precipitation nearly equals the above normal years. The mean monthly rainfall increases in the spring to a maximum in June. General storms provide the main source of precipitation during the spring months, while thunderstorms are the major factor during the summer months. Inadequate moisture received from March through June, often results in drought conditions throughout the summer months with thunderstorms providing only local relief. The frequency of thunderstorms increases to a maximum in July with a marked decrease in September. Hail is most frequent in May and June. Winds during thunderstorms have been recorded with gusts up to 80 mph.

Snow is an important factor in the production of winter wheat, and residual soil moisture often offsets the effects of subnormal spring precipitation. When snow is accompanied by strong winds it can become a dangerous enemy. As little as one inch of snow accompanied by strong winds can result in serious blocking of roads and highways. The heaviest snowfall is most likely to occur in March, although heavy snows have been recorded in every month from October through May. Snow may cover the ground about one third of the time from November through March.

Temperatures are typical of continental climates with January normally the coldest month and July the warmest. Winters are often modified by persistent foehn winds but polar outbreaks have been known to drop the temperature as much as 70 degrees in a 24-hour period. Low relative humidity during the summer months makes most nights comfortable even in the hottest weather.

Based on the 1951-1980 period, the average first occurrence of 32 degrees Fahrenheit in the fall is October 7 and the average last occurrence in the spring is May 4. The growing season is 156 days.

Goodland Renner Field *Sherman County*   Elevation: 3,645 ft.   Latitude: 39° 22' N   Longitude: 101° 42' W

	JAN	FEB	MAR	APR	MAY	JUN	JUL	AUG	SEP	OCT	NOV	DEC	YEAR
Mean Maximum Temp. (°F)	40.4	45.8	53.4	62.7	71.9	83.7	89.4	87.2	78.5	66.4	50.9	43.0	64.4
Mean Temp. (°F)	28.1	32.7	39.8	48.8	58.8	69.6	75.2	73.4	64.3	52.0	38.2	30.5	51.0
Mean Minimum Temp. (°F)	15.7	19.7	26.1	34.8	45.7	55.5	61.0	59.6	50.0	37.5	25.5	18.0	37.4
Extreme Maximum Temp. (°F)	78	81	87	96	98	107	106	108	102	94	84	79	108
Extreme Minimum Temp. (°F)	-20	-22	-8	4	24	36	43	42	19	7	-8	-27	-27
Days Maximum Temp. ≥ 90°F	0	0	0	0	1	9	17	14	6	0	0	0	47
Days Maximum Temp. ≤ 32°F	9	6	3	0	0	0	0	0	0	0	3	6	27
Days Minimum Temp. ≤ 32°F	30	26	24	12	1	0	0	0	1	8	24	30	156
Days Minimum Temp. ≤ 0°F	4	2	0	0	0	0	0	0	0	0	0	2	8
Heating Degree Days (base 65°F)	1,138	904	775	484	215	34	4	9	117	404	798	1,062	5,944
Cooling Degree Days (base 65°F)	0	0	0	5	32	179	327	283	106	8	0	0	940
Mean Precipitation (in.)	0.43	0.42	1.16	1.50	3.52	3.29	3.49	2.48	1.13	0.94	0.83	0.39	19.58
Maximum Precipitation (in.)	1.6	1.5	3.6	3.9	8.2	9.5	10.1	9.3	5.4	4.1	2.1	1.6	28.0
Minimum Precipitation (in.)	0	trace	0.1	trace	0.5	0.1	1.0	0.1	trace	trace	trace	trace	9.2
Maximum 24-hr. Precipitation (in.)	1.0	1.0	1.2	3.0	3.5	4.1	3.6	3.1	2.3	2.3	1.1	0.8	4.1
Days With ≥ 0.1" Precipitation	1	1	3	4	6	5	6	5	2	2	2	1	38
Days With ≥ 1.0" Precipitation	0	0	0	0	1	1	1	1	0	0	0	0	4
Mean Snowfall (in.)	7.2	5.4	9.0	5.4	0.6	0.1	trace	trace	0.4	3.2	5.9	5.3	42.5
Maximum Snowfall (in.)	19	24	27	22	7	0	0	0	6	18	23	17	86
Maximum 24-hr. Snowfall (in.)	12	8	12	9	7	0	0	0	4	11	15	9	15
Days With ≥ 1.0" Snow Depth	10	7	5	2	0	0	0	0	0	1	4	7	36
Thunderstorm Days	< 1	< 1	1	2	8	10	11	9	4	1	< 1	< 1	46
Foggy Days	7	8	9	8	9	6	5	7	7	6	7	6	85
Predominant Sky Cover	CLR	OVR	OVR	OVR	OVR	CLR	CLR	CLR	CLR	CLR	CLR	CLR	CLR
Mean Relative Humidity 6am (%)	76	79	79	77	80	78	78	81	78	74	76	75	78
Mean Relative Humidity 3pm (%)	51	49	44	39	44	39	36	38	36	35	44	50	42
Mean Dewpoint (°F)	16	19	23	32	44	52	57	56	46	33	24	17	35
Prevailing Wind Direction	WSW	NNW	NNW	SSE	SSE	SSE	SSE	SSE	SSE	SSE	NNW	WSW	SSE
Prevailing Wind Speed (mph)	10	16	18	16	16	15	14	13	13	13	16	10	14
Maximum Wind Gust (mph)	67	61	66	82	96	77	70	91	68	68	68	63	96

Topeka Municipal Airport

Topeka, is located near the geographical center of the United States, and the middle of the temperate zone. The city straddles the Kansas River about 60 miles above its junction with the Missouri River. The Kansas River flows in an easterly direction through northeastern Kansas. Near Topeka, the river valley ranges from two to four miles wide, and is bordered on both sides by rolling prairie uplands of some 200 to 300 feet. The city is built on both banks of the Kansas River and along two tributaries, Soldier Creek in north Topeka and Shunganunga Creek in the south and east part of town. Flooding is always a threat following periods of heavy rains but protective construction has reduced the problem.

Seventy percent of the annual precipitation normally falls during the six crop-growing months, April through September. The rains of this period are usually of short duration, predominantly of the thunderstorm type. They occur more frequently during the nighttime and early morning hours than at other times of the day. Excessive precipitation rates may occur with warm-season thunderstorms. Rainfall accumulations over eight inches in 24 hours have occurred in Topeka. Tornadoes have occurred in the area on several occasions and caused severe damage and numerous injuries.

Individual summers show wide departures from average conditions. Hottest summers may produce temperatures of 100 degrees or higher on more than 50 days. On the other hand, 25 percent of the summers pass with two or fewer 100 degree days. Similarly, precipitation has shown a wide range for June, July, and August, varying from under three inches to more than 27 inches during the three months. Summers are hot with low relative humidity and persistent southerly winds. Oppressively warm periods with high relative humidity are usually of short duration.

Winter temperatures average about 45 degrees cooler than summer. Cold spells are seldom prolonged. Winter precipitation is often in the form of snow, sleet, or glaze, but severe storms are not common.

In the transitional spring and fall seasons, the numerous days of fair weather are interspersed with short intervals of stormy weather. Strong, blustery winds are quite common in late winter and spring. Autumn is characteristically a season of warm days, cool nights, and infrequent precipitation, with cold air invasions gradually increasing in intensity as the season progresses.

Based on the 1951-1980 period, the average first occurrence of 32 degrees Fahrenheit in the fall is October 14 and the average last occurrence in the spring is April 21.

Topeka Municipal Airport *Shawnee County*   Elevation: 882 ft.   Latitude: 39° 04' N   Longitude: 95° 38' W

	JAN	FEB	MAR	APR	MAY	JUN	JUL	AUG	SEP	OCT	NOV	DEC	YEAR
Mean Maximum Temp. (°F)	37.0	43.5	55.5	66.3	75.5	84.7	89.4	88.0	80.3	68.9	53.3	41.5	65.3
Mean Temp. (°F)	27.0	33.1	44.1	54.6	64.5	74.0	78.5	76.7	68.2	56.5	42.8	31.8	54.3
Mean Minimum Temp. (°F)	17.0	22.5	32.7	42.8	53.4	63.2	67.6	65.3	56.0	44.1	32.3	22.2	43.2
Extreme Maximum Temp. (°F)	72	84	89	95	97	106	110	110	103	95	85	73	110
Extreme Minimum Temp. (°F)	-20	-23	-7	10	29	43	43	41	29	19	2	-26	-26
Days Maximum Temp. ≥ 90°F	0	0	0	0	1	8	16	14	5	0	0	0	44
Days Maximum Temp. ≤ 32°F	11	7	1	0	0	0	0	0	0	0	1	6	26
Days Minimum Temp. ≤ 32°F	29	22	16	4	0	0	0	0	0	4	16	27	118
Days Minimum Temp. ≤ 0°F	4	2	0	0	0	0	0	0	0	0	0	1	7
Heating Degree Days (base 65°F)	1,170	896	645	331	100	7	1	1	70	282	659	1,022	5,184
Cooling Degree Days (base 65°F)	0	0	3	24	88	286	441	367	172	26	1	0	1,408
Mean Precipitation (in.)	0.95	1.16	2.51	3.22	4.97	4.68	3.78	3.82	3.86	2.96	2.29	1.43	35.63
Maximum Precipitation (in.)	5.2	3.5	8.4	8.1	11.8	15.2	12.0	11.2	12.7	7.2	6.3	4.3	60.9
Minimum Precipitation (in.)	trace	trace	0.1	0.6	0.4	0.6	0.6	0.3	0.7	trace	trace	0	19.1
Maximum 24-hr. Precipitation (in.)	1.2	1.9	2.5	3.2	3.6	4.1	3.7	4.5	4.3	3.5	4.7	2.5	4.7
Days With ≥ 0.1" Precipitation	2	3	5	6	8	7	6	6	5	5	4	3	60
Days With ≥ 1.0" Precipitation	0	0	0	1	2	1	1	1	1	1	1	0	9
Mean Snowfall (in.)	6.2	4.9	2.6	0.7	trace	trace	trace	0.0	0.0	0.3	1.5	4.8	21.0
Maximum Snowfall (in.)	23	22	22	7	0	0	0	0	0	1	9	19	49
Maximum 24-hr. Snowfall (in.)	15	11	8	7	0	0	0	0	0	1	6	9	15
Days With ≥ 1.0" Snow Depth	10	7	2	0	0	0	0	0	0	0	1	5	25
Thunderstorm Days	< 1	1	3	5	9	10	9	8	6	3	1	< 1	55
Foggy Days	10	11	11	9	10	8	8	8	10	9	9	11	114
Predominant Sky Cover	OVR	OVR	OVR	OVR	OVR	OVR	CLR	CLR	CLR	CLR	OVR	OVR	OVR
Mean Relative Humidity 6am (%)	78	79	79	80	85	87	86	87	87	83	80	80	83
Mean Relative Humidity 3pm (%)	58	56	51	49	52	54	53	52	50	47	52	58	53
Mean Dewpoint (°F)	18	23	30	41	53	63	67	65	56	44	32	23	43
Prevailing Wind Direction	N	N	N	S	S	S	S	S	S	S	S	S	S
Prevailing Wind Speed (mph)	13	13	14	15	14	13	12	10	12	13	12	12	13
Maximum Wind Gust (mph)	53	59	62	64	67	82	77	67	61	59	58	54	82

Wichita Mid-Continent Airport

Wichita is in the Central Great Plains where masses of warm, moist air from the Gulf of Mexico collide with cold, dry air from the Arctic region to create a wide range of weather the year around. Summers are usually warm and humid, and can be very hot and dry. The winters are usually mild, with brief periods of very cold weather.

The elevation is just over 1,300 feet above sea level. The terrain is basically flat with natural tree areas mainly along the Arkansas River and its tributaries.

The temperature extremes for the period of weather records at Wichita range from more than 110 degrees to less than -20 degrees. Temperatures above 90 degrees occur an average of 63 days per year, while very cold temperatures below zero occur about two days per year.

Precipitation averages about 30 inches per year, with 70 percent of that falling from April through September during the growing season. The wettest years have recorded over 50 inches. The driest years less than 15 inches.

Thunderstorms occur mainly during the spring and early summer. They can be severe and cause damage from heavy rain, large hail, strong winds and tornadoes.

The city of Wichita is protected against floods from the Arkansas River and its local tributaries by the Wichita-Vally Center Flood Control Project, which is designed to protect against floods up to the 75 to 100 year frequency class.

Snowfall normally is 15 inches per year, falling from December through March. Monthly snowfalls in excess of 20 inches and 24-hour snowfalls of more than 13 inches have occurred.

The prevailing wind direction is south with the windiest months March and April. July has the least wind. Strong north winds often occur with the passage of cold fronts from late fall through early spring. Extremely low wind chill factors are experienced with very cold outbreaks during the mid winter. On rare occasions during the summer, strong, hot, dry southwest winds can do considerable damage to crops.

Wichita Mid-Continent Airport *Sedgwick County*   Elevation: 1,318 ft.   Latitude: 37° 39' N   Longitude: 97° 26' W

	JAN	FEB	MAR	APR	MAY	JUN	JUL	AUG	SEP	OCT	NOV	DEC	YEAR
Mean Maximum Temp. (°F)	39.9	47.3	57.3	67.3	76.2	87.2	93.0	91.4	82.1	70.2	54.8	43.9	67.5
Mean Temp. (°F)	29.9	36.1	45.7	55.6	65.3	75.8	81.3	79.8	70.7	58.4	44.3	34.0	56.4
Mean Minimum Temp. (°F)	19.9	24.9	34.2	43.9	54.3	64.4	69.5	68.1	59.3	46.5	33.7	24.1	45.2
Extreme Maximum Temp. (°F)	74	87	89	96	100	110	112	110	107	95	85	72	112
Extreme Minimum Temp. (°F)	-11	-21	2	15	31	44	51	49	31	18	1	-16	-21
Days Maximum Temp. ≥ 90°F	0	0	0	0	1	12	22	19	8	1	0	0	63
Days Maximum Temp. ≤ 32°F	9	5	1	0	0	0	0	0	0	0	1	5	21
Days Minimum Temp. ≤ 32°F	28	21	13	3	0	0	0	0	0	1	14	26	106
Days Minimum Temp. ≤0°F	2	1	0	0	0	0	0	0	0	0	0	1	4
Heating Degree Days (base 65°F)	1,082	810	593	296	84	5	0	0	47	233	615	955	4,720
Cooling Degree Days (base 65°F)	0	0	3	21	102	339	518	470	234	36	1	0	1,724
Mean Precipitation (in.)	0.82	0.94	2.60	2.68	4.12	4.24	3.20	3.01	3.06	2.35	1.79	1.32	30.13
Maximum Precipitation (in.)	6.3	3.3	9.2	6.3	9.6	10.5	13.4	7.9	9.5	6.1	5.9	4.7	50.5
Minimum Precipitation (in.)	trace	trace	trace	0.2	0.5	0.9	0	0.3	trace	0	trace	trace	12.1
Maximum 24-hr. Precipitation (in.)	1.8	1.3	2.6	2.3	3.7	4.6	3.5	3.8	3.3	4.1	2.8	2.6	4.6
Days With ≥ 0.1" Precipitation	2	3	5	5	7	6	5	5	5	4	3	3	53
Days With ≥ 1.0" Precipitation	0	0	1	1	1	1	1	1	1	1	1	0	9
Mean Snowfall (in.)	4.3	4.2	2.7	0.3	trace	trace	trace	trace	trace	trace	1.6	3.2	16.3
Maximum Snowfall (in.)	20	17	17	5	0	0	0	0	0	2	8	14	45
Maximum 24-hr. Snowfall (in.)	12	12	12	5	0	0	0	0	0	2	8	8	12
Days With ≥ 1.0" Snow Depth	7	5	1	0	0	0	0	0	0	0	1	3	17
Thunderstorm Days	< 1	1	3	5	9	10	8	8	6	3	1	< 1	54
Foggy Days	10	10	10	8	9	6	4	5	8	7	8	10	95
Predominant Sky Cover	OVR	OVR	OVR	OVR	OVR	OVR	CLR	CLR	CLR	CLR	CLR	OVR	CLR
Mean Relative Humidity 6am (%)	79	79	77	78	83	83	79	80	82	80	80	80	80
Mean Relative Humidity 3pm (%)	57	54	48	47	52	47	42	43	47	46	52	57	49
Mean Dewpoint (°F)	20	24	32	42	53	61	64	63	56	45	33	24	43
Prevailing Wind Direction	N	N	S	S	S	S	S	S	S	S	S	S	S
Prevailing Wind Speed (mph)	15	15	16	16	15	15	13	13	14	14	14	13	14
Maximum Wind Gust (mph)	56	61	82	71	75	83	83	68	59	55	63	53	83

Abilene 1 W *Dickinson County*   Elevation: 1,167 ft.   Latitude: 38° 55' N   Longitude: 97° 14' W

	JAN	FEB	MAR	APR	MAY	JUN	JUL	AUG	SEP	OCT	NOV	DEC	YEAR
Mean Maximum Temp. (°F)	39.8	46.6	57.0	67.9	77.1	87.4	93.3	91.2	82.5	70.7	54.8	43.8	67.7
Mean Temp. (°F)	28.8	34.9	44.7	55.2	65.2	75.1	80.7	78.6	69.8	57.7	43.7	33.3	55.6
Mean Minimum Temp. (°F)	17.7	22.8	32.3	42.5	53.3	62.8	68.1	66.0	57.1	44.7	32.6	22.6	43.5
Extreme Maximum Temp. (°F)	77	83	87	98	101	105	112	111	106	95	86	72	112
Extreme Minimum Temp. (°F)	-19	-22	-9	15	27	39	44	45	23	16	-6	-24	-24
Days Maximum Temp. ≥ 90°F	0	0	0	1	2	12	22	18	9	1	0	0	65
Days Maximum Temp. ≤ 32°F	9	5	1	0	0	0	0	0	0	0	1	5	21
Days Minimum Temp. ≤ 32°F	28	23	16	5	0	0	0	0	0	3	16	26	117
Days Minimum Temp. ≤ 0°F	3	2	0	0	0	0	0	0	0	0	0	1	6
Heating Degree Days (base 65°F)	1,116	842	626	311	89	8	0	0	55	253	633	978	4,911
Cooling Degree Days (base 65°F)	0	0	3	28	108	326	513	442	218	37	1	0	1,676
Mean Precipitation (in.)	0.82	1.01	2.47	2.80	4.74	4.41	4.24	3.89	2.70	2.60	1.95	1.04	32.67
Days With ≥ 0.1" Precipitation	2	2	5	5	7	6	5	5	4	4	3	2	50
Days With ≥ 1.0" Precipitation	0	0	1	1	2	1	1	1	1	1	1	0	10
Mean Snowfall (in.)	*4.7*	*3.8*	*2.0*	0.1	0.0	0.0	0.0	0.0	0.0	trace	0.9	*2.4*	*13.9*
Days With ≥ 1.0" Snow Depth	na	na	*0*	0	0	0	0	0	0	0	0	0	na

Alton 6 ESE *Osborne County*   Elevation: 1,617 ft.   Latitude: 39° 26' N   Longitude: 98° 51' W

	JAN	FEB	MAR	APR	MAY	JUN	JUL	AUG	SEP	OCT	NOV	DEC	YEAR
Mean Maximum Temp. (°F)	39.6	46.8	56.9	68.1	76.4	87.5	93.5	90.8	82.7	71.3	54.3	44.2	67.7
Mean Temp. (°F)	26.5	32.3	42.1	52.9	62.6	73.3	79.3	76.6	67.7	55.3	40.3	30.9	53.3
Mean Minimum Temp. (°F)	13.5	17.7	27.3	37.7	48.7	59.1	65.0	62.2	52.6	39.2	26.3	17.6	38.9
Extreme Maximum Temp. (°F)	80	87	92	106	102	113	112	110	109	100	88	*80*	*113*
Extreme Minimum Temp. (°F)	-24	-22	-12	9	25	33	41	41	26	6	-8	-31	-31
Days Maximum Temp. ≥ 90°F	0	0	0	1	2	13	*22*	*18*	9	1	0	0	*66*
Days Maximum Temp. ≤ 32°F	9	6	2	0	0	0	0	0	0	0	2	5	24
Days Minimum Temp. ≤ 32°F	30	26	22	9	1	0	0	0	1	8	22	*30*	*149*
Days Minimum Temp. ≤ 0°F	4	3	1	0	0	0	0	0	0	0	0	2	10
Heating Degree Days (base 65°F)	1,185	916	704	371	138	16	1	4	81	315	734	1,049	5,514
Cooling Degree Days (base 65°F)	0	0	1	17	65	262	437	353	168	18	0	0	1,321
Mean Precipitation (in.)	0.61	0.76	2.08	2.63	4.10	3.31	3.97	3.21	2.43	1.59	1.52	0.76	26.97
Days With ≥ 0.1" Precipitation	2	2	4	5	7	6	6	5	4	3	3	2	49
Days With ≥ 1.0" Precipitation	0	0	1	1	1	1	1	1	1	0	0	0	7
Mean Snowfall (in.)	4.9	5.0	3.1	0.9	0.0	0.0	0.0	0.0	0.1	0.2	2.1	*3.7*	*20.0*
Days With ≥ 1.0" Snow Depth	10	7	3	0	0	0	0	0	0	0	2	5	*27*

Anthony *Harper County*   Elevation: 1,318 ft.   Latitude: 37° 10' N   Longitude: 98° 05' W

	JAN	FEB	MAR	APR	MAY	JUN	JUL	AUG	SEP	OCT	NOV	DEC	YEAR
Mean Maximum Temp. (°F)	43.4	51.1	60.5	70.4	79.5	90.0	95.5	94.1	84.8	73.5	57.1	46.6	70.5
Mean Temp. (°F)	33.4	39.3	48.0	57.7	67.4	77.2	82.6	81.2	72.5	60.7	46.1	36.0	58.5
Mean Minimum Temp. (°F)	22.7	27.4	35.4	44.9	55.3	64.5	69.6	68.3	60.2	47.8	35.0	25.3	46.4
Extreme Maximum Temp. (°F)	72	90	92	97	102	108	110	110	106	96	83	77	110
Extreme Minimum Temp. (°F)	-12	-6	2	18	31	46	52	52	30	16	7	*-15*	*-15*
Days Maximum Temp. ≥ 90°F	0	0	0	0	3	17	25	23	10	1	0	0	79
Days Maximum Temp. ≤ 32°F	7	3	1	0	0	0	0	0	0	0	1	3	15
Days Minimum Temp. ≤ 32°F	26	19	12	2	0	0	0	0	0	1	12	*25*	*97*
Days Minimum Temp. ≤ 0°F	1	0	0	0	0	0	0	0	0	0	0	1	2
Heating Degree Days (base 65°F)	971	720	524	238	53	4	0	0	30	178	562	*897*	*4,177*
Cooling Degree Days (base 65°F)	0	0	4	23	138	366	552	513	264	46	1	0	1,907
Mean Precipitation (in.)	1.02	0.96	2.83	3.52	4.23	4.42	3.36	2.57	3.06	2.03	2.16	1.17	31.33
Days With ≥ 0.1" Precipitation	2	2	5	5	6	6	5	4	4	3	4	3	49
Days With ≥ 1.0" Precipitation	0	0	1	1	1	1	1	1	1	0	1	0	8
Mean Snowfall (in.)	*3.1*	*4.2*	*2.9*	trace	0.0	0.0	0.0	0.0	0.0	trace	1.2	2.3	*13.7*
Days With ≥ 1.0" Snow Depth	na	na	*1*	0	0	0	0	0	0	0	0	0	*1*	na

Ashland *Clark County*   Elevation: 1,968 ft.   Latitude: 37° 12' N   Longitude: 99° 46' W

	JAN	FEB	MAR	APR	MAY	JUN	JUL	AUG	SEP	OCT	NOV	DEC	YEAR
Mean Maximum Temp. (°F)	44.4	51.1	59.7	69.8	78.3	88.5	94.6	92.9	84.0	73.1	58.0	47.9	70.2
Mean Temp. (°F)	30.0	35.8	44.5	54.3	64.4	74.4	79.8	78.3	69.3	56.7	42.8	33.3	55.3
Mean Minimum Temp. (°F)	15.5	20.3	29.3	38.8	50.3	60.2	65.0	63.7	54.6	40.2	27.5	18.7	40.4
Extreme Maximum Temp. (°F)	84	90	93	102	104	112	112	111	107	99	90	77	112
Extreme Minimum Temp. (°F)	-19	-18	0	11	27	40	46	43	24	11	3	-17	-19
Days Maximum Temp. ≥ 90°F	0	0	0	1	3	15	24	22	11	2	0	0	78
Days Maximum Temp. ≤ 32°F	7	4	1	0	0	0	0	0	0	0	1	4	17
Days Minimum Temp. ≤ 32°F	31	25	20	8	0	0	0	0	0	6	21	29	140
Days Minimum Temp. ≤ 0°F	3	1	0	0	0	0	0	0	0	0	0	1	5
Heating Degree Days (base 65°F)	1,078	819	628	331	104	11	1	1	60	274	661	975	4,943
Cooling Degree Days (base 65°F)	0	0	1	18	95	303	471	434	204	22	1	0	1,549
Mean Precipitation (in.)	0.51	0.60	1.70	1.89	3.68	3.46	2.89	2.57	2.25	1.46	1.05	0.71	22.77
Days With ≥ 0.1" Precipitation	2	2	4	4	6	6	4	5	4	3	2	2	44
Days With ≥ 1.0" Precipitation	0	0	0	1	1	1	1	1	1	0	0	0	6
Mean Snowfall (in.)	*3.3*	2.2	1.7	0.5	0.0	0.0	0.0	0.0	0.0	0.2	0.3	2.4	*10.6*
Days With ≥ 1.0" Snow Depth	na	*1*	1	0	0	0	0	0	0	0	0	*1*	na

Atchison *Atchison County*   Elevation: 944 ft.   Latitude: 39° 34' N   Longitude: 95° 07' W

	JAN	FEB	MAR	APR	MAY	JUN	JUL	AUG	SEP	OCT	NOV	DEC	YEAR
Mean Maximum Temp. (°F)	36.1	43.5	55.0	66.6	75.5	84.3	89.1	87.5	79.6	68.4	52.4	40.6	64.9
Mean Temp. (°F)	27.2	33.7	44.4	55.6	65.1	74.0	78.7	76.7	68.5	57.5	43.2	32.0	54.7
Mean Minimum Temp. (°F)	18.3	23.8	33.8	44.5	54.7	63.6	68.2	65.9	57.5	46.5	34.0	23.4	44.5
Extreme Maximum Temp. (°F)	72	80	86	92	95	105	109	109	100	92	84	71	109
Extreme Minimum Temp. (°F)	-17	-16	-10	11	32	44	49	48	32	20	-2	-21	-21
Days Maximum Temp. ≥ 90°F	0	0	0	0	0	6	15	12	4	0	0	0	37
Days Maximum Temp. ≤ 32°F	12	7	1	0	0	0	0	0	0	0	0	0	29
Days Minimum Temp. ≤ 32°F	27	21	14	3	0	0	0	0	0	2	13	25	105
Days Minimum Temp. ≤ 0°F	3	2	0	0	0	0	0	0	0	0	0	1	6
Heating Degree Days (base 65°F)	1,165	879	634	303	80	6	1	1	59	254	649	1,016	5,047
Cooling Degree Days (base 65°F)	0	0	3	27	91	284	442	376	178	28	1	0	1,430
Mean Precipitation (in.)	0.97	1.02	2.38	3.35	5.12	4.63	4.50	4.06	4.66	3.17	2.42	1.46	37.74
Days With ≥ 0.1" Precipitation	3	3	5	6	8	7	6	6	6	5	4	3	62
Days With ≥ 1.0" Precipitation	0	0	0	1	2	1	2	1	1	1	1	0	10
Mean Snowfall (in.)	6.9	5.6	3.2	0.8	0.0	0.0	0.0	0.0	0.0	0.2	1.2	4.3	22.2
Days With ≥ 1.0" Snow Depth	12	9	3	0	0	0	0	0	0	0	1	6	31

Atwood 2 SW *Rawlins County*   Elevation: 2,860 ft.   Latitude: 39° 47' N   Longitude: 101° 05' W

	JAN	FEB	MAR	APR	MAY	JUN	JUL	AUG	SEP	OCT	NOV	DEC	YEAR
Mean Maximum Temp. (°F)	38.6	45.7	54.1	64.0	73.6	85.4	90.8	89.0	80.3	67.4	51.3	42.3	65.2
Mean Temp. (°F)	25.7	31.6	39.6	49.3	59.6	70.4	75.9	74.2	64.5	51.2	37.4	29.1	50.7
Mean Minimum Temp. (°F)	12.7	17.3	25.0	34.4	45.5	55.3	60.9	59.3	48.7	34.9	23.5	15.8	36.1
Extreme Maximum Temp. (°F)	74	83	88	96	102	107	109	106	104	95	86	75	109
Extreme Minimum Temp. (°F)	-25	-23	-13	11	23	32	40	39	21	8	-9	-34	-34
Days Maximum Temp. ≥ 90°F	0	0	0	0	2	11	19	16	7	1	0	0	56
Days Maximum Temp. ≤ 32°F	10	6	3	0	0	0	0	0	0	0	3	7	29
Days Minimum Temp. ≤ 32°F	31	27	25	*13*	2	0	0	0	1	13	26	30	*168*
Days Minimum Temp. ≤ 0°F	5	3	1	0	0	0	0	0	0	0	0	3	12
Heating Degree Days (base 65°F)	1,212	938	781	470	202	30	3	8	115	427	820	1,107	6,113
Cooling Degree Days (base 65°F)	0	0	0	5	41	192	341	291	102	5	0	0	977
Mean Precipitation (in.)	0.65	0.60	1.58	2.25	3.86	3.32	3.53	2.82	1.53	1.20	1.07	0.50	22.91
Days With ≥ 0.1" Precipitation	2	2	4	5	7	5	6	5	3	2	3	1	45
Days With ≥ 1.0" Precipitation	0	0	0	1	1	1	1	1	0	0	0	0	5
Mean Snowfall (in.)	*7.4*	*4.6*	*5.8*	*3.3*	0.0	0.0	0.0	0.0	0.3	1.1	*4.1*	*3.3*	*29.9*
Days With ≥ 1.0" Snow Depth	na	na	na	*1*	0	0	0	0	0	0	0	*1*	na	na

Belleville *Republic County*   Elevation: 1,538 ft.   Latitude: 39° 50' N   Longitude: 97° 38' W

	JAN	FEB	MAR	APR	MAY	JUN	JUL	AUG	SEP	OCT	NOV	DEC	YEAR
Mean Maximum Temp. (°F)	36.4	42.9	53.4	64.6	74.2	84.8	90.1	87.8	79.2	67.3	51.2	40.1	64.3
Mean Temp. (°F)	25.8	31.6	41.6	52.5	62.8	73.0	78.3	76.1	67.1	54.9	40.3	29.8	52.8
Mean Minimum Temp. (°F)	15.1	20.3	29.7	40.5	51.4	61.2	66.4	64.3	54.9	42.5	29.2	19.5	41.3
Extreme Maximum Temp. (°F)	78	85	87	97	99	106	111	109	103	94	85	73	111
Extreme Minimum Temp. (°F)	-19	-15	-11	14	30	40	46	47	25	14	-4	-25	-25
Days Maximum Temp. ≥ 90°F	0	0	0	0	1	9	17	13	5	0	0	0	45
Days Maximum Temp. ≤ 32°F	12	8	2	0	0	0	0	0	0	0	2	8	32
Days Minimum Temp. ≤ 32°F	30	25	19	6	0	0	0	0	0	4	19	29	132
Days Minimum Temp. ≤ 0°F	5	3	0	0	0	0	0	0	0	0	0	2	10
Heating Degree Days (base 65°F)	1,209	936	719	382	126	14	1	3	81	322	736	1,084	5,613
Cooling Degree Days (base 65°F)	0	0	1	17	64	255	420	348	153	17	1	0	1,276
Mean Precipitation (in.)	0.69	0.71	2.38	2.80	4.49	4.28	4.17	3.83	3.14	2.11	1.60	0.95	31.15
Days With ≥ 0.1" Precipitation	2	2	5	6	8	6	6	6	5	4	3	2	55
Days With ≥ 1.0" Precipitation	0	0	1	1	1	1	1	1	1	0	0	0	7
Mean Snowfall (in.)	4.9	*4.1*	*2.3*	0.8	0.0	0.0	0.0	0.0	0.0	0.3	2.1	3.0	*17.5*
Days With ≥ 1.0" Snow Depth	*6*	na	*1*	0	0	0	0	0	0	0	1	*2*	na

Beloit *Mitchell County*   Elevation: 1,459 ft.   Latitude: 39° 29' N   Longitude: 98° 06' W

	JAN	FEB	MAR	APR	MAY	JUN	JUL	AUG	SEP	OCT	NOV	DEC	YEAR
Mean Maximum Temp. (°F)	37.7	44.7	55.2	66.1	75.6	86.8	92.7	90.1	81.3	69.0	52.4	41.5	66.1
Mean Temp. (°F)	26.7	32.7	42.7	53.3	63.6	74.3	80.0	77.8	68.5	56.0	41.0	30.8	53.9
Mean Minimum Temp. (°F)	15.7	20.6	30.1	40.5	51.5	61.7	67.3	65.4	55.7	42.9	29.5	20.0	41.7
Extreme Maximum Temp. (°F)	77	86	88	100	101	112	112	112	105	97	85	73	112
Extreme Minimum Temp. (°F)	-20	-15	-7	14	29	40	46	45	27	16	-8	-26	-26
Days Maximum Temp. ≥ 90°F	0	0	0	1	2	12	21	17	8	1	0	0	62
Days Maximum Temp. ≤ 32°F	11	6	1	0	0	0	0	0	0	0	2	7	27
Days Minimum Temp. ≤ 32°F	30	25	19	6	0	0	0	0	0	4	19	29	132
Days Minimum Temp. ≤ 0°F	4	2	0	0	0	0	0	0	0	0	0	2	8
Heating Degree Days (base 65°F)	1,180	905	687	361	115	11	0	1	69	295	715	1,055	5,394
Cooling Degree Days (base 65°F)	0	0	1	20	78	298	477	409	191	23	1	0	1,498
Mean Precipitation (in.)	0.71	0.66	2.17	2.45	4.13	3.74	3.87	2.97	2.50	2.04	1.45	0.84	27.53
Days With ≥ 0.1" Precipitation	2	2	4	5	7	6	6	5	5	4	3	2	51
Days With ≥ 1.0" Precipitation	0	0	0	1	1	1	1	1	1	0	0	0	6
Mean Snowfall (in.)	5.4	5.1	3.3	1.0	0.0	0.0	0.0	0.0	0.0	0.3	1.4	3.3	19.8
Days With ≥ 1.0" Snow Depth	na	na	*1*	0	0	0	0	0	0	0	*1*	na	na

Bison *Rush County*   Elevation: 2,007 ft.   Latitude: 38° 31' N   Longitude: 99° 12' W

	JAN	FEB	MAR	APR	MAY	JUN	JUL	AUG	SEP	OCT	NOV	DEC	YEAR
Mean Maximum Temp. (°F)	41.2	47.7	57.0	67.5	76.8	87.9	94.2	92.1	83.3	71.7	55.2	45.0	68.3
Mean Temp. (°F)	28.4	34.0	42.9	53.2	63.4	74.1	79.7	77.8	68.9	56.5	41.6	32.2	54.4
Mean Minimum Temp. (°F)	15.5	20.2	28.8	39.0	50.0	60.2	65.1	63.5	54.5	41.2	28.0	19.4	40.5
Extreme Maximum Temp. (°F)	80	86	91	103	103	111	112	112	106	98	89	78	112
Extreme Minimum Temp. (°F)	-17	-15	-6	9	29	36	45	45	23	14	-3	-24	-24
Days Maximum Temp. ≥ 90°F	0	0	0	1	3	13	23	20	10	2	0	0	72
Days Maximum Temp. ≤ 32°F	9	5	1	0	0	0	0	0	0	0	2	5	22
Days Minimum Temp. ≤ 32°F	30	26	20	7	1	0	0	0	0	6	20	29	139
Days Minimum Temp. ≤ 0°F	3	2	0	0	0	0	0	0	0	0	0	2	7
Heating Degree Days (base 65°F)	1,128	869	679	364	122	15	0	3	69	287	696	1,009	5,241
Cooling Degree Days (base 65°F)	0	0	1	18	79	291	454	406	198	27	0	0	1,474
Mean Precipitation (in.)	0.65	0.80	1.96	2.26	3.61	3.41	3.14	2.63	2.04	1.37	1.17	0.76	23.80
Days With ≥ 0.1" Precipitation	2	2	4	5	6	6	5	5	4	2	3	2	46
Days With ≥ 1.0" Precipitation	0	0	0	0	1	1	1	1	0	0	0	0	4
Mean Snowfall (in.)	5.4	4.6	4.7	1.5	trace	0.0	0.0	0.0	trace	0.4	1.9	4.0	22.5
Days With ≥ 1.0" Snow Depth	6	5	2	0	0	0	0	0	0	0	1	4	18

Cassoday *Butler County*   Elevation: 1,459 ft.   Latitude: 38° 03' N   Longitude: 96° 38' W

	JAN	FEB	MAR	APR	MAY	JUN	JUL	AUG	SEP	OCT	NOV	DEC	YEAR
Mean Maximum Temp. (°F)	39.6	46.5	57.2	67.8	76.0	85.1	91.2	90.1	81.8	70.3	55.1	43.8	67.0
Mean Temp. (°F)	28.4	34.5	44.6	55.4	64.4	73.7	79.2	77.7	69.4	57.6	43.7	33.0	55.1
Mean Minimum Temp. (°F)	17.1	22.4	31.9	42.9	52.8	62.3	67.2	65.4	57.1	45.0	32.2	22.2	43.2
Extreme Maximum Temp. (°F)	75	81	86	94	97	109	110	109	104	94	84	74	110
Extreme Minimum Temp. (°F)	-20	-18	-4	13	27	42	46	45	27	15	-4	-22	-22
Days Maximum Temp. ≥ 90°F	0	0	0	0	0	8	18	17	7	0	0	0	50
Days Maximum Temp. ≤ 32°F	9	5	1	0	0	0	0	0	0	0	1	5	21
Days Minimum Temp. ≤ 32°F	29	23	16	5	0	0	0	0	0	3	15	27	118
Days Minimum Temp. ≤ 0°F	3	2	0	0	0	0	0	0	0	0	0	1	6
Heating Degree Days (base 65°F)	1,129	857	627	304	98	10	0	1	58	252	635	986	4,957
Cooling Degree Days (base 65°F)	0	0	2	21	82	274	446	399	201	26	1	0	1,452
Mean Precipitation (in.)	0.79	0.94	2.37	3.38	4.34	4.95	3.41	3.43	3.46	2.47	2.20	1.13	32.87
Days With ≥ 0.1" Precipitation	2	2	5	5	7	6	5	4	5	4	3	2	50
Days With ≥ 1.0" Precipitation	0	0	1	1	1	2	1	1	1	1	0	0	9
Mean Snowfall (in.)	na	2.4	1.3	0.3	0.0	0.0	0.0	0.0	0.0	trace	1.0	2.2	na
Days With ≥ 1.0" Snow Depth	na	na	0	0	0	0	0	0	0	0	0	na	na

Centralia *Nemaha County*   Elevation: 1,318 ft.   Latitude: 39° 43' N   Longitude: 96° 07' W

	JAN	FEB	MAR	APR	MAY	JUN	JUL	AUG	SEP	OCT	NOV	DEC	YEAR
Mean Maximum Temp. (°F)	35.7	42.8	54.0	65.5	75.1	84.5	89.7	88.0	79.7	68.3	51.5	39.9	64.6
Mean Temp. (°F)	25.9	32.0	42.5	53.6	63.7	73.2	78.1	76.3	67.9	56.2	41.5	30.5	53.4
Mean Minimum Temp. (°F)	16.0	21.2	30.9	41.6	52.2	61.8	66.6	64.6	55.9	44.0	31.4	21.0	42.3
Extreme Maximum Temp. (°F)	70	82	87	94	97	109	110	107	103	94	82	70	110
Extreme Minimum Temp. (°F)	-21	-21	-17	7	28	40	40	44	26	13	-5	-25	-25
Days Maximum Temp. ≥ 90°F	0	0	0	0	1	7	16	14	5	0	0	0	43
Days Maximum Temp. ≤ 32°F	12	8	2	0	0	0	0	0	0	0	2	8	32
Days Minimum Temp. ≤ 32°F	29	23	17	6	0	0	0	0	0	4	17	28	124
Days Minimum Temp. ≤ 0°F	5	2	0	0	0	0	0	0	0	0	0	2	9
Heating Degree Days (base 65°F)	1,208	926	693	357	111	11	1	2	73	290	700	1,063	5,435
Cooling Degree Days (base 65°F)	0	0	2	23	73	255	413	354	166	23	1	0	1,310
Mean Precipitation (in.)	0.86	0.94	2.55	3.24	4.90	4.57	4.58	3.83	4.11	2.68	2.13	1.06	35.45
Days With ≥ 0.1" Precipitation	2	3	5	6	8	7	6	6	5	5	4	3	60
Days With ≥ 1.0" Precipitation	0	0	1	1	1	1	1	1	1	1	0	0	8
Mean Snowfall (in.)	9.1	7.4	5.9	2.0	trace	trace	0.0	0.0	trace	0.7	3.2	6.7	35.0
Days With ≥ 1.0" Snow Depth	12	9	3	1	0	0	0	0	0	0	2	7	34

Chanute Martin Johnson Airport *Neosho County*   Elevation: 977 ft.   Latitude: 37° 40' N   Longitude: 95° 29' W

	JAN	FEB	MAR	APR	MAY	JUN	JUL	AUG	SEP	OCT	NOV	DEC	YEAR
Mean Maximum Temp. (°F)	40.0	46.5	57.6	68.1	75.7	84.7	90.7	89.4	80.5	69.9	55.7	44.5	67.0
Mean Temp. (°F)	30.3	35.8	46.4	56.6	65.2	74.3	79.5	78.0	69.4	58.2	45.3	34.9	56.2
Mean Minimum Temp. (°F)	20.5	25.1	35.2	45.1	54.7	63.9	68.3	66.5	58.3	46.4	34.8	25.2	45.3
Extreme Maximum Temp. (°F)	71	82	89	95	91	108	111	108	102	95	83	73	111
Extreme Minimum Temp. (°F)	-11	-13	3	18	31	45	49	45	30	17	1	-17	-17
Days Maximum Temp. ≥ 90°F	0	0	0	0	0	7	18	16	6	0	0	0	47
Days Maximum Temp. ≤ 32°F	9	5	1	0	0	0	0	0	0	0	1	5	21
Days Minimum Temp. ≤ 32°F	27	21	13	3	0	0	0	0	0	2	13	24	103
Days Minimum Temp. ≤ 0°F	2	1	0	0	0	0	0	0	0	0	0	1	4
Heating Degree Days (base 65°F)	1,070	817	572	269	77	5	0	1	55	235	586	927	4,614
Cooling Degree Days (base 65°F)	0	0	3	25	90	297	469	423	200	29	2	0	1,538
Mean Precipitation (in.)	1.30	1.75	3.20	4.10	5.53	5.09	4.15	4.10	4.14	3.86	2.99	1.96	42.17
Days With ≥ 0.1" Precipitation	3	4	5	6	7	7	5	5	6	5	5	4	62
Days With ≥ 1.0" Precipitation	0	0	1	1	2	2	1	1	1	1	1	1	12
Mean Snowfall (in.)	4.4	4.4	1.9	0.2	0.0	0.0	0.0	0.0	0.0	trace	1.4	1.9	14.2
Days With ≥ 1.0" Snow Depth	8	5	1	0	0	0	0	0	0	0	1	3	18

Cimarron *Gray County*   Elevation: 2,693 ft.   Latitude: 37° 49' N   Longitude: 100° 21' W

	JAN	FEB	MAR	APR	MAY	JUN	JUL	AUG	SEP	OCT	NOV	DEC	YEAR
Mean Maximum Temp. (°F)	43.3	50.2	58.5	68.1	76.4	87.1	92.6	90.5	83.0	71.5	55.5	46.6	68.6
Mean Temp. (°F)	29.8	35.7	43.7	53.3	62.8	73.2	78.4	76.4	68.4	56.1	41.4	32.9	54.3
Mean Minimum Temp. (°F)	16.3	21.2	28.9	38.4	49.2	59.2	64.1	62.3	53.7	40.7	27.3	19.1	40.0
Extreme Maximum Temp. (°F)	77	89	93	99	103	109	108	106	105	96	92	75	109
Extreme Minimum Temp. (°F)	-18	-15	-6	11	28	38	45	43	25	13	1	-21	-21
Days Maximum Temp. ≥ 90°F	0	0	0	1	2	13	22	19	10	1	0	0	68
Days Maximum Temp. ≤ 32°F	8	4	2	0	0	0	0	0	0	0	1	5	20
Days Minimum Temp. ≤ 32°F	31	25	20	8	1	0	0	0	0	5	22	30	142
Days Minimum Temp. ≤ 0°F	2	1	0	0	0	0	0	0	0	0	0	1	4
Heating Degree Days (base 65°F)	1,085	820	655	361	129	19	1	2	70	291	700	989	5,122
Cooling Degree Days (base 65°F)	0	0	1	15	64	258	421	372	180	20	0	0	1,331
Mean Precipitation (in.)	0.61	0.65	1.77	2.05	3.38	3.71	3.49	2.74	1.70	1.36	1.08	0.56	23.10
Days With ≥ 0.1" Precipitation	2	2	4	4	6	6	5	5	4	2	2	2	44
Days With ≥ 1.0" Precipitation	0	0	0	1	1	1	1	1	0	0	0	0	5
Mean Snowfall (in.)	5.0	3.3	5.1	1.0	trace	0.0	0.0	0.0	trace	0.5	1.9	3.7	20.5
Days With ≥ 1.0" Snow Depth	6	3	2	1	0	0	0	0	0	0	1	5	18

Clay Center *Clay County*   Elevation: 1,217 ft.   Latitude: 39° 24' N   Longitude: 97° 08' W

	JAN	FEB	MAR	APR	MAY	JUN	JUL	AUG	SEP	OCT	NOV	DEC	YEAR
Mean Maximum Temp. (°F)	38.5	45.9	57.1	68.6	77.6	87.4	92.7	90.9	82.3	70.6	53.6	42.3	67.3
Mean Temp. (°F)	28.0	34.3	44.7	55.8	65.5	75.3	80.5	78.7	69.8	57.9	42.9	32.2	55.5
Mean Minimum Temp. (°F)	17.5	22.7	32.3	43.0	53.5	63.1	68.3	66.4	57.3	45.1	32.3	22.2	43.6
Extreme Maximum Temp. (°F)	77	85	89	99	98	109	111	109	104	95	83	70	111
Extreme Minimum Temp. (°F)	-18	-19	-10	7	29	41	45	45	28	14	-6	-24	-24
Days Maximum Temp. ≥ 90°F	0	0	0	1	2	12	21	18	8	1	0	0	63
Days Maximum Temp. ≤ 32°F	10	6	1	0	0	0	0	0	0	0	1	6	24
Days Minimum Temp. ≤ 32°F	28	23	16	5	0	0	0	0	0	3	16	27	118
Days Minimum Temp. ≤ 0°F	3	2	0	0	0	0	0	0	0	0	0	1	6
Heating Degree Days (base 65°F)	1,140	860	624	298	84	7	0	1	56	246	656	1,008	4,980
Cooling Degree Days (base 65°F)	0	0	3	31	108	320	492	429	211	32	1	0	1,627
Mean Precipitation (in.)	0.81	0.82	2.35	2.76	4.97	3.93	3.94	3.57	3.42	2.26	1.71	0.96	31.50
Days With ≥ 0.1" Precipitation	3	2	5	6	8	7	6	6	5	4	4	3	59
Days With ≥ 1.0" Precipitation	0	0	1	1	1	1	1	1	1	1	0	0	8
Mean Snowfall (in.)	6.5	5.3	3.4	0.9	0.0	0.0	0.0	0.0	0.0	0.1	1.8	3.3	21.3
Days With ≥ 1.0" Snow Depth	11	7	2	0	0	0	0	0	0	0	2	5	27

Colby 1 SW *Thomas County*   Elevation: 3,169 ft.   Latitude: 39° 24' N   Longitude: 101° 04' W

	JAN	FEB	MAR	APR	MAY	JUN	JUL	AUG	SEP	OCT	NOV	DEC	YEAR
Mean Maximum Temp. (°F)	39.2	44.9	52.6	62.8	72.1	84.1	89.9	87.8	79.1	67.2	51.0	42.3	64.4
Mean Temp. (°F)	26.1	31.1	38.6	48.6	58.8	69.9	75.6	73.5	64.1	51.4	37.5	29.0	50.4
Mean Minimum Temp. (°F)	13.0	17.2	24.6	34.3	45.6	55.7	61.3	59.1	49.0	35.6	24.0	15.6	36.2
Extreme Maximum Temp. (°F)	76	81	87	98	102	110	109	106	104	94	84	76	110
Extreme Minimum Temp. (°F)	-23	-22	-13	5	23	33	42	41	21	7	-8	-32	-32
Days Maximum Temp. ≥ 90°F	0	0	0	0	1	9	17	15	7	1	0	0	50
Days Maximum Temp. ≤ 32°F	10	6	4	0	0	0	0	0	0	0	3	7	30
Days Minimum Temp. ≤ 32°F	31	27	26	13	2	0	0	0	1	10	26	31	167
Days Minimum Temp. ≤ 0°F	5	3	1	0	0	0	0	0	0	0	0	3	12
Heating Degree Days (base 65°F)	1,199	950	811	491	218	39	4	10	125	420	820	1,111	6,198
Cooling Degree Days (base 65°F)	0	0	0	5	33	190	337	284	109	6	0	0	964
Mean Precipitation (in.)	0.39	0.43	1.15	1.93	3.75	3.02	3.91	2.51	1.43	1.15	0.79	0.36	20.82
Days With ≥ 0.1" Precipitation	1	1	3	4	7	5	6	4	3	2	2	1	39
Days With ≥ 1.0" Precipitation	0	0	0	0	1	1	1	1	0	0	0	0	4
Mean Snowfall (in.)	5.1	4.8	7.5	3.5	0.3	trace	0.0	0.0	0.3	1.5	3.7	4.0	30.7
Days With ≥ 1.0" Snow Depth	11	7	4	1	0	0	0	0	0	1	4	7	35

Coldwater *Comanche County*   Elevation: 2,080 ft.   Latitude: 37° 16' N   Longitude: 99° 20' W

	JAN	FEB	MAR	APR	MAY	JUN	JUL	AUG	SEP	OCT	NOV	DEC	YEAR
Mean Maximum Temp. (°F)	44.6	52.4	60.7	70.6	78.7	88.4	93.9	92.3	83.8	73.0	57.5	47.7	70.3
Mean Temp. (°F)	32.7	39.2	47.3	57.0	66.0	75.8	80.9	79.3	70.8	59.5	45.2	35.9	57.5
Mean Minimum Temp. (°F)	20.6	25.7	33.8	43.4	53.4	62.9	67.8	66.2	57.8	45.9	32.9	24.1	44.5
Extreme Maximum Temp. (°F)	84	90	92	100	103	109	111	110	107	96	89	82	111
Extreme Minimum Temp. (°F)	-15	-14	2	17	29	42	50	51	29	15	3	-17	-17
Days Maximum Temp. ≥ 90°F	0	0	0	1	3	13	24	21	10	1	0	0	73
Days Maximum Temp. ≤ 32°F	7	3	1	0	0	0	0	0	0	0	1	4	16
Days Minimum Temp. ≤ 32°F	28	20	14	3	0	0	0	0	0	2	14	26	107
Days Minimum Temp. ≤ 0°F	1	1	0	0	0	0	0	0	0	0	0	1	3
Heating Degree Days (base 65°F)	994	722	547	264	77	6	0	0	44	207	589	894	4,344
Cooling Degree Days (base 65°F)	0	0	5	34	116	331	505	465	240	43	2	0	1,741
Mean Precipitation (in.)	0.69	0.82	1.85	2.10	3.81	3.82	3.10	3.17	2.29	1.92	1.35	0.89	25.81
Days With ≥ 0.1" Precipitation	2	2	4	4	6	5	4	4	4	3	2	2	42
Days With ≥ 1.0" Precipitation	0	0	1	1	1	1	1	1	1	0	0	0	6
Mean Snowfall (in.)	4.0	4.0	3.9	1.1	trace	0.0	0.0	0.0	trace	0.3	2.0	3.3	18.6
Days With ≥ 1.0" Snow Depth	3	1	1	0	0	0	0	0	0	0	1	2	8

Columbus 1 SW *Cherokee County*   Elevation: 898 ft.   Latitude: 37° 10' N   Longitude: 94° 51' W

	JAN	FEB	MAR	APR	MAY	JUN	JUL	AUG	SEP	OCT	NOV	DEC	YEAR
Mean Maximum Temp. (°F)	41.8	49.0	58.4	68.1	76.6	85.1	90.8	89.8	81.3	71.1	56.9	46.4	67.9
Mean Temp. (°F)	32.1	38.3	47.2	56.3	65.8	74.5	79.6	78.2	70.0	59.2	46.7	36.7	57.1
Mean Minimum Temp. (°F)	22.3	27.5	36.0	44.6	54.9	63.8	68.4	66.4	58.7	47.2	36.4	27.0	46.1
Extreme Maximum Temp. (°F)	72	85	90	97	91	101	109	105	103	94	84	74	109
Extreme Minimum Temp. (°F)	-15	-16	4	21	29	45	45	46	32	19	4	-15	-16
Days Maximum Temp. ≥ 90°F	0	0	0	0	0	8	19	17	5	0	0	0	49
Days Maximum Temp. ≤ 32°F	7	4	1	0	0	0	0	0	0	0	1	4	17
Days Minimum Temp. ≤ 32°F	26	20	12	3	0	0	0	0	0	2	11	22	96
Days Minimum Temp. ≤ 0°F	2	1	0	0	0	0	0	0	0	0	0	1	4
Heating Degree Days (base 65°F)	1,013	749	549	278	71	5	0	1	48	212	548	871	4,345
Cooling Degree Days (base 65°F)	0	0	4	21	100	296	464	421	204	35	4	0	1,549
Mean Precipitation (in.)	1.63	1.95	3.43	4.41	5.54	4.73	3.66	3.95	4.99	3.87	4.05	2.36	44.57
Days With ≥ 0.1" Precipitation	4	3	6	7	8	7	5	5	6	5	5	4	65
Days With ≥ 1.0" Precipitation	0	0	1	1	2	1	1	1	2	1	1	1	12
Mean Snowfall (in.)	3.9	2.4	2.0	trace	0.0	0.0	0.0	0.0	0.0	0.0	0.6	2.1	11.0
Days With ≥ 1.0" Snow Depth	7	3	1	0	0	0	0	0	0	0	0	3	14

Cottonwood Falls *Chase County*   Elevation: 1,240 ft.   Latitude: 38° 22' N   Longitude: 96° 33' W

	JAN	FEB	MAR	APR	MAY	JUN	JUL	AUG	SEP	OCT	NOV	DEC	YEAR
Mean Maximum Temp. (°F)	40.4	47.2	57.7	68.0	76.5	85.4	91.2	90.5	82.1	71.1	55.6	44.4	67.5
Mean Temp. (°F)	29.5	35.6	45.4	55.8	65.3	74.2	79.6	78.3	69.8	58.3	44.4	33.9	55.8
Mean Minimum Temp. (°F)	18.5	24.0	33.2	43.7	53.9	63.0	67.9	66.1	57.4	45.4	33.1	23.3	44.1
Extreme Maximum Temp. (°F)	77	83	85	94	97	111	113	111	107	97	86	75	113
Extreme Minimum Temp. (°F)	-14	-18	-3	11	28	42	47	46	29	13	-1	-22	-22
Days Maximum Temp. ≥ 90°F	0	0	0	1	1	8	19	17	7	1	0	0	54
Days Maximum Temp. ≤ 32°F	9	5	1	0	0	0	0	0	0	0	1	5	21
Days Minimum Temp. ≤ 32°F	28	22	15	4	0	0	0	0	0	3	15	26	113
Days Minimum Temp. ≤ 0°F	2	1	0	0	0	0	0	0	0	0	0	1	4
Heating Degree Days (base 65°F)	1,095	823	602	296	84	8	0	1	55	238	613	958	4,773
Cooling Degree Days (base 65°F)	0	0	3	28	93	290	462	415	209	34	2	0	1,536
Mean Precipitation (in.)	0.97	0.98	2.80	3.15	4.89	4.85	4.35	3.99	3.63	2.62	2.53	1.33	36.09
Days With ≥ 0.1" Precipitation	2	3	5	6	7	6	5	5	5	4	4	3	55
Days With ≥ 1.0" Precipitation	0	0	1	1	2	2	2	1	1	1	1	0	12
Mean Snowfall (in.)	4.9	3.6	1.7	0.6	0.0	0.0	0.0	0.0	0.0	0.2	1.1	2.9	15.0
Days With ≥ 1.0" Snow Depth	7	5	1	0	0	0	0	0	0	0	0	2	15

Council Grove Lake *Morris County*   Elevation: 1,318 ft.   Latitude: 38° 41' N   Longitude: 96° 31' W

	JAN	FEB	MAR	APR	MAY	JUN	JUL	AUG	SEP	OCT	NOV	DEC	YEAR
Mean Maximum Temp. (°F)	36.6	43.4	54.4	65.2	74.2	83.7	89.9	88.7	80.3	68.8	53.2	41.7	65.0
Mean Temp. (°F)	26.2	32.3	43.0	53.9	63.5	72.9	78.5	76.9	68.0	56.1	42.5	31.5	53.8
Mean Minimum Temp. (°F)	15.8	21.1	31.5	42.5	52.7	62.1	67.1	65.0	55.8	43.3	31.7	21.2	42.5
Extreme Maximum Temp. (°F)	76	80	86	95	99	112	114	110	105	94	85	75	114
Extreme Minimum Temp. (°F)	-17	-23	-9	6	30	41	46	46	28	15	-1	-24	-24
Days Maximum Temp. ≥ 90°F	0	0	0	0	1	7	16	15	6	0	0	0	45
Days Maximum Temp. ≤ 32°F	12	7	2	0	0	0	0	0	0	0	2	7	30
Days Minimum Temp. ≤ 32°F	30	24	17	4	0	0	0	0	0	4	16	28	123
Days Minimum Temp. ≤ 0°F	4	2	0	0	0	0	0	0	0	0	0	2	8
Heating Degree Days (base 65°F)	1,196	917	678	350	118	14	1	2	73	294	669	1,033	5,345
Cooling Degree Days (base 65°F)	0	0	2	25	74	262	437	380	176	24	1	0	1,381
Mean Precipitation (in.)	0.83	0.93	2.61	3.28	4.92	4.24	4.09	3.66	3.20	2.33	2.16	1.20	33.45
Days With ≥ 0.1" Precipitation	2	2	5	6	7	6	6	6	5	4	4	3	56
Days With ≥ 1.0" Precipitation	0	0	1	1	2	1	1	1	1	1	1	0	10
Mean Snowfall (in.)	5.1	3.5	1.5	0.4	0.0	0.0	0.0	0.0	0.0	0.3	1.1	3.5	15.4
Days With ≥ 1.0" Snow Depth	10	6	1	0	0	0	0	0	0	0	1	5	23

El Dorado *Butler County*   Elevation: 1,338 ft.   Latitude: 37° 49' N   Longitude: 96° 50' W

	JAN	FEB	MAR	APR	MAY	JUN	JUL	AUG	SEP	OCT	NOV	DEC	YEAR
Mean Maximum Temp. (°F)	41.6	48.6	58.7	68.9	77.1	85.9	91.3	89.9	82.0	71.2	56.1	45.2	68.1
Mean Temp. (°F)	30.7	36.9	46.6	56.8	66.0	74.9	80.0	78.4	70.5	59.1	45.2	34.8	56.7
Mean Minimum Temp. (°F)	19.9	25.1	34.4	44.7	54.7	63.8	68.7	66.8	58.9	46.9	34.3	24.4	45.2
Extreme Maximum Temp. (°F)	78	84	87	96	97	107	109	107	103	93	84	74	109
Extreme Minimum Temp. (°F)	-17	-16	0	14	29	43	48	46	28	15	-2	-18	-18
Days Maximum Temp. ≥ 90°F	0	0	0	0	1	9	19	17	7	0	0	0	53
Days Maximum Temp. ≤ 32°F	8	4	1	0	0	0	0	0	0	0	1	4	18
Days Minimum Temp. ≤ 32°F	28	21	14	3	0	0	0	0	0	2	14	25	107
Days Minimum Temp. ≤ 0°F	2	1	0	0	0	0	0	0	0	0	0	1	4
Heating Degree Days (base 65°F)	1,055	787	566	267	73	5	0	1	44	216	588	928	4,530
Cooling Degree Days (base 65°F)	0	0	3	29	109	312	479	423	221	36	1	0	1,613
Mean Precipitation (in.)	0.92	1.20	2.76	3.16	4.38	5.36	3.73	3.72	3.40	2.89	2.30	1.46	35.28
Days With ≥ 0.1" Precipitation	2	3	5	6	7	6	5	5	6	4	4	3	56
Days With ≥ 1.0" Precipitation	0	0	1	1	1	2	1	1	1	1	1	0	10
Mean Snowfall (in.)	2.9	3.6	1.8	trace	trace	0.0	0.0	0.0	0.0	trace	0.8	2.2	11.3
Days With ≥ 1.0" Snow Depth	1	na	1	0	0	0	0	0	0	0	0	1	na

Elk City Lake *Montgomery County*   Elevation: 846 ft.   Latitude: 37° 17' N   Longitude: 95° 47' W

	JAN	FEB	MAR	APR	MAY	JUN	JUL	AUG	SEP	OCT	NOV	DEC	YEAR
Mean Maximum Temp. (°F)	na	47.7	58.5	68.9	76.4	85.4	91.6	90.8	82.2	na	na	na	na
Mean Temp. (°F)	na	na	45.8	56.4	65.1	74.3	79.8	78.3	69.7	na	na	na	na
Mean Minimum Temp. (°F)	na	21.6	33.2	43.7	53.7	63.1	67.9	65.7	57.2	na	na	na	na
Extreme Maximum Temp. (°F)	71	81	87	99	92	104	110	108	105	97	85	75	110
Extreme Minimum Temp. (°F)	-18	-16	1	16	29	42	45	46	30	22	0	-16	-18
Days Maximum Temp. ≥ 90°F	0	0	0	0	0	9	20	19	7	1	0	0	56
Days Maximum Temp. ≤ 32°F	7	4	1	0	0	0	0	0	0	0	0	4	16
Days Minimum Temp. ≤ 32°F	25	20	13	4	0	0	0	0	0	3	13	23	101
Days Minimum Temp. ≤ 0°F	2	1	0	0	0	0	0	0	0	0	0	1	4
Heating Degree Days (base 65°F)	na	na	587	na	85	7	1	1	57	na	na	na	na
Cooling Degree Days (base 65°F)	na	na	na	na	93	298	483	439	211	na	na	na	na
Mean Precipitation (in.)	1.19	1.20	3.26	3.88	5.80	5.29	3.87	3.85	4.49	3.79	3.41	1.80	41.83
Days With ≥ 0.1" Precipitation	3	3	5	5	7	6	5	5	5	4	4	3	55
Days With ≥ 1.0" Precipitation	0	0	1	1	2	1	1	1	2	1	1	0	11
Mean Snowfall (in.)	na	na	0.9	0.0	0.0	0.0	0.0	0.0	0.0	0.0	trace	na	na
Days With ≥ 1.0" Snow Depth	na	na	0	0	0	0	0	0	0	0	0	na	na

Elkhart *Morton County*   Elevation: 3,599 ft.   Latitude: 37° 00' N   Longitude: 101° 53' W

	JAN	FEB	MAR	APR	MAY	JUN	JUL	AUG	SEP	OCT	NOV	DEC	YEAR
Mean Maximum Temp. (°F)	46.4	52.6	59.7	69.1	78.5	89.4	93.6	90.9	82.4	71.9	56.9	48.1	70.0
Mean Temp. (°F)	32.9	38.2	45.0	54.1	63.8	74.2	78.9	76.8	68.3	56.7	43.1	35.0	55.6
Mean Minimum Temp. (°F)	19.4	23.8	30.3	39.0	49.1	59.0	64.3	62.7	54.0	41.4	29.4	21.9	41.2
Extreme Maximum Temp. (°F)	83	85	89	95	103	110	109	108	104	96	91	80	110
Extreme Minimum Temp. (°F)	-22	-15	0	13	21	41	50	45	25	11	-7	-16	-22
Days Maximum Temp. ≥ 90°F	0	0	0	1	4	16	23	20	9	1	0	0	74
Days Maximum Temp. ≤ 32°F	6	3	1	0	0	0	0	0	0	0	1	4	15
Days Minimum Temp. ≤ 32°F	29	24	19	7	0	0	0	0	0	4	19	28	130
Days Minimum Temp. ≤ 0°F	1	1	0	0	0	0	0	0	0	0	0	1	3
Heating Degree Days (base 65°F)	989	751	613	333	107	11	1	2	63	274	648	922	4,714
Cooling Degree Days (base 65°F)	0	0	1	11	74	285	445	383	171	21	0	0	1,391
Mean Precipitation (in.)	0.52	0.50	1.26	1.74	2.74	2.26	2.82	2.85	1.73	1.00	0.83	0.47	18.72
Days With ≥ 0.1" Precipitation	2	2	3	3	5	5	5	5	3	2	2	1	38
Days With ≥ 1.0" Precipitation	0	0	0	0	1	0	1	1	0	0	0	0	3
Mean Snowfall (in.)	5.3	4.4	4.9	1.1	0.2	0.0	0.0	0.0	0.1	1.0	1.7	3.7	22.4
Days With ≥ 1.0" Snow Depth	na	na	2	0	0	0	0	0	0	0	1	2	na

Ellsworth *Ellsworth County*   Elevation: 1,528 ft.   Latitude: 38° 44' N   Longitude: 98° 13' W

	JAN	FEB	MAR	APR	MAY	JUN	JUL	AUG	SEP	OCT	NOV	DEC	YEAR
Mean Maximum Temp. (°F)	40.8	47.4	58.3	68.8	76.9	87.7	93.5	91.4	82.8	71.2	54.7	44.6	68.2
Mean Temp. (°F)	28.2	33.9	44.8	55.0	64.3	74.7	80.2	78.2	69.3	57.0	42.1	32.2	55.0
Mean Minimum Temp. (°F)	15.6	20.2	31.1	41.1	51.6	61.7	66.8	64.9	55.7	42.8	29.4	19.8	41.7
Extreme Maximum Temp. (°F)	77	89	92	101	97	112	112	110	105	96	87	74	112
Extreme Minimum Temp. (°F)	-25	-26	-5	10	28	40	43	43	24	11	-4	-28	-28
Days Maximum Temp. ≥ 90°F	0	0	0	1	2	13	22	19	9	1	0	0	67
Days Maximum Temp. ≤ 32°F	9	5	1	0	0	0	0	0	0	0	1	5	21
Days Minimum Temp. ≤ 32°F	29	24	17	7	1	0	0	0	0	5	19	28	130
Days Minimum Temp. ≤ 0°F	4	2	0	0	0	0	0	0	0	0	0	2	8
Heating Degree Days (base 65°F)	1,134	873	623	318	102	9	0	2	62	270	682	1,010	5,085
Cooling Degree Days (base 65°F)	0	0	3	25	80	298	468	406	199	25	1	0	1,505
Mean Precipitation (in.)	0.73	0.80	2.43	2.46	4.96	3.54	3.42	3.40	2.69	2.35	1.20	0.80	28.78
Days With ≥ 0.1" Precipitation	2	2	5	5	8	6	5	5	4	4	3	2	51
Days With ≥ 1.0" Precipitation	0	0	1	1	2	1	1	1	1	1	0	0	9
Mean Snowfall (in.)	6.3	na	2.2	0.4	0.0	0.0	0.0	0.0	0.0	0.4	1.2	3.2	na
Days With ≥ 1.0" Snow Depth	na	8	2	0	0	0	0	0	0	0	1	4	na

Eskridge *Wabaunsee County*   Elevation: 1,414 ft.   Latitude: 38° 52' N   Longitude: 96° 06' W

	JAN	FEB	MAR	APR	MAY	JUN	JUL	AUG	SEP	OCT	NOV	DEC	YEAR
Mean Maximum Temp. (°F)	36.7	43.3	55.0	65.7	74.4	83.7	89.5	88.1	79.8	68.4	52.4	41.2	64.8
Mean Temp. (°F)	26.8	32.4	43.3	54.0	63.6	72.8	77.9	76.2	67.8	56.4	41.9	31.3	53.7
Mean Minimum Temp. (°F)	16.8	21.4	31.4	42.2	52.7	61.9	66.2	64.3	55.8	44.3	31.5	21.4	42.5
Extreme Maximum Temp. (°F)	73	81	84	92	94	109	112	109	103	95	84	70	112
Extreme Minimum Temp. (°F)	-19	-16	-7	10	31	39	49	48	31	16	-1	-25	-25
Days Maximum Temp. ≥ 90°F	0	0	0	0	0	6	15	14	5	0	0	0	40
Days Maximum Temp. ≤ 32°F	11	7	1	0	0	0	0	0	0	0	2	6	27
Days Minimum Temp. ≤ 32°F	29	24	17	5	0	0	0	0	0	3	16	26	120
Days Minimum Temp. ≤ 0°F	3	2	0	0	0	0	0	0	0	0	0	2	7
Heating Degree Days (base 65°F)	1,180	915	669	343	109	11	1	3	72	282	685	1,038	5,308
Cooling Degree Days (base 65°F)	0	0	1	20	57	238	397	342	155	16	0	0	1,226
Mean Precipitation (in.)	0.90	0.96	2.82	3.26	5.42	4.75	3.34	4.03	3.94	2.53	2.40	1.33	35.68
Days With ≥ 0.1" Precipitation	3	2	5	6	8	7	5	6	6	5	4	3	60
Days With ≥ 1.0" Precipitation	0	0	1	1	2	2	1	1	1	1	1	0	11
Mean Snowfall (in.)	6.9	5.2	2.9	0.9	0.0	0.0	0.0	0.0	trace	0.4	2.4	3.8	22.5
Days With ≥ 1.0" Snow Depth	11	7	2	0	0	0	0	0	0	0	1	5	26

Eureka *Greenwood County*   Elevation: 1,040 ft.   Latitude: 37° 49' N   Longitude: 96° 17' W

	JAN	FEB	MAR	APR	MAY	JUN	JUL	AUG	SEP	OCT	NOV	DEC	YEAR
Mean Maximum Temp. (°F)	41.7	48.8	60.1	70.0	78.0	86.5	92.5	90.8	82.6	71.8	56.7	45.8	68.8
Mean Temp. (°F)	30.8	36.9	47.2	57.2	66.2	75.0	80.5	78.5	70.4	58.8	45.3	35.1	56.8
Mean Minimum Temp. (°F)	19.9	24.8	34.2	44.3	54.3	63.5	68.5	66.2	58.1	45.8	33.8	24.3	44.8
Extreme Maximum Temp. (°F)	75	85	87	99	95	110	112	111	105	95	85	73	112
Extreme Minimum Temp. (°F)	-13	-19	-1	14	29	44	47	46	28	15	0	-18	-19
Days Maximum Temp. ≥ 90°F	0	0	0	1	1	10	21	18	7	1	0	0	59
Days Maximum Temp. ≤ 32°F	8	4	1	0	0	0	0	0	0	0	1	4	18
Days Minimum Temp. ≤ 32°F	27	21	14	3	0	0	0	0	0	3	14	25	107
Days Minimum Temp. ≤ 0°F	2	1	0	0	0	0	0	0	0	0	0	1	4
Heating Degree Days (base 65°F)	1,053	789	550	261	68	5	0	0	46	222	588	920	4,502
Cooling Degree Days (base 65°F)	0	0	4	32	107	314	495	428	216	34	2	0	1,632
Mean Precipitation (in.)	1.16	1.43	2.75	3.39	4.66	5.09	3.77	4.09	3.61	3.19	2.85	1.74	37.73
Days With ≥ 0.1" Precipitation	3	4	6	6	7	7	5	6	5	5	4	3	61
Days With ≥ 1.0" Precipitation	0	0	1	1	2	2	1	1	1	1	1	0	11
Mean Snowfall (in.)	5.5	5.6	2.8	0.3	0.0	0.0	0.0	0.0	0.0	trace	1.6	3.9	19.7
Days With ≥ 1.0" Snow Depth	8	6	1	0	0	0	0	0	0	0	1	3	19

Fall River Lake *Greenwood County*   Elevation: 1,017 ft.   Latitude: 37° 39' N   Longitude: 96° 05' W

	JAN	FEB	MAR	APR	MAY	JUN	JUL	AUG	SEP	OCT	NOV	DEC	YEAR
Mean Maximum Temp. (°F)	39.7	46.3	57.0	68.0	75.6	84.2	90.5	90.0	81.3	70.7	56.4	45.0	67.1
Mean Temp. (°F)	28.8	34.8	45.1	56.2	64.9	73.6	79.1	77.9	69.1	57.7	44.8	34.0	55.5
Mean Minimum Temp. (°F)	17.8	23.2	33.2	44.3	54.0	63.0	67.8	65.8	56.9	44.7	33.2	23.0	43.9
Extreme Maximum Temp. (°F)	73	83	88	97	93	109	111	112	105	99	86	73	112
Extreme Minimum Temp. (°F)	-14	-18	-1	17	32	45	49	48	28	16	1	-18	-18
Days Maximum Temp. ≥ 90°F	0	0	0	1	0	6	17	17	7	1	0	0	49
Days Maximum Temp. ≤ 32°F	9	5	1	0	0	0	0	0	0	0	1	4	20
Days Minimum Temp. ≤ 32°F	28	23	15	3	0	0	0	0	0	2	14	24	109
Days Minimum Temp. ≤ 0°F	2	2	0	0	0	0	0	0	0	0	0	1	5
Heating Degree Days (base 65°F)	1,115	847	613	285	88	8	1	1	58	249	601	*961*	*4,827*
Cooling Degree Days (base 65°F)	0	0	3	26	88	272	451	410	183	26	2	*0*	*1,461*
Mean Precipitation (in.)	0.84	1.28	2.78	3.54	4.66	5.12	3.86	3.74	3.65	3.21	2.62	1.67	36.97
Days With ≥ 0.1" Precipitation	2	3	5	6	7	7	5	5	6	4	4	3	57
Days With ≥ 1.0" Precipitation	0	0	1	1	1	2	1	1	1	1	1	1	11
Mean Snowfall (in.)	na	na	0.7	0.0	0.0	0.0	0.0	0.0	0.0	0.0	0.5	na	na
Days With ≥ 1.0" Snow Depth	na	na	*0*	0	0	0	0	0	0	0	0	na	na

Florence *Marion County*   Elevation: 1,292 ft.   Latitude: 38° 15' N   Longitude: 96° 56' W

	JAN	FEB	MAR	APR	MAY	JUN	JUL	AUG	SEP	OCT	NOV	DEC	YEAR
Mean Maximum Temp. (°F)	40.6	47.8	58.3	68.6	77.1	86.5	92.4	91.0	82.3	71.5	55.8	44.8	68.0
Mean Temp. (°F)	29.7	36.0	45.8	56.1	65.2	74.7	80.2	78.6	69.9	58.5	44.5	34.0	56.1
Mean Minimum Temp. (°F)	18.8	24.1	33.3	43.6	53.4	62.8	67.9	66.2	57.5	45.5	33.1	23.2	44.1
Extreme Maximum Temp. (°F)	76	82	87	95	99	112	112	111	105	95	86	75	112
Extreme Minimum Temp. (°F)	-16	-20	-1	12	27	40	45	45	24	10	-2	-22	-22
Days Maximum Temp. ≥ 90°F	0	0	0	0	1	10	21	18	7	1	0	0	58
Days Maximum Temp. ≤ 32°F	9	5	1	0	0	0	0	0	0	0	1	4	20
Days Minimum Temp. ≤ 32°F	28	22	15	4	0	0	0	0	0	3	16	26	114
Days Minimum Temp. ≤ 0°F	2	2	0	0	0	0	0	0	0	0	0	1	5
Heating Degree Days (base 65°F)	1,088	813	591	287	86	7	1	1	53	231	610	953	4,721
Cooling Degree Days (base 65°F)	0	0	3	28	97	301	476	424	211	35	2	0	1,577
Mean Precipitation (in.)	0.82	0.92	2.47	2.92	4.66	4.55	3.68	3.34	3.40	2.50	2.13	1.08	32.47
Days With ≥ 0.1" Precipitation	2	2	4	5	7	6	5	5	5	4	3	2	50
Days With ≥ 1.0" Precipitation	0	0	1	1	2	2	1	1	1	1	1	0	11
Mean Snowfall (in.)	na	na	*0.6*	0.2	0.0	0.0	0.0	0.0	0.0	trace	0.7	na	na
Days With ≥ 1.0" Snow Depth	na	na	*0*	0	0	0	0	0	0	0	0	na	na

Fort Scott *Bourbon County*   Elevation: 843 ft.   Latitude: 37° 51' N   Longitude: 94° 43' W

	JAN	FEB	MAR	APR	MAY	JUN	JUL	AUG	SEP	OCT	NOV	DEC	YEAR
Mean Maximum Temp. (°F)	40.2	47.6	58.3	69.0	77.7	86.5	92.0	90.8	82.3	71.4	56.1	44.9	68.1
Mean Temp. (°F)	30.6	37.1	47.2	57.3	66.8	75.9	81.1	79.3	70.8	59.4	46.2	35.5	57.3
Mean Minimum Temp. (°F)	21.0	26.6	36.0	45.6	55.8	65.3	70.1	67.9	59.2	47.5	36.2	26.1	46.5
Extreme Maximum Temp. (°F)	73	82	91	97	96	105	110	106	102	95	84	74	110
Extreme Minimum Temp. (°F)	-14	-14	1	17	30	46	50	48	30	18	4	-18	-18
Days Maximum Temp. ≥ 90°F	0	0	0	0	1	11	22	19	8	1	0	0	62
Days Maximum Temp. ≤ 32°F	9	5	1	0	0	0	0	0	0	0	1	5	21
Days Minimum Temp. ≤ 32°F	26	20	12	3	0	0	0	0	0	2	12	23	98
Days Minimum Temp. ≤ 0°F	2	1	0	0	0	0	0	0	0	0	0	1	4
Heating Degree Days (base 65°F)	1,059	782	552	261	65	4	0	1	47	211	562	907	4,451
Cooling Degree Days (base 65°F)	0	0	6	33	121	335	503	445	220	38	4	0	1,705
Mean Precipitation (in.)	1.57	1.79	3.24	4.19	4.93	5.67	4.24	3.87	4.86	4.26	3.44	2.09	44.15
Days With ≥ 0.1" Precipitation	4	4	6	6	8	7	6	5	6	6	5	4	67
Days With ≥ 1.0" Precipitation	0	0	1	1	1	2	1	1	1	1	1	1	11
Mean Snowfall (in.)	5.4	4.3	1.7	trace	0.0	0.0	0.0	0.0	0.0	trace	1.2	2.6	15.2
Days With ≥ 1.0" Snow Depth	8	5	1	0	0	0	0	0	0	0	1	3	18

Garden City Exp. Station *Finney County*   Elevation: 2,867 ft.   Latitude: 38° 00' N   Longitude: 100° 49' W

	JAN	FEB	MAR	APR	MAY	JUN	JUL	AUG	SEP	OCT	NOV	DEC	YEAR
Mean Maximum Temp. (°F)	41.6	47.7	56.2	66.2	75.2	86.2	91.3	88.7	81.0	70.0	54.5	45.1	67.0
Mean Temp. (°F)	28.1	33.3	41.9	51.7	61.9	72.4	77.3	75.3	66.7	54.3	40.5	31.5	52.9
Mean Minimum Temp. (°F)	14.5	18.8	27.5	37.2	48.6	58.5	63.3	61.9	52.4	38.7	26.4	17.9	38.8
Extreme Maximum Temp. (°F)	78	86	91	99	103	108	106	104	103	95	88	77	108
Extreme Minimum Temp. (°F)	-22	-19	-7	9	29	38	45	44	25	12	-5	-17	-22
Days Maximum Temp. ≥ 90°F	0	0	0	1	2	12	20	16	8	1	0	0	60
Days Maximum Temp. ≤ 32°F	9	5	3	0	0	0	0	0	0	0	2	6	25
Days Minimum Temp. ≤ 32°F	31	27	22	9	1	0	0	0	0	7	24	30	151
Days Minimum Temp. ≤ 0°F	3	2	0	0	0	0	0	0	0	0	0	2	7
Heating Degree Days (base 65°F)	1,138	887	711	402	152	23	2	4	88	336	729	1,032	5,504
Cooling Degree Days (base 65°F)	0	0	0	12	64	247	395	342	157	14	0	0	1,231
Mean Precipitation (in.)	0.41	0.48	1.31	1.65	3.42	2.88	2.58	2.60	1.32	0.88	0.83	0.41	18.77
Days With ≥ 0.1" Precipitation	1	1	3	4	6	5	5	5	3	2	2	1	38
Days With ≥ 1.0" Precipitation	0	0	0	0	1	1	1	1	0	0	0	0	4
Mean Snowfall (in.)	4.3	3.8	5.0	1.2	trace	0.0	0.0	0.0	trace	0.7	2.2	*3.1*	*20.3*
Days With ≥ 1.0" Snow Depth	na	*3*	na	0	0	0	0	0	0	0	0	1	na

Garden City Municipal Airport *Finney County*   Elevation: 2,880 ft.   Latitude: 37° 56' N   Longitude: 100° 43' W

	JAN	FEB	MAR	APR	MAY	JUN	JUL	AUG	SEP	OCT	NOV	DEC	YEAR
Mean Maximum Temp. (°F)	42.1	49.0	58.0	68.3	76.5	87.8	93.3	91.0	82.3	70.8	54.9	45.4	68.3
Mean Temp. (°F)	28.9	34.7	43.5	53.6	63.2	73.9	79.1	77.3	68.2	55.7	40.9	32.1	54.3
Mean Minimum Temp. (°F)	15.6	20.3	29.1	38.8	49.9	60.0	64.9	63.6	54.0	40.5	26.9	18.6	40.2
Extreme Maximum Temp. (°F)	79	88	93	100	105	110	109	108	103	97	91	78	110
Extreme Minimum Temp. (°F)	-19	-17	-6	13	28	42	46	46	26	13	-5	-17	-19
Days Maximum Temp. ≥ 90°F	0	0	0	1	3	13	22	19	9	1	0	0	68
Days Maximum Temp. ≤ 32°F	9	5	2	0	0	0	0	0	0	0	2	6	24
Days Minimum Temp. ≤ 32°F	31	26	20	7	0	0	0	0	0	5	23	29	141
Days Minimum Temp. ≤ 0°F	3	1	0	0	0	0	0	0	0	0	0	1	5
Heating Degree Days (base 65°F)	1,111	849	659	351	125	14	1	2	72	302	716	1,015	5,217
Cooling Degree Days (base 65°F)	0	0	0	16	75	271	425	385	176	18	0	*0*	*1,366*
Mean Precipitation (in.)	0.40	0.52	1.59	1.86	3.20	3.13	3.27	2.53	1.42	0.90	0.89	0.45	20.16
Days With ≥ 0.1" Precipitation	1	2	3	4	6	5	5	5	3	2	2	1	39
Days With ≥ 1.0" Precipitation	0	0	0	0	1	1	1	1	0	0	0	0	4
Mean Snowfall (in.)	4.8	3.7	4.9	1.4	trace	trace	trace	0.0	0.1	0.5	2.4	3.1	20.9
Days With ≥ 1.0" Snow Depth	9	5	3	1	0	0	0	0	0	0	2	5	25

Garnett 1 E *Anderson County*   Elevation: 977 ft.   Latitude: 38° 17' N   Longitude: 95° 14' W

	JAN	FEB	MAR	APR	MAY	JUN	JUL	AUG	SEP	OCT	NOV	DEC	YEAR
Mean Maximum Temp. (°F)	40.3	47.1	58.3	68.6	77.0	85.3	91.0	89.7	81.7	70.7	55.5	44.5	67.5
Mean Temp. (°F)	30.0	36.0	46.3	56.4	65.6	74.2	79.6	78.0	69.9	58.7	45.1	34.7	56.2
Mean Minimum Temp. (°F)	19.8	24.8	34.2	44.2	54.0	63.1	68.1	66.3	58.0	46.6	34.7	24.9	44.9
Extreme Maximum Temp. (°F)	72	82	88	91	93	107	111	108	103	96	86	70	111
Extreme Minimum Temp. (°F)	-15	-17	-3	15	29	42	48	44	28	18	4	-23	-23
Days Maximum Temp. ≥ 90°F	0	0	0	0	1	8	19	17	6	0	0	0	51
Days Maximum Temp. ≤ 32°F	9	5	1	0	0	0	0	0	0	0	1	4	20
Days Minimum Temp. ≤ 32°F	27	21	14	3	0	0	0	0	0	2	13	24	104
Days Minimum Temp. ≤ 0°F	2	1	0	0	0	0	0	0	0	0	0	1	4
Heating Degree Days (base 65°F)	1,077	815	577	277	76	7	0	1	49	222	591	933	4,625
Cooling Degree Days (base 65°F)	0	0	3	27	97	291	460	410	203	32	2	0	1,525
Mean Precipitation (in.)	1.36	1.43	2.86	3.83	4.93	5.46	3.96	4.19	4.27	3.95	2.69	1.84	40.77
Days With ≥ 0.1" Precipitation	4	3	5	6	7	7	5	5	6	5	4	3	60
Days With ≥ 1.0" Precipitation	0	0	1	1	2	2	1	1	1	1	1	1	12
Mean Snowfall (in.)	5.6	4.6	2.1	0.1	0.0	0.0	0.0	0.0	0.0	0.2	1.1	3.6	17.3
Days With ≥ 1.0" Snow Depth	7	5	1	0	0	0	0	0	0	0	0	3	16

Girard *Crawford County*   Elevation: 984 ft.   Latitude: 37° 30' N   Longitude: 94° 50' W

	JAN	FEB	MAR	APR	MAY	JUN	JUL	AUG	SEP	OCT	NOV	DEC	YEAR
Mean Maximum Temp. (°F)	41.1	47.8	57.9	68.7	77.0	86.2	91.3	90.4	81.5	71.1	56.3	45.7	67.9
Mean Temp. (°F)	31.3	37.4	46.8	57.1	66.2	75.4	80.2	78.8	70.4	59.3	46.2	36.1	57.1
Mean Minimum Temp. (°F)	21.5	26.8	35.7	45.5	55.4	64.5	69.1	67.1	59.2	47.6	36.0	26.4	46.2
Extreme Maximum Temp. (°F)	72	80	89	97	93	103	110	107	103	94	81	75	110
Extreme Minimum Temp. (°F)	-12	-16	2	20	32	47	52	49	32	19	5	-18	-18
Days Maximum Temp. ≥ 90°F	0	0	0	0	1	10	20	18	6	0	0	0	55
Days Maximum Temp. ≤ 32°F	8	4	1	0	0	0	0	0	0	0	1	4	18
Days Minimum Temp. ≤ 32°F	26	20	12	2	0	0	0	0	0	1	12	23	96
Days Minimum Temp. ≤ 0°F	1	1	0	0	0	0	0	0	0	0	0	1	3
Heating Degree Days (base 65°F)	1,042	774	560	257	65	3	0	1	45	211	561	890	4,409
Cooling Degree Days (base 65°F)	0	0	4	25	104	322	480	437	210	37	3	0	1,622
Mean Precipitation (in.)	1.64	1.95	3.65	4.28	5.47	5.41	4.13	3.74	5.44	4.27	3.64	2.38	46.00
Days With ≥ 0.1" Precipitation	3	3	6	6	8	7	5	5	5	6	5	4	63
Days With ≥ 1.0" Precipitation	0	1	1	1	2	2	1	1	2	1	1	1	14
Mean Snowfall (in.)	*1.9*	*2.4*	0.7	trace	0.0	0.0	0.0	0.0	0.0	0.0	0.2	*0.8*	*6.0*
Days With ≥ 1.0" Snow Depth	na	na	*0*	0	0	0	0	0	0	0	0	*1*	na

Glen Elder Lake *Mitchell County*   Elevation: 1,499 ft.   Latitude: 39° 30' N   Longitude: 98° 19' W

	JAN	FEB	MAR	APR	MAY	JUN	JUL	AUG	SEP	OCT	NOV	DEC	YEAR
Mean Maximum Temp. (°F)	36.4	43.1	53.5	64.5	73.9	85.0	91.4	89.0	80.5	68.4	52.0	41.1	64.9
Mean Temp. (°F)	25.1	30.6	40.7	51.6	61.8	72.5	78.6	76.3	67.2	54.7	40.1	30.1	52.4
Mean Minimum Temp. (°F)	13.6	18.1	27.9	38.7	49.6	60.0	65.7	63.6	53.8	41.0	28.3	19.0	39.9
Extreme Maximum Temp. (°F)	70	81	87	100	97	108	111	109	104	95	83	74	111
Extreme Minimum Temp. (°F)	-22	-16	-10	13	28	41	46	45	25	14	-9	-27	-27
Days Maximum Temp. ≥ 90°F	0	0	0	0	1	9	19	16	7	1	0	0	53
Days Maximum Temp. ≤ 32°F	12	8	2	0	0	0	0	0	0	0	2	7	31
Days Minimum Temp. ≤ 32°F	31	26	21	7	0	0	0	0	0	5	21	30	141
Days Minimum Temp. ≤ 0°F	5	3	0	0	0	0	0	0	0	0	0	2	10
Heating Degree Days (base 65°F)	1,231	965	745	406	152	17	1	3	87	328	738	1,076	5,749
Cooling Degree Days (base 65°F)	0	0	1	13	58	245	427	358	163	16	0	0	1,281
Mean Precipitation (in.)	0.62	0.58	1.97	2.33	3.77	3.66	3.85	2.97	2.48	1.85	1.47	0.75	26.30
Days With ≥ 0.1" Precipitation	2	1	3	5	7	6	5	5	5	3	3	2	47
Days With ≥ 1.0" Precipitation	0	0	0	0	1	1	1	1	1	0	0	0	5
Mean Snowfall (in.)	*5.1*	3.3	2.5	0.4	0.0	0.0	0.0	0.0	0.0	0.1	1.7	*2.4*	*15.5*
Days With ≥ 1.0" Snow Depth	*11*	*7*	*2*	0	0	0	0	0	0	0	2	5	*27*

Great Bend *Barton County*   Elevation: 1,856 ft.   Latitude: 38° 22' N   Longitude: 98° 46' W

	JAN	FEB	MAR	APR	MAY	JUN	JUL	AUG	SEP	OCT	NOV	DEC	YEAR
Mean Maximum Temp. (°F)	41.9	49.1	58.3	69.2	78.0	88.6	94.1	92.0	83.4	72.1	55.7	45.2	69.0
Mean Temp. (°F)	30.9	36.8	45.7	56.1	65.8	76.0	81.3	79.4	70.5	58.8	44.2	34.3	56.6
Mean Minimum Temp. (°F)	19.8	24.4	33.0	43.0	53.5	63.3	68.4	66.7	57.7	45.5	32.5	23.3	44.3
Extreme Maximum Temp. (°F)	79	85	91	101	100	111	111	110	105	95	86	75	111
Extreme Minimum Temp. (°F)	-17	-16	-2	14	32	39	48	48	29	16	1	-21	-21
Days Maximum Temp. ≥ 90°F	0	0	0	1	3	15	23	21	10	1	0	0	74
Days Maximum Temp. ≤ 32°F	7	4	1	0	0	0	0	0	0	0	1	4	17
Days Minimum Temp. ≤ 32°F	28	22	15	4	0	0	0	0	0	2	15	27	113
Days Minimum Temp. ≤ 0°F	2	1	0	0	0	0	0	0	0	0	0	1	4
Heating Degree Days (base 65°F)	1,051	791	596	288	82	8	0	1	50	223	619	946	4,655
Cooling Degree Days (base 65°F)	0	0	3	30	113	336	504	446	227	36	2	0	1,696
Mean Precipitation (in.)	0.68	0.80	2.07	2.34	3.76	3.85	3.23	3.14	2.29	2.12	1.15	0.85	26.28
Days With ≥ 0.1" Precipitation	2	2	4	5	6	5	5	5	4	3	2	2	45
Days With ≥ 1.0" Precipitation	0	0	1	0	1	1	1	1	1	1	0	0	7
Mean Snowfall (in.)	5.2	5.1	3.2	0.8	0.0	0.0	0.0	0.0	0.0	0.5	1.0	3.3	19.1
Days With ≥ 1.0" Snow Depth	9	5	2	0	0	0	0	0	0	0	1	5	22

Greensburg *Kiowa County*   Elevation: 2,227 ft.   Latitude: 37° 37' N   Longitude: 99° 18' W

	JAN	FEB	MAR	APR	MAY	JUN	JUL	AUG	SEP	OCT	NOV	DEC	YEAR
Mean Maximum Temp. (°F)	41.0	47.9	57.0	67.1	76.5	86.7	92.4	90.5	80.9	69.8	54.4	44.4	67.4
Mean Temp. (°F)	29.8	35.6	44.1	54.2	64.3	74.3	79.8	77.8	68.6	56.8	42.4	33.1	55.1
Mean Minimum Temp. (°F)	18.5	23.3	31.2	41.2	52.1	61.8	67.2	65.1	56.3	43.7	30.3	21.7	42.7
Extreme Maximum Temp. (°F)	80	85	91	101	103	109	110	107	106	95	86	74	110
Extreme Minimum Temp. (°F)	-13	-12	-4	14	31	41	48	46	23	15	0	-20	-20
Days Maximum Temp. ≥ 90°F	0	0	0	1	3	12	21	18	7	1	0	0	63
Days Maximum Temp. ≤ 32°F	9	5	2	0	0	0	0	0	0	0	2	6	24
Days Minimum Temp. ≤ 32°F	29	23	17	5	0	0	0	0	0	3	18	28	123
Days Minimum Temp. ≤ 0°F	2	1	0	0	0	0	0	0	0	0	0	1	4
Heating Degree Days (base 65°F)	1,086	823	643	340	108	13	1	2	71	276	673	983	5,019
Cooling Degree Days (base 65°F)	0	0	2	23	92	286	468	405	188	24	1	0	1,489
Mean Precipitation (in.)	0.57	0.69	1.87	2.14	3.36	4.10	3.19	2.78	2.50	1.73	1.09	0.74	24.76
Days With ≥ 0.1" Precipitation	2	1	4	4	6	6	5	5	4	3	2	2	44
Days With ≥ 1.0" Precipitation	0	0	0	0	1	1	1	1	1	1	0	0	6
Mean Snowfall (in.)	4.3	3.7	3.6	0.5	0.0	0.0	0.0	0.0	0.0	0.5	1.4	3.4	17.4
Days With ≥ 1.0" Snow Depth	6	3	2	0	0	0	0	0	0	0	1	2	14

Hays 1 S *Ellis County*   Elevation: 2,007 ft.   Latitude: 38° 52' N   Longitude: 99° 20' W

	JAN	FEB	MAR	APR	MAY	JUN	JUL	AUG	SEP	OCT	NOV	DEC	YEAR
Mean Maximum Temp. (°F)	39.6	46.3	55.1	66.1	74.8	86.2	92.5	90.2	81.4	69.9	53.7	43.6	66.6
Mean Temp. (°F)	27.1	32.9	41.7	52.8	62.6	73.4	79.1	77.0	67.8	55.3	40.6	31.1	53.5
Mean Minimum Temp. (°F)	14.5	19.5	28.3	39.5	50.4	60.6	65.6	63.7	54.1	40.6	27.5	18.5	40.2
Extreme Maximum Temp. (°F)	79	88	90	107	101	110	113	111	106	100	87	79	113
Extreme Minimum Temp. (°F)	-19	-14	-6	11	28	36	45	44	25	9	-3	-20	-20
Days Maximum Temp. ≥ 90°F	0	0	0	1	2	11	20	18	9	1	0	0	62
Days Maximum Temp. ≤ 32°F	10	6	2	0	0	0	0	0	0	0	2	7	27
Days Minimum Temp. ≤ 32°F	31	26	20	7	0	0	0	0	1	6	22	30	143
Days Minimum Temp. ≤ 0°F	4	2	0	0	0	0	0	0	0	0	0	2	8
Heating Degree Days (base 65°F)	1,170	899	715	375	139	18	2	3	85	316	725	1,045	5,492
Cooling Degree Days (base 65°F)	0	0	1	19	76	283	448	388	185	23	0	0	1,423
Mean Precipitation (in.)	0.51	0.63	1.87	2.17	3.12	2.77	3.61	2.98	1.68	1.34	1.18	0.64	22.50
Days With ≥ 0.1" Precipitation	1	2	4	5	6	5	5	5	4	3	2	2	44
Days With ≥ 1.0" Precipitation	0	0	0	0	1	1	1	1	0	0	0	0	4
Mean Snowfall (in.)	4.7	4.3	4.5	1.1	0.0	0.0	0.0	0.0	0.1	0.3	1.8	4.0	20.8
Days With ≥ 1.0" Snow Depth	10	8	3	1	0	0	0	0	0	0	2	6	30

Healy *Lane County*   Elevation: 2,847 ft.   Latitude: 38° 36' N   Longitude: 100° 37' W

	JAN	FEB	MAR	APR	MAY	JUN	JUL	AUG	SEP	OCT	NOV	DEC	YEAR
Mean Maximum Temp. (°F)	42.2	48.5	57.1	66.9	75.8	87.4	93.0	90.6	81.8	70.4	54.2	45.5	67.8
Mean Temp. (°F)	28.7	34.2	42.4	52.0	62.1	73.3	78.4	76.5	67.2	54.8	40.5	32.1	53.5
Mean Minimum Temp. (°F)	15.2	19.8	27.6	37.1	48.3	59.0	63.7	62.4	52.4	39.2	26.8	18.6	39.2
Extreme Maximum Temp. (°F)	80	87	92	100	100	112	113	110	105	96	86	80	113
Extreme Minimum Temp. (°F)	-19	-21	-4	8	28	34	44	44	24	11	-8	-25	-25
Days Maximum Temp. ≥ 90°F	0	0	0	0	3	13	22	19	8	1	0	0	67
Days Maximum Temp. ≤ 32°F	8	5	2	0	0	0	0	0	0	0	0	0	22
Days Minimum Temp. ≤ 32°F	31	26	22	10	1	0	0	0	1	6	23	30	150
Days Minimum Temp. ≤ 0°F	3	2	0	0	0	0	0	0	0	0	0	2	7
Heating Degree Days (base 65°F)	1,117	863	694	393	144	19	1	3	83	324	728	1,014	5,383
Cooling Degree Days (base 65°F)	0	0	1	11	59	262	408	357	154	16	0	0	1,268
Mean Precipitation (in.)	0.57	0.61	1.51	1.90	3.32	2.84	3.23	2.76	1.78	1.17	1.17	0.51	21.37
Days With > 0.1" Precipitation	2	2	3	4	6	5	5	4	3	2	2	2	40
Days With ≥ 1.0" Precipitation	0	0	0	0	1	1	1	1	0	0	0	0	4
Mean Snowfall (in.)	4.8	4.7	5.8	2.7	trace	0.0	0.0	0.0	0.2	1.1	3.5	3.6	26.4
Days With ≥ 1.0" Snow Depth	10	7	4	1	0	0	0	0	0	1	3	7	33

Herington *Dickinson County*   Elevation: 1,348 ft.   Latitude: 38° 40' N   Longitude: 96° 57' W

	JAN	FEB	MAR	APR	MAY	JUN	JUL	AUG	SEP	OCT	NOV	DEC	YEAR
Mean Maximum Temp. (°F)	38.6	45.9	56.6	67.4	76.4	86.1	91.6	90.1	81.6	70.1	54.0	42.8	66.8
Mean Temp. (°F)	27.8	34.1	44.3	54.7	64.3	74.1	79.3	77.7	68.9	57.1	42.8	32.2	54.8
Mean Minimum Temp. (°F)	16.9	22.2	31.9	42.1	52.1	62.0	67.0	65.2	56.2	44.0	31.6	21.5	42.7
Extreme Maximum Temp. (°F)	78	82	86	96	99	111	111	109	105	95	87	75	111
Extreme Minimum Temp. (°F)	-19	-17	-9	8	26	38	44	46	28	11	-3	-23	-23
Days Maximum Temp. ≥ 90°F	0	0	0	0	1	10	20	17	7	1	0	0	56
Days Maximum Temp. ≤ 32°F	10	6	1	0	0	0	0	0	0	0	1	5	23
Days Minimum Temp. ≤ 32°F	29	23	16	5	0	0	0	0	0	4	16	27	120
Days Minimum Temp. ≤ 0°F	3	2	0	0	0	0	0	0	0	0	0	1	6
Heating Degree Days (base 65°F)	1,146	865	638	323	105	11	1	1	66	267	660	1,010	5,093
Cooling Degree Days (base 65°F)	0	0	2	24	84	289	458	400	193	27	1	0	1,478
Mean Precipitation (in.)	0.98	1.15	2.93	3.34	4.94	4.89	4.01	3.84	3.52	2.74	2.32	1.30	35.96
Days With ≥ 0.1" Precipitation	3	3	5	6	8	6	6	5	5	4	4	3	58
Days With ≥ 1.0" Precipitation	0	0	1	1	2	2	1	1	1	1	1	0	11
Mean Snowfall (in.)	6.9	5.2	4.0	1.6	0.0	0.0	0.0	0.0	0.0	0.3	2.5	4.6	25.1
Days With ≥ 1.0" Snow Depth	11	6	2	1	0	0	0	0	0	0	1	5	26

Holton 1 S *Jackson County*   Elevation: 1,118 ft.   Latitude: 39° 27' N   Longitude: 95° 44' W

	JAN	FEB	MAR	APR	MAY	JUN	JUL	AUG	SEP	OCT	NOV	DEC	YEAR
Mean Maximum Temp. (°F)	37.3	43.9	55.5	66.8	75.9	84.9	90.2	88.5	80.4	69.0	53.1	41.3	65.6
Mean Temp. (°F)	26.9	32.7	43.5	54.6	64.2	73.5	78.4	76.5	68.1	56.5	42.5	31.4	54.1
Mean Minimum Temp. (°F)	16.5	21.4	31.5	42.3	52.4	62.0	66.5	64.5	55.8	44.0	31.9	21.4	42.5
Extreme Maximum Temp. (°F)	71	81	88	93	96	109	110	110	102	93	85	71	110
Extreme Minimum Temp. (°F)	-21	-22	-21	5	22	40	43	46	29	14	-7	-23	-23
Days Maximum Temp. ≥ 90°F	0	0	0	0	1	8	16	14	5	0	0	0	44
Days Maximum Temp. ≤ 32°F	11	7	1	0	0	0	0	0	0	0	1	7	27
Days Minimum Temp. ≤ 32°F	28	23	17	5	0	0	0	0	0	4	16	27	120
Days Minimum Temp. ≤ 0°F	4	2	0	0	0	0	0	0	0	0	0	2	8
Heating Degree Days (base 65°F)	1,174	906	661	331	102	10	1	1	69	282	668	1,035	5,240
Cooling Degree Days (base 65°F)	0	0	4	27	84	273	431	376	177	27	1	0	1,400
Mean Precipitation (in.)	0.97	1.03	2.48	3.54	5.02	4.97	4.15	4.22	4.86	3.21	2.36	1.41	38.22
Days With ≥ 0.1" Precipitation	3	3	5	6	8	7	6	6	5	5	4	3	61
Days With ≥ 1.0" Precipitation	0	0	1	1	2	2	1	1	2	1	1	0	12
Mean Snowfall (in.)	6.3	4.5	2.5	0.3	trace	0.0	0.0	0.0	0.0	0.2	1.1	3.3	18.2
Days With ≥ 1.0" Snow Depth	na	na	1	0	0	0	0	0	0	0	0	1	3	na

Horton *Brown County*   Elevation: 1,026 ft.   Latitude: 39° 40' N   Longitude: 95° 31' W

	JAN	FEB	MAR	APR	MAY	JUN	JUL	AUG	SEP	OCT	NOV	DEC	YEAR
Mean Maximum Temp. (°F)	36.8	43.9	55.7	67.5	77.2	86.4	91.3	89.5	81.4	69.7	52.8	40.8	66.1
Mean Temp. (°F)	26.2	32.6	43.6	55.0	65.0	74.4	79.2	77.2	68.8	56.9	42.4	31.0	54.4
Mean Minimum Temp. (°F)	15.6	21.2	31.5	42.4	52.8	62.4	67.0	64.9	56.2	44.2	31.9	21.1	42.6
Extreme Maximum Temp. (°F)	71	82	89	95	95	107	110	109	102	96	84	71	110
Extreme Minimum Temp. (°F)	-22	-26	-18	3	28	42	44	45	28	15	-5	-27	-27
Days Maximum Temp. ≥ 90°F	0	0	0	0	2	11	19	16	6	0	0	0	54
Days Maximum Temp. ≤ 32°F	11	7	1	0	0	0	0	0	0	0	1	6	26
Days Minimum Temp. ≤ 32°F	29	24	17	6	0	0	0	0	0	4	16	27	123
Days Minimum Temp. ≤ 0°F	5	2	0	0	0	0	0	0	0	0	0	2	9
Heating Degree Days (base 65°F)	1,196	909	658	320	90	6	1	1	59	269	673	1,047	5,229
Cooling Degree Days (base 65°F)	0	0	3	28	96	299	456	392	186	27	1	0	1,488
Mean Precipitation (in.)	0.89	1.16	2.45	3.71	5.08	4.69	4.36	3.84	4.52	3.08	2.28	1.39	37.45
Days With ≥ 0.1" Precipitation	3	3	5	7	8	7	6	6	6	5	4	3	63
Days With ≥ 1.0" Precipitation	0	0	1	1	1	1	1	1	2	1	1	0	10
Mean Snowfall (in.)	4.7	4.6	2.5	0.4	0.0	0.0	0.0	0.0	0.0	0.1	1.0	2.6	15.9
Days With ≥ 1.0" Snow Depth	9	7	2	0	0	0	0	0	0	0	1	5	24

Howard 5 NE *Elk County*   Elevation: 1,099 ft.   Latitude: 37° 31' N   Longitude: 96° 12' W

	JAN	FEB	MAR	APR	MAY	JUN	JUL	AUG	SEP	OCT	NOV	DEC	YEAR
Mean Maximum Temp. (°F)	42.5	49.5	59.7	70.0	77.6	85.8	92.1	91.6	83.3	72.4	57.3	46.3	69.0
Mean Temp. (°F)	31.3	37.3	47.1	57.3	66.0	74.5	79.9	78.7	70.6	59.3	45.7	35.4	56.9
Mean Minimum Temp. (°F)	20.1	25.1	34.4	44.6	54.3	63.2	67.6	65.7	57.8	46.1	34.1	24.4	44.8
Extreme Maximum Temp. (°F)	74	84	86	97	96	107	110	108	107	96	85	74	110
Extreme Minimum Temp. (°F)	-16	-15	-2	15	28	43	47	43	27	13	-3	-17	-17
Days Maximum Temp. ≥ 90°F	0	0	0	1	1	9	21	20	8	1	0	0	61
Days Maximum Temp. ≤ 32°F	7	4	1	0	0	0	0	0	0	0	1	3	16
Days Minimum Temp. ≤ 32°F	28	21	13	3	0	0	0	0	0	3	14	25	107
Days Minimum Temp. ≤ 0°F	2	1	0	0	0	0	0	0	0	0	0	1	4
Heating Degree Days (base 65°F)	1,036	776	552	256	70	5	0	0	44	209	574	912	4,434
Cooling Degree Days (base 65°F)	0	0	4	31	108	303	479	439	225	37	3	0	1,629
Mean Precipitation (in.)	1.01	1.44	2.84	3.56	4.84	4.98	3.69	3.53	3.95	3.27	2.74	1.77	37.62
Days With ≥ 0.1" Precipitation	2	3	5	6	7	6	5	5	5	5	4	3	56
Days With ≥ 1.0" Precipitation	0	0	1	1	1	1	1	1	1	1	1	0	9
Mean Snowfall (in.)	5.0	3.5	2.0	0.1	0.0	0.0	0.0	0.0	0.0	trace	1.0	2.0	13.6
Days With ≥ 1.0" Snow Depth	8	5	1	0	0	0	0	0	0	0	1	3	18

Hoxie *Sheridan County*   Elevation: 2,703 ft.   Latitude: 39° 22' N   Longitude: 100° 27' W

	JAN	FEB	MAR	APR	MAY	JUN	JUL	AUG	SEP	OCT	NOV	DEC	YEAR
Mean Maximum Temp. (°F)	41.4	47.9	56.5	66.9	75.7	86.7	92.1	90.1	81.8	70.3	53.0	44.0	67.2
Mean Temp. (°F)	28.7	34.1	42.1	52.2	62.1	72.5	77.9	76.1	67.1	54.8	39.8	31.5	53.2
Mean Minimum Temp. (°F)	15.9	20.2	27.6	37.5	48.4	58.1	63.7	62.0	52.3	39.2	26.6	19.0	39.2
Extreme Maximum Temp. (°F)	79	85	91	100	98	109	109	109	105	97	88	77	109
Extreme Minimum Temp. (°F)	-20	-18	-6	10	28	36	45	42	25	9	-2	-28	-28
Days Maximum Temp. ≥ 90°F	0	0	0	1	2	12	20	18	9	1	0	0	63
Days Maximum Temp. ≤ 32°F	8	5	2	0	0	0	0	0	0	0	2	6	23
Days Minimum Temp. ≤ 32°F	30	26	22	9	1	0	0	0	1	7	23	29	148
Days Minimum Temp. ≤ 0°F	3	2	1	0	0	0	0	0	0	0	0	2	8
Heating Degree Days (base 65°F)	1,120	867	705	390	146	19	2	4	85	325	749	1,032	5,444
Cooling Degree Days (base 65°F)	0	0	1	13	58	239	393	343	147	13	0	0	1,207
Mean Precipitation (in.)	0.52	0.56	1.50	2.10	3.74	2.67	3.38	3.05	1.50	1.08	1.03	0.45	21.58
Days With ≥ 0.1" Precipitation	1	2	4	4	7	5	6	5	3	3	2	2	44
Days With ≥ 1.0" Precipitation	0	0	0	0	1	0	1	1	0	0	0	0	3
Mean Snowfall (in.)	5.4	4.8	6.2	2.1	0.0	0.0	0.0	0.0	0.3	1.5	2.7	3.9	26.9
Days With ≥ 1.0" Snow Depth	8	6	3	1	0	0	0	0	0	0	2	6	26

Hudson *Stafford County*   Elevation: 1,866 ft.   Latitude: 38° 06' N   Longitude: 98° 40' W

	JAN	FEB	MAR	APR	MAY	JUN	JUL	AUG	SEP	OCT	NOV	DEC	YEAR
Mean Maximum Temp. (°F)	41.6	48.7	58.2	68.8	77.7	88.9	94.3	92.1	82.8	71.3	55.4	45.1	68.7
Mean Temp. (°F)	30.9	36.9	46.0	56.2	65.8	76.1	81.4	79.5	70.6	58.8	44.3	34.6	56.8
Mean Minimum Temp. (°F)	20.2	25.1	33.7	43.6	53.8	63.4	68.5	66.8	58.4	46.1	33.2	24.2	44.7
Extreme Maximum Temp. (°F)	77	84	88	102	103	111	109	108	105	97	86	74	111
Extreme Minimum Temp. (°F)	-15	-15	-4	16	33	44	50	51	28	19	1	-18	-18
Days Maximum Temp. ≥ 90°F	0	0	0	1	3	15	24	20	9	1	0	0	73
Days Maximum Temp. ≤ 32°F	8	5	1	0	0	0	0	0	0	0	1	5	20
Days Minimum Temp. ≤ 32°F	28	21	14	3	0	0	0	0	0	2	14	26	108
Days Minimum Temp. ≤ 0°F	2	1	0	0	0	0	0	0	0	0	0	1	4
Heating Degree Days (base 65°F)	1,051	786	587	284	80	6	0	1	48	224	615	934	4,616
Cooling Degree Days (base 65°F)	0	0	3	31	116	355	527	470	239	37	1	0	1,779
Mean Precipitation (in.)	0.66	0.79	2.18	2.44	4.00	3.47	3.04	2.66	2.36	1.96	1.23	0.90	25.69
Days With ≥ 0.1" Precipitation	2	2	4	5	6	6	5	5	4	3	3	2	47
Days With ≥ 1.0" Precipitation	0	0	1	1	1	1	1	1	0	1	0	0	7
Mean Snowfall (in.)	5.2	4.7	3.2	1.0	0.0	0.0	0.0	0.0	trace	0.4	1.2	3.4	19.1
Days With ≥ 1.0" Snow Depth	5	4	1	0	0	0	0	0	0	0	1	3	14

Hugoton *Stevens County*   Elevation: 3,106 ft.   Latitude: 37° 10' N   Longitude: 101° 20' W

	JAN	FEB	MAR	APR	MAY	JUN	JUL	AUG	SEP	OCT	NOV	DEC	YEAR
Mean Maximum Temp. (°F)	45.1	51.3	59.1	68.3	77.2	88.1	92.7	90.3	81.8	71.5	56.9	47.7	69.2
Mean Temp. (°F)	31.8	37.2	44.5	53.9	63.8	74.2	79.1	77.0	68.3	56.8	43.1	34.3	55.3
Mean Minimum Temp. (°F)	18.3	22.9	30.0	39.5	50.3	60.3	65.4	63.6	54.9	42.0	29.0	20.9	41.4
Extreme Maximum Temp. (°F)	80	87	91	99	104	112	109	107	104	96	90	79	112
Extreme Minimum Temp. (°F)	-18	-13	-3	15	29	42	52	48	29	13	-4	-13	-18
Days Maximum Temp. ≥ 90°F	0	0	0	1	4	14	21	18	8	1	0	0	67
Days Maximum Temp. ≤ 32°F	7	3	1	0	0	0	0	0	0	0	1	4	16
Days Minimum Temp. ≤ 32°F	30	24	18	6	0	0	0	0	0	4	21	29	132
Days Minimum Temp. ≤ 0°F	2	1	0	0	0	0	0	0	0	0	0	1	4
Heating Degree Days (base 65°F)	1,022	779	629	341	115	13	1	1	65	273	651	946	4,836
Cooling Degree Days (base 65°F)	0	0	1	16	83	283	440	382	174	22	0	0	1,401
Mean Precipitation (in.)	0.41	0.38	1.16	1.67	3.00	2.81	2.67	2.13	1.70	1.07	0.87	0.44	18.31
Days With ≥ 0.1" Precipitation	1	1	3	3	5	5	5	4	3	2	2	1	35
Days With ≥ 1.0" Precipitation	0	0	0	0	1	1	1	0	0	0	0	0	3
Mean Snowfall (in.)	na	na	2.5	0.4	0.1	0.0	0.0	0.0	0.0	0.5	0.7	na	na
Days With ≥ 1.0" Snow Depth	na	na	0	0	0	0	0	0	0	0	0	na	na

Hutchinson 10 SW *Reno County* Elevation: 1,568 ft. Latitude: 37° 56' N Longitude: 98° 02' W

	JAN	FEB	MAR	APR	MAY	JUN	JUL	AUG	SEP	OCT	NOV	DEC	YEAR
Mean Maximum Temp. (°F)	40.4	47.4	56.9	66.9	75.8	87.4	93.3	91.5	82.6	70.8	54.7	44.2	67.7
Mean Temp. (°F)	29.4	35.4	44.9	54.6	64.3	75.0	80.4	78.7	69.8	57.6	43.4	33.5	55.6
Mean Minimum Temp. (°F)	18.4	23.3	32.8	42.1	52.7	62.6	67.5	65.8	56.9	44.3	32.0	22.8	43.4
Extreme Maximum Temp. (°F)	79	84	89	98	100	110	110	110	107	95	88	76	110
Extreme Minimum Temp. (°F)	-16	-19	-2	16	31	42	46	47	29	12	1	-18	-19
Days Maximum Temp. ≥ 90°F	0	0	0	0	1	13	22	19	9	1	0	0	65
Days Maximum Temp. ≤ 32°F	9	5	1	0	0	0	0	0	0	0	1	5	21
Days Minimum Temp. ≤ 32°F	29	23	15	4	0	0	0	0	0	3	16	27	117
Days Minimum Temp. ≤ 0°F	2	1	0	0	0	0	0	0	0	0	0	1	4
Heating Degree Days (base 65°F)	1,096	829	619	325	102	10	0	1	57	253	641	969	4,902
Cooling Degree Days (base 65°F)	0	0	1	19	83	309	476	428	209	27	1	0	1,553
Mean Precipitation (in.)	0.67	0.99	2.53	2.93	4.34	4.07	3.53	3.00	3.20	2.38	1.53	1.00	30.17
Days With > 0.1" Precipitation	2	2	4	4	7	5	5	5	4	3	3	2	46
Days With ≥ 1.0" Precipitation	0	0	1	1	1	1	1	1	1	1	0	0	8
Mean Snowfall (in.)	4.1	4.0	3.1	0.8	0.0	0.0	0.0	0.0	0.0	0.2	0.9	2.2	15.3
Days With ≥ 1.0" Snow Depth	8	5	2	0	0	0	0	0	0	0	1	4	20

Independence *Montgomery County* Elevation: 803 ft. Latitude: 37° 14' N Longitude: 95° 42' W

	JAN	FEB	MAR	APR	MAY	JUN	JUL	AUG	SEP	OCT	NOV	DEC	YEAR
Mean Maximum Temp. (°F)	42.9	49.8	59.9	70.2	77.7	86.5	92.1	91.4	82.6	72.0	57.9	47.2	69.2
Mean Temp. (°F)	32.3	38.3	48.0	58.1	66.7	75.6	80.7	79.5	71.0	59.8	46.8	36.7	57.8
Mean Minimum Temp. (°F)	21.7	26.9	36.1	45.9	55.7	64.7	69.3	67.4	59.4	47.5	35.7	26.1	46.3
Extreme Maximum Temp. (°F)	75	85	91	101	93	103	111	108	105	96	86	76	111
Extreme Minimum Temp. (°F)	-15	-14	2	18	32	43	50	50	29	19	5	-16	-16
Days Maximum Temp. ≥ 90°F	0	0	0	1	1	10	22	20	8	1	0	0	63
Days Maximum Temp. ≤ 32°F	7	4	1	0	0	0	0	0	0	0	0	4	16
Days Minimum Temp. ≤ 32°F	26	20	12	3	0	0	0	0	0	1	12	23	97
Days Minimum Temp. ≤ 0°F	1	1	0	0	0	0	0	0	0	0	0	1	3
Heating Degree Days (base 65°F)	1,007	746	525	236	60	3	0	0	42	198	542	872	4,231
Cooling Degree Days (base 65°F)	0	0	6	33	118	334	505	467	235	40	4	0	1,742
Mean Precipitation (in.)	1.46	1.81	3.66	4.11	5.81	5.35	3.34	3.73	4.81	4.01	3.24	2.19	43.52
Days With ≥ 0.1" Precipitation	3	3	6	7	8	6	5	5	6	5	5	4	63
Days With ≥ 1.0" Precipitation	0	0	1	1	2	2	1	1	2	1	1	1	13
Mean Snowfall (in.)	3.5	3.6	2.1	trace	0.0	0.0	0.0	0.0	0.0	trace	0.5	*2.4*	*12.1*
Days With ≥ 1.0" Snow Depth	7	4	1	0	0	0	0	0	0	0	0	3	15

Iola 1 W *Allen County* Elevation: 951 ft. Latitude: 37° 55' N Longitude: 95° 26' W

	JAN	FEB	MAR	APR	MAY	JUN	JUL	AUG	SEP	OCT	NOV	DEC	YEAR
Mean Maximum Temp. (°F)	40.8	47.7	58.6	69.3	77.2	85.8	91.0	89.6	81.7	71.1	56.0	45.0	67.8
Mean Temp. (°F)	31.0	37.0	47.1	57.5	66.4	75.3	80.2	78.4	70.4	59.4	46.1	35.6	57.0
Mean Minimum Temp. (°F)	21.1	26.3	35.6	45.6	55.6	64.8	69.4	67.2	59.1	47.7	36.1	26.1	46.2
Extreme Maximum Temp. (°F)	71	82	88	95	94	106	109	107	102	95	83	71	109
Extreme Minimum Temp. (°F)	-16	-19	2	19	31	45	50	46	30	18	3	-19	-19
Days Maximum Temp. ≥ 90°F	0	0	0	0	0	8	19	16	5	0	0	0	48
Days Maximum Temp. ≤ 32°F	8	4	1	0	0	0	0	0	0	0	1	4	18
Days Minimum Temp. ≤ 32°F	27	20	13	2	0	0	0	0	0	2	11	23	98
Days Minimum Temp. ≤ 0°F	2	1	0	0	0	0	0	0	0	0	0	1	4
Heating Degree Days (base 65°F)	1,047	783	551	251	64	3	0	0	44	206	563	906	4,418
Cooling Degree Days (base 65°F)	0	0	4	31	113	320	480	425	215	38	2	0	1,628
Mean Precipitation (in.)	1.35	1.47	3.15	3.90	5.19	5.35	4.45	4.03	4.58	3.76	3.09	1.73	42.05
Days With ≥ 0.1" Precipitation	3	3	6	6	7	7	6	5	6	5	5	3	62
Days With ≥ 1.0" Precipitation	0	0	1	1	1	2	2	1	1	1	1	0	11
Mean Snowfall (in.)	na	*1.9*	*1.1*	0.0	0.0	0.0	0.0	0.0	0.0	0.0	0.7	*1.2*	na
Days With ≥ 1.0" Snow Depth	na	na	*0*	0	0	0	0	0	0	0	0	2	na

John Redmond Lake *Coffey County* Elevation: 1,089 ft. Latitude: 38° 15' N Longitude: 95° 45' W

	JAN	FEB	MAR	APR	MAY	JUN	JUL	AUG	SEP	OCT	NOV	DEC	YEAR
Mean Maximum Temp. (°F)	*38.6*	44.1	55.6	66.3	75.0	84.1	89.9	88.8	80.7	69.3	*54.3*	na	na
Mean Temp. (°F)	*27.9*	32.9	43.8	54.5	64.0	73.3	78.5	76.9	68.5	56.6	*43.4*	na	na
Mean Minimum Temp. (°F)	*17.1*	22.0	31.9	42.6	53.0	62.4	67.1	65.1	56.4	43.9	*32.6*	23.2	*43.1*
Extreme Maximum Temp. (°F)	74	79	86	92	94	107	108	107	101	94	82	75	108
Extreme Minimum Temp. (°F)	-21	-22	0	13	30	39	47	47	29	13	-1	-21	-22
Days Maximum Temp. ≥ 90°F	0	0	0	0	0	7	16	15	5	0	0	0	43
Days Maximum Temp. ≤ 32°F	9	6	1	0	0	0	0	0	0	0	1	*5*	*22*
Days Minimum Temp. ≤ 32°F	28	23	16	4	0	0	0	0	0	3	*14*	25	*113*
Days Minimum Temp. ≤ 0°F	2	2	0	0	0	0	0	0	0	0	0	1	5
Heating Degree Days (base 65°F)	*1,152*	901	656	331	103	11	1	2	63	277	*636*	na	na
Cooling Degree Days (base 65°F)	*0*	0	2	18	78	268	432	375	181	22	*1*	0	*1,377*
Mean Precipitation (in.)	0.94	0.90	2.47	3.24	4.29	5.09	4.09	3.49	3.99	3.16	2.24	1.48	35.38
Days With ≥ 0.1" Precipitation	2	2	5	6	7	6	5	5	5	4	4	*3*	*54*
Days With ≥ 1.0" Precipitation	0	0	0	1	1	1	1	1	1	1	1	0	8
Mean Snowfall (in.)	*3.3*	*2.3*	1.4	trace	0.0	0.0	0.0	0.0	0.0	0.0	0.8	na	na
Days With ≥ 1.0" Snow Depth	na	*2*	1	0	0	0	0	0	0	0	0	na	na

Kanopolis Lake *Ellsworth County*   Elevation: 1,489 ft.   Latitude: 38° 36' N   Longitude: 97° 58' W

	JAN	FEB	MAR	APR	MAY	JUN	JUL	AUG	SEP	OCT	NOV	DEC	YEAR
Mean Maximum Temp. (°F)	38.3	44.6	54.7	65.4	74.6	85.5	91.9	90.1	81.1	69.6	53.7	42.5	66.0
Mean Temp. (°F)	27.1	32.6	42.3	53.0	62.9	73.3	79.0	77.0	67.9	56.1	41.9	31.5	53.7
Mean Minimum Temp. (°F)	15.7	20.5	29.8	40.6	51.0	61.0	66.0	63.9	54.6	42.5	30.0	20.4	41.3
Extreme Maximum Temp. (°F)	77	82	89	103	99	109	111	109	104	95	86	76	111
Extreme Minimum Temp. (°F)	-17	-18	-6	10	27	38	44	46	26	15	-3	-24	-24
Days Maximum Temp. ≥ 90°F	0	0	0	0	1	10	20	17	8	1	0	0	57
Days Maximum Temp. ≤ 32°F	11	7	2	0	0	0	0	0	0	0	2	7	29
Days Minimum Temp. ≤ 32°F	30	24	19	6	0	0	0	0	0	4	18	29	130
Days Minimum Temp. ≤ 0°F	4	2	0	0	0	0	0	0	0	0	0	2	8
Heating Degree Days (base 65°F)	1,170	910	697	367	130	16	1	2	79	295	688	1,031	5,386
Cooling Degree Days (base 65°F)	0	0	1	17	70	272	445	385	180	25	0	0	1,395
Mean Precipitation (in.)	0.55	0.79	2.21	2.42	4.18	3.72	3.38	3.42	2.59	2.08	1.46	0.77	27.57
Days With ≥ 0.1" Precipitation	1	2	4	5	7	6	5	4	4	3	3	2	46
Days With ≥ 1.0" Precipitation	0	0	1	1	1	1	1	1	1	1	0	0	8
Mean Snowfall (in.)	3.5	3.0	1.9	0.2	0.0	0.0	0.0	0.0	0.0	0.2	0.3	1.7	10.8
Days With ≥ 1.0" Snow Depth	9	6	2	0	0	0	0	0	0	0	1	3	21

Kingman *Kingman County*   Elevation: 1,558 ft.   Latitude: 37° 40' N   Longitude: 98° 07' W

	JAN	FEB	MAR	APR	MAY	JUN	JUL	AUG	SEP	OCT	NOV	DEC	YEAR
Mean Maximum Temp. (°F)	42.6	49.7	59.1	69.4	78.3	89.0	94.6	92.9	83.9	72.2	56.3	45.8	69.5
Mean Temp. (°F)	31.4	37.4	46.4	56.7	66.2	76.3	81.6	80.1	71.1	59.1	44.7	34.9	57.1
Mean Minimum Temp. (°F)	20.2	25.0	33.6	43.8	54.0	63.6	68.5	67.1	58.3	45.8	33.1	23.9	44.7
Extreme Maximum Temp. (°F)	76	84	91	97	101	110	112	111	109	100	88	74	112
Extreme Minimum Temp. (°F)	-14	-16	1	16	33	43	47	49	24	14	5	-17	-17
Days Maximum Temp. ≥ 90°F	0	0	0	1	2	15	24	21	10	1	0	0	74
Days Maximum Temp. ≤ 32°F	8	4	1	0	0	0	0	0	0	0	1	4	18
Days Minimum Temp. ≤ 32°F	28	21	15	4	0	0	0	0	0	2	15	26	111
Days Minimum Temp. ≤ 0°F	2	1	0	0	0	0	0	0	0	0	0	1	4
Heating Degree Days (base 65°F)	1,034	775	574	272	74	5	0	0	44	217	603	927	4,525
Cooling Degree Days (base 65°F)	0	0	3	29	115	348	519	474	237	36	1	0	1,762
Mean Precipitation (in.)	0.74	1.02	2.63	2.78	4.27	4.01	3.11	3.07	3.08	2.58	1.85	1.07	30.21
Days With ≥ 0.1" Precipitation	2	3	5	5	7	6	5	4	5	4	3	3	52
Days With ≥ 1.0" Precipitation	0	0	1	1	1	1	1	1	1	1	1	0	9
Mean Snowfall (in.)	4.1	3.8	2.8	0.4	0.0	0.0	0.0	0.0	0.0	0.1	1.2	2.3	14.7
Days With ≥ 1.0" Snow Depth	6	5	1	0	0	0	0	0	0	0	1	3	16

Kinsley *Edwards County*   Elevation: 2,165 ft.   Latitude: 37° 55' N   Longitude: 99° 24' W

	JAN	FEB	MAR	APR	MAY	JUN	JUL	AUG	SEP	OCT	NOV	DEC	YEAR
Mean Maximum Temp. (°F)	41.9	48.2	57.3	67.5	76.5	87.4	93.3	91.4	82.6	71.5	55.7	45.8	68.3
Mean Temp. (°F)	29.7	35.0	43.8	53.8	63.7	74.3	79.8	77.9	69.0	57.0	42.7	33.3	55.0
Mean Minimum Temp. (°F)	17.5	21.6	30.3	40.1	50.9	61.1	66.2	64.5	55.4	42.3	29.7	20.8	41.7
Extreme Maximum Temp. (°F)	78	88	92	99	103	110	109	109	106	97	90	77	110
Extreme Minimum Temp. (°F)	-15	-18	-2	12	31	42	48	47	26	16	1	-19	-19
Days Maximum Temp. ≥ 90°F	0	0	0	1	3	13	22	20	10	1	0	0	70
Days Maximum Temp. ≤ 32°F	8	5	2	0	0	0	0	0	0	0	1	5	21
Days Minimum Temp. ≤ 32°F	30	24	18	6	0	0	0	0	0	4	19	29	130
Days Minimum Temp. ≤ 0°F	3	2	0	0	0	0	0	0	0	0	0	1	6
Heating Degree Days (base 65°F)	1,087	842	651	347	117	14	1	2	67	270	663	974	5,035
Cooling Degree Days (base 65°F)	0	0	2	19	78	285	457	407	198	26	0	0	1,472
Mean Precipitation (in.)	0.67	0.84	2.23	2.51	3.82	3.52	3.47	3.52	1.99	1.82	1.20	0.97	26.56
Days With ≥ 0.1" Precipitation	2	2	4	4	6	6	5	5	4	3	3	2	46
Days With ≥ 1.0" Precipitation	0	0	1	1	1	1	1	1	0	1	0	0	7
Mean Snowfall (in.)	4.7	2.9	3.3	0.7	0.0	0.0	0.0	0.0	trace	0.2	0.7	2.8	15.3
Days With ≥ 1.0" Snow Depth	na	na	1	0	0	0	0	0	0	0	0	na	na

Kirwin Dam *Phillips County*   Elevation: 1,696 ft.   Latitude: 39° 40' N   Longitude: 99° 07' W

	JAN	FEB	MAR	APR	MAY	JUN	JUL	AUG	SEP	OCT	NOV	DEC	YEAR
Mean Maximum Temp. (°F)	37.4	44.6	53.8	65.3	74.6	86.0	91.8	89.7	79.9	68.8	51.9	43.2	65.6
Mean Temp. (°F)	24.7	30.5	39.8	51.0	61.1	71.8	77.4	75.1	64.9	53.1	38.4	30.4	51.5
Mean Minimum Temp. (°F)	12.0	16.4	25.7	36.7	47.6	57.6	63.0	60.6	49.6	37.2	24.8	17.6	37.4
Extreme Maximum Temp. (°F)	76	86	93	102	98	112	111	110	104	96	87	74	112
Extreme Minimum Temp. (°F)	-30	-20	-10	12	26	37	41	38	15	3	-10	-23	-30
Days Maximum Temp. ≥ 90°F	0	0	0	1	2	10	19	16	7	1	0	0	56
Days Maximum Temp. ≤ 32°F	11	7	2	0	0	0	0	0	0	0	2	6	28
Days Minimum Temp. ≤ 32°F	29	25	23	9	1	0	0	0	1	9	23	27	147
Days Minimum Temp. ≤ 0°F	5	3	1	0	0	0	0	0	0	0	0	1	10
Heating Degree Days (base 65°F)	1,242	959	768	421	167	21	2	5	112	375	793	1,065	5,930
Cooling Degree Days (base 65°F)	0	0	0	9	52	229	396	330	116	14	0	na	na
Mean Precipitation (in.)	0.46	0.65	2.01	2.28	4.12	2.88	3.11	2.89	2.39	1.58	1.26	0.58	24.21
Days With ≥ 0.1" Precipitation	1	1	4	5	7	5	5	5	4	3	2	1	43
Days With ≥ 1.0" Precipitation	0	0	0	1	1	1	1	1	1	0	0	0	6
Mean Snowfall (in.)	3.3	3.7	1.9	0.4	0.0	0.0	0.0	0.0	0.0	0.4	1.3	na	na
Days With ≥ 1.0" Snow Depth	na	3	1	0	0	0	0	0	0	0	0	3	na

Lakin *Kearny County*   Elevation: 2,995 ft.   Latitude: 37° 56' N   Longitude: 101° 15' W

	JAN	FEB	MAR	APR	MAY	JUN	JUL	AUG	SEP	OCT	NOV	DEC	YEAR
Mean Maximum Temp. (°F)	42.9	49.2	57.4	66.4	76.2	87.6	93.1	90.5	82.0	70.8	55.4	45.9	68.1
Mean Temp. (°F)	29.4	34.9	42.9	51.7	62.5	73.1	78.4	76.2	67.4	55.2	41.2	32.4	53.8
Mean Minimum Temp. (°F)	15.9	20.5	28.3	37.1	48.8	58.5	63.7	61.9	52.8	39.6	27.0	18.8	39.4
Extreme Maximum Temp. (°F)	80	86	91	99	107	112	110	106	104	98	87	77	112
Extreme Minimum Temp. (°F)	-20	-13	-6	9	29	40	50	44	24	11	-2	-15	-20
Days Maximum Temp. ≥ 90°F	0	0	0	1	3	13	22	19	9	1	0	0	68
Days Maximum Temp. ≤ 32°F	8	4	2	0	0	0	0	0	0	0	2	5	21
Days Minimum Temp. ≤ 32°F	30	26	21	9	0	0	0	0	0	6	22	29	143
Days Minimum Temp. ≤ 0°F	3	2	0	0	0	0	0	0	0	0	0	2	7
Heating Degree Days (base 65°F)	1,096	843	679	404	138	19	1	3	80	310	706	1,004	5,283
Cooling Degree Days (base 65°F)	0	0	0	10	71	268	430	374	170	18	0	0	1,341
Mean Precipitation (in.)	0.32	0.42	1.08	1.48	2.98	3.00	2.72	2.83	1.70	0.86	0.83	0.40	18.62
Days With > 0.1" Precipitation	1	1	3	3	6	5	5	5	3	2	2	1	37
Days With ≥ 1.0" Precipitation	0	0	0	0	1	1	1	1	0	0	0	0	4
Mean Snowfall (in.)	*3.9*	3.2	4.1	0.9	trace	0.0	0.0	0.0	trace	0.5	0.8	2.1	*15.5*
Days With ≥ 1.0" Snow Depth	na	*1*	*1*	0	0	0	0	0	0	0	0	*1*	na

Larned *Pawnee County*   Elevation: 1,994 ft.   Latitude: 38° 11' N   Longitude: 99° 06' W

	JAN	FEB	MAR	APR	MAY	JUN	JUL	AUG	SEP	OCT	NOV	DEC	YEAR
Mean Maximum Temp. (°F)	41.6	48.7	58.0	68.6	77.4	87.8	93.3	91.4	82.6	71.4	55.4	45.3	68.4
Mean Temp. (°F)	30.1	36.1	44.8	55.0	64.8	74.9	80.2	78.4	69.6	57.7	43.2	33.8	55.7
Mean Minimum Temp. (°F)	18.5	23.4	31.5	41.4	52.1	62.0	67.1	65.4	56.5	44.0	31.0	22.2	42.9
Extreme Maximum Temp. (°F)	78	88	93	101	101	111	109	109	105	95	87	76	111
Extreme Minimum Temp. (°F)	-14	-12	-1	14	32	43	47	48	26	16	0	-22	-22
Days Maximum Temp. ≥ 90°F	0	0	0	1	3	13	22	20	9	1	0	0	69
Days Maximum Temp. ≤ 32°F	9	5	2	0	0	0	0	0	0	0	1	5	22
Days Minimum Temp. ≤ 32°F	29	23	17	5	0	0	0	0	0	3	17	28	122
Days Minimum Temp. ≤ 0°F	2	1	0	0	0	0	0	0	0	0	0	1	4
Heating Degree Days (base 65°F)	1,076	811	623	318	99	11	0	2	61	254	647	961	4,863
Cooling Degree Days (base 65°F)	0	0	2	24	93	301	468	421	207	30	1	0	1,547
Mean Precipitation (in.)	0.62	0.75	1.89	2.12	3.26	3.70	3.66	3.00	2.16	1.60	1.18	0.79	24.73
Days With ≥ 0.1" Precipitation	2	2	4	4	6	6	5	5	4	3	3	2	46
Days With ≥ 1.0" Precipitation	0	0	0	1	1	1	1	1	0	0	0	0	5
Mean Snowfall (in.)	4.3	4.4	3.7	1.2	0.0	0.0	0.0	0.0	trace	0.5	0.7	2.5	17.3
Days With ≥ 1.0" Snow Depth	7	5	2	1	0	0	0	0	0	0	1	3	19

Lawrence *Douglas County*   Elevation: 977 ft.   Latitude: 38° 58' N   Longitude: 95° 16' W

	JAN	FEB	MAR	APR	MAY	JUN	JUL	AUG	SEP	OCT	NOV	DEC	YEAR
Mean Maximum Temp. (°F)	38.9	45.6	57.1	67.5	76.6	85.3	90.8	89.3	81.0	70.0	54.4	43.0	66.6
Mean Temp. (°F)	29.6	35.6	46.0	56.5	66.1	75.1	80.2	78.4	70.1	59.0	45.1	34.3	56.3
Mean Minimum Temp. (°F)	20.2	25.6	34.9	45.5	55.6	64.8	69.6	67.6	59.2	48.1	35.8	25.5	46.0
Extreme Maximum Temp. (°F)	71	82	86	94	95	107	108	107	100	97	84	70	108
Extreme Minimum Temp. (°F)	-16	-11	-7	13	31	45	51	45	34	20	2	-21	-21
Days Maximum Temp. ≥ 90°F	0	0	0	0	1	8	18	15	5	0	0	0	47
Days Maximum Temp. ≤ 32°F	10	6	1	0	0	0	0	0	0	0	1	6	24
Days Minimum Temp. ≤ 32°F	26	19	13	3	0	0	0	0	0	1	11	23	96
Days Minimum Temp. ≤ 0°F	2	1	0	0	0	0	0	0	0	0	0	1	4
Heating Degree Days (base 65°F)	1,092	823	584	280	71	5	0	1	47	218	592	946	4,659
Cooling Degree Days (base 65°F)	0	0	4	35	113	317	484	430	212	40	3	0	1,638
Mean Precipitation (in.)	1.26	1.13	2.62	3.65	5.42	5.55	3.96	3.87	4.79	3.30	2.52	1.84	39.91
Days With ≥ 0.1" Precipitation	3	3	5	7	8	7	5	5	6	5	4	4	62
Days With ≥ 1.0" Precipitation	0	0	0	1	2	2	1	1	2	1	1	0	11
Mean Snowfall (in.)	6.0	4.7	1.7	0.6	0.0	0.0	0.0	0.0	0.0	0.2	1.0	3.5	17.7
Days With ≥ 1.0" Snow Depth	9	6	1	0	0	0	0	0	0	0	1	4	21

Leavenworth *Leavenworth County*   Elevation: 869 ft.   Latitude: 39° 16' N   Longitude: 94° 55' W

	JAN	FEB	MAR	APR	MAY	JUN	JUL	AUG	SEP	OCT	NOV	DEC	YEAR
Mean Maximum Temp. (°F)	37.6	44.8	55.8	*67.3*	76.2	85.1	90.1	88.2	80.0	69.0	53.3	41.7	*65.8*
Mean Temp. (°F)	27.9	34.0	44.1	*55.3*	64.8	73.8	78.8	76.7	68.2	57.0	43.0	32.3	*54.7*
Mean Minimum Temp. (°F)	17.9	23.1	32.2	*43.1*	53.3	62.5	67.6	65.1	56.4	45.0	32.7	22.9	*43.5*
Extreme Maximum Temp. (°F)	69	81	86	93	92	106	108	108	99	92	84	70	108
Extreme Minimum Temp. (°F)	-17	-19	-10	4	30	42	45	43	30	18	-2	-27	-27
Days Maximum Temp. ≥ 90°F	0	0	0	0	0	8	17	14	4	0	0	0	43
Days Maximum Temp. ≤ 32°F	10	6	1	0	0	0	0	0	0	0	1	*6*	*24*
Days Minimum Temp. ≤ 32°F	28	22	16	*5*	0	0	0	0	0	3	15	26	*115*
Days Minimum Temp. ≤ 0°F	3	2	0	0	0	0	0	0	0	0	0	2	7
Heating Degree Days (base 65°F)	1,143	867	645	*311*	90	6	1	1	63	266	654	1,007	*5,054*
Cooling Degree Days (base 65°F)	0	0	3	28	83	276	443	372	167	27	1	0	1,400
Mean Precipitation (in.)	1.07	1.20	2.66	3.61	5.56	4.87	4.55	4.20	5.08	3.57	2.62	1.60	40.59
Days With ≥ 0.1" Precipitation	3	3	5	*7*	8	6	6	6	6	5	4	3	*62*
Days With ≥ 1.0" Precipitation	0	0	1	*1*	2	1	1	1	2	1	1	0	*11*
Mean Snowfall (in.)	na	na	na	trace	0.0	0.0	0.0	0.0	0.0	0.2	*0.5*	na	na
Days With ≥ 1.0" Snow Depth	na	na	na	0	0	0	0	0	0	0	na	na	na

Leoti 1 W *Wichita County*   Elevation: 3,307 ft.   Latitude: 38° 29' N   Longitude: 101° 22' W

	JAN	FEB	MAR	APR	MAY	JUN	JUL	AUG	SEP	OCT	NOV	DEC	YEAR
Mean Maximum Temp. (°F)	41.3	47.9	56.2	65.7	75.2	86.4	91.8	89.1	80.8	69.1	53.2	44.3	66.7
Mean Temp. (°F)	28.1	33.7	41.4	50.6	61.0	71.6	76.8	74.7	65.7	53.3	39.4	30.8	52.3
Mean Minimum Temp. (°F)	14.9	19.4	26.7	35.4	46.8	56.7	61.8	60.4	50.7	37.4	25.4	17.4	37.7
Extreme Maximum Temp. (°F)	78	83	90	93	101	108	111	105	103	94	84	80	111
Extreme Minimum Temp. (°F)	-20	-17	-7	6	22	32	42	42	24	9	-4	-16	-20
Days Maximum Temp. ≥ 90°F	0	0	0	0	2	13	20	17	7	1	0	0	60
Days Maximum Temp. ≤ 32°F	9	5	3	0	0	0	0	0	0	0	2	6	25
Days Minimum Temp. ≤ 32°F	31	27	23	12	1	0	0	0	1	8	25	30	158
Days Minimum Temp. ≤ 0°F	3	2	0	0	0	0	0	0	0	0	0	2	7
Heating Degree Days (base 65°F)	1,138	879	723	433	167	24	2	5	94	366	764	1,052	5,647
Cooling Degree Days (base 65°F)	0	0	0	7	46	209	363	313	122	7	0	0	1,067
Mean Precipitation (in.)	0.40	0.47	1.27	1.47	2.86	2.57	2.91	2.69	1.57	1.04	0.80	0.36	18.41
Days With ≥ 0.1" Precipitation	2	1	3	4	6	5	6	4	4	2	2	1	40
Days With ≥ 1.0" Precipitation	0	0	0	0	1	0	1	1	0	0	0	0	3
Mean Snowfall (in.)	*6.1*	*4.1*	*5.7*	2.5	0.1	0.0	0.0	0.0	0.2	1.3	2.6	*4.0*	*26.6*
Days With ≥ 1.0" Snow Depth	na	*6*	*4*	1	0	0	0	0	0	1	*2*	*6*	na

Liberal *Seward County*   Elevation: 2,831 ft.   Latitude: 37° 01' N   Longitude: 100° 56' W

	JAN	FEB	MAR	APR	MAY	JUN	JUL	AUG	SEP	OCT	NOV	DEC	YEAR
Mean Maximum Temp. (°F)	46.5	52.6	60.8	70.7	78.9	89.7	94.8	92.9	84.4	73.5	58.4	48.8	71.0
Mean Temp. (°F)	33.2	38.6	46.2	55.9	65.2	75.5	80.6	78.8	70.3	58.4	44.5	35.7	56.9
Mean Minimum Temp. (°F)	19.9	24.5	31.6	41.0	51.4	61.2	66.4	64.8	56.1	43.2	30.6	22.5	42.8
Extreme Maximum Temp. (°F)	84	87	93	103	105	114	112	109	106	98	87	77	114
Extreme Minimum Temp. (°F)	-13	-11	1	12	32	44	51	50	29	16	-2	-13	-13
Days Maximum Temp. ≥ 90°F	0	0	0	1	5	16	25	22	11	2	0	0	82
Days Maximum Temp. ≤ 32°F	6	3	1	0	0	0	0	0	0	0	1	4	15
Days Minimum Temp. ≤ 32°F	29	23	17	5	0	0	0	0	0	3	17	28	122
Days Minimum Temp. ≤ 0°F	1	1	0	0	0	0	0	0	0	0	0	1	3
Heating Degree Days (base 65°F)	978	739	578	291	94	10	1	1	51	233	609	902	4,487
Cooling Degree Days (base 65°F)	0	0	2	24	101	314	486	445	221	31	0	0	1,624
Mean Precipitation (in.)	0.52	0.56	1.36	1.60	3.09	2.64	2.84	2.26	1.82	1.34	0.92	0.53	19.48
Days With ≥ 0.1" Precipitation	2	2	3	3	5	5	5	4	3	2	2	2	38
Days With ≥ 1.0" Precipitation	0	0	0	0	1	1	1	1	0	0	0	0	4
Mean Snowfall (in.)	*4.2*	3.9	*5.3*	1.5	trace	0.0	0.0	0.0	trace	0.7	1.8	3.8	*21.2*
Days With ≥ 1.0" Snow Depth	na	na	*1*	0	0	0	0	0	0	0	0	*2*	na

Lincoln 1 ESE *Lincoln County*   Elevation: 1,377 ft.   Latitude: 39° 02' N   Longitude: 98° 07' W

	JAN	FEB	MAR	APR	MAY	JUN	JUL	AUG	SEP	OCT	NOV	DEC	YEAR
Mean Maximum Temp. (°F)	40.2	47.3	57.6	68.2	77.2	88.8	94.9	92.3	83.6	71.9	54.8	44.2	68.4
Mean Temp. (°F)	27.6	33.8	43.7	54.0	63.9	74.7	80.6	78.4	69.3	57.0	41.8	31.8	54.7
Mean Minimum Temp. (°F)	14.9	20.1	29.7	39.8	50.4	60.6	66.3	64.4	54.9	42.0	28.7	19.3	40.9
Extreme Maximum Temp. (°F)	81	87	91	104	102	112	112	112	105	98	87	77	112
Extreme Minimum Temp. (°F)	-23	-24	-11	11	26	35	44	44	26	10	-7	27	-27
Days Maximum Temp. ≥ 90°F	0	0	0	1	2	15	24	21	10	1	0	0	74
Days Maximum Temp. ≤ 32°F	9	5	1	0	0	0	0	0	0	0	1	5	21
Days Minimum Temp. ≤ 32°F	30	25	19	7	1	0	0	0	0	6	20	29	137
Days Minimum Temp. ≤ 0°F	4	2	0	0	0	0	0	0	0	0	0	2	8
Heating Degree Days (base 65°F)	1,154	876	656	342	115	11	0	2	63	273	691	1,022	5,205
Cooling Degree Days (base 65°F)	0	0	2	20	83	301	484	416	199	29	1	0	1,535
Mean Precipitation (in.)	0.76	0.80	2.33	2.43	4.74	3.16	3.98	3.78	2.57	2.00	1.56	0.84	28.95
Days With ≥ 0.1" Precipitation	2	2	5	5	8	6	6	6	5	3	3	2	53
Days With ≥ 1.0" Precipitation	0	0	1	0	1	1	1	1	1	0	0	0	6
Mean Snowfall (in.)	6.1	4.8	2.8	0.8	0.0	0.0	0.0	0.0	0.0	0.4	1.3	3.3	19.5
Days With ≥ 1.0" Snow Depth	9	7	3	1	0	0	0	0	0	0	2	5	27

Lovewell Lake *Jewell County*   Elevation: 1,601 ft.   Latitude: 39° 54' N   Longitude: 98° 02' W

	JAN	FEB	MAR	APR	MAY	JUN	JUL	AUG	SEP	OCT	NOV	DEC	YEAR
Mean Maximum Temp. (°F)	35.4	42.0	52.4	63.8	73.2	83.7	89.8	87.3	79.2	67.3	50.7	39.9	63.7
Mean Temp. (°F)	24.0	29.6	39.9	51.1	61.4	71.7	77.2	74.9	65.9	53.7	39.0	28.7	51.4
Mean Minimum Temp. (°F)	12.7	17.2	27.3	38.4	49.6	59.5	64.6	62.4	52.5	40.0	27.2	17.5	39.1
Extreme Maximum Temp. (°F)	79	79	86	98	97	107	108	108	104	94	81	73	108
Extreme Minimum Temp. (°F)	-22	-21	-13	9	29	41	44	45	25	14	-9	-29	-29
Days Maximum Temp. ≥ 90°F	0	0	0	0	1	8	16	13	6	0	0	0	44
Days Maximum Temp. ≤ 32°F	13	8	3	0	0	0	0	0	0	0	3	8	35
Days Minimum Temp. ≤ 32°F	31	26	22	8	0	0	0	0	0	6	*22*	30	*145*
Days Minimum Temp. ≤ 0°F	6	4	1	0	0	0	0	0	0	0	0	2	13
Heating Degree Days (base 65°F)	1,262	994	772	419	156	20	2	5	101	357	774	1,117	5,979
Cooling Degree Days (base 65°F)	0	0	1	11	52	224	385	313	140	12	0	0	1,138
Mean Precipitation (in.)	0.64	0.64	2.07	2.63	4.07	3.38	3.74	3.30	2.85	1.94	1.49	0.74	27.49
Days With ≥ 0.1" Precipitation	2	2	4	5	7	6	6	5	5	3	3	2	50
Days With ≥ 1.0" Precipitation	0	0	0	0	1	1	1	1	1	0	0	0	5
Mean Snowfall (in.)	5.9	4.6	3.2	0.8	0.0	0.0	0.0	0.0	trace	0.1	1.6	*4.1*	*20.3*
Days With ≥ 1.0" Snow Depth	14	9	3	1	0	0	0	0	0	0	3	8	38

Manhattan *Riley County*   Elevation: 1,062 ft.   Latitude: 39° 12' N   Longitude: 96° 35' W

	JAN	FEB	MAR	APR	MAY	JUN	JUL	AUG	SEP	OCT	NOV	DEC	YEAR
Mean Maximum Temp. (°F)	38.9	46.1	57.0	67.7	76.7	86.3	91.5	90.0	81.2	70.1	53.8	43.1	66.9
Mean Temp. (°F)	28.2	34.6	44.8	55.5	65.2	74.8	79.9	78.2	69.3	57.6	43.1	32.7	55.3
Mean Minimum Temp. (°F)	17.5	22.9	32.5	43.2	53.6	63.3	68.3	66.4	57.2	45.0	32.3	22.2	43.7
Extreme Maximum Temp. (°F)	73	84	88	97	100	109	110	108	103	94	85	73	110
Extreme Minimum Temp. (°F)	-15	-15	-10	7	27	41	46	47	26	13	-2	-22	-22
Days Maximum Temp. ≥ 90°F	0	0	0	1	1	10	20	16	7	1	0	0	56
Days Maximum Temp. ≤ 32°F	10	6	1	0	0	0	0	0	0	0	1	5	23
Days Minimum Temp. ≤ 32°F	29	22	16	5	0	0	0	0	0	3	16	27	118
Days Minimum Temp. ≤ 0°F	3	2	0	0	0	0	0	0	0	0	0	1	6
Heating Degree Days (base 65°F)	1,134	853	624	310	90	7	1	1	62	258	651	996	4,987
Cooling Degree Days (base 65°F)	0	0	4	32	99	307	474	412	200	34	1	0	1,563
Mean Precipitation (in.)	0.86	0.93	2.54	3.12	5.23	5.28	4.18	3.34	3.93	2.77	2.11	1.05	35.34
Days With ≥ 0.1" Precipitation	3	2	5	6	8	7	6	5	5	4	4	3	58
Days With ≥ 1.0" Precipitation	0	0	1	1	2	2	1	1	1	1	0	0	10
Mean Snowfall (in.)	5.9	4.5	2.7	0.5	0.0	0.0	0.0	0.0	0.0	trace	1.2	3.3	18.1
Days With ≥ 1.0" Snow Depth	10	7	2	0	0	0	0	0	0	0	1	4	24

Mankato *Jewell County*   Elevation: 1,751 ft.   Latitude: 39° 47' N   Longitude: 98° 13' W

	JAN	FEB	MAR	APR	MAY	JUN	JUL	AUG	SEP	OCT	NOV	DEC	YEAR
Mean Maximum Temp. (°F)	35.3	41.5	52.2	63.6	73.1	84.3	90.4	88.0	79.3	67.0	50.8	39.6	63.8
Mean Temp. (°F)	24.1	29.8	39.9	51.1	61.4	72.0	77.6	75.3	66.0	53.7	39.3	28.6	51.6
Mean Minimum Temp. (°F)	12.8	18.0	27.5	38.5	49.6	59.6	64.9	62.7	52.7	40.2	27.4	17.6	39.3
Extreme Maximum Temp. (°F)	76	80	87	99	100	106	110	110	104	96	84	75	110
Extreme Minimum Temp. (°F)	-25	-19	-13	12	24	39	47	46	22	10	-5	-23	-25
Days Maximum Temp. ≥ 90°F	0	0	0	0	1	8	17	13	6	0	0	0	45
Days Maximum Temp. ≤ 32°F	13	9	3	0	0	0	0	0	0	0	2	9	36
Days Minimum Temp. ≤ 32°F	30	26	21	8	1	0	0	0	0	6	21	29	142
Days Minimum Temp. ≤ 0°F	6	3	1	0	0	0	0	0	0	0	0	3	13
Heating Degree Days (base 65°F)	1,262	988	772	422	162	21	2	5	98	359	767	1,123	5,981
Cooling Degree Days (base 65°F)	0	0	1	13	54	227	392	325	137	13	0	0	1,162
Mean Precipitation (in.)	0.78	0.69	2.06	2.74	4.19	3.32	3.65	3.39	2.75	1.97	1.65	0.88	28.07
Days With ≥ 0.1" Precipitation	2	2	4	6	8	6	6	6	5	4	3	2	54
Days With ≥ 1.0" Precipitation	0	0	0	1	1	1	1	1	1	0	0	0	6
Mean Snowfall (in.)	6.7	5.9	*3.8*	1.0	0.0	0.0	0.0	0.0	0.0	0.4	2.8	*4.7*	*25.3*
Days With ≥ 1.0" Snow Depth	na	na	*2*	1	0	0	0	0	0	0	1	*5*	na

Marion Lake *Marion County*   Elevation: 1,368 ft.   Latitude: 38° 23' N   Longitude: 97° 05' W

	JAN	FEB	MAR	APR	MAY	JUN	JUL	AUG	SEP	OCT	NOV	DEC	YEAR
Mean Maximum Temp. (°F)	37.0	44.0	54.4	65.4	74.8	84.9	91.1	89.6	80.8	69.2	53.3	41.6	65.5
Mean Temp. (°F)	26.8	32.7	42.9	53.9	63.8	73.8	79.3	77.4	68.4	56.4	42.4	31.7	54.1
Mean Minimum Temp. (°F)	16.4	21.3	31.3	42.3	52.8	62.6	67.4	65.1	55.9	43.6	31.5	21.8	42.7
Extreme Maximum Temp. (°F)	75	78	86	95	98	105	109	109	105	93	83	71	109
Extreme Minimum Temp. (°F)	-16	-19	-5	11	29	42	48	48	28	14	4	-24	-24
Days Maximum Temp. ≥ 90°F	0	0	0	0	1	9	19	17	7	0	0	0	53
Days Maximum Temp. ≤ 32°F	11	6	2	0	0	0	0	0	0	0	1	6	26
Days Minimum Temp. ≤ 32°F	30	24	17	4	0	0	0	0	0	3	17	28	123
Days Minimum Temp. ≤ 0°F	3	2	0	0	0	0	0	0	0	0	0	1	6
Heating Degree Days (base 65°F)	1,180	906	679	345	110	12	1	2	71	283	671	1,024	5,284
Cooling Degree Days (base 65°F)	0	0	1	19	79	284	458	396	187	22	0	0	1,446
Mean Precipitation (in.)	0.72	0.81	2.48	3.05	4.71	4.47	3.97	3.94	3.51	2.50	2.10	1.09	33.35
Days With ≥ 0.1" Precipitation	2	2	4	5	7	6	5	5	5	4	3	2	50
Days With ≥ 1.0" Precipitation	0	0	1	1	1	2	1	1	1	0	1	0	9
Mean Snowfall (in.)	na	na	na	trace	0.0	0.0	0.0	0.0	0.0	0.0	0.2	na	na
Days With ≥ 1.0" Snow Depth	na	na	na	0	0	0	0	0	0	0	*0*	na	na

Marysville *Marshall County*   Elevation: 1,177 ft.   Latitude: 39° 50' N   Longitude: 96° 38' W

	JAN	FEB	MAR	APR	MAY	JUN	JUL	AUG	SEP	OCT	NOV	DEC	YEAR
Mean Maximum Temp. (°F)	34.8	41.9	53.1	64.8	74.9	84.9	89.9	87.9	79.5	67.6	51.1	39.7	64.2
Mean Temp. (°F)	24.1	30.3	41.2	52.6	63.2	73.3	78.2	76.1	66.9	54.5	40.1	29.2	52.5
Mean Minimum Temp. (°F)	13.4	18.7	29.3	40.3	51.4	61.6	66.4	64.2	54.3	41.3	29.1	18.6	40.7
Extreme Maximum Temp. (°F)	71	84	92	97	99	108	110	107	104	95	83	71	110
Extreme Minimum Temp. (°F)	-21	-22	-18	6	27	40	42	44	27	11	-3	-27	-27
Days Maximum Temp. ≥ 90°F	0	0	0	1	1	9	17	13	5	0	0	0	46
Days Maximum Temp. ≤ 32°F	13	8	2	0	0	0	0	0	0	0	2	8	33
Days Minimum Temp. ≤ 32°F	30	26	20	7	0	0	0	0	0	6	19	29	137
Days Minimum Temp. ≤ 0°F	5	3	0	0	0	0	0	0	0	0	0	2	10
Heating Degree Days (base 65°F)	1,261	972	733	385	129	13	1	3	88	337	740	1,103	5,765
Cooling Degree Days (base 65°F)	0	0	2	22	76	262	415	345	155	17	1	0	1,295
Mean Precipitation (in.)	0.71	0.72	2.44	2.89	4.71	4.91	4.42	3.90	3.39	2.29	1.68	0.92	32.98
Days With ≥ 0.1" Precipitation	2	2	5	6	8	6	6	6	6	4	3	2	56
Days With ≥ 1.0" Precipitation	0	0	1	1	1	2	1	1	1	1	0	0	8
Mean Snowfall (in.)	*4.9*	*3.7*	2.4	0.7	0.0	0.0	0.0	0.0	0.0	trace	0.7	*1.2*	*13.6*
Days With ≥ 1.0" Snow Depth	na	na	*0*	0	0	0	0	0	0	0	0	*1*	na

McDonald *Rawlins County*   Elevation: 3,362 ft.   Latitude: 39° 47' N   Longitude: 101° 22' W

	JAN	FEB	MAR	APR	MAY	JUN	JUL	AUG	SEP	OCT	NOV	DEC	YEAR
Mean Maximum Temp. (°F)	40.2	46.1	54.0	63.9	73.2	84.7	90.6	88.4	80.0	68.2	51.3	43.1	65.3
Mean Temp. (°F)	27.8	33.1	40.3	49.8	59.9	70.6	76.3	74.4	65.4	53.3	38.7	30.7	51.7
Mean Minimum Temp. (°F)	15.4	20.0	26.6	35.7	46.5	56.4	62.1	60.2	50.7	38.3	26.1	18.3	38.0
Extreme Maximum Temp. (°F)	76	81	89	95	100	107	109	107	104	95	84	77	109
Extreme Minimum Temp. (°F)	-20	-21	-6	7	26	35	44	44	21	9	-7	-26	-26
Days Maximum Temp. ≥ 90°F	0	0	0	0	1	10	18	16	7	1	0	0	53
Days Maximum Temp. ≤ 32°F	9	5	2	0	0	0	0	0	0	0	3	6	25
Days Minimum Temp. ≤ 32°F	30	26	23	11	1	0	0	0	1	7	23	30	152
Days Minimum Temp. ≤ 0°F	4	2	1	0	0	0	0	0	0	0	0	2	9
Heating Degree Days (base 65°F)	1,147	896	758	455	191	28	3	7	103	365	782	1,056	5,791
Cooling Degree Days (base 65°F)	0	0	0	6	37	193	351	298	120	10	0	0	1,015
Mean Precipitation (in.)	0.58	0.57	1.49	2.02	3.88	3.58	3.21	2.46	1.37	1.17	0.95	0.49	21.77
Days With ≥ 0.1" Precipitation	2	2	4	4	7	6	6	5	3	3	2	1	45
Days With ≥ 1.0" Precipitation	0	0	0	0	1	1	1	1	0	0	0	0	4
Mean Snowfall (in.)	8.0	6.1	10.3	5.6	0.3	0.0	0.0	0.0	0.7	2.6	6.3	6.1	46.0
Days With ≥ 1.0" Snow Depth	14	9	5	2	0	0	0	0	0	1	5	9	45

McPherson *McPherson County*   Elevation: 1,492 ft.   Latitude: 38° 23' N   Longitude: 97° 40' W

	JAN	FEB	MAR	APR	MAY	JUN	JUL	AUG	SEP	OCT	NOV	DEC	YEAR
Mean Maximum Temp. (°F)	40.0	47.3	57.6	68.0	76.7	87.3	93.3	91.4	82.9	71.3	54.8	43.9	67.9
Mean Temp. (°F)	29.6	35.8	45.3	55.5	64.9	75.1	80.7	79.0	70.4	58.6	43.9	33.7	56.1
Mean Minimum Temp. (°F)	19.3	24.2	33.0	42.9	53.0	62.9	68.1	66.6	58.0	45.8	33.0	23.5	44.2
Extreme Maximum Temp. (°F)	79	80	89	99	99	112	110	109	106	93	88	73	112
Extreme Minimum Temp. (°F)	-18	-20	-9	9	29	41	48	47	27	16	-3	-21	-21
Days Maximum Temp. ≥ 90°F	0	0	0	0	1	13	22	19	9	1	0	0	65
Days Maximum Temp. ≤ 32°F	9	5	1	0	0	0	0	0	0	0	1	5	21
Days Minimum Temp. ≤ 32°F	28	21	15	4	0	0	0	0	0	2	15	26	111
Days Minimum Temp. ≤ 0°F	2	1	0	0	0	0	0	0	0	0	0	1	4
Heating Degree Days (base 65°F)	1,090	817	606	301	91	8	0	1	50	230	625	963	4,782
Cooling Degree Days (base 65°F)	0	0	3	25	94	319	493	445	227	36	1	0	1,643
Mean Precipitation (in.)	0.70	1.00	2.65	2.77	4.81	4.61	3.72	3.61	3.05	2.23	1.72	0.94	31.81
Days With ≥ 0.1" Precipitation	2	2	5	5	7	7	5	5	5	4	3	2	52
Days With ≥ 1.0" Precipitation	0	0	1	1	1	2	1	1	1	1	0	0	9
Mean Snowfall (in.)	4.6	4.4	2.8	1.1	0.0	0.0	0.0	0.0	0.0	trace	1.0	2.5	16.4
Days With ≥ 1.0" Snow Depth	9	6	2	1	0	0	0	0	0	0	1	4	23

Meade *Meade County*   Elevation: 2,477 ft.   Latitude: 37° 17' N   Longitude: 100° 21' W

	JAN	FEB	MAR	APR	MAY	JUN	JUL	AUG	SEP	OCT	NOV	DEC	YEAR
Mean Maximum Temp. (°F)	45.5	52.6	60.7	70.7	78.9	89.2	94.7	92.9	84.6	73.6	57.9	48.6	70.8
Mean Temp. (°F)	32.0	37.8	45.7	55.6	65.0	75.0	80.2	78.6	70.1	58.0	43.7	34.9	56.4
Mean Minimum Temp. (°F)	18.5	22.9	30.7	40.4	50.9	60.8	65.5	64.3	55.2	42.2	29.4	21.2	41.8
Extreme Maximum Temp. (°F)	83	89	90	101	106	110	110	107	106	95	90	81	110
Extreme Minimum Temp. (°F)	-14	-13	-2	15	30	42	47	47	30	14	2	-17	-17
Days Maximum Temp. ≥ 90°F	0	0	0	1	4	15	24	22	11	2	0	0	79
Days Maximum Temp. ≤ 32°F	7	4	1	0	0	0	0	0	0	0	1	4	17
Days Minimum Temp. ≤ 32°F	30	24	17	5	0	0	0	0	0	4	19	29	128
Days Minimum Temp. ≤ 0°F	2	1	0	0	0	0	0	0	0	0	0	1	4
Heating Degree Days (base 65°F)	1,015	761	595	298	93	9	1	1	54	242	633	926	4,628
Cooling Degree Days (base 65°F)	0	0	1	22	95	303	473	435	211	26	0	0	1,566
Mean Precipitation (in.)	0.65	0.56	1.88	1.99	3.33	3.07	3.08	2.12	2.09	1.60	0.90	0.73	22.00
Days With ≥ 0.1" Precipitation	2	1	3	4	5	5	5	4	4	3	2	2	40
Days With ≥ 1.0" Precipitation	0	0	0	1	1	1	1	1	1	0	0	0	6
Mean Snowfall (in.)	4.5	4.1	4.9	1.0	trace	0.0	0.0	0.0	trace	0.3	1.9	3.9	20.6
Days With ≥ 1.0" Snow Depth	na	2	1	0	0	0	0	0	0	0	1	3	na

Medicine Lodge *Barber County*   Elevation: 1,499 ft.   Latitude: 37° 17' N   Longitude: 98° 34' W

	JAN	FEB	MAR	APR	MAY	JUN	JUL	AUG	SEP	OCT	NOV	DEC	YEAR
Mean Maximum Temp. (°F)	43.7	50.9	60.6	70.6	78.9	89.3	95.0	93.3	84.9	73.3	57.5	47.6	70.5
Mean Temp. (°F)	31.5	37.2	46.9	56.9	66.2	76.2	81.0	79.8	71.3	59.0	44.8	35.2	57.2
Mean Minimum Temp. (°F)	19.2	23.5	33.2	43.1	53.4	63.0	67.0	66.2	57.6	44.6	32.0	22.8	43.8
Extreme Maximum Temp. (°F)	76	89	96	99	103	107	110	113	113	99	90	78	113
Extreme Minimum Temp. (°F)	-15	-20	0	14	33	43	47	47	29	13	0	-18	-20
Days Maximum Temp. ≥ 90°F	0	0	0	1	3	16	24	22	11	2	0	0	79
Days Maximum Temp. ≤ 32°F	7	4	1	0	0	0	0	0	0	0	1	3	16
Days Minimum Temp. ≤ 32°F	29	23	14	4	0	0	0	0	0	3	16	26	115
Days Minimum Temp. ≤ 0°F	2	1	0	0	0	0	0	0	0	0	0	1	4
Heating Degree Days (base 65°F)	1,032	779	556	264	72	5	0	0	41	217	601	918	4,485
Cooling Degree Days (base 65°F)	0	0	2	26	115	347	507	468	245	35	1	0	1,746
Mean Precipitation (in.)	0.69	0.92	2.47	2.75	3.81	4.06	2.87	3.04	2.55	2.22	1.90	0.86	28.14
Days With ≥ 0.1" Precipitation	2	2	4	5	6	6	4	4	4	3	3	2	45
Days With ≥ 1.0" Precipitation	0	0	1	1	1	1	1	1	1	1	1	0	9
Mean Snowfall (in.)	3.7	4.3	3.0	0.6	0.0	0.0	0.0	0.0	0.0	0.1	1.0	2.3	15.0
Days With ≥ 1.0" Snow Depth	na	na	1	0	0	0	0	0	0	0	0	2	na

Milford Lake *Geary County*   Elevation: 1,207 ft.   Latitude: 39° 05' N   Longitude: 96° 53' W

	JAN	FEB	MAR	APR	MAY	JUN	JUL	AUG	SEP	OCT	NOV	DEC	YEAR
Mean Maximum Temp. (°F)	36.6	43.2	54.5	65.3	74.7	84.4	90.4	88.9	80.5	68.9	53.2	41.2	65.2
Mean Temp. (°F)	26.1	31.9	42.6	53.5	63.3	73.0	78.6	77.0	68.1	56.1	42.3	31.1	53.6
Mean Minimum Temp. (°F)	15.6	20.6	30.7	41.5	51.8	61.6	66.8	64.9	55.4	43.2	31.4	20.9	42.0
Extreme Maximum Temp. (°F)	75	79	88	96	100	108	110	108	103	94	83	75	110
Extreme Minimum Temp. (°F)	-17	-18	-9	8	29	41	47	49	31	15	-1	-21	-21
Days Maximum Temp. ≥ 90°F	0	0	0	0	1	8	17	14	6	0	0	0	46
Days Maximum Temp. ≤ 32°F	12	7	2	0	0	0	0	0	0	0	1	7	29
Days Minimum Temp. ≤ 32°F	30	24	18	5	0	0	0	0	0	4	17	28	126
Days Minimum Temp. ≤ 0°F	4	3	0	0	0	0	0	0	0	0	0	1	8
Heating Degree Days (base 65°F)	1,198	928	690	358	123	13	1	1	73	294	675	1,045	5,399
Cooling Degree Days (base 65°F)	0	0	3	20	76	259	439	380	175	23	1	0	1,376
Mean Precipitation (in.)	0.74	0.86	2.45	2.73	4.93	4.51	4.21	3.55	3.43	2.52	1.85	1.07	32.85
Days With ≥ 0.1" Precipitation	2	2	4	5	8	6	6	5	5	4	3	2	52
Days With ≥ 1.0" Precipitation	0	0	1	1	2	1	1	1	1	1	0	0	9
Mean Snowfall (in.)	4.6	2.8	1.2	0.5	0.0	0.0	0.0	0.0	0.0	0.0	0.6	1.7	11.4
Days With ≥ 1.0" Snow Depth	9	7	1	0	0	0	0	0	0	0	1	4	22

Minneapolis *Ottawa County*   Elevation: 1,309 ft.   Latitude: 39° 08' N   Longitude: 97° 42' W

	JAN	FEB	MAR	APR	MAY	JUN	JUL	AUG	SEP	OCT	NOV	DEC	YEAR
Mean Maximum Temp. (°F)	39.9	47.0	57.7	68.8	77.7	88.5	94.0	91.7	83.3	71.5	54.7	44.1	68.2
Mean Temp. (°F)	29.2	35.0	45.0	55.7	65.3	75.6	80.9	78.9	70.1	58.2	43.5	33.8	55.9
Mean Minimum Temp. (°F)	18.5	23.1	32.4	42.6	52.8	62.6	67.8	66.1	56.9	44.8	32.2	23.5	43.6
Extreme Maximum Temp. (°F)	80	87	89	101	99	113	112	109	106	96	86	72	113
Extreme Minimum Temp. (°F)	-18	-23	-11	12	30	41	48	48	30	16	-2	-24	-24
Days Maximum Temp. ≥ 90°F	0	0	0	1	2	14	23	20	9	1	0	0	70
Days Maximum Temp. ≤ 32°F	9	5	1	0	0	0	0	0	0	0	1	5	21
Days Minimum Temp. ≤ 32°F	29	22	16	5	0	0	0	0	0	3	15	27	117
Days Minimum Temp. ≤ 0°F	3	2	0	0	0	0	0	0	0	0	0	1	6
Heating Degree Days (base 65°F)	1,103	838	614	297	89	8	0	1	48	240	640	959	4,837
Cooling Degree Days (base 65°F)	0	0	2	29	104	329	504	439	217	37	1	0	1,662
Mean Precipitation (in.)	0.84	0.84	2.31	2.16	5.31	3.64	4.76	3.56	2.55	2.06	1.57	0.93	30.53
Days With ≥ 0.1" Precipitation	2	2	4	5	8	6	6	5	4	3	4	2	51
Days With ≥ 1.0" Precipitation	0	0	0	0	2	1	2	1	1	1	0	0	8
Mean Snowfall (in.)	6.2	4.8	2.9	0.6	0.0	0.0	0.0	0.0	0.0	0.2	1.5	2.7	18.9
Days With ≥ 1.0" Snow Depth	8	7	2	0	0	0	0	0	0	0	1	4	22

Mound City *Linn County*   Elevation: 839 ft.   Latitude: 38° 09' N   Longitude: 94° 49' W

	JAN	FEB	MAR	APR	MAY	JUN	JUL	AUG	SEP	OCT	NOV	DEC	YEAR
Mean Maximum Temp. (°F)	39.4	46.5	57.2	67.7	76.3	84.9	90.7	89.4	81.0	70.3	55.3	44.2	66.9
Mean Temp. (°F)	29.2	35.3	45.4	55.5	64.7	73.8	79.2	77.5	68.9	57.7	44.7	34.2	55.5
Mean Minimum Temp. (°F)	19.0	24.1	33.6	43.3	53.1	62.7	67.6	65.5	56.7	45.2	34.2	24.1	44.1
Extreme Maximum Temp. (°F)	71	81	87	93	95	106	112	110	103	95	84	72	112
Extreme Minimum Temp. (°F)	-17	-20	-4	16	27	43	44	43	28	17	3	-27	-27
Days Maximum Temp. ≥ 90°F	0	0	0	0	0	7	18	16	6	0	0	0	47
Days Maximum Temp. ≤ 32°F	9	5	1	0	0	0	0	0	0	0	1	5	21
Days Minimum Temp. ≤ 32°F	28	22	15	4	0	0	0	0	0	4	14	25	112
Days Minimum Temp. ≤ 0°F	2	1	0	0	0	0	0	0	0	0	0	1	4
Heating Degree Days (base 65°F)	1,101	832	603	305	94	9	1	3	64	251	604	950	4,817
Cooling Degree Days (base 65°F)	0	0	3	25	83	269	438	382	176	28	3	0	1,407
Mean Precipitation (in.)	1.58	1.74	3.31	4.19	5.09	5.00	3.74	3.83	4.72	3.68	3.26	1.94	42.08
Days With ≥ 0.1" Precipitation	4	4	5	6	8	7	5	5	6	6	6	4	66
Days With ≥ 1.0" Precipitation	0	0	1	1	2	2	1	1	1	1	1	0	11
Mean Snowfall (in.)	5.2	4.2	1.3	trace	0.0	0.0	0.0	0.0	0.0	trace	0.8	2.5	14.0
Days With ≥ 1.0" Snow Depth	na	na	1	0	0	0	0	0	0	0	0	2	na

Mound Valley 3 WSW *Labette County*   Elevation: 797 ft.   Latitude: 37° 11' N   Longitude: 95° 27' W

	JAN	FEB	MAR	APR	MAY	JUN	JUL	AUG	SEP	OCT	NOV	DEC	YEAR
Mean Maximum Temp. (°F)	42.5	48.6	58.9	69.0	77.2	85.8	91.6	91.2	82.1	71.7	57.1	46.5	68.5
Mean Temp. (°F)	31.5	37.0	46.8	56.6	65.8	74.7	79.8	78.5	70.1	58.5	45.8	35.9	56.8
Mean Minimum Temp. (°F)	20.1	25.1	34.7	44.2	54.4	63.6	68.1	65.8	57.9	45.3	34.4	25.2	44.9
Extreme Maximum Temp. (°F)	74	83	90	100	94	104	109	108	104	95	86	74	109
Extreme Minimum Temp. (°F)	-20	-16	3	18	28	40	47	45	27	15	2	-18	-20
Days Maximum Temp. ≥ 90°F	0	0	0	0	1	9	21	20	7	1	0	0	59
Days Maximum Temp. ≤ 32°F	7	4	1	0	0	0	0	0	0	0	1	4	17
Days Minimum Temp. ≤ 32°F	28	22	13	4	0	0	0	0	0	3	14	25	109
Days Minimum Temp. ≤ 0°F	2	1	0	0	0	0	0	0	0	0	0	1	4
Heating Degree Days (base 65°F)	1,032	785	560	273	73	6	0	1	50	229	573	894	4,476
Cooling Degree Days (base 65°F)	0	0	3	23	95	295	451	415	199	27	2	0	1,510
Mean Precipitation (in.)	1.57	1.75	3.61	4.23	5.87	5.36	3.68	4.11	5.22	4.34	3.54	2.25	45.53
Days With ≥ 0.1" Precipitation	3	3	5	6	8	7	5	5	6	5	5	4	62
Days With ≥ 1.0" Precipitation	0	0	1	1	2	2	1	2	2	1	1	1	14
Mean Snowfall (in.)	na	2.4	2.0	0.0	0.0	0.0	0.0	0.0	0.0	trace	0.6	1.8	na
Days With ≥ 1.0" Snow Depth	na	2	0	0	0	0	0	0	0	0	0	1	na

Ness City *Ness County* Elevation: 2,247 ft.   Latitude: 38° 27' N   Longitude: 99° 54' W

	JAN	FEB	MAR	APR	MAY	JUN	JUL	AUG	SEP	OCT	NOV	DEC	YEAR
Mean Maximum Temp. (°F)	41.9	49.1	57.4	68.3	77.5	88.5	93.8	92.0	83.1	71.5	55.2	45.6	68.7
Mean Temp. (°F)	28.7	34.9	43.1	53.6	63.6	74.2	79.4	77.4	68.2	55.7	41.1	32.3	54.4
Mean Minimum Temp. (°F)	15.5	20.6	28.7	38.8	49.7	59.8	64.9	62.9	53.2	39.8	27.1	19.0	40.0
Extreme Maximum Temp. (°F)	81	86	91	103	102	114	110	108	105	99	87	80	114
Extreme Minimum Temp. (°F)	-16	-18	-6	11	28	37	41	43	20	13	-3	-25	-25
Days Maximum Temp. ≥ 90°F	0	0	0	1	3	15	23	20	10	1	0	0	73
Days Maximum Temp. ≤ 32°F	8	5	2	0	0	0	0	0	0	0	1	5	21
Days Minimum Temp. ≤ 32°F	30	25	20	7	0	0	0	0	1	6	22	29	140
Days Minimum Temp. ≤ 0°F	3	2	0	0	0	0	0	0	0	0	0	1	6
Heating Degree Days (base 65°F)	1,118	844	675	353	117	14	1	2	74	304	709	1,006	5,217
Cooling Degree Days (base 65°F)	0	0	1	18	81	289	451	393	179	21	0	0	1,433
Mean Precipitation (in.)	0.55	0.66	1.85	1.96	3.07	3.04	3.41	2.67	1.77	1.19	1.12	0.56	21.85
Days With ≥ 0.1" Precipitation	1	2	4	4	6	5	5	5	3	2	2	2	41
Days With ≥ 1.0" Precipitation	0	0	0	0	1	1	1	1	1	0	0	0	5
Mean Snowfall (in.)	na	na	4.4	0.7	0.0	0.0	0.0	0.0	trace	0.1	1.5	2.4	na
Days With ≥ 1.0" Snow Depth	na	na	1	0	0	0	0	0	0	0	1	2	na

Newton 2 SW *Harvey County* Elevation: 1,446 ft.   Latitude: 38° 02' N   Longitude: 97° 23' W

	JAN	FEB	MAR	APR	MAY	JUN	JUL	AUG	SEP	OCT	NOV	DEC	YEAR
Mean Maximum Temp. (°F)	39.8	47.5	57.5	67.6	76.7	87.4	93.3	91.7	82.7	70.6	54.5	43.5	67.7
Mean Temp. (°F)	29.7	36.4	45.7	55.8	65.5	75.7	81.2	79.6	70.7	58.8	44.2	33.9	56.4
Mean Minimum Temp. (°F)	19.7	25.1	34.0	43.9	54.2	63.9	69.0	67.4	58.7	46.8	33.8	24.1	45.0
Extreme Maximum Temp. (°F)	75	81	89	95	99	109	111	110	106	93	84	72	111
Extreme Minimum Temp. (°F)	-17	-10	0	14	30	42	43	46	29	14	0	-20	-20
Days Maximum Temp. ≥ 90°F	0	0	0	0	1	13	23	19	9	1	0	0	66
Days Maximum Temp. ≤ 32°F	9	5	1	0	0	0	0	0	0	0	1	5	21
Days Minimum Temp. ≤ 32°F	28	21	14	3	0	0	0	0	0	2	14	26	108
Days Minimum Temp. ≤ 0°F	2	1	0	0	0	0	0	0	0	0	0	1	4
Heating Degree Days (base 65°F)	1,086	802	592	296	83	7	0	0	50	228	619	958	4,721
Cooling Degree Days (base 65°F)	0	0	3	26	104	336	511	461	230	38	1	0	1,710
Mean Precipitation (in.)	0.76	0.89	2.59	2.89	4.69	4.39	3.17	3.23	3.11	2.34	2.21	1.15	31.42
Days With ≥ 0.1" Precipitation	2	2	5	5	6	6	5	5	5	4	4	3	52
Days With ≥ 1.0" Precipitation	0	0	1	1	1	1	1	1	1	1	1	0	9
Mean Snowfall (in.)	2.9	3.7	1.2	0.3	0.0	0.0	0.0	0.0	0.0	trace	0.9	2.0	11.0
Days With ≥ 1.0" Snow Depth	na	na	0	0	0	0	0	0	0	0	0	1	na

Norton 9 SSE *Norton County* Elevation: 2,358 ft.   Latitude: 39° 44' N   Longitude: 99° 50' W

	JAN	FEB	MAR	APR	MAY	JUN	JUL	AUG	SEP	OCT	NOV	DEC	YEAR
Mean Maximum Temp. (°F)	39.1	45.5	54.7	65.5	74.2	85.8	91.9	90.0	81.2	69.2	52.2	42.5	66.0
Mean Temp. (°F)	26.8	32.3	40.8	51.3	61.1	71.8	77.5	75.7	66.5	54.3	39.4	30.2	52.3
Mean Minimum Temp. (°F)	14.5	19.2	26.9	37.0	48.0	57.6	63.2	61.4	51.7	39.4	26.6	17.9	38.6
Extreme Maximum Temp. (°F)	77	85	92	98	98	110	111	112	107	97	89	78	112
Extreme Minimum Temp. (°F)	-18	-16	-11	12	26	39	44	44	24	9	-5	-27	-27
Days Maximum Temp. ≥ 90°F	0	0	0	1	1	10	19	17	8	1	0	0	57
Days Maximum Temp. ≤ 32°F	10	6	2	0	0	0	0	0	0	0	2	7	27
Days Minimum Temp. ≤ 32°F	30	26	22	9	1	0	0	0	1	7	22	30	148
Days Minimum Temp. ≤ 0°F	4	2	1	0	0	0	0	0	0	0	0	2	9
Heating Degree Days (base 65°F)	1,176	916	744	416	162	22	1	4	91	340	761	1,071	5,704
Cooling Degree Days (base 65°F)	0	0	0	12	48	230	395	340	146	17	0	0	1,188
Mean Precipitation (in.)	0.60	0.56	1.67	2.20	3.91	2.67	3.31	2.77	1.76	1.33	1.15	0.49	22.42
Days With ≥ 0.1" Precipitation	2	1	4	4	7	5	6	5	4	3	2	2	45
Days With ≥ 1.0" Precipitation	0	0	0	1	1	1	1	1	0	0	0	0	5
Mean Snowfall (in.)	5.2	4.4	5.8	1.9	trace	0.0	0.0	0.0	0.4	1.0	3.6	4.2	26.5
Days With ≥ 1.0" Snow Depth	10	7	4	1	0	0	0	0	0	0	3	7	32

Norton Dam *Norton County* Elevation: 2,339 ft.   Latitude: 39° 49' N   Longitude: 99° 56' W

	JAN	FEB	MAR	APR	MAY	JUN	JUL	AUG	SEP	OCT	NOV	DEC	YEAR
Mean Maximum Temp. (°F)	37.4	43.9	52.8	63.9	72.8	84.3	90.8	88.4	79.5	68.0	50.9	41.8	64.5
Mean Temp. (°F)	24.8	30.5	39.0	50.1	59.9	70.7	76.9	74.7	65.1	52.8	38.3	29.2	50.9
Mean Minimum Temp. (°F)	12.2	17.1	25.3	36.2	47.0	57.1	63.0	61.2	50.6	37.7	24.6	15.9	37.3
Extreme Maximum Temp. (°F)	78	82	88	93	98	109	111	107	104	94	88	77	111
Extreme Minimum Temp. (°F)	-21	-18	-9	12	27	31	42	43	20	6	-7	-28	-28
Days Maximum Temp. ≥ 90°F	0	0	0	0	1	9	18	14	7	1	0	0	50
Days Maximum Temp. ≤ 32°F	11	7	3	0	0	0	0	0	0	0	3	7	31
Days Minimum Temp. ≤ 32°F	30	26	24	10	1	0	0	0	1	8	24	29	153
Days Minimum Temp. ≤ 0°F	5	3	1	0	0	0	0	0	0	0	0	3	12
Heating Degree Days (base 65°F)	1,240	958	801	449	193	29	3	6	112	381	810	1,104	6,086
Cooling Degree Days (base 65°F)	0	0	0	9	45	214	380	316	127	11	0	0	1,102
Mean Precipitation (in.)	0.41	0.43	1.63	2.75	4.49	3.31	3.54	3.26	1.97	1.52	1.16	0.43	24.90
Days With ≥ 0.1" Precipitation	1	1	3	5	7	6	6	5	4	3	2	1	44
Days With ≥ 1.0" Precipitation	0	0	0	1	1	1	1	1	0	0	0	0	5
Mean Snowfall (in.)	4.4	3.4	4.2	1.5	trace	0.0	0.0	0.0	0.0	0.7	1.3	2.8	18.3
Days With ≥ 1.0" Snow Depth	9	7	4	0	0	0	0	0	0	0	3	7	31

Norwich *Kingman County*   Elevation: 1,489 ft.   Latitude: 37° 27' N   Longitude: 97° 51' W

	JAN	FEB	MAR	APR	MAY	JUN	JUL	AUG	SEP	OCT	NOV	DEC	YEAR
Mean Maximum Temp. (°F)	42.4	49.3	59.3	69.3	77.9	88.6	94.9	93.5	84.4	72.6	56.6	45.5	69.5
Mean Temp. (°F)	32.3	38.2	47.4	57.2	66.6	76.5	82.2	80.9	72.4	60.6	46.1	35.8	58.0
Mean Minimum Temp. (°F)	22.2	27.1	35.3	45.0	55.2	64.4	69.3	68.2	60.2	48.4	35.5	26.1	46.4
Extreme Maximum Temp. (°F)	73	88	88	98	103	107	111	110	108	99	85	74	111
Extreme Minimum Temp. (°F)	-9	-11	3	18	35	46	53	53	33	20	5	-15	-15
Days Maximum Temp. ≥ 90°F	0	0	0	0	2	15	24	22	11	1	0	0	75
Days Maximum Temp. ≤ 32°F	7	4	1	0	0	0	0	0	0	0	1	3	16
Days Minimum Temp. ≤ 32°F	26	19	12	2	0	0	0	0	0	1	11	24	95
Days Minimum Temp. ≤ 0°F	1	1	0	0	0	0	0	0	0	0	0	1	3
Heating Degree Days (base 65°F)	1,006	749	542	254	62	4	0	0	33	184	562	898	4,294
Cooling Degree Days (base 65°F)	0	0	3	26	121	355	546	505	271	51	2	0	1,880
Mean Precipitation (in.)	0.78	0.94	2.48	2.91	4.12	4.18	2.81	3.01	2.99	2.37	2.03	0.96	29.58
Days With ≥ 0.1" Precipitation	2	2	4	5	6	6	5	4	4	4	3	2	47
Days With ≥ 1.0" Precipitation	0	0	1	1	1	1	1	1	1	1	1	0	9
Mean Snowfall (in.)	2.9	4.0	1.6	0.3	0.0	0.0	0.0	0.0	0.0	trace	0.4	1.9	11.1
Days With ≥ 1.0" Snow Depth	na	1	1	0	0	0	0	0	0	0	1	2	na

Oakley 4 W *Logan County*   Elevation: 3,097 ft.   Latitude: 39° 07' N   Longitude: 100° 57' W

	JAN	FEB	MAR	APR	MAY	JUN	JUL	AUG	SEP	OCT	NOV	DEC	YEAR
Mean Maximum Temp. (°F)	41.1	47.3	55.8	65.7	74.0	85.5	90.4	88.2	80.0	68.7	52.7	44.5	66.2
Mean Temp. (°F)	28.4	33.5	41.4	51.1	60.7	71.3	76.6	74.7	65.8	53.9	39.9	31.8	52.4
Mean Minimum Temp. (°F)	15.9	19.9	27.0	36.6	47.3	57.1	62.8	61.1	51.5	39.0	26.9	19.1	38.7
Extreme Maximum Temp. (°F)	78	82	92	96	101	107	108	105	103	94	83	78	108
Extreme Minimum Temp. (°F)	-14	-18	-7	7	27	33	46	44	23	9	-4	-21	-21
Days Maximum Temp. ≥ 90°F	0	0	0	0	1	10	18	15	6	0	0	0	50
Days Maximum Temp. ≤ 32°F	9	6	3	0	0	0	0	0	0	0	2	5	25
Days Minimum Temp. ≤ 32°F	30	26	23	10	1	0	0	0	0	7	22	29	148
Days Minimum Temp. ≤ 0°F	3	2	1	0	0	0	0	0	0	0	0	2	8
Heating Degree Days (base 65°F)	1,127	880	723	419	172	25	2	6	98	348	748	1,022	5,570
Cooling Degree Days (base 65°F)	0	0	0	9	42	207	355	304	124	9	0	0	1,050
Mean Precipitation (in.)	0.46	0.47	1.17	1.68	3.36	2.49	3.67	2.61	1.44	0.88	0.94	0.38	19.55
Days With ≥ 0.1" Precipitation	2	2	3	4	6	5	6	4	3	2	2	1	40
Days With ≥ 1.0" Precipitation	0	0	0	0	1	0	1	1	0	0	0	0	3
Mean Snowfall (in.)	5.1	4.8	6.0	2.5	trace	0.0	0.0	0.0	0.4	1.0	2.3	4.1	26.2
Days With ≥ 1.0" Snow Depth	8	6	3	1	0	0	0	0	0	0	2	5	25

Oberlin *Decatur County*   Elevation: 2,604 ft.   Latitude: 39° 50' N   Longitude: 100° 32' W

	JAN	FEB	MAR	APR	MAY	JUN	JUL	AUG	SEP	OCT	NOV	DEC	YEAR
Mean Maximum Temp. (°F)	40.6	47.0	55.4	66.1	75.0	86.5	91.9	89.8	81.5	69.6	52.2	43.6	66.6
Mean Temp. (°F)	27.4	32.8	40.7	51.2	61.2	71.9	77.4	75.4	65.9	53.3	38.6	30.2	52.1
Mean Minimum Temp. (°F)	14.1	18.5	25.9	36.2	47.2	57.1	62.8	60.8	50.3	36.9	24.9	16.8	37.6
Extreme Maximum Temp. (°F)	76	85	91	97	101	110	109	108	105	97	88	77	110
Extreme Minimum Temp. (°F)	-19	-19	-10	10	23	35	41	43	23	9	-8	-31	-31
Days Maximum Temp. ≥ 90°F	0	0	0	1	2	12	20	18	8	1	0	0	62
Days Maximum Temp. ≤ 32°F	9	5	2	0	0	0	0	0	0	0	3	6	25
Days Minimum Temp. ≤ 32°F	31	27	24	11	1	0	0	0	1	9	25	30	159
Days Minimum Temp. ≤ 0°F	4	2	1	0	0	0	0	0	0	0	0	2	9
Heating Degree Days (base 65°F)	1,160	904	747	418	164	22	2	5	99	366	785	1,073	5,745
Cooling Degree Days (base 65°F)	0	0	0	10	46	222	379	323	129	7	0	0	1,116
Mean Precipitation (in.)	0.49	0.60	1.62	2.22	3.67	3.35	3.79	2.76	1.60	1.11	1.02	0.48	22.71
Days With ≥ 0.1" Precipitation	1	2	4	4	7	5	6	5	4	2	2	1	43
Days With ≥ 1.0" Precipitation	0	0	0	0	1	1	1	1	0	0	0	0	4
Mean Snowfall (in.)	6.6	4.8	7.5	2.7	0.0	0.0	0.0	0.0	0.3	1.2	4.2	5.2	32.5
Days With ≥ 1.0" Snow Depth	na	na	na	1	0	0	0	0	0	0	0	1	na

Olathe 3 E *Johnson County*   Elevation: 1,053 ft.   Latitude: 38° 53' N   Longitude: 94° 46' W

	JAN	FEB	MAR	APR	MAY	JUN	JUL	AUG	SEP	OCT	NOV	DEC	YEAR
Mean Maximum Temp. (°F)	37.8	44.3	55.4	66.1	75.1	83.7	88.9	87.2	79.4	68.6	53.4	42.2	65.2
Mean Temp. (°F)	28.7	34.6	44.9	55.4	65.0	73.7	78.7	76.8	68.8	57.9	44.2	33.5	55.2
Mean Minimum Temp. (°F)	19.5	24.9	34.4	44.7	54.8	63.8	68.4	66.3	58.2	47.1	34.9	24.7	45.1
Extreme Maximum Temp. (°F)	69	81	85	91	94	105	108	106	99	93	84	69	108
Extreme Minimum Temp. (°F)	-16	-12	-8	13	30	43	48	46	33	18	3	-22	-22
Days Maximum Temp. ≥ 90°F	0	0	0	0	0	6	15	12	4	0	0	0	37
Days Maximum Temp. ≤ 32°F	10	6	1	0	0	0	0	0	0	0	1	6	24
Days Minimum Temp. ≤ 32°F	27	20	14	3	0	0	0	0	0	1	13	24	102
Days Minimum Temp. ≤ 0°F	3	1	0	0	0	0	0	0	0	0	0	1	5
Heating Degree Days (base 65°F)	1,119	851	618	304	84	7	1	1	55	246	619	970	4,875
Cooling Degree Days (base 65°F)	0	0	3	24	88	278	440	380	181	31	1	0	1,426
Mean Precipitation (in.)	1.26	1.20	2.68	3.95	5.47	5.22	3.88	3.60	5.00	3.40	2.94	1.78	40.38
Days With ≥ 0.1" Precipitation	3	3	5	7	9	7	6	6	6	5	5	3	65
Days With ≥ 1.0" Precipitation	0	0	1	1	2	2	1	1	2	1	1	0	12
Mean Snowfall (in.)	5.8	4.4	2.5	0.5	0.0	0.0	0.0	0.0	0.0	0.2	1.3	2.8	17.5
Days With ≥ 1.0" Snow Depth	11	7	2	0	0	0	0	0	0	0	1	5	26

Oskaloosa *Jefferson County*   Elevation: 1,112 ft.   Latitude: 39° 13' N   Longitude: 95° 19' W

	JAN	FEB	MAR	APR	MAY	JUN	JUL	AUG	SEP	OCT	NOV	DEC	YEAR
Mean Maximum Temp. (°F)	36.9	43.9	55.4	66.6	75.9	84.7	90.2	88.6	79.9	68.5	52.4	41.3	65.4
Mean Temp. (°F)	27.4	33.7	44.2	55.2	64.8	73.7	78.8	77.0	68.5	57.1	42.8	32.1	54.6
Mean Minimum Temp. (°F)	17.9	23.4	33.0	43.7	53.5	62.6	67.4	65.4	56.9	45.7	33.1	22.9	43.8
Extreme Maximum Temp. (°F)	70	82	86	91	93	109	110	108	102	95	84	70	110
Extreme Minimum Temp. (°F)	-20	-15	-11	10	28	43	48	45	29	16	-1	-24	-24
Days Maximum Temp. ≥ 90°F	0	0	0	0	1	7	17	15	5	0	0	0	45
Days Maximum Temp. ≤ 32°F	11	6	1	0	0	0	0	0	0	0	2	7	27
Days Minimum Temp. ≤ 32°F	28	22	15	4	0	0	0	0	0	2	14	26	111
Days Minimum Temp. ≤ 0°F	4	1	0	0	0	0	0	0	0	0	0	1	6
Heating Degree Days (base 65°F)	1,159	877	640	314	90	8	1	1	62	264	660	1,012	5,088
Cooling Degree Days (base 65°F)	0	0	2	24	81	271	432	375	169	24	1	0	1,379
Mean Precipitation (in.)	1.06	1.04	2.54	3.32	5.44	4.89	4.17	3.89	5.00	3.08	2.50	1.57	38.50
Days With ≥ 0.1" Precipitation	3	3	5	6	8	7	6	6	6	5	4	3	62
Days With ≥ 1.0" Precipitation	0	0	1	1	2	1	1	1	2	1	1	0	11
Mean Snowfall (in.)	5.5	4.4	2.8	0.6	0.0	0.0	0.0	0.0	0.0	0.3	1.1	3.6	18.3
Days With ≥ 1.0" Snow Depth	13	8	2	0	0	0	0	0	0	0	1	6	30

Ottawa *Franklin County*   Elevation: 898 ft.   Latitude: 38° 37' N   Longitude: 95° 17' W

	JAN	FEB	MAR	APR	MAY	JUN	JUL	AUG	SEP	OCT	NOV	DEC	YEAR
Mean Maximum Temp. (°F)	39.7	46.4	57.6	68.3	77.0	85.7	91.1	89.8	81.7	70.6	55.2	43.8	67.2
Mean Temp. (°F)	29.7	35.6	46.1	56.6	65.8	74.8	79.9	78.0	69.8	58.5	45.0	34.2	56.2
Mean Minimum Temp. (°F)	19.5	24.7	34.5	44.8	54.5	63.9	68.5	66.3	57.8	46.3	34.7	24.6	45.0
Extreme Maximum Temp. (°F)	73	84	86	95	95	108	109	108	101	95	86	73	109
Extreme Minimum Temp. (°F)	-15	-21	-6	19	30	42	47	45	28	17	4	-22	-22
Days Maximum Temp. ≥ 90°F	0	0	0	0	1	8	19	16	6	0	0	0	50
Days Maximum Temp. ≤ 32°F	9	5	1	0	0	0	0	0	0	0	1	5	21
Days Minimum Temp. ≤ 32°F	27	21	14	3	0	0	0	0	0	3	13	24	105
Days Minimum Temp. ≤ 0°F	3	1	0	0	0	0	0	0	0	0	0	1	5
Heating Degree Days (base 65°F)	1,089	825	583	276	74	5	0	1	49	229	598	946	4,675
Cooling Degree Days (base 65°F)	0	0	4	31	104	307	475	414	205	35	2	0	1,577
Mean Precipitation (in.)	1.29	1.22	2.88	3.72	5.49	5.09	3.57	3.77	4.42	3.34	2.89	1.75	39.43
Days With ≥ 0.1" Precipitation	3	3	5	7	8	7	6	6	6	5	5	4	65
Days With ≥ 1.0" Precipitation	0	0	1	1	2	1	1	1	2	1	1	0	11
Mean Snowfall (in.)	5.8	4.7	1.5	0.2	0.0	0.0	0.0	0.0	0.0	trace	0.9	3.0	16.1
Days With ≥ 1.0" Snow Depth	na	*1*	*0*	0	0	0	0	0	0	0	0	*1*	na

Paola *Miami County*   Elevation: 859 ft.   Latitude: 38° 35' N   Longitude: 94° 53' W

	JAN	FEB	MAR	APR	MAY	JUN	JUL	AUG	SEP	OCT	NOV	DEC	YEAR
Mean Maximum Temp. (°F)	39.3	46.2	57.1	68.2	76.8	85.2	90.6	89.1	80.8	69.9	54.6	43.1	66.7
Mean Temp. (°F)	29.4	35.5	45.7	56.2	65.4	74.3	79.3	77.4	69.1	57.8	44.5	33.7	55.7
Mean Minimum Temp. (°F)	19.5	24.7	34.3	44.1	54.0	63.3	67.9	65.6	57.3	45.7	34.5	24.3	44.6
Extreme Maximum Temp. (°F)	70	82	85	92	93	106	111	109	100	94	83	71	111
Extreme Minimum Temp. (°F)	-16	-20	-7	14	29	42	47	45	28	19	4	-21	-21
Days Maximum Temp. ≥ 90°F	0	0	0	0	0	7	18	15	5	0	0	0	45
Days Maximum Temp. ≤ 32°F	9	5	1	0	0	0	0	0	0	0	1	5	21
Days Minimum Temp. ≤ 32°F	27	21	14	4	0	0	0	0	0	3	13	25	107
Days Minimum Temp. ≤ 0°F	3	1	0	0	0	0	0	0	0	0	0	1	5
Heating Degree Days (base 65°F)	1,096	826	595	286	80	6	0	1	56	246	610	962	4,764
Cooling Degree Days (base 65°F)	0	0	3	28	99	297	457	397	190	29	2	0	1,502
Mean Precipitation (in.)	1.44	1.31	2.70	3.98	5.63	6.00	3.63	3.67	4.70	3.54	2.83	1.71	41.14
Days With ≥ 0.1" Precipitation	4	3	6	7	8	7	6	6	6	6	5	3	67
Days With ≥ 1.0" Precipitation	0	0	0	1	2	2	1	1	1	1	1	0	10
Mean Snowfall (in.)	5.5	4.5	2.0	0.3	0.0	0.0	0.0	0.0	0.0	0.1	0.7	2.4	15.5
Days With ≥ 1.0" Snow Depth	6	4	1	0	0	0	0	0	0	0	0	2	13

Parsons 2 NW *Labette County*   Elevation: 908 ft.   Latitude: 37° 22' N   Longitude: 95° 17' W

	JAN	FEB	MAR	APR	MAY	JUN	JUL	AUG	SEP	OCT	NOV	DEC	YEAR
Mean Maximum Temp. (°F)	40.6	47.7	57.7	67.8	76.3	85.3	91.3	90.3	81.3	70.6	55.9	45.3	67.5
Mean Temp. (°F)	30.8	37.1	46.7	56.4	65.7	74.6	80.0	78.3	69.9	58.5	45.8	35.6	56.6
Mean Minimum Temp. (°F)	20.9	26.3	35.7	45.0	55.0	64.0	68.6	66.4	58.5	46.5	35.6	25.9	45.7
Extreme Maximum Temp. (°F)	71	82	92	98	93	104	110	108	103	95	82	74	110
Extreme Minimum Temp. (°F)	-17	-16	-2	18	31	44	49	47	28	17	6	-17	-17
Days Maximum Temp. ≥ 90°F	0	0	0	0	0	9	19	18	6	0	0	0	52
Days Maximum Temp. ≤ 32°F	8	5	1	0	0	0	0	0	0	0	1	5	20
Days Minimum Temp. ≤ 32°F	27	21	12	3	0	0	0	0	0	2	12	23	100
Days Minimum Temp. ≤ 0°F	2	1	0	0	0	0	0	0	0	0	0	1	4
Heating Degree Days (base 65°F)	1,053	783	564	276	74	6	0	1	51	228	572	904	4,512
Cooling Degree Days (base 65°F)	0	0	3	21	92	295	462	413	196	27	2	0	1,511
Mean Precipitation (in.)	1.36	1.73	3.27	4.09	5.35	4.64	3.75	3.49	5.16	3.95	3.26	2.06	42.11
Days With ≥ 0.1" Precipitation	3	3	5	6	8	6	5	5	6	5	5	4	61
Days With ≥ 1.0" Precipitation	0	0	1	1	2	1	1	1	2	1	1	1	12
Mean Snowfall (in.)	*3.3*	*2.5*	1.4	trace	0.0	0.0	0.0	0.0	0.0	trace	0.4	*1.4*	*9.0*
Days With ≥ 1.0" Snow Depth	na	2	0	0	0	0	0	0	0	0	0	2	na

Perry Lake *Jefferson County*   Elevation: 958 ft.   Latitude: 39° 07' N   Longitude: 95° 25' W

	JAN	FEB	MAR	APR	MAY	JUN	JUL	AUG	SEP	OCT	NOV	DEC	YEAR
Mean Maximum Temp. (°F)	36.0	42.4	53.9	64.9	74.3	83.5	89.2	88.0	79.4	68.2	52.7	40.7	64.4
Mean Temp. (°F)	26.0	32.0	43.0	53.9	63.7	73.0	78.3	76.5	67.7	55.9	42.6	31.2	53.7
Mean Minimum Temp. (°F)	16.0	21.5	32.0	42.9	53.0	62.5	67.3	65.1	56.0	43.7	32.5	21.6	42.8
Extreme Maximum Temp. (°F)	72	78	88	93	96	110	111	112	101	94	84	74	112
Extreme Minimum Temp. (°F)	-18	-23	-9	9	29	41	45	45	28	13	1	-23	-23
Days Maximum Temp. ≥ 90°F	0	0	0	0	1	6	15	14	5	0	0	0	41
Days Maximum Temp. ≤ 32°F	12	8	2	0	0	0	0	0	0	0	2	7	31
Days Minimum Temp. ≤ 32°F	29	23	16	4	0	0	0	0	0	4	15	27	118
Days Minimum Temp. ≤ 0°F	4	2	0	0	0	0	0	0	0	0	0	1	7
Heating Degree Days (base 65°F)	1,201	926	678	348	113	12	1	2	76	298	665	1,043	5,363
Cooling Degree Days (base 65°F)	0	0	3	23	79	263	427	368	167	25	1	0	1,356
Mean Precipitation (in.)	0.95	0.89	2.40	3.42	5.30	5.12	3.81	3.75	4.64	3.00	2.42	1.53	37.23
Days With ≥ 0.1" Precipitation	2	2	5	6	8	7	6	6	6	5	4	3	60
Days With ≥ 1.0" Precipitation	0	0	1	1	2	2	1	1	1	1	1	0	11
Mean Snowfall (in.)	5.5	4.0	2.3	0.2	0.0	0.0	0.0	0.0	0.0	0.1	1.3	3.4	16.8
Days With ≥ 1.0" Snow Depth	11	6	2	0	0	0	0	0	0	0	1	5	25

Phillipsburg *Phillips County*   Elevation: 1,929 ft.   Latitude: 39° 45' N   Longitude: 99° 19' W

	JAN	FEB	MAR	APR	MAY	JUN	JUL	AUG	SEP	OCT	NOV	DEC	YEAR
Mean Maximum Temp. (°F)	38.6	44.5	55.4	66.8	75.6	87.5	93.4	91.4	82.1	69.7	52.1	42.0	66.6
Mean Temp. (°F)	26.0	31.1	41.8	52.8	62.5	73.7	79.2	77.1	67.1	54.4	39.1	29.5	52.9
Mean Minimum Temp. (°F)	13.4	17.6	28.2	38.7	49.4	59.8	64.9	62.7	52.1	39.0	26.1	17.0	39.1
Extreme Maximum Temp. (°F)	79	86	91	102	99	111	112	110	108	96	88	78	112
Extreme Minimum Temp. (°F)	-22	-16	-9	12	26	41	42	43	20	12	-7	-28	-28
Days Maximum Temp. ≥ 90°F	0	0	0	1	1	13	21	18	9	1	0	0	64
Days Maximum Temp. ≤ 32°F	10	6	2	0	0	0	0	0	0	0	2	7	27
Days Minimum Temp. ≤ 32°F	30	25	20	8	1	0	0	0	1	7	22	30	144
Days Minimum Temp. ≤ 0°F	4	3	1	0	0	0	0	0	0	0	0	2	10
Heating Degree Days (base 65°F)	1,201	951	715	374	135	14	1	3	84	336	770	1,094	5,678
Cooling Degree Days (base 65°F)	0	0	1	na	na	272	441	na	155	11	0	0	na
Mean Precipitation (in.)	0.42	0.47	2.02	2.31	4.12	3.06	3.20	2.73	2.27	1.37	1.02	0.48	23.47
Days With ≥ 0.1" Precipitation	1	1	4	5	7	5	5	5	4	3	2	2	44
Days With ≥ 1.0" Precipitation	0	0	1	1	1	1	1	1	0	0	0	0	6
Mean Snowfall (in.)	4.9	4.2	4.5	0.7	0.0	0.0	0.0	0.0	0.2	0.2	2.4	3.3	20.4
Days With ≥ 1.0" Snow Depth	na	4	na	0	0	0	0	0	0	0	1	na	na

Plainville 4 WNW *Rooks County*   Elevation: 2,080 ft.   Latitude: 39° 15' N   Longitude: 99° 23' W

	JAN	FEB	MAR	APR	MAY	JUN	JUL	AUG	SEP	OCT	NOV	DEC	YEAR
Mean Maximum Temp. (°F)	38.9	45.5	55.2	65.6	74.2	85.9	91.3	89.2	81.0	69.5	53.2	43.7	66.1
Mean Temp. (°F)	27.3	32.6	41.8	52.1	61.9	72.8	78.2	76.1	67.5	55.2	40.7	31.9	53.2
Mean Minimum Temp. (°F)	15.6	19.7	28.3	38.5	49.5	59.7	65.0	63.0	53.9	40.9	28.2	20.1	40.2
Extreme Maximum Temp. (°F)	77	85	92	102	101	113	112	107	107	95	85	78	113
Extreme Minimum Temp. (°F)	-17	-15	-5	11	28	40	45	45	29	6	-3	-29	-29
Days Maximum Temp. ≥ 90°F	0	0	0	1	1	11	19	15	7	1	0	0	55
Days Maximum Temp. ≤ 32°F	10	7	2	0	0	0	0	0	0	0	2	6	27
Days Minimum Temp. ≤ 32°F	30	26	20	8	0	0	0	0	0	5	21	29	139
Days Minimum Temp. ≤ 0°F	3	2	1	0	0	0	0	0	0	0	0	1	7
Heating Degree Days (base 65°F)	1,163	908	708	393	148	18	2	4	75	314	721	1,018	5,472
Cooling Degree Days (base 65°F)	0	0	1	15	56	247	401	335	155	15	0	0	1,225
Mean Precipitation (in.)	0.61	0.66	2.04	2.21	3.86	2.73	4.06	3.04	2.19	1.34	1.36	0.59	24.69
Days With ≥ 0.1" Precipitation	2	1	4	4	7	5	6	5	4	3	3	2	46
Days With ≥ 1.0" Precipitation	0	0	0	0	1	1	1	1	1	0	0	0	5
Mean Snowfall (in.)	4.8	5.6	5.1	1.6	0.0	0.0	0.0	0.0	trace	0.8	2.2	3.7	23.8
Days With ≥ 1.0" Snow Depth	10	8	4	1	0	0	0	0	0	0	2	6	31

Pomona Lake *Osage County*   Elevation: 1,062 ft.   Latitude: 38° 39' N   Longitude: 95° 34' W

	JAN	FEB	MAR	APR	MAY	JUN	JUL	AUG	SEP	OCT	NOV	DEC	YEAR
Mean Maximum Temp. (°F)	36.4	43.4	54.9	65.4	74.7	83.6	89.4	88.5	80.0	68.7	53.3	41.7	65.0
Mean Temp. (°F)	26.4	32.8	43.7	54.3	64.1	73.6	78.8	77.2	68.6	56.7	43.1	32.2	54.3
Mean Minimum Temp. (°F)	16.4	22.0	32.4	43.2	53.7	63.4	68.2	66.0	57.1	44.7	32.8	22.4	43.5
Extreme Maximum Temp. (°F)	73	79	86	92	95	108	110	108	102	94	85	71	110
Extreme Minimum Temp. (°F)	-15	-20	-7	13	32	43	51	50	32	18	3	-18	-20
Days Maximum Temp. ≥ 90°F	0	0	0	0	1	7	16	14	5	0	0	0	43
Days Maximum Temp. ≤ 32°F	11	7	1	0	0	0	0	0	0	0	1	7	27
Days Minimum Temp. ≤ 32°F	28	23	16	4	0	0	0	0	0	2	14	26	113
Days Minimum Temp. ≤ 0°F	3	2	0	0	0	0	0	0	0	0	0	1	6
Heating Degree Days (base 65°F)	1,190	904	655	337	102	9	1	2	63	276	653	1,011	5,203
Cooling Degree Days (base 65°F)	0	0	2	24	81	280	447	395	185	27	2	0	1,443
Mean Precipitation (in.)	1.11	1.08	2.77	3.72	5.19	4.90	3.39	3.62	4.53	2.82	2.81	1.56	37.50
Days With ≥ 0.1" Precipitation	3	3	5	7	8	7	6	5	6	5	4	3	62
Days With ≥ 1.0" Precipitation	0	0	1	1	2	2	1	1	2	1	1	0	12
Mean Snowfall (in.)	na	2.0	0.9	0.1	0.0	0.0	0.0	0.0	0.0	trace	0.5	1.1	na
Days With ≥ 1.0" Snow Depth	na	4	1	0	0	0	0	0	0	0	0	2	na

Pratt 4 W *Pratt County* Elevation: 1,938 ft. Latitude: 37° 41' N Longitude: 98° 48' W

	JAN	FEB	MAR	APR	MAY	JUN	JUL	AUG	SEP	OCT	NOV	DEC	YEAR
Mean Maximum Temp. (°F)	43.0	50.3	59.4	69.5	77.8	88.2	93.7	92.0	83.7	72.6	56.1	45.9	69.3
Mean Temp. (°F)	31.3	37.2	45.9	55.7	65.0	75.0	80.0	78.6	70.3	58.6	44.0	34.4	56.3
Mean Minimum Temp. (°F)	19.5	24.1	32.3	41.9	52.2	61.8	66.3	65.1	56.9	44.6	31.9	22.8	43.3
Extreme Maximum Temp. (°F)	80	88	90	106	107	112	112	110	110	98	87	74	112
Extreme Minimum Temp. (°F)	-13	-19	-2	16	31	41	45	47	26	14	1	-20	-20
Days Maximum Temp. ≥ 90°F	0	0	0	1	2	14	23	20	9	1	0	0	70
Days Maximum Temp. ≤ 32°F	8	4	1	0	0	0	0	0	0	0	1	4	18
Days Minimum Temp. ≤ 32°F	29	22	16	5	0	0	0	0	0	3	15	26	116
Days Minimum Temp. ≤ 0°F	2	1	0	0	0	0	0	0	0	0	0	1	4
Heating Degree Days (base 65°F)	1,039	778	588	294	89	8	0	1	47	228	623	944	4,639
Cooling Degree Days (base 65°F)	0	0	3	22	91	304	465	426	216	32	*0*	*0*	*1,559*
Mean Precipitation (in.)	0.65	0.87	2.27	2.80	3.79	3.71	3.20	3.00	2.60	2.12	1.36	0.96	27.33
Days With ≥ 0.1" Precipitation	2	2	4	4	6	6	5	5	4	3	3	2	46
Days With ≥ 1.0" Precipitation	0	0	1	1	1	1	1	1	1	1	0	0	8
Mean Snowfall (in.)	4.5	3.6	4.6	0.8	0.0	0.0	0.0	0.0	trace	trace	1.3	2.6	17.4
Days With ≥ 1.0" Snow Depth	*5*	4	2	0	0	0	0	0	0	0	1	2	*14*

Quinter *Gove County* Elevation: 2,677 ft. Latitude: 39° 04' N Longitude: 100° 14' W

	JAN	FEB	MAR	APR	MAY	JUN	JUL	AUG	SEP	OCT	NOV	DEC	YEAR
Mean Maximum Temp. (°F)	39.5	45.3	54.1	64.5	73.6	85.2	91.0	88.7	80.0	68.4	52.1	42.6	65.4
Mean Temp. (°F)	27.5	32.7	40.4	50.9	60.8	71.6	77.3	75.4	66.3	54.1	39.7	30.7	52.3
Mean Minimum Temp. (°F)	15.4	19.9	26.7	37.2	47.9	58.0	63.6	62.1	52.4	39.9	27.2	18.7	39.1
Extreme Maximum Temp. (°F)	79	84	91	99	98	107	109	107	104	95	87	76	109
Extreme Minimum Temp. (°F)	-13	-15	-6	11	29	38	46	48	26	12	0	-23	-23
Days Maximum Temp. ≥ 90°F	0	0	0	1	1	10	19	16	7	1	0	0	55
Days Maximum Temp. ≤ 32°F	10	6	3	0	0	0	0	0	0	0	3	7	29
Days Minimum Temp. ≤ 32°F	30	26	23	9	1	0	0	0	1	6	22	30	148
Days Minimum Temp. ≤ 0°F	4	2	0	0	0	0	0	0	0	0	0	2	8
Heating Degree Days (base 65°F)	1,157	906	756	427	171	24	2	5	96	343	752	1,057	5,696
Cooling Degree Days (base 65°F)	0	0	0	11	47	229	388	340	143	14	0	0	1,172
Mean Precipitation (in.)	0.56	0.68	1.75	2.18	3.96	2.87	4.09	3.37	1.83	1.28	1.17	0.53	24.27
Days With ≥ 0.1" Precipitation	2	2	4	5	7	6	6	5	3	3	2	2	47
Days With ≥ 1.0" Precipitation	0	0	0	0	1	1	1	1	0	0	0	0	4
Mean Snowfall (in.)	4.9	*4.8*	*6.0*	1.3	trace	0.0	0.0	0.0	0.1	1.3	2.0	*4.3*	*24.7*
Days With ≥ 1.0" Snow Depth	*2*	na	na	0	0	0	0	0	0	0	1	na	na

Russell Municipal Airport *Russell County* Elevation: 1,856 ft. Latitude: 38° 53' N Longitude: 98° 49' W

	JAN	FEB	MAR	APR	MAY	JUN	JUL	AUG	SEP	OCT	NOV	DEC	YEAR
Mean Maximum Temp. (°F)	38.7	45.1	55.3	65.6	74.5	86.3	92.3	89.8	80.4	68.6	53.0	42.7	66.0
Mean Temp. (°F)	27.8	33.2	43.2	53.4	63.2	74.2	79.9	77.8	68.2	56.0	41.5	31.8	54.2
Mean Minimum Temp. (°F)	16.9	21.4	31.0	41.2	51.9	62.1	67.4	65.7	55.9	43.2	29.9	20.9	42.3
Extreme Maximum Temp. (°F)	84	85	91	101	99	114	111	109	104	96	86	73	114
Extreme Minimum Temp. (°F)	-18	-16	-4	14	29	43	47	49	28	13	-3	-24	-24
Days Maximum Temp. ≥ 90°F	0	0	0	0	2	11	20	17	7	1	0	0	58
Days Maximum Temp. ≤ 32°F	10	6	2	0	0	0	0	0	0	0	2	6	26
Days Minimum Temp. ≤ 32°F	30	24	17	5	0	0	0	0	0	4	19	29	128
Days Minimum Temp. ≤ 0°F	3	2	0	0	0	0	0	0	0	0	0	1	6
Heating Degree Days (base 65°F)	1,143	890	671	359	125	13	1	2	77	297	698	1,023	5,299
Cooling Degree Days (base 65°F)	0	0	2	22	74	290	468	406	187	21	1	*0*	*1,471*
Mean Precipitation (in.)	0.70	0.72	2.23	2.96	3.98	3.07	3.51	3.43	2.15	1.54	1.18	0.90	26.37
Days With ≥ 0.1" Precipitation	2	2	4	5	7	6	5	6	4	3	3	2	49
Days With ≥ 1.0" Precipitation	0	0	1	1	1	1	1	1	1	0	0	0	7
Mean Snowfall (in.)	6.0	5.0	5.4	1.4	trace	trace	trace	trace	*trace*	0.5	2.3	*4.2*	*24.8*
Days With ≥ 1.0" Snow Depth	10	7	3	1	0	0	0	0	0	0	2	*5*	*28*

Russell Springs 4 W *Logan County* Elevation: 2,929 ft. Latitude: 38° 55' N Longitude: 101° 16' W

	JAN	FEB	MAR	APR	MAY	JUN	JUL	AUG	SEP	OCT	NOV	DEC	YEAR
Mean Maximum Temp. (°F)	43.1	49.6	58.0	68.0	76.5	87.6	93.1	91.1	83.0	71.2	54.3	46.0	68.5
Mean Temp. (°F)	28.6	34.4	42.4	52.4	62.0	72.3	77.9	76.0	66.8	54.0	39.2	31.0	53.1
Mean Minimum Temp. (°F)	14.0	19.1	26.8	36.8	47.4	56.9	62.6	60.8	50.6	36.8	24.3	16.1	37.7
Extreme Maximum Temp. (°F)	81	84	92	101	102	111	112	110	105	95	87	78	112
Extreme Minimum Temp. (°F)	-22	-19	-6	6	24	30	41	40	21	6	-7	-27	-27
Days Maximum Temp. ≥ 90°F	0	0	0	1	3	13	22	19	9	1	0	0	68
Days Maximum Temp. ≤ 32°F	8	4	1	0	0	0	0	0	0	0	2	5	20
Days Minimum Temp. ≤ 32°F	31	27	22	10	1	0	0	0	1	10	24	30	156
Days Minimum Temp. ≤ 0°F	4	2	0	0	0	0	0	0	0	0	0	2	8
Heating Degree Days (base 65°F)	1,124	858	694	384	146	19	2	3	84	343	767	1,048	5,472
Cooling Degree Days (base 65°F)	0	0	1	14	61	247	406	356	150	10	0	0	1,245
Mean Precipitation (in.)	0.41	0.44	1.36	1.49	3.17	2.61	3.28	2.45	1.40	0.92	0.88	0.33	18.74
Days With ≥ 0.1" Precipitation	1	1	3	4	6	4	6	4	3	2	2	1	37
Days With ≥ 1.0" Precipitation	0	0	0	0	1	0	1	1	0	0	0	0	3
Mean Snowfall (in.)	5.3	3.9	5.3	1.6	trace	0.0	0.0	0.0	0.2	0.8	2.7	4.4	24.2
Days With ≥ 1.0" Snow Depth	9	5	2	0	0	0	0	0	0	0	2	5	23

Saint Francis *Cheyenne County*   Elevation: 3,359 ft.   Latitude: 39° 46' N   Longitude: 101° 49' W

	JAN	FEB	MAR	APR	MAY	JUN	JUL	AUG	SEP	OCT	NOV	DEC	YEAR
Mean Maximum Temp. (°F)	41.5	47.7	55.2	65.0	74.6	86.1	91.6	89.7	81.3	69.5	52.9	44.4	66.6
Mean Temp. (°F)	28.0	33.4	40.8	50.2	60.5	71.2	76.8	74.8	65.5	53.0	38.8	30.6	52.0
Mean Minimum Temp. (°F)	14.5	19.0	26.4	35.4	46.4	56.2	61.9	59.8	49.7	36.5	24.7	16.8	37.3
Extreme Maximum Temp. (°F)	81	83	88	96	101	108	110	109	105	97	87	78	110
Extreme Minimum Temp. (°F)	-23	-22	-5	6	23	33	43	41	22	8	-6	-31	-31
Days Maximum Temp. ≥ 90°F	0	0	0	1	2	12	20	18	9	1	0	0	63
Days Maximum Temp. ≤ 32°F	8	5	3	0	0	0	0	0	0	0	3	6	25
Days Minimum Temp. ≤ 32°F	31	27	24	11	1	0	0	0	1	10	26	30	161
Days Minimum Temp. ≤ 0°F	4	2	1	0	0	0	0	0	0	0	0	2	9
Heating Degree Days (base 65°F)	1,139	885	744	444	179	27	3	6	100	373	780	1,060	5,740
Cooling Degree Days (base 65°F)	0	0	0	6	40	202	359	304	113	6	0	0	1,030
Mean Precipitation (in.)	0.51	0.48	1.16	1.72	3.18	2.56	2.93	2.14	1.15	1.00	0.77	0.41	18.01
Days With ≥ 0.1" Precipitation	2	2	3	4	7	5	6	4	3	2	2	1	41
Days With ≥ 1.0" Precipitation	0	0	0	0	1	0	1	0	0	0	0	0	2
Mean Snowfall (in.)	6.6	4.9	6.9	3.6	0.2	0.0	0.0	0.0	0.4	2.3	4.7	4.9	34.5
Days With ≥ 1.0" Snow Depth	10	5	3	1	0	0	0	0	0	1	3	5	28

Salina Municipal Airport *Saline County*   Elevation: 1,263 ft.   Latitude: 38° 49' N   Longitude: 97° 40' W

	JAN	FEB	MAR	APR	MAY	JUN	JUL	AUG	SEP	OCT	NOV	DEC	YEAR
Mean Maximum Temp. (°F)	38.4	44.8	56.0	66.2	75.4	86.7	92.9	90.7	81.1	69.2	53.5	42.7	66.5
Mean Temp. (°F)	28.4	33.8	44.7	54.7	64.5	75.2	81.0	79.2	69.6	57.3	43.1	32.8	55.4
Mean Minimum Temp. (°F)	18.3	22.8	33.4	43.1	53.4	63.6	69.2	67.6	58.0	45.3	32.6	22.8	44.2
Extreme Maximum Temp. (°F)	78	83	89	105	100	112	112	108	106	96	86	71	112
Extreme Minimum Temp. (°F)	-18	-19	-4	13	29	43	49	48	30	14	-3	-24	-24
Days Maximum Temp. ≥ 90°F	0	0	0	0	1	12	21	18	8	1	0	0	61
Days Maximum Temp. ≤ 32°F	10	6	1	0	0	0	0	0	0	0	1	6	24
Days Minimum Temp. ≤ 32°F	29	22	14	4	0	0	0	0	0	2	15	27	113
Days Minimum Temp. ≤ 0°F	2	2	0	0	0	0	0	0	0	0	0	1	5
Heating Degree Days (base 65°F)	1,125	874	626	324	99	8	0	1	61	264	653	992	5,027
Cooling Degree Days (base 65°F)	0	0	3	25	90	323	516	455	213	31	1	0	1,657
Mean Precipitation (in.)	0.83	0.98	2.57	3.18	5.03	4.27	4.26	3.56	2.72	2.42	1.55	1.00	32.37
Days With ≥ 0.1" Precipitation	2	2	5	5	8	6	5	5	5	4	3	3	53
Days With ≥ 1.0" Precipitation	0	0	1	1	1	1	1	1	1	1	0	0	8
Mean Snowfall (in.)	6.6	4.7	2.5	0.6	trace	trace	trace	trace	0.0	0.3	1.2	3.2	19.1
Days With ≥ 1.0" Snow Depth	11	8	2	0	0	0	0	0	0	0	1	4	26

Scott City *Scott County*   Elevation: 2,969 ft.   Latitude: 38° 29' N   Longitude: 100° 55' W

	JAN	FEB	MAR	APR	MAY	JUN	JUL	AUG	SEP	OCT	NOV	DEC	YEAR
Mean Maximum Temp. (°F)	42.8	49.2	57.5	67.5	76.4	87.7	92.4	90.2	82.3	71.1	54.5	45.6	68.1
Mean Temp. (°F)	29.3	34.8	42.6	52.2	62.1	72.9	77.8	75.9	67.3	55.2	40.7	32.2	53.6
Mean Minimum Temp. (°F)	15.8	20.4	27.6	36.8	47.8	58.0	63.1	61.6	52.2	39.3	26.8	18.8	39.0
Extreme Maximum Temp. (°F)	80	87	90	98	101	111	109	107	103	96	88	82	111
Extreme Minimum Temp. (°F)	-22	-15	-7	6	26	34	47	43	23	9	-2	-18	-22
Days Maximum Temp. ≥ 90°F	0	0	0	1	3	14	21	18	9	1	0	0	67
Days Maximum Temp. ≤ 32°F	8	5	2	0	0	0	0	0	0	0	2	5	22
Days Minimum Temp. ≤ 32°F	30	26	22	9	1	0	0	0	0	7	23	30	148
Days Minimum Temp. ≤ 0°F	3	2	0	0	0	0	0	0	0	0	0	2	7
Heating Degree Days (base 65°F)	1,100	846	687	388	142	19	2	3	78	311	723	1,009	5,308
Cooling Degree Days (base 65°F)	0	0	0	9	56	249	402	350	156	14	0	0	1,236
Mean Precipitation (in.)	0.69	0.63	1.44	1.70	3.02	2.91	3.16	2.65	1.77	1.01	1.12	0.59	20.69
Days With ≥ 0.1" Precipitation	2	2	3	4	6	5	5	5	3	2	2	2	41
Days With ≥ 1.0" Precipitation	0	0	0	0	1	1	1	1	0	0	0	0	4
Mean Snowfall (in.)	6.3	5.3	5.7	2.4	trace	0.0	0.0	0.0	trace	1.1	2.6	4.5	27.9
Days With ≥ 1.0" Snow Depth	11	6	4	1	0	0	0	0	0	1	3	7	33

Sedan *Chautauqua County*   Elevation: 879 ft.   Latitude: 37° 08' N   Longitude: 96° 11' W

	JAN	FEB	MAR	APR	MAY	JUN	JUL	AUG	SEP	OCT	NOV	DEC	YEAR
Mean Maximum Temp. (°F)	43.3	50.2	59.9	70.1	77.8	86.2	92.5	92.2	83.0	72.4	58.3	47.5	69.5
Mean Temp. (°F)	31.5	37.6	47.1	57.3	66.1	75.1	80.4	79.3	70.8	59.0	46.3	36.0	57.2
Mean Minimum Temp. (°F)	19.7	24.9	34.2	44.5	54.4	63.8	68.3	66.4	58.5	45.4	34.3	24.4	44.9
Extreme Maximum Temp. (°F)	76	88	90	99	95	103	111	110	107	96	86	76	111
Extreme Minimum Temp. (°F)	-16	-19	3	16	29	44	47	47	32	17	3	-15	-19
Days Maximum Temp. ≥ 90°F	0	0	0	1	1	10	22	21	9	1	0	0	65
Days Maximum Temp. ≤ 32°F	7	4	1	0	0	0	0	0	0	0	0	4	16
Days Minimum Temp. ≤ 32°F	28	21	14	3	0	0	0	0	0	3	14	25	108
Days Minimum Temp. ≤ 0°F	2	1	0	0	0	0	0	0	0	0	0	1	4
Heating Degree Days (base 65°F)	1,031	767	552	257	69	4	0	0	47	219	557	892	4,395
Cooling Degree Days (base 65°F)	0	0	4	29	106	312	494	461	232	36	4	0	1,678
Mean Precipitation (in.)	1.32	1.61	3.24	3.76	5.99	4.77	3.36	3.04	4.53	3.96	3.13	1.92	40.63
Days With ≥ 0.1" Precipitation	3	3	5	6	7	6	5	5	6	5	4	3	58
Days With ≥ 1.0" Precipitation	0	0	1	1	2	2	1	1	1	1	1	0	11
Mean Snowfall (in.)	3.4	3.4	2.0	trace	0.0	0.0	0.0	0.0	0.0	trace	0.5	1.8	11.1
Days With ≥ 1.0" Snow Depth	5	4	2	0	0	0	0	0	0	0	0	2	12

Sharon Springs *Wallace County*   Elevation: 3,448 ft.   Latitude: 38° 54' N   Longitude: 101° 45' W

	JAN	FEB	MAR	APR	MAY	JUN	JUL	AUG	SEP	OCT	NOV	DEC	YEAR
Mean Maximum Temp. (°F)	44.1	49.9	57.8	67.7	76.8	88.2	93.1	91.0	82.7	71.1	54.6	45.9	68.6
Mean Temp. (°F)	30.5	35.6	43.1	52.7	62.5	73.1	78.4	76.4	67.6	55.2	40.7	32.8	54.1
Mean Minimum Temp. (°F)	16.9	21.2	28.4	37.6	48.3	58.0	63.7	61.9	52.4	39.3	26.9	19.7	39.5
Extreme Maximum Temp. (°F)	78	82	87	98	101	112	109	107	103	95	87	82	112
Extreme Minimum Temp. (°F)	-20	-16	-3	11	25	34	44	44	22	10	-4	-22	-22
Days Maximum Temp. ≥ 90°F	0	0	0	0	2	14	22	19	8	1	0	0	66
Days Maximum Temp. ≤ 32°F	7	4	2	0	0	0	0	0	0	0	1	5	19
Days Minimum Temp. ≤ 32°F	30	25	21	9	1	0	0	0	1	6	23	29	145
Days Minimum Temp. ≤ 0°F	3	1	0	0	0	0	0	0	0	0	0	2	6
Heating Degree Days (base 65°F)	1,061	824	674	374	136	15	1	3	72	308	721	991	5,180
Cooling Degree Days (base 65°F)	0	0	1	10	64	254	413	364	158	13	0	0	1,277
Mean Precipitation (in.)	0.44	0.56	1.41	1.57	3.45	3.04	3.23	2.45	1.34	1.04	0.90	0.44	19.87
Days With ≥ 0.1" Precipitation	1	2	3	4	7	5	6	5	3	3	2	1	42
Days With ≥ 1.0" Precipitation	0	0	0	0	1	1	1	1	0	0	0	0	4
Mean Snowfall (in.)	4.8	4.0	7.1	2.3	0.2	0.0	0.0	0.0	0.2	1.3	3.0	3.5	26.4
Days With ≥ 1.0" Snow Depth	na	na	2	1	0	0	0	0	0	0	2	3	na

Smith Center *Smith County*   Elevation: 1,778 ft.   Latitude: 39° 47' N   Longitude: 98° 47' W

	JAN	FEB	MAR	APR	MAY	JUN	JUL	AUG	SEP	OCT	NOV	DEC	YEAR
Mean Maximum Temp. (°F)	38.1	45.2	55.4	67.2	76.2	87.5	93.1	90.7	82.1	69.8	51.9	41.4	66.6
Mean Temp. (°F)	27.0	33.2	42.7	54.1	63.9	74.6	80.0	77.8	68.8	56.3	40.6	30.8	54.1
Mean Minimum Temp. (°F)	15.9	21.1	30.0	40.8	51.5	61.6	66.8	64.9	55.4	42.8	29.2	20.0	41.7
Extreme Maximum Temp. (°F)	79	85	91	102	100	110	111	111	105	97	87	72	111
Extreme Minimum Temp. (°F)	-18	-17	-10	14	29	38	45	46	23	15	-6	-26	-26
Days Maximum Temp. ≥ 90°F	0	0	0	1	2	13	21	18	8	1	0	0	64
Days Maximum Temp. ≤ 32°F	10	6	2	0	0	0	0	0	0	0	2	6	26
Days Minimum Temp. ≤ 32°F	30	24	19	6	0	0	0	0	0	4	19	29	131
Days Minimum Temp. ≤ 0°F	3	2	0	0	0	0	0	0	0	0	0	1	6
Heating Degree Days (base 65°F)	1,171	892	686	342	110	10	0	2	66	286	725	1,055	5,345
Cooling Degree Days (base 65°F)	0	0	1	21	80	298	467	402	192	23	0	0	1,484
Mean Precipitation (in.)	0.47	0.48	1.93	2.41	3.93	3.13	3.21	3.18	2.38	1.64	1.31	0.55	24.62
Days With ≥ 0.1" Precipitation	2	1	4	5	7	6	5	5	4	3	3	2	47
Days With ≥ 1.0" Precipitation	0	0	0	1	1	1	1	1	1	0	0	0	6
Mean Snowfall (in.)	4.2	3.7	3.7	0.8	trace	0.0	0.0	0.0	0.2	0.5	2.0	3.0	18.1
Days With ≥ 1.0" Snow Depth	11	7	3	1	0	0	0	0	0	0	2	6	30

Sterling *Rice County*   Elevation: 1,633 ft.   Latitude: 38° 13' N   Longitude: 98° 12' W

	JAN	FEB	MAR	APR	MAY	JUN	JUL	AUG	SEP	OCT	NOV	DEC	YEAR
Mean Maximum Temp. (°F)	40.3	47.2	56.6	67.1	76.5	87.5	92.8	90.9	81.9	70.0	54.5	44.0	67.4
Mean Temp. (°F)	29.6	35.4	44.5	54.7	64.9	75.4	80.6	78.8	69.7	57.5	43.2	33.4	55.6
Mean Minimum Temp. (°F)	18.9	23.6	32.3	42.2	53.3	63.2	68.4	66.7	57.5	44.8	31.9	22.8	43.8
Extreme Maximum Temp. (°F)	76	84	91	102	101	112	108	112	105	95	89	73	112
Extreme Minimum Temp. (°F)	-12	-13	-3	17	32	42	49	44	30	16	3	-18	-18
Days Maximum Temp. ≥ 90°F	0	0	0	1	2	13	22	19	8	1	0	0	66
Days Maximum Temp. ≤ 32°F	9	5	1	0	0	0	0	0	0	0	1	6	22
Days Minimum Temp. ≤ 32°F	29	22	16	4	0	0	0	0	0	2	16	27	116
Days Minimum Temp. ≤ 0°F	2	1	0	0	0	0	0	0	0	0	0	1	4
Heating Degree Days (base 65°F)	1,090	829	631	323	94	8	0	1	57	257	648	973	4,911
Cooling Degree Days (base 65°F)	0	0	2	23	98	326	495	440	214	30	1	0	1,629
Mean Precipitation (in.)	0.73	0.96	2.53	2.49	4.31	3.85	3.60	3.09	2.73	2.27	1.38	0.94	28.88
Days With ≥ 0.1" Precipitation	2	2	5	5	7	6	5	5	4	4	3	2	50
Days With ≥ 1.0" Precipitation	0	0	1	1	1	1	1	1	1	1	0	0	8
Mean Snowfall (in.)	4.5	3.9	1.9	1.3	0.0	0.0	0.0	0.0	0.0	0.2	1.0	2.4	15.2
Days With ≥ 1.0" Snow Depth	7	5	1	0	0	0	0	0	0	0	1	2	16

Sublette *Haskell County*   Elevation: 2,919 ft.   Latitude: 37° 29' N   Longitude: 100° 50' W

	JAN	FEB	MAR	APR	MAY	JUN	JUL	AUG	SEP	OCT	NOV	DEC	YEAR
Mean Maximum Temp. (°F)	44.5	51.3	59.7	68.9	77.4	87.9	92.7	90.5	82.7	72.0	56.3	47.2	69.3
Mean Temp. (°F)	31.1	36.8	44.8	53.8	63.4	73.6	78.3	76.6	68.4	56.7	42.5	33.9	55.0
Mean Minimum Temp. (°F)	17.7	22.3	29.8	38.6	49.5	59.3	63.9	62.7	54.0	41.3	28.7	20.6	40.7
Extreme Maximum Temp. (°F)	80	88	92	98	104	110	107	107	102	94	88	75	110
Extreme Minimum Temp. (°F)	-24	-16	-2	13	28	42	49	46	25	13	-3	-14	-24
Days Maximum Temp. ≥ 90°F	0	0	0	1	3	14	22	19	9	1	0	0	69
Days Maximum Temp. ≤ 32°F	7	4	1	0	0	0	0	0	0	0	1	5	18
Days Minimum Temp. ≤ 32°F	30	24	19	7	1	0	0	0	0	4	21	29	135
Days Minimum Temp. ≤ 0°F	2	1	0	0	0	0	0	0	0	0	0	1	4
Heating Degree Days (base 65°F)	1,043	789	621	343	115	13	1	2	63	273	669	956	4,888
Cooling Degree Days (base 65°F)	0	0	1	13	70	264	413	373	172	20	0	0	1,326
Mean Precipitation (in.)	0.45	0.44	1.34	1.52	3.12	2.92	2.61	2.48	1.77	1.20	0.93	0.42	19.20
Days With ≥ 0.1" Precipitation	1	1	3	4	6	5	4	4	3	2	2	1	36
Days With ≥ 1.0" Precipitation	0	0	0	0	1	1	1	1	0	0	0	0	4
Mean Snowfall (in.)	4.3	3.6	4.9	1.0	trace	0.0	0.0	0.0	trace	0.8	2.2	3.5	20.3
Days With ≥ 1.0" Snow Depth	8	4	3	1	0	0	0	0	0	0	2	5	23

Syracuse *Hamilton County*   Elevation: 3,257 ft.   Latitude: 37° 59' N   Longitude: 101° 45' W

	JAN	FEB	MAR	APR	MAY	JUN	JUL	AUG	SEP	OCT	NOV	DEC	YEAR
Mean Maximum Temp. (°F)	44.6	51.8	59.7	69.0	77.6	88.9	93.8	91.8	83.8	72.7	56.8	47.4	69.8
Mean Temp. (°F)	29.2	35.7	43.6	52.8	62.7	73.3	78.6	76.8	67.8	55.3	40.9	31.9	54.0
Mean Minimum Temp. (°F)	13.7	19.6	27.5	36.6	47.7	57.7	63.3	61.7	51.8	37.8	24.9	16.4	38.2
Extreme Maximum Temp. (°F)	82	86	94	100	103	109	110	107	105	98	87	78	110
Extreme Minimum Temp. (°F)	-25	-17	-10	8	26	38	44	40	21	9	-8	-21	-25
Days Maximum Temp. ≥ 90°F	0	0	0	1	3	15	23	20	11	2	0	0	75
Days Maximum Temp. ≤ 32°F	7	3	1	0	0	0	0	0	0	0	1	4	16
Days Minimum Temp. ≤ 32°F	31	26	22	10	1	0	0	0	1	9	24	30	154
Days Minimum Temp. ≤ 0°F	4	1	0	0	0	0	0	0	0	0	0	2	7
Heating Degree Days (base 65°F)	1,104	822	656	370	134	15	1	2	71	308	717	1,020	5,220
Cooling Degree Days (base 65°F)	0	0	1	11	70	265	428	381	168	15	0	0	1,339
Mean Precipitation (in.)	0.42	0.45	1.10	1.24	2.44	2.48	2.65	2.43	1.33	0.92	0.70	0.40	16.56
Days With ≥ 0.1" Precipitation	1	1	3	3	5	5	5	4	3	2	2	1	35
Days With ≥ 1.0" Precipitation	0	0	0	0	1	1	1	1	0	0	0	0	4
Mean Snowfall (in.)	4.1	3.0	4.8	1.5	trace	0.0	0.0	0.0	0.2	0.8	2.1	3.5	20.0
Days With ≥ 1.0" Snow Depth	na	4	3	1	0	0	0	0	0	0	2	6	na

Toronto Lake *Woodson County*   Elevation: 948 ft.   Latitude: 37° 45' N   Longitude: 95° 56' W

	JAN	FEB	MAR	APR	MAY	JUN	JUL	AUG	SEP	OCT	NOV	DEC	YEAR
Mean Maximum Temp. (°F)	39.4	45.5	57.3	67.5	75.7	84.8	90.8	89.9	81.5	70.3	55.1	44.4	66.9
Mean Temp. (°F)	28.7	34.2	45.8	56.0	65.0	74.2	79.4	78.0	69.4	57.6	44.5	33.8	55.6
Mean Minimum Temp. (°F)	18.0	22.8	34.2	44.5	54.1	63.5	68.0	66.1	57.3	44.7	33.9	23.2	44.2
Extreme Maximum Temp. (°F)	73	80	88	96	93	103	110	109	102	94	85	73	110
Extreme Minimum Temp. (°F)	-13	-17	0	17	29	44	49	47	31	17	2	-18	-18
Days Maximum Temp. ≥ 90°F	0	0	0	0	0	7	18	17	6	1	0	0	49
Days Maximum Temp. ≤ 32°F	9	6	1	0	0	0	0	0	0	0	1	5	22
Days Minimum Temp. ≤ 32°F	28	23	13	3	0	0	0	0	0	3	13	25	108
Days Minimum Temp. ≤ 0°F	2	2	0	0	0	0	0	0	0	0	0	1	5
Heating Degree Days (base 65°F)	1,116	862	592	289	85	6	0	1	52	252	610	961	4,826
Cooling Degree Days (base 65°F)	0	0	3	25	91	297	464	418	194	25	2	0	1,519
Mean Precipitation (in.)	1.06	1.36	2.89	3.64	4.83	4.92	3.91	4.12	3.81	3.35	2.70	1.70	38.29
Days With ≥ 0.1" Precipitation	3	3	5	6	7	6	6	5	5	4	4	3	57
Days With ≥ 1.0" Precipitation	0	0	1	1	2	2	1	1	1	1	1	0	11
Mean Snowfall (in.)	na	na	0.3	0.0	0.0	0.0	0.0	0.0	0.0	0.0	0.2	na	na
Days With ≥ 1.0" Snow Depth	na	na	na	0	0	0	0	0	0	0	0	na	na

Tribune 1 W *Greeley County*   Elevation: 3,635 ft.   Latitude: 38° 28' N   Longitude: 101° 47' W

	JAN	FEB	MAR	APR	MAY	JUN	JUL	AUG	SEP	OCT	NOV	DEC	YEAR
Mean Maximum Temp. (°F)	42.6	48.9	56.6	66.2	75.0	86.5	92.0	89.6	81.6	69.8	53.7	45.3	67.3
Mean Temp. (°F)	28.4	33.8	41.2	50.2	60.1	70.8	76.3	74.3	65.5	53.1	39.2	31.0	52.0
Mean Minimum Temp. (°F)	14.2	18.7	25.8	34.2	45.1	55.1	60.5	59.0	49.3	36.3	24.7	16.7	36.6
Extreme Maximum Temp. (°F)	79	81	88	97	103	107	106	104	103	93	84	79	107
Extreme Minimum Temp. (°F)	-25	-23	-9	8	23	32	42	42	20	6	-4	-21	-25
Days Maximum Temp. ≥ 90°F	0	0	0	0	2	12	21	18	8	1	0	0	62
Days Maximum Temp. ≤ 32°F	8	4	2	0	0	0	0	0	0	0	2	5	21
Days Minimum Temp. ≤ 32°F	31	27	25	13	2	0	0	0	1	10	25	30	164
Days Minimum Temp. ≤ 0°F	3	2	0	0	0	0	0	0	0	0	0	2	7
Heating Degree Days (base 65°F)	1,128	874	730	441	183	26	2	5	97	369	766	1,047	5,668
Cooling Degree Days (base 65°F)	0	0	0	4	39	199	350	300	116	7	0	0	1,015
Mean Precipitation (in.)	0.43	0.52	1.16	1.28	2.78	2.67	3.06	2.12	1.35	0.94	0.62	0.36	17.29
Days With ≥ 0.1" Precipitation	1	1	3	3	6	5	5	4	3	2	2	1	36
Days With ≥ 1.0" Precipitation	0	0	0	0	1	1	1	0	0	0	0	0	3
Mean Snowfall (in.)	4.9	4.5	6.3	2.6	trace	0.0	0.0	0.0	0.2	1.2	2.6	3.7	26.0
Days With ≥ 1.0" Snow Depth	9	5	4	1	0	0	0	0	0	0	3	6	28

Troy 2 E *Doniphan County*   Elevation: 1,059 ft.   Latitude: 39° 47' N   Longitude: 95° 05' W

	JAN	FEB	MAR	APR	MAY	JUN	JUL	AUG	SEP	OCT	NOV	DEC	YEAR
Mean Maximum Temp. (°F)	35.0	42.1	54.1	66.1	75.6	84.3	88.3	86.7	79.7	68.5	51.7	39.3	64.3
Mean Temp. (°F)	25.8	32.2	43.1	54.5	64.6	73.5	77.5	75.5	67.8	56.6	42.1	30.6	53.6
Mean Minimum Temp. (°F)	16.7	22.2	32.0	42.8	53.6	62.6	66.7	64.2	55.9	44.7	32.5	21.9	43.0
Extreme Maximum Temp. (°F)	70	79	89	92	94	103	105	106	103	94	83	70	106
Extreme Minimum Temp. (°F)	-18	-18	-13	8	29	42	45	44	30	17	-7	-22	-22
Days Maximum Temp. ≥ 90°F	0	0	0	0	1	6	13	11	4	0	0	0	35
Days Maximum Temp. ≤ 32°F	12	8	1	0	0	0	0	0	0	0	2	8	31
Days Minimum Temp. ≤ 32°F	28	22	16	5	0	0	0	0	0	3	15	27	116
Days Minimum Temp. ≤ 0°F	4	2	0	0	0	0	0	0	0	0	0	2	8
Heating Degree Days (base 65°F)	1,207	921	675	332	93	8	1	2	67	277	681	1,059	5,323
Cooling Degree Days (base 65°F)	0	0	3	25	84	264	403	340	160	26	1	0	1,306
Mean Precipitation (in.)	0.90	1.08	2.51	3.39	5.23	4.71	4.43	4.01	4.78	3.01	2.30	1.33	37.68
Days With ≥ 0.1" Precipitation	3	3	5	7	8	6	6	6	6	5	4	3	62
Days With ≥ 1.0" Precipitation	0	0	1	1	2	1	2	1	1	1	1	0	11
Mean Snowfall (in.)	5.5	4.2	3.2	0.9	0.0	0.0	0.0	0.0	0.0	0.2	1.0	3.7	18.7
Days With ≥ 1.0" Snow Depth	12	8	2	0	0	0	0	0	0	0	1	6	29

Tuttle Creek Lake *Riley County*   Elevation: 1,056 ft.   Latitude: 39° 15' N   Longitude: 96° 36' W

	JAN	FEB	MAR	APR	MAY	JUN	JUL	AUG	SEP	OCT	NOV	DEC	YEAR
Mean Maximum Temp. (°F)	36.2	42.8	54.1	65.0	74.4	84.2	90.0	88.3	80.0	68.5	52.6	41.0	64.8
Mean Temp. (°F)	25.1	31.0	42.1	53.0	62.8	72.7	78.2	76.1	67.2	54.9	41.1	30.2	52.9
Mean Minimum Temp. (°F)	14.0	19.0	29.9	40.9	51.1	61.2	66.4	63.9	54.4	41.3	29.6	19.3	40.9
Extreme Maximum Temp. (°F)	73	79	87	97	98	111	111	110	103	94	83	74	111
Extreme Minimum Temp. (°F)	-20	-20	-16	2	26	40	42	44	29	11	-5	-28	-28
Days Maximum Temp. ≥ 90°F	0	0	0	0	1	8	16	14	6	0	0	0	45
Days Maximum Temp. ≤ 32°F	12	7	2	0	0	0	0	0	0	0	2	7	30
Days Minimum Temp. ≤ 32°F	30	25	19	7	0	0	0	0	0	6	19	29	135
Days Minimum Temp. ≤ 0°F	5	3	0	0	0	0	0	0	0	0	0	2	10
Heating Degree Days (base 65°F)	1,229	955	706	374	135	16	1	2	86	325	711	1,073	5,613
Cooling Degree Days (base 65°F)	0	0	3	23	75	254	422	361	163	20	1	0	1,322
Mean Precipitation (in.)	0.58	0.81	2.28	2.89	4.73	4.80	3.81	3.30	3.86	2.65	1.87	0.86	32.44
Days With ≥ 0.1" Precipitation	2	2	5	5	8	7	6	5	5	4	3	2	54
Days With ≥ 1.0" Precipitation	0	0	1	1	1	2	1	1	1	1	0	0	9
Mean Snowfall (in.)	3.4	2.7	1.8	trace	0.0	0.0	0.0	0.0	0.0	trace	0.6	1.6	10.1
Days With ≥ 1.0" Snow Depth	9	5	1	0	0	0	0	0	0	0	1	4	20

Ulysses *Grant County*   Elevation: 3,047 ft.   Latitude: 37° 35' N   Longitude: 101° 21' W

	JAN	FEB	MAR	APR	MAY	JUN	JUL	AUG	SEP	OCT	NOV	DEC	YEAR
Mean Maximum Temp. (°F)	45.6	50.9	59.5	69.0	78.0	88.6	93.8	91.3	83.8	72.7	56.8	47.6	69.8
Mean Temp. (°F)	30.6	35.5	43.6	52.8	63.1	73.7	78.7	76.7	68.4	55.8	41.6	32.7	54.4
Mean Minimum Temp. (°F)	15.5	20.2	27.6	36.4	48.2	58.7	63.6	62.1	52.8	38.8	26.3	17.7	39.0
Extreme Maximum Temp. (°F)	83	88	96	103	101	110	110	109	104	99	88	78	110
Extreme Minimum Temp. (°F)	-27	-19	-6	10	28	41	47	42	25	10	-8	-17	-27
Days Maximum Temp. ≥ 90°F	0	0	0	1	3	15	23	20	11	2	0	0	75
Days Maximum Temp. ≤ 32°F	6	4	2	0	0	0	0	0	0	0	1	5	18
Days Minimum Temp. ≤ 32°F	31	26	na	10	1	0	0	0	0	7	23	30	na
Days Minimum Temp. ≤ 0°F	2	1	0	0	0	0	0	0	0	0	0	2	5
Heating Degree Days (base 65°F)	1,060	825	658	372	123	15	1	3	66	298	694	996	5,111
Cooling Degree Days (base 65°F)	0	0	0	11	66	266	424	374	168	16	0	0	1,325
Mean Precipitation (in.)	0.41	0.44	0.99	1.53	2.71	2.67	2.14	2.90	1.53	0.87	0.83	0.32	17.34
Days With ≥ 0.1" Precipitation	1	1	3	3	5	5	4	4	3	2	2	1	34
Days With ≥ 1.0" Precipitation	0	0	0	0	1	1	0	1	0	0	0	0	3
Mean Snowfall (in.)	4.9	3.4	3.9	0.9	trace	0.0	0.0	0.0	trace	0.5	2.0	3.1	18.7
Days With ≥ 1.0" Snow Depth	5	4	2	0	0	0	0	0	0	0	1	4	16

Wakeeney *Trego County*   Elevation: 2,447 ft.   Latitude: 39° 02' N   Longitude: 99° 53' W

	JAN	FEB	MAR	APR	MAY	JUN	JUL	AUG	SEP	OCT	NOV	DEC	YEAR
Mean Maximum Temp. (°F)	39.6	45.6	54.5	65.0	74.3	85.6	91.6	89.4	80.4	68.9	52.6	42.9	65.9
Mean Temp. (°F)	27.6	33.0	41.5	51.8	61.9	72.6	78.3	76.2	66.7	54.6	40.2	31.1	53.0
Mean Minimum Temp. (°F)	15.6	20.2	28.4	38.6	49.4	59.6	64.9	62.9	53.0	40.3	27.8	19.2	40.0
Extreme Maximum Temp. (°F)	79	84	90	102	100	110	110	106	104	95	86	79	110
Extreme Minimum Temp. (°F)	-14	-14	-4	11	28	40	47	47	24	12	-4	-25	-25
Days Maximum Temp. ≥ 90°F	0	0	0	1	2	11	20	17	7	1	0	0	59
Days Maximum Temp. ≤ 32°F	10	6	3	0	0	0	0	0	0	0	2	7	28
Days Minimum Temp. ≤ 32°F	30	26	21	7	0	0	0	0	1	5	21	30	141
Days Minimum Temp. ≤ 0°F	4	2	0	0	0	0	0	0	0	0	0	2	8
Heating Degree Days (base 65°F)	1,151	899	724	401	152	22	2	4	93	332	736	1,045	5,561
Cooling Degree Days (base 65°F)	0	0	1	15	67	264	431	369	163	20	0	0	1,330
Mean Precipitation (in.)	0.68	0.74	1.81	2.16	3.71	2.65	3.56	3.04	2.13	1.26	1.30	0.65	23.69
Days With ≥ 0.1" Precipitation	2	2	4	4	6	6	5	5	4	2	3	2	45
Days With ≥ 1.0" Precipitation	0	0	0	0	1	1	1	1	1	0	0	0	5
Mean Snowfall (in.)	5.3	5.4	5.8	2.0	0.0	0.0	0.0	0.0	0.3	0.8	2.5	4.6	26.7
Days With ≥ 1.0" Snow Depth	9	7	3	1	0	0	0	0	0	0	2	5	27

Wamego *Pottawatomie County*   Elevation: 1,007 ft.   Latitude: 39° 13' N   Longitude: 96° 19' W

	JAN	FEB	MAR	APR	MAY	JUN	JUL	AUG	SEP	OCT	NOV	DEC	YEAR
Mean Maximum Temp. (°F)	38.8	46.0	57.3	68.7	77.3	85.9	91.0	89.8	81.7	70.3	54.4	43.0	67.0
Mean Temp. (°F)	28.2	34.5	45.1	56.1	65.4	74.5	79.4	77.8	69.3	57.8	43.6	32.7	55.4
Mean Minimum Temp. (°F)	17.5	23.0	32.8	43.3	53.4	63.0	67.7	65.7	57.0	45.0	32.7	22.4	43.6
Extreme Maximum Temp. (°F)	73	84	87	94	99	107	109	108	103	93	84	73	109
Extreme Minimum Temp. (°F)	-16	-22	-11	1	28	39	46	46	26	13	-3	-24	-24
Days Maximum Temp. ≥ 90°F	0	0	0	1	1	9	18	16	7	1	0	0	53
Days Maximum Temp. ≤ 32°F	10	6	1	0	0	0	0	0	0	0	1	5	23
Days Minimum Temp. ≤ 32°F	28	22	16	4	0	0	0	0	0	3	15	27	115
Days Minimum Temp. ≤ 0°F	3	2	0	0	0	0	0	0	0	0	0	2	7
Heating Degree Days (base 65°F)	1,135	854	616	291	83	7	0	1	57	251	638	994	4,927
Cooling Degree Days (base 65°F)	0	0	5	31	99	294	460	404	198	36	2	0	1,529
Mean Precipitation (in.)	0.87	0.94	2.39	2.90	4.93	4.88	4.13	3.54	3.87	2.60	2.15	1.23	34.43
Days With ≥ 0.1" Precipitation	3	2	5	5	7	6	6	5	5	4	4	3	55
Days With ≥ 1.0" Precipitation	0	0	1	1	2	2	1	1	1	1	1	0	11
Mean Snowfall (in.)	5.8	4.4	1.4	0.4	0.0	0.0	0.0	0.0	0.0	0.2	1.2	2.7	16.1
Days With ≥ 1.0" Snow Depth	11	6	1	0	0	0	0	0	0	0	1	4	23

Washington *Washington County*   Elevation: 1,302 ft.   Latitude: 39° 49' N   Longitude: 97° 03' W

	JAN	FEB	MAR	APR	MAY	JUN	JUL	AUG	SEP	OCT	NOV	DEC	YEAR
Mean Maximum Temp. (°F)	37.9	45.1	56.3	67.9	77.1	86.9	91.7	89.6	81.6	70.4	53.1	41.8	66.6
Mean Temp. (°F)	26.8	32.9	43.5	54.6	64.7	74.5	79.4	77.3	68.7	57.0	41.9	31.2	54.4
Mean Minimum Temp. (°F)	15.7	20.6	30.6	41.3	52.2	62.0	67.0	65.0	55.8	43.6	30.6	20.6	42.1
Extreme Maximum Temp. (°F)	75	85	87	98	96	107	109	107	103	93	82	70	109
Extreme Minimum Temp. (°F)	-21	-23	-18	5	28	40	44	45	26	13	-6	-29	-29
Days Maximum Temp. ≥ 90°F	0	0	0	1	1	11	19	16	7	0	0	0	55
Days Maximum Temp. ≤ 32°F	10	6	1	0	0	0	0	0	0	0	2	6	25
Days Minimum Temp. ≤ 32°F	29	24	18	6	0	0	0	0	0	4	18	28	127
Days Minimum Temp. ≤ 0°F	4	3	0	0	0	0	0	0	0	0	0	2	9
Heating Degree Days (base 65°F)	1,177	900	663	328	95	7	1	1	63	268	689	1,041	5,233
Cooling Degree Days (base 65°F)	0	0	2	25	89	292	455	391	185	28	1	0	1,468
Mean Precipitation (in.)	0.77	0.80	2.44	3.04	4.74	4.78	4.25	3.82	3.50	2.14	1.83	0.97	33.08
Days With ≥ 0.1" Precipitation	3	2	5	6	8	7	6	6	5	4	4	2	58
Days With ≥ 1.0" Precipitation	0	0	1	1	1	1	1	1	1	0	0	0	7
Mean Snowfall (in.)	7.1	5.3	3.0	0.5	0.0	0.0	0.0	0.0	0.0	0.1	1.4	4.3	21.7
Days With ≥ 1.0" Snow Depth	11	7	2	0	0	0	0	0	0	0	1	4	25

Webster Dam *Rooks County*   Elevation: 1,860 ft.   Latitude: 39° 24' N   Longitude: 99° 25' W

	JAN	FEB	MAR	APR	MAY	JUN	JUL	AUG	SEP	OCT	NOV	DEC	YEAR
Mean Maximum Temp. (°F)	39.4	45.1	55.2	66.4	75.4	87.0	93.0	90.5	81.5	69.5	52.7	42.8	66.5
Mean Temp. (°F)	26.2	31.3	41.3	52.1	62.0	72.8	78.5	76.2	66.6	54.1	39.2	30.1	52.5
Mean Minimum Temp. (°F)	13.1	17.3	27.1	37.8	48.5	58.6	63.8	61.9	51.8	38.7	25.7	17.3	38.5
Extreme Maximum Temp. (°F)	77	84	92	103	100	112	113	113	108	98	87	75	113
Extreme Minimum Temp. (°F)	-22	-20	-10	11	27	38	44	41	22	11	-8	-25	-25
Days Maximum Temp. ≥ 90°F	0	0	0	1	2	12	21	18	8	1	0	0	63
Days Maximum Temp. ≤ 32°F	10	7	2	0	0	0	0	0	0	0	2	6	27
Days Minimum Temp. ≤ 32°F	30	26	22	8	1	0	0	0	1	7	23	29	147
Days Minimum Temp. ≤ 0°F	5	3	1	0	0	0	0	0	0	0	0	2	11
Heating Degree Days (base 65°F)	1,195	946	728	398	152	18	2	4	94	345	766	1,075	5,723
Cooling Degree Days (base 65°F)	0	0	1	18	64	255	416	354	155	14	0	0	1,277
Mean Precipitation (in.)	0.52	0.64	1.79	2.35	4.12	2.71	3.66	3.14	2.06	1.37	1.25	0.61	24.22
Days With ≥ 0.1" Precipitation	1	2	4	4	7	5	5	4	3	2	2	44
Days With ≥ 1.0" Precipitation	0	0	0	0	1	1	1	1	0	0	0	0	4
Mean Snowfall (in.)	4.8	5.4	4.8	0.8	0.0	0.0	0.0	0.0	0.1	0.1	2.1	3.4	21.5
Days With ≥ 1.0" Snow Depth	na	4	2	0	0	0	0	0	0	0	1	na	na

Wellington *Sumner County*   Elevation: 1,217 ft.   Latitude: 37° 16' N   Longitude: 97° 25' W

	JAN	FEB	MAR	APR	MAY	JUN	JUL	AUG	SEP	OCT	NOV	DEC	YEAR
Mean Maximum Temp. (°F)	40.8	47.6	57.5	67.6	76.5	87.2	93.4	92.3	83.3	71.2	55.8	44.9	68.2
Mean Temp. (°F)	30.1	35.9	45.6	55.6	65.2	75.4	81.0	79.8	70.9	58.2	44.7	34.2	56.4
Mean Minimum Temp. (°F)	19.3	24.3	33.6	43.5	53.8	63.7	68.6	67.2	58.4	45.2	33.5	23.5	44.5
Extreme Maximum Temp. (°F)	73	88	90	99	99	107	110	111	106	97	86	74	111
Extreme Minimum Temp. (°F)	-14	-10	1	16	33	43	49	47	28	14	3	-15	-15
Days Maximum Temp. ≥ 90°F	0	0	0	0	1	13	22	21	10	1	0	0	68
Days Maximum Temp. ≤ 32°F	8	5	1	0	0	0	0	0	0	0	1	4	19
Days Minimum Temp. ≤ 32°F	29	22	14	3	0	0	0	0	0	3	15	27	113
Days Minimum Temp. ≤ 0°F	2	1	0	0	0	0	0	0	0	0	0	1	4
Heating Degree Days (base 65°F)	1,076	814	597	297	89	7	0	1	49	238	605	948	4,721
Cooling Degree Days (base 65°F)	0	0	2	19	100	328	510	471	241	33	2	0	1,706
Mean Precipitation (in.)	0.93	1.07	2.77	3.22	4.49	4.68	3.21	3.26	3.14	2.38	2.09	1.26	32.50
Days With ≥ 0.1" Precipitation	2	3	5	5	7	6	5	4	5	3	4	3	52
Days With ≥ 1.0" Precipitation	0	0	1	1	1	1	1	1	1	1	1	0	9
Mean Snowfall (in.)	3.6	4.0	2.3	trace	0.0	0.0	0.0	0.0	0.0	trace	1.0	2.4	13.3
Days With ≥ 1.0" Snow Depth	6	4	1	0	0	0	0	0	0	0	0	3	14

Wilson Lake *Russell County*   Elevation: 1,509 ft.   Latitude: 38° 58' N   Longitude: 98° 29' W

	JAN	FEB	MAR	APR	MAY	JUN	JUL	AUG	SEP	OCT	NOV	DEC	YEAR
Mean Maximum Temp. (°F)	39.0	45.2	55.1	66.2	75.4	86.5	92.8	90.4	81.6	70.0	54.1	43.1	66.6
Mean Temp. (°F)	27.8	33.0	42.5	53.3	63.4	74.0	79.8	77.5	68.3	56.3	42.2	32.2	54.2
Mean Minimum Temp. (°F)	16.6	20.8	30.0	40.5	51.4	61.4	66.8	64.6	54.9	42.7	30.3	21.2	41.7
Extreme Maximum Temp. (°F)	75	83	87	100	98	111	110	111	104	94	83	76	111
Extreme Minimum Temp. (°F)	-15	-17	-5	12	27	39	46	45	28	17	-5	-26	-26
Days Maximum Temp. ≥ 90°F	0	0	0	0	2	12	22	18	8	1	0	0	63
Days Maximum Temp. ≤ 32°F	10	6	2	0	0	0	0	0	0	0	2	6	26
Days Minimum Temp. ≤ 32°F	29	24	18	6	0	0	0	0	0	4	18	28	127
Days Minimum Temp. ≤ 0°F	3	2	0	0	0	0	0	0	0	0	0	1	6
Heating Degree Days (base 65°F)	1,147	896	691	360	122	15	1	3	75	288	678	1,011	5,287
Cooling Degree Days (base 65°F)	0	0	2	19	80	286	468	399	188	25	1	0	1,468
Mean Precipitation (in.)	0.50	0.56	1.96	2.31	3.98	3.15	3.50	3.56	2.22	1.85	1.27	0.61	25.47
Days With ≥ 0.1" Precipitation	1	2	3	5	7	6	5	5	4	3	3	2	46
Days With ≥ 1.0" Precipitation	0	0	0	0	1	1	1	1	0	1	0	0	5
Mean Snowfall (in.)	4.9	4.5	2.1	0.5	0.0	0.0	0.0	0.0	0.0	trace	0.9	2.5	15.4
Days With ≥ 1.0" Snow Depth	8	6	1	0	0	0	0	0	0	0	1	3	19

Winfield 1 *Cowley County*   Elevation: 1,177 ft.   Latitude: 37° 14' N   Longitude: 96° 58' W

	JAN	FEB	MAR	APR	MAY	JUN	JUL	AUG	SEP	OCT	NOV	DEC	YEAR
Mean Maximum Temp. (°F)	43.0	50.2	60.0	69.9	78.3	87.5	93.4	92.4	83.6	72.6	57.3	46.8	69.6
Mean Temp. (°F)	32.0	38.3	47.7	57.5	66.6	75.9	81.3	79.9	71.5	59.8	46.2	36.2	57.7
Mean Minimum Temp. (°F)	21.1	26.3	35.3	45.1	54.9	64.1	69.1	67.4	59.5	47.0	35.1	25.5	45.9
Extreme Maximum Temp. (°F)	75	88	91	98	98	109	110	112	106	94	85	75	112
Extreme Minimum Temp. (°F)	-25	-13	1	17	31	40	49	45	31	12	2	-15	-25
Days Maximum Temp. ≥ 90°F	0	0	0	1	1	13	23	22	9	1	0	0	70
Days Maximum Temp. ≤ 32°F	7	3	1	0	0	0	0	0	0	0	1	3	15
Days Minimum Temp. ≤ 32°F	27	20	13	3	0	0	0	0	0	2	12	24	101
Days Minimum Temp. ≤ 0°F	1	1	0	0	0	0	0	0	0	0	0	1	3
Heating Degree Days (base 65°F)	1,015	749	534	251	66	4	0	0	38	201	560	887	4,305
Cooling Degree Days (base 65°F)	0	0	5	31	120	332	513	474	241	41	2	0	1,759
Mean Precipitation (in.)	1.16	1.56	2.94	3.47	5.29	4.74	3.48	3.58	3.45	3.21	2.66	1.76	37.30
Days With ≥ 0.1" Precipitation	3	3	5	5	7	7	5	5	5	4	4	3	56
Days With ≥ 1.0" Precipitation	0	0	1	1	2	2	1	1	1	1	1	0	11
Mean Snowfall (in.)	*2.8*	3.6	1.5	trace	0.0	0.0	0.0	0.0	0.0	trace	0.9	2.1	*10.9*
Days With ≥ 1.0" Snow Depth	*5*	3	1	0	0	0	0	0	0	0	0	1	*10*

Winona *Logan County*   Elevation: 3,320 ft.   Latitude: 39° 04' N   Longitude: 101° 15' W

	JAN	FEB	MAR	APR	MAY	JUN	JUL	AUG	SEP	OCT	NOV	DEC	YEAR
Mean Maximum Temp. (°F)	40.3	46.6	54.7	64.4	73.6	85.0	90.7	89.0	80.4	68.2	52.1	43.6	65.7
Mean Temp. (°F)	27.9	33.2	40.5	49.9	60.0	70.8	76.5	75.1	66.0	53.6	39.3	31.1	52.0
Mean Minimum Temp. (°F)	15.4	19.7	26.2	35.4	46.4	56.6	62.3	61.2	51.5	38.9	26.5	18.5	38.2
Extreme Maximum Temp. (°F)	77	82	89	97	101	109	110	*107*	104	94	87	82	*110*
Extreme Minimum Temp. (°F)	-17	-19	-5	7	27	37	45	*45*	23	9	-3	-16	*-19*
Days Maximum Temp. ≥ 90°F	0	0	0	0	1	11	18	*16*	7	1	0	0	*54*
Days Maximum Temp. ≤ 32°F	10	5	3	0	0	0	0	0	0	0	3	7	28
Days Minimum Temp. ≤ 32°F	30	26	24	11	1	0	0	0	1	6	23	30	152
Days Minimum Temp. ≤ 0°F	3	2	0	0	0	0	0	0	0	0	0	2	7
Heating Degree Days (base 65°F)	1,144	890	754	453	189	32	4	6	98	359	763	1,044	5,736
Cooling Degree Days (base 65°F)	0	0	0	8	40	205	364	327	136	12	0	0	1,092
Mean Precipitation (in.)	0.40	0.38	1.18	1.47	3.47	2.81	3.50	2.71	1.39	1.19	0.80	0.41	19.71
Days With ≥ 0.1" Precipitation	*1*	1	3	3	6	5	6	*5*	3	2	2	1	*38*
Days With ≥ 1.0" Precipitation	0	0	0	0	1	1	1	1	0	0	0	0	4
Mean Snowfall (in.)	*5.8*	3.9	*6.1*	*3.0*	trace	0.0	0.0	0.0	0.3	1.3	3.1	4.4	*27.9*
Days With ≥ 1.0" Snow Depth	na	*3*	na	1	0	0	0	0	0	1	*1*	3	na

Yates Center *Woodson County*   Elevation: 1,049 ft.   Latitude: 37° 52' N   Longitude: 95° 44' W

	JAN	FEB	MAR	APR	MAY	JUN	JUL	AUG	SEP	OCT	NOV	DEC	YEAR
Mean Maximum Temp. (°F)	41.0	47.9	58.3	68.7	76.6	85.8	91.0	90.1	81.8	71.0	56.1	45.2	67.8
Mean Temp. (°F)	30.9	37.0	46.6	56.8	65.6	74.8	79.6	78.1	70.1	59.1	45.6	35.2	56.6
Mean Minimum Temp. (°F)	20.8	26.0	34.9	44.9	54.5	63.7	68.1	66.1	58.4	47.1	35.1	25.2	45.4
Extreme Maximum Temp. (°F)	71	84	87	95	93	108	111	110	103	96	85	74	111
Extreme Minimum Temp. (°F)	-15	-12	0	16	30	46	50	47	32	16	2	-20	-20
Days Maximum Temp. ≥ 90°F	0	0	0	0	0	8	18	17	6	1	0	0	50
Days Maximum Temp. ≤ 32°F	8	4	1	0	0	0	0	0	0	0	1	4	18
Days Minimum Temp. ≤ 32°F	27	20	13	3	0	0	0	0	0	1	12	24	100
Days Minimum Temp. ≤ 0°F	2	1	0	0	0	0	0	0	0	0	0	1	4
Heating Degree Days (base 65°F)	1,052	785	566	265	73	3	0	0	45	213	577	916	4,495
Cooling Degree Days (base 65°F)	0	0	3	24	93	*312*	457	413	208	33	2	0	*1,545*
Mean Precipitation (in.)	1.22	1.52	3.08	4.14	4.91	5.60	4.26	4.06	4.75	3.84	3.00	1.84	42.22
Days With ≥ 0.1" Precipitation	3	3	6	6	8	7	6	5	6	5	5	3	63
Days With ≥ 1.0" Precipitation	0	0	1	1	1	2	1	2	2	1	1	1	13
Mean Snowfall (in.)	*4.7*	4.5	2.1	0.1	0.0	0.0	0.0	0.0	0.0	0.2	0.8	3.1	*15.5*
Days With ≥ 1.0" Snow Depth	na	na	*0*	0	0	0	0	0	0	0	0	*1*	na

Note: See Appendix D for explanation of data.

KENTUCKY

PHYSICAL FEATURES. Kentucky has a land surface of 40,109 square miles. It is essentially an eroded plateau that slopes downward gradually to the southwest, with elevations ranging from about 400 feet above sea level at the western edge to 1,000 feet in the central districts, to above 4,000 feet near the southeastern border. There are seven major physiographic or natural regions.

The Bluegrass Region comprises about one-fifth of the State. The central area of this region is undulating to gently rolling. The outer area is more rolling and less uniform. Separating the two areas is a terrain that is hilly, with winding ridges and valleys and steep slopes.

The Knobs Region, named for its conical and flat-topped hills, comprises about one-tenth of the State. It forms a narrow crescent encircling the Bluegrass on the east, south, and west. Towards the Bluegrass the terrain is flat to rolling with scattered knobs and wide valleys, while the outer margin is rough.

The Eastern Mountains, also called the Cumberland Plateau, extends over the entire eastern fourth of the State. Ridges are high and sharp-crested there is little level land, and valleys are narrow. In the southeast the Pine and Cumberland Mountains comprise the highest and most rugged part of Kentucky.

The Pennyroyal Region or the Mississippean Plateaus Region is one of the three largest regions. Much of the surface is quite uniform, but as a whole is rather diverse. Much of the terrain is undulating to rolling. In some places it is hilly or cavernous. Subsurface drainage has created limestone sinks and karst terrain in much of the area.

The Western Coal Field is a small region. This area has extensive bottom lands in the valleys of the Ohio, Green, and Tradewater Rivers and many of their tributaries. There is also some undulating to gently rolling uplands.

The Cumberland-Tennessee Rivers Area is the smallest region. The topography is hilly and rough, except for the wide bottoms along the two major streams.

The Jackson Purchase is the extreme western area of Kentucky. In both elevation and relief it is lower than the other regions of the State, but it also has a varied surface. It is largely an upland plain which is mostly undulating to gently rolling, but is also level in places and hilly in others.

GENERAL CLIMATE. The climate of Kentucky is essentially continental in character, with rather wide extremes of temperature and precipitation. The State lies within the path of storms, in the belt of the westerly winds. The temperature generally varies as the storms move across the State. Thus in winter and summer, there are occasional cold and hot spells of short duration. In the spring and fall, the systems have a smaller frequency, temperatures are more consistent, and fewer extremes are experienced. Precipitation occurs with the systems which generally move from the west to east, or from summer thunderstorms. However, the greater portion of precipitation is due to the moisture-bearing low-pressure formations which move from southwest to northeast from the western Gulf of Mexico and frequently cross Kentucky. With warm moist tropical air predominating during the summer months, relative humidity remains consistently high during that season.

TEMPERATURE. The mean annual temperature ranges from 54°F. in the extreme north to 59°F. in the southwestern counties. July is usually the warmest month and January, the coldest. Extreme summer temperatures nearly always reach 100°F. or higher at most locations, but the frequencies of these high temperatures are low. Minimum temperatures of 0°F. or below can be expected during the months of December, January, and February at most locations, but the number of days with such temperatures is relatively small. Because of the State's geographic locations with reference to the center of the continent, the mid-winter cold waves from the Canadian Northwest usually have their intensity considerably modified by the time they reach Kentucky. In summer when the high pressure off the Florida coast is displaced westward from its normal position, extended periods of hot, sultry weather will occur. The spring and fall months are usually pleasant.

PRECIPITATION. Precipitation is generally plentiful. The fall season is generally the driest and the spring season the wettest. Approximately half of the average annual total occurs during the warm months of April to September. The average annual total in the State ranges from 36 inches in northern counties to 50 inches in the southern. Thunderstorms with high intensity rainfall are common during the spring and summer months, and rainfall during these storms in a 24-hour period frequently exceeds two to three inches, occasionally reaching five to six inches. Flash floods frequently result from the high intensity showers. Snowfall occurrence also varies from year to year but is common from November through March. Some snow has also been reported in the months of October and April. In some sections, the ground seldom remains covered with snow for more than a few days. The average annual snowfall for the State ranges from six to 10 inches in the southwest to 15 to 20 inches in the southeast.

WINDS. Winds in the State have an average velocity of seven to 12 m.p.h., and the prevailing direction is from south to southwest for the year. During the fall season some areas show a prevailing direction having a northerly component. The highest wind speeds usually range from 50 to 70 m.p.h., but in some storms (generally squalls attending thunderstorms), winds in gusts may occasionally exceed these speeds. A number of years may pass without a tornado, or several may visit the State in a single year. On the average, about one per year occurs somewhere in the State.

Thunderstorms may occur in any month, but they occur most frequently during the months March through September. The mean number of days with thunderstorms ranges approximately between 45 and 60. They are occasionally attended by damaging hail, but the area thus affected is nearly always small.

OTHER CLIMATIC ELEMENTS. Heavy fogs are rather rare in the State. The average number of days with heavy fogs varies between eight and 17 during the year with the majority occurring during the months of September through March inclusive.

The average date of the last spring freeze ranges from April 4 in the extreme west to May 5 in the mountain region in the extreme southeast; that of the first fall freeze, from October 11 in the Pennyroyal Region to October 30 near the lower Ohio River. The average length of the freeze-free period varies from 166 days on the southeastern plateau to 210 near the lower Ohio River.

The average number of days with clear and with partly cloudy skies is about the same and ranges between 115 and 120 days over the State. The number of days with cloudy skies averages about 130. The extreme northern section shows the greatest number of days with cloudy skies. The percentage of possible sunshine averages 35 to 50 for the winter months, 50 to 65 in the spring, 65 to 75 in the summer, and 55 to 65 in the fall. The largest percentage of possible sunshine is recorded in the extreme western section of the State.

The Ohio River forms the northern boundary and the Mississippi the western. All of the State is in the Ohio River Basin, except for a small section in the Jackson Purchase area that drains directly into the Mississippi. Kentucky lies in the path of rain producing lows moving from the west Gulf area northeastward. The flood season is in the winter and spring. Numerous flash floods occur from excessive rains and thunderstorms, particularly in the mountains of the eastern portion.

Kentucky

● Cities With Population ≥ 25,000
▲ Weather Stations

Portsmouth Sciotoville ▲
Ashland
Maysville Sewage Plant ▲
Grayson 3 SW ▲
Farmers 2 S ▲
West Liberty ▲
Jackson Julian Carroll Arpt ▲
Cincinnati Covington Airport ▲
●COVINGTON
Falmouth ▲
Williamstown 3 W ▲
Frankfort Lock 4 ▲
Lexington Bluegrass Field ▲
●LEXINGTON-FAYETTE
Warsaw Markland Dam ▲
Carrollton Lock 1 ▲
FRANKFORT ●
Shelbyville 1 E ▲
Dix Dam ▲
Danville ▲
●RICHMOND
Berea College ●
Gray Hawk ▲
Mount Vernon ▲
Manchester 4 W ▲
London-Corbin Arpt ▲
Barbourville ▲
Williamsburg ▲
Baxter ▲
Madison Sewage Plant ▲
Bardstown 5 E ▲
Bernheim Forest ▲
Hodgenville-Lincoln ▲
Greensburg ▲
Somerset 2 N ▲
JEFFERSONTOWN ●
LOUISVILLE ●
Louisville Standiford Field ▲
Monticello 3 NE ▲
Rough River Lake ▲
Leitchfield 2 N ▲
Nolin River Lake ▲
Mammoth Cave ▲
Glasgow ▲
Summer Shade ▲
Scottsville 3 SSW ▲
Barren River Lake ▲
Beaver Dam ▲
Bowling Green Warren Co Arpt ▲
BOWLING GREEN ●
OWENSBORO ●
HENDERSON ●
Henderson 7 SSW ▲
Madisonville ▲
Princeton 1 SE ▲
Hopkinsville WS ▲
●HOPKINSVILLE
PADUCAH ●
Paducah Walker Boat Yard ▲
Gilbertsville Kentucky Dam ▲
Mayfield Radio Wngo ▲
Murray ▲
Paducah Barkley Field ▲
Lovelaceville ▲
Bardwell 2 E ▲

Counties: BALLARD, CARLISLE, HICKMAN, FULTON, GRAVES, CALLOWAY, MARSHALL, McCRACKEN, LIVINGSTON, LYON, TRIGG, CRITTENDEN, CALDWELL, CHRISTIAN, TODD, LOGAN, SIMPSON, ALLEN, MONROE, CUMBERLAND, CLINTON, WAYNE, McCREARY, WHITLEY, KNOX, BELL, HARLAN, LETCHER, PIKE, FLOYD, KNOTT, PERRY, LESLIE, CLAY, LAUREL, PULASKI, RUSSELL, ADAIR, METCALFE, BARREN, WARREN, MUHLENBERG, HOPKINS, WEBSTER, UNION, HENDERSON, DAVIESS, HANCOCK, OHIO, BUTLER, EDMONSON, HART, GREEN, TAYLOR, CASEY, LINCOLN, ROCKCASTLE, JACKSON, OWSLEY, LEE, BREATHITT, MAGOFFIN, JOHNSON, MARTIN, LAWRENCE, BOYD, GREENUP, CARTER, ELLIOTT, MORGAN, WOLFE, POWELL, ESTILL, MADISON, GARRARD, BOYLE, MARION, WASHINGTON, NELSON, LARUE, GRAYSON, HARDIN, MEADE, BRECKINRIDGE, McLEAN, TRIMBLE, OLDHAM, HENRY, SHELBY, SPENCER, BULLITT, JEFFERSON, ANDERSON, FRANKLIN, WOODFORD, MERCER, JESSAMINE, FAYETTE, CLARK, MONTGOMERY, BATH, MENIFEE, FLEMING, NICHOLAS, BOURBON, SCOTT, OWEN, GALLATIN, CARROLL, BOONE, KENTON, CAMPBELL, PENDLETON, GRANT, HARRISON, ROBERTSON, MASON, LEWIS, ROWAN, BRACKEN

0   100 Miles
0   100 KM

Kentucky Weather Stations by County

County	Station Name
Allen	Barren River Lake Scottsville 3 SSW
Ballard	Lovelaceville
Barren	Glasgow
Boyd	Ashland
Boyle	Danville
Breathitt	Jackson Julian Carroll Airport
Breckinridge	Rough River Lake
Bullitt	Bernheim Forest
Caldwell	Princeton 1 SE
Calloway	Murray
Carlisle	Bardwell 2 E
Carroll	Carrollton Lock 1
Carter	Grayson 3 SW
Christian	Hopkinsville
Clay	Manchester 4 W
Edmonson	Mammoth Cave Nolin River Lake
Fayette	Lexington Bluegrass Field
Franklin	Frankfort Lock 4
Gallatin	Warsaw Markland Dam
Grant	Williamstown 3 W
Graves	Mayfield Radio Wngo
Grayson	Leitchfield 2 N
Green	Greensburg
Harlan	Baxter
Henderson	Henderson 7 SSW
Hopkins	Madisonville
Jackson	Gray Hawk
Jefferson	Louisville Standiford Field
Knox	Barbourville
Larue	Hodgenville-Lincoln
Laurel	London-Carbin Airport

County	Station Name
Livingston	Gilbertsville Kentucky Dam
Madison	Berea College
Marion	Bradfordsville
Mason	Maysville Sewage Plant
McCracken	Paducah Barkley Field Paducah Walker Boat Yard
Mercer	Dix Dam
Metcalfe	Summer Shade
Morgan	West Liberty
Nelson	Bardstown 5 E
Ohio	Beaver Dam
Pendleton	Falmouth
Pulaski	Somerset 2 N
Rockcastle	Mount Vernon
Rowan	Farmers 2 S
Shelby	Shelbyville 1 E
Warren	Bowling Green Warren Co. Airport
Wayne	Monticello 3 NE
Whitley	Williamsburg

Kentucky Weather Stations by City

City	Station Name	Miles
Bowling Green	Barren River Lake	18
	Bowling Green Warren Co. Airport	1
Covington	Cincinnati Covington Airport, OH	8
	Cincinnati Fernbank, OH	11
	Cincinnati Lunken Airport, OH	5
	Milford, OH	15
Frankfort	Frankfort Lock 4	3
	Lexington Bluegrass Field	18
	Shelbyville 1 E	18
Henderson	Evansville Museum, IN	9
	Evansville Regional Airport, IN	15
	Mount Vernon, IN	18
	Henderson 7 SSW	7
Hopkinsville	Hopkinsville	1
Jeffersontown	Louisville Standiford Field	9
Lexington-Fayette	Dix Dam	20
	Lexington Bluegrass Field	6
Louisville	Louisville Standiford Field	3
Paducah	Brookport Dam 52, IL	4
	Lovelaceville	13
	Mayfield Radio Wngo	20
	Paducah Barkley Field	8
	Paducah Walker Boat Yard	5
Richmond	Berea College	12

Note: Miles is the distance between the geographic center of the city and the weather station.

Kentucky Weather Stations by Elevation

Feet	Station Name
1,364	Jackson Julian Carroll Airport
1,250	Gray Hawk
1,187	London-Carbin Airport
1,161	Baxter
1,158	Mount Vernon
1,069	Berea College
1,049	Somerset 2 N
987	Barbourville
977	Monticello 3 NE
964	Lexington Bluegrass Field
938	Williamsburg
938	Williamstown 3 W
898	Danville
869	Dix Dam
869	Manchester 4 W
862	Summer Shade
849	Scottsville 3 SSW
830	West Liberty
787	Hodgenville-Lincoln
787	Mammoth Cave
777	Bardstown 5 E
767	Glasgow
728	Shelbyville 1 E
698	Grayson 3 SW
679	Farmers 2 S
679	Nolin River Lake
659	Bradfordsville
649	Falmouth
620	Barren River Lake
620	Leitchfield 2 N
587	Greensburg
557	Ashland
554	Rough River Lake
547	Bernheim Forest
524	Bowling Green Warren Co. Airport
524	Murray
518	Hopkinsville
515	Maysville Sewage Plant
498	Frankfort Lock 4
495	Princeton 1 SE
479	Louisville Standiford Field
465	Warsaw Markland Dam
449	Carrollton Lock 1
439	Beaver Dam
439	Madisonville
429	Henderson 7 SSW
410	Bardwell 2 E
406	Paducah Barkley Field
377	Mayfield Radio Wngo
367	Lovelaceville
357	Gilbertsville Kentucky Dam
337	Paducah Walker Boat Yard

Jackson Julian Carroll Airport

Jackson, County Seat of Breathitt County, is located on the leading edge of the Eastern Kentucky Coal Fields. The topography is mountainous, with 80 to 90 percent of the county area on a greater than 20 percent slope. The highest elevation is 1,547 feet above sea level. The terrain slopes gently westward into the Kentucky Bluegrass Region. To the east the mountains rise swiftly to heights of 4,000 to 5,000 feet above sea level.

The climate of Jackson and Eastern Kentucky is temperate and well suited to a variety of plant and animal life. The North Fork of the Kentucky River flows through Breathitt County westward into the Kentucky River and eventually into the Ohio River. There are numerous small creeks and streams in the county that are prone to flash flooding during periods of heavy rainfall.

Jackson is subject to sudden and large changes in temperature. Extremes of cold and heat are rare and usually of short duration. Temperatures above 100 degrees or below zero are extremely rare. Average daily temperatures range from about 32 degrees in the winter to the low 70s in the summer, and in the low 50s during the spring and fall months. January is the coldest month with an average temperature of 31 degrees. The warmest month is July, with an average temperature of 73 degrees.

Total annual precipitation for the Jackson area averages nearly 44 inches and is fairly evenly distributed throughout the year. The spring and summer seasons average nearly 12 inches each, while winter averages 11 inches and fall slightly over eight inches.

Jackson Julian Carroll Airport *Breathitt County*   Elevation: 1,364 ft.   Latitude: 37° 35' N   Longitude: 83° 19' W

	JAN	FEB	MAR	APR	MAY	JUN	JUL	AUG	SEP	OCT	NOV	DEC	YEAR
Mean Maximum Temp. (°F)	na	na	na	na	na	na	na	na	na	na	na	na	na
Mean Temp. (°F)	na	na	na	na	na	na	na	na	na	na	na	na	na
Mean Minimum Temp. (°F)	na	na	na	na	na	na	na	na	na	na	na	na	na
Extreme Maximum Temp. (°F)	na	na	na	na	na	na	na	na	na	na	na	na	na
Extreme Minimum Temp. (°F)	na	na	na	na	na	na	na	na	na	na	na	na	na
Days Maximum Temp. ≥ 90°F	na	na	na	na	na	na	na	na	na	na	na	na	na
Days Maximum Temp. ≤ 32°F	na	na	na	na	na	na	na	na	na	na	na	na	na
Days Minimum Temp. ≤ 32°F	na	na	na	na	na	na	na	na	na	na	na	na	na
Days Minimum Temp. ≤ 0°F	na	na	na	na	na	na	na	na	na	na	na	na	na
Heating Degree Days (base 65°F)	na	na	na	na	na	na	na	na	na	na	na	na	na
Cooling Degree Days (base 65°F)	0	0	9	36	94	229	345	293	143	28	3	1	1,181
Mean Precipitation (in.)	na	na	na	na	na	na	na	na	na	na	na	na	na
Maximum Precipitation (in.)	7.3	7.6	11.8	5.7	9.9	7.0	9.7	7.7	7.8	7.4	9.3	13.0	63.3
Minimum Precipitation (in.)	0.8	2.0	1.6	0.8	2.3	1.4	1.8	1.5	1.4	0.5	1.4	1.7	37.6
Maximum 24-hr. Precipitation (in.)	2.0	2.4	2.7	1.8	2.4	2.6	2.8	2.5	2.3	2.2	3.4	3.1	3.4
Days With ≥ 0.1" Precipitation	na	na	na	na	na	na	na	na	na	na	na	na	na
Days With ≥ 1.0" Precipitation	na	na	na	na	na	na	na	na	na	na	na	na	na
Mean Snowfall (in.)	na	na	na	na	na	na	na	na	na	na	na	na	na
Maximum Snowfall (in.)	26	21	22	18	1	0	0	0	0	2	5	12	44
Maximum 24-hr. Snowfall (in.)	15	12	20	8	1	0	0	0	0	2	4	4	20
Days With ≥ 1.0" Snow Depth	na	na	na	na	na	na	na	na	na	na	na	na	na
Thunderstorm Days	< 1	1	3	4	8	10	12	8	3	1	1	< 1	51
Foggy Days	15	13	15	11	17	19	24	25	19	13	13	15	199
Predominant Sky Cover	OVR	OVR	OVR	OVR	OVR	OVR	OVR	OVR	SCT	OVR	OVR	OVR	OVR
Mean Relative Humidity 7am (%)	77	75	72	69	81	86	89	91	89	82	75	78	80
Mean Relative Humidity 4pm (%)	59	56	49	44	57	59	62	60	59	52	54	62	56
Mean Dewpoint (°F)	24	26	31	39	52	62	66	65	57	45	35	28	44
Prevailing Wind Direction	SW	S	S	S	S	S	SSW	S	S	S	S	SW	S
Prevailing Wind Speed (mph)	9	9	9	8	7	6	6	6	6	7	8	8	7
Maximum Wind Gust (mph)	55	60	53	58	49	60	55	49	39	48	52	60	60

Lexington Bluegrass Field

Lexington, County Seat of Fayette County, is located in the heart of the famed Kentucky Blue Grass Region. Fayette County is a gently rolling plateau with the elevation varying between 900 and 1,050 feet above sea level. It is noted for its beauty, the fertility of its soil, excellent grass, stock farms, and burley tobacco. The soil has a high phosphorus content and this is very valuable in growing pasture grasses for the grazing of cattle and horses. Lexington has a decided continental climate with a rather large diurnal temperature range. The climate is temperate and well suited to a varied plant and animal life. There are no bodies of water close enough to have any effect on the climate. The closest river is the Kentucky which makes an arc about 15 to 20 miles to the southeast, south, and southwest on its course to the Ohio River. There are numerous small creeks that rise in the county and flow into the river. The reservoirs of the Lexington Water Company are about five miles southeast of the city and are the largest bodies of water in the area.

Lexington is subject to rather sudden and large changes in temperature with the spells generally of rather short duration. Temperatures above 100 degrees and below zero degrees are relatively rare. The average temperature for the winter is 35 degrees, spring 62 degrees, fall 50 degrees, and summer 74 degrees.

Precipitation is evenly distributed throughout the winter, spring, and summer, with about 12 inches recorded on the average for each of these seasons. The fall season averages nearly eight and a half inches. Snowfall amounts are variable and the ground does not retain snow cover more than a few days at a time.

The months of September and October are the most pleasant of the year. They have the least amount of precipitation, the greatest number of clear days, and generally comfortable temperatures are the rule during these months.

Based on the 1951-1980 period, the average first occurrence of 32 degrees Fahrenheit in the fall is October 25 and the average last occurrence in the spring is April 17.

Lexington Bluegrass Field *Fayette County*   Elevation: 964 ft.   Latitude: 38° 02' N   Longitude: 84° 36' W

	JAN	FEB	MAR	APR	MAY	JUN	JUL	AUG	SEP	OCT	NOV	DEC	YEAR
Mean Maximum Temp. (°F)	39.9	44.8	55.0	65.3	74.1	82.2	86.0	84.8	78.6	67.1	54.8	45.0	64.8
Mean Temp. (°F)	31.7	35.9	45.1	54.6	63.9	72.2	76.2	74.9	68.3	56.6	45.9	36.8	55.2
Mean Minimum Temp. (°F)	23.5	26.9	35.2	43.9	53.6	62.1	66.4	64.9	58.0	46.1	37.0	28.6	45.5
Extreme Maximum Temp. (°F)	73	80	82	87	92	101	103	103	97	87	83	75	103
Extreme Minimum Temp. (°F)	-20	-10	-1	18	32	42	47	45	34	20	4	-19	-20
Days Maximum Temp. ≥ 90°F	0	0	0	0	0	3	8	6	2	0	0	0	19
Days Maximum Temp. ≤ 32°F	9	6	1	0	0	0	0	0	0	0	0	5	21
Days Minimum Temp. ≤ 32°F	24	19	13	4	0	0	0	0	0	2	11	20	93
Days Minimum Temp. ≤ 0°F	2	1	0	0	0	0	0	0	0	0	0	0	3
Heating Degree Days (base 65°F)	1,025	816	614	323	114	12	1	2	50	276	569	867	4,669
Cooling Degree Days (base 65°F)	0	0	3	17	88	245	374	324	151	24	1	0	1,227
Mean Precipitation (in.)	3.25	3.23	4.43	3.83	4.79	4.58	4.81	3.74	3.12	2.75	3.46	4.09	46.08
Maximum Precipitation (in.)	16.6	10.1	10.4	9.3	10.8	11.7	10.6	11.2	9.7	6.1	6.9	10.2	60.1
Minimum Precipitation (in.)	0.4	0.7	1.0	1.2	1.2	0.6	0.8	0.6	0.2	0.3	0.4	0.6	32.1
Maximum 24-hr. Precipitation (in.)	2.7	3.1	3.5	2.8	3.0	5.0	4.3	3.6	4.1	2.7	2.6	3.3	5.0
Days With ≥ 0.1" Precipitation	7	6	9	7	8	8	7	6	5	5	7	7	82
Days With ≥ 1.0" Precipitation	1	1	1	1	1	1	2	1	1	1	1	1	13
Mean Snowfall (in.)	5.9	4.8	2.4	0.4	trace	trace	trace	trace	0.0	trace	0.5	1.9	15.9
Maximum Snowfall (in.)	22	16	18	6	trace	0	0	0	0	trace	10	11	39
Maximum 24-hr. Snowfall (in.)	10	7	7	5	trace	0	0	0	0	trace	8	8	10
Days With ≥ 1.0" Snow Depth	6	6	1	0	0	0	0	0	0	0	0	2	15
Thunderstorm Days	1	1	3	4	6	8	9	7	3	1	1	< 1	44
Foggy Days	14	12	12	9	12	13	16	18	15	12	12	13	158
Predominant Sky Cover	OVR	OVR	OVR	OVR	OVR	OVR	SCT	SCT	CLR	CLR	OVR	OVR	OVR
Mean Relative Humidity 7am (%)	81	80	77	75	79	81	84	86	86	83	81	81	81
Mean Relative Humidity 4pm (%)	67	61	55	51	54	55	56	55	54	53	60	66	57
Mean Dewpoint (°F)	25	26	33	42	52	61	65	64	57	45	35	28	45
Prevailing Wind Direction	S	S	S	S	S	S	S	S	S	S	S	S	S
Prevailing Wind Speed (mph)	12	10	12	12	9	8	7	7	8	8	10	12	9
Maximum Wind Gust (mph)	78	56	53	61	59	64	63	51	52	52	56	58	78

Louisville Standiford Field

Louisville is located on the south bank of the Ohio River, 604 miles below Pittsburgh, Pennsylvania, and 377 miles above the mouth of the river at Cairo, Illinois. The city is divided by Beargrass Creek and its south fork into two topographical types. The eastern portion is rolling, containing several creeks, and consists of plateaus and rolling hillsides. The highest elevation in this area is 565 feet. The western portion is mostly flat with an average elevation about 100 feet lower than the eastern area. Much of the western section lies in the flood plain of the Ohio River. Nearly all of the industries in the city are located in the western portion, while the eastern portion is almost entirely residential. A range of low hills about five miles northwest of Louisville, on the Indiana side of the Ohio River, present a partial barrier to arctic blasts in the winter months. During colder months, snow is frequently observed on the summits of these hills.

The climate of Louisville, while continental in type, is of a variable nature because of its position with respect to the paths of high and low pressure systems and the occasional influx of warm moist air from the Gulf of Mexico. As a whole, winters are moderately cold and summers are quite warm. Temperatures of 100 degrees or more in summer and zero degrees or less in winter are rare.

Thunderstorms with high rainfall intensities are common during the spring and summer months. The precipitation in Louisville is nonseasonal and varies from year to year. The fall months are usually the driest. Snowfall usually occurs from November through March. As with rainfall, amounts vary from year to year and month to month. Relative humidity remains rather high throughout the summer months. Cloud cover is about equally distributed throughout the year with the winter months showing somewhat of an increase in amount. The percentage of possible sunshine at Louisville varies from month to month with the greatest amount during the summer months as a result of the decreasing sky cover during that season. Heavy fog occurs only an average of 10 days during the year, generally in the months of September through March.

Based on the 1951-1980 period, the average date for the last occurrence in the spring of temperatures as low as 32 degrees is mid-April, and the first occurrence in the fall is generally in late October.

The prevailing direction of the wind has a southerly component.

Louisville Standiford Field *Jefferson County*   Elevation: 479 ft.   Latitude: 38° 11' N   Longitude: 85° 44' W

	JAN	FEB	MAR	APR	MAY	JUN	JUL	AUG	SEP	OCT	NOV	DEC	YEAR
Mean Maximum Temp. (°F)	40.9	46.3	56.6	67.4	76.1	84.1	88.0	86.7	80.3	68.9	56.4	46.1	66.5
Mean Temp. (°F)	32.9	37.3	46.7	56.6	65.9	74.3	78.5	77.1	70.2	58.2	47.5	38.1	56.9
Mean Minimum Temp. (°F)	24.8	28.3	36.8	45.7	55.6	64.5	69.0	67.3	60.1	47.5	38.5	30.0	47.3
Extreme Maximum Temp. (°F)	73	77	86	90	91	101	106	101	99	89	83	76	106
Extreme Minimum Temp. (°F)	-22	-5	1	22	32	45	50	46	37	24	7	-15	-22
Days Maximum Temp. ≥ 90°F	0	0	0	0	1	6	12	10	4	0	0	0	33
Days Maximum Temp. ≤ 32°F	8	4	1	0	0	0	0	0	0	0	0	4	17
Days Minimum Temp. ≤ 32°F	23	18	11	2	0	0	0	0	0	1	9	18	82
Days Minimum Temp. ≤ 0°F	1	0	0	0	0	0	0	0	0	0	0	0	1
Heating Degree Days (base 65°F)	990	775	566	272	81	6	0	0	34	234	522	828	4,308
Cooling Degree Days (base 65°F)	0	0	6	25	120	303	449	394	197	33	3	1	1,531
Mean Precipitation (in.)	3.11	3.15	4.44	4.18	4.85	3.80	4.29	3.57	2.99	2.92	3.76	3.69	44.75
Maximum Precipitation (in.)	11.4	9.0	14.9	11.1	11.6	10.1	10.0	8.8	10.5	6.5	9.1	8.9	59.8
Minimum Precipitation (in.)	0.4	0.8	1.0	0.8	1.4	0.5	1.0	0.2	0.3	0.4	0.7	0.6	30.4
Maximum 24-hr. Precipitation (in.)	3.0	3.7	7.0	4.1	4.6	5.1	5.1	3.1	4.3	2.6	3.6	2.8	7.0
Days With ≥ 0.1" Precipitation	6	6	9	8	8	7	6	6	6	5	7	7	81
Days With ≥ 1.0" Precipitation	1	1	1	1	1	1	1	1	1	1	1	1	12
Mean Snowfall (in.)	5.1	4.8	2.5	0.2	trace	trace	trace	trace	0.0	0.1	0.6	1.7	15.0
Maximum Snowfall (in.)	28	16	23	2	trace	0	0	0	0	2	13	9	43
Maximum 24-hr. Snowfall (in.)	16	11	12	1	trace	0	0	0	0	2	13	5	16
Days With ≥ 1.0" Snow Depth	6	5	1	0	0	0	0	0	0	0	0	2	14
Thunderstorm Days	1	1	3	4	7	7	8	7	3	2	2	1	46
Foggy Days	13	11	11	9	11	11	12	16	15	14	12	12	147
Predominant Sky Cover	OVR	OVR	OVR	OVR	OVR	SCT	SCT	SCT	CLR	CLR	OVR	OVR	OVR
Mean Relative Humidity 7am (%)	78	78	76	75	80	81	83	85	86	85	79	79	80
Mean Relative Humidity 4pm (%)	63	58	53	49	52	53	54	53	53	51	57	63	55
Mean Dewpoint (°F)	24	26	33	43	54	63	66	65	58	47	36	28	45
Prevailing Wind Direction	S	WNW	WNW	S	S	S	S	S	S	S	S	S	S
Prevailing Wind Speed (mph)	10	12	13	10	8	7	7	6	7	8	9	9	9
Maximum Wind Gust (mph)	60	60	60	84	60	73	84	59	55	44	58	56	84

Ashland *Boyd County*   Elevation: 557 ft.   Latitude: 38° 27' N   Longitude: 82° 37' W

	JAN	FEB	MAR	APR	MAY	JUN	JUL	AUG	SEP	OCT	NOV	DEC	YEAR
Mean Maximum Temp. (°F)	41.4	46.3	56.6	68.0	76.8	84.2	88.0	86.6	80.3	69.3	57.0	46.6	66.8
Mean Temp. (°F)	29.9	33.5	42.7	52.4	61.7	70.2	74.6	73.0	66.4	54.9	43.9	35.1	53.2
Mean Minimum Temp. (°F)	18.6	20.6	28.7	36.7	46.5	56.2	61.2	59.3	52.4	40.2	30.7	23.6	39.6
Extreme Maximum Temp. (°F)	77	78	88	92	94	102	104	105	99	88	83	82	105
Extreme Minimum Temp. (°F)	-25	-23	-8	16	22	30	34	33	27	16	2	-10	-25
Days Maximum Temp. ≥ 90°F	0	0	0	0	1	7	13	10	3	0	0	0	34
Days Maximum Temp. ≤ 32°F	8	4	1	0	0	0	0	0	0	0	0	4	17
Days Minimum Temp. ≤ 32°F	28	25	21	11	2	0	0	0	0	7	18	25	137
Days Minimum Temp. ≤ 0°F	3	1	0	0	0	0	0	0	0	0	0	1	5
Heating Degree Days (base 65°F)	1,083	884	687	382	154	24	2	5	71	319	627	920	5,158
Cooling Degree Days (base 65°F)	0	0	2	9	57	191	317	259	111	12	0	0	958
Mean Precipitation (in.)	3.19	2.98	3.74	3.32	4.47	4.01	4.64	3.77	2.83	3.02	3.42	3.71	43.10
Days With ≥ 0.1" Precipitation	8	7	9	8	9	8	8	6	5	6	7	7	88
Days With ≥ 1.0" Precipitation	0	1	1	0	1	1	1	1	1	1	1	1	10
Mean Snowfall (in.)	3.1	na	2.1	trace	0.0	0.0	0.0	0.0	0.0	trace	0.1	1.2	na
Days With ≥ 1.0" Snow Depth	6	6	1	0	0	0	0	0	0	0	0	1	14

Barbourville *Knox County*   Elevation: 987 ft.   Latitude: 36° 53' N   Longitude: 83° 53' W

	JAN	FEB	MAR	APR	MAY	JUN	JUL	AUG	SEP	OCT	NOV	DEC	YEAR
Mean Maximum Temp. (°F)	45.2	49.6	59.4	69.2	76.9	83.9	87.4	86.0	80.5	70.2	59.2	49.2	68.1
Mean Temp. (°F)	34.2	37.6	46.2	54.7	63.4	71.6	75.6	74.5	68.1	56.4	46.6	38.3	55.6
Mean Minimum Temp. (°F)	22.7	25.6	32.9	40.2	49.8	59.2	63.9	62.9	55.8	42.5	33.9	27.1	43.0
Extreme Maximum Temp. (°F)	76	80	84	91	91	100	101	102	98	88	83	78	102
Extreme Minimum Temp. (°F)	-22	-20	-5	19	30	38	46	44	34	19	6	-9	-22
Days Maximum Temp. ≥ 90°F	0	0	0	0	1	4	11	7	3	0	0	0	26
Days Maximum Temp. ≤ 32°F	4	3	0	0	0	0	0	0	0	0	0	3	10
Days Minimum Temp. ≤ 32°F	24	21	16	7	0	0	0	0	0	4	15	22	109
Days Minimum Temp. ≤ 0°F	2	1	0	0	0	0	0	0	0	0	0	0	3
Heating Degree Days (base 65°F)	948	766	579	314	113	12	0	2	43	285	548	821	4,431
Cooling Degree Days (base 65°F)	0	0	2	12	76	225	352	300	132	15	1	0	1,115
Mean Precipitation (in.)	4.14	3.87	4.79	4.20	5.31	4.45	4.53	4.23	3.76	3.14	4.35	4.38	51.15
Days With ≥ 0.1" Precipitation	8	7	9	8	9	8	8	7	6	6	8	8	92
Days With ≥ 1.0" Precipitation	1	1	1	1	1	1	1	1	1	1	1	1	12
Mean Snowfall (in.)	na	na	0.6	0.4	trace	0.0	0.0	0.0	0.0	0.0	trace	na	na
Days With ≥ 1.0" Snow Depth	na	na	0	0	0	0	0	0	0	0	0	0	na

Bardstown 5 E *Nelson County*   Elevation: 777 ft.   Latitude: 37° 49' N   Longitude: 85° 23' W

	JAN	FEB	MAR	APR	MAY	JUN	JUL	AUG	SEP	OCT	NOV	DEC	YEAR
Mean Maximum Temp. (°F)	42.3	48.3	57.7	68.2	76.4	84.0	87.9	86.9	81.0	70.1	57.1	47.6	67.3
Mean Temp. (°F)	33.2	38.0	46.8	56.1	64.6	72.7	76.7	75.3	69.0	57.9	46.9	38.5	56.3
Mean Minimum Temp. (°F)	24.1	27.5	35.7	44.0	52.7	61.4	65.4	63.6	56.9	45.5	36.6	29.4	45.2
Extreme Maximum Temp. (°F)	72	78	85	88	94	97	105	105	97	88	80	78	105
Extreme Minimum Temp. (°F)	-26	-9	-5	19	28	40	46	47	33	19	1	-20	-26
Days Maximum Temp. ≥ 90°F	0	0	0	0	0	5	12	10	4	0	0	0	31
Days Maximum Temp. ≤ 32°F	7	3	1	0	0	0	0	0	0	0	0	3	14
Days Minimum Temp. ≤ 32°F	23	19	13	5	0	0	0	0	0	3	11	19	93
Days Minimum Temp. ≤ 0°F	2	1	0	0	0	0	0	0	0	0	0	0	3
Heating Degree Days (base 65°F)	977	757	565	284	97	8	0	1	47	242	540	814	4,332
Cooling Degree Days (base 65°F)	0	0	4	21	89	247	382	332	164	29	1	1	1,270
Mean Precipitation (in.)	3.75	3.86	5.01	4.92	5.53	4.93	4.70	3.32	3.74	3.17	3.73	4.77	51.43
Days With ≥ 0.1" Precipitation	7	6	9	8	9	8	6	6	6	5	7	8	85
Days With ≥ 1.0" Precipitation	1	1	1	1	2	1	2	1	1	1	1	1	14
Mean Snowfall (in.)	na	na	na	trace	trace	0.0	0.0	0.0	0.0	trace	0.3	na	na
Days With ≥ 1.0" Snow Depth	na	na	na	0	0	0	0	0	0	0	0	na	na

Bardwell 2 E *Carlisle County*   Elevation: 410 ft.   Latitude: 36° 53' N   Longitude: 88° 58' W

	JAN	FEB	MAR	APR	MAY	JUN	JUL	AUG	SEP	OCT	NOV	DEC	YEAR
Mean Maximum Temp. (°F)	43.0	49.0	59.2	70.0	78.5	86.7	90.2	88.5	82.2	71.7	58.3	47.9	68.8
Mean Temp. (°F)	33.8	39.0	48.6	58.3	66.9	75.2	78.9	76.8	70.1	59.0	48.1	38.7	57.8
Mean Minimum Temp. (°F)	24.5	28.9	37.8	46.6	55.2	63.7	67.5	65.1	58.0	46.3	37.9	29.4	46.7
Extreme Maximum Temp. (°F)	73	77	84	90	95	102	104	102	100	91	82	77	104
Extreme Minimum Temp. (°F)	-21	-6	3	23	32	42	47	41	30	21	11	-12	-21
Days Maximum Temp. ≥ 90°F	0	0	0	0	2	10	19	14	5	0	0	0	50
Days Maximum Temp. ≤ 32°F	6	3	0	0	0	0	0	0	0	0	0	2	11
Days Minimum Temp. ≤ 32°F	23	17	11	3	0	0	0	0	0	2	10	19	85
Days Minimum Temp. ≤ 0°F	1	0	0	0	0	0	0	0	0	0	0	0	1
Heating Degree Days (base 65°F)	962	729	509	224	61	2	0	0	35	214	504	810	4,050
Cooling Degree Days (base 65°F)	0	0	7	29	125	320	453	389	194	34	2	1	1,554
Mean Precipitation (in.)	3.38	3.93	4.80	5.42	5.04	4.21	4.63	3.72	3.40	3.70	4.91	4.79	51.93
Days With ≥ 0.1" Precipitation	6	6	8	8	8	7	6	5	5	6	7	7	79
Days With ≥ 1.0" Precipitation	1	1	1	2	2	1	2	1	1	1	1	1	15
Mean Snowfall (in.)	4.6	3.8	1.6	trace	0.0	0.0	0.0	0.0	0.0	0.1	0.3	1.4	11.8
Days With ≥ 1.0" Snow Depth	7	4	0	0	0	0	0	0	0	0	0	1	12

Barren River Lake *Allen County*   Elevation: 620 ft.   Latitude: 36° 54' N   Longitude: 86° 08' W

	JAN	FEB	MAR	APR	MAY	JUN	JUL	AUG	SEP	OCT	NOV	DEC	YEAR
Mean Maximum Temp. (°F)	43.6	48.9	59.0	69.5	77.9	85.7	89.7	88.5	82.4	71.2	59.1	49.0	68.7
Mean Temp. (°F)	33.7	37.8	47.1	56.6	65.5	74.0	78.1	76.7	70.3	58.5	48.1	39.0	57.1
Mean Minimum Temp. (°F)	23.9	26.6	35.2	43.7	53.1	62.1	66.4	64.8	58.2	45.8	37.0	29.0	45.5
Extreme Maximum Temp. (°F)	74	82	86	94	94	104	106	104	102	90	84	80	106
Extreme Minimum Temp. (°F)	-19	-8	0	19	30	40	48	47	34	23	5	-15	-19
Days Maximum Temp. ≥ 90°F	0	0	0	0	2	10	18	14	7	0	0	0	51
Days Maximum Temp. ≤ 32°F	6	3	0	0	0	0	0	0	0	0	0	3	12
Days Minimum Temp. ≤ 32°F	23	20	14	4	0	0	0	0	0	3	11	19	94
Days Minimum Temp. ≤ 0°F	2	1	0	0	0	0	0	0	0	0	0	0	3
Heating Degree Days (base 65°F)	962	763	553	275	91	8	0	1	37	231	505	801	4,227
Cooling Degree Days (base 65°F)	0	0	7	32	119	292	436	380	199	40	4	1	1,510
Mean Precipitation (in.)	3.84	3.88	4.75	4.10	5.23	4.75	4.72	4.08	3.83	3.33	4.26	4.82	51.59
Days With ≥ 0.1" Precipitation	7	7	8	8	8	8	7	6	6	6	7	7	85
Days With ≥ 1.0" Precipitation	1	1	1	1	1	1	2	1	1	1	1	1	13
Mean Snowfall (in.)	3.2	2.4	1.0	trace	0.0	0.0	0.0	0.0	0.0	trace	0.2	0.8	7.6
Days With ≥ 1.0" Snow Depth	5	4	1	0	0	0	0	0	0	0	0	1	11

Baxter *Harlan County*   Elevation: 1,161 ft.   Latitude: 36° 51' N   Longitude: 83° 20' W

	JAN	FEB	MAR	APR	MAY	JUN	JUL	AUG	SEP	OCT	NOV	DEC	YEAR
Mean Maximum Temp. (°F)	43.8	48.4	57.8	67.9	75.6	82.4	86.0	84.9	79.0	68.4	57.9	48.4	66.7
Mean Temp. (°F)	33.8	37.2	45.3	54.1	62.9	70.8	74.8	73.7	67.6	55.9	46.0	38.1	55.0
Mean Minimum Temp. (°F)	23.7	26.0	32.9	40.2	50.0	59.0	63.6	62.5	56.2	43.4	34.1	27.8	43.3
Extreme Maximum Temp. (°F)	74	79	84	90	92	96	99	101	95	87	81	78	101
Extreme Minimum Temp. (°F)	-19	-12	1	21	25	35	46	42	36	19	4	-7	-19
Days Maximum Temp. ≥ 90°F	0	0	0	0	0	3	8	6	1	0	0	0	18
Days Maximum Temp. ≤ 32°F	5	3	1	0	0	0	0	0	0	0	0	3	12
Days Minimum Temp. ≤ 32°F	24	20	17	6	0	0	0	0	0	0	15	21	107
Days Minimum Temp. ≤ 0°F	2	1	0	0	0	0	0	0	0	0	0	1	4
Heating Degree Days (base 65°F)	962	778	604	330	120	14	1	2	47	286	564	827	4,535
Cooling Degree Days (base 65°F)	0	0	1	9	62	196	322	279	119	13	0	0	1,001
Mean Precipitation (in.)	4.43	4.04	4.90	4.23	5.22	4.70	4.55	4.30	3.32	3.30	4.13	4.39	51.51
Days With ≥ 0.1" Precipitation	9	8	10	8	9	8	9	7	6	6	8	8	96
Days With ≥ 1.0" Precipitation	1	1	1	1	2	1	1	1	1	1	1	1	13
Mean Snowfall (in.)	na	3.0	1.4	0.7	0.0	0.0	0.0	0.0	0.0	trace	0.4	0.8	na
Days With ≥ 1.0" Snow Depth	3	3	1	0	0	0	0	0	0	0	0	1	8

Beaver Dam *Ohio County*   Elevation: 439 ft.   Latitude: 37° 25' N   Longitude: 86° 52' W

	JAN	FEB	MAR	APR	MAY	JUN	JUL	AUG	SEP	OCT	NOV	DEC	YEAR
Mean Maximum Temp. (°F)	43.1	49.5	59.6	70.1	77.8	85.1	88.6	87.5	82.0	71.4	58.6	48.2	68.5
Mean Temp. (°F)	33.9	38.9	48.2	57.7	66.0	74.1	77.8	76.3	69.8	58.7	48.3	39.0	57.4
Mean Minimum Temp. (°F)	24.6	28.4	36.8	45.2	54.2	63.0	67.0	65.0	57.6	45.9	37.8	29.6	46.3
Extreme Maximum Temp. (°F)	72	81	85	90	91	100	104	101	100	90	82	78	104
Extreme Minimum Temp. (°F)	-23	-8	-2	21	30	39	47	42	32	20	5	-24	-24
Days Maximum Temp. ≥ 90°F	0	0	0	0	1	7	14	12	5	0	0	0	39
Days Maximum Temp. ≤ 32°F	6	3	0	0	0	0	0	0	0	0	0	3	12
Days Minimum Temp. ≤ 32°F	23	18	12	4	0	0	0	0	0	3	10	19	89
Days Minimum Temp. ≤ 0°F	2	1	0	0	0	0	0	0	0	0	0	0	3
Heating Degree Days (base 65°F)	958	729	522	245	74	5	0	1	36	225	499	801	4,095
Cooling Degree Days (base 65°F)	0	1	8	32	112	287	419	365	179	38	3	1	1,445
Mean Precipitation (in.)	3.53	4.28	4.64	4.44	5.05	3.77	4.08	3.10	3.68	3.37	4.31	4.51	48.76
Days With ≥ 0.1" Precipitation	6	6	8	7	8	7	7	5	5	5	7	7	78
Days With ≥ 1.0" Precipitation	1	1	1	1	2	1	1	1	1	1	1	1	13
Mean Snowfall (in.)	na	na	1.9	trace	0.0	0.0	0.0	0.0	0.0	0.1	0.2	1.0	na
Days With ≥ 1.0" Snow Depth	na	na	0	0	0	0	0	0	0	0	0	0	na

Berea College *Madison County*   Elevation: 1,069 ft.   Latitude: 37° 34' N   Longitude: 84° 18' W

	JAN	FEB	MAR	APR	MAY	JUN	JUL	AUG	SEP	OCT	NOV	DEC	YEAR
Mean Maximum Temp. (°F)	43.6	49.0	59.1	69.0	76.6	83.4	87.1	86.0	80.1	68.9	57.4	48.2	67.4
Mean Temp. (°F)	34.7	39.1	48.2	57.3	65.5	72.9	76.6	75.3	69.4	58.2	48.3	39.4	57.1
Mean Minimum Temp. (°F)	25.9	29.1	37.3	45.5	54.3	62.4	66.1	64.6	58.6	47.5	39.1	30.5	46.7
Extreme Maximum Temp. (°F)	75	80	85	90	91	96	102	100	97	85	81	78	102
Extreme Minimum Temp. (°F)	-21	-8	-3	21	32	43	47	42	31	22	7	-17	-21
Days Maximum Temp. ≥ 90°F	0	0	0	0	0	3	10	8	3	0	0	0	24
Days Maximum Temp. ≤ 32°F	6	3	0	0	0	0	0	0	0	0	0	3	12
Days Minimum Temp. ≤ 32°F	22	17	12	3	0	0	0	0	0	2	9	18	83
Days Minimum Temp. ≤ 0°F	1	0	0	0	0	0	0	0	0	0	0	0	1
Heating Degree Days (base 65°F)	932	726	523	258	85	7	0	1	38	234	499	787	4,090
Cooling Degree Days (base 65°F)	0	0	7	34	112	259	380	330	170	30	3	1	1,326
Mean Precipitation (in.)	3.01	3.01	4.28	4.04	5.10	4.55	4.09	4.19	3.98	3.14	3.71	4.02	47.12
Days With ≥ 0.1" Precipitation	6	6	9	8	8	8	7	7	6	6	6	7	85
Days With ≥ 1.0" Precipitation	1	1	1	1	1	1	1	1	1	1	1	1	12
Mean Snowfall (in.)	6.0	4.2	1.0	0.1	0.0	0.0	0.0	0.0	0.0	0.0	0.3	na	na
Days With ≥ 1.0" Snow Depth	6	4	1	0	0	0	0	0	0	0	0	1	12

Bernheim Forest *Bullitt County*   Elevation: 547 ft.   Latitude: 37° 55' N   Longitude: 85° 39' W

	JAN	FEB	MAR	APR	MAY	JUN	JUL	AUG	SEP	OCT	NOV	DEC	YEAR
Mean Maximum Temp. (°F)	43.6	49.7	60.2	70.6	78.6	85.8	89.6	88.9	83.1	72.0	59.1	49.0	69.2
Mean Temp. (°F)	33.7	38.4	47.8	57.0	65.7	73.4	77.4	76.2	69.9	58.6	48.1	39.1	57.1
Mean Minimum Temp. (°F)	23.8	27.0	35.3	43.4	52.6	60.9	65.1	63.4	56.7	45.1	37.1	29.2	45.0
Extreme Maximum Temp. (°F)	73	80	86	91	94	101	106	104	101	90	84	78	106
Extreme Minimum Temp. (°F)	-24	-10	-4	17	28	39	45	42	32	18	0	-19	-24
Days Maximum Temp. ≥ 90°F	0	0	0	0	1	8	17	14	6	0	0	0	46
Days Maximum Temp. ≤ 32°F	6	3	0	0	0	0	0	0	0	0	0	2	11
Days Minimum Temp. ≤ 32°F	23	20	14	5	0	0	0	0	0	4	11	19	96
Days Minimum Temp. ≤ 0°F	2	1	0	0	0	0	0	0	0	0	0	0	3
Heating Degree Days (base 65°F)	963	746	535	264	81	7	0	1	37	226	505	795	4,160
Cooling Degree Days (base 65°F)	0	1	7	32	116	278	421	375	195	38	3	1	1,467
Mean Precipitation (in.)	3.37	3.97	4.79	4.57	5.38	4.89	4.45	3.51	3.36	3.38	4.25	4.55	50.47
Days With ≥ 0.1" Precipitation	6	6	8	8	8	7	6	6	6	6	7	7	81
Days With ≥ 1.0" Precipitation	1	1	1	1	2	1	1	1	1	1	1	1	13
Mean Snowfall (in.)	3.8	2.7	1.0	trace	0.0	0.0	0.0	0.0	0.0	0.0	0.4	0.7	8.6
Days With ≥ 1.0" Snow Depth	5	4	1	0	0	0	0	0	0	0	0	1	11

Bowling Green Warren Co. Airport *Warren County*   Elevation: 524 ft.   Latitude: 36° 59' N   Longitude: 86° 26' W

	JAN	FEB	MAR	APR	MAY	JUN	JUL	AUG	SEP	OCT	NOV	DEC	YEAR
Mean Maximum Temp. (°F)	42.3	47.8	58.5	69.1	77.0	85.4	89.2	87.9	81.2	69.8	57.9	47.8	67.8
Mean Temp. (°F)	33.5	37.8	47.7	57.3	65.7	74.4	78.5	76.8	69.8	57.7	47.7	38.6	57.1
Mean Minimum Temp. (°F)	24.6	27.7	36.8	45.5	54.4	63.2	67.7	65.7	58.4	45.6	37.5	29.4	46.4
Extreme Maximum Temp. (°F)	74	79	85	90	94	102	107	103	104	89	83	78	107
Extreme Minimum Temp. (°F)	-15	-6	1	23	32	42	48	43	33	23	9	-14	-15
Days Maximum Temp. ≥ 90°F	0	0	0	0	1	8	16	13	5	0	0	0	43
Days Maximum Temp. ≤ 32°F	7	4	0	0	0	0	0	0	0	0	0	3	14
Days Minimum Temp. ≤ 32°F	23	19	11	3	0	0	0	0	0	2	11	20	89
Days Minimum Temp. ≤ 0°F	1	0	0	0	0	0	0	0	0	0	0	0	1
Heating Degree Days (base 65°F)	968	762	535	252	80	4	0	1	38	244	515	812	4,211
Cooling Degree Days (base 65°F)	0	0	5	26	106	291	440	377	174	25	2	1	1,447
Mean Precipitation (in.)	3.94	4.35	4.85	3.96	5.21	4.11	4.58	3.40	4.01	3.35	4.49	5.16	51.41
Days With ≥ 0.1" Precipitation	7	7	9	8	8	7	6	6	6	6	7	8	85
Days With ≥ 1.0" Precipitation	1	1	1	1	2	1	1	1	1	1	1	2	14
Mean Snowfall (in.)	4.2	4.0	1.1	trace	trace	trace	0.0	0.0	0.0	trace	0.2	0.9	10.4
Days With ≥ 1.0" Snow Depth	5	4	0	0	0	0	0	0	0	0	0	1	10

Bradfordsville *Marion County*   Elevation: 659 ft.   Latitude: 37° 29' N   Longitude: 85° 09' W

	JAN	FEB	MAR	APR	MAY	JUN	JUL	AUG	SEP	OCT	NOV	DEC	YEAR
Mean Maximum Temp. (°F)	42.6	47.5	57.5	68.2	76.4	84.2	88.3	87.1	81.7	70.5	58.3	48.0	67.5
Mean Temp. (°F)	32.6	36.2	45.1	54.6	63.5	72.0	76.5	74.8	68.5	56.4	46.5	37.7	55.4
Mean Minimum Temp. (°F)	22.5	24.7	32.7	41.0	50.5	59.8	64.7	62.4	55.3	42.3	34.6	27.5	43.2
Extreme Maximum Temp. (°F)	75	82	84	90	92	100	105	105	99	90	84	78	105
Extreme Minimum Temp. (°F)	-22	-14	-7	19	27	38	45	38	32	20	9	-17	-22
Days Maximum Temp. ≥ 90°F	0	0	0	0	1	6	14	10	5	0	0	0	36
Days Maximum Temp. ≤ 32°F	7	4	1	0	0	0	0	0	0	0	0	3	15
Days Minimum Temp. ≤ 32°F	24	21	17	7	1	0	0	0	0	6	13	21	110
Days Minimum Temp. ≤ 0°F	2	1	0	0	0	0	0	0	0	0	0	1	4
Heating Degree Days (base 65°F)	999	807	612	322	123	14	0	2	50	282	552	839	4,602
Cooling Degree Days (base 65°F)	0	0	4	15	82	236	376	316	146	22	2	1	1,200
Mean Precipitation (in.)	4.07	4.14	5.20	4.81	5.34	4.64	4.74	3.88	3.94	3.11	4.20	4.92	52.99
Days With ≥ 0.1" Precipitation	7	7	8	8	8	8	7	6	5	6	8	8	86
Days With ≥ 1.0" Precipitation	1	1	1	1	1	1	1	1	1	1	1	1	12
Mean Snowfall (in.)	na	5.7	2.0	0.1	trace	0.0	0.0	0.0	0.0	trace	0.3	1.6	na
Days With ≥ 1.0" Snow Depth	8	7	1	0	0	0	0	0	0	0	0	2	18

Carrollton Lock 1 *Carroll County*   Elevation: 449 ft.   Latitude: 38° 40' N   Longitude: 85° 09' W

	JAN	FEB	MAR	APR	MAY	JUN	JUL	AUG	SEP	OCT	NOV	DEC	YEAR
Mean Maximum Temp. (°F)	41.8	47.6	57.4	68.1	76.3	83.6	87.2	85.9	80.6	70.0	57.6	46.9	66.9
Mean Temp. (°F)	32.5	36.8	45.9	55.7	64.6	72.3	76.3	74.9	68.9	57.4	47.0	37.6	55.8
Mean Minimum Temp. (°F)	23.2	26.0	34.4	43.0	52.5	60.9	65.4	63.9	57.2	44.7	36.5	28.1	44.7
Extreme Maximum Temp. (°F)	71	80	85	89	93	104	105	103	99	90	84	75	105
Extreme Minimum Temp. (°F)	-22	-9	-5	20	30	39	47	42	35	20	3	-18	-22
Days Maximum Temp. ≥ 90°F	0	0	0	0	0	5	10	8	3	0	0	0	26
Days Maximum Temp. ≤ 32°F	7	3	0	0	0	0	0	0	0	0	0	3	13
Days Minimum Temp. ≤ 32°F	23	20	14	5	0	0	0	0	0	3	12	20	97
Days Minimum Temp. ≤ 0°F	2	1	0	0	0	0	0	0	0	0	0	1	4
Heating Degree Days (base 65°F)	1,000	790	589	293	96	10	0	2	43	255	534	845	4,457
Cooling Degree Days (base 65°F)	0	0	3	19	92	240	377	326	168	29	2	0	1,256
Mean Precipitation (in.)	3.02	2.90	4.18	4.28	4.94	4.43	3.96	3.89	2.96	3.07	3.48	3.63	44.74
Days With ≥ 0.1" Precipitation	6	5	8	8	8	8	7	6	5	6	7	6	80
Days With ≥ 1.0" Precipitation	1	1	1	1	1	1	1	1	1	1	1	1	12
Mean Snowfall (in.)	4.7	3.8	1.7	0.2	0.0	0.0	0.0	0.0	0.0	trace	0.2	1.3	11.9
Days With ≥ 1.0" Snow Depth	6	5	1	0	0	0	0	0	0	0	0	2	14

Danville *Boyle County*   Elevation: 898 ft.   Latitude: 37° 40' N   Longitude: 84° 46' W

	JAN	FEB	MAR	APR	MAY	JUN	JUL	AUG	SEP	OCT	NOV	DEC	YEAR
Mean Maximum Temp. (°F)	40.7	45.3	55.6	66.2	74.6	82.3	86.4	85.5	79.8	68.3	56.0	46.0	65.6
Mean Temp. (°F)	31.9	35.6	44.9	54.7	63.7	71.9	76.1	74.9	68.6	56.8	46.2	37.0	55.2
Mean Minimum Temp. (°F)	23.0	25.9	34.0	43.2	52.8	61.5	65.8	64.1	57.4	45.3	36.4	28.0	44.8
Extreme Maximum Temp. (°F)	75	79	85	90	92	100	103	103	100	90	83	75	103
Extreme Minimum Temp. (°F)	-20	-9	-1	19	32	41	49	42	36	21	5	-18	-20
Days Maximum Temp. ≥ 90°F	0	0	0	0	0	3	9	7	3	0	0	0	22
Days Maximum Temp. ≤ 32°F	8	5	1	0	0	0	0	0	0	0	0	4	18
Days Minimum Temp. ≤ 32°F	25	20	15	4	0	0	0	0	0	2	11	20	97
Days Minimum Temp. ≤ 0°F	2	0	0	0	0	0	0	0	0	0	0	0	2
Heating Degree Days (base 65°F)	1,020	822	621	320	115	14	1	1	47	271	560	861	4,653
Cooling Degree Days (base 65°F)	0	0	3	18	85	239	376	325	160	26	1	0	1,233
Mean Precipitation (in.)	3.65	3.86	4.93	4.13	4.94	4.78	4.90	3.43	3.42	3.19	3.72	4.37	49.32
Days With ≥ 0.1" Precipitation	7	7	9	8	8	7	7	6	5	6	7	7	84
Days With ≥ 1.0" Precipitation	1	1	1	1	1	1	1	1	1	1	1	1	12
Mean Snowfall (in.)	4.2	4.8	1.6	trace	trace	0.0	0.0	0.0	0.0	0.0	0.3	1.1	12.0
Days With ≥ 1.0" Snow Depth	6	5	1	0	0	0	0	0	0	0	0	1	13

Dix Dam *Mercer County*   Elevation: 869 ft.   Latitude: 37° 48' N   Longitude: 84° 43' W

	JAN	FEB	MAR	APR	MAY	JUN	JUL	AUG	SEP	OCT	NOV	DEC	YEAR
Mean Maximum Temp. (°F)	42.9	48.2	58.1	68.2	76.2	83.7	87.4	86.4	80.7	70.1	58.0	47.8	67.3
Mean Temp. (°F)	34.3	38.3	47.2	56.5	65.1	73.2	77.1	75.8	69.8	58.8	48.4	39.2	57.0
Mean Minimum Temp. (°F)	25.6	28.3	36.3	44.6	53.9	62.6	66.8	65.2	58.8	47.3	38.7	30.6	46.6
Extreme Maximum Temp. (°F)	73	80	83	89	92	101	104	102	97	88	84	76	104
Extreme Minimum Temp. (°F)	-18	-7	2	19	31	42	47	44	35	23	7	-17	-18
Days Maximum Temp. ≥ 90°F	0	0	0	0	0	4	10	9	3	0	0	0	26
Days Maximum Temp. ≤ 32°F	6	4	1	0	0	0	0	0	0	0	0	3	14
Days Minimum Temp. ≤ 32°F	22	18	12	3	0	0	0	0	0	2	9	18	84
Days Minimum Temp. ≤ 0°F	1	0	0	0	0	0	0	0	0	0	0	0	1
Heating Degree Days (base 65°F)	945	748	549	274	90	7	0	1	35	220	497	793	4,159
Cooling Degree Days (base 65°F)	0	0	3	23	99	263	395	349	179	35	2	1	1,349
Mean Precipitation (in.)	3.32	3.54	4.28	4.04	4.75	4.30	4.65	3.95	3.23	3.12	3.45	3.90	46.53
Days With ≥ 0.1" Precipitation	6	6	8	8	8	8	7	6	5	6	7	7	82
Days With ≥ 1.0" Precipitation	1	1	1	1	1	1	1	1	1	1	1	1	12
Mean Snowfall (in.)	na	na	na	trace	0.0	0.0	0.0	0.0	0.0	0.0	0.1	0.3	na
Days With ≥ 1.0" Snow Depth	6	4	0	0	0	0	0	0	0	0	0	1	11

Falmouth *Pendleton County*   Elevation: 649 ft.   Latitude: 38° 41' N   Longitude: 84° 20' W

	JAN	FEB	MAR	APR	MAY	JUN	JUL	AUG	SEP	OCT	NOV	DEC	YEAR
Mean Maximum Temp. (°F)	38.9	43.6	54.3	65.7	74.8	83.0	86.8	85.5	79.5	67.8	54.8	44.8	64.9
Mean Temp. (°F)	29.0	32.6	42.2	52.4	62.2	70.6	75.0	73.4	66.8	54.3	43.9	34.7	53.1
Mean Minimum Temp. (°F)	19.1	21.6	30.2	38.9	49.2	58.2	63.2	61.3	54.1	40.8	32.8	24.6	41.2
Extreme Maximum Temp. (°F)	71	77	84	93	95	100	101	103	99	89	83	76	103
Extreme Minimum Temp. (°F)	-30	-7	-3	17	23	34	41	41	29	17	0	-21	-30
Days Maximum Temp. ≥ 90°F	0	0	0	0	1	4	10	8	3	0	0	0	26
Days Maximum Temp. ≤ 32°F	10	6	1	0	0	0	0	0	0	0	0	4	21
Days Minimum Temp. ≤ 32°F	27	23	19	8	1	0	0	0	0	6	16	24	124
Days Minimum Temp. ≤ 0°F	3	2	0	0	0	0	0	0	0	0	0	1	6
Heating Degree Days (base 65°F)	1,109	908	700	382	145	20	1	5	67	336	628	933	5,234
Cooling Degree Days (base 65°F)	0	0	1	10	64	199	341	291	119	13	1	0	1,039
Mean Precipitation (in.)	2.83	2.68	3.71	4.11	4.56	4.24	4.49	3.73	2.95	2.87	3.46	3.36	42.99
Days With ≥ 0.1" Precipitation	6	6	7	7	8	7	7	6	5	6	7	7	79
Days With ≥ 1.0" Precipitation	1	1	1	1	1	1	1	1	1	1	1	1	12
Mean Snowfall (in.)	3.6	3.8	1.5	trace	0.0	0.0	0.0	0.0	0.0	trace	0.1	1.2	10.2
Days With ≥ 1.0" Snow Depth	5	na	1	0	0	0	0	0	0	0	0	1	na

Farmers 2 S *Rowan County*   Elevation: 679 ft.   Latitude: 38° 07' N   Longitude: 83° 33' W

	JAN	FEB	MAR	APR	MAY	JUN	JUL	AUG	SEP	OCT	NOV	DEC	YEAR
Mean Maximum Temp. (°F)	41.3	46.4	56.6	67.5	76.0	83.5	87.5	86.3	80.2	68.9	57.1	46.8	66.5
Mean Temp. (°F)	31.8	35.4	44.4	54.1	63.0	71.1	75.4	74.1	67.5	55.8	46.0	37.1	54.7
Mean Minimum Temp. (°F)	22.2	24.3	32.2	40.7	50.0	58.7	63.4	61.8	54.7	42.7	34.9	27.3	42.7
Extreme Maximum Temp. (°F)	77	80	89	92	95	101	105	103	99	90	82	79	105
Extreme Minimum Temp. (°F)	-26	-13	-7	17	28	37	45	35	32	17	9	-24	-26
Days Maximum Temp. ≥ 90°F	0	0	0	0	1	5	11	10	3	0	0	0	30
Days Maximum Temp. ≤ 32°F	8	4	1	0	0	0	0	0	0	0	0	4	17
Days Minimum Temp. ≤ 32°F	25	21	17	7	1	0	0	0	0	5	13	21	110
Days Minimum Temp. ≤ 0°F	2	1	0	0	0	0	0	0	0	0	0	1	4
Heating Degree Days (base 65°F)	1,023	830	636	338	131	19	1	3	59	298	565	859	4,762
Cooling Degree Days (base 65°F)	0	0	4	17	80	220	353	297	138	23	2	0	1,134
Mean Precipitation (in.)	3.33	3.24	4.09	4.03	4.94	4.41	5.41	3.82	3.32	3.19	3.51	4.06	47.35
Days With ≥ 0.1" Precipitation	7	6	9	8	9	8	8	6	5	6	7	8	87
Days With ≥ 1.0" Precipitation	1	1	1	1	1	1	2	1	1	1	1	1	13
Mean Snowfall (in.)	2.6	na	1.0	trace	0.0	0.0	0.0	0.0	0.0	0.0	trace	1.4	na
Days With ≥ 1.0" Snow Depth	7	5	1	0	0	0	0	0	0	0	0	2	15

Frankfort Lock 4 *Franklin County*   Elevation: 498 ft.   Latitude: 38° 14' N   Longitude: 84° 52' W

	JAN	FEB	MAR	APR	MAY	JUN	JUL	AUG	SEP	OCT	NOV	DEC	YEAR
Mean Maximum Temp. (°F)	40.7	45.6	55.5	66.4	75.1	82.9	87.5	86.3	80.2	68.8	56.5	45.9	66.0
Mean Temp. (°F)	31.0	34.7	43.5	53.2	62.5	71.1	75.8	74.4	67.7	55.7	45.3	36.1	54.3
Mean Minimum Temp. (°F)	21.3	23.8	31.3	40.0	49.9	59.2	64.1	62.4	55.1	42.4	34.1	26.2	42.5
Extreme Maximum Temp. (°F)	73	78	82	90	91	101	103	102	97	92	84	78	103
Extreme Minimum Temp. (°F)	-27	-10	-1	21	30	41	49	42	33	21	6	-17	-27
Days Maximum Temp. ≥ 90°F	0	0	0	0	0	4	11	9	3	0	0	0	27
Days Maximum Temp. ≤ 32°F	7	5	1	0	0	0	0	0	0	0	0	4	17
Days Minimum Temp. ≤ 32°F	26	23	19	6	0	0	0	0	0	4	14	22	114
Days Minimum Temp. ≤ 0°F	2	1	0	0	0	0	0	0	0	0	0	1	4
Heating Degree Days (base 65°F)	1,047	849	663	356	135	17	0	2	54	299	585	890	4,897
Cooling Degree Days (base 65°F)	0	0	2	9	63	205	354	302	132	17	1	0	1,085
Mean Precipitation (in.)	3.04	2.97	4.05	3.81	4.66	4.39	4.10	3.53	3.25	2.74	3.31	3.70	43.55
Days With ≥ 0.1" Precipitation	5	5	8	8	8	8	6	6	5	6	6	7	78
Days With ≥ 1.0" Precipitation	1	1	1	1	1	1	1	1	1	1	1	1	12
Mean Snowfall (in.)	na	2.8	0.5	trace	0.0	0.0	0.0	0.0	0.0	0.0	0.1	0.9	na
Days With ≥ 1.0" Snow Depth	4	6	1	0	0	0	0	0	0	0	0	1	12

Gilbertsville Kentucky Dam *Livingston County*   Elevation: 357 ft.   Latitude: 37° 01' N   Longitude: 88° 16' W

	JAN	FEB	MAR	APR	MAY	JUN	JUL	AUG	SEP	OCT	NOV	DEC	YEAR
Mean Maximum Temp. (°F)	44.4	50.3	60.9	71.7	80.1	88.9	92.6	91.4	84.9	73.0	59.9	49.0	70.6
Mean Temp. (°F)	35.4	40.2	50.1	60.0	68.6	77.4	81.5	79.8	73.1	61.1	50.5	40.1	59.8
Mean Minimum Temp. (°F)	26.4	30.0	39.2	48.2	57.0	65.9	70.2	68.1	61.3	49.2	40.8	31.1	48.9
Extreme Maximum Temp. (°F)	74	79	85	92	96	105	107	105	103	91	83	74	107
Extreme Minimum Temp. (°F)	-15	-9	9	27	36	46	52	46	36	25	13	-15	-15
Days Maximum Temp. ≥ 90°F	0	0	0	0	3	15	23	20	9	0	0	0	70
Days Maximum Temp. ≤ 32°F	5	2	0	0	0	0	0	0	0	0	0	2	9
Days Minimum Temp. ≤ 32°F	21	16	8	1	0	0	0	0	0	1	6	17	70
Days Minimum Temp. ≤ 0°F	1	0	0	0	0	0	0	0	0	0	0	0	1
Heating Degree Days (base 65°F)	912	696	463	190	38	1	0	0	19	164	434	766	3,683
Cooling Degree Days (base 65°F)	0	0	8	43	154	389	540	476	263	46	5	0	1,924
Mean Precipitation (in.)	3.65	4.36	4.58	4.66	4.84	4.10	4.41	4.22	3.38	3.20	4.73	4.56	50.69
Days With ≥ 0.1" Precipitation	6	6	9	7	8	6	6	5	5	5	7	7	77
Days With ≥ 1.0" Precipitation	1	1	1	1	1	1	1	1	1	1	2	1	13
Mean Snowfall (in.)	na	na	0.3	trace	0.0	0.0	0.0	0.0	0.0	trace	trace	0.5	na
Days With ≥ 1.0" Snow Depth	na	na	0	0	0	0	0	0	0	0	0	na	na

Glasgow *Barren County*   Elevation: 767 ft.   Latitude: 37° 00' N   Longitude: 85° 54' W

	JAN	FEB	MAR	APR	MAY	JUN	JUL	AUG	SEP	OCT	NOV	DEC	YEAR
Mean Maximum Temp. (°F)	43.4	49.5	59.6	70.1	78.2	85.7	88.8	87.6	81.5	69.7	57.6	48.4	68.3
Mean Temp. (°F)	34.6	39.5	48.4	57.7	66.2	74.2	77.6	76.2	69.9	57.8	47.7	39.5	57.4
Mean Minimum Temp. (°F)	25.7	29.4	37.2	45.2	54.1	62.5	66.4	64.7	58.3	45.8	37.8	30.6	46.5
Extreme Maximum Temp. (°F)	73	81	84	91	94	103	105	103	101	88	82	76	105
Extreme Minimum Temp. (°F)	-19	-6	-1	21	30	40	48	41	35	22	5	-15	-19
Days Maximum Temp. ≥ 90°F	0	0	0	0	1	8	15	11	4	0	0	0	39
Days Maximum Temp. ≤ 32°F	6	4	0	0	0	0	0	0	0	0	0	3	13
Days Minimum Temp. ≤ 32°F	22	18	12	4	0	0	0	0	0	3	10	18	87
Days Minimum Temp. ≤ 0°F	1	0	0	0	0	0	0	0	0	0	0	0	1
Heating Degree Days (base 65°F)	937	715	513	244	75	4	0	1	36	246	515	783	4,069
Cooling Degree Days (base 65°F)	0	1	7	33	128	301	427	372	194	34	2	1	1,500
Mean Precipitation (in.)	4.27	4.37	5.14	4.44	5.23	5.05	4.78	4.01	4.12	3.22	4.43	5.21	54.27
Days With ≥ 0.1" Precipitation	8	7	9	8	8	8	7	6	6	5	8	8	88
Days With ≥ 1.0" Precipitation	1	1	1	1	1	1	2	1	1	1	1	1	13
Mean Snowfall (in.)	4.9	4.0	1.2	0.1	0.0	0.0	0.0	0.0	0.0	0.0	0.3	1.1	11.6
Days With ≥ 1.0" Snow Depth	6	3	0	0	0	0	0	0	0	0	0	1	10

Gray Hawk *Jackson County*   Elevation: 1,250 ft.   Latitude: 37° 24' N   Longitude: 83° 57' W

	JAN	FEB	MAR	APR	MAY	JUN	JUL	AUG	SEP	OCT	NOV	DEC	YEAR
Mean Maximum Temp. (°F)	40.8	45.9	55.1	65.4	73.4	80.9	84.8	83.7	77.6	66.6	55.5	45.3	64.6
Mean Temp. (°F)	30.7	34.3	42.5	51.7	60.2	68.6	72.9	71.5	64.7	52.6	43.5	34.7	52.3
Mean Minimum Temp. (°F)	20.5	22.6	29.8	37.6	47.0	56.1	61.1	59.2	51.8	38.6	31.4	24.1	40.0
Extreme Maximum Temp. (°F)	73	77	82	90	89	96	101	101	95	86	80	76	101
Extreme Minimum Temp. (°F)	-35	-22	-12	14	27	30	42	35	30	18	-1	-16	-35
Days Maximum Temp. ≥ 90°F	0	0	0	0	0	1	6	4	2	0	0	0	13
Days Maximum Temp. ≤ 32°F	7	5	1	0	0	0	0	0	0	0	0	5	18
Days Minimum Temp. ≤ 32°F	25	23	20	10	2	0	0	0	0	9	17	24	130
Days Minimum Temp. ≤ 0°F	2	2	0	0	0	0	0	0	0	0	0	1	5
Heating Degree Days (base 65°F)	1,058	862	692	399	182	31	2	7	91	383	640	933	5,280
Cooling Degree Days (base 65°F)	0	0	1	5	40	151	270	217	90	8	0	0	782
Mean Precipitation (in.)	3.92	3.56	5.00	3.82	4.83	4.07	4.27	3.98	3.71	3.33	4.28	4.79	49.56
Days With ≥ 0.1" Precipitation	8	7	9	7	9	7	7	6	5	5	7	8	85
Days With ≥ 1.0" Precipitation	1	1	1	1	1	1	1	1	1	1	1	1	12
Mean Snowfall (in.)	5.9	4.5	2.6	0.7	trace	0.0	0.0	0.0	0.0	trace	0.5	1.8	16.0
Days With ≥ 1.0" Snow Depth	na	na	1	0	0	0	0	0	0	0	0	na	na

Grayson 3 SW *Carter County*   Elevation: 698 ft.   Latitude: 38° 18' N   Longitude: 82° 59' W

	JAN	FEB	MAR	APR	MAY	JUN	JUL	AUG	SEP	OCT	NOV	DEC	YEAR
Mean Maximum Temp. (°F)	41.6	45.9	55.7	66.8	75.5	82.7	86.7	85.6	79.6	68.8	57.0	46.7	66.0
Mean Temp. (°F)	30.6	33.6	42.0	51.8	61.1	69.5	74.1	72.7	65.8	53.8	43.8	35.3	52.9
Mean Minimum Temp. (°F)	19.6	21.2	28.2	36.8	46.7	56.3	61.5	59.9	52.0	38.7	30.6	24.0	39.6
Extreme Maximum Temp. (°F)	78	78	86	91	93	102	104	101	98	87	83	80	104
Extreme Minimum Temp. (°F)	-31	-22	-10	17	26	35	40	35	30	18	2	-18	-31
Days Maximum Temp. ≥ 90°F	0	0	0	0	1	4	10	8	3	0	0	0	26
Days Maximum Temp. ≤ 32°F	8	4	1	0	0	0	0	0	0	0	0	3	16
Days Minimum Temp. ≤ 32°F	26	24	21	11	2	0	0	0	0	10	18	24	136
Days Minimum Temp. ≤ 0°F	3	2	0	0	0	0	0	0	0	0	0	1	6
Heating Degree Days (base 65°F)	1,059	881	709	397	166	28	2	6	78	353	629	913	5,221
Cooling Degree Days (base 65°F)	0	0	1	7	50	173	302	249	100	12	1	0	895
Mean Precipitation (in.)	3.10	3.05	3.88	3.52	4.44	4.04	4.79	3.57	2.58	3.06	3.16	3.63	42.82
Days With ≥ 0.1" Precipitation	7	7	9	8	9	8	8	6	5	6	7	7	87
Days With ≥ 1.0" Precipitation	1	1	1	0	1	1	1	1	1	1	1	1	11
Mean Snowfall (in.)	5.6	4.5	2.6	trace	trace	0.0	trace	0.0	0.0	trace	0.5	1.4	14.6
Days With ≥ 1.0" Snow Depth	6	5	1	0	0	0	0	0	0	0	0	1	13

Greensburg *Green County*   Elevation: 587 ft.   Latitude: 37° 15' N   Longitude: 85° 30' W

	JAN	FEB	MAR	APR	MAY	JUN	JUL	AUG	SEP	OCT	NOV	DEC	YEAR
Mean Maximum Temp. (°F)	43.3	48.8	58.5	69.0	77.5	85.1	89.2	88.1	82.4	70.9	58.7	48.6	68.3
Mean Temp. (°F)	33.2	37.2	46.2	55.7	64.7	73.4	77.7	76.0	69.5	57.2	47.1	38.2	56.3
Mean Minimum Temp. (°F)	23.1	25.6	33.9	42.3	51.8	61.7	66.1	63.9	56.6	43.4	35.3	27.7	44.3
Extreme Maximum Temp. (°F)	77	80	85	97	93	99	105	105	98	93	84	78	105
Extreme Minimum Temp. (°F)	-16	-6	-4	19	30	40	49	43	33	21	2	-19	-19
Days Maximum Temp. ≥ 90°F	0	0	0	0	1	8	16	13	6	0	0	0	44
Days Maximum Temp. ≤ 32°F	6	3	1	0	0	0	0	0	0	0	0	3	13
Days Minimum Temp. ≤ 32°F	25	21	16	5	0	0	0	0	0	4	13	22	106
Days Minimum Temp. ≤ 0°F	2	1	0	0	0	0	0	0	0	0	0	0	3
Heating Degree Days (base 65°F)	979	779	579	295	101	8	0	1	39	261	535	826	4,403
Cooling Degree Days (base 65°F)	0	0	4	20	98	272	416	351	169	25	2	1	1,358
Mean Precipitation (in.)	4.10	4.33	5.04	4.33	5.63	4.83	4.65	4.01	4.15	3.23	4.19	4.91	53.40
Days With ≥ 0.1" Precipitation	7	7	9	7	8	8	7	6	6	6	7	8	86
Days With ≥ 1.0" Precipitation	1	1	1	1	1	1	1	1	1	1	1	2	13
Mean Snowfall (in.)	2.5	na	0.7	trace	0.0	0.0	0.0	0.0	0.0	0.0	0.2	0.8	na
Days With ≥ 1.0" Snow Depth	na	na	0	0	0	0	0	0	0	0	0	0	na

Henderson 7 SSW *Henderson County*   Elevation: 429 ft.   Latitude: 37° 45' N   Longitude: 87° 38' W

	JAN	FEB	MAR	APR	MAY	JUN	JUL	AUG	SEP	OCT	NOV	DEC	YEAR
Mean Maximum Temp. (°F)	41.3	47.2	57.9	68.8	77.5	85.3	88.4	87.5	81.6	70.8	57.2	46.1	67.5
Mean Temp. (°F)	32.9	37.8	47.5	57.5	66.4	74.6	78.0	76.4	70.1	59.0	47.9	37.9	57.2
Mean Minimum Temp. (°F)	24.4	28.3	37.0	46.1	55.3	63.8	67.6	65.3	58.4	47.0	38.6	29.5	46.8
Extreme Maximum Temp. (°F)	72	78	84	89	93	100	101	102	99	90	83	77	102
Extreme Minimum Temp. (°F)	-20	-7	-3	22	33	44	49	44	34	19	11	-15	-20
Days Maximum Temp. ≥ 90°F	0	0	0	0	1	7	14	11	4	0	0	0	37
Days Maximum Temp. ≤ 32°F	8	4	0	0	0	0	0	0	0	0	0	4	16
Days Minimum Temp. ≤ 32°F	23	17	12	3	0	0	0	0	0	2	9	19	85
Days Minimum Temp. ≤ 0°F	1	1	0	0	0	0	0	0	0	0	0	0	2
Heating Degree Days (base 65°F)	989	763	543	251	68	3	0	1	36	219	509	835	4,217
Cooling Degree Days (base 65°F)	0	0	7	30	122	302	420	368	189	39	3	1	1,481
Mean Precipitation (in.)	2.82	3.07	4.50	4.64	4.87	4.01	3.74	2.93	3.35	2.96	4.16	3.64	44.69
Days With ≥ 0.1" Precipitation	6	6	9	8	8	7	6	5	5	5	6	7	78
Days With ≥ 1.0" Precipitation	1	1	1	1	1	1	1	1	1	1	1	1	12
Mean Snowfall (in.)	5.2	4.6	2.5	0.4	0.0	0.0	0.0	0.0	0.0	0.1	0.4	2.0	15.2
Days With ≥ 1.0" Snow Depth	6	5	1	0	0	0	0	0	0	0	0	2	14

Hodgenville-Lincoln *Larue County*   Elevation: 787 ft.   Latitude: 37° 32' N   Longitude: 85° 44' W

	JAN	FEB	MAR	APR	MAY	JUN	JUL	AUG	SEP	OCT	NOV	DEC	YEAR
Mean Maximum Temp. (°F)	43.0	49.1	59.2	69.4	76.8	83.8	87.4	86.4	81.1	70.3	57.9	47.8	67.7
Mean Temp. (°F)	33.7	38.5	47.6	56.8	65.0	72.7	76.5	75.3	69.4	58.1	47.7	38.6	56.7
Mean Minimum Temp. (°F)	24.2	27.8	35.9	44.2	53.1	61.5	65.6	64.1	57.7	45.9	37.5	29.3	45.6
Extreme Maximum Temp. (°F)	72	77	85	87	91	99	107	104	99	90	82	78	107
Extreme Minimum Temp. (°F)	-25	-8	-3	20	29	40	47	43	35	21	3	-19	-25
Days Maximum Temp. ≥ 90°F	0	0	0	0	0	4	11	8	4	0	0	0	27
Days Maximum Temp. ≤ 32°F	6	3	0	0	0	0	0	0	0	0	0	3	12
Days Minimum Temp. ≤ 32°F	22	18	13	4	0	0	0	0	0	3	10	19	89
Days Minimum Temp. ≤ 0°F	2	1	0	0	0	0	0	0	0	0	0	0	3
Heating Degree Days (base 65°F)	966	743	539	263	90	10	0	1	40	235	513	811	4,211
Cooling Degree Days (base 65°F)	0	0	5	24	98	249	374	330	173	31	2	0	1,286
Mean Precipitation (in.)	3.62	4.21	4.65	4.58	5.30	4.40	4.45	3.73	4.04	3.47	4.43	4.75	51.63
Days With ≥ 0.1" Precipitation	6	6	8	7	8	7	7	6	6	5	7	6	79
Days With ≥ 1.0" Precipitation	1	1	1	1	2	1	1	1	1	1	1	1	13
Mean Snowfall (in.)	2.7	2.9	0.9	trace	0.0	0.0	0.0	0.0	0.0	0.0	0.4	1.1	8.0
Days With ≥ 1.0" Snow Depth	4	4	0	0	0	0	0	0	0	0	0	1	9

Hopkinsville *Christian County*   Elevation: 518 ft.   Latitude: 36° 51' N   Longitude: 87° 31' W

	JAN	FEB	MAR	APR	MAY	JUN	JUL	AUG	SEP	OCT	NOV	DEC	YEAR
Mean Maximum Temp. (°F)	41.3	46.7	58.4	69.0	77.1	85.3	89.1	87.9	81.9	70.7	58.2	47.2	67.7
Mean Temp. (°F)	32.1	36.0	47.0	56.8	65.3	73.7	77.7	76.2	69.9	57.9	47.5	37.7	56.5
Mean Minimum Temp. (°F)	22.8	25.3	35.5	44.5	53.4	62.1	66.3	64.5	57.7	45.1	36.7	28.1	45.2
Extreme Maximum Temp. (°F)	74	81	87	90	94	100	104	103	101	92	84	76	104
Extreme Minimum Temp. (°F)	-19	-3	3	21	30	44	50	48	32	20	11	-14	-19
Days Maximum Temp. ≥ 90°F	0	0	0	0	1	8	16	13	6	0	0	0	44
Days Maximum Temp. ≤ 32°F	8	4	0	0	0	0	0	0	0	0	0	3	15
Days Minimum Temp. ≤ 32°F	25	20	13	4	0	0	0	0	0	2	11	21	96
Days Minimum Temp. ≤ 0°F	1	0	0	0	0	0	0	0	0	0	0	1	2
Heating Degree Days (base 65°F)	1,013	812	555	272	86	6	0	1	41	242	522	840	4,390
Cooling Degree Days (base 65°F)	0	0	4	27	94	270	408	350	176	27	2	0	1,358
Mean Precipitation (in.)	4.13	4.35	5.11	4.51	4.91	3.99	4.06	3.35	3.48	3.55	4.79	5.31	51.54
Days With > 0.1" Precipitation	7	7	9	8	8	7	7	5	5	6	7	8	84
Days With ≥ 1.0" Precipitation	1	1	1	1	1	1	1	1	1	1	2	2	14
Mean Snowfall (in.)	3.6	4.0	1.0	trace	0.0	0.0	0.0	0.0	0.0	trace	0.2	0.9	9.7
Days With ≥ 1.0" Snow Depth	4	4	1	0	0	0	0	0	0	0	0	1	10

Leitchfield 2 N *Grayson County*   Elevation: 620 ft.   Latitude: 37° 31' N   Longitude: 86° 18' W

	JAN	FEB	MAR	APR	MAY	JUN	JUL	AUG	SEP	OCT	NOV	DEC	YEAR
Mean Maximum Temp. (°F)	41.9	47.5	57.6	68.2	76.4	83.8	87.5	86.2	80.2	69.4	57.0	46.7	66.9
Mean Temp. (°F)	32.4	36.8	46.1	55.6	64.3	72.5	76.4	74.8	68.4	56.8	46.3	37.3	55.6
Mean Minimum Temp. (°F)	22.9	26.1	34.5	43.0	52.3	61.1	65.4	63.3	56.6	44.1	35.6	27.8	44.4
Extreme Maximum Temp. (°F)	71	77	84	90	93	100	103	101	98	88	83	75	103
Extreme Minimum Temp. (°F)	-27	-9	-5	19	29	39	44	43	32	18	-1	-17	-27
Days Maximum Temp. ≥ 90°F	0	0	0	0	0	5	11	8	3	0	0	0	27
Days Maximum Temp. ≤ 32°F	7	4	1	0	0	0	0	0	0	0	0	3	15
Days Minimum Temp. ≤ 32°F	24	20	15	5	0	0	0	0	0	4	12	20	100
Days Minimum Temp. ≤ 0°F	2	1	0	0	0	0	0	0	0	0	0	0	3
Heating Degree Days (base 65°F)	1,002	784	584	291	100	9	0	1	48	269	555	852	4,495
Cooling Degree Days (base 65°F)	0	0	5	18	89	245	376	317	152	22	1	0	1,225
Mean Precipitation (in.)	3.45	4.14	4.58	4.36	4.82	4.14	4.80	3.57	3.69	3.34	4.15	4.68	49.72
Days With ≥ 0.1" Precipitation	6	6	8	8	8	7	7	6	6	6	7	7	82
Days With ≥ 1.0" Precipitation	1	1	1	1	1	1	2	1	1	1	1	1	13
Mean Snowfall (in.)	4.3	3.8	1.6	trace	0.0	0.0	0.0	0.0	0.0	trace	0.4	1.7	11.8
Days With ≥ 1.0" Snow Depth	na	na	0	0	0	0	0	0	0	0	0	0	na

London-Carbin Airport *Laurel County*   Elevation: 1,187 ft.   Latitude: 37° 05' N   Longitude: 84° 05' W

	JAN	FEB	MAR	APR	MAY	JUN	JUL	AUG	SEP	OCT	NOV	DEC	YEAR
Mean Maximum Temp. (°F)	43.0	48.7	58.5	68.6	75.6	82.7	86.2	84.9	78.9	68.4	58.1	48.5	66.8
Mean Temp. (°F)	33.8	38.1	47.1	56.3	64.0	71.8	75.8	74.3	68.1	56.4	47.5	39.0	56.0
Mean Minimum Temp. (°F)	24.5	27.4	35.7	43.8	52.3	60.8	65.4	63.8	57.3	44.4	36.7	29.4	45.1
Extreme Maximum Temp. (°F)	74	81	84	90	90	98	101	100	95	85	82	78	101
Extreme Minimum Temp. (°F)	-25	-11	-12	21	29	38	46	44	32	19	2	-11	-25
Days Maximum Temp. ≥ 90°F	0	0	0	0	0	3	8	6	1	0	0	0	18
Days Maximum Temp. ≤ 32°F	6	4	0	0	0	0	0	0	0	0	0	3	13
Days Minimum Temp. ≤ 32°F	22	19	12	4	0	0	0	0	0	3	12	19	91
Days Minimum Temp. ≤ 0°F	1	0	0	0	0	0	0	0	0	0	0	0	1
Heating Degree Days (base 65°F)	960	754	551	277	104	11	1	1	47	274	523	801	4,304
Cooling Degree Days (base 65°F)	0	0	3	22	86	239	370	307	143	17	2	1	1,190
Mean Precipitation (in.)	3.78	3.79	4.41	3.93	4.53	4.05	4.40	3.53	3.47	3.04	3.97	4.33	47.23
Days With ≥ 0.1" Precipitation	7	8	9	8	8	7	7	6	6	5	7	7	85
Days With ≥ 1.0" Precipitation	1	1	1	1	1	1	1	1	1	1	1	1	12
Mean Snowfall (in.)	5.7	4.8	1.6	0.5	0.0	0.0	0.0	0.0	0.0	0.0	0.5	1.6	14.7
Days With ≥ 1.0" Snow Depth	7	5	1	0	0	0	0	0	0	0	0	2	15

Lovelaceville *Ballard County*   Elevation: 367 ft.   Latitude: 36° 58' N   Longitude: 88° 50' W

	JAN	FEB	MAR	APR	MAY	JUN	JUL	AUG	SEP	OCT	NOV	DEC	YEAR
Mean Maximum Temp. (°F)	43.5	50.2	60.2	70.7	79.0	87.0	90.7	89.2	82.7	72.5	58.9	48.4	69.4
Mean Temp. (°F)	34.6	39.5	48.7	58.2	66.9	75.1	78.9	77.2	70.3	59.3	47.9	38.9	58.0
Mean Minimum Temp. (°F)	25.0	28.3	37.0	45.7	54.7	63.1	67.2	65.0	57.9	45.8	37.0	29.3	46.3
Extreme Maximum Temp. (°F)	73	77	85	90	94	104	104	104	101	93	85	78	104
Extreme Minimum Temp. (°F)	-23	-6	1	20	30	42	47	44	32	19	10	-11	-23
Days Maximum Temp. ≥ 90°F	0	0	0	0	2	12	20	15	6	0	0	0	55
Days Maximum Temp. ≤ 32°F	5	2	0	0	0	0	0	0	0	0	0	2	9
Days Minimum Temp. ≤ 32°F	23	18	12	3	0	0	0	0	0	3	11	19	89
Days Minimum Temp. ≤ 0°F	1	0	0	0	0	0	0	0	0	0	0	0	1
Heating Degree Days (base 65°F)	934	713	504	232	58	3	0	0	35	208	510	803	4,000
Cooling Degree Days (base 65°F)	0	0	7	32	131	323	460	401	204	36	4	1	1,599
Mean Precipitation (in.)	3.57	4.01	4.52	5.20	4.50	4.37	4.48	2.82	3.01	3.52	4.45	4.67	49.12
Days With ≥ 0.1" Precipitation	6	6	8	8	8	7	6	4	5	5	7	7	77
Days With ≥ 1.0" Precipitation	1	1	1	2	1	1	1	1	1	1	1	1	13
Mean Snowfall (in.)	3.1	na	0.9	0.0	0.0	0.0	0.0	0.0	0.0	0.1	trace	1.1	na
Days With ≥ 1.0" Snow Depth	na	4	0	0	0	0	0	0	0	0	0	1	na

Madisonville *Hopkins County*   Elevation: 439 ft.   Latitude: 37° 21' N   Longitude: 87° 31' W

	JAN	FEB	MAR	APR	MAY	JUN	JUL	AUG	SEP	OCT	NOV	DEC	YEAR
Mean Maximum Temp. (°F)	43.6	49.2	59.7	70.7	78.8	86.4	90.0	88.9	83.2	71.8	58.6	48.1	69.1
Mean Temp. (°F)	34.2	38.8	48.6	58.5	67.0	74.9	78.6	77.2	71.0	59.3	48.4	38.9	58.0
Mean Minimum Temp. (°F)	24.7	28.3	37.4	46.3	55.2	63.3	67.3	65.4	58.7	46.8	38.2	29.6	46.8
Extreme Maximum Temp. (°F)	74	78	85	91	95	102	104	102	101	91	85	79	104
Extreme Minimum Temp. (°F)	-20	-9	2	22	32	43	49	47	35	21	7	-14	-20
Days Maximum Temp. ≥ 90°F	0	0	0	0	2	9	18	15	7	0	0	0	51
Days Maximum Temp. ≤ 32°F	6	3	0	0	0	0	0	0	0	0	0	3	12
Days Minimum Temp. ≤ 32°F	23	18	11	3	0	0	0	0	0	3	10	19	87
Days Minimum Temp. ≤ 0°F	1	1	0	0	0	0	0	0	0	0	0	0	2
Heating Degree Days (base 65°F)	947	735	510	226	62	3	0	0	30	209	495	804	4,021
Cooling Degree Days (base 65°F)	0	0	8	39	140	319	447	404	220	43	3	1	1,624
Mean Precipitation (in.)	3.46	3.76	4.59	5.01	4.85	3.85	4.25	3.29	3.28	3.49	4.16	4.24	48.23
Days With ≥ 0.1" Precipitation	6	6	9	8	8	7	6	5	5	6	7	7	80
Days With ≥ 1.0" Precipitation	1	1	1	1	1	1	2	1	1	1	1	1	13
Mean Snowfall (in.)	3.1	2.3	1.0	trace	0.0	0.0	0.0	0.0	0.0	0.0	0.3	0.3	7.0
Days With ≥ 1.0" Snow Depth	5	4	1	0	0	0	0	0	0	0	0	1	11

Mammoth Cave *Edmonson County*   Elevation: 787 ft.   Latitude: 37° 11' N   Longitude: 86° 05' W

	JAN	FEB	MAR	APR	MAY	JUN	JUL	AUG	SEP	OCT	NOV	DEC	YEAR
Mean Maximum Temp. (°F)	43.5	49.9	59.8	70.3	77.9	84.6	88.2	87.1	81.4	70.8	58.4	48.7	68.4
Mean Temp. (°F)	34.0	39.0	47.9	57.1	65.1	72.6	76.6	75.3	69.1	58.0	47.9	39.1	56.8
Mean Minimum Temp. (°F)	24.4	28.0	35.9	43.9	52.3	60.5	64.9	63.5	56.8	45.3	37.4	29.5	45.2
Extreme Maximum Temp. (°F)	72	78	85	93	96	100	104	104	99	89	83	76	104
Extreme Minimum Temp. (°F)	-20	-10	-1	20	28	38	47	39	32	18	1	-18	-20
Days Maximum Temp. ≥ 90°F	0	0	0	0	0	6	13	11	4	0	0	0	34
Days Maximum Temp. ≤ 32°F	6	3	0	0	0	0	0	0	0	0	0	3	12
Days Minimum Temp. ≤ 32°F	23	18	13	5	0	0	0	0	0	4	11	19	93
Days Minimum Temp. ≤ 0°F	2	1	0	0	0	0	0	0	0	0	0	1	4
Heating Degree Days (base 65°F)	954	727	530	260	86	9	0	1	41	237	509	797	4,151
Cooling Degree Days (base 65°F)	0	0	7	30	102	249	387	339	164	31	2	1	1,312
Mean Precipitation (in.)	3.82	3.85	5.03	4.22	5.20	4.69	4.53	3.62	4.39	3.56	4.45	5.00	52.36
Days With ≥ 0.1" Precipitation	7	6	8	8	8	7	7	5	6	5	7	7	81
Days With ≥ 1.0" Precipitation	1	1	1	1	1	1	1	1	1	1	1	2	13
Mean Snowfall (in.)	4.6	4.3	1.5	trace	0.0	0.0	0.0	0.0	0.0	0.0	0.3	1.8	12.5
Days With ≥ 1.0" Snow Depth	6	5	1	0	0	0	0	0	0	0	0	1	13

Manchester 4 W *Clay County*   Elevation: 869 ft.   Latitude: 37° 09' N   Longitude: 83° 49' W

	JAN	FEB	MAR	APR	MAY	JUN	JUL	AUG	SEP	OCT	NOV	DEC	YEAR
Mean Maximum Temp. (°F)	45.7	50.5	60.3	70.0	76.7	82.7	86.2	85.0	80.0	70.5	59.9	50.3	68.2
Mean Temp. (°F)	34.2	38.1	46.4	55.0	63.3	70.6	74.7	73.4	67.5	56.2	46.5	38.6	55.4
Mean Minimum Temp. (°F)	23.0	25.4	32.6	39.7	49.6	58.3	63.1	61.9	54.8	41.5	33.1	26.8	42.5
Extreme Maximum Temp. (°F)	73	80	84	92	91	97	101	100	97	89	82	79	101
Extreme Minimum Temp. (°F)	-30	-22	-11	17	25	33	36	36	27	12	8	-7	-30
Days Maximum Temp. ≥ 90°F	0	0	0	0	0	2	8	5	2	0	0	0	17
Days Maximum Temp. ≤ 32°F	4	2	0	0	0	0	0	0	0	0	0	2	8
Days Minimum Temp. ≤ 32°F	23	21	16	8	1	0	0	0	0	6	15	22	112
Days Minimum Temp. ≤ 0°F	2	1	0	0	0	0	0	0	0	0	0	0	3
Heating Degree Days (base 65°F)	945	755	572	307	114	14	1	3	49	281	550	810	4,401
Cooling Degree Days (base 65°F)	0	0	2	11	68	191	321	264	118	13	1	0	989
Mean Precipitation (in.)	4.21	3.68	4.60	4.20	4.73	4.63	5.15	3.78	3.99	3.36	4.23	4.36	50.92
Days With ≥ 0.1" Precipitation	8	7	9	8	9	9	8	7	6	6	7	7	91
Days With ≥ 1.0" Precipitation	1	1	1	1	1	1	2	1	1	1	1	1	13
Mean Snowfall (in.)	4.7	3.2	1.8	0.3	0.0	0.0	0.0	0.0	0.0	0.0	0.3	1.6	11.9
Days With ≥ 1.0" Snow Depth	3	3	0	0	0	0	0	0	0	0	0	1	7

Mayfield Radio Wngo *Graves County*   Elevation: 377 ft.   Latitude: 36° 47' N   Longitude: 88° 38' W

	JAN	FEB	MAR	APR	MAY	JUN	JUL	AUG	SEP	OCT	NOV	DEC	YEAR
Mean Maximum Temp. (°F)	44.3	50.6	60.9	71.2	78.6	86.1	89.5	88.4	82.6	72.6	59.4	48.9	69.4
Mean Temp. (°F)	34.9	39.7	49.2	58.4	66.8	74.8	78.6	77.1	70.7	59.7	48.8	39.5	58.2
Mean Minimum Temp. (°F)	25.5	28.8	37.4	45.7	54.9	63.5	67.7	65.9	58.8	46.7	38.2	30.0	46.9
Extreme Maximum Temp. (°F)	74	79	85	90	93	101	103	101	100	91	83	78	103
Extreme Minimum Temp. (°F)	-18	-4	5	21	31	41	48	44	33	22	11	-12	-18
Days Maximum Temp. ≥ 90°F	0	0	0	0	1	8	17	13	5	0	0	0	44
Days Maximum Temp. ≤ 32°F	5	2	0	0	0	0	0	0	0	0	0	2	9
Days Minimum Temp. ≤ 32°F	22	18	11	3	0	0	0	0	0	2	10	18	84
Days Minimum Temp. ≤ 0°F	1	0	0	0	0	0	0	0	0	0	0	0	1
Heating Degree Days (base 65°F)	926	706	492	224	58	3	1	0	31	197	482	786	3,906
Cooling Degree Days (base 65°F)	0	1	8	34	125	315	450	400	209	42	4	1	1,589
Mean Precipitation (in.)	3.70	4.46	4.94	4.87	4.85	4.20	4.29	3.29	3.57	3.84	4.88	5.02	51.91
Days With ≥ 0.1" Precipitation	7	6	8	8	7	6	6	5	5	5	7	6	76
Days With ≥ 1.0" Precipitation	1	1	1	2	1	1	1	1	1	1	2	1	14
Mean Snowfall (in.)	2.7	na	0.9	trace	0.0	0.0	0.0	0.0	0.0	0.1	trace	0.7	na
Days With ≥ 1.0" Snow Depth	na	na	0	0	0	0	0	0	0	0	0	0	na

Maysville Sewage Plant *Mason County*   Elevation: 515 ft.   Latitude: 38° 41' N   Longitude: 83° 47' W

	JAN	FEB	MAR	APR	MAY	JUN	JUL	AUG	SEP	OCT	NOV	DEC	YEAR
Mean Maximum Temp. (°F)	39.6	44.4	54.6	65.6	74.8	83.2	87.2	86.1	80.0	68.3	55.7	45.2	65.4
Mean Temp. (°F)	30.5	33.6	42.5	52.5	62.0	71.1	75.4	74.2	67.7	55.6	44.8	35.6	53.8
Mean Minimum Temp. (°F)	20.9	22.8	30.6	39.4	49.2	58.9	63.7	62.3	55.3	43.0	33.9	26.0	42.2
Extreme Maximum Temp. (°F)	74	74	83	90	90	100	105	103	98	89	84	78	105
Extreme Minimum Temp. (°F)	-25	-8	1	19	29	37	46	39	34	19	5	-17	-25
Days Maximum Temp. ≥ 90°F	0	0	0	0	0	5	11	9	3	0	0	0	28
Days Maximum Temp. ≤ 32°F	9	6	1	0	0	0	0	0	0	0	0	4	20
Days Minimum Temp. ≤ 32°F	26	23	19	7	0	0	0	0	0	3	14	23	115
Days Minimum Temp. ≤ 0°F	1	1	0	0	0	0	0	0	0	0	0	1	3
Heating Degree Days (base 65°F)	1,063	880	691	377	144	18	1	3	55	299	600	904	5,035
Cooling Degree Days (base 65°F)	0	0	1	9	58	217	350	304	139	18	1	0	1,097
Mean Precipitation (in.)	3.46	3.11	4.23	4.22	4.77	3.93	4.44	3.75	3.06	2.87	3.42	3.90	45.16
Days With ≥ 0.1" Precipitation	7	6	8	9	9	8	7	6	5	6	7	8	86
Days With ≥ 1.0" Precipitation	1	1	1	1	1	1	1	1	1	1	1	1	12
Mean Snowfall (in.)	na	na	na	trace	trace	0.0	0.0	0.0	0.0	trace	*trace*	na	na
Days With ≥ 1.0" Snow Depth	na	na	*1*	0	0	0	0	0	0	0	*0*	na	na

Monticello 3 NE *Wayne County*   Elevation: 977 ft.   Latitude: 36° 52' N   Longitude: 84° 50' W

	JAN	FEB	MAR	APR	MAY	JUN	JUL	AUG	SEP	OCT	NOV	DEC	YEAR
Mean Maximum Temp. (°F)	44.7	49.7	58.9	68.5	76.1	83.2	86.7	85.9	80.5	70.1	58.7	49.0	67.7
Mean Temp. (°F)	35.0	38.8	47.1	55.6	64.1	72.1	75.8	74.6	68.7	57.5	47.7	39.2	56.4
Mean Minimum Temp. (°F)	25.3	27.8	35.2	42.7	52.1	60.9	64.9	63.2	56.9	44.7	36.6	29.3	45.0
Extreme Maximum Temp. (°F)	75	82	83	90	92	100	103	103	96	87	82	77	103
Extreme Minimum Temp. (°F)	-23	-14	-6	20	29	39	46	45	33	22	5	-11	-23
Days Maximum Temp. ≥ 90°F	0	0	0	0	0	3	9	7	3	0	0	0	22
Days Maximum Temp. ≤ 32°F	6	3	1	0	0	0	0	0	0	0	0	3	13
Days Minimum Temp. ≤ 32°F	23	19	14	6	0	0	0	0	0	4	12	19	97
Days Minimum Temp. ≤ 0°F	1	1	0	0	0	0	0	0	0	0	0	0	2
Heating Degree Days (base 65°F)	924	734	554	295	105	10	1	2	43	254	517	794	4,232
Cooling Degree Days (base 65°F)	0	0	5	18	82	229	357	308	152	28	2	1	1,182
Mean Precipitation (in.)	4.36	4.13	4.90	4.21	4.97	4.47	4.36	3.98	3.83	3.10	4.12	4.80	51.23
Days With ≥ 0.1" Precipitation	8	8	9	8	9	8	7	6	6	6	7	8	90
Days With ≥ 1.0" Precipitation	1	1	1	1	1	1	1	1	1	1	1	1	12
Mean Snowfall (in.)	6.0	5.4	2.6	0.1	0.0	0.0	0.0	0.0	0.0	trace	0.5	2.0	16.6
Days With ≥ 1.0" Snow Depth	na	*3*	*1*	0	0	0	0	0	0	0	0	2	na

Mount Vernon *Rockcastle County*   Elevation: 1,158 ft.   Latitude: 37° 21' N   Longitude: 84° 20' W

	JAN	FEB	MAR	APR	MAY	JUN	JUL	AUG	SEP	OCT	NOV	DEC	YEAR
Mean Maximum Temp. (°F)	42.5	47.6	57.5	67.6	75.6	82.6	86.2	85.5	79.8	69.0	57.2	47.4	66.5
Mean Temp. (°F)	33.1	37.0	46.1	55.2	63.8	71.6	75.5	74.2	68.1	56.5	46.6	38.0	55.5
Mean Minimum Temp. (°F)	23.6	26.4	34.6	42.8	52.1	60.6	64.8	62.9	56.3	44.0	36.0	28.4	44.4
Extreme Maximum Temp. (°F)	76	79	84	91	89	97	102	102	96	86	82	78	102
Extreme Minimum Temp. (°F)	-24	-11	-6	17	29	40	45	38	33	19	6	-16	-24
Days Maximum Temp. ≥ 90°F	0	0	0	0	0	2	8	7	3	0	0	0	20
Days Maximum Temp. ≤ 32°F	7	4	1	0	0	0	0	0	0	0	0	4	16
Days Minimum Temp. ≤ 32°F	24	20	14	5	0	0	0	0	0	5	12	20	100
Days Minimum Temp. ≤ 0°F	2	1	0	0	0	0	0	0	0	0	0	0	3
Heating Degree Days (base 65°F)	983	784	586	310	114	14	1	2	54	278	547	832	4,505
Cooling Degree Days (base 65°F)	0	0	4	20	81	218	342	292	138	21	2	1	1,119
Mean Precipitation (in.)	4.27	3.86	5.04	4.34	5.50	4.70	4.60	3.97	3.85	3.37	4.25	4.81	52.56
Days With ≥ 0.1" Precipitation	8	7	9	8	9	8	7	7	6	6	8	9	92
Days With ≥ 1.0" Precipitation	1	1	1	1	1	1	1	1	1	1	1	1	12
Mean Snowfall (in.)	6.9	6.0	1.8	0.2	trace	0.0	0.0	0.0	0.0	trace	0.5	1.9	17.3
Days With ≥ 1.0" Snow Depth	*6*	*6*	1	0	0	0	0	0	0	0	0	2	*15*

Murray *Calloway County*   Elevation: 524 ft.   Latitude: 36° 36' N   Longitude: 88° 18' W

	JAN	FEB	MAR	APR	MAY	JUN	JUL	AUG	SEP	OCT	NOV	DEC	YEAR
Mean Maximum Temp. (°F)	43.3	49.6	59.5	70.1	77.9	86.3	89.8	88.7	82.2	71.1	58.4	48.2	68.8
Mean Temp. (°F)	35.0	40.0	49.1	59.0	67.2	75.7	79.4	78.0	71.2	59.8	48.9	39.6	58.6
Mean Minimum Temp. (°F)	26.6	30.3	38.8	47.8	56.4	65.1	69.0	67.2	60.2	48.4	39.3	31.0	48.3
Extreme Maximum Temp. (°F)	74	78	88	90	95	104	105	105	101	90	81	77	105
Extreme Minimum Temp. (°F)	-16	-5	6	24	36	45	52	52	35	25	12	-13	-16
Days Maximum Temp. ≥ 90°F	0	0	0	0	1	9	17	13	5	0	0	0	45
Days Maximum Temp. ≤ 32°F	6	3	0	0	0	0	0	0	0	0	0	3	12
Days Minimum Temp. ≤ 32°F	22	16	10	2	0	0	0	0	0	1	8	18	77
Days Minimum Temp. ≤ 0°F	1	0	0	0	0	0	0	0	0	0	0	0	1
Heating Degree Days (base 65°F)	925	701	491	214	54	2	0	0	29	195	481	781	3,873
Cooling Degree Days (base 65°F)	0	0	8	37	125	335	468	424	216	39	3	1	1,656
Mean Precipitation (in.)	4.36	4.42	5.43	5.29	5.24	5.11	4.55	3.43	3.69	3.57	5.29	5.37	55.75
Days With ≥ 0.1" Precipitation	7	7	9	8	8	7	6	5	6	5	7	7	82
Days With ≥ 1.0" Precipitation	1	1	1	2	1	1	1	1	1	1	2	1	14
Mean Snowfall (in.)	4.8	3.9	1.0	trace	0.0	0.0	0.0	0.0	0.0	trace	0.2	*0.5*	*10.4*
Days With ≥ 1.0" Snow Depth	5	4	0	0	0	0	0	0	0	0	0	*1*	*10*

Nolin River Lake *Edmonson County*   Elevation: 679 ft.   Latitude: 37° 17' N   Longitude: 86° 15' W

	JAN	FEB	MAR	APR	MAY	JUN	JUL	AUG	SEP	OCT	NOV	DEC	YEAR
Mean Maximum Temp. (°F)	42.5	48.0	57.9	68.7	77.2	85.2	89.4	88.4	82.5	70.7	58.5	48.2	68.1
Mean Temp. (°F)	31.9	36.0	45.1	54.6	63.3	71.8	76.1	74.9	68.6	56.7	46.3	37.4	55.2
Mean Minimum Temp. (°F)	21.2	23.9	32.2	40.3	49.3	58.5	62.7	61.4	54.6	42.5	34.1	26.6	42.3
Extreme Maximum Temp. (°F)	72	79	85	93	94	104	109	105	102	92	86	78	109
Extreme Minimum Temp. (°F)	-20	-8	-1	17	29	34	45	43	29	20	3	-18	-20
Days Maximum Temp. ≥ 90°F	0	0	0	0	1	8	16	14	6	0	0	0	45
Days Maximum Temp. ≤ 32°F	7	4	1	0	0	0	0	0	0	0	0	3	15
Days Minimum Temp. ≤ 32°F	26	22	17	7	1	0	0	0	0	5	14	21	113
Days Minimum Temp. ≤ 0°F	2	1	0	0	0	0	0	0	0	0	0	1	4
Heating Degree Days (base 65°F)	1,020	813	616	324	123	15	1	1	49	273	557	847	4,639
Cooling Degree Days (base 65°F)	0	0	5	16	78	232	367	324	153	24	1	0	1,200
Mean Precipitation (in.)	3.91	4.12	4.78	4.39	5.26	4.32	4.45	3.39	4.07	3.46	4.33	5.09	51.57
Days With ≥ 0.1" Precipitation	7	7	9	8	8	8	7	6	6	6	7	8	87
Days With ≥ 1.0" Precipitation	1	1	1	1	1	1	1	1	1	1	1	2	13
Mean Snowfall (in.)	na	na	0.5	0.0	0.0	0.0	0.0	0.0	0.0	0.0	*trace*	0.4	na
Days With ≥ 1.0" Snow Depth	4	4	1	0	0	0	0	0	0	0	0	1	10

Paducah Barkley Field *McCracken County*   Elevation: 406 ft.   Latitude: 37° 03' N   Longitude: 88° 46' W

	JAN	FEB	MAR	APR	MAY	JUN	JUL	AUG	SEP	OCT	NOV	DEC	YEAR
Mean Maximum Temp. (°F)	41.9	47.9	58.1	68.9	77.5	85.9	89.5	88.0	81.6	70.8	57.5	47.1	67.9
Mean Temp. (°F)	33.3	38.4	48.0	57.9	66.9	75.5	79.3	77.2	70.3	58.8	47.9	38.3	57.6
Mean Minimum Temp. (°F)	24.7	28.7	37.8	46.8	56.2	65.1	69.1	66.4	58.9	46.8	38.2	29.4	47.3
Extreme Maximum Temp. (°F)	73	77	84	90	94	103	103	104	100	90	83	77	104
Extreme Minimum Temp. (°F)	-15	-8	5	24	34	44	52	44	35	22	10	-10	-15
Days Maximum Temp. ≥ 90°F	0	0	0	0	1	9	17	13	5	0	0	0	45
Days Maximum Temp. ≤ 32°F	7	3	1	0	0	0	0	0	0	0	0	3	14
Days Minimum Temp. ≤ 32°F	24	17	11	2	0	0	0	0	0	2	10	19	85
Days Minimum Temp. ≤ 0°F	1	0	0	0	0	0	0	0	0	0	0	0	1
Heating Degree Days (base 65°F)	974	746	527	243	63	2	0	0	35	222	511	822	4,145
Cooling Degree Days (base 65°F)	0	0	7	34	130	331	463	395	195	39	3	1	1,598
Mean Precipitation (in.)	3.29	3.86	4.33	5.08	4.71	4.55	4.30	3.02	3.54	3.55	4.45	4.41	49.09
Days With ≥ 0.1" Precipitation	6	6	8	8	7	6	6	5	5	5	7	7	76
Days With ≥ 1.0" Precipitation	1	1	1	1	1	1	1	1	1	1	1	1	12
Mean Snowfall (in.)	4.0	3.4	1.4	0.1	0.0	trace	trace	0.0	0.0	trace	trace	1.3	10.2
Days With ≥ 1.0" Snow Depth	6	4	1	0	0	0	0	0	0	0	0	1	12

Paducah Walker Boat Yard *McCracken County*   Elevation: 337 ft.   Latitude: 37° 03' N   Longitude: 88° 33' W

	JAN	FEB	MAR	APR	MAY	JUN	JUL	AUG	SEP	OCT	NOV	DEC	YEAR
Mean Maximum Temp. (°F)	41.2	46.9	57.7	69.1	*77.4*	*86.4*	*90.3*	88.6	81.9	70.4	57.6	46.6	*67.8*
Mean Temp. (°F)	32.6	37.1	47.5	57.9	*66.3*	*75.4*	*79.5*	77.6	70.7	58.6	47.8	37.8	*57.4*
Mean Minimum Temp. (°F)	23.9	27.4	37.4	46.7	*55.1*	*64.3*	*68.7*	66.5	59.4	46.9	37.9	28.9	*46.9*
Extreme Maximum Temp. (°F)	74	78	85	91	*96*	*100*	*105*	103	100	90	82	75	*105*
Extreme Minimum Temp. (°F)	-12	-1	8	27	*35*	*44*	*51*	47	37	23	11	-11	*-12*
Days Maximum Temp. ≥ 90°F	0	0	0	0	*2*	*10*	*19*	14	5	0	0	0	*50*
Days Maximum Temp. ≤ 32°F	8	5	1	0	*0*	0	0	0	0	0	0	3	*17*
Days Minimum Temp. ≤ 32°F	24	19	11	2	*0*	0	0	0	0	1	10	20	*87*
Days Minimum Temp. ≤ 0°F	1	0	0	0	*0*	0	0	0	0	0	0	0	*1*
Heating Degree Days (base 65°F)	997	780	540	243	*69*	*3*	*0*	1	33	225	514	838	*4,243*
Cooling Degree Days (base 65°F)	0	*0*	5	35	*117*	*327*	*467*	*409*	*201*	33	2	0	*1,596*
Mean Precipitation (in.)	3.09	3.72	4.29	4.64	4.45	3.58	3.98	3.11	3.40	3.25	4.50	4.28	46.29
Days With ≥ 0.1" Precipitation	6	6	8	7	*7*	*6*	6	5	5	6	7	7	*76*
Days With ≥ 1.0" Precipitation	1	1	1	2	*1*	*1*	1	1	1	1	1	1	*13*
Mean Snowfall (in.)	na	na	*1.1*	trace	0.0	0.0	0.0	0.0	0.0	trace	trace	*0.9*	na
Days With ≥ 1.0" Snow Depth	na	na	*0*	*0*	*0*	*0*	*0*	*0*	0	0	0	*1*	na

Princeton 1 SE *Caldwell County*   Elevation: 495 ft.   Latitude: 37° 07' N   Longitude: 87° 52' W

	JAN	FEB	MAR	APR	MAY	JUN	JUL	AUG	SEP	OCT	NOV	DEC	YEAR
Mean Maximum Temp. (°F)	44.0	50.1	60.4	70.5	78.2	86.0	89.8	88.7	82.9	72.1	59.2	48.9	69.2
Mean Temp. (°F)	34.7	39.8	49.2	58.7	66.7	75.0	78.8	77.4	71.1	59.8	49.1	39.6	58.3
Mean Minimum Temp. (°F)	25.3	29.4	37.9	46.8	55.2	63.9	67.9	66.1	59.2	47.4	39.0	30.4	47.4
Extreme Maximum Temp. (°F)	74	79	85	89	93	102	105	104	102	90	82	78	105
Extreme Minimum Temp. (°F)	-18	-6	2	22	31	42	50	44	34	19	10	-14	-18
Days Maximum Temp. ≥ 90°F	0	0	0	0	1	9	18	14	6	0	0	0	48
Days Maximum Temp. ≤ 32°F	6	3	0	0	0	0	0	0	0	0	0	2	11
Days Minimum Temp. ≤ 32°F	22	16	11	3	0	0	0	0	0	2	9	18	81
Days Minimum Temp. ≤ 0°F	1	1	0	0	0	0	0	0	0	0	0	0	2
Heating Degree Days (base 65°F)	934	706	494	223	63	3	0	0	29	200	475	780	3,907
Cooling Degree Days (base 65°F)	0	1	9	38	126	318	456	407	217	46	4	1	1,623
Mean Precipitation (in.)	3.84	4.44	4.73	4.70	4.96	4.10	4.42	3.72	3.23	3.54	4.74	5.08	51.50
Days With ≥ 0.1" Precipitation	7	7	9	8	8	7	6	5	5	6	7	8	83
Days With ≥ 1.0" Precipitation	1	1	1	1	1	1	2	1	1	1	1	1	13
Mean Snowfall (in.)	5.7	4.1	2.0	0.2	0.0	0.0	0.0	0.0	0.0	0.1	0.4	1.3	13.8
Days With ≥ 1.0" Snow Depth	na	*2*	*0*	0	0	0	0	0	0	0	0	1	na

Rough River Lake *Breckinridge County*   Elevation: 554 ft.   Latitude: 37° 37' N   Longitude: 86° 30' W

	JAN	FEB	MAR	APR	MAY	JUN	JUL	AUG	SEP	OCT	NOV	DEC	YEAR
Mean Maximum Temp. (°F)	40.7	46.4	56.5	67.6	76.1	84.5	88.7	87.7	81.4	69.5	57.0	46.4	66.9
Mean Temp. (°F)	30.4	34.7	44.2	54.2	62.9	71.7	76.0	74.4	67.6	55.4	45.3	35.7	54.4
Mean Minimum Temp. (°F)	20.0	23.1	31.8	40.8	49.8	59.0	63.3	61.0	53.7	41.3	33.6	25.1	41.9
Extreme Maximum Temp. (°F)	71	78	85	91	93	101	107	104	102	91	83	76	107
Extreme Minimum Temp. (°F)	-27	-13	-2	16	29	39	41	38	30	19	2	-18	-27
Days Maximum Temp. ≥ 90°F	0	0	0	0	1	7	15	12	5	0	0	0	40
Days Maximum Temp. ≤ 32°F	8	4	1	0	0	0	0	0	0	0	0	4	17
Days Minimum Temp. ≤ 32°F	26	22	18	7	1	0	0	0	0	8	15	23	120
Days Minimum Temp. ≤ 0°F	3	2	0	0	0	0	0	0	0	0	0	1	6
Heating Degree Days (base 65°F)	1,065	849	642	334	131	15	1	3	64	310	585	901	4,900
Cooling Degree Days (base 65°F)	0	0	4	16	68	219	356	300	135	20	1	0	1,119
Mean Precipitation (in.)	3.34	3.85	4.45	4.39	5.38	4.20	4.24	3.42	3.59	3.43	3.88	4.23	48.40
Days With ≥ 0.1" Precipitation	6	6	8	7	8	7	6	5	5	6	7	7	78
Days With ≥ 1.0" Precipitation	1	1	1	1	2	1	1	1	1	1	1	1	13
Mean Snowfall (in.)	2.0	2.7	1.2	0.1	0.0	0.0	0.0	0.0	0.0	trace	0.3	0.6	6.9
Days With ≥ 1.0" Snow Depth	3	4	1	0	0	0	0	0	0	0	0	1	9

Scottsville 3 SSW *Allen County*   Elevation: 849 ft.   Latitude: 36° 44' N   Longitude: 86° 13' W

	JAN	FEB	MAR	APR	MAY	JUN	JUL	AUG	SEP	OCT	NOV	DEC	YEAR
Mean Maximum Temp. (°F)	43.8	49.9	59.7	69.6	76.1	83.2	86.9	86.1	80.3	70.2	58.1	48.6	67.7
Mean Temp. (°F)	35.5	40.3	49.4	58.6	66.1	73.5	77.3	76.3	70.5	59.8	49.2	40.3	58.1
Mean Minimum Temp. (°F)	27.0	30.8	39.0	47.5	56.0	63.8	67.8	66.4	60.7	49.4	40.3	31.9	48.4
Extreme Maximum Temp. (°F)	74	81	86	89	90	99	102	100	99	89	83	77	102
Extreme Minimum Temp. (°F)	-18	-7	1	20	34	44	53	48	38	25	9	-15	-18
Days Maximum Temp. ≥ 90°F	0	0	0	0	0	3	9	8	3	0	0	0	23
Days Maximum Temp. ≤ 32°F	6	3	0	0	0	0	0	0	0	0	0	2	11
Days Minimum Temp. ≤ 32°F	20	16	10	2	0	0	0	0	0	1	7	16	72
Days Minimum Temp. ≤ 0°F	1	0	0	0	0	0	0	0	0	0	0	0	1
Heating Degree Days (base 65°F)	910	690	486	225	69	4	0	1	30	194	472	760	3,841
Cooling Degree Days (base 65°F)	0	0	8	37	113	270	404	366	198	41	4	1	1,442
Mean Precipitation (in.)	4.22	4.46	5.29	4.21	5.39	4.82	4.14	3.65	4.17	3.46	4.55	5.04	53.40
Days With ≥ 0.1" Precipitation	8	8	9	8	9	8	7	6	6	6	7	8	90
Days With ≥ 1.0" Precipitation	1	1	1	1	1	1	1	1	1	1	1	1	12
Mean Snowfall (in.)	4.2	4.1	1.2	trace	0.0	0.0	0.0	0.0	0.0	trace	0.1	1.1	10.7
Days With ≥ 1.0" Snow Depth	6	4	1	0	0	0	0	0	0	0	0	1	12

Shelbyville 1 E *Shelby County*   Elevation: 728 ft.   Latitude: 38° 12' N   Longitude: 85° 12' W

	JAN	FEB	MAR	APR	MAY	JUN	JUL	AUG	SEP	OCT	NOV	DEC	YEAR
Mean Maximum Temp. (°F)	39.4	45.3	55.2	65.9	75.3	83.1	87.2	85.8	79.9	68.3	55.6	44.8	65.5
Mean Temp. (°F)	29.3	33.6	42.6	52.1	62.1	70.5	74.7	73.1	66.2	54.1	43.8	34.4	53.0
Mean Minimum Temp. (°F)	19.1	21.8	29.9	38.3	48.7	57.7	62.3	60.2	52.4	39.8	32.2	24.0	40.5
Extreme Maximum Temp. (°F)	75	78	85	90	92	102	105	103	98	89	83	76	105
Extreme Minimum Temp. (°F)	-37	-17	-9	13	26	36	43	35	27	16	3	-21	-37
Days Maximum Temp. ≥ 90°F	0	0	0	0	1	5	11	8	3	0	0	0	28
Days Maximum Temp. ≤ 32°F	9	5	1	0	0	0	0	0	0	0	0	5	20
Days Minimum Temp. ≤ 32°F	27	23	20	9	1	0	0	0	1	9	16	23	129
Days Minimum Temp. ≤ 0°F	3	2	0	0	0	0	0	0	0	0	0	1	6
Heating Degree Days (base 65°F)	1,101	880	691	391	151	23	2	6	81	345	630	943	5,244
Cooling Degree Days (base 65°F)	0	0	2	9	65	194	320	259	112	13	1	0	975
Mean Precipitation (in.)	3.48	3.56	4.59	4.28	5.04	4.57	4.85	3.71	3.05	3.10	3.84	4.19	48.26
Days With ≥ 0.1" Precipitation	6	6	9	8	8	8	7	6	5	6	7	7	83
Days With ≥ 1.0" Precipitation	1	1	1	1	1	1	2	1	1	1	1	1	13
Mean Snowfall (in.)	5.0	3.7	1.6	trace	trace	0.0	0.0	0.0	0.0	trace	0.3	1.4	12.0
Days With ≥ 1.0" Snow Depth	6	5	1	0	0	0	0	0	0	0	0	2	14

Somerset 2 N *Pulaski County*   Elevation: 1,049 ft.   Latitude: 37° 07' N   Longitude: 84° 37' W

	JAN	FEB	MAR	APR	MAY	JUN	JUL	AUG	SEP	OCT	NOV	DEC	YEAR
Mean Maximum Temp. (°F)	43.7	48.9	58.3	68.5	75.7	82.8	86.3	85.2	79.3	69.2	57.1	48.1	66.9
Mean Temp. (°F)	34.4	38.3	46.9	55.9	64.0	71.8	75.5	74.1	68.0	56.7	46.8	38.8	55.9
Mean Minimum Temp. (°F)	25.0	27.7	35.4	43.3	52.3	60.7	64.7	63.0	56.6	44.2	36.4	29.6	44.9
Extreme Maximum Temp. (°F)	73	79	83	89	92	99	102	100	98	86	80	75	102
Extreme Minimum Temp. (°F)	-32	-14	-4	18	28	39	45	41	30	17	3	-16	-32
Days Maximum Temp. ≥ 90°F	0	0	0	0	0	3	8	6	2	0	0	0	19
Days Maximum Temp. ≤ 32°F	6	3	1	0	0	0	0	0	0	0	0	3	13
Days Minimum Temp. ≤ 32°F	22	18	14	5	0	0	0	0	0	4	12	19	94
Days Minimum Temp. ≤ 0°F	2	1	0	0	0	0	0	0	0	0	0	0	3
Heating Degree Days (base 65°F)	942	747	560	285	101	11	1	2	49	266	542	804	4,310
Cooling Degree Days (base 65°F)	0	0	4	20	82	229	356	295	135	19	1	0	1,141
Mean Precipitation (in.)	4.33	3.55	4.75	4.34	5.18	4.93	4.41	3.95	3.81	3.35	4.13	4.61	51.34
Days With ≥ 0.1" Precipitation	8	7	10	8	9	8	7	6	6	5	7	7	88
Days With ≥ 1.0" Precipitation	1	1	1	1	1	1	1	1	1	1	1	1	12
Mean Snowfall (in.)	4.5	3.2	0.8	trace	trace	0.0	0.0	0.0	0.0	0.0	0.2	1.7	10.4
Days With ≥ 1.0" Snow Depth	na	2	1	0	0	0	0	0	0	0	0	0	na

Summer Shade *Metcalfe County*   Elevation: 862 ft.   Latitude: 36° 53' N   Longitude: 85° 43' W

	JAN	FEB	MAR	APR	MAY	JUN	JUL	AUG	SEP	OCT	NOV	DEC	YEAR
Mean Maximum Temp. (°F)	43.9	49.6	59.3	69.2	76.4	83.8	87.2	86.0	80.1	69.4	58.3	48.8	67.7
Mean Temp. (°F)	34.3	38.9	47.9	56.8	64.9	72.6	76.4	75.0	68.9	57.5	47.6	39.2	56.7
Mean Minimum Temp. (°F)	24.8	28.2	36.4	44.4	53.4	61.5	65.5	63.9	57.7	45.5	36.8	29.5	45.6
Extreme Maximum Temp. (°F)	72	79	87	90	90	100	102	102	98	87	82	78	102
Extreme Minimum Temp. (°F)	-26	-18	-4	19	29	40	48	43	33	21	5	-15	-26
Days Maximum Temp. ≥ 90°F	0	0	0	0	0	4	11	8	2	0	0	0	25
Days Maximum Temp. ≤ 32°F	6	3	0	0	0	0	0	0	0	0	0	3	12
Days Minimum Temp. ≤ 32°F	23	18	12	5	0	0	0	0	0	4	12	19	93
Days Minimum Temp. ≤ 0°F	2	1	0	0	0	0	0	0	0	0	0	0	3
Heating Degree Days (base 65°F)	943	730	529	266	90	8	0	1	42	250	520	795	4,174
Cooling Degree Days (base 65°F)	0	0	6	26	100	254	383	329	162	28	2	1	1,291
Mean Precipitation (in.)	3.91	4.16	5.09	3.87	4.86	4.53	4.47	3.45	4.13	3.26	4.23	4.98	50.94
Days With ≥ 0.1" Precipitation	7	7	9	7	8	7	7	6	6	5	8	8	85
Days With ≥ 1.0" Precipitation	1	1	1	1	1	1	1	1	1	1	1	1	12
Mean Snowfall (in.)	4.6	4.1	1.1	0.1	0.0	0.0	0.0	0.0	0.0	trace	0.3	1.1	11.3
Days With ≥ 1.0" Snow Depth	6	4	1	0	0	0	0	0	0	0	0	1	12

Warsaw Markland Dam *Gallatin County*   Elevation: 465 ft.   Latitude: 38° 46' N   Longitude: 84° 58' W

	JAN	FEB	MAR	APR	MAY	JUN	JUL	AUG	SEP	OCT	NOV	DEC	YEAR
Mean Maximum Temp. (°F)	39.6	44.4	54.2	65.7	75.0	82.7	86.9	85.7	79.6	68.2	55.6	44.6	65.2
Mean Temp. (°F)	30.1	33.9	42.9	52.7	62.4	70.8	75.2	73.8	67.4	55.5	44.9	35.2	53.7
Mean Minimum Temp. (°F)	20.2	23.3	31.4	39.9	49.7	58.8	63.4	62.0	55.1	42.7	34.0	25.7	42.2
Extreme Maximum Temp. (°F)	71	77	84	89	92	102	104	104	97	92	82	76	104
Extreme Minimum Temp. (°F)	-23	-11	-9	20	28	38	44	41	30	18	2	-19	-23
Days Maximum Temp. ≥ 90°F	0	0	0	0	0	4	10	7	2	0	0	0	23
Days Maximum Temp. ≤ 32°F	9	5	1	0	0	0	0	0	0	0	0	4	19
Days Minimum Temp. ≤ 32°F	26	22	18	8	1	0	0	0	0	4	14	22	115
Days Minimum Temp. ≤ 0°F	2	1	0	0	0	0	0	0	0	0	0	1	4
Heating Degree Days (base 65°F)	1,076	873	682	372	140	19	1	3	59	304	599	919	5,047
Cooling Degree Days (base 65°F)	0	0	2	9	70	210	343	295	129	16	1	0	1,075
Mean Precipitation (in.)	2.96	2.83	4.12	4.27	4.63	4.80	3.88	3.66	3.10	3.00	3.45	3.49	44.19
Days With ≥ 0.1" Precipitation	6	6	8	8	8	7	6	6	5	6	7	7	80
Days With ≥ 1.0" Precipitation	1	1	1	1	1	1	1	1	1	1	1	1	12
Mean Snowfall (in.)	4.2	3.8	1.7	trace	0.0	0.0	0.0	0.0	0.0	trace	0.2	1.5	11.4
Days With ≥ 1.0" Snow Depth	5	5	1	0	0	0	0	0	0	0	0	1	12

West Liberty *Morgan County*   Elevation: 830 ft.   Latitude: 37° 55' N   Longitude: 83° 16' W

	JAN	FEB	MAR	APR	MAY	JUN	JUL	AUG	SEP	OCT	NOV	DEC	YEAR
Mean Maximum Temp. (°F)	42.3	47.8	57.3	68.4	76.2	83.3	87.3	86.1	80.2	69.8	57.8	47.7	67.0
Mean Temp. (°F)	30.4	34.5	43.0	52.7	61.3	69.8	74.2	72.8	66.0	54.0	44.0	*35.4*	*53.2*
Mean Minimum Temp. (°F)	18.8	21.1	28.7	36.9	46.5	56.1	61.0	59.4	51.6	38.3	30.4	*23.6*	*39.4*
Extreme Maximum Temp. (°F)	80	80	86	93	92	107	103	102	97	89	84	81	107
Extreme Minimum Temp. (°F)	-30	-22	-11	13	24	33	45	38	29	10	*6*	*-12*	*-30*
Days Maximum Temp. ≥ 90°F	0	0	0	0	1	5	11	8	3	0	0	0	28
Days Maximum Temp. ≤ 32°F	7	3	1	0	0	0	0	0	0	0	0	3	14
Days Minimum Temp. ≤ 32°F	27	24	20	10	2	0	0	0	0	10	*18*	*24*	*135*
Days Minimum Temp. ≤ 0°F	3	1	0	0	0	0	0	0	0	0	0	1	5
Heating Degree Days (base 65°F)	1,065	855	677	372	159	24	2	4	74	343	623	*910*	*5,108*
Cooling Degree Days (base 65°F)	0	0	2	8	50	180	303	249	99	9	0	0	900
Mean Precipitation (in.)	3.27	3.05	4.11	3.65	4.79	3.90	4.81	3.43	3.08	2.94	3.30	3.96	44.29
Days With ≥ 0.1" Precipitation	7	6	8	8	9	7	8	6	6	5	7	8	85
Days With ≥ 1.0" Precipitation	1	1	1	1	1	1	1	1	1	1	1	1	12
Mean Snowfall (in.)	na	na	*1.0*	trace	trace	0.0	0.0	0.0	0.0	trace	0.2	*0.6*	na
Days With ≥ 1.0" Snow Depth	6	5	1	0	0	0	0	0	0	0	0	2	14

Williamsburg *Whitley County*   Elevation: 938 ft.   Latitude: 36° 44' N   Longitude: 84° 09' W

	JAN	FEB	MAR	APR	MAY	JUN	JUL	AUG	SEP	OCT	NOV	DEC	YEAR
Mean Maximum Temp. (°F)	44.9	49.5	59.3	69.6	77.1	83.8	86.9	85.2	79.4	69.3	59.0	49.0	67.7
Mean Temp. (°F)	34.4	38.1	46.3	55.2	63.8	71.6	75.4	73.9	67.7	56.2	46.8	38.4	55.7
Mean Minimum Temp. (°F)	23.9	26.3	33.2	40.7	50.5	59.4	64.0	62.5	55.9	43.1	34.6	27.7	43.5
Extreme Maximum Temp. (°F)	75	82	86	92	92	96	101	99	97	87	81	77	101
Extreme Minimum Temp. (°F)	-21	-19	-4	19	30	40	48	42	31	23	*14*	-11	*-21*
Days Maximum Temp. ≥ 90°F	0	0	0	0	1	4	10	7	1	0	0	0	23
Days Maximum Temp. ≤ 32°F	5	3	1	0	0	0	0	0	0	0	0	2	11
Days Minimum Temp. ≤ 32°F	24	21	16	7	1	0	0	0	0	5	14	21	109
Days Minimum Temp. ≤ 0°F	1	0	0	0	0	0	0	0	0	0	0	0	1
Heating Degree Days (base 65°F)	940	754	576	307	111	13	0	2	51	283	538	820	4,395
Cooling Degree Days (base 65°F)	0	0	3	16	87	231	349	287	127	17	1	0	1,118
Mean Precipitation (in.)	4.21	4.01	4.99	4.12	5.06	4.30	4.14	4.50	4.02	3.21	4.18	4.40	51.14
Days With ≥ 0.1" Precipitation	9	8	9	8	9	7	8	7	6	6	7	8	92
Days With ≥ 1.0" Precipitation	1	1	1	1	1	1	1	1	1	1	1	1	12
Mean Snowfall (in.)	na	na	*2.2*	0.3	0.0	0.0	0.0	0.0	0.0	trace	*trace*	na	na
Days With ≥ 1.0" Snow Depth	na	na	na	0	0	0	0	0	0	0	*0*	na	na

Williamstown 3 W *Grant County*   Elevation: 938 ft.   Latitude: 38° 40' N   Longitude: 84° 37' W

	JAN	FEB	MAR	APR	MAY	JUN	JUL	AUG	SEP	OCT	NOV	DEC	YEAR
Mean Maximum Temp. (°F)	39.9	45.4	55.4	66.2	74.9	82.3	86.2	85.0	79.3	68.2	55.5	45.1	65.3
Mean Temp. (°F)	31.2	35.7	44.9	54.9	64.1	71.9	75.9	74.6	68.6	57.3	46.3	36.5	55.2
Mean Minimum Temp. (°F)	22.5	26.0	34.3	43.6	53.3	61.5	65.6	64.1	57.8	46.3	37.1	27.9	45.0
Extreme Maximum Temp. (°F)	71	75	83	89	91	102	104	104	98	86	83	74	104
Extreme Minimum Temp. (°F)	-23	-10	-1	15	32	41	50	42	32	22	4	-22	-23
Days Maximum Temp. ≥ 90°F	0	0	0	0	0	3	8	6	2	0	0	0	19
Days Maximum Temp. ≤ 32°F	8	5	1	0	0	0	0	0	0	0	0	4	18
Days Minimum Temp. ≤ 32°F	25	20	15	4	0	0	0	0	0	2	12	20	98
Days Minimum Temp. ≤ 0°F	2	1	0	0	0	0	0	0	0	0	0	1	4
Heating Degree Days (base 65°F)	1,039	820	621	314	106	12	1	2	46	256	557	876	4,650
Cooling Degree Days (base 65°F)	0	0	3	19	87	239	367	322	161	26	2	0	1,226
Mean Precipitation (in.)	2.92	2.77	4.44	4.44	4.72	4.38	4.06	3.91	3.15	3.10	3.51	3.58	44.98
Days With ≥ 0.1" Precipitation	7	6	9	9	9	7	7	6	5	5	8	8	86
Days With ≥ 1.0" Precipitation	0	1	1	1	1	1	1	1	1	1	1	1	11
Mean Snowfall (in.)	6.6	4.6	3.5	0.3	trace	0.0	0.0	0.0	0.0	0.2	0.7	2.6	18.5
Days With ≥ 1.0" Snow Depth	9	6	2	0	0	0	0	0	0	0	0	3	20

Note: See Appendix D for explanation of data.

LOUISIANA

PHYSICAL FEATURES. Louisiana extends roughly between latitudes 29.5° N. and 33° N. and from the 94th meridian eastward to the Mississippi River, and in the south to the Pearl River. Elevations increase gradually from the coast northward, rising to over 100 feet above sea level on uplands and 400 to 500 feet on some of the hills in the northwest.

Drainage in Louisiana is into the Gulf of Mexico. The Red River basin comprises the largest drainage area in the State. The Red joins with the Atchafalaya and Old Rivers, the latter forming an outlet to the Mississippi River. Southern Louisiana is mostly low and level with elevations generally less than 60 feet above mean Gulf level. The runoff is through numerous sluggish streams or bayous which flow through lakes and considerable marshland. The larger marshlands are mainly in the coastal area, extending farthest inland in the southeast. A great part of the southwestern region is drained through the Calcasieu River. The extreme southwestern part of the State drains into the Sabine River which forms more than half of the western boundary. The Pearl River drains a relatively small area in the southeast and forms the southeastern boundary.

GENERAL CLIMATE. The principal influences that determine the climate of Louisiana are its subtropical latitude and its proximity to the Gulf of Mexico. The marine tropical influence is evident from the fact that the average water temperatures of the Gulf along the Louisiana shore range from 64°F. in February to 84°F. in August.

In summer the prevailing southerly winds provide moist, semi-tropical weather often favorable for afternoon thundershowers. When westerly to northerly winds occur, periods of hotter and drier weather interrupt the prevailing moist condition. In the colder season the State is subjected alternately to tropical air and cold continental air, in periods of varying length. Although warmed by its southward journey, the cold air occasionally brings large and rather sudden drops in temperature, but conditions are usually less severe than farther west.

Louisiana is south of the usual track of winter storm centers, but occasionally one moves this far south. In some winters a succession of such centers will develop in the Gulf of Mexico and move over or near the State. The State is occasionally in the path of tropical storms or hurricanes.

From December to May the water of the Mississippi River is usually colder than the air temperature, which favors river fogs during this season, particularly with weak southerly winds. In the more southern sections, lakes also serve to modify the extremes of temperature and to increase fogginess over narrow strips along the shores.

PRECIPITATION. Mean annual precipitation ranges from 46 inches in Caddo Parish County to as much as 66 inches in parts of St. Mary, Assumption, Terrebonne, and Lafourche Parishes. A median line of 56 inches per year runs from Hackberry northward to Leesville, Montgomery, Winona, Luna, and southward to Harrisonburg and Deerpark on the Mississippi River. This line separates areas of lower precipitation averages to the north from areas of higher precipitation to the south.

During the summer months, seasonal rainfall usually increases from the northwest toward the southeast. In the winter this pattern is reversed with the heaviest seasonal precipitation in the area extending from the Carroll Parishes southwestward to Winn and southward to St. Landry, with the least in the lower Delta. During the summer months the rich source of moist tropical air results in almost daily showers in the coastal parishes; however, shower frequency diminishes with distance from the Gulf coast toward the northern parishes. In the winter months the northern portion of the State is invaded by cold air which tends to stall and become stationary. This sometimes produces prolonged rains over that area, while clear weather continues in the southern parishes. The pattern of spring rains is similar to that of winter, while fall rains are distributed in the same manner as summer rains. However, fall (September, October, and November) is the driest season of the year, with precipitation ranging from nine inches in the north to 15 inches in the southeast. Spring precipitation ranges from 13 inches on the coast to 18 inches in the central interior.

The heaviest rains of short duration are associated with thunderstorms, although tropical storms sometimes cause prolonged heavy rains. Rains of as much as 20 inches in one month have occurred at most weather stations, and falls of as much as 10 inches in 24 hours are not rare. Although Louisiana is one of the wettest states, droughts are not unknown, especially during the summer and fall. Snow and sleet are of little importance in Louisiana.

FLOODS. Flood producing rains may occur during any month of the year in Louisiana, although they are less likely during September, October, and November, the drier months, and are most frequent during late winter and early spring. Floods on the lower Mississippi and Atchafalaya result from runoff upstream, and rainfall within the State has little influence on these stages. Major floods can occur on the lower Red River from heavy rains in

Louisiana. Heavy rains cause several minor floods each year on the Sabine, Calcasieu, and Mermentau Rivers. A major flood on the Sabine occurs about once in four years. In the upper portions of the Calcasieu and Mermentau a major flood occurs about once in 10 years and in the lower portions not more than once in 25 years.

TEMPERATURE.   The average annual temperature ranges from 66°F. in northern divisions to 69°F. in southern divisions. The lowest January average is 49°F. in the northwest and north-central ranging upward to 57°F. in the southeast. The highest July average is 83°F. in the northwest and north-central, ranging downward to 81°F. in the east-central. This reversal of temperature distribution with warmer summers in the northern portion than in the southern portion, is due to the almost daily showers in the parishes near or on the Gulf of Mexico. This is further shown by the number of days with temperatures 90°F. or above. While Shreveport and Alexandria average 102 such days, Lake Charles and New Orleans average 86 and 57, respectively. In other words, at New Orleans, where there is a 50 percent expectancy of showers on any day in July, the temperature reaches or exceeds 90°F. about half as often as at Shreveport where summer showers are much less frequent. Temperatures above 110°F. and below 0°F. are rare. The average number of days with freezing temperatures (32°F.) or lower ranges from 24 at Shreveport to four at New Orleans. Near the mouth of the Mississippi River a freeze can be expected only about once in seven years.

STORMS.   Showers and thunderstorms occur on an average of 50 to 60 days a year in the northwest and north-central, 70 to 80 days a year in the south, and 60 to 70 days in central and northeast Louisiana. During fall, winter, and spring, these are often attended by high winds, but this is not the case during the summer. Thundershowers which move off Lake Pontchartrain at any season are usually attended by high winds. During late fall, winter, and early spring, thunder may occur at any time of day, but from late spring to early fall about 80 percent of all thundershowers occur between noon and midnight in the northern and between 6 a.m. and 6 p.m. in the southern half of the State.

Tropical cyclones are one of the hazards to life and property in Louisiana, especially in the parishes near the coast. About a third of the cyclones have been of hurricane intensity with winds of 74 miles per hour or more at some points. Most others are attended by gale winds. Almost one-half of all tropical cyclones and one-half of those reaching hurricane intensity have occurred in September.

Tornadoes have been reported in most years and in all months of the year. The largest number of tornadoes has occurred in April, followed by May, November, and March. Hurricanes and tornadoes affect only a relatively small area for a brief time and their frequency is quite low. Contrasting with these occasional adverse features are the mild and short winters, the abundant precipitation, the long growing (freeze-free) season, freedom from extreme summer heat, and the delightful spring and fall weather.

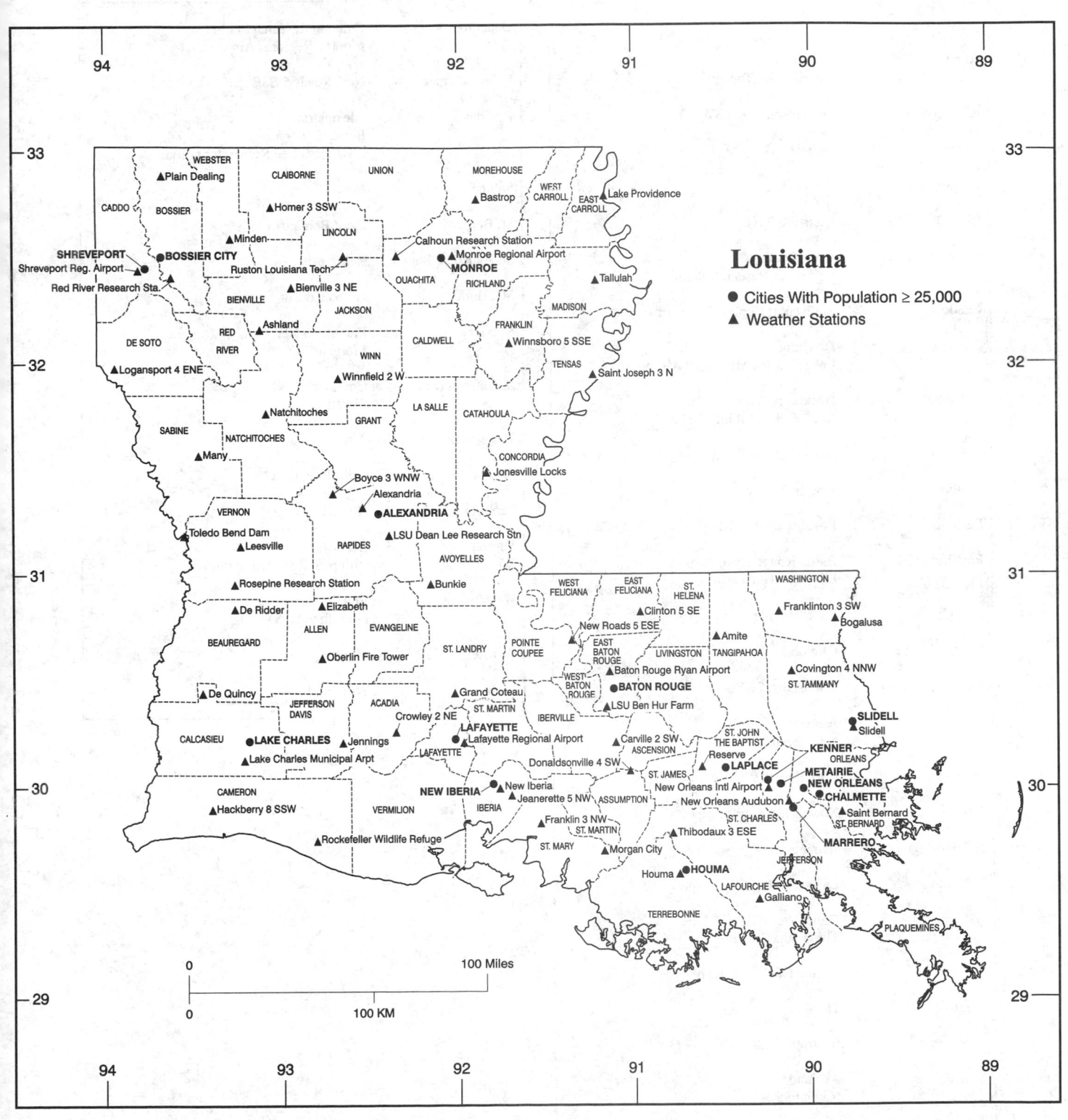

Louisiana

- ● Cities With Population ≥ 25,000
- ▲ Weather Stations

WEBSTER
▲Plain Dealing
CLAIBORNE
UNION
MOREHOUSE
WEST CARROLL
EAST CARROLL
▲Lake Providence

CADDO
BOSSIER
▲Homer 3 SSW
LINCOLN
▲Bastrop

SHREVEPORT
●BOSSIER CITY
▲Minden
Calhoun Research Station
▲Monroe Regional Airport
Shreveport Reg. Airport
Ruston Louisiana Tech
OUACHITA
●MONROE
RICHLAND
▲Tallulah

Red River Research Sta.
▲Bienville 3 NE
BIENVILLE
JACKSON
MADISON

▲Ashland
RED RIVER
FRANKLIN
▲Winnsboro 5 SSE

DE SOTO
WINN
CALDWELL
TENSAS

▲Logansport 4 ENE
▲Winnfield 2 W
▲Saint Joseph 3 N

SABINE
▲Natchitoches
GRANT
LA SALLE
CATAHOULA

NATCHITOCHES
▲Many
CONCORDIA
▲Jonesville Locks

Boyce 3 WNW
▲Alexandria

VERNON
●ALEXANDRIA

▲Toledo Bend Dam
▲LSU Dean Lee Research Stn
▲Leesville
RAPIDES
AVOYELLES

WEST FELICIANA
EAST FELICIANA
ST. HELENA
WASHINGTON

▲Rosepine Research Station
▲Bunkie
▲Clinton 5 SE
▲Franklinton 3 SW

▲De Ridder
▲Elizabeth
New Roads 5 ESE
▲Bogalusa

BEAUREGARD
ALLEN
EVANGELINE
POINTE COUPEE
EAST BATON ROUGE
LIVINGSTON
TANGIPAHOA
▲Amite

▲Oberlin Fire Tower
ST. LANDRY
WEST BATON ROUGE
▲Covington 4 NNW
ST. TAMMANY

▲De Quincy
▲Grand Coteau
Baton Rouge Ryan Airport

JEFFERSON DAVIS
ACADIA
Crowley 2 NE
ST. MARTIN
●BATON ROUGE
▲LSU Ben Hur Farm
IBERVILLE

CALCASIEU
●LAKE CHARLES
▲Jennings
LAFAYETTE
▲Lafayette Regional Airport
▲Carville 2 SW
ASCENSION
ST. JOHN THE BAPTIST
Reserve
SLIDELL
▲Slidell

▲Lake Charles Municipal Arpt
LAFAYETTE
Donaldsonville 4 SW
KENNER
●LAPLACE
METAIRIE

CAMERON
●NEW IBERIA
●New Iberia
ST. JAMES
New Orleans Intl Airport
●NEW ORLEANS
▲CHALMETTE

▲Hackberry 8 SSW
VERMILION
IBERIA
▲Jeanerette 5 NW
ASSUMPTION
New Orleans Audubon
▲Saint Bernard
ST. BERNARD

▲Rockefeller Wildlife Refuge
▲Franklin 3 NW
ST. MARTIN
▲Thibodaux 3 ESE
MARRERO

ST. MARY
▲Morgan City
JEFFERSON

Houma ▲●HOUMA
LAFOURCHE
▲Galliano

TERREBONNE
PLAQUEMINES

0   100 Miles

0   100 KM

Louisiana Weather Stations by Parish

Parish	Station Name
Acadia	Crowley 2 NE
Allen	Elizabeth Oberlin Fire Tower
Assumption	Donaldsonville 4 SW
Avoyelles	Bunkie
Beauregard	De Ridder
Bienville	Bienville 3 NE
Bossier	Plain Dealing Red River Research Station
Caddo	Shreveport Regional Airport
Calcasieu	De Quincy Lake Charles Municipal Airport
Cameron	Hackberry 8 SSW Rockefeller Wildlife Refuge
Catahoula	Jonesville Locks
Claiborne	Homer 3 SSW
De Soto	Logansport 4 ENE
East Baton Rouge	Baton Rouge Ryan Airport LSU Ben Hur Farm
East Carroll	Lake Providence
East Feliciana	Clinton 5 SE
Franklin	Winnsboro 5 SSE
Iberia	Jeanerette 5 NW New Iberia
Iberville	Carville 2 SW
Jefferson	New Orleans Int'l Airport
Jefferson Davis	Jennings
Lafayette	Lafayette Regional Airport
Lafourche	Galliano Thibodaux 3 ESE
Lincoln	Ruston Louisiana Tech
Madison	Tallulah
Morehouse	Bastrop
Natchitoches	Ashland Natchitoches
Orleans	New Orleans Audubon

Parish	Station Name
Ouachita	Calhoun Research Station Monroe Regional Airport
Pointe Coupee	New Roads 5 ESE
Rapides	Alexandria Boyce 3 WNW LSU Dean Lee Research Station
Sabine	Many
St. Bernard	Saint Bernard
St. John The Baptist	Reserve
St. Landry	Grand Coteau
St. Mary	Franklin 3 NW Morgan City
St. Tammany	Covington 4 NNW Slidell
Tangipahoa	Amite
Tensas	Saint Joseph 3 N
Terrebonne	Houma
Vernon	Leesville Rosepine Research Station
Washington	Bogalusa Franklinton 3 SW
Webster	Minden
Winn	Winnfield 2 W

Louisiana Weather Stations by City

City	Station Name	Miles
Alexandria	Alexandria	6
	Boyce 3 WNW	17
	LSU Dean Lee Research Station	8
Baton Rouge	Baton Rouge Ryan Airport	6
	Carville 2 SW	17
	LSU Ben Hur Farm	6
Bossier City	Red River Research Station	8
	Shreveport Regional Airport	9
Chalmette	New Orleans Int'l Airport	18
	New Orleans Audubon	10
	Saint Bernard	9
Houma	Houma	1
	Thibodaux 3 ESE	13
Kenner	New Orleans Int'l Airport	1
	New Orleans Audubon	10
Lafayette	Grand Coteau	15
	Lafayette Regional Airport	3
Lake Charles	Lake Charles Municipal Airport	7
Laplace	New Orleans Int'l Airport	15
	Reserve	8
Marrero	New Orleans Int'l Airport	12
	New Orleans Audubon	3
	Saint Bernard	17
Metairie	New Orleans Int'l Airport	4
	New Orleans Audubon	6
Monroe	Calhoun Research Station	15
	Monroe Regional Airport	4
New Iberia	Jeanerette 5 NW	7
	Lafayette Regional Airport	17
	New Iberia	3
New Orleans	New Orleans Int'l Airport	12
	New Orleans Audubon	6
	Saint Bernard	15
Shreveport	Red River Research Station	9
	Shreveport Regional Airport	2
Slidell	Slidell	1
	Picayune, MS	17

Note: Miles is the distance between the geographic center of the city and the weather station.

Louisiana Weather Stations by Elevation

Feet	Station Name
377	Homer 3 SSW
305	Bienville 3 NE
288	Plain Dealing
278	Ruston Louisiana Tech
259	Many
252	Shreveport Regional Airport
239	Ashland
236	Rosepine Research Station
209	Logansport 4 ENE
200	Clinton 5 SE
187	De Ridder
183	Minden
177	Calhoun Research Station
167	Amite
157	Winnfield 2 W
154	Red River Research Station
147	Bastrop
147	Elizabeth
144	Franklinton 3 SW
131	Monroe Regional Airport
127	Natchitoches
108	Boyce 3 WNW
98	Bogalusa
98	Lake Providence
85	Alexandria
82	Tallulah
78	Bunkie
78	De Quincy
78	Winnsboro 5 SSE
75	Saint Joseph 3 N
68	Jonesville Locks
68	LSU Dean Lee Research Station
62	Baton Rouge Ryan Airport
62	Oberlin Fire Tower
52	Grand Coteau
42	New Roads 5 ESE
39	Covington 4 NNW
36	Lafayette Regional Airport
29	Donaldsonville 4 SW
26	Leesville
22	Carville 2 SW
22	Crowley 2 NE
22	Jennings
22	New Iberia
19	Jeanerette 5 NW
19	LSU Ben Hur Farm
13	Houma
13	Lake Charles Municipal Airport
13	Reserve
13	Thibodaux 3 ESE
9	Franklin 3 NW
9	Slidell
3	Galliano
3	Hackberry 8 SSW
3	Morgan City

Feet	Station Name
3	New Orleans Int'l Airport
3	New Orleans Audubon
3	Rockefeller Wildlife Refuge
3	Saint Bernard

Baton Rouge Ryan Airport

Baton Rouge, the capital city, is located on the east side of the Mississippi River in the southeast section of the state, some 65 miles inland from the coast. The area is near the first evident relief north of the deltaic coastal plains. The National Weather Service Office is located at Ryan Airport, some 8 miles north of the downtown area. Elevations in East Baton Rouge Parish range from near 25 feet to more than 100 feet above sea level.

The general climate of Baton Rouge is humid subtropical, but the city is subject to significant polar influences during winter. Prevailing wind flow is from the southerly direction during much of the year. This maritime air from the Gulf of Mexico helps to temper summer heat, shorten winter cold spells, and provides abundant moisture and rainfall. Winds are usually rather light.

Rainfall is heavy and amounts are substantial in all seasons, with an early autumn low in September and October. Almost all rainfall is from brief convective showers. Occasionally during winter, slow moving cold fronts may produce rains lasting for a few days.

The winter months are normally mild with short cold spells. The typical pattern shows cold with rain on the first day, colder with clear skies on the second day, and warming on the third day. Freezing or sub-freezing temperatures occur several times annually, but temperatures nearly always rise above freezing during the day. The average date of the first freeze in the autumn is late November, and the average date of the last freeze in spring is late February, producing a mean freeze-free period of 273 days. Annual total snowfall averages only a fraction of an inch and many years pass with no measurable snow.

The summer months are consistently quite warm, but high temperatures rarely exceed 100 degrees. Scattered showers normally fall in the area on about one-half of the days in June, July, and August.

Except for three or four days per month, point rainfall totals are usually less than 0.5 inch. Summer relative humidity exceeds 80 percent for about 12 hours per day. High humidity may be experienced at any hour, but occurs mainly at night. Readings of 50 percent or less occur about two hours per day, usually in the afternoons. Temperatures in the spring are usually mild and pleasant and in the autumn they are generally delightful for outdoor activities.

Thunderstorms occur each month, most frequently in July and August. Severe local storms are most frequent during the spring months. Large damaging hail very rarely occurs and tornadoes are unusual. Hurricane centers have occasionally passed very near Baton Rouge.

Baton Rouge Ryan Airport *East Baton Rouge County*   Elevation: 62 ft.   Latitude: 30° 32' N   Longitude: 91° 09' W

	JAN	FEB	MAR	APR	MAY	JUN	JUL	AUG	SEP	OCT	NOV	DEC	YEAR
Mean Maximum Temp. (°F)	60.5	64.5	71.7	78.4	84.8	90.0	91.3	91.1	87.6	79.7	70.5	63.8	77.8
Mean Temp. (°F)	50.6	54.0	60.9	67.6	74.7	80.4	82.3	81.9	78.0	68.4	59.4	53.4	67.6
Mean Minimum Temp. (°F)	40.6	43.4	50.2	56.7	64.5	70.8	73.3	72.6	68.3	57.1	48.3	42.9	57.4
Extreme Maximum Temp. (°F)	82	85	88	92	97	101	100	100	99	94	87	85	101
Extreme Minimum Temp. (°F)	9	15	20	32	45	53	64	59	46	30	21	8	8
Days Maximum Temp. ≥ 90°F	0	0	0	0	5	19	24	23	13	1	0	0	85
Days Maximum Temp. ≤ 32°F	0	0	0	0	0	0	0	0	0	0	0	0	0
Days Minimum Temp. ≤ 32°F	8	4	1	0	0	0	0	0	0	0	2	6	21
Days Minimum Temp. ≤ 0°F	0	0	0	0	0	0	0	0	0	0	0	0	0
Heating Degree Days (base 65°F)	453	321	175	52	2	0	0	0	1	47	209	377	1,637
Cooling Degree Days (base 65°F)	11	17	54	133	316	472	548	539	395	161	49	23	2,718
Mean Precipitation (in.)	6.17	5.15	5.19	5.62	5.48	5.29	6.04	5.98	4.88	3.98	4.45	5.39	63.62
Maximum Precipitation (in.)	11.4	14.5	12.7	14.8	14.7	23.2	11.6	14.5	13.9	14.5	13.5	15.9	88.3
Minimum Precipitation (in.)	1.1	0.7	0.5	0.4	0.6	0.1	2.0	1.0	0.1	trace	0.1	1.9	38.3
Maximum 24-hr. Precipitation (in.)	4.2	4.5	5.3	12.+	4.8	4.9	4.3	7.9	6.3	4.8	6.2	7.2	12.+
Days With ≥ 0.1" Precipitation	7	6	7	5	6	7	9	8	7	4	5	7	78
Days With ≥ 1.0" Precipitation	2	2	2	2	2	1	2	2	2	2	1	2	22
Mean Snowfall (in.)	trace	0.2	trace	0.0	*trace*	*0.0*	0.0	0.0	0.0	0.0	trace	trace	*0.2*
Maximum Snowfall (in.)	2	3	trace	0	0	0	0	0	0	0	trace	trace	3
Maximum 24-hr. Snowfall (in.)	2	3	trace	0	0	0	0	0	0	0	trace	trace	3
Days With ≥ 1.0" Snow Depth	0	0	0	0	0	*0*	0	0	0	0	0	0	*0*
Thunderstorm Days	2	3	4	5	7	10	15	13	7	2	3	2	73
Foggy Days	17	14	16	17	19	17	16	18	18	17	16	17	202
Predominant Sky Cover	OVR	OVR	OVR	OVR	OVR	SCT	SCT	SCT	CLR	CLR	CLR	OVR	OVR
Mean Relative Humidity 6am (%)	85	85	86	89	91	91	92	93	91	89	88	86	89
Mean Relative Humidity 3pm (%)	59	55	52	52	54	57	62	61	59	51	53	57	56
Mean Dewpoint (°F)	42	44	49	57	64	70	72	72	68	57	49	44	57
Prevailing Wind Direction	N	N	S	SE	SE	SE	W	E	NE	NE	N	N	SE
Prevailing Wind Speed (mph)	10	10	12	10	9	8	7	7	7	7	9	10	9
Maximum Wind Gust (mph)	54	48	52	52	59	49	59	73	64	60	47	52	73

Lake Charles Municipal Airport

Lake Charles is located on the east side of the lake of the same name. The Calcasieu River enters and exits Lake Charles and several other lakes in the area on its way to the Gulf of Mexico. The terrain is flat, level coastal plain. Extensive marshes begin some 10 to 15 miles south and extend to the coast. Area elevations range from near sea level to about 25 feet above sea level. The National Weather Service Office is at the Lake Charles Municipal Airport, about seven miles south of the downtown area. Calcasieu Lake is only six miles southwest of the airport.

The general classification of the Lake Charles climate is humid subtropical with a strong maritime character. The climate is influenced to a large degree by the amount of water surface in the immediate area and the proximity of the Gulf of Mexico.

Prevailing wind flow is southerly during much of the year. The flow of air from the Gulf of Mexico helps to temper extremes of summer heat, shorten the duration of winter cold spells and provide a source of abundant rain. Winds are usually rather light.

Rainfall is heavy, with the normal annual total more than 50 inches. Amounts are substantial in all seasons. Almost all rainfall occurs from brief convective showers, except occasionally during winter when nearly continuous frontal rains may persist for a few days. In spite of the large normal rainfall amounts, dry spells of two or three weeks duration are not uncommon.

The winter months are normally mild with cold spells usually of short duration. Temperatures of 20 degrees and below are extremely rare, occurring only about one year in five.

Snow is a negligible. Many years pass without measurable snowfall. However, on rare occasions, as much as 22 inches of snow have fallen at Lake Charles. Freezing rain and sleet are only a little less uncommon than snow.

The summer weather is consistently quite warm and humid but the temperature rarely reaches the 100 degree mark. The humidity is often above 90 percent at night and seldom falls below 50 percent during the afternoons.

The spring and fall seasons are very mild and pleasant with only brief rains interrupting long periods of dry sunny weather.

Severe local storms may occur during any season but are most frequent in the spring. The area weather is occasionally influenced by tropical storms or hurricanes. Some of these storms may be accompanied by tornadoes.

Lake Charles Municipal Airport *Calcasieu County*   Elevation: 13 ft.   Latitude: 30° 07' N   Longitude: 93° 14' W

	JAN	FEB	MAR	APR	MAY	JUN	JUL	AUG	SEP	OCT	NOV	DEC	YEAR
Mean Maximum Temp. (°F)	60.3	64.2	70.9	77.4	84.0	88.9	90.9	91.2	87.6	80.4	70.6	63.8	77.5
Mean Temp. (°F)	51.2	54.6	61.2	67.8	75.0	80.6	82.6	82.3	78.4	69.5	60.3	54.2	68.1
Mean Minimum Temp. (°F)	42.0	45.0	51.4	58.0	66.0	72.2	74.1	73.3	69.0	58.6	50.0	44.5	58.7
Extreme Maximum Temp. (°F)	82	83	86	95	96	99	102	101	100	94	87	82	102
Extreme Minimum Temp. (°F)	15	17	25	34	49	56	63	59	48	30	23	11	11
Days Maximum Temp. ≥ 90°F	0	0	0	0	3	14	23	23	13	1	0	0	77
Days Maximum Temp. ≤ 32°F	0	0	0	0	0	0	0	0	0	0	0	0	0
Days Minimum Temp. ≤ 32°F	6	3	1	0	0	0	0	0	0	0	1	4	15
Days Minimum Temp. ≤ 0°F	0	0	0	0	0	0	0	0	0	0	0	0	0
Heating Degree Days (base 65°F)	431	299	161	44	1	0	0	0	1	36	188	352	1,513
Cooling Degree Days (base 65°F)	9	15	49	132	327	481	562	559	412	187	57	23	2,813
Mean Precipitation (in.)	5.54	3.35	3.64	3.52	6.01	6.04	5.00	4.92	5.99	4.46	4.27	4.67	57.41
Maximum Precipitation (in.)	14.3	6.8	9.0	10.9	14.8	25.3	13.2	17.4	20.0	17.3	14.1	13.3	75.8
Minimum Precipitation (in.)	0.8	0.6	0.3	0.5	0.3	0.8	0.5	0.8	0.4	trace	0.1	2.1	34.8
Maximum 24-hr. Precipitation (in.)	5.0	3.2	3.6	5.5	5.5	6.9	6.4	10.+	9.6	7.2	10.+	5.9	10.+
Days With ≥ 0.1" Precipitation	7	5	5	4	6	7	8	7	6	4	6	6	71
Days With ≥ 1.0" Precipitation	2	1	1	1	2	2	1	1	2	2	1	1	17
Mean Snowfall (in.)	0.2	trace	0.0	trace	trace	0.0	trace	0.0	0.0	0.0	trace	trace	0.2
Maximum Snowfall (in.)	4	2	trace	0	0	0	0	0	0	0	trace	trace	4
Maximum 24-hr. Snowfall (in.)	4	2	trace	0	0	0	0	0	0	0	trace	trace	4
Days With ≥ 1.0" Snow Depth	0	0	0	0	0	0	0	0	0	0	0	0	0
Thunderstorm Days	3	3	4	5	8	10	14	13	8	3	3	3	77
Foggy Days	18	16	18	17	18	13	11	16	17	18	16	18	196
Predominant Sky Cover	OVR	OVR	OVR	OVR	OVR	SCT	SCT	SCT	SCT	CLR	OVR	OVR	OVR
Mean Relative Humidity 6am (%)	87	87	89	91	93	93	94	94	93	91	89	88	91
Mean Relative Humidity 3pm (%)	64	59	59	59	60	62	64	62	60	52	57	63	60
Mean Dewpoint (°F)	43	45	52	59	66	72	74	73	69	59	52	46	59
Prevailing Wind Direction	N	N	S	S	S	S	S	ENE	ENE	NE	N	N	S
Prevailing Wind Speed (mph)	12	12	12	12	12	9	8	7	7	8	10	12	10
Maximum Wind Gust (mph)	51	62	59	70	61	61	66	56	59	62	69	53	70

New Orleans Int'l Airport

The New Orleans metropolitan area is virtually surrounded by water. Lake Pontchartrain borders the city on the north and is connected to the Gulf of Mexico through Lake Borgne on the east. In other directions there are bayous, lakes, and marshy delta land. The proximity of the Gulf of Mexico also has a great influence on the climate. Elevations in the city vary from a few feet below to a few feet above mean sea level. A massive levee system surrounding the city and along the Mississippi River offers protection against flooding from the river and tidal surges. The New Orleans International Airport is located 12 miles west of downtown New Orleans.

The climate of the city is humid with the surrounding water modifying the temperature. Almost daily sporadic afternoon thunderstorms from mid-June through September keep the temperature from rising much above 90 degrees. From about mid-November to mid-March, the area is subjected alternately to the southerly flow of warm tropical air and to the northerly flow of cold continental air in periods of varying lengths. The usual track of winter storms is to the north of New Orleans, but occasionally one moves this far south, bringing large and rather sudden drops in temperature. However, the cold spells seldom last over three or four days. The lowest temperatures observed are below 10 degrees.

During the winter and spring, the cold Mississippi River water enhances the formation of river fogs, particularly when light southerly winds bring warm, moist air into the area from the Gulf of Mexico. The nearby lakes and marshes also contribute to fog formation.

Rather frequent and sometimes very heavy rains are typical for this area. There are an average of 120 days of measurable rain per year and an annual average accumulation of over 60 inches. A fairly definite rainy period occurs from mid-December to mid-March. Precipitation during this period is most likely to be steady rain for two to three day periods. April, May, October, and November are generally dry, but there have been some extremely heavy showers in those months. Snowfall is rather infrequent and light.

While thunder occurs with most of the showers in the area, thunderstorms with damaging winds are infrequent. Damaging hail and tornadoes are extremely rare. However, waterspouts are observed quite often on nearby lakes. Hurricanes have effected the area.

The lower Mississippi River floods result from runoff upstream. Rainfall in the New Orleans area is pumped into the surrounding lakes and bayous. The average first occurrence of 32 degrees Fahrenheit in the fall is December 5 and the average last occurrence in the spring is February 20.

New Orleans Int'l Airport *Jefferson County*   Elevation: 3 ft.   Latitude: 30° 00' N   Longitude: 90° 15' W

	JAN	FEB	MAR	APR	MAY	JUN	JUL	AUG	SEP	OCT	NOV	DEC	YEAR
Mean Maximum Temp. (°F)	61.5	65.0	71.8	78.0	84.6	89.4	91.0	90.9	87.2	79.7	70.9	64.8	77.9
Mean Temp. (°F)	52.3	55.4	62.1	68.2	75.3	80.5	82.4	82.2	78.8	69.9	61.2	55.3	68.6
Mean Minimum Temp. (°F)	43.0	45.7	52.4	58.3	65.9	71.6	73.7	73.5	70.4	60.1	51.5	45.8	59.3
Extreme Maximum Temp. (°F)	83	85	89	92	95	99	101	102	101	94	87	84	102
Extreme Minimum Temp. (°F)	14	16	25	32	46	50	63	62	50	35	24	11	11
Days Maximum Temp. ≥ 90°F	0	0	0	0	3	16	21	22	10	1	0	0	73
Days Maximum Temp. ≤ 32°F	0	0	0	0	0	0	0	0	0	0	0	0	0
Days Minimum Temp. ≤ 32°F	5	3	0	0	0	0	0	0	0	0	1	3	12
Days Minimum Temp. ≤ 0°F	0	0	0	0	0	0	0	0	0	0	0	0	0
Heating Degree Days (base 65°F)	402	285	146	41	1	0	0	0	0	28	169	324	1,396
Cooling Degree Days (base 65°F)	13	21	58	136	340	476	554	551	420	194	65	30	2,858
Mean Precipitation (in.)	5.88	5.49	5.40	4.99	4.77	6.81	6.28	6.41	5.48	3.18	4.73	5.12	64.54
Maximum Precipitation (in.)	19.3	12.6	19.1	16.1	21.2	15.0	13.1	16.1	16.7	13.2	19.8	10.8	102.
Minimum Precipitation (in.)	0.5	0.1	0.2	0.3	0.9	0.2	1.9	1.7	0.2	0	0.2	1.5	39.0
Maximum 24-hr. Precipitation (in.)	4.6	4.8	7.9	6.4	12.+	4.1	4.3	4.8	5.4	4.2	11.+	6.5	12.+
Days With ≥ 0.1" Precipitation	7	6	6	5	6	8	10	9	7	4	6	6	80
Days With ≥ 1.0" Precipitation	2	2	2	1	2	3	2	2	2	1	2	2	23
Mean Snowfall (in.)	trace	trace	trace	trace	0.0	0.0	0.0	0.0	0.0	0.0	0.0	trace	trace
Maximum Snowfall (in.)	trace	2	trace	0	0	0	0	0	0	0	0	3	3
Maximum 24-hr. Snowfall (in.)	trace	2	trace	0	0	0	0	0	0	0	0	3	3
Days With ≥ 1.0" Snow Depth	0	0	0	0	0	0	0	0	0	0	0	0	0
Thunderstorm Days	2	3	4	5	6	10	16	13	7	2	2	2	72
Foggy Days	17	14	16	16	16	11	12	12	12	15	15	17	173
Predominant Sky Cover	OVR	OVR	OVR	OVR	SCT	SCT	SCT	SCT	SCT	CLR	CLR	OVR	OVR
Mean Relative Humidity 6am (%)	85	84	85	88	89	90	92	92	89	88	86	86	88
Mean Relative Humidity 3pm (%)	63	59	57	57	58	61	66	65	63	56	59	62	60
Mean Dewpoint (°F)	45	46	52	59	66	71	73	73	70	60	52	47	60
Prevailing Wind Direction	N	N	S	S	S	S	SW	NE	NE	NE	N	N	S
Prevailing Wind Speed (mph)	12	12	12	12	10	9	7	8	9	9	10	10	10
Maximum Wind Gust (mph)	63	67	62	62	69	67	79	66	112	60	55	69	112

Shreveport Regional Airport

Shreveport is located in the northwestern section of Louisiana, some 30 miles south of Arkansas and 15 miles east of Texas. A portion of the city is situated in the Red River bottom lands and the remainder in gently rolling hills that begin about 1 mile west of the river. The NOAA National Weather Service Office is at the Shreveport Regional Airport, about seven miles southwest of the downtown area. Elevations in the Shreveport area range from about 170 to 280 feet above sea level. The climate of Shreveport is transitional between the subtropical humid type prevalent to the south and the continental climates of the Great Plains and Middle West to the north. During winter, masses of moderate to severely cold air move periodically through the area. Rainfall is abundant with the normal annual total near 45 inches. Amounts are substantial from late autumn to spring and there is a summer-early autumn low amount with monthly averages less than three inches in August, September, and October.

The winter months are normally mild with cold spells generally of short duration. Freezing temperatures are recorded on an average of 34 days during the year. The average first occurrence of 32 degrees in the autumn is mid-November, and the last occurrence in the spring is early March Although temperatures have fallen below zero degrees, they normally drop below about 15 degrees in about one-half the years. Temperatures recorded at the NWS Office at the airport on clear, calm nights are normally two to five degrees warmer than those experienced in the river bottom lands. The summer months are consistently quite warm and humid with temperatures exceeding 100 degrees on about 10 days a year and exceeding 95 degrees about 45 days per year. Late afternoon humidity rarely drops below 55 percent.

Measurable snow occurs only once every other year on average. Many consecutive years may pass with no measurable snow. The heaviest snowstorms in the Shreveport area have produced more than 10 inches. More troublesome than the infrequent heavy snowfall are ice and sleet storms which may cause considerable damage to trees and utility lines, as well as make travel very difficult.

Thunderstorms occur each month, but are most frequent in spring and summer months. Severe local storms, including hailstorms, tornadoes, and local windstorms have occurred over small areas in all seasons, but are most frequent during the spring months, with a secondary peak from late November through early January. Large hail of a damaging nature is infrequent, although hail as large as grapefruit has fallen on a few occasions.

Shreveport Regional Airport *Caddo County*   Elevation: 252 ft.   Latitude: 32° 27' N   Longitude: 93° 49' W

	JAN	FEB	MAR	APR	MAY	JUN	JUL	AUG	SEP	OCT	NOV	DEC	YEAR
Mean Maximum Temp. (°F)	55.9	61.7	69.4	76.7	83.1	89.8	93.2	93.2	87.6	78.2	67.0	59.1	76.2
Mean Temp. (°F)	45.8	50.5	57.8	65.0	72.6	79.5	82.8	82.3	76.7	66.3	55.9	48.6	65.3
Mean Minimum Temp. (°F)	35.6	39.3	46.2	53.3	62.0	69.2	72.4	71.3	65.8	54.4	44.8	38.2	54.4
Extreme Maximum Temp. (°F)	84	89	92	94	102	102	107	108	105	96	88	82	108
Extreme Minimum Temp. (°F)	5	12	20	31	44	52	58	53	42	28	16	5	5
Days Maximum Temp. ≥ 90°F	0	0	0	0	4	18	26	25	15	2	0	0	90
Days Maximum Temp. ≤ 32°F	1	0	0	0	0	0	0	0	0	0	0	1	2
Days Minimum Temp. ≤ 32°F	13	7	2	0	0	0	0	0	0	0	3	10	35
Days Minimum Temp. ≤ 0°F	0	0	0	0	0	0	0	0	0	0	0	0	0
Heating Degree Days (base 65°F)	594	410	247	84	8	0	0	0	5	76	291	509	2,224
Cooling Degree Days (base 65°F)	4	9	31	93	258	452	574	563	370	123	25	10	2,512
Mean Precipitation (in.)	4.55	4.29	4.06	4.40	5.03	4.84	4.09	2.78	3.22	4.64	4.42	4.42	50.74
Maximum Precipitation (in.)	10.1	8.6	7.2	21.8	11.8	17.1	9.5	9.2	9.6	14.0	10.8	10.0	82.0
Minimum Precipitation (in.)	0.3	0.8	0.6	0.4	0.4	0.1	0.1	0.3	0.1	0	0.4	0.6	30.0
Maximum 24-hr. Precipitation (in.)	3.2	3.2	3.2	10.+	5.2	7.3	4.4	3.3	4.9	6.8	4.6	3.3	10.+
Days With ≥ 0.1" Precipitation	7	5	6	5	7	6	6	4	5	5	6	6	67
Days With ≥ 1.0" Precipitation	1	2	1	1	2	1	1	1	1	2	2	1	16
Mean Snowfall (in.)	0.8	0.4	trace	trace	trace	0.0	0.0	trace	0.0	trace	trace	0.2	1.4
Maximum Snowfall (in.)	12	4	4	trace	0	0	0	0	0	0	1	5	13
Maximum 24-hr. Snowfall (in.)	8	4	4	trace	0	0	0	0	0	0	1	5	8
Days With ≥ 1.0" Snow Depth	1	0	0	0	0	0	0	0	0	0	0	0	1
Thunderstorm Days	2	3	5	6	7	7	8	6	4	3	3	2	56
Foggy Days	13	10	9	9	9	6	5	7	9	11	11	12	111
Predominant Sky Cover	OVR	OVR	OVR	OVR	OVR	SCT	SCT	SCT	CLR	CLR	OVR	OVR	OVR
Mean Relative Humidity 6am (%)	84	83	83	87	90	91	91	91	90	89	86	85	88
Mean Relative Humidity 3pm (%)	57	53	50	52	55	54	53	50	51	49	52	57	53
Mean Dewpoint (°F)	36	39	45	54	62	69	71	70	65	55	45	39	54
Prevailing Wind Direction	S	S	S	S	S	S	S	S	SE	SE	S	S	S
Prevailing Wind Speed (mph)	12	12	13	12	10	9	8	8	7	8	10	10	10
Maximum Wind Gust (mph)	69	66	73	81	83	74	66	86	66	54	87	67	87

Alexandria *Rapides Parish*   Elevation: 85 ft.   Latitude: 31° 19' N   Longitude: 92° 33' W

	JAN	FEB	MAR	APR	MAY	JUN	JUL	AUG	SEP	OCT	NOV	DEC	YEAR
Mean Maximum Temp. (°F)	57.8	62.6	70.0	77.0	84.0	90.1	92.7	92.7	88.1	79.4	69.0	61.3	77.0
Mean Temp. (°F)	47.6	51.9	59.3	66.3	73.9	80.3	82.9	82.5	77.8	67.5	58.0	50.9	66.6
Mean Minimum Temp. (°F)	37.5	41.0	48.7	55.6	63.8	70.5	73.0	72.3	67.3	55.6	46.9	40.4	56.0
Extreme Maximum Temp. (°F)	81	85	90	94	99	102	103	107	101	96	88	83	107
Extreme Minimum Temp. (°F)	8	14	23	31	45	51	62	57	44	30	21	7	7
Days Maximum Temp. ≥ 90°F	0	0	0	0	4	18	25	25	15	2	0	0	89
Days Maximum Temp. ≤ 32°F	0	0	0	0	0	0	0	0	0	0	0	0	0
Days Minimum Temp. ≤ 32°F	11	6	1	0	0	0	0	0	0	0	2	7	27
Days Minimum Temp. ≤ 0°F	0	0	0	0	0	0	0	0	0	0	0	0	0
Heating Degree Days (base 65°F)	538	375	208	70	5	0	0	0	2	60	240	443	1,941
Cooling Degree Days (base 65°F)	5	13	40	114	298	475	575	566	400	147	35	12	2,680
Mean Precipitation (in.)	6.18	4.85	5.64	4.83	5.32	4.98	4.15	4.46	4.05	5.10	5.44	6.38	61.38
Days With ≥ 0.1" Precipitation	8	6	7	5	6	6	6	7	5	5	6	7	74
Days With ≥ 1.0" Precipitation	2	2	2	2	2	1	1	1	1	1	2	2	19
Mean Snowfall (in.)	0.3	trace	0.0	0.0	0.0	0.0	0.0	0.0	0.0	0.0	0.0	0.0	0.3
Days With ≥ 1.0" Snow Depth	0	0	0	0	0	0	0	0	0	0	0	0	0

Amite *Tangipahoa Parish*   Elevation: 167 ft.   Latitude: 30° 42' N   Longitude: 90° 32' W

	JAN	FEB	MAR	APR	MAY	JUN	JUL	AUG	SEP	OCT	NOV	DEC	YEAR
Mean Maximum Temp. (°F)	60.2	64.5	71.7	78.5	85.1	90.6	92.3	92.3	89.0	80.7	71.0	63.7	78.3
Mean Temp. (°F)	49.2	52.8	59.9	66.3	73.5	79.4	81.6	81.4	77.5	67.6	58.7	52.1	66.7
Mean Minimum Temp. (°F)	38.1	41.0	48.0	54.1	61.8	68.2	70.9	70.3	66.1	54.5	46.4	40.4	55.0
Extreme Maximum Temp. (°F)	81	84	89	94	97	104	103	102	102	95	89	84	104
Extreme Minimum Temp. (°F)	7	13	20	30	40	49	61	55	43	29	20	5	5
Days Maximum Temp. ≥ 90°F	0	0	0	0	6	20	25	25	17	2	0	0	95
Days Maximum Temp. ≤ 32°F	0	0	0	0	0	0	0	0	0	0	0	0	0
Days Minimum Temp. ≤ 32°F	11	7	2	0	0	0	0	0	0	0	3	9	32
Days Minimum Temp. ≤ 0°F	0	0	0	0	0	0	0	0	0	0	0	0	0
Heating Degree Days (base 65°F)	491	351	199	67	5	0	0	0	2	59	224	410	1,808
Cooling Degree Days (base 65°F)	5	13	45	105	272	436	521	517	376	147	41	15	2,493
Mean Precipitation (in.)	6.74	5.46	6.50	6.15	5.68	4.96	6.01	5.34	4.81	4.21	4.55	5.48	65.89
Days With ≥ 0.1" Precipitation	8	6	7	5	7	7	9	8	6	5	6	7	81
Days With ≥ 1.0" Precipitation	2	2	3	2	2	2	2	2	1	1	2	2	23
Mean Snowfall (in.)	0.1	0.1	trace	0.0	0.0	0.0	0.0	0.0	0.0	0.0	0.0	trace	0.2
Days With ≥ 1.0" Snow Depth	0	0	0	0	0	0	0	0	0	0	0	0	0

Ashland *Natchitoches Parish*   Elevation: 239 ft.   Latitude: 32° 10' N   Longitude: 93° 08' W

	JAN	FEB	MAR	APR	MAY	JUN	JUL	AUG	SEP	OCT	NOV	DEC	YEAR
Mean Maximum Temp. (°F)	55.0	60.9	68.6	76.2	82.5	89.3	92.7	92.8	87.3	77.6	66.9	58.5	75.7
Mean Temp. (°F)	43.9	48.5	56.0	63.3	70.8	77.8	81.1	80.5	75.1	64.2	54.4	46.9	63.5
Mean Minimum Temp. (°F)	32.7	36.2	43.4	50.3	59.1	66.4	69.4	68.3	62.9	50.7	41.8	35.4	51.4
Extreme Maximum Temp. (°F)	82	87	89	92	97	101	105	108	103	94	89	83	108
Extreme Minimum Temp. (°F)	5	10	11	24	38	45	54	48	38	24	14	2	2
Days Maximum Temp. ≥ 90°F	0	0	0	0	3	16	25	24	13	1	0	0	82
Days Maximum Temp. ≤ 32°F	1	0	0	0	0	0	0	0	0	0	0	1	2
Days Minimum Temp. ≤ 32°F	17	11	5	1	0	0	0	0	0	1	7	14	56
Days Minimum Temp. ≤ 0°F	0	0	0	0	0	0	0	0	0	0	0	0	0
Heating Degree Days (base 65°F)	651	464	295	122	18	0	0	0	11	113	328	558	2,560
Cooling Degree Days (base 65°F)	2	6	24	73	210	401	517	505	326	99	16	6	2,185
Mean Precipitation (in.)	5.46	5.12	4.85	4.35	5.36	4.36	4.30	3.12	3.51	4.18	4.28	5.34	54.23
Days With ≥ 0.1" Precipitation	8	6	7	5	6	6	6	5	5	5	6	7	72
Days With ≥ 1.0" Precipitation	2	2	2	1	2	1	1	1	1	1	2	2	18
Mean Snowfall (in.)	0.8	0.2	trace	trace	0.0	0.0	0.0	0.0	0.0	0.0	trace	trace	1.0
Days With ≥ 1.0" Snow Depth	0	0	0	0	0	0	0	0	0	0	0	0	0

Bastrop *Morehouse Parish*   Elevation: 147 ft.   Latitude: 32° 47' N   Longitude: 91° 54' W

	JAN	FEB	MAR	APR	MAY	JUN	JUL	AUG	SEP	OCT	NOV	DEC	YEAR
Mean Maximum Temp. (°F)	55.4	61.3	69.4	77.0	83.9	90.4	93.4	93.1	88.2	78.7	66.7	58.4	76.3
Mean Temp. (°F)	45.0	49.7	57.5	64.9	72.7	79.7	82.7	81.9	76.6	66.1	55.3	48.0	65.0
Mean Minimum Temp. (°F)	34.6	38.0	45.6	52.8	61.5	68.9	72.0	70.7	64.9	53.5	43.7	37.6	53.7
Extreme Maximum Temp. (°F)	84	86	93	94	98	101	105	105	105	96	89	83	105
Extreme Minimum Temp. (°F)	4	9	16	28	42	50	57	*51*	40	27	18	3	*3*
Days Maximum Temp. ≥ 90°F	0	0	0	0	5	19	26	25	15	2	0	0	92
Days Maximum Temp. ≤ 32°F	1	0	0	0	0	0	0	0	0	0	0	1	2
Days Minimum Temp. ≤ 32°F	14	9	3	0	0	0	0	0	0	0	4	11	41
Days Minimum Temp. ≤ 0°F	0	0	0	0	0	0	0	0	0	0	0	0	0
Heating Degree Days (base 65°F)	617	432	256	96	10	0	0	0	7	82	307	526	2,333
Cooling Degree Days (base 65°F)	2	8	26	90	248	443	557	531	349	118	19	7	2,398
Mean Precipitation (in.)	5.81	5.08	5.94	5.79	5.57	4.49	3.83	2.81	3.33	4.42	4.57	5.51	57.15
Days With ≥ 0.1" Precipitation	7	6	7	6	7	6	6	5	5	5	6	7	73
Days With ≥ 1.0" Precipitation	2	2	2	2	2	1	1	1	1	2	2	2	20
Mean Snowfall (in.)	*0.3*	trace	trace	0.0	0.0	0.0	0.0	0.0	0.0	0.0	trace	trace	*0.3*
Days With ≥ 1.0" Snow Depth	0	0	0	0	0	0	0	0	0	0	0	0	0

Bienville 3 NE *Bienville Parish*   Elevation: 305 ft.   Latitude: 32° 22' N   Longitude: 92° 57' W

	JAN	FEB	MAR	APR	MAY	JUN	JUL	AUG	SEP	OCT	NOV	DEC	YEAR
Mean Maximum Temp. (°F)	55.3	61.0	68.9	76.1	83.2	89.6	93.1	92.7	87.0	77.3	66.2	58.0	75.7
Mean Temp. (°F)	44.9	49.7	57.0	63.8	71.9	78.6	82.1	81.3	75.6	64.8	54.8	47.3	64.3
Mean Minimum Temp. (°F)	34.5	38.3	45.1	51.5	60.6	67.6	71.0	69.9	64.1	52.4	43.4	36.6	52.9
Extreme Maximum Temp. (°F)	81	87	93	93	101	102	106	109	103	96	85	82	109
Extreme Minimum Temp. (°F)	5	9	15	26	42	48	55	50	37	25	15	2	2
Days Maximum Temp. ≥ 90°F	0	0	0	0	4	17	26	24	13	1	0	0	85
Days Maximum Temp. ≤ 32°F	1	0	0	0	0	0	0	0	0	0	0	1	2
Days Minimum Temp. ≤ 32°F	15	9	3	1	0	0	0	0	0	0	5	13	46
Days Minimum Temp. ≤ 0°F	0	0	0	0	0	0	0	0	0	0	0	0	0
Heating Degree Days (base 65°F)	620	433	268	106	10	0	0	0	9	99	317	546	2,408
Cooling Degree Days (base 65°F)	2	7	24	78	229	418	537	518	340	101	18	6	2,278
Mean Precipitation (in.)	6.86	5.39	5.80	5.19	6.01	5.07	4.24	3.23	4.10	4.77	5.20	5.70	61.56
Days With ≥ 0.1" Precipitation	8	6	7	6	7	7	6	5	5	5	6	7	75
Days With ≥ 1.0" Precipitation	2	2	2	2	2	2	1	1	2	2	2	2	21
Mean Snowfall (in.)	0.5	*trace*	trace	0.0	0.0	0.0	0.0	0.0	0.0	0.0	trace	trace	*0.5*
Days With ≥ 1.0" Snow Depth	*0*	0	0	0	0	0	0	0	0	0	0	0	*0*

Bogalusa *Washington Parish*   Elevation: 98 ft.   Latitude: 30° 47' N   Longitude: 89° 52' W

	JAN	FEB	MAR	APR	MAY	JUN	JUL	AUG	SEP	OCT	NOV	DEC	YEAR
Mean Maximum Temp. (°F)	60.0	64.0	71.1	77.9	84.6	90.3	92.0	91.7	88.1	79.6	70.1	63.3	77.7
Mean Temp. (°F)	49.1	52.4	59.6	66.0	73.5	79.7	81.9	81.4	77.2	67.0	58.2	51.9	66.5
Mean Minimum Temp. (°F)	38.2	40.7	47.9	54.2	62.4	69.2	71.6	71.1	66.3	54.4	46.2	40.4	55.2
Extreme Maximum Temp. (°F)	86	83	91	93	98	100	105	101	101	94	87	84	105
Extreme Minimum Temp. (°F)	6	14	20	31	42	48	61	58	45	31	21	6	6
Days Maximum Temp. ≥ 90°F	0	0	0	0	6	17	25	24	15	2	0	0	89
Days Maximum Temp. ≤ 32°F	0	0	0	0	0	0	0	0	0	0	0	0	0
Days Minimum Temp. ≤ 32°F	11	7	2	0	0	0	0	0	0	0	3	9	32
Days Minimum Temp. ≤ 0°F	0	0	0	0	0	0	0	0	0	0	0	0	0
Heating Degree Days (base 65°F)	495	363	206	73	6	0	0	0	3	67	238	417	1,868
Cooling Degree Days (base 65°F)	7	14	43	100	279	446	536	524	369	142	38	19	2,517
Mean Precipitation (in.)	6.20	5.71	6.66	5.37	5.77	5.59	5.89	5.00	4.62	3.77	4.81	5.07	64.46
Days With ≥ 0.1" Precipitation	8	6	7	5	6	8	9	7	6	4	6	6	78
Days With ≥ 1.0" Precipitation	2	2	2	2	2	2	2	2	1	1	2	2	22
Mean Snowfall (in.)	0.2	trace	0.1	0.0	0.0	0.0	0.0	0.0	0.0	0.0	0.0	0.0	0.3
Days With ≥ 1.0" Snow Depth	0	0	0	0	0	0	0	0	0	0	0	0	0

Boyce 3 WNW *Rapides Parish*   Elevation: 108 ft.   Latitude: 31° 23' N   Longitude: 92° 43' W

	JAN	FEB	MAR	APR	MAY	JUN	JUL	AUG	SEP	OCT	NOV	DEC	YEAR
Mean Maximum Temp. (°F)	*57.3*	*62.6*	*70.2*	*77.7*	*84.4*	*90.3*	*93.2*	*92.7*	*87.8*	*78.6*	*68.1*	*60.5*	*77.0*
Mean Temp. (°F)	*47.8*	*52.7*	*59.6*	*67.0*	*74.5*	*80.7*	*83.5*	*82.8*	*77.6*	*67.5*	*57.9*	*50.9*	*66.9*
Mean Minimum Temp. (°F)	*38.3*	*42.7*	*48.8*	*56.1*	*64.4*	*70.9*	*73.7*	*72.9*	*67.3*	*56.3*	*47.8*	*41.2*	*56.7*
Extreme Maximum Temp. (°F)	*79*	*86*	*87*	*95*	*102*	*101*	*104*	*105*	*101*	*94*	*86*	*82*	*105*
Extreme Minimum Temp. (°F)	*9*	*15*	*23*	*31*	*43*	*55*	*59*	*56*	*43*	*30*	*23*	*7*	*7*
Days Maximum Temp. ≥ 90°F	*0*	*0*	*0*	*1*	*6*	*18*	*26*	*25*	*14*	*1*	*0*	*0*	*91*
Days Maximum Temp. ≤ 32°F	*0*	*0*	*0*	*0*	*0*	*0*	*0*	*0*	*0*	*0*	*0*	*0*	*0*
Days Minimum Temp. ≤ 32°F	*9*	*4*	*1*	*0*	*0*	*0*	*0*	*0*	*0*	*0*	*1*	*6*	*21*
Days Minimum Temp. ≤ 0°F	*0*	*0*	*0*	*0*	*0*	*0*	*0*	*0*	*0*	*0*	*0*	*0*	*0*
Heating Degree Days (base 65°F)	*531*	*353*	*200*	*54*	*3*	*0*	*0*	*0*	*2*	*57*	*233*	*440*	*1,873*
Cooling Degree Days (base 65°F)	*5*	*12*	*39*	*122*	*304*	*479*	*582*	*566*	*389*	*143*	*29*	*11*	*2,681*
Mean Precipitation (in.)	*6.03*	*4.65*	*5.47*	*4.83*	*4.98*	*4.43*	*4.25*	*3.90*	*4.42*	*4.59*	*5.75*	*5.81*	*59.11*
Days With ≥ 0.1" Precipitation	*8*	*6*	*6*	*5*	*6*	*6*	*6*	*6*	*5*	*5*	*6*	*7*	*72*
Days With ≥ 1.0" Precipitation	*2*	*2*	*2*	*2*	*2*	*1*	*1*	*1*	*1*	*2*	*2*	*2*	*20*
Mean Snowfall (in.)	*0.1*	*trace*	*trace*	*0.0*	*0.0*	*0.0*	*0.0*	*0.0*	*0.0*	*0.0*	*0.0*	*0.0*	*0.1*
Days With ≥ 1.0" Snow Depth	*0*	*0*	*0*	*0*	*0*	*0*	*0*	*0*	*0*	*0*	*0*	*0*	*0*

Bunkie *Avoyelles Parish*   Elevation: 78 ft.   Latitude: 30° 57' N   Longitude: 92° 10' W

	JAN	FEB	MAR	APR	MAY	JUN	JUL	AUG	SEP	OCT	NOV	DEC	YEAR
Mean Maximum Temp. (°F)	57.7	62.4	70.0	77.2	84.3	90.1	92.1	92.1	87.8	79.6	69.1	61.4	77.0
Mean Temp. (°F)	48.2	52.1	59.5	66.5	74.2	80.3	82.4	81.7	76.9	67.3	58.3	51.3	66.6
Mean Minimum Temp. (°F)	38.5	41.8	49.0	55.7	64.0	70.4	72.6	71.4	66.0	54.9	47.4	41.1	56.1
Extreme Maximum Temp. (°F)	80	85	88	93	99	100	103	105	100	96	88	82	105
Extreme Minimum Temp. (°F)	10	16	23	33	44	50	60	56	44	29	23	8	8
Days Maximum Temp. ≥ 90°F	0	0	0	1	5	18	24	23	14	2	0	0	87
Days Maximum Temp. ≤ 32°F	0	0	0	0	0	0	0	0	0	0	0	0	0
Days Minimum Temp. ≤ 32°F	10	5	1	0	0	0	0	0	0	0	2	7	25
Days Minimum Temp. ≤ 0°F	0	0	0	0	0	0	0	0	0	0	0	0	0
Heating Degree Days (base 65°F)	521	370	206	68	5	0	0	0	4	66	235	433	1,908
Cooling Degree Days (base 65°F)	5	12	43	117	304	464	548	534	362	146	39	14	2,588
Mean Precipitation (in.)	6.61	4.87	5.77	5.64	6.20	5.09	3.89	3.95	4.52	4.78	5.35	6.17	62.84
Days With ≥ 0.1" Precipitation	7	6	6	5	6	7	7	6	6	4	6	7	73
Days With ≥ 1.0" Precipitation	2	2	2	2	2	2	1	1	1	2	2	2	21
Mean Snowfall (in.)	trace	trace	0.0	0.0	0.0	0.0	0.0	0.0	0.0	0.0	trace	0.0	trace
Days With ≥ 1.0" Snow Depth	0	0	0	0	0	0	0	0	0	0	0	0	0

Calhoun Research Station *Ouachita Parish* Elevation: 177 ft. Latitude: 32° 31' N Longitude: 92° 21' W

	JAN	FEB	MAR	APR	MAY	JUN	JUL	AUG	SEP	OCT	NOV	DEC	YEAR
Mean Maximum Temp. (°F)	55.0	60.7	68.3	76.2	83.0	89.8	93.1	93.2	87.8	77.7	66.9	58.5	75.9
Mean Temp. (°F)	44.2	48.6	56.2	63.6	71.5	78.7	82.0	81.4	75.7	64.4	54.8	47.3	64.0
Mean Minimum Temp. (°F)	33.3	36.5	44.1	51.0	59.9	67.5	71.0	69.6	63.6	51.1	42.7	36.1	52.2
Extreme Maximum Temp. (°F)	83	86	89	94	96	102	105	108	104	96	87	84	108
Extreme Minimum Temp. (°F)	4	9	15	27	40	49	54	50	40	26	16	5	4
Days Maximum Temp. ≥ 90°F	0	0	0	0	4	18	25	25	14	2	0	0	88
Days Maximum Temp. ≤ 32°F	1	0	0	0	0	0	0	0	0	0	0	1	2
Days Minimum Temp. ≤ 32°F	16	11	4	1	0	0	0	0	0	0	5	13	50
Days Minimum Temp. ≤ 0°F	0	0	0	0	0	0	0	0	0	0	0	0	0
Heating Degree Days (base 65°F)	642	462	290	117	17	0	0	0	9	110	320	547	2,514
Cooling Degree Days (base 65°F)	2	8	26	80	230	423	547	528	338	99	20	7	2,308
Mean Precipitation (in.)	5.69	4.86	5.64	4.67	5.34	4.37	3.86	3.21	3.34	4.50	4.37	5.27	55.12
Days With ≥ 0.1" Precipitation	8	6	7	6	6	6	6	5	4	5	6	7	72
Days With ≥ 1.0" Precipitation	2	2	2	2	2	1	1	1	1	1	1	2	18
Mean Snowfall (in.)	0.5	0.1	trace	trace	0.0	0.0	0.0	0.0	0.0	0.0	trace	trace	0.6
Days With ≥ 1.0" Snow Depth	0	0	0	0	0	0	0	0	0	0	0	0	0

Carville 2 SW *Iberville Parish* Elevation: 22 ft. Latitude: 30° 12' N Longitude: 91° 07' W

	JAN	FEB	MAR	APR	MAY	JUN	JUL	AUG	SEP	OCT	NOV	DEC	YEAR
Mean Maximum Temp. (°F)	60.6	64.6	71.3	77.9	84.6	89.6	91.2	91.2	87.7	79.8	70.7	64.0	77.8
Mean Temp. (°F)	50.6	54.2	60.7	67.4	74.8	80.3	82.3	82.1	78.4	69.1	60.2	53.9	67.8
Mean Minimum Temp. (°F)	40.6	43.7	50.1	56.9	64.9	71.0	73.3	72.9	69.0	58.3	49.7	43.9	57.9
Extreme Maximum Temp. (°F)	82	84	86	91	96	98	100	100	97	95	87	82	100
Extreme Minimum Temp. (°F)	10	17	23	34	43	55	62	61	49	35	22	13	10
Days Maximum Temp. ≥ 90°F	0	0	0	0	3	17	23	23	13	1	0	0	80
Days Maximum Temp. ≤ 32°F	0	0	0	0	0	0	0	0	0	0	0	0	0
Days Minimum Temp. ≤ 32°F	7	3	1	0	0	0	0	0	0	0	1	4	16
Days Minimum Temp. ≤ 0°F	0	0	0	0	0	0	0	0	0	0	0	0	0
Heating Degree Days (base 65°F)	445	310	163	45	1	0	0	0	1	36	186	353	1,540
Cooling Degree Days (base 65°F)	4	11	35	122	316	468	548	544	404	168	47	18	2,685
Mean Precipitation (in.)	5.81	4.79	4.96	4.82	4.87	6.19	6.08	5.59	4.55	4.01	4.43	4.96	61.06
Days With ≥ 0.1" Precipitation	7	6	6	5	6	8	9	8	7	5	5	6	78
Days With ≥ 1.0" Precipitation	2	2	2	2	2	2	2	1	1	1	2	2	21
Mean Snowfall (in.)	trace	0.1	0.0	0.0	0.0	0.0	0.0	0.0	0.0	0.0	0.0	trace	0.1
Days With ≥ 1.0" Snow Depth	0	0	0	0	0	0	0	0	0	0	0	0	0

Clinton 5 SE *East Feliciana Parish* Elevation: 200 ft. Latitude: 30° 49' N Longitude: 90° 58' W

	JAN	FEB	MAR	APR	MAY	JUN	JUL	AUG	SEP	OCT	NOV	DEC	YEAR
Mean Maximum Temp. (°F)	58.4	62.9	70.1	76.7	83.4	89.0	91.1	91.2	87.4	78.8	69.6	62.0	76.7
Mean Temp. (°F)	47.6	52.0	58.8	65.4	72.8	78.7	81.1	80.8	76.6	66.7	58.3	51.1	65.8
Mean Minimum Temp. (°F)	36.8	41.0	47.5	53.9	62.2	68.3	71.0	70.4	65.8	54.6	46.9	40.1	54.9
Extreme Maximum Temp. (°F)	80	85	87	91	95	100	102	102	99	93	85	82	102
Extreme Minimum Temp. (°F)	6	11	18	28	43	48	60	58	43	28	20	1	1
Days Maximum Temp. ≥ 90°F	0	0	0	0	2	15	23	23	13	1	0	0	77
Days Maximum Temp. ≤ 32°F	0	0	0	0	0	0	0	0	0	0	0	0	0
Days Minimum Temp. ≤ 32°F	12	7	2	0	0	0	0	0	0	0	3	9	33
Days Minimum Temp. ≤ 0°F	0	0	0	0	0	0	0	0	0	0	0	0	0
Heating Degree Days (base 65°F)	536	373	220	80	6	0	0	0	4	70	233	440	1,962
Cooling Degree Days (base 65°F)	4	12	37	95	258	417	508	502	361	136	38	17	2,385
Mean Precipitation (in.)	6.84	5.54	5.44	6.14	5.60	5.07	5.26	5.35	4.16	4.41	4.76	5.18	63.75
Days With ≥ 0.1" Precipitation	8	7	7	5	7	7	8	8	6	4	6	7	80
Days With ≥ 1.0" Precipitation	2	2	2	2	2	2	1	1	1	1	2	2	20
Mean Snowfall (in.)	0.1	trace	0.0	0.0	0.0	0.0	0.0	0.0	0.0	0.0	0.0	0.0	0.1
Days With ≥ 1.0" Snow Depth	0	0	0	0	0	0	0	0	0	0	0	0	0

Covington 4 NNW *St. Tammany Parish* Elevation: 39 ft. Latitude: 30° 32' N Longitude: 90° 07' W

	JAN	FEB	MAR	APR	MAY	JUN	JUL	AUG	SEP	OCT	NOV	DEC	YEAR
Mean Maximum Temp. (°F)	61.6	65.9	72.6	78.6	85.0	90.0	91.6	91.4	87.7	80.1	70.7	64.8	78.3
Mean Temp. (°F)	50.6	54.0	60.6	66.5	73.4	79.0	81.2	81.0	77.2	67.8	59.1	53.7	67.0
Mean Minimum Temp. (°F)	39.6	42.0	48.5	54.3	61.8	68.0	70.7	70.5	66.5	55.4	47.5	42.4	55.6
Extreme Maximum Temp. (°F)	80	83	88	93	97	99	103	103	100	94	88	82	103
Extreme Minimum Temp. (°F)	7	10	17	28	40	46	58	57	41	29	21	11	7
Days Maximum Temp. ≥ 90°F	0	0	0	0	3	17	24	24	12	1	0	0	81
Days Maximum Temp. ≤ 32°F	0	0	0	0	0	0	0	0	0	0	0	0	0
Days Minimum Temp. ≤ 32°F	10	6	2	0	0	0	0	0	0	0	3	8	29
Days Minimum Temp. ≤ 0°F	0	0	0	0	0	0	0	0	0	0	0	0	0
Heating Degree Days (base 65°F)	448	319	179	61	4	0	0	0	2	53	213	365	1,644
Cooling Degree Days (base 65°F)	7	14	47	108	279	431	517	511	369	151	43	21	2,498
Mean Precipitation (in.)	5.70	5.55	6.50	5.28	5.72	5.11	6.80	5.59	4.72	3.55	4.60	5.22	64.34
Days With ≥ 0.1" Precipitation	8	6	7	5	6	7	10	8	6	4	5	6	78
Days With ≥ 1.0" Precipitation	2	2	2	2	2	2	2	1	2	1	2	2	22
Mean Snowfall (in.)	0.1	0.1	trace	trace	0.0	0.0	0.0	0.0	0.0	0.0	trace	trace	0.2
Days With ≥ 1.0" Snow Depth	0	0	0	0	0	0	0	0	0	0	0	0	0

Crowley 2 NE *Acadia Parish*   Elevation: 22 ft.   Latitude: 30° 15' N   Longitude: 92° 22' W

	JAN	FEB	MAR	APR	MAY	JUN	JUL	AUG	SEP	OCT	NOV	DEC	YEAR
Mean Maximum Temp. (°F)	59.3	63.1	70.3	77.4	84.2	89.4	90.9	91.2	87.8	80.4	70.2	63.0	77.3
Mean Temp. (°F)	49.7	53.0	60.3	67.4	74.8	80.3	81.9	81.5	77.9	68.8	59.7	52.9	67.3
Mean Minimum Temp. (°F)	40.0	42.9	50.3	57.3	65.4	71.2	72.8	71.9	67.9	57.1	49.0	42.8	57.4
Extreme Maximum Temp. (°F)	80	83	85	94	97	102	102	100	99	96	88	82	102
Extreme Minimum Temp. (°F)	10	15	22	36	46	54	62	60	45	29	22	9	9
Days Maximum Temp. ≥ 90°F	0	0	0	0	4	16	22	23	14	2	0	0	81
Days Maximum Temp. ≤ 32°F	0	0	0	0	0	0	0	0	0	0	0	0	0
Days Minimum Temp. ≤ 32°F	8	4	1	0	0	0	0	0	0	0	1	5	19
Days Minimum Temp. ≤ 0°F	0	0	0	0	0	0	0	0	0	0	0	0	0
Heating Degree Days (base 65°F)	476	343	183	53	3	0	0	0	2	48	205	387	1,700
Cooling Degree Days (base 65°F)	7	14	48	131	324	474	537	536	402	179	53	21	2,726
Mean Precipitation (in.)	6.27	4.20	4.49	4.37	5.79	5.42	5.73	5.24	5.02	4.33	4.74	5.10	60.70
Days With ≥ 0.1" Precipitation	7	6	6	5	6	7	9	8	7	5	6	6	78
Days With ≥ 1.0" Precipitation	2	1	1	1	2	2	2	2	2	2	2	1	20
Mean Snowfall (in.)	trace	trace	0.0	0.0	0.0	0.0	0.0	0.0	0.0	0.0	0.0	trace	trace
Days With ≥ 1.0" Snow Depth	0	0	0	0	0	0	0	0	0	0	0	0	0

De Quincy *Calcasieu Parish*   Elevation: 78 ft.   Latitude: 30° 26' N   Longitude: 93° 28' W

	JAN	FEB	MAR	APR	MAY	JUN	JUL	AUG	SEP	OCT	NOV	DEC	YEAR
Mean Maximum Temp. (°F)	59.7	63.5	70.8	77.8	84.6	89.9	92.3	92.4	88.1	79.9	70.4	63.3	77.7
Mean Temp. (°F)	48.6	51.7	59.2	65.8	73.3	79.2	81.6	81.4	76.9	67.1	58.5	51.8	66.3
Mean Minimum Temp. (°F)	37.4	39.8	47.4	53.9	62.0	68.4	70.9	70.3	65.7	54.4	46.4	40.3	54.7
Extreme Maximum Temp. (°F)	81	84	91	93	96	101	105	104	100	95	88	85	105
Extreme Minimum Temp. (°F)	10	14	21	31	41	50	61	56	43	28	19	9	9
Days Maximum Temp. ≥ 90°F	0	0	0	0	5	18	25	25	15	2	0	0	90
Days Maximum Temp. ≤ 32°F	0	0	0	0	0	0	0	0	0	0	0	0	0
Days Minimum Temp. ≤ 32°F	12	8	3	0	0	0	0	0	0	0	3	9	35
Days Minimum Temp. ≤ 0°F	0	0	0	0	0	0	0	0	0	0	0	0	0
Heating Degree Days (base 65°F)	510	379	209	na	5	0	0	0	4	66	229	417	na
Cooling Degree Days (base 65°F)	5	14	34	99	276	431	524	529	368	140	41	16	2,477
Mean Precipitation (in.)	5.74	3.88	4.34	3.45	5.25	5.86	5.29	5.21	6.01	5.46	5.04	5.64	61.17
Days With ≥ 0.1" Precipitation	8	6	7	4	6	7	8	8	7	5	6	7	79
Days With ≥ 1.0" Precipitation	2	1	1	1	2	2	2	2	2	2	2	2	21
Mean Snowfall (in.)	trace	trace	0.0	0.0	0.0	0.0	0.0	0.0	0.0	0.0	0.0	0.0	trace
Days With ≥ 1.0" Snow Depth	0	0	0	0	0	0	0	0	0	0	0	0	0

De Ridder *Beauregard Parish*   Elevation: 187 ft.   Latitude: 30° 50' N   Longitude: 93° 17' W

	JAN	FEB	MAR	APR	MAY	JUN	JUL	AUG	SEP	OCT	NOV	DEC	YEAR
Mean Maximum Temp. (°F)	59.1	63.8	71.0	77.5	84.1	89.5	92.2	92.2	88.0	79.7	69.6	62.4	77.4
Mean Temp. (°F)	48.3	52.2	59.4	66.1	73.5	79.3	81.9	81.6	77.0	67.3	58.0	51.2	66.3
Mean Minimum Temp. (°F)	37.5	40.5	47.7	54.6	62.7	69.1	71.6	71.0	66.1	54.9	46.4	39.9	55.2
Extreme Maximum Temp. (°F)	80	86	92	93	97	100	105	106	101	95	88	83	106
Extreme Minimum Temp. (°F)	10	15	21	30	42	50	62	54	41	28	20	7	7
Days Maximum Temp. ≥ 90°F	0	0	0	0	3	17	25	25	15	2	0	0	87
Days Maximum Temp. ≤ 32°F	0	0	0	0	0	0	0	0	0	0	0	0	0
Days Minimum Temp. ≤ 32°F	11	7	2	0	0	0	0	0	0	0	2	8	30
Days Minimum Temp. ≤ 0°F	0	0	0	0	0	0	0	0	0	0	0	0	0
Heating Degree Days (base 65°F)	516	367	205	69	5	0	0	0	3	62	238	433	1,898
Cooling Degree Days (base 65°F)	5	14	40	105	285	445	542	537	370	141	34	15	2,533
Mean Precipitation (in.)	6.24	4.72	5.27	3.99	5.36	5.26	5.24	4.25	4.85	4.45	4.96	6.67	61.26
Days With ≥ 0.1" Precipitation	8	6	7	5	6	7	8	6	6	5	6	7	77
Days With ≥ 1.0" Precipitation	2	2	2	1	2	2	2	1	1	1	2	2	20
Mean Snowfall (in.)	0.1	trace	trace	0.0	0.0	0.0	0.0	0.0	0.0	0.0	0.0	trace	0.1
Days With ≥ 1.0" Snow Depth	0	0	0	0	0	0	0	0	0	0	0	0	0

Donaldsonville 4 SW *Assumption Parish*   Elevation: 29 ft.   Latitude: 30° 04' N   Longitude: 91° 02' W

	JAN	FEB	MAR	APR	MAY	JUN	JUL	AUG	SEP	OCT	NOV	DEC	YEAR
Mean Maximum Temp. (°F)	61.4	64.7	71.5	78.1	84.5	89.4	91.1	91.1	87.8	79.9	71.4	64.7	78.0
Mean Temp. (°F)	51.4	54.3	61.0	67.8	74.8	80.5	82.3	82.0	78.5	69.0	60.8	54.2	68.0
Mean Minimum Temp. (°F)	41.3	43.8	50.5	57.3	65.0	71.5	73.5	72.9	69.2	58.1	50.2	43.7	58.1
Extreme Maximum Temp. (°F)	83	83	88	94	96	98	99	100	98	94	88	85	100
Extreme Minimum Temp. (°F)	10	15	24	33	45	56	62	60	49	34	25	9	9
Days Maximum Temp. ≥ 90°F	0	0	0	1	3	17	24	23	13	2	0	0	83
Days Maximum Temp. ≤ 32°F	0	0	0	0	0	0	0	0	0	0	0	0	0
Days Minimum Temp. ≤ 32°F	7	3	1	0	0	0	0	0	0	0	0	4	15
Days Minimum Temp. ≤ 0°F	0	0	0	0	0	0	0	0	0	0	0	0	0
Heating Degree Days (base 65°F)	427	311	169	48	2	0	0	0	1	43	178	352	1,531
Cooling Degree Days (base 65°F)	10	16	49	124	313	464	543	534	399	168	54	23	2,697
Mean Precipitation (in.)	5.73	4.65	5.28	5.21	4.62	5.55	6.56	5.63	5.46	4.00	4.18	4.95	61.82
Days With ≥ 0.1" Precipitation	7	6	6	5	6	8	10	9	7	4	6	6	80
Days With ≥ 1.0" Precipitation	2	2	1	2	2	2	2	2	2	1	1	2	21
Mean Snowfall (in.)	trace	trace	trace	0.0	0.0	0.0	0.0	0.0	0.0	0.0	0.0	trace	trace
Days With ≥ 1.0" Snow Depth	0	0	0	0	0	0	0	0	0	0	0	0	0

Elizabeth *Allen Parish*   Elevation: 147 ft.   Latitude: 30° 51' N   Longitude: 92° 47' W

	JAN	FEB	MAR	APR	MAY	JUN	JUL	AUG	SEP	OCT	NOV	DEC	YEAR
Mean Maximum Temp. (°F)	59.1	63.9	71.4	78.0	84.4	90.1	92.7	92.7	88.5	80.1	70.2	63.0	77.8
Mean Temp. (°F)	48.0	52.0	59.5	65.9	73.4	79.4	81.9	81.5	77.0	67.1	58.0	51.3	66.2
Mean Minimum Temp. (°F)	36.8	40.1	47.5	53.8	62.3	68.6	71.0	70.4	65.5	54.0	45.8	39.6	54.6
Extreme Maximum Temp. (°F)	81	86	91	93	99	101	105	104	100	95	90	83	105
Extreme Minimum Temp. (°F)	9	12	21	30	42	49	58	54	42	28	22	8	8
Days Maximum Temp. ≥ 90°F	0	0	0	0	4	18	26	25	16	0	0	0	91
Days Maximum Temp. ≤ 32°F	0	0	0	0	0	0	0	0	0	0	0	0	0
Days Minimum Temp. ≤ 32°F	13	7	2	0	0	0	0	0	0	0	3	9	34
Days Minimum Temp. ≤ 0°F	0	0	0	0	0	0	0	0	0	0	0	0	0
Heating Degree Days (base 65°F)	527	372	205	73	6	0	0	0	4	66	238	430	1,921
Cooling Degree Days (base 65°F)	5	14	40	104	277	443	536	531	370	138	35	15	2,508
Mean Precipitation (in.)	6.28	4.62	5.27	4.62	6.10	5.72	4.85	4.40	4.90	5.35	5.62	6.43	64.16
Days With ≥ 0.1" Precipitation	8	6	6	5	6	7	7	6	6	5	6	7	75
Days With ≥ 1.0" Precipitation	2	2	2	1	2	2	1	1	2	1	2	2	20
Mean Snowfall (in.)	0.2	trace	trace	0.0	0.0	0.0	0.0	0.0	0.0	0.0	0.0	trace	0.2
Days With ≥ 1.0" Snow Depth	0	0	0	0	0	0	0	0	0	0	0	0	0

Franklin 3 NW *St. Mary Parish*   Elevation: 9 ft.   Latitude: 29° 49' N   Longitude: 91° 33' W

	JAN	FEB	MAR	APR	MAY	JUN	JUL	AUG	SEP	OCT	NOV	DEC	YEAR
Mean Maximum Temp. (°F)	61.5	64.9	71.5	77.5	83.8	88.4	90.0	90.0	86.8	79.6	71.2	64.8	77.5
Mean Temp. (°F)	52.0	55.2	61.5	67.8	74.9	80.1	81.8	81.5	78.0	69.1	60.7	54.9	68.1
Mean Minimum Temp. (°F)	42.6	45.4	51.6	58.0	65.9	71.7	73.4	73.0	69.2	58.6	50.2	45.0	58.7
Extreme Maximum Temp. (°F)	82	82	86	92	95	98	100	98	98	93	89	84	100
Extreme Minimum Temp. (°F)	12	15	22	34	45	57	60	62	46	33	25	10	10
Days Maximum Temp. ≥ 90°F	0	0	0	0	2	12	19	19	10	1	0	0	63
Days Maximum Temp. ≤ 32°F	0	0	0	0	0	0	0	0	0	0	0	0	0
Days Minimum Temp. ≤ 32°F	5	3	1	0	0	0	0	0	0	0	1	3	13
Days Minimum Temp. ≤ 0°F	0	0	0	0	0	0	0	0	0	0	0	0	0
Heating Degree Days (base 65°F)	407	285	153	43	1	0	0	0	1	39	180	331	1,440
Cooling Degree Days (base 65°F)	10	14	52	126	314	456	527	523	391	173	55	24	2,665
Mean Precipitation (in.)	5.34	3.97	4.84	5.11	5.13	7.05	7.39	8.12	6.09	3.89	4.06	4.84	65.83
Days With ≥ 0.1" Precipitation	7	5	6	4	6	9	11	10	8	5	5	6	82
Days With ≥ 1.0" Precipitation	2	1	2	2	2	2	3	3	2	1	1	2	23
Mean Snowfall (in.)	trace	trace	0.0	0.0	0.0	0.0	0.0	0.0	0.0	0.0	0.0	trace	trace
Days With ≥ 1.0" Snow Depth	0	0	0	0	0	0	0	0	0	0	0	0	0

Franklinton 3 SW *Washington Parish*   Elevation: 144 ft.   Latitude: 30° 49' N   Longitude: 90° 11' W

	JAN	FEB	MAR	APR	MAY	JUN	JUL	AUG	SEP	OCT	NOV	DEC	YEAR
Mean Maximum Temp. (°F)	59.9	64.4	72.1	78.7	85.4	91.1	92.8	92.1	88.0	79.4	69.9	63.3	78.1
Mean Temp. (°F)	48.6	52.2	59.6	65.9	73.1	79.0	81.3	80.6	76.5	66.4	57.5	51.6	66.0
Mean Minimum Temp. (°F)	37.2	40.0	47.0	53.0	60.9	66.9	69.8	69.1	65.0	53.4	45.0	40.0	53.9
Extreme Maximum Temp. (°F)	85	86	89	96	99	101	103	104	101	96	89	84	104
Extreme Minimum Temp. (°F)	7	11	18	30	40	48	59	57	42	31	17	6	6
Days Maximum Temp. ≥ 90°F	0	0	0	1	7	21	25	24	14	2	0	0	94
Days Maximum Temp. ≤ 32°F	0	0	0	0	0	0	0	0	0	0	0	0	0
Days Minimum Temp. ≤ 32°F	12	8	3	0	0	0	0	0	0	0	4	10	37
Days Minimum Temp. ≤ 0°F	0	0	0	0	0	0	0	0	0	0	0	0	0
Heating Degree Days (base 65°F)	510	365	205	71	5	0	0	0	3	72	257	423	1,911
Cooling Degree Days (base 65°F)	6	12	43	102	275	432	529	506	356	131	42	16	2,450
Mean Precipitation (in.)	5.89	5.57	6.74	6.37	5.99	5.38	5.61	5.38	3.87	3.81	5.45	5.51	65.57
Days With ≥ 0.1" Precipitation	8	7	7	6	6	8	9	8	7	5	6	7	84
Days With ≥ 1.0" Precipitation	2	2	3	2	2	2	2	2	1	1	2	2	23
Mean Snowfall (in.)	0.2	0.1	trace	0.0	0.0	0.0	0.0	0.0	0.0	0.0	0.0	0.0	0.3
Days With ≥ 1.0" Snow Depth	0	0	0	0	0	0	0	0	0	0	0	0	0

Galliano *Lafourche Parish*   Elevation: 3 ft.   Latitude: 29° 27' N   Longitude: 90° 18' W

	JAN	FEB	MAR	APR	MAY	JUN	JUL	AUG	SEP	OCT	NOV	DEC	YEAR
Mean Maximum Temp. (°F)	62.3	65.2	71.2	76.9	83.3	88.1	90.0	89.8	86.7	79.5	71.6	65.5	77.5
Mean Temp. (°F)	52.8	55.7	61.9	67.9	74.7	80.0	81.9	81.9	78.8	70.0	62.0	55.9	68.6
Mean Minimum Temp. (°F)	43.3	46.2	52.6	58.9	66.2	71.8	73.8	74.0	70.8	60.4	52.3	46.2	59.7
Extreme Maximum Temp. (°F)	83	82	86	91	95	98	100	100	97	94	86	82	100
Extreme Minimum Temp. (°F)	14	19	26	35	48	50	65	62	52	34	24	10	10
Days Maximum Temp. ≥ 90°F	0	0	0	0	1	10	18	19	8	1	0	0	57
Days Maximum Temp. ≤ 32°F	0	0	0	0	0	0	0	0	0	0	0	0	0
Days Minimum Temp. ≤ 32°F	5	2	1	0	0	0	0	0	0	0	0	3	11
Days Minimum Temp. ≤ 0°F	0	0	0	0	0	0	0	0	0	0	0	0	0
Heating Degree Days (base 65°F)	386	271	143	42	1	0	0	0	0	28	150	302	1,323
Cooling Degree Days (base 65°F)	11	17	54	129	311	454	532	531	407	188	67	30	2,731
Mean Precipitation (in.)	5.90	4.56	5.68	4.44	6.00	5.65	7.78	7.50	6.37	3.84	4.48	4.03	66.23
Days With ≥ 0.1" Precipitation	7	6	6	4	5	8	11	10	8	4	5	5	79
Days With ≥ 1.0" Precipitation	2	2	2	1	2	2	2	2	2	1	2	1	21
Mean Snowfall (in.)	trace	trace	0.0	0.0	0.0	0.0	0.0	0.0	0.0	0.0	0.0	trace	trace
Days With ≥ 1.0" Snow Depth	0	0	0	0	0	0	0	0	0	0	0	0	0

Grand Coteau *St. Landry Parish*   Elevation: 52 ft.   Latitude: 30° 26' N   Longitude: 92° 02' W

	JAN	FEB	MAR	APR	MAY	JUN	JUL	AUG	SEP	OCT	NOV	DEC	YEAR
Mean Maximum Temp. (°F)	61.1	65.1	72.0	78.6	85.4	90.2	91.9	92.4	88.4	80.8	71.2	64.6	78.5
Mean Temp. (°F)	51.1	54.5	61.2	67.6	74.8	80.1	82.1	82.1	77.9	68.8	60.1	54.0	67.8
Mean Minimum Temp. (°F)	41.0	43.8	50.4	56.5	64.2	69.9	72.2	71.7	67.3	56.8	48.9	43.3	57.2
Extreme Maximum Temp. (°F)	80	82	86	93	99	100	101	104	101	96	89	84	104
Extreme Minimum Temp. (°F)	10	13	20	30	44	52	61	58	44	29	20	8	8
Days Maximum Temp. ≥ 90°F	0	0	0	0	5	19	24	25	15	2	0	0	90
Days Maximum Temp. ≤ 32°F	0	0	0	0	0	0	0	0	0	0	0	0	0
Days Minimum Temp. ≤ 32°F	8	4	1	0	0	0	0	0	0	0	2	6	21
Days Minimum Temp. ≤ 0°F	0	0	0	0	0	0	0	0	0	0	0	0	0
Heating Degree Days (base 65°F)	436	306	164	49	2	0	0	0	1	43	194	358	1,553
Cooling Degree Days (base 65°F)	11	18	54	136	321	466	547	556	396	169	53	23	2,750
Mean Precipitation (in.)	6.50	4.61	4.88	5.14	5.90	5.83	5.95	4.71	4.82	4.68	5.09	5.48	63.59
Days With ≥ 0.1" Precipitation	8	6	7	5	6	8	8	7	6	5	6	6	78
Days With ≥ 1.0" Precipitation	2	2	2	1	2	2	2	1	1	1	2	2	20
Mean Snowfall (in.)	trace	trace	trace	0.0	0.0	0.0	0.0	0.0	0.0	0.0	0.0	trace	trace
Days With ≥ 1.0" Snow Depth	0	0	0	0	0	0	0	0	0	0	0	0	0

Hackberry 8 SSW *Cameron Parish*   Elevation: 3 ft.   Latitude: 29° 53' N   Longitude: 93° 25' W

	JAN	FEB	MAR	APR	MAY	JUN	JUL	AUG	SEP	OCT	NOV	DEC	YEAR
Mean Maximum Temp. (°F)	58.9	62.8	69.2	75.6	82.2	87.8	90.1	90.3	87.0	79.3	70.1	62.6	76.3
Mean Temp. (°F)	51.1	54.6	61.3	68.2	75.4	81.3	83.0	82.9	79.4	70.7	61.6	54.4	68.7
Mean Minimum Temp. (°F)	43.2	46.3	53.4	60.9	68.5	74.7	75.9	75.5	71.8	62.0	53.0	46.2	60.9
Extreme Maximum Temp. (°F)	82	80	83	93	94	98	99	103	99	98	88	81	103
Extreme Minimum Temp. (°F)	13	20	25	37	47	60	63	66	50	32	20	12	12
Days Maximum Temp. ≥ 90°F	0	0	0	0	1	9	20	20	9	1	0	0	60
Days Maximum Temp. ≤ 32°F	0	0	0	0	0	0	0	0	0	0	0	0	0
Days Minimum Temp. ≤ 32°F	4	2	0	0	0	0	0	0	0	0	0	2	8
Days Minimum Temp. ≤ 0°F	0	0	0	0	0	0	0	0	0	0	0	0	0
Heating Degree Days (base 65°F)	431	295	149	35	2	0	0	0	0	30	161	337	1,440
Cooling Degree Days (base 65°F)	4	9	44	137	338	507	580	581	448	219	66	18	2,951
Mean Precipitation (in.)	5.74	3.51	3.88	3.98	4.92	6.58	6.58	5.56	5.61	4.58	4.30	4.49	59.73
Days With ≥ 0.1" Precipitation	7	6	5	4	6	7	8	8	6	5	5	6	73
Days With ≥ 1.0" Precipitation	2	1	1	1	2	2	2	2	2	2	1	1	19
Mean Snowfall (in.)	0.1	trace	0.0	0.0	0.0	0.0	0.0	0.0	0.0	0.0	0.0	0.0	0.1
Days With ≥ 1.0" Snow Depth	0	0	0	0	0	0	0	0	0	0	0	0	0

Homer 3 SSW *Claiborne Parish*   Elevation: 377 ft.   Latitude: 32° 45' N   Longitude: 93° 04' W

	JAN	FEB	MAR	APR	MAY	JUN	JUL	AUG	SEP	OCT	NOV	DEC	YEAR
Mean Maximum Temp. (°F)	54.0	59.3	67.3	75.1	81.8	88.3	92.0	92.3	86.6	76.6	65.6	57.4	74.7
Mean Temp. (°F)	43.4	47.6	55.2	62.8	70.5	77.5	81.2	80.7	74.9	64.0	54.0	46.4	63.2
Mean Minimum Temp. (°F)	32.6	36.0	43.2	50.6	59.2	66.7	70.4	69.2	63.2	51.3	42.3	35.4	51.7
Extreme Maximum Temp. (°F)	81	84	90	93	96	100	104	105	103	93	88	80	105
Extreme Minimum Temp. (°F)	2	9	16	27	40	50	55	50	40	26	15	1	1
Days Maximum Temp. ≥ 90°F	0	0	0	0	2	14	24	24	13	1	0	0	78
Days Maximum Temp. ≤ 32°F	1	1	0	0	0	0	0	0	0	0	0	1	3
Days Minimum Temp. ≤ 32°F	17	11	5	1	0	0	0	0	0	0	6	13	53
Days Minimum Temp. ≤ 0°F	0	0	0	0	0	0	0	0	0	0	0	0	0
Heating Degree Days (base 65°F)	666	489	314	124	20	0	0	0	13	114	339	574	2,653
Cooling Degree Days (base 65°F)	2	4	18	63	194	384	516	507	320	89	15	5	2,117
Mean Precipitation (in.)	5.22	4.83	5.22	4.93	4.96	4.70	4.24	2.88	3.87	4.35	5.02	4.83	55.05
Days With ≥ 0.1" Precipitation	7	6	7	6	7	6	6	5	5	5	6	7	73
Days With ≥ 1.0" Precipitation	2	2	1	2	2	2	2	1	1	2	2	2	21
Mean Snowfall (in.)	0.5	0.1	trace	0.0	0.0	0.0	0.0	0.0	0.0	0.0	0.0	0.2	0.8
Days With ≥ 1.0" Snow Depth	0	0	0	0	0	0	0	0	0	0	0	0	0

Houma *Terrebonne Parish*   Elevation: 13 ft.   Latitude: 29° 35' N   Longitude: 90° 44' W

	JAN	FEB	MAR	APR	MAY	JUN	JUL	AUG	SEP	OCT	NOV	DEC	YEAR
Mean Maximum Temp. (°F)	62.4	65.5	71.6	77.5	84.1	88.8	90.6	90.4	87.2	79.9	72.1	65.9	78.0
Mean Temp. (°F)	52.6	55.6	62.2	68.2	75.2	80.2	81.9	81.6	78.4	69.4	61.7	55.5	68.5
Mean Minimum Temp. (°F)	42.7	45.7	52.7	58.7	66.3	71.5	73.1	72.8	69.5	58.9	51.3	45.1	59.0
Extreme Maximum Temp. (°F)	82	86	86	92	94	96	99	99	100	97	87	84	100
Extreme Minimum Temp. (°F)	13	19	23	34	46	53	65	59	50	32	26	10	10
Days Maximum Temp. ≥ 90°F	0	0	0	0	3	14	21	20	11	1	0	0	70
Days Maximum Temp. ≤ 32°F	0	0	0	0	0	0	0	0	0	0	0	0	0
Days Minimum Temp. ≤ 32°F	6	3	1	0	0	0	0	0	0	0	1	4	15
Days Minimum Temp. ≤ 0°F	0	0	0	0	0	0	0	0	0	0	0	0	0
Heating Degree Days (base 65°F)	393	278	142	42	2	0	0	0	1	38	159	315	1,370
Cooling Degree Days (base 65°F)	14	21	62	135	334	464	539	533	408	189	69	30	2,798
Mean Precipitation (in.)	5.50	4.65	4.87	4.45	5.51	5.89	7.97	6.82	6.37	3.25	4.14	4.37	63.79
Days With ≥ 0.1" Precipitation	7	5	6	4	5	8	11	11	8	4	5	6	80
Days With ≥ 1.0" Precipitation	2	2	2	1	2	2	3	2	2	1	2	1	22
Mean Snowfall (in.)	trace	trace	0.0	0.0	0.0	0.0	0.0	0.0	0.0	0.0	0.0	0.1	0.1
Days With ≥ 1.0" Snow Depth	0	0	0	0	0	0	0	0	0	0	0	0	0

Jeanerette 5 NW *Iberia Parish*   Elevation: 19 ft.   Latitude: 29° 57' N   Longitude: 91° 43' W

	JAN	FEB	MAR	APR	MAY	JUN	JUL	AUG	SEP	OCT	NOV	DEC	YEAR
Mean Maximum Temp. (°F)	59.8	63.0	70.0	76.8	83.6	88.4	90.2	90.2	86.9	79.2	70.9	63.3	76.9
Mean Temp. (°F)	50.3	53.5	60.1	66.9	74.4	79.8	81.6	81.3	77.3	68.2	60.3	53.4	67.3
Mean Minimum Temp. (°F)	40.7	43.9	50.2	57.1	65.2	71.1	72.9	72.3	67.6	57.2	49.8	43.4	57.6
Extreme Maximum Temp. (°F)	80	80	85	93	93	97	100	99	98	93	86	82	100
Extreme Minimum Temp. (°F)	12	17	21	33	46	52	63	60	49	32	26	10	10
Days Maximum Temp. ≥ 90°F	0	0	0	0	2	13	21	20	10	1	0	0	67
Days Maximum Temp. ≤ 32°F	0	0	0	0	0	0	0	0	0	0	0	0	0
Days Minimum Temp. ≤ 32°F	7	3	1	0	0	0	0	0	0	0	1	5	17
Days Minimum Temp. ≤ 0°F	0	0	0	0	0	0	0	0	0	0	0	0	0
Heating Degree Days (base 65°F)	455	330	186	53	2	0	0	0	2	52	184	375	1,639
Cooling Degree Days (base 65°F)	6	12	44	118	301	450	520	512	375	160	51	22	2,571
Mean Precipitation (in.)	5.57	4.06	4.43	4.74	5.29	7.00	6.47	6.39	5.77	4.10	3.97	4.91	62.70
Days With ≥ 0.1" Precipitation	7	6	6	4	6	8	10	10	8	5	5	6	81
Days With ≥ 1.0" Precipitation	2	1	1	1	2	2	2	2	2	1	1	1	18
Mean Snowfall (in.)	trace	trace	0.0	0.0	0.0	0.0	0.0	0.0	0.0	0.0	0.0	trace	trace
Days With ≥ 1.0" Snow Depth	0	0	0	0	0	0	0	0	0	0	0	0	0

Jennings *Jefferson Davis Parish*   Elevation: 22 ft.   Latitude: 30° 12' N   Longitude: 92° 40' W

	JAN	FEB	MAR	APR	MAY	JUN	JUL	AUG	SEP	OCT	NOV	DEC	YEAR
Mean Maximum Temp. (°F)	58.9	63.1	70.4	77.4	84.1	88.9	90.7	91.1	87.8	79.9	69.8	62.4	77.1
Mean Temp. (°F)	49.7	53.3	60.3	67.1	74.6	80.0	81.8	81.7	78.0	68.8	59.6	52.8	67.3
Mean Minimum Temp. (°F)	40.4	43.3	50.1	56.6	65.0	71.0	72.9	72.1	68.1	57.6	49.2	43.2	57.5
Extreme Maximum Temp. (°F)	79	83	87	93	96	100	101	101	100	95	86	82	101
Extreme Minimum Temp. (°F)	11	18	22	33	46	52	60	58	46	30	22	10	10
Days Maximum Temp. ≥ 90°F	0	0	0	0	3	14	21	23	13	1	0	0	75
Days Maximum Temp. ≤ 32°F	0	0	0	0	0	0	0	0	0	0	0	0	0
Days Minimum Temp. ≤ 32°F	7	4	1	0	0	0	0	0	0	0	1	5	18
Days Minimum Temp. ≤ 0°F	0	0	0	0	0	0	0	0	0	0	0	0	0
Heating Degree Days (base 65°F)	476	337	185	56	3	0	0	0	2	50	208	390	1,707
Cooling Degree Days (base 65°F)	5	11	41	111	301	450	525	524	391	168	49	19	2,595
Mean Precipitation (in.)	6.19	3.91	4.56	3.93	5.61	5.39	5.47	4.95	5.88	4.52	4.90	5.27	60.58
Days With ≥ 0.1" Precipitation	7	6	6	4	6	7	9	7	7	5	6	7	77
Days With ≥ 1.0" Precipitation	2	1	1	1	2	2	2	1	1	2	2	2	19
Mean Snowfall (in.)	trace	trace	trace	0.0	0.0	0.0	0.0	0.0	0.0	0.0	0.0	trace	trace
Days With ≥ 1.0" Snow Depth	0	0	0	0	0	0	0	0	0	0	0	0	0

Jonesville Locks *Catahoula Parish*   Elevation: 68 ft.   Latitude: 31° 29' N   Longitude: 91° 51' W

	JAN	FEB	MAR	APR	MAY	JUN	JUL	AUG	SEP	OCT	NOV	DEC	YEAR
Mean Maximum Temp. (°F)	56.1	61.3	69.3	76.6	83.8	89.7	91.9	91.9	87.6	78.8	68.3	59.9	76.3
Mean Temp. (°F)	46.5	51.0	58.5	65.8	73.7	80.0	82.5	81.9	77.0	66.9	57.4	49.6	65.9
Mean Minimum Temp. (°F)	36.8	40.6	47.7	54.9	63.6	70.3	73.0	71.9	66.3	55.0	46.4	39.3	55.5
Extreme Maximum Temp. (°F)	80	85	88	95	96	103	102	104	101	96	88	83	104
Extreme Minimum Temp. (°F)	8	12	19	31	44	53	62	58	43	28	21	7	7
Days Maximum Temp. ≥ 90°F	0	0	0	0	4	18	24	23	14	1	0	0	84
Days Maximum Temp. ≤ 32°F	1	0	0	0	0	0	0	0	0	0	0	0	1
Days Minimum Temp. ≤ 32°F	11	6	1	0	0	0	0	0	0	0	2	8	28
Days Minimum Temp. ≤ 0°F	0	0	0	0	0	0	0	0	0	0	0	0	0
Heating Degree Days (base 65°F)	571	399	229	73	4	0	0	0	4	68	253	478	2,079
Cooling Degree Days (base 65°F)	3	10	31	101	283	461	556	542	377	140	29	10	2,543
Mean Precipitation (in.)	6.43	4.83	6.11	5.19	5.45	4.20	4.30	3.37	3.36	4.50	5.55	5.64	58.93
Days With ≥ 0.1" Precipitation	8	6	7	5	7	6	7	5	5	5	6	7	74
Days With ≥ 1.0" Precipitation	2	2	2	2	2	1	1	1	1	2	2	2	20
Mean Snowfall (in.)	trace	trace	0.0	0.0	0.0	0.0	0.0	0.0	0.0	0.0	0.0	0.0	trace
Days With ≥ 1.0" Snow Depth	0	0	0	0	0	0	0	0	0	0	0	0	0

LSU Ben Hur Farm *East Baton Rouge Parish*   Elevation: 19 ft.   Latitude: 30° 22' N   Longitude: 91° 10' W

	JAN	FEB	MAR	APR	MAY	JUN	JUL	AUG	SEP	OCT	NOV	DEC	YEAR
Mean Maximum Temp. (°F)	60.1	63.9	71.0	77.9	84.7	89.6	91.3	91.3	87.9	80.1	70.8	63.8	77.7
Mean Temp. (°F)	49.9	53.1	60.1	66.7	74.3	79.5	81.6	81.3	77.6	67.9	59.3	53.0	67.0
Mean Minimum Temp. (°F)	39.6	42.3	49.2	55.5	63.7	69.4	72.0	71.3	67.2	55.7	47.8	42.3	56.3
Extreme Maximum Temp. (°F)	82	84	88	92	96	98	100	102	98	95	87	84	102
Extreme Minimum Temp. (°F)	10	15	20	31	42	49	62	56	45	32	20	9	9
Days Maximum Temp. ≥ 90°F	0	0	0	0	5	18	24	23	14	2	0	0	86
Days Maximum Temp. ≤ 32°F	0	0	0	0	0	0	0	0	0	0	0	0	0
Days Minimum Temp. ≤ 32°F	9	5	1	0	0	0	0	0	0	0	2	7	24
Days Minimum Temp. ≤ 0°F	0	0	0	0	0	0	0	0	0	0	0	0	0
Heating Degree Days (base 65°F)	472	342	191	64	4	0	0	0	2	56	212	384	1,727
Cooling Degree Days (base 65°F)	7	14	47	119	304	451	533	525	390	159	50	21	2,620
Mean Precipitation (in.)	5.95	4.99	5.04	5.18	5.37	5.92	5.42	5.73	4.66	3.78	4.50	5.25	61.79
Days With ≥ 0.1" Precipitation	8	6	7	5	6	8	9	8	7	4	6	7	81
Days With ≥ 1.0" Precipitation	2	2	2	2	2	2	1	2	1	1	2	2	21
Mean Snowfall (in.)	trace	trace	0.0	0.0	0.0	0.0	0.0	0.0	0.0	0.0	0.0	0.0	trace
Days With ≥ 1.0" Snow Depth	0	0	0	0	0	0	0	0	0	0	0	0	0

LSU Dean Lee Research Station *Rapides Parish*   Elevation: 68 ft.   Latitude: 31° 11' N   Longitude: 92° 24' W

	JAN	FEB	MAR	APR	MAY	JUN	JUL	AUG	SEP	OCT	NOV	DEC	YEAR
Mean Maximum Temp. (°F)	57.0	61.9	69.9	77.1	84.1	90.1	92.6	92.5	88.4	79.4	69.1	60.9	76.9
Mean Temp. (°F)	46.9	51.4	58.9	65.9	73.7	80.0	82.5	81.7	76.9	66.5	57.7	50.2	66.0
Mean Minimum Temp. (°F)	36.9	40.8	47.8	54.7	63.2	69.9	72.3	70.9	65.5	53.6	46.3	39.5	55.1
Extreme Maximum Temp. (°F)	81	85	87	94	99	101	103	106	100	96	88	82	106
Extreme Minimum Temp. (°F)	9	15	23	29	45	52	61	52	42	28	20	7	7
Days Maximum Temp. ≥ 90°F	0	0	0	0	6	18	26	25	15	2	0	0	92
Days Maximum Temp. ≤ 32°F	1	0	0	0	0	0	0	0	0	0	0	0	1
Days Minimum Temp. ≤ 32°F	11	6	2	0	0	0	0	0	0	0	3	9	31
Days Minimum Temp. ≤ 0°F	0	0	0	0	0	0	0	0	0	0	0	0	0
Heating Degree Days (base 65°F)	556	389	221	72	6	0	0	0	4	76	243	463	2,030
Cooling Degree Days (base 65°F)	4	12	40	107	290	463	555	536	371	137	34	13	2,562
Mean Precipitation (in.)	6.37	5.07	5.34	4.53	5.26	4.58	4.48	4.01	4.39	4.60	6.24	6.25	61.12
Days With > 0.1" Precipitation	8	6	6	5	7	7	7	6	5	5	6	7	75
Days With ≥ 1.0" Precipitation	2	2	2	2	2	1	1	1	1	1	2	2	19
Mean Snowfall (in.)	0.2	trace	trace	0.0	trace	0.0	0.0	0.0	0.0	0.0	trace	0.0	0.2
Days With ≥ 1.0" Snow Depth	0	0	0	0	0	0	0	0	0	0	0	0	0

Lafayette Regional Airport *Lafayette Parish*   Elevation: 36 ft.   Latitude: 30° 12' N   Longitude: 91° 59' W

	JAN	FEB	MAR	APR	MAY	JUN	JUL	AUG	SEP	OCT	NOV	DEC	YEAR
Mean Maximum Temp. (°F)	60.5	64.3	71.4	78.1	84.8	89.7	91.1	91.1	87.6	79.9	70.8	64.2	77.8
Mean Temp. (°F)	51.3	54.6	61.6	68.1	75.4	80.7	82.5	82.3	78.4	69.2	60.3	54.4	68.2
Mean Minimum Temp. (°F)	41.9	44.9	51.8	58.0	65.9	71.7	73.9	73.5	69.0	58.4	49.8	44.6	58.6
Extreme Maximum Temp. (°F)	82	82	85	93	98	100	100	102	99	94	88	83	102
Extreme Minimum Temp. (°F)	10	16	22	33	46	54	63	60	48	32	26	9	9
Days Maximum Temp. ≥ 90°F	0	0	0	0	4	17	23	22	13	1	0	0	80
Days Maximum Temp. ≤ 32°F	0	0	0	0	0	0	0	0	0	0	0	0	0
Days Minimum Temp. ≤ 32°F	6	3	1	0	0	0	0	0	0	0	1	4	15
Days Minimum Temp. ≤ 0°F	0	0	0	0	0	0	0	0	0	0	0	0	0
Heating Degree Days (base 65°F)	432	301	158	44	1	0	0	0	1	39	191	348	1,515
Cooling Degree Days (base 65°F)	9	15	55	138	333	480	557	555	402	173	55	23	2,795
Mean Precipitation (in.)	6.21	4.36	4.55	4.74	5.35	5.98	6.60	5.19	5.23	4.29	4.35	5.63	62.48
Days With ≥ 0.1" Precipitation	7	6	6	5	6	8	10	8	7	5	6	7	81
Days With ≥ 1.0" Precipitation	2	2	1	2	2	2	2	1	2	1	1	2	20
Mean Snowfall (in.)	trace	trace	trace	trace	0.0	0.0	0.0	0.0	0.0	0.0	trace	trace	trace
Days With ≥ 1.0" Snow Depth	0	0	0	0	0	0	0	0	0	0	0	0	0

Lake Providence *East Carroll Parish*   Elevation: 98 ft.   Latitude: 32° 48' N   Longitude: 91° 10' W

	JAN	FEB	MAR	APR	MAY	JUN	JUL	AUG	SEP	OCT	NOV	DEC	YEAR
Mean Maximum Temp. (°F)	52.7	58.2	66.5	74.9	82.5	89.0	91.8	91.4	86.8	77.3	65.6	56.5	74.4
Mean Temp. (°F)	43.7	48.2	56.2	64.3	72.5	79.5	82.4	81.5	76.4	65.7	55.2	47.3	64.4
Mean Minimum Temp. (°F)	34.6	38.2	45.8	53.6	62.4	69.8	72.9	71.6	65.8	54.0	44.7	37.9	54.3
Extreme Maximum Temp. (°F)	79	85	88	94	97	102	104	104	101	97	88	80	104
Extreme Minimum Temp. (°F)	4	10	19	32	40	54	59	56	42	30	20	4	4
Days Maximum Temp. ≥ 90°F	0	0	0	0	4	15	23	22	12	1	0	0	77
Days Maximum Temp. ≤ 32°F	2	1	0	0	0	0	0	0	0	0	1	1	4
Days Minimum Temp. ≤ 32°F	14	8	2	0	0	0	0	0	0	0	3	10	37
Days Minimum Temp. ≤ 0°F	0	0	0	0	0	0	0	0	0	0	0	0	0
Heating Degree Days (base 65°F)	656	470	289	102	10	0	0	0	6	85	309	547	2,474
Cooling Degree Days (base 65°F)	2	5	20	84	249	442	557	528	351	113	19	5	2,375
Mean Precipitation (in.)	5.89	5.18	6.20	6.01	5.85	4.55	3.95	2.97	2.95	4.70	4.97	5.92	59.14
Days With ≥ 0.1" Precipitation	8	6	7	6	8	6	6	4	4	5	6	7	73
Days With ≥ 1.0" Precipitation	2	2	2	2	2	1	1	1	1	1	2	2	19
Mean Snowfall (in.)	0.5	0.2	trace	trace	0.0	0.0	0.0	0.0	0.0	0.0	trace	0.1	0.8
Days With ≥ 1.0" Snow Depth	1	0	0	0	0	0	0	0	0	0	0	0	1

Leesville *Vernon Parish*   Elevation: 26 ft.   Latitude: 31° 08' N   Longitude: 93° 15' W

	JAN	FEB	MAR	APR	MAY	JUN	JUL	AUG	SEP	OCT	NOV	DEC	YEAR
Mean Maximum Temp. (°F)	58.4	63.4	70.9	77.6	84.2	90.0	92.9	92.7	88.3	79.4	69.1	61.5	77.4
Mean Temp. (°F)	47.5	51.5	58.9	65.5	72.9	79.0	81.8	81.2	76.5	66.2	57.1	50.2	65.7
Mean Minimum Temp. (°F)	36.6	39.5	46.9	53.3	61.5	67.9	70.7	69.7	64.6	52.9	45.1	38.9	54.0
Extreme Maximum Temp. (°F)	81	86	91	93	99	101	106	108	104	95	88	83	108
Extreme Minimum Temp. (°F)	9	12	17	30	40	48	56	52	40	25	17	6	6
Days Maximum Temp. ≥ 90°F	0	0	0	0	5	18	25	25	15	2	0	0	90
Days Maximum Temp. ≤ 32°F	0	0	0	0	0	0	0	0	0	0	0	0	0
Days Minimum Temp. ≤ 32°F	13	9	3	1	0	0	0	0	0	0	4	11	41
Days Minimum Temp. ≤ 0°F	0	0	0	0	0	0	0	0	0	0	0	0	0
Heating Degree Days (base 65°F)	542	388	223	85	8	0	0	0	5	80	264	464	2,059
Cooling Degree Days (base 65°F)	5	14	43	104	266	434	534	521	356	125	34	15	2,451
Mean Precipitation (in.)	5.87	4.71	5.04	4.37	5.42	4.68	4.59	3.64	4.17	4.07	4.99	6.07	57.62
Days With ≥ 0.1" Precipitation	8	6	7	5	6	6	7	6	6	5	6	7	75
Days With ≥ 1.0" Precipitation	2	2	2	2	2	1	1	1	1	1	2	2	19
Mean Snowfall (in.)	0.2	trace	0.0	0.0	0.0	0.0	0.0	0.0	0.0	0.0	0.0	trace	0.2
Days With ≥ 1.0" Snow Depth	0	0	0	0	0	0	0	0	0	0	0	0	0

Logansport 4 ENE *De Soto Parish*   Elevation: 209 ft.   Latitude: 31° 59' N   Longitude: 93° 57' W

	JAN	FEB	MAR	APR	MAY	JUN	JUL	AUG	SEP	OCT	NOV	DEC	YEAR
Mean Maximum Temp. (°F)	57.2	63.0	71.2	78.1	84.1	90.2	93.6	93.8	88.4	79.2	67.8	60.4	77.2
Mean Temp. (°F)	45.8	50.4	58.0	65.1	72.1	78.7	81.8	81.4	76.1	65.5	55.5	48.7	64.9
Mean Minimum Temp. (°F)	34.3	37.7	44.8	52.1	60.2	67.1	69.8	68.9	63.8	51.9	43.1	36.9	52.5
Extreme Maximum Temp. (°F)	84	88	92	94	95	102	108	108	104	96	91	81	108
Extreme Minimum Temp. (°F)	4	13	17	25	39	46	53	49	38	25	14	0	0
Days Maximum Temp. ≥ 90°F	0	0	0	0	5	19	27	26	15	2	0	0	94
Days Maximum Temp. ≤ 32°F	0	0	0	0	0	0	0	0	0	0	0	1	1
Days Minimum Temp. ≤ 32°F	15	10	4	1	0	0	0	0	0	1	7	13	51
Days Minimum Temp. ≤ 0°F	0	0	0	0	0	0	0	0	0	0	0	0	0
Heating Degree Days (base 65°F)	595	413	240	86	9	0	0	0	8	92	306	506	2,255
Cooling Degree Days (base 65°F)	2	6	28	90	235	424	535	529	351	112	27	7	2,346
Mean Precipitation (in.)	4.63	4.35	4.04	4.06	5.39	4.51	3.67	2.73	3.37	4.59	4.54	4.64	50.52
Days With ≥ 0.1" Precipitation	8	6	6	5	7	6	5	4	4	5	6	6	68
Days With ≥ 1.0" Precipitation	1	2	1	1	2	1	1	1	1	2	2	2	17
Mean Snowfall (in.)	0.4	0.2	trace	0.0	0.0	0.0	0.0	0.0	0.0	0.0	0.0	trace	0.6
Days With ≥ 1.0" Snow Depth	0	0	0	0	0	0	0	0	0	0	0	0	0

Many *Sabine Parish*   Elevation: 259 ft.   Latitude: 31° 34' N   Longitude: 93° 29' W

	JAN	FEB	MAR	APR	MAY	JUN	JUL	AUG	SEP	OCT	NOV	DEC	YEAR
Mean Maximum Temp. (°F)	57.2	62.3	69.9	76.9	83.4	89.4	92.6	92.2	87.4	78.3	67.7	60.5	76.5
Mean Temp. (°F)	45.6	49.8	57.2	64.2	71.8	78.4	81.5	80.6	75.4	64.5	55.1	48.3	64.4
Mean Minimum Temp. (°F)	33.8	37.2	44.5	51.4	60.1	67.2	70.3	69.0	63.4	50.7	42.5	36.1	52.2
Extreme Maximum Temp. (°F)	82	88	90	94	100	100	104	105	104	94	87	85	105
Extreme Minimum Temp. (°F)	6	11	15	27	37	47	55	51	37	24	16	3	3
Days Maximum Temp. ≥ 90°F	0	0	0	0	4	17	25	24	13	1	0	0	84
Days Maximum Temp. ≤ 32°F	1	0	0	0	0	0	0	0	0	0	0	0	1
Days Minimum Temp. ≤ 32°F	16	11	4	1	0	0	0	0	0	1	6	14	53
Days Minimum Temp. ≤ 0°F	0	0	0	0	0	0	0	0	0	0	0	0	0
Heating Degree Days (base 65°F)	601	432	266	103	14	0	0	0	10	106	315	518	2,365
Cooling Degree Days (base 65°F)	3	9	31	85	239	417	527	508	330	102	22	9	2,282
Mean Precipitation (in.)	5.77	4.35	5.10	3.93	5.57	4.79	3.83	3.96	3.28	4.43	4.27	5.69	54.97
Days With ≥ 0.1" Precipitation	7	6	6	5	7	6	6	6	5	5	6	7	72
Days With ≥ 1.0" Precipitation	2	2	2	1	2	1	1	1	1	2	2	2	19
Mean Snowfall (in.)	0.3	trace	trace	0.0	0.0	0.0	0.0	0.0	0.0	0.0	trace	trace	0.3
Days With ≥ 1.0" Snow Depth	0	0	0	0	0	0	0	0	0	0	0	0	0

Minden *Webster Parish*   Elevation: 183 ft.   Latitude: 32° 36' N   Longitude: 93° 18' W

	JAN	FEB	MAR	APR	MAY	JUN	JUL	AUG	SEP	OCT	NOV	DEC	YEAR
Mean Maximum Temp. (°F)	55.0	60.6	68.1	75.8	82.6	89.2	92.5	92.7	87.3	77.6	66.7	58.2	75.5
Mean Temp. (°F)	43.9	48.5	55.9	63.5	71.5	78.7	82.1	81.6	75.8	64.8	54.6	46.9	64.0
Mean Minimum Temp. (°F)	32.8	36.3	43.6	51.2	60.3	68.1	71.6	70.5	64.3	51.9	42.5	35.6	52.4
Extreme Maximum Temp. (°F)	82	85	91	94	97	102	107	106	104	96	87	83	107
Extreme Minimum Temp. (°F)	5	12	17	25	40	49	57	52	42	27	15	2	2
Days Maximum Temp. ≥ 90°F	0	0	0	0	3	16	24	24	13	2	0	0	82
Days Maximum Temp. ≤ 32°F	1	0	0	0	0	0	0	0	0	0	0	1	2
Days Minimum Temp. ≤ 32°F	17	11	4	1	0	0	0	0	0	0	5	14	52
Days Minimum Temp. ≤ 0°F	0	0	0	0	0	0	0	0	0	0	0	0	0
Heating Degree Days (base 65°F)	650	466	298	113	15	0	0	0	10	102	324	558	2,536
Cooling Degree Days (base 65°F)	2	5	21	71	225	420	547	533	340	100	18	7	2,289
Mean Precipitation (in.)	5.23	4.79	4.86	4.99	5.16	4.79	4.29	2.86	3.67	4.23	5.13	4.82	54.82
Days With ≥ 0.1" Precipitation	7	6	7	6	7	6	6	5	5	5	6	7	73
Days With ≥ 1.0" Precipitation	2	2	1	1	2	1	1	1	1	2	2	2	19
Mean Snowfall (in.)	0.5	trace	trace	trace	0.0	0.0	0.0	0.0	0.0	0.0	trace	0.1	0.6
Days With ≥ 1.0" Snow Depth	0	0	0	0	0	0	0	0	0	0	0	0	0

Monroe Regional Airport *Ouachita Parish*   Elevation: 131 ft.   Latitude: 32° 31' N   Longitude: 92° 02' W

	JAN	FEB	MAR	APR	MAY	JUN	JUL	AUG	SEP	OCT	NOV	DEC	YEAR
Mean Maximum Temp. (°F)	54.3	60.2	68.1	76.2	83.8	90.6	92.6	92.0	87.2	78.1	66.6	58.2	75.7
Mean Temp. (°F)	45.0	49.9	57.6	65.2	73.6	80.4	82.6	81.5	76.1	65.5	55.5	48.2	65.1
Mean Minimum Temp. (°F)	35.6	39.7	47.0	54.1	63.3	70.1	72.5	71.0	65.0	52.9	44.3	38.2	54.5
Extreme Maximum Temp. (°F)	82	86	91	95	104	103	104	104	104	95	90	83	104
Extreme Minimum Temp. (°F)	4	12	18	32	43	51	54	54	41	30	19	5	4
Days Maximum Temp. ≥ 90°F	0	0	0	1	7	19	25	23	13	2	0	0	90
Days Maximum Temp. ≤ 32°F	1	1	0	0	0	0	0	0	0	0	0	0	2
Days Minimum Temp. ≤ 32°F	13	8	2	0	0	0	0	0	0	0	4	10	37
Days Minimum Temp. ≤ 0°F	0	0	0	0	0	0	0	0	0	0	0	0	0
Heating Degree Days (base 65°F)	618	425	256	87	7	0	0	0	7	92	303	520	2,315
Cooling Degree Days (base 65°F)	3	8	32	102	289	478	567	539	350	113	24	8	2,513
Mean Precipitation (in.)	5.29	4.51	5.42	4.70	5.42	4.36	3.60	2.89	3.36	4.20	4.20	5.05	53.00
Days With ≥ 0.1" Precipitation	7	6	7	6	6	6	6	5	5	5	6	6	71
Days With ≥ 1.0" Precipitation	2	2	2	2	2	1	1	1	1	1	1	2	18
Mean Snowfall (in.)	0.8	0.2	trace	trace	trace	0.0	trace	0.0	0.0	trace	trace	trace	1.0
Days With ≥ 1.0" Snow Depth	0	0	0	0	0	0	0	0	0	0	0	0	0

Morgan City *St. Mary Parish* Elevation: 3 ft. Latitude: 29° 41' N Longitude: 91° 11' W

	JAN	FEB	MAR	APR	MAY	JUN	JUL	AUG	SEP	OCT	NOV	DEC	YEAR
Mean Maximum Temp. (°F)	61.3	64.4	70.6	76.9	83.0	87.8	89.8	89.9	86.9	79.8	71.3	64.8	77.2
Mean Temp. (°F)	51.8	54.8	61.4	67.9	74.8	80.0	81.9	81.8	78.6	70.2	61.5	55.2	68.3
Mean Minimum Temp. (°F)	42.5	45.1	52.2	58.8	66.5	72.1	73.9	73.5	70.4	60.5	51.7	45.5	59.4
Extreme Maximum Temp. (°F)	81	84	86	92	93	97	102	99	99	92	91	82	102
Extreme Minimum Temp. (°F)	14	19	17	38	45	57	60	59	50	38	29	10	10
Days Maximum Temp. ≥ 90°F	0	0	0	0	1	10	18	18	9	1	0	0	57
Days Maximum Temp. ≤ 32°F	0	0	0	0	0	0	0	0	0	0	0	0	0
Days Minimum Temp. ≤ 32°F	5	2	0	0	0	0	0	0	0	0	0	3	10
Days Minimum Temp. ≤ 0°F	0	0	0	0	0	0	0	0	0	0	0	0	0
Heating Degree Days (base 65°F)	413	296	153	38	1	0	0	0	0	27	157	320	1,405
Cooling Degree Days (base 65°F)	8	14	49	122	311	457	533	532	417	195	61	22	2,721
Mean Precipitation (in.)	5.79	4.41	4.74	4.22	5.54	5.77	7.71	7.61	6.64	3.84	4.55	4.95	65.77
Days With ≥ 0.1" Precipitation	7	5	6	4	6	8	10	11	8	4	5	6	80
Days With ≥ 1.0" Precipitation	2	1	2	1	2	2	2	2	2	1	2	1	20
Mean Snowfall (in.)	trace	trace	0.0	0.0	0.0	0.0	0.0	0.0	0.0	0.0	0.0	trace	trace
Days With ≥ 1.0" Snow Depth	0	0	0	0	0	0	0	0	0	0	0	0	0

Natchitoches *Natchitoches Parish* Elevation: 127 ft. Latitude: 31° 46' N Longitude: 93° 06' W

	JAN	FEB	MAR	APR	MAY	JUN	JUL	AUG	SEP	OCT	NOV	DEC	YEAR
Mean Maximum Temp. (°F)	57.1	62.6	70.3	77.7	84.5	90.6	93.6	93.4	88.3	79.0	68.2	60.3	77.1
Mean Temp. (°F)	46.6	51.1	58.5	65.7	73.4	80.2	83.2	82.6	77.2	66.6	56.8	49.5	65.9
Mean Minimum Temp. (°F)	36.1	39.5	46.7	53.7	62.4	69.6	72.8	71.7	66.0	54.1	45.3	38.7	54.7
Extreme Maximum Temp. (°F)	83	89	93	94	100	104	105	107	104	97	88	83	107
Extreme Minimum Temp. (°F)	8	13	21	31	44	50	59	53	41	28	20	5	5
Days Maximum Temp. ≥ 90°F	0	0	0	1	6	20	26	26	15	2	0	0	96
Days Maximum Temp. ≤ 32°F	1	0	0	0	0	0	0	0	0	0	0	0	1
Days Minimum Temp. ≤ 32°F	12	7	2	0	0	0	0	0	0	0	3	10	34
Days Minimum Temp. ≤ 0°F	0	0	0	0	0	0	0	0	0	0	0	0	0
Heating Degree Days (base 65°F)	570	398	231	79	7	0	0	0	4	75	269	482	2,115
Cooling Degree Days (base 65°F)	3	10	33	97	271	459	576	560	371	124	26	9	2,539
Mean Precipitation (in.)	5.70	4.49	5.26	4.76	5.86	4.43	3.40	3.50	3.21	4.40	4.29	5.90	55.20
Days With ≥ 0.1" Precipitation	8	6	6	5	7	6	6	6	5	5	6	7	73
Days With ≥ 1.0" Precipitation	2	2	2	2	2	1	1	1	1	2	1	2	19
Mean Snowfall (in.)	0.6	trace	trace	0.0	0.0	0.0	0.0	0.0	0.0	0.0	trace	trace	0.6
Days With ≥ 1.0" Snow Depth	0	0	0	0	0	0	0	0	0	0	0	0	0

New Iberia *Iberia Parish* Elevation: 22 ft. Latitude: 29° 59' N Longitude: 91° 47' W

	JAN	FEB	MAR	APR	MAY	JUN	JUL	AUG	SEP	OCT	NOV	DEC	YEAR
Mean Maximum Temp. (°F)	61.0	64.6	71.4	78.0	84.4	89.2	91.1	90.8	87.6	79.9	71.2	64.6	77.8
Mean Temp. (°F)	51.3	54.5	61.4	68.0	75.1	80.3	82.3	81.9	78.4	69.2	60.6	54.6	68.1
Mean Minimum Temp. (°F)	41.4	44.4	51.3	58.0	65.8	71.3	73.3	73.0	69.1	58.5	50.0	44.5	58.4
Extreme Maximum Temp. (°F)	82	82	88	94	94	99	101	99	100	95	88	87	101
Extreme Minimum Temp. (°F)	11	17	19	33	45	54	65	61	48	32	23	9	9
Days Maximum Temp. ≥ 90°F	0	0	0	0	3	16	23	22	12	1	0	0	77
Days Maximum Temp. ≤ 32°F	0	0	0	0	0	0	0	0	0	0	0	0	0
Days Minimum Temp. ≤ 32°F	7	3	1	0	0	0	0	0	0	0	1	4	16
Days Minimum Temp. ≤ 0°F	0	0	0	0	0	0	0	0	0	0	0	0	0
Heating Degree Days (base 65°F)	431	304	159	43	2	0	0	0	1	40	180	340	1,500
Cooling Degree Days (base 65°F)	9	15	56	139	326	470	549	542	410	180	56	26	2,778
Mean Precipitation (in.)	5.17	4.09	4.40	4.60	5.18	6.08	7.03	6.15	5.79	4.26	4.07	4.86	61.68
Days With ≥ 0.1" Precipitation	7	6	6	5	6	8	9	9	7	4	5	6	78
Days With ≥ 1.0" Precipitation	2	1	2	1	2	2	2	2	2	1	1	1	19
Mean Snowfall (in.)	trace	trace	0.0	0.0	0.0	0.0	0.0	0.0	0.0	0.0	trace	trace	trace
Days With ≥ 1.0" Snow Depth	0	0	0	0	0	0	0	0	0	0	0	0	0

New Orleans Audubon *Orleans Parish* Elevation: 3 ft. Latitude: 29° 55' N Longitude: 90° 08' W

	JAN	FEB	MAR	APR	MAY	JUN	JUL	AUG	SEP	OCT	NOV	DEC	YEAR
Mean Maximum Temp. (°F)	62.3	65.9	72.4	78.6	85.1	90.0	91.4	91.4	87.9	80.4	71.6	65.6	78.6
Mean Temp. (°F)	53.8	57.0	63.5	69.5	76.6	81.8	83.4	83.4	80.0	71.5	62.8	56.9	70.0
Mean Minimum Temp. (°F)	45.2	48.1	54.6	60.4	68.1	73.5	75.4	75.4	72.2	62.6	53.9	48.2	61.5
Extreme Maximum Temp. (°F)	82	85	88	93	96	99	101	102	100	97	87	84	102
Extreme Minimum Temp. (°F)	16	20	28	37	51	54	67	64	52	37	29	12	12
Days Maximum Temp. ≥ 90°F	0	0	0	0	5	18	22	23	13	1	0	0	82
Days Maximum Temp. ≤ 32°F	0	0	0	0	0	0	0	0	0	0	0	0	0
Days Minimum Temp. ≤ 32°F	3	1	0	0	0	0	0	0	0	0	0	1	5
Days Minimum Temp. ≤ 0°F	0	0	0	0	0	0	0	0	0	0	0	0	0
Heating Degree Days (base 65°F)	360	243	117	28	1	0	0	0	0	17	139	282	1,187
Cooling Degree Days (base 65°F)	16	26	76	168	382	515	589	592	460	236	84	39	3,183
Mean Precipitation (in.)	5.59	4.72	5.45	4.97	5.26	6.18	7.14	6.45	6.06	2.96	4.66	4.64	64.08
Days With ≥ 0.1" Precipitation	7	6	6	5	6	8	11	10	8	4	6	6	83
Days With ≥ 1.0" Precipitation	2	2	2	1	2	2	2	2	2	1	2	2	22
Mean Snowfall (in.)	trace	trace	trace	0.0	0.0	0.0	0.0	0.0	0.0	0.0	0.0	trace	trace
Days With ≥ 1.0" Snow Depth	0	0	0	0	0	0	0	0	0	0	0	0	0

New Roads 5 ESE *Pointe Coupee Parish*   Elevation: 42 ft.   Latitude: 30° 41' N   Longitude: 91° 22' W

	JAN	FEB	MAR	APR	MAY	JUN	JUL	AUG	SEP	OCT	NOV	DEC	YEAR
Mean Maximum Temp. (°F)	58.8	63.1	70.5	77.0	83.9	89.1	91.0	90.8	86.9	79.0	70.0	62.2	76.9
Mean Temp. (°F)	48.8	52.7	59.6	66.2	73.9	79.6	81.7	81.3	77.1	67.4	59.0	51.6	66.6
Mean Minimum Temp. (°F)	38.7	42.3	48.7	55.4	63.8	69.9	72.3	71.7	67.2	55.7	48.0	41.0	56.2
Extreme Maximum Temp. (°F)	85	85	89	91	96	98	100	101	99	94	87	85	101
Extreme Minimum Temp. (°F)	8	14	23	32	43	51	62	60	47	30	22	8	8
Days Maximum Temp. ≥ 90°F	0	0	0	0	3	15	22	22	11	1	0	0	74
Days Maximum Temp. ≤ 32°F	0	0	0	0	0	0	0	0	0	0	0	0	0
Days Minimum Temp. ≤ 32°F	9	5	1	0	0	0	0	0	0	0	2	7	24
Days Minimum Temp. ≤ 0°F	0	0	0	0	0	0	0	0	0	0	0	0	0
Heating Degree Days (base 65°F)	501	350	198	64	3	0	0	0	2	57	216	423	1,814
Cooling Degree Days (base 65°F)	5	12	35	107	285	446	526	519	375	142	40	15	2,507
Mean Precipitation (in.)	6.75	5.73	5.13	5.66	5.47	4.59	4.80	5.27	4.88	3.85	4.87	5.40	62.40
Days With ≥ 0.1" Precipitation	8	7	6	6	6	7	8	8	6	4	6	7	79
Days With ≥ 1.0" Precipitation	2	2	2	2	2	1	1	2	1	1	2	2	20
Mean Snowfall (in.)	trace	trace	0.0	0.0	0.0	0.0	0.0	0.0	0.0	0.0	0.0	trace	trace
Days With ≥ 1.0" Snow Depth	0	0	0	0	0	0	0	0	0	0	0	0	0

Oberlin Fire Tower *Allen Parish*   Elevation: 62 ft.   Latitude: 30° 36' N   Longitude: 92° 47' W

	JAN	FEB	MAR	APR	MAY	JUN	JUL	AUG	SEP	OCT	NOV	DEC	YEAR
Mean Maximum Temp. (°F)	59.1	63.7	70.9	77.7	84.1	89.5	91.7	92.0	87.9	79.8	69.9	62.4	77.4
Mean Temp. (°F)	49.6	53.5	60.6	67.1	74.1	79.7	81.9	81.8	77.6	68.4	59.3	52.6	67.2
Mean Minimum Temp. (°F)	40.1	43.2	50.2	56.4	64.1	69.9	72.1	71.4	67.1	56.9	48.6	42.7	56.9
Extreme Maximum Temp. (°F)	82	83	87	93	97	100	102	105	101	95	90	83	105
Extreme Minimum Temp. (°F)	10	16	21	31	44	53	60	57	40	28	20	8	8
Days Maximum Temp. ≥ 90°F	0	0	0	0	3	16	24	24	14	2	0	0	83
Days Maximum Temp. ≤ 32°F	0	0	0	0	0	0	0	0	0	0	0	0	0
Days Minimum Temp. ≤ 32°F	8	5	1	0	0	0	0	0	0	0	2	6	22
Days Minimum Temp. ≤ 0°F	0	0	0	0	0	0	0	0	0	0	0	0	0
Heating Degree Days (base 65°F)	477	334	177	56	3	0	0	0	3	53	213	396	1,712
Cooling Degree Days (base 65°F)	6	15	47	122	296	451	535	534	383	162	45	18	2,614
Mean Precipitation (in.)	6.77	4.67	5.56	4.75	6.75	6.04	5.48	4.67	6.03	5.20	5.27	6.16	67.35
Days With ≥ 0.1" Precipitation	8	6	6	5	7	8	8	7	7	5	7	7	81
Days With ≥ 1.0" Precipitation	2	2	2	2	2	2	2	1	1	2	2	2	22
Mean Snowfall (in.)	trace	trace	0.0	0.0	0.0	0.0	0.0	0.0	0.0	0.0	0.0	0.0	trace
Days With ≥ 1.0" Snow Depth	0	0	0	0	0	0	0	0	0	0	0	0	0

Plain Dealing *Bossier Parish*   Elevation: 288 ft.   Latitude: 32° 54' N   Longitude: 93° 41' W

	JAN	FEB	MAR	APR	MAY	JUN	JUL	AUG	SEP	OCT	NOV	DEC	YEAR
Mean Maximum Temp. (°F)	54.4	60.1	68.0	75.7	82.2	89.1	92.9	92.8	87.2	77.2	65.7	57.8	75.3
Mean Temp. (°F)	42.8	47.3	54.8	62.2	70.3	77.6	81.3	80.7	75.0	63.8	53.4	45.9	62.9
Mean Minimum Temp. (°F)	31.1	34.4	41.6	48.7	58.4	66.0	69.5	68.6	62.8	50.3	40.9	34.0	50.5
Extreme Maximum Temp. (°F)	83	88	93	95	99	107	110	112	107	98	86	83	112
Extreme Minimum Temp. (°F)	3	4	13	28	36	49	55	51	38	22	11	0	0
Days Maximum Temp. ≥ 90°F	0	0	0	0	3	16	24	24	14	2	0	0	83
Days Maximum Temp. ≤ 32°F	1	0	0	0	0	0	0	0	0	0	0	1	2
Days Minimum Temp. ≤ 32°F	19	13	6	1	0	0	0	0	0	0	7	16	62
Days Minimum Temp. ≤ 0°F	0	0	0	0	0	0	0	0	0	0	0	0	0
Heating Degree Days (base 65°F)	683	497	326	136	22	0	0	0	12	116	358	588	2,738
Cooling Degree Days (base 65°F)	1	4	19	60	204	396	525	513	330	93	17	5	2,167
Mean Precipitation (in.)	4.83	4.21	4.60	4.35	4.31	5.12	3.80	3.77	3.31	4.81	4.98	4.73	52.82
Days With ≥ 0.1" Precipitation	7	6	6	6	6	6	5	5	5	5	7	7	71
Days With ≥ 1.0" Precipitation	2	1	1	1	1	2	1	2	1	2	2	2	18
Mean Snowfall (in.)	0.7	0.2	trace	trace	0.0	0.0	0.0	0.0	0.0	0.0	trace	0.3	1.2
Days With ≥ 1.0" Snow Depth	0	0	0	0	0	0	0	0	0	0	0	0	0

Red River Research Station *Bossier Parish*   Elevation: 154 ft.   Latitude: 32° 25' N   Longitude: 93° 38' W

	JAN	FEB	MAR	APR	MAY	JUN	JUL	AUG	SEP	OCT	NOV	DEC	YEAR
Mean Maximum Temp. (°F)	55.0	60.6	68.3	76.7	83.7	90.5	93.9	94.0	88.7	78.8	67.4	58.5	76.4
Mean Temp. (°F)	44.3	49.3	56.6	64.5	72.6	79.8	83.0	82.3	76.2	65.2	55.4	47.5	64.7
Mean Minimum Temp. (°F)	33.5	37.9	44.8	52.3	61.5	69.0	72.1	70.5	63.7	51.7	43.4	36.3	53.1
Extreme Maximum Temp. (°F)	81	87	88	95	99	103	105	108	104	97	87	83	108
Extreme Minimum Temp. (°F)	6	13	18	29	44	51	59	50	42	28	18	3	3
Days Maximum Temp. ≥ 90°F	0	0	0	1	5	20	27	26	16	2	0	0	97
Days Maximum Temp. ≤ 32°F	1	0	0	0	0	0	0	0	0	0	0	0	1
Days Minimum Temp. ≤ 32°F	16	9	3	0	0	0	0	0	0	0	5	13	46
Days Minimum Temp. ≤ 0°F	0	0	0	0	0	0	0	0	0	0	0	0	0
Heating Degree Days (base 65°F)	638	444	276	95	9	0	0	0	7	94	301	542	2,406
Cooling Degree Days (base 65°F)	2	6	23	87	257	454	570	551	355	112	22	6	2,445
Mean Precipitation (in.)	5.09	4.51	4.36	4.65	4.72	4.89	3.79	2.87	2.96	4.54	4.35	4.54	51.27
Days With ≥ 0.1" Precipitation	7	6	6	5	6	6	5	4	5	5	6	6	67
Days With ≥ 1.0" Precipitation	2	2	1	1	1	1	1	1	1	2	2	1	16
Mean Snowfall (in.)	0.3	trace	trace	0.0	0.0	0.0	0.0	0.0	0.0	0.0	trace	trace	0.3
Days With ≥ 1.0" Snow Depth	0	0	0	0	0	0	0	0	0	0	0	0	0

Reserve *St. John The Baptist Parish*   Elevation: 13 ft.   Latitude: 30° 05' N   Longitude: 90° 37' W

	JAN	FEB	MAR	APR	MAY	JUN	JUL	AUG	SEP	OCT	NOV	DEC	YEAR
Mean Maximum Temp. (°F)	61.3	64.9	71.5	78.0	84.4	89.3	91.2	90.9	87.5	79.6	70.9	64.7	77.8
Mean Temp. (°F)	51.0	54.3	61.0	67.3	74.3	79.9	81.9	81.6	78.1	68.7	60.2	54.0	67.7
Mean Minimum Temp. (°F)	40.8	43.6	50.5	56.6	64.1	70.5	72.5	72.3	68.7	57.8	49.5	43.3	57.5
Extreme Maximum Temp. (°F)	82	84	88	92	95	98	101	100	98	96	88	83	101
Extreme Minimum Temp. (°F)	11	16	23	34	42	53	62	60	45	33	25	9	9
Days Maximum Temp. ≥ 90°F	0	0	0	0	3	15	23	22	11	1	0	0	75
Days Maximum Temp. ≤ 32°F	0	0	0	0	0	0	0	0	0	0	0	0	0
Days Minimum Temp. ≤ 32°F	7	4	1	0	0	0	0	0	0	0	1	5	18
Days Minimum Temp. ≤ 0°F	0	0	0	0	0	0	0	0	0	0	0	0	0
Heating Degree Days (base 65°F)	434	317	168	49	2	0	0	0	1	42	186	355	1,554
Cooling Degree Days (base 65°F)	7	16	49	120	296	454	539	533	396	167	52	21	2,650
Mean Precipitation (in.)	6.18	5.47	5.92	5.06	5.50	6.69	6.58	5.40	5.63	3.54	4.41	4.70	65.08
Days With ≥ 0.1" Precipitation	8	6	6	5	6	8	10	8	7	5	5	6	80
Days With ≥ 1.0" Precipitation	2	2	2	2	2	3	2	1	2	1	2	2	23
Mean Snowfall (in.)	trace	0.1	0.0	0.0	0.0	0.0	0.0	0.0	0.0	0.0	0.0	trace	0.1
Days With ≥ 1.0" Snow Depth	0	0	0	0	0	0	0	0	0	0	0	0	0

Rockefeller Wildlife Refuge *Cameron Parish*   Elevation: 3 ft.   Latitude: 29° 44' N   Longitude: 92° 49' W

	JAN	FEB	MAR	APR	MAY	JUN	JUL	AUG	SEP	OCT	NOV	DEC	YEAR
Mean Maximum Temp. (°F)	60.0	63.4	70.2	76.4	83.1	88.4	90.3	90.7	87.7	80.3	71.0	63.8	77.1
Mean Temp. (°F)	51.3	54.5	61.3	67.8	75.1	80.6	82.5	82.4	79.0	70.1	61.5	54.7	68.4
Mean Minimum Temp. (°F)	42.5	45.6	52.4	59.3	67.0	72.8	74.7	73.9	70.2	59.9	51.9	45.5	59.6
Extreme Maximum Temp. (°F)	79	81	82	92	94	97	102	100	98	95	87	81	102
Extreme Minimum Temp. (°F)	14	19	24	36	46	52	63	62	51	31	25	10	10
Days Maximum Temp. ≥ 90°F	0	0	0	0	1	12	22	23	12	1	0	0	71
Days Maximum Temp. ≤ 32°F	0	0	0	0	0	0	0	0	0	0	0	0	0
Days Minimum Temp. ≤ 32°F	5	2	1	0	0	0	0	0	0	0	0	3	11
Days Minimum Temp. ≤ 0°F	0	0	0	0	0	0	0	0	0	0	0	0	0
Heating Degree Days (base 65°F)	427	300	154	40	2	0	0	0	1	32	162	335	1,453
Cooling Degree Days (base 65°F)	6	11	46	125	326	482	560	556	430	199	66	22	2,829
Mean Precipitation (in.)	5.90	3.55	3.75	3.96	5.09	5.33	7.13	6.81	6.36	4.94	4.48	5.14	62.44
Days With ≥ 0.1" Precipitation	7	5	5	4	5	7	9	9	6	4	5	6	72
Days With ≥ 1.0" Precipitation	2	1	1	1	2	2	2	2	2	2	1	2	20
Mean Snowfall (in.)	0.1	trace	0.0	0.0	0.0	0.0	0.0	0.0	0.0	0.0	0.0	trace	0.1
Days With ≥ 1.0" Snow Depth	0	0	0	0	0	0	0	0	0	0	0	0	0

Rosepine Research Station *Vernon Parish*   Elevation: 236 ft.   Latitude: 30° 57' N   Longitude: 93° 17' W

	JAN	FEB	MAR	APR	MAY	JUN	JUL	AUG	SEP	OCT	NOV	DEC	YEAR
Mean Maximum Temp. (°F)	58.5	63.4	70.5	77.3	84.4	90.3	93.2	93.6	89.2	80.1	70.0	61.9	77.7
Mean Temp. (°F)	47.2	51.7	58.5	65.3	73.1	79.2	81.9	81.7	77.0	66.8	57.9	50.4	65.9
Mean Minimum Temp. (°F)	35.8	39.9	46.5	53.3	61.7	68.0	70.5	69.8	64.8	53.4	45.9	38.8	54.0
Extreme Maximum Temp. (°F)	80	86	88	93	101	102	105	110	102	97	87	85	110
Extreme Minimum Temp. (°F)	8	12	18	30	42	49	57	51	42	26	18	6	6
Days Maximum Temp. ≥ 90°F	0	0	0	1	5	19	26	27	17	3	0	0	98
Days Maximum Temp. ≤ 32°F	0	0	0	0	0	0	0	0	0	0	0	0	0
Days Minimum Temp. ≤ 32°F	13	8	3	0	0	0	0	0	0	0	3	10	37
Days Minimum Temp. ≤ 0°F	0	0	0	0	0	0	0	0	0	0	0	0	0
Heating Degree Days (base 65°F)	549	381	227	79	6	0	0	0	4	72	239	458	2,015
Cooling Degree Days (base 65°F)	4	12	35	97	269	437	530	527	372	139	35	14	2,471
Mean Precipitation (in.)	5.77	4.49	5.34	4.16	5.43	4.78	5.27	4.08	4.38	4.38	4.90	6.11	59.09
Days With ≥ 0.1" Precipitation	8	6	6	5	6	7	8	6	6	5	6	7	76
Days With ≥ 1.0" Precipitation	2	1	2	2	2	1	2	1	1	1	2	2	19
Mean Snowfall (in.)	trace	trace	0.0	0.0	0.0	0.0	0.0	0.0	0.0	0.0	0.0	trace	trace
Days With ≥ 1.0" Snow Depth	0	0	0	0	0	0	0	0	0	0	0	0	0

Ruston Louisiana Tech *Lincoln Parish*   Elevation: 278 ft.   Latitude: 32° 31' N   Longitude: 92° 39' W

	JAN	FEB	MAR	APR	MAY	JUN	JUL	AUG	SEP	OCT	NOV	DEC	YEAR
Mean Maximum Temp. (°F)	55.1	60.5	68.2	76.1	82.8	89.6	92.9	92.8	87.2	77.4	66.6	58.5	75.6
Mean Temp. (°F)	44.2	48.7	56.1	63.8	71.5	78.6	81.7	81.1	75.6	64.7	54.8	47.4	64.0
Mean Minimum Temp. (°F)	33.3	36.8	44.0	51.4	60.2	67.5	70.4	69.4	63.9	52.0	43.0	36.2	52.3
Extreme Maximum Temp. (°F)	80	87	90	94	96	101	107	109	104	94	86	83	109
Extreme Minimum Temp. (°F)	4	9	16	28	39	51	55	49	42	25	19	0	0
Days Maximum Temp. ≥ 90°F	0	0	0	0	3	17	25	24	13	1	0	0	83
Days Maximum Temp. ≤ 32°F	1	0	0	0	0	0	0	0	0	0	0	1	2
Days Minimum Temp. ≤ 32°F	16	10	4	1	0	0	0	0	0	0	5	12	48
Days Minimum Temp. ≤ 0°F	0	0	0	0	0	0	0	0	0	0	0	0	0
Heating Degree Days (base 65°F)	629	458	290	108	14	0	0	0	9	101	318	545	2,472
Cooling Degree Days (base 65°F)	1	5	22	75	226	420	532	519	336	99	17	5	2,257
Mean Precipitation (in.)	5.65	4.89	5.13	4.60	5.43	4.28	4.11	2.94	3.44	4.27	4.58	5.35	54.67
Days With ≥ 0.1" Precipitation	8	6	7	6	6	6	6	5	5	5	6	7	73
Days With ≥ 1.0" Precipitation	2	2	2	2	2	1	1	1	1	2	2	2	20
Mean Snowfall (in.)	0.5	trace	0.0	trace	0.0	0.0	0.0	0.0	0.0	0.0	trace	trace	0.5
Days With ≥ 1.0" Snow Depth	0	0	0	0	0	0	0	0	0	0	0	0	0

Saint Bernard *St. Bernard Parish*   Elevation: 3 ft.   Latitude: 29° 52' N   Longitude: 89° 50' W

	JAN	FEB	MAR	APR	MAY	JUN	JUL	AUG	SEP	OCT	NOV	DEC	YEAR
Mean Maximum Temp. (°F)	63.1	66.6	72.8	78.6	85.2	89.8	91.3	90.9	87.3	79.9	71.6	65.7	78.6
Mean Temp. (°F)	53.2	56.3	62.5	68.7	75.7	80.7	82.5	82.3	78.9	70.3	62.0	55.8	69.1
Mean Minimum Temp. (°F)	43.3	46.0	52.4	58.8	66.2	71.6	73.6	73.6	70.4	60.6	52.3	45.9	59.6
Extreme Maximum Temp. (°F)	86	87	89	92	96	99	100	101	99	95	89	87	101
Extreme Minimum Temp. (°F)	11	17	22	36	47	54	64	63	50	35	27	10	10
Days Maximum Temp. ≥ 90°F	0	0	0	1	5	17	23	22	11	1	0	0	80
Days Maximum Temp. ≤ 32°F	0	0	0	0	0	0	0	0	0	0	0	0	0
Days Minimum Temp. ≤ 32°F	5	3	0	0	0	0	0	0	0	0	0	3	11
Days Minimum Temp. ≤ 0°F	0	0	0	0	0	0	0	0	0	0	0	0	0
Heating Degree Days (base 65°F)	376	261	135	34	1	0	0	0	0	25	153	307	1,292
Cooling Degree Days (base 65°F)	10	21	57	145	349	481	556	553	419	199	69	27	2,886
Mean Precipitation (in.)	5.20	5.06	6.26	4.93	5.04	5.17	6.97	6.24	6.51	3.11	5.09	4.31	63.89
Days With ≥ 0.1" Precipitation	7	6	6	4	6	7	9	9	8	4	5	5	76
Days With ≥ 1.0" Precipitation	2	2	2	1	2	2	2	2	1	2	2	1	21
Mean Snowfall (in.)	trace	trace	0.0	0.0	0.0	0.0	0.0	0.0	0.0	0.0	0.0	trace	trace
Days With ≥ 1.0" Snow Depth	0	0	0	0	0	0	0	0	0	0	0	0	0

Saint Joseph 3 N *Tensas Parish*   Elevation: 75 ft.   Latitude: 31° 57' N   Longitude: 91° 14' W

	JAN	FEB	MAR	APR	MAY	JUN	JUL	AUG	SEP	OCT	NOV	DEC	YEAR
Mean Maximum Temp. (°F)	55.8	60.5	68.5	76.4	83.7	90.0	92.3	92.1	87.9	78.7	68.3	59.8	76.2
Mean Temp. (°F)	46.1	50.0	57.9	65.4	73.5	80.0	82.5	81.7	76.8	66.3	57.1	49.6	65.6
Mean Minimum Temp. (°F)	36.3	39.5	47.2	54.5	63.2	69.9	72.6	71.2	65.7	53.8	45.8	39.4	54.9
Extreme Maximum Temp. (°F)	80	84	87	95	96	102	101	101	101	97	88	85	102
Extreme Minimum Temp. (°F)	6	12	18	30	41	52	59	55	41	29	20	5	5
Days Maximum Temp. ≥ 90°F	0	0	0	0	6	18	25	23	14	2	0	0	88
Days Maximum Temp. ≤ 32°F	1	0	0	0	0	0	0	0	0	0	0	1	2
Days Minimum Temp. ≤ 32°F	12	8	2	0	0	0	0	0	0	0	3	9	34
Days Minimum Temp. ≤ 0°F	0	0	0	0	0	0	0	0	0	0	0	0	0
Heating Degree Days (base 65°F)	583	424	246	84	8	0	0	0	6	83	264	480	2,178
Cooling Degree Days (base 65°F)	2	8	34	107	295	468	564	539	371	140	34	11	2,573
Mean Precipitation (in.)	6.29	4.97	6.24	5.28	5.42	3.84	3.83	3.52	3.11	3.82	4.74	5.60	56.66
Days With ≥ 0.1" Precipitation	8	6	7	5	6	6	6	6	5	5	6	7	73
Days With ≥ 1.0" Precipitation	2	2	2	2	2	1	1	1	1	1	2	2	19
Mean Snowfall (in.)	0.4	trace	trace	0.0	0.0	0.0	0.0	0.0	0.0	0.0	trace	trace	0.4
Days With ≥ 1.0" Snow Depth	0	3	0	0	0	0	0	0	0	0	0	0	3

Slidell *St. Tammany Parish*   Elevation: 9 ft.   Latitude: 30° 16' N   Longitude: 89° 46' W

	JAN	FEB	MAR	APR	MAY	JUN	JUL	AUG	SEP	OCT	NOV	DEC	YEAR
Mean Maximum Temp. (°F)	61.2	64.6	71.1	77.6	84.3	89.5	91.1	91.0	87.7	80.1	71.0	64.1	77.8
Mean Temp. (°F)	50.9	54.0	60.6	67.1	74.3	80.0	82.0	81.7	78.0	68.6	59.9	53.5	67.6
Mean Minimum Temp. (°F)	40.6	43.3	50.1	56.6	64.3	70.6	72.9	72.2	68.3	57.0	48.8	42.9	57.3
Extreme Maximum Temp. (°F)	81	83	88	92	95	98	102	103	99	93	88	83	103
Extreme Minimum Temp. (°F)	8	15	22	32	43	50	63	58	46	31	24	9	8
Days Maximum Temp. ≥ 90°F	0	0	0	0	3	16	23	22	13	1	0	0	78
Days Maximum Temp. ≤ 32°F	0	0	0	0	0	0	0	0	0	0	0	0	0
Days Minimum Temp. ≤ 32°F	8	5	1	0	0	0	0	0	0	0	2	6	22
Days Minimum Temp. ≤ 0°F	0	0	0	0	0	0	0	0	0	0	0	0	0
Heating Degree Days (base 65°F)	439	317	175	55	3	0	0	0	1	46	193	369	1,598
Cooling Degree Days (base 65°F)	7	13	47	120	309	463	543	535	399	168	49	20	2,673
Mean Precipitation (in.)	6.47	5.11	6.06	4.69	5.91	4.48	6.62	5.83	5.00	3.33	4.70	4.77	62.97
Days With ≥ 0.1" Precipitation	8	6	7	5	6	7	9	9	7	4	6	6	80
Days With ≥ 1.0" Precipitation	2	2	2	1	2	1	2	2	2	1	2	1	20
Mean Snowfall (in.)	trace	0.1	trace	0.0	trace	0.0	0.0	0.0	0.0	0.0	0.0	trace	0.1
Days With ≥ 1.0" Snow Depth	0	0	0	0	0	0	0	0	0	0	0	0	0

Tallulah *Madison Parish*   Elevation: 82 ft.   Latitude: 32° 24' N   Longitude: 91° 13' W

	JAN	FEB	MAR	APR	MAY	JUN	JUL	AUG	SEP	OCT	NOV	DEC	YEAR
Mean Maximum Temp. (°F)	54.2	59.4	67.6	75.5	82.6	89.2	91.7	91.4	86.8	77.5	66.4	57.9	75.0
Mean Temp. (°F)	44.3	48.7	56.7	64.2	72.1	79.0	81.7	81.0	75.7	64.8	55.2	47.5	64.2
Mean Minimum Temp. (°F)	34.3	38.1	45.7	52.9	61.6	68.8	71.6	70.5	64.5	52.0	43.9	37.1	53.4
Extreme Maximum Temp. (°F)	81	84	89	92	97	100	103	102	100	95	88	83	103
Extreme Minimum Temp. (°F)	3	10	11	28	42	48	56	56	40	28	20	4	3
Days Maximum Temp. ≥ 90°F	0	0	0	0	4	17	23	23	13	1	0	0	81
Days Maximum Temp. ≤ 32°F	1	1	0	0	0	0	0	0	0	0	0	1	3
Days Minimum Temp. ≤ 32°F	15	9	2	0	0	0	0	0	0	0	5	12	43
Days Minimum Temp. ≤ 0°F	0	0	0	0	0	0	0	0	0	0	0	0	0
Heating Degree Days (base 65°F)	639	458	280	108	13	0	0	0	8	102	311	539	2,458
Cooling Degree Days (base 65°F)	2	7	29	90	245	433	530	509	333	109	22	7	2,316
Mean Precipitation (in.)	6.13	4.94	6.26	5.29	5.94	4.65	4.04	3.24	3.08	4.01	4.84	6.05	58.47
Days With ≥ 0.1" Precipitation	8	6	7	5	8	6	7	5	4	5	6	7	74
Days With ≥ 1.0" Precipitation	2	2	2	2	2	1	1	1	1	1	1	2	18
Mean Snowfall (in.)	0.2	trace	trace	0.0	0.0	0.0	0.0	0.0	0.0	0.0	trace	trace	0.2
Days With ≥ 1.0" Snow Depth	0	0	0	0	0	0	0	0	0	0	0	0	0

Thibodaux 3 ESE *Lafourche Parish*   Elevation: 13 ft.   Latitude: 29° 46' N   Longitude: 90° 47' W

	JAN	FEB	MAR	APR	MAY	JUN	JUL	AUG	SEP	OCT	NOV	DEC	YEAR
Mean Maximum Temp. (°F)	62.4	66.0	72.6	78.7	85.1	89.8	91.4	91.1	87.9	80.6	72.8	65.8	78.7
Mean Temp. (°F)	52.1	55.9	61.9	68.2	75.3	80.3	82.2	81.8	78.2	69.2	61.9	55.3	68.5
Mean Minimum Temp. (°F)	41.8	45.8	51.3	57.7	65.4	70.8	72.9	72.4	68.5	57.8	51.0	44.7	58.4
Extreme Maximum Temp. (°F)	81	83	87	92	96	99	101	99	99	95	88	84	101
Extreme Minimum Temp. (°F)	12	19	23	34	46	51	63	59	48	31	25	9	9
Days Maximum Temp. ≥ 90°F	0	0	0	0	5	17	23	23	13	2	0	0	83
Days Maximum Temp. ≤ 32°F	0	0	0	0	0	0	0	0	0	0	0	0	0
Days Minimum Temp. ≤ 32°F	6	3	1	0	0	0	0	0	0	0	1	4	15
Days Minimum Temp. ≤ 0°F	0	0	0	0	0	0	0	0	0	0	0	0	0
Heating Degree Days (base 65°F)	405	271	146	39	1	0	0	0	1	39	155	323	1,380
Cooling Degree Days (base 65°F)	14	23	58	140	329	466	541	532	403	182	69	32	2,789
Mean Precipitation (in.)	6.51	5.28	5.42	5.21	6.69	7.08	7.91	7.00	5.27	4.07	4.64	5.16	70.24
Days With ≥ 0.1" Precipitation	8	6	6	5	7	8	11	10	8	5	6	6	86
Days With ≥ 1.0" Precipitation	2	2	2	1	2	2	3	2	1	1	2	2	22
Mean Snowfall (in.)	trace	trace	0.0	0.0	0.0	0.0	0.0	0.0	0.0	0.0	0.0	trace	trace
Days With ≥ 1.0" Snow Depth	0	0	0	0	0	0	0	0	0	0	0	0	0

Winnfield 2 W *Winn Parish*   Elevation: 157 ft.   Latitude: 31° 56' N   Longitude: 92° 41' W

	JAN	FEB	MAR	APR	MAY	JUN	JUL	AUG	SEP	OCT	NOV	DEC	YEAR
Mean Maximum Temp. (°F)	57.2	63.2	70.8	77.7	83.9	89.8	92.5	92.8	87.9	78.8	67.9	60.2	76.9
Mean Temp. (°F)	46.2	50.9	58.0	64.9	72.1	78.5	81.3	80.7	75.7	65.2	55.5	48.9	64.8
Mean Minimum Temp. (°F)	35.1	38.5	45.2	52.1	60.2	67.2	70.0	68.7	63.4	51.5	43.0	37.6	52.7
Extreme Maximum Temp. (°F)	82	86	90	93	97	101	104	109	102	95	87	83	109
Extreme Minimum Temp. (°F)	5	8	16	28	40	48	54	50	38	26	15	5	5
Days Maximum Temp. ≥ 90°F	0	0	0	0	4	17	25	24	14	1	0	0	85
Days Maximum Temp. ≤ 32°F	0	0	0	0	0	0	0	0	0	0	0	0	0
Days Minimum Temp. ≤ 32°F	15	9	4	1	0	0	0	0	0	1	6	12	48
Days Minimum Temp. ≤ 0°F	0	0	0	0	0	0	0	0	0	0	0	0	0
Heating Degree Days (base 65°F)	581	401	240	89	10	0	0	0	7	92	300	500	2,220
Cooling Degree Days (base 65°F)	3	10	31	94	247	424	527	518	341	111	22	8	2,336
Mean Precipitation (in.)	5.96	4.52	5.64	5.32	5.66	5.38	4.29	3.85	3.61	4.47	4.72	6.16	59.58
Days With ≥ 0.1" Precipitation	8	6	7	5	7	6	7	5	5	5	6	7	74
Days With ≥ 1.0" Precipitation	2	1	2	2	2	1	1	1	1	2	1	2	18
Mean Snowfall (in.)	0.8	0.1	trace	0.0	0.0	0.0	0.0	0.0	0.0	0.0	trace	0.1	1.0
Days With ≥ 1.0" Snow Depth	1	0	0	0	0	0	0	0	0	0	0	0	1

Winnsboro 5 SSE *Franklin Parish*   Elevation: 78 ft.   Latitude: 32° 06' N   Longitude: 91° 43' W

	JAN	FEB	MAR	APR	MAY	JUN	JUL	AUG	SEP	OCT	NOV	DEC	YEAR
Mean Maximum Temp. (°F)	54.9	60.0	68.0	76.1	83.4	90.2	92.9	92.8	88.3	78.7	67.4	58.7	76.0
Mean Temp. (°F)	45.0	49.3	57.1	64.8	72.8	79.7	82.4	81.6	76.5	65.5	56.0	48.5	64.9
Mean Minimum Temp. (°F)	35.1	38.5	46.1	53.4	62.1	69.1	71.9	70.4	64.6	52.3	44.7	38.2	53.9
Extreme Maximum Temp. (°F)	80	84	87	93	99	102	106	106	105	97	89	83	106
Extreme Minimum Temp. (°F)	5	12	18	29	41	48	56	55	38	27	19	5	5
Days Maximum Temp. ≥ 90°F	0	0	0	0	5	19	26	25	16	2	0	0	93
Days Maximum Temp. ≤ 32°F	1	1	0	0	0	0	0	0	0	0	0	1	3
Days Minimum Temp. ≤ 32°F	14	9	3	0	0	0	0	0	0	0	4	11	41
Days Minimum Temp. ≤ 0°F	0	0	0	0	0	0	0	0	0	0	0	0	0
Heating Degree Days (base 65°F)	616	443	266	99	12	0	0	0	8	93	291	513	2,341
Cooling Degree Days (base 65°F)	3	7	29	99	272	456	557	534	359	122	28	8	2,474
Mean Precipitation (in.)	5.92	4.99	5.81	5.40	5.34	4.54	3.56	3.24	3.00	4.19	4.99	5.73	56.71
Days With ≥ 0.1" Precipitation	8	6	7	5	6	6	6	5	4	5	6	7	71
Days With ≥ 1.0" Precipitation	2	2	2	2	2	1	1	1	1	1	1	2	18
Mean Snowfall (in.)	0.1	trace	trace	0.0	0.0	0.0	0.0	0.0	0.0	0.0	0.0	trace	0.1
Days With ≥ 1.0" Snow Depth	0	0	0	0	0	0	0	0	0	0	0	0	0

Note: See Appendix D for explanation of data.

MAINE

PHYSICAL FEATURES. Maine occupies 33,215 square miles. From near the 43d parallel, the State extends northward over 300 miles, spanning a full 4.5° of latitude. Its width from the 67th meridian extends westward over 4° of longitude, a span of over 200 miles. The terrain is hilly. Elevations are generally less than 500 feet above sea level over the southeastern one-half of the State. The northwestern one-half is a plateau ranging in elevation from 1,000 to 1,500 feet, but sloping downward to 500 feet in the northeast from 1,000 feet in the north (Aroostook County). A number of mountain peaks, extensions of the Appalachian chain, rise to heights from 3,000 to 5,000 feet mostly in the western and central portions of the State. Mt. Katahdin is the highest point. Its summit, at 5,268 feet, rises nearly 4,500 feet from a relatively low base elevation.

The great glaciers of the ice age were all-important in the physical formation of the State. They left "horsebacks" or ridges of glacial deposits, some as long as 150 miles in length. These ridges furnish both natural highway routes and abundant material for roadbuilding. The glaciers formed or left over 1,600 lakes, spread abundantly over the entire State. The largest of these lakes is Moosehead. The total water area of the State exceeds 2,200 square miles. Some flatland is found near the coast, especially near the mouths of the Androscoggin and Kennebec Rivers. Other tracts of flatland, often marshy, lie near lakes.

The coastal portion of the State has many inlets, bays, channels, fine harbors, rocky islands, and promontories. The extreme irregularity of the coast stretches the total coastline to about 2,400 miles, more than 10 times the distance from Kittery to Eastport. The southwestern portion of the coast has many beaches. The mid-coastal portion has many rugged hills and small mountains, some of which rise abruptly from the water, such as Mount Desert Island.

GENERAL CLIMATE. Maine's chief climatic characteristics include: (1) changeableness of the weather, (2) large ranges of temperature, both diurnal and annual, (3) great differences between the same seasons in different years, (4) equable distribution of precipitation, and (5) considerable diversity from place to place. The regional climatic influences are modified in Maine by varying distances from the ocean, by elevations, and by types of terrain. These modifying factors divide the State into three natural climatological divisions. The Northern Division contains slightly more than one-half of the State's area, with its southern boundary nearly parallel to the coast. It represents that area of the State least affected by ocean influences and most affected by higher elevations. In contrast, the Coastal Division is a strip roughly 20 to 30 miles in width. It is most affected by maritime influences and has the lowest average elevation above sea level. The remainder, known conveniently as the Southern Interior Division, covers nearly one-third of the State's area.

Maine lies in the "prevailing westerlies"—the belt of generally eastward air movement which encircles the globe in the middle latitudes. Embedded in this circulation are extensive masses of air originating in higher or lower latitudes and interacting to produce storm systems. Relative to most other sections of the country, a large number of such storms pass over or near Maine. The majority of air masses affecting this State belong to three types: (1) cold, dry air pouring down from subarctic North America, (2) warm, moist air streaming up on a long overland journey from the Gulf of Mexico and from subtropical waters eastward, and (3) cool, damp air moving in from the North Atlantic. Because the atmospheric flow is usually offshore, Maine is influenced more by the first two types than it is by the third.

The procession of contrasting air masses and the relatively frequent passage of storms bring about a roughly twice-weekly alternation from fair to cloudy or stormy conditions, attended by often abrupt changes in temperature, moisture, sunshine, wind direction, and wind speed. There is no regular or persistent rhythm to this sequence. It is interrupted by periods of time during which the same weather patterns continue for several days, and infrequently for several weeks. Maine weather, however, is distinguished for variety rather than for monotony. Changeability is also one of its features on a longer time-scale; that is, the same month or season will exhibit varying characteristics over the years—sometimes in close alternation, sometimes arranged in similar groups for successive years.

TEMPERATURE. The average annual temperature ranges from near 40°F. in the Northern Division, to 44°F. in the Southern Interior Division, and to nearly 45°F. in the Coastal Division. Summer temperatures are delightfully cool and are reasonably uniform over the State. Average temperatures vary much more in winter than in summer.

PRECIPITATION. Maine has precipitation rather evenly distributed throughout the year. The distribution is most regular in the Southern Interior Division. Along the Atlantic coast, summer thunderstorm activity is somewhat suppressed by the effects of the cool ocean, while winter precipitation is increased by coastal storms or "northeasters." In the Northern Division, these effects are reversed with increased thunderstorm activity in summer and with very little effect of coastal storms in winter. Precipitation totals in this Division are greater in summer.

Storm systems are the principal year-round moisture producers. Such systems are less active in the summer, but bands or patches of thunderstorm or shower activity take over much of this function. Though brief and often covering small areas, thunderstorms produce the heaviest local rainfall rates for short intervals. Many weather stations have received from one to two inches in an hour. Winter precipitation occurs mostly as snow, except in the Coastal Division where considerable rain or wet snow falls; stations in this Division, more than stations farther inland, are subject to occasional glazing, or "ice storm" conditions. Freezing rain coats streets, roads, and all exposed surfaces; on rare occasions, a heavy load of ice builds on trees and wires.

SNOWFALL. As a rule, average seasonal snowfall amounts increase northwestward from the coast. The Coastal Division snowfall totals range from 50 to 80 inches. The Southern Interior Division receives from 60 to 90 inches. The Northern Division totals range on the average from 90 to 110 inches. Local topography has a marked influence on snowfall, causing large variations within a short distance. The snowfall season usually begins in late October or in November and lasts into April and sometimes into May. Seasonal totals in the north do not vary as markedly as along the coast. Snow cover lasts throughout the season in the north. Along the coast, however, the snow cover may melt entirely in midwinter and then be replaced by a new cover. Melting is usually gradual enough to prevent serious flooding.

OTHER CLIMATIC FEATURES. The amount of possible sunshine averages from 50 to 60 percent in most of the southern half of the State. This percentage varies along the coast from near 50 to 60 percent. At higher elevations and over much of northern Maine, the average is near 45 percent. The average annual number of clear days ranges from 80 to 120 days in the southern half and from about 50 to 90 days in the northern half of the State.

Heavy fog is frequent and sometimes persistent along the coast, particularly in the eastern portion of the coast where it may occur on an average of one day out of six. Fog frequency and duration diminish inland. But short-duration heavy ground fogs of early morning occur frequently at susceptible places inland.

Prolonged dry spells, quite frequent in late summer or fall, create serious forest-fire hazards. Low humidities and lack of precipitation during some late summers cause the forest litter to become extremely inflammable.

WINDS AND STORMS. On a yearly basis, the wind direction is mostly from the west. During winter, north to northwest winds tend to prevail. In the summer, they are more often from the southwest or south. Topography has a strong influence on the prevailing direction. Parts of a major river valley, for example, may have a prevailing wind paralleling the valley. Along the coast in spring and summer, the sea breeze is important. On-shore local winds, blowing from the cool ocean, may come as far inland as 10 miles. They tend to retard spring growth, but are pleasingly cooling in summer.

Coastal storms or "northeasters" sometimes seriously affect the Coastal Division. They generate very strong winds and heavy rain or snow. They can produce abnormally high wind-driven tides, affecting beaches and coastal installations. In winter, these storms produce some of the heavier snowfalls along the coast. Occasionally, in summer or fall, a storm of tropical origin affects Maine. Usually the storm will be similar to the northeasters. But a few such storms may retain near or full hurricane force. Tornadoes are a phenomena not common in Maine. It is likely that several occur on the average each year. Fortunately, most tornadoes are very small, affecting a very localized area. About 80 percent of Maine's tornadoes occur between May 15 and September 15. The peak month is July. Thunderstorms and hailstorms have a similar frequency maximum from midspring to early fall. Thunderstorms occur in a range from 10 to 20 days a year in the Coastal Division and from 15 to 30 days a year elsewhere. The most severe storms are attended by hail.

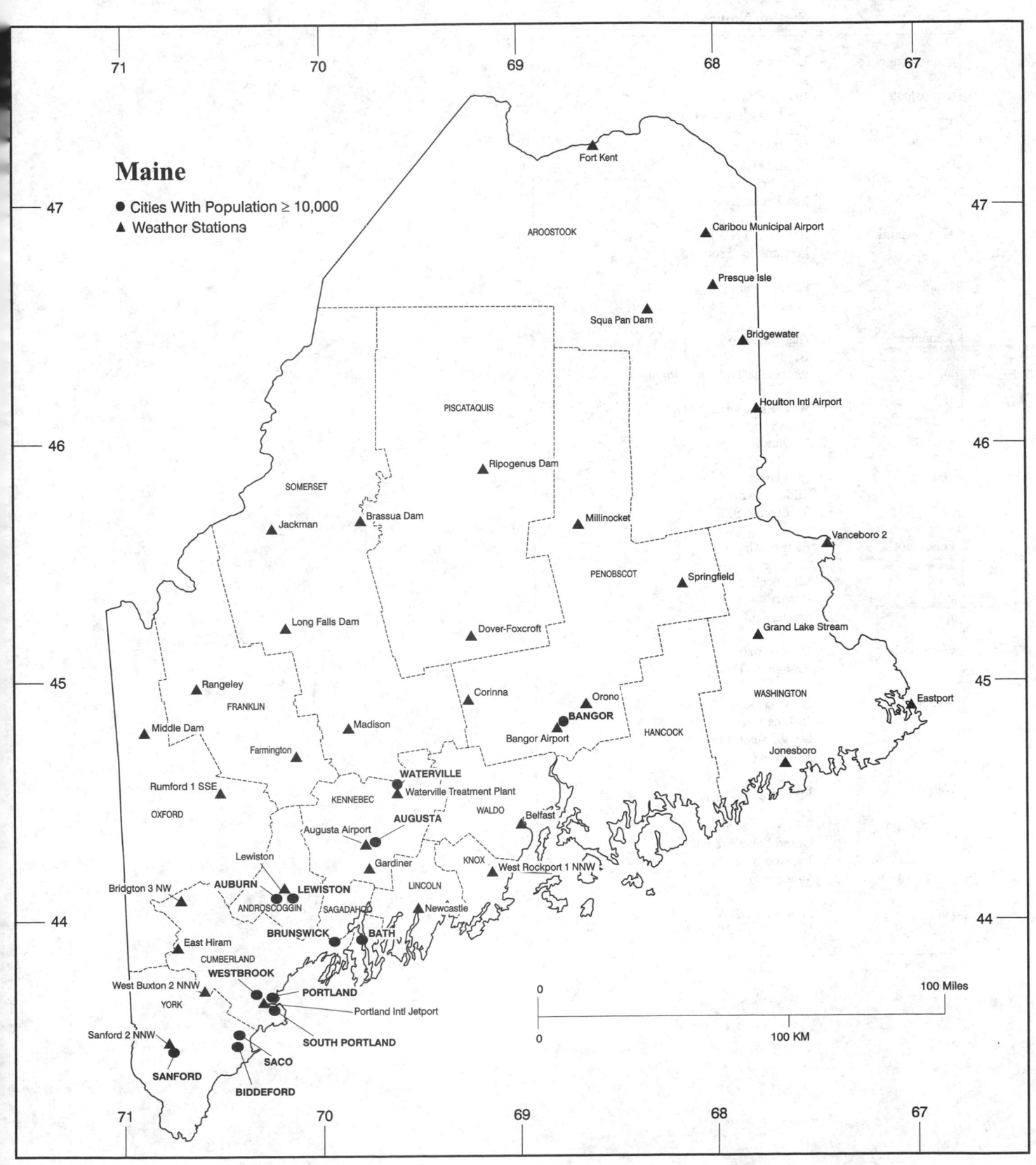

Maine

- ● Cities With Population ≥ 10,000
- ▲ Weather Stations

AROOSTOOK

PISCATAQUIS

SOMERSET

PENOBSCOT

FRANKLIN

WASHINGTON

OXFORD

KENNEBEC

WALDO

HANCOCK

KNOX

LINCOLN

SAGADAHOC

CUMBERLAND

YORK

Fort Kent

Caribou Municipal Airport

Presque Isle

Bridgewater

Houlton Intl Airport

Squa Pan Dam

Ripogenus Dam

Millinocket

Vanceboro 2

Springfield

Jackman

Brassua Dam

Grand Lake Stream

Long Falls Dam

Dover-Foxcroft

Rangeley

Corinna

Orono

Eastport

Middle Dam

Madison

BANGOR

Bangor Airport

Jonesboro

Farmington

Rumford 1 SSE

WATERVILLE

Waterville Treatment Plant

AUGUSTA

Augusta Airport

Belfast

Lewiston

Gardiner

West Rockport 1 NNW

Bridgton 3 NW

AUBURN

LEWISTON

ANDROSCOGGIN

Newcastle

BRUNSWICK

BATH

East Hiram

WESTBROOK

West Buxton 2 NNW

PORTLAND

Portland Intl Jetport

Sanford 2 NNW

SOUTH PORTLAND

SACO

SANFORD

BIDDEFORD

0   100 Miles

0   100 KM

Maine Weather Stations by County

County	Station Name
Androscoggin	Lewiston
Aroostook	Bridgewater
	Caribou Municipal Airport
	Fort Kent
	Houlton Int'l Airport
	Presque Isle
	Squa Pan Dam
	Van Buren 2
Cumberland	Bridgton 3 NW
	Portland Int'l Jetport
Franklin	Farmington
	Rangeley
Kennebec	Augusta Airport
	Gardiner
	Waterville Treatment Plant
Knox	West Rockport 1 NNW
Lincoln	Newcastle
Oxford	East Hiram
	Middle Dam
	Rumford 1 SSE
Penobscot	Bangor Airport
	Corinna
	Millinocket
	Orono
	Springfield
Piscataquis	Dover-Foxcroft
	Ripogenus Dam
Somerset	Brassua Dam
	Jackman
	Long Falls Dam
	Madison
Waldo	Belfast
Washington	Eastport
	Grand Lake Stream
	Jonesboro
	Vanceboro 2
York	Sanford 2 NNW
	West Buxton 2 NNW

Maine Weather Stations by City

City	Station Name	Miles
Auburn	Lewiston	1
Augusta	Augusta Airport	2
	Gardiner	7
	Waterville Treatment Plant	16
Bangor	Bangor Airport	2
	Orono	8
Bath	Newcastle	17
Biddeford	Portland Int'l Jetport	14
	Sanford 2 NNW	17
	West Buxton 2 NNW	17
Brunswick	Lewiston	18
Lewiston	Lewiston	1
Portland	Portland Int'l Jetport	2
	West Buxton 2 NNW	17
Saco	Portland Int'l Jetport	12
	Sanford 2 NNW	17
	West Buxton 2 NNW	16
Sanford	Sanford 2 NNW	2
	West Buxton 2 NNW	20
South Portland	Portland Int'l Jetport	2
	West Buxton 2 NNW	18
Waterville	Augusta Airport	18
	Waterville Treatment Plant	1
Westbrook	Portland Int'l Jetport	4
	West Buxton 2 NNW	13

Note: Miles is the distance between the geographic center of the city and the weather station.

Maine Weather Stations by Elevation

Feet	Station Name
1,528	Rangeley
1,459	Middle Dam
1,187	Jackman
1,158	Long Falls Dam
1,059	Brassua Dam
964	Ripogenus Dam
629	Rumford 1 SSE
623	Caribou Municipal Airport
606	Fort Kent
606	Squa Pan Dam
597	Presque Isle
557	Bridgton 3 NW
524	East Hiram
495	Houlton Int'l Airport
459	Dover-Foxcroft
456	Van Buren 2
439	Springfield
419	Bridgewater
419	Farmington
419	Vanceboro 2
377	West Rockport 1 NNW
357	Millinocket
347	Augusta Airport
288	Grand Lake Stream
278	Sanford 2 NNW
259	Madison
219	Corinna
187	Newcastle
183	Bangor Airport
183	Jonesboro
177	Lewiston
147	West Buxton 2 NNW
137	Gardiner
114	Orono
82	Eastport
72	Waterville Treatment Plant
42	Portland Int'l Jetport
29	Belfast

Caribou Municipal Airport

The Caribou Municipal Airport is located in Aroostook County, the largest and northernmost county in the state. The airport lies on top of high land which is about on the same level as most of the surrounding gently rolling hills. The Aroostook River, which runs about one mile to the east and southeast of the station, has little effect on the local weather. Even though Caribou is located only 150 miles from the Atlantic coast, its climate can be justly classed as a severe typical continental type. Winters are particularly long and windy, and seasonal snowfalls averaging over 100 inches are not unusual. While the extreme low temperatures may be less severe than one might expect, temperatures of zero or lower normally occur over 40 times per year. A study of heating degree day data will show the outstanding part that cold weather plays here.

Summers are cool and generally favored with abundant rainfall, which is one of the most important factors in the high yield of the potato and grain crops throughout the county. Caribou's location high up in the St. Lawrence Valley allows Aroostook County to come under the influence of the Summer Polar Front, resulting in practically no dry periods of more than 3 or 4 days in the growing season. The growing season at Caribou averages more than 120 days, with the average last freeze in the spring in mid-May and the average first freeze in autumn in late September.

Autumn climate is nearly ideal, with mostly sunny warm days and crisp cool nights predominating. Aroostook County, even with its relatively short growing season, provides profitable farming. The principal crops are potatoes, peas, a variety of grains, and some hardy vegetables.

Probably unknown to many victims of hay fever and similar afflictions, the immediate Caribou area offers sparkling visibility and relatively pollen-free air in the late summer months. This latter condition is principally due to the extremely high degree of cultivation of all available land.

Caribou Municipal Airport *Aroostook County* Elevation: 623 ft. Latitude: 46° 52' N Longitude: 68° 02' W

	JAN	FEB	MAR	APR	MAY	JUN	JUL	AUG	SEP	OCT	NOV	DEC	YEAR
Mean Maximum Temp. (°F)	19.1	23.2	34.0	47.0	62.6	71.9	76.6	74.3	64.0	51.5	37.5	24.6	48.9
Mean Temp. (°F)	9.4	13.1	24.6	38.2	51.7	61.0	65.9	63.6	53.9	42.9	30.6	16.3	39.3
Mean Minimum Temp. (°F)	-0.4	3.0	15.2	29.4	40.9	50.1	55.1	52.8	43.7	34.2	23.5	7.8	29.6
Extreme Maximum Temp. (°F)	53	59	66	86	96	93	95	95	90	78	67	54	96
Extreme Minimum Temp. (°F)	-33	-30	-21	1	18	31	39	34	23	14	-8	-31	-33
Days Maximum Temp. ≥ 90°F	0	0	0	0	0	0	1	0	0	0	0	0	1
Days Maximum Temp. ≤ 32°F	26	22	13	2	0	0	0	0	0	0	10	23	96
Days Minimum Temp. ≤ 32°F	31	28	29	20	4	0	0	0	2	14	25	30	183
Days Minimum Temp. ≤ 0°F	17	13	5	0	0	0	0	0	0	0	0	10	45
Heating Degree Days (base 65°F)	1,720	1,461	1,246	797	411	154	54	98	336	678	1,027	1,506	9,488
Cooling Degree Days (base 65°F)	0	0	0	0	4	38	85	58	10	0	0	0	195
Mean Precipitation (in.)	2.89	2.03	2.58	2.61	3.27	3.32	3.83	4.12	3.39	3.12	3.11	3.15	37.42
Maximum Precipitation (in.)	5.6	4.1	5.1	5.3	5.8	6.4	6.8	12.1	8.1	8.7	8.1	8.0	51.1
Minimum Precipitation (in.)	0.3	0.3	0.7	0.5	0.5	0.9	1.0	0.9	0.9	0.6	1.2	0.7	27.9
Maximum 24-hr. Precipitation (in.)	1.6	1.1	1.7	1.6	2.1	2.1	2.4	6.7	6.2	4.0	2.1	2.8	6.7
Days With ≥ 0.1" Precipitation	7	5	7	7	8	8	8	8	7	7	7	8	87
Days With ≥ 1.0" Precipitation	0	0	0	0	0	0	1	1	1	0	0	0	3
Mean Snowfall (in.)	25.7	20.1	19.8	9.9	0.6	trace	trace	trace	trace	1.0	11.7	24.9	113.7
Maximum Snowfall (in.)	45	41	47	36	11	trace	0	0	3	12	35	60	167
Maximum 24-hr. Snowfall (in.)	14	17	29	21	6	trace	0	0	2	9	21	19	29
Days With ≥ 1.0" Snow Depth	30	28	30	14	0	0	0	0	0	0	10	27	139
Thunderstorm Days	< 1	0	< 1	< 1	2	5	7	5	1	1	0	0	21
Foggy Days	8	6	8	11	10	12	14	15	14	13	12	9	132
Predominant Sky Cover	OVR	OVR	OVR	OVR	OVR	OVR	OVR	OVR	OVR	OVR	OVR	OVR	OVR
Mean Relative Humidity 7am (%)	75	74	76	75	74	78	83	86	87	86	84	80	80
Mean Relative Humidity 4pm (%)	68	63	60	56	51	55	58	59	61	65	74	73	62
Mean Dewpoint (°F)	4	5	15	27	38	50	56	54	46	36	25	11	31
Prevailing Wind Direction	NW	NW	NW	NW	NW	S	S	WSW	S	WSW	NW	NW	NW
Prevailing Wind Speed (mph)	16	16	17	16	16	10	9	10	10	12	15	16	14
Maximum Wind Gust (mph)	28	38	31	41	37	33	35	35	37	44	53	48	53

Portland Int'l Jetport

The Portland International Jetport is located two and three fourths miles west of the site of the former city office. The surrounding country is mostly open, rolling and sloping generally toward the Fore River, a body of brackish water about 1,000 feet wide at a distance of about one half mile from the station and forming one boundary (north through east) of the field. The airport is about five and a half miles west-northwest of the open ocean. A slight rise reaching an elevation of 100 feet, lying northwest of the field, cuts down the wind slightly from that direction. The older portion of the city is situated on a hill rising abruptly from sea level to 170 feet, one and a half miles east of the airport and on the opposite side of the Fore River. A line of low hills southeast of the airport, near the ocean, which reach a maximum height of 160 feet, shuts off sight of the ocean from the airport. Sebago Lake with an area of 44 square miles is situated about 15 miles to the northwest and 45 miles farther are the White Mountains, averaging 3,000 to 5,000 feet in height.

As a rule, Portland has very pleasant summers and falls, cold winters with frequent thaws, and disagreeable springs. Autumn has the greatest number of sunny days and the least cloudiness. Winters are quite severe, but begin late and then extend deeply into the normal springtime.

Heavy seasonal snowfalls, over 100 inches, normally occur about each 10 years. True blizzards are very rare. The White Mountains, to the northwest, keep considerable snow from reaching the Portland area and also moderate the temperature.

Winds are generally quite light with the highest velocities being confined mostly to March and November. Even in these months the occasional northeasterly gales have usually lost much of their severity before reaching the coast of Maine.

Temperatures well below zero are recorded frequently each winter. Cold waves sometimes come in on strong winds, but extremely low temperatures are generally accompanied by light winds.

The average freeze-free season at the airport station is 139 days. Mid-May is the average occurrence of the last freeze in spring, and the average occurrence of the first freeze in fall is late September. The freeze-free period is longer in the city proper, but may be even shorter at susceptible places further inland.

Daily maximum temperatures at the present airport site agree closely with those near the former intown office, but minimum temperatures on clear, quiet mornings range as much as 15 degrees lower at the airport.

Portland Int'l Jetport *Cumberland County* Elevation: 42 ft.   Latitude: 43° 39' N   Longitude: 70° 18' W

	JAN	FEB	MAR	APR	MAY	JUN	JUL	AUG	SEP	OCT	NOV	DEC	YEAR
Mean Maximum Temp. (°F)	30.6	33.9	41.7	52.5	63.3	73.0	79.2	77.7	69.2	58.3	47.3	36.3	55.2
Mean Temp. (°F)	21.4	24.5	33.1	43.4	53.7	62.9	69.1	67.7	59.3	48.3	38.8	27.6	45.8
Mean Minimum Temp. (°F)	12.2	15.1	24.6	34.3	44.0	52.8	59.0	57.7	49.3	38.3	30.2	18.9	36.4
Extreme Maximum Temp. (°F)	60	63	88	84	94	98	99	103	95	83	74	71	103
Extreme Minimum Temp. (°F)	-26	-25	-8	15	26	37	44	39	29	15	3	-20	-26
Days Maximum Temp. ≥ 90°F	0	0	0	0	0	1	2	1	0	0	0	0	4
Days Maximum Temp. ≤ 32°F	17	12	4	0	0	0	0	0	0	0	1	11	45
Days Minimum Temp. ≤ 32°F	30	26	25	12	1	0	0	0	0	9	19	28	150
Days Minimum Temp. ≤ 0°F	5	3	0	0	0	0	0	0	0	0	0	2	10
Heating Degree Days (base 65°F)	1,343	1,137	981	642	351	110	17	34	193	512	780	1,153	7,253
Cooling Degree Days (base 65°F)	0	0	0	0	8	58	156	127	28	1	0	0	378
Mean Precipitation (in.)	4.01	3.19	4.16	4.22	3.82	3.31	3.22	3.16	3.44	4.42	4.66	4.26	45.87
Maximum Precipitation (in.)	11.9	7.1	10.0	9.9	9.6	6.8	7.5	15.2	9.8	12.3	13.5	9.7	66.3
Minimum Precipitation (in.)	0.8	trace	0.8	1.0	0.5	0.8	0.6	0.5	0.3	0.6	0.9	1.0	26.3
Maximum 24-hr. Precipitation (in.)	3.6	3.2	3.5	5.2	3.3	4.0	2.5	7.8	7.5	7.5	4.7	3.5	7.8
Days With ≥ 0.1" Precipitation	7	5	7	7	7	6	6	5	6	6	7	8	77
Days With ≥ 1.0" Precipitation	1	1	1	1	1	1	1	1	1	1	1	1	12
Mean Snowfall (in.)	20.2	12.6	12.5	3.3	trace	0.0	0.0	0.0	trace	trace	3.2	14.7	66.5
Maximum Snowfall (in.)	62	61	49	16	2	0	0	0	trace	4	16	55	150
Maximum 24-hr. Snowfall (in.)	16	17	17	14	1	0	0	0	trace	4	9	22	22
Days With ≥ 1.0" Snow Depth	23	20	14	2	0	0	0	0	0	0	2	13	74
Thunderstorm Days	< 1	< 1	< 1	< 1	2	4	4	4	1	1	< 1	< 1	16
Foggy Days	10	9	12	14	15	16	17	17	16	15	14	12	167
Predominant Sky Cover	OVR	OVR	OVR	OVR	OVR	OVR	OVR	OVR	OVR	OVR	OVR	OVR	OVR
Mean Relative Humidity 7am (%)	75	75	74	73	75	78	80	83	86	84	82	78	79
Mean Relative Humidity 4pm (%)	62	59	60	58	61	63	62	63	64	64	66	65	62
Mean Dewpoint (°F)	13	14	22	32	43	53	59	58	51	40	31	18	36
Prevailing Wind Direction	N	NNW	N	S	S	S	S	S	S	N	W	N	S
Prevailing Wind Speed (mph)	9	10	10	12	12	10	10	10	10	9	9	9	10
Maximum Wind Gust (mph)	64	64	62	61	67	76	60	78	76	68	76	76	78

Augusta Airport *Kennebec County*   Elevation: 347 ft.   Latitude: 44° 19' N   Longitude: 69° 48' W

	JAN	FEB	MAR	APR	MAY	JUN	JUL	AUG	SEP	OCT	NOV	DEC	YEAR
Mean Maximum Temp. (°F)	27.9	31.7	40.4	52.6	65.3	74.2	79.6	78.0	68.9	57.2	44.9	33.1	54.5
Mean Temp. (°F)	19.4	22.9	32.2	43.8	55.4	64.4	70.3	68.6	59.7	48.6	37.8	25.4	45.7
Mean Minimum Temp. (°F)	10.9	14.1	23.9	35.0	45.5	54.7	60.9	59.1	50.5	39.9	30.6	17.6	36.9
Extreme Maximum Temp. (°F)	57	60	85	90	94	98	98	97	95	83	74	65	98
Extreme Minimum Temp. (°F)	-19	-18	-11	10	29	37	47	43	28	21	4	-12	-19
Days Maximum Temp. ≥ 90°F	0	0	0	0	0	1	2	1	0	0	0	0	4
Days Maximum Temp. ≤ 32°F	20	14	6	0	0	0	0	0	0	0	3	14	57
Days Minimum Temp. ≤ 32°F	29	26	24	11	0	0	0	0	0	6	18	28	142
Days Minimum Temp. ≤ 0°F	6	4	0	0	0	0	0	0	0	0	0	2	12
Heating Degree Days (base 65°F)	1,405	1,183	1,010	627	299	80	12	26	181	503	809	1,223	7,358
Cooling Degree Days (base 65°F)	0	0	0	0	9	69	178	140	30	1	0	0	427
Mean Precipitation (in.)	3.06	2.69	3.60	3.75	3.96	3.56	3.31	3.26	3.57	3.94	3.87	3.42	41.99
Days With ≥ 0.1" Precipitation	7	6	7	7	7	7	6	5	6	6	7	7	78
Days With ≥ 1.0" Precipitation	1	1	1	1	1	1	1	1	1	1	1	1	12
Mean Snowfall (in.)	19.3	13.6	14.4	5.0	trace	0.0	0.0	0.0	trace	0.1	3.9	15.4	71.7
Days With ≥ 1.0" Snow Depth	26	23	18	3	0	0	0	0	0	0	3	18	91

Bangor Airport *Penobscot County*   Elevation: 183 ft.   Latitude: 44° 48' N   Longitude: 68° 49' W

	JAN	FEB	MAR	APR	MAY	JUN	JUL	AUG	SEP	OCT	NOV	DEC	YEAR
Mean Maximum Temp. (°F)	26.5	29.8	39.2	51.6	64.5	73.2	78.7	77.2	68.1	56.7	44.5	31.8	53.5
Mean Temp. (°F)	17.3	20.2	30.6	42.4	54.0	63.0	68.7	67.3	58.4	47.6	36.9	23.3	44.1
Mean Minimum Temp. (°F)	7.9	10.7	22.0	33.2	43.6	52.8	58.7	57.3	48.6	38.4	29.3	14.8	34.8
Extreme Maximum Temp. (°F)	57	59	71	92	96	96	96	102	92	84	72	65	102
Extreme Minimum Temp. (°F)	-28	-27	-11	14	28	37	44	39	25	19	1	-23	-28
Days Maximum Temp. ≥ 90°F	0	0	0	0	0	1	2	1	0	0	0	0	4
Days Maximum Temp. ≤ 32°F	21	17	7	1	0	0	0	0	0	0	2	15	63
Days Minimum Temp. ≤ 32°F	29	27	26	14	1	0	0	0	0	8	20	29	154
Days Minimum Temp. ≤ 0°F	9	6	1	0	0	0	0	0	0	0	0	4	20
Heating Degree Days (base 65°F)	1,474	1,258	1,059	670	341	105	20	41	213	535	836	1,286	7,838
Cooling Degree Days (base 65°F)	0	0	0	0	8	57	152	124	23	1	0	0	365
Mean Precipitation (in.)	3.00	2.60	3.47	3.40	3.46	3.43	3.26	3.31	3.36	3.30	3.77	3.44	39.80
Days With ≥ 0.1" Precipitation	7	6	7	7	7	7	7	6	6	7	7	7	81
Days With ≥ 1.0" Precipitation	1	0	1	1	1	1	1	1	1	1	1	1	11
Mean Snowfall (in.)	17.9	15.5	12.8	4.4	trace	trace	0.0	0.0	trace	0.3	3.4	14.9	69.2
Days With ≥ 1.0" Snow Depth	25	23	19	3	0	0	0	0	0	0	3	17	90

Belfast *Waldo County*   Elevation: 29 ft.   Latitude: 44° 24' N   Longitude: 69° 00' W

	JAN	FEB	MAR	APR	MAY	JUN	JUL	AUG	SEP	OCT	NOV	DEC	YEAR
Mean Maximum Temp. (°F)	31.5	34.5	42.7	53.7	65.4	74.3	79.9	78.4	70.1	58.8	47.2	36.1	56.0
Mean Temp. (°F)	21.0	23.7	32.6	43.1	53.9	62.8	68.6	67.2	59.2	48.6	38.7	26.7	45.5
Mean Minimum Temp. (°F)	10.5	12.8	22.4	32.5	42.4	51.3	57.2	55.9	48.2	38.4	30.1	17.3	34.9
Extreme Maximum Temp. (°F)	58	60	82	82	95	96	96	96	90	82	73	65	96
Extreme Minimum Temp. (°F)	-27	-26	-15	12	26	35	44	35	25	20	2	-27	-27
Days Maximum Temp. ≥ 90°F	0	0	0	0	0	1	2	1	0	0	0	0	4
Days Maximum Temp. ≤ 32°F	16	11	4	0	0	0	0	0	0	0	1	10	42
Days Minimum Temp. ≤ 32°F	30	27	27	15	2	0	0	0	0	9	19	29	158
Days Minimum Temp. ≤ 0°F	8	5	1	0	0	0	0	0	0	0	0	3	17
Heating Degree Days (base 65°F)	1,357	1,160	998	649	342	102	16	31	186	501	783	1,180	7,305
Cooling Degree Days (base 65°F)	0	0	0	0	5	41	124	92	17	0	0	0	279
Mean Precipitation (in.)	3.97	3.15	4.34	4.45	4.10	3.84	3.13	3.15	4.15	4.37	4.73	4.33	47.71
Days With ≥ 0.1" Precipitation	5	5	6	7	7	6	6	6	6	6	7	6	73
Days With ≥ 1.0" Precipitation	1	1	1	1	1	1	1	1	1	1	1	1	12
Mean Snowfall (in.)	na	na	na	1.4	0.0	0.0	0.0	0.0	0.0	trace	1.9	na	na
Days With ≥ 1.0" Snow Depth	14	12	na	2	0	0	0	0	0	0	1	9	na

Brassua Dam *Somerset County*   Elevation: 1,059 ft.   Latitude: 45° 40' N   Longitude: 69° 49' W

	JAN	FEB	MAR	APR	MAY	JUN	JUL	AUG	SEP	OCT	NOV	DEC	YEAR
Mean Maximum Temp. (°F)	21.4	25.2	34.7	46.1	61.2	70.7	75.5	73.9	64.7	52.3	39.2	26.6	49.3
Mean Temp. (°F)	10.0	12.7	23.0	35.9	49.3	59.6	64.8	62.9	54.0	42.9	31.6	17.5	38.7
Mean Minimum Temp. (°F)	-1.3	0.2	11.3	25.7	37.5	48.5	54.1	51.9	43.4	33.5	23.9	8.2	28.1
Extreme Maximum Temp. (°F)	55	58	70	80	88	92	93	97	91	80	67	56	97
Extreme Minimum Temp. (°F)	-37	-33	-30	-2	19	28	34	32	20	15	-7	-30	-37
Days Maximum Temp. ≥ 90°F	0	0	0	0	0	0	0	0	0	0	0	0	0
Days Maximum Temp. ≤ 32°F	25	20	12	2	0	0	0	0	0	0	7	21	87
Days Minimum Temp. ≤ 32°F	31	28	30	25	10	0	0	0	3	15	25	30	197
Days Minimum Temp. ≤ 0°F	18	16	8	0	0	0	0	0	0	0	0	10	52
Heating Degree Days (base 65°F)	1,700	1,472	1,295	866	482	181	71	108	329	678	997	1,468	9,647
Cooling Degree Days (base 65°F)	0	0	0	0	2	29	68	49	8	0	0	0	156
Mean Precipitation (in.)	2.94	2.27	2.87	3.38	3.76	4.12	4.13	3.79	3.88	3.64	3.47	3.04	41.29
Days With ≥ 0.1" Precipitation	7	6	7	8	8	9	8	8	7	7	8	7	90
Days With ≥ 1.0" Precipitation	0	0	0	0	1	1	1	1	1	1	1	1	8
Mean Snowfall (in.)	24.5	20.0	20.2	10.1	0.2	trace	0.0	0.0	trace	1.1	9.3	23.1	108.5
Days With ≥ 1.0" Snow Depth	na	na	na	na	0	0	0	0	0	0	na	na	na

Bridgewater *Aroostook County*   Elevation: 419 ft.   Latitude: 46° 25' N   Longitude: 67° 51' W

	JAN	FEB	MAR	APR	MAY	JUN	JUL	AUG	SEP	OCT	NOV	DEC	YEAR
Mean Maximum Temp. (°F)	22.3	26.6	36.6	49.8	64.9	74.1	78.6	76.3	66.1	53.7	39.5	27.2	51.3
Mean Temp. (°F)	10.8	14.2	25.5	38.9	51.7	61.2	66.0	63.7	54.5	43.6	31.6	17.4	39.9
Mean Minimum Temp. (°F)	-0.8	1.7	14.3	27.9	38.5	48.2	53.3	51.1	42.8	33.4	23.5	7.5	28.5
Extreme Maximum Temp. (°F)	53	61	67	86	95	94	95	96	89	79	66	56	96
Extreme Minimum Temp. (°F)	-43	-38	-28	-1	18	24	33	29	19	12	-9	-38	-43
Days Maximum Temp. ≥ 90°F	0	0	0	0	0	1	1	1	0	0	0	0	3
Days Maximum Temp. ≤ 32°F	24	19	10	1	0	0	0	0	0	0	6	21	81
Days Minimum Temp. ≤ 32°F	30	28	29	22	8	1	0	0	4	15	25	30	192
Days Minimum Temp. ≤ 0°F	17	14	6	0	0	0	0	0	0	0	1	10	48
Heating Degree Days (base 65°F)	1,678	1,431	1,218	776	408	148	50	96	319	658	997	1,470	9,249
Cooling Degree Days (base 65°F)	0	0	0	0	4	36	84	64	10	0	0	0	198
Mean Precipitation (in.)	3.55	2.51	3.05	3.29	3.85	3.67	3.80	3.91	3.70	3.51	3.83	3.49	42.16
Days With ≥ 0.1" Precipitation	7	6	7	8	8	8	7	7	7	7	8	8	88
Days With ≥ 1.0" Precipitation	1	1	1	1	1	1	1	1	1	1	1	1	12
Mean Snowfall (in.)	22.0	17.3	15.3	6.7	trace	0.0	0.0	0.0	trace	0.5	8.2	20.3	90.3
Days With ≥ 1.0" Snow Depth	na	na	na	na	0	0	0	0	0	0	8	22	na

Bridgton 3 NW *Cumberland County*   Elevation: 557 ft.   Latitude: 44° 05' N   Longitude: 70° 44' W

	JAN	FEB	MAR	APR	MAY	JUN	JUL	AUG	SEP	OCT	NOV	DEC	YEAR
Mean Maximum Temp. (°F)	28.8	32.2	41.4	52.9	66.4	74.0	79.1	76.8	68.6	57.5	45.0	33.3	54.7
Mean Temp. (°F)	16.8	19.9	30.2	41.5	53.7	62.2	67.4	65.2	56.7	45.8	35.6	23.1	43.2
Mean Minimum Temp. (°F)	4.8	7.6	19.1	30.1	40.9	50.2	55.6	53.6	44.8	34.0	26.2	12.9	31.7
Extreme Maximum Temp. (°F)	58	63	76	89	93	95	96	100	90	83	75	68	100
Extreme Minimum Temp. (°F)	-26	-28	-17	9	23	28	36	29	19	15	-2	-25	-28
Days Maximum Temp. ≥ 90°F	0	0	0	0	0	1	1	0	0	0	0	0	2
Days Maximum Temp. ≤ 32°F	19	14	5	0	0	0	0	0	0	0	2	14	54
Days Minimum Temp. ≤ 32°F	31	28	29	21	4	0	0	0	2	14	24	30	183
Days Minimum Temp. ≤ 0°F	12	9	2	0	0	0	0	0	0	0	0	5	28
Heating Degree Days (base 65°F)	1,488	1,266	1,071	699	353	123	35	66	255	589	877	1,292	8,114
Cooling Degree Days (base 65°F)	0	0	0	0	6	42	109	72	14	0	0	0	243
Mean Precipitation (in.)	4.40	3.25	4.20	3.94	3.64	4.11	3.92	4.11	3.82	4.74	4.03	3.69	47.85
Days With ≥ 0.1" Precipitation	7	5	7	7	7	8	7	7	6	7	7	7	82
Days With ≥ 1.0" Precipitation	1	1	1	1	1	1	1	1	1	1	1	1	12
Mean Snowfall (in.)	22.6	15.9	14.6	5.2	trace	0.0	0.0	0.0	0.0	0.1	4.0	14.4	76.8
Days With ≥ 1.0" Snow Depth	na	na	na	na	0	0	0	0	0	0	na	na	na

Corinna *Penobscot County*   Elevation: 219 ft.   Latitude: 44° 55' N   Longitude: 69° 16' W

	JAN	FEB	MAR	APR	MAY	JUN	JUL	AUG	SEP	OCT	NOV	DEC	YEAR
Mean Maximum Temp. (°F)	26.0	30.4	39.8	52.8	66.7	74.9	79.7	78.1	68.9	57.3	43.8	31.2	54.1
Mean Temp. (°F)	13.6	17.4	28.7	41.4	53.9	62.7	67.8	65.8	56.7	45.4	34.5	20.4	42.3
Mean Minimum Temp. (°F)	1.1	4.4	17.4	29.9	41.1	50.4	55.9	53.4	44.4	33.4	25.0	9.7	30.5
Extreme Maximum Temp. (°F)	54	59	72	92	97	96	95	95	92	83	71	63	97
Extreme Minimum Temp. (°F)	-38	-32	-28	6	22	32	37	31	21	15	-8	-31	-38
Days Maximum Temp. ≥ 90°F	0	0	0	0	0	1	2	1	0	0	0	0	4
Days Maximum Temp. ≤ 32°F	22	16	7	0	0	0	0	0	0	0	3	16	64
Days Minimum Temp. ≤ 32°F	30	27	28	20	5	0	0	0	3	16	24	30	183
Days Minimum Temp. ≤ 0°F	16	11	3	0	0	0	0	0	0	0	0	8	38
Heating Degree Days (base 65°F)	1,587	1,338	1,120	703	347	115	30	59	258	602	910	1,375	8,444
Cooling Degree Days (base 65°F)	0	0	0	0	8	51	124	88	14	0	0	0	285
Mean Precipitation (in.)	3.35	2.64	3.61	3.70	3.80	3.89	3.42	3.63	3.81	3.81	3.79	3.44	42.89
Days With ≥ 0.1" Precipitation	7	6	7	8	8	8	7	6	7	7	8	7	86
Days With ≥ 1.0" Precipitation	1	0	1	1	1	1	1	1	1	1	1	1	11
Mean Snowfall (in.)	18.6	14.2	13.6	5.1	0.0	0.0	0.0	0.0	0.0	0.2	4.5	16.4	72.6
Days With ≥ 1.0" Snow Depth	29	27	25	5	0	0	0	0	0	0	4	21	111

Dover-Foxcroft *Piscataquis County*   Elevation: 459 ft.   Latitude: 45° 11' N   Longitude: 69° 15' W

	JAN	FEB	MAR	APR	MAY	JUN	JUL	AUG	SEP	OCT	NOV	DEC	YEAR
Mean Maximum Temp. (°F)	23.5	27.8	37.1	49.2	64.2	72.7	78.3	76.6	67.2	54.4	41.3	29.1	51.8
Mean Temp. (°F)	12.9	16.6	26.7	39.1	51.9	60.7	66.3	64.5	55.2	43.7	32.9	20.0	40.9
Mean Minimum Temp. (°F)	2.1	5.3	16.3	29.0	39.5	48.7	54.3	52.3	43.3	33.0	24.5	10.9	29.9
Extreme Maximum Temp. (°F)	57	57	69	84	93	96	94	93	91	81	68	63	96
Extreme Minimum Temp. (°F)	-31	-29	-18	4	23	32	38	32	23	15	-3	-28	-31
Days Maximum Temp. ≥ 90°F	0	0	0	0	0	0	1	1	0	0	0	0	2
Days Maximum Temp. ≤ 32°F	25	18	9	1	0	0	0	0	0	0	5	19	77
Days Minimum Temp. ≤ 32°F	31	28	30	22	5	0	0	0	3	16	25	30	190
Days Minimum Temp. ≤ 0°F	16	11	4	0	0	0	0	0	0	0	0	8	39
Heating Degree Days (base 65°F)	1,613	1,362	1,179	770	407	156	49	80	297	654	955	1,389	8,911
Cooling Degree Days (base 65°F)	0	0	0	0	3	36	96	69	11	0	0	0	215
Mean Precipitation (in.)	3.95	2.57	3.38	3.71	3.78	3.97	3.50	3.70	4.10	3.90	3.83	3.54	43.93
Days With ≥ 0.1" Precipitation	8	6	7	8	8	9	7	7	7	7	8	7	89
Days With ≥ 1.0" Precipitation	1	0	1	1	1	1	1	1	1	1	1	0	10
Mean Snowfall (in.)	26.0	19.3	18.8	7.8	0.1	0.0	0.0	0.0	0.0	0.6	6.9	19.6	99.1
Days With ≥ 1.0" Snow Depth	30	28	30	14	0	0	0	0	0	0	7	25	134

East Hiram *Oxford County*   Elevation: 524 ft.   Latitude: 43° 53' N   Longitude: 70° 45' W

	JAN	FEB	MAR	APR	MAY	JUN	JUL	AUG	SEP	OCT	NOV	DEC	YEAR
Mean Maximum Temp. (°F)	29.1	32.4	41.5	53.6	66.6	75.0	80.3	78.5	69.7	58.0	45.3	33.8	55.3
Mean Temp. (°F)	16.5	18.7	29.6	41.6	53.3	62.5	67.7	65.6	56.7	45.4	35.2	23.1	43.0
Mean Minimum Temp. (°F)	3.8	5.0	17.6	29.5	40.0	49.9	55.1	52.7	43.6	32.7	25.1	12.3	30.6
Extreme Maximum Temp. (°F)	60	64	79	92	94	94	98	102	92	86	74	69	102
Extreme Minimum Temp. (°F)	-35	-33	-22	8	22	30	36	30	23	12	-6	-25	-35
Days Maximum Temp. ≥ 90°F	0	0	0	0	1	1	2	1	0	0	0	0	5
Days Maximum Temp. ≤ 32°F	19	14	6	0	0	0	0	0	0	0	2	14	55
Days Minimum Temp. ≤ 32°F	31	28	29	21	6	0	0	0	4	17	24	30	190
Days Minimum Temp. ≤ 0°F	13	11	3	0	0	0	0	0	0	0	0	6	33
Heating Degree Days (base 65°F)	1,500	1,302	1,092	696	363	126	34	65	262	603	887	1,293	8,223
Cooling Degree Days (base 65°F)	0	0	0	0	7	52	121	86	18	1	0	0	285
Mean Precipitation (in.)	4.06	2.96	4.35	4.34	4.02	3.91	3.96	3.66	3.74	4.62	4.59	4.14	48.35
Days With ≥ 0.1" Precipitation	7	6	7	7	8	8	7	7	6	7	8	7	85
Days With ≥ 1.0" Precipitation	1	1	1	1	1	1	1	1	1	1	1	1	12
Mean Snowfall (in.)	23.6	14.8	13.9	4.9	trace	0.0	0.0	0.0	0.0	trace	4.2	17.2	78.6
Days With ≥ 1.0" Snow Depth	30	28	28	7	0	0	0	0	0	0	4	20	117

Eastport *Washington County*   Elevation: 82 ft.   Latitude: 44° 55' N   Longitude: 67° 00' W

	JAN	FEB	MAR	APR	MAY	JUN	JUL	AUG	SEP	OCT	NOV	DEC	YEAR
Mean Maximum Temp. (°F)	29.8	31.2	38.6	49.1	59.7	68.3	74.0	73.5	65.8	55.3	45.3	35.0	52.1
Mean Temp. (°F)	21.6	23.5	31.3	41.1	50.5	58.2	63.8	63.8	57.3	47.9	38.7	27.7	43.8
Mean Minimum Temp. (°F)	13.4	15.8	23.9	33.2	41.3	48.1	53.5	54.1	48.8	40.4	32.2	20.4	35.4
Extreme Maximum Temp. (°F)	58	65	79	84	93	93	98	94	89	79	68	60	98
Extreme Minimum Temp. (°F)	-16	-15	-13	8	29	34	41	40	31	19	6	-12	-16
Days Maximum Temp. ≥ 90°F	0	0	0	0	0	0	0	0	0	0	0	0	0
Days Maximum Temp. ≤ 32°F	17	15	6	0	0	0	0	0	0	0	0	2	11	51
Days Minimum Temp. ≤ 32°F	28	26	25	13	1	0	0	0	0	4	16	26	139
Days Minimum Temp. ≤ 0°F	5	2	0	0	0	0	0	0	0	0	0	1	8
Heating Degree Days (base 65°F)	1,339	1,165	1,038	709	444	208	70	69	230	524	781	1,148	7,725
Cooling Degree Days (base 65°F)	0	0	0	0	1	11	40	40	6	0	0	0	98
Mean Precipitation (in.)	4.21	3.16	4.08	3.52	3.79	3.42	3.04	3.10	3.77	3.89	4.20	4.44	44.62
Days With ≥ 0.1" Precipitation	7	6	7	7	7	7	6	5	6	7	7	8	80
Days With ≥ 1.0" Precipitation	1	1	1	1	1	1	1	1	1	1	1	1	12
Mean Snowfall (in.)	14.4	13.5	14.4	4.6	trace	0.0	0.0	0.0	0.0	trace	2.2	12.4	61.5
Days With ≥ 1.0" Snow Depth	*18*	18	16	3	0	0	0	0	0	0	2	*12*	*69*

Farmington *Franklin County*   Elevation: 419 ft.   Latitude: 44° 41' N   Longitude: 70° 09' W

	JAN	FEB	MAR	APR	MAY	JUN	JUL	AUG	SEP	OCT	NOV	DEC	YEAR
Mean Maximum Temp. (°F)	25.5	29.5	38.3	51.1	65.1	73.6	78.7	77.1	68.2	56.7	43.3	30.9	53.2
Mean Temp. (°F)	13.2	16.7	27.1	39.9	52.0	61.0	66.2	64.2	55.1	44.4	33.6	20.6	41.2
Mean Minimum Temp. (°F)	0.8	3.8	15.8	28.6	38.9	48.3	53.7	51.3	41.9	32.0	23.9	10.2	29.1
Extreme Maximum Temp. (°F)	56	61	74	90	95	98	95	101	92	87	73	65	101
Extreme Minimum Temp. (°F)	-39	-31	-25	0	23	27	36	29	20	12	-14	-26	-39
Days Maximum Temp. ≥ 90°F	0	0	0	0	0	1	1	1	0	0	0	0	3
Days Maximum Temp. ≤ 32°F	23	17	8	1	0	0	0	0	0	0	4	17	70
Days Minimum Temp. ≤ 32°F	31	28	29	22	7	0	0	0	6	17	25	30	195
Days Minimum Temp. ≤ 0°F	16	12	4	0	0	0	0	0	0	0	0	8	40
Heating Degree Days (base 65°F)	1,603	1,359	1,169	748	401	153	51	88	303	633	934	1,372	8,814
Cooling Degree Days (base 65°F)	0	0	0	0	4	40	95	71	10	0	0	0	220
Mean Precipitation (in.)	3.62	2.95	3.98	3.98	3.89	4.54	3.55	3.94	3.75	4.10	4.17	3.88	46.35
Days With ≥ 0.1" Precipitation	7	6	7	7	8	9	7	7	6	7	7	7	85
Days With ≥ 1.0" Precipitation	1	1	1	1	1	1	1	1	1	1	1	1	12
Mean Snowfall (in.)	21.7	16.7	16.4	7.4	trace	0.0	0.0	0.0	trace	0.4	6.3	18.9	87.8
Days With ≥ 1.0" Snow Depth	29	26	25	6	0	0	0	0	0	0	5	20	111

Fort Kent *Aroostook County*   Elevation: 606 ft.   Latitude: 47° 14' N   Longitude: 68° 37' W

	JAN	FEB	MAR	APR	MAY	JUN	JUL	AUG	SEP	OCT	NOV	DEC	YEAR
Mean Maximum Temp. (°F)	18.8	23.3	34.1	46.2	62.1	72.1	76.3	74.4	64.3	51.8	37.9	24.5	48.8
Mean Temp. (°F)	6.4	9.6	21.9	36.3	50.1	60.1	64.8	62.6	53.0	41.9	29.9	14.3	37.6
Mean Minimum Temp. (°F)	-6.2	-4.0	9.7	26.2	38.1	48.0	53.2	50.8	41.7	32.0	21.9	4.1	26.3
Extreme Maximum Temp. (°F)	53	59	70	83	92	92	94	93	89	80	71	53	94
Extreme Minimum Temp. (°F)	-38	-38	-33	-8	19	29	37	31	24	12	-11	-33	-38
Days Maximum Temp. ≥ 90°F	0	0	0	0	0	0	1	0	0	0	0	0	1
Days Maximum Temp. ≤ 32°F	26	22	13	2	0	0	0	0	0	0	9	23	95
Days Minimum Temp. ≤ 32°F	31	28	30	24	8	1	0	0	4	17	27	31	201
Days Minimum Temp. ≤ 0°F	21	18	9	0	0	0	0	0	0	0	1	13	62
Heating Degree Days (base 65°F)	1,816	1,560	1,329	855	460	179	76	121	362	708	1,047	1,565	10,078
Cooling Degree Days (base 65°F)	0	0	0	0	3	33	71	51	9	0	0	0	167
Mean Precipitation (in.)	2.66	1.80	2.19	2.67	3.24	3.56	3.79	4.11	3.56	3.19	2.90	2.79	36.46
Days With ≥ 0.1" Precipitation	7	5	5	7	8	8	9	9	7	7	7	7	86
Days With ≥ 1.0" Precipitation	0	0	0	0	1	1	1	1	1	0	0	0	5
Mean Snowfall (in.)	23.1	18.2	15.5	7.9	0.2	0.0	0.0	0.0	trace	0.9	10.0	19.9	95.7
Days With ≥ 1.0" Snow Depth	30	28	*30*	*15*	0	0	0	0	0	0	10	27	*140*

Gardiner *Kennebec County* Elevation: 137 ft.　Latitude: 44° 13' N　Longitude: 69° 47' W

	JAN	FEB	MAR	APR	MAY	JUN	JUL	AUG	SEP	OCT	NOV	DEC	YEAR
Mean Maximum Temp. (°F)	29.1	32.7	41.1	53.3	66.1	74.8	80.2	79.0	70.1	58.5	46.2	34.3	55.4
Mean Temp. (°F)	17.6	21.3	30.9	42.7	54.7	63.5	69.0	67.7	58.8	47.6	37.2	24.4	44.6
Mean Minimum Temp. (°F)	6.2	9.6	20.9	32.3	43.2	52.1	57.8	56.2	47.5	36.6	28.1	14.4	33.8
Extreme Maximum Temp. (°F)	59	62	76	90	94	96	96	103	95	82	77	67	103
Extreme Minimum Temp. (°F)	-34	-32	-15	9	27	33	40	35	23	17	-1	-24	-34
Days Maximum Temp. ≥ 90°F	0	0	0	0	0	1	2	1	0	0	0	0	4
Days Maximum Temp. ≤ 32°F	19	13	5	0	0	0	0	0	0	0	2	13	52
Days Minimum Temp. ≤ 32°F	31	27	27	16	2	0	0	0	1	11	21	30	166
Days Minimum Temp. ≤ 0°F	11	8	2	0	0	0	0	0	0	0	0	5	26
Heating Degree Days (base 65°F)	1,463	1,226	1,051	662	320	98	17	33	201	534	829	1,253	7,687
Cooling Degree Days (base 65°F)	0	0	0	0	7	60	149	120	22	0	0	0	358
Mean Precipitation (in.)	3.61	2.76	3.98	4.00	3.82	3.76	3.07	3.25	3.71	3.99	4.21	3.63	43.79
Days With ≥ 0.1" Precipitation	6	5	7	7	7	7	6	6	6	6	7	6	76
Days With ≥ 1.0" Precipitation	1	1	1	1	1	1	1	1	1	1	1	1	12
Mean Snowfall (in.)	*17.6*	12.0	12.1	2.9	trace	0.0	0.0	0.0	0.0	trace	*2.5*	*12.9*	*60.0*
Days With ≥ 1.0" Snow Depth	*26*	25	16	*2*	0	0	0	0	0	0	3	*15*	*87*

Grand Lake Stream *Washington County* Elevation: 288 ft.　Latitude: 45° 11' N　Longitude: 67° 47' W

	JAN	FEB	MAR	APR	MAY	JUN	JUL	AUG	SEP	OCT	NOV	DEC	YEAR
Mean Maximum Temp. (°F)	26.3	29.8	38.7	50.5	64.0	73.1	78.8	77.4	68.2	56.4	44.1	31.7	53.3
Mean Temp. (°F)	14.9	18.0	27.9	39.9	52.0	61.3	67.0	65.6	56.5	45.2	34.7	21.7	42.1
Mean Minimum Temp. (°F)	3.5	6.2	17.0	29.3	39.9	49.5	55.4	53.8	44.7	34.1	25.3	11.6	30.8
Extreme Maximum Temp. (°F)	58	68	72	80	95	96	95	101	94	84	73	62	101
Extreme Minimum Temp. (°F)	-28	-24	-20	3	23	33	39	38	26	17	-2	-27	-28
Days Maximum Temp. ≥ 90°F	0	0	0	0	0	1	1	1	0	0	0	0	3
Days Maximum Temp. ≤ 32°F	21	17	7	1	0	0	0	0	0	0	3	16	65
Days Minimum Temp. ≤ 32°F	31	28	29	22	4	0	0	0	1	15	24	30	184
Days Minimum Temp. ≤ 0°F	14	10	3	0	0	0	0	0	0	0	0	7	34
Heating Degree Days (base 65°F)	1,547	1,320	1,143	746	402	142	37	59	261	606	901	1,338	8,502
Cooling Degree Days (base 65°F)	0	0	0	0	3	37	105	83	12	0	0	0	240
Mean Precipitation (in.)	4.14	3.23	4.05	3.72	3.48	3.43	3.27	3.20	3.82	3.75	4.38	4.20	44.67
Days With ≥ 0.1" Precipitation	7	6	8	7	7	7	7	6	6	7	8	8	84
Days With ≥ 1.0" Precipitation	1	1	1	1	1	1	1	1	1	1	1	1	12
Mean Snowfall (in.)	na	na	na	na	0.0	0.0	0.0	0.0	0.0	trace	na	na	na
Days With ≥ 1.0" Snow Depth	na	na	na	na	0	0	0	0	0	0	na	na	na

Houlton Int'l Airport *Aroostook County* Elevation: 495 ft.　Latitude: 46° 08' N　Longitude: 67° 47' W

	JAN	FEB	MAR	APR	MAY	JUN	JUL	AUG	SEP	OCT	NOV	DEC	YEAR
Mean Maximum Temp. (°F)	22.1	26.4	36.2	48.8	64.3	73.8	78.9	76.6	66.0	53.6	40.3	27.3	51.2
Mean Temp. (°F)	11.1	14.6	25.6	38.2	51.7	61.2	66.6	64.2	54.1	43.2	31.8	17.7	40.0
Mean Minimum Temp. (°F)	-0.0	2.7	15.0	27.6	39.0	48.4	54.2	51.8	42.3	32.6	23.3	8.1	28.8
Extreme Maximum Temp. (°F)	55	62	71	86	96	96	97	99	91	82	70	56	99
Extreme Minimum Temp. (°F)	-41	-36	-30	-6	18	28	33	30	20	10	-14	-34	-41
Days Maximum Temp. ≥ 90°F	0	0	0	0	0	1	2	1	0	0	0	0	4
Days Maximum Temp. ≤ 32°F	24	19	10	1	0	0	0	0	0	0	7	21	82
Days Minimum Temp. ≤ 32°F	30	27	29	23	8	1	0	0	5	17	24	30	194
Days Minimum Temp. ≤ 0°F	16	14	5	0	0	0	0	0	0	0	1	10	46
Heating Degree Days (base 65°F)	1,666	1,420	1,214	796	413	158	50	89	331	671	989	1,461	9,258
Cooling Degree Days (base 65°F)	0	0	0	0	4	45	94	71	*13*	0	0	0	*227*
Mean Precipitation (in.)	3.14	2.28	2.72	2.86	3.26	3.66	3.47	3.89	3.48	3.44	3.61	3.38	39.19
Days With ≥ 0.1" Precipitation	7	6	7	7	8	8	7	7	6	7	7	8	85
Days With ≥ 1.0" Precipitation	0	0	0	0	1	1	1	1	1	1	1	0	7
Mean Snowfall (in.)	21.8	17.1	18.8	8.5	0.2	trace	0.0	trace	trace	0.9	7.9	21.2	96.4
Days With ≥ 1.0" Snow Depth	30	26	29	11	0	0	0	0	0	0	7	24	127

Jackman *Somerset County* Elevation: 1,187 ft.　Latitude: 45° 38' N　Longitude: 70° 16' W

	JAN	FEB	MAR	APR	MAY	JUN	JUL	AUG	SEP	OCT	NOV	DEC	YEAR
Mean Maximum Temp. (°F)	21.1	25.1	34.8	46.9	62.4	71.7	76.3	74.8	65.5	52.8	39.4	26.4	49.8
Mean Temp. (°F)	9.6	12.5	22.8	36.0	49.6	59.5	64.3	62.4	53.3	42.1	30.8	16.6	38.3
Mean Minimum Temp. (°F)	-2.0	-0.1	10.7	25.1	36.7	47.1	52.2	49.9	41.0	31.3	22.1	6.7	26.7
Extreme Maximum Temp. (°F)	58	59	70	80	97	92	95	97	91	82	67	61	97
Extreme Minimum Temp. (°F)	-38	-44	-30	-4	14	28	30	33	20	11	-15	-33	-44
Days Maximum Temp. ≥ 90°F	0	0	0	0	0	0	1	0	0	0	0	0	1
Days Maximum Temp. ≤ 32°F	25	20	12	2	0	0	0	0	0	0	8	21	88
Days Minimum Temp. ≤ 32°F	31	28	30	26	10	1	0	0	5	18	26	31	206
Days Minimum Temp. ≤ 0°F	19	16	8	0	0	0	0	0	0	0	1	11	55
Heating Degree Days (base 65°F)	1,715	1,478	1,304	862	475	185	80	119	353	705	1,020	1,496	9,792
Cooling Degree Days (base 65°F)	0	0	0	0	2	27	62	40	7	0	0	0	138
Mean Precipitation (in.)	2.77	2.12	2.58	2.98	3.25	3.98	4.12	3.83	3.79	3.31	3.35	3.00	39.08
Days With ≥ 0.1" Precipitation	7	5	7	7	8	9	9	8	8	7	8	8	91
Days With ≥ 1.0" Precipitation	0	0	0	0	1	1	1	1	1	1	1	0	6
Mean Snowfall (in.)	25.3	19.4	18.8	9.2	0.2	trace	0.0	0.0	trace	1.1	10.1	24.1	108.2
Days With ≥ 1.0" Snow Depth	30	28	29	13	0	0	0	0	0	1	9	26	136

Jonesboro *Washington County*   Elevation: 183 ft.   Latitude: 44° 39' N   Longitude: 67° 39' W

	JAN	FEB	MAR	APR	MAY	JUN	JUL	AUG	SEP	OCT	NOV	DEC	YEAR
Mean Maximum Temp. (°F)	28.4	31.2	38.8	50.0	61.2	69.8	75.6	75.3	67.4	56.5	45.6	34.4	52.9
Mean Temp. (°F)	17.9	20.5	29.6	40.7	50.9	59.4	65.1	64.6	56.8	46.5	36.8	24.7	42.8
Mean Minimum Temp. (°F)	7.4	9.9	20.4	31.2	40.6	48.9	54.5	53.9	46.0	36.4	28.1	14.9	32.7
Extreme Maximum Temp. (°F)	54	62	71	79	97	93	96	104	92	82	72	64	104
Extreme Minimum Temp. (°F)	-22	-21	-13	8	24	31	42	37	22	17	1	-26	-26
Days Maximum Temp. ≥ 90°F	0	0	0	0	0	1	1	1	0	0	0	0	3
Days Maximum Temp. ≤ 32°F	18	15	6	1	0	0	0	0	0	0	2	12	54
Days Minimum Temp. ≤ 32°F	29	26	27	18	3	0	0	0	1	11	21	29	165
Days Minimum Temp. ≤ 0°F	10	6	1	0	0	0	0	0	0	0	0	4	21
Heating Degree Days (base 65°F)	1,454	1,252	1,090	723	431	181	53	62	249	568	838	1,244	8,145
Cooling Degree Days (base 65°F)	0	0	0	0	2	18	63	55	9	0	0	0	147
Mean Precipitation (in.)	4.96	3.69	4.58	4.57	4.55	3.76	3.51	3.19	4.01	4.36	5.03	4.99	51.20
Days With ≥ 0.1" Precipitation	8	6	8	7	7	7	6	5	7	7	8	8	84
Days With ≥ 1.0" Precipitation	2	1	1	1	1	1	1	1	1	1	1	1	13
Mean Snowfall (in.)	16.1	14.5	14.2	5.1	trace	0.0	0.0	0.0	0.0	0.1	3.4	12.8	66.2
Days With ≥ 1.0" Snow Depth	22	21	19	5	0	0	0	0	0	0	0	4	15	86

Lewiston *Androscoggin County*   Elevation: 177 ft.   Latitude: 44° 06' N   Longitude: 70° 13' W

	JAN	FEB	MAR	APR	MAY	JUN	JUL	AUG	SEP	OCT	NOV	DEC	YEAR
Mean Maximum Temp. (°F)	29.2	32.9	41.4	53.5	66.6	75.7	81.3	79.4	70.0	58.4	45.6	34.1	55.7
Mean Temp. (°F)	20.4	23.7	32.9	44.2	56.3	65.5	71.4	69.7	60.8	49.5	38.5	26.6	46.6
Mean Minimum Temp. (°F)	11.5	14.5	24.4	34.9	45.9	55.2	61.4	60.0	51.5	40.5	31.3	19.1	37.5
Extreme Maximum Temp. (°F)	60	65	85	91	96	98	100	100	94	85	74	67	100
Extreme Minimum Temp. (°F)	-28	-20	-7	14	27	38	47	39	31	22	4	-17	-28
Days Maximum Temp. ≥ 90°F	0	0	0	0	1	2	4	2	0	0	0	0	9
Days Maximum Temp. ≤ 32°F	19	13	5	0	0	0	0	0	0	0	2	13	52
Days Minimum Temp. ≤ 32°F	30	27	25	11	0	0	0	0	0	5	17	28	143
Days Minimum Temp. ≤ 0°F	6	3	0	0	0	0	0	0	0	0	0	2	11
Heating Degree Days (base 65°F)	1,377	1,159	987	617	281	67	7	19	158	475	789	1,183	7,119
Cooling Degree Days (base 65°F)	0	0	0	0	15	92	216	173	41	1	0	0	538
Mean Precipitation (in.)	3.82	3.07	4.51	4.07	3.74	3.80	3.57	3.09	3.54	4.11	4.25	4.09	45.66
Days With ≥ 0.1" Precipitation	7	6	8	7	7	7	7	6	6	7	7	7	82
Days With ≥ 1.0" Precipitation	1	1	1	1	1	1	1	1	1	1	1	1	12
Mean Snowfall (in.)	20.2	13.8	13.2	3.9	trace	0.0	0.0	0.0	trace	trace	3.1	15.6	69.8
Days With ≥ 1.0" Snow Depth	na	24	na	1	0	0	0	0	0	0	0	3	na	na

Long Falls Dam *Somerset County*   Elevation: 1,158 ft.   Latitude: 45° 13' N   Longitude: 70° 12' W

	JAN	FEB	MAR	APR	MAY	JUN	JUL	AUG	SEP	OCT	NOV	DEC	YEAR
Mean Maximum Temp. (°F)	22.3	25.8	34.6	46.6	61.1	70.6	75.3	73.7	64.5	52.7	39.9	27.6	49.6
Mean Temp. (°F)	11.8	14.6	24.1	36.8	49.7	59.5	64.5	62.6	53.8	43.0	32.0	18.8	39.3
Mean Minimum Temp. (°F)	1.1	3.3	13.5	26.9	38.3	48.4	53.6	51.4	43.1	33.3	24.0	10.0	28.9
Extreme Maximum Temp. (°F)	56	60	69	83	90	92	92	98	92	80	68	62	98
Extreme Minimum Temp. (°F)	-37	-32	-23	0	21	30	35	35	22	14	-9	-25	-37
Days Maximum Temp. ≥ 90°F	0	0	0	0	0	0	0	0	0	0	0	0	0
Days Maximum Temp. ≤ 32°F	25	20	12	2	0	0	0	0	0	0	7	20	86
Days Minimum Temp. ≤ 32°F	31	28	30	24	8	0	0	0	3	16	25	30	195
Days Minimum Temp. ≤ 0°F	16	13	6	0	0	0	0	0	0	0	0	8	43
Heating Degree Days (base 65°F)	1,647	1,419	1,262	839	471	185	74	114	338	675	985	1,425	9,434
Cooling Degree Days (base 65°F)	0	0	0	0	3	29	67	49	8	0	0	0	156
Mean Precipitation (in.)	2.98	2.22	3.25	3.31	3.53	3.70	3.69	3.45	3.45	3.43	3.66	3.04	39.71
Days With ≥ 0.1" Precipitation	6	5	7	7	8	9	8	7	6	6	7	7	83
Days With ≥ 1.0" Precipitation	1	0	1	1	1	0	1	1	1	1	1	1	10
Mean Snowfall (in.)	24.2	19.8	21.1	10.6	trace	trace	0.0	0.0	trace	1.1	8.9	24.0	109.7
Days With ≥ 1.0" Snow Depth	na	na	na	na	1	0	0	0	0	0	na	na	na

Madison *Somerset County*   Elevation: 259 ft.   Latitude: 44° 48' N   Longitude: 69° 53' W

	JAN	FEB	MAR	APR	MAY	JUN	JUL	AUG	SEP	OCT	NOV	DEC	YEAR
Mean Maximum Temp. (°F)	26.5	30.4	39.1	51.1	64.7	73.8	79.1	77.5	68.4	56.8	43.8	31.5	53.6
Mean Temp. (°F)	14.4	17.7	28.1	40.8	52.9	62.3	67.6	65.6	56.7	45.7	35.0	21.7	42.4
Mean Minimum Temp. (°F)	2.4	4.9	17.0	30.5	41.0	50.7	56.1	53.8	45.0	34.6	26.1	11.9	31.2
Extreme Maximum Temp. (°F)	56	59	72	89	94	98	96	100	93	82	72	62	100
Extreme Minimum Temp. (°F)	-39	-33	-23	7	24	32	38	33	24	15	-5	-30	-39
Days Maximum Temp. ≥ 90°F	0	0	0	0	0	1	2	1	0	0	0	0	4
Days Maximum Temp. ≤ 32°F	22	16	7	1	0	0	0	0	0	0	3	16	65
Days Minimum Temp. ≤ 32°F	31	28	28	19	3	0	0	0	2	13	23	30	177
Days Minimum Temp. ≤ 0°F	14	11	3	0	0	0	0	0	0	0	0	7	35
Heating Degree Days (base 65°F)	1,562	1,330	1,138	719	374	123	32	61	256	592	893	1,336	8,416
Cooling Degree Days (base 65°F)	0	0	0	0	5	49	123	87	13	0	0	0	277
Mean Precipitation (in.)	3.15	2.42	3.17	3.25	3.59	3.68	3.12	3.26	3.28	3.54	3.60	3.37	39.43
Days With ≥ 0.1" Precipitation	7	6	7	7	7	8	7	7	6	7	7	7	83
Days With ≥ 1.0" Precipitation	1	0	1	1	1	1	0	1	1	1	1	1	10
Mean Snowfall (in.)	20.3	15.0	13.3	6.1	trace	0.0	0.0	0.0	0.0	0.2	4.6	18.3	77.8
Days With ≥ 1.0" Snow Depth	na	na	na	na	0	0	0	0	0	0	na	na	na

Middle Dam *Oxford County*   Elevation: 1,459 ft.   Latitude: 44° 47' N   Longitude: 70° 55' W

	JAN	FEB	MAR	APR	MAY	JUN	JUL	AUG	SEP	OCT	NOV	DEC	YEAR
Mean Maximum Temp. (°F)	23.3	26.5	35.8	47.1	61.9	71.0	75.8	74.1	65.0	53.1	40.0	27.9	50.1
Mean Temp. (°F)	11.4	13.6	23.9	36.5	49.8	59.4	64.2	62.5	53.9	42.8	31.6	18.0	39.0
Mean Minimum Temp. (°F)	-0.3	0.7	11.9	25.8	37.6	47.7	52.6	51.0	42.8	32.6	23.2	8.1	27.8
Extreme Maximum Temp. (°F)	59	62	71	84	90	94	92	96	89	80	70	62	96
Extreme Minimum Temp. (°F)	-34	-31	-24	-5	18	28	36	32	22	12	-9	-28	-34
Days Maximum Temp. ≥ 90°F	0	0	0	0	0	0	0	0	0	0	0	0	0
Days Maximum Temp. ≤ 32°F	24	19	11	1	0	0	0	0	0	0	7	20	82
Days Minimum Temp. ≤ 32°F	30	28	29	24	8	1	0	0	3	17	26	30	196
Days Minimum Temp. ≤ 0°F	16	16	8	0	0	0	0	0	0	0	0	9	49
Heating Degree Days (base 65°F)	1,659	1,444	1,268	849	470	187	79	114	334	681	995	1,452	9,532
Cooling Degree Days (base 65°F)	0	0	0	0	3	29	66	46	7	0	0	0	151
Mean Precipitation (in.)	2.58	1.91	2.69	2.69	3.21	3.92	3.72	4.04	3.50	3.37	3.12	2.56	37.31
Days With ≥ 0.1" Precipitation	6	5	7	7	7	9	8	8	7	7	7	7	85
Days With ≥ 1.0" Precipitation	0	0	0	0	1	1	1	1	1	1	0	0	6
Mean Snowfall (in.)	na	na	na	na	trace	0.0	0.0	0.0	trace	0.5	na	na	na
Days With ≥ 1.0" Snow Depth	na	na	na	na	0	0	0	0	0	0	na	na	na

Millinocket *Penobscot County*   Elevation: 357 ft.   Latitude: 45° 39' N   Longitude: 68° 42' W

	JAN	FEB	MAR	APR	MAY	JUN	JUL	AUG	SEP	OCT	NOV	DEC	YEAR
Mean Maximum Temp. (°F)	23.2	27.2	36.9	49.5	64.1	73.4	78.6	76.8	66.9	54.4	41.6	28.9	51.8
Mean Temp. (°F)	12.8	16.0	26.7	39.7	53.0	62.6	68.1	66.0	56.4	44.8	33.9	20.0	41.7
Mean Minimum Temp. (°F)	2.4	4.7	16.4	29.9	41.6	51.7	57.4	55.1	45.9	35.1	26.1	11.1	31.5
Extreme Maximum Temp. (°F)	54	62	70	87	96	96	96	100	92	81	68	61	100
Extreme Minimum Temp. (°F)	-35	-31	-22	2	21	33	41	32	22	15	-5	-26	-35
Days Maximum Temp. ≥ 90°F	0	0	0	0	0	1	2	1	0	0	0	0	4
Days Maximum Temp. ≤ 32°F	24	19	10	1	0	0	0	0	0	0	5	18	77
Days Minimum Temp. ≤ 32°F	30	28	29	20	4	0	0	0	1	13	23	30	178
Days Minimum Temp. ≤ 0°F	15	11	3	0	0	0	0	0	0	0	0	7	36
Heating Degree Days (base 65°F)	1,613	1,379	1,180	752	375	121	30	59	267	620	927	1,389	8,712
Cooling Degree Days (base 65°F)	0	0	0	0	6	57	130	97	16	0	0	0	306
Mean Precipitation (in.)	3.29	2.48	3.06	3.47	3.66	3.97	3.82	3.96	3.75	3.77	3.70	3.42	42.35
Days With ≥ 0.1" Precipitation	7	6	7	7	8	8	8	7	7	7	8	7	87
Days With ≥ 1.0" Precipitation	1	0	0	1	1	1	1	1	1	1	1	1	10
Mean Snowfall (in.)	22.3	17.6	17.8	6.9	0.0	0.0	0.0	0.0	0.0	0.4	6.8	19.7	91.5
Days With ≥ 1.0" Snow Depth	na	na	na	na	0	0	0	0	0	0	na	na	na

Newcastle *Lincoln County*   Elevation: 187 ft.   Latitude: 44° 03' N   Longitude: 69° 32' W

	JAN	FEB	MAR	APR	MAY	JUN	JUL	AUG	SEP	OCT	NOV	DEC	YEAR
Mean Maximum Temp. (°F)	29.5	32.9	41.2	53.0	65.0	72.9	78.5	76.8	67.5	56.7	45.3	34.2	54.5
Mean Temp. (°F)	21.1	24.2	32.8	43.4	54.5	62.9	68.7	67.3	58.8	48.4	38.3	26.6	45.6
Mean Minimum Temp. (°F)	12.7	15.5	24.3	33.9	44.0	52.8	58.8	57.8	50.2	40.1	31.2	19.0	36.7
Extreme Maximum Temp. (°F)	56	60	85	86	94	93	98	101	92	80	71	64	101
Extreme Minimum Temp. (°F)	-20	-18	-9	12	27	36	45	40	29	21	3	-20	-20
Days Maximum Temp. ≥ 90°F	0	0	0	0	0	0	1	0	0	0	0	0	1
Days Maximum Temp. ≤ 32°F	18	13	5	0	0	0	0	0	0	0	2	13	51
Days Minimum Temp. ≤ 32°F	30	26	25	13	1	0	0	0	0	6	17	28	146
Days Minimum Temp. ≤ 0°F	5	3	0	0	0	0	0	0	0	0	0	2	10
Heating Degree Days (base 65°F)	1,354	1,145	992	640	326	102	16	31	198	507	795	1,182	7,288
Cooling Degree Days (base 65°F)	0	0	0	0	7	47	134	105	19	0	0	0	312
Mean Precipitation (in.)	4.23	3.33	4.40	4.22	3.95	3.55	2.95	2.86	3.83	4.15	4.69	4.67	46.83
Days With ≥ 0.1" Precipitation	8	6	7	7	8	7	6	5	6	7	8	8	83
Days With ≥ 1.0" Precipitation	1	1	1	1	1	1	1	1	1	1	1	1	12
Mean Snowfall (in.)	20.3	14.4	13.2	4.4	trace	0.0	0.0	0.0	0.0	0.2	3.7	16.5	72.7
Days With ≥ 1.0" Snow Depth	25	23	18	2	0	0	0	0	0	0	3	16	87

Orono *Penobscot County*   Elevation: 114 ft.   Latitude: 44° 54' N   Longitude: 68° 40' W

	JAN	FEB	MAR	APR	MAY	JUN	JUL	AUG	SEP	OCT	NOV	DEC	YEAR
Mean Maximum Temp. (°F)	27.9	31.4	40.3	52.5	66.3	75.2	80.8	78.1	67.4	55.1	43.1	32.1	54.2
Mean Temp. (°F)	18.1	21.7	31.1	42.3	54.2	63.0	68.7	66.4	56.6	45.7	35.7	23.8	43.9
Mean Minimum Temp. (°F)	8.3	11.9	21.8	32.1	42.0	50.8	56.6	54.6	45.9	36.2	28.3	15.3	33.6
Extreme Maximum Temp. (°F)	58	58	78	86	99	100	102	98	96	78	67	64	102
Extreme Minimum Temp. (°F)	-20	-26	-14	12	22	36	40	37	22	19	-2	-22	-26
Days Maximum Temp. ≥ 90°F	0	0	0	0	0	2	4	2	0	0	0	0	8
Days Maximum Temp. ≤ 32°F	21	15	5	0	0	0	0	0	0	0	3	16	60
Days Minimum Temp. ≤ 32°F	30	27	27	17	2	0	0	0	1	11	22	29	166
Days Minimum Temp. ≤ 0°F	9	4	1	0	0	0	0	0	0	0	0	4	18
Heating Degree Days (base 65°F)	1,447	1,218	1,046	674	338	110	24	51	259	592	872	1,273	7,904
Cooling Degree Days (base 65°F)	0	0	0	0	6	55	139	94	15	0	0	0	309
Mean Precipitation (in.)	3.40	2.48	3.23	3.14	3.33	3.61	3.29	3.21	3.86	3.39	3.51	3.68	40.13
Days With ≥ 0.1" Precipitation	7	6	7	7	7	7	6	6	7	6	7	8	81
Days With ≥ 1.0" Precipitation	1	0	1	1	1	1	1	1	1	1	1	1	11
Mean Snowfall (in.)	19.6	14.3	12.8	4.3	trace	0.0	0.0	0.0	0.0	0.3	4.4	16.5	72.2
Days With ≥ 1.0" Snow Depth	na	na	na	1	0	0	0	0	0	0	2	na	na

Presque Isle *Aroostook County*   Elevation: 597 ft.   Latitude: 46° 39' N   Longitude: 68° 00' W

	JAN	FEB	MAR	APR	MAY	JUN	JUL	AUG	SEP	OCT	NOV	DEC	YEAR
Mean Maximum Temp. (°F)	21.0	25.1	35.4	48.4	64.7	73.8	78.0	76.1	66.0	53.1	38.7	26.0	50.5
Mean Temp. (°F)	11.1	14.9	25.8	38.7	52.7	61.9	66.6	64.6	55.4	44.0	31.7	17.6	40.4
Mean Minimum Temp. (°F)	1.2	4.7	16.0	29.0	40.6	49.9	55.2	53.2	44.7	35.0	24.7	9.1	30.3
Extreme Maximum Temp. (°F)	52	59	67	84	94	93	96	95	89	79	68	57	96
Extreme Minimum Temp. (°F)	-35	-33	-26	1	16	30	35	31	23	15	-6	-32	-35
Days Maximum Temp. ≥ 90°F	0	0	0	0	0	1	1	0	0	0	0	0	2
Days Maximum Temp. ≤ 32°F	25	21	11	1	0	0	0	0	0	0	8	22	88
Days Minimum Temp. ≤ 32°F	30	27	29	21	5	0	0	0	3	13	24	30	182
Days Minimum Temp. ≤ 0°F	16	12	5	0	0	0	0	0	0	0	0	8	41
Heating Degree Days (base 65°F)	1,666	1,410	1,210	782	385	136	45	81	297	643	992	1,465	9,112
Cooling Degree Days (base 65°F)	0	0	0	0	6	47	99	79	15	0	0	0	246
Mean Precipitation (in.)	2.49	1.68	2.13	2.27	3.43	3.50	3.73	3.94	3.52	3.40	2.73	2.50	35.32
Days With ≥ 0.1" Precipitation	6	5	6	6	8	8	8	8	7	7	7	7	83
Days With ≥ 1.0" Precipitation	0	0	0	0	0	1	1	1	1	0	0	0	4
Mean Snowfall (in.)	21.6	17.5	16.8	6.7	0.2	0.0	0.0	0.0	0.1	0.6	7.9	17.3	88.7
Days With ≥ 1.0" Snow Depth	28	27	28	10	0	0	0	0	0	0	0	9	24	126

Rangeley *Franklin County*   Elevation: 1,528 ft.   Latitude: 44° 58' N   Longitude: 70° 39' W

	JAN	FEB	MAR	APR	MAY	JUN	JUL	AUG	SEP	OCT	NOV	DEC	YEAR
Mean Maximum Temp. (°F)	21.9	26.1	35.6	47.3	62.3	71.3	76.0	74.0	65.0	52.8	39.6	27.3	49.9
Mean Temp. (°F)	9.7	12.2	22.7	36.1	49.6	59.1	64.1	62.1	53.6	42.3	31.2	17.1	38.3
Mean Minimum Temp. (°F)	-2.5	-1.7	9.8	24.9	36.9	47.0	52.0	50.2	42.1	31.7	22.7	6.8	26.7
Extreme Maximum Temp. (°F)	56	59	71	85	90	93	93	93	89	78	69	57	93
Extreme Minimum Temp. (°F)	-45	-38	-36	-9	18	28	33	30	19	15	-12	-33	-45
Days Maximum Temp. ≥ 90°F	0	0	0	0	0	0	0	0	0	0	0	0	0
Days Maximum Temp. ≤ 32°F	25	20	11	2	0	0	0	0	0	0	7	20	85
Days Minimum Temp. ≤ 32°F	30	28	30	25	10	1	0	0	4	18	25	31	202
Days Minimum Temp. ≤ 0°F	18	17	9	0	0	0	0	0	0	0	0	11	55
Heating Degree Days (base 65°F)	1,712	1,486	1,305	860	475	193	83	123	342	696	1,007	1,480	9,762
Cooling Degree Days (base 65°F)	0	0	0	0	2	24	57	39	6	0	0	0	128
Mean Precipitation (in.)	3.15	2.27	3.14	3.09	3.29	4.10	3.83	4.07	3.69	3.48	3.41	3.04	40.56
Days With ≥ 0.1" Precipitation	6	5	7	7	7	9	8	8	7	7	7	7	85
Days With ≥ 1.0" Precipitation	1	0	0	0	0	1	0	1	1	1	1	0	6
Mean Snowfall (in.)	28.0	21.0	22.1	10.4	0.3	trace	0.0	0.0	trace	1.3	10.1	24.8	118.0
Days With ≥ 1.0" Snow Depth	na	na	na	na	0	0	0	0	0	1	na	na	na

Ripogenus Dam *Piscataquis County*   Elevation: 964 ft.   Latitude: 45° 53' N   Longitude: 69° 11' W

	JAN	FEB	MAR	APR	MAY	JUN	JUL	AUG	SEP	OCT	NOV	DEC	YEAR
Mean Maximum Temp. (°F)	20.9	24.5	34.8	46.5	61.7	71.5	76.8	74.8	65.4	52.9	39.3	25.8	49.6
Mean Temp. (°F)	9.5	12.4	22.8	36.3	49.9	60.0	65.5	63.8	54.6	43.4	31.5	16.4	38.8
Mean Minimum Temp. (°F)	-1.8	0.2	10.8	26.0	38.2	48.5	54.2	52.7	43.7	33.7	23.8	6.9	28.1
Extreme Maximum Temp. (°F)	58	63	68	80	90	93	95	97	88	78	67	54	97
Extreme Minimum Temp. (°F)	-38	-31	-28	-4	18	33	39	35	24	16	-6	-30	-38
Days Maximum Temp. ≥ 90°F	0	0	0	0	0	0	1	0	0	0	0	0	1
Days Maximum Temp. ≤ 32°F	25	21	12	2	0	0	0	0	0	0	7	21	88
Days Minimum Temp. ≤ 32°F	31	28	30	24	7	0	0	0	2	14	26	30	192
Days Minimum Temp. ≤ 0°F	19	16	8	0	0	0	0	0	0	0	0	10	53
Heating Degree Days (base 65°F)	1,716	1,481	1,301	855	465	173	59	91	316	665	997	1,504	9,623
Cooling Degree Days (base 65°F)	0	0	0	0	2	28	79	60	9	0	0	0	178
Mean Precipitation (in.)	2.61	1.94	2.78	3.19	3.45	3.94	3.92	4.06	3.60	3.61	3.48	3.03	39.61
Days With ≥ 0.1" Precipitation	7	5	8	8	9	9	9	8	7	7	8	7	92
Days With ≥ 1.0" Precipitation	0	0	0	0	0	1	1	1	1	1	0	0	5
Mean Snowfall (in.)	25.3	20.3	20.3	8.7	trace	0.0	0.0	0.0	0.0	0.8	8.5	24.7	108.6
Days With ≥ 1.0" Snow Depth	na	na	na	na	0	0	0	0	0	0	na	na	na

Rumford 1 SSE *Oxford County*   Elevation: 629 ft.   Latitude: 44° 32' N   Longitude: 70° 32' W

	JAN	FEB	MAR	APR	MAY	JUN	JUL	AUG	SEP	OCT	NOV	DEC	YEAR
Mean Maximum Temp. (°F)	27.3	31.5	40.4	52.6	66.6	74.9	79.9	78.0	68.9	57.0	43.7	31.8	54.4
Mean Temp. (°F)	17.1	20.5	30.3	42.4	54.8	63.5	68.6	66.9	58.1	46.9	36.0	23.2	44.0
Mean Minimum Temp. (°F)	6.7	9.4	20.1	32.2	43.0	52.0	57.3	55.8	47.2	36.7	28.3	14.5	33.6
Extreme Maximum Temp. (°F)	55	61	81	90	96	98	98	100	92	83	73	67	100
Extreme Minimum Temp. (°F)	-36	-26	-23	8	26	34	40	37	25	20	-2	-17	-36
Days Maximum Temp. ≥ 90°F	0	0	0	0	1	1	2	1	0	0	0	0	5
Days Maximum Temp. ≤ 32°F	20	15	6	0	0	0	0	0	0	0	3	15	59
Days Minimum Temp. ≤ 32°F	30	27	27	16	2	0	0	0	1	10	21	29	163
Days Minimum Temp. ≤ 0°F	10	8	2	0	0	0	0	0	0	0	0	5	25
Heating Degree Days (base 65°F)	1,480	1,251	1,070	671	321	101	24	47	223	556	864	1,290	7,898
Cooling Degree Days (base 65°F)	0	0	0	0	11	62	144	115	23	0	0	0	355
Mean Precipitation (in.)	3.32	2.38	3.69	3.73	3.82	4.37	3.79	4.21	3.68	4.00	4.21	3.43	44.63
Days With ≥ 0.1" Precipitation	6	5	6	7	8	8	8	7	6	7	7	7	82
Days With ≥ 1.0" Precipitation	1	1	1	1	1	1	1	1	1	1	1	1	12
Mean Snowfall (in.)	22.8	15.3	15.2	6.8	trace	0.0	0.0	0.0	0.0	0.2	6.0	19.1	85.4
Days With ≥ 1.0" Snow Depth	30	27	29	10	0	0	0	0	0	0	5	22	123

Sanford 2 NNW *York County*   Elevation: 278 ft.   Latitude: 43° 28' N   Longitude: 70° 47' W

	JAN	FEB	MAR	APR	MAY	JUN	JUL	AUG	SEP	OCT	NOV	DEC	YEAR
Mean Maximum Temp. (°F)	32.4	36.4	45.3	57.4	70.1	78.3	83.2	81.3	72.8	61.6	48.3	36.9	58.7
Mean Temp. (°F)	21.9	25.2	34.5	45.2	56.7	65.4	70.7	69.1	60.7	49.6	38.9	27.7	47.1
Mean Minimum Temp. (°F)	11.5	14.0	23.6	32.9	43.4	52.5	58.2	56.8	48.5	37.5	29.4	18.4	35.5
Extreme Maximum Temp. (°F)	62	68	88	91	95	97	98	101	94	85	75	73	101
Extreme Minimum Temp. (°F)	-25	-24	-10	-10	22	31	41	34	27	16	-1	-18	-25
Days Maximum Temp. ≥ 90°F	0	0	0	0	1	2	4	2	0	0	0	0	9
Days Maximum Temp. ≤ 32°F	15	9	3	0	0	0	0	0	0	0	1	10	38
Days Minimum Temp. ≤ 32°F	30	26	26	15	2	0	0	0	1	11	20	29	160
Days Minimum Temp. ≤ 0°F	6	4	1	0	0	0	0	0	0	0	0	2	13
Heating Degree Days (base 65°F)	1,329	1,117	939	590	269	68	10	23	166	474	777	1,151	6,913
Cooling Degree Days (base 65°F)	0	0	0	1	17	89	197	156	44	2	0	0	506
Mean Precipitation (in.)	4.04	3.57	4.51	4.29	3.90	3.54	3.70	3.68	3.80	4.35	4.78	4.27	48.43
Days With ≥ 0.1" Precipitation	7	6	7	7	8	7	7	6	6	6	8	7	82
Days With ≥ 1.0" Precipitation	1	1	1	1	1	1	1	1	1	1	1	1	12
Mean Snowfall (in.)	na	na	na	1.7	trace	0.0	0.0	0.0	0.0	trace	2.2	na	na
Days With ≥ 1.0" Snow Depth	na	na	10	1	0	0	0	0	0	0	0	1	na

Springfield *Penobscot County*   Elevation: 439 ft.   Latitude: 45° 24' N   Longitude: 68° 10' W

	JAN	FEB	MAR	APR	MAY	JUN	JUL	AUG	SEP	OCT	NOV	DEC	YEAR
Mean Maximum Temp. (°F)	25.2	28.8	38.0	50.6	64.4	73.2	78.3	76.9	67.4	55.6	42.8	30.1	52.6
Mean Temp. (°F)	14.1	17.4	27.6	40.0	52.2	61.4	66.9	65.3	56.0	45.0	34.0	20.2	41.7
Mean Minimum Temp. (°F)	2.9	6.0	17.1	29.3	40.0	49.6	55.5	53.6	44.5	34.4	25.2	10.3	30.7
Extreme Maximum Temp. (°F)	56	65	74	87	94	95	93	98	89	81	70	61	98
Extreme Minimum Temp. (°F)	-31	-28	-19	4	20	28	36	31	20	13	-9	-29	-31
Days Maximum Temp. ≥ 90°F	0	0	0	0	0	1	1	1	0	0	0	0	3
Days Maximum Temp. ≤ 32°F	23	17	8	0	0	0	0	0	0	0	4	17	69
Days Minimum Temp. ≤ 32°F	31	27	28	21	6	0	0	0	3	15	24	30	185
Days Minimum Temp. ≤ 0°F	15	10	3	0	0	0	0	0	0	0	0	8	36
Heating Degree Days (base 65°F)	1,574	1,338	1,153	744	397	146	45	72	277	613	922	1,382	8,663
Cooling Degree Days (base 65°F)	0	0	0	0	5	44	110	91	12	1	0	0	263
Mean Precipitation (in.)	3.79	3.02	3.87	3.64	4.01	4.00	4.06	3.71	3.86	3.76	4.27	4.15	46.14
Days With ≥ 0.1" Precipitation	7	6	8	8	9	8	8	7	7	7	9	8	92
Days With ≥ 1.0" Precipitation	1	1	1	1	1	1	1	1	1	1	1	1	12
Mean Snowfall (in.)	25.3	21.9	21.0	8.6	trace	0.0	0.0	0.0	0.0	1.0	7.0	22.8	107.6
Days With ≥ 1.0" Snow Depth	28	28	29	12	0	0	0	0	0	0	6	21	124

Squa Pan Dam *Aroostook County*   Elevation: 606 ft.   Latitude: 46° 33' N   Longitude: 68° 20' W

	JAN	FEB	MAR	APR	MAY	JUN	JUL	AUG	SEP	OCT	NOV	DEC	YEAR
Mean Maximum Temp. (°F)	20.3	24.7	35.1	46.9	62.4	72.7	78.1	75.2	64.7	52.1	na	25.3	na
Mean Temp. (°F)	6.8	9.6	21.8	35.8	49.2	59.4	64.8	61.9	51.8	41.3	na	14.2	na
Mean Minimum Temp. (°F)	-6.7	-5.6	8.2	24.6	36.0	46.1	51.2	48.4	39.0	30.4	na	2.9	na
Extreme Maximum Temp. (°F)	56	65	68	84	94	95	96	96	88	79	67	55	96
Extreme Minimum Temp. (°F)	-44	-39	-33	-8	16	26	32	27	19	11	-15	-35	-44
Days Maximum Temp. ≥ 90°F	0	0	0	0	0	1	1	1	0	0	0	0	3
Days Maximum Temp. ≤ 32°F	26	21	11	1	0	0	0	0	0	0	6	22	87
Days Minimum Temp. ≤ 32°F	31	28	30	25	11	1	0	1	8	18	23	31	207
Days Minimum Temp. ≤ 0°F	21	19	10	0	0	0	0	0	0	0	1	14	65
Heating Degree Days (base 65°F)	1,801	1,561	1,334	870	487	195	79	137	395	728	na	1,572	na
Cooling Degree Days (base 65°F)	0	0	0	0	2	32	na	47	6	0	na	0	na
Mean Precipitation (in.)	2.82	2.13	2.45	2.63	3.45	3.45	3.55	3.94	3.29	3.40	2.99	3.09	37.19
Days With ≥ 0.1" Precipitation	6	6	6	7	8	7	7	6	6	6	6	8	80
Days With ≥ 1.0" Precipitation	0	0	0	0	0	0	1	1	1	0	0	0	3
Mean Snowfall (in.)	24.3	20.0	17.2	8.1	0.1	0.0	0.0	0.0	0.0	0.9	9.6	22.5	102.7
Days With ≥ 1.0" Snow Depth	31	28	30	23	2	0	0	0	0	0	8	27	149

Van Buren 2 *Aroostook County*   Elevation: 456 ft.   Latitude: 47° 10' N   Longitude: 67° 56' W

	JAN	FEB	MAR	APR	MAY	JUN	JUL	AUG	SEP	OCT	NOV	DEC	YEAR
Mean Maximum Temp. (°F)	18.8	23.0	33.7	46.7	62.6	72.0	76.3	74.5	64.5	51.8	38.4	25.5	49.0
Mean Temp. (°F)	5.5	8.7	21.7	36.6	50.3	59.9	64.6	62.6	53.0	41.8	30.1	14.7	37.4
Mean Minimum Temp. (°F)	-7.8	-5.6	9.6	26.4	37.9	47.8	53.0	50.6	41.4	31.7	21.8	3.8	25.9
Extreme Maximum Temp. (°F)	52	61	67	85	94	93	95	94	90	79	71	54	95
Extreme Minimum Temp. (°F)	-47	-44	-36	-5	18	28	36	26	19	13	-16	-35	-47
Days Maximum Temp. ≥ 90°F	0	0	0	0	0	1	1	0	0	0	0	0	2
Days Maximum Temp. ≤ 32°F	26	22	13	2	0	0	0	0	0	0	8	21	92
Days Minimum Temp. ≤ 32°F	31	28	30	24	8	1	0	0	5	18	26	31	202
Days Minimum Temp. ≤ 0°F	22	19	9	0	0	0	0	0	0	0	1	13	64
Heating Degree Days (base 65°F)	1,842	1,586	1,337	846	454	184	80	120	362	713	1,039	1,555	10,118
Cooling Degree Days (base 65°F)	0	0	0	0	3	37	74	51	9	0	0	0	174
Mean Precipitation (in.)	2.80	1.90	2.21	2.59	3.32	3.48	4.24	3.89	3.48	3.27	3.16	3.01	37.35
Days With ≥ 0.1" Precipitation	7	5	6	7	8	8	9	8	7	8	7	7	87
Days With ≥ 1.0" Precipitation	0	0	0	0	0	1	1	1	1	0	0	1	5
Mean Snowfall (in.)	24.7	17.9	13.4	5.7	trace	0.0	0.0	0.0	0.0	0.2	7.3	19.3	88.5
Days With ≥ 1.0" Snow Depth	31	28	31	16	0	0	0	0	0	0	9	26	141

Vanceboro 2 *Washington County*   Elevation: 419 ft.   Latitude: 45° 34' N   Longitude: 67° 26' W

	JAN	FEB	MAR	APR	MAY	JUN	JUL	AUG	SEP	OCT	NOV	DEC	YEAR
Mean Maximum Temp. (°F)	26.2	30.3	39.4	51.8	66.4	75.6	80.1	78.6	69.2	57.1	43.1	31.2	54.1
Mean Temp. (°F)	14.8	18.4	28.4	40.4	52.9	62.1	67.5	65.9	56.9	45.8	34.4	21.2	42.4
Mean Minimum Temp. (°F)	3.3	6.4	17.3	29.0	39.5	48.6	54.7	53.2	44.6	34.4	25.7	11.1	30.7
Extreme Maximum Temp. (°F)	54	66	69	88	97	96	96	98	94	80	71	60	98
Extreme Minimum Temp. (°F)	-35	-30	-19	0	15	29	38	31	26	12	-5	-32	-35
Days Maximum Temp. ≥ 90°F	0	0	0	0	0	1	2	1	0	0	0	0	4
Days Maximum Temp. ≤ 32°F	22	16	7	0	0	0	0	0	0	0	3	17	65
Days Minimum Temp. ≤ 32°F	30	27	29	21	6	0	0	0	2	14	23	30	182
Days Minimum Temp. ≤ 0°F	14	10	3	0	0	0	0	0	0	0	0	7	34
Heating Degree Days (base 65°F)	1,553	1,310	1,127	732	372	124	31	56	249	591	911	1,353	8,409
Cooling Degree Days (base 65°F)	0	0	0	0	4	42	109	92	14	1	0	0	262
Mean Precipitation (in.)	3.56	2.63	3.11	3.38	4.15	3.85	3.97	3.83	4.17	3.93	4.29	3.44	44.31
Days With ≥ 0.1" Precipitation	7	5	7	7	8	7	8	7	7	7	8	7	85
Days With ≥ 1.0" Precipitation	1	0	0	1	1	1	1	1	1	1	1	1	10
Mean Snowfall (in.)	18.8	14.5	14.8	4.7	0.1	0.0	0.0	0.0	0.0	0.2	5.2	17.4	75.7
Days With ≥ 1.0" Snow Depth	26	26	25	8	0	0	0	0	0	0	4	20	109

Waterville Treatment Plant *Kennebec County*   Elevation: 72 ft.   Latitude: 44° 32' N   Longitude: 69° 39' W

	JAN	FEB	MAR	APR	MAY	JUN	JUL	AUG	SEP	OCT	NOV	DEC	YEAR
Mean Maximum Temp. (°F)	30.3	34.6	43.2	55.6	68.9	77.3	82.2	80.5	71.5	59.9	46.8	34.9	57.1
Mean Temp. (°F)	18.8	22.5	32.1	43.5	55.6	64.5	69.8	68.2	59.5	48.3	37.4	24.9	45.4
Mean Minimum Temp. (°F)	7.2	10.3	21.0	31.4	42.2	51.7	57.4	55.7	47.4	36.7	27.9	14.8	33.7
Extreme Maximum Temp. (°F)	57	61	75	91	98	96	96	101	95	84	73	67	101
Extreme Minimum Temp. (°F)	-32	-28	-17	8	21	35	39	35	23	17	-1	-27	-32
Days Maximum Temp. ≥ 90°F	0	0	0	0	1	2	3	2	0	0	0	0	8
Days Maximum Temp. ≤ 32°F	17	11	4	0	0	0	0	0	0	0	1	11	44
Days Minimum Temp. ≤ 32°F	30	27	27	17	3	0	0	0	1	11	21	29	166
Days Minimum Temp. ≤ 0°F	10	7	2	0	0	0	0	0	0	0	0	4	23
Heating Degree Days (base 65°F)	1,427	1,195	1,014	639	297	77	13	29	185	510	821	1,236	7,443
Cooling Degree Days (base 65°F)	0	0	0	0	8	65	165	131	26	1	0	0	396
Mean Precipitation (in.)	3.09	2.39	3.64	3.32	3.67	3.77	3.47	3.41	3.80	3.95	3.56	3.10	41.17
Days With ≥ 0.1" Precipitation	6	5	6	7	7	7	7	6	6	7	7	6	77
Days With ≥ 1.0" Precipitation	1	0	1	1	1	1	1	1	1	1	1	1	11
Mean Snowfall (in.)	*16.6*	11.9	10.4	2.6	trace	0.0	0.0	0.0	0.0	trace	2.5	15.7	59.7
Days With ≥ 1.0" Snow Depth	27	25	16	2	0	0	0	0	0	0	3	19	92

West Buxton 2 NNW *York County*   Elevation: 147 ft.   Latitude: 43° 42' N   Longitude: 70° 37' W

	JAN	FEB	MAR	APR	MAY	JUN	JUL	AUG	SEP	OCT	NOV	DEC	YEAR
Mean Maximum Temp. (°F)	30.6	34.4	42.7	54.7	66.5	75.3	80.3	78.4	69.8	58.8	46.8	35.4	56.2
Mean Temp. (°F)	18.3	21.5	31.4	42.4	53.6	62.8	68.2	66.2	57.5	46.3	36.2	24.7	44.1
Mean Minimum Temp. (°F)	6.1	8.6	20.0	30.1	40.6	50.1	56.0	54.0	45.3	33.8	25.6	13.9	32.0
Extreme Maximum Temp. (°F)	59	63	88	94	94	95	98	98	93	84	74	70	98
Extreme Minimum Temp. (°F)	-34	-32	-18	11	20	32	38	30	23	12	-3	-31	-34
Days Maximum Temp. ≥ 90°F	0	0	0	0	0	1	2	1	0	0	0	0	4
Days Maximum Temp. ≤ 32°F	17	12	4	0	0	0	0	0	0	0	2	12	47
Days Minimum Temp. ≤ 32°F	31	28	28	19	5	0	0	0	2	15	23	30	181
Days Minimum Temp. ≤ 0°F	11	8	2	0	0	0	0	0	0	0	0	5	26
Heating Degree Days (base 65°F)	1,442	1,222	1,035	671	354	114	28	54	236	574	857	1,243	7,830
Cooling Degree Days (base 65°F)	0	0	0	0	7	55	134	101	21	0	0	0	318
Mean Precipitation (in.)	3.62	3.07	4.28	4.37	3.86	3.61	3.59	3.23	3.76	4.35	4.43	3.94	46.11
Days With ≥ 0.1" Precipitation	7	5	7	7	7	7	6	6	6	6	7	7	78
Days With ≥ 1.0" Precipitation	1	1	1	1	1	1	1	1	1	1	1	1	12
Mean Snowfall (in.)	na	na	na	na	0.0	0.0	0.0	0.0	0.0	trace	*1.1*	na	na
Days With ≥ 1.0" Snow Depth	na	na	na	1	0	0	0	0	0	0	2	na	na

West Rockport 1 NNW *Knox County*   Elevation: 377 ft.   Latitude: 44° 12' N   Longitude: 69° 09' W

	JAN	FEB	MAR	APR	MAY	JUN	JUL	AUG	SEP	OCT	NOV	DEC	YEAR
Mean Maximum Temp. (°F)	*29.1*	*31.7*	*39.4*	*50.6*	*62.4*	*70.6*	*76.4*	*75.0*	*66.7*	*56.1*	*45.6*	*35.0*	*53.2*
Mean Temp. (°F)	*19.7*	*22.3*	*30.9*	*41.9*	*52.9*	*61.5*	*67.4*	*66.2*	*58.1*	*47.6*	*37.7*	*26.3*	*44.4*
Mean Minimum Temp. (°F)	*10.2*	*12.8*	*22.3*	*33.2*	*43.5*	*52.3*	*58.4*	*57.4*	*49.5*	*39.1*	*29.8*	*17.6*	*35.5*
Extreme Maximum Temp. (°F)	*56*	*61*	*74*	*79*	*95*	*94*	*96*	*93*	*88*	*82*	*74*	*63*	*96*
Extreme Minimum Temp. (°F)	*-22*	*-15*	*-11*	*10*	*21*	*30*	*43*	*37*	*28*	*19*	*4*	*-25*	*-25*
Days Maximum Temp. ≥ 90°F	*0*	*0*	*0*	*0*	*0*	*0*	*1*	*0*	*0*	*0*	*0*	*0*	*1*
Days Maximum Temp. ≤ 32°F	*18*	*14*	*6*	*1*	*0*	*0*	*0*	*0*	*0*	*0*	*2*	*11*	*52*
Days Minimum Temp. ≤ 32°F	*29*	*26*	*26*	*13*	*1*	*0*	*0*	*0*	*0*	*6*	*19*	*28*	*148*
Days Minimum Temp. ≤ 0°F	*7*	*5*	*1*	*0*	*0*	*0*	*0*	*0*	*0*	*0*	*0*	*3*	*16*
Heating Degree Days (base 65°F)	*1,399*	*1,200*	*1,052*	*685*	*376*	*137*	*32*	*46*	*217*	*532*	*811*	*1,193*	*7,680*
Cooling Degree Days (base 65°F)	*0*	*0*	*0*	*0*	*6*	*41*	*111*	*91*	*18*	*0*	*0*	*0*	*267*
Mean Precipitation (in.)	*4.92*	*3.32*	*4.73*	*4.71*	*4.29*	*3.77*	*3.07*	*2.98*	*4.55*	*4.90*	*5.27*	*4.68*	*51.19*
Days With ≥ 0.1" Precipitation	*7*	*6*	*6*	*7*	*8*	*7*	*6*	*6*	*6*	*7*	*8*	*7*	*81*
Days With ≥ 1.0" Precipitation	*1*	*1*	*1*	*1*	*1*	*1*	*1*	*1*	*1*	*1*	*1*	*1*	*12*
Mean Snowfall (in.)	na	*12.0*	*11.0*	*2.7*	*trace*	*0.0*	*0.0*	*0.0*	*0.0*	*trace*	na	*8.2*	na
Days With ≥ 1.0" Snow Depth	na	na	*16*	*2*	*0*	*0*	*0*	*0*	*0*	*0*	*2*	na	na

Note: See Appendix D for explanation of data.

MARYLAND AND DISTRICT OF COLUMBIA

PHYSICAL FEATURES. The State of Maryland is on the east coast of the United States and lies in an east-west position between longitudes 75° and 79° W., spanning a distance of 240 miles. The latitude varies from about 38° to nearly 40° N., with a latitudinal width of approximately 125 miles in eastern portions which gradually narrows to about 1.5 miles in the Appalachian Mountain region near Hancock and increases again to 35 miles at the extreme western boundary. The total area of the State is 12,303 square miles, of which 9,887 square miles are land, 2,310 square miles are in the Chesapeake Bay and its tidal river waters, and 106 square miles are in Chincoteague Bay.

The Chesapeake Bay, elongated in a northerly direction, extends for about two-thirds of its length deep into Maryland. It virtually separates the State into two provinces except for a narrow neck of land about 10 miles wide in Cecil County, which bridges the gap between Chesapeake Bay and the State of Pennsylvania. That portion of the State east of Chesapeake Bay is commonly referred to as the Eastern Shore. The five southernmost counties between the Potomac River and Chesapeake Bay are commonly referred to as Southern Maryland. To the north and northwest of Southern Maryland, an area made up of six counties and located on the Piedmont, is an area commonly referred to as Northern-Central Maryland. The remainder of the State including roughly the Appalachian Mountain area or the three western counties is termed Western Maryland.

Although Maryland ranks as one of the smaller States with respect to size, it encompasses an extremely wide range of physiographic features which contribute to a comparatively wide range of climatic conditions. It extends across three well-defined physiographic belts which parallel the Atlantic coast in varying widths from New England to the southeastern United States. These physiographic provinces are the Coastal Plain, Piedmont province, and Appalachian province.

The land rises more or less gradually from the Atlantic Ocean across the Coastal Plain (which virtually includes the Eastern Shore and Southern Maryland) and then more rapidly across the Piedmont Plateau (northern-central Maryland) and the ridges of the Appalachian Mountains and finally reaches its highest point at 3,340 feet above mean sea level on Backbone Mountain in the Allegheny Plateau of Garrett County.

GENERAL CLIMATE. Since the general flow of the atmosphere in temperate latitudes is from west to east, the expansive North American Continent immediately to the west predisposes the Maryland area to a continental type of climate. This type of climate in middle latitudes is marked by well-defined seasons. Winter is the dormant season for plant growth based on low temperatures rather than drought. In spring and fall the changeableness of the weather is a striking feature. It is occasioned by a rapid succession of warm and cold fronts associated with cyclones and anticyclones which generally move from a westerly direction. Summers are warm to hot. The higher atmospheric humidity along the Atlantic coastal area causes the summer heat to be more oppressive and the winter cold more penetrating than for drier climates of the interior of the continent.

At times in winter the Appalachian Mountains afford a degree of protection from the icy blasts of cold Arctic air, particularly when a high pressure area attended by a coldwave approaches from the west. The modifying influences of the mountain barrier attending the passage of a storm area from the Ohio Valley is sometimes quite marked. The warming of the air as it descends the eastern slopes of the mountains may at times exceed 10°F.

The Allegheny Mountains contribute to the higher precipitation and heavy snowfall on the Allegheny Plateau. The formation of precipitation in the form of rain or snow is increased in storms or air masses which ascend the mountains from the Ohio Valley

TEMPERATURE. The winter climate on the Piedmont and Coastal plain sections of Maryland is intermediate between the cold of the Northeast and the mild weather of the South. Extremely cold air masses from the interior of the continent are moderated somewhat by passage over the Appalachian Mountains and in some instances by a short trajectory over the nearby ocean and bays. Weather on the Allegheny Plateau is frequently 10 to 15°F. colder than it is in eastern portions of the State and, at times, extremely low temperatures occur in winter. The average frost penetration ranges from about 5 inches or less in extreme southern portions of Maryland to more than 18 inches on the Allegheny Plateau.

Summer is characterized by considerable warm weather including at least several hot, humid periods. However, nights are usually quite comfortable. The average length of the freeze-free season based on a minimum temperature higher than 32°F. ranges from more than 225 days in extreme southern portions to fewer than 130 days on the Allegheny Plateau.

PRECIPITATION AND SNOWFALL. Although the heaviest precipitation occurs in the summer, this is the season when severe droughts are most frequent. Summer precipitation is less dependable and more variable than in winter. Average annual snowfall over Maryland ranges from a minimum of eight to 10 inches along the coastal areas of the Southern Eastern Shore division to a maximum well over 70 in the Garrett County area. Snow flurries fall as early as September on the Allegheny Plateau, and in October in extreme eastern portions of the State. The last snowfall in eastern portions usually occurs in April and on the Allegheny Plateau in May. Even in the warmest winters snow falls in Maryland; however, averages for a climatological division may be less than one inch for the season.

FLOODS. All of the State lies in the Atlantic drainage except for a portion of Garrett County in the western end of Maryland which drains into the Ohio Basin. The largest river in the State, the Potomac, forms the southern boundary through most of its length. The far eastern area is drained by many small streams and tidal estuaries into Chesapeake Bay and the Atlantic Ocean.

Minor or local flood damage can be expected every year in streams above the tidewater areas. Floods do occur in all months of the year, but the greatest frequency is in late winter and spring. Snow-melt at times is a factor. Intense convectional storms in summer occasionally cause local flash floods. Storms of tropical origin passing through the area in late summer and fall produce high water and occasionally damaging floods, mostly in tidewater areas. These are due to the heavy rains or strong easterly winds accompanying the storm, or a combination of both. Flooding from wind-driven tides at times extends upstream in the Potomac to the District of Columbia area. High water also results from persistent northeast winds along the coast caused by extra-tropical storms.

STORMS. Thunderstorms occur at a given station on an average of 30 days per year in extreme eastern portions of Maryland, and 40 days per year in western portions. They occur in all months of the year, but during the 4-month cold season from November through February, an average of less than one storm per month is observed. May, June, July, and August make up the thunderstorm season and include from 75 to 80 percent of the thunderstorms which occur annually. July is the peak of the season with about 25 percent of the annual total number of thunderstorms.

Hail at a given station occurs on an average of one day per year in extreme eastern portions and about two days per year in extreme western portions. The total number of days on which hail is observed at one or more weather stations in Maryland averages about 18 to 20 per year. Hail has been observed in all months of the year; however, occurrences in the 7-month period from September through March are infrequent. The number of days with hail at one or more weather stations increases from an average of one in April to about five in July, the peak of the hail season, and then decreases to an average of three in August. Although spring thunderstorms are much fewer in number than summer thunderstorms, they have a much greater tendency to occur with hail. Virtually all hailstorms occur between 2 p.m. and 9 p.m. Severe, devastating hailstorms occur somewhere in the State about once every five years on the average.

Tornadoes occur infrequently in Maryland, and of the ones that do occur most are small. Most tornadoes in Maryland tend to travel in the usual southwest to northeast direction, but few have been reported to travel southeastward or in a southerly direction. Usually paths are not more than a few miles in length; however, 10 to 15 percent of these storms maintain paths 20 miles or more in length.

RELATIVE HUMIDITY. Average relative humidity is lowest in the winter and early spring from February through April, and highest in the late summer and early from August through October.

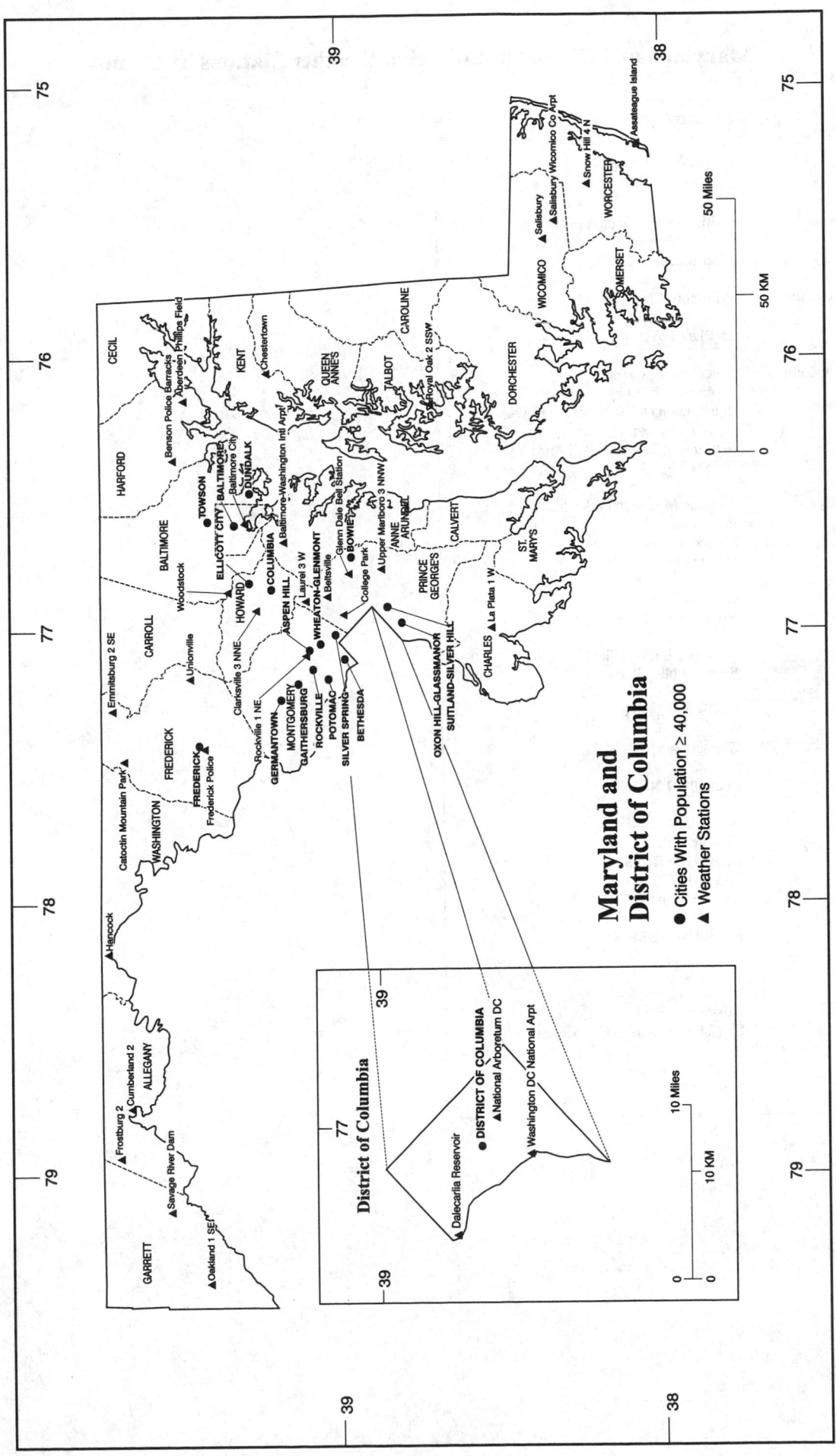

Maryland and
District of Columbia

● Cities With Population ≥ 40,000
▲ Weather Stations

District of Columbia

Maryland and District of Columbia Weather Stations by County

County	Station Name
Allegany	Cumberland 2 Frostburg 2
Anne Arundel	Baltimore-Washington Int'l Arpt.
Baltimore	Woodstock
Baltimore (City)	Baltimore City
Charles	La Plata 1 W
District of Columbia	Dalecarlia Reservoir National Arboretum Washington DC National Arpt., VA *See Virginia* Washington DC Dulles Int'l Arpt., VA *See Virginia*
Frederick	Catoctin Mountain Park Emmitsburg 2 SE Frederick Police Unionville
Garrett	Oakland 1 SE Savage River Dam
Harford	Aberdeen Phillips Field Benson Police Barracks
Howard	Clarksville 3 NNE
Kent	Chestertown
Montgomery	Rockville 1 NE
Prince George's	Beltsville College Park Glenn Dale Bell Station Laurel 3 W Upper Marlboro 3 NNW
Talbot	Royal Oak 2 SSW
Washington	Hancock
Wicomico	Salisbury Salisbury Wicomico Co. Airport
Worcester	Assateague Island Snow Hill 4 N

Maryland and District of Columbia Weather Stations by City

City	Station Name	Miles
Aspen Hill	Beltsville	11
	Clarksville 3 NNE	14
	College Park	10
	Dalecarlia Reservoir	11
	Glenn Dale Bell Station	17
	Laurel 3 W	10
	National Arboretum	14
	Rockville 1 NE	1
	Washington DC National Arpt., VA	16
Baltimore	Baltimore City	2
	Benson Police Barracks	18
	Clarksville 3 NNE	17
	Woodstock	13
	Baltimore-Washington Int'l Arpt.	11
Bethesda	Beltsville	13
	College Park	9
	Dalecarlia Reservoir	4
	Glenn Dale Bell Station	17
	Laurel 3 W	14
	National Arboretum	9
	Rockville 1 NE	8
	Upper Marlboro 3 NNW	20
	Washington DC Dulles Int'l Arpt., VA	18
	Washington DC National Arpt., VA	9
Bowie	Beltsville	9
	College Park	11
	Glenn Dale Bell Station	3
	Laurel 3 W	13
	National Arboretum	14
	Upper Marlboro 3 NNW	7
	Washington DC National Arpt., VA	17
	Baltimore-Washington Int'l Arpt.	15
Columbia	Baltimore City	14
	Beltsville	12
	Clarksville 3 NNE	5
	College Park	16
	Glenn Dale Bell Station	17
	Laurel 3 W	8
	Rockville 1 NE	15
	Woodstock	9
	Baltimore-Washington Int'l Arpt.	10
Dundalk	Baltimore City	6
	Benson Police Barracks	17
	Woodstock	20
	Baltimore-Washington Int'l Arpt.	12
Ellicott City	Baltimore City	12
	Beltsville	17
	Clarksville 3 NNE	6
	Laurel 3 W	12
	Rockville 1 NE	19
	Woodstock	5
	Baltimore-Washington Int'l Arpt.	11
Frederick	Catoctin Mountain Park	16
	Emmitsburg 2 SE	19
	Frederick Police	1
	Unionville	13

City	Station Name	Miles
Gaithersburg	Beltsville	18
	Clarksville 3 NNE	17
	College Park	17
	Dalecarlia Reservoir	14
	Laurel 3 W	16
	National Arboretum	19
	Rockville 1 NE	6
	Washington DC Dulles Int'l Arpt., VA	19
	Washington DC National Arpt., VA	20
Germantown	Clarksville 3 NNE	18
	Dalecarlia Reservoir	18
	Frederick Police	19
	Rockville 1 NE	10
	Unionville	19
	Washington DC Dulles Int'l Arpt., VA	20
Oxon Hill-Glassmanor	Beltsville	17
	College Park	12
	Dalecarlia Reservoir	12
	Glenn Dale Bell Station	15
	La Plata 1 W	19
	National Arboretum	7
	Upper Marlboro 3 NNW	11
	Washington DC National Arpt., VA	5
Potomac	Beltsville	16
	College Park	13
	Dalecarlia Reservoir	8
	Laurel 3 W	16
	National Arboretum	14
	Rockville 1 NE	7
	Washington DC Dulles Int'l Arpt., VA	16
	Washington DC National Arpt., VA	14
Rockville	Beltsville	15
	Clarksville 3 NNE	17
	College Park	13
	Dalecarlia Reservoir	10
	Laurel 3 W	13
	National Arboretum	15
	Rockville 1 NE	3
	Washington DC Dulles Int'l Arpt., VA	19
	Washington DC National Arpt., VA	16
Silver Spring	Beltsville	8
	Clarksville 3 NNE	17
	College Park	4
	Dalecarlia Reservoir	7
	Glenn Dale Bell Station	12
	Laurel 3 W	9
	National Arboretum	8
	Rockville 1 NE	8
	Upper Marlboro 3 NNW	16
	Washington DC National Arpt., VA	10
Suitland-Silver Hill	Beltsville	13
	College Park	9
	Dalecarlia Reservoir	12
	Glenn Dale Bell Station	10
	Laurel 3 W	17
	National Arboretum	5
	Rockville 1 NE	20
	Upper Marlboro 3 NNW	8

City	Station Name	Miles
Suitland-Silver Hill *(cont.)*	Washington DC National Arpt., VA	6
Towson	Baltimore City	8
	Benson Police Barracks	14
	Woodstock	14
	Baltimore-Washington Int'l Arpt.	16
Wheaton-Glenmont	Beltsville	9
	Clarksville 3 NNE	15
	College Park	8
	Dalecarlia Reservoir	9
	Glenn Dale Bell Station	15
	Laurel 3 W	9
	National Arboretum	11
	Rockville 1 NE	4
	Upper Marlboro 3 NNW	20
	Washington DC National Arpt., VA	13

Note: Miles is the distance between the geographic center of the city and the weather station.

Maryland and District of Columbia Weather Stations by Elevation

Feet	Station Name
2,417	Oakland 1 SE
2,165	Frostburg 2
1,607	Catoctin Mountain Park
1,492	Savage River Dam
728	Cumberland 2
459	Woodstock
439	Rockville 1 NE
429	Unionville
413	Emmitsburg 2 SE
396	Laurel 3 W
383	Hancock
377	Frederick Police
367	Clarksville 3 NNE
364	Benson Police Barracks
147	Baltimore-Washington Int'l Arpt.
147	Dalecarlia Reservoir
147	Glenn Dale Bell Station
144	Beltsville
137	La Plata 1 W
98	Upper Marlboro 3 NNW
88	College Park
59	Aberdeen Phillips Field
49	National Arboretum
49	Salisbury Wicomico Co. Airport
39	Chestertown
29	Snow Hill 4 N
13	Baltimore City
9	Assateague Island
9	Royal Oak 2 SSW
9	Salisbury

Baltimore-Washington Int'l Arpt.

Baltimore-Washington International Airport lies in a region about midway between the rigorous climates of the North and the mild climates of the South, and adjacent to the modifying influences of the Chesapeake Bay and Atlantic Ocean to the east and the Appalachian Mountains to the west. Since this region is near the average path of the low pressure systems which move across the country, changes in wind direction are frequent and contribute to the changeable character of the weather. The net effect of the mountains to the west and the bay and ocean to the east is to produce a more equable climate compared with other continental locations farther inland at the same latitude.

Rainfall distribution throughout the year is rather uniform, however, the greatest intensities are confined to the summer and early fall months, the season for hurricanes and severe thunderstorms. Moisture deficiencies for crops occur occasionally during the growing season, but severe droughts are rare. Rainfall during the growing season occurs principally in the form of thunderstorms, and rainfall totals during these months vary appreciably.

The average date for the last occurrence in spring of temperatures as low as 32 degrees is mid-April. The average date for the first occurrence in fall of temperatures as low as 32 degrees is late October. The freeze-free period is approximately 194 days.

In summer, the area is under the influence of the large semi-permanent high pressure system commonly known as the Bermuda High and centered over the Atlantic Ocean near 30 degrees N Latitude. This pressure system brings warm humid air to the area. The proximity of large water areas and the inflow of southerly winds contribute to high relative humidities during much of the year.

January is the coldest month, and July, the warmest. Snowfall occurs on about eleven days per year on the average, however, an average of only about six days annually produces snowfalls of one inch or greater. Snow is frequently mixed with rain and sleet, and snow seldom remains on the ground more than a few days.

Glaze or freezing rain which is hazardous to highway traffic occurs on an average of two to three times per year, generally in January or February. Some years pass without the occurrence of freezing rain, while in others it occurs on as many as eight to ten days. Sleet is observed on about five days annually with the greatest frequency of occurrence in January.

The annual prevailing wind direction is from the west. Winter and spring months have the highest average wind speed. Destructive velocities are rare and occur mostly during summer thunderstorms.

Baltimore-Washington Int'l Arpt. *Anne Arundel Co.*   Elevation: 147 ft.   Latitude: 39° 10' N   Longitude: 76° 41' W

	JAN	FEB	MAR	APR	MAY	JUN	JUL	AUG	SEP	OCT	NOV	DEC	YEAR
Mean Maximum Temp. (°F)	41.3	45.1	53.9	64.9	74.4	83.0	87.7	85.6	78.8	67.3	56.5	46.5	65.4
Mean Temp. (°F)	33.0	36.1	44.2	53.9	63.6	72.5	77.6	75.7	68.9	56.8	46.9	38.0	55.6
Mean Minimum Temp. (°F)	24.7	27.1	34.3	42.9	52.8	62.0	67.4	65.8	58.9	46.3	37.1	29.4	45.7
Extreme Maximum Temp. (°F)	75	79	89	93	98	101	104	105	100	89	83	77	105
Extreme Minimum Temp. (°F)	-7	-3	10	22	33	40	50	45	39	27	15	0	-7
Days Maximum Temp. ≥ 90°F	0	0	0	0	2	6	12	8	3	0	0	0	31
Days Maximum Temp. ≤ 32°F	6	4	1	0	0	0	0	0	0	0	0	3	14
Days Minimum Temp. ≤ 32°F	25	21	13	3	0	0	0	0	0	1	10	20	93
Days Minimum Temp. ≤ 0°F	0	0	0	0	0	0	0	0	0	0	0	0	0
Heating Degree Days (base 65°F)	984	809	643	339	113	11	0	1	38	269	540	831	4,578
Cooling Degree Days (base 65°F)	0	0	4	13	80	250	414	334	158	22	1	0	1,276
Mean Precipitation (in.)	3.38	3.06	3.89	2.98	3.85	3.38	3.81	3.68	3.81	3.25	3.23	3.39	41.71
Maximum Precipitation (in.)	7.8	7.2	8.6	8.1	8.7	9.9	8.2	18.3	8.6	8.1	7.7	7.4	59.0
Minimum Precipitation (in.)	0.3	0.4	0.9	0.4	0.4	0.1	0.3	0.8	0.2	trace	0.3	0.2	27.9
Maximum 24-hr. Precipitation (in.)	2.4	3.3	2.5	2.3	3.3	3.8	5.8	4.9	5.0	2.7	3.4	3.4	5.8
Days With ≥ 0.1" Precipitation	6	6	7	6	8	6	6	6	5	5	6	6	73
Days With ≥ 1.0" Precipitation	1	1	1	1	1	1	1	1	1	1	1	1	12
Mean Snowfall (in.)	6.4	6.4	2.5	trace	trace	0.0	trace	0.0	0.0	trace	0.6	1.9	17.8
Maximum Snowfall (in.)	25	33	22	1	trace	0	0	0	0	trace	8	20	53
Maximum 24-hr. Snowfall (in.)	12	23	11	1	trace	0	0	0	0	trace	8	9	23
Days With ≥ 1.0" Snow Depth	5	4	1	0	0	0	0	0	0	0	0	2	12
Thunderstorm Days	< 1	< 1	1	2	4	5	6	5	2	1	< 1	< 1	26
Foggy Days	11	10	12	10	14	13	14	15	14	13	11	11	148
Predominant Sky Cover	OVR	OVR	OVR	OVR	OVR	OVR	SCT	OVR	OVR	CLR	OVR	OVR	OVR
Mean Relative Humidity 7am (%)	72	71	72	72	77	79	80	83	85	83	78	74	77
Mean Relative Humidity 4pm (%)	56	52	49	47	52	53	53	55	55	54	55	57	53
Mean Dewpoint (°F)	22	23	29	39	51	60	65	64	58	46	35	26	43
Prevailing Wind Direction	WNW	WNW	WNW	WNW	W	W	W	W	W	W	WNW	WNW	WNW
Prevailing Wind Speed (mph)	13	14	14	13	9	8	8	7	7	8	12	13	10
Maximum Wind Gust (mph)	59	56	58	62	55	58	68	55	52	49	64	77	77

Aberdeen Phillips Field *Harford County*   Elevation: 59 ft.   Latitude: 39° 28' N   Longitude: 76° 10' W

	JAN	FEB	MAR	APR	MAY	JUN	JUL	AUG	SEP	OCT	NOV	DEC	YEAR
Mean Maximum Temp. (°F)	na	45.4	*53.8*	64.9	74.1	82.4	*86.8*	85.1	*79.0*	na	na	na	na
Mean Temp. (°F)	na	36.9	*44.3*	54.2	63.5	72.2	*76.8*	75.5	*69.1*	na	na	na	na
Mean Minimum Temp. (°F)	na	28.4	*34.7*	43.4	53.0	61.9	*66.9*	65.7	*58.8*	na	na	na	na
Extreme Maximum Temp. (°F)	70	79	88	93	94	97	100	100	98	88	81	74	100
Extreme Minimum Temp. (°F)	-10	-12	12	20	32	40	48	47	35	25	13	3	-12
Days Maximum Temp. ≥ 90°F	0	0	0	0	1	4	9	6	2	0	0	0	22
Days Maximum Temp. ≤ 32°F	5	3	0	0	0	0	0	0	0	0	0	2	10
Days Minimum Temp. ≤ 32°F	19	16	12	3	0	0	0	0	0	1	7	15	73
Days Minimum Temp. ≤ 0°F	0	0	0	0	0	0	0	0	0	0	0	0	0
Heating Degree Days (base 65°F)	na	789	*637*	330	113	11	*1*	1	*34*	na	na	na	na
Cooling Degree Days (base 65°F)	na	0	3	12	80	243	*399*	338	*165*	na	na	na	na
Mean Precipitation (in.)	3.25	2.75	3.53	3.40	4.43	4.15	4.34	4.08	4.42	3.43	3.25	3.33	44.36
Days With ≥ 0.1" Precipitation	*4*	*4*	4	5	6	5	5	4	4	3	4	*4*	52
Days With ≥ 1.0" Precipitation	1	1	1	1	1	1	1	1	1	1	1	1	12
Mean Snowfall (in.)	*4.0*	3.8	0.6	0.1	0.0	0.0	0.0	0.0	0.0	trace	0.1	0.9	*9.5*
Days With ≥ 1.0" Snow Depth	*3*	3	0	0	0	0	0	0	0	0	0	1	*7*

Assateague Island *Worcester County*   Elevation: 9 ft.   Latitude: 38° 04' N   Longitude: 75° 13' W

	JAN	FEB	MAR	APR	MAY	JUN	JUL	AUG	SEP	OCT	NOV	DEC	YEAR
Mean Maximum Temp. (°F)	44.7	46.5	53.1	61.7	70.1	79.0	83.8	83.6	78.8	68.7	59.2	50.0	64.9
Mean Temp. (°F)	36.0	37.9	44.1	52.8	61.8	70.7	75.8	75.7	70.8	60.0	50.3	41.4	56.4
Mean Minimum Temp. (°F)	27.7	29.3	35.1	44.0	53.5	62.3	67.7	67.7	62.7	51.2	41.3	32.7	47.9
Extreme Maximum Temp. (°F)	71	76	89	90	99	102	102	100	96	94	81	76	102
Extreme Minimum Temp. (°F)	-2	3	10	20	36	41	50	48	41	26	15	2	-2
Days Maximum Temp. ≥ 90°F	0	0	0	0	1	2	5	4	1	0	0	0	13
Days Maximum Temp. ≤ 32°F	3	2	0	0	0	0	0	0	0	0	0	1	6
Days Minimum Temp. ≤ 32°F	21	18	10	1	0	0	0	0	0	1	5	*14*	*70*
Days Minimum Temp. ≤ 0°F	0	0	0	0	0	0	0	0	0	0	0	0	0
Heating Degree Days (base 65°F)	891	759	641	363	135	13	0	1	15	181	437	725	4,161
Cooling Degree Days (base 65°F)	0	0	1	3	50	206	362	335	195	33	2	0	1,187
Mean Precipitation (in.)	4.37	3.60	4.42	3.35	3.61	2.87	3.61	4.15	3.66	3.37	3.21	3.22	43.44
Days With ≥ 0.1" Precipitation	7	*6*	8	6	7	5	6	5	5	5	6	6	*72*
Days With ≥ 1.0" Precipitation	1	1	1	1	1	1	1	1	1	1	1	1	12
Mean Snowfall (in.)	*1.9*	*2.2*	*0.4*	*trace*	*0.0*	0.0	0.0	0.0	0.0	0.0	trace	*0.5*	*5.0*
Days With ≥ 1.0" Snow Depth	*2*	*1*	*0*	0	0	0	0	0	0	0	0	0	*3*

Baltimore City *Baltimore (City) County*   Elevation: 13 ft.   Latitude: 39° 17' N   Longitude: 76° 37' W

	JAN	FEB	MAR	APR	MAY	JUN	JUL	AUG	SEP	OCT	NOV	DEC	YEAR
Mean Maximum Temp. (°F)	42.8	46.0	55.2	66.6	76.1	85.0	89.4	87.3	80.2	68.5	57.4	47.5	66.8
Mean Temp. (°F)	36.0	38.5	47.0	57.4	67.2	76.3	81.0	79.0	72.0	60.2	49.7	40.6	58.7
Mean Minimum Temp. (°F)	29.2	31.0	38.7	48.1	58.1	67.6	72.5	70.8	63.8	51.8	42.0	33.6	50.6
Extreme Maximum Temp. (°F)	75	84	97	98	99	104	104	105	102	94	86	85	105
Extreme Minimum Temp. (°F)	-4	7	13	21	40	48	58	52	40	30	20	6	-4
Days Maximum Temp. ≥ 90°F	0	0	0	1	3	8	16	12	4	0	0	0	44
Days Maximum Temp. ≤ 32°F	5	3	0	0	0	0	0	0	0	0	0	2	10
Days Minimum Temp. ≤ 32°F	19	16	7	1	0	0	0	0	0	0	4	13	60
Days Minimum Temp. ≤ 0°F	0	0	0	0	0	0	0	0	0	0	0	0	0
Heating Degree Days (base 65°F)	891	742	561	254	65	3	0	0	18	187	457	751	3,929
Cooling Degree Days (base 65°F)	0	0	11	33	148	368	523	442	234	47	3	2	1,811
Mean Precipitation (in.)	3.12	3.06	3.99	3.13	4.19	3.29	*4.00*	*4.17*	3.72	3.32	*3.59*	*3.75*	*43.33*
Days With ≥ 0.1" Precipitation	6	6	7	6	*8*	6	*6*	6	5	5	*6*	6	73
Days With ≥ 1.0" Precipitation	1	1	1	1	*1*	*1*	*1*	*1*	1	1	*1*	*1*	12
Mean Snowfall (in.)	na	na	na	na	na	na	na	na	na	na	na	na	na
Days With ≥ 1.0" Snow Depth	na	na	na	na	na	na	na	na	na	na	na	na	na

Beltsville *Prince George's County*   Elevation: 144 ft.   Latitude: 39° 02' N   Longitude: 76° 53' W

	JAN	FEB	MAR	APR	MAY	JUN	JUL	AUG	SEP	OCT	NOV	DEC	YEAR
Mean Maximum Temp. (°F)	41.3	44.7	53.5	64.4	74.1	82.5	87.2	85.7	79.1	67.5	56.7	46.2	65.2
Mean Temp. (°F)	31.8	35.0	43.0	52.7	62.7	71.4	76.3	74.7	67.9	55.6	46.1	37.0	54.5
Mean Minimum Temp. (°F)	22.3	25.2	32.6	41.0	51.2	60.2	65.3	63.7	56.7	43.7	35.4	27.7	43.7
Extreme Maximum Temp. (°F)	75	79	88	94	96	99	103	102	98	90	83	78	103
Extreme Minimum Temp. (°F)	-12	-12	6	21	30	37	45	38	35	22	13	-1	-12
Days Maximum Temp. ≥ 90°F	0	0	0	0	1	5	12	8	3	0	0	0	29
Days Maximum Temp. ≤ 32°F	6	4	1	0	0	0	0	0	0	0	0	3	14
Days Minimum Temp. ≤ 32°F	26	22	16	5	0	0	0	0	0	3	13	23	108
Days Minimum Temp. ≤ 0°F	1	0	0	0	0	0	0	0	0	0	0	0	1
Heating Degree Days (base 65°F)	1,021	840	678	371	133	19	1	3	50	300	563	861	4,840
Cooling Degree Days (base 65°F)	0	0	3	10	74	230	383	313	149	19	1	0	1,182
Mean Precipitation (in.)	3.34	2.72	3.90	3.43	4.58	3.52	4.01	3.70	4.29	3.74	3.46	3.36	44.05
Days With ≥ 0.1" Precipitation	*7*	6	7	7	8	6	7	6	6	5	5	6	*76*
Days With ≥ 1.0" Precipitation	1	0	1	1	1	1	1	1	1	1	1	1	11
Mean Snowfall (in.)	*5.8*	4.2	1.6	trace	0.0	0.0	0.0	0.0	0.0	0.0	0.6	*1.4*	*13.6*
Days With ≥ 1.0" Snow Depth	*5*	3	1	0	0	0	0	0	0	0	0	2	*11*

Benson Police Barracks *Harford County*   Elevation: 364 ft.   Latitude: 39° 30' N   Longitude: 76° 23' W

	JAN	FEB	MAR	APR	MAY	JUN	JUL	AUG	SEP	OCT	NOV	DEC	YEAR
Mean Maximum Temp. (°F)	41.5	46.1	55.2	66.8	76.3	83.8	88.0	86.3	80.3	69.1	57.9	46.4	66.5
Mean Temp. (°F)	32.0	35.5	43.8	54.0	64.1	72.0	76.6	74.9	68.5	56.8	46.9	37.0	55.2
Mean Minimum Temp. (°F)	22.4	24.9	32.5	41.3	51.8	60.3	65.2	63.6	56.6	44.6	36.1	27.3	43.9
Extreme Maximum Temp. (°F)	69	78	88	95	98	100	103	102	100	90	82	76	103
Extreme Minimum Temp. (°F)	-16	-2	5	17	30	42	48	43	32	24	11	-5	-16
Days Maximum Temp. ≥ 90°F	0	0	0	0	2	6	13	9	3	0	0	0	33
Days Maximum Temp. ≤ 32°F	6	3	0	0	0	0	0	0	0	0	0	2	11
Days Minimum Temp. ≤ 32°F	27	22	16	5	0	0	0	0	0	2	11	22	105
Days Minimum Temp. ≤ 0°F	1	0	0	0	0	0	0	0	0	0	0	0	1
Heating Degree Days (base 65°F)	1,020	826	651	336	102	11	1	2	40	264	538	860	4,651
Cooling Degree Days (base 65°F)	0	0	2	16	96	257	406	327	152	17	1	0	1,274
Mean Precipitation (in.)	3.60	2.94	4.34	3.93	5.05	4.37	4.96	4.52	4.22	3.66	4.12	3.82	49.53
Days With ≥ 0.1" Precipitation	7	6	8	7	9	7	8	7	6	6	7	6	84
Days With ≥ 1.0" Precipitation	1	1	1	1	2	1	1	1	1	1	1	1	13
Mean Snowfall (in.)	7.1	5.2	1.5	trace	0.0	0.0	0.0	0.0	0.0	trace	0.4	na	na
Days With ≥ 1.0" Snow Depth	8	7	2	0	0	0	0	0	0	0	0	2	19

Catoctin Mountain Park *Frederick County*   Elevation: 1,607 ft.   Latitude: 39° 39' N   Longitude: 77° 29' W

	JAN	FEB	MAR	APR	MAY	JUN	JUL	AUG	SEP	OCT	NOV	DEC	YEAR
Mean Maximum Temp. (°F)	36.2	39.8	49.3	62.0	71.0	77.2	80.6	78.7	72.2	62.4	51.3	41.1	60.2
Mean Temp. (°F)	28.6	31.6	40.0	51.2	60.9	68.2	72.3	70.7	64.3	53.7	43.5	33.8	51.6
Mean Minimum Temp. (°F)	21.0	23.4	30.6	40.3	50.7	59.1	63.9	62.6	56.3	45.0	35.7	26.5	42.9
Extreme Maximum Temp. (°F)	67	75	86	89	92	91	98	94	91	88	78	73	98
Extreme Minimum Temp. (°F)	-18	-5	1	12	26	34	48	42	34	21	6	-11	-18
Days Maximum Temp. ≥ 90°F	0	0	0	0	0	0	2	1	0	0	0	0	3
Days Maximum Temp. ≤ 32°F	11	8	2	0	0	0	0	0	0	0	1	6	28
Days Minimum Temp. ≤ 32°F	27	23	18	6	0	0	0	0	0	2	12	23	111
Days Minimum Temp. ≤ 0°F	1	1	0	0	0	0	0	0	0	0	0	0	2
Heating Degree Days (base 65°F)	1,121	936	771	420	170	34	4	10	90	351	639	961	5,507
Cooling Degree Days (base 65°F)	0	0	3	10	52	146	254	195	78	10	1	0	749
Mean Precipitation (in.)	3.91	3.37	4.29	4.01	5.05	4.70	3.83	3.76	4.89	4.09	3.96	3.46	49.32
Days With ≥ 0.1" Precipitation	7	6	7	8	9	8	7	6	7	6	6	6	83
Days With ≥ 1.0" Precipitation	1	1	1	1	1	1	1	1	1	1	1	1	12
Mean Snowfall (in.)	11.0	9.0	5.1	1.1	trace	0.0	0.0	0.0	0.0	0.2	2.6	4.0	33.0
Days With ≥ 1.0" Snow Depth	17	14	7	1	0	0	0	0	0	0	2	6	47

Chestertown *Kent County*   Elevation: 39 ft.   Latitude: 39° 13' N   Longitude: 76° 04' W

	JAN	FEB	MAR	APR	MAY	JUN	JUL	AUG	SEP	OCT	NOV	DEC	YEAR
Mean Maximum Temp. (°F)	40.9	44.3	53.4	64.6	74.5	83.0	87.4	86.0	79.3	67.8	56.6	46.1	65.3
Mean Temp. (°F)	32.8	35.6	43.8	53.8	63.7	72.5	77.3	75.6	68.8	57.1	47.0	37.7	55.5
Mean Minimum Temp. (°F)	24.7	26.9	34.3	43.0	52.9	61.9	67.0	65.2	58.3	46.2	37.3	29.3	45.6
Extreme Maximum Temp. (°F)	75	75	89	93	96	100	101	101	100	89	81	78	101
Extreme Minimum Temp. (°F)	-7	-5	10	21	33	43	50	44	35	26	13	2	-7
Days Maximum Temp. ≥ 90°F	0	0	0	0	1	5	12	8	3	0	0	0	29
Days Maximum Temp. ≤ 32°F	7	4	1	0	0	0	0	0	0	0	0	3	15
Days Minimum Temp. ≤ 32°F	25	21	14	2	0	0	0	0	0	1	9	20	92
Days Minimum Temp. ≤ 0°F	0	0	0	0	0	0	0	0	0	0	0	0	0
Heating Degree Days (base 65°F)	991	824	651	339	109	10	1	2	36	261	535	838	4,597
Cooling Degree Days (base 65°F)	0	0	3	11	84	258	413	342	156	25	1	0	1,293
Mean Precipitation (in.)	3.49	3.02	4.09	3.32	4.09	4.32	3.81	3.75	4.16	3.43	3.41	3.69	44.58
Days With ≥ 0.1" Precipitation	7	6	7	7	7	7	6	5	6	5	6	7	76
Days With ≥ 1.0" Precipitation	1	1	1	1	1	1	1	1	1	1	1	1	12
Mean Snowfall (in.)	5.4	6.1	1.8	0.1	0.0	0.0	0.0	0.0	0.0	trace	0.4	1.8	15.6
Days With ≥ 1.0" Snow Depth	7	5	1	0	0	0	0	0	0	0	0	2	15

Clarksville 3 NNE *Howard County*   Elevation: 367 ft.   Latitude: 39° 15' N   Longitude: 76° 56' W

	JAN	FEB	MAR	APR	MAY	JUN	JUL	AUG	SEP	OCT	NOV	DEC	YEAR
Mean Maximum Temp. (°F)	41.7	45.9	55.0	65.8	75.6	83.3	87.6	85.8	79.6	68.0	56.6	46.5	65.9
Mean Temp. (°F)	31.7	34.7	43.0	52.3	62.5	70.7	75.3	73.6	67.0	55.0	45.2	36.5	54.0
Mean Minimum Temp. (°F)	21.7	23.5	30.9	38.9	49.4	58.0	63.0	61.2	54.4	41.9	33.8	26.4	41.9
Extreme Maximum Temp. (°F)	74	80	89	93	96	100	103	103	99	88	84	78	103
Extreme Minimum Temp. (°F)	-18	-17	3	17	26	34	40	37	30	20	11	-6	-18
Days Maximum Temp. ≥ 90°F	0	0	0	0	1	5	11	7	3	0	0	0	27
Days Maximum Temp. ≤ 32°F	6	4	0	0	0	0	0	0	0	0	0	3	13
Days Minimum Temp. ≤ 32°F	26	23	18	8	1	0	0	0	0	6	15	22	119
Days Minimum Temp. ≤ 0°F	1	1	0	0	0	0	0	0	0	0	0	0	2
Heating Degree Days (base 65°F)	1,025	849	677	382	132	20	1	5	63	318	590	876	4,938
Cooling Degree Days (base 65°F)	0	0	3	8	66	206	349	274	128	14	1	0	1,049
Mean Precipitation (in.)	3.36	3.01	3.95	3.61	4.76	4.01	4.06	3.88	4.08	3.54	3.67	3.52	45.45
Days With ≥ 0.1" Precipitation	6	6	7	7	8	6	7	6	6	6	6	6	77
Days With ≥ 1.0" Precipitation	1	1	1	1	1	1	1	1	1	1	1	1	12
Mean Snowfall (in.)	7.9	6.8	2.4	0.2	0.0	0.0	0.0	0.0	0.0	trace	0.7	2.4	20.4
Days With ≥ 1.0" Snow Depth	9	6	1	0	0	0	0	0	0	0	0	2	18

College Park *Prince George's County*   Elevation: 88 ft.   Latitude: 38° 59' N   Longitude: 76° 57' W

	JAN	FEB	MAR	APR	MAY	JUN	JUL	AUG	SEP	OCT	NOV	DEC	YEAR
Mean Maximum Temp. (°F)	41.9	45.9	55.0	66.5	75.9	84.2	88.6	86.7	80.0	68.7	58.0	47.2	66.6
Mean Temp. (°F)	33.5	36.6	45.0	55.1	64.9	73.5	78.5	76.6	69.7	57.7	48.2	38.7	56.5
Mean Minimum Temp. (°F)	25.1	27.2	35.0	43.7	53.8	62.8	68.2	66.4	59.4	46.8	38.2	30.1	46.4
Extreme Maximum Temp. (°F)	74	82	92	96	100	101	104	104	99	93	85	77	104
Extreme Minimum Temp. (°F)	-7	-5	8	22	32	40	50	43	37	26	14	2	-7
Days Maximum Temp. ≥ 90°F	0	0	0	1	2	7	15	11	4	0	0	0	40
Days Maximum Temp. ≤ 32°F	6	3	0	0	0	0	0	0	0	0	0	3	12
Days Minimum Temp. ≤ 32°F	23	20	13	3	0	0	0	0	0	2	9	19	89
Days Minimum Temp. ≤ 0°F	0	0	0	0	0	0	0	0	0	0	0	1	1
Heating Degree Days (base 65°F)	970	798	618	312	97	9	0	3	34	245	502	810	4,398
Cooling Degree Days (base 65°F)	0	0	5	22	107	286	454	368	181	29	2	0	1,454
Mean Precipitation (in.)	3.25	2.79	3.64	3.28	4.69	3.65	4.53	4.06	3.81	3.60	3.51	3.34	44.15
Days With ≥ 0.1" Precipitation	6	6	7	6	8	6	6	6	6	5	5	5	72
Days With ≥ 1.0" Precipitation	0	0	1	1	1	1	1	1	1	1	1	1	10
Mean Snowfall (in.)	5.5	5.4	1.6	tracc	0.0	0.0	0.0	0.0	0.0	trace	0.7	1.3	14.5
Days With ≥ 1.0" Snow Depth	6	4	1	0	0	0	0	0	0	0	0	1	12

Cumberland 2 *Allegany County*   Elevation: 728 ft.   Latitude: 39° 38' N   Longitude: 78° 45' W

	JAN	FEB	MAR	APR	MAY	JUN	JUL	AUG	SEP	OCT	NOV	DEC	YEAR
Mean Maximum Temp. (°F)	39.6	45.3	55.2	67.2	76.5	84.0	88.1	86.5	79.1	67.7	55.7	44.5	65.8
Mean Temp. (°F)	30.3	34.6	43.1	53.8	63.1	71.1	75.6	73.9	66.4	54.4	44.7	35.1	53.8
Mean Minimum Temp. (°F)	20.9	23.9	31.0	40.3	49.8	58.0	63.0	61.3	53.7	41.1	33.6	25.6	41.8
Extreme Maximum Temp. (°F)	74	79	90	96	98	99	104	103	98	88	87	77	104
Extreme Minimum Temp. (°F)	-14	-3	3	20	25	39	46	40	31	20	10	-8	-14
Days Maximum Temp. ≥ 90°F	0	0	0	0	2	6	12	10	3	0	0	0	33
Days Maximum Temp. ≤ 32°F	8	4	1	0	0	0	0	0	0	0	0	3	16
Days Minimum Temp. ≤ 32°F	27	22	18	5	0	0	0	0	0	5	14	24	115
Days Minimum Temp. ≤ 0°F	1	0	0	0	0	0	0	0	0	0	0	0	1
Heating Degree Days (base 65°F)	1,069	852	675	346	126	16	1	4	67	331	605	921	5,013
Cooling Degree Days (base 65°F)	0	0	4	13	69	204	342	279	115	11	0	0	1,037
Mean Precipitation (in.)	2.93	2.30	3.43	3.11	3.88	2.97	3.57	3.36	3.20	2.77	2.91	2.57	37.00
Days With ≥ 0.1" Precipitation	6	5	8	7	8	7	7	6	6	6	6	5	77
Days With ≥ 1.0" Precipitation	1	0	1	1	1	1	1	1	1	1	1	1	11
Mean Snowfall (in.)	12.7	7.4	6.4	0.3	0.0	0.0	0.0	0.0	0.0	0.0	1.5	4.1	32.4
Days With ≥ 1.0" Snow Depth	15	10	5	0	0	0	0	0	0	0	1	5	36

Dalecarlia Reservoir *District of Columbia*   Elevation: 147 ft.   Latitude: 38° 56' N   Longitude: 77° 07' W

	JAN	FEB	MAR	APR	MAY	JUN	JUL	AUG	SEP	OCT	NOV	DEC	YEAR
Mean Maximum Temp. (°F)	43.9	48.2	57.5	69.0	77.6	85.3	89.2	87.5	81.0	69.9	58.8	48.7	68.0
Mean Temp. (°F)	33.6	37.5	45.5	55.8	65.1	73.2	77.7	76.3	69.5	57.5	47.4	38.5	56.5
Mean Minimum Temp. (°F)	23.6	26.5	33.3	42.3	52.3	61.2	66.1	65.0	58.0	45.0	36.0	28.2	44.8
Extreme Maximum Temp. (°F)	78	81	91	94	98	100	103	105	99	90	87	82	105
Extreme Minimum Temp. (°F)	-11	-10	7	19	27	40	44	41	35	22	9	-2	-11
Days Maximum Temp. ≥ 90°F	0	0	0	0	2	8	15	11	4	0	0	0	40
Days Maximum Temp. ≤ 32°F	4	2	0	0	0	0	0	0	0	0	0	2	8
Days Minimum Temp. ≤ 32°F	26	21	15	4	0	0	0	0	0	3	12	21	102
Days Minimum Temp. ≤ 0°F	0	0	0	0	0	0	0	0	0	0	0	0	0
Heating Degree Days (base 65°F)	967	769	602	292	90	9	0	1	35	251	524	817	4,357
Cooling Degree Days (base 65°F)	0	0	4	21	100	273	417	358	176	26	2	1	1,378
Mean Precipitation (in.)	3.45	3.03	4.11	3.56	4.42	3.62	4.33	3.84	4.18	3.60	3.55	3.48	45.17
Days With ≥ 0.1" Precipitation	7	6	7	7	9	6	8	6	6	6	6	7	81
Days With ≥ 1.0" Precipitation	1	1	1	1	1	1	1	1	1	1	1	1	12
Mean Snowfall (in.)	2.9	3.1	0.9	trace	0.0	0.0	0.0	0.0	0.0	0.0	trace	0.7	7.6
Days With ≥ 1.0" Snow Depth	4	3	0	0	0	0	0	0	0	0	0	0	7

Emmitsburg 2 SE *Frederick County*   Elevation: 413 ft.   Latitude: 39° 41' N   Longitude: 77° 18' W

	JAN	FEB	MAR	APR	MAY	JUN	JUL	AUG	SEP	OCT	NOV	DEC	YEAR
Mean Maximum Temp. (°F)	39.1	43.4	53.1	64.7	73.8	81.8	86.0	84.4	77.6	66.4	54.6	44.1	64.1
Mean Temp. (°F)	30.1	33.2	41.9	51.9	61.3	69.8	74.4	72.6	65.9	54.4	44.3	35.5	52.9
Mean Minimum Temp. (°F)	21.1	23.0	30.6	39.1	48.9	57.7	62.7	60.9	54.1	42.2	33.9	26.8	41.8
Extreme Maximum Temp. (°F)	72	78	85	91	92	97	101	103	98	88	82	77	103
Extreme Minimum Temp. (°F)	-27	-13	4	15	27	35	42	36	31	20	11	-4	-27
Days Maximum Temp. ≥ 90°F	0	0	0	0	0	3	8	6	2	0	0	0	19
Days Maximum Temp. ≤ 32°F	8	4	1	0	0	0	0	0	0	0	0	3	16
Days Minimum Temp. ≤ 32°F	27	23	19	7	1	0	0	0	0	5	14	23	119
Days Minimum Temp. ≤ 0°F	1	1	0	0	0	0	0	0	0	0	0	0	2
Heating Degree Days (base 65°F)	1,075	890	710	393	153	23	2	7	75	335	615	908	5,186
Cooling Degree Days (base 65°F)	0	0	2	7	49	180	319	251	108	13	0	0	929
Mean Precipitation (in.)	3.58	2.98	3.94	3.88	4.50	4.38	3.71	3.60	4.11	3.62	3.87	3.37	45.54
Days With ≥ 0.1" Precipitation	7	7	8	7	9	8	7	6	6	6	7	7	85
Days With ≥ 1.0" Precipitation	1	1	1	1	1	1	1	1	1	1	1	1	12
Mean Snowfall (in.)	10.9	9.6	5.3	0.7	0.0	0.0	0.0	0.0	0.0	0.1	1.4	3.7	31.7
Days With ≥ 1.0" Snow Depth	12	9	3	0	0	0	0	0	0	0	1	3	28

Frederick Police *Frederick County*   Elevation: 377 ft.   Latitude: 39° 25' N   Longitude: 77° 26' W

	JAN	FEB	MAR	APR	MAY	JUN	JUL	AUG	SEP	OCT	NOV	DEC	YEAR
Mean Maximum Temp. (°F)	41.2	45.5	55.3	67.1	76.3	84.5	88.9	86.7	79.6	68.0	56.8	45.9	66.3
Mean Temp. (°F)	32.9	36.3	44.9	55.6	65.0	73.4	78.0	76.2	69.1	57.3	47.6	37.8	56.2
Mean Minimum Temp. (°F)	24.9	27.1	34.4	44.1	53.6	62.2	67.1	65.6	58.4	46.5	38.3	29.6	46.0
Extreme Maximum Temp. (°F)	73	79	87	94	97	101	106	104	97	86	82	77	106
Extreme Minimum Temp. (°F)	-10	0	3	24	33	41	50	44	34	26	14	-8	-10
Days Maximum Temp. ≥ 90°F	0	0	0	1	2	7	14	10	3	0	0	0	37
Days Maximum Temp. ≤ 32°F	6	3	1	0	0	0	0	0	0	0	0	3	13
Days Minimum Temp. ≤ 32°F	23	19	13	2	0	0	0	0	0	0	0	20	87
Days Minimum Temp. ≤ 0°F	0	0	0	0	0	0	0	0	0	0	1	9	
Heating Degree Days (base 65°F)	987	802	622	294	91	9	0	1	39	254	516	838	4,453
Cooling Degree Days (base 65°F)	0	0	5	19	102	277	432	352	171	24	1	0	1,383
Mean Precipitation (in.)	3.14	2.49	3.57	3.28	4.15	3.60	3.52	2.93	3.80	3.36	3.15	3.32	40.31
Days With ≥ 0.1" Precipitation	7	6	7	7	8	7	6	6	6	5	6	6	77
Days With ≥ 1.0" Precipitation	1	0	1	1	1	1	1	1	1	1	1	1	11
Mean Snowfall (in.)	7.6	6.0	3.0	trace	0.0	0.0	0.0	0.0	0.0	0.0	0.3	1.6	18.5
Days With ≥ 1.0" Snow Depth	8	6	2	0	0	0	0	0	0	0	0	2	18

Frostburg 2 *Allegany County*   Elevation: 2,165 ft.   Latitude: 39° 40' N   Longitude: 78° 56' W

	JAN	FEB	MAR	APR	MAY	JUN	JUL	AUG	SEP	OCT	NOV	DEC	YEAR
Mean Maximum Temp. (°F)	33.0	36.6	45.5	57.1	66.8	74.8	79.1	77.6	70.6	59.2	48.2	37.7	57.2
Mean Temp. (°F)	25.3	28.1	36.0	46.7	56.4	64.3	68.8	67.4	60.6	49.4	40.0	30.2	47.8
Mean Minimum Temp. (°F)	17.6	19.5	26.5	36.2	46.0	53.8	58.4	57.2	50.5	39.6	31.7	22.7	38.3
Extreme Maximum Temp. (°F)	66	71	84	87	89	89	96	94	90	82	77	69	96
Extreme Minimum Temp. (°F)	-26	-10	-3	12	26	34	37	36	28	18	4	-16	-26
Days Maximum Temp. ≥ 90°F	0	0	0	0	0	0	1	1	0	0	0	0	2
Days Maximum Temp. ≤ 32°F	15	11	5	0	0	0	0	0	0	0	3	11	45
Days Minimum Temp. ≤ 32°F	29	25	23	10	1	0	0	0	0	6	17	26	137
Days Minimum Temp. ≤ 0°F	3	1	0	0	0	0	0	0	0	0	0	1	5
Heating Degree Days (base 65°F)	1,224	1,035	893	548	276	86	23	37	166	478	744	1,072	6,582
Cooling Degree Days (base 65°F)	0	0	1	3	19	75	158	120	40	2	0	0	418
Mean Precipitation (in.)	3.67	3.01	3.97	4.05	4.69	3.91	3.97	3.74	3.50	3.32	3.84	3.26	44.93
Days With ≥ 0.1" Precipitation	8	7	8	8	9	8	8	7	7	7	7	7	91
Days With ≥ 1.0" Precipitation	1	0	1	1	1	1	1	1	1	1	1	1	11
Mean Snowfall (in.)	28.3	20.0	17.1	3.4	trace	0.0	0.0	0.0	trace	0.4	7.5	17.4	94.1
Days With ≥ 1.0" Snow Depth	23	20	13	2	0	0	0	0	0	0	5	14	77

Glenn Dale Bell Station *Prince George's County*   Elevation: 147 ft.   Latitude: 38° 58' N   Longitude: 76° 48' W

	JAN	FEB	MAR	APR	MAY	JUN	JUL	AUG	SEP	OCT	NOV	DEC	YEAR
Mean Maximum Temp. (°F)	44.0	48.3	57.4	68.0	76.5	84.1	88.6	86.9	80.7	69.7	58.9	48.8	67.7
Mean Temp. (°F)	33.5	36.7	44.7	54.0	63.3	71.5	76.2	74.6	68.3	56.6	46.9	38.2	55.4
Mean Minimum Temp. (°F)	22.9	25.1	32.0	40.0	50.0	58.8	63.8	62.4	55.7	43.4	34.9	27.7	43.0
Extreme Maximum Temp. (°F)	75	80	95	95	97	102	102	104	98	89	85	79	104
Extreme Minimum Temp. (°F)	-11	-10	2	20	28	35	40	38	32	20	9	-3	-11
Days Maximum Temp. ≥ 90°F	0	0	0	1	2	7	14	10	4	0	0	0	38
Days Maximum Temp. ≤ 32°F	4	2	0	0	0	0	0	0	0	0	0	2	8
Days Minimum Temp. ≤ 32°F	26	21	17	7	1	0	0	0	0	5	13	21	111
Days Minimum Temp. ≤ 0°F	1	0	0	0	0	0	0	0	0	0	0	0	1
Heating Degree Days (base 65°F)	971	793	628	337	120	17	1	3	48	275	541	824	4,558
Cooling Degree Days (base 65°F)	0	0	5	14	74	227	376	308	150	21	2	0	1,177
Mean Precipitation (in.)	3.36	2.86	3.88	3.45	4.75	3.62	4.19	4.06	3.94	3.69	3.54	3.35	44.69
Days With ≥ 0.1" Precipitation	6	6	7	7	8	6	7	6	6	5	6	6	76
Days With ≥ 1.0" Precipitation	1	1	1	1	1	1	1	1	1	1	1	1	12
Mean Snowfall (in.)	5.0	4.8	1.8	trace	0.0	0.0	0.0	0.0	0.0	trace	0.9	1.6	14.1
Days With ≥ 1.0" Snow Depth	6	4	1	0	0	0	0	0	0	0	0	1	12

Hancock *Washington County*   Elevation: 383 ft.   Latitude: 39° 42' N   Longitude: 78° 11' W

	JAN	FEB	MAR	APR	MAY	JUN	JUL	AUG	SEP	OCT	NOV	DEC	YEAR
Mean Maximum Temp. (°F)	38.8	42.8	52.8	64.6	73.6	81.4	85.3	83.6	76.7	66.0	54.6	43.1	63.6
Mean Temp. (°F)	29.5	32.7	41.3	51.3	60.8	69.0	73.4	71.9	64.9	53.3	43.7	34.4	52.2
Mean Minimum Temp. (°F)	20.2	22.4	29.7	37.9	47.9	56.5	61.6	60.2	53.1	40.5	32.8	25.6	40.7
Extreme Maximum Temp. (°F)	74	81	89	92	100	98	102	102	99	90	83	77	102
Extreme Minimum Temp. (°F)	-27	-13	-3	18	26	33	40	33	30	17	10	-6	-27
Days Maximum Temp. ≥ 90°F	0	0	0	0	1	3	7	5	2	0	0	0	18
Days Maximum Temp. ≤ 32°F	8	5	1	0	0	0	0	0	0	0	0	4	18
Days Minimum Temp. ≤ 32°F	27	23	19	10	1	0	0	0	0	8	15	23	126
Days Minimum Temp. ≤ 0°F	1	1	0	0	0	0	0	0	0	0	0	0	2
Heating Degree Days (base 65°F)	1,093	907	729	415	173	33	4	10	90	366	632	943	5,395
Cooling Degree Days (base 65°F)	0	0	2	9	52	170	294	239	91	11	0	0	868
Mean Precipitation (in.)	2.64	2.27	3.15	3.26	3.98	3.55	4.01	3.34	3.17	3.41	3.38	2.84	39.00
Days With ≥ 0.1" Precipitation	6	5	7	7	8	7	7	6	6	5	6	5	75
Days With ≥ 1.0" Precipitation	0	0	0	1	1	1	1	1	1	1	1	1	9
Mean Snowfall (in.)	7.7	6.5	4.5	0.2	0.0	0.0	0.0	0.0	0.0	trace	1.2	2.3	22.4
Days With ≥ 1.0" Snow Depth	9	8	2	0	0	0	0	0	0	0	1	2	22

La Plata 1 W *Charles County*   Elevation: 137 ft.   Latitude: 38° 32' N   Longitude: 77° 00' W

	JAN	FEB	MAR	APR	MAY	JUN	JUL	AUG	SEP	OCT	NOV	DEC	YEAR
Mean Maximum Temp. (°F)	43.8	48.5	57.6	68.3	75.1	81.5	85.2	84.0	78.5	68.5	58.5	48.4	66.5
Mean Temp. (°F)	34.7	38.4	46.4	55.7	64.2	71.6	75.9	74.6	68.7	57.9	48.3	39.2	56.3
Mean Minimum Temp. (°F)	25.5	28.2	35.1	43.0	53.2	61.6	66.5	65.3	58.8	47.3	38.0	30.1	46.1
Extreme Maximum Temp. (°F)	75	81	91	95	96	96	99	99	103	87	86	77	103
Extreme Minimum Temp. (°F)	-8	-2	9	20	32	41	46	45	36	25	13	1	-8
Days Maximum Temp. ≥ 90°F	0	0	0	1	1	2	7	5	2	0	0	0	18
Days Maximum Temp. ≤ 32°F	4	2	0	0	0	0	0	0	0	0	0	2	8
Days Minimum Temp. ≤ 32°F	23	19	13	4	0	0	0	0	0	1	10	20	90
Days Minimum Temp. ≤ 0°F	0	0	0	0	0	0	0	0	0	0	0	0	0
Heating Degree Days (base 65°F)	934	746	578	294	101	13	1	2	39	238	500	791	4,237
Cooling Degree Days (base 65°F)	0	0	8	21	87	225	357	*301*	*149*	28	3	0	*1,179*
Mean Precipitation (in.)	3.30	2.96	3.81	3.25	4.16	3.89	4.14	4.53	4.04	3.57	3.54	3.32	44.51
Days With ≥ 0.1" Precipitation	7	6	7	6	7	6	6	6	6	5	6	6	74
Days With ≥ 1.0" Precipitation	1	1	1	1	1	1	1	2	1	1	1	1	13
Mean Snowfall (in.)	5.7	5.6	1.6	0.2	0.0	0.0	0.0	0.0	0.0	trace	0.6	1.9	15.6
Days With ≥ 1.0" Snow Depth	7	4	1	0	0	0	0	0	0	0	0	2	14

Laurel 3 W *Prince George's County*   Elevation: 396 ft.   Latitude: 39° 06' N   Longitude: 76° 54' W

	JAN	FEB	MAR	APR	MAY	JUN	JUL	AUG	SEP	OCT	NOV	DEC	YEAR
Mean Maximum Temp. (°F)	41.2	45.3	54.7	65.6	75.0	83.2	88.2	86.8	79.3	68.0	56.7	46.3	65.9
Mean Temp. (°F)	32.7	36.1	44.7	54.8	64.4	72.8	77.9	76.7	69.2	57.6	47.4	38.0	56.0
Mean Minimum Temp. (°F)	24.4	27.0	34.6	43.9	54.0	62.3	67.5	66.4	59.1	47.1	38.2	29.7	46.2
Extreme Maximum Temp. (°F)	73	79	89	94	97	101	104	102	99	89	83	78	104
Extreme Minimum Temp. (°F)	-12	0	8	22	35	41	50	45	38	11	10	0	-12
Days Maximum Temp. ≥ 90°F	0	0	0	0	1	6	13	10	3	0	0	0	33
Days Maximum Temp. ≤ 32°F	6	3	1	0	0	0	0	0	0	0	0	3	13
Days Minimum Temp. ≤ 32°F	25	20	12	2	0	0	0	0	0	1	9	20	89
Days Minimum Temp. ≤ 0°F	0	0	0	0	0	0	0	0	0	0	0	0	0
Heating Degree Days (base 65°F)	994	810	627	317	100	10	0	1	34	245	523	830	4,491
Cooling Degree Days (base 65°F)	0	0	6	18	100	267	436	374	166	25	2	0	1,394
Mean Precipitation (in.)	3.43	3.02	4.13	3.61	4.75	3.83	4.07	3.61	4.45	3.74	4.13	3.64	46.41
Days With ≥ 0.1" Precipitation	7	6	8	7	8	7	7	6	6	6	6	7	81
Days With ≥ 1.0" Precipitation	1	1	1	1	1	1	1	1	1	1	1	1	12
Mean Snowfall (in.)	na	*2.8*	1.2	trace	0.0	0.0	0.0	0.0	0.0	trace	0.7	0.8	na
Days With ≥ 1.0" Snow Depth	na	na	0	0	0	0	0	0	0	0	0	*0*	na

National Arboretum *District of Columbia*   Elevation: 49 ft.   Latitude: 38° 54' N   Longitude: 76° 59' W

	JAN	FEB	MAR	APR	MAY	JUN	JUL	AUG	SEP	OCT	NOV	DEC	YEAR
Mean Maximum Temp. (°F)	43.0	46.5	55.3	66.3	75.7	84.0	88.4	86.9	80.4	68.8	58.3	48.2	66.8
Mean Temp. (°F)	33.7	36.6	44.8	54.7	64.3	73.0	77.8	76.0	69.0	56.9	47.5	38.8	56.1
Mean Minimum Temp. (°F)	24.4	26.6	34.2	43.1	52.9	62.0	67.2	65.1	57.7	44.9	36.7	29.2	45.3
Extreme Maximum Temp. (°F)	76	80	90	94	98	101	104	104	100	90	85	81	104
Extreme Minimum Temp. (°F)	-10	0	12	18	34	42	47	42	34	22	10	0	-10
Days Maximum Temp. ≥ 90°F	0	0	0	0	1	7	14	11	4	0	0	0	37
Days Maximum Temp. ≤ 32°F	5	3	0	0	0	0	0	0	0	0	0	2	10
Days Minimum Temp. ≤ 32°F	25	21	13	2	0	0	0	0	0	2	10	21	94
Days Minimum Temp. ≤ 0°F	0	0	0	0	0	0	0	0	0	0	0	0	0
Heating Degree Days (base 65°F)	963	796	622	319	102	10	0	2	39	266	521	806	4,446
Cooling Degree Days (base 65°F)	0	0	5	16	89	265	421	345	158	21	1	1	1,322
Mean Precipitation (in.)	3.49	2.87	3.86	3.28	4.33	3.60	4.33	3.83	4.05	3.40	3.43	3.28	43.75
Days With ≥ 0.1" Precipitation	7	6	7	7	8	7	7	6	6	5	6	6	78
Days With ≥ 1.0" Precipitation	1	0	1	1	1	1	1	1	1	1	1	1	11
Mean Snowfall (in.)	*5.6*	4.7	1.1	trace	0.0	0.0	0.0	0.0	0.0	trace	*0.5*	0.9	*12.8*
Days With ≥ 1.0" Snow Depth	*5*	*4*	1	0	0	0	0	0	0	0	0	1	*11*

Oakland 1 SE *Garrett County*   Elevation: 2,417 ft.   Latitude: 39° 24' N   Longitude: 79° 24' W

	JAN	FEB	MAR	APR	MAY	JUN	JUL	AUG	SEP	OCT	NOV	DEC	YEAR
Mean Maximum Temp. (°F)	35.9	39.4	49.0	60.3	69.0	76.0	79.5	78.3	72.2	62.2	50.5	41.2	59.5
Mean Temp. (°F)	26.6	29.1	37.6	47.5	56.7	64.3	68.5	67.1	60.9	50.0	40.1	31.8	48.4
Mean Minimum Temp. (°F)	17.3	18.7	26.2	34.7	44.3	52.5	57.5	55.9	49.6	37.7	29.8	22.4	37.2
Extreme Maximum Temp. (°F)	71	69	81	87	89	89	95	97	90	81	75	72	97
Extreme Minimum Temp. (°F)	-25	-25	-19	3	19	31	33	32	27	12	-5	-22	-25
Days Maximum Temp. ≥ 90°F	0	0	0	0	0	0	0	1	0	0	0	0	1
Days Maximum Temp. ≤ 32°F	12	9	4	0	0	0	0	0	0	0	2	7	34
Days Minimum Temp. ≤ 32°F	28	25	23	14	4	0	0	0	1	10	19	26	150
Days Minimum Temp. ≤ 0°F	3	3	1	0	0	0	0	0	0	0	0	1	8
Heating Degree Days (base 65°F)	1,184	1,008	844	518	263	79	22	33	151	460	739	1,022	6,323
Cooling Degree Days (base 65°F)	0	0	1	1	14	73	157	110	35	2	0	0	393
Mean Precipitation (in.)	3.50	3.07	4.02	4.15	4.78	4.58	5.13	4.15	3.58	3.13	3.63	3.75	47.47
Days With ≥ 0.1" Precipitation	8	8	10	9	11	9	9	8	8	7	8	9	104
Days With ≥ 1.0" Precipitation	1	0	0	1	1	1	1	1	1	0	1	1	9
Mean Snowfall (in.)	25.9	21.0	16.8	4.8	trace	0.0	0.0	0.0	0.0	0.5	8.6	18.3	95.9
Days With ≥ 1.0" Snow Depth	*16*	*13*	*6*	1	0	0	0	0	0	0	3	9	*48*

Rockville 1 NE *Montgomery County*   Elevation: 439 ft.   Latitude: 39° 06' N   Longitude: 77° 06' W

	JAN	FEB	MAR	APR	MAY	JUN	JUL	AUG	SEP	OCT	NOV	DEC	YEAR
Mean Maximum Temp. (°F)	42.0	45.6	55.4	66.8	75.2	82.7	86.9	84.6	77.9	67.2	56.3	46.7	65.6
Mean Temp. (°F)	33.0	35.6	44.4	54.5	63.5	71.5	76.0	73.8	67.1	55.7	46.0	37.6	54.9
Mean Minimum Temp. (°F)	23.8	25.5	33.4	42.2	51.7	60.2	65.2	63.0	56.3	44.2	35.6	28.3	44.1
Extreme Maximum Temp. (°F)	75	82	89	95	96	98	101	100	96	87	85	78	101
Extreme Minimum Temp. (°F)	-13	-12	5	19	28	35	38	39	28	20	10	-1	-13
Days Maximum Temp. ≥ 90°F	0	0	0	0	1	4	10	6	2	0	0	0	23
Days Maximum Temp. ≤ 32°F	5	4	0	0	0	0	0	0	0	0	0	0	12
Days Minimum Temp. ≤ 32°F	24	21	*14*	4	0	0	0	0	0	3	12	21	*99*
Days Minimum Temp. ≤ 0°F	1	0	0	0	0	0	0	0	0	0	0	0	1
Heating Degree Days (base 65°F)	987	824	636	325	117	17	1	3	56	294	569	846	4,675
Cooling Degree Days (base 65°F)	0	0	6	16	81	237	379	297	133	17	1	0	1,167
Mean Precipitation (in.)	3.30	2.86	3.87	3.08	4.40	3.78	4.07	3.81	4.07	3.41	3.50	3.09	43.24
Days With ≥ 0.1" Precipitation	7	6	7	6	8	6	7	6	6	5	6	6	76
Days With ≥ 1.0" Precipitation	1	1	1	1	1	1	1	1	1	1	1	1	12
Mean Snowfall (in.)	*7.3*	4.1	2.7	trace	0.0	0.0	0.0	0.0	0.0	trace	0.6	1.8	*16.5*
Days With ≥ 1.0" Snow Depth	9	6	1	0	0	0	0	0	0	0	0	2	18

Royal Oak 2 SSW *Talbot County*   Elevation: 9 ft.   Latitude: 38° 43' N   Longitude: 76° 11' W

	JAN	FEB	MAR	APR	MAY	JUN	JUL	AUG	SEP	OCT	NOV	DEC	YEAR
Mean Maximum Temp. (°F)	43.0	46.2	55.0	65.6	74.7	82.9	87.3	85.8	79.8	68.8	58.2	48.2	66.3
Mean Temp. (°F)	35.3	37.8	45.9	55.5	65.1	73.6	78.2	76.4	70.3	59.3	49.5	40.3	57.3
Mean Minimum Temp. (°F)	27.5	29.4	36.7	45.4	55.3	64.3	69.0	67.0	60.7	49.7	40.9	32.5	48.2
Extreme Maximum Temp. (°F)	69	75	87	93	95	97	101	99	97	89	82	76	101
Extreme Minimum Temp. (°F)	-6	-3	13	23	36	43	51	45	38	27	18	4	-6
Days Maximum Temp. ≥ 90°F	0	0	0	0	1	4	10	7	2	0	0	0	24
Days Maximum Temp. ≤ 32°F	4	3	0	0	0	0	0	0	0	0	0	0	9
Days Minimum Temp. ≤ 32°F	22	18	10	1	0	0	0	0	0	1	6	16	74
Days Minimum Temp. ≤ 0°F	0	0	0	0	0	0	0	0	0	0	0	0	0
Heating Degree Days (base 65°F)	914	761	589	293	83	6	0	1	25	203	461	757	4,093
Cooling Degree Days (base 65°F)	0	0	3	14	93	280	436	358	186	34	2	0	1,406
Mean Precipitation (in.)	4.04	3.38	4.41	3.49	4.16	3.40	4.18	4.08	3.88	3.51	3.45	3.70	45.68
Days With ≥ 0.1" Precipitation	7	6	7	7	7	6	7	6	5	5	6	7	76
Days With ≥ 1.0" Precipitation	1	1	1	1	1	1	1	1	1	1	1	1	12
Mean Snowfall (in.)	5.1	5.4	1.4	trace	0.0	0.0	0.0	0.0	0.0	trace	0.4	1.3	13.6
Days With ≥ 1.0" Snow Depth	5	3	1	0	0	0	0	0	0	0	0	1	10

Salisbury *Wicomico County*   Elevation: 9 ft.   Latitude: 38° 22' N   Longitude: 75° 35' W

	JAN	FEB	MAR	APR	MAY	JUN	JUL	AUG	SEP	OCT	NOV	DEC	YEAR
Mean Maximum Temp. (°F)	46.0	48.7	57.1	67.2	75.7	83.1	87.4	85.8	80.4	70.1	60.4	50.6	67.7
Mean Temp. (°F)	37.1	39.2	46.8	55.9	64.8	72.9	77.8	76.2	70.3	59.2	50.3	41.5	57.7
Mean Minimum Temp. (°F)	28.1	29.7	36.5	44.5	54.0	62.7	68.0	66.6	60.1	48.3	40.1	32.3	47.6
Extreme Maximum Temp. (°F)	73	77	88	93	95	98	100	98	97	90	82	78	100
Extreme Minimum Temp. (°F)	-2	2	12	25	36	41	50	45	40	26	14	5	-2
Days Maximum Temp. ≥ 90°F	0	0	0	0	1	4	10	7	2	0	0	0	24
Days Maximum Temp. ≤ 32°F	3	2	0	0	0	0	0	0	0	0	0	2	7
Days Minimum Temp. ≤ 32°F	21	18	11	2	0	0	0	0	0	1	7	16	76
Days Minimum Temp. ≤ 0°F	0	0	0	0	0	0	0	0	0	0	0	0	0
Heating Degree Days (base 65°F)	859	722	561	285	86	8	0	1	23	206	441	722	3,914
Cooling Degree Days (base 65°F)	0	0	5	20	94	266	428	355	188	35	4	0	1,395
Mean Precipitation (in.)	3.95	3.47	4.47	3.37	3.67	3.54	4.54	4.76	3.85	3.49	3.17	3.54	45.82
Days With ≥ 0.1" Precipitation	7	6	8	7	7	7	7	6	5	5	6	7	78
Days With ≥ 1.0" Precipitation	1	1	1	1	1	1	1	2	1	1	1	1	13
Mean Snowfall (in.)	*1.9*	*1.0*	0.4	trace	0.0	0.0	0.0	0.0	0.0	trace	trace	0.5	*3.8*
Days With ≥ 1.0" Snow Depth	*3*	*1*	0	0	0	0	0	0	0	0	0	0	*4*

Salisbury Wicomico Co. Airport *Wicomico County*   Elevation: 49 ft.   Latitude: 38° 20' N   Longitude: 75° 31' W

	JAN	FEB	MAR	APR	MAY	JUN	JUL	AUG	SEP	OCT	NOV	DEC	YEAR
Mean Maximum Temp. (°F)	44.5	47.0	55.3	65.5	74.1	82.4	87.1	85.2	79.4	68.8	59.1	49.6	66.5
Mean Temp. (°F)	35.5	37.6	45.2	54.2	63.3	72.1	77.3	75.5	69.1	57.6	48.7	40.1	56.4
Mean Minimum Temp. (°F)	26.5	28.2	35.0	42.9	52.4	61.6	67.6	65.7	58.9	46.4	38.3	30.6	46.2
Extreme Maximum Temp. (°F)	73	79	88	94	95	99	102	98	99	92	82	77	102
Extreme Minimum Temp. (°F)	-6	-2	9	25	32	41	49	45	38	25	13	-1	-6
Days Maximum Temp. ≥ 90°F	0	0	0	0	1	4	11	7	2	0	0	0	25
Days Maximum Temp. ≤ 32°F	5	3	0	0	0	0	0	0	0	0	0	2	10
Days Minimum Temp. ≤ 32°F	23	19	14	4	0	0	0	0	0	2	10	19	91
Days Minimum Temp. ≤ 0°F	0	0	0	0	0	0	0	0	0	0	0	0	0
Heating Degree Days (base 65°F)	908	766	612	332	119	14	0	2	35	250	487	764	4,289
Cooling Degree Days (base 65°F)	0	0	4	14	76	240	407	325	161	30	3	0	1,260
Mean Precipitation (in.)	4.04	3.58	4.55	3.40	3.88	3.46	4.55	5.01	3.66	3.80	3.31	3.77	47.01
Days With ≥ 0.1" Precipitation	7	7	7	6	7	6	7	6	5	5	6	7	76
Days With ≥ 1.0" Precipitation	1	1	1	1	1	1	1	2	1	1	1	1	13
Mean Snowfall (in.)	3.5	3.9	1.3	0.2	0.0	trace	trace	trace	trace	trace	0.4	1.7	11.0
Days With ≥ 1.0" Snow Depth	3	3	1	0	0	0	0	0	0	0	0	1	8

Savage River Dam *Garrett County*   Elevation: 1,492 ft.   Latitude: 39° 31' N   Longitude: 79° 08' W

	JAN	FEB	MAR	APR	MAY	JUN	JUL	AUG	SEP	OCT	NOV	DEC	YEAR
Mean Maximum Temp. (°F)	34.8	38.5	47.9	59.7	69.4	76.9	80.9	79.9	73.3	61.8	50.1	39.7	59.4
Mean Temp. (°F)	26.4	29.0	37.5	48.0	57.7	65.6	70.0	68.6	62.1	50.4	40.7	31.5	49.0
Mean Minimum Temp. (°F)	17.9	19.4	27.0	36.2	45.9	54.2	59.0	57.2	50.7	39.0	31.3	23.4	38.4
Extreme Maximum Temp. (°F)	70	72	83	90	90	96	101	100	94	85	77	70	101
Extreme Minimum Temp. (°F)	-22	-16	-3	14	27	36	40	36	30	18	8	-12	-22
Days Maximum Temp. ≥ 90°F	0	0	0	0	0	0	2	2	0	0	0	0	4
Days Maximum Temp. ≤ 32°F	13	8	3	0	0	0	0	0	0	0	1	7	32
Days Minimum Temp. ≤ 32°F	29	25	23	10	1	0	0	0	0	8	18	26	140
Days Minimum Temp. ≤ 0°F	2	2	0	0	0	0	0	0	0	0	0	1	5
Heating Degree Days (base 65°F)	1,190	1,010	846	507	243	65	13	25	133	448	722	1,031	6,233
Cooling Degree Days (base 65°F)	0	0	0	2	22	94	191	147	49	3	0	0	508
Mean Precipitation (in.)	2.88	2.38	3.36	3.45	4.19	3.65	4.21	3.35	3.35	2.92	3.02	2.81	39.57
Days With ≥ 0.1" Precipitation	7	6	8	7	9	8	8	7	7	6	6	6	85
Days With ≥ 1.0" Precipitation	0	0	1	1	1	0	1	1	1	1	1	1	9
Mean Snowfall (in.)	*8.7*	*7.1*	4.2	0.9	0.0	0.0	0.0	0.0	0.0	trace	1.1	*3.3*	25.3
Days With ≥ 1.0" Snow Depth	18	15	6	1	0	0	0	0	0	0	2	9	51

Snow Hill 4 N *Worcester County*   Elevation: 29 ft.   Latitude: 38° 14' N   Longitude: 75° 23' W

	JAN	FEB	MAR	APR	MAY	JUN	JUL	AUG	SEP	OCT	NOV	DEC	YEAR
Mean Maximum Temp. (°F)	45.7	48.1	56.2	66.7	75.1	83.0	87.1	85.8	80.8	70.0	60.1	50.6	67.4
Mean Temp. (°F)	36.4	38.4	45.7	54.8	64.0	72.2	76.5	75.0	69.5	58.2	49.3	41.0	56.8
Mean Minimum Temp. (°F)	27.1	28.6	35.2	42.8	52.7	61.3	66.0	64.2	58.0	46.4	38.5	31.2	46.0
Extreme Maximum Temp. (°F)	71	78	88	94	98	100	102	99	99	91	84	78	102
Extreme Minimum Temp. (°F)	-5	-2	10	23	31	40	45	41	31	23	15	1	-5
Days Maximum Temp. ≥ 90°F	0	0	0	0	1	5	11	8	3	0	0	0	28
Days Maximum Temp. ≤ 32°F	4	2	0	0	0	0	0	0	0	0	0	1	7
Days Minimum Temp. ≤ 32°F	22	19	14	4	0	0	0	0	0	3	10	18	90
Days Minimum Temp. ≤ 0°F	0	0	0	0	0	0	0	0	0	0	0	0	0
Heating Degree Days (base 65°F)	879	745	594	316	106	13	0	2	33	234	468	739	4,129
Cooling Degree Days (base 65°F)	0	0	4	16	90	253	393	324	178	34	4	0	1,296
Mean Precipitation (in.)	3.97	3.45	4.55	3.22	3.64	3.30	4.46	5.28	3.68	3.48	3.32	3.45	45.80
Days With ≥ 0.1" Precipitation	7	6	8	6	7	6	7	6	5	5	6	7	76
Days With ≥ 1.0" Precipitation	1	1	1	1	1	1	1	2	1	1	1	1	13
Mean Snowfall (in.)	3.4	4.7	1.5	0.1	0.0	0.0	0.0	0.0	0.0	0.0	0.3	1.5	11.5
Days With ≥ 1.0" Snow Depth	2	3	1	0	0	0	0	0	0	0	0	1	7

Unionville *Frederick County*   Elevation: 429 ft.   Latitude: 39° 27' N   Longitude: 77° 11' W

	JAN	FEB	MAR	APR	MAY	JUN	JUL	AUG	SEP	OCT	NOV	DEC	YEAR
Mean Maximum Temp. (°F)	39.2	43.6	53.6	65.1	74.3	82.3	86.2	84.4	77.6	66.6	55.3	44.3	64.4
Mean Temp. (°F)	29.7	32.5	41.6	51.4	61.2	69.7	74.1	72.2	65.2	53.8	43.8	34.4	52.5
Mean Minimum Temp. (°F)	19.8	21.4	29.5	37.7	47.9	57.0	61.9	59.9	52.8	41.0	32.2	24.5	40.5
Extreme Maximum Temp. (°F)	72	79	85	93	96	99	103	101	97	88	82	78	103
Extreme Minimum Temp. (°F)	-22	-20	2	15	26	33	39	35	30	17	5	-6	-22
Days Maximum Temp. ≥ 90°F	0	0	0	0	1	4	9	6	2	0	0	0	22
Days Maximum Temp. ≤ 32°F	8	4	1	0	0	0	0	0	0	0	0	3	16
Days Minimum Temp. ≤ 32°F	*27*	24	20	10	1	0	0	0	0	7	16	24	*129*
Days Minimum Temp. ≤ 0°F	2	1	0	0	0	0	0	0	0	0	0	1	4
Heating Degree Days (base 65°F)	1,088	912	721	408	160	22	2	9	85	349	631	941	5,328
Cooling Degree Days (base 65°F)	0	0	1	7	50	182	316	240	97	11	*0*	*0*	*904*
Mean Precipitation (in.)	3.19	2.51	3.50	3.41	4.23	4.53	3.83	3.29	3.68	3.67	3.79	3.29	42.92
Days With ≥ 0.1" Precipitation	6	5	7	6	8	7	7	6	6	6	6	6	76
Days With ≥ 1.0" Precipitation	1	1	1	1	1	1	1	1	1	1	1	1	12
Mean Snowfall (in.)	*7.2*	*6.2*	*2.8*	trace	0.0	0.0	0.0	0.0	0.0	trace	0.7	*2.6*	*19.5*
Days With ≥ 1.0" Snow Depth	na	*4*	1	0	0	0	0	0	0	0	0	*2*	na

Upper Marlboro 3 NNW *Prince George's County*   Elevation: 98 ft.   Latitude: 38° 52' N   Longitude: 76° 47' W

	JAN	FEB	MAR	APR	MAY	JUN	JUL	AUG	SEP	OCT	NOV	DEC	YEAR
Mean Maximum Temp. (°F)	42.4	46.0	54.5	65.2	74.4	82.5	87.1	85.9	79.4	68.1	57.6	47.9	65.9
Mean Temp. (°F)	32.3	35.4	43.4	53.2	62.8	71.2	75.9	74.4	67.5	55.5	46.3	37.7	54.6
Mean Minimum Temp. (°F)	22.2	24.9	32.3	41.2	51.2	59.8	64.6	62.8	55.6	42.8	34.9	27.5	43.3
Extreme Maximum Temp. (°F)	75	80	89	94	97	100	102	102	99	91	85	80	102
Extreme Minimum Temp. (°F)	-12	-8	6	20	29	39	43	39	30	22	13	2	-12
Days Maximum Temp. ≥ 90°F	0	0	0	0	1	5	11	8	3	0	0	0	28
Days Maximum Temp. ≤ 32°F	6	4	0	0	0	0	0	0	0	0	0	2	12
Days Minimum Temp. ≤ 32°F	26	22	17	4	0	0	0	0	0	4	13	23	109
Days Minimum Temp. ≤ 0°F	1	0	0	0	0	0	0	0	0	0	0	0	1
Heating Degree Days (base 65°F)	1,006	829	666	360	132	19	1	4	56	304	557	839	4,773
Cooling Degree Days (base 65°F)	0	0	4	11	76	220	366	299	135	18	2	0	1,131
Mean Precipitation (in.)	3.40	2.79	3.76	3.38	4.34	3.81	4.03	3.87	3.85	3.83	3.41	3.28	43.75
Days With ≥ 0.1" Precipitation	7	6	7	7	8	7	8	6	6	5	6	6	79
Days With ≥ 1.0" Precipitation	1	1	1	1	1	1	1	1	1	1	1	1	12
Mean Snowfall (in.)	6.3	5.6	1.6	trace	0.0	0.0	0.0	0.0	0.0	0.1	0.5	0.9	15.0
Days With ≥ 1.0" Snow Depth	8	*5*	1	0	0	0	0	0	0	0	0	1	*15*

Woodstock *Baltimore County* Elevation: 459 ft. Latitude: 39° 20' N Longitude: 76° 52' W

	JAN	FEB	MAR	APR	MAY	JUN	JUL	AUG	SEP	OCT	NOV	DEC	YEAR
Mean Maximum Temp. (°F)	40.9	45.0	54.3	66.1	75.8	83.3	87.6	85.7	78.7	67.4	56.1	45.5	65.5
Mean Temp. (°F)	31.9	35.0	43.5	53.7	63.3	71.4	76.0	74.4	67.1	55.5	45.6	36.4	54.5
Mean Minimum Temp. (°F)	23.1	25.1	32.5	41.3	50.9	59.5	64.7	63.2	56.2	43.7	35.5	27.8	43.6
Extreme Maximum Temp. (°F)	72	79	90	93	97	98	102	101	100	87	83	77	102
Extreme Minimum Temp. (°F)	-13	-10	4	19	29	36	44	41	32	22	10	-3	-13
Days Maximum Temp. ≥ 90°F	0	0	0	0	1	5	12	8	2	0	0	0	28
Days Maximum Temp. ≤ 32°F	7	4	1	0	0	0	0	0	0	0	0	3	15
Days Minimum Temp. ≤ 32°F	26	22	16	5	0	0	0	0	0	4	13	22	108
Days Minimum Temp. ≤ 0°F	1	0	0	0	0	0	0	0	0	0	0	0	1
Heating Degree Days (base 65°F)	1,017	839	666	346	115	15	1	3	52	300	571	871	4,796
Cooling Degree Days (base 65°F)	0	0	4	14	74	229	379	303	137	19	1	0	1,160
Mean Precipitation (in.)	3.67	3.05	4.32	3.54	4.78	4.06	3.90	3.52	4.05	3.53	3.87	3.58	45.87
Days With ≥ 0.1" Precipitation	7	6	8	7	9	6	6	6	6	5	6	7	79
Days With ≥ 1.0" Precipitation	1	1	1	1	1	1	1	1	1	1	1	1	12
Mean Snowfall (in.)	8.4	7.3	3.4	0.2	0.0	0.0	0.0	0.0	0.0	trace	0.8	2.7	22.8
Days With ≥ 1.0" Snow Depth	9	7	2	0	0	0	0	0	0	0	0	3	21

Note: See Appendix D for explanation of data.

MASSACHUSETTS

PHYSICAL FEATURES. Massachusetts occupies 8,266 square miles, nearly one-eighth of New England's total area. Most of the State lies just above the 42nd parallel of latitude. Its north-south width is, roughly, 50 miles, except 100 miles in the eastern, Atlantic coast, portion. The east-west extension is barely 150 miles, excepting "the Cape." This is the familiar name of the long arm of land which reaches around the southern and eastern shores of Cape Cod Bay. Including the Cape, the State is nearly 200 miles in length.

The land surface is mountainous along the western border and generally hilly elsewhere. However, the Cape and some other sections of the coastal area consist of flat land with numerous marshes and some small lakes and ponds. In the west Mt. Greylock rises 3,491 feet above sea level, the highest peak in Massachusetts. The elevation is mostly over 1,000 feet west of the Connecticut River Valley. A number of peaks reach above 2,000 feet. Most of central Massachusetts lies between 500 and 1,000 feet. Eastern Massachusetts and the Connecticut River Valley are mostly less than 500 feet.

GENERAL CLIMATE. Climatic characteristics of Massachusetts includes: (1) changeableness in the weather, (2) large ranges of temperature, both daily and annual, (3) great differences between the same seasons in different years, (4) equable distribution of precipitation, and (5) considerable diversity from place to place. The regional New England climatic influences are modified in Massachusetts by varying distances from the ocean, elevations, and types of terrain. These modifying factors divide the State into three climatological divisions: (the Western Division, the Central Division, and the Coastal Division)

Massachusetts lies in the "prevailing westerlies," the belt of generally eastward air movement which encircles the globe in middle latitudes. Embedded in this circulation are extensive masses of air originating in higher or lower latitudes and interacting to produce storm systems. Relative to most other sections of the country, a large number of such storms pass over or near Massachusetts. The majority of air masses affecting this State belong to three types: (1) cold, dry air pouring down from subarctic North America, (2) warm, moist air streaming up on a long overland journey from the Gulf of Mexico and subtropical waters eastward, and (3) cool, damp air moving in from the North Atlantic. Because the atmospheric flow is usually offshore, Massachusetts is more influenced by the first two types than it is by the third. In other words, the adjacent ocean constitutes an important modifying factor, particularly on the immediate coast, but does not dominate the climate.

The procession of contrasting air masses and the relatively frequent passage of storm centers bring about a roughly twice-weekly alternation from fair to cloudy or stormy conditions, attended by often abrupt changes in temperature, moisture, sunshine, wind direction, and speed. There is no regular or persistent rhythm to this sequence, and it is interrupted by periods during which the weather patterns continue the same for several days, infrequently for several weeks. Massachusetts weather, however, is cited for variety rather than monotony. Changeability is also one of its features on a longer time-scale. That is, the same month or season will exhibit varying characteristics over the years, sometimes in close alternation, sometimes arranged in similar groups for successive years.

TEMPERATURE. Summer temperatures are delightfully comfortable for the most part, and summer averages are nearly uniform over the state. Hot days with maxima of 90°F. or higher generally average from five to 15 per year, varying not only from place to place but from year to year. They range, in frequency of occurrence, from only a few in cool summers to 25 or more in an occasional hot summer. The Cape and offshore islands are exceptions, averaging less than one day with a reading of 90°F. or higher per year.

Average temperatures vary from place to place more in winter than in summer. The diurnal temperature range in winter, though less than in summer, is still greater inland than along the coast. Days with subzero readings are rare on offshore islands. They average only a few per year near the coast, but increase in number of occurrences farther inland to from 5 to 15 annually.

PRECIPITATION. Massachusetts is fortunate in having its precipitation rather evenly distributed through the year. In this respect, the State is located in one of the relatively few areas of the world that does not have its "rainy" and "dry" seasons. Storm systems are the principal year-round moisture producers. But in the summer, when this activity ebbs, bands or patches of thunderstorms or showers tend to make up the difference. Though brief and often of small extent, the thunderstorms produce the heaviest local rainfall. Prolonged droughts are infrequent. Storms of a coastal nature make the Coastal Division the wettest in the winter season. Inland sections get the heavier rain in the warm season due, principally, to the higher frequency and greater intensity of convective showers and thunderstorms. The mountainous character of much of the Western Division is an additional cause for the heaviest annual totals being recorded in that part of the State.

SNOWFALL. Average annual amounts of snowfall increase rapidly from the coast westward. About 25 to 30 inches fall over Cape Cod, but up to 60 to 80 inches are recorded in the western part of the State. Topography has a marked influence on snowfall, causing much variation even in short distances. The average number of days with 1 inch or more of snowfall varies from about eight to 15 in the Coastal Division to mostly 20 to 30 in the Western Division. Most winters will have at least one snowstorm of five inches or more. The average number of days with snow on the ground also increases from shore to interior and with rise in elevation. There is little lasting snow cover in the coastal lowlands. In the Western Division the cover usually extends well into spring. Maximum snow depths usually occur in the middle part of February. Water stored in the snow over the watersheds makes an important contribution to the water supply. Melting is usually too gradual to threaten serious flooding.

FLOODS. The Connecticut River, the largest river system in New England, drains most of the western half of the State. Second in size in Massachusetts is the Merrimack River which occupies the northeast portion. The rest of the rivers are relatively small, most of them with headwaters in the State and flowing southward through Connecticut and Rhode Island, or directly to the coast in the east and southeast. Flooding occurs most often in spring, caused by combination of rain and melting snow. The Connecticut River shows a regular annual rise as the result of the melting of high elevation snow in northern and central New England, but extensive flooding does not occur unless the rise is accompanied by heavy rains. High flows and major floods occur from rainfall alone but less frequently. Some of the severest floods caused by heavy rains have been those associated with hurricanes or storms of tropical origin in late summer or fall, normally the low water season.

OTHER CLIMATIC FEATURES. The percentage of possible sunshine averages from 50 to 60 in most sections. Higher elevations are cloudier, reducing the Berkshire average to between 45 and 50 percent. The average annual number of clear days is between 90 and 120 for most of the State, with less in the Berkshires. Heavy fog is frequent and sometimes persistent south of Cape Cod. Nantucket Island has heavy fog on nearly 1 day out of 4. Fog frequency diminishes along the Massachusetts coast north of the Cape. Duration of fog also diminishes inland. But the shorter duration heavy ground fogs of early morning occur frequently at susceptible places inland. These, plus the fewer occurrences of other heavy fog, produce a frequency that also approaches this one day out of four in many localities. The number of days with fog varies from as low as about 15 up to nearly 100 per year over the State.

WINDS AND STORMS. The prevailing wind, on a yearly basis, comes from a westerly direction. It is more northwesterly in winter and southwesterly in summer. Along the coast in spring and summer the sea breeze is important. These onshore winds, blowing from the cool ocean, may come inland for 10 miles or so. They tend to retard the spring growth, but they are pleasantly cooling in summer. Coastal storms or "northeasters" are one of the State's most serious weather hazards. They generate very strong winds and heavy rain or snow. They can produce abnormally high, wind-driven tides. In winter, these storms produce the heaviest snow. Occasionally in summer or fall a storm of tropical origin affects Massachusetts. Often these will be similar to the northeasters. The few which retain full hurricane force cause widespread damage. Storms of tropical origin seriously affect Massachusetts about once in two years, on the average. Two such storms in the same year may be expected once in eight or 10 years.

Tornadoes are not common phenomena, yet, on a per unit area basis, Massachusetts ranks fairly high among the states. One or more may occur in Massachusetts each year. Four out of five tornadoes occur between May 15 and September 15. The peak month is July. Thunderstorms and hailstorms have a similar frequency maximum from midspring to early fall. Thunderstorms occur on about 20 to 30 days a year, and the most severe are attended by hail.

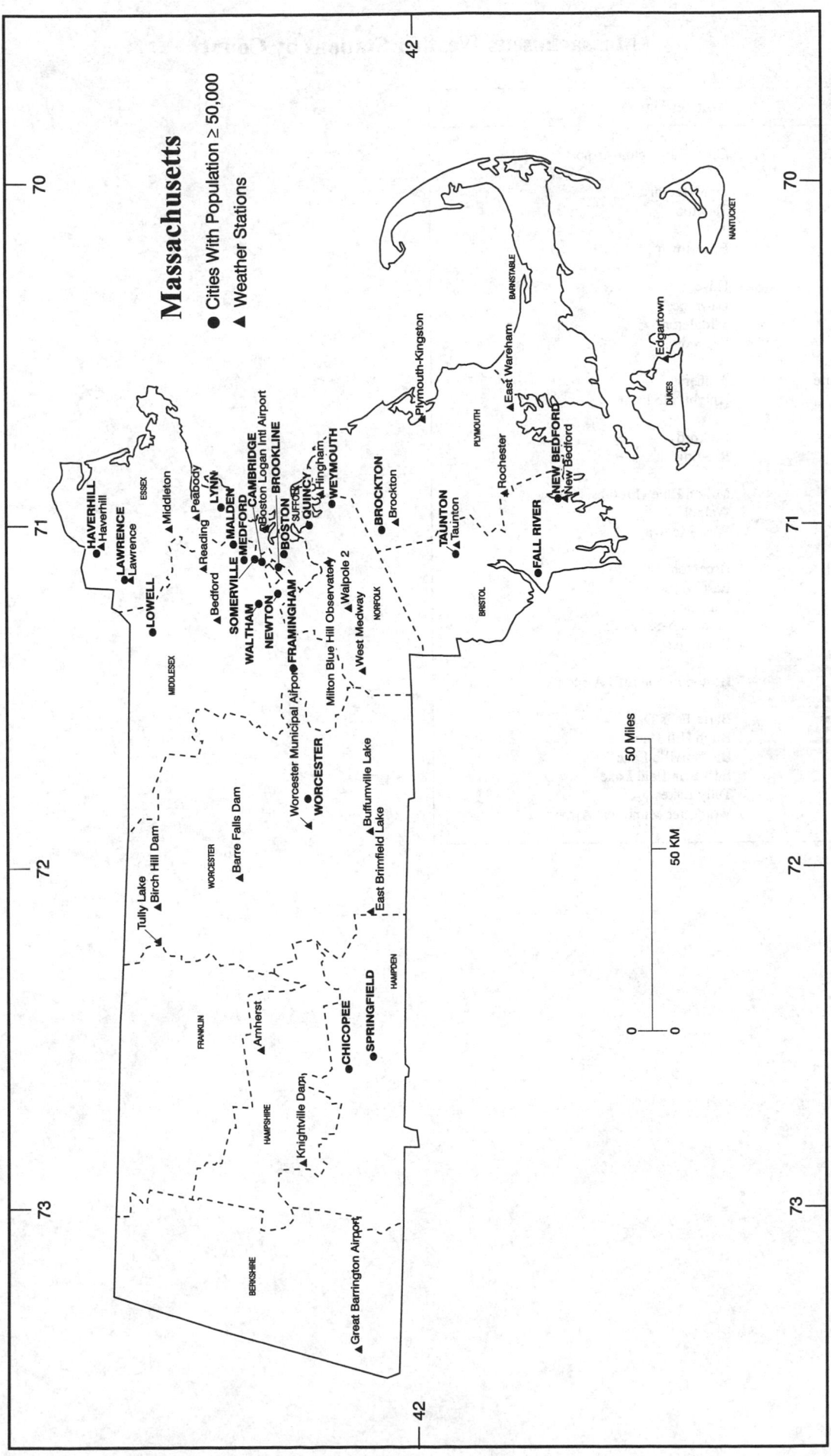

Massachusetts

● Cities With Population ≥ 50,000
▲ Weather Stations

Massachusetts Weather Stations by County

County	Station Name
Berkshire	Great Barrington Airport
Bristol	New Bedford Taunton
Dukes	Edgartown
Essex	Haverhill Lawrence Middleton Peabody
Hampshire	Amherst Knightville Dam
Middlesex	Bedford Reading
Norfolk	Milton Blue Hill Observatory Walpole 2 West Medway
Plymouth	Brockton East Wareham Hingham Plymouth-Kingston Rochester
Suffolk	Boston Logan Int'l Airport
Worcester	Barre Falls Dam Birch Hill Dam Buffumville Lake East Brimfield Lake Tully Lake Worcester Municipal Airport

Massachusetts Weather Stations by City

City	Station Name	Miles
Boston	Bedford	15
	Milton Blue Hill Observatory	7
	Boston Logan Int'l Airport	5
	Brockton	19
	Hingham	11
	Middleton	20
	Peabody	16
	Reading	14
	Walpole 2	13
Brockton	Milton Blue Hill Observatory	10
	Boston Logan Int'l Airport	20
	Brockton	3
	Hingham	12
	Plymouth-Kingston	18
	Taunton	13
	Walpole 2	13
Brookline	Bedford	13
	Milton Blue Hill Observatory	8
	Boston Logan Int'l Airport	6
	Hingham	13
	Middleton	19
	Peabody	16
	Reading	13
	Walpole 2	13
Cambridge	Bedford	11
	Milton Blue Hill Observatory	11
	Boston Logan Int'l Airport	5
	Hingham	14
	Middleton	16
	Peabody	13
	Reading	10
	Walpole 2	16
Chicopee	Hartford Bradley Int'l Airport, CT	17
	Amherst	15
	Knightville Dam	16
Fall River	New Bedford	12
	Rochester	13
	Taunton	15
	Newport Rose, RI	17
	Providence T F Green State Arpt., RI	15
Framingham	Bedford	15
	Milton Blue Hill Observatory	17
	Walpole 2	13
	West Medway	12
Haverhill	Haverhill	1
	Lawrence	7
	Middleton	13
	Peabody	18
	Reading	18
	Epping, NH	18
Lawrence	Bedford	16
	Haverhill	7
	Lawrence	0
	Middleton	10
	Peabody	15
	Reading	13

City	Station Name	Miles
Lawrence *(cont.)*	Nashua 2 NNW, NH	17
Lowell	Bedford	11
	Haverhill	15
	Lawrence	9
	Middleton	16
	Peabody	19
	Reading	13
	Nashua 2 NNW, NH	13
Lynn	Bedford	17
	Milton Blue Hill Observatory	19
	Boston Logan Int'l Airport	8
	Hingham	17
	Lawrence	19
	Middleton	9
	Peabody	4
	Reading	10
Malden	Bedford	12
	Milton Blue Hill Observatory	15
	Boston Logan Int'l Airport	5
	Hingham	15
	Lawrence	19
	Middleton	12
	Peabody	8
	Reading	7
Medford	Bedford	10
	Milton Blue Hill Observatory	14
	Boston Logan Int'l Airport	6
	Hingham	16
	Lawrence	20
	Middleton	13
	Peabody	10
	Reading	7
	Walpole 2	19
New Bedford	East Wareham	16
	New Bedford	1
	Rochester	9
	Taunton	19
Newton	Bedford	11
	Milton Blue Hill Observatory	9
	Boston Logan Int'l Airport	10
	Hingham	16
	Peabody	18
	Reading	13
	Walpole 2	12
	West Medway	18
Quincy	Milton Blue Hill Observatory	6
	Boston Logan Int'l Airport	7
	Brockton	15
	Hingham	5
	Peabody	19
	Reading	19
	Walpole 2	14
Somerville	Bedford	11
	Milton Blue Hill Observatory	12
	Boston Logan Int'l Airport	5
	Hingham	15

City	Station Name	Miles
Somerville *(cont.)*	Middleton	15
	Peabody	12
	Reading	9
	Walpole 2	17
Springfield	Hartford Bradley Int'l Airport, CT	14
	Amherst	19
Taunton	Brockton	11
	Rochester	12
	Taunton	1
	Walpole 2	20
Waltham	Bedford	7
	Milton Blue Hill Observatory	13
	Boston Logan Int'l Airport	11
	Hingham	19
	Middleton	19
	Peabody	17
	Reading	11
	Walpole 2	15
	West Medway	20
Weymouth	Milton Blue Hill Observatory	9
	Boston Logan Int'l Airport	12
	Brockton	11
	Hingham	2
	Plymouth-Kingston	20
	Walpole 2	16
Worcester	Barre Falls Dam	16
	Buffumville Lake	11
	East Brimfield Lake	20
	Worcester Municipal Airport	4

Note: Miles is the distance between the geographic center of the city and the weather station.

Massachusetts Weather Stations by Elevation

Feet	Station Name
984	Worcester Municipal Airport
908	Barre Falls Dam
862	Birch Hill Dam
816	Great Barrington Airport
688	Tully Lake
679	East Brimfield Lake
629	Milton Blue Hill Observatory
629	Knightville Dam
498	Buffumville Lake
209	West Medway
167	Peabody
164	Walpole 2
157	Bedford
147	Amherst
88	Middleton
88	Reading
78	Brockton
68	New Bedford
59	Lawrence
59	Rochester
42	Plymouth-Kingston
29	Hingham
19	Boston Logan Int'l Airport
19	East Wareham
19	Edgartown
19	Taunton
16	Haverhill

Boston Logan Int'l Airport

Three important influences are responsible for the main features of the Boston climate. First, the latitude places the city in the zone of prevailing west to east atmospheric flow. Both polar and tropical air masses influence the region. Secondly, Boston is situated on or near several tracks frequently followed by low pressure storm systems. The weather fluctuates regularly from fair to cloudy to stormy conditions and assures an adequate amount of precipitation. The third factor is the east-coast location of Boston. The ocean has a moderating influence on temperature extremes of winter and summer.

Hot summer afternoons are frequently relieved by the locally celebrated sea breeze, as air flows inland from the cool water surface to displace the warm air over the land. This refreshing east wind is more commonly experienced along the shore than in the interior of the city or the western suburbs. In winter, under appropriate conditions, the severity of cold waves is reduced by the nearness of the relatively warm ocean. The average last occurrence of freezing temperature in spring is early April and the first occurrence of freezing temperature in autumn is early November. In suburban areas, especially away from the coast, these dates are later in spring and earlier in autumn by up to one month in the more susceptible localities.

Boston has no dry season. Most growing seasons have several shorter dry spells during which irrigation for high-value crops may be useful. Much of the rainfall from June to September comes from showers and thunderstorms. During the rest of the year, low pressure systems pass more or less regularly and produce precipitation on an average of roughly one day in three. Coastal storms, or northeasters, are prolific producers of rain and snow. The main snow season extends from December through March. Periods when the ground is bare or nearly bare of snow may occur at any time in the winter.

Relative humidity has been known to fall as low as five percent but such desert dryness is very rare. Heavy fog occurs on an average of about two days per month with its prevalence increasing eastward from the interior of Boston Bay to the open waters beyond.

Although winds of 30 mph or higher may be expected on at least one day in every month of the year, gales are both more common and more severe in winter.

Boston Logan Int'l Airport *Suffolk County*   Elevation: 19 ft.   Latitude: 42° 22' N   Longitude: 71° 01' W

	JAN	FEB	MAR	APR	MAY	JUN	JUL	AUG	SEP	OCT	NOV	DEC	YEAR
Mean Maximum Temp. (°F)	36.3	38.6	46.1	56.2	66.8	76.7	82.4	80.2	72.6	61.8	51.8	41.7	59.3
Mean Temp. (°F)	29.2	31.4	38.7	48.4	58.6	68.0	74.0	72.4	64.8	54.2	44.9	34.8	51.6
Mean Minimum Temp. (°F)	22.0	24.1	31.3	40.6	50.2	59.4	65.6	64.5	56.9	46.5	37.9	27.8	43.9
Extreme Maximum Temp. (°F)	66	70	89	94	95	98	102	102	99	86	79	76	102
Extreme Minimum Temp. (°F)	-4	-3	6	16	35	45	50	47	39	28	15	-7	-7
Days Maximum Temp. ≥ 90°F	0	0	0	0	1	3	6	4	1	0	0	0	15
Days Maximum Temp. ≤ 32°F	11	7	2	0	0	0	0	0	0	0	0	5	25
Days Minimum Temp. ≤ 32°F	26	22	16	2	0	0	0	0	0	0	7	21	94
Days Minimum Temp. ≤ 0°F	0	0	0	0	0	0	0	0	0	0	0	0	0
Heating Degree Days (base 65°F)	1,103	943	808	494	226	45	4	7	80	336	597	931	5,574
Cooling Degree Days (base 65°F)	0	0	1	2	32	145	293	240	82	8	1	0	804
Mean Precipitation (in.)	3.87	3.37	3.88	3.53	3.24	3.15	2.93	3.43	3.46	3.78	3.96	3.80	42.40
Maximum Precipitation (in.)	10.5	7.8	11.0	9.5	13.4	13.2	8.1	17.1	8.3	8.7	8.9	9.7	62.3
Minimum Precipitation (in.)	0.6	0.7	0.6	1.2	0.5	0.5	0.5	0.8	0.3	0.3	0.6	0.8	23.7
Maximum 24-hr. Precipitation (in.)	2.5	2.6	3.5	3.3	4.5	3.0	2.4	7.1	5.6	3.3	3.3	4.2	7.1
Days With ≥ 0.1" Precipitation	7	6	7	6	7	6	6	6	6	6	7	7	77
Days With ≥ 1.0" Precipitation	1	1	1	1	1	1	1	1	1	1	1	1	12
Mean Snowfall (in.)	13.1	11.0	8.0	1.1	trace	0.0	0.0	trace	0.0	trace	1.4	7.5	42.1
Maximum Snowfall (in.)	36	41	39	13	1	0	0	0	0	trace	9	28	89
Maximum 24-hr. Snowfall (in.)	21	19	13	11	1	0	0	0	0	trace	6	13	21
Days With ≥ 1.0" Snow Depth	13	10	6	0	0	0	0	0	0	0	1	5	35
Thunderstorm Days	< 1	< 1	1	1	2	3	4	3	1	1	< 1	< 1	16
Foggy Days	10	9	11	11	13	12	12	13	11	12	11	10	135
Predominant Sky Cover	OVR	OVR	OVR	OVR	OVR	OVR	OVR	OVR	OVR	OVR	OVR	OVR	OVR
Mean Relative Humidity 7am (%)	68	68	69	68	71	72	73	76	78	77	74	70	72
Mean Relative Humidity 4pm (%)	58	56	57	56	58	58	57	60	61	59	61	60	58
Mean Dewpoint (°F)	17	18	25	34	45	55	61	60	54	43	34	22	39
Prevailing Wind Direction	WNW	WNW	WNW	WNW	SW	SW	SW	SW	SW	WNW	WNW	WNW	WNW
Prevailing Wind Speed (mph)	16	16	16	15	14	13	12	12	13	13	15	15	14
Maximum Wind Gust (mph)	69	79	81	76	70	84	60	100	87	58	86	78	100

Milton Blue Hill Observatory

The altitude of the Observatory and its proximity to Massachusetts Bay play major roles in determining the climate of Blue Hill. The elevation of 635 feet marks the summit as the highest point of a wooded range that extends east-northeast to west-southwest. The station lies at the southwest end of this range and has a three-quadrant unrestricted exposure, at approximately 400 feet above the surrounding terrain. The orographic effect created by this difference in elevation is responsible for lower temperatures, more precipitation, higher winds, more frequent occurrences of fog, and longer periods of snow cover than at nearby lower elevations. Eight miles to the northeast lies the nearest approach of Boston Harbor, and thus, the station is within range of the sea breeze.

Summer temperatures are generally comfortable. Winters at the summit are more severe than those experienced at surrounding areas. Average occurrence of last freezing temperature in the spring is late April and the first in the fall is late October. The freeze-free period is about 178 days. Records indicate that the freeze-free period at base stations is from six to seven weeks shorter than at the summit. This seeming paradox is due to temperature inversions, in which the colder air is found at lower elevations. This condition develops on clear, calm nights, and is responsible for the shorter freeze-free period in base areas.

Total precipitation is fairly evenly distributed throughout the year. Precipitation occurrences are most frequent January through March and least frequent August through October. Hourly precipitation occurrences indicate a coastal type distribution for the year as a whole, with maxima in the early morning and minima in the early afternoon. In the summer, however, convective action or the continental influence dominates, causing a late afternoon maximum. Coastal storms or northeasters are prolific producers of rain and snow.

The main snow season extends from November through early April. Nearly 14 percent of the annual total precipitation occurs as snow or sleet.

Wind velocities are higher in winter than in summer. Speeds average greatest from January through March and least in August. Surface contour is a factor in the stations, wind force, particularly from the southerly and westerly directions. These are the steepest slopes of the hill, and winds velocities increase. Peak winds have been recorded from these directions. Winds from the east-northeast and northeast are somewhat slowed by striking the lower range first.

Milton Blue Hill Observatory *Norfolk County*   Elevation: 629 ft.   Latitude: 42° 13' N   Longitude: 71° 07' W

	JAN	FEB	MAR	APR	MAY	JUN	JUL	AUG	SEP	OCT	NOV	DEC	YEAR
Mean Maximum Temp. (°F)	33.7	36.2	44.5	55.6	66.9	75.3	81.1	78.8	70.6	60.1	49.3	38.6	57.6
Mean Temp. (°F)	25.8	28.2	36.1	46.4	57.0	65.6	71.7	69.9	62.0	51.6	41.8	31.3	49.0
Mean Minimum Temp. (°F)	17.9	20.1	27.7	37.2	47.1	55.9	62.2	61.0	53.3	43.0	34.3	23.9	40.3
Extreme Maximum Temp. (°F)	65	68	89	94	92	95	100	101	93	85	78	74	101
Extreme Minimum Temp. (°F)	-10	-8	1	13	29	39	44	41	31	22	11	-12	-12
Days Maximum Temp. ≥ 90°F	0	0	0	0	0	1	3	1	0	0	0	0	5
Days Maximum Temp. ≤ 32°F	15	11	3	0	0	0	0	0	0	0	1	9	39
Days Minimum Temp. ≤ 32°F	28	25	22	7	0	0	0	0	0	3	13	25	123
Days Minimum Temp. ≤ 0°F	2	1	0	0	0	0	0	0	0	0	0	0	3
Heating Degree Days (base 65°F)	1,208	1,035	889	554	263	71	8	20	135	413	689	1,039	6,324
Cooling Degree Days (base 65°F)	0	0	1	1	22	100	227	177	54	4	0	0	586
Mean Precipitation (in.)	4.66	4.18	4.79	4.20	3.82	3.81	3.61	4.22	4.18	4.42	4.67	4.56	51.12
Maximum Precipitation (in.)	11.6	9.3	11.0	10.4	9.1	13.7	10.7	8.9	9.6	10.8	9.8	12.6	65.5
Minimum Precipitation (in.)	1.0	0.7	0.6	1.4	0.6	0.9	0.7	0.5	0.7	0.4	0.5	1.1	27.0
Maximum 24-hr. Precipitation (in.)	2.5	3.1	5.6	3.2	5.0	3.1	4.0	3.1	3.8	3.8	3.1	3.9	5.6
Days With ≥ 0.1" Precipitation	8	6	9	7	8	7	6	7	7	7	7	8	87
Days With ≥ 1.0" Precipitation	1	1	1	1	1	1	1	1	1	1	1	1	12
Mean Snowfall (in.)	15.4	12.9	11.2	3.5	0.3	trace	0.0	0.0	trace	0.3	3.1	11.2	57.9
Maximum Snowfall (in.)	46	65	41	14	8	0	0	0	0	7	14	27	124
Maximum 24-hr. Snowfall (in.)	19	27	14	12	5	0	0	0	0	7	11	15	27
Days With ≥ 1.0" Snow Depth	17	16	9	2	0	0	0	0	0	0	2	10	56
Thunderstorm Days	< 1	< 1	1	3	2	4	5	4	1	1	< 1	0	21
Foggy Days	12	8	17	13	9	12	15	14	14	13	11	12	150
Predominant Sky Cover	na	na	na	na	na	na	na	na	na	na	na	na	na
Mean Relative Humidity 7am (%)	na	na	na	na	na	na	na	na	na	na	na	na	na
Mean Relative Humidity 4pm (%)	na	na	na	na	na	na	na	na	na	na	na	na	na
Mean Dewpoint (°F)	na	na	na	na	na	na	na	na	na	na	na	na	na
Prevailing Wind Direction	na	na	na	na	na	na	na	na	na	na	na	na	na
Prevailing Wind Speed (mph)	na	na	na	na	na	na	na	na	na	na	na	na	na
Maximum Wind Gust (mph)	na	na	na	na	na	na	na	na	na	na	na	na	na

Worcester Municipal Airport

Worcester Municipal Airport is located on the crest of a hill, 1,000 feet above sea level. It is about 500 feet above and three and a half miles northwest of the city proper. The airport is surrounded by ridges and valleys with many of the valleys containing reservoirs. Only two of the ridges extend above the airport elevation. One is 400 feet higher and two and a half miles to the northwest, and the other is 1,000 feet higher and 15 miles to the north.

The proximity to the Atlantic Ocean, Long Island Sound, and the Berkshire Hills plays an important part in determining the weather and, hence, the climate of Worcester. Rapid weather changes occur when storms move up the east coast after developing off the Carolina Coast. In the majority of these cases, they pass to the south and east, resulting in northeast and easterly winds with rain or snow and fog. Storms developing in the Texas-Oklahoma area normally travel up the St. Lawrence River Valley and, depending on the movement and intensity, usually deposit little precipitation over the area. However, they do bring an influx of warm air into the region. Wintertime cold snaps are quite frequent, but temperatures are usually modified by the passage of the air over land and mountains before reaching the county. Summertime thunderstorms develop over the hills to the west, with a majority moving toward the northeast.

Airport site temperatures are moderate. The normal mean for the warmest month, July, is around 70 degrees. Though winters are reasonably cold, prolonged periods of severe cold weather are extremely rare. The three coldest months, December through February, have an average temperature of over 25 degrees. A review of Worcester Cooperative records since 1901 shows maximum temperatures above 100 degrees and minimum temperatures below -24 degrees.

Precipitation is usually plentiful and well distributed throughout the year. The annual snowfall for all Worcester sites since 1901, averages slightly less than 60 inches. The airport location averages slightly higher.

Based on the 1951-1980 period, the average first occurrence of 32 degrees Fahrenheit in the fall is October 17 and the average last occurrence in the spring is April 27.

Worcester Municipal Airport *Worcester County*   Elevation: 984 ft.   Latitude: 42° 16' N   Longitude: 71° 53' W

	JAN	FEB	MAR	APR	MAY	JUN	JUL	AUG	SEP	OCT	NOV	DEC	YEAR
Mean Maximum Temp. (°F)	31.1	33.9	42.7	54.4	66.4	74.1	79.4	77.3	68.9	58.5	46.9	36.0	55.8
Mean Temp. (°F)	23.4	25.8	34.2	45.1	56.4	64.6	70.2	68.5	60.2	49.7	39.5	28.8	47.2
Mean Minimum Temp. (°F)	15.6	17.7	25.6	35.7	46.3	54.9	61.0	59.6	51.3	40.9	31.9	21.4	38.5
Extreme Maximum Temp. (°F)	60	67	84	91	90	94	96	96	91	82	78	72	96
Extreme Minimum Temp. (°F)	-13	-11	-4	11	28	36	43	39	30	21	6	-11	-13
Days Maximum Temp. ≥ 90°F	0	0	0	0	0	1	1	1	0	0	0	0	3
Days Maximum Temp. ≤ 32°F	18	13	5	0	0	0	0	0	0	0	2	11	49
Days Minimum Temp. ≤ 32°F	29	26	25	10	1	0	0	0	0	4	17	27	139
Days Minimum Temp. ≤ 0°F	3	2	0	0	0	0	0	0	0	0	0	1	6
Heating Degree Days (base 65°F)	1,284	1,099	949	594	280	83	12	30	174	469	759	1,117	6,850
Cooling Degree Days (base 65°F)	0	0	1	1	20	78	180	142	37	2	0	0	461
Mean Precipitation (in.)	3.90	3.19	4.09	3.94	4.39	4.13	4.09	4.20	4.05	4.63	4.39	3.83	48.83
Maximum Precipitation (in.)	11.2	8.4	8.6	8.8	9.9	12.2	7.9	9.2	13.1	10.2	10.4	9.8	71.7
Minimum Precipitation (in.)	0.9	0.3	0.7	1.3	1.2	0.8	0.7	1.0	0.7	1.2	0.7	0.7	31.9
Maximum 24-hr. Precipitation (in.)	2.5	2.4	4.5	2.8	3.0	3.5	3.9	5.0	5.0	3.7	2.6	2.5	5.0
Days With ≥ 0.1" Precipitation	7	6	7	7	8	7	6	7	6	6	7	7	81
Days With ≥ 1.0" Precipitation	1	1	1	1	1	1	1	1	1	2	1	1	13
Mean Snowfall (in.)	15.5	13.5	*11.0*	3.3	*0.5*	*trace*	0.0	trace	trace	0.3	3.8	*12.3*	*60.2*
Maximum Snowfall (in.)	47	45	44	21	trace	0	0	0	trace	8	21	37	112
Maximum 24-hr. Snowfall (in.)	18	20	15	15	trace	0	0	0	trace	8	15	17	20
Days With ≥ 1.0" Snow Depth	18	18	10	1	*0*	0	0	0	0	0	3	11	*61*
Thunderstorm Days	< 1	< 1	1	1	3	5	6	4	2	1	< 1	< 1	23
Foggy Days	13	11	14	14	15	16	16	17	17	15	15	14	177
Predominant Sky Cover	OVR	OVR	OVR	OVR	OVR	OVR	OVR	OVR	OVR	OVR	OVR	OVR	OVR
Mean Relative Humidity 7am (%)	73	73	72	69	70	74	76	79	82	79	78	76	75
Mean Relative Humidity 4pm (%)	61	58	56	50	52	57	58	60	62	58	63	65	58
Mean Dewpoint (°F)	14	15	21	30	42	53	59	58	51	40	30	19	36
Prevailing Wind Direction	WNW	WNW	WNW	WNW	W	W	WSW	W	W	W	W	WNW	W
Prevailing Wind Speed (mph)	15	16	15	15	10	9	9	9	9	10	12	15	13
Maximum Wind Gust (mph)	67	69	69	64	61	58	59	69	71	60	69	73	73

Amherst *Hampshire County*   Elevation: 147 ft.   Latitude: 42° 23' N   Longitude: 72° 32' W

	JAN	FEB	MAR	APR	MAY	JUN	JUL	AUG	SEP	OCT	NOV	DEC	YEAR
Mean Maximum Temp. (°F)	34.4	37.8	46.7	59.3	71.3	79.3	84.1	82.2	74.2	63.0	50.8	39.0	60.2
Mean Temp. (°F)	23.6	26.8	35.8	46.7	58.2	66.7	71.5	69.6	61.5	50.3	40.3	29.4	48.4
Mean Minimum Temp. (°F)	12.7	15.6	24.9	34.1	45.0	54.0	58.9	57.1	48.7	37.6	29.8	19.7	36.5
Extreme Maximum Temp. (°F)	63	70	84	93	94	97	99	98	94	87	79	72	99
Extreme Minimum Temp. (°F)	-29	-23	-11	11	24	32	40	33	27	12	0	-20	-29
Days Maximum Temp. ≥ 90°F	0	0	0	0	1	2	5	3	1	0	0	0	12
Days Maximum Temp. ≤ 32°F	13	8	2	0	0	0	0	0	0	0	0	7	30
Days Minimum Temp. ≤ 32°F	30	26	25	13	2	0	0	0	1	11	19	28	155
Days Minimum Temp. ≤ 0°F	6	4	0	0	0	0	0	0	0	0	0	2	12
Heating Degree Days (base 65°F)	1,277	1,074	899	544	231	57	9	22	153	451	734	1,098	6,549
Cooling Degree Days (base 65°F)	0	0	0	2	24	109	215	164	52	3	0	0	569
Mean Precipitation (in.)	3.68	2.85	3.58	3.82	4.11	3.70	3.79	4.10	3.98	4.07	3.95	3.56	45.19
Days With ≥ 0.1" Precipitation	7	5	7	7	7	7	7	6	7	6	7	7	80
Days With ≥ 1.0" Precipitation	1	1	1	1	1	1	1	2	1	1	1	1	13
Mean Snowfall (in.)	11.7	8.3	6.3	1.7	0.0	0.0	0.0	0.0	0.0	trace	2.4	8.9	39.3
Days With ≥ 1.0" Snow Depth	22	18	9	1	0	0	0	0	0	0	2	12	64

Barre Falls Dam *Worcester County*   Elevation: 908 ft.   Latitude: 42° 26' N   Longitude: 72° 02' W

	JAN	FEB	MAR	APR	MAY	JUN	JUL	AUG	SEP	OCT	NOV	DEC	YEAR
Mean Maximum Temp. (°F)	*31.1*	*34.2*	*42.8*	*54.4*	66.9	74.8	79.7	77.6	69.7	*58.8*	*47.6*	na	na
Mean Temp. (°F)	*20.5*	*23.3*	*32.3*	*43.0*	54.2	62.4	67.4	65.3	57.1	*46.3*	*37.6*	na	na
Mean Minimum Temp. (°F)	*10.0*	*12.6*	*21.8*	*31.6*	41.5	50.1	55.1	53.0	44.4	*34.1*	*27.6*	na	na
Extreme Maximum Temp. (°F)	60	67	81	89	90	94	95	98	90	84	77	66	98
Extreme Minimum Temp. (°F)	-25	-22	-8	8	21	29	34	28	24	13	-7	-16	-25
Days Maximum Temp. ≥ 90°F	0	0	0	0	0	0	1	0	0	0	0	0	1
Days Maximum Temp. ≤ 32°F	16	12	4	0	0	0	0	0	0	0	1	10	43
Days Minimum Temp. ≤ 32°F	28	24	25	17	5	0	0	0	3	14	20	25	161
Days Minimum Temp. ≤ 0°F	7	4	1	0	0	0	0	0	0	0	0	3	15
Heating Degree Days (base 65°F)	*1,373*	*1,170*	*1,007*	*654*	337	122	37	71	252	*573*	*815*	na	na
Cooling Degree Days (base 65°F)	*0*	na	*0*	*0*	10	52	123	88	23	*1*	na	na	na
Mean Precipitation (in.)	3.69	2.69	3.52	3.77	3.89	3.81	3.94	4.56	3.78	4.16	3.87	3.49	45.17
Days With ≥ 0.1" Precipitation	7	6	8	8	8	7	7	7	7	7	8	8	88
Days With ≥ 1.0" Precipitation	1	1	1	1	1	1	1	1	1	2	1	1	13
Mean Snowfall (in.)	15.0	11.4	9.8	4.2	0.7	0.0	0.0	0.0	0.0	0.2	3.1	10.7	55.1
Days With ≥ 1.0" Snow Depth	22	21	16	3	0	0	0	0	0	0	3	13	78

Bedford *Middlesex County*   Elevation: 157 ft.   Latitude: 42° 29' N   Longitude: 71° 17' W

	JAN	FEB	MAR	APR	MAY	JUN	JUL	AUG	SEP	OCT	NOV	DEC	YEAR
Mean Maximum Temp. (°F)	34.8	37.9	46.5	58.0	69.4	77.4	82.8	80.9	72.5	61.8	50.7	39.5	59.4
Mean Temp. (°F)	25.2	28.0	36.4	46.9	57.7	66.1	71.7	70.0	61.4	50.4	41.0	30.5	48.8
Mean Minimum Temp. (°F)	15.5	18.1	26.4	35.7	45.9	54.7	60.4	58.9	50.3	39.0	31.2	21.5	38.1
Extreme Maximum Temp. (°F)	65	72	90	94	94	97	99	101	94	86	79	77	101
Extreme Minimum Temp. (°F)	-19	-14	-2	14	29	36	42	40	29	19	-1	-15	-19
Days Maximum Temp. ≥ 90°F	0	0	0	0	1	2	4	3	1	0	0	0	11
Days Maximum Temp. ≤ 32°F	13	8	2	0	0	0	0	0	0	0	1	7	31
Days Minimum Temp. ≤ 32°F	29	26	24	11	1	0	0	0	0	8	18	27	144
Days Minimum Temp. ≤ 0°F	3	2	0	0	0	0	0	0	0	0	0	1	6
Heating Degree Days (base 65°F)	1,228	1,037	879	539	244	63	8	20	149	448	713	1,062	6,390
Cooling Degree Days (base 65°F)	0	0	1	2	22	101	222	177	50	3	0	0	578
Mean Precipitation (in.)	4.16	3.37	4.20	3.90	3.79	3.59	3.76	3.60	3.84	4.11	4.34	4.09	46.75
Days With ≥ 0.1" Precipitation	7	6	8	7	8	7	6	6	6	6	7	7	81
Days With ≥ 1.0" Precipitation	1	1	1	1	1	1	1	1	1	1	1	1	12
Mean Snowfall (in.)	15.4	11.5	10.0	2.9	0.3	0.0	0.0	0.0	0.0	0.1	3.2	11.1	54.5
Days With ≥ 1.0" Snow Depth	20	17	10	1	0	0	0	0	0	0	3	11	62

Birch Hill Dam *Worcester County*   Elevation: 862 ft.   Latitude: 42° 38' N   Longitude: 72° 07' W

	JAN	FEB	MAR	APR	MAY	JUN	JUL	AUG	SEP	OCT	NOV	DEC	YEAR
Mean Maximum Temp. (°F)	*30.7*	*34.6*	43.1	55.1	67.7	76.0	81.0	79.1	70.6	*59.6*	na	*35.6*	na
Mean Temp. (°F)	*18.7*	*22.2*	31.9	43.0	54.5	63.0	68.1	66.0	57.3	*46.3*	na	*14.4*	na
Mean Minimum Temp. (°F)	*6.6*	*10.3*	20.7	30.8	41.3	49.9	55.1	52.9	44.1	*32.9*	na	*14.4*	na
Extreme Maximum Temp. (°F)	64	66	82	91	92	96	97	97	93	83	76	69	97
Extreme Minimum Temp. (°F)	-31	-28	-13	8	23	28	34	29	24	12	-5	-24	-31
Days Maximum Temp. ≥ 90°F	0	0	0	0	0	1	2	1	0	0	0	0	4
Days Maximum Temp. ≤ 32°F	15	11	4	0	0	0	0	0	0	0	1	10	41
Days Minimum Temp. ≤ 32°F	28	25	26	19	5	0	0	0	4	16	21	26	170
Days Minimum Temp. ≤ 0°F	9	7	1	0	0	0	0	0	0	0	0	4	21
Heating Degree Days (base 65°F)	*1,431*	*1,203*	1,019	655	330	116	34	61	248	*574*	na	na	na
Cooling Degree Days (base 65°F)	na	*0*	0	0	*11*	61	138	101	27	*1*	na	na	na
Mean Precipitation (in.)	3.73	2.79	3.79	3.64	3.71	3.73	4.15	3.94	3.49	3.91	4.17	3.62	44.67
Days With ≥ 0.1" Precipitation	7	6	8	7	8	7	7	6	6	6	8	7	83
Days With ≥ 1.0" Precipitation	1	1	1	1	1	1	1	1	1	1	1	1	12
Mean Snowfall (in.)	14.0	10.7	8.5	2.6	trace	0.0	0.0	0.0	0.0	0.1	3.1	10.2	49.2
Days With ≥ 1.0" Snow Depth	20	20	14	2	0	0	0	0	0	0	3	14	73

Brockton *Plymouth County*   Elevation: 78 ft.   Latitude: 42° 03' N   Longitude: 71° 00' W

	JAN	FEB	MAR	APR	MAY	JUN	JUL	AUG	SEP	OCT	NOV	DEC	YEAR
Mean Maximum Temp. (°F)	37.7	39.9	47.8	58.1	69.0	77.7	83.2	81.3	73.6	63.3	52.7	42.3	60.6
Mean Temp. (°F)	27.6	29.7	37.6	47.0	57.2	66.1	71.9	70.5	62.2	51.7	42.4	32.8	49.7
Mean Minimum Temp. (°F)	17.6	19.6	27.4	35.9	45.4	54.5	60.6	59.5	50.8	39.9	32.2	23.3	38.9
Extreme Maximum Temp. (°F)	68	69	87	93	95	98	100	101	98	87	79	78	101
Extreme Minimum Temp. (°F)	-15	-13	-2	20	26	35	40	38	28	19	3	-10	-15
Days Maximum Temp. ≥ 90°F	0	0	0	0	1	2	5	3	1	0	0	0	12
Days Maximum Temp. ≤ 32°F	10	7	1	0	0	0	0	0	0	0	0	5	23
Days Minimum Temp. ≤ 32°F	28	25	22	10	1	0	0	0	1	8	17	26	138
Days Minimum Temp. ≤ 0°F	2	1	0	0	0	0	0	0	0	0	0	0	3
Heating Degree Days (base 65°F)	1,154	990	841	534	255	64	8	16	134	412	672	991	6,071
Cooling Degree Days (base 65°F)	0	0	0	1	23	113	246	201	60	5	0	0	649
Mean Precipitation (in.)	4.09	3.65	4.35	4.10	3.43	3.50	3.55	4.29	3.93	4.39	4.46	4.35	48.09
Days With ≥ 0.1" Precipitation	7	6	7	6	7	6	5	6	6	6	7	7	76
Days With ≥ 1.0" Precipitation	1	1	1	1	1	1	1	1	1	1	1	1	12
Mean Snowfall (in.)	na	na	na	na	trace	0.0	0.0	0.0	0.0	trace	0.6	na	na
Days With ≥ 1.0" Snow Depth	na	na	na	na	0	0	0	0	0	0	0	na	na

Buffumville Lake *Worcester County*   Elevation: 498 ft.   Latitude: 42° 07' N   Longitude: 71° 54' W

	JAN	FEB	MAR	APR	MAY	JUN	JUL	AUG	SEP	OCT	NOV	DEC	YEAR
Mean Maximum Temp. (°F)	na	na	44.7	55.8	68.2	76.4	81.5	79.6	71.8	61.1	50.3	na	na
Mean Temp. (°F)	na	na	34.0	44.7	56.2	64.9	70.2	68.4	60.0	48.8	39.9	na	na
Mean Minimum Temp. (°F)	10.3	na	23.2	33.6	44.2	53.3	58.9	57.1	48.1	36.4	29.5	na	na
Extreme Maximum Temp. (°F)	62	68	83	92	91	94	98	98	95	85	79	72	98
Extreme Minimum Temp. (°F)	-28	-22	-5	2	25	35	40	34	23	15	-2	-16	-28
Days Maximum Temp. ≥ 90°F	0	0	0	0	0	1	3	1	0	0	0	0	5
Days Maximum Temp. ≤ 32°F	12	9	3	0	0	0	0	0	0	0	1	8	33
Days Minimum Temp. ≤ 32°F	26	23	24	13	2	0	0	0	1	10	17	24	140
Days Minimum Temp. ≤ 0°F	5	4	0	0	0	0	0	0	0	0	0	2	11
Heating Degree Days (base 65°F)	na	na	na	604	282	81	15	31	181	498	746	na	na
Cooling Degree Days (base 65°F)	na	na	na	1	16	86	191	145	39	na	na	na	na
Mean Precipitation (in.)	4.33	3.27	4.35	4.03	3.72	3.79	4.12	4.13	4.05	4.41	4.52	4.02	48.74
Days With ≥ 0.1" Precipitation	7	6	8	7	8	7	7	7	6	6	7	7	83
Days With ≥ 1.0" Precipitation	1	1	1	1	1	1	1	1	1	1	1	1	12
Mean Snowfall (in.)	11.8	9.5	7.9	3.2	trace	0.0	0.0	0.0	0.0	0.1	2.5	7.9	42.9
Days With ≥ 1.0" Snow Depth	18	15	10	1	0	0	0	0	0	0	2	10	56

East Brimfield Lake *Worcester County*   Elevation: 679 ft.   Latitude: 42° 07' N   Longitude: 72° 08' W

	JAN	FEB	MAR	APR	MAY	JUN	JUL	AUG	SEP	OCT	NOV	DEC	YEAR
Mean Maximum Temp. (°F)	33.2	35.8	44.8	56.7	68.9	77.0	82.0	79.8	71.7	61.0	49.4	37.9	58.2
Mean Temp. (°F)	22.6	24.9	34.2	45.3	56.6	65.2	70.4	68.5	60.2	49.0	39.5	28.5	47.1
Mean Minimum Temp. (°F)	11.9	13.9	23.5	33.8	44.2	53.4	58.7	57.2	48.7	37.1	29.5	19.1	35.9
Extreme Maximum Temp. (°F)	62	68	83	91	93	95	96	99	95	85	78	72	99
Extreme Minimum Temp. (°F)	-27	-24	-9	5	26	35	42	38	29	17	-1	-14	-27
Days Maximum Temp. ≥ 90°F	0	0	0	0	0	1	3	1	0	0	0	0	5
Days Maximum Temp. ≤ 32°F	15	11	3	0	0	0	0	0	0	0	1	8	38
Days Minimum Temp. ≤ 32°F	30	27	26	14	1	0	0	0	0	10	20	28	156
Days Minimum Temp. ≤ 0°F	6	4	0	0	0	0	0	0	0	0	0	1	11
Heating Degree Days (base 65°F)	1,309	1,126	948	587	273	74	13	29	176	489	759	1,124	6,907
Cooling Degree Days (base 65°F)	0	0	0	0	16	82	181	139	38	2	0	0	458
Mean Precipitation (in.)	4.27	3.24	4.23	4.11	3.74	3.63	3.62	3.94	3.95	4.17	4.33	4.01	47.24
Days With ≥ 0.1" Precipitation	7	7	8	7	8	7	7	7	6	6	8	8	86
Days With ≥ 1.0" Precipitation	1	1	1	1	1	1	1	1	1	1	1	1	12
Mean Snowfall (in.)	14.9	11.6	9.8	4.0	0.2	0.0	0.0	0.0	0.0	0.1	2.7	11.3	54.6
Days With ≥ 1.0" Snow Depth	19	17	10	2	0	0	0	0	0	0	2	11	61

East Wareham *Plymouth County*   Elevation: 19 ft.   Latitude: 41° 46' N   Longitude: 70° 40' W

	JAN	FEB	MAR	APR	MAY	JUN	JUL	AUG	SEP	OCT	NOV	DEC	YEAR
Mean Maximum Temp. (°F)	36.8	38.0	44.9	54.4	65.0	73.9	80.0	78.8	71.5	61.4	51.5	42.1	58.2
Mean Temp. (°F)	28.2	29.5	36.7	45.6	56.0	65.2	71.6	70.4	62.6	52.1	43.1	33.7	49.6
Mean Minimum Temp. (°F)	19.6	20.9	28.5	36.7	47.0	56.5	63.2	62.0	53.7	42.8	34.6	25.3	40.9
Extreme Maximum Temp. (°F)	64	64	75	89	94	93	98	100	90	85	77	70	100
Extreme Minimum Temp. (°F)	-15	-8	4	13	30	40	45	40	35	23	5	-7	-15
Days Maximum Temp. ≥ 90°F	0	0	0	0	0	0	1	1	0	0	0	0	2
Days Maximum Temp. ≤ 32°F	10	8	2	0	0	0	0	0	0	0	0	5	25
Days Minimum Temp. ≤ 32°F	27	24	22	9	0	0	0	0	0	4	14	24	124
Days Minimum Temp. ≤ 0°F	1	1	0	0	0	0	0	0	0	0	0	0	2
Heating Degree Days (base 65°F)	1,133	996	870	577	280	63	5	13	119	396	651	963	6,066
Cooling Degree Days (base 65°F)	0	0	0	0	9	77	217	186	55	4	0	0	548
Mean Precipitation (in.)	4.45	3.79	4.49	4.29	3.64	3.60	3.15	4.15	4.02	3.93	4.61	4.48	48.60
Days With ≥ 0.1" Precipitation	7	6	8	7	7	6	6	6	5	6	7	8	79
Days With ≥ 1.0" Precipitation	1	1	1	1	1	1	1	1	1	1	2	1	13
Mean Snowfall (in.)	10.3	9.7	5.2	1.3	trace	0.0	0.0	0.0	0.0	trace	1.2	4.9	32.6
Days With ≥ 1.0" Snow Depth	12	10	4	1	0	0	0	0	0	0	1	4	32

Edgartown *Dukes County*   Elevation: 19 ft.   Latitude: 41° 23' N   Longitude: 70° 31' W

	JAN	FEB	MAR	APR	MAY	JUN	JUL	AUG	SEP	OCT	NOV	DEC	YEAR
Mean Maximum Temp. (°F)	38.7	39.5	45.6	54.4	64.0	72.9	78.8	78.2	71.9	62.7	53.4	44.0	58.7
Mean Temp. (°F)	30.4	31.2	37.6	46.0	55.6	64.6	70.6	70.1	63.7	54.0	45.3	36.0	50.4
Mean Minimum Temp. (°F)	22.2	23.0	29.6	37.6	47.1	56.2	62.3	62.0	55.4	45.3	37.2	27.9	42.1
Extreme Maximum Temp. (°F)	62	64	79	90	90	93	95	96	88	80	74	67	96
Extreme Minimum Temp. (°F)	-5	-1	4	16	28	39	45	41	34	22	14	-2	-5
Days Maximum Temp. ≥ 90°F	0	0	0	0	0	0	1	0	0	0	0	0	1
Days Maximum Temp. ≤ 32°F	8	6	1	0	0	0	0	0	0	0	0	3	18
Days Minimum Temp. ≤ 32°F	27	23	20	7	0	0	0	0	0	2	10	22	111
Days Minimum Temp. ≤ 0°F	0	0	0	0	0	0	0	0	0	0	0	0	0
Heating Degree Days (base 65°F)	1,065	947	842	563	290	64	6	9	86	338	583	894	5,687
Cooling Degree Days (base 65°F)	0	0	0	0	6	64	190	168	56	4	0	0	488
Mean Precipitation (in.)	4.00	3.39	4.44	4.13	3.53	3.55	3.08	3.89	3.53	4.04	4.29	4.31	46.18
Days With ≥ 0.1" Precipitation	8	6	8	7	7	5	5	6	5	7	7	8	79
Days With ≥ 1.0" Precipitation	1	1	1	1	1	1	1	1	1	1	1	1	12
Mean Snowfall (in.)	na	na	na	0.4	0.0	0.0	0.0	0.0	0.0	trace	0.4	na	na
Days With ≥ 1.0" Snow Depth	na	na	na	0	0	0	0	0	0	0	0	na	na

Great Barrington Airport *Berkshire County*   Elevation: 816 ft.   Latitude: 42° 09' N   Longitude: 73° 25' W

	JAN	FEB	MAR	APR	MAY	JUN	JUL	AUG	SEP	OCT	NOV	DEC	YEAR
Mean Maximum Temp. (°F)	31.8	34.0	43.3	56.5	68.2	76.6	81.4	78.9	70.5	59.3	48.3	36.5	57.1
Mean Temp. (°F)	21.3	23.2	32.6	44.4	55.4	64.0	68.7	66.4	57.9	46.5	37.9	26.9	45.4
Mean Minimum Temp. (°F)	10.9	12.4	21.8	32.3	42.5	51.4	56.0	53.8	45.3	33.6	27.5	17.3	33.7
Extreme Maximum Temp. (°F)	60	67	83	94	91	94	99	93	95	85	80	70	99
Extreme Minimum Temp. (°F)	-27	-21	-8	14	23	29	36	31	22	13	1	-20	-27
Days Maximum Temp. ≥ 90°F	0	0	0	0	0	1	3	1	0	0	0	0	5
Days Maximum Temp. ≤ 32°F	16	12	5	0	0	0	0	0	0	0	1	10	44
Days Minimum Temp. ≤ 32°F	29	27	27	17	4	0	0	0	3	16	22	29	174
Days Minimum Temp. ≤ 0°F	7	6	1	0	0	0	0	0	0	0	0	3	17
Heating Degree Days (base 65°F)	1,347	1,175	998	614	308	94	27	52	231	568	806	1,173	7,393
Cooling Degree Days (base 65°F)	0	0	0	1	16	75	158	107	29	2	0	0	388
Mean Precipitation (in.)	3.90	2.88	3.65	3.76	4.72	3.52	4.10	4.76	4.33	4.14	4.05	3.48	47.29
Days With ≥ 0.1" Precipitation	7	6	7	8	9	7	8	8	7	7	8	7	89
Days With ≥ 1.0" Precipitation	1	0	1	1	1	1	1	1	1	1	1	1	11
Mean Snowfall (in.)	na	13.5	9.8	2.7	0.5	0.0	0.0	0.0	0.0	0.5	4.0	12.6	na
Days With ≥ 1.0" Snow Depth	na	na	na	na	0	0	0	0	0	0	2	na	na

Haverhill *Essex County*   Elevation: 16 ft.   Latitude: 42° 46' N   Longitude: 71° 04' W

	JAN	FEB	MAR	APR	MAY	JUN	JUL	AUG	SEP	OCT	NOV	DEC	YEAR
Mean Maximum Temp. (°F)	34.9	38.0	46.6	57.8	69.2	78.0	83.8	81.7	73.1	62.3	50.8	39.7	59.7
Mean Temp. (°F)	25.4	28.1	36.5	46.7	57.4	66.4	72.5	70.7	62.0	51.1	41.3	30.6	49.1
Mean Minimum Temp. (°F)	15.8	18.1	26.4	35.5	45.5	54.7	61.1	59.6	50.9	39.8	31.8	21.5	38.4
Extreme Maximum Temp. (°F)	66	73	90	94	94	101	102	103	95	88	82	76	103
Extreme Minimum Temp. (°F)	-21	-12	-3	15	26	36	41	36	29	21	-2	-12	-21
Days Maximum Temp. ≥ 90°F	0	0	0	0	1	2	6	4	1	0	0	0	14
Days Maximum Temp. ≤ 32°F	13	8	2	0	0	0	0	0	0	0	0	7	30
Days Minimum Temp. ≤ 32°F	29	26	23	11	1	0	0	0	0	7	17	27	141
Days Minimum Temp. ≤ 0°F	3	2	0	0	0	0	0	0	0	0	0	1	6
Heating Degree Days (base 65°F)	1,223	1,036	877	546	255	62	7	18	139	429	705	1,059	6,356
Cooling Degree Days (base 65°F)	0	0	1	1	19	93	222	181	49	3	0	0	569
Mean Precipitation (in.)	3.78	3.35	4.15	4.20	3.86	3.57	3.29	3.54	3.98	4.31	4.43	4.06	46.52
Days With ≥ 0.1" Precipitation	7	6	7	7	8	7	6	6	6	6	7	7	80
Days With ≥ 1.0" Precipitation	1	1	1	1	1	1	1	1	1	1	1	1	12
Mean Snowfall (in.)	15.9	11.5	9.2	2.6	trace	0.0	0.0	0.0	0.0	trace	2.9	10.1	52.2
Days With ≥ 1.0" Snow Depth	16	12	7	1	0	0	0	0	0	0	2	8	46

Hingham *Plymouth County*   Elevation: 29 ft.   Latitude: 42° 14' N   Longitude: 70° 55' W

	JAN	FEB	MAR	APR	MAY	JUN	JUL	AUG	SEP	OCT	NOV	DEC	YEAR
Mean Maximum Temp. (°F)	36.8	39.1	46.6	57.0	67.6	76.2	81.7	79.2	71.7	61.8	51.9	41.5	59.3
Mean Temp. (°F)	28.1	30.4	37.8	47.2	57.3	66.1	71.9	70.0	62.4	52.1	43.3	33.5	50.0
Mean Minimum Temp. (°F)	19.4	21.6	28.9	37.4	47.0	56.1	62.0	60.8	53.1	42.4	34.6	25.3	40.7
Extreme Maximum Temp. (°F)	67	69	89	92	93	96	100	100	94	86	78	77	100
Extreme Minimum Temp. (°F)	-13	-5	0	16	29	37	44	39	33	21	2	-8	-13
Days Maximum Temp. ≥ 90°F	0	0	0	0	0	1	4	2	0	0	0	0	7
Days Maximum Temp. ≤ 32°F	11	7	2	0	0	0	0	0	0	0	0	5	25
Days Minimum Temp. ≤ 32°F	27	24	20	8	1	0	0	0	0	4	14	24	122
Days Minimum Temp. ≤ 0°F	2	1	0	0	0	0	0	0	0	0	0	0	3
Heating Degree Days (base 65°F)	1,137	972	838	529	253	64	8	19	127	397	645	971	5,960
Cooling Degree Days (base 65°F)	0	0	1	2	21	106	229	181	58	5	1	0	604
Mean Precipitation (in.)	4.69	4.08	4.67	4.14	3.77	3.39	3.32	4.31	3.73	4.55	4.67	4.44	49.76
Days With ≥ 0.1" Precipitation	8	6	8	6	7	6	6	6	6	6	7	8	80
Days With ≥ 1.0" Precipitation	1	1	1	1	1	1	1	1	1	1	1	1	12
Mean Snowfall (in.)	14.1	11.8	8.2	1.9	trace	0.0	0.0	0.0	0.0	trace	1.8	8.2	46.0
Days With ≥ 1.0" Snow Depth	16	14	7	1	0	0	0	0	0	0	1	8	47

Knightville Dam *Hampshire County*   Elevation: 629 ft.   Latitude: 42° 17' N   Longitude: 72° 52' W

	JAN	FEB	MAR	APR	MAY	JUN	JUL	AUG	SEP	OCT	NOV	DEC	YEAR
Mean Maximum Temp. (°F)	31.7	34.9	43.6	56.3	69.0	76.7	81.6	79.8	71.4	60.7	48.8	na	na
Mean Temp. (°F)	20.4	23.3	32.5	44.2	55.6	63.8	68.7	66.9	58.3	47.6	na	na	na
Mean Minimum Temp. (°F)	9.0	11.6	21.3	32.0	42.1	50.8	55.8	54.1	45.1	34.3	na	na	na
Extreme Maximum Temp. (°F)	60	69	83	92	93	95	97	97	94	85	80	66	97
Extreme Minimum Temp. (°F)	-23	-25	-7	10	23	32	40	34	27	15	-6	-19	-25
Days Maximum Temp. ≥ 90°F	0	0	0	0	0	1	3	2	0	0	0	0	6
Days Maximum Temp. ≤ 32°F	15	11	4	0	0	0	0	0	0	0	1	9	40
Days Minimum Temp. ≤ 32°F	29	25	27	17	3	0	0	0	2	14	21	27	165
Days Minimum Temp. ≤ 0°F	7	5	1	0	0	0	0	0	0	0	0	3	16
Heating Degree Days (base 65°F)	1,377	1,171	1,001	620	300	96	24	46	220	535	na	na	na
Cooling Degree Days (base 65°F)	na	na	0	1	15	59	145	113	25	na	na	na	na
Mean Precipitation (in.)	3.76	3.26	4.13	4.26	4.40	3.53	4.04	4.41	3.81	4.15	4.30	4.09	48.14
Days With ≥ 0.1" Precipitation	6	6	7	7	8	6	7	6	6	6	7	7	79
Days With ≥ 1.0" Precipitation	1	1	1	1	1	1	1	1	1	1	1	1	12
Mean Snowfall (in.)	12.2	9.5	7.3	1.3	0.1	0.0	0.0	0.0	0.0	trace	2.4	9.6	42.4
Days With ≥ 1.0" Snow Depth	22	20	15	3	0	0	0	0	0	0	2	15	77

Lawrence *Essex County*   Elevation: 59 ft.   Latitude: 42° 42' N   Longitude: 71° 10' W

	JAN	FEB	MAR	APR	MAY	JUN	JUL	AUG	SEP	OCT	NOV	DEC	YEAR
Mean Maximum Temp. (°F)	34.1	37.2	45.4	56.8	68.5	77.5	83.0	81.6	72.9	61.9	51.0	39.5	59.1
Mean Temp. (°F)	24.7	27.8	36.2	47.1	58.0	67.0	72.7	71.1	62.5	51.2	41.9	31.0	49.3
Mean Minimum Temp. (°F)	15.4	18.2	26.9	37.3	47.5	56.5	62.3	60.5	51.9	40.5	32.7	22.5	39.3
Extreme Maximum Temp. (°F)	66	72	88	92	94	96	100	101	95	85	79	75	101
Extreme Minimum Temp. (°F)	-20	-9	2	15	28	35	46	43	31	24	4	-10	-20
Days Maximum Temp. ≥ 90°F	0	0	0	0	1	2	4	3	0	0	0	0	10
Days Maximum Temp. ≤ 32°F	14	9	3	0	0	0	0	0	0	0	1	7	34
Days Minimum Temp. ≤ 32°F	29	26	23	7	0	0	0	0	0	5	16	27	133
Days Minimum Temp. ≤ 0°F	3	1	0	0	0	0	0	0	0	0	0	1	5
Heating Degree Days (base 65°F)	1,241	1,045	888	534	236	52	5	13	125	422	688	1,047	6,296
Cooling Degree Days (base 65°F)	0	0	1	1	25	119	247	202	57	2	0	0	654
Mean Precipitation (in.)	4.20	3.23	3.91	4.02	3.73	3.46	3.20	3.26	3.77	3.97	4.05	3.66	44.46
Days With ≥ 0.1" Precipitation	7	6	7	7	7	6	6	5	6	6	7	6	76
Days With ≥ 1.0" Precipitation	1	1	1	1	1	1	1	1	1	1	1	1	12
Mean Snowfall (in.)	13.4	10.6	7.2	1.7	trace	0.0	0.0	0.0	0.0	trace	2.3	8.5	43.7
Days With ≥ 1.0" Snow Depth	na	na	6	0	0	0	0	0	0	0	1	5	na

Middleton *Essex County*   Elevation: 88 ft.   Latitude: 42° 36' N   Longitude: 71° 01' W

	JAN	FEB	MAR	APR	MAY	JUN	JUL	AUG	SEP	OCT	NOV	DEC	YEAR
Mean Maximum Temp. (°F)	36.8	39.5	46.9	57.5	68.7	77.5	83.0	81.3	73.9	63.6	52.3	41.2	60.2
Mean Temp. (°F)	26.8	29.2	36.9	46.9	57.6	66.7	72.4	70.7	63.0	52.5	42.9	32.1	49.8
Mean Minimum Temp. (°F)	16.8	18.9	26.8	36.3	46.5	55.8	61.7	60.0	51.9	41.2	33.4	23.0	39.4
Extreme Maximum Temp. (°F)	65	69	86	90	95	95	100	102	95	86	80	67	102
Extreme Minimum Temp. (°F)	-22	-15	-1	8	28	38	44	39	29	20	-3	-13	-22
Days Maximum Temp. ≥ 90°F	0	0	0	0	1	1	4	3	0	0	0	0	9
Days Maximum Temp. ≤ 32°F	10	6	1	0	0	0	0	0	0	0	0	6	23
Days Minimum Temp. ≤ 32°F	29	25	23	10	1	0	0	0	0	6	15	26	135
Days Minimum Temp. ≤ 0°F	3	1	0	0	0	0	0	0	0	0	0	1	5
Heating Degree Days (base 65°F)	1,177	1,004	865	538	245	58	7	16	119	387	657	1,013	6,086
Cooling Degree Days (base 65°F)	0	0	1	1	24	116	242	196	66	5	0	0	651
Mean Precipitation (in.)	3.70	3.21	3.88	4.03	3.60	3.55	3.32	3.40	3.70	4.12	4.41	3.97	44.89
Days With ≥ 0.1" Precipitation	7	6	7	7	8	6	6	6	6	6	7	7	79
Days With ≥ 1.0" Precipitation	1	1	1	1	1	1	1	1	1	1	1	1	12
Mean Snowfall (in.)	12.1	11.2	6.9	2.1	trace	0.0	0.0	0.0	0.0	trace	2.0	7.4	41.7
Days With ≥ 1.0" Snow Depth	12	11	6	0	0	0	0	0	0	0	1	8	38

New Bedford *Bristol County*   Elevation: 68 ft.   Latitude: 41° 38' N   Longitude: 70° 56' W

	JAN	FEB	MAR	APR	MAY	JUN	JUL	AUG	SEP	OCT	NOV	DEC	YEAR
Mean Maximum Temp. (°F)	37.6	38.9	45.9	55.7	66.5	75.8	82.1	81.0	73.6	63.2	52.8	42.8	59.7
Mean Temp. (°F)	30.2	31.5	38.5	47.9	58.2	67.5	74.0	73.1	65.7	55.1	45.6	35.5	51.9
Mean Minimum Temp. (°F)	22.7	24.1	31.1	39.9	49.8	59.1	65.9	65.1	57.8	47.1	38.3	28.1	44.1
Extreme Maximum Temp. (°F)	65	66	80	89	98	100	103	107	94	86	79	72	107
Extreme Minimum Temp. (°F)	-7	-6	6	16	32	44	50	44	36	27	11	-5	-7
Days Maximum Temp. ≥ 90°F	0	0	0	0	0	2	4	3	0	0	0	0	9
Days Maximum Temp. ≤ 32°F	10	7	2	0	0	0	0	0	0	0	0	4	23
Days Minimum Temp. ≤ 32°F	25	22	17	3	0	0	0	0	0	1	8	21	97
Days Minimum Temp. ≤ 0°F	1	0	0	0	0	0	0	0	0	0	0	0	1
Heating Degree Days (base 65°F)	1,072	940	814	509	225	40	2	5	68	309	578	910	5,472
Cooling Degree Days (base 65°F)	0	0	0	0	20	120	285	247	89	8	0	0	769
Mean Precipitation (in.)	4.61	4.08	4.67	4.29	3.64	3.96	3.38	4.71	3.87	4.02	4.68	4.73	50.64
Days With ≥ 0.1" Precipitation	8	7	8	7	7	6	6	6	6	6	7	9	83
Days With ≥ 1.0" Precipitation	1	1	1	1	1	1	1	1	1	1	1	1	12
Mean Snowfall (in.)	10.2	10.1	5.2	1.2	trace	0.0	0.0	0.0	0.0	trace	1.0	5.3	33.0
Days With ≥ 1.0" Snow Depth	na	na	na	0	0	0	0	0	0	0	0	na	na

Peabody *Essex County*   Elevation: 167 ft.   Latitude: 42° 32' N   Longitude: 70° 59' W

	JAN	FEB	MAR	APR	MAY	JUN	JUL	AUG	SEP	OCT	NOV	DEC	YEAR
Mean Maximum Temp. (°F)	34.6	37.3	45.6	56.4	67.6	77.2	82.8	80.8	72.3	60.8	50.3	39.0	58.7
Mean Temp. (°F)	26.5	28.9	37.1	47.0	57.6	66.8	72.5	70.8	62.5	51.8	42.4	31.3	49.6
Mean Minimum Temp. (°F)	18.4	20.4	28.6	37.5	47.5	56.4	62.3	60.8	52.7	42.6	34.5	23.5	40.4
Extreme Maximum Temp. (°F)	67	68	82	93	94	97	99	105	95	85	80	70	105
Extreme Minimum Temp. (°F)	-12	-11	2	18	29	39	45	39	30	23	7	-10	-12
Days Maximum Temp. ≥ 90°F	0	0	0	0	1	2	6	4	1	0	0	0	14
Days Maximum Temp. ≤ 32°F	13	9	2	0	0	0	0	0	0	0	1	8	33
Days Minimum Temp. ≤ 32°F	28	25	20	7	0	0	0	0	0	4	13	26	123
Days Minimum Temp. ≤ 0°F	2	1	0	0	0	0	0	0	0	0	0	1	4
Heating Degree Days (base 65°F)	1,186	1,014	857	538	251	57	8	16	127	408	671	1,040	6,173
Cooling Degree Days (base 65°F)	0	0	0	2	29	125	256	213	63	4	0	0	692
Mean Precipitation (in.)	3.91	3.48	4.13	4.29	3.74	3.29	3.34	4.22	3.81	3.85	4.76	4.49	47.31
Days With ≥ 0.1" Precipitation	6	6	7	7	8	7	6	6	6	7	7	7	80
Days With ≥ 1.0" Precipitation	1	1	1	1	1	1	1	1	1	1	1	1	12
Mean Snowfall (in.)	13.9	12.0	7.6	1.5	trace	0.0	0.0	0.0	0.0	trace	2.1	8.7	45.8
Days With ≥ 1.0" Snow Depth	17	15	8	1	0	0	0	0	0	0	0	2	9	52

Plymouth-Kingston *Plymouth County*   Elevation: 42 ft.   Latitude: 41° 59' N   Longitude: 70° 42' W

	JAN	FEB	MAR	APR	MAY	JUN	JUL	AUG	SEP	OCT	NOV	DEC	YEAR
Mean Maximum Temp. (°F)	37.6	39.7	46.9	56.1	66.9	76.2	82.1	80.0	72.8	62.8	52.9	42.9	59.7
Mean Temp. (°F)	27.5	29.3	36.7	45.8	56.0	65.5	71.6	70.0	62.4	52.1	43.1	33.3	49.4
Mean Minimum Temp. (°F)	17.4	18.8	26.5	35.4	45.1	54.7	61.0	59.9	51.9	41.4	33.1	23.6	39.1
Extreme Maximum Temp. (°F)	67	69	85	91	95	98	101	99	95	85	78	77	101
Extreme Minimum Temp. (°F)	-19	-15	0	16	25	35	42	41	32	22	3	-14	-19
Days Maximum Temp. ≥ 90°F	0	0	0	0	0	2	4	2	1	0	0	0	9
Days Maximum Temp. ≤ 32°F	9	7	1	0	0	0	0	0	0	0	0	4	21
Days Minimum Temp. ≤ 32°F	28	25	23	11	2	0	0	0	0	5	16	25	135
Days Minimum Temp. ≤ 0°F	2	2	0	0	0	0	0	0	0	0	0	1	5
Heating Degree Days (base 65°F)	1,155	1,002	870	572	287	74	10	20	127	398	652	977	6,144
Cooling Degree Days (base 65°F)	0	0	0	1	16	99	229	184	57	6	0	0	592
Mean Precipitation (in.)	4.68	4.12	4.71	4.42	3.72	3.56	3.28	4.08	4.56	4.24	4.79	4.50	50.66
Days With ≥ 0.1" Precipitation	8	7	8	7	8	6	6	6	6	7	7	8	84
Days With ≥ 1.0" Precipitation	1	1	1	1	1	1	1	1	1	1	1	1	12
Mean Snowfall (in.)	13.2	10.6	5.9	1.3	trace	0.0	0.0	0.0	0.0	trace	1.1	4.9	37.0
Days With ≥ 1.0" Snow Depth	12	10	4	1	0	0	0	0	0	0	1	5	33

Reading *Middlesex County*   Elevation: 88 ft.   Latitude: 42° 31' N   Longitude: 71° 08' W

	JAN	FEB	MAR	APR	MAY	JUN	JUL	AUG	SEP	OCT	NOV	DEC	YEAR
Mean Maximum Temp. (°F)	35.0	38.0	46.4	57.7	68.8	77.0	82.6	80.6	72.4	61.8	50.9	39.8	59.3
Mean Temp. (°F)	25.2	28.0	36.2	46.4	57.0	65.7	71.5	69.8	61.4	50.4	41.1	30.7	48.6
Mean Minimum Temp. (°F)	15.4	17.9	25.9	35.0	45.1	54.5	60.3	58.9	50.4	39.0	31.1	21.5	37.9
Extreme Maximum Temp. (°F)	66	72	92	93	94	96	99	105	95	87	80	78	105
Extreme Minimum Temp. (°F)	-19	-13	-4	15	26	36	42	39	30	17	-2	-14	-19
Days Maximum Temp. ≥ 90°F	0	0	0	0	1	2	5	3	1	0	0	0	12
Days Maximum Temp. ≤ 32°F	13	8	2	0	0	0	0	0	0	0	1	7	31
Days Minimum Temp. ≤ 32°F	29	26	24	12	1	0	0	0	0	8	18	27	145
Days Minimum Temp. ≤ 0°F	4	2	0	0	0	0	0	0	0	0	0	1	7
Heating Degree Days (base 65°F)	1,226	1,040	888	554	265	72	10	22	151	447	712	1,057	6,444
Cooling Degree Days (base 65°F)	0	0	1	2	23	100	217	177	52	3	0	0	575
Mean Precipitation (in.)	4.27	3.62	4.38	4.05	3.87	3.62	3.57	3.66	3.78	4.34	4.57	4.38	48.11
Days With ≥ 0.1" Precipitation	8	6	8	7	8	7	6	6	6	7	7	7	83
Days With ≥ 1.0" Precipitation	1	1	1	1	1	1	1	1	1	1	1	1	12
Mean Snowfall (in.)	16.3	12.8	11.1	3.3	0.3	0.0	0.0	0.0	0.0	0.1	3.1	11.8	58.8
Days With ≥ 1.0" Snow Depth	20	17	11	1	0	0	0	0	0	0	3	11	63

Rochester *Plymouth County*   Elevation: 59 ft.   Latitude: 41° 47' N   Longitude: 70° 55' W

	JAN	FEB	MAR	APR	MAY	JUN	JUL	AUG	SEP	OCT	NOV	DEC	YEAR
Mean Maximum Temp. (°F)	37.3	39.2	46.8	56.6	67.6	76.7	82.4	80.9	73.3	62.8	52.7	42.4	59.9
Mean Temp. (°F)	27.7	29.6	37.6	46.9	57.2	66.3	72.1	70.7	62.9	52.2	43.5	33.6	50.0
Mean Minimum Temp. (°F)	18.1	20.0	28.3	37.1	46.8	55.8	61.7	60.6	52.5	41.6	34.3	24.7	40.1
Extreme Maximum Temp. (°F)	67	68	82	92	97	99	102	100	97	86	77	75	102
Extreme Minimum Temp. (°F)	-12	-7	4	11	30	35	44	42	31	20	8	-8	-12
Days Maximum Temp. ≥ 90°F	0	0	0	0	0	2	4	2	1	0	0	0	9
Days Maximum Temp. ≤ 32°F	10	7	1	0	0	0	0	0	0	0	0	5	23
Days Minimum Temp. ≤ 32°F	28	25	22	8	0	0	0	0	0	5	15	25	128
Days Minimum Temp. ≤ 0°F	2	1	0	0	0	0	0	0	0	0	0	0	3
Heating Degree Days (base 65°F)	1,148	993	843	537	253	58	7	13	117	395	638	968	5,970
Cooling Degree Days (base 65°F)	0	0	0	1	21	114	247	204	67	6	0	0	660
Mean Precipitation (in.)	4.39	3.48	4.41	4.47	3.60	3.79	3.65	4.39	4.12	3.99	4.67	4.68	49.64
Days With ≥ 0.1" Precipitation	7	6	7	7	7	6	6	6	6	7	7	8	80
Days With ≥ 1.0" Precipitation	1	1	1	1	1	1	1	1	2	1	1	1	13
Mean Snowfall (in.)	na	7.5	3.2	0.9	trace	0.0	0.0	0.0	0.0	trace	0.9	4.9	na
Days With ≥ 1.0" Snow Depth	12	11	4	0	0	0	0	0	0	0	0	5	32

Taunton *Bristol County*   Elevation: 19 ft.   Latitude: 41° 54' N   Longitude: 71° 04' W

	JAN	FEB	MAR	APR	MAY	JUN	JUL	AUG	SEP	OCT	NOV	DEC	YEAR
Mean Maximum Temp. (°F)	37.0	39.3	47.5	58.4	69.5	78.0	83.3	81.5	73.6	62.5	52.2	41.5	60.4
Mean Temp. (°F)	27.0	29.3	37.3	47.0	57.4	66.3	71.8	70.4	62.2	50.9	42.2	32.1	49.5
Mean Minimum Temp. (°F)	17.0	19.3	27.1	35.5	45.3	54.5	60.2	59.2	50.6	39.3	32.2	22.7	38.6
Extreme Maximum Temp. (°F)	65	69	86	94	96	96	100	102	97	85	78	76	102
Extreme Minimum Temp. (°F)	-20	-13	-2	14	23	33	40	36	28	18	5	-13	-20
Days Maximum Temp. ≥ 90°F	0	0	0	0	1	2	5	3	0	0	0	0	11
Days Maximum Temp. ≤ 32°F	10	7	1	0	0	0	0	0	0	0	0	5	23
Days Minimum Temp. ≤ 32°F	29	25	23	11	1	0	0	0	1	8	18	27	143
Days Minimum Temp. ≤ 0°F	2	1	0	0	0	0	0	0	0	0	0	0	3
Heating Degree Days (base 65°F)	1,171	1,001	852	537	250	61	9	18	138	433	678	1,013	6,161
Cooling Degree Days (base 65°F)	0	0	0	1	20	113	233	200	62	4	0	0	633
Mean Precipitation (in.)	4.19	3.68	4.40	4.01	3.88	3.41	3.87	4.06	3.97	4.00	4.52	4.22	48.21
Days With ≥ 0.1" Precipitation	7	6	7	7	7	6	6	7	6	6	7	8	80
Days With ≥ 1.0" Precipitation	1	1	1	1	1	1	1	1	1	1	1	1	12
Mean Snowfall (in.)	10.3	9.2	4.7	1.5	trace	0.0	0.0	0.0	0.0	0.1	1.3	6.1	33.2
Days With ≥ 1.0" Snow Depth	13	11	5	1	0	0	0	0	0	0	0	6	36

Tully Lake *Worcester County*   Elevation: 688 ft.   Latitude: 42° 38' N   Longitude: 72° 13' W

	JAN	FEB	MAR	APR	MAY	JUN	JUL	AUG	SEP	OCT	NOV	DEC	YEAR
Mean Maximum Temp. (°F)	*30.1*	34.0	*43.4*	56.3	69.2	77.6	82.6	80.3	71.3	*59.4*	*46.9*	*34.4*	*57.1*
Mean Temp. (°F)	*19.1*	22.3	*32.4*	44.3	56.0	64.8	69.9	67.8	59.1	*47.6*	*37.6*	*25.4*	*45.5*
Mean Minimum Temp. (°F)	*7.9*	10.6	*21.5*	32.2	42.8	52.0	57.1	55.3	46.8	*35.7*	*28.3*	*16.2*	*33.9*
Extreme Maximum Temp. (°F)	60	64	83	94	95	98	99	99	93	82	76	66	99
Extreme Minimum Temp. (°F)	-27	-24	-9	12	25	34	40	34	29	18	0	-22	-27
Days Maximum Temp. ≥ 90°F	0	0	0	0	1	2	5	3	0	0	0	0	11
Days Maximum Temp. ≤ 32°F	16	11	3	0	0	0	0	0	0	0	1	10	41
Days Minimum Temp. ≤ 32°F	28	25	26	17	3	0	0	0	1	12	19	26	157
Days Minimum Temp. ≤ 0°F	8	6	1	0	0	0	0	0	0	0	0	3	18
Heating Degree Days (base 65°F)	*1,418*	1,201	*1,002*	616	290	83	18	39	204	*535*	*814*	*1,223*	*7,443*
Cooling Degree Days (base 65°F)	*0*	*0*	*0*	1	16	86	180	136	36	*2*	na	na	na
Mean Precipitation (in.)	3.82	2.94	3.77	3.72	3.91	3.85	4.20	4.29	3.78	3.85	4.04	3.59	45.76
Days With ≥ 0.1" Precipitation	7	6	7	7	8	7	7	7	6	7	8	7	84
Days With ≥ 1.0" Precipitation	1	1	1	1	1	1	1	1	1	1	1	1	12
Mean Snowfall (in.)	15.9	11.0	9.3	2.9	trace	0.0	0.0	0.0	0.0	trace	2.8	11.2	53.1
Days With ≥ 1.0" Snow Depth	23	22	17	2	0	0	0	0	0	0	3	15	82

Walpole 2 *Norfolk County*   Elevation: 164 ft.   Latitude: 42° 10' N   Longitude: 71° 15' W

	JAN	FEB	MAR	APR	MAY	JUN	JUL	AUG	SEP	OCT	NOV	DEC	YEAR
Mean Maximum Temp. (°F)	36.1	38.9	47.3	58.6	69.9	77.7	82.9	80.7	72.4	61.6	51.5	40.8	59.9
Mean Temp. (°F)	27.0	29.4	37.5	47.8	58.4	66.9	72.5	70.7	62.3	51.3	42.3	32.1	49.9
Mean Minimum Temp. (°F)	17.9	19.9	27.6	37.0	46.9	56.1	62.0	60.7	52.1	40.9	33.0	23.4	39.8
Extreme Maximum Temp. (°F)	66	70	90	96	95	97	101	102	97	86	78	76	102
Extreme Minimum Temp. (°F)	-19	-16	-4	14	28	37	42	39	32	20	4	-14	-19
Days Maximum Temp. ≥ 90°F	0	0	0	0	1	2	4	2	0	0	0	0	9
Days Maximum Temp. ≤ 32°F	11	7	2	0	0	0	0	0	0	0	0	6	26
Days Minimum Temp. ≤ 32°F	28	25	22	9	1	0	0	0	0	6	16	26	133
Days Minimum Temp. ≤ 0°F	2	1	0	0	0	0	0	0	0	0	0	1	4
Heating Degree Days (base 65°F)	1,171	998	848	513	227	53	6	16	133	421	675	1,012	6,073
Cooling Degree Days (base 65°F)	0	0	1	2	26	119	248	200	62	3	0	0	661
Mean Precipitation (in.)	4.42	3.32	4.00	4.15	3.29	3.28	3.70	4.16	3.82	4.07	4.28	4.21	46.70
Days With ≥ 0.1" Precipitation	7	6	7	6	7	6	6	7	6	6	7	7	78
Days With ≥ 1.0" Precipitation	1	1	1	1	1	1	1	1	1	1	1	1	12
Mean Snowfall (in.)	13.0	11.2	7.7	2.9	0.3	0.0	0.0	0.0	0.0	0.1	2.5	8.8	46.5
Days With ≥ 1.0" Snow Depth	17	14	9	1	0	0	0	0	0	0	2	9	52

West Medway *Norfolk County*   Elevation: 209 ft.   Latitude: 42° 08' N   Longitude: 71° 26' W

	JAN	FEB	MAR	APR	MAY	JUN	JUL	AUG	SEP	OCT	NOV	DEC	YEAR
Mean Maximum Temp. (°F)	36.6	39.4	47.6	58.5	69.8	78.4	84.0	82.3	74.4	63.7	52.5	41.3	60.7
Mean Temp. (°F)	24.7	27.4	36.0	46.3	56.9	65.8	71.4	69.6	61.0	49.8	40.9	30.5	48.4
Mean Minimum Temp. (°F)	12.8	15.5	24.5	34.1	44.0	53.2	58.8	56.8	47.6	36.0	29.2	19.7	36.0
Extreme Maximum Temp. (°F)	67	70	87	94	97	97	102	104	96	88	82	76	104
Extreme Minimum Temp. (°F)	-23	-20	-6	15	25	34	38	33	26	15	-2	-16	-23
Days Maximum Temp. ≥ 90°F	0	0	0	0	1	2	6	4	1	0	0	0	14
Days Maximum Temp. ≤ 32°F	11	7	1	0	0	0	0	0	0	0	0	6	25
Days Minimum Temp. ≤ 32°F	30	27	26	13	2	0	0	0	2	13	21	28	162
Days Minimum Temp. ≤ 0°F	5	3	0	0	0	0	0	0	0	0	0	1	9
Heating Degree Days (base 65°F)	1,242	1,054	891	556	263	71	12	25	162	467	717	1,062	6,522
Cooling Degree Days (base 65°F)	0	0	0	1	20	106	222	175	51	3	0	0	578
Mean Precipitation (in.)	4.42	3.47	4.08	4.35	3.60	3.74	3.58	4.27	4.07	4.29	4.62	4.08	48.57
Days With ≥ 0.1" Precipitation	7	6	7	6	7	6	6	6	6	6	7	7	77
Days With ≥ 1.0" Precipitation	1	1	1	1	1	1	1	1	1	1	1	1	12
Mean Snowfall (in.)	12.4	9.7	6.9	2.5	0.2	0.0	0.0	0.0	0.0	trace	1.8	7.9	41.4
Days With ≥ 1.0" Snow Depth	16	13	7	1	0	0	0	0	0	0	2	9	48

Note: See Appendix D for explanation of data.

MICHIGAN

PHYSICAL FEATURES. Michigan is located in the heart of the Great Lakes region and is composed of two large peninsulas. Many smaller peninsulas jut from these two peninsulas into the world's largest bodies of fresh water to give most of Michigan a quasi-marine type climate in spite of its midcontinent location.

The Upper Peninsula is long and narrow, lying primarily between 45° and 47° N. latitude. It averages only 75 miles in width and extends from Northern Wisconsin eastward over 300 miles into Northern Lake Huron. Lake Superior lies to the north while the northern portion of Lake Michigan forms the boundary to the southeast. Isle Royale, separated from the mainland, is located in Lake Superior about 50 miles northwest of the tip of the Keweenaw Peninsula. The Lower Peninsula, shaped like a mitten and occupying about 70 percent of Michigan's total land area, extends northward nearly 300 miles from the Indiana and Ohio border or about 42° N. latitude to the eastern end of the Upper Peninsula. Lake Michigan extends the entire length of the Lower Peninsula on the west while Lakes Huron, St. Clair and Erie form the eastern boundary. The total coastline for the state exceeds 3,100 miles. In addition, Michigan has over 11,000 smaller lakes with a total surface area of over 1,000 square miles. These lakes are scattered throughout 81 of the 83 counties while more than 36,000 miles of streams wind their way across the state.

While latitude, by determining the amount of solar insolation, is the major climatic control, the Great Lakes and variations in elevation play an important role in the amelioration of Michigan's climate. Because of its mid-latitude location, prevailing winds are from a westerly direction. During the summer months winds are predominantly from the southwest when the semi-permanent Bermuda High Pressure Center is located over the southeastern United States. During the winter months the prevailing winds are west to northwest, but change quite frequently for short periods as migrating cyclones and anticyclones move through the area.

The eastern half of the Upper Peninsula varies from level to gently rolling hills with elevation generally between 600 and 1,000 feet above sea level. The western tablelands rise to elevations generally between 1,400 and 1,600 feet with Porcupine Mountain, the State's highest point, 2,023 feet, located in Ontonagan County overlooking Lake Superior. The rugged hills extend northeastward from Ontonagan County through the center of the Keweenaw Peninsula and play an important role in the larger precipitation amounts received in this area.

The Lower Peninsula features range from quite level terrain in the southeast to gently rolling hills in the southwest with elevations generally between 800 and 1,000 feet. A series of sand dunes along the Lake Michigan shoreline rise to heights of nearly 400 feet above the lake level. These are the result of the prevailing westerly winds which blow across the lake. Tablelands cover the northern part of the Lower Peninsula and reach a maximum elevation of 1,700 feet in Osecola County near Cadillac. In the northwestern section of the Lower Peninsula a number of finger-like peninsulas extend into Grand Traverse Bay and Lake Michigan.

GENERAL CLIMATE. The lake effect imparts many interesting departures to Michigan's climate which one would not ordinarily expect to find at a midcontinental location. Because of the lake waters' slow response to temperature changes and the dominating westerly winds, the arrival of both summer and winter are retarded. In the spring, the cooler temperatures slow the development of vegetation until the danger of frost is past. In the fall, the warmer lake waters temper the first outbreaks of cold air allowing additional time for crops to mature. With the first cold air outbreaks in the fall, Michigan experiences a considerable increase in cloudiness. When cold air passes over the warmer lake water, a shallow layer of unstable, moisture-laden air develops in the lower levels of the atmosphere. This air, when forced to rise, produces the increased cloudiness and frequent snow flurry activity observed in the fall and early winter months.

On warm, summer days when prevailing winds are generally light, the lake's shore area frequently develops a localized wind pattern which may extend inland for only a few miles. This is frequently referred to as the "lake breeze." It develops when the much warmer air over the land masses begins to rise, allowing the cooler air over the lakes to move inland. At night this pattern may be reversed creating what is known as a "land breeze". A wind of this type may also be observed, but on a much smaller scale, along the shores of the larger inland lakes.

The length of Michigan's growing season or freeze-free period does not decrease in the normal manner from south to north. Instead, isolines for the length of the growing season follow closely the contours of the lake shores. The shortest average growing season, about 60 days, occurs in the interior section of the Western Upper Peninsula. The growing season increases to between 140 and 160 days, as one goes towards the lake shores. A similar pattern exists in the Lower Peninsula where the growing season in the northern tablelands averages only 70 days, but increases rapidly to 140 days near the lakes. Michigan's maximum average growing season, 170 days, is found in the southwest and southeastern corners of the state.

PRECIPITATION. Michigan averages about 31 inches of precipitation per year. About 55-60 percent of the annual total is recorded during the normal growing season. Summer precipitation falls primarily in the form of showers or thunderstorms, while a more steady type of precipitation of lighter intensity dominates the winter months. The annual number of thunderstorms observed decreases from about 40 in the south to around 25 in the Upper Peninsula area with nearly 50 percent of these recorded during the summer months, June through August.

The frequency of floods is quite low in Michigan with the greatest likelihood occurring in late winter or early spring when sudden warming and rain may be combined with snowmelt. Mild meteorological drought conditions are not uncommon in Michigan, but meteorological droughts reaching severe conditions are infrequent and generally of short duration. The normally even distribution of precipitation and higher humidities observed in Michigan are helpful in reducing the high demands for moisture.

SNOWFALL. Michigan receives some of the heaviest snowfall totals east of the Rockies except for isolated points in the New England States. The maximum average annual snowfall amounts of over 170 inches are located along the escarpment which rises abruptly to an elevation of over 1,400 feet above Lake Superior, at the western end of the Upper Peninsula. Another area with amounts exceeding 120 inches is centered in the western section of the tableland region of the Lower Peninsula. The prevailing westerlies, passing over the Great Lakes, become moisture laden in the lower levels and when forced upward by the land masses, drop much of their excessive moisture in the form of snow squalls in these areas.

STORMS. Damaging or dangerous storms do not occur as frequently in Michigan as in the states to the south and west. Recorded tornado occurrences have averaged four per year. About 90 percent of these tornadoes occurred in the southern one-half of the Lower Peninsula. Damaging wind storms and blizzards are not as frequent but do cause considerable damage from time to time. Hail is most frequently observed in the spring months. A higher frequency of hail is noted in the fall months over the northwestern section of the Lower Peninsula. This is attributed mainly to the strong lake influence in this region.

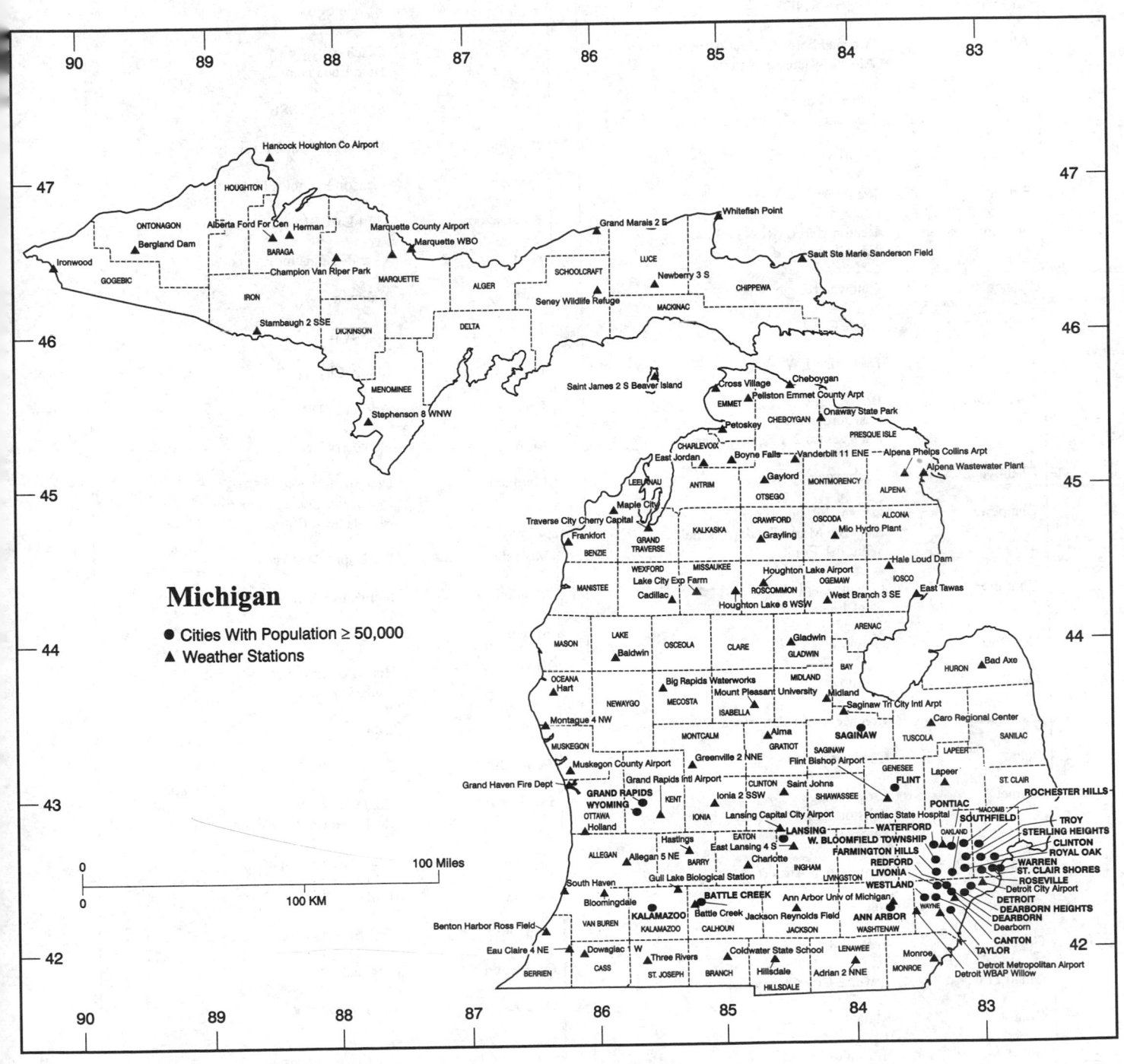

Michigan

● Cities With Population ≥ 50,000
▲ Weather Stations

Michigan Weather Stations by County

County	Station Name	County	Station Name
Alger	Grand Marais 2 E	Ingham	East Lansing 4 S
Allegan	Allegan 5 NE	Ionia	Ionia 2 SSW
Alpena	Alpena Phelps Collins Airport Alpena Wastewater Plant	Iosco	East Tawas Hale Loud Dam
Baraga	Alberta Ford Herman	Iron	Stambaugh 2 SSE
Barry	Hastings	Isabella	Mount Pleasant University
Benzie	Frankfort	Jackson	Jackson Reynolds Field
Berrien	Benton Harbor Ross Field Eau Claire 4 NE	Kalamazoo	Gull Lake Biological Station
Branch	Coldwater State School	Kent	Grand Rapids Int'l Airport
Calhoun	Battle Creek	Lake	Baldwin
Cass	Dowagiac 1 W	Lapeer	Lapeer WWTP
Charlevoix	Boyne Falls East Jordan Saint James 2 S Beaver Island	Leelanau	Maple City
Cheboygan	Cheboygan	Lenawee	Adrian 2 NNE
Chippewa	Detour Village Sault Ste Marie Sanderson Field Whitefish Point	Luce	Newberry 3 S
Clinton	Lansing Capital City Airport Saint Johns	Marquette	Champion Van Riper Park Marquette County Airport Marquette WBO
Crawford	Grayling	Mecosta	Big Rapids Waterworks
Delta	Fayette 4 SW	Menominee	Stephenson 8 WNW
Dickinson	Iron Mountain-Kingsford WWTP	Midland	Midland
Eaton	Charlotte	Missaukee	Houghton Lake 6 WSW Lake City Exp. Farm
Emmet	Cross Village Pellston Emmet County Airport Petoskey	Monroe	Monroe
Genesee	Flint Bishop Airport	Montcalm	Greenville 2 NNE
Gladwin	Gladwin	Muskegon	Montague 4 NW Muskegon County Airport
Gogebic	Ironwood	Oakland	Pontiac State Hospital
Grand Traverse	Traverse City Cherry Capital	Oceana	Hart
Gratiot	Alma	Ogemaw	West Branch 3 SE
Hillsdale	Hillsdale	Ontonagon	Bergland Dam
Houghton	Hancock Houghton Co. Airport	Oscoda	Mio Hydro Plant
Huron	Bad Axe Harbor Beach 1 SSE	Otsego	Gaylord Vanderbilt 11 ENE
		Ottawa	Grand Haven Fire Dept. Holland

County	Station Name
Presque Isle	Onaway State Park
Roscommon	Houghton Lake Airport
Saginaw	Saginaw Tri City Int'l Airport
Schoolcraft	Seney Wildlife Refuge
St. Clair	Port Huron
St. Joseph	Three Rivers
Tuscola	Caro Regional Center
Van Buren	Bloomingdale South Haven
Washtenaw	Ann Arbor Univ. of Michigan
Wayne	Dearborn Detroit City Airport Detroit Metropolitan Airport Detroit WBAP Willow Grosse Pointe Farms
Wexford	Cadillac

Michigan Weather Stations by City

City	Station Name	Miles
Ann Arbor	Ann Arbor Univ. of Michigan	2
	Detroit WBAP Willow	11
Battle Creek	Battle Creek	2
	Gull Lake Biological Station	11
Canton	Ann Arbor Univ. of Michigan	13
	Dearborn	12
	Detroit Metropolitan Airport	9
	Detroit WBAP Willow	7
Clinton	Detroit City Airport	12
	Grosse Pointe Farms	14
	Pontiac State Hospital	20
Dearborn	Dearborn	1
	Detroit City Airport	12
	Detroit Metropolitan Airport	10
	Grosse Pointe Farms	17
	Detroit WBAP Willow	17
Dearborn Heights	Dearborn	3
	Detroit City Airport	14
	Detroit Metropolitan Airport	9
	Grosse Pointe Farms	19
	Detroit WBAP Willow	15
Detroit	Dearborn	8
	Detroit City Airport	5
	Detroit Metropolitan Airport	17
	Grosse Pointe Farms	11
Farmington Hills	Dearborn	14
	Detroit City Airport	19
	Detroit Metropolitan Airport	19
	Pontiac State Hospital	12
	Detroit WBAP Willow	19
Flint	Flint Bishop Airport	5
Grand Rapids	Grand Rapids Int'l Airport	9
Kalamazoo	Battle Creek	18
	Gull Lake Biological Station	14
Lansing	Charlotte	18
	East Lansing 4 S	5
	Lansing Capital City Airport	5
Livonia	Ann Arbor Univ. of Michigan	19
	Dearborn	9
	Detroit City Airport	18
	Detroit Metropolitan Airport	12
	Pontiac State Hospital	18
	Detroit WBAP Willow	14
Pontiac	Pontiac State Hospital	1
Redford	Dearborn	6
	Detroit City Airport	14
	Detroit Metropolitan Airport	13
	Pontiac State Hospital	18
	Detroit WBAP Willow	17

City	Station Name	Miles
Rochester Hills	Detroit City Airport	19
	Pontiac State Hospital	7
Roseville	Dearborn	20
	Detroit City Airport	7
	Grosse Pointe Farms	9
Royal Oak	Dearborn	14
	Detroit City Airport	9
	Grosse Pointe Farms	15
	Pontiac State Hospital	12
Saginaw	Midland	19
	Saginaw Tri City Int'l Airport	10
Shelby	Detroit City Airport	17
	Pontiac State Hospital	13
Southfield	Dearborn	11
	Detroit City Airport	13
	Detroit Metropolitan Airport	19
	Grosse Pointe Farms	19
	Pontiac State Hospital	12
St. Clair Shores	Detroit City Airport	8
	Grosse Pointe Farms	8
Sterling Heights	Detroit City Airport	11
	Grosse Pointe Farms	15
	Pontiac State Hospital	15
Taylor	Dearborn	6
	Detroit City Airport	18
	Detroit Metropolitan Airport	4
	Detroit WBAP Willow	14
Troy	Dearborn	19
	Detroit City Airport	13
	Grosse Pointe Farms	18
	Pontiac State Hospital	9
Warren	Dearborn	16
	Detroit City Airport	5
	Grosse Pointe Farms	10
	Pontiac State Hospital	18
Waterford	Pontiac State Hospital	4
W. Bloomfield Twp.	Dearborn	19
	Pontiac State Hospital	7
Westland	Ann Arbor Univ. of Michigan	17
	Dearborn	8
	Detroit City Airport	20
	Detroit Metropolitan Airport	7
	Detroit WBAP Willow	10
Wyoming	Grand Rapids Int'l Airport	9

Note: Miles is the distance between the geographic center of the city and the weather station.

Michigan Weather Stations by Elevation

Feet	Station Name
1,738	Herman
1,564	Champion Van Riper Park
1,558	Stambaugh 2 SSE
1,427	Ironwood
1,414	Marquette County Airport
1,348	Gaylord
1,309	Alberta Ford
1,299	Bergland Dam
1,292	Cadillac
1,240	Lake City Exp. Farm
1,148	Houghton Lake Airport
1,138	Grayling
1,131	Houghton Lake 6 WSW
1,079	Hillsdale
1,072	Hancock Houghton Co. Airport
1,059	Iron Mountain-Kingsford WWTP
997	Jackson Reynolds Field
980	Coldwater State School
980	Pontiac State Hospital
958	Mio Hydro Plant
954	Battle Creek
928	Big Rapids Waterworks
921	Vanderbilt 11 ENE
908	Gull Lake Biological Station
898	Ann Arbor Univ. of Michigan
898	Charlotte
882	West Branch 3 SE
879	East Lansing 4 S
879	Greenville 2 NNE
869	Eau Claire 4 NE
849	Newberry 3 S
839	Lansing Capital City Airport
833	Baldwin
816	Hastings
816	Lapeer WWTP
813	Hale Loud Dam
807	Three Rivers
803	Ionia 2 SSW
793	Mount Pleasant University
784	Grand Rapids Int'l Airport
777	Detroit WBAP Willow
774	Gladwin
764	Flint Bishop Airport
757	Adrian 2 NNE
757	Alma
748	Allegan 5 NE
744	Fayette 4 SW
741	Cross Village
741	Saint Johns
738	Dowagiac 1 W
734	Boyne Falls
728	Maple City
725	Bloomingdale
718	Frankfort
715	Sault Ste Marie Sanderson Field

Feet	Station Name
711	Bad Axe
711	Pellston Emmet County Airport
708	Seney Wildlife Refuge
708	Stephenson 8 WNW
698	Hart
688	Alpena Phelps Collins Airport
688	Onaway State Park
675	Marquette WBO
669	Caro Regional Center
669	Saint James 2 S Beaver Island
659	Saginaw Tri City Int'l Airport
649	Montague 4 NW
639	Midland
629	Detroit Metropolitan Airport
626	Benton Harbor Ross Field
623	Detroit City Airport
623	Grand Marais 2 E
623	Muskegon County Airport
620	Grand Haven Fire Dept.
620	South Haven
620	Traverse City Cherry Capital
610	Grosse Pointe Farms
606	Holland
606	Petoskey
603	Dearborn
603	Whitefish Point
597	Harbor Beach 1 SSE
593	Detour Village
587	Alpena Wastewater Plant
587	Cheboygan
587	East Jordan
587	Monroe
587	Port Huron
583	East Tawas

Alpena Phelps Collins Airport

The city of Alpena lies on the northwest shore of Thunder Bay, eight miles from the open waters of Lake Huron. Lake Huron and Thunder Bay lie at an elevation of 580 feet above sea level. Generally, the land slopes up westward from the lakeshore to 689 feet at the airport. Farther to the west and southwest the land becomes higher and more rolling. A range of hills with tops 1,000 to 1,350 feet lies northwest to southeast about 25 miles southwest of the station.

Summer showers moving from the southwest weaken and sometimes dissipate as they approach Alpena. Winter storms often bring winds with an easterly component. Precipitation from these is increased by moisture and instability picked up from Lake Huron and by forced upslope flow.

The normal wintertime storm track is south of the city, and most passing storms bring snow. Rain, freezing rain, and sleet are uncommon, but not unknown, in winter. In summer, most storms pass to the north, often bringing brief showers to the area, but occasionally, heavy thunderstorms with damaging winds occur. The Great Lakes modify most climatic extremes. Precipitation amounts are distributed evenly throughout the year. The lake effect is most pronounced in early winter, before ice forms. Minimum temperatures during this season are higher than would be expected at this latitude.

Summers in Alpena are warm and sunny. Brief showers usually occur every few days, often falling on only part of the area. Hailstorms average less than one a year. During prolonged heat waves the highest temperatures in Michigan often occur in the forest area southwest of Alpena. Winter months are cloudy and marked by frequent snow flurries. Storms bring heavier snowfall. Snow cover is sufficiently deep and persistent to provide good protection for grasses and winter grains.

The climate along the immediate Lake Huron shore is semi-maritime and lacks the temperature extremes experienced just a few miles inland. Maximum temperatures near the lake shore average 1.6 degrees lower than those at the airport, minimum temperatures average five degrees higher. Afternoon lake breezes which are strongest in the late spring and early summer cause lake shore maximum temperatures to average 3.6 degrees lower during the month of May.

Freezing temperatures have occurred as late as late June and as early as late August. Principal crops in the area are hay, potatoes, berries, and apples.

Prevailing winds are from the northwest except during May and June when southeast winds predominate. Southeast winds are common in the afternoon during all the summer months.

Alpena Phelps Collins Airport *Alpena County*   Elevation: 688 ft.   Latitude: 45° 04' N   Longitude: 83° 35' W

	JAN	FEB	MAR	APR	MAY	JUN	JUL	AUG	SEP	OCT	NOV	DEC	YEAR
Mean Maximum Temp. (°F)	26.6	28.9	37.9	51.6	65.2	74.7	79.9	77.1	68.3	56.3	42.7	31.9	53.4
Mean Temp. (°F)	18.2	19.4	28.4	41.1	52.7	61.8	67.4	65.2	57.1	46.4	35.3	24.8	43.2
Mean Minimum Temp. (°F)	9.8	9.9	18.7	30.5	40.2	48.9	54.9	53.4	45.9	36.4	27.8	17.8	32.8
Extreme Maximum Temp. (°F)	52	65	76	90	93	103	102	102	94	88	76	65	103
Extreme Minimum Temp. (°F)	-28	-37	-17	5	23	29	35	30	25	16	-6	-18	-37
Days Maximum Temp. ≥ 90°F	0	0	0	0	0	2	3	1	0	0	0	0	6
Days Maximum Temp. ≤ 32°F	22	18	9	1	0	0	0	0	0	0	4	15	69
Days Minimum Temp. ≤ 32°F	30	27	28	18	6	0	0	0	2	11	22	29	173
Days Minimum Temp. ≤ 0°F	8	7	3	0	0	0	0	0	0	0	0	3	21
Heating Degree Days (base 65°F)	1,445	1,281	1,129	715	388	145	42	74	253	571	885	1,239	8,167
Cooling Degree Days (base 65°F)	0	0	0	0	3	14	57	130	91	22	1	0	318
Mean Precipitation (in.)	1.77	1.29	2.17	2.32	2.55	2.50	3.27	3.49	2.84	2.35	2.05	1.92	28.52
Maximum Precipitation (in.)	3.3	3.2	4.4	4.1	8.3	8.4	7.2	6.3	7.1	6.5	7.4	4.4	35.2
Minimum Precipitation (in.)	0.2	0.1	0.3	1.2	1.0	0.2	0.2	0.9	0.3	0.6	0.6	0.4	21.4
Maximum 24-hr. Precipitation (in.)	1.8	1.0	1.5	1.1	2.2	2.5	2.8	2.6	3.0	1.8	1.8	1.6	3.0
Days With ≥ 0.1" Precipitation	5	4	5	6	6	6	6	7	6	6	6	5	68
Days With ≥ 1.0" Precipitation	0	0	0	0	0	0	1	1	1	0	0	0	3
Mean Snowfall (in.)	22.3	16.0	13.6	5.7	0.3	0.0	trace	trace	trace	0.4	8.6	20.2	87.1
Maximum Snowfall (in.)	44	33	36	13	4	0	0	0	trace	4	35	46	146
Maximum 24-hr. Snowfall (in.)	16	11	17	11	4	0	0	0	trace	2	15	16	17
Days With ≥ 1.0" Snow Depth	30	27	22	5	0	0	0	0	0	0	7	21	112
Thunderstorm Days	< 1	< 1	1	2	4	5	7	6	4	1	< 1	< 1	30
Foggy Days	10	9	13	12	13	14	14	17	16	14	14	12	158
Predominant Sky Cover	OVR	OVR	OVR	OVR	OVR	OVR	OVR	OVR	OVR	OVR	OVR	OVR	OVR
Mean Relative Humidity 7am (%)	81	80	82	80	78	81	85	90	91	86	84	83	83
Mean Relative Humidity 4pm (%)	67	62	59	53	51	53	54	59	61	62	68	72	60
Mean Dewpoint (°F)	13	12	20	29	40	51	57	56	50	39	29	19	35
Prevailing Wind Direction	WNW	WNW	WNW	WNW	ESE	SE	WNW	SW	W	WSW	WNW	SW	WNW
Prevailing Wind Speed (mph)	10	9	10	10	9	8	8	7	7	8	9	8	9
Maximum Wind Gust (mph)	53	54	54	60	53	58	53	60	45	47	56	54	60

Detroit Metropolitan Airport

Detroit and the immediate suburbs, including nearby urban areas in Canada, occupy an area approximately 25 miles in radius. The waterway, consisting of the Detroit and St. Clair Rivers, Lake St. Clair, and the west end of Lake Erie, lies at an elevation of 568 to 580 feet above sea level. Nearly flat land slopes up gently from the waters edge northwestward for about 10 miles and then gives way to increasingly rolling terrain. The Irish Hills, parallel to and about 40 miles northwest of the waterway, have tops 1,000 to 1,250 feet above sea level. On the Canadian side of the waterway the land is relatively level.

Northwest winds in winter bring snow flurry accumulations to all of Michigan except in the Detroit Metropolitan area while summer showers moving from the northwest weaken and sometimes dissipate as they approach Detroit. On the other hand, much of the heaviest precipitation in winter comes from southeast winds, especially to the northwest suburbs of the city.

The climate of Detroit is influenced by its location with respect to major storm tracks and the influence of the Great Lakes. The normal wintertime storm track is south of the city, which brings on the average, about three inch snowfalls. Winter storms can bring combinations of rain, snow, freezing rain, and sleet with heavy snowfall accumulations possible at times. In summer, most storms pass to the north allowing for intervals of warm, humid, sunny skies with occasional thunderstorms followed by days of mild, dry, and fair weather. Temperatures of 90 degrees or higher are reached during each summer.

Local climatic variations are due largely to the immediate effect of Lake St. Clair and the urban heat island. On warm days in late spring or early summer, lake breezes often lower temperatures by 10 to 15 degrees in the eastern part of the city and the northeastern suburbs. The urban heat island effect shows up mainly at night where minimum temperatures at the Metropolitan Airport average four degrees lower than downtown Detroit. On humid summer nights or on very cold winter nights, this difference can exceed 10 degrees.

The growing season averages 180 days and has ranged from 145 days to 205 days. On average, the last freezing temperature occurs in late April while the average first freezing temperature occurs in late October. A freeze has occurred as late as mid-May and as early as late September.

Detroit Metropolitan Airport *Wayne County*   Elevation: 629 ft.   Latitude: 42° 13' N   Longitude: 83° 21' W

	JAN	FEB	MAR	APR	MAY	JUN	JUL	AUG	SEP	OCT	NOV	DEC	YEAR
Mean Maximum Temp. (°F)	30.9	34.2	44.8	57.9	70.3	79.0	83.5	81.5	73.9	61.3	47.8	36.2	58.4
Mean Temp. (°F)	23.8	26.6	36.1	47.7	59.3	68.3	73.0	71.3	63.5	51.5	40.3	29.6	49.2
Mean Minimum Temp. (°F)	16.7	18.9	27.4	37.5	48.2	57.6	62.4	61.0	53.2	41.6	32.7	22.9	40.0
Extreme Maximum Temp. (°F)	62	70	81	89	93	104	102	100	98	86	75	69	104
Extreme Minimum Temp. (°F)	-21	-15	-4	10	26	36	42	38	29	17	10	-10	-21
Days Maximum Temp. ≥ 90°F	0	0	0	0	1	3	5	3	1	0	0	0	13
Days Maximum Temp. ≤ 32°F	17	13	4	0	0	0	0	0	0	0	1	10	45
Days Minimum Temp. ≤ 32°F	29	25	22	9	1	0	0	0	0	4	16	26	132
Days Minimum Temp. ≤ 0°F	3	2	0	0	0	0	0	0	0	0	0	1	6
Heating Degree Days (base 65°F)	1,270	1,078	889	518	214	43	5	10	116	419	735	1,092	6,389
Cooling Degree Days (base 65°F)	0	0	0	6	44	155	271	216	78	5	0	0	775
Mean Precipitation (in.)	1.91	1.88	2.56	3.01	2.98	3.52	3.09	3.04	3.10	2.19	2.69	2.48	32.45
Maximum Precipitation (in.)	3.9	5.0	4.5	5.4	6.2	7.0	6.0	7.8	7.5	4.9	5.7	6.0	42.6
Minimum Precipitation (in.)	0.3	0.1	0.8	0.9	0.9	1.0	0.6	0.7	0.4	0.3	0.8	0.5	21.0
Maximum 24-hr. Precipitation (in.)	1.6	2.3	1.7	2.0	2.6	2.2	3.2	3.2	2.7	2.1	1.6	2.7	3.2
Days With ≥ 0.1" Precipitation	5	5	7	7	6	6	6	6	6	5	7	7	73
Days With ≥ 1.0" Precipitation	0	0	0	0	1	1	1	1	1	0	0	0	5
Mean Snowfall (in.)	11.9	9.2	7.3	1.7	trace	0.0	0.0	0.0	trace	0.2	2.8	10.1	43.2
Maximum Snowfall (in.)	30	21	16	9	trace	0	0	0	0	3	12	35	75
Maximum 24-hr. Snowfall (in.)	11	8	8	5	trace	0	0	0	0	3	6	18	18
Days With ≥ 1.0" Snow Depth	18	13	6	1	0	0	0	0	0	0	2	9	49
Thunderstorm Days	< 1	< 1	2	3	4	6	6	5	4	1	1	< 1	32
Foggy Days	12	11	13	11	12	12	13	17	15	15	14	14	159
Predominant Sky Cover	OVR	OVR	OVR	OVR	OVR	OVR	SCT	OVR	OVR	OVR	OVR	OVR	OVR
Mean Relative Humidity 7am (%)	80	79	79	78	78	79	82	86	87	84	82	81	81
Mean Relative Humidity 4pm (%)	67	63	58	53	51	52	52	54	54	55	64	69	58
Mean Dewpoint (°F)	17	18	26	35	46	56	61	60	53	42	32	22	39
Prevailing Wind Direction	WSW	SW	WNW	WSW	WSW	SW	SW	SW	SW	SW	SW	SW	SW
Prevailing Wind Speed (mph)	14	14	14	14	13	10	9	9	10	12	13	13	12
Maximum Wind Gust (mph)	66	64	64	66	61	94	71	69	54	52	58	61	94

Flint Bishop Airport

Flint, Michigan, is located in the Flint River Valley, in the center of Genesee County. Lake Huron lies approximately 65 miles to the east, while Saginaw Bay is about 40 miles to the north. The surrounding terrain is generally level with a slight rising tendency to a range of hills 15 to 20 miles southeast of the city.

Flint is generally under the climatic influence of the Great Lakes. Temperatures of 100 degrees or higher are rare and cold waves are less severe then expected. During the winter months, snow showers occur with strong northwesterly winds, and Lake Michigan, lying 120 miles to the west, causes a tempering effect upon cold waves coming from the northwest. The lake effect also results in delaying the coming of spring and prolonging warmer weather in late autumn. This results in conditions favorable for orchards and small fruit.

Precipitation is usually ample for growth and development of vegetation. The wettest periods normally occur in the late spring, early summer, and early fall. The driest period is normally during the winter, and although there is an occasional heavy snowfall, most of the snow occurs in the form of frequent light flurries.

Winter months are marked by considerable cloudiness and rather high relative humidity, while during the summer relative humidity is usually not excessive and sunshine is plentiful.

Violent windstorms associated with thunderstorms and squall lines occasionally hit this area. Tornadoes are infrequent but have caused extensive property damage and loss of life.

Weather changes are frequent throughout the year, since a majority of atmospheric disturbances moving eastward across the country pass near enough to affect the weather in Flint.

Flint Bishop Airport *Genesee County*   Elevation: 764 ft.   Latitude: 42° 58' N   Longitude: 83° 45' W

	JAN	FEB	MAR	APR	MAY	JUN	JUL	AUG	SEP	OCT	NOV	DEC	YEAR
Mean Maximum Temp. (°F)	29.0	32.1	42.6	56.0	68.8	77.6	82.0	79.5	71.8	59.6	46.3	34.5	56.7
Mean Temp. (°F)	21.9	24.4	34.0	45.9	57.5	66.5	71.0	69.0	61.4	50.0	39.0	27.9	47.4
Mean Minimum Temp. (°F)	14.8	16.6	25.4	35.8	46.1	55.3	60.0	58.4	50.8	40.3	31.7	21.3	38.0
Extreme Maximum Temp. (°F)	61	68	79	87	93	101	101	98	93	84	76	67	101
Extreme Minimum Temp. (°F)	-25	-19	-12	6	26	33	41	37	26	19	6	-12	-25
Days Maximum Temp. ≥ 90°F	0	0	0	0	0	2	3	2	1	0	0	0	8
Days Maximum Temp. ≤ 32°F	19	14	5	0	0	0	0	0	0	0	2	12	52
Days Minimum Temp. ≤ 32°F	29	25	23	11	2	0	0	0	0	6	17	27	140
Days Minimum Temp. ≤ 0°F	5	1	1	0	0	0	0	0	0	0	0	2	12
Heating Degree Days (base 65°F)	1,328	1,141	953	572	260	64	12	26	157	464	773	1,143	6,893
Cooling Degree Days (base 65°F)	0	0	1	6	36	117	212	161	52	4	0	0	589
Mean Precipitation (in.)	1.57	1.34	2.27	3.11	2.61	3.08	3.01	3.41	3.69	2.39	2.68	2.11	31.27
Maximum Precipitation (in.)	3.2	5.3	4.2	5.6	6.8	6.5	7.9	11.0	10.9	4.2	4.9	4.7	45.4
Minimum Precipitation (in.)	0.3	0.2	0.3	1.0	0.3	0.6	0.7	0.4	0.3	0.4	0.7	0.4	18.1
Maximum 24-hr. Precipitation (in.)	1.3	2.8	1.5	2.7	2.2	2.5	3.7	4.4	6.0	1.8	1.9	1.7	6.0
Days With ≥ 0.1" Precipitation	4	4	6	7	6	6	6	6	7	6	7	6	71
Days With ≥ 1.0" Precipitation	0	0	0	0	0	1	1	1	1	0	0	0	4
Mean Snowfall (in.)	13.0	9.4	8.0	2.7	trace	trace	trace	trace	trace	0.3	3.5	11.2	48.1
Maximum Snowfall (in.)	29	21	19	17	1	0	0	0	trace	4	16	25	84
Maximum 24-hr. Snowfall (in.)	15	10	13	12	1	0	0	0	trace	4	11	9	15
Days With ≥ 1.0" Snow Depth	22	17	9	1	0	0	0	0	0	0	2	14	65
Thunderstorm Days	< 1	< 1	1	3	4	6	6	6	4	1	1	< 1	32
Foggy Days	11	10	12	11	10	10	12	16	14	14	13	13	146
Predominant Sky Cover	OVR	OVR	OVR	OVR	OVR	OVR	OVR	OVR	OVR	OVR	OVR	OVR	OVR
Mean Relative Humidity 6am (%)	81	81	81	80	81	85	88	91	90	86	83	83	84
Mean Relative Humidity 3pm (%)	70	67	60	53	51	53	52	55	56	57	65	72	59
Mean Dewpoint (°F)	17	18	25	34	45	55	60	59	52	42	31	22	38
Prevailing Wind Direction	SW	WSW	WNW	WSW	WSW	WSW	SW	SW	S	S	SW	SW	SW
Prevailing Wind Speed (mph)	12	12	14	13	12	10	9	8	9	10	13	12	12
Maximum Wind Gust (mph)	61	54	69	68	56	76	73	71	63	49	63	69	76

Grand Rapids Int'l Airport

Grand Rapids, Michigan, is located in the west-central part of Kent County, in the picturesque Grand River valley about 30 air miles east of Lake Michigan. The Grand River, the longest stream in Michigan, flows through the city and bisects it into east and west sections. High hills rise on either side of the valley. Elevations range from 602 feet on the valley floor to 1,020 feet in the extreme southern part of Kent County, southwest of the airport.

Grand Rapids is under the natural climatic influence of Lake Michigan. In spring the cooling effect of Lake Michigan helps retard the growth of vegetation until the danger of frost has passed. The warming effect in the fall retards frost until most of the crops have matured. Fall is a colorful time of year in western Michigan, compensating for the late spring. During the winter, excessive cloudiness and numerous snow flurries occur with strong westerly winds. The tempering effect of Lake Michigan on cold waves coming in from the west and northwest is quite evident.

The tempering effect of the lake promotes the growth of a great variety of fruit trees and berries, especially apples, peaches, cherries, and blueberries. The intense cold of winter is modified, thus reducing winter kill of fruit trees. Summer days are pleasantly warm and most summer nights are quite comfortable, although there are about three weeks of hot, humid weather during most summers. Prolonged severe cold waves with below-zero temperatures are infrequent. The temperature usually rises to above zero during the daytime hours regardless of early morning readings.

July is the sunniest month and December is the month with the least sunshine. November through January is usually a period of excessive cloudiness and minimal sunshine.

Precipitation is usually ample for the growth and development of all vegetation. About one-half of the annual precipitation falls during the growing season, May through September. Droughts occur occasionally, but are seldom of protracted length. The snowfall season extends from mid-November to mid-March. Some winters have had continuous snow cover throughout this period, although there is usually a mid-winter thaw. The Grand River flows through the city and reaches critical heights a couple of times each year. Overflow is generally limited to the lowlands of the flood plain.

November is one of the windiest months and although violent windstorms are infrequent, gusts have on occasion exceeded 65 mph. Summer thunderstorms occasionally produce gusty winds over 60 mph.

Grand Rapids Int'l Airport *Kent County*   Elevation: 784 ft.   Latitude: 42° 53' N   Longitude: 85° 31' W

	JAN	FEB	MAR	APR	MAY	JUN	JUL	AUG	SEP	OCT	NOV	DEC	YEAR
Mean Maximum Temp. (°F)	29.2	32.4	42.8	56.7	69.8	78.7	82.7	80.1	72.1	59.9	45.9	34.2	57.0
Mean Temp. (°F)	22.4	24.8	34.0	46.2	58.1	67.2	71.8	69.6	61.6	50.1	38.6	28.0	47.7
Mean Minimum Temp. (°F)	15.5	17.1	25.3	35.8	46.3	55.7	60.7	59.0	51.0	40.2	31.3	21.7	38.3
Extreme Maximum Temp. (°F)	60	69	78	88	92	98	100	98	93	87	77	67	100
Extreme Minimum Temp. (°F)	-22	-19	-8	3	24	33	41	39	27	18	5	-18	-22
Days Maximum Temp. ≥ 90°F	0	0	0	0	1	2	4	2	0	0	0	0	9
Days Maximum Temp. ≤ 32°F	19	14	6	0	0	0	0	0	0	0	3	13	55
Days Minimum Temp. ≤ 32°F	29	26	24	11	2	0	0	0	0	6	18	28	144
Days Minimum Temp. ≤ 0°F	4	3	0	0	0	0	0	0	0	0	0	1	8
Heating Degree Days (base 65°F)	1,315	1,130	953	563	248	55	9	22	154	461	786	1,141	6,837
Cooling Degree Days (base 65°F)	0	0	1	7	39	130	230	178	57	4	0	0	646
Mean Precipitation (in.)	2.04	1.52	2.63	3.45	3.21	3.73	3.63	3.79	4.31	2.86	3.37	2.69	37.23
Maximum Precipitation (in.)	4.4	3.3	5.8	6.1	8.3	8.2	8.8	8.5	11.8	8.3	7.8	6.6	47.5
Minimum Precipitation (in.)	0.3	0.3	0.7	1.8	0.9	0.3	0.6	0.1	trace	trace	0.6	0.7	22.8
Maximum 24-hr. Precipitation (in.)	2.1	1.5	2.8	2.0	4.1	3.2	3.6	3.6	3.5	3.6	2.9	2.1	4.1
Days With ≥ 0.1" Precipitation	6	4	7	8	6	6	6	6	7	6	7	7	76
Days With ≥ 1.0" Precipitation	0	0	0	1	1	1	1	1	1	1	1	1	9
Mean Snowfall (in.)	21.3	11.8	9.3	2.8	trace	0.0	trace	trace	0.0	0.6	7.2	18.0	71.0
Maximum Snowfall (in.)	46	30	36	16	2	0	0	0	trace	8	27	51	118
Maximum 24-hr. Snowfall (in.)	16	9	10	12	1	0	0	0	trace	8	10	10	16
Days With ≥ 1.0" Snow Depth	24	18	9	1	0	0	0	0	0	0	4	17	73
Thunderstorm Days	< 1	< 1	2	4	4	6	6	5	4	2	1	< 1	34
Foggy Days	11	11	12	11	10	10	12	15	13	13	12	13	143
Predominant Sky Cover	OVR	OVR	OVR	OVR	OVR	OVR	OVR	OVR	OVR	OVR	OVR	OVR	OVR
Mean Relative Humidity 7am (%)	82	81	81	79	79	81	84	89	89	85	83	83	83
Mean Relative Humidity 4pm (%)	72	66	61	54	50	51	53	56	58	59	68	74	60
Mean Dewpoint (°F)	17	17	25	34	45	55	60	60	53	41	31	22	39
Prevailing Wind Direction	WSW	WSW	ENE	WSW	WSW	WSW	WSW	WSW	S	S	WSW	WSW	WSW
Prevailing Wind Speed (mph)	14	13	12	13	12	10	10	10	8	9	13	13	12
Maximum Wind Gust (mph)	62	62	71	68	68	63	61	61	61	48	78	62	78

Houghton Lake Airport

Houghton Lake is located in north-central lower Michigan. The present station is on the northeast shore of Houghton Lake, the largest inland lake in Michigan, with a circumference of about 32 miles. The Muskegon River source is Higgins Lake, eight miles to the north. It flows through Houghton Lake, then southwestward to Lake Michigan. The station lies within an elongated bowl shaped 1,000-foot plateau, which extends roughly 50 miles north, 75 miles southwest, and about 20 miles southeast of Houghton Lake. In the immediate area, the land is level to rolling, but there are hills and ridges from 100 to 300 feet higher in elevation surrounding the station. Soils are generally sand, or sandy loam supporting little agricultural production, but the area is rich in natural resources of forests, lakes, and streams.

The interior location diminishes the influence of the larger Great Lakes, which lie 70 to 80 miles east and west of Houghton Lake. Hence, the daily temperature range is larger, especially in summer, and temperature extremes are greater than are found nearer the shores of either Lake Michigan or Lake Huron. Temperatures reach the 100 degree mark about one summer out of ten, and at the other extreme, fall below zero an average of 22 times during the winter season.

Precipitation is normally a little heavier during the summer season. About 60 percent of the annual total falls in the six-month period from April through September. The heaviest precipitation occurs with summertime thunderstorms.

Snowfall averages above 80 inches per year at Houghton Lake, with considerable variation from year to year. Much heavier snows, averaging over 100 inches a season, fall within a 30- to 60-mile radius to the north and west of Houghton Lake. Seasonal totals have ranged from 24 inches to over 124 inches. Measurable amounts of snow have occurred in nine of the 12 months, and the average number of months with measurable snowfall is six.

Cloudiness is greatest in the late fall and early winter, while sunshine percentage is highest in the spring and summer. Cloudiness is increased in the late fall due to the moisture and warmth picked up by the westerly and northwesterly winds while crossing Lake Michigan.

The growing season is normally quite short, averaging about 90 days between spring and fall freezes.

Houghton Lake Airport *Roscommon County*   Elevation: 1,148 ft.   Latitude: 44° 22' N   Longitude: 84° 41' W

	JAN	FEB	MAR	APR	MAY	JUN	JUL	AUG	SEP	OCT	NOV	DEC	YEAR
Mean Maximum Temp. (°F)	25.6	29.0	38.8	52.9	66.9	75.4	79.8	76.8	68.0	55.7	41.8	30.6	53.4
Mean Temp. (°F)	17.5	19.5	28.9	42.3	54.7	63.3	67.9	65.5	57.5	46.5	35.0	23.9	43.5
Mean Minimum Temp. (°F)	9.3	9.9	18.8	31.6	42.5	51.1	55.9	54.2	46.9	37.3	28.2	17.3	33.6
Extreme Maximum Temp. (°F)	54	59	76	86	90	103	98	94	92	85	70	63	103
Extreme Minimum Temp. (°F)	-26	-34	-19	3	23	29	35	29	21	18	-5	-21	-34
Days Maximum Temp. ≥ 90°F	0	0	0	0	0	1	2	1	0	0	0	0	4
Days Maximum Temp. ≤ 32°F	24	18	9	1	0	0	0	0	0	0	5	18	75
Days Minimum Temp. ≤ 32°F	31	28	28	17	4	0	0	0	2	9	22	30	171
Days Minimum Temp. ≤ 0°F	8	8	3	0	0	0	0	0	0	0	0	3	22
Heating Degree Days (base 65°F)	1,467	1,280	1,114	678	332	113	38	70	243	566	893	1,266	8,060
Cooling Degree Days (base 65°F)	0	0	0	3	21	69	138	99	24	0	0	0	354
Mean Precipitation (in.)	1.60	1.22	2.08	2.30	2.49	2.98	2.72	3.69	3.23	2.33	2.19	1.79	28.62
Maximum Precipitation (in.)	3.1	3.4	5.7	4.7	6.0	6.7	5.3	7.2	9.5	8.1	5.1	4.5	37.7
Minimum Precipitation (in.)	0.6	0.3	0.6	1.0	0.4	0.8	0.5	0.8	trace	0.5	0.4	0.5	20.2
Maximum 24-hr. Precipitation (in.)	1.0	1.3	1.9	1.8	1.9	2.3	3.5	3.1	2.3	2.3	1.8	1.7	3.5
Days With ≥ 0.1" Precipitation	5	4	6	6	6	6	6	7	7	6	6	5	70
Days With ≥ 1.0" Precipitation	0	0	0	0	0	1	1	1	1	0	0	0	4
Mean Snowfall (in.)	19.1	12.8	11.5	4.1	0.3	0.0	trace	trace	trace	0.6	9.5	15.7	73.6
Maximum Snowfall (in.)	38	24	29	12	2	0	0	0	trace	4	42	30	117
Maximum 24-hr. Snowfall (in.)	15	7	12	6	2	0	0	0	trace	4	14	13	15
Days With ≥ 1.0" Snow Depth	30	27	19	3	0	0	0	0	0	0	7	22	108
Thunderstorm Days	< 1	< 1	1	2	4	5	6	6	4	1	1	< 1	30
Foggy Days	11	10	12	10	11	12	12	17	16	14	14	13	152
Predominant Sky Cover	OVR	OVR	OVR	OVR	OVR	OVR	OVR	OVR	OVR	OVR	OVR	OVR	OVR
Mean Relative Humidity 7am (%)	83	82	84	80	78	81	85	91	91	88	87	85	85
Mean Relative Humidity 4pm (%)	72	66	61	53	47	51	52	58	61	62	72	76	61
Mean Dewpoint (°F)	13	13	21	30	41	52	58	57	50	39	29	19	35
Prevailing Wind Direction	W	W	W	NW	W	W	SW	WSW	SW	SW	W	W	W
Prevailing Wind Speed (mph)	12	9	9	12	9	9	8	8	9	10	13	12	10
Maximum Wind Gust (mph)	62	48	61	61	60	58	58	59	48	54	61	43	62

Lansing Capital City Airport

The climate at Lansing alternates between continental and semi-marine, depending on meteorological conditions. The marine type is due to the influence of the Great Lakes and is governed by the force and direction of the wind. When there is little or no wind, the weather becomes continental in character, which means pronounced fluctuation in temperature, hot weather in summer and severe cold in winter. On the other hand, a strong wind from the Lakes may immediately transform the weather into a semi-marine type.

Since large bodies of water are less responsive to temperature changes, the Great Lakes hold the winter cold longer in the spring and the summer heat longer in the fall than do the land areas. This fact is illustrated by looking at some monthly mean temperatures at Lansing as compared to similar latitudes west of the Lakes. Such a comparison shows cooler summers and milder winters in Lansing because of the lake effect.

Based on the 1951-1980 period, the average first occurrence of 32 degrees Fahrenheit in the fall is September 30 and the average last occurrence in the spring is May 13.

Precipitation is fairly well distributed through the year, and no conspicuous annual variation is noted, although there is about one inch less per month in winter than in summer. The heavier amounts in summer occur in thunderstorms. The wettest months are May and June. Snowfall for Lansing is moderate, averaging about 52 inches per year.

There are almost twice as many cloudy days as clear days throughout the year. Much cloudiness prevails during the winter season, but sunshine is abundant during the summer months. Similarly, relative humidity remains rather high during the winter, but is only moderate in summer.

Tornadoes sometimes occur in this area, but their frequency is less than in states farther to the south and west. Destructive thunder and wind storms are not uncommon. Flooding of streams and rivers in the upper grand Basin occurs in about one year out of three, with floods causing considerable damage in about one year out of ten.

Lansing Capital City Airport *Clinton County* Elevation: 839 ft. Latitude: 42° 47' N Longitude: 84° 35' W

	JAN	FEB	MAR	APR	MAY	JUN	JUL	AUG	SEP	OCT	NOV	DEC	YEAR
Mean Maximum Temp. (°F)	29.1	32.3	42.9	56.5	69.4	78.3	82.5	80.2	72.3	59.8	45.9	34.3	57.0
Mean Temp. (°F)	21.6	23.9	33.6	45.8	57.2	66.5	70.8	68.8	60.8	49.4	38.2	27.3	47.0
Mean Minimum Temp. (°F)	14.0	15.5	24.3	34.9	45.0	54.5	59.0	57.3	49.3	38.9	30.4	20.3	37.0
Extreme Maximum Temp. (°F)	61	69	78	86	94	99	100	100	97	86	77	66	100
Extreme Minimum Temp. (°F)	-29	-25	-15	-2	22	32	37	35	22	16	4	-17	-29
Days Maximum Temp. ≥ 90°F	0	0	0	0	0	2	4	2	1	0	0	0	9
Days Maximum Temp. ≤ 32°F	19	14	6	0	0	0	0	0	0	0	3	13	55
Days Minimum Temp. ≤ 32°F	29	26	24	13	3	0	0	0	1	8	19	27	150
Days Minimum Temp. ≤ 0°F	5	4	1	0	0	0	0	0	0	0	0	2	12
Heating Degree Days (base 65°F)	1,340	1,154	967	577	270	67	16	33	174	483	797	1,161	7,039
Cooling Degree Days (base 65°F)	0	0	0	6	35	116	208	159	52	4	0	0	581
Mean Precipitation (in.)	1.61	1.43	2.37	3.08	2.57	3.63	2.70	3.45	3.43	2.36	2.68	2.22	31.53
Maximum Precipitation (in.)	3.6	4.2	4.4	5.2	6.6	10.2	6.4	9.8	8.3	5.6	5.4	4.7	39.6
Minimum Precipitation (in.)	0.4	0.2	0.9	1.1	0.6	0.2	0.5	0.2	trace	0.3	0.5	0.4	21.2
Maximum 24-hr. Precipitation (in.)	1.6	1.6	2.1	2.5	2.9	4.9	2.1	3.1	3.4	1.8	2.2	1.4	4.9
Days With ≥ 0.1" Precipitation	4	4	6	8	6	7	5	6	6	6	6	6	70
Days With ≥ 1.0" Precipitation	0	0	0	0	0	1	1	1	1	0	0	0	4
Mean Snowfall (in.)	14.3	10.7	8.8	3.0	trace	trace	0.0	0.0	trace	0.4	4.7	13.0	54.9
Maximum Snowfall (in.)	34	24	20	17	trace	0	0	0	trace	8	17	28	80
Maximum 24-hr. Snowfall (in.)	15	8	14	10	trace	0	0	0	trace	8	8	9	15
Days With ≥ 1.0" Snow Depth	23	17	10	1	0	0	0	0	0	0	3	16	70
Thunderstorm Days	< 1	< 1	1	3	4	6	6	6	4	1	1	< 1	32
Foggy Days	13	12	13	12	11	11	12	16	14	14	14	14	156
Predominant Sky Cover	OVR	OVR	OVR	OVR	OVR	OVR	SCT	OVR	OVR	OVR	OVR	OVR	OVR
Mean Relative Humidity 7am (%)	83	82	83	80	79	81	85	90	90	87	85	84	84
Mean Relative Humidity 4pm (%)	72	67	62	55	52	53	53	56	58	59	68	74	61
Mean Dewpoint (°F)	17	17	25	35	45	56	60	60	53	41	32	22	39
Prevailing Wind Direction	W	W	W	W	W	W	W	W	SSW	SW	SSW	SW	W
Prevailing Wind Speed (mph)	14	14	14	14	12	10	10	9	10	12	12	13	12
Maximum Wind Gust (mph)	60	52	64	70	62	69	64	54	48	55	60	62	70

Marquette County Airport

The Marquette County Airport lies about 7.5 miles southwest of the nearest shoreline of Lake Superior and about eight miles west of the city of Marquette. Lake Superior is the largest body of fresh water in the world and the deepest and coldest of the Great Lakes. An irregular northwest-southeast ridge line lies just to the east of the airport. There are several water storage basins in the vicinity of the station. One basin, about 20 miles long, is three miles northwest and another, about eight miles in diameter, is three miles west.

The climate is influenced considerably by the proximity of Lake Superior. As a consequence of the cool expanse of water in the summer, there is rarely a long period of sweltering hot weather. Periods of drought are extremely rare. In the winter, cold outbreaks are tempered considerably by the waters of Lake Superior if the lake is unfrozen. However, winds blowing across these relatively warmer waters pick up moisture and cause cloudy weather throughout the winter, as well as frequent periods of light snow. Lake-formed snow showers and snow squalls are intensified near the station by upslope winds, especially from the northwest through northeast. With a northeast through east wind, especially in autumn, the upslope condition will cause light snow at the airport, while along the lakeshore, only drizzle or no precipitation may occur.

The growing season averages 117 days. Precipitation is rather evenly distributed throughout the year, with an average precipitation of four inches or more in June and September and less than two inch averages only in January and February. One hundred inches or more of snow occur in nine of ten winter seasons.

Marquette County Airport *Marquette County*   Elevation: 1,414 ft.   Latitude: 46° 32' N   Longitude: 87° 33' W

	JAN	FEB	MAR	APR	MAY	JUN	JUL	AUG	SEP	OCT	NOV	DEC	YEAR
Mean Maximum Temp. (°F)	20.8	25.2	34.0	47.3	62.4	71.6	76.4	73.7	64.3	52.0	36.6	25.5	49.1
Mean Temp. (°F)	12.2	15.4	24.2	37.3	50.8	60.1	65.1	63.0	54.3	43.2	29.7	18.2	39.5
Mean Minimum Temp. (°F)	3.7	5.6	14.3	27.2	39.1	48.5	53.9	52.4	44.2	34.4	22.8	10.9	29.8
Extreme Maximum Temp. (°F)	53	61	68	92	93	96	99	95	92	87	73	59	99
Extreme Minimum Temp. (°F)	-32	-34	-24	-5	17	28	36	31	22	14	-13	-28	-34
Days Maximum Temp. ≥ 90°F	0	0	0	0	0	1	1	1	0	0	0	0	3
Days Maximum Temp. ≤ 32°F	27	21	14	3	0	0	0	0	0	1	11	24	101
Days Minimum Temp. ≤ 32°F	31	28	29	22	9	1	0	0	3	15	26	31	195
Days Minimum Temp. ≤ 0°F	12	11	5	0	0	0	0	0	0	0	1	7	36
Heating Degree Days (base 65°F)	1,631	1,396	1,260	827	450	185	80	118	332	669	1,051	1,445	9,444
Cooling Degree Days (base 65°F)	0	0	0	2	14	50	93	68	16	1	0	0	244
Mean Precipitation (in.)	2.62	1.84	3.05	2.81	3.20	3.12	3.13	3.45	3.90	3.69	3.22	2.44	36.47
Maximum Precipitation (in.)	4.5	3.6	6.1	6.6	7.9	12.3	5.6	8.6	7.6	7.6	8.3	6.9	51.6
Minimum Precipitation (in.)	0.6	0.5	0.3	0.9	0.1	0.6	0.6	0.6	1.2	0.9	1.0	0.4	22.7
Maximum 24-hr. Precipitation (in.)	2.2	1.5	2.0	3.1	2.9	4.1	2.5	2.4	2.6	2.9	2.2	2.3	4.1
Days With ≥ 0.1" Precipitation	7	5	7	6	6	7	6	7	8	8	7	7	81
Days With ≥ 1.0" Precipitation	0	0	1	0	1	1	1	1	1	1	1	0	8
Mean Snowfall (in.)	41.7	29.0	31.0	12.3	1.6	trace	0.0	trace	0.1	5.5	21.8	36.8	179.8
Maximum Snowfall (in.)	69	64	61	29	23	trace	0	0	2	19	49	83	269
Maximum 24-hr. Snowfall (in.)	23	18	21	16	14	trace	0	0	2	11	18	24	24
Days With ≥ 1.0" Snow Depth	31	28	30	16	1	0	0	0	0	3	16	30	155
Thunderstorm Days	< 1	< 1	1	1	3	6	6	5	4	2	< 1	< 1	28
Foggy Days	7	7	9	9	10	11	10	13	14	12	11	9	122
Predominant Sky Cover	na	na	na	na	na	na	na	na	na	na	na	na	na
Mean Relative Humidity 7am (%)	na	na	na	na	na	na	na	na	na	na	na	na	na
Mean Relative Humidity 4pm (%)	na	na	na	na	na	na	na	na	na	na	na	na	na
Mean Dewpoint (°F)	na	na	na	na	na	na	na	na	na	na	na	na	na
Prevailing Wind Direction	na	na	na	na	na	na	na	na	na	na	na	na	na
Prevailing Wind Speed (mph)	na	na	na	na	na	na	na	na	na	na	na	na	na
Maximum Wind Gust (mph)	na	na	na	na	na	na	na	na	na	na	na	na	na

Muskegon County Airport

Muskegon is located on the eastern shore of Lake Michigan approximately 100 miles north of the southern tip of the lake. The terrain is generally level with several sand dunes along the shoreline. Much of the soil is sandy and vegetation grows well, as evidenced by the trees and grass which grow on the dunes. Many crops grow in the area. Asparagus and celery are the principal truck- garden vegetables. A variety of fruits is raised and blueberries lead as a principal product. The main industry in this area is manufacturing with emphasis on foundry and machined products. The area is also a resort center due to features such as extensive sandy beaches, both on Lake Michigan and inland lakes.

Lake Michigan has a very decided effect upon the weather and climate of this area. The prevailing westerly winds tend to moderate the temperatures, resulting in warmer winters than further inland. In the summer the effect is just the opposite. The air temperature usually remains below the uncomfortable readings of the high 90s. Spring arrives about three to four weeks later than normal for this latitude. Autumn is also delayed, as is the cold of early winter.

Precipitation is fairly moderate, but snowfall is moderate to heavy. The heaviest snows occur during late December, January, and February. Precipitation is also influenced by the lake, especially during the winter. Instability in snow showers along the lakeshore vary enormously in intensity, resulting in traces of snow to more than a foot in 24 hours. The heavier snow squalls tend to concentrate over small sections of the shoreline, depending on their intensity and the direction of the wind. With strong winds most snowshowers will fall further inland, sometimes as much as 30 to 40 miles. Snowfall is likely to occur every day for weeks at a time. The daily accumulation of lake effect snow varies greatly. However, due to low water content of most of the storms, the snow settles rapidly.

Summertime thunderstorms have a tendency, as they move inland, to follow the Muskegon and Grand River Valleys. Thus, these areas are more often frequented by severe electrical storms which will pass without a drop of rain two to three miles from the immediate river valleys. Thunderstorms near the shoreline are most frequent at night. The afternoon convection-type storms seldom occur within five miles of the lake. Lake Michigan-spawned thunderstorms give shoreline areas a surprising number of occurrences.

Based on the 1951-1980 period, the average first occurrence of 32 degrees Fahrenheit in the fall is October 11 and the average last occurrence in the spring is May 8.

Muskegon County Airport *Muskegon County*   Elevation: 623 ft.   Latitude: 43° 10' N   Longitude: 86° 14' W

	JAN	FEB	MAR	APR	MAY	JUN	JUL	AUG	SEP	OCT	NOV	DEC	YEAR
Mean Maximum Temp. (°F)	29.2	31.8	41.7	54.6	67.1	75.9	80.4	78.4	70.5	58.6	45.4	34.5	55.7
Mean Temp. (°F)	23.3	25.1	33.6	45.1	56.3	65.3	70.4	68.9	60.9	49.9	38.9	28.9	47.2
Mean Minimum Temp. (°F)	17.4	18.4	25.5	35.6	45.6	54.7	60.4	59.3	51.3	41.2	32.4	23.4	38.8
Extreme Maximum Temp. (°F)	61	67	80	86	89	98	96	95	91	83	71	64	98
Extreme Minimum Temp. (°F)	-12	-19	-6	1	25	31	41	36	27	21	5	-15	-19
Days Maximum Temp. ≥ 90°F	0	0	0	0	0	1	1	1	0	0	0	0	3
Days Maximum Temp. ≤ 32°F	18	14	6	0	0	0	0	0	0	0	2	12	52
Days Minimum Temp. ≤ 32°F	29	26	24	11	2	0	0	0	1	6	16	26	141
Days Minimum Temp. ≤ 0°F	2	2	0	0	0	0	0	0	0	0	0	0	4
Heating Degree Days (base 65°F)	1,284	1,119	966	593	288	74	14	25	162	465	776	1,110	6,876
Cooling Degree Days (base 65°F)	0	0	0	4	25	94	197	158	46	2	0	0	526
Mean Precipitation (in.)	2.26	1.58	2.42	2.85	2.77	2.56	2.29	3.76	3.59	2.83	3.21	2.70	32.82
Maximum Precipitation (in.)	4.5	2.8	6.6	6.1	6.5	5.5	6.6	9.9	13.5	7.3	6.6	5.4	42.3
Minimum Precipitation (in.)	0.4	0.4	0.5	0.7	0.3	0.2	0.5	0.1	0.2	0.5	0.6	0.9	23.1
Maximum 24-hr. Precipitation (in.)	1.6	1.4	2.1	2.1	2.1	2.3	2.5	3.4	4.3	3.2	2.1	2.6	4.3
Days With ≥ 0.1" Precipitation	7	5	6	7	6	5	5	6	7	6	8	7	75
Days With ≥ 1.0" Precipitation	0	0	0	0	1	1	0	1	1	0	0	0	4
Mean Snowfall (in.)	35.5	18.7	10.9	3.2	trace	0.0	trace	0.0	trace	0.6	8.7	28.3	105.9
Maximum Snowfall (in.)	102	46	36	20	trace	0	0	0	trace	5	26	83	182
Maximum 24-hr. Snowfall (in.)	22	14	9	12	trace	0	0	0	trace	5	9	15	22
Days With ≥ 1.0" Snow Depth	26	21	11	1	0	0	0	0	0	0	4	19	82
Thunderstorm Days	< 1	< 1	2	3	4	6	6	6	5	2	1	< 1	35
Foggy Days	11	10	12	11	11	11	11	14	12	13	12	12	140
Predominant Sky Cover	OVR	OVR	OVR	OVR	OVR	OVR	CLR	OVR	OVR	OVR	OVR	OVR	OVR
Mean Relative Humidity 7am (%)	81	81	80	78	76	80	84	88	88	84	80	81	82
Mean Relative Humidity 4pm (%)	75	70	63	55	52	55	56	59	61	62	70	75	63
Mean Dewpoint (°F)	18	18	25	33	43	54	60	60	53	42	32	23	38
Prevailing Wind Direction	WNW	WNW	E	WNW	SW	SW	SW	SW	SSW	SSW	WNW	WNW	WNW
Prevailing Wind Speed (mph)	14	13	12	13	13	12	12	12	13	15	15	14	13
Maximum Wind Gust (mph)	62	67	59	63	54	55	58	63	54	55	59	56	67

Sault Ste. Marie Sanderson Field

Sault Ste. Marie is located at the extreme eastern tip of the Upper Peninsula of Michigan at the intersection of Lake Superior, Michigan, and Huron. Consequently, the regional climate is essentially maritime during ice-free periods of the year. Lake ice development usually begins in December and progresses to maximum coverage in February. As ice cover develops, the character of the regional climate gradually changes to continental polar by the time of maximum lake ice development. Lake Superior, to the northwest, is the largest, deepest, and coldest of the Great Lakes and is the dominant climatic control for the area. Water in the northern Great Lakes remains relatively cool during the summer and seldom freezes over during the winter. Therefore, temperatures are moderated throughout most of the year, whereas cloudiness and precipitation are increased.

Terrain on the Michigan side of the international border is nearly flat and lies 700 to 800 feet above sea level. Very little climatological influence is related to Michigan terrain. However, terrain on the Canadian side of the border rises rather abruptly to about 1,500 feet above sea level and this definite topographic influence increases the rain and snow shower activity over the Canadian hills.

Heavy fog occurrences reach a maximum in August, September, and October and form in response to the passage of relatively cold air masses over the warmer waters of the northern Great Lakes. Destructive tornadoes and thunderstorms have occurred on rare occasions.

Most summers pass without a temperature reaching 90 degrees. Winters are cold and snowy with total seasonal snowfall ranging from about 30 inches to more than 175 inches. November 21 is the average date for the appearance of the permanent winter snow cover which normally lasts until April 7.

Annual percent of possible sunshine is low but is especially low during late fall and early winter because of cloud cover produced by lake moisture evaporated into the cold air. Sunshine amounts increase as ice development increases in the winter season. Daylight during most of June and July lasts almost 16 hours, whereas winter daylight reaches a minimum of less than 9 hours a day in late December.

Based on the 1951-1980 period, the average first occurrence of 32 degrees Fahrenheit in the fall is September 27 and the average last occurrence in the spring is May 26.

Sault Ste. Marie Sanderson Field *Chippewa County* Elevation: 715 ft.   Latitude: 46° 28' N   Longitude: 84° 21' W

	JAN	FEB	MAR	APR	MAY	JUN	JUL	AUG	SEP	OCT	NOV	DEC	YEAR
Mean Maximum Temp. (°F)	21.4	24.2	33.1	47.8	63.0	70.9	75.8	74.1	64.7	52.8	38.9	27.3	49.5
Mean Temp. (°F)	13.1	15.1	24.3	38.3	51.1	58.6	63.9	63.2	54.8	44.4	32.4	20.3	40.0
Mean Minimum Temp. (°F)	4.8	6.0	15.5	28.7	39.2	46.4	52.0	52.3	44.8	36.0	25.8	13.3	30.4
Extreme Maximum Temp. (°F)	45	49	63	85	89	93	97	96	95	79	67	60	97
Extreme Minimum Temp. (°F)	-36	-35	-22	-2	22	26	36	29	25	16	-10	-31	-36
Days Maximum Temp. ≥ 90°F	0	0	0	0	0	0	1	0	0	0	0	0	1
Days Maximum Temp. ≤ 32°F	26	21	14	2	0	0	0	0	0	0	7	20	90
Days Minimum Temp. ≤ 32°F	31	28	29	21	7	1	0	0	2	11	22	30	182
Days Minimum Temp. ≤ 0°F	12	10	4	0	0	0	0	0	0	0	0	6	32
Heating Degree Days (base 65°F)	1,604	1,404	1,254	796	430	206	86	103	313	631	971	1,379	9,177
Cooling Degree Days (base 65°F)	0	0	0	1	5	23	62	55	12	0	0	0	158
Mean Precipitation (in.)	2.60	1.59	2.32	2.61	2.70	2.94	3.24	3.48	3.90	3.42	3.41	2.96	35.17
Maximum Precipitation (in.)	4.5	3.7	5.0	5.2	5.3	7.3	6.0	9.5	7.8	6.5	7.7	6.2	45.8
Minimum Precipitation (in.)	0.5	0.2	0.3	0.6	0.8	0.5	0.6	0.5	1.0	0.2	0.9	0.6	25.5
Maximum 24-hr. Precipitation (in.)	1.2	1.0	1.4	2.3	2.3	2.4	2.2	5.9	2.2	1.9	2.3	1.5	5.9
Days With ≥ 0.1" Precipitation	9	5	6	6	6	7	6	7	8	9	10	9	88
Days With ≥ 1.0" Precipitation	0	0	0	0	0	1	1	1	1	0	0	0	4
Mean Snowfall (in.)	34.9	19.3	15.0	7.3	0.3	0.0	trace	trace	trace	2.4	16.2	35.8	131.2
Maximum Snowfall (in.)	71	40	35	26	5	0	0	0	3	12	47	99	209
Maximum 24-hr. Snowfall (in.)	15	12	12	9	3	0	0	0	3	7	11	27	27
Days With ≥ 1.0" Snow Depth	30	28	29	11	0	0	0	0	0	1	11	28	138
Thunderstorm Days	< 1	< 1	1	1	3	6	6	5	4	2	< 1	< 1	28
Foggy Days	8	7	11	10	10	14	15	18	18	15	12	11	149
Predominant Sky Cover	OVR	OVR	OVR	OVR	OVR	OVR	OVR	OVR	OVR	OVR	OVR	OVR	OVR
Mean Relative Humidity 7am (%)	80	80	82	80	80	85	89	92	92	89	86	84	85
Mean Relative Humidity 4pm (%)	74	70	67	59	53	59	60	62	67	68	76	78	66
Mean Dewpoint (°F)	8	9	17	28	39	50	56	56	49	39	27	16	33
Prevailing Wind Direction	E	NW	NW	NW	WNW	WNW	WNW	NW	NW	ESE	ESE	E	NW
Prevailing Wind Speed (mph)	8	13	13	13	12	10	9	10	12	9	9	8	10
Maximum Wind Gust (mph)	61	56	59	58	55	52	54	56	55	61	71	60	71

Adrian 2 NNE *Lenawee County*   Elevation: 757 ft.   Latitude: 41° 55' N   Longitude: 84° 01' W

	JAN	FEB	MAR	APR	MAY	JUN	JUL	AUG	SEP	OCT	NOV	DEC	YEAR
Mean Maximum Temp. (°F)	31.8	34.6	45.4	58.3	70.5	79.9	83.5	81.3	74.0	61.7	47.9	36.3	58.8
Mean Temp. (°F)	23.4	25.5	35.4	46.8	58.0	67.5	71.4	69.2	61.7	50.1	38.9	28.5	48.0
Mean Minimum Temp. (°F)	15.0	16.6	25.3	35.2	45.6	55.0	59.3	56.9	49.4	38.3	29.8	20.7	37.3
Extreme Maximum Temp. (°F)	62	70	80	88	94	104	100	100	97	88	76	68	104
Extreme Minimum Temp. (°F)	-22	-18	-6	8	20	34	41	32	27	15	7	-14	-22
Days Maximum Temp. ≥ 90°F	0	0	0	0	0	3	5	3	1	0	0	0	12
Days Maximum Temp. ≤ 32°F	16	12	4	0	0	0	0	0	0	0	1	10	43
Days Minimum Temp. ≤ 32°F	29	26	24	12	1	0	0	0	1	8	20	28	149
Days Minimum Temp. ≤ 0°F	4	4	0	0	0	0	0	0	0	0	0	2	10
Heating Degree Days (base 65°F)	1,283	1,109	911	545	241	51	9	24	149	460	776	1,127	6,685
Cooling Degree Days (base 65°F)	0	0	1	4	33	129	222	161	54	3	0	0	607
Mean Precipitation (in.)	1.95	1.81	2.65	3.28	3.30	3.75	3.17	3.49	3.45	2.56	2.99	2.58	34.98
Days With ≥ 0.1" Precipitation	5	4	7	8	7	7	6	6	6	6	7	6	75
Days With ≥ 1.0" Precipitation	0	0	0	0	1	1	1	1	1	1	1	0	7
Mean Snowfall (in.)	8.5	6.4	4.7	0.8	0.0	0.0	0.0	0.0	0.0	0.1	2.7	6.9	30.1
Days With ≥ 1.0" Snow Depth	19	15	6	1	0	0	0	0	0	0	2	10	53

Alberta Ford *Baraga County*   Elevation: 1,309 ft.   Latitude: 46° 39' N   Longitude: 88° 29' W

	JAN	FEB	MAR	APR	MAY	JUN	JUL	AUG	SEP	OCT	NOV	DEC	YEAR
Mean Maximum Temp. (°F)	21.6	26.6	37.3	50.9	65.9	74.4	78.6	76.4	66.6	54.9	37.8	26.1	51.4
Mean Temp. (°F)	12.3	15.5	25.6	38.8	52.5	61.3	66.3	64.7	55.8	45.0	30.4	18.1	40.5
Mean Minimum Temp. (°F)	3.0	4.3	13.8	26.8	39.1	48.2	54.0	53.0	45.0	35.1	22.9	10.0	29.6
Extreme Maximum Temp. (°F)	52	61	69	94	94	98	100	99	97	88	75	60	100
Extreme Minimum Temp. (°F)	-35	-38	-27	-10	14	25	31	31	25	11	-14	-33	-38
Days Maximum Temp. ≥ 90°F	0	0	0	0	0	1	2	1	0	0	0	0	4
Days Maximum Temp. ≤ 32°F	26	20	10	2	0	0	0	0	0	0	10	22	90
Days Minimum Temp. ≤ 32°F	31	28	29	22	9	1	0	0	3	13	26	30	192
Days Minimum Temp. ≤ 0°F	13	11	7	1	0	0	0	0	0	0	1	7	40
Heating Degree Days (base 65°F)	1,630	1,394	1,216	780	400	159	63	91	293	612	1,031	1,449	9,118
Cooling Degree Days (base 65°F)	0	0	0	3	17	56	106	94	22	1	0	0	299
Mean Precipitation (in.)	1.69	1.26	2.18	2.19	3.46	3.39	3.95	3.94	3.80	3.24	2.90	1.85	33.85
Days With ≥ 0.1" Precipitation	6	4	5	6	7	7	7	7	8	8	7	5	77
Days With ≥ 1.0" Precipitation	0	0	0	0	1	1	1	1	1	0	1	0	6
Mean Snowfall (in.)	34.9	23.2	22.7	8.9	0.9	0.0	0.0	0.0	trace	3.7	22.4	30.3	147.0
Days With ≥ 1.0" Snow Depth	31	27	29	14	0	0	0	0	0	2	16	30	149

Allegan 5 NE *Allegan County*   Elevation: 748 ft.   Latitude: 42° 35' N   Longitude: 85° 47' W

	JAN	FEB	MAR	APR	MAY	JUN	JUL	AUG	SEP	OCT	NOV	DEC	YEAR
Mean Maximum Temp. (°F)	30.5	34.0	43.9	57.8	70.1	79.0	83.1	80.5	73.3	60.8	47.4	35.2	58.0
Mean Temp. (°F)	22.7	24.9	34.0	46.4	57.6	66.4	70.9	68.7	61.4	49.7	39.0	28.2	47.5
Mean Minimum Temp. (°F)	14.9	15.7	24.1	34.9	45.1	53.9	58.6	56.8	49.6	38.6	30.7	21.1	37.0
Extreme Maximum Temp. (°F)	60	70	79	88	94	99	100	97	93	89	76	68	100
Extreme Minimum Temp. (°F)	-21	-25	-10	0	23	32	39	36	26	18	6	-18	-25
Days Maximum Temp. ≥ 90°F	0	0	0	0	1	2	5	2	1	0	0	0	11
Days Maximum Temp. ≤ 32°F	17	13	5	0	0	0	0	0	0	0	2	11	48
Days Minimum Temp. ≤ 32°F	29	26	25	13	3	0	0	0	1	9	19	27	152
Days Minimum Temp. ≤ 0°F	4	4	1	0	0	0	0	0	0	0	0	1	10
Heating Degree Days (base 65°F)	1,304	1,126	954	560	260	68	17	30	159	472	773	1,134	6,857
Cooling Degree Days (base 65°F)	0	0	1	7	35	112	205	153	54	4	0	0	571
Mean Precipitation (in.)	2.89	1.81	2.73	3.44	3.37	4.07	3.63	3.91	4.21	3.02	3.68	3.12	39.88
Days With ≥ 0.1" Precipitation	8	6	7	8	7	6	6	7	7	7	8	8	85
Days With ≥ 1.0" Precipitation	0	0	0	1	1	1	1	1	1	0	1	0	7
Mean Snowfall (in.)	26.7	15.2	8.4	2.0	trace	0.0	0.0	0.0	0.0	0.4	7.3	21.7	81.7
Days With ≥ 1.0" Snow Depth	26	21	11	1	0	0	0	0	0	0	4	17	80

Alma *Gratiot County*   Elevation: 757 ft.   Latitude: 43° 23' N   Longitude: 84° 40' W

	JAN	FEB	MAR	APR	MAY	JUN	JUL	AUG	SEP	OCT	NOV	DEC	YEAR
Mean Maximum Temp. (°F)	28.7	32.1	42.2	56.3	69.9	78.7	83.3	80.6	72.4	59.9	45.4	33.8	56.9
Mean Temp. (°F)	21.0	23.4	32.6	45.2	57.4	66.5	71.0	68.6	60.6	49.1	37.3	26.9	46.6
Mean Minimum Temp. (°F)	13.2	14.6	22.8	34.0	45.0	54.2	58.8	56.7	48.8	38.2	29.1	19.9	36.3
Extreme Maximum Temp. (°F)	59	67	78	88	93	100	103	101	95	87	76	65	103
Extreme Minimum Temp. (°F)	-22	-16	-8	5	24	34	42	36	27	20	5	-10	-22
Days Maximum Temp. ≥ 90°F	0	0	0	0	1	3	6	3	1	0	0	0	14
Days Maximum Temp. ≤ 32°F	20	15	6	0	0	0	0	0	0	0	3	13	57
Days Minimum Temp. ≤ 32°F	30	27	27	14	2	0	0	0	1	8	21	29	159
Days Minimum Temp. ≤ 0°F	5	4	1	0	0	0	0	0	0	0	0	1	11
Heating Degree Days (base 65°F)	1,358	1,168	1,000	593	264	67	13	30	172	490	825	1,174	7,154
Cooling Degree Days (base 65°F)	0	0	0	5	31	108	202	145	42	2	0	0	535
Mean Precipitation (in.)	1.84	1.40	2.39	2.92	2.83	3.08	2.71	3.75	3.82	2.82	2.68	2.14	32.38
Days With ≥ 0.1" Precipitation	5	4	5	7	6	6	5	6	7	6	6	5	68
Days With ≥ 1.0" Precipitation	0	0	0	0	1	1	1	1	1	1	1	0	7
Mean Snowfall (in.)	11.2	7.3	7.2	2.1	trace	0.0	0.0	0.0	0.0	0.3	3.3	8.8	40.2
Days With ≥ 1.0" Snow Depth	25	22	12	0	0	0	0	0	0	0	3	16	79

Alpena Wastewater Plant *Alpena County*   Elevation: 587 ft.   Latitude: 45° 04' N   Longitude: 83° 26' W

	JAN	FEB	MAR	APR	MAY	JUN	JUL	AUG	SEP	OCT	NOV	DEC	YEAR
Mean Maximum Temp. (°F)	26.9	28.9	36.7	49.4	61.5	71.4	77.2	75.5	67.6	55.5	42.7	33.0	52.2
Mean Temp. (°F)	19.4	20.9	29.2	41.1	52.6	62.2	68.2	66.7	58.8	47.7	36.4	26.8	44.2
Mean Minimum Temp. (°F)	12.0	12.9	21.6	32.8	43.6	52.9	59.1	57.7	50.0	39.9	30.0	20.5	36.1
Extreme Maximum Temp. (°F)	52	62	75	85	92	100	100	98	92	86	75	65	100
Extreme Minimum Temp. (°F)	-21	-24	-6	11	28	35	41	36	29	22	2	-8	-24
Days Maximum Temp. ≥ 90°F	0	0	0	0	0	1	2	1	0	0	0	0	4
Days Maximum Temp. ≤ 32°F	22	18	9	1	0	0	0	0	0	0	3	13	66
Days Minimum Temp. ≤ 32°F	30	27	26	14	2	0	0	0	0	5	19	28	151
Days Minimum Temp. ≤ 0°F	5	4	1	0	0	0	0	0	0	0	0	1	11
Heating Degree Days (base 65°F)	1,405	1,239	1,104	711	387	132	30	49	206	530	853	1,178	7,824
Cooling Degree Days (base 65°F)	0	0	0	1	10	54	139	111	27	1	0	0	343
Mean Precipitation (in.)	1.72	1.27	1.88	2.12	2.77	2.56	3.30	3.42	3.17	2.45	1.96	1.88	28.50
Days With ≥ 0.1" Precipitation	5	4	5	6	6	6	6	7	7	6	6	6	70
Days With ≥ 1.0" Precipitation	0	0	0	0	0	1	1	1	1	0	0	0	4
Mean Snowfall (in.)	*16.0*	*10.8*	*9.6*	2.0	0.2	0.0	0.0	0.0	0.0	0.2	4.8	12.7	*56.3*
Days With ≥ 1.0" Snow Depth	28	26	20	2	0	0	0	0	0	0	4	16	96

Ann Arbor Univ. of Michigan *Washtenaw County*   Elevation: 898 ft.   Latitude: 42° 18' N   Longitude: 83° 43' W

	JAN	FEB	MAR	APR	MAY	JUN	JUL	AUG	SEP	OCT	NOV	DEC	YEAR
Mean Maximum Temp. (°F)	30.4	34.2	45.3	58.7	71.1	79.6	83.4	81.2	74.1	61.6	47.3	35.4	58.5
Mean Temp. (°F)	23.5	26.4	36.1	48.1	59.8	68.6	72.9	71.0	63.7	52.0	40.0	29.1	49.3
Mean Minimum Temp. (°F)	16.5	18.6	26.9	37.4	48.3	57.6	62.3	60.8	53.4	42.4	32.6	22.8	40.0
Extreme Maximum Temp. (°F)	60	67	80	87	91	101	100	97	94	88	75	67	101
Extreme Minimum Temp. (°F)	-22	-13	-3	7	25	36	45	39	30	20	8	-12	-22
Days Maximum Temp. ≥ 90°F	0	0	0	0	0	2	5	2	1	0	0	0	10
Days Maximum Temp. ≤ 32°F	18	13	4	0	0	0	0	0	0	0	2	12	49
Days Minimum Temp. ≤ 32°F	29	26	23	9	1	0	0	0	0	4	16	27	135
Days Minimum Temp. ≤ 0°F	3	2	0	0	0	0	0	0	0	0	0	1	6
Heating Degree Days (base 65°F)	1,280	1,082	889	509	204	40	5	13	113	403	743	1,106	6,387
Cooling Degree Days (base 65°F)	0	0	1	7	47	153	259	205	80	6	0	0	758
Mean Precipitation (in.)	2.22	2.01	2.83	3.33	2.91	3.26	3.15	3.61	3.30	2.49	3.03	2.72	34.86
Days With ≥ 0.1" Precipitation	6	5	6	8	6	7	7	7	6	5	7	7	77
Days With ≥ 1.0" Precipitation	0	0	0	1	0	1	1	1	1	0	0	0	5
Mean Snowfall (in.)	14.6	10.2	8.4	2.4	trace	0.0	0.0	0.0	trace	0.3	3.6	12.4	51.9
Days With ≥ 1.0" Snow Depth	21	17	7	1	0	0	0	0	0	0	2	14	62

Bad Axe *Huron County*   Elevation: 711 ft.   Latitude: 43° 49' N   Longitude: 83° 00' W

	JAN	FEB	MAR	APR	MAY	JUN	JUL	AUG	SEP	OCT	NOV	DEC	YEAR
Mean Maximum Temp. (°F)	27.8	30.2	39.6	53.2	66.7	76.3	81.0	78.5	70.6	58.5	44.8	32.9	55.0
Mean Temp. (°F)	20.7	22.4	31.2	43.3	55.3	64.8	69.6	67.5	60.2	49.2	37.9	26.8	45.7
Mean Minimum Temp. (°F)	13.6	14.6	22.7	33.4	43.8	53.1	58.2	56.4	49.6	39.9	30.9	20.7	36.4
Extreme Maximum Temp. (°F)	56	66	78	88	92	98	101	96	93	87	76	64	101
Extreme Minimum Temp. (°F)	-20	-18	-8	12	25	32	40	34	27	20	6	-7	-20
Days Maximum Temp. ≥ 90°F	0	0	0	0	0	2	3	1	0	0	0	0	6
Days Maximum Temp. ≤ 32°F	21	17	8	1	0	0	0	0	0	0	2	14	63
Days Minimum Temp. ≤ 32°F	30	27	27	15	2	0	0	0	0	6	19	29	155
Days Minimum Temp. ≤ 0°F	4	3	1	0	0	0	0	0	0	0	0	1	9
Heating Degree Days (base 65°F)	1,366	1,195	1,041	648	320	95	23	43	180	486	808	1,176	7,381
Cooling Degree Days (base 65°F)	0	0	0	4	21	88	169	120	37	2	0	0	441
Mean Precipitation (in.)	1.87	1.55	2.38	2.79	2.74	2.83	3.14	3.59	3.83	2.60	2.81	2.14	32.27
Days With ≥ 0.1" Precipitation	5	4	6	7	7	6	6	6	7	6	7	6	73
Days With ≥ 1.0" Precipitation	0	0	0	1	0	1	1	1	1	0	0	0	4
Mean Snowfall (in.)	13.0	9.3	9.9	3.0	trace	0.0	0.0	0.0	trace	0.6	5.0	10.9	51.7
Days With ≥ 1.0" Snow Depth	25	22	13	2	0	0	0	0	0	0	3	16	81

Baldwin *Lake County*   Elevation: 833 ft.   Latitude: 43° 54' N   Longitude: 85° 51' W

	JAN	FEB	MAR	APR	MAY	JUN	JUL	AUG	SEP	OCT	NOV	DEC	YEAR
Mean Maximum Temp. (°F)	28.6	32.3	42.5	56.1	69.5	*78.0*	82.2	79.9	71.5	59.1	44.8	33.3	*56.5*
Mean Temp. (°F)	19.5	21.3	30.6	43.5	55.7	*64.3*	68.4	66.5	58.2	47.1	35.7	25.2	*44.6*
Mean Minimum Temp. (°F)	10.3	10.3	18.6	30.9	41.7	*50.6*	54.6	52.9	45.0	35.0	26.4	16.9	*32.8*
Extreme Maximum Temp. (°F)	55	64	75	88	92	98	101	100	92	87	74	64	101
Extreme Minimum Temp. (°F)	-30	-38	-25	-8	16	26	35	29	21	11	-3	-24	-38
Days Maximum Temp. ≥ 90°F	0	0	0	0	0	2	3	2	0	0	0	0	7
Days Maximum Temp. ≤ 32°F	19	14	5	1	0	0	0	0	0	0	3	13	55
Days Minimum Temp. ≤ 32°F	30	27	27	17	6	1	0	0	2	13	22	29	174
Days Minimum Temp. ≤ 0°F	7	7	3	0	0	0	0	0	0	0	0	3	20
Heating Degree Days (base 65°F)	1,405	1,230	1,061	641	309	*96*	32	57	227	551	874	1,229	*7,712*
Cooling Degree Days (base 65°F)	0	0	0	5	*21*	*75*	144	111	27	0	0	0	*383*
Mean Precipitation (in.)	2.37	1.63	2.29	2.94	2.84	3.46	2.72	4.00	3.71	3.21	3.08	2.29	34.54
Days With ≥ 0.1" Precipitation	7	5	6	7	6	6	6	6	7	6	8	6	76
Days With ≥ 1.0" Precipitation	0	0	0	1	0	1	1	1	1	0	1	0	6
Mean Snowfall (in.)	25.7	17.4	10.0	2.0	trace	0.0	0.0	0.0	0.0	0.2	8.3	18.6	82.2
Days With ≥ 1.0" Snow Depth	29	25	16	2	0	0	0	0	0	0	6	21	99

Battle Creek *Calhoun County*   Elevation: 954 ft.   Latitude: 42° 18' N   Longitude: 85° 14' W

	JAN	FEB	MAR	APR	MAY	JUN	JUL	AUG	SEP	OCT	NOV	DEC	YEAR
Mean Maximum Temp. (°F)	30.6	34.6	45.4	58.9	71.1	79.5	83.1	80.9	73.1	61.0	46.9	35.4	58.4
Mean Temp. (°F)	22.9	26.0	35.5	47.5	58.7	67.6	71.7	69.7	62.0	50.6	39.0	28.4	48.3
Mean Minimum Temp. (°F)	15.2	17.3	25.5	36.0	46.4	55.6	60.2	58.4	50.8	40.1	31.0	21.2	38.1
Extreme Maximum Temp. (°F)	62	72	79	87	92	101	100	99	95	88	77	66	101
Extreme Minimum Temp. (°F)	-20	-19	-4	5	22	30	42	37	25	16	7	-18	-20
Days Maximum Temp. ≥ 90°F	0	0	0	0	0	2	4	2	1	0	0	0	9
Days Maximum Temp. ≤ 32°F	18	13	4	0	0	0	0	0	0	0	2	12	49
Days Minimum Temp. ≤ 32°F	30	26	24	11	2	0	0	0	1	7	19	28	148
Days Minimum Temp. ≤ 0°F	4	3	0	0	0	0	0	0	0	0	0	1	8
Heating Degree Days (base 65°F)	1,298	1,096	909	527	229	51	10	23	149	445	775	1,128	6,640
Cooling Degree Days (base 65°F)	0	0	1	7	39	133	221	176	60	3	0	0	640
Mean Precipitation (in.)	1.64	1.49	2.45	3.34	3.33	3.44	3.46	3.62	3.82	2.98	3.00	2.46	35.03
Days With ≥ 0.1" Precipitation	5	4	6	7	7	7	7	7	7	7	6	6	76
Days With ≥ 1.0" Precipitation	0	0	0	1	1	1	1	1	1	1	1	0	8
Mean Snowfall (in.)	14.5	9.7	6.1	2.2	trace	0.0	0.0	0.0	trace	0.4	5.5	13.3	51.7
Days With ≥ 1.0" Snow Depth	23	18	8	1	0	0	0	0	0	0	4	17	71

Benton Harbor Ross Field *Berrien County*   Elevation: 626 ft.   Latitude: 42° 08' N   Longitude: 86° 26' W

	JAN	FEB	MAR	APR	MAY	JUN	JUL	AUG	SEP	OCT	NOV	DEC	YEAR
Mean Maximum Temp. (°F)	31.8	35.7	46.0	57.6	69.3	78.7	82.6	80.7	74.0	62.7	48.8	37.0	58.7
Mean Temp. (°F)	24.9	27.6	36.6	47.2	57.9	67.5	71.8	69.8	62.9	52.2	40.6	30.1	49.1
Mean Minimum Temp. (°F)	17.6	19.4	27.3	36.8	46.4	56.2	61.0	58.8	51.5	41.6	32.4	23.0	39.3
Extreme Maximum Temp. (°F)	62	71	84	88	93	99	104	100	94	87	77	69	104
Extreme Minimum Temp. (°F)	-17	-13	-3	9	24	31	39	37	23	15	8	-15	-17
Days Maximum Temp. ≥ 90°F	0	0	0	0	0	3	5	3	1	0	0	0	12
Days Maximum Temp. ≤ 32°F	16	11	3	0	0	0	0	0	0	0	2	9	41
Days Minimum Temp. ≤ 32°F	29	25	23	10	2	0	0	0	1	5	16	26	137
Days Minimum Temp. ≤ 0°F	2	1	0	0	0	0	0	0	0	0	0	1	4
Heating Degree Days (base 65°F)	1,236	1,052	875	537	260	62	15	25	132	399	727	1,075	6,395
Cooling Degree Days (base 65°F)	0	0	1	9	44	139	230	173	69	7	0	0	672
Mean Precipitation (in.)	2.08	1.63	2.48	3.70	3.26	3.46	3.26	3.53	4.20	3.11	3.27	2.65	36.63
Days With ≥ 0.1" Precipitation	6	5	6	8	7	7	6	6	7	7	7	7	79
Days With ≥ 1.0" Precipitation	0	0	0	1	1	1	1	1	1	1	1	0	8
Mean Snowfall (in.)	26.2	18.8	7.9	1.1	trace	0.0	0.0	0.0	trace	0.4	3.6	19.9	77.9
Days With ≥ 1.0" Snow Depth	19	14	5	0	0	0	0	0	0	0	2	12	52

Bergland Dam *Ontonagon County*   Elevation: 1,299 ft.   Latitude: 46° 35' N   Longitude: 89° 33' W

	JAN	FEB	MAR	APR	MAY	JUN	JUL	AUG	SEP	OCT	NOV	DEC	YEAR
Mean Maximum Temp. (°F)	19.8	25.3	35.5	49.7	64.3	73.3	77.7	75.7	65.7	53.4	36.9	25.0	50.2
Mean Temp. (°F)	9.5	12.9	22.6	37.2	50.6	60.3	64.9	62.8	54.0	42.8	28.9	16.3	38.6
Mean Minimum Temp. (°F)	-0.8	0.5	9.6	24.6	36.9	47.2	52.0	49.9	42.3	32.4	20.8	7.5	26.9
Extreme Maximum Temp. (°F)	53	58	69	89	92	98	97	97	98	86	73	59	98
Extreme Minimum Temp. (°F)	-38	-40	-31	-11	15	27	32	31	21	12	-13	-30	-40
Days Maximum Temp. ≥ 90°F	0	0	0	0	0	0	2	1	0	0	0	0	3
Days Maximum Temp. ≤ 32°F	27	20	12	2	0	0	0	0	0	0	11	23	95
Days Minimum Temp. ≤ 32°F	31	28	30	25	11	1	0	0	4	18	27	31	206
Days Minimum Temp. ≤ 0°F	16	14	9	1	0	0	0	0	0	0	1	9	50
Heating Degree Days (base 65°F)	1,716	1,468	1,308	830	450	178	79	118	339	681	1,077	1,506	9,750
Cooling Degree Days (base 65°F)	0	0	0	1	11	46	76	57	14	0	0	0	205
Mean Precipitation (in.)	2.85	1.58	2.40	2.31	3.56	3.87	3.85	3.95	3.79	3.59	3.52	2.90	38.17
Days With ≥ 0.1" Precipitation	9	5	7	6	8	8	8	7	9	9	10	9	95
Days With ≥ 1.0" Precipitation	0	0	0	0	1	1	1	1	0	1	1	0	6
Mean Snowfall (in.)	44.0	24.5	24.9	9.1	1.4	0.0	0.0	0.0	0.1	3.5	27.7	41.2	176.4
Days With ≥ 1.0" Snow Depth	31	28	31	15	1	0	0	0	0	2	18	29	155

Big Rapids Waterworks *Mecosta County*   Elevation: 928 ft.   Latitude: 43° 42' N   Longitude: 85° 29' W

	JAN	FEB	MAR	APR	MAY	JUN	JUL	AUG	SEP	OCT	NOV	DEC	YEAR
Mean Maximum Temp. (°F)	28.4	32.4	41.8	55.6	69.2	77.9	82.3	79.3	70.9	58.5	44.3	33.2	56.1
Mean Temp. (°F)	19.8	22.5	31.3	43.8	56.2	65.1	69.7	67.2	58.9	47.5	35.7	25.7	45.3
Mean Minimum Temp. (°F)	11.0	12.6	20.7	32.2	43.3	52.2	57.1	55.0	47.0	36.5	27.8	18.0	34.4
Extreme Maximum Temp. (°F)	58	63	76	86	92	99	100	101	92	87	75	63	101
Extreme Minimum Temp. (°F)	-25	-29	-15	1	22	30	38	32	24	16	-1	-18	-29
Days Maximum Temp. ≥ 90°F	0	0	0	0	0	2	4	2	0	0	0	0	8
Days Maximum Temp. ≤ 32°F	21	14	6	0	0	0	0	0	0	0	3	14	58
Days Minimum Temp. ≤ 32°F	30	27	27	16	4	0	0	0	1	11	22	29	167
Days Minimum Temp. ≤ 0°F	6	5	1	0	0	0	0	0	0	0	0	3	15
Heating Degree Days (base 65°F)	1,396	1,193	1,040	632	291	81	21	45	209	538	861	1,213	7,520
Cooling Degree Days (base 65°F)	0	0	0	2	24	90	176	121	31	1	0	0	445
Mean Precipitation (in.)	2.15	1.51	2.42	2.91	3.14	3.20	2.62	4.17	3.95	2.99	3.04	2.34	34.44
Days With ≥ 0.1" Precipitation	6	4	6	7	7	6	5	7	8	7	7	6	76
Days With ≥ 1.0" Precipitation	0	0	0	0	1	1	1	1	1	0	0	0	5
Mean Snowfall (in.)	20.6	13.1	9.9	2.3	trace	0.0	0.0	0.0	trace	0.4	6.6	16.4	69.3
Days With ≥ 1.0" Snow Depth	28	24	14	1	0	0	0	0	0	0	5	21	93

Bloomingdale *Van Buren County*　Elevation: 725 ft.　Latitude: 42° 23' N　Longitude: 85° 58' W

	JAN	FEB	MAR	APR	MAY	JUN	JUL	AUG	SEP	OCT	NOV	DEC	YEAR
Mean Maximum Temp. (°F)	30.4	33.9	44.1	56.8	69.4	78.6	82.6	80.8	73.1	61.0	47.3	35.8	57.8
Mean Temp. (°F)	22.7	25.1	34.2	45.7	57.0	66.2	70.3	68.6	61.0	49.7	38.8	28.6	47.3
Mean Minimum Temp. (°F)	15.0	16.2	24.2	34.6	44.6	53.7	57.9	56.4	48.9	38.4	30.3	21.3	36.8
Extreme Maximum Temp. (°F)	62	71	79	87	92	98	101	100	94	89	78	68	101
Extreme Minimum Temp. (°F)	-18	-23	-7	5	24	31	39	36	26	16	8	-18	-23
Days Maximum Temp. ≥ 90°F	0	0	0	0	0	3	5	3	1	0	0	0	12
Days Maximum Temp. ≤ 32°F	17	13	5	0	0	0	0	0	0	0	2	10	47
Days Minimum Temp. ≤ 32°F	30	26	25	14	3	0	0	0	1	9	20	28	156
Days Minimum Temp. ≤ 0°F	4	3	1	0	0	0	0	0	0	0	0	1	9
Heating Degree Days (base 65°F)	1,304	1,121	950	579	280	76	21	34	169	472	779	1,123	6,908
Cooling Degree Days (base 65°F)	0	0	1	8	36	118	197	161	56	4	0	0	581
Mean Precipitation (in.)	2.60	1.76	2.73	3.58	3.36	3.56	3.96	3.57	4.44	3.05	3.64	3.33	39.58
Days With ≥ 0.1" Precipitation	8	6	7	9	7	6	6	7	7	7	9	9	88
Days With ≥ 1.0" Precipitation	0	0	0	1	1	1	1	1	1	1	1	0	8
Mean Snowfall (in.)	29.9	14.3	7.4	1.5	trace	0.0	0.0	0.0	0.0	0.4	8.1	22.8	84.4
Days With ≥ 1.0" Snow Depth	25	19	9	1	0	0	0	0	0	0	5	19	78

Boyne Falls *Charlevoix County*　Elevation: 734 ft.　Latitude: 45° 10' N　Longitude: 84° 55' W

	JAN	FEB	MAR	APR	MAY	JUN	JUL	AUG	SEP	OCT	NOV	DEC	YEAR
Mean Maximum Temp. (°F)	27.5	31.1	41.3	55.8	69.9	78.1	82.2	79.6	70.8	59.0	44.0	32.5	56.0
Mean Temp. (°F)	19.5	20.9	30.1	43.2	55.3	64.2	68.7	66.8	59.0	48.5	36.5	25.6	44.9
Mean Minimum Temp. (°F)	11.4	10.6	18.9	30.6	40.8	50.3	55.1	53.9	47.2	37.9	28.9	18.6	33.7
Extreme Maximum Temp. (°F)	56	59	78	89	94	98	98	99	95	86	76	64	99
Extreme Minimum Temp. (°F)	-32	-35	-19	-2	20	27	33	28	24	15	-3	-26	-35
Days Maximum Temp. ≥ 90°F	0	0	0	0	1	2	4	2	0	0	0	0	9
Days Maximum Temp. ≤ 32°F	21	16	6	0	0	0	0	0	0	0	3	15	61
Days Minimum Temp. ≤ 32°F	30	27	27	18	8	1	0	0	2	9	21	29	172
Days Minimum Temp. ≤ 0°F	6	7	3	0	0	0	0	0	0	0	0	2	18
Heating Degree Days (base 65°F)	1,405	1,239	1,074	652	320	102	31	54	211	509	850	1,216	7,663
Cooling Degree Days (base 65°F)	0	0	0	6	27	87	153	126	41	3	0	0	443
Mean Precipitation (in.)	2.35	1.37	2.00	2.29	2.58	2.59	3.19	3.57	4.09	3.43	2.91	2.45	32.82
Days With ≥ 0.1" Precipitation	8	5	6	6	7	6	6	7	9	8	9	9	86
Days With ≥ 1.0" Precipitation	0	0	0	0	0	0	1	1	1	1	0	0	4
Mean Snowfall (in.)	33.6	19.9	12.4	4.6	0.4	0.0	0.0	0.0	trace	0.9	14.3	30.2	116.3
Days With ≥ 1.0" Snow Depth	30	27	22	4	0	0	0	0	0	0	8	24	115

Cadillac *Wexford County*　Elevation: 1,292 ft.　Latitude: 44° 16' N　Longitude: 85° 24' W

	JAN	FEB	MAR	APR	MAY	JUN	JUL	AUG	SEP	OCT	NOV	DEC	YEAR
Mean Maximum Temp. (°F)	25.5	28.6	38.0	52.0	66.1	74.7	79.0	76.5	68.0	55.6	41.8	30.5	53.0
Mean Temp. (°F)	17.5	18.8	27.5	41.0	53.3	62.2	66.8	64.7	56.5	45.6	34.3	23.5	42.6
Mean Minimum Temp. (°F)	9.4	8.9	17.0	30.0	40.4	49.8	54.6	52.7	44.8	35.6	26.7	16.3	32.2
Extreme Maximum Temp. (°F)	55	57	75	86	91	95	99	95	88	84	73	62	99
Extreme Minimum Temp. (°F)	-30	-34	-19	-3	20	26	32	26	19	16	-7	-25	-34
Days Maximum Temp. ≥ 90°F	0	0	0	0	0	1	2	1	0	0	0	0	4
Days Maximum Temp. ≤ 32°F	24	18	10	2	0	0	0	0	0	0	6	18	78
Days Minimum Temp. ≤ 32°F	31	28	28	19	8	1	0	0	4	13	23	30	185
Days Minimum Temp. ≤ 0°F	8	8	4	0	0	0	0	0	0	0	0	4	24
Heating Degree Days (base 65°F)	1,467	1,300	1,157	716	374	139	55	87	272	595	916	1,281	8,359
Cooling Degree Days (base 65°F)	0	0	0	4	15	65	123	87	21	1	0	0	316
Mean Precipitation (in.)	1.80	1.34	2.05	2.71	2.75	3.03	3.13	3.75	4.05	3.18	2.72	2.02	32.53
Days With ≥ 0.1" Precipitation	6	4	6	7	7	6	6	7	8	7	7	6	77
Days With ≥ 1.0" Precipitation	0	0	0	0	0	1	1	1	1	0	0	0	4
Mean Snowfall (in.)	*25.7*	na	*13.1*	3.2	trace	0.0	0.0	0.0	trace	0.5	8.5	*20.9*	na
Days With ≥ 1.0" Snow Depth	*24*	na	*14*	3	0	0	0	0	0	0	*5*	*20*	na

Caro Regional Center *Tuscola County*　Elevation: 669 ft.　Latitude: 43° 27' N　Longitude: 83° 24' W

	JAN	FEB	MAR	APR	MAY	JUN	JUL	AUG	SEP	OCT	NOV	DEC	YEAR
Mean Maximum Temp. (°F)	29.3	32.4	43.4	57.5	71.0	79.7	*84.1*	*81.1*	73.0	60.8	46.1	34.0	*57.7*
Mean Temp. (°F)	21.5	23.7	33.8	45.8	57.6	66.3	*71.1*	*68.7*	61.1	50.1	38.4	27.4	*47.1*
Mean Minimum Temp. (°F)	13.8	15.0	24.1	34.0	44.1	52.8	*58.1*	*56.1*	49.1	39.3	30.7	20.7	*36.5*
Extreme Maximum Temp. (°F)	60	67	79	88	94	100	101	*98*	95	87	76	65	*101*
Extreme Minimum Temp. (°F)	-25	-24	-15	9	24	31	35	32	25	12	1	-16	-25
Days Maximum Temp. ≥ 90°F	0	0	0	0	1	3	6	2	1	0	0	0	13
Days Maximum Temp. ≤ 32°F	19	14	5	0	0	0	0	0	0	0	2	12	52
Days Minimum Temp. ≤ 32°F	29	26	25	14	4	0	0	0	1	8	18	27	152
Days Minimum Temp. ≤ 0°F	6	4	1	0	0	0	0	0	0	0	0	2	13
Heating Degree Days (base 65°F)	1,342	1,161	962	577	263	70	*14*	*33*	166	463	791	1,160	*7,002*
Cooling Degree Days (base 65°F)	0	0	1	6	38	*110*	*216*	*156*	50	4	0	0	*581*
Mean Precipitation (in.)	1.67	1.20	2.36	2.84	2.87	3.32	2.90	3.26	4.34	2.59	2.68	2.04	32.07
Days With ≥ 0.1" Precipitation	5	4	6	7	7	7	6	6	7	6	7	6	74
Days With ≥ 1.0" Precipitation	0	0	0	0	0	1	1	1	1	0	0	0	4
Mean Snowfall (in.)	11.1	6.6	5.5	1.1	trace	0.0	0.0	0.0	0.0	trace	2.5	9.0	35.8
Days With ≥ 1.0" Snow Depth	23	19	8	1	0	0	0	0	0	0	2	14	67

Champion Van Riper Park *Marquette County* Elevation: 1,564 ft. Latitude: 46° 31' N Longitude: 87° 59' W

	JAN	FEB	MAR	APR	MAY	JUN	JUL	AUG	SEP	OCT	NOV	DEC	YEAR
Mean Maximum Temp. (°F)	21.9	27.4	37.4	51.5	66.1	74.3	78.6	76.1	66.6	54.5	37.6	26.1	51.5
Mean Temp. (°F)	11.0	14.7	24.0	37.6	50.6	59.4	64.3	62.3	54.1	43.3	29.0	16.9	38.9
Mean Minimum Temp. (°F)	0.0	1.8	10.5	23.6	35.0	44.4	49.9	48.5	41.4	31.9	20.4	7.7	26.3
Extreme Maximum Temp. (°F)	54	61	69	92	90	95	98	96	94	86	73	60	98
Extreme Minimum Temp. (°F)	-40	-44	-33	-16	12	17	27	27	18	10	-13	-38	-44
Days Maximum Temp. ≥ 90°F	0	0	0	0	0	1	1	0	0	0	0	0	2
Days Maximum Temp. ≤ 32°F	27	19	9	2	0	0	0	0	0	0	10	23	90
Days Minimum Temp. ≤ 32°F	31	28	30	24	14	3	0	1	6	18	27	31	213
Days Minimum Temp. ≤ 0°F	15	12	8	1	0	0	0	0	0	0	1	9	46
Heating Degree Days (base 65°F)	1,670	1,417	1,265	818	451	194	92	128	335	667	1,072	1,485	9,594
Cooling Degree Days (base 65°F)	0	0	0	2	8	33	74	52	11	0	0	0	180
Mean Precipitation (in.)	1.82	1.31	2.24	2.43	3.19	3.26	3.80	3.81	3.96	3.36	2.55	1.85	33.58
Days With ≥ 0.1" Precipitation	5	4	6	5	7	7	7	7	9	8	7	6	78
Days With ≥ 1.0" Precipitation	0	0	0	0	0	1	1	1	1	1	0	0	5
Mean Snowfall (in.)	29.8	18.2	21.9	8.8	1.1	0.0	0.0	0.0	trace	4.8	*19.9*	27.2	*131.7*
Days With ≥ 1.0" Snow Depth	31	28	30	16	1	0	0	0	0	2	17	30	155

Charlotte *Eaton County* Elevation: 898 ft. Latitude: 42° 33' N Longitude: 84° 50' W

	JAN	FEB	MAR	APR	MAY	JUN	JUL	AUG	SEP	OCT	NOV	DEC	YEAR
Mean Maximum Temp. (°F)	29.5	33.0	43.2	56.4	69.4	78.4	82.1	79.9	72.7	60.4	46.3	34.5	57.1
Mean Temp. (°F)	21.3	23.6	33.3	45.2	57.1	66.1	69.9	67.8	60.5	49.2	37.8	27.0	46.6
Mean Minimum Temp. (°F)	13.1	14.2	23.2	34.0	44.8	53.9	57.7	55.7	48.3	37.9	29.3	19.5	36.0
Extreme Maximum Temp. (°F)	60	70	78	88	92	99	100	101	94	88	77	66	101
Extreme Minimum Temp. (°F)	-25	-22	-12	3	20	30	39	33	24	15	4	-20	-25
Days Maximum Temp. ≥ 90°F	0	0	0	0	0	1	4	2	0	0	0	0	7
Days Maximum Temp. ≤ 32°F	19	14	6	0	0	0	0	0	0	0	3	12	54
Days Minimum Temp. ≤ 32°F	30	27	26	14	3	0	0	0	1	10	20	28	159
Days Minimum Temp. ≤ 0°F	6	5	1	0	0	0	0	0	0	0	0	2	14
Heating Degree Days (base 65°F)	1,348	1,162	978	592	272	69	20	39	176	487	809	1,169	7,121
Cooling Degree Days (base 65°F)	0	0	1	4	34	108	180	135	44	3	0	0	509
Mean Precipitation (in.)	1.67	1.33	2.44	3.27	3.09	3.52	3.24	3.75	3.77	2.85	2.80	2.28	34.01
Days With ≥ 0.1" Precipitation	5	4	6	8	6	7	7	7	6	6	7	6	75
Days With ≥ 1.0" Precipitation	0	0	0	0	1	1	1	1	1	1	0	0	6
Mean Snowfall (in.)	14.1	8.8	7.5	2.2	trace	0.0	0.0	0.0	0.0	0.4	3.5	11.3	47.8
Days With ≥ 1.0" Snow Depth	23	18	9	1	0	0	0	0	0	0	3	16	70

Cheboygan *Cheboygan County* Elevation: 587 ft. Latitude: 45° 39' N Longitude: 84° 28' W

	JAN	FEB	MAR	APR	MAY	JUN	JUL	AUG	SEP	OCT	NOV	DEC	YEAR
Mean Maximum Temp. (°F)	26.4	28.9	36.9	49.2	62.6	72.1	77.7	76.1	67.8	56.0	42.7	31.9	52.4
Mean Temp. (°F)	17.7	18.9	27.2	39.6	51.7	61.4	67.5	66.1	58.2	47.1	35.7	24.9	43.0
Mean Minimum Temp. (°F)	8.9	8.9	17.3	30.0	40.7	50.6	57.3	56.2	48.5	38.1	28.7	17.8	33.6
Extreme Maximum Temp. (°F)	58	58	74	86	88	96	98	98	92	86	72	64	98
Extreme Minimum Temp. (°F)	-27	-28	-25	3	17	30	40	36	26	19	2	-15	-28
Days Maximum Temp. ≥ 90°F	0	0	0	0	0	1	1	1	0	0	0	0	3
Days Maximum Temp. ≤ 32°F	23	18	9	1	0	0	0	0	0	0	4	15	70
Days Minimum Temp. ≤ 32°F	30	28	29	18	4	0	0	0	0	7	21	29	166
Days Minimum Temp. ≤ 0°F	8	8	3	0	0	0	0	0	0	0	0	2	21
Heating Degree Days (base 65°F)	1,461	1,297	1,164	756	411	146	37	56	225	550	872	1,237	8,212
Cooling Degree Days (base 65°F)	0	0	0	0	4	45	123	101	25	2	0	0	300
Mean Precipitation (in.)	1.72	1.17	1.89	2.45	2.62	2.52	3.31	2.95	3.85	2.91	2.37	2.17	29.93
Days With ≥ 0.1" Precipitation	6	3	5	6	6	5	5	6	8	7	6	6	69
Days With ≥ 1.0" Precipitation	0	0	0	0	0	1	1	1	0	0	0	3
Mean Snowfall (in.)	26.5	16.0	11.7	3.7	trace	0.0	0.0	0.0	0.0	trace	7.7	23.6	89.2
Days With ≥ 1.0" Snow Depth	29	27	21	4	0	0	0	0	0	0	*8*	22	*111*

Coldwater State School *Branch County* Elevation: 980 ft. Latitude: 41° 57' N Longitude: 85° 00' W

	JAN	FEB	MAR	APR	MAY	JUN	JUL	AUG	SEP	OCT	NOV	DEC	YEAR
Mean Maximum Temp. (°F)	30.2	34.0	44.4	57.4	69.9	78.9	82.4	80.3	73.0	60.7	46.4	35.1	57.7
Mean Temp. (°F)	22.3	25.5	35.0	46.7	58.4	67.4	71.3	69.1	61.8	50.2	38.5	27.8	47.8
Mean Minimum Temp. (°F)	14.4	16.9	25.5	35.9	46.8	56.0	60.1	57.9	50.4	39.6	30.6	20.5	37.9
Extreme Maximum Temp. (°F)	61	67	78	86	91	102	100	101	95	87	75	67	102
Extreme Minimum Temp. (°F)	-23	-17	-6	6	24	35	40	36	29	16	4	-15	-23
Days Maximum Temp. ≥ 90°F	0	0	0	0	0	2	4	2	1	0	0	0	9
Days Maximum Temp. ≤ 32°F	18	13	5	0	0	0	0	0	0	0	2	12	50
Days Minimum Temp. ≤ 32°F	29	26	24	12	2	0	0	0	0	7	19	28	147
Days Minimum Temp. ≤ 0°F	5	3	0	0	0	0	0	0	0	0	0	2	10
Heating Degree Days (base 65°F)	1,316	1,109	925	550	239	53	11	27	152	458	788	1,146	6,774
Cooling Degree Days (base 65°F)	0	0	1	5	42	136	222	168	60	4	0	0	638
Mean Precipitation (in.)	1.78	1.69	2.53	3.17	3.71	3.61	3.98	3.90	3.50	2.82	2.68	2.43	35.80
Days With ≥ 0.1" Precipitation	5	4	6	8	7	7	7	7	7	6	6	7	77
Days With ≥ 1.0" Precipitation	0	0	0	0	1	1	1	1	1	1	0	0	6
Mean Snowfall (in.)	16.2	10.3	7.9	1.9	trace	0.0	0.0	0.0	trace	0.6	5.2	13.5	55.6
Days With ≥ 1.0" Snow Depth	21	16	7	1	0	0	0	0	0	0	3	14	62

Cross Village *Emmet County*   Elevation: 741 ft.   Latitude: 45° 38' N   Longitude: 85° 02' W

	JAN	FEB	MAR	APR	MAY	JUN	JUL	AUG	SEP	OCT	NOV	DEC	YEAR
Mean Maximum Temp. (°F)	26.6	29.3	38.5	51.5	64.6	72.0	76.9	75.6	68.2	56.8	42.9	32.0	52.9
Mean Temp. (°F)	19.5	20.4	28.9	41.1	52.8	61.2	67.0	66.2	59.4	48.8	36.9	26.4	44.1
Mean Minimum Temp. (°F)	12.5	11.4	19.3	30.6	40.9	50.4	57.1	56.8	50.4	40.7	30.9	20.8	35.1
Extreme Maximum Temp. (°F)	55	59	76	89	90	90	95	93	90	82	73	65	95
Extreme Minimum Temp. (°F)	-27	-29	-19	2	22	31	38	35	27	18	6	-20	-29
Days Maximum Temp. ≥ 90°F	0	0	0	0	0	0	0	0	0	0	0	0	0
Days Maximum Temp. ≤ 32°F	23	18	8	1	0	0	0	0	0	0	3	15	68
Days Minimum Temp. ≤ 32°F	30	27	27	18	6	0	0	0	0	4	17	28	157
Days Minimum Temp. ≤ 0°F	6	6	2	0	0	0	0	0	0	0	0	1	15
Heating Degree Days (base 65°F)	1,402	1,255	1,112	712	382	147	41	50	193	498	836	1,189	7,817
Cooling Degree Days (base 65°F)	0	0	0	3	9	43	113	99	30	1	0	0	298
Mean Precipitation (in.)	1.78	1.08	1.91	2.40	2.44	2.47	2.21	3.25	3.51	2.77	2.38	2.04	28.24
Days With ≥ 0.1" Precipitation	5	4	5	6	6	5	5	7	7	7	7	6	70
Days With ≥ 1.0" Precipitation	0	0	0	0	0	0	0	1	1	0	0	0	2
Mean Snowfall (in.)	23.7	15.4	11.0	4.3	0.2	0.0	0.0	0.0	trace	0.3	5.4	18.0	78.3
Days With ≥ 1.0" Snow Depth	29	28	23	5	0	0	0	0	0	0	6	21	112

Dearborn *Wayne County*   Elevation: 603 ft.   Latitude: 42° 19' N   Longitude: 83° 14' W

	JAN	FEB	MAR	APR	MAY	JUN	JUL	AUG	SEP	OCT	NOV	DEC	YEAR
Mean Maximum Temp. (°F)	31.4	35.0	45.0	58.4	71.2	80.1	84.4	82.6	75.1	62.3	48.7	37.0	59.3
Mean Temp. (°F)	23.8	26.6	35.9	47.7	59.4	68.5	73.2	71.5	63.8	51.7	40.5	29.8	49.4
Mean Minimum Temp. (°F)	16.2	18.2	26.6	37.0	47.6	56.9	62.0	60.3	52.4	41.0	32.3	22.7	39.4
Extreme Maximum Temp. (°F)	62	70	81	90	92	104	102	100	99	86	76	69	104
Extreme Minimum Temp. (°F)	-20	-12	-4	10	23	36	45	40	29	19	8	-9	-20
Days Maximum Temp. ≥ 90°F	0	0	0	0	0	3	6	4	1	0	0	0	14
Days Maximum Temp. ≤ 32°F	16	12	4	0	0	0	0	0	0	0	1	10	43
Days Minimum Temp. ≤ 32°F	29	25	23	10	1	0	0	0	0	5	16	26	135
Days Minimum Temp. ≤ 0°F	3	2	0	0	0	0	0	0	0	0	0	1	6
Heating Degree Days (base 65°F)	1,269	1,077	898	519	214	44	5	13	115	414	728	1,083	6,379
Cooling Degree Days (base 65°F)	0	0	1	7	45	149	264	214	79	6	0	0	765
Mean Precipitation (in.)	1.90	1.90	2.67	3.27	2.88	3.56	3.10	2.77	3.40	2.50	2.80	2.45	33.20
Days With ≥ 0.1" Precipitation	5	5	6	8	6	7	6	5	6	5	7	6	72
Days With ≥ 1.0" Precipitation	0	0	0	0	0	1	1	1	1	1	0	0	5
Mean Snowfall (in.)	10.8	7.6	4.8	0.8	0.0	0.0	0.0	0.0	0.0	trace	1.7	7.3	33.0
Days With ≥ 1.0" Snow Depth	20	16	6	1	0	0	0	0	0	0	2	11	56

Detour Village *Chippewa County*   Elevation: 593 ft.   Latitude: 46° 00' N   Longitude: 83° 54' W

	JAN	FEB	MAR	APR	MAY	JUN	JUL	AUG	SEP	OCT	NOV	DEC	YEAR
Mean Maximum Temp. (°F)	24.2	26.5	35.0	47.4	61.0	70.3	76.1	74.7	65.5	53.6	41.6	30.9	50.6
Mean Temp. (°F)	16.0	17.3	26.0	38.7	51.0	60.3	66.4	65.9	57.5	46.4	35.6	24.1	42.1
Mean Minimum Temp. (°F)	7.7	8.0	17.1	29.9	40.9	50.2	56.7	57.0	49.5	39.2	29.5	17.4	33.6
Extreme Maximum Temp. (°F)	45	52	60	83	88	94	98	95	91	80	68	58	98
Extreme Minimum Temp. (°F)	-27	-39	-32	1	22	32	38	36	27	19	2	-24	-39
Days Maximum Temp. ≥ 90°F	0	0	0	0	0	0	1	0	0	0	0	0	1
Days Maximum Temp. ≤ 32°F	24	20	11	2	0	0	0	0	0	0	4	16	77
Days Minimum Temp. ≤ 32°F	31	28	29	19	4	0	0	0	0	5	19	29	164
Days Minimum Temp. ≤ 0°F	10	9	3	0	0	0	0	0	0	0	0	3	25
Heating Degree Days (base 65°F)	1,515	1,343	1,202	783	430	163	44	51	236	571	877	1,261	8,476
Cooling Degree Days (base 65°F)	0	0	0	0	3	30	99	93	18	0	0	0	243
Mean Precipitation (in.)	1.88	1.22	2.20	2.34	2.59	2.55	3.22	2.95	4.01	2.68	2.41	2.01	30.06
Days With ≥ 0.1" Precipitation	7	4	6	6	6	6	7	7	8	7	7	7	78
Days With ≥ 1.0" Precipitation	0	0	0	0	0	0	1	1	1	0	0	0	3
Mean Snowfall (in.)	19.1	13.2	13.1	3.6	trace	0.0	0.0	0.0	0.0	trace	5.1	15.6	69.7
Days With ≥ 1.0" Snow Depth	29	27	26	9	0	0	0	0	0	0	5	20	116

Detroit City Airport *Wayne County*   Elevation: 623 ft.   Latitude: 42° 25' N   Longitude: 83° 01' W

	JAN	FEB	MAR	APR	MAY	JUN	JUL	AUG	SEP	OCT	NOV	DEC	YEAR
Mean Maximum Temp. (°F)	30.8	33.5	44.3	57.2	70.2	78.8	83.4	81.0	73.2	60.6	48.1	36.3	58.1
Mean Temp. (°F)	24.9	27.1	36.7	48.3	60.4	69.3	74.5	72.5	64.8	52.9	42.0	30.8	50.4
Mean Minimum Temp. (°F)	19.1	20.7	29.1	39.4	50.6	59.8	65.6	63.9	56.3	45.1	35.7	25.3	42.6
Extreme Maximum Temp. (°F)	61	66	82	89	93	103	102	99	97	84	75	68	103
Extreme Minimum Temp. (°F)	-17	-7	5	17	30	41	42	46	34	24	14	-5	-17
Days Maximum Temp. ≥ 90°F	0	0	0	0	1	3	5	3	1	0	0	0	13
Days Maximum Temp. ≤ 32°F	16	14	5	0	0	0	0	0	0	0	1	10	46
Days Minimum Temp. ≤ 32°F	27	24	19	7	0	0	0	0	0	2	11	23	113
Days Minimum Temp. ≤ 0°F	1	1	0	0	0	0	0	0	0	0	0	0	2
Heating Degree Days (base 65°F)	1,234	1,064	870	504	196	37	3	8	97	378	685	1,052	6,128
Cooling Degree Days (base 65°F)	0	0	0	10	63	165	312	249	96	7	0	0	902
Mean Precipitation (in.)	na	na	na	na	na	na	na	na	na	na	na	na	na
Days With ≥ 0.1" Precipitation	na	na	na	na	na	na	na	na	na	na	na	na	na
Days With ≥ 1.0" Precipitation	na	na	na	na	na	na	na	na	na	na	na	na	na
Mean Snowfall (in.)	na	na	na	na	na	na	na	na	na	na	na	na	na
Days With ≥ 1.0" Snow Depth	na	na	na	na	na	na	na	na	na	na	na	na	na

Detroit WBAP Willow *Wayne County* Elevation: 777 ft. Latitude: 42° 14' N Longitude: 83° 32' W

	JAN	FEB	MAR	APR	MAY	JUN	JUL	AUG	SEP	OCT	NOV	DEC	YEAR
Mean Maximum Temp. (°F)	31.0	35.0	45.9	59.2	71.8	80.6	84.4	81.9	74.7	62.2	47.9	36.3	59.2
Mean Temp. (°F)	24.2	27.3	36.9	48.8	60.6	69.6	73.8	71.7	64.3	52.6	40.6	30.1	50.0
Mean Minimum Temp. (°F)	17.3	19.7	27.9	38.3	49.4	58.6	63.2	61.4	53.9	42.8	33.2	23.8	40.8
Extreme Maximum Temp. (°F)	62	69	80	87	92	102	100	98	96	86	75	68	102
Extreme Minimum Temp. (°F)	-20	-9	0	10	28	38	47	38	33	21	9	-10	-20
Days Maximum Temp. ≥ 90°F	0	0	0	0	1	3	6	3	1	0	0	0	14
Days Maximum Temp. ≤ 32°F	17	12	4	0	0	0	0	0	0	0	2	10	45
Days Minimum Temp. ≤ 32°F	29	25	22	8	0	0	0	0	0	3	15	26	128
Days Minimum Temp. ≤ 0°F	3	2	0	0	0	0	0	0	0	0	0	1	6
Heating Degree Days (base 65°F)	1,259	1,057	865	487	185	31	3	9	103	386	725	1,076	6,186
Cooling Degree Days (base 65°F)	0	0	1	8	56	180	293	228	88	6	0	0	860
Mean Precipitation (in.)	1.76	1.64	2.52	3.08	3.06	3.15	2.95	3.23	3.41	2.33	2.83	2.41	32.37
Days With ≥ 0.1" Precipitation	5	4	6	7	6	6	6	6	6	5	7	6	70
Days With ≥ 1.0" Precipitation	0	0	0	0	1	1	1	1	1	0	0	0	5
Mean Snowfall (in.)	10.8	7.0	5.5	1.1	trace	0.0	0.0	0.0	0.0	trace	2.1	9.0	35.5
Days With ≥ 1.0" Snow Depth	20	15	7	1	0	0	0	0	0	0	2	12	57

Dowagiac 1 W *Cass County* Elevation: 738 ft. Latitude: 41° 59' N Longitude: 86° 08' W

	JAN	FEB	MAR	APR	MAY	JUN	JUL	AUG	SEP	OCT	NOV	DEC	YEAR
Mean Maximum Temp. (°F)	31.4	35.4	45.6	58.4	70.5	79.6	83.6	81.4	74.3	62.3	48.3	36.7	59.0
Mean Temp. (°F)	23.0	26.6	35.7	47.3	58.5	67.6	71.7	69.6	62.2	50.9	39.6	29.0	48.5
Mean Minimum Temp. (°F)	14.5	17.4	25.7	36.1	46.3	55.5	59.8	57.8	50.1	39.5	30.7	21.2	37.9
Extreme Maximum Temp. (°F)	62	71	80	88	92	101	103	100	95	88	77	69	103
Extreme Minimum Temp. (°F)	-21	-23	-6	6	25	30	38	38	26	17	8	-20	-23
Days Maximum Temp. ≥ 90°F	0	0	0	0	1	3	6	3	1	0	0	0	14
Days Maximum Temp. ≤ 32°F	17	11	4	0	0	0	0	0	0	0	1	9	42
Days Minimum Temp. ≤ 32°F	30	26	24	12	2	0	0	0	1	7	19	28	149
Days Minimum Temp. ≤ 0°F	4	3	0	0	0	0	0	0	0	0	0	1	8
Heating Degree Days (base 65°F)	1,296	1,077	904	534	243	57	14	24	146	436	758	1,109	6,598
Cooling Degree Days (base 65°F)	0	0	1	7	45	144	232	174	63	5	0	0	671
Mean Precipitation (in.)	2.66	1.98	2.69	3.55	3.58	3.68	3.76	3.87	4.12	3.57	3.44	3.07	39.97
Days With ≥ 0.1" Precipitation	8	6	7	8	7	7	7	7	7	7	8	9	88
Days With ≥ 1.0" Precipitation	0	0	0	1	1	1	1	1	1	1	1	0	8
Mean Snowfall (in.)	21.3	12.7	6.2	1.3	trace	0.0	0.0	0.0	0.0	trace	6.0	16.7	64.2
Days With ≥ 1.0" Snow Depth	23	18	7	1	0	0	0	0	0	0	4	15	68

East Jordan *Charlevoix County* Elevation: 587 ft. Latitude: 45° 09' N Longitude: 85° 08' W

	JAN	FEB	MAR	APR	MAY	JUN	JUL	AUG	SEP	OCT	NOV	DEC	YEAR
Mean Maximum Temp. (°F)	28.5	31.6	40.9	54.7	68.7	77.3	81.1	78.8	70.9	59.4	44.8	33.5	55.8
Mean Temp. (°F)	20.5	21.4	30.0	42.7	54.6	63.3	68.0	66.1	58.9	48.7	37.0	26.8	44.9
Mean Minimum Temp. (°F)	12.5	11.1	19.2	30.7	40.6	49.3	55.0	53.5	46.9	37.9	29.2	20.0	33.8
Extreme Maximum Temp. (°F)	55	57	79	88	93	96	97	98	93	86	75	64	98
Extreme Minimum Temp. (°F)	-36	-41	-24	0	19	29	35	30	24	15	2	-31	-41
Days Maximum Temp. ≥ 90°F	0	0	0	0	0	2	3	1	0	0	0	0	6
Days Maximum Temp. ≤ 32°F	20	16	7	1	0	0	0	0	0	0	3	13	60
Days Minimum Temp. ≤ 32°F	30	27	27	17	6	1	0	0	1	9	20	29	167
Days Minimum Temp. ≤ 0°F	5	7	3	0	0	0	0	0	0	0	0	1	16
Heating Degree Days (base 65°F)	1,374	1,225	1,078	665	336	110	35	59	209	503	833	1,178	7,605
Cooling Degree Days (base 65°F)	0	0	0	3	22	68	140	112	33	2	0	0	380
Mean Precipitation (in.)	2.07	1.22	1.63	2.37	2.58	2.73	3.09	3.46	4.19	3.59	2.83	2.38	32.14
Days With ≥ 0.1" Precipitation	7	4	5	6	6	6	6	7	9	8	8	8	80
Days With ≥ 1.0" Precipitation	0	0	0	0	0	0	1	1	1	1	0	0	4
Mean Snowfall (in.)	33.9	18.0	10.2	2.5	0.2	0.0	0.0	0.0	0.0	0.4	10.0	29.6	104.8
Days With ≥ 1.0" Snow Depth	29	27	22	3	0	0	0	0	0	0	8	24	113

East Lansing 4 S *Ingham County* Elevation: 879 ft. Latitude: 42° 40' N Longitude: 84° 29' W

	JAN	FEB	MAR	APR	MAY	JUN	JUL	AUG	SEP	OCT	NOV	DEC	YEAR
Mean Maximum Temp. (°F)	29.0	32.3	42.9	56.4	69.1	78.2	82.4	80.3	72.7	60.2	46.2	34.3	57.0
Mean Temp. (°F)	21.4	23.9	33.6	45.8	57.4	66.6	70.8	68.8	61.1	49.5	38.2	27.3	47.0
Mean Minimum Temp. (°F)	13.7	15.4	24.3	35.2	45.7	54.9	59.1	57.2	49.5	38.8	30.2	20.2	37.0
Extreme Maximum Temp. (°F)	61	64	80	86	91	98	101	100	93	88	75	67	101
Extreme Minimum Temp. (°F)	-20	-19	-7	3	24	34	41	33	26	19	4	-12	-20
Days Maximum Temp. ≥ 90°F	0	0	0	0	0	2	4	2	1	0	0	0	9
Days Maximum Temp. ≤ 32°F	19	14	6	0	0	0	0	0	0	0	3	13	55
Days Minimum Temp. ≤ 32°F	30	26	25	13	2	0	0	0	1	8	20	28	153
Days Minimum Temp. ≤ 0°F	4	4	1	0	0	0	0	0	0	0	0	1	10
Heating Degree Days (base 65°F)	1,346	1,156	966	573	264	65	15	31	165	478	798	1,163	7,020
Cooling Degree Days (base 65°F)	0	0	1	4	35	111	202	154	49	3	0	0	559
Mean Precipitation (in.)	1.53	1.38	2.18	3.25	2.56	3.20	3.09	3.31	3.35	2.48	2.60	2.00	30.93
Days With ≥ 0.1" Precipitation	4	4	6	8	6	6	6	6	6	6	6	5	69
Days With ≥ 1.0" Precipitation	0	0	0	0	0	1	1	1	1	0	0	0	4
Mean Snowfall (in.)	*11.3*	*8.1*	5.1	1.4	0.0	0.0	0.0	0.0	0.0	0.2	*2.2*	*9.0*	*37.3*
Days With ≥ 1.0" Snow Depth	22	18	9	1	0	0	0	0	0	0	3	15	68

East Tawas *Iosco County*   Elevation: 583 ft.   Latitude: 44° 17' N   Longitude: 83° 30' W

	JAN	FEB	MAR	APR	MAY	JUN	JUL	AUG	SEP	OCT	NOV	DEC	YEAR
Mean Maximum Temp. (°F)	28.6	31.1	39.8	52.0	65.5	74.7	79.9	77.7	70.1	57.9	44.8	34.1	54.7
Mean Temp. (°F)	20.1	21.7	30.5	42.2	54.1	63.2	68.4	66.7	59.3	48.1	36.9	26.8	44.8
Mean Minimum Temp. (°F)	11.4	12.3	21.1	32.4	42.7	51.6	57.0	55.7	48.3	38.0	29.1	19.4	34.9
Extreme Maximum Temp. (°F)	52	58	74	91	92	101	102	95	95	81	76	65	102
Extreme Minimum Temp. (°F)	-19	-26	-18	7	23	28	35	31	26	16	1	-19	-26
Days Maximum Temp. ≥ 90°F	0	0	0	0	0	1	2	1	0	0	0	0	4
Days Maximum Temp. ≤ 32°F	20	15	6	1	0	0	0	0	0	0	2	12	56
Days Minimum Temp. ≤ 32°F	30	27	27	15	3	0	0	0	1	9	20	29	161
Days Minimum Temp. ≤ 0°F	7	6	2	0	0	0	0	0	0	0	0	2	17
Heating Degree Days (base 65°F)	1,387	1,214	1,063	677	346	114	29	50	195	517	835	1,177	7,604
Cooling Degree Days (base 65°F)	0	0	0	1	16	72	153	119	33	1	0	0	395
Mean Precipitation (in.)	2.05	1.30	2.13	2.61	2.69	3.08	2.91	3.34	3.42	2.59	2.52	2.04	30.68
Days With ≥ 0.1" Precipitation	5	4	5	6	7	6	6	7	6	6	6	6	70
Days With ≥ 1.0" Precipitation	0	0	0	0	1	1	1	1	1	0	0	0	5
Mean Snowfall (in.)	17.9	11.9	9.9	2.5	0.1	0.0	0.0	0.0	trace	trace	3.3	10.5	56.1
Days With ≥ 1.0" Snow Depth	28	26	19	2	0	0	0	0	0	0	3	14	92

Eau Claire 4 NE *Berrien County*   Elevation: 869 ft.   Latitude: 42° 01' N   Longitude: 86° 15' W

	JAN	FEB	MAR	APR	MAY	JUN	JUL	AUG	SEP	OCT	NOV	DEC	YEAR
Mean Maximum Temp. (°F)	30.6	34.8	45.9	58.9	70.9	79.9	83.6	81.3	73.9	61.8	47.8	35.8	58.8
Mean Temp. (°F)	23.8	27.4	37.1	48.6	59.9	69.1	73.3	71.5	64.2	52.8	40.6	29.5	49.8
Mean Minimum Temp. (°F)	16.9	19.9	28.3	38.2	48.9	58.3	62.9	61.6	54.4	43.7	33.4	23.2	40.8
Extreme Maximum Temp. (°F)	62	71	82	87	92	100	103	101	94	89	76	68	103
Extreme Minimum Temp. (°F)	-22	-13	-1	10	24	36	44	43	33	21	8	-12	-22
Days Maximum Temp. ≥ 90°F	0	0	0	0	0	3	5	3	1	0	0	0	12
Days Maximum Temp. ≤ 32°F	18	12	4	0	0	0	0	0	0	0	2	11	47
Days Minimum Temp. ≤ 32°F	29	25	22	9	1	0	0	0	0	2	15	27	130
Days Minimum Temp. ≤ 0°F	3	1	0	0	0	0	0	0	0	0	0	1	5
Heating Degree Days (base 65°F)	1,271	1,056	858	495	208	40	5	10	105	380	725	1,094	6,247
Cooling Degree Days (base 65°F)	0	0	1	9	58	178	281	229	91	8	0	0	855
Mean Precipitation (in.)	2.02	1.56	2.55	3.40	3.44	3.47	3.35	3.69	3.79	3.14	3.25	2.74	36.40
Days With ≥ 0.1" Precipitation	6	5	7	8	7	7	6	6	7	7	8	7	81
Days With ≥ 1.0" Precipitation	0	0	0	1	1	1	1	1	1	1	1	0	8
Mean Snowfall (in.)	25.9	15.1	8.4	1.8	trace	0.0	0.0	0.0	0.0	0.4	7.6	21.6	80.8
Days With ≥ 1.0" Snow Depth	23	19	8	1	0	0	0	0	0	0	4	17	72

Fayette 4 SW *Delta County*   Elevation: 744 ft.   Latitude: 45° 40' N   Longitude: 86° 43' W

	JAN	FEB	MAR	APR	MAY	JUN	JUL	AUG	SEP	OCT	NOV	DEC	YEAR
Mean Maximum Temp. (°F)	24.4	26.8	35.9	47.8	60.9	69.6	75.2	74.1	65.5	54.6	41.3	29.7	50.5
Mean Temp. (°F)	17.4	19.3	28.3	39.5	51.2	60.2	66.5	66.0	58.2	47.8	35.6	23.7	42.8
Mean Minimum Temp. (°F)	10.4	11.6	20.6	31.1	41.5	50.7	57.8	57.9	50.9	41.0	30.0	17.8	35.1
Extreme Maximum Temp. (°F)	45	49	63	78	89	90	90	93	82	76	61	57	93
Extreme Minimum Temp. (°F)	-24	-25	-12	5	25	33	40	38	30	24	0	-19	-25
Days Maximum Temp. ≥ 90°F	0	0	0	0	0	0	0	0	0	0	0	0	0
Days Maximum Temp. ≤ 32°F	24	19	9	1	0	0	0	0	0	0	4	18	75
Days Minimum Temp. ≤ 32°F	31	28	28	17	3	0	0	0	0	4	19	29	159
Days Minimum Temp. ≤ 0°F	6	5	1	0	0	0	0	0	0	0	0	2	14
Heating Degree Days (base 65°F)	1,469	1,286	1,132	758	423	161	36	44	212	526	874	1,273	8,194
Cooling Degree Days (base 65°F)	0	0	0	0	1	29	98	94	18	0	0	0	240
Mean Precipitation (in.)	1.51	1.01	2.10	2.33	2.76	2.57	2.85	3.50	3.28	2.78	2.41	1.76	28.86
Days With ≥ 0.1" Precipitation	5	4	5	5	6	6	7	7	7	6	6	5	69
Days With ≥ 1.0" Precipitation	0	0	0	0	0	0	1	1	1	0	0	0	3
Mean Snowfall (in.)	15.7	9.8	9.6	2.6	trace	0.0	0.0	0.0	0.0	0.2	na	13.5	na
Days With ≥ 1.0" Snow Depth	26	26	18	4	0	0	0	0	0	0	na	na	na

Frankfort *Benzie County*   Elevation: 718 ft.   Latitude: 44° 39' N   Longitude: 86° 13' W

	JAN	FEB	MAR	APR	MAY	JUN	JUL	AUG	SEP	OCT	NOV	DEC	YEAR
Mean Maximum Temp. (°F)	27.7	30.1	38.8	51.3	64.0	72.5	77.2	75.3	68.0	56.9	43.5	32.6	53.2
Mean Temp. (°F)	22.2	23.9	31.5	42.7	53.8	62.5	67.8	67.0	59.9	49.4	37.7	27.4	45.5
Mean Minimum Temp. (°F)	16.7	17.6	24.2	34.0	43.6	52.4	58.4	58.6	51.6	41.8	31.8	22.2	37.7
Extreme Maximum Temp. (°F)	56	58	73	86	88	94	93	95	91	82	69	62	95
Extreme Minimum Temp. (°F)	-15	-12	0	11	25	30	40	40	31	23	5	-3	-15
Days Maximum Temp. ≥ 90°F	0	0	0	0	0	0	0	0	0	0	0	0	0
Days Maximum Temp. ≤ 32°F	21	16	8	1	0	0	0	0	0	0	3	14	63
Days Minimum Temp. ≤ 32°F	30	27	26	14	2	0	0	0	0	3	17	28	147
Days Minimum Temp. ≤ 0°F	2	1	0	0	0	0	0	0	0	0	0	0	3
Heating Degree Days (base 65°F)	1,319	1,155	1,030	665	353	125	28	35	182	480	813	1,158	7,343
Cooling Degree Days (base 65°F)	0	0	0	2	13	62	130	111	34	1	0	0	353
Mean Precipitation (in.)	2.80	1.98	2.37	2.57	2.69	3.18	3.00	3.42	4.17	3.30	2.97	2.79	35.24
Days With ≥ 0.1" Precipitation	10	7	7	6	6	6	6	6	7	7	8	9	85
Days With ≥ 1.0" Precipitation	0	0	0	0	0	1	1	1	1	1	0	0	5
Mean Snowfall (in.)	37.4	22.0	14.7	4.4	0.2	0.0	0.0	0.0	trace	0.5	9.0	27.5	115.7
Days With ≥ 1.0" Snow Depth	29	27	22	3	0	0	0	0	0	0	7	23	111

Gaylord *Otsego County*   Elevation: 1,348 ft.   Latitude: 45° 02' N   Longitude: 84° 40' W

	JAN	FEB	MAR	APR	MAY	JUN	JUL	AUG	SEP	OCT	NOV	DEC	YEAR
Mean Maximum Temp. (°F)	25.1	28.9	39.0	53.2	67.9	76.4	80.3	77.5	68.5	56.5	41.4	29.9	53.7
Mean Temp. (°F)	17.4	19.5	28.5	41.6	54.6	63.5	67.9	65.8	57.5	46.7	34.1	23.2	43.4
Mean Minimum Temp. (°F)	9.5	10.0	18.0	29.9	41.2	50.6	55.4	54.0	46.6	36.8	26.8	16.4	32.9
Extreme Maximum Temp. (°F)	53	58	74	88	92	95	97	95	91	85	75	62	97
Extreme Minimum Temp. (°F)	-32	-37	-27	-4	22	26	33	26	22	14	-3	-27	-37
Days Maximum Temp. ≥ 90°F	0	0	0	0	0	1	2	1	0	0	0	0	4
Days Maximum Temp. ≤ 32°F	24	18	9	1	0	0	0	0	0	0	6	19	77
Days Minimum Temp. ≤ 32°F	31	28	28	19	6	1	0	0	2	11	23	29	178
Days Minimum Temp. ≤ 0°F	7	7	3	0	0	0	0	0	0	0	0	3	20
Heating Degree Days (base 65°F)	1,471	1,280	1,124	699	338	112	38	64	244	563	920	1,290	8,143
Cooling Degree Days (base 65°F)	0	0	0	3	19	70	129	96	24	0	0	0	341
Mean Precipitation (in.)	3.06	2.00	2.52	2.44	2.80	2.72	3.33	3.74	3.90	3.53	3.32	3.17	36.53
Days With ≥ 0.1" Precipitation	10	7	7	7	7	6	6	7	9	9	10	10	95
Days With ≥ 1.0" Precipitation	0	0	0	0	0	0	1	1	1	0	0	0	3
Mean Snowfall (in.)	39.0	23.9	19.1	6.9	1.0	0.0	0.0	0.0	trace	2.7	22.1	34.7	149.4
Days With ≥ 1.0" Snow Depth	31	28	26	6	0	0	0	0	0	1	12	26	130

Gladwin *Gladwin County*   Elevation: 774 ft.   Latitude: 43° 59' N   Longitude: 84° 29' W

	JAN	FEB	MAR	APR	MAY	JUN	JUL	AUG	SEP	OCT	NOV	DEC	YEAR
Mean Maximum Temp. (°F)	28.3	32.1	41.9	55.9	70.0	78.8	83.1	80.2	71.7	59.5	44.7	33.8	56.7
Mean Temp. (°F)	19.2	22.1	31.4	43.9	56.3	65.3	69.8	67.5	59.2	47.9	36.2	26.2	45.4
Mean Minimum Temp. (°F)	10.0	12.1	20.8	31.8	42.6	51.7	56.5	54.7	46.6	36.1	27.7	18.6	34.1
Extreme Maximum Temp. (°F)	57	63	79	90	92	102	101	97	94	86	74	63	102
Extreme Minimum Temp. (°F)	-23	-27	-14	8	22	30	36	31	25	11	-1	-19	-27
Days Maximum Temp. ≥ 90°F	0	0	0	0	1	3	5	2	0	0	0	0	11
Days Maximum Temp. ≤ 32°F	21	15	6	0	0	0	0	0	0	0	3	14	59
Days Minimum Temp. ≤ 32°F	30	28	28	17	4	0	0	0	2	11	22	29	171
Days Minimum Temp. ≤ 0°F	8	6	2	0	0	0	0	0	0	0	0	2	18
Heating Degree Days (base 65°F)	1,414	1,203	1,035	631	291	79	21	42	202	525	858	1,197	7,498
Cooling Degree Days (base 65°F)	0	0	0	3	28	94	178	128	33	1	0	0	465
Mean Precipitation (in.)	1.93	1.25	2.27	2.50	2.83	3.24	2.97	3.60	3.53	2.71	2.52	2.09	31.44
Days With ≥ 0.1" Precipitation	5	4	5	6	6	6	6	7	7	6	6	6	70
Days With ≥ 1.0" Precipitation	0	0	0	0	0	1	1	1	1	1	1	0	6
Mean Snowfall (in.)	15.0	9.2	9.0	1.9	trace	0.0	0.0	0.0	0.0	0.3	4.0	10.8	50.2
Days With ≥ 1.0" Snow Depth	27	24	16	2	0	0	0	0	0	0	3	19	91

Grand Haven Fire Dept. *Ottawa County*   Elevation: 620 ft.   Latitude: 43° 04' N   Longitude: 86° 13' W

	JAN	FEB	MAR	APR	MAY	JUN	JUL	AUG	SEP	OCT	NOV	DEC	YEAR
Mean Maximum Temp. (°F)	30.6	33.0	43.1	55.3	67.3	75.8	80.2	78.4	71.5	59.8	46.9	35.6	56.5
Mean Temp. (°F)	24.8	26.5	35.5	46.5	57.6	66.3	71.7	70.1	63.0	52.0	40.7	30.1	48.7
Mean Minimum Temp. (°F)	19.0	20.0	27.8	37.6	47.8	56.8	63.1	61.8	54.4	44.2	34.4	24.5	40.9
Extreme Maximum Temp. (°F)	59	60	81	85	91	91	95	93	88	83	72	66	95
Extreme Minimum Temp. (°F)	-11	-10	1	14	27	37	46	39	31	24	10	-9	-11
Days Maximum Temp. ≥ 90°F	0	0	0	0	0	0	1	0	0	0	0	0	1
Days Maximum Temp. ≤ 32°F	17	13	4	0	0	0	0	0	0	0	1	9	44
Days Minimum Temp. ≤ 32°F	29	25	22	8	0	0	0	0	0	2	13	25	124
Days Minimum Temp. ≤ 0°F	1	1	0	0	0	0	0	0	0	0	0	0	2
Heating Degree Days (base 65°F)	1,241	1,080	908	555	257	60	9	16	120	401	722	1,075	6,444
Cooling Degree Days (base 65°F)	0	0	0	7	34	112	243	195	65	3	0	0	659
Mean Precipitation (in.)	2.03	1.30	2.40	2.81	2.91	2.99	2.51	3.57	3.66	2.72	3.28	2.64	32.82
Days With ≥ 0.1" Precipitation	7	4	6	7	6	6	5	6	6	6	7	7	73
Days With ≥ 1.0" Precipitation	0	0	0	1	1	1	0	1	1	0	0	0	5
Mean Snowfall (in.)	24.1	13.2	5.8	1.7	trace	0.0	0.0	0.0	0.0	0.2	5.5	19.9	70.4
Days With ≥ 1.0" Snow Depth	23	20	9	1	0	0	0	0	0	0	2	15	70

Grand Marais 2 E *Alger County*   Elevation: 623 ft.   Latitude: 46° 40' N   Longitude: 85° 57' W

	JAN	FEB	MAR	APR	MAY	JUN	JUL	AUG	SEP	OCT	NOV	DEC	YEAR
Mean Maximum Temp. (°F)	25.1	28.0	36.6	49.1	62.0	71.1	75.9	75.6	67.3	55.5	40.9	30.2	51.4
Mean Temp. (°F)	17.8	19.4	27.0	38.6	49.7	58.3	63.6	63.9	56.7	46.0	33.9	23.5	41.5
Mean Minimum Temp. (°F)	10.5	10.8	17.3	28.0	37.3	45.5	51.3	52.2	46.1	36.5	26.9	16.7	31.6
Extreme Maximum Temp. (°F)	48	56	69	87	90	97	99	97	95	84	71	57	99
Extreme Minimum Temp. (°F)	-25	-31	-22	-1	17	27	30	30	24	16	-4	-17	-31
Days Maximum Temp. ≥ 90°F	0	0	0	0	0	1	2	1	0	0	0	0	4
Days Maximum Temp. ≤ 32°F	25	19	10	1	0	0	0	0	0	0	5	18	78
Days Minimum Temp. ≤ 32°F	31	28	29	22	11	2	0	0	2	10	24	31	190
Days Minimum Temp. ≤ 0°F	5	5	2	0	0	0	0	0	0	0	0	2	14
Heating Degree Days (base 65°F)	1,458	1,282	1,171	788	479	228	111	97	263	584	927	1,281	8,669
Cooling Degree Days (base 65°F)	0	0	0	0	1	9	36	75	70	21	1	0	213
Mean Precipitation (in.)	2.32	1.21	1.44	1.35	2.62	2.88	3.04	2.93	3.56	3.05	2.37	2.18	28.95
Days With ≥ 0.1" Precipitation	8	4	4	4	6	6	6	6	8	8	7	8	75
Days With ≥ 1.0" Precipitation	0	0	0	0	1	1	1	1	1	0	0	0	5
Mean Snowfall (in.)	47.9	27.9	16.1	5.0	0.4	0.0	0.0	0.0	trace	0.7	13.0	39.4	150.4
Days With ≥ 1.0" Snow Depth	30	27	28	15	0	0	0	0	0	0	11	27	138

Grayling *Crawford County*   Elevation: 1,138 ft.   Latitude: 44° 39' N   Longitude: 84° 42' W

	JAN	FEB	MAR	APR	MAY	JUN	JUL	AUG	SEP	OCT	NOV	DEC	YEAR
Mean Maximum Temp. (°F)	25.3	28.2	38.1	52.5	67.2	76.2	80.3	77.6	68.6	56.1	42.0	30.6	53.6
Mean Temp. (°F)	15.9	17.3	26.5	40.4	53.2	62.4	66.9	64.5	56.0	44.9	33.5	22.6	42.0
Mean Minimum Temp. (°F)	6.5	6.3	14.9	28.3	39.1	48.6	53.5	51.3	43.3	33.6	25.0	14.7	30.4
Extreme Maximum Temp. (°F)	57	60	76	89	94	98	100	97	91	85	73	63	100
Extreme Minimum Temp. (°F)	-34	-42	-27	-2	18	23	33	26	16	11	-8	-26	-42
Days Maximum Temp. ≥ 90°F	0	0	0	0	0	2	3	1	0	0	0	0	6
Days Maximum Temp. ≤ 32°F	24	19	9	2	0	0	0	0	0	0	6	17	77
Days Minimum Temp. ≤ 32°F	31	28	29	20	9	1	0	0	4	16	24	30	192
Days Minimum Temp. ≤ 0°F	10	10	5	0	0	0	0	0	0	0	0	5	30
Heating Degree Days (base 65°F)	1,515	1,342	1,187	734	378	136	54	90	285	619	936	1,307	8,583
Cooling Degree Days (base 65°F)	0	0	0	3	18	64	121	83	20	1	0	0	310
Mean Precipitation (in.)	1.74	1.27	1.98	2.65	3.07	3.37	3.82	3.77	4.14	3.46	2.47	1.82	33.56
Days With ≥ 0.1" Precipitation	6	4	5	6	7	7	7	7	8	8	7	5	77
Days With ≥ 1.0" Precipitation	0	0	0	0	1	1	1	1	1	0	0	0	5
Mean Snowfall (in.)	*31.5*	19.6	15.1	3.9	0.1	0.0	0.0	0.0	0.0	0.9	11.0	24.4	*106.5*
Days With ≥ 1.0" Snow Depth	29	28	25	6	0	0	0	0	0	1	9	25	123

Greenville 2 NNE *Montcalm County*   Elevation: 879 ft.   Latitude: 43° 12' N   Longitude: 85° 15' W

	JAN	FEB	MAR	APR	MAY	JUN	JUL	AUG	SEP	OCT	NOV	DEC	YEAR
Mean Maximum Temp. (°F)	28.7	32.6	43.3	57.9	70.5	79.4	83.5	81.0	73.0	60.7	45.9	33.9	57.5
Mean Temp. (°F)	20.9	23.8	33.2	45.9	57.7	66.6	70.8	68.7	60.9	49.6	37.6	26.6	46.9
Mean Minimum Temp. (°F)	13.1	14.8	23.1	34.0	44.8	53.7	58.0	56.4	48.8	38.5	29.1	19.2	36.1
Extreme Maximum Temp. (°F)	60	70	78	85	92	99	101	101	92	87	75	65	101
Extreme Minimum Temp. (°F)	-26	-23	-11	5	20	30	39	35	24	16	2	-13	-26
Days Maximum Temp. ≥ 90°F	0	0	0	0	0	2	5	3	1	0	0	0	11
Days Maximum Temp. ≤ 32°F	20	15	5	0	0	0	0	0	0	0	3	14	57
Days Minimum Temp. ≤ 32°F	30	27	26	14	3	0	0	0	1	9	21	29	160
Days Minimum Temp. ≤ 0°F	5	4	1	0	0	0	0	0	0	0	0	2	12
Heating Degree Days (base 65°F)	1,360	1,159	978	570	254	61	14	30	167	473	817	1,185	7,068
Cooling Degree Days (base 65°F)	0	0	1	5	32	110	199	151	49	2	0	0	549
Mean Precipitation (in.)	1.82	1.42	2.38	2.97	3.26	3.40	2.83	4.21	3.77	3.04	3.15	2.45	34.70
Days With ≥ 0.1" Precipitation	5	4	6	7	7	6	6	7	7	6	7	6	74
Days With ≥ 1.0" Precipitation	0	0	0	0	1	1	1	1	1	0	1	0	6
Mean Snowfall (in.)	20.5	12.7	10.4	2.6	trace	0.0	0.0	0.0	0.0	0.4	5.8	16.3	68.7
Days With ≥ 1.0" Snow Depth	25	20	12	1	0	0	0	0	0	0	3	17	78

Grosse Pointe Farms *Wayne County*   Elevation: 610 ft.   Latitude: 42° 23' N   Longitude: 82° 54' W

	JAN	FEB	MAR	APR	MAY	JUN	JUL	AUG	SEP	OCT	NOV	DEC	YEAR
Mean Maximum Temp. (°F)	32.2	35.1	44.7	57.7	70.3	79.5	83.9	81.2	74.2	61.6	48.8	37.3	58.9
Mean Temp. (°F)	25.3	27.6	36.2	47.8	59.7	69.0	73.9	72.0	64.9	53.1	41.6	30.9	50.2
Mean Minimum Temp. (°F)	18.2	20.1	27.6	37.9	48.9	58.5	63.9	62.7	55.5	44.4	34.4	24.5	41.4
Extreme Maximum Temp. (°F)	59	65	81	90	93	105	102	100	95	83	75	69	105
Extreme Minimum Temp. (°F)	-17	-12	-4	12	27	38	45	43	33	23	4	-10	-17
Days Maximum Temp. ≥ 90°F	0	0	0	0	0	3	6	3	1	0	0	0	13
Days Maximum Temp. ≤ 32°F	15	11	4	0	0	0	0	0	0	0	1	8	39
Days Minimum Temp. ≤ 32°F	28	25	23	8	0	0	0	0	0	2	13	25	124
Days Minimum Temp. ≤ 0°F	2	1	0	0	0	0	0	0	0	0	0	0	3
Heating Degree Days (base 65°F)	1,224	1,048	886	516	205	38	3	8	92	371	694	1,049	6,134
Cooling Degree Days (base 65°F)	0	0	1	6	47	164	291	234	92	7	0	0	842
Mean Precipitation (in.)	1.77	1.77	2.46	3.17	2.91	3.40	3.36	3.48	3.40	2.61	2.86	2.38	33.57
Days With ≥ 0.1" Precipitation	5	4	6	8	7	7	6	7	7	5	7	6	75
Days With ≥ 1.0" Precipitation	0	0	0	0	1	1	1	1	1	0	1	0	6
Mean Snowfall (in.)	9.2	6.7	2.9	0.7	trace	0.0	0.0	0.0	0.0	trace	1.0	5.9	26.4
Days With ≥ 1.0" Snow Depth	19	16	6	1	0	0	0	0	0	0	1	9	52

Gull Lake Biological Station *Kalamazoo County*   Elevation: 908 ft.   Latitude: 42° 24' N   Longitude: 85° 23' W

	JAN	FEB	MAR	APR	MAY	JUN	JUL	AUG	SEP	OCT	NOV	DEC	YEAR
Mean Maximum Temp. (°F)	31.0	35.1	46.0	59.4	71.9	80.9	84.5	82.2	74.9	62.6	48.1	36.1	59.4
Mean Temp. (°F)	23.4	26.2	35.9	47.9	59.7	68.9	73.1	71.1	63.8	52.3	40.4	29.2	49.3
Mean Minimum Temp. (°F)	15.7	17.2	25.8	36.5	47.4	56.9	61.6	60.0	52.6	42.0	32.6	22.3	39.2
Extreme Maximum Temp. (°F)	61	70	78	85	94	99	103	100	95	88	74	66	103
Extreme Minimum Temp. (°F)	-20	-19	-8	4	24	34	44	39	29	18	9	-15	-20
Days Maximum Temp. ≥ 90°F	0	0	0	0	1	3	6	2	1	0	0	0	13
Days Maximum Temp. ≤ 32°F	17	12	3	0	0	0	0	0	0	0	1	11	44
Days Minimum Temp. ≤ 32°F	29	25	23	11	2	0	0	0	0	5	16	27	138
Days Minimum Temp. ≤ 0°F	4	3	1	0	0	0	0	0	0	0	0	1	9
Heating Degree Days (base 65°F)	1,284	1,089	895	510	207	38	5	13	113	393	733	1,102	6,382
Cooling Degree Days (base 65°F)	0	0	1	5	49	168	269	220	82	7	0	0	801
Mean Precipitation (in.)	2.04	1.71	2.65	3.78	3.33	3.77	3.73	3.82	4.17	3.15	3.28	2.86	38.29
Days With ≥ 0.1" Precipitation	6	5	6	9	7	7	7	7	7	7	7	7	82
Days With ≥ 1.0" Precipitation	0	0	0	1	1	1	1	1	1	1	1	1	9
Mean Snowfall (in.)	18.3	10.7	5.4	1.4	trace	0.0	0.0	0.0	0.0	0.4	4.0	15.2	55.4
Days With ≥ 1.0" Snow Depth	23	18	8	1	0	0	0	0	0	0	3	17	70

Hale Loud Dam *Iosco County*   Elevation: 813 ft.   Latitude: 44° 28' N   Longitude: 83° 43' W

	JAN	FEB	MAR	APR	MAY	JUN	JUL	AUG	SEP	OCT	NOV	DEC	YEAR
Mean Maximum Temp. (°F)	28.2	31.2	41.1	54.7	68.1	76.4	80.9	78.3	70.4	58.4	44.3	32.8	55.4
Mean Temp. (°F)	18.8	20.5	30.1	42.9	55.0	63.8	68.8	66.6	59.0	47.9	36.3	25.3	44.6
Mean Minimum Temp. (°F)	9.4	9.7	19.0	30.9	41.8	51.2	56.6	54.9	47.6	37.3	28.3	17.8	33.7
Extreme Maximum Temp. (°F)	55	63	77	87	92	99	98	94	90	85	74	64	99
Extreme Minimum Temp. (°F)	-31	-40	-23	0	24	30	39	33	27	12	-4	-26	-40
Days Maximum Temp. ≥ 90°F	0	0	0	0	0	1	3	1	0	0	0	0	5
Days Maximum Temp. ≤ 32°F	21	16	7	0	0	0	0	0	0	0	3	14	61
Days Minimum Temp. ≤ 32°F	30	27	28	17	5	0	0	0	1	10	21	29	168
Days Minimum Temp. ≤ 0°F	9	8	3	0	0	0	0	0	0	0	0	3	23
Heating Degree Days (base 65°F)	1,425	1,252	1,075	660	324	101	26	48	205	526	854	1,223	7,719
Cooling Degree Days (base 65°F)	0	0	0	3	20	75	159	113	32	1	0	0	403
Mean Precipitation (in.)	1.73	1.13	1.77	2.24	2.41	2.98	3.19	3.54	3.34	2.46	2.27	1.68	28.74
Days With ≥ 0.1" Precipitation	5	3	5	6	6	6	6	7	6	6	6	5	67
Days With ≥ 1.0" Precipitation	0	0	0	0	0	1	1	1	1	0	0	0	4
Mean Snowfall (in.)	13.9	8.3	7.6	1.6	0.2	0.0	0.0	0.0	trace	trace	3.4	8.7	43.7
Days With ≥ 1.0" Snow Depth	29	27	23	6	0	0	0	0	0	0	5	20	110

Hancock Houghton Co. Airport *Houghton County*   Elevation: 1,072 ft.   Latitude: 47° 10' N   Longitude: 88° 30' W

	JAN	FEB	MAR	APR	MAY	JUN	JUL	AUG	SEP	OCT	NOV	DEC	YEAR
Mean Maximum Temp. (°F)	20.8	23.6	32.3	46.3	61.4	70.5	75.7	73.3	63.0	51.3	36.3	25.6	48.3
Mean Temp. (°F)	14.8	16.5	25.1	38.2	51.3	60.3	65.8	64.5	55.1	44.3	31.1	20.2	40.6
Mean Minimum Temp. (°F)	8.6	9.5	17.9	30.1	41.2	50.0	55.9	55.5	47.1	37.3	25.8	14.8	32.8
Extreme Maximum Temp. (°F)	43	51	65	88	91	96	102	97	91	82	71	53	102
Extreme Minimum Temp. (°F)	-26	-23	-17	3	22	32	37	38	26	17	1	-15	-26
Days Maximum Temp. ≥ 90°F	0	0	0	0	0	1	1	0	0	0	0	0	2
Days Maximum Temp. ≤ 32°F	27	22	15	3	0	0	0	0	0	1	10	23	101
Days Minimum Temp. ≤ 32°F	30	28	29	19	4	0	0	0	1	8	24	30	173
Days Minimum Temp. ≤ 0°F	7	7	2	0	0	0	0	0	0	0	0	3	19
Heating Degree Days (base 65°F)	1,552	1,364	1,229	798	429	176	63	87	306	635	1,010	1,381	9,030
Cooling Degree Days (base 65°F)	0	0	0	1	14	44	98	79	15	1	0	0	252
Mean Precipitation (in.)	4.16	2.29	2.40	1.71	2.62	2.85	3.07	2.73	3.32	2.59	2.86	3.48	34.08
Days With ≥ 0.1" Precipitation	13	7	6	5	6	6	6	6	7	7	8	12	89
Days With ≥ 1.0" Precipitation	0	0	0	0	0	0	1	1	1	0	0	0	3
Mean Snowfall (in.)	70.5	34.2	23.7	7.7	1.1	trace	trace	trace	0.1	3.8	23.8	57.7	222.6
Days With ≥ 1.0" Snow Depth	31	28	30	15	1	0	0	0	0	2	15	29	151

Harbor Beach 1 SSE *Huron County*   Elevation: 597 ft.   Latitude: 43° 50' N   Longitude: 82° 38' W

	JAN	FEB	MAR	APR	MAY	JUN	JUL	AUG	SEP	OCT	NOV	DEC	YEAR
Mean Maximum Temp. (°F)	28.7	30.6	38.8	50.5	62.8	72.1	78.0	76.6	69.9	57.9	45.3	34.2	53.8
Mean Temp. (°F)	21.4	23.0	31.2	42.1	53.2	62.5	68.4	67.3	60.5	49.4	38.3	27.9	45.4
Mean Minimum Temp. (°F)	14.1	15.4	23.5	33.6	43.7	52.8	58.8	58.0	51.0	40.8	31.3	21.5	37.0
Extreme Maximum Temp. (°F)	55	68	77	88	92	97	100	96	94	85	75	65	100
Extreme Minimum Temp. (°F)	-19	-13	-12	14	27	33	41	35	32	21	6	-8	-19
Days Maximum Temp. ≥ 90°F	0	0	0	0	0	1	2	1	0	0	0	0	4
Days Maximum Temp. ≤ 32°F	20	16	8	1	0	0	0	0	0	0	2	12	59
Days Minimum Temp. ≤ 32°F	30	27	27	14	1	0	0	0	0	4	18	28	149
Days Minimum Temp. ≤ 0°F	4	3	1	0	0	0	0	0	0	0	0	1	9
Heating Degree Days (base 65°F)	1,344	1,178	1,042	684	375	132	30	39	167	479	794	1,143	7,407
Cooling Degree Days (base 65°F)	0	0	0	2	17	59	142	113	35	1	0	0	369
Mean Precipitation (in.)	2.67	2.00	2.46	2.80	2.84	2.62	2.97	3.47	3.97	2.71	3.05	2.72	34.28
Days With ≥ 0.1" Precipitation	8	6	7	7	7	7	6	6	7	6	8	8	83
Days With ≥ 1.0" Precipitation	0	0	0	1	1	0	0	1	1	0	0	0	4
Mean Snowfall (in.)	na	*12.8*	*10.6*	3.1	0.2	0.0	0.0	0.0	trace	0.2	3.8	*15.9*	na
Days With ≥ 1.0" Snow Depth	25	22	16	2	0	0	0	0	0	0	3	*14*	*82*

Hart *Oceana County*   Elevation: 698 ft.   Latitude: 43° 41' N   Longitude: 86° 21' W

	JAN	FEB	MAR	APR	MAY	JUN	JUL	AUG	SEP	OCT	NOV	DEC	YEAR
Mean Maximum Temp. (°F)	28.8	31.6	40.7	54.2	67.1	75.9	80.3	78.0	70.2	58.3	45.1	34.1	55.4
Mean Temp. (°F)	22.2	24.0	32.2	44.3	55.7	64.8	69.4	67.8	60.2	49.2	38.1	28.1	46.3
Mean Minimum Temp. (°F)	15.5	16.3	23.6	34.5	44.2	53.7	58.5	57.6	50.1	40.1	31.0	22.1	37.3
Extreme Maximum Temp. (°F)	59	65	77	84	90	97	97	94	90	87	71	68	97
Extreme Minimum Temp. (°F)	-14	-22	-8	1	24	30	40	37	26	22	4	-16	-22
Days Maximum Temp. ≥ 90°F	0	0	0	0	0	1	2	1	0	0	0	0	4
Days Maximum Temp. ≤ 32°F	20	15	6	1	0	0	0	0	0	0	3	12	57
Days Minimum Temp. ≤ 32°F	30	26	25	13	3	0	0	0	1	6	19	27	150
Days Minimum Temp. ≤ 0°F	3	3	1	0	0	0	0	0	0	0	0	1	8
Heating Degree Days (base 65°F)	1,321	1,152	1,010	617	309	88	25	37	182	487	801	1,136	7,165
Cooling Degree Days (base 65°F)	0	0	0	4	23	85	163	127	39	2	0	0	443
Mean Precipitation (in.)	2.59	1.72	2.41	2.88	2.84	3.31	2.90	3.95	3.82	3.59	3.30	2.63	35.94
Days With ≥ 0.1" Precipitation	9	5	6	6	6	6	6	7	7	7	8	8	81
Days With ≥ 1.0" Precipitation	0	0	0	0	1	1	1	1	1	1	0	0	6
Mean Snowfall (in.)	31.1	19.0	9.0	2.1	trace	0.0	0.0	0.0	0.0	0.2	5.4	21.7	88.5
Days With ≥ 1.0" Snow Depth	26	22	13	0	0	0	0	0	0	0	4	18	84

Hastings *Barry County*   Elevation: 816 ft.   Latitude: 42° 39' N   Longitude: 85° 17' W

	JAN	FEB	MAR	APR	MAY	JUN	JUL	AUG	SEP	OCT	NOV	DEC	YEAR
Mean Maximum Temp. (°F)	30.3	34.0	44.2	57.6	70.1	79.1	83.0	80.9	73.4	61.1	47.0	35.2	58.0
Mean Temp. (°F)	22.1	24.5	33.9	46.3	57.7	66.9	71.0	69.0	61.3	49.7	38.5	27.7	47.4
Mean Minimum Temp. (°F)	13.8	14.9	23.6	34.9	45.3	54.6	58.9	57.1	49.2	38.3	30.0	20.3	36.8
Extreme Maximum Temp. (°F)	62	70	79	87	91	99	102	102	93	90	76	68	102
Extreme Minimum Temp. (°F)	-22	-20	-8	1	23	31	40	38	26	15	6	-22	-22
Days Maximum Temp. ≥ 90°F	0	0	0	0	0	3	4	2	1	0	0	0	10
Days Maximum Temp. ≤ 32°F	19	13	5	0	0	0	0	0	0	0	2	12	51
Days Minimum Temp. ≤ 32°F	30	27	25	13	3	0	0	0	1	9	20	28	156
Days Minimum Temp. ≤ 0°F	5	4	1	0	0	0	0	0	0	0	0	2	12
Heating Degree Days (base 65°F)	1,323	1,137	957	562	256	63	14	29	164	472	787	1,149	6,913
Cooling Degree Days (base 65°F)	0	0	1	8	36	122	211	164	45	4	0	0	601
Mean Precipitation (in.)	1.96	1.52	2.48	3.34	2.87	4.00	3.20	3.71	3.87	2.99	3.03	2.44	35.41
Days With ≥ 0.1" Precipitation	6	4	6	8	7	7	6	7	7	6	7	6	77
Days With ≥ 1.0" Precipitation	0	0	0	0	0	1	1	1	1	1	1	0	6
Mean Snowfall (in.)	17.4	10.4	7.4	2.3	trace	0.0	0.0	0.0	0.0	0.5	4.9	12.9	55.8
Days With ≥ 1.0" Snow Depth	24	19	9	1	0	0	0	0	0	0	3	17	73

Herman *Baraga County*   Elevation: 1,738 ft.   Latitude: 46° 40' N   Longitude: 88° 21' W

	JAN	FEB	MAR	APR	MAY	JUN	JUL	AUG	SEP	OCT	NOV	DEC	YEAR
Mean Maximum Temp. (°F)	20.1	25.9	36.0	50.4	64.9	72.9	76.8	74.2	64.8	53.2	36.3	24.6	50.0
Mean Temp. (°F)	11.7	15.5	24.8	38.3	51.7	60.1	64.6	62.5	54.1	43.5	29.0	17.2	39.4
Mean Minimum Temp. (°F)	3.1	5.1	13.5	26.2	38.3	47.3	52.4	50.8	43.3	33.8	21.7	9.7	28.8
Extreme Maximum Temp. (°F)	54	61	69	91	90	96	96	95	95	86	73	58	96
Extreme Minimum Temp. (°F)	-36	-40	-32	-17	12	22	27	27	20	7	-12	-37	-40
Days Maximum Temp. ≥ 90°F	0	0	0	0	0	0	1	0	0	0	0	0	1
Days Maximum Temp. ≤ 32°F	27	20	12	2	0	0	0	0	0	1	12	25	99
Days Minimum Temp. ≤ 32°F	31	27	29	22	11	2	0	1	5	15	27	31	201
Days Minimum Temp. ≤ 0°F	12	11	6	1	0	0	0	0	0	0	1	7	38
Heating Degree Days (base 65°F)	1,649	1,390	1,240	796	423	183	87	127	337	660	1,074	1,476	9,442
Cooling Degree Days (base 65°F)	0	0	0	2	14	46	84	58	14	1	0	0	219
Mean Precipitation (in.)	2.43	1.59	2.68	2.33	3.56	3.63	4.25	4.05	4.17	3.61	3.33	2.63	38.26
Days With ≥ 0.1" Precipitation	9	5	7	6	8	8	8	7	9	9	9	8	93
Days With ≥ 1.0" Precipitation	0	0	1	0	1	1	1	1	1	1	0	0	7
Mean Snowfall (in.)	55.0	34.0	35.9	14.9	3.5	trace	0.0	0.0	0.2	8.5	34.6	49.3	235.9
Days With ≥ 1.0" Snow Depth	31	28	30	18	1	0	0	0	0	4	20	30	162

Hillsdale *Hillsdale County*   Elevation: 1,079 ft.   Latitude: 41° 56' N   Longitude: 84° 38' W

	JAN	FEB	MAR	APR	MAY	JUN	JUL	AUG	SEP	OCT	NOV	DEC	YEAR
Mean Maximum Temp. (°F)	29.7	33.6	44.0	57.1	69.3	78.5	82.1	80.2	72.9	60.6	46.8	35.0	57.5
Mean Temp. (°F)	21.5	24.4	34.3	46.0	57.4	66.7	70.5	68.4	61.2	49.7	38.2	27.5	47.2
Mean Minimum Temp. (°F)	13.3	15.1	24.5	34.8	45.5	54.8	58.8	56.6	49.4	38.7	29.6	20.1	36.8
Extreme Maximum Temp. (°F)	59	69	79	86	90	104	99	99	95	88	76	68	104
Extreme Minimum Temp. (°F)	-22	-20	-10	3	23	32	36	34	26	15	5	-19	-22
Days Maximum Temp. ≥ 90°F	0	0	0	0	0	1	4	2	0	0	0	0	7
Days Maximum Temp. ≤ 32°F	18	13	5	0	0	0	0	0	0	0	3	11	50
Days Minimum Temp. ≤ 32°F	30	26	25	13	3	0	0	0	1	9	19	28	154
Days Minimum Temp. ≤ 0°F	5	4	1	0	0	0	0	0	0	0	0	2	12
Heating Degree Days (base 65°F)	1,342	1,141	946	569	261	61	18	32	163	471	796	1,153	6,953
Cooling Degree Days (base 65°F)	0	0	1	5	33	116	200	145	52	3	0	0	555
Mean Precipitation (in.)	2.09	1.80	2.88	3.28	3.73	4.17	3.67	3.58	3.65	2.83	2.99	2.63	37.30
Days With ≥ 0.1" Precipitation	6	5	7	9	8	7	7	7	7	7	7	7	84
Days With ≥ 1.0" Precipitation	0	0	0	0	1	1	1	1	1	0	0	0	5
Mean Snowfall (in.)	14.8	10.7	7.4	1.6	trace	0.0	0.0	0.0	0.0	0.3	4.5	12.0	51.3
Days With ≥ 1.0" Snow Depth	18	15	7	1	0	0	0	0	0	0	3	11	55

Holland *Ottawa County*   Elevation: 606 ft.   Latitude: 42° 47' N   Longitude: 86° 07' W

	JAN	FEB	MAR	APR	MAY	JUN	JUL	AUG	SEP	OCT	NOV	DEC	YEAR
Mean Maximum Temp. (°F)	31.2	34.9	44.8	57.3	69.6	78.8	82.9	81.2	73.3	61.1	47.7	36.4	58.3
Mean Temp. (°F)	24.3	27.0	35.5	46.7	57.9	66.9	71.6	70.0	62.6	51.3	40.2	29.8	48.7
Mean Minimum Temp. (°F)	17.4	19.1	26.3	36.1	46.3	55.1	60.2	58.8	51.8	41.6	32.6	23.1	39.0
Extreme Maximum Temp. (°F)	62	72	78	90	93	101	100	98	94	86	77	67	101
Extreme Minimum Temp. (°F)	-18	-16	-5	5	25	29	40	40	27	19	10	-11	-18
Days Maximum Temp. ≥ 90°F	0	0	0	0	1	3	4	2	0	0	0	0	10
Days Maximum Temp. ≤ 32°F	17	11	4	0	0	0	0	0	0	0	1	9	42
Days Minimum Temp. ≤ 32°F	29	26	24	12	2	0	0	0	0	5	16	27	141
Days Minimum Temp. ≤ 0°F	2	1	0	0	0	0	0	0	0	0	0	0	3
Heating Degree Days (base 65°F)	1,254	1,066	907	551	256	64	16	21	133	423	738	1,085	6,514
Cooling Degree Days (base 65°F)	0	0	1	9	42	132	240	191	68	6	0	0	689
Mean Precipitation (in.)	2.04	1.36	2.13	3.16	3.24	3.68	3.53	3.49	3.98	2.94	3.21	2.92	35.68
Days With ≥ 0.1" Precipitation	6	4	5	7	6	6	6	6	7	7	7	7	74
Days With ≥ 1.0" Precipitation	0	0	0	1	1	1	1	1	1	0	1	0	7
Mean Snowfall (in.)	28.2	15.5	6.8	1.9	trace	0.0	0.0	0.0	0.0	0.3	5.4	21.3	79.4
Days With ≥ 1.0" Snow Depth	22	19	8	1	0	0	0	0	0	0	3	15	68

Houghton Lake 6 WSW *Missaukee County*   Elevation: 1,131 ft.   Latitude: 44° 19' N   Longitude: 84° 54' W

	JAN	FEB	MAR	APR	MAY	JUN	JUL	AUG	SEP	OCT	NOV	DEC	YEAR
Mean Maximum Temp. (°F)	26.0	29.5	39.4	53.2	67.3	76.3	81.0	78.0	69.3	56.5	42.5	31.1	54.2
Mean Temp. (°F)	16.9	18.7	28.1	41.5	53.5	62.3	66.8	64.2	56.0	45.0	34.0	23.2	42.5
Mean Minimum Temp. (°F)	7.6	7.9	16.6	29.8	39.6	48.3	52.6	50.4	42.7	33.5	25.3	15.3	30.8
Extreme Maximum Temp. (°F)	54	60	77	88	93	102	102	96	92	85	74	64	102
Extreme Minimum Temp. (°F)	-30	-38	-20	1	18	22	30	24	18	12	-6	-24	-38
Days Maximum Temp. ≥ 90°F	0	0	0	0	0	2	4	1	0	0	0	0	7
Days Maximum Temp. ≤ 32°F	23	17	8	1	0	0	0	0	0	0	5	17	71
Days Minimum Temp. ≤ 32°F	31	28	29	19	8	1	0	1	5	16	25	30	193
Days Minimum Temp. ≤ 0°F	10	9	4	0	0	0	0	0	0	0	0	4	27
Heating Degree Days (base 65°F)	1,487	1,301	1,139	702	369	136	55	94	282	614	924	1,289	8,392
Cooling Degree Days (base 65°F)	0	0	0	3	16	60	116	82	18	1	0	0	296
Mean Precipitation (in.)	1.55	1.20	1.57	2.30	2.57	3.21	2.85	3.77	3.56	2.76	2.30	1.75	29.39
Days With ≥ 0.1" Precipitation	5	4	5	6	6	6	6	7	7	6	6	5	69
Days With ≥ 1.0" Precipitation	0	0	0	0	0	0	1	1	1	0	0	0	3
Mean Snowfall (in.)	na	9.7	na	1.5	trace	0.0	0.0	0.0	0.0	0.3	5.9	na	na
Days With ≥ 1.0" Snow Depth	na	25	19	3	0	0	0	0	0	0	na	na	na

Ionia 2 SSW *Ionia County*   Elevation: 803 ft.   Latitude: 42° 57' N   Longitude: 85° 05' W

	JAN	FEB	MAR	APR	MAY	JUN	JUL	AUG	SEP	OCT	NOV	DEC	YEAR
Mean Maximum Temp. (°F)	29.4	33.0	43.5	57.3	70.6	79.7	83.5	81.0	73.3	60.6	46.2	34.3	57.7
Mean Temp. (°F)	21.4	24.0	33.4	45.7	58.0	67.0	71.1	68.8	61.1	49.5	37.9	27.2	47.1
Mean Minimum Temp. (°F)	13.4	14.9	23.5	33.9	45.3	54.3	58.6	56.6	48.9	38.4	29.5	20.1	36.4
Extreme Maximum Temp. (°F)	60	69	80	87	95	100	103	101	97	89	77	66	103
Extreme Minimum Temp. (°F)	-21	-18	-6	6	23	31	40	36	27	16	4	-14	-21
Days Maximum Temp. ≥ 90°F	0	0	0	0	1	3	6	3	1	0	0	0	14
Days Maximum Temp. ≤ 32°F	19	14	5	0	0	0	0	0	0	0	2	13	53
Days Minimum Temp. ≤ 32°F	30	27	25	14	2	0	0	0	1	8	20	29	156
Days Minimum Temp. ≤ 0°F	5	4	0	0	0	0	0	0	0	0	0	1	10
Heating Degree Days (base 65°F)	1,344	1,151	972	579	248	59	13	30	161	476	807	1,165	7,005
Cooling Degree Days (base 65°F)	0	0	1	6	32	120	203	148	45	2	0	0	557
Mean Precipitation (in.)	2.08	1.80	2.83	3.09	3.09	3.47	2.91	4.22	3.88	3.04	2.92	2.49	35.82
Days With ≥ 0.1" Precipitation	6	4	6	7	7	6	6	7	6	6	6	6	73
Days With ≥ 1.0" Precipitation	0	0	0	0	1	1	1	1	1	1	1	0	7
Mean Snowfall (in.)	14.5	9.4	8.1	1.8	trace	0.0	0.0	0.0	0.0	0.3	4.1	12.9	51.1
Days With ≥ 1.0" Snow Depth	25	21	12	1	0	0	0	0	0	0	3	19	81

Iron Mountain-Kingsford WWTP *Dickinson County*   Elevation: 1,059 ft.   Latitude: 45° 47' N   Longitude: 88° 05' W

	JAN	FEB	MAR	APR	MAY	JUN	JUL	AUG	SEP	OCT	NOV	DEC	YEAR
Mean Maximum Temp. (°F)	23.3	28.9	38.6	53.5	67.5	76.2	80.1	77.6	68.3	56.0	39.9	27.9	53.2
Mean Temp. (°F)	12.4	17.3	27.5	41.3	54.2	63.3	67.9	65.8	56.8	45.3	31.6	19.0	41.9
Mean Minimum Temp. (°F)	1.4	5.7	16.3	29.2	40.8	50.4	55.6	54.0	45.2	34.6	23.1	10.2	30.5
Extreme Maximum Temp. (°F)	51	61	70	94	95	100	100	97	98	88	75	64	100
Extreme Minimum Temp. (°F)	-33	-39	-24	-6	16	29	36	34	22	12	-10	-26	-39
Days Maximum Temp. ≥ 90°F	0	0	0	0	0	2	3	1	0	0	0	0	6
Days Maximum Temp. ≤ 32°F	26	18	8	1	0	0	0	0	0	0	7	21	81
Days Minimum Temp. ≤ 32°F	31	28	29	20	6	0	0	0	2	14	26	30	186
Days Minimum Temp. ≤ 0°F	15	11	4	0	0	0	0	0	0	0	1	8	39
Heating Degree Days (base 65°F)	1,627	1,341	1,156	705	349	115	39	64	263	605	997	1,418	8,679
Cooling Degree Days (base 65°F)	0	0	0	2	18	77	133	103	22	1	0	0	356
Mean Precipitation (in.)	1.39	0.86	1.69	2.17	3.18	3.41	3.56	3.71	3.59	2.79	2.03	1.52	29.90
Days With ≥ 0.1" Precipitation	5	3	4	5	6	8	7	8	7	6	5	4	68
Days With ≥ 1.0" Precipitation	0	0	0	0	1	1	1	1	1	0	0	0	5
Mean Snowfall (in.)	16.9	9.0	11.3	4.2	0.8	0.0	0.0	0.0	trace	0.3	6.4	15.5	64.4
Days With ≥ 1.0" Snow Depth	31	28	22	4	0	0	0	0	0	0	7	27	119

Ironwood *Gogebic County*   Elevation: 1,427 ft.   Latitude: 46° 28' N   Longitude: 90° 11' W

	JAN	FEB	MAR	APR	MAY	JUN	JUL	AUG	SEP	OCT	NOV	DEC	YEAR
Mean Maximum Temp. (°F)	19.4	25.6	35.4	50.0	64.3	73.0	76.9	74.8	65.2	53.1	36.7	24.5	49.9
Mean Temp. (°F)	9.5	14.5	24.6	39.0	52.3	61.4	65.8	63.6	54.8	43.6	29.0	16.1	39.5
Mean Minimum Temp. (°F)	-0.4	3.3	13.7	28.0	40.2	49.7	54.5	52.4	44.3	34.1	21.1	7.6	29.0
Extreme Maximum Temp. (°F)	55	62	72	88	90	97	97	94	95	86	74	59	97
Extreme Minimum Temp. (°F)	-41	-37	-34	-12	16	26	35	30	22	5	-18	-36	-41
Days Maximum Temp. ≥ 90°F	0	0	0	0	0	0	1	1	0	0	0	0	2
Days Maximum Temp. ≤ 32°F	27	20	12	2	0	0	0	0	0	1	11	24	97
Days Minimum Temp. ≤ 32°F	31	28	29	21	8	1	0	0	3	14	26	31	192
Days Minimum Temp. ≤ 0°F	16	12	6	1	0	0	0	0	0	0	2	10	47
Heating Degree Days (base 65°F)	1,717	1,421	1,246	775	404	160	70	105	320	657	1,073	1,511	9,459
Cooling Degree Days (base 65°F)	0	0	0	2	15	55	93	68	17	0	0	0	250
Mean Precipitation (in.)	2.07	1.20	1.98	2.11	3.13	4.01	3.98	3.68	3.88	3.45	2.96	2.08	34.53
Days With ≥ 0.1" Precipitation	6	4	5	6	7	8	8	7	9	8	7	6	81
Days With ≥ 1.0" Precipitation	0	0	0	0	1	1	1	1	1	1	0	0	6
Mean Snowfall (in.)	45.6	24.3	22.2	9.6	2.1	0.0	0.0	0.0	0.3	5.2	27.5	40.3	177.1
Days With ≥ 1.0" Snow Depth	31	28	28	11	1	0	0	0	0	2	17	30	148

Jackson Reynolds Field *Jackson County*   Elevation: 997 ft.   Latitude: 42° 16' N   Longitude: 84° 28' W

	JAN	FEB	MAR	APR	MAY	JUN	JUL	AUG	SEP	OCT	NOV	DEC	YEAR
Mean Maximum Temp. (°F)	29.3	33.0	44.0	57.4	69.8	79.2	82.8	80.5	72.8	60.2	46.8	34.7	57.5
Mean Temp. (°F)	22.5	25.1	35.0	47.1	58.4	67.8	72.0	69.9	62.2	50.4	39.2	28.2	48.2
Mean Minimum Temp. (°F)	15.4	17.2	26.0	36.7	47.1	56.5	61.2	59.2	51.6	40.5	31.5	21.6	38.7
Extreme Maximum Temp. (°F)	60	69	79	88	94	101	103	96	100	87	77	68	103
Extreme Minimum Temp. (°F)	-20	-17	-7	3	23	34	40	37	27	16	6	-14	-20
Days Maximum Temp. ≥ 90°F	0	0	0	0	0	3	5	2	1	0	0	0	11
Days Maximum Temp. ≤ 32°F	19	14	5	0	0	0	0	0	0	0	3	12	53
Days Minimum Temp. ≤ 32°F	29	25	23	10	2	0	0	0	0	6	17	27	139
Days Minimum Temp. ≤ 0°F	4	3	0	0	0	0	0	0	0	0	0	2	9
Heating Degree Days (base 65°F)	1,312	1,120	923	540	239	51	9	23	147	453	767	1,135	6,719
Cooling Degree Days (base 65°F)	0	0	1	7	37	135	229	180	63	4	0	0	656
Mean Precipitation (in.)	1.41	1.22	2.08	2.73	2.77	3.20	3.36	3.35	3.49	2.31	2.56	2.06	30.54
Days With ≥ 0.1" Precipitation	4	4	5	7	6	7	6	6	7	6	6	6	70
Days With ≥ 1.0" Precipitation	0	0	0	0	0	1	1	1	1	0	0	0	4
Mean Snowfall (in.)	12.5	7.2	6.3	1.5	trace	trace	0.0	0.0	0.0	0.2	2.1	9.3	39.1
Days With ≥ 1.0" Snow Depth	23	17	8	1	0	0	0	0	0	0	3	15	67

Lake City Exp. Farm *Missaukee County*   Elevation: 1,240 ft.   Latitude: 44° 19' N   Longitude: 85° 12' W

	JAN	FEB	MAR	APR	MAY	JUN	JUL	AUG	SEP	OCT	NOV	DEC	YEAR
Mean Maximum Temp. (°F)	25.7	29.1	38.6	52.7	66.7	75.6	80.1	77.4	68.6	56.3	42.0	30.8	53.6
Mean Temp. (°F)	17.1	18.9	27.9	41.6	53.7	62.7	67.2	65.0	56.7	45.7	34.1	23.2	42.8
Mean Minimum Temp. (°F)	8.5	8.6	17.2	30.4	40.7	49.6	54.2	52.5	44.7	35.0	26.2	15.6	31.9
Extreme Maximum Temp. (°F)	54	58	72	87	92	99	99	95	89	84	72	62	99
Extreme Minimum Temp. (°F)	-28	-35	-20	2	22	27	31	27	22	16	-7	-25	-35
Days Maximum Temp. ≥ 90°F	0	0	0	0	0	1	2	1	0	0	0	0	4
Days Maximum Temp. ≤ 32°F	24	17	9	1	0	0	0	0	0	0	5	18	74
Days Minimum Temp. ≤ 32°F	31	28	28	19	6	0	0	0	3	14	23	30	182
Days Minimum Temp. ≤ 0°F	8	8	4	0	0	0	0	0	0	0	0	4	24
Heating Degree Days (base 65°F)	1,478	1,296	1,143	699	359	125	45	76	263	594	919	1,288	8,285
Cooling Degree Days (base 65°F)	0	0	0	2	14	60	117	81	17	1	0	0	292
Mean Precipitation (in.)	1.57	1.19	2.03	2.80	2.73	2.98	2.90	3.61	3.81	2.99	2.49	1.82	30.92
Days With ≥ 0.1" Precipitation	5	3	5	7	6	6	6	7	8	7	6	5	71
Days With ≥ 1.0" Precipitation	0	0	0	0	0	1	1	1	1	0	0	0	4
Mean Snowfall (in.)	20.0	14.8	11.9	4.2	0.5	0.0	0.0	0.0	trace	1.3	9.1	15.6	77.4
Days With ≥ 1.0" Snow Depth	30	27	22	4	0	0	0	0	0	0	8	24	115

Lapeer WWTP *Lapeer County*   Elevation: 816 ft.   Latitude: 43° 04' N   Longitude: 83° 18' W

	JAN	FEB	MAR	APR	MAY	JUN	JUL	AUG	SEP	OCT	NOV	DEC	YEAR
Mean Maximum Temp. (°F)	29.3	33.2	43.6	57.5	69.8	78.5	82.6	80.1	72.9	60.6	46.6	34.7	57.5
Mean Temp. (°F)	21.5	24.5	33.7	46.2	57.5	66.2	70.7	68.3	61.3	50.1	38.5	27.5	47.2
Mean Minimum Temp. (°F)	13.5	15.7	23.7	34.9	45.2	53.9	58.7	56.5	49.6	39.3	30.4	20.2	36.8
Extreme Maximum Temp. (°F)	61	68	79	86	92	100	100	96	93	89	76	65	100
Extreme Minimum Temp. (°F)	-26	-24	-15	7	24	32	36	29	26	17	2	-13	-26
Days Maximum Temp. ≥ 90°F	0	0	0	0	0	2	4	2	1	0	0	0	9
Days Maximum Temp. ≤ 32°F	19	14	5	0	0	0	0	0	0	0	2	12	52
Days Minimum Temp. ≤ 32°F	30	26	25	14	2	0	0	0	1	7	18	28	151
Days Minimum Temp. ≤ 0°F	5	4	1	0	0	0	0	0	0	0	0	2	12
Heating Degree Days (base 65°F)	1,343	1,140	963	565	263	69	17	35	160	460	791	1,157	6,963
Cooling Degree Days (base 65°F)	0	0	1	6	39	107	206	146	52	3	0	0	560
Mean Precipitation (in.)	1.50	1.13	1.98	2.81	2.79	3.13	3.03	3.44	3.73	2.65	2.70	1.87	30.76
Days With ≥ 0.1" Precipitation	4	4	6	6	6	7	6	7	7	5	6	5	69
Days With ≥ 1.0" Precipitation	0	0	0	1	0	1	1	1	1	0	0	0	5
Mean Snowfall (in.)	*9.5*	*7.8*	*6.7*	1.1	trace	0.0	0.0	0.0	0.0	trace	*1.9*	*9.3*	*36.3*
Days With ≥ 1.0" Snow Depth	*20*	*17*	*7*	0	0	0	0	0	0	0	*2*	*15*	*61*

Maple City *Leelanau County*   Elevation: 728 ft.   Latitude: 44° 51' N   Longitude: 85° 51' W

	JAN	FEB	MAR	APR	MAY	JUN	JUL	AUG	SEP	OCT	NOV	DEC	YEAR
Mean Maximum Temp. (°F)	28.3	31.8	40.6	54.2	67.8	77.2	81.4	79.3	70.7	59.0	44.6	33.4	55.7
Mean Temp. (°F)	21.6	23.4	31.1	43.1	54.8	64.1	69.2	67.8	60.2	49.5	37.6	27.2	45.8
Mean Minimum Temp. (°F)	14.9	14.9	21.5	31.8	41.7	51.1	57.0	56.3	49.6	39.8	30.5	21.0	35.8
Extreme Maximum Temp. (°F)	55	58	76	90	92	98	102	98	94	86	73	65	102
Extreme Minimum Temp. (°F)	-13	-24	-12	7	21	25	34	35	27	21	2	-12	-24
Days Maximum Temp. ≥ 90°F	0	0	0	0	0	2	3	2	0	0	0	0	7
Days Maximum Temp. ≤ 32°F	20	15	6	1	0	0	0	0	0	0	2	13	57
Days Minimum Temp. ≤ 32°F	30	27	27	16	6	0	0	0	1	6	19	28	160
Days Minimum Temp. ≤ 0°F	3	4	1	0	0	0	0	0	0	0	0	1	9
Heating Degree Days (base 65°F)	1,338	1,169	1,044	658	338	104	27	42	182	480	816	1,165	7,363
Cooling Degree Days (base 65°F)	0	0	0	0	6	25	86	163	41	3	0	0	469
Mean Precipitation (in.)	2.86	1.79	2.17	2.56	2.68	2.93	2.96	3.31	4.05	3.31	3.22	2.81	34.65
Days With ≥ 0.1" Precipitation	10	6	6	6	7	6	6	7	8	8	9	10	89
Days With ≥ 1.0" Precipitation	0	0	0	0	0	1	1	1	1	0	0	0	4
Mean Snowfall (in.)	51.0	29.2	16.2	3.8	trace	0.0	0.0	0.0	trace	0.3	12.9	38.0	151.4
Days With ≥ 1.0" Snow Depth	na	*25*	*20*	4	0	0	0	0	0	0	0	*21*	na

Marquette WBO *Marquette County*   Elevation: 675 ft.   Latitude: 46° 34' N   Longitude: 87° 24' W

	JAN	FEB	MAR	APR	MAY	JUN	JUL	AUG	SEP	OCT	NOV	DEC	YEAR
Mean Maximum Temp. (°F)	25.0	28.6	36.2	47.9	60.4	69.5	75.7	74.6	66.2	54.7	40.3	29.5	50.7
Mean Temp. (°F)	18.0	20.9	28.7	39.8	50.8	59.8	66.4	65.9	57.8	47.1	34.3	23.4	42.7
Mean Minimum Temp. (°F)	10.9	13.2	21.1	31.6	41.1	50.1	57.0	57.1	49.3	39.4	28.4	17.2	34.7
Extreme Maximum Temp. (°F)	49	62	71	91	93	99	104	99	97	85	74	60	104
Extreme Minimum Temp. (°F)	-22	-24	-11	4	23	31	41	40	30	19	-2	-13	-24
Days Maximum Temp. ≥ 90°F	0	0	0	0	0	1	2	1	0	0	0	0	4
Days Maximum Temp. ≤ 32°F	24	18	11	2	0	0	0	0	0	0	6	18	79
Days Minimum Temp. ≤ 32°F	31	27	28	17	3	0	0	0	0	6	21	30	163
Days Minimum Temp. ≤ 0°F	5	4	1	0	0	0	0	0	0	0	0	2	12
Heating Degree Days (base 65°F)	1,451	1,239	1,120	751	446	193	63	66	239	551	913	1,283	8,315
Cooling Degree Days (base 65°F)	0	0	0	2	10	46	108	100	28	1	0	0	295
Mean Precipitation (in.)	2.03	1.32	2.15	2.41	2.77	2.71	2.77	2.98	3.57	3.04	2.59	1.95	30.29
Days With ≥ 0.1" Precipitation	7	4	5	6	6	6	6	6	8	7	7	6	74
Days With ≥ 1.0" Precipitation	0	0	0	0	1	1	0	1	1	0	0	0	4
Mean Snowfall (in.)	31.0	19.3	20.0	7.7	1.1	0.0	0.0	0.0	0.2	1.7	12.0	25.2	118.2
Days With ≥ 1.0" Snow Depth	31	28	29	11	0	0	0	0	0	1	11	28	139

Midland *Midland County*   Elevation: 639 ft.   Latitude: 43° 37' N   Longitude: 84° 13' W

	JAN	FEB	MAR	APR	MAY	JUN	JUL	AUG	SEP	OCT	NOV	DEC	YEAR
Mean Maximum Temp. (°F)	29.5	32.7	43.2	57.5	70.8	79.8	84.0	81.1	73.4	60.8	46.3	34.5	57.8
Mean Temp. (°F)	22.5	24.8	33.9	46.5	58.5	67.7	72.2	69.9	62.1	50.7	38.9	28.0	48.0
Mean Minimum Temp. (°F)	15.4	16.9	24.7	35.4	46.2	55.6	60.4	58.5	50.7	40.8	31.5	21.6	38.1
Extreme Maximum Temp. (°F)	59	67	78	88	95	103	100	98	95	87	75	64	103
Extreme Minimum Temp. (°F)	-19	-15	-10	10	25	32	39	33	28	18	3	-11	-19
Days Maximum Temp. ≥ 90°F	0	0	0	0	1	3	6	2	1	0	0	0	13
Days Maximum Temp. ≤ 32°F	19	14	5	0	0	0	0	0	0	0	2	12	52
Days Minimum Temp. ≤ 32°F	30	26	25	12	2	0	0	0	0	6	17	28	146
Days Minimum Temp. ≤ 0°F	3	3	0	0	0	0	0	0	0	0	0	1	7
Heating Degree Days (base 65°F)	1,313	1,128	956	554	238	53	9	22	145	440	775	1,140	6,773
Cooling Degree Days (base 65°F)	0	0	1	6	42	140	249	192	66	4	0	0	700
Mean Precipitation (in.)	1.57	1.21	2.27	2.82	2.74	2.97	2.54	3.64	3.89	2.60	2.51	1.86	30.62
Days With ≥ 0.1" Precipitation	4	3	5	7	6	6	5	6	6	6	5	5	64
Days With ≥ 1.0" Precipitation	0	0	0	0	1	1	0	1	1	1	0	0	5
Mean Snowfall (in.)	na	na	na	0.4	0.0	0.0	0.0	0.0	0.0	trace	na	na	na
Days With ≥ 1.0" Snow Depth	22	18	7	0	0	0	0	0	0	0	2	na	na

Mio Hydro Plant *Oscoda County*   Elevation: 958 ft.   Latitude: 44° 40' N   Longitude: 84° 08' W

	JAN	FEB	MAR	APR	MAY	JUN	JUL	AUG	SEP	OCT	NOV	DEC	YEAR
Mean Maximum Temp. (°F)	27.4	30.8	40.6	54.3	68.2	76.9	81.8	79.0	70.2	58.0	43.8	32.4	55.3
Mean Temp. (°F)	17.9	19.8	29.2	42.4	54.5	63.5	68.6	66.2	57.9	47.0	35.7	24.5	43.9
Mean Minimum Temp. (°F)	8.3	8.9	17.8	30.4	40.8	50.1	55.4	53.4	45.6	35.9	27.5	16.4	32.5
Extreme Maximum Temp. (°F)	60	61	77	88	93	103	101	96	93	85	74	63	103
Extreme Minimum Temp. (°F)	-29	-38	-22	3	22	29	37	24	25	16	-8	-25	-38
Days Maximum Temp. ≥ 90°F	0	0	0	0	1	2	4	2	0	0	0	0	9
Days Maximum Temp. ≤ 32°F	22	17	7	1	0	0	0	0	0	0	3	15	65
Days Minimum Temp. ≤ 32°F	31	28	28	18	7	0	0	0	2	11	22	30	177
Days Minimum Temp. ≤ 0°F	9	9	3	0	0	0	0	0	0	0	0	4	25
Heating Degree Days (base 65°F)	1,454	1,269	1,102	676	340	111	31	58	230	554	873	1,251	7,949
Cooling Degree Days (base 65°F)	0	0	0	3	20	73	152	106	23	0	0	0	377
Mean Precipitation (in.)	1.58	1.17	1.79	2.08	2.32	2.57	2.97	3.44	2.95	2.30	1.90	1.68	26.75
Days With ≥ 0.1" Precipitation	5	4	5	6	6	6	6	7	7	6	6	5	69
Days With ≥ 1.0" Precipitation	0	0	0	0	0	0	1	1	1	0	0	0	3
Mean Snowfall (in.)	15.1	8.1	9.2	2.5	0.3	0.0	0.0	0.0	trace	0.2	4.0	11.0	50.4
Days With ≥ 1.0" Snow Depth	29	26	22	5	0	0	0	0	0	0	7	21	110

Monroe *Monroe County*   Elevation: 587 ft.   Latitude: 41° 55' N   Longitude: 83° 24' W

	JAN	FEB	MAR	APR	MAY	JUN	JUL	AUG	SEP	OCT	NOV	DEC	YEAR
Mean Maximum Temp. (°F)	31.5	34.9	44.8	57.9	70.5	80.7	85.2	83.0	75.1	61.6	48.1	37.0	59.2
Mean Temp. (°F)	24.1	26.9	36.2	48.0	60.0	70.0	74.6	72.6	64.6	51.9	40.4	30.0	49.9
Mean Minimum Temp. (°F)	16.6	18.9	27.6	38.1	49.4	59.3	63.9	62.1	53.9	42.1	32.6	23.1	40.6
Extreme Maximum Temp. (°F)	62	69	81	90	95	106	104	102	98	87	76	69	106
Extreme Minimum Temp. (°F)	-18	-11	2	11	26	40	48	42	33	21	6	-12	-18
Days Maximum Temp. ≥ 90°F	0	0	0	0	1	5	8	5	1	0	0	0	20
Days Maximum Temp. ≤ 32°F	16	12	3	0	0	0	0	0	0	0	1	9	41
Days Minimum Temp. ≤ 32°F	29	25	22	8	0	0	0	0	0	4	16	26	130
Days Minimum Temp. ≤ 0°F	3	1	0	0	0	0	0	0	0	0	0	1	5
Heating Degree Days (base 65°F)	1,262	1,068	887	512	201	33	3	7	99	406	733	1,076	6,287
Cooling Degree Days (base 65°F)	0	0	1	8	54	200	320	253	90	7	0	0	933
Mean Precipitation (in.)	1.83	1.74	2.70	3.23	3.06	3.58	3.01	3.37	3.03	2.27	2.89	2.49	33.20
Days With ≥ 0.1" Precipitation	5	5	6	8	7	7	6	6	6	5	7	6	74
Days With ≥ 1.0" Precipitation	0	0	1	0	1	1	1	1	1	0	0	0	6
Mean Snowfall (in.)	na	5.7	5.4	1.0	0.0	0.0	0.0	0.0	0.0	trace	na	na	na
Days With ≥ 1.0" Snow Depth	na	na	na	0	0	0	0	0	0	0	na	na	na

Montague 4 NW *Muskegon County*   Elevation: 649 ft.   Latitude: 43° 28' N   Longitude: 86° 25' W

	JAN	FEB	MAR	APR	MAY	JUN	JUL	AUG	SEP	OCT	NOV	DEC	YEAR
Mean Maximum Temp. (°F)	29.5	32.7	42.5	55.0	67.3	75.5	79.5	77.7	70.3	58.8	45.6	34.7	55.8
Mean Temp. (°F)	23.0	25.3	33.6	44.1	55.0	63.7	68.3	67.1	60.1	49.4	38.5	28.6	46.4
Mean Minimum Temp. (°F)	16.4	17.5	24.3	33.1	42.6	51.8	57.2	56.4	49.8	40.0	31.4	22.3	36.9
Extreme Maximum Temp. (°F)	59	64	78	84	88	96	94	92	90	85	70	64	96
Extreme Minimum Temp. (°F)	-17	-27	-17	0	18	27	37	32	24	17	5	-13	-27
Days Maximum Temp. ≥ 90°F	0	0	0	0	0	0	1	0	0	0	0	0	1
Days Maximum Temp. ≤ 32°F	18	13	5	0	0	0	0	0	0	0	2	11	49
Days Minimum Temp. ≤ 32°F	30	26	25	15	5	0	0	0	1	7	18	27	154
Days Minimum Temp. ≤ 0°F	2	2	1	0	0	0	0	0	0	0	0	0	5
Heating Degree Days (base 65°F)	1,295	1,116	968	624	322	102	30	45	180	480	786	1,122	7,070
Cooling Degree Days (base 65°F)	0	0	0	3	15	67	140	119	38	2	0	0	384
Mean Precipitation (in.)	1.73	1.06	2.36	3.09	2.56	2.83	2.77	4.21	3.49	3.33	3.13	1.76	32.32
Days With ≥ 0.1" Precipitation	4	3	6	7	6	6	5	6	7	7	7	5	69
Days With ≥ 1.0" Precipitation	0	0	0	1	0	1	1	1	1	1	1	0	7
Mean Snowfall (in.)	25.8	14.5	5.6	1.6	trace	0.0	0.0	0.0	0.0	0.1	4.1	19.0	70.7
Days With ≥ 1.0" Snow Depth	26	21	10	1	0	0	0	0	0	0	3	17	78

Mount Pleasant University *Isabella County*   Elevation: 793 ft.   Latitude: 43° 35' N   Longitude: 84° 46' W

	JAN	FEB	MAR	APR	MAY	JUN	JUL	AUG	SEP	OCT	NOV	DEC	YEAR
Mean Maximum Temp. (°F)	27.9	30.5	41.2	55.1	*69.1*	77.9	82.5	80.1	*71.3*	*58.9*	45.0	33.0	*56.1*
Mean Temp. (°F)	20.5	22.2	31.9	44.5	*56.9*	66.1	70.8	68.6	*60.2*	*49.1*	*37.4*	26.4	*46.2*
Mean Minimum Temp. (°F)	13.1	13.8	22.4	33.8	*44.7*	54.2	59.0	57.1	*48.9*	*38.8*	29.5	19.7	*36.3*
Extreme Maximum Temp. (°F)	57	62	77	88	*92*	100	100	100	93	*87*	75	67	*100*
Extreme Minimum Temp. (°F)	-19	-17	-9	10	*25*	34	43	36	27	18	2	-14	*-19*
Days Maximum Temp. ≥ 90°F	0	0	0	0	*0*	2	4	2	0	*0*	0	0	*8*
Days Maximum Temp. ≤ 32°F	20	16	6	1	*0*	0	0	0	0	*0*	3	14	*60*
Days Minimum Temp. ≤ 32°F	30	27	27	15	*2*	0	0	0	1	6	20	29	*157*
Days Minimum Temp. ≤ 0°F	4	4	1	0	*0*	0	0	0	0	0	0	1	*10*
Heating Degree Days (base 65°F)	1,372	1,203	1,021	614	*275*	67	14	31	*183*	*491*	821	1,190	*7,282*
Cooling Degree Days (base 65°F)	*0*	0	*0*	4	*31*	102	*207*	154	39	*2*	*0*	0	*539*
Mean Precipitation (in.)	1.50	1.13	2.22	3.08	2.69	3.51	2.75	3.71	3.70	*3.00*	2.79	1.93	*32.01*
Days With ≥ 0.1" Precipitation	4	3	5	7	*6*	6	5	6	6	6	6	5	*65*
Days With ≥ 1.0" Precipitation	0	0	0	1	1	1	0	1	1	1	1	0	7
Mean Snowfall (in.)	na	*4.7*	na	*1.7*	*trace*	0.0	0.0	0.0	0.0	*trace*	na	na	na
Days With ≥ 1.0" Snow Depth	na	na	na	*1*	0	0	0	0	0	*0*	na	na	na

Newberry 3 S *Luce County*   Elevation: 849 ft.   Latitude: 46° 19' N   Longitude: 85° 30' W

	JAN	FEB	MAR	APR	MAY	JUN	JUL	AUG	SEP	OCT	NOV	DEC	YEAR
Mean Maximum Temp. (°F)	22.9	26.2	35.0	49.0	63.4	71.8	76.6	74.4	65.2	53.4	39.5	28.1	50.5
Mean Temp. (°F)	15.1	17.3	25.9	38.9	51.5	59.8	65.0	63.8	55.4	44.8	32.8	21.3	41.0
Mean Minimum Temp. (°F)	7.2	8.4	16.7	28.8	39.5	47.8	53.4	53.0	45.5	36.1	26.0	14.4	31.4
Extreme Maximum Temp. (°F)	46	50	65	82	93	94	97	92	89	78	71	60	97
Extreme Minimum Temp. (°F)	-26	-27	-18	0	21	28	32	33	24	15	-10	-20	-27
Days Maximum Temp. ≥ 90°F	0	0	0	0	0	0	1	0	0	0	0	0	1
Days Maximum Temp. ≤ 32°F	26	20	12	2	0	0	0	0	0	0	7	20	87
Days Minimum Temp. ≤ 32°F	31	28	29	21	7	1	0	0	2	12	24	30	185
Days Minimum Temp. ≤ 0°F	9	8	3	0	0	0	0	0	0	0	0	4	24
Heating Degree Days (base 65°F)	1,541	1,340	1,205	776	421	180	72	94	297	620	960	1,350	8,856
Cooling Degree Days (base 65°F)	0	0	0	0	6	36	84	66	16	0	0	0	208
Mean Precipitation (in.)	*2.07*	1.22	1.95	1.94	2.70	3.04	3.32	3.53	3.66	3.17	2.54	2.11	*31.25*
Days With ≥ 0.1" Precipitation	6	*4*	5	5	6	6	6	7	8	7	7	6	73
Days With ≥ 1.0" Precipitation	0	0	0	0	0	1	1	1	1	0	0	0	4
Mean Snowfall (in.)	33.1	19.7	15.4	6.3	0.1	0.0	0.0	0.0	trace	0.8	12.4	26.9	114.7
Days With ≥ 1.0" Snow Depth	na	*26*	*25*	*8*	0	0	0	0	0	1	6	21	na

Onaway State Park *Presque Isle County*   Elevation: 688 ft.   Latitude: 45° 26' N   Longitude: 84° 14' W

	JAN	FEB	MAR	APR	MAY	JUN	JUL	AUG	SEP	OCT	NOV	DEC	YEAR
Mean Maximum Temp. (°F)	27.4	31.0	40.5	54.2	68.7	77.5	82.0	79.5	70.8	58.9	44.1	32.5	55.6
Mean Temp. (°F)	18.8	20.5	29.4	42.5	55.4	64.3	69.3	67.3	59.5	48.9	36.8	25.4	44.8
Mean Minimum Temp. (°F)	10.1	10.0	18.3	30.9	42.0	51.0	56.5	55.2	48.1	38.9	29.5	18.5	34.1
Extreme Maximum Temp. (°F)	55	61	77	91	94	98	100	98	95	89	77	63	100
Extreme Minimum Temp. (°F)	-30	-35	-22	3	24	30	38	33	24	19	0	-21	-35
Days Maximum Temp. ≥ 90°F	0	0	0	0	0	2	4	2	0	0	0	0	8
Days Maximum Temp. ≤ 32°F	22	16	6	0	0	0	0	0	0	0	3	14	61
Days Minimum Temp. ≤ 32°F	31	28	28	18	5	0	0	0	1	7	20	29	167
Days Minimum Temp. ≤ 0°F	7	7	3	0	0	0	0	0	0	0	0	2	19
Heating Degree Days (base 65°F)	1,427	1,250	1,095	672	314	92	20	42	195	494	839	1,219	7,659
Cooling Degree Days (base 65°F)	0	0	0	0	5	21	81	166	131	37	2	0	443
Mean Precipitation (in.)	1.86	1.26	2.14	2.47	2.78	2.67	3.34	3.32	3.58	2.78	2.32	2.10	30.62
Days With ≥ 0.1" Precipitation	5	4	5	6	6	6	6	7	8	7	7	6	73
Days With ≥ 1.0" Precipitation	0	0	0	0	0	0	1	1	1	0	0	0	3
Mean Snowfall (in.)	25.4	16.4	15.0	5.0	0.2	0.0	0.0	0.0	0.0	0.3	10.0	20.6	92.9
Days With ≥ 1.0" Snow Depth	30	28	22	5	0	0	0	0	0	0	7	23	115

Pellston Emmet County Airport *Emmet County*   Elevation: 711 ft.   Latitude: 45° 34' N   Longitude: 84° 47' W

	JAN	FEB	MAR	APR	MAY	JUN	JUL	AUG	SEP	OCT	NOV	DEC	YEAR
Mean Maximum Temp. (°F)	25.6	28.1	37.3	51.4	65.9	74.9	79.3	76.8	67.5	55.8	41.9	30.9	53.0
Mean Temp. (°F)	17.0	17.7	27.1	40.5	53.1	62.0	67.1	65.0	56.6	46.1	34.9	24.0	42.6
Mean Minimum Temp. (°F)	8.3	7.2	16.8	29.6	40.2	49.1	54.7	53.1	45.7	36.3	27.9	17.0	32.2
Extreme Maximum Temp. (°F)	53	56	75	91	94	99	98	98	93	85	74	64	99
Extreme Minimum Temp. (°F)	-35	-37	-30	-5	20	28	35	29	21	15	-3	-28	-37
Days Maximum Temp. ≥ 90°F	0	0	0	0	0	1	2	1	0	0	0	0	4
Days Maximum Temp. ≤ 32°F	24	18	9	1	0	0	0	0	0	0	5	17	74
Days Minimum Temp. ≤ 32°F	31	27	28	20	7	1	0	0	3	11	22	29	179
Days Minimum Temp. ≤ 0°F	9	10	4	0	0	0	0	0	0	0	0	3	26
Heating Degree Days (base 65°F)	1,483	1,331	1,168	730	379	138	46	78	267	582	896	1,265	8,363
Cooling Degree Days (base 65°F)	0	0	0	4	15	59	122	90	23	1	0	0	314
Mean Precipitation (in.)	2.41	1.58	2.28	2.63	2.72	2.52	2.83	3.18	4.14	3.27	2.95	2.54	33.05
Days With ≥ 0.1" Precipitation	8	5	5	6	6	6	5	7	8	8	8	7	79
Days With ≥ 1.0" Precipitation	0	0	0	0	1	0	1	1	1	1	0	0	5
Mean Snowfall (in.)	34.2	20.4	13.5	5.4	0.3	0.0	trace	trace	trace	0.8	12.2	28.1	114.9
Days With ≥ 1.0" Snow Depth	30	28	25	7	0	0	0	0	0	0	8	23	121

Petoskey *Emmet County*   Elevation: 606 ft.   Latitude: 45° 22' N   Longitude: 84° 59' W

	JAN	FEB	MAR	APR	MAY	JUN	JUL	AUG	SEP	OCT	NOV	DEC	YEAR
Mean Maximum Temp. (°F)	27.4	29.3	37.8	49.5	61.8	70.5	76.0	75.2	68.1	56.9	43.6	33.0	52.4
Mean Temp. (°F)	20.9	21.1	29.2	40.7	52.1	61.2	67.4	66.7	59.6	49.2	37.7	27.5	44.4
Mean Minimum Temp. (°F)	14.4	12.8	20.6	31.8	42.2	52.0	58.7	58.0	51.0	41.5	31.7	22.0	36.4
Extreme Maximum Temp. (°F)	56	59	79	89	93	96	94	95	93	84	73	64	96
Extreme Minimum Temp. (°F)	-21	-25	-19	2	28	34	40	36	28	23	6	-18	-25
Days Maximum Temp. ≥ 90°F	0	0	0	0	0	0	1	1	0	0	0	0	2
Days Maximum Temp. ≤ 32°F	22	17	9	1	0	0	0	0	0	0	3	13	65
Days Minimum Temp. ≤ 32°F	31	27	27	16	2	0	0	0	0	3	17	27	150
Days Minimum Temp. ≤ 0°F	3	5	2	0	0	0	0	0	0	0	0	1	11
Heating Degree Days (base 65°F)	1,359	1,234	1,103	724	401	151	38	47	191	485	814	1,155	7,702
Cooling Degree Days (base 65°F)	0	0	0	2	6	42	111	104	32	2	0	0	299
Mean Precipitation (in.)	2.05	1.21	2.00	2.51	2.66	2.70	3.23	3.43	3.83	3.20	2.51	2.19	31.52
Days With ≥ 0.1" Precipitation	7	4	5	6	6	6	6	7	8	8	7	7	77
Days With ≥ 1.0" Precipitation	0	0	0	0	0	0	1	1	1	0	0	0	3
Mean Snowfall (in.)	39.7	21.9	12.1	4.1	0.2	0.0	0.0	0.0	trace	0.4	10.6	31.6	120.6
Days With ≥ 1.0" Snow Depth	na	na	na	na	0	0	0	0	0	0	na	na	na

Pontiac State Hospital *Oakland County*   Elevation: 980 ft.   Latitude: 42° 39' N   Longitude: 83° 18' W

	JAN	FEB	MAR	APR	MAY	JUN	JUL	AUG	SEP	OCT	NOV	DEC	YEAR
Mean Maximum Temp. (°F)	29.8	33.5	44.5	58.0	70.5	79.3	83.4	81.3	73.6	60.5	46.4	34.4	57.9
Mean Temp. (°F)	22.8	25.4	35.1	47.1	59.0	68.0	72.4	70.7	63.2	51.0	39.2	28.1	48.5
Mean Minimum Temp. (°F)	15.7	17.3	25.7	36.1	47.5	56.6	61.3	60.0	52.6	41.7	31.8	21.6	39.0
Extreme Maximum Temp. (°F)	61	65	78	87	92	102	104	101	96	85	76	64	104
Extreme Minimum Temp. (°F)	-21	-12	-5	8	25	34	41	40	31	19	8	-11	-21
Days Maximum Temp. ≥ 90°F	0	0	0	0	0	2	5	2	1	0	0	0	10
Days Maximum Temp. ≤ 32°F	18	13	5	0	0	0	0	0	0	0	2	12	50
Days Minimum Temp. ≤ 32°F	30	26	24	11	1	0	0	0	0	4	17	28	141
Days Minimum Temp. ≤ 0°F	3	2	0	0	0	0	0	0	0	0	0	1	6
Heating Degree Days (base 65°F)	1,302	1,111	918	538	225	46	6	15	122	433	768	1,139	6,623
Cooling Degree Days (base 65°F)	0	0	1	6	46	141	248	202	74	6	0	0	724
Mean Precipitation (in.)	1.42	1.48	2.26	2.66	2.69	3.11	2.78	3.14	3.01	2.64	2.73	2.29	30.21
Days With ≥ 0.1" Precipitation	4	4	5	6	6	6	6	6	6	6	7	6	68
Days With ≥ 1.0" Precipitation	0	0	0	0	0	1	0	1	0	0	0	0	2
Mean Snowfall (in.)	9.1	6.3	4.5	1.6	trace	0.0	0.0	0.0	0.0	0.1	2.2	7.5	31.3
Days With ≥ 1.0" Snow Depth	20	17	7	1	0	0	0	0	0	0	2	13	60

Port Huron *St. Clair County*   Elevation: 587 ft.   Latitude: 42° 59' N   Longitude: 82° 25' W

	JAN	FEB	MAR	APR	MAY	JUN	JUL	AUG	SEP	OCT	NOV	DEC	YEAR
Mean Maximum Temp. (°F)	30.4	33.0	42.3	54.7	67.0	77.0	81.9	80.5	72.9	60.4	46.9	35.7	56.9
Mean Temp. (°F)	23.2	25.3	33.9	45.0	56.5	66.3	72.0	70.7	63.0	51.3	39.7	29.0	48.0
Mean Minimum Temp. (°F)	16.1	17.6	25.5	35.3	45.9	55.6	62.0	60.9	53.1	42.1	32.3	22.2	39.1
Extreme Maximum Temp. (°F)	59	64	80	87	95	102	102	101	95	86	76	66	102
Extreme Minimum Temp. (°F)	-19	-11	-2	13	28	35	43	40	32	20	10	-7	-19
Days Maximum Temp. ≥ 90°F	0	0	0	0	1	2	4	2	1	0	0	0	10
Days Maximum Temp. ≤ 32°F	17	13	6	0	0	0	0	0	0	0	2	11	49
Days Minimum Temp. ≤ 32°F	29	26	25	10	0	0	0	0	0	3	16	27	136
Days Minimum Temp. ≤ 0°F	3	2	0	0	0	0	0	0	0	0	0	1	6
Heating Degree Days (base 65°F)	1,288	1,115	956	596	286	67	8	14	121	425	754	1,110	6,740
Cooling Degree Days (base 65°F)	0	0	0	3	29	114	239	202	70	5	0	0	662
Mean Precipitation (in.)	1.77	1.56	2.26	2.95	2.70	3.23	2.80	3.02	3.39	2.47	2.86	2.05	31.06
Days With ≥ 0.1" Precipitation	5	4	6	7	7	7	7	6	7	6	7	6	75
Days With ≥ 1.0" Precipitation	0	0	0	0	0	1	0	1	1	0	0	0	3
Mean Snowfall (in.)	10.0	8.3	4.7	1.3	trace	0.0	0.0	0.0	0.0	0.5	1.5	7.9	34.2
Days With ≥ 1.0" Snow Depth	18	15	5	1	0	0	0	0	0	0	1	10	50

Saginaw Tri City Int'l Airport *Saginaw County*　Elevation: 659 ft.　Latitude: 43° 32' N　Longitude: 84° 05' W

	JAN	FEB	MAR	APR	MAY	JUN	JUL	AUG	SEP	OCT	NOV	DEC	YEAR
Mean Maximum Temp. (°F)	27.6	30.2	40.7	55.0	68.3	77.5	82.0	78.9	71.0	58.6	44.8	32.9	55.6
Mean Temp. (°F)	21.2	23.3	33.0	45.5	57.6	66.8	71.3	68.7	60.9	49.4	37.9	27.0	46.9
Mean Minimum Temp. (°F)	14.7	16.3	25.3	36.0	46.8	56.0	60.6	58.4	50.6	40.1	31.0	21.0	38.1
Extreme Maximum Temp. (°F)	60	63	78	87	94	103	101	97	94	88	75	64	103
Extreme Minimum Temp. (°F)	-22	-17	-7	12	25	36	40	37	27	21	-2	-7	-22
Days Maximum Temp. ≥ 90°F	0	0	0	0	0	2	4	2	1	0	0	0	9
Days Maximum Temp. ≤ 32°F	21	16	7	0	0	0	0	0	0	0	3	14	61
Days Minimum Temp. ≤ 32°F	29	26	24	10	1	0	0	0	0	5	18	28	141
Days Minimum Temp. ≤ 0°F	4	3	0	0	0	0	0	0	0	0	0	1	8
Heating Degree Days (base 65°F)	1,349	1,172	984	583	260	61	11	30	166	482	807	1,172	7,077
Cooling Degree Days (base 65°F)	0	0	0	5	36	119	215	149	46	3	0	0	573
Mean Precipitation (in.)	1.72	1.54	2.47	2.82	2.80	3.02	2.54	3.26	4.02	2.57	2.70	2.12	31.58
Days With > 0.1" Precipitation	5	4	6	7	6	6	5	6	7	6	6	6	70
Days With ≥ 1.0" Precipitation	0	0	0	0	1	1	1	1	1	0	1	0	6
Mean Snowfall (in.)	11.4	8.0	8.4	2.2	trace	trace	trace	trace	trace	0.2	3.6	11.0	44.8
Days With ≥ 1.0" Snow Depth	22	18	9	1	0	0	0	0	0	0	2	13	65

Saint James 2 S Beaver Island *Charlevoix County*　Elevation: 669 ft.　Latitude: 45° 43' N　Longitude: 85° 31' W

	JAN	FEB	MAR	APR	MAY	JUN	JUL	AUG	SEP	OCT	NOV	DEC	YEAR
Mean Maximum Temp. (°F)	26.0	27.2	36.0	48.2	61.7	70.7	75.7	74.4	66.5	55.1	41.8	32.1	51.3
Mean Temp. (°F)	19.9	19.7	28.2	39.4	51.3	60.3	66.2	65.6	58.4	47.8	36.5	27.0	43.3
Mean Minimum Temp. (°F)	13.7	12.1	20.4	30.7	40.8	49.8	56.5	56.9	50.2	40.3	31.1	21.8	35.4
Extreme Maximum Temp. (°F)	51	52	68	82	84	91	94	93	90	78	69	59	94
Extreme Minimum Temp. (°F)	-23	-25	-20	7	21	31	36	36	28	21	7	-10	-25
Days Maximum Temp. ≥ 90°F	0	0	0	0	0	0	0	0	0	0	0	0	0
Days Maximum Temp. ≤ 32°F	22	19	11	1	0	0	0	0	0	0	4	14	71
Days Minimum Temp. ≤ 32°F	30	28	28	17	4	0	0	0	0	4	17	28	156
Days Minimum Temp. ≤ 0°F	4	5	1	0	0	0	0	0	0	0	0	0	10
Heating Degree Days (base 65°F)	1,392	1,273	1,134	760	421	163	44	51	210	529	850	1,172	7,999
Cooling Degree Days (base 65°F)	0	0	0	0	3	35	93	86	20	0	0	0	237
Mean Precipitation (in.)	2.40	1.22	2.12	2.53	2.83	2.55	2.74	3.12	3.67	3.15	2.58	2.24	31.15
Days With ≥ 0.1" Precipitation	6	4	4	5	6	6	6	6	7	6	6	6	68
Days With ≥ 1.0" Precipitation	0	0	0	0	1	0	1	1	1	0	0	0	4
Mean Snowfall (in.)	28.0	15.6	12.2	4.4	0.2	0.0	0.0	0.0	trace	trace	6.3	19.6	86.3
Days With ≥ 1.0" Snow Depth	na	na	na	4	0	0	0	0	0	0	2	na	na

Saint Johns *Clinton County*　Elevation: 741 ft.　Latitude: 43° 01' N　Longitude: 84° 33' W

	JAN	FEB	MAR	APR	MAY	JUN	JUL	AUG	SEP	OCT	NOV	DEC	YEAR
Mean Maximum Temp. (°F)	29.6	33.0	43.9	57.6	70.8	79.4	83.6	81.1	73.8	61.3	46.9	34.9	58.0
Mean Temp. (°F)	21.9	24.5	34.3	46.4	58.5	67.4	71.8	69.4	62.1	50.6	38.6	27.8	47.8
Mean Minimum Temp. (°F)	14.0	15.9	24.6	35.2	46.3	55.4	59.8	57.8	50.3	39.9	30.3	20.5	37.5
Extreme Maximum Temp. (°F)	61	69	79	89	92	98	100	100	95	88	76	66	100
Extreme Minimum Temp. (°F)	-25	-17	-10	7	24	34	41	38	27	18	0	-10	-25
Days Maximum Temp. ≥ 90°F	0	0	0	0	0	2	5	2	1	0	0	0	10
Days Maximum Temp. ≤ 32°F	19	14	5	0	0	0	0	0	0	0	2	12	52
Days Minimum Temp. ≤ 32°F	30	26	25	13	2	0	0	0	1	7	19	28	151
Days Minimum Temp. ≤ 0°F	4	3	0	0	0	0	0	0	0	0	0	1	8
Heating Degree Days (base 65°F)	1,331	1,136	946	558	236	54	10	24	145	445	787	1,148	6,820
Cooling Degree Days (base 65°F)	0	0	1	6	40	124	223	163	58	4	0	0	619
Mean Precipitation (in.)	1.67	1.36	2.29	3.24	2.93	3.36	3.00	3.74	3.77	2.95	2.58	1.94	32.83
Days With ≥ 0.1" Precipitation	5	4	5	8	6	6	6	7	7	6	6	5	71
Days With ≥ 1.0" Precipitation	0	0	0	0	1	1	1	1	1	1	0	0	6
Mean Snowfall (in.)	13.7	9.2	7.1	2.2	trace	0.0	0.0	0.0	0.0	0.2	2.9	10.0	45.3
Days With ≥ 1.0" Snow Depth	20	15	7	1	0	0	0	0	0	0	2	11	56

Seney Wildlife Refuge *Schoolcraft County*　Elevation: 708 ft.　Latitude: 46° 17' N　Longitude: 85° 57' W

	JAN	FEB	MAR	APR	MAY	JUN	JUL	AUG	SEP	OCT	NOV	DEC	YEAR
Mean Maximum Temp. (°F)	24.9	29.1	38.0	51.6	66.4	74.9	80.5	77.4	68.4	56.0	41.7	30.4	53.3
Mean Temp. (°F)	15.7	18.1	26.7	40.6	53.7	61.8	67.5	65.2	57.5	46.7	34.5	23.0	42.6
Mean Minimum Temp. (°F)	6.3	7.2	15.5	29.6	40.8	48.7	54.4	53.1	46.7	37.3	27.3	15.7	31.9
Extreme Maximum Temp. (°F)	46	54	68	83	95	93	100	96	91	82	70	58	100
Extreme Minimum Temp. (°F)	-29	-41	-31	-1	22	24	35	30	25	17	-9	-33	-41
Days Maximum Temp. ≥ 90°F	0	0	0	0	0	1	2	1	0	0	0	0	4
Days Maximum Temp. ≤ 32°F	22	16	8	1	0	0	0	0	0	0	4	16	67
Days Minimum Temp. ≤ 32°F	28	25	26	18	5	0	0	0	1	10	20	26	159
Days Minimum Temp. ≤ 0°F	10	9	5	0	0	0	0	0	0	0	0	4	28
Heating Degree Days (base 65°F)	1,524	1,322	1,182	726	358	137	40	69	238	561	907	1,294	8,358
Cooling Degree Days (base 65°F)	0	na	0	0	12	54	133	87	21	0	0	na	na
Mean Precipitation (in.)	2.01	1.19	1.89	1.91	2.66	2.97	3.81	3.18	3.42	3.14	2.50	2.03	30.71
Days With ≥ 0.1" Precipitation	6	3	5	5	6	6	7	6	7	6	6	5	68
Days With ≥ 1.0" Precipitation	0	0	0	0	0	1	1	1	1	0	0	0	4
Mean Snowfall (in.)	30.0	17.6	14.4	3.4	0.3	0.0	0.0	0.0	trace	1.1	10.8	23.6	101.2
Days With ≥ 1.0" Snow Depth	26	23	24	10	0	0	0	0	0	1	8	20	112

South Haven *Van Buren County* Elevation: 620 ft. Latitude: 42° 24' N Longitude: 86° 17' W

	JAN	FEB	MAR	APR	MAY	JUN	JUL	AUG	SEP	OCT	NOV	DEC	YEAR
Mean Maximum Temp. (°F)	31.6	34.7	43.9	55.0	66.0	75.1	79.2	78.4	72.1	61.6	48.1	36.8	56.9
Mean Temp. (°F)	25.3	28.0	36.3	46.5	56.9	66.2	70.9	70.2	63.5	53.2	41.4	31.0	49.1
Mean Minimum Temp. (°F)	19.0	21.4	28.7	37.9	47.8	57.2	62.6	61.9	54.7	44.9	34.7	25.0	41.3
Extreme Maximum Temp. (°F)	63	71	81	87	91	97	94	95	89	85	76	68	97
Extreme Minimum Temp. (°F)	-14	-13	1	13	24	36	39	38	30	17	5	-5	-14
Days Maximum Temp. ≥ 90°F	0	0	0	0	0	0	1	1	0	0	0	0	2
Days Maximum Temp. ≤ 32°F	16	12	4	0	0	0	0	0	0	0	1	8	41
Days Minimum Temp. ≤ 32°F	28	24	21	7	1	0	0	0	0	2	12	24	119
Days Minimum Temp. ≤ 0°F	1	1	0	0	0	0	0	0	0	0	0	0	2
Heating Degree Days (base 65°F)	1,223	1,037	883	552	275	70	14	17	111	366	700	1,048	6,296
Cooling Degree Days (base 65°F)	0	0	0	4	31	118	221	203	76	8	0	0	661
Mean Precipitation (in.)	*2.13*	*1.52*	2.07	3.32	3.07	3.15	3.46	3.61	4.09	2.85	3.40	*2.71*	*35.38*
Days With ≥ 0.1" Precipitation	*7*	*4*	6	7	7	6	6	7	7	7	7	*7*	*78*
Days With ≥ 1.0" Precipitation	*0*	*0*	0	1	1	1	1	1	1	0	1	*0*	*7*
Mean Snowfall (in.)	na	na	4.0	1.2	0.0	0.0	0.0	0.0	0.0	0.2	*2.3*	na	na
Days With ≥ 1.0" Snow Depth	*16*	14	4	1	0	0	0	0	0	0	*2*	na	na

Stambaugh 2 SSE *Iron County* Elevation: 1,558 ft. Latitude: 46° 03' N Longitude: 88° 37' W

	JAN	FEB	MAR	APR	MAY	JUN	JUL	AUG	SEP	OCT	NOV	DEC	YEAR
Mean Maximum Temp. (°F)	21.3	27.0	36.8	51.8	66.0	74.1	77.9	75.5	66.3	54.3	37.7	25.8	51.2
Mean Temp. (°F)	9.6	13.8	24.3	38.9	51.7	60.3	64.5	62.3	53.8	43.0	29.0	16.2	39.0
Mean Minimum Temp. (°F)	-2.2	0.6	11.8	25.9	37.4	46.5	51.1	49.1	41.2	31.6	20.2	6.5	26.6
Extreme Maximum Temp. (°F)	55	62	71	92	90	97	98	94	95	88	74	59	98
Extreme Minimum Temp. (°F)	-42	-45	-31	-12	14	25	29	28	18	8	-15	-41	-45
Days Maximum Temp. ≥ 90°F	0	0	0	0	0	0	1	0	0	0	0	0	1
Days Maximum Temp. ≤ 32°F	27	20	11	2	0	0	0	0	0	0	10	23	93
Days Minimum Temp. ≤ 32°F	31	28	29	23	11	2	0	1	7	18	27	31	208
Days Minimum Temp. ≤ 0°F	16	14	7	1	0	0	0	0	0	0	2	10	50
Heating Degree Days (base 65°F)	1,715	1,442	1,256	777	415	173	87	125	343	676	1,074	1,508	9,591
Cooling Degree Days (base 65°F)	0	0	0	2	8	37	69	48	10	0	0	0	174
Mean Precipitation (in.)	1.12	0.83	1.62	2.17	3.31	3.61	3.95	3.74	3.86	2.89	2.13	1.35	30.58
Days With ≥ 0.1" Precipitation	4	2	4	6	7	8	8	7	8	7	5	4	70
Days With ≥ 1.0" Precipitation	0	0	0	0	1	1	1	1	1	1	0	0	6
Mean Snowfall (in.)	17.8	10.6	12.6	5.7	0.8	0.0	0.0	trace	trace	1.8	10.2	17.1	76.6
Days With ≥ 1.0" Snow Depth	31	28	27	7	0	0	0	0	0	1	11	29	134

Stephenson 8 WNW *Menominee County* Elevation: 708 ft. Latitude: 45° 27' N Longitude: 87° 45' W

	JAN	FEB	MAR	APR	MAY	JUN	JUL	AUG	SEP	OCT	NOV	DEC	YEAR
Mean Maximum Temp. (°F)	24.5	29.0	39.4	53.7	67.5	76.4	80.3	77.9	69.0	56.9	41.3	29.3	53.8
Mean Temp. (°F)	13.6	17.5	28.6	41.9	54.0	63.1	67.4	65.5	56.9	45.7	32.5	20.3	42.2
Mean Minimum Temp. (°F)	2.7	6.0	17.6	30.0	40.4	49.7	54.6	53.0	44.7	34.5	23.6	11.3	30.7
Extreme Maximum Temp. (°F)	52	58	76	91	93	98	99	96	94	87	76	61	99
Extreme Minimum Temp. (°F)	-39	-45	-21	2	19	28	32	30	21	13	-13	-31	-45
Days Maximum Temp. ≥ 90°F	0	0	0	0	0	2	3	1	0	0	0	0	6
Days Maximum Temp. ≤ 32°F	24	18	8	1	0	0	0	0	0	0	6	19	76
Days Minimum Temp. ≤ 32°F	31	28	28	19	7	1	0	0	3	14	25	30	186
Days Minimum Temp. ≤ 0°F	14	10	4	0	0	0	0	0	0	0	1	7	36
Heating Degree Days (base 65°F)	1,588	1,334	1,123	688	351	120	43	66	259	591	970	1,378	8,511
Cooling Degree Days (base 65°F)	0	0	0	2	16	69	113	86	20	0	0	0	306
Mean Precipitation (in.)	1.45	0.92	1.92	2.30	3.30	3.31	3.72	3.72	3.58	2.74	2.48	1.76	31.20
Days With ≥ 0.1" Precipitation	5	3	5	6	7	7	7	7	7	6	6	5	71
Days With ≥ 1.0" Precipitation	0	0	0	0	1	1	1	1	1	1	1	0	7
Mean Snowfall (in.)	18.0	8.8	11.6	3.7	0.6	0.0	0.0	0.0	trace	0.5	5.7	15.7	64.6
Days With ≥ 1.0" Snow Depth	29	27	20	4	0	0	0	0	0	0	5	22	107

Three Rivers *St. Joseph County* Elevation: 807 ft. Latitude: 41° 56' N Longitude: 85° 38' W

	JAN	FEB	MAR	APR	MAY	JUN	JUL	AUG	SEP	OCT	NOV	DEC	YEAR
Mean Maximum Temp. (°F)	30.9	35.1	46.1	59.3	71.6	80.7	84.2	81.8	74.8	62.6	48.2	36.4	59.3
Mean Temp. (°F)	23.1	26.3	36.2	47.8	59.3	68.4	72.2	70.0	62.7	51.2	39.7	29.0	48.8
Mean Minimum Temp. (°F)	15.2	17.4	26.3	36.3	46.9	56.2	60.3	58.2	50.6	39.8	31.2	21.6	38.3
Extreme Maximum Temp. (°F)	61	72	80	87	92	103	102	100	96	88	76	68	103
Extreme Minimum Temp. (°F)	-23	-18	-4	7	25	34	41	35	27	16	4	-15	-23
Days Maximum Temp. ≥ 90°F	0	0	0	0	1	3	6	3	1	0	0	0	14
Days Maximum Temp. ≤ 32°F	17	12	4	0	0	0	0	0	0	0	2	10	45
Days Minimum Temp. ≤ 32°F	29	26	23	11	1	0	0	0	1	7	18	27	143
Days Minimum Temp. ≤ 0°F	4	3	0	0	0	0	0	0	0	0	0	1	8
Heating Degree Days (base 65°F)	1,293	1,086	886	516	218	45	9	19	135	426	752	1,109	6,494
Cooling Degree Days (base 65°F)	0	0	1	7	45	153	244	182	69	5	0	0	706
Mean Precipitation (in.)	1.94	1.60	2.62	3.33	3.56	3.64	3.98	3.82	3.63	3.04	2.93	2.52	36.61
Days With ≥ 0.1" Precipitation	5	5	6	8	7	6	7	6	7	6	7	6	76
Days With ≥ 1.0" Precipitation	0	0	0	1	1	1	1	1	1	1	0	0	7
Mean Snowfall (in.)	8.9	5.7	5.4	1.5	trace	0.0	0.0	0.0	0.0	0.4	3.4	7.3	32.6
Days With ≥ 1.0" Snow Depth	21	16	8	1	0	0	0	0	0	0	3	14	63

Traverse City Cherry Capital *Grand Traverse County*   Elevation: 620 ft.   Latitude: 44° 44' N   Longitude: 85° 35' W

	JAN	FEB	MAR	APR	MAY	JUN	JUL	AUG	SEP	OCT	NOV	DEC	YEAR
Mean Maximum Temp. (°F)	27.1	29.0	39.0	52.9	66.7	76.5	81.2	78.6	69.7	57.8	43.3	32.0	54.5
Mean Temp. (°F)	20.7	20.7	30.1	42.4	54.1	64.3	69.6	67.8	59.7	48.8	36.9	26.4	45.1
Mean Minimum Temp. (°F)	14.3	12.4	21.1	31.9	41.5	52.0	57.9	56.9	49.7	39.6	30.4	20.7	35.7
Extreme Maximum Temp. (°F)	56	60	78	90	95	101	99	98	93	88	75	63	101
Extreme Minimum Temp. (°F)	-21	-37	-16	3	24	31	37	32	27	22	3	-26	-37
Days Maximum Temp. ≥ 90°F	0	0	0	0	1	2	4	2	0	0	0	0	9
Days Maximum Temp. ≤ 32°F	22	17	9	1	0	0	0	0	0	0	4	15	68
Days Minimum Temp. ≤ 32°F	30	27	26	17	6	0	0	0	0	6	19	28	159
Days Minimum Temp. ≤ 0°F	4	5	2	0	0	0	0	0	0	0	0	1	12
Heating Degree Days (base 65°F)	1,364	1,245	1,075	676	353	103	23	40	192	501	838	1,190	7,600
Cooling Degree Days (base 65°F)	0	0	0	5	23	87	172	138	40	3	0	0	468
Mean Precipitation (in.)	2.95	1.77	1.95	2.59	2.28	3.21	3.17	3.39	3.81	3.01	2.79	2.69	33.61
Days With ≥ 0.1" Precipitation	8	6	6	6	5	5	5	6	7	7	8	7	76
Days With ≥ 1.0" Precipitation	0	0	0	0	0	1	1	1	1	1	0	0	5
Mean Snowfall (in.)	30.8	19.1	10.4	2.7	0.1	trace	0.0	0.0	trace	0.4	9.2	24.1	96.8
Days With ≥ 1.0" Snow Depth	28	26	18	2	0	0	0	0	0	0	7	21	102

Vanderbilt 11 ENE *Otsego County*   Elevation: 921 ft.   Latitude: 45° 10' N   Longitude: 84° 26' W

	JAN	FEB	MAR	APR	MAY	JUN	JUL	AUG	SEP	OCT	NOV	DEC	YEAR
Mean Maximum Temp. (°F)	25.1	28.0	37.7	52.2	67.4	76.4	80.3	77.3	67.5	55.1	41.0	30.0	53.2
Mean Temp. (°F)	15.0	15.6	25.4	39.4	52.0	61.1	65.4	63.0	54.5	43.8	32.9	21.8	40.8
Mean Minimum Temp. (°F)	4.9	3.2	13.0	26.5	36.6	45.8	50.4	48.8	41.5	32.6	24.7	13.6	28.5
Extreme Maximum Temp. (°F)	55	60	75	90	95	100	100	96	92	83	75	62	100
Extreme Minimum Temp. (°F)	-36	-43	-27	-6	16	25	29	24	18	10	-8	-31	-43
Days Maximum Temp. ≥ 90°F	0	0	0	0	1	2	3	1	0	0	0	0	7
Days Maximum Temp. ≤ 32°F	24	19	10	1	0	0	0	0	0	0	6	18	78
Days Minimum Temp. ≤ 32°F	31	28	29	22	13	3	0	1	7	17	24	30	205
Days Minimum Temp. ≤ 0°F	12	12	6	0	0	0	0	0	0	0	0	6	36
Heating Degree Days (base 65°F)	1,544	1,390	1,219	765	413	165	76	117	327	650	958	1,333	8,957
Cooling Degree Days (base 65°F)	0	0	0	3	17	58	107	75	17	1	0	0	278
Mean Precipitation (in.)	2.24	1.40	2.09	2.35	2.85	2.42	3.48	3.51	3.57	2.94	2.41	2.27	31.53
Days With ≥ 0.1" Precipitation	7	4	6	6	6	5	7	7	8	8	7	7	78
Days With ≥ 1.0" Precipitation	0	0	0	0	1	0	1	1	1	0	0	0	4
Mean Snowfall (in.)	27.5	16.7	12.7	4.9	0.5	0.0	0.0	0.0	trace	0.8	11.6	23.1	97.8
Days With ≥ 1.0" Snow Depth	30	28	29	10	0	0	0	0	0	0	10	26	133

West Branch 3 SE *Ogemaw County*   Elevation: 882 ft.   Latitude: 44° 15' N   Longitude: 84° 12' W

	JAN	FEB	MAR	APR	MAY	JUN	JUL	AUG	SEP	OCT	NOV	DEC	YEAR
Mean Maximum Temp. (°F)	27.4	30.8	40.4	54.5	68.2	76.8	81.2	78.6	70.1	57.9	43.9	32.5	55.2
Mean Temp. (°F)	17.8	20.2	29.7	42.8	55.0	63.9	68.5	66.3	58.1	46.5	35.3	24.5	44.1
Mean Minimum Temp. (°F)	8.3	9.6	19.0	31.1	41.8	50.9	55.8	54.0	46.0	35.1	26.8	16.5	32.9
Extreme Maximum Temp. (°F)	57	61	78	91	91	103	100	97	93	86	76	63	103
Extreme Minimum Temp. (°F)	-25	-30	-19	7	19	28	39	31	25	16	-8	-21	-30
Days Maximum Temp. ≥ 90°F	0	0	0	0	0	2	3	1	0	0	0	0	6
Days Maximum Temp. ≤ 32°F	21	16	7	1	0	0	0	0	0	0	3	15	63
Days Minimum Temp. ≤ 32°F	31	28	29	17	5	0	0	0	2	14	23	30	179
Days Minimum Temp. ≤ 0°F	9	8	3	0	0	0	0	0	0	0	0	3	23
Heating Degree Days (base 65°F)	1,456	1,259	1,089	662	323	103	29	55	227	567	883	1,248	7,901
Cooling Degree Days (base 65°F)	0	0	0	2	21	74	147	106	24	0	0	0	374
Mean Precipitation (in.)	1.66	1.18	1.99	2.41	2.92	3.10	3.12	3.74	3.59	2.58	2.42	1.86	30.57
Days With ≥ 0.1" Precipitation	5	4	5	6	6	6	6	7	7	5	6	5	68
Days With ≥ 1.0" Precipitation	0	0	0	0	1	1	1	1	1	0	0	0	5
Mean Snowfall (in.)	14.9	9.4	8.8	2.0	0.1	0.0	0.0	0.0	0.0	0.3	4.9	10.8	51.2
Days With ≥ 1.0" Snow Depth	29	26	19	2	0	0	0	0	0	0	5	19	100

Whitefish Point *Chippewa County*   Elevation: 603 ft.   Latitude: 46° 45' N   Longitude: 84° 59' W

	JAN	FEB	MAR	APR	MAY	JUN	JUL	AUG	SEP	OCT	NOV	DEC	YEAR
Mean Maximum Temp. (°F)	23.8	26.1	34.2	44.8	57.1	65.7	71.9	72.3	64.7	52.9	39.8	29.5	48.6
Mean Temp. (°F)	17.3	17.7	25.3	36.6	47.2	55.3	61.6	63.1	56.4	45.9	34.3	23.8	40.4
Mean Minimum Temp. (°F)	10.7	9.3	16.5	28.3	37.2	44.9	51.3	53.8	48.1	38.9	28.8	18.1	32.1
Extreme Maximum Temp. (°F)	43	50	61	78	85	89	96	94	90	82	68	53	96
Extreme Minimum Temp. (°F)	-23	-27	-23	-1	22	29	33	33	26	19	-5	-14	-27
Days Maximum Temp. ≥ 90°F	0	0	0	0	0	0	0	0	0	0	0	0	0
Days Maximum Temp. ≤ 32°F	26	20	12	1	0	0	0	0	0	0	6	18	83
Days Minimum Temp. ≤ 32°F	31	28	29	21	7	1	0	0	0	6	20	29	172
Days Minimum Temp. ≤ 0°F	5	8	3	0	0	0	0	0	0	0	0	2	18
Heating Degree Days (base 65°F)	1,473	1,330	1,222	847	546	291	133	98	262	586	914	1,269	8,971
Cooling Degree Days (base 65°F)	0	0	0	0	0	9	39	54	13	0	0	0	115
Mean Precipitation (in.)	3.06	1.85	1.98	2.07	2.79	2.96	3.33	3.43	3.27	3.22	2.95	3.17	34.08
Days With ≥ 0.1" Precipitation	10	6	5	5	6	7	7	7	7	9	9	11	89
Days With ≥ 1.0" Precipitation	0	0	0	0	1	1	1	1	0	0	0	0	4
Mean Snowfall (in.)	40.8	22.2	14.0	4.8	trace	0.0	0.0	0.0	trace	0.9	12.9	37.1	132.7
Days With ≥ 1.0" Snow Depth	31	28	31	17	0	0	0	0	0	0	9	25	141

Note: See Appendix D for explanation of data.

MINNESOTA

PHYSICAL FEATURES. The State of Minnesota covers 84,068 square miles, of which 4,059 square miles is water (15,291 lakes greater than 10 acres). It extends about 400 miles south to north between latitudes 43° 30' and 49° N., and averages 275 miles east to west between longitudes 89° 30' and 97° W.

Elevations are less than 1,200 feet near each of the three major rivers—the Red, the Minnesota, and the Mississippi (except in the northern part). There are three areas at elevations greater than 1,600 feet: the Iron Range, paralleling the north shore of Lake Superior; the Coteau Des Prairies (also known as Buffalo Ridge), extending out of South Dakota across the southwest portion of the State; and a small area in the Lake Itasca region. The highest point above sea level is at 2,301 feet, Eagle Mountain, in the extreme northeast; and the lowest is at 602 feet, the surface of Lake Superior. Minnesota can be considered to have a continental divide in three directions; drainage is toward Hudson Bay to the north; toward the Atlantic Ocean to the east; and toward the Gulf of Mexico to the south.

GENERAL CLIMATE. Minnesota has a continental-type climate. The State is subject to frequent outbreaks of continental polar air throughout the year, with occasional Arctic outbreaks during the cold season. Occasional periods of prolonged heat occur during summer, particularly in the southern portion when warm air pushes northward from the Gulf of Mexico and the southwestern United States. Pacific Ocean air masses that move across the Western United States produce comparatively mild and dry weather at all seasons.

PRECIPITATION. Although the total precipitation is important, its distribution during the growing season is even more significant. For the most part, native vegetation grows for seven months (April to October) and row crops grow for five months (May through September). During the latter five-month period, approximately two-thirds of the annual precipitation occurs. Mean annual precipitation is 32 inches in extreme southeast Minnesota, an amount which gradually decreases to 19 inches in the extreme northwest portion of the State.

SNOWFALL. Seasonal snowfall averages near 70 inches along the north shore of Lake Superior in northeast Minnesota, gradually decreases to 40 inches along the Iowa border in the south, and measures 30 inches along the North Dakota and South Dakota borders in the west.

DROUGHT. Conditions of moderate droughts or worse are expected on the average at least once in four to five years, except in southwest Minnesota when they occur about once in every three years. Severe or extreme drought conditions occur on the average about once in every eight to nine years, except in the western divisions where they occur about once in every six years. Generally, the more severe droughts tend to persist or recur several years in succession.

STORMS. Thunderstorm winds generally cause more damage to property than any other weather factor. The annual frequency of thunderstorm days is about 45 days in southern Minnesota, decreasing to about 30 days along the Canadian border. Generally, 80 percent or more of these storms occur during the heavier rainfall months—from May through September. Damaging local windstorms, tornadoes, hail, and heavy rains generally occur with the stronger and more well-developed thunderstorms.

The month with the greatest frequency of tornadoes is June, followed by July, and then May. During these 3 months, nearly 75 percent of all tornadoes occur. Tornadoes have never been reported in December, January, and February. The southern one-half of Minnesota has three to four times as many tornadoes as does the northern one-half of the State.

The frequency of hailstorms shows a high of four to five days annually in southwestern Minnesota, decreasing to near two days in the northern portion of the State. The month with the most hail is July, with June next, and then August. During these three months, over 80 percent of the hail occurs. The size of the hail reported is generally in the marble-to-golfball category, with several reports annually of baseball-size and larger.

Heavy snowfalls of greater than four inches are common any time from mid-November through mid-April. Heavy snowfalls with blizzard conditions affect the State on the average about two times each winter. (Blizzard conditions involve snow, temperatures of 20°F. or less, and wind velocities of 35 m.p.h. and greater.)

Freezing rain and glaze storms are not numerous, but do coat the roads several times each season in Minnesota. The more severe ice storms cause extensive damage; such storms are not as common in the far north as they are in southern and southeastern portions of the State.

FLOODS. Major floods on the larger rivers occur on the average one or two years out of 10. Floods show the greatest frequency in April during the spring breakup of snow cover and frozen ground. Local flash flooding is most common in the hilly terrain and narrow valleys of southeast Minnesota, partly because of the intensive rainstorms in the southern portion of the State.

SUNSHINE. Sunshine amounts vary from a low in November of nearly 40 percent of possible sunshine hours to a high of about 70 percent in July, with an annual average of 58 percent. Hours of sunlight varies from near 8.5 hours in December to about 16 hours in June.

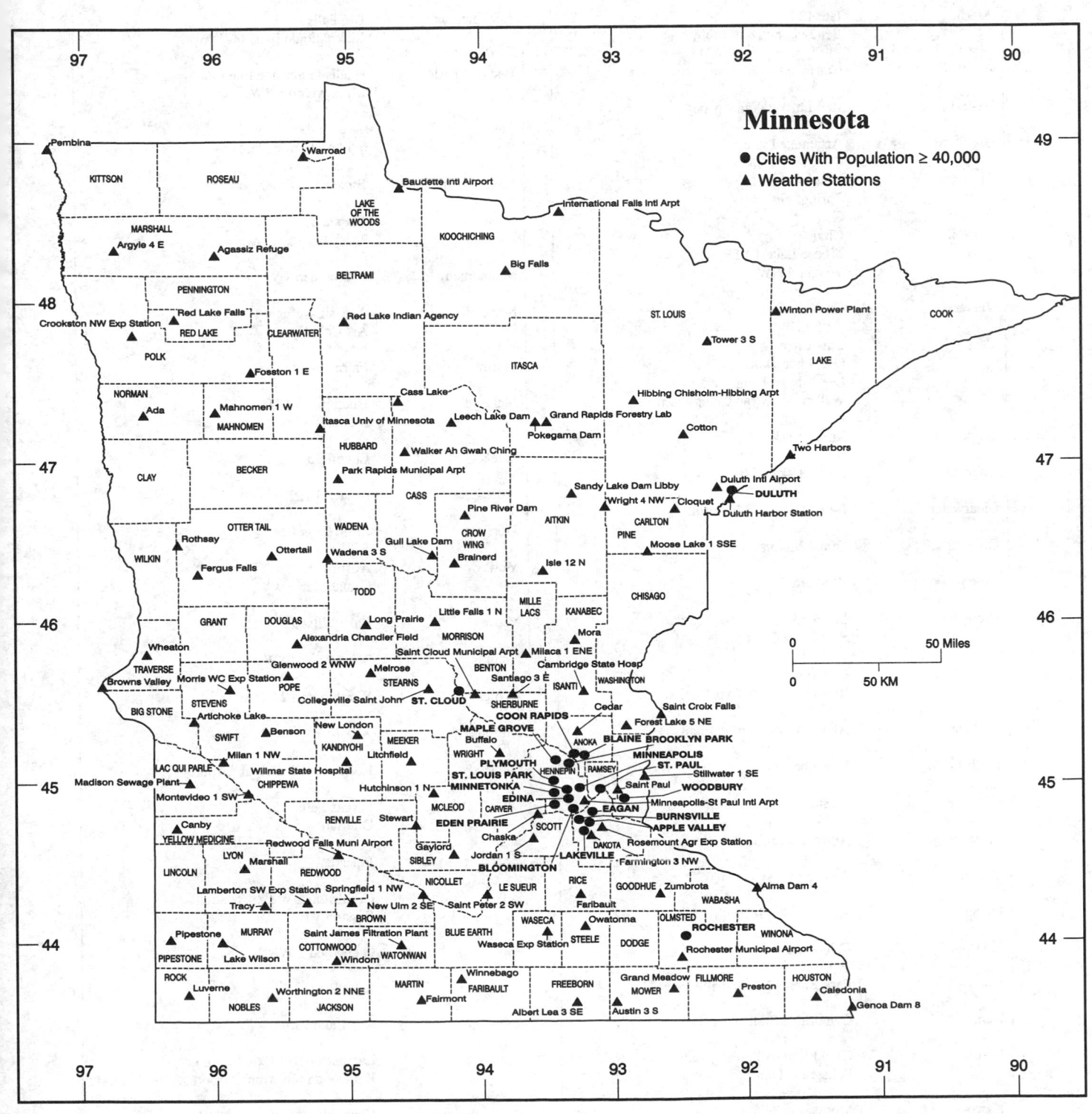

Minnesota

● Cities With Population ≥ 40,000
▲ Weather Stations

Pembina ▲
Warroad ▲
KITTSON
ROSEAU
Baudette Intl Airport ▲
LAKE OF THE WOODS
International Falls Intl Arpt ▲
KOOCHICHING
MARSHALL
Argyle 4 E ▲
Agassiz Refuge ▲
Big Falls ▲
BELTRAMI
Winton Power Plant ▲
ST. LOUIS
COOK
PENNINGTON
Red Lake Falls ▲
Crookston NW Exp Station ▲
RED LAKE
CLEARWATER
Red Lake Indian Agency ▲
Tower 3 S ▲
LAKE
POLK
Fosston 1 E ▲
ITASCA
Hibbing Chisholm-Hibbing Arpt ▲
NORMAN
Ada ▲
Mahnomen 1 W ▲
MAHNOMEN
Cass Lake ▲
Leech Lake Dam ▲
Grand Rapids Forestry Lab ▲
Cotton ▲
CLAY
BECKER
Itasca Univ of Minnesota ▲
Pokegama Dam ▲
Two Harbors ▲
HUBBARD
Walker Ah Gwah Ching ▲
Sandy Lake Dam Libby ▲
Duluth Intl Airport ▲
● DULUTH
Park Rapids Municipal Arpt ▲
CASS
Wright 4 NW ▲
Cloquet ▲
Duluth Harbor Station ▲
CARLTON
Pine River Dam ▲
AITKIN
PINE
Rothsay ▲
OTTER TAIL
WADENA
CROW WING
Moose Lake 1 SSE ▲
WILKIN
Ottertail ▲
Wadena 3 S ▲
Gull Lake Dam ▲
Brainerd ▲
Isle 12 N ▲
Fergus Falls ▲
CHISAGO
TODD
MILLE LACS
KANABEC
GRANT
DOUGLAS
Long Prairie ▲
Little Falls 1 N ▲
Mora ▲
Wheaton ▲
Alexandria Chandler Field ▲
MORRISON
TRAVERSE
Glenwood 2 WNW ▲
Melrose ▲
Saint Cloud Municipal Arpt ▲
Milaca 1 ENE ▲
Cambridge State Hosp ▲
Browns Valley ▲
Morris WC Exp Station ▲
BENTON
ISANTI
WASHINGTON
POPE
STEARNS
Santiago 3 E ▲
Saint Croix Falls ▲
BIG STONE
Collegeville Saint John ▲
● ST. CLOUD
SHERBURNE
Cedar ▲
Forest Lake 5 NE ▲
Artichoke Lake ▲
● COON RAPIDS
SWIFT
Benson ▲
New London ▲
● MAPLE GROVE
Buffalo ▲
● BLAINE ● BROOKLYN PARK
● ANOKA
Milan 1 NW ▲
KANDIYOHI
MEEKER
WRIGHT
● MINNEAPOLIS ● ST. PAUL
LAC QUI PARLE
Litchfield ▲
● PLYMOUTH
Stillwater 1 SE ▲
Willmar State Hospital ▲
● ST. LOUIS PARK
HENNEPIN
RAMSEY
Madison Sewage Plant ▲
Hutchinson 1 N ▲
● MINNETONKA
Saint Paul ▲
● WOODBURY
CHIPPEWA
● EDINA
Minneapolis-St Paul Intl Arpt ▲
Montevideo 1 SW ▲
CARVER
● EAGAN
Canby ▲
MCLEOD
● EDEN PRAIRIE
● BURNSVILLE
YELLOW MEDICINE
Stewart ▲
SCOTT
● APPLE VALLEY
RENVILLE
DAKOTA
LYON
Redwood Falls Muni Airport ▲
Chaska ▲
Rosemount Agr Exp Station ▲
Marshall ▲
Gaylord ▲
Jordan 1 S ▲
● LAKEVILLE
LINCOLN
REDWOOD
SIBLEY
● BLOOMINGTON
Farmington 3 NW ▲
Lamberton SW Exp Station ▲
Springfield 1 NW ▲
NICOLLET
RICE
GOODHUE
Zumbrota ▲
Tracy ▲
New Ulm 2 SE ▲
LE SUEUR
Alma Dam 4 ▲
BROWN
Saint Peter 2 SW ▲
Faribault ▲
WABASHA
Pipestone ▲
Saint James Filtration Plant ▲
WASECA
Owatonna ▲
OLMSTED
● ROCHESTER
PIPESTONE
COTTONWOOD
Windom ▲
WATONWAN
Waseca Exp Station ▲
STEELE
DODGE
WINONA
Lake Wilson ▲
BLUE EARTH
Rochester Municipal Airport ▲
ROCK
Winnebago ▲
FILLMORE
HOUSTON
Luverne ▲
Worthington 2 NNE ▲
MARTIN
FARIBAULT
FREEBORN
Grand Meadow ▲
Preston ▲
Caledonia ▲
Fairmont ▲
MOWER
Genoa Dam 8 ▲
NOBLES
JACKSON
Albert Lea 3 SE ▲
Austin 3 S ▲

0   50 Miles
0   50 KM

Minnesota Weather Stations by County

County	Station Name
Aitkin	Isle 12 N
	Sandy Lake Dam Libby
Anoka	Cedar
Beltrami	Red Lake Indian Agency
Big Stone	Artichoke Lake
Brown	New Ulm 2 SE
	Springfield 1 NW
Carlton	Cloquet
	Moose Lake 1 SSE
	Wright 4 NW
Carver	Chaska
Cass	Cass Lake
	Gull Lake Dam
	Leech Lake Dam
	Walker Ah Gwah Ching
Chippewa	Milan 1 NW
Chisago	Forest Lake 5 NE
Clearwater	Itasca Univ. of Minnesota
Cook	Grand Marais
Cottonwood	Windom
Crow Wing	Brainerd
	Pine River Dam
Dakota	Farmington 3 NW
	Rosemount Agr. Exp. Station
Douglas	Alexandria Chandler Field
Faribault	Winnebago
Fillmore	Preston
Freeborn	Albert Lea 3 SE
Goodhue	Zumbrota
Hennepin	Minneapolis-St Paul Int'l Arpt.
Houston	Caledonia
Hubbard	Park Rapids Municipal Airport
Isanti	Cambridge State Hosp
Itasca	Grand Rapids Forestry Lab
	Pokegama Dam
Kanabec	Mora
Kandiyohi	New London
	Willmar State Hospital

County	Station Name
Koochiching	Big Falls
	International Falls Int'l Arpt.
Lac Qui Parle	Madison Sewage Plant
	Montevideo 1 SW
Lake	Two Harbors
	Winton Power Plant
Lake Of The Woods	Baudette Int'l Airport
Lyon	Marshall
	Tracy
Mahnomen	Mahnomen 1 W
Marshall	Agassiz Refuge
	Argyle 4 E
Martin	Fairmont
McLeod	Hutchinson 1 N
	Stewart
Meeker	Litchfield
Mille Lacs	Milaca 1 ENE
Morrison	Little Falls 1 N
Mower	Austin 3 S
	Grand Meadow
Murray	Lake Wilson
Nicollet	Saint Peter 2 SW
Nobles	Worthington 2 NNE
Norman	Ada
Olmsted	Rochester Municipal Airport
Otter Tail	Fergus Falls
	Ottertail
Pipestone	Pipestone
Polk	Crookston NW Exp. Station
	Fosston 1 E
Pope	Glenwood 2 WNW
Ramsey	Saint Paul
Red Lake	Red Lake Falls
Redwood	Lamberton SW Exp. Station
	Redwood Falls Muni Airport
Rice	Faribault
Rock	Luverne

County	Station Name
Roseau	Warroad
Scott	Jordan 1 S
Sherburne	Saint Cloud Municipal Airport Santiago 3 E
Sibley	Gaylord
St. Louis	Cotton Duluth Harbor Station Duluth Int'l Airport Hibbing Chisholm-Hibbing Airport Tower 3 S
Stearns	Collegeville Saint John Melrose
Steele	Owatonna
Stevens	Morris WC Exp. Station
Swift	Benson
Todd	Long Prairie
Traverse	Browns Valley Wheaton
Wadena	Wadena 3 S
Waseca	Waseca Exp. Station
Washington	Stillwater 1 SE
Watonwan	Saint James Filtration Plant
Wilkin	Rothsay
Wright	Buffalo
Yellow Medicine	Canby

Minnesota Weather Stations by City

City	Station Name	Miles
Apple Valley	Chaska	19
	Farmington 3 NW	6
	Minneapolis-St Paul Int'l Arpt.	10
	Rosemount Agr. Exp. Station	6
	Saint Paul	18
Blaine	Cedar	11
	Forest Lake 5 NE	20
	Minneapolis-St Paul Int'l Arpt.	19
	Saint Paul	19
Bloomington	Chaska	13
	Farmington 3 NW	13
	Jordan 1 S	19
	Minneapolis-St Paul Int'l Arpt.	6
	Rosemount Agr. Exp. Station	13
	Saint Paul	18
Brooklyn Park	Cedar	16
	Minneapolis-St Paul Int'l Arpt.	16
Burnsville	Chaska	15
	Farmington 3 NW	8
	Jordan 1 S	18
	Minneapolis-St Paul Int'l Arpt.	9
	Rosemount Agr. Exp. Station	9
	Saint Paul	19
Coon Rapids	Cedar	10
Duluth	Duluth Harbor Station	2
	Duluth Int'l Airport	6
	Superior, WI	8
Eagan	Farmington 3 NW	10
	Minneapolis-St Paul Int'l Arpt.	6
	Rosemount Agr. Exp. Station	7
	Saint Paul	13
Eden Prairie	Chaska	7
	Farmington 3 NW	19
	Jordan 1 S	16
	Minneapolis-St Paul Int'l Arpt.	11
	Rosemount Agr. Exp. Station	20
Edina	Chaska	13
	Farmington 3 NW	18
	Minneapolis-St Paul Int'l Arpt.	6
	Rosemount Agr. Exp. Station	17
	Saint Paul	19
Lakeville	Chaska	18
	Farmington 3 NW	3
	Jordan 1 S	19
	Minneapolis-St Paul Int'l Arpt.	13
	Rosemount Agr. Exp. Station	7
Maple Grove	Cedar	16
	Minneapolis-St Paul Int'l Arpt.	19
Minneapolis	Chaska	19
	Minneapolis-St Paul Int'l Arpt.	6
	Rosemount Agr. Exp. Station	19
	Saint Paul	14

City	Station Name	Miles
Minnetonka	Chaska	11
	Minneapolis-St Paul Int'l Arpt.	12
Plymouth	Chaska	16
	Minneapolis-St Paul Int'l Arpt.	14
Rochester	Rochester Municipal Airport	9
St. Cloud	Collegeville Saint John	11
	Saint Cloud Municipal Airport	6
	Santiago 3 E	19
St. Louis Park	Chaska	15
	Minneapolis-St Paul Int'l Arpt.	8
	Saint Paul	19
St. Paul	Minneapolis-St Paul Int'l Arpt.	8
	Rosemount Agr. Exp. Station	16
	Saint Paul	6
	Stillwater 1 SE	17
Woodbury	Minneapolis-St Paul Int'l Arpt.	14
	Rosemount Agr. Exp. Station	16
	Saint Paul	3
	Stillwater 1 SE	12
	River Falls, WI	17

Note: Miles is the distance between the geographic center of the city and the weather station.

Minnesota Weather Stations by Elevation

Feet	Station Name
1,702	Pipestone
1,646	Lake Wilson
1,568	Worthington 2 NNE
1,499	Luverne
1,489	Itasca Univ. of Minnesota
1,459	Tower 3 S
1,433	Park Rapids Municipal Airport
1,430	Duluth Int'l Airport
1,414	Alexandria Chandler Field
1,407	Walker Ah Gwah Ching
1,400	Tracy
1,374	Windom
1,348	Grand Meadow
1,348	Wadena 3 S
1,345	Hibbing Chisholm-Hibbing Airport
1,335	Winton Power Plant
1,328	Cotton
1,309	Fosston 1 E
1,309	Grand Rapids Forestry Lab
1,299	Leech Lake Dam
1,295	Cass Lake
1,295	Rochester Municipal Airport
1,292	Wright 4 NW
1,289	Long Prairie
1,282	Isle 12 N
1,279	Pokegama Dam
1,263	Cloquet
1,250	Fergus Falls
1,250	Pine River Dam
1,240	Canby
1,240	New London
1,233	Sandy Lake Dam Libby
1,227	Albert Lea 3 SE
1,223	Collegeville Saint John
1,217	Big Falls
1,217	Red Lake Indian Agency
1,213	Austin 3 S
1,213	Gull Lake Dam
1,207	Melrose
1,204	Rothsay
1,200	Mahnomen 1 W
1,197	Glenwood 2 WNW
1,184	Fairmont
1,177	Brainerd
1,177	International Falls Int'l Arpt.
1,174	Caledonia
1,151	Marshall
1,151	Waseca Exp. Station
1,148	Owatonna
1,141	Agassiz Refuge
1,141	Lamberton SW Exp. Station
1,138	Morris WC Exp. Station
1,131	Litchfield
1,125	Willmar State Hospital
1,118	Little Falls 1 N

Feet	Station Name
1,108	Moose Lake 1 SSE
1,108	Winnebago
1,099	Saint James Filtration Plant
1,092	Hutchinson 1 N
1,092	Milaca 1 ENE
1,079	Baudette Int'l Airport
1,079	Madison Sewage Plant
1,072	Artichoke Lake
1,072	Red Lake Falls
1,066	Warroad
1,062	Springfield 1 NW
1,040	Benson
1,040	Stewart
1,026	Saint Cloud Municipal Airport
1,023	Redwood Falls Muni Airport
1,017	Gaylord
1,017	Milan 1 NW
1,017	Santiago 3 E
1,017	Wheaton
1,003	Mora
984	Browns Valley
984	Montevideo 1 SW
984	Zumbrota
977	Buffalo
977	Farmington 3 NW
977	Ottertail
958	Cambridge State Hosp
958	Forest Lake 5 NE
948	Rosemount Agr. Exp. Station
938	Faribault
928	Jordan 1 S
928	Preston
908	Ada
905	Cedar
898	Saint Paul
885	Crookston NW Exp. Station
869	Argyle 4 E
859	New Ulm 2 SE
849	Saint Peter 2 SW
833	Minneapolis-St Paul Int'l Arpt.
718	Chaska
711	Stillwater 1 SE
623	Two Harbors
610	Grand Marais
606	Duluth Harbor Station

Duluth Int'l Airport

Duluth, Minnesota is located at the western tip of Lake Superior. The city, about 20 miles long, lies at the base of a range of hills that rise abruptly to 600 - 800 feet above the level of Lake Superior. The range runs in a northeast and southwest direction. Two or three miles from the lake the land becomes a slightly rolling plateau.

Duluth in the summer is known as the Air Conditioned City. Being situated below high terrain and along the lake, any easterly component winds automatically cool the city. However, with westerly flow in the summer, the wind generally abates at night, thus, allowing cool lake air to move back into the city area near the lake.

An important influence on the climate is the passage of a succession of high and low pressure systems west and east. The proximity of Lake Superior, which is the largest and coldest of the Great Lakes, modifies the local weather. Summer temperatures are cooler and winter temperatures are warmer. The lake effect at Duluth is most prevalent when low pressure systems pass to the south creating easterly winds. In the summer, warm, moist air flowing over the cold lake surface has a stabilizing effect that results in cool, cloudy weather over Duluth. However, during the winter cold air flowing over the warm open lake surface absorbs moisture that is later precipitated over Duluth as snow. The lake effect is further reflected from the low frequency of severe storms such as wind, hail, tornadoes, freezing rain (glaze), and blizzards when compared to other areas that are a further distance from the lake.

Easterly component winds at Duluth occur 40 to 50 percent of the time from March through August and 20 to 25 percent of the time from November through February. During the winter 60 to 70 percent of the winds are from a westerly component.

The climate of Duluth is predominantly continental with significant local Lake Superior effects. Duluth averages 143 days between the last occurrence of 32 degrees in mid-May and the first in early October. At the Duluth Airport about six miles away from the lake, the average first and last occurrences of 32 degrees are late May and late September, giving a freeze-free period of 123 days.

Ice in the harbor forms about mid-November and generally is gone by mid-April. The shipping season can vary from year to year depending on temperatures and the winds that move the ice around. In most years there is little or no shipping during February and March on Lake Superior.

Duluth Int'l Airport *St. Louis County*   Elevation: 1,430 ft.   Latitude: 46° 50' N   Longitude: 92° 13' W

	JAN	FEB	MAR	APR	MAY	JUN	JUL	AUG	SEP	OCT	NOV	DEC	YEAR
Mean Maximum Temp. (°F)	16.5	23.0	32.9	48.3	62.5	71.0	76.2	73.6	63.9	51.4	34.2	21.5	47.9
Mean Temp. (°F)	7.7	14.0	24.6	38.8	51.5	60.0	65.6	63.6	54.5	43.1	27.6	13.8	38.7
Mean Minimum Temp. (°F)	-1.2	5.0	16.3	29.3	40.5	48.9	54.8	53.6	45.0	34.7	20.9	6.1	29.5
Extreme Maximum Temp. (°F)	47	55	71	84	90	94	97	94	95	84	71	53	97
Extreme Minimum Temp. (°F)	-39	-39	-29	-5	19	27	35	32	23	8	-18	-34	-39
Days Maximum Temp. ≥ 90°F	0	0	0	0	0	0	1	1	0	0	0	0	2
Days Maximum Temp. ≤ 32°F	28	22	15	2	0	0	0	0	0	1	13	26	107
Days Minimum Temp. ≤ 32°F	31	28	29	19	5	0	0	0	2	12	26	31	183
Days Minimum Temp. ≤ 0°F	17	11	4	0	0	0	0	0	0	0	2	11	45
Heating Degree Days (base 65°F)	1,774	1,435	1,245	780	418	174	64	100	324	672	1,116	1,583	9,685
Cooling Degree Days (base 65°F)	0	0	0	0	8	32	89	68	12	0	0	0	209
Mean Precipitation (in.)	1.12	0.80	1.64	2.15	2.95	4.17	4.21	4.10	4.12	2.58	2.06	0.98	30.88
Maximum Precipitation (in.)	4.7	2.4	5.1	5.8	7.7	8.0	8.5	10.3	9.4	7.5	5.0	3.7	43.4
Minimum Precipitation (in.)	0.1	0.1	0.2	0.2	0.1	0.5	1.1	0.7	0.2	0.3	0.2	0.2	19.8
Maximum 24-hr. Precipitation (in.)	1.2	0.8	2.2	2.6	3.0	3.4	3.4	3.1	3.8	2.8	2.2	1.9	3.8
Days With ≥ 0.1" Precipitation	3	3	5	5	6	8	7	7	7	5	5	3	64
Days With ≥ 1.0" Precipitation	0	0	0	0	0	1	1	1	1	0	0	0	4
Mean Snowfall (in.)	19.3	11.3	13.6	6.6	0.4	trace	trace	trace	0.1	1.6	15.2	15.2	83.3
Maximum Snowfall (in.)	47	32	46	32	8	0	0	0	2	10	50	44	169
Maximum 24-hr. Snowfall (in.)	16	13	17	12	4	0	0	0	2	8	24	23	24
Days With ≥ 1.0" Snow Depth	31	28	29	11	0	0	0	0	0	1	14	28	142
Thunderstorm Days	< 1	< 1	1	2	4	7	8	7	4	1	< 1	< 1	34
Foggy Days	10	9	10	9	10	12	11	14	13	12	10	12	132
Predominant Sky Cover	OVR	OVR	OVR	OVR	OVR	OVR	OVR	OVR	OVR	OVR	OVR	OVR	OVR
Mean Relative Humidity 6am (%)	77	77	79	77	76	82	86	89	89	83	82	80	81
Mean Relative Humidity 3pm (%)	66	62	61	53	50	56	56	59	60	58	67	70	60
Mean Dewpoint (°F)	1	5	15	26	37	49	55	54	46	34	21	8	29
Prevailing Wind Direction	NW	NW	E	E	E	ESE	WNW	ESE	WNW	WNW	WNW	NW	NW
Prevailing Wind Speed (mph)	14	13	15	15	13	10	10	9	12	13	14	13	13
Maximum Wind Gust (mph)	58	55	71	60	71	69	64	56	60	70	55	54	71

International Falls Int'l Arpt.

Situated on the Canadian border, International Falls is subjected to frequent outbreaks of continental polar air throughout most of the year. These are tempered to mildness during June, July, and August, when the land and lake areas to the north and northwest have been warmed by long days of sunshine. Periods of fine, mild weather occur, interspersed with showers and an occasional three or four day period of cloudy, rainy weather. The area of small lakes, covering up to 30 percent of the area to the north and northwest, supplies a good deal of the moisture for the late afternoon and evening showers and stores heat that tempers southward flow of cold air during September and October. This prolongs the fall season until early November. In November the water surfaces freeze and snow returns to International Falls. From December through February, temperatures fall below zero on most days and occasionally fail to rise above zero for a week or more.

In winter, frost penetrates into the ground to depths of 36 to 60 inches. If winter begins abruptly so that a heavy blanket of snow covers the ground before protracted freezing occurs, it may freeze to only a few inches deep. This is very important to loggers, who depend upon deep soil freezing for road foundations into otherwise inaccessible places. The wide expanse of deep snow and ice prolongs winter. The transition to summer is rapid after the spring thaw. Spring lasts only about a month.

By June 1st, the ground generally is warm enough for successful planting, but vigilance against freezing temperatures is required through most of June. Crops that do not mature by September 1st have little chance of providing a harvest. Heaviest precipitation coincides with the growing season.

Based on the 1951-1980 period, the average first occurrence of 32 degrees Fahrenheit in the fall is September 15 and the average last occurrence in the spring is May 26.

Heavy deposits of glaze occur only about once a year at International Falls. Occasional storms that intensify over the southern plateau or plains states and move rapidly northeastward, drawing up moist gulf air, bring the most violent weather changes. They often produce severe thunderstorms and windstorms in early fall and blizzards with heavy snowfall and drifting in winter. Quite often such a storm brings an abrupt end to fall weather. During winter, a variation of 100 miles in the paths of such storms as they approach the border is of tremendous importance to local transportation and road maintenance.

Surrounding terrain is generally level. Forests of varying density and swampland surround the station for many miles to the east, south, and west. Rainy Lake, approximately 300 square miles in area, lies to the north. The lake is five miles from the station at its closest point.

International Falls Int'l Arpt. *Koochiching County*   Elevation: 1,177 ft.   Latitude: 48° 34' N   Longitude: 93° 24' W

	JAN	FEB	MAR	APR	MAY	JUN	JUL	AUG	SEP	OCT	NOV	DEC	YEAR
Mean Maximum Temp. (°F)	12.7	21.0	33.4	50.6	65.8	74.0	78.2	75.8	64.4	51.2	32.1	17.9	48.1
Mean Temp. (°F)	2.1	9.9	22.8	39.2	53.2	62.0	66.3	64.0	53.4	41.8	24.4	8.6	37.3
Mean Minimum Temp. (°F)	-8.5	-1.2	12.1	27.7	40.5	50.0	54.4	52.0	42.5	32.3	16.7	-0.7	26.5
Extreme Maximum Temp. (°F)	48	55	65	90	93	99	98	95	95	84	73	48	99
Extreme Minimum Temp. (°F)	-45	-45	-29	-11	19	28	34	30	23	2	-32	-40	-45
Days Maximum Temp. ≥ 90°F	0	0	0	0	0	1	2	1	0	0	0	0	4
Days Maximum Temp. ≤ 32°F	29	22	13	2	0	0	0	0	0	1	16	27	110
Days Minimum Temp. ≤ 32°F	31	28	29	21	6	0	0	0	4	17	28	31	195
Days Minimum Temp. ≤ 0°F	21	15	7	0	0	0	0	0	0	0	4	16	63
Heating Degree Days (base 65°F)	1,950	1,553	1,302	769	377	133	51	96	351	713	1,211	1,747	10,253
Cooling Degree Days (base 65°F)	0	0	0	1	17	50	94	75	9	1	0	0	247
Mean Precipitation (in.)	0.85	0.65	0.97	1.39	2.57	3.91	3.33	3.08	3.06	2.08	1.30	0.73	23.92
Maximum Precipitation (in.)	3.0	1.8	3.1	3.3	6.7	7.4	9.5	6.7	7.4	4.8	3.5	1.7	32.6
Minimum Precipitation (in.)	0.1	0.1	0.2	0.1	0.2	0.7	1.1	0.6	0.3	0.1	0.2	0.2	17.2
Maximum 24-hr. Precipitation (in.)	0.9	0.9	1.3	1.4	2.7	3.2	4.2	2.5	3.3	2.3	1.4	1.2	4.2
Days With ≥ 0.1" Precipitation	2	2	3	4	6	8	7	6	6	5	4	2	55
Days With ≥ 1.0" Precipitation	0	0	0	0	0	1	1	1	1	0	0	0	4
Mean Snowfall (in.)	15.3	10.6	9.1	5.7	0.3	trace	trace	trace	0.1	2.5	13.6	13.8	71.0
Maximum Snowfall (in.)	43	32	32	23	13	trace	0	0	2	9	30	44	132
Maximum 24-hr. Snowfall (in.)	14	10	13	14	7	trace	0	0	1	5	12	9	14
Days With ≥ 1.0" Snow Depth	31	28	25	9	0	0	0	0	0	1	17	29	140
Thunderstorm Days	< 1	0	< 1	1	4	7	9	7	4	1	< 1	< 1	33
Foggy Days	7	6	6	6	6	7	8	7	10	10	8	7	8	90
Predominant Sky Cover	OVR	OVR	OVR	OVR	OVR	OVR	OVR	OVR	OVR	OVR	OVR	OVR	OVR
Mean Relative Humidity 7am (%)	74	75	77	74	72	77	84	88	89	85	84	79	80
Mean Relative Humidity 4pm (%)	65	60	55	47	45	52	54	56	59	58	69	70	58
Mean Dewpoint (°F)	-3	2	14	25	38	50	56	55	45	33	19	3	28
Prevailing Wind Direction	W	W	WNW	NW	NW	S	WNW	S	S	S	WNW	WNW	WNW
Prevailing Wind Speed (mph)	9	9	12	12	12	9	9	8	9	9	12	10	10
Maximum Wind Gust (mph)	55	46	52	60	59	58	63	67	48	46	49	44	67

Minneapolis-St. Paul Int'l Arpt.

The Twin Cities of Minneapolis and St. Paul are located at the confluence of the Mississippi and Minnesota Rivers over the heart of an artesian water basin. Its flat or gently rolling terrain varies little in elevation from that of the official observation station at International Airport. Numerous lakes dot the surrounding area. Minneapolis alone boasts of 22 lakes within the city park system. The largest body of water, nearly 15,000 acres, is Lake Minnetonka, located about 15 miles west of the airport. Most bodies of water are relatively small and shallow and are ice covered during winter.

The climate of the Minneapolis-St. Paul area is predominantly continental. Seasonal temperature variations are quite large. Temperatures range from less than -30 degrees to over 100 degrees. The growing season is 166 days. Because of this favorable growing season, all crops generally mature before the autumn freeze occurs.

The Twin Cities lie near the northern edge of the influx of moisture from the Gulf of Mexico. Severe storms such as blizzards, freezing rain (glaze), tornadoes, wind and hail storms do occur. The total annual precipitation is important. Even more significant is its proper distribution during the growing season. During the five month growing season, May through September, the major crops produced are corn, soybeans, small grains, and hay. During this period, the normal rainfall is over 16 inches, approximately 65 percent of the annual precipitation. Winter snowfall is nearly 48 inches. Winter recreational weather is excellent because of the dry snow. These conditions exist from about Christmas into early March. Snow depths average six to eight inches in the city and eight to 10 inches in the suburbs during this period.

Floods occur along the Mississippi River due to spring snow melt, excessive rainfall, or both. Occasionally an ice jam forms and creates a local flood condition. The flood problem at St. Paul is complicated because the Minnesota River empties into the Mississippi River between the two cities. Consequently, high water or flooding on the Minnesota River creates a greater flood potential at St. Paul. Flood stage at St. Paul can be expected on the average once in every eight years.

Minneapolis-St. Paul Int'l Arpt. *Hennepin County*   Elevation: 833 ft.   Latitude: 44° 53' N   Longitude: 93° 14' W

	JAN	FEB	MAR	APR	MAY	JUN	JUL	AUG	SEP	OCT	NOV	DEC	YEAR
Mean Maximum Temp. (°F)	21.3	27.9	39.8	56.8	69.9	79.0	83.4	80.4	71.0	58.2	40.0	26.6	54.5
Mean Temp. (°F)	12.7	19.6	31.5	46.5	59.2	68.5	73.2	70.6	61.0	48.5	32.4	19.0	45.2
Mean Minimum Temp. (°F)	4.0	11.3	23.1	36.2	48.4	57.9	63.1	60.7	50.8	38.8	24.8	11.2	35.8
Extreme Maximum Temp. (°F)	57	60	83	95	96	102	105	101	98	90	77	68	105
Extreme Minimum Temp. (°F)	-34	-32	-11	5	25	35	43	40	26	13	-16	-29	-34
Days Maximum Temp. ≥ 90°F	0	0	0	0	1	3	6	3	1	0	0	0	14
Days Maximum Temp. ≤ 32°F	24	17	8	0	0	0	0	0	0	0	8	20	77
Days Minimum Temp. ≤ 32°F	31	27	25	10	1	0	0	0	0	7	24	30	155
Days Minimum Temp. ≤ 0°F	13	7	2	0	0	0	0	0	0	0	1	7	30
Heating Degree Days (base 65°F)	1,619	1,277	1,032	553	217	41	6	18	173	508	970	1,422	7,836
Cooling Degree Days (base 65°F)	0	0	0	5	41	153	264	197	59	3	0	0	722
Mean Precipitation (in.)	1.03	0.75	1.89	2.37	3.25	4.23	3.96	4.02	2.72	2.24	1.95	0.97	29.38
Maximum Precipitation (in.)	3.6	2.1	4.8	5.9	8.0	9.8	17.9	9.3	6.9	5.7	5.3	4.3	39.9
Minimum Precipitation (in.)	0.1	0.1	0.3	0.2	0.6	0.2	0.6	0.4	0.4	trace	0.1	0.2	16.2
Maximum 24-hr. Precipitation (in.)	1.2	1.1	1.6	2.2	2.4	2.9	9.1	7.3	2.6	2.2	2.0	1.3	9.1
Days With ≥ 0.1" Precipitation	4	3	5	6	7	7	6	6	6	5	5	3	63
Days With ≥ 1.0" Precipitation	0	0	0	0	1	1	1	1	1	0	0	0	5
Mean Snowfall (in.)	13.2	7.9	10.6	3.2	trace	trace	trace	trace	trace	0.6	9.9	9.7	55.1
Maximum Snowfall (in.)	46	27	40	22	3	0	0	0	trace	8	47	33	102
Maximum 24-hr. Snowfall (in.)	17	9	15	14	3	0	0	0	trace	8	19	12	19
Days With ≥ 1.0" Snow Depth	27	24	15	2	0	0	0	0	0	0	7	21	96
Thunderstorm Days	< 1	< 1	1	3	5	8	7	7	4	2	1	< 1	38
Foggy Days	10	9	9	7	7	5	5	8	8	8	9	11	96
Predominant Sky Cover	OVR	OVR	OVR	OVR	OVR	OVR	SCT	CLR	OVR	OVR	OVR	OVR	OVR
Mean Relative Humidity 6am (%)	75	76	77	75	75	79	82	84	85	81	80	79	79
Mean Relative Humidity 3pm (%)	65	62	58	48	47	50	50	52	53	52	63	68	56
Mean Dewpoint (°F)	5	10	21	32	43	55	60	59	50	38	24	12	34
Prevailing Wind Direction	NW	NW	NW	NW	SE	SE	S	SE	S	NW	NW	NW	NW
Prevailing Wind Speed (mph)	14	14	13	14	10	10	10	9	12	14	14	13	13
Maximum Wind Gust (mph)	67	55	60	61	67	66	63	71	54	53	66	48	71

Rochester Municipal Airport

Rochester, Minnesota, is in the Zumbro River Valley. The south branch of the Zumbro flows through Rochester. Within the city of Rochester three creeks flow into the south branch. Terrain around Rochester is rolling, and the elevation ranges from 1,000 to 1,300 feet above sea level.

The National Weather Service station is located eight miles south of Rochester on a ridge 300 feet above the city elevation. Temperatures from radiation cooling on clear, calm nights can sometimes be much lower in the city.

The succession of high and low pressure systems over Rochester brings a variety of weather that is changeable and stimulating. The weather pattern is continental with four definite seasons. Winters are cold, but summers are pleasant.

The season-to-season temperature variation is quite large. The average temperature for a warm winter is 20 degrees and for a cold winter it is 12 degrees. The average temperature for a warm summer is 70 degrees and a cold summer is 67 degrees, which indicates that summer temperatures are not as variable as those during the winter. The average growing season is about 140 days.

Rochester lies near the northern edge of the influx of moisture from the Gulf of Mexico. Severe storms such as blizzards, freezing rain (glaze), tornadoes, wind, and hail storms do occur. During the five month growing season, May through September, the major crops of corn, soybeans, small grains, and hay are produced. During this period, the normal rainfall is over 18 inches, approximately 65 percent of the annual precipitation.

Snowfall averages above 45 inches per season. The snow season usually begins in November. About one year in ten the first one inch or more of snow will occur the latter part of October.

Rolling terrain and the thunderstorm probability make the south branch of the Zumbro River and its tributaries susceptible to flash flooding. Some flooding can occur with the spring snowmelt. In some instances the snowmelt is complicated with moderate spring rainfall.

Rochester Municipal Airport *Olmsted County*   Elevation: 1,295 ft.   Latitude: 43° 54' N   Longitude: 92° 30' W

	JAN	FEB	MAR	APR	MAY	JUN	JUL	AUG	SEP	OCT	NOV	DEC	YEAR
Mean Maximum Temp. (°F)	20.4	26.7	38.7	55.3	68.4	77.8	81.3	78.6	70.0	57.6	39.7	25.8	53.3
Mean Temp. (°F)	11.9	18.4	30.5	45.0	57.3	66.8	70.7	68.3	59.4	47.4	31.7	18.1	43.8
Mean Minimum Temp. (°F)	3.3	10.1	22.2	34.7	46.1	55.7	60.1	57.9	48.7	37.1	23.7	10.4	34.2
Extreme Maximum Temp. (°F)	55	63	79	91	92	101	102	99	95	93	75	62	102
Extreme Minimum Temp. (°F)	-32	-35	-13	5	22	35	43	40	24	11	-20	-33	-35
Days Maximum Temp. ≥ 90°F	0	0	0	0	0	2	3	2	0	0	0	0	7
Days Maximum Temp. ≤ 32°F	25	18	9	1	0	0	0	0	0	0	8	22	83
Days Minimum Temp. ≤ 32°F	31	27	26	12	2	0	0	0	1	10	24	30	163
Days Minimum Temp. ≤ 0°F	13	8	2	0	0	0	0	0	0	0	1	8	32
Heating Degree Days (base 65°F)	1,643	1,310	1,063	598	263	59	14	34	205	543	992	1,448	8,172
Cooling Degree Days (base 65°F)	0	0	0	4	27	116	190	139	44	3	0	0	523
Mean Precipitation (in.)	0.94	0.75	1.91	3.05	3.51	3.71	4.57	4.20	3.22	2.34	1.98	0.99	31.17
Maximum Precipitation (in.)	2.5	2.2	4.0	6.5	8.4	9.3	12.3	9.5	10.5	6.1	5.9	2.8	43.9
Minimum Precipitation (in.)	0.1	trace	0.2	0.9	1.2	0.9	0.5	0.6	0.3	trace	0.1	0.2	15.4
Maximum 24-hr. Precipitation (in.)	1.4	1.1	1.8	3.8	2.1	4.0	7.5	2.9	6.0	2.8	2.3	1.0	7.5
Days With ≥ 0.1" Precipitation	3	2	5	7	7	7	7	7	6	5	4	3	63
Days With ≥ 1.0" Precipitation	0	0	0	0	1	1	1	1	1	0	0	0	5
Mean Snowfall (in.)	11.8	7.9	8.9	4.2	trace	trace	trace	trace	trace	0.9	7.1	10.4	51.2
Maximum Snowfall (in.)	27	19	35	16	1	0	0	0	1	5	23	31	89
Maximum 24-hr. Snowfall (in.)	15	9	11	13	1	0	0	0	1	5	11	10	15
Days With ≥ 1.0" Snow Depth	28	24	16	3	0	0	0	0	0	0	7	24	102
Thunderstorm Days	< 1	< 1	1	3	6	8	8	7	5	2	1	< 1	41
Foggy Days	11	10	12	10	10	8	9	11	11	9	12	13	126
Predominant Sky Cover	OVR	OVR	OVR	OVR	OVR	OVR	OVR	OVR	OVR	OVR	OVR	OVR	OVR
Mean Relative Humidity 6am (%)	80	81	82	80	80	82	86	88	87	82	83	83	83
Mean Relative Humidity 3pm (%)	72	68	65	54	52	53	56	57	56	54	66	74	61
Mean Dewpoint (°F)	7	12	22	33	45	55	60	59	50	38	25	14	35
Prevailing Wind Direction	NW	NW	NW	NW	S	S	S	S	S	S	WNW	NW	S
Prevailing Wind Speed (mph)	15	15	15	15	14	14	12	12	13	14	15	15	14
Maximum Wind Gust (mph)	69	56	90	85	76	82	74	78	64	62	67	56	90

Saint Cloud Municipal Airport

St. Cloud is located in central Minnesota on the banks of the Mississippi River. The topography is gently rolling terrain with numerous lakes and wooded areas.

The climate is influenced by atmospheric moisture flowing into the state from the Gulf of Mexico and the Pacific coast. Air masses carrying moisture which is eventually released as precipitation may travel nearly 1,500 miles. Due to this long trek, a minor change in the wind system can result in the area receiving well below or well above the normal precipitation. Rainfall is generally ample for farm and garden crops. Although the total amount is important, its distribution during the average 140 day growing season from mid-May to the end of September is even more significant. Thunderstorms are the principal source of rainfall during this period.

Spring, summer, and fall are very pleasant. Prolonged periods of hot and humid weather are infrequent. Extremely hot days with temperatures of 100 degrees or higher occur only once every five to ten years and rarely are temperatures this high recorded on successive days. Tornadoes and severe local storms are common.

Winter is cold, but not unpleasant, since strong winds and high humidities are generally absent on the coldest days. Cold Canadian air masses are prevalent throughout the winter season. The normal winter will have five to ten days with temperatures in the -20 to -30 degree range. Heavy snowfalls do occur, but the northern location limits the numerous heavy snowfalls that occur just a short distance to the south. Snowfalls of three inches or more in a 24 hour period occur only on an average of four times per year. Snow generally remains on the ground from the onset of the winter season until spring. Blizzards occur on the average of once per year with a severe blizzard once every three or four years. Ice storms are infrequent because temperatures are usually too cold and the transition period from season to season is rather abrupt.

Saint Cloud Municipal Airport *Sherburne County*   Elevation: 1,026 ft.   Latitude: 45° 33' N   Longitude: 94° 03' W

	JAN	FEB	MAR	APR	MAY	JUN	JUL	AUG	SEP	OCT	NOV	DEC	YEAR
Mean Maximum Temp. (°F)	19.0	26.1	37.9	55.4	69.2	77.8	82.1	79.2	69.5	56.8	37.9	24.2	52.9
Mean Temp. (°F)	8.6	16.0	28.2	43.8	56.6	65.5	70.1	67.4	57.7	45.6	29.1	15.0	42.0
Mean Minimum Temp. (°F)	-1.7	5.8	18.4	32.1	44.0	53.2	58.0	55.5	45.8	34.4	20.4	5.8	31.0
Extreme Maximum Temp. (°F)	56	57	78	96	94	102	102	99	98	90	75	61	102
Extreme Minimum Temp. (°F)	-43	-40	-20	-3	21	32	40	33	18	5	-17	-41	-43
Days Maximum Temp. ≥ 90°F	0	0	0	0	1	2	4	2	1	0	0	0	10
Days Maximum Temp. ≤ 32°F	26	18	9	1	0	0	0	0	0	0	10	23	87
Days Minimum Temp. ≤ 32°F	31	28	28	16	3	0	0	0	2	14	27	31	180
Days Minimum Temp. ≤ 0°F	17	11	4	0	0	0	0	0	0	0	2	11	45
Heating Degree Days (base 65°F)	1,745	1,380	1,135	632	280	75	17	45	246	596	1,070	1,546	8,767
Cooling Degree Days (base 65°F)	0	0	0	2	27	97	180	128	33	2	0	0	469
Mean Precipitation (in.)	0.75	0.57	1.48	2.20	2.95	4.53	3.34	3.95	2.96	2.36	1.53	0.69	27.31
Maximum Precipitation (in.)	2.5	2.8	3.4	5.5	8.0	10.5	8.0	7.5	9.5	6.2	3.7	2.0	39.3
Minimum Precipitation (in.)	0.1	trace	0.1	0	0.3	0	0.2	0.5	0.1	0.1	0.1	0.1	14.9
Maximum 24-hr. Precipitation (in.)	0.6	1.8	1.1	2.5	3.2	3.5	2.3	4.6	3.6	3.2	2.0	0.7	4.6
Days With ≥ 0.1" Precipitation	3	2	4	5	7	8	6	7	6	5	4	2	59
Days With ≥ 1.0" Precipitation	0	0	0	0	0	1	1	1	1	1	0	0	5
Mean Snowfall (in.)	10.2	7.0	8.4	2.8	0.1	0.0	0.0	0.0	trace	0.6	9.1	8.4	46.6
Maximum Snowfall (in.)	30	22	52	11	3	0	0	0	trace	6	25	25	82
Maximum 24-hr. Snowfall (in.)	9	12	15	7	3	0	0	0	trace	5	11	10	15
Days With ≥ 1.0" Snow Depth	28	25	18	2	0	0	0	0	0	0	8	23	104
Thunderstorm Days	0	< 1	1	3	6	9	9	9	4	2	< 1	0	43
Foggy Days	11	10	11	9	9	9	10	14	12	12	11	14	132
Predominant Sky Cover	OVR	OVR	OVR	OVR	OVR	OVR	CLR	OVR	OVR	OVR	OVR	OVR	OVR
Mean Relative Humidity 6am (%)	77	79	81	81	81	85	88	91	90	85	83	80	84
Mean Relative Humidity 3pm (%)	66	63	60	48	46	51	51	54	54	53	64	69	57
Mean Dewpoint (°F)	2	8	19	30	42	54	59	58	48	37	23	10	32
Prevailing Wind Direction	WNW	NW	NW	NW	NW	S	S	S	S	NW	WNW	WNW	NW
Prevailing Wind Speed (mph)	10	10	12	13	12	10	9	9	9	12	12	10	10
Maximum Wind Gust (mph)	58	46	46	78	51	63	63	48	51	46	53	46	78

Ada *Norman County* Elevation: 908 ft. Latitude: 47° 18' N Longitude: 96° 31' W

	JAN	FEB	MAR	APR	MAY	JUN	JUL	AUG	SEP	OCT	NOV	DEC	YEAR
Mean Maximum Temp. (°F)	16.6	24.0	35.9	55.5	70.7	78.7	83.3	82.2	71.3	56.9	36.0	22.2	52.8
Mean Temp. (°F)	6.5	13.9	26.6	43.7	57.3	66.5	70.9	69.3	58.7	45.7	27.5	13.3	41.7
Mean Minimum Temp. (°F)	-3.6	3.9	17.2	31.9	43.9	54.3	58.6	56.3	46.0	34.3	18.9	4.3	30.5
Extreme Maximum Temp. (°F)	53	54	75	100	96	98	105	104	98	90	73	55	105
Extreme Minimum Temp. (°F)	-43	-43	-30	-8	20	34	40	33	20	8	-28	-32	-43
Days Maximum Temp. ≥ 90°F	0	0	0	0	1	3	5	5	1	0	0	0	15
Days Maximum Temp. ≤ 32°F	26	18	10	1	0	0	0	0	0	1	12	24	92
Days Minimum Temp. ≤ 32°F	31	28	28	16	4	0	0	0	2	13	27	31	180
Days Minimum Temp. ≤ 0°F	18	12	5	0	0	0	0	0	0	0	2	13	50
Heating Degree Days (base 65°F)	1,813	1,440	1,184	631	264	60	15	33	223	596	1,119	1,599	8,977
Cooling Degree Days (base 65°F)	0	0	0	3	38	113	202	169	39	1	0	0	565
Mean Precipitation (in.)	0.83	0.58	1.06	1.72	3.03	4.36	3.22	2.71	2.41	2.13	0.94	0.67	23.66
Days With ≥ 0.1" Precipitation	3	2	3	4	6	7	6	5	5	4	3	2	50
Days With ≥ 1.0" Precipitation	0	0	0	0	1	1	1	1	1	1	0	0	6
Mean Snowfall (in.)	na	5.5	na	1.3	trace	0.0	0.0	0.0	0.0	0.7	na	8.2	na
Days With ≥ 1.0" Snow Depth	na	na	12	2	0	0	0	0	0	0	6	na	na

Agassiz Refuge *Marshall County* Elevation: 1,141 ft. Latitude: 48° 18' N Longitude: 95° 59' W

	JAN	FEB	MAR	APR	MAY	JUN	JUL	AUG	SEP	OCT	NOV	DEC	YEAR
Mean Maximum Temp. (°F)	14.2	22.0	34.6	53.1	68.7	76.2	80.1	78.8	68.2	54.8	33.5	19.4	50.3
Mean Temp. (°F)	3.7	11.0	23.8	41.2	55.9	64.3	68.3	66.3	56.0	43.7	25.2	10.2	39.1
Mean Minimum Temp. (°F)	-6.7	0.0	13.0	29.3	43.1	52.3	56.6	53.6	43.7	32.6	16.8	0.9	27.9
Extreme Maximum Temp. (°F)	43	54	70	94	94	98	99	97	94	86	70	52	99
Extreme Minimum Temp. (°F)	-43	-46	-30	-12	21	32	38	31	19	1	-29	-35	-46
Days Maximum Temp. ≥ 90°F	0	0	0	0	1	1	2	2	0	0	0	0	6
Days Maximum Temp. ≤ 32°F	28	21	12	1	0	0	0	0	0	1	14	26	103
Days Minimum Temp. ≤ 32°F	31	28	29	20	4	0	0	0	3	15	28	31	189
Days Minimum Temp. ≤ 0°F	20	14	7	0	0	0	0	0	0	0	3	15	59
Heating Degree Days (base 65°F)	1,899	1,522	1,271	707	299	90	26	61	287	653	1,188	1,697	9,700
Cooling Degree Days (base 65°F)	0	0	0	2	27	77	140	117	22	1	0	0	386
Mean Precipitation (in.)	0.61	0.45	0.73	1.25	2.82	3.53	3.59	3.03	2.57	1.74	1.05	0.53	21.90
Days With ≥ 0.1" Precipitation	2	1	2	3	6	7	7	6	5	4	3	2	48
Days With ≥ 1.0" Precipitation	0	0	0	0	1	1	1	1	1	0	0	0	5
Mean Snowfall (in.)	9.3	5.4	6.0	2.1	trace	0.0	0.0	0.0	trace	1.1	7.9	7.7	39.5
Days With ≥ 1.0" Snow Depth	31	28	25	6	0	0	0	0	0	1	15	28	134

Albert Lea 3 SE *Freeborn County* Elevation: 1,227 ft. Latitude: 43° 37' N Longitude: 93° 18' W

	JAN	FEB	MAR	APR	MAY	JUN	JUL	AUG	SEP	OCT	NOV	DEC	YEAR
Mean Maximum Temp. (°F)	21.5	27.6	39.3	55.5	69.4	79.2	82.6	79.9	71.8	59.1	40.5	26.6	54.4
Mean Temp. (°F)	12.5	18.9	30.9	45.4	58.6	68.3	72.0	69.4	60.5	48.1	32.1	18.3	44.6
Mean Minimum Temp. (°F)	2.9	9.4	22.2	34.9	47.3	57.2	61.4	58.9	49.1	36.7	23.5	9.6	34.4
Extreme Maximum Temp. (°F)	58	64	82	92	94	102	101	101	98	94	78	67	102
Extreme Minimum Temp. (°F)	-29	-33	-16	3	24	34	44	39	27	13	-18	-29	-33
Days Maximum Temp. ≥ 90°F	0	0	0	0	0	4	5	3	1	0	0	0	13
Days Maximum Temp. ≤ 32°F	24	17	9	1	0	0	0	0	0	0	8	21	80
Days Minimum Temp. ≤ 32°F	31	28	27	11	1	0	0	0	1	10	25	31	165
Days Minimum Temp. ≤ 0°F	14	9	2	0	0	0	0	0	0	0	1	8	34
Heating Degree Days (base 65°F)	1,625	1,298	1,049	588	232	44	10	26	182	516	979	1,443	7,992
Cooling Degree Days (base 65°F)	0	0	0	5	38	147	229	168	53	3	0	0	643
Mean Precipitation (in.)	0.84	0.63	2.01	3.44	4.12	4.65	4.18	4.38	3.16	2.66	1.93	0.96	32.96
Days With ≥ 0.1" Precipitation	3	2	5	7	8	7	7	7	6	5	4	3	64
Days With ≥ 1.0" Precipitation	0	0	0	1	1	1	1	1	1	1	0	0	7
Mean Snowfall (in.)	10.6	6.0	6.9	3.4	trace	0.0	0.0	0.0	0.0	0.5	4.8	8.5	40.7
Days With ≥ 1.0" Snow Depth	25	20	12	2	0	0	0	0	0	0	6	19	84

Alexandria Chandler Field *Douglas County* Elevation: 1,414 ft. Latitude: 45° 52' N Longitude: 95° 23' W

	JAN	FEB	MAR	APR	MAY	JUN	JUL	AUG	SEP	OCT	NOV	DEC	YEAR
Mean Maximum Temp. (°F)	17.5	23.7	36.2	53.5	67.9	76.4	81.5	78.5	68.2	55.0	36.3	22.1	51.4
Mean Temp. (°F)	8.0	14.5	27.6	43.5	57.2	66.2	71.3	68.7	58.3	45.6	28.9	14.0	42.0
Mean Minimum Temp. (°F)	-1.5	5.3	18.9	33.4	46.5	56.0	61.0	58.8	48.3	36.2	21.5	5.9	32.5
Extreme Maximum Temp. (°F)	58	58	71	95	93	102	101	104	98	86	76	55	104
Extreme Minimum Temp. (°F)	-38	-33	-20	-2	25	39	44	41	24	13	-15	-32	-38
Days Maximum Temp. ≥ 90°F	0	0	0	0	0	2	4	3	1	0	0	0	10
Days Maximum Temp. ≤ 32°F	27	20	11	1	0	0	0	0	0	0	11	25	95
Days Minimum Temp. ≤ 32°F	30	28	28	14	1	0	0	0	1	10	26	31	169
Days Minimum Temp. ≤ 0°F	16	11	3	0	0	0	0	0	0	0	1	11	42
Heating Degree Days (base 65°F)	1,766	1,420	1,153	642	263	64	11	32	232	594	1,075	1,575	8,827
Cooling Degree Days (base 65°F)	0	0	0	3	33	107	209	154	31	2	0	0	539
Mean Precipitation (in.)	0.94	0.66	1.51	2.11	2.96	4.34	3.20	3.58	2.72	2.23	1.22	0.59	26.06
Days With ≥ 0.1" Precipitation	3	2	4	5	6	7	6	6	5	4	3	2	53
Days With ≥ 1.0" Precipitation	0	0	0	0	1	1	1	1	1	1	0	0	6
Mean Snowfall (in.)	10.1	6.7	9.2	2.9	trace	trace	0.0	trace	trace	0.8	7.0	6.0	42.7
Days With ≥ 1.0" Snow Depth	29	26	21	3	0	0	0	0	0	0	10	24	113

Argyle 4 E *Marshall County*   Elevation: 869 ft.   Latitude: 48° 20' N   Longitude: 96° 44' W

	JAN	FEB	MAR	APR	MAY	JUN	JUL	AUG	SEP	OCT	NOV	DEC	YEAR
Mean Maximum Temp. (°F)	12.3	20.0	32.5	52.3	68.8	76.5	80.7	80.2	69.0	55.0	33.8	18.9	50.0
Mean Temp. (°F)	1.8	9.0	22.3	40.3	54.9	63.8	67.7	66.1	55.6	43.1	24.7	9.5	38.2
Mean Minimum Temp. (°F)	-8.7	-2.0	12.0	28.3	41.1	51.0	54.6	51.9	42.2	31.2	15.6	0.1	26.4
Extreme Maximum Temp. (°F)	45	49	68	98	98	100	105	104	100	92	75	54	105
Extreme Minimum Temp. (°F)	-43	-48	-38	-18	19	31	37	30	19	4	-34	-35	-48
Days Maximum Temp. ≥ 90°F	0	0	0	0	1	2	3	4	1	0	0	0	11
Days Maximum Temp. ≤ 32°F	28	22	14	2	0	0	0	0	0	1	14	25	106
Days Minimum Temp. ≤ 32°F	31	28	30	20	7	0	0	0	4	17	29	31	197
Days Minimum Temp. ≤ 0°F	22	16	8	1	0	0	0	0	0	0	4	16	67
Heating Degree Days (base 65°F)	1,959	1,580	1,319	735	330	104	36	66	297	673	1,203	1,718	10,020
Cooling Degree Days (base 65°F)	0	0	0	3	25	76	124	112	21	1	0	0	362
Mean Precipitation (in.)	0.78	0.58	0.92	1.13	2.27	3.17	3.09	2.43	2.29	1.52	0.95	0.63	19.76
Days With ≥ 0.1" Precipitation	3	2	3	3	5	7	6	5	5	4	3	2	48
Days With ≥ 1.0" Precipitation	0	0	0	0	0	1	1	0	1	0	0	0	3
Mean Snowfall (in.)	10.2	6.5	6.4	1.9	trace	0.0	0.0	0.0	trace	0.9	7.3	7.6	40.8
Days With ≥ 1.0" Snow Depth	28	24	17	4	0	0	0	0	0	0	9	20	102

Artichoke Lake *Big Stone County*   Elevation: 1,072 ft.   Latitude: 45° 23' N   Longitude: 96° 09' W

	JAN	FEB	MAR	APR	MAY	JUN	JUL	AUG	SEP	OCT	NOV	DEC	YEAR
Mean Maximum Temp. (°F)	19.7	26.4	37.0	55.0	69.3	77.6	82.0	79.5	70.3	57.5	37.9	24.8	53.1
Mean Temp. (°F)	10.0	17.1	28.5	44.6	58.4	67.2	71.5	69.2	59.6	47.2	29.6	16.1	43.2
Mean Minimum Temp. (°F)	-0.1	7.4	19.8	34.1	47.4	56.6	60.9	58.7	48.9	36.7	21.3	7.3	33.3
Extreme Maximum Temp. (°F)	63	60	75	97	95	106	108	103	97	91	78	60	108
Extreme Minimum Temp. (°F)	-33	-36	-19	-1	22	37	41	36	24	11	-17	-31	-36
Days Maximum Temp. ≥ 90°F	0	0	0	0	0	2	5	3	1	0	0	0	11
Days Maximum Temp. ≤ 32°F	25	17	9	1	0	0	0	0	0	0	10	22	84
Days Minimum Temp. ≤ 32°F	31	27	27	13	1	0	0	0	1	10	26	31	167
Days Minimum Temp. ≤ 0°F	16	10	3	0	0	0	0	0	0	0	2	11	42
Heating Degree Days (base 65°F)	1,704	1,350	1,126	609	236	52	11	28	199	550	1,055	1,510	8,430
Cooling Degree Days (base 65°F)	0	0	0	4	39	119	208	162	44	3	0	0	579
Mean Precipitation (in.)	0.87	0.62	1.54	2.05	2.53	3.69	3.89	3.04	1.95	2.22	1.16	0.47	24.03
Days With ≥ 0.1" Precipitation	3	2	4	5	6	7	6	5	4	4	3	2	51
Days With ≥ 1.0" Precipitation	0	0	0	0	0	1	1	1	0	1	0	0	4
Mean Snowfall (in.)	10.0	6.6	8.0	2.5	trace	0.0	0.0	0.0	trace	0.9	6.6	5.4	40.0
Days With ≥ 1.0" Snow Depth	27	22	16	2	0	0	0	0	0	0	8	20	95

Austin 3 S *Mower County*   Elevation: 1,213 ft.   Latitude: 43° 37' N   Longitude: 93° 00' W

	JAN	FEB	MAR	APR	MAY	JUN	JUL	AUG	SEP	OCT	NOV	DEC	YEAR
Mean Maximum Temp. (°F)	21.7	28.3	40.4	57.2	70.2	79.4	82.3	80.0	72.5	59.9	40.8	26.6	54.9
Mean Temp. (°F)	12.7	19.4	32.0	46.4	58.7	68.2	71.4	69.1	61.0	48.9	32.8	18.5	44.9
Mean Minimum Temp. (°F)	3.7	10.4	23.6	35.6	47.3	56.9	60.6	58.1	49.3	38.0	24.7	10.4	34.9
Extreme Maximum Temp. (°F)	55	62	79	90	94	100	99	98	97	92	77	65	100
Extreme Minimum Temp. (°F)	-35	-34	-18	6	24	35	42	38	23	13	-25	-31	-35
Days Maximum Temp. ≥ 90°F	0	0	0	0	0	2	4	2	1	0	0	0	9
Days Maximum Temp. ≤ 32°F	24	17	8	1	0	0	0	0	0	0	8	21	79
Days Minimum Temp. ≤ 32°F	31	27	26	12	1	0	0	0	1	9	23	30	160
Days Minimum Temp. ≤ 0°F	13	8	2	0	0	0	0	0	0	0	1	8	32
Heating Degree Days (base 65°F)	1,616	1,282	1,016	556	224	41	12	27	173	494	961	1,436	7,838
Cooling Degree Days (base 65°F)	0	0	0	4	35	144	216	158	58	3	0	0	618
Mean Precipitation (in.)	*0.93*	0.49	1.59	3.08	3.99	3.94	4.46	4.37	3.50	2.48	1.90	*0.91*	*31.64*
Days With ≥ 0.1" Precipitation	na	*1*	3	7	7	8	7	7	6	5	3	*2*	na
Days With ≥ 1.0" Precipitation	*0*	0	0	1	1	1	1	1	1	1	1	*0*	*8*
Mean Snowfall (in.)	na	6.5	*5.9*	2.8	trace	0.0	0.0	0.0	0.0	0.3	4.6	*9.0*	na
Days With ≥ 1.0" Snow Depth	na	*20*	*12*	1	0	0	0	0	0	0	4	*19*	na

Baudette Int'l Airport *Lake Of The Woods County*   Elevation: 1,079 ft.   Latitude: 48° 43' N   Longitude: 94° 36' W

	JAN	FEB	MAR	APR	MAY	JUN	JUL	AUG	SEP	OCT	NOV	DEC	YEAR
Mean Maximum Temp. (°F)	15.1	23.8	35.6	53.2	68.2	76.1	80.1	78.2	67.9	54.4	34.4	20.2	50.6
Mean Temp. (°F)	3.6	11.4	23.6	40.8	55.0	63.7	68.0	65.8	55.9	44.0	26.1	10.5	39.0
Mean Minimum Temp. (°F)	-7.8	-1.0	11.5	28.5	41.8	51.2	55.8	53.3	43.9	33.5	17.8	0.7	27.4
Extreme Maximum Temp. (°F)	47	54	67	91	94	98	98	101	95	86	75	51	101
Extreme Minimum Temp. (°F)	-49	-46	-34	-19	21	20	36	28	23	2	-29	-40	-49
Days Maximum Temp. ≥ 90°F	0	0	0	0	0	1	2	2	0	0	0	0	5
Days Maximum Temp. ≤ 32°F	28	20	12	2	0	0	0	0	0	1	13	26	102
Days Minimum Temp. ≤ 32°F	31	28	29	20	5	0	0	0	2	14	28	31	188
Days Minimum Temp. ≤ 0°F	21	15	8	0	0	0	0	0	0	0	3	15	62
Heating Degree Days (base 65°F)	1,902	1,510	1,278	719	325	99	29	66	286	646	1,160	1,687	9,707
Cooling Degree Days (base 65°F)	0	0	0	0	1	22	70	128	18	0	0	0	346
Mean Precipitation (in.)	0.58	0.41	0.67	1.18	2.69	3.58	3.37	3.23	2.73	2.17	1.02	0.57	22.20
Days With ≥ 0.1" Precipitation	2	1	2	3	6	8	7	6	6	5	3	2	51
Days With ≥ 1.0" Precipitation	0	0	0	0	0	1	1	1	1	0	0	0	4
Mean Snowfall (in.)	9.5	*6.3*	*5.2*	2.8	trace	0.0	0.0	0.0	trace	1.0	9.6	*8.8*	*43.2*
Days With ≥ 1.0" Snow Depth	*13*	na	na	*1*	0	0	0	0	0	0	na	*9*	na

Benson *Swift County*   Elevation: 1,040 ft.   Latitude: 45° 19' N   Longitude: 95° 37' W

	JAN	FEB	MAR	APR	MAY	JUN	JUL	AUG	SEP	OCT	NOV	DEC	YEAR
Mean Maximum Temp. (°F)	19.5	26.8	38.7	56.8	71.1	79.5	83.4	80.9	72.0	58.7	38.6	25.4	54.3
Mean Temp. (°F)	10.3	17.8	29.9	45.7	59.2	68.2	72.3	69.9	60.5	47.8	30.4	17.0	44.1
Mean Minimum Temp. (°F)	0.9	8.6	21.0	34.5	47.2	56.8	61.1	58.9	49.0	36.9	22.1	8.5	33.8
Extreme Maximum Temp. (°F)	63	59	76	97	96	104	102	103	99	90	81	60	104
Extreme Minimum Temp. (°F)	-35	-35	-16	0	25	37	41	39	23	12	-15	-26	-35
Days Maximum Temp. ≥ 90°F	0	0	0	0	1	3	6	4	1	0	0	0	15
Days Maximum Temp. ≤ 32°F	25	17	8	1	0	0	0	0	0	0	9	22	82
Days Minimum Temp. ≤ 32°F	31	27	26	13	2	0	0	0	1	10	26	31	167
Days Minimum Temp. ≤ 0°F	15	9	2	0	0	0	0	0	0	0	1	9	36
Heating Degree Days (base 65°F)	1,695	1,329	1,081	578	217	44	8	24	182	528	1,031	1,483	8,200
Cooling Degree Days (base 65°F)	0	0	0	4	46	145	234	184	54	4	0	0	671
Mean Precipitation (in.)	0.87	0.69	1.67	2.20	3.00	4.54	4.03	3.99	2.64	2.52	1.47	0.62	28.24
Days With ≥ 0.1" Precipitation	3	2	4	5	7	7	6	6	5	4	3	2	54
Days With ≥ 1.0" Precipitation	0	0	0	0	0	1	1	1	1	1	0	0	5
Mean Snowfall (in.)	10.2	7.1	8.5	2.0	trace	0.0	0.0	0.0	trace	0.5	6.6	6.5	41.4
Days With ≥ 1.0" Snow Depth	28	24	18	2	0	0	0	0	0	0	9	21	102

Big Falls *Koochiching County*   Elevation: 1,217 ft.   Latitude: 48° 12' N   Longitude: 93° 48' W

	JAN	FEB	MAR	APR	MAY	JUN	JUL	AUG	SEP	OCT	NOV	DEC	YEAR
Mean Maximum Temp. (°F)	15.7	26.1	38.5	54.8	69.4	76.8	80.6	78.5	67.5	54.9	na	20.9	na
Mean Temp. (°F)	3.4	12.6	25.5	41.2	54.5	63.4	66.9	64.6	54.7	na	na	na	na
Mean Minimum Temp. (°F)	-8.8	-0.4	12.6	27.3	39.7	49.3	53.0	50.8	41.9	na	na	na	na
Extreme Maximum Temp. (°F)	49	60	68	91	92	99	101	99	97	85	75	51	101
Extreme Minimum Temp. (°F)	-51	-48	-34	-10	18	26	32	29	20	3	-33	-44	-51
Days Maximum Temp. ≥ 90°F	0	0	0	0	1	1	3	2	0	0	0	0	7
Days Maximum Temp. ≤ 32°F	26	19	10	1	0	0	0	0	0	0	10	24	90
Days Minimum Temp. ≤ 32°F	28	26	26	21	8	1	0	0	4	15	21	27	177
Days Minimum Temp. ≤ 0°F	17	13	6	1	0	0	0	0	0	0	3	13	53
Heating Degree Days (base 65°F)	1,914	1,474	1,221	706	338	105	43	88	317	na	na	na	na
Cooling Degree Days (base 65°F)	0	0	0	1	21	67	106	82	12	na	na	na	na
Mean Precipitation (in.)	0.88	0.64	1.07	1.66	2.79	4.21	3.72	3.30	3.25	2.40	1.37	0.86	26.15
Days With ≥ 0.1" Precipitation	2	2	3	4	6	8	7	6	6	5	3	3	55
Days With ≥ 1.0" Precipitation	0	0	0	0	0	1	1	1	1	0	0	0	4
Mean Snowfall (in.)	12.4	8.7	9.5	4.3	0.3	0.0	0.0	trace	trace	1.4	10.0	11.6	58.2
Days With ≥ 1.0" Snow Depth	na	17	21	6	0	0	0	0	0	0	7	na	na

Brainerd *Crow Wing County*   Elevation: 1,177 ft.   Latitude: 46° 22' N   Longitude: 94° 12' W

	JAN	FEB	MAR	APR	MAY	JUN	JUL	AUG	SEP	OCT	NOV	DEC	YEAR
Mean Maximum Temp. (°F)	19.0	26.6	37.4	54.1	68.4	76.3	80.9	78.2	67.9	55.3	37.0	23.3	52.0
Mean Temp. (°F)	6.3	13.7	26.1	42.1	55.7	64.2	68.9	66.0	55.7	43.8	27.7	12.9	40.3
Mean Minimum Temp. (°F)	-7.1	-0.1	14.5	29.8	42.5	51.7	56.5	53.6	43.6	32.0	18.2	2.5	28.2
Extreme Maximum Temp. (°F)	56	57	75	94	92	100	102	100	96	88	73	57	102
Extreme Minimum Temp. (°F)	-48	-54	-33	-12	20	32	36	29	18	4	-23	-43	-54
Days Maximum Temp. ≥ 90°F	0	0	0	0	0	1	3	2	0	0	0	0	6
Days Maximum Temp. ≤ 32°F	26	18	9	1	0	0	0	0	0	0	11	24	89
Days Minimum Temp. ≤ 32°F	31	28	29	19	4	0	0	0	4	17	28	31	191
Days Minimum Temp. ≤ 0°F	19	13	5	0	0	0	0	0	0	0	2	14	53
Heating Degree Days (base 65°F)	1,809	1,438	1,198	678	304	96	26	64	294	653	1,112	1,609	9,281
Cooling Degree Days (base 65°F)	0	0	0	2	20	79	146	104	21	1	0	0	373
Mean Precipitation (in.)	0.79	0.58	1.42	2.06	3.09	4.15	3.95	3.48	2.83	2.69	1.64	0.69	27.37
Days With ≥ 0.1" Precipitation	3	2	4	5	6	8	7	6	6	4	4	2	57
Days With ≥ 1.0" Precipitation	0	0	0	0	1	1	1	1	1	1	0	0	6
Mean Snowfall (in.)	13.3	6.0	9.7	2.1	trace	0.0	0.0	0.0	0.0	0.5	7.1	8.1	46.8
Days With ≥ 1.0" Snow Depth	na	na	na	3	0	0	0	0	0	0	10	na	na

Browns Valley *Traverse County*   Elevation: 984 ft.   Latitude: 45° 36' N   Longitude: 96° 50' W

	JAN	FEB	MAR	APR	MAY	JUN	JUL	AUG	SEP	OCT	NOV	DEC	YEAR
Mean Maximum Temp. (°F)	20.6	27.4	38.4	56.4	70.9	79.1	84.9	82.4	72.5	58.7	39.4	26.3	54.8
Mean Temp. (°F)	10.7	17.6	29.1	44.8	58.5	67.3	72.9	70.2	60.1	46.9	30.1	17.1	43.8
Mean Minimum Temp. (°F)	0.7	7.8	19.6	33.1	46.0	55.4	60.8	57.8	47.5	35.1	20.9	7.8	32.7
Extreme Maximum Temp. (°F)	63	65	79	100	96	107	109	107	100	93	79	60	109
Extreme Minimum Temp. (°F)	-40	-41	-18	-3	20	35	44	37	19	9	-19	-32	-41
Days Maximum Temp. ≥ 90°F	0	0	0	0	1	4	9	6	2	0	0	0	22
Days Maximum Temp. ≤ 32°F	23	17	9	1	0	0	0	0	0	0	9	20	79
Days Minimum Temp. ≤ 32°F	31	27	27	15	2	0	0	0	1	12	26	31	172
Days Minimum Temp. ≤ 0°F	16	10	4	0	0	0	0	0	0	0	2	10	42
Heating Degree Days (base 65°F)	1,681	1,332	1,107	605	238	57	10	26	198	557	1,040	1,482	8,333
Cooling Degree Days (base 65°F)	0	0	0	6	44	137	251	201	52	4	0	0	695
Mean Precipitation (in.)	0.89	0.64	1.71	2.10	2.35	3.40	3.26	2.87	1.92	1.79	1.08	0.50	22.51
Days With ≥ 0.1" Precipitation	3	2	4	5	6	6	6	5	4	3	3	2	49
Days With ≥ 1.0" Precipitation	0	0	0	0	0	1	1	1	0	0	0	0	3
Mean Snowfall (in.)	10.8	7.6	9.1	2.4	0.0	0.0	0.0	0.0	0.0	0.3	6.8	5.7	42.7
Days With ≥ 1.0" Snow Depth	na	na	na	na	0	0	0	0	0	0	0	na	na

Buffalo *Wright County*   Elevation: 977 ft.   Latitude: 45° 11' N   Longitude: 93° 52' W

	JAN	FEB	MAR	APR	MAY	JUN	JUL	AUG	SEP	OCT	NOV	DEC	YEAR
Mean Maximum Temp. (°F)	20.7	27.8	38.9	56.6	70.7	79.3	83.5	80.7	71.6	58.7	39.0	25.3	54.4
Mean Temp. (°F)	11.1	18.1	29.5	45.3	58.7	67.8	72.3	69.7	60.3	48.1	31.2	17.1	44.1
Mean Minimum Temp. (°F)	1.5	8.5	20.1	33.9	46.6	56.3	61.1	58.7	49.0	37.4	23.3	8.8	33.8
Extreme Maximum Temp. (°F)	56	60	80	94	93	102	105	102	96	89	77	64	105
Extreme Minimum Temp. (°F)	-38	-36	-14	3	24	34	43	39	26	14	-16	-33	-38
Days Maximum Temp. ≥ 90°F	0	0	0	0	1	3	6	3	1	0	0	0	14
Days Maximum Temp. ≤ 32°F	25	16	8	0	0	0	0	0	0	0	9	22	80
Days Minimum Temp. ≤ 32°F	31	27	26	13	2	0	0	0	1	9	25	31	165
Days Minimum Temp. ≤ 0°F	15	9	3	0	0	0	0	0	0	0	1	9	37
Heating Degree Days (base 65°F)	1,666	1,317	1,093	589	228	48	9	24	184	521	1,008	1,481	8,168
Cooling Degree Days (base 65°F)	0	0	0	4	36	135	234	169	47	3	0	0	628
Mean Precipitation (in.)	0.78	0.61	1.56	2.42	3.19	4.37	3.84	4.25	3.03	2.34	1.82	0.76	28.97
Days With ≥ 0.1" Precipitation	2	2	4	5	7	7	6	6	6	5	4	3	57
Days With ≥ 1.0" Precipitation	0	0	0	0	1	1	1	1	1	1	0	0	6
Mean Snowfall (in.)	9.7	6.2	8.8	2.6	0.1	0.0	0.0	0.0	trace	0.2	7.6	8.2	43.4
Days With ≥ 1.0" Snow Depth	29	26	18	3	0	0	0	0	0	0	9	24	109

Caledonia *Houston County*   Elevation: 1,174 ft.   Latitude: 43° 38' N   Longitude: 91° 30' W

	JAN	FEB	MAR	APR	MAY	JUN	JUL	AUG	SEP	OCT	NOV	DEC	YEAR
Mean Maximum Temp. (°F)	22.7	29.0	40.7	56.3	68.5	78.2	81.9	79.4	70.9	58.8	40.9	27.7	54.6
Mean Temp. (°F)	13.1	19.2	31.3	45.2	57.2	67.1	71.0	68.7	59.7	48.1	32.6	19.3	44.4
Mean Minimum Temp. (°F)	3.7	9.7	21.9	34.2	46.0	55.8	60.0	57.9	48.5	37.2	24.2	10.8	34.1
Extreme Maximum Temp. (°F)	57	57	82	93	90	97	101	102	91	91	75	62	102
Extreme Minimum Temp. (°F)	-32	-35	-13	2	23	37	43	39	24	13	-16	-28	-35
Days Maximum Temp. ≥ 90°F	0	0	0	0	0	2	4	2	0	0	0	0	8
Days Maximum Temp. ≤ 32°F	24	16	7	0	0	0	0	0	0	0	7	20	74
Days Minimum Temp. ≤ 32°F	31	28	25	12	2	0	0	0	1	10	24	31	164
Days Minimum Temp. ≤ 0°F	13	8	2	0	0	0	0	0	0	0	1	7	31
Heating Degree Days (base 65°F)	1,602	1,287	1,035	591	265	55	15	*30*	196	522	968	1,413	*7,979*
Cooling Degree Days (base 65°F)	0	0	0	5	26	124	204	151	43	2	0	0	555
Mean Precipitation (in.)	0.92	0.82	1.98	3.80	3.80	4.42	4.71	4.71	3.72	2.53	2.37	1.27	35.05
Days With ≥ 0.1" Precipitation	3	2	4	7	8	7	7	7	6	5	5	3	64
Days With ≥ 1.0" Precipitation	0	0	0	1	1	1	1	1	1	0	1	0	7
Mean Snowfall (in.)	10.6	8.0	7.9	3.3	trace	0.0	0.0	0.0	0.0	0.2	5.6	9.2	44.8
Days With ≥ 1.0" Snow Depth	na	na	na	na	0	0	0	0	0	0	4	na	na

Cambridge State Hosp *Isanti County*   Elevation: 958 ft.   Latitude: 45° 34' N   Longitude: 93° 14' W

	JAN	FEB	MAR	APR	MAY	JUN	JUL	AUG	SEP	OCT	NOV	DEC	YEAR
Mean Maximum Temp. (°F)	18.7	26.4	37.4	54.6	68.6	76.8	81.2	78.1	68.4	56.1	37.7	24.7	52.4
Mean Temp. (°F)	8.8	16.5	28.0	43.6	56.9	65.5	70.1	67.3	57.7	45.7	29.4	15.9	42.1
Mean Minimum Temp. (°F)	-1.2	6.7	18.6	32.7	45.0	54.1	59.0	56.5	46.9	35.2	21.1	7.2	31.8
Extreme Maximum Temp. (°F)	52	58	70	92	98	99	102	100	97	85	72	60	102
Extreme Minimum Temp. (°F)	-41	-41	-18	0	22	32	42	39	24	8	-14	-41	-41
Days Maximum Temp. ≥ 90°F	0	0	0	0	0	2	4	2	0	0	0	0	8
Days Maximum Temp. ≤ 32°F	26	18	9	1	0	0	0	0	0	0	10	23	87
Days Minimum Temp. ≤ 32°F	31	27	28	15	2	0	0	0	2	12	26	31	174
Days Minimum Temp. ≤ 0°F	17	9	3	0	0	0	0	0	0	0	2	10	41
Heating Degree Days (base 65°F)	1,741	1,364	1,140	638	275	73	19	46	245	592	1,061	1,517	8,711
Cooling Degree Days (base 65°F)	0	0	0	3	30	90	175	125	32	1	0	0	456
Mean Precipitation (in.)	1.00	0.57	1.38	2.17	3.23	4.49	4.25	4.14	3.05	2.49	1.85	0.82	29.44
Days With ≥ 0.1" Precipitation	3	2	4	4	7	8	6	7	6	6	4	3	60
Days With ≥ 1.0" Precipitation	0	0	0	0	1	1	1	1	1	1	0	0	6
Mean Snowfall (in.)	*10.1*	5.5	7.9	1.9	trace	0.0	0.0	0.0	0.0	0.4	6.5	7.1	*39.4*
Days With ≥ 1.0" Snow Depth	29	26	20	2	0	0	0	0	0	0	8	22	107

Canby *Yellow Medicine County*   Elevation: 1,240 ft.   Latitude: 44° 43' N   Longitude: 96° 17' W

	JAN	FEB	MAR	APR	MAY	JUN	JUL	AUG	SEP	OCT	NOV	DEC	YEAR
Mean Maximum Temp. (°F)	22.6	29.2	40.2	57.6	71.5	81.1	85.5	83.0	73.5	60.4	40.5	27.8	56.1
Mean Temp. (°F)	12.9	19.8	30.9	45.8	59.2	68.9	73.5	71.2	61.4	48.6	31.5	18.7	45.2
Mean Minimum Temp. (°F)	3.2	10.4	21.6	34.1	46.8	56.7	61.5	59.3	49.3	36.8	22.5	9.5	34.3
Extreme Maximum Temp. (°F)	68	67	78	98	95	107	105	108	99	94	82	64	108
Extreme Minimum Temp. (°F)	-31	-29	-17	7	24	36	42	39	22	12	-14	-27	-31
Days Maximum Temp. ≥ 90°F	0	0	0	0	1	5	10	6	2	0	0	0	24
Days Maximum Temp. ≤ 32°F	23	16	8	0	0	0	0	0	0	0	8	19	74
Days Minimum Temp. ≤ 32°F	31	27	27	13	2	0	0	0	1	11	25	31	168
Days Minimum Temp. ≤ 0°F	14	8	2	0	0	0	0	0	0	0	1	8	33
Heating Degree Days (base 65°F)	1,612	1,270	1,050	573	219	42	8	20	168	506	999	1,431	7,898
Cooling Degree Days (base 65°F)	0	0	0	7	46	155	262	208	62	4	0	0	744
Mean Precipitation (in.)	0.87	0.73	1.77	2.36	2.85	4.12	3.32	2.84	2.46	2.22	1.64	0.67	25.85
Days With ≥ 0.1" Precipitation	3	2	4	5	6	6	6	5	5	4	3	2	51
Days With ≥ 1.0" Precipitation	0	0	0	1	1	1	1	1	1	0	0	0	6
Mean Snowfall (in.)	8.7	6.2	9.2	3.2	trace	0.0	0.0	0.0	trace	0.8	8.0	6.2	42.3
Days With ≥ 1.0" Snow Depth	26	23	17	2	0	0	0	0	0	1	9	21	99

Cass Lake *Cass County*   Elevation: 1,295 ft.   Latitude: 47° 23' N   Longitude: 94° 37' W

	JAN	FEB	MAR	APR	MAY	JUN	JUL	AUG	SEP	OCT	NOV	DEC	YEAR
Mean Maximum Temp. (°F)	16.2	24.0	36.0	51.5	66.7	75.1	79.4	77.3	66.4	53.3	34.7	21.4	50.2
Mean Temp. (°F)	3.3	10.3	24.0	39.2	53.5	62.9	67.4	65.2	55.1	42.8	25.5	10.3	38.3
Mean Minimum Temp. (°F)	-9.6	-3.4	12.0	26.8	40.2	50.6	55.3	53.1	43.7	32.1	16.2	-0.9	26.3
Extreme Maximum Temp. (°F)	53	60	73	96	93	98	104	101	98	87	74	53	104
Extreme Minimum Temp. (°F)	-48	-48	-34	-13	16	27	33	26	17	2	-30	-46	-48
Days Maximum Temp. ≥ 90°F	0	0	0	0	0	1	3	2	0	0	0	0	6
Days Maximum Temp. ≤ 32°F	27	20	11	1	0	0	0	0	0	1	14	24	98
Days Minimum Temp. ≤ 32°F	30	28	29	22	8	1	0	0	4	17	28	30	197
Days Minimum Temp. ≤ 0°F	21	16	7	0	0	0	0	0	0	0	4	16	64
Heating Degree Days (base 65°F)	1,910	1,540	1,265	770	369	125	47	82	310	683	1,178	1,694	9,973
Cooling Degree Days (base 65°F)	0	0	0	2	18	68	123	100	17	0	0	0	328
Mean Precipitation (in.)	0.82	0.63	1.27	1.89	2.63	3.86	4.28	3.23	2.83	2.62	1.31	0.68	26.05
Days With ≥ 0.1" Precipitation	2	2	3	5	6	7	8	6	6	5	3	2	55
Days With ≥ 1.0" Precipitation	0	0	0	0	0	1	1	1	0	1	0	0	4
Mean Snowfall (in.)	11.3	7.2	8.7	3.0	trace	0.0	0.0	0.0	0.0	0.7	8.2	8.6	47.7
Days With ≥ 1.0" Snow Depth	na	na	na	4	0	0	0	0	0	0	na	na	na

Cedar *Anoka County*   Elevation: 905 ft.   Latitude: 45° 19' N   Longitude: 93° 17' W

	JAN	FEB	MAR	APR	MAY	JUN	JUL	AUG	SEP	OCT	NOV	DEC	YEAR
Mean Maximum Temp. (°F)	21.3	28.6	40.5	58.1	71.3	78.9	82.8	79.8	71.3	59.0	39.6	26.3	54.8
Mean Temp. (°F)	11.3	18.3	30.4	46.0	58.7	67.0	71.4	68.8	60.1	48.1	31.3	17.8	44.1
Mean Minimum Temp. (°F)	1.2	8.0	20.4	33.9	46.0	55.0	60.0	57.7	48.9	37.1	22.9	9.2	33.4
Extreme Maximum Temp. (°F)	53	58	83	93	94	99	103	98	98	87	76	64	103
Extreme Minimum Temp. (°F)	-40	-39	-17	1	23	31	38	38	22	6	-18	-31	-40
Days Maximum Temp. ≥ 90°F	0	0	0	0	1	2	5	2	1	0	0	0	11
Days Maximum Temp. ≤ 32°F	24	16	7	0	0	0	0	0	0	0	8	21	76
Days Minimum Temp. ≤ 32°F	31	27	26	14	2	0	0	0	1	10	25	31	167
Days Minimum Temp. ≤ 0°F	15	9	3	0	0	0	0	0	0	0	1	9	37
Heating Degree Days (base 65°F)	1,663	1,313	1,065	568	230	55	12	31	189	521	1,005	1,458	8,110
Cooling Degree Days (base 65°F)	0	0	0	6	40	119	208	148	46	3	0	0	570
Mean Precipitation (in.)	1.06	0.72	1.84	2.48	3.56	4.19	4.32	4.77	3.37	2.55	2.10	0.85	31.81
Days With ≥ 0.1" Precipitation	3	2	4	6	7	7	8	8	6	5	5	3	64
Days With ≥ 1.0" Precipitation	0	0	0	0	1	1	1	2	1	1	0	0	7
Mean Snowfall (in.)	13.2	7.3	10.5	2.9	trace	0.0	0.0	0.0	trace	0.5	9.9	9.1	53.4
Days With ≥ 1.0" Snow Depth	29	25	20	3	0	0	0	0	0	0	9	25	111

Chaska *Carver County*   Elevation: 718 ft.   Latitude: 44° 48' N   Longitude: 93° 35' W

	JAN	FEB	MAR	APR	MAY	JUN	JUL	AUG	SEP	OCT	NOV	DEC	YEAR
Mean Maximum Temp. (°F)	23.9	30.6	42.0	59.5	72.7	81.9	85.5	82.4	73.4	61.0	41.5	28.2	56.9
Mean Temp. (°F)	13.8	20.6	32.4	47.8	60.3	69.7	73.8	71.2	62.0	49.8	33.1	19.7	46.2
Mean Minimum Temp. (°F)	3.6	10.6	22.7	35.9	47.8	57.4	62.1	59.9	50.4	38.6	24.8	11.1	35.4
Extreme Maximum Temp. (°F)	60	61	81	95	95	102	107	105	96	87	80	70	107
Extreme Minimum Temp. (°F)	-37	-37	-14	6	26	39	45	41	25	13	-14	-35	-37
Days Maximum Temp. ≥ 90°F	0	0	0	0	1	4	8	4	1	0	0	0	18
Days Maximum Temp. ≤ 32°F	22	14	6	0	0	0	0	0	0	0	6	18	66
Days Minimum Temp. ≤ 32°F	31	27	25	11	1	0	0	0	1	8	24	30	158
Days Minimum Temp. ≤ 0°F	13	8	2	0	0	0	0	0	0	0	1	7	31
Heating Degree Days (base 65°F)	1,585	1,250	1,004	517	190	29	4	14	150	470	949	1,399	7,561
Cooling Degree Days (base 65°F)	0	0	0	6	54	177	283	217	72	5	0	0	814
Mean Precipitation (in.)	0.91	0.60	1.84	2.46	3.70	4.19	4.47	4.46	3.10	2.32	2.06	0.81	30.92
Days With ≥ 0.1" Precipitation	3	2	5	5	7	7	7	7	6	5	4	2	60
Days With ≥ 1.0" Precipitation	0	0	0	0	1	1	1	1	1	1	0	0	6
Mean Snowfall (in.)	11.0	6.3	8.6	2.1	trace	0.0	0.0	0.0	trace	0.1	7.5	8.0	43.6
Days With ≥ 1.0" Snow Depth	27	24	14	1	0	0	0	0	0	0	7	18	91

Cloquet *Carlton County*   Elevation: 1,263 ft.   Latitude: 46° 42' N   Longitude: 92° 32' W

	JAN	FEB	MAR	APR	MAY	JUN	JUL	AUG	SEP	OCT	NOV	DEC	YEAR
Mean Maximum Temp. (°F)	18.5	26.1	36.6	52.7	67.7	76.0	80.3	77.4	67.3	54.2	35.6	23.0	51.3
Mean Temp. (°F)	8.5	15.3	26.2	40.4	53.3	62.0	67.3	65.2	56.0	44.2	28.1	14.3	40.1
Mean Minimum Temp. (°F)	-1.5	4.4	15.7	28.2	38.8	47.9	54.3	53.0	44.7	34.1	20.5	5.6	28.8
Extreme Maximum Temp. (°F)	50	57	73	85	92	96	101	95	96	86	70	54	101
Extreme Minimum Temp. (°F)	-42	-41	-30	-3	18	25	36	32	19	5	-20	-35	-42
Days Maximum Temp. ≥ 90°F	0	0	0	0	0	1	3	1	0	0	0	0	5
Days Maximum Temp. ≤ 32°F	27	19	10	1	0	0	0	0	0	0	12	25	94
Days Minimum Temp. ≤ 32°F	31	28	29	22	7	1	0	0	3	14	27	31	193
Days Minimum Temp. ≤ 0°F	17	11	5	0	0	0	0	0	0	0	2	12	47
Heating Degree Days (base 65°F)	1,749	1,399	1,198	730	366	127	39	70	282	639	1,101	1,566	9,266
Cooling Degree Days (base 65°F)	0	0	0	0	10	45	116	88	17	0	0	0	276
Mean Precipitation (in.)	1.17	0.77	1.69	2.06	3.25	4.19	4.27	4.28	4.09	2.77	2.08	1.06	31.68
Days With ≥ 0.1" Precipitation	3	2	5	5	7	8	8	7	7	5	5	3	65
Days With ≥ 1.0" Precipitation	0	0	0	0	1	1	1	1	1	1	0	0	6
Mean Snowfall (in.)	16.1	9.9	10.6	3.6	0.1	0.0	0.0	0.0	trace	0.8	11.0	13.3	65.4
Days With ≥ 1.0" Snow Depth	31	28	28	9	0	0	0	0	0	0	16	29	141

Collegeville Saint John *Stearns County*   Elevation: 1,223 ft.   Latitude: 45° 35' N   Longitude: 94° 24' W

	JAN	FEB	MAR	APR	MAY	JUN	JUL	AUG	SEP	OCT	NOV	DEC	YEAR
Mean Maximum Temp. (°F)	19.8	27.1	38.7	56.2	70.3	78.5	82.6	79.8	70.5	57.9	38.4	24.7	53.7
Mean Temp. (°F)	10.5	17.9	29.5	45.2	58.7	67.5	71.9	69.5	60.3	48.1	30.8	16.7	43.9
Mean Minimum Temp. (°F)	1.2	8.5	20.2	34.3	47.1	56.4	61.2	59.3	50.0	38.3	23.3	8.6	34.0
Extreme Maximum Temp. (°F)	54	56	75	95	95	101	103	100	97	89	78	61	103
Extreme Minimum Temp. (°F)	-36	-37	-17	2	25	37	44	40	25	13	-11	-35	-37
Days Maximum Temp. ≥ 90°F	0	0	0	0	0	2	4	2	1	0	0	0	9
Days Maximum Temp. ≤ 32°F	25	17	8	0	0	0	0	0	0	0	10	23	83
Days Minimum Temp. ≤ 32°F	31	27	26	13	1	0	0	0	0	8	25	31	162
Days Minimum Temp. ≤ 0°F	15	9	3	0	0	0	0	0	0	0	1	9	37
Heating Degree Days (base 65°F)	1,686	1,326	1,094	591	226	47	8	24	185	521	1,018	1,493	8,219
Cooling Degree Days (base 65°F)	0	0	0	4	41	131	234	181	50	4	0	0	645
Mean Precipitation (in.)	0.89	0.68	1.77	2.25	3.48	4.71	3.51	3.80	3.22	2.60	1.68	0.71	29.30
Days With ≥ 0.1" Precipitation	3	2	4	5	7	8	6	7	6	5	4	2	59
Days With ≥ 1.0" Precipitation	0	0	0	0	1	1	1	1	1	1	0	0	6
Mean Snowfall (in.)	12.2	7.4	9.7	3.2	trace	trace	0.0	0.0	trace	0.4	9.0	8.4	50.3
Days With ≥ 1.0" Snow Depth	29	26	19	3	0	0	0	0	0	0	9	23	109

Cotton *St. Louis County*   Elevation: 1,328 ft.   Latitude: 47° 10' N   Longitude: 92° 28' W

	JAN	FEB	MAR	APR	MAY	JUN	JUL	AUG	SEP	OCT	NOV	DEC	YEAR
Mean Maximum Temp. (°F)	18.2	26.1	37.3	52.3	na	74.3	78.5	76.0	66.2	53.4	35.3	22.3	na
Mean Temp. (°F)	5.5	12.9	25.0	39.2	na	60.7	65.3	63.1	54.2	42.7	26.1	11.8	na
Mean Minimum Temp. (°F)	-7.1	-0.4	12.7	26.1	na	47.0	52.1	50.2	42.0	31.8	16.9	1.3	na
Extreme Maximum Temp. (°F)	52	59	72	87	93	96	100	96	97	82	72	52	100
Extreme Minimum Temp. (°F)	-50	-46	-40	-14	15	26	31	23	19	-2	-30	-44	-50
Days Maximum Temp. ≥ 90°F	0	0	0	0	0	1	1	1	0	0	0	0	3
Days Maximum Temp. ≤ 32°F	28	19	10	1	0	0	0	0	0	1	13	25	97
Days Minimum Temp. ≤ 32°F	31	28	29	23	8	2	0	1	6	17	28	31	204
Days Minimum Temp. ≤ 0°F	20	14	7	1	0	0	0	0	0	0	3	15	60
Heating Degree Days (base 65°F)	1,840	1,467	1,234	768	na	159	67	111	331	685	1,161	1,646	na
Cooling Degree Days (base 65°F)	0	0	0	0	na	38	77	61	11	0	0	0	na
Mean Precipitation (in.)	*0.81*	0.55	1.05	2.03	na	4.29	5.03	3.50	3.23	2.44	1.65	0.75	na
Days With ≥ 0.1" Precipitation	3	2	3	5	5	8	8	6	7	5	4	3	59
Days With ≥ 1.0" Precipitation	0	0	0	0	0	1	1	1	1	0	0	0	4
Mean Snowfall (in.)	11.4	6.7	*7.8*	3.0	trace	0.0	0.0	0.0	trace	0.7	10.8	10.2	*50.6*
Days With ≥ 1.0" Snow Depth	31	28	24	6	0	0	0	0	0	0	14	28	131

Crookston NW Exp. Station *Polk County*   Elevation: 885 ft.   Latitude: 47° 48' N   Longitude: 96° 36' W

	JAN	FEB	MAR	APR	MAY	JUN	JUL	AUG	SEP	OCT	NOV	DEC	YEAR
Mean Maximum Temp. (°F)	14.0	21.3	33.3	53.0	69.0	77.0	81.4	80.4	69.4	55.2	33.9	20.1	50.7
Mean Temp. (°F)	4.2	11.5	24.4	42.0	56.5	65.3	69.5	67.9	57.3	44.3	25.8	11.2	40.0
Mean Minimum Temp. (°F)	-5.6	1.6	15.4	31.1	43.9	53.6	57.5	55.4	45.1	33.4	17.6	2.3	29.3
Extreme Maximum Temp. (°F)	49	49	70	96	95	99	104	104	98	88	73	56	104
Extreme Minimum Temp. (°F)	-41	-45	-31	-10	18	34	39	33	20	5	-30	-35	-45
Days Maximum Temp. ≥ 90°F	0	0	0	0	1	2	4	4	1	0	0	0	12
Days Maximum Temp. ≤ 32°F	28	22	13	2	0	0	0	0	0	1	14	26	106
Days Minimum Temp. ≤ 32°F	31	28	28	18	4	0	0	0	3	14	28	31	185
Days Minimum Temp. ≤ 0°F	20	14	6	0	0	0	0	0	0	0	3	14	57
Heating Degree Days (base 65°F)	1,891	1,509	1,254	684	290	80	24	45	259	635	1,171	1,664	9,506
Cooling Degree Days (base 65°F)	0	0	0	3	33	91	159	136	27	1	0	0	450
Mean Precipitation (in.)	0.54	0.50	0.78	1.34	2.58	3.44	3.04	2.92	2.28	1.82	0.88	0.51	20.63
Days With ≥ 0.1" Precipitation	2	1	2	3	5	6	6	6	5	4	2	1	43
Days With ≥ 1.0" Precipitation	0	0	0	0	0	1	1	1	1	0	0	0	4
Mean Snowfall (in.)	9.8	6.5	6.4	1.7	0.1	0.0	0.0	0.0	0.0	0.5	6.6	7.3	38.9
Days With ≥ 1.0" Snow Depth	29	24	17	3	0	0	0	0	0	0	11	24	108

Duluth Harbor Station *St. Louis County*   Elevation: 606 ft.   Latitude: 46° 46' N   Longitude: 92° 05' W

	JAN	FEB	MAR	APR	MAY	JUN	JUL	AUG	SEP	OCT	NOV	DEC	YEAR
Mean Maximum Temp. (°F)	19.3	24.9	33.3	45.2	55.4	66.2	74.2	72.6	64.1	52.3	36.9	24.7	47.4
Mean Temp. (°F)	11.2	16.8	26.5	38.4	48.0	57.7	66.3	65.8	57.3	46.3	31.5	18.0	40.3
Mean Minimum Temp. (°F)	3.0	8.6	19.7	31.6	40.7	49.4	58.3	58.9	50.4	40.1	26.1	11.3	33.2
Extreme Maximum Temp. (°F)	48	54	67	78	90	91	97	93	92	85	67	56	97
Extreme Minimum Temp. (°F)	-32	-37	-17	-14	22	30	41	40	29	14	-10	-27	-37
Days Maximum Temp. ≥ 90°F	0	0	0	0	0	0	0	0	0	0	0	0	0
Days Maximum Temp. ≤ 32°F	27	21	13	2	0	0	0	0	0	0	9	22	94
Days Minimum Temp. ≤ 32°F	31	28	28	15	2	0	0	0	0	3	22	30	159
Days Minimum Temp. ≤ 0°F	14	8	2	0	0	0	0	0	0	0	1	7	32
Heating Degree Days (base 65°F)	1,665	1,357	1,186	791	522	229	56	57	240	574	997	1,452	9,126
Cooling Degree Days (base 65°F)	0	0	0	0	4	19	*112*	102	16	0	0	0	*253*
Mean Precipitation (in.)	*0.88*	*0.55*	*1.35*	*1.50*	*2.49*	*3.46*	*3.59*	*3.69*	*3.70*	*2.23*	*1.47*	*0.85*	*25.76*
Days With ≥ 0.1" Precipitation	na	*2*	*4*	*4*	na	*6*	*5*	*6*	*6*	*4*	*4*	*2*	na
Days With ≥ 1.0" Precipitation	*0*	*0*	*0*	*0*	*1*	*1*	*1*	*1*	*1*	*0*	*0*	*0*	*5*
Mean Snowfall (in.)	*10.4*	na	*7.0*	*1.7*	trace	trace	trace	0.0	trace	*0.1*	*4.0*	na	na
Days With ≥ 1.0" Snow Depth	na	na	*20*	4	0	0	0	0	0	0	*5*	na	na

Fairmont *Martin County*   Elevation: 1,184 ft.   Latitude: 43° 38' N   Longitude: 94° 28' W

	JAN	FEB	MAR	APR	MAY	JUN	JUL	AUG	SEP	OCT	NOV	DEC	YEAR
Mean Maximum Temp. (°F)	22.2	28.7	40.4	56.5	70.6	80.0	82.9	80.5	72.4	59.4	40.5	26.9	55.1
Mean Temp. (°F)	13.3	20.0	31.8	46.4	59.7	69.2	72.5	70.2	61.6	49.1	32.5	18.8	45.4
Mean Minimum Temp. (°F)	4.4	11.3	23.2	36.3	48.8	58.3	62.1	59.9	50.7	38.7	24.4	10.6	35.7
Extreme Maximum Temp. (°F)	64	63	79	90	94	100	100	100	97	91	79	65	100
Extreme Minimum Temp. (°F)	-33	-28	-17	9	27	39	42	41	27	14	-13	-24	-33
Days Maximum Temp. ≥ 90°F	0	0	0	0	1	3	5	3	1	0	0	0	13
Days Maximum Temp. ≤ 32°F	23	16	8	1	0	0	0	0	0	0	8	21	77
Days Minimum Temp. ≤ 32°F	31	27	26	10	1	0	0	0	1	7	24	31	158
Days Minimum Temp. ≤ 0°F	13	7	2	0	0	0	0	0	0	0	1	8	31
Heating Degree Days (base 65°F)	1,599	1,265	1,022	556	205	35	7	18	156	491	969	1,427	7,750
Cooling Degree Days (base 65°F)	0	0	0	5	44	167	251	193	61	5	0	0	726
Mean Precipitation (in.)	0.78	0.69	1.96	3.18	3.90	4.39	4.18	4.19	2.73	2.43	2.02	0.99	31.44
Days With ≥ 0.1" Precipitation	2	2	4	6	7	7	7	6	6	4	4	2	57
Days With ≥ 1.0" Precipitation	0	0	0	1	1	1	1	1	1	1	0	0	7
Mean Snowfall (in.)	9.5	6.2	8.3	3.2	trace	0.0	0.0	0.0	0.0	0.6	6.0	8.7	42.5
Days With ≥ 1.0" Snow Depth	26	20	12	2	0	0	0	0	0	0	7	20	87

Faribault *Rice County*   Elevation: 938 ft.   Latitude: 44° 18' N   Longitude: 93° 16' W

	JAN	FEB	MAR	APR	MAY	JUN	JUL	AUG	SEP	OCT	NOV	DEC	YEAR
Mean Maximum Temp. (°F)	21.9	28.4	39.9	56.6	70.0	79.4	83.1	80.4	72.0	59.6	40.9	27.3	55.0
Mean Temp. (°F)	11.8	18.3	30.5	45.2	58.0	67.5	71.6	69.1	60.4	48.3	32.2	18.4	44.3
Mean Minimum Temp. (°F)	1.6	8.1	21.0	33.8	45.9	55.6	60.1	57.9	48.8	36.9	23.5	9.5	33.5
Extreme Maximum Temp. (°F)	58	65	81	93	94	102	102	104	99	92	78	68	104
Extreme Minimum Temp. (°F)	-40	-36	-17	0	24	33	41	38	24	11	-15	-36	-40
Days Maximum Temp. ≥ 90°F	0	0	0	0	1	3	6	3	1	0	0	0	14
Days Maximum Temp. ≤ 32°F	24	16	8	1	0	0	0	0	0	0	7	20	76
Days Minimum Temp. ≤ 32°F	31	28	26	14	2	0	0	0	1	11	25	30	168
Days Minimum Temp. ≤ 0°F	15	9	3	0	0	0	0	0	0	0	1	8	36
Heating Degree Days (base 65°F)	1,646	1,315	1,063	592	250	55	11	30	188	517	978	1,437	8,082
Cooling Degree Days (base 65°F)	0	0	0	5	34	135	216	159	52	4	0	0	605
Mean Precipitation (in.)	1.04	0.69	1.94	2.85	3.70	4.03	4.33	4.38	3.35	2.36	2.06	1.00	31.73
Days With ≥ 0.1" Precipitation	3	2	5	6	8	7	6	7	6	5	5	3	63
Days With ≥ 1.0" Precipitation	0	0	0	1	1	1	1	1	1	1	0	0	7
Mean Snowfall (in.)	10.7	6.5	8.2	3.0	0.0	0.0	0.0	0.0	0.0	trace	5.8	8.6	42.8
Days With ≥ 1.0" Snow Depth	28	24	16	2	0	0	0	0	0	0	7	21	98

Farmington 3 NW *Dakota County*   Elevation: 977 ft.   Latitude: 44° 40' N   Longitude: 93° 11' W

	JAN	FEB	MAR	APR	MAY	JUN	JUL	AUG	SEP	OCT	NOV	DEC	YEAR
Mean Maximum Temp. (°F)	21.2	28.1	40.1	57.8	71.2	79.6	83.0	80.2	71.6	59.3	40.2	26.5	54.9
Mean Temp. (°F)	12.3	19.3	31.3	46.7	59.5	68.3	71.9	69.3	60.6	48.7	32.2	18.4	44.9
Mean Minimum Temp. (°F)	3.3	10.4	22.4	35.7	47.8	57.0	60.7	58.2	49.5	38.1	24.2	10.3	34.8
Extreme Maximum Temp. (°F)	59	59	79	93	94	102	104	101	96	91	77	67	104
Extreme Minimum Temp. (°F)	-36	-33	-15	5	24	38	40	40	25	12	-19	-35	-36
Days Maximum Temp. ≥ 90°F	0	0	0	0	1	3	5	3	1	0	0	0	13
Days Maximum Temp. ≤ 32°F	24	16	7	0	0	0	0	0	0	0	8	20	75
Days Minimum Temp. ≤ 32°F	31	27	25	11	1	0	0	0	1	9	24	30	159
Days Minimum Temp. ≤ 0°F	13	8	2	0	0	0	0	0	0	0	1	8	32
Heating Degree Days (base 65°F)	1,631	1,286	1,039	547	210	40	8	24	180	502	977	1,438	7,882
Cooling Degree Days (base 65°F)	0	0	0	5	46	152	232	171	58	4	0	0	668
Mean Precipitation (in.)	0.89	0.70	1.98	2.71	3.70	4.37	4.04	4.44	3.25	2.35	2.07	1.02	31.52
Days With ≥ 0.1" Precipitation	3	2	5	6	8	8	7	7	6	5	5	3	65
Days With ≥ 1.0" Precipitation	0	0	0	0	1	1	1	1	1	1	0	0	6
Mean Snowfall (in.)	*10.6*	7.1	9.0	3.1	trace	0.0	0.0	0.0	trace	0.2	7.9	8.0	*45.9*
Days With ≥ 1.0" Snow Depth	29	23	15	1	0	0	0	0	0	0	8	22	98

Fergus Falls *Otter Tail County*   Elevation: 1,250 ft.   Latitude: 46° 18' N   Longitude: 96° 07' W

	JAN	FEB	MAR	APR	MAY	JUN	JUL	AUG	SEP	OCT	NOV	DEC	YEAR
Mean Maximum Temp. (°F)	16.3	22.9	35.1	53.2	68.2	76.2	80.7	79.2	69.4	56.0	36.0	22.2	51.3
Mean Temp. (°F)	6.6	13.3	26.2	42.7	56.9	65.7	70.2	68.3	58.3	45.6	28.1	13.6	41.3
Mean Minimum Temp. (°F)	-3.2	3.7	17.3	32.2	45.6	55.1	59.7	57.4	47.1	35.0	20.2	5.0	31.3
Extreme Maximum Temp. (°F)	55	56	73	94	92	99	101	102	96	88	74	54	102
Extreme Minimum Temp. (°F)	-38	-40	-23	-2	23	31	42	40	22	10	-20	-35	-40
Days Maximum Temp. ≥ 90°F	0	0	0	0	0	2	4	3	1	0	0	0	10
Days Maximum Temp. ≤ 32°F	27	20	11	1	0	0	0	0	0	0	12	24	95
Days Minimum Temp. ≤ 32°F	31	28	28	16	2	0	0	0	1	12	27	31	176
Days Minimum Temp. ≤ 0°F	18	12	4	0	0	0	0	0	0	0	2	12	48
Heating Degree Days (base 65°F)	1,808	1,455	1,194	664	271	73	18	39	235	598	1,100	1,588	9,043
Cooling Degree Days (base 65°F)	0	0	0	3	30	98	177	146	36	1	0	0	491
Mean Precipitation (in.)	1.00	0.55	1.47	1.54	2.67	3.79	3.26	3.20	2.21	2.12	1.14	0.51	23.46
Days With ≥ 0.1" Precipitation	2	2	4	4	6	7	6	5	4	4	3	2	49
Days With ≥ 1.0" Precipitation	0	0	0	0	0	1	1	1	1	0	0	0	4
Mean Snowfall (in.)	13.3	5.8	8.0	1.7	trace	0.0	0.0	0.0	0.0	0.3	7.3	7.9	44.3
Days With ≥ 1.0" Snow Depth	27	23	15	2	0	0	0	0	0	0	9	19	95

Forest Lake 5 NE *Chisago County*   Elevation: 958 ft.   Latitude: 45° 21' N   Longitude: 92° 55' W

	JAN	FEB	MAR	APR	MAY	JUN	JUL	AUG	SEP	OCT	NOV	DEC	YEAR
Mean Maximum Temp. (°F)	21.8	29.1	40.5	57.4	70.6	78.4	82.1	79.7	70.8	58.8	40.3	26.7	54.7
Mean Temp. (°F)	12.0	19.2	30.8	46.1	59.0	67.5	71.8	69.6	60.6	48.9	32.4	18.3	44.7
Mean Minimum Temp. (°F)	2.2	9.2	21.0	34.7	47.4	56.6	61.4	59.6	50.4	38.9	24.3	9.8	34.6
Extreme Maximum Temp. (°F)	50	57	76	88	91	99	104	102	92	86	75	65	104
Extreme Minimum Temp. (°F)	-38	-37	-17	2	22	37	45	41	27	13	-14	-37	-38
Days Maximum Temp. ≥ 90°F	0	0	0	0	1	2	3	2	0	0	0	0	8
Days Maximum Temp. ≤ 32°F	23	15	7	0	0	0	0	0	0	0	7	21	73
Days Minimum Temp. ≤ 32°F	31	27	26	13	1	0	0	0	0	7	24	31	160
Days Minimum Temp. ≤ 0°F	14	9	2	0	0	0	0	0	0	0	1	8	34
Heating Degree Days (base 65°F)	1,641	1,289	1,054	565	218	47	8	23	178	497	973	1,444	7,937
Cooling Degree Days (base 65°F)	0	0	0	4	44	144	239	196	59	4	0	0	690
Mean Precipitation (in.)	0.96	0.75	1.61	2.41	3.50	4.56	4.54	4.60	3.26	2.69	1.94	0.95	31.77
Days With ≥ 0.1" Precipitation	3	3	4	6	7	8	7	7	7	6	5	3	66
Days With ≥ 1.0" Precipitation	0	0	0	0	1	1	1	1	1	1	0	0	6
Mean Snowfall (in.)	10.4	6.5	8.9	3.0	trace	0.0	0.0	0.0	trace	0.3	8.6	8.9	46.6
Days With ≥ 1.0" Snow Depth	30	27	21	3	0	0	0	0	0	0	9	24	114

Fosston 1 E *Polk County*   Elevation: 1,309 ft.   Latitude: 47° 34' N   Longitude: 95° 43' W

	JAN	FEB	MAR	APR	MAY	JUN	JUL	AUG	SEP	OCT	NOV	DEC	YEAR
Mean Maximum Temp. (°F)	13.8	21.7	34.5	52.2	67.7	75.6	79.8	78.5	67.7	54.5	33.9	20.2	50.0
Mean Temp. (°F)	3.0	10.6	24.1	40.5	54.8	63.5	67.3	65.7	55.3	43.4	25.4	10.8	38.7
Mean Minimum Temp. (°F)	-7.9	-0.5	13.7	28.7	41.9	51.3	54.8	52.9	42.8	32.3	16.8	1.4	27.4
Extreme Maximum Temp. (°F)	46	52	70	96	94	98	100	103	97	88	72	55	103
Extreme Minimum Temp. (°F)	-50	-53	-35	-9	19	31	34	28	19	4	-24	-40	-53
Days Maximum Temp. ≥ 90°F	0	0	0	0	0	1	3	2	1	0	0	0	7
Days Maximum Temp. ≤ 32°F	28	21	12	2	0	0	0	0	0	1	14	25	103
Days Minimum Temp. ≤ 32°F	31	28	29	21	6	0	0	0	4	17	28	31	195
Days Minimum Temp. ≤ 0°F	21	15	6	0	0	0	0	0	0	0	3	14	59
Heating Degree Days (base 65°F)	1,923	1,532	1,263	730	333	107	44	70	307	663	1,183	1,676	9,831
Cooling Degree Days (base 65°F)	0	0	0	2	24	61	109	91	15	1	0	0	303
Mean Precipitation (in.)	0.64	0.49	0.94	1.45	2.62	4.34	4.02	3.51	2.81	2.46	0.94	0.56	24.78
Days With ≥ 0.1" Precipitation	2	2	3	4	6	8	7	7	5	5	3	2	54
Days With ≥ 1.0" Precipitation	0	0	0	0	0	1	1	1	1	0	0	0	4
Mean Snowfall (in.)	9.6	5.9	7.3	2.2	0.2	0.0	0.0	0.0	trace	1.1	8.0	7.3	41.6
Days With ≥ 1.0" Snow Depth	26	23	19	4	0	0	0	0	0	1	10	21	104

Gaylord *Sibley County*   Elevation: 1,017 ft.   Latitude: 44° 33' N   Longitude: 94° 13' W

	JAN	FEB	MAR	APR	MAY	JUN	JUL	AUG	SEP	OCT	NOV	DEC	YEAR
Mean Maximum Temp. (°F)	21.3	28.3	39.8	57.2	71.6	80.8	84.4	81.2	72.6	59.8	40.1	26.7	55.3
Mean Temp. (°F)	12.0	19.1	30.9	46.3	59.8	69.2	73.1	70.1	60.9	48.7	31.9	18.3	45.0
Mean Minimum Temp. (°F)	2.7	10.0	21.9	35.3	48.0	57.5	61.8	59.0	49.2	37.6	23.7	9.8	34.7
Extreme Maximum Temp. (°F)	53	61	83	93	97	103	105	104	98	88	77	65	105
Extreme Minimum Temp. (°F)	-32	-34	-13	5	26	38	44	42	23	14	-16	-34	-34
Days Maximum Temp. ≥ 90°F	0	0	0	0	1	4	7	3	1	0	0	0	16
Days Maximum Temp. ≤ 32°F	24	16	8	0	0	0	0	0	0	0	8	20	76
Days Minimum Temp. ≤ 32°F	31	27	26	12	1	0	0	0	1	9	24	31	162
Days Minimum Temp. ≤ 0°F	14	8	2	0	0	0	0	0	0	0	1	8	33
Heating Degree Days (base 65°F)	1,640	1,288	1,052	561	202	35	6	19	169	501	985	1,443	7,901
Cooling Degree Days (base 65°F)	0	0	0	6	48	166	264	189	52	3	0	0	728
Mean Precipitation (in.)	0.67	0.61	1.60	2.61	3.39	4.68	3.60	4.40	3.02	2.19	1.71	0.72	29.20
Days With ≥ 0.1" Precipitation	2	2	4	5	7	7	6	6	5	4	3	2	53
Days With ≥ 1.0" Precipitation	0	0	0	1	1	1	1	1	1	1	0	0	7
Mean Snowfall (in.)	9.1	5.7	9.3	1.8	trace	0.0	0.0	0.0	0.0	0.3	5.4	8.3	39.9
Days With ≥ 1.0" Snow Depth	*24*	*19*	13	1	0	0	0	0	0	0	5	15	*77*

Glenwood 2 WNW *Pope County*   Elevation: 1,197 ft.   Latitude: 45° 40' N   Longitude: 95° 27' W

	JAN	FEB	MAR	APR	MAY	JUN	JUL	AUG	SEP	OCT	NOV	DEC	YEAR
Mean Maximum Temp. (°F)	20.2	26.7	37.7	56.5	70.0	78.5	82.7	80.5	71.2	58.6	39.0	25.4	53.9
Mean Temp. (°F)	10.4	17.1	28.5	44.6	57.5	66.0	70.7	68.6	58.9	47.0	30.0	16.3	43.0
Mean Minimum Temp. (°F)	0.6	7.5	19.3	32.5	44.9	53.9	58.7	56.7	46.5	35.3	20.9	7.2	32.0
Extreme Maximum Temp. (°F)	50	58	78	98	93	102	103	102	93	87	77	*60*	*103*
Extreme Minimum Temp. (°F)	-34	-35	-20	-3	25	34	42	36	24	11	-22	*-32*	*-35*
Days Maximum Temp. ≥ 90°F	0	0	0	0	0	2	5	3	1	0	0	0	11
Days Maximum Temp. ≤ 32°F	25	17	10	1	0	0	0	0	0	0	9	22	84
Days Minimum Temp. ≤ 32°F	31	28	28	16	2	0	0	0	2	12	27	31	177
Days Minimum Temp. ≤ 0°F	16	10	3	0	0	0	0	0	0	0	2	10	41
Heating Degree Days (base 65°F)	1,690	1,350	1,125	610	254	66	14	30	216	554	1,045	1,504	8,458
Cooling Degree Days (base 65°F)	0	0	0	4	29	101	187	149	39	1	0	0	510
Mean Precipitation (in.)	0.62	0.45	1.25	1.78	3.34	4.05	3.31	3.39	2.31	2.57	1.23	0.41	24.71
Days With ≥ 0.1" Precipitation	2	1	3	5	7	7	6	6	4	5	*3*	2	*51*
Days With ≥ 1.0" Precipitation	0	0	0	0	1	1	1	1	0	1	0	0	5
Mean Snowfall (in.)	*9.4*	5.4	7.3	2.2	trace	0.0	0.0	0.0	0.0	0.4	5.6	*5.8*	*36.1*
Days With ≥ 1.0" Snow Depth	26	23	*16*	*1*	0	0	0	0	0	0	9	*21*	*96*

Grand Marais *Cook County*   Elevation: 610 ft.   Latitude: 47° 44' N   Longitude: 90° 22' W

	JAN	FEB	MAR	APR	MAY	JUN	JUL	AUG	SEP	OCT	NOV	DEC	YEAR
Mean Maximum Temp. (°F)	22.4	26.6	34.6	45.7	55.1	62.8	69.5	70.6	62.4	51.4	37.8	27.4	47.2
Mean Temp. (°F)	13.6	17.8	26.9	38.0	46.6	53.4	60.4	62.4	54.8	44.3	31.4	19.6	39.1
Mean Minimum Temp. (°F)	4.7	9.1	19.1	30.2	38.0	43.9	51.2	54.1	47.2	37.0	25.0	11.8	30.9
Extreme Maximum Temp. (°F)	47	58	67	81	87	93	94	90	87	79	67	51	94
Extreme Minimum Temp. (°F)	-33	-33	-17	-8	23	32	38	35	28	13	-14	-22	-33
Days Maximum Temp. ≥ 90°F	0	0	0	0	0	0	0	0	0	0	0	0	0
Days Maximum Temp. ≤ 32°F	25	19	11	1	0	0	0	0	0	0	7	19	82
Days Minimum Temp. ≤ 32°F	31	28	28	18	4	0	0	0	1	9	23	30	172
Days Minimum Temp. ≤ 0°F	13	8	2	0	0	0	0	0	0	0	1	7	31
Heating Degree Days (base 65°F)	1,591	1,327	1,176	803	566	345	158	107	304	637	1,000	1,401	9,415
Cooling Degree Days (base 65°F)	0	0	0	0	0	2	23	37	5	0	0	0	67
Mean Precipitation (in.)	0.76	0.56	1.12	1.35	2.59	3.39	3.54	3.04	3.50	2.77	1.74	0.83	25.19
Days With ≥ 0.1" Precipitation	3	2	3	3	6	7	7	6	6	6	4	3	56
Days With ≥ 1.0" Precipitation	0	0	0	0	0	1	1	1	1	1	0	0	5
Mean Snowfall (in.)	17.5	7.9	7.7	1.8	trace	0.0	0.0	0.0	0.0	0.2	3.9	12.6	51.6
Days With ≥ 1.0" Snow Depth	31	28	29	8	0	0	0	0	0	0	6	23	125

Grand Meadow *Mower County*   Elevation: 1,348 ft.   Latitude: 43° 42' N   Longitude: 92° 34' W

	JAN	FEB	MAR	APR	MAY	JUN	JUL	AUG	SEP	OCT	NOV	DEC	YEAR
Mean Maximum Temp. (°F)	20.3	26.6	37.8	54.2	68.0	77.8	81.2	79.0	70.9	58.3	40.2	25.9	53.3
Mean Temp. (°F)	11.3	17.7	29.4	44.0	57.1	66.9	70.7	68.3	59.6	47.6	31.9	17.8	43.5
Mean Minimum Temp. (°F)	2.2	8.7	21.0	33.9	46.0	56.0	60.1	57.6	48.3	36.9	23.5	9.7	33.7
Extreme Maximum Temp. (°F)	55	63	75	91	94	102	100	101	97	92	76	62	102
Extreme Minimum Temp. (°F)	-32	-35	-16	1	22	34	40	39	26	10	-16	-29	-35
Days Maximum Temp. ≥ 90°F	0	0	0	0	0	2	3	2	1	0	0	0	8
Days Maximum Temp. ≤ 32°F	26	18	9	1	0	0	0	0	0	0	8	22	84
Days Minimum Temp. ≤ 32°F	31	28	27	14	2	0	0	0	1	10	24	31	168
Days Minimum Temp. ≤ 0°F	14	9	2	0	0	0	0	0	0	0	1	8	34
Heating Degree Days (base 65°F)	1,663	1,331	1,096	627	272	59	16	35	200	536	987	1,456	8,278
Cooling Degree Days (base 65°F)	0	0	0	5	31	127	196	151	48	3	0	0	561
Mean Precipitation (in.)	1.01	0.74	1.87	3.42	4.18	4.17	4.79	4.89	3.60	2.60	2.14	1.01	34.42
Days With ≥ 0.1" Precipitation	3	2	4	7	8	8	7	7	6	5	4	3	64
Days With ≥ 1.0" Precipitation	0	0	0	1	1	1	1	1	1	1	0	0	7
Mean Snowfall (in.)	*13.5*	8.2	*7.4*	2.6	0.0	0.0	0.0	0.0	0.0	0.4	5.4	9.4	*46.9*
Days With ≥ 1.0" Snow Depth	na	na	na	*1*	0	0	0	0	0	0	na	na	na

Grand Rapids Forestry Lab *Itasca County*   Elevation: 1,309 ft.   Latitude: 47° 15' N   Longitude: 93° 30' W

	JAN	FEB	MAR	APR	MAY	JUN	JUL	AUG	SEP	OCT	NOV	DEC	YEAR
Mean Maximum Temp. (°F)	17.3	25.8	37.4	53.8	68.2	76.3	80.3	78.0	67.3	54.5	35.4	22.0	51.4
Mean Temp. (°F)	6.3	13.8	26.1	41.4	54.7	63.5	67.8	65.5	55.6	44.1	27.3	12.5	39.9
Mean Minimum Temp. (°F)	-4.7	1.8	14.8	29.0	41.2	50.6	55.3	53.0	43.8	33.6	19.1	3.0	28.4
Extreme Maximum Temp. (°F)	51	59	69	93	93	96	100	100	97	84	71	53	100
Extreme Minimum Temp. (°F)	-43	-41	-29	-5	19	30	34	31	22	5	-23	-40	-43
Days Maximum Temp. ≥ 90°F	0	0	0	0	0	1	2	1	0	0	0	0	4
Days Maximum Temp. ≤ 32°F	28	19	10	1	0	0	0	0	0	1	13	24	96
Days Minimum Temp. ≤ 32°F	31	28	29	20	5	0	0	0	3	15	28	31	190
Days Minimum Temp. ≤ 0°F	19	13	6	0	0	0	0	0	0	0	2	14	54
Heating Degree Days (base 65°F)	1,818	1,442	1,198	703	331	106	35	68	295	643	1,126	1,622	9,387
Cooling Degree Days (base 65°F)	0	0	0	2	19	70	128	97	16	0	0	0	332
Mean Precipitation (in.)	1.01	0.60	1.24	1.84	2.78	4.58	4.64	3.57	3.06	2.78	1.51	0.89	28.50
Days With ≥ 0.1" Precipitation	3	2	4	5	7	8	8	7	7	6	4	3	64
Days With ≥ 1.0" Precipitation	0	0	0	0	0	1	1	1	1	1	0	0	5
Mean Snowfall (in.)	14.4	7.5	9.0	3.4	0.5	0.0	0.0	0.0	trace	1.1	9.5	11.3	56.7
Days With ≥ 1.0" Snow Depth	*24*	21	*19*	4	0	0	0	0	0	0	na	*22*	na

Gull Lake Dam *Cass County*   Elevation: 1,213 ft.   Latitude: 46° 25' N   Longitude: 94° 22' W

	JAN	FEB	MAR	APR	MAY	JUN	JUL	AUG	SEP	OCT	NOV	DEC	YEAR
Mean Maximum Temp. (°F)	18.0	25.8	36.7	53.7	68.1	76.1	80.3	77.9	68.0	55.3	36.1	22.7	51.6
Mean Temp. (°F)	7.6	14.9	26.4	41.9	55.8	65.0	69.6	67.3	57.6	45.4	28.3	13.8	41.1
Mean Minimum Temp. (°F)	-2.6	4.0	16.0	30.0	43.5	53.9	58.9	56.7	47.1	35.4	20.5	4.9	30.7
Extreme Maximum Temp. (°F)	55	56	71	95	90	96	101	102	96	84	73	57	102
Extreme Minimum Temp. (°F)	-41	-45	-21	-4	22	36	42	39	23	7	-20	-38	-45
Days Maximum Temp. ≥ 90°F	0	0	0	0	0	1	3	2	0	0	0	0	6
Days Maximum Temp. ≤ 32°F	27	18	10	1	0	0	0	0	0	0	11	24	91
Days Minimum Temp. ≤ 32°F	30	28	28	19	3	0	0	0	1	12	26	30	177
Days Minimum Temp. ≤ 0°F	17	12	4	0	0	0	0	0	0	0	2	11	46
Heating Degree Days (base 65°F)	1,774	1,410	1,192	688	299	77	21	42	245	601	1,094	1,581	9,024
Cooling Degree Days (base 65°F)	0	0	0	2	19	80	165	119	24	0	0	0	409
Mean Precipitation (in.)	0.78	0.53	1.41	1.78	3.04	4.23	3.86	3.66	2.64	2.69	1.30	0.55	26.47
Days With ≥ 0.1" Precipitation	3	2	4	5	6	8	7	7	5	4	3	2	56
Days With ≥ 1.0" Precipitation	0	0	0	0	1	1	1	1	1	1	0	0	6
Mean Snowfall (in.)	na	na	9.6	2.8	0.2	0.0	0.0	0.0	0.0	0.6	na	na	na
Days With ≥ 1.0" Snow Depth	na	na	na	7	0	0	0	0	0	0	na	na	na

Hibbing Chisholm-Hibbing Airport *St. Louis County*   Elevation: 1,345 ft.   Latitude: 47° 23' N   Longitude: 92° 51' W

	JAN	FEB	MAR	APR	MAY	JUN	JUL	AUG	SEP	OCT	NOV	DEC	YEAR
Mean Maximum Temp. (°F)	15.6	23.2	34.5	50.7	65.1	73.1	77.2	75.0	64.5	51.7	33.3	20.5	48.7
Mean Temp. (°F)	5.0	12.3	24.2	39.1	52.2	60.9	65.5	63.2	53.3	41.8	25.4	11.4	37.8
Mean Minimum Temp. (°F)	-5.5	1.3	13.8	27.5	39.2	48.6	53.7	51.3	42.1	31.8	17.4	2.2	26.9
Extreme Maximum Temp. (°F)	48	57	64	89	92	97	100	95	94	82	72	53	100
Extreme Minimum Temp. (°F)	-50	-44	-37	-4	19	30	35	29	20	0	-27	-38	-50
Days Maximum Temp. ≥ 90°F	0	0	0	0	0	1	1	1	0	0	0	0	3
Days Maximum Temp. ≤ 32°F	28	21	13	2	0	0	0	0	0	1	14	27	106
Days Minimum Temp. ≤ 32°F	30	28	29	22	8	0	0	0	5	17	28	31	198
Days Minimum Temp. ≤ 0°F	19	13	6	0	0	0	0	0	0	0	3	14	55
Heating Degree Days (base 65°F)	1,859	1,485	1,258	770	400	154	62	107	356	713	1,182	1,659	10,005
Cooling Degree Days (base 65°F)	0	0	0	0	7	39	80	59	9	0	0	0	194
Mean Precipitation (in.)	0.78	0.58	0.98	1.52	2.58	4.24	4.69	3.40	3.19	2.56	1.34	0.77	26.63
Days With ≥ 0.1" Precipitation	2	2	3	4	6	9	8	6	7	5	4	3	59
Days With ≥ 1.0" Precipitation	0	0	0	0	0	1	1	1	1	1	0	0	5
Mean Snowfall (in.)	15.0	8.5	10.0	4.1	0.3	trace	trace	trace	trace	1.0	11.5	11.6	62.0
Days With ≥ 1.0" Snow Depth	31	28	25	6	0	0	0	0	0	1	14	28	133

Hutchinson 1 N *McLeod County*   Elevation: 1,092 ft.   Latitude: 44° 56' N   Longitude: 94° 22' W

	JAN	FEB	MAR	APR	MAY	JUN	JUL	AUG	SEP	OCT	NOV	DEC	YEAR
Mean Maximum Temp. (°F)	20.9	27.7	39.4	56.8	70.7	79.6	83.2	80.7	72.3	59.4	39.7	25.9	54.7
Mean Temp. (°F)	10.9	18.1	30.4	45.9	59.1	68.3	72.3	69.7	60.7	48.2	31.4	17.2	44.3
Mean Minimum Temp. (°F)	0.9	8.4	21.3	34.9	47.4	56.9	61.3	58.6	49.0	37.0	23.0	8.4	33.9
Extreme Maximum Temp. (°F)	61	60	80	95	95	102	102	104	98	89	81	65	104
Extreme Minimum Temp. (°F)	-39	-36	-15	3	25	37	44	41	22	12	-18	-34	-39
Days Maximum Temp. ≥ 90°F	0	0	0	0	1	3	5	3	1	0	0	0	13
Days Maximum Temp. ≤ 32°F	24	17	8	0	0	0	0	0	0	0	8	22	79
Days Minimum Temp. ≤ 32°F	31	27	26	12	1	0	0	0	1	10	25	31	164
Days Minimum Temp. ≤ 0°F	15	9	2	0	0	0	0	0	0	0	1	9	36
Heating Degree Days (base 65°F)	1,673	1,320	1,067	572	220	43	8	23	176	517	1,003	1,478	8,100
Cooling Degree Days (base 65°F)	0	0	0	5	43	146	239	173	51	3	0	0	660
Mean Precipitation (in.)	0.77	0.50	1.64	2.22	3.12	4.47	3.72	4.07	2.43	2.03	1.72	0.74	27.43
Days With ≥ 0.1" Precipitation	2	1	4	5	7	8	6	7	5	4	4	2	55
Days With ≥ 1.0" Precipitation	0	0	0	0	1	1	1	1	1	0	0	0	5
Mean Snowfall (in.)	9.6	5.1	7.9	2.3	trace	0.0	trace	0.0	trace	0.2	7.2	7.1	39.4
Days With ≥ 1.0" Snow Depth	*26*	22	14	1	0	0	0	0	0	0	7	20	*90*

Isle 12 N *Aitkin County*   Elevation: 1,282 ft.   Latitude: 46° 19' N   Longitude: 93° 32' W

	JAN	FEB	MAR	APR	MAY	JUN	JUL	AUG	SEP	OCT	NOV	DEC	YEAR
Mean Maximum Temp. (°F)	17.1	24.8	36.1	51.8	66.1	74.7	78.7	76.5	67.1	54.4	35.9	22.0	50.4
Mean Temp. (°F)	6.2	13.2	25.4	40.6	54.1	63.4	67.9	65.8	56.4	44.4	28.1	12.7	39.8
Mean Minimum Temp. (°F)	-4.8	1.5	14.6	29.5	42.0	52.0	56.9	55.0	45.7	34.3	20.2	3.4	29.2
Extreme Maximum Temp. (°F)	56	56	71	93	89	96	99	99	96	85	72	51	99
Extreme Minimum Temp. (°F)	-45	-44	-26	-6	19	28	34	31	18	4	-25	-46	-46
Days Maximum Temp. ≥ 90°F	0	0	0	0	0	1	2	1	0	0	0	0	4
Days Maximum Temp. ≤ 32°F	28	19	10	1	0	0	0	0	0	0	12	25	95
Days Minimum Temp. ≤ 32°F	31	28	28	19	5	0	0	0	2	*13*	27	31	*184*
Days Minimum Temp. ≤ 0°F	19	13	5	0	0	0	0	0	0	0	2	13	52
Heating Degree Days (base 65°F)	1,822	1,461	1,221	725	347	106	37	64	273	632	1,101	1,618	9,407
Cooling Degree Days (base 65°F)	0	0	0	2	14	66	134	94	19	0	0	0	329
Mean Precipitation (in.)	*0.62*	0.47	1.18	1.98	2.82	4.40	4.88	3.82	2.91	2.32	1.53	*0.74*	27.67
Days With ≥ 0.1" Precipitation	2	*2*	*4*	5	6	8	8	7	6	4	4	2	*58*
Days With ≥ 1.0" Precipitation	0	0	0	1	1	1	1	1	1	1	0	0	6
Mean Snowfall (in.)	12.0	*6.1*	na	2.2	trace	0.0	0.0	0.0	0.0	0.7	*5.2*	6.4	na
Days With ≥ 1.0" Snow Depth	na	na	na	4	0	0	0	0	0	0	*5*	22	na

Itasca Univ. of Minnesota *Clearwater County*   Elevation: 1,489 ft.   Latitude: 47° 13' N   Longitude: 95° 12' W

	JAN	FEB	MAR	APR	MAY	JUN	JUL	AUG	SEP	OCT	NOV	DEC	YEAR
Mean Maximum Temp. (°F)	16.4	24.8	36.4	53.0	67.7	75.6	79.9	78.1	67.2	53.9	34.3	21.1	50.7
Mean Temp. (°F)	4.6	12.0	24.5	40.0	54.0	62.9	67.4	65.4	55.1	43.1	25.8	11.2	38.8
Mean Minimum Temp. (°F)	-7.2	-0.8	12.6	27.0	40.2	50.2	54.8	52.6	43.0	32.2	17.3	1.4	26.9
Extreme Maximum Temp. (°F)	53	63	71	96	93	95	100	101	97	84	74	54	101
Extreme Minimum Temp. (°F)	-46	-52	-34	-15	19	28	38	33	21	5	-29	-40	-52
Days Maximum Temp. ≥ 90°F	0	0	0	0	0	1	3	2	0	0	0	0	6
Days Maximum Temp. ≤ 32°F	28	19	11	1	0	0	0	0	0	1	14	25	99
Days Minimum Temp. ≤ 32°F	31	28	29	23	8	0	0	0	4	17	28	31	199
Days Minimum Temp. ≤ 0°F	20	15	7	0	0	0	0	0	0	0	3	14	59
Heating Degree Days (base 65°F)	1,871	1,492	1,248	744	353	118	41	72	310	672	1,170	1,662	9,753
Cooling Degree Days (base 65°F)	0	0	0	2	15	59	112	88	14	0	0	0	290
Mean Precipitation (in.)	0.91	0.60	1.32	1.80	2.77	4.23	3.88	3.55	3.01	2.61	1.30	0.77	26.75
Days With ≥ 0.1" Precipitation	3	2	3	4	6	8	7	6	6	5	3	3	56
Days With ≥ 1.0" Precipitation	0	0	0	0	0	1	1	1	1	1	0	0	5
Mean Snowfall (in.)	11.8	7.0	9.2	3.2	trace	0.0	0.0	0.0	trace	1.3	8.7	8.5	49.7
Days With ≥ 1.0" Snow Depth	31	28	27	7	0	0	0	0	0	1	14	28	136

Jordan 1 S *Scott County*   Elevation: 928 ft.   Latitude: 44° 39' N   Longitude: 93° 37' W

	JAN	FEB	MAR	APR	MAY	JUN	JUL	AUG	SEP	OCT	NOV	DEC	YEAR
Mean Maximum Temp. (°F)	21.9	28.3	39.9	57.6	70.8	79.2	82.6	79.6	71.4	59.2	40.3	26.9	54.8
Mean Temp. (°F)	11.4	18.1	30.1	45.5	58.2	67.0	70.7	67.8	59.3	47.4	31.2	17.5	43.7
Mean Minimum Temp. (°F)	0.9	7.9	20.2	33.3	45.6	54.7	58.7	56.0	47.2	35.7	22.1	8.0	32.5
Extreme Maximum Temp. (°F)	59	61	80	93	95	102	105	101	95	90	77	67	105
Extreme Minimum Temp. (°F)	-41	-36	-21	3	18	34	39	33	20	3	-20	-41	-41
Days Maximum Temp. ≥ 90°F	0	0	0	0	1	3	5	2	1	0	0	0	12
Days Maximum Temp. ≤ 32°F	24	16	7	0	0	0	0	0	0	0	8	20	75
Days Minimum Temp. ≤ 32°F	31	28	27	14	3	0	0	0	2	12	26	31	174
Days Minimum Temp. ≤ 0°F	15	10	3	0	0	0	0	0	0	0	1	10	39
Heating Degree Days (base 65°F)	1,658	1,319	1,075	583	241	56	13	39	208	540	1,007	1,469	8,208
Cooling Degree Days (base 65°F)	0	0	0	0	33	120	192	134	42	3	0	0	529
Mean Precipitation (in.)	0.75	0.50	1.62	2.45	3.42	4.40	3.93	4.66	3.10	2.28	1.71	0.74	29.56
Days With ≥ 0.1" Precipitation	2	2	4	5	7	7	7	7	6	4	4	2	57
Days With ≥ 1.0" Precipitation	0	0	0	0	1	1	1	1	1	0	0	0	5
Mean Snowfall (in.)	na	3.3	3.9	1.5	trace	0.0	0.0	0.0	trace	0.1	2.2	5.3	na
Days With ≥ 1.0" Snow Depth	na	na	na	0	0	0	0	0	0	0	0	4	na

Lake Wilson *Murray County*   Elevation: 1,646 ft.   Latitude: 44° 00' N   Longitude: 95° 57' W

	JAN	FEB	MAR	APR	MAY	JUN	JUL	AUG	SEP	OCT	NOV	DEC	YEAR
Mean Maximum Temp. (°F)	22.6	28.8	40.5	56.8	70.7	79.6	83.5	80.3	72.8	59.8	40.2	26.9	55.2
Mean Temp. (°F)	13.3	19.7	31.2	45.6	58.7	67.8	72.2	69.3	60.8	48.2	31.4	18.4	44.7
Mean Minimum Temp. (°F)	4.0	10.6	21.9	34.3	46.6	56.0	60.9	58.2	48.9	36.5	22.6	9.8	34.2
Extreme Maximum Temp. (°F)	64	63	80	91	96	105	104	100	101	92	79	64	105
Extreme Minimum Temp. (°F)	-29	-26	-17	5	23	36	45	41	23	10	-16	-28	-29
Days Maximum Temp. ≥ 90°F	0	0	0	0	0	3	6	3	1	0	0	0	13
Days Maximum Temp. ≤ 32°F	23	16	8	1	0	0	0	0	0	0	8	20	76
Days Minimum Temp. ≤ 32°F	31	27	26	13	2	0	0	0	1	11	25	31	167
Days Minimum Temp. ≤ 0°F	13	8	2	0	0	0	0	0	0	0	1	8	32
Heating Degree Days (base 65°F)	1,599	1,271	1,041	581	226	47	11	28	176	516	1,001	1,440	7,937
Cooling Degree Days (base 65°F)	0	0	0	0	5	40	139	230	168	57	3	0	642
Mean Precipitation (in.)	0.69	0.66	2.02	2.86	3.11	3.94	3.28	3.82	2.73	2.00	1.52	0.67	27.30
Days With ≥ 0.1" Precipitation	2	2	4	6	7	7	5	5	5	4	3	2	52
Days With ≥ 1.0" Precipitation	0	0	0	0	1	1	1	1	1	1	0	0	6
Mean Snowfall (in.)	9.1	6.3	9.4	2.6	trace	0.0	0.0	0.0	trace	0.8	7.7	7.4	43.3
Days With ≥ 1.0" Snow Depth	na	19	na	1	0	0	0	0	0	0	7	16	na

Lamberton SW Exp. Station *Redwood County*   Elevation: 1,141 ft.   Latitude: 44° 15' N   Longitude: 95° 19' W

	JAN	FEB	MAR	APR	MAY	JUN	JUL	AUG	SEP	OCT	NOV	DEC	YEAR
Mean Maximum Temp. (°F)	21.9	28.1	39.3	56.2	71.0	80.4	83.3	80.8	73.1	60.2	40.6	27.0	55.2
Mean Temp. (°F)	11.8	18.3	30.2	44.9	58.7	68.5	71.9	69.1	60.2	47.7	31.1	17.6	44.2
Mean Minimum Temp. (°F)	1.7	8.5	21.1	33.6	46.3	56.6	60.3	57.4	47.3	35.2	21.6	8.2	33.2
Extreme Maximum Temp. (°F)	66	65	78	95	98	106	105	106	102	91	81	68	106
Extreme Minimum Temp. (°F)	-34	-30	-23	3	22	35	40	39	20	10	-15	-31	-34
Days Maximum Temp. ≥ 90°F	0	0	0	0	2	5	6	4	2	0	0	0	19
Days Maximum Temp. ≤ 32°F	23	16	9	1	0	0	0	0	0	0	8	19	76
Days Minimum Temp. ≤ 32°F	31	28	27	14	2	0	0	0	2	13	25	31	173
Days Minimum Temp. ≤ 0°F	15	9	2	0	0	0	0	0	0	0	2	9	37
Heating Degree Days (base 65°F)	1,646	1,314	1,072	601	238	46	13	32	192	535	1,009	1,465	8,163
Cooling Degree Days (base 65°F)	0	0	0	6	49	159	228	165	53	5	0	0	665
Mean Precipitation (in.)	0.65	0.49	1.78	2.76	3.14	3.90	3.57	3.33	2.67	2.00	1.42	0.58	26.29
Days With ≥ 0.1" Precipitation	2	2	4	6	6	6	6	6	5	4	3	2	52
Days With ≥ 1.0" Precipitation	0	0	0	1	1	1	1	1	1	0	0	0	6
Mean Snowfall (in.)	9.7	6.0	8.6	2.8	0.0	0.0	0.0	0.0	0.0	0.3	7.1	7.2	41.7
Days With ≥ 1.0" Snow Depth	24	19	11	2	0	0	0	0	0	0	8	19	83

Leech Lake Dam *Cass County*   Elevation: 1,299 ft.   Latitude: 47° 15' N   Longitude: 94° 13' W

	JAN	FEB	MAR	APR	MAY	JUN	JUL	AUG	SEP	OCT	NOV	DEC	YEAR
Mean Maximum Temp. (°F)	17.1	26.5	37.7	53.7	67.8	75.9	79.8	77.8	67.6	54.7	35.4	22.4	51.4
Mean Temp. (°F)	6.1	14.8	26.4	41.5	55.1	64.1	68.5	66.2	56.6	44.6	27.6	13.3	40.4
Mean Minimum Temp. (°F)	-4.8	2.3	15.0	29.2	42.3	52.3	57.2	54.6	45.5	34.5	19.7	4.1	29.3
Extreme Maximum Temp. (°F)	53	60	69	94	91	95	99	100	95	83	72	54	100
Extreme Minimum Temp. (°F)	-42	-46	-28	-9	21	33	40	31	24	3	-22	-38	-46
Days Maximum Temp. ≥ 90°F	0	0	0	0	0	1	2	1	0	0	0	0	4
Days Maximum Temp. ≤ 32°F	27	18	10	1	0	0	0	0	0	1	13	25	95
Days Minimum Temp. ≤ 32°F	31	28	29	20	5	0	0	0	2	13	27	31	186
Days Minimum Temp. ≤ 0°F	19	13	5	0	0	0	0	0	0	0	2	13	52
Heating Degree Days (base 65°F)	1,825	1,415	1,189	700	322	92	27	56	268	627	1,117	1,600	9,238
Cooling Degree Days (base 65°F)	0	0	0	2	19	71	139	104	19	0	0	0	354
Mean Precipitation (in.)	0.76	0.49	1.03	1.63	2.60	3.82	4.36	3.55	2.79	2.60	1.14	0.72	25.49
Days With ≥ 0.1" Precipitation	3	2	3	4	6	7	8	6	6	5	3	3	56
Days With ≥ 1.0" Precipitation	0	0	0	0	0	1	1	1	0	1	0	0	4
Mean Snowfall (in.)	12.3	6.8	7.9	2.7	trace	0.0	0.0	0.0	trace	0.8	6.9	9.1	46.5
Days With ≥ 1.0" Snow Depth	30	25	22	7	0	0	0	0	0	1	13	27	125

Litchfield *Meeker County*   Elevation: 1,131 ft.   Latitude: 45° 08' N   Longitude: 94° 32' W

	JAN	FEB	MAR	APR	MAY	JUN	JUL	AUG	SEP	OCT	NOV	DEC	YEAR
Mean Maximum Temp. (°F)	20.7	27.9	39.6	57.3	71.4	80.1	83.7	81.0	72.4	59.5	39.2	25.6	54.9
Mean Temp. (°F)	11.0	18.3	30.3	45.9	59.3	68.5	72.5	69.9	60.7	48.5	31.0	17.2	44.4
Mean Minimum Temp. (°F)	1.3	8.6	20.9	34.5	47.2	56.8	61.2	58.8	48.9	37.4	22.8	8.7	33.9
Extreme Maximum Temp. (°F)	60	58	77	93	93	101	104	104	98	87	78	62	104
Extreme Minimum Temp. (°F)	-37	-37	-17	-1	25	35	43	39	24	11	-14	-34	-37
Days Maximum Temp. ≥ 90°F	0	0	0	0	1	3	6	4	1	0	0	0	15
Days Maximum Temp. ≤ 32°F	24	16	7	0	0	0	0	0	0	0	9	22	78
Days Minimum Temp. ≤ 32°F	31	28	26	13	2	0	0	0	1	9	26	31	167
Days Minimum Temp. ≤ 0°F	15	9	3	0	0	0	0	0	0	0	2	9	38
Heating Degree Days (base 65°F)	1,671	1,315	1,070	571	217	43	6	22	177	509	1,012	1,477	8,090
Cooling Degree Days (base 65°F)	0	0	0	5	46	148	234	175	50	3	0	0	661
Mean Precipitation (in.)	0.80	0.62	1.54	2.35	3.36	4.96	4.06	3.69	2.94	2.25	1.48	0.66	28.71
Days With ≥ 0.1" Precipitation	3	2	3	5	6	7	6	6	5	4	4	2	53
Days With ≥ 1.0" Precipitation	0	0	0	0	1	1	1	1	1	1	0	0	6
Mean Snowfall (in.)	10.3	6.2	8.3	2.3	trace	0.0	0.0	0.0	0.0	0.3	*9.1*	*7.5*	*44.0*
Days With ≥ 1.0" Snow Depth	na	16	14	1	0	0	0	0	0	0	na	na	na

Little Falls 1 N *Morrison County*   Elevation: 1,118 ft.   Latitude: 46° 00' N   Longitude: 94° 21' W

	JAN	FEB	MAR	APR	MAY	JUN	JUL	AUG	SEP	OCT	NOV	DEC	YEAR
Mean Maximum Temp. (°F)	20.0	27.8	39.4	57.2	71.4	79.5	83.8	81.3	71.9	58.5	38.4	24.7	54.5
Mean Temp. (°F)	9.4	16.8	28.8	44.6	58.1	67.0	71.5	69.0	59.6	47.3	29.9	15.6	43.1
Mean Minimum Temp. (°F)	-1.2	5.7	18.0	31.9	44.8	54.4	59.2	56.6	47.3	35.9	21.3	6.4	31.7
Extreme Maximum Temp. (°F)	54	58	75	95	95	99	102	101	99	89	75	59	102
Extreme Minimum Temp. (°F)	-41	-38	-28	-5	22	35	40	36	17	5	-19	-42	-42
Days Maximum Temp. ≥ 90°F	0	0	0	0	1	3	6	4	1	0	0	0	15
Days Maximum Temp. ≤ 32°F	26	17	7	0	0	0	0	0	0	0	9	23	82
Days Minimum Temp. ≤ 32°F	31	28	27	16	3	0	0	0	2	12	27	31	177
Days Minimum Temp. ≤ 0°F	17	10	4	0	0	0	0	0	0	0	2	11	44
Heating Degree Days (base 65°F)	1,720	1,358	1,117	608	242	53	11	30	199	546	1,046	1,528	8,458
Cooling Degree Days (base 65°F)	0	0	0	3	37	123	225	169	43	2	0	0	602
Mean Precipitation (in.)	0.79	0.53	1.44	1.96	3.04	4.26	3.46	3.44	2.80	2.54	1.44	0.61	26.31
Days With ≥ 0.1" Precipitation	2	2	4	5	7	8	7	6	5	4	4	2	56
Days With ≥ 1.0" Precipitation	0	0	0	0	1	1	1	1	1	1	0	0	6
Mean Snowfall (in.)	12.7	7.4	9.2	2.3	trace	0.0	0.0	0.0	trace	0.6	8.2	8.4	48.8
Days With ≥ 1.0" Snow Depth	*18*	19	17	3	0	0	0	0	0	0	7	15	*79*

Long Prairie *Todd County*   Elevation: 1,289 ft.   Latitude: 45° 59' N   Longitude: 94° 52' W

	JAN	FEB	MAR	APR	MAY	JUN	JUL	AUG	SEP	OCT	NOV	DEC	YEAR
Mean Maximum Temp. (°F)	18.8	26.8	37.9	55.9	70.1	78.2	82.6	80.2	70.5	57.8	37.6	23.9	53.3
Mean Temp. (°F)	8.8	16.4	28.0	44.0	57.4	66.3	70.7	68.4	58.8	46.7	29.3	15.2	42.5
Mean Minimum Temp. (°F)	-1.2	5.7	17.9	32.1	44.8	54.3	58.7	56.5	47.0	35.6	21.0	6.5	31.6
Extreme Maximum Temp. (°F)	56	59	74	95	94	100	103	102	95	89	76	58	103
Extreme Minimum Temp. (°F)	-40	-44	-26	-7	19	32	38	34	19	4	-16	-39	-44
Days Maximum Temp. ≥ 90°F	0	0	0	0	0	2	5	3	0	0	0	0	10
Days Maximum Temp. ≤ 32°F	26	17	9	1	0	0	0	0	0	0	10	23	86
Days Minimum Temp. ≤ 32°F	31	28	28	16	3	0	0	0	2	12	27	31	178
Days Minimum Temp. ≤ 0°F	17	11	4	0	0	0	0	0	0	0	2	11	45
Heating Degree Days (base 65°F)	1,739	1,365	1,142	625	262	65	15	38	218	563	1,063	1,539	8,634
Cooling Degree Days (base 65°F)	0	0	0	3	33	112	195	156	40	2	0	0	541
Mean Precipitation (in.)	1.27	0.80	1.96	2.28	3.13	4.28	3.97	3.45	2.93	2.64	1.70	0.90	29.31
Days With ≥ 0.1" Precipitation	4	2	5	5	6	8	7	6	5	4	4	3	59
Days With ≥ 1.0" Precipitation	0	0	0	0	1	1	1	1	1	1	0	0	6
Mean Snowfall (in.)	13.0	7.5	10.2	3.0	trace	0.0	0.0	0.0	trace	0.8	8.2	8.5	51.2
Days With ≥ 1.0" Snow Depth	30	27	23	5	0	0	0	0	0	0	10	25	120

Luverne *Rock County*   Elevation: 1,499 ft.   Latitude: 43° 40' N   Longitude: 96° 12' W

	JAN	FEB	MAR	APR	MAY	JUN	JUL	AUG	SEP	OCT	NOV	DEC	YEAR
Mean Maximum Temp. (°F)	23.8	30.7	43.0	59.2	71.9	81.4	84.9	82.6	74.7	61.7	41.2	28.4	57.0
Mean Temp. (°F)	13.9	20.7	32.9	46.8	59.1	69.1	72.8	70.6	61.6	49.0	31.8	19.1	45.6
Mean Minimum Temp. (°F)	4.0	10.8	22.8	34.3	46.2	56.7	60.8	58.4	48.5	36.2	22.4	9.7	34.2
Extreme Maximum Temp. (°F)	65	66	85	94	94	104	106	103	104	91	78	66	106
Extreme Minimum Temp. (°F)	-37	-32	-20	6	23	34	40	38	20	9	-16	-28	-37
Days Maximum Temp. ≥ 90°F	0	0	0	0	1	4	9	5	2	0	0	0	21
Days Maximum Temp. ≤ 32°F	22	14	6	0	0	0	0	0	0	0	7	19	68
Days Minimum Temp. ≤ 32°F	31	28	26	13	2	0	0	0	2	11	26	31	170
Days Minimum Temp. ≤ 0°F	13	7	1	0	0	0	0	0	0	0	1	8	30
Heating Degree Days (base 65°F)	1,581	1,244	987	544	215	35	8	20	160	493	988	1,418	7,693
Cooling Degree Days (base 65°F)	0	0	0	5	40	158	240	192	59	5	0	0	699
Mean Precipitation (in.)	0.62	0.66	2.19	2.60	3.28	4.31	3.62	3.28	2.66	2.28	1.74	0.79	28.03
Days With ≥ 0.1" Precipitation	2	2	5	6	7	7	6	5	5	4	4	2	55
Days With ≥ 1.0" Precipitation	0	0	0	0	1	1	1	1	1	1	0	0	6
Mean Snowfall (in.)	10.0	6.7	9.5	2.0	trace	0.0	0.0	0.0	trace	0.9	7.5	8.1	44.7
Days With ≥ 1.0" Snow Depth	26	21	13	2	0	0	0	0	0	0	8	19	89

Madison Sewage Plant *Lac Qui Parle County*   Elevation: 1,079 ft.   Latitude: 45° 00' N   Longitude: 96° 11' W

	JAN	FEB	MAR	APR	MAY	JUN	JUL	AUG	SEP	OCT	NOV	DEC	YEAR
Mean Maximum Temp. (°F)	23.0	29.9	41.1	58.7	73.1	81.9	85.8	83.7	75.4	62.6	42.1	28.8	57.2
Mean Temp. (°F)	12.7	19.8	31.2	46.3	59.8	69.4	73.3	70.9	61.7	49.7	32.3	19.1	45.5
Mean Minimum Temp. (°F)	2.4	9.6	21.2	33.9	46.4	56.9	60.8	58.1	47.7	36.7	22.5	9.3	33.8
Extreme Maximum Temp. (°F)	67	66	76	94	96	105	110	110	100	94	80	63	110
Extreme Minimum Temp. (°F)	-35	-36	-20	0	21	38	41	34	17	11	-16	-35	-36
Days Maximum Temp. ≥ 90°F	0	0	0	0	1	5	10	7	3	0	0	0	26
Days Maximum Temp. ≤ 32°F	22	15	7	0	0	0	0	0	0	0	6	18	68
Days Minimum Temp. ≤ 32°F	31	28	27	13	2	0	0	0	1	10	26	31	169
Days Minimum Temp. ≤ 0°F	15	8	2	0	0	0	0	0	0	0	1	9	35
Heating Degree Days (base 65°F)	1,618	1,271	1,041	559	202	33	6	20	160	475	973	1,416	7,774
Cooling Degree Days (base 65°F)	0	0	0	5	52	177	267	217	67	7	0	0	792
Mean Precipitation (in.)	0.75	0.63	1.49	2.24	2.93	3.84	3.45	2.99	2.13	2.58	1.31	0.45	24.79
Days With ≥ 0.1" Precipitation	2	2	4	5	6	7	6	6	5	4	3	1	51
Days With ≥ 1.0" Precipitation	0	0	0	0	1	1	1	1	0	1	0	0	5
Mean Snowfall (in.)	8.6	6.9	8.4	2.3	trace	0.0	0.0	0.0	trace	0.5	5.8	5.1	37.6
Days With ≥ 1.0" Snow Depth	na	na	8	1	0	0	0	0	0	0	na	na	na

Mahnomen 1 W *Mahnomen County*   Elevation: 1,200 ft.   Latitude: 47° 19' N   Longitude: 95° 59' W

	JAN	FEB	MAR	APR	MAY	JUN	JUL	AUG	SEP	OCT	NOV	DEC	YEAR
Mean Maximum Temp. (°F)	15.4	22.6	35.2	54.1	69.6	76.6	80.8	80.3	70.0	55.9	34.2	20.7	51.3
Mean Temp. (°F)	5.1	12.5	25.6	42.5	56.6	64.7	68.7	67.5	57.6	45.0	26.2	11.7	40.3
Mean Minimum Temp. (°F)	-5.1	2.2	15.9	30.8	43.5	52.7	56.6	54.7	45.2	34.1	18.2	2.8	29.3
Extreme Maximum Temp. (°F)	51	50	70	96	93	97	102	103	98	87	72	55	103
Extreme Minimum Temp. (°F)	-44	-48	-34	-10	19	32	37	31	21	5	-35	-39	-48
Days Maximum Temp. ≥ 90°F	0	0	0	0	0	1	3	4	1	0	0	0	9
Days Maximum Temp. ≤ 32°F	27	20	12	1	0	0	0	0	0	1	14	25	100
Days Minimum Temp. ≤ 32°F	31	28	28	18	5	0	0	0	3	14	27	31	185
Days Minimum Temp. ≤ 0°F	19	13	5	0	0	0	0	0	0	0	3	14	54
Heating Degree Days (base 65°F)	1,854	1,482	1,216	671	283	88	28	51	253	616	1,156	1,648	9,346
Cooling Degree Days (base 65°F)	0	0	0	3	30	85	149	144	36	2	0	0	449
Mean Precipitation (in.)	0.89	0.64	1.08	1.57	2.52	4.24	3.28	3.05	2.44	2.26	1.02	0.70	23.69
Days With ≥ 0.1" Precipitation	3	2	3	4	6	8	6	6	5	5	3	2	53
Days With ≥ 1.0" Precipitation	0	0	0	0	0	1	1	1	0	0	0	0	3
Mean Snowfall (in.)	10.2	6.5	7.5	2.6	trace	0.0	0.0	0.0	trace	1.4	7.9	7.6	43.7
Days With ≥ 1.0" Snow Depth	31	28	21	4	0	0	0	0	0	1	12	27	124

Marshall *Lyon County*   Elevation: 1,151 ft.   Latitude: 44° 28' N   Longitude: 95° 47' W

	JAN	FEB	MAR	APR	MAY	JUN	JUL	AUG	SEP	OCT	NOV	DEC	YEAR
Mean Maximum Temp. (°F)	22.5	29.0	40.1	56.8	71.0	80.5	83.7	81.5	72.7	59.8	40.5	26.7	55.4
Mean Temp. (°F)	12.9	19.5	31.1	45.9	59.2	69.2	72.6	70.3	61.0	48.5	31.9	18.0	45.0
Mean Minimum Temp. (°F)	3.0	10.0	21.9	34.8	47.5	57.5	61.6	59.1	49.3	36.9	23.1	9.6	34.5
Extreme Maximum Temp. (°F)	67	65	79	94	99	106	109	105	100	92	78	64	109
Extreme Minimum Temp. (°F)	-30	-30	-13	3	23	32	42	40	24	9	-15	-27	-30
Days Maximum Temp. ≥ 90°F	0	0	0	0	1	4	7	5	2	0	0	0	19
Days Maximum Temp. ≤ 32°F	22	16	8	1	0	0	0	0	0	0	8	20	75
Days Minimum Temp. ≤ 32°F	31	27	26	13	1	0	0	0	1	10	25	30	164
Days Minimum Temp. ≤ 0°F	14	8	2	0	0	0	0	0	0	0	1	9	34
Heating Degree Days (base 65°F)	1,612	1,279	1,046	570	218	37	8	23	177	511	987	1,453	7,921
Cooling Degree Days (base 65°F)	0	0	0	5	49	173	242	190	67	6	0	0	732
Mean Precipitation (in.)	0.82	0.56	1.84	2.40	3.06	3.69	3.51	3.18	2.37	2.06	1.60	0.78	25.87
Days With ≥ 0.1" Precipitation	2	2	4	5	6	6	6	5	5	4	4	2	51
Days With ≥ 1.0" Precipitation	0	0	0	1	1	1	1	1	1	1	0	0	7
Mean Snowfall (in.)	9.5	5.7	8.4	1.8	trace	0.0	0.0	0.0	0.0	0.8	7.6	8.3	42.1
Days With ≥ 1.0" Snow Depth	14	16	8	1	0	0	0	0	0	0	4	12	55

Melrose *Stearns County*   Elevation: 1,207 ft.   Latitude: 45° 41' N   Longitude: 94° 50' W

	JAN	FEB	MAR	APR	MAY	JUN	JUL	AUG	SEP	OCT	NOV	DEC	YEAR
Mean Maximum Temp. (°F)	19.6	27.0	38.6	56.7	71.1	79.4	83.7	80.9	71.4	58.4	38.1	24.6	54.1
Mean Temp. (°F)	9.4	16.8	28.8	44.7	58.3	67.2	71.6	69.2	59.6	47.0	29.6	15.7	43.2
Mean Minimum Temp. (°F)	-0.8	6.6	19.1	32.6	45.4	55.1	59.5	57.4	47.8	35.6	20.9	6.7	32.2
Extreme Maximum Temp. (°F)	59	57	74	95	96	102	103	101	98	90	77	58	103
Extreme Minimum Temp. (°F)	-39	-38	-18	-3	23	34	38	38	20	8	-19	-36	-39
Days Maximum Temp. ≥ 90°F	0	0	0	0	0	3	5	3	1	0	0	0	12
Days Maximum Temp. ≤ 32°F	25	17	8	0	0	0	0	0	0	0	10	23	83
Days Minimum Temp. ≤ 32°F	31	28	28	16	3	0	0	0	2	12	26	31	177
Days Minimum Temp. ≤ 0°F	16	10	3	0	0	0	0	0	0	0	2	10	41
Heating Degree Days (base 65°F)	1,722	1,356	1,114	606	238	53	9	29	201	552	1,057	1,525	8,462
Cooling Degree Days (base 65°F)	0	0	0	3	37	130	225	172	45	3	0	0	615
Mean Precipitation (in.)	0.87	0.60	1.59	2.24	3.26	4.33	3.44	3.48	2.81	2.54	1.47	0.62	27.25
Days With ≥ 0.1" Precipitation	3	2	4	5	7	7	6	6	5	5	4	2	56
Days With ≥ 1.0" Precipitation	0	0	0	0	1	1	1	1	1	1	0	0	6
Mean Snowfall (in.)	11.3	6.8	7.9	2.1	trace	0.0	0.0	0.0	0.0	0.4	6.7	6.5	41.7
Days With ≥ 1.0" Snow Depth	na	na	na	0	0	0	0	0	0	0	0	na	na

Milaca 1 ENE *Mille Lacs County*   Elevation: 1,092 ft.   Latitude: 45° 48' N   Longitude: 93° 40' W

	JAN	FEB	MAR	APR	MAY	JUN	JUL	AUG	SEP	OCT	NOV	DEC	YEAR
Mean Maximum Temp. (°F)	19.4	26.9	37.8	55.1	68.8	77.2	81.7	79.2	69.9	56.9	38.2	24.6	53.0
Mean Temp. (°F)	8.8	16.4	28.1	43.7	56.6	65.5	70.2	67.5	58.1	45.9	29.7	15.4	42.2
Mean Minimum Temp. (°F)	-1.6	5.8	18.4	32.3	44.3	53.8	58.5	55.9	46.2	34.6	21.2	6.1	31.3
Extreme Maximum Temp. (°F)	52	56	73	94	93	103	104	100	98	90	72	61	104
Extreme Minimum Temp. (°F)	-38	-48	-18	-2	23	33	42	38	22	5	-17	-39	-48
Days Maximum Temp. ≥ 90°F	0	0	0	0	0	2	4	2	0	0	0	0	8
Days Maximum Temp. ≤ 32°F	26	17	8	1	0	0	0	0	0	0	9	23	84
Days Minimum Temp. ≤ 32°F	30	28	28	16	3	0	0	0	2	13	27	31	178
Days Minimum Temp. ≤ 0°F	16	11	3	0	0	0	0	0	0	0	2	11	43
Heating Degree Days (base 65°F)	1,738	1,369	1,137	635	277	73	17	41	233	587	1,053	1,533	8,693
Cooling Degree Days (base 65°F)	0	0	0	0	4	24	101	185	129	30	1	0	474
Mean Precipitation (in.)	0.74	0.56	1.39	2.06	3.16	4.30	3.98	4.00	2.93	2.41	1.59	0.78	27.90
Days With ≥ 0.1" Precipitation	2	2	4	5	7	8	7	6	6	5	4	2	58
Days With ≥ 1.0" Precipitation	0	0	0	0	1	1	1	1	1	1	0	0	6
Mean Snowfall (in.)	*12.3*	6.0	*6.1*	1.6	trace	0.0	0.0	0.0	0.0	0.3	*6.0*	7.9	*40.2*
Days With ≥ 1.0" Snow Depth	na	na	na	*1*	0	0	0	0	0	0	na	na	na

Milan 1 NW *Chippewa County*   Elevation: 1,017 ft.   Latitude: 45° 08' N   Longitude: 95° 56' W

	JAN	FEB	MAR	APR	MAY	JUN	JUL	AUG	SEP	OCT	NOV	DEC	YEAR
Mean Maximum Temp. (°F)	21.1	28.0	39.6	57.6	71.7	80.4	84.6	82.1	73.0	59.8	39.6	26.2	55.3
Mean Temp. (°F)	10.5	17.8	29.9	45.6	58.9	67.9	72.0	69.4	59.8	47.4	30.0	16.4	43.8
Mean Minimum Temp. (°F)	-0.2	7.5	20.2	33.6	46.0	55.4	59.3	56.7	46.6	34.9	20.4	6.6	32.2
Extreme Maximum Temp. (°F)	66	61	77	97	97	105	107	107	101	93	80	63	107
Extreme Minimum Temp. (°F)	-38	-35	-22	-3	16	34	37	34	19	9	-19	-35	-38
Days Maximum Temp. ≥ 90°F	0	0	0	0	1	4	8	5	2	0	0	0	20
Days Maximum Temp. ≤ 32°F	23	16	8	0	0	0	0	0	0	0	9	20	76
Days Minimum Temp. ≤ 32°F	31	28	27	14	2	0	0	0	2	13	27	31	175
Days Minimum Temp. ≤ 0°F	16	10	3	0	0	0	0	0	0	0	2	11	42
Heating Degree Days (base 65°F)	1,688	1,329	1,080	579	225	47	9	30	200	541	1,044	1,500	8,272
Cooling Degree Days (base 65°F)	0	0	0	5	45	139	222	170	48	4	0	0	633
Mean Precipitation (in.)	0.73	0.61	1.49	2.18	2.73	3.85	3.92	3.14	2.36	2.34	1.15	0.44	24.94
Days With ≥ 0.1" Precipitation	2	2	4	5	6	7	6	6	5	4	3	1	51
Days With ≥ 1.0" Precipitation	0	0	0	0	0	1	1	1	1	1	0	0	5
Mean Snowfall (in.)	11.2	7.9	9.1	2.6	trace	0.0	0.0	0.0	trace	0.7	6.7	6.6	44.8
Days With ≥ 1.0" Snow Depth	26	22	16	2	0	0	0	0	0	0	7	19	92

Montevideo 1 SW *Lac Qui Parle County*   Elevation: 984 ft.   Latitude: 44° 56' N   Longitude: 95° 45' W

	JAN	FEB	MAR	APR	MAY	JUN	JUL	AUG	SEP	OCT	NOV	DEC	YEAR
Mean Maximum Temp. (°F)	21.1	28.1	39.9	57.7	71.9	80.5	84.4	82.3	73.5	60.5	39.8	26.6	55.5
Mean Temp. (°F)	11.3	18.5	30.8	46.1	59.5	68.6	72.6	70.2	60.9	48.6	31.0	17.7	44.6
Mean Minimum Temp. (°F)	1.4	8.9	21.6	34.3	47.0	56.6	60.6	58.1	48.2	36.6	22.1	8.8	33.7
Extreme Maximum Temp. (°F)	69	64	78	100	96	105	110	110	103	92	77	63	110
Extreme Minimum Temp. (°F)	-37	-34	-20	0	23	37	35	35	21	12	-19	-32	-37
Days Maximum Temp. ≥ 90°F	0	0	0	0	1	4	8	5	2	0	0	0	20
Days Maximum Temp. ≤ 32°F	23	16	8	1	0	0	0	0	0	0	9	20	77
Days Minimum Temp. ≤ 32°F	31	28	26	13	2	0	0	0	1	11	26	31	169
Days Minimum Temp. ≤ 0°F	15	9	2	0	0	0	0	0	0	0	1	10	37
Heating Degree Days (base 65°F)	1,663	1,309	1,054	568	212	39	10	23	174	509	1,014	1,460	8,035
Cooling Degree Days (base 65°F)	0	0	0	7	49	151	245	192	52	5	0	0	701
Mean Precipitation (in.)	0.94	0.89	1.60	2.32	3.15	4.24	3.38	3.23	2.37	2.09	1.42	0.68	26.31
Days With ≥ 0.1" Precipitation	3	2	4	5	7	7	6	5	5	4	4	1	53
Days With ≥ 1.0" Precipitation	0	0	0	0	1	1	1	1	1	0	0	0	5
Mean Snowfall (in.)	10.6	*7.9*	9.7	2.0	trace	0.0	0.0	0.0	trace	0.6	8.5	7.4	*46.7*
Days With ≥ 1.0" Snow Depth	*22*	18	12	1	0	0	0	0	0	0	7	17	*77*

Moose Lake 1 SSE *Carlton County*   Elevation: 1,108 ft.   Latitude: 46° 26' N   Longitude: 92° 45' W

	JAN	FEB	MAR	APR	MAY	JUN	JUL	AUG	SEP	OCT	NOV	DEC	YEAR
Mean Maximum Temp. (°F)	19.3	27.0	37.7	53.9	68.0	76.3	81.1	78.0	68.3	55.8	36.8	23.7	52.2
Mean Temp. (°F)	8.1	15.1	26.7	41.0	53.4	62.1	67.7	65.6	56.4	44.8	28.5	14.2	40.3
Mean Minimum Temp. (°F)	-3.2	3.2	15.6	28.0	38.6	47.7	54.3	53.1	44.3	33.7	20.2	4.6	28.3
Extreme Maximum Temp. (°F)	54	57	73	92	90	94	101	98	97	87	72	57	101
Extreme Minimum Temp. (°F)	-53	-41	-32	-8	16	26	34	31	18	5	-31	-46	-53
Days Maximum Temp. ≥ 90°F	0	0	0	0	0	1	3	1	0	0	0	0	5
Days Maximum Temp. ≤ 32°F	27	18	9	1	0	0	0	0	0	0	11	25	91
Days Minimum Temp. ≤ 32°F	31	28	29	21	8	0	0	0	3	14	27	31	192
Days Minimum Temp. ≤ 0°F	17	12	5	0	0	0	0	0	0	0	2	12	48
Heating Degree Days (base 65°F)	1,763	1,406	1,181	716	364	128	32	66	274	621	1,088	1,572	9,211
Cooling Degree Days (base 65°F)	0	0	0	1	9	50	126	101	22	0	0	0	309
Mean Precipitation (in.)	0.94	0.64	1.46	1.98	3.07	4.43	4.34	3.96	3.56	2.59	1.86	0.85	29.68
Days With ≥ 0.1" Precipitation	3	2	4	5	7	8	7	7	7	6	4	3	63
Days With ≥ 1.0" Precipitation	0	0	0	0	1	1	1	1	1	1	0	0	6
Mean Snowfall (in.)	9.5	5.3	7.2	3.4	trace	0.0	0.0	0.0	0.0	0.7	7.2	7.2	40.5
Days With ≥ 1.0" Snow Depth	22	18	16	2	0	0	0	0	0	0	7	20	89

Mora *Kanabec County*   Elevation: 1,003 ft.   Latitude: 45° 53' N   Longitude: 93° 18' W

	JAN	FEB	MAR	APR	MAY	JUN	JUL	AUG	SEP	OCT	NOV	DEC	YEAR
Mean Maximum Temp. (°F)	20.0	27.6	39.0	55.6	69.6	77.8	82.0	79.7	69.8	57.3	38.5	24.8	53.5
Mean Temp. (°F)	7.2	15.3	27.4	42.8	55.6	64.1	68.5	66.3	56.5	44.8	28.5	13.7	40.9
Mean Minimum Temp. (°F)	-5.6	2.7	15.9	29.9	41.6	50.4	54.9	52.8	43.3	32.1	18.6	2.6	28.3
Extreme Maximum Temp. (°F)	53	57	76	94	93	99	102	104	97	91	74	59	104
Extreme Minimum Temp. (°F)	-46	-46	-22	-4	17	23	33	27	13	4	-25	-52	-52
Days Maximum Temp. ≥ 90°F	0	0	0	0	0	2	4	2	0	0	0	0	8
Days Maximum Temp. ≤ 32°F	26	17	8	1	0	0	0	0	0	0	9	23	84
Days Minimum Temp. ≤ 32°F	31	28	29	18	6	0	0	0	4	16	27	31	190
Days Minimum Temp. ≤ 0°F	19	12	5	0	0	0	0	0	0	0	2	13	51
Heating Degree Days (base 65°F)	1,790	1,399	1,158	662	305	95	32	58	273	619	1,089	1,585	9,065
Cooling Degree Days (base 65°F)	0	0	0	2	19	74	132	100	22	1	0	0	350
Mean Precipitation (in.)	0.83	0.64	1.65	2.19	3.23	3.94	3.95	3.93	3.07	2.55	1.80	0.78	28.56
Days With ≥ 0.1" Precipitation	3	2	4	5	7	8	7	7	6	5	4	2	60
Days With ≥ 1.0" Precipitation	0	0	0	0	1	1	1	1	1	1	0	0	6
Mean Snowfall (in.)	11.3	6.5	8.0	1.8	trace	0.0	0.0	0.0	0.0	0.3	7.2	8.1	43.2
Days With ≥ 1.0" Snow Depth	30	24	17	2	0	0	0	0	0	0	8	26	107

Morris WC Exp. Station *Stevens County*   Elevation: 1,138 ft.   Latitude: 45° 35' N   Longitude: 95° 53' W

	JAN	FEB	MAR	APR	MAY	JUN	JUL	AUG	SEP	OCT	NOV	DEC	YEAR
Mean Maximum Temp. (°F)	17.2	24.0	35.5	53.9	68.8	77.4	81.3	79.7	70.3	57.2	37.3	23.5	52.2
Mean Temp. (°F)	7.5	14.5	27.0	43.4	57.2	66.4	70.3	68.2	58.1	45.5	28.6	14.6	41.8
Mean Minimum Temp. (°F)	-2.3	5.0	18.5	32.9	45.5	55.3	59.2	56.5	45.9	33.7	19.9	5.6	31.3
Extreme Maximum Temp. (°F)	60	59	73	98	97	104	102	103	96	89	78	60	104
Extreme Minimum Temp. (°F)	-37	-34	-18	0	21	34	40	36	20	7	-18	-32	-37
Days Maximum Temp. ≥ 90°F	0	0	0	0	1	2	4	3	1	0	0	0	11
Days Maximum Temp. ≤ 32°F	26	19	11	1	0	0	0	0	0	0	11	23	91
Days Minimum Temp. ≤ 32°F	31	28	28	15	2	0	0	0	2	14	27	31	178
Days Minimum Temp. ≤ 0°F	17	11	4	0	0	0	0	0	0	0	2	12	46
Heating Degree Days (base 65°F)	1,780	1,420	1,171	643	269	67	17	40	237	601	1,084	1,560	8,889
Cooling Degree Days (base 65°F)	0	0	0	3	36	115	187	145	38	2	0	0	526
Mean Precipitation (in.)	0.83	0.66	1.54	2.12	2.81	3.94	3.94	3.26	2.18	2.40	1.23	0.56	25.47
Days With ≥ 0.1" Precipitation	3	2	4	5	6	7	6	5	5	4	3	2	52
Days With ≥ 1.0" Precipitation	0	0	0	0	0	1	1	1	1	1	0	0	5
Mean Snowfall (in.)	11.6	7.8	9.7	3.3	trace	0.0	0.0	0.0	trace	0.9	7.3	6.9	47.5
Days With ≥ 1.0" Snow Depth	30	26	20	3	0	0	0	0	0	1	10	22	112

New London *Kandiyohi County*   Elevation: 1,240 ft.   Latitude: 45° 18' N   Longitude: 94° 56' W

	JAN	FEB	MAR	APR	MAY	JUN	JUL	AUG	SEP	OCT	NOV	DEC	YEAR
Mean Maximum Temp. (°F)	20.5	28.1	39.7	57.8	71.8	79.7	83.6	80.9	72.1	58.4	38.6	25.2	54.7
Mean Temp. (°F)	10.4	18.2	29.8	45.8	59.5	68.1	72.5	70.0	60.9	47.5	30.3	16.6	44.1
Mean Minimum Temp. (°F)	0.2	8.3	19.8	33.9	47.1	56.4	61.3	59.0	49.7	36.6	22.1	7.9	33.5
Extreme Maximum Temp. (°F)	60	56	76	95	95	102	104	102	99	88	78	58	104
Extreme Minimum Temp. (°F)	-38	-39	-18	0	20	37	46	41	25	10	-17	-35	-39
Days Maximum Temp. ≥ 90°F	0	0	0	0	1	3	6	3	1	0	0	0	14
Days Maximum Temp. ≤ 32°F	25	16	8	0	0	0	0	0	0	0	10	22	81
Days Minimum Temp. ≤ 32°F	31	28	27	14	2	0	0	0	1	10	25	31	169
Days Minimum Temp. ≤ 0°F	16	9	3	0	0	0	0	0	0	0	2	10	40
Heating Degree Days (base 65°F)	1,685	1,316	1,085	573	209	43	5	19	172	537	1,033	1,496	8,173
Cooling Degree Days (base 65°F)	0	0	0	4	44	141	241	184	51	3	0	0	668
Mean Precipitation (in.)	1.09	0.68	2.07	2.51	3.55	5.67	4.14	3.98	3.60	2.41	1.60	0.85	32.15
Days With ≥ 0.1" Precipitation	4	3	5	6	7	8	7	6	6	5	4	3	64
Days With ≥ 1.0" Precipitation	0	0	0	0	1	2	1	1	1	1	0	0	7
Mean Snowfall (in.)	12.1	7.1	10.7	3.2	trace	0.0	0.0	0.0	trace	0.6	9.9	9.1	52.7
Days With ≥ 1.0" Snow Depth	28	24	18	2	0	0	0	0	0	0	9	22	103

New Ulm 2 SE *Brown County*   Elevation: 859 ft.   Latitude: 44° 18' N   Longitude: 94° 27' W

	JAN	FEB	MAR	APR	MAY	JUN	JUL	AUG	SEP	OCT	NOV	DEC	YEAR
Mean Maximum Temp. (°F)	22.8	29.6	41.5	58.7	72.2	80.9	84.0	81.3	73.4	61.1	41.2	27.5	56.2
Mean Temp. (°F)	13.3	20.3	32.4	47.3	60.1	69.2	72.9	70.3	61.8	49.8	32.9	19.1	45.8
Mean Minimum Temp. (°F)	3.7	10.9	23.3	35.8	47.9	57.5	61.8	59.3	50.2	38.4	24.6	10.7	35.3
Extreme Maximum Temp. (°F)	65	63	82	95	94	103	105	100	99	89	80	67	105
Extreme Minimum Temp. (°F)	-37	-33	-18	6	27	35	43	41	23	12	-17	-36	-37
Days Maximum Temp. ≥ 90°F	0	0	0	0	1	4	7	4	1	0	0	0	17
Days Maximum Temp. ≤ 32°F	23	15	7	0	0	0	0	0	0	0	7	20	72
Days Minimum Temp. ≤ 32°F	31	27	25	11	1	0	0	0	1	9	23	30	158
Days Minimum Temp. ≤ 0°F	14	8	2	0	0	0	0	0	0	0	1	8	33
Heating Degree Days (base 65°F)	1,601	1,257	1,004	531	197	35	8	20	155	471	956	1,418	7,653
Cooling Degree Days (base 65°F)	0	0	0	6	47	160	248	184	61	5	0	0	711
Mean Precipitation (in.)	0.72	0.64	2.06	2.66	3.22	4.44	4.00	3.88	2.89	2.28	1.84	0.75	29.38
Days With ≥ 0.1" Precipitation	2	2	5	6	7	7	6	6	6	4	4	2	57
Days With ≥ 1.0" Precipitation	0	0	0	1	1	1	1	1	1	1	0	0	7
Mean Snowfall (in.)	9.6	6.3	8.8	2.2	trace	0.0	0.0	0.0	trace	0.5	7.3	7.9	42.6
Days With ≥ 1.0" Snow Depth	25	21	12	1	0	0	0	0	0	0	6	19	84

Ottertail *Otter Tail County*   Elevation: 977 ft.   Latitude: 46° 25' N   Longitude: 95° 34' W

	JAN	FEB	MAR	APR	MAY	JUN	JUL	AUG	SEP	OCT	NOV	DEC	YEAR
Mean Maximum Temp. (°F)	18.0	25.5	37.3	54.9	69.5	77.5	82.0	79.9	69.9	56.7	36.7	23.4	52.6
Mean Temp. (°F)	7.5	14.8	27.2	43.4	57.7	66.6	71.2	69.1	59.2	46.6	28.7	14.2	42.2
Mean Minimum Temp. (°F)	-3.0	4.1	17.0	31.9	45.7	55.5	60.3	58.2	48.5	36.5	20.6	4.9	31.7
Extreme Maximum Temp. (°F)	56	59	71	94	92	98	102	101	97	87	71	56	102
Extreme Minimum Temp. (°F)	-40	-45	-28	-7	24	36	40	36	25	10	-21	-38	-45
Days Maximum Temp. ≥ 90°F	0	0	0	0	0	2	4	3	1	0	0	0	10
Days Maximum Temp. ≤ 32°F	26	18	9	1	0	0	0	0	0	0	11	24	89
Days Minimum Temp. ≤ 32°F	31	28	28	16	3	0	0	0	1	10	26	31	174
Days Minimum Temp. ≤ 0°F	18	12	4	0	0	0	0	0	0	0	2	12	48
Heating Degree Days (base 65°F)	1,781	1,413	1,167	644	254	58	11	29	211	565	1,084	1,572	8,789
Cooling Degree Days (base 65°F)	0	0	0	3	35	117	214	172	42	2	0	0	585
Mean Precipitation (in.)	0.86	0.59	1.37	2.05	3.11	4.57	3.89	3.33	2.45	2.51	1.11	0.54	26.38
Days With ≥ 0.1" Precipitation	3	3	4	5	7	8	7	6	5	5	4	3	60
Days With ≥ 1.0" Precipitation	0	0	0	0	1	1	1	1	0	1	0	0	5
Mean Snowfall (in.)	14.0	8.8	10.5	4.0	trace	trace	0.0	0.0	trace	1.4	9.9	8.6	57.2
Days With ≥ 1.0" Snow Depth	31	27	20	3	0	0	0	0	0	0	12	25	118

Owatonna *Steele County*   Elevation: 1,148 ft.   Latitude: 44° 06' N   Longitude: 93° 14' W

	JAN	FEB	MAR	APR	MAY	JUN	JUL	AUG	SEP	OCT	NOV	DEC	YEAR
Mean Maximum Temp. (°F)	22.3	29.2	41.3	58.2	71.6	81.1	84.3	81.8	73.8	60.9	41.4	27.5	56.1
Mean Temp. (°F)	13.1	19.9	31.7	46.5	59.5	69.1	72.9	70.5	62.0	49.6	32.9	19.1	45.6
Mean Minimum Temp. (°F)	3.8	10.4	22.1	34.9	47.3	57.1	61.3	59.2	50.1	38.2	24.3	10.7	34.9
Extreme Maximum Temp. (°F)	58	65	81	92	96	102	102	102	98	93	78	67	102
Extreme Minimum Temp. (°F)	-35	-34	-16	0	24	35	43	36	23	13	-15	-32	-35
Days Maximum Temp. ≥ 90°F	0	0	0	0	1	4	7	4	1	0	0	0	17
Days Maximum Temp. ≤ 32°F	23	16	7	1	0	0	0	0	0	0	7	20	74
Days Minimum Temp. ≤ 32°F	31	27	26	13	2	0	0	0	1	9	24	30	163
Days Minimum Temp. ≤ 0°F	13	8	2	0	0	0	0	0	0	0	1	8	32
Heating Degree Days (base 65°F)	1,606	1,270	1,023	554	216	39	7	19	154	478	956	1,417	7,739
Cooling Degree Days (base 65°F)	0	0	0	7	50	169	255	199	71	6	0	0	757
Mean Precipitation (in.)	1.00	0.57	1.91	2.99	3.91	3.84	4.57	4.36	3.27	2.39	1.84	0.97	31.62
Days With ≥ 0.1" Precipitation	3	2	5	7	8	7	7	7	5	5	4	3	63
Days With ≥ 1.0" Precipitation	0	0	0	0	1	1	1	1	1	0	0	0	5
Mean Snowfall (in.)	10.3	6.0	7.6	2.9	trace	0.0	0.0	0.0	0.0	0.6	5.2	8.3	40.9
Days With ≥ 1.0" Snow Depth	27	22	15	2	0	0	0	0	0	0	7	21	94

Park Rapids Municipal Airport *Hubbard County*   Elevation: 1,433 ft.   Latitude: 46° 54' N   Longitude: 95° 04' W

	JAN	FEB	MAR	APR	MAY	JUN	JUL	AUG	SEP	OCT	NOV	DEC	YEAR
Mean Maximum Temp. (°F)	16.4	24.9	36.7	54.3	68.8	76.7	80.9	79.0	68.5	55.2	34.4	20.9	51.4
Mean Temp. (°F)	5.5	13.4	25.9	41.7	55.5	64.2	68.5	66.6	56.6	44.2	26.0	11.4	40.0
Mean Minimum Temp. (°F)	-5.6	1.8	15.0	29.0	42.1	51.6	56.1	54.2	44.6	33.1	17.5	1.9	28.5
Extreme Maximum Temp. (°F)	51	61	69	96	92	96	100	101	99	87	72	55	101
Extreme Minimum Temp. (°F)	-45	-51	-32	-8	19	31	35	31	17	2	-29	-46	-51
Days Maximum Temp. ≥ 90°F	0	0	0	0	0	1	3	2	1	0	0	0	7
Days Maximum Temp. ≤ 32°F	28	19	11	1	0	0	0	0	0	1	14	26	100
Days Minimum Temp. ≤ 32°F	31	28	29	20	6	0	0	0	3	16	28	31	192
Days Minimum Temp. ≤ 0°F	19	13	5	0	0	0	0	0	0	0	3	14	54
Heating Degree Days (base 65°F)	1,845	1,455	1,207	694	308	95	27	57	274	639	1,164	1,657	9,422
Cooling Degree Days (base 65°F)	0	0	0	1	21	79	141	119	25	1	0	0	387
Mean Precipitation (in.)	0.65	0.48	1.17	1.87	2.78	4.17	3.98	3.69	2.84	2.68	1.12	0.61	26.04
Days With ≥ 0.1" Precipitation	3	2	4	4	7	8	7	6	5	5	3	2	56
Days With ≥ 1.0" Precipitation	0	0	0	0	1	1	1	1	1	1	0	0	6
Mean Snowfall (in.)	11.9	6.7	10.1	3.4	0.2	0.0	trace	0.0	trace	1.3	7.1	8.2	48.9
Days With ≥ 1.0" Snow Depth	31	28	24	6	0	0	0	0	0	1	13	28	131

Pine River Dam *Crow Wing County*   Elevation: 1,250 ft.   Latitude: 46° 40' N   Longitude: 94° 07' W

	JAN	FEB	MAR	APR	MAY	JUN	JUL	AUG	SEP	OCT	NOV	DEC	YEAR
Mean Maximum Temp. (°F)	19.3	27.5	38.5	55.1	69.6	77.7	81.9	79.5	69.3	56.8	37.6	23.8	53.0
Mean Temp. (°F)	7.4	15.0	26.6	41.9	56.0	64.9	69.5	67.0	57.4	45.5	28.6	13.9	41.2
Mean Minimum Temp. (°F)	-4.6	2.5	14.8	28.7	42.3	52.1	57.1	54.5	45.4	34.2	19.6	4.0	29.2
Extreme Maximum Temp. (°F)	57	58	69	96	92	97	103	101	96	85	76	57	103
Extreme Minimum Temp. (°F)	-47	-45	-30	-6	21	32	38	32	20	5	-25	-45	-47
Days Maximum Temp. ≥ 90°F	0	0	0	0	0	2	4	2	0	0	0	0	8
Days Maximum Temp. ≤ 32°F	26	17	9	1	0	0	0	0	0	0	10	23	86
Days Minimum Temp. ≤ 32°F	31	28	29	21	4	0	0	0	2	14	28	31	188
Days Minimum Temp. ≤ 0°F	19	12	5	0	0	0	0	0	0	0	2	12	50
Heating Degree Days (base 65°F)	1,786	1,408	1,182	686	297	80	22	47	247	598	1,085	1,579	9,017
Cooling Degree Days (base 65°F)	0	0	0	2	24	89	173	128	25	1	0	0	442
Mean Precipitation (in.)	1.02	0.63	1.65	2.11	3.07	4.21	4.28	3.49	2.83	2.78	1.76	0.79	28.62
Days With ≥ 0.1" Precipitation	3	2	4	5	7	8	7	6	6	5	4	3	60
Days With ≥ 1.0" Precipitation	0	0	0	0	1	1	1	1	1	1	0	0	6
Mean Snowfall (in.)	12.3	6.8	8.1	2.8	0.3	0.0	0.0	0.0	trace	0.5	na	7.6	na
Days With ≥ 1.0" Snow Depth	15	16	15	2	0	0	0	0	0	0	7	15	70

Pipestone *Pipestone County*   Elevation: 1,702 ft.   Latitude: 44° 01' N   Longitude: 96° 20' W

	JAN	FEB	MAR	APR	MAY	JUN	JUL	AUG	SEP	OCT	NOV	DEC	YEAR
Mean Maximum Temp. (°F)	21.4	28.2	40.3	57.2	70.5	79.7	84.1	82.0	73.1	60.1	39.8	26.9	55.3
Mean Temp. (°F)	10.8	17.8	30.0	44.7	57.5	66.8	71.1	68.8	59.2	46.4	29.6	16.7	43.3
Mean Minimum Temp. (°F)	0.1	7.3	19.7	32.2	44.5	53.9	58.1	55.6	45.2	32.6	19.4	6.4	31.2
Extreme Maximum Temp. (°F)	64	66	81	93	96	106	105	106	102	92	78	61	106
Extreme Minimum Temp. (°F)	-36	-36	-21	-2	20	32	32	25	15	8	-21	-33	-36
Days Maximum Temp. ≥ 90°F	0	0	0	0	1	3	8	5	2	0	0	0	19
Days Maximum Temp. ≤ 32°F	24	16	8	1	0	0	0	0	0	0	9	20	78
Days Minimum Temp. ≤ 32°F	31	28	27	16	3	0	0	0	3	16	27	31	182
Days Minimum Temp. ≤ 0°F	15	9	3	0	0	0	0	0	0	0	2	10	39
Heating Degree Days (base 65°F)	1,677	1,329	1,077	606	257	63	18	37	219	574	1,055	1,493	8,405
Cooling Degree Days (base 65°F)	0	0	0	5	32	120	200	153	46	3	0	0	559
Mean Precipitation (in.)	0.54	0.48	1.75	2.43	3.17	4.00	3.38	3.09	2.79	2.29	1.51	0.61	26.04
Days With ≥ 0.1" Precipitation	1	2	4	6	7	7	6	5	5	4	3	2	52
Days With ≥ 1.0" Precipitation	0	0	0	1	1	1	1	1	1	1	0	0	6
Mean Snowfall (in.)	5.9	5.0	6.5	3.4	trace	0.0	0.0	0.0	trace	0.8	6.3	6.1	34.0
Days With ≥ 1.0" Snow Depth	13	na	7	1	0	0	0	0	0	0	5	10	na

Pokegama Dam *Itasca County*   Elevation: 1,279 ft.   Latitude: 47° 15' N   Longitude: 93° 35' W

	JAN	FEB	MAR	APR	MAY	JUN	JUL	AUG	SEP	OCT	NOV	DEC	YEAR
Mean Maximum Temp. (°F)	na	na	na	54.5	68.5	76.1	79.9	77.7	67.5	na	na	na	na
Mean Temp. (°F)	na	na	na	42.0	55.3	63.8	68.2	66.1	56.4	na	na	na	na
Mean Minimum Temp. (°F)	na	na	na	29.4	42.0	51.5	56.4	54.5	45.2	na	na	na	na
Extreme Maximum Temp. (°F)	53	60	71	92	90	94	99	98	95	83	72	54	99
Extreme Minimum Temp. (°F)	-44	-40	-26	-8	18	31	39	34	23	6	-22	-36	-44
Days Maximum Temp. ≥ 90°F	0	0	0	0	0	1	2	1	0	0	0	0	4
Days Maximum Temp. ≤ 32°F	22	16	8	1	0	0	0	0	0	0	10	20	77
Days Minimum Temp. ≤ 32°F	25	23	24	17	5	0	0	0	2	11	22	25	154
Days Minimum Temp. ≤ 0°F	14	10	4	0	0	0	0	0	0	0	2	11	41
Heating Degree Days (base 65°F)	na	na	na	684	315	96	30	57	273	na	na	na	na
Cooling Degree Days (base 65°F)	na	na	na	na	20	69	133	102	17	na	na	na	na
Mean Precipitation (in.)	0.89	0.57	1.20	1.70	2.77	4.51	4.65	3.70	3.15	2.73	1.43	0.87	28.17
Days With ≥ 0.1" Precipitation	3	2	3	4	6	8	8	6	7	5	4	3	59
Days With ≥ 1.0" Precipitation	0	0	0	0	0	1	1	1	1	1	0	0	5
Mean Snowfall (in.)	11.7	6.8	9.0	2.2	0.1	0.0	0.0	0.0	trace	1.1	7.3	8.9	47.1
Days With ≥ 1.0" Snow Depth	29	27	23	6	0	0	0	0	0	1	14	28	128

Preston *Fillmore County*   Elevation: 928 ft.   Latitude: 43° 40' N   Longitude: 92° 05' W

	JAN	FEB	MAR	APR	MAY	JUN	JUL	AUG	SEP	OCT	NOV	DEC	YEAR
Mean Maximum Temp. (°F)	23.8	30.3	41.8	57.4	69.5	79.3	83.0	80.6	72.8	60.7	42.5	28.8	55.9
Mean Temp. (°F)	13.2	19.6	31.5	45.4	56.8	66.6	70.7	68.1	59.9	48.3	32.8	19.4	44.4
Mean Minimum Temp. (°F)	2.7	8.8	21.3	33.4	44.2	53.7	58.3	55.5	47.0	35.7	23.1	10.0	32.8
Extreme Maximum Temp. (°F)	55	65	82	91	91	100	101	98	96	92	76	63	101
Extreme Minimum Temp. (°F)	-39	-45	-16	-8	22	31	35	32	20	8	-19	-35	-45
Days Maximum Temp. ≥ 90°F	0	0	0	0	0	2	5	2	1	0	0	0	10
Days Maximum Temp. ≤ 32°F	22	15	6	0	0	0	0	0	0	0	6	18	67
Days Minimum Temp. ≤ 32°F	31	27	26	14	4	0	0	0	2	12	24	30	170
Days Minimum Temp. ≤ 0°F	13	8	2	0	0	0	0	0	0	0	1	8	32
Heating Degree Days (base 65°F)	1,601	1,268	1,031	588	274	62	18	39	196	516	958	1,407	7,958
Cooling Degree Days (base 65°F)	0	0	0	6	23	114	197	141	48	4	0	0	533
Mean Precipitation (in.)	1.00	0.83	1.93	3.32	3.87	4.32	4.66	4.56	3.67	2.44	2.11	1.25	33.96
Days With ≥ 0.1" Precipitation	3	2	4	7	7	7	7	7	6	5	4	4	63
Days With ≥ 1.0" Precipitation	0	0	0	1	1	1	1	1	1	0	0	0	6
Mean Snowfall (in.)	11.1	6.7	7.1	2.1	trace	0.0	0.0	0.0	0.0	trace	4.6	10.0	41.6
Days With ≥ 1.0" Snow Depth	26	22	12	1	0	0	0	0	0	0	4	21	86

Red Lake Falls *Red Lake County*   Elevation: 1,072 ft.   Latitude: 47° 54' N   Longitude: 96° 17' W

	JAN	FEB	MAR	APR	MAY	JUN	JUL	AUG	SEP	OCT	NOV	DEC	YEAR
Mean Maximum Temp. (°F)	14.2	21.4	34.5	54.2	69.5	77.4	81.5	80.0	69.1	55.2	33.9	19.8	50.9
Mean Temp. (°F)	4.1	11.3	25.0	42.7	56.6	65.1	69.2	67.2	57.0	44.3	25.8	10.8	39.9
Mean Minimum Temp. (°F)	-5.9	1.2	15.5	31.2	43.8	52.7	56.8	54.4	44.8	33.4	17.7	1.8	28.9
Extreme Maximum Temp. (°F)	48	50	71	97	95	97	104	102	96	86	71	55	104
Extreme Minimum Temp. (°F)	-46	-46	-29	-10	19	31	38	28	18	5	-29	-35	-46
Days Maximum Temp. ≥ 90°F	0	0	0	0	1	2	3	3	1	0	0	0	10
Days Maximum Temp. ≤ 32°F	28	21	11	1	0	0	0	0	0	1	13	25	100
Days Minimum Temp. ≤ 32°F	31	28	28	17	4	0	0	0	3	14	27	31	183
Days Minimum Temp. ≤ 0°F	20	14	6	0	0	0	0	0	0	0	3	14	57
Heating Degree Days (base 65°F)	1,886	1,512	1,233	664	285	79	22	54	264	635	1,169	1,676	9,479
Cooling Degree Days (base 65°F)	0	0	0	3	35	87	154	137	27	1	0	0	444
Mean Precipitation (in.)	0.68	0.53	0.97	1.35	2.60	3.73	3.38	3.66	2.58	1.84	0.98	0.51	22.81
Days With ≥ 0.1" Precipitation	2	2	3	3	6	7	6	7	5	4	3	2	50
Days With ≥ 1.0" Precipitation	0	0	0	0	0	1	1	1	1	0	0	0	4
Mean Snowfall (in.)	11.5	8.0	8.4	2.2	trace	0.0	0.0	0.0	trace	0.9	9.5	8.7	49.2
Days With ≥ 1.0" Snow Depth	31	28	21	3	0	0	0	0	0	0	15	27	125

Red Lake Indian Agency *Beltrami County* Elevation: 1,217 ft. Latitude: 47° 53' N Longitude: 95° 01' W

	JAN	FEB	MAR	APR	MAY	JUN	JUL	AUG	SEP	OCT	NOV	DEC	YEAR
Mean Maximum Temp. (°F)	13.8	21.6	33.4	49.8	64.9	73.4	77.7	76.2	65.1	52.5	33.9	20.1	48.5
Mean Temp. (°F)	3.3	10.4	23.0	39.2	53.8	63.0	67.6	65.7	55.1	43.0	25.8	10.5	38.4
Mean Minimum Temp. (°F)	-7.2	-0.8	12.4	28.4	42.7	52.6	57.5	55.3	44.9	33.5	17.7	0.9	28.2
Extreme Maximum Temp. (°F)	51	59	71	95	92	100	99	100	95	86	75	55	100
Extreme Minimum Temp. (°F)	-43	-44	-30	-17	21	32	40	34	22	-3	-23	-38	-44
Days Maximum Temp. ≥ 90°F	0	0	0	0	0	1	1	1	0	0	0	0	3
Days Maximum Temp. ≤ 32°F	28	21	13	2	0	0	0	0	0	1	14	25	104
Days Minimum Temp. ≤ 32°F	31	28	30	21	5	0	0	0	2	14	28	30	189
Days Minimum Temp. ≤ 0°F	21	15	7	0	0	0	0	0	0	0	3	15	61
Heating Degree Days (base 65°F)	1,912	1,539	1,298	771	361	115	36	67	310	675	1,169	1,687	9,940
Cooling Degree Days (base 65°F)	0	0	0	2	20	63	121	102	15	0	0	0	323
Mean Precipitation (in.)	0.57	0.37	0.78	1.21	2.53	3.71	4.16	3.32	2.63	2.07	0.83	0.38	22.56
Days With ≥ 0.1" Precipitation	2	1	2	3	6	7	7	6	6	4	2	1	47
Days With ≥ 1.0" Precipitation	0	0	0	0	0	1	1	1	1	0	0	0	4
Mean Snowfall (in.)	10.6	5.9	6.6	2.2	trace	0.0	0.0	0.0	0.0	1.1	8.0	7.7	42.1
Days With ≥ 1.0" Snow Depth	30	28	24	5	0	0	0	0	0	1	12	24	124

Redwood Falls Muni Airport *Redwood County* Elevation: 1,023 ft. Latitude: 44° 33' N Longitude: 95° 05' W

	JAN	FEB	MAR	APR	MAY	JUN	JUL	AUG	SEP	OCT	NOV	DEC	YEAR
Mean Maximum Temp. (°F)	21.9	28.1	40.0	57.5	71.6	80.8	84.6	81.9	73.1	59.9	40.4	26.8	55.5
Mean Temp. (°F)	12.8	19.6	31.8	47.1	60.4	69.7	73.5	71.0	61.8	49.1	32.3	18.5	45.6
Mean Minimum Temp. (°F)	3.7	11.0	23.5	36.6	49.1	58.6	62.4	60.1	50.4	38.3	24.2	10.1	35.7
Extreme Maximum Temp. (°F)	68	64	79	96	100	105	107	104	103	92	82	64	107
Extreme Minimum Temp. (°F)	-34	-30	-14	8	26	37	43	40	27	13	-15	-29	-34
Days Maximum Temp. ≥ 90°F	0	0	0	0	1	5	8	5	2	0	0	0	21
Days Maximum Temp. ≤ 32°F	23	17	8	1	0	0	0	0	0	0	0	0	77
Days Minimum Temp. ≤ 32°F	30	27	23	9	1	0	0	0	1	8	23	30	152
Days Minimum Temp. ≤ 0°F	14	8	2	0	0	0	0	0	0	0	1	8	33
Heating Degree Days (base 65°F)	1,611	1,277	1,024	536	191	30	5	18	155	491	974	1,436	7,748
Cooling Degree Days (base 65°F)	0	0	0	5	52	170	265	201	61	5	0	0	759
Mean Precipitation (in.)	0.68	0.57	1.65	2.56	3.08	4.04	3.77	3.59	2.59	1.98	1.64	0.62	26.77
Days With ≥ 0.1" Precipitation	2	2	4	6	7	7	6	6	5	4	3	2	54
Days With ≥ 1.0" Precipitation	0	0	0	0	1	1	1	1	1	1	0	0	6
Mean Snowfall (in.)	6.8	4.9	7.8	2.0	trace	trace	0.0	0.0	trace	0.4	6.6	6.2	34.7
Days With ≥ 1.0" Snow Depth	25	21	15	1	0	0	0	0	0	0	8	20	90

Rosemount Agr. Exp. Station *Dakota County* Elevation: 948 ft. Latitude: 44° 43' N Longitude: 93° 06' W

	JAN	FEB	MAR	APR	MAY	JUN	JUL	AUG	SEP	OCT	NOV	DEC	YEAR
Mean Maximum Temp. (°F)	21.7	28.7	40.6	58.4	71.6	80.1	83.7	81.0	72.6	60.2	40.8	27.4	55.6
Mean Temp. (°F)	11.9	18.8	31.0	46.3	59.1	68.2	72.2	69.7	61.1	49.0	32.2	18.9	44.9
Mean Minimum Temp. (°F)	2.1	8.9	21.4	34.3	46.5	56.2	60.6	58.4	49.5	37.7	23.6	10.4	34.1
Extreme Maximum Temp. (°F)	57	58	81	93	96	100	105	103	97	91	77	66	105
Extreme Minimum Temp. (°F)	-38	-37	-15	4	24	36	42	40	24	12	-18	-31	-38
Days Maximum Temp. ≥ 90°F	0	0	0	0	1	3	6	3	1	0	0	0	14
Days Maximum Temp. ≤ 32°F	24	16	7	0	0	0	0	0	0	0	7	20	74
Days Minimum Temp. ≤ 32°F	31	27	26	13	2	0	0	0	1	9	24	31	164
Days Minimum Temp. ≤ 0°F	14	9	2	0	0	0	0	0	0	0	1	8	34
Heating Degree Days (base 65°F)	1,642	1,299	1,045	557	219	42	8	21	166	496	977	1,422	7,894
Cooling Degree Days (base 65°F)	0	0	0	4	41	147	236	180	58	4	0	0	670
Mean Precipitation (in.)	1.20	0.83	2.29	2.93	4.03	4.55	4.55	4.58	3.65	2.69	2.30	1.10	34.70
Days With ≥ 0.1" Precipitation	4	3	5	7	8	7	7	7	7	6	5	3	69
Days With ≥ 1.0" Precipitation	0	0	0	1	1	1	1	2	1	1	1	0	9
Mean Snowfall (in.)	10.8	6.3	9.2	2.1	trace	0.0	0.0	0.0	0.0	0.2	7.3	8.3	44.2
Days With ≥ 1.0" Snow Depth	28	25	17	2	0	0	0	0	0	0	8	23	103

Rothsay *Wilkin County* Elevation: 1,204 ft. Latitude: 46° 29' N Longitude: 96° 16' W

	JAN	FEB	MAR	APR	MAY	JUN	JUL	AUG	SEP	OCT	NOV	DEC	YEAR
Mean Maximum Temp. (°F)	16.1	24.3	36.3	55.6	70.2	78.3	82.3	80.8	70.9	57.2	36.0	22.1	52.5
Mean Temp. (°F)	6.6	15.1	27.5	44.4	58.0	66.9	70.9	69.3	59.3	46.7	27.9	13.5	42.2
Mean Minimum Temp. (°F)	-2.8	5.8	18.7	33.1	45.7	55.4	59.5	57.8	47.6	36.1	19.7	4.9	31.8
Extreme Maximum Temp. (°F)	55	55	73	98	95	99	102	105	98	88	77	55	105
Extreme Minimum Temp. (°F)	-39	-37	-24	-5	19	35	40	35	21	10	-21	-34	-39
Days Maximum Temp. ≥ 90°F	0	0	0	0	0	2	5	4	1	0	0	0	12
Days Maximum Temp. ≤ 32°F	27	19	10	1	0	0	0	0	0	0	12	25	94
Days Minimum Temp. ≤ 32°F	31	28	27	15	3	0	0	0	2	11	26	31	174
Days Minimum Temp. ≤ 0°F	18	11	4	0	0	0	0	0	0	0	2	12	47
Heating Degree Days (base 65°F)	1,808	1,405	1,155	616	248	55	15	30	213	562	1,107	1,592	8,806
Cooling Degree Days (base 65°F)	0	0	0	4	38	112	196	166	43	2	0	0	561
Mean Precipitation (in.)	0.72	0.49	1.25	1.63	2.88	3.51	3.79	2.75	2.21	2.20	1.02	0.48	22.93
Days With ≥ 0.1" Precipitation	2	2	3	4	6	7	6	5	5	4	3	2	49
Days With ≥ 1.0" Precipitation	0	0	0	0	0	1	1	1	1	1	0	0	5
Mean Snowfall (in.)	11.6	6.2	*7.9*	2.3	trace	0.0	0.0	0.0	trace	0.9	*7.9*	6.3	*43.1*
Days With ≥ 1.0" Snow Depth	28	20	15	2	0	0	0	0	0	0	10	20	95

Saint James Filtration Plant *Watonwan County*   Elevation: 1,099 ft.   Latitude: 43° 59' N   Longitude: 94° 37' W

	JAN	FEB	MAR	APR	MAY	JUN	JUL	AUG	SEP	OCT	NOV	DEC	YEAR
Mean Maximum Temp. (°F)	22.6	29.4	41.0	57.7	71.8	81.2	83.9	81.5	74.0	61.1	41.4	27.7	56.1
Mean Temp. (°F)	13.4	20.2	32.0	46.5	59.7	69.4	72.6	70.3	61.7	49.3	32.7	19.1	45.6
Mean Minimum Temp. (°F)	4.0	11.0	22.8	35.2	47.6	57.5	61.2	59.1	49.6	37.4	24.0	10.6	35.0
Extreme Maximum Temp. (°F)	64	63	84	93	94	104	105	104	98	90	81	68	105
Extreme Minimum Temp. (°F)	-30	-30	-17	6	26	36	40	38	25	13	-13	-27	-30
Days Maximum Temp. ≥ 90°F	0	0	0	0	1	5	7	4	1	0	0	0	18
Days Maximum Temp. ≤ 32°F	23	15	7	1	0	0	0	0	0	0	8	19	73
Days Minimum Temp. ≤ 32°F	31	27	25	12	1	0	0	0	1	10	24	31	162
Days Minimum Temp. ≤ 0°F	13	8	2	0	0	0	0	0	0	0	1	8	32
Heating Degree Days (base 65°F)	1,598	1,259	1,017	555	208	36	8	19	158	487	962	1,416	7,723
Cooling Degree Days (base 65°F)	0	0	0	6	48	168	250	188	64	5	0	0	729
Mean Precipitation (in.)	0.49	0.39	1.73	2.80	3.34	4.41	3.84	3.61	2.86	2.17	1.47	0.65	27.76
Days With ≥ 0.1" Precipitation	2	1	4	6	7	7	6	6	5	4	3	2	53
Days With ≥ 1.0" Precipitation	0	0	0	1	1	1	1	1	1	1	0	0	7
Mean Snowfall (in.)	9.7	5.5	8.7	2.4	trace	0.0	0.0	0.0	0.0	0.6	6.2	7.7	40.8
Days With ≥ 1.0" Snow Depth	na	16	10	1	0	0	0	0	0	0	0	3	na

Saint Paul *Ramsey County*   Elevation: 898 ft.   Latitude: 44° 57' N   Longitude: 92° 59' W

	JAN	FEB	MAR	APR	MAY	JUN	JUL	AUG	SEP	OCT	NOV	DEC	YEAR
Mean Maximum Temp. (°F)	22.2	29.3	41.0	58.0	70.9	79.1	83.5	80.8	71.7	59.2	40.1	26.9	55.2
Mean Temp. (°F)	13.6	20.5	31.9	46.9	59.5	68.4	73.2	70.7	61.6	49.4	32.7	19.4	45.7
Mean Minimum Temp. (°F)	5.0	11.7	22.8	35.8	48.1	57.6	62.8	60.6	51.4	39.5	25.2	11.9	36.1
Extreme Maximum Temp. (°F)	57	59	83	93	92	100	105	103	95	88	75	66	105
Extreme Minimum Temp. (°F)	-29	-32	-12	3	24	36	45	42	28	15	-10	-29	-32
Days Maximum Temp. ≥ 90°F	0	0	0	0	0	2	5	3	1	0	0	0	11
Days Maximum Temp. ≤ 32°F	24	16	7	0	0	0	0	0	0	0	8	20	75
Days Minimum Temp. ≤ 32°F	31	27	25	11	1	0	0	0	0	7	23	30	155
Days Minimum Temp. ≤ 0°F	12	7	1	0	0	0	0	0	0	0	1	7	28
Heating Degree Days (base 65°F)	1,589	1,252	1,019	541	210	42	5	16	159	481	963	1,408	7,685
Cooling Degree Days (base 65°F)	0	0	0	6	46	151	269	206	63	4	0	0	745
Mean Precipitation (in.)	1.00	0.74	1.96	2.62	3.70	4.88	4.35	4.35	3.23	2.62	2.13	1.01	32.59
Days With ≥ 0.1" Precipitation	3	2	5	6	7	7	7	6	6	5	4	3	61
Days With ≥ 1.0" Precipitation	0	0	0	0	1	1	1	1	1	1	0	0	6
Mean Snowfall (in.)	12.1	7.4	9.9	3.0	trace	0.0	0.0	0.0	trace	0.4	9.2	9.8	51.8
Days With ≥ 1.0" Snow Depth	29	25	16	2	0	0	0	0	0	0	8	23	103

Saint Peter 2 SW *Nicollet County*   Elevation: 849 ft.   Latitude: 44° 18' N   Longitude: 93° 58' W

	JAN	FEB	MAR	APR	MAY	JUN	JUL	AUG	SEP	OCT	NOV	DEC	YEAR
Mean Maximum Temp. (°F)	22.8	29.2	41.5	58.1	71.7	80.5	84.0	81.3	73.1	60.7	41.2	27.9	56.0
Mean Temp. (°F)	12.7	19.2	31.8	46.4	59.5	68.7	72.7	70.2	61.2	48.9	32.8	19.0	45.3
Mean Minimum Temp. (°F)	2.6	9.4	21.9	34.6	47.1	56.9	61.3	59.0	49.1	36.9	24.1	10.0	34.4
Extreme Maximum Temp. (°F)	60	64	83	94	99	104	102	102	96	91	79	69	104
Extreme Minimum Temp. (°F)	-38	-34	-15	4	24	37	44	39	25	9	-15	-32	-38
Days Maximum Temp. ≥ 90°F	0	0	0	0	1	4	7	3	1	0	0	0	16
Days Maximum Temp. ≤ 32°F	22	15	7	1	0	0	0	0	0	0	7	18	70
Days Minimum Temp. ≤ 32°F	31	27	26	12	1	0	0	0	1	9	23	30	160
Days Minimum Temp. ≤ 0°F	14	9	2	0	0	0	0	0	0	0	1	8	34
Heating Degree Days (base 65°F)	1,617	1,288	1,023	558	213	41	8	20	168	498	961	1,421	7,816
Cooling Degree Days (base 65°F)	0	0	0	7	48	162	254	196	68	4	0	0	739
Mean Precipitation (in.)	0.87	0.51	1.93	2.42	3.40	4.77	3.93	4.04	2.89	2.33	1.66	0.85	29.60
Days With ≥ 0.1" Precipitation	3	2	4	5	7	7	6	6	5	4	4	2	55
Days With ≥ 1.0" Precipitation	0	0	0	0	1	1	1	1	1	1	0	0	6
Mean Snowfall (in.)	8.9	3.8	5.9	1.4	trace	0.0	0.0	0.0	0.0	trace	4.1	6.6	30.7
Days With ≥ 1.0" Snow Depth	17	13	8	1	0	0	0	0	0	0	3	11	53

Sandy Lake Dam Libby *Aitkin County*   Elevation: 1,233 ft.   Latitude: 46° 48' N   Longitude: 93° 19' W

	JAN	FEB	MAR	APR	MAY	JUN	JUL	AUG	SEP	OCT	NOV	DEC	YEAR
Mean Maximum Temp. (°F)	19.2	26.8	38.3	54.4	68.2	76.3	80.1	77.7	68.3	56.2	na	na	na
Mean Temp. (°F)	7.7	14.8	26.9	42.0	55.3	64.0	68.3	66.4	57.2	45.6	na	na	na
Mean Minimum Temp. (°F)	-3.8	2.7	15.5	29.5	42.4	51.7	56.5	54.7	45.9	34.9	na	3.2	na
Extreme Maximum Temp. (°F)	51	57	72	90	91	95	102	101	95	84	74	54	102
Extreme Minimum Temp. (°F)	-49	-44	-29	-7	18	32	36	28	24	3	-25	-40	-49
Days Maximum Temp. ≥ 90°F	0	0	0	0	0	1	3	1	0	0	0	0	5
Days Maximum Temp. ≤ 32°F	25	16	8	1	0	0	0	0	0	0	9	21	80
Days Minimum Temp. ≤ 32°F	29	26	26	19	4	0	0	0	2	12	23	27	168
Days Minimum Temp. ≤ 0°F	17	11	5	0	0	0	0	0	0	0	2	12	47
Heating Degree Days (base 65°F)	1,773	1,414	1,173	683	312	95	32	56	255	596	na	na	na
Cooling Degree Days (base 65°F)	0	0	0	1	18	75	137	110	24	na	na	na	na
Mean Precipitation (in.)	0.86	0.53	1.20	1.77	2.94	4.48	4.54	3.77	3.07	2.46	1.25	0.70	27.57
Days With ≥ 0.1" Precipitation	3	2	3	5	7	8	8	6	6	4	3	2	57
Days With ≥ 1.0" Precipitation	0	0	0	0	0	1	1	1	1	1	0	0	5
Mean Snowfall (in.)	15.6	8.3	9.7	3.1	0.2	0.0	0.0	0.0	trace	1.0	8.3	10.8	57.0
Days With ≥ 1.0" Snow Depth	28	25	24	7	0	0	0	0	0	0	10	25	119

Santiago 3 E *Sherburne County*   Elevation: 1,017 ft.   Latitude: 45° 33' N   Longitude: 93° 46' W

	JAN	FEB	MAR	APR	MAY	JUN	JUL	AUG	SEP	OCT	NOV	DEC	YEAR
Mean Maximum Temp. (°F)	21.3	28.8	40.1	57.9	71.5	79.7	83.9	81.0	71.6	59.1	39.5	26.2	55.0
Mean Temp. (°F)	10.1	17.4	29.5	45.1	57.9	66.4	70.7	68.0	58.7	46.8	30.0	16.3	43.1
Mean Minimum Temp. (°F)	-1.3	5.6	18.6	32.3	44.4	52.9	57.4	55.0	45.8	34.4	20.5	6.3	31.0
Extreme Maximum Temp. (°F)	55	58	74	96	95	104	105	101	97	90	75	62	105
Extreme Minimum Temp. (°F)	-41	-39	-24	-2	22	31	38	35	18	5	-16	-41	-41
Days Maximum Temp. ≥ 90°F	0	0	0	0	1	3	6	4	1	0	0	0	15
Days Maximum Temp. ≤ 32°F	24	16	7	0	0	0	0	0	0	0	0	0	77
Days Minimum Temp. ≤ 32°F	31	28	28	16	4	0	0	0	3	14	27	31	182
Days Minimum Temp. ≤ 0°F	16	11	3	0	0	0	0	0	0	0	2	11	43
Heating Degree Days (base 65°F)	1,698	1,342	1,094	594	247	63	15	39	221	563	1,039	1,506	8,421
Cooling Degree Days (base 65°F)	0	0	0	4	36	110	193	140	38	3	0	0	524
Mean Precipitation (in.)	1.12	0.83	1.72	2.46	3.25	4.45	4.18	4.63	2.91	2.65	1.82	0.87	30.89
Days With ≥ 0.1" Precipitation	3	2	4	5	7	7	7	7	6	5	4	3	60
Days With ≥ 1.0" Precipitation	0	0	0	0	1	1	1	1	1	1	1	0	7
Mean Snowfall (in.)	12.5	7.1	8.7	2.3	trace	0.0	0.0	0.0	trace	0.1	8.1	8.5	47.3
Days With ≥ 1.0" Snow Depth	29	26	19	2	0	0	0	0	0	0	9	25	110

Springfield 1 NW *Brown County*   Elevation: 1,062 ft.   Latitude: 44° 15' N   Longitude: 94° 59' W

	JAN	FEB	MAR	APR	MAY	JUN	JUL	AUG	SEP	OCT	NOV	DEC	YEAR
Mean Maximum Temp. (°F)	21.4	27.6	39.0	56.2	71.3	80.5	83.2	80.3	72.9	60.0	40.3	26.7	55.0
Mean Temp. (°F)	11.7	18.3	30.3	45.1	58.9	68.7	71.8	68.8	60.2	47.9	31.4	17.7	44.2
Mean Minimum Temp. (°F)	1.9	8.9	21.5	34.0	46.6	56.8	60.3	57.3	47.4	35.7	22.4	8.7	33.5
Extreme Maximum Temp. (°F)	67	63	79	95	100	104	103	105	101	91	83	67	105
Extreme Minimum Temp. (°F)	-32	-29	-18	-1	24	35	40	38	20	11	-16	-32	-32
Days Maximum Temp. ≥ 90°F	0	0	0	0	2	5	6	3	1	0	0	0	17
Days Maximum Temp. ≤ 32°F	23	16	9	1	0	0	0	0	0	0	8	20	77
Days Minimum Temp. ≤ 32°F	31	28	26	14	2	0	0	0	2	12	26	31	172
Days Minimum Temp. ≤ 0°F	15	9	2	0	0	0	0	0	0	0	2	9	37
Heating Degree Days (base 65°F)	1,650	1,314	1,070	596	232	43	11	32	192	529	1,001	1,461	8,131
Cooling Degree Days (base 65°F)	0	0	0	6	48	157	224	157	52	5	0	0	649
Mean Precipitation (in.)	0.64	0.61	2.01	2.83	3.06	3.91	3.50	3.31	2.56	2.10	1.73	0.60	26.86
Days With ≥ 0.1" Precipitation	2	2	4	6	6	7	6	6	5	4	3	2	53
Days With ≥ 1.0" Precipitation	0	0	0	1	1	1	1	1	1	1	1	0	8
Mean Snowfall (in.)	9.1	5.9	9.5	3.0	trace	0.0	0.0	0.0	trace	0.7	7.7	7.9	43.8
Days With ≥ 1.0" Snow Depth	24	19	12	1	0	0	0	0	0	0	7	17	80

Stewart *McLeod County*   Elevation: 1,040 ft.   Latitude: 44° 44' N   Longitude: 94° 30' W

	JAN	FEB	MAR	APR	MAY	JUN	JUL	AUG	SEP	OCT	NOV	DEC	YEAR
Mean Maximum Temp. (°F)	20.6	27.7	39.7	57.5	71.5	80.7	84.4	81.4	73.3	60.3	40.2	25.8	55.3
Mean Temp. (°F)	10.9	18.3	30.8	46.2	59.4	69.0	73.0	70.1	61.2	48.9	31.8	17.2	44.7
Mean Minimum Temp. (°F)	1.2	8.8	21.8	34.9	47.2	57.3	61.5	58.8	49.1	37.5	23.4	8.5	34.2
Extreme Maximum Temp. (°F)	62	61	76	93	95	104	102	106	99	87	75	66	106
Extreme Minimum Temp. (°F)	-35	-34	-14	4	26	38	42	40	21	13	-15	-30	-35
Days Maximum Temp. ≥ 90°F	0	0	0	0	1	4	7	3	1	0	0	0	16
Days Maximum Temp. ≤ 32°F	24	17	8	0	0	0	0	0	0	0	8	21	78
Days Minimum Temp. ≤ 32°F	31	27	26	12	2	0	0	0	1	10	25	30	164
Days Minimum Temp. ≤ 0°F	15	9	2	0	0	0	0	0	0	0	1	9	36
Heating Degree Days (base 65°F)	1,673	1,313	1,055	562	215	36	6	20	167	496	990	1,479	8,012
Cooling Degree Days (base 65°F)	0	0	0	5	41	161	260	188	57	3	0	0	715
Mean Precipitation (in.)	0.85	0.62	1.79	2.60	3.05	4.29	3.95	4.37	2.69	2.14	1.89	0.74	28.98
Days With ≥ 0.1" Precipitation	3	2	4	6	8	7	6	7	6	5	4	2	60
Days With ≥ 1.0" Precipitation	0	0	0	1	1	1	1	1	1	1	0	0	6
Mean Snowfall (in.)	11.3	7.4	9.6	3.0	trace	0.0	0.0	0.0	0.0	0.3	8.5	8.6	48.7
Days With ≥ 1.0" Snow Depth	25	21	16	2	0	0	0	0	0	0	7	21	92

Stillwater 1 SE *Washington County*   Elevation: 711 ft.   Latitude: 45° 02' N   Longitude: 92° 47' W

	JAN	FEB	MAR	APR	MAY	JUN	JUL	AUG	SEP	OCT	NOV	DEC	YEAR
Mean Maximum Temp. (°F)	23.1	30.2	41.6	58.4	71.7	80.4	84.9	82.0	72.4	59.9	41.4	27.7	56.2
Mean Temp. (°F)	13.3	20.2	31.6	46.9	59.7	68.8	73.5	70.9	61.5	49.5	33.3	19.3	45.7
Mean Minimum Temp. (°F)	3.2	9.8	21.6	35.2	47.8	57.2	62.0	59.8	50.6	39.0	25.1	10.8	35.2
Extreme Maximum Temp. (°F)	54	60	83	94	94	101	106	104	94	90	78	67	106
Extreme Minimum Temp. (°F)	-40	-36	-13	4	22	34	45	44	26	15	-15	-39	-40
Days Maximum Temp. ≥ 90°F	0	0	0	0	1	3	7	4	1	0	0	0	16
Days Maximum Temp. ≤ 32°F	22	14	6	0	0	0	0	0	0	0	6	19	67
Days Minimum Temp. ≤ 32°F	31	27	26	12	1	0	0	0	1	7	24	30	159
Days Minimum Temp. ≤ 0°F	13	9	2	0	0	0	0	0	0	0	1	8	33
Heating Degree Days (base 65°F)	1,599	1,261	1,029	544	202	37	4	13	158	479	944	1,412	7,682
Cooling Degree Days (base 65°F)	0	0	0	5	44	158	277	212	66	4	0	0	766
Mean Precipitation (in.)	1.00	0.68	1.79	2.93	3.54	4.84	4.68	4.89	3.68	2.77	2.14	0.92	33.86
Days With ≥ 0.1" Precipitation	3	2	4	6	7	8	7	6	6	5	5	3	62
Days With ≥ 1.0" Precipitation	0	0	0	1	1	1	1	2	1	1	0	0	8
Mean Snowfall (in.)	*11.2*	na	na	*0.9*	0.0	0.0	0.0	0.0	0.0	trace	na	na	na
Days With ≥ 1.0" Snow Depth	na	*21*	*14*	*1*	0	0	0	0	0	0	na	na	na

Tower 3 S *St. Louis County*   Elevation: 1,459 ft.   Latitude: 47° 45' N   Longitude: 92° 17' W

	JAN	FEB	MAR	APR	MAY	JUN	JUL	AUG	SEP	OCT	NOV	DEC	YEAR
Mean Maximum Temp. (°F)	15.6	23.8	35.6	50.9	65.5	73.5	77.5	75.3	64.6	51.8	34.1	20.8	49.1
Mean Temp. (°F)	2.3	9.4	22.1	37.1	50.2	58.8	63.1	61.0	51.5	40.2	24.1	8.9	35.7
Mean Minimum Temp. (°F)	-11.1	-5.2	8.5	23.4	34.9	44.1	48.7	46.6	38.3	28.6	14.0	-3.0	22.3
Extreme Maximum Temp. (°F)	52	58	69	87	95	97	98	97	95	81	75	52	98
Extreme Minimum Temp. (°F)	-57	-60	-42	-22	10	21	24	21	14	-7	-33	-52	-60
Days Maximum Temp. ≥ 90°F	0	0	0	0	0	1	2	1	0	0	0	0	4
Days Maximum Temp. ≤ 32°F	28	21	12	2	0	0	0	0	0	1	14	26	104
Days Minimum Temp. ≤ 32°F	31	28	30	25	14	4	1	2	10	21	29	31	226
Days Minimum Temp. ≤ 0°F	22	17	9	1	0	0	0	0	0	0	5	17	71
Heating Degree Days (base 65°F)	1,943	1,570	1,325	830	461	208	112	161	408	761	1,220	1,734	10,733
Cooling Degree Days (base 65°F)	0	0	0	1	8	29	58	40	7	0	0	0	143
Mean Precipitation (in.)	0.80	0.70	0.97	1.64	3.04	4.42	4.36	4.18	4.04	3.04	1.35	0.62	29.16
Days With ≥ 0.1" Precipitation	2	2	3	4	7	8	9	8	8	6	3	2	62
Days With ≥ 1.0" Precipitation	0	0	0	0	1	1	1	1	1	1	0	0	6
Mean Snowfall (in.)	15.2	9.9	10.8	5.6	0.5	0.0	0.0	0.0	trace	2.6	12.6	11.1	68.3
Days With ≥ 1.0" Snow Depth	17	18	16	5	0	0	0	0	0	1	11	18	86

Tracy *Lyon County*   Elevation: 1,400 ft.   Latitude: 44° 14' N   Longitude: 95° 38' W

	JAN	FEB	MAR	APR	MAY	JUN	JUL	AUG	SEP	OCT	NOV	DEC	YEAR
Mean Maximum Temp. (°F)	21.3	27.4	38.3	54.7	69.4	79.1	82.9	80.3	71.5	58.6	39.5	26.5	54.1
Mean Temp. (°F)	11.9	18.5	30.0	44.5	58.3	68.2	72.3	69.6	60.0	47.5	31.1	17.6	44.1
Mean Minimum Temp. (°F)	2.5	9.5	21.6	34.4	47.1	57.3	61.5	58.8	48.7	36.5	22.6	8.9	34.1
Extreme Maximum Temp. (°F)	65	63	78	93	98	104	103	104	100	90	79	66	104
Extreme Minimum Temp. (°F)	-32	-30	-17	3	22	36	44	39	22	13	-11	-30	-32
Days Maximum Temp. ≥ 90°F	0	0	0	0	1	3	6	4	1	0	0	0	15
Days Maximum Temp. ≤ 32°F	23	17	10	1	0	0	0	0	0	0	9	20	80
Days Minimum Temp. ≤ 32°F	31	27	26	13	1	0	0	0	1	10	25	31	165
Days Minimum Temp. ≤ 0°F	15	9	2	0	0	0	0	0	0	0	1	9	36
Heating Degree Days (base 65°F)	1,641	1,309	1,080	613	243	48	11	28	192	538	1,009	1,465	8,177
Cooling Degree Days (base 65°F)	0	0	0	6	42	153	237	179	53	4	0	0	674
Mean Precipitation (in.)	0.65	0.51	1.99	2.77	3.25	4.04	3.22	3.10	2.87	2.08	1.68	0.65	26.81
Days With ≥ 0.1" Precipitation	2	2	5	6	6	7	6	5	5	4	4	2	54
Days With ≥ 1.0" Precipitation	0	0	0	1	1	1	1	1	1	0	0	0	6
Mean Snowfall (in.)	8.4	4.8	10.3	3.8	trace	0.0	0.0	0.0	trace	1.0	8.2	7.6	44.1
Days With ≥ 1.0" Snow Depth	25	22	16	3	0	0	0	0	0	1	9	21	97

Two Harbors *Lake County*   Elevation: 623 ft.   Latitude: 47° 02' N   Longitude: 91° 40' W

	JAN	FEB	MAR	APR	MAY	JUN	JUL	AUG	SEP	OCT	NOV	DEC	YEAR
Mean Maximum Temp. (°F)	22.5	27.4	35.8	47.8	57.8	66.9	74.0	73.4	65.3	53.7	38.9	27.6	49.3
Mean Temp. (°F)	13.6	18.6	27.9	39.2	48.2	56.1	63.7	64.6	56.6	45.6	32.2	19.7	40.5
Mean Minimum Temp. (°F)	4.7	9.7	19.9	30.7	38.6	45.3	53.4	55.6	47.8	37.5	25.5	11.9	31.7
Extreme Maximum Temp. (°F)	49	57	69	81	87	96	94	98	88	86	71	57	98
Extreme Minimum Temp. (°F)	-34	-36	-19	-15	23	31	37	39	22	0	-13	-26	-36
Days Maximum Temp. ≥ 90°F	0	0	0	0	0	0	1	0	0	0	0	0	1
Days Maximum Temp. ≤ 32°F	25	18	10	1	0	0	0	0	0	0	7	20	81
Days Minimum Temp. ≤ 32°F	31	27	28	16	4	0	0	0	1	8	22	30	167
Days Minimum Temp. ≤ 0°F	13	8	2	0	0	0	0	0	0	0	1	7	31
Heating Degree Days (base 65°F)	1,589	1,305	1,145	766	514	268	92	72	257	594	978	1,397	8,977
Cooling Degree Days (base 65°F)	0	0	0	0	1	10	68	75	11	0	0	0	165
Mean Precipitation (in.)	0.96	0.71	1.59	2.15	2.97	4.04	4.31	3.92	4.06	2.62	2.05	1.08	30.46
Days With ≥ 0.1" Precipitation	3	2	4	5	6	8	7	7	7	6	5	3	63
Days With ≥ 1.0" Precipitation	0	0	0	0	1	1	1	1	1	1	0	0	6
Mean Snowfall (in.)	na	na	7.7	2.5	trace	0.0	0.0	0.0	0.0	trace	na	na	na
Days With ≥ 1.0" Snow Depth	26	25	19	4	0	0	0	0	0	0	7	21	102

Wadena 3 S *Wadena County*   Elevation: 1,348 ft.   Latitude: 46° 24' N   Longitude: 95° 09' W

	JAN	FEB	MAR	APR	MAY	JUN	JUL	AUG	SEP	OCT	NOV	DEC	YEAR
Mean Maximum Temp. (°F)	15.7	22.9	34.4	52.4	66.9	74.3	78.6	77.0	67.1	54.6	35.2	21.5	50.0
Mean Temp. (°F)	5.2	12.0	24.3	40.9	54.7	63.6	67.8	65.8	55.8	43.6	26.7	12.2	39.4
Mean Minimum Temp. (°F)	-5.3	1.1	14.3	29.4	42.5	52.9	56.9	54.6	44.5	32.6	18.0	2.9	28.7
Extreme Maximum Temp. (°F)	55	57	71	96	91	96	101	102	96	89	74	55	102
Extreme Minimum Temp. (°F)	-41	-43	-28	-7	21	36	37	36	17	6	-21	-42	-43
Days Maximum Temp. ≥ 90°F	0	0	0	0	0	1	2	2	0	0	0	0	5
Days Maximum Temp. ≤ 32°F	28	20	12	1	0	0	0	0	0	0	13	25	99
Days Minimum Temp. ≤ 32°F	31	28	29	20	5	0	0	0	3	16	28	31	191
Days Minimum Temp. ≤ 0°F	19	14	5	0	0	0	0	0	0	0	2	14	54
Heating Degree Days (base 65°F)	1,852	1,493	1,254	716	330	105	35	64	294	656	1,144	1,633	9,576
Cooling Degree Days (base 65°F)	0	0	0	1	18	68	123	94	20	1	0	0	325
Mean Precipitation (in.)	0.94	0.57	1.57	2.03	2.92	4.24	3.52	3.11	2.60	2.68	1.43	0.59	26.20
Days With ≥ 0.1" Precipitation	3	2	4	5	6	8	7	6	5	4	3	2	55
Days With ≥ 1.0" Precipitation	0	0	0	0	1	1	1	1	0	1	0	0	5
Mean Snowfall (in.)	12.1	7.0	9.7	3.2	trace	0.0	0.0	0.0	trace	1.3	8.1	6.9	48.3
Days With ≥ 1.0" Snow Depth	29	26	21	4	0	0	0	0	0	1	10	25	116

Walker Ah Gwah Ching *Cass County*   Elevation: 1,407 ft.   Latitude: 47° 04' N   Longitude: 94° 34' W

	JAN	FEB	MAR	APR	MAY	JUN	JUL	AUG	SEP	OCT	NOV	DEC	YEAR
Mean Maximum Temp. (°F)	16.8	24.9	36.1	52.7	67.3	74.9	79.1	76.6	66.1	53.7	34.6	21.7	50.4
Mean Temp. (°F)	7.1	14.7	26.4	41.8	55.6	64.1	68.5	66.3	56.1	44.6	27.5	13.3	40.5
Mean Minimum Temp. (°F)	-2.6	4.5	16.7	30.8	43.9	53.2	57.9	56.0	46.3	35.5	20.3	4.8	30.6
Extreme Maximum Temp. (°F)	51	59	70	94	91	95	100	103	97	85	72	53	103
Extreme Minimum Temp. (°F)	-39	-44	-28	-6	20	32	41	35	25	9	-22	-36	-44
Days Maximum Temp. ≥ 90°F	0	0	0	0	0	1	2	1	0	0	0	0	4
Days Maximum Temp. ≤ 32°F	28	19	11	1	0	0	0	0	0	1	13	25	98
Days Minimum Temp. ≤ 32°F	31	28	28	18	3	0	0	0	2	12	27	31	180
Days Minimum Temp. ≤ 0°F	18	11	4	0	0	0	0	0	0	0	2	12	47
Heating Degree Days (base 65°F)	1,792	1,417	1,190	691	307	92	27	57	280	625	1,120	1,600	9,198
Cooling Degree Days (base 65°F)	0	0	0	2	23	75	145	111	19	0	0	0	375
Mean Precipitation (in.)	0.80	0.57	1.33	2.07	2.86	3.98	4.14	3.51	2.90	2.81	1.31	0.79	27.07
Days With ≥ 0.1" Precipitation	3	2	3	5	7	8	7	6	6	5	4	3	59
Days With ≥ 1.0" Precipitation	0	0	0	0	0	1	1	1	1	1	0	0	5
Mean Snowfall (in.)	*11.3*	6.6	8.4	2.0	trace	0.0	0.0	0.0	trace	0.5	7.7	8.9	*45.4*
Days With ≥ 1.0" Snow Depth	29	27	24	6	0	0	0	0	0	0	11	25	122

Warroad *Roseau County*   Elevation: 1,066 ft.   Latitude: 48° 55' N   Longitude: 95° 19' W

	JAN	FEB	MAR	APR	MAY	JUN	JUL	AUG	SEP	OCT	NOV	DEC	YEAR
Mean Maximum Temp. (°F)	12.5	20.8	32.6	49.7	64.8	73.9	78.5	76.9	65.9	52.6	32.7	18.2	48.3
Mean Temp. (°F)	1.7	9.3	21.7	38.2	53.2	63.0	67.4	65.3	54.8	42.7	24.6	8.8	37.6
Mean Minimum Temp. (°F)	-9.2	-2.3	10.8	26.8	41.5	51.9	56.3	53.7	43.7	32.7	16.4	-0.7	26.8
Extreme Maximum Temp. (°F)	45	50	60	93	93	98	100	101	94	85	73	50	101
Extreme Minimum Temp. (°F)	-43	-46	-31	-11	20	31	37	32	22	2	-29	-36	-46
Days Maximum Temp. ≥ 90°F	0	0	0	0	0	1	2	1	0	0	0	0	4
Days Maximum Temp. ≤ 32°F	29	22	14	2	0	0	0	0	0	1	15	26	109
Days Minimum Temp. ≤ 32°F	31	28	30	22	6	0	0	0	3	16	28	31	195
Days Minimum Temp. ≤ 0°F	21	16	8	0	0	0	0	0	0	0	4	16	65
Heating Degree Days (base 65°F)	1,963	1,571	1,335	797	377	116	38	73	316	684	1,207	1,739	10,216
Cooling Degree Days (base 65°F)	0	0	0	1	18	65	119	95	13	0	0	0	311
Mean Precipitation (in.)	0.64	0.52	0.73	1.23	2.48	3.66	3.69	2.74	2.68	1.82	1.07	0.63	21.89
Days With ≥ 0.1" Precipitation	2	2	2	3	6	7	7	5	6	4	3	3	50
Days With ≥ 1.0" Precipitation	0	0	0	0	0	1	1	1	0	0	0	0	3
Mean Snowfall (in.)	*7.9*	*4.8*	na	2.7	trace	0.0	0.0	0.0	trace	0.6	na	na	na
Days With ≥ 1.0" Snow Depth	*14*	*15*	na	*3*	0	0	0	0	0	0	na	*11*	na

Waseca Exp. Station *Waseca County*   Elevation: 1,151 ft.   Latitude: 44° 04' N   Longitude: 93° 31' W

	JAN	FEB	MAR	APR	MAY	JUN	JUL	AUG	SEP	OCT	NOV	DEC	YEAR
Mean Maximum Temp. (°F)	20.1	26.6	38.2	55.0	69.4	78.8	81.9	79.5	71.7	58.8	39.9	25.6	53.8
Mean Temp. (°F)	10.5	17.5	29.8	44.8	58.3	67.9	71.3	68.9	60.1	47.6	31.5	16.9	43.7
Mean Minimum Temp. (°F)	0.9	8.3	21.4	34.5	47.2	56.9	60.6	58.2	48.5	36.3	23.0	8.2	33.7
Extreme Maximum Temp. (°F)	58	63	79	92	96	102	102	103	97	93	79	68	103
Extreme Minimum Temp. (°F)	-36	-35	-20	5	24	37	41	38	22	13	-21	-35	-36
Days Maximum Temp. ≥ 90°F	0	0	0	0	1	3	4	2	1	0	0	0	11
Days Maximum Temp. ≤ 32°F	25	18	9	1	0	0	0	0	0	0	9	22	84
Days Minimum Temp. ≤ 32°F	31	28	27	12	2	0	0	0	1	12	25	30	168
Days Minimum Temp. ≤ 0°F	15	9	3	0	0	0	0	0	0	0	1	10	38
Heating Degree Days (base 65°F)	1,685	1,338	1,085	605	245	54	13	31	193	539	1,000	1,486	8,274
Cooling Degree Days (base 65°F)	0	0	0	5	44	153	217	166	56	5	0	0	646
Mean Precipitation (in.)	1.34	0.90	2.49	3.31	3.90	4.02	4.48	4.54	3.37	2.61	2.33	1.31	34.60
Days With ≥ 0.1" Precipitation	4	2	6	8	8	7	7	7	6	5	5	3	68
Days With ≥ 1.0" Precipitation	0	0	0	0	1	1	1	1	1	1	1	0	7
Mean Snowfall (in.)	12.9	7.8	10.2	4.1	trace	0.0	0.0	0.0	0.0	0.6	8.4	10.7	54.7
Days With ≥ 1.0" Snow Depth	28	23	16	3	0	0	0	0	0	0	9	24	103

Wheaton *Traverse County*   Elevation: 1,017 ft.   Latitude: 45° 48' N   Longitude: 96° 30' W

	JAN	FEB	MAR	APR	MAY	JUN	JUL	AUG	SEP	OCT	NOV	DEC	YEAR
Mean Maximum Temp. (°F)	20.5	27.7	39.1	57.7	72.1	80.4	85.1	83.6	74.2	60.8	39.9	26.1	55.6
Mean Temp. (°F)	10.7	18.0	29.8	45.8	59.2	68.3	72.7	71.0	61.4	48.7	31.0	17.0	44.5
Mean Minimum Temp. (°F)	0.8	8.2	20.4	33.8	46.3	56.1	60.3	58.4	48.5	36.6	21.9	7.8	33.3
Extreme Maximum Temp. (°F)	61	66	79	98	94	106	104	104	100	93	77	59	106
Extreme Minimum Temp. (°F)	-33	-33	-18	2	23	37	39	39	26	10	-15	-30	-33
Days Maximum Temp. ≥ 90°F	0	0	0	0	1	4	8	6	2	0	0	0	21
Days Maximum Temp. ≤ 32°F	24	17	8	0	0	0	0	0	0	0	8	20	77
Days Minimum Temp. ≤ 32°F	31	28	27	14	2	0	0	0	1	10	26	31	170
Days Minimum Temp. ≤ 0°F	16	9	3	0	0	0	0	0	0	0	1	9	38
Heating Degree Days (base 65°F)	1,681	1,323	1,086	574	215	40	7	18	166	503	1,014	1,484	8,111
Cooling Degree Days (base 65°F)	0	0	0	5	44	145	250	209	59	5	0	0	717
Mean Precipitation (in.)	0.90	0.53	1.50	1.95	2.60	3.74	3.05	2.50	2.10	1.93	1.08	0.52	22.40
Days With ≥ 0.1" Precipitation	3	2	4	4	6	6	5	5	4	4	3	2	48
Days With ≥ 1.0" Precipitation	0	0	0	0	0	1	1	1	0	1	0	0	4
Mean Snowfall (in.)	11.0	6.1	*8.7*	2.3	trace	0.0	0.0	0.0	0.0	0.3	5.4	*6.4*	*40.2*
Days With ≥ 1.0" Snow Depth	na	na	na	1	0	0	0	0	0	0	na	na	na

Willmar State Hospital *Kandiyohi County*   Elevation: 1,125 ft.   Latitude: 45° 08' N   Longitude: 95° 01' W

	JAN	FEB	MAR	APR	MAY	JUN	JUL	AUG	SEP	OCT	NOV	DEC	YEAR
Mean Maximum Temp. (°F)	19.7	26.3	37.8	55.5	69.9	78.7	82.3	80.0	71.6	58.4	38.5	24.9	53.6
Mean Temp. (°F)	9.9	16.9	29.0	44.8	58.5	67.7	71.6	69.1	60.0	47.4	30.3	16.1	43.4
Mean Minimum Temp. (°F)	-0.2	6.9	20.2	34.1	47.0	56.6	60.9	58.2	48.4	36.4	22.0	7.1	33.1
Extreme Maximum Temp. (°F)	62	60	74	94	95	103	101	105	99	89	80	61	105
Extreme Minimum Temp. (°F)	-41	-36	-17	1	24	36	44	38	19	8	-18	-34	-41
Days Maximum Temp. ≥ 90°F	0	0	0	0	0	2	5	3	1	0	0	0	11
Days Maximum Temp. ≤ 32°F	25	18	9	1	0	0	0	0	0	0	10	22	85
Days Minimum Temp. ≤ 32°F	31	28	27	13	1	0	0	0	1	10	26	31	168
Days Minimum Temp. ≤ 0°F	16	10	3	0	0	0	0	0	0	0	2	10	41
Heating Degree Days (base 65°F)	1,704	1,355	1,110	602	235	49	9	25	191	541	1,036	1,510	8,367
Cooling Degree Days (base 65°F)	0	0	0	4	39	133	214	155	42	2	0	0	589
Mean Precipitation (in.)	0.79	0.60	1.53	2.21	3.20	5.18	3.78	3.83	2.87	2.24	1.50	0.64	28.37
Days With ≥ 0.1" Precipitation	2	2	4	5	7	7	6	6	5	4	3	2	53
Days With ≥ 1.0" Precipitation	0	0	0	0	0	1	1	1	1	1	0	0	5
Mean Snowfall (in.)	11.6	7.2	9.5	2.3	trace	0.0	0.0	0.0	trace	0.4	8.3	7.9	47.2
Days With ≥ 1.0" Snow Depth	na	na	na	0	0	0	0	0	0	0	na	na	na

Windom *Cottonwood County*   Elevation: 1,374 ft.   Latitude: 43° 53' N   Longitude: 95° 06' W

	JAN	FEB	MAR	APR	MAY	JUN	JUL	AUG	SEP	OCT	NOV	DEC	YEAR
Mean Maximum Temp. (°F)	22.7	29.1	40.5	56.5	71.1	80.4	84.2	81.1	73.1	60.1	40.6	27.4	55.6
Mean Temp. (°F)	13.0	19.5	31.2	45.3	58.9	68.5	72.8	70.0	61.1	48.1	31.8	18.6	44.9
Mean Minimum Temp. (°F)	3.2	9.9	21.8	34.1	46.7	56.6	61.3	58.8	49.0	36.1	22.9	9.8	34.2
Extreme Maximum Temp. (°F)	65	64	80	93	96	103	103	105	100	90	80	64	105
Extreme Minimum Temp. (°F)	-36	-31	-17	6	27	33	43	41	22	9	-17	-28	-36
Days Maximum Temp. ≥ 90°F	0	0	0	0	1	4	8	4	1	0	0	0	18
Days Maximum Temp. ≤ 32°F	23	16	8	1	0	0	0	0	0	0	8	19	75
Days Minimum Temp. ≤ 32°F	31	28	27	13	2	0	0	0	1	11	25	31	169
Days Minimum Temp. ≤ 0°F	14	8	2	0	0	0	0	0	0	0	1	8	33
Heating Degree Days (base 65°F)	1,608	1,279	1,041	588	226	43	9	23	171	520	990	1,434	7,932
Cooling Degree Days (base 65°F)	0	0	0	6	38	149	243	176	55	3	0	0	670
Mean Precipitation (in.)	0.80	0.55	2.14	2.94	3.51	4.36	4.00	3.51	2.75	1.99	1.77	0.76	29.08
Days With ≥ 0.1" Precipitation	2	2	5	7	8	7	6	5	5	4	4	2	57
Days With ≥ 1.0" Precipitation	0	0	0	1	1	1	1	1	1	1	0	0	7
Mean Snowfall (in.)	9.3	5.8	9.4	3.2	0.0	0.0	0.0	0.0	trace	0.9	6.9	7.6	43.1
Days With ≥ 1.0" Snow Depth	27	21	15	3	0	0	0	0	0	0	8	22	96

Winnebago *Faribault County*   Elevation: 1,108 ft.   Latitude: 43° 46' N   Longitude: 94° 10' W

	JAN	FEB	MAR	APR	MAY	JUN	JUL	AUG	SEP	OCT	NOV	DEC	YEAR
Mean Maximum Temp. (°F)	20.6	27.4	38.9	55.4	69.4	78.8	82.2	79.6	71.6	59.0	40.1	25.9	54.1
Mean Temp. (°F)	11.5	18.5	30.2	44.8	58.1	68.0	71.8	69.2	60.4	47.9	31.8	17.7	44.2
Mean Minimum Temp. (°F)	2.4	9.5	21.5	34.1	46.8	57.2	61.3	58.9	49.1	36.8	23.5	9.5	34.2
Extreme Maximum Temp. (°F)	59	63	78	92	94	102	101	103	97	92	80	67	103
Extreme Minimum Temp. (°F)	-30	-32	-13	8	26	39	44	44	25	14	-13	-29	-32
Days Maximum Temp. ≥ 90°F	0	0	0	0	1	3	5	2	1	0	0	0	12
Days Maximum Temp. ≤ 32°F	24	17	9	1	0	0	0	0	0	0	9	21	81
Days Minimum Temp. ≤ 32°F	31	28	27	13	1	0	0	0	1	10	25	31	167
Days Minimum Temp. ≤ 0°F	15	9	2	0	0	0	0	0	0	0	1	9	36
Heating Degree Days (base 65°F)	1,654	1,309	1,072	604	247	49	11	26	184	527	989	1,460	8,132
Cooling Degree Days (base 65°F)	0	0	0	5	41	147	223	164	50	4	0	0	634
Mean Precipitation (in.)	0.86	0.64	1.85	2.96	3.90	4.46	4.14	4.05	2.83	2.52	1.83	0.96	31.00
Days With ≥ 0.1" Precipitation	3	2	5	6	8	7	7	7	5	5	4	3	62
Days With ≥ 1.0" Precipitation	0	0	0	1	1	1	1	1	1	1	0	0	7
Mean Snowfall (in.)	11.1	6.2	8.2	3.1	trace	0.0	0.0	0.0	0.0	0.4	6.7	9.4	45.1
Days With ≥ 1.0" Snow Depth	28	20	14	2	0	0	0	0	0	0	7	22	93

Winton Power Plant *Lake County*   Elevation: 1,335 ft.   Latitude: 47° 56' N   Longitude: 91° 46' W

	JAN	FEB	MAR	APR	MAY	JUN	JUL	AUG	SEP	OCT	NOV	DEC	YEAR
Mean Maximum Temp. (°F)	14.7	22.5	35.2	50.4	65.7	73.3	78.1	75.3	63.5	50.5	32.3	18.5	48.3
Mean Temp. (°F)	3.8	10.7	23.4	38.8	53.3	61.9	67.1	64.6	54.1	42.1	25.4	9.4	37.9
Mean Minimum Temp. (°F)	-7.2	-1.4	11.7	27.1	40.9	50.7	56.0	53.9	44.6	33.7	18.5	0.3	27.4
Extreme Maximum Temp. (°F)	49	55	64	86	91	100	96	97	97	79	70	50	100
Extreme Minimum Temp. (°F)	-44	-40	-35	-11	15	31	40	34	24	7	-24	-40	-44
Days Maximum Temp. ≥ 90°F	0	0	0	0	0	1	2	1	0	0	0	0	4
Days Maximum Temp. ≤ 32°F	28	22	12	2	0	0	0	0	0	1	15	27	107
Days Minimum Temp. ≤ 32°F	31	28	29	22	6	0	0	0	2	15	27	30	190
Days Minimum Temp. ≤ 0°F	20	15	7	1	0	0	0	0	0	0	2	15	60
Heating Degree Days (base 65°F)	1,897	1,529	1,284	782	373	131	41	82	333	703	1,181	1,721	10,057
Cooling Degree Days (base 65°F)	0	0	0	0	17	43	112	81	8	0	na	na	na
Mean Precipitation (in.)	0.98	0.73	1.23	1.72	2.94	4.16	3.74	3.89	3.73	2.60	1.67	0.98	28.37
Days With ≥ 0.1" Precipitation	3	2	4	4	7	8	8	8	8	6	5	3	66
Days With ≥ 1.0" Precipitation	0	0	0	0	0	1	1	1	1	0	0	0	4
Mean Snowfall (in.)	na	7.2	na	2.5	0.3	0.0	0.0	0.0	trace	0.6	na	na	na
Days With ≥ 1.0" Snow Depth	31	27	29	12	0	0	0	0	0	1	16	30	146

Worthington 2 NNE *Nobles County*   Elevation: 1,568 ft.   Latitude: 43° 39' N   Longitude: 95° 35' W

	JAN	FEB	MAR	APR	MAY	JUN	JUL	AUG	SEP	OCT	NOV	DEC	YEAR
Mean Maximum Temp. (°F)	21.5	27.7	39.3	55.1	69.0	78.6	82.6	79.7	71.8	59.1	39.8	26.3	54.2
Mean Temp. (°F)	12.2	18.6	30.2	44.1	57.2	67.1	71.3	68.3	59.5	47.1	30.8	17.7	43.7
Mean Minimum Temp. (°F)	2.9	9.5	21.0	33.1	45.4	55.5	59.9	56.7	47.1	34.9	21.7	9.1	33.1
Extreme Maximum Temp. (°F)	63	64	79	91	99	103	103	104	101	92	79	64	104
Extreme Minimum Temp. (°F)	-29	-30	-13	5	24	37	42	39	24	10	-11	-28	-30
Days Maximum Temp. ≥ 90°F	0	0	0	0	1	3	6	3	1	0	0	0	14
Days Maximum Temp. ≤ 32°F	24	17	9	1	0	0	0	0	0	0	9	21	81
Days Minimum Temp. ≤ 32°F	31	28	27	15	2	0	0	0	2	13	26	31	175
Days Minimum Temp. ≤ 0°F	14	9	2	0	0	0	0	0	0	0	1	8	34
Heating Degree Days (base 65°F)	1,632	1,305	1,073	624	267	59	13	39	206	552	1,020	1,460	8,250
Cooling Degree Days (base 65°F)	0	0	0	5	31	131	208	148	49	3	0	0	575
Mean Precipitation (in.)	0.72	0.55	1.99	2.76	3.38	4.58	3.62	3.56	2.64	1.88	1.61	0.69	27.98
Days With ≥ 0.1" Precipitation	2	2	5	6	7	7	6	6	5	4	3	2	55
Days With ≥ 1.0" Precipitation	0	0	0	1	1	1	1	1	1	0	0	0	5
Mean Snowfall (in.)	8.2	*5.6*	*7.5*	3.2	trace	0.0	0.0	0.0	trace	1.0	6.4	*7.1*	*39.0*
Days With ≥ 1.0" Snow Depth	25	20	*14*	3	0	0	0	0	0	1	10	20	*93*

Wright 4 NW *Carlton County*   Elevation: 1,292 ft.   Latitude: 46° 43' N   Longitude: 93° 04' W

	JAN	FEB	MAR	APR	MAY	JUN	JUL	AUG	SEP	OCT	NOV	DEC	YEAR
Mean Maximum Temp. (°F)	18.0	25.8	36.7	53.1	67.2	74.9	79.1	76.7	66.9	54.5	35.6	22.5	50.9
Mean Temp. (°F)	7.2	14.4	26.0	40.8	53.4	61.6	66.4	64.5	55.4	44.1	27.5	13.4	39.6
Mean Minimum Temp. (°F)	-3.7	3.0	15.3	28.5	39.6	48.3	53.7	52.3	44.0	33.7	19.4	4.2	28.2
Extreme Maximum Temp. (°F)	54	62	74	93	94	95	100	100	97	82	72	55	100
Extreme Minimum Temp. (°F)	-52	-45	-28	-12	18	27	33	28	18	1	-28	-47	-52
Days Maximum Temp. ≥ 90°F	0	0	0	0	0	0	2	1	0	0	0	0	3
Days Maximum Temp. ≤ 32°F	27	19	10	1	0	0	0	0	0	1	12	25	95
Days Minimum Temp. ≤ 32°F	31	28	29	21	8	1	0	0	4	14	27	31	194
Days Minimum Temp. ≤ 0°F	18	12	5	0	0	0	0	0	0	0	2	13	50
Heating Degree Days (base 65°F)	1,790	1,424	1,203	721	362	134	50	84	298	642	1,117	1,597	9,422
Cooling Degree Days (base 65°F)	0	0	0	1	11	41	99	81	16	1	0	0	250
Mean Precipitation (in.)	0.95	0.64	1.39	2.12	3.24	4.28	4.20	3.97	3.38	2.69	1.70	0.85	29.41
Days With ≥ 0.1" Precipitation	3	2	4	5	7	8	8	7	7	6	4	3	64
Days With ≥ 1.0" Precipitation	0	0	0	0	1	1	1	1	1	1	0	0	6
Mean Snowfall (in.)	14.1	7.7	9.7	4.6	0.3	0.0	0.0	0.0	trace	1.6	11.0	10.2	59.2
Days With ≥ 1.0" Snow Depth	31	28	25	7	0	0	0	0	0	1	12	28	132

Zumbrota *Goodhue County*   Elevation: 984 ft.   Latitude: 44° 18' N   Longitude: 92° 40' W

	JAN	FEB	MAR	APR	MAY	JUN	JUL	AUG	SEP	OCT	NOV	DEC	YEAR
Mean Maximum Temp. (°F)	23.0	29.3	41.6	58.3	71.2	80.1	83.8	81.3	73.1	61.1	42.0	28.2	56.1
Mean Temp. (°F)	12.8	18.9	31.5	46.2	58.3	67.6	71.5	69.3	60.8	49.0	33.0	19.3	44.9
Mean Minimum Temp. (°F)	2.5	8.5	21.4	33.9	45.5	55.0	59.3	57.2	48.4	36.9	23.9	10.4	33.6
Extreme Maximum Temp. (°F)	57	63	82	92	92	102	103	103	98	92	78	65	103
Extreme Minimum Temp. (°F)	-39	-37	-17	-1	22	32	40	34	21	11	-17	-40	-40
Days Maximum Temp. ≥ 90°F	0	0	0	0	0	3	6	3	1	0	0	0	13
Days Maximum Temp. ≤ 32°F	23	15	6	0	0	0	0	0	0	0	6	19	69
Days Minimum Temp. ≤ 32°F	31	27	26	14	3	0	0	0	2	11	24	30	168
Days Minimum Temp. ≤ 0°F	14	9	3	0	0	0	0	0	0	0	1	8	35
Heating Degree Days (base 65°F)	1,615	1,297	1,030	564	239	54	13	29	178	495	954	1,410	7,878
Cooling Degree Days (base 65°F)	0	0	0	6	40	143	224	173	63	5	0	0	654
Mean Precipitation (in.)	1.01	0.71	1.99	3.26	3.97	4.33	4.37	4.24	3.51	2.69	2.23	0.98	33.29
Days With ≥ 0.1" Precipitation	3	2	5	7	8	7	7	7	6	5	5	3	65
Days With ≥ 1.0" Precipitation	0	0	0	1	1	1	1	1	1	1	0	0	7
Mean Snowfall (in.)	10.7	6.7	7.8	3.0	0.0	0.0	0.0	0.0	0.0	0.5	5.9	8.4	43.0
Days With ≥ 1.0" Snow Depth	na	*12*	*8*	1	0	0	0	0	0	0	0	*4*	*12*	na

Note: See Appendix D for explanation of data.

MISSISSIPPI

PHYSICAL FEATURES. The State of Mississippi extends on the west from the Mississippi River to about longitude 88° W., between latitude 31° and 35° N; and from the Pearl River on the west to about 88.5° W. longitude below latitude 31° N. The southern boundary of this area, a sort of "panhandle," is Mississippi Sound, which is an arm of the Gulf of Mexico. Land areas near the coast line, in contrast to those of Louisiana, are sharply defined, with the land rising to elevations of 10 to 20 feet behind the beaches. The coast is cut by numerous bays. A string of islands parallels the coast a few miles offshore. The waters of Mississippi Sound provide a natural air conditioning to ameliorate the summer heat. Thus Biloxi has an average of only 55 days with temperature 90°F. or higher, while only 40 miles inland Wiggins averages 105 such days.

A triangular area comprising nearly one-third of the State, with its apex in Rankin County and its base on the coast, is composed of rolling hills at from 200 to 500 feet above sea level. The "Delta" region in the northwest extends from the Yazoo-Tallahatchie River system westward to the Mississippi River. Between the Delta and the upland prairie the land is broken by a series of ridges and valleys which are oriented in a general southwest-northeast direction. These extend from the Tennessee border to the lower Mississippi River. From Vicksburg to Natchez these ridges stop abruptly at the river forming high bluffs along its left bank. The valleys form natural paths for the northeastward passage of tornadoes and for southward drainage of cold winter air. On clear, cold nights temperatures in these valleys are lower, sometimes as much as 20°F., than on the nearby hilltops.

GENERAL CLIMATE. In its broader aspects the climate of Mississippi is determined by the huge land mass to the north, its subtropical latitude, and the Gulf of Mexico to the south, but modifications are introduced by the varied topography.

The prevailing southerly winds provide a moist, semitropical climate, with conditions often favorable for afternoon thundershowers. When the pressure distribution is altered so as to bring westerly or northerly winds, periods of hotter and drier weather interrupt the prevailing moist condition. The high humidity, combined with hot days and nights in the interior from May to September, produces discomfort at times. The principal relief is by thunderstorms, sometimes accompanied by locally violent and destructive winds.

In the colder season the State is alternately subjected to warm tropical air and cold continental air, in periods of varying length. However, cold spells seldom last over three or four days. The ground rarely freezes, and then mostly only in the extreme north and only a few inches deep. Although slowly warmed by its southward journey, the cold air occasionally brings large and rather sudden drops in temperature. In winter the Atlantic High is also sometimes located far enough west to serve as a barrier to cold air approaching the State. Most frequently this produces a pattern of warm, clear weather over the southern part of the State with cold, rainy weather to the north of the "front," but occasionally the entire State will be under the balmy influence of this subtropical anticyclone.

Mississippi is south of the average track of winter cyclones, but occasionally one moves over the State. In some winters a succession of such cyclones will develop in the Gulf of Mexico or in Texas and move over or near the State. The State is also occasionally in the path of tropical storms or hurricanes.

FLOODS. All of the State is in the Gulf of Mexico drainage. Main rivers which flow directly into the Gulf include the Tombigbee in the northeast portion, and the Pascagoula and Pearl which forms the southwestern boundary. The Mississippi River forms most of the western boundary. The flood season in Mississippi is from November through June (the period of greatest rainfall), with March and April being the months of greatest frequency. The season of high flows in the main Mississippi River is during the first six months of the year. In other streams flooding sometimes occurs during the summer from persistent thundershower rains, or during the late summer and early fall from heavy rains associated with tropical storms originating in the Gulf of Mexico.

PRECIPITATION. Mean annual precipitation ranges from about 50 inches in the northwest to 65 inches in the southeast. During the freeze-free season rainfall ranges from 23 to 25 inches in the Delta districts to 36 to 38 inches in the southeast. During the winter the precipitation maximum is centered over the northern and western counties (16 to 18 inches) with the minimum (13 inches) on the coast. In summer the maximum shifts to the coastal counties (19 to 21 inches) and the minimum to the Delta counties (nine to 11 inches). The spring and fall patterns are very similar to the summer pattern. The fall months are the driest of the year, precipitation ranging from about eight to 13 inches. Fall is the most agreeable season of the year, with cool nights and mild, clear, sunny days persisting for several days, and even weeks, at a time.

While snowfall is not of much economic importance, it is not such a rare event in Mississippi as is generally believed. Measurable snow or sleet falls on some part of the State most years.

TEMPERATURE. The normal annual temperature ranges from 62°F. in the northern border counties to 68°F. in the coastal counties. The lowest January normal is 43°F. in the north-central area, ranging upward to 54°F. in the coastal district. The highest July normal is 84°F. in the upper Delta, ranging downward to 80 to 81°F. in parts of central and north-central districts. Temperatures of 90°F. or higher occur on an average of 55 days per year on the immediate Gulf coast under the ameliorating effect of the relatively cooler Gulf waters. There is a rapid increase in number of days 90°F. or higher inland from the coast, reaching a maximum of 105 such days in Stone County. Temperatures of 32°F. (freezing) or lower occur on an average of 11 days a year on the immediate Gulf coast, increasing to a maximum of 60 days in Panola County. Temperatures exceed 100°F. at one or more weather stations each summer. They drop to zero or lower in Mississippi on an average of once in five years and to 32°F. or lower on the Gulf coast almost every winter.

STORMS. Thunderstorms occur on an average of 50 to 60 days a year in the northern districts and 70 to 80 days a year near the coast. Thundershowers occur more frequently in July than any other month, with the least in December. Those in late fall, winter, and early spring are more apt to be attended by high winds than in summer. However, in the interior in summer after a spell of unusually high temperatures, thunderstorms may develop with local violence.

A hazard to life and property in Mississippi is the tropical cyclone which occurs from June to November. While these storms generally move into the State on the coast, they have on occasion entered as far north as Meridian and Greenville after crossing part of Alabama or Louisiana. These latter storms are usually weakened considerably by passage over land. Hurricanes which move inland over southeast Louisiana may be as damaging on the Mississippi coast as those which cross the coast line. This is especially true of those moving from the southeast because of the usually more severe winds in the northeast quadrant and because of the high seas which move across Mississippi Sound and pile up on the shore. Those which move westward offshore often cause tide and wind damage on the coast. Those which move northeastward across or south of the Louisiana Delta and move inland between Mobile and Panama City are usually less damaging because winds are offshore and tides are subnormal. Hurricanes which move inland on the Alabama coast may affect Mississippi only slightly because of less intense and offshore winds in their western portions.

About a fourth of the tropical cyclones which affect Mississippi are of hurricane intensity with winds of 74 m.p.h. or higher at some point. One-half of all hurricanes occur in September and twice as many tropical cyclones occur in August and September as during June, July, October, and November combined.

Tornadoes occur in all months in Mississippi, but the largest number of reported tornadoes occur in March, while April, February, and May rank high. Tornadoes may occur at any place in Mississippi, but are least likely in the tier of counties within the "panhandle" below 31 N. latitude; this, however, is the area where hurricanes are most likely to occur.

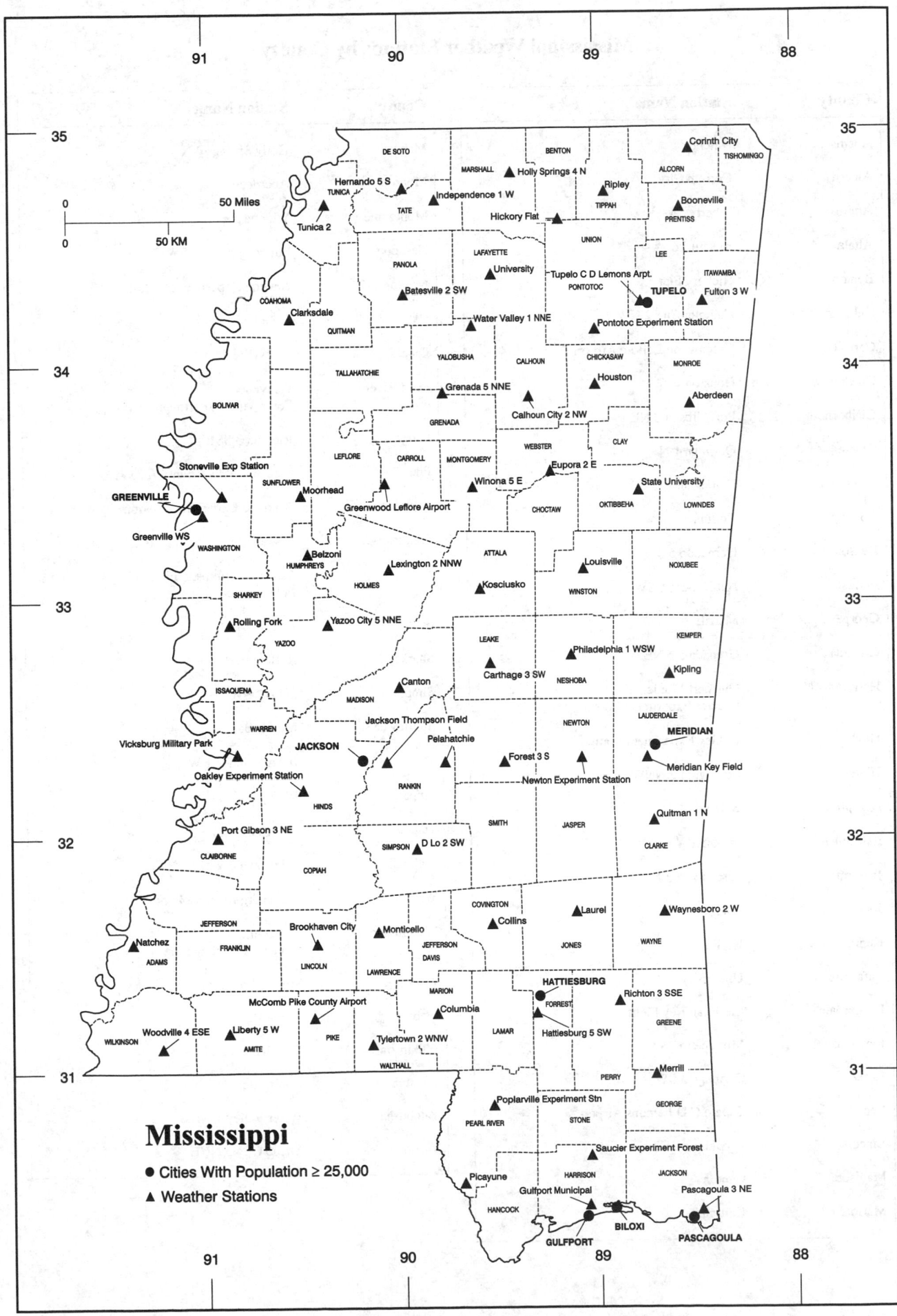

Mississippi

● Cities With Population ≥ 25,000
▲ Weather Stations

Mississippi Weather Stations by County

County	Station Name
Adams	Natchez
Alcorn	Corinth City
Amite	Liberty 5 W
Attala	Kosciusko
Benton	Hickory Flat
Calhoun	Calhoun City 2 NW
Carroll	Greenwood Leflore Airport
Chickasaw	Houston
Claiborne	Port Gibson 3 NE
Clarke	Quitman 1 N
Coahoma	Clarksdale
Covington	Collins
De Soto	Hernando 5 S
Forrest	Hattiesburg 5 SW
George	Merrill
Grenada	Grenada 5 NNE
Harrison	Gulfport Municipal Saucier Experiment Forest
Hinds	Oakley Experiment Station
Holmes	Lexington 2 NNW
Humphreys	Belzoni
Itawamba	Fulton 3 W
Jackson	Pascagoula 3 NE
Jones	Laurel
Kemper	Kipling
Lafayette	University
Lauderdale	Meridian Key Field
Lawrence	Monticello
Leake	Carthage 3 SW
Lee	Tupelo C D Lemons Airport
Lincoln	Brookhaven City
Madison	Canton
Marion	Columbia

County	Station Name
Marshall	Holly Springs 4 N
Monroe	Aberdeen
Montgomery	Winona 5 E
Neshoba	Philadelphia 1 WSW
Newton	Newton Experiment Station
Oktibbeha	State University
Panola	Batesville 2 SW
Pearl River	Picayune Poplarville Experiment Station
Perry	Richton 3 SSE
Pike	McComb Pike County Airport
Pontotoc	Pontotoc Experiment Station
Prentiss	Booneville
Rankin	Jackson Thompson Field Pelahatchie
Scott	Forest 3 S
Sharkey	Rolling Fork
Simpson	D Lo 2 SW
Sunflower	Moorhead
Tate	Independence 1 W
Tippah	Ripley
Tunica	Tunica 2
Walthall	Tylertown 2 WNW
Warren	Vicksburg Military Park
Washington	Greenville Stoneville Exp. Station
Wayne	Waynesboro 2 W
Webster	Eupora 2 E
Wilkinson	Woodville 4 ESE
Winston	Louisville
Yalobusha	Water Valley 1 NNE
Yazoo	Yazoo City 5 NNE

Mississippi Weather Stations by City

City	Station Name	Miles
Biloxi	Gulfport Municipal	8
	Saucier Experiment Forest	17
Greenville	Greenville	2
	Stoneville Exp. Station	8
Gulfport	Gulfport Municipal	2
	Saucier Experiment Forest	17
Hattiesburg	Hattiesburg 5 SW	5
Jackson	Jackson Thompson Field	7
Meridian	Meridian Key Field	4
Pascagoula	Pascagoula 3 NE	4
Tupelo	Fulton 3 W	16
	Pontotoc Experiment Station	17
	Tupelo C D Lemons Airport	2

Note: Miles is the distance between the geographic center of the city and the weather station.

Mississippi Weather Stations by Elevation

Feet	Station Name
580	Louisville
518	Ripley
488	Booneville
482	Holly Springs 4 N
479	Forest 3 S
439	Eupora 2 E
439	Tylertown 2 WNW
433	Brookhaven City
410	Kosciusko
410	McComb Pike County Airport
410	Philadelphia 1 WSW
403	Pontotoc Experiment Station
396	Hickory Flat
396	Woodville 4 ESE
387	Winona 5 E
383	Corinth City
383	Hattiesburg 5 SW
377	Hernando 5 S
377	University
374	Water Valley 1 NNE
367	Carthage 3 SW
367	Pelahatchie
360	Tupelo C D Lemons Airport
347	Fulton 3 W
347	Newton Experiment Station
344	Independence 1 W
344	Liberty 5 W
334	D Lo 2 SW
314	Kipling
314	Lexington 2 NNW
311	Poplarville Experiment Station
308	Jackson Thompson Field
298	Quitman 1 N
291	Meridian Key Field
288	Collins
278	Grenada 5 NNE
269	Houston
265	Calhoun City 2 NW
252	Vicksburg Military Park
226	Saucier Experiment Forest
223	Canton
223	Laurel
219	Batesville 2 SW
203	Monticello
203	Oakley Experiment Station
200	Waynesboro 2 W
196	Aberdeen
196	Tunica 2
193	Natchez
183	State University
170	Clarksdale
164	Richton 3 SSE
154	Columbia
154	Greenwood Leflore Airport
131	Greenville

Feet	Station Name
124	Stoneville Exp. Station
118	Port Gibson 3 NE
114	Moorhead
108	Belzoni
104	Rolling Fork
104	Yazoo City 5 NNE
59	Picayune
49	Merrill
22	Gulfport Municipal
9	Pascagoula 3 NE

Jackson Thompson Field

Jackson is located on the west bank of the Pearl River, about 45 miles east of the Mississippi River and 150 miles north of the Gulf of Mexico. The nearby terrain is gently rolling with no topographic features that appreciably influence the weather. The National Weather Service Office is nearly seven miles east-northeast of the Jackson Post Office and over five miles southwest of the Ross Barnett Reservoir.

The climate is significantly humid during most of the year, with relatively short mild winters and long warm summers. The Gulf of Mexico has a moderating effect on the climate. Cold spells are fairly frequent in winter, but are usually of short duration. Temperatures occasionally exceed 80 degrees in mid-winter. In summer, temperatures reach 90 degrees or higher on about two-thirds of the days, 100 degree readings are infrequent. Extended periods of very hot weather are rare.

Snowfall averages less than two inches per season. Rainfall is abundant and fairly well-distributed throughout the year.

Thunderstorms can be expected on an average of 65 days a year, usually occurring in each month. They are most frequent in summer when they occur on about one-third of the days.

Jackson Thompson Field *Rankin County*   Elevation: 308 ft.   Latitude: 32° 19' N   Longitude: 90° 05' W

	JAN	FEB	MAR	APR	MAY	JUN	JUL	AUG	SEP	OCT	NOV	DEC	YEAR
Mean Maximum Temp. (°F)	56.0	61.2	69.2	76.6	83.5	90.1	92.2	91.9	87.3	77.8	67.6	59.7	76.1
Mean Temp. (°F)	45.4	49.6	57.2	64.3	72.2	79.2	81.9	81.3	76.3	65.1	55.6	48.8	64.7
Mean Minimum Temp. (°F)	34.8	37.9	45.2	52.0	60.8	68.2	71.6	70.7	65.1	52.3	43.5	37.9	53.3
Extreme Maximum Temp. (°F)	82	85	89	94	96	105	106	104	104	95	88	84	106
Extreme Minimum Temp. (°F)	2	10	15	27	38	47	55	55	41	26	17	4	2
Days Maximum Temp. ≥ 90°F	0	0	0	0	5	18	24	23	13	1	0	0	84
Days Maximum Temp. ≤ 32°F	1	0	0	0	0	0	0	0	0	0	0	0	1
Days Minimum Temp. ≤ 32°F	14	10	4	0	0	0	0	0	0	0	5	12	45
Days Minimum Temp. ≤ 0°F	0	0	0	0	0	0	0	0	0	0	0	0	0
Heating Degree Days (base 65°F)	605	436	268	105	11	0	0	0	6	96	301	505	2,333
Cooling Degree Days (base 65°F)	3	8	31	88	245	437	538	520	344	106	24	10	2,354
Mean Precipitation (in.)	5.67	4.54	5.78	5.81	4.85	3.71	4.71	3.84	3.33	3.68	4.87	5.35	56.14
Maximum Precipitation (in.)	14.1	10.3	15.1	15.9	10.8	8.2	13.3	8.3	9.6	9.1	10.0	17.7	92.8
Minimum Precipitation (in.)	0.8	1.4	2.0	1.2	0.3	0.1	1.0	0.6	0.6	0.5	0.5	0.9	38.9
Maximum 24-hr. Precipitation (in.)	4.7	3.3	3.8	4.9	3.2	3.2	4.9	4.0	4.6	7.0	3.5	4.9	7.0
Days With ≥ 0.1" Precipitation	8	6	7	6	7	5	7	6	5	5	6	7	75
Days With ≥ 1.0" Precipitation	2	2	2	2	2	1	1	1	1	1	2	2	19
Mean Snowfall (in.)	0.5	trace	trace	trace	0.0	0.0	0.0	0.0	0.0	0.0	trace	0.2	0.7
Maximum Snowfall (in.)	6	4	5	1	0	0	0	0	0	0	trace	3	9
Maximum 24-hr. Snowfall (in.)	6	4	5	1	0	0	0	0	0	0	trace	2	6
Days With ≥ 1.0" Snow Depth	0	0	0	0	0	0	0	0	0	0	0	0	0
Thunderstorm Days	2	3	6	6	7	9	13	10	5	2	3	2	68
Foggy Days	16	13	16	15	18	18	18	22	20	17	15	16	204
Predominant Sky Cover	OVR	OVR	OVR	OVR	OVR	SCT	SCT	SCT	CLR	CLR	OVR	OVR	OVR
Mean Relative Humidity 6am (%)	87	87	87	91	92	92	94	95	94	93	90	87	91
Mean Relative Humidity 3pm (%)	59	54	51	50	53	53	57	55	54	49	52	58	54
Mean Dewpoint (°F)	37	38	46	54	62	68	72	71	66	54	46	40	55
Prevailing Wind Direction	N	N	S	SSE	SSE	S	SSW	SE	SE	SE	SSE	SSE	SSE
Prevailing Wind Speed (mph)	10	10	10	10	9	8	7	7	8	8	9	10	9
Maximum Wind Gust (mph)	59	53	68	63	60	63	67	56	52	51	69	48	69

Meridian Key Field

Mild winters and warm summers describe the general temperature pattern for Meridian. However, the terrain features exert a pronounced influence, particularly during the winter months. The hills to the north, east, and west leave Meridian in a valley. During periods of near calm winds, cold air drainage brings temperatures which may be as much as 10 degrees lower than for other locations in the area. January is usually the coldest month, followed closely by December and February. Sub-zero temperatures are very rare. Summer temperatures are consistently warm. Prolonged periods with above 100 degrees readings are rare.

Precipitation is distributed evenly throughout the year. The widespread rains of the winter months reach a maximum in March. Spring showers reach a minimum in May, followed by localized summer thunderstorms in July and August. The driest period of the year is in late September and October, followed by the onset of winter-type precipitation in late November. This pattern is ideally suited to agricultural operations since the spring rains are conducive to crop growth in the early stages and the dry period in the fall is ideal for harvesting operations. Summer thunderstorms are highly localized and occur on one in three days during July and August.

The long growing season averages 235 days, nearly eight months. The average date of the first occurrence of a temperature as low as 32 degrees in autumn is November 7, and the occurrence of 32 degrees before October 20 is very rare. The average date of the last occurrence of 32 degrees in spring is March 19, although 32 degrees has been recorded in late April. Some portions of the area not affected by cold air drainage may have slightly longer average growing seasons.

The nearby Gulf of Mexico provides an abundant supply of moisture to the Meridian area and results in high humidities for prolonged periods. Humidities of greater than 90 percent occur nightly during every month except for short periods during the autumn and winter when cool continental air is flowing from the north. Lowest humidities are observed during the early afternoons, but seldom reach below 40 percent except for short periods.

March is generally the windiest month of the year due to the frequent occurrence of late winter and spring storms across the Gulf States. October has the lowest average wind speed. Prevailing winds are from the north and northeast during the autumn and winter months, and from the south and southwest during the spring and summer. Local thunderstorms produce short periods of high winds during the spring and summer months and can be quite destructive. Severe thunderstorms and tornadoes have caused considerable loss of life and property in this area. The highest sustained wind speed recorded was 50 mph, but there have been short periods with winds in excess of 50 mph.

Fifty years of record show that December, January, and February receive the smallest amount of possible sunshine. About 40 to 45 percent of the days during these months are cloudy. Sunshine reaches a maximum during the dry period in the fall, September and October. These months are characterized by long periods of cloudless skies.

Thunderstorms normally occur during every month in the year, but most occur during the summer months. These summer thunderstorms provide most of the precipitation during the crop growing season.

Meridian Key Field *Lauderdale County*   Elevation: 291 ft.   Latitude: 32° 20' N   Longitude: 88° 45' W

	JAN	FEB	MAR	APR	MAY	JUN	JUL	AUG	SEP	OCT	NOV	DEC	YEAR
Mean Maximum Temp. (°F)	56.9	61.9	69.7	76.9	83.5	89.7	92.4	92.2	87.6	77.7	68.1	60.5	76.4
Mean Temp. (°F)	45.7	49.7	57.0	63.8	71.5	78.3	81.4	81.0	76.0	64.6	55.4	49.1	64.5
Mean Minimum Temp. (°F)	34.5	37.4	44.2	50.6	59.4	66.9	70.4	69.8	64.4	51.4	42.7	37.6	52.4
Extreme Maximum Temp. (°F)	82	85	90	95	96	104	107	104	105	96	86	84	107
Extreme Minimum Temp. (°F)	4	8	15	28	38	42	56	55	40	28	16	2	2
Days Maximum Temp. ≥ 90°F	0	0	0	0	4	16	24	24	13	1	0	0	82
Days Maximum Temp. ≤ 32°F	0	0	0	0	0	0	0	0	0	0	0	0	0
Days Minimum Temp. ≤ 32°F	15	10	4	1	0	0	0	0	0	0	6	12	48
Days Minimum Temp. ≤ 0°F	0	0	0	0	0	0	0	0	0	0	0	0	0
Heating Degree Days (base 65°F)	595	431	270	106	14	0	0	0	5	102	301	496	2,320
Cooling Degree Days (base 65°F)	3	8	26	79	228	414	523	510	334	100	21	10	2,256
Mean Precipitation (in.)	5.91	5.40	6.96	5.62	4.84	3.94	5.59	3.49	3.59	3.59	4.81	5.35	59.09
Maximum Precipitation (in.)	11.4	15.9	16.5	16.8	9.8	8.9	15.3	10.3	10.2	10.6	13.9	14.8	79.0
Minimum Precipitation (in.)	1.2	1.7	1.3	0.9	0.3	0.7	1.1	0.7	0.1	0	0.4	1.1	35.3
Maximum 24-hr. Precipitation (in.)	5.3	7.5	6.5	5.6	3.4	2.7	6.9	4.8	4.5	5.3	4.2	8.0	8.0
Days With ≥ 0.1" Precipitation	8	6	8	6	7	7	8	6	5	4	7	7	79
Days With ≥ 1.0" Precipitation	2	2	2	2	2	1	2	1	1	1	2	2	20
Mean Snowfall (in.)	0.4	trace	0.2	0.1	trace	0.0	trace	0.0	0.0	0.0	trace	trace	0.7
Maximum Snowfall (in.)	7	3	6	3	0	0	0	0	0	0	trace	18	20
Maximum 24-hr. Snowfall (in.)	5	3	5	2	0	0	0	0	0	0	trace	14	14
Days With ≥ 1.0" Snow Depth	0	0	0	0	0	0	0	0	0	0	0	0	0
Thunderstorm Days	2	3	5	6	6	8	12	9	4	2	2	2	61
Foggy Days	15	13	14	15	17	16	18	20	18	17	15	15	193
Predominant Sky Cover	OVR	OVR	OVR	OVR	OVR	SCT	BRK	SCT	CLR	CLR	CLR	OVR	OVR
Mean Relative Humidity 6am (%)	87	86	87	90	91	91	93	93	92	91	88	87	90
Mean Relative Humidity 3pm (%)	56	51	47	46	50	52	57	54	53	48	49	55	52
Mean Dewpoint (°F)	37	39	44	52	61	67	71	70	65	54	45	39	54
Prevailing Wind Direction	S	S	S	S	S	S	S	S	N	N	S	S	S
Prevailing Wind Speed (mph)	8	9	10	9	8	7	6	6	7	8	8	9	8
Maximum Wind Gust (mph)	49	55	64	52	51	64	66	56	69	44	55	68	69

Tupelo C D Lemons Airport

Tupelo is located in the Black Prairie physiographic region of Mississippi. The surface is flat to gently undulating, underlain by soft limestone which has weathered into dark, fertile soils. The Black Prairie is largely devoid of trees, although precipitation in the region is more than sufficient for forest growth. The Black Prairie is bordered by the Fall Line Hills on the east and the Pontotoc Ridge on the west, thus being situated as a low, flat region from 20 to 25 miles wide trending northwest-southeast in the northeastern corner of Mississippi.

Agricultural interests are varied, but the region is a major producer of soybeans and livestock. Tupelo is the dominant urban center of the region, and population is projected to continue to increase in the future. Manufacturing and industry are growing rapidly in the area, enhanced by recent completion of the Tenn-Tom Waterway. Water supply for the growing municipal and industrial demand has been identified as a potential problem in the region as ground water is being used faster than it can be replenished by natural processes.

Average annual precipitation of over 50 inches is well distributed throughout the year. On average, about half the annual total falls between April and September, with March being the wettest month and October the driest month. There is a 90 percent probability that the freeze-free period will be longer than six months, with a 50 percent chance for a freeze before the end of October and after the first of April. Maximum temperatures over 90 degrees are expected on 78 days between May and September, with freezes expected on 66 days between October and March.

Record temperatures of over 105 degrees and below -10 degrees have been observed at Tupelo. Snow is not infrequent during the winter, although amounts average less than two and one-half inches each year. However, accumulations greater than 10 inches have been recorded. Frontal passages are common features of the climate from fall through spring, and there are seasonal occurrences of thunderstorms. Tornadoes, though quite rare, have occurred in the region, particularly during late spring. Precipitation amounts of one-half inch or more are expected on 37 days each year, with one-tenth inch or more expected on 73 days. Daily totals of precipitation have exceeded six inches on several occasions.

Tupelo C D Lemons Airport *Lee County*   Elevation: 360 ft.   Latitude: 34° 16' N   Longitude: 88° 46' W

	JAN	FEB	MAR	APR	MAY	JUN	JUL	AUG	SEP	OCT	NOV	DEC	YEAR
Mean Maximum Temp. (°F)	50.7	56.7	65.3	74.4	81.4	88.4	91.6	91.0	85.6	75.2	63.4	54.8	73.2
Mean Temp. (°F)	40.8	45.3	53.4	61.5	69.5	77.1	80.7	79.7	73.8	62.1	51.9	44.5	61.7
Mean Minimum Temp. (°F)	30.8	33.8	41.5	48.5	57.6	65.7	69.8	68.3	62.0	49.0	40.3	34.2	50.1
Extreme Maximum Temp. (°F)	80	84	86	93	98	101	105	105	104	92	85	79	105
Extreme Minimum Temp. (°F)	-6	4	7	23	30	43	52	51	35	24	11	-3	-6
Days Maximum Temp. ≥ 90°F	0	0	0	0	3	13	22	20	9	1	0	0	68
Days Maximum Temp. ≤ 32°F	2	1	0	0	0	0	0	0	0	0	0	1	4
Days Minimum Temp. ≤ 32°F	18	13	6	2	0	0	0	0	0	2	8	15	64
Days Minimum Temp. ≤ 0°F	0	0	0	0	0	0	0	0	0	0	0	0	0
Heating Degree Days (base 65°F)	745	553	365	153	28	0	0	0	13	145	396	630	3,028
Cooling Degree Days (base 65°F)	0	1	12	55	186	385	513	477	282	66	8	2	1,987
Mean Precipitation (in.)	5.05	4.72	6.47	4.98	6.08	4.80	3.73	2.75	3.32	3.66	4.79	6.22	56.57
Maximum Precipitation (in.)	7.0	10.9	9.3	12.2	17.6	11.1	6.5	6.2	6.3	7.9	9.6	14.5	81.0
Minimum Precipitation (in.)	0.3	2.3	2.1	0.5	1.3	0.2	0.5	0.6	0.6	0.4	1.5	1.6	37.6
Maximum 24-hr. Precipitation (in.)	2.1	4.5	3.8	3.7	7.9	3.7	3.6	2.8	3.1	3.3	3.7	5.0	7.9
Days With ≥ 0.1" Precipitation	8	6	8	7	8	7	7	5	5	5	7	8	81
Days With ≥ 1.0" Precipitation	2	1	2	2	2	1	1	1	1	1	2	2	18
Mean Snowfall (in.)	0.9	0.5	0.1	trace	trace	0.0	trace	0.0	0.0	trace	trace	0.2	1.7
Maximum Snowfall (in.)	7	5	2	trace	0	0	0	0	0	trace	trace	2	10
Maximum 24-hr. Snowfall (in.)	5	3	2	trace	0	0	0	0	0	trace	trace	2	5
Days With ≥ 1.0" Snow Depth	1	1	0	0	0	0	0	0	0	0	0	0	2
Thunderstorm Days	1	2	4	5	8	9	9	7	4	3	3	2	57
Foggy Days	15	14	14	12	19	20	19	22	19	19	15	15	203
Predominant Sky Cover	OVR	OVR	OVR	OVR	OVR	SCT	SCT	SCT	SCT	CLR	OVR	OVR	OVR
Mean Relative Humidity 6am (%)	82	82	81	85	88	89	91	92	91	89	84	82	86
Mean Relative Humidity 3pm (%)	57	55	49	47	54	54	54	53	52	50	53	59	53
Mean Dewpoint (°F)	32	35	41	49	59	67	70	69	63	52	42	35	51
Prevailing Wind Direction	N	N	S	S	S	S	S	N	N	N	SSE	S	S
Prevailing Wind Speed (mph)	9	9	9	9	8	7	7	7	7	7	9	8	8
Maximum Wind Gust (mph)	48	51	51	51	47	58	45	52	45	79	56	47	79

Aberdeen *Monroe County*   Elevation: 196 ft.   Latitude: 33° 50' N   Longitude: 88° 31' W

	JAN	FEB	MAR	APR	MAY	JUN	JUL	AUG	SEP	OCT	NOV	DEC	YEAR
Mean Maximum Temp. (°F)	53.0	58.0	66.9	75.3	82.0	88.2	91.5	90.4	85.1	75.4	64.8	56.9	74.0
Mean Temp. (°F)	43.0	47.0	55.0	62.8	70.5	77.5	81.2	80.1	74.5	63.4	53.5	46.4	62.9
Mean Minimum Temp. (°F)	33.0	36.0	43.0	50.2	59.0	66.8	70.8	69.8	63.9	51.3	42.2	35.9	51.8
Extreme Maximum Temp. (°F)	80	87	87	94	96	102	104	104	99	92	85	84	104
Extreme Minimum Temp. (°F)	0	5	14	28	35	48	55	50	40	29	17	-5	-5
Days Maximum Temp. ≥ 90°F	0	0	0	0	3	13	21	19	7	0	0	0	63
Days Maximum Temp. ≤ 32°F	2	0	0	0	0	0	0	0	0	0	0	0	2
Days Minimum Temp. ≤ 32°F	16	11	4	1	0	0	0	0	0	0	6	13	51
Days Minimum Temp. ≤ 0°F	0	0	0	0	0	0	0	0	0	0	0	0	0
Heating Degree Days (base 65°F)	676	504	319	128	18	0	0	0	9	117	349	572	2,692
Cooling Degree Days (base 65°F)	1	3	16	64	199	387	521	484	296	79	9	4	2,063
Mean Precipitation (in.)	5.41	4.66	6.17	5.04	5.58	4.32	3.97	3.04	3.72	4.11	4.49	5.18	55.69
Days With ≥ 0.1" Precipitation	8	7	7	6	7	7	7	5	6	5	7	7	79
Days With ≥ 1.0" Precipitation	2	2	2	2	2	1	1	1	1	1	1	2	18
Mean Snowfall (in.)	0.6	0.2	0.2	trace	0.0	0.0	0.0	0.0	0.0	0.0	trace	trace	1.0
Days With ≥ 1.0" Snow Depth	1	0	0	0	0	0	0	0	0	0	0	0	1

Batesville 2 SW *Panola County*   Elevation: 219 ft.   Latitude: 34° 18' N   Longitude: 89° 59' W

	JAN	FEB	MAR	APR	MAY	JUN	JUL	AUG	SEP	OCT	NOV	DEC	YEAR
Mean Maximum Temp. (°F)	49.3	55.0	63.9	72.9	80.6	87.7	91.0	90.4	85.5	75.4	63.3	54.0	72.4
Mean Temp. (°F)	39.0	43.5	52.0	60.5	69.0	76.6	79.9	78.3	72.6	61.5	51.1	43.3	60.6
Mean Minimum Temp. (°F)	28.7	32.0	40.1	48.1	57.4	65.5	68.8	66.2	59.7	47.6	38.8	32.5	48.8
Extreme Maximum Temp. (°F)	79	79	86	93	99	102	106	103	100	96	86	82	106
Extreme Minimum Temp. (°F)	-8	3	14	24	35	44	50	51	38	27	8	-2	-8
Days Maximum Temp. ≥ 90°F	0	0	0	0	2	12	21	19	10	1	0	0	65
Days Maximum Temp. ≤ 32°F	3	1	0	0	0	0	0	0	0	0	0	1	5
Days Minimum Temp. ≤ 32°F	21	16	8	2	0	0	0	0	0	0	2	10	17	76
Days Minimum Temp. ≤ 0°F	0	0	0	0	0	0	0	0	0	0	0	0	0
Heating Degree Days (base 65°F)	798	601	404	181	38	1	0	0	22	163	421	669	3,298
Cooling Degree Days (base 65°F)	0	1	10	53	180	367	480	433	254	65	9	3	1,855
Mean Precipitation (in.)	4.69	4.29	6.02	5.32	5.58	5.07	4.21	2.86	3.26	3.73	5.36	5.87	56.26
Days With ≥ 0.1" Precipitation	7	6	7	6	7	6	6	4	5	5	7	7	73
Days With ≥ 1.0" Precipitation	1	2	2	2	2	2	1	1	1	1	2	2	19
Mean Snowfall (in.)	*0.7*	0.3	trace	0.0	0.0	0.0	0.0	0.0	0.0	0.0	0.0	trace	*1.0*
Days With ≥ 1.0" Snow Depth	0	0	0	0	0	0	0	0	0	0	0	0	0

Belzoni *Humphreys County*   Elevation: 108 ft.   Latitude: 33° 12' N   Longitude: 90° 29' W

	JAN	FEB	MAR	APR	MAY	JUN	JUL	AUG	SEP	OCT	NOV	DEC	YEAR
Mean Maximum Temp. (°F)	51.7	57.6	66.3	75.3	83.3	90.2	92.8	92.4	87.7	77.7	65.7	56.0	74.7
Mean Temp. (°F)	42.6	47.4	55.7	64.0	72.5	79.5	82.2	81.0	75.6	64.7	54.6	46.3	63.8
Mean Minimum Temp. (°F)	33.5	37.1	45.1	52.7	61.6	68.8	71.6	69.6	63.4	51.7	43.4	36.6	52.9
Extreme Maximum Temp. (°F)	80	83	88	95	100	105	107	104	102	97	89	82	107
Extreme Minimum Temp. (°F)	2	6	14	30	41	50	56	53	41	26	17	1	1
Days Maximum Temp. ≥ 90°F	0	0	0	1	6	18	24	23	15	2	0	0	89
Days Maximum Temp. ≤ 32°F	2	1	0	0	0	0	0	0	0	0	0	1	4
Days Minimum Temp. ≤ 32°F	*14*	*8*	3	0	0	0	0	0	0	0	3	*10*	*38*
Days Minimum Temp. ≤ 0°F	0	0	0	0	0	0	0	0	0	0	0	0	0
Heating Degree Days (base 65°F)	685	494	304	110	12	0	0	0	9	103	321	*576*	*2,614*
Cooling Degree Days (base 65°F)	1	3	22	90	261	452	549	517	335	107	19	5	2,361
Mean Precipitation (in.)	5.85	4.52	6.34	5.76	6.11	4.07	5.19	3.18	2.87	4.02	4.98	5.70	58.59
Days With ≥ 0.1" Precipitation	7	6	7	6	7	6	6	5	4	5	6	7	72
Days With ≥ 1.0" Precipitation	2	2	2	2	2	1	2	1	1	1	2	2	20
Mean Snowfall (in.)	trace	trace	0.0	0.0	0.0	0.0	0.0	0.0	0.0	0.0	0.0	0.0	trace
Days With ≥ 1.0" Snow Depth	0	0	0	0	0	0	0	0	0	0	0	0	0

Booneville *Prentiss County*   Elevation: 488 ft.   Latitude: 34° 40' N   Longitude: 88° 34' W

	JAN	FEB	MAR	APR	MAY	JUN	JUL	AUG	SEP	OCT	NOV	DEC	YEAR
Mean Maximum Temp. (°F)	47.9	53.5	62.9	71.8	78.8	85.8	89.4	88.8	83.2	72.6	61.2	52.1	70.7
Mean Temp. (°F)	38.4	43.0	51.9	60.1	68.2	75.7	79.5	78.4	72.3	60.6	50.8	42.5	60.1
Mean Minimum Temp. (°F)	28.9	32.4	40.8	48.4	57.5	65.6	69.5	68.0	61.3	48.6	40.3	32.9	49.5
Extreme Maximum Temp. (°F)	79	83	85	93	92	100	106	105	98	92	84	79	106
Extreme Minimum Temp. (°F)	-8	1	11	27	36	45	54	50	40	28	11	-6	-8
Days Maximum Temp. ≥ 90°F	0	0	0	0	1	8	16	14	6	0	0	0	45
Days Maximum Temp. ≤ 32°F	3	2	0	0	0	0	0	0	0	0	0	2	7
Days Minimum Temp. ≤ 32°F	19	14	7	1	0	0	0	0	0	1	8	16	66
Days Minimum Temp. ≤ 0°F	0	0	0	0	0	0	0	0	0	0	0	0	0
Heating Degree Days (base 65°F)	819	614	409	185	42	1	0	0	22	177	424	691	3,384
Cooling Degree Days (base 65°F)	0	1	10	45	149	337	467	432	243	49	5	1	1,739
Mean Precipitation (in.)	5.34	4.49	6.32	5.41	6.24	4.48	4.10	3.50	3.63	3.65	5.41	6.28	58.85
Days With ≥ 0.1" Precipitation	7	6	8	7	8	7	7	6	6	5	7	8	82
Days With ≥ 1.0" Precipitation	2	1	2	2	2	1	1	1	1	1	2	2	19
Mean Snowfall (in.)	1.1	1.0	trace	trace	trace	0.0	0.0	0.0	0.0	trace	trace	0.3	2.4
Days With ≥ 1.0" Snow Depth	1	1	0	0	0	0	0	0	0	0	0	0	2

Brookhaven City *Lincoln County*   Elevation: 433 ft.   Latitude: 31° 33' N   Longitude: 90° 27' W

	JAN	FEB	MAR	APR	MAY	JUN	JUL	AUG	SEP	OCT	NOV	DEC	YEAR
Mean Maximum Temp. (°F)	57.0	62.1	69.5	76.4	82.5	88.7	90.9	90.9	86.8	77.7	67.9	60.8	75.9
Mean Temp. (°F)	46.1	50.2	57.3	63.9	71.1	77.9	80.4	79.8	75.2	64.6	55.9	49.5	64.3
Mean Minimum Temp. (°F)	35.1	38.2	45.1	51.5	59.6	66.8	69.8	68.6	63.5	51.6	43.8	38.2	52.7
Extreme Maximum Temp. (°F)	80	83	89	91	98	101	102	101	102	94	85	81	102
Extreme Minimum Temp. (°F)	3	10	14	26	39	44	58	51	40	27	19	5	3
Days Maximum Temp. ≥ 90°F	0	0	0	0	2	14	22	21	11	1	0	0	71
Days Maximum Temp. ≤ 32°F	0	0	0	0	0	0	0	0	0	0	0	0	0
Days Minimum Temp. ≤ 32°F	15	9	4	1	0	0	0	0	0	0	5	12	46
Days Minimum Temp. ≤ 0°F	0	0	0	0	0	0	0	0	0	0	0	0	0
Heating Degree Days (base 65°F)	582	418	262	105	13	0	0	0	6	101	290	482	2,259
Cooling Degree Days (base 65°F)	1	6	25	71	203	385	480	463	306	95	20	8	2,063
Mean Precipitation (in.)	6.50	5.82	6.37	6.36	5.58	4.08	4.69	4.69	3.76	3.43	4.61	6.01	61.90
Days With ≥ 0.1" Precipitation	8	7	7	6	7	7	8	7	6	4	6	7	80
Days With ≥ 1.0" Precipitation	2	2	3	2	2	1	1	1	1	1	2	2	20
Mean Snowfall (in.)	0.2	trace	0.1	0.0	0.0	0.0	0.0	0.0	0.0	0.0	trace	trace	0.3
Days With ≥ 1.0" Snow Depth	0	0	0	0	0	0	0	0	0	0	0	0	0

Calhoun City 2 NW *Calhoun County*   Elevation: 265 ft.   Latitude: 33° 52' N   Longitude: 89° 21' W

	JAN	FEB	MAR	APR	MAY	JUN	JUL	AUG	SEP	OCT	NOV	DEC	YEAR
Mean Maximum Temp. (°F)	52.7	58.7	67.2	75.3	81.7	88.0	91.5	90.9	86.2	77.1	65.7	56.7	74.3
Mean Temp. (°F)	41.9	46.7	54.6	62.1	69.6	76.7	80.4	79.3	73.9	63.1	53.6	45.9	62.3
Mean Minimum Temp. (°F)	31.0	34.6	42.0	49.2	57.5	65.3	69.4	67.7	61.4	49.1	41.0	35.0	50.3
Extreme Maximum Temp. (°F)	80	86	87	92	95	101	104	103	102	95	85	80	104
Extreme Minimum Temp. (°F)	-6	3	10	26	33	44	52	50	37	27	12	-8	-8
Days Maximum Temp. ≥ 90°F	0	0	0	0	2	12	22	21	10	1	0	0	68
Days Maximum Temp. ≤ 32°F	2	1	0	0	0	0	0	0	0	0	0	1	4
Days Minimum Temp. ≤ 32°F	18	13	7	1	0	0	0	0	0	1	8	14	62
Days Minimum Temp. ≤ 0°F	0	0	0	0	0	0	0	0	0	0	0	0	0
Heating Degree Days (base 65°F)	711	514	332	139	24	0	0	0	11	120	348	588	2,787
Cooling Degree Days (base 65°F)	1	4	19	58	177	360	495	458	272	72	11	3	1,930
Mean Precipitation (in.)	5.35	4.37	5.76	5.70	5.32	4.54	4.22	3.42	3.52	3.22	4.77	5.78	55.97
Days With ≥ 0.1" Precipitation	6	6	7	6	7	6	6	5	5	4	6	7	71
Days With ≥ 1.0" Precipitation	2	2	2	2	2	1	1	1	1	1	2	2	19
Mean Snowfall (in.)	0.7	0.4	trace	0.0	0.0	0.0	0.0	0.0	0.0	0.0	trace	trace	1.1
Days With ≥ 1.0" Snow Depth	0	0	0	0	0	0	0	0	0	0	0	0	0

Canton *Madison County*   Elevation: 223 ft.   Latitude: 32° 38' N   Longitude: 90° 01' W

	JAN	FEB	MAR	APR	MAY	JUN	JUL	AUG	SEP	OCT	NOV	DEC	YEAR
Mean Maximum Temp. (°F)	54.8	59.5	68.3	75.9	83.1	90.0	92.7	92.3	87.6	77.8	67.7	58.7	75.7
Mean Temp. (°F)	43.8	47.7	56.3	63.3	71.5	78.5	81.3	80.5	75.1	64.0	54.9	47.1	63.7
Mean Minimum Temp. (°F)	32.6	35.8	44.2	50.7	60.0	66.9	69.8	68.6	62.6	50.1	42.1	35.4	51.6
Extreme Maximum Temp. (°F)	81	84	89	95	98	103	104	103	103	93	89	84	104
Extreme Minimum Temp. (°F)	1	9	15	28	39	46	52	53	37	26	15	2	1
Days Maximum Temp. ≥ 90°F	0	0	0	0	4	18	25	24	14	1	0	0	86
Days Maximum Temp. ≤ 32°F	2	1	0	0	0	0	0	0	0	0	0	0	3
Days Minimum Temp. ≤ 32°F	17	11	4	1	0	0	0	0	0	1	6	15	55
Days Minimum Temp. ≤ 0°F	0	0	0	0	0	0	0	0	0	0	0	0	0
Heating Degree Days (base 65°F)	654	488	291	116	15	0	0	0	11	117	317	555	2,564
Cooling Degree Days (base 65°F)	2	7	30	71	233	422	521	500	315	96	22	7	2,226
Mean Precipitation (in.)	5.99	5.00	6.17	5.60	5.62	3.28	3.74	3.31	3.05	4.10	5.21	5.47	56.54
Days With ≥ 0.1" Precipitation	8	6	7	6	7	5	6	5	5	5	6	7	73
Days With ≥ 1.0" Precipitation	2	2	2	2	2	1	1	1	1	1	2	2	19
Mean Snowfall (in.)	0.2	trace	trace	0.0	0.0	0.0	0.0	0.0	0.0	0.0	trace	0.3	0.5
Days With ≥ 1.0" Snow Depth	0	0	0	0	0	0	0	0	0	0	0	0	0

Carthage 3 SW *Leake County*   Elevation: 367 ft.   Latitude: 32° 44' N   Longitude: 89° 33' W

	JAN	FEB	MAR	APR	MAY	JUN	JUL	AUG	SEP	OCT	NOV	DEC	YEAR
Mean Maximum Temp. (°F)	54.7	59.8	68.0	75.7	82.4	89.0	91.9	91.6	87.1	77.1	66.9	58.4	75.2
Mean Temp. (°F)	43.4	47.4	55.4	62.5	70.3	77.3	80.7	79.9	74.7	63.2	53.8	46.7	62.9
Mean Minimum Temp. (°F)	32.1	35.0	42.7	49.4	58.2	65.6	69.4	68.2	62.3	49.1	40.7	34.9	50.6
Extreme Maximum Temp. (°F)	81	86	89	94	96	103	104	105	104	94	87	82	105
Extreme Minimum Temp. (°F)	0	6	13	26	38	44	54	53	38	27	16	1	0
Days Maximum Temp. ≥ 90°F	0	0	0	0	3	16	24	23	13	1	0	0	80
Days Maximum Temp. ≤ 32°F	2	0	0	0	0	0	0	0	0	0	0	0	2
Days Minimum Temp. ≤ 32°F	18	13	6	1	0	0	0	0	0	1	8	15	62
Days Minimum Temp. ≤ 0°F	0	0	0	0	0	0	0	0	0	0	0	0	0
Heating Degree Days (base 65°F)	664	497	314	134	22	0	0	0	11	131	346	566	2,685
Cooling Degree Days (base 65°F)	2	6	23	65	197	380	499	471	297	82	17	7	2,046
Mean Precipitation (in.)	5.94	4.95	6.23	5.67	5.48	3.54	4.57	3.72	3.36	3.60	5.02	5.44	57.52
Days With ≥ 0.1" Precipitation	9	6	8	6	7	6	8	6	5	5	6	8	80
Days With ≥ 1.0" Precipitation	2	2	2	2	2	1	1	1	1	1	2	2	19
Mean Snowfall (in.)	0.6	trace	trace	trace	0.0	0.0	0.0	0.0	0.0	0.0	trace	trace	0.6
Days With ≥ 1.0" Snow Depth	0	0	0	0	0	0	0	0	0	0	0	0	0

Clarksdale *Coahoma County* Elevation: 170 ft.   Latitude: 34° 12' N   Longitude: 90° 34' W

	JAN	FEB	MAR	APR	MAY	JUN	JUL	AUG	SEP	OCT	NOV	DEC	YEAR
Mean Maximum Temp. (°F)	48.0	53.7	62.8	72.7	81.3	88.9	91.5	90.1	85.2	75.2	62.3	52.6	72.0
Mean Temp. (°F)	39.6	44.5	52.8	62.1	71.0	78.7	81.6	79.9	74.4	63.5	52.4	44.0	62.1
Mean Minimum Temp. (°F)	31.2	35.1	42.8	51.5	60.7	68.5	71.6	69.7	63.5	51.8	42.5	35.4	52.0
Extreme Maximum Temp. (°F)	80	80	85	94	100	102	105	104	100	93	87	81	105
Extreme Minimum Temp. (°F)	-1	6	17	29	41	54	58	52	40	30	16	-2	-2
Days Maximum Temp. ≥ 90°F	0	0	0	0	4	15	22	18	10	1	0	0	70
Days Maximum Temp. ≤ 32°F	4	2	0	0	0	0	0	0	0	0	0	1	7
Days Minimum Temp. ≤ 32°F	18	11	4	0	0	0	0	0	0	0	5	13	51
Days Minimum Temp. ≤ 0°F	0	0	0	0	0	0	0	0	0	0	0	0	0
Heating Degree Days (base 65°F)	781	574	380	145	22	0	0	0	13	123	381	645	3,064
Cooling Degree Days (base 65°F)	0	1	9	60	217	419	521	472	299	82	9	3	2,092
Mean Precipitation (in.)	5.16	4.79	5.54	5.13	5.12	4.93	4.18	2.71	2.98	3.31	5.22	5.35	54.42
Days With ≥ 0.1" Precipitation	8	6	8	6	7	6	6	4	5	5	6	7	74
Days With ≥ 1.0" Precipitation	1	2	2	2	2	2	1	1	1	1	2	2	19
Mean Snowfall (in.)	0.8	0.5	trace	0.0	0.0	0.0	0.0	0.0	0.0	0.0	0.0	0.1	1.4
Days With ≥ 1.0" Snow Depth	0	0	0	0	0	0	0	0	0	0	0	0	0

Collins *Covington County* Elevation: 288 ft.   Latitude: 31° 38' N   Longitude: 89° 33' W

	JAN	FEB	MAR	APR	MAY	JUN	JUL	AUG	SEP	OCT	NOV	DEC	YEAR
Mean Maximum Temp. (°F)	58.6	63.7	71.0	77.3	82.8	88.6	90.7	90.4	86.4	77.6	68.4	61.7	76.4
Mean Temp. (°F)	47.5	51.5	58.6	65.0	71.8	78.0	80.7	80.2	75.8	65.3	56.6	50.5	65.1
Mean Minimum Temp. (°F)	36.3	39.3	46.1	52.6	60.6	67.5	70.7	69.9	65.1	53.0	44.8	39.3	53.8
Extreme Maximum Temp. (°F)	81	85	90	94	95	100	102	101	100	92	87	83	102
Extreme Minimum Temp. (°F)	3	11	16	28	38	47	55	54	42	29	19	2	2
Days Maximum Temp. ≥ 90°F	0	0	0	0	2	14	22	22	11	1	0	0	72
Days Maximum Temp. ≤ 32°F	0	0	0	0	0	0	0	0	0	0	0	0	0
Days Minimum Temp. ≤ 32°F	12	8	3	0	0	0	0	0	0	0	5	11	39
Days Minimum Temp. ≤ 0°F	0	0	0	0	0	0	0	0	0	0	0	0	0
Heating Degree Days (base 65°F)	541	383	226	84	9	0	0	0	4	86	270	454	2,057
Cooling Degree Days (base 65°F)	3	10	33	90	234	404	503	484	327	105	27	13	2,233
Mean Precipitation (in.)	6.00	4.86	6.49	5.32	5.84	4.10	4.98	4.27	4.11	3.80	4.70	5.25	59.72
Days With ≥ 0.1" Precipitation	8	6	7	5	6	7	8	7	5	5	6	7	77
Days With ≥ 1.0" Precipitation	2	2	2	2	2	1	2	1	1	1	2	2	20
Mean Snowfall (in.)	0.2	trace	0.1	trace	0.0	0.0	0.0	0.0	0.0	0.0	trace	trace	0.3
Days With ≥ 1.0" Snow Depth	0	0	0	0	0	0	0	0	0	0	0	0	0

Columbia *Marion County* Elevation: 154 ft.   Latitude: 31° 15' N   Longitude: 89° 50' W

	JAN	FEB	MAR	APR	MAY	JUN	JUL	AUG	SEP	OCT	NOV	DEC	YEAR
Mean Maximum Temp. (°F)	59.7	64.2	71.7	78.2	84.8	90.8	92.7	92.6	88.4	79.8	70.0	62.8	78.0
Mean Temp. (°F)	48.4	52.1	59.5	65.8	73.2	79.5	81.9	81.5	77.0	66.7	57.6	51.3	66.2
Mean Minimum Temp. (°F)	37.2	40.0	47.2	53.4	61.6	68.1	71.0	70.4	65.6	53.5	45.1	39.7	54.4
Extreme Maximum Temp. (°F)	82	86	90	94	98	101	105	104	102	95	91	84	105
Extreme Minimum Temp. (°F)	4	11	16	30	39	46	55	58	41	30	19	5	4
Days Maximum Temp. ≥ 90°F	0	0	0	0	6	20	25	25	15	2	0	0	93
Days Maximum Temp. ≤ 32°F	0	0	0	0	0	0	0	0	0	0	0	0	0
Days Minimum Temp. ≤ 32°F	12	8	2	0	0	0	0	0	0	0	4	11	37
Days Minimum Temp. ≤ 0°F	0	0	0	0	0	0	0	0	0	0	0	0	0
Heating Degree Days (base 65°F)	514	368	209	76	5	0	0	0	3	71	248	433	1,927
Cooling Degree Days (base 65°F)	5	11	41	101	268	440	533	528	365	132	31	15	2,470
Mean Precipitation (in.)	7.08	5.46	6.54	5.83	5.64	4.97	5.68	4.67	4.11	3.62	4.75	5.94	64.29
Days With ≥ 0.1" Precipitation	8	7	8	6	7	7	9	7	6	4	6	8	83
Days With ≥ 1.0" Precipitation	2	2	2	2	2	1	2	1	1	1	2	2	20
Mean Snowfall (in.)	0.2	trace	0.1	trace	0.0	0.0	0.0	0.0	0.0	0.0	0.0	trace	0.3
Days With ≥ 1.0" Snow Depth	0	0	0	0	0	0	0	0	0	0	0	0	0

Corinth City *Alcorn County* Elevation: 383 ft.   Latitude: 34° 55' N   Longitude: 88° 31' W

	JAN	FEB	MAR	APR	MAY	JUN	JUL	AUG	SEP	OCT	NOV	DEC	YEAR
Mean Maximum Temp. (°F)	49.7	55.6	64.9	74.4	81.1	88.3	92.0	91.0	85.3	75.3	63.2	53.9	72.9
Mean Temp. (°F)	39.6	44.3	52.9	61.7	69.4	77.0	80.7	79.2	73.1	61.7	51.6	43.7	61.3
Mean Minimum Temp. (°F)	29.5	33.0	40.9	48.9	57.8	65.5	69.3	67.4	60.9	48.1	40.0	33.2	49.6
Extreme Maximum Temp. (°F)	79	86	87	94	96	104	107	106	103	94	84	78	107
Extreme Minimum Temp. (°F)	-10	-1	12	25	35	45	52	52	36	26	12	-6	-10
Days Maximum Temp. ≥ 90°F	0	0	0	0	3	14	23	20	9	0	0	0	69
Days Maximum Temp. ≤ 32°F	3	1	0	0	0	0	0	0	0	0	0	1	5
Days Minimum Temp. ≤ 32°F	19	14	7	1	0	0	0	0	0	2	8	16	67
Days Minimum Temp. ≤ 0°F	0	0	0	0	0	0	0	0	0	0	0	0	0
Heating Degree Days (base 65°F)	780	579	382	154	31	1	0	0	19	154	403	653	3,156
Cooling Degree Days (base 65°F)	1	1	14	59	181	373	507	461	265	62	8	2	1,934
Mean Precipitation (in.)	4.84	4.41	6.11	5.34	5.75	4.05	4.24	3.13	4.14	3.61	5.38	5.69	56.69
Days With ≥ 0.1" Precipitation	7	7	8	7	7	7	6	5	6	5	7	8	80
Days With ≥ 1.0" Precipitation	1	1	2	2	2	1	1	1	1	1	2	2	17
Mean Snowfall (in.)	1.2	1.1	trace	trace	0.0	0.0	0.0	0.0	0.0	trace	trace	0.3	2.6
Days With ≥ 1.0" Snow Depth	1	0	0	0	0	0	0	0	0	0	0	0	1

D Lo 2 SW *Simpson County*   Elevation: 334 ft.   Latitude: 31° 57' N   Longitude: 89° 56' W

	JAN	FEB	MAR	APR	MAY	JUN	JUL	AUG	SEP	OCT	NOV	DEC	YEAR
Mean Maximum Temp. (°F)	56.2	60.9	68.9	76.1	82.6	89.0	91.2	90.9	86.6	77.3	67.7	59.9	75.6
Mean Temp. (°F)	44.3	48.1	55.8	62.7	70.4	77.2	80.1	79.4	74.3	63.0	54.1	47.4	63.1
Mean Minimum Temp. (°F)	32.4	35.1	42.6	49.3	58.2	65.4	68.9	67.7	62.0	48.7	40.4	34.9	50.5
Extreme Maximum Temp. (°F)	81	85	90	92	95	103	104	103	101	95	89	83	104
Extreme Minimum Temp. (°F)	0	9	14	25	37	44	54	50	37	27	14	3	0
Days Maximum Temp. ≥ 90°F	0	0	0	0	2	15	22	21	11	1	0	0	72
Days Maximum Temp. ≤ 32°F	1	0	0	0	0	0	0	0	0	0	0	0	1
Days Minimum Temp. ≤ 32°F	17	13	6	1	0	0	0	0	0	2	9	16	64
Days Minimum Temp. ≤ 0°F	0	0	0	0	0	0	0	0	0	0	0	0	0
Heating Degree Days (base 65°F)	636	477	304	130	21	0	0	0	11	134	340	547	2,600
Cooling Degree Days (base 65°F)	2	6	25	67	204	381	486	469	298	89	19	9	2,055
Mean Precipitation (in.)	5.89	5.29	6.26	6.03	5.39	4.15	5.14	4.26	3.57	3.45	4.93	5.86	60.22
Days With ≥ 0.1" Precipitation	8	6	7	6	7	7	8	7	5	4	6	7	78
Days With ≥ 1.0" Precipitation	2	2	2	2	2	1	1	1	1	1	2	2	19
Mean Snowfall (in.)	0.2	trace	0.1	trace	0.0	0.0	0.0	0.0	0.0	0.0	trace	0.1	0.4
Days With ≥ 1.0" Snow Depth	0	0	0	0	0	0	0	0	0	0	0	0	0

Eupora 2 E *Webster County*   Elevation: 439 ft.   Latitude: 33° 33' N   Longitude: 89° 14' W

	JAN	FEB	MAR	APR	MAY	JUN	JUL	AUG	SEP	OCT	NOV	DEC	YEAR
Mean Maximum Temp. (°F)	54.0	59.9	68.2	76.2	82.5	88.8	91.6	91.0	86.2	76.7	66.0	57.6	74.9
Mean Temp. (°F)	43.1	47.6	55.3	62.7	70.1	77.1	80.2	79.0	73.7	62.9	53.5	46.4	62.6
Mean Minimum Temp. (°F)	32.2	35.1	42.4	49.1	57.7	65.3	68.6	66.9	61.3	49.0	40.9	35.3	50.3
Extreme Maximum Temp. (°F)	83	85	90	97	96	102	104	103	102	96	88	81	104
Extreme Minimum Temp. (°F)	-4	3	11	25	34	42	50	50	37	26	12	-4	-4
Days Maximum Temp. ≥ 90°F	0	0	0	0	3	14	23	20	10	1	0	0	71
Days Maximum Temp. ≤ 32°F	2	0	0	0	0	0	0	0	0	0	0	0	2
Days Minimum Temp. ≤ 32°F	17	13	7	2	0	0	0	0	0	2	8	14	63
Days Minimum Temp. ≤ 0°F	0	0	0	0	0	0	0	0	0	0	0	0	0
Heating Degree Days (base 65°F)	672	490	314	130	22	0	0	0	12	128	351	570	2,689
Cooling Degree Days (base 65°F)	1	4	20	69	191	371	487	449	280	72	13	4	1,961
Mean Precipitation (in.)	5.65	4.55	6.69	5.52	5.25	4.28	4.09	3.17	3.66	4.09	4.87	5.95	57.77
Days With ≥ 0.1" Precipitation	7	6	7	6	7	6	7	5	5	5	6	7	74
Days With ≥ 1.0" Precipitation	2	2	2	2	2	1	1	1	1	1	2	2	19
Mean Snowfall (in.)	0.6	0.1	trace	trace	0.0	0.0	0.0	0.0	0.0	trace	trace	trace	0.7
Days With ≥ 1.0" Snow Depth	0	0	0	0	0	0	0	0	0	0	0	0	0

Forest 3 S *Scott County*   Elevation: 479 ft.   Latitude: 32° 19' N   Longitude: 89° 29' W

	JAN	FEB	MAR	APR	MAY	JUN	JUL	AUG	SEP	OCT	NOV	DEC	YEAR
Mean Maximum Temp. (°F)	56.6	62.7	69.9	76.6	82.9	89.1	91.3	91.1	87.0	77.9	68.0	60.2	76.1
Mean Temp. (°F)	45.1	49.8	56.6	63.2	70.5	77.1	80.1	79.5	74.7	64.1	55.0	48.5	63.7
Mean Minimum Temp. (°F)	33.5	36.8	43.2	49.6	58.2	65.0	68.7	67.8	62.5	50.4	42.1	36.7	51.2
Extreme Maximum Temp. (°F)	81	85	89	93	96	104	103	101	102	94	89	84	104
Extreme Minimum Temp. (°F)	-1	6	7	26	30	43	52	52	38	27	13	0	-1
Days Maximum Temp. ≥ 90°F	0	0	0	0	2	15	23	22	11	1	0	0	74
Days Maximum Temp. ≤ 32°F	1	0	0	0	0	0	0	0	0	0	0	0	1
Days Minimum Temp. ≤ 32°F	16	11	6	1	0	0	0	0	0	1	7	13	55
Days Minimum Temp. ≤ 0°F	0	0	0	0	0	0	0	0	0	0	0	0	0
Heating Degree Days (base 65°F)	612	427	279	116	15	0	0	0	7	106	311	511	2,384
Cooling Degree Days (base 65°F)	2	5	24	65	201	375	482	467	299	89	20	6	2,035
Mean Precipitation (in.)	6.06	5.63	6.59	5.83	4.95	4.36	5.71	4.37	3.76	3.95	5.26	5.85	62.32
Days With ≥ 0.1" Precipitation	8	7	8	6	7	6	8	6	5	5	6	7	79
Days With ≥ 1.0" Precipitation	2	2	2	2	2	1	2	2	1	1	2	2	21
Mean Snowfall (in.)	0.4	0.0	trace	0.0	0.0	0.0	0.0	0.0	0.0	0.0	0.0	0.0	0.4
Days With ≥ 1.0" Snow Depth	0	0	0	0	0	0	0	0	0	0	0	0	0

Fulton 3 W *Itawamba County*   Elevation: 347 ft.   Latitude: 34° 16' N   Longitude: 88° 27' W

	JAN	FEB	MAR	APR	MAY	JUN	JUL	AUG	SEP	OCT	NOV	DEC	YEAR
Mean Maximum Temp. (°F)	52.0	57.9	66.8	75.4	81.9	88.5	91.8	91.3	85.9	75.7	64.3	55.7	73.9
Mean Temp. (°F)	41.7	46.3	54.3	62.1	69.6	76.6	80.2	79.2	73.6	62.4	52.8	45.4	62.0
Mean Minimum Temp. (°F)	31.4	34.6	41.8	48.6	57.2	64.7	68.6	67.0	61.3	49.1	41.2	35.1	50.1
Extreme Maximum Temp. (°F)	79	85	86	94	95	102	108	104	101	92	85	78	108
Extreme Minimum Temp. (°F)	-9	4	9	25	31	42	51	48	36	27	9	-4	-9
Days Maximum Temp. ≥ 90°F	0	0	0	0	3	13	22	21	9	0	0	0	68
Days Maximum Temp. ≤ 32°F	2	1	0	0	0	0	0	0	0	0	0	1	4
Days Minimum Temp. ≤ 32°F	17	13	7	2	0	0	0	0	0	2	8	14	63
Days Minimum Temp. ≤ 0°F	0	0	0	0	0	0	0	0	0	0	0	0	0
Heating Degree Days (base 65°F)	716	525	342	141	26	1	0	0	13	138	369	603	2,874
Cooling Degree Days (base 65°F)	1	3	18	58	184	365	491	453	273	68	9	4	1,927
Mean Precipitation (in.)	5.44	5.04	6.61	5.32	6.42	4.49	4.46	3.75	4.05	3.71	5.06	6.22	60.57
Days With ≥ 0.1" Precipitation	8	7	8	7	8	7	7	5	6	5	7	8	83
Days With ≥ 1.0" Precipitation	2	2	2	2	2	1	1	1	1	1	2	2	19
Mean Snowfall (in.)	0.6	0.7	0.1	trace	0.0	0.0	0.0	0.0	0.0	0.0	trace	0.1	1.5
Days With ≥ 1.0" Snow Depth	0	0	0	0	0	0	0	0	0	0	0	0	0

Greenville *Washington County*   Elevation: 131 ft.   Latitude: 33° 23' N   Longitude: 91° 01' W

	JAN	FEB	MAR	APR	MAY	JUN	JUL	AUG	SEP	OCT	NOV	DEC	YEAR
Mean Maximum Temp. (°F)	52.2	58.3	66.5	75.4	83.4	90.3	92.9	91.9	87.0	77.6	65.3	56.7	74.8
Mean Temp. (°F)	42.9	47.9	55.9	64.1	72.6	79.9	82.7	81.3	75.5	64.9	54.4	47.0	64.1
Mean Minimum Temp. (°F)	33.5	37.5	45.1	52.8	61.8	69.4	72.4	70.6	64.0	52.2	43.5	37.1	53.3
Extreme Maximum Temp. (°F)	80	82	89	97	100	103	108	105	103	96	88	83	108
Extreme Minimum Temp. (°F)	0	8	16	31	42	51	55	54	42	27	17	1	0
Days Maximum Temp. ≥ 90°F	0	0	0	0	5	18	24	22	13	1	0	0	83
Days Maximum Temp. ≤ 32°F	2	1	0	0	0	0	0	0	0	0	0	1	4
Days Minimum Temp. ≤ 32°F	15	9	2	0	0	0	0	0	0	0	4	11	41
Days Minimum Temp. ≤ 0°F	0	0	0	0	0	0	0	0	0	0	0	0	0
Heating Degree Days (base 65°F)	680	479	299	107	12	0	0	0	9	97	327	557	2,567
Cooling Degree Days (base 65°F)	1	3	18	82	251	451	559	517	324	92	15	5	2,318
Mean Precipitation (in.)	5.29	4.86	5.83	5.32	5.23	4.47	3.99	2.36	2.77	3.65	5.36	5.13	54.26
Days With ≥ 0.1" Precipitation	7	6	7	6	6	6	5	4	4	5	6	7	69
Days With ≥ 1.0" Precipitation	2	2	2	2	2	1	1	1	1	1	2	2	19
Mean Snowfall (in.)	0.3	trace	trace	0.0	0.0	0.0	0.0	0.0	0.0	0.0	trace	0.0	0.3
Days With ≥ 1.0" Snow Depth	0	0	0	0	0	0	0	0	0	0	0	0	0

Greenwood Leflore Airport *Carroll County*   Elevation: 154 ft.   Latitude: 33° 30' N   Longitude: 90° 05' W

	JAN	FEB	MAR	APR	MAY	JUN	JUL	AUG	SEP	OCT	NOV	DEC	YEAR
Mean Maximum Temp. (°F)	52.1	57.7	66.3	74.6	82.2	89.4	91.8	91.5	86.4	76.4	65.4	56.5	74.2
Mean Temp. (°F)	43.0	47.6	55.8	63.5	71.9	79.1	81.9	81.0	75.4	64.5	54.5	47.0	63.8
Mean Minimum Temp. (°F)	33.8	37.4	45.3	52.3	61.5	68.8	72.0	70.5	64.3	52.5	43.6	37.5	53.3
Extreme Maximum Temp. (°F)	82	82	88	94	97	103	105	102	102	93	89	83	105
Extreme Minimum Temp. (°F)	-2	8	15	28	43	49	56	52	40	28	17	2	-2
Days Maximum Temp. ≥ 90°F	0	0	0	0	4	16	23	22	12	1	0	0	78
Days Maximum Temp. ≤ 32°F	2	1	0	0	0	0	0	0	0	0	0	1	4
Days Minimum Temp. ≤ 32°F	15	10	3	0	0	0	0	0	0	0	5	12	45
Days Minimum Temp. ≤ 0°F	0	0	0	0	0	0	0	0	0	0	0	0	0
Heating Degree Days (base 65°F)	678	489	301	121	14	0	0	0	12	107	329	556	2,607
Cooling Degree Days (base 65°F)	2	6	24	83	241	444	546	520	327	102	22	7	2,324
Mean Precipitation (in.)	4.99	4.28	5.85	5.18	5.45	4.44	4.29	2.55	3.27	3.96	4.83	5.41	54.50
Days With ≥ 0.1" Precipitation	7	6	8	6	7	5	6	4	5	5	6	7	72
Days With ≥ 1.0" Precipitation	2	1	2	2	2	1	1	1	1	1	2	2	18
Mean Snowfall (in.)	0.8	trace	trace	trace	trace	trace	trace	0.0	0.0	0.0	trace	trace	0.8
Days With ≥ 1.0" Snow Depth	1	0	0	0	0	0	0	0	0	0	0	0	1

Grenada 5 NNE *Grenada County*   Elevation: 278 ft.   Latitude: 33° 53' N   Longitude: 89° 47' W

	JAN	FEB	MAR	APR	MAY	JUN	JUL	AUG	SEP	OCT	NOV	DEC	YEAR
Mean Maximum Temp. (°F)	51.4	56.8	65.8	74.4	81.1	87.9	91.3	90.5	85.6	75.5	64.6	56.0	73.4
Mean Temp. (°F)	40.9	45.1	53.7	61.8	69.5	76.9	80.5	79.1	73.5	62.3	52.5	45.1	61.7
Mean Minimum Temp. (°F)	30.2	33.4	41.5	49.1	57.9	65.8	69.5	67.7	61.3	49.0	40.3	34.2	50.0
Extreme Maximum Temp. (°F)	83	84	88	93	98	104	103	103	99	97	87	82	104
Extreme Minimum Temp. (°F)	-4	4	12	22	37	46	53	51	39	25	15	1	-4
Days Maximum Temp. ≥ 90°F	0	0	0	0	2	13	22	19	10	1	0	0	67
Days Maximum Temp. ≤ 32°F	2	1	0	0	0	0	0	0	0	0	0	1	4
Days Minimum Temp. ≤ 32°F	19	15	7	1	0	0	0	0	0	1	8	15	66
Days Minimum Temp. ≤ 0°F	0	0	0	0	0	0	0	0	0	0	0	0	0
Heating Degree Days (base 65°F)	744	558	359	151	31	1	0	0	14	146	379	612	2,995
Cooling Degree Days (base 65°F)	1	2	13	53	170	358	487	443	260	67	10	4	1,868
Mean Precipitation (in.)	5.50	4.72	6.28	5.85	4.96	4.93	4.73	3.19	3.98	3.77	5.22	6.00	59.13
Days With ≥ 0.1" Precipitation	8	7	8	6	7	6	6	5	5	5	7	8	78
Days With ≥ 1.0" Precipitation	2	2	2	2	1	2	2	1	1	1	2	2	20
Mean Snowfall (in.)	0.4	0.2	0.1	0.0	0.0	0.0	0.0	0.0	0.0	0.0	trace	trace	0.7
Days With ≥ 1.0" Snow Depth	0	0	0	0	0	0	0	0	0	0	0	0	0

Gulfport Municipal *Harrison County*   Elevation: 22 ft.   Latitude: 30° 25' N   Longitude: 89° 04' W

	JAN	FEB	MAR	APR	MAY	JUN	JUL	AUG	SEP	OCT	NOV	DEC	YEAR
Mean Maximum Temp. (°F)	60.5	64.1	70.0	76.5	83.5	88.8	91.1	90.7	87.2	79.5	70.2	63.3	77.1
Mean Temp. (°F)	51.4	54.7	60.8	67.4	74.9	80.2	82.4	82.0	78.3	69.4	60.6	54.3	68.0
Mean Minimum Temp. (°F)	42.2	45.3	51.6	58.2	66.1	71.6	73.6	73.2	69.5	59.3	50.9	45.1	58.9
Extreme Maximum Temp. (°F)	80	80	86	94	96	99	103	102	100	93	84	82	103
Extreme Minimum Temp. (°F)	4	15	22	34	46	52	65	61	46	35	25	9	4
Days Maximum Temp. ≥ 90°F	0	0	0	0	2	12	20	20	9	1	0	0	64
Days Maximum Temp. ≤ 32°F	0	0	0	0	0	0	0	0	0	0	0	0	0
Days Minimum Temp. ≤ 32°F	6	3	1	0	0	0	0	0	0	0	1	4	15
Days Minimum Temp. ≤ 0°F	0	0	0	0	0	0	0	0	0	0	0	0	0
Heating Degree Days (base 65°F)	420	294	164	46	1	0	0	0	1	33	174	342	1,475
Cooling Degree Days (base 65°F)	3	8	41	116	313	454	547	536	398	172	44	14	2,646
Mean Precipitation (in.)	6.66	5.59	6.13	5.16	5.87	5.10	7.09	6.05	6.08	2.96	4.40	4.95	66.04
Days With ≥ 0.1" Precipitation	8	7	7	5	6	7	9	9	7	3	6	6	80
Days With ≥ 1.0" Precipitation	2	2	2	2	2	2	2	2	2	1	1	2	22
Mean Snowfall (in.)	trace	0.0	trace	0.0	0.0	0.0	0.0	0.0	0.0	0.0	0.0	trace	trace
Days With ≥ 1.0" Snow Depth	0	0	0	0	0	0	0	0	0	0	0	0	0

Hattiesburg 5 SW *Forrest County*   Elevation: 383 ft.   Latitude: 31° 15' N   Longitude: 89° 20' W

	JAN	FEB	MAR	APR	MAY	JUN	JUL	AUG	SEP	OCT	NOV	DEC	YEAR
Mean Maximum Temp. (°F)	58.5	63.0	70.5	77.3	83.8	89.5	91.7	91.5	87.5	78.8	69.3	61.8	76.9
Mean Temp. (°F)	47.6	51.2	58.7	65.4	72.6	78.9	81.5	81.2	76.8	66.1	57.3	50.5	65.7
Mean Minimum Temp. (°F)	36.6	39.4	46.8	53.4	61.4	68.3	71.3	70.9	66.0	53.4	45.2	39.3	54.3
Extreme Maximum Temp. (°F)	80	84	89	93	96	99	102	101	102	94	90	83	102
Extreme Minimum Temp. (°F)	4	12	17	31	40	49	58	58	44	32	20	4	4
Days Maximum Temp. ≥ 90°F	0	0	0	0	4	16	24	23	13	1	0	0	81
Days Maximum Temp. ≤ 32°F	0	0	0	0	0	0	0	0	0	0	0	0	0
Days Minimum Temp. ≤ 32°F	12	8	2	0	0	0	0	0	0	0	3	11	36
Days Minimum Temp. ≤ 0°F	0	0	0	0	0	0	0	0	0	0	0	0	0
Heating Degree Days (base 65°F)	539	391	226	82	9	0	0	0	3	79	254	456	2,039
Cooling Degree Days (base 65°F)	4	10	38	97	260	427	524	518	359	127	29	13	2,406
Mean Precipitation (in.)	7.03	5.19	6.35	5.48	5.41	4.33	5.72	4.94	4.11	3.71	5.01	5.35	62.63
Days With ≥ 0.1" Precipitation	8	6	7	6	6	6	8	7	6	5	6	7	78
Days With ≥ 1.0" Precipitation	2	2	2	2	2	1	2	1	1	1	2	2	20
Mean Snowfall (in.)	0.2	trace	0.1	0.0	0.0	0.0	0.0	0.0	0.0	0.0	0.0	trace	0.3
Days With ≥ 1.0" Snow Depth	0	0	0	0	0	0	0	0	0	0	0	0	0

Hernando 5 S *De Soto County*   Elevation: 377 ft.   Latitude: 34° 45' N   Longitude: 89° 59' W

	JAN	FEB	MAR	APR	MAY	JUN	JUL	AUG	SEP	OCT	NOV	DEC	YEAR
Mean Maximum Temp. (°F)	48.7	54.8	63.9	73.3	80.4	87.6	90.8	89.7	84.2	74.1	61.9	52.8	71.9
Mean Temp. (°F)	39.6	44.9	53.5	62.3	70.0	77.6	81.0	79.5	73.6	62.9	52.2	43.9	61.7
Mean Minimum Temp. (°F)	30.7	35.0	43.0	51.2	59.6	67.5	71.1	69.2	62.9	51.7	42.5	35.0	51.6
Extreme Maximum Temp. (°F)	78	80	85	92	98	99	106	102	100	96	82	81	106
Extreme Minimum Temp. (°F)	-6	3	14	28	40	49	54	51	41	26	13	-5	-6
Days Maximum Temp. ≥ 90°F	0	0	0	0	1	11	19	17	7	0	0	0	55
Days Maximum Temp. ≤ 32°F	3	1	0	0	0	0	0	0	0	0	0	1	5
Days Minimum Temp. ≤ 32°F	18	12	5	1	0	0	0	0	0	0	6	13	55
Days Minimum Temp. ≤ 0°F	0	0	0	0	0	0	0	0	0	0	0	0	0
Heating Degree Days (base 65°F)	781	561	364	140	24	0	0	0	14	134	387	649	3,054
Cooling Degree Days (base 65°F)	0	1	14	61	188	389	506	461	271	69	8	2	1,970
Mean Precipitation (in.)	4.51	4.32	5.63	6.00	5.57	4.98	3.69	3.21	3.35	3.59	4.95	5.69	55.49
Days With ≥ 0.1" Precipitation	7	6	8	7	8	6	6	4	5	5	6	8	76
Days With ≥ 1.0" Precipitation	1	1	2	2	2	2	1	1	1	1	2	2	18
Mean Snowfall (in.)	2.0	0.7	0.2	0.0	0.0	0.0	0.0	0.0	0.0	trace	0.1	0.1	3.1
Days With ≥ 1.0" Snow Depth	1	1	0	0	0	0	0	0	0	0	0	0	2

Hickory Flat *Benton County*   Elevation: 396 ft.   Latitude: 34° 37' N   Longitude: 89° 11' W

	JAN	FEB	MAR	APR	MAY	JUN	JUL	AUG	SEP	OCT	NOV	DEC	YEAR
Mean Maximum Temp. (°F)	50.7	56.5	65.5	74.6	81.3	88.0	91.4	90.8	85.5	75.5	63.3	54.6	73.1
Mean Temp. (°F)	40.3	44.9	53.1	61.4	69.2	76.4	80.1	78.9	73.2	62.0	51.7	44.2	61.3
Mean Minimum Temp. (°F)	30.0	33.2	40.7	48.0	57.0	64.9	68.7	67.0	60.8	48.5	40.1	33.7	49.4
Extreme Maximum Temp. (°F)	80	82	85	93	95	100	108	104	103	93	84	78	108
Extreme Minimum Temp. (°F)	-10	-1	8	22	32	43	52	50	35	25	12	-5	-10
Days Maximum Temp. ≥ 90°F	0	0	0	0	2	12	21	20	9	0	0	0	64
Days Maximum Temp. ≤ 32°F	2	1	0	0	0	0	0	0	0	0	0	1	4
Days Minimum Temp. ≤ 32°F	19	14	8	2	0	0	0	0	0	2	9	15	69
Days Minimum Temp. ≤ 0°F	0	0	0	0	0	0	0	0	0	0	0	0	0
Heating Degree Days (base 65°F)	758	562	375	157	32	1	0	0	15	148	400	641	3,089
Cooling Degree Days (base 65°F)	0	1	12	51	172	358	477	446	260	62	8	3	1,850
Mean Precipitation (in.)	5.19	4.65	6.23	5.64	5.58	4.72	4.57	3.67	3.92	3.52	5.33	6.07	59.09
Days With ≥ 0.1" Precipitation	8	6	8	7	8	6	7	6	5	5	6	8	80
Days With ≥ 1.0" Precipitation	2	2	2	2	2	1	2	1	1	1	2	2	20
Mean Snowfall (in.)	1.7	1.3	0.1	trace	0.0	0.0	0.0	0.0	0.0	0.0	trace	0.4	3.5
Days With ≥ 1.0" Snow Depth	2	1	0	0	0	0	0	0	0	0	0	0	3

Holly Springs 4 N *Marshall County*   Elevation: 482 ft.   Latitude: 34° 49' N   Longitude: 89° 26' W

	JAN	FEB	MAR	APR	MAY	JUN	JUL	AUG	SEP	OCT	NOV	DEC	YEAR
Mean Maximum Temp. (°F)	47.4	53.0	62.0	71.5	78.7	85.9	89.6	88.9	83.5	73.3	61.6	51.9	70.6
Mean Temp. (°F)	37.4	41.9	50.5	59.2	67.3	75.1	79.0	77.5	71.4	59.8	49.9	41.4	59.2
Mean Minimum Temp. (°F)	27.4	30.8	38.9	46.8	55.8	64.2	68.3	66.0	59.2	46.3	38.1	31.0	47.7
Extreme Maximum Temp. (°F)	78	80	85	92	95	100	106	104	100	93	84	78	106
Extreme Minimum Temp. (°F)	-5	0	11	24	33	43	50	46	36	25	11	-6	-6
Days Maximum Temp. ≥ 90°F	0	0	0	0	1	8	18	15	7	0	0	0	49
Days Maximum Temp. ≤ 32°F	4	2	0	0	0	0	0	0	0	0	0	2	8
Days Minimum Temp. ≤ 32°F	22	17	10	2	0	0	0	0	0	3	11	18	83
Days Minimum Temp. ≤ 0°F	0	0	0	0	0	0	0	0	0	0	0	0	0
Heating Degree Days (base 65°F)	847	647	451	211	58	3	0	0	30	200	454	724	3,625
Cooling Degree Days (base 65°F)	0	1	9	41	145	325	456	407	223	48	7	1	1,663
Mean Precipitation (in.)	4.77	4.23	6.04	5.46	5.57	4.94	4.66	3.49	3.65	4.01	5.31	5.63	57.76
Days With ≥ 0.1" Precipitation	8	7	8	7	8	6	6	5	5	5	7	7	79
Days With ≥ 1.0" Precipitation	1	1	2	2	2	2	2	1	1	1	2	2	19
Mean Snowfall (in.)	1.2	0.9	trace	0.0	0.0	0.0	0.0	0.0	0.0	0.0	trace	trace	2.1
Days With ≥ 1.0" Snow Depth	1	1	0	0	0	0	0	0	0	0	0	0	2

Houston *Chickasaw County* Elevation: 269 ft. Latitude: 33° 55' N Longitude: 89° 00' W

	JAN	FEB	MAR	APR	MAY	JUN	JUL	AUG	SEP	OCT	NOV	DEC	YEAR
Mean Maximum Temp. (°F)	49.8	55.8	64.7	73.3	80.3	87.2	90.7	89.6	84.4	74.5	63.3	54.8	72.4
Mean Temp. (°F)	39.9	44.2	52.6	60.6	68.5	76.0	79.6	78.2	72.5	61.2	51.3	44.1	60.7
Mean Minimum Temp. (°F)	29.9	32.5	40.5	47.8	56.7	64.8	68.6	66.8	60.6	47.8	39.3	33.4	49.0
Extreme Maximum Temp. (°F)	80	86	86	95	96	101	105	104	100	93	86	78	105
Extreme Minimum Temp. (°F)	-5	4	10	23	33	43	52	49	38	26	12	1	-5
Days Maximum Temp. ≥ 90°F	0	0	0	0	2	11	20	17	7	0	0	0	57
Days Maximum Temp. ≤ 32°F	2	1	0	0	0	0	0	0	0	0	0	1	4
Days Minimum Temp. ≤ 32°F	20	15	7	2	0	0	0	0	0	2	10	16	72
Days Minimum Temp. ≤ 0°F	0	0	0	0	0	0	0	0	0	0	0	0	0
Heating Degree Days (base 65°F)	774	582	389	173	38	2	0	0	18	166	413	643	3,198
Cooling Degree Days (base 65°F)	1	1	10	44	158	347	468	417	236	56	6	2	1,746
Mean Precipitation (in.)	5.16	4.66	6.69	5.51	5.65	5.37	3.97	3.33	3.81	3.61	5.08	6.19	59.03
Days With ≥ 0.1" Precipitation	7	6	8	6	7	7	6	5	5	5	7	8	77
Days With ≥ 1.0" Precipitation	2	1	2	2	2	2	1	1	1	1	2	2	19
Mean Snowfall (in.)	1.2	0.4	trace	trace	0.0	0.0	0.0	0.0	0.0	0.0	trace	trace	1.6
Days With ≥ 1.0" Snow Depth	1	1	0	0	0	0	0	0	0	0	0	0	2

Independence 1 W *Tate County* Elevation: 344 ft. Latitude: 34° 42' N Longitude: 89° 49' W

	JAN	FEB	MAR	APR	MAY	JUN	JUL	AUG	SEP	OCT	NOV	DEC	YEAR
Mean Maximum Temp. (°F)	47.4	52.9	61.8	71.4	78.9	86.3	89.6	88.9	83.6	73.3	61.2	51.8	70.6
Mean Temp. (°F)	38.1	42.6	51.2	59.9	68.1	75.9	79.3	78.1	72.2	60.7	50.5	42.3	59.9
Mean Minimum Temp. (°F)	28.9	32.2	40.4	48.3	57.3	65.5	69.1	67.2	60.7	48.0	39.7	32.9	49.2
Extreme Maximum Temp. (°F)	77	80	84	93	97	101	105	105	100	93	83	77	105
Extreme Minimum Temp. (°F)	-8	-1	11	24	35	45	53	50	37	23	14	-5	-8
Days Maximum Temp. ≥ 90°F	0	0	0	0	2	9	17	15	7	0	0	0	50
Days Maximum Temp. ≤ 32°F	4	2	0	0	0	0	0	0	0	0	0	2	8
Days Minimum Temp. ≤ 32°F	20	16	8	1	0	0	0	0	0	1	9	16	71
Days Minimum Temp. ≤ 0°F	0	0	0	0	0	0	0	0	0	0	0	0	0
Heating Degree Days (base 65°F)	826	627	431	196	46	2	0	0	24	180	437	697	3,466
Cooling Degree Days (base 65°F)	0	1	9	45	149	337	450	414	237	52	8	1	1,703
Mean Precipitation (in.)	4.43	4.03	5.23	4.98	5.55	4.84	3.93	3.20	3.54	3.30	4.70	5.17	52.90
Days With ≥ 0.1" Precipitation	7	6	8	7	8	6	6	5	5	5	6	8	77
Days With ≥ 1.0" Precipitation	1	1	1	2	2	2	1	1	1	1	2	2	17
Mean Snowfall (in.)	1.4	0.9	0.1	0.0	0.0	0.0	0.0	0.0	0.0	0.0	trace	0.1	2.5
Days With ≥ 1.0" Snow Depth	0	0	0	0	0	0	0	0	0	0	0	0	0

Kipling *Kemper County* Elevation: 314 ft. Latitude: 32° 41' N Longitude: 88° 38' W

	JAN	FEB	MAR	APR	MAY	JUN	JUL	AUG	SEP	OCT	NOV	DEC	YEAR
Mean Maximum Temp. (°F)	55.3	60.8	68.9	76.3	82.4	88.7	91.1	90.9	86.5	76.8	67.0	59.3	75.3
Mean Temp. (°F)	44.1	48.3	55.7	62.7	70.0	76.9	79.9	79.3	74.4	63.1	54.2	47.6	63.0
Mean Minimum Temp. (°F)	32.8	35.7	42.6	49.1	57.7	65.0	68.8	67.7	62.3	49.5	41.3	36.0	50.7
Extreme Maximum Temp. (°F)	81	83	90	94	97	100	104	104	102	92	84	82	104
Extreme Minimum Temp. (°F)	-3	8	10	26	35	44	51	51	38	27	14	0	-3
Days Maximum Temp. ≥ 90°F	0	0	0	0	2	13	21	21	11	1	0	0	69
Days Maximum Temp. ≤ 32°F	1	0	0	0	0	0	0	0	0	0	0	0	1
Days Minimum Temp. ≤ 32°F	16	12	7	1	0	0	0	0	0	2	8	13	59
Days Minimum Temp. ≤ 0°F	0	0	0	0	0	0	0	0	0	0	0	0	0
Heating Degree Days (base 65°F)	644	470	303	124	20	0	0	0	10	122	333	542	2,568
Cooling Degree Days (base 65°F)	1	6	22	57	189	372	479	460	291	74	17	7	1,975
Mean Precipitation (in.)	5.48	5.07	6.54	5.81	5.36	4.02	4.64	3.19	3.32	3.36	4.20	5.07	56.06
Days With ≥ 0.1" Precipitation	8	6	8	6	7	7	7	6	5	4	5	7	76
Days With ≥ 1.0" Precipitation	2	2	2	2	1	1	1	1	1	1	2	2	18
Mean Snowfall (in.)	0.5	trace	0.2	trace	0.0	0.0	0.0	0.0	0.0	0.0	trace	trace	0.7
Days With ≥ 1.0" Snow Depth	0	0	0	0	0	0	0	0	0	0	0	0	0

Kosciusko *Attala County* Elevation: 410 ft. Latitude: 33° 03' N Longitude: 89° 36' W

	JAN	FEB	MAR	APR	MAY	JUN	JUL	AUG	SEP	OCT	NOV	DEC	YEAR
Mean Maximum Temp. (°F)	53.4	59.1	67.6	75.2	81.8	88.8	91.7	91.4	86.8	76.9	65.8	57.1	74.6
Mean Temp. (°F)	42.2	46.5	54.5	61.9	69.7	77.0	80.3	79.5	74.2	63.0	53.0	45.7	62.3
Mean Minimum Temp. (°F)	30.9	33.8	41.3	48.5	57.6	65.1	68.7	67.5	61.5	49.1	40.2	34.2	49.9
Extreme Maximum Temp. (°F)	81	84	90	94	95	100	105	103	104	94	88	80	105
Extreme Minimum Temp. (°F)	-1	11	10	24	39	41	55	52	39	27	15	3	-1
Days Maximum Temp. ≥ 90°F	0	0	0	0	3	15	23	22	12	1	0	0	76
Days Maximum Temp. ≤ 32°F	2	0	0	0	0	0	0	0	0	0	0	1	3
Days Minimum Temp. ≤ 32°F	18	14	7	1	0	0	0	0	0	1	8	16	65
Days Minimum Temp. ≤ 0°F	0	0	0	0	0	0	0	0	0	0	0	0	0
Heating Degree Days (base 65°F)	702	519	336	145	25	1	0	0	13	130	365	597	2,833
Cooling Degree Days (base 65°F)	1	2	17	57	184	380	499	470	298	84	12	5	2,009
Mean Precipitation (in.)	6.36	5.14	6.81	5.97	5.48	3.59	5.37	3.66	3.46	4.14	5.25	5.81	61.04
Days With ≥ 0.1" Precipitation	8	6	8	6	7	6	7	6	5	5	6	7	77
Days With ≥ 1.0" Precipitation	2	2	2	2	2	1	1	1	1	1	2	2	19
Mean Snowfall (in.)	0.8	trace	trace	0.0	0.0	0.0	0.0	0.0	0.0	0.0	0.0	0.2	1.0
Days With ≥ 1.0" Snow Depth	0	0	0	0	0	0	0	0	0	0	0	0	0

Laurel *Jones County*   Elevation: 223 ft.   Latitude: 31° 41' N   Longitude: 89° 07' W

	JAN	FEB	MAR	APR	MAY	JUN	JUL	AUG	SEP	OCT	NOV	DEC	YEAR
Mean Maximum Temp. (°F)	57.3	61.8	69.6	76.8	83.1	89.2	91.4	91.0	86.7	77.6	68.2	60.4	76.1
Mean Temp. (°F)	46.4	50.0	57.4	64.2	71.5	78.1	80.9	80.4	75.6	64.7	55.8	49.0	64.5
Mean Minimum Temp. (°F)	35.5	38.0	45.1	51.6	59.8	67.0	70.3	69.7	64.4	51.8	43.4	37.7	52.9
Extreme Maximum Temp. (°F)	80	85	88	94	98	101	104	101	101	93	87	83	104
Extreme Minimum Temp. (°F)	3	10	17	31	42	45	55	57	40	31	20	3	3
Days Maximum Temp. ≥ 90°F	0	0	0	0	3	15	22	21	11	1	0	0	73
Days Maximum Temp. ≤ 32°F	0	0	0	0	0	0	0	0	0	0	0	0	0
Days Minimum Temp. ≤ 32°F	14	10	3	0	0	0	0	0	0	0	5	12	44
Days Minimum Temp. ≤ 0°F	0	0	0	0	0	0	0	0	0	0	0	0	0
Heating Degree Days (base 65°F)	574	425	259	98	12	0	0	0	5	99	291	498	2,261
Cooling Degree Days (base 65°F)	3	7	28	79	225	403	505	489	323	100	21	9	2,192
Mean Precipitation (in.)	6.15	4.66	6.08	5.24	5.31	3.93	5.49	4.28	4.32	3.45	4.63	5.21	58.75
Days With ≥ 0.1" Precipitation	8	6	7	6	7	6	9	6	5	4	6	7	77
Days With ≥ 1.0" Precipitation	2	2	2	2	2	1	1	1	1	1	2	2	19
Mean Snowfall (in.)	trace	trace	trace	trace	0.0	0.0	0.0	0.0	0.0	0.0	0.0	0.0	trace
Days With ≥ 1.0" Snow Depth	0	0	0	0	0	0	0	0	0	0	0	0	0

Lexington 2 NNW *Holmes County*   Elevation: 314 ft.   Latitude: 33° 08' N   Longitude: 90° 04' W

	JAN	FEB	MAR	APR	MAY	JUN	JUL	AUG	SEP	OCT	NOV	DEC	YEAR
Mean Maximum Temp. (°F)	53.9	59.4	67.8	75.1	81.8	88.1	90.7	90.6	86.0	76.6	66.1	57.4	74.5
Mean Temp. (°F)	43.3	47.5	55.5	62.3	69.9	76.7	79.7	79.2	74.0	63.4	53.9	46.7	62.7
Mean Minimum Temp. (°F)	32.6	35.5	43.1	49.5	57.9	65.1	68.8	67.7	62.0	50.1	41.7	36.0	50.8
Extreme Maximum Temp. (°F)	81	84	87	91	95	100	104	101	100	95	89	87	104
Extreme Minimum Temp. (°F)	-2	2	9	22	36	44	50	51	37	26	13	-4	-4
Days Maximum Temp. ≥ 90°F	0	0	0	0	2	13	20	21	10	1	0	0	67
Days Maximum Temp. ≤ 32°F	1	0	0	0	0	0	0	0	0	0	0	1	2
Days Minimum Temp. ≤ 32°F	16	11	6	2	0	0	0	0	0	1	7	13	56
Days Minimum Temp. ≤ 0°F	0	0	0	0	0	0	0	0	0	0	0	0	0
Heating Degree Days (base 65°F)	669	492	308	137	22	0	0	0	11	121	339	565	2,664
Cooling Degree Days (base 65°F)	1	4	21	61	182	358	468	450	276	78	14	6	1,919
Mean Precipitation (in.)	5.70	4.82	6.02	5.64	5.00	4.36	3.96	3.08	2.93	3.88	5.06	5.78	56.23
Days With ≥ 0.1" Precipitation	7	6	7	6	7	6	6	5	5	5	6	7	73
Days With ≥ 1.0" Precipitation	2	2	2	2	2	1	1	1	1	1	1	2	18
Mean Snowfall (in.)	0.7	trace	trace	trace	0.0	0.0	0.0	0.0	0.0	trace	trace	trace	0.7
Days With ≥ 1.0" Snow Depth	0	0	0	0	0	0	0	0	0	0	0	0	0

Liberty 5 W *Amite County*   Elevation: 344 ft.   Latitude: 31° 10' N   Longitude: 90° 54' W

	JAN	FEB	MAR	APR	MAY	JUN	JUL	AUG	SEP	OCT	NOV	DEC	YEAR
Mean Maximum Temp. (°F)	57.3	61.9	69.8	76.5	83.3	89.5	91.4	91.3	87.1	78.5	68.3	60.4	76.3
Mean Temp. (°F)	45.9	49.5	57.1	63.6	71.2	77.9	80.3	79.7	75.1	64.7	55.7	48.5	64.1
Mean Minimum Temp. (°F)	34.5	37.0	44.4	50.6	59.0	66.1	69.1	68.0	63.1	50.9	42.9	36.6	51.8
Extreme Maximum Temp. (°F)	80	85	87	91	98	100	103	102	100	95	87	83	103
Extreme Minimum Temp. (°F)	4	4	15	26	38	42	58	51	40	25	15	3	3
Days Maximum Temp. ≥ 90°F	0	0	0	0	3	16	22	22	11	2	0	0	76
Days Maximum Temp. ≤ 32°F	0	0	0	0	0	0	0	0	0	0	0	0	0
Days Minimum Temp. ≤ 32°F	15	11	4	1	0	0	0	0	0	0	6	13	50
Days Minimum Temp. ≤ 0°F	0	0	0	0	0	0	0	0	0	0	0	0	0
Heating Degree Days (base 65°F)	587	438	264	113	15	0	0	0	8	102	296	521	2,344
Cooling Degree Days (base 65°F)	3	5	24	65	214	390	478	460	304	101	19	7	2,070
Mean Precipitation (in.)	6.77	5.60	6.81	5.43	5.23	4.87	4.94	4.68	4.58	3.42	4.73	5.74	62.80
Days With ≥ 0.1" Precipitation	8	6	7	5	6	6	8	7	6	4	6	6	75
Days With ≥ 1.0" Precipitation	2	2	2	2	2	1	1	1	1	1	2	2	19
Mean Snowfall (in.)	trace	trace	trace	0.0	0.0	0.0	0.0	0.0	0.0	0.0	0.0	0.0	trace
Days With ≥ 1.0" Snow Depth	0	0	0	0	0	0	0	0	0	0	0	0	0

Louisville *Winston County*   Elevation: 580 ft.   Latitude: 33° 08' N   Longitude: 89° 04' W

	JAN	FEB	MAR	APR	MAY	JUN	JUL	AUG	SEP	OCT	NOV	DEC	YEAR
Mean Maximum Temp. (°F)	51.8	57.2	65.9	73.7	80.4	87.0	89.5	89.1	84.3	74.6	64.2	56.1	72.8
Mean Temp. (°F)	41.7	46.0	54.4	61.8	69.6	76.5	79.4	78.7	73.6	62.7	53.2	45.6	61.9
Mean Minimum Temp. (°F)	31.6	34.7	42.8	49.8	58.7	66.0	69.2	68.3	62.8	50.8	42.2	35.1	51.0
Extreme Maximum Temp. (°F)	79	87	88	92	95	101	104	100	100	95	85	82	104
Extreme Minimum Temp. (°F)	-3	3	12	26	39	47	55	52	41	28	14	-3	-3
Days Maximum Temp. ≥ 90°F	0	0	0	0	1	10	17	16	7	0	0	0	51
Days Maximum Temp. ≤ 32°F	2	1	0	0	0	0	0	0	0	0	0	1	4
Days Minimum Temp. ≤ 32°F	18	13	5	1	0	0	0	0	0	0	6	14	57
Days Minimum Temp. ≤ 0°F	0	0	0	0	0	0	0	0	0	0	0	0	0
Heating Degree Days (base 65°F)	716	534	338	147	28	1	0	0	15	134	360	598	2,871
Cooling Degree Days (base 65°F)	1	4	15	53	182	356	468	444	280	74	12	3	1,892
Mean Precipitation (in.)	5.94	5.20	6.63	6.07	5.15	3.83	5.66	3.47	3.74	3.78	4.79	5.37	59.63
Days With ≥ 0.1" Precipitation	8	7	7	6	7	6	8	5	5	4	6	7	76
Days With ≥ 1.0" Precipitation	2	2	2	2	2	1	2	1	1	1	2	2	20
Mean Snowfall (in.)	0.3	trace	0.0	trace	0.0	0.0	0.0	0.0	0.0	0.0	0.0	0.2	0.5
Days With ≥ 1.0" Snow Depth	0	0	0	0	0	0	0	0	0	0	0	0	0

McComb Pike County Airport *Pike County* Elevation: 410 ft. Latitude: 31° 14' N Longitude: 90° 28' W

	JAN	FEB	MAR	APR	MAY	JUN	JUL	AUG	SEP	OCT	NOV	DEC	YEAR
Mean Maximum Temp. (°F)	58.9	63.3	70.7	77.3	83.7	89.8	91.7	91.5	87.2	78.7	69.0	62.0	77.0
Mean Temp. (°F)	47.9	51.5	58.5	65.0	72.2	78.3	80.7	80.4	76.2	66.2	57.0	50.8	65.4
Mean Minimum Temp. (°F)	36.8	39.7	46.3	52.7	60.6	66.9	69.7	69.3	65.2	53.7	45.0	39.6	53.8
Extreme Maximum Temp. (°F)	86	84	88	95	100	100	102	103	102	93	86	82	103
Extreme Minimum Temp. (°F)	2	9	14	28	41	46	59	55	43	27	16	4	2
Days Maximum Temp. ≥ 90°F	0	0	0	0	3	17	23	23	12	1	0	0	79
Days Maximum Temp. ≤ 32°F	0	0	0	0	0	0	0	0	0	0	0	0	0
Days Minimum Temp. ≤ 32°F	13	8	3	0	0	0	0	0	0	0	4	10	38
Days Minimum Temp. ≤ 0°F	0	0	0	0	0	0	0	0	0	0	0	0	0
Heating Degree Days (base 65°F)	530	384	229	84	7	0	0	0	3	75	262	445	2,019
Cooling Degree Days (base 65°F)	6	11	35	91	247	414	507	498	348	126	31	13	2,327
Mean Precipitation (in.)	6.70	5.58	6.62	5.75	5.51	4.81	5.54	5.24	4.70	3.60	4.94	5.89	64.88
Days With ≥ 0.1" Precipitation	8	6	7	6	7	7	9	8	6	5	6	7	82
Days With ≥ 1.0" Precipitation	2	2	2	2	2	2	2	1	2	1	2	2	22
Mean Snowfall (in.)	0.1	0.1	trace	trace	0.0	trace	0.0	trace	0.0	0.0	trace	trace	0.2
Days With ≥ 1.0" Snow Depth	0	0	0	0	0	0	0	0	0	0	0	0	0

Merrill *George County* Elevation: 49 ft. Latitude: 30° 59' N Longitude: 88° 43' W

	JAN	FEB	MAR	APR	MAY	JUN	JUL	AUG	SEP	OCT	NOV	DEC	YEAR
Mean Maximum Temp. (°F)	59.7	64.5	72.1	78.7	85.2	90.7	92.5	92.0	88.7	80.1	70.4	62.9	78.1
Mean Temp. (°F)	47.4	50.9	58.7	64.7	71.7	77.9	80.4	79.8	75.8	64.9	56.1	49.8	64.8
Mean Minimum Temp. (°F)	35.1	37.3	45.3	50.7	58.2	65.0	68.2	67.5	62.7	49.6	41.8	36.6	51.5
Extreme Maximum Temp. (°F)	81	85	90	95	97	105	103	101	100	95	90	86	105
Extreme Minimum Temp. (°F)	-6	10	17	25	36	42	52	52	39	20	19	7	-6
Days Maximum Temp. ≥ 90°F	0	0	0	1	6	20	25	24	15	2	0	0	93
Days Maximum Temp. ≤ 32°F	0	0	0	0	0	0	0	0	0	0	0	0	0
Days Minimum Temp. ≤ 32°F	16	11	4	0	0	0	0	0	0	2	8	15	56
Days Minimum Temp. ≤ 0°F	0	0	0	0	0	0	0	0	0	0	0	0	0
Heating Degree Days (base 65°F)	545	401	227	88	11	0	0	0	5	101	288	477	2,143
Cooling Degree Days (base 65°F)	3	9	39	82	229	391	486	465	319	104	25	12	2,164
Mean Precipitation (in.)	6.84	5.74	6.89	5.10	6.40	4.83	6.76	4.96	5.06	3.27	5.27	5.34	66.46
Days With ≥ 0.1" Precipitation	8	7	7	5	7	7	10	8	6	4	6	6	81
Days With ≥ 1.0" Precipitation	2	2	2	2	2	2	2	2	2	1	2	2	23
Mean Snowfall (in.)	0.2	0.0	0.0	0.0	0.0	0.0	0.0	0.0	0.0	0.0	0.0	0.0	0.2
Days With ≥ 1.0" Snow Depth	0	0	0	0	0	0	0	0	0	0	0	0	0

Monticello *Lawrence County* Elevation: 203 ft. Latitude: 31° 36' N Longitude: 90° 08' W

	JAN	FEB	MAR	APR	MAY	JUN	JUL	AUG	SEP	OCT	NOV	DEC	YEAR
Mean Maximum Temp. (°F)	57.7	62.7	70.7	77.4	84.1	90.5	92.6	92.3	87.9	78.3	68.4	61.1	77.0
Mean Temp. (°F)	46.0	49.7	57.5	64.2	71.8	78.5	81.2	80.7	75.9	64.3	55.2	48.9	64.5
Mean Minimum Temp. (°F)	34.3	36.7	44.2	51.0	59.4	66.5	69.7	69.1	63.9	50.4	42.0	36.7	52.0
Extreme Maximum Temp. (°F)	82	86	90	92	98	104	103	104	101	96	88	85	104
Extreme Minimum Temp. (°F)	5	11	10	28	40	47	56	56	42	17	15	6	5
Days Maximum Temp. ≥ 90°F	0	0	0	0	5	19	25	24	14	2	0	0	89
Days Maximum Temp. ≤ 32°F	0	0	0	0	0	0	0	0	0	0	0	0	0
Days Minimum Temp. ≤ 32°F	15	11	4	1	0	0	0	0	0	1	7	14	53
Days Minimum Temp. ≤ 0°F	0	0	0	0	0	0	0	0	0	0	0	0	0
Heating Degree Days (base 65°F)	585	432	260	102	12	0	0	0	6	109	308	501	2,315
Cooling Degree Days (base 65°F)	3	7	31	82	236	419	518	507	337	100	21	10	2,271
Mean Precipitation (in.)	6.39	5.52	6.79	6.10	6.05	4.52	4.74	4.08	3.75	3.69	4.78	5.79	62.20
Days With ≥ 0.1" Precipitation	8	7	7	6	7	7	8	6	6	4	6	7	79
Days With ≥ 1.0" Precipitation	2	2	2	2	2	1	1	1	1	1	2	2	19
Mean Snowfall (in.)	0.2	trace	trace	0.0	0.0	0.0	0.0	0.0	0.0	0.0	0.0	0.0	0.2
Days With ≥ 1.0" Snow Depth	0	0	0	0	0	0	0	0	0	0	0	0	0

Moorhead *Sunflower County* Elevation: 114 ft. Latitude: 33° 27' N Longitude: 90° 31' W

	JAN	FEB	MAR	APR	MAY	JUN	JUL	AUG	SEP	OCT	NOV	DEC	YEAR
Mean Maximum Temp. (°F)	51.9	57.7	66.2	75.1	82.7	89.6	92.3	91.6	86.6	76.8	64.6	55.8	74.2
Mean Temp. (°F)	43.2	48.1	56.0	64.4	72.6	79.7	82.5	81.3	76.0	65.4	54.6	46.9	64.2
Mean Minimum Temp. (°F)	34.4	38.4	45.8	53.8	62.4	69.6	72.7	71.0	65.3	53.9	44.6	38.0	54.2
Extreme Maximum Temp. (°F)	81	82	87	94	99	105	107	104	101	96	86	83	107
Extreme Minimum Temp. (°F)	1	7	16	28	42	51	55	54	42	29	14	0	0
Days Maximum Temp. ≥ 90°F	0	0	0	0	4	16	23	21	13	1	0	0	78
Days Maximum Temp. ≤ 32°F	2	1	0	0	0	0	0	0	0	0	0	1	4
Days Minimum Temp. ≤ 32°F	14	9	3	0	0	0	0	0	0	0	4	10	40
Days Minimum Temp. ≤ 0°F	0	0	0	0	0	0	0	0	0	0	0	0	0
Heating Degree Days (base 65°F)	671	476	294	102	10	0	0	0	8	91	324	560	2,536
Cooling Degree Days (base 65°F)	1	4	21	89	256	455	561	531	350	111	17	6	2,402
Mean Precipitation (in.)	5.35	4.65	5.97	5.45	5.22	4.43	4.84	2.70	3.35	3.61	4.99	5.95	56.51
Days With ≥ 0.1" Precipitation	7	6	7	6	7	6	6	5	4	4	6	7	71
Days With ≥ 1.0" Precipitation	2	2	2	2	2	2	1	1	1	2	2	2	21
Mean Snowfall (in.)	0.8	0.3	trace	0.0	0.0	0.0	0.0	0.0	0.0	0.0	trace	trace	1.1
Days With ≥ 1.0" Snow Depth	1	0	0	0	0	0	0	0	0	0	0	0	1

Natchez *Adams County*   Elevation: 193 ft.   Latitude: 31° 33' N   Longitude: 91° 23' W

	JAN	FEB	MAR	APR	MAY	JUN	JUL	AUG	SEP	OCT	NOV	DEC	YEAR
Mean Maximum Temp. (°F)	58.6	63.4	70.9	77.5	83.7	89.2	91.2	91.1	87.1	78.9	68.8	61.7	76.8
Mean Temp. (°F)	48.6	52.5	59.8	66.3	73.1	79.2	81.7	81.3	76.7	67.0	58.0	51.5	66.3
Mean Minimum Temp. (°F)	38.6	41.6	48.6	55.0	62.5	69.1	72.2	71.3	66.3	55.1	47.1	41.3	55.7
Extreme Maximum Temp. (°F)	80	82	87	90	99	99	101	99	99	93	86	83	101
Extreme Minimum Temp. (°F)	6	12	19	32	42	49	60	56	43	30	20	5	5
Days Maximum Temp. ≥ 90°F	0	0	0	0	3	16	24	23	11	1	0	0	78
Days Maximum Temp. ≤ 32°F	0	0	0	0	0	0	0	0	0	0	0	0	0
Days Minimum Temp. ≤ 32°F	11	6	2	0	0	0	0	0	0	0	3	8	30
Days Minimum Temp. ≤ 0°F	0	0	0	0	0	0	0	0	0	0	0	0	0
Heating Degree Days (base 65°F)	510	359	199	69	5	0	0	0	3	64	241	426	1,876
Cooling Degree Days (base 65°F)	7	14	40	108	264	430	526	515	352	129	37	14	2,436
Mean Precipitation (in.)	6.48	5.11	6.70	6.03	5.54	4.51	4.08	4.02	3.87	4.36	5.26	6.46	62.42
Days With ≥ 0.1" Precipitation	8	7	8	6	7	6	7	6	5	5	6	8	79
Days With ≥ 1.0" Precipitation	2	2	2	2	2	2	1	1	1	1	2	2	20
Mean Snowfall (in.)	0.5	trace	trace	0.0	0.0	0.0	0.0	0.0	0.0	0.0	trace	trace	0.5
Days With ≥ 1.0" Snow Depth	0	0	0	0	0	0	0	0	0	0	0	0	0

Newton Experiment Station *Newton County*   Elevation: 347 ft.   Latitude: 32° 20' N   Longitude: 89° 05' W

	JAN	FEB	MAR	APR	MAY	JUN	JUL	AUG	SEP	OCT	NOV	DEC	YEAR
Mean Maximum Temp. (°F)	55.2	60.3	68.3	75.4	82.2	88.8	91.8	91.2	86.7	77.1	66.9	58.9	75.2
Mean Temp. (°F)	44.1	48.0	55.7	62.5	70.4	77.3	80.5	79.8	74.6	63.3	54.1	47.4	63.1
Mean Minimum Temp. (°F)	32.8	35.7	43.1	49.6	58.5	65.7	69.2	68.2	62.4	49.4	41.3	35.8	51.0
Extreme Maximum Temp. (°F)	80	83	88	93	96	100	104	103	102	94	88	82	104
Extreme Minimum Temp. (°F)	0	6	14	26	38	44	53	53	39	28	16	1	0
Days Maximum Temp. ≥ 90°F	0	0	0	0	2	14	23	21	11	1	0	0	72
Days Maximum Temp. ≤ 32°F	1	0	0	0	0	0	0	0	0	0	0	0	1
Days Minimum Temp. ≤ 32°F	17	12	5	1	0	0	0	0	0	1	7	14	57
Days Minimum Temp. ≤ 0°F	0	0	0	0	0	0	0	0	0	0	0	0	0
Heating Degree Days (base 65°F)	644	478	302	131	19	1	0	0	9	126	335	548	2,593
Cooling Degree Days (base 65°F)	1	4	19	59	191	381	493	469	294	79	14	7	2,011
Mean Precipitation (in.)	5.83	5.28	6.50	5.83	4.17	3.84	4.86	3.89	3.60	3.71	4.91	5.26	57.68
Days With ≥ 0.1" Precipitation	8	6	8	6	7	7	8	6	5	4	7	7	79
Days With ≥ 1.0" Precipitation	2	2	2	2	1	1	1	1	1	1	2	2	18
Mean Snowfall (in.)	0.4	trace	trace	0.0	0.0	0.0	0.0	0.0	0.0	0.0	0.0	0.0	0.4
Days With ≥ 1.0" Snow Depth	0	0	0	0	0	0	0	0	0	0	0	0	0

Oakley Experiment Station *Hinds County*   Elevation: 203 ft.   Latitude: 32° 12' N   Longitude: 90° 31' W

	JAN	FEB	MAR	APR	MAY	JUN	JUL	AUG	SEP	OCT	NOV	DEC	YEAR
Mean Maximum Temp. (°F)	55.3	60.4	68.4	75.5	82.6	88.9	91.8	91.5	87.1	77.7	67.1	59.0	75.4
Mean Temp. (°F)	44.6	48.9	56.7	63.6	71.7	78.2	81.1	80.2	75.1	64.1	54.7	47.9	63.9
Mean Minimum Temp. (°F)	33.8	37.4	45.0	51.6	60.8	67.4	70.4	68.8	63.1	50.5	42.3	36.7	52.3
Extreme Maximum Temp. (°F)	80	85	88	91	95	101	102	104	100	96	88	83	104
Extreme Minimum Temp. (°F)	2	9	12	27	39	48	55	50	37	27	17	1	1
Days Maximum Temp. ≥ 90°F	0	0	0	0	3	15	24	22	13	1	0	0	78
Days Maximum Temp. ≤ 32°F	1	0	0	0	0	0	0	0	0	0	0	0	1
Days Minimum Temp. ≤ 32°F	16	10	4	1	0	0	0	0	0	1	6	13	51
Days Minimum Temp. ≤ 0°F	0	0	0	0	0	0	0	0	0	0	0	0	0
Heating Degree Days (base 65°F)	630	453	282	118	15	0	0	0	11	116	324	531	2,480
Cooling Degree Days (base 65°F)	3	7	29	83	239	406	515	487	317	100	21	9	2,216
Mean Precipitation (in.)	6.25	4.84	6.30	5.70	4.83	4.67	3.86	3.86	3.00	3.68	4.88	5.34	57.21
Days With ≥ 0.1" Precipitation	8	6	7	6	7	6	6	6	5	4	6	7	74
Days With ≥ 1.0" Precipitation	2	2	2	2	2	2	1	1	1	1	2	2	20
Mean Snowfall (in.)	0.5	trace	trace	trace	0.0	0.0	0.0	0.0	0.0	0.0	trace	trace	0.5
Days With ≥ 1.0" Snow Depth	0	0	0	0	0	0	0	0	0	0	0	0	0

Pascagoula 3 NE *Jackson County*   Elevation: 9 ft.   Latitude: 30° 24' N   Longitude: 88° 29' W

	JAN	FEB	MAR	APR	MAY	JUN	JUL	AUG	SEP	OCT	NOV	DEC	YEAR
Mean Maximum Temp. (°F)	59.7	63.2	69.0	75.8	82.6	87.9	89.8	89.7	86.8	79.0	70.1	63.1	76.4
Mean Temp. (°F)	50.6	53.5	60.0	66.9	74.0	79.9	81.8	81.5	78.2	68.7	60.1	53.6	67.4
Mean Minimum Temp. (°F)	41.3	43.9	51.0	57.9	65.3	71.8	73.8	73.3	69.5	58.4	50.2	44.1	58.4
Extreme Maximum Temp. (°F)	77	79	83	92	97	100	104	101	100	92	86	81	104
Extreme Minimum Temp. (°F)	6	14	22	32	41	51	62	58	47	32	25	6	6
Days Maximum Temp. ≥ 90°F	0	0	0	0	1	10	17	17	9	0	0	0	54
Days Maximum Temp. ≤ 32°F	0	0	0	0	0	0	0	0	0	0	0	0	0
Days Minimum Temp. ≤ 32°F	8	5	1	0	0	0	0	0	0	0	1	5	20
Days Minimum Temp. ≤ 0°F	0	0	0	0	0	0	0	0	0	0	0	0	0
Heating Degree Days (base 65°F)	445	326	180	58	4	0	0	0	1	44	186	363	1,607
Cooling Degree Days (base 65°F)	3	5	27	92	255	422	514	506	375	149	39	15	2,402
Mean Precipitation (in.)	6.24	5.40	6.32	4.56	6.01	5.52	7.51	6.81	6.37	4.02	4.92	4.31	67.99
Days With ≥ 0.1" Precipitation	7	6	6	4	6	6	9	8	7	4	6	6	75
Days With ≥ 1.0" Precipitation	2	2	2	1	2	2	2	2	2	1	2	1	21
Mean Snowfall (in.)	trace	0.0	trace	0.0	0.0	0.0	0.0	0.0	0.0	0.0	0.0	0.0	trace
Days With ≥ 1.0" Snow Depth	0	0	0	0	0	0	0	0	0	0	0	0	0

Pelahatchie *Rankin County*   Elevation: 367 ft.   Latitude: 32° 19' N   Longitude: 89° 47' W

	JAN	FEB	MAR	APR	MAY	JUN	JUL	AUG	SEP	OCT	NOV	DEC	YEAR
Mean Maximum Temp. (°F)	57.6	63.2	70.6	77.9	83.9	90.0	92.6	92.1	88.1	79.4	68.6	61.3	77.1
Mean Temp. (°F)	45.9	50.1	57.6	64.6	71.5	78.1	81.0	80.3	75.8	65.4	55.8	49.5	64.6
Mean Minimum Temp. (°F)	34.2	36.9	44.6	51.3	59.1	66.1	69.3	68.5	63.4	51.4	42.9	37.6	52.1
Extreme Maximum Temp. (°F)	80	84	90	91	98	101	104	105	103	95	87	83	105
Extreme Minimum Temp. (°F)	0	8	13	27	38	45	51	52	37	28	15	6	0
Days Maximum Temp. ≥ 90°F	0	0	0	0	4	18	25	24	14	1	0	0	86
Days Maximum Temp. ≤ 32°F	1	0	0	0	0	0	0	0	0	0	0	0	1
Days Minimum Temp. ≤ 32°F	15	11	5	1	0	0	0	0	0	1	7	12	52
Days Minimum Temp. ≤ 0°F	0	0	0	0	0	0	0	0	0	0	0	0	0
Heating Degree Days (base 65°F)	589	421	254	93	12	0	0	0	6	87	292	485	2,239
Cooling Degree Days (base 65°F)	3	8	30	na	226	403	509	487	326	115	22	11	na
Mean Precipitation (in.)	6.26	4.95	6.80	5.69	5.30	3.99	5.12	4.15	3.54	4.08	5.01	6.29	61.18
Days With ≥ 0.1" Precipitation	8	6	8	6	7	6	8	6	6	5	6	8	80
Days With ≥ 1.0" Precipitation	2	2	3	2	2	1	1	1	1	2	2	2	21
Mean Snowfall (in.)	trace	0.0	trace	0.0	0.0	0.0	0.0	0.0	0.0	0.0	0.0	0.0	trace
Days With ≥ 1.0" Snow Depth	0	0	0	0	0	0	0	0	0	0	0	0	0

Philadelphia 1 WSW *Neshoba County*   Elevation: 410 ft.   Latitude: 32° 46' N   Longitude: 89° 08' W

	JAN	FEB	MAR	APR	MAY	JUN	JUL	AUG	SEP	OCT	NOV	DEC	YEAR
Mean Maximum Temp. (°F)	54.3	59.4	67.8	75.2	81.6	88.3	90.9	90.6	86.1	76.3	66.4	58.0	74.6
Mean Temp. (°F)	43.4	47.6	55.5	62.7	70.2	77.4	80.5	79.9	74.8	63.0	54.1	46.8	63.0
Mean Minimum Temp. (°F)	32.6	35.7	43.3	50.2	58.8	66.4	70.1	69.2	63.4	49.7	41.8	35.7	51.4
Extreme Maximum Temp. (°F)	82	85	89	93	96	101	102	103	102	95	88	84	103
Extreme Minimum Temp. (°F)	0	5	14	27	37	44	55	54	40	24	16	0	0
Days Maximum Temp. ≥ 90°F	0	0	0	0	2	13	20	19	10	1	0	0	65
Days Maximum Temp. ≤ 32°F	1	1	0	0	0	0	0	0	0	0	0	1	3
Days Minimum Temp. ≤ 32°F	17	12	4	1	0	0	0	0	0	1	7	14	56
Days Minimum Temp. ≤ 0°F	0	0	0	0	0	0	0	0	0	0	0	0	0
Heating Degree Days (base 65°F)	663	490	307	128	23	0	0	0	10	129	334	561	2,645
Cooling Degree Days (base 65°F)	1	5	20	66	199	389	501	485	311	81	14	6	2,078
Mean Precipitation (in.)	6.29	5.34	6.36	5.62	5.21	4.03	4.83	3.77	3.29	3.55	5.18	5.40	58.87
Days With ≥ 0.1" Precipitation	9	6	7	6	7	6	7	6	5	4	6	7	76
Days With ≥ 1.0" Precipitation	2	2	2	2	2	1	1	1	1	1	2	2	19
Mean Snowfall (in.)	0.3	trace	0.2	trace	0.0	0.0	0.0	0.0	0.0	0.0	0.0	trace	0.5
Days With ≥ 1.0" Snow Depth	0	0	0	0	0	0	0	0	0	0	0	0	0

Picayune *Pearl River County*   Elevation: 59 ft.   Latitude: 30° 31' N   Longitude: 89° 42' W

	JAN	FEB	MAR	APR	MAY	JUN	JUL	AUG	SEP	OCT	NOV	DEC	YEAR
Mean Maximum Temp. (°F)	61.7	65.4	71.7	77.8	84.3	89.7	91.5	91.1	87.7	79.9	71.0	64.8	78.0
Mean Temp. (°F)	50.4	53.5	60.1	65.9	73.4	79.1	81.3	81.0	77.0	67.5	59.0	53.3	66.8
Mean Minimum Temp. (°F)	38.9	41.5	48.7	54.0	62.4	68.5	71.1	70.8	66.3	55.1	46.8	41.4	55.5
Extreme Maximum Temp. (°F)	80	83	88	92	98	101	103	101	99	93	88	87	103
Extreme Minimum Temp. (°F)	7	11	20	29	43	47	60	59	42	30	22	8	7
Days Maximum Temp. ≥ 90°F	0	0	0	0	3	16	23	22	12	2	0	0	78
Days Maximum Temp. ≤ 32°F	0	0	0	0	0	0	0	0	0	0	0	0	0
Days Minimum Temp. ≤ 32°F	10	6	2	0	0	0	0	0	0	0	3	9	30
Days Minimum Temp. ≤ 0°F	0	0	0	0	0	0	0	0	0	0	0	0	0
Heating Degree Days (base 65°F)	454	329	189	66	4	0	0	0	3	60	215	378	1,698
Cooling Degree Days (base 65°F)	6	11	37	91	263	422	508	500	357	142	39	19	2,395
Mean Precipitation (in.)	6.02	5.45	6.70	5.17	5.45	5.00	6.74	5.39	5.12	3.46	4.45	5.67	64.62
Days With ≥ 0.1" Precipitation	8	7	7	5	6	7	10	8	7	4	6	7	82
Days With ≥ 1.0" Precipitation	2	2	3	2	2	2	2	2	2	1	2	2	24
Mean Snowfall (in.)	trace	0.1	0.0	0.0	0.0	0.0	0.0	0.0	0.0	0.0	0.0	0.0	0.1
Days With ≥ 1.0" Snow Depth	0	0	0	0	0	0	0	0	0	0	0	0	0

Pontotoc Experiment Station *Pontotoc County*   Elevation: 403 ft.   Latitude: 34° 09' N   Longitude: 89° 00' W

	JAN	FEB	MAR	APR	MAY	JUN	JUL	AUG	SEP	OCT	NOV	DEC	YEAR
Mean Maximum Temp. (°F)	49.5	54.7	63.6	72.5	80.0	86.9	90.5	90.0	84.6	74.3	62.8	53.8	71.9
Mean Temp. (°F)	39.5	43.9	52.3	60.8	69.0	76.2	79.8	78.8	73.0	61.7	51.7	43.6	60.9
Mean Minimum Temp. (°F)	29.4	33.0	41.0	49.0	57.9	65.4	69.1	67.5	61.4	49.1	40.6	33.3	49.7
Extreme Maximum Temp. (°F)	79	84	85	93	96	101	105	104	101	94	85	79	105
Extreme Minimum Temp. (°F)	-6	2	12	24	36	48	53	48	39	26	12	-7	-7
Days Maximum Temp. ≥ 90°F	0	0	0	0	2	11	19	18	8	0	0	0	58
Days Maximum Temp. ≤ 32°F	3	1	0	0	0	0	0	0	0	0	0	1	5
Days Minimum Temp. ≤ 32°F	19	14	7	1	0	0	0	0	0	1	7	15	64
Days Minimum Temp. ≤ 0°F	0	0	0	0	0	0	0	0	0	0	0	0	0
Heating Degree Days (base 65°F)	785	592	396	172	36	1	0	0	18	154	398	659	3,211
Cooling Degree Days (base 65°F)	0	1	11	50	174	354	478	445	261	61	7	2	1,844
Mean Precipitation (in.)	5.30	4.82	6.23	5.64	5.41	5.04	4.51	3.24	4.07	3.66	4.66	6.16	58.74
Days With ≥ 0.1" Precipitation	7	7	8	7	8	7	7	5	5	5	7	8	81
Days With ≥ 1.0" Precipitation	2	2	2	2	2	2	1	1	1	1	2	2	20
Mean Snowfall (in.)	0.3	0.5	trace	0.0	0.0	0.0	0.0	0.0	0.0	0.0	trace	trace	0.8
Days With ≥ 1.0" Snow Depth	0	0	0	0	0	0	0	0	0	0	0	0	0

Poplarville Experiment Station *Pearl River County*   Elevation: 311 ft.   Latitude: 30° 51' N   Longitude: 89° 33' W

	JAN	FEB	MAR	APR	MAY	JUN	JUL	AUG	SEP	OCT	NOV	DEC	YEAR
Mean Maximum Temp. (°F)	60.8	64.7	71.4	77.7	84.4	89.9	91.4	91.4	87.7	79.7	70.5	63.6	77.8
Mean Temp. (°F)	50.1	53.4	60.1	66.3	73.7	79.5	81.3	81.1	77.1	67.8	59.2	53.0	66.9
Mean Minimum Temp. (°F)	39.4	42.1	48.7	54.9	62.9	68.9	71.1	70.7	66.5	55.9	47.8	42.2	55.9
Extreme Maximum Temp. (°F)	84	87	87	93	98	100	103	103	100	94	86	82	103
Extreme Minimum Temp. (°F)	3	10	15	30	41	49	62	57	45	28	21	5	3
Days Maximum Temp. ≥ 90°F	0	0	0	0	4	17	23	23	13	1	0	0	81
Days Maximum Temp. ≤ 32°F	0	0	0	0	0	0	0	0	0	0	0	0	0
Days Minimum Temp. ≤ 32°F	9	6	2	0	0	0	0	0	0	0	2	7	26
Days Minimum Temp. ≤ 0°F	0	0	0	0	0	0	0	0	0	0	0	0	0
Heating Degree Days (base 65°F)	461	333	188	64	4	0	0	0	2	53	209	385	1,699
Cooling Degree Days (base 65°F)	5	10	39	100	277	437	512	512	365	142	37	17	2,453
Mean Precipitation (in.)	6.07	5.82	6.70	5.41	5.58	4.63	6.62	5.26	4.20	3.70	4.52	5.26	63.77
Days With ≥ 0.1" Precipitation	8	7	7	6	7	7	10	8	7	5	6	7	85
Days With ≥ 1.0" Precipitation	2	2	2	2	2	1	2	1	1	1	2	2	20
Mean Snowfall (in.)	trace	trace	0.2	0.0	0.0	0.0	0.0	0.0	0.0	0.0	0.0	0.0	0.2
Days With ≥ 1.0" Snow Depth	0	0	0	0	0	0	0	0	0	0	0	0	0

Port Gibson 3 NE *Claiborne County*   Elevation: 118 ft.   Latitude: 32° 00' N   Longitude: 90° 57' W

	JAN	FEB	MAR	APR	MAY	JUN	JUL	AUG	SEP	OCT	NOV	DEC	YEAR
Mean Maximum Temp. (°F)	56.3	61.1	69.0	76.2	82.8	88.8	91.2	91.2	86.8	77.6	67.6	59.6	75.7
Mean Temp. (°F)	44.7	48.8	56.5	63.5	71.2	77.7	80.5	80.0	75.1	64.0	54.8	47.8	63.7
Mean Minimum Temp. (°F)	33.1	36.4	44.0	50.8	59.5	66.4	69.7	68.7	63.2	50.3	42.0	35.9	51.7
Extreme Maximum Temp. (°F)	82	87	89	94	96	100	101	100	101	93	87	84	101
Extreme Minimum Temp. (°F)	0	13	15	26	40	45	55	53	39	28	15	4	0
Days Maximum Temp. ≥ 90°F	0	0	0	0	3	15	23	22	12	1	0	0	76
Days Maximum Temp. ≤ 32°F	1	0	0	0	0	0	0	0	0	0	0	0	1
Days Minimum Temp. ≤ 32°F	17	11	4	1	0	0	0	0	0	0	6	15	54
Days Minimum Temp. ≤ 0°F	0	0	0	0	0	0	0	0	0	0	0	0	0
Heating Degree Days (base 65°F)	625	457	286	117	15	0	0	0	10	113	319	535	2,477
Cooling Degree Days (base 65°F)	3	6	30	79	218	389	492	477	312	93	20	8	2,127
Mean Precipitation (in.)	6.42	4.98	6.45	5.70	5.55	4.74	4.23	3.19	3.39	4.04	4.82	5.83	59.34
Days With ≥ 0.1" Precipitation	8	6	7	6	7	6	7	5	5	5	6	7	75
Days With ≥ 1.0" Precipitation	2	2	2	2	2	2	1	1	1	1	2	2	20
Mean Snowfall (in.)	0.4	trace	trace	0.0	0.0	0.0	0.0	0.0	0.0	0.0	trace	trace	0.4
Days With ≥ 1.0" Snow Depth	0	0	0	0	0	0	0	0	0	0	0	0	0

Quitman 1 N *Clarke County*   Elevation: 298 ft.   Latitude: 32° 04' N   Longitude: 88° 43' W

	JAN	FEB	MAR	APR	MAY	JUN	JUL	AUG	SEP	OCT	NOV	DEC	YEAR
Mean Maximum Temp. (°F)	56.5	61.5	69.5	76.9	83.4	89.7	91.8	91.4	87.0	77.5	68.7	60.1	76.1
Mean Temp. (°F)	44.9	48.7	56.4	63.3	70.9	77.7	80.4	79.6	74.8	63.5	55.6	48.2	63.7
Mean Minimum Temp. (°F)	33.2	35.9	43.2	49.6	58.3	65.7	68.9	67.9	62.7	49.3	42.5	36.3	51.1
Extreme Maximum Temp. (°F)	80	84	89	94	97	104	104	102	102	92	92	83	104
Extreme Minimum Temp. (°F)	0	7	11	27	35	42	53	54	39	22	17	2	0
Days Maximum Temp. ≥ 90°F	0	0	0	0	4	17	23	22	13	1	0	0	80
Days Maximum Temp. ≤ 32°F	1	0	0	0	0	0	0	0	0	0	0	0	1
Days Minimum Temp. ≤ 32°F	16	12	6	1	0	0	0	0	0	1	7	13	56
Days Minimum Temp. ≤ 0°F	0	0	0	0	0	0	0	0	0	0	0	0	0
Heating Degree Days (base 65°F)	620	460	286	120	17	0	0	0	10	124	303	523	2,463
Cooling Degree Days (base 65°F)	2	6	24	71	211	391	488	463	298	80	17	9	2,060
Mean Precipitation (in.)	6.24	5.03	6.83	5.26	4.34	4.13	4.99	3.34	3.59	3.37	4.35	4.98	56.45
Days With ≥ 0.1" Precipitation	7	6	7	6	6	6	8	6	5	4	6	6	73
Days With ≥ 1.0" Precipitation	2	2	2	2	2	1	1	1	1	1	2	1	18
Mean Snowfall (in.)	0.3	trace	0.1	trace	0.0	0.0	0.0	0.0	0.0	0.0	0.0	trace	0.4
Days With ≥ 1.0" Snow Depth	0	0	0	0	0	0	0	0	0	0	0	0	0

Richton 3 SSE *Perry County*   Elevation: 164 ft.   Latitude: 31° 18' N   Longitude: 88° 54' W

	JAN	FEB	MAR	APR	MAY	JUN	JUL	AUG	SEP	OCT	NOV	DEC	YEAR
Mean Maximum Temp. (°F)	59.1	63.4	70.7	77.3	83.7	89.5	91.6	91.3	87.8	79.3	69.5	62.2	77.1
Mean Temp. (°F)	46.5	50.1	57.4	63.6	71.0	77.5	80.1	79.6	75.5	64.7	55.7	49.4	64.3
Mean Minimum Temp. (°F)	34.1	36.7	44.0	49.8	58.3	65.3	68.6	67.8	63.1	50.1	41.9	36.6	51.4
Extreme Maximum Temp. (°F)	81	83	90	94	97	105	103	102	100	96	89	83	105
Extreme Minimum Temp. (°F)	3	8	14	26	33	43	53	54	40	25	16	5	3
Days Maximum Temp. ≥ 90°F	0	0	0	0	4	16	23	23	14	2	0	0	82
Days Maximum Temp. ≤ 32°F	0	0	0	0	0	0	0	0	0	0	0	0	0
Days Minimum Temp. ≤ 32°F	16	11	5	1	0	0	0	0	0	1	8	14	56
Days Minimum Temp. ≤ 0°F	0	0	0	0	0	0	0	0	0	0	0	0	0
Heating Degree Days (base 65°F)	572	423	259	110	15	0	0	0	6	103	297	488	2,273
Cooling Degree Days (base 65°F)	4	8	30	69	218	387	482	465	321	107	26	13	2,130
Mean Precipitation (in.)	6.64	5.20	6.57	5.09	5.08	3.90	6.25	4.08	4.72	3.10	4.97	5.15	60.75
Days With ≥ 0.1" Precipitation	8	7	7	6	6	7	9	7	6	4	6	7	80
Days With ≥ 1.0" Precipitation	2	2	2	2	2	1	2	1	1	1	2	2	20
Mean Snowfall (in.)	0.2	0.1	0.1	trace	0.0	0.0	0.0	0.0	0.0	0.0	0.0	trace	0.4
Days With ≥ 1.0" Snow Depth	0	0	0	0	0	0	0	0	0	0	0	0	0

Ripley *Tippah County* Elevation: 518 ft. Latitude: 34° 44' N Longitude: 88° 57' W

	JAN	FEB	MAR	APR	MAY	JUN	JUL	AUG	SEP	OCT	NOV	DEC	YEAR
Mean Maximum Temp. (°F)	47.5	53.0	62.3	72.0	79.4	86.7	90.3	89.7	83.9	72.8	61.1	51.6	70.9
Mean Temp. (°F)	37.6	41.8	50.5	59.2	67.7	75.5	79.3	78.2	72.0	59.9	49.8	41.5	59.4
Mean Minimum Temp. (°F)	27.6	30.5	38.6	46.5	56.0	64.2	68.3	66.6	60.0	47.0	38.3	31.3	47.9
Extreme Maximum Temp. (°F)	79	82	85	92	96	99	108	105	101	92	85	77	108
Extreme Minimum Temp. (°F)	-10	-1	10	24	33	42	52	48	35	26	10	-6	-10
Days Maximum Temp. ≥ 90°F	0	0	0	0	1	11	18	17	8	0	0	0	55
Days Maximum Temp. ≤ 32°F	4	2	0	0	0	0	0	0	0	0	0	2	8
Days Minimum Temp. ≤ 32°F	21	17	10	2	0	0	0	0	0	2	10	18	80
Days Minimum Temp. ≤ 0°F	0	0	0	0	0	0	0	0	0	0	0	0	0
Heating Degree Days (base 65°F)	843	650	452	209	51	2	0	0	25	196	457	722	3,607
Cooling Degree Days (base 65°F)	0	1	8	40	143	327	456	418	228	45	5	1	1,672
Mean Precipitation (in.)	5.07	4.72	6.20	5.73	5.41	4.78	4.58	3.04	3.74	3.58	5.49	6.14	58.48
Days With ≥ 0.1" Precipitation	8	7	8	7	8	7	7	5	6	5	7	8	83
Days With ≥ 1.0" Precipitation	1	1	2	2	2	2	1	1	1	1	2	2	18
Mean Snowfall (in.)	1.0	1.1	trace	0.0	0.0	0.0	0.0	0.0	0.0	0.0	trace	0.2	2.3
Days With ≥ 1.0" Snow Depth	0	0	0	0	0	0	0	0	0	0	0	0	0

Rolling Fork *Sharkey County* Elevation: 104 ft. Latitude: 32° 54' N Longitude: 90° 53' W

	JAN	FEB	MAR	APR	MAY	JUN	JUL	AUG	SEP	OCT	NOV	DEC	YEAR
Mean Maximum Temp. (°F)	52.2	58.4	66.5	75.4	83.0	89.8	92.6	92.3	87.4	77.6	66.1	56.6	74.8
Mean Temp. (°F)	42.4	47.4	55.2	63.6	72.0	79.1	82.1	80.9	75.2	64.3	54.4	46.2	63.6
Mean Minimum Temp. (°F)	32.5	36.5	43.9	51.9	60.9	68.4	71.6	69.5	63.0	51.1	42.6	35.7	52.3
Extreme Maximum Temp. (°F)	77	84	89	94	99	103	104	103	102	97	87	83	104
Extreme Minimum Temp. (°F)	4	8	14	27	41	49	58	51	40	25	11	-2	-2
Days Maximum Temp. ≥ 90°F	0	0	0	0	5	18	25	23	14	2	0	0	87
Days Maximum Temp. ≤ 32°F	2	1	0	0	0	0	0	0	0	0	0	1	4
Days Minimum Temp. ≤ 32°F	17	10	4	0	0	0	0	0	0	0	5	14	50
Days Minimum Temp. ≤ 0°F	0	0	0	0	0	0	0	0	0	0	0	0	0
Heating Degree Days (base 65°F)	696	494	317	118	15	0	0	0	11	112	331	583	2,677
Cooling Degree Days (base 65°F)	1	5	20	82	242	432	540	501	321	102	17	7	2,270
Mean Precipitation (in.)	5.77	4.71	6.09	5.55	5.20	4.33	4.16	2.80	3.03	4.07	4.67	5.60	55.98
Days With ≥ 0.1" Precipitation	7	6	7	6	7	6	6	4	4	5	6	7	71
Days With ≥ 1.0" Precipitation	2	2	2	2	2	2	1	1	1	2	2	2	21
Mean Snowfall (in.)	0.2	trace	0.0	0.0	0.0	0.0	0.0	0.0	0.0	0.0	trace	trace	0.2
Days With ≥ 1.0" Snow Depth	0	0	0	0	0	0	0	0	0	0	0	0	0

Saucier Experiment Forest *Harrison County* Elevation: 226 ft. Latitude: 30° 38' N Longitude: 89° 03' W

	JAN	FEB	MAR	APR	MAY	JUN	JUL	AUG	SEP	OCT	NOV	DEC	YEAR
Mean Maximum Temp. (°F)	61.3	65.3	72.1	78.3	84.5	89.7	91.3	90.7	87.1	79.6	70.5	64.2	77.9
Mean Temp. (°F)	51.1	54.5	61.0	67.0	73.8	79.5	81.5	81.1	77.3	68.5	59.9	54.0	67.4
Mean Minimum Temp. (°F)	40.9	43.6	50.0	55.8	63.1	69.2	71.7	71.5	67.5	57.4	49.2	43.7	57.0
Extreme Maximum Temp. (°F)	81	83	87	94	95	100	102	101	98	92	86	82	102
Extreme Minimum Temp. (°F)	4	11	19	30	43	52	60	60	45	29	22	7	4
Days Maximum Temp. ≥ 90°F	0	0	0	0	3	16	23	22	10	1	0	0	75
Days Maximum Temp. ≤ 32°F	0	0	0	0	0	0	0	0	0	0	0	0	0
Days Minimum Temp. ≤ 32°F	8	5	1	0	0	0	0	0	0	0	1	5	20
Days Minimum Temp. ≤ 0°F	0	0	0	0	0	0	0	0	0	0	0	0	0
Heating Degree Days (base 65°F)	431	303	164	49	2	0	0	0	1	41	191	355	1,537
Cooling Degree Days (base 65°F)	6	13	48	114	289	442	525	515	376	162	46	19	2,555
Mean Precipitation (in.)	6.67	5.73	7.27	5.14	6.60	5.42	7.63	6.86	6.12	3.26	5.02	5.39	71.11
Days With ≥ 0.1" Precipitation	8	7	7	5	7	8	11	10	7	4	6	6	86
Days With ≥ 1.0" Precipitation	2	2	3	2	2	2	2	2	2	1	2	2	24
Mean Snowfall (in.)	trace	trace	trace	0.0	0.0	0.0	0.0	0.0	0.0	0.0	0.0	0.0	trace
Days With ≥ 1.0" Snow Depth	0	0	0	0	0	0	0	0	0	0	0	0	0

State University *Oktibbeha County* Elevation: 183 ft. Latitude: 33° 28' N Longitude: 88° 47' W

	JAN	FEB	MAR	APR	MAY	JUN	JUL	AUG	SEP	OCT	NOV	DEC	YEAR
Mean Maximum Temp. (°F)	51.6	56.9	65.8	74.1	81.3	88.2	91.5	91.0	85.7	75.5	64.8	55.8	73.5
Mean Temp. (°F)	41.4	45.9	54.4	62.2	70.3	77.7	81.3	80.1	74.5	63.1	53.6	45.4	62.5
Mean Minimum Temp. (°F)	31.4	34.9	42.9	50.2	59.4	67.1	71.0	69.2	63.2	50.7	42.3	34.9	51.4
Extreme Maximum Temp. (°F)	80	88	88	93	99	103	108	105	103	94	85	82	108
Extreme Minimum Temp. (°F)	-6	4	13	28	40	41	57	53	41	27	14	-8	-8
Days Maximum Temp. ≥ 90°F	0	0	0	0	3	13	21	20	9	1	0	0	67
Days Maximum Temp. ≤ 32°F	2	1	0	0	0	0	0	0	0	0	0	1	4
Days Minimum Temp. ≤ 32°F	18	12	5	1	0	0	0	0	0	0	5	14	55
Days Minimum Temp. ≤ 0°F	0	0	0	0	0	0	0	0	0	0	0	0	0
Heating Degree Days (base 65°F)	724	535	339	140	22	1	0	0	11	125	348	605	2,850
Cooling Degree Days (base 65°F)	1	3	16	57	198	389	519	482	297	69	13	2	2,046
Mean Precipitation (in.)	5.55	4.96	6.18	5.70	5.08	4.02	4.43	3.60	3.65	3.48	4.42	5.28	56.35
Days With ≥ 0.1" Precipitation	8	7	8	6	7	7	7	6	5	5	7	7	80
Days With ≥ 1.0" Precipitation	2	2	2	2	2	1	1	1	1	1	1	2	18
Mean Snowfall (in.)	0.3	0.1	trace	0.0	0.0	0.0	0.0	0.0	0.0	0.0	trace	0.0	0.4
Days With ≥ 1.0" Snow Depth	0	0	0	0	0	0	0	0	0	0	0	0	0

Stoneville Exp. Station *Washington County*   Elevation: 124 ft.   Latitude: 33° 27' N   Longitude: 90° 55' W

	JAN	FEB	MAR	APR	MAY	JUN	JUL	AUG	SEP	OCT	NOV	DEC	YEAR
Mean Maximum Temp. (°F)	49.8	55.6	64.4	73.7	82.1	89.1	91.5	90.8	85.6	76.1	63.4	54.4	73.1
Mean Temp. (°F)	41.1	46.0	54.3	63.2	72.0	79.3	82.0	80.5	74.5	63.8	53.2	45.4	62.9
Mean Minimum Temp. (°F)	32.4	36.4	44.2	52.6	61.9	69.5	72.3	70.2	63.4	51.6	42.9	36.3	52.8
Extreme Maximum Temp. (°F)	79	83	90	*93*	98	101	104	104	100	94	87	80	*104*
Extreme Minimum Temp. (°F)	3	12	16	*32*	42	52	58	52	42	28	18	4	*3*
Days Maximum Temp. ≥ 90°F	0	0	0	0	5	16	22	20	10	1	0	0	74
Days Maximum Temp. ≤ 32°F	3	1	0	0	0	0	0	0	0	0	0	1	5
Days Minimum Temp. ≤ 32°F	17	10	3	0	0	0	0	0	0	0	5	12	47
Days Minimum Temp. ≤ 0°F	0	0	0	0	0	0	0	0	0	0	0	0	0
Heating Degree Days (base 65°F)	734	531	340	127	16	0	0	0	13	119	362	605	2,847
Cooling Degree Days (base 65°F)	1	2	16	79	246	442	539	494	295	87	13	4	2,218
Mean Precipitation (in.)	5.27	4.36	5.63	5.06	5.12	3.90	3.88	2.21	3.20	3.64	5.18	5.30	52.75
Days With ≥ 0.1" Precipitation	7	6	7	6	7	6	6	4	5	5	6	7	72
Days With ≥ 1.0" Precipitation	2	2	2	2	2	1	1	1	1	1	2	2	19
Mean Snowfall (in.)	0.9	0.2	trace	trace	0.0	0.0	0.0	0.0	0.0	0.0	trace	trace	1.1
Days With ≥ 1.0" Snow Depth	1	0	0	0	0	0	0	0	0	0	0	0	1

Tunica 2 *Tunica County*   Elevation: 196 ft.   Latitude: 34° 41' N   Longitude: 90° 23' W

	JAN	FEB	MAR	APR	MAY	JUN	JUL	AUG	SEP	OCT	NOV	DEC	YEAR
Mean Maximum Temp. (°F)	47.5	53.0	62.3	72.3	80.7	88.5	91.7	90.2	84.8	74.6	61.8	51.9	71.6
Mean Temp. (°F)	38.8	43.5	52.3	61.9	70.3	78.2	81.6	79.4	73.4	62.3	51.7	43.4	61.4
Mean Minimum Temp. (°F)	30.1	34.0	42.3	51.4	60.0	67.9	71.4	68.6	61.9	50.0	41.6	34.5	51.1
Extreme Maximum Temp. (°F)	78	79	85	93	98	101	105	105	100	96	85	80	105
Extreme Minimum Temp. (°F)	-4	2	13	27	39	49	55	50	37	28	15	-3	-4
Days Maximum Temp. ≥ 90°F	0	0	0	0	3	15	22	19	9	1	0	0	69
Days Maximum Temp. ≤ 32°F	4	2	0	0	0	0	0	0	0	0	0	2	8
Days Minimum Temp. ≤ 32°F	19	13	5	1	0	0	0	0	0	0	6	14	58
Days Minimum Temp. ≤ 0°F	0	0	0	0	0	0	0	0	0	0	0	0	0
Heating Degree Days (base 65°F)	805	601	398	151	28	0	0	0	18	145	401	665	3,212
Cooling Degree Days (base 65°F)	0	1	11	65	205	411	526	462	275	68	9	2	2,035
Mean Precipitation (in.)	4.59	4.06	5.58	5.69	5.65	5.16	3.85	2.64	2.68	3.64	5.17	5.61	54.32
Days With ≥ 0.1" Precipitation	7	6	8	7	7	6	5	4	5	5	6	7	73
Days With ≥ 1.0" Precipitation	1	1	2	2	2	2	1	1	1	1	2	2	18
Mean Snowfall (in.)	1.0	0.7	0.1	0.0	0.0	0.0	0.0	0.0	0.0	0.0	trace	trace	1.8
Days With ≥ 1.0" Snow Depth	0	0	0	0	0	0	0	0	0	0	0	0	0

Tylertown 2 WNW *Walthall County*   Elevation: 439 ft.   Latitude: 31° 07' N   Longitude: 90° 10' W

	JAN	FEB	MAR	APR	MAY	JUN	JUL	AUG	SEP	OCT	NOV	DEC	YEAR
Mean Maximum Temp. (°F)	60.0	64.4	71.5	77.4	83.6	89.3	91.1	91.1	87.5	79.3	69.4	62.8	77.3
Mean Temp. (°F)	49.3	52.9	59.7	65.7	72.7	78.6	80.9	80.6	76.8	67.2	58.2	52.1	66.2
Mean Minimum Temp. (°F)	38.6	41.2	47.8	53.9	61.7	67.9	70.6	70.1	66.0	55.0	46.9	41.4	55.1
Extreme Maximum Temp. (°F)	82	84	87	92	96	101	104	101	102	93	86	82	104
Extreme Minimum Temp. (°F)	3	9	15	28	41	48	58	55	43	29	18	4	3
Days Maximum Temp. ≥ 90°F	0	0	0	0	2	15	22	22	11	1	0	0	73
Days Maximum Temp. ≤ 32°F	0	0	0	0	0	0	0	0	0	0	0	0	0
Days Minimum Temp. ≤ 32°F	11	7	3	0	0	0	0	0	0	0	3	9	33
Days Minimum Temp. ≤ 0°F	0	0	0	0	0	0	0	0	0	0	0	0	0
Heating Degree Days (base 65°F)	487	347	199	73	5	0	0	0	2	61	235	409	1,818
Cooling Degree Days (base 65°F)	6	13	38	97	255	415	506	499	358	138	39	16	2,380
Mean Precipitation (in.)	6.73	5.49	6.35	5.70	5.83	4.84	6.20	4.89	4.03	4.05	4.60	5.62	64.33
Days With ≥ 0.1" Precipitation	8	6	7	6	7	7	9	8	6	4	6	7	81
Days With ≥ 1.0" Precipitation	2	2	2	2	2	1	2	1	1	1	2	2	20
Mean Snowfall (in.)	0.2	trace	trace	0.0	0.0	0.0	0.0	0.0	0.0	0.0	0.0	trace	0.2
Days With ≥ 1.0" Snow Depth	0	0	0	0	0	0	0	0	0	0	0	0	0

University *Lafayette County*   Elevation: 377 ft.   Latitude: 34° 23' N   Longitude: 89° 32' W

	JAN	FEB	MAR	APR	MAY	JUN	JUL	AUG	SEP	OCT	NOV	DEC	YEAR
Mean Maximum Temp. (°F)	49.5	54.8	63.8	73.1	80.4	87.6	90.9	90.1	84.8	74.4	63.0	54.0	72.2
Mean Temp. (°F)	38.9	43.2	51.7	60.3	68.5	76.3	80.0	78.6	72.7	60.9	51.2	43.0	60.4
Mean Minimum Temp. (°F)	28.2	31.4	39.7	47.4	56.6	65.0	69.0	67.1	60.5	47.3	39.3	32.0	48.6
Extreme Maximum Temp. (°F)	80	81	87	93	96	103	104	104	101	96	85	79	104
Extreme Minimum Temp. (°F)	-13	-5	7	21	31	43	50	48	34	24	9	-1	-13
Days Maximum Temp. ≥ 90°F	0	0	0	0	2	12	20	17	9	0	0	0	60
Days Maximum Temp. ≤ 32°F	3	1	0	0	0	0	0	0	0	0	0	1	5
Days Minimum Temp. ≤ 32°F	20	16	9	3	0	0	0	0	0	3	10	17	78
Days Minimum Temp. ≤ 0°F	0	0	0	0	0	0	0	0	0	0	0	0	0
Heating Degree Days (base 65°F)	802	612	415	188	46	2	0	0	23	177	418	677	3,360
Cooling Degree Days (base 65°F)	1	1	12	54	176	373	496	452	263	59	9	2	1,898
Mean Precipitation (in.)	5.25	4.66	5.99	5.37	5.83	4.57	4.08	3.48	3.63	3.97	5.17	5.91	57.91
Days With ≥ 0.1" Precipitation	8	7	8	7	8	6	6	5	5	5	7	8	80
Days With ≥ 1.0" Precipitation	1	1	2	2	2	2	1	1	1	1	2	2	18
Mean Snowfall (in.)	1.2	0.9	trace	0.0	0.0	0.0	0.0	0.0	0.0	0.0	trace	0.1	2.2
Days With ≥ 1.0" Snow Depth	1	1	0	0	0	0	0	0	0	0	0	0	2

Vicksburg Military Park *Warren County*　Elevation: 252 ft.　Latitude: 32° 21' N　Longitude: 90° 51' W

	JAN	FEB	MAR	APR	MAY	JUN	JUL	AUG	SEP	OCT	NOV	DEC	YEAR
Mean Maximum Temp. (°F)	57.9	63.1	71.0	77.8	84.0	89.8	92.0	91.7	87.6	78.9	68.7	60.9	77.0
Mean Temp. (°F)	46.7	50.7	58.1	65.2	72.3	78.7	81.4	80.8	76.3	66.3	57.1	49.9	65.3
Mean Minimum Temp. (°F)	35.3	38.2	45.2	52.5	60.5	67.6	70.7	69.9	65.0	53.6	45.5	38.8	53.6
Extreme Maximum Temp. (°F)	81	86	90	94	97	102	102	101	100	96	91	85	102
Extreme Minimum Temp. (°F)	3	8	14	25	42	50	54	51	41	28	17	2	2
Days Maximum Temp. ≥ 90°F	0	0	0	0	3	17	25	23	13	1	0	0	82
Days Maximum Temp. ≤ 32°F	1	0	0	0	0	0	0	0	0	0	0	0	1
Days Minimum Temp. ≤ 32°F	13	9	3	0	0	0	0	0	0	0	0	3	10	38
Days Minimum Temp. ≤ 0°F	0	0	0	0	0	0	0	0	0	0	0	0	0
Heating Degree Days (base 65°F)	567	406	239	84	6	0	0	0	4	73	262	470	2,111
Cooling Degree Days (base 65°F)	2	8	34	98	245	423	516	498	347	122	37	10	2,340
Mean Precipitation (in.)	6.28	4.92	6.42	5.50	5.44	4.23	4.31	3.21	3.28	4.13	4.99	5.70	58.41
Days With ≥ 0.1" Precipitation	8	6	7	6	6	6	6	5	5	5	6	7	73
Days With ≥ 1.0" Precipitation	2	2	2	2	2	1	1	1	1	1	2	2	19
Mean Snowfall (in.)	0.3	trace	trace	0.0	0.0	0.0	0.0	0.0	0.0	0.0	0.0	trace	0.3
Days With ≥ 1.0" Snow Depth	0	0	0	0	0	0	0	0	0	0	0	0	0

Water Valley 1 NNE *Yalobusha County*　Elevation: 374 ft.　Latitude: 34° 10' N　Longitude: 89° 38' W

	JAN	FEB	MAR	APR	MAY	JUN	JUL	AUG	SEP	OCT	NOV	DEC	YEAR
Mean Maximum Temp. (°F)	50.7	56.1	64.9	73.5	80.2	87.1	90.4	90.5	85.9	75.8	64.5	55.1	72.9
Mean Temp. (°F)	39.5	43.8	52.2	60.4	68.4	76.1	79.8	79.0	73.5	62.0	51.9	43.5	60.8
Mean Minimum Temp. (°F)	28.2	31.5	39.5	47.2	56.5	65.1	69.2	67.5	61.1	48.2	39.3	32.0	48.8
Extreme Maximum Temp. (°F)	82	83	87	94	96	102	106	104	103	97	89	81	106
Extreme Minimum Temp. (°F)	-8	2	9	24	35	42	52	49	37	27	12	-4	-8
Days Maximum Temp. ≥ 90°F	0	0	0	0	2	10	20	19	11	1	0	0	63
Days Maximum Temp. ≤ 32°F	2	1	0	0	0	0	0	0	0	0	0	1	4
Days Minimum Temp. ≤ 32°F	21	16	9	2	0	0	0	0	0	1	9	18	76
Days Minimum Temp. ≤ 0°F	0	0	0	0	0	0	0	0	0	0	0	0	0
Heating Degree Days (base 65°F)	785	593	400	182	41	1	0	0	17	153	397	661	3,230
Cooling Degree Days (base 65°F)	0	2	12	48	160	350	476	450	271	69	11	3	1,852
Mean Precipitation (in.)	5.22	4.70	6.36	5.65	5.57	4.85	4.42	3.45	3.30	3.81	5.32	6.12	58.77
Days With ≥ 0.1" Precipitation	8	7	8	6	7	7	7	5	5	5	6	8	79
Days With ≥ 1.0" Precipitation	1	2	2	2	2	1	1	1	1	1	2	2	18
Mean Snowfall (in.)	1.4	0.9	0.1	0.0	0.0	0.0	0.0	0.0	0.0	trace	0.1	0.3	2.8
Days With ≥ 1.0" Snow Depth	1	1	0	0	0	0	0	0	0	0	0	0	2

Waynesboro 2 W *Wayne County*　Elevation: 200 ft.　Latitude: 31° 41' N　Longitude: 88° 40' W

	JAN	FEB	MAR	APR	MAY	JUN	JUL	AUG	SEP	OCT	NOV	DEC	YEAR
Mean Maximum Temp. (°F)	58.5	64.0	71.9	78.3	84.2	90.0	92.0	91.9	87.8	79.1	69.2	61.9	77.4
Mean Temp. (°F)	46.9	50.9	58.3	64.5	71.2	77.7	80.4	80.1	75.4	64.7	55.7	49.6	64.6
Mean Minimum Temp. (°F)	35.3	37.8	44.7	50.6	58.1	65.3	68.7	68.2	63.0	50.2	42.1	37.3	51.8
Extreme Maximum Temp. (°F)	81	87	90	92	97	102	106	102	102	94	88	*83*	*106*
Extreme Minimum Temp. (°F)	0	9	14	26	35	42	53	54	39	27	16	*6*	*0*
Days Maximum Temp. ≥ 90°F	0	0	0	0	4	18	24	24	13	1	0	0	84
Days Maximum Temp. ≤ 32°F	0	0	0	0	0	0	0	0	0	0	0	0	0
Days Minimum Temp. ≤ 32°F	14	10	5	1	0	0	0	0	0	1	8	13	52
Days Minimum Temp. ≤ 0°F	0	0	0	0	0	0	0	0	0	0	0	0	0
Heating Degree Days (base 65°F)	557	399	234	95	13	0	0	0	6	98	294	479	2,175
Cooling Degree Days (base 65°F)	3	9	29	82	211	389	487	484	313	99	19	8	2,133
Mean Precipitation (in.)	6.64	4.85	6.12	4.75	5.14	4.62	5.31	3.49	4.42	3.08	4.80	5.35	58.57
Days With ≥ 0.1" Precipitation	8	6	7	5	7	7	8	6	6	4	6	7	77
Days With ≥ 1.0" Precipitation	2	2	2	2	2	2	1	1	1	1	2	2	21
Mean Snowfall (in.)	trace	trace	0.3	0.0	0.0	0.0	0.0	0.0	0.0	0.0	0.0	trace	0.3
Days With ≥ 1.0" Snow Depth	0	0	0	0	0	0	0	0	0	0	0	0	0

Winona 5 E *Montgomery County*　Elevation: 387 ft.　Latitude: 33° 29' N　Longitude: 89° 38' W

	JAN	FEB	MAR	APR	MAY	JUN	JUL	AUG	SEP	OCT	NOV	DEC	YEAR
Mean Maximum Temp. (°F)	51.8	57.0	65.4	73.2	79.8	86.5	89.6	89.6	84.8	75.3	64.8	55.9	72.8
Mean Temp. (°F)	40.2	44.1	52.0	59.4	67.5	74.9	78.5	77.7	72.2	60.9	51.4	43.8	60.2
Mean Minimum Temp. (°F)	28.6	31.2	38.5	45.5	55.2	63.2	67.4	65.8	59.6	46.4	38.0	31.7	47.6
Extreme Maximum Temp. (°F)	79	84	86	92	94	100	104	103	99	94	87	82	104
Extreme Minimum Temp. (°F)	-6	0	9	24	35	40	49	50	37	26	12	-2	-6
Days Maximum Temp. ≥ 90°F	0	0	0	0	1	9	17	17	8	1	0	0	53
Days Maximum Temp. ≤ 32°F	2	1	0	0	0	0	0	0	0	0	0	1	4
Days Minimum Temp. ≤ 32°F	21	17	10	3	0	0	0	0	0	3	11	18	83
Days Minimum Temp. ≤ 0°F	0	0	0	0	0	0	0	0	0	0	0	0	0
Heating Degree Days (base 65°F)	762	584	406	198	44	2	0	0	20	172	408	651	3,247
Cooling Degree Days (base 65°F)	1	1	9	37	132	313	433	404	234	52	8	3	1,627
Mean Precipitation (in.)	5.38	4.68	6.46	5.40	5.00	4.35	4.59	3.34	3.44	3.67	4.92	6.08	57.31
Days With ≥ 0.1" Precipitation	8	6	7	6	7	6	7	5	5	5	6	7	75
Days With ≥ 1.0" Precipitation	1	2	2	2	1	1	1	1	1	1	2	2	17
Mean Snowfall (in.)	0.7	0.1	0.2	trace	0.0	0.0	0.0	0.0	0.0	0.0	trace	trace	1.0
Days With ≥ 1.0" Snow Depth	0	0	0	0	0	0	0	0	0	0	0	0	0

Woodville 4 ESE *Wilkinson County*   Elevation: 396 ft.   Latitude: 31° 06' N   Longitude: 91° 14' W

	JAN	FEB	MAR	APR	MAY	JUN	JUL	AUG	SEP	OCT	NOV	DEC	YEAR
Mean Maximum Temp. (°F)	59.5	64.0	71.4	78.1	84.1	89.2	91.0	91.0	87.2	79.0	69.8	62.6	77.2
Mean Temp. (°F)	49.1	52.8	59.8	66.3	73.2	78.6	81.0	80.8	76.5	67.2	58.5	52.0	66.3
Mean Minimum Temp. (°F)	38.7	41.5	48.2	54.4	62.2	68.1	70.9	70.5	65.7	55.4	47.2	41.4	55.4
Extreme Maximum Temp. (°F)	82	90	88	90	97	100	100	103	99	94	87	82	103
Extreme Minimum Temp. (°F)	6	11	19	29	40	51	55	56	44	29	18	4	4
Days Maximum Temp. ≥ 90°F	0	0	0	0	3	15	22	22	11	1	0	0	74
Days Maximum Temp. ≤ 32°F	0	0	0	0	0	0	0	0	0	0	0	0	0
Days Minimum Temp. ≤ 32°F	10	6	2	0	0	0	0	0	0	0	2	7	27
Days Minimum Temp. ≤ 0°F	0	0	0	0	0	0	0	0	0	0	0	0	0
Heating Degree Days (base 65°F)	493	349	197	65	4	0	0	0	4	59	226	409	1,806
Cooling Degree Days (base 65°F)	6	13	39	108	272	421	512	505	355	141	38	14	2,424
Mean Precipitation (in.)	7.02	5.70	7.13	6.13	5.84	5.54	5.78	4.64	5.14	3.79	5.21	6.27	68.19
Days With ≥ 0.1" Precipitation	8	7	8	6	7	8	8	7	7	4	6	8	84
Days With ≥ 1.0" Precipitation	2	2	2	2	2	2	2	1	2	1	2	2	22
Mean Snowfall (in.)	trace	trace	0.0	0.0	0.0	0.0	0.0	0.0	0.0	0.0	trace	trace	trace
Days With ≥ 1.0" Snow Depth	0	0	0	0	0	0	0	0	0	0	0	0	0

Yazoo City 5 NNE *Yazoo County*   Elevation: 104 ft.   Latitude: 32° 54' N   Longitude: 90° 23' W

	JAN	FEB	MAR	APR	MAY	JUN	JUL	AUG	SEP	OCT	NOV	DEC	YEAR
Mean Maximum Temp. (°F)	54.5	59.9	68.1	76.2	83.3	90.2	92.4	92.1	87.4	77.5	66.6	58.1	75.5
Mean Temp. (°F)	45.0	49.5	57.2	64.9	72.8	79.7	82.3	81.6	76.5	65.8	55.7	48.4	64.9
Mean Minimum Temp. (°F)	35.4	39.0	46.2	53.5	62.3	69.1	72.2	71.1	65.6	54.0	44.8	38.5	54.3
Extreme Maximum Temp. (°F)	84	87	90	94	98	102	106	103	101	96	88	84	106
Extreme Minimum Temp. (°F)	3	13	15	28	39	51	54	54	42	30	18	2	2
Days Maximum Temp. ≥ 90°F	0	0	0	0	5	19	24	23	14	2	0	0	87
Days Maximum Temp. ≤ 32°F	1	0	0	0	0	0	0	0	0	0	0	0	1
Days Minimum Temp. ≤ 32°F	14	8	3	0	0	0	0	0	0	0	4	10	39
Days Minimum Temp. ≤ 0°F	0	0	0	0	0	0	0	0	0	0	0	0	0
Heating Degree Days (base 65°F)	618	438	269	98	10	0	0	0	6	88	300	518	2,345
Cooling Degree Days (base 65°F)	3	8	32	100	268	451	552	529	356	122	26	10	2,457
Mean Precipitation (in.)	6.27	5.25	6.70	5.83	5.53	4.00	4.44	3.43	2.84	4.43	4.96	6.22	59.90
Days With ≥ 0.1" Precipitation	8	7	8	6	7	5	6	5	5	5	6	7	75
Days With ≥ 1.0" Precipitation	2	2	3	2	2	1	2	1	1	2	2	2	22
Mean Snowfall (in.)	trace	trace	trace	0.0	0.0	0.0	0.0	0.0	0.0	0.0	trace	trace	trace
Days With ≥ 1.0" Snow Depth	0	0	0	0	0	0	0	0	0	0	0	0	0

Note: See Appendix D for explanation of data.

MISSOURI

PHYSICAL FEATURES. Missouri's three main terrain features are the rolling prairies of the area north of the Missouri River and in the west-central counties, the Ozarks, and the southeast lowlands, commonly called the "Bootheel." The flat lowlands of the Bootheel counties are about 250 feet above sea level. The highest elevation in the State is 1,772 feet above sea level on Taum Sauk Mountain in Iron County, in the eastern Ozarks, but the largest area of high elevation is in the central Ozarks, in Webster County, where elevations of 1,600 to 1,700 feet are common. The northwestern part of Missouri has extensive areas above 1,000 feet and some over 1,200. The northeastern part of the State slopes down to about 700 feet above sea level near the Mississippi River. The terrain varies from rugged areas bordering some of the larger streams, with deep valleys and steep hills, to broad, rolling uplands.

GENERAL CLIMATE. Missouri is an inland state, thus its climate is essentially continental. There are frequent changes in the weather, both from day to day and from season to season. Missouri is in the path of cold air moving down out of Canada, warm, moist air coming up from the Gulf of Mexico, and dry air from the west.

Annual precipitation in Missouri averages from near 50 inches in the southeastern corner to about 32 inches in the northwest. In the southeastern counties much of the precipitation comes during the fall, winter, and early spring months. In most of the western and northern counties the winter months are comparatively dry, with most of the precipitation coming in the spring, summer, and fall months.

Snow has been known to fall in Missouri as early as October, and as late as May. However, most of it falls in December, January, and February. As one would expect, the northern counties usually get the most snow. North of the Missouri River the winter snowfall averages 18 to 22 inches. This average figure tapers off to eight to 12 inches in the southernmost counties. It is unusual for snow to stay on the ground for more than a week or two before it melts. Winter precipitation usually is in the form of rain or snow, or both. Conditions sometimes are on the borderline between rain and snow, and in these situations freezing drizzle or freezing rain occurs. This does not usually happen more than twice in a winter season.

Spring, summer, and early fall precipitation comes largely in the form of showers or thunderstorms. Thunderstorms have been observed in Missouri during the winter months, but they are most frequent from April to July. Occasionally, these produce some very heavy rains. Measurable precipitation occurs on an average of about 100 days a year. About half of these will be days with thunderstorms.

The river drainage in Missouri is wholly, either directly or indirectly, into the Mississippi River which forms the eastern boundary of the State. The northern part of the western boundary is formed by the Missouri River which then flows eastward across the State from Kansas City, entering the Mississippi just above St. Louis. Most of northern Missouri is drained by tributaries of the Missouri River, the principal ones being the Grand, Charlton, One Hundred and Two, and the Nodaway Rivers. The principal southern tributaries of the Missouri are the Osage and the Gasconade. Important tributaries which drain directly into the Mississippi within the borders of the State are the Fox, Wyaconda, Fabius, and Salt Rivers in the northeast, and the Meramec River which enters the Mississippi just below St. Louis.

Tributary flooding resulting from heavy rains may be expected once or twice in most years, and flash flooding along minor streams following heavy thunderstorm rains, occur most frequently in the spring and early summer, April to July, but may occur during any month. Serious flooding occurs less frequently along the main stems of the Missouri and Mississippi Rivers and usually occurs during the spring and early summer. Main stem flooding may be caused by prolonged periods of heavy rains, ice jams, or upstream flood crests synchronized with high tributary discharge.

On the average the amount of water that falls in Missouri on a square mile in a year varies from near 600 million gallons in the northwest corner to over 800 million gallons in the southeast. Some of this water runs off into the rivers and streams, some is consumed by animal life, and large amounts are evaporated back into the atmosphere, or transpired by growing vegetation. During years when precipitation comes in a fairly normal manner, moisture is stored in the top layers of the soil during the winter and early spring, when evaporation and transpiration are low. During the summer months the loss of water by evaporation and transpiration is high, and if rainfall fails to occur at frequent intervals, drought will result. Nearly every year some areas have short periods of drought in Missouri.

Tornadoes have been observed during every month of the year, with about 70 percent occurring during the four months, March through June. Over 25 percent of the total number were reported during May for the month of greatest frequency. Paths of the Missouri tornadoes have been short, averaging only nine and a half miles. The width of tornado paths averages slightly less than 300 yards.

TEMPERATURE. Because of its inland location, Missouri is subject to frequent changes in temperature. While winters are cold and summers are hot, prolonged periods of very cold or very hot weather are unusual. Occasional periods of mild, above freezing temperatures are noted almost every winter. Conversely, during the peak of the summer season, occasional periods of dry, cool weather break up stretches of hot, humid weather.

Temperatures over 100°F. are rare, but they have occurred in every section of the State. In the summer, temperatures rise to 90°F. or higher on an average of 40 to 50 days in the west and north, and 55 to 60 days in the southeast. Temperatures below zero are infrequent, but have occurred in every county in Missouri. On the average there are two to five days a year with below zero temperatures in the northern counties, and one to two days in the southern counties, although there are some winters when temperatures do not go below zero at all.

In winter there is an average of about 110 days with temperatures below 32°F. in the northern half, the West Central Plains, and East Ozarks, about 100 days in the West Ozarks, and about 70 such days in the Bootheel counties. The average date of the first occurrence of temperatures 28 to 32°F. in the fall would come as early as mid-October in the northernmost counties and high elevations of the Ozarks, and as early as the third week in October over much of the rest of the State, except the Bootheel where the average date of the first freeze is in early November. About one year in 20, the first freeze would come as early as mid-September in the northern counties and late September in the rest of the State, except the Bootheel where it would occur as early as the third week in October.

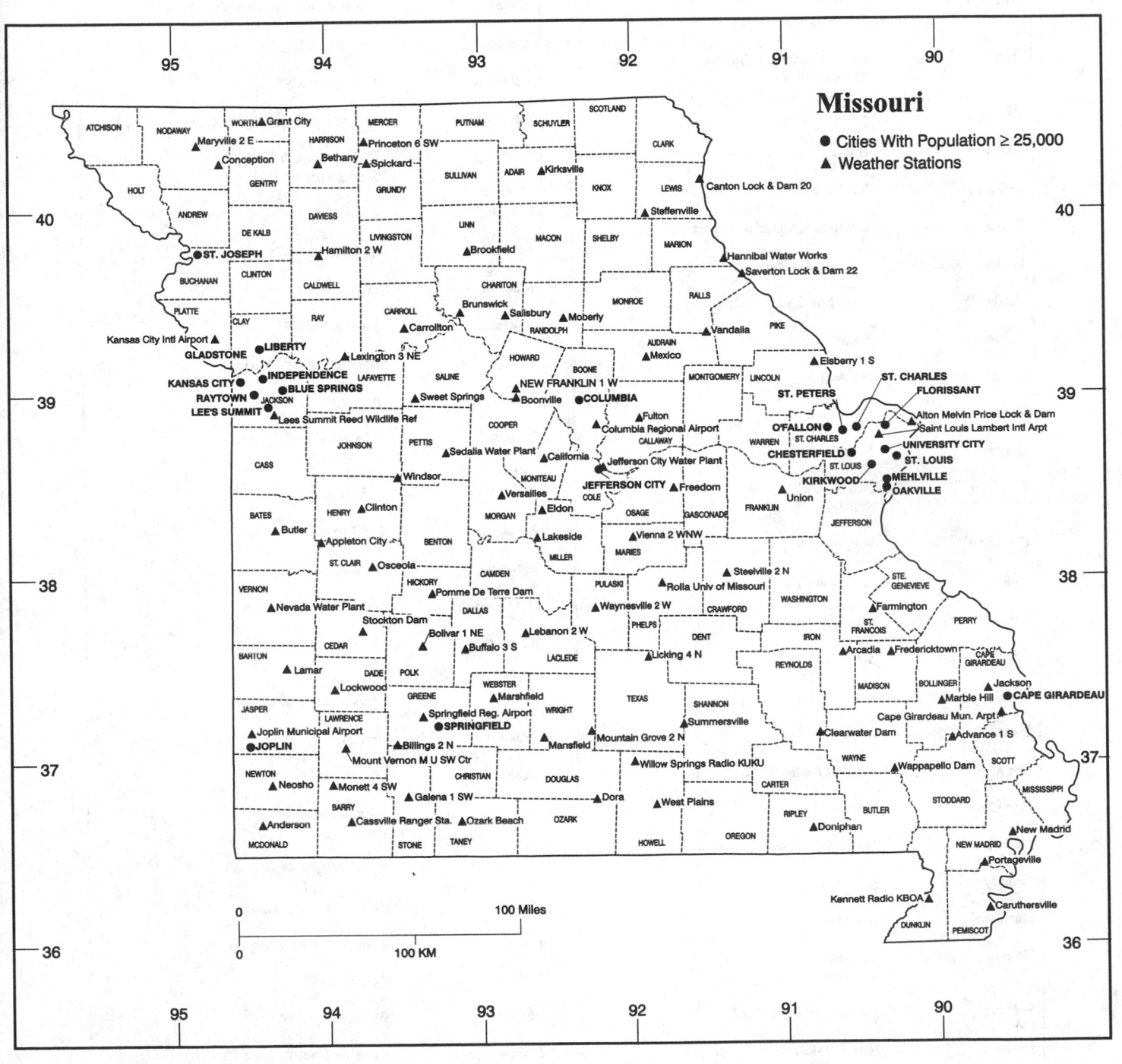

Missouri

- ● Cities With Population ≥ 25,000
- ▲ Weather Stations

Missouri Weather Stations by County

County	Station Name
Adair	Kirksville
Audrain	Mexico
	Vandalia
Barry	Cassville Ranger Station
	Monett 4 SW
Barton	Lamar
Bates	Butler
Bollinger	Marble Hill
Boone	Columbia Regional Airport
Butler	Wappapello Dam
Caldwell	Hamilton 2 W
Callaway	Fulton
Cape Girardeau	Jackson
Carroll	Carrollton
Cedar	Stockton Dam
Chariton	Brunswick
	Salisbury
Christian	Billings 2 N
Cole	Jefferson City Water Plant
Cooper	Boonville
Crawford	Steelville 2 N
Dade	Lockwood
Dallas	Buffalo 3 S
Dunklin	Kennett Radio KBOA
Franklin	Union
Greene	Springfield Regional Airport
Grundy	Spickard
Harrison	Bethany
Henry	Clinton
	Windsor
Hickory	Pomme De Terre Dam
Howard	New Franklin 1 W
Howell	West Plains
	Willow Springs Radio KUKU
Iron	Arcadia

County	Station Name
Jackson	Lees Summit Reed Wildlife Refuge
Jasper	Joplin Municipal Airport
Laclede	Lebanon 2 W
Lafayette	Lexington 3 NE
Lawrence	Mount Vernon M U SW Center
Lewis	Canton Lock & Dam 20
	Steffenville
Lincoln	Elsberry 1 S
Linn	Brookfield
Madison	Fredericktown
Maries	Vienna 2 WNW
Marion	Hannibal Water Works
McDonald	Anderson
Mercer	Princeton 6 SW
Miller	Eldon
	Lakeside
Moniteau	California
Morgan	Versailles
New Madrid	New Madrid
Newton	Neosho
Nodaway	Conception
	Maryville 2 E
Osage	Freedom
Ozark	Dora
Pemiscot	Caruthersville
	Portageville
Pettis	Sedalia Water Plant
Phelps	Rolla Univ. of Missouri
Platte	Kansas City Int'l Airport
Polk	Bolivar 1 NE
Pulaski	Waynesville 2 W
Ralls	Saverton Lock & Dam 22
Randolph	Moberly
Ripley	Doniphan

County	Station Name
Saline	Sweet Springs
Scott	Cape Girardeau Municipal Airport
St. Clair	Appleton City Osceola
St. Francois	Farmington
St. Louis	Saint Louis Lambert Int'l Arpt.
Stoddard	Advance 1 S
Stone	Galena 1 SW
Taney	Ozark Beach
Texas	Licking 4 N Summersville
Vernon	Nevada Water Plant
Wayne	Clearwater Dam
Webster	Marshfield
Worth	Grant City
Wright	Mansfield Mountain Grove 2 N

Missouri Weather Stations by City

City	Station Name	Miles
Blue Springs	Lees Summit Reed Wildlife Refuge	10
Cape Girardeau	Anna 2 NNE, IL	20
	Cape Girardeau Municipal Airport	6
	Jackson	8
Chesterfield	Saint Louis Lambert Int'l Arpt.	12
Columbia	Columbia Regional Airport	11
Florissant	Alton Melvin Price Lock & Dam, IL	10
	Saint Louis Lambert Int'l Arpt.	4
Gladstone	Leavenworth, KS	20
	Kansas City Int'l Airport	10
Independence	Lees Summit Reed Wildlife Refuge	14
Jefferson City	Columbia Regional Airport	17
	Jefferson City Water Plant	1
Joplin	Columbus 1 SW, KS	20
	Joplin Municipal Airport	5
	Neosho	16
Kansas City	Olathe 3 E, KS	17
	Kansas City Int'l Airport	19
	Lees Summit Reed Wildlife Refuge	17
Kirkwood	Saint Louis Lambert Int'l Arpt.	12
Lee's Summit	Lees Summit Reed Wildlife Refuge	3
Liberty	Kansas City Int'l Airport	16
Mehlville	Waterloo, IL	15
	Saint Louis Lambert Int'l Arpt.	17
O'Fallon	Saint Louis Lambert Int'l Arpt.	18
Oakville	Waterloo, IL	13
Raytown	Olathe 3 E, KS	18
	Lees Summit Reed Wildlife Refuge	10
Springfield	Billings 2 N	17
	Springfield Regional Airport	6
St. Charles	Alton Melvin Price Lock & Dam, IL	20
	Saint Louis Lambert Int'l Arpt.	8
St. Joseph	Troy 2 E, KS	14
St. Louis	Alton Melvin Price Lock & Dam, IL	14
	Saint Louis Lambert Int'l Arpt.	10
St. Peters	Saint Louis Lambert Int'l Arpt.	13
University City	Alton Melvin Price Lock & Dam, IL	14
	Saint Louis Lambert Int'l Arpt.	6

Note: Miles is the distance between the geographic center of the city and the weather station.

Missouri Weather Stations by Elevation

Feet	Station Name
1,519	Mansfield
1,489	Marshfield
1,450	Mountain Grove 2 N
1,377	Monett 4 SW
1,351	Billings 2 N
1,338	Cassville Ranger Station
1,309	Willow Springs Radio KUKU
1,276	Lebanon 2 W
1,256	Springfield Regional Airport
1,187	Mount Vernon M U SW Center
1,177	Licking 4 N
1,177	Summersville
1,164	Rolla Univ. of Missouri
1,148	Buffalo 3 S
1,128	Grant City
1,105	Conception
1,099	Galena 1 SW
1,079	Lockwood
1,069	Arcadia
1,049	Anderson
1,033	Bolivar 1 NE
1,026	Versailles
1,010	Neosho
1,007	West Plains
997	Lees Summit Reed Wildlife Refuge
987	Dora
984	Maryville 2 E
977	Joplin Municipal Airport
977	Lamar
977	Princeton 6 SW
971	Kansas City Int'l Airport
967	Kirksville
948	Bethany
928	Eldon
921	Stockton Dam
898	Farmington
898	Hamilton 2 W
898	Pomme De Terre Dam
889	Columbia Regional Airport
889	Waynesville 2 W
872	Spickard
869	California
869	Fulton
839	Moberly
839	Windsor
823	Lexington 3 NE
816	Nevada Water Plant
800	Clinton
800	Mexico
797	Appleton City
787	Butler
777	Sedalia Water Plant
767	Vienna 2 WNW
764	Brookfield
764	Osceola

Feet	Station Name
757	Vandalia
744	Freedom
728	Salisbury
711	Hannibal Water Works
702	Carrollton
698	Fredericktown
698	Ozark Beach
698	Steelville 2 N
688	Steffenville
679	Sweet Springs
669	Boonville
669	Jefferson City Water Plant
659	Brunswick
659	Clearwater Dam
639	New Franklin 1 W
590	Lakeside
567	Saint Louis Lambert Int'l Arpt.
538	Union
488	Canton Lock & Dam 20
469	Saverton Lock & Dam 22
449	Elsberry 1 S
439	Jackson
410	Wappapello Dam
387	Marble Hill
357	Advance 1 S
334	Cape Girardeau Municipal Airport
328	Doniphan
308	New Madrid
278	Caruthersville
278	Portageville
269	Kennett Radio KBOA

Columbia Regional Airport

Columbia, Missouri, with its interior continental location, experiences moderately cold winters and warm summers that are often humid.

There are usually a few days of temperatures below zero during the winter months, but there have been several winters when this did not occur. Periods of cold weather are usually interrupted by periods of at least a few mild days. It is not uncommon to find some days with temperatures in the 60s in the midst of the winter months. Some snow falls each winter, but it is very unlikely that a snow cover will persist for more than three weeks. Most of the time when snow does fall, it stays on the ground for less than a week. March is the month in which substantial amounts of snowfall are most likely.

Temperatures of 100 degrees or more occur in most summers, but there have been several summers when temperatures failed to reach this high. The late spring and early summer months produce more frequent and larger amounts of rain than the other months of the year. Thus, in addition to being warm, these months are often quite humid. By late summer smaller amounts of rain fall and rains occur less frequently, so by mid-August, the moisture in the top two feet of soil is often depleted.

Based on the 1951-1980 period, the average occurrence of the last temperature as cold as 32 degrees in spring is early April, and the first 32 degree temperature in the fall occurs in late October.

Columbia Regional Airport *Boone County*   Elevation: 889 ft.   Latitude: 38° 49' N   Longitude: 92° 13' W

	JAN	FEB	MAR	APR	MAY	JUN	JUL	AUG	SEP	OCT	NOV	DEC	YEAR
Mean Maximum Temp. (°F)	36.3	42.7	54.0	65.2	74.1	83.2	88.5	87.0	78.8	67.3	52.9	41.3	64.3
Mean Temp. (°F)	27.7	33.4	43.8	54.5	63.7	72.8	77.7	76.0	67.8	56.3	43.6	32.8	54.2
Mean Minimum Temp. (°F)	19.0	24.1	33.6	43.7	53.3	62.4	66.9	64.9	56.7	45.2	34.3	24.3	44.0
Extreme Maximum Temp. (°F)	74	82	85	90	92	103	111	110	101	93	83	76	111
Extreme Minimum Temp. (°F)	-19	-15	-5	19	29	40	48	42	32	22	0	-20	-20
Days Maximum Temp. ≥ 90°F	0	0	0	0	0	5	14	12	4	0	0	0	35
Days Maximum Temp. ≤ 32°F	12	7	1	0	0	0	0	0	0	0	1	7	28
Days Minimum Temp. ≤ 32°F	27	21	15	3	0	0	0	0	0	2	13	25	106
Days Minimum Temp. ≤ 0°F	3	1	0	0	0	0	0	0	0	0	0	1	5
Heating Degree Days (base 65°F)	1,151	885	653	328	108	10	1	2	68	285	635	991	5,117
Cooling Degree Days (base 65°F)	0	0	4	19	74	257	409	354	152	18	1	0	1,288
Mean Precipitation (in.)	1.71	2.10	3.17	4.40	5.01	3.94	3.73	3.59	3.66	3.15	3.46	2.50	40.42
Maximum Precipitation (in.)	4.8	6.2	10.1	11.7	12.3	10.3	12.1	9.0	12.1	6.1	10.4	7.0	62.5
Minimum Precipitation (in.)	0	0.1	0.8	1.4	1.6	0.3	0.2	0.2	0.4	1.0	0.4	0.6	23.3
Maximum 24-hr. Precipitation (in.)	1.8	2.4	3.9	3.8	4.8	3.2	5.9	4.3	2.8	2.4	2.8	2.7	5.9
Days With ≥ 0.1" Precipitation	4	4	6	7	8	6	5	5	6	6	6	4	67
Days With ≥ 1.0" Precipitation	0	0	1	1	1	1	1	1	1	1	1	1	10
Mean Snowfall (in.)	7.0	7.2	3.5	0.8	trace	trace	trace	0.0	0.0	*trace*	2.3	4.5	*25.3*
Maximum Snowfall (in.)	24	20	18	7	0	0	0	0	0	trace	8	18	49
Maximum 24-hr. Snowfall (in.)	18	12	6	7	0	0	0	0	0	trace	8	11	18
Days With ≥ 1.0" Snow Depth	12	8	3	0	0	0	0	0	0	0	1	6	30
Thunderstorm Days	1	1	3	5	8	8	8	7	5	3	2	1	52
Foggy Days	11	11	11	9	11	9	8	12	12	10	11	13	128
Predominant Sky Cover	OVR	OVR	OVR	OVR	OVR	OVR	CLR	CLR	CLR	OVR	OVR	OVR	OVR
Mean Relative Humidity 6am (%)	80	80	79	79	85	86	87	89	88	84	82	81	83
Mean Relative Humidity 3pm (%)	62	59	53	52	57	56	53	52	54	53	59	64	56
Mean Dewpoint (°F)	19	23	32	42	53	62	66	64	57	45	34	24	43
Prevailing Wind Direction	WNW	WNW	S	S	S	S	S	S	S	S	S	WNW	S
Prevailing Wind Speed (mph)	13	12	13	12	10	9	8	8	9	10	10	12	10
Maximum Wind Gust (mph)	53	63	66	69	70	96	73	62	58	48	61	71	96

Kansas City Int'l Airport

The National Weather Service Office at Kansas City is very near the geographical center of the United States. The surrounding terrain is gently rolling. It has a modified continental climate. There are no natural topographic obstructions to prevent the free sweep of air from all directions. The influx of moist air from the Gulf of Mexico, or dry air from the semi-arid regions of the southwest, determine whether wet or dry conditions will prevail. There is often conflict between the warm moist gulf air and the cold polar continental air from the north in this area.

Early spring brings a period of frequent and rapid fluctuations in weather, with the fluctuations generally less frequent as spring progresses. The summer season is characterized by warm days and mild nights, with moderate humidities. July is the warmest month. The fall season is normally mild and usually includes a period near the middle of the season characterized by mild, sunny days, and cool nights. Winters are not severely cold. January is the coldest month. Falls of snow to a depth of 10 inches or more are comparatively rare. The distribution of measurable snow normally extends from November to April.

Nearly 60 percent of the annual precipitation occurs during the six months from April through September. More than 75 percent of the annual moisture normally falls during the growing season. The frequency and distribution of precipitation over a normal day is also important. The maximum frequency of precipitation, from April through October, occurs during the six hours following midnight and the minimum frequency occurs during the six hours following noon.

Kansas City Int'l Airport *Platte County*   Elevation: 971 ft.   Latitude: 39° 18' N   Longitude: 94° 43' W

	JAN	FEB	MAR	APR	MAY	JUN	JUL	AUG	SEP	OCT	NOV	DEC	YEAR
Mean Maximum Temp. (°F)	35.4	42.1	53.8	64.6	74.2	83.4	88.8	86.6	78.4	67.0	51.8	39.9	63.8
Mean Temp. (°F)	26.6	32.7	43.5	54.1	64.1	73.3	78.7	76.4	67.8	56.4	42.7	31.3	54.0
Mean Minimum Temp. (°F)	17.7	23.3	33.2	43.6	53.9	63.2	68.4	66.1	57.1	45.6	33.6	22.7	44.0
Extreme Maximum Temp. (°F)	69	77	86	93	95	105	107	109	102	92	82	70	109
Extreme Minimum Temp. (°F)	-17	-19	-10	12	30	42	51	43	31	17	1	-23	-23
Days Maximum Temp. ≥ 90°F	0	0	0	0	0	6	15	11	3	0	0	0	35
Days Maximum Temp. ≤ 32°F	12	7	2	0	0	0	0	0	0	0	2	8	31
Days Minimum Temp. ≤ 32°F	28	21	15	4	0	0	0	0	0	2	13	26	109
Days Minimum Temp. ≤ 0°F	4	2	0	0	0	0	0	0	0	0	0	2	8
Heating Degree Days (base 65°F)	1,184	905	662	342	105	8	0	2	71	286	664	1,038	5,267
Cooling Degree Days (base 65°F)	0	0	3	23	82	268	427	363	166	25	1	0	1,358
Mean Precipitation (in.)	1.19	1.29	2.52	3.56	5.47	4.47	4.37	3.70	4.79	3.36	2.30	1.64	38.66
Maximum Precipitation (in.)	5.5	6.8	6.7	10.6	11.0	11.0	11.4	11.6	16.2	11.9	9.5	4.1	60.3
Minimum Precipitation (in.)	trace	trace	0.1	0.5	0.7	0.3	0.4	0.3	0.2	0.2	trace	trace	19.2
Maximum 24-hr. Precipitation (in.)	2.3	2.0	2.7	4.7	4.7	3.9	4.6	7.4	6.1	4.5	5.7	2.6	7.4
Days With ≥ 0.1" Precipitation	3	3	6	7	8	7	6	6	6	5	5	3	65
Days With ≥ 1.0" Precipitation	0	0	0	1	1	1	1	1	1	1	1	0	8
Mean Snowfall (in.)	5.9	5.0	2.6	0.9	trace	trace	trace	0.0	trace	0.3	1.4	4.0	20.1
Maximum Snowfall (in.)	31	21	40	7	2	0	0	0	0	3	9	17	63
Maximum 24-hr. Snowfall (in.)	12	12	21	7	2	0	0	0	0	3	9	9	21
Days With ≥ 1.0" Snow Depth	11	7	2	0	0	0	0	0	0	0	1	5	26
Thunderstorm Days	< 1	1	3	5	8	9	8	8	6	3	1	< 1	52
Foggy Days	8	7	6	5	6	4	4	4	6	7	6	8	71
Predominant Sky Cover	OVR	OVR	OVR	OVR	OVR	OVR	CLR	CLR	CLR	CLR	OVR	OVR	OVR
Mean Relative Humidity 6am (%)	74	74	73	73	77	79	78	79	80	75	74	75	76
Mean Relative Humidity 3pm (%)	57	55	49	47	49	51	49	49	48	46	51	57	51
Mean Dewpoint (°F)	18	23	29	41	53	62	66	64	56	44	32	24	43
Prevailing Wind Direction	SSW	SSW	S	S	S	S	S	S	S	S	S	SSW	S
Prevailing Wind Speed (mph)	10	10	13	14	13	12	12	10	12	12	12	10	12
Maximum Wind Gust (mph)	55	52	33	54	49	58	54	55	44	45	53	35	58

Saint Louis Lambert Int'l Arpt.

Saint Louis is located at the confluence of the Missouri and Mississippi Rivers and near the geographical center of the United States. Thus, with a somewhat modified continental climate, it is in the enviable position of being able to enjoy the changes of a four-season climate without the undue hardship of prolonged periods of extreme heat or high humidity. To the south is the warm, moist air of the Gulf of Mexico, and to the north, in Canada, is a favored region of cold air masses. The alternate invasion of Saint Louis by air masses from these sources, and the conflict along the frontal zones where they come together, produce a variety of weather conditions, none of which are likely to persist to the point of monotony.

Winters are brisk and stimulating, seldom severe. Records since 1870 show that temperatures drop to zero or below an average of two or three days per year. Temperatures remain as cold as 32 degrees or lower less than 25 days in most years. Snowfall has averaged a little over 18 inches per winter season. Snowfall of an inch or more is received on five to ten days in most years.

The long-term record for Saint Louis (since 1870) indicates that temperatures of 90 degrees or higher occur on about 35-40 days a year. Extremely hot days of 100 degrees or more are expected on no more than five days per year.

Normal annual precipitation for the Saint Louis area, is a little less than 34 inches. The three winter months are the driest, with an average total of about six inches of precipitation. The spring months of March through May are normally the wettest with normal total precipitation of just under 10 and a half inches. It is not unusual to have extended dry periods of one to two weeks during the growing season.

Thunderstorms occur normally on between 40 and 50 days per year. During any year, there are usually a few of these that can be classified as severe storms with hail and damaging winds. Tornadoes have produced extensive damage and loss of life in the Saint Louis area.

Saint Louis Lambert Int'l Arpt. *St. Louis County*   Elevation: 567 ft.   Latitude: 38° 45' N   Longitude: 90° 22' W

	JAN	FEB	MAR	APR	MAY	JUN	JUL	AUG	SEP	OCT	NOV	DEC	YEAR
Mean Maximum Temp. (°F)	37.7	44.0	55.0	66.7	76.3	85.0	89.4	87.4	80.1	68.4	54.3	42.8	65.6
Mean Temp. (°F)	29.5	35.1	45.3	56.4	66.2	75.3	79.8	77.7	70.1	58.2	45.6	34.7	56.2
Mean Minimum Temp. (°F)	21.2	26.1	35.5	46.0	56.0	65.5	70.2	68.1	60.0	47.9	36.9	26.5	46.7
Extreme Maximum Temp. (°F)	76	85	89	93	94	102	107	107	104	92	85	76	107
Extreme Minimum Temp. (°F)	-18	-12	-1	22	31	45	51	47	36	23	7	-16	-18
Days Maximum Temp. ≥ 90°F	0	0	0	0	1	9	16	12	5	0	0	0	43
Days Maximum Temp. ≤ 32°F	11	7	1	0	0	0	0	0	0	0	1	6	26
Days Minimum Temp. ≤ 32°F	26	19	13	3	0	0	0	0	0	1	10	22	94
Days Minimum Temp. ≤ 0°F	2	1	0	0	0	0	0	0	0	0	0	1	4
Heating Degree Days (base 65°F)	1,095	840	610	287	79	6	0	0	43	241	578	934	4,713
Cooling Degree Days (base 65°F)	0	0	7	35	125	336	486	425	209	41	4	0	1,668
Mean Precipitation (in.)	2.10	2.20	3.61	3.93	3.99	3.65	3.85	3.08	3.05	2.75	3.64	2.86	38.71
Maximum Precipitation (in.)	8.0	5.0	6.7	10.3	12.9	10.5	12.7	14.8	10.0	7.1	9.9	7.8	55.0
Minimum Precipitation (in.)	0.1	0.3	0.8	1.0	1.0	0.4	0.6	0.1	trace	0.2	0.1	trace	20.6
Maximum 24-hr. Precipitation (in.)	4.2	2.4	2.4	4.8	5.6	3.9	4.7	4.3	4.6	2.9	3.1	2.8	5.6
Days With ≥ 0.1" Precipitation	4	5	7	7	7	6	5	5	5	5	6	5	67
Days With ≥ 1.0" Precipitation	0	0	0	1	1	1	1	1	1	1	1	1	9
Mean Snowfall (in.)	7.0	4.8	3.2	0.8	trace	trace	trace	0.0	0.0	trace	1.5	4.3	21.6
Maximum Snowfall (in.)	24	21	22	7	0	0	0	0	0	trace	11	26	49
Maximum 24-hr. Snowfall (in.)	11	10	10	5	0	0	0	0	0	trace	8	12	12
Days With ≥ 1.0" Snow Depth	10	6	2	0	0	0	0	0	0	0	1	4	23
Thunderstorm Days	1	1	3	6	7	8	7	6	4	2	2	1	48
Foggy Days	13	13	13	11	11	9	9	13	13	12	12	14	143
Predominant Sky Cover	OVR	OVR	OVR	OVR	OVR	OVR	SCT	CLR	CLR	CLR	OVR	OVR	OVR
Mean Relative Humidity 6am (%)	80	80	80	77	81	82	83	86	86	82	80	81	82
Mean Relative Humidity 3pm (%)	62	58	54	49	51	51	51	51	50	50	56	63	54
Mean Dewpoint (°F)	22	25	33	42	53	62	66	65	57	46	35	26	44
Prevailing Wind Direction	WNW	WNW	WNW	WNW	S	S	S	S	S	S	WNW	WNW	S
Prevailing Wind Speed (mph)	13	13	14	14	10	10	9	8	9	10	13	13	12
Maximum Wind Gust (mph)	62	66	66	83	59	76	62	63	56	78	64	56	83

Springfield Regional Airport

The entire metropolitan area, airport, and surrounding territory consists of comparatively flat or very gently rolling tableland, practically atop the crest of the Missouri Ozark Mountain plateau. The average elevation of the city proper is slightly over 1,300 feet above sea level. There are no serious problems of instrumental exposure.

As a result of this advantageous location, the city and surrounding territory enjoy what is described as a plateau climate. The winter season in the Ozarks has temperatures considerably milder than in the upland, plain or prairie, and in the summer the Ozarks are appreciably cooler.

The city of Springfield also occupies a unique location with regard to natural water drainage. The line separating two major water sheds crosses the north-central part of the city. Drainage north of this line flows north into the Gasconade and Missouri Rivers. To the south of the line, drainage is to the south into the White and Mississippi Rivers.

The average annual temperature range is over 140 degrees with lowest temperatures below -25 and and highest temperatures above 115 degrees.

The growing season extends over a period of 199 days. Agriculture is greatly diversified, practically every farm product of the temperate zone is grown in this area. It is a noted livestock and poultry production and distribution center. The climate permits green pasturage the year around in varying quantity, resulting in ever increasing cattle production for both meat and dairy products.

The air is remarkably free from palls of industrial smoke, and the altitude of the city also tends to prevent other than few amounts of either radiation or advection fogs.

Springfield Regional Airport *Greene County*   Elevation: 1,256 ft.   Latitude: 37° 14' N   Longitude: 93° 23' W

	JAN	FEB	MAR	APR	MAY	JUN	JUL	AUG	SEP	OCT	NOV	DEC	YEAR
Mean Maximum Temp. (°F)	41.3	47.5	57.2	67.3	75.4	84.2	89.4	88.7	80.1	69.2	55.7	45.9	66.8
Mean Temp. (°F)	31.5	37.0	46.1	55.7	64.5	73.3	78.3	77.2	69.0	57.8	45.7	36.2	56.0
Mean Minimum Temp. (°F)	21.6	26.4	35.0	44.1	53.6	62.4	67.1	65.7	57.9	46.3	35.6	26.4	45.2
Extreme Maximum Temp. (°F)	73	81	87	91	93	99	108	106	99	93	81	77	108
Extreme Minimum Temp. (°F)	-13	-17	0	19	30	43	44	46	31	18	5	-16	-17
Days Maximum Temp. ≥ 90°F	0	0	0	0	0	6	17	15	4	0	0	0	42
Days Maximum Temp. ≤ 32°F	8	4	1	0	0	0	0	0	0	0	1	4	18
Days Minimum Temp. ≤ 32°F	25	20	13	3	0	0	0	0	0	2	12	22	97
Days Minimum Temp. ≤ 0°F	2	1	0	0	0	0	0	0	0	0	0	1	4
Heating Degree Days (base 65°F)	1,032	784	581	294	95	8	1	1	58	245	574	888	4,561
Cooling Degree Days (base 65°F)	0	0	3	22	89	270	430	397	182	26	2	0	1,421
Mean Precipitation (in.)	2.09	2.24	3.85	4.45	4.54	4.95	3.35	3.48	5.08	3.54	4.40	3.19	45.16
Maximum Precipitation (in.)	6.8	5.7	9.0	10.6	13.4	11.3	18.8	8.6	17.5	8.7	12.2	8.8	63.2
Minimum Precipitation (in.)	0.1	0.4	0.5	0.1	1.5	0.2	0.3	0.5	0.2	0.4	0.2	0.1	25.2
Maximum 24-hr. Precipitation (in.)	3.8	3.1	2.9	3.4	4.2	4.8	4.5	3.4	5.0	5.5	6.3	3.7	6.3
Days With ≥ 0.1" Precipitation	4	5	7	7	8	7	5	5	6	6	6	5	71
Days With ≥ 1.0" Precipitation	0	0	1	1	1	1	1	1	2	1	1	1	11
Mean Snowfall (in.)	6.6	4.4	3.6	0.4	trace	trace	trace	0.0	0.0	trace	1.7	3.3	20.0
Maximum Snowfall (in.)	23	19	24	7	0	0	0	0	0	1	20	15	35
Maximum 24-hr. Snowfall (in.)	9	12	16	7	0	0	0	0	0	1	11	6	16
Days With ≥ 1.0" Snow Depth	10	5	2	0	0	0	0	0	0	0	1	3	21
Thunderstorm Days	1	1	4	6	8	9	8	8	5	3	2	1	56
Foggy Days	12	12	11	9	10	9	8	10	11	10	10	12	124
Predominant Sky Cover	OVR	OVR	OVR	OVR	OVR	OVR	CLR	CLR	CLR	CLR	OVR	OVR	OVR
Mean Relative Humidity 6am (%)	79	80	79	79	85	87	87	88	87	82	80	80	83
Mean Relative Humidity 3pm (%)	59	55	52	50	56	56	53	50	52	50	54	59	54
Mean Dewpoint (°F)	22	26	33	43	54	63	66	64	57	46	34	26	45
Prevailing Wind Direction	SSE	SSE	SSE	SSE	SSE	SSE	SSE	SSE	SSE	SSE	SSE	SSE	SSE
Prevailing Wind Speed (mph)	13	13	14	13	12	10	9	9	10	12	13	13	12
Maximum Wind Gust (mph)	52	52	52	56	60	55	73	59	52	68	53	115	115

Advance 1 S *Stoddard County*   Elevation: 357 ft.   Latitude: 37° 06' N   Longitude: 89° 54' W

	JAN	FEB	MAR	APR	MAY	JUN	JUL	AUG	SEP	OCT	NOV	DEC	YEAR
Mean Maximum Temp. (°F)	41.3	47.7	57.3	68.0	77.3	86.0	90.1	88.5	81.8	71.1	57.3	45.6	67.7
Mean Temp. (°F)	32.2	37.4	46.5	56.3	65.8	74.6	78.7	76.4	68.9	57.4	46.4	36.4	56.4
Mean Minimum Temp. (°F)	23.0	27.0	35.6	44.5	54.1	63.3	67.2	64.2	56.0	43.7	35.4	27.2	45.1
Extreme Maximum Temp. (°F)	72	79	82	90	95	102	105	103	101	91	85	75	105
Extreme Minimum Temp. (°F)	-20	-13	9	25	32	41	51	40	32	20	6	-11	-20
Days Maximum Temp. ≥ 90°F	0	0	0	0	1	10	19	14	6	0	0	0	50
Days Maximum Temp. ≤ 32°F	7	4	0	0	0	0	0	0	0	0	0	3	14
Days Minimum Temp. ≤ 32°F	26	20	14	3	0	0	0	0	0	5	13	22	103
Days Minimum Temp. ≤ 0°F	1	1	0	0	0	0	0	0	0	0	0	1	3
Heating Degree Days (base 65°F)	1,012	775	570	279	76	4	0	1	50	256	554	880	4,457
Cooling Degree Days (base 65°F)	0	0	4	23	107	300	433	360	166	22	2	0	1,417
Mean Precipitation (in.)	3.24	3.30	4.32	5.13	4.99	3.83	4.06	3.04	3.15	3.43	4.57	3.90	46.96
Days With ≥ 0.1" Precipitation	5	5	7	7	7	6	6	5	5	6	6	6	71
Days With ≥ 1.0" Precipitation	1	1	1	2	1	1	1	1	1	1	2	1	14
Mean Snowfall (in.)	2.8	3.9	1.4	trace	0.0	0.0	0.0	0.0	0.0	trace	0.4	1.3	9.8
Days With ≥ 1.0" Snow Depth	4	3	1	0	0	0	0	0	0	0	0	2	10

Anderson *McDonald County*   Elevation: 1,049 ft.   Latitude: 36° 39' N   Longitude: 94° 26' W

	JAN	FEB	MAR	APR	MAY	JUN	JUL	AUG	SEP	OCT	NOV	DEC	YEAR
Mean Maximum Temp. (°F)	44.5	50.9	60.4	70.5	76.3	83.6	89.0	88.1	79.8	70.7	58.4	48.6	68.4
Mean Temp. (°F)	33.2	38.7	47.8	57.4	64.7	72.7	77.6	76.1	68.6	58.1	46.9	37.4	56.6
Mean Minimum Temp. (°F)	21.9	26.5	35.2	44.2	53.1	61.7	66.1	64.1	57.3	45.3	35.3	26.1	44.7
Extreme Maximum Temp. (°F)	76	86	90	93	90	98	107	105	101	92	86	76	107
Extreme Minimum Temp. (°F)	-21	-21	-1	19	30	42	44	42	27	17	0	-18	-21
Days Maximum Temp. ≥ 90°F	0	0	0	0	0	4	15	13	4	0	0	0	36
Days Maximum Temp. ≤ 32°F	6	3	0	0	0	0	0	0	0	0	0	3	12
Days Minimum Temp. ≤ 32°F	25	20	13	4	0	0	0	0	0	4	13	23	102
Days Minimum Temp. ≤ 0°F	2	1	0	0	0	0	0	0	0	0	0	1	4
Heating Degree Days (base 65°F)	979	736	531	251	87	8	1	2	57	236	540	850	4,278
Cooling Degree Days (base 65°F)	0	0	5	27	82	247	398	358	170	24	2	0	1,313
Mean Precipitation (in.)	2.00	1.98	3.74	4.17	4.74	4.50	3.11	3.66	5.00	3.64	4.32	3.00	43.86
Days With ≥ 0.1" Precipitation	4	4	6	7	8	7	4	5	6	5	5	5	66
Days With ≥ 1.0" Precipitation	0	0	1	1	1	1	1	1	2	1	2	1	12
Mean Snowfall (in.)	4.5	3.0	2.8	trace	0.0	0.0	0.0	0.0	0.0	trace	1.1	2.3	13.7
Days With ≥ 1.0" Snow Depth	7	4	1	0	0	0	0	0	0	0	0	3	15

Appleton City *St. Clair County*   Elevation: 797 ft.   Latitude: 38° 11' N   Longitude: 94° 02' W

	JAN	FEB	MAR	APR	MAY	JUN	JUL	AUG	SEP	OCT	NOV	DEC	YEAR
Mean Maximum Temp. (°F)	39.6	46.4	57.6	68.2	76.7	85.2	90.8	89.7	81.1	70.0	55.2	44.2	67.1
Mean Temp. (°F)	29.4	35.5	45.9	55.9	65.1	73.9	78.7	77.2	69.0	57.6	44.8	34.4	55.6
Mean Minimum Temp. (°F)	19.2	24.5	34.0	43.7	53.5	62.6	66.7	64.7	56.8	45.3	34.4	24.5	44.1
Extreme Maximum Temp. (°F)	71	81	86	94	94	104	112	111	104	95	87	73	112
Extreme Minimum Temp. (°F)	-17	-19	-4	17	28	44	46	44	31	19	4	-22	-22
Days Maximum Temp. ≥ 90°F	0	0	0	0	1	8	19	16	5	0	0	0	49
Days Maximum Temp. ≤ 32°F	9	5	1	0	0	0	0	0	0	0	1	4	20
Days Minimum Temp. ≤ 32°F	28	21	15	4	0	0	0	0	0	3	14	25	110
Days Minimum Temp. ≤ 0°F	2	1	0	0	0	0	0	0	0	0	0	1	4
Heating Degree Days (base 65°F)	1,096	827	590	291	83	6	1	1	57	248	599	943	4,742
Cooling Degree Days (base 65°F)	0	0	3	23	87	277	434	379	174	22	1	0	1,400
Mean Precipitation (in.)	1.62	1.79	3.19	4.33	4.96	4.65	3.60	3.81	4.60	3.92	3.51	2.29	42.27
Days With ≥ 0.1" Precipitation	4	4	6	6	8	7	5	5	6	6	5	4	66
Days With ≥ 1.0" Precipitation	0	0	1	1	1	1	1	1	1	1	1	0	9
Mean Snowfall (in.)	5.9	4.1	1.9	0.1	0.0	0.0	0.0	0.0	0.0	trace	1.0	3.0	16.0
Days With ≥ 1.0" Snow Depth	11	6	1	0	0	0	0	0	0	0	1	5	24

Arcadia *Iron County*   Elevation: 1,069 ft.   Latitude: 37° 34' N   Longitude: 90° 37' W

	JAN	FEB	MAR	APR	MAY	JUN	JUL	AUG	SEP	OCT	NOV	DEC	YEAR
Mean Maximum Temp. (°F)	41.4	47.9	59.0	70.5	77.4	84.5	89.1	87.8	80.1	70.3	56.2	46.2	67.5
Mean Temp. (°F)	31.1	36.3	46.5	57.0	64.5	72.1	76.7	75.3	67.6	57.2	45.6	36.4	55.5
Mean Minimum Temp. (°F)	20.7	24.7	33.9	43.5	51.6	59.7	64.3	62.7	55.2	44.1	34.9	26.6	43.5
Extreme Maximum Temp. (°F)	75	85	87	93	91	99	110	102	99	91	83	76	110
Extreme Minimum Temp. (°F)	-20	-13	-6	18	28	36	43	37	28	15	5	-11	-20
Days Maximum Temp. ≥ 90°F	0	0	0	0	0	5	15	12	3	0	0	0	35
Days Maximum Temp. ≤ 32°F	8	4	1	0	0	0	0	0	0	0	0	3	16
Days Minimum Temp. ≤ 32°F	26	21	15	5	1	0	0	0	0	5	13	22	108
Days Minimum Temp. ≤ 0°F	2	1	0	0	0	0	0	0	0	0	0	1	4
Heating Degree Days (base 65°F)	1,045	804	570	261	92	9	1	2	62	257	578	879	4,560
Cooling Degree Days (base 65°F)	0	0	2	28	83	226	369	335	135	17	1	0	1,196
Mean Precipitation (in.)	2.35	2.49	4.18	4.72	5.05	4.07	3.60	4.55	3.93	3.61	5.64	3.71	47.90
Days With ≥ 0.1" Precipitation	5	5	7	8	8	7	6	6	5	6	7	5	75
Days With ≥ 1.0" Precipitation	0	0	1	1	1	1	1	1	1	1	2	1	11
Mean Snowfall (in.)	4.3	3.5	1.8	0.6	0.0	0.0	0.0	0.0	0.0	trace	1.1	1.9	13.2
Days With ≥ 1.0" Snow Depth	na	na	1	0	0	0	0	0	0	0	0	1	na

Bethany *Harrison County*   Elevation: 948 ft.   Latitude: 40° 15' N   Longitude: 94° 02' W

	JAN	FEB	MAR	APR	MAY	JUN	JUL	AUG	SEP	OCT	NOV	DEC	YEAR
Mean Maximum Temp. (°F)	32.8	39.6	51.4	63.8	74.0	83.4	88.3	86.2	78.0	66.4	49.9	37.5	62.6
Mean Temp. (°F)	23.4	29.6	40.5	52.4	62.7	72.3	77.0	74.8	66.1	54.4	40.4	28.8	51.9
Mean Minimum Temp. (°F)	14.0	19.5	29.5	40.9	51.5	61.2	65.6	63.2	54.2	42.4	30.8	20.0	41.1
Extreme Maximum Temp. (°F)	63	76	88	91	92	102	107	106	100	90	80	69	107
Extreme Minimum Temp. (°F)	-29	-26	-14	9	28	42	42	41	30	14	-9	-25	-29
Days Maximum Temp. ≥ 90°F	0	0	0	0	0	6	14	10	3	0	0	0	33
Days Maximum Temp. ≤ 32°F	14	9	2	0	0	0	0	0	0	0	2	10	37
Days Minimum Temp. ≤ 32°F	29	24	19	6	0	0	0	0	0	5	18	28	129
Days Minimum Temp. ≤ 0°F	6	3	0	0	0	0	0	0	0	0	0	2	11
Heating Degree Days (base 65°F)	1,282	995	754	390	129	14	1	5	93	336	732	1,116	5,847
Cooling Degree Days (base 65°F)	0	0	2	17	57	227	375	311	131	14	0	0	1,134
Mean Precipitation (in.)	1.06	1.24	2.55	3.58	4.74	4.01	5.16	4.36	4.29	3.09	2.40	1.49	37.97
Days With ≥ 0.1" Precipitation	3	3	5	7	8	6	6	6	6	5	5	3	63
Days With ≥ 1.0" Precipitation	0	0	1	1	1	1	2	1	1	1	1	0	10
Mean Snowfall (in.)	8.1	5.9	3.3	1.6	0.0	0.0	0.0	0.0	0.0	trace	1.7	4.9	25.5
Days With ≥ 1.0" Snow Depth	*10*	*7*	1	0	0	0	0	0	0	0	1	*4*	*23*

Billings 2 N *Christian County*   Elevation: 1,351 ft.   Latitude: 37° 05' N   Longitude: 93° 33' W

	JAN	FEB	MAR	APR	MAY	JUN	JUL	AUG	SEP	OCT	NOV	DEC	YEAR
Mean Maximum Temp. (°F)	40.3	47.1	56.5	66.9	74.6	82.7	88.7	88.6	na	na	55.6	45.0	na
Mean Temp. (°F)	29.8	35.7	44.8	54.6	63.5	72.1	77.4	76.4	na	na	44.5	34.7	na
Mean Minimum Temp. (°F)	19.3	24.3	33.0	42.2	52.2	61.3	66.2	64.1	na	na	33.4	24.3	na
Extreme Maximum Temp. (°F)	70	79	84	91	92	100	109	108	101	*94*	83	75	*109*
Extreme Minimum Temp. (°F)	-17	-15	0	19	29	41	47	44	*34*	17	3	-15	*-17*
Days Maximum Temp. ≥ 90°F	0	0	0	0	0	4	14	14	*3*	0	0	0	*35*
Days Maximum Temp. ≤ 32°F	9	5	1	0	0	0	0	0	0	0	1	5	21
Days Minimum Temp. ≤ 32°F	28	22	15	4	0	0	0	0	0	3	14	25	111
Days Minimum Temp. ≤ 0°F	2	1	0	0	0	0	0	0	0	0	0	1	4
Heating Degree Days (base 65°F)	1,083	820	622	324	113	12	2	3	na	na	610	934	na
Cooling Degree Days (base 65°F)	0	0	3	17	71	235	398	368	na	*20*	1	0	na
Mean Precipitation (in.)	1.97	1.94	3.71	4.13	4.41	4.60	3.32	3.69	4.97	3.37	4.30	3.05	43.46
Days With ≥ 0.1" Precipitation	4	4	6	7	7	7	5	5	5	*5*	6	5	*66*
Days With ≥ 1.0" Precipitation	0	0	1	1	1	1	1	1	1	1	1	1	10
Mean Snowfall (in.)	6.2	4.0	3.6	0.5	0.0	0.0	0.0	0.0	0.0	trace	1.4	2.8	18.5
Days With ≥ 1.0" Snow Depth	9	5	2	0	0	0	0	0	0	0	1	3	20

Bolivar 1 NE *Polk County*   Elevation: 1,033 ft.   Latitude: 37° 37' N   Longitude: 93° 23' W

	JAN	FEB	MAR	APR	MAY	JUN	JUL	AUG	SEP	OCT	NOV	DEC	YEAR
Mean Maximum Temp. (°F)	40.7	46.5	56.9	67.5	75.5	84.0	89.8	89.0	80.7	70.1	56.0	46.1	66.9
Mean Temp. (°F)	29.5	34.9	44.9	55.0	63.6	72.6	77.6	76.2	67.9	56.6	44.6	35.2	54.9
Mean Minimum Temp. (°F)	18.2	23.2	32.9	42.6	51.7	61.2	65.4	63.4	55.1	43.1	33.0	24.3	42.8
Extreme Maximum Temp. (°F)	70	80	86	91	95	102	107	105	100	93	82	75	107
Extreme Minimum Temp. (°F)	-18	-19	-4	16	28	40	44	36	19	18	-1	-19	-19
Days Maximum Temp. ≥ 90°F	0	0	0	0	0	7	18	15	5	0	0	0	45
Days Maximum Temp. ≤ 32°F	9	5	1	0	0	0	0	0	0	0	1	4	20
Days Minimum Temp. ≤ 32°F	28	22	16	5	0	0	0	0	1	5	15	24	116
Days Minimum Temp. ≤ 0°F	3	2	0	0	0	0	0	0	0	0	0	1	6
Heating Degree Days (base 65°F)	1,095	844	620	315	111	11	2	3	73	275	608	916	4,873
Cooling Degree Days (base 65°F)	0	0	4	20	73	250	400	359	160	19	1	0	1,286
Mean Precipitation (in.)	1.95	2.28	3.92	4.56	5.08	4.72	3.57	3.44	4.77	4.34	4.15	3.05	45.83
Days With ≥ 0.1" Precipitation	4	4	7	7	8	7	5	5	6	6	6	5	70
Days With ≥ 1.0" Precipitation	0	0	1	1	1	1	1	1	2	1	1	1	11
Mean Snowfall (in.)	na	na	*trace*	*0.0*	0.0	0.0	0.0	0.0	0.0	0.0	0.0	na	na
Days With ≥ 1.0" Snow Depth	na	na	na	*0*	0	0	0	0	0	0	0	na	na

Boonville *Cooper County*   Elevation: 669 ft.   Latitude: 38° 58' N   Longitude: 92° 45' W

	JAN	FEB	MAR	APR	MAY	JUN	JUL	AUG	SEP	OCT	NOV	DEC	YEAR
Mean Maximum Temp. (°F)	36.1	42.2	53.7	65.4	75.0	83.9	89.4	87.6	79.7	68.2	53.3	41.2	64.7
Mean Temp. (°F)	27.2	32.5	43.3	54.6	64.4	73.7	78.6	76.4	68.2	56.5	43.6	32.5	54.3
Mean Minimum Temp. (°F)	18.2	22.8	32.8	43.8	53.8	63.3	67.8	65.2	56.6	44.7	33.9	23.7	43.9
Extreme Maximum Temp. (°F)	74	78	86	90	95	103	110	107	100	92	82	74	110
Extreme Minimum Temp. (°F)	-18	-12	-5	20	33	43	50	45	32	23	0	-22	-22
Days Maximum Temp. ≥ 90°F	0	0	0	0	1	7	17	14	5	0	0	0	44
Days Maximum Temp. ≤ 32°F	12	7	2	0	0	0	0	0	0	0	1	7	29
Days Minimum Temp. ≤ 32°F	28	22	15	3	0	0	0	0	0	3	13	26	110
Days Minimum Temp. ≤ 0°F	3	2	0	0	0	0	0	0	0	0	0	1	6
Heating Degree Days (base 65°F)	1,166	912	670	330	101	9	1	2	67	283	637	1,001	5,179
Cooling Degree Days (base 65°F)	0	0	4	25	92	287	443	372	167	25	2	0	1,417
Mean Precipitation (in.)	1.61	1.76	3.08	4.34	5.38	4.67	3.66	4.19	4.43	3.48	3.80	2.55	42.95
Days With ≥ 0.1" Precipitation	4	4	6	7	8	6	6	6	6	5	6	4	68
Days With ≥ 1.0" Precipitation	0	0	1	1	1	2	1	1	2	1	1	1	12
Mean Snowfall (in.)	7.2	6.1	2.9	0.4	0.0	0.0	0.0	0.0	0.0	trace	1.5	3.9	22.0
Days With ≥ 1.0" Snow Depth	*9*	*6*	1	0	0	0	0	0	0	0	1	*4*	*21*

Brookfield *Linn County*   Elevation: 764 ft.   Latitude: 39° 46' N   Longitude: 93° 04' W

	JAN	FEB	MAR	APR	MAY	JUN	JUL	AUG	SEP	OCT	NOV	DEC	YEAR
Mean Maximum Temp. (°F)	34.4	41.6	53.8	65.9	75.0	83.9	88.6	86.9	79.6	68.2	51.9	39.3	64.1
Mean Temp. (°F)	25.6	31.9	43.1	54.4	64.2	73.3	77.8	75.9	68.2	56.8	42.6	30.9	53.7
Mean Minimum Temp. (°F)	16.7	22.2	32.2	42.9	53.3	62.6	67.0	64.8	56.9	45.3	33.2	22.5	43.3
Extreme Maximum Temp. (°F)	70	79	86	91	91	103	109	108	99	92	81	70	109
Extreme Minimum Temp. (°F)	-21	-18	-10	13	29	41	46	43	30	16	-6	-24	-24
Days Maximum Temp. ≥ 90°F	0	0	0	0	0	6	14	11	3	0	0	0	34
Days Maximum Temp. ≤ 32°F	13	7	1	0	0	0	0	0	0	0	2	8	31
Days Minimum Temp. ≤ 32°F	28	22	16	4	0	0	0	0	0	3	15	26	114
Days Minimum Temp. ≤ 0°F	5	2	0	0	0	0	0	0	0	0	0	2	9
Heating Degree Days (base 65°F)	1,216	927	677	335	103	10	1	1	63	272	667	1,049	5,321
Cooling Degree Days (base 65°F)	0	0	4	23	77	259	407	347	166	22	1	0	1,306
Mean Precipitation (in.)	1.48	1.41	2.68	3.75	4.96	4.02	4.56	4.10	4.55	3.38	2.94	2.02	39.85
Days With ≥ 0.1" Precipitation	4	4	6	7	8	7	6	6	7	5	5	4	69
Days With ≥ 1.0" Precipitation	0	0	1	1	1	1	2	1	1	1	1	0	10
Mean Snowfall (in.)	*4.8*	*3.2*	1.7	0.5	0.0	0.0	0.0	0.0	0.0	trace	1.2	*2.4*	*13.8*
Days With ≥ 1.0" Snow Depth	*14*	*8*	2	0	0	0	0	0	0	0	1	6	*31*

Brunswick *Chariton County*   Elevation: 659 ft.   Latitude: 39° 26' N   Longitude: 93° 07' W

	JAN	FEB	MAR	APR	MAY	JUN	JUL	AUG	SEP	OCT	NOV	DEC	YEAR
Mean Maximum Temp. (°F)	34.8	41.3	53.1	65.2	74.2	82.8	87.7	85.8	78.4	67.2	52.2	40.0	63.6
Mean Temp. (°F)	25.4	31.2	42.2	53.6	63.3	72.4	77.0	74.7	66.8	55.4	42.3	30.9	52.9
Mean Minimum Temp. (°F)	15.9	21.0	31.2	42.0	52.4	61.9	66.3	63.7	55.0	43.5	32.4	21.7	42.2
Extreme Maximum Temp. (°F)	69	81	86	91	94	102	108	106	98	93	83	71	108
Extreme Minimum Temp. (°F)	-22	-17	-3	14	30	40	48	42	30	20	-7	-25	-25
Days Maximum Temp. ≥ 90°F	0	0	0	0	0	5	13	10	3	0	0	0	31
Days Maximum Temp. ≤ 32°F	13	7	2	0	0	0	0	0	0	0	2	7	31
Days Minimum Temp. ≤ 32°F	29	23	18	5	0	0	0	0	0	4	15	27	121
Days Minimum Temp. ≤ 0°F	4	3	0	0	0	0	0	0	0	0	0	2	9
Heating Degree Days (base 65°F)	1,222	949	703	356	119	12	1	5	83	309	674	1,052	5,485
Cooling Degree Days (base 65°F)	0	0	3	18	64	228	368	304	132	15	1	0	1,133
Mean Precipitation (in.)	1.56	1.47	2.66	3.68	5.03	4.34	3.72	3.85	3.96	3.28	3.23	1.88	38.66
Days With ≥ 0.1" Precipitation	4	4	6	7	8	7	5	5	6	5	6	4	67
Days With ≥ 1.0" Precipitation	0	0	1	1	1	1	1	1	1	1	1	0	9
Mean Snowfall (in.)	na	na	1.8	trace	0.0	0.0	0.0	0.0	0.0	trace	1.1	2.3	na
Days With ≥ 1.0" Snow Depth	na	na	*1*	0	0	0	0	0	0	0	1	*2*	na

Buffalo 3 S *Dallas County*   Elevation: 1,148 ft.   Latitude: 37° 36' N   Longitude: 93° 06' W

	JAN	FEB	MAR	APR	MAY	JUN	JUL	AUG	SEP	OCT	NOV	DEC	YEAR
Mean Maximum Temp. (°F)	41.2	48.0	58.5	68.9	75.6	83.5	89.1	88.4	80.1	69.3	55.5	45.6	67.0
Mean Temp. (°F)	31.1	37.1	46.7	56.6	64.3	72.5	77.4	76.3	68.4	57.5	45.3	35.5	55.7
Mean Minimum Temp. (°F)	21.1	26.1	34.9	44.3	52.9	61.4	65.6	64.1	56.7	45.7	35.1	25.5	44.5
Extreme Maximum Temp. (°F)	72	82	84	91	90	101	109	106	99	92	81	77	109
Extreme Minimum Temp. (°F)	-19	-16	-4	16	28	36	44	39	24	17	3	-28	-28
Days Maximum Temp. ≥ 90°F	0	0	0	0	0	4	15	13	4	0	0	0	36
Days Maximum Temp. ≤ 32°F	8	4	1	0	0	0	0	0	0	0	1	4	18
Days Minimum Temp. ≤ 32°F	26	19	13	4	0	0	0	0	0	3	13	22	100
Days Minimum Temp. ≤ 0°F	2	1	0	0	0	0	0	0	0	0	0	1	4
Heating Degree Days (base 65°F)	1,043	783	562	272	98	9	1	3	63	252	586	908	4,580
Cooling Degree Days (base 65°F)	0	0	3	26	76	233	382	352	163	23	1	0	1,259
Mean Precipitation (in.)	1.85	2.09	3.59	4.26	4.90	4.18	3.00	3.91	4.87	4.07	4.39	2.84	43.95
Days With ≥ 0.1" Precipitation	4	4	6	7	8	7	5	6	6	6	6	5	70
Days With ≥ 1.0" Precipitation	0	0	1	1	1	1	1	1	2	1	1	1	11
Mean Snowfall (in.)	5.1	3.8	2.6	0.2	0.0	0.0	0.0	0.0	0.0	trace	1.4	3.0	16.1
Days With ≥ 1.0" Snow Depth	10	6	2	0	0	0	0	0	0	0	1	4	23

Butler *Bates County*   Elevation: 787 ft.   Latitude: 38° 15' N   Longitude: 94° 20' W

	JAN	FEB	MAR	APR	MAY	JUN	JUL	AUG	SEP	OCT	NOV	DEC	YEAR
Mean Maximum Temp. (°F)	39.8	47.5	58.0	68.5	76.7	85.2	90.7	89.4	81.7	70.9	55.7	44.4	67.4
Mean Temp. (°F)	29.5	36.2	46.0	56.2	65.0	74.0	79.2	77.4	69.5	58.2	45.1	34.4	55.9
Mean Minimum Temp. (°F)	19.2	24.8	33.9	43.8	53.3	62.8	67.5	65.3	57.2	45.4	34.4	24.4	44.3
Extreme Maximum Temp. (°F)	71	78	87	91	95	104	111	108	101	93	83	75	111
Extreme Minimum Temp. (°F)	-19	-24	-6	12	28	41	45	44	29	18	3	-26	-26
Days Maximum Temp. ≥ 90°F	0	0	0	0	0	8	19	16	6	0	0	0	49
Days Maximum Temp. ≤ 32°F	9	5	1	0	0	0	0	0	0	0	1	4	20
Days Minimum Temp. ≤ 32°F	27	21	14	4	0	0	0	0	0	4	14	24	108
Days Minimum Temp. ≤ 0°F	3	1	0	0	0	0	0	0	0	0	0	1	5
Heating Degree Days (base 65°F)	1,093	807	587	286	89	6	1	1	54	237	593	941	4,695
Cooling Degree Days (base 65°F)	0	0	5	28	100	294	459	405	200	34	3	0	1,528
Mean Precipitation (in.)	1.72	1.70	3.09	4.23	4.97	5.28	3.92	3.87	4.61	3.60	3.33	2.00	42.32
Days With ≥ 0.1" Precipitation	4	3	6	7	8	7	6	6	6	6	5	4	68
Days With ≥ 1.0" Precipitation	0	0	1	1	1	2	1	1	2	1	1	1	11
Mean Snowfall (in.)	4.6	2.3	1.0	trace	0.0	0.0	0.0	0.0	0.0	0.0	0.6	*1.5*	*10.0*
Days With ≥ 1.0" Snow Depth	na	na	*1*	0	0	0	0	0	0	0	0	na	na

California *Moniteau County*   Elevation: 869 ft.   Latitude: 38° 38' N   Longitude: 92° 34' W

	JAN	FEB	MAR	APR	MAY	JUN	JUL	AUG	SEP	OCT	NOV	DEC	YEAR
Mean Maximum Temp. (°F)	39.7	46.7	57.5	68.2	76.4	84.6	90.2	89.0	81.4	70.5	56.0	44.1	67.0
Mean Temp. (°F)	30.1	36.1	46.4	56.6	65.5	74.1	79.3	77.8	69.7	58.4	45.9	34.9	56.2
Mean Minimum Temp. (°F)	20.4	25.4	35.0	44.9	54.5	63.6	68.3	66.5	58.2	46.5	35.7	25.7	45.4
Extreme Maximum Temp. (°F)	75	82	85	92	94	103	109	108	102	96	83	75	109
Extreme Minimum Temp. (°F)	-17	-14	-8	19	30	43	48	45	30	22	-1	-21	-21
Days Maximum Temp. ≥ 90°F	0	0	0	0	0	7	18	15	5	0	0	0	45
Days Maximum Temp. ≤ 32°F	9	5	1	0	0	0	0	0	0	0	1	5	21
Days Minimum Temp. ≤ 32°F	26	20	13	3	0	0	0	0	0	2	12	23	99
Days Minimum Temp. ≤ 0°F	3	1	0	0	0	0	0	0	0	0	0	1	5
Heating Degree Days (base 65°F)	1,076	810	577	279	81	6	0	1	50	234	571	926	4,611
Cooling Degree Days (base 65°F)	0	0	7	32	99	290	448	400	193	33	3	0	1,505
Mean Precipitation (in.)	1.53	1.84	3.18	4.25	5.34	3.82	3.66	3.40	4.09	3.39	3.49	2.32	40.31
Days With ≥ 0.1" Precipitation	4	4	6	7	8	6	5	5	6	6	6	4	67
Days With ≥ 1.0" Precipitation	0	0	1	1	2	1	1	1	1	1	1	1	11
Mean Snowfall (in.)	3.9	4.1	1.4	0.2	0.0	0.0	0.0	0.0	0.0	0.0	1.1	2.3	13.0
Days With ≥ 1.0" Snow Depth	na	3	0	0	0	0	0	0	0	0	0	2	na

Canton Lock & Dam 20 *Lewis County*   Elevation: 488 ft.   Latitude: 40° 09' N   Longitude: 91° 31' W

	JAN	FEB	MAR	APR	MAY	JUN	JUL	AUG	SEP	OCT	NOV	DEC	YEAR
Mean Maximum Temp. (°F)	33.8	39.3	51.7	64.3	74.8	84.1	88.7	86.1	78.8	67.6	52.0	39.1	63.4
Mean Temp. (°F)	25.0	30.0	41.5	53.5	64.2	73.6	78.0	75.5	67.5	56.0	42.5	30.6	53.1
Mean Minimum Temp. (°F)	16.1	20.6	31.3	42.7	53.6	63.0	67.2	64.7	56.2	44.3	33.0	22.0	42.9
Extreme Maximum Temp. (°F)	70	78	89	95	96	103	110	108	104	94	82	73	110
Extreme Minimum Temp. (°F)	-20	-20	-10	15	33	42	49	44	32	20	-6	-18	-20
Days Maximum Temp. ≥ 90°F	0	0	0	0	1	7	14	9	3	0	0	0	34
Days Maximum Temp. ≤ 32°F	13	8	2	0	0	0	0	0	0	0	1	8	32
Days Minimum Temp. ≤ 32°F	29	24	17	4	0	0	0	0	0	3	15	26	118
Days Minimum Temp. ≤ 0°F	5	3	0	0	0	0	0	0	0	0	0	2	10
Heating Degree Days (base 65°F)	1,234	982	725	358	108	9	1	2	70	294	670	1,059	5,512
Cooling Degree Days (base 65°F)	0	0	4	20	84	271	411	343	152	21	1	0	1,307
Mean Precipitation (in.)	1.50	1.57	2.89	3.63	5.30	3.55	4.24	3.86	4.46	2.69	3.16	2.09	38.94
Days With ≥ 0.1" Precipitation	4	4	6	7	8	6	6	6	6	6	5	4	68
Days With ≥ 1.0" Precipitation	0	0	0	1	1	1	1	1	1	1	1	0	8
Mean Snowfall (in.)	na	na	1.1	trace	0.0	0.0	0.0	0.0	0.0	0.0	0.4	na	na
Days With ≥ 1.0" Snow Depth	na	na	1	0	0	0	0	0	0	0	0	na	na

Cape Girardeau Municipal Airport *Scott County*   Elevation: 334 ft.   Latitude: 37° 14' N   Longitude: 89° 35' W

	JAN	FEB	MAR	APR	MAY	JUN	JUL	AUG	SEP	OCT	NOV	DEC	YEAR
Mean Maximum Temp. (°F)	40.3	46.4	57.2	68.8	77.8	86.5	90.2	88.3	80.9	70.2	56.6	45.4	67.4
Mean Temp. (°F)	31.9	37.2	47.4	58.0	67.3	76.0	79.9	77.7	70.0	58.5	47.2	37.1	57.4
Mean Minimum Temp. (°F)	23.4	28.0	37.5	47.2	56.7	65.5	69.6	67.0	59.0	46.7	37.7	28.8	47.3
Extreme Maximum Temp. (°F)	72	78	94	91	97	103	105	104	99	92	82	76	105
Extreme Minimum Temp. (°F)	-18	-8	4	25	34	43	50	45	33	23	8	-11	-18
Days Maximum Temp. ≥ 90°F	0	0	0	0	2	11	19	14	5	0	0	0	51
Days Maximum Temp. ≤ 32°F	8	4	1	0	0	0	0	0	0	0	0	4	17
Days Minimum Temp. ≤ 32°F	25	18	11	2	0	0	0	0	0	2	10	20	88
Days Minimum Temp. ≤ 0°F	1	0	0	0	0	0	0	0	0	0	0	0	1
Heating Degree Days (base 65°F)	1,019	778	543	237	58	2	0	1	41	228	530	858	4,295
Cooling Degree Days (base 65°F)	0	0	5	34	136	345	482	414	191	31	2	1	1,641
Mean Precipitation (in.)	3.15	3.40	4.59	4.49	5.09	3.79	3.48	3.35	3.48	3.30	4.51	4.31	46.94
Days With ≥ 0.1" Precipitation	6	5	7	7	8	7	6	5	5	5	7	7	75
Days With ≥ 1.0" Precipitation	1	1	1	1	1	1	1	1	1	1	1	1	12
Mean Snowfall (in.)	4.4	4.3	2.1	trace	trace	trace	0.0	0.0	0.0	0.1	0.3	1.8	13.0
Days With ≥ 1.0" Snow Depth	7	5	1	0	0	0	0	0	0	0	0	2	15

Carrollton *Carroll County*   Elevation: 702 ft.   Latitude: 39° 21' N   Longitude: 93° 29' W

	JAN	FEB	MAR	APR	MAY	JUN	JUL	AUG	SEP	OCT	NOV	DEC	YEAR
Mean Maximum Temp. (°F)	35.9	42.7	55.1	67.1	76.8	85.7	90.3	88.1	80.0	68.2	52.5	40.7	65.2
Mean Temp. (°F)	26.8	32.8	44.0	55.1	65.0	74.1	78.6	76.4	68.1	56.5	42.9	32.0	54.3
Mean Minimum Temp. (°F)	17.7	22.8	32.8	43.1	53.1	62.5	66.9	64.5	56.2	44.7	33.3	23.3	43.4
Extreme Maximum Temp. (°F)	69	80	87	93	98	105	110	108	100	93	81	71	110
Extreme Minimum Temp. (°F)	-20	-19	-8	14	29	43	47	43	28	21	-5	-24	-24
Days Maximum Temp. ≥ 90°F	0	0	0	0	1	10	18	13	4	0	0	0	46
Days Maximum Temp. ≤ 32°F	11	7	1	0	0	0	0	0	0	0	1	6	26
Days Minimum Temp. ≤ 32°F	28	23	16	4	0	0	0	0	0	3	14	25	113
Days Minimum Temp. ≤ 0°F	4	2	0	0	0	0	0	0	0	0	0	1	7
Heating Degree Days (base 65°F)	1,178	903	647	316	89	6	1	1	63	279	657	1,016	5,156
Cooling Degree Days (base 65°F)	0	0	3	26	95	294	440	371	165	21	1	0	1,416
Mean Precipitation (in.)	1.51	1.62	2.86	4.15	5.07	4.50	4.23	4.09	4.68	3.54	3.01	2.22	41.48
Days With ≥ 0.1" Precipitation	4	4	6	7	8	6	6	6	6	5	5	4	67
Days With ≥ 1.0" Precipitation	0	0	1	1	1	1	1	1	1	1	1	0	9
Mean Snowfall (in.)	7.5	6.1	3.2	0.7	0.0	0.0	0.0	0.0	0.0	0.2	1.4	3.7	22.8
Days With ≥ 1.0" Snow Depth	12	9	2	0	0	0	0	0	0	0	1	5	29

Caruthersville *Pemiscot County*   Elevation: 278 ft.   Latitude: 36° 10' N   Longitude: 89° 40' W

	JAN	FEB	MAR	APR	MAY	JUN	JUL	AUG	SEP	OCT	NOV	DEC	YEAR
Mean Maximum Temp. (°F)	42.9	48.9	58.6	69.5	78.6	86.9	90.5	88.5	82.4	72.2	58.9	48.2	68.8
Mean Temp. (°F)	34.3	39.4	48.5	58.6	68.2	76.3	80.3	78.1	71.5	60.2	49.0	39.5	58.7
Mean Minimum Temp. (°F)	25.6	30.0	38.4	47.6	57.7	65.8	70.0	67.7	60.5	48.2	39.0	30.7	48.4
Extreme Maximum Temp. (°F)	74	77	84	89	95	102	107	103	99	93	83	78	107
Extreme Minimum Temp. (°F)	-13	-3	11	21	38	45	54	48	37	27	13	-9	-13
Days Maximum Temp. ≥ 90°F	0	0	0	0	2	12	19	14	6	0	0	0	53
Days Maximum Temp. ≤ 32°F	6	3	0	0	0	0	0	0	0	0	0	2	11
Days Minimum Temp. ≤ 32°F	23	16	9	1	0	0	0	0	0	1	8	18	76
Days Minimum Temp. ≤ 0°F	1	0	0	0	0	0	0	0	0	0	0	0	1
Heating Degree Days (base 65°F)	945	715	508	223	46	2	0	0	26	188	478	786	3,917
Cooling Degree Days (base 65°F)	0	0	5	34	151	350	484	419	218	43	3	1	1,708
Mean Precipitation (in.)	3.41	3.79	4.84	5.09	4.85	4.63	3.91	3.10	3.23	3.70	4.78	4.83	50.16
Days With ≥ 0.1" Precipitation	6	6	8	7	7	7	6	5	5	5	7	7	76
Days With ≥ 1.0" Precipitation	1	1	1	2	1	1	1	1	1	1	1	1	13
Mean Snowfall (in.)	2.1	1.8	0.4	trace	0.0	0.0	0.0	0.0	0.0	trace	0.2	0.4	4.9
Days With ≥ 1.0" Snow Depth	na	0	0	0	0	0	0	0	0	0	0	0	na

Cassville Ranger Station *Barry County*   Elevation: 1,338 ft.   Latitude: 36° 40' N   Longitude: 93° 51' W

	JAN	FEB	MAR	APR	MAY	JUN	JUL	AUG	SEP	OCT	NOV	DEC	YEAR
Mean Maximum Temp. (°F)	42.1	48.2	57.8	68.2	75.5	83.7	88.5	88.7	80.6	69.8	na	na	na
Mean Temp. (°F)	30.5	35.9	45.7	55.3	63.6	72.2	76.6	75.8	68.2	56.4	na	na	na
Mean Minimum Temp. (°F)	19.2	23.7	33.5	42.4	51.6	60.6	64.6	62.8	55.9	42.8	na	na	na
Extreme Maximum Temp. (°F)	75	78	86	90	90	101	106	104	102	92	83	78	106
Extreme Minimum Temp. (°F)	-19	-22	-2	17	29	37	43	43	30	19	2	-15	-22
Days Maximum Temp. ≥ 90°F	0	0	0	0	0	4	13	13	4	0	0	0	34
Days Maximum Temp. ≤ 32°F	6	4	1	0	0	0	0	0	0	0	1	3	15
Days Minimum Temp. ≤ 32°F	25	20	15	5	0	0	0	0	0	5	13	21	104
Days Minimum Temp. ≤ 0°F	2	1	0	0	0	0	0	0	0	0	0	1	4
Heating Degree Days (base 65°F)	1,065	817	593	303	112	12	2	3	63	281	na	na	na
Cooling Degree Days (base 65°F)	na	na	3	17	na	234	364	358	166	na	na	na	na
Mean Precipitation (in.)	1.99	2.39	4.26	4.78	4.90	4.55	3.36	3.50	4.83	3.44	4.41	3.53	45.94
Days With ≥ 0.1" Precipitation	4	4	6	6	7	6	5	5	5	5	5	4	62
Days With ≥ 1.0" Precipitation	0	1	1	1	1	1	1	1	2	1	1	1	12
Mean Snowfall (in.)	2.4	2.6	2.9	0.3	0.0	0.0	0.0	0.0	0.0	0.0	0.7	2.0	10.9
Days With ≥ 1.0" Snow Depth	na	2	1	0	0	0	0	0	0	0	0	1	na

Clearwater Dam *Wayne County*   Elevation: 659 ft.   Latitude: 37° 08' N   Longitude: 90° 46' W

	JAN	FEB	MAR	APR	MAY	JUN	JUL	AUG	SEP	OCT	NOV	DEC	YEAR
Mean Maximum Temp. (°F)	41.7	48.2	58.2	70.1	78.1	85.9	91.0	89.0	81.3	70.0	56.8	46.0	68.0
Mean Temp. (°F)	30.8	36.1	45.7	56.7	65.3	73.7	78.5	76.5	68.8	56.7	45.4	35.2	55.8
Mean Minimum Temp. (°F)	19.8	23.9	33.2	43.2	52.4	61.4	66.0	63.9	56.3	43.4	33.9	24.4	43.5
Extreme Maximum Temp. (°F)	76	83	87	94	94	102	110	109	102	92	84	76	110
Extreme Minimum Temp. (°F)	-18	-7	4	20	32	41	48	41	34	19	5	-13	-18
Days Maximum Temp. ≥ 90°F	0	0	0	1	1	10	19	15	5	0	0	0	51
Days Maximum Temp. ≤ 32°F	7	4	0	0	0	0	0	0	0	0	0	3	14
Days Minimum Temp. ≤ 32°F	27	21	16	4	0	0	0	0	0	4	14	22	108
Days Minimum Temp. ≤ 0°F	2	1	0	0	0	0	0	0	0	0	0	1	4
Heating Degree Days (base 65°F)	1,054	811	594	271	83	6	1	1	50	271	583	917	4,642
Cooling Degree Days (base 65°F)	0	0	4	28	99	289	441	383	167	21	2	0	1,434
Mean Precipitation (in.)	3.10	2.88	4.57	4.62	4.57	3.66	3.87	3.63	3.32	3.25	4.80	3.99	46.26
Days With ≥ 0.1" Precipitation	5	5	7	7	7	6	6	5	5	5	6	6	70
Days With ≥ 1.0" Precipitation	1	1	1	1	1	1	1	1	1	1	1	1	12
Mean Snowfall (in.)	na	na	0.4	0.0	0.0	0.0	0.0	0.0	0.0	trace	0.2	0.4	na
Days With ≥ 1.0" Snow Depth	4	4	1	0	0	0	0	0	0	0	0	1	10

Clinton *Henry County*   Elevation: 800 ft.   Latitude: 38° 22' N   Longitude: 93° 46' W

	JAN	FEB	MAR	APR	MAY	JUN	JUL	AUG	SEP	OCT	NOV	DEC	YEAR
Mean Maximum Temp. (°F)	37.9	44.6	55.6	66.7	75.5	84.3	90.3	89.0	80.4	69.6	54.7	43.3	66.0
Mean Temp. (°F)	27.5	33.2	43.7	54.3	63.9	73.3	78.6	76.7	68.0	56.5	43.8	33.0	54.4
Mean Minimum Temp. (°F)	17.1	21.8	31.8	41.9	52.3	62.1	66.8	64.3	55.5	43.3	32.9	22.7	42.7
Extreme Maximum Temp. (°F)	71	79	85	91	94	102	107	107	100	95	84	74	107
Extreme Minimum Temp. (°F)	-21	-20	-4	18	28	42	45	43	29	20	0	-31	-31
Days Maximum Temp. ≥ 90°F	0	0	0	0	0	7	17	16	5	0	0	0	45
Days Maximum Temp. ≤ 32°F	10	6	1	0	0	0	0	0	0	0	1	5	23
Days Minimum Temp. ≤ 32°F	28	23	17	5	0	0	0	0	0	4	15	26	118
Days Minimum Temp. ≤ 0°F	3	2	0	0	0	0	0	0	0	0	0	1	6
Heating Degree Days (base 65°F)	1,155	890	654	336	111	9	1	2	72	283	631	986	5,130
Cooling Degree Days (base 65°F)	0	0	2	20	80	265	434	374	165	23	2	0	1,365
Mean Precipitation (in.)	1.60	1.96	3.25	4.32	5.57	5.09	3.76	4.02	4.71	3.73	3.67	2.17	43.85
Days With ≥ 0.1" Precipitation	4	4	7	7	8	7	5	5	6	6	5	4	68
Days With ≥ 1.0" Precipitation	0	0	1	2	2	1	1	1	1	1	1	0	11
Mean Snowfall (in.)	6.3	3.6	1.7	trace	0.0	0.0	0.0	0.0	0.0	trace	1.3	2.4	15.3
Days With ≥ 1.0" Snow Depth	na	na	1	0	0	0	0	0	0	0	0	na	na

Conception *Nodaway County*   Elevation: 1,105 ft.   Latitude: 40° 15' N   Longitude: 94° 41' W

	JAN	FEB	MAR	APR	MAY	JUN	JUL	AUG	SEP	OCT	NOV	DEC	YEAR
Mean Maximum Temp. (°F)	31.9	38.4	50.4	62.5	72.9	82.8	87.6	86.0	78.0	65.9	49.5	37.1	61.9
Mean Temp. (°F)	22.6	28.6	39.9	51.6	62.3	72.0	76.5	74.4	65.8	54.0	39.7	28.1	51.3
Mean Minimum Temp. (°F)	13.2	18.7	29.3	40.6	51.7	61.1	65.3	62.7	53.6	42.1	29.9	19.2	40.6
Extreme Maximum Temp. (°F)	69	78	86	92	91	104	108	105	100	94	82	70	108
Extreme Minimum Temp. (°F)	-24	-21	-11	8	28	40	45	41	15	16	-5	-23	-24
Days Maximum Temp. ≥ 90°F	0	0	0	0	0	5	13	10	4	0	0	0	32
Days Maximum Temp. ≤ 32°F	15	10	3	0	0	0	0	0	0	0	2	10	40
Days Minimum Temp. ≤ 32°F	29	24	20	6	0	0	0	0	0	5	19	28	131
Days Minimum Temp. ≤ 0°F	7	3	0	0	0	0	0	0	0	0	0	3	13
Heating Degree Days (base 65°F)	1,311	1,023	774	410	141	15	2	5	97	351	754	1,137	6,020
Cooling Degree Days (base 65°F)	0	0	2	15	62	228	359	300	125	14	0	0	1,105
Mean Precipitation (in.)	0.83	1.10	2.62	3.37	4.86	4.12	4.90	4.21	4.54	2.79	2.41	1.34	37.09
Days With ≥ 0.1" Precipitation	3	3	6	7	8	6	6	6	6	5	5	3	64
Days With ≥ 1.0" Precipitation	0	0	1	1	1	1	1	1	1	1	1	0	9
Mean Snowfall (in.)	6.2	5.3	3.9	1.2	0.0	0.0	0.0	0.0	0.0	trace	1.4	3.9	21.9
Days With ≥ 1.0" Snow Depth	13	9	3	1	0	0	0	0	0	0	2	7	35

Doniphan *Ripley County*   Elevation: 328 ft.   Latitude: 36° 37' N   Longitude: 90° 49' W

	JAN	FEB	MAR	APR	MAY	JUN	JUL	AUG	SEP	OCT	NOV	DEC	YEAR
Mean Maximum Temp. (°F)	43.9	50.7	59.7	70.6	78.9	86.7	91.8	90.0	82.9	72.6	59.0	47.8	69.6
Mean Temp. (°F)	32.2	37.6	46.5	56.6	65.4	73.9	78.6	76.6	69.0	57.3	46.1	36.2	56.3
Mean Minimum Temp. (°F)	20.5	24.5	33.3	42.6	51.9	60.9	65.4	63.2	55.1	42.0	33.0	24.5	43.1
Extreme Maximum Temp. (°F)	76	84	86	94	94	105	110	108	102	93	85	78	110
Extreme Minimum Temp. (°F)	-19	-11	6	18	30	35	47	38	32	17	2	-14	-19
Days Maximum Temp. ≥ 90°F	0	0	0	0	2	11	21	17	7	0	0	0	58
Days Maximum Temp. ≤ 32°F	5	2	0	0	0	0	0	0	0	0	0	2	9
Days Minimum Temp. ≤ 32°F	26	21	16	6	0	0	0	0	0	7	15	23	114
Days Minimum Temp. ≤ 0°F	2	1	0	0	0	0	0	0	0	0	0	1	4
Heating Degree Days (base 65°F)	1,011	768	569	269	81	5	1	1	48	255	563	887	4,458
Cooling Degree Days (base 65°F)	0	0	3	21	97	284	439	382	171	22	1	0	1,420
Mean Precipitation (in.)	3.42	3.33	5.02	5.28	4.88	3.11	3.54	4.03	3.75	3.56	5.40	4.39	49.71
Days With ≥ 0.1" Precipitation	6	6	8	7	8	5	5	5	5	5	7	7	74
Days With ≥ 1.0" Precipitation	1	1	1	2	1	1	1	1	1	1	2	1	14
Mean Snowfall (in.)	4.3	3.8	2.2	trace	0.0	0.0	0.0	0.0	0.0	trace	0.7	1.1	12.1
Days With ≥ 1.0" Snow Depth	5	4	1	0	0	0	0	0	0	0	0	1	11

Dora *Ozark County*   Elevation: 987 ft.   Latitude: 36° 47' N   Longitude: 92° 14' W

	JAN	FEB	MAR	APR	MAY	JUN	JUL	AUG	SEP	OCT	NOV	DEC	YEAR
Mean Maximum Temp. (°F)	43.3	50.3	59.5	70.0	76.5	83.9	89.7	89.0	81.2	71.2	58.3	47.8	68.4
Mean Temp. (°F)	31.6	37.6	46.3	56.2	64.1	72.3	77.6	76.5	68.7	57.2	45.8	36.1	55.8
Mean Minimum Temp. (°F)	19.8	24.5	33.1	42.3	51.7	60.7	65.5	63.8	56.1	42.9	33.3	24.6	43.2
Extreme Maximum Temp. (°F)	76	82	87	94	95	102	109	107	103	94	88	78	109
Extreme Minimum Temp. (°F)	-19	-9	2	14	26	38	46	41	26	16	5	-21	-21
Days Maximum Temp. ≥ 90°F	0	0	0	0	0	5	17	15	5	0	0	0	42
Days Maximum Temp. ≤ 32°F	7	3	1	0	0	0	0	0	0	0	0	3	14
Days Minimum Temp. ≤ 32°F	27	22	15	5	0	0	0	0	0	5	15	24	113
Days Minimum Temp. ≤ 0°F	2	1	0	0	0	0	0	0	0	0	0	1	4
Heating Degree Days (base 65°F)	1,029	767	575	281	98	10	1	2	56	258	565	890	4,532
Cooling Degree Days (base 65°F)	0	0	3	22	74	235	402	370	166	17	1	0	1,290
Mean Precipitation (in.)	2.32	2.59	4.02	4.53	4.82	4.06	3.15	3.12	4.25	3.70	4.88	3.67	45.11
Days With ≥ 0.1" Precipitation	4	4	6	6	7	6	4	4	5	5	6	5	62
Days With ≥ 1.0" Precipitation	1	1	1	1	2	1	1	1	1	1	2	1	14
Mean Snowfall (in.)	4.6	3.0	2.0	0.3	0.0	0.0	0.0	0.0	0.0	trace	0.7	2.1	12.7
Days With ≥ 1.0" Snow Depth	6	4	1	0	0	0	0	0	0	0	0	2	13

Eldon *Miller County*   Elevation: 928 ft.   Latitude: 38° 21' N   Longitude: 92° 35' W

	JAN	FEB	MAR	APR	MAY	JUN	JUL	AUG	SEP	OCT	NOV	DEC	YEAR
Mean Maximum Temp. (°F)	39.7	47.1	57.0	67.9	76.4	84.5	90.1	89.1	80.3	69.7	55.5	44.5	66.8
Mean Temp. (°F)	29.5	36.1	45.5	56.1	65.2	73.6	79.0	77.3	68.7	57.8	45.2	34.5	55.7
Mean Minimum Temp. (°F)	19.0	24.4	34.0	44.3	53.9	62.6	67.8	65.5	57.0	45.9	34.9	24.4	44.5
Extreme Maximum Temp. (°F)	73	82	85	95	93	103	109	108	99	91	84	77	109
Extreme Minimum Temp. (°F)	-28	-14	-7	18	30	39	50	43	33	23	4	-25	-28
Days Maximum Temp. ≥ 90°F	0	0	0	0	1	7	18	16	5	0	0	0	47
Days Maximum Temp. ≤ 32°F	9	5	1	0	0	0	0	0	0	0	1	5	21
Days Minimum Temp. ≤ 32°F	27	22	14	3	0	0	0	0	0	2	13	24	105
Days Minimum Temp. ≤ 0°F	3	1	0	0	0	0	0	0	0	0	0	1	5
Heating Degree Days (base 65°F)	1,093	808	602	292	82	8	1	2	62	245	591	937	4,723
Cooling Degree Days (base 65°F)	0	0	4	27	86	269	439	384	165	26	2	0	1,402
Mean Precipitation (in.)	1.68	1.87	3.19	4.27	5.17	4.35	3.74	3.41	4.46	3.60	3.69	2.66	42.09
Days With ≥ 0.1" Precipitation	3	4	6	7	7	6	5	5	5	5	6	5	64
Days With ≥ 1.0" Precipitation	0	0	1	1	1	1	1	1	1	1	1	1	10
Mean Snowfall (in.)	4.1	3.4	1.9	0.2	0.0	0.0	0.0	0.0	0.0	trace	1.3	3.0	13.9
Days With ≥ 1.0" Snow Depth	8	5	1	0	0	0	0	0	0	0	1	4	19

Elsberry 1 S *Lincoln County*   Elevation: 449 ft.   Latitude: 39° 09' N   Longitude: 90° 47' W

	JAN	FEB	MAR	APR	MAY	JUN	JUL	AUG	SEP	OCT	NOV	DEC	YEAR
Mean Maximum Temp. (°F)	37.4	43.8	55.6	68.0	77.1	85.7	90.1	87.8	80.3	69.1	54.7	42.1	66.0
Mean Temp. (°F)	27.3	33.0	43.8	55.2	64.5	73.5	77.8	75.6	67.8	56.3	44.1	32.7	54.3
Mean Minimum Temp. (°F)	17.2	22.1	32.0	42.4	51.8	61.2	65.5	63.3	55.2	43.4	33.5	23.3	42.6
Extreme Maximum Temp. (°F)	74	79	88	94	94	103	108	109	105	92	82	76	109
Extreme Minimum Temp. (°F)	-24	-24	-14	19	29	38	40	39	29	18	-7	-23	-24
Days Maximum Temp. ≥ 90°F	0	0	0	1	2	10	17	12	5	0	0	0	47
Days Maximum Temp. ≤ 32°F	11	6	1	0	0	0	0	0	0	0	1	6	25
Days Minimum Temp. ≤ 32°F	28	22	17	5	0	0	0	0	0	5	14	24	115
Days Minimum Temp. ≤ 0°F	4	2	0	0	0	0	0	0	0	0	0	1	7
Heating Degree Days (base 65°F)	1,162	899	655	314	103	9	1	2	63	286	622	994	5,110
Cooling Degree Days (base 65°F)	0	0	6	27	95	278	417	349	153	22	1	0	1,348
Mean Precipitation (in.)	2.00	1.97	3.51	3.99	4.15	3.42	3.28	3.25	3.42	2.90	3.48	2.99	38.36
Days With ≥ 0.1" Precipitation	5	4	7	7	8	6	6	5	6	6	6	6	72
Days With ≥ 1.0" Precipitation	0	0	1	1	1	1	1	1	1	1	1	1	10
Mean Snowfall (in.)	6.8	4.6	2.9	0.7	0.0	0.0	0.0	0.0	0.0	trace	1.2	4.0	20.2
Days With ≥ 1.0" Snow Depth	na	na	*1*	0	0	0	0	0	0	0	*0*	na	na

Farmington *St. Francois County*   Elevation: 898 ft.   Latitude: 37° 48' N   Longitude: 90° 25' W

	JAN	FEB	MAR	APR	MAY	JUN	JUL	AUG	SEP	OCT	NOV	DEC	YEAR
Mean Maximum Temp. (°F)	38.7	45.2	55.4	67.0	75.1	83.2	88.0	86.7	79.1	68.4	54.7	43.7	65.4
Mean Temp. (°F)	28.9	34.3	44.2	55.0	63.2	71.8	76.4	74.6	66.9	55.5	44.1	34.0	54.1
Mean Minimum Temp. (°F)	19.1	23.4	33.0	42.9	51.2	60.3	64.8	62.4	54.6	42.6	33.5	24.3	42.7
Extreme Maximum Temp. (°F)	73	83	86	92	91	101	104	105	100	91	84	76	105
Extreme Minimum Temp. (°F)	-23	-17	-9	19	29	39	43	46	27	16	5	-17	-23
Days Maximum Temp. ≥ 90°F	0	0	0	0	0	5	14	10	3	0	0	0	32
Days Maximum Temp. ≤ 32°F	10	5	1	0	0	0	0	0	0	0	1	5	22
Days Minimum Temp. ≤ 32°F	27	22	16	5	0	0	0	0	0	5	15	24	114
Days Minimum Temp. ≤ 0°F	2	2	0	0	0	0	0	0	0	0	0	1	5
Heating Degree Days (base 65°F)	1,112	860	642	316	123	14	2	3	76	306	621	954	5,029
Cooling Degree Days (base 65°F)	0	0	3	19	71	226	371	314	133	18	0	0	1,155
Mean Precipitation (in.)	2.28	2.44	3.99	4.22	4.38	3.54	3.69	4.06	3.50	2.98	4.40	3.48	42.96
Days With ≥ 0.1" Precipitation	5	5	7	7	8	6	6	6	5	5	7	5	72
Days With ≥ 1.0" Precipitation	0	1	1	1	1	1	1	1	1	1	1	1	11
Mean Snowfall (in.)	*3.4*	4.2	2.3	0.1	0.0	0.0	0.0	0.0	0.0	trace	0.9	2.2	*13.1*
Days With ≥ 1.0" Snow Depth	*5*	5	1	0	0	0	0	0	0	0	1	2	*14*

Fredericktown *Madison County*   Elevation: 698 ft.   Latitude: 37° 34' N   Longitude: 90° 18' W

	JAN	FEB	MAR	APR	MAY	JUN	JUL	AUG	SEP	OCT	NOV	DEC	YEAR
Mean Maximum Temp. (°F)	40.6	46.9	56.8	68.1	76.8	84.8	89.8	88.2	80.9	69.7	56.4	45.1	67.0
Mean Temp. (°F)	29.5	34.9	44.6	54.9	63.7	72.2	77.0	75.0	67.3	55.3	44.7	34.5	54.5
Mean Minimum Temp. (°F)	18.5	22.8	32.4	41.7	50.6	59.5	64.1	61.7	53.6	40.7	33.0	23.9	41.9
Extreme Maximum Temp. (°F)	74	83	87	92	93	103	109	109	100	91	85	75	109
Extreme Minimum Temp. (°F)	-24	-17	-6	12	24	34	42	36	23	16	3	-18	-24
Days Maximum Temp. ≥ 90°F	0	0	0	0	1	8	17	13	5	0	0	0	44
Days Maximum Temp. ≤ 32°F	8	4	1	0	0	0	0	0	0	0	0	4	17
Days Minimum Temp. ≤ 32°F	27	22	16	7	1	0	0	0	0	8	15	24	120
Days Minimum Temp. ≤ 0°F	3	2	0	0	0	0	0	0	0	0	0	1	6
Heating Degree Days (base 65°F)	1,092	845	628	317	117	14	2	4	74	312	603	938	4,946
Cooling Degree Days (base 65°F)	0	0	3	19	82	239	387	323	142	16	1	0	1,212
Mean Precipitation (in.)	2.72	2.52	4.20	4.61	4.74	3.77	3.67	4.05	3.26	3.21	4.74	3.90	45.39
Days With ≥ 0.1" Precipitation	5	5	7	7	7	6	5	5	5	5	6	6	69
Days With ≥ 1.0" Precipitation	1	1	1	1	1	1	1	1	1	1	2	1	13
Mean Snowfall (in.)	5.1	3.9	2.2	0.2	0.0	0.0	0.0	0.0	0.0	0.1	0.9	2.2	14.6
Days With ≥ 1.0" Snow Depth	9	6	2	0	0	0	0	0	0	0	0	3	20

Freedom *Osage County*   Elevation: 744 ft.   Latitude: 38° 28' N   Longitude: 91° 42' W

	JAN	FEB	MAR	APR	MAY	JUN	JUL	AUG	SEP	OCT	NOV	DEC	YEAR
Mean Maximum Temp. (°F)	39.9	46.6	57.5	68.2	76.2	84.3	89.7	88.5	80.7	69.9	55.6	44.7	66.8
Mean Temp. (°F)	29.6	35.3	45.2	55.6	63.9	72.5	77.5	75.8	68.0	56.8	45.0	34.6	55.0
Mean Minimum Temp. (°F)	19.2	24.0	32.9	42.9	51.6	60.7	65.2	63.1	55.2	43.8	34.4	24.5	43.1
Extreme Maximum Temp. (°F)	75	84	87	94	93	106	111	109	103	92	85	77	111
Extreme Minimum Temp. (°F)	-20	-17	-6	17	27	38	45	37	28	17	2	-21	-21
Days Maximum Temp. ≥ 90°F	0	0	0	0	1	7	17	14	5	0	0	0	44
Days Maximum Temp. ≤ 32°F	9	5	1	0	0	0	0	0	0	0	1	5	21
Days Minimum Temp. ≤ 32°F	27	22	16	5	0	0	0	0	0	5	13	24	112
Days Minimum Temp. ≤ 0°F	3	2	0	0	0	0	0	0	0	0	0	1	6
Heating Degree Days (base 65°F)	1,091	832	611	303	106	14	2	3	67	272	594	936	4,831
Cooling Degree Days (base 65°F)	0	0	5	22	73	240	388	334	150	22	2	0	1,236
Mean Precipitation (in.)	1.63	1.95	3.28	3.89	4.84	4.26	3.19	3.74	4.05	3.43	3.67	2.75	40.68
Days With ≥ 0.1" Precipitation	4	4	6	7	8	6	5	5	6	6	6	5	68
Days With ≥ 1.0" Precipitation	0	0	1	1	1	1	1	1	2	1	1	1	11
Mean Snowfall (in.)	*3.8*	4.5	*1.4*	trace	0.0	0.0	0.0	0.0	0.0	0.0	1.5	na	na
Days With ≥ 1.0" Snow Depth	na	na	*0*	0	0	0	0	0	0	0	0	na	na

Fulton *Callaway County*   Elevation: 869 ft.   Latitude: 38° 51' N   Longitude: 91° 56' W

	JAN	FEB	MAR	APR	MAY	JUN	JUL	AUG	SEP	OCT	NOV	DEC	YEAR
Mean Maximum Temp. (°F)	36.0	42.5	53.6	65.1	73.8	82.7	87.9	86.6	79.2	67.8	53.2	41.2	64.1
Mean Temp. (°F)	26.8	32.4	42.6	53.7	62.8	71.9	77.0	75.2	67.6	55.8	43.2	32.1	53.4
Mean Minimum Temp. (°F)	17.6	22.2	31.6	42.3	51.7	61.1	66.0	63.7	55.8	43.7	33.2	22.9	42.6
Extreme Maximum Temp. (°F)	73	77	85	91	92	101	108	106	99	92	82	76	108
Extreme Minimum Temp. (°F)	-19	-15	-7	20	28	42	48	43	31	19	0	-21	-21
Days Maximum Temp. ≥ 90°F	0	0	0	0	0	4	13	11	4	0	0	0	32
Days Maximum Temp. ≤ 32°F	13	7	2	0	0	0	0	0	0	0	1	7	30
Days Minimum Temp. ≤ 32°F	28	23	17	4	0	0	0	0	0	4	15	26	117
Days Minimum Temp. ≤ 0°F	4	2	0	0	0	0	0	0	0	0	0	2	8
Heating Degree Days (base 65°F)	1,177	915	690	352	129	14	2	3	71	297	647	1,013	5,310
Cooling Degree Days (base 65°F)	0	0	4	18	64	228	376	320	140	16	1	0	1,167
Mean Precipitation (in.)	1.84	2.09	3.10	4.10	5.09	3.91	4.01	3.51	3.89	3.21	3.81	2.71	41.27
Days With ≥ 0.1" Precipitation	5	4	6	7	8	7	6	5	6	6	6	5	71
Days With ≥ 1.0" Precipitation	0	1	1	1	1	1	1	1	1	1	1	1	11
Mean Snowfall (in.)	6.9	5.9	3.3	0.6	0.0	0.0	0.0	0.0	0.0	trace	1.6	4.4	22.7
Days With ≥ 1.0" Snow Depth	11	6	2	0	0	0	0	0	0	0	1	5	25

Galena 1 SW *Stone County*   Elevation: 1,099 ft.   Latitude: 36° 48' N   Longitude: 93° 29' W

	JAN	FEB	MAR	APR	MAY	JUN	JUL	AUG	SEP	OCT	NOV	DEC	YEAR
Mean Maximum Temp. (°F)	43.8	50.4	59.7	70.1	76.3	84.1	89.2	88.6	80.6	70.9	57.9	48.2	68.3
Mean Temp. (°F)	32.3	37.7	46.7	56.3	64.0	72.1	76.9	75.8	68.3	57.3	45.7	36.6	55.8
Mean Minimum Temp. (°F)	20.7	24.9	33.6	42.3	51.7	60.2	64.6	63.1	56.0	43.6	33.5	24.9	43.3
Extreme Maximum Temp. (°F)	72	83	89	92	91	99	106	104	103	91	83	77	106
Extreme Minimum Temp. (°F)	-21	-16	2	18	28	38	45	40	28	17	1	-18	-21
Days Maximum Temp. ≥ 90°F	0	0	0	0	0	5	17	15	4	0	0	0	41
Days Maximum Temp. ≤ 32°F	6	3	1	0	0	0	0	0	0	0	0	3	13
Days Minimum Temp. ≤ 32°F	27	22	16	6	0	0	0	0	0	5	14	24	114
Days Minimum Temp. ≤ 0°F	2	1	0	0	0	0	0	0	0	0	0	1	4
Heating Degree Days (base 65°F)	1,007	765	566	279	102	9	1	3	60	252	575	875	4,494
Cooling Degree Days (base 65°F)	0	0	5	21	77	237	383	351	161	18	2	0	1,255
Mean Precipitation (in.)	2.18	2.36	4.05	4.45	4.53	4.61	3.66	3.32	4.79	3.53	4.58	3.43	45.49
Days With ≥ 0.1" Precipitation	4	4	7	7	7	7	5	5	6	5	6	5	68
Days With ≥ 1.0" Precipitation	0	1	1	1	1	1	1	1	2	1	2	1	13
Mean Snowfall (in.)	*3.3*	na	1.1	0.1	0.0	0.0	0.0	0.0	0.0	0.0	0.5	1.3	na
Days With ≥ 1.0" Snow Depth	*1*	na	1	0	0	0	0	0	0	0	0	*1*	na

Grant City *Worth County*   Elevation: 1,128 ft.   Latitude: 40° 29' N   Longitude: 94° 24' W

	JAN	FEB	MAR	APR	MAY	JUN	JUL	AUG	SEP	OCT	NOV	DEC	YEAR
Mean Maximum Temp. (°F)	32.6	39.3	51.7	64.9	74.4	83.7	87.8	85.9	78.1	66.4	49.8	37.2	62.6
Mean Temp. (°F)	23.2	29.4	40.7	53.2	63.2	72.4	76.7	74.5	*66.4*	54.6	40.3	28.4	*51.9*
Mean Minimum Temp. (°F)	13.8	19.3	29.7	41.4	52.0	61.0	65.4	63.1	*54.7*	42.7	30.7	19.6	*41.1*
Extreme Maximum Temp. (°F)	70	75	89	94	92	107	108	105	99	92	81	70	108
Extreme Minimum Temp. (°F)	-25	-27	-19	7	28	40	43	42	26	14	-6	-25	-27
Days Maximum Temp. ≥ 90°F	0	0	0	0	0	5	12	10	3	0	0	0	30
Days Maximum Temp. ≤ 32°F	14	9	2	0	0	0	0	0	0	0	2	10	37
Days Minimum Temp. ≤ 32°F	30	24	19	6	0	0	0	0	0	5	18	28	130
Days Minimum Temp. ≤ 0°F	6	3	0	0	0	0	0	0	0	0	0	3	12
Heating Degree Days (base 65°F)	1,289	1,000	747	365	118	11	1	3	*83*	331	735	1,128	*5,811*
Cooling Degree Days (base 65°F)	0	0	2	18	66	228	*358*	301	*133*	13	0	0	*1,119*
Mean Precipitation (in.)	0.84	1.05	2.34	3.16	4.50	4.05	4.57	3.75	4.13	2.94	2.35	1.38	35.06
Days With ≥ 0.1" Precipitation	2	3	5	6	8	6	6	6	6	5	5	3	61
Days With ≥ 1.0" Precipitation	0	0	1	1	1	1	2	1	1	1	1	0	10
Mean Snowfall (in.)	6.2	5.3	4.0	1.5	0.0	0.0	0.0	0.0	0.0	0.2	2.4	4.2	23.8
Days With ≥ 1.0" Snow Depth	12	10	4	1	0	0	0	0	0	0	2	7	36

Hamilton 2 W *Caldwell County*   Elevation: 898 ft.   Latitude: 39° 45' N   Longitude: 94° 02' W

	JAN	FEB	MAR	APR	MAY	JUN	JUL	AUG	SEP	OCT	NOV	DEC	YEAR
Mean Maximum Temp. (°F)	33.6	39.7	51.9	63.6	73.5	83.1	88.1	86.4	78.3	66.8	51.1	38.7	62.9
Mean Temp. (°F)	22.9	28.4	40.1	51.3	61.6	71.2	76.1	74.0	65.3	53.1	40.0	28.3	51.0
Mean Minimum Temp. (°F)	12.2	17.1	28.1	38.9	49.7	59.3	64.2	61.6	52.3	39.4	28.8	17.8	39.1
Extreme Maximum Temp. (°F)	67	77	86	92	93	102	107	108	100	91	82	72	108
Extreme Minimum Temp. (°F)	-27	-27	-17	9	25	34	43	40	27	14	-10	-27	-27
Days Maximum Temp. ≥ 90°F	0	0	0	0	0	6	14	11	3	0	0	0	34
Days Maximum Temp. ≤ 32°F	13	9	2	0	0	0	0	0	0	0	2	9	35
Days Minimum Temp. ≤ 32°F	30	26	21	9	1	0	0	0	1	8	20	29	145
Days Minimum Temp. ≤ 0°F	6	4	0	0	0	0	0	0	0	0	0	3	13
Heating Degree Days (base 65°F)	1,299	1,027	768	420	155	20	3	7	104	373	744	1,133	6,053
Cooling Degree Days (base 65°F)	0	0	2	16	51	210	355	295	116	11	0	0	1,056
Mean Precipitation (in.)	1.07	1.17	2.68	3.65	4.91	4.09	3.78	3.75	4.75	3.24	2.42	1.66	37.17
Days With ≥ 0.1" Precipitation	3	3	6	7	8	7	6	6	6	5	5	3	65
Days With ≥ 1.0" Precipitation	0	0	1	1	1	1	1	1	1	1	1	0	9
Mean Snowfall (in.)	*2.9*	*3.1*	*1.7*	trace	0.0	0.0	0.0	0.0	0.0	trace	0.5	*1.8*	*10.0*
Days With ≥ 1.0" Snow Depth	na	na	*0*	0	0	0	0	0	0	0	0	na	na

Hannibal Water Works *Marion County*   Elevation: 711 ft.   Latitude: 39° 43' N   Longitude: 91° 22' W

	JAN	FEB	MAR	APR	MAY	JUN	JUL	AUG	SEP	OCT	NOV	DEC	YEAR
Mean Maximum Temp. (°F)	33.0	39.6	51.2	63.8	73.7	82.6	87.0	84.8	77.6	66.4	51.3	38.3	62.4
Mean Temp. (°F)	24.5	30.4	41.4	53.5	63.6	72.5	77.0	74.7	66.9	55.4	42.4	30.1	52.7
Mean Minimum Temp. (°F)	15.9	21.1	31.6	43.1	53.4	62.3	66.8	64.5	56.2	44.4	33.4	21.9	42.9
Extreme Maximum Temp. (°F)	70	81	87	93	93	103	108	105	99	91	81	74	108
Extreme Minimum Temp. (°F)	-21	-19	-4	16	30	45	48	43	32	21	1	-21	-21
Days Maximum Temp. ≥ 90°F	0	0	0	0	1	5	12	7	3	0	0	0	28
Days Maximum Temp. ≤ 32°F	14	9	2	0	0	0	0	0	0	0	2	9	36
Days Minimum Temp. ≤ 32°F	28	23	18	4	0	0	0	0	0	2	14	26	115
Days Minimum Temp. ≤ 0°F	5	2	0	0	0	0	0	0	0	0	0	2	9
Heating Degree Days (base 65°F)	1,250	972	727	361	120	13	1	4	77	310	673	1,074	5,582
Cooling Degree Days (base 65°F)	0	0	4	20	79	249	383	324	139	18	1	0	1,217
Mean Precipitation (in.)	1.73	2.06	3.19	3.99	4.89	3.46	4.25	4.27	3.52	3.21	3.46	2.61	40.64
Days With ≥ 0.1" Precipitation	5	4	7	7	7	6	6	6	6	6	6	5	71
Days With ≥ 1.0" Precipitation	0	0	1	1	1	1	2	1	1	1	1	1	11
Mean Snowfall (in.)	7.2	5.5	3.1	1.0	0.0	0.0	0.0	0.0	0.0	trace	1.4	4.6	22.8
Days With ≥ 1.0" Snow Depth	14	12	3	0	0	0	0	0	0	0	1	6	36

Jackson *Cape Girardeau County*   Elevation: 439 ft.   Latitude: 37° 22' N   Longitude: 89° 40' W

	JAN	FEB	MAR	APR	MAY	JUN	JUL	AUG	SEP	OCT	NOV	DEC	YEAR
Mean Maximum Temp. (°F)	41.7	48.4	58.9	70.6	79.3	87.7	91.5	89.7	82.9	72.1	57.4	45.9	68.8
Mean Temp. (°F)	32.4	38.1	47.8	58.4	67.2	75.9	79.8	77.6	70.7	59.2	47.3	36.9	57.6
Mean Minimum Temp. (°F)	23.0	27.8	36.6	46.2	55.2	64.1	68.1	65.7	58.4	46.3	37.3	27.9	46.4
Extreme Maximum Temp. (°F)	76	77	85	92	95	103	106	104	100	91	87	73	106
Extreme Minimum Temp. (°F)	-21	-16	-1	21	32	40	49	40	32	21	6	-16	-21
Days Maximum Temp. ≥ 90°F	0	0	0	0	3	13	21	16	6	0	0	0	59
Days Maximum Temp. ≤ 32°F	7	3	0	0	0	0	0	0	0	0	0	3	13
Days Minimum Temp. ≤ 32°F	24	18	12	3	0	0	0	0	0	3	11	20	91
Days Minimum Temp. ≤ 0°F	1	0	0	0	0	0	0	0	0	0	0	1	2
Heating Degree Days (base 65°F)	1,005	753	532	226	60	2	0	1	34	211	525	864	4,213
Cooling Degree Days (base 65°F)	0	0	4	35	137	345	479	408	205	36	2	0	1,651
Mean Precipitation (in.)	2.96	3.31	4.88	4.93	5.13	4.01	3.79	3.38	3.46	3.34	4.70	3.84	47.73
Days With ≥ 0.1" Precipitation	6	5	7	8	8	6	6	5	5	6	7	6	75
Days With ≥ 1.0" Precipitation	1	1	1	1	2	1	1	1	1	1	1	1	13
Mean Snowfall (in.)	na	3.2	2.1	trace	0.0	0.0	0.0	0.0	0.0	trace	0.5	1.3	na
Days With ≥ 1.0" Snow Depth	na	1	0	0	0	0	0	0	0	0	0	0	na

Jefferson City Water Plant *Cole County*   Elevation: 669 ft.   Latitude: 38° 35' N   Longitude: 92° 11' W

	JAN	FEB	MAR	APR	MAY	JUN	JUL	AUG	SEP	OCT	NOV	DEC	YEAR
Mean Maximum Temp. (°F)	38.8	45.4	56.1	66.8	75.7	84.3	89.8	88.3	80.9	69.6	55.2	43.7	66.2
Mean Temp. (°F)	28.4	34.0	44.0	54.5	64.0	72.9	78.1	76.2	68.2	56.5	44.2	33.4	54.5
Mean Minimum Temp. (°F)	18.0	22.5	32.0	42.2	52.2	61.6	66.4	64.0	55.5	43.3	33.0	23.1	42.8
Extreme Maximum Temp. (°F)	73	85	87	93	93	103	110	110	100	93	84	78	110
Extreme Minimum Temp. (°F)	-18	-13	-4	17	29	38	44	42	30	14	3	-21	-21
Days Maximum Temp. ≥ 90°F	0	0	0	0	1	7	17	14	5	0	0	0	44
Days Maximum Temp. ≤ 32°F	10	6	1	0	0	0	0	0	0	0	1	6	24
Days Minimum Temp. ≤ 32°F	28	23	17	4	0	0	0	0	0	4	15	25	116
Days Minimum Temp. ≤ 0°F	3	2	0	0	0	0	0	0	0	0	0	1	6
Heating Degree Days (base 65°F)	1,126	869	645	330	106	10	1	2	63	281	619	972	5,024
Cooling Degree Days (base 65°F)	0	0	4	22	76	257	418	356	158	21	1	0	1,313
Mean Precipitation (in.)	1.61	1.91	3.19	3.97	4.84	4.14	3.62	3.33	3.72	3.34	3.50	2.64	39.81
Days With ≥ 0.1" Precipitation	4	4	6	7	8	7	6	5	6	6	6	4	69
Days With ≥ 1.0" Precipitation	0	0	1	1	1	1	1	1	1	1	1	1	10
Mean Snowfall (in.)	5.5	3.7	1.9	0.2	0.0	0.0	0.0	0.0	0.0	0.0	1.1	2.6	15.0
Days With ≥ 1.0" Snow Depth	4	4	1	0	0	0	0	0	0	0	0	1	10

Joplin Municipal Airport *Jasper County*   Elevation: 977 ft.   Latitude: 37° 09' N   Longitude: 94° 30' W

	JAN	FEB	MAR	APR	MAY	JUN	JUL	AUG	SEP	OCT	NOV	DEC	YEAR
Mean Maximum Temp. (°F)	42.0	48.4	58.7	69.2	76.6	85.0	90.4	89.4	80.7	70.6	56.6	46.6	67.8
Mean Temp. (°F)	32.7	38.4	48.1	58.0	66.2	74.9	80.1	78.6	70.1	59.4	46.8	37.3	57.5
Mean Minimum Temp. (°F)	23.4	28.3	37.4	46.7	55.8	64.8	69.7	67.7	59.4	48.1	37.1	27.9	47.2
Extreme Maximum Temp. (°F)	77	87	90	96	94	100	108	106	100	93	83	75	108
Extreme Minimum Temp. (°F)	-12	-12	3	19	31	44	50	47	30	18	7	-15	-15
Days Maximum Temp. ≥ 90°F	0	0	0	0	0	7	19	16	5	0	0	0	47
Days Maximum Temp. ≤ 32°F	8	4	1	0	0	0	0	0	0	0	1	4	18
Days Minimum Temp. ≤ 32°F	24	18	10	2	0	0	0	0	0	2	10	21	87
Days Minimum Temp. ≤ 0°F	1	1	0	0	0	0	0	0	0	0	0	1	3
Heating Degree Days (base 65°F)	993	746	523	244	71	4	0	1	50	214	542	853	4,241
Cooling Degree Days (base 65°F)	0	1	7	39	115	319	486	441	210	45	4	0	1,667
Mean Precipitation (in.)	1.80	2.22	3.55	4.57	5.09	5.43	3.29	3.92	5.44	3.87	4.03	3.02	46.23
Days With ≥ 0.1" Precipitation	4	4	6	7	8	8	5	6	6	5	5	5	69
Days With ≥ 1.0" Precipitation	0	0	1	1	2	1	1	2	2	1	1	1	12
Mean Snowfall (in.)	4.5	3.3	2.1	trace	trace	0.0	0.0	trace	trace	trace	0.6	2.6	13.1
Days With ≥ 1.0" Snow Depth	7	4	1	0	0	0	0	0	0	0	0	3	15

Kennett Radio KBOA *Dunklin County*   Elevation: 269 ft.   Latitude: 36° 13' N   Longitude: 90° 04' W

	JAN	FEB	MAR	APR	MAY	JUN	JUL	AUG	SEP	OCT	NOV	DEC	YEAR
Mean Maximum Temp. (°F)	44.0	50.5	60.3	71.4	80.3	88.8	92.8	90.7	84.1	73.8	59.8	48.9	70.5
Mean Temp. (°F)	34.7	40.2	49.5	59.5	68.7	77.1	81.1	78.7	71.8	60.4	49.1	39.6	59.2
Mean Minimum Temp. (°F)	25.4	29.9	38.6	47.6	57.2	65.4	69.4	66.7	59.3	46.9	38.3	30.3	47.9
Extreme Maximum Temp. (°F)	74	79	86	93	97	105	112	107	106	96	87	78	112
Extreme Minimum Temp. (°F)	-12	-4	0	27	37	43	50	46	34	24	12	-6	-12
Days Maximum Temp. ≥ 90°F	0	0	0	0	3	15	23	18	8	1	0	0	68
Days Maximum Temp. ≤ 32°F	5	2	0	0	0	0	0	0	0	0	0	2	9
Days Minimum Temp. ≤ 32°F	23	17	10	1	0	0	0	0	0	2	9	19	81
Days Minimum Temp. ≤ 0°F	1	0	0	0	0	0	0	0	0	0	0	0	1
Heating Degree Days (base 65°F)	932	693	480	201	42	1	0	0	30	188	475	781	3,823
Cooling Degree Days (base 65°F)	0	0	6	39	164	374	521	449	236	49	5	1	1,844
Mean Precipitation (in.)	3.29	3.71	4.85	5.11	5.27	4.08	3.59	2.83	3.52	4.11	4.71	4.62	49.69
Days With ≥ 0.1" Precipitation	6	6	8	8	7	6	5	4	5	5	7	7	74
Days With ≥ 1.0" Precipitation	1	1	1	2	2	1	1	1	1	1	1	1	14
Mean Snowfall (in.)	3.9	3.1	0.6	trace	0.0	0.0	0.0	0.0	0.0	0.0	0.3	0.9	8.8
Days With ≥ 1.0" Snow Depth	3	2	0	0	0	0	0	0	0	0	0	1	6

Kirksville *Adair County*   Elevation: 967 ft.   Latitude: 40° 12' N   Longitude: 92° 34' W

	JAN	FEB	MAR	APR	MAY	JUN	JUL	AUG	SEP	OCT	NOV	DEC	YEAR
Mean Maximum Temp. (°F)	32.6	39.1	50.8	63.8	73.1	82.0	86.9	84.8	77.0	65.5	50.1	37.3	61.9
Mean Temp. (°F)	24.0	29.9	40.7	52.7	62.4	71.5	76.3	74.1	66.1	54.8	41.1	29.1	51.9
Mean Minimum Temp. (°F)	15.3	20.7	30.5	41.5	51.6	61.1	65.6	63.4	55.2	44.0	31.9	21.0	41.8
Extreme Maximum Temp. (°F)	69	78	85	90	92	102	105	105	97	92	78	70	105
Extreme Minimum Temp. (°F)	-23	-20	-7	13	30	41	46	40	30	19	-4	-22	-23
Days Maximum Temp. ≥ 90°F	0	0	0	0	0	3	11	8	2	0	0	0	24
Days Maximum Temp. ≤ 32°F	15	9	2	0	0	0	0	0	0	0	2	10	38
Days Minimum Temp. ≤ 32°F	28	23	18	5	0	0	0	0	0	4	16	27	121
Days Minimum Temp. ≤ 0°F	5	3	0	0	0	0	0	0	0	0	0	2	10
Heating Degree Days (base 65°F)	1,265	984	748	379	137	15	2	5	88	327	712	1,105	5,767
Cooling Degree Days (base 65°F)	0	0	2	16	58	214	355	296	127	16	0	0	1,084
Mean Precipitation (in.)	0.95	1.10	2.45	3.48	5.08	4.28	4.55	3.97	4.26	3.25	2.78	1.71	37.86
Days With ≥ 0.1" Precipitation	2	3	5	7	8	6	5	6	6	5	5	3	61
Days With ≥ 1.0" Precipitation	0	0	1	1	1	2	1	1	1	1	1	0	10
Mean Snowfall (in.)	6.1	4.8	2.7	1.0	0.0	0.0	0.0	0.0	0.0	trace	1.7	3.6	19.9
Days With ≥ 1.0" Snow Depth	na	na	1	0	0	0	0	0	0	0	0	na	na

Lakeside *Miller County*   Elevation: 590 ft.   Latitude: 38° 12' N   Longitude: 92° 37' W

	JAN	FEB	MAR	APR	MAY	JUN	JUL	AUG	SEP	OCT	NOV	DEC	YEAR
Mean Maximum Temp. (°F)	40.3	46.6	56.6	67.8	76.0	84.1	89.8	88.6	80.4	70.1	56.6	45.6	66.9
Mean Temp. (°F)	30.2	35.4	44.8	55.5	64.1	72.9	78.0	76.6	68.8	57.8	46.2	35.8	55.5
Mean Minimum Temp. (°F)	19.5	23.8	33.0	43.0	52.2	61.6	66.2	64.6	57.2	45.2	35.7	25.9	44.0
Extreme Maximum Temp. (°F)	72	81	85	94	92	103	107	105	100	93	83	77	107
Extreme Minimum Temp. (°F)	-15	-12	-1	22	32	41	45	45	34	24	6	-10	-15
Days Maximum Temp. ≥ 90°F	0	0	0	0	1	7	17	15	5	0	0	0	45
Days Maximum Temp. ≤ 32°F	9	5	1	0	0	0	0	0	0	0	1	4	20
Days Minimum Temp. ≤ 32°F	27	22	16	4	0	0	0	0	0	2	11	23	105
Days Minimum Temp. ≤ 0°F	2	1	0	0	0	0	0	0	0	0	0	1	4
Heating Degree Days (base 65°F)	1,073	828	621	302	100	8	1	1	57	243	560	897	4,691
Cooling Degree Days (base 65°F)	0	0	3	22	78	257	422	377	176	25	2	0	1,362
Mean Precipitation (in.)	1.70	1.83	3.25	4.28	4.95	4.05	3.78	3.74	4.19	3.58	3.74	2.48	41.57
Days With ≥ 0.1" Precipitation	4	4	6	7	8	7	5	5	5	6	6	4	67
Days With ≥ 1.0" Precipitation	0	0	1	1	1	1	1	1	1	1	1	1	10
Mean Snowfall (in.)	*4.0*	3.0	1.1	0.1	0.0	0.0	0.0	0.0	0.0	0.0	0.7	*2.2*	*11.1*
Days With ≥ 1.0" Snow Depth	6	4	1	0	0	0	0	0	0	0	0	2	13

Lamar *Barton County*   Elevation: 977 ft.   Latitude: 37° 30' N   Longitude: 94° 16' W

	JAN	FEB	MAR	APR	MAY	JUN	JUL	AUG	SEP	OCT	NOV	DEC	YEAR
Mean Maximum Temp. (°F)	40.3	46.8	57.0	67.6	75.4	83.8	89.3	88.6	80.5	70.5	56.3	45.4	66.8
Mean Temp. (°F)	30.3	36.0	45.5	55.7	64.6	73.4	78.6	77.1	69.0	58.3	45.6	35.4	55.8
Mean Minimum Temp. (°F)	20.2	25.2	33.9	43.8	53.8	62.9	67.8	65.5	57.5	46.0	34.8	25.5	44.7
Extreme Maximum Temp. (°F)	73	80	89	92	91	100	107	105	102	93	85	75	107
Extreme Minimum Temp. (°F)	-15	-11	1	20	31	43	48	45	32	19	6	-18	-18
Days Maximum Temp. ≥ 90°F	0	0	0	0	0	6	17	15	5	0	0	0	43
Days Maximum Temp. ≤ 32°F	9	5	1	0	0	0	0	0	0	0	1	5	21
Days Minimum Temp. ≤ 32°F	28	21	14	3	0	0	0	0	0	2	13	24	105
Days Minimum Temp. ≤ 0°F	2	1	0	0	0	0	0	0	0	0	0	1	4
Heating Degree Days (base 65°F)	1,070	813	602	297	94	9	1	2	61	234	579	910	4,672
Cooling Degree Days (base 65°F)	0	0	4	21	85	268	430	387	186	29	3	0	1,413
Mean Precipitation (in.)	1.91	2.14	4.01	4.67	5.33	5.35	4.41	3.73	5.51	4.21	4.33	2.89	48.49
Days With ≥ 0.1" Precipitation	5	4	7	7	8	8	5	5	7	5	6	5	72
Days With ≥ 1.0" Precipitation	0	0	1	1	2	2	1	1	2	1	1	1	13
Mean Snowfall (in.)	*4.2*	2.9	1.9	trace	0.0	0.0	0.0	0.0	0.0	trace	0.9	2.8	*12.7*
Days With ≥ 1.0" Snow Depth	na	*1*	1	0	0	0	0	0	0	0	0	*1*	na

Lebanon 2 W *Laclede County*   Elevation: 1,276 ft.   Latitude: 37° 41' N   Longitude: 92° 42' W

	JAN	FEB	MAR	APR	MAY	JUN	JUL	AUG	SEP	OCT	NOV	DEC	YEAR
Mean Maximum Temp. (°F)	40.9	47.6	58.2	68.9	76.7	84.5	89.7	88.9	80.5	69.9	55.8	45.7	67.3
Mean Temp. (°F)	31.2	37.0	46.7	56.8	65.1	73.3	78.2	77.0	69.0	58.1	45.8	36.1	56.2
Mean Minimum Temp. (°F)	21.5	26.3	35.1	44.7	53.3	62.0	66.7	65.0	57.4	46.2	35.8	26.5	45.0
Extreme Maximum Temp. (°F)	71	81	84	92	92	102	108	105	101	93	82	76	108
Extreme Minimum Temp. (°F)	-19	-17	-6	19	26	40	43	43	28	20	5	-17	-19
Days Maximum Temp. ≥ 90°F	0	0	0	0	0	6	17	15	4	0	0	0	42
Days Maximum Temp. ≤ 32°F	8	4	1	0	0	0	0	0	0	0	1	4	18
Days Minimum Temp. ≤ 32°F	26	20	14	4	0	0	0	0	0	3	12	22	101
Days Minimum Temp. ≤ 0°F	2	1	0	0	0	0	0	0	0	0	0	1	4
Heating Degree Days (base 65°F)	1,041	785	566	268	86	7	1	1	55	238	571	889	4,508
Cooling Degree Days (base 65°F)	0	0	4	30	94	263	420	381	175	29	3	0	1,399
Mean Precipitation (in.)	1.81	2.14	3.56	4.49	4.61	4.19	3.66	3.31	4.45	3.81	4.27	2.56	42.86
Days With ≥ 0.1" Precipitation	4	4	6	7	7	6	5	5	6	6	6	4	66
Days With ≥ 1.0" Precipitation	0	0	1	1	1	1	1	1	1	1	1	1	10
Mean Snowfall (in.)	5.2	3.2	1.8	0.2	0.0	0.0	0.0	0.0	0.0	trace	1.3	1.9	13.6
Days With ≥ 1.0" Snow Depth	7	4	1	0	0	0	0	0	0	0	1	2	15

Lees Summit Reed Wildlife Refuge *Jackson County*   Elevation: 997 ft.   Latitude: 38° 53' N   Longitude: 94° 20' W

	JAN	FEB	MAR	APR	MAY	JUN	JUL	AUG	SEP	OCT	NOV	DEC	YEAR
Mean Maximum Temp. (°F)	37.8	44.8	56.3	67.2	75.9	84.6	89.6	88.3	80.2	69.5	53.5	42.3	65.8
Mean Temp. (°F)	27.6	33.9	44.4	55.1	64.2	73.0	77.8	76.1	67.9	57.0	43.1	32.5	54.4
Mean Minimum Temp. (°F)	17.5	23.0	32.4	43.0	52.6	61.4	65.9	63.8	55.6	44.3	32.9	22.7	42.9
Extreme Maximum Temp. (°F)	71	80	87	91	91	103	108	107	100	94	82	70	108
Extreme Minimum Temp. (°F)	-19	-15	-5	11	28	35	48	43	29	7	-19	-25	-25
Days Maximum Temp. ≥ 90°F	0	0	0	0	0	7	17	14	5	0	0	0	43
Days Maximum Temp. ≤ 32°F	10	6	1	0	0	0	0	0	0	0	1	6	24
Days Minimum Temp. ≤ 32°F	28	22	16	5	0	0	0	0	0	4	15	26	116
Days Minimum Temp. ≤ 0°F	4	2	0	0	0	0	0	0	0	0	0	2	8
Heating Degree Days (base 65°F)	1,153	872	635	312	96	10	1	3	70	266	650	1,000	5,068
Cooling Degree Days (base 65°F)	0	0	2	23	73	254	400	349	160	21	1	0	1,283
Mean Precipitation (in.)	1.30	1.46	2.77	3.97	5.22	5.39	4.08	3.98	4.91	3.54	2.91	1.89	41.42
Days With ≥ 0.1" Precipitation	3	3	6	7	8	7	6	6	6	6	5	4	67
Days With ≥ 1.0" Precipitation	0	0	1	1	1	2	1	1	1	1	1	0	10
Mean Snowfall (in.)	5.6	5.1	1.8	0.3	0.0	0.0	0.0	0.0	0.0	trace	0.7	2.3	15.8
Days With ≥ 1.0" Snow Depth	8	6	1	0	0	0	0	0	0	0	0	3	18

Lexington 3 NE *Lafayette County*   Elevation: 823 ft.   Latitude: 39° 12' N   Longitude: 93° 52' W

	JAN	FEB	MAR	APR	MAY	JUN	JUL	AUG	SEP	OCT	NOV	DEC	YEAR
Mean Maximum Temp. (°F)	35.6	41.8	54.1	65.6	75.1	84.1	88.8	86.7	79.3	68.0	52.6	41.4	64.4
Mean Temp. (°F)	26.1	31.9	43.0	54.5	64.1	73.3	77.9	75.6	67.5	56.2	42.7	32.2	53.8
Mean Minimum Temp. (°F)	16.7	22.0	32.0	43.1	53.1	62.5	67.0	64.3	55.8	44.3	32.7	22.9	43.0
Extreme Maximum Temp. (°F)	70	77	86	91	96	102	109	108	99	92	82	71	109
Extreme Minimum Temp. (°F)	-18	-14	-7	15	30	42	49	41	30	22	-5	-22	-22
Days Maximum Temp. ≥ 90°F	0	0	0	0	1	7	15	12	4	0	0	0	39
Days Maximum Temp. ≤ 32°F	12	8	1	0	0	0	0	0	0	0	1	7	29
Days Minimum Temp. ≤ 32°F	29	23	16	4	0	0	0	0	0	3	15	26	116
Days Minimum Temp. ≤ 0°F	4	2	0	0	0	0	0	0	0	0	0	1	7
Heating Degree Days (base 65°F)	1,198	928	677	332	106	10	1	3	73	289	664	1,010	5,291
Cooling Degree Days (base 65°F)	0	0	3	21	73	252	394	322	143	19	1	0	1,228
Mean Precipitation (in.)	1.50	1.52	2.72	3.76	4.98	4.21	4.58	3.85	4.92	3.41	2.90	2.01	40.36
Days With ≥ 0.1" Precipitation	4	4	6	7	8	7	6	6	6	5	5	4	68
Days With ≥ 1.0" Precipitation	0	0	0	1	1	1	1	1	2	1	1	0	9
Mean Snowfall (in.)	6.4	4.8	2.6	0.7	0.0	0.0	0.0	0.0	0.0	trace	1.1	3.1	18.7
Days With ≥ 1.0" Snow Depth	9	7	2	0	0	0	0	0	0	0	1	3	22

Licking 4 N *Texas County*   Elevation: 1,177 ft.   Latitude: 37° 33' N   Longitude: 91° 53' W

	JAN	FEB	MAR	APR	MAY	JUN	JUL	AUG	SEP	OCT	NOV	DEC	YEAR
Mean Maximum Temp. (°F)	39.4	45.7	55.7	66.8	75.1	82.6	88.4	87.2	78.8	68.3	54.8	44.0	65.6
Mean Temp. (°F)	28.8	34.5	44.3	54.6	63.4	71.6	76.8	75.4	67.2	55.7	44.2	33.9	54.2
Mean Minimum Temp. (°F)	18.2	23.3	32.7	42.4	51.7	60.5	65.1	63.5	55.5	43.0	33.6	23.7	42.8
Extreme Maximum Temp. (°F)	71	80	85	90	91	98	108	106	99	91	84	76	108
Extreme Minimum Temp. (°F)	-24	-19	-7	16	25	36	42	38	28	19	2	-19	-24
Days Maximum Temp. ≥ 90°F	0	0	0	0	0	4	14	12	3	0	0	0	33
Days Maximum Temp. ≤ 32°F	10	6	1	0	0	0	0	0	0	0	1	5	23
Days Minimum Temp. ≤ 32°F	27	22	16	6	1	0	0	0	0	6	15	25	118
Days Minimum Temp. ≤ 0°F	3	2	0	0	0	0	0	0	0	0	0	1	6
Heating Degree Days (base 65°F)	1,115	855	639	327	120	17	3	5	78	300	618	958	5,035
Cooling Degree Days (base 65°F)	0	0	3	20	76	222	378	334	145	16	1	0	1,195
Mean Precipitation (in.)	2.31	2.50	3.98	4.59	4.82	4.58	3.44	3.36	4.35	3.79	4.40	3.40	45.52
Days With ≥ 0.1" Precipitation	5	5	8	7	8	7	5	5	6	6	7	5	74
Days With ≥ 1.0" Precipitation	1	1	1	1	1	2	1	1	1	1	1	1	13
Mean Snowfall (in.)	5.7	3.7	3.1	0.1	0.0	0.0	0.0	0.0	0.0	trace	0.8	2.4	15.8
Days With ≥ 1.0" Snow Depth	9	5	2	0	0	0	0	0	0	0	0	3	19

Lockwood *Dade County*   Elevation: 1,079 ft.   Latitude: 37° 23' N   Longitude: 93° 57' W

	JAN	FEB	MAR	APR	MAY	JUN	JUL	AUG	SEP	OCT	NOV	DEC	YEAR
Mean Maximum Temp. (°F)	41.7	48.5	58.3	68.6	76.6	84.9	90.5	89.8	81.5	70.9	56.6	46.4	67.9
Mean Temp. (°F)	31.8	37.7	47.0	56.6	65.5	74.2	79.4	78.1	70.0	59.0	46.4	36.5	56.8
Mean Minimum Temp. (°F)	21.8	26.9	35.7	44.6	54.3	63.3	68.3	66.2	58.4	47.1	36.1	26.7	45.8
Extreme Maximum Temp. (°F)	74	81	86	91	92	101	108	105	103	93	87	75	108
Extreme Minimum Temp. (°F)	-16	-12	2	18	29	44	47	47	32	18	6	-17	-17
Days Maximum Temp. ≥ 90°F	0	0	0	0	0	7	19	17	5	0	0	0	48
Days Maximum Temp. ≤ 32°F	7	4	1	0	0	0	0	0	0	0	1	4	17
Days Minimum Temp. ≤ 32°F	26	20	12	3	0	0	0	0	0	2	11	22	96
Days Minimum Temp. ≤ 0°F	2	1	0	0	0	0	0	0	0	0	0	1	4
Heating Degree Days (base 65°F)	1,023	765	556	273	81	6	0	1	50	217	554	876	4,402
Cooling Degree Days (base 65°F)	0	0	5	26	99	289	459	419	205	35	3	0	1,540
Mean Precipitation (in.)	1.92	2.23	3.69	4.49	4.89	5.12	3.93	3.93	5.06	3.99	4.22	2.96	46.43
Days With ≥ 0.1" Precipitation	4	4	6	7	8	7	5	5	6	5	5	5	67
Days With ≥ 1.0" Precipitation	0	0	1	1	1	2	1	1	2	1	1	1	12
Mean Snowfall (in.)	5.4	3.8	3.6	trace	0.0	0.0	0.0	0.0	0.0	trace	0.9	2.8	16.5
Days With ≥ 1.0" Snow Depth	9	5	2	0	0	0	0	0	0	0	1	3	20

Mansfield *Wright County*   Elevation: 1,519 ft.   Latitude: 37° 07' N   Longitude: 92° 35' W

	JAN	FEB	MAR	APR	MAY	JUN	JUL	AUG	SEP	OCT	NOV	DEC	YEAR
Mean Maximum Temp. (°F)	41.6	*47.7*	57.6	68.2	76.0	83.8	89.2	88.4	80.1	69.7	55.0	45.9	*66.9*
Mean Temp. (°F)	30.2	*35.8*	44.8	54.9	63.6	71.7	76.7	75.3	67.4	56.7	43.9	*35.1*	*54.7*
Mean Minimum Temp. (°F)	18.6	*23.6*	31.9	41.6	51.1	59.4	64.1	62.1	54.7	43.7	32.8	24.3	*42.3*
Extreme Maximum Temp. (°F)	72	*82*	85	92	92	100	106	104	99	92	*80*	*73*	*106*
Extreme Minimum Temp. (°F)	-25	-16	-1	10	28	*35*	43	35	24	16	-5	*-20*	-25
Days Maximum Temp. ≥ 90°F	0	0	0	0	0	5	16	14	4	0	0	0	39
Days Maximum Temp. ≤ 32°F	8	*4*	1	0	0	0	0	0	0	0	1	4	*18*
Days Minimum Temp. ≤ 32°F	27	21	16	6	0	0	0	0	0	4	15	24	113
Days Minimum Temp. ≤ 0°F	3	1	0	0	0	0	0	0	0	0	0	1	5
Heating Degree Days (base 65°F)	1,071	*816*	621	311	105	11	1	4	68	270	626	*919*	*4,823*
Cooling Degree Days (base 65°F)	0	*0*	2	10	55	200	362	319	130	18	0	*0*	*1,095*
Mean Precipitation (in.)	2.00	*2.36*	4.01	4.24	4.54	4.54	3.34	3.09	4.61	3.75	4.54	3.35	*44.37*
Days With ≥ 0.1" Precipitation	4	4	6	6	8	7	5	5	6	6	6	5	68
Days With ≥ 1.0" Precipitation	0	1	1	1	1	1	1	1	2	1	2	1	13
Mean Snowfall (in.)	*5.8*	*4.1*	2.8	0.3	0.0	0.0	0.0	0.0	0.0	trace	0.7	*1.9*	*15.6*
Days With ≥ 1.0" Snow Depth	na	na	*1*	0	0	0	0	0	0	0	0	*0*	na

Marble Hill *Bollinger County*   Elevation: 387 ft.   Latitude: 37° 18' N   Longitude: 89° 58' W

	JAN	FEB	MAR	APR	MAY	JUN	JUL	AUG	SEP	OCT	NOV	DEC	YEAR
Mean Maximum Temp. (°F)	42.1	48.6	58.9	69.5	77.9	85.4	89.4	88.2	81.8	71.5	57.4	46.5	68.1
Mean Temp. (°F)	31.7	37.2	46.7	56.5	65.2	73.2	77.4	75.7	68.7	57.5	46.0	36.4	56.0
Mean Minimum Temp. (°F)	21.3	25.7	34.5	43.5	52.5	61.0	65.3	63.1	55.6	43.3	34.5	26.2	43.9
Extreme Maximum Temp. (°F)	73	79	85	90	93	101	102	104	100	90	88	74	104
Extreme Minimum Temp. (°F)	-23	-16	-4	18	28	36	44	37	29	13	5	-12	-23
Days Maximum Temp. ≥ 90°F	0	0	0	0	1	8	16	13	5	0	0	0	43
Days Maximum Temp. ≤ 32°F	7	3	0	0	0	0	0	0	0	0	0	3	13
Days Minimum Temp. ≤ 32°F	26	20	14	5	0	0	0	0	0	6	14	22	107
Days Minimum Temp. ≤ 0°F	2	1	0	0	0	0	0	0	0	0	0	1	4
Heating Degree Days (base 65°F)	1,024	779	566	270	83	7	0	2	49	252	567	880	4,479
Cooling Degree Days (base 65°F)	0	0	4	18	92	257	386	340	159	23	1	0	1,280
Mean Precipitation (in.)	3.15	3.09	5.00	4.71	4.56	4.10	4.12	3.80	3.63	3.47	4.70	4.29	48.62
Days With ≥ 0.1" Precipitation	6	5	8	7	8	7	5	6	5	6	7	6	76
Days With ≥ 1.0" Precipitation	1	1	1	1	1	1	1	1	1	1	2	1	13
Mean Snowfall (in.)	4.3	4.6	2.1	trace	0.0	0.0	0.0	0.0	0.0	0.1	0.6	1.8	13.5
Days With ≥ 1.0" Snow Depth	3	2	1	0	0	0	0	0	0	0	0	*1*	7

Marshfield *Webster County*   Elevation: 1,489 ft.   Latitude: 37° 20' N   Longitude: 92° 55' W

	JAN	FEB	MAR	APR	MAY	JUN	JUL	AUG	SEP	OCT	NOV	DEC	YEAR
Mean Maximum Temp. (°F)	40.8	47.0	56.9	67.3	75.4	83.2	88.4	87.7	79.3	68.7	55.2	45.2	66.3
Mean Temp. (°F)	31.1	36.6	45.9	56.0	64.7	72.9	77.9	76.9	68.8	57.8	45.5	35.7	55.8
Mean Minimum Temp. (°F)	21.2	26.1	34.9	44.6	54.0	62.6	67.4	66.1	58.3	46.9	35.7	26.1	45.3
Extreme Maximum Temp. (°F)	72	82	88	91	95	100	105	103	100	91	80	75	105
Extreme Minimum Temp. (°F)	-20	-12	-2	19	29	43	47	47	31	19	4	-18	-20
Days Maximum Temp. ≥ 90°F	0	0	0	0	0	4	14	13	3	0	0	0	34
Days Maximum Temp. ≤ 32°F	8	4	1	0	0	0	0	0	0	0	1	4	18
Days Minimum Temp. ≤ 32°F	26	20	13	3	0	0	0	0	0	2	12	23	99
Days Minimum Temp. ≤ 0°F	2	1	0	0	0	0	0	0	0	0	0	1	4
Heating Degree Days (base 65°F)	1,045	797	588	288	91	9	1	1	56	243	581	902	4,602
Cooling Degree Days (base 65°F)	0	0	3	23	86	257	412	384	175	25	1	0	1,366
Mean Precipitation (in.)	2.21	2.09	3.77	4.29	4.73	4.33	3.67	3.10	4.47	3.76	4.20	3.08	43.70
Days With ≥ 0.1" Precipitation	5	5	7	7	8	6	5	5	6	6	6	5	71
Days With ≥ 1.0" Precipitation	1	0	1	1	1	1	1	1	2	1	1	1	12
Mean Snowfall (in.)	na	*3.4*	1.3	0.1	0.0	0.0	0.0	0.0	0.0	0.0	0.6	*1.4*	na
Days With ≥ 1.0" Snow Depth	na	na	1	0	0	0	0	0	0	0	0	*0*	na

Maryville 2 E *Nodaway County*   Elevation: 984 ft.   Latitude: 40° 21' N   Longitude: 94° 50' W

	JAN	FEB	MAR	APR	MAY	JUN	JUL	AUG	SEP	OCT	NOV	DEC	YEAR
Mean Maximum Temp. (°F)	32.3	38.6	50.2	62.9	73.4	83.1	87.6	85.4	77.9	66.3	49.7	36.9	62.0
Mean Temp. (°F)	21.9	27.8	38.6	50.6	61.6	71.2	75.6	73.1	64.8	53.0	38.9	27.1	50.4
Mean Minimum Temp. (°F)	11.5	16.6	27.0	38.3	49.6	59.2	63.6	60.8	51.6	39.6	28.1	17.3	38.6
Extreme Maximum Temp. (°F)	69	78	89	96	94	103	107	105	103	94	84	69	107
Extreme Minimum Temp. (°F)	-32	-28	-17	4	30	38	42	42	22	16	-11	-28	-32
Days Maximum Temp. ≥ 90°F	0	0	0	0	1	7	13	9	4	0	0	0	34
Days Maximum Temp. ≤ 32°F	15	9	3	0	0	0	0	0	0	0	3	10	40
Days Minimum Temp. ≤ 32°F	30	26	22	8	0	0	0	0	1	7	21	29	144
Days Minimum Temp. ≤ 0°F	7	4	1	0	0	0	0	0	0	0	0	4	16
Heating Degree Days (base 65°F)	1,330	1,044	812	437	155	21	3	7	111	380	779	1,167	6,246
Cooling Degree Days (base 65°F)	0	0	1	15	53	216	348	271	115	13	0	0	1,032
Mean Precipitation (in.)	0.86	0.94	2.34	3.21	4.69	4.12	5.14	3.89	4.24	3.01	2.33	1.30	36.07
Days With ≥ 0.1" Precipitation	3	3	5	6	8	7	7	6	6	5	5	3	64
Days With ≥ 1.0" Precipitation	0	0	1	1	1	2	2	1	1	1	1	0	11
Mean Snowfall (in.)	*4.8*	3.4	2.5	0.9	0.0	0.0	0.0	0.0	0.0	trace	0.8	3.6	*16.0*
Days With ≥ 1.0" Snow Depth	na	2	1	0	0	0	0	0	0	0	0	1	na

Mexico *Audrain County*   Elevation: 800 ft.   Latitude: 39° 11' N   Longitude: 91° 53' W

	JAN	FEB	MAR	APR	MAY	JUN	JUL	AUG	SEP	OCT	NOV	DEC	YEAR
Mean Maximum Temp. (°F)	34.8	41.0	52.9	65.2	74.5	83.9	89.2	87.1	79.1	67.6	53.2	40.5	64.1
Mean Temp. (°F)	25.2	30.4	41.7	53.5	63.2	72.6	77.5	75.2	66.9	55.2	42.9	31.0	52.9
Mean Minimum Temp. (°F)	15.5	19.8	30.4	41.7	51.9	61.3	65.8	63.3	54.7	42.8	32.5	21.5	41.8
Extreme Maximum Temp. (°F)	72	75	86	93	94	103	109	108	99	92	82	73	109
Extreme Minimum Temp. (°F)	-20	-18	-8	18	28	42	46	41	30	20	3	-25	-25
Days Maximum Temp. ≥ 90°F	0	0	0	0	0	6	16	12	4	0	0	0	38
Days Maximum Temp. ≤ 32°F	13	8	2	0	0	0	0	0	0	0	2	7	32
Days Minimum Temp. ≤ 32°F	29	24	19	5	0	0	0	0	0	4	16	26	123
Days Minimum Temp. ≤ 0°F	5	3	0	0	0	0	0	0	0	0	0	2	10
Heating Degree Days (base 65°F)	1,227	971	718	360	124	13	1	3	81	314	659	1,048	5,519
Cooling Degree Days (base 65°F)	0	0	3	21	72	256	405	343	145	15	1	0	1,261
Mean Precipitation (in.)	1.66	1.74	3.12	4.05	5.28	4.31	3.53	3.48	3.86	3.05	3.60	2.60	40.28
Days With ≥ 0.1" Precipitation	4	4	7	7	9	7	6	6	6	5	7	5	73
Days With ≥ 1.0" Precipitation	0	0	1	1	1	1	1	1	1	1	1	1	10
Mean Snowfall (in.)	7.1	5.8	3.3	0.4	0.0	0.0	0.0	0.0	0.0	trace	1.7	4.2	22.5
Days With ≥ 1.0" Snow Depth	8	5	1	0	0	0	0	0	0	0	1	3	*18*

Moberly *Randolph County*   Elevation: 839 ft.   Latitude: 39° 24' N   Longitude: 92° 26' W

	JAN	FEB	MAR	APR	MAY	JUN	JUL	AUG	SEP	OCT	NOV	DEC	YEAR
Mean Maximum Temp. (°F)	36.0	42.4	54.4	66.6	75.7	84.4	89.4	87.3	79.4	68.2	53.0	41.0	64.8
Mean Temp. (°F)	27.2	33.0	44.0	55.5	65.0	73.9	78.6	76.5	68.6	57.4	43.9	32.7	54.7
Mean Minimum Temp. (°F)	18.5	23.6	33.6	44.3	54.3	63.4	67.8	65.6	57.7	46.5	34.8	24.4	44.5
Extreme Maximum Temp. (°F)	72	82	87	92	92	102	109	107	98	91	80	71	109
Extreme Minimum Temp. (°F)	-21	-15	-8	17	31	44	48	45	34	18	1	-20	-21
Days Maximum Temp. ≥ 90°F	0	0	0	0	0	6	16	12	4	0	0	0	38
Days Maximum Temp. ≤ 32°F	12	7	1	0	0	0	0	0	0	0	1	6	27
Days Minimum Temp. ≤ 32°F	27	22	15	4	0	0	0	0	0	2	13	24	107
Days Minimum Temp. ≤ 0°F	3	1	0	0	0	0	0	0	0	0	0	1	5
Heating Degree Days (base 65°F)	1,164	896	650	308	88	6	1	1	57	257	627	994	5,049
Cooling Degree Days (base 65°F)	0	0	6	33	98	290	446	382	177	28	2	0	1,462
Mean Precipitation (in.)	1.66	1.81	3.10	4.24	4.99	4.13	3.89	3.70	4.25	3.22	3.04	2.31	40.34
Days With ≥ 0.1" Precipitation	4	4	6	7	8	6	5	6	6	5	6	4	67
Days With ≥ 1.0" Precipitation	0	0	1	1	1	1	1	1	1	1	1	1	10
Mean Snowfall (in.)	*7.1*	5.0	2.0	0.4	0.0	0.0	0.0	0.0	0.0	trace	1.1	2.9	*18.5*
Days With ≥ 1.0" Snow Depth	na	na	0	0	0	0	0	0	0	0	0	na	na

Monett 4 SW *Barry County*   Elevation: 1,377 ft.   Latitude: 36° 52' N   Longitude: 93° 58' W

	JAN	FEB	MAR	APR	MAY	JUN	JUL	AUG	SEP	OCT	NOV	DEC	YEAR
Mean Maximum Temp. (°F)	41.1	48.3	57.3	66.8	74.4	82.5	*88.6*	*87.7*	79.3	68.9	*55.6*	45.1	*66.3*
Mean Temp. (°F)	31.6	38.0	46.7	55.8	64.3	72.5	78.1	76.7	68.9	58.0	46.0	35.8	56.0
Mean Minimum Temp. (°F)	22.1	27.6	36.0	44.8	54.1	62.4	*67.6*	65.6	*58.3*	47.0	*36.3*	26.6	*45.7*
Extreme Maximum Temp. (°F)	74	79	85	90	90	100	*106*	*103*	103	*93*	*81*	75	*106*
Extreme Minimum Temp. (°F)	-16	-14	0	19	29	44	*50*	*47*	32	*17*	*4*	-13	*-16*
Days Maximum Temp. ≥ 90°F	0	0	0	0	0	3	*14*	*12*	4	0	*0*	0	*33*
Days Maximum Temp. ≤ 32°F	8	4	1	0	0	0	*0*	*0*	0	0	*1*	5	*19*
Days Minimum Temp. ≤ 32°F	25	18	12	3	0	0	*0*	*0*	0	1	*11*	22	*92*
Days Minimum Temp. ≤ 0°F	2	1	0	0	0	0	*0*	*0*	0	0	*0*	1	*4*
Heating Degree Days (base 65°F)	1,029	757	565	290	96	9	*0*	*1*	57	241	566	897	*4,508*
Cooling Degree Days (base 65°F)	0	0	4	20	82	254	421	387	187	27	*1*	0	*1,383*
Mean Precipitation (in.)	2.03	2.09	4.09	4.57	5.03	5.43	*3.06*	*3.66*	*5.00*	3.94	*4.27*	2.91	*46.08*
Days With ≥ 0.1" Precipitation	4	4	7	7	8	7	*4*	*5*	6	6	*5*	5	*68*
Days With ≥ 1.0" Precipitation	0	0	1	1	1	2	*1*	*1*	2	1	*1*	1	*12*
Mean Snowfall (in.)	*4.6*	3.3	2.0	trace	0.0	0.0	*0.0*	*0.0*	0.0	trace	*1.1*	1.8	*12.8*
Days With ≥ 1.0" Snow Depth	*6*	4	1	0	0	0	*0*	*0*	0	0	*1*	2	*14*

Mount Vernon M U SW Center *Lawrence County* Elevation: 1,187 ft. Latitude: 37° 04' N Longitude: 93° 53' W

	JAN	FEB	MAR	APR	MAY	JUN	JUL	AUG	SEP	OCT	NOV	DEC	YEAR
Mean Maximum Temp. (°F)	40.9	47.1	56.7	66.7	74.6	83.0	89.0	88.4	79.9	69.3	56.0	45.8	66.4
Mean Temp. (°F)	30.3	36.2	45.5	55.1	63.9	72.4	77.7	76.6	68.4	57.1	45.3	35.5	55.3
Mean Minimum Temp. (°F)	19.7	25.2	34.3	43.5	53.1	61.8	66.4	64.7	56.9	44.9	34.6	25.0	44.2
Extreme Maximum Temp. (°F)	74	79	85	89	90	100	106	105	103	91	82	75	106
Extreme Minimum Temp. (°F)	-16	-18	1	18	29	41	43	44	28	16	4	-17	-18
Days Maximum Temp. ≥ 90°F	0	0	0	0	0	5	15	14	4	0	0	0	38
Days Maximum Temp. ≤ 32°F	8	5	1	0	0	0	0	0	0	0	1	4	19
Days Minimum Temp. ≤ 32°F	27	21	14	4	0	0	0	0	0	4	14	24	108
Days Minimum Temp. ≤ 0°F	2	1	0	0	0	0	0	0	0	0	0	1	4
Heating Degree Days (base 65°F)	1,069	807	600	312	110	13	2	3	68	263	586	909	4,742
Cooling Degree Days (base 65°F)	0	0	3	21	83	250	408	376	174	23	2	0	1,340
Mean Precipitation (in.)	1.87	1.93	3.79	4.21	4.66	5.31	3.17	4.02	5.57	3.57	4.43	2.94	45.47
Days With ≥ 0.1" Precipitation	4	4	7	6	7	8	5	5	7	6	6	5	70
Days With ≥ 1.0" Precipitation	0	0	1	1	1	2	1	1	2	1	2	1	13
Mean Snowfall (in.)	na	3.3	2.4	trace	0.0	0.0	0.0	0.0	0.0	0.0	0.8	2.4	na
Days With ≥ 1.0" Snow Depth	na	3	1	0	0	0	0	0	0	0	0	2	na

Mountain Grove 2 N *Wright County* Elevation: 1,450 ft. Latitude: 37° 09' N Longitude: 92° 16' W

	JAN	FEB	MAR	APR	MAY	JUN	JUL	AUG	SEP	OCT	NOV	DEC	YEAR
Mean Maximum Temp. (°F)	39.9	46.7	56.2	66.7	74.6	82.5	87.9	87.2	79.2	68.7	54.7	44.5	65.7
Mean Temp. (°F)	30.4	36.2	45.2	55.3	63.8	72.0	76.9	75.6	67.9	57.0	44.8	35.0	55.0
Mean Minimum Temp. (°F)	20.8	25.7	34.2	43.9	52.9	61.4	65.9	63.9	56.5	45.2	34.8	25.6	44.2
Extreme Maximum Temp. (°F)	70	80	83	89	89	98	104	103	99	90	81	75	104
Extreme Minimum Temp. (°F)	-19	-10	-1	20	29	43	46	41	27	19	4	-19	-19
Days Maximum Temp. ≥ 90°F	0	0	0	0	0	3	13	12	3	0	0	0	31
Days Maximum Temp. ≤ 32°F	9	5	1	0	0	0	0	0	0	0	1	5	21
Days Minimum Temp. ≤ 32°F	27	20	14	4	0	0	0	0	0	3	13	23	104
Days Minimum Temp. ≤ 0°F	2	1	0	0	0	0	0	0	0	0	0	1	4
Heating Degree Days (base 65°F)	1,067	807	609	304	106	12	1	3	66	262	600	922	4,759
Cooling Degree Days (base 65°F)	0	0	2	17	67	222	374	338	150	18	1	0	1,189
Mean Precipitation (in.)	2.28	2.55	4.28	4.52	4.82	4.18	3.75	3.43	4.28	3.68	4.51	3.60	45.88
Days With ≥ 0.1" Precipitation	5	4	7	7	8	7	5	6	6	5	6	5	71
Days With ≥ 1.0" Precipitation	0	1	1	1	1	1	1	1	1	1	2	1	12
Mean Snowfall (in.)	5.0	2.9	2.6	0.5	0.0	0.0	0.0	0.0	0.0	trace	1.2	2.0	14.2
Days With ≥ 1.0" Snow Depth	10	6	3	0	0	0	0	0	0	0	1	4	24

Neosho *Newton County* Elevation: 1,010 ft. Latitude: 36° 52' N Longitude: 94° 22' W

	JAN	FEB	MAR	APR	MAY	JUN	JUL	AUG	SEP	OCT	NOV	DEC	YEAR
Mean Maximum Temp. (°F)	44.1	50.9	60.4	70.5	77.7	85.4	90.8	90.2	82.0	72.1	58.4	48.7	69.3
Mean Temp. (°F)	33.0	38.9	47.9	57.4	65.6	73.8	78.7	77.3	69.6	58.8	47.1	37.6	57.1
Mean Minimum Temp. (°F)	21.8	26.8	35.4	44.3	53.5	62.1	66.5	64.3	57.2	45.5	35.4	26.6	44.9
Extreme Maximum Temp. (°F)	76	87	89	95	93	100	107	105	105	92	85	76	107
Extreme Minimum Temp. (°F)	-18	-16	-2	17	29	38	44	40	27	17	4	-15	-18
Days Maximum Temp. ≥ 90°F	0	0	0	0	0	7	20	18	6	0	0	0	51
Days Maximum Temp. ≤ 32°F	6	3	0	0	0	0	0	0	0	0	1	3	13
Days Minimum Temp. ≤ 32°F	26	20	13	4	0	0	0	0	0	4	13	22	102
Days Minimum Temp. ≤ 0°F	2	1	0	0	0	0	0	0	0	0	0	1	4
Heating Degree Days (base 65°F)	986	732	530	256	78	7	1	2	53	223	535	842	4,245
Cooling Degree Days (base 65°F)	0	0	7	32	99	275	430	389	189	31	4	0	1,456
Mean Precipitation (in.)	1.95	2.21	3.87	4.49	4.97	4.90	3.20	3.67	5.21	4.10	4.36	2.99	45.92
Days With ≥ 0.1" Precipitation	4	4	6	7	8	7	5	5	6	5	5	5	67
Days With ≥ 1.0" Precipitation	0	0	1	1	2	2	1	1	2	1	1	1	13
Mean Snowfall (in.)	4.2	2.6	3.4	trace	0.0	0.0	0.0	0.0	0.0	trace	0.7	1.9	12.8
Days With ≥ 1.0" Snow Depth	na	na	0	0	0	0	0	0	0	0	0	0	na

Nevada Water Plant *Vernon County* Elevation: 816 ft. Latitude: 37° 50' N Longitude: 94° 22' W

	JAN	FEB	MAR	APR	MAY	JUN	JUL	AUG	SEP	OCT	NOV	DEC	YEAR
Mean Maximum Temp. (°F)	41.1	47.9	58.5	69.2	77.4	85.6	91.3	90.1	81.6	71.3	56.6	45.6	68.0
Mean Temp. (°F)	30.4	36.4	46.6	56.7	65.6	74.3	79.1	77.4	69.2	58.3	45.7	35.3	56.2
Mean Minimum Temp. (°F)	19.6	24.9	34.7	43.9	53.7	62.8	66.8	64.7	56.9	45.2	34.7	25.0	44.4
Extreme Maximum Temp. (°F)	72	82	89	95	94	103	110	107	102	94	84	74	110
Extreme Minimum Temp. (°F)	-20	-21	-3	17	28	42	44	43	25	19	1	-25	-25
Days Maximum Temp. ≥ 90°F	0	0	0	0	1	9	20	17	6	0	0	0	53
Days Maximum Temp. ≤ 32°F	8	5	1	0	0	0	0	0	0	0	1	4	19
Days Minimum Temp. ≤ 32°F	27	21	14	4	0	0	0	0	0	4	14	24	108
Days Minimum Temp. ≤ 0°F	2	1	0	0	0	0	0	0	0	0	0	1	4
Heating Degree Days (base 65°F)	1,067	800	568	275	79	6	1	1	58	236	575	914	4,580
Cooling Degree Days (base 65°F)	0	0	5	27	102	289	444	390	185	29	3	0	1,474
Mean Precipitation (in.)	1.66	1.93	3.57	4.52	5.31	5.60	3.86	4.06	4.39	4.21	3.54	2.36	45.01
Days With ≥ 0.1" Precipitation	4	4	6	6	8	7	5	5	7	6	5	4	67
Days With ≥ 1.0" Precipitation	0	1	1	1	2	2	1	1	1	1	1	1	13
Mean Snowfall (in.)	4.9	3.2	2.0	trace	0.0	0.0	0.0	0.0	0.0	trace	0.8	2.5	13.4
Days With ≥ 1.0" Snow Depth	9	5	1	0	0	0	0	0	0	0	0	3	18

New Franklin 1 W *Howard County*   Elevation: 639 ft.   Latitude: 39° 01' N   Longitude: 92° 45' W

	JAN	FEB	MAR	APR	MAY	JUN	JUL	AUG	SEP	OCT	NOV	DEC	YEAR
Mean Maximum Temp. (°F)	37.3	43.8	55.2	66.4	75.8	84.5	89.8	87.8	80.2	69.3	54.3	42.3	65.6
Mean Temp. (°F)	27.6	33.3	44.2	55.0	64.7	73.8	78.5	76.3	68.3	57.0	44.3	33.0	54.7
Mean Minimum Temp. (°F)	17.8	22.7	33.1	43.5	53.6	63.0	67.2	64.7	56.4	44.5	34.3	23.7	43.7
Extreme Maximum Temp. (°F)	72	81	85	92	92	104	109	106	99	94	83	73	109
Extreme Minimum Temp. (°F)	-24	-21	-12	18	29	43	48	43	31	22	-5	-22	-24
Days Maximum Temp. ≥ 90°F	0	0	0	0	0	7	16	13	5	0	0	0	41
Days Maximum Temp. ≤ 32°F	11	6	1	0	0	0	0	0	0	0	1	5	24
Days Minimum Temp. ≤ 32°F	28	23	16	3	0	0	0	0	0	3	13	25	111
Days Minimum Temp. ≤ 0°F	3	2	0	0	0	0	0	0	0	0	0	1	6
Heating Degree Days (base 65°F)	1,154	888	642	319	93	7	1	2	66	268	616	985	5,041
Cooling Degree Days (base 65°F)	0	0	3	24	87	277	425	352	162	22	2	0	1,354
Mean Precipitation (in.)	1.58	1.70	3.00	3.98	4.90	4.00	3.41	4.24	4.02	3.17	2.88	2.13	39.01
Days With ≥ 0.1" Precipitation	4	4	6	7	8	7	5	6	6	6	5	4	68
Days With ≥ 1.0" Precipitation	0	0	1	1	1	1	1	1	1	1	1	1	10
Mean Snowfall (in.)	na	3.9	1.4	0.1	0.0	0.0	0.0	0.0	0.0	0.0	1.1	2.3	na
Days With ≥ 1.0" Snow Depth	8	6	1	0	0	0	0	0	0	0	1	4	20

New Madrid *New Madrid County*   Elevation: 308 ft.   Latitude: 36° 35' N   Longitude: 89° 31' W

	JAN	FEB	MAR	APR	MAY	JUN	JUL	AUG	SEP	OCT	NOV	DEC	YEAR
Mean Maximum Temp. (°F)	41.2	47.1	57.0	68.5	78.2	86.9	91.2	89.5	82.9	71.6	57.3	46.6	68.2
Mean Temp. (°F)	33.0	38.0	47.5	58.0	67.7	76.3	80.5	78.3	71.1	59.4	47.9	37.9	58.0
Mean Minimum Temp. (°F)	24.7	28.9	37.9	47.4	57.2	65.5	69.8	67.0	59.4	47.1	38.5	29.3	47.7
Extreme Maximum Temp. (°F)	71	77	84	94	94	104	106	104	101	92	85	74	106
Extreme Minimum Temp. (°F)	-14	-4	8	25	35	47	53	42	35	25	13	-11	-14
Days Maximum Temp. ≥ 90°F	0	0	0	0	2	11	20	17	7	0	0	0	57
Days Maximum Temp. ≤ 32°F	7	4	0	0	0	0	0	0	0	0	0	3	14
Days Minimum Temp. ≤ 32°F	24	18	10	1	0	0	0	0	0	2	8	19	82
Days Minimum Temp. ≤ 0°F	1	0	0	0	0	0	0	0	0	0	0	0	1
Heating Degree Days (base 65°F)	986	756	539	234	55	3	0	1	33	207	508	832	4,154
Cooling Degree Days (base 65°F)	0	0	4	31	146	353	500	432	218	42	2	0	1,728
Mean Precipitation (in.)	3.23	3.69	4.77	5.48	5.11	4.25	4.03	2.70	3.41	3.87	4.85	4.85	50.24
Days With ≥ 0.1" Precipitation	5	6	8	8	7	6	6	4	5	5	7	7	74
Days With ≥ 1.0" Precipitation	1	1	1	2	2	1	1	1	1	1	2	1	15
Mean Snowfall (in.)	1.9	1.7	0.3	0.0	0.0	0.0	0.0	0.0	0.0	0.0	trace	0.4	4.3
Days With ≥ 1.0" Snow Depth	na	na	0	0	0	0	0	0	0	0	0	na	na

Osceola *St. Clair County*   Elevation: 764 ft.   Latitude: 38° 03' N   Longitude: 93° 42' W

	JAN	FEB	MAR	APR	MAY	JUN	JUL	AUG	SEP	OCT	NOV	DEC	YEAR
Mean Maximum Temp. (°F)	40.4	47.1	58.0	68.6	76.7	85.3	90.9	89.8	80.9	70.2	55.9	44.9	67.4
Mean Temp. (°F)	30.6	36.5	46.7	56.8	65.4	74.2	79.4	77.9	69.5	58.4	45.9	35.5	56.4
Mean Minimum Temp. (°F)	20.7	25.8	35.4	45.0	54.0	63.1	67.8	66.0	58.0	46.5	35.9	26.0	45.3
Extreme Maximum Temp. (°F)	76	83	90	92	94	104	110	106	102	94	84	74	110
Extreme Minimum Temp. (°F)	-18	-20	-2	19	27	41	44	46	29	20	0	-25	-25
Days Maximum Temp. ≥ 90°F	0	0	0	0	1	9	19	17	6	0	0	0	52
Days Maximum Temp. ≤ 32°F	9	5	1	0	0	0	0	0	0	0	1	4	20
Days Minimum Temp. ≤ 32°F	26	20	13	3	0	0	0	0	0	3	12	22	99
Days Minimum Temp. ≤ 0°F	2	1	0	0	0	0	0	0	0	0	0	1	4
Heating Degree Days (base 65°F)	1,061	799	566	270	80	5	1	1	52	231	570	909	4,545
Cooling Degree Days (base 65°F)	0	0	7	31	100	300	465	412	194	32	4	0	1,545
Mean Precipitation (in.)	1.74	1.96	3.04	4.38	4.69	4.50	3.31	4.11	4.26	3.96	3.62	2.51	42.08
Days With ≥ 0.1" Precipitation	4	4	6	7	7	7	5	5	6	6	5	5	67
Days With ≥ 1.0" Precipitation	0	0	1	1	1	2	1	1	1	1	1	1	11
Mean Snowfall (in.)	5.9	4.3	1.8	0.3	0.0	0.0	0.0	0.0	0.0	trace	1.1	2.9	16.3
Days With ≥ 1.0" Snow Depth	8	5	1	0	0	0	0	0	0	0	0	3	17

Ozark Beach *Taney County*   Elevation: 698 ft.   Latitude: 36° 40' N   Longitude: 93° 08' W

	JAN	FEB	MAR	APR	MAY	JUN	JUL	AUG	SEP	OCT	NOV	DEC	YEAR
Mean Maximum Temp. (°F)	44.6	50.7	60.0	70.5	77.9	86.0	91.3	90.3	82.5	72.4	59.3	48.9	69.5
Mean Temp. (°F)	32.5	37.5	46.3	55.8	64.1	72.7	77.3	76.0	68.8	57.7	46.5	37.2	56.0
Mean Minimum Temp. (°F)	20.3	24.3	32.5	41.1	50.1	59.4	63.5	61.8	55.0	42.9	33.7	25.4	42.5
Extreme Maximum Temp. (°F)	74	81	87	94	93	103	109	107	104	94	85	78	109
Extreme Minimum Temp. (°F)	-15	-12	5	20	32	40	49	40	32	22	6	-12	-15
Days Maximum Temp. ≥ 90°F	0	0	0	0	1	10	21	18	7	1	0	0	58
Days Maximum Temp. ≤ 32°F	5	3	0	0	0	0	0	0	0	0	0	3	11
Days Minimum Temp. ≤ 32°F	27	23	17	5	0	0	0	0	0	4	15	24	115
Days Minimum Temp. ≤ 0°F	2	0	0	0	0	0	0	0	0	0	0	1	3
Heating Degree Days (base 65°F)	1,003	769	575	284	96	8	1	2	49	240	550	856	4,433
Cooling Degree Days (base 65°F)	0	0	2	14	73	243	390	355	163	17	1	0	1,258
Mean Precipitation (in.)	2.26	2.40	4.00	4.02	4.31	4.48	3.45	3.19	4.40	3.12	4.58	3.14	43.35
Days With ≥ 0.1" Precipitation	4	4	7	7	8	7	5	5	6	5	6	5	69
Days With ≥ 1.0" Precipitation	1	1	1	1	1	1	1	1	1	1	2	1	13
Mean Snowfall (in.)	3.7	2.5	2.2	trace	0.0	0.0	0.0	0.0	0.0	trace	0.7	1.2	10.3
Days With ≥ 1.0" Snow Depth	4	3	1	0	0	0	0	0	0	0	0	1	9

Pomme De Terre Dam *Hickory County* Elevation: 898 ft. Latitude: 37° 54' N Longitude: 93° 19' W

	JAN	FEB	MAR	APR	MAY	JUN	JUL	AUG	SEP	OCT	NOV	DEC	YEAR
Mean Maximum Temp. (°F)	na	na	56.4	67.1	76.0	84.3	90.4	89.4	80.5	69.7	55.5	na	na
Mean Temp. (°F)	na	na	44.9	55.4	64.7	73.7	79.1	77.7	69.1	57.7	45.5	na	na
Mean Minimum Temp. (°F)	na	23.5	33.2	43.7	53.3	63.0	67.9	65.9	57.6	45.6	35.5	na	na
Extreme Maximum Temp. (°F)	69	79	86	92	94	106	111	107	103	93	83	72	111
Extreme Minimum Temp. (°F)	-17	-21	-3	18	30	41	46	45	30	20	4	-22	-22
Days Maximum Temp. ≥ 90°F	0	0	0	0	1	7	18	16	5	0	0	0	47
Days Maximum Temp. ≤ 32°F	7	5	1	0	0	0	0	0	0	0	1	4	18
Days Minimum Temp. ≤ 32°F	23	19	15	4	0	0	0	0	0	3	12	21	97
Days Minimum Temp. ≤ 0°F	2	1	0	0	0	0	0	0	0	0	0	1	4
Heating Degree Days (base 65°F)	na	na	619	305	95	10	1	1	63	251	580	na	na
Cooling Degree Days (base 65°F)	na	na	2	24	91	279	453	404	192	29	2	na	na
Mean Precipitation (in.)	1.65	1.95	3.29	4.18	4.96	4.00	3.76	3.18	4.45	3.80	3.44	2.54	41.20
Days With ≥ 0.1" Precipitation	3	3	6	7	8	7	6	5	6	6	5	3	65
Days With ≥ 1.0" Precipitation	0	0	1	1	1	1	1	1	1	1	1	0	9
Mean Snowfall (in.)	na	na	1.0	0.1	0.0	0.0	0.0	0.0	0.0	0.0	0.5	1.6	na
Days With ≥ 1.0" Snow Depth	na	na	1	0	0	0	0	0	0	0	0	1	na

Portageville *Pemiscot County* Elevation: 278 ft. Latitude: 36° 25' N Longitude: 89° 42' W

	JAN	FEB	MAR	APR	MAY	JUN	JUL	AUG	SEP	OCT	NOV	DEC	YEAR
Mean Maximum Temp. (°F)	41.6	47.7	57.4	68.9	78.1	86.7	90.3	88.1	81.7	71.6	57.8	46.9	68.1
Mean Temp. (°F)	33.8	38.9	48.3	58.7	68.0	76.5	80.2	77.8	71.0	59.8	48.7	38.9	58.4
Mean Minimum Temp. (°F)	26.0	30.1	39.1	48.5	57.9	66.3	70.1	67.6	60.3	48.0	39.6	30.9	48.7
Extreme Maximum Temp. (°F)	73	76	82	92	96	105	106	102	100	91	83	77	106
Extreme Minimum Temp. (°F)	-15	-3	11	28	37	47	52	50	38	25	13	-9	-15
Days Maximum Temp. ≥ 90°F	0	0	0	0	2	11	19	13	5	0	0	0	50
Days Maximum Temp. ≤ 32°F	7	4	1	0	0	0	0	0	0	0	0	3	15
Days Minimum Temp. ≤ 32°F	22	17	9	1	0	0	0	0	0	1	7	18	75
Days Minimum Temp. ≤ 0°F	1	0	0	0	0	0	0	0	0	0	0	0	1
Heating Degree Days (base 65°F)	960	730	516	220	51	2	0	0	32	198	486	802	3,997
Cooling Degree Days (base 65°F)	0	0	6	36	156	364	494	423	219	44	4	1	1,747
Mean Precipitation (in.)	3.11	3.46	4.46	5.17	4.75	4.35	3.54	2.92	3.28	3.72	4.40	4.42	47.58
Days With ≥ 0.1" Precipitation	6	5	8	8	7	7	6	4	5	5	6	7	74
Days With ≥ 1.0" Precipitation	1	1	1	1	1	1	1	1	1	1	1	1	12
Mean Snowfall (in.)	3.8	3.0	1.3	trace	0.0	0.0	0.0	0.0	0.0	trace	0.3	1.3	9.7
Days With ≥ 1.0" Snow Depth	5	3	0	0	0	0	0	0	0	0	0	1	9

Princeton 6 SW *Mercer County* Elevation: 977 ft. Latitude: 40° 22' N Longitude: 93° 44' W

	JAN	FEB	MAR	APR	MAY	JUN	JUL	AUG	SEP	OCT	NOV	DEC	YEAR
Mean Maximum Temp. (°F)	33.3	39.4	51.6	64.1	73.4	82.5	87.1	85.3	77.2	65.8	49.8	37.2	62.2
Mean Temp. (°F)	23.8	29.3	40.8	52.6	62.4	71.5	75.9	73.8	65.6	54.1	40.0	28.2	51.5
Mean Minimum Temp. (°F)	14.3	19.2	30.0	41.1	51.2	60.5	64.6	62.3	54.0	42.3	30.2	19.1	40.7
Extreme Maximum Temp. (°F)	72	75	87	92	93	106	107	110	100	90	80	70	110
Extreme Minimum Temp. (°F)	-26	-24	-13	10	28	41	42	35	25	15	-5	-25	-26
Days Maximum Temp. ≥ 90°F	0	0	0	0	0	4	12	9	3	0	0	0	28
Days Maximum Temp. ≤ 32°F	14	9	2	0	0	0	0	0	0	0	2	10	37
Days Minimum Temp. ≤ 32°F	29	24	18	6	0	0	0	0	0	5	18	28	128
Days Minimum Temp. ≤ 0°F	6	3	0	0	0	0	0	0	0	0	0	3	12
Heating Degree Days (base 65°F)	1,271	1,000	744	379	136	14	1	5	93	343	744	1,135	5,865
Cooling Degree Days (base 65°F)	0	0	1	16	53	210	337	282	114	12	0	0	1,025
Mean Precipitation (in.)	0.86	1.05	2.37	3.63	4.56	3.97	4.97	4.01	4.08	3.08	2.23	1.47	36.28
Days With ≥ 0.1" Precipitation	3	3	5	7	8	7	6	6	6	6	5	4	66
Days With ≥ 1.0" Precipitation	0	0	0	1	1	1	2	1	1	1	0	0	8
Mean Snowfall (in.)	na	na	0.5	0.7	0.0	0.0	0.0	0.0	0.0	trace	0.7	na	na
Days With ≥ 1.0" Snow Depth	na	na	0	0	0	0	0	0	0	0	0	na	na

Rolla Univ. of Missouri *Phelps County* Elevation: 1,164 ft. Latitude: 37° 57' N Longitude: 91° 47' W

	JAN	FEB	MAR	APR	MAY	JUN	JUL	AUG	SEP	OCT	NOV	DEC	YEAR
Mean Maximum Temp. (°F)	39.9	45.7	55.1	66.1	75.0	83.7	89.1	88.0	79.2	68.8	54.8	43.5	65.7
Mean Temp. (°F)	30.9	35.7	44.8	55.5	64.8	73.6	78.7	77.1	68.5	57.8	45.6	34.8	55.6
Mean Minimum Temp. (°F)	21.3	25.6	34.5	44.9	54.4	63.4	68.2	66.2	58.0	46.6	36.4	26.0	45.5
Extreme Maximum Temp. (°F)	72	81	86	93	92	100	108	106	100	92	83	77	108
Extreme Minimum Temp. (°F)	-19	-14	3	22	34	45	51	46	33	22	5	-19	-19
Days Maximum Temp. ≥ 90°F	0	0	0	0	1	6	16	13	4	0	0	0	40
Days Maximum Temp. ≤ 32°F	9	6	1	0	0	0	0	0	0	0	1	6	23
Days Minimum Temp. ≤ 32°F	26	20	15	3	0	0	0	0	0	1	11	23	99
Days Minimum Temp. ≤ 0°F	2	1	0	0	0	0	0	0	0	0	0	1	4
Heating Degree Days (base 65°F)	1,052	820	624	308	93	8	1	2	62	249	578	931	4,728
Cooling Degree Days (base 65°F)	0	0	5	30	96	271	436	383	174	30	3	0	1,428
Mean Precipitation (in.)	2.28	2.34	3.62	4.36	4.90	4.14	4.45	3.88	3.91	3.52	4.47	3.35	45.22
Days With ≥ 0.1" Precipitation	5	5	7	8	8	7	6	5	5	6	6	5	73
Days With ≥ 1.0" Precipitation	1	0	1	1	1	1	1	1	1	1	1	1	11
Mean Snowfall (in.)	6.3	4.8	2.9	0.5	0.0	0.0	0.0	0.0	0.0	trace	1.7	4.2	20.4
Days With ≥ 1.0" Snow Depth	9	6	2	0	0	0	0	0	0	0	1	5	23

Salisbury *Chariton County*   Elevation: 728 ft.   Latitude: 39° 25' N   Longitude: 92° 49' W

	JAN	FEB	MAR	APR	MAY	JUN	JUL	AUG	SEP	OCT	NOV	DEC	YEAR
Mean Maximum Temp. (°F)	34.9	41.9	53.6	65.1	75.1	83.7	88.4	86.8	79.2	68.0	52.6	40.6	64.2
Mean Temp. (°F)	25.6	31.8	42.8	53.8	63.8	72.7	77.3	75.2	67.2	55.8	42.8	31.6	53.4
Mean Minimum Temp. (°F)	16.2	21.7	31.9	42.4	52.4	61.8	66.1	63.4	55.1	43.7	32.8	22.5	42.5
Extreme Maximum Temp. (°F)	72	81	86	93	95	104	109	107	100	93	82	71	109
Extreme Minimum Temp. (°F)	-21	-21	-8	16	29	40	46	36	25	20	-8	-28	-28
Days Maximum Temp. ≥ 90°F	0	0	0	0	0	6	14	11	4	0	0	0	35
Days Maximum Temp. ≤ 32°F	13	7	2	0	0	0	0	0	0	0	1	7	30
Days Minimum Temp. ≤ 32°F	29	23	17	5	0	0	0	0	0	4	15	26	119
Days Minimum Temp. ≤ 0°F	4	2	0	0	0	0	0	0	0	0	0	2	8
Heating Degree Days (base 65°F)	1,215	931	685	352	111	12	1	4	77	299	662	1,029	5,378
Cooling Degree Days (base 65°F)	0	0	3	21	77	249	387	324	143	22	1	0	1,227
Mean Precipitation (in.)	1.56	1.74	2.84	3.95	5.24	4.44	3.94	3.92	4.74	3.30	3.16	2.25	41.08
Days With ≥ 0.1" Precipitation	4	4	6	7	9	7	6	6	6	5	6	5	71
Days With ≥ 1.0" Precipitation	0	0	0	1	1	1	1	2	1	1	1	1	10
Mean Snowfall (in.)	7.2	5.0	2.8	0.6	0.0	0.0	0.0	0.0	0.0	trace	1.5	4.1	21.2
Days With ≥ 1.0" Snow Depth	10	7	2	0	0	0	0	0	0	0	1	3	23

Saverton Lock & Dam 22 *Ralls County*   Elevation: 469 ft.   Latitude: 39° 38' N   Longitude: 91° 15' W

	JAN	FEB	MAR	APR	MAY	JUN	JUL	AUG	SEP	OCT	NOV	DEC	YEAR
Mean Maximum Temp. (°F)	34.7	40.5	52.2	64.6	74.6	83.8	88.7	86.4	78.7	67.3	52.5	40.2	63.7
Mean Temp. (°F)	26.1	31.4	42.3	54.1	64.3	73.6	78.4	76.2	68.3	56.8	43.7	32.0	53.9
Mean Minimum Temp. (°F)	17.5	22.2	32.3	43.7	53.9	63.4	68.1	66.0	57.9	46.3	34.8	23.7	44.1
Extreme Maximum Temp. (°F)	72	82	88	93	96	105	107	106	100	91	81	74	107
Extreme Minimum Temp. (°F)	-22	-19	-11	22	35	45	50	48	36	25	4	-18	-22
Days Maximum Temp. ≥ 90°F	0	0	0	0	1	7	15	10	4	0	0	0	37
Days Maximum Temp. ≤ 32°F	13	8	2	0	0	0	0	0	0	0	1	7	31
Days Minimum Temp. ≤ 32°F	28	23	17	3	0	0	0	0	0	1	13	25	110
Days Minimum Temp. ≤ 0°F	4	2	0	0	0	0	0	0	0	0	0	2	8
Heating Degree Days (base 65°F)	1,200	945	702	344	104	9	0	1	57	271	636	1,019	5,288
Cooling Degree Days (base 65°F)	0	0	4	20	80	267	420	361	160	21	1	0	1,334
Mean Precipitation (in.)	1.35	1.66	2.99	3.87	4.76	3.38	3.69	3.81	3.95	2.97	3.24	2.27	37.94
Days With ≥ 0.1" Precipitation	4	4	6	7	8	6	6	6	6	6	6	4	69
Days With ≥ 1.0" Precipitation	0	0	1	1	2	1	1	1	1	1	1	1	11
Mean Snowfall (in.)	3.0	3.4	1.8	0.1	0.0	0.0	0.0	0.0	0.0	trace	0.4	2.7	11.4
Days With ≥ 1.0" Snow Depth	9	7	2	0	0	0	0	0	0	0	0	4	22

Sedalia Water Plant *Pettis County*   Elevation: 777 ft.   Latitude: 38° 40' N   Longitude: 93° 13' W

	JAN	FEB	MAR	APR	MAY	JUN	JUL	AUG	SEP	OCT	NOV	DEC	YEAR
Mean Maximum Temp. (°F)	36.9	43.0	54.2	65.4	74.4	83.4	88.8	87.4	79.5	68.1	53.6	42.1	64.7
Mean Temp. (°F)	26.5	32.0	42.7	53.4	62.9	72.2	77.1	75.0	66.9	55.2	42.7	32.2	53.2
Mean Minimum Temp. (°F)	16.1	21.0	31.2	41.3	51.3	61.0	65.3	62.5	54.2	42.2	31.8	22.2	41.7
Extreme Maximum Temp. (°F)	71	77	84	91	91	105	107	107	99	93	81	74	107
Extreme Minimum Temp. (°F)	-23	-27	-17	17	28	41	44	39	28	20	-6	-28	-28
Days Maximum Temp. ≥ 90°F	0	0	0	0	0	6	16	13	5	0	0	0	40
Days Maximum Temp. ≤ 32°F	11	7	1	0	0	0	0	0	0	0	1	6	26
Days Minimum Temp. ≤ 32°F	29	24	18	6	0	0	0	0	1	6	17	26	127
Days Minimum Temp. ≤ 0°F	4	2	0	0	0	0	0	0	0	0	0	1	7
Heating Degree Days (base 65°F)	1,187	925	686	362	129	15	2	4	86	317	663	1,011	5,387
Cooling Degree Days (base 65°F)	0	0	3	18	63	235	380	312	135	16	1	0	1,163
Mean Precipitation (in.)	1.57	1.72	3.01	4.15	5.30	4.95	4.32	3.63	4.09	3.61	3.50	2.28	42.13
Days With ≥ 0.1" Precipitation	4	4	6	7	8	7	5	5	6	6	6	5	69
Days With ≥ 1.0" Precipitation	0	0	0	1	2	2	1	1	1	1	1	0	10
Mean Snowfall (in.)	4.3	3.4	1.0	0.5	0.0	0.0	0.0	0.0	0.0	0.0	1.1	1.5	11.8
Days With ≥ 1.0" Snow Depth	6	5	1	0	0	0	0	0	0	0	1	2	15

Spickard *Grundy County*   Elevation: 872 ft.   Latitude: 40° 15' N   Longitude: 93° 43' W

	JAN	FEB	MAR	APR	MAY	JUN	JUL	AUG	SEP	OCT	NOV	DEC	YEAR
Mean Maximum Temp. (°F)	32.7	39.2	51.5	63.7	73.3	83.2	88.2	86.3	78.1	66.8	50.1	37.7	62.6
Mean Temp. (°F)	22.9	29.0	40.4	52.0	62.0	71.8	76.4	74.1	65.5	54.0	39.9	28.0	51.3
Mean Minimum Temp. (°F)	13.0	18.7	29.2	40.2	50.7	60.3	64.5	62.0	52.9	41.1	29.6	18.3	40.0
Extreme Maximum Temp. (°F)	64	76	88	93	94	103	107	107	98	91	81	69	107
Extreme Minimum Temp. (°F)	-30	-24	-15	8	29	38	43	37	27	14	-9	-28	-30
Days Maximum Temp. ≥ 90°F	0	0	0	0	0	6	13	10	3	0	0	0	32
Days Maximum Temp. ≤ 32°F	14	9	2	0	0	0	0	0	0	0	2	9	36
Days Minimum Temp. ≤ 32°F	30	25	19	7	0	0	0	0	1	6	19	28	135
Days Minimum Temp. ≤ 0°F	6	3	0	0	0	0	0	0	0	0	0	3	12
Heating Degree Days (base 65°F)	1,299	1,012	759	399	144	17	2	6	100	351	748	1,141	5,978
Cooling Degree Days (base 65°F)	0	0	2	14	54	218	358	296	119	12	0	0	1,073
Mean Precipitation (in.)	1.03	1.02	2.59	3.49	4.90	4.19	4.88	3.75	4.05	3.18	2.42	1.62	37.12
Days With ≥ 0.1" Precipitation	3	3	6	6	8	7	6	5	7	5	5	4	65
Days With ≥ 1.0" Precipitation	0	0	0	1	1	1	2	1	1	1	1	0	9
Mean Snowfall (in.)	5.6	4.3	2.9	0.3	0.0	0.0	0.0	0.0	0.0	0.0	0.8	3.0	16.9
Days With ≥ 1.0" Snow Depth	na	9	3	0	0	0	0	0	0	0	0	4	na

Steelville 2 N *Crawford County*   Elevation: 698 ft.   Latitude: 38° 00' N   Longitude: 91° 22' W

	JAN	FEB	MAR	APR	MAY	JUN	JUL	AUG	SEP	OCT	NOV	DEC	YEAR
Mean Maximum Temp. (°F)	40.2	46.8	57.1	68.9	76.9	84.3	89.4	87.9	80.1	69.5	56.3	44.8	66.9
Mean Temp. (°F)	28.1	33.5	42.9	53.6	62.2	70.9	75.8	74.0	65.9	54.2	43.1	32.9	53.1
Mean Minimum Temp. (°F)	16.0	20.2	28.6	38.3	47.5	57.3	62.1	60.1	51.6	38.9	29.8	20.8	39.3
Extreme Maximum Temp. (°F)	75	84	89	95	94	102	111	110	100	92	85	76	111
Extreme Minimum Temp. (°F)	-31	-22	-15	13	22	32	43	37	24	13	-3	-29	-31
Days Maximum Temp. ≥ 90°F	0	0	0	1	1	7	17	12	5	0	0	0	43
Days Maximum Temp. ≤ 32°F	9	5	1	0	0	0	0	0	0	0	1	5	21
Days Minimum Temp. ≤ 32°F	28	24	20	10	2	0	0	0	1	10	18	25	138
Days Minimum Temp. ≤ 0°F	4	2	0	0	0	0	0	0	0	0	0	2	8
Heating Degree Days (base 65°F)	1,137	883	682	356	144	22	3	6	95	341	652	989	5,310
Cooling Degree Days (base 65°F)	0	0	4	17	62	205	345	292	119	12	1	0	1,057
Mean Precipitation (in.)	2.06	2.29	3.54	4.34	4.56	3.90	3.79	3.69	3.65	3.40	3.90	2.86	41.98
Days With ≥ 0.1" Precipitation	4	4	7	7	7	6	6	5	5	6	7	5	69
Days With ≥ 1.0" Precipitation	0	0	1	1	1	1	1	1	1	1	1	1	10
Mean Snowfall (in.)	5.1	3.4	1.9	0.1	0.0	0.0	0.0	0.0	0.0	trace	0.8	2.6	13.9
Days With ≥ 1.0" Snow Depth	8	5	1	0	0	0	0	0	0	0	1	3	18

Steffenville *Lewis County*   Elevation: 688 ft.   Latitude: 39° 58' N   Longitude: 91° 53' W

	JAN	FEB	MAR	APR	MAY	JUN	JUL	AUG	SEP	OCT	NOV	DEC	YEAR
Mean Maximum Temp. (°F)	33.9	40.2	52.9	65.0	74.1	83.1	88.0	86.2	79.0	67.1	51.9	38.8	63.4
Mean Temp. (°F)	24.8	30.4	42.1	53.5	63.0	72.3	76.9	74.7	67.1	55.4	42.3	30.3	52.7
Mean Minimum Temp. (°F)	15.6	20.6	31.2	41.9	51.9	61.5	65.8	63.2	55.1	43.7	32.6	21.7	42.1
Extreme Maximum Temp. (°F)	73	74	86	91	91	103	105	106	99	94	79	70	106
Extreme Minimum Temp. (°F)	-21	-20	-5	15	29	43	46	39	28	17	3	-26	-26
Days Maximum Temp. ≥ 90°F	0	0	0	0	0	5	12	10	3	0	0	0	30
Days Maximum Temp. ≤ 32°F	13	8	2	0	0	0	0	0	0	0	2	8	33
Days Minimum Temp. ≤ 32°F	28	23	18	5	0	0	0	0	0	4	16	26	120
Days Minimum Temp. ≤ 0°F	6	3	0	0	0	0	0	0	0	0	0	2	11
Heating Degree Days (base 65°F)	1,241	969	707	361	124	11	1	4	76	310	676	1,069	5,549
Cooling Degree Days (base 65°F)	0	0	4	21	69	243	382	328	149	21	1	0	1,218
Mean Precipitation (in.)	1.32	1.38	2.73	3.40	4.92	3.36	3.91	3.59	3.95	3.04	3.09	2.02	36.71
Days With ≥ 0.1" Precipitation	3	3	5	7	8	6	7	6	6	5	5	4	65
Days With ≥ 1.0" Precipitation	0	0	0	1	2	1	1	1	1	1	1	1	10
Mean Snowfall (in.)	7.0	5.2	2.4	0.8	0.0	0.0	0.0	0.0	0.0	trace	1.4	3.9	20.7
Days With ≥ 1.0" Snow Depth	14	10	2	0	0	0	0	0	0	0	1	6	33

Stockton Dam *Cedar County*   Elevation: 921 ft.   Latitude: 37° 42' N   Longitude: 93° 46' W

	JAN	FEB	MAR	APR	MAY	JUN	JUL	AUG	SEP	OCT	NOV	DEC	YEAR
Mean Maximum Temp. (°F)	39.8	45.7	56.6	67.1	76.0	84.3	90.2	89.6	80.8	70.0	55.6	45.0	66.7
Mean Temp. (°F)	30.1	35.3	45.6	55.8	65.3	74.1	79.5	78.4	69.7	58.3	45.7	35.6	56.1
Mean Minimum Temp. (°F)	20.5	24.9	34.1	44.4	54.4	63.8	69.0	67.1	58.6	46.5	36.0	26.0	45.4
Extreme Maximum Temp. (°F)	70	80	87	91	93	104	108	107	103	92	83	75	108
Extreme Minimum Temp. (°F)	-16	-15	-1	19	30	42	47	47	31	19	5	-18	-18
Days Maximum Temp. ≥ 90°F	0	0	0	0	1	7	18	17	6	0	0	0	49
Days Maximum Temp. ≤ 32°F	8	5	1	0	0	0	0	0	0	0	1	5	20
Days Minimum Temp. ≤ 32°F	27	21	13	3	0	0	0	0	0	2	12	22	100
Days Minimum Temp. ≤ 0°F	2	1	0	0	0	0	0	0	0	0	0	1	4
Heating Degree Days (base 65°F)	1,076	831	597	290	87	9	1	1	58	236	573	905	4,664
Cooling Degree Days (base 65°F)	0	0	2	19	106	290	462	431	207	34	3	0	1,554
Mean Precipitation (in.)	1.76	2.33	3.51	4.03	5.14	4.73	3.65	3.96	4.61	4.27	3.70	2.72	44.41
Days With ≥ 0.1" Precipitation	4	4	6	7	8	7	5	5	6	6	5	4	67
Days With ≥ 1.0" Precipitation	0	0	1	1	2	1	1	1	1	1	1	1	11
Mean Snowfall (in.)	*3.2*	*2.4*	0.8	trace	0.0	0.0	0.0	0.0	0.0	0.0	0.8	1.2	*8.4*
Days With ≥ 1.0" Snow Depth	na	na	1	0	0	0	0	0	0	0	0	na	na

Summersville *Texas County*   Elevation: 1,177 ft.   Latitude: 37° 11' N   Longitude: 91° 39' W

	JAN	FEB	MAR	APR	MAY	JUN	JUL	AUG	SEP	OCT	NOV	DEC	YEAR
Mean Maximum Temp. (°F)	42.3	48.6	58.6	69.3	75.9	83.9	89.2	87.9	80.2	70.1	56.2	*46.2*	*67.4*
Mean Temp. (°F)	31.9	37.6	46.7	56.7	64.1	72.5	77.5	75.8	68.3	57.6	45.8	*36.6*	*55.9*
Mean Minimum Temp. (°F)	21.5	26.6	34.6	44.1	52.3	61.0	65.7	63.7	56.4	45.1	35.3	*27.1*	*44.4*
Extreme Maximum Temp. (°F)	75	80	85	90	90	100	107	103	99	91	83	75	107
Extreme Minimum Temp. (°F)	-19	-11	-2	21	30	40	44	39	30	19	4	-10	-19
Days Maximum Temp. ≥ 90°F	0	0	0	0	0	4	15	13	3	0	0	0	35
Days Maximum Temp. ≤ 32°F	7	4	1	0	0	0	0	0	0	0	1	3	16
Days Minimum Temp. ≤ 32°F	25	19	13	4	0	0	0	0	0	3	12	20	96
Days Minimum Temp. ≤ 0°F	2	1	0	0	0	0	0	0	0	0	0	0	3
Heating Degree Days (base 65°F)	1,018	766	565	265	99	8	1	1	56	246	571	*873*	*4,469*
Cooling Degree Days (base 65°F)	0	0	*4*	23	73	247	408	354	158	22	1	*0*	*1,290*
Mean Precipitation (in.)	2.04	2.24	4.19	3.98	4.94	4.24	3.61	3.38	4.10	3.54	3.77	*3.18*	*43.21*
Days With ≥ 0.1" Precipitation	4	4	6	6	7	6	4	4	6	5	5	4	61
Days With ≥ 1.0" Precipitation	0	1	1	1	1	1	1	1	1	1	1	1	11
Mean Snowfall (in.)	5.2	*3.6*	2.8	0.1	0.0	0.0	0.0	0.0	0.0	trace	0.8	*1.9*	*14.4*
Days With ≥ 1.0" Snow Depth	5	5	*1*	0	0	0	0	0	0	0	0	1	*12*

Sweet Springs *Saline County*   Elevation: 679 ft.   Latitude: 38° 58' N   Longitude: 93° 25' W

	JAN	FEB	MAR	APR	MAY	JUN	JUL	AUG	SEP	OCT	NOV	DEC	YEAR
Mean Maximum Temp. (°F)	37.7	44.6	56.4	67.9	76.9	85.4	90.6	88.9	80.8	69.3	54.2	42.4	66.3
Mean Temp. (°F)	28.3	34.3	45.2	55.8	65.2	74.1	78.8	76.8	68.6	57.2	44.2	33.4	55.1
Mean Minimum Temp. (°F)	18.7	23.9	33.9	43.7	53.4	62.7	67.0	64.7	56.3	44.9	34.1	24.3	44.0
Extreme Maximum Temp. (°F)	72	83	88	93	92	106	110	109	101	96	84	73	110
Extreme Minimum Temp. (°F)	-24	-22	-10	17	30	42	46	42	30	21	-8	-23	-24
Days Maximum Temp. ≥ 90°F	0	0	0	0	1	8	18	14	5	0	0	0	46
Days Maximum Temp. ≤ 32°F	10	6	1	0	0	0	0	0	0	0	1	6	24
Days Minimum Temp. ≤ 32°F	27	22	15	4	0	0	0	0	0	4	14	24	110
Days Minimum Temp. ≤ 0°F	3	2	0	0	0	0	0	0	0	0	0	1	6
Heating Degree Days (base 65°F)	1,132	861	612	297	84	6	1	1	60	262	620	973	4,909
Cooling Degree Days (base 65°F)	0	0	5	29	95	287	441	374	171	24	2	0	1,428
Mean Precipitation (in.)	1.48	1.79	3.06	4.34	5.00	3.99	3.85	3.93	4.60	3.41	3.24	2.25	40.94
Days With > 0.1" Precipitation	3	4	6	7	8	7	5	6	6	6	5	4	67
Days With ≥ 1.0" Precipitation	0	0	1	1	1	1	1	1	1	1	1	1	10
Mean Snowfall (in.)	7.2	6.0	3.6	0.7	trace	trace	0.0	0.0	0.0	trace	1.9	4.2	23.6
Days With ≥ 1.0" Snow Depth	10	7	1	0	0	0	0	0	0	0	1	4	23

Union *Franklin County*   Elevation: 538 ft.   Latitude: 38° 27' N   Longitude: 91° 00' W

	JAN	FEB	MAR	APR	MAY	JUN	JUL	AUG	SEP	OCT	NOV	DEC	YEAR
Mean Maximum Temp. (°F)	40.8	47.5	58.2	69.7	77.8	86.0	90.8	89.2	81.7	70.9	56.7	45.3	67.9
Mean Temp. (°F)	30.4	36.0	45.9	56.5	65.1	73.7	78.5	76.7	68.7	57.4	45.5	35.3	55.8
Mean Minimum Temp. (°F)	19.9	24.5	33.6	43.3	52.2	61.4	66.1	64.1	55.6	43.9	34.2	25.2	43.7
Extreme Maximum Temp. (°F)	76	85	88	94	94	104	107	109	103	95	86	77	109
Extreme Minimum Temp. (°F)	-26	-20	-10	18	28	35	44	41	29	19	5	-23	-26
Days Maximum Temp. ≥ 90°F	0	0	0	0	1	9	19	16	6	0	0	0	51
Days Maximum Temp. ≤ 32°F	8	4	1	0	0	0	0	0	0	0	1	4	18
Days Minimum Temp. ≤ 32°F	26	21	15	5	0	0	0	0	0	5	14	23	109
Days Minimum Temp. ≤ 0°F	3	1	0	0	0	0	0	0	0	0	0	1	5
Heating Degree Days (base 65°F)	1,067	812	592	280	87	7	1	1	53	254	581	915	4,650
Cooling Degree Days (base 65°F)	0	0	6	31	98	288	444	386	175	26	3	0	1,457
Mean Precipitation (in.)	2.20	2.32	3.76	4.18	4.18	4.07	3.65	3.67	3.86	3.29	4.12	3.10	42.40
Days With ≥ 0.1" Precipitation	5	5	8	7	7	7	6	6	5	6	7	5	74
Days With ≥ 1.0" Precipitation	0	1	1	1	1	1	1	1	1	1	1	1	11
Mean Snowfall (in.)	5.7	4.4	2.7	0.6	0.0	0.0	0.0	0.0	0.0	trace	1.4	3.6	18.4
Days With ≥ 1.0" Snow Depth	9	6	2	0	0	0	0	0	0	0	1	4	22

Vandalia *Audrain County*   Elevation: 757 ft.   Latitude: 39° 19' N   Longitude: 91° 29' W

	JAN	FEB	MAR	APR	MAY	JUN	JUL	AUG	SEP	OCT	NOV	DEC	YEAR
Mean Maximum Temp. (°F)	35.2	42.1	53.7	65.2	75.1	84.2	89.3	87.4	79.7	68.3	53.3	41.5	64.6
Mean Temp. (°F)	26.3	32.2	42.7	53.7	63.7	72.9	77.7	75.8	67.6	56.1	43.5	32.7	53.7
Mean Minimum Temp. (°F)	17.3	22.2	31.8	42.1	52.3	61.6	66.1	64.1	55.4	43.8	33.7	23.8	42.9
Extreme Maximum Temp. (°F)	71	81	84	91	91	105	108	106	99	92	80	*72*	*108*
Extreme Minimum Temp. (°F)	-20	-16	-8	19	29	40	45	45	31	20	-1	*-24*	*-24*
Days Maximum Temp. ≥ 90°F	0	0	0	0	1	7	15	12	4	0	0	0	39
Days Maximum Temp. ≤ 32°F	12	7	1	0	0	0	0	0	0	0	1	6	27
Days Minimum Temp. ≤ 32°F	28	23	17	5	0	0	0	0	0	4	14	25	116
Days Minimum Temp. ≤ 0°F	4	2	0	0	0	0	0	0	0	0	0	1	7
Heating Degree Days (base 65°F)	1,193	921	686	353	112	12	1	2	68	292	639	995	5,274
Cooling Degree Days (base 65°F)	*0*	0	*3*	16	*70*	251	*400*	343	140	19	1	*0*	*1,243*
Mean Precipitation (in.)	1.78	1.76	3.13	3.91	5.10	4.15	4.07	3.92	3.44	2.84	3.28	2.44	39.82
Days With ≥ 0.1" Precipitation	4	*4*	6	7	8	6	5	5	5	5	6	5	*66*
Days With ≥ 1.0" Precipitation	0	0	1	1	1	1	1	1	1	1	1	1	10
Mean Snowfall (in.)	*5.5*	4.6	2.7	0.7	0.0	0.0	0.0	0.0	0.0	trace	1.7	*4.4*	*19.6*
Days With ≥ 1.0" Snow Depth	*9*	*6*	2	0	0	0	0	0	0	0	1	*3*	*21*

Versailles *Morgan County*   Elevation: 1,026 ft.   Latitude: 38° 26' N   Longitude: 92° 51' W

	JAN	FEB	MAR	APR	MAY	JUN	JUL	AUG	SEP	OCT	NOV	DEC	YEAR
Mean Maximum Temp. (°F)	40.2	46.7	57.7	68.2	75.6	82.7	88.6	87.1	79.4	69.3	55.6	44.8	66.3
Mean Temp. (°F)	30.1	35.7	45.9	56.1	64.4	72.4	77.8	76.1	68.2	57.5	45.2	34.9	55.4
Mean Minimum Temp. (°F)	19.9	24.7	33.9	43.9	53.1	62.1	67.0	65.0	57.0	45.5	34.8	25.0	44.3
Extreme Maximum Temp. (°F)	73	83	84	92	90	99	109	106	98	94	83	75	109
Extreme Minimum Temp. (°F)	-18	-18	-8	18	28	42	45	43	30	20	0	-23	-23
Days Maximum Temp. ≥ 90°F	0	0	0	0	0	3	13	11	3	0	0	0	30
Days Maximum Temp. ≤ 32°F	9	5	1	0	0	0	0	0	0	0	1	4	20
Days Minimum Temp. ≤ 32°F	26	21	15	4	0	0	0	0	0	3	13	24	106
Days Minimum Temp. ≤ 0°F	3	1	0	0	0	0	0	0	0	0	0	1	5
Heating Degree Days (base 65°F)	1,076	820	591	290	92	10	1	2	62	252	590	927	4,713
Cooling Degree Days (base 65°F)	0	0	5	28	77	239	401	346	158	23	1	0	1,278
Mean Precipitation (in.)	1.77	2.04	3.32	4.47	5.17	4.13	3.89	3.83	4.07	4.04	3.78	2.59	43.10
Days With ≥ 0.1" Precipitation	4	4	6	7	8	7	5	5	5	6	6	4	67
Days With ≥ 1.0" Precipitation	0	1	1	1	1	1	1	1	1	1	1	1	11
Mean Snowfall (in.)	na	*2.1*	0.5	trace	0.0	0.0	0.0	0.0	0.0	trace	1.1	*1.2*	na
Days With ≥ 1.0" Snow Depth	11	7	2	0	0	0	0	0	0	0	1	5	26

Vienna 2 WNW *Maries County*   Elevation: 767 ft.   Latitude: 38° 12' N   Longitude: 91° 59' W

	JAN	FEB	MAR	APR	MAY	JUN	JUL	AUG	SEP	OCT	NOV	DEC	YEAR
Mean Maximum Temp. (°F)	38.9	45.3	55.6	66.8	75.5	83.5	89.0	88.0	79.9	69.1	55.3	44.0	65.9
Mean Temp. (°F)	28.4	34.0	43.9	54.3	63.4	71.9	76.9	75.4	67.2	55.6	44.1	33.8	54.1
Mean Minimum Temp. (°F)	17.8	22.7	32.1	41.8	51.1	60.3	64.9	62.8	54.4	42.1	32.9	23.4	42.2
Extreme Maximum Temp. (°F)	72	81	85	93	91	102	110	108	101	93	84	78	110
Extreme Minimum Temp. (°F)	-27	-22	-11	18	27	36	44	40	27	17	1	-27	-27
Days Maximum Temp. ≥ 90°F	0	0	0	0	0	5	16	13	5	0	0	0	39
Days Maximum Temp. ≤ 32°F	10	5	1	0	0	0	0	0	0	0	1	5	22
Days Minimum Temp. ≤ 32°F	28	23	17	6	1	0	0	0	0	6	16	25	122
Days Minimum Temp. ≤ 0°F	3	1	0	0	0	0	0	0	0	0	0	1	5
Heating Degree Days (base 65°F)	1,129	869	653	336	122	16	2	3	80	304	621	962	5,097
Cooling Degree Days (base 65°F)	0	0	4	22	75	230	382	334	143	17	2	0	1,209
Mean Precipitation (in.)	1.97	2.18	3.69	4.29	4.89	4.53	3.92	3.81	4.09	3.51	4.11	3.08	44.07
Days With ≥ 0.1" Precipitation	5	4	7	7	8	7	5	5	6	5	6	5	70
Days With ≥ 1.0" Precipitation	0	0	1	1	1	1	1	1	1	1	1	1	10
Mean Snowfall (in.)	5.6	3.6	2.7	0.3	0.0	0.0	0.0	0.0	0.0	0.0	1.7	3.6	17.5
Days With ≥ 1.0" Snow Depth	11	6	2	0	0	0	0	0	0	0	1	4	24

Wappapello Dam *Butler County*   Elevation: 410 ft.   Latitude: 36° 56' N   Longitude: 90° 17' W

	JAN	FEB	MAR	APR	MAY	JUN	JUL	AUG	SEP	OCT	NOV	DEC	YEAR
Mean Maximum Temp. (°F)	*41.2*	48.3	57.9	69.8	78.0	86.3	91.2	89.4	82.2	71.1	57.9	*46.7*	*68.3*
Mean Temp. (°F)	*31.4*	37.6	46.9	58.3	67.0	75.6	80.1	78.1	70.8	58.9	47.4	*37.4*	*57.4*
Mean Minimum Temp. (°F)	*21.5*	26.9	36.2	46.7	55.8	64.8	68.9	66.7	59.5	46.7	36.8	*28.0*	*46.5*
Extreme Maximum Temp. (°F)	73	80	86	92	94	103	110	108	102	93	83	73	110
Extreme Minimum Temp. (°F)	-15	-8	5	24	36	46	51	48	38	22	8	-10	-15
Days Maximum Temp. ≥ 90°F	0	0	0	0	2	10	20	16	6	0	0	0	54
Days Maximum Temp. ≤ 32°F	6	3	0	0	0	0	0	0	0	0	0	2	11
Days Minimum Temp. ≤ 32°F	24	19	12	2	0	0	0	0	0	1	10	19	87
Days Minimum Temp. ≤ 0°F	1	0	0	0	0	0	0	0	0	0	0	0	1
Heating Degree Days (base 65°F)	*1,035*	767	558	229	60	2	0	0	30	215	524	*848*	*4,268*
Cooling Degree Days (base 65°F)	na	0	4	32	124	336	492	434	214	32	2	na	na
Mean Precipitation (in.)	3.51	3.31	4.78	4.84	4.47	3.86	3.78	3.31	3.56	3.57	4.97	3.97	47.93
Days With ≥ 0.1" Precipitation	5	5	7	7	7	6	6	5	5	5	6	5	69
Days With ≥ 1.0" Precipitation	1	1	1	2	1	1	1	1	1	1	2	1	14
Mean Snowfall (in.)	*2.6*	*1.8*	0.9	0.0	0.0	0.0	0.0	0.0	0.0	0.0	0.3	0.7	*6.3*
Days With ≥ 1.0" Snow Depth	na	2	1	0	0	0	0	0	0	0	0	*0*	na

Waynesville 2 W *Pulaski County*   Elevation: 889 ft.   Latitude: 37° 49' N   Longitude: 92° 14' W

	JAN	FEB	MAR	APR	MAY	JUN	JUL	AUG	SEP	OCT	NOV	DEC	YEAR
Mean Maximum Temp. (°F)	44.1	50.3	60.5	70.7	77.0	83.9	89.2	88.3	80.9	71.7	58.5	48.2	68.6
Mean Temp. (°F)	31.4	36.8	46.3	56.1	63.9	71.9	76.8	75.4	67.8	57.1	45.7	36.1	55.4
Mean Minimum Temp. (°F)	18.6	23.3	32.1	41.5	50.7	59.8	64.3	62.4	54.6	42.5	32.9	23.9	42.2
Extreme Maximum Temp. (°F)	77	83	86	95	90	100	109	106	100	94	85	78	109
Extreme Minimum Temp. (°F)	-23	-17	-10	13	25	35	42	36	24	15	2	-25	-25
Days Maximum Temp. ≥ 90°F	0	0	0	0	0	5	16	14	5	0	0	0	40
Days Maximum Temp. ≤ 32°F	6	3	0	0	0	0	0	0	0	0	0	3	12
Days Minimum Temp. ≤ 32°F	27	22	17	7	1	0	0	0	0	6	16	24	120
Days Minimum Temp. ≤ 0°F	3	2	0	0	0	0	0	0	0	0	0	1	6
Heating Degree Days (base 65°F)	1,036	789	578	287	107	13	1	3	68	261	573	890	4,606
Cooling Degree Days (base 65°F)	0	0	5	24	75	224	374	331	148	20	2	0	1,203
Mean Precipitation (in.)	2.21	2.36	4.05	4.20	4.74	4.31	3.69	3.66	4.30	3.92	4.32	3.30	45.06
Days With ≥ 0.1" Precipitation	5	5	7	8	8	7	5	6	6	6	6	5	74
Days With ≥ 1.0" Precipitation	1	1	1	1	1	1	1	1	1	1	1	1	12
Mean Snowfall (in.)	7.7	4.6	3.2	0.4	0.0	0.0	0.0	0.0	0.0	trace	1.8	2.5	20.2
Days With ≥ 1.0" Snow Depth	9	5	2	0	0	0	0	0	0	0	1	3	20

West Plains *Howell County*   Elevation: 1,007 ft.   Latitude: 36° 45' N   Longitude: 91° 50' W

	JAN	FEB	MAR	APR	MAY	JUN	JUL	AUG	SEP	OCT	NOV	DEC	YEAR
Mean Maximum Temp. (°F)	42.8	49.2	58.5	68.9	76.4	84.0	89.6	88.4	80.5	70.5	57.1	46.9	67.7
Mean Temp. (°F)	32.1	37.5	46.3	56.1	64.4	72.6	77.7	76.2	68.6	57.4	45.7	36.4	55.9
Mean Minimum Temp. (°F)	21.3	25.7	34.1	43.3	52.4	61.0	65.8	64.0	56.7	44.3	34.4	25.8	44.1
Extreme Maximum Temp. (°F)	76	82	85	91	94	102	107	105	101	93	84	77	107
Extreme Minimum Temp. (°F)	-18	-9	4	19	31	39	46	40	32	21	5	-13	-18
Days Maximum Temp. ≥ 90°F	0	0	0	0	0	6	17	14	4	0	0	0	41
Days Maximum Temp. ≤ 32°F	7	3	1	0	0	0	0	0	0	0	0	3	14
Days Minimum Temp. ≤ 32°F	27	21	15	4	0	0	0	0	0	4	13	23	107
Days Minimum Temp. ≤ 0°F	2	0	0	0	0	0	0	0	0	0	0	0	2
Heating Degree Days (base 65°F)	1,014	771	575	280	91	7	1	1	52	248	573	881	4,494
Cooling Degree Days (base 65°F)	0	0	2	18	79	242	410	366	164	18	1	0	1,300
Mean Precipitation (in.)	2.57	2.87	4.85	4.62	4.54	4.33	3.10	3.25	4.07	3.55	4.84	3.98	46.57
Days With ≥ 0.1" Precipitation	5	5	7	7	8	7	5	5	6	5	6	6	72
Days With ≥ 1.0" Precipitation	1	1	1	1	1	1	1	1	1	1	2	1	13
Mean Snowfall (in.)	3.7	3.4	2.6	0.2	0.0	0.0	0.0	0.0	0.0	trace	0.7	1.9	12.5
Days With ≥ 1.0" Snow Depth	6	3	1	0	0	0	0	0	0	0	0	1	11

Willow Springs Radio KUKU *Howell County*   Elevation: 1,309 ft.   Latitude: 36° 59' N   Longitude: 91° 59' W

	JAN	FEB	MAR	APR	MAY	JUN	JUL	AUG	SEP	OCT	NOV	DEC	YEAR
Mean Maximum Temp. (°F)	41.8	48.3	57.9	68.4	76.0	83.3	88.8	88.1	79.8	69.7	55.9	45.8	67.0
Mean Temp. (°F)	31.8	37.4	46.3	56.1	64.2	72.2	77.1	76.1	68.4	57.5	45.4	36.1	55.7
Mean Minimum Temp. (°F)	21.7	26.5	34.6	43.7	52.3	60.9	65.4	64.1	56.9	45.3	35.0	26.4	44.4
Extreme Maximum Temp. (°F)	74	82	85	90	92	101	106	102	100	91	83	75	106
Extreme Minimum Temp. (°F)	-15	-12	1	17	24	36	43	45	31	20	3	-16	-16
Days Maximum Temp. ≥ 90°F	0	0	0	0	0	4	14	13	3	0	0	0	34
Days Maximum Temp. ≤ 32°F	7	4	1	0	0	0	0	0	0	0	1	4	17
Days Minimum Temp. ≤ 32°F	26	19	14	4	0	0	0	0	0	3	13	23	102
Days Minimum Temp. ≤ 0°F	2	1	0	0	0	0	0	0	0	0	0	1	4
Heating Degree Days (base 65°F)	1,022	772	575	281	97	8	1	1	54	247	580	889	4,527
Cooling Degree Days (base 65°F)	0	0	4	21	82	241	400	371	164	22	1	0	1,306
Mean Precipitation (in.)	2.10	2.32	4.17	4.64	4.77	4.04	3.19	3.03	3.50	3.76	4.16	3.45	43.13
Days With ≥ 0.1" Precipitation	4	4	7	6	8	6	5	5	5	5	5	4	64
Days With ≥ 1.0" Precipitation	0	1	1	2	1	1	1	1	1	1	1	1	12
Mean Snowfall (in.)	*3.9*	2.1	2.4	0.3	0.0	0.0	0.0	0.0	0.0	trace	0.6	1.6	*10.9*
Days With ≥ 1.0" Snow Depth	*5*	3	1	0	0	0	0	0	0	0	0	1	*10*

Windsor *Henry County*   Elevation: 839 ft.   Latitude: 38° 32' N   Longitude: 93° 32' W

	JAN	FEB	MAR	APR	MAY	JUN	JUL	AUG	SEP	OCT	NOV	DEC	YEAR
Mean Maximum Temp. (°F)	36.2	43.6	54.6	65.8	75.1	83.3	89.3	87.7	79.6	68.7	53.7	42.6	65.0
Mean Temp. (°F)	26.1	33.0	43.1	53.8	63.6	72.4	77.6	75.5	67.4	55.9	43.1	32.7	53.7
Mean Minimum Temp. (°F)	16.1	22.2	31.5	41.6	52.1	61.5	65.9	63.3	55.2	43.1	32.5	22.8	42.3
Extreme Maximum Temp. (°F)	70	78	85	91	91	102	109	108	99	95	82	73	109
Extreme Minimum Temp. (°F)	-19	-19	-10	17	29	37	46	43	29	17	-2	-18	-19
Days Maximum Temp. ≥ 90°F	0	0	0	0	0	5	16	14	5	0	0	0	40
Days Maximum Temp. ≤ 32°F	11	6	1	0	0	0	0	0	0	0	1	6	25
Days Minimum Temp. ≤ 32°F	29	23	18	5	0	0	0	0	0	4	16	26	121
Days Minimum Temp. ≤ 0°F	4	2	0	0	0	0	0	0	0	0	0	1	7
Heating Degree Days (base 65°F)	1,199	900	675	346	112	13	1	3	77	294	650	994	5,264
Cooling Degree Days (base 65°F)	0	0	3	14	74	244	410	333	152	17	1	0	1,248
Mean Precipitation (in.)	*1.61*	1.81	3.13	4.12	4.78	4.56	3.73	3.63	4.57	3.67	3.48	2.13	*41.22*
Days With ≥ 0.1" Precipitation	na	3	5	7	7	6	5	5	6	6	5	4	na
Days With ≥ 1.0" Precipitation	*0*	0	1	1	1	1	1	1	1	1	1	1	*10*
Mean Snowfall (in.)	5.5	*4.5*	*1.7*	0.1	0.0	0.0	0.0	0.0	0.0	0.0	1.0	3.4	*16.2*
Days With ≥ 1.0" Snow Depth	na	na	na	0	0	0	0	0	0	0	*0*	na	na

Note: See Appendix D for explanation of data.

MONTANA

PHYSICAL FEATURES. Montana, with an area of 146,316 square miles, is the fourth largest State of the Union. Climatic variations are large. The half of the State southwest of a line from the southeastern corner to the Canadian Border north of Cut Bank in Glacier County is very mountainous, while the northeastern half is very much like Great Plains country, broken occasionally by wide valleys and isolated groups of hills. The extent of the climatic variations one should expect is indicated by the range in elevation of from 1,800 feet above sea level where the Kootenai River enters Idaho to 12,850 feet at Granite Peak near Yellowstone Park. Half the State lies over 4,000 feet above sea level.

The Continental Divide traverses the western half of the State in roughly a north-south direction. To the west of the Divide, Montana is drained by the Kootenai, Clark Fork, and Flathead Rivers into the Pacific Ocean through the Columbia River. Many of the tributary streams in this region have their origin in the high elevations of the western slopes of the Rockies. Most streams traverse narrow canyons, at least through parts of their length, affording many valuable waterpower sites. A relatively small area located between the Hudson Bay Divide and the Rocky Mountains is drained by the St. Mary River, which finds its way to the Hudson Bay through the Saskatchewan River. The remainder of the State is drained by the Missouri River, which is formed by the confluence of the Gallatin, Madison, and Jefferson Rivers at Three Forks, travels northward through deep canyons in the Big Belt Mountains, and flows through the lower lying northeastern portion of the State. The Yellowstone River, the principal tributary of the Missouri in Montana and which has its source in Wyoming, drains the southeastern section of the State and has its confluence with the Missouri just east of the Montana - North Dakota line.

GENERAL CLIMATE. The Continental Divide exerts a marked influence on the climate of adjacent areas. West of the Divide the climate might be termed a modified north Pacific coast type, while to the east, climatic characteristics are decidedly continental. On the west of the mountain barrier winters are milder, precipitation is more evenly distributed throughout the year, summers are cooler in general, and winds are lighter than on the eastern side. There is more cloudiness in the west in all seasons, humidity runs a bit higher, and the growing season is shorter than in the eastern plains areas.

Cold waves, which cover parts of Montana on the average of six to 12 times a winter, are confined mostly to the sections northeast of a Glacier Park - Miles City line. A few of these cold waves cover the entire area east of the Divide, and one or two a season will cover the State all the way from the Dakotas to Idaho. With temperatures well below 0 and sometimes strong winds with blowing snow, these cold waves can be very inconvenient and even dangerous. In small areas ideally situated for radiation cooling, low temperatures can fall to -50°F. or lower.

During the summer months hot weather occurs fairly often in the eastern parts of the State. Temperatures of over 100 sometimes occur in the lower elevation areas west of the Divide during the summer, but hot spells are less frequent and of shorter duration than in the plains sections. Hot spells nowhere become oppressive, however, because summer nights almost invariably are cool and pleasant. In the areas with elevations above 4,000 feet, extremely hot weather is almost unknown. Summer days, however, are usually warm enough for light summer clothing.

Winters, while usually cold, have few extended cold spells. Between cold waves there are periods, sometimes longer than 10 days, of mild but often windy weather. These warm, windy winter periods occur almost entirely along the eastern slopes of the Divide and are popularly known as "chinook" weather. The so-called "chinook" belt extends from the Browning-Shelby area southeastward to the Yellowstone Valley above Billings. Through this belt, "chinook" winds frequently reach speeds of 25 to 50 m.p.h. or more and can persist, with little interruptions, for several days.

Most Montana lakes freeze over every winter, but Flathead Lake, between Polson and Kalispell, freezes over completely only during the coldest winters, and one year in 10. All rivers carry floating ice during the late winter or early spring. Few streams freeze solid; water generally continues to flow beneath the ice. During coldest winters "anchor" ice, which builds from the bottom of shallow streams, on rare occasions causes some flooding.

PRECIPITATION. Precipitation varies widely and depends largely upon topographic influences. Areas adjacent to mountain ranges in general are the wettest, although there are a few exceptions where the "rain-shadow" effect appears. Generally, nearly half the annual long-term average total falls in the three months, May through July.

SNOWFALL. Annual snowfall varies from quite heavy, 300 inches, in some parts of the mountains in the western half of the State, to around 20 inches at some stations in the two northern Divisions east of the Continental Divide. Most snow falls during the November-March period, but heavy snowstorms can occur as early as mid-September or as late as May 1 in the higher southwestern half of the State. In eastern sections early or late season snows are not very common. Mountain snowpacks in the wetter areas often exceed 100 inches in depth as the annual snow season approaches its end around April 1 to 15.

The greatest volume of flow of Montana's rivers occurs during the spring and early summer months with the melting of the winter snowpack. Heavy rains falling during the spring thaw constitute a serious flood threat. Ice jams, which occur during the spring breakup, usually in March, cause backwater flooding. Flash-floods, although restricted in scope, are probably the most numerous and result from locally heavy rainstorms in the spring and summer.

STORMS. Severe storms of several types can occur, but the most troublesome are hailstorms. Their occurrence is limited mainly to July and August, infrequently in June and September. Tornadoes develop infrequently and occur almost entirely east of the Divide, largely in the eastern third of the State. Severe windstorms of a general nature are rare but can occur locally, mainly east of the Divide, from a few to several times a year. Drought in its most severe form is practically unknown, but dry years do occur in some sections. All parts of the State rarely suffer from dryness at the same time.

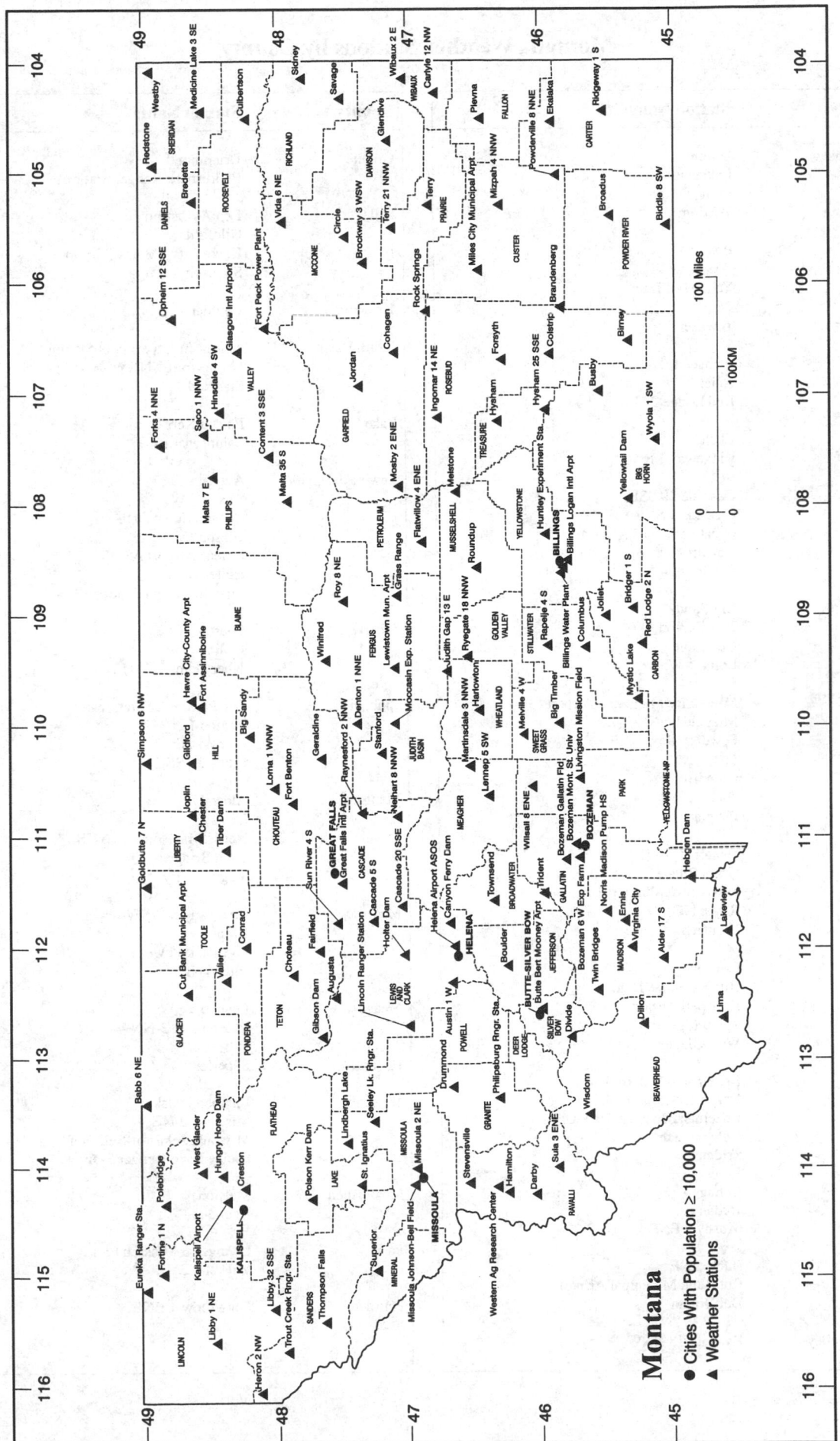

Montana

● Cities With Population ≥ 10,000
▲ Weather Stations

Montana Weather Stations by County

County	Station Name
Beaverhead	Dillon
	Lakeview
	Lima
	Wisdom
Big Horn	Busby
	Wyola 1 SW
	Yellowtail Dam
Broadwater	Townsend
Carbon	Bridger 1 S
	Joliet
	Red Lodge 2 N
Carter	Ekalaka
	Ridgeway 1 S
Cascade	Cascade 20 SSE
	Cascade 5 S
	Great Falls Int'l Airport
	Neihart 8 NNW
	Sun River 4 S
Chouteau	Big Sandy
	Fort Benton
	Geraldine
	Loma 1 WNW
Custer	Miles City Municipal Airport
	Mizpah 4 NNW
	Powderville 8 NNE
Dawson	Glendive
Fallon	Plevna
Fergus	Denton 1 NNE
	Grass Range
	Lewistown Municipal Airport
	Roy 8 NE
	Winifred
Flathead	Creston
	Hungry Horse Dam
	Kalispell Airport
	Polebridge
	West Glacier
Gallatin	Bozeman 6 W Exp. Farm
	Bozeman Gallatin Field
	Bozeman Montana State Univ.
	Hebgen Dam
	Trident
Garfield	Cohagen
	Jordan
	Mosby 2 ENE
Glacier	Babb 6 NE
	Cut Bank Municipal Airport
	Del Bonita
Golden Valley	Ryegate 18 NNW

County	Station Name
Granite	Drummond
	Philipsburg Ranger Station
Hill	Fort Assinniboine
	Gildford
	Havre City-County Airport
	Simpson 6 NW
Jefferson	Boulder
Judith Basin	Moccasin Experiment Station
	Raynesford 2 NNW
	Stanford
Lake	Polson Kerr Dam
	Saint Ignatius
Lewis And Clark	Augusta
	Austin 1 W
	Canyon Ferry Dam
	Gibson Dam
	Helena Airport ASOS
	Holter Dam
	Lincoln Ranger Station
Liberty	Chester
	Joplin
	Tiber Dam
Lincoln	Eureka Ranger Station
	Fortine 1 N
	Libby 1 NE
	Libby 32 SSE
Madison	Alder 17 S
	Ennis
	Norris Madison Pump HS
	Twin Bridges
	Virginia City
McCone	Brockway 3 WSW
	Circle
	Fort Peck Power Plant
	Vida 6 NE
Meagher	Lennep 5 SW
	Martinsdale 3 NNW
Mineral	Superior
Missoula	Lindbergh Lake
	Missoula 2 NE
	Missoula Johnson-Bell Field
	Seeley Lake Ranger Station
Musselshell	Melstone
	Roundup
Park	Livingston Mission Field
	Wilsall 8 ENE
Petroleum	Flatwillow 4 ENE

County	Station Name
Phillips	Content 3 SSE
	Forks 4 NNE
	Malta 35 S
	Malta 7 E
	Saco 1 NNW
Pondera	Conrad
	Valier
Powder River	Biddle 8 SW
	Broadus
Prairie	Terry
	Terry 21 NNW
Ravalli	Darby
	Hamilton
	Stevensville
	Sula 3 ENE
	Western Agr. Research Station
Richland	Savage
	Sidney
Roosevelt	Bredette
	Culbertson
Rosebud	Birney
	Brandenberg
	Colstrip
	Forsyth
	Ingomar 14 NE
	Rock Springs
Sanders	Heron 2 NW
	Thompson Falls
	Trout Creek Ranger Station
Sheridan	Medicine Lake 3 SE
	Raymond Border Station
	Redstone
	Westby
Silver Bow	Butte Bert Mooney Airport
	Divide
Stillwater	Columbus
	Mystic Lake
	Rapelje 4 S
Sweet Grass	Big Timber
	Melville 4 W
Teton	Choteau
	Fairfield
Toole	Goldbutte 7 N
	Sweetgrass
Treasure	Hysham
	Hysham 25 SSE
Valley	Glasgow Int'l Airport
	Hinsdale 4 SW
	Opheim 10 N

County	Station Name
Valley (cont.)	Opheim 12 SSE
Wheatland	Harlowton
	Judith Gap 13 E
Wibaux	Carlyle 12 NW
	Wibaux 2 E
Yellowstone	Billings Logan Int'l Airport
	Billings Water Plant
	Huntley Experiment Station

Montana Weather Stations by City

City	Station Name	Miles
Billings	Billings Water Plant	3
	Billings Logan Int'l Airport	1
	Huntley Experiment Station	17
Bozeman	Bozeman Gallatin Field	10
	Bozeman Montana State Univ.	0
	Bozeman 6 W Exp. Farm	5
Butte-Silver Bow	Butte Bert Mooney Airport	2
	Divide	20
Great Falls	Great Falls Int'l Airport	5
Helena	Austin 1 W	12
	Canyon Ferry Dam	15
	Helena Airport ASOS	3
Kalispell	Creston	9
	Hungry Horse Dam	17
	Kalispell Airport	9
Missoula	Missoula 2 NE	3
	Missoula Johnson-Bell Field	6

Note: Miles is the distance between the geographic center of the city and the weather station.

Montana Weather Stations by Elevation

Feet	Station Name
6,709	Lakeview
6,555	Mystic Lake
6,486	Hebgen Dam
6,272	Lima
6,059	Wisdom
5,849	Alder 17 S
5,833	Wilsall 8 ENE
5,770	Virginia City
5,597	Lennep 5 SW
5,538	Butte Bert Mooney Airport
5,498	Red Lodge 2 N
5,364	Melville 4 W
5,347	Divide
5,269	Philipsburg Ranger Station
5,229	Neihart 8 NNW
5,226	Dillon
5,098	Judith Gap 13 E
4,950	Ennis
4,911	Bozeman Montana State Univ.
4,901	Boulder
4,858	Stanford
4,799	Martinsdale 3 NNW
4,790	Austin 1 W
4,773	Bozeman 6 W Exp. Farm
4,744	Norris Madison Pump HS
4,652	Livingston Mission Field
4,622	Twin Bridges
4,599	Cascade 20 SSE
4,589	Gibson Dam
4,573	Lincoln Ranger Station
4,471	Sula 3 ENE
4,438	Ryegate 18 NNW
4,425	Bozeman Gallatin Field
4,333	Del Bonita
4,317	Lindbergh Lake
4,297	Babb 6 NE
4,297	Moccasin Experiment Station
4,212	Raynesford 2 NNW
4,160	Harlowton
4,143	Lewistown Municipal Airport
4,124	Rapelje 4 S
4,097	Big Timber
4,097	Seeley Lake Ranger Station
4,068	Augusta
4,035	Trident
3,999	Drummond
3,982	Fairfield
3,877	Darby
3,845	Choteau
3,838	Townsend
3,835	Cut Bank Municipal Airport
3,825	Helena Airport ASOS
3,809	Valier
3,727	Wyola 1 SW
3,697	Joliet

Feet	Station Name
3,677	Bridger 1 S
3,671	Canyon Ferry Dam
3,661	Great Falls Int'l Airport
3,618	Denton 1 NNE
3,599	Libby 32 SSE
3,599	Sun River 4 S
3,595	Biddle 8 SW
3,595	Western Agr. Research Station
3,582	Columbus
3,566	Billings Logan Int'l Airport
3,549	Conrad
3,526	Hamilton
3,517	Polebridge
3,497	Goldbutte 7 N
3,487	Grass Range
3,484	Holter Dam
3,464	Sweetgrass
3,444	Roy 8 NE
3,428	Busby
3,421	Ekalaka
3,418	Missoula 2 NE
3,372	Stevensville
3,359	Cascade 5 S
3,323	Joplin
3,316	Ridgeway 1 S
3,303	Yellowtail Dam
3,254	Terry 21 NNW
3,241	Winifred
3,225	Roundup
3,215	Colstrip
3,188	Missoula Johnson-Bell Field
3,162	Chester
3,159	Birney
3,159	Hungry Horse Dam
3,152	West Glacier
3,136	Flatwillow 4 ENE
3,129	Geraldine
3,097	Billings Water Plant
3,097	Hysham 25 SSE
3,031	Broadus
3,028	Carlyle 12 NW
3,021	Rock Springs
2,998	Fortine 1 N
2,988	Huntley Experiment Station
2,979	Opheim 10 N
2,969	Kalispell Airport
2,949	Opheim 12 SSE
2,939	Creston
2,919	Melstone
2,896	Saint Ignatius
2,847	Tiber Dam
2,818	Gildford
2,798	Powderville 8 NNE
2,791	Ingomar 14 NE
2,788	Mosby 2 ENE

Feet	Station Name
2,778	Plevna
2,769	Big Sandy
2,769	Brandenberg
2,739	Simpson 6 NW
2,729	Polson Kerr Dam
2,713	Cohagen
2,709	Superior
2,687	Bredette
2,677	Jordan
2,673	Hinsdale 4 SW
2,667	Wibaux 2 E
2,657	Hysham
2,647	Malta 35 S
2,634	Fort Benton
2,627	Brockway 3 WSW
2,627	Miles City Municipal Airport
2,611	Fort Assinniboine
2,598	Forks 4 NNE
2,582	Havre City-County Airport
2,578	Loma 1 WNW
2,529	Eureka Ranger Station
2,513	Forsyth
2,477	Mizpah 4 NNW
2,437	Circle
2,398	Vida 6 NE
2,378	Thompson Falls
2,355	Trout Creek Ranger Station
2,349	Raymond Border Station
2,339	Content 3 SSE
2,293	Glasgow Int'l Airport
2,247	Terry
2,244	Malta 7 E
2,237	Heron 2 NW
2,168	Saco 1 NNW
2,109	Redstone
2,103	Westby
2,093	Libby 1 NE
2,073	Glendive
2,066	Fort Peck Power Plant
1,984	Savage
1,952	Medicine Lake 3 SE
1,919	Culbertson
1,919	Sidney

Billings Logan Int'l Airport

Billings, Montana, at an elevation of 3,100 to 3,600 feet above sea level, is situated in the borderline area between the Great Plains and the Rocky Mountains, and has a semi-arid climate which takes on some of the characteristics of both regions. With irrigation and the favorable distribution of the precipitation a variety of crops successfully grow in the area.

About a third of the annual precipitation falls during May and June, with June being the wettest month. The period of least precipitation is from November through February. These four months normally produce less than 20 percent of the annual precipitation. The heaviest snows occur during the spring and fall months when the temperature and moisture conditions are most favorable. Heavy snows of 6 inches or more also occur during November and December. The occurrence of thawing periods normally prevents the snow from accumulating to great depths on the ground. Thunderstorms are most frequent during the summer months. These storms are frequently accompanied by strong, gusty winds and occasionally by hail. Destructive hailstorms, however, are rather infrequent.

Winter is usually cold, though not extremely so, and generally affords several mild periods of a week to several weeks in length. The winter cold periods are ushered in by moderately strong north to northeast winds and snow. The coldest temperatures occur after the snow ends and the sky clears. True blizzard conditions are not observed very often in town, but in the surrounding rural areas, blizzard conditions may develop several times during the winter. Cold weather improves with the onset of moderate to strong southwest winds. This wind is sometimes a foehn condition (chinook), but is more often a drainage wind moving down the Yellowstone Valley which transports warmer air of Pacific origin to the area.

Spring brings a period of frequent and rapid fluctuations in the weather. It is usually cloudy and cool with frequent periods of rain and/or snow. As the season progresses, snows become less frequent until late May and June when rain is the rule. The last freezing temperatures in spring usually occur before mid-May though they have occurred as late as late June.

The summer season is characterized by warm days with abundant sunshine and low humidities. The nights are cool because of the altitude and the cool air drainage into the valley from the higher terrain. Frequent thunderstorms bring threatening afternoon cloudiness but usually only small amounts of rain.

The first freezing temperatures of the fall season occur in late September, but they have been noted as early as late August. The change to severe winter weather usually arrives after the middle of November. There have been years when the more severe type of winter weather have been delayed until late in December.

Billings Logan Int'l Airport *Yellowstone County*   Elevation: 3,566 ft.   Latitude: 45° 48' N   Longitude: 108° 33' W

	JAN	FEB	MAR	APR	MAY	JUN	JUL	AUG	SEP	OCT	NOV	DEC	YEAR
Mean Maximum Temp. (°F)	32.6	39.4	47.0	57.0	67.2	78.0	85.8	85.0	72.4	59.9	43.9	35.2	58.6
Mean Temp. (°F)	23.6	29.7	36.5	45.7	55.4	65.1	71.8	70.9	59.5	48.4	34.7	26.4	47.3
Mean Minimum Temp. (°F)	14.6	19.9	26.1	34.3	43.5	52.1	57.7	56.8	46.6	36.8	25.4	17.6	36.0
Extreme Maximum Temp. (°F)	67	71	79	90	95	105	105	103	103	90	77	69	105
Extreme Minimum Temp. (°F)	-30	-28	-19	5	22	36	41	35	22	-7	-19	-32	-32
Days Maximum Temp. ≥ 90°F	0	0	0	0	0	4	12	11	2	0	0	0	29
Days Maximum Temp. ≤ 32°F	13	8	4	1	0	0	0	0	0	1	6	11	44
Days Minimum Temp. ≤ 32°F	27	24	23	12	2	0	0	0	1	9	22	27	147
Days Minimum Temp. ≤ 0°F	8	4	1	0	0	0	0	0	0	0	1	4	18
Heating Degree Days (base 65°F)	1,277	991	876	574	306	86	18	23	203	512	902	1,190	6,958
Cooling Degree Days (base 65°F)	0	0	0	2	18	94	237	223	50	4	0	0	628
Mean Precipitation (in.)	*0.90*	*0.67*	*1.20*	*1.83*	*2.75*	*1.66*	*0.99*	*0.86*	*1.39*	*1.34*	*0.83*	*0.82*	*15.24*
Maximum Precipitation (in.)	2.3	1.8	2.7	4.4	7.7	5.7	5.1	3.5	4.0	3.8	2.3	2.0	26.8
Minimum Precipitation (in.)	0.1	0	0.2	0.1	0.4	0.2	trace	0	0.1	trace	trace	0	7.9
Maximum 24-hr. Precipitation (in.)	1.2	0.6	0.9	2.5	2.8	1.9	2.1	1.9	2.2	1.7	1.1	1.0	2.8
Days With ≥ 0.1" Precipitation	2	2	3	5	6	5	3	2	3	4	3	2	40
Days With ≥ 1.0" Precipitation	0	0	0	0	0	0	0	0	0	0	0	0	0
Mean Snowfall (in.)	na	na	na	na	na	na	na	na	na	na	na	na	na
Maximum Snowfall (in.)	28	22	27	42	16	2	0	trace	9	23	25	29	127
Maximum 24-hr. Snowfall (in.)	14	8	11	24	15	2	0	trace	6	10	13	14	24
Days With ≥ 1.0" Snow Depth	17	11	9	3	0	0	0	0	0	2	8	15	65
Thunderstorm Days	< 1	< 1	< 1	1	4	7	7	6	2	< 1	0	< 1	27
Foggy Days	5	5	6	6	4	2	1	1	3	4	5	5	47
Predominant Sky Cover	OVR	OVR	OVR	OVR	OVR	BRK	CLR	CLR	CLR	OVR	OVR	OVR	OVR
Mean Relative Humidity 5am (%)	64	66	69	68	71	72	64	61	64	63	65	64	66
Mean Relative Humidity 5pm (%)	56	53	48	42	42	41	32	30	37	42	53	56	44
Mean Dewpoint (°F)	10	15	20	27	37	45	47	45	38	30	20	13	29
Prevailing Wind Direction	SW	SW	SW	SW	SW	SW	SW	SW	SW	SW	SW	SW	SW
Prevailing Wind Speed (mph)	15	14	12	10	10	9	9	9	10	12	13	14	12
Maximum Wind Gust (mph)	63	74	58	69	60	61	69	71	61	61	73	64	74

Glasgow Int'l Airport

Founded in the days of national expansion as a railroad shop town, Glasgow is situated in the valley of the Milk River, about 20 miles upstream from where the Milk River joins the Missouri. It lies on the natural route from the plains to Marias Pass in the northern Rockies. The city is located on the valley floor at an average elevation of about 2,100 feet above sea level. Hills rise sharply from the northern edge of the city to flat tableland about 200 feet higher than the valley. The Weather Service Office is located on this flat land about 1 mile north-northeast of the city. A gradual incline commences 3 to 4 miles to the south and southwest of the city and reaches to the rolling hills which separate the Milk River drainage from the Fort Peck Reservoir on the Missouri. The northern shore of Fort Peck Reservoir lies about 15 miles south of Glasgow. The reservoir's average width south of Glasgow is about 10 miles.

The climate in the Glasgow area is continental with a large annual range in temperature and limited precipitation. Fort Peck Reservoir, to the south, seems to have little climatic effect as far north as Glasgow, except for brief periods of morning fog in the late fall which occasionally drift northward from the lake before it freezes. Seventy-eight percent of the annual precipitation falls from April through September, with May and June accounting for about 38 percent of the annual total. This distribution of precipitation helps to make the climate quite favorable for the growing of small grains. Winter precipitation nearly always falls as snow, but as a rule, although snow seldom accumulates to any great depth, it usually is formed into drifts in the open, unprotected areas. Blizzards during the winter months occur occasionally, but usually are of short duration. Glasgow itself is well protected from most strong winds and blizzard conditions by hills to the north of the city, but occasionally the unprotected surrounding areas feel the full brunt of these winter storms.

Glasgow has a wide range of temperature. Winters are quite cold, but mild winter weather occasionally does occur, sometimes caused when the chinook or foehn wind, which descends the eastern slopes of the Rocky Mountains, reaches as far east as Glasgow. Very cold spells also occur, at least once each winter, but as a rule, these last only a few days. Summers are characterized by warm, sunny weather which can last for several weeks at a time. Sunny weather predominates during the warmer season, but interruptions in the form of clouds and showers do occur, usually in the afternoons and evenings. A few days of hot weather in July and August occur at times, but hot days are seldom oppressive because they are usually accompanied by low humidity.

Glasgow Int'l Airport *Valley County*   Elevation: 2,293 ft.   Latitude: 48° 13' N   Longitude: 106° 37' W

	JAN	FEB	MAR	APR	MAY	JUN	JUL	AUG	SEP	OCT	NOV	DEC	YEAR
Mean Maximum Temp. (°F)	20.4	28.8	41.2	56.8	68.2	77.7	84.1	83.8	70.9	57.7	38.6	26.0	54.5
Mean Temp. (°F)	11.0	19.3	30.8	44.6	55.6	64.8	70.4	69.8	57.5	45.3	28.7	16.3	42.8
Mean Minimum Temp. (°F)	1.5	9.8	20.3	32.2	43.0	51.8	56.5	55.7	44.1	32.9	18.7	6.5	31.1
Extreme Maximum Temp. (°F)	57	71	79	91	102	108	104	108	103	90	79	59	108
Extreme Minimum Temp. (°F)	-40	-38	-27	-3	20	32	41	37	15	-6	-26	-38	-40
Days Maximum Temp. ≥ 90°F	0	0	0	0	1	3	9	9	2	0	0	0	24
Days Maximum Temp. ≤ 32°F	22	15	7	1	0	0	0	0	0	1	9	19	74
Days Minimum Temp. ≤ 32°F	31	28	28	15	2	0	0	0	2	13	27	31	177
Days Minimum Temp. ≤ 0°F	14	8	2	0	0	0	0	0	0	0	3	10	37
Heating Degree Days (base 65°F)	1,672	1,285	1,054	608	303	85	20	35	249	604	1,083	1,505	8,503
Cooling Degree Days (base 65°F)	0	0	0	2	21	90	196	200	34	1	0	0	544
Mean Precipitation (in.)	*0.33*	*0.27*	*0.44*	*0.68*	*1.85*	*1.92*	*1.59*	*1.17*	*1.03*	*0.58*	*0.31*	*0.40*	*10.57*
Maximum Precipitation (in.)	1.4	1.4	1.4	2.6	4.9	6.9	5.9	5.7	4.1	1.8	1.3	1.5	19.0
Minimum Precipitation (in.)	trace	trace	0	trace	trace	0.1	trace	trace	trace	trace	trace	trace	6.7
Maximum 24-hr. Precipitation (in.)	0.7	0.6	0.8	1.0	2.3	2.3	2.5	3.0	1.6	1.1	0.4	0.4	3.0
Days With ≥ 0.1" Precipitation	1	1	1	2	5	5	4	3	2	2	1	1	28
Days With ≥ 1.0" Precipitation	0	0	0	0	0	0	0	0	0	0	0	0	0
Mean Snowfall (in.)	na	na	na	na	na	na	na	na	na	na	na	na	na
Maximum Snowfall (in.)	24	21	15	14	11	1	0	0	2	8	17	15	58
Maximum 24-hr. Snowfall (in.)	7	8	9	11	10	1	0	0	2	5	10	7	11
Days With ≥ 1.0" Snow Depth	26	18	12	2	0	0	0	0	0	1	7	19	85
Thunderstorm Days	< 1	0	< 1	1	4	7	8	6	2	< 1	< 1	0	28
Foggy Days	8	6	6	3	3	2	1	1	2	2	5	7	46
Predominant Sky Cover	OVR	OVR	OVR	OVR	OVR	SCT	SCT	SCT	CLR	OVR	OVR	OVR	OVR
Mean Relative Humidity 5am (%)	77	80	81	75	73	75	73	68	72	74	79	79	75
Mean Relative Humidity 5pm (%)	74	71	58	41	39	39	33	31	37	46	65	74	51
Mean Dewpoint (°F)	4	11	20	27	37	46	49	46	38	30	19	10	28
Prevailing Wind Direction	ESE	ESE	ESE	ESE	ESE	ESE	ESE	ESE	ESE	ESE	ESE	ESE	ESE
Prevailing Wind Speed (mph)	13	13	13	13	13	13	12	13	13	12	12	12	13
Maximum Wind Gust (mph)	61	68	59	63	63	62	86	73	59	61	73	61	86

Great Falls Int'l Airport

The city of Great Falls is located along the main stem of the Missouri River at its confluence with the Sun River. The Weather Service Office is located at the Municipal Airport on a plateau between the Sun and Missouri Rivers. This plateau is about 200 feet higher than most of the immediate valley area, and the airport is about two miles southwest of the Sun and Missouri River Junction. Except to the north and northeast, the valley is encircled by mountain ranges, which lie about 30 miles away from east to south, 40 miles to the southwest, and 60 to 100 miles distant from west to northwest. The combination of valleys and plateaus in the immediate area, contributes to marked temperature differences between the airport and the city proper, either on calm, clear mornings, or when chinook winds reach the airport before they are felt at the lower elevations in town.

Summertime in the area generally is quite pleasant, with cool nights, moderately warm and sunny days, and very little hot, humid weather. Most of the summer rainfall occurs in showers or thunderstorms, and steady rains may occur during late spring or early summer. At the airport, freezing temperatures do not occur in July or August and very rarely in June. Frost occurs frequently in April and October, but more often in the valleys than on the surrounding hills or plateaus.

Winters are not as cold as is usually expected of a continental location at this latitude, largely as a result of the chinook winds for which this area is noted. While sub-zero weather is experienced normally several times during a winter, the coldest weather seldom lasts more than a few days at a time, and is usually terminated by southwest chinook winds which can produce sharp temperature rises of 40 degrees or more in 24 hours.

As a result of recurring chinooks throughout the winter season, snow seldom lies on the ground for more than a few days. In fact, the ground usually is bare, or nearly bare, of snow most of the winter, except in the surrounding mountains and higher foothills. On the other hand, invasions of cold air from the polar regions occur a few times each winter, and sharp temperature falls from above freezing to below zero within 24 hours are observed occasionally.

Precipitation generally falls as snow during late fall, winter, and early spring, although rain can occur in any month. Late spring, summer, and early fall precipitation is almost always rain, but some hail is observed occasionally during summer thunderstorms.

Although average annual precipitation at Great Falls would normally classify the area as semi- arid, it is important to note that about 70 percent of the annual total falls normally during the April to September growing season. The combination of ideal temperatures during the peak of the growing season, long hours of summer sunshine, and adequate precipitation during the six critical months, makes the climate very favorable for dryland farming. Heavy fog occurs about one day per month, but each case lasts only a small part of the day. Although the average windspeed is relatively high, strong winds over 70 mph are seldom observed. Visibility normally is excellent.

Great Falls Int'l Airport *Cascade County*   Elevation: 3,661 ft.   Latitude: 47° 28' N   Longitude: 111° 23' W

	JAN	FEB	MAR	APR	MAY	JUN	JUL	AUG	SEP	OCT	NOV	DEC	YEAR
Mean Maximum Temp. (°F)	31.8	38.0	45.1	55.4	65.1	74.7	82.6	81.9	70.1	58.3	42.6	34.4	56.7
Mean Temp. (°F)	22.1	27.5	34.3	43.6	52.8	61.5	67.7	67.0	56.5	46.3	33.2	25.1	44.8
Mean Minimum Temp. (°F)	12.4	17.0	23.4	31.8	40.4	48.3	52.7	52.0	43.0	34.4	23.7	15.6	32.9
Extreme Maximum Temp. (°F)	67	70	78	89	93	101	105	104	98	91	76	63	105
Extreme Minimum Temp. (°F)	-33	-35	-20	-6	21	31	36	30	20	-11	-25	-42	-42
Days Maximum Temp. ≥ 90°F	0	0	0	0	0	2	7	7	1	0	0	0	17
Days Maximum Temp. ≤ 32°F	13	8	5	1	0	0	0	0	0	1	6	11	45
Days Minimum Temp. ≤ 32°F	27	24	25	16	4	0	0	0	3	13	22	27	161
Days Minimum Temp. ≤ 0°F	9	5	2	0	0	0	0	0	0	0	2	6	24
Heating Degree Days (base 65°F)	1,325	1,052	946	636	381	151	44	59	271	574	948	1,233	7,620
Cooling Degree Days (base 65°F)	0	0	0	2	9	41	113	119	22	2	0	0	308
Mean Precipitation (in.)	*0.78*	*0.58*	*1.16*	*1.39*	*2.57*	*2.10*	*1.30*	*1.74*	*1.29*	*0.85*	*0.63*	*0.81*	*15.20*
Maximum Precipitation (in.)	2.0	2.2	2.2	4.6	8.1	5.4	4.7	4.9	3.2	3.4	2.3	1.9	25.2
Minimum Precipitation (in.)	0	trace	0.1	0	0.7	0.5	trace	trace	0.1	trace	trace	trace	9.0
Maximum 24-hr. Precipitation (in.)	0.7	0.9	1.1	2.2	2.5	2.3	1.6	1.9	1.6	1.1	0.6	0.6	2.5
Days With ≥ 0.1" Precipitation	3	2	3	4	6	5	4	4	3	3	2	2	41
Days With ≥ 1.0" Precipitation	0	0	0	0	0	0	0	0	0	0	0	0	0
Mean Snowfall (in.)	na	na	na	na	na	na	na	na	na	na	na	na	na
Maximum Snowfall (in.)	23	26	24	35	12	11	0	8	10	17	22	23	117
Maximum 24-hr. Snowfall (in.)	8	11	12	17	10	8	0	7	6	7	7	7	17
Days With ≥ 1.0" Snow Depth	15	11	9	3	0	0	0	0	0	2	8	13	61
Thunderstorm Days	< 1	< 1	< 1	1	3	7	7	6	1	< 1	< 1	< 1	25
Foggy Days	6	6	6	5	4	3	1	1	3	3	5	5	48
Predominant Sky Cover	OVR	OVR	OVR	OVR	OVR	OVR	SCT	SCT	OVR	OVR	OVR	OVR	OVR
Mean Relative Humidity 5am (%)	67	67	69	68	70	71	66	64	66	63	64	65	67
Mean Relative Humidity 5pm (%)	61	55	50	41	40	40	30	30	36	43	55	59	45
Mean Dewpoint (°F)	10	14	19	25	34	42	44	42	36	29	20	13	27
Prevailing Wind Direction	SW	SW	SW	SW	SW	SW	SW	SW	SW	SW	SW	SW	SW
Prevailing Wind Speed (mph)	20	18	16	15	13	13	12	12	13	16	18	20	15
Maximum Wind Gust (mph)	70	66	66	62	61	75	77	74	61	67	82	68	82

Havre City-County Airport

Havre, Montana, is located in a level valley formed by the Milk River, which courses through the city from west to east. Most of the city lies on the south side of the river. On the north side, hills rise abruptly to about 200 feet above the valley floor. The land mass north to the Canadian border is gently rolling and increases slightly in elevation. During winter months, frequent invasions of cold polar continental air move down across these rolling plains, bringing snow and sub-zero temperatures.

The Bearpaw Mountains extend from 15 to 30 miles south of Havre. Most of the peaks are from 4,000 to 5,000 feet above sea level, and several are above 6,000 feet. The highest is Old Baldy, 6,916 feet above sea level.

Winters are cold in the Havre area, but snow cover is seldom more than a few inches, and usually some ground is bare. Spells of mild weather do occur at least a few times each winter, arriving with sometimes fresh to strong southwest to west foehn winds. During winter months, rain rarely falls. Winter precipitation is almost always in the form of snow. The transition from winter to spring conditions is fairly rapid in the usual year, but cold snaps and snow can occur as late as early May or as early as September.

Summers are characterized by warm weather, seldom exceeding 95 degrees. Daytime warmest readings usually run from the 80s to the mid-90s during most of July and August, but summer relative humidities are seldom as high as 50 percent during afternoon hours. Summertime night temperatures are rarely oppressively warm. Most spring and summer precipitation falls as showers, but occasionally steady rains lasting several hours are observed in May and June, and again in September. Fall seasons are characterized by much clear weather, although cold snaps of a day or two, with some snow, can occur as early as mid-September.

Havre City-County Airport *Hill County*   Elevation: 2,582 ft.   Latitude: 48° 33' N   Longitude: 109° 46' W

	JAN	FEB	MAR	APR	MAY	JUN	JUL	AUG	SEP	OCT	NOV	DEC	YEAR
Mean Maximum Temp. (°F)	25.4	33.4	44.1	57.6	68.1	77.1	84.2	83.7	71.4	59.0	40.5	30.1	56.2
Mean Temp. (°F)	14.9	22.4	32.6	44.5	54.9	63.3	68.8	68.1	56.6	44.9	29.3	19.2	43.3
Mean Minimum Temp. (°F)	4.4	11.3	21.0	31.4	41.6	49.5	53.4	52.5	41.8	30.8	18.0	8.3	30.3
Extreme Maximum Temp. (°F)	68	74	77	91	98	105	106	107	101	90	78	64	107
Extreme Minimum Temp. (°F)	-42	-44	-30	-14	24	29	39	33	18	-21	-30	-50	-50
Days Maximum Temp. ≥ 90°F	0	0	0	0	0	4	9	10	2	0	0	0	25
Days Maximum Temp. ≤ 32°F	17	11	6	1	0	0	0	0	0	1	8	14	58
Days Minimum Temp. ≤ 32°F	30	26	27	16	3	0	0	0	4	17	26	30	179
Days Minimum Temp. ≤ 0°F	13	7	2	0	0	0	0	0	0	0	4	9	35
Heating Degree Days (base 65°F)	1,550	1,197	999	610	316	108	30	46	265	618	1,066	1,414	8,219
Cooling Degree Days (base 65°F)	0	0	0	1	12	57	139	142	20	1	0	0	372
Mean Precipitation (in.)	*0.52*	*0.37*	*0.75*	*0.94*	*1.94*	*1.62*	*1.31*	*1.28*	*1.13*	*0.55*	*0.44*	*0.57*	*11.42*
Maximum Precipitation (in.)	2.3	1.0	2.0	2.6	5.0	4.7	5.4	3.6	5.8	2.1	1.2	2.0	18.5
Minimum Precipitation (in.)	trace	0.1	trace	0.1	0.3	0.2	trace	trace	trace	trace	trace	trace	7.0
Maximum 24-hr. Precipitation (in.)	0.5	0.4	1.4	1.5	2.1	2.0	2.1	2.3	1.9	0.8	0.4	0.6	2.3
Days With ≥ 0.1" Precipitation	2	1	2	3	5	5	4	3	3	2	2	2	34
Days With ≥ 1.0" Precipitation	0	0	0	0	0	0	0	0	0	0	0	0	0
Mean Snowfall (in.)	na	na	na	na	na	na	na	na	na	na	na	na	na
Maximum Snowfall (in.)	41	19	30	33	31	trace	0	trace	6	12	19	25	100
Maximum 24-hr. Snowfall (in.)	11	6	20	16	21	trace	0	trace	6	8	7	5	21
Days With ≥ 1.0" Snow Depth	21	14	10	3	0	0	0	0	0	1	8	16	73
Thunderstorm Days	0	< 1	0	< 1	3	5	6	5	1	< 1	0	0	20
Foggy Days	3	4	4	3	2	1	< 1	1	1	2	3	3	27
Predominant Sky Cover	OVR	OVR	OVR	OVR	OVR	BRK	CLR	CLR	OVR	OVR	OVR	OVR	OVR
Mean Relative Humidity 5am (%)	74	76	79	75	74	75	72	68	73	73	76	75	74
Mean Relative Humidity 5pm (%)	68	63	53	40	38	37	31	29	35	44	62	69	48
Mean Dewpoint (°F)	7	12	21	27	36	44	46	44	37	29	19	10	28
Prevailing Wind Direction	SW	SW	SW	SW	SW	SW	WSW	WSW	WSW	SW	SW	SW	SW
Prevailing Wind Speed (mph)	15	14	13	12	10	10	9	9	9	12	13	14	12
Maximum Wind Gust (mph)	60	53	58	63	58	69	53	70	55	60	78	67	78

Helena Airport ASOS

Helena is located on the south side of an intermountain valley bounded on the west and south by the main chain of the Continental Divide. The valley is approximately 25 miles in width from north to south and 35 miles long from east to west. The average height of the mountains above the valley floor is about 3,000 feet.

The climate of Helena may be described as modified continental. Factors that enter into modifying the continental climate are invasion by Pacific Ocean air masses, drainage of cool air into the valley from the surrounding mountains, and the protecting mountain shield.

The mountains to the north and east sometimes deflect shallow masses of invading cold Arctic air to the east. Following periods of extreme cold, when the return circulation of maritime air has brought warming to most of the eastern part of the state, cold air may remain trapped in the valley for several days before being replaced by warmer air. During these periods of transition from cold-to-warm temperatures, inversions are often quite pronounced.

As may be expected in a northern latitude, cold waves may occur from November through February, with temperatures occasionally dropping to zero or lower.

Summertime temperatures are moderate, with maximum readings generally under 90 degrees and very seldom reaching 100 degrees. Like all mountain stations, there is usually a marked change in temperature from day to night. During the summer this tends to produce an agreeable combination of fairly warm days and cool nights.

Most of the precipitation falls from April through July from frequent showers or thunderstorms, but usually with some steady rains in June, the wettest month of the year. Like summer, fall and winter months are relatively dry. During the April to September growing season, precipitation varies considerably.

Thunderstorms are rather frequent from May through August. Snow can be expected from September through May, but amounts during the spring and fall are usually light, and snow on the ground ordinarily lasts only a day or two. During the winter months snow may remain on the ground for several weeks at a time.

In winter, hours of sunshine are more than would be expected at a mountain location.

Due to the sheltering influence of the mountains, Foehn (Chinook) winds are not as pronounced as might be expected. Strong winds can occur at any time throughout the year, but generally do not last more than a few hours at a time.

Based on the 1951-1980 period, the average first occurrence of 32 degrees Fahrenheit in the fall is September 18 and the average last occurrence in the spring is May 18.

Helena Airport ASOS *Lewis And Clark County*   Elevation: 3,825 ft.   Latitude: 46° 36' N   Longitude: 111° 58' W

	JAN	FEB	MAR	APR	MAY	JUN	JUL	AUG	SEP	OCT	NOV	DEC	YEAR
Mean Maximum Temp. (°F)	30.1	37.2	46.2	56.3	65.7	74.8	83.0	82.2	70.6	58.1	41.6	31.5	56.4
Mean Temp. (°F)	19.9	26.5	34.7	43.7	52.7	61.1	67.6	66.5	55.9	44.5	31.0	21.5	43.8
Mean Minimum Temp. (°F)	9.7	15.7	23.2	31.0	39.7	47.5	52.2	50.7	41.0	31.0	20.4	11.4	31.1
Extreme Maximum Temp. (°F)	62	69	77	86	92	100	102	103	96	87	75	64	103
Extreme Minimum Temp. (°F)	-37	-42	-20	5	20	30	36	28	18	-8	-27	-37	-42
Days Maximum Temp. ≥ 90°F	0	0	0	0	0	2	8	7	1	0	0	0	18
Days Maximum Temp. ≤ 32°F	14	8	3	1	0	0	0	0	0	1	6	14	47
Days Minimum Temp. ≤ 32°F	29	27	27	17	4	0	0	0	4	17	27	30	182
Days Minimum Temp. ≤ 0°F	9	4	1	0	0	0	0	0	0	0	2	6	22
Heating Degree Days (base 65°F)	1,392	1,081	932	634	377	151	39	52	281	628	1,013	1,343	7,923
Cooling Degree Days (base 65°F)	0	0	0	0	5	42	133	118	16	0	0	0	314
Mean Precipitation (in.)	*0.56*	*0.44*	*0.72*	*0.95*	*1.65*	*1.74*	*1.32*	*1.33*	*1.10*	*0.64*	*0.47*	*0.52*	*11.44*
Maximum Precipitation (in.)	2.8	1.2	1.6	3.0	6.1	4.3	4.7	4.2	3.4	2.7	1.5	1.5	20.9
Minimum Precipitation (in.)	trace	trace	trace	0.1	0.3	0.1	0.1	trace	0.1	trace	trace	trace	6.3
Maximum 24-hr. Precipitation (in.)	0.6	0.5	0.6	1.0	2.1	1.8	1.4	1.8	1.6	0.8	0.6	0.5	2.1
Days With ≥ 0.1" Precipitation	2	1	2	3	5	5	4	4	3	2	2	1	34
Days With ≥ 1.0" Precipitation	0	0	0	0	0	0	0	0	0	0	0	0	0
Mean Snowfall (in.)	na	na	na	na	na	na	na	na	na	na	na	na	na
Maximum Snowfall (in.)	36	20	22	21	13	3	trace	6	14	11	33	23	92
Maximum 24-hr. Snowfall (in.)	9	8	9	13	13	3	trace	3	13	7	19	10	19
Days With ≥ 1.0" Snow Depth	18	11	7	1	0	0	0	0	0	1	6	14	58
Thunderstorm Days	< 1	< 1	< 1	1	4	7	8	8	2	< 1	< 1	< 1	30
Foggy Days	3	2	2	2	1	1	< 1	1	1	2	3	5	23
Predominant Sky Cover	OVR	OVR	OVR	OVR	OVR	OVR	CLR	CLR	CLR	OVR	OVR	OVR	OVR
Mean Relative Humidity 5am (%)	72	73	73	71	73	73	68	68	73	74	73	73	72
Mean Relative Humidity 5pm (%)	63	56	48	40	39	39	30	30	36	44	58	66	46
Mean Dewpoint (°F)	10	15	19	26	34	41	44	43	36	29	20	13	28
Prevailing Wind Direction	W	W	W	W	W	W	W	W	W	W	W	W	W
Prevailing Wind Speed (mph)	10	10	12	12	12	12	10	9	10	10	10	10	10
Maximum Wind Gust (mph)	68	63	60	58	69	64	81	61	54	60	61	58	81

Kalispell Airport

The climate of the Flathead Valley is influenced by the topography. The high mountains to the east form an effective barrier to many severe winter cold waves that move into areas east of the Rockies from Alberta. The mountains to the east rise abruptly 4,500 feet above the valley floor. The mountain snows and spring rains assure an adequate supply of water for the area.

In addition to Flathead Lake, the valley contains many smaller lakes, three rivers, and numerous streams and sloughs. Until late in the winter when a large portion of the lakes and sloughs become frozen, this water surface tends to limit temperature extremes. This effect is most noticeable in the southern end of the valley, because of the influence of Flathead Lake. Due to its size, Flathead Lake seldom freezes over.

The weather at the airport is considerably different in some respects from the weather in Kalispell. Generally there is more cloudiness at the airport since it is closer to the mountains to the east and north. Moist air moving in from the west and southwest, lifting and cooling as it moves over the mountains, is the major cause. On average there is more precipitation on the east side of the valley than on the west side. Average snowfall during the winter at the airport is 68 inches and in Kalispell it is 49 inches.

The annual prevailing wind direction at Kalispell is from the west. At the airport it is from the south. Wind speeds average considerably stronger at the airport than in Kalispell.

In the winter, when a cold wave moving down the east side of the Continental Divide does come over the mountains, the airport is in direct line of the pass the cold air comes through. During these cold waves the wind is from the northeast and will usually have speeds reaching 30 to 40 mph. The strongest gusts reported during these storms exceed 80 mph. As the cold air moves down the valley it spreads out, decreasing the wind velocity, and mixes with the warmer air of the valley. Unless these cold strong winds persist for three or four days, the wind in the lower part of the valley will be from the northwest, because of the influence of Flathead Lake and the mountains to the west. This wind is always much stronger in the northeast end of the valley where the airport is located than any other place in the valley.

Kalispell Airport *Flathead County*   Elevation: 2,969 ft.   Latitude: 48° 19' N   Longitude: 114° 15' W

	JAN	FEB	MAR	APR	MAY	JUN	JUL	AUG	SEP	OCT	NOV	DEC	YEAR
Mean Maximum Temp. (°F)	28.7	35.2	44.7	55.7	64.8	72.1	80.2	80.5	68.9	55.2	38.7	30.2	54.6
Mean Temp. (°F)	21.1	26.8	34.8	43.6	51.9	58.6	64.4	64.0	53.6	42.2	31.2	23.2	42.9
Mean Minimum Temp. (°F)	13.5	18.4	24.8	31.4	38.9	45.1	48.4	47.5	38.3	29.2	23.6	16.1	31.3
Extreme Maximum Temp. (°F)	51	64	72	84	94	95	102	99	97	86	69	57	102
Extreme Minimum Temp. (°F)	-37	-30	-10	12	20	26	30	31	16	-3	-17	-35	-37
Days Maximum Temp. ≥ 90°F	0	0	0	0	0	1	5	6	0	0	0	0	12
Days Maximum Temp. ≤ 32°F	17	8	3	0	0	0	0	0	0	1	6	17	52
Days Minimum Temp. ≤ 32°F	29	26	27	18	5	1	0	0	6	21	25	29	187
Days Minimum Temp. ≤ 0°F	6	3	0	0	0	0	0	0	0	0	1	4	14
Heating Degree Days (base 65°F)	1,355	1,072	931	636	404	204	80	89	338	700	1,008	1,289	8,106
Cooling Degree Days (base 65°F)	0	0	0	0	5	16	56	62	5	0	0	0	144
Mean Precipitation (in.)	*1.55*	*1.18*	*1.06*	*1.14*	*2.00*	*2.05*	*1.29*	*1.40*	*1.20*	*0.82*	*1.39*	*1.67*	*16.75*
Maximum Precipitation (in.)	3.1	2.0	3.0	2.4	4.8	5.3	6.0	3.8	4.0	3.0	4.4	4.4	23.9
Minimum Precipitation (in.)	0.2	0.4	0.1	0.3	0.4	0.4	trace	trace	trace	trace	0.3	0.3	11.1
Maximum 24-hr. Precipitation (in.)	1.0	0.6	0.8	1.6	1.4	2.7	2.1	1.7	1.1	0.9	1.1	1.3	2.7
Days With ≥ 0.1" Precipitation	5	4	4	4	6	6	4	4	3	5	6	55
Days With ≥ 1.0" Precipitation	0	0	0	0	0	0	0	0	0	0	0	0	0
Mean Snowfall (in.)	na	na	na	na	na	na	na	na	na	na	na	na	na
Maximum Snowfall (in.)	35	21	19	11	9	6	0	trace	3	11	39	52	115
Maximum 24-hr. Snowfall (in.)	12	7	7	7	8	6	0	trace	3	5	9	12	12
Days With ≥ 1.0" Snow Depth	24	19	9	1	0	0	0	0	0	1	8	19	81
Thunderstorm Days	0	< 1	< 1	1	3	5	6	5	2	< 1	< 1	< 1	22
Foggy Days	12	9	6	3	3	4	3	3	5	9	12	13	82
Predominant Sky Cover	OVR	OVR	OVR	OVR	OVR	OVR	CLR	CLR	OVR	OVR	OVR	OVR	OVR
Mean Relative Humidity 5am (%)	81	81	80	77	79	83	83	81	83	85	84	84	82
Mean Relative Humidity 5pm (%)	75	67	54	43	42	46	37	36	42	54	73	79	54
Mean Dewpoint (°F)	15	20	23	29	37	44	47	45	39	32	25	19	31
Prevailing Wind Direction	S	S	S	S	S	S	S	S	S	S	S	S	S
Prevailing Wind Speed (mph)	9	8	9	9	9	9	8	8	8	8	8	9	9
Maximum Wind Gust (mph)	66	49	52	51	52	62	51	69	49	54	60	62	69

Miles City Municipal Airport

Miles City is located on the western edge of the northern great plains in a shallow part of the Yellowstone Valley. The Tongue River runs south from its confluence with the Yellowstone just west of the city. To the north the river bluffs are from 200 to 300 feet above the valley floor. There are no nearby mountain ranges to influence climatic conditions. Temperatures range from very cold in winter to quite warm in summer, which is characteristic of continental locations. The climate is classed as semi-arid with less than 10 inches of rainfall in about one year in seven.

The temperature has ranged from less than -65 degrees to more than 110 degrees. Cold waves with temperatures of zero or lower occur frequently during the winter. They are usually accompanied by northerly winds and snow, and last two to four days. Periods of several days with zero or lower can be expected during the winter months. Spring and fall are cool with temperatures of 90 degrees or above rarely occurring. High temperatures of 90 degrees or more do occur frequently in July and August, but humidities are low.

About 70 percent of the precipitation falls during the growing season, April through September, with greatest monthly amounts usually falling during May and June. Precipitation during the spring and summer often falls during periods of shower or thunderstorm activity, however, general rains also are frequent in late spring and early summer. Measurable snowfall can be expected as late as May and as early as September.

Sunny growing seasons, with May and June rainfall being the heaviest of the year, encourage rapid crop development. Crops grown in this area seldom have difficulty in reaching maturity, although hail sometimes causes local damage during the middle of the summer.

Based on the 1951-1980 period, the average first occurrence of 32 degrees Fahrenheit in the fall is September 29 and the average last occurrence in the spring is May 7.

Miles City Municipal Airport *Custer County*   Elevation: 2,627 ft.   Latitude: 46° 26' N   Longitude: 105° 53' W

	JAN	FEB	MAR	APR	MAY	JUN	JUL	AUG	SEP	OCT	NOV	DEC	YEAR
Mean Maximum Temp. (°F)	26.7	35.1	45.6	58.3	69.4	80.0	87.8	86.8	73.8	59.8	42.1	31.1	58.1
Mean Temp. (°F)	16.9	24.8	34.5	46.4	57.2	67.2	74.0	72.9	60.3	47.5	32.0	21.0	46.2
Mean Minimum Temp. (°F)	7.1	14.4	23.4	34.4	44.9	54.4	60.1	58.9	46.7	35.1	21.8	10.9	34.3
Extreme Maximum Temp. (°F)	72	73	81	92	100	106	109	110	106	95	81	67	110
Extreme Minimum Temp. (°F)	-37	-36	-28	5	23	36	44	36	19	-8	-25	-38	-38
Days Maximum Temp. ≥ 90°F	0	0	0	0	1	6	14	13	3	0	0	0	37
Days Maximum Temp. ≤ 32°F	17	10	5	1	0	0	0	0	0	1	7	14	55
Days Minimum Temp. ≤ 32°F	30	27	26	12	2	0	0	0	2	11	26	30	166
Days Minimum Temp. ≤ 0°F	11	6	2	0	0	0	0	0	0	0	2	7	28
Heating Degree Days (base 65°F)	1,486	1,129	938	555	264	62	11	17	193	538	984	1,357	7,534
Cooling Degree Days (base 65°F)	0	0	0	3	30	134	294	280	62	3	0	0	806
Mean Precipitation (in.)	*0.52*	*0.39*	*0.55*	*1.41*	*2.39*	*2.49*	*1.35*	*1.19*	*1.40*	*1.09*	*0.54*	na	na
Maximum Precipitation (in.)	1.8	1.3	1.8	4.2	6.8	5.2	4.5	4.0	4.0	6.3	2.2	1.8	20.3
Minimum Precipitation (in.)	0	trace	0.1	trace	0.2	0.7	trace	trace	trace	trace	trace	trace	5.3
Maximum 24-hr. Precipitation (in.)	0.5	0.8	0.7	2.1	2.3	2.7	2.2	1.7	1.6	2.1	1.2	0.5	2.7
Days With ≥ 0.1" Precipitation	2	1	2	4	6	6	4	3	3	3	2	1	37
Days With ≥ 1.0" Precipitation	0	0	0	0	0	0	0	0	0	0	0	0	0
Mean Snowfall (in.)	na	na	na	na	na	na	na	na	na	na	na	na	na
Maximum Snowfall (in.)	17	19	18	17	12	trace	0	0	7	13	19	18	66
Maximum 24-hr. Snowfall (in.)	8	10	6	15	8	trace	0	0	7	10	8	7	15
Days With ≥ 1.0" Snow Depth	23	14	10	2	0	0	0	0	0	1	6	16	72
Thunderstorm Days	0	< 1	< 1	1	4	8	7	6	2	< 1	< 1	0	28
Foggy Days	6	6	7	4	4	2	1	1	2	3	5	6	47
Predominant Sky Cover	OVR	OVR	OVR	OVR	OVR	SCT	SCT	CLR	CLR	CLR	OVR	OVR	OVR
Mean Relative Humidity 5am (%)	75	79	80	75	76	76	68	66	70	73	78	77	74
Mean Relative Humidity 5pm (%)	70	67	57	43	42	40	31	30	38	46	63	70	50
Mean Dewpoint (°F)	7	14	21	29	39	48	50	48	40	32	22	13	30
Prevailing Wind Direction	SSE	SSE	NW	NW	SE	NW	SE	SE	NW	SSE	SSE	SSE	SSE
Prevailing Wind Speed (mph)	8	8	14	16	12	13	10	10	14	8	8	8	10
Maximum Wind Gust (mph)	na	na	na	na	na	na	na	na	na	na	na	na	na

Missoula Johnson-Bell Field

Missoula is situated in the heart of the Montana Rocky Mountains in the extreme north portion of the Bitterroot Valley, and about five miles east of the confluence of the Bitterroot and Clark Fork Rivers. The Clark Fork Valley begins at Missoula and extends about 20 miles west-northwestward. The Bitterroot Valley extends about 70 miles due southward from Missoula. The Continental Divide is 60 to 80 miles east of Missoula, and the Bitterroot Range is only about 20 miles away to the southwest. These two mountain ranges have a marked effect on the climate of Missoula.

The prevailing flow of air aloft over western Montana is from the west and southwest during spring and summer months, and from the west and northwest during the winter months. Since this air must pass over the Bitterroot Range, it loses much of its moisture on the western slopes of these mountains. As a result, Missoula receives only between 12 inches and 15 inches of precipitation annually. This small amount of precipitation makes for a semi-arid climate. There is sufficient irrigation water, however, from the nearby mountains. The heaviest precipitation, of about two inches, is received in each month of May and June.

Generally the spring months are cool and a little damp, with almost daily shower activity during May and June. There are about 137 growing days each year. The summer months are dry with moderate temperatures and cool nights. Seldom does the temperature reach 100 degrees. Oppressively warm nighttime temperatures are unknown.

In the winter, the Continental Divide shields the Missoula area from much of the severely cold air which moves down the continent from arctic regions. Because of this shielding effect, many of the cold waves which sweep down over eastern Montana miss the Missoula area entirely. Under certain conditions, however, the cold Arctic air does break over the Continental Divide, and moves with force into the Bitterroot and Clark Fork Valleys. When this happens, Missoula experiences severe blizzard conditions. The cold air is funnelled to the city through Hell Gate which is the mouth of the Clark Fork River canyon at Missoula. Locally these blizzards are referred to as Hell Gate Blizzards. After the valleys of western Montana are filled with the cold air, prolonged cold spells may occur. January is the coldest month, although periods of sub-zero weather occur occasionally in December and February. Rarely, there are brief periods of sub-zero weather in November and March. During the winter months the sunshine is limited to about 30 percent of the possible amount.

Missoula Johnson-Bell Field *Missoula County*   Elevation: 3,188 ft.   Latitude: 46° 55' N   Longitude: 114° 06' W

	JAN	FEB	MAR	APR	MAY	JUN	JUL	AUG	SEP	OCT	NOV	DEC	YEAR
Mean Maximum Temp. (°F)	30.9	37.5	47.9	57.7	66.2	74.6	83.5	83.3	71.5	57.4	40.3	30.3	56.7
Mean Temp. (°F)	23.6	29.0	37.4	45.0	52.7	60.3	66.9	66.3	56.0	44.4	32.3	23.5	44.8
Mean Minimum Temp. (°F)	16.3	20.6	26.9	32.3	39.3	46.0	50.3	49.3	40.4	31.4	24.2	16.5	32.8
Extreme Maximum Temp. (°F)	56	66	75	87	95	98	105	101	98	85	73	59	105
Extreme Minimum Temp. (°F)	-28	-27	-9	15	21	30	31	30	20	0	-11	-30	-30
Days Maximum Temp. ≥ 90°F	0	0	0	0	0	3	9	9	1	0	0	0	22
Days Maximum Temp. ≤ 32°F	15	7	1	0	0	0	0	0	0	0	6	17	46
Days Minimum Temp. ≤ 32°F	29	26	25	16	5	0	0	0	4	17	26	29	177
Days Minimum Temp. ≤ 0°F	4	2	0	0	0	0	0	0	0	0	1	3	10
Heating Degree Days (base 65°F)	1,276	1,009	848	594	376	172	51	57	275	632	976	1,282	7,548
Cooling Degree Days (base 65°F)	0	0	0	0	5	34	109	103	12	0	0	0	263
Mean Precipitation (in.)	*1.14*	*0.78*	*1.02*	*0.90*	*2.04*	*1.63*	*0.98*	*1.20*	*1.06*	*0.68*	*0.88*	*1.11*	*13.42*
Maximum Precipitation (in.)	2.9	2.2	2.1	3.0	7.4	4.2	2.5	3.3	3.6	3.5	2.5	3.1	19.3
Minimum Precipitation (in.)	0.2	0.2	0.2	0.1	0.3	0.3	0.1	trace	0	trace	0.2	0.3	8.6
Maximum 24-hr. Precipitation (in.)	0.8	1.0	0.8	1.6	1.8	1.5	1.6	1.1	1.3	1.0	0.5	0.7	1.8
Days With ≥ 0.1" Precipitation	4	2	3	3	6	5	3	3	3	2	3	4	41
Days With ≥ 1.0" Precipitation	0	0	0	0	0	0	0	0	0	0	0	0	0
Mean Snowfall (in.)	na	na	na	na	na	na	na	na	na	na	na	na	na
Maximum Snowfall (in.)	43	20	16	8	8	trace	0	0	trace	5	16	32	78
Maximum 24-hr. Snowfall (in.)	11	14	7	7	7	trace	0	0	trace	5	5	10	14
Days With ≥ 1.0" Snow Depth	23	14	5	0	0	0	0	0	0	0	5	19	66
Thunderstorm Days	< 1	< 1	< 1	1	3	5	6	6	2	< 1	< 1	0	23
Foggy Days	12	9	4	2	2	2	1	1	3	6	11	14	67
Predominant Sky Cover	OVR	OVR	OVR	OVR	OVR	OVR	CLR	CLR	CLR	OVR	OVR	OVR	OVR
Mean Relative Humidity 5am (%)	85	85	83	79	82	83	77	74	81	85	86	86	82
Mean Relative Humidity 5pm (%)	76	66	52	41	42	42	31	30	38	50	71	79	51
Mean Dewpoint (°F)	17	21	25	29	37	44	45	44	39	33	25	19	32
Prevailing Wind Direction	ESE	WNW	NW	NW	NW	NW	NW	NW	NW	NW	NW	ESE	NW
Prevailing Wind Speed (mph)	9	7	8	9	9	9	9	9	8	8	7	8	8
Maximum Wind Gust (mph)	58	46	67	63	56	67	76	67	54	61	55	76	76

Alder 17 S *Madison County*   Elevation: 5,849 ft.   Latitude: 45° 04' N   Longitude: 112° 03' W

	JAN	FEB	MAR	APR	MAY	JUN	JUL	AUG	SEP	OCT	NOV	DEC	YEAR
Mean Maximum Temp. (°F)	32.3	37.1	43.3	51.8	61.2	70.3	78.9	78.4	68.1	56.8	40.9	32.6	54.3
Mean Temp. (°F)	22.4	26.5	32.4	39.6	48.1	56.0	62.4	61.8	52.5	43.0	30.4	22.8	41.5
Mean Minimum Temp. (°F)	12.6	15.8	21.5	27.3	34.9	41.7	45.9	45.1	36.9	29.1	19.7	13.0	28.6
Extreme Maximum Temp. (°F)	58	61	70	80	84	95	93	95	89	83	72	59	95
Extreme Minimum Temp. (°F)	-31	-30	-17	-2	11	23	24	27	8	-9	-23	-41	-41
Days Maximum Temp. ≥ 90°F	0	0	0	0	0	0	1	1	0	0	0	0	2
Days Maximum Temp. ≤ 32°F	14	7	3	1	0	0	0	0	0	1	7	14	47
Days Minimum Temp. ≤ 32°F	30	27	28	22	11	3	0	1	8	20	26	30	206
Days Minimum Temp. ≤ 0°F	6	3	1	0	0	0	0	0	0	0	2	5	17
Heating Degree Days (base 65°F)	1,313	1,081	1,003	756	519	273	108	125	372	675	1,033	1,302	8,560
Cooling Degree Days (base 65°F)	0	0	0	0	0	9	35	31	3	0	0	0	78
Mean Precipitation (in.)	0.36	0.30	0.73	1.11	2.33	2.40	1.57	1.50	1.30	0.93	0.60	0.40	13.53
Days With ≥ 0.1" Precipitation	1	1	2	4	7	7	5	5	4	3	2	1	42
Days With ≥ 1.0" Precipitation	0	0	0	0	0	0	0	0	0	0	0	0	0
Mean Snowfall (in.)	7.5	5.7	10.6	9.1	*3.5*	0.3	0.0	trace	0.7	*3.4*	*7.1*	7.5	*55.4*
Days With ≥ 1.0" Snow Depth	na	na	na	2	0	0	0	0	0	*1*	na	na	na

Augusta *Lewis And Clark County*   Elevation: 4,068 ft.   Latitude: 47° 30' N   Longitude: 112° 24' W

	JAN	FEB	MAR	APR	MAY	JUN	JUL	AUG	SEP	OCT	NOV	DEC	YEAR
Mean Maximum Temp. (°F)	36.0	41.5	47.6	57.2	66.2	74.8	82.0	82.0	72.0	61.2	44.2	36.9	58.5
Mean Temp. (°F)	24.0	28.6	34.7	43.4	52.1	60.2	65.7	64.9	55.8	46.5	32.9	25.5	44.5
Mean Minimum Temp. (°F)	11.9	15.6	21.8	29.7	37.9	45.5	49.3	47.7	39.6	31.7	21.6	14.1	30.5
Extreme Maximum Temp. (°F)	66	72	75	86	90	96	101	101	95	90	74	67	101
Extreme Minimum Temp. (°F)	-39	-42	-26	-8	16	29	33	26	14	-17	-27	-47	-47
Days Maximum Temp. ≥ 90°F	0	0	0	0	0	2	6	6	1	0	0	0	15
Days Maximum Temp. ≤ 32°F	10	6	3	1	0	0	0	0	0	1	4	7	32
Days Minimum Temp. ≤ 32°F	27	24	25	19	7	0	0	0	6	16	23	27	174
Days Minimum Temp. ≤ 0°F	9	5	2	0	0	0	0	0	0	0	3	6	25
Heating Degree Days (base 65°F)	1,268	1,023	931	641	397	169	57	71	283	570	956	1,218	7,584
Cooling Degree Days (base 65°F)	0	0	0	0	4	26	74	72	15	2	0	0	193
Mean Precipitation (in.)	0.50	0.44	0.66	1.19	2.59	2.29	1.50	1.51	1.27	0.82	0.51	0.53	13.81
Days With ≥ 0.1" Precipitation	2	2	2	3	6	5	4	4	3	2	2	2	37
Days With ≥ 1.0" Precipitation	0	0	0	0	0	1	0	0	0	0	0	0	1
Mean Snowfall (in.)	na	na	na	na	na	na	na	na	na	na	na	na	na
Days With ≥ 1.0" Snow Depth	na	na	na	na	0	0	0	0	0	*0*	na	na	na

Austin 1 W *Lewis And Clark County*   Elevation: 4,790 ft.   Latitude: 46° 38' N   Longitude: 112° 16' W

	JAN	FEB	MAR	APR	MAY	JUN	JUL	AUG	SEP	OCT	NOV	DEC	YEAR
Mean Maximum Temp. (°F)	29.9	35.3	42.8	52.3	61.9	70.7	78.9	78.6	67.3	54.6	38.2	30.8	53.4
Mean Temp. (°F)	20.8	25.8	32.1	40.3	48.9	56.8	63.4	63.0	53.3	43.0	29.6	22.2	41.6
Mean Minimum Temp. (°F)	11.7	16.3	21.4	28.4	35.9	43.0	47.9	47.4	39.1	31.4	20.9	13.6	29.7
Extreme Maximum Temp. (°F)	56	62	70	80	86	99	97	96	92	80	67	59	99
Extreme Minimum Temp. (°F)	-33	-38	-26	-6	21	27	31	26	13	-9	-21	-41	-41
Days Maximum Temp. ≥ 90°F	0	0	0	0	0	0	2	1	0	0	0	0	3
Days Maximum Temp. ≤ 32°F	15	8	4	1	0	0	0	0	0	1	8	15	52
Days Minimum Temp. ≤ 32°F	30	27	28	22	9	1	0	0	6	16	27	30	196
Days Minimum Temp. ≤ 0°F	8	4	1	0	0	0	0	0	0	0	2	5	20
Heating Degree Days (base 65°F)	1,365	1,101	1,013	733	493	252	95	102	351	674	1,056	1,321	8,556
Cooling Degree Days (base 65°F)	0	0	0	0	1	10	44	44	6	0	0	0	105
Mean Precipitation (in.)	1.07	0.76	1.00	1.45	2.43	2.17	1.66	1.47	1.42	1.10	1.19	1.09	16.81
Days With ≥ 0.1" Precipitation	4	3	4	5	7	6	4	4	4	4	4	4	53
Days With ≥ 1.0" Precipitation	0	0	0	0	0	0	0	0	0	0	0	0	0
Mean Snowfall (in.)	na	na	na	na	na	na	na	na	na	na	na	na	na
Days With ≥ 1.0" Snow Depth	*21*	na	*9*	2	0	0	0	0	0	2	7	16	na

Babb 6 NE *Glacier County*   Elevation: 4,297 ft.   Latitude: 48° 56' N   Longitude: 113° 22' W

	JAN	FEB	MAR	APR	MAY	JUN	JUL	AUG	SEP	OCT	NOV	DEC	YEAR
Mean Maximum Temp. (°F)	*32.6*	37.0	42.4	51.7	61.7	69.1	75.7	76.1	*65.8*	55.7	40.5	na	na
Mean Temp. (°F)	*21.1*	25.1	31.0	39.6	48.4	55.5	60.3	60.2	*51.1*	42.9	*30.2*	na	na
Mean Minimum Temp. (°F)	*9.3*	13.1	19.6	27.5	35.1	41.7	44.8	44.1	*36.3*	30.1	*19.5*	na	na
Extreme Maximum Temp. (°F)	62	70	68	85	88	91	96	97	93	87	72	70	97
Extreme Minimum Temp. (°F)	-47	-41	-31	-15	18	24	29	21	7	-15	-31	-43	-47
Days Maximum Temp. ≥ 90°F	0	0	0	0	0	0	1	1	0	0	0	0	2
Days Maximum Temp. ≤ 32°F	11	7	5	1	0	0	0	0	0	1	5	*10*	*40*
Days Minimum Temp. ≤ 32°F	27	25	27	22	11	2	0	1	9	*18*	*24*	25	*191*
Days Minimum Temp. ≤ 0°F	9	6	3	0	0	0	0	0	0	0	3	7	28
Heating Degree Days (base 65°F)	*1,355*	1,120	1,045	756	508	284	159	157	*414*	679	*1,052*	na	na
Cooling Degree Days (base 65°F)	0	0	0	0	1	5	18	25	2	0	*0*	na	na
Mean Precipitation (in.)	na	na	na	na	na	na	na	na	na	na	na	na	na
Days With ≥ 0.1" Precipitation	3	2	3	4	6	6	4	5	4	3	3	2	45
Days With ≥ 1.0" Precipitation	0	0	0	0	1	1	0	0	0	0	0	0	2
Mean Snowfall (in.)	na	na	na	na	na	na	na	na	na	na	na	na	na
Days With ≥ 1.0" Snow Depth	na	na	na	*0*	na	na	0	0	0	na	na	na	na

Biddle 8 SW *Powder River County* Elevation: 3,595 ft. Latitude: 45° 02' N Longitude: 105° 29' W

	JAN	FEB	MAR	APR	MAY	JUN	JUL	AUG	SEP	OCT	NOV	DEC	YEAR
Mean Maximum Temp. (°F)	33.4	39.6	47.7	58.2	68.4	78.6	86.8	86.6	74.9	61.5	45.2	35.7	59.7
Mean Temp. (°F)	21.1	27.1	34.8	44.5	54.4	64.0	71.0	70.1	59.0	46.9	32.9	23.5	45.8
Mean Minimum Temp. (°F)	8.8	14.6	21.8	30.8	40.5	49.4	55.1	53.5	43.1	32.2	20.5	11.3	31.8
Extreme Maximum Temp. (°F)	69	72	78	90	96	107	109	105	104	89	79	69	109
Extreme Minimum Temp. (°F)	-32	-37	-27	0	21	31	36	31	13	-17	-24	-43	-43
Days Maximum Temp. ≥ 90°F	0	0	0	0	0	4	12	12	3	0	0	0	31
Days Maximum Temp. ≤ 32°F	12	7	4	1	0	0	0	0	0	0	5	10	39
Days Minimum Temp. ≤ 32°F	31	27	27	*17*	5	0	0	0	3	16	27	29	*182*
Days Minimum Temp. ≤ 0°F	9	4	2	0	0	0	0	0	0	0	2	6	23
Heating Degree Days (base 65°F)	1,355	1,063	931	610	331	100	19	23	214	557	957	1,280	7,440
Cooling Degree Days (base 65°F)	0	0	0	1	13	79	218	197	42	1	0	0	551
Mean Precipitation (in.)	0.46	0.39	0.88	1.56	2.68	2.51	1.58	0.98	1.41	1.27	0.59	0.53	14.84
Days With ≥ 0.1" Precipitation	2	2	3	5	6	5	4	3	3	3	2	2	40
Days With ≥ 1.0" Precipitation	0	0	0	0	0	0	0	0	0	0	0	0	0
Mean Snowfall (in.)	7.3	5.7	7.4	*5.4*	0.8	0.0	0.0	0.0	0.8	2.4	5.1	*7.2*	*42.1*
Days With ≥ 1.0" Snow Depth	25	14	9	*2*	0	0	0	0	0	1	8	17	*76*

Big Sandy *Chouteau County* Elevation: 2,769 ft. Latitude: 48° 08' N Longitude: 110° 04' W

	JAN	FEB	MAR	APR	MAY	JUN	JUL	AUG	SEP	OCT	NOV	DEC	YEAR
Mean Maximum Temp. (°F)	29.5	36.7	48.1	60.7	70.9	79.6	86.5	86.2	74.1	62.3	43.5	*32.9*	*59.2*
Mean Temp. (°F)	17.3	24.0	34.7	45.9	55.8	64.2	69.5	68.5	57.3	46.6	30.8	*20.7*	*44.6*
Mean Minimum Temp. (°F)	5.1	11.3	21.4	31.0	40.5	48.6	52.5	50.9	40.5	30.8	18.1	*8.6*	*29.9*
Extreme Maximum Temp. (°F)	62	76	78	91	96	103	103	106	99	90	78	64	106
Extreme Minimum Temp. (°F)	-42	-45	-31	-8	17	28	37	25	17	-7	-33	-50	-50
Days Maximum Temp. ≥ 90°F	0	0	0	0	1	4	12	12	2	0	0	0	31
Days Maximum Temp. ≤ 32°F	15	9	4	1	0	0	0	0	0	1	6	11	47
Days Minimum Temp. ≤ 32°F	30	27	27	17	5	0	0	0	5	16	26	28	181
Days Minimum Temp. ≤ 0°F	12	7	2	0	0	0	0	0	0	0	3	8	32
Heating Degree Days (base 65°F)	1,455	1,152	931	569	296	97	30	39	247	562	1,019	*1,368*	7,765
Cooling Degree Days (base 65°F)	0	0	0	2	22	76	170	150	24	*0*	0	*0*	*444*
Mean Precipitation (in.)	0.61	0.37	0.61	1.12	2.55	2.64	1.71	1.36	1.42	0.76	0.51	0.51	14.17
Days With ≥ 0.1" Precipitation	2	1	*2*	3	6	5	4	4	4	2	2	1	*36*
Days With ≥ 1.0" Precipitation	0	0	0	0	1	1	0	0	0	0	0	0	2
Mean Snowfall (in.)	na	na	na	na	*0.2*	*0.0*	*0.0*	*0.0*	*trace*	na	na	na	na
Days With ≥ 1.0" Snow Depth	na	na	na	na	*0*	*0*	*0*	*0*	*0*	na	na	na	na

Big Timber *Sweet Grass County* Elevation: 4,097 ft. Latitude: 45° 50' N Longitude: 109° 57' W

	JAN	FEB	MAR	APR	MAY	JUN	JUL	AUG	SEP	OCT	NOV	DEC	YEAR
Mean Maximum Temp. (°F)	36.7	42.2	49.3	58.6	68.2	78.2	86.2	85.7	73.8	61.3	45.4	38.0	60.3
Mean Temp. (°F)	26.3	30.8	36.9	45.1	53.9	62.8	69.2	68.3	57.6	47.4	35.1	28.3	46.8
Mean Minimum Temp. (°F)	15.8	19.4	24.4	31.5	39.6	47.4	52.2	50.9	41.3	33.5	24.8	18.5	33.3
Extreme Maximum Temp. (°F)	64	69	77	87	92	104	104	102	98	88	75	65	104
Extreme Minimum Temp. (°F)	-32	-32	-26	-1	21	29	36	29	16	-9	-26	-38	-38
Days Maximum Temp. ≥ 90°F	0	0	0	0	0	4	12	11	2	0	0	0	29
Days Maximum Temp. ≤ 32°F	9	6	3	0	0	0	0	0	0	0	4	8	30
Days Minimum Temp. ≤ 32°F	26	23	24	17	4	0	0	0	4	14	23	26	161
Days Minimum Temp. ≤ 0°F	7	4	1	0	0	0	0	0	0	0	1	4	17
Heating Degree Days (base 65°F)	1,194	959	866	592	341	117	25	30	236	540	888	1,133	6,921
Cooling Degree Days (base 65°F)	0	0	0	0	6	56	162	146	23	1	0	0	394
Mean Precipitation (in.)	0.67	0.47	0.93	1.85	2.86	2.61	1.54	1.25	1.34	1.38	0.73	0.70	16.33
Days With ≥ 0.1" Precipitation	2	2	3	5	6	6	4	3	4	3	3	2	43
Days With ≥ 1.0" Precipitation	0	0	0	0	0	1	0	0	0	0	0	0	1
Mean Snowfall (in.)	na	na	na	na	na	na	na	na	na	na	na	na	na
Days With ≥ 1.0" Snow Depth	na	na	na	na	*0*	*0*	*0*	*0*	*0*	na	na	na	na

Billings Water Plant *Yellowstone County* Elevation: 3,097 ft. Latitude: 45° 46' N Longitude: 108° 29' W

	JAN	FEB	MAR	APR	MAY	JUN	JUL	AUG	SEP	OCT	NOV	DEC	YEAR
Mean Maximum Temp. (°F)	37.5	44.3	52.8	62.2	71.7	81.2	88.3	87.8	77.0	65.2	48.5	39.2	63.0
Mean Temp. (°F)	25.4	31.1	38.8	47.7	57.1	65.9	71.9	70.8	60.4	49.7	36.1	27.3	48.5
Mean Minimum Temp. (°F)	13.1	17.8	24.7	33.2	42.4	50.5	55.4	53.8	43.8	34.2	23.7	15.3	34.0
Extreme Maximum Temp. (°F)	70	73	81	90	95	103	104	104	100	92	80	69	104
Extreme Minimum Temp. (°F)	-33	-35	-25	5	24	32	37	33	22	-10	-24	-41	-41
Days Maximum Temp. ≥ 90°F	0	0	0	0	1	6	15	14	3	0	0	0	39
Days Maximum Temp. ≤ 32°F	10	6	2	0	0	0	0	0	0	0	4	7	29
Days Minimum Temp. ≤ 32°F	29	26	25	14	2	0	0	0	2	12	25	29	164
Days Minimum Temp. ≤ 0°F	7	4	1	0	0	0	0	0	0	0	1	4	17
Heating Degree Days (base 65°F)	1,221	950	805	513	255	69	10	16	173	468	860	1,163	6,503
Cooling Degree Days (base 65°F)	0	0	0	1	19	105	232	216	46	2	0	0	621
Mean Precipitation (in.)	0.62	0.47	0.86	1.58	2.48	2.00	1.18	0.92	1.41	1.32	0.65	0.57	14.06
Days With ≥ 0.1" Precipitation	2	2	3	4	6	5	3	3	3	3	2	2	38
Days With ≥ 1.0" Precipitation	0	0	0	0	0	0	0	0	0	0	0	0	0
Mean Snowfall (in.)	na	na	na	na	na	na	na	na	na	na	na	na	na
Days With ≥ 1.0" Snow Depth	na	na	na	na	*0*	*0*	*0*	*0*	*0*	na	na	na	na

Birney *Rosebud County*   Elevation: 3,159 ft.   Latitude: 45° 19' N   Longitude: 106° 31' W

	JAN	FEB	MAR	APR	MAY	JUN	JUL	AUG	SEP	OCT	NOV	DEC	YEAR
Mean Maximum Temp. (°F)	34.0	41.9	51.5	62.8	72.6	82.0	89.5	88.5	77.2	63.9	45.2	35.6	62.1
Mean Temp. (°F)	19.8	27.5	36.8	46.8	56.4	65.7	71.6	70.1	59.3	47.4	32.1	22.0	46.3
Mean Minimum Temp. (°F)	5.8	13.1	22.0	30.7	40.3	49.4	53.8	51.7	41.5	30.8	19.0	8.4	30.5
Extreme Maximum Temp. (°F)	69	75	81	90	99	108	107	106	102	94	76	70	108
Extreme Minimum Temp. (°F)	-40	-40	-27	-1	21	31	33	31	13	-18	-27	-46	-46
Days Maximum Temp. ≥ 90°F	0	0	0	0	1	7	17	15	4	0	0	0	44
Days Maximum Temp. ≤ 32°F	12	6	2	0	0	0	0	0	0	0	4	10	34
Days Minimum Temp. ≤ 32°F	30	27	27	17	5	0	0	0	4	18	28	30	186
Days Minimum Temp. ≤ 0°F	10	5	2	0	0	0	0	0	0	0	2	7	26
Heating Degree Days (base 65°F)	1,392	1,053	868	541	273	73	11	18	198	540	980	1,324	7,271
Cooling Degree Days (base 65°F)	0	0	0	1	17	107	235	208	41	1	0	0	610
Mean Precipitation (in.)	0.59	0.39	0.87	1.40	2.19	2.47	1.33	0.96	1.05	1.11	0.72	0.56	13.64
Days With ≥ 0.1" Precipitation	2	1	3	4	5	5	4	2	3	3	2	2	36
Days With ≥ 1.0" Precipitation	0	0	0	0	0	0	0	0	0	0	0	0	0
Mean Snowfall (in.)	7.3	5.5	3.1	2.6	0.3	0.0	0.0	0.0	0.4	0.5	3.7	5.7	29.1
Days With ≥ 1.0" Snow Depth	17	11	6	1	0	0	0	0	0	0	4	13	52

Boulder *Jefferson County*   Elevation: 4,901 ft.   Latitude: 46° 14' N   Longitude: 112° 07' W

	JAN	FEB	MAR	APR	MAY	JUN	JUL	AUG	SEP	OCT	NOV	DEC	YEAR
Mean Maximum Temp. (°F)	34.0	39.4	46.2	55.2	64.5	73.7	82.0	81.9	71.0	59.4	42.3	34.6	57.0
Mean Temp. (°F)	22.1	27.0	33.4	41.2	49.9	58.2	64.8	64.0	53.9	43.5	30.4	22.8	42.6
Mean Minimum Temp. (°F)	10.1	14.6	20.6	27.2	35.2	42.8	47.6	46.1	36.7	27.6	18.4	10.9	28.2
Extreme Maximum Temp. (°F)	58	65	72	83	89	96	96	99	93	87	71	62	99
Extreme Minimum Temp. (°F)	-33	-39	-22	-6	17	24	31	19	11	-14	-26	-42	-42
Days Maximum Temp. ≥ 90°F	0	0	0	0	0	1	5	4	0	0	0	0	10
Days Maximum Temp. ≤ 32°F	11	6	3	1	0	0	0	0	0	0	5	11	37
Days Minimum Temp. ≤ 32°F	30	27	29	23	11	2	0	1	8	22	28	30	211
Days Minimum Temp. ≤ 0°F	8	4	1	0	0	0	0	0	0	0	3	6	22
Heating Degree Days (base 65°F)	1,325	1,066	973	707	463	216	73	83	333	658	1,032	1,303	8,232
Cooling Degree Days (base 65°F)	0	0	0	0	1	18	68	58	7	0	0	0	152
Mean Precipitation (in.)	0.42	0.30	0.55	0.79	2.00	2.02	1.53	1.43	1.08	0.57	0.55	0.42	11.66
Days With ≥ 0.1" Precipitation	1	1	2	3	6	6	5	4	3	2	2	2	37
Days With ≥ 1.0" Precipitation	0	0	0	0	0	0	0	0	0	0	0	0	0
Mean Snowfall (in.)	na	na	na	na	na	na	na	na	na	na	na	na	na
Days With ≥ 1.0" Snow Depth	na	na	na	na	0	0	0	0	0	na	na	na	na

Bozeman 6 W Exp. Farm *Gallatin County*   Elevation: 4,773 ft.   Latitude: 45° 41' N   Longitude: 111° 09' W

	JAN	FEB	MAR	APR	MAY	JUN	JUL	AUG	SEP	OCT	NOV	DEC	YEAR
Mean Maximum Temp. (°F)	na	na	na	na	na	na	na	na	na	na	na	na	na
Mean Temp. (°F)	na	na	na	na	na	na	na	na	na	na	na	na	na
Mean Minimum Temp. (°F)	na	na	na	na	na	na	na	na	na	na	na	na	na
Extreme Maximum Temp. (°F)	61	64	75	81	86	98	97	97	94	85	75	63	98
Extreme Minimum Temp. (°F)	-32	-35	-20	-3	16	28	32	26	13	-10	-23	-39	-39
Days Maximum Temp. ≥ 90°F	0	0	0	0	0	1	3	3	1	0	0	0	8
Days Maximum Temp. ≤ 32°F	12	7	3	0	0	0	0	0	0	0	6	12	40
Days Minimum Temp. ≤ 32°F	29	26	27	19	7	1	0	0	5	17	26	29	186
Days Minimum Temp. ≤ 0°F	7	4	1	0	0	0	0	0	0	0	2	5	19
Heating Degree Days (base 65°F)	1,311	1,052	944	666	420	197	64	72	303	617	998	1,286	7,930
Cooling Degree Days (base 65°F)	0	0	0	0	2	21	74	67	11	0	0	0	175
Mean Precipitation (in.)	na	na	na	na	na	na	na	na	na	na	na	na	na
Days With ≥ 0.1" Precipitation	2	2	4	5	7	7	4	4	4	4	3	2	48
Days With ≥ 1.0" Precipitation	0	0	0	0	0	0	0	0	0	0	0	0	0
Mean Snowfall (in.)	na	na	na	na	na	na	na	na	na	na	na	na	na
Days With ≥ 1.0" Snow Depth	24	17	14	4	1	0	0	0	0	3	11	20	94

Bozeman Gallatin Field *Gallatin County*   Elevation: 4,425 ft.   Latitude: 45° 47' N   Longitude: 111° 10' W

	JAN	FEB	MAR	APR	MAY	JUN	JUL	AUG	SEP	OCT	NOV	DEC	YEAR
Mean Maximum Temp. (°F)	29.6	36.0	44.4	54.8	64.5	74.6	83.3	82.8	70.2	58.0	40.8	31.0	55.8
Mean Temp. (°F)	18.4	24.6	32.7	41.9	50.9	59.5	66.2	65.5	54.3	43.5	29.2	19.4	42.2
Mean Minimum Temp. (°F)	7.2	13.2	21.0	29.0	37.4	44.3	48.9	48.1	38.4	28.8	17.5	7.8	28.5
Extreme Maximum Temp. (°F)	58	66	75	85	88	100	102	102	95	87	74	63	102
Extreme Minimum Temp. (°F)	-38	-43	-31	-5	18	29	30	27	15	-10	-27	-46	-46
Days Maximum Temp. ≥ 90°F	0	0	0	0	0	2	8	8	1	0	0	0	19
Days Maximum Temp. ≤ 32°F	15	9	4	1	0	0	0	0	0	1	7	15	52
Days Minimum Temp. ≤ 32°F	30	27	29	21	7	1	0	0	6	21	28	30	200
Days Minimum Temp. ≤ 0°F	10	5	2	0	0	0	0	0	0	0	3	8	28
Heating Degree Days (base 65°F)	1,435	1,135	994	685	430	186	56	62	321	661	1,069	1,408	8,442
Cooling Degree Days (base 65°F)	0	0	0	0	2	25	97	84	8	0	0	0	216
Mean Precipitation (in.)	0.55	0.54	1.05	1.41	2.46	2.29	1.26	1.16	1.52	1.13	0.77	0.56	14.70
Days With ≥ 0.1" Precipitation	2	2	4	5	7	6	4	4	4	4	3	2	47
Days With ≥ 1.0" Precipitation	0	0	0	0	0	0	0	0	0	0	0	0	0
Mean Snowfall (in.)	6.5	5.5	8.7	6.9	2.0	trace	trace	trace	0.6	2.1	5.8	6.3	44.4
Days With ≥ 1.0" Snow Depth	24	15	13	3	0	0	0	0	0	1	10	21	87

Bozeman Montana State Univ. *Gallatin County*   Elevation: 4,911 ft.   Latitude: 45° 40' N   Longitude: 111° 03' W

	JAN	FEB	MAR	APR	MAY	JUN	JUL	AUG	SEP	OCT	NOV	DEC	YEAR
Mean Maximum Temp. (°F)	33.3	38.6	45.7	55.0	64.4	73.8	81.7	81.7	70.7	59.0	42.2	34.1	56.7
Mean Temp. (°F)	23.6	28.4	34.9	43.1	52.0	60.2	66.9	66.3	56.4	46.1	32.5	24.5	44.6
Mean Minimum Temp. (°F)	13.8	18.2	24.0	31.2	39.4	46.6	52.0	50.8	41.9	33.1	22.8	14.8	32.4
Extreme Maximum Temp. (°F)	61	63	73	81	86	96	97	97	93	88	73	63	97
Extreme Minimum Temp. (°F)	-26	-31	-17	1	19	29	34	30	16	-5	-18	-32	-32
Days Maximum Temp. ≥ 90°F	0	0	0	0	0	1	4	3	1	0	0	0	9
Days Maximum Temp. ≤ 32°F	12	7	3	1	0	0	0	0	0	1	6	12	42
Days Minimum Temp. ≤ 32°F	29	26	26	17	5	1	0	0	3	14	25	29	175
Days Minimum Temp. ≤ 0°F	6	3	1	0	0	0	0	0	0	0	1	4	15
Heating Degree Days (base 65°F)	1,278	1,027	928	650	401	174	48	52	269	579	969	1,249	7,624
Cooling Degree Days (base 65°F)	0	0	0	0	4	36	113	103	18	1	0	0	275
Mean Precipitation (in.)	0.79	0.71	1.48	1.94	3.37	2.56	1.37	1.37	2.01	1.54	1.09	0.73	18.96
Days With ≥ 0.1" Precipitation	3	2	5	6	8	7	4	4	5	4	3	3	54
Days With ≥ 1.0" Precipitation	0	0	0	0	0	0	0	0	0	0	0	0	0
Mean Snowfall (in.)	na	na	na	na	na	na	na	na	na	na	na	na	na
Days With ≥ 1.0" Snow Depth	29	22	17	5	1	0	0	0	0	3	14	27	118

Brandenberg *Rosebud County*   Elevation: 2,769 ft.   Latitude: 45° 49' N   Longitude: 106° 13' W

	JAN	FEB	MAR	APR	MAY	JUN	JUL	AUG	SEP	OCT	NOV	DEC	YEAR
Mean Maximum Temp. (°F)	31.9	39.5	48.6	60.2	70.7	80.8	89.1	88.2	75.3	61.5	44.3	34.6	60.4
Mean Temp. (°F)	20.0	27.1	35.7	46.0	55.9	65.4	71.6	70.3	58.7	46.9	32.6	23.1	46.1
Mean Minimum Temp. (°F)	8.1	14.5	22.6	31.8	41.1	49.9	54.1	52.4	42.0	32.3	20.9	11.5	31.8
Extreme Maximum Temp. (°F)	67	72	82	91	101	111	108	109	102	92	81	69	111
Extreme Minimum Temp. (°F)	-36	-39	-28	-2	20	28	34	30	19	-12	-25	-44	-44
Days Maximum Temp. ≥ 90°F	0	0	0	0	1	6	16	15	3	0	0	0	41
Days Maximum Temp. ≤ 32°F	13	8	3	0	0	0	0	0	0	0	5	11	40
Days Minimum Temp. ≤ 32°F	30	27	27	16	5	0	0	0	4	15	27	30	181
Days Minimum Temp. ≤ 0°F	10	5	2	0	0	0	0	0	0	0	2	6	25
Heating Degree Days (base 65°F)	1,390	1,065	903	565	290	78	13	21	216	555	965	1,294	7,355
Cooling Degree Days (base 65°F)	0	0	0	1	19	103	234	212	38	1	0	0	608
Mean Precipitation (in.)	0.67	0.48	0.81	1.65	2.36	2.33	1.14	0.99	1.22	1.37	0.72	0.61	14.35
Days With ≥ 0.1" Precipitation	2	2	2	4	6	6	3	3	3	4	2	2	39
Days With ≥ 1.0" Precipitation	0	0	0	0	0	0	0	0	0	0	0	0	0
Mean Snowfall (in.)	9.0	6.1	6.5	4.7	0.7	0.0	0.0	0.0	0.8	1.7	6.2	8.4	44.1
Days With ≥ 1.0" Snow Depth	23	15	8	2	0	0	0	0	0	1	8	20	77

Bredette *Roosevelt County*   Elevation: 2,687 ft.   Latitude: 48° 33' N   Longitude: 105° 16' W

	JAN	FEB	MAR	APR	MAY	JUN	JUL	AUG	SEP	OCT	NOV	DEC	YEAR
Mean Maximum Temp. (°F)	19.5	27.3	38.9	54.9	67.8	77.5	83.2	82.9	70.0	56.3	36.1	24.1	53.2
Mean Temp. (°F)	10.5	18.2	28.9	42.9	54.8	64.1	69.0	68.5	56.8	44.6	27.2	15.1	41.7
Mean Minimum Temp. (°F)	1.4	9.1	18.9	30.8	41.8	50.5	54.8	54.0	43.5	32.8	18.1	6.1	30.2
Extreme Maximum Temp. (°F)	52	65	76	91	100	107	105	108	103	95	76	55	108
Extreme Minimum Temp. (°F)	-36	-36	-21	-12	19	31	39	33	18	-6	-24	-37	-37
Days Maximum Temp. ≥ 90°F	0	0	0	0	1	3	7	8	2	0	0	0	21
Days Maximum Temp. ≤ 32°F	23	15	9	1	0	0	0	0	0	1	11	20	80
Days Minimum Temp. ≤ 32°F	31	28	28	17	4	0	0	0	3	13	27	31	182
Days Minimum Temp. ≤ 0°F	15	9	3	0	0	0	0	0	0	0	3	11	41
Heating Degree Days (base 65°F)	1,688	1,316	1,111	658	327	98	29	47	270	622	1,129	1,543	8,838
Cooling Degree Days (base 65°F)	0	0	0	2	21	81	161	171	33	2	0	0	471
Mean Precipitation (in.)	0.28	0.21	0.50	0.87	1.89	2.73	2.38	1.41	1.24	0.71	0.36	0.35	12.93
Days With ≥ 0.1" Precipitation	1	1	2	3	5	6	5	4	3	2	1	1	34
Days With ≥ 1.0" Precipitation	0	0	0	0	0	0	0	0	0	0	0	0	0
Mean Snowfall (in.)	na	na	na	na	na	na	na	na	na	na	na	na	na
Days With ≥ 1.0" Snow Depth	30	22	13	3	0	0	0	0	0	1	9	24	102

Bridger 1 S *Carbon County*   Elevation: 3,677 ft.   Latitude: 45° 17' N   Longitude: 108° 55' W

	JAN	FEB	MAR	APR	MAY	JUN	JUL	AUG	SEP	OCT	NOV	DEC	YEAR
Mean Maximum Temp. (°F)	33.7	41.2	50.6	59.8	70.1	79.5	87.0	86.3	75.6	62.7	45.6	35.9	60.6
Mean Temp. (°F)	23.0	29.5	37.5	46.0	55.5	63.9	70.1	69.0	59.0	48.1	34.3	25.4	46.8
Mean Minimum Temp. (°F)	12.2	17.9	24.4	32.1	40.8	48.3	53.1	51.8	42.3	33.4	22.7	14.8	32.8
Extreme Maximum Temp. (°F)	65	70	78	87	93	102	105	102	100	90	76	72	105
Extreme Minimum Temp. (°F)	-28	-32	-18	5	20	30	36	28	18	-8	-17	-37	-37
Days Maximum Temp. ≥ 90°F	0	0	0	0	1	5	13	11	3	0	0	0	33
Days Maximum Temp. ≤ 32°F	12	6	2	0	0	0	0	0	0	0	4	10	34
Days Minimum Temp. ≤ 32°F	29	25	25	16	4	0	0	0	3	14	24	28	168
Days Minimum Temp. ≤ 0°F	7	4	1	0	0	0	0	0	0	0	2	5	19
Heating Degree Days (base 65°F)	1,297	995	846	564	301	100	19	24	208	519	914	1,222	7,009
Cooling Degree Days (base 65°F)	0	0	0	1	14	74	181	157	38	1	0	0	466
Mean Precipitation (in.)	0.76	0.55	1.08	1.75	2.42	1.70	0.86	0.74	1.31	1.26	0.72	0.58	13.73
Days With ≥ 0.1" Precipitation	2	2	3	4	5	4	2	2	3	3	3	2	35
Days With ≥ 1.0" Precipitation	0	0	0	0	1	0	0	0	0	0	0	0	1
Mean Snowfall (in.)	8.6	6.2	9.6	7.2	1.2	0.0	0.0	0.0	1.1	na	5.7	6.6	na
Days With ≥ 1.0" Snow Depth	21	15	7	3	0	0	0	0	0	na	na	16	na

Broadus *Powder River County*   Elevation: 3,031 ft.   Latitude: 45° 27' N   Longitude: 105° 24' W

	JAN	FEB	MAR	APR	MAY	JUN	JUL	AUG	SEP	OCT	NOV	DEC	YEAR
Mean Maximum Temp. (°F)	32.1	39.6	48.1	59.3	69.2	79.2	86.8	86.2	74.4	61.6	45.1	35.1	59.7
Mean Temp. (°F)	19.3	26.6	34.7	45.1	55.1	64.8	71.0	69.7	58.0	46.1	32.2	22.3	45.4
Mean Minimum Temp. (°F)	6.4	13.3	21.2	30.9	41.0	50.3	55.1	53.1	41.6	30.6	19.2	9.5	31.0
Extreme Maximum Temp. (°F)	69	75	81	93	101	108	108	106	104	95	80	68	108
Extreme Minimum Temp. (°F)	-36	-40	-30	-5	20	31	35	28	16	-12	-26	-47	-47
Days Maximum Temp. ≥ 90°F	0	0	0	0	1	5	13	12	4	0	0	0	35
Days Maximum Temp. ≤ 32°F	13	8	4	1	0	0	0	0	0	0	5	11	42
Days Minimum Temp. ≤ 32°F	31	27	28	17	4	0	0	0	4	18	28	31	188
Days Minimum Temp. ≤ 0°F	10	6	2	0	0	0	0	0	0	0	2	7	27
Heating Degree Days (base 65°F)	1,413	1,079	934	590	313	86	17	27	235	578	980	1,317	7,569
Cooling Degree Days (base 65°F)	0	0	0	2	18	90	227	201	36	1	0	0	575
Mean Precipitation (in.)	0.51	0.40	0.87	1.57	2.42	2.15	1.52	0.90	1.08	1.14	0.61	0.51	13.68
Days With > 0.1" Precipitation	2	1	3	4	6	5	4	3	3	3	2	2	38
Days With ≥ 1.0" Precipitation	0	0	0	0	0	0	0	0	0	0	0	0	0
Mean Snowfall (in.)	na	na	na	na	na	na	na	na	na	na	na	na	na
Days With ≥ 1.0" Snow Depth	21	13	8	1	0	0	0	0	0	1	6	16	66

Brockway 3 WSW *McCone County*   Elevation: 2,627 ft.   Latitude: 47° 17' N   Longitude: 105° 49' W

	JAN	FEB	MAR	APR	MAY	JUN	JUL	AUG	SEP	OCT	NOV	DEC	YEAR
Mean Maximum Temp. (°F)	25.9	33.4	44.0	57.6	68.8	78.7	85.7	85.4	73.1	59.9	41.4	30.3	57.0
Mean Temp. (°F)	15.2	22.5	32.2	44.1	54.8	64.2	69.7	69.1	57.4	45.4	29.8	19.1	43.6
Mean Minimum Temp. (°F)	4.3	11.6	20.2	30.5	40.6	49.6	53.7	52.8	41.6	30.9	18.2	7.9	30.2
Extreme Maximum Temp. (°F)	68	71	77	91	101	110	106	108	103	94	78	68	110
Extreme Minimum Temp. (°F)	-42	-38	-36	-9	12	30	33	28	14	-10	-35	-42	-42
Days Maximum Temp. ≥ 90°F	0	0	0	0	1	4	11	11	2	0	0	0	29
Days Maximum Temp. ≤ 32°F	*18*	11	*6*	1	0	0	0	0	0	1	7	*15*	*59*
Days Minimum Temp. ≤ 32°F	31	27	28	18	5	0	0	0	4	*17*	27	30	*187*
Days Minimum Temp. ≤ 0°F	*11*	7	3	0	0	0	0	0	0	0	3	8	*32*
Heating Degree Days (base 65°F)	1,544	1,196	1,009	622	328	99	29	41	255	600	1,044	1,417	8,184
Cooling Degree Days (base 65°F)	0	0	0	1	18	86	182	192	35	1	0	0	515
Mean Precipitation (in.)	0.24	0.16	0.42	1.03	1.91	2.30	1.63	1.19	1.26	0.81	0.27	0.25	11.47
Days With ≥ 0.1" Precipitation	1	1	1	3	5	5	3	3	3	2	1	1	29
Days With ≥ 1.0" Precipitation	0	0	0	0	0	1	0	0	0	0	0	0	1
Mean Snowfall (in.)	na	na	na	na	*0.0*	*0.0*	*0.0*	*0.0*	*trace*	na	na	na	na
Days With ≥ 1.0" Snow Depth	na	na	na	na	*0*	*0*	0	*0*	*0*	na	na	na	na

Busby *Big Horn County*   Elevation: 3,428 ft.   Latitude: 45° 32' N   Longitude: 106° 58' W

	JAN	FEB	MAR	APR	MAY	JUN	JUL	AUG	SEP	OCT	NOV	DEC	YEAR
Mean Maximum Temp. (°F)	31.5	38.2	47.3	59.1	68.9	78.7	87.3	87.1	75.1	61.6	44.7	34.3	59.5
Mean Temp. (°F)	18.4	24.7	33.8	44.4	53.7	62.8	69.2	68.3	57.4	45.5	31.3	21.1	44.2
Mean Minimum Temp. (°F)	5.2	11.1	20.3	29.7	38.5	46.8	51.0	49.5	39.6	29.4	17.9	7.8	28.9
Extreme Maximum Temp. (°F)	69	70	79	87	95	104	105	104	101	90	82	68	105
Extreme Minimum Temp. (°F)	-45	-47	-33	4	20	28	33	29	12	-21	-33	-52	-52
Days Maximum Temp. ≥ 90°F	0	0	0	0	0	4	*13*	13	3	0	0	0	*33*
Days Maximum Temp. ≤ 32°F	13	8	3	1	0	0	0	0	0	0	5	11	41
Days Minimum Temp. ≤ 32°F	31	28	29	19	7	0	0	0	6	20	28	30	198
Days Minimum Temp. ≤ 0°F	11	7	2	0	0	0	0	0	0	0	3	7	30
Heating Degree Days (base 65°F)	1,440	1,133	960	613	348	117	24	33	245	597	1,004	1,357	7,871
Cooling Degree Days (base 65°F)	0	0	0	0	6	59	164	157	27	0	0	0	413
Mean Precipitation (in.)	0.76	0.52	0.86	1.42	2.39	2.39	1.25	0.82	1.44	1.37	0.89	0.67	14.78
Days With ≥ 0.1" Precipitation	3	2	3	5	6	6	3	3	4	4	3	2	44
Days With ≥ 1.0" Precipitation	0	0	0	0	0	0	0	0	0	0	0	0	0
Mean Snowfall (in.)	na	na	na	na	na	na	na	na	na	na	na	na	na
Days With ≥ 1.0" Snow Depth	28	21	15	2	0	0	0	0	0	1	9	22	98

Butte Bert Mooney Airport *Silver Bow County*   Elevation: 5,538 ft.   Latitude: 45° 58' N   Longitude: 112° 30' W

	JAN	FEB	MAR	APR	MAY	JUN	JUL	AUG	SEP	OCT	NOV	DEC	YEAR
Mean Maximum Temp. (°F)	29.5	34.6	41.7	51.1	60.8	70.7	79.5	79.0	67.6	55.4	39.3	29.9	53.3
Mean Temp. (°F)	17.7	22.2	29.9	38.7	47.6	56.1	62.6	61.6	51.5	40.8	27.6	17.9	39.5
Mean Minimum Temp. (°F)	5.7	9.7	18.1	26.2	34.3	41.4	45.6	44.1	35.3	26.1	15.8	5.8	25.7
Extreme Maximum Temp. (°F)	56	61	69	80	87	94	97	97	93	83	70	58	97
Extreme Minimum Temp. (°F)	-42	-44	-28	-16	9	26	28	23	8	-23	-32	-52	-52
Days Maximum Temp. ≥ 90°F	0	0	0	0	0	0	3	3	0	0	0	0	6
Days Maximum Temp. ≤ 32°F	16	10	6	1	0	0	0	0	0	1	8	17	59
Days Minimum Temp. ≤ 32°F	30	27	30	25	12	3	0	1	11	26	28	30	223
Days Minimum Temp. ≤ 0°F	11	7	3	0	0	0	0	0	0	0	4	11	36
Heating Degree Days (base 65°F)	1,459	1,203	1,081	782	533	270	104	127	402	744	1,116	1,455	9,276
Cooling Degree Days (base 65°F)	0	0	0	0	0	0	8	38	29	3	0	0	78
Mean Precipitation (in.)	*0.49*	*0.41*	*0.86*	na	*1.88*	*1.73*	na	*1.36*	*1.25*	*0.68*	*0.55*	*0.44*	na
Days With ≥ 0.1" Precipitation	1	1	3	3	6	6	5	4	3	3	2	2	39
Days With ≥ 1.0" Precipitation	0	0	0	0	0	0	0	0	0	0	0	0	0
Mean Snowfall (in.)	na	na	na	na	na	na	na	na	na	na	na	na	na
Days With ≥ 1.0" Snow Depth	27	21	16	5	1	0	0	0	0	2	11	24	107

Canyon Ferry Dam *Lewis And Clark County* Elevation: 3,671 ft. Latitude: 46° 39' N Longitude: 111° 44' W

	JAN	FEB	MAR	APR	MAY	JUN	JUL	AUG	SEP	OCT	NOV	DEC	YEAR
Mean Maximum Temp. (°F)	31.2	37.4	46.4	57.2	66.7	75.7	83.3	83.2	71.7	59.0	42.7	33.4	57.3
Mean Temp. (°F)	22.5	27.4	35.7	44.9	53.5	61.7	67.7	67.4	57.5	47.0	34.2	25.2	45.4
Mean Minimum Temp. (°F)	13.8	17.5	25.0	32.5	40.3	47.7	52.1	51.5	43.3	35.0	25.7	16.9	33.4
Extreme Maximum Temp. (°F)	57	68	75	85	91	95	100	99	93	84	69	62	100
Extreme Minimum Temp. (°F)	-30	-32	-21	6	23	33	37	30	24	-2	-14	-31	-32
Days Maximum Temp. ≥ 90°F	0	0	0	0	0	1	7	6	0	0	0	0	14
Days Maximum Temp. ≤ 32°F	13	8	3	0	0	0	0	0	0	0	4	12	40
Days Minimum Temp. ≤ 32°F	28	26	25	15	3	0	0	0	2	11	22	28	160
Days Minimum Temp. ≤ 0°F	7	4	1	0	0	0	0	0	0	0	0	1	4	17
Heating Degree Days (base 65°F)	1,312	1,055	899	598	351	134	36	39	234	550	917	1,228	7,353
Cooling Degree Days (base 65°F)	0	0	0	0	3	39	114	117	16	0	0	0	289
Mean Precipitation (in.)	0.45	0.31	0.59	0.97	1.95	1.79	1.48	1.29	1.15	0.64	0.46	0.45	11.53
Days With ≥ 0.1" Precipitation	1	1	2	3	5	5	4	3	3	2	2	2	33
Days With ≥ 1.0" Precipitation	0	0	0	0	0	0	0	0	0	0	0	0	0
Mean Snowfall (in.)	na	na	na	na	0.0	0.0	0.0	0.0	0.0	na	na	na	na
Days With ≥ 1.0" Snow Depth	na	na	na	na	0	0	0	0	0	na	na	na	na

Carlyle 12 NW *Wibaux County* Elevation: 3,028 ft. Latitude: 46° 45' N Longitude: 104° 17' W

	JAN	FEB	MAR	APR	MAY	JUN	JUL	AUG	SEP	OCT	NOV	DEC	YEAR
Mean Maximum Temp. (°F)	25.7	32.8	42.4	55.5	66.7	76.2	83.5	83.4	71.7	58.6	40.5	30.0	55.6
Mean Temp. (°F)	15.7	22.6	31.3	42.9	53.8	63.2	69.3	68.7	57.9	46.0	30.5	20.2	43.5
Mean Minimum Temp. (°F)	5.7	12.3	20.1	30.3	40.9	50.2	55.1	54.0	44.0	33.4	20.5	10.3	31.4
Extreme Maximum Temp. (°F)	62	69	77	91	99	107	106	103	103	92	78	62	107
Extreme Minimum Temp. (°F)	-38	-35	-23	-8	20	30	34	31	15	-8	-23	-39	-39
Days Maximum Temp. ≥ 90°F	0	0	0	0	0	2	7	9	2	0	0	0	20
Days Maximum Temp. ≤ 32°F	18	11	7	1	0	0	0	0	0	1	8	16	62
Days Minimum Temp. ≤ 32°F	30	27	28	18	5	0	0	0	3	13	26	30	180
Days Minimum Temp. ≤ 0°F	12	7	3	0	0	0	0	0	0	0	2	8	32
Heating Degree Days (base 65°F)	1,525	1,193	1,040	656	352	111	29	40	244	585	1,030	1,386	8,191
Cooling Degree Days (base 65°F)	0	0	0	1	14	69	176	175	39	1	0	0	475
Mean Precipitation (in.)	0.51	0.44	0.74	1.53	2.35	2.63	1.89	1.57	1.52	1.30	0.60	0.50	15.58
Days With ≥ 0.1" Precipitation	2	2	3	4	6	6	4	3	4	3	2	2	41
Days With ≥ 1.0" Precipitation	0	0	0	0	1	1	0	0	0	0	0	0	2
Mean Snowfall (in.)	10.0	7.9	8.2	5.4	1.4	0.0	0.0	0.0	0.7	2.2	6.1	7.8	49.7
Days With ≥ 1.0" Snow Depth	na	na	na	na	0	0	0	0	0	0	na	na	na

Cascade 20 SSE *Cascade County* Elevation: 4,599 ft. Latitude: 47° 00' N Longitude: 111° 35' W

	JAN	FEB	MAR	APR	MAY	JUN	JUL	AUG	SEP	OCT	NOV	DEC	YEAR
Mean Maximum Temp. (°F)	35.7	40.4	45.9	54.4	63.5	72.1	79.8	80.2	69.7	58.6	43.5	36.9	56.7
Mean Temp. (°F)	23.7	28.0	33.2	41.0	49.3	56.8	61.7	61.7	52.7	44.0	32.4	25.5	42.5
Mean Minimum Temp. (°F)	11.6	15.6	20.5	27.5	34.9	41.5	43.7	43.1	35.8	29.3	21.3	14.1	28.2
Extreme Maximum Temp. (°F)	64	65	74	82	86	95	95	99	96	88	73	63	99
Extreme Minimum Temp. (°F)	-37	-44	-28	-10	14	21	27	21	6	-16	-27	-45	-45
Days Maximum Temp. ≥ 90°F	0	0	0	0	0	1	3	4	1	0	0	0	9
Days Maximum Temp. ≤ 32°F	10	6	3	1	0	0	0	0	0	1	4	9	34
Days Minimum Temp. ≤ 32°F	27	25	27	22	11	3	1	1	11	20	23	27	198
Days Minimum Temp. ≤ 0°F	9	5	2	0	0	0	0	0	0	0	3	6	25
Heating Degree Days (base 65°F)	1,277	1,039	978	713	482	250	124	129	365	646	971	1,217	8,191
Cooling Degree Days (base 65°F)	0	0	0	0	1	10	30	35	5	0	0	0	81
Mean Precipitation (in.)	0.51	0.37	0.75	1.23	2.71	2.54	1.65	1.45	1.47	0.91	0.54	0.45	14.58
Days With ≥ 0.1" Precipitation	2	1	3	4	6	6	4	4	4	3	2	2	41
Days With ≥ 1.0" Precipitation	0	0	0	0	0	0	0	0	0	0	0	0	0
Mean Snowfall (in.)	na	na	na	na	1.5	0.0	0.0	0.0	0.2	na	na	na	na
Days With ≥ 1.0" Snow Depth	na	na	na	na	0	0	0	0	0	na	na	na	na

Cascade 5 S *Cascade County* Elevation: 3,359 ft. Latitude: 47° 13' N Longitude: 111° 43' W

	JAN	FEB	MAR	APR	MAY	JUN	JUL	AUG	SEP	OCT	NOV	DEC	YEAR
Mean Maximum Temp. (°F)	35.4	41.1	47.9	57.4	66.6	75.3	83.1	82.9	72.0	61.0	45.1	37.6	58.8
Mean Temp. (°F)	24.7	29.8	35.9	44.6	53.3	61.3	66.7	66.0	56.4	47.6	35.0	27.6	45.7
Mean Minimum Temp. (°F)	13.9	18.4	23.8	31.8	39.9	47.3	50.2	49.0	40.7	34.1	24.9	17.5	32.6
Extreme Maximum Temp. (°F)	70	69	77	89	92	101	104	103	99	94	77	66	104
Extreme Minimum Temp. (°F)	-42	-44	-30	-11	20	30	33	29	15	-16	-32	-45	-45
Days Maximum Temp. ≥ 90°F	0	0	0	0	0	3	7	8	2	0	0	0	20
Days Maximum Temp. ≤ 32°F	10	6	4	1	0	0	0	0	0	1	4	8	34
Days Minimum Temp. ≤ 32°F	25	22	24	16	5	0	0	0	5	14	20	24	155
Days Minimum Temp. ≤ 0°F	8	5	2	0	0	0	0	0	0	0	3	6	24
Heating Degree Days (base 65°F)	1,246	990	897	605	361	143	45	61	271	536	892	1,155	7,202
Cooling Degree Days (base 65°F)	0	0	0	1	5	35	99	102	21	3	0	0	266
Mean Precipitation (in.)	0.59	0.51	1.16	1.67	2.93	2.15	1.46	1.73	1.71	1.01	0.62	0.63	16.17
Days With ≥ 0.1" Precipitation	2	2	4	4	6	6	4	4	4	3	2	2	43
Days With ≥ 1.0" Precipitation	0	0	0	0	0	0	0	0	0	0	0	0	0
Mean Snowfall (in.)	na	na	na	na	na	na	na	na	na	na	na	na	na
Days With ≥ 1.0" Snow Depth	11	9	8	3	0	0	0	0	0	2	7	11	51

Chester *Liberty County*   Elevation: 3,162 ft.   Latitude: 48° 31' N   Longitude: 110° 58' W

	JAN	FEB	MAR	APR	MAY	JUN	JUL	AUG	SEP	OCT	NOV	DEC	YEAR
Mean Maximum Temp. (°F)	28.5	35.9	45.7	58.4	68.4	76.5	83.1	82.8	72.0	60.3	41.3	31.5	57.0
Mean Temp. (°F)	16.0	22.4	32.1	43.5	53.7	61.6	66.7	66.0	55.4	44.2	28.5	18.8	42.4
Mean Minimum Temp. (°F)	3.5	8.9	18.4	28.5	39.0	46.6	50.4	49.1	38.7	28.1	15.6	6.0	27.7
Extreme Maximum Temp. (°F)	66	74	77	88	94	100	99	102	96	89	75	64	102
Extreme Minimum Temp. (°F)	-44	-44	-28	-19	19	27	32	28	13	-17	-29	-52	-52
Days Maximum Temp. ≥ 90°F	0	0	0	0	0	2	7	7	1	0	0	0	17
Days Maximum Temp. ≤ 32°F	15	10	5	1	0	0	0	0	0	1	7	13	52
Days Minimum Temp. ≤ 32°F	30	28	29	21	6	0	0	0	7	21	28	31	201
Days Minimum Temp. ≤ 0°F	13	8	2	0	0	0	0	0	0	0	4	10	37
Heating Degree Days (base 65°F)	1,516	1,198	1,014	639	352	139	50	63	295	639	1,090	1,429	8,424
Cooling Degree Days (base 65°F)	0	0	0	1	10	43	109	108	13	0	0	0	284
Mean Precipitation (in.)	0.40	0.26	0.50	0.74	1.84	2.35	1.60	1.26	0.82	0.48	0.38	0.42	11.05
Days With ≥ 0.1" Precipitation	2	1	2	2	5	6	4	4	2	2	1	2	33
Days With ≥ 1.0" Precipitation	0	0	0	0	0	0	0	0	0	0	0	0	0
Mean Snowfall (in.)	na	na	na	na	*0.0*	*0.0*	*0.0*	*0.0*	*0.0*	na	na	na	na
Days With ≥ 1.0" Snow Depth	na	na	na	na	*0*	*0*	*0*	*0*	*0*	na	na	na	na

Choteau *Teton County*   Elevation: 3,845 ft.   Latitude: 47° 49' N   Longitude: 112° 12' W

	JAN	FEB	MAR	APR	MAY	JUN	JUL	AUG	SEP	OCT	NOV	DEC	YEAR
Mean Maximum Temp. (°F)	34.3	40.0	46.6	56.3	66.2	74.2	81.5	81.3	71.1	60.3	43.8	36.7	57.7
Mean Temp. (°F)	23.8	28.7	35.1	44.0	53.3	61.1	66.7	66.3	57.0	47.7	34.0	26.9	45.4
Mean Minimum Temp. (°F)	13.2	17.3	23.6	31.6	40.4	48.0	51.9	51.2	42.9	35.0	24.2	17.1	33.0
Extreme Maximum Temp. (°F)	66	72	74	86	91	97	101	102	92	90	75	69	102
Extreme Minimum Temp. (°F)	-36	-34	-30	-3	22	29	28	31	21	-6	-25	-35	-36
Days Maximum Temp. ≥ 90°F	0	0	0	0	0	1	5	5	1	0	0	0	12
Days Maximum Temp. ≤ 32°F	11	7	4	1	0	0	0	0	0	1	4	8	36
Days Minimum Temp. ≤ 32°F	27	24	25	16	4	0	0	0	3	12	23	26	160
Days Minimum Temp. ≤ 0°F	8	5	2	0	0	0	0	0	0	0	2	5	22
Heating Degree Days (base 65°F)	1,275	1,021	920	624	362	152	49	60	257	534	924	1,176	7,354
Cooling Degree Days (base 65°F)	0	0	0	1	9	40	101	107	28	4	0	0	290
Mean Precipitation (in.)	0.25	0.21	0.35	0.77	2.01	2.04	1.45	1.42	1.00	*0.48*	*0.17*	*0.21*	*10.36*
Days With ≥ 0.1" Precipitation	1	1	1	2	5	5	4	4	3	2	1	1	30
Days With ≥ 1.0" Precipitation	0	0	0	0	0	0	0	0	0	0	0	0	0
Mean Snowfall (in.)	na	na	na	na	na	na	na	na	na	na	na	na	na
Days With ≥ 1.0" Snow Depth	*12*	*8*	na	*2*	0	0	0	0	0	*1*	na	na	na

Circle *McCone County*   Elevation: 2,437 ft.   Latitude: 47° 25' N   Longitude: 105° 35' W

	JAN	FEB	MAR	APR	MAY	JUN	JUL	AUG	SEP	OCT	NOV	DEC	YEAR
Mean Maximum Temp. (°F)	24.7	33.3	43.0	57.1	68.7	79.1	85.9	85.5	72.7	59.3	41.0	29.7	56.7
Mean Temp. (°F)	13.9	22.3	31.5	44.2	55.4	65.0	70.6	69.9	57.6	45.5	30.0	18.8	43.7
Mean Minimum Temp. (°F)	3.1	11.3	20.0	31.3	42.0	50.8	55.2	54.2	42.4	31.8	19.0	7.8	30.7
Extreme Maximum Temp. (°F)	65	70	77	92	101	107	108	109	105	94	79	67	109
Extreme Minimum Temp. (°F)	-42	-35	-39	-2	18	30	38	27	15	-9	-31	-46	-46
Days Maximum Temp. ≥ 90°F	0	0	0	0	1	4	12	12	3	0	0	0	32
Days Maximum Temp. ≤ 32°F	18	11	7	1	0	0	0	0	0	1	8	16	62
Days Minimum Temp. ≤ 32°F	31	27	28	17	4	0	0	0	4	16	27	30	184
Days Minimum Temp. ≤ 0°F	13	7	3	0	0	0	0	0	0	0	2	10	35
Heating Degree Days (base 65°F)	1,580	1,201	1,031	618	312	89	25	38	253	597	1,044	1,428	8,216
Cooling Degree Days (base 65°F)	0	0	0	1	22	96	208	208	41	2	0	0	578
Mean Precipitation (in.)	0.46	0.35	0.64	1.22	1.97	2.37	1.86	1.30	1.39	0.95	0.44	0.43	13.38
Days With ≥ 0.1" Precipitation	1	1	2	3	5	5	4	3	3	3	2	2	34
Days With ≥ 1.0" Precipitation	0	0	0	0	0	0	0	0	0	0	0	0	0
Mean Snowfall (in.)	na	na	na	na	na	na	na	na	na	na	na	na	na
Days With ≥ 1.0" Snow Depth	*16*	*11*	*7*	1	0	0	0	0	0	1	4	*12*	*52*

Cohagen *Garfield County*   Elevation: 2,713 ft.   Latitude: 47° 03' N   Longitude: 106° 37' W

	JAN	FEB	MAR	APR	MAY	JUN	JUL	AUG	SEP	OCT	NOV	DEC	YEAR
Mean Maximum Temp. (°F)	29.5	37.4	47.5	60.0	70.1	79.9	87.2	87.1	75.0	62.0	43.8	33.5	59.4
Mean Temp. (°F)	17.2	24.7	34.1	45.1	55.2	64.5	70.3	69.6	58.0	46.4	31.2	21.0	44.8
Mean Minimum Temp. (°F)	4.9	12.0	20.6	30.1	40.2	49.1	53.3	52.1	41.0	30.8	18.5	8.5	30.1
Extreme Maximum Temp. (°F)	68	74	78	91	102	109	106	109	104	93	80	69	109
Extreme Minimum Temp. (°F)	-40	-42	-35	-11	14	29	36	28	13	-16	-29	-42	-42
Days Maximum Temp. ≥ 90°F	0	0	0	0	1	5	13	13	3	0	0	0	35
Days Maximum Temp. ≤ 32°F	15	9	5	1	0	0	0	0	0	0	6	12	48
Days Minimum Temp. ≤ 32°F	30	27	28	19	6	0	0	0	5	17	27	30	189
Days Minimum Temp. ≤ 0°F	12	7	2	0	0	0	0	0	0	0	3	9	33
Heating Degree Days (base 65°F)	1,477	1,132	953	591	310	89	21	32	233	570	1,009	1,359	7,776
Cooling Degree Days (base 65°F)	0	0	0	1	15	86	197	193	34	2	0	0	528
Mean Precipitation (in.)	0.45	0.26	0.49	1.08	2.12	2.10	1.60	1.05	1.34	0.90	0.42	0.45	12.26
Days With ≥ 0.1" Precipitation	2	1	2	3	5	6	4	3	3	2	2	2	35
Days With ≥ 1.0" Precipitation	0	0	0	0	0	0	0	0	0	0	0	0	0
Mean Snowfall (in.)	6.1	4.2	4.8	3.7	1.1	0.0	0.0	0.0	0.2	1.1	3.7	6.1	31.0
Days With ≥ 1.0" Snow Depth	21	13	10	2	0	0	0	0	0	1	7	17	71

Colstrip *Rosebud County* Elevation: 3,215 ft. Latitude: 45° 54' N Longitude: 106° 38' W

	JAN	FEB	MAR	APR	MAY	JUN	JUL	AUG	SEP	OCT	NOV	DEC	YEAR
Mean Maximum Temp. (°F)	34.0	40.8	47.9	58.4	68.7	78.5	86.1	85.8	73.8	60.5	45.1	36.2	59.7
Mean Temp. (°F)	21.9	28.5	35.3	45.4	55.2	64.5	70.6	69.8	58.8	47.0	33.9	24.4	46.3
Mean Minimum Temp. (°F)	9.7	16.1	23.3	32.2	41.7	50.5	55.1	53.8	43.7	33.5	22.7	12.5	32.9
Extreme Maximum Temp. (°F)	64	72	80	90	97	103	104	104	101	92	80	68	104
Extreme Minimum Temp. (°F)	-29	-36	-18	3	22	32	35	33	19	-8	-20	*-38*	*-38*
Days Maximum Temp. ≥ 90°F	0	0	0	0	1	4	12	12	3	0	0	0	32
Days Maximum Temp. ≤ 32°F	11	7	4	1	0	0	0	0	0	1	*5*	*10*	*39*
Days Minimum Temp. ≤ 32°F	29	26	26	15	4	0	0	0	2	13	25	29	169
Days Minimum Temp. ≤ 0°F	9	4	2	0	0	0	0	0	0	0	2	*6*	*23*
Heating Degree Days (base 65°F)	1,326	1,027	894	585	310	97	22	30	217	553	927	1,253	7,241
Cooling Degree Days (base 65°F)	0	0	0	0	1	14	85	196	189	41	2	0	528
Mean Precipitation (in.)	0.60	0.43	0.86	1.38	2.58	2.46	1.33	1.08	1.31	1.34	0.64	0.47	14.48
Days With ≥ 0.1" Precipitation	2	2	3	4	6	6	3	3	3	3	2	2	39
Days With ≥ 1.0" Precipitation	0	0	0	0	0	0	0	0	0	0	0	0	0
Mean Snowfall (in.)	na	na	na	na	na	na	na	na	na	na	na	na	na
Days With ≥ 1.0" Snow Depth	*19*	*12*	*8*	*3*	0	0	0	0	*0*	2	*8*	*16*	*68*

Columbus *Stillwater County* Elevation: 3,582 ft. Latitude: 45° 38' N Longitude: 109° 16' W

	JAN	FEB	MAR	APR	MAY	JUN	JUL	AUG	SEP	OCT	NOV	DEC	YEAR
Mean Maximum Temp. (°F)	36.1	43.0	50.7	60.0	69.6	79.1	86.3	85.5	74.5	62.8	46.1	37.3	60.9
Mean Temp. (°F)	23.1	29.3	37.0	45.5	54.8	63.4	69.5	68.2	57.9	47.2	33.7	24.9	46.2
Mean Minimum Temp. (°F)	10.1	15.5	23.3	31.0	40.0	47.6	52.5	50.8	41.2	31.5	21.3	12.5	31.5
Extreme Maximum Temp. (°F)	67	72	83	87	92	101	105	101	99	92	76	70	105
Extreme Minimum Temp. (°F)	-36	-35	-27	-1	18	29	34	31	20	-9	-23	-42	-42
Days Maximum Temp. ≥ 90°F	0	0	0	0	0	4	11	10	2	0	0	0	27
Days Maximum Temp. ≤ 32°F	10	6	2	0	0	0	0	0	0	0	4	9	31
Days Minimum Temp. ≤ 32°F	30	26	27	17	4	0	0	0	3	16	26	30	179
Days Minimum Temp. ≤ 0°F	9	4	1	0	0	0	0	0	0	0	2	5	21
Heating Degree Days (base 65°F)	1,293	1,005	860	578	314	102	20	28	225	545	934	1,236	7,140
Cooling Degree Days (base 65°F)	0	0	0	0	7	58	161	138	21	0	0	0	385
Mean Precipitation (in.)	0.72	0.58	1.11	1.89	3.00	1.90	1.35	1.06	1.48	1.32	0.68	0.67	15.76
Days With ≥ 0.1" Precipitation	3	2	4	5	6	5	3	3	3	3	2	3	42
Days With ≥ 1.0" Precipitation	0	0	0	0	1	0	0	0	0	0	0	0	1
Mean Snowfall (in.)	na	na	na	na	na	na	na	na	na	na	na	na	na
Days With ≥ 1.0" Snow Depth	na	na	na	na	0	0	0	0	0	*1*	na	na	na

Conrad *Pondera County* Elevation: 3,549 ft. Latitude: 48° 10' N Longitude: 111° 57' W

	JAN	FEB	MAR	APR	MAY	JUN	JUL	AUG	SEP	OCT	NOV	DEC	YEAR
Mean Maximum Temp. (°F)	31.9	38.1	45.8	57.3	66.8	74.4	80.6	80.7	70.3	59.7	42.7	34.5	56.9
Mean Temp. (°F)	19.3	25.0	32.5	42.6	52.2	59.7	64.5	64.2	54.2	44.3	30.0	22.2	42.6
Mean Minimum Temp. (°F)	6.6	11.9	19.1	28.0	37.5	45.0	48.4	47.6	38.0	29.0	17.3	9.7	28.2
Extreme Maximum Temp. (°F)	65	72	73	88	91	96	101	102	93	91	74	65	102
Extreme Minimum Temp. (°F)	-42	-37	-27	-11	18	29	31	25	17	-16	-32	-46	-46
Days Maximum Temp. ≥ 90°F	0	0	0	0	0	1	4	4	1	0	0	0	10
Days Maximum Temp. ≤ 32°F	13	8	4	1	0	0	0	0	0	1	6	11	44
Days Minimum Temp. ≤ 32°F	29	27	29	21	8	1	0	0	7	20	27	30	199
Days Minimum Temp. ≤ 0°F	11	7	2	0	0	0	0	0	0	0	3	8	31
Heating Degree Days (base 65°F)	1,414	1,124	1,001	664	393	177	76	85	326	633	1,044	1,323	8,260
Cooling Degree Days (base 65°F)	0	0	0	0	4	22	65	69	8	0	0	0	168
Mean Precipitation (in.)	0.46	0.33	0.67	1.07	2.13	2.25	1.37	1.51	1.02	0.56	0.48	0.45	12.30
Days With ≥ 0.1" Precipitation	1	1	2	3	5	5	4	4	3	2	2	2	34
Days With ≥ 1.0" Precipitation	0	0	0	0	0	0	0	0	0	0	0	0	0
Mean Snowfall (in.)	na	na	na	na	na	na	na	na	na	na	na	na	na
Days With ≥ 1.0" Snow Depth	na	na	na	na	*0*	*0*	*0*	*0*	*0*	*1*	na	na	na

Content 3 SSE *Phillips County* Elevation: 2,339 ft. Latitude: 47° 59' N Longitude: 107° 33' W

	JAN	FEB	MAR	APR	MAY	JUN	JUL	AUG	SEP	OCT	NOV	DEC	YEAR
Mean Maximum Temp. (°F)	26.9	34.3	45.0	58.5	69.2	78.2	85.0	85.0	72.2	59.7	41.8	31.1	57.2
Mean Temp. (°F)	15.7	22.8	32.8	44.6	55.2	64.0	69.4	68.8	56.8	45.4	30.1	19.4	43.8
Mean Minimum Temp. (°F)	4.5	11.3	20.5	30.7	41.2	49.6	53.7	52.5	41.3	31.1	18.3	7.7	30.2
Extreme Maximum Temp. (°F)	67	73	79	92	100	106	105	107	103	90	79	66	107
Extreme Minimum Temp. (°F)	-42	-45	-39	-5	15	27	33	32	16	-11	-30	-49	-49
Days Maximum Temp. ≥ 90°F	0	0	0	0	1	4	10	11	2	0	0	0	28
Days Maximum Temp. ≤ 32°F	17	11	5	1	0	0	0	0	0	1	7	14	56
Days Minimum Temp. ≤ 32°F	30	27	27	17	4	0	0	0	4	16	27	30	182
Days Minimum Temp. ≤ 0°F	12	7	2	0	0	0	0	0	0	0	3	9	33
Heating Degree Days (base 65°F)	1,522	1,187	993	605	311	101	28	39	264	601	1,041	1,407	8,099
Cooling Degree Days (base 65°F)	0	0	0	1	17	78	172	169	27	1	0	0	465
Mean Precipitation (in.)	0.37	0.24	0.53	1.02	2.20	2.34	1.64	1.23	1.04	0.70	0.36	0.37	12.04
Days With ≥ 0.1" Precipitation	2	1	*3*	*3*	6	6	4	3	2	2	2	2	*36*
Days With ≥ 1.0" Precipitation	0	0	0	*0*	0	0	0	0	0	0	0	0	*0*
Mean Snowfall (in.)	na	na	na	na	0.1	0.0	0.0	0.0	trace	*0.5*	na	na	na
Days With ≥ 1.0" Snow Depth	na	na	na	na	0	0	0	0	0	na	na	na	na

Creston *Flathead County*   Elevation: 2,939 ft.   Latitude: 48° 11' N   Longitude: 114° 08' W

	JAN	FEB	MAR	APR	MAY	JUN	JUL	AUG	SEP	OCT	NOV	DEC	YEAR
Mean Maximum Temp. (°F)	na	na	na	na	na	na	na	na	na	na	na	na	na
Mean Temp. (°F)	na	na	na	na	na	na	na	na	na	na	na	na	na
Mean Minimum Temp. (°F)	15.1	19.0	25.1	31.5	39.0	45.5	48.8	47.1	38.1	29.9	24.4	17.7	31.7
Extreme Maximum Temp. (°F)	53	62	71	85	93	93	97	97	96	80	67	56	97
Extreme Minimum Temp. (°F)	-32	-25	-15	13	20	30	32	31	18	0	-17	-33	-33
Days Maximum Temp. ≥ 90°F	0	0	0	0	0	0	2	3	0	0	0	0	5
Days Maximum Temp. ≤ 32°F	15	7	2	0	0	0	0	0	0	0	5	15	44
Days Minimum Temp. ≤ 32°F	29	26	27	17	4	0	0	0	6	20	25	29	183
Days Minimum Temp. ≤ 0°F	5	3	0	0	0	0	0	0	0	0	1	3	12
Heating Degree Days (base 65°F)	1,305	1,050	931	648	414	215	94	99	353	686	978	1,242	8,015
Cooling Degree Days (base 65°F)	0	0	0	0	4	17	55	52	4	0	0	0	132
Mean Precipitation (in.)	na	na	na	na	na	na	na	na	na	na	na	na	na
Days With ≥ 0.1" Precipitation	5	5	5	5	7	8	5	4	5	4	5	6	64
Days With ≥ 1.0" Precipitation	0	0	0	0	0	0	0	0	0	0	0	0	0
Mean Snowfall (in.)	na	na	na	na	na	na	na	na	na	na	na	na	na
Days With ≥ 1.0" Snow Depth	23	18	9	1	0	0	0	0	0	1	8	20	80

Culbertson *Roosevelt County*   Elevation: 1,919 ft.   Latitude: 48° 09' N   Longitude: 104° 31' W

	JAN	FEB	MAR	APR	MAY	JUN	JUL	AUG	SEP	OCT	NOV	DEC	YEAR
Mean Maximum Temp. (°F)	21.4	30.7	43.1	59.6	71.4	80.5	86.1	85.9	73.3	60.2	39.2	26.4	56.5
Mean Temp. (°F)	9.9	19.1	30.4	44.3	55.9	64.8	69.5	68.7	56.9	44.9	27.4	15.0	42.2
Mean Minimum Temp. (°F)	-1.6	7.4	17.7	29.0	40.4	49.0	52.9	51.4	40.5	29.6	15.5	3.4	27.9
Extreme Maximum Temp. (°F)	54	67	80	94	103	109	108	107	104	95	80	60	109
Extreme Minimum Temp. (°F)	-43	-43	-29	-12	14	28	33	30	15	-8	-31	-48	-48
Days Maximum Temp. ≥ 90°F	0	0	0	0	1	5	10	11	2	0	0	0	29
Days Maximum Temp. ≤ 32°F	21	13	7	1	0	0	0	0	0	0	9	19	70
Days Minimum Temp. ≤ 32°F	31	28	29	20	6	0	0	0	5	19	28	31	197
Days Minimum Temp. ≤ 0°F	16	9	3	0	0	0	0	0	0	0	4	12	44
Heating Degree Days (base 65°F)	1,706	1,291	1,065	615	295	83	23	42	260	616	1,123	1,547	8,666
Cooling Degree Days (base 65°F)	0	0	0	1	23	89	178	181	28	1	0	0	501
Mean Precipitation (in.)	*0.31*	*0.22*	*0.48*	na	na	na	na	*1.19*	*1.81*	*0.82*	*0.35*	*0.38*	na
Days With ≥ 0.1" Precipitation	1	1	2	3	6	6	5	3	3	2	1	1	34
Days With ≥ 1.0" Precipitation	0	0	0	0	0	1	1	0	0	0	0	0	2
Mean Snowfall (in.)	na	na	na	na	na	na	na	na	na	na	na	na	na
Days With ≥ 1.0" Snow Depth	28	20	12	1	0	0	0	0	0	*1*	8	20	*90*

Cut Bank Municipal Airport *Glacier County*   Elevation: 3,835 ft.   Latitude: 48° 36' N   Longitude: 112° 22' W

	JAN	FEB	MAR	APR	MAY	JUN	JUL	AUG	SEP	OCT	NOV	DEC	YEAR
Mean Maximum Temp. (°F)	28.6	34.4	41.4	52.4	62.2	70.5	77.7	77.5	67.1	55.7	39.0	31.4	53.2
Mean Temp. (°F)	18.6	23.7	30.6	40.7	50.0	58.1	63.6	63.1	53.3	43.2	29.2	21.7	41.3
Mean Minimum Temp. (°F)	8.5	12.9	19.9	28.9	37.8	45.6	49.4	48.6	39.5	30.7	19.4	11.9	29.4
Extreme Maximum Temp. (°F)	63	71	72	86	91	95	101	103	95	88	72	62	103
Extreme Minimum Temp. (°F)	-38	-44	-31	-5	18	30	32	31	18	-14	-24	-40	-44
Days Maximum Temp. ≥ 90°F	0	0	0	0	0	1	2	3	1	0	0	0	7
Days Maximum Temp. ≤ 32°F	14	10	7	2	0	0	0	0	0	2	8	13	56
Days Minimum Temp. ≤ 32°F	28	26	28	20	7	0	0	0	6	18	25	28	186
Days Minimum Temp. ≤ 0°F	11	7	2	0	0	0	0	0	0	0	4	8	32
Heating Degree Days (base 65°F)	1,430	1,162	1,059	722	459	221	95	112	350	669	1,068	1,337	8,684
Cooling Degree Days (base 65°F)	0	0	0	0	2	18	58	64	8	1	0	0	151
Mean Precipitation (in.)	*0.47*	*0.31*	*0.60*	*0.86*	*2.33*	na	*1.28*	na	*1.21*	*0.46*	*0.40*	*0.33*	na
Days With ≥ 0.1" Precipitation	1	1	2	3	5	5	4	4	3	1	1	1	31
Days With ≥ 1.0" Precipitation	0	0	0	0	0	0	0	0	0	0	0	0	0
Mean Snowfall (in.)	na	na	na	na	na	na	na	na	na	na	na	na	na
Days With ≥ 1.0" Snow Depth	16	13	10	3	0	0	0	0	0	2	9	13	66

Darby *Ravalli County*   Elevation: 3,877 ft.   Latitude: 46° 01' N   Longitude: 114° 11' W

	JAN	FEB	MAR	APR	MAY	JUN	JUL	AUG	SEP	OCT	NOV	DEC	YEAR
Mean Maximum Temp. (°F)	36.0	42.4	50.5	58.3	67.3	75.4	83.7	83.7	73.0	61.6	44.9	36.5	59.4
Mean Temp. (°F)	27.2	31.9	38.5	44.9	52.9	59.9	65.7	65.4	56.5	47.1	35.1	27.6	46.1
Mean Minimum Temp. (°F)	18.3	21.4	26.5	31.5	38.5	44.4	47.7	47.1	39.9	32.5	25.1	18.6	32.6
Extreme Maximum Temp. (°F)	61	70	78	84	95	98	103	101	97	88	74	61	103
Extreme Minimum Temp. (°F)	-28	-28	-10	8	19	28	31	27	19	0	-12	-34	-34
Days Maximum Temp. ≥ 90°F	0	0	0	0	0	2	8	8	1	0	0	0	19
Days Maximum Temp. ≤ 32°F	10	5	1	0	0	0	0	0	0	0	3	8	27
Days Minimum Temp. ≤ 32°F	28	25	25	17	5	1	0	0	4	15	24	28	172
Days Minimum Temp. ≤ 0°F	4	2	0	0	0	0	0	0	0	0	1	2	9
Heating Degree Days (base 65°F)	1,167	927	814	597	374	175	61	63	262	549	892	1,154	7,035
Cooling Degree Days (base 65°F)	0	0	0	0	6	28	93	89	17	0	0	0	233
Mean Precipitation (in.)	1.54	1.06	0.98	1.18	2.04	2.03	1.16	1.23	1.15	1.05	1.50	1.53	16.45
Days With ≥ 0.1" Precipitation	5	4	3	4	6	6	3	4	4	3	5	5	52
Days With ≥ 1.0" Precipitation	0	0	0	0	0	0	0	0	0	0	0	0	0
Mean Snowfall (in.)	na	na	na	na	na	na	na	na	na	na	na	na	na
Days With ≥ 1.0" Snow Depth	na	na	na	na	*0*	*0*	*0*	*0*	*0*	na	na	na	na

Del Bonita *Glacier County* Elevation: 4,333 ft. Latitude: 49° 00' N Longitude: 112° 47' W

	JAN	FEB	MAR	APR	MAY	JUN	JUL	AUG	SEP	OCT	NOV	DEC	YEAR
Mean Maximum Temp. (°F)	28.4	33.9	40.5	52.1	62.6	69.8	76.2	76.8	67.1	55.6	38.1	30.5	52.6
Mean Temp. (°F)	18.3	23.5	30.0	39.9	49.7	57.0	61.8	61.9	53.0	43.0	28.4	21.0	40.6
Mean Minimum Temp. (°F)	8.1	13.0	19.4	27.7	36.8	44.0	47.4	47.0	38.9	30.3	18.6	11.3	28.6
Extreme Maximum Temp. (°F)	62	69	66	83	90	91	97	95	92	83	73	60	97
Extreme Minimum Temp. (°F)	-43	-38	-24	-9	17	28	31	24	11	-11	-28	-38	-43
Days Maximum Temp. ≥ 90°F	0	0	0	0	0	0	1	1	0	0	0	0	2
Days Maximum Temp. ≤ 32°F	15	10	6	1	0	0	0	0	0	2	8	14	56
Days Minimum Temp. ≤ 32°F	29	26	28	22	9	1	0	0	7	18	27	29	196
Days Minimum Temp. ≤ 0°F	10	6	2	0	0	0	0	0	0	0	0	3	7	28
Heating Degree Days (base 65°F)	1,444	1,166	1,079	746	469	247	129	133	361	676	1,093	1,357	8,900
Cooling Degree Days (base 65°F)	0	0	0	0	2	13	37	48	9	1	0	0	110
Mean Precipitation (in.)	0.46	0.37	0.74	1.28	2.59	3.02	1.71	1.84	1.46	0.53	0.56	0.37	14.93
Days With ≥ 0.1" Precipitation	2	1	2	4	6	6	4	4	4	2	2	1	38
Days With ≥ 1.0" Precipitation	0	0	0	0	1	1	0	0	0	0	0	0	2
Mean Snowfall (in.)	8.9	6.9	11.8	11.4	2.5	trace	0.0	0.2	2.2	6.4	9.6	9.0	68.9
Days With ≥ 1.0" Snow Depth	18	na	10	5	0	0	0	0	0	3	11	16	na

Denton 1 NNE *Fergus County* Elevation: 3,618 ft. Latitude: 47° 20' N Longitude: 109° 57' W

	JAN	FEB	MAR	APR	MAY	JUN	JUL	AUG	SEP	OCT	NOV	DEC	YEAR
Mean Maximum Temp. (°F)	33.1	39.5	47.0	57.2	66.3	75.0	82.5	82.7	71.7	60.4	44.3	36.2	58.0
Mean Temp. (°F)	20.0	25.6	33.1	42.4	51.4	59.5	64.7	64.2	54.2	44.0	30.5	22.8	42.7
Mean Minimum Temp. (°F)	6.9	11.7	19.2	27.6	36.4	44.0	46.7	45.7	36.6	27.5	16.7	9.4	27.4
Extreme Maximum Temp. (°F)	70	72	77	88	93	99	100	104	99	89	78	67	104
Extreme Minimum Temp. (°F)	-47	-45	-35	-14	17	25	28	22	12	-22	-33	-50	-50
Days Maximum Temp. ≥ 90°F	0	0	0	0	0	1	6	7	1	0	0	0	15
Days Maximum Temp. ≤ 32°F	12	8	4	1	0	0	0	0	0	1	4	9	39
Days Minimum Temp. ≤ 32°F	29	27	28	21	9	1	0	1	9	21	27	29	202
Days Minimum Temp. ≤ 0°F	11	7	2	0	0	0	0	0	0	0	3	8	31
Heating Degree Days (base 65°F)	1,389	1,106	983	671	417	182	73	82	326	645	1,029	1,302	8,205
Cooling Degree Days (base 65°F)	0	0	0	0	3	23	63	67	8	0	0	0	164
Mean Precipitation (in.)	0.50	0.34	0.70	1.16	2.76	2.66	1.89	1.78	1.45	0.92	0.47	0.51	15.14
Days With ≥ 0.1" Precipitation	2	1	3	3	7	6	4	4	4	3	2	2	41
Days With ≥ 1.0" Precipitation	0	0	0	0	0	0	0	0	0	0	0	0	0
Mean Snowfall (in.)	na	na	na	na	na	na	na	na	na	na	na	na	na
Days With ≥ 1.0" Snow Depth	10	8	na	1	0	0	0	0	0	na	5	8	na

Dillon *Beaverhead County* Elevation: 5,226 ft. Latitude: 45° 13' N Longitude: 112° 38' W

	JAN	FEB	MAR	APR	MAY	JUN	JUL	AUG	SEP	OCT	NOV	DEC	YEAR
Mean Maximum Temp. (°F)	34.7	40.9	48.1	57.1	66.7	75.5	83.7	82.4	72.3	60.7	43.8	34.6	58.4
Mean Temp. (°F)	24.0	28.9	35.5	43.0	51.6	59.5	65.6	64.1	55.4	45.8	32.6	24.1	44.2
Mean Minimum Temp. (°F)	13.3	16.9	22.8	28.8	36.5	43.4	47.3	45.8	38.4	30.7	21.3	13.7	29.9
Extreme Maximum Temp. (°F)	59	65	73	83	90	93	98	99	94	86	71	63	99
Extreme Minimum Temp. (°F)	-31	-34	-18	-3	18	28	32	25	12	-7	-24	-37	-37
Days Maximum Temp. ≥ 90°F	0	0	0	0	0	1	6	4	0	0	0	0	11
Days Maximum Temp. ≤ 32°F	11	5	2	0	0	0	0	0	0	0	4	11	33
Days Minimum Temp. ≤ 32°F	30	27	27	21	8	1	0	0	6	17	26	30	193
Days Minimum Temp. ≤ 0°F	6	3	1	0	0	0	0	0	0	0	2	5	17
Heating Degree Days (base 65°F)	1,265	1,011	907	654	409	178	51	71	287	587	967	1,261	7,648
Cooling Degree Days (base 65°F)	0	0	0	0	2	18	73	52	7	0	0	0	152
Mean Precipitation (in.)	na	na	na	na	na	na	na	na	na	na	na	na	na
Days With ≥ 0.1" Precipitation	1	1	2	4	6	5	3	3	3	2	1	1	32
Days With ≥ 1.0" Precipitation	0	0	0	0	0	0	0	0	0	0	0	0	0
Mean Snowfall (in.)	na	na	na	na	na	na	na	na	na	na	na	na	na
Days With ≥ 1.0" Snow Depth	na	na	na	na	0	0	0	0	0	na	na	na	na

Divide *Silver Bow County* Elevation: 5,347 ft. Latitude: 45° 45' N Longitude: 112° 45' W

	JAN	FEB	MAR	APR	MAY	JUN	JUL	AUG	SEP	OCT	NOV	DEC	YEAR
Mean Maximum Temp. (°F)	31.4	36.6	43.1	52.0	61.4	70.7	78.7	77.6	67.3	56.3	40.3	31.3	53.9
Mean Temp. (°F)	20.6	24.8	31.9	39.5	48.3	56.5	62.6	61.6	52.2	42.3	29.4	21.0	40.9
Mean Minimum Temp. (°F)	9.8	13.0	20.7	27.0	35.0	42.0	46.5	45.6	37.0	28.3	18.6	10.5	27.8
Extreme Maximum Temp. (°F)	55	59	70	80	86	93	98	96	90	82	71	59	98
Extreme Minimum Temp. (°F)	-34	-35	-18	0	17	26	24	26	8	-5	-19	-35	-35
Days Maximum Temp. ≥ 90°F	0	0	0	0	0	0	1	1	0	0	0	0	2
Days Maximum Temp. ≤ 32°F	14	8	4	1	0	0	0	0	0	1	6	15	49
Days Minimum Temp. ≤ 32°F	30	28	29	23	10	2	0	0	8	22	28	30	210
Days Minimum Temp. ≤ 0°F	7	4	1	0	0	0	0	0	0	0	2	5	19
Heating Degree Days (base 65°F)	1,371	1,129	1,018	758	513	259	105	124	380	698	1,061	1,364	8,780
Cooling Degree Days (base 65°F)	0	0	0	0	1	10	38	26	1	0	0	0	76
Mean Precipitation (in.)	0.45	0.41	0.79	0.97	1.89	2.13	1.35	1.41	1.19	0.68	0.58	0.54	12.39
Days With ≥ 0.1" Precipitation	1	1	3	3	5	6	4	4	3	2	2	2	36
Days With ≥ 1.0" Precipitation	0	0	0	0	0	0	0	0	0	0	0	0	0
Mean Snowfall (in.)	na	na	na	na	na	na	na	na	na	na	na	na	na
Days With ≥ 1.0" Snow Depth	17	10	5	2	0	0	0	0	0	1	6	15	56

Drummond *Granite County*   Elevation: 3,999 ft.   Latitude: 46° 38' N   Longitude: 113° 12' W

	JAN	FEB	MAR	APR	MAY	JUN	JUL	AUG	SEP	OCT	NOV	DEC	YEAR
Mean Maximum Temp. (°F)	31.3	38.4	48.0	58.0	66.8	75.2	83.5	83.1	72.2	59.0	41.1	31.0	57.3
Mean Temp. (°F)	21.4	27.1	35.2	43.0	51.1	58.8	64.2	63.4	54.1	43.5	30.6	21.6	42.8
Mean Minimum Temp. (°F)	11.5	15.7	22.3	28.0	35.3	42.4	44.9	43.7	35.8	27.9	20.1	12.2	28.3
Extreme Maximum Temp. (°F)	57	67	78	84	93	97	101	101	96	82	73	59	101
Extreme Minimum Temp. (°F)	-35	-39	-23	5	9	20	27	27	13	-3	-22	-43	-43
Days Maximum Temp. ≥ 90°F	0	0	0	0	0	2	8	8	1	0	0	0	19
Days Maximum Temp. ≤ 32°F	13	6	2	0	0	0	0	0	0	0	5	15	41
Days Minimum Temp. ≤ 32°F	30	27	28	21	11	2	1	1	10	22	27	30	210
Days Minimum Temp. ≤ 0°F	7	4	1	0	0	0	0	0	0	0	2	6	20
Heating Degree Days (base 65°F)	1,347	1,065	916	653	427	199	76	87	326	660	1,025	1,340	8,121
Cooling Degree Days (base 65°F)	0	0	0	0	2	18	55	47	5	0	0	0	127
Mean Precipitation (in.)	0.84	0.59	0.78	0.99	1.95	1.74	1.27	1.32	1.06	0.73	0.78	0.83	12.88
Days With ≥ 0.1" Precipitation	3	2	3	3	6	5	4	4	3	3	3	3	42
Days With ≥ 1.0" Precipitation	0	0	0	0	0	0	0	0	0	0	0	0	0
Mean Snowfall (in.)	7.9	5.5	5.8	4.3	2.1	0.0	0.0	0.1	0.5	1.6	6.0	7.6	41.4
Days With ≥ 1.0" Snow Depth	22	15	6	1	0	0	0	0	0	0	7	18	69

Ekalaka *Carter County*   Elevation: 3,421 ft.   Latitude: 45° 53' N   Longitude: 104° 33' W

	JAN	FEB	MAR	APR	MAY	JUN	JUL	AUG	SEP	OCT	NOV	DEC	YEAR
Mean Maximum Temp. (°F)	29.4	35.9	44.7	56.9	68.1	77.8	85.4	84.4	72.3	59.0	41.9	32.6	57.4
Mean Temp. (°F)	18.4	25.0	32.8	43.9	54.6	63.9	70.3	69.2	57.7	45.6	31.0	21.6	44.5
Mean Minimum Temp. (°F)	7.4	14.0	20.9	30.8	40.9	50.0	55.2	54.0	43.1	32.2	20.1	10.6	31.6
Extreme Maximum Temp. (°F)	65	66	76	87	97	105	105	102	103	88	77	66	105
Extreme Minimum Temp. (°F)	-35	-35	-28	-6	13	31	33	26	15	0	-25	-43	-43
Days Maximum Temp. ≥ 90°F	0	0	0	0	0	3	10	9	2	0	0	0	24
Days Maximum Temp. ≤ 32°F	16	9	5	1	0	0	0	0	0	0	7	13	51
Days Minimum Temp. ≤ 32°F	30	27	27	17	5	0	0	0	4	14	26	30	180
Days Minimum Temp. ≤ 0°F	10	5	2	0	0	0	0	0	0	0	2	7	26
Heating Degree Days (base 65°F)	1,440	1,125	990	626	331	105	26	37	251	595	1,016	1,339	7,881
Cooling Degree Days (base 65°F)	0	0	0	1	16	85	203	183	38	1	0	0	527
Mean Precipitation (in.)	0.62	0.49	0.80	1.77	2.74	3.16	1.86	1.25	1.57	1.60	0.72	0.58	17.16
Days With ≥ 0.1" Precipitation	2	1	3	4	6	6	4	3	3	3	2	2	39
Days With ≥ 1.0" Precipitation	0	0	0	0	0	1	0	0	0	0	0	0	1
Mean Snowfall (in.)	na	na	na	na	na	na	na	na	na	na	na	na	na
Days With ≥ 1.0" Snow Depth	na	na	na	na	0	0	0	0	0	na	na	na	na

Ennis *Madison County*   Elevation: 4,950 ft.   Latitude: 45° 21' N   Longitude: 111° 43' W

	JAN	FEB	MAR	APR	MAY	JUN	JUL	AUG	SEP	OCT	NOV	DEC	YEAR
Mean Maximum Temp. (°F)	33.2	38.8	46.1	55.6	65.4	74.5	82.3	81.5	71.1	59.3	42.5	33.5	57.0
Mean Temp. (°F)	24.0	28.4	34.9	42.5	51.1	59.0	65.0	63.8	54.7	45.2	32.9	24.7	43.9
Mean Minimum Temp. (°F)	14.9	17.9	23.7	29.4	36.8	43.4	47.7	46.1	38.2	31.1	23.2	15.9	30.7
Extreme Maximum Temp. (°F)	61	65	73	85	88	94	96	96	92	87	72	60	96
Extreme Minimum Temp. (°F)	-30	-31	-22	0	16	27	31	28	10	-12	-19	-32	-32
Days Maximum Temp. ≥ 90°F	0	0	0	0	0	1	4	3	0	0	0	0	8
Days Maximum Temp. ≤ 32°F	13	6	3	0	0	0	0	0	0	0	5	12	39
Days Minimum Temp. ≤ 32°F	28	25	25	20	9	1	0	0	7	17	23	28	183
Days Minimum Temp. ≤ 0°F	6	3	1	0	0	0	0	0	0	0	1	4	15
Heating Degree Days (base 65°F)	1,264	1,028	926	668	424	190	58	73	308	607	952	1,244	7,742
Cooling Degree Days (base 65°F)	0	0	0	0	0	15	67	46	6	0	0	0	134
Mean Precipitation (in.)	0.46	0.43	0.85	1.30	2.19	2.27	1.42	1.35	1.23	0.95	0.62	0.48	13.55
Days With ≥ 0.1" Precipitation	1	2	3	4	6	6	4	4	4	3	2	2	41
Days With ≥ 1.0" Precipitation	0	0	0	0	0	0	0	0	0	0	0	0	0
Mean Snowfall (in.)	na	na	na	na	na	na	na	na	na	na	na	na	na
Days With ≥ 1.0" Snow Depth	na	na	na	na	0	0	0	0	0	na	na	na	na

Eureka Ranger Station *Lincoln County*   Elevation: 2,529 ft.   Latitude: 48° 54' N   Longitude: 115° 04' W

	JAN	FEB	MAR	APR	MAY	JUN	JUL	AUG	SEP	OCT	NOV	DEC	YEAR
Mean Maximum Temp. (°F)	29.5	37.9	48.8	59.1	68.7	76.0	83.9	83.8	72.2	57.0	39.7	30.7	57.3
Mean Temp. (°F)	22.3	29.2	37.8	46.0	54.6	61.4	67.0	66.3	56.4	44.8	32.8	24.4	45.2
Mean Minimum Temp. (°F)	15.0	20.4	26.7	32.9	40.4	46.7	50.0	48.8	40.5	32.5	25.8	18.2	33.2
Extreme Maximum Temp. (°F)	55	66	71	89	94	97	104	105	97	86	68	55	105
Extreme Minimum Temp. (°F)	-34	-30	-14	8	22	27	33	30	18	2	-23	-35	-35
Days Maximum Temp. ≥ 90°F	0	0	0	0	0	3	10	10	1	0	0	0	24
Days Maximum Temp. ≤ 32°F	16	6	1	0	0	0	0	0	0	0	5	16	44
Days Minimum Temp. ≤ 32°F	28	24	23	14	4	0	0	0	4	16	22	27	162
Days Minimum Temp. ≤ 0°F	6	3	0	0	0	0	0	0	0	0	1	4	14
Heating Degree Days (base 65°F)	1,320	1,006	837	563	322	145	49	58	264	621	960	1,251	7,396
Cooling Degree Days (base 65°F)	0	0	0	0	0	9	43	116	110	17	0	0	295
Mean Precipitation (in.)	1.16	0.78	0.78	0.91	1.86	2.12	1.51	1.24	1.08	0.99	1.32	1.14	14.89
Days With ≥ 0.1" Precipitation	4	3	3	3	5	6	4	3	3	3	4	4	45
Days With ≥ 1.0" Precipitation	0	0	0	0	0	0	0	0	0	0	0	0	0
Mean Snowfall (in.)	*11.4*	*7.2*	*4.2*	*1.1*	trace	0.0	0.0	0.0	trace	*0.4*	na	*12.7*	na
Days With ≥ 1.0" Snow Depth	na	na	na	na	0	0	0	0	0	0	na	na	na

Fairfield *Teton County*   Elevation: 3,982 ft.   Latitude: 47° 37' N   Longitude: 111° 59' W

	JAN	FEB	MAR	APR	MAY	JUN	JUL	AUG	SEP	OCT	NOV	DEC	YEAR
Mean Maximum Temp. (°F)	33.1	39.5	46.4	56.2	65.4	73.2	79.8	80.5	70.6	59.8	43.2	35.5	56.9
Mean Temp. (°F)	23.0	28.2	34.6	43.7	52.7	60.3	65.5	65.7	56.5	46.9	33.2	25.7	44.7
Mean Minimum Temp. (°F)	12.9	16.9	22.8	31.1	40.0	47.3	51.1	50.8	42.3	34.0	23.2	15.8	32.3
Extreme Maximum Temp. (°F)	62	70	76	85	91	97	98	99	96	89	72	65	99
Extreme Minimum Temp. (°F)	-34	-35	-25	-8	23	32	35	31	19	-9	-26	-35	-35
Days Maximum Temp. ≥ 90°F	0	0	0	0	0	1	3	4	1	0	0	0	9
Days Maximum Temp. ≤ 32°F	12	7	4	1	0	0	0	0	0	1	5	9	39
Days Minimum Temp. ≤ 32°F	27	24	26	18	4	0	0	0	3	13	24	27	166
Days Minimum Temp. ≤ 0°F	8	5	1	0	0	0	0	0	0	0	2	5	21
Heating Degree Days (base 65°F)	1,293	1,033	934	635	381	168	66	69	271	555	946	1,210	7,561
Cooling Degree Days (base 65°F)	0	0	0	0	1	8	29	85	97	25	2	0	247
Mean Precipitation (in.)	*0.39*	*0.26*	*0.63*	*1.05*	*2.50*	*1.93*	*1.44*	*1.80*	*1.19*	*0.61*	na	*0.36*	na
Days With ≥ 0.1" Precipitation	1	1	2	3	6	5	4	4	3	2	1	1	33
Days With ≥ 1.0" Precipitation	0	0	0	0	0	0	0	0	0	0	0	0	0
Mean Snowfall (in.)	na	na	na	na	na	na	na	na	na	na	na	na	na
Days With ≥ 1.0" Snow Depth	15	11	9	4	0	0	0	0	0	2	7	13	61

Flatwillow 4 ENE *Petroleum County*   Elevation: 3,136 ft.   Latitude: 46° 51' N   Longitude: 108° 19' W

	JAN	FEB	MAR	APR	MAY	JUN	JUL	AUG	SEP	OCT	NOV	DEC	YEAR
Mean Maximum Temp. (°F)	34.3	41.0	48.9	59.3	69.3	78.4	85.7	85.7	74.3	62.7	45.9	37.4	60.2
Mean Temp. (°F)	22.2	28.2	35.8	45.3	54.6	63.6	69.3	68.9	58.4	48.0	33.6	25.2	46.1
Mean Minimum Temp. (°F)	10.1	15.3	22.8	31.2	39.9	48.8	52.9	51.9	42.4	33.4	21.3	13.0	31.9
Extreme Maximum Temp. (°F)	68	76	80	90	95	104	103	105	102	92	79	69	105
Extreme Minimum Temp. (°F)	-42	-37	-24	-7	13	30	35	30	14	-8	-27	-40	-42
Days Maximum Temp. ≥ 90°F	0	0	0	0	1	4	11	12	3	0	0	0	31
Days Maximum Temp. ≤ 32°F	11	7	3	1	0	0	0	0	0	0	5	9	36
Days Minimum Temp. ≤ 32°F	29	26	26	17	5	0	0	0	3	14	25	29	174
Days Minimum Temp. ≤ 0°F	9	5	1	0	0	0	0	0	0	0	2	6	23
Heating Degree Days (base 65°F)	1,320	1,033	898	586	325	99	25	30	223	521	934	1,228	7,222
Cooling Degree Days (base 65°F)	0	0	0	0	1	10	66	164	168	34	3	0	446
Mean Precipitation (in.)	*0.53*	*0.36*	*0.72*	*1.30*	*2.73*	*2.28*	*1.46*	*1.38*	*1.12*	*0.93*	*0.46*	*0.50*	13.77
Days With ≥ 0.1" Precipitation	2	1	3	4	6	6	4	3	3	3	2	2	39
Days With ≥ 1.0" Precipitation	0	0	0	0	0	0	0	0	0	0	0	0	0
Mean Snowfall (in.)	na	na	na	na	na	na	na	na	na	na	na	na	na
Days With ≥ 1.0" Snow Depth	na	na	5	2	0	0	0	0	0	1	4	na	na

Forks 4 NNE *Phillips County*   Elevation: 2,598 ft.   Latitude: 48° 47' N   Longitude: 107° 27' W

	JAN	FEB	MAR	APR	MAY	JUN	JUL	AUG	SEP	OCT	NOV	DEC	YEAR
Mean Maximum Temp. (°F)	21.4	*27.5*	41.7	56.7	68.6	*77.6*	83.7	83.4	71.1	57.9	37.8	*25.5*	*54.4*
Mean Temp. (°F)	11.1	*16.8*	30.1	43.3	54.6	*63.1*	68.3	67.7	56.1	44.4	27.2	*15.1*	*41.5*
Mean Minimum Temp. (°F)	0.7	*6.0*	18.6	29.9	40.5	*48.7*	52.8	51.9	41.1	30.8	16.5	*4.7*	*28.5*
Extreme Maximum Temp. (°F)	58	*69*	77	88	99	106	104	107	101	91	74	*58*	*107*
Extreme Minimum Temp. (°F)	-42	*-37*	-27	-11	16	30	34	33	14	-12	*-29*	*-42*	*-42*
Days Maximum Temp. ≥ 90°F	0	*0*	0	0	1	3	7	9	2	0	0	*0*	*22*
Days Maximum Temp. ≤ 32°F	21	*15*	7	1	0	0	0	0	0	1	*9*	*19*	*73*
Days Minimum Temp. ≤ 32°F	30	*27*	29	19	5	0	0	0	5	17	28	*30*	*190*
Days Minimum Temp. ≤ 0°F	15	*10*	3	0	0	0	0	0	0	0	4	*10*	*42*
Heating Degree Days (base 65°F)	1,670	*1,356*	1,073	644	331	*115*	35	55	284	634	1,128	*1,542*	*8,867*
Cooling Degree Days (base 65°F)	0	*0*	*0*	*1*	19	*74*	148	155	*29*	*0*	*0*	*0*	*426*
Mean Precipitation (in.)	0.34	*0.30*	0.55	0.82	2.17	2.64	2.15	1.22	1.10	0.62	0.44	*0.38*	*12.73*
Days With ≥ 0.1" Precipitation	1	*1*	2	*2*	5	5	5	3	3	2	2	*1*	*32*
Days With ≥ 1.0" Precipitation	0	*0*	0	0	0	1	0	0	0	0	0	*0*	*1*
Mean Snowfall (in.)	5.4	*4.4*	*4.9*	*1.8*	*0.9*	0.0	0.0	0.0	*trace*	*1.7*	4.6	*4.9*	*28.6*
Days With ≥ 1.0" Snow Depth	26	*21*	*15*	3	0	0	0	0	*0*	2	9	*21*	*97*

Forsyth *Rosebud County*   Elevation: 2,513 ft.   Latitude: 46° 16' N   Longitude: 106° 41' W

	JAN	FEB	MAR	APR	MAY	JUN	JUL	AUG	SEP	OCT	NOV	DEC	YEAR
Mean Maximum Temp. (°F)	*31.9*	*40.1*	*49.9*	*62.1*	*71.8*	*80.9*	*88.2*	*87.1*	*76.0*	62.7	45.3	*34.9*	*60.9*
Mean Temp. (°F)	*19.6*	*27.0*	*36.6*	*47.7*	*57.5*	*66.3*	*72.2*	*70.8*	*60.1*	47.9	33.0	*23.0*	*46.8*
Mean Minimum Temp. (°F)	*7.3*	*13.9*	*23.2*	*33.3*	*43.0*	*51.6*	*56.2*	*54.5*	*44.2*	32.9	20.6	*11.0*	*32.7*
Extreme Maximum Temp. (°F)	*70*	*73*	*81*	*91*	*99*	*106*	*107*	*105*	*102*	93	82	*70*	*107*
Extreme Minimum Temp. (°F)	*-38*	*-38*	*-27*	*6*	*24*	*34*	*41*	*32*	*19*	-11	-27	*-44*	*-44*
Days Maximum Temp. ≥ 90°F	*0*	*0*	*0*	*0*	*1*	*6*	*14*	*14*	*4*	0	0	*0*	*39*
Days Maximum Temp. ≤ 32°F	*14*	*8*	*3*	*0*	*0*	*0*	*0*	*0*	*0*	0	5	*11*	*41*
Days Minimum Temp. ≤ 32°F	*30*	*26*	*26*	*13*	*3*	*0*	*0*	*0*	*2*	14	26	*30*	*170*
Days Minimum Temp. ≤ 0°F	*10*	*6*	*2*	*0*	*0*	*0*	*0*	*0*	*0*	0	2	*7*	*27*
Heating Degree Days (base 65°F)	*1,403*	*1,066*	*874*	*513*	*246*	*65*	*9*	*18*	*181*	526	954	*1,298*	*7,153*
Cooling Degree Days (base 65°F)	*0*	*0*	*0*	*1*	*20*	*109*	*239*	*216*	*40*	1	0	*0*	*626*
Mean Precipitation (in.)	*0.48*	*0.37*	*0.86*	*1.33*	*2.41*	*2.16*	*1.51*	*1.20*	*1.51*	1.09	0.76	*0.54*	*14.22*
Days With ≥ 0.1" Precipitation	*2*	*1*	*3*	*4*	*6*	*5*	*4*	*3*	*3*	3	3	*2*	*39*
Days With ≥ 1.0" Precipitation	*0*	*0*	*0*	*0*	*1*	*0*	*0*	*0*	*0*	0	0	*0*	*1*
Mean Snowfall (in.)	na	na	na	na	*0.8*	*0.0*	*0.0*	*0.0*	*0.3*	1.3	na	na	na
Days With ≥ 1.0" Snow Depth	na	na	na	na	*0*	*0*	*0*	*0*	*0*	na	na	na	na

Fort Assinniboine *Hill County*   Elevation: 2,611 ft.   Latitude: 48° 30' N   Longitude: 109° 48' W

	JAN	FEB	MAR	APR	MAY	JUN	JUL	AUG	SEP	OCT	NOV	DEC	YEAR
Mean Maximum Temp. (°F)	27.4	35.3	46.6	60.0	70.4	79.4	86.0	86.2	74.0	61.1	42.0	31.8	58.3
Mean Temp. (°F)	17.2	23.0	33.7	45.6	55.7	64.7	70.2	69.2	57.6	na	30.8	20.2	na
Mean Minimum Temp. (°F)	6.0	12.2	21.3	31.2	41.0	49.1	52.9	51.9	42.0	32.3	19.7	9.9	30.8
Extreme Maximum Temp. (°F)	68	75	77	91	98	108	103	108	101	91	78	64	108
Extreme Minimum Temp. (°F)	-37	-38	-29	-11	21	30	38	31	19	-21	-28	-44	-44
Days Maximum Temp. ≥ 90°F	0	0	0	0	1	4	11	12	3	0	0	0	31
Days Maximum Temp. ≤ 32°F	16	10	5	1	0	0	0	0	0	1	7	13	53
Days Minimum Temp. ≤ 32°F	29	26	27	16	4	0	0	0	4	15	25	29	175
Days Minimum Temp. ≤ 0°F	12	7	2	0	0	0	0	0	0	0	3	8	32
Heating Degree Days (base 65°F)	1,492	1,159	955	576	295	91	24	34	231	559	1,018	1,363	7,797
Cooling Degree Days (base 65°F)	0	0	0	2	17	76	165	171	30	2	0	0	463
Mean Precipitation (in.)	na	na	na	na	na	na	na	na	na	na	na	na	na
Days With ≥ 0.1" Precipitation	2	1	2	3	5	5	5	3	3	2	2	2	35
Days With ≥ 1.0" Precipitation	0	0	0	0	0	0	0	0	0	0	0	0	0
Mean Snowfall (in.)	na	na	na	na	na	na	na	na	na	na	na	na	na
Days With ≥ 1.0" Snow Depth	25	17	9	2	0	0	0	0	0	1	7	16	77

Fort Benton *Chouteau County*   Elevation: 2,634 ft.   Latitude: 47° 49' N   Longitude: 110° 40' W

	JAN	FEB	MAR	APR	MAY	JUN	JUL	AUG	SEP	OCT	NOV	DEC	YEAR
Mean Maximum Temp. (°F)	33.3	40.7	49.8	61.0	70.6	78.9	85.3	85.0	74.2	63.0	45.7	36.5	60.3
Mean Temp. (°F)	21.5	27.7	36.4	46.5	55.9	64.0	68.9	68.2	57.8	47.5	33.3	24.7	46.0
Mean Minimum Temp. (°F)	9.5	14.6	22.9	32.0	41.2	49.0	52.3	51.3	41.3	31.9	20.9	12.9	31.7
Extreme Maximum Temp. (°F)	71	77	82	93	97	104	103	106	100	94	79	67	106
Extreme Minimum Temp. (°F)	-39	-37	-24	-8	21	30	35	29	17	-15	-29	-45	-45
Days Maximum Temp. ≥ 90°F	0	0	0	0	1	4	10	10	3	0	0	0	28
Days Maximum Temp. ≤ 32°F	12	8	3	1	0	0	0	0	0	0	5	10	39
Days Minimum Temp. ≤ 32°F	28	25	25	15	3	0	0	0	4	16	25	28	169
Days Minimum Temp. ≤ 0°F	10	6	2	0	0	0	0	0	0	0	3	6	27
Heating Degree Days (base 65°F)	1,345	1,048	881	550	285	90	23	36	230	537	942	1,244	7,211
Cooling Degree Days (base 65°F)	0	0	0	1	15	69	154	155	24	1	0	0	419
Mean Precipitation (in.)	0.58	0.39	0.86	1.24	2.38	2.46	1.37	1.53	1.21	0.79	0.54	0.52	13.87
Days With ≥ 0.1" Precipitation	2	2	2	3	5	6	4	4	3	3	2	2	38
Days With ≥ 1.0" Precipitation	0	0	0	0	0	0	0	0	0	0	0	0	0
Mean Snowfall (in.)	na	na	na	na	na	na	na	na	na	na	na	na	na
Days With ≥ 1.0" Snow Depth	14	10	6	1	0	0	0	0	0	1	6	12	50

Fort Peck Power Plant *McCone County*   Elevation: 2,066 ft.   Latitude: 48° 01' N   Longitude: 106° 24' W

	JAN	FEB	MAR	APR	MAY	JUN	JUL	AUG	SEP	OCT	NOV	DEC	YEAR
Mean Maximum Temp. (°F)	24.5	32.5	44.1	58.7	70.5	80.6	86.8	86.5	73.9	60.9	42.2	30.5	57.7
Mean Temp. (°F)	14.5	22.3	33.0	46.0	57.3	66.7	71.9	71.3	59.7	48.6	32.4	20.3	45.3
Mean Minimum Temp. (°F)	4.4	11.9	21.8	33.2	43.9	52.8	56.9	56.0	45.4	36.2	22.4	10.0	32.9
Extreme Maximum Temp. (°F)	58	69	79	91	100	107	105	107	103	89	78	63	107
Extreme Minimum Temp. (°F)	-35	-38	-28	-1	20	34	41	33	15	-4	-24	-38	-38
Days Maximum Temp. ≥ 90°F	0	0	0	0	1	5	12	12	2	0	0	0	32
Days Maximum Temp. ≤ 32°F	19	12	6	1	0	0	0	0	0	0	6	15	59
Days Minimum Temp. ≤ 32°F	30	27	26	13	2	0	0	0	2	10	24	30	164
Days Minimum Temp. ≤ 0°F	13	7	2	0	0	0	0	0	0	0	2	8	32
Heating Degree Days (base 65°F)	1,562	1,201	985	566	255	56	10	21	194	504	973	1,381	7,708
Cooling Degree Days (base 65°F)	0	0	0	1	26	119	233	235	47	2	0	0	663
Mean Precipitation (in.)	0.28	0.17	0.38	0.98	1.98	2.13	1.72	1.08	1.21	0.69	0.26	0.30	11.18
Days With ≥ 0.1" Precipitation	1	1	1	2	5	5	4	3	3	2	1	1	29
Days With ≥ 1.0" Precipitation	0	0	0	0	0	0	1	0	0	0	0	0	1
Mean Snowfall (in.)	na	na	na	na	na	na	na	na	na	na	na	na	na
Days With ≥ 1.0" Snow Depth	na	na	na	na	0	0	0	0	0	na	na	na	na

Fortine 1 N *Lincoln County*   Elevation: 2,998 ft.   Latitude: 48° 47' N   Longitude: 114° 55' W

	JAN	FEB	MAR	APR	MAY	JUN	JUL	AUG	SEP	OCT	NOV	DEC	YEAR
Mean Maximum Temp. (°F)	28.8	37.1	46.9	57.6	67.0	74.2	81.7	81.7	70.8	56.1	38.2	29.9	55.8
Mean Temp. (°F)	21.2	28.2	35.9	44.1	52.1	59.0	64.4	64.0	54.2	42.9	30.9	23.2	43.3
Mean Minimum Temp. (°F)	13.6	19.2	24.9	30.6	37.1	43.7	47.2	46.2	37.5	29.6	23.5	16.4	30.8
Extreme Maximum Temp. (°F)	55	64	73	88	96	96	100	100	95	86	67	56	100
Extreme Minimum Temp. (°F)	-38	-29	-12	5	17	24	28	28	16	1	-27	-38	-38
Days Maximum Temp. ≥ 90°F	0	0	0	0	0	2	7	6	1	0	0	0	16
Days Maximum Temp. ≤ 32°F	17	7	2	0	0	0	0	0	0	0	7	17	50
Days Minimum Temp. ≤ 32°F	29	26	26	19	8	1	0	0	8	20	25	29	191
Days Minimum Temp. ≤ 0°F	7	3	1	0	0	0	0	0	0	0	1	4	16
Heating Degree Days (base 65°F)	1,354	1,036	895	621	397	193	80	84	323	679	1,018	1,291	7,971
Cooling Degree Days (base 65°F)	0	0	0	0	4	16	67	61	6	0	0	0	154
Mean Precipitation (in.)	1.13	0.78	0.88	1.09	1.89	2.35	1.85	1.33	1.19	0.90	1.36	1.23	15.98
Days With ≥ 0.1" Precipitation	4	3	3	3	6	7	5	4	4	4	5	4	52
Days With ≥ 1.0" Precipitation	0	0	0	0	0	0	0	0	0	0	0	0	0
Mean Snowfall (in.)	na	na	na	na	na	na	na	na	na	na	na	na	na
Days With ≥ 1.0" Snow Depth	23	16	6	0	0	0	0	0	0	1	8	21	75

Geraldine *Chouteau County*   Elevation: 3,129 ft.   Latitude: 47° 36' N   Longitude: 110° 16' W

	JAN	FEB	MAR	APR	MAY	JUN	JUL	AUG	SEP	OCT	NOV	DEC	YEAR
Mean Maximum Temp. (°F)	33.9	40.4	47.9	58.3	68.2	77.1	84.6	84.8	73.3	61.5	44.9	37.1	59.3
Mean Temp. (°F)	21.9	28.0	35.5	44.9	54.5	62.8	68.4	68.2	57.7	47.1	33.2	25.3	45.6
Mean Minimum Temp. (°F)	9.9	15.5	23.0	31.5	40.7	48.4	52.2	51.6	42.1	32.8	21.4	13.5	31.9
Extreme Maximum Temp. (°F)	70	73	77	91	95	103	102	105	98	92	81	68	105
Extreme Minimum Temp. (°F)	-36	-36	-23	-6	20	29	32	28	17	-14	-26	-41	-41
Days Maximum Temp. ≥ 90°F	0	0	0	0	0	3	10	10	2	0	0	0	25
Days Maximum Temp. ≤ 32°F	12	7	4	1	0	0	0	0	0	1	5	9	39
Days Minimum Temp. ≤ 32°F	27	24	25	16	4	0	0	0	4	14	23	27	164
Days Minimum Temp. ≤ 0°F	10	6	2	0	0	0	0	0	0	0	3	6	27
Heating Degree Days (base 65°F)	1,333	1,040	909	596	330	112	31	40	240	548	949	1,224	7,352
Cooling Degree Days (base 65°F)	0	0	0	0	1	13	57	152	161	31	2	0	417
Mean Precipitation (in.)	0.77	0.48	1.01	1.37	2.81	2.53	1.83	1.68	1.38	0.89	0.63	0.66	16.04
Days With ≥ 0.1" Precipitation	3	2	3	4	6	6	4	4	4	3	2	2	43
Days With ≥ 1.0" Precipitation	0	0	0	0	1	0	0	0	0	0	0	0	1
Mean Snowfall (in.)	na	na	na	na	na	na	na	na	na	na	na	na	na
Days With ≥ 1.0" Snow Depth	14	8	6	1	0	0	0	0	0	1	6	11	47

Gibson Dam *Lewis And Clark County*   Elevation: 4,589 ft.   Latitude: 47° 36' N   Longitude: 112° 45' W

	JAN	FEB	MAR	APR	MAY	JUN	JUL	AUG	SEP	OCT	NOV	DEC	YEAR
Mean Maximum Temp. (°F)	33.8	38.5	43.4	51.9	60.8	69.1	76.9	77.0	67.2	56.5	41.2	34.4	54.2
Mean Temp. (°F)	23.5	27.7	32.5	40.2	48.2	55.8	61.5	61.1	52.5	44.2	32.0	25.1	42.0
Mean Minimum Temp. (°F)	13.1	17.0	21.6	28.4	35.6	42.5	46.1	45.2	37.8	31.8	22.7	15.7	29.8
Extreme Maximum Temp. (°F)	62	64	71	81	85	91	96	98	94	88	70	65	98
Extreme Minimum Temp. (°F)	-34	-39	-26	-8	18	28	30	26	9	-10	-35	-39	-39
Days Maximum Temp. ≥ 90°F	0	0	0	0	0	0	1	1	0	0	0	0	2
Days Maximum Temp. ≤ 32°F	11	6	4	1	0	0	0	0	0	1	5	11	39
Days Minimum Temp. ≤ 32°F	28	25	27	22	9	1	0	1	6	17	23	27	186
Days Minimum Temp. ≤ 0°F	8	5	2	0	0	0	0	0	0	0	2	5	22
Heating Degree Days (base 65°F)	1,281	1,045	1,001	738	513	277	127	139	370	638	985	1,231	8,345
Cooling Degree Days (base 65°F)	0	0	0	0	1	7	24	24	3	0	0	0	59
Mean Precipitation (in.)	*1.00*	*0.71*	*0.91*	*1.43*	*2.91*	*2.46*	*1.53*	*1.86*	*1.48*	*0.96*	*0.88*	*0.87*	*17.00*
Days With ≥ 0.1" Precipitation	3	2	3	4	7	7	4	4	4	3	3	3	47
Days With ≥ 1.0" Precipitation	0	0	0	0	1	0	0	0	0	0	0	0	1
Mean Snowfall (in.)	na	na	na	na	na	na	na	na	na	na	na	na	na
Days With ≥ 1.0" Snow Depth	15	11	10	3	0	0	0	0	1	2	7	11	60

Gildford *Hill County*   Elevation: 2,818 ft.   Latitude: 48° 34' N   Longitude: 110° 18' W

	JAN	FEB	MAR	APR	MAY	JUN	JUL	AUG	SEP	OCT	NOV	DEC	YEAR
Mean Maximum Temp. (°F)	26.6	34.1	44.2	57.4	68.2	76.5	83.4	83.0	71.1	58.9	40.5	30.7	56.2
Mean Temp. (°F)	15.7	22.6	32.1	43.7	54.0	62.2	67.4	66.8	55.8	44.6	29.0	19.4	42.8
Mean Minimum Temp. (°F)	4.7	10.9	19.9	29.9	39.9	47.8	51.4	50.5	40.3	30.3	17.5	8.2	29.3
Extreme Maximum Temp. (°F)	64	75	76	89	95	103	103	106	98	89	76	64	106
Extreme Minimum Temp. (°F)	-39	-44	-33	-16	18	29	36	29	16	-20	-27	-44	-44
Days Maximum Temp. ≥ 90°F	0	0	0	0	0	3	7	8	1	0	0	0	19
Days Maximum Temp. ≤ 32°F	16	11	6	1	0	0	0	0	0	1	8	14	57
Days Minimum Temp. ≤ 32°F	30	27	28	19	5	0	0	0	5	17	27	30	188
Days Minimum Temp. ≤ 0°F	13	8	2	0	0	0	0	0	0	0	4	9	36
Heating Degree Days (base 65°F)	1,527	1,195	1,015	633	341	127	40	57	285	626	1,073	1,409	8,328
Cooling Degree Days (base 65°F)	0	0	0	0	9	48	117	119	15	1	0	0	309
Mean Precipitation (in.)	0.35	0.22	0.47	0.80	1.98	2.29	1.42	1.33	1.07	0.58	0.37	0.35	11.23
Days With ≥ 0.1" Precipitation	1	1	1	2	5	5	4	4	3	2	1	1	30
Days With ≥ 1.0" Precipitation	0	0	0	0	0	1	0	0	0	0	0	0	1
Mean Snowfall (in.)	na	na	na	na	0.2	0.0	0.0	trace	trace	*0.1*	na	na	na
Days With ≥ 1.0" Snow Depth	na	na	na	na	0	0	0	0	0	*1*	na	na	na

Glendive *Dawson County*   Elevation: 2,073 ft.   Latitude: 47° 06' N   Longitude: 104° 43' W

	JAN	FEB	MAR	APR	MAY	JUN	JUL	AUG	SEP	OCT	NOV	DEC	YEAR
Mean Maximum Temp. (°F)	26.2	34.8	45.5	59.8	71.4	81.4	88.2	88.0	75.5	61.9	42.3	30.7	58.8
Mean Temp. (°F)	15.2	23.3	33.5	46.5	58.0	67.7	73.4	72.5	60.5	48.2	31.7	20.0	45.9
Mean Minimum Temp. (°F)	4.1	11.8	21.4	33.2	44.5	54.1	58.6	57.0	45.4	34.4	21.0	9.3	32.9
Extreme Maximum Temp. (°F)	57	71	81	93	102	110	110	109	106	94	80	68	110
Extreme Minimum Temp. (°F)	-41	-41	-28	0	23	37	42	36	22	0	-27	-42	-42
Days Maximum Temp. ≥ 90°F	0	0	0	0	2	6	15	15	4	0	0	0	42
Days Maximum Temp. ≤ 32°F	18	11	6	1	0	0	0	0	0	0	7	15	58
Days Minimum Temp. ≤ 32°F	31	27	27	14	2	0	0	0	2	12	27	31	173
Days Minimum Temp. ≤ 0°F	13	7	2	0	0	0	0	0	0	0	2	8	32
Heating Degree Days (base 65°F)	1,540	1,171	971	550	244	52	11	16	186	517	994	1,388	7,640
Cooling Degree Days (base 65°F)	0	0	0	2	33	129	268	256	53	2	0	0	743
Mean Precipitation (in.)	*0.42*	*0.27*	*0.59*	*1.20*	*2.19*	*2.51*	*1.39*	*1.44*	*1.66*	*0.89*	*0.44*	*0.41*	*13.41*
Days With ≥ 0.1" Precipitation	2	1	2	3	5	6	4	3	3	2	2	1	34
Days With ≥ 1.0" Precipitation	0	0	0	0	0	0	0	0	0	0	0	0	0
Mean Snowfall (in.)	na	na	na	na	na	na	na	na	na	na	na	na	na
Days With ≥ 1.0" Snow Depth	23	16	8	1	0	0	0	0	0	1	7	18	74

Goldbutte 7 N *Toole County*   Elevation: 3,497 ft.   Latitude: 48° 59' N   Longitude: 111° 24' W

	JAN	FEB	MAR	APR	MAY	JUN	JUL	AUG	SEP	OCT	NOV	DEC	YEAR
Mean Maximum Temp. (°F)	31.4	36.6	44.2	55.8	65.5	73.3	79.8	79.7	68.9	57.5	41.2	33.5	55.6
Mean Temp. (°F)	20.0	24.9	32.5	42.8	52.0	59.4	64.4	63.9	54.2	44.5	30.4	22.8	42.7
Mean Minimum Temp. (°F)	8.5	13.2	20.6	29.8	38.4	45.5	49.0	48.1	39.5	31.4	19.6	12.0	29.6
Extreme Maximum Temp. (°F)	65	73	72	86	93	98	98	102	97	88	74	67	102
Extreme Minimum Temp. (°F)	-40	-36	-30	-15	13	27	31	28	9	-19	-30	-43	-43
Days Maximum Temp. ≥ 90°F	0	0	0	0	0	1	4	4	1	0	0	0	10
Days Maximum Temp. ≤ 32°F	13	9	6	1	0	0	0	0	0	1	6	11	47
Days Minimum Temp. ≤ 32°F	28	25	27	19	7	1	0	1	6	16	25	28	183
Days Minimum Temp. ≤ 0°F	11	7	3	0	0	0	0	0	0	0	3	8	32
Heating Degree Days (base 65°F)	1,391	1,125	1,002	659	400	187	83	96	328	630	1,032	1,304	8,237
Cooling Degree Days (base 65°F)	0	0	0	0	6	24	68	69	13	1	0	0	181
Mean Precipitation (in.)	0.41	0.32	0.67	1.12	2.17	2.75	1.49	1.77	1.47	0.75	0.51	0.41	13.84
Days With ≥ 0.1" Precipitation	1	1	2	3	5	6	3	4	4	3	2	1	35
Days With ≥ 1.0" Precipitation	0	0	0	0	0	1	0	0	0	0	0	0	1
Mean Snowfall (in.)	na	na	na	na	na	na	na	na	na	na	na	na	na
Days With ≥ 1.0" Snow Depth	7	6	7	2	0	0	0	0	0	2	6	7	37

Grass Range *Fergus County*   Elevation: 3,487 ft.   Latitude: 47° 02' N   Longitude: 108° 48' W

	JAN	FEB	MAR	APR	MAY	JUN	JUL	AUG	SEP	OCT	NOV	DEC	YEAR
Mean Maximum Temp. (°F)	36.8	42.4	49.2	58.7	68.6	77.7	84.4	84.4	73.4	62.5	46.8	39.6	60.4
Mean Temp. (°F)	23.9	29.1	35.9	44.7	54.0	62.3	67.7	67.3	57.1	47.4	33.9	26.7	45.8
Mean Minimum Temp. (°F)	11.0	15.7	22.5	30.6	39.2	46.9	50.9	50.1	40.8	32.3	21.0	13.8	31.2
Extreme Maximum Temp. (°F)	74	73	80	94	97	103	104	105	99	90	85	70	105
Extreme Minimum Temp. (°F)	-38	-34	-22	-5	21	29	31	29	15	-9	-23	-39	-39
Days Maximum Temp. ≥ 90°F	0	0	0	0	1	3	9	9	2	0	0	0	24
Days Maximum Temp. ≤ 32°F	10	6	3	1	0	0	0	0	0	0	4	8	32
Days Minimum Temp. ≤ 32°F	29	26	27	18	5	0	0	0	4	15	25	29	178
Days Minimum Temp. ≤ 0°F	9	5	2	0	0	0	0	0	0	0	2	5	23
Heating Degree Days (base 65°F)	1,268	1,009	896	605	343	126	40	43	249	539	927	1,180	7,225
Cooling Degree Days (base 65°F)	0	0	0	1	10	55	131	127	22	1	0	0	347
Mean Precipitation (in.)	0.81	0.30	1.01	1.47	3.18	2.68	2.05	1.63	1.27	0.92	0.61	0.62	16.55
Days With ≥ 0.1" Precipitation	2	1	4	4	6	6	5	4	4	3	2	2	43
Days With ≥ 1.0" Precipitation	0	0	0	0	1	0	0	0	0	0	0	0	1
Mean Snowfall (in.)	na	na	na	na	na	na	na	na	na	na	na	na	na
Days With ≥ 1.0" Snow Depth	na	na	na	na	0	0	0	0	0	na	na	na	na

Hamilton *Ravalli County*   Elevation: 3,526 ft.   Latitude: 46° 14' N   Longitude: 114° 10' W

	JAN	FEB	MAR	APR	MAY	JUN	JUL	AUG	SEP	OCT	NOV	DEC	YEAR
Mean Maximum Temp. (°F)	35.3	41.9	50.3	58.7	67.2	75.1	83.4	82.9	71.9	59.6	43.8	34.9	58.8
Mean Temp. (°F)	26.4	31.4	38.5	45.7	53.4	60.5	66.5	65.8	56.2	45.6	34.0	26.3	45.9
Mean Minimum Temp. (°F)	17.4	20.9	26.7	32.6	39.6	45.8	49.6	48.6	40.4	31.5	24.2	17.6	32.9
Extreme Maximum Temp. (°F)	63	71	76	87	95	99	102	100	98	84	76	64	102
Extreme Minimum Temp. (°F)	-28	-30	-11	11	21	32	31	30	18	4	-14	-31	-31
Days Maximum Temp. ≥ 90°F	0	0	0	0	0	2	8	7	1	0	0	0	18
Days Maximum Temp. ≤ 32°F	10	5	1	0	0	0	0	0	0	0	4	11	31
Days Minimum Temp. ≤ 32°F	27	25	25	15	4	0	0	0	4	17	25	28	170
Days Minimum Temp. ≤ 0°F	4	2	0	0	0	0	0	0	0	0	1	3	10
Heating Degree Days (base 65°F)	1,191	943	814	573	357	164	51	58	269	595	922	1,195	7,132
Cooling Degree Days (base 65°F)	0	0	0	0	7	33	107	94	13	0	0	0	254
Mean Precipitation (in.)	1.15	0.81	0.96	0.99	1.79	1.63	1.05	1.21	1.12	0.72	1.04	1.00	13.47
Days With ≥ 0.1" Precipitation	4	3	3	3	5	5	3	3	3	2	3	4	41
Days With ≥ 1.0" Precipitation	0	0	0	0	0	0	0	0	0	0	0	0	0
Mean Snowfall (in.)	na	na	na	na	na	na	na	na	na	na	na	na	na
Days With ≥ 1.0" Snow Depth	13	na	na	na	0	0	0	0	0	0	na	na	na

Harlowton *Wheatland County*   Elevation: 4,160 ft.   Latitude: 46° 26' N   Longitude: 109° 50' W

	JAN	FEB	MAR	APR	MAY	JUN	JUL	AUG	SEP	OCT	NOV	DEC	YEAR
Mean Maximum Temp. (°F)	35.3	41.1	47.5	56.9	66.5	75.7	82.9	82.6	71.5	60.4	43.9	36.4	58.4
Mean Temp. (°F)	24.1	28.8	34.6	43.1	52.1	60.7	66.3	65.6	55.5	45.8	32.8	25.9	44.6
Mean Minimum Temp. (°F)	13.0	16.5	21.7	29.2	37.6	45.6	49.6	48.5	39.4	31.2	21.6	15.3	30.8
Extreme Maximum Temp. (°F)	69	67	75	86	89	98	98	100	98	90	75	64	100
Extreme Minimum Temp. (°F)	-36	-35	-29	-2	16	28	33	24	10	-8	-23	-38	-38
Days Maximum Temp. ≥ 90°F	0	0	0	0	0	2	6	6	1	0	0	0	15
Days Maximum Temp. ≤ 32°F	10	6	3	1	0	0	0	0	0	0	4	9	33
Days Minimum Temp. ≤ 32°F	28	25	27	20	7	0	0	0	5	16	25	28	181
Days Minimum Temp. ≤ 0°F	8	4	1	0	0	0	0	0	0	0	2	5	20
Heating Degree Days (base 65°F)	1,261	1,016	935	652	395	157	48	58	289	588	959	1,207	7,565
Cooling Degree Days (base 65°F)	0	0	0	0	3	35	93	86	12	0	0	0	229
Mean Precipitation (in.)	0.46	0.42	0.73	1.31	2.31	2.70	1.73	1.61	1.22	0.77	0.52	0.49	14.27
Days With ≥ 0.1" Precipitation	1	1	2	4	6	6	5	4	3	2	2	2	38
Days With ≥ 1.0" Precipitation	0	0	0	0	0	1	0	0	0	0	0	0	1
Mean Snowfall (in.)	na	na	na	na	na	na	na	na	na	na	na	na	na
Days With ≥ 1.0" Snow Depth	10	8	5	1	0	0	0	0	0	0	1	5	9	39

Hebgen Dam *Gallatin County*   Elevation: 6,486 ft.   Latitude: 44° 52' N   Longitude: 111° 20' W

	JAN	FEB	MAR	APR	MAY	JUN	JUL	AUG	SEP	OCT	NOV	DEC	YEAR
Mean Maximum Temp. (°F)	22.1	28.0	37.1	46.8	58.6	69.4	77.7	77.2	66.5	52.3	33.4	22.1	49.3
Mean Temp. (°F)	12.4	16.5	25.0	34.7	45.2	54.1	60.7	60.0	50.9	40.1	25.6	13.3	36.5
Mean Minimum Temp. (°F)	2.7	5.0	12.9	22.5	31.7	38.7	43.6	42.7	35.2	27.8	17.7	4.5	23.8
Extreme Maximum Temp. (°F)	43	48	60	75	88	92	92	90	87	82	59	45	92
Extreme Minimum Temp. (°F)	-40	-42	-31	-13	13	20	29	28	12	-9	-18	-37	-42
Days Maximum Temp. ≥ 90°F	0	0	0	0	0	0	0	0	0	0	0	0	0
Days Maximum Temp. ≤ 32°F	27	19	8	1	0	0	0	0	0	1	14	27	97
Days Minimum Temp. ≤ 32°F	31	28	31	27	17	4	0	1	9	24	29	31	232
Days Minimum Temp. ≤ 0°F	13	10	5	0	0	0	0	0	0	0	2	12	42
Heating Degree Days (base 65°F)	1,626	1,364	1,234	902	609	322	138	156	417	767	1,177	1,597	10,309
Cooling Degree Days (base 65°F)	0	0	0	0	0	1	9	6	0	0	0	0	16
Mean Precipitation (in.)	2.92	2.27	2.77	*1.87*	2.75	3.13	*2.12*	1.90	1.94	1.69	2.72	3.27	*29.35*
Days With ≥ 0.1" Precipitation	11	8	8	6	8	8	6	5	5	5	8	10	88
Days With ≥ 1.0" Precipitation	0	0	0	0	0	0	0	0	0	0	0	0	0
Mean Snowfall (in.)	na	na	na	na	na	na	na	na	na	na	na	na	na
Days With ≥ 1.0" Snow Depth	31	27	31	23	4	0	0	0	0	3	21	31	171

Heron 2 NW *Sanders County*   Elevation: 2,237 ft.   Latitude: 48° 04' N   Longitude: 115° 59' W

	JAN	FEB	MAR	APR	MAY	JUN	JUL	AUG	SEP	OCT	NOV	DEC	YEAR
Mean Maximum Temp. (°F)	31.6	37.4	46.1	57.2	66.6	73.3	80.7	80.3	69.5	55.0	39.4	32.0	55.8
Mean Temp. (°F)	25.7	30.0	36.3	44.6	52.4	58.7	63.8	63.1	54.5	43.8	33.8	26.7	44.4
Mean Minimum Temp. (°F)	19.7	22.6	26.5	31.9	38.2	44.0	46.8	45.7	39.4	32.5	28.1	21.4	33.1
Extreme Maximum Temp. (°F)	51	59	69	88	93	97	100	98	93	78	65	53	100
Extreme Minimum Temp. (°F)	-33	-21	-8	14	20	29	31	29	20	10	-12	-32	-33
Days Maximum Temp. ≥ 90°F	0	0	0	0	0	1	5	5	0	0	0	0	11
Days Maximum Temp. ≤ 32°F	13	5	1	0	0	0	0	0	0	0	4	14	37
Days Minimum Temp. ≤ 32°F	29	26	26	17	6	1	0	0	4	16	22	29	176
Days Minimum Temp. ≤ 0°F	3	1	0	0	0	0	0	0	0	0	0	2	6
Heating Degree Days (base 65°F)	1,213	981	882	607	385	199	84	98	312	651	929	1,180	7,521
Cooling Degree Days (base 65°F)	0	0	0	0	3	15	49	46	3	0	0	0	116
Mean Precipitation (in.)	*4.50*	*3.42*	*2.72*	*2.14*	*2.68*	*2.48*	*1.31*	*1.62*	*1.71*	*1.86*	*4.49*	*4.51*	*33.44*
Days With ≥ 0.1" Precipitation	11	9	8	7	8	7	4	4	5	6	11	12	92
Days With ≥ 1.0" Precipitation	1	1	0	0	0	0	0	0	0	0	1	0	3
Mean Snowfall (in.)	na	na	na	na	na	na	na	na	na	na	na	na	na
Days With ≥ 1.0" Snow Depth	29	26	18	1	0	0	0	0	0	0	9	25	108

Hinsdale 4 SW *Valley County*   Elevation: 2,673 ft.   Latitude: 48° 21' N   Longitude: 107° 09' W

	JAN	FEB	MAR	APR	MAY	JUN	JUL	AUG	SEP	OCT	NOV	DEC	YEAR
Mean Maximum Temp. (°F)	23.0	30.1	41.8	56.5	67.7	76.8	83.1	82.9	70.4	57.4	38.6	27.0	54.6
Mean Temp. (°F)	14.5	21.5	32.1	44.8	55.5	64.3	69.9	69.4	57.8	46.2	30.1	18.6	43.7
Mean Minimum Temp. (°F)	6.0	12.8	22.3	33.2	43.3	51.7	56.6	55.8	45.2	34.9	21.5	10.1	32.8
Extreme Maximum Temp. (°F)	58	69	78	90	101	107	105	106	101	87	76	62	107
Extreme Minimum Temp. (°F)	-33	-34	-21	-3	24	31	39	37	20	-4	-25	-37	-37
Days Maximum Temp. ≥ 90°F	0	0	0	0	1	3	7	8	1	0	0	0	20
Days Maximum Temp. ≤ 32°F	20	14	7	1	0	0	0	0	0	1	9	17	69
Days Minimum Temp. ≤ 32°F	29	26	26	14	2	0	0	0	2	11	25	29	164
Days Minimum Temp. ≤ 0°F	12	7	2	0	0	0	0	0	0	0	2	8	31
Heating Degree Days (base 65°F)	1,562	1,224	1,014	599	306	94	24	39	244	580	1,041	1,434	8,161
Cooling Degree Days (base 65°F)	0	0	0	2	21	83	190	193	39	2	0	0	530
Mean Precipitation (in.)	0.40	0.34	0.73	1.24	2.74	2.85	1.88	1.55	1.41	0.91	0.62	0.46	15.13
Days With ≥ 0.1" Precipitation	1	1	2	3	5	6	4	4	3	2	2	1	34
Days With ≥ 1.0" Precipitation	0	0	0	0	1	1	0	0	0	0	0	0	2
Mean Snowfall (in.)	na	na	na	na	*trace*	0.0	0.0	0.0	0.0	na	na	na	na
Days With ≥ 1.0" Snow Depth	na	na	na	na	*0*	0	0	0	0	na	na	na	na

Holter Dam *Lewis And Clark County*   Elevation: 3,484 ft.   Latitude: 46° 59' N   Longitude: 112° 01' W

	JAN	FEB	MAR	APR	MAY	JUN	JUL	AUG	SEP	OCT	NOV	DEC	YEAR
Mean Maximum Temp. (°F)	35.4	40.7	47.8	57.2	67.1	76.3	84.3	84.2	72.3	60.2	45.1	37.4	59.0
Mean Temp. (°F)	27.0	31.6	37.7	45.9	54.7	63.1	69.1	68.8	59.0	49.9	37.6	29.9	47.9
Mean Minimum Temp. (°F)	18.6	22.5	27.5	34.6	42.3	49.9	54.0	53.3	45.6	39.5	30.1	22.2	36.7
Extreme Maximum Temp. (°F)	63	68	75	86	93	98	101	100	95	87	77	65	101
Extreme Minimum Temp. (°F)	-36	-31	-22	4	21	29	35	34	22	0	-21	-34	-36
Days Maximum Temp. ≥ 90°F	0	0	0	0	0	3	8	9	1	0	0	0	21
Days Maximum Temp. ≤ 32°F	10	5	3	1	0	0	0	0	0	0	3	7	29
Days Minimum Temp. ≤ 32°F	24	20	21	11	2	0	0	0	2	7	15	22	124
Days Minimum Temp. ≤ 0°F	6	3	1	0	0	0	0	0	0	0	1	4	15
Heating Degree Days (base 65°F)	1,172	936	841	566	318	109	24	28	203	465	814	1,083	6,559
Cooling Degree Days (base 65°F)	0	0	0	0	1	9	56	153	160	32	4	0	415
Mean Precipitation (in.)	0.41	0.25	0.51	1.26	2.33	1.97	1.47	1.36	1.19	0.69	0.39	0.34	12.17
Days With ≥ 0.1" Precipitation	1	1	2	4	6	5	3	4	3	2	1	1	33
Days With ≥ 1.0" Precipitation	0	0	0	0	0	0	0	0	0	0	0	0	0
Mean Snowfall (in.)	na	na	na	na	na	na	na	na	na	na	na	na	na
Days With ≥ 1.0" Snow Depth	na	na	na	*1*	*0*	*0*	*0*	*0*	*0*	*1*	na	*12*	na

Hungry Horse Dam *Flathead County* Elevation: 3,159 ft.   Latitude: 48° 21' N   Longitude: 114° 01' W

	JAN	FEB	MAR	APR	MAY	JUN	JUL	AUG	SEP	OCT	NOV	DEC	YEAR
Mean Maximum Temp. (°F)	29.3	34.5	42.8	53.4	64.0	72.1	80.0	79.8	66.3	52.1	37.4	30.8	53.5
Mean Temp. (°F)	22.7	26.7	33.5	42.5	51.8	59.2	65.2	64.7	53.6	42.4	31.4	24.8	43.2
Mean Minimum Temp. (°F)	15.9	18.8	24.1	31.7	39.7	46.2	50.3	49.6	40.7	32.7	25.4	18.8	32.8
Extreme Maximum Temp. (°F)	55	62	67	86	95	96	100	98	97	77	64	59	100
Extreme Minimum Temp. (°F)	-26	-26	-16	5	25	31	35	31	20	5	-14	-20	-26
Days Maximum Temp. ≥ 90°F	0	0	0	0	0	1	5	5	0	0	0	0	11
Days Maximum Temp. ≤ 32°F	16	9	3	0	0	0	0	0	0	1	7	16	52
Days Minimum Temp. ≤ 32°F	29	26	27	17	3	0	0	0	3	16	24	29	174
Days Minimum Temp. ≤ 0°F	5	3	1	0	0	0	0	0	0	0	1	2	12
Heating Degree Days (base 65°F)	1,306	1,076	971	668	406	201	81	85	342	696	1,001	1,239	8,072
Cooling Degree Days (base 65°F)	0	0	0	0	7	30	96	88	7	0	0	0	228
Mean Precipitation (in.)	na	na	na	na	na	na	na	na	na	na	na	na	na
Days With ≥ 0.1" Precipitation	8	7	7	6	8	7	5	5	5	6	8	9	81
Days With ≥ 1.0" Precipitation	0	0	0	0	0	0	0	0	0	0	1	0	1
Mean Snowfall (in.)	na	na	na	na	na	na	na	na	na	na	na	na	na
Days With ≥ 1.0" Snow Depth	24	19	17	3	0	0	0	0	0	na	10	20	na

Huntley Experiment Station *Yellowstone County* Elevation: 2,988 ft.   Latitude: 45° 56' N   Longitude: 108° 15' W

	JAN	FEB	MAR	APR	MAY	JUN	JUL	AUG	SEP	OCT	NOV	DEC	YEAR
Mean Maximum Temp. (°F)	na	na	na	na	na	na	na	na	na	na	na	na	na
Mean Temp. (°F)	na	na	na	na	na	na	na	na	na	na	na	na	na
Mean Minimum Temp. (°F)	na	na	na	na	na	na	na	na	na	na	na	na	na
Extreme Maximum Temp. (°F)	67	74	82	89	93	105	105	104	102	93	81	67	105
Extreme Minimum Temp. (°F)	-38	-29	-29	0	22	27	36	35	17	-15	-31	-47	-47
Days Maximum Temp. ≥ 90°F	0	0	0	0	1	4	11	11	2	0	0	0	29
Days Maximum Temp. ≤ 32°F	11	7	3	1	0	0	0	0	0	0	4	9	35
Days Minimum Temp. ≤ 32°F	30	27	27	18	4	0	0	0	4	19	28	29	186
Days Minimum Temp. ≤ 0°F	9	5	2	0	0	0	0	0	0	0	2	6	24
Heating Degree Days (base 65°F)	1,340	1,047	897	580	315	108	28	33	241	571	956	1,271	7,387
Cooling Degree Days (base 65°F)	0	0	0	1	11	68	158	149	28	1	0	0	416
Mean Precipitation (in.)	na	na	na	na	na	na	na	na	na	na	na	na	na
Days With ≥ 0.1" Precipitation	2	2	3	5	6	5	4	3	4	3	2	2	41
Days With ≥ 1.0" Precipitation	0	0	0	0	0	0	0	0	0	0	0	0	0
Mean Snowfall (in.)	na	na	na	na	na	na	na	na	na	na	na	na	na
Days With ≥ 1.0" Snow Depth	20	12	9	2	0	0	0	0	0	1	8	17	69

Hysham *Treasure County* Elevation: 2,657 ft.   Latitude: 46° 18' N   Longitude: 107° 14' W

	JAN	FEB	MAR	APR	MAY	JUN	JUL	AUG	SEP	OCT	NOV	DEC	YEAR
Mean Maximum Temp. (°F)	32.7	40.5	50.4	61.6	71.5	81.0	87.8	87.2	75.9	63.4	45.5	35.7	61.1
Mean Temp. (°F)	20.9	27.9	37.0	47.2	56.9	66.0	71.6	70.6	59.7	48.3	33.5	24.1	47.0
Mean Minimum Temp. (°F)	9.0	15.1	23.4	32.7	42.3	51.1	55.4	54.0	43.4	33.1	21.5	12.5	32.8
Extreme Maximum Temp. (°F)	72	75	82	92	100	106	106	105	105	93	79	70	106
Extreme Minimum Temp. (°F)	-37	-38	-25	6	23	31	37	32	19	-9	-31	-46	-46
Days Maximum Temp. ≥ 90°F	0	0	0	0	1	6	15	13	3	0	0	0	38
Days Maximum Temp. ≤ 32°F	13	8	3	0	0	0	0	0	0	0	5	10	39
Days Minimum Temp. ≤ 32°F	29	26	26	15	3	0	0	0	3	14	26	29	171
Days Minimum Temp. ≤ 0°F	10	5	2	0	0	0	0	0	0	0	2	6	25
Heating Degree Days (base 65°F)	1,363	1,043	863	529	260	63	12	17	188	512	939	1,261	7,050
Cooling Degree Days (base 65°F)	0	0	0	1	19	102	222	203	37	2	0	0	586
Mean Precipitation (in.)	0.53	0.34	0.83	1.37	2.55	1.92	1.45	0.93	1.41	1.20	0.60	0.49	13.62
Days With ≥ 0.1" Precipitation	2	1	3	4	6	5	3	3	3	3	3	2	38
Days With ≥ 1.0" Precipitation	0	0	0	0	1	0	0	0	0	0	0	0	1
Mean Snowfall (in.)	9.3	4.4	6.0	3.6	1.1	0.0	0.0	0.0	0.4	1.7	6.4	7.4	40.3
Days With ≥ 1.0" Snow Depth	na	na	na	0	0	0	0	0	0	0	6.4	na	na

Hysham 25 SSE *Treasure County* Elevation: 3,097 ft.   Latitude: 45° 56' N   Longitude: 107° 08' W

	JAN	FEB	MAR	APR	MAY	JUN	JUL	AUG	SEP	OCT	NOV	DEC	YEAR
Mean Maximum Temp. (°F)	31.5	38.6	46.7	57.5	67.9	78.4	87.2	86.7	74.5	61.2	44.3	35.2	59.1
Mean Temp. (°F)	18.4	25.6	33.9	43.8	53.4	62.9	69.7	68.5	57.4	45.3	31.3	22.0	44.3
Mean Minimum Temp. (°F)	5.3	12.5	21.1	30.0	38.8	47.3	52.1	50.1	40.1	29.4	18.3	8.8	29.5
Extreme Maximum Temp. (°F)	61	71	80	88	99	107	107	108	103	93	81	68	108
Extreme Minimum Temp. (°F)	-44	-45	-30	-2	19	28	31	27	16	-15	-31	-50	-50
Days Maximum Temp. ≥ 90°F	0	0	0	0	0	4	14	13	3	0	0	0	34
Days Maximum Temp. ≤ 32°F	13	8	5	1	0	0	0	0	0	1	6	10	44
Days Minimum Temp. ≤ 32°F	30	27	28	18	6	1	0	0	5	20	28	30	193
Days Minimum Temp. ≤ 0°F	11	6	2	0	0	0	0	0	0	0	3	7	29
Heating Degree Days (base 65°F)	1,440	1,107	956	632	360	126	31	47	254	604	1,004	1,327	7,888
Cooling Degree Days (base 65°F)	0	0	0	0	10	74	180	178	34	1	0	0	477
Mean Precipitation (in.)	0.65	0.48	0.95	1.50	2.24	2.29	1.52	0.84	1.36	1.20	0.77	0.62	14.42
Days With ≥ 0.1" Precipitation	2	2	3	4	6	6	4	3	3	4	3	2	42
Days With ≥ 1.0" Precipitation	0	0	0	0	0	0	0	0	0	0	0	0	0
Mean Snowfall (in.)	11.4	6.8	9.0	6.7	1.6	trace	0.0	0.0	1.0	2.9	7.2	10.9	57.5
Days With ≥ 1.0" Snow Depth	21	14	9	3	0	0	0	0	0	2	8	17	74

Ingomar 14 NE *Rosebud County*   Elevation: 2,791 ft.   Latitude: 46° 44' N   Longitude: 107° 12' W

	JAN	FEB	MAR	APR	MAY	JUN	JUL	AUG	SEP	OCT	NOV	DEC	YEAR
Mean Maximum Temp. (°F)	30.3	38.2	48.3	60.1	70.4	80.1	88.1	87.8	75.6	62.5	44.2	34.2	60.0
Mean Temp. (°F)	17.1	24.8	34.5	45.3	55.5	64.9	71.4	70.3	58.4	46.3	30.8	20.7	45.0
Mean Minimum Temp. (°F)	3.8	11.3	20.6	30.4	40.4	49.6	54.6	52.7	41.2	29.9	17.4	7.2	29.9
Extreme Maximum Temp. (°F)	70	77	79	90	99	107	105	108	102	92	78	69	108
Extreme Minimum Temp. (°F)	-45	-45	-31	0	18	28	33	30	13	-17	-32	-54	-54
Days Maximum Temp. ≥ 90°F	0	0	0	0	1	5	15	14	3	0	0	0	38
Days Maximum Temp. ≤ 32°F	15	9	4	1	0	0	0	0	0	0	6	12	47
Days Minimum Temp. ≤ 32°F	30	27	28	18	4	0	0	0	4	19	28	30	188
Days Minimum Temp. ≤ 0°F	13	7	2	0	0	0	0	0	0	0	0	3	9	34
Heating Degree Days (base 65°F)	1,481	1,130	940	586	302	84	14	24	222	575	1,021	1,368	7,747
Cooling Degree Days (base 65°F)	0	0	0	0	13	88	213	200	33	0	0	0	547
Mean Precipitation (in.)	0.42	0.26	0.51	1.10	2.27	2.30	1.44	0.93	1.28	0.79	0.46	0.47	12.23
Days With ≥ 0.1" Precipitation	2	1	2	3	6	5	3	2	3	2	2	2	33
Days With ≥ 1.0" Precipitation	0	0	0	0	0	0	0	0	0	0	0	0	0
Mean Snowfall (in.)	8.6	4.7	5.4	3.5	1.2	0.0	0.0	0.0	0.5	1.5	5.7	7.8	38.9
Days With ≥ 1.0" Snow Depth	18	13	7	1	0	0	0	0	0	1	7	15	62

Joliet *Carbon County*   Elevation: 3,697 ft.   Latitude: 45° 29' N   Longitude: 108° 59' W

	JAN	FEB	MAR	APR	MAY	JUN	JUL	AUG	SEP	OCT	NOV	DEC	YEAR
Mean Maximum Temp. (°F)	35.5	42.6	50.4	59.6	69.5	79.2	86.6	85.7	74.6	62.6	45.5	37.4	60.8
Mean Temp. (°F)	23.6	29.8	36.8	45.2	54.5	63.2	69.5	68.2	58.0	47.7	33.7	25.9	46.3
Mean Minimum Temp. (°F)	11.7	17.1	23.2	30.8	39.4	47.1	52.4	50.7	41.4	32.7	21.8	14.3	31.9
Extreme Maximum Temp. (°F)	63	73	78	87	93	102	104	101	99	90	75	69	104
Extreme Minimum Temp. (°F)	-37	-35	-20	-4	18	29	33	29	18	-10	-19	-39	-39
Days Maximum Temp. ≥ 90°F	0	0	0	0	0	4	12	11	2	0	0	0	29
Days Maximum Temp. ≤ 32°F	11	5	2	0	0	0	0	0	0	0	4	8	30
Days Minimum Temp. ≤ 32°F	29	26	26	18	5	0	0	0	3	14	25	29	175
Days Minimum Temp. ≤ 0°F	8	4	1	0	0	0	0	0	0	0	2	5	20
Heating Degree Days (base 65°F)	1,278	986	868	587	326	108	20	30	226	532	935	1,206	7,102
Cooling Degree Days (base 65°F)	0	0	0	0	8	60	165	139	25	0	0	0	397
Mean Precipitation (in.)	0.75	0.59	1.29	2.01	3.10	1.79	1.12	1.07	1.43	1.54	0.71	0.65	16.05
Days With ≥ 0.1" Precipitation	3	2	4	5	6	5	3	3	4	3	3	3	44
Days With ≥ 1.0" Precipitation	0	0	0	0	1	0	0	0	0	0	0	0	1
Mean Snowfall (in.)	10.9	7.0	10.1	7.1	0.8	0.0	0.0	0.0	0.9	4.3	7.4	9.6	58.1
Days With ≥ 1.0" Snow Depth	22	13	8	3	0	0	0	0	0	2	8	18	74

Joplin *Liberty County*   Elevation: 3,323 ft.   Latitude: 48° 34' N   Longitude: 110° 46' W

	JAN	FEB	MAR	APR	MAY	JUN	JUL	AUG	SEP	OCT	NOV	DEC	YEAR
Mean Maximum Temp. (°F)	27.2	33.8	43.8	56.0	66.9	74.9	81.9	82.0	70.3	58.4	39.6	30.2	55.4
Mean Temp. (°F)	16.4	22.4	31.9	42.8	53.0	60.7	66.3	66.1	55.2	44.5	28.7	19.7	42.3
Mean Minimum Temp. (°F)	5.5	11.0	19.9	29.5	39.0	46.5	50.6	50.1	40.0	30.6	17.7	9.2	29.1
Extreme Maximum Temp. (°F)	66	72	74	88	94	101	100	103	98	88	75	62	103
Extreme Minimum Temp. (°F)	-36	-35	-25	-11	19	30	32	28	18	-14	-25	-48	-48
Days Maximum Temp. ≥ 90°F	0	0	0	0	0	2	6	7	1	0	0	0	16
Days Maximum Temp. ≤ 32°F	16	11	5	1	0	0	0	0	0	1	8	14	56
Days Minimum Temp. ≤ 32°F	30	27	29	19	6	0	0	0	5	17	27	30	190
Days Minimum Temp. ≤ 0°F	12	7	2	0	0	0	0	0	0	0	3	8	32
Heating Degree Days (base 65°F)	1,503	1,195	1,020	660	373	160	57	68	303	630	1,078	1,400	8,447
Cooling Degree Days (base 65°F)	0	0	0	1	10	40	103	116	19	1	0	0	290
Mean Precipitation (in.)	0.28	0.19	0.42	0.73	2.03	2.16	1.30	1.30	0.89	0.47	0.31	0.25	10.33
Days With ≥ 0.1" Precipitation	1	1	1	2	5	6	4	4	2	2	1	1	30
Days With ≥ 1.0" Precipitation	0	0	0	0	0	0	0	0	0	0	0	0	0
Mean Snowfall (in.)	na	na	na	na	na	na	na	na	na	na	na	na	na
Days With ≥ 1.0" Snow Depth	12	na	na	2	0	0	0	0	0	0	3	9	na

Jordan *Garfield County*   Elevation: 2,677 ft.   Latitude: 47° 19' N   Longitude: 106° 55' W

	JAN	FEB	MAR	APR	MAY	JUN	JUL	AUG	SEP	OCT	NOV	DEC	YEAR
Mean Maximum Temp. (°F)	28.6	36.9	48.0	60.8	71.9	81.9	88.8	88.8	76.1	62.7	*43.4*	32.4	*60.0*
Mean Temp. (°F)	16.2	24.0	34.3	45.8	56.4	66.0	71.6	70.9	58.8	46.8	*30.8*	19.9	*45.1*
Mean Minimum Temp. (°F)	3.7	11.4	20.6	30.8	40.9	50.1	54.4	53.0	41.5	30.9	*18.1*	7.3	*30.2*
Extreme Maximum Temp. (°F)	68	74	79	91	102	108	107	109	105	95	78	70	109
Extreme Minimum Temp. (°F)	-40	-40	-34	-1	18	30	34	29	13	-5	-32	-46	-46
Days Maximum Temp. ≥ 90°F	0	0	0	0	2	6	15	15	4	0	0	0	42
Days Maximum Temp. ≤ 32°F	15	9	4	0	0	0	0	0	0	0	5	13	46
Days Minimum Temp. ≤ 32°F	30	27	27	17	5	0	0	0	4	17	26	29	182
Days Minimum Temp. ≤ 0°F	13	7	2	0	0	0	0	0	0	0	3	8	33
Heating Degree Days (base 65°F)	1,508	1,153	947	570	279	70	14	24	215	558	*1,020*	1,393	*7,751*
Cooling Degree Days (base 65°F)	0	0	0	1	24	113	228	229	39	2	0	0	636
Mean Precipitation (in.)	0.53	0.34	0.60	1.05	2.23	2.28	1.69	1.19	1.27	0.88	0.44	0.52	13.02
Days With ≥ 0.1" Precipitation	2	1	2	3	5	5	4	3	3	2	2	2	34
Days With ≥ 1.0" Precipitation	0	0	0	0	0	0	0	0	0	0	0	0	0
Mean Snowfall (in.)	na	na	na	na	na	na	na	na	na	na	na	na	na
Days With ≥ 1.0" Snow Depth	na	na	na	na	*0*	*0*	*0*	*0*	*0*	na	na	na	na

Judith Gap 13 E *Wheatland County*   Elevation: 5,098 ft.   Latitude: 46° 40' N   Longitude: 109° 29' W

	JAN	FEB	MAR	APR	MAY	JUN	JUL	AUG	SEP	OCT	NOV	DEC	YEAR
Mean Maximum Temp. (°F)	32.3	37.5	43.2	52.4	61.9	70.3	77.1	77.3	66.3	56.2	41.3	33.9	54.1
Mean Temp. (°F)	20.8	25.6	31.1	39.3	48.2	56.2	61.9	61.8	52.1	42.7	29.9	22.7	41.0
Mean Minimum Temp. (°F)	9.2	13.6	18.9	26.2	34.6	42.0	46.6	46.3	37.8	29.0	18.4	11.5	27.8
Extreme Maximum Temp. (°F)	65	67	69	81	85	94	94	98	91	88	73	60	98
Extreme Minimum Temp. (°F)	-35	-35	-26	-9	17	25	30	25	10	-10	-24	*-39*	*-39*
Days Maximum Temp. ≥ 90°F	0	0	0	0	0	0	1	1	0	0	0	0	2
Days Maximum Temp. ≤ 32°F	13	8	5	1	0	0	0	0	0	1	6	11	*45*
Days Minimum Temp. ≤ 32°F	30	27	30	24	12	3	0	0	7	20	27	30	*210*
Days Minimum Temp. ≤ 0°F	9	5	2	0	0	0	0	0	0	0	2	6	24
Heating Degree Days (base 65°F)	1,366	1,107	1,044	765	513	267	125	129	386	686	1,048	1,306	8,742
Cooling Degree Days (base 65°F)	0	0	0	0	0	11	34	36	5	0	0	0	86
Mean Precipitation (in.)	0.66	0.47	0.90	1.36	2.46	2.70	2.15	1.72	1.27	0.74	0.50	0.60	15.53
Days With ≥ 0.1" Precipitation	3	2	3	4	6	7	5	4	4	2	2	2	44
Days With ≥ 1.0" Precipitation	0	0	0	0	0	0	0	0	0	0	0	0	0
Mean Snowfall (in.)	na	na	na	na	0.4	0.0	0.0	0.0	0.3	na	na	na	na
Days With ≥ 1.0" Snow Depth	na	na	na	na	na	0	0	0	0	na	na	na	na

Lakeview *Beaverhead County*   Elevation: 6,709 ft.   Latitude: 44° 36' N   Longitude: 111° 49' W

	JAN	FEB	MAR	APR	MAY	JUN	JUL	AUG	SEP	OCT	NOV	DEC	YEAR
Mean Maximum Temp. (°F)	*22.9*	*28.4*	*35.9*	46.8	*57.7*	*67.8*	76.0	*75.4*	*66.0*	*53.1*	na	na	na
Mean Temp. (°F)	*11.2*	*15.9*	*23.6*	34.3	*43.8*	*52.0*	58.4	*57.3*	48.6	38.3	na	na	na
Mean Minimum Temp. (°F)	*-0.5*	*3.4*	*11.3*	21.7	*29.9*	*36.2*	40.7	*39.2*	31.5	23.4	na	na	na
Extreme Maximum Temp. (°F)	50	48	59	75	80	91	93	94	89	79	61	47	94
Extreme Minimum Temp. (°F)	-43	-41	-26	-13	9	19	19	20	4	-16	-34	-45	-45
Days Maximum Temp. ≥ 90°F	0	0	0	0	0	0	0	0	0	0	0	0	0
Days Maximum Temp. ≤ 32°F	22	15	8	1	0	0	0	0	0	0	10	19	76
Days Minimum Temp. ≤ 32°F	28	25	28	26	18	8	2	3	14	24	25	26	227
Days Minimum Temp. ≤ 0°F	13	11	6	1	0	0	0	0	0	0	5	12	48
Heating Degree Days (base 65°F)	*1,665*	*1,382*	*1,276*	914	*650*	*384*	201	*233*	485	822	na	na	na
Cooling Degree Days (base 65°F)	na	na	*0*	*0*	*0*	2	4	na	na	na	na	na	na
Mean Precipitation (in.)	0.88	0.91	1.84	1.57	2.60	2.84	1.91	1.61	1.91	1.35	1.27	1.17	19.86
Days With ≥ 0.1" Precipitation	2	3	5	4	6	6	5	4	3	3	3	3	47
Days With ≥ 1.0" Precipitation	0	0	0	0	0	0	0	0	0	0	0	0	0
Mean Snowfall (in.)	na	na	*16.7*	na	*4.3*	*0.7*	0.0	trace	*1.9*	*3.5*	na	na	na
Days With ≥ 1.0" Snow Depth	27	25	27	20	2	0	0	0	0	3	16	24	*144*

Lennep 5 SW *Meagher County*   Elevation: 5,597 ft.   Latitude: 46° 22' N   Longitude: 110° 36' W

	JAN	FEB	MAR	APR	MAY	JUN	JUL	AUG	SEP	OCT	NOV	DEC	YEAR
Mean Maximum Temp. (°F)	29.8	33.5	39.5	49.0	58.8	68.0	75.5	76.0	65.3	53.5	37.6	30.2	51.4
Mean Temp. (°F)	20.5	23.7	29.2	37.3	45.9	54.2	60.0	60.0	50.7	40.8	28.2	21.2	39.3
Mean Minimum Temp. (°F)	11.2	13.8	18.9	25.5	33.0	40.3	44.4	43.9	35.8	28.2	18.7	12.3	27.2
Extreme Maximum Temp. (°F)	59	63	66	79	83	90	92	92	89	81	69	57	92
Extreme Minimum Temp. (°F)	-34	-44	-30	-10	14	22	28	20	10	-14	-25	-40	-44
Days Maximum Temp. ≥ 90°F	0	0	0	0	0	0	0	0	0	0	0	0	0
Days Maximum Temp. ≤ 32°F	16	11	7	2	0	0	0	0	0	1	9	16	62
Days Minimum Temp. ≤ 32°F	30	28	29	25	16	3	1	1	9	21	28	30	221
Days Minimum Temp. ≤ 0°F	7	5	2	0	0	0	0	0	0	0	2	5	21
Heating Degree Days (base 65°F)	1,373	1,162	1,102	826	586	323	167	167	423	742	1,099	1,352	9,322
Cooling Degree Days (base 65°F)	0	0	0	0	0	4	18	14	2	0	0	0	38
Mean Precipitation (in.)	1.00	0.73	0.97	1.30	2.50	2.66	1.88	1.56	1.38	1.07	0.90	0.89	16.84
Days With ≥ 0.1" Precipitation	4	3	4	5	7	7	5	5	4	3	3	4	54
Days With ≥ 1.0" Precipitation	0	0	0	0	0	0	0	0	0	0	0	0	0
Mean Snowfall (in.)	na	na	na	na	na	trace	0.0	0.0	0.1	na	na	na	na
Days With ≥ 1.0" Snow Depth	na	na	na	na	na	0	0	0	0	na	na	na	na

Lewistown Municipal Airport *Fergus County*   Elevation: 4,143 ft.   Latitude: 47° 03' N   Longitude: 109° 27' W

	JAN	FEB	MAR	APR	MAY	JUN	JUL	AUG	SEP	OCT	NOV	DEC	YEAR
Mean Maximum Temp. (°F)	31.1	36.2	42.5	52.8	62.6	71.7	79.5	80.1	68.6	57.2	42.3	34.2	54.9
Mean Temp. (°F)	20.6	25.7	31.8	41.1	50.3	58.6	64.6	64.7	54.5	44.3	31.5	23.7	42.6
Mean Minimum Temp. (°F)	10.0	15.1	21.2	29.4	37.8	45.4	49.6	49.3	40.4	31.3	20.7	13.1	30.3
Extreme Maximum Temp. (°F)	73	69	73	83	89	96	97	102	97	86	78	66	102
Extreme Minimum Temp. (°F)	-34	-37	-25	-6	22	30	34	28	17	-9	-30	-42	-42
Days Maximum Temp. ≥ 90°F	0	0	0	0	0	1	4	5	1	0	0	0	11
Days Maximum Temp. ≤ 32°F	14	9	6	2	0	0	0	0	0	1	6	11	49
Days Minimum Temp. ≤ 32°F	29	26	27	20	7	1	0	0	4	17	25	29	185
Days Minimum Temp. ≤ 0°F	10	5	2	0	0	0	0	0	0	0	2	6	25
Heating Degree Days (base 65°F)	1,373	1,104	1,021	710	451	208	79	84	320	636	998	1,276	8,260
Cooling Degree Days (base 65°F)	0	0	0	0	2	24	75	84	14	1	0	0	200
Mean Precipitation (in.)	0.93	0.60	1.18	1.39	3.01	2.88	2.06	1.92	1.37	1.08	0.74	0.82	17.98
Days With ≥ 0.1" Precipitation	3	2	4	4	7	7	6	5	4	3	3	3	51
Days With ≥ 1.0" Precipitation	0	0	0	0	1	0	0	0	0	0	0	0	1
Mean Snowfall (in.)	na	na	na	na	na	na	na	na	na	na	na	na	na
Days With ≥ 1.0" Snow Depth	23	17	16	7	1	0	0	0	0	3	10	19	96

Libby 1 NE *Lincoln County*   Elevation: 2,093 ft.   Latitude: 48° 24' N   Longitude: 115° 32' W

	JAN	FEB	MAR	APR	MAY	JUN	JUL	AUG	SEP	OCT	NOV	DEC	YEAR
Mean Maximum Temp. (°F)	32.1	40.5	50.9	61.3	71.0	78.6	86.0	86.5	74.5	58.4	40.6	32.1	59.4
Mean Temp. (°F)	25.0	31.6	38.7	46.3	54.8	61.7	67.1	66.7	57.0	45.8	34.1	26.3	46.3
Mean Minimum Temp. (°F)	17.9	22.6	26.4	31.3	38.4	44.7	48.1	47.0	39.4	33.1	27.6	20.5	33.1
Extreme Maximum Temp. (°F)	55	59	73	90	97	100	108	107	105	82	69	55	108
Extreme Minimum Temp. (°F)	-30	-21	-10	6	19	26	30	27	17	3	-14	-31	-31
Days Maximum Temp. ≥ 90°F	0	0	0	0	1	4	12	13	2	0	0	0	32
Days Maximum Temp. ≤ 32°F	13	4	0	0	0	0	0	0	0	0	4	14	35
Days Minimum Temp. ≤ 32°F	30	26	25	18	7	1	0	0	5	14	22	30	178
Days Minimum Temp. ≤ 0°F	4	1	0	0	0	0	0	0	0	0	0	2	7
Heating Degree Days (base 65°F)	1,234	938	809	556	318	138	47	51	246	590	920	1,194	7,041
Cooling Degree Days (base 65°F)	0	0	0	0	10	47	119	118	16	0	0	0	310
Mean Precipitation (in.)	1.99	1.49	1.31	1.02	1.64	1.66	1.30	1.01	1.05	1.41	2.45	2.32	18.65
Days With ≥ 0.1" Precipitation	6	4	5	4	5	5	3	3	3	4	8	7	57
Days With ≥ 1.0" Precipitation	0	0	0	0	0	0	0	0	0	0	0	0	0
Mean Snowfall (in.)	na	na	na	na	na	na	na	na	na	na	na	na	na
Days With ≥ 1.0" Snow Depth	29	23	11	1	0	0	0	0	0	0	7	21	92

Libby 32 SSE *Lincoln County*   Elevation: 3,599 ft.   Latitude: 47° 58' N   Longitude: 115° 14' W

	JAN	FEB	MAR	APR	MAY	JUN	JUL	AUG	SEP	OCT	NOV	DEC	YEAR
Mean Maximum Temp. (°F)	30.0	36.1	43.9	53.6	63.2	70.4	77.8	78.3	67.8	54.2	37.2	29.5	53.5
Mean Temp. (°F)	21.7	26.2	32.8	40.4	48.2	54.8	59.7	59.5	50.4	40.5	29.3	21.9	40.4
Mean Minimum Temp. (°F)	13.3	16.2	21.6	27.1	33.3	39.3	41.6	40.4	33.0	26.7	21.4	14.3	27.4
Extreme Maximum Temp. (°F)	51	59	69	84	89	92	96	96	95	81	65	51	96
Extreme Minimum Temp. (°F)	-34	-38	-23	4	18	23	26	23	11	-11	-26	-43	-43
Days Maximum Temp. ≥ 90°F	0	0	0	0	0	0	2	2	0	0	0	0	4
Days Maximum Temp. ≤ 32°F	15	7	2	0	0	0	0	0	0	1	7	17	49
Days Minimum Temp. ≤ 32°F	30	28	30	24	15	5	2	4	15	24	27	30	234
Days Minimum Temp. ≤ 0°F	6	3	1	0	0	0	0	0	0	0	2	5	17
Heating Degree Days (base 65°F)	1,338	1,091	991	732	513	304	177	182	431	754	1,065	1,329	8,907
Cooling Degree Days (base 65°F)	0	0	0	0	0	1	8	8	0	0	0	0	17
Mean Precipitation (in.)	2.86	2.22	1.87	1.50	2.14	2.26	1.28	1.27	1.32	1.85	3.14	3.01	24.72
Days With ≥ 0.1" Precipitation	8	6	7	5	7	6	4	3	4	6	9	9	74
Days With ≥ 1.0" Precipitation	0	0	0	0	0	0	0	0	0	0	0	0	0
Mean Snowfall (in.)	21.4	15.5	11.9	5.2	0.8	0.1	0.0	0.2	0.1	2.8	17.2	23.2	98.4
Days With ≥ 1.0" Snow Depth	30	28	26	8	0	0	0	0	0	1	16	30	139

Lima *Beaverhead County*   Elevation: 6,272 ft.   Latitude: 44° 38' N   Longitude: 112° 35' W

	JAN	FEB	MAR	APR	MAY	JUN	JUL	AUG	SEP	OCT	NOV	DEC	YEAR
Mean Maximum Temp. (°F)	27.8	33.2	41.5	51.5	61.2	70.8	79.2	78.4	68.6	55.8	38.2	28.2	52.9
Mean Temp. (°F)	17.4	21.9	29.8	38.1	46.8	55.2	61.7	60.8	51.9	41.3	27.4	18.0	39.2
Mean Minimum Temp. (°F)	7.0	10.5	18.0	24.7	32.5	39.5	44.2	43.1	35.1	26.7	16.5	7.9	25.5
Extreme Maximum Temp. (°F)	51	56	66	76	85	92	94	94	87	80	67	54	94
Extreme Minimum Temp. (°F)	-35	-36	-17	-7	11	20	24	23	6	-14	-24	-44	-44
Days Maximum Temp. ≥ 90°F	0	0	0	0	0	0	1	1	0	0	0	0	2
Days Maximum Temp. ≤ 32°F	20	11	4	1	0	0	0	0	0	1	9	20	66
Days Minimum Temp. ≤ 32°F	31	28	30	25	16	4	1	1	11	24	28	31	230
Days Minimum Temp. ≤ 0°F	9	5	1	0	0	0	0	0	0	0	3	7	25
Heating Degree Days (base 65°F)	1,469	1,211	1,085	799	557	293	120	140	389	729	1,122	1,450	9,364
Cooling Degree Days (base 65°F)	0	0	0	0	0	4	24	14	1	0	0	0	43
Mean Precipitation (in.)	0.40	0.33	0.67	1.10	2.16	1.97	1.60	1.39	1.16	0.93	0.48	0.44	12.63
Days With ≥ 0.1" Precipitation	1	1	2	4	6	6	5	4	4	3	2	2	40
Days With ≥ 1.0" Precipitation	0	0	0	0	0	0	0	0	0	0	0	0	0
Mean Snowfall (in.)	na	na	na	na	na	na	na	na	na	na	na	na	na
Days With ≥ 1.0" Snow Depth	27	20	11	4	1	0	0	0	0	3	10	23	99

Lincoln Ranger Station *Lewis And Clark County*   Elevation: 4,573 ft.   Latitude: 46° 57' N   Longitude: 112° 39' W

	JAN	FEB	MAR	APR	MAY	JUN	JUL	AUG	SEP	OCT	NOV	DEC	YEAR
Mean Maximum Temp. (°F)	30.7	36.8	44.7	54.2	63.6	72.2	80.3	80.5	69.4	56.2	38.8	31.3	54.9
Mean Temp. (°F)	20.9	26.2	32.9	40.7	48.7	56.1	61.4	60.8	51.2	41.7	29.2	21.9	41.0
Mean Minimum Temp. (°F)	11.0	15.4	21.4	27.1	33.8	39.8	42.6	41.1	33.1	27.1	19.6	12.4	27.0
Extreme Maximum Temp. (°F)	56	62	72	82	91	94	100	100	93	82	68	55	100
Extreme Minimum Temp. (°F)	-42	-43	-25	-5	15	24	27	21	10	-13	-24	-48	-48
Days Maximum Temp. ≥ 90°F	0	0	0	0	0	1	4	4	1	0	0	0	10
Days Maximum Temp. ≤ 32°F	15	7	2	0	0	0	0	0	0	1	6	15	46
Days Minimum Temp. ≤ 32°F	30	26	28	24	14	4	1	3	15	23	27	29	224
Days Minimum Temp. ≤ 0°F	7	5	2	0	0	0	0	0	0	0	3	6	23
Heating Degree Days (base 65°F)	1,362	1,091	987	723	498	271	133	145	409	718	1,067	1,331	8,735
Cooling Degree Days (base 65°F)	0	0	0	0	0	1	8	27	22	2	0	0	60
Mean Precipitation (in.)	1.95	1.28	1.12	1.35	2.33	2.04	1.34	1.58	1.25	1.24	1.40	1.99	18.87
Days With ≥ 0.1" Precipitation	6	5	4	4	7	6	4	5	4	4	5	7	61
Days With ≥ 1.0" Precipitation	0	0	0	0	0	0	0	0	0	0	0	0	0
Mean Snowfall (in.)	na	na	na	na	na	na	na	na	na	na	na	na	na
Days With ≥ 1.0" Snow Depth	25	23	22	7	1	0	0	0	0	2	12	24	116

Lindbergh Lake *Missoula County*   Elevation: 4,317 ft.   Latitude: 47° 25' N   Longitude: 113° 43' W

	JAN	FEB	MAR	APR	MAY	JUN	JUL	AUG	SEP	OCT	NOV	DEC	YEAR
Mean Maximum Temp. (°F)	29.3	35.3	42.3	51.6	61.7	69.8	77.7	78.0	67.1	53.1	36.2	29.1	52.6
Mean Temp. (°F)	21.4	26.1	32.2	40.2	49.1	56.6	62.7	62.5	52.9	42.3	29.6	22.1	41.5
Mean Minimum Temp. (°F)	13.5	16.9	22.2	28.7	36.4	43.4	47.6	46.9	38.7	31.4	22.8	15.0	30.3
Extreme Maximum Temp. (°F)	55	61	70	81	87	97	99	96	91	83	65	53	99
Extreme Minimum Temp. (°F)	-34	-40	-26	3	21	29	28	28	18	-3	-16	-37	-40
Days Maximum Temp. ≥ 90°F	0	0	0	0	0	1	2	2	0	0	0	0	5
Days Maximum Temp. ≤ 32°F	18	9	3	0	0	0	0	0	0	1	9	19	59
Days Minimum Temp. ≤ 32°F	30	28	29	22	9	1	0	0	5	18	27	30	199
Days Minimum Temp. ≤ 0°F	6	3	1	0	0	0	0	0	0	0	1	3	14
Heating Degree Days (base 65°F)	1,346	1,092	1,010	738	488	257	112	115	361	698	1,057	1,325	8,599
Cooling Degree Days (base 65°F)	0	0	0	0	2	9	42	41	6	0	0	0	100
Mean Precipitation (in.)	3.20	2.22	1.97	1.69	2.33	2.36	1.40	1.43	1.57	1.86	3.18	3.24	26.45
Days With ≥ 0.1" Precipitation	10	7	8	6	7	7	5	4	5	6	9	10	84
Days With ≥ 1.0" Precipitation	0	0	0	0	0	0	0	0	0	0	0	0	0
Mean Snowfall (in.)	36.2	23.0	21.3	7.8	1.8	trace	0.0	trace	0.1	4.7	24.4	33.4	152.7
Days With ≥ 1.0" Snow Depth	31	28	31	21	3	0	0	0	0	2	18	31	165

Livingston Mission Field *Park County*   Elevation: 4,652 ft.   Latitude: 45° 42' N   Longitude: 110° 27' W

	JAN	FEB	MAR	APR	MAY	JUN	JUL	AUG	SEP	OCT	NOV	DEC	YEAR
Mean Maximum Temp. (°F)	35.2	40.4	46.7	55.2	64.7	74.3	83.2	83.2	71.7	59.7	43.6	36.6	57.9
Mean Temp. (°F)	26.8	30.7	36.0	43.2	51.8	60.4	67.2	66.5	56.5	47.0	35.1	28.3	45.8
Mean Minimum Temp. (°F)	17.8	21.1	25.2	31.2	38.8	46.5	51.1	49.7	41.2	34.3	26.2	19.7	33.6
Extreme Maximum Temp. (°F)	67	70	75	83	89	99	100	100	99	88	77	62	100
Extreme Minimum Temp. (°F)	-32	-33	-20	-2	19	27	35	28	10	-11	-21	-41	-41
Days Maximum Temp. ≥ 90°F	0	0	0	0	0	1	8	8	2	0	0	0	19
Days Maximum Temp. ≤ 32°F	11	6	4	1	0	0	0	0	0	1	5	10	38
Days Minimum Temp. ≤ 32°F	25	22	24	17	6	0	0	0	4	13	21	25	157
Days Minimum Temp. ≤ 0°F	6	3	1	0	0	0	0	0	0	0	1	4	15
Heating Degree Days (base 65°F)	1,178	961	892	647	404	164	44	49	268	553	891	1,130	7,181
Cooling Degree Days (base 65°F)	0	0	0	0	3	31	125	109	22	2	0	0	292
Mean Precipitation (in.)	0.64	0.46	0.87	1.59	2.90	2.45	1.62	1.37	1.55	1.21	0.75	0.56	15.97
Days With ≥ 0.1" Precipitation	2	2	3	5	7	6	4	4	3	3	2	2	44
Days With ≥ 1.0" Precipitation	0	0	0	0	0	0	0	0	0	0	0	0	0
Mean Snowfall (in.)	na	na	na	na	na	na	na	na	na	na	na	na	na
Days With ≥ 1.0" Snow Depth	11	8	9	5	1	0	0	0	0	2	8	10	54

Loma 1 WNW *Chouteau County*   Elevation: 2,578 ft.   Latitude: 47° 57' N   Longitude: 110° 32' W

	JAN	FEB	MAR	APR	MAY	JUN	JUL	AUG	SEP	OCT	NOV	DEC	YEAR
Mean Maximum Temp. (°F)	31.9	39.7	49.0	60.6	70.6	79.5	86.9	86.2	74.5	62.6	45.1	35.6	60.2
Mean Temp. (°F)	18.9	25.8	35.3	45.9	55.7	64.3	70.0	68.8	57.8	46.6	31.9	22.5	45.3
Mean Minimum Temp. (°F)	5.8	11.9	21.5	31.1	40.8	49.1	52.9	51.3	41.0	30.6	18.6	9.4	30.3
Extreme Maximum Temp. (°F)	72	76	81	95	99	107	108	111	102	94	80	67	111
Extreme Minimum Temp. (°F)	-54	-50	-29	-12	21	31	37	30	15	-17	-33	-54	-54
Days Maximum Temp. ≥ 90°F	0	0	0	0	1	5	13	12	3	0	0	0	34
Days Maximum Temp. ≤ 32°F	13	8	4	1	0	0	0	0	0	1	5	10	42
Days Minimum Temp. ≤ 32°F	29	27	27	17	4	0	0	0	5	18	27	30	184
Days Minimum Temp. ≤ 0°F	12	7	2	0	0	0	0	0	0	0	3	8	32
Heating Degree Days (base 65°F)	1,426	1,100	916	569	293	88	22	36	234	563	988	1,312	7,547
Cooling Degree Days (base 65°F)	0	0	0	1	15	71	174	165	24	1	0	0	451
Mean Precipitation (in.)	0.62	0.38	0.76	1.18	2.16	2.36	1.39	1.54	1.14	0.72	0.53	0.49	13.27
Days With ≥ 0.1" Precipitation	2	2	2	3	5	6	4	4	3	2	2	2	37
Days With ≥ 1.0" Precipitation	0	0	0	0	0	0	0	0	0	0	0	0	0
Mean Snowfall (in.)	na	na	na	na	na	na	na	na	na	na	na	na	na
Days With ≥ 1.0" Snow Depth	18	13	8	2	0	0	0	0	0	1	7	15	64

Malta 35 S *Phillips County*   Elevation: 2,647 ft.   Latitude: 47° 51' N   Longitude: 107° 57' W

	JAN	FEB	MAR	APR	MAY	JUN	JUL	AUG	SEP	OCT	NOV	DEC	YEAR
Mean Maximum Temp. (°F)	27.9	35.6	45.9	58.4	68.7	78.1	85.6	86.0	73.2	60.4	41.6	32.1	57.8
Mean Temp. (°F)	15.9	23.2	33.3	44.1	54.4	63.7	69.3	69.3	57.1	45.4	29.7	20.0	43.8
Mean Minimum Temp. (°F)	4.0	10.7	20.6	29.8	40.1	49.2	52.9	52.5	40.9	30.4	17.8	7.8	29.7
Extreme Maximum Temp. (°F)	62	75	80	87	97	107	104	109	103	91	81	68	109
Extreme Minimum Temp. (°F)	-41	-45	-35	-6	14	29	35	32	15	-10	-32	-51	-51
Days Maximum Temp. ≥ 90°F	0	0	0	0	1	4	11	13	2	0	0	0	31
Days Maximum Temp. ≤ 32°F	16	10	5	1	0	0	0	0	0	0	8	13	53
Days Minimum Temp. ≤ 32°F	29	26	27	19	5	0	0	0	5	17	28	30	186
Days Minimum Temp. ≤ 0°F	12	8	2	0	0	0	0	0	0	0	3	9	34
Heating Degree Days (base 65°F)	1,518	1,175	974	621	330	107	26	36	257	600	1,053	1,391	8,088
Cooling Degree Days (base 65°F)	0	0	0	0	10	76	167	181	28	1	0	0	463
Mean Precipitation (in.)	0.36	0.27	0.64	1.11	2.40	2.31	1.82	1.28	1.11	0.54	0.40	0.38	12.62
Days With ≥ 0.1" Precipitation	1	1	2	3	6	5	4	3	2	2	2	1	32
Days With ≥ 1.0" Precipitation	0	0	0	0	0	0	0	0	0	0	0	0	0
Mean Snowfall (in.)	6.8	4.3	6.2	5.5	1.3	0.0	0.0	0.0	0.1	1.4	5.0	5.2	35.8
Days With ≥ 1.0" Snow Depth	19	13	8	3	0	0	0	0	0	1	6	16	66

Malta 7 E *Phillips County*   Elevation: 2,244 ft.   Latitude: 48° 24' N   Longitude: 107° 44' W

	JAN	FEB	MAR	APR	MAY	JUN	JUL	AUG	SEP	OCT	NOV	DEC	YEAR
Mean Maximum Temp. (°F)	25.2	33.6	45.7	60.8	71.1	79.6	85.5	84.8	73.7	61.3	41.1	29.6	57.7
Mean Temp. (°F)	13.2	21.0	32.3	45.6	56.1	64.5	69.3	68.1	57.2	45.6	28.6	17.4	43.2
Mean Minimum Temp. (°F)	1.1	8.3	18.9	30.4	41.0	49.4	53.2	51.4	40.6	30.0	16.1	5.2	28.8
Extreme Maximum Temp. (°F)	61	74	82	94	101	106	107	108	103	90	79	63	108
Extreme Minimum Temp. (°F)	-42	-44	-36	-4	21	29	37	31	11	-11	-36	-45	-45
Days Maximum Temp. ≥ 90°F	0	0	0	0	1	5	10	10	2	0	0	0	28
Days Maximum Temp. ≤ 32°F	19	12	5	1	0	0	0	0	0	1	8	15	61
Days Minimum Temp. ≤ 32°F	31	27	29	18	4	0	0	0	4	19	28	31	191
Days Minimum Temp. ≤ 0°F	14	8	2	0	0	0	0	0	0	0	0	3	10	37
Heating Degree Days (base 65°F)	1,602	1,239	1,008	578	289	89	26	46	251	594	1,086	1,471	8,279
Cooling Degree Days (base 65°F)	0	0	0	2	21	88	171	163	26	1	0	0	472
Mean Precipitation (in.)	0.35	0.28	0.60	0.92	2.28	2.58	1.86	1.29	1.19	0.78	0.53	0.42	13.08
Days With ≥ 0.1" Precipitation	1	1	2	3	5	5	4	3	3	2	2	1	32
Days With ≥ 1.0" Precipitation	0	0	0	0	0	1	0	0	0	0	0	0	1
Mean Snowfall (in.)	na	na	na	na	na	na	na	na	na	na	na	na	na
Days With ≥ 1.0" Snow Depth	15	na	na	1	0	0	0	0	0	0	5	12	na

Martinsdale 3 NNW *Meagher County*   Elevation: 4,799 ft.   Latitude: 46° 30' N   Longitude: 110° 20' W

	JAN	FEB	MAR	APR	MAY	JUN	JUL	AUG	SEP	OCT	NOV	DEC	YEAR
Mean Maximum Temp. (°F)	35.1	40.3	46.1	55.9	65.2	73.3	79.4	80.1	70.4	59.8	43.4	36.1	57.1
Mean Temp. (°F)	23.8	28.0	33.2	41.3	49.9	57.5	62.5	62.0	53.3	44.5	31.9	25.3	42.8
Mean Minimum Temp. (°F)	12.5	15.6	20.3	26.7	34.6	41.7	45.5	43.8	36.2	29.2	20.3	14.4	28.4
Extreme Maximum Temp. (°F)	68	65	76	85	88	97	95	96	93	87	76	63	97
Extreme Minimum Temp. (°F)	-38	-40	-26	-7	10	19	26	22	8	-16	-23	-42	-42
Days Maximum Temp. ≥ 90°F	0	0	0	0	0	1	2	2	0	0	0	0	5
Days Maximum Temp. ≤ 32°F	11	6	3	1	0	0	0	0	0	0	4	10	35
Days Minimum Temp. ≤ 32°F	29	26	28	24	11	2	0	1	9	19	26	29	204
Days Minimum Temp. ≤ 0°F	7	4	2	0	0	0	0	0	0	0	2	5	20
Heating Degree Days (base 65°F)	1,271	1,039	978	702	463	226	105	113	347	628	991	1,226	8,089
Cooling Degree Days (base 65°F)	0	0	0	0	0	13	37	30	4	0	0	0	84
Mean Precipitation (in.)	0.51	0.33	0.71	1.18	2.26	2.25	1.90	1.55	1.23	0.74	0.54	0.49	13.69
Days With ≥ 0.1" Precipitation	2	1	2	4	6	6	5	4	3	2	2	2	39
Days With ≥ 1.0" Precipitation	0	0	0	0	0	0	0	0	0	0	0	0	0
Mean Snowfall (in.)	na	na	na	na	na	na	na	na	na	na	na	na	na
Days With ≥ 1.0" Snow Depth	9	6	6	2	0	0	0	0	0	1	6	8	38

Medicine Lake 3 SE *Sheridan County*   Elevation: 1,952 ft.   Latitude: 48° 29' N   Longitude: 104° 27' W

	JAN	FEB	MAR	APR	MAY	JUN	JUL	AUG	SEP	OCT	NOV	DEC	YEAR
Mean Maximum Temp. (°F)	20.4	29.6	41.6	57.4	69.7	79.0	84.7	84.4	72.2	59.1	38.4	25.8	55.2
Mean Temp. (°F)	9.7	18.7	29.9	44.0	56.1	65.2	70.0	69.1	57.5	45.5	27.7	15.2	42.4
Mean Minimum Temp. (°F)	-1.0	7.9	18.1	30.6	42.4	51.4	55.2	53.8	42.8	31.8	17.1	4.4	29.5
Extreme Maximum Temp. (°F)	51	68	75	92	101	107	105	104	101	91	74	59	107
Extreme Minimum Temp. (°F)	-38	40	-28	-15	15	29	39	34	17	-2	-31	-46	-46
Days Maximum Temp. ≥ 90°F	0	0	0	0	1	4	8	10	2	0	0	0	25
Days Maximum Temp. ≤ 32°F	22	14	7	1	0	0	0	0	0	1	9	19	73
Days Minimum Temp. ≤ 32°F	31	28	29	18	4	0	0	0	3	16	28	31	188
Days Minimum Temp. ≤ 0°F	16	9	3	0	0	0	0	0	0	0	4	11	43
Heating Degree Days (base 65°F)	1,712	1,301	1,082	624	292	80	21	37	247	598	1,113	1,542	8,649
Cooling Degree Days (base 65°F)	0	0	0	2	25	98	181	181	28	1	0	0	516
Mean Precipitation (in.)	na	na	na	na	na	na	na	na	na	na	na	na	na
Days With ≥ 0.1" Precipitation	1	1	2	3	6	6	5	4	3	2	1	1	35
Days With ≥ 1.0" Precipitation	0	0	0	0	0	0	1	0	0	0	0	0	1
Mean Snowfall (in.)	na	na	na	na	na	na	na	na	na	na	na	na	na
Days With ≥ 1.0" Snow Depth	26	17	10	3	0	0	0	0	0	0	8	20	84

Melstone *Musselshell County*   Elevation: 2,919 ft.   Latitude: 46° 36' N   Longitude: 107° 52' W

	JAN	FEB	MAR	APR	MAY	JUN	JUL	AUG	SEP	OCT	NOV	DEC	YEAR
Mean Maximum Temp. (°F)	33.3	40.7	49.1	59.9	70.1	80.2	87.7	87.2	75.5	62.5	44.9	35.9	60.6
Mean Temp. (°F)	22.2	28.7	36.6	46.3	56.1	65.5	71.6	70.9	59.9	48.4	33.7	24.9	47.1
Mean Minimum Temp. (°F)	11.1	16.7	24.0	32.7	42.1	50.8	55.3	54.5	44.3	34.2	22.5	13.8	33.5
Extreme Maximum Temp. (°F)	69	76	80	89	97	105	105	105	103	92	79	69	105
Extreme Minimum Temp. (°F)	-38	-36	-22	1	24	32	38	32	18	-9	-27	-43	-43
Days Maximum Temp. ≥ 90°F	0	0	0	0	1	6	14	13	3	0	0	0	37
Days Maximum Temp. ≤ 32°F	12	7	3	1	0	0	0	0	0	0	5	10	38
Days Minimum Temp. ≤ 32°F	28	25	25	15	3	0	0	0	2	12	23	28	161
Days Minimum Temp. ≤ 0°F	9	5	1	0	0	0	0	0	0	0	2	6	23
Heating Degree Days (base 65°F)	1,321	1,017	875	555	283	75	15	20	188	513	937	1,227	7,026
Cooling Degree Days (base 65°F)	0	0	0	1	18	98	224	218	46	3	0	0	608
Mean Precipitation (in.)	0.62	0.43	0.83	na	3.01	2.27	1.17	1.34	1.66	1.01	na	0.60	na
Days With ≥ 0.1" Precipitation	3	2	3	4	6	7	4	3	3	3	2	2	42
Days With ≥ 1.0" Precipitation	0	0	0	0	1	0	0	0	0	0	0	0	1
Mean Snowfall (in.)	na	na	na	na	na	na	na	na	na	na	na	na	na
Days With ≥ 1.0" Snow Depth	17	11	7	2	0	0	0	0	0	1	6	13	57

Melville 4 W *Sweet Grass County*   Elevation: 5,364 ft.   Latitude: 46° 06' N   Longitude: 110° 03' W

	JAN	FEB	MAR	APR	MAY	JUN	JUL	AUG	SEP	OCT	NOV	DEC	YEAR
Mean Maximum Temp. (°F)	33.9	37.7	42.4	50.6	60.0	68.5	75.6	75.5	65.6	55.5	41.3	35.4	53.5
Mean Temp. (°F)	22.4	25.9	30.7	38.5	47.4	55.5	61.4	61.0	51.9	42.5	30.1	23.8	40.9
Mean Minimum Temp. (°F)	10.7	14.0	19.0	26.3	34.8	42.4	47.2	46.4	38.1	29.5	18.9	12.3	28.3
Extreme Maximum Temp. (°F)	62	64	71	78	82	89	93	92	90	82	74	62	93
Extreme Minimum Temp. (°F)	-38	-45	-31	-12	9	26	31	26	10	-12	-26	-41	-45
Days Maximum Temp. ≥ 90°F	0	0	0	0	0	0	1	0	0	0	0	0	1
Days Maximum Temp. ≤ 32°F	12	7	6	2	0	0	0	0	0	1	7	11	46
Days Minimum Temp. ≤ 32°F	30	27	29	24	11	2	0	0	7	19	27	30	206
Days Minimum Temp. ≤ 0°F	8	5	2	0	0	0	0	0	0	0	3	6	24
Heating Degree Days (base 65°F)	1,316	1,098	1,055	790	536	286	134	141	392	689	1,040	1,270	8,747
Cooling Degree Days (base 65°F)	0	0	0	0	0	7	30	21	5	0	0	0	63
Mean Precipitation (in.)	0.61	0.53	1.17	1.97	2.90	2.95	2.15	1.63	1.45	1.13	0.76	0.55	17.80
Days With ≥ 0.1" Precipitation	2	2	4	6	7	7	6	4	4	3	3	2	50
Days With ≥ 1.0" Precipitation	0	0	0	0	0	1	0	0	0	0	0	0	1
Mean Snowfall (in.)	na	na	na	na	na	0.0	0.0	0.0	1.7	na	na	na	na
Days With ≥ 1.0" Snow Depth	na	na	na	na	0	0	0	0	0	na	na	na	na

Missoula 2 NE *Missoula County*   Elevation: 3,418 ft.   Latitude: 46° 54' N   Longitude: 113° 58' W

	JAN	FEB	MAR	APR	MAY	JUN	JUL	AUG	SEP	OCT	NOV	DEC	YEAR
Mean Maximum Temp. (°F)	32.2	38.9	47.5	56.4	65.1	73.2	82.0	82.2	70.6	56.7	40.4	31.6	56.4
Mean Temp. (°F)	24.7	30.1	37.4	44.7	52.4	59.7	66.4	66.2	56.2	44.8	32.8	24.6	45.0
Mean Minimum Temp. (°F)	17.3	21.3	27.1	32.9	39.7	46.2	50.7	50.1	41.8	32.9	25.2	17.5	33.6
Extreme Maximum Temp. (°F)	58	65	75	87	93	97	104	99	97	83	73	61	104
Extreme Minimum Temp. (°F)	-27	-23	-4	16	21	30	30	31	21	2	-10	-30	-30
Days Maximum Temp. ≥ 90°F	0	0	0	0	0	2	7	8	1	0	0	0	18
Days Maximum Temp. ≤ 32°F	13	6	1	0	0	0	0	0	0	0	5	15	40
Days Minimum Temp. ≤ 32°F	29	26	24	14	4	0	0	0	3	14	24	29	167
Days Minimum Temp. ≤ 0°F	4	2	0	0	0	0	0	0	0	0	1	2	9
Heating Degree Days (base 65°F)	1,242	978	850	604	388	186	62	63	272	620	958	1,246	7,469
Cooling Degree Days (base 65°F)	0	0	0	0	6	32	110	110	18	0	0	0	276
Mean Precipitation (in.)	1.41	1.00	1.23	1.45	2.41	2.17	1.34	1.22	1.24	1.03	1.22	1.44	17.16
Days With ≥ 0.1" Precipitation	5	3	4	4	6	6	4	4	4	3	4	5	52
Days With ≥ 1.0" Precipitation	0	0	0	0	0	0	0	0	0	0	0	0	0
Mean Snowfall (in.)	14.0	8.8	8.0	2.2	0.5	trace	0.0	0.0	trace	1.2	7.9	13.4	56.0
Days With ≥ 1.0" Snow Depth	25	17	6	0	0	0	0	0	0	0	7	22	77

Mizpah 4 NNW *Custer County*   Elevation: 2,477 ft.   Latitude: 46° 17' N   Longitude: 105° 18' W

	JAN	FEB	MAR	APR	MAY	JUN	JUL	AUG	SEP	OCT	NOV	DEC	YEAR
Mean Maximum Temp. (°F)	28.2	36.5	47.3	60.2	71.0	80.9	89.3	88.7	76.3	62.2	43.5	32.5	59.7
Mean Temp. (°F)	15.5	24.0	34.4	46.1	56.5	66.0	72.5	71.2	59.2	46.5	31.1	19.7	45.2
Mean Minimum Temp. (°F)	2.7	11.4	21.4	31.8	42.0	51.0	55.5	53.5	42.1	30.7	18.7	6.9	30.7
Extreme Maximum Temp. (°F)	69	73	80	92	101	110	110	110	106	95	80	66	110
Extreme Minimum Temp. (°F)	-45	-45	-38	-4	21	30	37	31	16	-11	-29	-49	-49
Days Maximum Temp. ≥ 90°F	0	0	0	0	1	5	16	15	4	0	0	0	41
Days Maximum Temp. ≤ 32°F	16	10	4	1	0	0	0	0	0	0	6	13	50
Days Minimum Temp. ≤ 32°F	31	27	27	16	4	0	0	0	5	18	28	31	187
Days Minimum Temp. ≤ 0°F	13	6	2	0	0	0	0	0	0	0	2	9	32
Heating Degree Days (base 65°F)	1,532	1,153	944	564	277	70	12	21	210	569	1,010	1,400	7,762
Cooling Degree Days (base 65°F)	0	0	0	1	25	116	263	242	48	1	0	0	696
Mean Precipitation (in.)	0.45	0.27	0.58	1.42	2.35	2.27	1.60	1.17	1.30	1.12	0.52	0.38	13.43
Days With ≥ 0.1" Precipitation	1	1	2	3	5	5	4	3	3	3	2	1	33
Days With ≥ 1.0" Precipitation	0	0	0	0	0	0	0	0	0	0	0	0	0
Mean Snowfall (in.)	5.8	3.2	4.6	3.3	0.7	0.0	0.0	0.0	0.5	1.2	4.4	5.7	29.4
Days With ≥ 1.0" Snow Depth	23	16	8	1	0	0	0	0	0	1	6	18	73

Moccasin Experiment Station *Judith Basin County*   Elevation: 4,297 ft.   Latitude: 47° 03' N   Longitude: 109° 57' W

	JAN	FEB	MAR	APR	MAY	JUN	JUL	AUG	SEP	OCT	NOV	DEC	YEAR
Mean Maximum Temp. (°F)	na	na	na	na	na	na	na	na	na	na	na	na	na
Mean Temp. (°F)	na	na	na	na	na	na	na	na	na	na	na	na	na
Mean Minimum Temp. (°F)	na	na	na	na	na	na	na	na	na	na	na	na	na
Extreme Maximum Temp. (°F)	69	71	73	84	89	97	99	101	96	90	79	67	101
Extreme Minimum Temp. (°F)	-38	-34	-24	-3	21	30	31	29	16	-7	-27	-37	-38
Days Maximum Temp. ≥ 90°F	0	0	0	0	0	1	3	4	1	0	0	0	9
Days Maximum Temp. ≤ 32°F	12	8	6	2	0	0	0	0	0	1	6	10	45
Days Minimum Temp. ≤ 32°F	29	26	28	20	6	0	0	0	4	16	25	28	182
Days Minimum Temp. ≤ 0°F	9	5	2	0	0	0	0	0	0	0	2	6	24
Heating Degree Days (base 65°F)	1,326	1,085	1,010	712	449	208	80	81	317	621	978	1,240	8,107
Cooling Degree Days (base 65°F)	0	0	0	0	4	26	85	98	22	2	0	0	237
Mean Precipitation (in.)	na	na	na	na	na	na	na	na	na	na	na	na	na
Days With ≥ 0.1" Precipitation	2	2	3	4	7	7	5	5	4	3	2	2	46
Days With ≥ 1.0" Precipitation	0	0	0	0	0	0	0	0	0	0	0	0	0
Mean Snowfall (in.)	na	na	na	na	na	na	na	na	na	na	na	na	na
Days With ≥ 1.0" Snow Depth	18	14	14	6	1	0	0	0	1	3	9	15	81

Mosby 2 ENE *Garfield County*   Elevation: 2,788 ft.   Latitude: 47° 01' N   Longitude: 107° 49' W

	JAN	FEB	MAR	APR	MAY	JUN	JUL	AUG	SEP	OCT	NOV	DEC	YEAR
Mean Maximum Temp. (°F)	*32.0*	38.9	48.5	59.3	69.3	79.9	87.8	*87.3*	*74.3*	63.1	*45.9*	36.1	*60.2*
Mean Temp. (°F)	*20.1*	26.4	36.2	46.1	55.9	65.7	72.0	*71.2*	59.1	48.7	*33.9*	24.1	*46.6*
Mean Minimum Temp. (°F)	*8.3*	13.9	23.7	32.7	42.4	51.3	56.0	*55.1*	43.8	34.3	*21.9*	12.1	*33.0*
Extreme Maximum Temp. (°F)	65	76	80	90	99	107	105	108	101	94	80	72	108
Extreme Minimum Temp. (°F)	-40	-39	-24	-5	21	31	33	34	20	1	-27	-43	-43
Days Maximum Temp. ≥ 90°F	0	0	0	0	1	5	14	13	3	0	0	0	36
Days Maximum Temp. ≤ 32°F	12	8	3	1	0	0	0	0	0	0	5	9	38
Days Minimum Temp. ≤ 32°F	27	25	25	14	3	0	0	0	2	11	23	27	157
Days Minimum Temp. ≤ 0°F	10	5	1	0	0	0	0	0	0	0	2	6	24
Heating Degree Days (base 65°F)	*1,386*	1,084	887	563	294	76	16	*20*	*211*	*500*	*925*	1,261	*7,223*
Cooling Degree Days (base 65°F)	na	0	0	1	18	100	*220*	na	*36*	*2*	*0*	*0*	na
Mean Precipitation (in.)	0.54	0.33	0.67	1.18	2.63	2.13	1.64	1.14	1.28	0.87	0.44	0.43	13.28
Days With ≥ 0.1" Precipitation	2	1	2	3	6	5	4	3	3	2	2	1	34
Days With ≥ 1.0" Precipitation	0	0	0	0	1	0	0	0	0	0	0	0	1
Mean Snowfall (in.)	*5.5*	3.3	*3.6*	2.9	1.0	0.0	0.0	0.0	0.1	1.6	2.9	*5.3*	*26.2*
Days With ≥ 1.0" Snow Depth	na	*10*	*5*	1	0	0	0	0	0	0	0	3	9	na

Mystic Lake *Stillwater County*   Elevation: 6,555 ft.   Latitude: 45° 15' N   Longitude: 109° 44' W

	JAN	FEB	MAR	APR	MAY	JUN	JUL	AUG	SEP	OCT	NOV	DEC	YEAR
Mean Maximum Temp. (°F)	34.0	37.3	42.2	49.3	58.5	67.8	74.7	74.5	64.9	54.4	40.3	33.9	52.6
Mean Temp. (°F)	25.4	28.0	32.2	38.6	47.5	56.2	62.5	62.5	53.3	44.2	32.4	26.1	42.4
Mean Minimum Temp. (°F)	16.8	18.8	22.1	27.9	36.5	44.6	50.2	50.3	41.7	34.0	24.5	18.4	32.1
Extreme Maximum Temp. (°F)	59	61	65	76	79	91	90	89	86	78	66	58	91
Extreme Minimum Temp. (°F)	-29	-38	-18	-7	15	28	29	29	11	-8	-18	-35	-38
Days Maximum Temp. ≥ 90°F	0	0	0	0	0	0	0	0	0	0	0	0	0
Days Maximum Temp. ≤ 32°F	12	8	5	2	0	0	0	0	0	1	6	12	46
Days Minimum Temp. ≤ 32°F	27	25	26	21	10	1	0	0	5	14	23	27	179
Days Minimum Temp. ≤ 0°F	5	3	1	0	0	0	0	0	0	0	2	4	15
Heating Degree Days (base 65°F)	1,222	1,038	1,011	784	536	269	117	115	355	638	972	1,198	8,255
Cooling Degree Days (base 65°F)	0	0	0	0	0	13	50	46	12	0	0	0	121
Mean Precipitation (in.)	*1.27*	*1.23*	*2.27*	*2.69*	*3.92*	2.63	2.26	*1.85*	*2.29*	*1.91*	*1.51*	*1.26*	*25.09*
Days With ≥ 0.1" Precipitation	5	4	7	7	9	8	8	6	6	5	5	5	75
Days With ≥ 1.0" Precipitation	0	0	0	0	0	0	0	0	0	0	0	0	0
Mean Snowfall (in.)	na	na	na	na	na	na	na	na	na	na	na	na	na
Days With ≥ 1.0" Snow Depth	23	21	23	15	5	0	0	0	2	7	17	21	134

Neihart 8 NNW *Cascade County*   Elevation: 5,229 ft.   Latitude: 47° 02' N   Longitude: 110° 47' W

	JAN	FEB	MAR	APR	MAY	JUN	JUL	AUG	SEP	OCT	NOV	DEC	YEAR
Mean Maximum Temp. (°F)	34.1	38.7	44.0	52.4	61.5	70.7	78.4	78.9	68.5	57.2	41.5	35.0	55.1
Mean Temp. (°F)	22.9	27.1	31.9	39.4	47.8	55.9	61.7	61.9	52.8	43.6	31.0	24.3	41.7
Mean Minimum Temp. (°F)	11.6	15.5	19.7	26.5	34.0	41.0	45.0	44.8	37.1	29.9	20.4	13.6	28.3
Extreme Maximum Temp. (°F)	67	64	69	82	85	96	94	96	93	89	73	59	96
Extreme Minimum Temp. (°F)	-39	-46	-30	-19	11	25	28	27	4	-9	-26	-44	-46
Days Maximum Temp. ≥ 90°F	0	0	0	0	0	0	2	2	0	0	0	0	4
Days Maximum Temp. ≤ 32°F	11	7	4	1	0	0	0	0	0	1	5	11	40
Days Minimum Temp. ≤ 32°F	29	26	28	24	13	2	0	1	8	18	26	29	204
Days Minimum Temp. ≤ 0°F	8	5	2	0	0	0	0	0	0	0	3	5	23
Heating Degree Days (base 65°F)	1,299	1,064	1,020	760	526	276	129	130	365	657	1,013	1,255	8,494
Cooling Degree Days (base 65°F)	0	0	0	0	0	12	40	45	9	1	0	0	107
Mean Precipitation (in.)	0.96	0.66	1.39	1.89	3.50	3.30	2.27	2.15	1.97	1.36	0.98	1.00	21.43
Days With ≥ 0.1" Precipitation	4	3	5	5	7	8	6	6	5	4	3	4	60
Days With ≥ 1.0" Precipitation	0	0	0	0	1	1	0	0	0	0	0	0	2
Mean Snowfall (in.)	na	*11.7*	*21.9*	*16.4*	*6.4*	*0.4*	0.0	trace	*2.7*	*10.0*	na	na	na
Days With ≥ 1.0" Snow Depth	29	25	23	10	2	0	0	0	1	5	12	24	*131*

Norris Madison Pump HS *Madison County*   Elevation: 4,744 ft.   Latitude: 45° 29' N   Longitude: 111° 38' W

	JAN	FEB	MAR	APR	MAY	JUN	JUL	AUG	SEP	OCT	NOV	DEC	YEAR
Mean Maximum Temp. (°F)	35.4	40.4	46.8	55.6	65.3	74.8	83.5	83.2	72.6	59.9	43.9	35.9	58.1
Mean Temp. (°F)	27.3	31.5	37.1	44.6	53.4	61.7	68.8	68.3	58.8	48.4	35.8	28.2	47.0
Mean Minimum Temp. (°F)	19.2	22.5	27.3	33.4	41.4	48.5	54.0	53.5	44.9	36.8	27.7	20.6	35.8
Extreme Maximum Temp. (°F)	62	65	70	83	87	96	98	100	93	88	73	59	100
Extreme Minimum Temp. (°F)	-20	-30	-9	7	21	33	39	33	17	-10	-26	-30
Days Maximum Temp. ≥ 90°F	0	0	0	0	0	1	7	6	1	0	0	0	15
Days Maximum Temp. ≤ 32°F	10	5	2	0	0	0	0	0	0	0	4	10	31
Days Minimum Temp. ≤ 32°F	26	23	22	14	2	0	0	0	2	8	19	26	142
Days Minimum Temp. ≤ 0°F	4	2	0	0	0	0	0	0	0	0	1	2	9
Heating Degree Days (base 65°F)	1,162	939	857	606	358	141	30	31	211	509	869	1,133	6,846
Cooling Degree Days (base 65°F)	0	0	0	0	6	45	155	153	35	1	0	0	395
Mean Precipitation (in.)	*0.51*	*0.45*	*1.32*	*1.73*	*3.23*	2.57	*1.55*	*1.56*	*1.94*	*1.26*	*0.78*	*0.55*	*17.45*
Days With ≥ 0.1" Precipitation	2	2	4	5	8	7	5	5	5	4	3	2	52
Days With ≥ 1.0" Precipitation	0	0	0	0	0	0	0	0	0	0	0	0	0
Mean Snowfall (in.)	na	na	na	na	na	na	na	na	na	na	na	na	na
Days With ≥ 1.0" Snow Depth	na	na	na	*3*	0	0	0	0	0	*1*	9	na	na

Opheim 10 N *Valley County*   Elevation: 2,979 ft.   Latitude: 49° 00' N   Longitude: 106° 23' W

	JAN	FEB	MAR	APR	MAY	JUN	JUL	AUG	SEP	OCT	NOV	DEC	YEAR
Mean Maximum Temp. (°F)	18.8	26.4	38.3	55.0	67.1	76.0	81.3	81.9	69.5	56.3	36.0	24.3	52.6
Mean Temp. (°F)	8.0	15.7	26.9	41.0	52.2	61.1	65.4	65.0	53.5	42.1	24.9	13.0	39.1
Mean Minimum Temp. (°F)	-2.9	5.0	15.5	26.9	37.3	46.1	49.5	48.1	37.5	27.8	13.6	1.7	25.5
Extreme Maximum Temp. (°F)	56	64	73	91	98	105	103	104	98	89	76	55	105
Extreme Minimum Temp. (°F)	-48	-46	-35	-18	8	20	31	25	2	-19	-33	-47	-48
Days Maximum Temp. ≥ 90°F	0	0	0	0	0	2	5	7	1	0	0	0	15
Days Maximum Temp. ≤ 32°F	23	16	9	1	0	0	0	0	0	1	11	20	81
Days Minimum Temp. ≤ 32°F	31	28	30	23	9	1	0	1	8	21	28	31	211
Days Minimum Temp. ≤ 0°F	17	11	5	0	0	0	0	0	0	0	5	14	52
Heating Degree Days (base 65°F)	1,766	1,388	1,175	714	400	154	70	85	349	705	1,198	1,608	9,612
Cooling Degree Days (base 65°F)	0	0	0	0	10	48	89	97	12	0	0	0	256
Mean Precipitation (in.)	0.28	0.25	0.38	0.62	2.03	2.71	2.25	1.24	1.26	0.64	0.26	0.31	12.23
Days With ≥ 0.1" Precipitation	1	1	1	2	6	6	5	3	3	2	1	1	32
Days With ≥ 1.0" Precipitation	0	0	0	0	0	1	0	0	0	0	0	0	1
Mean Snowfall (in.)	na	na	na	na	*0.6*	*trace*	0.0	0.0	*trace*	na	na	na	na
Days With ≥ 1.0" Snow Depth	na	na	na	na	*0*	0	0	0	0	na	na	na	na

Opheim 12 SSE *Valley County*   Elevation: 2,949 ft.   Latitude: 48° 42' N   Longitude: 106° 19' W

	JAN	FEB	MAR	APR	MAY	JUN	JUL	AUG	SEP	OCT	NOV	DEC	YEAR
Mean Maximum Temp. (°F)	18.8	26.2	38.0	53.4	65.8	74.8	80.6	80.6	67.9	54.7	35.7	23.1	51.6
Mean Temp. (°F)	8.4	15.8	27.1	40.5	51.9	60.9	65.7	65.1	53.2	41.5	24.8	12.3	38.9
Mean Minimum Temp. (°F)	-2.1	5.4	16.1	27.6	38.0	47.0	50.7	49.5	38.6	28.1	13.9	1.4	26.2
Extreme Maximum Temp. (°F)	53	66	75	89	98	105	102	105	100	91	74	54	105
Extreme Minimum Temp. (°F)	-40	-41	-32	-9	15	24	34	28	8	-14	-28	-41	-41
Days Maximum Temp. ≥ 90°F	0	0	0	0	0	2	5	6	1	0	0	0	14
Days Maximum Temp. ≤ 32°F	24	16	10	2	0	0	0	0	0	2	11	22	87
Days Minimum Temp. ≤ 32°F	31	28	30	22	8	0	0	0	6	21	29	31	206
Days Minimum Temp. ≤ 0°F	16	10	4	0	0	0	0	0	0	0	5	14	49
Heating Degree Days (base 65°F)	1,752	1,384	1,169	728	405	155	65	86	356	724	1,200	1,631	9,655
Cooling Degree Days (base 65°F)	0	0	0	0	7	43	89	103	11	0	0	0	253
Mean Precipitation (in.)	0.24	0.19	0.39	0.87	1.91	2.53	2.06	1.24	1.21	0.64	0.30	0.27	11.85
Days With ≥ 0.1" Precipitation	1	0	1	2	5	6	5	3	3	2	1	1	30
Days With ≥ 1.0" Precipitation	0	0	0	0	0	0	0	0	0	0	0	0	0
Mean Snowfall (in.)	na	na	na	na	na	na	na	na	na	na	na	na	na
Days With ≥ 1.0" Snow Depth	29	23	18	4	1	0	0	0	0	2	10	24	111

Philipsburg Ranger Station *Granite County*   Elevation: 5,269 ft.   Latitude: 46° 18' N   Longitude: 113° 18' W

	JAN	FEB	MAR	APR	MAY	JUN	JUL	AUG	SEP	OCT	NOV	DEC	YEAR
Mean Maximum Temp. (°F)	33.0	38.0	44.9	53.4	62.2	70.8	79.2	79.7	69.3	58.1	41.7	33.1	55.3
Mean Temp. (°F)	23.5	27.4	33.4	40.3	47.9	55.4	61.0	60.7	51.9	43.1	31.3	23.5	41.6
Mean Minimum Temp. (°F)	14.0	16.7	21.9	27.1	33.7	40.0	42.8	41.7	34.5	28.0	20.9	14.0	27.9
Extreme Maximum Temp. (°F)	57	64	72	80	90	92	96	97	92	86	73	62	97
Extreme Minimum Temp. (°F)	-34	-38	-23	0	8	24	25	21	8	-9	-20	-38	-38
Days Maximum Temp. ≥ 90°F	0	0	0	0	0	0	2	3	0	0	0	0	5
Days Maximum Temp. ≤ 32°F	12	7	3	0	0	0	0	0	0	0	5	13	40
Days Minimum Temp. ≤ 32°F	28	26	27	23	14	3	1	2	12	23	25	29	213
Days Minimum Temp. ≤ 0°F	6	4	1	0	0	0	0	0	0	0	2	5	18
Heating Degree Days (base 65°F)	1,279	1,056	973	736	522	289	140	148	388	673	1,004	1,281	8,489
Cooling Degree Days (base 65°F)	0	0	0	0	1	7	25	25	3	0	0	0	61
Mean Precipitation (in.)	0.59	0.50	0.88	1.50	2.51	2.25	1.38	1.62	1.48	1.01	0.71	0.61	15.04
Days With ≥ 0.1" Precipitation	2	2	3	5	7	7	5	5	4	3	3	2	48
Days With ≥ 1.0" Precipitation	0	0	0	0	0	0	0	0	0	0	0	0	0
Mean Snowfall (in.)	na	na	na	na	na	na	na	na	na	na	na	na	na
Days With ≥ 1.0" Snow Depth	*19*	*14*	*8*	2	0	0	0	0	0	*1*	na	na	na

Plevna *Fallon County*   Elevation: 2,778 ft.   Latitude: 46° 25' N   Longitude: 104° 31' W

	JAN	FEB	MAR	APR	MAY	JUN	JUL	AUG	SEP	OCT	NOV	DEC	YEAR
Mean Maximum Temp. (°F)	28.3	35.4	45.5	58.7	70.0	80.3	88.3	87.4	75.4	61.5	42.9	31.9	58.8
Mean Temp. (°F)	15.5	23.5	32.7	44.6	55.5	65.2	71.6	70.1	58.7	46.2	30.4	19.4	44.4
Mean Minimum Temp. (°F)	2.9	11.4	19.8	30.5	40.9	50.0	54.9	52.8	41.9	30.8	18.1	6.8	30.1
Extreme Maximum Temp. (°F)	66	70	79	90	99	110	109	105	105	93	79	64	110
Extreme Minimum Temp. (°F)	-49	-39	-32	-9	16	28	35	29	12	-15	-32	-45	-49
Days Maximum Temp. ≥ 90°F	0	0	0	0	1	5	14	13	3	0	0	0	36
Days Maximum Temp. ≤ 32°F	16	10	5	1	0	0	0	0	0	1	6	13	52
Days Minimum Temp. ≤ 32°F	30	27	28	18	5	0	0	0	4	17	28	31	188
Days Minimum Temp. ≤ 0°F	*11*	6	3	0	0	0	0	0	0	0	2	*8*	*30*
Heating Degree Days (base 65°F)	1,530	1,166	994	607	309	85	18	29	225	586	1,032	1,408	7,989
Cooling Degree Days (base 65°F)	0	0	0	1	22	104	231	202	43	1	0	0	604
Mean Precipitation (in.)	0.56	0.41	0.76	1.40	2.38	2.43	1.80	1.44	1.42	1.25	0.52	0.41	14.78
Days With ≥ 0.1" Precipitation	2	1	2	3	6	5	4	3	3	3	2	2	36
Days With ≥ 1.0" Precipitation	0	0	0	0	0	0	0	0	0	0	0	0	0
Mean Snowfall (in.)	na	na	na	na	na	na	na	na	na	na	na	na	na
Days With ≥ 1.0" Snow Depth	na	na	na	na	*0*	*0*	*0*	0	*0*	na	na	na	na

Polebridge *Flathead County*　Elevation: 3,517 ft.　Latitude: 48° 46' N　Longitude: 114° 17' W

	JAN	FEB	MAR	APR	MAY	JUN	JUL	AUG	SEP	OCT	NOV	DEC	YEAR
Mean Maximum Temp. (°F)	29.0	36.1	43.7	54.0	63.1	70.7	78.5	78.9	68.1	55.0	37.8	29.2	53.7
Mean Temp. (°F)	17.9	23.3	30.6	39.4	47.7	54.7	*59.5*	59.0	49.5	39.4	27.7	18.9	*39.0*
Mean Minimum Temp. (°F)	6.7	10.5	17.5	24.8	32.2	38.7	*40.9*	39.0	31.2	23.8	17.6	8.5	24.3
Extreme Maximum Temp. (°F)	50	60	67	83	91	94	*97*	97	95	85	65	53	97
Extreme Minimum Temp. (°F)	-44	-42	-30	-6	11	24	*25*	26	11	-13	-35	-48	*-48*
Days Maximum Temp. ≥ 90°F	0	0	0	0	0	0	3	3	0	0	0	0	*6*
Days Maximum Temp. ≤ 32°F	17	7	2	0	0	0	0	0	0	1	7	18	52
Days Minimum Temp. ≤ 32°F	31	28	30	27	17	5	2	4	*18*	*28*	28	30	*248*
Days Minimum Temp. ≤ 0°F	10	6	2	0	0	0	0	0	0	0	0	3	8	29
Heating Degree Days (base 65°F)	1,456	1,171	1,059	759	531	307	*179*	192	457	786	1,112	1,424	*9,433*
Cooling Degree Days (base 65°F)	0	0	0	0	0	4	17	11	0	0	0	0	32
Mean Precipitation (in.)	2.30	1.78	1.46	1.17	1.75	2.28	1.60	1.34	1.22	1.33	2.46	2.51	21.20
Days With ≥ 0.1" Precipitation	7	6	5	4	6	6	5	4	4	4	7	8	66
Days With ≥ 1.0" Precipitation	0	0	0	0	0	0	0	0	0	0	0	0	0
Mean Snowfall (in.)	na	na	na	na	na	na	na	na	na	na	na	na	na
Days With ≥ 1.0" Snow Depth	30	27	26	9	0	0	0	0	0	*1*	15	28	*136*

Polson Kerr Dam *Lake County*　Elevation: 2,729 ft.　Latitude: 47° 41' N　Longitude: 114° 14' W

	JAN	FEB	MAR	APR	MAY	JUN	JUL	AUG	SEP	OCT	NOV	DEC	YEAR
Mean Maximum Temp. (°F)	32.6	38.8	47.8	57.8	66.2	73.1	82.0	82.4	71.0	57.6	41.4	33.4	57.0
Mean Temp. (°F)	26.4	31.0	37.9	46.1	53.9	60.6	67.2	67.4	57.3	46.5	34.7	27.6	46.4
Mean Minimum Temp. (°F)	20.2	23.1	28.1	34.3	41.5	48.1	52.5	52.3	43.6	35.2	27.9	21.7	35.7
Extreme Maximum Temp. (°F)	57	67	75	82	88	95	100	99	95	82	71	59	100
Extreme Minimum Temp. (°F)	-21	-20	-9	18	25	33	34	36	22	6	-10	-22	-22
Days Maximum Temp. ≥ 90°F	0	0	0	0	0	1	6	6	0	0	0	0	13
Days Maximum Temp. ≤ 32°F	13	6	1	0	0	0	0	0	0	0	4	13	37
Days Minimum Temp. ≤ 32°F	27	24	23	12	2	0	0	0	2	11	22	27	150
Days Minimum Temp. ≤ 0°F	3	1	0	0	0	0	0	0	0	0	0	1	5
Heating Degree Days (base 65°F)	1,190	955	832	561	343	155	43	42	238	567	904	1,154	6,984
Cooling Degree Days (base 65°F)	0	0	0	0	6	32	122	132	18	0	0	0	310
Mean Precipitation (in.)	1.01	0.79	0.84	1.13	2.23	2.18	1.41	1.15	1.19	1.00	1.08	1.06	15.07
Days With ≥ 0.1" Precipitation	3	3	3	4	6	6	4	4	4	3	4	4	48
Days With ≥ 1.0" Precipitation	0	0	0	0	0	0	0	0	0	0	0	0	0
Mean Snowfall (in.)	na	na	na	na	na	na	na	na	na	na	na	na	na
Days With ≥ 1.0" Snow Depth	21	*15*	*7*	0	0	0	0	0	0	0	na	*15*	na

Powderville 8 NNE *Custer County*　Elevation: 2,798 ft.　Latitude: 45° 51' N　Longitude: 105° 02' W

	JAN	FEB	MAR	APR	MAY	JUN	JUL	AUG	SEP	OCT	NOV	DEC	YEAR
Mean Maximum Temp. (°F)	29.8	37.8	47.6	59.8	70.9	81.6	89.9	89.1	76.9	61.7	44.0	33.6	60.2
Mean Temp. (°F)	17.4	25.3	34.2	45.7	56.3	66.4	73.1	72.2	59.9	46.4	31.6	21.1	45.8
Mean Minimum Temp. (°F)	5.0	13.1	21.0	31.6	41.6	51.2	56.3	54.8	42.7	31.1	19.2	8.4	31.3
Extreme Maximum Temp. (°F)	68	71	82	91	102	108	109	108	105	93	79	67	109
Extreme Minimum Temp. (°F)	-36	-39	-34	-2	19	32	37	31	16	-13	-28	-45	-45
Days Maximum Temp. ≥ 90°F	0	0	0	0	1	6	17	16	5	0	0	0	45
Days Maximum Temp. ≤ 32°F	15	9	4	1	0	0	0	0	0	0	6	12	47
Days Minimum Temp. ≤ 32°F	31	27	28	*16*	4	0	0	0	4	*16*	28	31	*185*
Days Minimum Temp. ≤ 0°F	11	6	2	0	0	0	0	0	0	0	2	8	29
Heating Degree Days (base 65°F)	1,471	1,115	948	572	283	66	11	14	197	571	995	1,356	7,599
Cooling Degree Days (base 65°F)	0	0	0	2	22	119	274	255	53	1	0	0	726
Mean Precipitation (in.)	0.49	0.40	0.55	1.60	2.34	2.71	1.60	1.07	1.41	1.38	0.56	0.41	14.52
Days With ≥ 0.1" Precipitation	na	*1*	*2*	4	5	5	4	3	3	*3*	na	*1*	na
Days With ≥ 1.0" Precipitation	0	0	0	0	0	1	0	0	0	0	0	0	1
Mean Snowfall (in.)	*6.2*	*4.2*	na	na	na	*0.0*	*0.0*	*0.0*	0.2	*0.8*	na	na	na
Days With ≥ 1.0" Snow Depth	na	na	na	na	*0*	0	0	0	0	*1*	na	na	na

Rapelje 4 S *Stillwater County*　Elevation: 4,124 ft.　Latitude: 45° 55' N　Longitude: 109° 15' W

	JAN	FEB	MAR	APR	MAY	JUN	JUL	AUG	SEP	OCT	NOV	DEC	YEAR
Mean Maximum Temp. (°F)	35.6	41.3	48.0	57.9	67.4	77.9	86.0	85.8	74.2	61.8	45.1	37.3	59.9
Mean Temp. (°F)	24.0	28.8	35.1	44.0	52.9	62.1	68.7	68.2	57.8	47.1	33.5	26.0	45.7
Mean Minimum Temp. (°F)	12.3	16.3	22.2	30.0	38.4	46.3	51.3	50.6	41.4	32.2	21.9	14.7	31.5
Extreme Maximum Temp. (°F)	66	71	80	87	92	101	105	103	101	93	77	67	105
Extreme Minimum Temp. (°F)	-37	-39	-30	-3	10	28	34	27	17	-14	-25	-38	-39
Days Maximum Temp. ≥ 90°F	0	0	0	0	0	4	12	12	3	0	0	0	31
Days Maximum Temp. ≤ 32°F	11	6	4	1	0	0	0	0	0	1	5	9	37
Days Minimum Temp. ≤ 32°F	28	26	27	19	6	0	0	0	4	15	25	28	178
Days Minimum Temp. ≤ 0°F	9	5	2	0	0	0	0	0	0	0	2	6	24
Heating Degree Days (base 65°F)	1,266	1,016	920	624	373	132	34	38	238	551	940	1,204	7,336
Cooling Degree Days (base 65°F)	0	0	0	0	7	50	151	147	31	2	0	0	388
Mean Precipitation (in.)	*0.68*	*0.63*	*1.10*	1.64	2.83	1.90	*1.68*	*1.39*	*1.43*	1.34	0.72	0.59	15.93
Days With ≥ 0.1" Precipitation	2	2	3	5	6	5	4	3	3	3	2	2	40
Days With ≥ 1.0" Precipitation	0	0	0	0	0	0	0	0	0	0	0	0	0
Mean Snowfall (in.)	na	na	na	na	na	na	na	na	na	na	na	na	na
Days With ≥ 1.0" Snow Depth	na	na	na	*2*	0	0	0	0	0	*1*	na	na	na

Raymond Border Station *Sheridan County*   Elevation: 2,349 ft.   Latitude: 49° 00' N   Longitude: 104° 35' W

	JAN	FEB	MAR	APR	MAY	JUN	JUL	AUG	SEP	OCT	NOV	DEC	YEAR
Mean Maximum Temp. (°F)	19.2	27.7	39.3	56.3	68.8	77.8	83.1	83.2	71.5	58.4	36.4	24.3	53.8
Mean Temp. (°F)	9.1	17.2	28.2	43.0	54.7	63.8	68.3	67.6	56.8	44.9	26.5	14.1	41.2
Mean Minimum Temp. (°F)	-1.1	6.9	17.1	29.5	40.6	49.9	53.6	52.0	42.0	31.3	16.4	3.8	28.5
Extreme Maximum Temp. (°F)	54	68	77	91	101	106	104	107	100	93	74	58	107
Extreme Minimum Temp. (°F)	-38	-41	-25	-15	16	29	38	32	19	-5	-29	-41	-41
Days Maximum Temp. ≥ 90°F	0	0	0	0	1	3	7	9	2	0	0	0	22
Days Maximum Temp. ≤ 32°F	23	15	9	1	0	0	0	0	0	1	11	20	80
Days Minimum Temp. ≤ 32°F	30	27	29	19	5	0	0	0	4	17	27	31	189
Days Minimum Temp. ≤ 0°F	16	10	4	0	0	0	0	0	0	0	4	12	46
Heating Degree Days (base 65°F)	1,735	1,343	1,133	656	330	102	35	56	267	616	1,152	1,576	9,001
Cooling Degree Days (base 65°F)	0	0	0	1	18	79	147	152	28	2	0	0	427
Mean Precipitation (in.)	0.21	0.15	0.41	0.90	2.02	2.85	2.31	1.45	1.43	0.69	0.25	0.28	12.95
Days With ≥ 0.1" Precipitation	1	0	2	3	6	6	5	4	4	2	1	1	35
Days With ≥ 1.0" Precipitation	0	0	0	0	0	1	0	0	0	0	0	0	1
Mean Snowfall (in.)	na	na	na	na	0.5	0.0	0.0	0.0	trace	na	na	na	na
Days With ≥ 1.0" Snow Depth	na	na	na	na	0	0	0	0	0	0	na	na	na

Raynesford 2 NNW *Judith Basin County*   Elevation: 4,212 ft.   Latitude: 47° 18' N   Longitude: 110° 45' W

	JAN	FEB	MAR	APR	MAY	JUN	JUL	AUG	SEP	OCT	NOV	DEC	YEAR
Mean Maximum Temp. (°F)	34.0	38.7	44.9	54.8	63.7	72.1	79.5	80.3	69.7	58.5	43.2	36.2	56.3
Mean Temp. (°F)	23.4	27.7	33.7	42.3	50.9	58.9	64.6	64.9	55.4	45.8	32.9	25.9	43.9
Mean Minimum Temp. (°F)	12.7	16.7	22.5	29.9	38.0	45.6	49.7	49.5	41.1	33.1	22.5	15.6	31.4
Extreme Maximum Temp. (°F)	69	68	75	85	89	98	99	99	96	89	75	65	99
Extreme Minimum Temp. (°F)	-38	-35	-24	-10	19	30	31	29	16	-10	-25	-38	-38
Days Maximum Temp. ≥ 90°F	0	0	0	0	0	1	3	4	1	0	0	0	9
Days Maximum Temp. ≤ 32°F	11	8	4	1	0	0	0	0	0	1	5	9	39
Days Minimum Temp. ≤ 32°F	27	24	26	19	7	0	0	0	5	14	23	27	172
Days Minimum Temp. ≤ 0°F	9	5	2	0	0	0	0	0	0	0	2	5	23
Heating Degree Days (base 65°F)	1,285	1,047	963	673	434	200	78	81	299	589	958	1,206	7,813
Cooling Degree Days (base 65°F)	0	0	0	0	3	25	76	93	22	2	0	0	221
Mean Precipitation (in.)	0.80	0.63	1.25	1.58	3.06	2.87	1.93	1.69	1.71	1.21	0.83	0.88	18.44
Days With ≥ 0.1" Precipitation	3	2	4	4	7	7	4	4	5	4	3	3	50
Days With ≥ 1.0" Precipitation	0	0	0	0	0	0	0	0	0	0	0	0	0
Mean Snowfall (in.)	13.1	7.7	12.8	7.2	2.3	0.1	0.0	0.0	0.6	3.6	5.1	11.7	64.2
Days With ≥ 1.0" Snow Depth	22	16	14	5	1	0	0	0	0	4	11	20	93

Red Lodge 2 N *Carbon County*   Elevation: 5,498 ft.   Latitude: 45° 13' N   Longitude: 109° 14' W

	JAN	FEB	MAR	APR	MAY	JUN	JUL	AUG	SEP	OCT	NOV	DEC	YEAR
Mean Maximum Temp. (°F)	33.0	36.9	43.0	51.9	61.6	71.4	78.6	78.3	67.2	55.3	40.7	34.5	54.4
Mean Temp. (°F)	22.6	26.4	32.0	40.2	49.2	57.7	64.1	63.6	53.7	43.6	30.8	24.3	42.3
Mean Minimum Temp. (°F)	12.1	15.9	20.9	28.4	36.9	44.1	49.6	48.8	40.1	31.8	21.0	14.2	30.3
Extreme Maximum Temp. (°F)	60	64	71	80	87	95	97	95	91	82	71	63	97
Extreme Minimum Temp. (°F)	-33	-42	-16	-2	16	26	31	28	11	-13	-20	-42	-42
Days Maximum Temp. ≥ 90°F	0	0	0	0	0	0	2	1	0	0	0	0	3
Days Maximum Temp. ≤ 32°F	13	8	5	2	0	0	0	0	0	1	7	12	48
Days Minimum Temp. ≤ 32°F	29	27	28	20	9	2	0	0	5	16	25	29	190
Days Minimum Temp. ≤ 0°F	7	4	2	0	0	0	0	0	0	0	2	5	20
Heating Degree Days (base 65°F)	1,309	1,084	1,017	738	483	233	86	94	344	657	1,019	1,255	8,319
Cooling Degree Days (base 65°F)	0	0	0	0	2	20	64	55	11	0	0	0	152
Mean Precipitation (in.)	1.55	1.30	2.74	3.31	4.23	2.26	1.51	1.51	2.47	2.02	1.53	1.34	25.77
Days With ≥ 0.1" Precipitation	4	3	6	7	7	6	5	4	5	4	4	4	59
Days With ≥ 1.0" Precipitation	0	0	0	1	1	0	0	0	0	0	0	0	2
Mean Snowfall (in.)	na	na	na	na	na	na	na	na	na	na	na	na	na
Days With ≥ 1.0" Snow Depth	28	23	21	10	2	0	0	0	1	5	16	24	130

Redstone *Sheridan County*   Elevation: 2,109 ft.   Latitude: 48° 50' N   Longitude: 104° 57' W

	JAN	FEB	MAR	APR	MAY	JUN	JUL	AUG	SEP	OCT	NOV	DEC	YEAR
Mean Maximum Temp. (°F)	21.4	29.6	40.8	57.0	69.6	78.8	84.4	84.1	71.4	58.0	37.7	26.1	54.9
Mean Temp. (°F)	9.4	17.9	28.6	42.2	54.1	63.4	67.8	66.7	54.9	43.0	25.9	14.2	40.7
Mean Minimum Temp. (°F)	-2.7	6.1	16.3	27.3	38.7	47.8	51.1	49.3	38.5	28.5	14.2	2.2	26.5
Extreme Maximum Temp. (°F)	62	68	79	92	102	105	105	110	104	96	80	60	110
Extreme Minimum Temp. (°F)	-43	-44	-33	-27	11	23	34	28	9	-12	-32	-52	-52
Days Maximum Temp. ≥ 90°F	0	0	0	0	1	4	9	9	2	0	0	0	25
Days Maximum Temp. ≤ 32°F	21	14	8	1	0	0	0	0	0	1	10	18	73
Days Minimum Temp. ≤ 32°F	31	28	30	21	8	1	0	1	8	21	28	31	208
Days Minimum Temp. ≤ 0°F	17	10	4	0	0	0	0	0	0	0	5	14	50
Heating Degree Days (base 65°F)	1,723	1,327	1,123	678	344	110	38	62	313	675	1,166	1,573	9,132
Cooling Degree Days (base 65°F)	0	0	0	0	13	71	126	131	16	0	0	0	357
Mean Precipitation (in.)	0.32	0.21	0.60	0.85	2.04	2.54	2.09	1.57	1.35	0.75	0.33	0.34	12.99
Days With ≥ 0.1" Precipitation	1	1	2	3	6	6	5	4	3	2	1	1	35
Days With ≥ 1.0" Precipitation	0	0	0	0	0	0	0	0	0	0	0	0	0
Mean Snowfall (in.)	na	na	na	na	na	na	na	na	na	na	na	na	na
Days With ≥ 1.0" Snow Depth	22	13	8	2	0	0	0	0	0	1	7	17	70

Ridgeway 1 S *Carter County*   Elevation: 3,316 ft.   Latitude: 45° 30' N   Longitude: 104° 27' W

	JAN	FEB	MAR	APR	MAY	JUN	JUL	AUG	SEP	OCT	NOV	DEC	YEAR
Mean Maximum Temp. (°F)	28.4	35.0	43.4	56.4	67.4	76.9	84.4	84.3	72.6	59.7	42.4	32.4	56.9
Mean Temp. (°F)	16.0	23.0	31.4	43.6	54.2	63.5	69.9	68.9	57.2	45.1	30.1	19.8	43.6
Mean Minimum Temp. (°F)	3.5	10.8	19.4	30.7	40.9	50.1	55.3	53.4	41.7	30.4	17.8	7.2	30.1
Extreme Maximum Temp. (°F)	68	69	77	90	97	101	108	103	103	91	80	65	108
Extreme Minimum Temp. (°F)	-37	-39	-36	-6	19	26	35	28	10	-22	-28	-51	-51
Days Maximum Temp. ≥ 90°F	0	0	0	0	0	3	9	9	2	0	0	0	23
Days Maximum Temp. ≤ 32°F	16	10	6	1	0	0	0	0	0	0	6	14	53
Days Minimum Temp. ≤ 32°F	31	28	29	18	4	0	0	0	4	17	28	31	190
Days Minimum Temp. ≤ 0°F	11	6	2	0	0	0	0	0	0	0	2	8	29
Heating Degree Days (base 65°F)	1,515	1,177	1,034	638	340	110	28	36	260	611	1,041	1,394	8,184
Cooling Degree Days (base 65°F)	0	0	0	1	12	73	187	170	32	1	0	0	476
Mean Precipitation (in.)	0.46	0.36	0.71	1.48	2.49	2.49	1.73	1.12	1.21	1.24	0.53	0.45	14.27
Days With ≥ 0.1" Precipitation	1	1	2	4	6	6	4	3	3	3	2	1	36
Days With ≥ 1.0" Precipitation	0	0	0	0	0	0	0	0	0	0	0	0	0
Mean Snowfall (in.)	6.5	4.8	8.4	5.3	0.6	0.0	0.0	0.0	0.7	2.0	5.0	5.6	38.9
Days With ≥ 1.0" Snow Depth	na	na	na	na	0	0	0	0	0	na	na	na	na

Rock Springs *Rosebud County*   Elevation: 3,021 ft.   Latitude: 46° 49' N   Longitude: 106° 15' W

	JAN	FEB	MAR	APR	MAY	JUN	JUL	AUG	SEP	OCT	NOV	DEC	YEAR
Mean Maximum Temp. (°F)	26.8	33.9	44.5	57.0	67.5	77.3	85.1	84.7	72.3	59.3	41.6	30.8	56.7
Mean Temp. (°F)	16.3	23.2	32.8	43.9	54.2	63.5	69.9	69.3	57.5	45.7	30.7	20.0	43.9
Mean Minimum Temp. (°F)	5.8	12.5	21.0	30.8	40.8	49.7	54.7	53.8	42.6	32.2	19.7	9.1	31.0
Extreme Maximum Temp. (°F)	68	72	76	88	100	107	106	105	101	91	76	68	107
Extreme Minimum Temp. (°F)	-34	-35	-26	-5	16	30	35	29	12	-10	-25	-40	-40
Days Maximum Temp. ≥ 90°F	0	0	0	0	0	3	10	10	2	0	0	0	25
Days Maximum Temp. ≤ 32°F	17	11	6	1	0	0	0	0	0	1	7	14	57
Days Minimum Temp. ≤ 32°F	30	27	28	17	4	0	0	0	3	15	27	30	181
Days Minimum Temp. ≤ 0°F	11	7	2	0	0	0	0	0	0	0	2	8	30
Heating Degree Days (base 65°F)	1,507	1,175	992	627	341	109	25	37	248	591	1,024	1,391	8,067
Cooling Degree Days (base 65°F)	0	0	0	0	13	74	182	187	32	1	0	0	489
Mean Precipitation (in.)	0.30	0.17	0.34	1.09	2.19	2.34	1.51	0.87	1.20	0.86	0.35	0.25	11.47
Days With ≥ 0.1" Precipitation	1	0	1	3	5	6	4	3	3	2	1	1	30
Days With ≥ 1.0" Precipitation	0	0	0	0	0	0	0	0	0	0	0	0	0
Mean Snowfall (in.)	na	na	na	na	na	na	na	na	na	na	na	na	na
Days With ≥ 1.0" Snow Depth	na	na	na	na	0	0	0	0	0	na	na	na	na

Roundup *Musselshell County*   Elevation: 3,225 ft.   Latitude: 46° 27' N   Longitude: 108° 33' W

	JAN	FEB	MAR	APR	MAY	JUN	JUL	AUG	SEP	OCT	NOV	DEC	YEAR
Mean Maximum Temp. (°F)	36.4	43.1	50.7	60.3	70.4	80.1	87.2	87.0	75.5	63.5	46.5	37.9	61.6
Mean Temp. (°F)	24.4	30.2	37.4	46.3	56.1	65.1	70.9	69.9	59.2	48.4	34.6	26.3	47.4
Mean Minimum Temp. (°F)	12.4	17.3	23.9	32.4	41.6	50.1	54.6	53.0	42.8	33.3	22.7	14.8	33.2
Extreme Maximum Temp. (°F)	70	73	80	91	95	105	109	106	102	90	77	70	109
Extreme Minimum Temp. (°F)	-40	-41	-24	1	22	31	37	30	15	-7	-23	-44	-44
Days Maximum Temp. ≥ 90°F	0	0	0	0	1	5	13	13	3	0	0	0	35
Days Maximum Temp. ≤ 32°F	10	6	3	1	0	0	0	0	0	0	4	8	32
Days Minimum Temp. ≤ 32°F	28	25	25	16	3	0	0	0	3	14	24	28	166
Days Minimum Temp. ≤ 0°F	8	4	1	0	0	0	0	0	0	0	1	5	19
Heating Degree Days (base 65°F)	1,252	976	849	554	283	81	18	24	204	510	907	1,196	6,854
Cooling Degree Days (base 65°F)	0	0	0	1	14	85	206	183	37	2	0	0	528
Mean Precipitation (in.)	0.43	0.37	0.63	1.30	2.39	2.16	1.62	1.28	1.29	1.05	0.35	0.46	13.33
Days With ≥ 0.1" Precipitation	1	1	2	4	6	5	4	3	3	3	1	2	35
Days With ≥ 1.0" Precipitation	0	0	0	0	0	0	0	0	0	0	0	0	0
Mean Snowfall (in.)	na	na	na	na	na	na	na	na	na	na	na	na	na
Days With ≥ 1.0" Snow Depth	na	na	na	na	0	0	0	0	0	na	na	na	na

Roy 8 NE *Fergus County*   Elevation: 3,444 ft.   Latitude: 47° 26' N   Longitude: 108° 51' W

	JAN	FEB	MAR	APR	MAY	JUN	JUL	AUG	SEP	OCT	NOV	DEC	YEAR
Mean Maximum Temp. (°F)	31.2	37.8	46.1	57.1	67.4	77.0	84.5	84.7	72.7	61.0	43.9	34.6	58.2
Mean Temp. (°F)	19.4	25.5	33.9	44.0	53.9	62.8	68.8	68.4	57.3	46.5	31.8	22.6	44.6
Mean Minimum Temp. (°F)	7.4	13.2	21.7	30.9	40.4	48.5	53.0	52.0	41.9	32.0	19.6	10.5	30.9
Extreme Maximum Temp. (°F)	69	72	78	90	96	103	102	107	103	92	78	68	107
Extreme Minimum Temp. (°F)	-41	-39	-33	-5	20	31	36	30	16	-11	-27	-41	-41
Days Maximum Temp. ≥ 90°F	0	0	0	0	0	3	9	11	2	0	0	0	25
Days Maximum Temp. ≤ 32°F	14	9	5	1	0	0	0	0	0	1	6	11	47
Days Minimum Temp. ≤ 32°F	29	26	27	17	4	0	0	0	3	15	26	30	177
Days Minimum Temp. ≤ 0°F	11	6	2	0	0	0	0	0	0	0	3	8	30
Heating Degree Days (base 65°F)	1,411	1,109	958	622	344	117	30	39	247	568	991	1,311	7,747
Cooling Degree Days (base 65°F)	0	0	0	0	10	57	154	154	27	2	0	0	404
Mean Precipitation (in.)	0.51	0.33	0.82	1.23	2.81	2.34	1.93	1.54	1.19	0.75	0.45	0.49	14.39
Days With ≥ 0.1" Precipitation	2	1	3	3	6	6	5	4	3	2	2	2	39
Days With ≥ 1.0" Precipitation	0	0	0	0	0	0	0	0	0	0	0	0	0
Mean Snowfall (in.)	na	na	na	na	na	na	na	na	na	na	na	na	na
Days With ≥ 1.0" Snow Depth	17	12	10	3	0	0	0	0	0	1	6	15	64

Ryegate 18 NNW *Golden Valley County*   Elevation: 4,438 ft.   Latitude: 46° 31' N   Longitude: 109° 21' W

	JAN	FEB	MAR	APR	MAY	JUN	JUL	AUG	SEP	OCT	NOV	DEC	YEAR
Mean Maximum Temp. (°F)	33.3	39.2	45.5	55.6	64.9	74.3	81.5	81.8	70.5	59.3	43.4	35.4	57.1
Mean Temp. (°F)	21.6	26.9	32.9	42.0	51.0	59.5	65.6	65.4	54.8	44.5	31.2	23.9	43.3
Mean Minimum Temp. (°F)	9.9	14.5	20.3	28.3	36.9	44.6	49.6	49.0	39.0	29.6	19.0	12.2	29.4
Extreme Maximum Temp. (°F)	66	73	76	86	88	100	102	99	98	94	77	66	102
Extreme Minimum Temp. (°F)	-36	-41	-26	-10	20	27	32	28	10	-8	-26	-37	-41
Days Maximum Temp. ≥ 90°F	0	0	0	0	0	2	5	6	1	0	0	0	14
Days Maximum Temp. ≤ 32°F	13	8	4	1	0	0	0	0	0	1	5	11	43
Days Minimum Temp. ≤ 32°F	30	26	29	21	8	1	0	0	6	19	27	30	197
Days Minimum Temp. ≤ 0°F	9	5	2	0	0	0	0	0	0	0	2	6	24
Heating Degree Days (base 65°F)	1,339	1,071	988	686	430	188	64	71	313	630	1,007	1,270	8,057
Cooling Degree Days (base 65°F)	0	0	0	0	2	32	94	99	16	1	0	0	244
Mean Precipitation (in.)	0.54	0.30	0.61	1.11	2.01	2.31	1.84	1.46	1.11	0.76	0.49	0.48	13.02
Days With ≥ 0.1" Precipitation	2	1	2	4	6	6	5	4	3	2	2	2	39
Days With ≥ 1.0" Precipitation	0	0	0	0	0	0	0	0	0	0	0	0	0
Mean Snowfall (in.)	8.6	4.5	7.3	4.7	1.2	0.0	0.0	0.0	0.6	3.0	5.7	7.5	43.1
Days With ≥ 1.0" Snow Depth	*14*	8	7	1	0	0	0	0	0	1	6	11	*48*

Saco 1 NNW *Phillips County*   Elevation: 2,168 ft.   Latitude: 48° 28' N   Longitude: 107° 21' W

	JAN	FEB	MAR	APR	MAY	JUN	JUL	AUG	SEP	OCT	NOV	DEC	YEAR
Mean Maximum Temp. (°F)	22.7	31.0	42.9	58.7	69.4	77.3	84.0	83.4	72.1	59.0	40.2	27.6	55.7
Mean Temp. (°F)	10.5	18.7	30.2	44.0	54.8	63.4	68.8	67.6	56.1	43.8	27.6	15.2	41.7
Mean Minimum Temp. (°F)	-1.7	6.5	17.5	29.2	40.1	49.5	53.5	51.7	40.1	28.7	15.1	2.8	27.7
Extreme Maximum Temp. (°F)	60	72	79	92	100	104	102	105	100	89	81	62	105
Extreme Minimum Temp. (°F)	-48	-45	-34	-5	14	28	34	32	17	-9	-37	-48	-48
Days Maximum Temp. ≥ 90°F	0	0	0	0	1	3	7	9	1	0	0	0	21
Days Maximum Temp. ≤ 32°F	20	13	6	1	0	0	0	0	0	1	8	17	66
Days Minimum Temp. ≤ 32°F	30	28	29	20	5	0	0	0	5	21	28	30	196
Days Minimum Temp. ≤ 0°F	15	10	3	0	0	0	0	0	0	0	4	12	44
Heating Degree Days (base 65°F)	1,689	1,304	1,070	624	321	102	23	47	276	651	1,104	1,531	8,742
Cooling Degree Days (base 65°F)	0	0	0	0	12	63	149	136	17	0	0	0	377
Mean Precipitation (in.)	0.37	0.31	0.56	0.78	1.89	2.51	1.58	1.08	1.16	0.67	0.56	0.41	11.88
Days With ≥ 0.1" Precipitation	1	1	2	2	4	5	3	3	3	2	2	2	30
Days With ≥ 1.0" Precipitation	0	0	0	0	0	1	0	0	0	0	0	0	1
Mean Snowfall (in.)	na	na	na	na	na	*0.0*	*0.0*	*0.0*	*0.0*	na	na	na	na
Days With ≥ 1.0" Snow Depth	na	na	na	na	*0*	*0*	*0*	*0*	*0*	na	na	na	na

Saint Ignatius *Lake County*   Elevation: 2,896 ft.   Latitude: 47° 19' N   Longitude: 114° 06' W

	JAN	FEB	MAR	APR	MAY	JUN	JUL	AUG	SEP	OCT	NOV	DEC	YEAR
Mean Maximum Temp. (°F)	33.6	39.6	49.3	59.1	67.8	75.6	83.4	83.5	71.6	58.2	42.3	34.2	58.2
Mean Temp. (°F)	26.2	30.9	38.3	46.0	53.8	61.0	66.6	66.0	56.3	45.6	34.3	27.1	46.0
Mean Minimum Temp. (°F)	18.8	22.1	27.3	33.0	39.8	46.3	49.6	48.5	41.0	32.9	26.3	20.0	33.8
Extreme Maximum Temp. (°F)	62	68	82	85	93	97	102	102	98	87	73	61	102
Extreme Minimum Temp. (°F)	-30	-29	-15	14	22	30	33	32	19	0	-15	-28	-30
Days Maximum Temp. ≥ 90°F	0	0	0	0	0	2	8	8	1	0	0	0	19
Days Maximum Temp. ≤ 32°F	12	6	1	0	0	0	0	0	0	0	4	12	35
Days Minimum Temp. ≤ 32°F	26	24	23	14	4	0	0	0	3	15	23	26	158
Days Minimum Temp. ≤ 0°F	4	2	0	0	0	0	0	0	0	0	1	2	9
Heating Degree Days (base 65°F)	1,197	958	821	563	344	153	51	54	264	596	914	1,168	7,083
Cooling Degree Days (base 65°F)	0	0	0	0	5	35	107	98	13	0	0	0	258
Mean Precipitation (in.)	1.00	0.74	1.24	1.45	2.62	2.36	*1.46*	1.35	1.38	1.14	1.01	1.00	*16.75*
Days With ≥ 0.1" Precipitation	3	3	4	4	7	6	4	4	4	4	3	3	49
Days With ≥ 1.0" Precipitation	0	0	0	0	0	0	0	0	0	0	0	0	0
Mean Snowfall (in.)	na	na	na	na	na	na	na	na	na	na	na	na	na
Days With ≥ 1.0" Snow Depth	18	11	5	0	0	0	0	0	0	1	6	15	56

Savage *Richland County*   Elevation: 1,984 ft.   Latitude: 47° 27' N   Longitude: 104° 20' W

	JAN	FEB	MAR	APR	MAY	JUN	JUL	AUG	SEP	OCT	NOV	DEC	YEAR
Mean Maximum Temp. (°F)	24.5	33.3	44.8	59.4	71.7	80.5	87.1	86.6	74.5	60.6	41.2	29.0	57.8
Mean Temp. (°F)	13.9	22.4	32.7	45.6	57.5	66.5	71.9	70.8	59.3	47.1	30.8	18.6	44.8
Mean Minimum Temp. (°F)	3.2	11.3	20.5	31.7	43.3	52.4	56.6	55.0	44.2	33.5	20.3	8.2	31.7
Extreme Maximum Temp. (°F)	57	70	83	93	102	109	109	106	103	91	76	66	109
Extreme Minimum Temp. (°F)	-40	-37	-31	-11	21	31	42	32	19	0	-22	-42	-42
Days Maximum Temp. ≥ 90°F	0	0	0	0	1	5	12	13	3	0	0	0	34
Days Maximum Temp. ≤ 32°F	19	12	6	1	0	0	0	0	0	0	8	16	62
Days Minimum Temp. ≤ 32°F	30	27	27	16	3	0	0	0	2	13	26	31	175
Days Minimum Temp. ≤ 0°F	14	7	2	0	0	0	0	0	0	0	2	9	34
Heating Degree Days (base 65°F)	1,581	1,199	996	577	251	58	11	22	203	548	1,019	1,433	7,898
Cooling Degree Days (base 65°F)	0	0	0	0	2	32	119	238	44	1	0	0	663
Mean Precipitation (in.)	*0.33*	*0.24*	*0.55*	*1.17*	*2.18*	na	*1.78*	*1.24*	*1.74*	*0.89*	*0.39*	*0.40*	na
Days With ≥ 0.1" Precipitation	1	1	2	3	5	5	4	3	3	2	2	1	32
Days With ≥ 1.0" Precipitation	0	0	0	0	0	1	0	0	0	0	0	0	1
Mean Snowfall (in.)	na	na	na	na	na	na	na	na	na	na	na	na	na
Days With ≥ 1.0" Snow Depth	23	16	8	2	0	0	0	0	0	1	7	18	75

Seeley Lake Ranger Station *Missoula County*   Elevation: 4,097 ft.   Latitude: 47° 13' N   Longitude: 113° 31' W

	JAN	FEB	MAR	APR	MAY	JUN	JUL	AUG	SEP	OCT	NOV	DEC	YEAR
Mean Maximum Temp. (°F)	29.8	36.6	44.2	53.7	63.5	71.9	80.5	81.4	70.2	56.5	38.4	29.3	54.7
Mean Temp. (°F)	20.1	25.1	32.4	40.6	49.2	56.7	62.2	62.2	52.9	42.8	30.1	20.9	41.3
Mean Minimum Temp. (°F)	10.5	13.6	20.5	27.4	34.9	41.4	43.9	43.0	35.6	29.0	21.7	12.4	27.8
Extreme Maximum Temp. (°F)	51	60	67	86	93	94	98	98	92	84	65	56	98
Extreme Minimum Temp. (°F)	-42	-45	-25	3	17	27	28	27	16	-10	-20	-44	-45
Days Maximum Temp. ≥ 90°F	0	0	0	0	0	1	4	6	1	0	0	0	12
Days Maximum Temp. ≤ 32°F	17	7	2	0	0	0	0	0	0	0	7	20	53
Days Minimum Temp. ≤ 32°F	30	28	30	24	12	2	1	1	10	22	28	30	218
Days Minimum Temp. ≤ 0°F	8	5	2	0	0	0	0	0	0	0	1	6	22
Heating Degree Days (base 65°F)	1,384	1,119	1,005	727	484	254	119	115	359	682	1,042	1,363	8,653
Cooling Degree Days (base 65°F)	0	0	0	0	2	9	37	39	4	0	0	0	91
Mean Precipitation (in.)	2.57	1.70	1.34	1.08	2.02	2.21	1.27	1.38	1.30	1.34	2.30	2.59	21.10
Days With ≥ 0.1" Precipitation	8	5	5	4	6	6	4	4	4	4	7	8	65
Days With ≥ 1.0" Precipitation	0	0	0	0	0	0	0	0	0	0	0	0	0
Mean Snowfall (in.)	na	na	na	na	na	na	na	na	na	na	na	na	na
Days With ≥ 1.0" Snow Depth	30	27	27	9	0	0	0	0	0	1	15	29	138

Sidney *Richland County*   Elevation: 1,919 ft.   Latitude: 47° 44' N   Longitude: 104° 09' W

	JAN	FEB	MAR	APR	MAY	JUN	JUL	AUG	SEP	OCT	NOV	DEC	YEAR
Mean Maximum Temp. (°F)	23.9	32.7	44.8	60.1	72.0	80.3	85.8	85.1	73.2	59.7	40.1	28.4	57.2
Mean Temp. (°F)	13.2	21.6	32.2	45.3	57.1	65.8	70.5	69.3	58.0	46.0	29.5	17.9	43.9
Mean Minimum Temp. (°F)	2.4	10.5	19.6	30.5	42.2	51.2	55.1	53.4	42.8	32.4	18.8	7.3	30.5
Extreme Maximum Temp. (°F)	55	68	81	95	102	105	106	105	101	91	77	68	106
Extreme Minimum Temp. (°F)	-39	-35	-28	-17	19	31	39	30	19	0	-24	-40	-40
Days Maximum Temp. ≥ 90°F	0	0	0	0	1	4	10	11	2	0	0	0	28
Days Maximum Temp. ≤ 32°F	20	12	6	1	0	0	0	0	0	0	8	17	64
Days Minimum Temp. ≤ 32°F	31	28	28	18	4	0	0	0	3	15	27	31	185
Days Minimum Temp. ≤ 0°F	14	8	3	0	0	0	0	0	0	0	3	10	38
Heating Degree Days (base 65°F)	1,603	1,220	1,010	584	265	64	13	31	232	581	1,059	1,456	8,118
Cooling Degree Days (base 65°F)	0	0	0	2	30	105	204	192	34	1	0	0	568
Mean Precipitation (in.)	na	na	na	na	na	na	na	na	na	na	na	na	na
Days With ≥ 0.1" Precipitation	1	1	2	3	6	6	5	3	3	2	2	1	35
Days With ≥ 1.0" Precipitation	0	0	0	0	0	0	0	0	0	0	0	0	0
Mean Snowfall (in.)	na	na	na	na	na	na	na	na	na	na	na	na	na
Days With ≥ 1.0" Snow Depth	25	18	9	2	0	0	0	0	0	1	8	20	83

Simpson 6 NW *Hill County*   Elevation: 2,739 ft.   Latitude: 48° 59' N   Longitude: 110° 18' W

	JAN	FEB	MAR	APR	MAY	JUN	JUL	AUG	SEP	OCT	NOV	DEC	YEAR
Mean Maximum Temp. (°F)	23.7	31.9	43.4	58.0	69.7	78.0	84.8	84.6	72.8	58.8	39.0	28.6	56.1
Mean Temp. (°F)	12.5	19.7	30.9	43.6	54.2	62.3	67.7	67.2	55.8	43.7	27.2	16.9	41.8
Mean Minimum Temp. (°F)	1.3	7.9	18.4	29.0	38.7	46.6	50.5	49.6	38.8	28.6	15.3	5.2	27.5
Extreme Maximum Temp. (°F)	63	73	77	89	97	104	104	108	101	89	74	62	108
Extreme Minimum Temp. (°F)	-45	-46	-33	-18	16	28	33	29	15	-20	-32	-47	-47
Days Maximum Temp. ≥ 90°F	0	0	0	0	1	4	10	10	2	0	0	0	27
Days Maximum Temp. ≤ 32°F	18	12	6	1	0	0	0	0	0	1	9	16	63
Days Minimum Temp. ≤ 32°F	29	26	28	20	6	1	0	0	6	20	28	30	194
Days Minimum Temp. ≤ 0°F	14	9	3	0	0	0	0	0	0	0	4	11	41
Heating Degree Days (base 65°F)	1,627	1,273	1,049	637	335	126	38	53	285	658	1,131	1,488	8,700
Cooling Degree Days (base 65°F)	0	0	0	0	10	54	130	132	18	1	0	0	345
Mean Precipitation (in.)	0.29	0.23	0.46	0.67	1.71	2.20	1.57	1.46	1.12	0.47	0.38	0.32	10.88
Days With ≥ 0.1" Precipitation	1	1	2	2	4	5	4	4	2	2	2	1	30
Days With ≥ 1.0" Precipitation	0	0	0	0	0	0	0	0	0	0	0	0	0
Mean Snowfall (in.)	na	na	na	na	na	na	na	na	na	na	na	na	na
Days With ≥ 1.0" Snow Depth	20	15	10	2	0	0	0	0	0	1	7	15	70

Stanford *Judith Basin County*   Elevation: 4,858 ft.   Latitude: 47° 09' N   Longitude: 110° 13' W

	JAN	FEB	MAR	APR	MAY	JUN	JUL	AUG	SEP	OCT	NOV	DEC	YEAR
Mean Maximum Temp. (°F)	36.2	40.2	45.8	55.4	64.5	73.0	80.1	80.6	70.2	59.3	44.6	38.3	57.4
Mean Temp. (°F)	24.7	28.4	33.9	42.6	51.3	59.3	65.1	65.2	55.6	45.9	33.3	26.7	44.3
Mean Minimum Temp. (°F)	13.1	16.5	22.0	29.9	38.1	45.6	50.0	49.7	41.0	32.4	21.9	15.1	31.3
Extreme Maximum Temp. (°F)	70	73	75	84	89	101	98	100	97	87	78	69	101
Extreme Minimum Temp. (°F)	-35	-35	-25	-5	20	27	29	29	16	-11	-24	-40	-40
Days Maximum Temp. ≥ 90°F	0	0	0	0	0	1	3	4	1	0	0	0	9
Days Maximum Temp. ≤ 32°F	10	7	5	1	0	0	0	0	0	1	5	8	37
Days Minimum Temp. ≤ 32°F	27	25	26	19	7	0	0	0	5	15	24	26	174
Days Minimum Temp. ≤ 0°F	8	5	2	0	0	0	0	0	0	0	2	5	22
Heating Degree Days (base 65°F)	1,245	1,029	957	664	420	191	72	78	298	586	945	1,180	7,665
Cooling Degree Days (base 65°F)	0	0	0	1	5	32	92	105	24	2	0	0	261
Mean Precipitation (in.)	0.71	0.52	0.98	1.55	2.99	2.85	2.12	1.87	1.42	0.98	0.63	0.65	17.27
Days With ≥ 0.1" Precipitation	2	2	4	4	7	7	5	5	4	3	2	3	48
Days With ≥ 1.0" Precipitation	0	0	0	0	0	0	0	0	0	0	0	0	0
Mean Snowfall (in.)	na	na	na	na	na	na	na	na	na	na	na	na	na
Days With ≥ 1.0" Snow Depth	15	12	10	3	1	0	0	0	0	2	7	12	62

Stevensville *Ravalli County*   Elevation: 3,372 ft.   Latitude: 46° 31' N   Longitude: 114° 05' W

	JAN	FEB	MAR	APR	MAY	JUN	JUL	AUG	SEP	OCT	NOV	DEC	YEAR
Mean Maximum Temp. (°F)	34.0	41.3	50.6	59.8	68.4	76.1	83.9	83.8	72.9	60.0	43.4	34.0	59.0
Mean Temp. (°F)	25.5	30.9	38.2	45.3	53.2	60.5	65.7	65.0	55.6	45.2	33.7	25.5	45.4
Mean Minimum Temp. (°F)	16.9	20.4	25.7	30.8	37.9	44.9	47.5	46.1	38.3	30.4	23.9	17.0	31.6
Extreme Maximum Temp. (°F)	63	70	78	88	94	97	100	99	96	84	74	64	100
Extreme Minimum Temp. (°F)	-30	-33	-14	13	18	29	30	27	16	-2	-12	-35	-35
Days Maximum Temp. ≥ 90°F	0	0	0	0	0	2	8	8	1	0	0	0	19
Days Maximum Temp. ≤ 32°F	11	5	1	0	0	0	0	0	0	0	3	12	32
Days Minimum Temp. ≤ 32°F	28	25	26	18	7	0	0	0	6	19	25	29	183
Days Minimum Temp. ≤ 0°F	4	2	0	0	0	0	0	0	0	0	1	3	10
Heating Degree Days (base 65°F)	1,220	957	823	585	363	158	54	60	282	607	933	1,217	7,259
Cooling Degree Days (base 65°F)	0	0	0	0	5	28	87	72	9	0	0	0	201
Mean Precipitation (in.)	1.18	0.83	0.78	0.89	1.51	1.55	0.83	1.04	0.98	0.63	1.13	1.12	12.47
Days With ≥ 0.1" Precipitation	4	3	3	3	5	5	2	3	3	2	4	3	40
Days With ≥ 1.0" Precipitation	0	0	0	0	0	0	0	0	0	0	0	0	0
Mean Snowfall (in.)	na	na	na	na	na	na	na	na	na	na	na	na	na
Days With ≥ 1.0" Snow Depth	*17*	*10*	na	na	*0*	*0*	*0*	*0*	*0*	*0*	na	*14*	na

Sula 3 ENE *Ravalli County*   Elevation: 4,471 ft.   Latitude: 45° 51' N   Longitude: 113° 56' W

	JAN	FEB	MAR	APR	MAY	JUN	JUL	AUG	SEP	OCT	NOV	DEC	YEAR
Mean Maximum Temp. (°F)	33.6	40.7	48.2	56.3	64.8	72.9	81.4	81.6	72.1	60.0	43.1	33.1	57.3
Mean Temp. (°F)	21.8	27.4	34.5	41.3	48.7	55.6	60.9	60.4	51.8	42.3	31.0	21.8	41.5
Mean Minimum Temp. (°F)	9.8	14.0	20.8	26.3	32.5	38.2	40.5	39.1	31.5	24.5	18.9	10.5	25.5
Extreme Maximum Temp. (°F)	58	67	73	83	90	95	97	98	92	87	72	59	98
Extreme Minimum Temp. (°F)	-40	-40	-21	3	10	20	21	14	10	-10	-28	-45	-45
Days Maximum Temp. ≥ 90°F	0	0	0	0	0	1	4	5	1	0	0	0	11
Days Maximum Temp. ≤ 32°F	12	5	1	0	0	0	0	0	0	0	4	14	36
Days Minimum Temp. ≤ 32°F	30	27	29	24	15	6	3	5	17	26	28	30	240
Days Minimum Temp. ≤ 0°F	8	5	1	0	0	0	0	0	0	0	2	7	23
Heating Degree Days (base 65°F)	1,336	1,057	940	704	498	280	139	150	392	699	1,013	1,332	8,540
Cooling Degree Days (base 65°F)	0	0	0	0	0	4	18	15	1	0	0	0	38
Mean Precipitation (in.)	0.94	0.79	1.00	1.49	2.28	2.28	1.45	1.41	1.24	1.13	1.20	0.98	16.19
Days With ≥ 0.1" Precipitation	3	3	4	5	7	7	4	4	4	4	4	4	53
Days With ≥ 1.0" Precipitation	0	0	0	0	0	0	0	0	0	0	0	0	0
Mean Snowfall (in.)	*6.4*	na	na	na	*0.2*	*trace*	*0.0*	*0.0*	*0.6*	na	na	na	na
Days With ≥ 1.0" Snow Depth	*27*	na	*11*	na	*0*	*0*	*0*	*0*	*0*	*1*	na	*25*	na

Sun River 4 S *Cascade County*   Elevation: 3,599 ft.   Latitude: 47° 29' N   Longitude: 111° 44' W

	JAN	FEB	MAR	APR	MAY	JUN	JUL	AUG	SEP	OCT	NOV	DEC	YEAR
Mean Maximum Temp. (°F)	34.8	40.7	47.1	57.2	66.2	74.5	81.6	80.9	70.9	60.1	44.2	36.9	57.9
Mean Temp. (°F)	23.5	28.6	34.5	43.7	52.4	60.5	65.8	64.8	55.7	46.4	33.5	26.1	44.6
Mean Minimum Temp. (°F)	12.1	16.5	21.8	30.3	38.6	46.4	49.8	48.6	40.4	32.8	22.9	15.1	31.3
Extreme Maximum Temp. (°F)	65	73	78	88	93	99	101	102	96	91	74	64	102
Extreme Minimum Temp. (°F)	-46	-45	-29	-16	18	27	33	28	16	-19	-30	-48	-48
Days Maximum Temp. ≥ 90°F	0	0	0	0	0	2	5	5	1	0	0	0	13
Days Maximum Temp. ≤ 32°F	10	7	4	1	0	0	0	0	0	1	4	8	35
Days Minimum Temp. ≤ 32°F	26	23	25	18	6	1	0	0	5	15	22	26	167
Days Minimum Temp. ≤ 0°F	9	5	2	0	0	0	0	0	0	0	3	6	25
Heating Degree Days (base 65°F)	1,282	1,023	941	631	387	162	56	74	287	570	938	1,203	7,554
Cooling Degree Days (base 65°F)	0	0	0	1	4	31	82	82	14	2	0	0	216
Mean Precipitation (in.)	0.42	0.35	0.68	1.26	2.24	2.08	1.51	1.51	1.05	0.78	0.48	0.43	12.79
Days With ≥ 0.1" Precipitation	1	1	2	3	5	5	4	4	3	3	2	1	34
Days With ≥ 1.0" Precipitation	0	0	0	0	0	0	0	0	0	0	0	0	0
Mean Snowfall (in.)	na	na	na	na	na	na	na	na	na	na	na	na	na
Days With ≥ 1.0" Snow Depth	13	10	7	2	0	0	0	0	0	*1*	6	10	*49*

Superior *Mineral County*   Elevation: 2,709 ft.   Latitude: 47° 12' N   Longitude: 114° 53' W

	JAN	FEB	MAR	APR	MAY	JUN	JUL	AUG	SEP	OCT	NOV	DEC	YEAR
Mean Maximum Temp. (°F)	34.4	42.3	51.6	60.5	69.5	76.9	85.2	85.4	74.6	60.5	42.7	33.6	59.8
Mean Temp. (°F)	27.0	32.4	39.4	46.5	54.3	61.3	67.4	67.2	57.8	46.8	34.8	27.2	46.8
Mean Minimum Temp. (°F)	19.5	22.4	27.2	32.4	39.1	45.7	49.5	49.0	41.0	33.0	26.9	20.5	33.9
Extreme Maximum Temp. (°F)	58	68	79	90	97	98	102	103	100	84	74	56	103
Extreme Minimum Temp. (°F)	-28	-22	-3	16	22	20	33	33	20	5	-5	-24	-28
Days Maximum Temp. ≥ 90°F	0	0	0	0	1	4	11	11	2	0	0	0	29
Days Maximum Temp. ≤ 32°F	10	4	1	0	0	0	0	0	0	0	3	12	30
Days Minimum Temp. ≤ 32°F	28	25	25	16	5	0	0	0	3	15	22	28	167
Days Minimum Temp. ≤ 0°F	3	1	0	0	0	0	0	0	0	0	0	1	5
Heating Degree Days (base 65°F)	1,171	915	786	549	330	147	43	41	225	557	899	1,166	6,829
Cooling Degree Days (base 65°F)	0	0	0	0	7	38	118	119	21	0	0	0	303
Mean Precipitation (in.)	1.41	1.01	1.27	1.17	1.75	1.78	1.05	1.35	1.08	1.10	1.66	1.45	16.08
Days With ≥ 0.1" Precipitation	5	3	5	4	5	5	3	4	3	4	6	5	52
Days With ≥ 1.0" Precipitation	0	0	0	0	0	0	0	0	0	0	0	0	0
Mean Snowfall (in.)	na	na	na	na	na	na	na	na	na	na	na	na	na
Days With ≥ 1.0" Snow Depth	*18*	*11*	*3*	*0*	0	0	*0*	0	0	0	*4*	na	na

Sweetgrass *Toole County* Elevation: 3,464 ft.   Latitude: 49° 00' N   Longitude: 111° 58' W

	JAN	FEB	MAR	APR	MAY	JUN	JUL	AUG	SEP	OCT	NOV	DEC	YEAR
Mean Maximum Temp. (°F)	30.0	35.9	44.1	56.0	66.6	74.2	80.8	80.7	70.0	59.0	41.0	32.4	55.9
Mean Temp. (°F)	19.4	24.7	32.8	43.5	53.5	61.2	66.4	66.0	56.0	45.9	30.4	21.9	43.5
Mean Minimum Temp. (°F)	8.5	13.4	21.3	30.9	40.4	48.1	51.9	51.3	41.9	32.7	19.8	11.3	31.0
Extreme Maximum Temp. (°F)	62	70	68	84	91	96	100	101	95	88	74	67	101
Extreme Minimum Temp. (°F)	-34	-35	-21	-7	19	30	36	30	19	-12	-26	-44	-44
Days Maximum Temp. ≥ 90°F	0	0	0	0	0	1	4	5	1	0	0	0	11
Days Maximum Temp. ≤ 32°F	13	9	5	1	0	0	0	0	0	1	6	11	46
Days Minimum Temp. ≤ 32°F	27	24	25	17	4	0	0	0	4	14	25	28	168
Days Minimum Temp. ≤ 0°F	10	6	2	0	0	0	0	0	0	0	3	7	28
Heating Degree Days (base 65°F)	1,410	1,133	992	640	357	146	55	68	283	588	1,032	1,328	8,032
Cooling Degree Days (base 65°F)	0	0	0	1	9	36	97	109	22	2	0	0	276
Mean Precipitation (in.)	0.31	0.23	0.57	1.01	2.58	3.21	2.03	2.08	1.49	0.64	0.45	0.31	14.91
Days With ≥ 0.1" Precipitation	1	1	2	3	5	6	5	5	3	2	1	1	35
Days With ≥ 1.0" Precipitation	0	0	0	0	1	1	0	0	0	0	0	0	2
Mean Snowfall (in.)	na	na	na	na	trace	0.0	0.0	0.0	*0.1*	na	na	na	na
Days With ≥ 1.0" Snow Depth	na	na	na	*0*	0	0	0	0	0	na	na	na	na

Terry *Prairie County* Elevation: 2,247 ft.   Latitude: 46° 48' N   Longitude: 105° 18' W

	JAN	FEB	MAR	APR	MAY	JUN	JUL	AUG	SEP	OCT	NOV	DEC	YEAR
Mean Maximum Temp. (°F)	26.2	34.9	45.3	58.8	70.2	80.5	87.5	87.4	74.7	60.6	43.1	31.9	58.4
Mean Temp. (°F)	13.4	21.9	31.7	44.4	55.8	65.7	71.2	70.0	57.6	44.9	29.8	18.4	43.7
Mean Minimum Temp. (°F)	0.5	8.8	18.3	29.8	41.1	50.8	54.9	52.5	40.3	29.2	16.9	5.1	29.0
Extreme Maximum Temp. (°F)	58	73	79	91	102	110	109	111	106	94	79	69	111
Extreme Minimum Temp. (°F)	-44	-41	-31	-5	19	30	38	28	15	-9	-31	-43	-44
Days Maximum Temp. ≥ 90°F	0	0	0	0	1	5	14	14	4	0	0	0	38
Days Maximum Temp. ≤ 32°F	16	11	5	1	0	0	0	0	0	1	6	*15*	*55*
Days Minimum Temp. ≤ 32°F	30	27	29	18	4	0	0	0	5	20	29	30	192
Days Minimum Temp. ≤ 0°F	13	7	3	0	0	0	0	0	0	0	2	*10*	*35*
Heating Degree Days (base 65°F)	1,596	1,211	1,026	613	299	78	20	33	251	616	1,053	1,439	8,235
Cooling Degree Days (base 65°F)	0	0	0	1	21	112	216	214	35	1	0	0	600
Mean Precipitation (in.)	na	*0.26*	0.43	1.11	1.96	2.17	1.55	1.29	1.31	0.95	0.45	0.25	na
Days With ≥ 0.1" Precipitation	na	na	1	3	5	5	3	3	3	2	*1*	*1*	na
Days With ≥ 1.0" Precipitation	na	*0*	0	0	0	0	0	0	0	0	0	0	na
Mean Snowfall (in.)	na	na	na	na	0.0	0.0	0.0	0.0	0.3	na	na	na	na
Days With ≥ 1.0" Snow Depth	na	na	na	na	*0*	0	0	0	*0*	na	na	na	na

Terry 21 NNW *Prairie County* Elevation: 3,254 ft.   Latitude: 47° 04' N   Longitude: 105° 30' W

	JAN	FEB	MAR	APR	MAY	JUN	JUL	AUG	SEP	OCT	NOV	DEC	YEAR
Mean Maximum Temp. (°F)	25.6	32.4	42.0	54.9	65.8	75.4	82.6	82.3	70.2	57.0	39.6	29.4	54.8
Mean Temp. (°F)	15.0	21.8	30.6	42.1	52.8	62.1	68.1	67.5	56.0	43.9	28.9	18.8	42.3
Mean Minimum Temp. (°F)	4.4	11.1	19.2	29.2	39.7	48.9	53.6	52.7	41.7	30.8	18.1	8.1	29.8
Extreme Maximum Temp. (°F)	65	67	74	87	96	103	103	102	99	89	75	66	103
Extreme Minimum Temp. (°F)	-36	-33	-34	-5	18	26	34	28	14	-14	-26	-37	-37
Days Maximum Temp. ≥ 90°F	0	0	0	0	0	2	6	7	1	0	0	0	16
Days Maximum Temp. ≤ 32°F	19	12	7	1	0	0	0	0	0	1	8	16	64
Days Minimum Temp. ≤ 32°F	31	28	29	20	6	0	0	0	5	17	28	30	194
Days Minimum Temp. ≤ 0°F	12	7	3	0	0	0	0	0	0	0	3	9	34
Heating Degree Days (base 65°F)	1,546	1,215	1,059	681	379	131	37	49	287	648	1,077	1,427	8,536
Cooling Degree Days (base 65°F)	0	0	0	0	9	54	140	140	24	0	0	0	367
Mean Precipitation (in.)	0.46	0.25	0.54	1.27	2.24	2.60	1.82	1.22	1.36	1.10	0.45	0.44	13.75
Days With ≥ 0.1" Precipitation	2	1	2	3	5	6	4	3	3	3	2	*2*	*36*
Days With ≥ 1.0" Precipitation	0	0	0	0	0	1	0	0	0	0	0	0	1
Mean Snowfall (in.)	na	na	na	na	*trace*	0.0	0.0	0.0	0.4	na	na	na	na
Days With ≥ 1.0" Snow Depth	na	na	na	na	0	0	0	0	0	na	na	na	na

Thompson Falls *Sanders County* Elevation: 2,378 ft.   Latitude: 47° 35' N   Longitude: 115° 21' W

	JAN	FEB	MAR	APR	MAY	JUN	JUL	AUG	SEP	OCT	NOV	DEC	YEAR
Mean Maximum Temp. (°F)	34.7	42.4	52.1	62.1	71.0	78.1	86.9	87.4	76.0	60.8	42.9	34.6	60.8
Mean Temp. (°F)	28.0	33.2	40.2	47.8	55.6	62.4	68.6	68.5	59.0	47.4	35.8	28.6	47.9
Mean Minimum Temp. (°F)	21.1	24.1	28.3	33.5	40.2	46.6	50.2	49.6	41.8	34.1	28.6	22.6	35.0
Extreme Maximum Temp. (°F)	58	71	77	93	99	100	106	106	105	88	74	54	106
Extreme Minimum Temp. (°F)	-22	-15	0	20	24	32	35	33	20	10	-7	-30	-30
Days Maximum Temp. ≥ 90°F	0	0	0	0	1	5	14	14	3	0	0	0	37
Days Maximum Temp. ≤ 32°F	9	3	0	0	0	0	0	0	0	0	2	9	23
Days Minimum Temp. ≤ 32°F	28	25	23	14	3	0	0	0	3	12	21	28	157
Days Minimum Temp. ≤ 0°F	2	1	0	0	0	0	0	0	0	0	0	1	4
Heating Degree Days (base 65°F)	1,142	891	761	510	294	123	35	33	197	539	870	1,121	6,516
Cooling Degree Days (base 65°F)	0	0	0	0	1	14	51	153	154	28	0	0	401
Mean Precipitation (in.)	*2.59*	*1.92*	*1.81*	*1.52*	*2.21*	*2.16*	*1.27*	*1.24*	*1.17*	*1.51*	*2.48*	*2.57*	*22.45*
Days With ≥ 0.1" Precipitation	8	6	7	5	6	6	3	3	4	5	8	8	69
Days With ≥ 1.0" Precipitation	0	0	0	0	0	0	0	0	0	0	0	0	0
Mean Snowfall (in.)	na	na	na	na	na	na	na	na	na	na	na	na	na
Days With ≥ 1.0" Snow Depth	*24*	14	*5*	*0*	0	0	0	0	0	*0*	na	*17*	na

Tiber Dam *Liberty County*   Elevation: 2,847 ft.   Latitude: 48° 19' N   Longitude: 111° 05' W

	JAN	FEB	MAR	APR	MAY	JUN	JUL	AUG	SEP	OCT	NOV	DEC	YEAR
Mean Maximum Temp. (°F)	*30.3*	38.4	47.4	59.8	70.0	78.8	85.0	85.4	73.9	63.0	45.2	33.9	*59.2*
Mean Temp. (°F)	*18.4*	25.5	34.3	45.1	55.3	63.6	68.4	68.1	57.4	47.2	32.5	22.0	*44.8*
Mean Minimum Temp. (°F)	*6.8*	12.6	21.2	30.3	40.5	48.3	51.7	50.8	40.9	31.3	19.7	10.1	*30.4*
Extreme Maximum Temp. (°F)	70	74	76	89	95	103	102	106	99	94	78	65	106
Extreme Minimum Temp. (°F)	-42	-35	-26	-13	18	32	36	29	16	-13	-28	-43	-43
Days Maximum Temp. ≥ 90°F	0	0	0	0	1	4	10	10	2	0	0	0	27
Days Maximum Temp. ≤ 32°F	12	8	4	1	0	0	0	0	0	0	4	10	39
Days Minimum Temp. ≤ 32°F	26	25	26	17	3	0	0	0	4	15	24	28	168
Days Minimum Temp. ≤ 0°F	10	6	2	0	0	0	0	0	0	0	2	8	28
Heating Degree Days (base 65°F)	*1,442*	1,111	946	593	305	100	31	38	241	548	969	1,327	*7,651*
Cooling Degree Days (base 65°F)	na	*0*	*0*	1	12	64	*127*	138	*19*	1	*0*	0	na
Mean Precipitation (in.)	0.37	0.24	0.53	0.90	1.71	2.19	1.30	1.32	0.84	0.59	0.39	0.33	10.71
Days With ≥ 0.1" Precipitation	1	1	1	3	5	5	3	3	2	2	1	1	28
Days With ≥ 1.0" Precipitation	0	0	0	0	0	0	0	0	0	0	0	0	0
Mean Snowfall (in.)	na	na	na	na	*0.0*	*0.0*	*0.0*	*0.0*	*0.0*	na	na	na	na
Days With ≥ 1.0" Snow Depth	na	na	na	na	0	0	0	0	0	na	na	na	na

Townsend *Broadwater County*   Elevation: 3,838 ft.   Latitude: 46° 20' N   Longitude: 111° 32' W

	JAN	FEB	MAR	APR	MAY	JUN	JUL	AUG	SEP	OCT	NOV	DEC	YEAR
Mean Maximum Temp. (°F)	34.1	40.5	49.1	58.6	67.5	75.2	82.0	82.1	71.6	60.3	44.5	35.1	58.4
Mean Temp. (°F)	23.0	28.3	36.3	44.7	53.3	60.9	66.4	65.6	55.8	45.7	33.2	24.1	44.8
Mean Minimum Temp. (°F)	11.9	16.1	23.3	30.8	39.1	46.6	50.8	49.0	39.9	30.9	21.9	13.1	31.1
Extreme Maximum Temp. (°F)	64	72	77	88	93	100	99	98	99	88	75	65	100
Extreme Minimum Temp. (°F)	-32	-38	-25	6	19	27	34	25	14	-11	-27	-37	-38
Days Maximum Temp. ≥ 90°F	0	0	0	0	0	2	5	5	1	0	0	0	13
Days Maximum Temp. ≤ 32°F	12	6	2	0	0	0	0	0	0	0	4	11	35
Days Minimum Temp. ≤ 32°F	29	26	27	17	5	0	0	0	5	18	25	29	181
Days Minimum Temp. ≤ 0°F	8	4	1	0	0	0	0	0	0	0	2	6	21
Heating Degree Days (base 65°F)	1,296	1,029	882	602	359	153	51	59	282	593	947	1,261	7,514
Cooling Degree Days (base 65°F)	0	0	0	0	4	34	93	85	13	0	0	0	229
Mean Precipitation (in.)	0.37	0.24	0.57	0.71	1.74	2.02	1.41	1.34	1.04	0.56	0.40	0.35	10.75
Days With ≥ 0.1" Precipitation	1	1	2	2	5	6	4	4	3	2	1	1	32
Days With ≥ 1.0" Precipitation	0	0	0	0	0	0	0	0	0	0	0	0	0
Mean Snowfall (in.)	na	na	na	na	na	na	na	na	na	na	na	na	na
Days With ≥ 1.0" Snow Depth	na	na	na	na	*0*	*0*	0	*0*	*0*	*0*	na	na	na

Trident *Gallatin County*   Elevation: 4,035 ft.   Latitude: 45° 57' N   Longitude: 111° 28' W

	JAN	FEB	MAR	APR	MAY	JUN	JUL	AUG	SEP	OCT	NOV	DEC	YEAR
Mean Maximum Temp. (°F)	34.2	40.9	48.7	58.6	68.4	77.6	85.5	85.3	73.6	61.0	44.2	35.3	59.4
Mean Temp. (°F)	23.0	29.1	36.5	45.0	54.1	62.4	68.5	67.6	57.0	46.3	32.8	24.2	45.5
Mean Minimum Temp. (°F)	11.8	17.3	24.3	31.3	39.9	47.2	51.5	49.8	40.3	31.5	21.5	13.0	31.6
Extreme Maximum Temp. (°F)	63	68	78	88	94	102	104	103	96	86	77	65	104
Extreme Minimum Temp. (°F)	-29	-37	-26	4	22	32	32	27	16	-6	-23	-34	-37
Days Maximum Temp. ≥ 90°F	0	0	0	0	0	4	11	11	2	0	0	0	28
Days Maximum Temp. ≤ 32°F	12	6	2	0	0	0	0	0	0	0	5	11	36
Days Minimum Temp. ≤ 32°F	29	26	26	17	4	0	0	0	4	17	25	29	177
Days Minimum Temp. ≤ 0°F	7	4	1	0	0	0	0	0	0	0	2	5	19
Heating Degree Days (base 65°F)	1,297	1,007	876	595	334	123	30	37	249	573	960	1,259	7,340
Cooling Degree Days (base 65°F)	0	0	0	0	6	51	146	128	18	1	0	0	350
Mean Precipitation (in.)	0.36	0.31	0.72	1.18	2.26	2.00	1.55	1.17	1.50	0.87	0.54	0.27	12.73
Days With ≥ 0.1" Precipitation	1	1	2	4	6	6	4	4	4	3	2	1	38
Days With ≥ 1.0" Precipitation	0	0	0	0	0	0	0	0	0	0	0	0	0
Mean Snowfall (in.)	na	na	na	na	na	na	na	na	na	na	na	na	na
Days With ≥ 1.0" Snow Depth	*15*	*7*	*5*	*1*	0	0	0	0	0	*1*	*6*	*15*	*50*

Trout Creek Ranger Station *Sanders County*   Elevation: 2,355 ft.   Latitude: 47° 52' N   Longitude: 115° 37' W

	JAN	FEB	MAR	APR	MAY	JUN	JUL	AUG	SEP	OCT	NOV	DEC	YEAR
Mean Maximum Temp. (°F)	34.0	41.0	50.2	60.1	69.1	75.9	84.1	85.2	74.6	59.6	42.1	33.9	59.1
Mean Temp. (°F)	26.8	31.9	38.6	45.8	53.3	59.5	64.9	65.0	56.7	46.1	35.3	27.7	46.0
Mean Minimum Temp. (°F)	19.6	22.7	27.0	31.5	37.4	43.1	45.7	44.9	38.8	32.5	28.4	21.5	32.8
Extreme Maximum Temp. (°F)	57	69	75	92	96	97	105	104	101	89	67	52	105
Extreme Minimum Temp. (°F)	-33	-23	-6	9	18	27	27	28	19	5	-8	-33	-33
Days Maximum Temp. ≥ 90°F	0	0	0	0	1	3	10	11	2	0	0	0	27
Days Maximum Temp. ≤ 32°F	10	3	0	0	0	0	0	0	0	0	2	10	25
Days Minimum Temp. ≤ 32°F	28	25	24	18	8	1	0	0	5	16	20	28	173
Days Minimum Temp. ≤ 0°F	3	2	0	0	0	0	0	0	0	0	0	2	7
Heating Degree Days (base 65°F)	1,177	930	812	570	363	183	74	71	255	581	887	1,150	7,053
Cooling Degree Days (base 65°F)	0	0	0	0	6	24	79	83	15	0	0	0	207
Mean Precipitation (in.)	3.80	2.74	2.24	1.84	2.32	2.25	1.43	1.41	1.36	2.01	3.97	3.96	29.33
Days With ≥ 0.1" Precipitation	10	8	7	6	7	6	4	4	4	6	10	10	82
Days With ≥ 1.0" Precipitation	1	0	0	0	0	0	0	0	0	0	1	0	2
Mean Snowfall (in.)	na	na	na	na	na	na	na	na	na	na	na	na	na
Days With ≥ 1.0" Snow Depth	25	20	8	0	0	0	0	0	0	0	6	18	77

Twin Bridges *Madison County*   Elevation: 4,622 ft.   Latitude: 45° 33' N   Longitude: 112° 20' W

	JAN	FEB	MAR	APR	MAY	JUN	JUL	AUG	SEP	OCT	NOV	DEC	YEAR
Mean Maximum Temp. (°F)	34.4	40.6	48.2	57.3	66.6	75.6	83.3	82.2	71.8	60.3	43.8	34.5	58.2
Mean Temp. (°F)	23.0	27.9	35.0	42.6	51.2	59.1	64.7	62.9	53.5	43.7	31.6	23.2	43.2
Mean Minimum Temp. (°F)	11.5	15.2	21.8	27.8	35.7	42.6	46.0	43.6	35.2	27.1	19.4	11.9	28.2
Extreme Maximum Temp. (°F)	57	64	78	85	90	95	97	97	95	86	72	62	97
Extreme Minimum Temp. (°F)	-29	-32	-17	2	15	24	28	23	10	-3	-22	-35	-35
Days Maximum Temp. ≥ 90°F	0	0	0	0	0	2	6	5	0	0	0	0	13
Days Maximum Temp. ≤ 32°F	11	5	2	0	0	0	0	0	0	0	4	11	33
Days Minimum Temp. ≤ 32°F	30	27	28	22	10	2	0	1	11	23	27	30	211
Days Minimum Temp. ≤ 0°F	7	3	1	0	0	0	0	0	0	0	0	2	18
Heating Degree Days (base 65°F)	1,298	1,042	924	666	422	186	61	90	339	652	995	1,289	7,964
Cooling Degree Days (base 65°F)	0	0	0	0	1	14	57	32	3	0	0	0	107
Mean Precipitation (in.)	0.20	0.18	0.48	0.83	1.87	1.82	1.22	1.06	1.10	0.54	0.36	0.23	9.89
Days With ≥ 0.1" Precipitation	0	1	2	3	6	5	4	3	3	2	1	1	31
Days With ≥ 1.0" Precipitation	0	0	0	0	0	0	0	0	0	0	0	0	0
Mean Snowfall (in.)	na	na	na	na	0.0	0.0	0.0	0.1	trace	*trace*	na	na	na
Days With ≥ 1.0" Snow Depth	na	na	na	na	0	0	0	0	0	*0*	na	na	na

Valier *Pondera County*   Elevation: 3,809 ft.   Latitude: 48° 19' N   Longitude: 112° 15' W

	JAN	FEB	MAR	APR	MAY	JUN	JUL	AUG	SEP	OCT	NOV	DEC	YEAR
Mean Maximum Temp. (°F)	32.1	37.8	44.8	55.6	65.3	73.2	79.8	80.1	69.9	59.0	41.8	34.2	56.1
Mean Temp. (°F)	21.1	26.3	33.0	42.8	52.2	60.1	65.5	65.3	55.8	46.1	31.6	24.0	43.6
Mean Minimum Temp. (°F)	10.1	14.6	21.3	30.0	39.2	46.9	51.1	50.4	41.6	33.1	21.3	13.7	31.1
Extreme Maximum Temp. (°F)	63	69	69	85	91	95	100	100	93	88	73	64	100
Extreme Minimum Temp. (°F)	-39	-37	-23	-7	21	31	32	28	18	-9	-25	-35	-39
Days Maximum Temp. ≥ 90°F	0	0	0	0	0	1	3	4	0	0	0	0	8
Days Maximum Temp. ≤ 32°F	12	8	4	1	0	0	0	0	0	1	5	10	41
Days Minimum Temp. ≤ 32°F	29	25	27	19	5	0	0	0	4	14	24	28	175
Days Minimum Temp. ≤ 0°F	10	6	2	0	0	0	0	0	0	0	3	6	27
Heating Degree Days (base 65°F)	1,358	1,088	984	659	392	169	63	70	284	581	997	1,265	7,910
Cooling Degree Days (base 65°F)	0	0	0	0	5	27	83	92	18	1	0	0	226
Mean Precipitation (in.)	na	na	na	na	na	na	na	na	na	na	na	na	na
Days With ≥ 0.1" Precipitation	1	1	2	3	5	6	4	4	3	2	1	1	33
Days With ≥ 1.0" Precipitation	0	0	0	0	0	1	0	0	0	0	0	0	1
Mean Snowfall (in.)	na	na	na	na	na	na	na	na	na	na	na	na	na
Days With ≥ 1.0" Snow Depth	14	11	9	*3*	0	0	0	0	0	1	8	*12*	*58*

Vida 6 NE *McCone County*   Elevation: 2,398 ft.   Latitude: 47° 53' N   Longitude: 105° 27' W

	JAN	FEB	MAR	APR	MAY	JUN	JUL	AUG	SEP	OCT	NOV	DEC	YEAR
Mean Maximum Temp. (°F)	24.4	32.5	43.2	58.0	69.2	79.0	84.9	84.6	72.4	59.0	40.3	29.1	56.4
Mean Temp. (°F)	13.0	21.4	31.8	44.4	55.4	64.9	69.8	69.0	57.5	45.5	29.5	18.3	43.4
Mean Minimum Temp. (°F)	2.2	10.6	20.1	31.1	41.6	50.8	54.6	53.3	42.5	32.0	18.5	7.5	30.4
Extreme Maximum Temp. (°F)	61	71	78	95	103	108	106	108	103	95	80	62	108
Extreme Minimum Temp. (°F)	-37	-36	-33	-8	20	29	37	32	14	-4	-25	*-39*	*-39*
Days Maximum Temp. ≥ 90°F	0	0	0	0	1	4	9	10	2	0	0	0	26
Days Maximum Temp. ≤ 32°F	19	12	6	1	0	0	0	0	0	1	8	16	63
Days Minimum Temp. ≤ 32°F	30	27	26	16	*4*	0	0	0	3	15	27	30	*178*
Days Minimum Temp. ≤ 0°F	13	7	3	0	0	0	0	0	0	0	3	9	35
Heating Degree Days (base 65°F)	1,609	1,224	1,024	614	305	81	23	41	252	596	1,059	*1,440*	*8,268*
Cooling Degree Days (base 65°F)	0	0	0	2	18	92	176	182	31	1	0	0	502
Mean Precipitation (in.)	0.47	*0.31*	0.69	1.21	*2.13*	2.74	1.80	1.31	1.43	0.90	0.51	0.48	*13.98*
Days With ≥ 0.1" Precipitation	1	1	2	3	5	5	4	3	3	2	2	1	32
Days With ≥ 1.0" Precipitation	0	0	0	0	0	0	0	0	0	0	0	0	0
Mean Snowfall (in.)	na	na	na	na	na	na	na	na	na	na	na	na	na
Days With ≥ 1.0" Snow Depth	na	*8*	5	1	0	0	0	0	0	*1*	*4*	*12*	na

Virginia City *Madison County*   Elevation: 5,770 ft.   Latitude: 45° 18' N   Longitude: 111° 57' W

	JAN	FEB	MAR	APR	MAY	JUN	JUL	AUG	SEP	OCT	NOV	DEC	YEAR
Mean Maximum Temp. (°F)	33.8	38.2	44.0	52.5	61.8	71.4	79.6	79.2	68.7	57.3	41.7	34.0	55.2
Mean Temp. (°F)	23.0	26.7	32.5	40.0	48.8	57.0	63.9	63.1	53.5	43.6	30.8	23.3	42.2
Mean Minimum Temp. (°F)	12.2	15.2	20.9	27.5	35.8	42.7	48.1	46.9	38.3	29.8	19.9	12.6	29.1
Extreme Maximum Temp. (°F)	57	63	70	79	84	93	98	96	90	83	70	59	98
Extreme Minimum Temp. (°F)	-28	-34	-13	-5	12	25	27	24	11	-10	-18	-38	-38
Days Maximum Temp. ≥ 90°F	0	0	0	0	0	0	1	1	0	0	0	0	2
Days Maximum Temp. ≤ 32°F	12	6	3	1	0	0	0	0	0	1	5	12	40
Days Minimum Temp. ≤ 32°F	30	27	29	23	10	2	0	1	7	19	27	30	205
Days Minimum Temp. ≤ 0°F	6	3	1	0	0	0	0	0	0	0	2	5	17
Heating Degree Days (base 65°F)	1,297	1,075	1,001	743	497	248	86	100	344	659	1,019	1,286	8,355
Cooling Degree Days (base 65°F)	0	0	0	0	0	0	10	52	41	6	0	0	109
Mean Precipitation (in.)	0.69	0.51	1.04	1.48	2.47	2.40	1.80	1.49	1.36	1.02	0.95	0.66	15.87
Days With ≥ 0.1" Precipitation	3	2	3	4	7	6	4	5	4	3	3	3	47
Days With ≥ 1.0" Precipitation	0	0	0	0	0	0	0	0	0	0	0	0	0
Mean Snowfall (in.)	na	na	na	na	na	na	na	na	na	na	na	na	na
Days With ≥ 1.0" Snow Depth	na	na	na	na	1	0	0	0	0	*1*	na	na	na

West Glacier *Flathead County*   Elevation: 3,152 ft.   Latitude: 48° 30' N   Longitude: 113° 59' W

	JAN	FEB	MAR	APR	MAY	JUN	JUL	AUG	SEP	OCT	NOV	DEC	YEAR
Mean Maximum Temp. (°F)	29.0	34.7	42.8	53.6	64.3	71.8	78.6	78.4	66.8	52.9	36.9	29.5	53.3
Mean Temp. (°F)	22.2	26.8	33.5	42.0	51.0	57.9	63.3	62.7	52.7	42.2	30.9	23.7	42.4
Mean Minimum Temp. (°F)	15.3	18.8	24.1	30.4	37.6	44.0	47.9	46.8	38.6	31.4	24.9	17.9	31.5
Extreme Maximum Temp. (°F)	50	55	66	83	90	91	99	95	95	77	65	51	99
Extreme Minimum Temp. (°F)	-32	-27	-11	7	23	28	31	26	18	-3	-17	-32	-32
Days Maximum Temp. ≥ 90°F	0	0	0	0	0	0	2	2	0	0	0	0	4
Days Maximum Temp. ≤ 32°F	16	7	2	0	0	0	0	0	0	0	7	18	50
Days Minimum Temp. ≤ 32°F	30	27	28	20	6	1	0	0	5	18	25	30	190
Days Minimum Temp. ≤ 0°F	5	3	1	0	0	0	0	0	0	0	1	3	13
Heating Degree Days (base 65°F)	1,322	1,074	972	683	429	220	95	107	364	701	1,016	1,273	8,256
Cooling Degree Days (base 65°F)	0	0	0	0	2	13	47	44	3	0	0	0	109
Mean Precipitation (in.)	*3.15*	*2.25*	*1.77*	*1.69*	*2.76*	*3.07*	*1.93*	*1.79*	*1.90*	*1.79*	*3.25*	*3.23*	*28.58*
Days With ≥ 0.1" Precipitation	9	7	7	5	7	8	5	5	6	6	9	10	84
Days With ≥ 1.0" Precipitation	0	0	0	0	0	0	0	0	0	0	0	0	0
Mean Snowfall (in.)	na	na	na	na	na	na	na	na	na	na	na	na	na
Days With ≥ 1.0" Snow Depth	31	28	30	12	0	0	0	0	0	1	16	29	147

Westby *Sheridan County*   Elevation: 2,103 ft.   Latitude: 48° 52' N   Longitude: 104° 03' W

	JAN	FEB	MAR	APR	MAY	JUN	JUL	AUG	SEP	OCT	NOV	DEC	YEAR
Mean Maximum Temp. (°F)	16.8	25.7	37.3	54.4	67.6	76.7	*81.5*	82.3	70.2	56.2	36.1	22.8	*52.3*
Mean Temp. (°F)	6.2	15.0	26.2	41.4	54.1	63.6	*67.8*	67.4	55.7	43.0	26.0	12.4	*39.9*
Mean Minimum Temp. (°F)	-4.5	4.3	15.0	28.3	40.7	50.4	*54.0*	52.5	41.2	29.7	15.7	1.9	*27.4*
Extreme Maximum Temp. (°F)	52	66	77	91	102	103	107	108	103	92	73	55	108
Extreme Minimum Temp. (°F)	-37	-38	-28	-18	18	31	*41*	34	18	-5	-26	-42	*-42*
Days Maximum Temp. ≥ 90°F	0	0	0	0	1	3	5	7	2	0	0	0	*18*
Days Maximum Temp. ≤ 32°F	25	16	10	1	0	0	0	0	0	1	12	21	86
Days Minimum Temp. ≤ 32°F	31	28	30	21	5	0	0	0	4	na	28	31	na
Days Minimum Temp. ≤ 0°F	18	11	5	0	0	0	0	0	0	0	3	13	50
Heating Degree Days (base 65°F)	1,822	1,406	1,196	703	346	105	*39*	55	291	678	1,165	1,627	*9,433*
Cooling Degree Days (base 65°F)	0	0	0	0	13	61	*104*	136	20	0	0	0	*334*
Mean Precipitation (in.)	0.41	0.28	0.58	0.99	1.79	2.94	2.48	1.53	1.34	0.75	0.33	0.43	13.85
Days With ≥ 0.1" Precipitation	1	1	2	3	5	6	5	3	3	2	1	1	33
Days With ≥ 1.0" Precipitation	0	0	0	0	0	1	1	0	0	0	0	0	2
Mean Snowfall (in.)	5.3	4.1	*5.6*	*2.8*	0.7	0.0	0.0	0.0	trace	*0.8*	*4.2*	*5.8*	*29.3*
Days With ≥ 1.0" Snow Depth	na	*17*	*12*	*3*	0	0	0	0	0	na	*5*	*17*	na

Western Agr. Research Station *Ravalli County*   Elevation: 3,595 ft.   Latitude: 46° 19' N   Longitude: 114° 07' W

	JAN	FEB	MAR	APR	MAY	JUN	JUL	AUG	SEP	OCT	NOV	DEC	YEAR
Mean Maximum Temp. (°F)	na	na	na	na	na	na	na	na	na	na	na	na	na
Mean Temp. (°F)	na	na	na	na	na	na	na	na	na	na	na	na	na
Mean Minimum Temp. (°F)	na	na	na	na	na	na	na	na	na	na	na	na	na
Extreme Maximum Temp. (°F)	63	70	78	88	95	97	102	101	95	83	76	63	102
Extreme Minimum Temp. (°F)	-26	-30	-11	9	17	29	31	27	18	0	-14	-32	-32
Days Maximum Temp. ≥ 90°F	0	0	0	0	0	3	7	7	0	0	0	0	17
Days Maximum Temp. ≤ 32°F	10	4	1	0	0	0	0	0	0	0	3	11	29
Days Minimum Temp. ≤ 32°F	27	25	24	17	5	0	0	0	4	16	24	27	169
Days Minimum Temp. ≤ 0°F	4	2	0	0	0	0	0	0	0	0	1	3	10
Heating Degree Days (base 65°F)	1,202	933	811	577	362	162	48	58	270	584	933	1,210	7,150
Cooling Degree Days (base 65°F)	0	0	0	0	5	32	101	89	11	0	0	0	238
Mean Precipitation (in.)	na	na	na	na	na	na	na	na	na	na	na	na	na
Days With ≥ 0.1" Precipitation	2	2	2	3	5	5	3	3	3	2	2	2	34
Days With ≥ 1.0" Precipitation	0	0	0	0	0	0	0	0	0	0	0	0	0
Mean Snowfall (in.)	na	na	na	na	na	na	na	na	na	na	na	na	na
Days With ≥ 1.0" Snow Depth	na	na	na	na	0	0	0	0	0	0	na	na	na

Wibaux 2 E *Wibaux County*   Elevation: 2,667 ft.   Latitude: 46° 59' N   Longitude: 104° 09' W

	JAN	FEB	MAR	APR	MAY	JUN	JUL	AUG	SEP	OCT	NOV	DEC	YEAR
Mean Maximum Temp. (°F)	24.6	32.3	42.7	56.3	68.2	78.0	85.3	85.0	72.5	58.7	39.9	29.0	56.0
Mean Temp. (°F)	13.2	21.0	30.5	42.5	53.8	63.2	68.7	68.2	56.4	44.4	28.5	17.6	42.3
Mean Minimum Temp. (°F)	1.6	9.5	18.2	28.7	39.4	48.3	52.1	51.4	40.2	30.0	17.0	6.2	28.5
Extreme Maximum Temp. (°F)	60	69	78	92	101	109	108	105	104	93	78	62	109
Extreme Minimum Temp. (°F)	-42	-36	-32	-11	18	26	31	27	13	-7	-26	-42	-42
Days Maximum Temp. ≥ 90°F	0	0	0	0	1	3	10	11	2	0	0	0	27
Days Maximum Temp. ≤ 32°F	19	12	7	1	0	0	0	0	0	1	8	16	64
Days Minimum Temp. ≤ 32°F	31	27	29	20	6	1	0	0	5	19	28	31	197
Days Minimum Temp. ≤ 0°F	14	8	3	0	0	0	0	0	0	0	3	11	39
Heating Degree Days (base 65°F)	1,604	1,238	1,063	668	351	113	34	45	279	633	1,089	1,465	8,582
Cooling Degree Days (base 65°F)	0	0	0	1	13	68	156	155	29	1	0	0	423
Mean Precipitation (in.)	0.32	0.27	0.58	1.34	2.41	2.60	2.01	1.54	1.54	1.22	0.44	0.24	14.51
Days With ≥ 0.1" Precipitation	1	1	2	4	6	6	5	3	4	3	1	1	37
Days With ≥ 1.0" Precipitation	0	0	0	0	1	0	0	0	0	0	0	0	1
Mean Snowfall (in.)	na	na	na	na	na	na	na	na	na	na	na	na	na
Days With ≥ 1.0" Snow Depth	*8*	na	na	*1*	0	0	0	0	0	*1*	*6*	*9*	na

Wilsall 8 ENE *Park County*   Elevation: 5,833 ft.   Latitude: 46° 02' N   Longitude: 110° 31' W

	JAN	FEB	MAR	APR	MAY	JUN	JUL	AUG	SEP	OCT	NOV	DEC	YEAR
Mean Maximum Temp. (°F)	33.3	37.3	42.9	51.0	60.9	70.2	78.2	78.5	67.5	55.9	40.7	34.1	54.2
Mean Temp. (°F)	22.6	26.2	31.4	38.8	47.7	55.9	62.2	62.0	52.6	43.0	30.6	23.9	41.4
Mean Minimum Temp. (°F)	11.7	15.1	20.0	26.5	34.5	41.5	46.0	45.5	37.6	29.9	20.4	13.6	28.5
Extreme Maximum Temp. (°F)	61	62	70	79	83	92	95	94	92	83	70	59	95
Extreme Minimum Temp. (°F)	-35	-42	-23	-10	13	25	30	26	10	-11	-22	-41	-42
Days Maximum Temp. ≥ 90°F	0	0	0	0	0	0	1	1	0	0	0	0	2
Days Maximum Temp. ≤ 32°F	13	7	4	1	0	0	0	0	0	1	6	12	44
Days Minimum Temp. ≤ 32°F	30	27	28	23	12	2	0	0	7	19	26	30	204
Days Minimum Temp. ≤ 0°F	7	3	2	0	0	0	0	0	0	0	2	4	18
Heating Degree Days (base 65°F)	1,310	1,089	1,033	780	529	275	113	116	370	676	1,027	1,268	8,586
Cooling Degree Days (base 65°F)	0	0	0	0	0	8	34	30	5	0	0	0	77
Mean Precipitation (in.)	0.94	0.75	1.52	2.10	3.52	3.20	2.01	1.74	1.88	1.42	1.07	0.90	21.05
Days With ≥ 0.1" Precipitation	3	3	5	7	9	8	6	5	5	4	4	3	62
Days With ≥ 1.0" Precipitation	0	0	0	0	0	0	0	0	0	0	0	0	0
Mean Snowfall (in.)	16.7	12.8	18.8	15.1	6.4	0.3	0.0	trace	2.4	5.6	11.2	15.0	104.3
Days With ≥ 1.0" Snow Depth	22	18	19	8	1	0	0	0	0	2	9	20	99

Winifred *Fergus County*   Elevation: 3,241 ft.   Latitude: 47° 34' N   Longitude: 109° 23' W

	JAN	FEB	MAR	APR	MAY	JUN	JUL	AUG	SEP	OCT	NOV	DEC	YEAR
Mean Maximum Temp. (°F)	31.3	38.2	46.1	56.8	66.8	76.2	83.7	84.2	72.2	60.2	43.6	34.9	57.8
Mean Temp. (°F)	19.4	25.9	33.8	43.6	53.3	61.9	67.5	67.1	56.2	45.2	31.3	22.6	44.0
Mean Minimum Temp. (°F)	7.5	13.5	21.5	30.3	39.6	47.6	51.2	50.0	40.2	30.1	18.9	10.3	30.1
Extreme Maximum Temp. (°F)	67	71	76	90	95	102	100	107	100	89	80	65	107
Extreme Minimum Temp. (°F)	-42	-38	-28	-10	20	30	33	29	15	-17	-31	-43	-43
Days Maximum Temp. ≥ 90°F	0	0	0	0	0	3	9	10	2	0	0	0	24
Days Maximum Temp. ≤ 32°F	13	8	5	1	0	0	0	0	0	1	6	11	45
Days Minimum Temp. ≤ 32°F	29	26	27	19	5	0	0	0	5	18	27	29	185
Days Minimum Temp. ≤ 0°F	11	6	2	0	0	0	0	0	0	0	3	7	29
Heating Degree Days (base 65°F)	1,410	1,100	959	637	365	135	43	54	279	607	1,004	1,310	7,903
Cooling Degree Days (base 65°F)	0	0	0	0	9	50	125	132	23	1	0	0	340
Mean Precipitation (in.)	0.73	0.43	0.86	1.38	2.82	2.81	1.75	1.72	1.31	0.82	0.59	0.71	15.93
Days With ≥ 0.1" Precipitation	3	2	3	4	6	6	5	4	3	3	2	3	44
Days With ≥ 1.0" Precipitation	0	0	0	0	1	0	0	0	0	0	0	0	1
Mean Snowfall (in.)	na	na	na	na	na	na	na	na	na	na	na	na	na
Days With ≥ 1.0" Snow Depth	na	na	na	na	0	0	0	0	0	na	na	na	na

Wisdom *Beaverhead County*   Elevation: 6,059 ft.   Latitude: 45° 37' N   Longitude: 113° 27' W

	JAN	FEB	MAR	APR	MAY	JUN	JUL	AUG	SEP	OCT	NOV	DEC	YEAR
Mean Maximum Temp. (°F)	27.1	31.9	39.9	49.3	59.7	69.0	77.8	77.5	67.3	55.1	37.3	27.5	51.6
Mean Temp. (°F)	14.4	17.9	26.3	35.1	44.2	52.5	57.7	56.1	47.3	37.6	24.9	15.2	35.8
Mean Minimum Temp. (°F)	1.7	3.8	12.7	20.8	28.6	35.9	37.6	34.7	27.2	20.0	12.4	2.8	19.8
Extreme Maximum Temp. (°F)	51	55	65	77	85	91	93	93	89	79	65	53	93
Extreme Minimum Temp. (°F)	-49	-52	-33	-18	9	19	23	11	3	-23	-30	-55	-55
Days Maximum Temp. ≥ 90°F	0	0	0	0	0	0	1	0	0	0	0	0	1
Days Maximum Temp. ≤ 32°F	19	13	5	1	0	0	0	0	0	1	9	21	69
Days Minimum Temp. ≤ 32°F	30	28	31	29	22	9	5	12	22	29	29	31	277
Days Minimum Temp. ≤ 0°F	13	11	5	1	0	0	0	0	0	1	5	13	49
Heating Degree Days (base 65°F)	1,564	1,325	1,193	891	639	371	222	270	526	844	1,198	1,539	10,582
Cooling Degree Days (base 65°F)	0	0	0	0	0	1	3	2	0	0	0	0	6
Mean Precipitation (in.)	0.59	0.49	0.67	0.96	1.71	1.80	1.33	1.13	1.04	0.68	0.78	0.69	11.87
Days With ≥ 0.1" Precipitation	2	2	2	3	6	6	4	4	3	2	3	2	39
Days With ≥ 1.0" Precipitation	0	0	0	0	0	0	0	0	0	0	0	0	0
Mean Snowfall (in.)	na	na	na	na	na	na	na	na	na	na	na	na	na
Days With ≥ 1.0" Snow Depth	na	na	na	na	na	0	0	0	0	na	na	na	na

Wyola 1 SW *Big Horn County*   Elevation: 3,727 ft.   Latitude: 45° 07' N   Longitude: 107° 24' W

	JAN	FEB	MAR	APR	MAY	JUN	JUL	AUG	SEP	OCT	NOV	DEC	YEAR
Mean Maximum Temp. (°F)	35.6	41.5	49.9	60.1	69.5	78.8	86.2	86.3	74.7	62.7	46.2	37.7	60.8
Mean Temp. (°F)	21.8	27.1	35.5	44.6	53.5	62.3	68.2	67.3	57.0	46.1	32.8	23.9	45.0
Mean Minimum Temp. (°F)	7.7	12.7	21.1	29.2	37.4	45.9	50.0	48.2	39.1	29.4	19.1	10.0	29.2
Extreme Maximum Temp. (°F)	69	74	80	89	94	101	104	105	96	92	79	71	105
Extreme Minimum Temp. (°F)	-42	-36	-25	-4	19	28	33	27	15	-18	-25	-46	-46
Days Maximum Temp. ≥ 90°F	0	0	0	0	0	4	11	12	2	0	0	0	29
Days Maximum Temp. ≤ 32°F	10	6	2	0	0	0	0	0	0	0	4	9	31
Days Minimum Temp. ≤ 32°F	30	27	28	20	8	1	0	0	6	20	27	30	197
Days Minimum Temp. ≤ 0°F	9	5	2	0	0	0	0	0	0	0	2	7	25
Heating Degree Days (base 65°F)	1,335	1,063	908	607	352	121	29	37	256	581	959	1,268	7,516
Cooling Degree Days (base 65°F)	0	0	0	0	3	50	134	109	26	1	0	0	323
Mean Precipitation (in.)	0.77	0.70	1.20	2.01	2.74	2.36	1.50	0.83	1.63	1.65	0.99	0.74	17.12
Days With ≥ 0.1" Precipitation	3	3	4	6	6	5	4	2	4	4	3	3	47
Days With ≥ 1.0" Precipitation	0	0	0	0	0	0	0	0	0	0	0	0	0
Mean Snowfall (in.)	na	na	na	na	na	na	na	na	na	na	na	na	na
Days With ≥ 1.0" Snow Depth	na	na	na	1	0	0	0	0	0	1	4	na	na

Yellowtail Dam *Big Horn County*   Elevation: 3,303 ft.   Latitude: 45° 19' N   Longitude: 107° 56' W

	JAN	FEB	MAR	APR	MAY	JUN	JUL	AUG	SEP	OCT	NOV	DEC	YEAR
Mean Maximum Temp. (°F)	38.8	44.8	52.2	61.8	71.6	81.7	89.9	90.1	78.2	65.5	48.7	41.2	63.7
Mean Temp. (°F)	28.4	33.7	40.3	49.3	58.4	67.5	74.0	73.6	63.2	52.4	38.7	31.3	50.9
Mean Minimum Temp. (°F)	18.0	22.5	28.4	36.8	45.1	53.2	58.0	57.1	48.1	39.3	28.5	21.3	38.0
Extreme Maximum Temp. (°F)	68	72	80	89	97	104	107	107	103	93	78	72	107
Extreme Minimum Temp. (°F)	-30	-32	-16	8	26	35	40	37	24	-7	-14	-28	-32
Days Maximum Temp. ≥ 90°F	0	0	0	0	1	7	18	18	5	0	0	0	49
Days Maximum Temp. ≤ 32°F	9	5	2	0	0	0	0	0	0	0	4	7	27
Days Minimum Temp. ≤ 32°F	24	21	20	9	1	0	0	0	1	7	18	24	125
Days Minimum Temp. ≤ 0°F	5	3	1	0	0	0	0	0	0	0	1	3	13
Heating Degree Days (base 65°F)	1,129	878	759	469	226	53	7	9	132	396	785	1,040	5,883
Cooling Degree Days (base 65°F)	0	0	1	7	30	135	293	290	88	11	0	0	855
Mean Precipitation (in.)	na	na	na	na	na	na	na	na	na	na	na	na	na
Days With ≥ 0.1" Precipitation	3	2	5	6	6	5	3	3	4	4	3	3	47
Days With ≥ 1.0" Precipitation	0	0	0	0	1	0	0	0	0	0	0	0	1
Mean Snowfall (in.)	na	na	na	na	na	na	na	na	na	na	na	na	na
Days With ≥ 1.0" Snow Depth	na	na	na	na	*0*	0	0	0	*0*	na	na	na	na

Note: See Appendix D for explanation of data.

NEBRASKA

PHYSICAL FEATURES. Nebraska, one of the Great Plains States, is located in the north-central portion of the United States. The area of the State is 76,653 square miles, of which about 600 are water. On the eastern boundary, along the Missouri River, the elevation rises from less than 900 feet in the southeast to 1,200 feet in the northeast. The elevation also increases westward to about 3,000 feet in the southwest and 5,000 feet in the northwest. The landscape changes from level or gently rolling prairie in the east, to rounded sandhills in the north-central part, and thence westward to high plains.

All of Nebraska is drained by the Missouri River System. The direction of flow is mostly west to east, but in the southeastern section the flow is from northwest to southeast. The Missouri River forms the eastern boundary of the State and a part of the northern boundary. The major tributary is the Platte River, with its two main branches which rise in the high elevations of Colorado. Other important tributaries are the Niobrara River in the north and the Republican and Big Blue Rivers in the south.

Greatest volume of flow occurs during May, June, and July, the months of heaviest rainfall. Although the heaviest snowfall occurs in February and March, it usually does not accumulate to any considerable depth and so the resultant runoff does not materially affect river stages.

GENERAL CLIMATE. The climate is typical of the interior of large continents in middle latitudes; that is, rather light rainfall, low humidity, hot summers, cold winters, great variations in temperature and rainfall from year to year, and frequent changes in weather from day to day. The rapid changes in weather are brought about by invasion of large masses of air of different characteristics, such as warm, moist air from the Gulf of Mexico; hot, dry air from the Southwest; cool, dry air from the north Pacific Ocean; and cold, dry air from northwestern Canada.

The Rocky Mountains to the west have a profound influence on the climate of Nebraska. Air crossing the mountains from the west loses much of its moisture on the windward side and becomes warmer and drier as it descends on the eastern slopes; therefore, no significant amount of moisture which falls as rain or snow reaches the State from the Pacific Ocean. The moisture supply for precipitation comes from the Gulf of Mexico. The remoteness from the source of supply is one of the reasons for the wide variation in rainfall from year to year. Moist air from the Gulf is often deflected eastward before it reaches Nebraska. Downslope winds from the Rocky Mountains occasionally cause large, rapid changes to higher temperatures, particularly during the winter.

Although hot nights in summer occur rather frequently in the east, they are almost unknown in the higher elevations of the western, less humid, part of the State where rapid cooling after sunset generally occurs.

TEMPERATURE. The mean annual temperature varies from about 53°F. along the eastern half of the southern border to about 45°F. in the northwest corner. Maximum temperatures above 100°F. have occurred throughout the State in the months of June, July, August, and September. Temperatures of 110°F. or higher have been recorded over most of the State, except in parts of the northwest. Minimum temperatures of zero or below occur on an average about 10 days a year in the southeast and 25 days in the northwest. Minima below -40°F. have been recorded a few times at northern and western weather stations. Although the winter climate is classed as cold, there are frequent periods of mild, pleasant weather.

The average date of the last freeze (32°F.) in spring ranges from about April 25 in the extreme southeast to about May 21 in a small area in the northwest portion, while the first in the fall varies from about October 6 in the southeast to about September 20 in the extreme northwest. Hence the average length of the growing season (freeze-free season) ranges from 164 days in the southeast to 122 in the northwest.

PRECIPITATION. The average annual precipitation in the eastern third of the State is about 27 inches; in the central third, about 22 inches; and in the western third, about 18 inches. The amount decreases rather uniformly from 33 inches in the southeast corner to about 14 inches in a small area near the western border. On the average nearly 80 percent of the yearly total falls in the six months from April to September. During July and August, rainfall normally diminishes slowly in the east portion. In the west it decreases more rapidly, so that the August average is only a little over one-half the June average in many localities.

Excessive rates of rainfall for short periods occur frequently in summer thundershowers. In some seasons thundershowers are numerous and well distributed, but sometimes they are scattered and infrequent. The result is great variability in the monthly amounts of rainfall in different years and also in the annual amounts from year to year. In dry years, periods of 15 to 20 days without appreciable rain may occur in June, July, and August; and under such conditions, hot, dry winds often cause serious and extensive damage to crops. The precipitation records show successions of wet and dry epochs.

Floods may be expected once or twice in most years in smaller streams in the eastern third of the State, but less frequently over the west and central portions, and are generally caused by short duration, high intensity rainfall. Severe flooding occurs infrequently on the Missouri and is usually caused by rapid melting of heavy snowpacks in the upper portion of the basin, attended by moderate to heavy rains.

The average seasonal snowfall is approximately 29 inches. Snowfall usually increases during the late winter and reaches a maximum in March over most of the State. The higher regions in the west portion frequently have heavy snows in April, and occasionally in May.

OTHER CLIMATIC ELEMENTS. Sunshine for the year averages about 65 percent of the possible amount, ranging from about 55 percent in December to nearly 80 percent in July.

There are frequent changes in wind direction at all seasons of the year, but the prevailing direction is from the south or southeast from May to September, and from the northwest or north during the remainder of the year, except that westerly winds predominate in the southwest portion during the autumn and winter months. The average is about nine m.p.h.

A few tornadoes occur within the State nearly every year; the average is about 10 per year. Although tornadoes are usually very small, both in width and in length of path, there is almost total destruction where the whirling funnel cloud touches the ground.

The number of hailstorms averages between 20 and 25 per year, occurring mostly in June, July, and August.

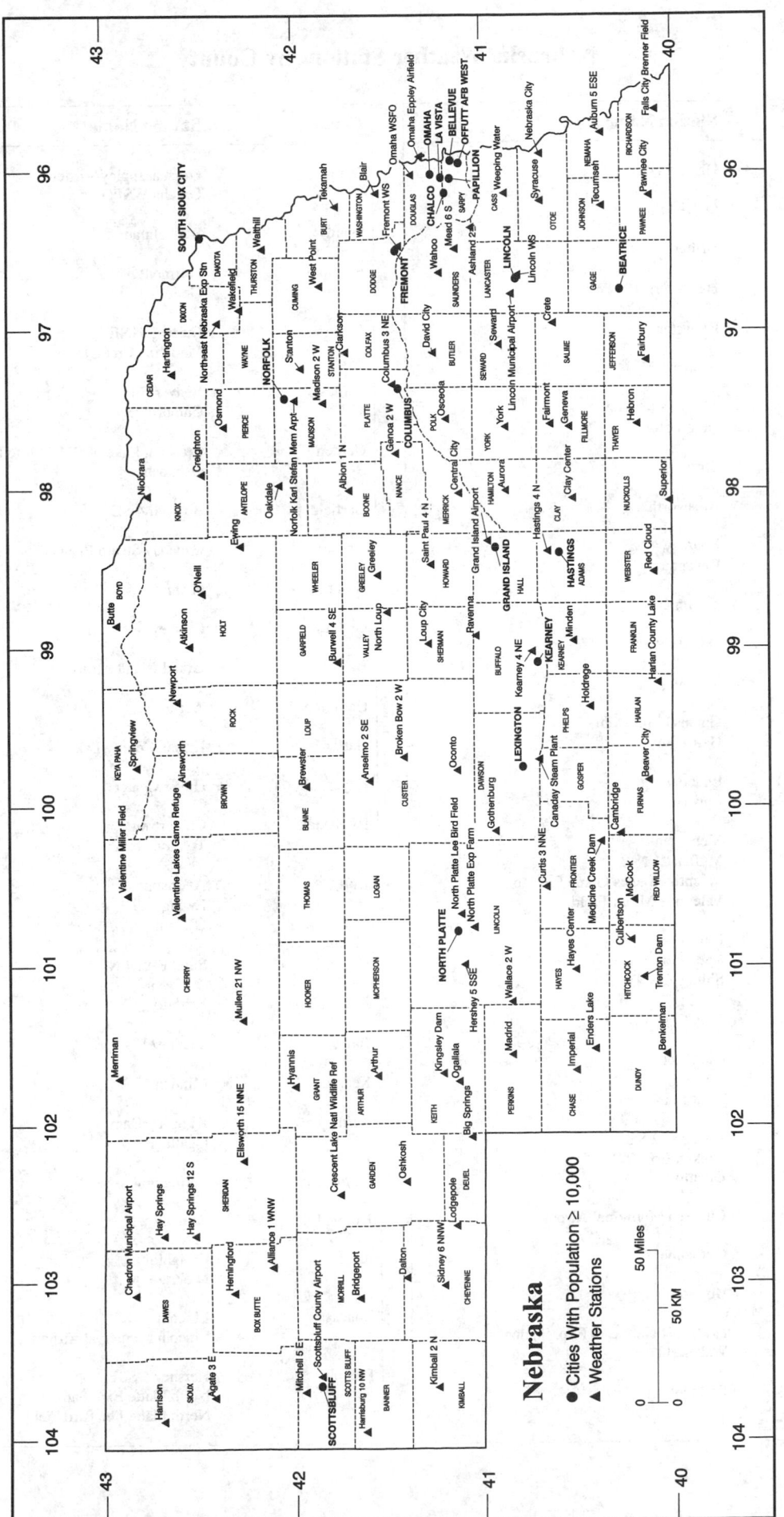

Nebraska

- ● Cities With Population ≥ 10,000
- ▲ Weather Stations

Nebraska Weather Stations by County

County	Station Name
Adams	Hastings 4 N
Antelope	Oakdale
Arthur	Arthur
Banner	Harrisburg 10 NW
Blaine	Brewster
Boone	Albion 1 N
Box Butte	Alliance 1 WNW
	Hemingford
Boyd	Butte
Brown	Ainsworth
Buffalo	Kearney 4 NE
	Ravenna
Burt	Tekamah
Butler	David City
Cass	Weeping Water
Cedar	Gavins Point Dam
	Hartington
Chase	Enders Lake
	Imperial
Cherry	Merriman
	Mullen 21 NW
	Valentine Lakes Game Refuge
	Valentine Miller Field
Cheyenne	Dalton
	Lodgepole
	Sidney 6 NNW
Clay	Clay Center
Colfax	Clarkson
Cuming	West Point
Custer	Anselmo 2 SE
	Broken Bow 2 W
	Oconto
Dawes	Chadron Municipal Airport
Dawson	Gothenburg
Deuel	Big Springs
Dixon	Northeast Nebraska Exp. Station
	Wakefield
Dodge	Fremont

County	Station Name
Douglas	Omaha Eppley Airfield
	Omaha WSFO
Dundy	Benkelman
Fillmore	Fairmont
	Geneva
Frontier	Curtis 3 NNE
	Medicine Creek Dam
Furnas	Beaver City
	Cambridge
Garden	Crescent Lake Nat'l Wildlife Ref
	Oshkosh
Garfield	Burwell 4 SE
Gosper	Canaday Steam Plant
Grant	Hyannis
Greeley	Greeley
Hall	Grand Island Airport
Hamilton	Aurora
Harlan	Harlan County Lake
Hayes	Hayes Center
Hitchcock	Culbertson
	Trenton Dam
Holt	Atkinson
	Ewing
	O'Neill
Howard	Saint Paul 4 N
Jefferson	Fairbury
Johnson	Tecumseh
Kearney	Minden
Keith	Kingsley Dam
	Ogallala
Keya Paha	Springview
Kimball	Kimball 2 N
Knox	Creighton
	Niobrara
Lancaster	Lincoln
	Lincoln Municipal Airport
Lincoln	Hershey 5 SSE
	North Platte Exp. Farm
	North Platte Lee Bird Field

County	Station Name
Lincoln (cont.)	Wallace 2 W
Madison	Madison 2 W
	Norfolk Karl Stefan Mem. Arpt.
Merrick	Central City
Morrill	Bridgeport
Nance	Genoa 2 W
Nemaha	Auburn 5 ESE
Nuckolls	Superior
Otoe	Nebraska City
	Syracuse
Pawnee	Pawnee City
Perkins	Madrid
Phelps	Holdrege
Pierce	Osmond
Platte	Columbus 3 NE
Polk	Osceola
Red Willow	McCook
Richardson	Falls City Brenner Field
Rock	Newport
Saline	Crete
Saunders	Ashland 2
	Mead 6 S
	Wahoo
Scotts Bluff	Mitchell 5 E
	Scottsbluff County Airport
Seward	Seward
Sheridan	Ellsworth 15 NNE
	Hay Springs
	Hay Springs 12 S
Sherman	Loup City
Sioux	Agate 3 E
	Harrison
Stanton	Stanton
Thayer	Hebron
Thurston	Walthill
Valley	North Loup
Washington	Blair

County	Station Name
Webster	Red Cloud
York	York

Nebraska Weather Stations by City

City	Station Name	Miles
Bellevue	Glenwood 3 SW, IA	13
	Omaha Eppley Airfield	12
	Omaha WSFO	16
Chalco	Ashland 2	15
	Mead 6 S	19
	Omaha Eppley Airfield	15
	Omaha WSFO	14
Columbus	Columbus 3 NE	3
	David City	17
Fremont	Blair	20
	Fremont	1
	Wahoo	17
Grand Island	Aurora	19
	Grand Island Airport	4
	Hastings 4 N	19
Hastings	Clay Center	19
	Hastings 4 N	4
Kearney	Kearney 4 NE	4
	Minden	15
La Vista	Glenwood 3 SW, IA	19
	Ashland 2	19
	Omaha Eppley Airfield	12
	Omaha WSFO	13
Lexington	Canaday Steam Plant	6
Lincoln	Crete	20
	Lincoln Municipal Airport	5
	Lincoln	1
Norfolk	Madison 2 W	14
	Norfolk Karl Stefan Mem. Arpt.	4
	Stanton	11
North Platte	Hershey 5 SSE	11
	North Platte Lee Bird Field	6
	North Platte Exp. Farm	6
Offutt AFB West	Glenwood 3 SW, IA	12
	Omaha Eppley Airfield	14
	Omaha WSFO	17
Omaha	Omaha Eppley Airfield	7
	Omaha WSFO	8
Papillion	Glenwood 3 SW, IA	18
	Ashland 2	18
	Omaha Eppley Airfield	13
	Omaha WSFO	15
Scottsbluff	Mitchell 5 E	6
	Scottsbluff County Airport	3
South Sioux City	Sioux City Municipal Airport, IA	6

Note: Miles is the distance between the geographic center of the city and the weather station.

Nebraska Weather Stations by Elevation

Feet	Station Name
4,849	Harrison
4,757	Kimball 2 N
4,668	Agate 3 E
4,547	Harrisburg 10 NW
4,317	Sidney 6 NNW
4,271	Dalton
4,268	Hemingford
4,078	Mitchell 5 E
3,992	Alliance 1 WNW
3,969	Ellsworth 15 NNE
3,943	Scottsbluff County Airport
3,854	Hay Springs
3,832	Lodgepole
3,818	Crescent Lake Nat'l Wildlife Ref
3,802	Hay Springs 12 S
3,769	Hyannis
3,664	Bridgeport
3,497	Arthur
3,448	Mullen 21 NW
3,379	Oshkosh
3,369	Big Springs
3,316	Kingsley Dam
3,297	Chadron Municipal Airport
3,274	Imperial
3,248	Merriman
3,228	Ogallala
3,198	Madrid
3,097	Wallace 2 W
3,077	Enders Lake
3,038	Hayes Center
3,024	Benkelman
3,021	North Platte Exp. Farm
2,949	Hershey 5 SSE
2,926	Valentine Lakes Game Refuge
2,808	Trenton Dam
2,775	North Platte Lee Bird Field
2,719	Curtis 3 NNE
2,604	Anselmo 2 SE
2,598	Culbertson
2,588	Valentine Miller Field
2,582	Gothenburg
2,578	Oconto
2,572	McCook
2,509	Ainsworth
2,500	Broken Bow 2 W
2,493	Brewster
2,493	Springview
2,385	Medicine Creek Dam
2,358	Canaday Steam Plant
2,319	Holdrege
2,257	Cambridge
2,227	Newport
2,158	Beaver City
2,158	Minden
2,129	Kearney 4 NE

Feet	Station Name
2,122	Burwell 4 SE
2,109	Atkinson
2,063	Loup City
2,047	Ravenna
2,017	Greeley
1,998	Harlan County Lake
1,988	O'Neill
1,958	North Loup
1,938	Hastings 4 N
1,847	Ewing
1,837	Grand Island Airport
1,811	Butte
1,784	Aurora
1,774	Saint Paul 4 N
1,758	Albion 1 N
1,748	Clay Center
1,719	Red Cloud
1,706	Oakdale
1,692	Central City
1,673	Madison 2 W
1,660	Osceola
1,646	Osmond
1,637	Fairmont
1,627	Creighton
1,627	Geneva
1,607	David City
1,607	York
1,587	Genoa 2 W
1,578	Superior
1,548	Clarkson
1,548	Norfolk Karl Stefan Mem. Arpt.
1,489	Stanton
1,479	Hebron
1,459	Northeast Nebraska Exp. Station
1,450	Columbus 3 NE
1,437	Seward
1,433	Crete
1,387	Wakefield
1,377	Niobrara
1,368	Hartington
1,312	Fairbury
1,309	Omaha WSFO
1,309	West Point
1,269	Wahoo
1,253	Gavins Point Dam
1,217	Lincoln
1,217	Walthill
1,207	Pawnee City
1,187	Lincoln Municipal Airport
1,177	Fremont
1,154	Mead 6 S
1,148	Tecumseh
1,099	Syracuse
1,099	Weeping Water
1,089	Blair

Feet	Station Name
1,079	Nebraska City
1,069	Ashland 2
1,036	Tekamah
980	Omaha Eppley Airfield
977	Falls City Brenner Field
928	Auburn 5 ESE

Grand Island Airport

The Grand Island Weather Service Office is located at the Hall County Regional Airport, three miles northeast of downtown Grand Island. It is situated just west of the mid-point of the north-south runway. The site is less than 50 miles from the geographical center of the contiguous United States and in the shallow Platte River valley. The complex of the Loup River and its tributaries converge approximately 15 miles northwest of the station, then flows eastward across the state. The terrain immediately surrounding the station is flat, sandy, and loam. Just to the north is the southern boundary of the Nebraska sandhills. The terrain slopes gently upward from the Missouri River valley in eastern Nebraska to the Rocky Mountains of Colorado and Wyoming.

The climate is primarily continental in nature with occasional incursions of maritime tropical air from the Gulf of Mexico and modified maritime polar air from the Pacific Ocean. Wintertime outbreaks of cold, dry, Arctic air from Canada are common, usually accompanied by strong biting winds.

The east-west upslope produces periods of fog and low stratus when winds have an easterly component, and the characteristics of a Chinook, with warm dry air, when the component is westerly. Dry-season dust storms occur occasionally with these Chinook winds. These have been reduced in recent years by increased farm irrigation. Growing season humidities have also been increased by the expanding irrigation projects. Summers are usually hot and dry with temperatures often reaching 100 degrees or more. Late spring and early summer is the peak season for severe thunderstorms with frequent hail and tornados occasionally occurring. Winters are punctuated by occasional severe blizzards and have wide variations in temperatures that range from mild to bitterly cold.

Based on the 1951-1980 period, the average first occurrence of 32 degrees Fahrenheit in the fall is October 9 and the average last occurrence in the spring is April 29.

Grand Island Airport *Hall County*   Elevation: 1,837 ft.   Latitude: 40° 58' N   Longitude: 98° 19' W

	JAN	FEB	MAR	APR	MAY	JUN	JUL	AUG	SEP	OCT	NOV	DEC	YEAR
Mean Maximum Temp. (°F)	33.0	39.4	49.9	62.6	72.6	83.7	88.0	85.7	77.6	65.2	48.1	37.0	61.9
Mean Temp. (°F)	22.6	28.6	38.5	50.3	61.1	71.6	76.3	74.0	64.8	52.2	37.2	26.7	50.3
Mean Minimum Temp. (°F)	12.1	17.8	26.9	37.9	49.5	59.4	64.5	62.4	52.0	39.2	26.2	16.4	38.7
Extreme Maximum Temp. (°F)	76	80	90	96	101	107	108	110	104	95	82	73	110
Extreme Minimum Temp. (°F)	-26	-21	-12	7	26	39	42	43	23	9	-11	-26	-26
Days Maximum Temp. ≥ 90°F	0	0	0	1	1	8	13	10	5	0	0	0	38
Days Maximum Temp. ≤ 32°F	15	10	4	0	0	0	0	0	0	0	4	11	44
Days Minimum Temp. ≤ 32°F	31	26	22	8	1	0	0	0	0	7	23	30	148
Days Minimum Temp. ≤ 0°F	7	4	1	0	0	0	0	0	0	0	0	3	15
Heating Degree Days (base 65°F)	1,308	1,020	817	447	168	22	2	7	111	398	827	1,181	6,308
Cooling Degree Days (base 65°F)	0	0	1	14	52	218	353	288	116	10	0	0	1,052
Mean Precipitation (in.)	0.53	0.65	2.01	2.65	4.08	3.73	2.99	3.13	2.58	1.44	1.36	0.64	25.79
Maximum Precipitation (in.)	1.6	3.4	6.6	7.3	8.9	14.0	10.4	8.7	9.0	3.6	3.8	2.2	38.2
Minimum Precipitation (in.)	trace	0.1	trace	0.1	0.4	0.5	0.6	0.7	0.2	0	trace	trace	13.6
Maximum 24-hr. Precipitation (in.)	0.8	1.9	2.0	2.6	2.9	4.2	4.6	4.1	5.6	2.2	1.5	1.2	5.6
Days With ≥ 0.1" Precipitation	2	2	4	5	7	6	6	5	5	3	3	2	50
Days With ≥ 1.0" Precipitation	0	0	0	1	1	1	1	1	1	0	0	0	6
Mean Snowfall (in.)	6.1	5.8	6.8	1.5	trace	trace	trace	trace	0.2	1.0	4.5	6.2	32.1
Maximum Snowfall (in.)	18	22	21	9	4	0	0	0	4	10	17	26	58
Maximum 24-hr. Snowfall (in.)	9	12	12	6	4	0	0	0	4	9	10	11	12
Days With ≥ 1.0" Snow Depth	15	11	5	1	0	0	0	0	0	0	4	9	45
Thunderstorm Days	< 1	< 1	1	4	7	10	9	8	5	2	< 1	< 1	46
Foggy Days	7	8	9	8	9	6	7	9	8	7	7	8	93
Predominant Sky Cover	OVR	OVR	OVR	OVR	OVR	OVR	CLR	CLR	CLR	CLR	OVR	OVR	OVR
Mean Relative Humidity 6am (%)	78	79	80	78	82	82	83	85	83	79	79	79	81
Mean Relative Humidity 3pm (%)	59	57	52	45	49	46	47	47	45	42	50	57	50
Mean Dewpoint (°F)	13	18	25	35	48	57	62	60	50	38	26	17	38
Prevailing Wind Direction	NNW	NNW	NNW	S	S	S	S	S	S	S	S	NNW	S
Prevailing Wind Speed (mph)	16	16	17	15	15	14	13	13	13	13	12	15	14
Maximum Wind Gust (mph)	55	60	64	67	76	78	71	68	66	58	62	58	78

Lincoln Municipal Airport

Lincoln is near the center of Lancaster County in southeastern Nebraska. The surrounding area is gently rolling prairie. The western edge of the city is in the flat valley of Salt Creek, which receives a number of tributaries in or near the city and flows northeastward to the lower Platte. The terrain slopes upward to the west and is sufficient to cause instability in moist easterly winds in the Lincoln area. Precipitation with westerly winds is infrequent since they are downslope. The upward slope to the west is a part of the general rise in elevation that begins at the Missouri River 45 miles east of Lincoln and culminates in the Continental Divide about 575 miles to the west. The chinook or foehn effect often produces rapid rises in temperature here during the winter with a shift of the wind to westerly.

The maximum temperature has exceeded 110 degrees. Hot winds, combining unusual wind force and high temperatures, occasionally cause serious injury to crops.

The majority of winter outbreaks of severely cold air from northwestern Canada move over the Lincoln area. The temperature has remained below zero degrees for more than eight consecutive days. The center of some of the cold air masses move southward far enough to the east that their full effect is usually not felt here.

Normally the crop season, April through September, receives over three-fourths of the annual precipitation. Nighttime thunderstorms are predominant in the summer months, so that the needed moisture is received during much of the growing season at a time of least interference with outdoor work.

Annual snowfall is about 25 inches, although the annual snowfall has exceeded 59 inches. Much of the snow is light and melts rapidly. However, at times a considerable amount accumulates on the ground and has exceeded a depth of 21 inches.

In the summer the higher winds are associated with thunderstorms. Lincoln has been relatively free from tornadoes and more than slight hail damage seldom occurs. There is much sunshine, averaging 64 percent of the possible duration. Moderate to low humidities are at comfortable levels except for short periods during the summer when warm, moist, tropical air occasionally reaches this area.

Lincoln Municipal Airport *Lancaster County*   Elevation: 1,187 ft.   Latitude: 40° 50' N   Longitude: 96° 46' W

	JAN	FEB	MAR	APR	MAY	JUN	JUL	AUG	SEP	OCT	NOV	DEC	YEAR
Mean Maximum Temp. (°F)	32.9	39.2	51.2	63.6	73.8	84.4	89.4	86.5	78.2	66.0	49.0	36.9	62.6
Mean Temp. (°F)	22.3	28.3	39.3	51.2	62.0	72.4	77.8	75.1	65.7	53.1	38.1	26.6	51.0
Mean Minimum Temp. (°F)	11.5	17.3	27.5	38.9	50.1	60.4	66.2	63.6	53.3	40.1	27.1	16.3	39.4
Extreme Maximum Temp. (°F)	73	77	89	97	99	107	108	107	101	93	85	70	108
Extreme Minimum Temp. (°F)	-33	-24	-19	3	24	39	45	41	26	8	-5	-27	-33
Days Maximum Temp. ≥ 90°F	0	0	0	0	1	8	15	11	4	0	0	0	39
Days Maximum Temp. ≤ 32°F	15	10	3	0	0	0	0	0	0	0	3	11	42
Days Minimum Temp. ≤ 32°F	30	26	21	8	1	0	0	0	0	6	22	30	144
Days Minimum Temp. ≤ 0°F	7	4	1	0	0	0	0	0	0	0	0	3	15
Heating Degree Days (base 65°F)	1,319	1,030	790	420	146	16	1	4	97	374	801	1,184	6,182
Cooling Degree Days (base 65°F)	0	0	1	16	60	250	399	323	132	14	0	0	1,195
Mean Precipitation (in.)	0.70	0.60	2.36	2.99	4.21	3.56	3.50	3.48	3.04	1.92	1.55	0.86	28.77
Maximum Precipitation (in.)	3.1	3.5	6.6	7.2	8.0	9.8	12.5	8.6	8.3	5.4	3.8	3.4	42.2
Minimum Precipitation (in.)	trace	0.1	0.1	0.3	0.9	0.6	0.4	0.1	0.3	trace	trace	trace	17.9
Maximum 24-hr. Precipitation (in.)	1.4	1.7	1.8	2.3	2.4	4.2	5.4	2.9	4.7	4.1	1.5	2.1	5.4
Days With ≥ 0.1" Precipitation	2	2	5	6	7	6	6	5	5	4	3	2	53
Days With ≥ 1.0" Precipitation	0	0	0	1	1	1	1	1	1	0	0	0	6
Mean Snowfall (in.)	5.9	4.9	5.3	1.8	trace	trace	trace	trace	trace	0.7	2.9	5.3	26.8
Maximum Snowfall (in.)	15	14	21	8	trace	0	0	0	1	3	9	20	59
Maximum 24-hr. Snowfall (in.)	8	7	8	6	trace	0	0	0	1	3	8	10	10
Days With ≥ 1.0" Snow Depth	16	11	5	1	0	0	0	0	0	0	3	9	45
Thunderstorm Days	< 1	< 1	2	4	7	9	8	8	5	2	1	< 1	46
Foggy Days	9	10	11	8	9	7	6	9	8	7	9	11	104
Predominant Sky Cover	OVR	OVR	OVR	OVR	OVR	OVR	CLR	CLR	CLR	CLR	OVR	OVR	OVR
Mean Relative Humidity 6am (%)	78	81	81	80	83	83	83	86	84	80	80	80	82
Mean Relative Humidity 3pm (%)	61	60	55	47	51	49	48	51	49	46	54	60	53
Mean Dewpoint (°F)	14	19	27	38	50	59	64	63	53	41	28	19	40
Prevailing Wind Direction	N	N	N	N	S	S	S	S	S	S	S	NNW	S
Prevailing Wind Speed (mph)	12	13	14	13	13	12	10	10	10	10	9	14	12
Maximum Wind Gust (mph)	63	55	60	64	55	84	62	79	55	58	59	53	84

Norfolk Karl Stefan Mem. Arpt.

Norfolk is located in northeastern Nebraska, in the valley of the Elkhorn River. The city of Norfolk lies at an average elevation of 1,550 feet above sea level. The surrounding country is moderately rolling in all directions. The terrain becomes more level to the south and southwest. Norfolk is situated near the western limit of the Corn Belt. To the east the climate and soils are favorable for diversified farming and dairying. To the west precipitation becomes lighter, and the farming country gives way to the grazing lands of the Great Plains. There are no local topographic features of sufficient importance to affect the climate of the area.

Northeast Nebraska has a climate typical of the interior of large continents in middle latitudes. The rainfall is moderate. Summers are hot and winters cold, and there are great variations in temperature and precipitation from day to day and from season to season. Most of the moisture which falls over this area is brought in from the Gulf of Mexico. The rapid changes in temperature are caused by the interchange of warm air from the south and southwest with cold air from the north. The rapid day to day changes in weather conditions produce an invigorating and healthful climate in northeast Nebraska.

Daily temperature ranges of 30 to 40 degrees are not uncommon. Summertime precipitation is almost wholly in the form of showers and thunderstorms. Practically all precipitation in the colder months is in the form of snow. As a rule, nearly 85 percent of the snowfall occurs from December to March and the ground is covered by snow during this period.

Norfolk is subject to the strong and persistent winds which prevail over the Great Plains states. Winds of 40 to 50 mph are not uncommon in this area, and gusts up to 100 mph have been recorded at Norfolk. Prevailing winds are from the south and southwest from May through September, with prevailing northwesterly winds during the remainder of the year.

Based on the 1951-1980 period, the average first occurrence of 32 degrees Fahrenheit in the fall is October 5 and the average last occurrence in the spring is May 1.

Norfolk Karl Stefan Mem. Arpt. *Madison County*   Elevation: 1,548 ft.   Latitude: 41° 59' N   Longitude: 97° 26' W

	JAN	FEB	MAR	APR	MAY	JUN	JUL	AUG	SEP	OCT	NOV	DEC	YEAR
Mean Maximum Temp. (°F)	30.3	36.4	47.5	61.2	72.6	82.7	86.9	84.4	76.3	63.8	45.9	33.9	60.2
Mean Temp. (°F)	20.0	26.2	36.7	49.4	60.9	70.9	75.4	73.2	63.8	51.2	35.7	24.2	49.0
Mean Minimum Temp. (°F)	9.8	15.9	25.8	37.6	49.2	59.0	63.9	61.9	51.2	38.6	25.5	14.4	37.7
Extreme Maximum Temp. (°F)	71	74	88	95	99	106	108	107	101	95	82	70	108
Extreme Minimum Temp. (°F)	-27	-26	-14	2	24	38	42	40	26	11	-13	-30	-30
Days Maximum Temp. ≥ 90°F	0	0	0	1	1	7	12	8	3	0	0	0	32
Days Maximum Temp. ≤ 32°F	16	11	5	0	0	0	0	0	0	0	4	14	50
Days Minimum Temp. ≤ 32°F	31	26	23	9	1	0	0	0	1	8	24	30	153
Days Minimum Temp. ≤ 0°F	9	4	1	0	0	0	0	0	0	0	1	4	19
Heating Degree Days (base 65°F)	1,389	1,091	872	472	172	26	3	9	127	428	873	1,260	6,722
Cooling Degree Days (base 65°F)	0	0	0	15	51	204	324	267	99	8	0	0	968
Mean Precipitation (in.)	0.57	0.73	1.98	2.64	3.95	4.18	3.61	2.80	2.48	1.73	1.38	0.65	26.70
Maximum Precipitation (in.)	2.3	3.2	7.3	7.5	8.6	12.2	9.1	6.0	8.1	4.6	4.0	2.3	36.2
Minimum Precipitation (in.)	0.1	trace	trace	0.2	1.0	0.5	0.3	0.5	0.3	trace	trace	0.1	15.8
Maximum 24-hr. Precipitation (in.)	1.3	2.4	2.4	1.5	3.4	5.4	3.3	5.1	3.9	2.1	1.5	1.1	5.4
Days With ≥ 0.1" Precipitation	1	2	4	6	8	6	6	5	5	4	3	2	52
Days With ≥ 1.0" Precipitation	0	0	0	1	1	1	1	1	1	0	0	0	6
Mean Snowfall (in.)	5.9	5.5	6.0	2.7	trace	trace	trace	trace	trace	0.7	4.6	6.0	31.4
Maximum Snowfall (in.)	16	23	21	13	trace	0	0	0	1	7	23	19	64
Maximum 24-hr. Snowfall (in.)	13	19	10	10	trace	0	0	0	1	6	14	9	19
Days With ≥ 1.0" Snow Depth	17	12	7	1	0	0	0	0	0	0	4	15	56
Thunderstorm Days	< 1	< 1	1	4	8	10	10	9	5	2	1	< 1	50
Foggy Days	8	10	11	9	9	7	8	11	9	8	8	9	107
Predominant Sky Cover	OVR	OVR	OVR	OVR	OVR	OVR	CLR	CLR	CLR	CLR	OVR	OVR	OVR
Mean Relative Humidity 6am (%)	76	79	81	79	81	82	84	86	84	79	79	78	81
Mean Relative Humidity 3pm (%)	60	60	55	44	46	46	47	49	46	43	52	61	51
Mean Dewpoint (°F)	11	16	25	34	46	56	62	61	50	43	37	25	37
Prevailing Wind Direction	NNW	NNW	NNW	NNW	S	S	S	S	S	NNW	NNW	NNW	NNW
Prevailing Wind Speed (mph)	17	17	18	18	16	15	14	14	14	16	18	17	16
Maximum Wind Gust (mph)	64	62	71	74	62	76	78	82	81	61	84	64	84

North Platte Lee Bird Field

The climate of North Platte is characterized throughout the year by frequent rapid changes in the weather. During the winter, most North Pacific lows cross the country north of North Platte. The passage usually brings little or no snowfall, and only a moderate drop in temperature. Only when there is a major outbreak of cold air from Canada does the temperature fall to zero or below. The duration of below-zero temperature is hardly more than two mornings, and by the third or fourth day the temperature is ordinarily rising to the 40s or higher. Snowfall at the onset of a cold outbreak is usually less than two inches.

Only when a low moves from the middle Rockies through Nebraska, allowing easterly winds to draw moist air into the low circulation, does snowfall of appreciable amounts occur. Few of these storms move slowly enough, or are intense enough, to deposit much precipitation in the North Platte area. However, during some winters the cold outbreak and intense low from the mid-Rockies combine to produce severe cold and snow several inches in depth, with blizzard conditions following. During and after these snowfalls and blizzards, rail and highway traffic may be stalled until the snow is cleared. Widespread loss of unsheltered livestock and wild life results from such conditions.

The sudden and frequent weather changes of the winter continue through spring with decreasing intensity of temperature changes but increasing precipitation. The summer and fall months bring frequent changes from hot to cool weather. Most summer and fall precipitation is associated with thunderstorms, so the amounts are extremely variable. The surrounding area is occasionally damaged by locally severe winds and hailstorms.

Temperatures may reach into the upper 90s and lower 100s frequently during the summer months, but the elevation and clear skies bring rapid cooling after sunset to lows in the 60s or below by daybreak. Since the humidity is generally low, the extremely hot days of summer are not uncomfortable.

Based on the 1951-1980 period, the average first occurrence of 32 degrees Fahrenheit in the fall is September 24 and the average last occurrence in the spring is May 11.

North Platte Lee Bird Field *Lincoln County*   Elevation: 2,775 ft.   Latitude: 41° 07' N   Longitude: 100° 40' W

	JAN	FEB	MAR	APR	MAY	JUN	JUL	AUG	SEP	OCT	NOV	DEC	YEAR
Mean Maximum Temp. (°F)	35.7	42.4	50.9	61.8	71.4	81.7	87.5	85.9	77.4	65.2	48.7	39.1	62.3
Mean Temp. (°F)	22.8	28.8	37.3	47.8	58.1	68.1	73.9	72.1	62.1	49.5	35.0	25.7	48.4
Mean Minimum Temp. (°F)	9.8	15.2	23.7	33.7	44.8	54.5	60.1	58.3	46.6	33.7	21.2	12.2	34.5
Extreme Maximum Temp. (°F)	73	76	86	98	102	106	108	104	102	94	82	75	108
Extreme Minimum Temp. (°F)	-23	-22	-14	7	19	30	39	35	17	10	-13	-34	-34
Days Maximum Temp. ≥ 90°F	0	0	0	0	1	6	13	11	4	0	0	0	35
Days Maximum Temp. ≤ 32°F	12	7	4	0	0	0	0	0	0	0	4	9	36
Days Minimum Temp. ≤ 32°F	31	28	26	14	2	0	0	0	2	14	28	31	176
Days Minimum Temp. ≤ 0°F	7	3	1	0	0	0	0	0	0	0	1	4	16
Heating Degree Days (base 65°F)	1,303	1,016	852	514	231	44	6	13	156	478	894	1,214	6,721
Cooling Degree Days (base 65°F)	0	0	0	6	26	148	292	248	78	3	0	0	801
Mean Precipitation (in.)	0.39	0.50	1.23	2.00	3.35	3.26	3.13	2.09	1.35	1.18	0.77	0.41	19.66
Maximum Precipitation (in.)	2.2	2.0	4.4	5.0	8.0	10.5	7.0	7.2	6.0	2.9	2.9	1.2	33.4
Minimum Precipitation (in.)	trace	trace	0	0.1	0.8	0.3	0.4	0.1	trace	0	trace	trace	10.5
Maximum 24-hr. Precipitation (in.)	1.3	1.1	1.8	2.2	2.2	3.6	3.1	3.8	2.5	1.3	1.1	0.7	3.8
Days With ≥ 0.1" Precipitation	1	1	3	5	7	6	6	4	3	3	2	1	42
Days With ≥ 1.0" Precipitation	0	0	0	0	1	1	1	0	0	0	0	0	3
Mean Snowfall (in.)	4.9	4.7	5.8	2.7	trace	trace	trace	trace	0.1	1.4	4.6	4.3	28.5
Maximum Snowfall (in.)	21	21	22	15	6	trace	0	0	3	16	18	14	49
Maximum 24-hr. Snowfall (in.)	12	9	12	9	6	trace	0	0	3	9	9	8	12
Days With ≥ 1.0" Snow Depth	12	7	4	1	0	0	0	0	0	1	4	8	37
Thunderstorm Days	< 1	< 1	1	3	7	10	11	9	4	1	< 1	0	46
Foggy Days	6	7	8	7	7	5	5	7	7	6	7	6	78
Predominant Sky Cover	OVR	OVR	OVR	OVR	OVR	OVR	SCT	SCT	CLR	CLR	OVR	OVR	OVR
Mean Relative Humidity 6am (%)	79	80	81	80	84	85	84	85	83	81	81	80	82
Mean Relative Humidity 3pm (%)	54	51	47	41	46	46	44	43	40	38	45	51	45
Mean Dewpoint (°F)	13	17	23	32	45	55	59	58	47	35	23	16	35
Prevailing Wind Direction	NW	NW	N	N	SSE	SSE	SSE	SSE	S	NW	NW	NW	NW
Prevailing Wind Speed (mph)	10	10	15	15	14	13	12	12	12	10	12	10	12
Maximum Wind Gust (mph)	60	61	76	76	73	73	68	74	58	68	60	63	76

Omaha Eppley Airfield

Omaha, Nebraska, is situated on the west bank of the Missouri River. The river level at Omaha is normally about 965 feet above sea level and the rolling hills in and around Omaha rise to about 1,300 feet above sea level. The climate is typically continental with relatively warm summers and cold, dry winters. It is situated midway between two distinctive climatic zones, the humid east and the dry west. Fluctuations between these two zones produce weather conditions for periods that are characteristic of either zone, or combinations of both. Omaha is also affected by most low pressure systems that cross the country. This causes periodic and rapid changes in weather, especially during the winter months.

Most of the precipitation in Omaha falls during sharp showers or thunderstorms, and these occur mostly during the growing season from April to September. Of the total precipitation, about 75 percent falls during this six-month period. The rain occurs mostly as evening or nighttime showers and thunderstorms. Although winters are relatively cold, precipitation is light, with only 10 percent of the total annual precipitation falling during the winter months.

Sunshine is fairly abundant, ranging around 50 percent of the possible in the winter to 75 percent of the possible in the summer.

Omaha Eppley Airfield *Douglas County*   Elevation: 980 ft.   Latitude: 41° 19' N   Longitude: 95° 54' W

	JAN	FEB	MAR	APR	MAY	JUN	JUL	AUG	SEP	OCT	NOV	DEC	YEAR
Mean Maximum Temp. (°F)	31.4	37.7	50.1	63.2	73.7	83.8	87.6	85.3	77.1	64.9	48.1	35.4	61.5
Mean Temp. (°F)	21.4	27.8	39.0	51.4	62.3	72.3	76.8	74.5	65.3	53.0	38.3	26.1	50.7
Mean Minimum Temp. (°F)	11.4	17.8	27.9	39.6	50.8	60.7	65.9	63.7	53.5	40.9	28.4	16.7	39.8
Extreme Maximum Temp. (°F)	67	78	89	97	98	104	110	107	103	95	83	69	110
Extreme Minimum Temp. (°F)	-23	-21	-11	5	27	38	44	44	25	13	-6	-23	-23
Days Maximum Temp. ≥ 90°F	0	0	0	1	1	7	12	9	3	0	0	0	33
Days Maximum Temp. ≤ 32°F	15	10	3	0	0	0	0	0	0	0	0	3	42
Days Minimum Temp. ≤ 32°F	30	26	21	7	1	0	0	0	0	0	6	21	30	142
Days Minimum Temp. ≤ 0°F	7	4	1	0	0	0	0	0	0	0	0	4	16
Heating Degree Days (base 65°F)	1,346	1,044	800	416	144	16	1	5	102	379	796	1,201	6,250
Cooling Degree Days (base 65°F)	0	0	1	16	59	226	362	296	116	11	1	0	1,088
Mean Precipitation (in.)	0.76	0.76	2.13	2.94	4.43	3.85	3.76	3.27	3.31	2.35	1.79	0.92	30.27
Maximum Precipitation (in.)	3.7	3.0	6.0	6.4	10.3	9.9	10.3	10.2	13.8	5.0	4.7	5.4	44.8
Minimum Precipitation (in.)	trace	0.1	0.1	0.4	0.6	1.0	0.4	0.6	0.4	trace	trace	trace	18.4
Maximum 24-hr. Precipitation (in.)	1.5	1.8	1.7	2.2	4.2	4.1	3.2	3.8	6.2	3.1	2.0	1.5	6.2
Days With ≥ 0.1" Precipitation	2	2	5	6	8	7	6	5	5	4	4	2	56
Days With ≥ 1.0" Precipitation	0	0	0	1	1	1	1	1	1	1	0	0	7
Mean Snowfall (in.)	6.4	5.7	4.7	1.2	trace	trace	trace	0.0	trace	0.5	3.3	4.9	26.7
Maximum Snowfall (in.)	23	25	27	10	1	0	0	0	trace	4	12	20	59
Maximum 24-hr. Snowfall (in.)	12	18	10	9	1	0	0	0	trace	4	8	10	18
Days With ≥ 1.0" Snow Depth	15	12	5	1	0	0	0	0	0	0	3	9	45
Thunderstorm Days	< 1	< 1	2	4	7	9	9	8	5	2	1	< 1	47
Foggy Days	11	11	12	9	10	8	8	12	11	10	10	12	124
Predominant Sky Cover	OVR	OVR	OVR	OVR	OVR	OVR	SCT	CLR	CLR	CLR	OVR	OVR	OVR
Mean Relative Humidity 6am (%)	78	80	79	77	80	82	84	87	86	81	80	80	81
Mean Relative Humidity 3pm (%)	61	59	54	46	49	50	52	54	51	47	55	62	53
Mean Dewpoint (°F)	13	18	26	37	49	60	65	63	54	41	29	19	40
Prevailing Wind Direction	NNW	NNW	NNW	SSE	SSE	SSE	SSE	SSE	SSE	SSE	SSE	SSE	SSE
Prevailing Wind Speed (mph)	15	14	15	12	12	10	9	9	10	9	9	9	12
Maximum Wind Gust (mph)	58	61	60	70	66	64	64	73	55	53	61	53	73

Omaha WSFO

Omaha, Nebraska, is situated on the west bank of the Missouri River. The river level at Omaha is normally about 965 feet above sea level and the rolling hills in and around Omaha rise to about 1,300 feet above sea level. The climate is typically continental with relatively warm summers and cold, dry winters. It is situated midway between two distinctive climatic zones, the humid east and the dry west. Fluctuations between these two zones produce weather conditions for periods that are characteristic of either zone, or combinations of both. Omaha is also affected by most low pressure systems that cross the country. This causes periodic and rapid changes in weather, especially during the winter months.

Most of the precipitation in Omaha falls during sharp showers or thunderstorms, and these occur mostly during the growing season from April to September. Of the total precipitation, about 75 percent falls during this six-month period. The rain occurs mostly as evening or nighttime showers and thunderstorms. Although winters are relatively cold, precipitation is light, with only 10 percent of the total annual precipitation falling during the winter months.

Sunshine is fairly abundant, ranging around 50 percent of the possible in the winter to 75 percent of the possible in the summer.

Omaha WSFO *Douglas County*   Elevation: 1,309 ft.   Latitude: 41° 22' N   Longitude: 96° 01' W

	JAN	FEB	MAR	APR	MAY	JUN	JUL	AUG	SEP	OCT	NOV	DEC	YEAR
Mean Maximum Temp. (°F)	30.2	36.7	48.3	61.8	72.3	82.0	85.7	83.5	75.6	63.6	46.6	34.3	60.0
Mean Temp. (°F)	21.3	27.8	38.4	51.2	62.2	71.7	76.3	74.0	65.5	53.2	38.0	26.1	50.5
Mean Minimum Temp. (°F)	12.4	18.8	28.4	40.4	52.1	61.5	66.5	64.4	55.1	42.8	29.3	17.9	40.8
Extreme Maximum Temp. (°F)	66	76	88	96	98	104	107	106	99	93	81	68	107
Extreme Minimum Temp. (°F)	-22	-25	-13	7	26	40	44	44	28	13	-3	-24	-25
Days Maximum Temp. ≥ 90°F	0	0	0	0	0	4	10	6	2	0	0	0	22
Days Maximum Temp. ≤ 32°F	16	11	4	0	0	0	0	0	0	0	4	13	48
Days Minimum Temp. ≤ 32°F	30	25	20	6	0	0	0	0	0	4	18	29	132
Days Minimum Temp. ≤ 0°F	7	3	0	0	0	0	0	0	0	0	0	3	13
Heating Degree Days (base 65°F)	1,349	1,046	820	424	144	17	2	6	99	371	804	1,199	6,281
Cooling Degree Days (base 65°F)	0	0	2	17	63	222	365	297	126	13	0	0	1,105
Mean Precipitation (in.)	0.76	0.74	2.32	3.12	4.64	3.79	3.61	3.01	3.13	2.56	1.64	0.93	30.25
Maximum Precipitation (in.)	1.6	2.4	5.3	7.1	9.0	8.8	9.7	7.9	14.1	5.3	5.1	4.4	41.7
Minimum Precipitation (in.)	trace	0.1	0.1	0.3	0.5	0.9	1.1	0.6	1.0	0.1	trace	0.1	21.3
Maximum 24-hr. Precipitation (in.)	0.9	0.9	2.0	2.2	3.1	2.6	3.7	2.8	5.3	2.7	2.2	2.7	5.3
Days With ≥ 0.1" Precipitation	2	2	5	6	8	6	6	5	6	4	3	3	56
Days With ≥ 1.0" Precipitation	0	0	0	1	1	1	1	1	1	1	0	0	7
Mean Snowfall (in.)	7.2	5.4	5.1	1.7	trace	0.0	trace	0.0	trace	0.9	3.6	4.4	28.3
Maximum Snowfall (in.)	17	22	18	10	1	0	0	0	trace	6	14	19	74
Maximum 24-hr. Snowfall (in.)	9	8	9	9	1	0	0	0	trace	6	9	8	9
Days With ≥ 1.0" Snow Depth	16	12	6	1	0	0	0	0	0	0	3	9	47
Thunderstorm Days	< 1	< 1	2	3	7	9	9	8	6	2	1	< 1	47
Foggy Days	8	10	11	9	10	6	7	10	8	8	10	10	107
Predominant Sky Cover	OVR	OVR	OVR	OVR	OVR	OVR	CLR	CLR	CLR	CLR	OVR	OVR	OVR
Mean Relative Humidity 6am (%)	75	77	78	76	79	79	85	87	84	78	78	77	79
Mean Relative Humidity 3pm (%)	58	58	54	47	51	51	57	57	54	50	61	64	55
Mean Dewpoint (°F)	16	18	29	37	50	58	64	62	54	39	27	18	39
Prevailing Wind Direction	NW	NW	SSE	NW	SSE	SSE	SSE	SSE	S	S	NW	NW	SSE
Prevailing Wind Speed (mph)	14	13	10	14	10	10	9	9	10	10	14	14	12
Maximum Wind Gust (mph)	59	53	54	55	55	51	73	55	48	48	49	47	73

Scottsbluff County Airport

Scottsbluff is located in the North Platte river valley that extends from central Wyoming southeast across western Nebraska. The valley is approximately 20 miles wide in the vicinity of Scottsbluff with a range of hills both to the north and south, parallel to the river. To the south the hills average 600 to 700 feet above the river with some projections upward to 1,000 feet. To the north, rolling hills range from 300 to 400 feet higher than the river.

Due to the protection of the higher hills to the south, southerly winds in the valley are rare. Prevailing winds are west to northwest during the winter months and east to southeast during the summer months. West to northwest winds are intensified by the funneling action of the valley and velocities of 30 to 50 mph are common during the winter and early spring. Quite often these winds are warmed by the downslope (chinook) effect from the higher elevations to the west and bring rapid warming and melting of the snow. Outbreaks of Arctic air bring cold wave conditions about five times each season. Snow with strong winds causing blowing and drifting snow occur several times each winter with a severe blizzard of extended duration occurring about once every thirty years. Easterly winds during the winter and early spring cause upslope conditions with low cloudiness and precipitation.

The average temperature is in the upper 40s. Summertime highs generally range from the 80s to the 90s with lows around 60. Summer temperatures of 100 degrees are reached or exceeded at least once each summer. In winter, highs average about 40 degrees with lows in the teens. Temperatures of zero or below occur about 15 times each winter.

Most of the precipitation occurs as thunderstorms during the spring and summer months. Severe thunderstorms with destructive hail are quite common during the late spring and summer. Tornadoes are infrequent and usually of short duration.

The Platte River in the vicinity of Scottsbluff is a wide shallow stream and has very little effect on the climate. Water stored in numerous upstream reservoirs is used for extensive irrigation in the valley. Lowland flooding occurs when heavy rains fall upstream and a greater than normal amount of water is being released from the upstream reservoirs.

Based on the 1951-1980 period, the average first occurrence of 32 degrees Fahrenheit in the fall is September 29 and the average last occurrence in the spring is May 7.

Scottsbluff County Airport *Scotts Bluff County* Elevation: 3,943 ft. Latitude: 41° 52' N Longitude: 103° 36' W

	JAN	FEB	MAR	APR	MAY	JUN	JUL	AUG	SEP	OCT	NOV	DEC	YEAR
Mean Maximum Temp. (°F)	38.1	44.4	51.5	60.9	71.2	82.4	89.0	87.3	77.7	64.8	49.0	40.2	63.0
Mean Temp. (°F)	25.2	30.8	37.8	46.8	57.3	67.7	73.8	72.0	61.8	49.0	35.6	26.8	48.7
Mean Minimum Temp. (°F)	12.3	17.1	24.1	32.6	43.4	53.1	58.5	56.6	45.7	33.3	22.1	13.4	34.3
Extreme Maximum Temp. (°F)	74	74	83	93	94	106	109	104	102	91	80	77	109
Extreme Minimum Temp. (°F)	-25	-27	-21	-8	15	33	41	40	19	-6	-11	-42	-42
Days Maximum Temp. ≥ 90°F	0	0	0	0	1	8	16	13	5	0	0	0	43
Days Maximum Temp. ≤ 32°F	10	6	3	1	0	0	0	0	0	0	4	8	32
Days Minimum Temp. ≤ 32°F	30	27	27	15	2	0	0	0	2	13	27	30	173
Days Minimum Temp. ≤ 0°F	6	3	1	0	0	0	0	0	0	0	1	5	16
Heating Degree Days (base 65°F)	1,227	960	837	542	251	52	6	10	156	489	877	1,176	6,583
Cooling Degree Days (base 65°F)	0	0	0	2	21	135	280	240	67	1	0	0	746
Mean Precipitation (in.)	0.54	0.56	1.16	1.77	2.70	2.71	2.11	1.19	1.15	0.98	0.80	0.57	16.24
Maximum Precipitation (in.)	1.3	1.9	2.6	3.9	7.3	6.6	4.8	3.4	4.2	3.0	2.1	1.5	24.8
Minimum Precipitation (in.)	trace	trace	0.2	0.3	0.3	0.6	0.2	0.1	trace	trace	trace	trace	7.7
Maximum 24-hr. Precipitation (in.)	0.7	0.9	1.4	1.3	2.3	3.2	2.5	1.8	2.6	1.1	1.4	0.9	3.2
Days With ≥ 0.1" Precipitation	2	2	4	5	6	6	5	3	3	3	2	2	43
Days With ≥ 1.0" Precipitation	0	0	0	0	0	1	0	0	0	0	0	0	1
Mean Snowfall (in.)	6.9	6.0	9.1	5.6	0.6	trace	trace	trace	0.5	2.7	6.6	7.1	45.1
Maximum Snowfall (in.)	24	23	24	18	8	trace	0	0	5	22	19	18	67
Maximum 24-hr. Snowfall (in.)	9	10	12	8	3	trace	0	0	5	7	8	11	12
Days With ≥ 1.0" Snow Depth	13	7	5	2	0	0	0	0	0	1	5	11	44
Thunderstorm Days	0	0	< 1	2	8	11	11	8	4	1	< 1	< 1	45
Foggy Days	3	3	5	4	4	3	2	3	4	3	4	3	41
Predominant Sky Cover	OVR	OVR	OVR	OVR	OVR	CLR	CLR	CLR	CLR	CLR	OVR	OVR	OVR
Mean Relative Humidity 6am (%)	73	76	77	76	77	76	75	80	78	76	75	75	76
Mean Relative Humidity 3pm (%)	50	45	43	38	40	37	34	34	32	34	43	51	40
Mean Dewpoint (°F)	13	17	22	29	41	49	54	53	42	31	21	16	32
Prevailing Wind Direction	WNW	WNW	WNW	WNW	ESE	ESE	ESE	ESE	ESE	NW	WNW	WNW	WNW
Prevailing Wind Speed (mph)	14	13	14	15	13	12	10	10	10	12	13	13	13
Maximum Wind Gust (mph)	74	62	61	63	63	70	68	66	54	54	56	56	74

Valentine Miller Field

Valentine, located near the northern edge of the Sandhills and cattle country of Nebraska, is near the extreme northern border of the state. The city lies in the valley of the Niobrara River, a branch of the Missouri River, about 160 miles above the junction with the Missouri. It is the county seat of Cherry County and had its beginning in the fall of 1882.

The inland location offers a wide variety of weather. The high afternoon temperatures during the two warmest months, July and August, average nearly 90 degrees and the corresponding humidity averages about 40 percent. Uncomfortably warm nights are few with low morning temperatures averaging about 60 degrees. The temperature seldom reaches 100 degrees or more during the summer. The two coldest months are January and February. The minimum temperature generally reaches -20 degrees or colder once each winter.

Valentines location frequently places it in the path of cold Canadian air mass outbreaks during the cold season, alternating with mild, dry air moving across the Rockies from the Pacific. One or two bitterly cold days usually occur each winter when the temperature will stay below zero throughout the day. Blizzards are not frequent, but at least one is likely each winter season. An occasional severe blizzard occurs about once in every three or four winters. Blowing and drifting snow reduce visibility to zero and bring outdoor activities and travel to a complete stop. Lives may be lost for anyone caught away from shelter, and there is usually loss of livestock which varies with the intensity and duration of the storm. Temperatures below 32 degrees have occurred as late as mid-June and as early as early September, and low temperature records in the 30s have occurred during the summer with light frost in low places. However, these are rare occurrences and temperatures below 50 degrees are not common in July and August.

About 65 percent of the annual precipitation falls during the growing season, May through September, and is predominantly the nighttime thunderstorm type with June being the wettest month.

The spring and fall seasons have mostly pleasant days, with the fall season having the most uniform character with lighter winds and gradually falling temperatures as the season progresses. In the spring the weather is windy and extremely variable, with summer-like days mixed with some of cold of winter. The widest extremes of temperature occur in March.

Some of the damaging weather elements other than blizzards, are high winds, which dig blow outs in the sand hills, and an occasional hailstorm. Tornadoes occasionally occur but seldom do much damage.

Valentine Miller Field *Cherry County*   Elevation: 2,588 ft.   Latitude: 42° 52' N   Longitude: 100° 33' W

	JAN	FEB	MAR	APR	MAY	JUN	JUL	AUG	SEP	OCT	NOV	DEC	YEAR
Mean Maximum Temp. (°F)	33.2	39.0	47.6	59.4	71.1	81.9	88.2	86.7	76.9	63.3	46.1	36.6	60.8
Mean Temp. (°F)	20.2	26.1	34.7	46.0	57.6	67.9	74.0	72.3	61.7	48.4	33.3	23.5	47.1
Mean Minimum Temp. (°F)	7.2	13.2	21.8	32.6	44.2	53.9	59.6	57.9	46.4	33.4	20.5	10.3	33.4
Extreme Maximum Temp. (°F)	72	78	85	100	99	110	114	106	104	96	86	74	114
Extreme Minimum Temp. (°F)	-30	-31	-29	3	21	33	38	34	17	-1	-19	-39	-39
Days Maximum Temp. ≥ 90°F	0	0	0	0	1	7	14	13	6	0	0	0	41
Days Maximum Temp. ≤ 32°F	14	9	5	1	0	0	0	0	0	0	6	11	46
Days Minimum Temp. ≤ 32°F	31	28	27	15	3	0	0	0	2	14	27	31	178
Days Minimum Temp. ≤ 0°F	10	5	1	0	0	0	0	0	0	0	2	6	24
Heating Degree Days (base 65°F)	1,384	1,091	932	567	250	54	9	17	172	512	944	1,281	7,213
Cooling Degree Days (base 65°F)	0	0	0	6	31	142	289	249	81	4	0	0	802
Mean Precipitation (in.)	0.30	0.44	1.10	1.98	3.15	2.98	3.31	2.22	1.62	1.19	0.72	0.34	19.35
Maximum Precipitation (in.)	0.8	1.3	4.2	4.0	6.7	7.1	9.0	6.7	5.9	3.8	2.6	1.8	32.7
Minimum Precipitation (in.)	trace	0.1	0.2	0.3	0.4	0.4	0.3	0.4	0.3	trace	trace	trace	10.6
Maximum 24-hr. Precipitation (in.)	0.5	0.7	1.6	1.2	2.2	3.0	3.4	3.2	2.4	1.8	1.1	1.2	3.4
Days With ≥ 0.1" Precipitation	1	2	3	5	7	6	6	4	4	3	2	1	44
Days With ≥ 1.0" Precipitation	0	0	0	0	1	1	1	1	0	0	0	0	4
Mean Snowfall (in.)	4.7	6.1	8.4	5.0	0.1	trace	0.0	trace	0.7	1.7	6.3	4.9	37.9
Maximum Snowfall (in.)	15	16	51	30	3	0	0	0	18	12	35	23	84
Maximum 24-hr. Snowfall (in.)	7	8	17	9	3	0	0	0	18	6	14	18	18
Days With ≥ 1.0" Snow Depth	13	12	7	2	0	0	0	0	0	1	6	12	53
Thunderstorm Days	0	< 1	1	4	10	15	19	17	10	1	< 1	0	77
Foggy Days	4	7	12	10	9	9	6	9	10	7	9	6	98
Predominant Sky Cover	OVR	OVR	OVR	OVR	OVR	OVR	SCT	SCT	CLR	CLR	OVR	CLR	OVR
Mean Relative Humidity 6am (%)	73	74	77	75	76	77	76	78	74	74	74	73	75
Mean Relative Humidity 3pm (%)	54	51	47	40	41	40	39	40	35	38	47	51	43
Mean Dewpoint (°F)	10	14	22	30	41	51	55	54	43	31	20	12	32
Prevailing Wind Direction	NW	NNW	NNW	NNW	SSE	SSE	S	S	S	WNW	WNW	WNW	WNW
Prevailing Wind Speed (mph)	13	13	13	13	15	13	12	13	13	8	8	8	12
Maximum Wind Gust (mph)	na	na	na	na	na	na	na	na	na	54	40	51	54

Agate 3 E *Sioux County*   Elevation: 4,668 ft.   Latitude: 42° 25' N   Longitude: 103° 44' W

	JAN	FEB	MAR	APR	MAY	JUN	JUL	AUG	SEP	OCT	NOV	DEC	YEAR
Mean Maximum Temp. (°F)	37.1	42.7	50.4	59.8	70.2	80.5	87.9	87.2	77.4	64.7	48.1	38.2	62.0
Mean Temp. (°F)	22.4	27.8	35.2	43.7	54.1	63.6	69.9	68.7	58.4	46.2	32.6	22.7	45.4
Mean Minimum Temp. (°F)	7.6	12.9	20.0	27.7	37.9	46.6	51.9	50.2	39.4	27.5	17.0	7.2	28.8
Extreme Maximum Temp. (°F)	69	72	80	90	92	106	108	102	98	90	79	69	108
Extreme Minimum Temp. (°F)	-34	-37	-27	-17	13	21	29	27	5	-11	-19	-44	-44
Days Maximum Temp. ≥ 90°F	0	0	0	0	0	5	14	13	4	0	0	0	36
Days Maximum Temp. ≤ 32°F	9	6	3	1	0	0	0	0	0	0	4	9	32
Days Minimum Temp. ≤ 32°F	30	28	29	22	8	1	0	0	7	22	29	31	207
Days Minimum Temp. ≤ 0°F	8	5	1	0	0	0	0	0	0	0	2	7	23
Heating Degree Days (base 65°F)	1,316	1,044	912	633	336	101	18	24	220	577	966	1,308	7,455
Cooling Degree Days (base 65°F)	0	0	0	0	7	67	182	151	29	1	0	0	437
Mean Precipitation (in.)	0.27	0.28	0.58	1.23	2.80	2.31	1.99	1.61	1.28	1.00	0.38	0.26	13.99
Days With ≥ 0.1" Precipitation	1	1	2	3	6	5	5	4	3	3	1	1	35
Days With ≥ 1.0" Precipitation	0	0	0	0	1	0	0	0	0	0	0	0	1
Mean Snowfall (in.)	3.9	4.2	5.6	4.8	1.0	trace	0.0	0.0	0.5	2.1	4.6	4.8	31.5
Days With ≥ 1.0" Snow Depth	15	9	5	2	0	0	0	0	0	1	6	13	51

Ainsworth *Brown County*   Elevation: 2,509 ft.   Latitude: 42° 33' N   Longitude: 99° 51' W

	JAN	FEB	MAR	APR	MAY	JUN	JUL	AUG	SEP	OCT	NOV	DEC	YEAR
Mean Maximum Temp. (°F)	33.3	39.3	48.4	60.4	71.4	81.5	87.2	85.4	76.7	64.2	46.1	36.8	60.9
Mean Temp. (°F)	22.9	28.6	36.9	48.1	59.4	69.2	74.7	73.1	63.8	51.6	35.9	26.5	49.2
Mean Minimum Temp. (°F)	12.4	17.9	25.5	35.8	47.2	56.8	62.1	60.6	50.8	39.0	25.6	16.2	37.5
Extreme Maximum Temp. (°F)	69	76	86	97	95	103	107	102	100	92	84	72	107
Extreme Minimum Temp. (°F)	-24	-26	-20	7	24	35	42	43	25	7	-13	-30	-30
Days Maximum Temp. ≥ 90°F	0	0	0	0	0	5	12	9	4	0	0	0	30
Days Maximum Temp. ≤ 32°F	13	9	4	0	0	0	0	0	0	0	5	11	42
Days Minimum Temp. ≤ 32°F	29	25	23	11	1	0	0	0	1	7	22	29	148
Days Minimum Temp. ≤ 0°F	7	4	1	0	0	0	0	0	0	0	1	4	17
Heating Degree Days (base 65°F)	1,299	1,021	863	507	204	34	6	10	127	418	867	1,188	6,544
Cooling Degree Days (base 65°F)	0	0	0	10	37	160	305	261	95	9	0	0	877
Mean Precipitation (in.)	0.41	0.56	1.45	2.35	3.37	3.25	3.49	2.63	2.51	1.49	1.01	0.42	22.94
Days With ≥ 0.1" Precipitation	1	2	3	5	7	6	6	5	4	3	2	1	45
Days With ≥ 1.0" Precipitation	0	0	0	0	1	1	1	1	1	0	0	0	5
Mean Snowfall (in.)	5.5	5.7	8.7	5.4	trace	trace	0.0	0.0	0.3	1.9	7.6	5.7	40.8
Days With ≥ 1.0" Snow Depth	17	12	7	2	0	0	0	0	0	1	7	13	59

Albion 1 N *Boone County*   Elevation: 1,758 ft.   Latitude: 41° 42' N   Longitude: 98° 00' W

	JAN	FEB	MAR	APR	MAY	JUN	JUL	AUG	SEP	OCT	NOV	DEC	YEAR
Mean Maximum Temp. (°F)	31.5	37.7	47.8	61.1	72.0	82.4	87.0	84.7	77.0	64.6	46.2	35.3	60.6
Mean Temp. (°F)	20.2	26.2	35.9	48.1	59.4	69.7	74.3	72.2	63.0	50.4	34.9	24.3	48.2
Mean Minimum Temp. (°F)	8.9	14.6	23.9	35.0	46.7	56.9	61.6	59.7	49.0	36.2	23.6	13.3	35.8
Extreme Maximum Temp. (°F)	72	78	90	95	99	105	106	105	101	94	82	71	106
Extreme Minimum Temp. (°F)	-29	-25	-16	3	21	37	39	40	21	8	-13	-27	-29
Days Maximum Temp. ≥ 90°F	0	0	0	0	1	6	12	9	4	0	0	0	32
Days Maximum Temp. ≤ 32°F	16	10	5	0	0	0	0	0	0	0	4	12	47
Days Minimum Temp. ≤ 32°F	31	27	25	12	2	0	0	0	1	10	25	31	164
Days Minimum Temp. ≤ 0°F	9	5	1	0	0	0	0	0	0	0	1	4	20
Heating Degree Days (base 65°F)	1,382	1,091	896	507	207	35	7	13	139	451	896	1,255	6,879
Cooling Degree Days (base 65°F)	0	0	0	8	38	181	292	240	87	7	0	0	853
Mean Precipitation (in.)	0.43	0.66	2.22	2.74	4.13	3.90	3.55	3.06	2.66	1.77	1.52	0.55	27.19
Days With ≥ 0.1" Precipitation	1	2	4	6	8	6	6	5	5	4	3	2	52
Days With ≥ 1.0" Precipitation	0	0	1	1	1	1	1	1	1	0	0	0	7
Mean Snowfall (in.)	5.1	6.0	6.4	2.1	0.0	0.0	0.0	0.0	trace	0.5	4.4	6.1	30.6
Days With ≥ 1.0" Snow Depth	15	12	6	1	0	0	0	0	0	0	4	12	50

Alliance 1 WNW *Box Butte County*   Elevation: 3,992 ft.   Latitude: 42° 07' N   Longitude: 102° 54' W

	JAN	FEB	MAR	APR	MAY	JUN	JUL	AUG	SEP	OCT	NOV	DEC	YEAR
Mean Maximum Temp. (°F)	36.2	42.8	49.0	58.5	68.9	80.2	87.5	86.0	75.7	63.0	47.3	38.8	61.2
Mean Temp. (°F)	23.3	29.4	35.8	45.0	55.7	66.2	72.6	71.0	60.4	47.8	34.2	25.7	47.3
Mean Minimum Temp. (°F)	10.4	16.0	22.4	31.5	42.5	52.1	57.7	55.8	45.1	32.5	21.0	12.8	33.3
Extreme Maximum Temp. (°F)	70	72	82	90	93	105	110	104	102	91	80	71	110
Extreme Minimum Temp. (°F)	-27	-28	-25	-12	19	28	40	39	18	-8	-11	-42	-42
Days Maximum Temp. ≥ 90°F	0	0	0	0	0	5	14	11	3	0	0	0	33
Days Maximum Temp. ≤ 32°F	11	7	4	1	0	0	0	0	0	0	5	9	37
Days Minimum Temp. ≤ 32°F	30	27	28	17	3	0	0	0	2	15	27	30	179
Days Minimum Temp. ≤ 0°F	7	3	1	0	0	0	0	0	0	0	1	4	16
Heating Degree Days (base 65°F)	1,288	999	898	594	297	72	11	16	187	527	915	1,212	7,016
Cooling Degree Days (base 65°F)	0	0	0	1	17	110	259	218	61	1	0	0	667
Mean Precipitation (in.)	0.37	0.31	0.77	1.66	2.95	2.85	2.10	1.57	1.37	0.87	0.55	0.36	15.73
Days With ≥ 0.1" Precipitation	1	1	2	4	7	6	5	4	3	2	2	1	38
Days With ≥ 1.0" Precipitation	0	0	0	0	1	1	1	0	0	0	0	0	3
Mean Snowfall (in.)	na	3.6	6.4	3.0	trace	trace	0.0	0.0	0.2	1.8	4.7	na	na
Days With ≥ 1.0" Snow Depth	10	6	4	1	0	0	0	0	0	1	6	7	35

Anselmo 2 SE *Custer County* Elevation: 2,604 ft. Latitude: 41° 36' N Longitude: 99° 50' W

	JAN	FEB	MAR	APR	MAY	JUN	JUL	AUG	SEP	OCT	NOV	DEC	YEAR
Mean Maximum Temp. (°F)	34.9	41.4	50.6	62.1	72.4	82.2	87.5	85.5	77.1	65.0	47.5	37.9	62.0
Mean Temp. (°F)	22.3	28.4	37.1	47.8	58.5	68.4	73.7	71.9	62.3	49.8	34.8	25.5	48.4
Mean Minimum Temp. (°F)	9.7	15.2	23.4	33.3	44.6	54.6	59.9	58.2	47.5	34.7	22.0	13.2	34.7
Extreme Maximum Temp. (°F)	72	78	88	93	97	105	108	109	101	92	82	71	109
Extreme Minimum Temp. (°F)	-32	-28	-24	5	18	32	35	36	16	5	-19	-32	-32
Days Maximum Temp. ≥ 90°F	0	0	0	0	1	6	13	10	4	0	0	0	34
Days Maximum Temp. ≤ 32°F	12	8	4	0	0	0	0	0	0	0	4	10	38
Days Minimum Temp. ≤ 32°F	31	27	26	15	3	0	0	0	2	13	26	31	174
Days Minimum Temp. ≤ 0°F	8	4	1	0	0	0	0	0	0	0	1	5	19
Heating Degree Days (base 65°F)	1,320	1,027	860	515	226	44	7	13	152	466	898	1,220	6,748
Cooling Degree Days (base 65°F)	0	0	0	7	32	146	274	230	78	4	0	0	771
Mean Precipitation (in.)	0.48	0.58	1.65	2.67	3.69	4.01	3.47	2.80	2.40	1.50	1.25	0.50	25.00
Days With ≥ 0.1" Precipitation	1	2	4	5	7	6	6	5	4	3	3	1	47
Days With ≥ 1.0" Precipitation	0	0	0	1	1	1	1	1	1	0	0	0	6
Mean Snowfall (in.)	6.0	5.3	7.9	3.7	trace	0.0	0.0	0.0	0.1	1.5	7.2	6.2	37.9
Days With ≥ 1.0" Snow Depth	16	11	6	2	0	0	0	0	0	1	7	12	55

Arthur *Arthur County* Elevation: 3,497 ft. Latitude: 41° 34' N Longitude: 101° 41' W

	JAN	FEB	MAR	APR	MAY	JUN	JUL	AUG	SEP	OCT	NOV	DEC	YEAR
Mean Maximum Temp. (°F)	36.0	42.0	49.6	59.9	70.1	80.3	86.9	85.2	75.9	63.7	47.8	39.1	61.4
Mean Temp. (°F)	23.3	28.8	36.2	46.2	56.6	66.5	72.8	71.2	61.1	48.4	34.6	26.1	47.7
Mean Minimum Temp. (°F)	10.0	15.4	22.7	32.3	43.2	52.7	58.6	57.0	46.4	33.0	21.4	12.8	33.8
Extreme Maximum Temp. (°F)	71	76	81	93	95	104	106	104	100	91	80	69	106
Extreme Minimum Temp. (°F)	-25	-29	-23	-1	17	32	37	36	14	-1	-12	-33	-33
Days Maximum Temp. ≥ 90°F	0	0	0	0	0	5	13	10	3	0	0	0	31
Days Maximum Temp. ≤ 32°F	11	7	4	0	0	0	0	0	0	0	5	9	36
Days Minimum Temp. ≤ 32°F	31	28	27	15	3	0	0	0	2	14	27	31	178
Days Minimum Temp. ≤ 0°F	8	4	1	0	0	0	0	0	0	0	1	5	19
Heating Degree Days (base 65°F)	1,287	1,017	887	566	270	65	10	17	173	510	904	1,199	6,905
Cooling Degree Days (base 65°F)	0	0	0	3	21	121	264	228	70	2	0	0	709
Mean Precipitation (in.)	0.34	0.39	1.13	1.89	3.32	2.73	3.22	1.84	1.68	1.02	0.69	0.37	18.62
Days With ≥ 0.1" Precipitation	1	2	3	4	6	6	6	4	4	2	2	1	41
Days With ≥ 1.0" Precipitation	0	0	0	0	1	0	1	0	0	0	0	0	2
Mean Snowfall (in.)	5.5	4.6	8.3	4.9	0.2	trace	trace	trace	0.3	1.3	5.3	4.8	35.2
Days With ≥ 1.0" Snow Depth	16	10	8	2	0	0	0	0	0	1	7	13	57

Ashland 2 *Saunders County* Elevation: 1,069 ft. Latitude: 41° 03' N Longitude: 96° 21' W

	JAN	FEB	MAR	APR	MAY	JUN	JUL	AUG	SEP	OCT	NOV	DEC	YEAR
Mean Maximum Temp. (°F)	31.9	38.5	49.7	62.8	73.0	83.1	87.7	85.6	77.8	65.8	48.8	36.1	61.7
Mean Temp. (°F)	21.0	27.3	38.1	50.6	61.4	71.7	76.5	74.2	65.2	52.8	38.1	26.3	50.3
Mean Minimum Temp. (°F)	10.1	16.0	26.5	38.4	49.7	60.3	65.2	62.8	52.6	39.8	27.3	16.5	38.8
Extreme Maximum Temp. (°F)	72	79	90	97	100	104	110	110	104	95	85	72	110
Extreme Minimum Temp. (°F)	-33	-25	-16	3	27	41	41	42	25	11	-6	-26	-33
Days Maximum Temp. ≥ 90°F	0	0	0	1	1	7	12	10	5	0	0	0	36
Days Maximum Temp. ≤ 32°F	16	10	4	0	0	0	0	0	0	0	3	12	45
Days Minimum Temp. ≤ 32°F	31	26	22	8	1	0	0	0	1	7	22	30	148
Days Minimum Temp. ≤ 0°F	8	5	1	0	0	0	0	0	0	0	0	4	18
Heating Degree Days (base 65°F)	1,357	1,057	824	438	166	20	3	7	111	382	801	1,194	6,360
Cooling Degree Days (base 65°F)	0	0	1	16	57	229	363	292	125	12	0	0	1,095
Mean Precipitation (in.)	0.74	0.66	2.00	3.00	4.77	3.65	3.59	4.08	2.74	2.29	1.70	0.89	30.11
Days With ≥ 0.1" Precipitation	2	2	5	6	8	6	5	5	5	4	4	2	54
Days With ≥ 1.0" Precipitation	0	0	0	1	1	1	1	1	1	1	0	0	7
Mean Snowfall (in.)	5.9	5.1	3.9	1.0	0.0	0.0	0.0	0.0	0.0	0.7	2.7	4.6	23.9
Days With ≥ 1.0" Snow Depth	na	na	na	0	0	0	0	0	0	0	0	na	na

Atkinson *Holt County* Elevation: 2,109 ft. Latitude: 42° 32' N Longitude: 98° 59' W

	JAN	FEB	MAR	APR	MAY	JUN	JUL	AUG	SEP	OCT	NOV	DEC	YEAR
Mean Maximum Temp. (°F)	32.4	38.1	48.1	61.1	72.1	81.8	87.1	85.7	77.2	64.4	45.9	35.3	60.8
Mean Temp. (°F)	21.7	27.2	36.4	48.4	59.7	69.3	74.4	72.8	63.5	51.0	35.3	24.9	48.7
Mean Minimum Temp. (°F)	10.5	16.3	24.7	35.7	47.3	56.7	61.7	59.9	49.7	37.5	24.6	14.5	36.6
Extreme Maximum Temp. (°F)	71	77	85	94	96	107	109	106	101	93	82	73	109
Extreme Minimum Temp. (°F)	-25	-28	-18	1	23	37	41	41	24	10	-11	-29	-29
Days Maximum Temp. ≥ 90°F	0	0	0	0	0	5	12	10	4	0	0	0	31
Days Maximum Temp. ≤ 32°F	14	10	4	0	0	0	0	0	0	0	5	12	45
Days Minimum Temp. ≤ 32°F	29	26	24	11	1	0	0	0	1	9	23	30	154
Days Minimum Temp. ≤ 0°F	8	4	1	0	0	0	0	0	0	0	1	5	19
Heating Degree Days (base 65°F)	1,339	1,061	878	499	197	33	6	12	133	436	884	1,236	6,714
Cooling Degree Days (base 65°F)	0	0	0	10	45	177	317	274	101	9	0	0	933
Mean Precipitation (in.)	0.49	0.62	1.70	2.69	3.63	3.67	3.43	2.47	2.48	1.81	1.15	0.54	24.68
Days With ≥ 0.1" Precipitation	1	2	4	6	7	7	6	5	5	4	3	2	52
Days With ≥ 1.0" Precipitation	0	0	0	0	1	1	1	1	1	1	0	0	6
Mean Snowfall (in.)	5.6	5.3	7.9	4.0	0.0	0.0	0.0	0.0	0.1	1.4	6.7	6.4	37.4
Days With ≥ 1.0" Snow Depth	na	9	na	1	0	0	0	0	0	1	4	na	na

Auburn 5 ESE *Nemaha County*   Elevation: 928 ft.   Latitude: 40° 22' N   Longitude: 95° 45' W

	JAN	FEB	MAR	APR	MAY	JUN	JUL	AUG	SEP	OCT	NOV	DEC	YEAR
Mean Maximum Temp. (°F)	33.8	40.5	52.6	65.4	75.4	85.3	89.1	87.2	79.7	67.7	50.6	38.1	63.8
Mean Temp. (°F)	23.7	30.0	41.2	53.2	63.8	73.7	77.7	75.6	67.3	55.2	40.3	28.5	52.5
Mean Minimum Temp. (°F)	13.7	19.5	29.7	40.9	52.2	62.0	66.3	63.9	54.8	42.7	30.0	18.9	41.2
Extreme Maximum Temp. (°F)	70	81	91	99	101	109	110	109	103	98	84	71	110
Extreme Minimum Temp. (°F)	-22	-23	-21	7	26	40	43	38	23	13	-4	-27	-27
Days Maximum Temp. ≥ 90°F	0	0	0	1	1	9	15	12	6	1	0	0	45
Days Maximum Temp. ≤ 32°F	15	9	3	0	0	0	0	0	0	0	0	3	40
Days Minimum Temp. ≤ 32°F	30	25	20	7	1	0	0	0	0	6	19	29	137
Days Minimum Temp. ≤ 0°F	6	3	0	0	0	0	0	0	0	0	0	3	12
Heating Degree Days (base 65°F)	1,272	981	734	371	113	10	1	3	81	318	734	1,124	5,742
Cooling Degree Days (base 65°F)	0	0	3	25	83	276	405	336	161	24	1	0	1,314
Mean Precipitation (in.)	0.84	1.06	2.47	2.97	4.39	3.53	4.37	3.56	3.70	2.58	2.01	1.07	32.55
Days With ≥ 0.1" Precipitation	2	3	5	6	7	6	6	5	5	5	4	3	57
Days With ≥ 1.0" Precipitation	0	0	1	1	1	1	1	1	1	1	0	0	8
Mean Snowfall (in.)	7.5	6.5	5.6	2.1	0.0	0.0	0.0	0.0	trace	0.7	2.6	5.5	30.5
Days With ≥ 1.0" Snow Depth	16	12	4	1	0	0	0	0	0	0	2	9	44

Aurora *Hamilton County*   Elevation: 1,784 ft.   Latitude: 40° 52' N   Longitude: 98° 00' W

	JAN	FEB	MAR	APR	MAY	JUN	JUL	AUG	SEP	OCT	NOV	DEC	YEAR
Mean Maximum Temp. (°F)	32.8	39.3	49.5	62.7	73.0	83.6	87.5	85.2	77.6	65.5	48.0	36.6	61.8
Mean Temp. (°F)	22.5	28.5	38.3	50.5	61.6	71.7	75.9	73.6	64.9	52.6	37.4	26.7	50.3
Mean Minimum Temp. (°F)	12.2	17.7	27.0	38.2	50.1	59.7	64.2	62.0	52.0	39.5	26.7	16.8	38.8
Extreme Maximum Temp. (°F)	70	79	89	95	98	107	106	108	101	93	83	71	108
Extreme Minimum Temp. (°F)	-21	-20	-11	10	29	39	47	44	24	4	-9	-28	-28
Days Maximum Temp. ≥ 90°F	0	0	0	1	1	8	13	10	4	0	0	0	37
Days Maximum Temp. ≤ 32°F	15	10	4	0	0	0	0	0	0	0	4	11	44
Days Minimum Temp. ≤ 32°F	30	26	22	8	0	0	0	0	1	6	22	30	145
Days Minimum Temp. ≤ 0°F	7	3	1	0	0	0	0	0	0	0	0	3	14
Heating Degree Days (base 65°F)	1,310	1,024	822	440	158	22	3	6	110	389	821	1,181	6,286
Cooling Degree Days (base 65°F)	0	0	1	13	54	214	335	267	107	8	0	0	999
Mean Precipitation (in.)	0.64	0.61	2.21	3.12	4.78	4.18	3.25	3.27	2.68	1.95	1.64	0.77	29.10
Days With ≥ 0.1" Precipitation	2	2	5	5	8	6	6	5	5	4	3	2	53
Days With ≥ 1.0" Precipitation	0	0	0	1	1	1	1	1	1	1	0	0	7
Mean Snowfall (in.)	6.0	5.7	6.3	2.1	0.0	0.0	0.0	0.0	0.2	0.9	4.4	6.2	31.8
Days With ≥ 1.0" Snow Depth	na	*11*	5	1	0	0	0	0	0	0	3	*11*	na

Beaver City *Furnas County*   Elevation: 2,158 ft.   Latitude: 40° 08' N   Longitude: 99° 50' W

	JAN	FEB	MAR	APR	MAY	JUN	JUL	AUG	SEP	OCT	NOV	DEC	YEAR
Mean Maximum Temp. (°F)	40.8	48.1	57.7	68.8	77.3	88.4	93.9	92.3	84.1	72.2	53.8	43.6	68.4
Mean Temp. (°F)	26.9	33.1	42.2	52.8	62.6	73.1	78.5	76.6	67.3	54.8	39.4	29.8	53.1
Mean Minimum Temp. (°F)	12.9	18.1	26.7	36.8	47.9	57.7	63.1	60.9	50.4	37.3	24.9	16.1	37.7
Extreme Maximum Temp. (°F)	80	83	92	101	100	111	112	111	107	98	89	75	112
Extreme Minimum Temp. (°F)	-26	-24	-12	10	21	34	40	37	16	1	-13	-34	-34
Days Maximum Temp. ≥ 90°F	0	0	0	1	2	14	22	20	11	2	0	0	72
Days Maximum Temp. ≤ 32°F	9	5	1	0	0	0	0	0	0	0	2	6	23
Days Minimum Temp. ≤ 32°F	30	26	23	10	2	0	0	0	1	10	24	30	156
Days Minimum Temp. ≤ 0°F	5	3	1	0	0	0	0	0	0	0	0	3	12
Heating Degree Days (base 65°F)	1,174	893	699	374	135	14	1	3	77	325	763	1,083	5,541
Cooling Degree Days (base 65°F)	0	0	0	17	68	263	422	373	163	15	0	0	1,321
Mean Precipitation (in.)	0.62	0.63	1.96	2.19	3.69	3.46	3.08	2.76	2.00	1.34	1.28	0.63	23.64
Days With ≥ 0.1" Precipitation	2	2	4	5	7	6	5	5	4	3	3	2	48
Days With ≥ 1.0" Precipitation	0	0	0	0	1	1	1	1	0	0	0	0	4
Mean Snowfall (in.)	5.9	5.1	6.2	1.8	0.0	0.0	0.0	0.0	0.4	0.2	3.8	5.5	28.9
Days With ≥ 1.0" Snow Depth	12	8	4	1	0	0	0	0	0	0	3	8	36

Benkelman *Dundy County*   Elevation: 3,024 ft.   Latitude: 40° 03' N   Longitude: 101° 33' W

	JAN	FEB	MAR	APR	MAY	JUN	JUL	AUG	SEP	OCT	NOV	DEC	YEAR
Mean Maximum Temp. (°F)	40.4	46.5	54.4	64.7	74.1	85.4	91.2	89.3	80.6	69.0	52.7	43.7	66.0
Mean Temp. (°F)	26.0	31.6	39.6	49.6	59.9	70.7	76.4	74.4	64.5	51.8	37.8	29.0	51.0
Mean Minimum Temp. (°F)	11.6	16.7	24.8	34.4	45.7	56.0	61.7	59.3	48.4	34.6	22.8	14.3	35.9
Extreme Maximum Temp. (°F)	77	81	88	97	99	107	110	106	106	96	88	77	110
Extreme Minimum Temp. (°F)	-27	-21	-9	8	21	35	43	39	21	8	-11	-34	-34
Days Maximum Temp. ≥ 90°F	0	0	0	1	2	11	19	17	8	1	0	0	59
Days Maximum Temp. ≤ 32°F	9	5	3	0	0	0	0	0	0	0	3	6	26
Days Minimum Temp. ≤ 32°F	31	28	25	13	2	0	0	0	2	12	27	31	171
Days Minimum Temp. ≤ 0°F	6	3	1	0	0	0	0	0	0	0	0	3	13
Heating Degree Days (base 65°F)	1,203	936	780	463	195	30	4	8	119	407	811	1,108	6,064
Cooling Degree Days (base 65°F)	0	0	0	8	44	209	366	313	116	7	0	0	1,063
Mean Precipitation (in.)	0.58	0.51	1.39	1.85	3.27	2.92	3.03	2.09	1.34	1.09	0.82	0.49	19.38
Days With ≥ 0.1" Precipitation	2	1	3	4	6	6	5	4	3	3	2	2	41
Days With ≥ 1.0" Precipitation	0	0	0	0	1	1	1	0	0	0	0	0	3
Mean Snowfall (in.)	7.0	3.7	6.4	1.8	trace	0.0	0.0	0.0	0.4	1.3	4.2	5.0	29.8
Days With ≥ 1.0" Snow Depth	11	7	*4*	1	0	0	0	0	0	0	1	2	*33*

Big Springs *Deuel County* Elevation: 3,369 ft. Latitude: 41° 04' N Longitude: 102° 04' W

	JAN	FEB	MAR	APR	MAY	JUN	JUL	AUG	SEP	OCT	NOV	DEC	YEAR
Mean Maximum Temp. (°F)	37.5	44.4	52.0	61.8	71.1	81.1	87.5	85.6	77.1	65.0	49.4	40.3	62.7
Mean Temp. (°F)	24.6	30.5	38.2	47.7	57.9	67.7	73.8	71.8	62.2	49.6	35.9	27.0	48.9
Mean Minimum Temp. (°F)	11.6	16.5	24.3	33.7	44.7	54.2	59.9	58.0	47.3	34.1	22.2	13.6	35.0
Extreme Maximum Temp. (°F)	73	78	84	92	96	102	106	101	98	92	80	73	106
Extreme Minimum Temp. (°F)	-33	-23	-13	-10	21	35	42	36	23	5	-10	-37	-37
Days Maximum Temp. ≥ 90°F	0	0	0	0	0	5	13	10	3	0	0	0	31
Days Maximum Temp. ≤ 32°F	10	6	3	0	0	0	0	0	0	0	4	8	31
Days Minimum Temp. ≤ 32°F	30	27	26	13	2	0	0	0	1	12	27	31	169
Days Minimum Temp. ≤ 0°F	6	3	1	0	0	0	0	0	0	0	1	4	15
Heating Degree Days (base 65°F)	1,247	967	824	513	238	52	6	12	144	471	866	1,173	6,513
Cooling Degree Days (base 65°F)	0	0	0	2	23	130	272	226	63	2	0	0	718
Mean Precipitation (in.)	0.42	0.39	1.27	1.98	3.18	2.71	2.19	1.91	1.19	0.76	0.63	0.46	17.09
Days With ≥ 0.1" Precipitation	1	2	3	4	6	5	5	4	3	2	2	1	38
Days With ≥ 1.0" Precipitation	0	0	0	0	1	0	0	0	0	0	0	0	1
Mean Snowfall (in.)	na	na	na	0.6	0.1	0.0	0.0	0.0	trace	trace	2.2	na	na
Days With ≥ 1.0" Snow Depth	na	na	na	0	0	0	0	0	0	0	0	na	na

Blair *Washington County* Elevation: 1,089 ft. Latitude: 41° 33' N Longitude: 96° 08' W

	JAN	FEB	MAR	APR	MAY	JUN	JUL	AUG	SEP	OCT	NOV	DEC	YEAR
Mean Maximum Temp. (°F)	30.5	36.1	48.2	62.1	72.9	82.3	86.2	83.8	76.1	64.6	47.3	34.6	60.4
Mean Temp. (°F)	20.6	26.3	37.6	50.5	61.4	71.3	75.5	73.1	64.5	52.5	37.4	25.6	49.7
Mean Minimum Temp. (°F)	10.7	16.4	26.8	38.8	49.9	60.2	64.7	62.3	52.7	40.3	27.5	16.5	38.9
Extreme Maximum Temp. (°F)	70	77	86	98	97	104	108	105	99	94	85	68	108
Extreme Minimum Temp. (°F)	-21	-24	-9	8	26	40	43	41	27	12	-6	-24	-24
Days Maximum Temp. ≥ 90°F	0	0	0	0	1	6	10	7	2	0	0	0	26
Days Maximum Temp. ≤ 32°F	16	12	4	0	0	0	0	0	0	0	4	13	49
Days Minimum Temp. ≤ 32°F	30	26	22	8	1	0	0	0	0	6	21	30	144
Days Minimum Temp. ≤ 0°F	8	4	1	0	0	0	0	0	0	0	0	3	16
Heating Degree Days (base 65°F)	1,369	1,086	845	443	161	23	3	8	115	392	820	1,215	6,480
Cooling Degree Days (base 65°F)	0	0	0	16	55	211	331	261	107	11	0	0	992
Mean Precipitation (in.)	0.72	0.72	2.68	3.07	4.06	4.37	3.55	3.14	3.16	2.35	1.53	0.92	30.27
Days With ≥ 0.1" Precipitation	2	2	5	6	8	7	6	5	5	4	3	2	55
Days With ≥ 1.0" Precipitation	0	0	1	1	1	1	1	1	1	1	0	0	8
Mean Snowfall (in.)	6.2	5.8	4.9	1.5	0.0	0.0	0.0	0.0	0.0	0.5	2.2	5.4	26.5
Days With ≥ 1.0" Snow Depth	na	na	4	0	0	0	0	0	0	0	2	na	na

Brewster *Blaine County* Elevation: 2,493 ft. Latitude: 41° 56' N Longitude: 99° 52' W

	JAN	FEB	MAR	APR	MAY	JUN	JUL	AUG	SEP	OCT	NOV	DEC	YEAR
Mean Maximum Temp. (°F)	33.3	39.1	48.4	59.7	70.7	81.2	87.8	85.8	76.6	64.5	46.9	36.6	60.9
Mean Temp. (°F)	20.7	26.4	35.5	46.5	57.5	67.7	73.9	71.9	61.5	49.2	34.2	24.0	47.4
Mean Minimum Temp. (°F)	8.2	13.7	22.6	33.2	44.2	54.1	60.0	57.9	46.4	34.0	21.4	11.7	33.9
Extreme Maximum Temp. (°F)	72	81	86	93	99	108	109	105	100	93	82	73	109
Extreme Minimum Temp. (°F)	-34	-35	-26	2	19	35	38	37	18	6	-20	-35	-35
Days Maximum Temp. ≥ 90°F	0	0	0	0	1	5	13	11	5	0	0	0	35
Days Maximum Temp. ≤ 32°F	14	9	5	1	0	0	0	0	0	0	5	11	45
Days Minimum Temp. ≤ 32°F	31	27	26	15	3	0	0	0	2	13	27	31	175
Days Minimum Temp. ≤ 0°F	9	4	1	0	0	0	0	0	0	0	1	5	20
Heating Degree Days (base 65°F)	1,367	1,084	905	553	253	53	9	17	170	486	918	1,263	7,078
Cooling Degree Days (base 65°F)	0	0	0	4	23	134	292	249	69	3	0	0	774
Mean Precipitation (in.)	0.40	0.63	1.28	2.01	3.62	3.87	3.14	3.02	1.70	1.30	1.00	0.55	22.52
Days With ≥ 0.1" Precipitation	1	1	3	5	6	6	5	4	3	3	2	1	40
Days With ≥ 1.0" Precipitation	0	0	0	0	1	1	1	1	0	0	0	0	4
Mean Snowfall (in.)	5.7	4.6	5.1	2.6	0.0	0.0	0.0	0.0	trace	1.1	5.6	4.4	29.1
Days With ≥ 1.0" Snow Depth	na	7	na	1	0	0	0	0	0	1	4	na	na

Bridgeport *Morrill County* Elevation: 3,664 ft. Latitude: 41° 40' N Longitude: 103° 06' W

	JAN	FEB	MAR	APR	MAY	JUN	JUL	AUG	SEP	OCT	NOV	DEC	YEAR
Mean Maximum Temp. (°F)	39.5	46.5	54.2	63.6	73.7	84.5	90.9	89.1	80.1	67.7	50.6	41.8	65.2
Mean Temp. (°F)	26.0	32.0	39.4	48.4	59.0	69.2	75.1	73.3	63.4	50.7	36.5	28.0	50.1
Mean Minimum Temp. (°F)	12.4	17.5	24.7	33.2	44.3	53.7	59.4	57.4	46.6	33.7	22.4	14.2	35.0
Extreme Maximum Temp. (°F)	75	74	82	95	93	106	108	104	102	90	79	73	108
Extreme Minimum Temp. (°F)	-28	-30	-23	-11	18	34	43	40	16	-1	-11	-42	-42
Days Maximum Temp. ≥ 90°F	0	0	0	0	1	10	19	17	6	0	0	0	53
Days Maximum Temp. ≤ 32°F	9	4	2	0	0	0	0	0	0	0	3	6	24
Days Minimum Temp. ≤ 32°F	30	27	26	14	2	0	0	0	2	14	27	30	172
Days Minimum Temp. ≤ 0°F	6	3	1	0	0	0	0	0	0	0	1	4	15
Heating Degree Days (base 65°F)	1,203	925	786	494	208	37	3	6	124	438	847	1,140	6,211
Cooling Degree Days (base 65°F)	0	0	0	3	32	169	328	283	86	2	0	0	903
Mean Precipitation (in.)	0.37	0.35	0.91	1.67	2.84	2.74	2.45	1.62	1.42	0.93	0.61	0.33	16.24
Days With ≥ 0.1" Precipitation	1	1	2	4	6	6	5	4	3	3	2	1	38
Days With ≥ 1.0" Precipitation	0	0	0	0	1	1	1	0	0	0	0	0	3
Mean Snowfall (in.)	6.8	5.9	7.5	3.8	0.3	0.0	0.0	0.0	0.5	1.9	6.0	7.0	39.7
Days With ≥ 1.0" Snow Depth	12	6	4	1	0	0	0	0	0	1	4	10	38

Broken Bow 2 W *Custer County* Elevation: 2,500 ft. Latitude: 41° 25' N Longitude: 99° 41' W

	JAN	FEB	MAR	APR	MAY	JUN	JUL	AUG	SEP	OCT	NOV	DEC	YEAR
Mean Maximum Temp. (°F)	35.1	41.0	49.9	61.4	71.1	81.3	86.7	85.0	77.0	65.2	47.7	38.3	61.6
Mean Temp. (°F)	22.5	28.0	36.5	47.2	57.8	68.0	73.4	71.6	62.1	50.0	34.7	25.6	48.1
Mean Minimum Temp. (°F)	9.8	15.0	23.0	33.0	44.6	54.6	60.1	58.1	47.3	34.8	21.7	12.9	34.6
Extreme Maximum Temp. (°F)	72	79	86	91	95	105	106	104	102	92	80	71	106
Extreme Minimum Temp. (°F)	-33	-27	-20	3	18	33	37	36	16	2	-23	-29	-33
Days Maximum Temp. ≥ 90°F	0	0	0	0	0	5	12	10	4	0	0	0	31
Days Maximum Temp. ≤ 32°F	12	8	4	0	0	0	0	0	0	0	5	10	39
Days Minimum Temp. ≤ 32°F	31	27	26	14	3	0	0	0	2	13	27	30	173
Days Minimum Temp. ≤ 0°F	8	4	1	0	0	0	0	0	0	0	1	5	19
Heating Degree Days (base 65°F)	1,313	1,039	879	532	242	48	9	16	158	461	901	1,216	6,814
Cooling Degree Days (base 65°F)	0	0	0	5	25	133	260	210	73	4	0	0	710
Mean Precipitation (in.)	0.41	0.47	1.46	2.29	3.44	4.02	3.54	2.42	2.03	1.39	0.94	0.36	22.77
Days With ≥ 0.1" Precipitation	1	2	4	5	8	7	6	5	4	3	2	1	48
Days With ≥ 1.0" Precipitation	0	0	0	0	1	1	1	1	0	0	0	0	4
Mean Snowfall (in.)	4.9	4.6	6.4	2.6	0.0	0.0	0.0	0.0	0.1	0.6	4.8	5.2	29.2
Days With ≥ 1.0" Snow Depth	10	5	4	1	0	0	0	0	0	0	3	7	30

Burwell 4 SE *Garfield County* Elevation: 2,122 ft. Latitude: 41° 46' N Longitude: 99° 05' W

	JAN	FEB	MAR	APR	MAY	JUN	JUL	AUG	SEP	OCT	NOV	DEC	YEAR
Mean Maximum Temp. (°F)	35.2	41.0	50.2	62.3	72.8	82.8	87.7	86.1	77.1	65.0	47.0	37.2	62.0
Mean Temp. (°F)	23.3	28.9	37.4	48.6	59.8	69.6	74.6	73.0	62.9	50.7	35.1	25.4	49.1
Mean Minimum Temp. (°F)	11.4	16.8	24.5	34.8	46.7	56.5	61.4	59.9	48.6	36.4	23.0	13.5	36.1
Extreme Maximum Temp. (°F)	71	79	87	94	95	105	108	107	100	93	79	70	108
Extreme Minimum Temp. (°F)	-32	-29	-19	1	23	30	37	40	19	6	-16	-30	-32
Days Maximum Temp. ≥ 90°F	0	0	0	0	1	7	13	11	4	0	0	0	36
Days Maximum Temp. ≤ 32°F	13	8	4	0	0	0	0	0	0	0	4	10	39
Days Minimum Temp. ≤ 32°F	31	27	25	13	2	0	0	0	1	10	26	31	166
Days Minimum Temp. ≤ 0°F	7	4	1	0	0	0	0	0	0	0	1	5	18
Heating Degree Days (base 65°F)	1,286	1,014	849	492	195	30	5	10	142	441	892	1,221	6,577
Cooling Degree Days (base 65°F)	0	0	0	9	42	183	317	270	94	6	0	0	921
Mean Precipitation (in.)	0.44	0.56	1.36	2.55	3.46	3.74	3.09	2.85	2.32	1.71	1.08	0.46	23.62
Days With ≥ 0.1" Precipitation	1	2	3	5	7	7	5	5	4	4	2	1	46
Days With ≥ 1.0" Precipitation	0	0	0	0	1	1	1	1	1	0	0	0	5
Mean Snowfall (in.)	5.2	4.5	5.9	3.0	trace	0.0	0.0	0.0	trace	1.0	4.7	4.8	29.1
Days With ≥ 1.0" Snow Depth	16	10	5	1	0	0	0	0	0	0	6	12	50

Butte *Boyd County* Elevation: 1,811 ft. Latitude: 42° 55' N Longitude: 98° 51' W

	JAN	FEB	MAR	APR	MAY	JUN	JUL	AUG	SEP	OCT	NOV	DEC	YEAR
Mean Maximum Temp. (°F)	31.3	37.9	48.3	61.6	72.6	82.6	88.0	86.5	77.4	64.4	45.7	34.6	60.9
Mean Temp. (°F)	20.7	27.0	36.7	49.0	60.3	70.1	75.5	73.8	64.1	51.4	35.4	24.4	49.0
Mean Minimum Temp. (°F)	10.1	16.1	25.0	36.4	47.9	57.6	62.9	61.1	50.7	38.4	24.9	14.1	37.1
Extreme Maximum Temp. (°F)	70	78	87	96	95	106	107	106	102	93	82	72	107
Extreme Minimum Temp. (°F)	-25	-26	-20	5	24	37	41	39	24	10	-9	-30	-30
Days Maximum Temp. ≥ 90°F	0	0	0	0	1	5	13	11	4	0	0	0	34
Days Maximum Temp. ≤ 32°F	15	10	4	0	0	0	0	0	0	0	5	12	46
Days Minimum Temp. ≤ 32°F	30	26	24	11	1	0	0	0	1	8	24	30	155
Days Minimum Temp. ≤ 0°F	8	4	1	0	0	0	0	0	0	0	1	5	19
Heating Degree Days (base 65°F)	1,367	1,065	871	483	185	28	4	8	123	422	883	1,253	6,692
Cooling Degree Days (base 65°F)	0	0	0	12	48	183	328	285	105	8	0	0	969
Mean Precipitation (in.)	0.47	0.59	1.84	2.71	3.94	3.50	3.32	2.83	2.55	1.89	1.11	0.45	25.20
Days With ≥ 0.1" Precipitation	1	2	4	6	7	6	6	5	4	3	3	2	49
Days With ≥ 1.0" Precipitation	0	0	0	1	1	1	1	1	1	1	0	0	7
Mean Snowfall (in.)	5.7	5.3	7.5	2.4	0.0	0.0	0.0	0.0	trace	1.1	6.2	5.6	33.8
Days With ≥ 1.0" Snow Depth	na	na	na	0	0	0	0	0	0	0	3	na	na

Cambridge *Furnas County* Elevation: 2,257 ft. Latitude: 40° 17' N Longitude: 100° 10' W

	JAN	FEB	MAR	APR	MAY	JUN	JUL	AUG	SEP	OCT	NOV	DEC	YEAR
Mean Maximum Temp. (°F)	39.3	46.3	54.9	65.9	74.5	85.3	90.2	88.6	80.8	69.1	52.0	42.2	65.8
Mean Temp. (°F)	26.0	32.1	40.6	50.9	61.0	71.4	76.6	74.7	65.5	52.8	38.1	28.9	51.5
Mean Minimum Temp. (°F)	12.6	17.9	26.2	36.0	47.4	57.5	62.9	60.8	50.0	36.3	24.2	15.6	37.3
Extreme Maximum Temp. (°F)	76	81	90	96	100	111	107	110	107	95	84	78	111
Extreme Minimum Temp. (°F)	-23	-17	-11	13	23	36	42	42	18	8	-10	-35	-35
Days Maximum Temp. ≥ 90°F	0	0	0	1	1	9	17	15	7	1	0	0	51
Days Maximum Temp. ≤ 32°F	10	6	2	0	0	0	0	0	0	0	2	7	27
Days Minimum Temp. ≤ 32°F	31	27	24	11	1	0	0	0	1	10	25	30	160
Days Minimum Temp. ≤ 0°F	5	3	1	0	0	0	0	0	0	0	0	3	12
Heating Degree Days (base 65°F)	1,204	922	751	425	165	22	3	6	101	380	800	1,113	5,892
Cooling Degree Days (base 65°F)	0	0	0	9	42	212	358	306	117	6	0	0	1,050
Mean Precipitation (in.)	0.43	0.52	1.49	2.12	3.62	3.55	3.23	2.69	1.49	1.12	1.16	0.50	21.92
Days With ≥ 0.1" Precipitation	1	2	4	4	7	5	5	5	3	2	3	1	42
Days With ≥ 1.0" Precipitation	0	0	0	1	1	1	1	1	0	0	0	0	5
Mean Snowfall (in.)	5.2	4.7	4.8	1.6	0.0	0.0	0.0	0.0	0.2	0.4	4.4	5.7	27.0
Days With ≥ 1.0" Snow Depth	11	9	3	1	0	0	0	0	0	0	3	8	35

Canaday Steam Plant *Gosper County*   Elevation: 2,358 ft.   Latitude: 40° 42' N   Longitude: 99° 42' W

	JAN	FEB	MAR	APR	MAY	JUN	JUL	AUG	SEP	OCT	NOV	DEC	YEAR
Mean Maximum Temp. (°F)	35.1	41.3	50.3	62.1	72.0	82.6	87.1	85.0	77.2	65.4	48.7	38.7	62.1
Mean Temp. (°F)	23.5	29.3	38.1	49.2	60.0	70.2	75.1	73.0	63.8	51.5	36.9	27.2	49.8
Mean Minimum Temp. (°F)	11.9	17.2	25.9	36.3	48.0	57.8	63.0	60.8	50.3	37.5	24.9	15.7	37.4
Extreme Maximum Temp. (°F)	75	79	88	93	98	107	106	105	103	93	83	74	107
Extreme Minimum Temp. (°F)	-20	-17	-11	11	23	38	45	42	24	13	-12	-27	-27
Days Maximum Temp. ≥ 90°F	0	0	0	0	1	7	12	9	4	0	0	0	33
Days Maximum Temp. ≤ 32°F	13	9	4	0	0	0	0	0	0	0	4	9	39
Days Minimum Temp. ≤ 32°F	31	27	23	10	1	0	0	0	1	8	24	30	155
Days Minimum Temp. ≤ 0°F	7	3	1	0	0	0	0	0	0	0	0	3	14
Heating Degree Days (base 65°F)	1,280	1,003	827	475	191	31	4	10	125	419	838	1,166	6,369
Cooling Degree Days (base 65°F)	0	0	0	8	40	182	312	257	97	6	0	0	902
Mean Precipitation (in.)	0.42	0.38	1.41	2.12	3.79	3.36	3.54	2.84	1.76	1.27	1.01	0.42	22.32
Days With ≥ 0.1" Precipitation	1	1	4	4	7	6	5	5	4	3	2	1	43
Days With ≥ 1.0" Precipitation	0	0	0	0	1	1	1	1	0	0	0	0	4
Mean Snowfall (in.)	4.6	3.0	3.1	0.9	0.0	0.0	0.0	0.0	trace	0.3	2.5	4.1	18.5
Days With ≥ 1.0" Snow Depth	10	7	3	1	0	0	0	0	0	0	3	5	29

Central City *Merrick County*   Elevation: 1,692 ft.   Latitude: 41° 07' N   Longitude: 98° 01' W

	JAN	FEB	MAR	APR	MAY	JUN	JUL	AUG	SEP	OCT	NOV	DEC	YEAR
Mean Maximum Temp. (°F)	34.4	41.2	52.1	65.0	74.7	84.3	87.8	85.8	79.0	67.4	49.2	37.9	63.2
Mean Temp. (°F)	24.1	30.3	40.3	52.3	62.9	72.6	76.6	74.7	66.6	54.5	38.7	28.0	51.8
Mean Minimum Temp. (°F)	13.7	19.3	28.5	39.6	51.1	60.9	65.3	63.6	54.1	41.6	28.1	18.1	40.3
Extreme Maximum Temp. (°F)	74	79	90	95	99	105	105	105	101	93	83	71	105
Extreme Minimum Temp. (°F)	-22	-19	-15	9	26	41	43	44	25	9	-10	-26	-26
Days Maximum Temp. ≥ 90°F	0	0	0	1	1	8	13	10	4	0	0	0	37
Days Maximum Temp. ≤ 32°F	14	9	3	0	0	0	0	0	0	0	3	9	38
Days Minimum Temp. ≤ 32°F	30	25	20	7	0	0	0	0	0	5	20	29	136
Days Minimum Temp. ≤ 0°F	6	3	0	0	0	0	0	0	0	0	0	3	12
Heating Degree Days (base 65°F)	1,262	974	760	391	126	14	2	5	84	332	784	1,140	5,874
Cooling Degree Days (base 65°F)	0	0	1	20	68	240	361	308	142	14	0	0	1,154
Mean Precipitation (in.)	0.59	0.62	2.05	2.91	4.38	3.45	3.50	2.78	2.91	1.72	1.49	0.68	27.08
Days With ≥ 0.1" Precipitation	2	2	4	5	7	5	6	5	4	3	3	2	48
Days With ≥ 1.0" Precipitation	0	0	0	1	1	1	1	1	1	0	0	0	6
Mean Snowfall (in.)	4.0	4.2	4.5	0.9	0.0	0.0	0.0	0.0	trace	0.7	3.2	5.1	22.6
Days With ≥ 1.0" Snow Depth	16	11	5	0	0	0	0	0	0	0	4	11	47

Chadron Municipal Airport *Dawes County*   Elevation: 3,297 ft.   Latitude: 42° 50' N   Longitude: 103° 05' W

	JAN	FEB	MAR	APR	MAY	JUN	JUL	AUG	SEP	OCT	NOV	DEC	YEAR
Mean Maximum Temp. (°F)	34.9	41.2	49.5	58.9	69.8	81.3	88.9	88.3	77.6	63.9	47.0	38.2	61.6
Mean Temp. (°F)	22.9	28.7	36.5	45.9	56.7	67.3	74.1	73.2	62.4	49.2	34.8	25.8	48.1
Mean Minimum Temp. (°F)	10.8	16.1	23.5	32.8	43.4	53.2	59.2	58.1	47.0	34.3	22.4	13.4	34.5
Extreme Maximum Temp. (°F)	70	76	83	93	93	107	109	108	104	93	81	72	109
Extreme Minimum Temp. (°F)	-27	-27	-26	-11	21	34	38	39	17	-7	-20	-40	-40
Days Maximum Temp. ≥ 90°F	0	0	0	0	1	6	15	15	6	0	0	0	43
Days Maximum Temp. ≤ 32°F	12	7	4	1	0	0	0	0	0	1	5	9	39
Days Minimum Temp. ≤ 32°F	30	26	25	15	3	0	0	0	2	12	25	29	167
Days Minimum Temp. ≤ 0°F	8	4	1	0	0	0	0	0	0	0	1	5	19
Heating Degree Days (base 65°F)	1,300	1,018	876	568	273	59	7	10	159	488	900	1,209	6,867
Cooling Degree Days (base 65°F)	0	0	0	3	24	131	301	280	91	4	0	0	834
Mean Precipitation (in.)	0.46	0.38	0.82	1.89	3.04	2.76	2.09	1.72	1.44	1.07	0.56	0.42	16.65
Days With ≥ 0.1" Precipitation	1	1	2	5	6	6	5	3	3	3	2	1	38
Days With ≥ 1.0" Precipitation	0	0	0	0	1	0	0	0	0	0	0	0	1
Mean Snowfall (in.)	6.3	5.6	8.3	4.1	0.4	0.0	0.0	0.0	0.2	2.6	5.5	7.6	40.6
Days With ≥ 1.0" Snow Depth	17	10	7	2	0	0	0	0	0	1	6	12	55

Clarkson *Colfax County*   Elevation: 1,548 ft.   Latitude: 41° 43' N   Longitude: 97° 08' W

	JAN	FEB	MAR	APR	MAY	JUN	JUL	AUG	SEP	OCT	NOV	DEC	YEAR
Mean Maximum Temp. (°F)	30.1	37.2	48.3	62.3	73.1	83.4	86.9	84.4	76.3	63.8	45.9	34.3	60.5
Mean Temp. (°F)	19.8	26.5	36.9	49.6	61.0	71.1	75.2	72.9	63.7	51.1	35.7	24.6	49.0
Mean Minimum Temp. (°F)	9.4	15.7	25.6	36.9	48.8	58.8	63.5	61.3	51.0	38.3	25.4	14.8	37.5
Extreme Maximum Temp. (°F)	75	76	90	97	99	106	106	106	98	92	79	68	106
Extreme Minimum Temp. (°F)	-31	-24	-16	7	22	37	40	40	21	8	-12	-27	-31
Days Maximum Temp. ≥ 90°F	0	0	0	1	1	7	12	8	3	0	0	0	32
Days Maximum Temp. ≤ 32°F	17	10	4	0	0	0	0	0	0	0	4	13	48
Days Minimum Temp. ≤ 32°F	31	27	23	10	1	0	0	0	1	8	24	30	155
Days Minimum Temp. ≤ 0°F	8	4	1	0	0	0	0	0	0	0	1	4	18
Heating Degree Days (base 65°F)	1,394	1,081	863	466	171	23	4	10	128	431	873	1,247	6,691
Cooling Degree Days (base 65°F)	0	0	0	14	52	205	321	255	96	6	0	0	949
Mean Precipitation (in.)	0.64	0.72	2.18	2.87	4.70	4.24	3.33	3.16	2.74	2.20	1.53	0.84	29.15
Days With ≥ 0.1" Precipitation	2	2	4	5	7	6	5	5	5	4	3	2	50
Days With ≥ 1.0" Precipitation	0	0	0	1	2	2	1	1	1	1	0	0	9
Mean Snowfall (in.)	5.5	4.4	5.1	1.9	0.0	0.0	0.0	0.0	0.1	0.9	4.0	6.2	28.1
Days With ≥ 1.0" Snow Depth	13	8	3	1	0	0	0	0	0	0	3	9	37

Clay Center *Clay County*   Elevation: 1,748 ft.   Latitude: 40° 31' N   Longitude: 98° 03' W

	JAN	FEB	MAR	APR	MAY	JUN	JUL	AUG	SEP	OCT	NOV	DEC	YEAR
Mean Maximum Temp. (°F)	33.5	39.5	50.3	62.0	71.8	82.6	87.6	85.5	77.9	65.7	48.8	37.3	61.9
Mean Temp. (°F)	22.5	28.3	38.2	49.5	59.9	70.2	75.1	72.9	64.3	52.0	37.3	26.8	49.8
Mean Minimum Temp. (°F)	11.4	17.0	26.0	36.7	48.0	57.8	62.6	60.3	50.7	38.2	25.7	16.2	37.5
Extreme Maximum Temp. (°F)	76	80	89	95	96	106	106	107	102	94	81	76	107
Extreme Minimum Temp. (°F)	-30	-24	-15	3	24	35	42	42	21	9	-11	-39	-39
Days Maximum Temp. ≥ 90°F	0	0	0	0	1	6	13	9	4	0	0	0	33
Days Maximum Temp. ≤ 32°F	14	10	3	0	0	0	0	0	0	0	4	11	42
Days Minimum Temp. ≤ 32°F	30	26	23	10	1	0	0	0	1	8	23	30	152
Days Minimum Temp. ≤ 0°F	8	4	1	0	0	0	0	0	0	0	0	3	16
Heating Degree Days (base 65°F)	1,314	1,029	826	468	189	31	4	9	120	405	822	1,179	6,396
Cooling Degree Days (base 65°F)	0	0	1	10	41	198	328	262	111	9	0	0	960
Mean Precipitation (in.)	0.40	0.45	1.79	3.15	4.75	3.89	4.14	3.41	2.62	1.93	1.40	0.61	28.54
Days With ≥ 0.1" Precipitation	1	*1*	3	5	7	5	5	5	4	3	2	2	*43*
Days With ≥ 1.0" Precipitation	0	0	0	1	1	1	1	1	1	0	0	0	6
Mean Snowfall (in.)	*4.7*	*3.9*	na	1.1	0.0	0.0	0.0	0.0	trace	0.2	2.7	*4.1*	na
Days With ≥ 1.0" Snow Depth	*10*	8	*4*	0	0	0	0	0	0	0	*2*	*6*	*30*

Columbus 3 NE *Platte County*   Elevation: 1,450 ft.   Latitude: 41° 28' N   Longitude: 97° 20' W

	JAN	FEB	MAR	APR	MAY	JUN	JUL	AUG	SEP	OCT	NOV	DEC	YEAR
Mean Maximum Temp. (°F)	30.7	37.1	48.7	62.3	73.4	84.0	87.9	85.2	77.0	63.8	45.9	34.4	60.9
Mean Temp. (°F)	21.1	27.2	38.0	50.7	62.3	72.5	76.7	74.3	65.2	52.2	36.4	25.3	50.2
Mean Minimum Temp. (°F)	11.4	17.3	27.3	39.1	51.1	61.0	65.5	63.5	53.4	40.6	26.8	16.1	39.4
Extreme Maximum Temp. (°F)	69	76	91	96	99	108	110	105	99	93	78	68	110
Extreme Minimum Temp. (°F)	-23	-20	-11	4	27	40	41	44	24	14	-7	-24	-24
Days Maximum Temp. ≥ 90°F	0	0	0	1	1	8	13	9	4	0	0	0	36
Days Maximum Temp. ≤ 32°F	16	11	4	0	0	0	0	0	0	0	4	13	48
Days Minimum Temp. ≤ 32°F	31	26	22	7	0	0	0	0	0	6	22	30	144
Days Minimum Temp. ≤ 0°F	7	4	0	0	0	0	0	0	0	0	0	4	15
Heating Degree Days (base 65°F)	1,355	1,060	830	435	144	17	2	6	106	399	852	1,225	6,431
Cooling Degree Days (base 65°F)	0	0	1	17	67	253	380	308	127	11	0	0	1,164
Mean Precipitation (in.)	0.53	0.70	1.98	2.92	4.42	4.09	3.55	3.22	2.82	2.12	1.51	0.73	28.59
Days With ≥ 0.1" Precipitation	2	2	4	6	8	6	6	5	5	4	3	2	53
Days With ≥ 1.0" Precipitation	0	0	0	1	1	1	1	1	1	1	0	0	6
Mean Snowfall (in.)	4.7	5.4	4.6	1.3	0.0	0.0	0.0	0.0	trace	1.0	3.4	4.9	25.3
Days With ≥ 1.0" Snow Depth	17	13	5	1	0	0	0	0	0	0	3	12	51

Creighton *Knox County*   Elevation: 1,627 ft.   Latitude: 42° 28' N   Longitude: 97° 54' W

	JAN	FEB	MAR	APR	MAY	JUN	JUL	AUG	SEP	OCT	NOV	DEC	YEAR
Mean Maximum Temp. (°F)	31.5	38.3	49.2	63.0	73.8	84.0	88.3	86.3	78.2	65.5	46.5	34.9	61.6
Mean Temp. (°F)	20.9	27.4	37.5	50.1	61.3	71.2	75.8	73.6	64.5	52.3	36.1	24.7	49.6
Mean Minimum Temp. (°F)	10.2	16.5	25.8	37.1	48.8	58.4	63.0	60.8	50.8	38.9	25.7	14.4	37.5
Extreme Maximum Temp. (°F)	73	78	87	94	96	107	105	104	103	93	80	68	107
Extreme Minimum Temp. (°F)	-30	-26	-17	-1	22	38	39	40	24	9	-10	-31	-31
Days Maximum Temp. ≥ 90°F	0	0	0	1	1	8	14	11	4	0	0	0	39
Days Maximum Temp. ≤ 32°F	15	10	4	0	0	0	0	0	0	0	4	12	45
Days Minimum Temp. ≤ 32°F	30	26	23	10	1	0	0	0	1	8	23	30	152
Days Minimum Temp. ≤ 0°F	8	4	1	0	0	0	0	0	0	0	1	5	19
Heating Degree Days (base 65°F)	1,363	1,055	846	454	164	24	3	8	116	397	860	1,243	6,533
Cooling Degree Days (base 65°F)	0	0	1	15	60	223	348	290	113	12	0	0	1,062
Mean Precipitation (in.)	0.49	0.59	1.82	2.71	3.86	3.75	3.24	3.16	2.29	1.75	1.37	0.68	25.71
Days With ≥ 0.1" Precipitation	1	2	4	6	7	6	6	5	4	4	3	2	50
Days With ≥ 1.0" Precipitation	0	0	0	1	1	1	1	1	1	0	0	0	6
Mean Snowfall (in.)	na	na	na	*1.6*	trace	0.0	0.0	0.0	0.0	0.3	na	na	na
Days With ≥ 1.0" Snow Depth	na	na	na	0	0	0	0	0	0	0	na	na	na

Crescent Lake Nat'l Wildlife Ref *Garden County*   Elevation: 3,818 ft.   Latitude: 41° 46' N   Longitude: 102° 26' W

	JAN	FEB	MAR	APR	MAY	JUN	JUL	AUG	SEP	OCT	NOV	DEC	YEAR
Mean Maximum Temp. (°F)	36.8	43.6	50.7	60.4	70.1	80.2	86.9	85.5	76.6	64.8	49.0	40.3	62.1
Mean Temp. (°F)	23.2	29.5	36.9	46.5	56.7	66.1	72.2	70.5	60.8	48.7	35.1	26.5	47.7
Mean Minimum Temp. (°F)	9.6	15.3	23.1	32.5	43.2	51.9	57.6	55.5	44.9	32.5	21.2	12.6	33.3
Extreme Maximum Temp. (°F)	74	78	85	91	90	102	104	102	99	92	82	75	104
Extreme Minimum Temp. (°F)	-30	-25	-21	-14	18	30	38	36	11	-8	-15	-46	-46
Days Maximum Temp. ≥ 90°F	0	0	0	0	0	4	13	10	3	0	0	0	30
Days Maximum Temp. ≤ 32°F	10	6	3	1	0	0	0	0	0	0	4	8	32
Days Minimum Temp. ≤ 32°F	29	27	26	15	3	0	0	0	3	15	27	30	175
Days Minimum Temp. ≤ 0°F	7	4	1	0	0	0	0	0	0	0	1	5	18
Heating Degree Days (base 65°F)	1,291	996	865	549	267	67	10	18	177	502	888	1,189	6,819
Cooling Degree Days (base 65°F)	0	0	0	2	18	108	248	202	62	3	0	0	643
Mean Precipitation (in.)	0.30	0.36	0.92	1.73	3.15	2.88	2.30	1.70	1.66	1.05	0.63	0.30	16.98
Days With ≥ 0.1" Precipitation	1	1	3	4	6	6	5	4	3	3	2	1	39
Days With ≥ 1.0" Precipitation	0	0	0	0	1	1	0	0	0	0	0	0	2
Mean Snowfall (in.)	5.4	4.8	8.0	3.6	0.4	0.0	0.0	0.0	0.3	1.9	5.2	5.4	35.0
Days With ≥ 1.0" Snow Depth	*10*	7	5	1	0	0	0	0	0	1	3	8	*35*

Crete *Saline County*   Elevation: 1,433 ft.   Latitude: 40° 37' N   Longitude: 96° 57' W

	JAN	FEB	MAR	APR	MAY	JUN	JUL	AUG	SEP	OCT	NOV	DEC	YEAR
Mean Maximum Temp. (°F)	34.4	41.3	52.4	64.9	74.5	84.8	88.6	86.5	79.0	67.6	49.6	38.4	63.5
Mean Temp. (°F)	24.2	30.4	40.9	52.6	62.9	72.9	77.0	75.0	66.7	55.1	39.4	28.7	52.1
Mean Minimum Temp. (°F)	13.9	19.5	29.3	40.2	51.3	60.9	65.2	63.5	54.4	42.5	29.2	19.0	40.7
Extreme Maximum Temp. (°F)	73	84	88	95	97	105	105	106	102	92	82	71	106
Extreme Minimum Temp. (°F)	-25	-21	-15	6	26	39	41	44	25	8	-5	-25	-25
Days Maximum Temp. ≥ 90°F	0	0	0	0	1	8	14	11	4	0	0	0	38
Days Maximum Temp. ≤ 32°F	13	9	2	0	0	0	0	0	0	0	3	9	36
Days Minimum Temp. ≤ 32°F	30	25	19	7	0	0	0	0	0	5	19	29	134
Days Minimum Temp. ≤ 0°F	6	3	0	0	0	0	0	0	0	0	0	3	12
Heating Degree Days (base 65°F)	1,259	971	742	383	126	13	1	4	83	319	761	1,119	5,781
Cooling Degree Days (base 65°F)	0	0	1	18	64	248	374	315	144	17	0	0	1,181
Mean Precipitation (in.)	0.62	0.61	2.17	2.69	4.58	3.63	3.79	3.18	3.67	2.34	1.57	0.78	29.63
Days With ≥ 0.1" Precipitation	2	2	4	6	8	6	5	5	5	4	3	2	52
Days With ≥ 1.0" Precipitation	0	0	1	1	1	1	1	1	1	1	0	0	8
Mean Snowfall (in.)	5.1	4.8	4.3	0.9	trace	0.0	0.0	0.0	trace	0.6	3.1	4.4	23.2
Days With ≥ 1.0" Snow Depth	16	10	4	0	0	0	0	0	0	0	3	8	41

Culbertson *Hitchcock County*   Elevation: 2,598 ft.   Latitude: 40° 14' N   Longitude: 100° 50' W

	JAN	FEB	MAR	APR	MAY	JUN	JUL	AUG	SEP	OCT	NOV	DEC	YEAR
Mean Maximum Temp. (°F)	38.0	44.7	53.4	64.0	73.6	84.7	90.4	88.5	79.9	67.7	50.9	41.3	64.8
Mean Temp. (°F)	24.7	30.5	38.6	48.8	59.4	69.9	75.6	73.8	64.1	51.1	36.7	27.7	50.1
Mean Minimum Temp. (°F)	11.2	16.2	23.8	33.6	45.1	55.1	60.9	59.0	48.2	34.5	22.4	14.1	35.3
Extreme Maximum Temp. (°F)	77	80	89	94	100	107	108	107	104	96	83	76	108
Extreme Minimum Temp. (°F)	-25	-21	-10	10	21	33	38	39	20	11	-12	-34	-34
Days Maximum Temp. ≥ 90°F	0	0	0	1	1	10	18	15	7	1	0	0	53
Days Maximum Temp. ≤ 32°F	10	6	3	0	0	0	0	0	0	0	3	8	30
Days Minimum Temp. ≤ 32°F	31	28	27	14	2	0	0	0	2	13	28	31	176
Days Minimum Temp. ≤ 0°F	6	3	1	0	0	0	0	0	0	0	1	3	14
Heating Degree Days (base 65°F)	1,242	969	811	485	205	33	4	8	123	429	843	1,149	6,301
Cooling Degree Days (base 65°F)	0	0	0	6	39	187	341	293	105	5	0	0	976
Mean Precipitation (in.)	0.54	0.54	1.37	2.10	3.36	3.33	3.24	2.70	1.39	1.23	1.04	0.47	21.31
Days With ≥ 0.1" Precipitation	1	2	4	4	7	6	6	5	3	2	2	1	43
Days With ≥ 1.0" Precipitation	0	0	0	1	1	1	1	1	0	0	0	0	5
Mean Snowfall (in.)	6.7	4.8	6.6	2.6	0.0	0.0	0.0	0.0	0.3	1.0	4.4	5.0	31.4
Days With ≥ 1.0" Snow Depth	13	8	5	1	0	0	0	0	0	1	4	9	41

Curtis 3 NNE *Frontier County*   Elevation: 2,719 ft.   Latitude: 40° 40' N   Longitude: 100° 30' W

	JAN	FEB	MAR	APR	MAY	JUN	JUL	AUG	SEP	OCT	NOV	DEC	YEAR
Mean Maximum Temp. (°F)	38.6	45.2	53.4	65.0	73.7	84.2	90.2	88.5	80.1	68.1	50.0	42.2	64.9
Mean Temp. (°F)	24.6	30.7	38.5	49.3	59.4	69.7	75.2	73.3	63.6	50.9	35.8	27.9	49.9
Mean Minimum Temp. (°F)	10.1	15.8	23.7	33.7	44.9	55.1	60.3	58.2	47.0	33.8	21.5	13.5	34.8
Extreme Maximum Temp. (°F)	74	80	87	94	100	107	110	106	102	95	85	74	110
Extreme Minimum Temp. (°F)	-26	-29	-17	8	17	35	39	34	21	9	-18	-31	-31
Days Maximum Temp. ≥ 90°F	0	0	0	1	1	8	17	14	6	1	0	0	48
Days Maximum Temp. ≤ 32°F	10	6	3	0	0	0	0	0	0	0	3	7	29
Days Minimum Temp. ≤ 32°F	31	27	26	14	3	0	0	0	2	14	27	30	174
Days Minimum Temp. ≤ 0°F	7	3	1	0	0	0	0	0	0	0	1	4	16
Heating Degree Days (base 65°F)	1,246	964	814	469	202	32	4	9	129	433	869	1,146	6,317
Cooling Degree Days (base 65°F)	0	0	0	6	34	173	316	267	90	4	0	0	890
Mean Precipitation (in.)	0.42	0.48	1.30	1.88	3.33	3.36	2.85	2.39	1.57	1.17	0.83	0.36	19.94
Days With ≥ 0.1" Precipitation	1	1	3	4	6	6	5	4	4	3	2	1	40
Days With ≥ 1.0" Precipitation	0	0	0	0	1	1	1	1	0	0	0	0	4
Mean Snowfall (in.)	5.9	4.6	5.2	1.9	0.0	0.0	0.0	0.0	0.2	0.7	3.6	4.6	26.7
Days With ≥ 1.0" Snow Depth	11	7	4	1	0	0	0	0	0	0	3	7	33

Dalton *Cheyenne County*   Elevation: 4,271 ft.   Latitude: 41° 25' N   Longitude: 102° 58' W

	JAN	FEB	MAR	APR	MAY	JUN	JUL	AUG	SEP	OCT	NOV	DEC	YEAR
Mean Maximum Temp. (°F)	38.6	44.2	50.6	59.9	69.8	80.5	87.4	85.7	76.5	64.1	48.7	41.0	62.3
Mean Temp. (°F)	26.4	31.3	37.2	45.9	55.8	65.8	72.1	70.4	61.0	49.0	36.1	28.7	48.3
Mean Minimum Temp. (°F)	14.2	18.3	23.7	31.8	41.7	51.0	56.7	55.0	45.4	34.0	23.4	16.3	34.3
Extreme Maximum Temp. (°F)	73	75	82	89	93	101	103	102	98	89	78	78	103
Extreme Minimum Temp. (°F)	-24	-26	-16	-7	21	33	41	39	15	-2	-8	-32	-32
Days Maximum Temp. ≥ 90°F	0	0	0	0	0	5	14	11	3	0	0	0	33
Days Maximum Temp. ≤ 32°F	9	6	4	1	0	0	0	0	0	0	4	7	31
Days Minimum Temp. ≤ 32°F	30	26	27	16	3	0	0	0	2	12	25	29	170
Days Minimum Temp. ≤ 0°F	5	3	1	0	0	0	0	0	0	0	1	4	14
Heating Degree Days (base 65°F)	1,189	946	855	567	289	71	9	17	166	489	861	1,120	6,579
Cooling Degree Days (base 65°F)	0	0	0	1	12	96	225	184	48	1	0	0	567
Mean Precipitation (in.)	0.47	0.56	1.33	2.09	3.37	3.05	2.46	1.93	1.46	1.13	0.83	0.49	19.17
Days With ≥ 0.1" Precipitation	2	2	3	5	7	6	5	4	3	3	2	2	44
Days With ≥ 1.0" Precipitation	0	0	0	0	1	1	1	0	0	0	0	0	3
Mean Snowfall (in.)	8.1	7.5	11.1	6.6	0.5	0.0	0.0	0.0	0.2	2.3	7.2	7.1	50.6
Days With ≥ 1.0" Snow Depth	na	4	4	1	0	0	0	0	0	1	4	5	na

David City *Butler County*   Elevation: 1,607 ft.   Latitude: 41° 15' N   Longitude: 97° 08' W

	JAN	FEB	MAR	APR	MAY	JUN	JUL	AUG	SEP	OCT	NOV	DEC	YEAR
Mean Maximum Temp. (°F)	30.6	37.1	48.4	61.9	72.8	83.2	87.5	85.1	77.1	64.8	47.0	34.7	60.9
Mean Temp. (°F)	20.8	26.9	37.4	50.0	61.1	71.5	76.1	73.7	64.9	52.7	37.0	25.4	49.8
Mean Minimum Temp. (°F)	11.0	16.5	26.3	38.0	49.4	59.7	64.6	62.3	52.6	40.5	27.1	16.0	38.7
Extreme Maximum Temp. (°F)	71	79	89	96	99	106	105	105	101	92	82	68	106
Extreme Minimum Temp. (°F)	-25	-23	-14	5	25	40	43	42	18	6	-7	-27	-27
Days Maximum Temp. ≥ 90°F	0	0	0	1	1	7	13	9	4	0	0	0	35
Days Maximum Temp. ≤ 32°F	16	11	4	0	0	0	0	0	0	0	4	12	47
Days Minimum Temp. ≤ 32°F	31	26	22	8	1	0	0	0	0	6	21	30	145
Days Minimum Temp. ≤ 0°F	8	4	0	0	0	0	0	0	0	0	0	4	16
Heating Degree Days (base 65°F)	1,364	1,071	850	456	169	25	3	8	111	388	833	1,221	6,499
Cooling Degree Days (base 65°F)	0	0	1	14	51	217	345	276	115	11	0	0	1,030
Mean Precipitation (in.)	0.64	0.66	2.29	3.11	4.62	4.50	3.04	3.49	3.16	2.01	1.62	0.84	29.98
Days With ≥ 0.1" Precipitation	2	2	5	6	8	7	6	6	5	4	3	2	56
Days With ≥ 1.0" Precipitation	0	0	1	1	1	1	1	1	1	1	1	0	9
Mean Snowfall (in.)	6.2	6.0	6.2	2.2	0.0	0.0	0.0	0.0	0.2	0.9	4.2	5.6	31.5
Days With ≥ 1.0" Snow Depth	na	9	6	1	0	0	0	0	0	0	2	10	na

Ellsworth 15 NNE *Sheridan County*   Elevation: 3,969 ft.   Latitude: 42° 16' N   Longitude: 102° 13' W

	JAN	FEB	MAR	APR	MAY	JUN	JUL	AUG	SEP	OCT	NOV	DEC	YEAR
Mean Maximum Temp. (°F)	33.9	40.0	47.7	57.8	68.3	78.6	85.6	84.8	75.1	62.4	46.2	37.2	59.8
Mean Temp. (°F)	21.4	27.1	34.8	44.5	55.0	64.9	71.4	70.3	60.1	47.6	33.4	24.4	46.2
Mean Minimum Temp. (°F)	8.9	14.3	21.9	31.2	41.6	51.1	57.2	55.8	45.1	32.6	20.5	11.5	32.6
Extreme Maximum Temp. (°F)	67	74	83	91	91	104	106	103	99	92	79	69	106
Extreme Minimum Temp. (°F)	-28	-32	-22	-10	18	32	38	35	12	-5	-17	-42	-42
Days Maximum Temp. ≥ 90°F	0	0	0	0	0	3	11	10	3	0	0	0	27
Days Maximum Temp. ≤ 32°F	13	8	5	1	0	0	0	0	0	0	6	10	43
Days Minimum Temp. ≤ 32°F	31	27	27	17	4	0	0	0	3	14	27	31	181
Days Minimum Temp. ≤ 0°F	8	4	1	0	0	0	0	0	0	0	1	5	19
Heating Degree Days (base 65°F)	1,345	1,064	928	608	316	88	17	22	195	535	942	1,253	7,313
Cooling Degree Days (base 65°F)	0	0	0	2	12	86	218	194	53	1	0	0	566
Mean Precipitation (in.)	0.31	0.44	0.82	1.98	3.04	3.04	2.85	1.75	1.73	1.29	0.53	0.28	18.06
Days With ≥ 0.1" Precipitation	1	1	2	5	6	6	6	4	4	3	2	1	41
Days With ≥ 1.0" Precipitation	0	0	0	0	1	1	1	0	0	0	0	0	3
Mean Snowfall (in.)	5.7	5.0	7.6	4.9	0.2	0.0	0.0	0.0	0.5	2.0	5.7	4.5	36.1
Days With ≥ 1.0" Snow Depth	na	5	3	2	0	0	0	0	0	0	3	5	na

Enders Lake *Chase County*   Elevation: 3,077 ft.   Latitude: 40° 25' N   Longitude: 101° 31' W

	JAN	FEB	MAR	APR	MAY	JUN	JUL	AUG	SEP	OCT	NOV	DEC	YEAR
Mean Maximum Temp. (°F)	37.9	44.2	51.9	62.2	72.0	83.0	89.5	87.9	79.4	66.6	*49.7*	*40.7*	*63.8*
Mean Temp. (°F)	24.3	30.0	37.5	47.6	57.9	68.4	74.5	72.6	63.1	49.9	*35.6*	*26.7*	*49.0*
Mean Minimum Temp. (°F)	10.6	15.6	23.1	33.0	43.7	53.7	59.4	57.3	46.8	33.2	*21.5*	*12.7*	*34.2*
Extreme Maximum Temp. (°F)	72	79	85	93	99	104	110	107	104	94	82	76	110
Extreme Minimum Temp. (°F)	-26	-22	-14	4	16	33	36	37	20	9	-10	-38	-38
Days Maximum Temp. ≥ 90°F	0	0	0	0	1	7	17	14	6	1	0	0	46
Days Maximum Temp. ≤ 32°F	10	6	3	0	0	0	0	0	0	0	3	7	29
Days Minimum Temp. ≤ 32°F	31	28	27	14	3	0	0	0	2	14	25	28	172
Days Minimum Temp. ≤ 0°F	6	4	1	0	0	0	0	0	0	0	0	3	14
Heating Degree Days (base 65°F)	1,257	983	845	517	240	44	7	12	139	464	*873*	*1,180*	*6,561*
Cooling Degree Days (base 65°F)	0	0	0	3	25	145	303	249	92	3	*0*	*0*	*820*
Mean Precipitation (in.)	0.45	0.45	1.23	2.01	3.21	3.21	2.96	2.56	1.25	1.13	0.77	0.40	19.63
Days With ≥ 0.1" Precipitation	1	1	3	4	6	5	5	4	3	2	2	1	37
Days With ≥ 1.0" Precipitation	0	0	0	0	1	1	1	1	0	0	0	0	4
Mean Snowfall (in.)	6.2	4.0	6.2	2.4	trace	0.0	0.0	0.0	0.0	0.7	4.5	4.7	28.7
Days With ≥ 1.0" Snow Depth	13	8	4	1	0	0	0	0	0	0	4	9	39

Ewing *Holt County*   Elevation: 1,847 ft.   Latitude: 42° 16' N   Longitude: 98° 21' W

	JAN	FEB	MAR	APR	MAY	JUN	JUL	AUG	SEP	OCT	NOV	DEC	YEAR
Mean Maximum Temp. (°F)	32.3	38.8	49.0	62.3	72.9	82.6	87.0	85.3	77.3	65.2	46.5	35.7	61.2
Mean Temp. (°F)	20.8	27.1	37.0	49.3	60.5	70.0	74.8	73.0	63.7	51.4	35.5	24.6	49.0
Mean Minimum Temp. (°F)	9.2	15.4	24.8	36.3	48.0	57.4	62.5	60.6	50.1	37.7	24.4	13.5	36.7
Extreme Maximum Temp. (°F)	73	78	86	96	94	105	106	104	100	92	80	69	106
Extreme Minimum Temp. (°F)	-31	-32	-21	0	23	34	38	39	21	10	-11	-32	-32
Days Maximum Temp. ≥ 90°F	0	0	0	0	1	5	12	9	4	0	0	0	31
Days Maximum Temp. ≤ 32°F	15	10	4	0	0	0	0	0	0	0	4	12	45
Days Minimum Temp. ≤ 32°F	31	27	24	11	1	0	0	0	1	10	24	30	159
Days Minimum Temp. ≤ 0°F	9	4	1	0	0	0	0	0	0	0	1	5	20
Heating Degree Days (base 65°F)	1,365	1,064	863	473	180	29	6	10	127	420	879	1,247	6,663
Cooling Degree Days (base 65°F)	0	0	0	12	47	185	310	265	95	8	0	0	922
Mean Precipitation (in.)	0.51	0.53	1.75	2.64	3.73	3.83	3.31	3.01	2.30	1.70	1.18	0.55	25.04
Days With ≥ 0.1" Precipitation	1	2	4	6	7	6	6	6	5	4	3	2	52
Days With ≥ 1.0" Precipitation	0	0	0	0	1	1	1	1	1	0	0	0	5
Mean Snowfall (in.)	5.2	5.2	6.3	3.1	0.0	0.0	0.0	0.0	trace	0.7	5.0	5.9	31.4
Days With ≥ 1.0" Snow Depth	17	12	6	1	0	0	0	0	0	0	5	13	54

Fairbury *Jefferson County*   Elevation: 1,312 ft.   Latitude: 40° 08' N   Longitude: 97° 11' W

	JAN	FEB	MAR	APR	MAY	JUN	JUL	AUG	SEP	OCT	NOV	DEC	YEAR
Mean Maximum Temp. (°F)	34.2	40.9	52.0	64.0	73.6	83.7	89.2	86.9	78.8	67.0	50.2	38.6	63.3
Mean Temp. (°F)	23.3	29.0	39.5	51.1	61.4	71.5	77.0	74.9	65.7	53.5	38.8	28.2	51.2
Mean Minimum Temp. (°F)	12.4	17.1	27.1	38.0	49.2	59.3	64.8	62.8	52.6	39.9	27.2	17.7	39.0
Extreme Maximum Temp. (°F)	78	79	89	97	96	106	112	106	105	96	83	72	112
Extreme Minimum Temp. (°F)	-23	-20	-18	9	28	40	42	43	25	13	-9	-26	-26
Days Maximum Temp. ≥ 90°F	0	0	0	1	1	7	15	12	5	0	0	0	41
Days Maximum Temp. ≤ 32°F	14	9	3	0	0	0	0	0	0	0	3	9	38
Days Minimum Temp. ≤ 32°F	30	26	22	9	1	0	0	0	0	7	22	30	147
Days Minimum Temp. ≤ 0°F	7	4	1	0	0	0	0	0	0	0	0	3	15
Heating Degree Days (base 65°F)	1,286	1,010	783	426	158	21	2	4	104	363	781	1,135	6,073
Cooling Degree Days (base 65°F)	0	0	1	15	51	222	380	309	131	12	0	0	1,121
Mean Precipitation (in.)	0.74	0.72	2.32	2.78	4.28	4.09	4.36	3.99	3.14	2.02	1.65	0.91	31.00
Days With ≥ 0.1" Precipitation	2	2	5	6	8	6	6	6	5	4	3	2	55
Days With ≥ 1.0" Precipitation	0	0	0	1	1	1	1	1	1	0	0	0	6
Mean Snowfall (in.)	6.6	5.8	4.6	1.1	0.0	0.0	0.0	0.0	trace	0.4	3.0	4.9	26.4
Days With ≥ 1.0" Snow Depth	15	10	4	1	0	0	0	0	0	0	0	3	8	41

Fairmont *Fillmore County*   Elevation: 1,637 ft.   Latitude: 40° 38' N   Longitude: 97° 35' W

	JAN	FEB	MAR	APR	MAY	JUN	JUL	AUG	SEP	OCT	NOV	DEC	YEAR
Mean Maximum Temp. (°F)	33.9	40.4	51.6	64.2	74.1	84.3	88.1	86.0	79.0	66.9	49.3	38.2	63.0
Mean Temp. (°F)	23.3	29.2	39.7	51.2	62.1	72.1	76.4	74.1	66.0	53.8	38.3	27.9	51.2
Mean Minimum Temp. (°F)	12.6	17.9	27.7	38.2	50.1	59.9	64.6	62.2	52.9	40.6	27.3	17.4	39.3
Extreme Maximum Temp. (°F)	75	80	90	96	98	105	104	104	100	93	82	71	105
Extreme Minimum Temp. (°F)	-25	-20	-15	7	28	40	43	33	26	10	-8	-26	-26
Days Maximum Temp. ≥ 90°F	0	0	0	0	1	8	14	11	5	0	0	0	39
Days Maximum Temp. ≤ 32°F	13	9	3	0	0	0	0	0	0	0	3	10	38
Days Minimum Temp. ≤ 32°F	30	26	21	8	0	0	0	0	0	5	22	30	142
Days Minimum Temp. ≤ 0°F	6	3	1	0	0	0	0	0	0	0	0	3	13
Heating Degree Days (base 65°F)	1,287	1,006	780	417	142	17	2	7	94	353	793	1,145	6,043
Cooling Degree Days (base 65°F)	0	0	0	13	58	226	361	286	128	10	0	0	1,082
Mean Precipitation (in.)	0.65	0.66	2.39	2.77	4.43	3.78	3.40	3.14	2.91	2.11	1.61	0.80	28.65
Days With ≥ 0.1" Precipitation	2	2	5	5	8	6	6	5	5	3	3	2	52
Days With ≥ 1.0" Precipitation	0	0	0	1	1	1	1	1	1	1	0	0	7
Mean Snowfall (in.)	6.8	5.8	6.5	1.6	0.0	0.0	0.0	0.0	0.1	0.8	4.0	6.1	31.7
Days With ≥ 1.0" Snow Depth	*16*	*13*	6	1	0	0	0	0	0	0	4	10	*50*

Falls City Brenner Field *Richardson County*   Elevation: 977 ft.   Latitude: 40° 05' N   Longitude: 95° 36' W

	JAN	FEB	MAR	APR	MAY	JUN	JUL	AUG	SEP	OCT	NOV	DEC	YEAR
Mean Maximum Temp. (°F)	34.9	41.7	53.3	65.6	75.8	85.5	90.1	87.9	79.9	68.1	51.4	39.4	64.5
Mean Temp. (°F)	24.9	30.9	41.4	53.1	63.8	73.4	77.7	75.3	66.9	55.2	40.7	29.5	52.7
Mean Minimum Temp. (°F)	14.9	19.9	29.6	40.6	51.7	61.2	65.3	62.7	53.9	42.3	30.0	19.6	41.0
Extreme Maximum Temp. (°F)	71	80	90	96	97	107	109	109	104	96	83	71	109
Extreme Minimum Temp. (°F)	-20	-18	-17	8	29	39	41	41	25	12	-4	-29	-29
Days Maximum Temp. ≥ 90°F	0	0	0	0	1	10	17	14	5	0	0	0	47
Days Maximum Temp. ≤ 32°F	13	8	2	0	0	0	0	0	0	0	2	9	34
Days Minimum Temp. ≤ 32°F	30	24	19	6	0	0	0	0	0	5	18	28	130
Days Minimum Temp. ≤ 0°F	5	2	0	0	0	0	0	0	0	0	0	2	9
Heating Degree Days (base 65°F)	1,236	958	725	371	113	12	2	4	85	318	722	1,093	5,639
Cooling Degree Days (base 65°F)	0	0	2	20	72	254	394	314	143	18	0	0	1,217
Mean Precipitation (in.)	0.84	0.91	2.39	3.23	4.59	3.76	5.11	4.37	4.13	2.59	2.30	1.01	35.23
Days With ≥ 0.1" Precipitation	3	3	4	6	8	6	6	6	6	4	4	2	58
Days With ≥ 1.0" Precipitation	0	0	0	1	1	1	2	1	1	1	1	0	9
Mean Snowfall (in.)	6.3	5.0	3.6	1.1	0.0	0.0	0.0	0.0	0.0	0.2	1.2	3.6	21.0
Days With ≥ 1.0" Snow Depth	14	10	4	0	0	0	0	0	0	0	2	6	36

Fremont *Dodge County*   Elevation: 1,177 ft.   Latitude: 41° 26' N   Longitude: 96° 28' W

	JAN	FEB	MAR	APR	MAY	JUN	JUL	AUG	SEP	OCT	NOV	DEC	YEAR
Mean Maximum Temp. (°F)	32.4	39.0	50.8	64.7	75.2	84.9	88.1	85.8	78.5	66.2	48.5	36.1	62.5
Mean Temp. (°F)	22.4	28.7	39.6	52.2	63.1	72.8	76.6	74.3	66.0	53.8	38.6	27.0	51.3
Mean Minimum Temp. (°F)	12.3	18.4	28.3	39.7	50.9	60.6	65.0	62.7	53.5	41.3	28.7	17.7	39.9
Extreme Maximum Temp. (°F)	72	77	90	95	98	105	108	107	100	92	84	70	108
Extreme Minimum Temp. (°F)	-27	-20	-10	3	24	40	44	42	24	11	-6	-24	-27
Days Maximum Temp. ≥ 90°F	0	0	0	1	2	9	13	10	4	0	0	0	39
Days Maximum Temp. ≤ 32°F	15	10	3	0	0	0	0	0	0	0	3	11	42
Days Minimum Temp. ≤ 32°F	30	25	20	6	1	0	0	0	0	6	19	29	136
Days Minimum Temp. ≤ 0°F	7	3	0	0	0	0	0	0	0	0	0	3	13
Heating Degree Days (base 65°F)	1,315	1,017	783	392	126	13	1	5	90	355	784	1,173	6,054
Cooling Degree Days (base 65°F)	0	0	1	18	73	254	374	307	135	14	0	0	1,176
Mean Precipitation (in.)	0.78	0.71	2.27	2.85	4.43	4.43	3.23	3.25	3.20	2.35	1.60	0.92	30.02
Days With ≥ 0.1" Precipitation	2	2	5	6	8	7	6	5	5	4	3	2	55
Days With ≥ 1.0" Precipitation	0	0	1	1	1	1	1	1	1	1	0	0	8
Mean Snowfall (in.)	6.6	6.1	6.1	2.1	trace	0.0	0.0	0.0	0.0	0.8	4.2	6.1	32.0
Days With ≥ 1.0" Snow Depth	17	11	5	1	0	0	0	0	0	0	4	11	49

Gavins Point Dam *Cedar County*   Elevation: 1,253 ft.   Latitude: 42° 51' N   Longitude: 97° 28' W

	JAN	FEB	MAR	APR	MAY	JUN	JUL	AUG	SEP	OCT	NOV	DEC	YEAR
Mean Maximum Temp. (°F)	27.5	32.8	44.6	59.2	71.1	81.1	86.3	84.2	75.0	61.9	43.7	31.2	58.2
Mean Temp. (°F)	17.4	22.8	34.6	48.1	59.9	69.6	74.7	72.8	63.0	50.1	34.5	21.8	47.4
Mean Minimum Temp. (°F)	7.3	12.8	24.5	36.8	48.6	58.1	63.2	61.5	50.9	38.2	25.2	12.2	36.6
Extreme Maximum Temp. (°F)	73	78	86	95	95	109	108	108	104	90	79	63	109
Extreme Minimum Temp. (°F)	-30	-26	-10	6	28	37	44	43	26	12	-13	-28	-30
Days Maximum Temp. ≥ 90°F	0	0	0	0	1	5	12	9	3	0	0	0	30
Days Maximum Temp. ≤ 32°F	18	13	6	0	0	0	0	0	0	0	6	16	59
Days Minimum Temp. ≤ 32°F	31	27	24	10	1	0	0	0	1	8	23	30	155
Days Minimum Temp. ≤ 0°F	11	6	1	0	0	0	0	0	0	0	1	5	24
Heating Degree Days (base 65°F)	1,471	1,185	936	512	199	35	7	12	142	460	909	1,335	7,203
Cooling Degree Days (base 65°F)	0	0	0	13	44	170	290	250	82	4	0	0	853
Mean Precipitation (in.)	0.46	0.54	1.98	2.51	3.92	3.66	2.99	3.06	2.30	1.86	1.26	0.69	25.23
Days With ≥ 0.1" Precipitation	1	1	4	5	6	6	5	5	5	4	3	2	47
Days With ≥ 1.0" Precipitation	0	0	0	0	1	1	1	1	0	0	0	0	4
Mean Snowfall (in.)	na	na	na	na	0.0	0.0	0.0	0.0	0.0	0.1	na	na	na
Days With ≥ 1.0" Snow Depth	na	na	na	na	0	0	0	0	0	0	na	na	na

Geneva *Fillmore County*   Elevation: 1,627 ft.   Latitude: 40° 32' N   Longitude: 97° 36' W

	JAN	FEB	MAR	APR	MAY	JUN	JUL	AUG	SEP	OCT	NOV	DEC	YEAR
Mean Maximum Temp. (°F)	34.6	41.2	52.0	64.6	74.0	83.9	87.9	85.5	78.3	66.4	49.5	38.2	63.0
Mean Temp. (°F)	24.3	30.4	40.4	52.2	62.7	72.4	76.6	74.6	66.2	54.3	39.2	28.5	51.8
Mean Minimum Temp. (°F)	14.0	19.6	28.7	39.8	51.3	60.8	65.4	63.5	54.0	42.1	28.7	18.8	40.6
Extreme Maximum Temp. (°F)	76	81	89	96	97	105	105	106	103	93	82	70	106
Extreme Minimum Temp. (°F)	-21	-18	-12	11	27	41	43	45	25	11	-6	-26	-26
Days Maximum Temp. ≥ 90°F	0	0	0	0	1	7	13	10	4	0	0	0	35
Days Maximum Temp. ≤ 32°F	13	8	3	0	0	0	0	0	0	0	3	9	36
Days Minimum Temp. ≤ 32°F	30	25	20	6	0	0	0	0	0	4	20	29	134
Days Minimum Temp. ≤ 0°F	6	3	0	0	0	0	0	0	0	0	0	2	11
Heating Degree Days (base 65°F)	1,256	970	757	392	131	15	2	5	89	338	769	1,125	5,849
Cooling Degree Days (base 65°F)	0	0	1	17	64	234	364	301	133	14	0	0	1,128
Mean Precipitation (in.)	0.62	0.55	2.24	2.95	4.75	4.13	3.62	3.46	3.17	2.16	1.63	0.65	29.93
Days With ≥ 0.1" Precipitation	2	2	4	6	8	6	6	5	5	3	3	2	52
Days With ≥ 1.0" Precipitation	0	0	0	1	1	1	1	1	1	0	0	0	6
Mean Snowfall (in.)	5.4	5.6	5.3	1.5	0.0	0.0	0.0	0.0	0.1	0.4	2.3	3.9	24.5
Days With ≥ 1.0" Snow Depth	11	10	4	1	0	0	0	0	0	0	2	7	35

Genoa 2 W *Nance County*   Elevation: 1,587 ft.   Latitude: 41° 27' N   Longitude: 97° 46' W

	JAN	FEB	MAR	APR	MAY	JUN	JUL	AUG	SEP	OCT	NOV	DEC	YEAR
Mean Maximum Temp. (°F)	33.1	39.6	50.4	63.9	73.8	83.6	87.2	85.2	78.1	66.0	47.9	36.4	62.1
Mean Temp. (°F)	21.9	28.1	38.3	50.5	61.3	71.0	75.0	73.1	64.5	52.2	36.7	25.8	49.9
Mean Minimum Temp. (°F)	10.8	16.5	26.0	37.1	48.6	58.3	62.7	60.9	50.9	38.2	25.5	15.1	37.6
Extreme Maximum Temp. (°F)	74	80	91	97	99	108	107	106	101	95	82	71	108
Extreme Minimum Temp. (°F)	-30	-26	-18	-1	23	37	40	37	21	9	-12	-27	-30
Days Maximum Temp. ≥ 90°F	0	0	0	1	1	7	12	9	4	0	0	0	34
Days Maximum Temp. ≤ 32°F	15	9	3	0	0	0	0	0	0	0	3	11	41
Days Minimum Temp. ≤ 32°F	31	26	24	10	1	0	0	0	1	9	23	30	155
Days Minimum Temp. ≤ 0°F	8	4	1	0	0	0	0	0	0	0	1	4	18
Heating Degree Days (base 65°F)	1,329	1,036	823	439	161	21	3	8	112	400	842	1,209	6,383
Cooling Degree Days (base 65°F)	0	0	0	14	52	206	312	259	105	8	0	0	956
Mean Precipitation (in.)	0.60	0.76	2.22	2.64	4.23	4.33	3.53	3.05	2.59	1.76	1.61	0.79	28.11
Days With ≥ 0.1" Precipitation	2	2	5	5	7	6	6	5	5	4	3	2	52
Days With ≥ 1.0" Precipitation	0	0	0	1	1	1	1	1	0	0	0	0	5
Mean Snowfall (in.)	5.3	5.7	5.6	2.0	0.0	trace	0.0	trace	trace	1.0	5.4	6.6	31.6
Days With ≥ 1.0" Snow Depth	17	12	7	1	0	0	0	0	0	0	4	13	54

Gothenburg *Dawson County*   Elevation: 2,582 ft.   Latitude: 40° 56' N   Longitude: 100° 09' W

	JAN	FEB	MAR	APR	MAY	JUN	JUL	AUG	SEP	OCT	NOV	DEC	YEAR
Mean Maximum Temp. (°F)	36.4	43.1	52.1	63.3	72.8	83.8	88.4	86.5	77.8	65.7	48.7	39.7	63.2
Mean Temp. (°F)	24.4	30.3	38.9	49.6	60.1	70.5	75.3	73.5	63.8	51.3	36.4	27.5	50.1
Mean Minimum Temp. (°F)	12.3	17.5	25.6	35.7	47.4	57.2	62.2	60.3	49.8	36.9	23.9	15.2	37.0
Extreme Maximum Temp. (°F)	73	78	85	93	100	107	109	105	102	91	83	75	109
Extreme Minimum Temp. (°F)	-23	-23	-15	9	23	34	43	41	20	9	-14	-30	-30
Days Maximum Temp. ≥ 90°F	0	0	0	0	1	8	14	12	4	0	0	0	39
Days Maximum Temp. ≤ 32°F	11	7	3	0	0	0	0	0	0	0	3	8	32
Days Minimum Temp. ≤ 32°F	31	27	24	11	1	0	0	0	1	9	26	30	160
Days Minimum Temp. ≤ 0°F	6	3	1	0	0	0	0	0	0	0	1	3	14
Heating Degree Days (base 65°F)	1,252	973	804	464	184	25	3	7	122	421	854	1,155	6,264
Cooling Degree Days (base 65°F)	0	0	0	8	39	187	317	270	87	3	0	0	911
Mean Precipitation (in.)	0.41	0.50	1.37	2.24	3.67	3.74	3.19	2.75	1.56	1.34	0.84	0.44	22.05
Days With ≥ 0.1" Precipitation	1	2	3	4	7	6	6	5	4	3	2	1	44
Days With ≥ 1.0" Precipitation	0	0	0	0	1	1	1	1	0	0	0	0	4
Mean Snowfall (in.)	na	na	3.7	1.0	0.0	0.0	0.0	0.0	0.0	0.2	1.9	na	na
Days With ≥ 1.0" Snow Depth	na	na	2	0	0	0	0	0	0	0	2	na	na

Greeley *Greeley County* Elevation: 2,017 ft. Latitude: 41° 33' N Longitude: 98° 32' W

	JAN	FEB	MAR	APR	MAY	JUN	JUL	AUG	SEP	OCT	NOV	DEC	YEAR
Mean Maximum Temp. (°F)	32.8	39.5	49.7	62.5	72.5	82.9	87.5	85.8	78.2	66.0	47.7	36.9	61.8
Mean Temp. (°F)	20.7	27.3	36.8	48.6	59.2	69.3	74.2	72.2	63.2	50.7	35.4	25.0	48.6
Mean Minimum Temp. (°F)	8.6	15.0	23.9	34.7	45.9	55.8	60.8	58.6	48.2	35.5	23.0	13.1	35.3
Extreme Maximum Temp. (°F)	75	81	88	96	96	105	107	108	102	95	82	73	108
Extreme Minimum Temp. (°F)	-31	-28	-15	6	22	35	36	35	19	4	-16	-26	-31
Days Maximum Temp. ≥ 90°F	0	0	0	1	1	6	12	10	4	0	0	0	34
Days Maximum Temp. ≤ 32°F	15	9	4	0	0	0	0	0	0	0	4	11	43
Days Minimum Temp. ≤ 32°F	31	27	25	12	2	0	0	0	1	11	26	31	166
Days Minimum Temp. ≤ 0°F	9	4	1	0	0	0	0	0	0	0	1	5	20
Heating Degree Days (base 65°F)	1,367	1,058	867	492	207	36	6	11	136	439	882	1,233	6,734
Cooling Degree Days (base 65°F)	0	0	0	8	30	166	286	232	86	3	0	0	811
Mean Precipitation (in.)	0.43	0.57	1.97	2.71	3.87	3.93	3.69	2.79	2.49	1.59	1.41	0.56	26.01
Days With ≥ 0.1" Precipitation	1	2	4	5	7	7	6	5	5	3	3	2	50
Days With ≥ 1.0" Precipitation	0	0	1	1	1	1	1	1	1	0	0	0	7
Mean Snowfall (in.)	na	na	na	0.7	0.0	0.0	0.0	0.0	0.0	0.6	na	na	na
Days With ≥ 1.0" Snow Depth	na	na	na	0	0	0	0	0	0	0	na	na	na

Harlan County Lake *Harlan County* Elevation: 1,998 ft. Latitude: 40° 05' N Longitude: 99° 13' W

	JAN	FEB	MAR	APR	MAY	JUN	JUL	AUG	SEP	OCT	NOV	DEC	YEAR
Mean Maximum Temp. (°F)	35.9	41.3	52.0	63.4	72.5	83.3	89.5	87.2	78.7	67.0	50.0	39.7	63.4
Mean Temp. (°F)	23.5	28.5	38.9	50.1	60.3	70.7	76.5	74.2	64.8	52.5	37.5	27.6	50.4
Mean Minimum Temp. (°F)	11.1	16.2	25.7	36.8	48.0	58.1	63.5	61.2	50.8	38.0	25.0	15.4	37.5
Extreme Maximum Temp. (°F)	77	79	89	97	97	106	107	108	104	93	86	78	108
Extreme Minimum Temp. (°F)	-24	-17	-12	10	26	34	40	43	21	3	-10	-35	-35
Days Maximum Temp. ≥ 90°F	0	0	0	0	1	7	16	13	5	0	0	0	42
Days Maximum Temp. ≤ 32°F	12	8	3	0	0	0	0	0	0	0	3	8	34
Days Minimum Temp. ≤ 32°F	30	27	23	10	1	0	0	0	1	8	25	30	155
Days Minimum Temp. ≤ 0°F	6	4	1	0	0	0	0	0	0	0	0	3	14
Heating Degree Days (base 65°F)	1,279	1,026	801	448	182	27	3	7	113	387	817	1,153	6,243
Cooling Degree Days (base 65°F)	0	0	1	10	42	209	369	304	119	7	0	0	1,061
Mean Precipitation (in.)	0.37	0.43	1.72	2.09	4.17	3.15	3.69	3.15	2.32	1.40	0.96	0.39	23.84
Days With ≥ 0.1" Precipitation	1	1	3	4	7	5	6	5	4	3	2	1	42
Days With ≥ 1.0" Precipitation	0	0	0	0	1	1	1	1	1	0	0	0	5
Mean Snowfall (in.)	4.4	3.7	*3.5*	0.4	0.0	0.0	0.0	0.0	0.2	0.8	*2.0*	*3.6*	*18.6*
Days With ≥ 1.0" Snow Depth	9	*6*	*3*	0	0	0	0	0	0	0	*2*	*5*	*25*

Harrisburg 10 NW *Banner County* Elevation: 4,547 ft. Latitude: 41° 38' N Longitude: 103° 57' W

	JAN	FEB	MAR	APR	MAY	JUN	JUL	AUG	SEP	OCT	NOV	DEC	YEAR
Mean Maximum Temp. (°F)	38.4	43.7	49.9	58.8	68.8	79.6	86.4	85.2	75.6	63.4	49.0	41.0	61.6
Mean Temp. (°F)	25.2	30.1	36.2	44.4	54.5	64.4	70.6	69.1	59.2	47.0	34.7	27.2	46.9
Mean Minimum Temp. (°F)	12.1	16.5	22.4	30.0	40.1	49.2	54.8	53.0	42.6	30.6	20.2	13.4	32.1
Extreme Maximum Temp. (°F)	70	72	81	89	95	103	104	103	100	90	81	74	104
Extreme Minimum Temp. (°F)	-31	-31	-23	-16	18	27	36	34	13	-10	-23	-44	-44
Days Maximum Temp. ≥ 90°F	0	0	0	0	0	4	11	9	3	0	0	0	27
Days Maximum Temp. ≤ 32°F	9	6	3	1	0	0	0	0	0	1	4	7	31
Days Minimum Temp. ≤ 32°F	30	27	28	19	5	0	0	0	4	18	27	30	188
Days Minimum Temp. ≤ 0°F	6	4	1	0	0	0	0	0	0	0	1	5	17
Heating Degree Days (base 65°F)	1,227	979	886	612	328	92	17	23	207	551	904	1,166	6,992
Cooling Degree Days (base 65°F)	0	0	0	0	11	83	200	167	41	1	0	0	503
Mean Precipitation (in.)	0.40	0.43	1.03	1.65	2.57	2.33	2.01	1.39	1.15	1.00	0.61	0.38	14.95
Days With ≥ 0.1" Precipitation	1	1	3	5	6	5	5	4	3	3	2	2	40
Days With ≥ 1.0" Precipitation	0	0	0	0	1	0	0	0	0	0	0	0	1
Mean Snowfall (in.)	7.9	6.4	9.7	6.5	0.7	0.0	0.0	0.0	0.3	2.9	7.1	8.1	49.6
Days With ≥ 1.0" Snow Depth	16	11	9	4	0	0	0	0	0	2	9	15	66

Harrison *Sioux County* Elevation: 4,849 ft. Latitude: 42° 41' N Longitude: 103° 53' W

	JAN	FEB	MAR	APR	MAY	JUN	JUL	AUG	SEP	OCT	NOV	DEC	YEAR
Mean Maximum Temp. (°F)	32.1	37.4	44.7	54.1	64.8	76.2	84.4	83.3	72.5	59.3	43.4	35.1	57.3
Mean Temp. (°F)	20.7	26.1	32.8	41.7	52.1	62.6	69.6	68.4	57.7	45.2	31.6	23.4	44.3
Mean Minimum Temp. (°F)	9.2	14.6	20.9	29.2	39.2	48.9	54.8	53.4	42.8	31.1	19.8	11.7	31.3
Extreme Maximum Temp. (°F)	65	67	76	86	88	103	104	100	97	89	75	66	104
Extreme Minimum Temp. (°F)	-26	-28	-17	-5	15	26	36	37	13	-8	-16	-39	-39
Days Maximum Temp. ≥ 90°F	0	0	0	0	0	2	9	7	2	0	0	0	20
Days Maximum Temp. ≤ 32°F	14	9	6	2	0	0	0	0	0	1	7	12	51
Days Minimum Temp. ≤ 32°F	31	27	29	20	6	0	0	0	4	16	27	30	190
Days Minimum Temp. ≤ 0°F	8	4	1	0	0	0	0	0	0	0	2	5	20
Heating Degree Days (base 65°F)	1,368	1,094	991	694	399	128	29	33	245	606	995	1,283	7,865
Cooling Degree Days (base 65°F)	0	0	0	0	5	60	180	150	33	0	0	0	428
Mean Precipitation (in.)	0.41	0.40	1.09	2.16	3.43	2.58	1.96	1.34	1.53	1.31	0.65	0.46	17.32
Days With ≥ 0.1" Precipitation	2	1	3	5	7	5	5	4	3	3	2	2	42
Days With ≥ 1.0" Precipitation	0	0	0	0	1	0	0	0	0	0	0	0	1
Mean Snowfall (in.)	7.5	6.3	9.6	8.0	0.9	trace	0.0	0.0	0.7	4.0	6.8	7.6	51.4
Days With ≥ 1.0" Snow Depth	*10*	7	7	3	0	0	0	0	0	1	5	*9*	*42*

Hartington *Cedar County*   Elevation: 1,368 ft.   Latitude: 42° 37' N   Longitude: 97° 16' W

	JAN	FEB	MAR	APR	MAY	JUN	JUL	AUG	SEP	OCT	NOV	DEC	YEAR
Mean Maximum Temp. (°F)	29.9	37.0	48.3	62.5	73.9	83.5	87.8	85.7	77.9	65.1	45.6	33.8	60.9
Mean Temp. (°F)	20.0	26.5	36.9	49.8	61.4	71.2	75.6	73.7	64.9	52.5	35.3	24.2	49.4
Mean Minimum Temp. (°F)	10.0	16.0	25.6	37.2	48.9	58.8	63.4	61.7	51.9	39.8	24.9	14.5	37.7
Extreme Maximum Temp. (°F)	74	76	86	97	99	106	107	106	103	94	81	71	107
Extreme Minimum Temp. (°F)	-27	-27	-13	1	24	39	42	39	25	9	-13	-26	-27
Days Maximum Temp. ≥ 90°F	0	0	0	0	1	7	13	10	4	0	0	0	35
Days Maximum Temp. ≤ 32°F	16	11	4	0	0	0	0	0	0	0	4	13	48
Days Minimum Temp. ≤ 32°F	29	26	23	9	1	0	0	0	0	7	23	30	148
Days Minimum Temp. ≤ 0°F	9	5	1	0	0	0	0	0	0	0	1	5	21
Heating Degree Days (base 65°F)	1,388	1,080	863	460	162	22	3	7	111	392	885	1,259	6,632
Cooling Degree Days (base 65°F)	0	0	0	13	54	203	318	269	112	10	0	0	979
Mean Precipitation (in.)	0.51	0.55	2.14	2.72	3.79	4.13	3.14	2.71	2.42	1.97	1.44	0.64	26.16
Days With ≥ 0.1" Precipitation	2	2	4	6	7	6	5	5	4	4	3	2	50
Days With ≥ 1.0" Precipitation	0	0	0	0	1	1	1	1	1	0	0	0	5
Mean Snowfall (in.)	7.0	5.8	6.0	2.7	0.0	trace	0.0	0.0	0.0	0.3	6.0	6.3	34.1
Days With ≥ 1.0" Snow Depth	na	na	na	0	0	0	0	0	0	0	na	na	na

Hastings 4 N *Adams County*   Elevation: 1,938 ft.   Latitude: 40° 39' N   Longitude: 98° 23' W

	JAN	FEB	MAR	APR	MAY	JUN	JUL	AUG	SEP	OCT	NOV	DEC	YEAR
Mean Maximum Temp. (°F)	34.3	40.9	51.0	63.5	73.7	84.5	88.9	86.5	78.5	66.0	48.7	37.6	62.8
Mean Temp. (°F)	23.8	29.9	39.2	50.9	61.9	72.1	76.6	74.3	65.5	53.2	37.9	27.5	51.1
Mean Minimum Temp. (°F)	13.3	18.9	27.3	38.3	50.1	59.8	64.3	62.0	52.4	40.3	27.1	17.4	39.3
Extreme Maximum Temp. (°F)	76	80	89	96	99	109	109	109	102	94	82	71	109
Extreme Minimum Temp. (°F)	-22	-18	-15	9	30	40	47	46	26	4	-4	-23	-23
Days Maximum Temp. ≥ 90°F	0	0	0	1	1	9	15	11	5	0	0	0	42
Days Maximum Temp. ≤ 32°F	13	9	3	0	0	0	0	0	0	0	3	10	38
Days Minimum Temp. ≤ 32°F	30	26	22	7	0	0	0	0	0	6	22	30	143
Days Minimum Temp. ≤ 0°F	6	3	1	0	0	0	0	0	0	0	0	3	13
Heating Degree Days (base 65°F)	1,270	984	796	426	147	17	2	5	99	372	805	1,157	6,080
Cooling Degree Days (base 65°F)	0	0	1	13	55	230	362	294	122	12	0	0	1,089
Mean Precipitation (in.)	0.55	0.62	2.05	2.97	4.58	3.55	3.66	3.22	2.83	1.67	1.41	0.71	27.82
Days With ≥ 0.1" Precipitation	2	2	4	6	8	6	6	6	4	3	3	2	52
Days With ≥ 1.0" Precipitation	0	0	0	1	1	1	1	1	1	0	0	0	6
Mean Snowfall (in.)	5.0	5.4	5.8	1.4	trace	0.0	0.0	0.0	0.2	1.0	3.5	5.7	28.0
Days With ≥ 1.0" Snow Depth	13	10	4	1	0	0	0	0	0	0	4	8	40

Hay Springs *Sheridan County*   Elevation: 3,854 ft.   Latitude: 42° 41' N   Longitude: 102° 42' W

	JAN	FEB	MAR	APR	MAY	JUN	JUL	AUG	SEP	OCT	NOV	DEC	YEAR
Mean Maximum Temp. (°F)	34.8	42.2	49.3	58.7	69.7	79.5	86.4	85.7	76.7	63.5	46.5	38.5	61.0
Mean Temp. (°F)	22.4	29.3	36.0	45.0	55.8	65.4	71.8	70.8	60.7	47.9	33.7	25.6	47.0
Mean Minimum Temp. (°F)	10.0	16.3	22.6	31.2	41.8	51.3	57.1	55.8	44.8	32.2	20.9	12.6	33.1
Extreme Maximum Temp. (°F)	72	73	81	90	91	101	110	103	99	*90*	82	70	*110*
Extreme Minimum Temp. (°F)	-26	-29	-20	-17	22	32	36	37	15	-5	-17	-28	-29
Days Maximum Temp. ≥ 90°F	0	0	0	0	0	4	12	11	4	0	0	0	31
Days Maximum Temp. ≤ 32°F	12	7	4	1	0	0	0	0	0	0	5	9	38
Days Minimum Temp. ≤ 32°F	30	27	28	18	4	0	0	0	2	15	27	30	181
Days Minimum Temp. ≤ 0°F	9	4	1	0	0	0	0	0	0	0	1	5	20
Heating Degree Days (base 65°F)	1,314	1,003	892	595	291	77	14	17	177	524	931	1,216	7,051
Cooling Degree Days (base 65°F)	0	0	0	1	13	88	219	199	54	1	0	0	575
Mean Precipitation (in.)	0.55	0.55	1.37	2.50	3.05	2.91	3.02	1.99	1.40	1.37	0.82	0.53	20.06
Days With ≥ 0.1" Precipitation	2	2	4	6	7	7	6	4	4	3	3	2	50
Days With ≥ 1.0" Precipitation	0	0	0	0	1	0	1	0	0	0	0	0	2
Mean Snowfall (in.)	*8.9*	na	*9.2*	6.4	trace	0.0	0.0	0.0	0.3	3.4	8.4	*8.0*	na
Days With ≥ 1.0" Snow Depth	na	na	na	*2*	0	0	0	0	0	1	*6*	na	na

Hay Springs 12 S *Sheridan County*   Elevation: 3,802 ft.   Latitude: 42° 31' N   Longitude: 102° 42' W

	JAN	FEB	MAR	APR	MAY	JUN	JUL	AUG	SEP	OCT	NOV	DEC	YEAR
Mean Maximum Temp. (°F)	35.8	42.1	49.9	59.9	70.7	81.1	87.2	85.9	76.9	64.2	47.1	38.4	61.6
Mean Temp. (°F)	22.4	28.1	35.7	45.0	55.9	65.8	71.5	70.1	60.1	47.6	33.2	24.6	46.7
Mean Minimum Temp. (°F)	9.0	14.2	21.4	30.0	41.1	50.4	55.8	54.3	43.2	31.0	19.3	10.8	31.7
Extreme Maximum Temp. (°F)	69	73	83	93	92	104	108	102	99	93	82	71	108
Extreme Minimum Temp. (°F)	-34	-31	-21	-15	17	32	37	36	14	-9	-18	-42	-42
Days Maximum Temp. ≥ 90°F	0	0	0	0	1	6	13	11	4	0	0	0	35
Days Maximum Temp. ≤ 32°F	11	6	3	1	0	0	0	0	0	0	5	9	35
Days Minimum Temp. ≤ 32°F	31	27	29	19	5	0	0	0	4	18	28	31	192
Days Minimum Temp. ≤ 0°F	8	4	1	0	0	0	0	0	0	0	1	5	19
Heating Degree Days (base 65°F)	1,315	1,035	901	595	288	73	10	17	186	532	946	1,247	7,145
Cooling Degree Days (base 65°F)	0	0	0	1	16	99	220	190	44	1	0	0	571
Mean Precipitation (in.)	0.31	0.29	0.77	1.84	2.90	2.97	2.57	1.93	1.38	1.06	0.49	0.28	16.79
Days With ≥ 0.1" Precipitation	1	1	2	5	6	6	6	4	3	3	2	1	40
Days With ≥ 1.0" Precipitation	0	0	0	0	0	1	0	0	0	0	0	0	1
Mean Snowfall (in.)	6.0	5.1	7.0	5.8	0.5	0.0	0.0	0.0	0.5	2.4	5.8	5.9	39.0
Days With ≥ 1.0" Snow Depth	13	9	5	2	0	0	0	0	0	1	5	10	45

Hayes Center *Hayes County*   Elevation: 3,038 ft.   Latitude: 40° 31' N   Longitude: 101° 01' W

	JAN	FEB	MAR	APR	MAY	JUN	JUL	AUG	SEP	OCT	NOV	DEC	YEAR
Mean Maximum Temp. (°F)	37.8	43.8	51.6	62.2	71.8	82.6	88.6	86.8	77.9	66.0	49.9	41.0	63.3
Mean Temp. (°F)	26.1	31.2	38.5	48.6	58.9	69.2	74.9	73.1	63.8	51.7	37.5	29.0	50.2
Mean Minimum Temp. (°F)	13.9	18.5	25.4	35.0	45.9	55.7	61.1	59.4	49.6	37.3	25.1	16.8	37.0
Extreme Maximum Temp. (°F)	74	80	86	93	98	104	109	105	102	94	85	75	109
Extreme Minimum Temp. (°F)	-21	-17	-9	7	24	37	46	45	25	11	-6	-27	-27
Days Maximum Temp. ≥ 90°F	0	0	0	0	1	7	15	12	5	0	0	0	40
Days Maximum Temp. ≤ 32°F	10	7	4	0	0	0	0	0	0	0	3	8	32
Days Minimum Temp. ≤ 32°F	30	26	24	12	1	0	0	0	1	8	23	30	155
Days Minimum Temp. ≤ 0°F	5	3	1	0	0	0	0	0	0	0	0	3	12
Heating Degree Days (base 65°F)	1,199	948	814	490	214	37	5	10	126	412	817	1,109	6,181
Cooling Degree Days (base 65°F)	0	0	0	6	31	168	316	270	99	6	0	0	896
Mean Precipitation (in.)	0.51	0.57	1.53	2.17	3.21	3.49	3.14	2.64	1.42	1.36	0.91	0.49	21.44
Days With ≥ 0.1" Precipitation	1	2	4	5	7	6	6	5	3	3	2	1	45
Days With ≥ 1.0" Precipitation	0	0	0	0	1	1	1	1	0	0	0	0	4
Mean Snowfall (in.)	7.0	6.1	8.1	4.2	trace	0.0	0.0	0.0	trace	1.7	4.8	5.0	36.9
Days With ≥ 1.0" Snow Depth	14	10	6	2	0	0	0	0	0	1	5	10	48

Hebron *Thayer County*   Elevation: 1,479 ft.   Latitude: 40° 11' N   Longitude: 97° 35' W

	JAN	FEB	MAR	APR	MAY	JUN	JUL	AUG	SEP	OCT	NOV	DEC	YEAR
Mean Maximum Temp. (°F)	33.9	40.9	51.7	64.0	73.6	84.3	89.6	87.2	79.3	67.2	50.1	38.4	63.4
Mean Temp. (°F)	23.4	29.3	39.8	51.7	62.0	72.5	77.7	75.3	66.3	53.8	39.0	28.2	51.6
Mean Minimum Temp. (°F)	12.9	17.7	27.9	39.4	50.3	60.6	65.7	63.4	53.2	40.2	27.8	17.9	39.8
Extreme Maximum Temp. (°F)	78	80	89	98	100	105	110	109	105	95	83	73	110
Extreme Minimum Temp. (°F)	-21	-16	-15	9	28	39	44	45	25	12	-6	-26	-26
Days Maximum Temp. ≥ 90°F	0	0	0	1	1	8	16	12	6	0	0	0	44
Days Maximum Temp. ≤ 32°F	14	9	3	0	0	0	0	0	0	0	3	9	38
Days Minimum Temp. ≤ 32°F	30	26	21	8	1	0	0	0	0	6	22	29	143
Days Minimum Temp. ≤ 0°F	6	3	1	0	0	0	0	0	0	0	0	2	12
Heating Degree Days (base 65°F)	1,283	1,000	775	407	151	19	2	5	98	354	773	1,136	6,003
Cooling Degree Days (base 65°F)	0	0	1	17	60	241	396	323	143	12	0	0	1,193
Mean Precipitation (in.)	0.75	0.66	2.34	2.68	4.61	3.90	3.95	3.56	2.90	1.99	1.61	0.91	29.86
Days With ≥ 0.1" Precipitation	2	2	4	5	8	6	5	6	5	4	3	2	52
Days With ≥ 1.0" Precipitation	0	0	0	1	1	1	1	1	1	0	0	0	6
Mean Snowfall (in.)	5.7	4.8	5.4	1.2	0.0	0.0	0.0	0.0	trace	0.8	3.1	4.8	25.8
Days With ≥ 1.0" Snow Depth	16	11	4	1	0	0	0	0	0	0	3	9	44

Hemingford *Box Butte County*   Elevation: 4,268 ft.   Latitude: 42° 19' N   Longitude: 103° 04' W

	JAN	FEB	MAR	APR	MAY	JUN	JUL	AUG	SEP	OCT	NOV	DEC	YEAR
Mean Maximum Temp. (°F)	35.4	41.0	47.6	56.7	67.3	78.6	86.1	84.7	74.7	62.0	46.3	38.5	59.9
Mean Temp. (°F)	24.5	29.7	35.9	44.6	55.1	65.6	72.2	70.7	60.9	48.8	35.2	27.3	47.5
Mean Minimum Temp. (°F)	13.6	18.3	24.1	32.5	42.8	52.4	58.1	56.7	47.0	35.6	24.1	16.1	35.1
Extreme Maximum Temp. (°F)	70	71	80	89	91	103	107	102	97	90	78	70	107
Extreme Minimum Temp. (°F)	-23	-25	-13	-6	19	33	41	42	20	-3	-12	-35	-35
Days Maximum Temp. ≥ 90°F	0	0	0	0	0	4	12	10	3	0	0	0	29
Days Maximum Temp. ≤ 32°F	12	7	4	1	0	0	0	0	0	1	5	9	39
Days Minimum Temp. ≤ 32°F	30	26	26	15	3	0	0	0	2	10	24	29	165
Days Minimum Temp. ≤ 0°F	6	3	1	0	0	0	0	0	0	0	1	4	15
Heating Degree Days (base 65°F)	1,250	992	895	605	314	81	14	20	178	498	888	1,161	6,896
Cooling Degree Days (base 65°F)	0	0	0	2	15	101	242	210	64	4	0	0	638
Mean Precipitation (in.)	0.43	0.39	1.05	1.89	3.41	2.63	2.34	1.58	1.34	1.03	0.58	0.37	17.04
Days With ≥ 0.1" Precipitation	1	1	3	5	6	6	5	4	3	3	2	1	40
Days With ≥ 1.0" Precipitation	0	0	0	0	1	1	0	0	0	0	0	0	2
Mean Snowfall (in.)	7.1	6.5	9.8	8.3	0.8	0.0	0.0	0.0	0.8	3.9	7.3	7.0	51.5
Days With ≥ 1.0" Snow Depth	20	13	11	5	0	0	0	0	0	2	10	17	78

Hershey 5 SSE *Lincoln County*   Elevation: 2,949 ft.   Latitude: 41° 06' N   Longitude: 100° 59' W

	JAN	FEB	MAR	APR	MAY	JUN	JUL	AUG	SEP	OCT	NOV	DEC	YEAR
Mean Maximum Temp. (°F)	35.8	43.0	51.5	62.4	72.4	*82.9*	*87.9*	86.5	78.0	66.6	49.4	39.7	*63.0*
Mean Temp. (°F)	23.7	29.8	37.8	48.3	59.0	*69.1*	*74.1*	72.4	62.9	51.2	36.3	27.1	*49.3*
Mean Minimum Temp. (°F)	11.5	16.5	24.1	34.1	45.5	*55.3*	60.2	58.3	47.8	35.7	23.1	14.4	*35.5*
Extreme Maximum Temp. (°F)	73	79	84	95	98	*107*	110	106	102	93	86	75	*110*
Extreme Minimum Temp. (°F)	-23	-23	-15	7	23	*33*	43	41	22	9	-7	-31	*-31*
Days Maximum Temp. ≥ 90°F	0	0	0	0	1	*6*	13	11	5	0	0	0	*36*
Days Maximum Temp. ≤ 32°F	12	7	4	0	0	0	0	0	0	0	4	8	35
Days Minimum Temp. ≤ 32°F	31	27	26	14	2	0	0	0	1	10	26	31	168
Days Minimum Temp. ≤ 0°F	7	3	1	0	0	0	0	0	0	0	1	4	16
Heating Degree Days (base 65°F)	1,275	988	835	500	211	*35*	*7*	10	138	425	856	1,169	*6,449*
Cooling Degree Days (base 65°F)	0	0	0	6	28	*155*	*290*	255	88	5	0	0	*827*
Mean Precipitation (in.)	0.51	0.43	1.12	1.92	3.19	*3.18*	3.01	2.21	1.39	1.24	0.72	0.37	*19.29*
Days With ≥ 0.1" Precipitation	1	1	3	4	7	*6*	6	4	3	3	2	1	*41*
Days With ≥ 1.0" Precipitation	0	0	0	0	1	*1*	1	1	0	0	0	0	*4*
Mean Snowfall (in.)	5.0	4.5	5.7	2.8	trace	0.0	0.0	0.0	0.1	1.2	4.9	4.7	28.9
Days With ≥ 1.0" Snow Depth	14	8	5	1	0	0	0	0	0	1	5	10	44

Holdrege *Phelps County*   Elevation: 2,319 ft.   Latitude: 40° 26' N   Longitude: 99° 22' W

	JAN	FEB	MAR	APR	MAY	JUN	JUL	AUG	SEP	OCT	NOV	DEC	YEAR
Mean Maximum Temp. (°F)	34.7	41.4	50.6	62.7	72.4	83.3	87.8	85.6	77.8	65.7	48.4	38.3	62.4
Mean Temp. (°F)	23.9	29.9	38.4	49.7	60.3	70.6	75.3	73.3	64.6	52.5	37.2	27.7	50.3
Mean Minimum Temp. (°F)	13.1	18.4	26.2	36.7	48.1	57.9	62.8	61.0	51.4	39.2	26.0	17.0	38.1
Extreme Maximum Temp. (°F)	74	78	88	95	98	108	108	105	103	94	82	73	108
Extreme Minimum Temp. (°F)	-21	-19	-12	11	27	40	42	45	26	8	-11	-29	-29
Days Maximum Temp. ≥ 90°F	0	0	0	0	1	7	13	10	4	0	0	0	35
Days Maximum Temp. ≤ 32°F	13	8	3	0	0	0	0	0	0	0	3	10	37
Days Minimum Temp. ≤ 32°F	31	26	23	10	1	0	0	0	1	6	23	30	151
Days Minimum Temp. ≤ 0°F	6	3	1	0	0	0	0	0	0	0	0	3	13
Heating Degree Days (base 65°F)	1,267	985	817	460	182	27	4	8	112	390	827	1,151	6,230
Cooling Degree Days (base 65°F)	0	0	1	10	41	190	322	264	104	7	0	0	939
Mean Precipitation (in.)	0.51	0.48	1.99	2.33	4.45	3.73	3.95	3.25	2.12	1.41	1.26	0.48	25.96
Days With ≥ 0.1" Precipitation	1	2	4	5	8	6	6	5	5	3	3	2	50
Days With ≥ 1.0" Precipitation	0	0	0	0	1	1	1	1	1	0	0	0	5
Mean Snowfall (in.)	5.6	4.8	6.2	2.2	0.0	0.0	0.0	0.0	0.3	1.0	4.2	4.6	28.9
Days With ≥ 1.0" Snow Depth	16	10	5	1	0	0	0	0	0	0	4	10	46

Hyannis *Grant County*   Elevation: 3,769 ft.   Latitude: 42° 00' N   Longitude: 101° 45' W

	JAN	FEB	MAR	APR	MAY	JUN	JUL	AUG	SEP	OCT	NOV	DEC	YEAR
Mean Maximum Temp. (°F)	35.1	40.9	48.8	60.1	70.0	80.6	86.5	85.0	75.9	63.1	na	39.3	na
Mean Temp. (°F)	23.3	28.1	35.9	46.3	56.7	66.7	72.2	70.8	na	48.2	na	26.7	na
Mean Minimum Temp. (°F)	11.3	15.3	23.0	32.4	43.4	52.7	57.8	56.5	na	33.3	21.6	14.1	na
Extreme Maximum Temp. (°F)	71	75	82	93	93	104	105	102	100	90	80	70	105
Extreme Minimum Temp. (°F)	-26	-25	-17	0	20	30	38	36	12	-5	-16	-34	-34
Days Maximum Temp. ≥ 90°F	0	0	0	0	0	4	12	9	3	0	0	0	28
Days Maximum Temp. ≤ 32°F	11	7	4	0	0	0	0	0	0	0	4	9	35
Days Minimum Temp. ≤ 32°F	29	27	26	15	3	0	0	0	2	13	25	30	170
Days Minimum Temp. ≤ 0°F	7	4	1	0	0	0	0	0	0	0	1	4	17
Heating Degree Days (base 65°F)	1,288	1,035	896	558	267	58	10	16	na	515	na	1,179	na
Cooling Degree Days (base 65°F)	0	0	0	3	20	120	243	208	na	1	na	0	na
Mean Precipitation (in.)	0.36	0.48	1.30	1.89	3.46	3.03	3.02	2.19	1.38	1.24	0.74	0.35	19.44
Days With ≥ 0.1" Precipitation	1	1	3	5	6	6	6	4	3	3	2	1	41
Days With ≥ 1.0" Precipitation	0	0	0	0	1	1	1	1	0	0	0	0	4
Mean Snowfall (in.)	4.8	4.9	7.8	4.8	0.2	0.0	0.0	0.0	0.5	1.0	6.1	5.0	35.1
Days With ≥ 1.0" Snow Depth	na	10	7	2	0	0	0	0	0	1	6	12	na

Imperial *Chase County*   Elevation: 3,274 ft.   Latitude: 40° 31' N   Longitude: 101° 39' W

	JAN	FEB	MAR	APR	MAY	JUN	JUL	AUG	SEP	OCT	NOV	DEC	YEAR
Mean Maximum Temp. (°F)	39.1	46.0	53.6	63.9	73.5	83.9	89.8	87.9	79.7	67.5	50.4	41.7	64.8
Mean Temp. (°F)	26.7	32.6	39.9	49.6	60.1	70.2	75.9	74.1	64.9	52.2	37.6	29.2	51.1
Mean Minimum Temp. (°F)	14.4	19.1	26.0	35.2	46.7	56.5	61.9	60.2	50.1	37.0	24.7	16.6	37.4
Extreme Maximum Temp. (°F)	72	78	86	95	98	104	107	104	102	94	83	74	107
Extreme Minimum Temp. (°F)	-22	-22	-10	6	22	37	44	41	20	6	-8	-34	-34
Days Maximum Temp. ≥ 90°F	0	0	0	0	1	8	17	14	6	0	0	0	46
Days Maximum Temp. ≤ 32°F	9	5	3	0	0	0	0	0	0	0	3	7	27
Days Minimum Temp. ≤ 32°F	30	27	24	12	1	0	0	0	1	9	25	30	159
Days Minimum Temp. ≤ 0°F	4	2	1	0	0	0	0	0	0	0	0	3	10
Heating Degree Days (base 65°F)	1,179	908	773	461	184	28	3	5	102	393	815	1,104	5,955
Cooling Degree Days (base 65°F)	0	0	0	5	41	186	344	293	108	4	0	0	981
Mean Precipitation (in.)	0.52	0.49	1.39	1.93	3.28	3.20	2.83	2.49	1.30	1.15	0.78	0.44	19.80
Days With ≥ 0.1" Precipitation	2	1	3	4	6	6	5	4	3	3	2	1	40
Days With ≥ 1.0" Precipitation	0	0	0	0	1	1	1	1	0	0	0	0	4
Mean Snowfall (in.)	5.7	4.5	7.7	3.5	0.2	0.0	0.0	0.0	0.2	1.9	5.2	4.8	33.7
Days With ≥ 1.0" Snow Depth	13	8	5	1	0	0	0	0	0	1	5	10	43

Kearney 4 NE *Buffalo County*   Elevation: 2,129 ft.   Latitude: 40° 44' N   Longitude: 99° 01' W

	JAN	FEB	MAR	APR	MAY	JUN	JUL	AUG	SEP	OCT	NOV	DEC	YEAR
Mean Maximum Temp. (°F)	34.3	40.7	50.1	62.4	72.3	83.1	87.8	85.6	77.6	65.6	48.3	37.8	62.1
Mean Temp. (°F)	22.8	28.5	37.6	49.1	60.0	70.4	75.2	72.9	63.7	51.4	36.4	26.5	49.5
Mean Minimum Temp. (°F)	11.2	16.2	25.0	35.9	47.7	57.7	62.4	60.1	49.8	37.2	24.4	15.2	36.9
Extreme Maximum Temp. (°F)	77	79	89	95	100	108	108	105	101	93	83	72	108
Extreme Minimum Temp. (°F)	-21	-21	-17	5	24	36	42	40	19	6	-13	-30	-30
Days Maximum Temp. ≥ 90°F	0	0	0	1	1	7	14	10	5	0	0	0	38
Days Maximum Temp. ≤ 32°F	13	9	4	0	0	0	0	0	0	0	4	10	40
Days Minimum Temp. ≤ 32°F	31	27	24	11	1	0	0	0	1	9	25	31	160
Days Minimum Temp. ≤ 0°F	8	4	1	0	0	0	0	0	0	0	0	3	16
Heating Degree Days (base 65°F)	1,303	1,024	842	478	192	30	4	11	129	419	853	1,187	6,472
Cooling Degree Days (base 65°F)	0	0	1	10	44	194	323	261	101	6	0	0	940
Mean Precipitation (in.)	0.52	0.56	2.00	2.45	4.16	3.66	3.35	2.92	2.15	1.51	1.18	0.60	25.06
Days With ≥ 0.1" Precipitation	1	1	4	5	8	6	6	5	4	3	3	2	48
Days With ≥ 1.0" Precipitation	0	0	0	1	1	1	1	1	1	0	0	0	6
Mean Snowfall (in.)	5.5	5.2	6.2	2.0	0.0	0.0	0.0	0.0	0.2	0.8	4.4	6.1	30.4
Days With ≥ 1.0" Snow Depth	na	6	4	1	0	0	0	0	0	0	2	na	na

Kimball 2 N *Kimball County*   Elevation: 4,757 ft.   Latitude: 41° 15' N   Longitude: 103° 40' W

	JAN	FEB	MAR	APR	MAY	JUN	JUL	AUG	SEP	OCT	NOV	DEC	YEAR
Mean Maximum Temp. (°F)	38.8	43.9	49.9	58.7	68.8	80.2	87.0	85.3	76.0	63.6	48.8	41.0	61.8
Mean Temp. (°F)	25.9	30.5	36.4	44.8	55.0	65.5	71.7	69.8	60.0	47.9	35.3	27.7	47.5
Mean Minimum Temp. (°F)	12.9	17.0	22.9	30.9	41.2	50.7	56.4	54.4	44.0	32.1	21.7	14.3	33.2
Extreme Maximum Temp. (°F)	72	73	81	90	95	105	103	102	99	91	83	73	105
Extreme Minimum Temp. (°F)	-26	-27	-10	-11	23	33	41	38	14	3	-13	-35	-35
Days Maximum Temp. ≥ 90°F	0	0	0	0	0	5	13	10	4	0	0	0	32
Days Maximum Temp. ≤ 32°F	9	6	4	1	0	0	0	0	0	1	4	8	33
Days Minimum Temp. ≤ 32°F	31	27	28	18	3	0	0	0	2	15	27	30	181
Days Minimum Temp. ≤ 0°F	5	3	1	0	0	0	0	0	0	0	1	4	14
Heating Degree Days (base 65°F)	1,206	969	879	599	313	78	11	18	187	524	884	1,151	6,819
Cooling Degree Days (base 65°F)	0	0	0	0	11	100	229	183	48	2	0	0	573
Mean Precipitation (in.)	0.41	0.30	1.13	1.57	2.90	2.64	2.85	1.89	1.39	0.91	0.61	0.49	17.09
Days With ≥ 0.1" Precipitation	1	1	3	4	7	6	5	5	3	3	2	2	42
Days With ≥ 1.0" Precipitation	0	0	0	0	0	0	1	0	0	0	0	0	1
Mean Snowfall (in.)	6.9	4.1	10.6	5.8	0.7	0.0	0.0	0.0	0.4	2.6	6.9	7.6	45.6
Days With ≥ 1.0" Snow Depth	11	6	6	2	0	0	0	0	0	1	5	10	41

Kingsley Dam *Keith County*   Elevation: 3,316 ft.   Latitude: 41° 13' N   Longitude: 101° 40' W

	JAN	FEB	MAR	APR	MAY	JUN	JUL	AUG	SEP	OCT	NOV	DEC	YEAR
Mean Maximum Temp. (°F)	36.8	43.9	51.9	62.5	72.2	82.7	89.2	87.6	78.6	66.2	49.5	39.9	63.4
Mean Temp. (°F)	26.0	31.6	39.0	49.2	59.4	69.5	75.6	74.0	64.7	52.7	38.4	29.3	50.8
Mean Minimum Temp. (°F)	15.1	19.1	26.1	35.8	46.7	56.2	61.9	60.3	50.8	39.0	27.3	18.7	38.1
Extreme Maximum Temp. (°F)	70	75	84	93	100	103	108	104	102	93	80	68	108
Extreme Minimum Temp. (°F)	-22	-18	-15	5	26	36	44	40	24	7	-4	-25	-25
Days Maximum Temp. ≥ 90°F	0	0	0	0	1	7	16	14	5	0	0	0	43
Days Maximum Temp. ≤ 32°F	10	6	3	0	0	0	0	0	0	0	3	8	30
Days Minimum Temp. ≤ 32°F	30	26	24	10	1	0	0	0	1	6	21	29	148
Days Minimum Temp. ≤ 0°F	5	3	1	0	0	0	0	0	0	0	0	3	12
Heating Degree Days (base 65°F)	1,203	938	797	472	200	32	3	7	106	380	791	1,100	6,029
Cooling Degree Days (base 65°F)	0	0	0	5	36	169	334	297	107	6	0	0	954
Mean Precipitation (in.)	0.50	0.57	1.41	1.90	3.37	3.14	2.58	1.87	1.47	0.98	0.82	0.42	19.03
Days With ≥ 0.1" Precipitation	2	2	3	5	6	6	5	4	3	3	2	1	42
Days With ≥ 1.0" Precipitation	0	0	0	0	1	1	1	0	0	0	0	0	3
Mean Snowfall (in.)	6.4	5.9	8.9	3.1	0.3	0.0	0.0	0.0	0.1	0.5	5.8	5.4	36.4
Days With ≥ 1.0" Snow Depth	13	7	5	1	0	0	0	0	0	0	4	10	40

Lincoln *Lancaster County*   Elevation: 1,217 ft.   Latitude: 40° 48' N   Longitude: 96° 39' W

	JAN	FEB	MAR	APR	MAY	JUN	JUL	AUG	SEP	OCT	NOV	DEC	YEAR
Mean Maximum Temp. (°F)	32.8	38.4	50.3	63.1	73.7	84.6	88.8	86.4	77.9	66.1	48.5	37.1	62.3
Mean Temp. (°F)	23.4	28.5	39.6	51.9	62.8	73.7	75.5	76.0	66.7	54.4	38.9	28.2	51.6
Mean Minimum Temp. (°F)	13.9	18.6	28.9	40.6	51.9	62.7	67.7	65.5	55.3	42.8	29.2	19.4	41.4
Extreme Maximum Temp. (°F)	72	83	89	99	99	109	108	107	103	95	81	*74*	*109*
Extreme Minimum Temp. (°F)	-22	-19	-10	10	28	42	46	46	29	8	-1	*-27*	*-27*
Days Maximum Temp. ≥ 90°F	0	0	0	1	1	9	14	11	4	0	0	0	40
Days Maximum Temp. ≤ 32°F	14	10	3	0	0	0	0	0	0	0	3	10	40
Days Minimum Temp. ≤ 32°F	30	25	19	6	0	0	0	0	0	4	19	29	132
Days Minimum Temp. ≤ 0°F	6	3	0	0	0	0	0	0	0	0	0	2	11
Heating Degree Days (base 65°F)	1,285	1,025	781	407	135	15	1	4	86	339	777	1,134	5,989
Cooling Degree Days (base 65°F)	0	0	1	21	69	271	415	341	*139*	*14*	0	*0*	*1,271*
Mean Precipitation (in.)	0.59	0.69	2.23	2.83	4.58	3.78	3.97	3.66	3.14	2.28	1.57	0.86	30.18
Days With ≥ 0.1" Precipitation	2	2	4	5	7	6	5	5	5	3	3	2	49
Days With ≥ 1.0" Precipitation	0	0	1	1	2	1	1	1	1	1	0	0	9
Mean Snowfall (in.)	5.4	4.8	4.0	1.2	trace	trace	0.0	0.0	trace	0.9	3.0	4.5	23.8
Days With ≥ 1.0" Snow Depth	14	10	4	1	0	0	0	0	0	0	*2*	*6*	*37*

Lodgepole *Cheyenne County*   Elevation: 3,832 ft.   Latitude: 41° 09' N   Longitude: 102° 38' W

	JAN	FEB	MAR	APR	MAY	JUN	JUL	AUG	SEP	OCT	NOV	DEC	YEAR
Mean Maximum Temp. (°F)	40.7	47.4	54.6	63.9	73.9	85.0	91.7	90.0	80.9	68.4	51.1	42.4	65.8
Mean Temp. (°F)	27.2	32.9	39.7	48.5	58.8	69.0	75.4	73.8	63.9	51.7	37.2	28.8	50.6
Mean Minimum Temp. (°F)	13.7	18.3	24.6	33.0	43.5	52.8	59.1	57.4	46.8	34.7	23.1	15.2	35.2
Extreme Maximum Temp. (°F)	69	77	83	93	96	107	107	105	101	91	80	71	107
Extreme Minimum Temp. (°F)	-23	-25	-17	-7	17	34	42	39	15	-1	-11	-34	-34
Days Maximum Temp. ≥ 90°F	0	0	0	0	1	10	20	18	7	0	0	0	56
Days Maximum Temp. ≤ 32°F	7	4	2	0	0	0	0	0	0	0	2	6	21
Days Minimum Temp. ≤ 32°F	30	27	26	14	2	0	0	0	2	11	26	30	168
Days Minimum Temp. ≤ 0°F	5	3	1	0	0	0	0	0	0	0	1	3	13
Heating Degree Days (base 65°F)	1,165	898	777	492	215	38	3	6	119	409	827	1,118	6,067
Cooling Degree Days (base 65°F)	0	0	0	3	32	166	337	296	98	3	0	0	935
Mean Precipitation (in.)	0.41	0.46	1.31	1.85	3.18	3.04	2.54	2.13	1.38	0.95	0.74	0.43	18.42
Days With ≥ 0.1" Precipitation	1	1	3	4	6	6	5	5	3	3	2	2	41
Days With ≥ 1.0" Precipitation	0	0	0	0	1	1	0	0	0	0	0	0	2
Mean Snowfall (in.)	5.2	5.4	7.8	3.7	0.3	0.0	0.0	0.0	0.2	1.0	*6.1*	6.1	*35.8*
Days With ≥ 1.0" Snow Depth	11	6	4	1	0	0	0	0	0	0	*4*	*9*	*35*

Loup City *Sherman County*   Elevation: 2,063 ft.   Latitude: 41° 17' N   Longitude: 98° 58' W

	JAN	FEB	MAR	APR	MAY	JUN	JUL	AUG	SEP	OCT	NOV	DEC	YEAR
Mean Maximum Temp. (°F)	33.8	40.0	49.6	61.9	71.9	81.7	87.2	85.3	77.0	65.6	48.3	38.0	61.7
Mean Temp. (°F)	21.3	27.4	37.1	48.5	59.4	69.1	74.5	72.6	62.8	50.7	35.9	25.7	48.8
Mean Minimum Temp. (°F)	8.7	14.8	24.4	35.1	46.8	56.5	61.9	59.9	48.6	35.9	23.4	13.4	35.8
Extreme Maximum Temp. (°F)	75	80	90	93	97	103	105	103	103	94	80	73	105
Extreme Minimum Temp. (°F)	-23	-25	-14	9	24	35	42	39	14	6	-16	-26	-26
Days Maximum Temp. ≥ 90°F	0	0	0	0	1	5	13	10	4	0	0	0	33
Days Maximum Temp. ≤ 32°F	14	10	4	0	0	0	0	0	0	0	4	10	42
Days Minimum Temp. ≤ 32°F	31	27	25	12	1	0	0	0	2	10	25	31	164
Days Minimum Temp. ≤ 0°F	9	4	1	0	0	0	0	0	0	0	1	4	19
Heating Degree Days (base 65°F)	1,349	1,055	859	494	205	39	6	11	143	440	867	1,210	6,678
Cooling Degree Days (base 65°F)	0	0	0	9	33	156	296	249	85	4	0	0	832
Mean Precipitation (in.)	0.55	0.66	2.26	3.03	3.96	3.84	3.45	2.73	2.39	1.54	1.51	0.73	26.65
Days With ≥ 0.1" Precipitation	1	2	4	6	8	7	6	5	4	3	3	2	51
Days With ≥ 1.0" Precipitation	0	0	1	1	1	1	1	1	1	0	0	0	7
Mean Snowfall (in.)	7.1	5.8	7.3	1.8	0.0	0.0	0.0	0.0	0.1	1.0	5.6	7.1	35.8
Days With ≥ 1.0" Snow Depth	na	na	na	0	0	0	0	0	0	0	0	na	na	na

Madison 2 W *Madison County*   Elevation: 1,673 ft.   Latitude: 41° 50' N   Longitude: 97° 27' W

	JAN	FEB	MAR	APR	MAY	JUN	JUL	AUG	SEP	OCT	NOV	DEC	YEAR
Mean Maximum Temp. (°F)	30.4	37.0	47.7	61.5	72.6	82.9	87.0	84.6	77.0	64.8	46.3	34.8	60.6
Mean Temp. (°F)	19.6	26.0	36.1	48.8	60.2	70.5	74.7	72.5	63.4	50.9	35.3	24.3	48.5
Mean Minimum Temp. (°F)	8.7	14.9	24.4	35.9	47.8	58.0	62.4	60.3	49.7	36.9	24.2	13.7	36.4
Extreme Maximum Temp. (°F)	71	76	89	94	98	104	104	104	100	93	81	72	104
Extreme Minimum Temp. (°F)	-30	-26	-17	-2	23	35	38	38	19	8	-12	-28	-30
Days Maximum Temp. ≥ 90°F	0	0	0	0	1	7	11	9	4	0	0	0	32
Days Maximum Temp. ≤ 32°F	17	11	4	0	0	0	0	0	0	0	4	12	48
Days Minimum Temp. ≤ 32°F	31	27	25	10	1	0	0	0	1	10	25	30	160
Days Minimum Temp. ≤ 0°F	9	5	1	0	0	0	0	0	0	0	1	4	20
Heating Degree Days (base 65°F)	1,401	1,096	890	491	189	31	5	12	136	438	886	1,258	6,833
Cooling Degree Days (base 65°F)	0	0	0	10	41	184	288	230	85	6	0	0	844
Mean Precipitation (in.)	0.51	0.60	1.98	2.67	4.14	4.09	3.60	3.16	2.37	1.84	1.42	0.67	27.05
Days With ≥ 0.1" Precipitation	1	2	4	6	8	6	6	5	4	4	3	2	51
Days With ≥ 1.0" Precipitation	0	0	0	1	1	1	1	1	1	0	0	0	6
Mean Snowfall (in.)	4.3	4.4	4.6	1.4	0.0	0.0	0.0	0.0	trace	0.5	3.9	5.9	25.0
Days With ≥ 1.0" Snow Depth	11	8	4	0	0	0	0	0	0	0	3	10	36

Madrid *Perkins County*   Elevation: 3,198 ft.   Latitude: 40° 51' N   Longitude: 101° 33' W

	JAN	FEB	MAR	APR	MAY	JUN	JUL	AUG	SEP	OCT	NOV	DEC	YEAR
Mean Maximum Temp. (°F)	38.1	45.4	53.3	64.0	74.1	85.5	91.4	89.5	80.9	68.2	50.0	41.0	65.1
Mean Temp. (°F)	25.5	31.8	39.4	49.3	60.0	70.6	76.2	74.4	64.9	52.1	36.9	28.1	50.7
Mean Minimum Temp. (°F)	12.9	18.0	25.3	34.5	45.8	55.6	60.8	59.2	48.8	35.9	23.7	15.2	36.3
Extreme Maximum Temp. (°F)	72	77	84	97	98	106	109	106	101	92	81	73	109
Extreme Minimum Temp. (°F)	-23	-22	-12	2	21	34	43	41	22	5	-13	-33	-33
Days Maximum Temp. ≥ 90°F	0	0	0	0	1	11	20	17	7	0	0	0	56
Days Maximum Temp. ≤ 32°F	10	5	3	0	0	0	0	0	0	0	3	7	28
Days Minimum Temp. ≤ 32°F	30	27	25	13	2	0	0	0	1	10	26	30	164
Days Minimum Temp. ≤ 0°F	6	3	1	0	0	0	0	0	0	0	0	3	13
Heating Degree Days (base 65°F)	1,217	932	788	470	191	27	3	5	104	399	838	1,136	6,110
Cooling Degree Days (base 65°F)	0	0	0	6	44	191	346	299	106	4	0	0	996
Mean Precipitation (in.)	0.46	0.49	1.36	1.88	3.37	3.45	3.10	2.51	1.35	1.13	0.81	0.39	20.30
Days With ≥ 0.1" Precipitation	2	1	3	4	6	6	6	4	3	2	2	1	40
Days With ≥ 1.0" Precipitation	0	0	0	0	1	1	1	1	0	0	0	0	4
Mean Snowfall (in.)	6.9	5.8	8.8	3.9	trace	0.0	0.0	0.0	0.1	1.4	5.8	6.3	39.0
Days With ≥ 1.0" Snow Depth	11	6	4	1	0	0	0	0	0	0	4	7	33

McCook *Red Willow County*   Elevation: 2,572 ft.   Latitude: 40° 13' N   Longitude: 100° 35' W

	JAN	FEB	MAR	APR	MAY	JUN	JUL	AUG	SEP	OCT	NOV	DEC	YEAR
Mean Maximum Temp. (°F)	38.5	44.7	52.5	63.8	73.0	84.2	90.0	87.6	79.1	67.1	51.0	41.4	64.4
Mean Temp. (°F)	26.2	31.8	39.3	49.9	60.1	70.7	76.5	74.3	65.0	52.3	38.0	29.1	51.1
Mean Minimum Temp. (°F)	13.9	18.8	25.9	36.0	47.2	57.2	63.0	61.0	50.9	37.5	24.9	16.7	37.7
Extreme Maximum Temp. (°F)	75	82	89	96	100	108	109	106	104	93	84	77	109
Extreme Minimum Temp. (°F)	-20	-18	-8	12	23	37	46	44	23	13	-7	-27	-27
Days Maximum Temp. ≥ 90°F	0	0	0	0	1	9	17	14	6	0	0	0	47
Days Maximum Temp. ≤ 32°F	10	7	3	0	0	0	0	0	0	0	3	8	31
Days Minimum Temp. ≤ 32°F	31	27	24	11	1	0	0	0	1	8	24	30	157
Days Minimum Temp. ≤ 0°F	4	3	1	0	0	0	0	0	0	0	0	3	11
Heating Degree Days (base 65°F)	1,196	930	792	454	186	28	3	7	108	395	804	1,107	6,010
Cooling Degree Days (base 65°F)	0	0	0	8	42	201	349	297	112	6	0	0	1,015
Mean Precipitation (in.)	0.47	0.58	1.41	2.22	3.20	3.23	3.26	2.74	1.35	1.23	1.02	0.54	21.25
Days With ≥ 0.1" Precipitation	2	2	3	4	7	5	5	5	3	3	2	1	42
Days With ≥ 1.0" Precipitation	0	0	0	1	1	1	1	1	0	0	0	0	5
Mean Snowfall (in.)	*7.2*	4.9	6.6	*3.2*	trace	0.0	0.0	0.0	0.2	0.9	4.6	5.6	*33.2*
Days With ≥ 1.0" Snow Depth	*12*	9	*4*	*1*	0	0	0	0	0	0	3	8	*37*

Mead 6 S *Saunders County*   Elevation: 1,154 ft.   Latitude: 41° 08' N   Longitude: 96° 29' W

	JAN	FEB	MAR	APR	MAY	JUN	JUL	AUG	SEP	OCT	NOV	DEC	YEAR
Mean Maximum Temp. (°F)	31.4	37.7	49.5	63.0	73.4	83.9	87.8	85.2	77.7	65.7	48.1	36.7	61.7
Mean Temp. (°F)	20.5	26.7	38.0	50.6	61.5	71.8	75.9	73.3	64.8	52.5	37.3	26.6	50.0
Mean Minimum Temp. (°F)	9.6	15.8	26.5	38.2	49.5	59.6	63.9	61.3	51.7	39.2	26.7	16.5	38.2
Extreme Maximum Temp. (°F)	71	78	90	97	99	108	107	105	102	94	86	69	108
Extreme Minimum Temp. (°F)	-35	-29	-18	3	23	37	39	38	26	9	-7	-27	-35
Days Maximum Temp. ≥ 90°F	0	0	0	1	1	8	13	9	4	0	0	0	36
Days Maximum Temp. ≤ 32°F	15	11	4	0	0	0	0	0	0	0	3	10	43
Days Minimum Temp. ≤ 32°F	31	27	22	9	1	0	0	0	1	7	22	29	149
Days Minimum Temp. ≤ 0°F	9	4	1	0	0	0	0	0	0	0	0	3	17
Heating Degree Days (base 65°F)	1,373	1,074	833	441	165	20	3	9	114	392	823	1,183	6,430
Cooling Degree Days (base 65°F)	0	0	1	19	59	230	343	267	116	9	0	0	1,044
Mean Precipitation (in.)	0.48	0.49	1.81	2.74	4.22	3.92	3.23	3.46	2.99	2.22	1.57	0.68	27.81
Days With ≥ 0.1" Precipitation	2	1	4	6	7	6	5	5	5	4	3	2	50
Days With ≥ 1.0" Precipitation	0	0	0	0	1	1	1	1	1	1	0	0	6
Mean Snowfall (in.)	4.3	3.8	3.1	0.9	0.0	0.0	0.0	0.0	0.0	0.5	2.8	4.0	19.4
Days With ≥ 1.0" Snow Depth	14	11	5	1	0	0	0	0	0	0	0	3	8	42

Medicine Creek Dam *Frontier County*   Elevation: 2,385 ft.   Latitude: 40° 23' N   Longitude: 100° 13' W

	JAN	FEB	MAR	APR	MAY	JUN	JUL	AUG	SEP	OCT	NOV	DEC	YEAR
Mean Maximum Temp. (°F)	36.9	43.2	52.0	63.2	72.2	83.2	88.8	87.2	78.6	67.1	50.2	40.3	63.6
Mean Temp. (°F)	23.9	29.6	38.4	49.1	59.4	69.9	75.4	73.4	63.6	51.2	36.6	27.2	49.8
Mean Minimum Temp. (°F)	10.8	15.9	24.7	35.0	46.6	56.6	61.9	59.6	48.6	35.3	22.9	14.0	36.0
Extreme Maximum Temp. (°F)	75	81	88	95	98	109	109	107	106	96	85	78	109
Extreme Minimum Temp. (°F)	-27	-26	-12	10	25	36	42	42	19	9	-10	-35	-35
Days Maximum Temp. ≥ 90°F	0	0	0	1	1	8	15	13	6	1	0	0	45
Days Maximum Temp. ≤ 32°F	11	8	3	0	0	0	0	0	0	0	3	8	33
Days Minimum Temp. ≤ 32°F	30	27	25	12	1	0	0	0	2	11	26	31	165
Days Minimum Temp. ≤ 0°F	6	4	1	0	0	0	0	0	0	0	1	4	16
Heating Degree Days (base 65°F)	1,263	993	820	477	202	33	4	8	131	425	846	1,165	6,367
Cooling Degree Days (base 65°F)	0	0	0	9	36	184	326	276	96	6	0	0	933
Mean Precipitation (in.)	0.39	0.49	1.40	2.01	3.43	3.64	3.14	2.69	1.47	1.16	1.01	0.41	21.24
Days With ≥ 0.1" Precipitation	1	1	3	4	7	5	6	4	3	3	2	1	40
Days With ≥ 1.0" Precipitation	0	0	0	0	1	1	1	1	0	0	0	0	4
Mean Snowfall (in.)	3.9	4.1	3.6	1.2	0.0	0.0	0.0	0.0	0.0	trace	*2.1*	*3.8*	*18.7*
Days With ≥ 1.0" Snow Depth	10	7	4	1	0	0	0	0	0	0	3	8	33

Merriman *Cherry County*   Elevation: 3,248 ft.   Latitude: 42° 55' N   Longitude: 101° 42' W

	JAN	FEB	MAR	APR	MAY	JUN	JUL	AUG	SEP	OCT	NOV	DEC	YEAR
Mean Maximum Temp. (°F)	33.5	40.2	48.2	59.0	70.3	80.8	87.8	86.7	77.3	64.0	46.4	37.2	61.0
Mean Temp. (°F)	22.0	28.1	35.8	46.1	57.2	67.0	73.3	71.9	61.8	49.3	34.4	25.5	47.7
Mean Minimum Temp. (°F)	10.5	15.8	23.4	33.1	44.0	53.2	58.7	57.0	46.3	34.4	22.3	13.8	34.4
Extreme Maximum Temp. (°F)	69	75	84	95	97	109	108	107	105	94	84	70	109
Extreme Minimum Temp. (°F)	-29	-32	-21	4	19	32	38	33	18	-1	-22	-36	-36
Days Maximum Temp. ≥ 90°F	0	0	0	0	1	6	14	12	6	1	0	0	40
Days Maximum Temp. ≤ 32°F	13	8	5	1	0	0	0	0	0	0	5	10	42
Days Minimum Temp. ≤ 32°F	30	26	26	14	3	0	0	0	2	12	25	30	168
Days Minimum Temp. ≤ 0°F	8	4	1	0	0	0	0	0	0	0	1	5	19
Heating Degree Days (base 65°F)	1,327	1,037	898	564	263	67	11	19	171	486	913	1,218	6,974
Cooling Degree Days (base 65°F)	0	0	0	5	29	131	275	243	82	6	0	0	771
Mean Precipitation (in.)	0.34	0.43	0.97	1.93	2.97	3.27	2.90	1.89	1.61	1.18	0.67	0.31	18.47
Days With ≥ 0.1" Precipitation	1	1	3	5	6	6	6	4	3	3	2	1	41
Days With ≥ 1.0" Precipitation	0	0	0	0	1	1	1	0	0	0	0	0	3
Mean Snowfall (in.)	4.2	4.6	7.6	5.1	0.2	trace	trace	trace	0.3	2.6	6.5	4.3	35.4
Days With ≥ 1.0" Snow Depth	15	11	7	3	0	0	0	0	0	1	7	14	58

Minden *Kearney County*   Elevation: 2,158 ft.   Latitude: 40° 31' N   Longitude: 98° 57' W

	JAN	FEB	MAR	APR	MAY	JUN	JUL	AUG	SEP	OCT	NOV	DEC	YEAR
Mean Maximum Temp. (°F)	36.7	43.6	53.9	65.4	74.5	84.9	89.6	87.2	80.0	68.2	50.2	39.7	64.5
Mean Temp. (°F)	25.0	31.0	40.6	51.6	61.9	71.9	76.8	74.6	66.1	54.0	38.3	28.4	51.7
Mean Minimum Temp. (°F)	13.2	18.6	27.3	37.8	49.3	58.9	63.9	62.0	52.1	39.7	26.5	17.2	38.9
Extreme Maximum Temp. (°F)	78	80	88	96	99	107	108	107	107	94	82	74	108
Extreme Minimum Temp. (°F)	-21	-20	-13	9	24	37	44	42	20	1	-15	-31	-31
Days Maximum Temp. ≥ 90°F	0	0	0	1	1	8	16	13	5	0	0	0	44
Days Maximum Temp. ≤ 32°F	11	7	2	0	0	0	0	0	0	0	3	8	31
Days Minimum Temp. ≤ 32°F	30	26	21	9	1	0	0	0	1	6	22	30	146
Days Minimum Temp. ≤ 0°F	6	3	1	0	0	0	0	0	0	0	0	3	13
Heating Degree Days (base 65°F)	1,234	955	749	407	145	18	2	5	90	348	793	1,126	5,872
Cooling Degree Days (base 65°F)	0	0	1	15	57	228	373	307	132	13	0	0	1,126
Mean Precipitation (in.)	0.42	0.48	1.95	2.24	4.18	3.31	3.82	3.18	2.31	1.51	1.25	0.50	25.15
Days With ≥ 0.1" Precipitation	1	1	4	5	7	6	6	5	4	3	3	1	46
Days With ≥ 1.0" Precipitation	0	0	0	0	1	1	1	1	1	0	0	0	5
Mean Snowfall (in.)	5.1	4.6	5.5	2.6	trace	0.0	0.0	0.0	0.3	0.9	3.7	4.2	26.9
Days With ≥ 1.0" Snow Depth	15	10	5	1	0	0	0	0	0	0	3	10	44

Mitchell 5 E *Scotts Bluff County*   Elevation: 4,078 ft.   Latitude: 41° 57' N   Longitude: 103° 42' W

	JAN	FEB	MAR	APR	MAY	JUN	JUL	AUG	SEP	OCT	NOV	DEC	YEAR
Mean Maximum Temp. (°F)	37.1	43.1	50.0	59.7	70.4	81.7	86.9	84.7	76.3	64.2	*48.1*	39.6	*61.8*
Mean Temp. (°F)	24.8	29.8	36.9	45.8	56.5	67.4	72.2	69.9	60.4	48.4	*35.1*	26.5	*47.8*
Mean Minimum Temp. (°F)	12.4	16.5	23.8	31.8	42.6	52.9	57.4	55.0	44.5	32.5	22.1	13.5	33.7
Extreme Maximum Temp. (°F)	73	71	82	92	96	105	108	102	99	90	78	70	108
Extreme Minimum Temp. (°F)	-28	-27	-17	-13	15	36	43	39	18	-3	-12	-41	-41
Days Maximum Temp. ≥ 90°F	0	0	0	0	1	7	12	8	3	0	0	0	31
Days Maximum Temp. ≤ 32°F	10	7	3	1	0	0	0	0	0	0	3	8	32
Days Minimum Temp. ≤ 32°F	30	27	27	16	3	0	0	0	2	15	26	30	176
Days Minimum Temp. ≤ 0°F	6	3	1	0	0	0	0	0	0	0	1	4	15
Heating Degree Days (base 65°F)	1,239	988	863	572	274	59	10	17	178	509	*889*	1,185	*6,783*
Cooling Degree Days (base 65°F)	0	0	0	1	21	138	241	189	51	1	*0*	0	*642*
Mean Precipitation (in.)	0.29	0.26	0.65	1.31	2.78	2.38	1.92	1.09	1.08	0.78	0.57	0.25	13.36
Days With ≥ 0.1" Precipitation	1	1	2	4	5	5	5	3	3	2	2	1	34
Days With ≥ 1.0" Precipitation	0	0	0	0	1	0	0	0	0	0	0	0	1
Mean Snowfall (in.)	*5.0*	*4.2*	*5.6*	3.0	0.2	0.0	0.0	0.0	0.2	1.9	na	na	na
Days With ≥ 1.0" Snow Depth	na	5	5	1	0	0	0	0	0	1	na	na	na

Mullen 21 NW *Cherry County*   Elevation: 3,448 ft.   Latitude: 42° 16' N   Longitude: 101° 20' W

	JAN	FEB	MAR	APR	MAY	JUN	JUL	AUG	SEP	OCT	NOV	DEC	YEAR
Mean Maximum Temp. (°F)	33.2	39.8	47.2	57.7	69.3	79.8	86.4	85.3	76.0	62.9	46.5	*37.9*	*60.1*
Mean Temp. (°F)	21.3	27.5	34.6	44.6	55.9	65.7	71.8	70.7	60.4	47.9	33.7	*25.5*	*46.6*
Mean Minimum Temp. (°F)	9.3	15.2	21.9	31.4	42.4	51.5	57.1	56.1	44.7	32.8	20.9	*13.1*	*33.0*
Extreme Maximum Temp. (°F)	70	76	84	96	92	102	106	102	101	95	86	75	106
Extreme Minimum Temp. (°F)	-26	-30	-17	3	18	31	36	30	15	-2	-18	-34	-34
Days Maximum Temp. ≥ 90°F	0	0	0	0	0	4	12	11	4	0	0	0	31
Days Maximum Temp. ≤ 32°F	13	8	6	1	0	0	0	0	0	0	6	10	44
Days Minimum Temp. ≤ 32°F	31	27	27	17	3	0	0	0	3	14	27	31	180
Days Minimum Temp. ≤ 0°F	9	4	1	0	0	0	0	0	0	0	1	4	19
Heating Degree Days (base 65°F)	1,350	1,051	937	608	292	80	17	22	194	544	915	*1,218*	*7,228*
Cooling Degree Days (base 65°F)	0	0	0	3	17	105	230	209	65	3	0	0	632
Mean Precipitation (in.)	0.62	0.59	1.63	2.64	3.44	3.44	3.31	2.31	1.85	1.54	1.27	0.59	23.23
Days With ≥ 0.1" Precipitation	*2*	2	5	6	7	6	6	5	4	3	3	*2*	*51*
Days With ≥ 1.0" Precipitation	0	0	0	1	1	1	1	0	0	0	0	0	4
Mean Snowfall (in.)	8.2	6.2	12.8	9.5	0.3	trace	trace	trace	1.1	3.2	10.1	7.9	59.3
Days With ≥ 1.0" Snow Depth	18	12	10	4	0	0	0	0	0	2	10	15	71

Nebraska City *Otoe County*   Elevation: 1,079 ft.   Latitude: 40° 41' N   Longitude: 95° 53' W

	JAN	FEB	MAR	APR	MAY	JUN	JUL	AUG	SEP	OCT	NOV	DEC	YEAR
Mean Maximum Temp. (°F)	32.1	38.7	50.3	63.0	73.4	83.3	87.1	85.1	77.6	65.8	49.2	36.7	61.9
Mean Temp. (°F)	22.2	28.3	39.1	51.1	61.9	71.8	76.1	73.9	65.5	53.5	39.1	27.5	50.8
Mean Minimum Temp. (°F)	12.3	17.9	27.9	39.1	50.3	60.2	65.0	62.6	53.4	41.2	29.0	18.3	39.8
Extreme Maximum Temp. (°F)	71	77	89	91	92	106	108	106	102	92	83	69	108
Extreme Minimum Temp. (°F)	-22	-20	-11	4	27	42	43	44	28	14	-3	-23	-23
Days Maximum Temp. ≥ 90°F	0	0	0	0	1	6	12	9	4	0	0	0	32
Days Maximum Temp. ≤ 32°F	15	10	3	0	0	0	0	0	0	0	3	11	42
Days Minimum Temp. ≤ 32°F	30	26	21	7	0	0	0	0	0	5	20	29	138
Days Minimum Temp. ≤ 0°F	7	3	0	0	0	0	0	0	0	0	0	3	13
Heating Degree Days (base 65°F)	1,320	1,029	796	425	149	17	3	5	100	361	770	1,155	6,130
Cooling Degree Days (base 65°F)	0	0	1	15	54	222	351	280	123	12	0	0	1,058
Mean Precipitation (in.)	0.87	0.95	2.44	3.49	4.36	3.72	5.11	3.64	3.48	2.67	1.91	1.25	33.89
Days With ≥ 0.1" Precipitation	2	3	5	6	8	6	6	6	5	4	4	3	58
Days With ≥ 1.0" Precipitation	0	0	1	1	1	1	2	1	1	1	0	0	9
Mean Snowfall (in.)	7.5	7.0	3.9	1.5	0.0	0.0	0.0	0.0	0.0	0.3	1.7	5.0	26.9
Days With ≥ 1.0" Snow Depth	13	10	5	1	0	0	0	0	0	0	2	6	37

Newport *Rock County*   Elevation: 2,227 ft.   Latitude: 42° 36' N   Longitude: 99° 20' W

	JAN	FEB	MAR	APR	MAY	JUN	JUL	AUG	SEP	OCT	NOV	DEC	YEAR
Mean Maximum Temp. (°F)	31.2	37.4	46.7	59.0	70.8	81.6	87.7	86.1	76.6	63.4	45.6	35.4	60.1
Mean Temp. (°F)	20.4	26.5	35.6	47.4	59.0	69.1	74.7	73.0	63.1	50.3	34.9	24.6	48.2
Mean Minimum Temp. (°F)	9.6	15.5	24.4	35.7	47.1	56.5	61.6	59.9	49.6	37.1	24.1	13.7	36.2
Extreme Maximum Temp. (°F)	72	78	86	96	97	107	109	107	102	94	84	73	109
Extreme Minimum Temp. (°F)	-28	-29	-20	4	23	36	41	40	22	7	-15	-32	-32
Days Maximum Temp. ≥ 90°F	0	0	0	0	1	6	14	11	5	1	0	0	38
Days Maximum Temp. ≤ 32°F	16	11	5	1	0	0	0	0	0	0	6	12	51
Days Minimum Temp. ≤ 32°F	30	27	24	11	1	0	0	0	1	9	24	30	157
Days Minimum Temp. ≤ 0°F	9	5	1	0	0	0	0	0	0	0	1	5	21
Heating Degree Days (base 65°F)	1,377	1,082	905	530	219	42	8	14	147	458	896	1,247	6,925
Cooling Degree Days (base 65°F)	0	0	0	9	41	168	310	266	96	8	0	0	898
Mean Precipitation (in.)	0.51	0.73	1.67	2.48	3.87	3.63	3.63	2.29	2.64	1.81	1.20	0.63	25.09
Days With ≥ 0.1" Precipitation	2	2	4	6	7	6	6	4	5	4	3	2	51
Days With ≥ 1.0" Precipitation	0	0	0	0	1	1	1	0	1	0	0	0	4
Mean Snowfall (in.)	5.9	6.5	9.1	6.2	trace	trace	trace	trace	0.3	2.4	8.0	7.1	45.5
Days With ≥ 1.0" Snow Depth	19	15	9	3	0	0	0	0	0	1	8	16	71

Niobrara *Knox County*   Elevation: 1,377 ft.   Latitude: 42° 45' N   Longitude: 98° 02' W

	JAN	FEB	MAR	APR	MAY	JUN	JUL	AUG	SEP	OCT	NOV	DEC	YEAR
Mean Maximum Temp. (°F)	31.0	37.7	48.5	62.9	74.2	83.7	88.2	86.6	78.1	65.0	45.4	34.4	61.3
Mean Temp. (°F)	20.5	27.0	37.2	50.1	61.4	70.9	75.8	74.3	64.8	52.0	35.6	24.5	49.5
Mean Minimum Temp. (°F)	9.9	16.3	25.8	37.2	48.6	58.0	63.2	61.7	51.5	38.9	25.7	14.5	37.6
Extreme Maximum Temp. (°F)	70	78	85	97	95	109	109	107	100	95	83	74	109
Extreme Minimum Temp. (°F)	-31	-29	-16	1	21	36	39	40	25	12	-14	-33	-33
Days Maximum Temp. ≥ 90°F	0	0	0	1	1	8	13	11	4	0	0	0	38
Days Maximum Temp. ≤ 32°F	16	10	4	0	0	0	0	0	0	0	4	13	47
Days Minimum Temp. ≤ 32°F	30	26	23	10	1	0	0	0	1	8	23	30	152
Days Minimum Temp. ≤ 0°F	9	4	1	0	0	0	0	0	0	0	1	5	20
Heating Degree Days (base 65°F)	1,375	1,066	856	454	163	24	3	6	112	405	878	1,250	6,592
Cooling Degree Days (base 65°F)	0	0	0	16	65	211	354	307	122	11	0	0	1,086
Mean Precipitation (in.)	0.35	0.46	1.49	2.64	3.45	3.19	3.22	2.56	2.21	1.69	1.04	0.37	22.67
Days With ≥ 0.1" Precipitation	1	1	3	5	6	6	5	5	4	3	3	1	43
Days With ≥ 1.0" Precipitation	0	0	0	1	1	1	1	1	0	0	0	0	5
Mean Snowfall (in.)	4.9	5.1	5.7	1.8	trace	0.0	0.0	0.0	0.0	0.5	4.6	5.4	28.0
Days With ≥ 1.0" Snow Depth	19	12	7	1	0	0	0	0	0	0	5	15	59

North Loup *Valley County*   Elevation: 1,958 ft.   Latitude: 41° 30' N   Longitude: 98° 46' W

	JAN	FEB	MAR	APR	MAY	JUN	JUL	AUG	SEP	OCT	NOV	DEC	YEAR
Mean Maximum Temp. (°F)	33.9	40.1	50.3	63.2	72.5	82.2	85.9	83.9	76.5	65.2	47.6	37.2	61.5
Mean Temp. (°F)	22.4	28.4	37.9	49.8	60.3	70.1	74.3	72.4	63.5	51.5	36.1	26.0	49.4
Mean Minimum Temp. (°F)	10.8	16.6	25.5	36.3	48.1	57.9	62.7	60.8	50.6	37.8	24.5	14.6	37.2
Extreme Maximum Temp. (°F)	75	77	87	94	95	103	105	103	102	92	79	72	105
Extreme Minimum Temp. (°F)	-30	-28	-18	2	24	36	38	40	20	7	-13	-27	-30
Days Maximum Temp. ≥ 90°F	0	0	0	0	0	5	10	7	2	0	0	0	24
Days Maximum Temp. ≤ 32°F	14	9	3	0	0	0	0	0	0	0	4	10	40
Days Minimum Temp. ≤ 32°F	31	26	24	11	1	0	0	0	1	9	25	30	158
Days Minimum Temp. ≤ 0°F	7	4	1	0	0	0	0	0	0	0	1	4	17
Heating Degree Days (base 65°F)	1,317	1,028	832	458	178	26	4	9	124	416	862	1,204	6,458
Cooling Degree Days (base 65°F)	0	0	0	10	41	183	291	243	88	5	0	0	861
Mean Precipitation (in.)	0.47	0.58	1.87	2.61	3.59	3.79	3.43	3.08	2.37	1.49	1.26	0.59	25.13
Days With ≥ 0.1" Precipitation	2	2	4	6	7	7	6	5	5	3	3	2	52
Days With ≥ 1.0" Precipitation	0	0	0	1	1	1	1	1	1	0	0	0	6
Mean Snowfall (in.)	4.8	5.0	5.7	1.7	0.0	0.0	0.0	0.0	trace	0.9	4.9	6.7	29.7
Days With ≥ 1.0" Snow Depth	15	11	5	1	0	0	0	0	0	0	4	11	47

North Platte Exp. Farm *Lincoln County*   Elevation: 3,021 ft.   Latitude: 41° 03' N   Longitude: 100° 45' W

	JAN	FEB	MAR	APR	MAY	JUN	JUL	AUG	SEP	OCT	NOV	DEC	YEAR
Mean Maximum Temp. (°F)	34.1	41.1	49.4	60.6	70.3	81.1	87.9	86.2	77.4	64.6	47.7	38.3	61.6
Mean Temp. (°F)	22.9	28.7	36.9	47.5	57.8	68.1	74.3	72.5	62.9	50.4	35.7	26.6	48.7
Mean Minimum Temp. (°F)	11.6	16.4	24.4	34.3	45.2	55.0	60.5	58.8	48.4	36.1	23.7	14.9	35.8
Extreme Maximum Temp. (°F)	71	77	84	93	96	103	108	105	102	92	83	72	108
Extreme Minimum Temp. (°F)	-21	-20	-14	8	13	37	44	37	20	9	-8	-36	-36
Days Maximum Temp. ≥ 90°F	0	0	0	0	1	5	14	12	5	0	0	0	37
Days Maximum Temp. ≤ 32°F	13	8	4	0	0	0	0	0	0	0	5	10	40
Days Minimum Temp. ≤ 32°F	31	27	25	13	2	0	0	0	1	10	25	30	164
Days Minimum Temp. ≤ 0°F	7	4	1	0	0	0	0	0	0	0	1	4	17
Heating Degree Days (base 65°F)	1,300	1,018	863	523	241	46	6	13	142	451	871	1,184	6,658
Cooling Degree Days (base 65°F)	0	0	0	6	22	142	290	247	84	4	0	0	795
Mean Precipitation (in.)	0.36	0.50	1.15	1.95	3.47	3.31	2.89	2.21	1.56	1.29	0.76	0.37	19.82
Days With ≥ 0.1" Precipitation	1	1	3	5	7	6	6	4	3	3	2	1	42
Days With ≥ 1.0" Precipitation	0	0	0	0	1	1	1	0	0	0	0	0	3
Mean Snowfall (in.)	5.8	5.2	6.6	3.4	trace	0.0	0.0	0.0	0.2	1.4	5.1	5.1	32.8
Days With ≥ 1.0" Snow Depth	na	na	na	0	0	0	0	0	0	0	na	na	na

Northeast Nebraska Exp. Station *Dixon County*   Elevation: 1,459 ft.   Latitude: 42° 23' N   Longitude: 96° 57' W

	JAN	FEB	MAR	APR	MAY	JUN	JUL	AUG	SEP	OCT	NOV	DEC	YEAR
Mean Maximum Temp. (°F)	27.5	33.3	45.2	59.8	71.0	81.3	85.3	82.9	74.9	62.8	44.1	31.7	58.3
Mean Temp. (°F)	16.8	22.6	34.2	47.2	58.8	69.3	73.3	70.9	61.7	49.3	33.6	21.5	46.6
Mean Minimum Temp. (°F)	6.0	11.9	23.1	34.7	46.6	57.3	61.3	59.0	48.4	35.7	23.0	11.3	34.9
Extreme Maximum Temp. (°F)	71	72	86	95	96	107	107	103	100	93	79	69	107
Extreme Minimum Temp. (°F)	-31	-28	-16	-4	21	37	38	37	22	7	-14	-28	-31
Days Maximum Temp. ≥ 90°F	0	0	0	0	1	5	9	6	2	0	0	0	23
Days Maximum Temp. ≤ 32°F	18	13	6	0	0	0	0	0	0	0	6	15	58
Days Minimum Temp. ≤ 32°F	31	28	26	13	2	0	0	0	2	11	26	31	170
Days Minimum Temp. ≤ 0°F	11	7	1	0	0	0	0	0	0	0	1	6	26
Heating Degree Days (base 65°F)	1,489	1,191	949	534	225	37	8	20	165	487	937	1,343	7,385
Cooling Degree Days (base 65°F)	0	0	0	9	38	172	262	210	71	6	0	0	768
Mean Precipitation (in.)	0.48	0.69	1.96	2.76	4.20	3.98	2.92	2.59	2.74	2.00	1.51	0.68	26.51
Days With ≥ 0.1" Precipitation	1	2	4	6	8	6	5	5	5	4	3	2	51
Days With ≥ 1.0" Precipitation	0	0	0	1	1	1	1	1	1	1	0	0	7
Mean Snowfall (in.)	4.2	4.8	*4.4*	1.5	trace	0.0	0.0	0.0	0.0	0.7	4.1	5.2	*24.9*
Days With ≥ 1.0" Snow Depth	*16*	*13*	7	1	0	0	0	0	0	0	5	*13*	55

O'Neill *Holt County* Elevation: 1,988 ft. Latitude: 42° 28' N Longitude: 98° 39' W

	JAN	FEB	MAR	APR	MAY	JUN	JUL	AUG	SEP	OCT	NOV	DEC	YEAR
Mean Maximum Temp. (°F)	30.0	36.8	47.2	60.5	72.0	82.4	88.1	86.3	76.9	63.8	44.7	34.0	60.2
Mean Temp. (°F)	19.5	25.9	35.4	47.8	59.3	69.4	74.8	73.1	63.1	50.4	34.2	23.7	48.1
Mean Minimum Temp. (°F)	9.0	14.9	23.6	35.0	46.6	56.4	61.6	59.8	49.2	37.0	23.7	13.3	35.8
Extreme Maximum Temp. (°F)	70	75	85	100	95	108	110	104	101	94	82	72	110
Extreme Minimum Temp. (°F)	-28	-27	-18	0	22	36	39	41	20	10	-11	-32	-32
Days Maximum Temp. ≥ 90°F	0	0	0	0	1	7	14	11	4	0	0	0	37
Days Maximum Temp. ≤ 32°F	16	11	5	1	0	0	0	0	0	0	6	13	52
Days Minimum Temp. ≤ 32°F	30	27	25	13	1	0	0	0	1	10	25	30	162
Days Minimum Temp. ≤ 0°F	9	5	1	0	0	0	0	0	0	0	1	5	21
Heating Degree Days (base 65°F)	1,404	1,099	910	518	209	37	7	11	145	452	916	1,274	6,982
Cooling Degree Days (base 65°F)	0	0	0	9	39	175	320	267	93	5	0	0	908
Mean Precipitation (in.)	0.50	0.52	1.72	2.49	3.71	3.41	3.46	2.52	2.25	1.71	1.17	0.56	24.02
Days With ≥ 0.1" Precipitation	1	2	4	5	7	6	6	5	5	4	3	2	50
Days With ≥ 1.0" Precipitation	0	0	0	0	1	1	1	1	1	0	0	0	5
Mean Snowfall (in.)	4.7	5.0	6.3	3.8	0.0	0.0	0.0	0.0	trace	1.2	4.5	5.5	31.0
Days With ≥ 1.0" Snow Depth	16	11	8	2	0	0	0	0	0	1	5	14	57

Oakdale *Antelope County* Elevation: 1,706 ft. Latitude: 42° 04' N Longitude: 97° 58' W

	JAN	FEB	MAR	APR	MAY	JUN	JUL	AUG	SEP	OCT	NOV	DEC	YEAR
Mean Maximum Temp. (°F)	30.8	36.8	46.8	60.0	70.9	81.0	85.8	83.6	75.6	63.7	46.1	34.9	59.7
Mean Temp. (°F)	19.2	25.2	35.4	47.8	59.1	69.1	73.9	71.7	62.0	49.6	34.6	23.6	47.6
Mean Minimum Temp. (°F)	7.6	13.4	23.9	35.5	47.2	57.1	61.9	59.7	48.4	35.5	23.1	12.2	35.5
Extreme Maximum Temp. (°F)	74	76	88	94	98	105	105	105	101	93	81	70	105
Extreme Minimum Temp. (°F)	-28	-29	-21	-1	24	33	38	36	17	9	-16	-33	-33
Days Maximum Temp. ≥ 90°F	0	0	0	0	1	5	10	8	3	0	0	0	27
Days Maximum Temp. ≤ 32°F	16	11	5	0	0	0	0	0	0	0	5	13	50
Days Minimum Temp. ≤ 32°F	31	27	25	11	1	0	0	0	2	11	26	31	165
Days Minimum Temp. ≤ 0°F	10	5	1	0	0	0	0	0	0	0	1	5	22
Heating Degree Days (base 65°F)	1,415	1,119	912	519	217	42	8	16	162	475	904	1,279	7,068
Cooling Degree Days (base 65°F)	0	0	0	10	38	163	276	227	79	5	0	0	798
Mean Precipitation (in.)	0.49	0.62	1.83	2.74	3.83	4.04	3.28	2.96	2.26	1.77	1.33	0.62	25.77
Days With ≥ 0.1" Precipitation	2	2	4	6	7	6	6	5	4	4	3	2	51
Days With ≥ 1.0" Precipitation	0	0	0	1	1	1	1	1	1	0	0	0	6
Mean Snowfall (in.)	5.0	5.4	6.3	2.8	0.0	trace	trace	0.0	trace	0.7	5.2	6.0	31.4
Days With ≥ 1.0" Snow Depth	17	12	6	1	0	0	0	0	0	0	5	14	55

Oconto *Custer County* Elevation: 2,578 ft. Latitude: 41° 08' N Longitude: 99° 46' W

	JAN	FEB	MAR	APR	MAY	JUN	JUL	AUG	SEP	OCT	NOV	DEC	YEAR
Mean Maximum Temp. (°F)	35.7	42.1	51.3	62.8	72.2	82.3	87.3	85.7	78.1	65.7	48.4	39.8	62.6
Mean Temp. (°F)	23.5	29.4	38.1	48.8	59.2	69.1	74.0	72.6	63.7	51.2	36.1	27.6	49.4
Mean Minimum Temp. (°F)	11.3	16.7	24.8	34.6	46.2	55.8	60.7	59.3	49.2	36.7	23.7	15.3	36.2
Extreme Maximum Temp. (°F)	73	78	87	92	97	106	106	106	102	93	80	74	106
Extreme Minimum Temp. (°F)	-30	-27	-22	7	18	33	39	38	20	4	-15	-29	-30
Days Maximum Temp. ≥ 90°F	0	0	0	0	0	5	12	10	4	0	0	0	31
Days Maximum Temp. ≤ 32°F	12	8	3	0	0	0	0	0	0	0	4	8	35
Days Minimum Temp. ≤ 32°F	31	26	25	12	2	0	0	0	1	10	25	30	162
Days Minimum Temp. ≤ 0°F	7	3	1	0	0	0	0	0	0	0	1	3	15
Heating Degree Days (base 65°F)	1,280	996	828	487	205	33	6	10	122	425	861	1,154	6,407
Cooling Degree Days (base 65°F)	0	0	0	7	32	165	290	245	85	5	0	0	829
Mean Precipitation (in.)	0.55	0.43	1.60	1.97	3.72	3.50	3.12	2.47	1.84	1.32	0.98	0.49	21.99
Days With ≥ 0.1" Precipitation	2	2	4	5	7	5	5	5	4	3	2	2	46
Days With ≥ 1.0" Precipitation	0	0	0	0	1	1	1	1	0	0	0	0	4
Mean Snowfall (in.)	5.6	na	na	2.1	0.0	0.0	0.0	0.0	0.1	1.0	4.6	na	na
Days With ≥ 1.0" Snow Depth	na	na	na	1	0	0	0	0	0	0	2	na	na

Ogallala *Keith County* Elevation: 3,228 ft. Latitude: 41° 08' N Longitude: 101° 43' W

	JAN	FEB	MAR	APR	MAY	JUN	JUL	AUG	SEP	OCT	NOV	DEC	YEAR
Mean Maximum Temp. (°F)	36.4	43.5	51.2	61.9	71.9	82.8	89.7	87.5	78.1	65.6	49.8	40.3	63.2
Mean Temp. (°F)	23.9	29.9	37.7	47.9	58.5	68.9	75.1	72.9	62.7	49.9	36.2	27.1	49.2
Mean Minimum Temp. (°F)	11.4	16.2	24.1	33.8	45.0	54.9	60.4	58.2	47.2	34.1	22.6	14.0	35.2
Extreme Maximum Temp. (°F)	74	77	85	95	98	105	109	105	103	93	80	73	109
Extreme Minimum Temp. (°F)	-23	-23	-13	-2	22	37	39	38	19	6	-6	-36	-36
Days Maximum Temp. ≥ 90°F	0	0	0	0	1	8	17	14	5	0	0	0	45
Days Maximum Temp. ≤ 32°F	11	7	3	0	0	0	0	0	0	0	3	8	32
Days Minimum Temp. ≤ 32°F	30	27	26	14	2	0	0	0	2	12	26	31	170
Days Minimum Temp. ≤ 0°F	6	3	1	0	0	0	0	0	0	0	0	3	13
Heating Degree Days (base 65°F)	1,267	985	840	511	226	43	5	10	145	465	856	1,168	6,521
Cooling Degree Days (base 65°F)	0	0	0	5	32	169	328	267	87	3	0	0	891
Mean Precipitation (in.)	0.50	0.38	1.40	1.97	3.46	2.81	2.77	1.99	1.24	0.97	0.76	0.51	18.76
Days With ≥ 0.1" Precipitation	1	1	4	4	6	6	5	4	3	3	2	1	40
Days With ≥ 1.0" Precipitation	0	0	0	0	1	1	1	1	0	0	0	0	4
Mean Snowfall (in.)	6.1	4.6	8.0	2.8	0.2	0.0	0.0	trace	0.2	0.5	4.0	3.4	29.8
Days With ≥ 1.0" Snow Depth	na	na	na	1	0	0	0	0	0	0	1	na	na

Osceola *Polk County*   Elevation: 1,660 ft.   Latitude: 41° 11' N   Longitude: 97° 33' W

	JAN	FEB	MAR	APR	MAY	JUN	JUL	AUG	SEP	OCT	NOV	DEC	YEAR
Mean Maximum Temp. (°F)	32.9	39.7	50.9	64.1	74.2	84.5	87.9	86.0	78.7	66.3	48.2	36.5	62.5
Mean Temp. (°F)	22.4	28.7	39.1	51.1	62.1	72.1	76.0	74.1	65.5	53.2	37.5	26.5	50.7
Mean Minimum Temp. (°F)	11.9	17.6	27.2	38.0	49.9	59.7	64.1	62.0	52.2	40.1	26.7	16.5	38.8
Extreme Maximum Temp. (°F)	73	81	90	97	100	105	106	107	103	94	81	71	107
Extreme Minimum Temp. (°F)	-28	-24	-16	3	25	40	38	40	22	5	-12	-29	-29
Days Maximum Temp. ≥ 90°F	0	0	0	1	1	8	14	10	4	0	0	0	38
Days Maximum Temp. ≤ 32°F	15	9	3	0	0	0	0	0	0	0	3	11	41
Days Minimum Temp. ≤ 32°F	30	26	22	9	1	0	0	0	1	7	22	30	148
Days Minimum Temp. ≤ 0°F	7	4	1	0	0	0	0	0	0	0	1	3	16
Heating Degree Days (base 65°F)	1,314	1,020	798	423	145	17	2	6	99	369	820	1,186	6,199
Cooling Degree Days (base 65°F)	0	0	1	16	59	231	346	289	120	10	0	0	1,072
Mean Precipitation (in.)	0.62	0.65	2.27	3.06	4.64	4.05	3.36	3.17	2.71	1.96	1.69	0.79	28.97
Days With ≥ 0.1" Precipitation	2	2	4	6	8	6	5	5	5	4	3	2	52
Days With ≥ 1.0" Precipitation	0	0	1	1	1	1	1	1	1	0	0	0	7
Mean Snowfall (in.)	5.9	5.7	5.8	1.7	trace	0.0	0.0	0.0	0.1	0.9	4.3	5.6	30.0
Days With ≥ 1.0" Snow Depth	*13*	10	*3*	1	0	0	0	0	0	0	4	*8*	*39*

Oshkosh *Garden County*   Elevation: 3,379 ft.   Latitude: 41° 25' N   Longitude: 102° 21' W

	JAN	FEB	MAR	APR	MAY	JUN	JUL	AUG	SEP	OCT	NOV	DEC	YEAR
Mean Maximum Temp. (°F)	37.9	45.1	52.5	62.8	72.0	82.5	88.7	87.0	78.4	66.6	50.0	41.0	63.7
Mean Temp. (°F)	24.1	30.7	37.9	47.5	57.8	67.7	73.7	71.9	62.2	49.6	35.5	26.5	48.8
Mean Minimum Temp. (°F)	10.2	16.1	23.2	32.2	43.6	52.9	58.6	56.7	45.8	32.6	20.9	12.0	33.7
Extreme Maximum Temp. (°F)	75	76	85	95	94	107	109	107	101	92	82	76	109
Extreme Minimum Temp. (°F)	-27	-29	-19	-9	14	29	38	35	14	-5	-11	-47	-47
Days Maximum Temp. ≥ 90°F	0	0	0	0	1	7	14	12	4	0	0	0	38
Days Maximum Temp. ≤ 32°F	10	5	2	0	0	0	0	0	0	0	3	8	28
Days Minimum Temp. ≤ 32°F	31	27	27	16	2	0	0	0	2	15	28	31	179
Days Minimum Temp. ≤ 0°F	7	3	1	0	0	0	0	0	0	0	1	5	17
Heating Degree Days (base 65°F)	1,263	963	833	520	238	48	5	10	146	471	879	1,187	6,563
Cooling Degree Days (base 65°F)	0	0	0	2	22	135	280	241	72	1	0	0	753
Mean Precipitation (in.)	0.26	0.34	1.04	1.78	3.14	2.64	2.71	1.71	1.44	0.95	0.63	0.34	16.98
Days With ≥ 0.1" Precipitation	1	1	3	4	6	5	5	4	3	2	2	1	37
Days With ≥ 1.0" Precipitation	0	0	0	0	1	1	1	0	0	0	0	0	3
Mean Snowfall (in.)	4.3	3.6	5.4	2.4	0.3	0.0	0.0	0.0	0.2	0.8	4.7	4.5	26.2
Days With ≥ 1.0" Snow Depth	12	7	4	1	0	0	0	0	0	0	5	9	38

Osmond *Pierce County*   Elevation: 1,646 ft.   Latitude: 42° 21' N   Longitude: 97° 36' W

	JAN	FEB	MAR	APR	MAY	JUN	JUL	AUG	SEP	OCT	NOV	DEC	YEAR
Mean Maximum Temp. (°F)	30.4	37.3	48.2	62.4	74.1	84.3	88.3	86.0	77.9	65.1	45.7	34.1	61.1
Mean Temp. (°F)	19.2	26.3	36.7	49.3	61.3	71.4	75.6	73.4	64.2	51.5	35.1	23.8	49.0
Mean Minimum Temp. (°F)	8.4	15.2	25.1	36.4	48.3	58.4	62.9	60.7	50.5	37.9	24.3	13.4	36.8
Extreme Maximum Temp. (°F)	72	75	87	95	98	106	106	108	101	92	80	68	108
Extreme Minimum Temp. (°F)	-32	-27	-20	-3	22	35	38	32	22	10	-13	-28	-32
Days Maximum Temp. ≥ 90°F	0	0	0	1	1	8	14	10	4	0	0	0	38
Days Maximum Temp. ≤ 32°F	16	11	4	0	0	0	0	0	0	0	5	13	49
Days Minimum Temp. ≤ 32°F	31	26	24	11	1	0	0	0	1	9	25	30	158
Days Minimum Temp. ≤ 0°F	9	5	1	0	0	0	0	0	0	0	1	5	21
Heating Degree Days (base 65°F)	1,412	1,086	871	475	165	23	3	9	121	419	892	1,271	6,747
Cooling Degree Days (base 65°F)	0	0	0	12	53	218	331	269	101	7	0	0	991
Mean Precipitation (in.)	0.44	0.74	1.84	2.78	3.70	3.79	3.25	2.89	2.42	1.67	1.38	0.53	25.43
Days With ≥ 0.1" Precipitation	1	2	4	6	7	6	5	5	4	3	3	2	48
Days With ≥ 1.0" Precipitation	0	0	0	1	1	1	1	1	1	0	0	0	6
Mean Snowfall (in.)	na	*5.6*	*4.9*	2.1	0.0	0.0	0.0	0.0	trace	0.6	5.0	*5.8*	na
Days With ≥ 1.0" Snow Depth	*14*	*11*	*6*	1	0	0	0	0	0	0	*3*	*13*	*48*

Pawnee City *Pawnee County*   Elevation: 1,207 ft.   Latitude: 40° 07' N   Longitude: 96° 09' W

•	JAN	FEB	MAR	APR	MAY	JUN	JUL	AUG	SEP	OCT	NOV	DEC	YEAR
Mean Maximum Temp. (°F)	35.7	43.0	54.4	67.1	76.5	86.1	90.7	89.1	80.4	68.8	51.8	39.7	65.3
Mean Temp. (°F)	25.7	32.1	42.8	54.9	64.8	74.2	78.8	76.9	67.9	56.1	41.5	30.2	53.8
Mean Minimum Temp. (°F)	15.6	21.2	31.2	42.6	53.1	62.2	66.9	64.8	55.4	43.5	31.1	20.5	42.3
Extreme Maximum Temp. (°F)	73	84	91	96	96	109	110	108	105	95	83	70	110
Extreme Minimum Temp. (°F)	-24	-22	-17	7	27	42	41	45	28	11	-3	-25	-25
Days Maximum Temp. ≥ 90°F	0	0	0	1	1	10	18	15	6	0	0	0	51
Days Maximum Temp. ≤ 32°F	12	7	1	0	0	0	0	0	0	0	2	8	30
Days Minimum Temp. ≤ 32°F	28	23	17	4	0	0	0	0	0	4	17	27	120
Days Minimum Temp. ≤ 0°F	5	2	0	0	0	0	0	0	0	0	0	3	10
Heating Degree Days (base 65°F)	1,215	922	684	323	97	8	1	1	72	290	699	1,074	5,386
Cooling Degree Days (base 65°F)	0	0	3	28	88	280	434	376	166	22	1	0	1,398
Mean Precipitation (in.)	0.78	0.81	2.29	2.92	4.14	4.23	4.18	3.89	3.83	2.36	1.80	1.02	32.25
Days With ≥ 0.1" Precipitation	2	2	4	5	7	5	5	6	5	4	3	2	50
Days With ≥ 1.0" Precipitation	0	0	1	1	1	1	1	1	1	1	0	0	8
Mean Snowfall (in.)	6.3	5.2	*3.2*	0.7	0.0	0.0	0.0	0.0	0.0	0.2	1.4	4.4	*21.4*
Days With ≥ 1.0" Snow Depth	8	*4*	2	0	0	0	0	0	0	0	0	*3*	*17*

Ravenna *Buffalo County*   Elevation: 2,047 ft.   Latitude: 41° 02' N   Longitude: 98° 55' W

	JAN	FEB	MAR	APR	MAY	JUN	JUL	AUG	SEP	OCT	NOV	DEC	YEAR
Mean Maximum Temp. (°F)	35.1	41.5	51.7	63.8	73.6	83.7	88.0	86.0	78.0	66.2	48.7	38.3	62.9
Mean Temp. (°F)	22.8	28.9	38.4	49.9	60.5	70.6	75.4	73.4	64.0	51.6	36.4	26.3	49.9
Mean Minimum Temp. (°F)	10.5	16.1	25.1	35.9	47.4	57.5	62.7	60.8	49.9	37.0	24.0	14.2	36.8
Extreme Maximum Temp. (°F)	75	80	90	94	98	106	106	104	102	93	83	74	106
Extreme Minimum Temp. (°F)	-27	-26	-18	5	18	35	37	38	20	4	-15	-31	-31
Days Maximum Temp. ≥ 90°F	0	0	0	1	1	8	13	11	4	0	0	0	38
Days Maximum Temp. ≤ 32°F	12	8	3	0	0	0	0	0	0	0	4	10	37
Days Minimum Temp. ≤ 32°F	31	27	24	11	2	0	0	0	2	10	25	30	162
Days Minimum Temp. ≤ 0°F	7	4	1	0	0	0	0	0	0	0	1	4	17
Heating Degree Days (base 65°F)	1,301	1,014	817	456	178	27	4	8	124	416	851	1,194	6,390
Cooling Degree Days (base 65°F)	0	0	0	10	43	194	323	269	98	7	0	0	944
Mean Precipitation (in.)	0.50	0.53	2.08	2.71	4.18	4.20	3.36	2.90	2.19	1.56	1.39	0.57	26.17
Days With ≥ 0.1" Precipitation	2	2	4	5	8	6	6	5	4	3	3	2	50
Days With ≥ 1.0" Precipitation	0	0	1	1	1	1	1	1	1	0	0	0	7
Mean Snowfall (in.)	5.6	5.0	4.9	1.0	0.0	0.0	0.0	0.0	0.1	0.9	4.0	*5.3*	*26.8*
Days With ≥ 1.0" Snow Depth	na	na	*1*	0	0	0	0	0	0	0	*1*	na	na

Red Cloud *Webster County*   Elevation: 1,719 ft.   Latitude: 40° 06' N   Longitude: 98° 31' W

	JAN	FEB	MAR	APR	MAY	JUN	JUL	AUG	SEP	OCT	NOV	DEC	YEAR
Mean Maximum Temp. (°F)	35.6	42.2	52.5	64.6	74.1	85.1	90.5	88.0	79.6	67.5	50.4	39.9	64.2
Mean Temp. (°F)	23.1	28.9	38.7	50.4	60.8	71.4	76.8	74.4	64.8	52.1	37.3	27.6	50.5
Mean Minimum Temp. (°F)	10.5	15.8	24.9	36.2	47.5	57.7	63.1	60.6	49.9	36.7	24.2	15.2	36.9
Extreme Maximum Temp. (°F)	77	83	92	100	99	109	109	111	106	96	83	76	111
Extreme Minimum Temp. (°F)	-28	-20	-12	9	25	34	38	39	20	2	-9	-36	-36
Days Maximum Temp. ≥ 90°F	0	0	0	0	1	9	17	14	6	1	0	0	48
Days Maximum Temp. ≤ 32°F	12	8	3	0	0	0	0	0	0	0	3	8	34
Days Minimum Temp. ≤ 32°F	31	27	24	11	2	0	0	0	2	10	25	30	162
Days Minimum Temp. ≤ 0°F	7	4	1	0	0	0	0	0	0	0	0	3	15
Heating Degree Days (base 65°F)	1,294	1,013	808	440	174	24	3	7	115	402	824	1,153	6,257
Cooling Degree Days (base 65°F)	0	0	0	9	44	215	368	296	115	8	0	0	1,055
Mean Precipitation (in.)	0.52	0.51	1.93	2.35	4.36	3.31	3.86	3.28	2.59	1.67	1.42	0.62	26.42
Days With ≥ 0.1" Precipitation	2	2	4	5	8	6	6	5	4	3	3	2	50
Days With ≥ 1.0" Precipitation	0	0	0	1	1	1	1	1	1	0	0	0	6
Mean Snowfall (in.)	*5.1*	*3.8*	3.4	0.8	0.0	0.0	0.0	0.0	0.2	0.7	*2.3*	*3.7*	*20.0*
Days With ≥ 1.0" Snow Depth	*13*	*9*	3	1	0	0	0	0	0	0	*3*	*7*	*36*

Saint Paul 4 N *Howard County*   Elevation: 1,774 ft.   Latitude: 41° 16' N   Longitude: 98° 28' W

	JAN	FEB	MAR	APR	MAY	JUN	JUL	AUG	SEP	OCT	NOV	DEC	YEAR
Mean Maximum Temp. (°F)	33.4	40.3	50.0	62.8	72.2	82.3	86.4	84.6	76.9	64.8	47.4	36.7	61.5
Mean Temp. (°F)	22.6	28.9	38.4	50.4	60.8	70.8	75.1	73.3	64.3	52.0	36.5	26.2	49.9
Mean Minimum Temp. (°F)	11.6	17.5	26.8	38.0	49.4	59.2	63.8	62.0	51.6	39.1	25.7	15.6	38.4
Extreme Maximum Temp. (°F)	74	79	89	95	100	103	105	105	103	93	80	73	105
Extreme Minimum Temp. (°F)	-28	-27	-15	6	26	40	42	43	22	11	-10	-29	-29
Days Maximum Temp. ≥ 90°F	0	0	0	0	1	6	11	8	4	0	0	0	30
Days Maximum Temp. ≤ 32°F	14	9	3	0	0	0	0	0	0	0	4	11	41
Days Minimum Temp. ≤ 32°F	31	26	23	8	1	0	0	0	1	7	24	30	151
Days Minimum Temp. ≤ 0°F	7	3	1	0	0	0	0	0	0	0	1	3	15
Heating Degree Days (base 65°F)	1,310	1,012	818	441	169	23	4	8	117	405	847	1,198	6,352
Cooling Degree Days (base 65°F)	0	0	1	13	49	208	329	283	112	8	0	0	1,003
Mean Precipitation (in.)	0.42	0.57	2.00	2.62	4.18	3.75	3.10	2.75	2.56	1.51	1.22	0.53	25.21
Days With ≥ 0.1" Precipitation	1	2	4	5	7	6	6	5	4	3	2	1	46
Days With ≥ 1.0" Precipitation	0	0	1	1	1	1	1	1	1	0	0	0	7
Mean Snowfall (in.)	na	na	na	*0.8*	0.0	0.0	0.0	0.0	trace	0.5	*3.4*	na	na
Days With ≥ 1.0" Snow Depth	na	*5*	na	0	0	0	0	0	0	0	na	na	na

Seward *Seward County*   Elevation: 1,437 ft.   Latitude: 40° 54' N   Longitude: 97° 05' W

	JAN	FEB	MAR	APR	MAY	JUN	JUL	AUG	SEP	OCT	NOV	DEC	YEAR
Mean Maximum Temp. (°F)	33.4	40.1	51.5	65.0	74.9	85.3	89.3	86.6	78.5	66.6	48.8	37.3	63.1
Mean Temp. (°F)	23.6	29.7	40.2	52.6	63.2	73.4	77.7	75.2	66.6	54.6	38.8	28.0	52.0
Mean Minimum Temp. (°F)	13.7	19.2	28.9	40.2	51.5	61.3	66.0	63.9	54.6	42.5	28.8	18.7	40.8
Extreme Maximum Temp. (°F)	74	80	90	97	98	106	107	106	100	92	85	69	107
Extreme Minimum Temp. (°F)	-27	-24	-19	5	27	42	42	42	20	6	-5	-24	-27
Days Maximum Temp. ≥ 90°F	0	0	0	1	1	10	15	12	4	0	0	0	43
Days Maximum Temp. ≤ 32°F	14	9	3	0	0	0	0	0	0	0	3	10	39
Days Minimum Temp. ≤ 32°F	30	25	19	6	0	0	0	0	0	5	19	29	133
Days Minimum Temp. ≤ 0°F	6	3	0	0	0	0	0	0	0	0	0	3	12
Heating Degree Days (base 65°F)	1,279	990	762	382	121	12	1	4	83	330	779	1,139	5,882
Cooling Degree Days (base 65°F)	0	0	1	20	72	263	400	330	145	16	0	0	1,247
Mean Precipitation (in.)	0.62	0.53	2.07	2.67	4.55	3.62	3.44	3.40	2.83	2.06	1.57	0.71	28.07
Days With ≥ 0.1" Precipitation	2	2	4	6	8	6	5	5	5	4	3	2	52
Days With ≥ 1.0" Precipitation	0	0	0	1	1	1	1	1	1	0	0	0	6
Mean Snowfall (in.)	5.1	4.8	4.6	1.1	trace	0.0	0.0	0.0	trace	0.6	2.9	4.3	23.4
Days With ≥ 1.0" Snow Depth	16	12	5	1	0	0	0	0	0	0	3	8	45

Sidney 6 NNW *Cheyenne County*   Elevation: 4,317 ft.   Latitude: 41° 13' N   Longitude: 103° 01' W

	JAN	FEB	MAR	APR	MAY	JUN	JUL	AUG	SEP	OCT	NOV	DEC	YEAR
Mean Maximum Temp. (°F)	37.1	43.3	49.5	58.5	68.4	79.8	87.1	85.4	76.2	63.1	48.0	40.2	61.4
Mean Temp. (°F)	24.2	29.7	35.7	44.1	54.4	64.8	71.5	69.7	60.3	47.6	34.5	26.9	46.9
Mean Minimum Temp. (°F)	11.4	16.0	21.9	29.7	40.3	49.9	55.8	54.0	44.2	32.0	20.9	13.7	32.5
Extreme Maximum Temp. (°F)	74	75	81	91	93	103	108	104	101	94	78	75	108
Extreme Minimum Temp. (°F)	-24	-30	-20	-7	16	29	39	35	13	-2	-19	-39	-39
Days Maximum Temp. ≥ 90°F	0	0	0	0	0	5	13	10	4	0	0	0	32
Days Maximum Temp. ≤ 32°F	10	6	4	1	0	0	0	0	0	1	5	8	35
Days Minimum Temp. ≤ 32°F	30	27	28	19	4	0	0	0	3	16	27	30	184
Days Minimum Temp. ≤ 0°F	6	3	1	0	0	0	0	0	0	0	1	4	15
Heating Degree Days (base 65°F)	1,258	990	902	622	331	88	15	23	187	535	908	1,174	7,033
Cooling Degree Days (base 65°F)	0	0	0	1	8	86	223	180	55	2	0	0	555
Mean Precipitation (in.)	0.29	0.34	0.96	1.51	2.93	2.88	2.38	1.87	1.26	0.82	0.57	0.24	16.05
Days With ≥ 0.1" Precipitation	1	1	3	4	7	6	5	4	3	2	2	1	39
Days With ≥ 1.0" Precipitation	0	0	0	0	1	1	0	0	0	0	0	0	2
Mean Snowfall (in.)	4.1	3.9	6.9	2.3	trace	0.0	0.0	0.0	0.2	1.1	3.2	3.2	24.9
Days With ≥ 1.0" Snow Depth	na	na	na	1	0	0	0	0	0	0	2	na	na

Springview *Keya Paha County*   Elevation: 2,493 ft.   Latitude: 42° 49' N   Longitude: 99° 45' W

	JAN	FEB	MAR	APR	MAY	JUN	JUL	AUG	SEP	OCT	NOV	DEC	YEAR
Mean Maximum Temp. (°F)	30.7	36.5	45.3	57.6	69.4	80.2	86.5	84.8	75.5	62.2	44.4	34.8	59.0
Mean Temp. (°F)	19.9	25.6	34.1	46.1	57.7	68.0	73.8	71.9	62.1	49.3	34.0	24.0	47.2
Mean Minimum Temp. (°F)	9.1	14.8	22.8	34.6	46.0	55.8	61.0	59.1	48.6	36.3	23.4	13.2	35.4
Extreme Maximum Temp. (°F)	68	76	86	94	99	106	110	105	101	95	84	75	110
Extreme Minimum Temp. (°F)	-23	-27	-21	7	22	35	39	40	24	7	-14	-31	-31
Days Maximum Temp. ≥ 90°F	0	0	0	0	0	5	12	10	4	0	0	0	31
Days Maximum Temp. ≤ 32°F	15	11	7	1	0	0	0	0	0	0	7	13	54
Days Minimum Temp. ≤ 32°F	30	27	26	13	2	0	0	0	1	10	24	30	163
Days Minimum Temp. ≤ 0°F	9	5	1	0	0	0	0	0	0	0	1	5	21
Heating Degree Days (base 65°F)	1,391	1,105	952	567	248	52	10	20	165	488	925	1,266	7,189
Cooling Degree Days (base 65°F)	0	0	0	7	31	142	279	237	84	7	0	0	787
Mean Precipitation (in.)	0.36	0.50	1.43	2.27	3.80	3.56	3.39	2.35	2.43	1.41	0.82	0.36	22.68
Days With ≥ 0.1" Precipitation	1	1	3	5	7	7	6	5	4	3	2	1	45
Days With ≥ 1.0" Precipitation	0	0	0	0	1	1	1	1	1	0	0	0	5
Mean Snowfall (in.)	4.8	5.6	7.9	5.1	trace	0.0	0.0	0.0	0.1	1.6	5.5	5.3	35.9
Days With ≥ 1.0" Snow Depth	9	8	6	2	0	0	0	0	0	1	3	7	36

Stanton *Stanton County*   Elevation: 1,489 ft.   Latitude: 41° 57' N   Longitude: 97° 14' W

	JAN	FEB	MAR	APR	MAY	JUN	JUL	AUG	SEP	OCT	NOV	DEC	YEAR
Mean Maximum Temp. (°F)	31.0	38.0	49.2	63.3	73.8	83.5	87.2	85.0	77.4	65.1	46.6	34.8	61.2
Mean Temp. (°F)	20.7	27.2	37.8	50.4	61.4	71.1	75.3	73.3	64.6	52.3	36.3	24.9	49.6
Mean Minimum Temp. (°F)	10.4	16.5	26.2	37.5	49.0	58.7	63.4	61.6	51.7	39.5	25.9	15.0	38.0
Extreme Maximum Temp. (°F)	72	73	90	95	98	105	104	105	100	90	83	71	105
Extreme Minimum Temp. (°F)	-25	-27	-17	5	24	36	40	39	22	10	-13	-33	-33
Days Maximum Temp. ≥ 90°F	0	0	0	1	1	7	13	9	3	0	0	0	34
Days Maximum Temp. ≤ 32°F	16	10	4	0	0	0	0	0	0	0	4	13	47
Days Minimum Temp. ≤ 32°F	31	26	22	9	1	0	0	0	1	8	23	30	151
Days Minimum Temp. ≤ 0°F	8	4	1	0	0	0	0	0	0	0	1	4	18
Heating Degree Days (base 65°F)	1,366	1,060	838	443	160	22	4	8	113	396	856	1,236	6,502
Cooling Degree Days (base 65°F)	0	0	0	15	53	205	318	266	106	9	0	0	972
Mean Precipitation (in.)	0.57	0.74	2.20	2.98	4.58	4.23	3.84	3.03	2.55	1.91	1.60	0.78	29.01
Days With ≥ 0.1" Precipitation	2	2	4	6	8	7	6	5	5	4	3	2	54
Days With ≥ 1.0" Precipitation	0	0	1	1	1	1	1	1	1	1	1	0	9
Mean Snowfall (in.)	5.0	5.3	5.0	2.1	0.0	0.0	0.0	0.0	trace	0.8	3.2	5.5	26.9
Days With ≥ 1.0" Snow Depth	na	11	5	0	0	0	0	0	0	0	3	12	na

Superior *Nuckolls County*   Elevation: 1,578 ft.   Latitude: 40° 01' N   Longitude: 98° 04' W

	JAN	FEB	MAR	APR	MAY	JUN	JUL	AUG	SEP	OCT	NOV	DEC	YEAR
Mean Maximum Temp. (°F)	36.7	43.6	54.3	66.3	75.5	85.8	90.6	88.5	80.1	67.8	51.2	40.4	65.1
Mean Temp. (°F)	25.9	32.0	42.0	53.4	63.5	73.5	78.4	76.3	67.3	54.9	40.1	29.9	53.1
Mean Minimum Temp. (°F)	15.0	20.2	29.7	40.4	51.5	61.2	66.0	64.2	54.4	41.9	28.9	19.3	41.1
Extreme Maximum Temp. (°F)	78	83	92	99	100	106	107	106	103	95	82	71	107
Extreme Minimum Temp. (°F)	-20	-17	-10	10	29	40	44	46	25	12	-7	-30	-30
Days Maximum Temp. ≥ 90°F	0	0	0	1	1	10	18	14	6	0	0	0	50
Days Maximum Temp. ≤ 32°F	11	7	2	0	0	0	0	0	0	0	2	7	29
Days Minimum Temp. ≤ 32°F	30	25	19	6	0	0	0	0	0	5	19	29	133
Days Minimum Temp. ≤ 0°F	5	2	0	0	0	0	0	0	0	0	0	2	9
Heating Degree Days (base 65°F)	1,206	927	706	359	115	11	1	2	78	322	741	1,082	5,550
Cooling Degree Days (base 65°F)	0	0	1	20	76	274	426	363	162	16	0	0	1,338
Mean Precipitation (in.)	0.67	0.70	2.23	2.73	4.45	3.40	3.56	3.16	2.72	2.00	1.75	0.88	28.25
Days With ≥ 0.1" Precipitation	2	2	4	5	8	6	6	5	4	3	3	2	50
Days With ≥ 1.0" Precipitation	0	0	1	1	1	1	1	1	1	0	1	0	8
Mean Snowfall (in.)	6.1	5.4	4.3	1.3	trace	0.0	0.0	trace	0.1	0.5	3.4	4.9	26.0
Days With ≥ 1.0" Snow Depth	15	9	4	1	0	0	0	0	0	0	3	9	41

Syracuse *Otoe County*   Elevation: 1,099 ft.   Latitude: 40° 41' N   Longitude: 96° 11' W

	JAN	FEB	MAR	APR	MAY	JUN	JUL	AUG	SEP	OCT	NOV	DEC	YEAR
Mean Maximum Temp. (°F)	33.0	39.5	51.2	64.0	74.4	84.8	89.2	86.8	79.2	66.9	49.8	37.4	63.0
Mean Temp. (°F)	22.1	28.1	39.2	51.4	62.2	72.6	77.2	74.7	65.8	53.3	38.7	27.3	51.0
Mean Minimum Temp. (°F)	11.1	16.7	27.1	38.7	50.0	60.4	65.1	62.5	52.4	39.6	27.6	17.0	39.0
Extreme Maximum Temp. (°F)	71	83	89	96	98	107	108	107	102	95	83	71	108
Extreme Minimum Temp. (°F)	-30	-23	-22	6	26	38	41	43	23	7	-6	-26	-30
Days Maximum Temp. ≥ 90°F	0	0	0	1	1	9	15	12	5	0	0	0	43
Days Maximum Temp. ≤ 32°F	15	10	3	0	0	0	0	0	0	0	3	10	41
Days Minimum Temp. ≤ 32°F	30	26	22	8	1	0	0	0	1	8	21	29	146
Days Minimum Temp. ≤ 0°F	7	4	1	0	0	0	0	0	0	0	0	3	15
Heating Degree Days (base 65°F)	1,325	1,036	795	419	147	17	2	5	103	371	783	1,164	6,167
Cooling Degree Days (base 65°F)	0	0	1	18	63	247	384	309	135	13	0	0	1,170
Mean Precipitation (in.)	0.71	0.77	2.37	2.88	4.41	3.33	4.36	3.50	3.33	2.38	1.77	0.82	30.63
Days With ≥ 0.1" Precipitation	2	2	5	6	8	6	6	6	5	4	4	2	56
Days With ≥ 1.0" Precipitation	0	0	1	1	1	1	1	1	1	1	0	0	8
Mean Snowfall (in.)	6.3	5.6	4.7	1.1	0.0	0.0	0.0	0.0	0.0	0.6	2.0	4.0	24.3
Days With ≥ 1.0" Snow Depth	13	7	3	0	0	0	0	0	0	0	1	5	29

Tecumseh *Johnson County*   Elevation: 1,148 ft.   Latitude: 40° 22' N   Longitude: 96° 13' W

	JAN	FEB	MAR	APR	MAY	JUN	JUL	AUG	SEP	OCT	NOV	DEC	YEAR
Mean Maximum Temp. (°F)	33.2	39.8	51.2	63.5	73.9	84.3	89.0	87.0	78.9	67.0	50.2	38.0	63.0
Mean Temp. (°F)	22.4	28.5	39.6	51.3	62.1	72.4	77.2	74.9	65.8	53.4	39.2	27.7	51.2
Mean Minimum Temp. (°F)	11.6	17.0	28.0	39.2	50.3	60.4	65.3	62.8	52.7	39.7	28.1	17.3	39.4
Extreme Maximum Temp. (°F)	72	79	89	96	98	107	109	108	105	93	84	71	109
Extreme Minimum Temp. (°F)	-25	-24	-18	2	25	37	41	39	23	11	-7	-29	-29
Days Maximum Temp. ≥ 90°F	0	0	0	1	1	8	15	12	5	0	0	0	42
Days Maximum Temp. ≤ 32°F	14	9	3	0	0	0	0	0	0	0	3	10	39
Days Minimum Temp. ≤ 32°F	30	26	21	8	1	0	0	0	1	7	21	30	145
Days Minimum Temp. ≤ 0°F	7	4	1	0	0	0	0	0	0	0	0	3	15
Heating Degree Days (base 65°F)	1,313	1,026	781	420	149	18	2	6	104	368	768	1,150	6,105
Cooling Degree Days (base 65°F)	0	0	2	19	63	242	388	316	135	14	0	0	1,179
Mean Precipitation (in.)	0.89	0.97	2.67	2.91	4.54	3.54	4.52	3.62	3.45	2.36	2.01	1.07	32.55
Days With ≥ 0.1" Precipitation	3	3	5	6	7	6	7	6	5	5	4	3	60
Days With ≥ 1.0" Precipitation	0	0	1	1	1	1	1	1	1	1	1	0	9
Mean Snowfall (in.)	7.8	6.9	5.0	1.3	0.0	0.0	0.0	0.0	0.0	0.5	2.3	5.0	28.8
Days With ≥ 1.0" Snow Depth	14	11	4	1	0	0	0	0	0	0	2	8	40

Tekamah *Burt County*   Elevation: 1,036 ft.   Latitude: 41° 46' N   Longitude: 96° 13' W

	JAN	FEB	MAR	APR	MAY	JUN	JUL	AUG	SEP	OCT	NOV	DEC	YEAR
Mean Maximum Temp. (°F)	30.4	37.0	48.5	62.8	74.4	84.5	88.0	85.5	78.2	65.7	47.5	34.4	61.4
Mean Temp. (°F)	20.3	27.3	37.7	50.7	62.6	72.4	76.2	73.8	65.1	52.8	37.4	25.0	50.1
Mean Minimum Temp. (°F)	10.2	17.1	26.9	38.6	50.6	60.4	64.4	62.0	52.1	39.8	27.3	15.6	38.8
Extreme Maximum Temp. (°F)	69	75	90	96	99	107	110	104	100	94	82	70	110
Extreme Minimum Temp. (°F)	-24	-25	-13	5	27	39	43	42	26	12	-11	-26	-26
Days Maximum Temp. ≥ 90°F	0	0	0	1	2	8	13	9	4	0	0	0	37
Days Maximum Temp. ≤ 32°F	16	11	4	0	0	0	0	0	0	0	4	13	48
Days Minimum Temp. ≤ 32°F	30	26	21	7	0	0	0	0	0	6	22	30	142
Days Minimum Temp. ≤ 0°F	8	4	1	0	0	0	0	0	0	0	1	4	18
Heating Degree Days (base 65°F)	1,380	1,059	836	438	143	17	2	6	104	384	821	1,233	6,423
Cooling Degree Days (base 65°F)	0	0	0	15	67	233	342	273	111	10	0	0	1,052
Mean Precipitation (in.)	0.76	0.70	2.25	3.15	4.25	3.80	3.47	3.51	3.42	2.34	1.57	0.81	30.03
Days With ≥ 0.1" Precipitation	2	2	4	6	8	7	6	5	5	4	4	2	55
Days With ≥ 1.0" Precipitation	0	0	1	1	1	1	1	1	1	1	0	0	8
Mean Snowfall (in.)	6.8	6.0	4.8	1.2	0.0	0.0	0.0	0.0	0.0	0.5	2.5	5.1	26.9
Days With ≥ 1.0" Snow Depth	na	na	3	0	0	0	0	0	0	0	1	na	na

Trenton Dam *Hitchcock County*   Elevation: 2,808 ft.   Latitude: 40° 10' N   Longitude: 101° 04' W

	JAN	FEB	MAR	APR	MAY	JUN	JUL	AUG	SEP	OCT	NOV	DEC	YEAR
Mean Maximum Temp. (°F)	38.7	45.3	53.5	64.3	73.2	83.9	90.1	88.7	79.9	68.0	51.3	41.6	64.9
Mean Temp. (°F)	25.6	31.2	39.3	49.9	59.6	70.2	76.2	74.5	64.9	52.3	38.0	28.4	50.8
Mean Minimum Temp. (°F)	12.5	17.1	25.1	35.5	46.0	56.4	62.2	60.1	49.8	36.5	24.7	15.5	36.8
Extreme Maximum Temp. (°F)	74	79	89	101	99	106	110	107	105	95	85	75	110
Extreme Minimum Temp. (°F)	-24	-20	-10	10	23	37	42	44	25	10	-8	-31	-31
Days Maximum Temp. ≥ 90°F	0	0	0	0	1	8	17	16	7	1	0	0	50
Days Maximum Temp. ≤ 32°F	10	6	3	0	0	0	0	0	0	0	3	7	29
Days Minimum Temp. ≤ 32°F	31	27	25	12	2	0	0	0	1	9	25	31	163
Days Minimum Temp. ≤ 0°F	5	3	1	0	0	0	0	0	0	0	0	3	12
Heating Degree Days (base 65°F)	1,214	948	789	453	198	31	4	6	113	394	805	1,127	6,082
Cooling Degree Days (base 65°F)	0	0	0	7	41	199	361	315	123	7	0	0	1,053
Mean Precipitation (in.)	0.52	0.48	1.34	2.07	3.48	3.33	3.30	2.52	1.50	1.19	1.04	0.47	21.24
Days With ≥ 0.1" Precipitation	2	2	4	4	7	6	6	5	3	3	2	1	45
Days With ≥ 1.0" Precipitation	0	0	0	1	1	1	1	1	0	0	0	0	5
Mean Snowfall (in.)	6.4	3.7	6.0	2.4	trace	0.0	0.0	0.0	0.2	1.0	4.3	4.8	28.8
Days With ≥ 1.0" Snow Depth	12	6	4	1	0	0	0	0	0	0	4	8	35

Valentine Lakes Game Refuge *Cherry County*   Elevation: 2,926 ft.   Latitude: 42° 35' N   Longitude: 100° 41' W

	JAN	FEB	MAR	APR	MAY	JUN	JUL	AUG	SEP	OCT	NOV	DEC	YEAR
Mean Maximum Temp. (°F)	34.6	40.7	48.6	59.8	70.8	81.1	86.9	85.2	76.5	63.8	46.5	37.3	61.0
Mean Temp. (°F)	23.3	28.9	36.5	47.3	58.4	68.1	73.6	71.9	62.5	50.5	35.4	26.2	48.6
Mean Minimum Temp. (°F)	12.0	17.0	24.2	34.8	45.9	54.9	60.2	58.6	48.5	37.1	24.3	15.2	36.1
Extreme Maximum Temp. (°F)	69	76	82	97	96	105	109	103	99	92	83	73	109
Extreme Minimum Temp. (°F)	-27	-29	-30	5	23	30	41	39	23	4	-13	-29	-30
Days Maximum Temp. ≥ 90°F	0	0	0	0	0	5	12	9	3	0	0	0	29
Days Maximum Temp. ≤ 32°F	12	8	4	1	0	0	0	0	0	0	5	10	40
Days Minimum Temp. ≤ 32°F	29	26	24	13	2	0	0	0	1	9	23	29	156
Days Minimum Temp. ≤ 0°F	7	4	1	0	0	0	0	0	0	0	1	4	17
Heating Degree Days (base 65°F)	1,287	1,012	878	528	228	50	10	13	148	449	881	1,196	6,680
Cooling Degree Days (base 65°F)	0	0	0	7	28	135	265	223	79	5	0	0	742
Mean Precipitation (in.)	0.37	0.48	1.23	2.43	3.60	3.14	3.98	2.54	1.82	1.40	0.97	0.48	22.44
Days With ≥ 0.1" Precipitation	1	2	3	5	7	6	6	5	4	3	2	2	46
Days With ≥ 1.0" Precipitation	0	0	0	0	1	1	1	1	0	0	0	0	4
Mean Snowfall (in.)	5.4	6.3	8.4	5.4	trace	0.0	0.0	0.0	0.7	1.5	8.2	5.2	41.1
Days With ≥ 1.0" Snow Depth	12	10	6	2	0	0	0	0	0	1	7	9	47

Wahoo *Saunders County*   Elevation: 1,269 ft.   Latitude: 41° 13' N   Longitude: 96° 38' W

	JAN	FEB	MAR	APR	MAY	JUN	JUL	AUG	SEP	OCT	NOV	DEC	YEAR
Mean Maximum Temp. (°F)	32.1	38.8	50.4	63.6	74.4	84.3	88.1	85.5	78.4	66.6	48.5	37.4	62.3
Mean Temp. (°F)	21.8	27.8	38.7	50.9	61.9	72.0	76.0	73.3	65.0	53.0	37.8	27.4	50.5
Mean Minimum Temp. (°F)	11.4	16.8	27.0	38.1	49.4	59.7	64.0	61.3	51.7	39.4	27.1	17.3	38.6
Extreme Maximum Temp. (°F)	71	76	89	95	98	105	108	106	101	92	82	68	108
Extreme Minimum Temp. (°F)	-31	-21	-14	3	23	40	40	42	27	10	-6	-23	-31
Days Maximum Temp. ≥ 90°F	0	0	0	0	1	8	14	9	4	0	0	0	36
Days Maximum Temp. ≤ 32°F	15	10	3	0	0	0	0	0	0	0	3	10	41
Days Minimum Temp. ≤ 32°F	30	26	22	9	1	0	0	0	1	7	22	29	147
Days Minimum Temp. ≤ 0°F	7	4	1	0	0	0	0	0	0	0	0	2	14
Heating Degree Days (base 65°F)	1,334	1,041	810	430	150	18	2	7	106	376	809	1,160	6,243
Cooling Degree Days (base 65°F)	0	0	1	13	55	231	344	261	115	9	0	0	1,029
Mean Precipitation (in.)	0.72	0.81	2.45	3.54	5.00	4.35	3.70	4.31	3.69	2.69	1.94	0.90	34.10
Days With ≥ 0.1" Precipitation	3	2	5	8	9	8	7	7	6	5	5	3	68
Days With ≥ 1.0" Precipitation	0	0	1	1	1	1	1	2	1	1	0	0	9
Mean Snowfall (in.)	8.1	7.0	6.9	2.0	trace	0.0	0.0	0.0	trace	0.9	3.8	7.5	36.2
Days With ≥ 1.0" Snow Depth	na	na	na	0	0	0	0	0	0	0	na	na	na

Wakefield *Dixon County*   Elevation: 1,387 ft.   Latitude: 42° 16' N   Longitude: 96° 52' W

	JAN	FEB	MAR	APR	MAY	JUN	JUL	AUG	SEP	OCT	NOV	DEC	YEAR
Mean Maximum Temp. (°F)	29.8	36.8	48.4	62.8	73.8	83.6	87.1	84.8	77.4	65.1	46.2	33.6	60.8
Mean Temp. (°F)	19.3	26.0	36.8	49.8	61.3	71.2	75.0	72.8	64.2	51.9	35.8	23.7	49.0
Mean Minimum Temp. (°F)	8.7	15.2	25.2	36.7	48.8	58.7	62.9	60.8	51.0	38.6	25.3	13.7	37.1
Extreme Maximum Temp. (°F)	71	72	88	96	97	108	107	104	100	92	82	70	108
Extreme Minimum Temp. (°F)	-34	-30	-18	-4	19	37	40	37	20	8	-13	-28	-34
Days Maximum Temp. ≥ 90°F	0	0	0	1	1	7	12	8	3	0	0	0	32
Days Maximum Temp. ≤ 32°F	17	11	4	0	0	0	0	0	0	0	4	13	49
Days Minimum Temp. ≤ 32°F	31	26	24	10	1	0	0	0	1	8	23	30	154
Days Minimum Temp. ≤ 0°F	9	5	1	0	0	0	0	0	0	0	1	5	21
Heating Degree Days (base 65°F)	1,412	1,094	867	461	164	22	3	9	117	408	870	1,276	6,703
Cooling Degree Days (base 65°F)	0	0	0	14	60	220	323	263	105	10	0	0	995
Mean Precipitation (in.)	0.68	0.79	2.38	3.13	4.04	3.99	3.31	2.77	2.75	2.15	1.74	0.84	28.57
Days With ≥ 0.1" Precipitation	2	2	4	7	8	7	6	5	5	4	3	2	55
Days With ≥ 1.0" Precipitation	0	0	0	1	1	1	1	1	1	1	0	0	7
Mean Snowfall (in.)	7.0	6.2	7.0	2.5	trace	trace	trace	0.0	trace	0.9	5.3	7.8	36.7
Days With ≥ 1.0" Snow Depth	19	11	6	1	0	0	0	0	0	0	4	16	57

Wallace 2 W *Lincoln County*   Elevation: 3,097 ft.   Latitude: 40° 51' N   Longitude: 101° 13' W

	JAN	FEB	MAR	APR	MAY	JUN	JUL	AUG	SEP	OCT	NOV	DEC	YEAR
Mean Maximum Temp. (°F)	36.2	43.3	51.4	62.5	71.8	82.3	88.4	86.7	78.4	66.0	48.7	39.4	62.9
Mean Temp. (°F)	23.7	29.8	37.4	47.6	57.8	68.1	73.8	72.2	62.6	50.0	35.3	26.5	48.7
Mean Minimum Temp. (°F)	11.2	16.1	23.4	32.7	43.8	53.8	59.2	57.6	46.8	34.0	21.8	13.6	34.5
Extreme Maximum Temp. (°F)	71	78	84	94	97	105	109	107	101	92	81	72	109
Extreme Minimum Temp. (°F)	-26	-24	-19	3	20	34	40	37	15	4	-20	-33	-33
Days Maximum Temp. ≥ 90°F	0	0	0	0	0	6	14	11	5	0	0	0	36
Days Maximum Temp. ≤ 32°F	11	7	4	0	0	0	0	0	0	0	4	9	35
Days Minimum Temp. ≤ 32°F	31	27	27	15	3	0	0	0	2	13	27	31	176
Days Minimum Temp. ≤ 0°F	7	3	1	0	0	0	0	0	0	0	1	4	16
Heating Degree Days (base 65°F)	1,274	988	847	518	238	44	6	9	143	460	884	1,186	6,597
Cooling Degree Days (base 65°F)	0	0	0	2	23	138	283	242	78	2	0	0	768
Mean Precipitation (in.)	0.31	0.41	1.16	1.67	3.33	3.13	2.82	2.42	1.33	1.15	0.62	0.35	18.70
Days With ≥ 0.1" Precipitation	1	1	3	4	7	6	5	4	3	3	2	1	40
Days With ≥ 1.0" Precipitation	0	0	0	0	1	1	1	1	0	0	0	0	4
Mean Snowfall (in.)	4.5	4.5	6.9	2.3	trace	0.0	0.0	0.0	0.2	1.4	4.4	4.2	28.4
Days With ≥ 1.0" Snow Depth	13	8	6	2	0	0	0	0	0	1	5	10	45

Walthill *Thurston County*   Elevation: 1,217 ft.   Latitude: 42° 09' N   Longitude: 96° 29' W

	JAN	FEB	MAR	APR	MAY	JUN	JUL	AUG	SEP	OCT	NOV	DEC	YEAR
Mean Maximum Temp. (°F)	31.0	37.2	49.3	63.8	74.7	84.8	87.9	86.0	78.6	66.1	46.3	33.9	61.6
Mean Temp. (°F)	20.7	26.5	37.4	50.1	61.5	71.6	75.2	73.6	65.0	52.5	36.0	24.0	49.5
Mean Minimum Temp. (°F)	10.2	15.8	25.4	36.3	48.3	58.3	62.4	61.1	51.4	38.9	25.7	14.1	37.3
Extreme Maximum Temp. (°F)	69	72	89	95	96	107	108	103	98	92	82	76	108
Extreme Minimum Temp. (°F)	-33	-28	-19	6	22	35	37	36	20	8	-14	-27	-33
Days Maximum Temp. ≥ 90°F	0	0	0	1	1	8	13	9	3	0	0	0	35
Days Maximum Temp. ≤ 32°F	15	10	3	0	0	0	0	0	0	0	3	13	44
Days Minimum Temp. ≤ 32°F	30	26	23	11	1	0	0	0	1	8	23	30	153
Days Minimum Temp. ≤ 0°F	8	5	1	0	0	0	0	0	0	0	0	5	19
Heating Degree Days (base 65°F)	1,369	1,077	850	455	162	23	3	8	109	390	864	1,263	6,573
Cooling Degree Days (base 65°F)	0	0	0	13	64	222	328	279	114	11	0	0	1,031
Mean Precipitation (in.)	0.67	0.72	2.25	3.13	4.30	4.09	3.82	3.12	2.90	2.28	1.53	0.83	29.64
Days With ≥ 0.1" Precipitation	2	2	4	5	7	7	6	5	5	4	3	2	52
Days With ≥ 1.0" Precipitation	0	0	0	1	1	1	1	1	1	1	0	0	7
Mean Snowfall (in.)	6.0	5.5	5.9	2.4	0.0	0.0	0.0	0.0	0.0	0.9	4.6	5.8	31.1
Days With ≥ 1.0" Snow Depth	na	na	na	1	0	0	0	0	0	0	4	na	na

Weeping Water *Cass County*   Elevation: 1,099 ft.   Latitude: 40° 52' N   Longitude: 96° 08' W

	JAN	FEB	MAR	APR	MAY	JUN	JUL	AUG	SEP	OCT	NOV	DEC	YEAR
Mean Maximum Temp. (°F)	32.9	39.7	51.0	64.3	74.0	83.5	87.2	84.9	77.2	66.0	48.9	36.6	62.2
Mean Temp. (°F)	22.4	28.8	39.5	51.9	62.2	71.8	76.1	73.9	65.3	53.4	38.4	26.7	50.9
Mean Minimum Temp. (°F)	11.8	17.9	28.0	39.5	50.4	60.1	64.8	62.8	53.4	40.8	27.8	16.7	39.5
Extreme Maximum Temp. (°F)	70	76	89	96	97	104	107	106	102	93	82	69	107
Extreme Minimum Temp. (°F)	-26	-25	-15	5	25	39	41	43	24	12	-5	-29	-29
Days Maximum Temp. ≥ 90°F	0	0	0	1	1	6	12	9	3	0	0	0	32
Days Maximum Temp. ≤ 32°F	15	9	2	0	0	0	0	0	0	0	3	11	40
Days Minimum Temp. ≤ 32°F	30	25	21	7	1	0	0	0	0	6	21	29	140
Days Minimum Temp. ≤ 0°F	7	3	1	0	0	0	0	0	0	0	0	3	14
Heating Degree Days (base 65°F)	1,315	1,014	785	402	140	15	2	6	101	364	791	1,184	6,119
Cooling Degree Days (base 65°F)	0	0	1	17	56	219	344	275	114	11	0	0	1,037
Mean Precipitation (in.)	0.89	0.87	2.44	3.17	4.88	4.13	4.57	3.92	3.36	2.60	1.83	1.05	33.71
Days With ≥ 0.1" Precipitation	2	2	5	6	8	6	6	6	5	4	4	3	57
Days With ≥ 1.0" Precipitation	0	0	1	1	1	1	1	1	1	1	0	0	8
Mean Snowfall (in.)	7.7	na	3.9	1.1	0.0	0.0	0.0	0.0	0.0	0.7	2.0	na	na
Days With ≥ 1.0" Snow Depth	na	na	4	0	0	0	0	0	0	0	1	na	na

West Point *Cuming County*   Elevation: 1,309 ft.   Latitude: 41° 51' N   Longitude: 96° 43' W

	JAN	FEB	MAR	APR	MAY	JUN	JUL	AUG	SEP	OCT	NOV	DEC	YEAR
Mean Maximum Temp. (°F)	29.3	35.7	47.0	61.2	72.6	82.7	86.8	84.2	76.3	64.0	45.9	33.4	59.9
Mean Temp. (°F)	19.0	25.2	36.1	49.2	60.7	70.9	75.3	72.8	63.5	51.0	35.7	23.7	48.6
Mean Minimum Temp. (°F)	8.6	14.5	25.2	37.1	48.7	59.1	63.8	61.3	50.7	37.9	25.4	13.9	37.2
Extreme Maximum Temp. (°F)	68	75	89	94	98	105	107	104	101	91	80	68	107
Extreme Minimum Temp. (°F)	-26	-25	-17	3	24	36	41	41	22	10	-8	-27	-27
Days Maximum Temp. ≥ 90°F	0	0	0	0	1	7	12	8	3	0	0	0	31
Days Maximum Temp. ≤ 32°F	17	12	5	0	0	0	0	0	0	0	4	14	52
Days Minimum Temp. ≤ 32°F	31	27	24	9	1	0	0	0	1	9	24	30	156
Days Minimum Temp. ≤ 0°F	9	5	1	0	0	0	0	0	0	0	1	4	20
Heating Degree Days (base 65°F)	1,423	1,119	889	479	180	28	4	10	133	435	873	1,274	6,847
Cooling Degree Days (base 65°F)	0	0	0	13	47	204	320	249	90	7	0	0	930
Mean Precipitation (in.)	0.62	0.76	2.25	3.07	4.35	4.44	3.60	3.48	2.76	2.24	1.65	0.84	30.06
Days With ≥ 0.1" Precipitation	2	2	5	6	8	7	6	6	5	4	3	2	56
Days With ≥ 1.0" Precipitation	0	0	1	1	1	1	1	1	1	1	0	0	8
Mean Snowfall (in.)	6.4	6.3	5.8	2.0	0.0	0.0	0.0	0.0	trace	0.5	4.4	6.7	32.1
Days With ≥ 1.0" Snow Depth	17	13	7	1	0	0	0	0	0	0	4	13	55

York *York County*   Elevation: 1,607 ft.   Latitude: 40° 52' N   Longitude: 97° 36' W

	JAN	FEB	MAR	APR	MAY	JUN	JUL	AUG	SEP	OCT	NOV	DEC	YEAR
Mean Maximum Temp. (°F)	33.1	39.5	49.9	62.9	73.7	84.9	88.8	86.2	78.2	66.0	48.5	37.1	62.4
Mean Temp. (°F)	23.0	28.8	38.8	50.9	62.2	73.0	77.3	74.8	65.9	53.5	38.0	27.4	51.1
Mean Minimum Temp. (°F)	12.8	18.0	27.6	38.8	50.8	61.1	65.9	63.3	53.6	40.9	27.5	17.6	39.8
Extreme Maximum Temp. (°F)	75	81	90	96	98	108	108	108	100	94	83	73	108
Extreme Minimum Temp. (°F)	-23	-18	-13	3	29	40	43	46	26	11	-6	-24	-24
Days Maximum Temp. ≥ 90°F	0	0	0	1	1	9	15	11	5	0	0	0	42
Days Maximum Temp. ≤ 32°F	15	9	3	0	0	0	0	0	0	0	4	10	41
Days Minimum Temp. ≤ 32°F	30	26	21	7	0	0	0	0	0	5	21	30	140
Days Minimum Temp. ≤ 0°F	6	3	0	0	0	0	0	0	0	0	0	3	12
Heating Degree Days (base 65°F)	1,296	1,017	807	428	145	15	2	5	96	363	802	1,158	6,134
Cooling Degree Days (base 65°F)	0	0	1	14	61	251	386	303	131	12	0	0	1,159
Mean Precipitation (in.)	0.75	0.65	2.34	2.74	4.61	3.83	3.69	3.32	2.61	1.91	1.76	0.79	29.00
Days With ≥ 0.1" Precipitation	2	2	5	5	8	6	5	6	5	4	3	2	53
Days With ≥ 1.0" Precipitation	0	0	1	1	1	1	1	1	1	1	0	0	7
Mean Snowfall (in.)	7.0	6.1	6.4	1.3	0.0	0.0	0.0	0.0	trace	0.7	4.0	6.0	31.5
Days With ≥ 1.0" Snow Depth	na	6	na	0	0	0	0	0	0	0	2	na	na

Note: See Appendix D for explanation of data.

NEVADA

PHYSICAL FEATURES. Nevada is primarily a plateau area. The eastern part has an average elevation of between 5,000 and 6,000 feet above sea level; the western portion between 3,800 and 5,000 feet, the lower limit being in the vicinity of Pyramid Lake and Carson Sink; and the southern part generally between 2,000 and 3,000 feet. From the lower elevations of the west portion there is a fairly rapid rise westward to the summits of the eastern ranges of the Sierra Nevada. The southwestern part slopes down toward Death Valley, California, and the southern portion toward the channel of the Colorado River, the elevation of which is less than 1,000 feet above sea level. The extreme northeastern part slopes northerly, draining into the Snake River and thence into the Columbia.

On the Nevada plateau there are many mountain ranges, most of them 50 to 100 miles long, running generally north and south. The only east-west range is in the northeast. It forms the southern limit of the Columbia River Basin. With the exception of this small drainage area and another limited region in the southeast which drains into the Colorado River, the State lies within the confines of the Great Basin, and the waters of its streams disappear into sinks or flow into lakes with no outlets.

GENERAL CLIMATE. Nevada lies just east and to the leeward of the Sierra Nevada Range, a massive mountain barrier which has a marked influence on the climate of the State. One of the greatest contrasts in precipitation found within a short distance in the United States occurs between the western, or California, slopes of the Sierras and the valleys just to the east of this range. The prevailing winds are from the west, and as moist air associated with storms from the Pacific Ocean ascends the western slopes of the Sierras, a large portion of the original moisture falls as precipitation. As the air descends the eastern slope, it is warmed by compression, so that very little precipitation occurs. The effects of this mountain barrier are felt not only in the extreme western part, but generally throughout the State, with the result that the lowlands of Nevada are largely desert or semidesert.

With its varied and rugged topography—its mountain ranges, narrow valleys and low, sage-covered deserts, ranging in elevation from about 1,500 to more than 10,000 feet—Nevada presents wide local variations of temperature and rainfall. The most striking climatic features are bright sunshine, small annual precipitation in the valleys and deserts, heavy snowfall in the higher mountains, dryness and purity of air, and phenomenally large daily ranges of temperature.

TEMPERATURE. The mean annual temperatures vary from the middle 40s in the northeastern part to around 50°F. in the west, and to the middle 60s in the south. In the northeastern portion summers are short and hot, winters long and cold. In the west, the summers are also short and hot, but the winters are only moderately cold; while in the south the summers are long and hot and the winters short and mild. Prolonged periods of extremely cold weather are rare, due primarily to the mountains east and north of the State which act as a barrier to the intensely cold continental Arctic air masses.

In Nevada there is relatively strong insolation of heat during the day and rapid nighttime cooling, because of the clear air, resulting in wide daily ranges in temperature. Even after the hottest days, the nights are usually cool. At Reno the average range between the highest and the lowest daily temperatures is 29°F. in January, increasing month by month to 45°F. in July. In summer temperatures above 100°F. occur rather frequently in the extreme southern portion and occasionally over the remainder of the State. However, the humidity is normally low so that corresponding temperatures are less disagreeable in Nevada than in more humid climates.

PRECIPITATION. Nevada's precipitation mostly occurs during the winter season and on the average is less than in any other State. Precipitation is lightest over the lower parts of the western plateau, a series of long valleys extending from the State border opposite Death Valley in California northward to the Idaho line. Over the more southerly of those valleys the average annual precipitation is less than 5 inches. From this low average it ranges upward to 18 inches in Lamoille Canyon on the western side of the Ruby Mountains of northeast Nevada, and up to about 28 inches at Marlette Lake high in the most easterly range of the Sierras. Variations in precipitation are due mainly to differences in elevation and exposure to precipitation-bearing winds. The average annual number of days with measurable precipitation varies considerably.

Snowfall is usually heavy in the mountains, particularly in the north. Mountain snowfall forms the main source of water for streamflow. In years when winter and spring snowfall is light, the result is a shortage of water. Melting of the mountain snowpack in the spring usually causes some flooding in northern and extreme western streams during the period April to June, but damaging floods of this type are infrequent. Rain floods in which snowmelt is also a factor usually occur from November to March. Heavy summer thunderstorms cause flooding in local streams, but they usually occur over sparsely settled mountainous areas and, therefore, are seldom destructive.

OTHER CLIMATIC ELEMENTS. The State has a generous supply of sunshine, the average percentage of the possible amount at northern and central locations being generally between 65 and 75 percent and at southern locations above 80 percent.

The low humidity and abundant sunshine produce rapid evaporation. Annual amounts in the extreme southern portion of the State, as measured in evaporation pans, average over 100 inches. In northern and central sections amounts average roughly half as much.

Winds are generally light. Storms with high winds rarely occur, and still more rarely cause appreciable damage, except locally along the east slope of the Sierras. The prevailing wind direction is west, although at a few stations, because of local topography, it is south or southwest.

Dust or sandstorms occur occasionally, particularly over the southern part during the spring months when storms are moving through the region more frequently than at other seasons of the year.

Thunderstorms are infrequent, the average annual number being 12 at Winnemucca, 13 at Reno and Las Vegas, 22 at Elko, and 30 at Ely. Summer thunderstorms develop occasionally into heavy local downpours of rain. These storms, locally termed cloudbursts, may bring to a locality as much rain in a few hours as would normally fall in several months. Tornadoes are extremely rare.

Over the northern and central portions of the State, freezes continue until late in spring and being early in autumn. The shortest freeze-free season is in the extreme northeast, and the longest in the extreme south, the range being from less than 100 days at several weather stations in the northeast to around 140 in the west, and to over 225 in the extreme south.

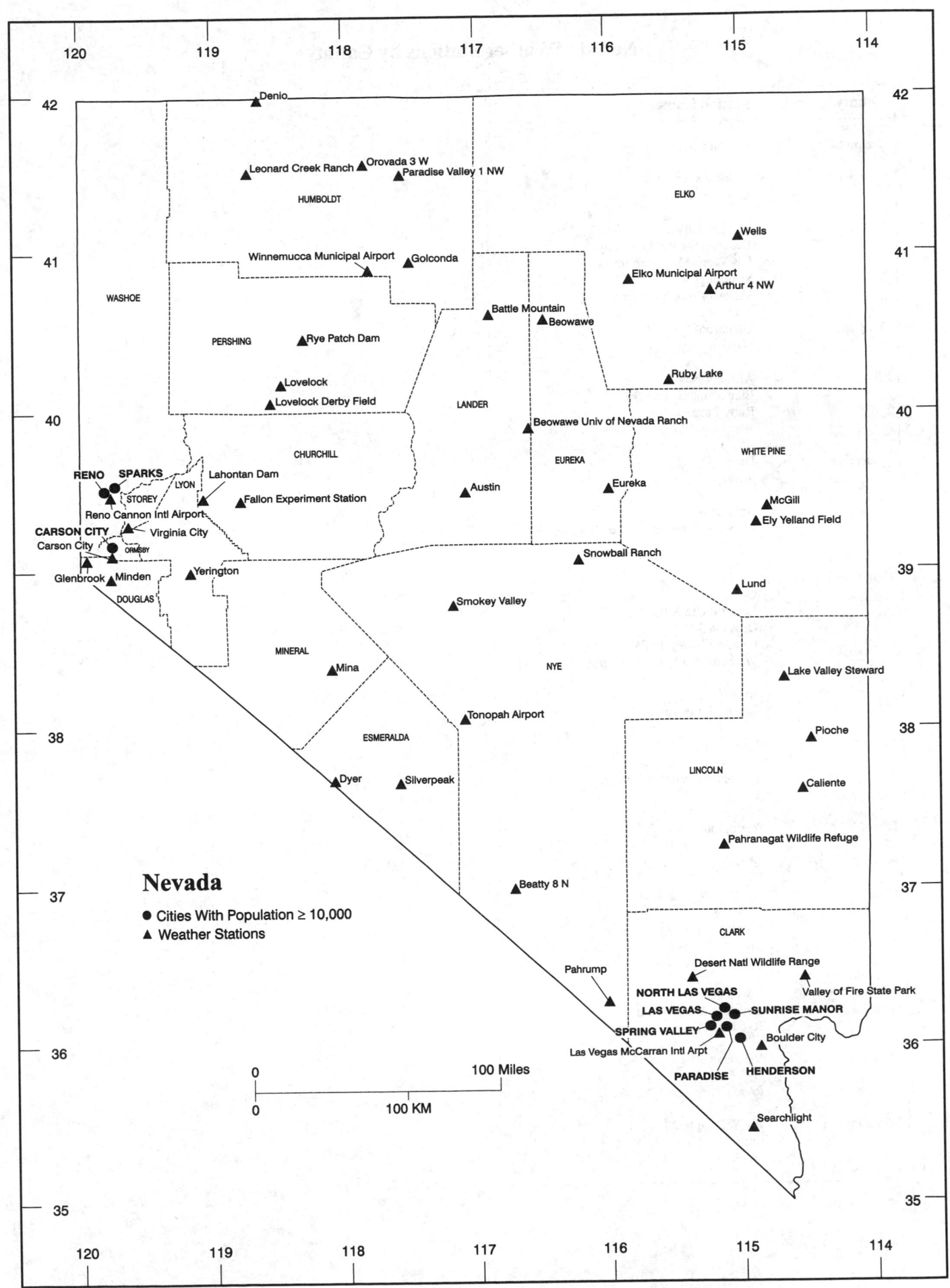

Nevada

● Cities With Population ≥ 10,000
▲ Weather Stations

Denio

Leonard Creek Ranch
Orovada 3 W
Paradise Valley 1 NW
HUMBOLDT

ELKO

Wells

Winnemucca Municipal Airport
Golconda

Elko Municipal Airport
Arthur 4 NW

WASHOE

PERSHING

Rye Patch Dam

Battle Mountain
Beowawe

Ruby Lake

Lovelock
Lovelock Derby Field

LANDER

CHURCHILL

Beowawe Univ of Nevada Ranch

WHITE PINE

EUREKA

RENO SPARKS
Lahontan Dam
STOREY LYON
Reno Cannon Intl Airport
Virginia City
CARSON CITY
Carson City
ORMSBY
Glenbrook Minden
DOUGLAS

Fallon Experiment Station

Austin

Eureka

McGill
Ely Yelland Field

Yerington

Snowball Ranch

Lund

Smokey Valley

MINERAL

Mina

NYE

Lake Valley Steward

Tonopah Airport

Pioche

ESMERALDA

LINCOLN

Dyer Silverpeak

Caliente

Pahranagat Wildlife Refuge

Beatty 8 N

CLARK

Pahrump

Desert Natl Wildlife Range

NORTH LAS VEGAS
Valley of Fire State Park
LAS VEGAS SUNRISE MANOR
SPRING VALLEY
Las Vegas McCarran Intl Arpt Boulder City
PARADISE HENDERSON

Searchlight

0 _____ 100 Miles
0 _____ 100 KM

Nevada Weather Stations by County

County	Station Name
Carson City	Carson City
Churchill	Fallon Experiment Station
	Lahontan Dam
Clark	Boulder City
	Desert Nat'l Wildlife Range
	Las Vegas McCarran Int'l Arpt.
	Searchlight
	Valley of Fire State Park
Douglas	Glenbrook
	Minden
Elko	Arthur 4 NW
	Elko Municipal Airport
	Ruby Lake
	Wells
Esmeralda	Dyer
	Silverpeak
Eureka	Beowawe
	Beowawe Univ. of Nevada Ranch
	Eureka
Humboldt	Denio
	Golconda
	Leonard Creek Ranch
	Orovada 3 W
	Paradise Valley 1 NW
	Winnemucca Municipal Airport
Lander	Austin
	Battle Mountain
Lincoln	Caliente
	Lake Valley Steward
	Pahranagat Wildlife Refuge
	Pioche
Lyon	Yerington
Mineral	Mina
Nye	Beatty 8 N
	Pahrump
	Smokey Valley
	Snowball Ranch
	Tonopah Airport
Pershing	Lovelock
	Lovelock Derby Field
	Rye Patch Dam
Storey	Virginia City
Washoe	Reno Cannon Int'l Airport
White Pine	Ely Yelland Field
	Lund
	McGill

Nevada Weather Stations by City

City	Station Name	Miles
Carson City	Carson City	1
	Glenbrook	12
	Minden	14
	Virginia City	11
Henderson	Boulder City	10
	Las Vegas McCarran Int'l Arpt.	9
Las Vegas	Las Vegas McCarran Int'l Arpt.	7
North Las Vegas	Las Vegas McCarran Int'l Arpt.	9
Paradise	Boulder City	18
	Las Vegas McCarran Int'l Arpt.	2
Reno	Boca, CA	18
	Reno Cannon Int'l Airport	4
	Virginia City	18
Sparks	Reno Cannon Int'l Airport	5
	Virginia City	18
Spring Valley	Las Vegas McCarran Int'l Arpt.	5
Sunrise Manor	Boulder City	18
	Las Vegas McCarran Int'l Arpt.	9

Note: Miles is the distance between the geographic center of the city and the weather station.

Nevada Weather Stations by Elevation

Feet	Station Name
7,158	Snowball Ranch
6,604	Austin
6,538	Eureka
6,348	Glenbrook
6,348	Lake Valley Steward
6,338	Virginia City
6,299	Arthur 4 NW
6,299	McGill
6,259	Ely Yelland Field
6,177	Pioche
6,007	Ruby Lake
5,738	Beowawe Univ. of Nevada Ranch
5,698	Wells
5,623	Smokey Valley
5,567	Lund
5,429	Tonopah Airport
5,078	Elko Municipal Airport
4,898	Dyer
4,708	Minden
4,698	Beowawe
4,671	Paradise Valley 1 NW
4,648	Carson City
4,547	Mina
4,537	Battle Mountain
4,412	Golconda
4,402	Reno Cannon Int'l Airport
4,399	Caliente
4,379	Yerington
4,294	Winnemucca Municipal Airport
4,258	Silverpeak
4,222	Leonard Creek Ranch
4,199	Orovada 3 W
4,189	Denio
4,146	Lahontan Dam
4,133	Rye Patch Dam
3,973	Lovelock
3,963	Fallon Experiment Station
3,897	Lovelock Derby Field
3,549	Beatty 8 N
3,540	Searchlight
3,398	Pahranagat Wildlife Refuge
2,919	Desert Nat'l Wildlife Range
2,673	Pahrump
2,522	Boulder City
2,125	Las Vegas McCarran Int'l Arpt.
1,998	Valley of Fire State Park

Elko Municipal Airport

Elko is located in the Humbolt River Valley of northeastern Nevada. Weather observations are taken at the Flight Service Station which is located at the Municipal Airport on the west side of town. The elevation at the airport is just above 5,000 feet.

The Ruby mountain range, with many peaks near or exceeding 10,000 feet in height, dominates the landscape from about 40 miles northeast through 40 miles southeast of Elko. The immediate terrain consists of sagebrush-covered valleys and hills. The highest hills are approximately 2,500 feet above the valley floors. A few areas, mostly in the higher mountains, are covered with sparse stands of juniper, aspen, pinion pine, and spruce. The only heavily forested area in northeastern Nevada is in the Jarbidge Wilderness Area north of Elko near the Idaho border.

Because of the high elevation and proximity of the mountains, there is a wide range between the normal high and low temperatures. High radiative cooling at night makes cool nights the rule, even in mid summer.

Normal precipitation is light, especially during the summer months when the precipitation falls mostly as light showers which do not contribute much toward crop growth. The precipitation that falls between November and June (rain and snow) is critical to agriculture in the area. Not only is the precipitation that falls directly on the fields a benefit to farmers and ranchers, but the runoff from snowfall that accumulates in the mountains is used for irrigation.

The principal crop in northeast Nevada is hay. Cattle ranching is a major industry within the area. The ranges ordinarily furnish excellent summer pasture for cattle. Hay crops are needed for winter feeding.

Mining is another major industry. Many of the mines are located in the mountains at rather high elevations and are affected by daily weather. This is especially true during the winter when snow and rain may cause poor or impassable road conditions, thereby halting mining operations.

Transportation by air, rail, or road is seldom affected by the weather for more than short periods.

Based on the 1951-1980 period, the average first occurrence of 32 degrees Fahrenheit in the fall is September 8 and the average last occurrence in the spring is June 5.

Elko Municipal Airport *Elko County*   Elevation: 5,078 ft.   Latitude: 40° 50' N   Longitude: 115° 48' W

	JAN	FEB	MAR	APR	MAY	JUN	JUL	AUG	SEP	OCT	NOV	DEC	YEAR
Mean Maximum Temp. (°F)	36.9	43.1	51.1	58.9	68.6	79.7	89.6	88.2	78.0	64.9	48.4	38.0	62.1
Mean Temp. (°F)	25.5	31.4	38.5	44.2	52.7	61.7	69.3	67.7	58.1	46.6	34.9	26.0	46.4
Mean Minimum Temp. (°F)	14.1	19.6	25.8	29.6	36.7	43.6	48.9	47.1	38.2	28.3	21.3	13.8	30.6
Extreme Maximum Temp. (°F)	64	70	75	86	92	104	107	107	98	88	78	65	107
Extreme Minimum Temp. (°F)	-21	-29	-4	4	15	23	30	20	15	1	-11	-33	-33
Days Maximum Temp. ≥ 90°F	0	0	0	0	0	5	18	14	3	0	0	0	40
Days Maximum Temp. ≤ 32°F	9	4	1	0	0	0	0	0	0	0	2	8	24
Days Minimum Temp. ≤ 32°F	29	26	25	20	8	1	0	0	8	22	26	29	194
Days Minimum Temp. ≤ 0°F	5	2	0	0	0	0	0	0	0	0	1	4	12
Heating Degree Days (base 65°F)	1,217	943	816	616	378	138	21	35	219	562	897	1,204	7,046
Cooling Degree Days (base 65°F)	0	0	0	0	2	40	151	120	21	0	0	0	334
Mean Precipitation (in.)	1.17	0.81	0.98	0.80	1.06	0.71	0.31	0.51	0.70	0.68	1.08	0.98	9.79
Maximum Precipitation (in.)	3.3	1.9	2.4	2.2	4.1	2.6	2.3	4.6	3.2	1.9	2.8	4.2	18.3
Minimum Precipitation (in.)	trace	0.1	trace	trace	trace	trace	0	trace	0	trace	trace	trace	4.8
Maximum 24-hr. Precipitation (in.)	1.3	0.7	0.8	0.8	1.7	1.0	1.0	4.1	2.3	1.0	1.3	1.6	4.1
Days With ≥ 0.1" Precipitation	3	3	3	3	4	3	1	1	2	2	4	3	32
Days With ≥ 1.0" Precipitation	0	0	0	0	0	0	0	0	0	0	0	0	0
Mean Snowfall (in.)	9.3	5.9	4.3	2.8	1.2	trace	trace	trace	trace	0.9	5.0	7.8	37.2
Maximum Snowfall (in.)	27	25	23	16	11	trace	0	0	2	6	17	33	85
Maximum 24-hr. Snowfall (in.)	16	9	8	9	8	trace	0	0	2	5	6	9	16
Days With ≥ 1.0" Snow Depth	12	5	2	1	0	0	0	0	0	0	3	8	31
Thunderstorm Days	< 1	< 1	< 1	1	3	4	5	4	2	< 1	< 1	< 1	19
Foggy Days	5	3	3	1	1	< 1	< 1	< 1	< 1	1	2	4	20
Predominant Sky Cover	OVR	OVR	OVR	OVR	OVR	CLR	CLR	CLR	CLR	CLR	OVR	OVR	CLR
Mean Relative Humidity 7am (%)	79	80	77	64	58	52	42	45	53	66	77	79	64
Mean Relative Humidity 4pm (%)	61	54	44	33	31	26	18	18	22	29	48	61	37
Mean Dewpoint (°F)	16	21	23	25	31	36	37	35	30	25	22	17	26
Prevailing Wind Direction	SW	WSW	SW	WSW	SW	SW	SW	SW	SW	WSW	SW	SW	SW
Prevailing Wind Speed (mph)	9	9	9	10	9	9	9	9	9	9	9	9	9
Maximum Wind Gust (mph)	na	na	na	na	na	na	na	na	na	na	na	na	na

Ely Yelland Field

Ely, Nevada, is located within but near the southern rim of the Great Basin. The neighboring terrain consists of alternate mountain ranges and sagebrush covered valleys. Principal cover on the mountains is juniper, pinion, and, at higher elevations, white fir, and white pine. Valley floors in this region are near 6,000 feet above sea level. This high elevation is conducive to sharp nighttime radiation, which produces pleasant summer nights but also reduces the season that is free from freezing temperatures.

The Ely weather station is near the center of Steptoe Valley, which is five miles wide at this point. The mountains of the Egan Range to the west and the Schell Creek Range to the east range up to 4,000 feet above the station elevation and prevent strong surface winds from these directions. A very pronounced drainage wind sweeps down the valley during the morning hours. More precipitation is noted near the mountains than is measured in the center of the valley.

Because of low annual precipitation, farming is limited to areas that can be irrigated from mountain streams or wells. The livestock industry is predominant in agriculture. Cultivated crops consist almost entirely of grains and forage.

The mountain ranges provide fairly good summer pastures for cattle and the lowlands provide food for a good portion of the winter in dry or snow-softened desert plants. All stock, however, has to be finished for market in the feed yards. Sheep share the mountain pastures with cattle in the summer, and as winter approaches move out on the wide flat valleys. These browsers eat snow for water and consume a wide variety of desert plants, including the lowly sagebrush. It is not uncommon for bands of sheep to spend an entire winter without supplemental feed.

Based on the 1951-1980 period, the average first occurrence of 32 degrees Fahrenheit in the fall is September 6 and the average last occurrence in the spring is June 16.

Ely Yelland Field *White Pine County*   Elevation: 6,259 ft.   Latitude: 39° 18' N   Longitude: 114° 51' W

	JAN	FEB	MAR	APR	MAY	JUN	JUL	AUG	SEP	OCT	NOV	DEC	YEAR
Mean Maximum Temp. (°F)	40.0	44.2	49.8	57.5	67.2	78.9	87.2	85.1	75.6	63.0	49.1	40.7	61.5
Mean Temp. (°F)	25.2	29.9	35.8	41.8	50.2	59.8	67.3	65.8	56.5	45.3	33.8	25.5	44.8
Mean Minimum Temp. (°F)	10.3	15.6	21.8	26.1	33.3	40.5	47.5	46.4	37.3	27.6	18.5	10.3	27.9
Extreme Maximum Temp. (°F)	63	67	71	82	90	96	101	97	93	85	75	66	101
Extreme Minimum Temp. (°F)	-26	-30	-10	-5	14	18	28	27	16	-3	-15	-29	-30
Days Maximum Temp. ≥ 90°F	0	0	0	0	0	3	12	7	1	0	0	0	23
Days Maximum Temp. ≤ 32°F	7	3	1	0	0	0	0	0	0	0	2	7	20
Days Minimum Temp. ≤ 32°F	31	27	29	24	14	3	0	0	8	23	28	31	218
Days Minimum Temp. ≤ 0°F	7	3	1	0	0	0	0	0	0	0	1	6	18
Heating Degree Days (base 65°F)	1,228	984	898	689	450	175	24	43	256	603	928	1,217	7,495
Cooling Degree Days (base 65°F)	0	0	0	0	0	23	103	79	8	0	0	0	213
Mean Precipitation (in.)	0.72	0.69	1.05	0.92	1.24	0.69	0.66	0.90	0.94	0.95	0.67	0.55	9.98
Maximum Precipitation (in.)	2.1	2.2	2.4	3.4	3.3	3.5	2.3	2.5	5.0	3.7	1.8	2.1	15.5
Minimum Precipitation (in.)	trace	trace	0.1	trace	trace	trace	trace	trace	trace	0	trace	trace	4.2
Maximum 24-hr. Precipitation (in.)	0.9	1.4	0.7	0.8	1.4	1.4	1.2	1.0	2.5	1.1	1.2	0.8	2.5
Days With ≥ 0.1" Precipitation	2	3	4	3	3	2	2	2	2	3	2	2	30
Days With ≥ 1.0" Precipitation	0	0	0	0	0	0	0	0	0	0	0	0	0
Mean Snowfall (in.)	8.8	6.9	9.5	6.0	3.1	0.1	trace	trace	0.6	2.9	6.0	6.9	50.8
Maximum Snowfall (in.)	25	20	25	25	12	2	trace	trace	6	12	17	22	101
Maximum 24-hr. Snowfall (in.)	12	10	9	6	8	2	trace	trace	4	7	12	9	12
Days With ≥ 1.0" Snow Depth	16	12	5	2	0	0	0	0	0	1	5	12	53
Thunderstorm Days	< 1	< 1	1	1	4	5	8	8	3	1	< 1	< 1	31
Foggy Days	2	1	2	1	1	< 1	< 1	< 1	1	1	1	1	11
Predominant Sky Cover	OVR	OVR	OVR	OVR	BRK	CLR	CLR	CLR	CLR	CLR	CLR	CLR	CLR
Mean Relative Humidity 7am (%)	73	74	71	60	53	45	40	46	52	64	71	72	60
Mean Relative Humidity 4pm (%)	55	50	43	34	31	24	21	23	24	31	46	54	36
Mean Dewpoint (°F)	13	17	20	22	27	31	35	36	29	24	18	13	24
Prevailing Wind Direction	S	S	S	S	S	S	S	S	S	S	S	S	S
Prevailing Wind Speed (mph)	13	13	13	13	12	12	10	12	12	12	12	12	12
Maximum Wind Gust (mph)	59	52	64	62	63	60	61	60	61	61	59	56	64

Las Vegas McCarran Int'l Arpt.

Las Vegas is situated near the center of a broad desert valley, which is almost surrounded by mountains ranging from 2,000 to 10,000 feet higher than the floor of the valley. This Vegas Valley, comprising about 600 square miles, runs from northwest to southeast, and slopes gradually upward on each side toward the surrounding mountains. Weather observations are taken at McCarran Airport, seven miles south of downtown Las Vegas, and about five miles southwest and 300 feet higher than the lower portions of the valley. Since mountains encircle the valley, drainage winds are usually downslope toward the center, or lowest portion of the valley. This condition also affects minimum temperatures, which in lower portions of the valley can be from 15 to 25 degrees colder than recorded at the airport on clear, calm nights.

The four seasons are well defined. Summers display desert conditions, with maximum temperatures usually in the 100 degree range. The proximity of the mountains contributes to the relatively cool summer nights, with the majority of minimum temperatures in the mid 70s. During about two weeks almost every summer warm, moist air predominates in this area, and causes scattered thunderstorms, occasionally quite severe, together with higher than average humidity. Soil erosion, especially near the mountains and foothills surrounding the valley, is evidence of the intensity of some of the thunderstorm activity. Winters, on the whole, are mild and pleasant. Daytime temperatures average near 60 degrees with mostly clear skies. The spring and fall seasons are generally considered most ideal, although rather sharp temperature changes can occur during these months. There are very few days during the spring and fall months when outdoor activities are affected in any degree by the weather.

The Sierra Nevada Mountains of California and the Spring Mountains immediately west of the Vegas Valley, the latter rising to elevations over 10,000 feet above the valley floor, act as effective barriers to moisture moving eastward from the Pacific Ocean. It is mainly these barriers that result in a minimum of dark overcast and rainy days. Rainy days average less than one in June to three per month in the winter months.

Strong winds, associated with major storms, usually reach this valley from the southwest or through the pass from the northwest. Winds over 50 mph are infrequent but, when they do occur, are probably the most provoking of the elements experienced in the Vegas Valley, because of the blowing dust and sand associated with them.

The average first occurrence of 32 degrees Fahrenheit in the fall is November 21 and the average last occurrence in the spring is March 7.

Las Vegas McCarran Int'l Arpt. *Clark County*   Elevation: 2,125 ft.   Latitude: 36° 05' N   Longitude: 115° 09' W

	JAN	FEB	MAR	APR	MAY	JUN	JUL	AUG	SEP	OCT	NOV	DEC	YEAR
Mean Maximum Temp. (°F)	56.9	63.1	69.4	77.7	87.7	98.8	104.1	101.8	93.7	80.8	66.2	57.1	79.8
Mean Temp. (°F)	46.1	51.6	57.5	64.9	74.6	84.9	90.6	88.7	80.6	67.9	54.5	46.2	67.3
Mean Minimum Temp. (°F)	35.3	40.1	45.6	52.1	61.4	70.9	77.1	75.5	67.4	54.9	42.8	35.3	54.9
Extreme Maximum Temp. (°F)	77	87	89	99	108	115	116	116	110	103	87	77	116
Extreme Minimum Temp. (°F)	12	16	23	31	42	48	60	60	47	26	22	11	11
Days Maximum Temp. ≥ 90°F	0	0	0	3	15	26	30	30	22	6	0	0	132
Days Maximum Temp. ≤ 32°F	0	0	0	0	0	0	0	0	0	0	0	0	0
Days Minimum Temp. ≤ 32°F	9	3	1	0	0	0	0	0	0	0	2	9	24
Days Minimum Temp. ≤ 0°F	0	0	0	0	0	0	0	0	0	0	0	0	0
Heating Degree Days (base 65°F)	578	371	242	90	14	1	0	0	1	56	312	575	2,240
Cooling Degree Days (base 65°F)	0	2	19	111	325	599	794	756	483	154	5	0	3,248
Mean Precipitation (in.)	0.59	0.67	0.59	0.15	0.24	0.08	0.46	0.48	0.31	0.21	0.33	0.41	4.52
Maximum Precipitation (in.)	3.0	2.5	4.8	2.4	1.0	1.0	2.5	2.6	1.6	1.2	2.2	1.7	9.9
Minimum Precipitation (in.)	0	0	0	0	0	0	0	0	0	0	0	0	0.6
Maximum 24-hr. Precipitation (in.)	0.7	1.3	1.2	1.0	0.8	0.8	1.4	2.6	1.1	1.0	1.1	0.9	2.6
Days With ≥ 0.1" Precipitation	2	2	2	1	1	0	1	1	1	1	1	1	14
Days With ≥ 1.0" Precipitation	0	0	0	0	0	0	0	0	0	0	0	0	0
Mean Snowfall (in.)	0.9	0.1	trace	trace	0.0	0.0	0.0	trace	0.0	0.0	trace	trace	1.0
Maximum Snowfall (in.)	17	1	trace	trace	0	0	0	0	0	0	4	2	17
Maximum 24-hr. Snowfall (in.)	7	1	trace	trace	0	0	0	0	0	0	3	2	7
Days With ≥ 1.0" Snow Depth	0	0	0	0	0	0	0	0	0	0	0	0	0
Thunderstorm Days	< 1	< 1	< 1	< 1	1	1	4	4	2	< 1	< 1	< 1	12
Foggy Days	2	1	< 1	< 1	< 1	0	< 1	< 1	< 1	< 1	1	1	5
Predominant Sky Cover	CLR	CLR	CLR	CLR	CLR	CLR	CLR	CLR	CLR	CLR	CLR	CLR	CLR
Mean Relative Humidity 7am (%)	59	53	43	31	27	20	26	31	30	36	47	56	38
Mean Relative Humidity 4pm (%)	32	26	21	15	13	10	14	16	15	18	26	31	20
Mean Dewpoint (°F)	23	24	23	24	28	30	40	43	36	29	25	22	29
Prevailing Wind Direction	WSW	WSW	SW	SW	SW	SW	SW	SW	SW	WSW	WSW	WSW	SW
Prevailing Wind Speed (mph)	8	8	14	15	15	15	13	13	12	8	8	8	12
Maximum Wind Gust (mph)	54	73	82	69	73	63	75	90	73	56	70	55	90

Reno Cannon Int'l Airport

At an elevation of 4,400 feet above mean sea level, Reno is located at the west edge of Truckee Meadows in a semi-arid plateau lying in the lee of the Sierra Nevada Mountain Range. To the west, the Sierras rise to elevations of 9,000 to 11,000 feet. Hills to the east reach 6,000 to 7,000 feet. The Truckee River, flowing from the Sierras eastward through Reno, drains into Pyramid Lake to the northeast of the city.

The daily temperatures on the whole are mild, but the difference between the high and low often exceeds 45 degrees. While the afternoon high may exceed 90 degrees, a light wrap is often needed shortly after sunset. Nights with low temperatures over 60 degrees are rare. Afternoon temperatures in winter are moderate.

Based on the 1951-1980 period, the average first occurrence of 32 degrees Fahrenheit in the fall is September 16 and the average last occurrence in the spring is June 1.

More than half of the precipitation in Reno occurs mainly as mixed rain and snow, and falls from December to March. Although there is an average of about 25 inches of snow a year, it seldom remains on the ground for more than three or four days at a time. Summer rain comes mainly as brief thunderstorms in the middle and late afternoons. While precipitation is scarce, considerable water is available from the high altitude reservoirs in the Sierra Nevada, where precipitation is heavy.

Humidity is very low during the summer months, and moderately low during the winter. Fogs are rare, and are usually confined to the early morning hours of midwinter. Sunshine is abundant throughout the year.

Reno Cannon Int'l Airport *Washoe County*   Elevation: 4,402 ft.   Latitude: 39° 29' N   Longitude: 119° 46' W

	JAN	FEB	MAR	APR	MAY	JUN	JUL	AUG	SEP	OCT	NOV	DEC	YEAR
Mean Maximum Temp. (°F)	45.1	51.5	56.8	63.4	72.5	82.5	91.2	89.7	81.1	69.2	55.0	45.5	67.0
Mean Temp. (°F)	33.4	38.4	42.9	48.2	56.3	64.4	71.3	69.7	61.9	51.5	40.8	33.1	51.0
Mean Minimum Temp. (°F)	21.7	25.2	29.0	32.8	40.0	46.3	51.3	49.6	42.7	33.7	26.6	20.6	35.0
Extreme Maximum Temp. (°F)	68	75	80	89	96	103	104	105	100	91	77	68	105
Extreme Minimum Temp. (°F)	-11	-16	0	15	19	29	33	32	23	8	3	-16	-16
Days Maximum Temp. ≥ 90°F	0	0	0	0	1	7	20	17	5	0	0	0	50
Days Maximum Temp. ≤ 32°F	3	1	0	0	0	0	0	0	0	0	0	3	7
Days Minimum Temp. ≤ 32°F	28	24	22	15	4	0	0	0	3	13	24	28	161
Days Minimum Temp. ≤ 0°F	1	0	0	0	0	0	0	0	0	0	0	1	2
Heating Degree Days (base 65°F)	972	746	677	499	276	88	11	19	128	413	719	983	5,531
Cooling Degree Days (base 65°F)	0	0	0	1	15	86	229	195	53	2	0	0	581
Mean Precipitation (in.)	1.04	1.04	0.85	0.36	0.61	0.49	0.25	0.24	0.44	0.42	0.84	0.93	7.51
Maximum Precipitation (in.)	4.1	4.8	2.9	2.0	2.9	1.5	1.1	1.6	2.3	2.1	3.1	5.3	13.2
Minimum Precipitation (in.)	trace	trace	trace	trace	trace	0	0	0	0	0	0	trace	3.3
Maximum 24-hr. Precipitation (in.)	1.6	1.8	1.1	1.6	1.8	0.6	0.8	0.9	0.8	1.5	1.6	2.0	2.0
Days With ≥ 0.1" Precipitation	3	3	3	1	2	2	1	1	1	1	2	2	22
Days With ≥ 1.0" Precipitation	0	0	0	0	0	0	0	0	0	0	0	0	0
Mean Snowfall (in.)	5.0	5.3	3.3	1.0	0.7	trace	0.0	0.0	trace	0.5	2.9	4.7	23.4
Maximum Snowfall (in.)	23	24	29	8	14	trace	0	0	2	5	17	26	64
Maximum 24-hr. Snowfall (in.)	11	18	14	4	9	trace	0	0	2	4	15	15	18
Days With ≥ 1.0" Snow Depth	7	3	1	0	0	0	0	0	0	0	2	4	17
Thunderstorm Days	0	< 1	< 1	< 1	2	3	3	3	1	1	0	0	13
Foggy Days	6	2	1	< 1	1	< 1	< 1	< 1	< 1	< 1	2	5	17
Predominant Sky Cover	OVR	OVR	OVR	OVR	CLR	CLR	CLR	CLR	CLR	CLR	CLR	OVR	CLR
Mean Relative Humidity 7am (%)	79	77	71	61	55	50	49	54	63	72	77	80	66
Mean Relative Humidity 4pm (%)	51	41	34	27	26	22	19	19	21	27	41	51	32
Mean Dewpoint (°F)	21	23	24	26	32	36	40	39	35	30	25	22	29
Prevailing Wind Direction	S	S	WNW	WNW	WNW	WNW	WNW	WNW	WNW	S	S	S	WNW
Prevailing Wind Speed (mph)	9	10	12	13	13	14	14	13	12	7	9	9	12
Maximum Wind Gust (mph)	90	83	71	64	70	67	67	70	54	81	81	81	90

Winnemucca Municipal Airport

Winnemucca lies at an elevation about 4300 feet above sea level and is effectively cut off by the Sierra Nevada Mountains from the moisture source of the Pacific Ocean. Winnemucca has a climate marked by warm days, cool nights, and light precipitation. Sixty-six percent of the annual rainfall occurs as rain and snow between December and May. The winter snow pack in the surrounding mountains is generally sufficient for essential summertime irrigation. Reservoirs along the streams hold surplus water for less favorable years. As a result of the characteristic dryness of the climate, the neighboring valleys and hills are covered with sagebrush, and trees are found only along streams and in other places where water is sufficient the year round. Though it is heavier in the mountains, snowfall at Winnemucca itself has had measurable amounts fall in every month except July, August and September. During the winter months, snow on the ground permits grazing in many desert regions where there is no other source of stock water. Grazing in the summer months is restricted to mountain range tracts where there is sufficient water. Streams in many areas have been stocked with fish and provide good fishing each year.

Temperatures in this plateau area tend to rise sharply right after sunrise and remain comparatively high during the daylight hours, then drop rapidly about sundown. Daily temperature variations of 50 degrees are not uncommon.

Based on the 1951-1980 period, the average first occurrence of 32 degrees Fahrenheit in the fall is September 10 and the average last occurrence in the spring is June 8.

Winnemucca Municipal Airport *Humboldt County*   Elevation: 4,294 ft.   Latitude: 40° 54' N   Longitude: 117° 48' W

	JAN	FEB	MAR	APR	MAY	JUN	JUL	AUG	SEP	OCT	NOV	DEC	YEAR
Mean Maximum Temp. (°F)	41.9	49.0	55.4	62.6	72.5	83.1	92.8	91.1	80.6	67.6	52.0	42.3	65.9
Mean Temp. (°F)	30.1	36.1	40.9	46.3	55.2	64.3	72.2	69.9	60.0	48.5	37.5	29.5	49.2
Mean Minimum Temp. (°F)	18.3	23.2	26.4	29.9	37.9	45.4	51.5	48.7	39.4	29.3	23.0	16.7	32.5
Extreme Maximum Temp. (°F)	68	74	81	90	96	106	106	108	101	91	77	67	108
Extreme Minimum Temp. (°F)	-19	-28	-3	6	14	25	29	28	15	5	-8	-37	-37
Days Maximum Temp. ≥ 90°F	0	0	0	0	2	10	22	20	6	0	0	0	60
Days Maximum Temp. ≤ 32°F	6	1	0	0	0	0	0	0	0	0	1	5	13
Days Minimum Temp. ≤ 32°F	28	24	24	19	8	1	0	0	6	20	25	28	183
Days Minimum Temp. ≤ 0°F	3	1	0	0	0	0	0	0	0	0	0	3	7
Heating Degree Days (base 65°F)	1,075	809	740	555	308	102	11	21	172	505	817	1,093	6,208
Cooling Degree Days (base 65°F)	0	0	0	1	12	76	226	177	32	0	0	0	524
Mean Precipitation (in.)	0.85	0.57	0.84	0.84	1.03	0.75	0.28	0.34	0.51	0.61	0.82	0.84	8.28
Maximum Precipitation (in.)	2.7	2.2	1.7	2.9	3.4	2.9	1.7	1.7	1.5	2.2	2.7	3.7	14.5
Minimum Precipitation (in.)	trace	0	0.1	0.1	trace	0	0	0	0	trace	trace	trace	3.1
Maximum 24-hr. Precipitation (in.)	0.7	0.7	0.6	0.8	0.9	1.4	0.9	0.7	0.8	1.6	1.6	0.9	1.6
Days With ≥ 0.1" Precipitation	3	2	3	3	3	2	1	1	2	2	3	3	28
Days With ≥ 1.0" Precipitation	0	0	0	0	0	0	0	0	0	0	0	0	0
Mean Snowfall (in.)	4.5	3.6	*3.7*	2.2	*0.6*	*trace*	*0.0*	*trace*	*trace*	*0.5*	*2.4*	4.7	*22.2*
Maximum Snowfall (in.)	19	14	23	12	5	trace	0	0	1	7	20	18	51
Maximum 24-hr. Snowfall (in.)	8	9	8	7	3	trace	0	0	1	4	6	6	9
Days With ≥ 1.0" Snow Depth	9	4	1	0	0	0	0	0	0	0	2	6	22
Thunderstorm Days	0	< 1	< 1	1	3	3	3	3	2	1	< 1	< 1	16
Foggy Days	4	2	1	1	< 1	< 1	< 1	< 1	< 1	1	2	3	14
Predominant Sky Cover	OVR	OVR	OVR	OVR	OVR	CLR	CLR	CLR	CLR	CLR	OVR	OVR	CLR
Mean Relative Humidity 7am (%)	79	78	72	59	52	45	35	38	47	62	76	80	60
Mean Relative Humidity 4pm (%)	57	46	38	29	27	22	15	16	20	28	45	58	33
Mean Dewpoint (°F)	20	23	23	24	30	34	35	33	29	26	24	21	27
Prevailing Wind Direction	S	S	S	W	W	W	W	W	NE	S	S	S	S
Prevailing Wind Speed (mph)	9	8	8	10	10	10	10	10	10	7	8	9	9
Maximum Wind Gust (mph)	59	62	64	58	49	85	56	78	56	43	54	62	85

Arthur 4 NW *Elko County* Elevation: 6,299 ft. Latitude: 40° 47' N Longitude: 115° 11' W

	JAN	FEB	MAR	APR	MAY	JUN	JUL	AUG	SEP	OCT	NOV	DEC	YEAR
Mean Maximum Temp. (°F)	35.3	39.0	45.5	53.8	63.3	73.4	82.1	81.4	71.9	60.1	44.8	36.1	57.2
Mean Temp. (°F)	24.9	28.5	34.7	41.3	49.6	58.1	65.6	64.9	56.1	45.8	33.6	25.6	44.1
Mean Minimum Temp. (°F)	14.5	17.8	23.7	28.8	35.8	42.7	49.1	48.3	40.2	31.5	22.2	15.0	30.8
Extreme Maximum Temp. (°F)	59	63	70	83	84	92	95	93	89	88	70	60	95
Extreme Minimum Temp. (°F)	-20	-19	-2	5	17	25	31	29	19	2	-8	-26	-26
Days Maximum Temp. ≥ 90°F	0	0	0	0	0	0	2	1	0	0	0	0	3
Days Maximum Temp. ≤ 32°F	11	6	2	0	0	0	0	0	0	0	4	10	33
Days Minimum Temp. ≤ 32°F	30	27	27	21	10	1	0	0	4	17	27	30	194
Days Minimum Temp. ≤ 0°F	4	2	0	0	0	0	0	0	0	0	1	3	10
Heating Degree Days (base 65°F)	1,234	1,026	931	702	472	213	49	58	266	588	937	1,215	7,691
Cooling Degree Days (base 65°F)	0	0	0	0	0	10	75	65	6	0	0	0	156
Mean Precipitation (in.)	1.62	1.34	1.44	1.24	1.59	0.96	0.59	0.75	1.10	1.15	1.66	1.47	14.91
Days With ≥ 0.1" Precipitation	5	4	5	4	5	3	2	2	3	3	5	4	45
Days With ≥ 1.0" Precipitation	0	0	0	0	0	0	0	0	0	0	0	0	0
Mean Snowfall (in.)	10.8	8.2	6.7	2.5	1.1	0.0	0.0	0.0	trace	1.2	7.2	9.9	47.6
Days With ≥ 1.0" Snow Depth	21	17	13	3	1	0	0	0	0	1	9	15	80

Austin *Lander County* Elevation: 6,604 ft. Latitude: 39° 30' N Longitude: 117° 04' W

	JAN	FEB	MAR	APR	MAY	JUN	JUL	AUG	SEP	OCT	NOV	DEC	YEAR
Mean Maximum Temp. (°F)	42.0	45.4	49.5	56.1	65.7	77.5	87.2	85.7	76.1	63.7	49.7	42.5	61.7
Mean Temp. (°F)	31.1	34.1	37.8	43.2	51.8	61.8	70.5	69.2	60.5	49.7	38.2	31.5	48.3
Mean Minimum Temp. (°F)	20.1	22.7	26.1	30.2	37.7	46.0	53.8	52.7	44.9	35.6	26.6	20.5	34.7
Extreme Maximum Temp. (°F)	64	70	71	83	90	97	99	99	93	85	75	65	99
Extreme Minimum Temp. (°F)	-11	-15	-6	11	19	23	36	33	24	5	0	-19	-19
Days Maximum Temp. ≥ 90°F	0	0	0	0	0	2	11	9	1	0	0	0	23
Days Maximum Temp. ≤ 32°F	4	2	1	0	0	0	0	0	0	0	2	5	14
Days Minimum Temp. ≤ 32°F	28	25	24	18	8	1	0	0	2	10	22	28	166
Days Minimum Temp. ≤ 0°F	1	0	0	0	0	0	0	0	0	0	0	1	2
Heating Degree Days (base 65°F)	1,045	867	835	649	410	147	14	26	165	470	798	1,031	6,457
Cooling Degree Days (base 65°F)	0	0	0	0	7	57	190	173	41	2	0	0	470
Mean Precipitation (in.)	1.40	1.08	1.85	1.71	1.91	0.89	0.53	0.66	0.81	1.02	1.23	1.25	14.34
Days With ≥ 0.1" Precipitation	4	3	5	4	4	3	1	2	2	3	4	4	39
Days With ≥ 1.0" Precipitation	0	0	0	0	0	0	0	0	0	0	0	0	0
Mean Snowfall (in.)	13.8	10.1	15.5	12.4	6.1	0.6	0.0	0.0	0.4	2.9	7.8	10.3	79.9
Days With ≥ 1.0" Snow Depth	14	9	7	4	1	0	0	0	0	1	5	11	52

Battle Mountain *Lander County* Elevation: 4,537 ft. Latitude: 40° 37' N Longitude: 116° 53' W

	JAN	FEB	MAR	APR	MAY	JUN	JUL	AUG	SEP	OCT	NOV	DEC	YEAR
Mean Maximum Temp. (°F)	41.6	49.0	56.0	63.3	73.4	84.1	93.6	92.0	81.7	68.3	52.2	42.3	66.4
Mean Temp. (°F)	29.6	35.7	41.3	47.0	56.1	65.0	72.6	70.4	61.0	49.1	37.7	29.2	49.6
Mean Minimum Temp. (°F)	17.3	22.4	26.7	30.6	38.9	45.8	51.6	48.9	40.2	29.9	23.2	16.1	32.6
Extreme Maximum Temp. (°F)	67	72	80	90	96	102	109	106	100	95	80	67	109
Extreme Minimum Temp. (°F)	-23	-25	-2	8	18	26	31	30	11	3	-8	-39	-39
Days Maximum Temp. ≥ 90°F	0	0	0	0	2	10	24	22	7	0	0	0	65
Days Maximum Temp. ≤ 32°F	5	1	0	0	0	0	0	0	0	0	1	5	12
Days Minimum Temp. ≤ 32°F	28	25	24	19	6	1	0	0	5	19	25	28	180
Days Minimum Temp. ≤ 0°F	4	1	0	0	0	0	0	0	0	0	0	3	8
Heating Degree Days (base 65°F)	1,092	821	726	535	283	86	8	17	154	485	812	1,105	6,124
Cooling Degree Days (base 65°F)	0	0	0	1	17	91	249	205	45	1	0	0	609
Mean Precipitation (in.)	0.87	0.63	0.80	0.93	1.23	0.83	0.28	0.34	0.68	0.65	0.72	0.74	8.70
Days With ≥ 0.1" Precipitation	3	2	3	3	3	2	1	1	2	2	2	2	26
Days With ≥ 1.0" Precipitation	0	0	0	0	0	0	0	0	0	0	0	0	0
Mean Snowfall (in.)	5.3	3.2	2.2	1.9	trace	trace	0.0	0.0	trace	0.4	1.9	5.1	20.0
Days With ≥ 1.0" Snow Depth	9	4	1	0	0	0	0	0	0	0	1	5	20

Beatty 8 N *Nye County* Elevation: 3,549 ft. Latitude: 37° 00' N Longitude: 116° 43' W

	JAN	FEB	MAR	APR	MAY	JUN	JUL	AUG	SEP	OCT	NOV	DEC	YEAR
Mean Maximum Temp. (°F)	53.6	58.3	63.3	71.4	80.4	90.4	96.6	95.1	88.0	77.4	63.3	54.7	74.4
Mean Temp. (°F)	41.3	45.2	49.4	55.9	64.4	72.9	78.8	77.4	71.0	61.1	48.6	41.5	58.9
Mean Minimum Temp. (°F)	29.0	32.0	35.5	40.4	48.4	55.3	61.0	59.6	54.0	44.5	33.9	28.3	43.5
Extreme Maximum Temp. (°F)	74	83	83	94	101	107	112	109	104	100	88	75	112
Extreme Minimum Temp. (°F)	4	5	16	19	32	35	42	43	32	22	7	2	2
Days Maximum Temp. ≥ 90°F	0	0	0	0	4	17	28	27	14	3	0	0	93
Days Maximum Temp. ≤ 32°F	0	0	0	0	0	0	0	0	0	0	0	0	0
Days Minimum Temp. ≤ 32°F	22	15	10	4	0	0	0	0	0	1	13	23	88
Days Minimum Temp. ≤ 0°F	0	0	0	0	0	0	0	0	0	0	0	0	0
Heating Degree Days (base 65°F)	728	553	478	276	92	12	0	0	16	153	485	721	3,514
Cooling Degree Days (base 65°F)	0	0	0	14	87	263	450	416	209	40	0	0	1,479
Mean Precipitation (in.)	0.78	0.95	1.09	0.40	0.39	0.22	0.42	0.37	0.48	0.27	0.43	0.48	6.28
Days With ≥ 0.1" Precipitation	3	3	3	1	1	1	1	1	1	1	1	1	18
Days With ≥ 1.0" Precipitation	0	0	0	0	0	0	0	0	0	0	0	0	0
Mean Snowfall (in.)	0.6	0.3	0.4	trace	trace	0.0	0.0	0.0	0.0	0.0	0.4	0.8	2.5
Days With ≥ 1.0" Snow Depth	1	1	0	0	0	0	0	0	0	0	0	1	3

Beowawe *Eureka County*   Elevation: 4,698 ft.   Latitude: 40° 35' N   Longitude: 116° 28' W

	JAN	FEB	MAR	APR	MAY	JUN	JUL	AUG	SEP	OCT	NOV	DEC	YEAR
Mean Maximum Temp. (°F)	39.4	46.3	54.2	61.2	71.3	82.0	91.5	89.9	80.1	66.7	50.1	40.1	64.4
Mean Temp. (°F)	27.0	33.7	40.2	45.6	54.4	63.2	71.0	69.1	59.8	48.0	36.4	27.6	48.0
Mean Minimum Temp. (°F)	14.8	20.9	26.2	29.8	37.5	44.4	50.5	48.3	39.5	29.4	22.6	14.9	31.6
Extreme Maximum Temp. (°F)	67	72	78	90	96	105	108	106	97	90	78	65	108
Extreme Minimum Temp. (°F)	-22	-36	-3	10	15	25	33	25	17	1	-8	-43	-43
Days Maximum Temp. ≥ 90°F	0	0	0	0	1	8	20	18	5	0	0	0	52
Days Maximum Temp. ≤ 32°F	8	2	0	0	0	0	0	0	0	0	1	6	17
Days Minimum Temp. ≤ 32°F	29	26	25	18	8	1	0	0	5	20	25	29	186
Days Minimum Temp. ≤ 0°F	5	1	0	0	0	0	0	0	0	0	0	3	9
Heating Degree Days (base 65°F)	1,172	877	761	576	331	115	13	29	180	520	851	1,153	6,578
Cooling Degree Days (base 65°F)	0	0	0	0	13	59	180	155	32	0	0	0	439
Mean Precipitation (in.)	0.85	0.61	0.82	0.81	1.28	0.80	0.27	0.46	0.60	0.66	0.84	0.82	8.82
Days With ≥ 0.1" Precipitation	3	2	3	2	3	2	1	1	2	2	3	3	27
Days With ≥ 1.0" Precipitation	0	0	0	0	0	0	0	0	0	0	0	0	0
Mean Snowfall (in.)	6.1	2.8	1.4	1.1	0.1	0.0	0.0	0.0	0.0	0.3	1.5	4.2	17.5
Days With ≥ 1.0" Snow Depth	na	3	0	0	0	0	0	0	0	0	1	na	na

Beowawe Univ. of Nevada Ranch *Eureka County*   Elevation: 5,738 ft.   Latitude: 39° 54' N   Longitude: 116° 35' W

	JAN	FEB	MAR	APR	MAY	JUN	JUL	AUG	SEP	OCT	NOV	DEC	YEAR
Mean Maximum Temp. (°F)	40.4	45.9	51.4	58.7	67.8	78.4	87.3	86.0	77.6	66.2	51.5	42.2	62.8
Mean Temp. (°F)	27.2	32.8	38.5	44.2	52.0	60.8	68.3	66.7	58.3	47.7	36.5	28.3	46.8
Mean Minimum Temp. (°F)	13.9	19.6	25.6	29.6	36.1	43.1	49.2	47.3	39.0	29.1	21.5	14.3	30.7
Extreme Maximum Temp. (°F)	64	70	75	83	89	100	101	100	93	89	75	66	101
Extreme Minimum Temp. (°F)	-27	-26	0	6	18	23	29	27	18	4	-10	-31	-31
Days Maximum Temp. ≥ 90°F	0	0	0	0	0	3	12	9	1	0	0	0	25
Days Maximum Temp. ≤ 32°F	6	2	0	0	0	0	0	0	0	0	1	5	14
Days Minimum Temp. ≤ 32°F	29	25	26	20	10	2	0	0	6	21	27	29	195
Days Minimum Temp. ≤ 0°F	5	2	0	0	0	0	0	0	0	0	1	4	12
Heating Degree Days (base 65°F)	1,167	903	814	619	398	157	23	39	208	530	846	1,132	6,836
Cooling Degree Days (base 65°F)	0	0	0	0	2	36	129	107	16	0	0	0	290
Mean Precipitation (in.)	1.02	0.76	1.34	1.15	1.51	0.87	0.51	0.56	0.78	0.90	0.98	0.82	11.20
Days With ≥ 0.1" Precipitation	4	3	4	4	4	3	2	2	2	3	3	3	37
Days With ≥ 1.0" Precipitation	0	0	0	0	0	0	0	0	0	0	0	0	0
Mean Snowfall (in.)	na	5.0	na	4.3	1.6	trace	0.0	0.0	trace	0.6	2.6	5.4	na
Days With ≥ 1.0" Snow Depth	na	na	na	na	0	0	0	0	0	0	na	na	na

Boulder City *Clark County*   Elevation: 2,522 ft.   Latitude: 35° 59' N   Longitude: 114° 51' W

	JAN	FEB	MAR	APR	MAY	JUN	JUL	AUG	SEP	OCT	NOV	DEC	YEAR
Mean Maximum Temp. (°F)	55.3	61.3	68.3	76.6	86.1	96.7	101.9	99.8	92.2	79.9	64.9	55.7	78.2
Mean Temp. (°F)	47.2	52.3	57.9	65.2	74.0	84.0	89.4	87.7	80.5	69.1	55.7	47.5	67.5
Mean Minimum Temp. (°F)	39.2	43.3	47.5	53.6	61.8	71.2	76.8	75.5	68.8	58.2	46.5	39.3	56.8
Extreme Maximum Temp. (°F)	75	84	89	97	111	112	116	111	107	99	86	73	116
Extreme Minimum Temp. (°F)	16	16	29	33	37	41	56	61	43	30	4	9	4
Days Maximum Temp. ≥ 90°F	0	0	0	2	12	25	30	30	20	5	0	0	124
Days Maximum Temp. ≤ 32°F	0	0	0	0	0	0	0	0	0	0	0	0	0
Days Minimum Temp. ≤ 32°F	4	2	0	0	0	0	0	0	0	0	0	4	10
Days Minimum Temp. ≤ 0°F	0	0	0	0	0	0	0	0	0	0	0	0	0
Heating Degree Days (base 65°F)	544	355	237	94	19	1	0	0	1	50	281	535	2,117
Cooling Degree Days (base 65°F)	0	3	24	123	321	577	764	730	488	193	11	0	3,234
Mean Precipitation (in.)	0.75	0.76	0.94	0.25	0.22	0.12	0.57	1.01	0.62	0.28	0.51	0.48	6.51
Days With ≥ 0.1" Precipitation	2	2	2	1	1	0	2	2	1	1	1	1	16
Days With ≥ 1.0" Precipitation	0	0	0	0	0	0	0	0	0	0	0	0	0
Mean Snowfall (in.)	0.0	0.0	trace	0.0	0.0	0.0	0.0	0.0	0.0	0.0	0.0	0.0	trace
Days With ≥ 1.0" Snow Depth	0	0	0	0	0	0	0	0	0	0	0	0	0

Caliente *Lincoln County*   Elevation: 4,399 ft.   Latitude: 37° 37' N   Longitude: 114° 31' W

	JAN	FEB	MAR	APR	MAY	JUN	JUL	AUG	SEP	OCT	NOV	DEC	YEAR
Mean Maximum Temp. (°F)	46.7	53.7	60.1	68.0	77.8	88.9	95.1	93.0	84.8	73.2	57.9	47.9	70.6
Mean Temp. (°F)	32.7	38.7	44.7	51.2	60.1	69.5	76.0	74.3	65.6	54.2	41.9	33.3	53.5
Mean Minimum Temp. (°F)	18.8	23.7	29.2	34.3	42.3	50.1	56.9	55.6	46.4	35.2	25.8	18.6	36.4
Extreme Maximum Temp. (°F)	69	81	90	92	97	106	109	106	100	93	82	71	109
Extreme Minimum Temp. (°F)	-14	-19	12	18	24	33	40	35	29	13	2	-18	-19
Days Maximum Temp. ≥ 90°F	0	0	0	0	2	15	25	23	9	1	0	0	75
Days Maximum Temp. ≤ 32°F	1	1	0	0	0	0	0	0	0	0	0	1	3
Days Minimum Temp. ≤ 32°F	29	25	22	12	2	0	0	0	0	10	26	30	156
Days Minimum Temp. ≤ 0°F	1	0	0	0	0	0	0	0	0	0	0	1	2
Heating Degree Days (base 65°F)	994	736	624	409	174	26	1	1	61	332	686	976	5,020
Cooling Degree Days (base 65°F)	0	0	0	1	29	170	353	313	95	3	0	0	964
Mean Precipitation (in.)	0.93	0.97	1.39	0.71	0.73	0.33	0.78	1.01	0.78	0.78	0.83	0.52	9.76
Days With ≥ 0.1" Precipitation	3	2	4	2	2	1	2	3	2	2	2	2	27
Days With ≥ 1.0" Precipitation	0	0	0	0	0	0	0	0	0	0	0	0	0
Mean Snowfall (in.)	na	1.8	0.9	trace	trace	0.0	0.0	0.0	trace	trace	0.7	2.1	na
Days With ≥ 1.0" Snow Depth	na	1	0	0	0	0	0	0	0	0	1	1	na

Carson City *Carson City County*   Elevation: 4,648 ft.   Latitude: 39° 09' N   Longitude: 119° 46' W

	JAN	FEB	MAR	APR	MAY	JUN	JUL	AUG	SEP	OCT	NOV	DEC	YEAR
Mean Maximum Temp. (°F)	45.3	50.6	56.3	62.6	71.3	80.6	89.0	87.7	79.5	68.6	54.8	45.7	66.0
Mean Temp. (°F)	33.4	37.7	42.7	47.7	55.4	63.3	69.9	68.3	60.7	50.8	40.5	33.1	50.3
Mean Minimum Temp. (°F)	21.4	24.8	29.2	32.7	39.5	45.9	50.6	48.9	41.9	33.0	26.3	20.5	34.6
Extreme Maximum Temp. (°F)	69	76	78	88	93	100	102	103	97	90	77	70	103
Extreme Minimum Temp. (°F)	-16	-22	5	12	19	28	33	31	21	6	-4	-19	-22
Days Maximum Temp. ≥ 90°F	0	0	0	0	0	5	16	13	2	0	0	0	36
Days Maximum Temp. ≤ 32°F	3	1	0	0	0	0	0	0	0	0	0	3	7
Days Minimum Temp. ≤ 32°F	27	23	21	15	5	1	0	0	3	14	23	27	159
Days Minimum Temp. ≤ 0°F	1	0	0	0	0	0	0	0	0	0	0	1	2
Heating Degree Days (base 65°F)	974	763	683	514	299	101	14	23	148	434	727	983	5,663
Cooling Degree Days (base 65°F)	0	0	0	0	9	55	170	142	31	0	0	0	407
Mean Precipitation (in.)	1.90	1.63	1.25	0.41	0.51	0.39	0.22	0.31	0.53	0.68	1.35	1.37	10.55
Days With ≥ 0.1" Precipitation	4	3	3	1	1	1	1	1	1	2	3	3	24
Days With ≥ 1.0" Precipitation	0	0	0	0	0	0	0	0	0	0	0	0	0
Mean Snowfall (in.)	*5.3*	4.1	1.8	0.5	0.2	0.0	0.0	0.0	0.1	0.1	*1.0*	*3.1*	*16.2*
Days With ≥ 1.0" Snow Depth	*4*	2	1	0	0	0	0	0	0	0	*1*	2	*10*

Denio *Humboldt County*   Elevation: 4,189 ft.   Latitude: 41° 59' N   Longitude: 118° 38' W

	JAN	FEB	MAR	APR	MAY	JUN	JUL	AUG	SEP	OCT	NOV	DEC	YEAR
Mean Maximum Temp. (°F)	40.9	47.3	54.0	62.0	71.0	81.0	90.9	89.2	79.3	66.8	50.8	41.4	64.6
Mean Temp. (°F)	31.2	36.0	41.1	47.0	54.6	63.5	71.6	69.9	60.4	50.0	38.6	30.9	49.6
Mean Minimum Temp. (°F)	21.4	24.7	28.1	31.9	38.1	45.9	52.2	50.5	41.5	33.4	26.4	20.3	34.5
Extreme Maximum Temp. (°F)	65	76	78	90	96	102	105	107	99	92	75	63	107
Extreme Minimum Temp. (°F)	-21	-25	0	11	15	27	29	30	18	6	-4	-25	-25
Days Maximum Temp. ≥ 90°F	0	0	0	0	1	7	19	17	4	0	0	0	48
Days Maximum Temp. ≤ 32°F	5	2	0	0	0	0	0	0	0	0	1	5	13
Days Minimum Temp. ≤ 32°F	27	23	22	16	7	1	0	0	4	14	22	27	163
Days Minimum Temp. ≤ 0°F	1	0	0	0	0	0	0	0	0	0	0	1	2
Heating Degree Days (base 65°F)	1,042	811	735	534	324	113	14	23	169	460	785	1,050	6,060
Cooling Degree Days (base 65°F)	0	0	0	1	12	72	220	190	42	2	0	0	539
Mean Precipitation (in.)	0.94	0.80	1.12	1.02	1.17	0.89	0.28	0.50	0.56	0.60	1.14	0.92	9.94
Days With ≥ 0.1" Precipitation	3	3	4	3	4	3	1	1	2	2	4	3	33
Days With ≥ 1.0" Precipitation	0	0	0	0	0	0	0	0	0	0	0	0	0
Mean Snowfall (in.)	*4.6*	3.1	2.7	*0.8*	0.2	0.2	0.0	0.0	trace	0.5	3.9	5.0	*21.0*
Days With ≥ 1.0" Snow Depth	6	2	*1*	0	0	0	0	0	0	0	1	*3*	*13*

Desert Nat'l Wildlife Range *Clark County*   Elevation: 2,919 ft.   Latitude: 36° 26' N   Longitude: 115° 22' W

	JAN	FEB	MAR	APR	MAY	JUN	JUL	AUG	SEP	OCT	NOV	DEC	YEAR
Mean Maximum Temp. (°F)	57.2	62.5	68.6	76.2	85.8	96.7	101.9	99.9	92.0	80.2	66.0	57.3	78.7
Mean Temp. (°F)	43.3	47.8	53.5	60.2	69.1	78.5	84.4	82.7	75.0	63.5	50.9	43.3	62.7
Mean Minimum Temp. (°F)	29.4	33.1	38.4	44.0	52.3	60.2	66.7	65.6	57.9	46.6	35.8	29.2	46.6
Extreme Maximum Temp. (°F)	80	87	90	98	104	112	115	114	107	100	86	78	115
Extreme Minimum Temp. (°F)	0	10	20	25	32	41	47	45	39	19	16	3	0
Days Maximum Temp. ≥ 90°F	0	0	0	2	12	25	30	30	19	5	0	0	123
Days Maximum Temp. ≤ 32°F	0	0	0	0	0	0	0	0	0	0	0	0	0
Days Minimum Temp. ≤ 32°F	22	13	5	1	0	0	0	0	0	1	9	22	73
Days Minimum Temp. ≤ 0°F	0	0	0	0	0	0	0	0	0	0	0	0	0
Heating Degree Days (base 65°F)	665	478	351	171	39	3	0	0	4	108	415	667	2,901
Cooling Degree Days (base 65°F)	0	0	2	39	178	412	601	566	311	62	1	0	2,172
Mean Precipitation (in.)	0.47	0.54	0.77	0.28	0.27	0.14	0.50	0.42	0.42	0.28	0.31	0.40	4.80
Days With ≥ 0.1" Precipitation	1	1	2	1	1	1	1	1	1	1	1	1	13
Days With ≥ 1.0" Precipitation	0	0	0	0	0	0	0	0	0	0	0	0	0
Mean Snowfall (in.)	0.5	trace	0.0	0.0	0.0	0.0	0.0	0.0	0.0	trace	0.0	trace	0.5
Days With ≥ 1.0" Snow Depth	0	0	0	0	0	0	0	0	0	0	0	0	0

Dyer *Esmeralda County*   Elevation: 4,898 ft.   Latitude: 37° 41' N   Longitude: 118° 05' W

	JAN	FEB	MAR	APR	MAY	JUN	JUL	AUG	SEP	OCT	NOV	DEC	YEAR
Mean Maximum Temp. (°F)	46.7	53.7	59.8	67.0	76.1	86.2	92.9	90.7	82.7	71.3	57.0	47.3	69.3
Mean Temp. (°F)	32.1	38.2	44.0	49.8	58.4	67.4	73.7	71.5	63.5	52.5	40.5	32.1	52.0
Mean Minimum Temp. (°F)	17.4	22.8	28.2	32.5	40.7	48.5	54.6	52.3	44.2	33.6	23.9	16.9	34.6
Extreme Maximum Temp. (°F)	69	76	81	90	95	103	105	105	99	93	82	69	105
Extreme Minimum Temp. (°F)	-21	-23	-2	10	19	30	37	35	21	5	-3	-15	-23
Days Maximum Temp. ≥ 90°F	0	0	0	0	2	12	24	19	6	0	0	0	63
Days Maximum Temp. ≤ 32°F	2	1	0	0	0	0	0	0	0	0	0	1	4
Days Minimum Temp. ≤ 32°F	29	24	22	15	4	0	0	0	2	14	25	30	165
Days Minimum Temp. ≤ 0°F	2	0	0	0	0	0	0	0	0	0	0	1	3
Heating Degree Days (base 65°F)	1,015	750	644	450	216	44	1	5	91	383	728	1,013	5,340
Cooling Degree Days (base 65°F)	0	0	0	1	25	127	278	220	55	2	0	0	708
Mean Precipitation (in.)	0.36	0.43	0.57	0.41	0.64	0.35	0.45	0.41	0.49	0.37	0.41	0.29	5.18
Days With ≥ 0.1" Precipitation	1	1	2	1	2	1	1	1	1	1	1	1	14
Days With ≥ 1.0" Precipitation	0	0	0	0	0	0	0	0	0	0	0	0	0
Mean Snowfall (in.)	2.5	1.9	1.8	1.0	0.3	trace	0.0	0.0	trace	0.1	1.2	1.1	9.9
Days With ≥ 1.0" Snow Depth	3	1	0	0	0	0	0	0	0	0	0	1	5

Eureka *Eureka County*   Elevation: 6,538 ft.   Latitude: 39° 31' N   Longitude: 115° 58' W

	JAN	FEB	MAR	APR	MAY	JUN	JUL	AUG	SEP	OCT	NOV	DEC	YEAR
Mean Maximum Temp. (°F)	37.6	42.0	47.7	55.6	65.2	76.4	85.0	83.2	74.0	61.8	46.8	38.7	59.5
Mean Temp. (°F)	27.5	31.4	36.3	42.4	51.0	60.7	69.0	67.7	59.1	48.0	35.6	28.2	46.4
Mean Minimum Temp. (°F)	17.3	20.7	24.8	29.2	36.8	44.9	52.8	52.2	44.1	34.1	24.5	17.6	33.2
Extreme Maximum Temp. (°F)	58	64	70	80	87	95	98	97	90	83	72	63	98
Extreme Minimum Temp. (°F)	-13	-18	-9	7	15	23	33	32	21	3	-5	-21	-21
Days Maximum Temp. ≥ 90°F	0	0	0	0	0	1	6	4	0	0	0	0	11
Days Maximum Temp. ≤ 32°F	9	4	1	1	0	0	0	0	0	0	3	7	25
Days Minimum Temp. ≤ 32°F	29	26	25	20	10	1	0	0	2	13	24	29	179
Days Minimum Temp. ≤ 0°F	2	1	0	0	0	0	0	0	0	0	0	2	5
Heating Degree Days (base 65°F)	1,157	944	883	672	430	164	20	30	196	521	875	1,135	7,027
Cooling Degree Days (base 65°F)	0	0	0	0	3	35	135	121	24	0	0	0	318
Mean Precipitation (in.)	1.00	0.83	1.46	1.19	1.54	0.78	0.61	0.86	1.03	1.01	1.02	0.90	12.23
Days With ≥ 0.1" Precipitation	3	3	4	3	4	2	2	2	2	2	3	2	32
Days With ≥ 1.0" Precipitation	0	0	0	0	0	0	0	0	0	0	0	0	0
Mean Snowfall (in.)	*8.4*	4.6	9.4	5.8	3.4	0.1	0.0	0.0	0.7	1.9	5.9	7.5	*47.7*
Days With ≥ 1.0" Snow Depth	na	na	na	2	1	0	0	0	0	1	na	na	na

Fallon Experiment Station *Churchill County*   Elevation: 3,963 ft.   Latitude: 39° 27' N   Longitude: 118° 47' W

	JAN	FEB	MAR	APR	MAY	JUN	JUL	AUG	SEP	OCT	NOV	DEC	YEAR
Mean Maximum Temp. (°F)	44.3	52.4	58.9	64.6	73.1	82.4	90.5	89.0	80.0	68.5	54.9	45.4	67.0
Mean Temp. (°F)	32.1	38.3	44.0	49.3	57.3	65.3	72.2	70.4	61.8	51.2	40.4	32.1	51.2
Mean Minimum Temp. (°F)	19.8	24.2	29.1	34.0	41.5	48.2	53.8	51.7	43.5	33.8	25.8	18.8	35.4
Extreme Maximum Temp. (°F)	71	76	83	90	97	101	104	104	100	89	77	69	104
Extreme Minimum Temp. (°F)	-15	-27	1	15	26	32	36	35	23	12	3	-21	-27
Days Maximum Temp. ≥ 90°F	0	0	0	0	1	8	20	16	4	0	0	0	49
Days Maximum Temp. ≤ 32°F	4	1	0	0	0	0	0	0	0	0	0	3	8
Days Minimum Temp. ≤ 32°F	28	24	21	13	2	0	0	0	2	13	23	28	154
Days Minimum Temp. ≤ 0°F	1	0	0	0	0	0	0	0	0	0	0	1	2
Heating Degree Days (base 65°F)	1,014	746	641	463	247	76	8	15	132	423	732	1,013	5,510
Cooling Degree Days (base 65°F)	0	0	0	1	18	89	236	198	49	1	0	0	592
Mean Precipitation (in.)	0.51	0.46	0.50	0.55	0.67	0.59	0.18	0.26	0.36	0.42	0.39	0.35	5.24
Days With ≥ 0.1" Precipitation	2	1	1	2	2	1	1	1	1	1	1	1	15
Days With ≥ 1.0" Precipitation	0	0	0	0	0	0	0	0	0	0	0	0	0
Mean Snowfall (in.)	*2.8*	*1.4*	*1.2*	0.2	trace	0.0	0.0	0.0	0.0	trace	0.5	*1.5*	*7.6*
Days With ≥ 1.0" Snow Depth	*6*	*1*	0	0	0	0	0	0	0	0	*0*	*2*	*9*

Glenbrook *Douglas County*   Elevation: 6,348 ft.   Latitude: 39° 05' N   Longitude: 119° 57' W

	JAN	FEB	MAR	APR	MAY	JUN	JUL	AUG	SEP	OCT	NOV	DEC	YEAR
Mean Maximum Temp. (°F)	42.2	44.0	47.5	53.3	61.5	70.8	78.4	78.0	72.1	61.3	48.8	42.5	58.4
Mean Temp. (°F)	33.0	34.4	37.1	41.5	48.6	56.7	63.4	63.4	58.0	48.8	39.0	33.5	46.5
Mean Minimum Temp. (°F)	23.8	24.8	26.7	29.6	35.7	42.6	48.4	48.7	43.8	36.3	29.3	24.4	34.5
Extreme Maximum Temp. (°F)	61	68	67	76	83	88	94	93	95	82	70	60	95
Extreme Minimum Temp. (°F)	-3	-6	5	11	17	26	30	27	16	9	6	-10	-10
Days Maximum Temp. ≥ 90°F	0	0	0	0	0	0	0	1	0	0	0	0	1
Days Maximum Temp. ≤ 32°F	3	2	1	0	0	0	0	0	0	0	1	3	10
Days Minimum Temp. ≤ 32°F	29	26	27	21	9	2	0	0	1	8	20	27	170
Days Minimum Temp. ≤ 0°F	0	0	0	0	0	0	0	0	0	0	0	0	0
Heating Degree Days (base 65°F)	985	857	857	699	501	249	83	83	210	496	775	969	6,764
Cooling Degree Days (base 65°F)	0	0	0	0	0	5	33	36	5	0	0	0	79
Mean Precipitation (in.)	2.96	2.60	2.43	0.91	0.79	0.58	0.32	0.48	0.76	1.12	2.20	2.29	17.44
Days With ≥ 0.1" Precipitation	6	5	5	3	2	2	1	1	2	3	4	4	38
Days With ≥ 1.0" Precipitation	1	1	0	0	0	0	0	0	0	0	0	1	3
Mean Snowfall (in.)	11.7	*15.1*	11.9	4.5	1.3	0.2	0.0	0.0	trace	0.8	6.0	*11.7*	*63.2*
Days With ≥ 1.0" Snow Depth	na	na	na	*1*	0	0	0	0	0	*0*	*4*	na	na

Golconda *Humboldt County*   Elevation: 4,412 ft.   Latitude: 40° 57' N   Longitude: 117° 29' W

	JAN	FEB	MAR	APR	MAY	JUN	JUL	AUG	SEP	OCT	NOV	DEC	YEAR
Mean Maximum Temp. (°F)	41.4	48.3	55.0	62.3	71.7	83.3	92.5	90.9	80.9	68.1	51.6	41.2	65.6
Mean Temp. (°F)	30.6	36.4	41.9	47.4	55.8	65.7	73.4	71.5	61.7	50.6	38.9	30.1	50.3
Mean Minimum Temp. (°F)	19.8	24.4	28.7	32.3	39.8	47.9	54.3	52.1	42.5	33.0	26.1	18.9	35.0
Extreme Maximum Temp. (°F)	67	70	79	88	98	103	106	105	99	91	76	68	106
Extreme Minimum Temp. (°F)	-10	-20	4	11	21	27	31	34	20	5	-3	-33	-33
Days Maximum Temp. ≥ 90°F	0	0	0	0	1	9	22	20	6	0	0	0	58
Days Maximum Temp. ≤ 32°F	6	1	0	0	0	0	0	0	0	0	1	5	13
Days Minimum Temp. ≤ 32°F	27	23	22	15	5	0	0	0	3	14	23	28	160
Days Minimum Temp. ≤ 0°F	1	0	0	0	0	0	0	0	0	0	0	2	3
Heating Degree Days (base 65°F)	1,058	801	711	524	293	81	8	14	*142*	442	777	1,075	*5,926*
Cooling Degree Days (base 65°F)	0	0	0	1	16	100	264	229	*57*	2	0	0	*669*
Mean Precipitation (in.)	0.68	0.60	0.79	0.64	1.03	0.71	0.27	0.36	0.47	0.50	0.81	0.77	7.63
Days With ≥ 0.1" Precipitation	3	2	3	2	3	2	1	1	1	2	3	3	26
Days With ≥ 1.0" Precipitation	0	0	0	0	0	0	0	0	0	0	0	0	0
Mean Snowfall (in.)	na	*2.2*	*0.9*	trace	trace	0.0	0.0	0.0	0.0	0.3	*1.6*	*2.1*	na
Days With ≥ 1.0" Snow Depth	na	na	*0*	0	0	0	0	0	0	0	na	*3*	na

Lahontan Dam *Churchill County*   Elevation: 4,146 ft.   Latitude: 39° 28' N   Longitude: 119° 04' W

	JAN	FEB	MAR	APR	MAY	JUN	JUL	AUG	SEP	OCT	NOV	DEC	YEAR
Mean Maximum Temp. (°F)	44.4	51.8	58.7	65.7	75.1	84.8	93.9	92.6	82.8	70.5	55.4	45.7	68.4
Mean Temp. (°F)	33.6	39.7	46.0	52.3	61.2	69.9	78.4	77.1	67.6	56.2	43.3	34.4	55.0
Mean Minimum Temp. (°F)	23.1	27.6	33.4	38.9	47.3	54.9	62.8	61.5	52.3	41.9	31.1	23.0	41.5
Extreme Maximum Temp. (°F)	68	75	80	89	100	105	108	106	100	92	76	69	108
Extreme Minimum Temp. (°F)	-13	-17	6	20	24	32	31	35	29	16	9	-15	-17
Days Maximum Temp. ≥ 90°F	0	0	0	0	2	10	24	22	8	0	0	0	66
Days Maximum Temp. ≤ 32°F	4	1	0	0	0	0	0	0	0	0	0	3	8
Days Minimum Temp. ≤ 32°F	27	20	14	6	1	0	0	0	0	3	16	27	114
Days Minimum Temp. ≤ 0°F	1	0	0	0	0	0	0	0	0	0	0	1	2
Heating Degree Days (base 65°F)	965	707	582	382	173	41	2	3	60	283	646	942	4,786
Cooling Degree Days (base 65°F)	0	0	0	8	69	198	433	398	155	15	0	0	1,276
Mean Precipitation (in.)	0.55	0.48	0.57	0.42	0.59	0.49	0.32	0.44	0.38	0.31	0.50	0.45	5.50
Days With ≥ 0.1" Precipitation	2	1	2	1	2	1	1	1	1	1	2	1	16
Days With ≥ 1.0" Precipitation	0	0	0	0	0	0	0	0	0	0	0	0	0
Mean Snowfall (in.)	na	na	0.6	0.2	trace	0.0	0.0	0.0	trace	trace	0.1	1.3	na
Days With ≥ 1.0" Snow Depth	na	1	0	0	0	0	0	0	0	0	0	0	na

Lake Valley Steward *Lincoln County*   Elevation: 6,348 ft.   Latitude: 38° 19' N   Longitude: 114° 39' W

	JAN	FEB	MAR	APR	MAY	JUN	JUL	AUG	SEP	OCT	NOV	DEC	YEAR
Mean Maximum Temp. (°F)	39.1	42.5	48.3	57.0	66.1	77.8	85.1	82.6	74.0	62.1	48.3	41.2	60.3
Mean Temp. (°F)	29.6	32.8	37.9	45.1	53.5	64.1	71.6	69.3	60.8	49.7	37.9	31.2	48.6
Mean Minimum Temp. (°F)	20.1	23.1	27.5	33.0	40.7	50.4	58.0	56.1	47.7	37.4	27.6	21.3	36.9
Extreme Maximum Temp. (°F)	62	69	83	80	89	98	100	110	90	91	72	62	110
Extreme Minimum Temp. (°F)	-10	-13	0	5	15	28	34	34	24	7	-2	-7	-13
Days Maximum Temp. ≥ 90°F	0	0	0	0	0	2	6	4	0	0	0	0	12
Days Maximum Temp. ≤ 32°F	7	4	1	0	0	0	0	0	0	0	2	5	19
Days Minimum Temp. ≤ 32°F	30	25	23	14	5	0	0	0	1	8	21	28	155
Days Minimum Temp. ≤ 0°F	1	0	0	0	0	0	0	0	0	0	0	0	1
Heating Degree Days (base 65°F)	1,090	903	832	592	360	102	11	18	154	467	805	1,040	6,374
Cooling Degree Days (base 65°F)	0	0	0	0	6	74	196	155	31	1	0	0	463
Mean Precipitation (in.)	1.54	1.82	1.99	1.02	1.38	0.68	1.20	1.44	1.19	1.26	1.08	0.96	15.56
Days With ≥ 0.1" Precipitation	4	4	5	3	4	2	3	3	3	3	3	3	40
Days With ≥ 1.0" Precipitation	0	0	0	0	0	0	0	0	0	0	0	0	0
Mean Snowfall (in.)	12.9	13.0	na	4.0	1.5	0.0	0.0	0.0	1.1	1.6	6.8	8.5	na
Days With ≥ 1.0" Snow Depth	na	na	na	na	0	0	0	0	0	na	na	na	na

Leonard Creek Ranch *Humboldt County*   Elevation: 4,222 ft.   Latitude: 41° 31' N   Longitude: 118° 43' W

	JAN	FEB	MAR	APR	MAY	JUN	JUL	AUG	SEP	OCT	NOV	DEC	YEAR
Mean Maximum Temp. (°F)	39.8	47.5	55.1	63.4	73.0	82.6	92.0	90.1	80.4	67.1	50.7	40.3	65.2
Mean Temp. (°F)	30.2	36.7	42.8	49.0	57.7	66.0	74.0	72.4	63.6	52.4	39.6	30.6	51.2
Mean Minimum Temp. (°F)	20.5	25.9	30.5	34.6	42.3	49.4	55.8	54.6	46.8	37.6	28.4	20.7	37.3
Extreme Maximum Temp. (°F)	63	71	78	90	97	103	107	107	100	91	75	63	107
Extreme Minimum Temp. (°F)	-7	-14	5	15	20	30	37	35	25	9	0	-19	-19
Days Maximum Temp. ≥ 90°F	0	0	0	0	2	8	21	18	5	0	0	0	54
Days Maximum Temp. ≤ 32°F	6	1	0	0	0	0	0	0	0	0	1	5	13
Days Minimum Temp. ≤ 32°F	28	22	19	12	3	0	0	0	1	8	20	27	140
Days Minimum Temp. ≤ 0°F	1	0	0	0	0	0	0	0	0	0	0	1	2
Heating Degree Days (base 65°F)	1,072	793	681	474	249	78	8	14	113	389	756	1,062	5,689
Cooling Degree Days (base 65°F)	0	0	0	2	29	108	286	249	85	5	0	0	764
Mean Precipitation (in.)	1.17	0.94	1.03	0.76	0.82	0.82	0.35	0.41	0.52	0.54	0.98	1.11	9.45
Days With ≥ 0.1" Precipitation	4	3	3	3	3	2	1	1	2	2	3	4	31
Days With ≥ 1.0" Precipitation	0	0	0	0	0	0	0	0	0	0	0	0	0
Mean Snowfall (in.)	4.8	na	1.0	0.6	0.2	0.1	0.0	0.0	0.0	0.6	1.3	5.9	na
Days With ≥ 1.0" Snow Depth	11	4	0	0	0	0	0	0	0	0	1	7	23

Lovelock *Pershing County*   Elevation: 3,973 ft.   Latitude: 40° 11' N   Longitude: 118° 28' W

	JAN	FEB	MAR	APR	MAY	JUN	JUL	AUG	SEP	OCT	NOV	DEC	YEAR
Mean Maximum Temp. (°F)	42.6	51.3	58.6	65.5	74.7	83.8	92.4	90.8	81.7	69.0	53.6	43.6	67.3
Mean Temp. (°F)	31.0	38.0	43.7	49.7	58.5	66.5	74.0	71.9	63.4	52.1	39.6	31.2	51.6
Mean Minimum Temp. (°F)	19.3	24.6	28.8	33.9	42.3	49.2	55.5	52.9	45.2	35.0	25.5	18.7	35.9
Extreme Maximum Temp. (°F)	67	76	81	91	97	106	107	105	98	92	76	68	107
Extreme Minimum Temp. (°F)	-12	-21	5	12	23	33	37	36	28	12	1	-23	-23
Days Maximum Temp. ≥ 90°F	0	0	0	0	1	9	22	20	5	0	0	0	57
Days Maximum Temp. ≤ 32°F	5	1	0	0	0	0	0	0	0	0	0	3	9
Days Minimum Temp. ≤ 32°F	29	24	21	12	2	0	0	0	1	11	24	29	153
Days Minimum Temp. ≤ 0°F	1	0	0	0	0	0	0	0	0	0	0	1	2
Heating Degree Days (base 65°F)	1,047	757	652	452	221	63	5	9	99	398	756	1,042	5,501
Cooling Degree Days (base 65°F)	0	0	0	1	23	106	263	219	54	3	0	0	669
Mean Precipitation (in.)	0.56	0.46	0.47	0.62	0.61	0.63	0.17	0.27	0.48	0.47	0.51	0.55	5.80
Days With ≥ 0.1" Precipitation	2	2	2	2	2	2	1	1	1	2	2	2	21
Days With ≥ 1.0" Precipitation	0	0	0	0	0	0	0	0	0	0	0	0	0
Mean Snowfall (in.)	3.8	1.4	0.9	0.4	trace	0.0	0.0	0.0	0.0	0.1	0.6	1.8	9.0
Days With ≥ 1.0" Snow Depth	4	2	0	0	0	0	0	0	0	0	0	2	8

Lovelock Derby Field *Pershing County*   Elevation: 3,897 ft.   Latitude: 40° 04' N   Longitude: 118° 33' W

	JAN	FEB	MAR	APR	MAY	JUN	JUL	AUG	SEP	OCT	NOV	DEC	YEAR
Mean Maximum Temp. (°F)	42.6	50.8	57.9	64.6	74.4	84.4	94.4	92.1	82.5	69.3	53.9	43.2	67.5
Mean Temp. (°F)	30.1	36.9	42.8	49.0	58.4	67.0	75.3	72.6	63.6	51.3	38.6	29.8	51.3
Mean Minimum Temp. (°F)	17.6	22.9	27.7	33.3	42.3	49.6	56.1	53.0	44.6	33.3	23.2	16.3	35.0
Extreme Maximum Temp. (°F)	66	73	81	91	97	106	107	105	99	91	76	67	107
Extreme Minimum Temp. (°F)	-19	-25	-2	8	25	30	39	32	24	6	-3	-28	-28
Days Maximum Temp. ≥ 90°F	0	0	0	0	2	10	24	21	8	0	0	0	65
Days Maximum Temp. ≤ 32°F	5	1	0	0	0	0	0	0	0	0	0	4	10
Days Minimum Temp. ≤ 32°F	29	25	22	13	2	0	0	0	2	13	25	29	160
Days Minimum Temp. ≤ 0°F	2	0	0	0	0	0	0	0	0	0	0	2	4
Heating Degree Days (base 65°F)	1,074	787	680	475	227	61	3	9	102	420	786	1,085	5,709
Cooling Degree Days (base 65°F)	0	0	0	1	29	120	316	253	72	3	0	0	794
Mean Precipitation (in.)	0.54	0.44	0.53	0.52	0.56	0.58	0.15	0.33	0.38	0.31	0.41	0.57	5.32
Days With ≥ 0.1" Precipitation	2	1	2	1	2	2	0	1	1	1	1	2	16
Days With ≥ 1.0" Precipitation	0	0	0	0	0	0	0	0	0	0	0	0	0
Mean Snowfall (in.)	2.4	1.1	0.3	0.4	trace	trace	0.0	trace	0.0	trace	0.5	3.0	7.7
Days With ≥ 1.0" Snow Depth	5	1	0	0	0	0	0	0	0	0	0	3	9

Lund *White Pine County*   Elevation: 5,567 ft.   Latitude: 38° 52' N   Longitude: 115° 00' W

	JAN	FEB	MAR	APR	MAY	JUN	JUL	AUG	SEP	OCT	NOV	DEC	YEAR
Mean Maximum Temp. (°F)	42.3	47.8	53.9	61.5	70.6	81.2	88.6	86.8	78.7	67.2	52.5	44.1	64.6
Mean Temp. (°F)	28.4	33.7	39.0	45.1	53.5	62.3	69.2	67.7	59.8	49.2	37.1	29.5	47.9
Mean Minimum Temp. (°F)	14.6	19.5	24.1	28.7	36.3	43.5	49.8	48.5	40.8	31.2	21.7	14.9	31.1
Extreme Maximum Temp. (°F)	64	75	78	83	92	99	102	101	93	90	75	68	102
Extreme Minimum Temp. (°F)	-15	-12	-2	-3	17	23	33	34	22	5	-6	-18	-18
Days Maximum Temp. ≥ 90°F	0	0	0	0	0	5	14	10	2	0	0	0	31
Days Maximum Temp. ≤ 32°F	5	2	0	0	0	0	0	0	0	0	1	4	12
Days Minimum Temp. ≤ 32°F	31	27	27	22	9	1	0	0	3	17	28	31	196
Days Minimum Temp. ≤ 0°F	3	1	0	0	0	0	0	0	0	0	0	2	6
Heating Degree Days (base 65°F)	1,126	878	800	591	352	118	15	25	168	482	830	1,093	6,478
Cooling Degree Days (base 65°F)	0	0	0	0	2	44	148	123	20	0	0	0	337
Mean Precipitation (in.)	0.88	0.82	1.26	0.86	1.17	0.88	0.76	1.08	0.94	0.96	0.77	0.67	11.05
Days With ≥ 0.1" Precipitation	2	2	4	2	3	2	2	3	2	2	2	2	28
Days With ≥ 1.0" Precipitation	0	0	0	0	0	0	0	0	0	0	0	0	0
Mean Snowfall (in.)	na	2.7	3.7	2.2	0.7	0.0	0.0	0.0	0.0	0.3	2.0	3.0	na
Days With ≥ 1.0" Snow Depth	na	na	na	0	0	0	0	0	0	0	0	na	na

McGill *White Pine County*   Elevation: 6,299 ft.   Latitude: 39° 24' N   Longitude: 114° 46' W

	JAN	FEB	MAR	APR	MAY	JUN	JUL	AUG	SEP	OCT	NOV	DEC	YEAR
Mean Maximum Temp. (°F)	38.9	43.0	48.9	56.1	66.0	77.3	85.4	83.6	74.3	62.5	48.3	40.1	60.4
Mean Temp. (°F)	27.4	31.4	36.8	42.9	51.7	61.6	69.6	68.1	58.7	47.7	35.9	28.2	46.7
Mean Minimum Temp. (°F)	15.9	19.7	24.6	29.7	37.3	45.9	53.7	52.6	43.0	32.9	23.5	16.3	32.9
Extreme Maximum Temp. (°F)	61	67	72	80	88	94	99	95	90	84	75	64	99
Extreme Minimum Temp. (°F)	-15	-21	-4	9	18	28	35	31	23	4	-7	-16	-21
Days Maximum Temp. ≥ 90°F	0	0	0	0	0	2	7	4	0	0	0	0	13
Days Maximum Temp. ≤ 32°F	8	4	1	0	0	0	0	0	0	0	3	7	23
Days Minimum Temp. ≤ 32°F	30	26	26	20	8	1	0	0	2	14	25	29	181
Days Minimum Temp. ≤ 0°F	3	2	0	0	0	0	0	0	0	0	0	2	7
Heating Degree Days (base 65°F)	1,158	943	869	656	408	146	14	25	203	530	866	1,133	6,951
Cooling Degree Days (base 65°F)	0	0	0	0	1	50	160	139	22	0	0	0	372
Mean Precipitation (in.)	0.53	0.48	0.67	0.86	1.16	0.75	0.72	0.71	0.95	0.91	0.57	0.38	8.69
Days With ≥ 0.1" Precipitation	2	1	2	2	3	2	2	2	2	3	2	1	24
Days With ≥ 1.0" Precipitation	0	0	0	0	0	0	0	0	0	0	0	0	0
Mean Snowfall (in.)	na	na	1.5	1.2	0.1	trace	0.0	0.0	trace	0.5	1.1	2.0	na
Days With ≥ 1.0" Snow Depth	na	9	3	2	0	0	0	0	0	0	3	7	na

Mina *Mineral County*   Elevation: 4,547 ft.   Latitude: 38° 23' N   Longitude: 118° 06' W

	JAN	FEB	MAR	APR	MAY	JUN	JUL	AUG	SEP	OCT	NOV	DEC	YEAR
Mean Maximum Temp. (°F)	46.0	52.8	59.2	65.7	75.4	86.2	94.4	92.8	83.6	71.0	56.2	46.7	69.2
Mean Temp. (°F)	34.5	40.0	45.7	51.5	60.8	70.7	78.3	76.4	67.1	55.1	43.2	34.7	54.8
Mean Minimum Temp. (°F)	23.0	27.1	32.2	37.3	46.1	55.2	62.2	59.9	50.5	39.2	30.3	22.6	40.5
Extreme Maximum Temp. (°F)	71	76	80	90	97	105	108	105	100	93	78	69	108
Extreme Minimum Temp. (°F)	-6	-9	0	17	26	33	42	42	30	16	7	-23	-23
Days Maximum Temp. ≥ 90°F	0	0	0	0	2	13	26	23	8	0	0	0	72
Days Maximum Temp. ≤ 32°F	2	1	0	0	0	0	0	0	0	0	0	2	5
Days Minimum Temp. ≤ 32°F	26	22	16	8	1	0	0	0	0	6	19	26	124
Days Minimum Temp. ≤ 0°F	0	0	0	0	0	0	0	0	0	0	0	0	0
Heating Degree Days (base 65°F)	938	699	591	402	178	35	1	2	57	309	646	934	4,792
Cooling Degree Days (base 65°F)	0	0	0	5	58	213	417	375	132	8	0	0	1,208
Mean Precipitation (in.)	0.45	0.43	0.67	0.60	0.75	0.55	0.52	0.40	0.41	0.45	0.41	0.33	5.97
Days With ≥ 0.1" Precipitation	1	1	2	2	2	1	1	1	1	1	1	1	15
Days With ≥ 1.0" Precipitation	0	0	0	0	0	0	0	0	0	0	0	0	0
Mean Snowfall (in.)	2.9	2.4	2.4	1.0	0.4	0.0	0.0	0.0	0.0	0.5	0.9	1.5	12.0
Days With ≥ 1.0" Snow Depth	na	na	0	0	0	0	0	0	0	0	0	na	na

Minden *Douglas County*   Elevation: 4,708 ft.   Latitude: 38° 58' N   Longitude: 119° 46' W

	JAN	FEB	MAR	APR	MAY	JUN	JUL	AUG	SEP	OCT	NOV	DEC	YEAR
Mean Maximum Temp. (°F)	45.6	51.7	57.2	63.4	72.1	81.7	90.0	89.1	81.4	70.2	56.1	46.8	67.1
Mean Temp. (°F)	31.6	36.6	41.4	46.4	54.2	62.3	68.7	67.4	60.0	49.8	39.5	31.9	49.2
Mean Minimum Temp. (°F)	17.6	21.6	25.5	29.4	36.2	42.9	47.4	45.6	38.7	29.3	22.8	16.9	31.1
Extreme Maximum Temp. (°F)	71	74	82	90	95	105	107	105	99	92	79	70	107
Extreme Minimum Temp. (°F)	-20	-24	-1	9	19	24	29	28	20	3	-7	-22	-24
Days Maximum Temp. ≥ 90°F	0	0	0	0	0	6	18	16	5	1	0	0	46
Days Maximum Temp. ≤ 32°F	3	1	0	0	0	0	0	0	0	0	0	2	6
Days Minimum Temp. ≤ 32°F	29	26	26	20	9	2	0	0	6	21	27	28	194
Days Minimum Temp. ≤ 0°F	2	0	0	0	0	0	0	0	0	0	0	2	4
Heating Degree Days (base 65°F)	1,028	794	726	552	332	119	21	32	165	465	758	1,020	6,012
Cooling Degree Days (base 65°F)	0	0	0	0	4	45	139	117	28	0	0	0	333
Mean Precipitation (in.)	1.49	1.18	1.10	0.34	0.45	0.44	0.23	0.34	0.40	0.57	0.95	1.04	8.53
Days Wlth ≥ 0.1" Precipitation	4	3	3	1	1	1	1	1	1	2	2	3	23
Days With ≥ 1.0" Precipitation	0	0	0	0	0	0	0	0	0	0	0	0	0
Mean Snowfall (in.)	*5.4*	*3.6*	*3.1*	1.0	0.3	0.1	0.0	0.0	0.0	0.2	na	na	na
Days With ≥ 1.0" Snow Depth	*4*	*2*	*1*	0	0	0	0	0	0	0	na	na	na

Orovada 3 W *Humboldt County*   Elevation: 4,199 ft.   Latitude: 41° 34' N   Longitude: 117° 50' W

	JAN	FEB	MAR	APR	MAY	JUN	JUL	AUG	SEP	OCT	NOV	DEC	YEAR
Mean Maximum Temp. (°F)	40.1	47.3	53.4	60.7	70.4	80.9	90.2	89.3	79.2	66.6	50.5	40.5	64.1
Mean Temp. (°F)	30.0	35.6	40.6	46.3	54.7	63.5	70.8	69.4	60.0	49.4	37.9	29.7	49.0
Mean Minimum Temp. (°F)	19.8	23.9	27.7	31.8	38.9	45.9	51.3	49.5	40.7	32.2	25.3	18.8	33.8
Extreme Maximum Temp. (°F)	64	71	79	89	96	102	104	105	99	93	76	67	105
Extreme Minimum Temp. (°F)	-17	-16	3	9	18	28	33	25	15	1	-7	-33	-33
Days Maximum Temp. ≥ 90°F	0	0	0	0	1	7	19	17	5	0	0	0	49
Days Maximum Temp. ≤ 32°F	6	2	0	0	0	0	0	0	0	0	1	5	14
Days Minimum Temp. ≤ 32°F	27	24	22	16	5	1	0	0	4	15	23	28	165
Days Minimum Temp. ≤ 0°F	2	1	0	0	0	0	0	0	0	0	0	2	5
Heating Degree Days (base 65°F)	1,079	822	749	556	324	114	21	26	176	476	807	1,089	6,239
Cooling Degree Days (base 65°F)	0	0	0	0	11	65	180	161	33	1	0	0	451
Mean Precipitation (in.)	0.96	0.72	1.16	1.29	1.20	1.07	0.32	0.49	0.71	0.75	1.02	0.89	10.58
Days With ≥ 0.1" Precipitation	3	2	4	4	3	3	1	1	2	2	4	3	32
Days With ≥ 1.0" Precipitation	0	0	0	0	0	0	0	0	0	0	0	0	0
Mean Snowfall (in.)	*3.9*	2.0	2.4	2.0	trace	0.0	0.0	0.0	trace	0.5	*2.1*	*3.8*	*16.7*
Days With ≥ 1.0" Snow Depth	*3*	*1*	*0*	0	0	0	0	0	0	0	*1*	na	na

Pahranagat Wildlife Refuge *Lincoln County*   Elevation: 3,398 ft.   Latitude: 37° 16' N   Longitude: 115° 07' W

	JAN	FEB	MAR	APR	MAY	JUN	JUL	AUG	SEP	OCT	NOV	DEC	YEAR
Mean Maximum Temp. (°F)	52.6	58.7	64.8	72.4	82.2	92.7	98.4	96.5	89.2	76.9	62.2	*53.1*	*75.0*
Mean Temp. (°F)	39.7	45.0	50.3	56.7	65.8	75.0	81.1	79.5	71.5	60.2	47.5	*39.8*	*59.4*
Mean Minimum Temp. (°F)	26.8	31.3	35.8	41.0	49.4	57.3	63.8	62.3	53.9	43.5	32.8	*26.5*	*43.7*
Extreme Maximum Temp. (°F)	75	83	86	95	102	110	112	111	106	102	86	74	112
Extreme Minimum Temp. (°F)	6	4	16	19	31	38	46	44	35	19	9	-1	-1
Days Maximum Temp. ≥ 90°F	0	0	0	1	5	19	28	27	15	3	0	0	98
Days Maximum Temp. ≤ 32°F	0	0	0	0	0	0	0	0	0	0	0	0	0
Days Minimum Temp. ≤ 32°F	25	16	8	3	0	0	0	0	0	2	14	25	93
Days Minimum Temp. ≤ 0°F	0	0	0	0	0	0	0	0	0	0	0	0	0
Heating Degree Days (base 65°F)	*775*	558	448	254	71	6	0	0	14	179	518	*774*	*3,597*
Cooling Degree Days (base 65°F)	0	0	0	17	110	334	517	479	235	40	0	0	1,732
Mean Precipitation (in.)	0.69	0.64	0.87	0.57	0.49	0.21	0.41	0.68	0.38	0.56	0.56	0.47	6.53
Days With ≥ 0.1" Precipitation	2	2	3	2	2	1	1	1	1	1	2	1	19
Days With ≥ 1.0" Precipitation	0	0	0	0	0	0	0	0	0	0	0	0	0
Mean Snowfall (in.)	0.6	0.2	0.1	trace	0.0	0.0	0.0	0.0	0.0	trace	0.3	0.5	1.7
Days With ≥ 1.0" Snow Depth	0	0	0	0	0	0	0	0	0	0	0	0	0

Pahrump *Nye County*   Elevation: 2,673 ft.   Latitude: 36° 17' N   Longitude: 116° 00' W

	JAN	FEB	MAR	APR	MAY	JUN	JUL	AUG	SEP	OCT	NOV	DEC	YEAR
Mean Maximum Temp. (°F)	57.6	62.9	67.8	75.1	84.2	94.8	100.6	99.0	91.9	80.5	66.9	57.9	78.3
Mean Temp. (°F)	42.7	47.8	52.9	59.2	68.0	77.5	83.8	82.1	74.2	62.3	50.2	42.3	61.9
Mean Minimum Temp. (°F)	27.7	32.6	37.9	43.2	51.8	60.1	66.9	65.1	56.5	44.1	33.5	26.6	45.5
Extreme Maximum Temp. (°F)	77	85	89	97	104	112	115	112	107	101	87	77	115
Extreme Minimum Temp. (°F)	5	6	16	18	30	38	50	46	35	19	11	-2	-2
Days Maximum Temp. ≥ 90°F	0	0	0	2	9	24	30	30	20	5	0	0	120
Days Maximum Temp. ≤ 32°F	0	0	0	0	0	0	0	0	0	0	0	0	0
Days Minimum Temp. ≤ 32°F	24	15	7	1	0	0	0	0	0	2	13	24	86
Days Minimum Temp. ≤ 0°F	0	0	0	0	0	0	0	0	0	0	0	0	0
Heating Degree Days (base 65°F)	685	480	370	193	54	4	0	0	8	129	439	702	3,064
Cooling Degree Days (base 65°F)	0	0	2	32	151	372	573	537	292	52	0	0	2,011
Mean Precipitation (in.)	0.73	0.79	0.78	0.30	0.29	0.09	0.40	0.40	0.31	0.18	0.38	0.47	5.12
Days With ≥ 0.1" Precipitation	2	2	2	1	1	0	1	1	1	1	1	1	14
Days With ≥ 1.0" Precipitation	0	0	0	0	0	0	0	0	0	0	0	1	0
Mean Snowfall (in.)	trace	trace	trace	trace	0.0	0.0	0.0	0.0	0.0	trace	trace	trace	trace
Days With ≥ 1.0" Snow Depth	0	0	0	0	0	0	0	0	0	0	0	0	0

Paradise Valley 1 NW *Humboldt County*   Elevation: 4,671 ft.   Latitude: 41° 30' N   Longitude: 117° 33' W

	JAN	FEB	MAR	APR	MAY	JUN	JUL	AUG	SEP	OCT	NOV	DEC	YEAR
Mean Maximum Temp. (°F)	40.2	46.6	53.6	61.3	70.3	80.6	89.8	88.8	79.5	67.2	50.2	40.9	64.1
Mean Temp. (°F)	28.6	34.1	39.8	45.4	53.1	61.4	68.7	67.4	58.8	48.5	36.6	28.7	47.6
Mean Minimum Temp. (°F)	17.0	21.6	26.0	29.4	35.8	42.2	47.5	46.0	38.0	29.7	22.9	16.4	31.0
Extreme Maximum Temp. (°F)	61	70	77	87	94	102	104	104	99	92	75	63	104
Extreme Minimum Temp. (°F)	-18	-21	-1	11	14	25	30	25	16	4	-9	-32	-32
Days Maximum Temp. ≥ 90°F	0	0	0	0	1	5	18	16	4	0	0	0	44
Days Maximum Temp. ≤ 32°F	5	1	0	0	0	0	0	0	0	0	1	4	11
Days Minimum Temp. ≤ 32°F	29	26	25	21	10	2	0	0	6	20	26	29	194
Days Minimum Temp. ≤ 0°F	3	1	0	0	0	0	0	0	0	0	0	2	6
Heating Degree Days (base 65°F)	1,121	865	774	583	366	141	24	38	199	505	846	1,120	6,582
Cooling Degree Days (base 65°F)	0	0	0	0	5	37	138	119	22	0	0	0	321
Mean Precipitation (in.)	1.42	1.09	1.08	0.68	0.89	0.79	0.34	0.32	0.62	0.69	1.43	1.49	10.84
Days With ≥ 0.1" Precipitation	4	4	4	2	3	2	1	1	2	2	4	5	34
Days With ≥ 1.0" Precipitation	0	0	0	0	0	0	0	0	0	0	0	0	0
Mean Snowfall (in.)	7.5	4.1	2.3	0.8	0.1	0.0	0.0	0.0	trace	0.4	*3.7*	7.4	*26.3*
Days With ≥ 1.0" Snow Depth	13	6	1	0	0	0	0	0	0	0	4	9	33

Pioche *Lincoln County*   Elevation: 6,177 ft.   Latitude: 37° 56' N   Longitude: 114° 27' W

	JAN	FEB	MAR	APR	MAY	JUN	JUL	AUG	SEP	OCT	NOV	DEC	YEAR
Mean Maximum Temp. (°F)	41.9	46.6	51.8	59.6	68.8	79.9	86.7	85.0	76.6	65.1	51.2	44.1	63.1
Mean Temp. (°F)	32.0	35.5	40.5	47.1	56.1	66.0	72.7	71.3	63.1	52.1	40.1	33.2	50.8
Mean Minimum Temp. (°F)	21.7	24.4	29.2	34.5	43.3	52.1	58.6	57.6	49.7	39.2	29.0	22.3	38.5
Extreme Maximum Temp. (°F)	66	72	77	82	89	99	102	97	93	86	74	67	102
Extreme Minimum Temp. (°F)	-5	-15	5	13	21	30	43	43	27	4	2	-5	-15
Days Maximum Temp. ≥ 90°F	0	0	0	0	0	4	11	8	0	0	0	0	23
Days Maximum Temp. ≤ 32°F	5	2	0	0	0	0	0	0	0	0	1	3	11
Days Minimum Temp. ≤ 32°F	29	24	21	12	3	0	0	0	0	7	19	28	143
Days Minimum Temp. ≤ 0°F	1	0	0	0	0	0	0	0	0	0	0	0	1
Heating Degree Days (base 65°F)	1,017	825	753	531	282	71	4	7	103	397	739	979	5,708
Cooling Degree Days (base 65°F)	0	0	0	0	14	101	237	223	55	5	0	0	636
Mean Precipitation (in.)	1.50	1.46	1.86	0.96	1.17	0.56	1.11	1.31	0.92	1.08	1.04	1.04	14.01
Days With ≥ 0.1" Precipitation	4	3	5	3	3	1	3	3	2	3	2	3	35
Days With ≥ 1.0" Precipitation	0	0	0	0	0	0	0	0	0	0	0	0	0
Mean Snowfall (in.)	na	na	*2.1*	1.2	trace	0.1	0.0	0.0	0.0	0.6	na	na	na
Days With ≥ 1.0" Snow Depth	na	na	na	0	0	0	0	0	0	0	*1*	na	na

Ruby Lake *Elko County*   Elevation: 6,007 ft.   Latitude: 40° 12' N   Longitude: 115° 30' W

	JAN	FEB	MAR	APR	MAY	JUN	JUL	AUG	SEP	OCT	NOV	DEC	YEAR
Mean Maximum Temp. (°F)	39.1	43.4	50.1	57.1	66.8	78.1	86.7	85.7	75.6	*63.7*	48.9	39.7	*61.2*
Mean Temp. (°F)	27.0	31.3	38.2	44.0	52.6	61.9	69.4	67.9	58.4	*47.5*	36.1	27.5	*46.8*
Mean Minimum Temp. (°F)	14.9	19.0	26.1	30.9	38.4	45.6	52.0	50.1	41.2	31.2	23.3	15.3	32.3
Extreme Maximum Temp. (°F)	62	67	72	81	94	95	100	97	92	86	74	64	100
Extreme Minimum Temp. (°F)	-23	-23	-9	10	21	25	34	30	18	3	-6	-29	-29
Days Maximum Temp. ≥ 90°F	0	0	0	0	0	3	na	7	1	0	0	0	na
Days Maximum Temp. ≤ 32°F	7	3	1	0	0	0	0	0	0	0	2	6	19
Days Minimum Temp. ≤ 32°F	29	*26*	*25*	na	7	1	0	0	4	*18*	*25*	29	na
Days Minimum Temp. ≤ 0°F	4	2	0	0	0	0	0	0	0	0	0	*2*	*8*
Heating Degree Days (base 65°F)	1,171	945	824	624	380	134	14	24	206	*536*	865	1,155	*6,878*
Cooling Degree Days (base 65°F)	0	0	0	0	3	49	154	116	15	0	0	0	337
Mean Precipitation (in.)	1.59	1.11	1.43	1.19	1.43	0.87	0.46	0.75	0.99	1.21	1.53	1.33	13.89
Days With ≥ 0.1" Precipitation	5	3	4	4	4	3	2	2	2	3	4	4	40
Days With ≥ 1.0" Precipitation	0	0	0	0	0	0	0	0	0	0	0	0	0
Mean Snowfall (in.)	12.6	*7.7*	*6.1*	4.4	1.3	trace	0.0	0.0	0.2	1.2	6.1	*9.8*	*49.4*
Days With ≥ 1.0" Snow Depth	na	na	na	*1*	0	0	0	0	0	1	*5*	na	na

Rye Patch Dam *Pershing County*   Elevation: 4,133 ft.   Latitude: 40° 28' N   Longitude: 118° 18' W

	JAN	FEB	MAR	APR	MAY	JUN	JUL	AUG	SEP	OCT	NOV	DEC	YEAR
Mean Maximum Temp. (°F)	42.5	50.8	57.9	65.1	74.8	84.9	94.1	92.7	83.3	70.4	53.9	43.9	67.9
Mean Temp. (°F)	30.2	36.8	42.4	48.1	56.8	65.4	72.8	71.0	62.4	50.8	*39.0*	30.4	*50.5*
Mean Minimum Temp. (°F)	17.7	22.7	26.8	31.1	38.8	46.0	51.4	49.3	41.5	31.2	*24.2*	16.9	*33.1*
Extreme Maximum Temp. (°F)	67	75	81	92	98	105	106	108	101	94	79	65	108
Extreme Minimum Temp. (°F)	-12	-21	-10	8	18	27	30	30	17	5	-4	-23	-23
Days Maximum Temp. ≥ 90°F	0	0	0	0	2	11	24	23	9	1	0	0	70
Days Maximum Temp. ≤ 32°F	5	1	0	0	0	0	0	0	0	0	0	3	9
Days Minimum Temp. ≤ 32°F	29	25	24	18	6	1	0	0	4	17	23	28	175
Days Minimum Temp. ≤ 0°F	2	0	0	0	0	0	0	0	0	0	0	2	4
Heating Degree Days (base 65°F)	1,074	789	694	499	266	80	8	14	122	435	*772*	1,066	*5,819*
Cooling Degree Days (base 65°F)	0	0	0	1	22	97	251	210	56	2	*0*	0	*639*
Mean Precipitation (in.)	0.80	0.67	0.95	0.95	1.01	0.93	0.28	0.35	0.54	0.69	0.78	0.79	8.74
Days With ≥ 0.1" Precipitation	3	3	3	3	3	2	1	1	2	2	2	3	28
Days With ≥ 1.0" Precipitation	0	0	0	0	0	0	0	0	0	0	0	0	0
Mean Snowfall (in.)	na	*0.4*	na	*trace*	trace	0.0	0.0	0.0	trace	0.0	na	na	na
Days With ≥ 1.0" Snow Depth	na	na	na	0	0	0	0	0	0	0	*0*	na	na

Searchlight *Clark County*   Elevation: 3,540 ft.   Latitude: 35° 28' N   Longitude: 114° 55' W

	JAN	FEB	MAR	APR	MAY	JUN	JUL	AUG	SEP	OCT	NOV	DEC	YEAR
Mean Maximum Temp. (°F)	54.1	59.2	65.2	73.1	82.7	93.3	97.8	95.9	88.6	77.1	63.3	54.2	75.4
Mean Temp. (°F)	45.2	49.1	53.7	60.3	69.2	79.4	84.5	82.9	75.8	65.2	52.9	45.2	63.6
Mean Minimum Temp. (°F)	36.2	38.9	42.1	47.5	55.8	65.4	71.2	69.8	63.0	53.2	42.4	36.2	51.8
Extreme Maximum Temp. (°F)	77	81	90	94	102	108	111	107	104	98	83	75	111
Extreme Minimum Temp. (°F)	9	11	22	29	31	40	52	55	41	23	21	8	8
Days Maximum Temp. ≥ 90°F	0	0	0	0	6	21	29	28	14	2	0	0	100
Days Maximum Temp. ≤ 32°F	0	0	0	0	0	0	0	0	0	0	0	0	0
Days Minimum Temp. ≤ 32°F	9	5	2	1	0	0	0	0	0	0	3	9	29
Days Minimum Temp. ≤ 0°F	0	0	0	0	0	0	0	0	0	0	0	0	0
Heating Degree Days (base 65°F)	608	443	350	178	42	3	0	0	6	96	360	607	2,693
Cooling Degree Days (base 65°F)	0	1	6	57	183	428	599	569	344	111	5	0	2,303
Mean Precipitation (in.)	0.97	1.09	1.07	0.34	0.23	0.08	0.98	1.18	0.72	0.49	0.48	0.71	8.34
Days With ≥ 0.1" Precipitation	2	3	3	1	1	0	2	2	2	1	1	2	20
Days With ≥ 1.0" Precipitation	0	0	0	0	0	0	0	0	0	0	0	0	0
Mean Snowfall (in.)	0.3	trace	0.1	trace	0.0	0.0	0.0	0.0	0.0	0.0	trace	0.2	0.6
Days With ≥ 1.0" Snow Depth	0	0	0	0	0	0	0	0	0	0	0	0	0

Silverpeak *Esmeralda County*   Elevation: 4,258 ft.   Latitude: 37° 40' N   Longitude: 117° 35' W

	JAN	FEB	MAR	APR	MAY	JUN	JUL	AUG	SEP	OCT	NOV	DEC	YEAR
Mean Maximum Temp. (°F)	46.7	54.6	61.3	69.1	78.9	89.8	97.0	95.1	86.0	72.8	57.1	46.1	71.2
Mean Temp. (°F)	32.8	39.5	46.7	53.7	63.3	73.2	79.6	77.4	68.3	55.4	41.8	31.8	55.3
Mean Minimum Temp. (°F)	18.8	24.4	32.0	38.2	47.8	56.7	62.2	59.8	50.5	37.9	26.5	17.4	39.3
Extreme Maximum Temp. (°F)	72	77	84	89	101	107	111	111	104	104	79	68	111
Extreme Minimum Temp. (°F)	-22	-21	4	11	26	35	41	36	28	12	-2	-14	-22
Days Maximum Temp. ≥ 90°F	0	0	0	0	5	17	28	26	11	1	0	0	88
Days Maximum Temp. ≤ 32°F	2	0	0	0	0	0	0	0	0	0	0	2	4
Days Minimum Temp. ≤ 32°F	29	24	16	6	1	0	0	0	0	8	23	30	137
Days Minimum Temp. ≤ 0°F	1	0	0	0	0	0	0	0	0	0	0	1	2
Heating Degree Days (base 65°F)	992	714	563	340	123	18	0	1	43	303	690	1,022	4,809
Cooling Degree Days (base 65°F)	0	0	0	9	75	257	441	383	135	8	0	0	1,308
Mean Precipitation (in.)	0.35	0.34	0.63	0.34	0.40	0.27	0.40	0.42	0.53	0.35	0.29	0.16	4.48
Days With ≥ 0.1" Precipitation	1	1	2	1	1	1	1	1	1	1	1	1	13
Days With ≥ 1.0" Precipitation	0	0	0	0	0	0	0	0	0	0	0	0	0
Mean Snowfall (in.)	0.5	*1.4*	0.6	0.1	trace	0.0	0.0	0.0	0.0	0.2	trace	*0.1*	*2.9*
Days With ≥ 1.0" Snow Depth	*0*	na	0	0	0	0	0	0	0	0	0	*0*	na

Smokey Valley *Nye County*   Elevation: 5,623 ft.   Latitude: 38° 47' N   Longitude: 117° 10' W

	JAN	FEB	MAR	APR	MAY	JUN	JUL	AUG	SEP	OCT	NOV	DEC	YEAR
Mean Maximum Temp. (°F)	43.2	49.9	56.1	63.5	73.1	83.6	91.0	88.8	80.2	68.4	53.7	44.0	66.3
Mean Temp. (°F)	29.6	35.7	41.2	47.2	56.0	65.4	72.4	70.4	61.6	50.7	38.5	29.8	49.9
Mean Minimum Temp. (°F)	15.9	21.1	26.3	30.9	38.9	47.1	53.6	52.0	43.0	33.0	23.2	15.5	33.4
Extreme Maximum Temp. (°F)	66	71	76	85	93	100	102	101	94	89	76	67	102
Extreme Minimum Temp. (°F)	-14	-12	-8	6	20	26	34	33	23	7	-5	-31	-31
Days Maximum Temp. ≥ 90°F	0	0	0	0	0	8	20	15	3	0	0	0	46
Days Maximum Temp. ≤ 32°F	3	1	0	0	0	0	0	0	0	0	1	3	8
Days Minimum Temp. ≤ 32°F	28	24	24	*18*	*5*	1	0	0	2	14	25	29	*170*
Days Minimum Temp. ≤ 0°F	2	1	0	0	0	0	0	0	0	0	0	2	5
Heating Degree Days (base 65°F)	1,091	*828*	731	528	280	73	3	10	132	437	792	1,085	*5,990*
Cooling Degree Days (base 65°F)	0	0	0	0	11	92	241	196	43	1	0	0	584
Mean Precipitation (in.)	0.59	0.59	0.89	0.56	0.70	0.48	0.64	0.74	0.64	0.59	0.51	0.35	7.28
Days With ≥ 0.1" Precipitation	2	2	2	2	2	2	2	2	2	2	1	1	22
Days With ≥ 1.0" Precipitation	0	0	0	0	0	0	0	0	0	0	0	0	0
Mean Snowfall (in.)	na	na	na	0.8	0.0	0.0	0.0	0.0	0.0	0.0	*0.9*	na	na
Days With ≥ 1.0" Snow Depth	na	na	na	0	0	0	0	0	0	0	*0*	na	na

Snowball Ranch *Nye County*   Elevation: 7,158 ft.   Latitude: 39° 04' N   Longitude: 116° 12' W

	JAN	FEB	MAR	APR	MAY	JUN	JUL	AUG	SEP	OCT	NOV	DEC	YEAR
Mean Maximum Temp. (°F)	40.1	43.2	48.1	55.1	64.1	73.9	81.4	79.4	72.1	61.5	48.9	41.2	59.1
Mean Temp. (°F)	27.0	30.2	35.2	40.8	48.6	57.0	64.4	62.7	55.4	45.8	34.8	27.9	44.1
Mean Minimum Temp. (°F)	13.9	17.1	22.2	26.4	33.1	39.9	47.3	45.9	38.7	30.1	20.6	14.4	29.1
Extreme Maximum Temp. (°F)	62	67	69	77	83	91	93	91	86	83	72	63	93
Extreme Minimum Temp. (°F)	-21	-18	-12	7	15	21	29	29	17	0	-9	-24	-24
Days Maximum Temp. ≥ 90°F	0	0	0	0	0	0	1	0	0	0	0	0	1
Days Maximum Temp. ≤ 32°F	6	3	1	0	0	0	0	0	0	0	2	6	18
Days Minimum Temp. ≤ 32°F	31	28	29	24	14	4	0	0	5	19	28	31	213
Days Minimum Temp. ≤ 0°F	3	2	0	0	0	0	0	0	0	0	1	3	9
Heating Degree Days (base 65°F)	1,171	977	918	721	501	242	58	92	283	588	899	1,144	7,594
Cooling Degree Days (base 65°F)	0	0	0	0	0	6	45	27	2	0	0	0	80
Mean Precipitation (in.)	0.55	0.57	0.98	0.74	1.01	0.64	0.95	0.97	0.90	0.69	0.52	0.35	8.87
Days With ≥ 0.1" Precipitation	2	2	3	3	3	2	2	3	2	2	2	1	27
Days With ≥ 1.0" Precipitation	0	0	0	0	0	0	0	0	0	0	0	0	0
Mean Snowfall (in.)	8.5	7.3	9.0	4.8	2.2	0.4	0.0	0.0	0.2	1.8	4.3	5.4	43.9
Days With ≥ 1.0" Snow Depth	3	2	2	1	0	0	0	0	0	0	1	2	11

Tonopah Airport *Nye County*   Elevation: 5,429 ft.   Latitude: 38° 04' N   Longitude: 117° 05' W

	JAN	FEB	MAR	APR	MAY	JUN	JUL	AUG	SEP	OCT	NOV	DEC	YEAR
Mean Maximum Temp. (°F)	43.9	49.9	55.6	63.4	73.2	84.2	91.2	89.0	80.1	68.0	53.3	44.6	66.4
Mean Temp. (°F)	31.7	37.0	42.1	48.6	57.7	67.4	74.0	71.9	63.8	52.5	39.7	32.0	51.5
Mean Minimum Temp. (°F)	19.5	24.1	28.6	33.6	42.2	50.6	56.6	54.8	47.4	36.9	25.9	19.4	36.6
Extreme Maximum Temp. (°F)	67	75	76	88	94	101	103	103	95	90	77	66	103
Extreme Minimum Temp. (°F)	-10	-9	4	16	24	27	40	38	25	13	4	-10	-10
Days Maximum Temp. ≥ 90°F	0	0	0	0	1	9	21	15	3	0	0	0	49
Days Maximum Temp. ≤ 32°F	3	1	0	0	0	0	0	0	0	0	1	3	8
Days Minimum Temp. ≤ 32°F	30	25	23	13	3	0	0	0	0	8	25	30	157
Days Minimum Temp. ≤ 0°F	1	0	0	0	0	0	0	0	0	0	0	1	2
Heating Degree Days (base 65°F)	1,024	783	702	487	237	52	2	6	92	384	754	1,016	5,539
Cooling Degree Days (base 65°F)	0	0	0	1	21	134	286	235	65	3	0	0	745
Mean Precipitation (in.)	0.47	0.47	0.68	0.41	0.62	0.33	0.55	0.53	0.49	0.44	0.43	0.30	5.72
Days With ≥ 0.1" Precipitation	2	2	2	1	2	1	1	1	2	1	1	1	17
Days With ≥ 1.0" Precipitation	0	0	0	0	0	0	0	0	0	0	0	0	0
Mean Snowfall (in.)	4.0	2.9	2.9	1.4	0.4	tracc	0.0	trace	trace	0.2	1.8	2.6	16.2
Days With ≥ 1.0" Snow Depth	4	2	1	0	0	0	0	0	0	0	1	2	10

Valley of Fire State Park *Clark County*   Elevation: 1,998 ft.   Latitude: 36° 26' N   Longitude: 114° 31' W

	JAN	FEB	MAR	APR	MAY	JUN	JUL	AUG	SEP	OCT	NOV	DEC	YEAR
Mean Maximum Temp. (°F)	56.3	62.2	69.3	78.5	88.9	100.0	105.2	103.3	95.3	82.5	66.6	56.8	80.4
Mean Temp. (°F)	47.3	52.4	58.2	66.2	76.1	86.6	92.5	90.5	82.8	70.5	56.4	47.5	68.9
Mean Minimum Temp. (°F)	38.1	42.6	47.1	53.9	63.3	73.1	79.7	77.7	70.3	58.4	46.1	38.1	57.4
Extreme Maximum Temp. (°F)	74	87	90	100	109	117	117	115	110	102	87	74	117
Extreme Minimum Temp. (°F)	19	18	29	29	42	48	60	62	49	38	19	12	12
Days Maximum Temp. ≥ 90°F	0	0	0	4	16	27	31	30	24	7	0	0	139
Days Maximum Temp. ≤ 32°F	0	0	0	0	0	0	0	0	0	0	0	0	0
Days Minimum Temp. ≤ 32°F	4	2	0	0	0	0	0	0	0	0	1	4	11
Days Minimum Temp. ≤ 0°F	0	0	0	0	0	0	0	0	0	0	0	0	0
Heating Degree Days (base 65°F)	544	352	222	78	11	1	0	0	1	34	263	536	2,042
Cooling Degree Days (base 65°F)	0	3	21	135	367	650	853	807	541	204	12	0	3,593
Mean Precipitation (in.)	0.98	1.01	0.99	0.25	0.19	0.10	0.61	0.72	0.53	0.40	0.50	0.55	6.83
Days With ≥ 0.1" Precipitation	2	2	3	1	1	0	1	1	1	1	1	2	16
Days With ≥ 1.0" Precipitation	0	0	0	0	0	0	0	0	0	0	0	0	0
Mean Snowfall (in.)	trace	0.2	trace	0.0	0.0	0.0	0.0	0.0	0.0	0.0	trace	0.1	0.3
Days With ≥ 1.0" Snow Depth	0	0	0	0	0	0	0	0	0	0	0	0	0

Virginia City *Storey County*   Elevation: 6,338 ft.   Latitude: 39° 18' N   Longitude: 119° 38' W

	JAN	FEB	MAR	APR	MAY	JUN	JUL	AUG	SEP	OCT	NOV	DEC	YEAR
Mean Maximum Temp. (°F)	40.7	43.8	48.7	54.8	64.0	73.6	82.8	81.6	72.9	61.7	48.8	41.6	59.6
Mean Temp. (°F)	32.2	35.2	39.3	44.4	53.0	62.1	70.5	69.5	61.3	51.0	39.6	33.1	49.3
Mean Minimum Temp. (°F)	23.7	26.5	29.8	34.0	42.0	50.5	58.2	57.3	49.6	40.2	30.3	24.5	38.9
Extreme Maximum Temp. (°F)	63	70	71	79	109	92	98	100	91	84	72	64	109
Extreme Minimum Temp. (°F)	-1	-9	4	10	15	28	36	35	21	11	9	-11	-11
Days Maximum Temp. ≥ 90°F	0	0	0	0	0	0	5	3	0	0	0	0	8
Days Maximum Temp. ≤ 32°F	6	3	1	0	0	0	0	0	0	0	2	5	17
Days Minimum Temp. ≤ 32°F	26	21	19	13	5	1	0	0	1	7	18	26	137
Days Minimum Temp. ≤ 0°F	0	0	0	0	0	0	0	0	0	0	0	0	0
Heating Degree Days (base 65°F)	1,010	835	792	611	374	147	25	31	157	432	756	983	6,153
Cooling Degree Days (base 65°F)	0	0	0	0	12	62	202	181	56	6	0	0	519
Mean Precipitation (in.)	2.18	2.16	1.96	0.74	0.88	0.75	0.33	0.40	0.63	0.86	1.75	1.87	14.51
Days With ≥ 0.1" Precipitation	5	5	5	2	3	2	1	1	2	2	4	4	36
Days With ≥ 1.0" Precipitation	0	0	0	0	0	0	0	0	0	0	0	0	0
Mean Snowfall (in.)	14.5	15.3	9.8	2.2	1.4	0.1	trace	trace	0.3	0.8	7.1	13.2	64.7
Days With ≥ 1.0" Snow Depth	16	14	6	2	1	0	0	0	0	1	5	11	56

Wells *Elko County*   Elevation: 5,698 ft.   Latitude: 41° 06' N   Longitude: 114° 58' W

	JAN	FEB	MAR	APR	MAY	JUN	JUL	AUG	SEP	OCT	NOV	DEC	YEAR
Mean Maximum Temp. (°F)	35.7	40.8	48.3	56.4	66.1	77.2	86.5	85.0	74.7	61.8	46.2	36.7	59.6
Mean Temp. (°F)	23.9	28.7	35.8	42.1	50.4	59.5	67.3	65.6	56.1	44.7	33.1	24.3	44.3
Mean Minimum Temp. (°F)	11.9	16.7	23.3	27.7	34.7	41.8	47.9	46.1	37.4	27.5	20.0	11.7	28.9
Extreme Maximum Temp. (°F)	62	66	72	83	89	98	99	98	93	83	73	61	99
Extreme Minimum Temp. (°F)	-25	-27	-17	4	14	21	29	22	14	-9	-15	-36	-36
Days Maximum Temp. ≥ 90°F	0	0	0	0	0	2	11	7	0	0	0	0	20
Days Maximum Temp. ≤ 32°F	11	5	1	0	0	0	0	0	0	0	3	9	29
Days Minimum Temp. ≤ 32°F	30	27	28	23	12	3	0	1	8	23	27	30	212
Days Minimum Temp. ≤ 0°F	6	3	0	0	0	0	0	0	0	0	1	6	16
Heating Degree Days (base 65°F)	1,269	1,018	898	680	445	182	31	52	269	623	949	1,256	7,672
Cooling Degree Days (base 65°F)	0	0	0	0	1	23	103	80	9	0	0	0	216
Mean Precipitation (in.)	0.94	0.82	1.03	0.92	1.25	0.95	0.46	0.41	0.96	0.78	1.03	0.87	10.42
Days With ≥ 0.1" Precipitation	3	3	4	3	4	3	1	1	2	3	3	3	33
Days With ≥ 1.0" Precipitation	0	0	0	0	0	0	0	0	0	0	0	0	0
Mean Snowfall (in.)	9.5	8.2	7.8	4.1	1.7	trace	0.0	0.0	0.1	1.2	6.0	9.5	48.1
Days With ≥ 1.0" Snow Depth	19	14	6	1	0	0	0	0	0	1	6	16	63

Yerington *Lyon County*   Elevation: 4,379 ft.   Latitude: 39° 00' N   Longitude: 119° 10' W

	JAN	FEB	MAR	APR	MAY	JUN	JUL	AUG	SEP	OCT	NOV	DEC	YEAR
Mean Maximum Temp. (°F)	46.0	53.5	59.7	66.4	74.9	84.3	91.9	90.5	82.3	70.3	56.1	46.6	68.5
Mean Temp. (°F)	33.1	38.9	44.6	50.4	58.5	66.7	73.2	71.6	63.6	53.0	41.2	32.9	52.3
Mean Minimum Temp. (°F)	20.2	24.1	29.5	34.4	42.0	49.2	54.5	52.7	44.9	35.6	26.2	19.2	36.0
Extreme Maximum Temp. (°F)	71	76	83	92	97	101	103	105	99	89	78	69	105
Extreme Minimum Temp. (°F)	-14	-23	4	11	18	30	35	37	25	7	2	-17	-23
Days Maximum Temp. ≥ 90°F	0	0	0	0	1	9	22	20	6	0	0	0	58
Days Maximum Temp. ≤ 32°F	3	1	0	0	0	0	0	0	0	0	0	2	6
Days Minimum Temp. ≤ 32°F	28	24	20	12	3	0	0	0	1	10	24	28	150
Days Minimum Temp. ≤ 0°F	1	0	0	0	0	0	0	0	0	0	0	1	2
Heating Degree Days (base 65°F)	981	733	625	431	218	56	4	10	96	368	706	988	5,216
Cooling Degree Days (base 65°F)	0	0	0	1	27	114	264	235	70	2	0	0	713
Mean Precipitation (in.)	0.49	0.54	0.58	0.41	0.76	0.53	0.30	0.35	0.25	0.41	0.37	0.37	5.36
Days With ≥ 0.1" Precipitation	2	2	2	1	2	1	1	1	1	1	1	1	16
Days With ≥ 1.0" Precipitation	0	0	0	0	0	0	0	0	0	0	0	0	0
Mean Snowfall (in.)	*1.5*	*1.5*	*0.8*	trace	trace	trace	0.0	0.0	0.1	0.2	*0.4*	*0.4*	*4.9*
Days With ≥ 1.0" Snow Depth	na	na	*0*	0	0	0	0	0	0	0	*1*	na	na

Note: See Appendix D for explanation of data.

NEW HAMPSHIRE

PHYSICAL FEATURES. New Hampshire occupies 9,304 square miles. From below the 43d parallel of latitude it extends nearly 200 miles northward to beyond the 45th parallel. At its southern border, New Hampshire extends westward from the Atlantic coastline for nearly 100 miles. It narrows to less than 20 miles in width at its northern tip. The eastern border lies near 71 W. longitude. Its western border is the Connecticut River, except in the extreme north.

The terrain is hilly to mountainous. Elevations of less than 500 feet above sea level are found only in the coastal area of the southeast, the Merrimac River Valley, and the central and southern portions of the Connecticut River Valley. Elsewhere the general elevation is from 500 to 1,500 feet, excepting up to near 2,500 feet in the extreme north. Numerous hills and mountains extend to heights of 2,000 to 4,000 feet above sea level over most of the State except in the southeast. Many White Mountain peaks rise above 4,000 feet; Mt. Washington reaches 6,288 feet above sea level. This is the highest mountain in the northeastern United States.

The glacier of the great Ice Age accounts for much of the topography, including many of the 1,300 lakes and ponds. The largest is Lake Winnepesaukee which covers an area of 71 square miles in the central part of the State. Inland waters cover about 280 square miles. The two principal rivers in the State are the Connecticut and the Merrimack Rivers, both of which flow in a southerly direction.

GENERAL CLIMATE. Characteristics of New Hampshire climate are: (1) changeableness of the weather, (2) large range of temperature, both daily and annual, (3) great differences between the same seasons in different years, (4) equable distribution of precipitation, and (5) considerable diversity from place to place. The regional climatic influences are modified in New Hampshire by varying distances from the ocean, elevations, and types of terrain. The State has been divided into two climatological divisions (Northern and Southern) which take into account the main features of these modifying factors.

New Hampshire lies in the "prevailing westerlies", the belt of generally eastward air movement which encircles the globe in middle latitudes. Embedded in this circulation are extensive masses of air originating in higher or lower latitudes and interacting to produce low-pressure storm systems. Relative to most other sections of the country, a large number of such storms pass over or near New Hampshire. The majority of air masses affecting this State belong to three types: (1) cold, dry air pouring down from subarctic North America, (2) warm, moist air streaming up on a long overland journey from the Gulf of Mexico and eastward, and (3) cool, damp air moving in from the North Atlantic. Because the atmospheric flow is usually offshore, New Hampshire is more influenced by the first two types than it is by the third.

The procession of contrasting air masses and the relatively frequent passage of storms bring about approximately twice-weekly alternation from fair to cloudy or stormy conditions, often attended by abrupt changes in temperature, moisture, sunshine, wind direction and speed. There is no regular or persistent rhythm to this sequence, and it is interrupted by periods during which the weather patterns continue the same for several days, infrequently for several weeks. New Hampshire weather, however, is cited for variety rather than monotony.

The Northern Division is the area least affected by the ocean influences and most affected by higher elevations as well as by its more northerly latitude. In the Southern Division, lower elevation and latitude tend to cause higher temperatures, though this is modified seasonally by ocean influences.

TEMPERATURE. The annual temperature averages near 41°F. in the Northern Division and near 46°F. in the Southern. Summer temperatures are comfortable for the most part. They are reasonably uniform over the State, excepting topographical extremes. Hot days with maxima of 90°F. or higher average from only a few per year in the extreme north to 5 to 15 per year over most of the rest of the State. Average temperatures vary from place to place more in the winter than in summer. Days with subzero readings are relatively few along the immediate coast but are common inland. They average from 25 to 50 in number per year in most of the Northern Division and from 10 to 25 in the Southern Division. The average date of the last freezing temperature in spring ranges from early in June at the colder locations to late in April at a few southern stations. For most of the State the growing season begins in May and usually ends in the latter part of September.

PRECIPITATION. New Hampshire is fortunate in having its precipitation rather evenly distributed through the year. Low pressure, or frontal, storm systems are the principal year-round moisture producers. This activity ebbs somewhat in summer, but thunderstorms are of increased activity at this time, tending to make up the difference. Though brief and often of small extent, the thunderstorms produce the heaviest local rainfall intensities. Rains of one to two inches in one hour can be expected at least once in a 10-year period. Prolonged droughts are infrequent; shorter dry spells in summer are fairly common. Widespread floods are infrequent. Floods occur most often in the spring when they are caused by a combination of rain and melting snow.

Total annual precipitation averages near 44 inches in the Northern Division and 41 inches in the Southern. The distribution is quite uniform over the Southern Division. The mountainous character of much of central and northern New Hampshire, and the generally higher elevations there, account for the greater annual totals and variability from place to place. Considerable rain or wet snow falls along the coast in winter, while farther inland snow is more generally the rule. Occasionally freezing rain occurs, coating exposed surfaces with troublesome ice. This problem is less frequent in northern New Hampshire. Most areas can expect at least one occurrence of glaze in the season. Measurable amounts of precipitation fall on an average of one day in three. Frequency is higher at higher elevations and in extreme northern New Hampshire, up to 140 to 150 days per year.

SNOWFALL. Average annual amounts of snowfall in the Southern Division increase from around 50 inches near the coast to 60 to 80 inches inland. Totals vary greatly in the Northern Division. Along the Connecticut River in the southern portion, totals average near 60 inches but increase to over 100 inches at the higher elevations of the northern and western portions. The summit of Mt. Washington receives nearly 185 inches. Bethlehem, only about 20 miles to the west, receives only about 70 inches per year. The number of days with one inch or more of snowfall varies from near 20 per season over much of the Southern Division up to 30 to 40 in the Northern Division and even to 50 or more at the highest elevations.

Snow cover is continuous through the whole winter season as a rule. Most frequent exceptions are found along the immediate coast and sometimes in extreme southern New Hampshire. Snow cover reaches its maximum depth, on the average, during the latter half of February in the Southern Division. In the Northern Division, the greatest depth comes in early March. Water stored in the snow makes an important contribution to a continuous water supply. The spring melting is usually too gradual to produce serious flooding.

OTHER CLIMATIC ELEMENTS. Sunshine averages over 50 percent of the possible amount in the Southern Division. and the lower elevations of the Northern Division. Higher elevations and peaks are cloudier, especially in winter, reducing the percentage to less than 50 percent generally. Mt. Washington reports an average of only 33 percent. Persistent fogs are sometimes experienced along the coast and on the higher elevations inland. Duration of fogs diminishes inland over flat and valley locations. But the shorter duration heavy ground fogs of early morning occur frequently at susceptible places in these areas. The number of days with fog probably varies from about 20 to 90 per year over the State.

The prevailing wind, on a yearly basis, comes from a westerly direction. It is predominantly from the northwest in winter and from the southwest in summer. Along the coast in spring and summer the sea breeze is important. These onshore winds, from the cool ocean, may come inland for 10 miles or so.

Coastal storms or "northeasters" can be a serious weather hazard in southeastern New Hampshire, decreasing in importance northward. They generate very strong winds and heavy rain or snow. They can produce abnormally high wind-driven tides. Occasionally in summer or fall storms of tropical origin affect New Hampshire. These may be similar (except for snow) to the northeasters. Only a very few retain near or full hurricane force. Tornadoes are not common phenomena, yet many years may have one or more. Most tornadoes are small, affecting a very localized area. About 80 percent of tornadoes occur between May 15 and September 15. Thunder and hailstorms have a similar frequency maximum from mid-spring to early fall. Thunderstorms occur on 15 to 30 days per year. The most severe are attended by hail.

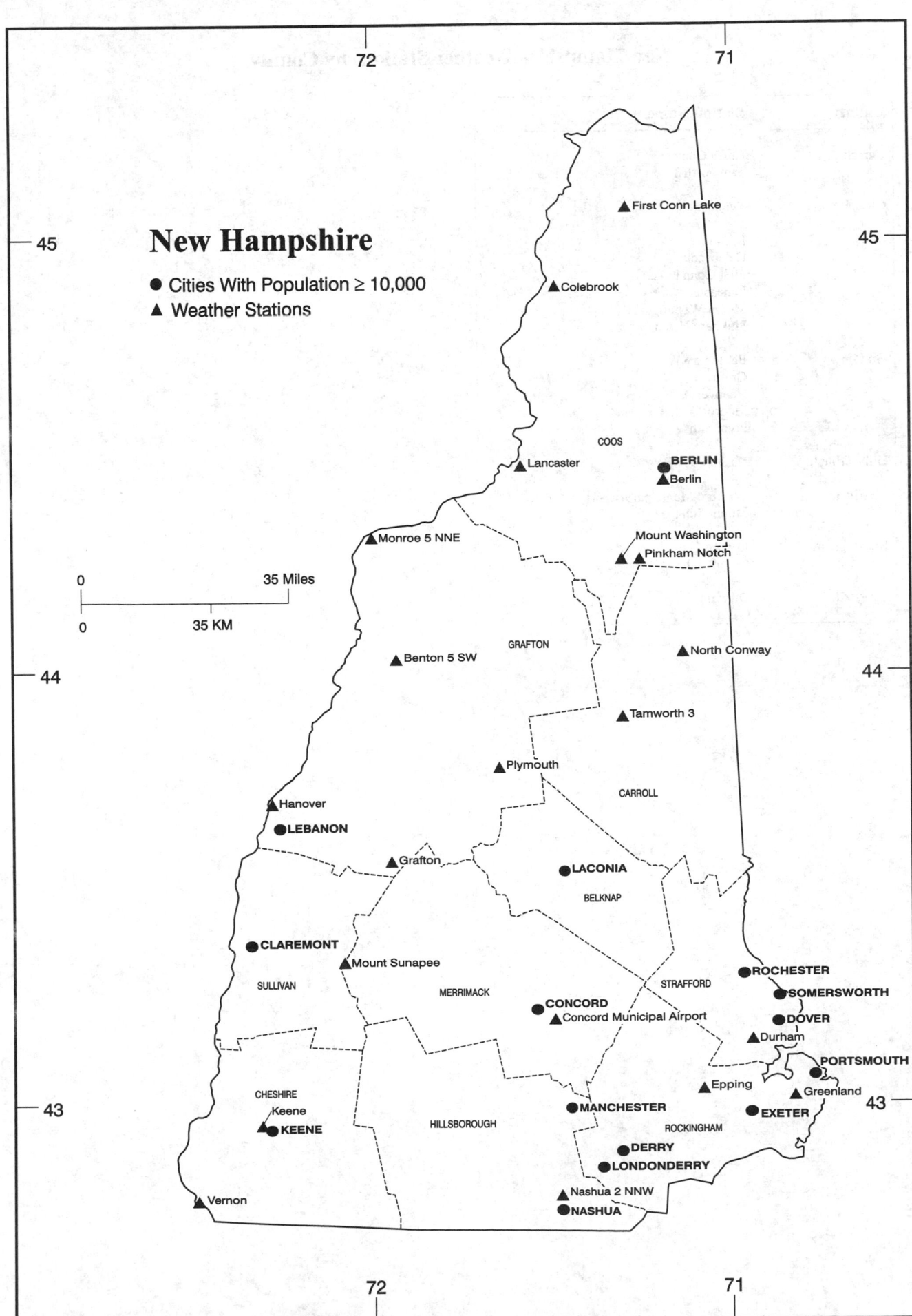

New Hampshire

● Cities With Population ≥ 10,000
▲ Weather Stations

▲ First Conn Lake

▲ Colebrook

COOS

▲ Lancaster

● BERLIN
▲ Berlin

▲ Monroe 5 NNE

Mount Washington
▲ ▲ Pinkham Notch

0   35 Miles

0   35 KM

▲ Benton 5 SW

GRAFTON

▲ North Conway

▲ Tamworth 3

▲ Plymouth

CARROLL

▲ Hanover
● LEBANON

▲ Grafton

● LACONIA

BELKNAP

● CLAREMONT

▲ Mount Sunapee

● ROCHESTER

● SOMERSWORTH

SULLIVAN

MERRIMACK

STRAFFORD

● CONCORD
▲ Concord Municipal Airport

● DOVER
▲ Durham

PORTSMOUTH
●

CHESHIRE

Keene

HILLSBOROUGH

● MANCHESTER

▲ Epping

▲ Greenland

● EXETER

▲● KEENE

ROCKINGHAM

● DERRY
● LONDONDERRY

▲ Vernon

▲ Nashua 2 NNW
● NASHUA

New Hampshire Weather Stations by County

County	Station Name
Carroll	North Conway
	Tamworth 3
Cheshire	Keene
Coos	Berlin
	Colebrook
	First Conn Lake
	Lancaster
	Mount Washington
	Pinkham Notch
Grafton	Benton 5 SW
	Grafton
	Hanover
	Monroe 5 NNE
	Plymouth
Hillsborough	Nashua 2 NNW
Merrimack	Concord Municipal Airport
	Mount Sunapee
Rockingham	Epping
	Greenland
Strafford	Durham

New Hampshire Weather Stations by City

City	Station Name	Miles
Berlin	Berlin	2
	Lancaster	20
	Mount Washington	16
	Pinkham Notch	15
Claremont	Mount Sunapee	13
	Bellows Falls, VT	17
	Cavendish, VT	13
Concord	Concord Municipal Airport	3
Derry	Haverhill, MA	15
	Lawrence, MA	15
	Epping	15
	Nashua 2 NNW	11
Dover	Sanford 2 NNW, ME	20
	Durham	5
	Epping	15
	Greenland	12
Exeter	Haverhill, MA	16
	Durham	12
	Epping	8
	Greenland	7
Keene	Keene	2
	Bellows Falls, VT	16
	Vernon, VT	17
Laconia	Plymouth	19
Lebanon	Grafton	16
	Hanover	4
Londonderry	Haverhill, MA	16
	Lawrence, MA	14
	Epping	19
	Nashua 2 NNW	8
Manchester	Concord Municipal Airport	15
	Epping	19
	Nashua 2 NNW	14
Nashua	Lawrence, MA	16
	Nashua 2 NNW	2
Portsmouth	Durham	10
	Epping	16
	Greenland	4
Rochester	Sanford 2 NNW, ME	15
	Durham	11
	Epping	20
Somersworth	Sanford 2 NNW, ME	16
	Durham	8
	Epping	18
	Greenland	16

Note: Miles is the distance between the geographic center of the city and the weather station.

New Hampshire Weather Stations by Elevation

Feet	Station Name
6,259	Mount Washington
2,007	Pinkham Notch
1,660	First Conn Lake
1,269	Mount Sunapee
1,197	Benton 5 SW
1,040	Colebrook
928	Berlin
859	Lancaster
830	Grafton
787	Tamworth 3
659	Monroe 5 NNE
659	Plymouth
600	Hanover
528	North Conway
508	Keene
344	Concord Municipal Airport
157	Epping
127	Nashua 2 NNW
82	Greenland
78	Durham

Concord Municipal Airport

Concord, the Capital of New Hampshire, is situated near the geographical center of New England at an altitude of approximately 300 feet above sea level on the Merrimack River. Its surroundings are hilly with many lakes and ponds. The countryside is generously wooded, mostly on land reclaimed from fields which were formerly cleared for farming. From the coast about 50 miles to the southeast, the terrain slopes gently upward to the city. West of the city, the land rises some 2,000 feet higher in only half that distance. Mount Washington, at an elevation of 6,288 feet is in the White Mountains 75 miles north of town.

Northwesterly winds are prevalent. They bring cold, dry air during the winter and pleasantly cool, dry air in the summer. Stronger southerly winds occur during July and August, and easterly winds usually accompany summer and winter storms. Winter breezes are somewhat lighter, and winds are frequently calm during the night and early morning hours. Low temperatures, as a rule, do not interrupt normal out-of-doors activity because winds are calm or light, producing a low wind chill factor.

Very hot summer weather is infrequent. During any month, temperatures considerably above the average maxima and much below the normal minima are observed.

The average amount of precipitation for the warmer half of the year differs little from that for the colder half. Precipitation occurrences average approximately one day of three for the year, with a somewhat higher frequency for the April-May period, offsetting the lower frequency of August-October. The more significant rains and heavier snowfalls are associated with easterly winds, especially northeasterly winds. The first snowfall of an inch or more is likely to come between the middle of November and the middle of December. The snow cover normally lasts from mid-December until the last week of March, but bare ground is not rare in the winter, nor is a snowscape rare earlier or later in the season. Rain, sleet, or freezing rain may also occur.

Agriculture is neither intensive nor large-scale in the vicinity of the station. Potatoes and other frost-resistant vegetables, hardy fruits such as apples, forage for the dairy industry, and maple sugar are the principal crops.

Based on the 1951-1980 period, the average first occurrence of 32 degrees Fahrenheit in the fall is September 22 and the average last occurrence in the spring is May 23. Freezing temperatures have occurred as late as June and as early as August.

Concord Municipal Airport *Merrimack County*   Elevation: 344 ft.   Latitude: 43° 12' N   Longitude: 71° 30' W

	JAN	FEB	MAR	APR	MAY	JUN	JUL	AUG	SEP	OCT	NOV	DEC	YEAR
Mean Maximum Temp. (°F)	30.1	33.8	43.1	56.7	69.4	77.7	82.7	80.5	71.6	60.1	47.3	35.3	57.4
Mean Temp. (°F)	19.5	23.0	32.7	44.4	55.9	64.7	69.9	67.9	59.1	47.5	37.3	25.5	45.6
Mean Minimum Temp. (°F)	8.8	12.1	22.3	32.0	42.4	51.7	57.1	55.3	46.5	34.9	27.2	15.7	33.8
Extreme Maximum Temp. (°F)	63	67	89	95	96	98	101	101	95	87	78	73	101
Extreme Minimum Temp. (°F)	-33	-27	-13	11	23	30	37	30	26	10	-5	-21	-33
Days Maximum Temp. ≥ 90°F	0	0	0	0	1	2	5	3	0	0	0	0	11
Days Maximum Temp. ≤ 32°F	18	13	5	0	0	0	0	0	0	0	2	12	50
Days Minimum Temp. ≤ 32°F	30	27	26	17	5	0	0	0	2	14	22	29	172
Days Minimum Temp. ≤ 0°F	9	6	1	0	0	0	0	0	0	0	0	4	20
Heating Degree Days (base 65°F)	1,404	1,181	994	615	294	87	20	41	205	537	825	1,218	7,421
Cooling Degree Days (base 65°F)	0	0	0	1	17	81	181	139	37	1	0	0	457
Mean Precipitation (in.)	2.90	2.40	3.02	3.03	3.34	3.07	3.31	3.25	3.15	3.50	3.56	2.96	37.49
Maximum Precipitation (in.)	8.1	7.8	7.8	5.9	9.5	7.8	6.5	7.3	7.8	8.8	7.4	7.5	49.3
Minimum Precipitation (in.)	0.4	trace	0.9	1.0	0.6	0.6	1.0	1.0	0.4	0.9	0.8	0.8	24.2
Maximum 24-hr. Precipitation (in.)	2.0	2.1	2.3	2.0	2.4	2.4	2.4	3.8	4.1	4.0	2.5	2.0	4.1
Days With ≥ 0.1" Precipitation	7	5	7	7	7	7	6	6	6	6	7	6	77
Days With ≥ 1.0" Precipitation	1	1	1	1	1	0	1	1	1	1	1	1	11
Mean Snowfall (in.)	18.5	12.9	11.3	3.1	trace	trace	0.0	0.0	trace	trace	4.2	13.9	63.9
Maximum Snowfall (in.)	45	50	38	15	1	0	0	0	trace	2	18	38	128
Maximum 24-hr. Snowfall (in.)	16	14	16	13	1	0	0	0	trace	2	9	12	16
Days With ≥ 1.0" Snow Depth	25	22	15	2	0	0	0	0	0	0	4	17	85
Thunderstorm Days	< 1	< 1	< 1	1	2	4	5	4	2	1	< 1	< 1	19
Foggy Days	11	10	13	13	15	17	17	20	21	17	15	13	182
Predominant Sky Cover	OVR	OVR	OVR	OVR	OVR	OVR	OVR	OVR	OVR	OVR	OVR	OVR	OVR
Mean Relative Humidity 7am (%)	76	76	76	75	76	80	83	87	89	87	83	79	81
Mean Relative Humidity 4pm (%)	59	54	52	46	47	51	51	53	55	53	61	63	54
Mean Dewpoint (°F)	12	13	21	31	42	54	59	58	50	39	29	17	35
Prevailing Wind Direction	NW	NW	NW	NW	NW	NW	NW	NW	NW	NW	NW	NW	NW
Prevailing Wind Speed (mph)	12	12	12	12	10	10	9	9	9	10	10	12	10
Maximum Wind Gust (mph)	53	60	56	61	52	59	53	45	52	48	53	58	61

Mount Washington

The Mount Washington Observatory is located at the summit of Mount Washington, New Hampshire, highest mountain of the Presidential range. The weather is very severe most of the year, conditions approximating those that would be encountered at a much higher latitude. The upper limits of timberline extend to 4,500 to 5,000 feet.

Prevailing winds are from the west and west-northwest, although the most severe storms are usually from the southeast. Winds are stronger at the summit than at the same elevation at a distance from the mountain, due to the Bernouilli effect. Mount Washington is near the mid-point of a 60-mile-long mountain front trending northeast to southwest. Wind speeds in excess of 100 mph are not uncommon, and the stations highest measured wind, 231 mph, still stands as a world record.

The station is in the clouds approximately 55 percent of the time. This is due partly to the effect of orographic uplift and partly due to the fact that the summit is often above the cloud base when there are low clouds in the area.

Minimum temperatures are not extreme compared to some U. S. valley stations. Annual temperature variations are not as great as they are in the surrounding lowlands, which may actually be colder than the summit when there is a strong inversion. Rime or glaze icing occurs often in winter, when the mountain is frequently in supercooled clouds.

Because of its severe climate, Mount Washington has for many years been used as a natural laboratory for cloud physics research and for the development and testing of instruments, aircraft components, and structures which are required to withstand high winds and icing conditions.

Mount Washington *Coos County*   Elevation: 6,259 ft.   Latitude: 44° 16' N   Longitude: 71° 18' W

	JAN	FEB	MAR	APR	MAY	JUN	JUL	AUG	SEP	OCT	NOV	DEC	YEAR
Mean Maximum Temp. (°F)	13.1	14.2	20.7	29.3	41.6	50.2	54.2	52.9	45.8	36.2	27.1	18.1	33.6
Mean Temp. (°F)	4.5	6.1	13.2	22.9	35.6	44.4	48.9	47.5	40.2	30.2	20.4	10.0	27.0
Mean Minimum Temp. (°F)	-4.1	-2.1	5.6	16.4	29.5	38.5	43.5	42.1	34.6	24.2	13.6	1.8	20.3
Extreme Maximum Temp. (°F)	47	43	55	60	66	67	70	72	69	57	52	45	72
Extreme Minimum Temp. (°F)	-44	-39	-32	-20	2	13	25	20	9	-2	-17	-37	-44
Days Maximum Temp. ≥ 90°F	0	0	0	0	0	0	0	0	0	0	0	0	0
Days Maximum Temp. ≤ 32°F	29	26	25	19	6	1	0	0	2	11	20	27	166
Days Minimum Temp. ≤ 32°F	31	28	30	28	19	7	2	3	12	24	28	31	243
Days Minimum Temp. ≤ 0°F	19	16	11	2	0	0	0	0	0	0	4	13	65
Heating Degree Days (base 65°F)	1,872	1,662	1,602	1,258	906	612	492	535	736	1,072	1,332	1,703	13,782
Cooling Degree Days (base 65°F)	0	0	0	0	0	0	0	0	0	0	0	0	0
Mean Precipitation (in.)	8.46	7.85	9.67	8.35	8.15	8.31	7.81	8.12	8.63	7.67	10.45	8.96	102.43
Maximum Precipitation (in.)	18.2	25.6	16.0	15.2	18.8	16.0	15.5	20.7	15.5	21.3	19.6	17.9	130.
Minimum Precipitation (in.)	1.3	1.0	2.7	2.2	1.8	2.4	2.7	2.8	2.7	2.2	3.2	1.5	56.2
Maximum 24-hr. Precipitation (in.)	4.4	8.4	4.5	8.2	3.4	5.4	5.8	6.6	5.1	9.7	4.9	7.4	9.7
Days With ≥ 0.1" Precipitation	16	13	15	13	13	12	12	11	12	12	15	16	160
Days With ≥ 1.0" Precipitation	2	2	3	2	2	2	2	2	3	2	3	2	27
Mean Snowfall (in.)	52.5	44.5	56.3	42.5	12.8	1.1	trace	0.1	2.4	12.5	39.7	51.0	315.4
Maximum Snowfall (in.)	95	124	98	111	52	8	1	3	8	34	87	92	449
Maximum 24-hr. Snowfall (in.)	23	28	27	23	23	5	1	2	8	15	20	26	28
Days With ≥ 1.0" Snow Depth	30	28	31	27	11	1	0	0	1	9	20	29	187
Thunderstorm Days	< 1	< 1	< 1	1	2	3	4	3	1	1	< 1	< 1	15
Foggy Days	29	25	28	26	25	26	29	29	27	26	27	29	326
Predominant Sky Cover	na	na	na	na	na	na	na	na	na	na	na	na	na
Mean Relative Humidity 7am (%)	na	na	na	na	na	na	na	na	na	na	na	na	na
Mean Relative Humidity 4pm (%)	na	na	na	na	na	na	na	na	na	na	na	na	na
Mean Dewpoint (°F)	na	na	na	na	na	na	na	na	na	na	na	na	na
Prevailing Wind Direction	na	na	na	na	na	na	na	na	na	na	na	na	na
Prevailing Wind Speed (mph)	na	na	na	na	na	na	na	na	na	na	na	na	na
Maximum Wind Gust (mph)	153	166	148	229	129	127	119	142	174	150	229	178	229

Benton 5 SW *Grafton County*   Elevation: 1,197 ft.   Latitude: 44° 02' N   Longitude: 71° 56' W

	JAN	FEB	MAR	APR	MAY	JUN	JUL	AUG	SEP	OCT	NOV	DEC	YEAR
Mean Maximum Temp. (°F)	27.0	30.0	39.1	52.0	65.8	73.7	78.0	75.7	67.0	55.9	43.0	31.6	53.2
Mean Temp. (°F)	17.1	19.8	29.4	41.6	54.1	62.3	66.7	64.6	56.3	45.8	35.0	22.9	43.0
Mean Minimum Temp. (°F)	7.3	9.5	19.6	31.1	42.4	50.8	55.3	53.4	45.6	35.7	26.8	14.1	32.6
Extreme Maximum Temp. (°F)	59	63	78	88	89	93	95	94	88	81	71	64	95
Extreme Minimum Temp. (°F)	-29	-26	-17	4	21	30	37	32	23	15	-2	-28	-29
Days Maximum Temp. ≥ 90°F	0	0	0	0	0	0	1	0	0	0	0	0	1
Days Maximum Temp. ≤ 32°F	20	17	8	1	0	0	0	0	0	0	5	16	67
Days Minimum Temp. ≤ 32°F	30	27	28	18	4	0	0	0	2	12	22	30	173
Days Minimum Temp. ≤ 0°F	11	8	2	0	0	0	0	0	0	0	0	5	26
Heating Degree Days (base 65°F)	1,479	1,273	1,098	697	340	125	44	77	269	589	895	1,299	8,185
Cooling Degree Days (base 65°F)	0	0	0	0	1	8	49	102	71	16	0	0	247
Mean Precipitation (in.)	2.57	1.97	2.57	2.67	3.38	3.78	3.85	4.18	3.67	3.59	3.41	2.48	38.12
Days With ≥ 0.1" Precipitation	6	5	7	7	8	8	8	7	7	7	7	7	84
Days With ≥ 1.0" Precipitation	0	0	0	0	1	1	1	1	1	1	1	0	7
Mean Snowfall (in.)	16.1	12.8	13.8	5.5	trace	0.0	0.0	0.0	trace	0.4	5.7	15.4	69.7
Days With ≥ 1.0" Snow Depth	28	25	21	5	0	0	0	0	0	0	7	21	107

Berlin *Coos County*   Elevation: 928 ft.   Latitude: 44° 27' N   Longitude: 71° 11' W

	JAN	FEB	MAR	APR	MAY	JUN	JUL	AUG	SEP	OCT	NOV	DEC	YEAR
Mean Maximum Temp. (°F)	26.4	29.6	38.8	51.4	66.0	*74.3*	78.9	*76.9*	68.3	56.2	43.2	31.2	*53.4*
Mean Temp. (°F)	15.1	17.9	27.8	40.6	53.5	*62.4*	66.8	*64.8*	56.1	45.1	34.4	21.4	*42.2*
Mean Minimum Temp. (°F)	3.9	6.2	16.8	29.8	40.9	*50.4*	54.7	*52.6*	44.0	34.0	25.6	11.7	*30.9*
Extreme Maximum Temp. (°F)	65	64	77	89	93	*95*	98	96	91	82	72	67	98
Extreme Minimum Temp. (°F)	-32	-29	-28	3	24	*32*	35	33	25	8	-4	-26	*-32*
Days Maximum Temp. ≥ 90°F	0	0	0	0	0	1	2	1	0	0	0	0	4
Days Maximum Temp. ≤ 32°F	21	16	9	1	0	0	0	0	0	0	4	17	68
Days Minimum Temp. ≤ 32°F	31	28	28	19	5	0	0	0	3	14	23	30	181
Days Minimum Temp. ≤ 0°F	13	11	4	0	0	0	0	0	0	0	0	7	35
Heating Degree Days (base 65°F)	1,541	1,323	1,145	724	360	*127*	46	*81*	274	611	912	1,345	*8,489*
Cooling Degree Days (base 65°F)	0	0	0	0	8	55	113	83	17	1	0	0	277
Mean Precipitation (in.)	2.77	2.18	2.89	3.09	3.35	3.92	3.68	4.12	3.57	4.08	3.65	2.98	40.28
Days With ≥ 0.1" Precipitation	6	5	7	7	8	9	8	7	7	7	7	7	*85*
Days With ≥ 1.0" Precipitation	1	0	0	1	1	1	1	1	1	1	1	0	9
Mean Snowfall (in.)	19.9	16.7	15.9	5.5	trace	0.0	0.0	0.0	trace	0.2	5.6	18.8	82.6
Days With ≥ 1.0" Snow Depth	30	27	24	6	0	0	0	0	0	0	5	22	114

Colebrook *Coos County*   Elevation: 1,040 ft.   Latitude: 44° 54' N   Longitude: 71° 29' W

	JAN	FEB	MAR	APR	MAY	JUN	JUL	AUG	SEP	OCT	NOV	DEC	YEAR
Mean Maximum Temp. (°F)	24.5	28.4	38.0	51.1	65.7	73.1	77.5	75.1	66.5	55.0	41.7	29.1	52.1
Mean Temp. (°F)	12.8	15.9	26.5	39.3	52.1	60.6	65.0	63.0	54.9	44.2	33.1	19.5	40.6
Mean Minimum Temp. (°F)	1.1	3.4	15.0	27.4	38.3	48.0	52.5	50.8	43.3	33.3	24.3	9.8	28.9
Extreme Maximum Temp. (°F)	61	61	79	86	90	92	94	95	94	81	71	62	95
Extreme Minimum Temp. (°F)	-38	-40	-29	-5	19	27	31	29	18	7	-13	-38	-40
Days Maximum Temp. ≥ 90°F	0	0	0	0	0	0	0	0	0	0	0	0	0
Days Maximum Temp. ≤ 32°F	22	17	10	1	0	0	0	0	0	0	6	18	74
Days Minimum Temp. ≤ 32°F	31	27	29	22	9	1	0	0	4	15	24	30	192
Days Minimum Temp. ≤ 0°F	15	13	6	0	0	0	0	0	0	0	1	8	43
Heating Degree Days (base 65°F)	1,613	1,381	1,186	765	401	162	71	110	308	638	950	1,404	8,989
Cooling Degree Days (base 65°F)	0	0	0	0	7	35	83	57	11	0	0	0	193
Mean Precipitation (in.)	2.80	1.98	2.64	2.48	3.71	4.23	4.16	4.54	3.75	3.48	3.38	2.87	40.02
Days With ≥ 0.1" Precipitation	6	6	6	7	8	9	8	9	7	8	8	8	90
Days With ≥ 1.0" Precipitation	0	0	0	0	1	1	1	1	1	1	0	0	6
Mean Snowfall (in.)	21.2	*16.7*	14.8	4.8	trace	0.0	0.0	0.0	trace	0.5	8.9	21.6	*88.5*
Days With ≥ 1.0" Snow Depth	29	28	25	7	0	0	0	0	0	0	9	25	123

Durham *Strafford County*   Elevation: 78 ft.   Latitude: 43° 09' N   Longitude: 70° 57' W

	JAN	FEB	MAR	APR	MAY	JUN	JUL	AUG	SEP	OCT	NOV	DEC	YEAR
Mean Maximum Temp. (°F)	33.3	36.9	45.5	57.6	69.2	78.0	83.4	81.3	73.1	61.8	49.3	37.7	58.9
Mean Temp. (°F)	22.8	26.1	34.8	45.4	56.1	65.1	70.5	68.6	60.5	49.5	39.3	28.2	47.2
Mean Minimum Temp. (°F)	12.3	15.3	24.0	33.1	42.9	52.1	57.5	55.8	47.8	37.2	29.3	18.7	35.5
Extreme Maximum Temp. (°F)	62	71	89	91	94	96	99	102	95	86	76	74	102
Extreme Minimum Temp. (°F)	-30	-21	-12	14	22	30	37	32	24	14	-7	-22	-30
Days Maximum Temp. ≥ 90°F	0	0	0	0	1	2	5	3	1	0	0	0	12
Days Maximum Temp. ≤ 32°F	14	9	3	0	0	0	0	0	0	0	1	9	36
Days Minimum Temp. ≤ 32°F	30	26	25	15	3	0	0	0	2	10	19	28	158
Days Minimum Temp. ≤ 0°F	6	3	1	0	0	0	0	0	0	0	0	2	12
Heating Degree Days (base 65°F)	1,301	1,091	930	584	288	77	13	31	171	475	764	1,133	6,858
Cooling Degree Days (base 65°F)	0	0	0	1	16	88	193	147	44	2	0	0	491
Mean Precipitation (in.)	3.04	2.83	3.47	4.01	3.60	3.41	3.22	3.41	3.48	4.11	4.42	3.60	42.60
Days With ≥ 0.1" Precipitation	7	5	7	7	8	7	6	6	6	6	7	7	79
Days With ≥ 1.0" Precipitation	1	1	1	1	1	1	1	1	1	1	1	1	12
Mean Snowfall (in.)	14.9	9.5	8.7	2.0	0.0	0.0	0.0	0.0	0.0	0.1	2.6	11.9	49.7
Days With ≥ 1.0" Snow Depth	22	19	12	1	0	0	0	0	0	0	2	15	71

Epping *Rockingham County*   Elevation: 157 ft.   Latitude: 43° 02' N   Longitude: 71° 05' W

	JAN	FEB	MAR	APR	MAY	JUN	JUL	AUG	SEP	OCT	NOV	DEC	YEAR
Mean Maximum Temp. (°F)	32.7	36.5	45.2	57.2	69.4	78.0	83.1	80.8	72.5	61.2	48.8	37.1	58.5
Mean Temp. (°F)	22.7	26.0	34.7	45.3	56.3	65.2	70.4	68.5	60.1	49.0	39.1	28.0	47.1
Mean Minimum Temp. (°F)	12.6	15.4	24.2	33.2	43.1	52.3	57.7	56.0	47.7	36.8	29.3	18.8	35.6
Extreme Maximum Temp. (°F)	63	70	89	91	94	96	99	100	94	85	77	76	100
Extreme Minimum Temp. (°F)	-28	-29	-10	9	18	32	37	32	23	14	-5	-22	-29
Days Maximum Temp. ≥ 90°F	0	0	0	0	1	2	4	2	1	0	0	0	10
Days Maximum Temp. ≤ 32°F	15	10	3	0	0	0	0	0	0	0	1	10	39
Days Minimum Temp. ≤ 32°F	30	26	25	15	3	0	0	0	2	11	20	29	161
Days Minimum Temp. ≤ 0°F	6	4	0	0	0	0	0	0	0	0	0	2	12
Heating Degree Days (base 65°F)	1,306	1,096	931	587	282	76	15	32	181	490	772	1,141	6,909
Cooling Degree Days (base 65°F)	0	0	0	1	18	91	192	144	42	1	0	0	489
Mean Precipitation (in.)	3.51	3.09	3.69	4.09	3.61	3.58	3.36	3.43	3.83	4.09	4.26	3.88	44.42
Days With ≥ 0.1" Precipitation	7	6	7	7	7	7	7	6	6	6	7	7	80
Days With ≥ 1.0" Precipitation	1	1	1	1	1	1	1	1	1	1	1	1	12
Mean Snowfall (in.)	16.3	11.1	10.3	3.0	0.0	0.0	0.0	0.0	0.0	trace	3.1	12.4	56.2
Days With ≥ 1.0" Snow Depth	na	na	na	1	0	0	0	0	0	0	1	na	na

First Conn Lake *Coos County*   Elevation: 1,660 ft.   Latitude: 45° 05' N   Longitude: 71° 17' W

	JAN	FEB	MAR	APR	MAY	JUN	JUL	AUG	SEP	OCT	NOV	DEC	YEAR
Mean Maximum Temp. (°F)	20.6	23.9	33.7	45.8	60.6	69.3	73.7	71.7	63.1	51.2	37.7	25.8	48.1
Mean Temp. (°F)	8.8	10.9	21.4	35.2	48.7	58.0	62.7	60.4	52.1	41.2	29.7	16.1	37.1
Mean Minimum Temp. (°F)	-3.0	-2.3	9.0	24.5	36.8	46.7	51.5	49.1	41.1	31.3	21.7	6.3	26.1
Extreme Maximum Temp. (°F)	60	58	69	82	86	90	89	91	86	79	69	59	91
Extreme Minimum Temp. (°F)	-44	-40	-29	-10	18	25	29	28	18	8	-11	-33	-44
Days Maximum Temp. ≥ 90°F	0	0	0	0	0	0	0	0	0	0	0	0	0
Days Maximum Temp. ≤ 32°F	25	22	15	3	0	0	0	0	0	1	10	23	99
Days Minimum Temp. ≤ 32°F	31	28	30	25	10	1	0	0	5	18	26	31	205
Days Minimum Temp. ≤ 0°F	18	17	10	1	0	0	0	0	0	0	1	11	58
Heating Degree Days (base 65°F)	1,738	1,525	1,346	889	502	222	112	162	387	731	1,052	1,512	10,178
Cooling Degree Days (base 65°F)	0	0	0	0	1	19	43	27	4	0	0	0	94
Mean Precipitation (in.)	3.00	2.30	2.95	3.02	4.01	4.78	4.63	4.84	4.28	3.82	3.83	3.30	44.76
Days With ≥ 0.1" Precipitation	8	6	8	8	9	10	9	10	9	9	10	9	105
Days With ≥ 1.0" Precipitation	0	0	0	0	1	1	1	1	1	1	0	0	6
Mean Snowfall (in.)	33.3	26.3	27.0	11.5	1.1	0.0	0.0	0.0	trace	1.9	17.0	33.3	151.4
Days With ≥ 1.0" Snow Depth	31	28	31	22	2	0	0	0	0	1	14	29	158

Grafton *Grafton County*   Elevation: 830 ft.   Latitude: 43° 34' N   Longitude: 71° 57' W

	JAN	FEB	MAR	APR	MAY	JUN	JUL	AUG	SEP	OCT	NOV	DEC	YEAR
Mean Maximum Temp. (°F)	28.0	31.8	40.9	53.7	67.2	75.1	79.9	77.4	68.9	57.5	44.5	32.8	54.8
Mean Temp. (°F)	16.3	19.3	29.2	40.9	53.1	61.6	66.4	64.3	55.9	45.1	34.8	22.5	42.5
Mean Minimum Temp. (°F)	4.6	6.8	17.6	28.1	38.9	48.1	52.8	51.2	42.9	32.6	25.0	12.2	30.1
Extreme Maximum Temp. (°F)	60	63	80	92	92	94	95	97	90	83	74	70	97
Extreme Minimum Temp. (°F)	-40	-36	-25	3	19	27	31	28	21	9	-4	-29	-40
Days Maximum Temp. ≥ 90°F	0	0	0	0	0	1	2	1	0	0	0	0	4
Days Maximum Temp. ≤ 32°F	20	14	7	0	0	0	0	0	0	0	3	15	59
Days Minimum Temp. ≤ 32°F	31	27	29	21	9	1	0	0	6	17	24	30	195
Days Minimum Temp. ≤ 0°F	12	10	3	0	0	0	0	0	0	0	0	6	31
Heating Degree Days (base 65°F)	1,503	1,285	1,102	715	369	141	53	88	281	612	900	1,310	8,359
Cooling Degree Days (base 65°F)	0	0	0	0	6	43	99	69	14	0	0	0	231
Mean Precipitation (in.)	2.86	2.37	2.94	3.10	3.72	3.69	3.89	3.68	3.40	4.03	3.41	2.98	40.07
Days With ≥ 0.1" Precipitation	6	5	7	6	7	7	6	7	6	6	7	7	77
Days With ≥ 1.0" Precipitation	0	0	1	1	1	1	1	1	1	1	1	0	9
Mean Snowfall (in.)	21.5	14.9	13.9	5.4	trace	0.0	0.0	0.0	trace	0.3	6.1	16.8	78.9
Days With ≥ 1.0" Snow Depth	na	na	na	3	0	0	0	0	0	0	3	na	na

Greenland *Rockingham County*   Elevation: 82 ft.   Latitude: 43° 01' N   Longitude: 70° 50' W

	JAN	FEB	MAR	APR	MAY	JUN	JUL	AUG	SEP	OCT	NOV	DEC	YEAR
Mean Maximum Temp. (°F)	34.2	37.5	45.7	56.6	68.4	77.3	82.9	80.8	72.4	61.4	50.2	39.1	58.9
Mean Temp. (°F)	24.5	27.3	35.6	45.5	56.2	65.1	70.6	68.7	60.7	49.9	40.7	29.9	47.9
Mean Minimum Temp. (°F)	14.8	17.1	25.3	34.3	44.0	52.9	58.2	56.5	48.8	38.4	31.1	20.7	36.8
Extreme Maximum Temp. (°F)	62	72	89	93	94	96	101	104	95	86	78	75	104
Extreme Minimum Temp. (°F)	-26	-15	-6	13	15	33	38	33	23	17	-6	-17	-26
Days Maximum Temp. ≥ 90°F	0	0	0	0	1	2	4	3	1	0	0	0	11
Days Maximum Temp. ≤ 32°F	13	9	2	0	0	0	0	0	0	0	0	7	31
Days Minimum Temp. ≤ 32°F	29	26	23	13	3	0	0	0	1	9	18	27	149
Days Minimum Temp. ≤ 0°F	4	2	0	0	0	0	0	0	0	0	0	2	8
Heating Degree Days (base 65°F)	1,249	1,057	907	581	288	79	13	31	168	463	724	1,081	6,641
Cooling Degree Days (base 65°F)	0	0	1	1	18	87	190	147	46	2	0	0	492
Mean Precipitation (in.)	4.40	3.26	4.34	4.22	3.56	3.58	3.29	3.56	3.99	4.51	4.72	4.33	47.76
Days With ≥ 0.1" Precipitation	7	5	8	7	7	7	6	6	6	6	7	7	79
Days With ≥ 1.0" Precipitation	1	1	1	1	1	1	1	1	1	1	1	1	12
Mean Snowfall (in.)	17.5	10.7	9.5	2.5	0.0	0.0	0.0	0.0	0.0	trace	2.6	10.6	53.4
Days With ≥ 1.0" Snow Depth	20	19	11	1	0	0	0	0	0	0	2	12	65

Hanover *Grafton County* Elevation: 600 ft. Latitude: 43° 42' N Longitude: 72° 17' W

	JAN	FEB	MAR	APR	MAY	JUN	JUL	AUG	SEP	OCT	NOV	DEC	YEAR
Mean Maximum Temp. (°F)	28.7	33.4	42.7	56.5	70.1	77.9	82.8	80.5	70.9	58.2	45.4	32.9	56.7
Mean Temp. (°F)	18.5	22.3	32.1	44.4	56.9	65.3	70.4	68.5	59.9	47.9	37.2	24.2	45.6
Mean Minimum Temp. (°F)	8.3	11.1	21.6	32.4	43.6	52.6	58.1	56.5	48.9	37.5	29.0	15.5	34.6
Extreme Maximum Temp. (°F)	63	62	86	93	96	98	101	103	93	84	74	70	103
Extreme Minimum Temp. (°F)	-27	-26	-11	10	24	30	40	36	24	17	3	-27	-27
Days Maximum Temp. ≥ 90°F	0	0	0	0	1	2	5	2	0	0	0	0	10
Days Maximum Temp. ≤ 32°F	19	13	4	0	0	0	0	0	0	0	2	13	51
Days Minimum Temp. ≤ 32°F	30	27	27	16	3	0	0	0	1	10	20	27	161
Days Minimum Temp. ≤ 0°F	9	7	2	0	0	0	0	0	0	0	0	4	22
Heating Degree Days (base 65°F)	1,435	1,200	1,014	613	265	72	13	28	180	525	826	1,262	7,433
Cooling Degree Days (base 65°F)	0	0	0	2	18	86	196	150	37	1	0	0	490
Mean Precipitation (in.)	2.85	2.30	2.86	2.95	3.44	3.36	3.59	3.69	3.61	3.46	3.35	2.90	38.36
Days With ≥ 0.1" Precipitation	7	5	6	6	7	7	7	6	7	6	7	7	78
Days With ≥ 1.0" Precipitation	0	0	0	0	1	0	1	1	1	1	1	0	6
Mean Snowfall (in.)	18.8	12.1	11.2	2.0	0.0	0.0	0.0	0.0	trace	trace	4.0	15.7	63.8
Days With ≥ 1.0" Snow Depth	25	25	19	2	0	0	0	0	0	0	4	19	94

Keene *Cheshire County* Elevation: 508 ft. Latitude: 42° 57' N Longitude: 72° 19' W

	JAN	FEB	MAR	APR	MAY	JUN	JUL	AUG	SEP	OCT	NOV	DEC	YEAR
Mean Maximum Temp. (°F)	31.5	35.4	44.4	57.8	70.8	78.6	83.2	81.1	72.4	61.1	48.2	36.2	58.4
Mean Temp. (°F)	21.0	24.0	33.4	45.1	57.0	65.3	70.2	68.5	60.0	48.7	38.5	26.7	46.5
Mean Minimum Temp. (°F)	10.4	12.6	22.2	32.3	43.1	52.1	57.1	55.8	47.5	36.3	28.8	17.3	34.6
Extreme Maximum Temp. (°F)	60	63	87	93	93	96	99	98	92	86	76	70	99
Extreme Minimum Temp. (°F)	-27	-24	-13	12	23	33	40	30	24	16	3	-23	-27
Days Maximum Temp. ≥ 90°F	0	0	0	0	1	2	4	2	1	0	0	0	10
Days Maximum Temp. ≤ 32°F	16	11	4	0	0	0	0	0	0	0	1	10	42
Days Minimum Temp. ≤ 32°F	30	26	26	16	4	0	0	0	2	13	21	29	167
Days Minimum Temp. ≤ 0°F	8	6	1	0	0	0	0	0	0	0	0	3	18
Heating Degree Days (base 65°F)	1,358	1,151	975	593	262	72	17	32	182	501	788	1,180	7,111
Cooling Degree Days (base 65°F)	0	0	0	1	19	82	178	141	39	2	0	0	462
Mean Precipitation (in.)	3.32	2.44	3.27	3.28	3.87	3.46	3.78	3.93	3.51	3.52	3.54	3.18	41.10
Days With ≥ 0.1" Precipitation	7	6	7	7	7	7	7	7	6	6	8	6	81
Days With ≥ 1.0" Precipitation	1	0	1	1	1	1	1	1	1	1	1	0	10
Mean Snowfall (in.)	16.1	10.6	10.2	2.9	trace	0.0	0.0	0.0	0.0	trace	3.3	11.4	54.5
Days With ≥ 1.0" Snow Depth	26	24	18	2	0	0	0	0	0	0	3	18	91

Lancaster *Coos County* Elevation: 859 ft. Latitude: 44° 29' N Longitude: 71° 35' W

	JAN	FEB	MAR	APR	MAY	JUN	JUL	AUG	SEP	OCT	NOV	DEC	YEAR
Mean Maximum Temp. (°F)	25.8	30.1	39.9	53.2	68.0	75.7	79.9	77.7	68.7	56.7	42.7	30.3	54.1
Mean Temp. (°F)	14.0	17.1	28.0	40.7	53.7	62.0	66.5	64.8	56.2	45.0	33.8	20.5	41.9
Mean Minimum Temp. (°F)	2.2	4.1	16.0	28.2	39.3	48.2	53.0	51.9	43.6	33.3	24.9	10.7	29.6
Extreme Maximum Temp. (°F)	62	63	78	90	91	95	95	94	93	82	73	62	95
Extreme Minimum Temp. (°F)	-39	-40	-26	0	18	28	32	28	21	8	-9	-36	-40
Days Maximum Temp. ≥ 90°F	0	0	0	0	0	1	1	0	0	0	0	0	2
Days Maximum Temp. ≤ 32°F	22	16	7	1	0	0	0	0	0	0	5	17	68
Days Minimum Temp. ≤ 32°F	30	28	29	22	8	1	0	0	3	15	24	30	190
Days Minimum Temp. ≤ 0°F	14	12	5	0	0	0	0	0	0	0	0	7	38
Heating Degree Days (base 65°F)	1,576	1,347	1,140	722	354	131	48	76	273	613	928	1,373	8,581
Cooling Degree Days (base 65°F)	0	0	0	0	7	45	102	75	14	0	0	0	243
Mean Precipitation (in.)	2.55	1.78	2.36	2.60	3.34	4.02	3.97	4.40	3.48	3.23	3.14	2.72	37.59
Days With ≥ 0.1" Precipitation	6	5	7	7	9	9	9	8	7	7	8	7	89
Days With ≥ 1.0" Precipitation	0	0	0	0	1	1	1	1	1	1	0	0	6
Mean Snowfall (in.)	17.5	13.8	12.9	4.1	trace	0.0	0.0	0.0	trace	0.2	5.8	16.6	70.9
Days With ≥ 1.0" Snow Depth	29	27	25	5	0	0	0	0	0	0	6	23	115

Monroe 5 NNE *Grafton County* Elevation: 659 ft. Latitude: 44° 19' N Longitude: 72° 00' W

	JAN	FEB	MAR	APR	MAY	JUN	JUL	AUG	SEP	OCT	NOV	DEC	YEAR
Mean Maximum Temp. (°F)	24.7	28.7	38.9	52.2	66.2	74.8	79.6	77.4	67.7	55.5	42.3	29.6	53.1
Mean Temp. (°F)	13.4	15.8	27.5	40.9	53.6	62.7	67.6	65.8	56.6	45.1	34.1	20.3	41.9
Mean Minimum Temp. (°F)	2.1	2.8	16.0	29.6	41.1	50.5	55.6	54.1	45.5	34.6	25.8	10.9	30.7
Extreme Maximum Temp. (°F)	61	63	79	90	93	96	99	97	90	82	72	65	99
Extreme Minimum Temp. (°F)	-36	-33	-19	-1	23	31	36	33	25	13	-3	-32	-36
Days Maximum Temp. ≥ 90°F	0	0	0	0	0	1	2	1	0	0	0	0	4
Days Maximum Temp. ≤ 32°F	23	17	8	1	0	0	0	0	0	0	5	18	72
Days Minimum Temp. ≤ 32°F	31	28	29	20	5	0	0	0	1	14	23	30	181
Days Minimum Temp. ≤ 0°F	15	13	5	0	0	0	0	0	0	0	0	7	40
Heating Degree Days (base 65°F)	1,595	1,383	1,156	717	357	120	38	67	261	612	921	1,381	8,608
Cooling Degree Days (base 65°F)	0	0	0	0	9	52	123	95	17	0	0	0	296
Mean Precipitation (in.)	2.48	1.78	2.27	2.56	2.97	3.98	3.60	4.08	3.43	3.37	3.21	2.63	36.36
Days With ≥ 0.1" Precipitation	6	5	6	7	7	9	8	8	7	7	8	7	85
Days With ≥ 1.0" Precipitation	0	0	0	0	0	1	1	1	1	1	0	0	5
Mean Snowfall (in.)	18.0	13.3	10.8	3.0	trace	0.0	0.0	0.0	0.0	trace	4.1	16.6	65.8
Days With ≥ 1.0" Snow Depth	na	na	na	na	0	0	0	0	0	0	na	na	na

Mount Sunapee — *Merrimack County*   Elevation: 1,269 ft.   Latitude: 43° 20' N   Longitude: 72° 05' W

	JAN	FEB	MAR	APR	MAY	JUN	JUL	AUG	SEP	OCT	NOV	DEC	YEAR
Mean Maximum Temp. (°F)	29.5	32.7	41.6	54.3	67.9	75.2	79.6	77.5	68.9	58.1	45.1	33.8	55.3
Mean Temp. (°F)	20.8	23.4	32.1	43.6	56.0	64.3	68.9	67.3	58.8	48.2	37.2	26.0	45.5
Mean Minimum Temp. (°F)	12.0	14.0	22.6	32.8	44.1	53.3	58.1	56.6	48.8	38.3	29.2	18.1	35.6
Extreme Maximum Temp. (°F)	60	61	82	88	88	93	98	93	87	84	72	67	98
Extreme Minimum Temp. (°F)	-18	-20	-11	10	25	32	39	30	25	16	5	-23	-23
Days Maximum Temp. ≥ 90°F	0	0	0	0	0	0	1	0	0	0	0	0	1
Days Maximum Temp. ≤ 32°F	19	14	6	0	0	0	0	0	0	0	2	14	55
Days Minimum Temp. ≤ 32°F	30	26	26	15	2	0	0	0	1	8	20	29	157
Days Minimum Temp. ≤ 0°F	6	4	1	0	0	0	0	0	0	0	0	2	13
Heating Degree Days (base 65°F)	1,364	1,169	1,012	638	291	91	21	42	206	516	829	1,204	7,383
Cooling Degree Days (base 65°F)	0	0	0	1	18	77	151	122	28	2	0	0	399
Mean Precipitation (in.)	3.02	2.71	3.34	3.69	4.18	3.81	3.81	4.00	3.74	4.24	3.96	3.15	43.65
Days With ≥ 0.1" Precipitation	6	4	6	7	8	8	7	7	7	6	7	6	79
Days With ≥ 1.0" Precipitation	1	1	1	1	1	1	1	1	1	1	1	1	12
Mean Snowfall (in.)	19.5	16.3	13.6	5.0	trace	0.0	0.0	0.0	0.0	trace	3.8	14.3	72.5
Days With ≥ 1.0" Snow Depth	na	na	na	na	0	0	0	0	0	0	0	1	na

Nashua 2 NNW — *Hillsborough County*   Elevation: 127 ft.   Latitude: 42° 47' N   Longitude: 71° 29' W

	JAN	FEB	MAR	APR	MAY	JUN	JUL	AUG	SEP	OCT	NOV	DEC	YEAR
Mean Maximum Temp. (°F)	33.1	36.5	45.1	57.1	69.2	77.4	82.6	80.6	72.2	61.1	49.5	37.7	58.5
Mean Temp. (°F)	22.7	25.6	34.6	45.4	56.8	65.4	70.6	68.8	60.5	49.1	39.4	28.3	47.3
Mean Minimum Temp. (°F)	12.1	14.7	24.0	33.6	44.3	53.3	58.5	57.0	48.8	37.0	29.2	18.8	35.9
Extreme Maximum Temp. (°F)	64	70	85	92	93	97	99	100	95	85	77	73	100
Extreme Minimum Temp. (°F)	-24	-22	-8	13	25	34	40	34	27	14	1	-15	-24
Days Maximum Temp. ≥ 90°F	0	0	0	0	1	2	4	2	1	0	0	0	10
Days Maximum Temp. ≤ 32°F	15	10	3	0	0	0	0	0	0	0	1	9	38
Days Minimum Temp. ≤ 32°F	30	27	27	15	2	0	0	0	0	11	20	29	161
Days Minimum Temp. ≤ 0°F	5	3	0	0	0	0	0	0	0	0	0	2	10
Heating Degree Days (base 65°F)	1,306	1,105	937	584	267	73	13	31	170	489	763	1,131	6,869
Cooling Degree Days (base 65°F)	0	0	0	1	19	93	201	162	46	1	0	0	523
Mean Precipitation (in.)	3.78	3.12	4.02	3.79	3.67	3.81	3.57	3.89	3.59	3.94	4.15	3.70	45.03
Days With ≥ 0.1" Precipitation	7	6	7	7	7	7	7	6	6	6	8	7	81
Days With ≥ 1.0" Precipitation	1	1	1	1	1	1	1	1	1	1	1	1	12
Mean Snowfall (in.)	15.4	12.0	11.0	2.7	0.0	0.0	0.0	0.0	0.0	trace	3.1	12.2	56.4
Days With ≥ 1.0" Snow Depth	na	14	na	0	0	0	0	0	0	0	0	na	na

North Conway — *Carroll County*   Elevation: 528 ft.   Latitude: 44° 03' N   Longitude: 71° 08' W

	JAN	FEB	MAR	APR	MAY	JUN	JUL	AUG	SEP	OCT	NOV	DEC	YEAR
Mean Maximum Temp. (°F)	29.3	33.8	41.9	54.4	68.2	76.8	81.8	79.6	70.6	58.7	46.1	34.4	56.3
Mean Temp. (°F)	18.3	21.8	31.1	43.1	55.4	64.4	69.4	67.2	58.0	46.4	36.6	24.6	44.7
Mean Minimum Temp. (°F)	7.3	9.7	20.2	31.7	42.5	52.0	57.0	54.7	45.3	34.1	27.1	14.8	33.0
Extreme Maximum Temp. (°F)	59	64	77	92	98	102	100	103	94	85	77	71	103
Extreme Minimum Temp. (°F)	-29	-21	-10	10	24	31	40	35	26	16	1	-19	-29
Days Maximum Temp. ≥ 90°F	0	0	0	0	1	3	4	2	0	0	0	0	10
Days Maximum Temp. ≤ 32°F	18	12	6	0	0	0	0	0	0	0	2	13	51
Days Minimum Temp. ≤ 32°F	31	28	28	17	3	0	0	0	2	15	23	30	177
Days Minimum Temp. ≤ 0°F	10	7	2	0	0	0	0	0	0	0	0	5	24
Heating Degree Days (base 65°F)	1,442	1,214	1,044	651	307	92	20	43	227	570	846	1,245	7,701
Cooling Degree Days (base 65°F)	0	0	0	0	14	83	170	123	27	1	0	0	418
Mean Precipitation (in.)	4.33	2.99	3.98	4.10	3.84	4.01	4.00	4.24	3.85	4.57	4.39	3.63	47.93
Days With ≥ 0.1" Precipitation	7	6	7	7	7	8	7	7	7	7	8	7	85
Days With ≥ 1.0" Precipitation	1	1	1	1	1	1	1	1	1	1	1	1	12
Mean Snowfall (in.)	24.1	16.0	16.2	5.1	trace	0.0	0.0	0.0	trace	0.3	4.5	18.0	84.2
Days With ≥ 1.0" Snow Depth	29	27	25	5	0	0	0	0	0	0	4	21	111

Pinkham Notch — *Coos County*   Elevation: 2,007 ft.   Latitude: 44° 16' N   Longitude: 71° 15' W

	JAN	FEB	MAR	APR	MAY	JUN	JUL	AUG	SEP	OCT	NOV	DEC	YEAR
Mean Maximum Temp. (°F)	25.0	27.4	35.6	47.1	61.3	69.3	74.1	71.9	63.3	52.8	40.5	30.0	49.8
Mean Temp. (°F)	14.6	16.9	25.5	37.3	50.3	58.8	63.6	61.3	53.0	42.6	32.0	20.7	39.7
Mean Minimum Temp. (°F)	4.1	6.3	15.4	27.5	39.2	48.2	53.0	50.7	42.7	32.4	23.4	11.3	29.5
Extreme Maximum Temp. (°F)	58	62	70	86	88	90	93	91	85	80	70	65	93
Extreme Minimum Temp. (°F)	-28	-27	-18	-6	19	26	33	32	21	3	-5	-21	-28
Days Maximum Temp. ≥ 90°F	0	0	0	0	0	0	0	0	0	0	0	0	0
Days Maximum Temp. ≤ 32°F	23	19	12	2	0	0	0	0	0	0	7	18	81
Days Minimum Temp. ≤ 32°F	31	28	30	22	6	0	0	0	3	17	25	30	192
Days Minimum Temp. ≤ 0°F	13	10	4	0	0	0	0	0	0	0	0	6	33
Heating Degree Days (base 65°F)	1,556	1,352	1,218	825	455	201	91	139	358	686	983	1,367	9,231
Cooling Degree Days (base 65°F)	0	0	0	0	3	23	53	30	5	0	0	0	114
Mean Precipitation (in.)	5.01	3.61	4.93	4.84	4.75	5.23	4.55	5.14	4.87	5.57	5.56	4.79	58.85
Days With ≥ 0.1" Precipitation	8	7	9	8	9	10	9	8	8	8	9	9	102
Days With ≥ 1.0" Precipitation	1	1	1	1	1	1	1	2	1	1	1	1	14
Mean Snowfall (in.)	29.3	22.0	27.0	12.9	0.3	0.0	0.0	0.0	trace	1.0	12.6	28.8	133.9
Days With ≥ 1.0" Snow Depth	30	28	30	17	1	0	0	0	0	1	9	27	142

Plymouth *Grafton County*   Elevation: 659 ft.   Latitude: 43° 47' N   Longitude: 71° 39' W

	JAN	FEB	MAR	APR	MAY	JUN	JUL	AUG	SEP	OCT	NOV	DEC	YEAR
Mean Maximum Temp. (°F)	27.2	31.4	40.5	53.4	67.0	75.2	80.2	78.0	68.5	57.4	44.3	32.0	54.6
Mean Temp. (°F)	15.9	19.0	29.0	41.2	53.1	61.8	66.8	64.7	55.7	44.8	34.5	22.2	42.4
Mean Minimum Temp. (°F)	4.6	6.6	17.5	29.0	39.0	48.3	53.4	51.3	42.8	32.1	24.7	12.4	30.1
Extreme Maximum Temp. (°F)	57	62	79	92	93	95	97	98	91	83	73	65	98
Extreme Minimum Temp. (°F)	-35	-28	-20	8	22	26	35	31	23	15	-5	-23	-35
Days Maximum Temp. ≥ 90°F	0	0	0	0	0	1	2	1	0	0	0	0	4
Days Maximum Temp. ≤ 32°F	21	15	6	0	0	0	0	0	0	0	3	15	60
Days Minimum Temp. ≤ 32°F	31	28	30	21	7	1	0	0	4	18	25	30	195
Days Minimum Temp. ≤ 0°F	13	10	3	0	0	0	0	0	0	0	0	6	32
Heating Degree Days (base 65°F)	1,517	1,292	1,109	707	371	135	46	79	287	620	908	1,320	8,391
Cooling Degree Days (base 65°F)	0	0	0	0	6	42	106	74	14	0	0	0	242
Mean Precipitation (in.)	3.67	2.84	3.56	3.27	3.84	3.79	4.21	4.09	3.48	4.13	4.12	3.55	44.55
Days With ≥ 0.1" Precipitation	7	6	7	7	8	8	7	7	7	7	8	7	86
Days With ≥ 1.0" Precipitation	1	1	1	1	1	1	1	1	1	1	1	1	12
Mean Snowfall (in.)	20.9	14.3	13.7	4.3	trace	0.0	0.0	0.0	0.0	trace	4.6	17.4	75.2
Days With ≥ 1.0" Snow Depth	22	20	19	7	0	0	0	0	0	0	4	17	89

Tamworth 3 *Carroll County*   Elevation: 787 ft.   Latitude: 43° 54' N   Longitude: 71° 18' W

	JAN	FEB	MAR	APR	MAY	JUN	JUL	AUG	SEP	OCT	NOV	DEC	YEAR
Mean Maximum Temp. (°F)	28.0	32.1	40.7	53.1	66.9	74.8	79.9	77.5	68.1	56.4	44.6	32.9	54.6
Mean Temp. (°F)	16.4	19.7	29.5	41.1	53.1	61.6	66.4	64.0	54.9	44.1	35.2	22.8	42.4
Mean Minimum Temp. (°F)	4.7	7.2	18.2	29.1	39.2	48.3	52.8	50.4	41.6	31.7	25.6	12.6	30.1
Extreme Maximum Temp. (°F)	55	59	76	91	93	96	98	98	89	81	73	65	98
Extreme Minimum Temp. (°F)	-29	-27	-15	5	20	28	34	30	18	16	-6	-29	-29
Days Maximum Temp. ≥ 90°F	0	0	0	0	0	1	2	1	0	0	0	0	4
Days Maximum Temp. ≤ 32°F	20	14	6	0	0	0	0	0	0	0	2	14	56
Days Minimum Temp. ≤ 32°F	31	28	29	21	8	1	0	0	6	18	24	30	196
Days Minimum Temp. ≤ 0°F	12	10	3	0	0	0	0	0	0	0	0	6	31
Heating Degree Days (base 65°F)	1,502	1,274	1,093	711	372	143	53	92	306	641	888	1,303	8,378
Cooling Degree Days (base 65°F)	0	0	0	0	6	46	103	66	12	0	0	0	233
Mean Precipitation (in.)	4.46	3.12	4.16	4.13	4.33	4.33	4.45	4.68	4.11	4.56	4.44	3.86	50.63
Days With ≥ 0.1" Precipitation	7	6	7	8	8	9	7	7	7	7	8	7	88
Days With ≥ 1.0" Precipitation	1	1	1	1	1	1	1	1	1	1	1	1	12
Mean Snowfall (in.)	23.2	15.0	15.7	5.3	trace	0.0	0.0	0.0	0.0	0.1	4.8	17.9	82.0
Days With ≥ 1.0" Snow Depth	29	28	28	7	0	0	0	0	0	0	5	22	119

Note: See Appendix D for explanation of data.

NEW JERSEY

PHYSICAL FEATURES. New Jersey, though one of the smaller states, has a varied topography. In the northwestern part a section comprising about one-fifth of the area of the State is known as the Highlands and Kittatinny Valley. This region is traversed by several low mountain ridges extending northeasterly across the State with valleys and rolling hills between. The highest of these ranges is the Kittatinny, which rises from the banks of the Delaware River at the famous Delaware Water Gap. To the eastward the region is studded with numerous lakes, some of the largest of which are Lakes Hopatcong, Mohawk, and Greenwood. Elevations up to 1,800 feet above sea level are found in the Kittatinny Mountains near the New York State line.

South and east of the Highlands is a region of about equal area known as the Red Sandstone Plain, or the Piedmont of New Jersey. It is generally hilly in its northwestern part, becoming rolling and then flat toward the south and southeast. At its northeastern corner are the Palisades, cliffs which rise abruptly from the Hudson River to heights of 200 to 500 feet. The seacoast section extends from Sandy Hook to Cape May, or about 125 miles. This area is characterized by long stretches of sandy beaches. Tidewater marshes become numerous toward the south.

In the southern interior a region known as the Pines is covered with scrubby forests of pine and some oak. The land is low and some of it is swampy. In fact, most of the State that lies south of a line connecting Jersey City and Trenton is low and flat with few elevations higher than 100 feet above mean sea level, these being mainly in Monmouth County.

About 30 percent of the area of New Jersey drains into the Delaware River and Delaware Bay, which form the western boundary. Nearly half of Sussex County, in the northwest, drains northward through the Wallkill River into the Hudson River of New York. The remainder of the State drains directly into the Atlantic Ocean through the Passaic, Hackensack, and Raritan Rivers in the north, and a number of small rivers and streams in the south.

GENERAL CLIMATE. The extreme length of the State is 166 miles and its greatest width only about 65. The difference in climate is quite marked between the southern tip at Cape May and the northern extremity in the Kittatinny Mountains. The former locality is almost surrounded by water and is fairly well removed from the influence of the frequent storms that cross the Great Lakes region and move out the St. Lawrence Valley. The northern extremity is well within the zone of influence of these storms and, in addition, lies at elevations varying from 800 to 1,800 feet. The influence of these high elevations on the temperature is considerable. The differences between these two localities are particularly marked in the winter, Cape May having a normal January temperature about the same as that of southwestern Virginia, while that of Layton, in the extreme northwest, is similar to that of the northern area of Ohio. Since the prevailing winds are mostly offshore, the ocean influence does not have full effect.

TEMPERATURE. Temperature differences between the northern and southern parts of the State are greatest in winter and least in summer. Nearly every weather station has registered readings of 100°F. or higher at some time, and all of them have records of zero or below. In the northern Highland area, the average date of last freeze (32°F.) in spring is about May 2, and that of the first in fall, October 12. On the seacoast corresponding dates are April 6 and November 9, while in the central and southern interior the dates are April 23 and October 19. Freeze-free days in the northern Highlands average 163, with 217 along the seacoast and 179 in the central and southern interior.

PRECIPITATION. Northern New Jersey is near enough to the paths of the storms which cross the Great Lakes region and pass down the St. Lawrence Valley to receive part of its precipitation from that source. However, the heaviest general rains are produced by coastal storms of tropical origin. The centers of these storms usually pass some distance offshore, with heaviest rainfall and strongest wind near the coast. On several occasions tropical storms have moved inland along the south Atlantic coast, and then moved northward either through or to the west of New Jersey. The damage by high tides to coastal installations during the passage of a tropical storm is often severe, whether the storm passes offshore or inland.

The average annual precipitation ranges from about 40 inches along the southeast coast to 51 inches in north-central parts of the State. In other sections the annual averages are mostly between 43 and 47 inches. Rainfall is well distributed during the warm months. Heavy 24-hour falls of seven or eight inches are occasionally recorded. Brief periods of drought during the growing season are not uncommon, but prolonged droughts are relatively rare, occurring on the average once in 15 years. Flooding in New Jersey is usually caused by heavy general rains, at times associated with storms of tropical origin. Local flooding results from ice gorging.

The season during which measurable quantities of snow are likely to fall extends from about October 15 to April 20 in the Highlands, and from about November 15 to March 15 in the vicinity of Cape May. Average seasonal amounts range from about 13 inches at Cape May to nearly 50 inches in the Highlands. Snowfalls of 10 or more inches in a single storm are occasional occurrences.

The number of days a month with measurable precipitation averages eight for each of the fall months (September, October, and November) and nine to 12 for the other months of the year; the average yearly number is 120. Midday relative humidity averages 68 percent along the seacoast and 57 percent or less at inland locations.

Normally, sunshine varies from slightly over one-half of the possible amount in the northern counties to about 60 percent in the south. The prevailing wind is from the northwest from October to April, inclusive, and from the southwest for the other months of the year.

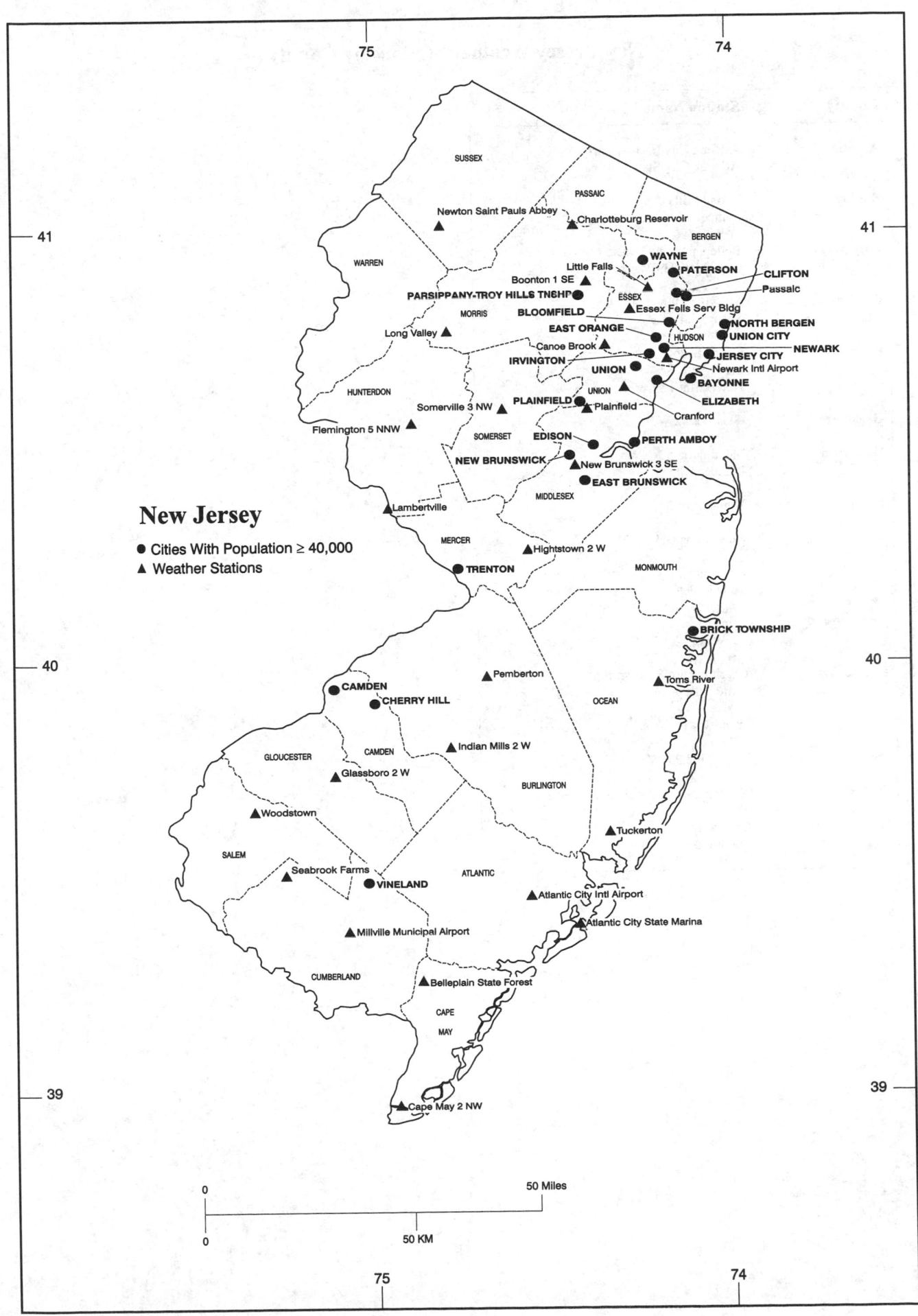

New Jersey

● Cities With Population ≥ 40,000
▲ Weather Stations

SUSSEX

PASSAIC

BERGEN

WARREN

Newton Saint Pauls Abbey ▲

▲ Charlotteburg Reservoir

● WAYNE

Little Falls

● PATERSON

CLIFTON

Boonton 1 SE ▲

Passaic

PARSIPPANY-TROY HILLS TNSHP ●

Essex

MORRIS

▲ Essex Fells Serv Bldg

BLOOMFIELD ●

NORTH BERGEN

Long Valley ▲

EAST ORANGE ●

UNION CITY

HUDSON

NEWARK

Canoe Brook ▲

IRVINGTON

Newark Intl Airport

HUNTERDON

UNION ●

BAYONNE

UNION

ELIZABETH

Somerville 3 NW ▲

PLAINFIELD ●

▲ Plainfield

Cranford

Flemington 5 NNW ▲

SOMERSET

EDISON ●

PERTH AMBOY ●

NEW BRUNSWICK ●

▲ New Brunswick 3 SE

EAST BRUNSWICK ●

MIDDLESEX

Lambertville ▲

MERCER

▲ Hightstown 2 W

MONMOUTH

● TRENTON

● **BRICK TOWNSHIP**

Pemberton ▲

▲ Toms River

OCEAN

● **CAMDEN**

● **CHERRY HILL**

GLOUCESTER

CAMDEN

▲ Indian Mills 2 W

BURLINGTON

Glassboro 2 W ▲

▲ Woodstown

SALEM

▲ Tuckerton

Seabrook Farms ▲

ATLANTIC

● **VINELAND**

▲ Atlantic City Intl Airport

▲ Millville Municipal Airport

▲ Atlantic City State Marina

CUMBERLAND

▲ Belleplain State Forest

CAPE

MAY

▲ Cape May 2 NW

0

50 Miles

0

50 KM

New Jersey Weather Stations by County

County	Station Name
Atlantic	Atlantic City Int'l Airport Atlantic City State Marina
Burlington	Indian Mills 2 W Pemberton
Cape May	Belleplain State Forest Cape May 2 NW
Cumberland	Millville Municipal Airport Seabrook Farms
Essex	Canoe Brook Essex Fells Serv Bldg Newark Int'l Airport
Gloucester	Glassboro 2 W
Hunterdon	Flemington 5 NNW Lambertville
Mercer	Hightstown 2 W
Middlesex	New Brunswick 3 SE
Morris	Boonton 1 SE Long Valley
Ocean	Toms River Tuckerton
Passaic	Charlotteburg Reservoir Little Falls
Salem	Woodstown
Somerset	Somerville 3 NW
Sussex	Newton Saint Pauls Abbey
Union	Cranford Plainfield

New Jersey Weather Stations by City

City	Station Name	Miles
Bayonne	Canoe Brook	13
	Cranford	10
	Essex Fells Serv Bldg	14
	Little Falls	16
	Newark Int'l Airport	5
	Plainfield	15
	New York Avenue V Brooklyn, NY	8
	New York Central Park Observatory, NY	11
	New York JFK Int'l Airport, NY	17
	New York Laguardia Airport, NY	15
Bloomfield	Boonton 1 SE	13
	Canoe Brook	9
	Cranford	12
	Essex Fells Serv Bldg	5
	Little Falls	6
	Newark Int'l Airport	6
	Plainfield	18
	New York Avenue V Brooklyn, NY	18
	New York Central Park Observatory, NY	12
	New York Laguardia Airport, NY	16
Brick Township	Toms River	10
Camden	Glassboro 2 W	14
	Indian Mills 2 W	19
	Marcus Hook, PA	19
	Philadelphia Int'l Airport, PA	9
Cherry Hill	Glassboro 2 W	13
	Indian Mills 2 W	13
	Pemberton	17
	Philadelphia Int'l Airport, PA	13
Clifton	Boonton 1 SE	13
	Canoe Brook	13
	Charlotteburg Reservoir	18
	Cranford	17
	Essex Fells Serv Bldg	7
	Little Falls	4
	Newark Int'l Airport	11
	Dobbs Ferry Ardsley, NY	19
	New York Central Park Observatory, NY	11
	New York Laguardia Airport, NY	15
East Brunswick	Cranford	16
	Hightstown 2 W	14
	New Brunswick 3 SE	3
	Plainfield	12
	Somerville 3 NW	17
East Orange	Boonton 1 SE	14
	Canoe Brook	7
	Cranford	9
	Essex Fells Serv Bldg	6
	Little Falls	8
	Newark Int'l Airport	4
	Plainfield	15
	New York Avenue V Brooklyn, NY	16
	New York Central Park Observatory, NY	13
	New York Laguardia Airport, NY	17
Edison	Canoe Brook	16
	Cranford	10

City	Station Name	Miles
Edison (cont.)	Hightstown 2 W	20
	Newark Int'l Airport	18
	New Brunswick 3 SE	4
	Plainfield	6
	Somerville 3 NW	14
Elizabeth	Boonton 1 SE	19
	Canoe Brook	9
	Cranford	5
	Essex Fells Serv Bldg	12
	Little Falls	15
	Newark Int'l Airport	4
	New Brunswick 3 SE	18
	Plainfield	11
	New York Avenue V Brooklyn, NY	13
	New York Central Park Observatory, NY	15
	New York Laguardia Airport, NY	19
Irvington	Boonton 1 SE	15
	Canoe Brook	6
	Cranford	6
	Essex Fells Serv Bldg	8
	Little Falls	11
	Newark Int'l Airport	3
	Plainfield	12
	New York Avenue V Brooklyn, NY	16
	New York Central Park Observatory, NY	14
	New York Laguardia Airport, NY	19
Jersey City	Canoe Brook	15
	Cranford	13
	Essex Fells Serv Bldg	14
	Little Falls	14
	Newark Int'l Airport	6
	Plainfield	19
	New York Avenue V Brooklyn, NY	10
	New York Central Park Observatory, NY	7
	New York JFK Int'l Airport, NY	15
	New York Laguardia Airport, NY	10
New Brunswick	Canoe Brook	19
	Cranford	14
	Hightstown 2 W	17
	New Brunswick 3 SE	2
	Plainfield	8
	Somerville 3 NW	12
Newark	Boonton 1 SE	16
	Canoe Brook	8
	Cranford	8
	Essex Fells Serv Bldg	8
	Little Falls	10
	Newark Int'l Airport	2
	Plainfield	15
	New York Avenue V Brooklyn, NY	14
	New York Central Park Observatory, NY	12
	New York Laguardia Airport, NY	16
North Bergen	Canoe Brook	17
	Cranford	18
	Essex Fells Serv Bldg	14
	Little Falls	13
	Newark Int'l Airport	10
	Dobbs Ferry Ardsley, NY	17

City	Station Name	Miles
North Bergen (cont.)	New York Avenue V Brooklyn, NY	14
	New York Central Park Observatory, NY	3
	New York JFK Int'l Airport, NY	15
	New York Laguardia Airport, NY	7
Parsippany-Troy Hills Twp.	Boonton 1 SE	3
	Canoe Brook	9
	Charlotteburg Reservoir	12
	Cranford	16
	Essex Fells Serv Bldg	8
	Little Falls	10
	Long Valley	20
	Newark Int'l Airport	16
	Plainfield	18
Passaic	Boonton 1 SE	14
	Canoe Brook	14
	Charlotteburg Reservoir	20
	Cranford	17
	Essex Fells Serv Bldg	8
	Little Falls	6
	Newark Int'l Airport	10
	Dobbs Ferry Ardsley, NY	18
	New York Avenue V Brooklyn, NY	19
	New York Central Park Observatory, NY	10
	New York Laguardia Airport, NY	14
Paterson	Boonton 1 SE	12
	Canoe Brook	15
	Charlotteburg Reservoir	16
	Cranford	20
	Essex Fells Serv Bldg	9
	Little Falls	4
	Newark Int'l Airport	14
	Dobbs Ferry Ardsley, NY	18
	New York Central Park Observatory, NY	14
	New York Laguardia Airport, NY	17
Perth Amboy	Canoe Brook	17
	Cranford	9
	Newark Int'l Airport	15
	New Brunswick 3 SE	9
	Plainfield	9
	Somerville 3 NW	20
	New York Avenue V Brooklyn, NY	16
Plainfield	Boonton 1 SE	20
	Canoe Brook	10
	Cranford	7
	Essex Fells Serv Bldg	17
	Newark Int'l Airport	14
	New Brunswick 3 SE	10
	Plainfield	1
	Somerville 3 NW	11
Trenton	Hightstown 2 W	11
	Lambertville	14
	Pemberton	18
Union	Boonton 1 SE	16
	Canoe Brook	6
	Cranford	4
	Essex Fells Serv Bldg	9
	Little Falls	13
	Newark Int'l Airport	5

City	Station Name	Miles
Union (cont.)	New Brunswick 3 SE	18
	Plainfield	10
	New York Avenue V Brooklyn, NY	16
	New York Central Park Observatory, NY	17
Union City	Canoe Brook	17
	Cranford	16
	Essex Fells Serv Bldg	14
	Little Falls	13
	Newark Int'l Airport	9
	Dobbs Ferry Ardsley, NY	19
	New York Avenue V Brooklyn, NY	12
	New York Central Park Observatory, NY	4
	New York JFK Int'l Airport, NY	15
	New York Laguardia Airport, NY	8
Vineland	Belleplain State Forest	18
	Glassboro 2 W	18
	Millville Municipal Airport	8
	Seabrook Farms	12
	Woodstown	20
Wayne	Boonton 1 SE	9
	Canoe Brook	15
	Charlotteburg Reservoir	11
	Essex Fells Serv Bldg	8
	Little Falls	4
	Newark Int'l Airport	16
	New York Central Park Observatory, NY	18

Note: Miles is the distance between the geographic center of the city and the weather station.

New Jersey Weather Stations by Elevation

Feet	Station Name
757	Charlotteburg Reservoir
597	Newton Saint Pauls Abbey
547	Long Valley
347	Essex Fells Serv Bldg
278	Boonton 1 SE
259	Flemington 5 NNW
177	Canoe Brook
157	Somerville 3 NW
147	Little Falls
98	Glassboro 2 W
98	Hightstown 2 W
98	Indian Mills 2 W
98	Toms River
88	Plainfield
88	Seabrook Farms
85	New Brunswick 3 SE
72	Cranford
68	Millville Municipal Airport
65	Lambertville
59	Atlantic City Int'l Airport
59	Pemberton
49	Woodstown
29	Belleplain State Forest
19	Cape May 2 NW
19	Tuckerton
9	Atlantic City State Marina
9	Newark Int'l Airport

Atlantic City Int'l Airport

The Atlantic City National Weather Service Office is located at the National Aviation Facilities Experimental Center, Pomona, which is about 10 miles west-northwest of Atlantic City and the Atlantic Ocean. The surrounding terrain is fairly flat at an elevation of 50 to 60 feet above sea level. Vegetation in the area consists of scrub pine and low underbrush, but clearing for the air facility has been quite extensive. Bays and salt marshes are as near as 6 miles east of the airport. Atlantic City is located on Abescon Island on the southeast coast of New Jersey. Surrounding terrain, composed of tidal marshes and beach sand, is flat and lies slightly above sea level. The climate is principally continental in character. However, the moderating influence of the Atlantic Ocean is apparent throughout the year, being more marked in the city than at the airport. As a result, summers are relatively cooler and winters milder than elsewhere at the same latitude.

Land and sea breezes, local circulations resulting from the differential heating and cooling of the land and sea, often prevail. These winds occur when moderate or intense storms are not present in the area, thus enabling the local circulation to overcome the general wind pattern. During the warm season sea breezes in the late morning and afternoon hours prevent excessive heating. Frequently, the temperature at Atlantic City during the afternoon hours in the summer averages several degrees lower than at the airport and the airport averages several degrees lower than localities farther inland. On occasions, sea breezes have lowered the temperature as much as 15 to 20 degrees within a half hour. However, the major effect of the sea breeze at the airport is preventing the temperature from rising above the 80's. Because the change in ocean temperature lags behind the air temperature from season to season, the weather tends to remain comparatively mild late into the fall, but on the other hand, warming is retarded in the spring. Normal ocean temperatures range from an average near 37 degrees in January to near 72 degrees in August.

Precipitation is moderate and well distributed throughout the year, with June the driest month and August the wettest. Tropical storms or hurricanes occasionally bring excessive rainfall to the area. The bulk of winter precipitation results from storms which move northeastward along or near the east coast of the United States. Snowfall is considerably less than elsewhere at the same latitude and does not remain long on the ground. Precipitation, often beginning as snow, will frequently become mixed with or change to rain while continuing as snow over more interior sections. In addition, ice storms and resultant glaze are relatively infrequent.

Atlantic City Int'l Airport *Atlantic County*   Elevation: 59 ft.   Latitude: 39° 27' N   Longitude: 74° 34' W

	JAN	FEB	MAR	APR	MAY	JUN	JUL	AUG	SEP	OCT	NOV	DEC	YEAR
Mean Maximum Temp. (°F)	41.8	44.1	51.5	61.3	71.1	80.0	85.1	83.4	76.8	66.3	56.1	46.6	63.7
Mean Temp. (°F)	32.5	34.5	41.6	50.6	60.5	69.6	75.3	73.5	66.4	55.2	45.9	37.1	53.6
Mean Minimum Temp. (°F)	23.1	24.9	31.5	39.8	49.8	59.2	65.5	63.5	56.0	44.0	35.7	27.5	43.4
Extreme Maximum Temp. (°F)	72	75	87	92	96	100	101	100	99	87	81	77	101
Extreme Minimum Temp. (°F)	-9	-11	5	20	26	37	42	40	34	20	10	-2	-11
Days Maximum Temp. ≥ 90°F	0	0	0	0	1	3	8	5	1	0	0	0	18
Days Maximum Temp. ≤ 32°F	6	4	0	0	0	0	0	0	0	0	0	3	13
Days Minimum Temp. ≤ 32°F	25	21	17	6	0	0	0	0	0	3	12	22	106
Days Minimum Temp. ≤ 0°F	1	0	0	0	0	0	0	0	0	0	0	0	1
Heating Degree Days (base 65°F)	1,000	855	721	431	180	29	1	5	66	313	568	859	5,028
Cooling Degree Days (base 65°F)	0	0	1	6	52	184	347	272	118	18	1	0	999
Mean Precipitation (in.)	3.47	2.96	3.99	3.59	3.39	2.75	3.73	4.15	3.02	2.95	3.23	3.09	40.32
Maximum Precipitation (in.)	7.1	5.8	9.3	7.6	6.7	6.4	13.1	12.0	6.3	6.6	9.6	7.3	50.4
Minimum Precipitation (in.)	0.6	0.8	0.7	0.8	0.5	0.7	0.5	0.4	0.4	0.1	0.7	0.6	25.3
Maximum 24-hr. Precipitation (in.)	2.5	2.6	2.7	2.9	4.1	2.8	6.5	6.4	3.9	2.5	2.8	1.9	6.5
Days With ≥ 0.1" Precipitation	7	6	7	7	7	6	6	6	5	5	6	6	74
Days With ≥ 1.0" Precipitation	1	1	1	1	1	1	1	1	1	1	1	1	12
Mean Snowfall (in.)	*4.8*	*5.1*	*1.1*	*0.4*	*trace*	*trace*	*trace*	*0.0*	*0.0*	*trace*	*0.3*	*1.6*	*13.3*
Maximum Snowfall (in.)	20	35	18	4	trace	0	0	0	0	trace	8	9	50
Maximum 24-hr. Snowfall (in.)	14	17	12	4	trace	0	0	0	0	trace	8	7	17
Days With ≥ 1.0" Snow Depth	*4*	*3*	*1*	*0*	*0*	*0*	*0*	0	*0*	*0*	*0*	*1*	*9*
Thunderstorm Days	< 1	< 1	1	2	4	5	7	5	2	1	1	< 1	28
Foggy Days	12	11	13	13	15	16	19	19	16	14	12	12	172
Predominant Sky Cover	OVR	OVR	OVR	OVR	OVR	OVR	OVR	OVR	OVR	OVR	OVR	OVR	OVR
Mean Relative Humidity 7am (%)	78	78	78	77	79	81	84	87	87	87	83	79	81
Mean Relative Humidity 4pm (%)	60	57	55	54	57	58	60	62	61	59	61	61	59
Mean Dewpoint (°F)	22	23	30	38	50	60	65	65	58	47	37	27	44
Prevailing Wind Direction	WNW	WNW	WNW	S	S	S	S	S	N	NW	WNW	WNW	WNW
Prevailing Wind Speed (mph)	14	14	15	12	12	10	10	9	8	10	13	14	12
Maximum Wind Gust (mph)	78	64	68	67	55	64	81	62	83	58	69	71	83

Atlantic City State Marina

The Atlantic City State Marina is located on Abescon Island on the southeast coast of New Jersey. Surrounding terrain, composed of tidal marshes and beach sand, is flat and lies slightly above sea level. The climate is principally continental in character. However, the moderating influence of the Atlantic Ocean is apparent throughout the year, being more marked in the city than at the airport. As a result, summers are relatively cooler and winters milder than elsewhere at the same latitude.

Land and sea breezes, local circulations resulting from the differential heating and cooling of the land and sea, often prevail. These winds occur when moderate or intense storms are not present in the area, thus enabling the local circulation to overcome the general wind pattern. During the warm season sea breezes in the late morning and afternoon hours prevent excessive heating. Frequently, the temperature at Atlantic City during the afternoon hours in the summer averages several degrees lower than at the airport and the airport averages several degrees lower than localities farther inland. On occasions, sea breezes have lowered the temperature as much as 15 to 20 degrees within a half hour. However, the major effect of the sea breeze at the airport is preventing the temperature from rising above the 80s. Because the change in ocean temperature lags behind the air temperature from season to season, the weather tends to remain comparatively mild late into the fall, but on the other hand, warming is retarded in the spring. Normal ocean temperatures range from an average near 37 degrees in January to near 72 degrees in August.

Precipitation is moderate and well distributed throughout the year, with June the driest month and August the wettest. Tropical storms or hurricanes occasionally bring excessive rainfall to the area. The bulk of winter precipitation results from storms which move northeastward along or near the east coast of the United States. Snowfall is considerably less than elsewhere at the same latitude and does not remain long on the ground. Precipitation, often beginning as snow, will frequently become mixed with or change to rain while continuing as snow over more interior sections. In addition, ice storms and resultant glaze are relatively infrequent.

Atlantic City State Marina *Atlantic County*   Elevation: 9 ft.   Latitude: 39° 23' N   Longitude: 74° 26' W

	JAN	FEB	MAR	APR	MAY	JUN	JUL	AUG	SEP	OCT	NOV	DEC	YEAR
Mean Maximum Temp. (°F)	40.7	42.9	49.1	57.6	66.2	74.7	80.6	79.9	74.1	64.4	55.0	46.8	61.0
Mean Temp. (°F)	34.3	36.4	42.7	51.1	60.1	68.7	74.7	74.2	68.2	57.9	48.5	40.4	54.8
Mean Minimum Temp. (°F)	27.9	29.9	36.3	44.5	54.0	62.8	68.7	68.4	62.2	51.4	41.9	33.8	48.5
Extreme Maximum Temp. (°F)	69	72	82	90	93	97	101	102	92	89	78	74	102
Extreme Minimum Temp. (°F)	-3	4	12	22	38	45	53	50	42	27	19	4	-3
Days Maximum Temp. ≥ 90°F	0	0	0	0	0	0	3	1	0	0	0	0	4
Days Maximum Temp. ≤ 32°F	6	4	0	0	0	0	0	0	0	0	0	2	12
Days Minimum Temp. ≤ 32°F	21	16	9	1	0	0	0	0	0	0	4	13	64
Days Minimum Temp. ≤ 0°F	0	0	0	0	0	0	0	0	0	0	0	0	0
Heating Degree Days (base 65°F)	944	801	683	413	176	21	1	1	31	231	490	757	4,549
Cooling Degree Days (base 65°F)	0	0	0	1	38	158	334	301	145	23	1	0	1,001
Mean Precipitation (in.)	3.44	2.96	3.77	3.21	3.04	2.43	3.20	3.82	2.78	2.82	2.97	3.38	37.82
Maximum Precipitation (in.)	8.4	6.9	8.5	6.9	8.8	7.3	11.1	14.8	5.8	5.9	8.9	6.8	62.2
Minimum Precipitation (in.)	0.3	0.8	0.7	0.8	0.3	0.3	0.3	0.9	0.5	trace	0.8	0.7	27.5
Maximum 24-hr. Precipitation (in.)	2.5	2.5	3.3	4.0	3.1	3.6	6.6	7.3	3.0	2.9	3.7	3.3	7.3
Days With ≥ 0.1" Precipitation	7	6	7	7	6	5	5	5	5	5	6	6	70
Days With ≥ 1.0" Precipitation	1	1	1	1	0	1	1	1	1	1	1	1	11
Mean Snowfall (in.)	na	na	na	na	na	na	na	na	na	na	na	na	na
Maximum Snowfall (in.)	13	13	10	1	0	0	0	0	0	0	3	5	29
Maximum 24-hr. Snowfall (in.)	11	9	8	1	0	0	0	0	0	0	3	4	11
Days With ≥ 1.0" Snow Depth	na	na	na	na	na	na	na	na	na	na	na	na	na
Thunderstorm Days	0	< 1	2	2	5	5	6	2	1	1	0	0	24
Foggy Days	7	7	12	9	13	15	12	11	7	13	18	10	134
Predominant Sky Cover	na	na	na	na	na	na	na	na	na	na	na	na	na
Mean Relative Humidity 7am (%)	na	na	na	na	na	na	na	na	na	na	na	na	na
Mean Relative Humidity 4pm (%)	na	na	na	na	na	na	na	na	na	na	na	na	na
Mean Dewpoint (°F)	na	na	na	na	na	na	na	na	na	na	na	na	na
Prevailing Wind Direction	na	na	na	na	na	na	na	na	na	na	na	na	na
Prevailing Wind Speed (mph)	na	na	na	na	na	na	na	na	na	na	na	na	na
Maximum Wind Gust (mph)	67	69	87	63	53	51	52	71	67	67	67	67	87

Newark Int'l Airport

Terrain in vicinity of the station is flat and rather marshy. To the northwest are ridges oriented roughly in a south-southwest to north-northeast direction. They rise to an elevation of about 200 feet at 4.5 to five miles and to 500 to 600 feet at seven to eight miles. All winds between west-northwest and north-northwest are downslope and therefore are subject to some adiabatic temperature increase. This effect is evident in the rapid improvement which normally occurs with shift of wind to westerly, following a coastal storm or frontal passage. The drying effect of the downslope winds accounts for the relatively few local thunderstorms occurring at the station, compared to areas to the west. Easterly winds, particularly southeasterly, moderate the temperature because of the influence of the Atlantic Ocean.

Temperature falls of five to 15 degrees, depending on the season, are not uncommon when the wind backs from southwesterly to southeasterly. Periods of very hot weather, lasting as long as a week, are associated with a west-southwest air flow which has a long trajectory over land. Extremes of cold are related to rapidly moving outbreaks of cold air traveling southeastward from the Hudson Bay region. Temperatures of zero or below occur in one winter out of four, but are much more common several miles to the west of the station. Average dates of the last occurrence in spring and the first occurrence in autumn of temperatures as low as 32 degrees are in mid-April and the end of October or early November. Areas to the west of the station experience a growing season at least a month shorter than that at the airport.

A considerable amount of precipitation is realized from the Northeasters of the Atlantic coast. These storms, more typical of the fall and winter, generally last for a period of two days and commonly produce between one and two inches of precipitation. Storms producing four inches or more of snow occur from two to five times a winter. Snowstorms producing eight inches or more have occurred in about one-half the winters. As many as three such storms have been experienced in one winter. The frequency and intensity of snow storms and the duration of snow cover increase dramatically within a few miles to the west of the station.

Newark Int'l Airport *Essex County*   Elevation: 9 ft.   Latitude: 40° 43' N   Longitude: 74° 11' W

	JAN	FEB	MAR	APR	MAY	JUN	JUL	AUG	SEP	OCT	NOV	DEC	YEAR
Mean Maximum Temp. (°F)	38.7	41.9	50.9	62.1	72.7	81.4	86.5	84.6	77.0	65.8	54.8	44.1	63.4
Mean Temp. (°F)	31.6	34.2	42.5	53.0	63.4	72.5	78.0	76.3	68.6	57.2	47.1	37.1	55.1
Mean Minimum Temp. (°F)	24.3	26.5	34.1	43.7	54.2	63.6	69.4	68.0	60.2	48.5	39.4	30.2	46.8
Extreme Maximum Temp. (°F)	70	74	86	94	99	102	105	100	100	88	81	76	105
Extreme Minimum Temp. (°F)	-8	-1	7	16	36	46	54	45	41	29	16	-1	-8
Days Maximum Temp. ≥ 90°F	0	0	0	0	2	5	10	7	2	0	0	0	26
Days Maximum Temp. ≤ 32°F	9	5	1	0	0	0	0	0	0	0	0	4	19
Days Minimum Temp. ≤ 32°F	24	20	12	1	0	0	0	0	0	0	6	18	81
Days Minimum Temp. ≤ 0°F	1	0	0	0	0	0	0	0	0	0	0	0	1
Heating Degree Days (base 65°F)	1,030	863	693	365	114	11	0	1	38	255	531	857	4,758
Cooling Degree Days (base 65°F)	0	0	3	9	78	259	423	359	156	21	1	0	1,309
Mean Precipitation (in.)	3.89	3.02	4.21	3.92	4.36	3.37	4.60	4.00	3.92	3.22	3.94	3.53	45.98
Maximum Precipitation (in.)	10.1	5.9	11.1	11.1	10.2	6.4	10.0	11.8	10.3	8.2	11.5	9.5	65.5
Minimum Precipitation (in.)	0.4	0.8	1.1	0.9	0.5	0.1	0.9	0.4	0.1	0.2	0.5	0.3	26.1
Maximum 24-hr. Precipitation (in.)	2.9	2.4	2.7	2.8	4.0	3.0	3.5	5.9	4.7	4.0	6.7	2.8	6.7
Days With ≥ 0.1" Precipitation	7	6	7	7	7	6	7	6	6	5	6	7	77
Days With ≥ 1.0" Precipitation	1	1	1	1	1	1	1	1	1	1	1	1	12
Mean Snowfall (in.)	8.4	8.2	4.4	0.8	trace	0.0	0.0	0.0	trace	trace	0.6	2.5	24.9
Maximum Snowfall (in.)	27	33	26	14	trace	0	0	0	0	trace	9	29	66
Maximum 24-hr. Snowfall (in.)	14	18	13	13	trace	0	0	0	0	trace	9	29	26
Days With ≥ 1.0" Snow Depth	10	7	2	0	0	0	0	0	0	0	0	2	21
Thunderstorm Days	< 1	< 1	2	3	6	9	11	8	4	2	1	< 1	46
Foggy Days	9	9	10	9	11	10	9	10	11	11	9	10	118
Predominant Sky Cover	OVR	OVR	OVR	OVR	OVR	OVR	OVR	OVR	OVR	OVR	OVR	OVR	OVR
Mean Relative Humidity 7am (%)	73	71	69	67	70	71	72	76	79	78	76	74	73
Mean Relative Humidity 4pm (%)	58	54	51	48	51	51	52	54	55	53	57	59	54
Mean Dewpoint (°F)	21	21	27	36	48	57	63	63	56	45	35	25	42
Prevailing Wind Direction	WSW	NW	NW	NW	SW	SW	SW	SW	SW	SW	SW	WNW	SW
Prevailing Wind Speed (mph)	12	16	16	16	10	9	9	9	8	9	9	14	12
Maximum Wind Gust (mph)	62	60	67	62	58	83	69	68	67	55	63	61	83

Belleplain State Forest *Cape May County*   Elevation: 29 ft.   Latitude: 39° 15' N   Longitude: 74° 52' W

	JAN	FEB	MAR	APR	MAY	JUN	JUL	AUG	SEP	OCT	NOV	DEC	YEAR
Mean Maximum Temp. (°F)	43.9	46.7	54.9	65.7	74.8	82.3	86.7	85.0	79.3	68.7	58.6	48.9	66.3
Mean Temp. (°F)	33.6	35.7	43.1	52.5	61.9	70.3	75.6	73.8	67.6	56.5	47.2	38.4	54.7
Mean Minimum Temp. (°F)	23.2	24.6	31.3	39.3	49.0	58.4	64.4	62.6	55.9	44.3	35.8	27.8	43.0
Extreme Maximum Temp. (°F)	72	74	88	93	96	99	103	100	97	88	82	78	103
Extreme Minimum Temp. (°F)	-14	-9	5	14	24	38	43	38	33	21	9	-9	-14
Days Maximum Temp. ≥ 90°F	0	0	0	0	1	4	9	6	2	0	0	0	22
Days Maximum Temp. ≤ 32°F	4	2	0	0	0	0	0	0	0	0	0	2	8
Days Minimum Temp. ≤ 32°F	25	21	18	8	1	0	0	0	0	5	13	21	112
Days Minimum Temp. ≤ 0°F	1	0	0	0	0	0	0	0	0	0	0	0	1
Heating Degree Days (base 65°F)	967	822	673	376	145	24	1	4	52	276	528	818	4,686
Cooling Degree Days (base 65°F)	0	0	2	7	57	196	348	274	131	22	1	0	1,038
Mean Precipitation (in.)	3.80	3.01	4.08	3.72	3.65	2.90	3.63	5.19	3.67	3.82	3.34	3.51	44.32
Days With ≥ 0.1" Precipitation	7	6	7	7	7	5	6	6	5	5	6	6	73
Days With ≥ 1.0" Precipitation	1	1	1	1	1	1	1	2	1	1	1	1	13
Mean Snowfall (in.)	3.2	4.3	1.0	trace	0.0	0.0	0.0	0.0	0.0	trace	0.2	0.8	9.5
Days With ≥ 1.0" Snow Depth	4	2	0	0	0	0	0	0	0	0	0	1	7

Boonton 1 SE *Morris County*   Elevation: 278 ft.   Latitude: 40° 54' N   Longitude: 74° 24' W

	JAN	FEB	MAR	APR	MAY	JUN	JUL	AUG	SEP	OCT	NOV	DEC	YEAR
Mean Maximum Temp. (°F)	35.7	38.8	48.1	59.7	70.8	78.9	83.9	82.4	75.0	63.6	52.4	41.1	60.9
Mean Temp. (°F)	26.9	29.3	38.5	49.2	59.7	68.1	73.1	71.5	63.8	52.2	42.9	32.8	50.7
Mean Minimum Temp. (°F)	17.9	19.7	28.7	38.7	48.5	57.3	62.3	60.7	52.5	40.6	33.4	24.4	40.4
Extreme Maximum Temp. (°F)	65	69	82	92	96	95	100	97	94	83	78	68	100
Extreme Minimum Temp. (°F)	-15	-8	5	17	28	38	47	40	32	20	9	-6	-15
Days Maximum Temp. ≥ 90°F	0	0	0	0	0	2	5	3	1	0	0	0	11
Days Maximum Temp. ≤ 32°F	11	8	1	0	0	0	0	0	0	0	0	5	25
Days Minimum Temp. ≤ 32°F	29	25	21	6	0	0	0	0	0	6	14	25	126
Days Minimum Temp. ≤ 0°F	2	1	0	0	0	0	0	0	0	0	0	0	3
Heating Degree Days (base 65°F)	1,176	1,002	817	471	194	35	4	8	103	395	656	992	5,853
Cooling Degree Days (base 65°F)	0	0	0	3	38	142	274	219	73	5	0	0	754
Mean Precipitation (in.)	3.92	3.06	4.15	4.40	4.79	4.62	4.70	4.05	4.64	4.17	4.45	3.87	50.82
Days With ≥ 0.1" Precipitation	6	6	7	8	8	8	7	7	6	6	6	6	81
Days With ≥ 1.0" Precipitation	1	1	1	1	1	1	2	1	1	1	2	1	14
Mean Snowfall (in.)	8.9	9.0	5.1	0.8	0.0	0.0	0.0	0.0	0.0	trace	0.8	3.6	28.2
Days With ≥ 1.0" Snow Depth	na	na	3	0	0	0	0	0	0	0	0	0	na

Canoe Brook *Essex County*   Elevation: 177 ft.   Latitude: 40° 45' N   Longitude: 74° 21' W

	JAN	FEB	MAR	APR	MAY	JUN	JUL	AUG	SEP	OCT	NOV	DEC	YEAR
Mean Maximum Temp. (°F)	37.8	40.8	49.7	61.2	71.9	80.4	85.6	83.8	76.5	65.3	53.9	43.0	62.5
Mean Temp. (°F)	27.9	30.2	39.1	49.5	59.8	68.7	74.0	72.3	64.7	52.9	43.4	33.6	51.3
Mean Minimum Temp. (°F)	17.9	19.5	28.5	37.8	47.6	57.0	62.3	60.7	52.9	40.5	33.0	24.2	40.2
Extreme Maximum Temp. (°F)	69	75	89	94	95	100	103	99	99	88	80	76	103
Extreme Minimum Temp. (°F)	-15	-15	-1	18	25	36	44	39	31	19	10	-8	-15
Days Maximum Temp. ≥ 90°F	0	0	0	0	1	3	8	6	2	0	0	0	20
Days Maximum Temp. ≤ 32°F	9	6	1	0	0	0	0	0	0	0	0	5	21
Days Minimum Temp. ≤ 32°F	29	25	21	8	1	0	0	0	0	6	16	26	132
Days Minimum Temp. ≤ 0°F	2	1	0	0	0	0	0	0	0	0	0	0	3
Heating Degree Days (base 65°F)	1,149	981	802	468	198	37	4	8	94	378	645	971	5,735
Cooling Degree Days (base 65°F)	0	0	2	5	41	163	303	245	93	8	0	0	860
Mean Precipitation (in.)	4.06	3.09	4.21	4.22	4.66	4.35	4.61	4.77	4.97	4.26	4.49	3.78	51.47
Days With ≥ 0.1" Precipitation	7	6	7	7	8	7	7	6	6	6	6	6	79
Days With ≥ 1.0" Precipitation	1	1	1	1	1	1	1	1	1	1	1	1	12
Mean Snowfall (in.)	8.7	7.8	4.5	0.8	0.0	0.0	0.0	0.0	0.0	trace	0.6	3.2	25.6
Days With ≥ 1.0" Snow Depth	14	11	4	0	0	0	0	0	0	0	0	3	32

Cape May 2 NW *Cape May County*   Elevation: 19 ft.   Latitude: 38° 57' N   Longitude: 74° 56' W

	JAN	FEB	MAR	APR	MAY	JUN	JUL	AUG	SEP	OCT	NOV	DEC	YEAR
Mean Maximum Temp. (°F)	41.4	43.1	50.3	59.7	69.1	78.0	83.7	82.7	77.1	66.3	56.2	46.9	62.9
Mean Temp. (°F)	34.2	35.7	42.6	51.5	60.8	69.8	75.6	74.6	68.9	58.0	48.6	39.5	55.0
Mean Minimum Temp. (°F)	27.0	28.3	34.9	43.2	52.6	61.6	67.4	66.5	60.5	49.6	41.0	32.0	47.0
Extreme Maximum Temp. (°F)	68	71	82	88	95	96	100	96	95	88	78	76	100
Extreme Minimum Temp. (°F)	-2	-1	10	22	33	43	53	45	40	30	20	6	-2
Days Maximum Temp. ≥ 90°F	0	0	0	0	0	1	5	3	1	0	0	0	10
Days Maximum Temp. ≤ 32°F	6	4	1	0	0	0	0	0	0	0	0	2	13
Days Minimum Temp. ≤ 32°F	22	19	11	2	0	0	0	0	0	1	5	16	76
Days Minimum Temp. ≤ 0°F	0	0	0	0	0	0	0	0	0	0	0	0	0
Heating Degree Days (base 65°F)	947	821	688	402	158	17	0	2	31	233	486	785	4,570
Cooling Degree Days (base 65°F)	0	0	0	3	44	184	355	306	157	24	1	0	1,074
Mean Precipitation (in.)	3.64	3.06	4.09	3.48	3.61	3.00	3.16	3.63	3.19	3.56	3.24	3.56	41.22
Days With ≥ 0.1" Precipitation	7	7	7	7	7	5	5	5	5	5	6	7	73
Days With ≥ 1.0" Precipitation	1	1	1	1	1	1	1	1	1	1	1	1	12
Mean Snowfall (in.)	4.0	6.2	1.7	trace	0.0	0.0	0.0	0.0	0.0	trace	0.3	1.3	13.5
Days With ≥ 1.0" Snow Depth	3	5	1	0	0	0	0	0	0	0	0	1	10

Charlotteburg Reservoir *Passaic County*   Elevation: 757 ft.   Latitude: 41° 02' N   Longitude: 74° 26' W

	JAN	FEB	MAR	APR	MAY	JUN	JUL	AUG	SEP	OCT	NOV	DEC	YEAR
Mean Maximum Temp. (°F)	35.1	37.9	46.8	58.3	69.4	77.3	82.6	80.8	73.4	62.8	51.4	40.2	59.7
Mean Temp. (°F)	25.4	27.5	36.2	46.9	57.4	65.7	70.8	68.9	61.3	50.5	41.3	31.1	48.6
Mean Minimum Temp. (°F)	15.6	16.9	25.5	35.5	45.2	54.0	58.9	57.0	49.1	38.1	31.2	22.0	37.4
Extreme Maximum Temp. (°F)	65	74	85	92	94	95	100	97	94	85	79	73	100
Extreme Minimum Temp. (°F)	-24	-12	2	13	24	34	41	36	29	20	9	-11	-24
Days Maximum Temp. ≥ 90°F	0	0	0	0	0	1	4	2	0	0	0	0	7
Days Maximum Temp. ≤ 32°F	12	9	2	0	0	0	0	0	0	0	0	7	30
Days Minimum Temp. ≤ 32°F	29	26	25	11	1	0	0	0	1	9	18	27	147
Days Minimum Temp. ≤ 0°F	3	2	0	0	0	0	0	0	0	0	0	1	6
Heating Degree Days (base 65°F)	1,222	1,054	888	540	253	66	11	25	151	446	704	1,044	6,404
Cooling Degree Days (base 65°F)	0	0	0	3	24	99	208	152	46	3	0	0	535
Mean Precipitation (in.)	4.23	3.38	4.56	4.55	4.75	4.44	4.62	4.56	5.10	4.38	4.66	3.99	53.22
Days With ≥ 0.1" Precipitation	7	6	7	7	8	7	7	7	6	6	6	6	80
Days With ≥ 1.0" Precipitation	1	1	1	2	1	1	2	1	2	1	2	1	16
Mean Snowfall (in.)	10.2	9.7	7.1	1.9	trace	0.0	0.0	0.0	0.0	0.1	0.9	4.6	34.5
Days With ≥ 1.0" Snow Depth	14	13	6	1	0	0	0	0	0	0	1	5	40

Cranford *Union County*   Elevation: 72 ft.   Latitude: 40° 39' N   Longitude: 74° 18' W

	JAN	FEB	MAR	APR	MAY	JUN	JUL	AUG	SEP	OCT	NOV	DEC	YEAR
Mean Maximum Temp. (°F)	40.1	43.7	52.5	63.7	73.9	82.1	87.0	84.8	77.5	66.6	55.6	44.6	64.3
Mean Temp. (°F)	30.8	33.5	41.4	51.2	61.2	70.0	75.2	73.3	66.1	54.7	45.2	35.8	53.2
Mean Minimum Temp. (°F)	21.4	23.3	30.3	38.7	48.5	57.9	63.4	61.8	54.6	42.8	34.8	27.0	42.0
Extreme Maximum Temp. (°F)	70	75	90	96	96	98	102	99	99	87	80	76	102
Extreme Minimum Temp. (°F)	-10	-6	1	12	24	32	42	39	33	22	14	-5	-10
Days Maximum Temp. ≥ 90°F	0	0	0	0	1	5	11	6	2	0	0	0	25
Days Maximum Temp. ≤ 32°F	7	4	1	0	0	0	0	0	0	0	0	3	15
Days Minimum Temp. ≤ 32°F	26	23	18	7	1	0	0	0	0	4	13	23	115
Days Minimum Temp. ≤ 0°F	1	0	0	0	0	0	0	0	0	0	0	0	1
Heating Degree Days (base 65°F)	1,055	883	726	413	158	24	1	5	70	322	587	897	5,141
Cooling Degree Days (base 65°F)	0	0	2	5	49	188	337	266	107	11	0	0	965
Mean Precipitation (in.)	3.99	3.13	4.18	4.21	4.84	4.14	5.22	4.30	4.48	4.01	4.47	3.96	50.93
Days With ≥ 0.1" Precipitation	7	6	7	7	8	7	7	7	6	6	7	7	82
Days With ≥ 1.0" Precipitation	1	1	1	1	2	1	1	1	1	1	1	1	13
Mean Snowfall (in.)	7.2	6.6	3.7	0.4	0.0	0.0	0.0	0.0	0.0	trace	0.5	2.2	20.6
Days With ≥ 1.0" Snow Depth	12	9	3	0	0	0	0	0	0	0	0	2	26

Essex Fells Serv Bldg *Essex County*   Elevation: 347 ft.   Latitude: 40° 50' N   Longitude: 74° 17' W

	JAN	FEB	MAR	APR	MAY	JUN	JUL	AUG	SEP	OCT	NOV	DEC	YEAR
Mean Maximum Temp. (°F)	36.8	40.1	49.2	60.7	71.5	79.5	84.7	82.9	75.6	64.5	53.1	41.6	61.7
Mean Temp. (°F)	27.8	30.7	38.7	49.3	59.7	68.1	*73.4*	71.6	64.0	52.8	43.3	33.0	*51.0*
Mean Minimum Temp. (°F)	18.6	20.6	28.2	37.8	47.8	56.6	62.1	60.0	52.3	41.0	33.4	24.3	40.2
Extreme Maximum Temp. (°F)	67	75	89	94	92	96	101	98	99	87	83	74	101
Extreme Minimum Temp. (°F)	-14	-4	0	15	26	38	45	36	32	21	12	-6	-14
Days Maximum Temp. ≥ 90°F	0	0	0	0	1	2	6	4	1	0	0	0	14
Days Maximum Temp. ≤ 32°F	10	7	1	0	0	0	0	0	0	0	0	5	23
Days Minimum Temp. ≤ 32°F	28	25	22	7	0	0	0	0	0	5	15	26	128
Days Minimum Temp. ≤ 0°F	1	0	0	0	0	0	0	0	0	0	0	0	1
Heating Degree Days (base 65°F)	1,148	962	808	470	195	38	*3*	9	102	380	645	985	*5,745*
Cooling Degree Days (base 65°F)	0	0	1	4	36	137	274	214	76	7	0	0	749
Mean Precipitation (in.)	4.11	3.17	4.06	4.58	4.86	4.51	4.85	4.41	4.70	4.06	4.39	4.02	51.72
Days With ≥ 0.1" Precipitation	6	5	6	7	8	7	7	7	6	5	6	6	76
Days With ≥ 1.0" Precipitation	1	1	1	2	1	1	1	1	2	1	1	1	14
Mean Snowfall (in.)	*5.6*	*4.1*	*3.6*	0.7	0.0	0.0	0.0	0.0	0.0	trace	0.3	*2.4*	*16.7*
Days With ≥ 1.0" Snow Depth	na	na	*1*	0	0	0	0	0	0	0	0	1	na

Flemington 5 NNW *Hunterdon County*   Elevation: 259 ft.   Latitude: 40° 34' N   Longitude: 74° 53' W

	JAN	FEB	MAR	APR	MAY	JUN	JUL	AUG	SEP	OCT	NOV	DEC	YEAR
Mean Maximum Temp. (°F)	37.2	40.5	49.6	61.6	72.3	80.7	85.9	83.9	76.4	65.2	53.6	42.6	62.5
Mean Temp. (°F)	27.8	30.2	38.7	49.3	59.6	68.4	74.0	71.9	64.5	52.8	43.0	33.5	51.1
Mean Minimum Temp. (°F)	18.2	19.9	27.8	36.9	46.9	56.0	62.0	59.9	52.5	40.4	32.3	24.4	39.8
Extreme Maximum Temp. (°F)	67	73	88	94	95	96	104	101	100	86	81	75	104
Extreme Minimum Temp. (°F)	-18	-10	-6	18	26	34	45	38	29	19	10	-9	-18
Days Maximum Temp. ≥ 90°F	0	0	0	0	1	3	9	5	2	0	0	0	20
Days Maximum Temp. ≤ 32°F	10	7	1	0	0	0	0	0	0	0	0	5	23
Days Minimum Temp. ≤ 32°F	28	25	22	9	1	0	0	0	0	7	17	26	135
Days Minimum Temp. ≤ 0°F	2	1	0	0	0	0	0	0	0	0	0	0	3
Heating Degree Days (base 65°F)	1,148	976	810	470	195	35	3	10	94	377	653	968	5,739
Cooling Degree Days (base 65°F)	0	0	1	4	38	144	301	234	85	7	0	0	814
Mean Precipitation (in.)	4.24	3.07	4.18	4.11	4.82	4.31	4.67	3.95	4.43	3.97	3.90	3.93	49.58
Days With ≥ 0.1" Precipitation	7	6	7	7	8	7	7	6	6	6	6	6	80
Days With ≥ 1.0" Precipitation	1	1	1	1	1	1	2	1	1	1	1	1	13
Mean Snowfall (in.)	9.9	8.4	5.4	1.0	0.0	0.0	0.0	0.0	0.0	trace	0.6	3.5	28.8
Days With ≥ 1.0" Snow Depth	14	9	4	0	0	0	0	0	0	0	0	4	31

Glassboro 2 W *Gloucester County*   Elevation: 98 ft.   Latitude: 39° 44' N   Longitude: 75° 06' W

	JAN	FEB	MAR	APR	MAY	JUN	JUL	AUG	SEP	OCT	NOV	DEC	YEAR
Mean Maximum Temp. (°F)	39.3	42.4	51.2	62.1	72.3	81.0	85.8	84.2	77.3	65.8	55.3	44.8	63.5
Mean Temp. (°F)	31.3	33.9	42.1	52.0	62.1	71.0	76.2	74.6	67.5	55.6	46.4	36.9	54.1
Mean Minimum Temp. (°F)	23.2	25.3	33.0	42.0	51.7	60.9	66.6	64.9	57.8	45.5	37.4	28.9	44.8
Extreme Maximum Temp. (°F)	71	75	85	93	95	100	101	99	99	86	80	73	101
Extreme Minimum Temp. (°F)	-8	-2	5	18	31	43	51	45	38	23	15	1	-8
Days Maximum Temp. ≥ 90°F	0	0	0	0	1	4	8	5	2	0	0	0	20
Days Maximum Temp. ≤ 32°F	8	5	1	0	0	0	0	0	0	0	0	3	17
Days Minimum Temp. ≤ 32°F	26	22	15	3	0	0	0	0	0	1	10	21	98
Days Minimum Temp. ≤ 0°F	1	0	0	0	0	0	0	0	0	0	0	0	1
Heating Degree Days (base 65°F)	1,038	872	704	393	143	19	1	3	51	299	554	866	4,943
Cooling Degree Days (base 65°F)	0	0	2	8	61	215	370	300	131	17	1	0	1,105
Mean Precipitation (in.)	3.64	2.83	4.15	3.89	4.22	3.75	4.36	4.28	3.44	3.59	3.69	3.79	45.63
Days With ≥ 0.1" Precipitation	7	6	7	7	8	6	7	6	5	5	6	7	77
Days With ≥ 1.0" Precipitation	1	1	1	1	1	1	1	1	1	1	1	1	12
Mean Snowfall (in.)	na	na	*trace*	trace	0.0	0.0	0.0	0.0	0.0	trace	*trace*	1.2	na
Days With ≥ 1.0" Snow Depth	na	na	*1*	0	0	0	0	0	0	0	0	3	na

Hightstown 2 W *Mercer County*   Elevation: 98 ft.   Latitude: 40° 16' N   Longitude: 74° 34' W

	JAN	FEB	MAR	APR	MAY	JUN	JUL	AUG	SEP	OCT	NOV	DEC	YEAR
Mean Maximum Temp. (°F)	38.6	41.4	50.2	61.4	72.0	80.6	85.5	83.7	76.7	65.5	54.6	43.8	62.8
Mean Temp. (°F)	30.0	32.4	40.7	50.5	60.7	69.4	74.6	72.9	65.7	54.2	45.0	35.5	52.6
Mean Minimum Temp. (°F)	21.4	23.4	31.1	39.6	49.3	58.2	63.7	62.0	54.5	42.9	35.3	27.2	42.4
Extreme Maximum Temp. (°F)	70	75	88	93	95	98	102	97	98	88	80	76	102
Extreme Minimum Temp. (°F)	-12	-8	4	18	28	39	45	40	33	23	11	-5	-12
Days Maximum Temp. ≥ 90°F	0	0	0	0	1	3	8	5	1	0	0	0	18
Days Maximum Temp. ≤ 32°F	9	6	1	0	0	0	0	0	0	0	0	4	20
Days Minimum Temp. ≤ 32°F	27	23	18	6	0	0	0	0	0	4	13	23	114
Days Minimum Temp. ≤ 0°F	1	0	0	0	0	0	0	0	0	0	0	0	1
Heating Degree Days (base 65°F)	1,076	913	749	435	173	30	3	7	79	338	595	907	5,305
Cooling Degree Days (base 65°F)	0	0	1	6	48	173	317	249	101	12	1	0	908
Mean Precipitation (in.)	3.70	2.77	3.96	4.00	4.33	3.97	4.82	4.71	4.14	3.47	3.75	3.68	47.30
Days With ≥ 0.1" Precipitation	7	6	7	7	8	7	7	6	6	6	6	7	80
Days With ≥ 1.0" Precipitation	1	1	1	1	1	1	2	1	1	1	1	1	13
Mean Snowfall (in.)	7.1	7.4	3.6	0.9	trace	0.0	0.0	0.0	0.0	trace	0.4	2.6	22.0
Days With ≥ 1.0" Snow Depth	9	7	3	0	0	0	0	0	0	0	0	3	22

Indian Mills 2 W *Burlington County*   Elevation: 98 ft.   Latitude: 39° 48' N   Longitude: 74° 47' W

	JAN	FEB	MAR	APR	MAY	JUN	JUL	AUG	SEP	OCT	NOV	DEC	YEAR
Mean Maximum Temp. (°F)	41.2	44.7	53.2	64.6	74.8	82.8	87.5	85.7	78.8	67.8	57.0	46.4	65.4
Mean Temp. (°F)	31.5	34.2	42.1	51.9	61.9	70.3	75.4	73.6	66.6	55.3	45.9	36.7	53.8
Mean Minimum Temp. (°F)	21.8	23.6	30.9	39.0	48.9	57.8	63.2	61.5	54.5	42.7	34.7	26.9	42.1
Extreme Maximum Temp. (°F)	72	77	90	95	97	100	103	100	99	90	82	76	103
Extreme Minimum Temp. (°F)	-18	-12	-3	18	24	36	40	36	31	18	12	-4	-18
Days Maximum Temp. ≥ 90°F	0	0	0	0	2	5	11	8	2	0	0	0	28
Days Maximum Temp. ≤ 32°F	7	4	0	0	0	0	0	0	0	0	0	2	13
Days Minimum Temp. ≤ 32°F	26	22	18	8	1	0	0	0	0	6	14	22	117
Days Minimum Temp. ≤ 0°F	1	0	0	0	0	0	0	0	0	0	0	0	1
Heating Degree Days (base 65°F)	1,032	865	706	398	150	22	1	5	66	313	570	871	4,999
Cooling Degree Days (base 65°F)	0	0	2	10	64	198	343	275	122	19	2	0	1,035
Mean Precipitation (in.)	4.02	3.06	4.35	4.01	3.98	3.58	4.31	4.92	3.52	3.41	3.67	4.01	46.84
Days With ≥ 0.1" Precipitation	7	6	7	7	8	6	7	6	5	5	6	7	77
Days With ≥ 1.0" Precipitation	1	1	1	1	1	1	1	1	1	1	1	1	12
Mean Snowfall (in.)	6.7	5.2	2.3	0.6	0.0	0.0	0.0	0.0	0.0	trace	0.3	2.1	17.2
Days With ≥ 1.0" Snow Depth	7	5	1	0	0	0	0	0	0	0	0	2	15

Lambertville *Hunterdon County*   Elevation: 65 ft.   Latitude: 40° 22' N   Longitude: 74° 57' W

	JAN	FEB	MAR	APR	MAY	JUN	JUL	AUG	SEP	OCT	NOV	DEC	YEAR
Mean Maximum Temp. (°F)	39.7	43.1	52.4	63.9	74.8	83.0	87.6	85.8	78.6	67.2	55.4	44.4	64.6
Mean Temp. (°F)	30.3	33.0	41.4	51.4	62.0	70.7	75.7	73.9	66.6	54.8	44.9	35.3	53.3
Mean Minimum Temp. (°F)	21.1	22.9	30.4	38.8	49.2	58.4	63.7	62.0	54.6	42.5	34.3	26.2	42.0
Extreme Maximum Temp. (°F)	69	75	88	95	95	98	103	100	100	88	82	75	103
Extreme Minimum Temp. (°F)	-11	-9	1	13	25	38	45	39	32	22	12	-1	-11
Days Maximum Temp. ≥ 90°F	0	0	0	0	1	5	11	8	2	0	0	0	27
Days Maximum Temp. ≤ 32°F	8	4	0	0	0	0	0	0	0	0	0	3	15
Days Minimum Temp. ≤ 32°F	27	23	19	8	0	0	0	0	0	5	14	23	119
Days Minimum Temp. ≤ 0°F	1	1	0	0	0	0	0	0	0	0	0	0	2
Heating Degree Days (base 65°F)	1,068	896	726	410	141	18	1	4	65	322	597	913	5,161
Cooling Degree Days (base 65°F)	0	0	1	7	57	199	346	280	117	15	0	0	1,022
Mean Precipitation (in.)	3.96	2.90	4.23	4.08	4.56	4.15	5.01	4.28	4.47	3.62	3.87	3.84	48.97
Days With ≥ 0.1" Precipitation	7	6	8	7	8	7	7	7	6	6	6	7	82
Days With ≥ 1.0" Precipitation	1	1	1	1	1	1	2	1	1	1	1	1	13
Mean Snowfall (in.)	7.4	6.1	3.3	0.7	0.0	0.0	0.0	0.0	0.0	trace	0.5	2.4	20.4
Days With ≥ 1.0" Snow Depth	10	6	2	0	0	0	0	0	0	0	0	2	20

Little Falls *Passaic County*   Elevation: 147 ft.   Latitude: 40° 53' N   Longitude: 74° 14' W

	JAN	FEB	MAR	APR	MAY	JUN	JUL	AUG	SEP	OCT	NOV	DEC	YEAR
Mean Maximum Temp. (°F)	37.6	40.7	49.4	61.2	71.7	80.5	85.8	83.5	75.8	64.6	53.7	42.6	62.3
Mean Temp. (°F)	28.9	31.5	39.8	50.6	60.9	69.9	75.2	73.4	65.3	53.6	44.4	34.3	52.3
Mean Minimum Temp. (°F)	20.1	22.2	30.2	39.9	49.9	59.2	64.6	63.1	54.8	42.5	35.0	25.9	42.3
Extreme Maximum Temp. (°F)	67	75	88	95	96	96	103	99	98	87	83	74	103
Extreme Minimum Temp. (°F)	-10	-6	3	17	30	40	40	43	33	23	14	-6	-10
Days Maximum Temp. ≥ 90°F	0	0	0	0	1	4	8	4	1	0	0	0	18
Days Maximum Temp. ≤ 32°F	10	6	1	0	0	0	0	0	0	0	0	5	22
Days Minimum Temp. ≤ 32°F	28	23	19	5	0	0	0	0	0	4	12	24	115
Days Minimum Temp. ≤ 0°F	1	0	0	0	0	0	0	0	0	0	0	0	1
Heating Degree Days (base 65°F)	1,115	942	776	434	172	27	2	5	80	355	613	948	5,469
Cooling Degree Days (base 65°F)	0	0	2	6	51	187	335	270	96	7	0	0	954
Mean Precipitation (in.)	4.07	3.10	4.32	4.42	4.93	4.42	4.43	4.46	5.23	4.04	4.44	3.83	51.69
Days With ≥ 0.1" Precipitation	7	6	7	7	8	7	7	6	6	6	6	7	80
Days With ≥ 1.0" Precipitation	1	1	1	1	1	1	1	1	2	1	1	1	13
Mean Snowfall (in.)	na	na	2.3	trace	0.0	0.0	0.0	0.0	0.0	0.0	trace	na	na
Days With ≥ 1.0" Snow Depth	na	6	2	0	0	0	0	0	0	0	0	na	na

Long Valley *Morris County*   Elevation: 547 ft.   Latitude: 40° 47' N   Longitude: 74° 47' W

	JAN	FEB	MAR	APR	MAY	JUN	JUL	AUG	SEP	OCT	NOV	DEC	YEAR
Mean Maximum Temp. (°F)	36.3	39.4	48.1	59.8	69.9	77.2	81.9	79.9	72.3	62.6	52.2	41.1	60.0
Mean Temp. (°F)	26.5	28.8	37.0	47.4	57.6	65.5	70.5	68.8	61.0	50.4	41.5	31.7	48.9
Mean Minimum Temp. (°F)	16.6	18.1	25.8	35.0	45.2	53.7	59.1	57.7	49.6	38.2	30.7	22.3	37.7
Extreme Maximum Temp. (°F)	68	76	85	93	93	94	99	95	95	87	80	73	99
Extreme Minimum Temp. (°F)	-18	-12	-2	15	26	34	40	35	26	19	4	-11	-18
Days Maximum Temp. ≥ 90°F	0	0	0	0	0	1	3	1	0	0	0	0	5
Days Maximum Temp. ≤ 32°F	11	7	2	0	0	0	0	0	0	0	0	6	26
Days Minimum Temp. ≤ 32°F	29	26	25	12	2	0	0	0	0	10	19	27	150
Days Minimum Temp. ≤ 0°F	3	2	0	0	0	0	0	0	0	0	0	1	6
Heating Degree Days (base 65°F)	1,187	1,016	862	525	244	66	11	22	157	448	699	1,024	6,261
Cooling Degree Days (base 65°F)	0	0	0	2	21	89	201	148	43	3	0	0	507
Mean Precipitation (in.)	4.19	3.28	4.18	4.60	4.87	4.71	5.04	4.82	4.91	4.28	4.42	3.98	53.28
Days With ≥ 0.1" Precipitation	7	6	7	7	9	7	8	7	7	6	6	7	84
Days With ≥ 1.0" Precipitation	1	1	1	1	1	1	1	2	2	1	1	1	14
Mean Snowfall (in.)	10.5	8.9	6.3	1.9	0.0	0.0	0.0	0.0	0.0	0.2	1.0	4.9	33.7
Days With ≥ 1.0" Snow Depth	na	na	na	0	0	0	0	0	0	0	0	na	na

Millville Municipal Airport *Cumberland County*   Elevation: 68 ft.   Latitude: 39° 22' N   Longitude: 75° 04' W

	JAN	FEB	MAR	APR	MAY	JUN	JUL	AUG	SEP	OCT	NOV	DEC	YEAR
Mean Maximum Temp. (°F)	41.1	43.8	52.1	62.8	72.7	81.2	86.0	84.4	77.7	66.7	56.4	46.3	64.3
Mean Temp. (°F)	32.5	34.6	42.4	52.0	62.0	70.9	76.4	74.8	67.8	56.1	46.6	37.5	54.5
Mean Minimum Temp. (°F)	24.0	25.4	32.7	41.1	51.2	60.6	66.8	65.1	57.9	45.5	36.9	28.7	44.6
Extreme Maximum Temp. (°F)	71	75	86	91	96	99	101	101	97	90	82	77	101
Extreme Minimum Temp. (°F)	-10	-6	5	20	30	40	44	44	37	23	12	2	-10
Days Maximum Temp. ≥ 90°F	0	0	0	0	1	3	9	5	2	0	0	0	20
Days Maximum Temp. ≤ 32°F	7	5	1	0	0	0	0	0	0	0	0	3	16
Days Minimum Temp. ≤ 32°F	25	21	16	5	0	0	0	0	0	2	11	21	101
Days Minimum Temp. ≤ 0°F	0	0	0	0	0	0	0	0	0	0	0	0	0
Heating Degree Days (base 65°F)	999	852	694	392	144	18	1	2	47	288	546	845	4,828
Cooling Degree Days (base 65°F)	0	0	2	7	61	208	378	306	137	21	1	0	1,121
Mean Precipitation (in.)	3.55	3.22	4.32	3.66	3.92	3.32	3.59	4.24	3.37	3.20	3.28	3.62	43.29
Days With ≥ 0.1" Precipitation	6	6	7	7	7	6	6	5	5	5	6	6	72
Days With ≥ 1.0" Precipitation	1	1	1	1	1	1	1	1	1	1	1	1	12
Mean Snowfall (in.)	5.0	4.7	1.4	0.3	trace	0.0	trace	0.0	0.0	trace	0.2	1.6	13.2
Days With ≥ 1.0" Snow Depth	5	5	1	0	0	0	0	0	0	0	0	2	13

New Brunswick 3 SE *Middlesex County*   Elevation: 85 ft.   Latitude: 40° 28' N   Longitude: 74° 26' W

	JAN	FEB	MAR	APR	MAY	JUN	JUL	AUG	SEP	OCT	NOV	DEC	YEAR
Mean Maximum Temp. (°F)	38.0	41.0	49.7	60.8	71.3	79.9	85.2	83.4	76.5	65.3	54.3	43.5	62.4
Mean Temp. (°F)	29.5	31.9	40.3	50.3	60.5	69.4	74.8	73.1	65.7	54.2	44.9	35.1	52.5
Mean Minimum Temp. (°F)	21.0	22.8	30.8	39.7	49.6	58.7	64.4	62.8	54.9	43.0	35.3	26.7	42.5
Extreme Maximum Temp. (°F)	70	75	88	94	95	97	103	100	98	88	80	76	103
Extreme Minimum Temp. (°F)	-13	-7	6	16	30	40	45	40	35	25	13	-7	-13
Days Maximum Temp. ≥ 90°F	0	0	0	0	1	3	7	4	1	0	0	0	16
Days Maximum Temp. ≤ 32°F	9	6	1	0	0	0	0	0	0	0	0	4	20
Days Minimum Temp. ≤ 32°F	27	23	19	5	0	0	0	0	0	3	12	23	112
Days Minimum Temp. ≤ 0°F	1	0	0	0	0	0	0	0	0	0	0	0	1
Heating Degree Days (base 65°F)	1,093	927	761	441	177	29	2	5	73	339	598	919	5,364
Cooling Degree Days (base 65°F)	0	0	1	4	44	172	323	260	103	11	0	0	918
Mean Precipitation (in.)	4.03	3.00	4.11	4.15	4.50	3.89	4.96	4.36	4.29	3.47	4.03	3.87	48.66
Days With ≥ 0.1" Precipitation	7	6	7	6	8	7	7	6	6	6	6	7	79
Days With ≥ 1.0" Precipitation	1	1	1	1	1	1	2	1	1	1	1	1	13
Mean Snowfall (in.)	8.9	8.3	4.5	1.0	trace	0.0	0.0	0.0	0.0	trace	0.6	3.1	26.4
Days With ≥ 1.0" Snow Depth	12	9	3	0	0	0	0	0	0	0	0	3	27

Newton Saint Pauls Abbey *Sussex County*   Elevation: 597 ft.   Latitude: 41° 02' N   Longitude: 74° 48' W

	JAN	FEB	MAR	APR	MAY	JUN	JUL	AUG	SEP	OCT	NOV	DEC	YEAR
Mean Maximum Temp. (°F)	34.2	37.5	46.5	58.6	69.9	78.0	83.0	80.9	73.2	62.1	50.3	39.1	59.4
Mean Temp. (°F)	24.2	26.8	35.9	47.0	57.5	66.1	71.0	69.0	61.1	49.7	40.0	30.1	48.2
Mean Minimum Temp. (°F)	14.2	16.1	25.2	35.3	45.1	54.2	59.0	57.1	49.0	37.2	29.7	21.0	36.9
Extreme Maximum Temp. (°F)	65	71	83	91	95	96	101	95	95	85	80	72	101
Extreme Minimum Temp. (°F)	-26	-17	-5	14	24	33	40	35	27	16	7	-11	-26
Days Maximum Temp. ≥ 90°F	0	0	0	0	0	2	5	2	1	0	0	0	10
Days Maximum Temp. ≤ 32°F	12	9	2	0	0	0	0	0	0	0	1	7	31
Days Minimum Temp. ≤ 32°F	28	26	24	12	2	0	0	0	1	11	20	27	151
Days Minimum Temp. ≤ 0°F	4	3	0	0	0	0	0	0	0	0	0	1	8
Heating Degree Days (base 65°F)	1,258	1,072	896	537	249	63	12	25	158	471	743	1,077	6,561
Cooling Degree Days (base 65°F)	0	0	1	3	24	105	216	159	48	3	0	0	559
Mean Precipitation (in.)	3.50	2.76	3.65	4.08	4.32	4.47	4.34	4.41	4.55	3.82	3.94	3.41	47.25
Days With ≥ 0.1" Precipitation	7	6	7	7	8	7	7	6	7	6	7	6	81
Days With ≥ 1.0" Precipitation	1	0	1	1	1	1	1	1	1	1	1	1	11
Mean Snowfall (in.)	11.1	9.9	7.4	2.0	trace	0.0	0.0	0.0	0.0	0.1	1.9	5.4	37.8
Days With ≥ 1.0" Snow Depth	17	14	7	1	0	0	0	0	0	0	1	8	48

Pemberton *Burlington County*   Elevation: 59 ft.   Latitude: 39° 58' N   Longitude: 74° 41' W

	JAN	FEB	MAR	APR	MAY	JUN	JUL	AUG	SEP	OCT	NOV	DEC	YEAR
Mean Maximum Temp. (°F)	41.6	45.2	53.5	64.0	74.8	82.4	87.0	85.5	79.1	68.2	57.3	46.5	65.4
Mean Temp. (°F)	31.8	34.6	42.3	51.4	61.7	69.9	74.8	73.7	67.0	55.7	46.3	37.1	53.9
Mean Minimum Temp. (°F)	22.0	24.0	31.0	38.7	48.6	57.3	62.6	61.9	54.8	43.1	35.3	27.6	42.2
Extreme Maximum Temp. (°F)	70	77	91	93	95	98	104	101	98	91	82	75	104
Extreme Minimum Temp. (°F)	-17	-12	-2	16	25	36	41	37	32	20	8	-2	-17
Days Maximum Temp. ≥ 90°F	0	0	0	0	1	5	10	8	2	0	0	0	26
Days Maximum Temp. ≤ 32°F	6	3	0	0	0	0	0	0	0	0	0	2	11
Days Minimum Temp. ≤ 32°F	26	22	18	8	1	0	0	0	0	6	13	21	115
Days Minimum Temp. ≤ 0°F	1	1	0	0	0	0	0	0	0	0	0	0	2
Heating Degree Days (base 65°F)	1,023	852	701	409	149	25	2	5	61	300	556	858	4,941
Cooling Degree Days (base 65°F)	0	0	3	6	58	185	329	280	131	18	2	0	1,012
Mean Precipitation (in.)	3.88	2.90	4.20	3.83	4.29	4.09	4.51	5.14	3.66	3.50	3.53	3.84	47.37
Days With ≥ 0.1" Precipitation	7	6	8	7	8	7	6	6	6	5	6	7	79
Days With ≥ 1.0" Precipitation	1	1	1	1	1	1	1	2	1	1	1	1	13
Mean Snowfall (in.)	5.9	5.7	2.5	0.5	0.0	0.0	0.0	0.0	0.0	trace	0.3	2.0	16.9
Days With ≥ 1.0" Snow Depth	7	5	2	0	0	0	0	0	0	0	0	2	16

Plainfield *Union County*   Elevation: 88 ft.   Latitude: 40° 36' N   Longitude: 74° 24' W

	JAN	FEB	MAR	APR	MAY	JUN	JUL	AUG	SEP	OCT	NOV	DEC	YEAR
Mean Maximum Temp. (°F)	37.9	42.3	51.8	62.9	73.7	81.7	86.6	84.9	77.4	65.9	53.9	42.7	63.5
Mean Temp. (°F)	30.1	33.3	41.7	51.5	61.9	70.4	75.5	73.9	66.4	54.8	44.8	35.3	53.3
Mean Minimum Temp. (°F)	22.3	24.2	31.5	40.2	50.0	59.0	64.2	62.8	55.4	43.7	35.7	27.8	43.1
Extreme Maximum Temp. (°F)	68	76	91	97	99	100	104	100	100	88	82	74	104
Extreme Minimum Temp. (°F)	-8	-4	5	18	29	40	45	40	33	23	14	-3	-8
Days Maximum Temp. ≥ 90°F	0	0	0	0	2	5	10	7	2	0	0	0	26
Days Maximum Temp. ≤ 32°F	10	5	1	0	0	0	0	0	0	0	0	4	20
Days Minimum Temp. ≤ 32°F	26	23	17	5	0	0	0	0	0	3	12	22	108
Days Minimum Temp. ≤ 0°F	1	0	0	0	0	0	0	0	0	0	0	0	1
Heating Degree Days (base 65°F)	1,074	889	718	405	145	20	2	4	64	320	599	913	5,153
Cooling Degree Days (base 65°F)	0	0	2	7	57	195	344	282	112	12	0	0	1,011
Mean Precipitation (in.)	3.99	3.05	4.11	3.97	4.66	3.96	5.29	4.23	4.47	3.98	4.10	3.69	49.50
Days With ≥ 0.1" Precipitation	7	6	8	7	8	7	7	7	6	6	6	7	82
Days With ≥ 1.0" Precipitation	1	1	1	1	1	1	2	1	1	1	1	1	13
Mean Snowfall (in.)	9.2	8.7	4.4	0.6	trace	0.0	0.0	0.0	0.0	trace	0.6	3.1	26.6
Days With ≥ 1.0" Snow Depth	13	10	3	0	0	0	0	0	0	0	0	3	29

Seabrook Farms *Cumberland County*   Elevation: 88 ft.   Latitude: 39° 30' N   Longitude: 75° 14' W

	JAN	FEB	MAR	APR	MAY	JUN	JUL	AUG	SEP	OCT	NOV	DEC	YEAR
Mean Maximum Temp. (°F)	40.9	43.1	51.7	62.5	72.3	81.5	85.9	84.5	78.0	66.9	55.7	45.6	64.0
Mean Temp. (°F)	32.5	34.3	42.5	52.1	61.9	71.3	76.1	74.6	67.5	56.1	46.5	37.4	54.4
Mean Minimum Temp. (°F)	24.1	25.5	33.3	41.6	51.5	61.1	66.4	64.6	57.1	45.3	37.3	29.1	44.7
Extreme Maximum Temp. (°F)	70	74	86	92	95	100	100	100	98	88	80	74	100
Extreme Minimum Temp. (°F)	-13	0	9	24	33	41	49	44	36	24	15	5	-13
Days Maximum Temp. ≥ 90°F	0	0	0	0	1	4	8	5	2	0	0	0	20
Days Maximum Temp. ≤ 32°F	7	5	1	0	0	0	0	0	0	0	0	3	16
Days Minimum Temp. ≤ 32°F	25	21	15	4	0	0	0	0	0	2	10	21	98
Days Minimum Temp. ≤ 0°F	0	0	0	0	0	0	0	0	0	0	0	0	0
Heating Degree Days (base 65°F)	1,000	859	692	392	146	17	1	2	51	286	550	850	4,846
Cooling Degree Days (base 65°F)	0	0	3	8	63	228	376	303	132	19	1	0	1,133
Mean Precipitation (in.)	4.05	2.85	4.17	3.35	3.96	3.28	4.35	4.31	3.71	3.52	3.30	3.84	44.69
Days With ≥ 0.1" Precipitation	7	6	7	6	7	6	7	6	6	5	6	6	75
Days With ≥ 1.0" Precipitation	1	1	1	1	1	1	1	1	1	1	1	1	12
Mean Snowfall (in.)	na	na	na	0.4	0.0	0.0	0.0	0.0	0.0	0.0	0.2	na	na
Days With ≥ 1.0" Snow Depth	na	na	na	0	0	0	0	0	0	0	0	na	na

Somerville 3 NW *Somerset County*   Elevation: 157 ft.   Latitude: 40° 36' N   Longitude: 74° 38' W

	JAN	FEB	MAR	APR	MAY	JUN	JUL	AUG	SEP	OCT	NOV	DEC	YEAR
Mean Maximum Temp. (°F)	36.8	39.8	49.3	60.9	71.6	79.9	85.0	82.8	75.4	64.0	53.2	41.8	61.7
Mean Temp. (°F)	27.6	29.8	38.6	49.1	59.4	68.1	73.4	71.6	63.9	52.3	43.0	33.0	50.8
Mean Minimum Temp. (°F)	18.3	19.8	27.8	37.2	47.2	56.3	61.7	60.2	52.4	40.5	32.7	24.1	39.9
Extreme Maximum Temp. (°F)	68	75	83	94	94	96	103	97	99	85	80	73	103
Extreme Minimum Temp. (°F)	-16	-10	2	18	26	37	45	38	32	21	10	-7	-16
Days Maximum Temp. ≥ 90°F	0	0	0	0	1	2	7	4	1	0	0	0	15
Days Maximum Temp. ≤ 32°F	10	7	1	0	0	0	0	0	0	0	0	5	23
Days Minimum Temp. ≤ 32°F	28	25	22	9	1	0	0	0	0	6	17	26	134
Days Minimum Temp. ≤ 0°F	2	1	0	0	0	0	0	0	0	0	0	0	3
Heating Degree Days (base 65°F)	1,154	988	813	475	200	35	4	9	103	392	653	986	5,812
Cooling Degree Days (base 65°F)	0	0	0	3	35	140	278	217	76	7	0	0	756
Mean Precipitation (in.)	3.77	2.83	3.88	4.07	4.39	4.16	4.83	4.39	4.33	3.90	3.89	3.70	48.14
Days With ≥ 0.1" Precipitation	7	6	7	7	8	7	8	7	6	6	6	7	82
Days With ≥ 1.0" Precipitation	1	0	1	1	1	1	1	1	1	1	1	1	11
Mean Snowfall (in.)	8.8	8.4	5.1	1.4	0.0	0.0	0.0	0.0	0.0	trace	0.7	3.1	27.5
Days With ≥ 1.0" Snow Depth	13	11	4	0	0	0	0	0	0	0	0	4	32

Toms River *Ocean County*   Elevation: 98 ft.   Latitude: 39° 57' N   Longitude: 74° 13' W

	JAN	FEB	MAR	APR	MAY	JUN	JUL	AUG	SEP	OCT	NOV	DEC	YEAR
Mean Maximum Temp. (°F)	41.6	43.8	51.8	62.1	72.4	80.9	86.3	84.6	78.2	67.2	57.2	46.7	64.4
Mean Temp. (°F)	31.3	33.1	41.0	50.2	60.6	69.3	74.9	73.1	66.3	54.7	45.9	36.3	53.0
Mean Minimum Temp. (°F)	20.8	22.3	30.0	38.3	48.8	57.6	63.4	61.7	54.2	42.3	34.5	25.9	41.7
Extreme Maximum Temp. (°F)	72	75	87	93	99	102	105	101	99	91	85	76	105
Extreme Minimum Temp. (°F)	-19	-8	3	12	28	39	46	39	33	21	9	-3	-19
Days Maximum Temp. ≥ 90°F	0	0	0	0	1	4	10	7	2	0	0	0	24
Days Maximum Temp. ≤ 32°F	6	4	0	0	0	0	0	0	0	0	0	2	12
Days Minimum Temp. ≤ 32°F	27	23	19	8	0	0	0	0	0	5	14	24	120
Days Minimum Temp. ≤ 0°F	1	1	0	0	0	0	0	0	0	0	0	0	2
Heating Degree Days (base 65°F)	1,039	895	739	442	179	31	2	5	65	322	568	882	5,169
Cooling Degree Days (base 65°F)	0	0	2	4	53	174	328	255	109	11	1	0	937
Mean Precipitation (in.)	4.13	3.30	4.38	4.17	4.15	3.50	4.39	4.98	3.78	3.65	4.08	4.12	48.63
Days With ≥ 0.1" Precipitation	7	6	7	7	7	7	7	6	6	6	7	7	80
Days With ≥ 1.0" Precipitation	1	1	1	1	1	1	1	2	1	1	1	1	13
Mean Snowfall (in.)	na	2.2	0.4	trace	0.0	0.0	0.0	0.0	0.0	0.0	trace	na	na
Days With ≥ 1.0" Snow Depth	na	na	0	0	0	0	0	0	0	0	0	na	na

Tuckerton *Ocean County*   Elevation: 19 ft.   Latitude: 39° 36' N   Longitude: 74° 21' W

	JAN	FEB	MAR	APR	MAY	JUN	JUL	AUG	SEP	OCT	NOV	DEC	YEAR
Mean Maximum Temp. (°F)	41.3	43.7	51.7	61.6	71.5	80.4	85.5	84.1	77.6	66.7	57.0	46.7	64.0
Mean Temp. (°F)	32.1	34.0	41.8	50.9	60.9	70.1	75.7	74.3	67.6	56.1	47.0	37.4	54.0
Mean Minimum Temp. (°F)	22.9	24.3	31.9	40.1	50.4	59.8	65.8	64.5	57.5	45.5	37.0	28.0	44.0
Extreme Maximum Temp. (°F)	74	74	87	92	97	101	104	100	98	87	85	76	104
Extreme Minimum Temp. (°F)	-7	-4	5	19	27	38	45	41	35	25	10	-2	-7
Days Maximum Temp. ≥ 90°F	0	0	0	0	1	4	9	6	2	0	0	0	22
Days Maximum Temp. ≤ 32°F	6	4	0	0	0	0	0	0	0	0	0	2	12
Days Minimum Temp. ≤ 32°F	25	22	17	6	0	0	0	0	0	2	11	21	104
Days Minimum Temp. ≤ 0°F	1	0	0	0	0	0	0	0	0	0	0	0	1
Heating Degree Days (base 65°F)	1,012	868	712	423	166	22	1	4	53	287	534	849	4,931
Cooling Degree Days (base 65°F)	0	0	0	6	55	199	362	297	135	20	1	0	1,075
Mean Precipitation (in.)	3.86	3.20	4.46	4.12	3.60	3.08	4.11	4.84	3.23	3.27	3.82	3.73	45.32
Days With ≥ 0.1" Precipitation	7	6	7	6	7	6	6	7	5	5	6	6	74
Days With ≥ 1.0" Precipitation	1	1	1	1	1	1	1	1	1	1	1	1	12
Mean Snowfall (in.)	6.1	6.7	2.0	0.4	trace	0.0	0.0	0.0	0.0	trace	0.4	2.3	17.9
Days With ≥ 1.0" Snow Depth	6	5	2	0	0	0	0	0	0	0	0	2	15

Woodstown *Salem County*   Elevation: 49 ft.   Latitude: 39° 39' N   Longitude: 75° 19' W

	JAN	FEB	MAR	APR	MAY	JUN	JUL	AUG	SEP	OCT	NOV	DEC	YEAR
Mean Maximum Temp. (°F)	41.3	44.4	53.8	65.5	75.5	83.7	88.2	86.2	79.4	67.8	56.9	46.2	65.8
Mean Temp. (°F)	32.5	34.8	43.2	53.1	63.1	71.9	76.7	74.7	68.1	56.6	47.0	37.4	54.9
Mean Minimum Temp. (°F)	23.7	25.0	32.5	40.7	50.7	60.0	65.2	63.4	56.7	45.3	37.0	28.6	44.1
Extreme Maximum Temp. (°F)	71	76	88	93	96	101	102	102	99	90	80	75	102
Extreme Minimum Temp. (°F)	-13	-6	-3	18	29	43	43	42	35	20	8	-2	-13
Days Maximum Temp. ≥ 90°F	0	0	0	0	2	6	13	9	2	0	0	0	32
Days Maximum Temp. ≤ 32°F	6	4	0	0	0	0	0	0	0	0	0	3	13
Days Minimum Temp. ≤ 32°F	25	22	16	5	0	0	0	0	0	3	11	21	103
Days Minimum Temp. ≤ 0°F	1	0	0	0	0	0	0	0	0	0	0	0	1
Heating Degree Days (base 65°F)	1,001	848	673	359	119	13	1	2	47	273	537	847	4,720
Cooling Degree Days (base 65°F)	0	0	2	10	72	237	388	310	145	23	1	0	1,188
Mean Precipitation (in.)	3.72	2.83	4.07	3.80	3.94	3.89	4.40	4.21	3.85	3.50	3.57	3.71	45.49
Days With ≥ 0.1" Precipitation	7	5	7	7	7	6	7	6	6	5	6	6	75
Days With ≥ 1.0" Precipitation	1	1	1	1	1	1	1	1	1	1	1	1	12
Mean Snowfall (in.)	5.7	5.0	2.6	0.5	trace	0.0	0.0	0.0	0.0	0.1	0.3	2.3	16.5
Days With ≥ 1.0" Snow Depth	7	6	1	0	0	0	0	0	0	0	0	3	17

Note: See Appendix D for explanation of data.

NEW MEXICO

PHYSICAL FEATURES. New Mexico, with a total area of 121,666 square miles, is in the southwestern part of the country. The State, approximately 350 miles square, lies mostly between latitudes 32° and 37° N. and longitudes 103° and 109° W. The State's topography consists mainly of high plateaus or mesas, with numerous mountain ranges, canyons, valleys, and normally dry arroyos. Average elevation is about 5,700 feet above sea level. The lowest point is upstream from the Red Bluff Reservoir at 2,817 feet where the Pecos River flows into Texas. The highest point is Wheeler Peak at 13,161 feet above sea level. The principal sources of moisture for the scant rains and snows that fall on the State are the Pacific Ocean, 500 miles to the west, and the Gulf of Mexico, 500 miles to the southeast.

New Mexico is divided into three major areas by mountain ranges and highlands, oriented in a general north-south direction, which merge in the north. The Northern Mountains and Central Highlands, between longitudes 105° and 106° W., are the western boundary of the Northeastern and Southeastern Plains which slope gradually eastward and southeastward. The northern part of these eastern plains lies within the Arkansas River Basin and is drained mostly by the Canadian River and the Cimarron River. West of the mountain ranges that form the Continental Divide, whose height decreases to a markedly lower elevation in southern New Mexico, rivers drain into the Gulf of California through the Colorado River system. Between the Northern Mountains and the Central Highland system and the Continental Divide system is the Rio Grande Valley which widens toward the south.

GENERAL CLIMATE. New Mexico has a mild, arid or semiarid, continental climate characterized by light precipitation totals, abundant sunshine, low relative humidities, and a relatively large annual and diurnal temperature range. The highest mountains have climate characteristics common to the Rocky Mountains.

Location and topography play major roles in determining the climate of New Mexico, particularly true for any specific locality. Both the ruggedness of the terrain and its direction of slope are important. The eastern plains open to the Great Plains of Texas and Oklahoma and to their northward extension into central Canada. At times during winter months, cold continental air masses move southward out of central Canada and invade this area, producing blizzard and cold-wave conditions. These air masses occasionally cross the Central Highlands, which greatly modify and warm the air masses before they reach the Rio Grande Valley.

PRECIPITATION. Average annual precipitation ranges from less than 10 inches over much of the southern desert and the Rio Grande and San Juan Valleys, to more than 20 inches at higher elevations in the State. A wide variation in annual totals is characteristic of arid and semiarid climates.

Summer rains fall almost entirely during brief, but frequently intense, thunderstorms. The general southeasterly circulation from the Gulf of Mexico brings moisture for these storms into the State, and strong surface heating combined with orographic lifting as the air moves over higher terrain causes convective air currents and condensation. July and August are the rainiest months over most of the State, with from 30 to 40 percent of the year's total moisture falling at that time. The San Juan Valley area is least affected by this summer circulation, receiving about 25 percent of its annual rainfall during July and August. During the warmest six months of the year, May through October, total precipitation averages from 60 percent of the annual total in the Northwestern Plateau to 80 percent of the annual total in the eastern plains.

Winter precipitation is caused mainly by frontal activity associated with the general movement of Pacific Ocean storms across the country from west to east. As these storms move inland, much of the moisture is precipitated over the coastal and inland mountain ranges of California, Nevada, Arizona, and Utah. Much of the remaining moisture falls on the western slope of the Continental Divide and over northern and high central mountain ranges. Winter is the driest season in New Mexico except for the portion west of the Continental Divide. This dryness is most noticeable in the Central Valley and on eastern slopes of the mountains.

Much of the winter precipitation falls as snow in the mountain areas, but it may occur as either rain or snow in the valleys. Average annual snowfall ranges from about 3 inches at the Southern Desert and Southeastern Plains stations to well over 100 inches at Northern Mountain stations. It may exceed 300 inches in the highest mountains of the north.

FLOODS. General floods are seldom widespread in New Mexico. Heavy summer thunderstorms may bring several inches of rain to small areas in a short time. Because of the rough terrain and sparse vegetation in many areas, run-offs from these storms frequently cause local flash floods. Normally dry arroyos may overflow their banks for several hours, halting traffic where water crosses highways, and damaging bridges, culverts, and roadways. Snowmelt during April to June, especially in combination with a warm rain, and heavy general rains during August to October may occasionally cause flooding of the larger rivers.

TEMPERATURE. Elevation is a greater factor in determining the temperature of any specific locality than its latitude. During the summer months, individual daytime temperatures quite often exceed 100 at elevations below 5,000 feet; but the average monthly maximum temperatures during July, the warmest month, range from slightly above 90°F. at lower elevations to the upper 70s at high elevations. Warmest days quite often occur in June before the thunderstorm season sets in; during July and August, afternoon convective storms tend to shut off afternoon solar insolation, lowering temperatures before they reach their potential daily high. A preponderance of clear skies and low relative humidity permits rapid cooling by radiation from the earth after sundown; consequently, nights are usually comfortable in summer.

In January, the coldest month, average daytime temperatures range from the middle 50s in the southern and central valleys to the middle 30s in the higher elevations of the north. Minimum temperatures below freezing are common in all sections of the State during the winter, but subzero temperatures are rare except in the mountains. The freeze-free season ranges from more than 200 days in the southern valleys to less than 80 days in the northern mountains where some high mountain valleys have freezes in summer months.

SEVERE STORMS. On rare occasions, a tropical hurricane may cause heavy rain in eastern and central New Mexico as it moves inland from the western part of the Gulf of Mexico. Also on rare occasions, a tropical storm moving inland from the Gulf of California area may cause heavy rain to fall in southwestern New Mexico. Tornadoes are occasionally reported in New Mexico, most frequently during afternoon and early evening hours from May through August.

Thunderstorms are relatively frequent in summer, averaging in numbers from 40 in the south to more than 70 in the northeast, the latter area having the second greatest thunderstorm frequency in the country. Occasionally, these heavy thunderstorms are accompanied by hail, with the greatest hail frequency occurring near and to the east of Los Alamos.

OTHER CLIMATIC ELEMENTS. Plentiful sunshine occurs in New Mexico, with from 75 to 80 percent of the possible sunshine being received. In winter, this prevalence is particularly noticeable with from 70 to 75 percent of the possible sunshine being received. It is not uncommon for as much as 90 percent of the possible sunshine to occur in November and in some of the spring months. The average number of hours of annual sunshine ranges from near 3,700 in the southwest to 2,800 in the north-central portions.

Average relative humidities are lower in the valleys but higher in the mountains because of the lower mountain temperatures. Relative humidity ranges from an average of near 65 percent at about sunrise to near 30 percent in midafternoon; however, afternoon humidities in warmer months are often less than 20 percent and occasionally may go as low as four percent. The prevalent low relative humidities during periods of extreme temperatures ease the effect of summer and winter temperatures on comfort.

Wind speeds over the State are usually moderate, although relatively strong winds often accompany occasional frontal activity during late winter and spring months and sometimes occur just in advance of thunderstorms. Frontal winds may exceed 30 m.p.h. for several hours and reach peak speeds of more than 50 m.p.h. Spring is the windy season. Blowing dust and serious soil erosion of unprotected fields may be a problem during dry spells. Winds are generally stronger in the eastern plains than in other parts of the State. Winds generally predominate from the southeast in summer and from the west in winter, but local surface wind directions will vary greatly because of local topography and mountain and valley breezes.

Potential evaporation in New Mexico is much greater than average annual precipitation.

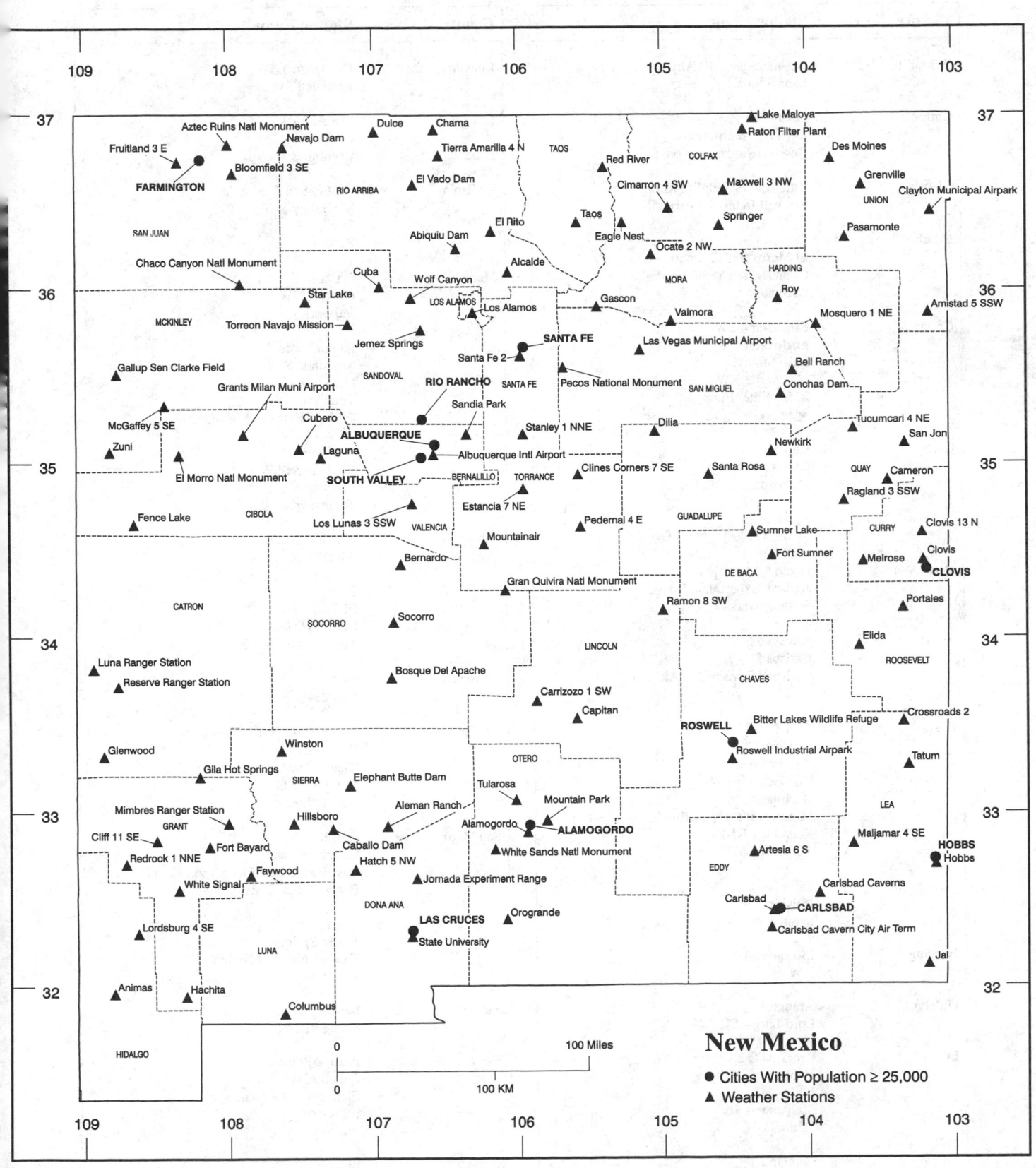

New Mexico

● Cities With Population ≥ 25,000
▲ Weather Stations

New Mexico Weather Stations by County

County	Station Name
Bernalillo	Albuquerque Int'l Airport
	Sandia Park
Catron	Glenwood
	Luna Ranger Station
	Reserve Ranger Station
Chaves	Bitter Lakes Wildlife Refuge
	Roswell Industrial Airpark
Cibola	Cubero
	El Morro Nat'l Monument
	Grants Milan Muni Airport
	Laguna
Colfax	Cimarron 4 SW
	Eagle Nest
	Lake Maloya
	Maxwell 3 NW
	Raton Filter Plant
	Springer
Curry	Clovis
	Clovis 13 N
	Melrose
Debaca	Fort Sumner
	Sumner Lake
Dona Ana	Hatch 5 NW
	Jornada Experiment Range
	State University
Eddy	Artesia 6 S
	Carlsbad
	Carlsbad Cavern City Air Term
	Carlsbad Caverns
Grant	Cliff 11 SE
	Faywood
	Fort Bayard
	Gila Hot Springs
	Hachita
	Mimbres Ranger Station
	Redrock 1 NNE
	White Signal
Guadalupe	Dilia
	Newkirk
	Santa Rosa
Harding	Mosquero 1 NE
	Roy
Hidalgo	Animas
	Lordsburg 4 SE
Lea	Crossroads 2
	Hobbs
	Jal
	Maljamar 4 SE
	Tatum
Lincoln	Capitan

County	Station Name
Lincoln (cont.)	Carrizozo 1 SW
	Ramon 8 SW
Los Alamos	Los Alamos
Luna	Columbus
McKinley	Gallup Sen Clarke Field
	McGaffey 5 SE
	Star Lake
	Zuni
Mora	Gascon
	Ocate 2 NW
	Valmora
Otero	Alamogordo
	Mountain Park
	Orogrande
	Tularosa
	White Sands Nat'l Monument
Quay	Cameron
	Ragland 3 SSW
	San Jon
	Tucumcari 4 NE
Rio Arriba	Abiquiu Dam
	Alcalde
	Chama
	Dulce
	El Rito
	El Vado Dam
	Tierra Amarilla 4 N
Roosevelt	Elida
	Portales
San Juan	Aztec Ruins Nat'l Monument
	Bloomfield 3 SE
	Chaco Canyon Nat'l Monument
	Fruitland 3 E
	Navajo Dam
San Miguel	Bell Ranch
	Conchas Dam
	Las Vegas Municipal Airport
	Pecos National Monument
Sandoval	Cuba
	Jemez Springs
	Torreon Navajo Mission
	Wolf Canyon
Santa Fe	Santa Fe 2
	Stanley 1 NNE
Sierra	Aleman Ranch
	Caballo Dam
	Elephant Butte Dam
	Hillsboro
	Winston
Socorro	Bernardo

County	Station Name
Socorro *(cont.)*	Bosque Del Apache
	Gran Quivira Nat'l Monument
	Socorro
Taos	Red River
	Taos
Torrance	Clines Corners 7 SE
	Estancia 7 NE
	Mountainair
	Pedernal 4 E
Union	Amistad 5 SSW
	Clayton Municipal Airpark
	Des Moines
	Grenville
	Pasamonte
Valencia	Fence Lake
	Los Lunas 3 SSW

New Mexico Weather Stations by City

City	Station Name	Miles
Alamogordo	Alamogordo	1
	Mountain Park	8
	Tularosa	13
	White Sands Nat'l Monument	16
Albuquerque	Albuquerque Int'l Airport	4
	Sandia Park	13
Carlsbad	Carlsbad	1
	Carlsbad Cavern City Air Term	6
	Carlsbad Caverns	20
Clovis	Clovis	0
	Clovis 13 N	13
	Portales	19
Farmington	Aztec Ruins Nat'l Monument	12
	Bloomfield 3 SE	14
	Fruitland 3 E	9
Hobbs	Hobbs	1
Las Cruces	State University	2
Rio Rancho	Albuquerque Int'l Airport	15
	Sandia Park	19
Roswell	Bitter Lakes Wildlife Refuge	9
	Roswell Industrial Airpark	6
Santa Fe	Pecos National Monument	18
	Santa Fe 2	4
South Valley	Albuquerque Int'l Airport	5
	Los Lunas 3 SSW	19

Note: Miles is the distance between the geographic center of the city and the weather station.

New Mexico Weather Stations by Elevation

Feet	Station Name
8,674	Red River
8,277	Eagle Nest
8,248	Gascon
8,218	Wolf Canyon
7,998	McGaffey 5 SE
7,847	Chama
7,654	Ocate 2 NW
7,463	Tierra Amarilla 4 N
7,421	Los Alamos
7,398	Lake Maloya
7,224	El Morro Nat'l Monument
7,053	Fence Lake
7,047	Luna Ranger Station
7,043	Cuba
7,007	Sandia Park
6,961	Taos
6,929	Raton Filter Plant
6,922	Clines Corners 7 SE
6,876	Pecos National Monument
6,870	El Rito
6,863	Las Vegas Municipal Airport
6,791	Dulce
6,778	Mountain Park
6,738	El Vado Dam
6,715	Santa Fe 2
6,699	Torreon Navajo Mission
6,633	Star Lake
6,617	Des Moines
6,597	Gran Quivira Nat'l Monument
6,538	Cimarron 4 SW
6,519	Grants Milan Muni Airport
6,496	Mountainair
6,463	Capitan
6,463	Gallup Sen Clarke Field
6,377	Abiquiu Dam
6,377	Stanley 1 NNE
6,309	Valmora
6,309	Zuni
6,263	Jemez Springs
6,236	Mimbres Ranger Station
6,197	Pedernal 4 E
6,194	Cubero
6,194	Winston
6,171	Chaco Canyon Nat'l Monument
6,141	Fort Bayard
6,118	Estancia 7 NE
6,066	White Signal
6,017	Maxwell 3 NW
6,000	Grenville
5,921	Springer
5,875	Roy
5,846	Reserve Ranger Station
5,816	Laguna
5,803	Bloomfield 3 SE
5,767	Navajo Dam

Feet	Station Name
5,679	Alcalde
5,649	Pasamonte
5,643	Aztec Ruins Nat'l Monument
5,597	Gila Hot Springs
5,462	Mosquero 1 NE
5,403	Carrizozo 1 SW
5,324	Ramon 8 SW
5,308	Albuquerque Int'l Airport
5,269	Hillsboro
5,219	Fruitland 3 E
5,190	Faywood
5,147	Dilia
5,059	Ragland 3 SSW
4,957	Clayton Municipal Airpark
4,839	Los Lunas 3 SSW
4,773	Cliff 11 SE
4,750	Glenwood
4,734	Bernardo
4,599	Santa Rosa
4,596	Melrose
4,583	Socorro
4,576	Cameron
4,573	Elephant Butte Dam
4,560	Newkirk
4,520	Aleman Ranch
4,511	Bosque Del Apache
4,504	Hachita
4,498	Bell Ranch
4,442	Amistad 5 SSW
4,432	Clovis 13 N
4,429	Tularosa
4,416	Animas
4,402	Carlsbad Caverns
4,353	Elida
4,347	Alamogordo
4,304	Sumner Lake
4,288	Clovis
4,265	Jornada Experiment Range
4,248	Lordsburg 4 SE
4,242	Conchas Dam
4,229	San Jon
4,189	Caballo Dam
4,179	Orogrande
4,146	Crossroads 2
4,097	Tatum
4,084	Tucumcari 4 NE
4,064	Columbus
4,048	Redrock 1 NNE
4,038	Hatch 5 NW
4,022	Fort Sumner
4,009	Portales
3,999	Maljamar 4 SE
3,992	White Sands Nat'l Monument
3,877	State University
3,661	Bitter Lakes Wildlife Refuge

Feet	Station Name
3,648	Roswell Industrial Airpark
3,612	Hobbs
3,316	Artesia 6 S
3,231	Carlsbad Cavern City Air Term
3,120	Carlsbad
3,057	Jal

Albuquerque Int'l Airport

The Albuquerque metropolitan area is largely situated in the Rio Grande Valley and on the mesas and piedmont slopes which rise either side of the valley floor. The Rio Grande flows from north to south through the area. The Sandia and Manzano Mountains rise abruptly at the eastern edge of the city with Tijeras Canyon separating the two ranges. The climate of Albuquerque is best described as arid continental with abundant sunshine, low humidity, scant precipitation, and a wide yet tolerable seasonal range of temperatures. Sunny days and low humidity are renowned features of the climate. More than three-fourths of the daylight hours have sunshine, even in the winter months. The air is normally dry and muggy days are rare. The combination of dry air and plentiful solar radiation allows widespread use of energy-efficient devices such as evaporative coolers and solar collectors.

Precipitation within the valley area is adequate only for native desert vegetation and deep-rooted imports. However, irrigation supports successful farming and fruit growing in the Rio Grande Valley.

Meager amounts of precipitation fall in the winter, much of it as snow. Snowfalls of an inch or more occur about four times a year in the Rio Grande Valley, while the mountains receive substantial snowfall on occasion. Snow seldom remains on the ground more than 24 hours in the city proper. However, snow cover on the east slopes of the Sandias is sufficient for skiing during most winters.

Nearly half of the annual precipitation in Albuquerque results from afternoon and evening thunderstorms during the summer. Thunderstorm frequency increases rapidly around July 1st, peaks during August, then tapers off by the end of September. Hailstorms are infrequent and tornadoes rare.

High temperatures during the winter are near 50 degrees with only a few days on which the temperature fails to rise above the freezing mark. In the summer, daytime maxima are about 90 degrees, but with the large daily range, the nights usually are comfortably cool.

The growing season in Albuquerque and adjacent suburbs ranges from around 170 days in the Rio Grande Valley to about 200 days in parts of the northeast section of the city.

Sustained winds of 12 mph or less occur approximately 80 percent of the time at the Albuquerque International Airport. Late winter and spring storms along with occasional east winds out of Tijeras Canyon are the main sources of strong wind conditions. Blowing dust, the least attractive feature of the climate, often accompanies the occasional strong winds of winter and spring.

Albuquerque Int'l Airport *Bernalillo County*   Elevation: 5,308 ft.   Latitude: 35° 03' N   Longitude: 106° 36' W

	JAN	FEB	MAR	APR	MAY	JUN	JUL	AUG	SEP	OCT	NOV	DEC	YEAR
Mean Maximum Temp. (°F)	47.5	54.6	62.4	70.4	79.6	90.2	92.3	89.0	82.1	70.8	57.4	48.0	70.4
Mean Temp. (°F)	35.5	41.4	48.0	55.3	64.6	74.7	78.5	76.1	68.9	57.2	44.6	36.1	56.7
Mean Minimum Temp. (°F)	23.5	28.1	33.5	40.1	49.5	59.2	64.7	63.2	55.8	43.5	31.7	24.1	43.1
Extreme Maximum Temp. (°F)	69	76	85	89	96	107	105	101	100	91	77	68	107
Extreme Minimum Temp. (°F)	-17	5	10	19	28	40	52	50	37	21	-7	-7	-17
Days Maximum Temp. ≥ 90°F	0	0	0	0	2	17	22	16	4	0	0	0	61
Days Maximum Temp. ≤ 32°F	2	0	0	0	0	0	0	0	0	0	0	2	4
Days Minimum Temp. ≤ 32°F	28	21	13	4	0	0	0	0	0	2	16	28	112
Days Minimum Temp. ≤ 0°F	0	0	0	0	0	0	0	0	0	0	0	0	0
Heating Degree Days (base 65°F)	907	661	521	290	80	4	0	0	29	246	607	890	4,235
Cooling Degree Days (base 65°F)	0	0	0	9	82	307	424	358	160	9	0	0	1,349
Mean Precipitation (in.)	0.48	0.44	0.58	0.50	0.61	0.64	1.28	1.78	1.08	0.92	0.59	0.49	9.39
Maximum Precipitation (in.)	1.3	1.8	2.2	1.8	2.5	2.6	3.3	3.3	2.6	3.1	1.9	1.8	13.1
Minimum Precipitation (in.)	0	trace	trace	trace	trace	trace	0.1	trace	trace	0	0	0	4.1
Maximum 24-hr. Precipitation (in.)	0.9	0.8	0.9	1.7	1.0	1.6	1.6	1.8	1.9	1.7	1.4	0.8	1.9
Days With ≥ 0.1" Precipitation	2	2	2	1	2	2	4	4	3	3	2	2	29
Days With ≥ 1.0" Precipitation	0	0	0	0	0	0	0	0	0	0	0	0	0
Mean Snowfall (in.)	3.0	2.2	1.8	0.9	trace	trace	trace	trace	trace	0.3	1.1	2.4	11.7
Maximum Snowfall (in.)	10	10	14	8	trace	0	0	0	trace	3	8	15	34
Maximum 24-hr. Snowfall (in.)	5	5	9	7	trace	0	0	0	trace	3	4	9	9
Days With ≥ 1.0" Snow Depth	2	1	0	0	0	0	0	0	0	0	1	2	6
Thunderstorm Days	< 1	< 1	1	1	4	5	10	10	5	2	1	< 1	39
Foggy Days	3	2	2	1	< 1	< 1	< 1	< 1	1	2	2	3	16
Predominant Sky Cover	CLR	CLR	CLR	CLR	CLR	CLR	SCT	SCT	CLR	CLR	CLR	CLR	CLR
Mean Relative Humidity 5am (%)	68	64	55	48	48	45	59	66	61	59	63	68	59
Mean Relative Humidity 5pm (%)	41	32	25	19	19	18	27	30	29	29	35	43	29
Mean Dewpoint (°F)	18	20	20	22	29	36	49	51	43	32	23	19	30
Prevailing Wind Direction	N	N	N	S	S	S	ESE	SE	SE	N	N	N	N
Prevailing Wind Speed (mph)	9	9	9	10	10	10	12	8	8	8	8	9	9
Maximum Wind Gust (mph)	70	63	77	67	70	68	73	67	61	62	63	71	77

Clayton Municipal Airpark

Clayton is located on the high plains of northeastern New Mexico some 90 miles southeast of the eastern slope of the Rocky Mountains. The climate is semi-arid. Nearly 80 percent of the rainfall occurs from May through October in sudden thunderstorms which form over the mountains northwest of Clayton and drift southeastward. This makes the growing of small grains and the raising of range cattle profitable. Native grasses in the area remain nutritious even in winter.

The climate of Clayton is characteristic of that found in the higher-altitude sections of the continental southwest. Temperatures are mostly moderate. While daytime temperatures in summer are moderately warm, 90 degrees or slightly higher about half the time in July, hot days recording temperatures of 100 degrees or more, only occur about once a year. Minimum temperatures range from the teens in January to the 60s in July. With clear nocturnal skies and an altitude of about 5,000 feet, summer nights in Clayton are usually comfortable for sleeping. While winter minima are generally below freezing, zero temperatures only occur about three times a year.

From June through August nearly all precipitation is from scattered thunderstorms. As late summer and fall give way to winter, showery precipitation becomes less frequent and copious. Occasional winter snows, caused in part by upslope movement of air from the Gulf of Mexico, supply some winter moisture.

Blizzards are rare but high winds and cold temperatures frequent winter storms and can produce blizzard conditions. These storms may often close highways and, unless proper precautions are taken, they may also cause loss of life and livestock.

Based on the 1951-1980 period, the average first occurrence of 32 degrees Fahrenheit in the fall is October 16 and the average last occurrence in the spring is May 1.

Clayton Municipal Airpark *Union County*   Elevation: 4,957 ft.   Latitude: 36° 27' N   Longitude: 103° 09' W

	JAN	FEB	MAR	APR	MAY	JUN	JUL	AUG	SEP	OCT	NOV	DEC	YEAR
Mean Maximum Temp. (°F)	46.8	51.0	57.9	66.3	73.7	83.8	87.3	84.9	77.5	68.2	55.5	47.7	66.7
Mean Temp. (°F)	33.1	37.0	43.3	51.8	59.9	69.7	73.8	71.9	64.5	54.3	41.9	34.4	53.0
Mean Minimum Temp. (°F)	19.3	23.0	28.7	37.2	46.1	55.5	60.2	58.9	51.4	40.3	28.2	21.0	39.2
Extreme Maximum Temp. (°F)	80	78	86	90	95	102	100	98	97	90	85	80	102
Extreme Minimum Temp. (°F)	-13	-12	2	12	29	40	49	46	26	12	-10	-14	-14
Days Maximum Temp. ≥ 90°F	0	0	0	0	1	8	12	8	2	0	0	0	31
Days Maximum Temp. ≤ 32°F	5	3	1	0	0	0	0	0	0	0	2	4	15
Days Minimum Temp. ≤ 32°F	30	24	22	8	1	0	0	0	0	5	20	28	138
Days Minimum Temp. ≤ 0°F	1	1	0	0	0	0	0	0	0	0	0	1	3
Heating Degree Days (base 65°F)	982	783	665	394	178	26	4	5	96	332	687	943	5,095
Cooling Degree Days (base 65°F)	na	na	na	na	na	na	na	na	na	na	na	na	na
Mean Precipitation (in.)	0.29	0.30	0.63	0.98	2.10	2.25	2.77	2.62	1.70	0.78	0.58	0.33	15.33
Maximum Precipitation (in.)	1.1	1.6	2.3	3.1	6.8	5.0	7.8	5.8	5.2	4.5	2.1	1.1	25.7
Minimum Precipitation (in.)	trace	trace	trace	trace	0.3	0.2	0.4	0.3	trace	trace	trace	0	8.8
Maximum 24-hr. Precipitation (in.)	0.6	0.9	0.9	1.9	4.7	2.5	2.6	4.1	2.9	3.7	1.5	0.6	4.7
Days With ≥ 0.1" Precipitation	1	1	2	3	5	5	5	5	4	2	2	1	36
Days With ≥ 1.0" Precipitation	0	0	0	0	0	0	1	1	0	0	0	0	2
Mean Snowfall (in.)	4.5	3.6	5.2	2.2	0.7	trace	0.0	trace	0.3	1.0	3.4	4.6	25.5
Maximum Snowfall (in.)	12	16	16	11	8	0	0	0	5	8	15	12	49
Maximum 24-hr. Snowfall (in.)	8	9	9	11	6	0	0	0	3	6	12	8	12
Days With ≥ 1.0" Snow Depth	6	4	na	1	0	0	0	0	0	0	3	6	na
Thunderstorm Days	0	1	1	3	10	14	16	16	5	3	0	<1	69
Foggy Days	4	5	7	4	4	3	2	3	5	4	1	3	45
Predominant Sky Cover	CLR	CLR	OVR	CLR	OVR	CLR	CLR	CLR	CLR	CLR	CLR	CLR	CLR
Mean Relative Humidity 5am (%)	64	64	64	65	71	71	76	77	73	64	64	62	68
Mean Relative Humidity 5pm (%)	46	41	35	31	35	34	41	41	40	40	46	51	40
Mean Dewpoint (°F)	15	17	20	26	38	47	54	54	45	33	23	17	33
Prevailing Wind Direction	W	W	W	SW	SW	SW	SW	SW	SW	SSW	W	W	SW
Prevailing Wind Speed (mph)	13	13	14	17	15	15	13	13	14	14	12	13	14
Maximum Wind Gust (mph)	na	na	na	na	na	na	na	na	na	na	na	na	na

Roswell Industrial Airpark

The climate at Roswell conforms to the basic trend of the four seasons, but shows certain deviations related to geography. Higher landmasses almost surround the valley location, with a long, gradual descent from points southwest through west and north. The topography acts to modify air masses, especially the cold outbreaks in wintertime. Downslope warming of air, as well as air interchange within a tempering environment, often prevents sharp cooling. Moreover, the elevation of 3,600 feet is high enough to moderate the heat and humidity compared to locations to the south and east.

Summer moves into a wet phase that delivers the most important rain of the year. Rather frequent showers and thunderstorms from June through September account for over half of the annual precipitation. Storm clouds that build up from the heat of the day, overspread the sky on many afternoons, retarding a further rise in temperature. At the same time, relative humidity shows moderation, ranging from about 70 percent in early morning to 30 percent in the mid-afternoon. Temperatures are quite warm on most summer days with readings of 100 degrees or higher occurring on 10 days in an average year.

Rainfall tapers off markedly in the fall with decline in storm activity. This leaves usually agreeable conditions because of low wind movement and mostly clear skies. Frosty nights alternate with warm days. Relative humidity reaches rather low levels in autumn, but dryness is not as rigorous as in the spring.

In winter, sub-freezing at night is tempered by considerable warming during the day. Zero or lower temperatures occur on only one day in an average winter. Sub-zero cold spells are of short duration. Winter is the season of least precipitation.

Spring ushers in the driest season of the year with respect to relative humidity. Wind movement shows a large increase, especially from the plateau areas of the west. Most of the 60 days a year with winds of 25 mph or more occur from February to May. Destructive storms seldom strike the city, but minor damage results from thundersqualls or hailstorms about once a year. Rain is most erratic in spring, ranging from none of consequence in some years, to excessive amounts in others.

Roswell Industrial Airpark *Chaves County*   Elevation: 3,648 ft.   Latitude: 33° 18' N   Longitude: 104° 32' W

	JAN	FEB	MAR	APR	MAY	JUN	JUL	AUG	SEP	OCT	NOV	DEC	YEAR
Mean Maximum Temp. (°F)	54.1	60.6	68.6	76.4	84.8	93.3	94.0	91.7	84.8	76.0	64.0	55.4	75.3
Mean Temp. (°F)	40.2	45.9	53.1	60.8	70.0	78.4	80.9	79.0	71.9	61.4	49.3	41.0	61.0
Mean Minimum Temp. (°F)	26.2	31.1	37.4	45.1	55.0	63.4	67.7	66.2	58.9	46.7	34.6	26.5	46.6
Extreme Maximum Temp. (°F)	82	85	93	99	104	114	111	106	103	96	88	81	114
Extreme Minimum Temp. (°F)	-9	3	13	23	34	47	59	54	40	14	4	-8	-9
Days Maximum Temp. ≥ 90°F	0	0	0	1	9	22	25	22	10	2	0	0	91
Days Maximum Temp. ≤ 32°F	2	1	0	0	0	0	0	0	0	0	0	2	5
Days Minimum Temp. ≤ 32°F	25	16	7	2	0	0	0	0	0	1	12	24	87
Days Minimum Temp. ≤ 0°F	0	0	0	0	0	0	0	0	0	0	0	0	0
Heating Degree Days (base 65°F)	764	533	367	161	27	0	0	0	23	146	464	738	3,223
Cooling Degree Days (base 65°F)	0	1	4	41	189	412	504	448	243	42	1	0	1,885
Mean Precipitation (in.)	0.42	0.44	0.36	0.62	1.39	1.68	2.04	2.40	2.03	1.23	0.48	0.60	13.69
Maximum Precipitation (in.)	1.6	2.0	2.0	2.5	4.6	5.0	6.9	6.5	6.6	5.5	1.9	2.7	24.8
Minimum Precipitation (in.)	trace	0	0	trace	trace	trace	trace	0.3	0	0	0	0	4.5
Maximum 24-hr. Precipitation (in.)	1.1	1.0	1.3	1.5	2.6	3.0	4.3	3.6	3.4	3.5	1.1	0.6	4.3
Days With ≥ 0.1" Precipitation	1	1	1	2	3	3	3	5	4	2	1	2	28
Days With ≥ 1.0" Precipitation	0	0	0	0	0	0	0	1	0	0	0	0	1
Mean Snowfall (in.)	3.1	2.6	0.9	0.4	trace	trace	0.0	0.0	trace	0.3	1.1	3.4	11.8
Maximum Snowfall (in.)	17	17	5	5	trace	0	0	0	0	4	12	15	30
Maximum 24-hr. Snowfall (in.)	8	12	4	3	trace	0	0	0	0	3	7	9	12
Days With ≥ 1.0" Snow Depth	2	1	0	0	0	0	0	0	0	0	1	2	6
Thunderstorm Days	< 1	< 1	1	2	5	6	8	8	4	2	1	< 1	37
Foggy Days	6	5	3	2	2	1	1	2	5	5	4	5	41
Predominant Sky Cover	CLR	CLR	CLR	CLR	CLR	SCT	SCT	SCT	CLR	CLR	CLR	CLR	CLR
Mean Relative Humidity 5am (%)	67	64	54	51	57	61	67	70	71	67	65	66	63
Mean Relative Humidity 5pm (%)	39	33	25	22	24	25	31	34	37	35	37	41	32
Mean Dewpoint (°F)	21	23	24	29	39	49	56	56	51	39	28	22	37
Prevailing Wind Direction	S	S	S	S	S	S	S	S	S	S	S	S	S
Prevailing Wind Speed (mph)	9	9	10	12	12	12	10	9	9	9	9	9	10
Maximum Wind Gust (mph)	58	62	75	62	66	89	60	68	69	58	55	62	89

Abiquiu Dam *Rio Arriba County*   Elevation: 6,377 ft.   Latitude: 36° 14' N   Longitude: 106° 26' W

	JAN	FEB	MAR	APR	MAY	JUN	JUL	AUG	SEP	OCT	NOV	DEC	YEAR
Mean Maximum Temp. (°F)	*41.3*	47.0	54.6	62.4	72.0	82.8	86.5	84.0	77.4	66.7	52.9	43.4	*64.3*
Mean Temp. (°F)	*29.0*	34.1	41.5	48.3	57.6	67.5	72.1	70.2	63.2	52.2	40.0	30.7	*50.5*
Mean Minimum Temp. (°F)	*16.7*	21.2	28.3	34.2	43.3	52.2	57.6	56.3	48.9	37.8	26.9	18.1	*36.8*
Extreme Maximum Temp. (°F)	60	70	85	83	89	100	100	96	94	85	77	67	100
Extreme Minimum Temp. (°F)	-25	-15	4	11	24	31	37	39	20	14	-8	-18	-25
Days Maximum Temp. ≥ 90°F	0	0	0	0	0	5	9	5	1	0	0	0	20
Days Maximum Temp. ≤ 32°F	*4*	1	0	0	0	0	0	0	0	0	1	3	*9*
Days Minimum Temp. ≤ 32°F	30	27	24	12	1	0	0	0	0	7	24	30	155
Days Minimum Temp. ≤ 0°F	1	0	0	0	0	0	0	0	0	0	0	1	2
Heating Degree Days (base 65°F)	*1,108*	862	719	494	230	39	2	6	93	389	744	1,057	*5,743*
Cooling Degree Days (base 65°F)	0	0	0	0	11	122	232	182	47	0	0	0	594
Mean Precipitation (in.)	0.35	0.24	0.59	0.61	0.99	0.76	1.68	1.99	1.23	0.83	0.55	0.29	10.11
Days With ≥ 0.1" Precipitation	1	1	2	2	3	2	5	6	3	3	2	1	31
Days With ≥ 1.0" Precipitation	0	0	0	0	0	0	0	0	0	0	0	0	0
Mean Snowfall (in.)	*2.1*	*1.4*	0.8	0.6	trace	0.0	0.0	0.0	0.0	trace	0.3	*2.1*	7.3
Days With ≥ 1.0" Snow Depth	*1*	*1*	1	0	0	0	0	0	0	0	0	*1*	*4*

Alamogordo *Otero County*   Elevation: 4,347 ft.   Latitude: 32° 53' N   Longitude: 105° 57' W

	JAN	FEB	MAR	APR	MAY	JUN	JUL	AUG	SEP	OCT	NOV	DEC	YEAR
Mean Maximum Temp. (°F)	56.2	61.7	68.6	76.4	85.2	94.3	93.7	90.7	85.8	76.5	64.9	56.8	75.9
Mean Temp. (°F)	43.0	47.8	53.9	61.1	70.0	78.8	80.0	77.7	72.4	62.2	50.8	43.3	61.7
Mean Minimum Temp. (°F)	29.7	33.9	39.3	45.7	54.7	63.1	66.3	64.7	58.9	47.8	36.7	29.8	47.5
Extreme Maximum Temp. (°F)	75	81	89	95	100	110	109	105	101	94	84	75	110
Extreme Minimum Temp. (°F)	4	11	14	24	35	41	53	53	40	24	0	6	0
Days Maximum Temp. ≥ 90°F	0	0	0	1	8	24	24	20	9	1	0	0	87
Days Maximum Temp. ≤ 32°F	0	0	0	0	0	0	0	0	0	0	0	0	0
Days Minimum Temp. ≤ 32°F	21	13	6	1	0	0	0	0	0	1	9	21	72
Days Minimum Temp. ≤ 0°F	0	0	0	0	0	0	0	0	0	0	0	0	0
Heating Degree Days (base 65°F)	676	479	338	146	18	0	0	0	10	122	419	666	2,874
Cooling Degree Days (base 65°F)	0	0	2	38	185	425	480	410	237	44	1	0	1,822
Mean Precipitation (in.)	0.78	0.54	0.46	0.31	0.64	0.90	2.20	2.31	1.87	1.39	0.73	0.98	13.11
Days With ≥ 0.1" Precipitation	2	2	1	1	2	2	5	6	5	3	2	3	34
Days With ≥ 1.0" Precipitation	0	0	0	0	0	0	0	0	0	0	0	0	0
Mean Snowfall (in.)	1.8	0.5	0.2	0.1	0.0	0.0	0.0	0.0	0.0	trace	0.3	1.4	4.3
Days With ≥ 1.0" Snow Depth	*0*	0	0	0	0	0	0	0	0	0	0	0	*0*

Alcalde *Rio Arriba County*   Elevation: 5,679 ft.   Latitude: 36° 06' N   Longitude: 106° 04' W

	JAN	FEB	MAR	APR	MAY	JUN	JUL	AUG	SEP	OCT	NOV	DEC	YEAR
Mean Maximum Temp. (°F)	45.3	52.2	59.8	67.5	76.8	86.5	89.3	86.7	80.6	70.6	56.5	*46.4*	*68.2*
Mean Temp. (°F)	30.6	36.8	43.2	50.0	58.6	67.6	72.2	70.3	62.9	51.9	40.0	*31.4*	*51.3*
Mean Minimum Temp. (°F)	15.9	21.2	26.6	32.5	40.4	48.5	55.1	53.9	45.1	33.2	23.4	*16.4*	*34.4*
Extreme Maximum Temp. (°F)	70	73	80	88	96	101	102	100	95	90	79	68	102
Extreme Minimum Temp. (°F)	-34	-4	4	12	20	33	39	34	23	9	-11	-11	-34
Days Maximum Temp. ≥ 90°F	0	0	0	0	1	11	16	10	2	0	0	0	40
Days Maximum Temp. ≤ 32°F	2	0	0	0	0	0	0	0	0	0	0	1	3
Days Minimum Temp. ≤ 32°F	29	26	25	15	3	0	0	0	1	15	26	27	167
Days Minimum Temp. ≤ 0°F	1	0	0	0	0	0	0	0	0	0	0	0	1
Heating Degree Days (base 65°F)	1,059	792	668	442	201	28	1	6	96	400	743	*1,034*	*5,470*
Cooling Degree Days (base 65°F)	*0*	0	0	0	11	118	233	183	39	0	0	*0*	*584*
Mean Precipitation (in.)	0.40	0.38	0.58	0.65	0.90	0.83	1.42	1.82	1.29	0.97	0.79	0.40	10.43
Days With ≥ 0.1" Precipitation	1	1	2	2	2	2	4	4	3	2	2	1	26
Days With ≥ 1.0" Precipitation	0	0	0	0	0	0	0	0	0	0	0	0	0
Mean Snowfall (in.)	2.6	2.7	2.0	0.2	trace	0.0	0.0	0.0	0.0	0.3	1.1	*1.2*	*10.1*
Days With ≥ 1.0" Snow Depth	na	*1*	0	0	0	0	0	0	0	0	*0*	*1*	na

Aleman Ranch *Sierra County*   Elevation: 4,520 ft.   Latitude: 32° 55' N   Longitude: 106° 56' W

	JAN	FEB	MAR	APR	MAY	JUN	JUL	AUG	SEP	OCT	NOV	DEC	YEAR
Mean Maximum Temp. (°F)	54.6	60.4	67.2	74.9	83.3	92.8	92.7	89.8	84.4	74.9	63.2	54.3	74.4
Mean Temp. (°F)	39.5	44.0	49.7	56.6	65.3	74.7	77.7	75.6	69.4	58.6	47.1	39.6	58.2
Mean Minimum Temp. (°F)	24.3	27.5	32.2	38.3	47.2	56.4	62.7	61.4	54.4	42.4	31.1	24.8	41.9
Extreme Maximum Temp. (°F)	77	81	87	93	100	109	107	104	100	90	82	75	109
Extreme Minimum Temp. (°F)	-1	5	8	12	26	37	47	49	37	18	0	-6	-6
Days Maximum Temp. ≥ 90°F	0	0	0	0	5	21	23	18	7	0	0	0	74
Days Maximum Temp. ≤ 32°F	0	0	0	0	0	0	0	0	0	0	0	0	0
Days Minimum Temp. ≤ 32°F	27	21	16	7	0	0	0	0	0	3	18	26	118
Days Minimum Temp. ≤ 0°F	0	0	0	0	0	0	0	0	0	0	0	0	0
Heating Degree Days (base 65°F)	784	587	466	252	57	2	0	0	19	203	529	781	3,680
Cooling Degree Days (base 65°F)	0	0	0	9	80	301	408	345	162	12	0	0	1,317
Mean Precipitation (in.)	0.48	0.39	0.31	0.19	0.54	0.61	2.32	2.29	1.50	1.08	0.64	0.86	11.21
Days With ≥ 0.1" Precipitation	2	1	1	1	1	2	6	5	4	3	2	3	31
Days With ≥ 1.0" Precipitation	0	0	0	0	0	0	0	0	0	0	0	0	0
Mean Snowfall (in.)	2.1	0.7	0.5	0.1	trace	0.0	0.0	0.0	0.0	0.0	0.5	2.8	6.7
Days With ≥ 1.0" Snow Depth	1	0	0	0	0	0	0	0	0	0	0	2	3

Amistad 5 SSW *Union County* Elevation: 4,442 ft. Latitude: 35° 52' N Longitude: 103° 10' W

	JAN	FEB	MAR	APR	MAY	JUN	JUL	AUG	SEP	OCT	NOV	DEC	YEAR
Mean Maximum Temp. (°F)	49.0	54.5	62.0	69.9	78.3	87.9	91.1	88.7	81.9	71.9	59.3	50.3	70.4
Mean Temp. (°F)	34.0	38.6	45.6	53.3	62.5	72.0	76.2	74.4	67.0	55.9	43.8	35.5	54.9
Mean Minimum Temp. (°F)	19.0	22.7	29.1	36.6	46.7	56.1	61.2	60.0	51.9	39.8	28.3	20.6	39.3
Extreme Maximum Temp. (°F)	78	81	91	95	100	108	107	103	102	93	88	80	108
Extreme Minimum Temp. (°F)	-16	-11	3	10	28	37	49	42	29	6	-11	-12	-16
Days Maximum Temp. ≥ 90°F	0	0	0	0	3	14	19	16	6	0	0	0	58
Days Maximum Temp. ≤ 32°F	4	2	1	0	0	0	0	0	0	0	1	3	11
Days Minimum Temp. ≤ 32°F	30	25	20	9	1	0	0	0	0	6	21	28	140
Days Minimum Temp. ≤ 0°F	1	1	0	0	0	0	0	0	0	0	0	1	3
Heating Degree Days (base 65°F)	954	737	595	350	122	13	1	1	63	286	629	908	4,659
Cooling Degree Days (base 65°F)	0	0	0	5	51	224	356	310	132	9	0	0	1,087
Mean Precipitation (in.)	0.28	0.31	0.65	0.95	2.22	1.84	2.79	2.76	1.66	1.07	0.62	0.38	15.53
Days With ≥ 0.1" Precipitation	1	1	2	3	4	4	5	5	3	2	2	1	33
Days With ≥ 1.0" Precipitation	0	0	0	0	1	0	1	1	0	0	0	0	3
Mean Snowfall (in.)	2.7	3.0	2.1	0.8	0.2	0.0	0.0	0.0	0.0	0.3	0.6	3.5	13.2
Days With ≥ 1.0" Snow Depth	na	0	0	0	0	0	0	0	0	0	0	na	na

Animas *Hidalgo County* Elevation: 4,416 ft. Latitude: 31° 57' N Longitude: 108° 49' W

	JAN	FEB	MAR	APR	MAY	JUN	JUL	AUG	SEP	OCT	NOV	DEC	YEAR
Mean Maximum Temp. (°F)	57.8	63.2	69.7	77.5	86.4	95.5	94.4	91.5	87.4	78.4	66.3	57.8	77.2
Mean Temp. (°F)	42.3	46.5	51.8	58.3	67.2	76.3	78.9	76.7	71.8	61.4	49.5	42.4	60.2
Mean Minimum Temp. (°F)	26.6	29.6	33.8	39.1	48.0	57.0	63.3	61.8	56.1	44.4	32.6	26.9	43.3
Extreme Maximum Temp. (°F)	81	82	92	97	104	110	108	105	101	95	85	77	110
Extreme Minimum Temp. (°F)	-1	3	12	18	28	37	48	50	39	19	10	-19	-19
Days Maximum Temp. ≥ 90°F	0	0	0	1	9	26	25	22	12	2	0	0	97
Days Maximum Temp. ≤ 32°F	0	0	0	0	0	0	0	0	0	0	0	0	0
Days Minimum Temp. ≤ 32°F	24	19	13	6	1	0	0	0	0	2	15	24	104
Days Minimum Temp. ≤ 0°F	0	0	0	0	0	0	0	0	0	0	0	0	0
Heating Degree Days (base 65°F)	698	516	403	205	40	1	0	0	9	139	458	695	3,164
Cooling Degree Days (base 65°F)	0	0	0	15	119	347	437	376	229	34	0	0	1,557
Mean Precipitation (in.)	0.72	0.56	0.50	0.21	0.25	0.47	2.20	2.37	1.45	1.23	0.71	1.13	11.80
Days With ≥ 0.1" Precipitation	2	2	2	1	1	1	5	4	3	3	2	3	29
Days With ≥ 1.0" Precipitation	0	0	0	0	0	0	0	0	0	0	0	0	0
Mean Snowfall (in.)	1.9	0.9	0.6	0.2	0.0	0.0	0.0	0.0	0.0	trace	0.5	1.6	5.7
Days With ≥ 1.0" Snow Depth	1	0	0	0	0	0	0	0	0	0	0	1	2

Artesia 6 S *Eddy County* Elevation: 3,316 ft. Latitude: 32° 46' N Longitude: 104° 23' W

	JAN	FEB	MAR	APR	MAY	JUN	JUL	AUG	SEP	OCT	NOV	DEC	YEAR
Mean Maximum Temp. (°F)	56.2	62.2	69.8	77.7	85.6	93.1	93.7	91.7	85.2	76.9	65.7	57.5	76.3
Mean Temp. (°F)	39.0	44.1	51.3	59.0	68.2	76.4	78.8	77.0	69.9	59.4	48.0	39.9	59.3
Mean Minimum Temp. (°F)	21.7	25.9	32.8	40.3	50.9	59.7	63.9	62.1	54.7	42.0	30.2	22.3	42.2
Extreme Maximum Temp. (°F)	85	86	93	100	106	113	108	105	103	97	89	83	113
Extreme Minimum Temp. (°F)	-9	1	9	16	31	42	54	50	36	18	-10	-13	-13
Days Maximum Temp. ≥ 90°F	0	0	0	2	10	22	25	22	11	2	0	0	94
Days Maximum Temp. ≤ 32°F	2	1	0	0	0	0	0	0	0	0	0	1	4
Days Minimum Temp. ≤ 32°F	29	23	15	5	0	0	0	0	0	3	19	28	122
Days Minimum Temp. ≤ 0°F	1	0	0	0	0	0	0	0	0	0	0	0	1
Heating Degree Days (base 65°F)	800	585	421	201	40	2	0	0	34	189	504	772	3,548
Cooling Degree Days (base 65°F)	0	0	3	29	158	366	451	398	196	25	1	0	1,627
Mean Precipitation (in.)	0.40	0.45	0.30	0.51	1.33	1.78	1.36	2.23	2.58	1.22	0.57	0.56	13.29
Days With ≥ 0.1" Precipitation	1	2	1	1	3	3	3	5	4	3	1	2	29
Days With ≥ 1.0" Precipitation	0	0	0	0	0	0	0	0	1	0	0	0	1
Mean Snowfall (in.)	2.3	1.5	0.5	0.6	trace	0.0	0.0	0.0	0.0	trace	0.9	2.3	8.1
Days With ≥ 1.0" Snow Depth	3	1	0	0	0	0	0	0	0	0	1	2	7

Aztec Ruins Nat'l Monument *San Juan County* Elevation: 5,643 ft. Latitude: 36° 50' N Longitude: 108° 00' W

	JAN	FEB	MAR	APR	MAY	JUN	JUL	AUG	SEP	OCT	NOV	DEC	YEAR
Mean Maximum Temp. (°F)	43.0	50.5	59.0	67.4	77.0	87.5	91.8	89.1	81.7	69.6	54.5	44.1	67.9
Mean Temp. (°F)	29.4	35.8	42.6	49.5	58.4	67.9	73.9	72.2	64.2	52.6	39.7	30.6	51.4
Mean Minimum Temp. (°F)	15.8	21.1	26.1	31.5	39.8	48.2	56.0	55.4	46.6	35.6	24.9	17.0	34.8
Extreme Maximum Temp. (°F)	69	74	82	88	92	102	105	101	98	92	76	65	105
Extreme Minimum Temp. (°F)	-23	-16	4	11	12	24	40	36	22	13	-5	-18	-23
Days Maximum Temp. ≥ 90°F	0	0	0	0	1	12	22	16	3	0	0	0	54
Days Maximum Temp. ≤ 32°F	3	0	0	0	0	0	0	0	0	0	0	3	6
Days Minimum Temp. ≤ 32°F	30	26	25	16	4	0	0	0	1	10	25	30	167
Days Minimum Temp. ≤ 0°F	2	0	0	0	0	0	0	0	0	0	0	1	3
Heating Degree Days (base 65°F)	1,097	817	687	458	207	34	1	2	79	378	750	1,058	5,568
Cooling Degree Days (base 65°F)	0	0	0	0	13	137	284	245	67	0	0	0	746
Mean Precipitation (in.)	0.97	0.82	0.96	0.73	0.74	0.35	1.01	1.26	1.07	1.17	0.94	0.73	10.75
Days With ≥ 0.1" Precipitation	3	3	3	2	2	1	3	3	3	3	3	2	31
Days With ≥ 1.0" Precipitation	0	0	0	0	0	0	0	0	0	0	0	0	0
Mean Snowfall (in.)	5.1	2.6	0.6	0.1	trace	0.0	0.0	0.0	0.0	0.2	0.7	3.9	13.2
Days With ≥ 1.0" Snow Depth	na	1	0	0	0	0	0	0	0	0	0	4	na

Bell Ranch *San Miguel County* Elevation: 4,498 ft. Latitude: 35° 32' N Longitude: 104° 06' W

	JAN	FEB	MAR	APR	MAY	JUN	JUL	AUG	SEP	OCT	NOV	DEC	YEAR
Mean Maximum Temp. (°F)	*52.7*	*58.1*	65.7	73.0	80.9	90.1	91.9	89.9	83.1	74.1	62.5	na	na
Mean Temp. (°F)	*35.3*	*40.2*	47.2	55.3	64.3	73.6	77.5	75.8	68.2	57.1	45.2	na	na
Mean Minimum Temp. (°F)	*17.9*	*22.3*	28.8	37.5	47.6	57.1	63.1	61.6	53.2	40.1	27.9	na	na
Extreme Maximum Temp. (°F)	78	80	89	94	98	107	105	102	100	91	87	79	107
Extreme Minimum Temp. (°F)	-26	-8	5	19	28	35	51	47	31	11	-3	-20	-26
Days Maximum Temp. ≥ 90°F	0	0	0	0	4	17	21	18	6	0	0	0	66
Days Maximum Temp. ≤ 32°F	2	1	0	0	0	0	0	0	0	0	0	1	4
Days Minimum Temp. ≤ 32°F	27	23	21	8	1	0	0	0	0	5	22	24	131
Days Minimum Temp. ≤ 0°F	1	0	0	0	0	0	0	0	0	0	0	1	2
Heating Degree Days (base 65°F)	*913*	*693*	544	290	84	5	0	1	39	246	586	na	na
Cooling Degree Days (base 65°F)	*0*	*0*	0	7	76	277	400	*353*	*150*	10	0	na	na
Mean Precipitation (in.)	0.29	0.32	0.60	0.82	1.56	2.17	2.49	2.60	1.73	1.00	0.74	0.37	14.69
Days With ≥ 0.1" Precipitation	1	1	2	2	3	4	5	4	3	2	1	1	29
Days With ≥ 1.0" Precipitation	0	0	0	0	0	0	1	1	0	0	0	0	2
Mean Snowfall (in.)	na	2.5	*2.2*	0.5	0.0	0.0	0.0	trace	0.0	0.5	1.5	2.9	na
Days With ≥ 1.0" Snow Depth	na	*0*	*0*	0	0	0	0	0	0	0	0	*0*	na

Bernardo *Socorro County* Elevation: 4,734 ft. Latitude: 34° 25' N Longitude: 106° 50' W

	JAN	FEB	MAR	APR	MAY	JUN	JUL	AUG	SEP	OCT	NOV	DEC	YEAR
Mean Maximum Temp. (°F)	52.6	59.5	67.5	75.6	84.2	93.9	95.6	92.5	86.0	75.7	62.7	53.0	74.9
Mean Temp. (°F)	*35.6*	41.5	48.5	55.2	64.6	72.7	77.4	75.3	68.1	56.8	44.7	36.2	*56.4*
Mean Minimum Temp. (°F)	*19.1*	23.6	29.2	35.0	45.0	51.6	59.5	58.3	50.3	37.7	26.7	19.9	*38.0*
Extreme Maximum Temp. (°F)	84	81	89	96	103	113	111	109	103	96	82	75	113
Extreme Minimum Temp. (°F)	*-20*	*-3*	*3*	7	20	25	40	39	26	7	*3*	-3	*-20*
Days Maximum Temp. ≥ 90°F	0	0	0	1	8	23	26	22	10	1	0	0	91
Days Maximum Temp. ≤ 32°F	1	0	0	0	0	0	0	0	0	0	0	1	2
Days Minimum Temp. ≤ 32°F	*28*	23	19	12	3	0	0	0	1	9	22	27	*144*
Days Minimum Temp. ≤ 0°F	*1*	0	0	0	0	0	0	0	0	0	0	0	*1*
Heating Degree Days (base 65°F)	*903*	657	506	296	92	11	0	1	38	259	602	886	*4,251*
Cooling Degree Days (base 65°F)	*0*	0	0	12	119	308	447	387	173	11	0	0	*1,457*
Mean Precipitation (in.)	0.31	0.29	0.30	0.33	0.57	0.52	1.44	1.79	1.38	1.00	0.40	0.47	8.80
Days With ≥ 0.1" Precipitation	1	1	1	1	2	1	4	5	3	2	1	2	24
Days With ≥ 1.0" Precipitation	0	0	0	0	0	0	0	0	0	0	0	0	0
Mean Snowfall (in.)	*1.3*	0.7	0.3	0.2	0.0	0.0	0.0	0.0	0.0	0.3	0.2	1.5	*4.5*
Days With ≥ 1.0" Snow Depth	0	0	0	0	0	0	0	0	0	0	0	0	0

Bitter Lakes Wildlife Refuge *Chaves County* Elevation: 3,661 ft. Latitude: 33° 28' N Longitude: 104° 24' W

	JAN	FEB	MAR	APR	MAY	JUN	JUL	AUG	SEP	OCT	NOV	DEC	YEAR
Mean Maximum Temp. (°F)	*54.4*	61.2	69.5	77.8	85.8	94.2	95.1	93.2	86.1	76.8	65.0	56.4	*76.3*
Mean Temp. (°F)	*37.4*	43.2	50.7	58.9	67.8	76.6	79.3	77.5	70.3	58.7	46.8	38.5	*58.8*
Mean Minimum Temp. (°F)	20.5	25.1	31.8	40.0	49.7	59.0	63.4	61.8	54.5	40.6	28.6	20.5	41.3
Extreme Maximum Temp. (°F)	84	89	95	98	106	114	110	107	106	99	89	83	114
Extreme Minimum Temp. (°F)	-18	-1	5	16	27	41	40	40	30	10	1	-11	-18
Days Maximum Temp. ≥ 90°F	0	0	0	3	10	22	25	24	12	2	0	0	98
Days Maximum Temp. ≤ 32°F	1	1	0	0	0	0	0	0	0	0	0	2	4
Days Minimum Temp. ≤ 32°F	27	22	16	5	0	0	0	0	0	5	19	27	121
Days Minimum Temp. ≤ 0°F	1	0	0	0	0	0	0	0	0	0	0	1	2
Heating Degree Days (base 65°F)	846	607	438	203	47	3	0	0	34	211	538	814	*3,741*
Cooling Degree Days (base 65°F)	*0*	*0*	2	28	146	373	462	417	215	23	0	*0*	*1,666*
Mean Precipitation (in.)	0.41	0.46	0.35	0.50	1.26	1.71	2.13	2.54	1.98	1.26	0.62	0.56	13.78
Days With ≥ 0.1" Precipitation	1	1	1	1	2	3	3	4	4	3	1	2	26
Days With ≥ 1.0" Precipitation	0	0	0	0	0	0	1	1	0	0	0	0	2
Mean Snowfall (in.)	2.5	2.0	0.4	trace	0.0	0.0	0.0	0.0	0.0	0.2	0.7	2.2	8.0
Days With ≥ 1.0" Snow Depth	1	1	0	0	0	0	0	0	0	0	0	1	3

Bloomfield 3 SE *San Juan County* Elevation: 5,803 ft. Latitude: 36° 40' N Longitude: 107° 58' W

	JAN	FEB	MAR	APR	MAY	JUN	JUL	AUG	SEP	OCT	NOV	DEC	YEAR
Mean Maximum Temp. (°F)	41.1	49.2	58.1	66.8	76.7	88.0	91.4	88.6	80.8	68.7	53.6	43.1	67.2
Mean Temp. (°F)	29.7	36.7	43.9	51.0	60.6	70.6	75.7	73.8	66.0	53.9	40.7	31.4	52.8
Mean Minimum Temp. (°F)	18.4	24.1	29.7	35.2	44.4	53.2	60.0	58.9	51.1	39.2	27.7	19.9	38.5
Extreme Maximum Temp. (°F)	64	70	80	87	95	103	105	103	98	90	74	67	105
Extreme Minimum Temp. (°F)	-17	-15	5	16	26	34	48	38	30	17	-5	-16	-17
Days Maximum Temp. ≥ 90°F	0	0	0	0	1	13	21	14	3	0	0	0	52
Days Maximum Temp. ≤ 32°F	5	1	0	0	0	0	0	0	0	0	0	3	9
Days Minimum Temp. ≤ 32°F	29	25	21	11	1	0	0	0	0	5	22	29	143
Days Minimum Temp. ≤ 0°F	1	0	0	0	0	0	0	0	0	0	0	1	2
Heating Degree Days (base 65°F)	1,087	793	648	414	155	16	0	1	51	339	724	1,035	5,263
Cooling Degree Days (base 65°F)	0	0	0	1	30	187	335	281	86	2	0	0	922
Mean Precipitation (in.)	0.61	0.60	0.78	0.61	0.60	0.35	1.02	1.29	0.96	1.08	0.84	0.51	9.25
Days With ≥ 0.1" Precipitation	2	2	3	2	2	1	3	3	3	3	2	2	28
Days With ≥ 1.0" Precipitation	0	0	0	0	0	0	0	0	0	0	0	0	0
Mean Snowfall (in.)	3.3	1.9	1.3	0.4	trace	0.0	0.0	0.0	0.0	0.2	0.6	3.3	11.0
Days With ≥ 1.0" Snow Depth	5	2	*0*	0	0	0	0	0	0	0	0	*2*	*9*

Bosque Del Apache *Socorro County*   Elevation: 4,511 ft.   Latitude: 33° 46' N   Longitude: 106° 54' W

	JAN	FEB	MAR	APR	MAY	JUN	JUL	AUG	SEP	OCT	NOV	DEC	YEAR
Mean Maximum Temp. (°F)	55.5	62.4	69.7	77.5	85.9	94.7	95.7	93.0	87.4	78.2	65.9	55.3	76.8
Mean Temp. (°F)	37.8	43.4	50.1	56.8	65.5	73.7	77.6	76.0	69.1	58.3	46.3	37.5	57.7
Mean Minimum Temp. (°F)	20.0	24.4	30.5	36.1	45.1	52.8	59.5	58.9	50.7	38.3	26.6	19.5	38.5
Extreme Maximum Temp. (°F)	75	85	91	97	106	111	111	105	102	94	88	76	111
Extreme Minimum Temp. (°F)	-8	-1	9	17	24	31	42	45	31	12	-10	-4	-10
Days Maximum Temp. ≥ 90°F	0	0	0	1	10	24	27	24	13	2	0	0	101
Days Maximum Temp. ≤ 32°F	0	0	0	0	0	0	0	0	0	0	0	0	0
Days Minimum Temp. ≤ 32°F	28	23	18	9	1	0	0	0	0	7	22	29	137
Days Minimum Temp. ≤ 0°F	0	0	0	0	0	0	0	0	0	0	0	0	0
Heating Degree Days (base 65°F)	837	593	456	247	58	4	0	0	23	214	548	839	3,819
Cooling Degree Days (base 65°F)	0	0	1	12	95	284	409	364	169	12	0	0	1,346
Mean Precipitation (in.)	0.39	0.43	0.32	0.22	0.55	0.59	1.36	1.85	1.44	1.25	0.55	0.67	9.62
Days With ≥ 0.1" Precipitation	1	1	1	1	2	1	3	4	3	2	1	2	22
Days With ≥ 1.0" Precipitation	0	0	0	0	0	0	0	0	0	0	0	0	0
Mean Snowfall (in.)	0.9	1.0	trace	0.2	0.0	0.0	0.0	0.0	0.0	0.2	0.1	2.6	5.0
Days With ≥ 1.0" Snow Depth	0	0	0	0	0	0	0	0	0	0	0	1	1

Caballo Dam *Sierra County*   Elevation: 4,189 ft.   Latitude: 32° 54' N   Longitude: 107° 18' W

	JAN	FEB	MAR	APR	MAY	JUN	JUL	AUG	SEP	OCT	NOV	DEC	YEAR
Mean Maximum Temp. (°F)	56.7	62.3	69.1	76.5	84.9	94.8	95.1	92.2	86.8	77.6	66.2	56.8	76.6
Mean Temp. (°F)	41.3	46.1	52.3	59.0	67.6	77.2	80.3	78.0	71.8	61.0	49.9	41.7	60.5
Mean Minimum Temp. (°F)	25.8	29.9	35.4	41.5	50.2	59.6	65.3	63.7	56.8	44.4	33.5	26.5	44.4
Extreme Maximum Temp. (°F)	78	83	90	95	102	111	109	104	102	94	87	77	111
Extreme Minimum Temp. (°F)	4	0	13	23	32	38	50	47	41	22	10	3	0
Days Maximum Temp. ≥ 90°F	0	0	0	1	9	24	26	23	12	2	0	0	97
Days Maximum Temp. ≤ 32°F	0	0	0	0	0	0	0	0	0	0	0	0	0
Days Minimum Temp. ≤ 32°F	27	18	10	3	0	0	0	0	0	2	13	26	99
Days Minimum Temp. ≤ 0°F	0	0	0	0	0	0	0	0	0	0	0	0	0
Heating Degree Days (base 65°F)	727	527	388	191	39	1	0	0	12	150	446	716	3,197
Cooling Degree Days (base 65°F)	0	0	1	21	136	384	486	414	229	33	0	0	1,704
Mean Precipitation (in.)	0.48	0.36	0.23	0.15	0.46	0.73	2.04	2.33	1.61	1.15	0.61	0.78	10.93
Days With ≥ 0.1" Precipitation	2	1	1	1	1	2	5	5	4	3	2	2	29
Days With ≥ 1.0" Precipitation	0	0	0	0	0	0	0	1	0	0	0	0	1
Mean Snowfall (in.)	0.2	trace	trace	0.0	0.0	0.0	0.0	0.0	0.0	0.0	0.3	0.6	1.1
Days With ≥ 1.0" Snow Depth	0	0	0	0	0	0	0	0	0	0	0	0	0

Cameron *Quay County*   Elevation: 4,576 ft.   Latitude: 34° 54' N   Longitude: 103° 27' W

	JAN	FEB	MAR	APR	MAY	JUN	JUL	AUG	SEP	OCT	NOV	DEC	YEAR
Mean Maximum Temp. (°F)	48.8	54.2	62.6	70.5	79.0	87.5	89.6	86.9	80.3	70.8	57.8	49.9	69.8
Mean Temp. (°F)	35.5	40.1	46.8	54.3	63.4	72.2	75.0	73.1	66.5	56.3	44.2	36.9	55.4
Mean Minimum Temp. (°F)	22.2	25.8	31.1	38.1	47.7	56.7	60.5	59.3	52.6	41.8	30.6	23.8	40.8
Extreme Maximum Temp. (°F)	77	79	88	93	102	106	104	100	99	92	84	74	106
Extreme Minimum Temp. (°F)	-15	-10	2	13	24	38	45	47	28	10	-5	-9	-15
Days Maximum Temp. ≥ 90°F	0	0	0	0	3	13	17	12	4	0	0	0	49
Days Maximum Temp. ≤ 32°F	4	2	0	0	0	0	0	0	0	0	1	3	10
Days Minimum Temp. ≤ 32°F	27	22	17	7	1	0	0	0	0	4	17	26	121
Days Minimum Temp. ≤ 0°F	1	0	0	0	0	0	0	0	0	0	0	1	2
Heating Degree Days (base 65°F)	907	697	556	320	106	11	1	2	59	271	617	864	4,411
Cooling Degree Days (base 65°F)	0	0	0	6	65	233	329	273	114	9	0	0	1,029
Mean Precipitation (in.)	0.54	0.64	0.84	1.16	1.88	2.72	2.83	3.37	2.23	1.44	0.88	0.67	19.20
Days With ≥ 0.1" Precipitation	2	2	2	3	4	5	5	6	4	3	2	2	40
Days With ≥ 1.0" Precipitation	0	0	0	0	0	1	1	1	0	0	0	0	3
Mean Snowfall (in.)	na	na	1.4	0.8	trace	0.0	0.0	0.0	0.0	0.6	1.6	3.5	na
Days With ≥ 1.0" Snow Depth	na	na	0	0	0	0	0	0	0	0	0	1	na

Capitan *Lincoln County*   Elevation: 6,463 ft.   Latitude: 33° 32' N   Longitude: 105° 36' W

	JAN	FEB	MAR	APR	MAY	JUN	JUL	AUG	SEP	OCT	NOV	DEC	YEAR
Mean Maximum Temp. (°F)	48.4	53.1	59.4	67.5	75.2	84.5	84.2	81.0	76.2	68.2	57.2	49.5	67.0
Mean Temp. (°F)	35.6	39.0	43.7	50.7	58.7	67.1	68.8	66.9	61.5	52.4	43.0	36.2	52.0
Mean Minimum Temp. (°F)	22.4	24.8	27.9	33.9	42.1	49.6	53.3	52.7	46.8	36.7	28.7	23.0	36.8
Extreme Maximum Temp. (°F)	73	73	79	85	91	101	98	97	91	85	79	71	101
Extreme Minimum Temp. (°F)	-4	-6	2	8	25	33	42	41	30	8	2	-15	-15
Days Maximum Temp. ≥ 90°F	0	0	0	0	0	7	5	1	0	0	0	0	13
Days Maximum Temp. ≤ 32°F	1	1	0	0	0	0	0	0	0	0	0	2	4
Days Minimum Temp. ≤ 32°F	28	23	23	14	3	0	0	0	0	8	20	27	146
Days Minimum Temp. ≤ 0°F	0	0	0	0	0	0	0	0	0	0	0	0	0
Heating Degree Days (base 65°F)	904	729	654	422	202	29	4	14	111	382	654	884	4,989
Cooling Degree Days (base 65°F)	0	0	0	1	15	99	129	79	14	0	0	0	337
Mean Precipitation (in.)	0.77	0.72	0.52	0.64	1.39	1.64	2.88	3.79	2.50	1.25	0.79	0.97	17.86
Days With ≥ 0.1" Precipitation	2	2	2	2	3	4	7	9	6	3	2	3	45
Days With ≥ 1.0" Precipitation	0	0	0	0	0	0	0	1	0	0	0	0	1
Mean Snowfall (in.)	na	7.2	4.6	2.8	0.4	0.0	0.0	0.0	0.0	1.6	2.3	9.4	na
Days With ≥ 1.0" Snow Depth	5	3	1	0	0	0	0	0	0	0	1	5	15

Carlsbad *Eddy County* Elevation: 3,120 ft. Latitude: 32° 26' N Longitude: 104° 15' W

	JAN	FEB	MAR	APR	MAY	JUN	JUL	AUG	SEP	OCT	NOV	DEC	YEAR
Mean Maximum Temp. (°F)	57.8	63.9	71.8	79.4	87.1	94.8	95.5	93.5	87.1	79.3	67.5	59.1	78.1
Mean Temp. (°F)	42.9	48.0	55.2	62.8	71.6	79.5	81.6	80.0	73.3	63.2	51.8	44.1	62.8
Mean Minimum Temp. (°F)	27.9	32.1	38.5	46.2	56.0	64.1	67.7	66.5	59.5	46.8	36.1	29.0	47.5
Extreme Maximum Temp. (°F)	86	88	95	99	105	114	111	106	105	99	90	82	114
Extreme Minimum Temp. (°F)	-6	10	13	25	32	43	54	51	41	21	0	3	-6
Days Maximum Temp. ≥ 90°F	0	0	0	3	*13*	23	*26*	24	14	3	0	0	*106*
Days Maximum Temp. ≤ 32°F	1	0	0	0	0	0	0	0	0	0	0	0	1
Days Minimum Temp. ≤ 32°F	23	15	6	1	0	0	0	0	0	1	9	*20*	75
Days Minimum Temp. ≤ 0°F	0	0	0	0	0	0	0	0	0	0	0	0	0
Heating Degree Days (base 65°F)	679	473	310	122	18	1	0	0	21	*111*	391	*640*	2,766
Cooling Degree Days (base 65°F)	0	1	9	64	238	457	539	488	284	66	3	0	2,149
Mean Precipitation (in.)	0.44	0.53	0.27	0.57	1.29	1.56	1.78	2.04	2.99	1.32	0.60	0.63	14.02
Days With ≥ 0.1" Precipitation	1	2	1	1	2	3	3	4	4	3	1	1	26
Days With ≥ 1.0" Precipitation	0	0	0	0	0	0	0	1	1	0	0	0	2
Mean Snowfall (in.)	*0.8*	0.9	0.2	0.0	0.0	0.0	0.0	0.0	0.0	0.0	0.4	*0.4*	*2.7*
Days With ≥ 1.0" Snow Depth	*0*	*0*	0	0	0	0	0	0	0	0	0	*0*	*0*

Carlsbad Cavern City Air Term *Eddy County* Elevation: 3,231 ft. Latitude: 32° 20' N Longitude: 104° 16' W

	JAN	FEB	MAR	APR	MAY	JUN	JUL	AUG	SEP	OCT	NOV	DEC	YEAR
Mean Maximum Temp. (°F)	56.8	63.1	70.9	79.1	87.5	95.3	95.3	93.0	86.2	77.5	65.8	58.1	77.4
Mean Temp. (°F)	42.7	48.0	55.0	63.0	72.0	79.9	81.8	79.8	73.1	62.9	51.2	43.8	62.8
Mean Minimum Temp. (°F)	28.5	32.9	39.1	46.8	56.5	64.5	68.2	66.6	59.9	48.2	36.5	29.4	48.1
Extreme Maximum Temp. (°F)	86	87	95	100	107	113	113	108	104	99	90	83	113
Extreme Minimum Temp. (°F)	-2	-2	11	20	34	45	58	55	40	22	-1	-4	-4
Days Maximum Temp. ≥ 90°F	0	0	1	3	14	24	26	24	13	3	0	1	2
Days Maximum Temp. ≤ 32°F	1	0	0	0	0	0	0	0	0	0	0	0	0
Days Minimum Temp. ≤ 32°F	22	14	7	1	0	0	0	0	0	1	9	21	75
Days Minimum Temp. ≤ 0°F	0	0	0	0	0	0	0	0	0	0	0	0	0
Heating Degree Days (base 65°F)	686	475	313	122	15	0	0	0	20	120	410	651	2,812
Cooling Degree Days (base 65°F)	0	2	10	68	248	462	536	482	279	65	3	0	2,155
Mean Precipitation (in.)	0.41	0.46	0.28	0.51	1.45	1.55	1.79	2.37	2.96	1.07	0.57	0.66	14.08
Days With ≥ 0.1" Precipitation	1	1	1	1	3	3	3	4	4	3	1	2	27
Days With ≥ 1.0" Precipitation	0	0	0	0	0	0	0	1	1	0	0	0	2
Mean Snowfall (in.)	1.9	1.7	0.6	0.5	trace	trace	trace	trace	trace	trace	0.7	2.5	7.9
Days With ≥ 1.0" Snow Depth	1	1	0	0	0	0	0	0	0	0	0	1	3

Carlsbad Caverns *Eddy County* Elevation: 4,402 ft. Latitude: 32° 32' N Longitude: 103° 56' W

	JAN	FEB	MAR	APR	MAY	JUN	JUL	AUG	SEP	OCT	NOV	DEC	YEAR
Mean Maximum Temp. (°F)	55.2	59.4	66.6	74.3	82.2	90.0	90.1	88.1	81.8	73.9	63.8	56.5	73.5
Mean Temp. (°F)	43.7	47.6	54.2	61.5	69.7	76.8	77.8	76.4	70.5	62.5	52.3	45.3	61.5
Mean Minimum Temp. (°F)	32.4	36.1	41.7	48.5	57.2	63.7	65.4	64.6	59.2	51.0	41.1	34.2	49.6
Extreme Maximum Temp. (°F)	81	84	90	95	101	110	106	103	98	94	86	79	110
Extreme Minimum Temp. (°F)	2	4	12	21	34	44	46	52	34	15	8	2	2
Days Maximum Temp. ≥ 90°F	0	0	0	1	6	17	18	15	6	1	0	0	64
Days Maximum Temp. ≤ 32°F	2	1	0	0	0	0	0	0	0	0	0	2	5
Days Minimum Temp. ≤ 32°F	15	9	5	1	0	0	0	0	0	0	*5*	13	*48*
Days Minimum Temp. ≤ 0°F	0	0	0	0	0	0	0	0	0	0	0	0	0
Heating Degree Days (base 65°F)	654	486	340	154	34	3	0	2	38	137	381	605	2,834
Cooling Degree Days (base 65°F)	0	2	11	58	196	373	423	377	217	69	7	1	1,734
Mean Precipitation (in.)	0.42	0.50	0.29	0.53	1.52	2.15	2.10	2.62	3.78	1.26	0.49	0.57	16.23
Days With ≥ 0.1" Precipitation	1	2	1	1	3	4	4	5	5	3	1	1	31
Days With ≥ 1.0" Precipitation	0	0	0	0	0	0	0	1	1	0	0	0	2
Mean Snowfall (in.)	1.4	1.1	0.5	trace	0.0	0.0	0.0	0.0	0.0	0.1	0.3	1.8	5.2
Days With ≥ 1.0" Snow Depth	*1*	1	0	0	0	0	0	0	0	0	0	0	*2*

Carrizozo 1 SW *Lincoln County* Elevation: 5,403 ft. Latitude: 33° 38' N Longitude: 105° 53' W

	JAN	FEB	MAR	APR	MAY	JUN	JUL	AUG	SEP	OCT	NOV	DEC	YEAR
Mean Maximum Temp. (°F)	52.0	57.3	64.4	72.4	81.1	90.6	90.9	88.0	82.6	73.3	61.1	52.6	72.2
Mean Temp. (°F)	37.4	41.9	48.0	55.0	64.1	73.0	75.6	73.3	67.4	57.0	45.3	37.7	56.3
Mean Minimum Temp. (°F)	22.6	26.4	31.6	37.6	46.9	55.5	60.2	58.5	52.1	40.6	29.5	22.8	40.4
Extreme Maximum Temp. (°F)	71	79	87	97	101	108	105	103	98	91	80	74	108
Extreme Minimum Temp. (°F)	-18	0	7	15	28	40	46	43	32	12	-7	-15	-18
Days Maximum Temp. ≥ 90°F	0	0	0	0	4	18	19	14	5	0	0	0	60
Days Maximum Temp. ≤ 32°F	1	0	0	0	0	0	0	0	0	0	0	1	2
Days Minimum Temp. ≤ 32°F	28	22	17	8	1	0	0	0	0	5	20	27	128
Days Minimum Temp. ≤ 0°F	0	0	0	0	0	0	0	0	0	0	0	0	0
Heating Degree Days (base 65°F)	850	648	520	301	86	4	0	1	37	249	583	838	4,117
Cooling Degree Days (base 65°F)	0	0	0	6	69	256	335	275	118	9	0	0	1,068
Mean Precipitation (in.)	0.71	0.60	0.67	0.42	0.75	0.87	2.24	2.47	1.62	1.32	0.81	0.85	13.33
Days With ≥ 0.1" Precipitation	2	2	2	1	2	3	5	6	4	3	2	3	35
Days With ≥ 1.0" Precipitation	0	0	0	0	0	0	0	0	0	0	0	0	0
Mean Snowfall (in.)	2.3	1.8	1.5	0.6	trace	0.0	0.0	0.0	0.0	0.2	1.0	*1.6*	*9.0*
Days With ≥ 1.0" Snow Depth	na	*0*	0	0	0	0	0	0	0	0	0	*0*	na

Chaco Canyon Nat'l Monument *San Juan County*   Elevation: 6,171 ft.   Latitude: 36° 02' N   Longitude: 107° 55' W

	JAN	FEB	MAR	APR	MAY	JUN	JUL	AUG	SEP	OCT	NOV	DEC	YEAR
Mean Maximum Temp. (°F)	42.8	49.1	57.8	66.1	75.8	86.2	89.8	87.1	80.1	68.6	54.1	44.1	66.8
Mean Temp. (°F)	27.8	33.9	40.5	47.4	56.8	66.3	72.2	70.2	62.2	50.1	37.7	28.8	49.5
Mean Minimum Temp. (°F)	12.8	18.7	23.2	28.6	37.7	46.3	54.5	53.4	44.3	31.5	21.3	13.4	32.1
Extreme Maximum Temp. (°F)	69	70	85	86	93	103	104	100	97	85	75	67	104
Extreme Minimum Temp. (°F)	-37	-26	-17	1	14	25	34	36	19	7	-35	-37	-37
Days Maximum Temp. ≥ 90°F	0	0	0	0	0	9	17	9	1	0	0	0	36
Days Maximum Temp. ≤ 32°F	4	1	0	0	0	0	0	0	0	0	0	3	8
Days Minimum Temp. ≤ 32°F	30	27	27	20	8	1	0	0	2	17	26	29	187
Days Minimum Temp. ≤ 0°F	5	1	0	0	0	0	0	0	0	0	0	4	10
Heating Degree Days (base 65°F)	1,146	870	752	522	255	52	1	5	111	457	812	1,115	6,098
Cooling Degree Days (base 65°F)	0	0	0	0	8	100	226	180	33	0	0	0	547
Mean Precipitation (in.)	0.59	0.54	0.58	0.52	0.69	0.47	1.23	1.31	1.20	1.02	0.76	0.53	9.44
Days With ≥ 0.1" Precipitation	2	2	2	2	2	1	3	4	3	3	2	2	28
Days With ≥ 1.0" Precipitation	0	0	0	0	0	0	0	0	0	0	0	0	0
Mean Snowfall (in.)	3.4	3.1	1.6	0.8	trace	0.0	0.0	0.0	0.0	0.7	1.6	3.3	14.5
Days With ≥ 1.0" Snow Depth	na	1	1	0	0	0	0	0	0	0	1	2	na

Chama *Rio Arriba County*   Elevation: 7,847 ft.   Latitude: 36° 55' N   Longitude: 106° 35' W

	JAN	FEB	MAR	APR	MAY	JUN	JUL	AUG	SEP	OCT	NOV	DEC	YEAR
Mean Maximum Temp. (°F)	36.9	41.1	47.2	55.7	65.0	75.9	80.3	77.6	71.3	60.9	46.6	38.5	58.1
Mean Temp. (°F)	20.9	25.2	31.8	39.3	47.8	56.6	62.3	61.0	54.1	43.7	31.3	23.1	41.4
Mean Minimum Temp. (°F)	4.7	9.3	16.3	22.8	30.5	37.3	44.3	44.4	36.8	26.5	16.0	7.6	24.7
Extreme Maximum Temp. (°F)	57	61	69	75	81	92	92	92	88	79	71	60	92
Extreme Minimum Temp. (°F)	-30	-29	-14	-7	9	18	28	30	16	-2	-16	-30	-30
Days Maximum Temp. ≥ 90°F	0	0	0	0	0	0	1	0	0	0	0	0	1
Days Maximum Temp. ≤ 32°F	9	3	1	0	0	0	0	0	0	0	3	7	23
Days Minimum Temp. ≤ 32°F	31	28	31	27	19	7	1	0	8	26	29	31	238
Days Minimum Temp. ≤ 0°F	10	5	2	0	0	0	0	0	0	0	2	7	26
Heating Degree Days (base 65°F)	1,361	1,116	1,019	760	526	248	88	123	321	653	1,005	1,293	8,513
Cooling Degree Days (base 65°F)	0	0	0	0	0	3	10	7	1	0	0	0	21
Mean Precipitation (in.)	1.90	1.79	2.19	1.49	1.45	1.14	2.14	2.85	2.21	2.08	1.91	1.63	22.78
Days With ≥ 0.1" Precipitation	5	5	6	4	4	3	6	8	5	5	5	5	61
Days With ≥ 1.0" Precipitation	0	0	0	0	0	0	0	0	0	0	0	0	0
Mean Snowfall (in.)	26.0	21.1	18.0	5.7	0.7	trace	0.0	0.0	0.0	3.9	12.6	19.5	107.5
Days With ≥ 1.0" Snow Depth	27	25	22	5	0	0	0	0	0	2	9	22	112

Cimarron 4 SW *Colfax County*   Elevation: 6,538 ft.   Latitude: 36° 28' N   Longitude: 104° 57' W

	JAN	FEB	MAR	APR	MAY	JUN	JUL	AUG	SEP	OCT	NOV	DEC	YEAR
Mean Maximum Temp. (°F)	46.2	50.3	55.9	62.9	71.4	80.8	83.5	80.7	75.9	67.8	55.3	48.0	64.9
Mean Temp. (°F)	31.0	34.6	40.2	46.8	55.3	64.2	67.7	65.7	59.8	50.5	39.2	32.4	49.0
Mean Minimum Temp. (°F)	15.8	18.9	24.4	30.5	39.2	47.5	51.8	50.6	43.8	33.3	23.1	16.7	33.0
Extreme Maximum Temp. (°F)	75	75	79	83	89	98	99	94	91	88	77	75	99
Extreme Minimum Temp. (°F)	-22	-21	-2	-1	19	31	41	38	16	-5	-18	-17	-22
Days Maximum Temp. ≥ 90°F	0	0	0	0	0	3	5	1	0	0	0	0	9
Days Maximum Temp. ≤ 32°F	3	2	0	0	0	0	0	0	0	0	1	3	9
Days Minimum Temp. ≤ 32°F	30	26	27	18	4	0	0	0	2	13	26	30	176
Days Minimum Temp. ≤ 0°F	2	1	0	0	0	0	0	0	0	0	0	2	5
Heating Degree Days (base 65°F)	1,047	852	763	541	297	72	14	30	159	441	767	1,003	5,986
Cooling Degree Days (base 65°F)	0	0	0	0	5	52	97	56	10	0	0	0	220
Mean Precipitation (in.)	0.48	0.56	0.88	1.23	2.13	2.18	2.65	3.40	2.04	0.97	0.73	0.43	17.68
Days With ≥ 0.1" Precipitation	1	2	3	3	4	5	7	7	5	2	2	1	42
Days With ≥ 1.0" Precipitation	0	0	0	0	0	0	0	1	0	0	0	0	1
Mean Snowfall (in.)	6.2	8.5	5.6	6.0	1.0	0.0	0.0	0.0	0.2	2.2	5.8	6.0	41.5
Days With ≥ 1.0" Snow Depth	4	4	2	1	0	0	0	0	0	1	2	5	19

Cliff 11 SE *Grant County*   Elevation: 4,773 ft.   Latitude: 32° 50' N   Longitude: 108° 31' W

	JAN	FEB	MAR	APR	MAY	JUN	JUL	AUG	SEP	OCT	NOV	DEC	YEAR
Mean Maximum Temp. (°F)	55.6	60.2	66.0	73.6	82.0	91.8	92.1	89.4	84.9	75.4	64.1	55.8	74.3
Mean Temp. (°F)	38.7	42.4	47.3	53.3	61.6	71.0	75.3	73.5	67.7	56.8	45.6	38.5	56.0
Mean Minimum Temp. (°F)	21.9	24.5	28.6	33.1	41.1	50.0	58.5	57.5	50.3	38.0	26.8	21.2	37.6
Extreme Maximum Temp. (°F)	78	83	87	92	100	106	106	104	100	94	83	75	106
Extreme Minimum Temp. (°F)	-10	4	9	15	22	32	41	38	31	15	8	-9	-10
Days Maximum Temp. ≥ 90°F	0	0	0	0	4	20	21	16	7	0	0	0	68
Days Maximum Temp. ≤ 32°F	0	0	0	0	0	0	0	0	0	0	0	0	0
Days Minimum Temp. ≤ 32°F	28	24	22	15	3	0	0	0	0	8	24	28	152
Days Minimum Temp. ≤ 0°F	0	0	0	0	0	0	0	0	0	0	0	0	0
Heating Degree Days (base 65°F)	807	633	541	345	124	10	0	0	25	254	577	814	4,130
Cooling Degree Days (base 65°F)	0	0	0	1	25	188	312	265	107	3	0	0	901
Mean Precipitation (in.)	1.15	1.16	0.91	0.37	0.50	0.45	2.82	2.76	1.94	1.52	0.90	1.27	15.75
Days With ≥ 0.1" Precipitation	3	3	3	1	2	1	6	7	4	3	2	3	38
Days With ≥ 1.0" Precipitation	0	0	0	0	0	0	0	0	0	0	0	0	0
Mean Snowfall (in.)	1.4	1.0	0.8	0.3	trace	0.0	0.0	0.0	0.0	trace	0.3	0.5	4.3
Days With ≥ 1.0" Snow Depth	1	0	0	0	0	0	0	0	0	0	0	0	1

Clines Corners 7 SE *Torrance County*   Elevation: 6,922 ft.   Latitude: 34° 56' N   Longitude: 105° 35' W

	JAN	FEB	MAR	APR	MAY	JUN	JUL	AUG	SEP	OCT	NOV	DEC	YEAR
Mean Maximum Temp. (°F)	42.3	48.4	55.1	63.0	72.0	81.8	83.5	80.6	74.5	64.8	52.4	44.5	63.6
Mean Temp. (°F)	30.9	35.3	40.6	47.3	56.2	65.3	68.9	66.8	60.3	50.4	39.5	32.5	49.5
Mean Minimum Temp. (°F)	19.4	22.2	26.1	31.4	40.3	48.8	54.3	53.0	46.2	35.9	26.6	20.5	35.4
Extreme Maximum Temp. (°F)	68	70	77	82	88	100	95	93	90	82	72	68	100
Extreme Minimum Temp. (°F)	-29	-10	-6	7	21	29	42	40	22	0	-18	-12	-29
Days Maximum Temp. ≥ 90°F	0	0	0	0	0	4	4	1	0	0	0	0	9
Days Maximum Temp. ≤ 32°F	4	2	0	0	0	0	0	0	0	0	1	3	10
Days Minimum Temp. ≤ 32°F	29	25	25	16	5	0	0	0	1	9	22	28	160
Days Minimum Temp. ≤ 0°F	1	0	0	0	0	0	0	0	0	0	0	1	2
Heating Degree Days (base 65°F)	1,052	832	750	526	273	60	6	19	148	445	758	1,001	5,870
Cooling Degree Days (base 65°F)	0	0	0	0	9	83	*148*	*94*	*16*	*0*	*0*	0	*350*
Mean Precipitation (in.)	0.99	0.83	1.00	0.97	1.58	1.60	2.72	3.12	2.25	1.47	1.05	0.99	18.57
Days With ≥ 0.1" Precipitation	3	3	4	3	4	4	7	8	5	3	3	3	50
Days With ≥ 1.0" Precipitation	0	0	0	0	0	0	0	1	1	0	0	0	2
Mean Snowfall (in.)	*8.8*	7.0	5.4	3.8	0.8	0.0	0.0	0.0	trace	2.3	5.6	9.6	*43.3*
Days With ≥ 1.0" Snow Depth	9	5	2	1	0	0	0	0	0	1	3	8	29

Clovis *Curry County*   Elevation: 4,288 ft.   Latitude: 34° 25' N   Longitude: 103° 12' W

	JAN	FEB	MAR	APR	MAY	JUN	JUL	AUG	SEP	OCT	NOV	DEC	YEAR
Mean Maximum Temp. (°F)	50.2	55.8	63.5	71.4	79.9	88.4	90.4	88.0	81.6	72.3	60.5	52.1	71.2
Mean Temp. (°F)	36.8	41.5	48.1	55.9	65.1	73.8	76.9	75.0	68.2	57.9	46.5	38.7	57.0
Mean Minimum Temp. (°F)	23.4	27.2	32.8	40.4	50.3	59.2	63.3	62.0	54.8	43.5	32.6	25.1	42.9
Extreme Maximum Temp. (°F)	79	83	91	97	100	110	108	104	100	94	85	76	110
Extreme Minimum Temp. (°F)	-7	-4	7	15	30	40	51	52	33	13	-1	-7	-7
Days Maximum Temp. ≥ 90°F	0	0	0	1	4	15	19	14	6	0	0	0	59
Days Maximum Temp. ≤ 32°F	4	2	1	0	0	0	0	0	0	0	1	3	11
Days Minimum Temp. ≤ 32°F	27	21	15	5	0	0	0	0	0	2	14	25	109
Days Minimum Temp. ≤ 0°F	0	0	0	0	0	0	0	0	0	0	0	1	1
Heating Degree Days (base 65°F)	866	656	517	279	83	8	1	1	52	233	547	810	4,053
Cooling Degree Days (base 65°F)	0	0	1	13	97	284	388	335	164	19	0	0	1,301
Mean Precipitation (in.)	0.48	0.42	0.62	1.03	1.94	2.67	2.62	3.45	2.27	1.56	0.71	0.67	18.44
Days With ≥ 0.1" Precipitation	2	2	2	2	4	5	5	6	4	3	2	2	39
Days With ≥ 1.0" Precipitation	0	0	0	0	0	1	1	1	1	0	0	0	4
Mean Snowfall (in.)	3.8	3.3	1.2	0.3	0.0	0.0	0.0	0.0	0.0	0.4	1.7	3.6	14.3
Days With ≥ 1.0" Snow Depth	4	3	1	0	0	0	0	0	0	0	1	3	12

Clovis 13 N *Curry County*   Elevation: 4,432 ft.   Latitude: 34° 36' N   Longitude: 103° 13' W

	JAN	FEB	MAR	APR	MAY	JUN	JUL	AUG	SEP	OCT	NOV	DEC	YEAR
Mean Maximum Temp. (°F)	52.3	57.9	65.7	73.3	81.2	89.9	91.3	88.8	83.1	74.3	61.6	53.8	72.8
Mean Temp. (°F)	37.7	42.1	48.5	55.9	64.9	73.6	76.4	74.5	68.4	58.4	46.7	39.4	57.2
Mean Minimum Temp. (°F)	23.0	26.2	31.3	38.5	48.5	57.2	61.4	60.2	53.5	42.6	31.7	24.9	41.6
Extreme Maximum Temp. (°F)	79	82	88	94	102	108	106	101	102	93	85	78	108
Extreme Minimum Temp. (°F)	-10	-4	4	13	25	40	48	46	28	11	0	-8	-10
Days Maximum Temp. ≥ 90°F	0	0	0	1	5	17	20	16	7	0	0	0	66
Days Maximum Temp. ≤ 32°F	2	1	0	0	0	0	0	0	0	0	0	1	4
Days Minimum Temp. ≤ 32°F	27	22	17	6	0	0	0	0	0	3	16	25	116
Days Minimum Temp. ≤ 0°F	0	0	0	0	0	0	0	0	0	0	0	0	0
Heating Degree Days (base 65°F)	840	642	504	274	78	7	0	0	40	212	542	786	3,925
Cooling Degree Days (base 65°F)	0	0	1	9	88	278	375	317	158	16	0	0	1,242
Mean Precipitation (in.)	0.33	0.34	0.58	0.98	2.25	2.30	2.49	3.23	2.17	1.58	0.58	0.50	17.33
Days With ≥ 0.1" Precipitation	1	1	1	2	4	4	5	5	4	3	1	1	32
Days With ≥ 1.0" Precipitation	0	0	0	0	1	1	0	1	1	0	0	0	4
Mean Snowfall (in.)	na	*0.9*	*0.4*	0.4	0.0	0.0	0.0	0.0	0.0	0.3	0.3	*1.3*	na
Days With ≥ 1.0" Snow Depth	*0*	*0*	0	0	0	0	0	0	0	0	0	na	na

Columbus *Luna County*   Elevation: 4,064 ft.   Latitude: 31° 50' N   Longitude: 107° 38' W

	JAN	FEB	MAR	APR	MAY	JUN	JUL	AUG	SEP	OCT	NOV	DEC	YEAR
Mean Maximum Temp. (°F)	58.6	64.4	71.3	79.1	87.6	96.6	95.7	92.7	88.3	78.9	67.3	58.4	78.2
Mean Temp. (°F)	44.1	49.0	54.9	61.9	70.8	80.0	81.5	79.1	74.0	63.4	51.9	44.2	62.9
Mean Minimum Temp. (°F)	29.5	33.5	38.5	44.8	54.0	63.5	67.3	65.4	59.6	47.8	36.3	29.9	47.5
Extreme Maximum Temp. (°F)	79	86	91	98	104	111	109	105	102	96	86	80	111
Extreme Minimum Temp. (°F)	5	5	13	22	32	44	54	52	40	17	2	6	2
Days Maximum Temp. ≥ 90°F	0	0	0	1	12	27	27	24	14	2	0	0	107
Days Maximum Temp. ≤ 32°F	0	0	0	0	0	0	0	0	0	0	0	0	0
Days Minimum Temp. ≤ 32°F	20	13	6	2	0	0	0	0	0	1	9	20	71
Days Minimum Temp. ≤ 0°F	0	0	0	0	0	0	0	0	0	0	0	0	0
Heating Degree Days (base 65°F)	642	446	309	129	13	0	0	0	7	104	389	638	2,677
Cooling Degree Days (base 65°F)	0	0	3	54	225	476	535	456	303	69	2	0	2,123
Mean Precipitation (in.)	0.56	0.44	0.27	0.28	0.26	0.32	2.14	1.94	1.37	1.07	0.55	0.85	10.05
Days With ≥ 0.1" Precipitation	2	1	1	1	1	1	5	4	4	3	2	2	27
Days With ≥ 1.0" Precipitation	0	0	0	0	0	0	0	0	0	0	0	0	0
Mean Snowfall (in.)	*0.8*	0.3	trace	0.2	0.0	0.0	0.0	0.0	0.0	0.0	0.3	0.9	*2.5*
Days With ≥ 1.0" Snow Depth	0	0	0	0	0	0	0	0	0	0	0	0	0

Conchas Dam *San Miguel County*   Elevation: 4,242 ft.   Latitude: 35° 24' N   Longitude: 104° 11' W

	JAN	FEB	MAR	APR	MAY	JUN	JUL	AUG	SEP	OCT	NOV	DEC	YEAR
Mean Maximum Temp. (°F)	52.4	57.7	64.7	72.0	80.8	90.5	93.4	91.2	84.0	74.6	62.3	53.8	73.1
Mean Temp. (°F)	37.8	42.6	49.6	57.3	66.4	75.8	79.5	77.6	70.4	59.8	47.8	39.6	58.7
Mean Minimum Temp. (°F)	23.1	27.5	34.5	42.5	52.0	61.0	65.6	64.0	56.7	45.1	33.2	25.3	44.2
Extreme Maximum Temp. (°F)	80	82	91	97	106	114	107	107	103	93	86	78	114
Extreme Minimum Temp. (°F)	-8	-5	9	17	32	41	51	46	35	16	2	-10	-10
Days Maximum Temp. ≥ 90°F	0	0	0	1	5	18	24	21	9	1	0	0	79
Days Maximum Temp. ≤ 32°F	3	1	0	0	0	0	0	0	0	0	0	2	6
Days Minimum Temp. ≤ 32°F	28	21	12	3	0	0	0	0	0	2	14	26	106
Days Minimum Temp. ≤ 0°F	0	0	0	0	0	0	0	0	0	0	0	0	0
Heating Degree Days (base 65°F)	831	624	471	242	64	5	0	1	36	186	510	782	3,752
Cooling Degree Days (base 65°F)	0	0	1	19	114	334	468	406	213	31	0	0	1,586
Mean Precipitation (in.)	0.41	0.39	0.73	0.92	1.63	1.90	2.59	2.61	1.71	1.07	0.75	0.44	15.15
Days With ≥ 0.1" Precipitation	1	1	2	2	3	4	5	6	3	2	1	1	31
Days With ≥ 1.0" Precipitation	0	0	0	0	0	0	1	1	0	0	0	0	2
Mean Snowfall (in.)	*3.1*	3.2	0.8	0.4	0.2	0.0	0.0	0.0	0.0	0.4	0.9	3.0	*12.0*
Days With ≥ 1.0" Snow Depth	*2*	1	0	0	0	0	0	0	0	0	0	1	*4*

Crossroads 2 *Lea County*   Elevation: 4,146 ft.   Latitude: 33° 31' N   Longitude: 103° 21' W

	JAN	FEB	MAR	APR	MAY	JUN	JUL	AUG	SEP	OCT	NOV	DEC	YEAR
Mean Maximum Temp. (°F)	54.2	59.5	67.4	75.0	82.9	*90.6*	91.5	89.0	82.9	74.7	63.0	55.8	*73.9*
Mean Temp. (°F)	38.8	43.2	50.0	57.6	66.6	*74.7*	77.0	75.0	68.7	58.8	47.3	40.2	*58.1*
Mean Minimum Temp. (°F)	23.3	26.8	32.6	40.1	50.2	58.8	62.4	60.9	54.5	42.8	31.5	24.6	42.4
Extreme Maximum Temp. (°F)	78	83	90	97	101	109	108	103	102	97	85	78	109
Extreme Minimum Temp. (°F)	-12	-5	6	18	30	*43*	52	48	32	10	5	-8	*-12*
Days Maximum Temp. ≥ 90°F	0	0	0	1	6	16	20	16	7	1	0	0	67
Days Maximum Temp. ≤ 32°F	2	1	0	0	0	0	0	0	0	0	0	2	5
Days Minimum Temp. ≤ 32°F	27	21	14	5	0	0	0	0	0	3	16	25	111
Days Minimum Temp. ≤ 0°F	0	0	0	0	0	0	0	0	0	0	0	0	0
Heating Degree Days (base 65°F)	807	609	459	233	54	*3*	0	1	41	204	524	761	*3,696*
Cooling Degree Days (base 65°F)	0	0	1	15	*115*	*305*	396	333	160	16	1	0	*1,342*
Mean Precipitation (in.)	0.34	0.38	0.39	0.63	2.00	1.96	2.70	2.91	2.41	1.32	0.60	0.49	16.13
Days With ≥ 0.1" Precipitation	1	1	1	2	4	4	4	5	4	2	1	1	30
Days With ≥ 1.0" Precipitation	0	0	0	0	1	0	1	1	1	0	0	0	4
Mean Snowfall (in.)	*0.7*	*0.7*	0.3	0.0	0.0	0.0	0.0	0.0	0.0	0.1	*0.7*	*1.5*	*4.0*
Days With ≥ 1.0" Snow Depth	*0*	*0*	0	0	0	0	0	0	0	0	0	*0*	*0*

Cuba *Sandoval County*   Elevation: 7,043 ft.   Latitude: 36° 01' N   Longitude: 106° 58' W

	JAN	FEB	MAR	APR	MAY	JUN	JUL	AUG	SEP	OCT	NOV	DEC	YEAR
Mean Maximum Temp. (°F)	na	*45.9*	*53.4*	61.3	70.5	81.2	84.9	82.6	75.9	65.5	52.3	*44.1*	na
Mean Temp. (°F)	na	na	*37.1*	43.4	52.2	61.0	67.0	65.5	57.8	46.5	35.0	*27.2*	na
Mean Minimum Temp. (°F)	na	na	*20.8*	25.6	33.8	40.8	48.9	48.6	39.7	27.4	17.7	*10.3*	na
Extreme Maximum Temp. (°F)	66	68	76	80	88	98	100	98	94	84	75	69	100
Extreme Minimum Temp. (°F)	-32	-38	-10	-6	16	20	31	29	15	4	-30	-32	-38
Days Maximum Temp. ≥ 90°F	0	0	0	0	0	3	5	2	0	0	0	0	10
Days Maximum Temp. ≤ 32°F	3	2	0	0	0	0	0	0	0	0	1	2	8
Days Minimum Temp. ≤ 32°F	27	24	26	24	13	4	0	0	5	24	29	28	204
Days Minimum Temp. ≤ 0°F	7	3	0	0	0	0	0	0	0	0	1	4	15
Heating Degree Days (base 65°F)	na	na	*853*	*645*	391	143	20	35	215	568	892	*1,162*	na
Cooling Degree Days (base 65°F)	na	*0*	*0*	0	*0*	24	84	59	7	0	0	*0*	na
Mean Precipitation (in.)	0.91	0.57	0.86	0.71	0.92	0.82	1.94	2.27	1.43	1.12	0.88	0.56	12.99
Days With ≥ 0.1" Precipitation	2	2	2	2	2	2	5	6	4	3	2	2	34
Days With ≥ 1.0" Precipitation	0	0	0	0	0	0	0	0	0	0	0	0	0
Mean Snowfall (in.)	*9.1*	*4.9*	*3.4*	*1.7*	trace	0.0	0.0	0.0	0.0	0.6	*2.5*	*5.6*	*27.8*
Days With ≥ 1.0" Snow Depth	na	*5*	*1*	*0*	0	0	0	0	0	0	0	*2*	na

Cubero *Cibola County*   Elevation: 6,194 ft.   Latitude: 35° 05' N   Longitude: 107° 31' W

	JAN	FEB	MAR	APR	MAY	JUN	JUL	AUG	SEP	OCT	NOV	DEC	YEAR
Mean Maximum Temp. (°F)	*46.9*	52.6	*59.4*	67.8	76.4	*87.1*	89.4	85.8	80.0	69.8	56.6	48.0	68.3
Mean Temp. (°F)	*32.5*	37.2	*42.9*	50.4	58.9	68.5	72.7	70.3	63.4	52.3	40.7	33.0	51.9
Mean Minimum Temp. (°F)	*18.0*	21.6	*26.4*	33.0	41.4	49.9	56.0	54.8	46.8	34.7	24.6	17.8	35.4
Extreme Maximum Temp. (°F)	*67*	75	*80*	87	97	*103*	103	100	98	89	78	*69*	*103*
Extreme Minimum Temp. (°F)	*-13*	-7	*6*	11	23	*31*	42	40	26	11	3	*-13*	*-13*
Days Maximum Temp. ≥ 90°F	*0*	0	*0*	0	1	*12*	16	8	1	0	0	*0*	38
Days Maximum Temp. ≤ 32°F	*1*	0	*0*	0	0	*0*	0	0	0	0	0	*2*	3
Days Minimum Temp. ≤ 32°F	*30*	26	*25*	15	3	*0*	0	0	0	11	26	*29*	165
Days Minimum Temp. ≤ 0°F	*1*	0	*0*	0	0	*0*	0	0	0	0	0	*1*	2
Heating Degree Days (base 65°F)	*1,002*	779	*678*	431	195	27	*0*	*4*	81	389	724	986	5,296
Cooling Degree Days (base 65°F)	*0*	0	*0*	1	14	134	239	174	39	0	0	0	601
Mean Precipitation (in.)	*0.68*	na	na	*0.57*	na	na	na	*1.97*	*1.48*	*1.10*	*0.66*	na	na
Days With ≥ 0.1" Precipitation	na	na	na	na	na	na	na	5	4	3	2	na	na
Days With ≥ 1.0" Precipitation	na	na	na	na	na	na	na	0	0	0	0	na	na
Mean Snowfall (in.)	*5.6*	na	na	na	na	*0.0*	*0.0*	0.0	0.0	0.5	1.2	na	na
Days With ≥ 1.0" Snow Depth	na	na	*0*	*0*	*0*	*0*	*0*	0	0	0	0	na	na

Des Moines *Union County* Elevation: 6,617 ft. Latitude: 36° 45' N Longitude: 103° 50' W

	JAN	FEB	MAR	APR	MAY	JUN	JUL	AUG	SEP	OCT	NOV	DEC	YEAR
Mean Maximum Temp. (°F)	44.4	48.2	54.2	62.4	69.9	79.8	83.2	80.9	75.1	65.9	52.1	45.1	63.4
Mean Temp. (°F)	30.7	34.1	39.9	47.5	55.7	65.6	70.0	68.0	61.4	51.3	38.6	31.9	49.6
Mean Minimum Temp. (°F)	16.9	19.9	25.6	32.6	41.6	51.4	56.7	55.1	47.6	36.6	25.0	18.6	35.6
Extreme Maximum Temp. (°F)	69	72	81	84	88	98	97	92	90	84	78	74	98
Extreme Minimum Temp. (°F)	-21	-18	-4	6	20	30	44	41	21	-2	-11	-16	-21
Days Maximum Temp. ≥ 90°F	0	0	0	0	0	2	3	1	0	0	0	0	6
Days Maximum Temp. ≤ 32°F	5	3	1	0	0	0	0	0	0	0	3	4	16
Days Minimum Temp. ≤ 32°F	30	26	24	15	4	0	0	0	1	10	23	29	162
Days Minimum Temp. ≤ 0°F	2	1	0	0	0	0	0	0	0	0	0	2	5
Heating Degree Days (base 65°F)	1,057	867	769	518	286	68	9	18	138	420	786	1,019	5,955
Cooling Degree Days (base 65°F)	0	0	0	1	6	94	171	120	36	0	0	0	428
Mean Precipitation (in.)	0.43	0.51	1.13	1.01	2.27	2.09	2.98	2.90	2.08	1.03	0.89	0.54	17.86
Days With ≥ 0.1" Precipitation	1	1	3	3	5	5	6	6	4	2	2	2	40
Days With ≥ 1.0" Precipitation	0	0	0	0	0	0	1	0	0	0	0	0	1
Mean Snowfall (in.)	4.1	4.6	7.9	3.7	2.2	trace	0.0	0.0	0.5	2.1	6.1	5.5	36.7
Days With ≥ 1.0" Snow Depth	10	7	6	3	1	0	0	0	0	1	6	8	42

Dilia *Guadalupe County* Elevation: 5,147 ft. Latitude: 35° 11' N Longitude: 105° 03' W

	JAN	FEB	MAR	APR	MAY	JUN	JUL	AUG	SEP	OCT	NOV	DEC	YEAR
Mean Maximum Temp. (°F)	50.9	56.1	62.7	70.4	78.8	88.4	90.6	88.3	81.7	72.4	60.3	52.2	71.1
Mean Temp. (°F)	36.2	40.3	46.2	53.3	62.3	71.4	75.1	73.3	66.4	56.1	44.9	37.4	55.2
Mean Minimum Temp. (°F)	21.4	24.5	29.7	36.1	45.7	54.4	59.6	58.2	51.0	39.7	29.5	22.6	39.4
Extreme Maximum Temp. (°F)	77	80	86	92	97	107	105	103	99	90	82	77	107
Extreme Minimum Temp. (°F)	-21	-8	1	10	28	32	40	42	28	10	-4	-28	-28
Days Maximum Temp. ≥ 90°F	0	0	0	0	2	14	19	14	4	0	0	0	53
Days Maximum Temp. ≤ 32°F	2	1	0	0	0	0	0	0	0	0	0	1	4
Days Minimum Temp. ≤ 32°F	28	24	20	10	1	0	0	0	0	5	20	27	135
Days Minimum Temp. ≤ 0°F	1	0	0	0	0	0	0	0	0	0	0	1	2
Heating Degree Days (base 65°F)	886	691	576	349	116	10	1	1	52	275	595	848	4,400
Cooling Degree Days (base 65°F)	0	0	0	4	41	212	326	277	101	4	0	0	965
Mean Precipitation (in.)	0.63	0.50	0.69	0.90	1.37	1.53	2.72	2.78	1.96	1.18	0.78	0.76	15.80
Days With ≥ 0.1" Precipitation	2	1	2	2	3	3	6	6	4	3	2	2	36
Days With ≥ 1.0" Precipitation	0	0	0	0	0	0	1	1	1	0	0	0	3
Mean Snowfall (in.)	6.9	4.5	5.4	1.4	0.5	0.0	0.0	trace	trace	1.0	3.0	8.5	31.2
Days With ≥ 1.0" Snow Depth	na	1	1	0	0	0	0	0	0	0	1	3	na

Dulce *Rio Arriba County* Elevation: 6,791 ft. Latitude: 36° 56' N Longitude: 107° 00' W

	JAN	FEB	MAR	APR	MAY	JUN	JUL	AUG	SEP	OCT	NOV	DEC	YEAR
Mean Maximum Temp. (°F)	40.8	45.9	53.0	61.5	70.4	80.7	84.8	82.4	75.9	65.5	51.3	42.4	62.9
Mean Temp. (°F)	23.8	29.4	36.7	43.2	51.2	59.3	65.6	64.7	57.0	46.4	34.6	25.7	44.8
Mean Minimum Temp. (°F)	6.8	12.8	20.3	24.8	31.6	37.8	46.3	46.9	38.0	27.2	18.0	9.0	26.6
Extreme Maximum Temp. (°F)	62	67	74	83	87	97	97	97	92	84	74	65	97
Extreme Minimum Temp. (°F)	-36	-25	-15	1	13	20	29	30	17	5	-18	-38	-38
Days Maximum Temp. ≥ 90°F	0	0	0	0	0	2	5	2	0	0	0	0	9
Days Maximum Temp. ≤ 32°F	4	1	0	0	0	0	0	0	0	0	1	3	9
Days Minimum Temp. ≤ 32°F	31	27	29	26	18	7	1	0	7	24	28	31	229
Days Minimum Temp. ≤ 0°F	9	4	0	0	0	0	0	0	0	0	1	6	20
Heating Degree Days (base 65°F)	1,269	997	871	647	422	177	34	48	236	570	903	1,211	7,385
Cooling Degree Days (base 65°F)	0	0	0	0	0	13	61	55	4	0	0	0	133
Mean Precipitation (in.)	1.35	1.20	1.58	1.13	1.43	0.78	1.80	2.56	1.76	1.69	1.43	1.19	17.90
Days With ≥ 0.1" Precipitation	4	4	5	3	4	2	5	6	4	5	4	4	50
Days With ≥ 1.0" Precipitation	0	0	0	0	0	0	0	0	0	0	0	0	0
Mean Snowfall (in.)	15.2	11.4	7.2	2.5	trace	0.0	0.0	0.0	0.0	1.1	5.9	12.5	55.8
Days With ≥ 1.0" Snow Depth	20	15	6	0	0	0	0	0	0	0	5	14	60

Eagle Nest *Colfax County* Elevation: 8,277 ft. Latitude: 36° 23' N Longitude: 105° 16' W

	JAN	FEB	MAR	APR	MAY	JUN	JUL	AUG	SEP	OCT	NOV	DEC	YEAR
Mean Maximum Temp. (°F)	36.9	41.0	46.8	54.5	64.0	73.9	77.4	75.1	69.8	60.8	47.5	38.9	57.2
Mean Temp. (°F)	19.0	23.7	31.5	38.5	47.1	55.2	60.0	58.5	52.0	42.2	31.2	21.7	40.1
Mean Minimum Temp. (°F)	1.0	6.4	16.1	22.5	30.1	36.5	42.5	41.9	34.2	23.5	14.8	4.4	22.8
Extreme Maximum Temp. (°F)	62	66	70	76	80	91	91	89	85	81	71	68	91
Extreme Minimum Temp. (°F)	-47	-39	-25	-12	7	19	26	26	12	-4	-38	-41	-47
Days Maximum Temp. ≥ 90°F	0	0	0	0	0	0	0	0	0	0	0	0	0
Days Maximum Temp. ≤ 32°F	8	4	2	1	0	0	0	0	0	0	3	8	26
Days Minimum Temp. ≤ 32°F	30	28	29	27	20	7	1	1	11	27	29	30	240
Days Minimum Temp. ≤ 0°F	14	9	2	0	0	0	0	0	0	0	2	11	38
Heating Degree Days (base 65°F)	1,419	1,158	1,032	787	548	288	151	195	383	701	1,006	1,336	9,004
Cooling Degree Days (base 65°F)	0	0	0	0	0	0	1	2	1	0	0	0	4
Mean Precipitation (in.)	0.68	0.74	1.21	1.02	1.34	1.40	2.48	2.88	1.37	0.96	0.84	0.67	15.59
Days With ≥ 0.1" Precipitation	2	2	3	3	4	4	7	8	4	3	3	2	45
Days With ≥ 1.0" Precipitation	0	0	0	0	0	0	0	0	0	0	0	0	0
Mean Snowfall (in.)	10.8	11.6	12.2	5.9	2.4	trace	0.0	0.0	0.3	2.8	7.5	9.4	62.9
Days With ≥ 1.0" Snow Depth	14	na	8	2	0	0	0	0	0	1	5	12	na

El Morro Nat'l Monument *Cibola County*   Elevation: 7,224 ft.   Latitude: 35° 03' N   Longitude: 108° 21' W

	JAN	FEB	MAR	APR	MAY	JUN	JUL	AUG	SEP	OCT	NOV	DEC	YEAR
Mean Maximum Temp. (°F)	43.5	47.8	54.2	62.7	72.2	82.6	84.8	81.9	76.5	66.3	52.9	45.1	64.2
Mean Temp. (°F)	28.5	33.3	38.9	45.2	53.5	62.6	67.9	66.1	59.6	48.8	37.2	30.1	47.6
Mean Minimum Temp. (°F)	13.4	18.8	23.6	27.8	34.8	42.6	50.9	50.1	42.7	31.3	21.5	14.9	31.0
Extreme Maximum Temp. (°F)	68	72	77	80	90	104	98	96	92	87	78	69	104
Extreme Minimum Temp. (°F)	-32	-14	-10	3	13	25	34	33	23	8	-20	-32	-32
Days Maximum Temp. ≥ 90°F	0	0	0	0	0	4	6	2	0	0	0	0	12
Days Maximum Temp. ≤ 32°F	3	1	0	0	0	0	0	0	0	0	1	2	7
Days Minimum Temp. ≤ 32°F	31	27	29	23	11	2	0	0	2	18	27	30	200
Days Minimum Temp. ≤ 0°F	4	1	0	0	0	0	0	0	0	0	0	2	8
Heating Degree Days (base 65°F)	1,126	888	802	585	350	103	10	25	164	496	827	1,076	6,452
Cooling Degree Days (base 65°F)	0	0	0	0	1	35	97	69	9	0	0	0	211
Mean Precipitation (in.)	1.23	0.96	1.26	0.81	0.79	0.61	1.92	2.79	1.55	1.29	1.02	1.01	15.24
Days With ≥ 0.1" Precipitation	3	3	4	3	3	2	5	7	4	4	3	3	44
Days With ≥ 1.0" Precipitation	0	0	0	0	0	0	0	0	0	0	0	0	0
Mean Snowfall (in.)	13.0	8.5	8.1	3.6	0.7	0.0	0.0	0.0	trace	2.1	6.5	9.7	52.2
Days With ≥ 1.0" Snow Depth	17	9	2	1	0	0	0	0	0	0	3	8	40

El Rito *Rio Arriba County*   Elevation: 6,870 ft.   Latitude: 36° 20' N   Longitude: 106° 11' W

	JAN	FEB	MAR	APR	MAY	JUN	JUL	AUG	SEP	OCT	NOV	DEC	YEAR
Mean Maximum Temp. (°F)	41.4	46.9	54.0	62.2	71.1	81.0	84.5	82.1	76.5	66.2	51.9	42.8	63.4
Mean Temp. (°F)	29.0	34.0	39.9	47.1	55.3	64.0	69.0	67.4	61.3	51.2	38.9	30.4	48.9
Mean Minimum Temp. (°F)	16.5	20.9	25.8	31.9	39.5	46.9	53.4	52.5	46.0	36.2	25.7	17.8	34.4
Extreme Maximum Temp. (°F)	65	68	80	82	90	98	99	95	92	88	73	66	99
Extreme Minimum Temp. (°F)	-20	-9	-1	5	19	26	33	39	25	1	-10	-10	-20
Days Maximum Temp. ≥ 90°F	0	0	0	0	0	3	4	1	0	0	0	0	8
Days Maximum Temp. ≤ 32°F	4	2	0	0	0	0	0	0	0	0	1	3	10
Days Minimum Temp. ≤ 32°F	30	27	26	16	4	1	0	0	1	8	24	30	167
Days Minimum Temp. ≤ 0°F	1	0	0	0	0	0	0	0	0	0	0	1	2
Heating Degree Days (base 65°F)	1,110	869	771	532	296	80	5	13	125	421	778	1,068	6,068
Cooling Degree Days (base 65°F)	0	0	0	0	4	54	136	101	23	1	0	0	319
Mean Precipitation (in.)	0.74	0.55	0.91	0.79	0.95	0.92	1.71	2.23	1.33	1.14	0.96	0.57	12.80
Days With ≥ 0.1" Precipitation	2	2	3	2	3	3	5	6	4	3	3	2	38
Days With ≥ 1.0" Precipitation	0	0	0	0	0	0	0	0	0	0	0	0	0
Mean Snowfall (in.)	7.6	6.7	4.8	1.7	0.0	0.0	0.0	0.0	trace	1.2	4.0	6.7	32.7
Days With ≥ 1.0" Snow Depth	na	na	0	0	0	0	0	0	0	0	1	1	na

El Vado Dam *Rio Arriba County*   Elevation: 6,738 ft.   Latitude: 36° 36' N   Longitude: 106° 44' W

	JAN	FEB	MAR	APR	MAY	JUN	JUL	AUG	SEP	OCT	NOV	DEC	YEAR
Mean Maximum Temp. (°F)	39.9	44.9	51.3	59.5	69.3	80.4	84.8	82.0	75.4	65.0	51.0	42.1	62.1
Mean Temp. (°F)	23.1	28.9	36.2	42.5	51.3	60.2	66.5	65.0	57.2	46.4	34.8	26.2	44.9
Mean Minimum Temp. (°F)	6.3	12.9	21.1	25.5	33.2	40.0	48.0	47.9	38.9	27.6	18.5	10.3	27.5
Extreme Maximum Temp. (°F)	64	67	75	81	89	97	98	95	90	90	77	64	98
Extreme Minimum Temp. (°F)	-45	-35	-11	4	14	24	30	31	17	5	-19	-24	-45
Days Maximum Temp. ≥ 90°F	0	0	0	0	0	2	6	2	0	0	0	0	10
Days Maximum Temp. ≤ 32°F	5	2	0	0	0	0	0	0	0	0	1	4	12
Days Minimum Temp. ≤ 32°F	31	27	29	25	14	4	0	0	6	24	28	31	219
Days Minimum Temp. ≤ 0°F	10	4	0	0	0	0	0	0	0	0	0	5	19
Heating Degree Days (base 65°F)	1,292	1,012	884	668	419	156	25	48	233	571	900	1,196	7,404
Cooling Degree Days (base 65°F)	0	0	0	0	1	21	79	61	6	0	0	0	168
Mean Precipitation (in.)	0.90	0.74	0.98	0.99	1.25	0.87	1.79	2.58	1.68	1.38	1.10	0.79	15.05
Days With ≥ 0.1" Precipitation	3	3	3	3	4	3	5	7	5	4	4	3	47
Days With ≥ 1.0" Precipitation	0	0	0	0	0	0	0	0	0	0	0	0	0
Mean Snowfall (in.)	12.1	7.3	5.0	2.3	trace	0.0	0.0	0.0	0.0	1.0	5.0	8.4	41.1
Days With ≥ 1.0" Snow Depth	21	16	7	1	0	0	0	0	0	0	4	11	60

Elephant Butte Dam *Sierra County*   Elevation: 4,573 ft.   Latitude: 33° 09' N   Longitude: 107° 11' W

	JAN	FEB	MAR	APR	MAY	JUN	JUL	AUG	SEP	OCT	NOV	DEC	YEAR
Mean Maximum Temp. (°F)	54.1	60.1	67.2	75.0	83.6	93.1	93.5	90.5	85.1	75.5	63.5	53.9	74.6
Mean Temp. (°F)	41.4	46.4	52.9	60.1	69.0	78.3	80.4	78.0	72.2	61.6	50.1	41.6	61.0
Mean Minimum Temp. (°F)	28.7	32.7	38.5	45.1	54.4	63.4	67.3	65.4	59.3	47.7	36.7	29.2	47.4
Extreme Maximum Temp. (°F)	75	83	89	94	101	111	109	104	101	92	84	78	111
Extreme Minimum Temp. (°F)	2	12	18	26	36	46	57	53	42	22	9	5	2
Days Maximum Temp. ≥ 90°F	0	0	0	1	5	22	24	19	9	0	0	0	80
Days Maximum Temp. ≤ 32°F	0	0	0	0	0	0	0	0	0	0	0	1	1
Days Minimum Temp. ≤ 32°F	24	14	5	1	0	0	0	0	0	0	1	8	23	76
Days Minimum Temp. ≤ 0°F	0	0	0	0	0	0	0	0	0	0	0	0	0
Heating Degree Days (base 65°F)	724	517	370	169	26	1	0	0	11	137	441	721	3,117
Cooling Degree Days (base 65°F)	0	0	2	33	169	413	487	411	235	36	0	0	1,786
Mean Precipitation (in.)	0.42	0.33	0.26	0.15	0.49	0.64	1.68	2.23	1.58	1.18	0.65	0.77	10.38
Days With ≥ 0.1" Precipitation	1	1	1	1	1	1	4	5	3	3	2	2	25
Days With ≥ 1.0" Precipitation	0	0	0	0	0	0	0	0	0	0	0	0	0
Mean Snowfall (in.)	1.0	0.2	0.2	trace	0.0	0.0	0.0	0.0	0.0	0.0	0.3	0.3	0.9	2.9
Days With ≥ 1.0" Snow Depth	0	0	0	0	0	0	0	0	0	0	0	0	0

Elida *Roosevelt County*   Elevation: 4,353 ft.   Latitude: 33° 57' N   Longitude: 103° 39' W

	JAN	FEB	MAR	APR	MAY	JUN	JUL	AUG	SEP	OCT	NOV	DEC	YEAR
Mean Maximum Temp. (°F)	52.1	57.5	65.4	73.7	81.9	90.2	91.2	89.3	83.4	74.1	61.8	53.4	72.8
Mean Temp. (°F)	37.6	42.2	49.0	57.0	66.1	74.6	77.1	75.4	69.1	58.8	46.7	38.9	57.7
Mean Minimum Temp. (°F)	23.2	27.0	32.6	40.2	50.3	58.9	62.9	61.4	54.7	43.5	31.7	24.4	42.6
Extreme Maximum Temp. (°F)	78	83	90	98	102	112	111	105	104	96	85	77	112
Extreme Minimum Temp. (°F)	-18	-2	4	15	27	34	41	42	27	10	2	-11	-18
Days Maximum Temp. ≥ 90°F	0	0	0	1	5	17	19	17	8	1	0	0	68
Days Maximum Temp. ≤ 32°F	3	1	0	0	0	0	0	0	0	0	0	2	6
Days Minimum Temp. ≤ 32°F	26	20	14	5	1	0	0	0	0	3	16	25	110
Days Minimum Temp. ≤ 0°F	0	0	0	0	0	0	0	0	0	0	0	0	0
Heating Degree Days (base 65°F)	843	639	490	251	68	7	1	1	44	211	543	803	3,901
Cooling Degree Days (base 65°F)	0	0	1	17	120	313	395	345	178	28	0	0	1,397
Mean Precipitation (in.)	0.51	0.39	0.42	0.71	1.50	2.24	3.07	2.53	2.14	1.21	0.73	0.53	15.98
Days With ≥ 0.1" Precipitation	1	1	1	1	3	4	5	4	4	2	2	1	29
Days With ≥ 1.0" Precipitation	0	0	0	0	0	1	1	1	1	0	0	0	4
Mean Snowfall (in.)	2.9	1.8	0.9	0.5	0.0	0.0	0.0	0.0	0.0	0.5	1.5	2.9	11.0
Days With ≥ 1.0" Snow Depth	na	na	0	0	0	0	0	0	0	0	0	2	na

Estancia 7 NE *Torrance County*   Elevation: 6,118 ft.   Latitude: 34° 51' N   Longitude: 105° 58' W

	JAN	FEB	MAR	APR	MAY	JUN	JUL	AUG	SEP	OCT	NOV	DEC	YEAR
Mean Maximum Temp. (°F)	46.8	53.1	60.4	68.3	77.1	87.3	89.2	86.1	80.0	70.2	57.3	48.0	68.7
Mean Temp. (°F)	32.0	37.1	43.0	49.7	58.5	67.4	71.5	69.3	62.5	51.6	40.5	32.1	51.3
Mean Minimum Temp. (°F)	17.1	21.0	25.5	31.0	39.8	47.5	53.7	52.5	45.0	33.0	23.7	16.3	33.8
Extreme Maximum Temp. (°F)	71	77	84	88	93	104	102	98	96	89	78	70	104
Extreme Minimum Temp. (°F)	-37	-17	-1	7	17	29	40	38	22	4	-22	-23	-37
Days Maximum Temp. ≥ 90°F	0	0	0	0	1	11	16	8	2	0	0	0	38
Days Maximum Temp. ≤ 32°F	3	1	0	0	0	0	0	0	0	0	0	2	6
Days Minimum Temp. ≤ 32°F	30	26	25	18	5	0	0	0	1	14	25	30	174
Days Minimum Temp. ≤ 0°F	2	0	0	0	0	0	0	0	0	0	0	2	4
Heating Degree Days (base 65°F)	1,016	782	675	453	207	32	1	4	99	408	728	1,012	5,417
Cooling Degree Days (base 65°F)	0	0	0	0	13	118	213	160	34	0	0	0	538
Mean Precipitation (in.)	0.66	0.52	0.71	0.56	1.25	1.04	2.43	2.39	1.87	1.44	0.85	0.92	14.64
Days With ≥ 0.1" Precipitation	2	2	2	2	3	2	6	6	4	3	2	3	37
Days With ≥ 1.0" Precipitation	0	0	0	0	0	0	0	0	0	0	0	0	0
Mean Snowfall (in.)	5.9	4.6	2.6	0.8	trace	0.0	0.0	0.0	0.0	1.3	2.1	6.9	24.2
Days With ≥ 1.0" Snow Depth	na	3	1	0	0	0	0	0	0	0	1	7	na

Faywood *Grant County*   Elevation: 5,190 ft.   Latitude: 32° 38' N   Longitude: 107° 52' W

	JAN	FEB	MAR	APR	MAY	JUN	JUL	AUG	SEP	OCT	NOV	DEC	YEAR
Mean Maximum Temp. (°F)	55.5	59.9	65.7	73.6	81.9	91.1	90.9	88.3	83.6	74.2	63.4	55.7	73.7
Mean Temp. (°F)	40.9	44.6	49.5	56.2	64.3	73.2	73.8	73.8	68.6	58.5	47.8	41.2	57.9
Mean Minimum Temp. (°F)	26.2	29.2	33.3	38.7	46.5	55.3	60.8	59.2	53.6	42.7	32.1	26.7	42.0
Extreme Maximum Temp. (°F)	79	80	87	92	97	105	104	100	98	93	82	74	105
Extreme Minimum Temp. (°F)	3	10	9	19	30	35	46	40	30	18	8	0	0
Days Maximum Temp. ≥ 90°F	0	0	0	0	2	18	18	12	4	0	0	0	54
Days Maximum Temp. ≤ 32°F	0	0	0	0	0	0	0	0	0	0	0	0	0
Days Minimum Temp. ≤ 32°F	26	19	14	5	0	0	0	0	0	2	15	25	106
Days Minimum Temp. ≤ 0°F	0	0	0	0	0	0	0	0	0	0	0	0	0
Heating Degree Days (base 65°F)	741	570	473	264	74	3	0	0	21	207	510	731	3,594
Cooling Degree Days (base 65°F)	0	0	0	7	60	252	334	268	131	12	0	0	1,064
Mean Precipitation (in.)	0.79	0.61	0.46	0.18	0.38	0.74	2.49	2.60	1.77	1.41	0.89	1.14	13.46
Days With ≥ 0.1" Precipitation	2	2	1	1	1	2	6	6	4	3	2	3	33
Days With ≥ 1.0" Precipitation	0	0	0	0	0	0	0	0	0	0	0	0	0
Mean Snowfall (in.)	0.7	0.6	0.3	0.0	0.0	0.0	0.0	0.0	0.0	0.1	0.1	1.5	3.3
Days With ≥ 1.0" Snow Depth	0	0	0	0	0	0	0	0	0	0	0	0	0

Fence Lake *Valencia County*   Elevation: 7,053 ft.   Latitude: 34° 39' N   Longitude: 108° 40' W

	JAN	FEB	MAR	APR	MAY	JUN	JUL	AUG	SEP	OCT	NOV	DEC	YEAR
Mean Maximum Temp. (°F)	45.0	49.8	56.1	64.4	74.0	84.3	86.1	83.1	77.8	67.3	54.8	46.6	65.8
Mean Temp. (°F)	30.1	34.4	39.6	45.9	54.4	63.8	68.7	66.7	60.4	49.4	38.1	31.1	48.6
Mean Minimum Temp. (°F)	15.2	19.0	23.0	27.2	34.7	43.1	51.3	50.4	43.0	31.5	21.4	15.5	31.3
Extreme Maximum Temp. (°F)	69	70	79	86	93	98	101	96	92	85	76	68	101
Extreme Minimum Temp. (°F)	-40	-17	-11	8	12	22	36	34	20	9	-14	-27	-40
Days Maximum Temp. ≥ 90°F	0	0	0	0	0	7	9	3	0	0	0	0	19
Days Maximum Temp. ≤ 32°F	2	1	0	0	0	0	0	0	0	0	1	2	6
Days Minimum Temp. ≤ 32°F	31	27	29	24	11	2	0	0	2	17	28	30	201
Days Minimum Temp. ≤ 0°F	3	1	0	0	0	0	0	0	0	0	0	2	6
Heating Degree Days (base 65°F)	1,074	857	782	568	324	84	5	17	144	476	800	1,045	6,176
Cooling Degree Days (base 65°F)	0	0	0	0	2	52	122	84	12	0	0	0	272
Mean Precipitation (in.)	0.99	0.87	1.18	0.69	0.54	0.57	2.17	2.44	1.55	1.37	0.97	0.85	14.19
Days With ≥ 0.1" Precipitation	4	3	4	2	2	2	6	7	4	3	3	3	43
Days With ≥ 1.0" Precipitation	0	0	0	0	0	0	0	0	0	0	0	0	0
Mean Snowfall (in.)	6.2	4.4	5.4	2.2	0.2	0.0	0.0	0.0	0.0	1.3	4.0	5.5	29.2
Days With ≥ 1.0" Snow Depth	na	2	2	0	0	0	0	0	0	0	1	2	na

Fort Bayard *Grant County* Elevation: 6,141 ft. Latitude: 32° 48' N Longitude: 108° 09' W

	JAN	FEB	MAR	APR	MAY	JUN	JUL	AUG	SEP	OCT	NOV	DEC	YEAR
Mean Maximum Temp. (°F)	52.3	56.1	61.5	69.5	77.9	87.7	87.0	84.5	80.3	71.2	60.2	52.6	70.1
Mean Temp. (°F)	39.2	42.3	46.7	53.0	61.3	71.1	72.9	71.0	66.2	56.8	46.0	39.6	55.5
Mean Minimum Temp. (°F)	25.8	28.3	31.8	36.6	44.7	54.4	58.7	57.4	52.1	42.3	31.8	26.5	40.9
Extreme Maximum Temp. (°F)	73	76	84	95	95	106	104	97	95	89	79	73	106
Extreme Minimum Temp. (°F)	-4	7	10	17	25	35	42	38	33	20	6	-1	-4
Days Maximum Temp. ≥ 90°F	0	0	0	0	1	12	11	4	1	0	0	0	29
Days Maximum Temp. ≤ 32°F	0	0	0	0	0	0	0	0	0	0	0	0	0
Days Minimum Temp. ≤ 32°F	26	21	17	9	1	0	0	0	0	3	16	25	118
Days Minimum Temp. ≤ 0°F	0	0	0	0	0	0	0	0	0	0	0	0	0
Heating Degree Days (base 65°F)	794	636	561	355	136	10	1	2	39	253	563	782	4,132
Cooling Degree Days (base 65°F)	0	0	0	3	31	204	245	196	85	5	0	0	769
Mean Precipitation (in.)	0.93	0.79	0.54	0.21	0.59	0.72	3.67	3.14	1.94	1.55	0.90	1.18	16.16
Days With ≥ 0.1" Precipitation	3	2	2	1	2	2	8	7	5	3	2	3	40
Days With ≥ 1.0" Precipitation	0	0	0	0	0	0	0	0	0	0	0	0	0
Mean Snowfall (in.)	1.6	1.0	0.4	trace	0.0	0.0	0.0	0.0	0.0	trace	0.4	1.1	4.5
Days With ≥ 1.0" Snow Depth	na	0	0	0	0	0	0	0	0	0	0	0	na

Fort Sumner *Debaca County* Elevation: 4,022 ft. Latitude: 34° 28' N Longitude: 104° 15' W

	JAN	FEB	MAR	APR	MAY	JUN	JUL	AUG	SEP	OCT	NOV	DEC	YEAR
Mean Maximum Temp. (°F)	52.9	58.2	66.1	73.2	81.0	89.2	91.1	88.8	82.5	73.5	62.4	53.9	72.7
Mean Temp. (°F)	37.7	42.3	49.3	56.6	65.5	73.9	77.0	75.3	68.3	57.7	46.6	38.4	57.4
Mean Minimum Temp. (°F)	22.5	26.5	32.5	39.9	49.9	58.5	62.9	61.7	54.1	41.8	30.6	22.8	42.0
Extreme Maximum Temp. (°F)	80	84	92	96	98	107	105	103	99	95	87	80	107
Extreme Minimum Temp. (°F)	-26	-4	8	20	30	40	51	48	32	12	0	-18	-26
Days Maximum Temp. ≥ 90°F	0	0	0	0	4	16	20	16	6	0	0	0	62
Days Maximum Temp. ≤ 32°F	2	1	0	0	0	0	0	0	0	0	0	2	5
Days Minimum Temp. ≤ 32°F	27	21	16	5	0	0	0	0	0	3	18	27	117
Days Minimum Temp. ≤ 0°F	0	0	0	0	0	0	0	0	0	0	0	0	0
Heating Degree Days (base 65°F)	838	633	481	256	65	5	0	1	43	234	547	818	3,921
Cooling Degree Days (base 65°F)	0	0	1	10	88	278	384	334	153	12	0	0	1,260
Mean Precipitation (in.)	0.48	0.45	0.49	0.96	1.33	1.73	2.31	3.20	2.16	1.56	0.66	0.61	15.94
Days With ≥ 0.1" Precipitation	2	1	2	2	3	3	4	5	4	3	2	2	33
Days With ≥ 1.0" Precipitation	0	0	0	0	0	0	0	1	0	0	0	0	1
Mean Snowfall (in.)	3.5	2.6	0.8	0.4	0.0	0.0	0.0	0.0	0.0	0.2	1.2	3.1	11.8
Days With ≥ 1.0" Snow Depth	3	1	0	0	0	0	0	0	0	0	0	3	7

Fruitland 3 E *San Juan County* Elevation: 5,219 ft. Latitude: 36° 44' N Longitude: 108° 21' W

	JAN	FEB	MAR	APR	MAY	JUN	JUL	AUG	SEP	OCT	NOV	DEC	YEAR
Mean Maximum Temp. (°F)	42.6	51.1	60.2	68.5	77.9	87.8	91.5	89.1	81.9	69.8	54.7	44.7	68.3
Mean Temp. (°F)	30.3	36.8	43.9	50.8	59.4	68.7	74.6	72.9	64.7	52.8	40.3	31.7	52.2
Mean Minimum Temp. (°F)	17.9	22.5	27.5	33.0	40.9	49.5	57.6	56.8	47.5	35.7	25.8	18.7	36.1
Extreme Maximum Temp. (°F)	66	73	82	88	96	102	106	100	99	90	77	73	106
Extreme Minimum Temp. (°F)	-17	-11	3	8	11	32	40	32	23	14	2	-15	-17
Days Maximum Temp. ≥ 90°F	0	0	0	0	1	12	22	16	3	0	0	0	54
Days Maximum Temp. ≤ 32°F	4	1	0	0	0	0	0	0	0	0	0	3	8
Days Minimum Temp. ≤ 32°F	29	25	23	14	4	0	0	0	1	11	24	29	160
Days Minimum Temp. ≤ 0°F	1	0	0	0	0	0	0	0	0	0	0	1	2
Heating Degree Days (base 65°F)	1,068	789	648	420	181	26	0	2	71	374	733	1,026	5,338
Cooling Degree Days (base 65°F)	0	0	0	1	19	147	319	273	76	1	0	0	836
Mean Precipitation (in.)	0.70	0.62	0.73	0.60	0.48	0.26	0.73	1.01	0.92	0.91	0.77	0.59	8.32
Days With ≥ 0.1" Precipitation	2	2	3	2	2	1	2	3	3	3	3	2	28
Days With ≥ 1.0" Precipitation	0	0	0	0	0	0	0	0	0	0	0	0	0
Mean Snowfall (in.)	4.0	3.5	1.0	0.4	0.0	0.0	0.0	0.0	0.0	0.4	1.5	3.2	14.0
Days With ≥ 1.0" Snow Depth	na	na	1	0	0	0	0	0	0	0	0	1	na

Gallup Sen Clarke Field *McKinley County* Elevation: 6,463 ft. Latitude: 35° 31' N Longitude: 108° 47' W

	JAN	FEB	MAR	APR	MAY	JUN	JUL	AUG	SEP	OCT	NOV	DEC	YEAR
Mean Maximum Temp. (°F)	44.0	49.1	55.7	64.2	73.4	84.4	87.2	84.8	78.5	67.8	54.3	45.4	65.7
Mean Temp. (°F)	28.7	33.8	39.2	45.9	54.9	64.5	70.2	68.7	61.2	49.0	37.2	29.2	48.5
Mean Minimum Temp. (°F)	13.3	18.4	22.7	27.5	36.4	44.5	53.3	52.5	43.8	30.1	19.9	13.1	31.3
Extreme Maximum Temp. (°F)	67	73	79	84	91	98	100	97	93	87	78	66	100
Extreme Minimum Temp. (°F)	-20	-19	-10	6	12	23	31	35	20	5	-26	-34	-34
Days Maximum Temp. ≥ 90°F	0	0	0	0	0	7	10	5	1	0	0	0	23
Days Maximum Temp. ≤ 32°F	3	1	0	0	0	0	0	0	0	0	1	3	8
Days Minimum Temp. ≤ 32°F	31	27	28	22	9	2	0	0	3	19	27	30	198
Days Minimum Temp. ≤ 0°F	4	1	0	0	0	0	0	0	0	0	0	3	8
Heating Degree Days (base 65°F)	1,119	875	792	567	307	75	3	7	130	491	829	1,102	6,297
Cooling Degree Days (base 65°F)	0	0	0	0	2	64	171	138	21	0	0	0	396
Mean Precipitation (in.)	0.88	0.72	0.87	0.55	0.66	0.47	1.59	2.06	1.14	1.01	0.95	0.74	11.64
Days With ≥ 0.1" Precipitation	3	3	3	2	2	1	4	5	3	3	2	3	34
Days With ≥ 1.0" Precipitation	0	0	0	0	0	0	0	0	0	0	0	0	0
Mean Snowfall (in.)	7.1	6.2	4.2	2.8	0.9	trace	trace	trace	trace	0.8	4.6	6.1	32.7
Days With ≥ 1.0" Snow Depth	8	4	4	1	0	0	0	0	0	0	2	6	23

Gascon *Mora County* Elevation: 8,248 ft. Latitude: 35° 54' N Longitude: 105° 27' W

	JAN	FEB	MAR	APR	MAY	JUN	JUL	AUG	SEP	OCT	NOV	DEC	YEAR
Mean Maximum Temp. (°F)	43.0	44.7	48.6	54.6	63.1	72.8	75.1	72.8	68.0	60.2	50.2	44.1	58.1
Mean Temp. (°F)	29.5	31.3	35.3	40.5	48.3	56.9	60.1	58.5	53.4	45.1	36.0	30.4	43.8
Mean Minimum Temp. (°F)	15.9	17.9	22.0	26.3	33.5	40.9	45.0	44.0	38.8	29.9	21.8	16.7	29.4
Extreme Maximum Temp. (°F)	71	70	78	78	80	90	90	89	82	79	74	68	90
Extreme Minimum Temp. (°F)	-26	-17	-8	-5	12	23	35	29	15	-1	-19	-21	-26
Days Maximum Temp. ≥ 90°F	0	0	0	0	0	0	0	0	0	0	0	0	0
Days Maximum Temp. ≤ 32°F	5	3	1	1	0	0	0	0	0	0	2	4	16
Days Minimum Temp. ≤ 32°F	30	27	28	24	14	2	0	0	4	20	27	30	206
Days Minimum Temp. ≤ 0°F	2	1	0	0	0	0	0	0	0	0	0	2	5
Heating Degree Days (base 65°F)	1,095	944	913	729	510	242	150	196	341	611	862	1,067	7,660
Cooling Degree Days (base 65°F)	0	0	0	0	0	6	3	1	0	0	0	0	10
Mean Precipitation (in.)	1.03	1.13	1.95	1.86	2.11	2.10	3.75	4.18	2.26	1.56	1.34	1.06	24.33
Days With ≥ 0.1" Precipitation	3	3	4	4	5	5	8	9	5	3	3	3	55
Days With ≥ 1.0" Precipitation	0	0	0	0	0	0	1	1	0	0	0	0	2
Mean Snowfall (in.)	20.4	20.7	28.8	19.3	4.9	trace	trace	0.0	0.4	9.1	14.7	21.1	139.4
Days With ≥ 1.0" Snow Depth	12	8	7	3	0	0	0	0	0	2	6	11	49

Gila Hot Springs *Grant County* Elevation: 5,597 ft. Latitude: 33° 12' N Longitude: 108° 13' W

	JAN	FEB	MAR	APR	MAY	JUN	JUL	AUG	SEP	OCT	NOV	DEC	YEAR
Mean Maximum Temp. (°F)	54.8	59.2	64.7	71.8	79.6	88.8	88.5	85.5	81.7	73.4	63.1	55.0	72.2
Mean Temp. (°F)	37.0	40.6	45.1	50.8	58.2	66.5	71.0	69.4	63.8	53.8	43.4	37.0	53.0
Mean Minimum Temp. (°F)	19.1	21.9	25.6	29.8	36.8	44.1	53.5	53.2	45.8	34.1	23.6	19.0	33.9
Extreme Maximum Temp. (°F)	76	79	85	89	96	104	103	100	98	91	81	73	104
Extreme Minimum Temp. (°F)	-15	0	4	12	21	29	38	38	30	13	6	-13	-15
Days Maximum Temp. ≥ 90°F	0	0	0	0	2	13	14	6	2	0	0	0	37
Days Maximum Temp. ≤ 32°F	0	0	0	0	0	0	0	0	0	0	0	0	0
Days Minimum Temp. ≤ 32°F	29	26	27	21	7	1	0	0	1	14	26	29	181
Days Minimum Temp. ≤ 0°F	0	0	0	0	0	0	0	0	0	0	0	0	0
Heating Degree Days (base 65°F)	863	683	609	418	207	36	1	2	66	342	642	862	4,731
Cooling Degree Days (base 65°F)	0	0	0	0	5	85	185	151	34	0	0	0	460
Mean Precipitation (in.)	1.07	1.07	0.90	0.39	0.68	0.62	2.83	3.29	2.02	1.68	1.07	1.30	16.92
Days With ≥ 0.1" Precipitation	3	3	3	1	2	2	7	8	5	4	2	3	43
Days With ≥ 1.0" Precipitation	0	0	0	0	0	0	0	0	0	0	0	0	0
Mean Snowfall (in.)	3.3	1.2	0.5	trace	trace	0.0	trace	0.0	0.0	0.4	0.3	1.5	7.2
Days With ≥ 1.0" Snow Depth	2	1	0	0	0	0	0	0	0	0	0	1	4

Glenwood *Catron County* Elevation: 4,750 ft. Latitude: 33° 19' N Longitude: 108° 53' W

	JAN	FEB	MAR	APR	MAY	JUN	JUL	AUG	SEP	OCT	NOV	DEC	YEAR
Mean Maximum Temp. (°F)	56.1	60.5	65.7	73.5	81.4	91.0	91.5	88.8	84.9	75.4	64.1	56.2	74.1
Mean Temp. (°F)	40.8	44.4	48.9	55.2	62.6	71.9	75.7	73.8	68.7	58.4	47.3	40.8	57.4
Mean Minimum Temp. (°F)	25.4	28.3	32.1	36.9	43.8	52.7	59.8	58.8	52.4	41.3	30.4	25.4	40.6
Extreme Maximum Temp. (°F)	78	80	86	93	99	108	106	103	99	92	83	77	108
Extreme Minimum Temp. (°F)	3	9	11	21	22	35	43	45	33	20	12	-3	-3
Days Maximum Temp. ≥ 90°F	0	0	0	0	3	18	20	14	6	0	0	0	61
Days Maximum Temp. ≤ 32°F	0	0	0	0	0	0	0	0	0	0	0	0	0
Days Minimum Temp. ≤ 32°F	26	21	17	8	1	0	0	0	0	3	19	26	121
Days Minimum Temp. ≤ 0°F	0	0	0	0	0	0	0	0	0	0	0	0	0
Heating Degree Days (base 65°F)	745	575	491	291	102	7	0	0	17	207	524	742	3,701
Cooling Degree Days (base 65°F)	0	0	0	5	42	235	342	292	135	8	0	0	1,059
Mean Precipitation (in.)	1.24	1.38	1.14	0.52	0.83	0.68	2.76	2.70	1.66	1.78	1.14	1.55	17.38
Days With ≥ 0.1" Precipitation	3	3	3	1	2	2	6	7	4	3	2	3	39
Days With ≥ 1.0" Precipitation	0	0	0	0	0	0	0	0	0	0	0	0	0
Mean Snowfall (in.)	*0.5*	*0.4*	trace	0.0	0.0	0.0	0.0	0.0	0.0	0.0	0.0	0.2	*1.1*
Days With ≥ 1.0" Snow Depth	*0*	*0*	0	0	0	0	0	0	0	0	0	0	*0*

Gran Quivira Nat'l Monument *Socorro County* Elevation: 6,597 ft. Latitude: 34° 16' N Longitude: 106° 06' W

	JAN	FEB	MAR	APR	MAY	JUN	JUL	AUG	SEP	OCT	NOV	DEC	YEAR
Mean Maximum Temp. (°F)	48.5	54.1	61.2	69.4	78.2	87.8	89.0	85.9	80.4	71.0	57.8	49.6	69.4
Mean Temp. (°F)	35.0	39.6	45.2	52.1	60.5	69.9	72.5	70.4	64.5	54.9	43.0	35.8	53.6
Mean Minimum Temp. (°F)	21.4	24.9	29.1	34.7	43.3	52.0	55.9	54.8	48.7	38.5	28.4	22.0	37.8
Extreme Maximum Temp. (°F)	71	75	84	88	95	104	102	100	98	89	78	71	104
Extreme Minimum Temp. (°F)	-26	-5	3	5	23	37	45	40	29	2	-9	-13	-26
Days Maximum Temp. ≥ 90°F	0	0	0	0	1	13	15	8	2	0	0	0	39
Days Maximum Temp. ≤ 32°F	2	1	0	0	0	0	0	0	0	0	0	1	4
Days Minimum Temp. ≤ 32°F	29	24	21	12	2	0	0	0	0	6	20	28	142
Days Minimum Temp. ≤ 0°F	0	0	0	0	0	0	0	0	0	0	0	0	0
Heating Degree Days (base 65°F)	924	712	606	383	151	17	0	4	66	310	652	896	4,721
Cooling Degree Days (base 65°F)	0	0	0	2	23	179	249	191	64	2	0	0	710
Mean Precipitation (in.)	0.77	0.76	0.75	0.69	1.02	1.09	2.77	3.49	2.20	1.53	0.94	0.96	16.97
Days With ≥ 0.1" Precipitation	3	3	2	2	2	3	7	8	5	3	2	3	43
Days With ≥ 1.0" Precipitation	0	0	0	0	0	0	0	1	0	0	0	0	1
Mean Snowfall (in.)	*5.3*	*5.0*	2.5	0.5	0.0	0.0	0.0	0.0	trace	0.6	2.0	5.3	*21.2*
Days With ≥ 1.0" Snow Depth	na	na	*0*	0	0	0	0	0	0	0	0	0	na

Grants Milan Muni Airport *Cibola County* Elevation: 6,519 ft. Latitude: 35° 10' N Longitude: 107° 54' W

	JAN	FEB	MAR	APR	MAY	JUN	JUL	AUG	SEP	OCT	NOV	DEC	YEAR
Mean Maximum Temp. (°F)	46.3	52.5	59.2	67.6	76.2	86.6	88.3	85.4	79.6	69.2	56.4	47.4	67.9
Mean Temp. (°F)	30.6	36.0	42.1	48.8	57.5	66.7	71.5	69.2	62.2	50.9	39.6	31.3	50.5
Mean Minimum Temp. (°F)	14.9	19.4	24.8	29.9	38.8	46.9	54.6	53.0	44.8	32.7	22.7	15.1	33.1
Extreme Maximum Temp. (°F)	70	75	82	89	94	103	102	99	94	89	78	71	103
Extreme Minimum Temp. (°F)	-31	-6	-3	9	15	28	37	35	20	10	-22	-33	-33
Days Maximum Temp. ≥ 90°F	0	0	0	0	1	11	14	7	1	0	0	0	34
Days Maximum Temp. ≤ 32°F	3	1	0	0	0	0	0	0	0	0	0	2	6
Days Minimum Temp. ≤ 32°F	30	27	26	19	6	0	0	0	1	15	27	30	181
Days Minimum Temp. ≤ 0°F	3	0	0	0	0	0	0	0	0	0	0	2	5
Heating Degree Days (base 65°F)	1,059	814	704	480	233	42	1	7	107	429	756	1,039	5,671
Cooling Degree Days (base 65°F)	0	0	0	0	10	107	221	166	34	0	0	0	538
Mean Precipitation (in.)	0.57	0.44	0.57	0.50	0.67	0.53	1.68	2.15	1.45	1.11	0.67	0.65	10.99
Days With ≥ 0.1" Precipitation	2	1	2	2	2	2	5	6	4	3	2	2	33
Days With ≥ 1.0" Precipitation	0	0	0	0	0	0	0	0	0	0	0	0	0
Mean Snowfall (in.)	na	1.5	0.7	0.3	trace	0.0	0.0	0.0	0.0	0.4	0.7	2.7	na
Days With ≥ 1.0" Snow Depth	na	0	0	0	0	0	0	0	0	0	0	1	na

Grenville *Union County* Elevation: 6,000 ft. Latitude: 36° 36' N Longitude: 103° 37' W

	JAN	FEB	MAR	APR	MAY	JUN	JUL	AUG	SEP	OCT	NOV	DEC	YEAR
Mean Maximum Temp. (°F)	46.3	50.6	57.2	64.9	72.9	82.5	86.4	84.1	77.9	68.6	55.5	47.3	66.2
Mean Temp. (°F)	31.6	35.2	41.3	48.4	57.3	66.6	71.0	69.4	62.6	52.3	40.4	32.9	50.8
Mean Minimum Temp. (°F)	17.0	19.8	25.3	31.9	41.7	50.7	55.6	54.6	47.3	35.9	25.3	18.5	35.3
Extreme Maximum Temp. (°F)	77	76	82	87	97	102	100	98	100	88	82	76	102
Extreme Minimum Temp. (°F)	-21	-19	-1	7	19	34	42	40	21	2	-20	-15	-21
Days Maximum Temp. ≥ 90°F	0	0	0	0	1	6	10	6	1	0	0	0	24
Days Maximum Temp. ≤ 32°F	5	3	1	0	0	0	0	0	0	0	1	4	14
Days Minimum Temp. ≤ 32°F	30	27	26	16	3	0	0	0	1	10	23	30	166
Days Minimum Temp. ≤ 0°F	2	1	0	0	0	0	0	0	0	0	0	1	4
Heating Degree Days (base 65°F)	1,028	835	728	492	245	52	7	8	111	389	731	987	5,613
Cooling Degree Days (base 65°F)	0	0	0	0	13	105	198	156	49	1	0	0	522
Mean Precipitation (in.)	0.25	0.33	0.73	1.23	2.41	1.98	3.14	2.89	1.96	0.87	0.60	0.26	16.65
Days With ≥ 0.1" Precipitation	1	1	2	3	5	5	7	6	4	2	2	1	39
Days With ≥ 1.0" Precipitation	0	0	0	0	0	0	1	1	0	0	0	0	2
Mean Snowfall (in.)	1.6	1.8	2.9	1.2	0.1	0.0	0.0	0.0	0.2	0.4	1.1	1.9	11.2
Days With ≥ 1.0" Snow Depth	na	na	0	0	0	0	0	0	0	0	0	0	na

Hachita *Grant County* Elevation: 4,504 ft. Latitude: 31° 56' N Longitude: 108° 19' W

	JAN	FEB	MAR	APR	MAY	JUN	JUL	AUG	SEP	OCT	NOV	DEC	YEAR
Mean Maximum Temp. (°F)	58.4	63.4	69.9	77.5	85.8	94.9	94.2	91.4	87.6	77.9	66.7	58.1	77.2
Mean Temp. (°F)	42.6	46.6	52.0	58.4	67.1	76.2	79.1	76.8	71.9	61.2	50.0	42.7	60.4
Mean Minimum Temp. (°F)	26.7	29.5	34.0	39.2	48.2	57.6	63.8	62.2	56.1	44.4	33.2	27.3	43.5
Extreme Maximum Temp. (°F)	78	83	90	96	102	110	108	105	101	95	85	81	110
Extreme Minimum Temp. (°F)	6	5	13	20	25	38	51	50	37	20	12	-9	-9
Days Maximum Temp. ≥ 90°F	0	0	0	1	9	25	26	22	13	2	0	0	98
Days Maximum Temp. ≤ 32°F	0	0	0	0	0	0	0	0	0	0	0	0	0
Days Minimum Temp. ≤ 32°F	24	19	13	6	0	0	0	0	0	2	14	24	102
Days Minimum Temp. ≤ 0°F	0	0	0	0	0	0	0	0	0	0	0	0	0
Heating Degree Days (base 65°F)	689	514	397	207	43	1	0	0	8	143	444	683	3,129
Cooling Degree Days (base 65°F)	0	0	0	19	129	355	447	384	233	33	0	0	1,600
Mean Precipitation (in.)	0.65	0.53	0.45	0.18	0.24	0.43	2.70	2.21	1.25	1.05	0.66	1.13	11.48
Days With ≥ 0.1" Precipitation	2	2	2	1	1	1	6	5	3	3	2	3	31
Days With ≥ 1.0" Precipitation	0	0	0	0	0	0	0	0	0	0	0	0	0
Mean Snowfall (in.)	1.2	0.9	0.5	0.5	0.0	0.0	0.0	0.0	0.0	trace	0.3	1.8	5.2
Days With ≥ 1.0" Snow Depth	0	0	0	0	0	0	0	0	0	0	0	0	0

Hatch 5 NW *Dona Ana County* Elevation: 4,038 ft. Latitude: 32° 40' N Longitude: 107° 09' W

	JAN	FEB	MAR	APR	MAY	JUN	JUL	AUG	SEP	OCT	NOV	DEC	YEAR
Mean Maximum Temp. (°F)	59.5	64.3	70.9	78.2	86.6	95.4	95.3	93.1	88.1	79.1	68.3	60.0	78.2
Mean Temp. (°F)	41.8	45.9	52.3	58.8	67.2	75.7	78.8	77.0	71.0	60.1	49.0	42.2	60.0
Mean Minimum Temp. (°F)	24.1	27.4	33.6	39.4	48.0	56.0	62.2	60.8	53.8	41.1	29.6	24.3	41.7
Extreme Maximum Temp. (°F)	80	84	91	98	101	113	107	105	101	96	85	79	113
Extreme Minimum Temp. (°F)	2	9	9	21	28	23	48	47	36	20	2	6	2
Days Maximum Temp. ≥ 90°F	0	0	0	1	11	26	27	25	14	2	0	0	106
Days Maximum Temp. ≤ 32°F	0	0	0	0	0	0	0	0	0	0	0	0	0
Days Minimum Temp. ≤ 32°F	27	21	14	6	0	0	0	0	0	4	21	27	120
Days Minimum Temp. ≤ 0°F	0	0	0	0	0	0	0	0	0	0	0	0	0
Heating Degree Days (base 65°F)	712	533	388	193	37	1	0	0	12	169	474	701	3,220
Cooling Degree Days (base 65°F)	0	0	1	14	122	329	431	389	201	21	0	0	1,508
Mean Precipitation (in.)	0.62	0.40	0.23	0.16	0.48	0.58	1.96	2.25	1.49	1.15	0.60	0.84	10.76
Days With ≥ 0.1" Crecipitation	2	1	1	1	1	1	5	5	4	3	2	2	28
Days With ≥ 1.0" Precipitation	0	0	0	0	0	0	0	0	0	0	0	0	0
Mean Snowfall (in.)	1.4	0.4	0.3	0.2	0.0	0.0	0.0	0.0	0.0	0.0	0.6	0.7	3.6
Days With ≥ 1.0" Snow Depth	na	0	0	0	0	0	0	0	0	0	0	0	na

Hillsboro *Sierra County*   Elevation: 5,269 ft.   Latitude: 32° 56' N   Longitude: 107° 34' W

	JAN	FEB	MAR	APR	MAY	JUN	JUL	AUG	SEP	OCT	NOV	DEC	YEAR
Mean Maximum Temp. (°F)	54.9	60.0	66.3	73.6	81.7	91.0	90.7	87.9	82.7	73.9	63.0	54.6	73.4
Mean Temp. (°F)	39.7	44.0	49.7	56.2	64.1	73.0	75.6	73.3	67.4	57.5	46.9	39.7	57.3
Mean Minimum Temp. (°F)	24.5	27.9	33.0	38.7	46.4	54.8	60.4	58.8	52.1	41.1	30.7	24.7	41.1
Extreme Maximum Temp. (°F)	80	80	86	91	98	107	105	100	98	92	83	75	107
Extreme Minimum Temp. (°F)	1	5	8	20	28	39	46	47	35	19	5	-5	-5
Days Maximum Temp. ≥ 90°F	0	0	0	0	3	18	18	12	4	0	0	0	55
Days Maximum Temp. ≤ 32°F	0	0	0	0	0	0	0	0	0	0	0	0	0
Days Minimum Temp. ≤ 32°F	26	21	15	6	0	0	0	0	0	3	18	26	115
Days Minimum Temp. ≤ 0°F	0	0	0	0	0	0	0	0	0	0	0	0	0
Heating Degree Days (base 65°F)	778	587	466	264	76	4	0	0	29	231	536	778	3,749
Cooling Degree Days (base 65°F)	0	0	0	6	56	244	334	271	103	5	0	0	1,019
Mean Precipitation (in.)	0.64	0.49	0.29	0.24	0.66	0.79	2.49	2.85	2.39	1.48	0.68	1.05	14.05
Days With ≥ 0.1" Precipitation	2	1	1	1	2	2	6	6	4	3	1	2	31
Days With ≥ 1.0" Precipitation	0	0	0	0	0	0	0	0	0	0	0	0	0
Mean Snowfall (in.)	2.3	1.5	0.4	0.1	0.0	0.0	0.0	0.0	0.0	0.8	0.7	2.1	7.9
Days With ≥ 1.0" Snow Depth	2	0	0	0	0	0	0	0	0	0	0	1	3

Hobbs *Lea County*   Elevation: 3,612 ft.   Latitude: 32° 42' N   Longitude: 103° 08' W

	JAN	FEB	MAR	APR	MAY	JUN	JUL	AUG	SEP	OCT	NOV	DEC	YEAR
Mean Maximum Temp. (°F)	56.6	62.8	70.5	78.4	85.8	92.8	93.4	91.1	85.2	77.2	65.7	58.4	76.5
Mean Temp. (°F)	42.8	47.9	54.7	62.5	70.6	77.9	80.0	78.3	72.2	63.1	51.6	44.5	62.2
Mean Minimum Temp. (°F)	29.0	33.0	38.8	46.6	55.4	63.0	66.6	65.4	59.2	48.9	37.5	30.3	47.8
Extreme Maximum Temp. (°F)	82	87	95	98	107	114	108	104	103	97	86	80	114
Extreme Minimum Temp. (°F)	-1	-2	11	24	34	42	55	51	32	18	4	-1	-2
Days Maximum Temp. ≥ 90°F	0	0	0	2	10	22	25	21	10	1	0	0	91
Days Maximum Temp. ≤ 32°F	1	1	0	0	0	0	0	0	0	0	0	1	3
Days Minimum Temp. ≤ 32°F	20	14	7	1	0	0	0	0	0	1	8	18	69
Days Minimum Temp. ≤ 0°F	0	0	0	0	0	0	0	0	0	0	0	0	0
Heating Degree Days (base 65°F)	681	477	322	125	21	1	0	1	22	115	396	628	2,789
Cooling Degree Days (base 65°F)	0	1	8	56	214	413	496	442	253	64	2	0	1,949
Mean Precipitation (in.)	0.51	0.66	0.43	0.80	2.60	1.93	2.41	2.51	3.24	1.39	0.81	0.72	18.01
Days With ≥ 0.1" Precipitation	2	2	1	2	4	3	4	4	5	2	2	2	33
Days With ≥ 1.0" Precipitation	0	0	0	0	1	1	1	1	1	0	0	0	5
Mean Snowfall (in.)	2.0	1.6	0.4	0.4	0.0	0.0	0.0	0.0	0.0	0.2	1.0	1.1	6.7
Days With ≥ 1.0" Snow Depth	*0*	0	0	0	0	0	0	0	0	0	0	*0*	*0*

Jal *Lea County*   Elevation: 3,057 ft.   Latitude: 32° 07' N   Longitude: 103° 11' W

	JAN	FEB	MAR	APR	MAY	JUN	JUL	AUG	SEP	OCT	NOV	DEC	YEAR
Mean Maximum Temp. (°F)	59.4	65.9	73.7	81.5	88.3	94.5	95.1	93.3	87.2	79.6	68.3	61.4	79.0
Mean Temp. (°F)	43.8	49.4	56.5	64.5	72.5	79.6	81.7	80.1	73.8	64.3	52.7	45.5	63.7
Mean Minimum Temp. (°F)	28.3	33.0	39.2	47.3	56.7	64.7	68.2	66.9	60.3	49.1	37.0	29.5	48.4
Extreme Maximum Temp. (°F)	85	89	98	101	105	111	110	108	105	99	89	84	111
Extreme Minimum Temp. (°F)	0	-8	10	22	28	40	58	55	37	20	8	3	-8
Days Maximum Temp. ≥ 90°F	0	0	1	5	15	24	26	24	14	3	0	0	112
Days Maximum Temp. ≤ 32°F	1	0	0	0	0	0	0	0	0	0	0	0	1
Days Minimum Temp. ≤ 32°F	22	14	6	2	0	0	0	0	0	1	10	20	75
Days Minimum Temp. ≤ 0°F	0	0	0	0	0	0	0	0	0	0	0	0	0
Heating Degree Days (base 65°F)	649	434	270	93	12	0	0	0	16	90	367	598	2,529
Cooling Degree Days (base 65°F)	0	1	12	77	254	442	528	484	285	80	3	0	2,166
Mean Precipitation (in.)	0.41	0.50	0.37	0.58	1.71	1.70	1.84	2.01	2.46	1.20	0.62	0.58	13.98
Days With ≥ 0.1" Precipitation	1	2	1	1	3	3	3	3	4	2	1	1	25
Days With ≥ 1.0" Precipitation	0	0	0	0	1	1	1	1	1	0	0	0	5
Mean Snowfall (in.)	1.4	0.4	0.4	trace	0.0	0.0	0.0	0.0	0.0	trace	0.9	0.8	3.9
Days With ≥ 1.0" Snow Depth	1	0	0	0	0	0	0	0	0	0	0	0	1

Jemez Springs *Sandoval County*   Elevation: 6,263 ft.   Latitude: 35° 46' N   Longitude: 106° 41' W

	JAN	FEB	MAR	APR	MAY	JUN	JUL	AUG	SEP	OCT	NOV	DEC	YEAR
Mean Maximum Temp. (°F)	46.1	51.6	58.0	66.4	75.2	85.8	88.3	85.2	79.3	69.0	55.7	47.1	67.3
Mean Temp. (°F)	32.9	37.7	43.4	50.4	58.6	68.1	71.9	69.9	63.5	53.3	41.7	34.0	52.1
Mean Minimum Temp. (°F)	19.6	23.8	28.7	34.3	42.1	50.4	55.5	54.5	47.7	37.6	27.8	20.9	36.9
Extreme Maximum Temp. (°F)	67	74	78	83	94	101	101	98	93	90	76	69	101
Extreme Minimum Temp. (°F)	-18	-4	3	10	24	31	41	40	26	15	-7	-8	-18
Days Maximum Temp. ≥ 90°F	0	0	0	0	0	9	14	6	1	0	0	0	30
Days Maximum Temp. ≤ 32°F	2	0	0	0	0	0	0	0	0	0	0	1	3
Days Minimum Temp. ≤ 32°F	30	25	23	12	2	0	0	0	0	7	23	30	152
Days Minimum Temp. ≤ 0°F	1	0	0	0	0	0	0	0	0	0	0	0	1
Heating Degree Days (base 65°F)	990	763	663	432	201	30	1	4	80	355	691	954	5,164
Cooling Degree Days (base 65°F)	0	0	0	0	0	129	226	167	46	0	0	0	580
Mean Precipitation (in.)	1.29	0.89	1.21	0.96	1.13	0.99	2.56	3.04	1.93	1.43	1.22	0.94	17.59
Days With ≥ 0.1" Precipitation	3	3	3	3	3	3	7	8	5	4	3	3	48
Days With ≥ 1.0" Precipitation	0	0	0	0	0	0	0	0	0	0	0	0	0
Mean Snowfall (in.)	9.7	6.0	4.5	2.3	0.2	trace	0.0	0.0	0.0	0.3	2.9	6.3	32.2
Days With ≥ 1.0" Snow Depth	*12*	4	1	0	0	0	0	0	0	0	1	6	*24*

Jornada Experiment Range *Dona Ana County*   Elevation: 4,265 ft.   Latitude: 32° 37' N   Longitude: 106° 44' W

	JAN	FEB	MAR	APR	MAY	JUN	JUL	AUG	SEP	OCT	NOV	DEC	YEAR
Mean Maximum Temp. (°F)	56.6	61.8	68.7	76.3	85.0	94.2	94.9	91.7	86.5	77.2	65.4	56.5	76.2
Mean Temp. (°F)	38.9	43.5	49.6	56.6	65.4	74.6	78.8	76.4	70.2	58.7	46.7	39.0	58.2
Mean Minimum Temp. (°F)	21.2	25.1	30.6	36.9	45.8	55.1	62.6	60.9	53.8	40.1	27.9	21.4	40.1
Extreme Maximum Temp. (°F)	80	83	89	94	101	110	107	106	100	94	85	76	110
Extreme Minimum Temp. (°F)	-11	5	4	14	23	36	47	45	34	15	-3	-12	-12
Days Maximum Temp. ≥ 90°F	0	0	0	1	7	24	25	21	11	1	0	0	90
Days Maximum Temp. ≤ 32°F	0	0	0	0	0	0	0	0	0	0	0	0	0
Days Minimum Temp. ≤ 32°F	27	22	18	9	1	0	0	0	0	5	21	26	129
Days Minimum Temp. ≤ 0°F	0	0	0	0	0	0	0	0	0	0	0	0	0
Heating Degree Days (base 65°F)	801	600	470	254	63	3	0	0	18	205	543	800	3,757
Cooling Degree Days (base 65°F)	0	0	0	10	89	301	432	368	182	15	0	0	1,397
Mean Precipitation (in.)	0.58	0.39	0.28	0.22	0.48	0.78	2.13	2.49	1.36	1.06	0.56	0.90	11.23
Days With ≥ 0.1" Precipitation	2	1	1	1	1	1	5	5	3	3	2	3	28
Days With ≥ 1.0" Precipitation	0	0	0	0	0	0	0	0	0	0	0	0	0
Mean Snowfall (in.)	1.2	0.3	0.1	0.0	0.0	0.0	0.0	0.0	0.0	0.0	0.2	1.3	3.1
Days With ≥ 1.0" Snow Depth	0	0	0	0	0	0	0	0	0	0	0	1	1

Laguna *Cibola County*   Elevation: 5,816 ft.   Latitude: 35° 02' N   Longitude: 107° 22' W

	JAN	FEB	MAR	APR	MAY	JUN	JUL	AUG	SEP	OCT	NOV	DEC	YEAR
Mean Maximum Temp. (°F)	47.5	53.6	*60.5*	68.5	77.5	88.3	90.1	87.1	80.8	70.5	58.1	48.8	*69.3*
Mean Temp. (°F)	33.6	38.7	*44.7*	51.4	60.5	70.5	74.4	72.5	65.3	54.2	42.8	34.5	*53.6*
Mean Minimum Temp. (°F)	19.7	23.8	*28.8*	34.3	43.5	52.7	58.7	57.9	49.8	37.8	27.5	20.1	*37.9*
Extreme Maximum Temp. (°F)	70	78	82	94	94	103	102	99	96	90	77	72	103
Extreme Minimum Temp. (°F)	-16	-4	5	13	24	31	44	45	26	15	-9	-6	-16
Days Maximum Temp. ≥ 90°F	0	0	0	0	1	14	17	11	2	0	0	0	45
Days Maximum Temp. ≤ 32°F	1	0	0	0	0	0	0	0	0	0	0	1	2
Days Minimum Temp. ≤ 32°F	29	25	21	12	2	0	0	0	0	7	21	28	145
Days Minimum Temp. ≤ 0°F	1	0	0	0	0	0	0	0	0	0	0	0	1
Heating Degree Days (base 65°F)	967	736	*623*	402	159	15	1	2	60	331	660	942	*4,898*
Cooling Degree Days (base 65°F)	0	0	*0*	3	29	190	301	257	81	2	0	0	*863*
Mean Precipitation (in.)	0.55	0.42	0.40	0.39	0.72	0.52	1.79	2.11	1.56	1.16	0.45	0.52	10.59
Days With ≥ 0.1" Precipitation	2	1	1	1	2	1	5	5	4	2	1	2	27
Days With ≥ 1.0" Precipitation	0	0	0	0	0	0	0	0	0	0	0	0	0
Mean Snowfall (in.)	4.2	2.1	0.7	0.7	trace	0.0	0.0	0.0	0.0	0.7	0.6	3.4	12.4
Days With ≥ 1.0" Snow Depth	3	1	0	0	0	0	0	0	0	0	0	3	7

Lake Maloya *Colfax County*   Elevation: 7,398 ft.   Latitude: 36° 59' N   Longitude: 104° 22' W

	JAN	FEB	MAR	APR	MAY	JUN	JUL	AUG	SEP	OCT	NOV	DEC	YEAR
Mean Maximum Temp. (°F)	41.4	44.2	49.6	56.2	65.6	74.9	78.6	76.1	70.0	61.0	48.7	41.8	59.0
Mean Temp. (°F)	25.1	28.0	34.1	40.7	50.3	58.9	63.2	61.4	54.8	45.4	34.2	26.7	43.6
Mean Minimum Temp. (°F)	8.6	11.7	18.1	25.2	35.0	42.8	47.6	46.7	39.6	29.7	19.7	11.5	28.0
Extreme Maximum Temp. (°F)	67	68	76	82	86	92	91	89	85	82	72	70	92
Extreme Minimum Temp. (°F)	-30	-23	-14	-6	16	25	33	34	18	-6	-17	-20	-30
Days Maximum Temp. ≥ 90°F	0	0	0	0	0	0	0	0	0	0	0	0	0
Days Maximum Temp. ≤ 32°F	6	4	2	1	0	0	0	0	0	0	3	6	22
Days Minimum Temp. ≤ 32°F	31	28	31	26	9	1	0	0	4	20	29	31	210
Days Minimum Temp. ≤ 0°F	6	4	1	0	0	0	0	0	0	0	1	4	16
Heating Degree Days (base 65°F)	1,229	1,037	953	722	448	186	69	109	299	601	917	1,181	7,751
Cooling Degree Days (base 65°F)	0	0	0	0	0	9	16	5	1	0	0	0	31
Mean Precipitation (in.)	0.91	1.09	1.81	2.02	3.02	2.54	3.60	3.71	2.18	1.44	1.52	0.79	24.63
Days With ≥ 0.1" Precipitation	3	3	5	5	7	6	8	9	5	4	3	3	61
Days With ≥ 1.0" Precipitation	0	0	0	0	1	0	1	1	1	0	0	0	4
Mean Snowfall (in.)	14.8	16.3	21.6	14.1	2.1	trace	0.0	0.0	0.6	4.9	16.0	15.6	106.0
Days With ≥ 1.0" Snow Depth	*11*	na	*6*	*5*	0	0	0	0	0	1	*6*	na	na

Las Vegas Municipal Airport *San Miguel County*   Elevation: 6,863 ft.   Latitude: 35° 39' N   Longitude: 105° 09' W

	JAN	FEB	MAR	APR	MAY	JUN	JUL	AUG	SEP	OCT	NOV	DEC	YEAR
Mean Maximum Temp. (°F)	45.6	49.7	55.5	62.5	71.1	80.7	83.1	80.7	74.9	65.9	54.5	47.0	64.3
Mean Temp. (°F)	32.1	35.8	41.0	47.5	56.1	65.1	68.5	66.7	60.7	51.1	40.4	33.4	49.9
Mean Minimum Temp. (°F)	18.6	21.9	26.5	32.4	41.0	49.5	53.8	52.7	46.5	36.3	26.4	19.7	35.4
Extreme Maximum Temp. (°F)	72	74	81	84	90	99	98	94	91	86	80	73	99
Extreme Minimum Temp. (°F)	-21	-15	-4	0	17	32	37	39	23	3	-10	-14	-21
Days Maximum Temp. ≥ 90°F	0	0	0	0	0	4	4	1	0	0	0	0	9
Days Maximum Temp. ≤ 32°F	4	2	1	0	0	0	0	0	0	0	1	3	11
Days Minimum Temp. ≤ 32°F	29	25	25	15	3	0	0	0	1	9	23	29	159
Days Minimum Temp. ≤ 0°F	1	1	0	0	0	0	0	0	0	0	0	1	3
Heating Degree Days (base 65°F)	1,011	817	737	520	276	62	11	23	140	425	730	973	5,725
Cooling Degree Days (base 65°F)	0	0	0	1	8	77	129	89	21	1	0	0	326
Mean Precipitation (in.)	0.38	0.37	0.74	0.97	1.87	2.10	3.38	3.61	2.23	1.16	0.77	0.52	18.10
Days With ≥ 0.1" Precipitation	1	1	2	2	4	5	7	8	5	3	2	2	42
Days With ≥ 1.0" Precipitation	0	0	0	0	0	0	1	1	0	0	0	0	2
Mean Snowfall (in.)	7.1	6.2	7.2	4.1	0.9	trace	trace	trace	trace	2.3	4.4	7.3	39.5
Days With ≥ 1.0" Snow Depth	10	6	3	2	0	0	0	0	0	1	3	8	33

Lordsburg 4 SE *Hidalgo County*   Elevation: 4,248 ft.   Latitude: 32° 18' N   Longitude: 108° 39' W

	JAN	FEB	MAR	APR	MAY	JUN	JUL	AUG	SEP	OCT	NOV	DEC	YEAR
Mean Maximum Temp. (°F)	58.4	63.6	69.9	78.1	86.8	96.3	96.0	93.4	88.8	78.9	66.8	58.2	77.9
Mean Temp. (°F)	41.7	45.5	51.2	57.8	66.8	76.6	80.0	77.8	71.9	60.5	48.3	41.6	60.0
Mean Minimum Temp. (°F)	25.0	27.4	32.3	37.5	46.8	56.9	63.9	62.2	55.0	42.2	29.7	25.0	42.0
Extreme Maximum Temp. (°F)	77	83	93	98	104	114	110	107	104	97	86	76	114
Extreme Minimum Temp. (°F)	2	3	11	12	24	37	49	42	36	19	8	-14	-14
Days Maximum Temp. ≥ 90°F	0	0	0	1	11	26	28	25	15	3	0	0	109
Days Maximum Temp. ≤ 32°F	0	0	0	0	0	0	0	0	0	0	0	0	0
Days Minimum Temp. ≤ 32°F	26	21	17	8	1	0	0	0	0	3	19	25	120
Days Minimum Temp. ≤ 0°F	0	0	0	0	0	0	0	0	0	0	0	0	0
Heating Degree Days (base 65°F)	716	544	421	221	46	1	0	0	11	161	496	719	3,336
Cooling Degree Days (base 65°F)	0	0	0	14	125	366	476	415	238	33	0	0	1,667
Mean Precipitation (in.)	0.92	0.78	0.79	0.27	0.38	0.43	1.99	1.90	1.27	1.26	0.78	1.29	12.06
Days With ≥ 0.1" Precipitation	3	2	3	1	1	1	5	5	3	3	2	3	32
Days With ≥ 1.0" Precipitation	0	0	0	0	0	0	0	0	0	0	0	0	0
Mean Snowfall (in.)	1.1	0.8	0.5	0.1	0.0	0.0	0.0	0.0	0.0	0.0	0.3	1.2	4.0
Days With ≥ 1.0" Snow Depth	0	0	0	0	0	0	0	0	0	0	0	0	0

Los Alamos *Los Alamos County*   Elevation: 7,421 ft.   Latitude: 35° 52' N   Longitude: 106° 19' W

	JAN	FEB	MAR	APR	MAY	JUN	JUL	AUG	SEP	OCT	NOV	DEC	YEAR
Mean Maximum Temp. (°F)	39.3	44.1	50.6	58.5	67.6	78.2	80.5	77.5	71.5	61.2	48.5	40.7	59.8
Mean Temp. (°F)	28.5	33.0	38.8	45.7	54.7	64.6	67.5	65.3	59.2	48.9	37.3	29.9	47.8
Mean Minimum Temp. (°F)	17.6	21.8	26.9	32.9	41.7	51.0	54.6	53.1	46.8	36.6	26.1	19.0	35.7
Extreme Maximum Temp. (°F)	62	69	73	79	86	95	94	91	88	84	71	64	95
Extreme Minimum Temp. (°F)	-16	-9	2	8	24	32	40	31	25	6	-14	-13	-16
Days Maximum Temp. ≥ 90°F	0	0	0	0	0	1	1	0	0	0	0	0	2
Days Maximum Temp. ≤ 32°F	6	3	1	0	0	0	0	0	0	0	2	5	17
Days Minimum Temp. ≤ 32°F	31	27	25	14	3	0	0	0	0	8	24	30	162
Days Minimum Temp. ≤ 0°F	1	0	0	0	0	0	0	0	0	0	0	0	1
Heating Degree Days (base 65°F)	1,125	898	808	572	318	78	18	38	180	493	824	1,081	6,433
Cooling Degree Days (base 65°F)	0	0	0	0	6	72	104	54	11	0	0	0	247
Mean Precipitation (in.)	0.95	0.75	1.31	1.04	1.44	1.44	3.00	3.45	2.12	1.42	1.14	0.91	18.97
Days With ≥ 0.1" Precipitation	2	2	4	3	4	3	8	8	5	3	2	2	46
Days With ≥ 1.0" Precipitation	0	0	0	0	0	0	0	0	0	0	0	0	0
Mean Snowfall (in.)	14.2	9.1	11.0	4.9	0.9	0.0	0.0	0.0	trace	2.9	4.9	11.0	58.9
Days With ≥ 1.0" Snow Depth	23	11	4	1	0	0	0	0	0	1	3	13	56

Los Lunas 3 SSW *Valencia County*   Elevation: 4,839 ft.   Latitude: 34° 46' N   Longitude: 106° 45' W

	JAN	FEB	MAR	APR	MAY	JUN	JUL	AUG	SEP	OCT	NOV	DEC	YEAR
Mean Maximum Temp. (°F)	51.1	58.4	65.8	73.1	81.1	90.5	92.5	89.9	84.1	73.8	60.9	51.3	72.7
Mean Temp. (°F)	35.0	40.9	47.7	54.3	62.9	71.8	76.3	74.5	67.3	55.8	43.5	35.1	55.4
Mean Minimum Temp. (°F)	18.8	23.3	29.6	35.5	44.6	53.1	60.1	59.1	50.5	37.7	26.1	18.9	38.1
Extreme Maximum Temp. (°F)	74	79	86	93	98	107	104	101	98	93	80	74	107
Extreme Minimum Temp. (°F)	-25	4	9	16	26	37	45	44	32	15	-15	-5	-25
Days Maximum Temp. ≥ 90°F	0	0	0	0	3	17	24	18	6	0	0	0	68
Days Maximum Temp. ≤ 32°F	1	0	0	0	0	0	0	0	0	0	0	1	2
Days Minimum Temp. ≤ 32°F	30	25	20	11	1	0	0	0	0	7	24	29	147
Days Minimum Temp. ≤ 0°F	1	0	0	0	0	0	0	0	0	0	0	0	1
Heating Degree Days (base 65°F)	925	674	529	315	100	6	0	1	33	282	637	919	4,421
Cooling Degree Days (base 65°F)	0	0	0	3	51	233	369	323	121	3	0	0	1,103
Mean Precipitation (in.)	0.44	0.42	0.51	0.49	0.60	0.51	1.33	1.92	1.41	1.03	0.56	0.52	9.74
Days With ≥ 0.1" Precipitation	2	1	1	1	2	1	4	4	3	3	1	2	25
Days With ≥ 1.0" Precipitation	0	0	0	0	0	0	0	0	0	0	0	0	0
Mean Snowfall (in.)	1.6	0.8	0.1	0.3	0.0	0.0	0.0	0.0	0.0	0.3	0.5	2.2	5.8
Days With ≥ 1.0" Snow Depth	0	0	0	0	0	0	0	0	0	0	0	1	1

Luna Ranger Station *Catron County*   Elevation: 7,047 ft.   Latitude: 33° 49' N   Longitude: 108° 57' W

	JAN	FEB	MAR	APR	MAY	JUN	JUL	AUG	SEP	OCT	NOV	DEC	YEAR
Mean Maximum Temp. (°F)	49.0	52.1	57.0	64.4	72.4	82.2	83.2	80.2	76.2	68.0	57.1	50.0	66.0
Mean Temp. (°F)	30.6	33.8	38.2	43.3	50.9	59.2	64.8	63.2	57.3	47.5	37.1	31.0	46.4
Mean Minimum Temp. (°F)	12.2	15.6	19.4	22.1	29.4	36.2	46.4	46.1	38.4	27.0	17.0	12.0	26.8
Extreme Maximum Temp. (°F)	70	73	76	83	90	97	97	93	91	85	78	73	97
Extreme Minimum Temp. (°F)	-32	-12	-5	-5	10	20	28	31	21	2	-7	-32	-32
Days Maximum Temp. ≥ 90°F	0	0	0	0	0	4	4	1	0	0	0	0	9
Days Maximum Temp. ≤ 32°F	1	0	0	0	0	0	0	0	0	0	0	1	2
Days Minimum Temp. ≤ 32°F	31	27	30	27	22	10	1	0	7	24	29	30	238
Days Minimum Temp. ≤ 0°F	3	2	0	0	0	0	0	0	0	0	0	3	8
Heating Degree Days (base 65°F)	1,060	873	823	646	429	179	37	66	226	536	830	1,048	6,753
Cooling Degree Days (base 65°F)	0	0	0	0	0	12	34	17	1	0	0	0	64
Mean Precipitation (in.)	1.01	0.94	0.89	0.40	0.76	0.61	3.16	3.62	2.17	1.78	1.06	1.06	17.46
Days With ≥ 0.1" Precipitation	3	3	2	1	2	2	8	9	5	4	2	3	44
Days With ≥ 1.0" Precipitation	0	0	0	0	0	0	1	0	0	0	0	0	1
Mean Snowfall (in.)	3.4	3.3	1.9	0.4	0.0	0.0	0.0	0.0	0.0	0.2	0.8	4.9	14.9
Days With ≥ 1.0" Snow Depth	3	3	1	0	0	0	0	0	0	0	0	4	11

Maljamar 4 SE *Lea County*   Elevation: 3,999 ft.   Latitude: 32° 49' N   Longitude: 103° 42' W

	JAN	FEB	MAR	APR	MAY	JUN	JUL	AUG	SEP	OCT	NOV	DEC	YEAR
Mean Maximum Temp. (°F)	56.1	62.2	70.2	78.5	86.5	94.4	95.3	93.0	86.6	77.6	65.4	57.7	77.0
Mean Temp. (°F)	40.6	45.5	52.6	60.6	69.2	77.3	79.6	78.0	71.4	61.3	49.5	42.0	60.6
Mean Minimum Temp. (°F)	25.0	28.8	35.0	42.7	51.9	60.1	63.7	62.8	56.3	45.1	33.5	26.2	44.3
Extreme Maximum Temp. (°F)	82	84	92	100	109	116	111	109	106	98	86	79	116
Extreme Minimum Temp. (°F)	-8	0	4	19	30	41	50	50	30	16	-4	-3	-8
Days Maximum Temp. ≥ 90°F	0	0	0	2	11	22	26	23	13	2	0	0	99
Days Maximum Temp. ≤ 32°F	1	1	0	0	0	0	0	0	0	0	0	1	3
Days Minimum Temp. ≤ 32°F	25	18	11	3	0	0	0	0	0	2	13	24	96
Days Minimum Temp. ≤ 0°F	0	0	0	0	0	0	0	0	0	0	0	0	0
Heating Degree Days (base 65°F)	751	544	380	162	28	2	0	0	26	149	458	707	3,207
Cooling Degree Days (base 65°F)	0	0	3	37	186	404	488	443	245	51	1	0	1,858
Mean Precipitation (in.)	0.44	0.50	0.39	0.53	1.93	1.73	2.29	2.80	3.16	1.11	0.75	0.65	16.28
Days With ≥ 0.1" Precipitation	1	2	1	2	3	4	5	5	5	2	2	2	34
Days With ≥ 1.0" Precipitation	0	0	0	0	1	1	0	1	1	0	0	0	4
Mean Snowfall (in.)	2.2	1.6	0.6	0.3	0.0	0.0	0.0	0.0	0.0	0.2	0.8	2.0	7.7
Days With ≥ 1.0" Snow Depth	1	0	0	0	0	0	0	0	0	0	0	1	2

Maxwell 3 NW *Colfax County*   Elevation: 6,017 ft.   Latitude: 36° 34' N   Longitude: 104° 34' W

	JAN	FEB	MAR	APR	MAY	JUN	JUL	AUG	SEP	OCT	NOV	DEC	YEAR
Mean Maximum Temp. (°F)	45.9	51.6	57.8	64.8	72.9	81.8	85.7	83.4	77.5	68.0	55.7	47.0	66.0
Mean Temp. (°F)	28.8	33.3	40.1	46.7	55.8	64.2	69.1	67.4	60.9	50.1	38.6	30.0	48.7
Mean Minimum Temp. (°F)	11.6	14.9	22.3	28.8	38.6	46.6	52.4	51.3	44.2	32.1	21.4	13.1	31.5
Extreme Maximum Temp. (°F)	75	78	84	88	93	100	98	96	95	89	81	76	100
Extreme Minimum Temp. (°F)	-28	-26	-7	1	19	28	39	40	16	-3	-24	-20	-28
Days Maximum Temp. ≥ 90°F	0	0	0	0	0	5	9	4	1	0	0	0	19
Days Maximum Temp. ≤ 32°F	5	2	1	0	0	0	0	0	0	0	1	4	13
Days Minimum Temp. ≤ 32°F	30	27	28	20	6	0	0	0	2	16	27	30	186
Days Minimum Temp. ≤ 0°F	3	2	0	0	0	0	0	0	0	0	0	3	8
Heating Degree Days (base 65°F)	1,118	886	767	542	283	73	7	17	139	456	786	1,074	6,148
Cooling Degree Days (base 65°F)	0	0	0	0	5	59	143	109	24	0	0	0	340
Mean Precipitation (in.)	0.27	0.25	0.51	0.68	2.25	2.14	2.39	3.19	2.01	0.96	0.57	0.25	15.47
Days With ≥ 0.1" Precipitation	1	1	2	2	4	4	5	6	3	2	1	1	32
Days With ≥ 1.0" Precipitation	0	0	0	0	0	0	1	1	1	0	0	0	3
Mean Snowfall (in.)	4.1	3.9	2.6	1.4	0.8	0.0	0.0	0.0	0.2	1.4	3.0	3.8	21.2
Days With ≥ 1.0" Snow Depth	na	2	1	0	0	0	0	0	0	0	1	na	na

McGaffey 5 SE *McKinley County*   Elevation: 7,998 ft.   Latitude: 35° 20' N   Longitude: 108° 27' W

	JAN	FEB	MAR	APR	MAY	JUN	JUL	AUG	SEP	OCT	NOV	DEC	YEAR
Mean Maximum Temp. (°F)	39.1	42.4	47.7	55.2	65.3	76.7	79.9	77.0	71.8	62.0	49.1	40.9	58.9
Mean Temp. (°F)	23.6	27.3	33.0	39.4	48.2	57.8	63.1	61.3	55.1	44.7	33.0	25.4	42.7
Mean Minimum Temp. (°F)	8.1	12.2	18.2	23.5	31.1	38.9	46.2	45.6	38.3	27.4	16.9	9.8	26.3
Extreme Maximum Temp. (°F)	69	65	71	78	83	93	94	90	85	80	74	65	94
Extreme Minimum Temp. (°F)	-32	-25	-14	-3	10	19	28	32	18	0	-21	-30	-32
Days Maximum Temp. ≥ 90°F	0	0	0	0	0	1	1	0	0	0	0	0	2
Days Maximum Temp. ≤ 32°F	7	4	1	0	0	0	0	0	0	0	2	5	19
Days Minimum Temp. ≤ 32°F	31	28	31	27	17	4	0	0	5	24	29	31	227
Days Minimum Temp. ≤ 0°F	8	4	1	0	0	0	0	0	0	0	2	6	21
Heating Degree Days (base 65°F)	1,276	1,057	987	762	513	217	75	115	292	621	955	1,222	8,092
Cooling Degree Days (base 65°F)	0	0	0	0	0	7	19	8	0	0	0	0	34
Mean Precipitation (in.)	1.86	1.60	2.03	1.23	1.05	0.65	2.40	2.79	1.79	1.62	1.80	1.51	20.33
Days With ≥ 0.1" Precipitation	4	4	5	4	3	2	6	7	5	4	4	3	51
Days With ≥ 1.0" Precipitation	0	0	0	0	0	0	0	0	0	0	0	0	0
Mean Snowfall (in.)	na	na	na	4.6	0.4	trace	0.0	0.0	trace	2.6	7.6	9.2	na
Days With ≥ 1.0" Snow Depth	na	na	na	2	0	0	0	0	0	0	na	na	na

Melrose *Curry County*   Elevation: 4,596 ft.   Latitude: 34° 26' N   Longitude: 103° 37' W

	JAN	FEB	MAR	APR	MAY	JUN	JUL	AUG	SEP	OCT	NOV	DEC	YEAR
Mean Maximum Temp. (°F)	51.8	57.4	65.0	73.0	81.3	89.5	90.9	88.4	82.6	73.1	61.0	52.9	72.3
Mean Temp. (°F)	37.6	42.1	48.5	56.2	65.4	74.0	76.8	75.0	68.5	58.1	46.4	38.8	57.3
Mean Minimum Temp. (°F)	23.3	26.8	31.9	39.4	49.4	58.5	62.8	61.5	54.5	43.0	31.7	24.5	42.3
Extreme Maximum Temp. (°F)	78	81	90	96	100	108	107	105	101	95	85	77	108
Extreme Minimum Temp. (°F)	-14	-8	3	14	26	41	51	48	30	12	0	-13	-14
Days Maximum Temp. ≥ 90°F	0	0	0	0	5	16	19	14	6	0	0	0	60
Days Maximum Temp. ≤ 32°F	2	1	0	0	0	0	0	0	0	0	0	2	5
Days Minimum Temp. ≤ 32°F	27	21	16	5	0	0	0	0	0	3	16	26	114
Days Minimum Temp. ≤ 0°F	0	0	0	0	0	0	0	0	0	0	0	0	0
Heating Degree Days (base 65°F)	844	639	505	265	70	5	0	1	40	223	551	807	3,950
Cooling Degree Days (base 65°F)	0	0	0	10	95	294	391	340	162	16	0	0	1,308
Mean Precipitation (in.)	0.43	0.46	0.62	0.97	1.68	2.11	3.01	3.35	2.12	1.50	0.62	0.60	17.47
Days With ≥ 0.1" Precipitation	1	1	2	2	4	4	5	6	4	3	2	2	36
Days With ≥ 1.0" Precipitation	0	0	0	0	0	0	1	1	0	0	0	0	3
Mean Snowfall (in.)	3.6	3.3	1.5	1.0	trace	0.0	0.0	0.0	0.0	0.7	1.8	4.0	15.9
Days With ≥ 1.0" Snow Depth	3	2	0	0	0	0	0	0	0	0	1	2	8

Mimbres Ranger Station *Grant County*   Elevation: 6,236 ft.   Latitude: 32° 56' N   Longitude: 108° 01' W

	JAN	FEB	MAR	APR	MAY	JUN	JUL	AUG	SEP	OCT	NOV	DEC	YEAR
Mean Maximum Temp. (°F)	*52.4*	56.6	61.9	70.0	77.9	87.8	86.7	83.8	*80.0*	71.2	*60.4*	*53.5*	*70.2*
Mean Temp. (°F)	*36.2*	39.2	43.4	49.6	57.0	66.3	69.6	67.6	*62.3*	52.7	*42.3*	*36.9*	*51.9*
Mean Minimum Temp. (°F)	*20.0*	22.1	24.9	29.1	36.2	45.0	52.6	51.5	*44.5*	34.2	*24.2*	*20.3*	*33.7*
Extreme Maximum Temp. (°F)	72	78	83	90	94	103	101	97	97	89	79	74	103
Extreme Minimum Temp. (°F)	-17	2	3	12	19	29	37	34	25	14	0	-9	-17
Days Maximum Temp. ≥ 90°F	0	0	0	0	1	12	10	3	1	0	0	0	27
Days Maximum Temp. ≤ 32°F	0	0	0	0	0	0	0	0	0	0	0	0	0
Days Minimum Temp. ≤ 32°F	28	24	27	21	9	1	0	0	1	12	25	28	176
Days Minimum Temp. ≤ 0°F	0	0	0	0	0	0	0	0	0	0	0	0	0
Heating Degree Days (base 65°F)	*884*	721	662	457	245	40	3	9	*99*	374	*674*	*864*	*5,032*
Cooling Degree Days (base 65°F)	*0*	0	*0*	0	6	89	158	*111*	24	0	*0*	*0*	*388*
Mean Precipitation (in.)	0.93	0.82	0.74	0.30	0.71	0.67	3.67	3.82	2.37	1.74	1.09	1.20	18.06
Days With ≥ 0.1" Precipitation	2	2	2	1	2	2	8	8	4	3	2	3	39
Days With ≥ 1.0" Precipitation	0	0	0	0	0	1	1	0	0	0	0	0	2
Mean Snowfall (in.)	*2.1*	2.0	1.9	0.2	trace	0.0	0.0	0.0	0.0	0.5	0.9	*3.1*	*10.7*
Days With ≥ 1.0" Snow Depth	*2*	*1*	0	0	0	0	0	0	0	0	0	*1*	*4*

Mosquero 1 NE *Harding County*   Elevation: 5,462 ft.   Latitude: 35° 48' N   Longitude: 103° 56' W

	JAN	FEB	MAR	APR	MAY	JUN	JUL	AUG	SEP	OCT	NOV	DEC	YEAR
Mean Maximum Temp. (°F)	46.9	51.9	59.7	67.5	75.7	84.9	87.5	84.6	78.7	69.3	56.2	47.5	67.5
Mean Temp. (°F)	33.0	37.2	43.9	51.2	60.0	69.4	73.2	71.1	64.6	54.0	41.8	33.9	52.8
Mean Minimum Temp. (°F)	19.0	22.5	28.1	34.8	44.3	53.8	58.9	57.5	50.4	38.7	27.4	20.3	38.0
Extreme Maximum Temp. (°F)	76	78	86	94	96	103	102	100	98	90	82	78	103
Extreme Minimum Temp. (°F)	-18	-12	3	8	26	36	43	42	22	0	-16	-15	-18
Days Maximum Temp. ≥ 90°F	0	0	0	0	1	9	12	6	1	0	0	0	29
Days Maximum Temp. ≤ 32°F	4	2	0	0	0	0	0	0	0	0	1	3	10
Days Minimum Temp. ≤ 32°F	30	25	22	11	1	0	0	0	0	6	22	29	146
Days Minimum Temp. ≤ 0°F	1	1	0	0	0	0	0	0	0	0	0	1	3
Heating Degree Days (base 65°F)	987	778	647	410	171	25	2	5	80	336	688	956	5,085
Cooling Degree Days (base 65°F)	0	0	0	2	26	160	269	201	74	2	0	0	734
Mean Precipitation (in.)	0.38	0.35	0.73	1.06	2.00	2.16	2.61	2.94	1.84	1.08	0.78	0.46	16.39
Days With ≥ 0.1" Precipitation	1	1	2	2	4	5	5	6	3	3	2	1	35
Days With ≥ 1.0" Precipitation	0	0	0	0	0	0	1	1	0	0	0	0	2
Mean Snowfall (in.)	4.1	3.3	3.8	2.2	0.8	0.0	0.0	0.0	trace	1.6	3.2	4.7	23.7
Days With ≥ 1.0" Snow Depth	6	3	1	0	0	0	0	0	0	0	0	6	18

Mountain Park *Otero County*   Elevation: 6,778 ft.   Latitude: 32° 57' N   Longitude: 105° 49' W

	JAN	FEB	MAR	APR	MAY	JUN	JUL	AUG	SEP	OCT	NOV	DEC	YEAR
Mean Maximum Temp. (°F)	48.5	52.3	58.4	65.7	73.3	81.9	80.9	78.6	74.6	66.9	56.3	49.8	65.6
Mean Temp. (°F)	37.1	40.3	44.9	51.4	59.0	67.8	68.6	66.9	62.5	54.0	44.0	38.2	52.9
Mean Minimum Temp. (°F)	25.6	28.2	31.3	37.1	44.6	53.6	56.3	55.1	50.5	41.1	31.7	26.6	40.1
Extreme Maximum Temp. (°F)	69	71	80	85	93	98	95	92	92	83	76	70	98
Extreme Minimum Temp. (°F)	-5	2	9	13	24	35	42	41	28	17	0	-5	-5
Days Maximum Temp. ≥ 90°F	0	0	0	0	0	3	1	0	0	0	0	0	4
Days Maximum Temp. ≤ 32°F	1	1	0	0	0	0	0	0	0	0	0	1	3
Days Minimum Temp. ≤ 32°F	26	21	17	8	1	0	0	0	0	4	16	25	118
Days Minimum Temp. ≤ 0°F	0	0	0	0	0	0	0	0	0	0	0	0	0
Heating Degree Days (base 65°F)	859	692	617	401	194	30	9	20	97	334	621	824	4,698
Cooling Degree Days (base 65°F)	0	0	0	1	16	126	132	95	30	1	0	0	401
Mean Precipitation (in.)	1.18	1.20	0.97	0.56	1.06	1.34	3.54	4.20	2.71	1.88	1.27	1.51	21.42
Days With ≥ 0.1" Precipitation	3	4	3	1	3	3	8	9	6	3	3	3	49
Days With ≥ 1.0" Precipitation	0	0	0	0	0	1	1	0	0	0	0	0	2
Mean Snowfall (in.)	3.7	3.9	3.3	1.1	trace	0.0	0.0	0.0	0.0	1.2	1.6	4.2	19.0
Days With ≥ 1.0" Snow Depth	3	2	*0*	0	0	0	0	0	0	0	0	*2*	*7*

Mountainair *Torrance County*   Elevation: 6,496 ft.   Latitude: 34° 32' N   Longitude: 106° 15' W

	JAN	FEB	MAR	APR	MAY	JUN	JUL	AUG	SEP	OCT	NOV	DEC	YEAR
Mean Maximum Temp. (°F)	46.0	52.3	58.9	66.8	75.2	85.4	87.2	84.0	78.4	68.6	56.7	47.0	67.2
Mean Temp. (°F)	32.6	37.8	43.2	49.3	57.8	67.4	70.8	68.6	62.7	52.3	41.4	33.2	51.4
Mean Minimum Temp. (°F)	19.2	23.2	27.3	31.8	40.4	49.2	54.3	53.3	46.9	36.0	26.0	19.4	35.6
Extreme Maximum Temp. (°F)	67	72	79	84	94	102	101	97	95	90	77	66	102
Extreme Minimum Temp. (°F)	-25	-6	0	8	13	30	38	35	21	1	-10	-14	-25
Days Maximum Temp. ≥ 90°F	0	0	0	0	0	9	11	4	0	0	0	0	24
Days Maximum Temp. ≤ 32°F	2	1	0	0	0	0	0	0	0	0	0	2	5
Days Minimum Temp. ≤ 32°F	29	26	24	16	4	0	0	0	1	9	23	28	160
Days Minimum Temp. ≤ 0°F	1	0	0	0	0	0	0	0	0	0	0	1	2
Heating Degree Days (base 65°F)	996	763	668	464	226	36	2	8	97	387	702	979	5,328
Cooling Degree Days (base 65°F)	0	0	0	1	13	120	199	137	40	*1*	0	0	*511*
Mean Precipitation (in.)	0.76	0.62	0.77	0.60	0.89	0.82	2.70	2.72	2.05	1.48	0.76	0.97	15.14
Days With ≥ 0.1" Precipitation	2	2	2	2	2	2	6	6	4	3	2	2	35
Days With ≥ 1.0" Precipitation	0	0	0	0	0	0	1	1	0	0	0	0	2
Mean Snowfall (in.)	6.4	4.6	4.1	1.3	0.4	0.0	0.0	0.0	0.0	0.5	1.3	6.1	24.7
Days With ≥ 1.0" Snow Depth	na	2	*0*	0	0	0	0	0	0	0	0	*2*	na

Navajo Dam *San Juan County* Elevation: 5,767 ft. Latitude: 36° 49' N Longitude: 107° 37' W

	JAN	FEB	MAR	APR	MAY	JUN	JUL	AUG	SEP	OCT	NOV	DEC	YEAR
Mean Maximum Temp. (°F)	39.8	47.0	56.0	64.4	74.3	85.4	90.6	87.9	79.5	67.5	51.5	41.1	65.4
Mean Temp. (°F)	29.2	35.1	42.6	49.6	59.0	69.3	75.2	73.3	65.1	53.3	39.9	30.8	51.9
Mean Minimum Temp. (°F)	18.5	23.1	29.1	34.8	43.7	53.0	59.9	58.7	50.7	39.1	28.2	20.5	38.3
Extreme Maximum Temp. (°F)	60	69	80	88	96	102	103	104	99	89	72	60	104
Extreme Minimum Temp. (°F)	-16	-6	8	18	20	33	40	40	30	18	9	-16	-16
Days Maximum Temp. ≥ 90°F	0	0	0	0	0	9	20	13	2	0	0	0	44
Days Maximum Temp. ≤ 32°F	5	1	0	0	0	0	0	0	0	0	1	4	11
Days Minimum Temp. ≤ 32°F	30	27	23	11	2	0	0	0	0	5	22	29	149
Days Minimum Temp. ≤ 0°F	1	0	0	0	0	0	0	0	0	0	0	0	1
Heating Degree Days (base 65°F)	1,104	838	684	457	195	28	1	3	67	362	746	1,053	5,538
Cooling Degree Days (base 65°F)	0	0	0	1	21	168	332	288	85	2	0	0	897
Mean Precipitation (in.)	1.09	0.99	1.31	1.03	0.95	0.50	1.34	1.76	1.24	1.32	1.21	1.06	13.80
Days With ≥ 0.1" Precipitation	3	3	4	3	3	1	3	5	3	3	4	3	38
Days With ≥ 1.0" Precipitation	0	0	0	0	0	0	0	0	0	0	0	0	0
Mean Snowfall (in.)	na	3.2	0.4	trace	trace	0.0	0.0	0.0	0.0	0.3	0.8	2.5	na
Days With ≥ 1.0" Snow Depth	7	3	0	0	0	0	0	0	0	0	0	2	12

Newkirk *Guadalupe County* Elevation: 4,560 ft. Latitude: 35° 04' N Longitude: 104° 15' W

	JAN	FEB	MAR	APR	MAY	JUN	JUL	AUG	SEP	OCT	NOV	DEC	YEAR
Mean Maximum Temp. (°F)	52.3	57.9	65.2	72.9	81.8	90.9	92.8	90.2	84.0	74.2	61.7	53.1	73.1
Mean Temp. (°F)	37.4	41.9	48.5	56.1	65.3	74.5	77.9	76.0	69.2	58.4	46.6	38.5	57.5
Mean Minimum Temp. (°F)	22.4	25.9	31.8	39.2	48.8	58.0	63.1	61.7	54.3	42.5	31.5	23.8	41.9
Extreme Maximum Temp. (°F)	82	80	88	97	102	108	105	104	100	93	86	81	108
Extreme Minimum Temp. (°F)	-17	-8	6	8	26	36	49	45	29	9	-7	-19	-19
Days Maximum Temp. ≥ 90°F	0	0	0	0	5	18	23	18	7	0	0	0	71
Days Maximum Temp. ≤ 32°F	2	1	0	0	0	0	0	0	0	0	0	2	5
Days Minimum Temp. ≤ 32°F	27	21	15	7	1	0	0	0	0	4	17	25	117
Days Minimum Temp. ≤ 0°F	1	0	0	0	0	0	0	0	0	0	0	0	1
Heating Degree Days (base 65°F)	850	645	504	271	75	6	0	1	36	218	546	816	3,968
Cooling Degree Days (base 65°F)	0	0	1	12	90	293	415	352	175	17	0	0	1,355
Mean Precipitation (in.)	0.37	0.39	0.62	0.99	1.49	1.63	2.72	2.73	1.72	1.29	0.65	0.52	15.12
Days With ≥ 0.1" Precipitation	1	1	2	2	3	4	5	6	4	2	2	2	34
Days With ≥ 1.0" Precipitation	0	0	0	0	0	0	1	0	0	0	0	0	1
Mean Snowfall (in.)	4.7	4.6	1.8	1.7	0.2	0.0	0.0	0.0	0.0	0.8	2.0	5.8	21.6
Days With ≥ 1.0" Snow Depth	3	2	0	0	0	0	0	0	0	0	0	2	7

Ocate 2 NW *Mora County* Elevation: 7,654 ft. Latitude: 36° 12' N Longitude: 105° 04' W

	JAN	FEB	MAR	APR	MAY	JUN	JUL	AUG	SEP	OCT	NOV	DEC	YEAR
Mean Maximum Temp. (°F)	45.2	48.4	53.3	60.4	68.9	78.1	80.9	78.4	73.2	64.3	53.0	46.2	62.5
Mean Temp. (°F)	29.7	32.7	37.2	43.7	52.3	60.7	64.6	63.1	57.1	47.1	36.9	30.4	46.3
Mean Minimum Temp. (°F)	13.9	16.9	21.0	27.0	35.6	43.1	48.3	47.6	40.9	29.9	20.8	14.5	30.0
Extreme Maximum Temp. (°F)	70	71	74	82	85	97	97	92	90	83	77	74	97
Extreme Minimum Temp. (°F)	-29	-21	-9	-4	9	24	31	35	14	-8	-31	-26	-31
Days Maximum Temp. ≥ 90°F	0	0	0	0	0	1	1	0	0	0	0	0	2
Days Maximum Temp. ≤ 32°F	3	2	1	0	0	0	0	0	0	0	1	3	10
Days Minimum Temp. ≤ 32°F	30	26	28	22	9	1	0	0	3	19	27	30	195
Days Minimum Temp. ≤ 0°F	3	2	1	0	0	0	0	0	0	0	1	3	10
Heating Degree Days (base 65°F)	1,089	905	856	632	386	139	41	72	235	547	835	1,067	6,804
Cooling Degree Days (base 65°F)	0	0	0	0	2	15	32	21	4	0	0	0	74
Mean Precipitation (in.)	0.37	0.34	0.72	1.09	2.10	2.29	3.69	3.76	2.07	1.02	0.66	0.44	18.55
Days With ≥ 0.1" Precipitation	1	1	2	3	5	5	8	9	4	3	2	2	45
Days With ≥ 1.0" Precipitation	0	0	0	0	0	1	1	1	0	0	0	0	3
Mean Snowfall (in.)	6.3	6.3	7.2	5.2	1.1	trace	trace	trace	trace	3.0	4.2	6.0	39.3
Days With ≥ 1.0" Snow Depth	na	1	1	1	0	0	0	0	0	0	1	na	na

Orogrande *Otero County* Elevation: 4,179 ft. Latitude: 32° 23' N Longitude: 106° 06' W

	JAN	FEB	MAR	APR	MAY	JUN	JUL	AUG	SEP	OCT	NOV	DEC	YEAR
Mean Maximum Temp. (°F)	56.9	62.9	69.7	77.2	85.9	95.3	95.2	92.2	86.9	77.8	66.2	57.4	77.0
Mean Temp. (°F)	42.2	47.3	53.1	60.2	68.7	78.3	80.2	77.9	72.5	61.9	50.4	42.4	61.3
Mean Minimum Temp. (°F)	27.5	31.9	36.3	43.3	51.4	61.2	65.3	63.6	58.0	46.0	34.5	27.3	45.5
Extreme Maximum Temp. (°F)	78	82	90	97	102	110	109	106	103	95	84	75	110
Extreme Minimum Temp. (°F)	2	6	14	22	33	44	52	53	40	21	3	2	2
Days Maximum Temp. ≥ 90°F	0	0	0	1	10	25	26	23	12	1	0	0	98
Days Maximum Temp. ≤ 32°F	0	0	0	0	0	0	0	0	0	0	0	0	0
Days Minimum Temp. ≤ 32°F	23	16	9	2	0	0	0	0	0	1	11	23	85
Days Minimum Temp. ≤ 0°F	0	0	0	0	0	0	0	0	0	0	0	0	0
Heating Degree Days (base 65°F)	701	491	365	165	28	0	0	0	12	128	432	694	3,016
Cooling Degree Days (base 65°F)	0	0	1	33	160	417	484	415	245	41	0	0	1,796
Mean Precipitation (in.)	0.55	0.34	0.21	0.25	0.61	1.06	2.20	2.49	1.92	1.38	0.55	0.90	12.46
Days With ≥ 0.1" Precipitation	2	1	1	1	1	2	5	5	4	2	1	2	27
Days With ≥ 1.0" Precipitation	0	0	0	0	0	0	1	0	0	0	0	0	1
Mean Snowfall (in.)	1.4	0.4	trace	0.4	0.0	0.0	0.0	0.0	0.0	0.1	0.4	1.2	3.9
Days With ≥ 1.0" Snow Depth	0	0	0	0	0	0	0	0	0	0	0	0	0

Pasamonte *Union County*   Elevation: 5,649 ft.   Latitude: 36° 18' N   Longitude: 103° 44' W

	JAN	FEB	MAR	APR	MAY	JUN	JUL	AUG	SEP	OCT	NOV	DEC	YEAR
Mean Maximum Temp. (°F)	45.9	50.3	57.3	65.0	73.8	83.5	87.7	85.0	77.6	67.9	55.5	47.1	66.4
Mean Temp. (°F)	31.1	35.0	41.4	48.8	58.0	67.5	72.1	70.2	62.7	52.0	40.1	32.5	51.0
Mean Minimum Temp. (°F)	16.3	19.6	25.4	32.5	42.2	51.5	56.4	55.3	47.8	36.0	24.7	17.8	35.5
Extreme Maximum Temp. (°F)	77	76	86	89	96	103	102	99	97	89	83	78	103
Extreme Minimum Temp. (°F)	-17	-18	0	8	21	33	39	42	26	0	-15	-23	-23
Days Maximum Temp. ≥ 90°F	0	0	0	0	1	8	13	8	2	0	0	0	32
Days Maximum Temp. ≤ 32°F	5	3	1	0	0	0	0	0	0	0	2	4	15
Days Minimum Temp. ≤ 32°F	31	27	25	15	3	0	0	0	1	10	25	30	167
Days Minimum Temp. ≤ 0°F	2	1	0	0	0	0	0	0	0	0	0	2	5
Heating Degree Days (base 65°F)	1,043	840	726	482	226	43	5	8	115	397	740	1,001	5,626
Cooling Degree Days (base 65°F)	0	0	0	2	16	119	226	176	52	1	0	0	592
Mean Precipitation (in.)	0.25	0.31	0.69	1.02	2.29	1.84	3.17	3.15	1.82	0.89	0.58	0.26	16.27
Days With ≥ 0.1" Precipitation	1	1	2	3	4	5	6	7	4	2	2	1	38
Days With ≥ 1.0" Precipitation	0	0	0	0	1	0	1	1	0	0	0	0	3
Mean Snowfall (in.)	3.4	3.3	3.6	2.4	0.5	0.0	0.0	0.0	trace	1.1	2.9	3.1	20.3
Days With ≥ 1.0" Snow Depth	4	3	2	1	0	0	0	0	0	1	2	4	17

Pecos National Monument *San Miguel County*   Elevation: 6,876 ft.   Latitude: 35° 33' N   Longitude: 105° 41' W

	JAN	FEB	MAR	APR	MAY	JUN	JUL	AUG	SEP	OCT	NOV	DEC	YEAR
Mean Maximum Temp. (°F)	46.7	49.8	54.9	62.5	71.7	82.4	84.4	81.7	75.8	66.8	54.5	48.2	64.9
Mean Temp. (°F)	31.1	34.9	39.8	46.4	55.0	65.0	68.6	66.6	60.2	50.4	39.2	32.6	49.2
Mean Minimum Temp. (°F)	15.4	20.0	24.5	30.3	38.3	47.7	52.7	51.4	44.4	33.9	23.9	17.0	33.3
Extreme Maximum Temp. (°F)	70	75	78	82	93	100	98	95	92	86	78	70	100
Extreme Minimum Temp. (°F)	-27	-19	-10	9	15	25	38	36	20	6	-23	-18	-27
Days Maximum Temp. ≥ 90°F	0	0	0	0	0	4	6	2	0	0	0	0	12
Days Maximum Temp. ≤ 32°F	2	1	0	0	0	0	0	0	0	0	1	1	5
Days Minimum Temp. ≤ 32°F	30	27	27	19	7	0	0	0	1	13	27	30	181
Days Minimum Temp. ≤ 0°F	2	1	0	0	0	0	0	0	0	0	0	2	5
Heating Degree Days (base 65°F)	1,046	844	777	551	309	64	12	24	152	446	768	997	5,990
Cooling Degree Days (base 65°F)	0	0	0	0	6	69	131	85	14	0	0	0	305
Mean Precipitation (in.)	0.71	0.63	0.92	0.78	1.29	1.32	3.25	3.55	2.07	1.26	1.02	0.57	17.37
Days With ≥ 0.1" Precipitation	2	2	3	2	3	3	8	8	5	3	3	2	44
Days With ≥ 1.0" Precipitation	0	0	0	0	0	0	1	1	0	0	0	0	2
Mean Snowfall (in.)	*5.3*	*3.3*	2.8	1.7	trace	0.0	0.0	0.0	0.0	0.6	*2.6*	3.6	*19.9*
Days With ≥ 1.0" Snow Depth	na	*2*	*1*	1	0	0	0	0	0	0	*1*	*4*	na

Pedernal 4 E *Torrance County*   Elevation: 6,197 ft.   Latitude: 34° 38' N   Longitude: 105° 34' W

	JAN	FEB	MAR	APR	MAY	JUN	JUL	AUG	SEP	OCT	NOV	DEC	YEAR
Mean Maximum Temp. (°F)	43.0	49.5	57.4	65.3	74.2	84.6	87.0	84.3	78.0	67.9	54.9	45.0	65.9
Mean Temp. (°F)	30.5	35.5	41.5	48.3	57.3	67.1	70.9	69.0	62.5	51.9	40.2	31.8	50.5
Mean Minimum Temp. (°F)	18.1	21.4	25.6	31.2	40.4	49.5	54.7	53.7	46.9	35.8	25.5	18.6	35.1
Extreme Maximum Temp. (°F)	69	73	80	85	92	105	103	100	97	89	76	69	105
Extreme Minimum Temp. (°F)	-29	-13	-2	1	15	25	41	40	24	0	-10	-15	-29
Days Maximum Temp. ≥ 90°F	0	0	0	0	0	8	12	6	1	0	0	0	27
Days Maximum Temp. ≤ 32°F	6	2	1	0	0	0	0	0	0	0	1	4	14
Days Minimum Temp. ≤ 32°F	30	26	26	17	4	0	0	0	1	10	24	30	168
Days Minimum Temp. ≤ 0°F	1	1	0	0	0	0	0	0	0	0	0	1	3
Heating Degree Days (base 65°F)	1,061	828	721	494	243	43	4	10	108	401	736	1,023	5,672
Cooling Degree Days (base 65°F)	0	0	0	0	12	116	203	150	42	1	0	0	524
Mean Precipitation (in.)	0.42	0.39	0.43	0.43	0.98	1.29	1.96	2.73	1.55	1.06	0.57	0.59	12.40
Days With ≥ 0.1" Precipitation	1	1	1	1	2	2	5	6	4	2	2	1	28
Days With ≥ 1.0" Precipitation	0	0	0	0	0	0	0	1	0	0	0	0	1
Mean Snowfall (in.)	*4.3*	*4.1*	*2.2*	1.0	0.3	0.0	0.0	0.0	0.0	0.6	*1.8*	*6.4*	*20.7*
Days With ≥ 1.0" Snow Depth	*6*	*3*	*1*	0	0	0	0	0	0	0	1	*4*	*15*

Portales *Roosevelt County*   Elevation: 4,009 ft.   Latitude: 34° 10' N   Longitude: 103° 21' W

	JAN	FEB	MAR	APR	MAY	JUN	JUL	AUG	SEP	OCT	NOV	DEC	YEAR
Mean Maximum Temp. (°F)	53.8	59.3	67.2	75.1	83.0	90.6	91.5	89.1	84.0	75.0	62.6	54.5	73.8
Mean Temp. (°F)	38.3	42.9	49.8	57.8	66.7	75.2	77.7	75.8	69.7	59.1	47.0	39.1	58.3
Mean Minimum Temp. (°F)	22.7	26.5	32.4	40.4	50.4	59.8	63.9	62.5	55.3	43.2	31.4	23.7	42.7
Extreme Maximum Temp. (°F)	80	82	88	93	100	108	105	102	99	95	84	75	108
Extreme Minimum Temp. (°F)	-17	0	5	10	28	40	50	46	29	12	-1	-12	-17
Days Maximum Temp. ≥ 90°F	0	0	0	0	6	18	21	17	7	0	0	0	69
Days Maximum Temp. ≤ 32°F	2	1	0	0	0	0	0	0	0	0	0	2	5
Days Minimum Temp. ≤ 32°F	28	22	15	5	0	0	0	0	0	3	16	26	115
Days Minimum Temp. ≤ 0°F	0	0	0	0	0	0	0	0	0	0	0	0	0
Heating Degree Days (base 65°F)	821	618	465	227	52	3	0	1	30	194	534	797	3,742
Cooling Degree Days (base 65°F)	0	0	0	15	114	322	410	354	184	18	0	0	1,417
Mean Precipitation (in.)	0.51	0.41	0.51	0.77	1.64	2.42	2.61	3.26	2.04	1.45	0.72	0.65	16.99
Days With ≥ 0.1" Precipitation	2	1	1	2	3	4	5	6	4	3	2	2	35
Days With ≥ 1.0" Precipitation	0	0	0	0	0	1	1	1	0	0	0	0	3
Mean Snowfall (in.)	1.9	2.4	0.8	0.2	0.0	0.0	0.0	0.0	0.0	0.2	0.9	2.7	9.1
Days With ≥ 1.0" Snow Depth	2	*0*	0	0	0	0	0	0	0	0	0	*1*	*3*

Ragland 3 SSW *Quay County*　Elevation: 5,059 ft.　Latitude: 34° 47' N　Longitude: 103° 45' W

	JAN	FEB	MAR	APR	MAY	JUN	JUL	AUG	SEP	OCT	NOV	DEC	YEAR
Mean Maximum Temp. (°F)	49.0	54.9	62.7	71.0	79.2	88.5	89.9	87.2	80.4	71.2	58.4	50.0	70.2
Mean Temp. (°F)	35.4	40.2	46.6	54.5	63.2	72.4	75.3	73.4	66.5	56.4	44.6	36.6	55.4
Mean Minimum Temp. (°F)	21.8	25.6	30.4	38.0	47.2	56.2	60.7	59.6	52.6	41.4	30.7	23.1	40.6
Extreme Maximum Temp. (°F)	77	80	88	94	98	106	105	102	100	92	84	77	106
Extreme Minimum Temp. (°F)	-13	-9	4	14	28	39	42	46	29	9	-7	-12	-13
Days Maximum Temp. ≥ 90°F	0	0	0	0	3	14	17	12	4	0	0	0	50
Days Maximum Temp. ≤ 32°F	3	2	0	0	0	0	0	0	0	0	1	3	9
Days Minimum Temp. ≤ 32°F	28	23	19	7	0	0	0	0	0	3	17	27	124
Days Minimum Temp. ≤ 0°F	1	0	0	0	0	0	0	0	0	0	0	1	2
Heating Degree Days (base 65°F)	910	693	564	313	103	10	1	1	58	267	606	874	4,400
Cooling Degree Days (base 65°F)	0	0	0	4	54	240	340	276	112	6	0	0	1,032
Mean Precipitation (in.)	0.49	0.55	0.74	1.11	1.70	2.17	3.18	3.23	2.41	1.27	0.77	0.58	18.20
Days With ≥ 0.1" Precipitation	2	2	2	2	4	4	5	6	4	3	2	2	38
Days With ≥ 1.0" Precipitation	0	0	0	0	0	1	1	1	1	0	0	0	4
Mean Snowfall (in.)	4.5	4.4	2.4	2.6	trace	0.0	0.0	0.0	0.0	0.4	1.9	4.3	20.5
Days With ≥ 1.0" Snow Depth	5	2	1	1	0	0	0	0	0	0	1	4	14

Ramon 8 SW *Lincoln County*　Elevation: 5,324 ft.　Latitude: 34° 09' N　Longitude: 105° 00' W

	JAN	FEB	MAR	APR	MAY	JUN	JUL	AUG	SEP	OCT	NOV	DEC	YEAR
Mean Maximum Temp. (°F)	51.3	57.0	64.1	71.3	79.7	88.6	90.0	87.7	81.1	71.9	60.5	52.1	71.3
Mean Temp. (°F)	36.6	40.8	46.7	53.7	62.7	71.4	74.5	72.9	66.0	55.9	44.8	37.4	55.3
Mean Minimum Temp. (°F)	21.9	24.5	29.4	36.1	45.7	54.1	59.0	58.0	50.9	39.8	29.0	22.7	39.2
Extreme Maximum Temp. (°F)	76	79	86	92	98	106	106	104	100	91	82	77	106
Extreme Minimum Temp. (°F)	-25	-8	-3	8	23	36	44	43	27	7	-11	-14	-25
Days Maximum Temp. ≥ 90°F	0	0	0	0	3	14	17	12	3	0	0	0	49
Days Maximum Temp. ≤ 32°F	2	1	0	0	0	0	0	0	0	0	0	2	5
Days Minimum Temp. ≤ 32°F	27	22	20	9	1	0	0	0	0	5	18	25	127
Days Minimum Temp. ≤ 0°F	1	0	0	0	0	0	0	0	0	0	0	1	2
Heating Degree Days (base 65°F)	872	672	558	334	111	10	0	2	54	281	600	850	4,344
Cooling Degree Days (base 65°F)	0	0	0	4	51	212	302	254	93	7	0	0	923
Mean Precipitation (in.)	0.47	0.44	0.52	0.82	1.36	1.62	1.90	2.19	1.93	1.20	0.60	0.65	13.70
Days With ≥ 0.1" Precipitation	2	1	2	2	3	3	4	5	4	2	1	2	31
Days With ≥ 1.0" Precipitation	0	0	0	0	0	0	0	0	0	0	0	0	0
Mean Snowfall (in.)	5.2	4.8	2.6	1.4	0.1	0.0	0.0	0.0	0.0	0.9	1.4	5.6	22.0
Days With ≥ 1.0" Snow Depth	3	1	0	0	0	0	0	0	0	0	0	1	5

Raton Filter Plant *Colfax County*　Elevation: 6,929 ft.　Latitude: 36° 55' N　Longitude: 104° 26' W

	JAN	FEB	MAR	APR	MAY	JUN	JUL	AUG	SEP	OCT	NOV	DEC	YEAR
Mean Maximum Temp. (°F)	44.5	47.8	53.3	59.9	68.6	78.3	82.5	79.9	73.8	64.9	52.9	45.6	62.7
Mean Temp. (°F)	31.6	34.7	39.6	46.1	55.2	64.6	68.8	67.0	60.4	50.9	40.1	33.0	49.3
Mean Minimum Temp. (°F)	18.6	21.5	25.9	32.2	41.7	50.8	55.0	53.9	46.9	36.9	27.2	20.3	35.9
Extreme Maximum Temp. (°F)	74	72	79	83	90	97	95	93	89	83	78	72	97
Extreme Minimum Temp. (°F)	-13	-14	3	7	20	31	41	40	24	5	-8	-10	-14
Days Maximum Temp. ≥ 90°F	0	0	0	0	0	2	3	0	0	0	0	0	5
Days Maximum Temp. ≤ 32°F	5	3	1	0	0	0	0	0	0	0	1	4	14
Days Minimum Temp. ≤ 32°F	30	26	25	15	3	0	0	0	1	8	21	28	157
Days Minimum Temp. ≤ 0°F	1	1	0	0	0	0	0	0	0	0	0	1	3
Heating Degree Days (base 65°F)	1,029	849	780	561	303	78	11	23	156	430	740	986	5,946
Cooling Degree Days (base 65°F)	0	0	0	0	6	69	134	91	23	0	0	0	323
Mean Precipitation (in.)	0.49	0.50	0.97	1.22	2.59	1.92	2.90	3.64	1.67	1.11	0.69	0.58	18.28
Days With ≥ 0.1" Precipitation	2	1	3	3	6	5	7	8	4	3	2	2	46
Days With ≥ 1.0" Precipitation	0	0	0	0	1	0	0	1	0	0	0	0	2
Mean Snowfall (in.)	7.0	5.7	6.0	3.3	0.7	trace	0.0	0.0	0.2	1.6	4.4	6.6	35.5
Days With ≥ 1.0" Snow Depth	3	2	1	1	0	0	0	0	0	0	1	3	11

Red River *Taos County*　Elevation: 8,674 ft.　Latitude: 36° 42' N　Longitude: 105° 24' W

	JAN	FEB	MAR	APR	MAY	JUN	JUL	AUG	SEP	OCT	NOV	DEC	YEAR
Mean Maximum Temp. (°F)	37.0	40.5	45.9	53.6	62.9	73.0	76.2	73.7	68.2	58.1	44.8	38.0	56.0
Mean Temp. (°F)	21.5	25.4	31.5	38.1	46.4	54.7	58.9	57.4	51.5	41.8	30.3	23.1	40.1
Mean Minimum Temp. (°F)	6.0	10.3	17.1	22.5	29.9	36.3	41.6	41.0	34.7	25.4	15.8	8.1	24.1
Extreme Maximum Temp. (°F)	58	61	66	76	80	88	90	84	82	80	67	60	90
Extreme Minimum Temp. (°F)	-36	-25	-15	-11	2	24	31	26	18	-2	-23	-26	-36
Days Maximum Temp. ≥ 90°F	0	0	0	0	0	0	0	0	0	0	0	0	0
Days Maximum Temp. ≤ 32°F	8	5	2	1	0	0	0	0	0	0	3	8	27
Days Minimum Temp. ≤ 32°F	31	28	30	28	22	7	0	1	11	27	29	31	245
Days Minimum Temp. ≤ 0°F	9	6	2	0	0	0	0	0	0	0	2	8	27
Heating Degree Days (base 65°F)	1,341	1,111	1,031	801	569	303	181	229	399	712	1,034	1,292	9,003
Cooling Degree Days (base 65°F)	0	0	0	0	0	0	0	0	0	0	0	0	0
Mean Precipitation (in.)	1.07	1.17	2.07	1.88	2.02	1.53	2.71	3.03	1.85	1.80	1.72	1.17	22.02
Days With ≥ 0.1" Precipitation	4	4	6	5	5	5	8	9	6	5	5	3	65
Days With ≥ 1.0" Precipitation	0	0	0	0	0	0	0	0	0	0	0	0	0
Mean Snowfall (in.)	19.6	21.4	36.0	24.8	8.9	0.2	0.0	0.0	0.9	10.9	22.8	19.4	164.9
Days With ≥ 1.0" Snow Depth	25	21	18	7	1	0	0	0	0	3	13	21	109

Redrock 1 NNE *Grant County* Elevation: 4,048 ft. Latitude: 32° 42' N Longitude: 108° 44' W

	JAN	FEB	MAR	APR	MAY	JUN	JUL	AUG	SEP	OCT	NOV	DEC	YEAR
Mean Maximum Temp. (°F)	58.2	63.1	69.2	76.9	85.2	94.7	94.7	91.7	87.4	77.6	66.5	58.3	76.9
Mean Temp. (°F)	41.8	45.8	50.7	56.7	64.7	73.9	78.6	77.0	71.1	59.9	48.3	41.7	59.2
Mean Minimum Temp. (°F)	25.3	28.4	32.2	36.5	44.2	53.0	62.5	62.2	54.8	42.2	30.1	25.0	41.4
Extreme Maximum Temp. (°F)	79	82	89	93	101	109	107	105	102	96	86	76	109
Extreme Minimum Temp. (°F)	9	8	12	20	26	34	44	46	37	20	11	-3	-3
Days Maximum Temp. ≥ 90°F	0	0	0	1	8	24	26	22	12	1	0	0	94
Days Maximum Temp. ≤ 32°F	0	0	0	0	0	0	0	0	0	0	0	0	0
Days Minimum Temp. ≤ 32°F	26	20	17	9	1	0	0	0	0	4	19	26	122
Days Minimum Temp. ≤ 0°F	0	0	0	0	0	0	0	0	0	0	0	0	0
Heating Degree Days (base 65°F)	714	538	437	248	66	3	0	0	8	170	494	716	3,394
Cooling Degree Days (base 65°F)	0	0	0	7	67	273	423	381	203	18	0	0	1,372
Mean Precipitation (in.)	0.98	0.93	0.74	0.25	0.45	0.41	2.46	2.58	1.71	1.36	0.74	1.17	13.78
Days With ≥ 0.1" Precipitation	3	3	2	1	1	2	6	5	4	3	2	3	35
Days With ≥ 1.0" Precipitation	0	0	0	0	0	0	0	1	0	0	0	0	1
Mean Snowfall (in.)	1.0	0.6	0.3	trace	trace	0.0	trace	0.0	0.0	trace	0.2	1.1	3.2
Days With ≥ 1.0" Snow Depth	0	0	0	0	0	0	0	0	0	0	0	1	1

Reserve Ranger Station *Catron County* Elevation: 5,846 ft. Latitude: 33° 43' N Longitude: 108° 47' W

	JAN	FEB	MAR	APR	MAY	JUN	JUL	AUG	SEP	OCT	NOV	DEC	YEAR
Mean Maximum Temp. (°F)	52.5	*56.1*	61.6	69.3	77.0	87.4	*88.2*	85.8	*81.0*	na	*61.0*	53.8	na
Mean Temp. (°F)	34.4	*37.2*	42.1	47.8	55.6	65.0	*70.3*	68.5	*62.4*	na	*41.6*	34.9	na
Mean Minimum Temp. (°F)	16.2	*18.5*	22.6	26.6	34.0	42.5	*52.4*	51.3	*43.9*	na	*22.1*	16.0	na
Extreme Maximum Temp. (°F)	71	79	88	91	97	104	104	101	95	90	83	75	104
Extreme Minimum Temp. (°F)	-18	-6	0	11	15	26	35	37	27	8	-7	-23	-23
Days Maximum Temp. ≥ 90°F	0	0	0	0	1	12	14	7	2	0	0	0	36
Days Maximum Temp. ≤ 32°F	0	0	0	0	0	0	0	0	0	0	0	0	0
Days Minimum Temp. ≤ 32°F	29	24	27	23	12	2	0	0	1	16	25	27	186
Days Minimum Temp. ≤ 0°F	1	0	0	0	0	0	0	0	0	0	0	1	2
Heating Degree Days (base 65°F)	943	*779*	702	509	288	66	*4*	8	*100*	na	*695*	927	na
Cooling Degree Days (base 65°F)	0	na	0	0	*3*	74	*174*	134	*31*	na	*0*	na	na
Mean Precipitation (in.)	1.07	1.11	1.10	0.47	0.64	0.72	2.42	2.94	1.98	1.79	1.22	1.21	16.67
Days With ≥ 0.1" Precipitation	3	2	3	1	2	2	6	7	5	3	2	2	38
Days With ≥ 1.0" Precipitation	0	0	0	0	0	0	0	0	0	0	0	0	0
Mean Snowfall (in.)	2.5	1.6	1.0	0.5	0.0	0.0	0.0	0.0	0.0	trace	0.2	*2.0*	7.8
Days With ≥ 1.0" Snow Depth	2	1	1	0	0	0	0	0	0	0	0	1	5

Roy *Harding County* Elevation: 5,875 ft. Latitude: 35° 57' N Longitude: 104° 12' W

	JAN	FEB	MAR	APR	MAY	JUN	JUL	AUG	SEP	OCT	NOV	DEC	YEAR
Mean Maximum Temp. (°F)	46.4	51.1	57.5	65.0	73.5	82.6	85.6	83.4	76.8	67.4	55.4	47.0	66.0
Mean Temp. (°F)	32.3	36.6	42.4	49.4	58.6	67.5	71.5	69.8	63.1	52.6	41.3	33.5	51.6
Mean Minimum Temp. (°F)	18.3	22.1	27.3	33.8	43.7	52.4	57.3	56.2	49.4	37.7	27.2	19.9	37.1
Extreme Maximum Temp. (°F)	75	78	83	86	94	101	99	96	94	89	82	77	101
Extreme Minimum Temp. (°F)	-17	-12	4	6	24	37	46	42	28	7	-15	-17	-17
Days Maximum Temp. ≥ 90°F	0	0	0	0	0	6	8	3	1	0	0	0	18
Days Maximum Temp. ≤ 32°F	4	2	0	0	0	0	0	0	0	0	1	3	10
Days Minimum Temp. ≤ 32°F	30	25	22	12	2	0	0	0	0	7	22	29	149
Days Minimum Temp. ≤ 0°F	1	1	0	0	0	0	0	0	0	0	0	1	3
Heating Degree Days (base 65°F)	1,006	794	694	462	208	42	4	9	97	379	704	971	5,370
Cooling Degree Days (base 65°F)	0	0	0	1	18	116	211	167	47	1	0	0	561
Mean Precipitation (in.)	0.37	0.43	0.75	0.89	1.85	1.99	2.81	3.33	1.79	1.07	0.54	0.48	16.30
Days With ≥ 0.1" Precipitation	1	1	2	2	4	4	6	6	4	2	1	2	35
Days With ≥ 1.0" Precipitation	0	0	0	0	0	0	1	1	0	0	0	0	2
Mean Snowfall (in.)	na	*3.6*	*0.6*	0.5	trace	0.0	trace	trace	0.0	0.1	1.2	na	na
Days With ≥ 1.0" Snow Depth	na	*2*	0	0	0	0	0	0	0	0	1	na	na

San Jon *Quay County* Elevation: 4,229 ft. Latitude: 35° 07' N Longitude: 103° 20' W

	JAN	FEB	MAR	APR	MAY	JUN	JUL	AUG	SEP	OCT	NOV	DEC	YEAR
Mean Maximum Temp. (°F)	52.3	57.7	65.6	73.4	82.1	91.3	93.4	90.9	84.2	74.4	62.1	53.2	73.4
Mean Temp. (°F)	37.8	42.6	49.8	57.6	66.8	76.1	79.5	77.4	70.3	59.6	47.4	39.1	58.7
Mean Minimum Temp. (°F)	23.3	27.5	34.0	41.7	51.5	60.9	65.5	63.9	56.4	44.7	32.7	25.0	43.9
Extreme Maximum Temp. (°F)	80	82	91	97	104	110	106	105	104	97	87	79	110
Extreme Minimum Temp. (°F)	-14	-12	7	11	29	41	50	48	32	11	-1	-13	-14
Days Maximum Temp. ≥ 90°F	0	0	0	1	6	19	24	20	9	1	0	0	80
Days Maximum Temp. ≤ 32°F	2	1	0	0	0	0	0	0	0	0	0	2	5
Days Minimum Temp. ≤ 32°F	26	20	13	5	0	0	0	0	0	3	15	25	107
Days Minimum Temp. ≤ 0°F	1	0	0	0	0	0	0	0	0	0	0	1	2
Heating Degree Days (base 65°F)	836	625	467	241	61	5	0	0	35	195	522	795	3,782
Cooling Degree Days (base 65°F)	0	0	3	25	120	338	463	395	206	34	0	0	1,584
Mean Precipitation (in.)	0.57	0.55	0.92	1.23	1.98	2.25	2.77	3.41	1.90	1.42	0.84	0.56	18.40
Days With ≥ 0.1" Precipitation	2	1	2	2	4	4	5	5	4	3	2	2	36
Days With ≥ 1.0" Precipitation	0	0	0	0	0	1	1	1	0	0	0	0	3
Mean Snowfall (in.)	5.0	3.7	2.5	1.4	trace	0.0	0.0	0.0	0.0	0.7	1.4	3.7	18.4
Days With ≥ 1.0" Snow Depth	*2*	*2*	0	0	0	0	0	0	0	0	0	*1*	5

Sandia Park　*Bernalillo County*　Elevation: 7,007 ft.　Latitude: 35° 10' N　Longitude: 106° 22' W

	JAN	FEB	MAR	APR	MAY	JUN	JUL	AUG	SEP	OCT	NOV	DEC	YEAR
Mean Maximum Temp. (°F)	43.0	47.9	53.8	62.2	71.3	82.1	84.0	80.7	74.7	64.6	51.7	43.8	63.3
Mean Temp. (°F)	30.7	35.2	40.6	47.6	56.1	65.4	68.6	66.5	60.5	50.1	38.8	31.5	49.3
Mean Minimum Temp. (°F)	18.3	22.5	27.3	33.0	40.8	48.7	53.1	52.1	46.2	35.5	26.0	19.1	35.2
Extreme Maximum Temp. (°F)	64	69	75	83	89	99	100	95	91	85	74	65	100
Extreme Minimum Temp. (°F)	-17	-6	3	5	25	32	38	39	21	6	-11	-21	-21
Days Maximum Temp. ≥ 90°F	0	0	0	0	0	5	6	1	0	0	0	0	12
Days Maximum Temp. ≤ 32°F	3	1	0	0	0	0	0	0	0	0	1	3	8
Days Minimum Temp. ≤ 32°F	30	26	25	15	3	0	0	0	1	11	24	29	164
Days Minimum Temp. ≤ 0°F	2	0	0	0	0	0	0	0	0	0	0	1	3
Heating Degree Days (base 65°F)	1,057	834	751	516	274	63	12	26	147	457	778	1,032	5,947
Cooling Degree Days (base 65°F)	0	0	0	0	5	64	114	67	13	0	0	0	263
Mean Precipitation (in.)	1.47	1.19	1.53	0.95	1.20	1.13	3.10	2.95	1.92	1.71	1.43	1.18	19.76
Days With ≥ 0.1" Precipitation	4	3	4	2	3	3	7	7	4	4	3	3	47
Days With ≥ 1.0" Precipitation	0	0	0	0	0	0	1	0	0	0	0	0	1
Mean Snowfall (in.)	15.5	11.1	10.5	5.0	0.7	trace	0.0	0.0	trace	2.8	7.5	11.3	64.4
Days With ≥ 1.0" Snow Depth	na	na	na	1	0	0	0	0	0	0	0	3	8	na

Santa Fe 2　*Santa Fe County*　Elevation: 6,715 ft.　Latitude: 35° 37' N　Longitude: 105° 59' W

	JAN	FEB	MAR	APR	MAY	JUN	JUL	AUG	SEP	OCT	NOV	DEC	YEAR
Mean Maximum Temp. (°F)	42.1	47.9	55.1	63.6	72.4	82.8	85.6	83.2	76.9	66.8	53.0	43.8	64.4
Mean Temp. (°F)	30.2	35.5	41.4	48.6	57.2	66.9	70.6	68.8	62.2	51.9	39.6	31.4	50.4
Mean Minimum Temp. (°F)	18.3	23.1	27.6	33.3	42.0	51.0	55.6	54.3	47.5	36.9	26.3	19.0	36.2
Extreme Maximum Temp. (°F)	65	73	77	84	95	99	99	95	94	87	75	65	99
Extreme Minimum Temp. (°F)	-14	-10	6	10	23	33	38	36	27	5	-12	-17	-17
Days Maximum Temp. ≥ 90°F	0	0	0	0	0	5	7	3	1	0	0	0	16
Days Maximum Temp. ≤ 32°F	4	2	0	0	0	0	0	0	0	0	1	3	10
Days Minimum Temp. ≤ 32°F	30	26	24	13	3	0	0	0	0	7	24	30	157
Days Minimum Temp. ≤ 0°F	1	0	0	0	0	0	0	0	0	0	0	1	2
Heating Degree Days (base 65°F)	1,072	827	725	487	242	42	4	9	111	402	752	1,033	5,706
Cooling Degree Days (base 65°F)	0	0	0	0	11	109	190	142	38	0	0	0	490
Mean Precipitation (in.)	0.65	0.54	0.90	0.74	1.32	1.29	2.18	2.15	1.71	1.21	1.02	0.65	14.36
Days With ≥ 0.1" Precipitation	2	2	3	2	3	3	5	6	4	3	3	2	38
Days With ≥ 1.0" Precipitation	0	0	0	0	0	0	0	0	0	0	0	0	0
Mean Snowfall (in.)	na	na	2.9	0.8	0.0	0.0	0.0	0.0	0.0	1.0	2.7	3.6	na
Days With ≥ 1.0" Snow Depth	na	na	1	0	0	0	0	0	0	0	1	2	na

Santa Rosa　*Guadalupe County*　Elevation: 4,599 ft.　Latitude: 34° 56' N　Longitude: 104° 41' W

	JAN	FEB	MAR	APR	MAY	JUN	JUL	AUG	SEP	OCT	NOV	DEC	YEAR
Mean Maximum Temp. (°F)	54.1	59.4	66.3	73.7	82.2	90.7	92.2	90.1	84.2	75.3	62.9	54.6	73.8
Mean Temp. (°F)	39.4	43.6	49.8	56.9	65.7	74.2	77.3	75.5	69.0	58.7	47.7	40.1	58.2
Mean Minimum Temp. (°F)	24.8	27.9	33.2	40.1	49.1	57.6	62.4	60.8	53.8	42.2	32.4	25.6	42.5
Extreme Maximum Temp. (°F)	81	86	89	94	98	109	106	104	100	95	85	79	109
Extreme Minimum Temp. (°F)	-19	-3	6	13	32	38	49	46	29	15	3	-17	-19
Days Maximum Temp. ≥ 90°F	0	0	0	0	4	18	23	18	6	1	0	0	70
Days Maximum Temp. ≤ 32°F	2	1	0	0	0	0	0	0	0	0	0	1	4
Days Minimum Temp. ≤ 32°F	25	19	15	5	0	0	0	0	0	3	16	24	107
Days Minimum Temp. ≤ 0°F	0	0	0	0	0	0	0	0	0	0	0	0	0
Heating Degree Days (base 65°F)	786	597	466	245	60	3	0	0	27	202	514	765	3,665
Cooling Degree Days (base 65°F)	0	0	0	10	87	282	392	335	158	12	1	0	1,277
Mean Precipitation (in.)	0.42	0.44	0.60	0.90	1.41	1.70	2.43	2.90	1.92	1.13	0.83	0.71	15.39
Days With ≥ 0.1" Precipitation	2	1	2	2	3	4	5	6	4	3	2	2	36
Days With ≥ 1.0" Precipitation	0	0	0	0	0	0	1	1	0	0	0	0	2
Mean Snowfall (in.)	3.2	2.8	1.1	1.0	0.1	0.0	0.0	trace	0.0	0.6	1.7	4.4	14.9
Days With ≥ 1.0" Snow Depth	2	1	0	0	0	0	0	0	0	0	1	3	7

Socorro　*Socorro County*　Elevation: 4,583 ft.　Latitude: 34° 05' N　Longitude: 106° 53' W

	JAN	FEB	MAR	APR	MAY	JUN	JUL	AUG	SEP	OCT	NOV	DEC	YEAR
Mean Maximum Temp. (°F)	53.0	60.3	67.8	75.5	83.3	92.1	93.2	90.5	84.7	75.3	62.5	52.7	74.2
Mean Temp. (°F)	37.1	42.9	49.6	56.4	64.5	73.0	76.7	74.6	67.8	57.1	45.2	37.5	56.9
Mean Minimum Temp. (°F)	21.2	25.5	31.3	37.2	45.9	53.8	60.1	58.6	50.7	39.0	27.9	22.3	39.5
Extreme Maximum Temp. (°F)	76	81	88	95	101	109	107	103	100	91	82	75	109
Extreme Minimum Temp. (°F)	-12	2	9	17	23	35	45	43	34	14	-13	-6	-13
Days Maximum Temp. ≥ 90°F	0	0	0	0	5	21	24	19	7	0	0	0	76
Days Maximum Temp. ≤ 32°F	1	0	0	0	0	0	0	0	0	0	0	1	2
Days Minimum Temp. ≤ 32°F	27	22	18	9	1	0	0	0	0	6	22	27	132
Days Minimum Temp. ≤ 0°F	0	0	0	0	0	0	0	0	0	0	0	0	0
Heating Degree Days (base 65°F)	858	617	471	259	70	3	0	0	30	243	587	847	3,985
Cooling Degree Days (base 65°F)	0	0	0	11	75	261	380	324	131	7	0	0	1,189
Mean Precipitation (in.)	0.35	0.37	0.34	0.34	0.52	0.60	1.48	2.23	1.65	1.16	0.47	0.56	10.07
Days With ≥ 0.1" Precipitation	1	1	1	1	1	1	4	5	4	3	1	2	25
Days With ≥ 1.0" Precipitation	0	0	0	0	0	0	0	0	0	0	0	0	0
Mean Snowfall (in.)	1.0	1.7	0.3	0.2	0.0	0.0	0.0	0.0	0.0	0.4	0.7	3.2	7.5
Days With ≥ 1.0" Snow Depth	1	0	0	0	0	0	0	0	0	0	0	2	3

Springer *Colfax County*   Elevation: 5,921 ft.   Latitude: 36° 22' N   Longitude: 104° 36' W

	JAN	FEB	MAR	APR	MAY	JUN	JUL	AUG	SEP	OCT	NOV	DEC	YEAR
Mean Maximum Temp. (°F)	47.8	53.5	60.4	67.0	75.4	84.9	87.8	85.6	79.9	70.8	57.3	48.0	68.2
Mean Temp. (°F)	30.5	35.5	42.2	48.9	58.0	66.9	70.8	69.2	62.6	51.9	39.8	31.1	50.6
Mean Minimum Temp. (°F)	13.2	17.5	24.0	30.7	40.5	48.9	53.8	52.7	45.3	32.9	22.1	14.1	33.0
Extreme Maximum Temp. (°F)	74	78	84	90	95	104	103	99	96	90	82	78	104
Extreme Minimum Temp. (°F)	-27	-26	-3	5	17	31	35	41	21	-5	-22	-27	-27
Days Maximum Temp. ≥ 90°F	0	0	0	0	1	9	13	7	2	0	0	0	32
Days Maximum Temp. ≤ 32°F	4	1	0	0	0	0	0	0	0	0	1	3	9
Days Minimum Temp. ≤ 32°F	30	27	27	18	4	0	0	0	1	15	27	30	179
Days Minimum Temp. ≤ 0°F	3	1	0	0	0	0	0	0	0	0	0	3	7
Heating Degree Days (base 65°F)	1,062	826	699	478	222	36	3	5	101	401	751	1,045	5,629
Cooling Degree Days (base 65°F)	0	0	0	0	11	91	187	140	36	0	0	0	465
Mean Precipitation (in.)	0.34	0.35	0.76	0.99	1.96	2.00	2.51	3.37	2.08	1.07	0.67	0.34	16.44
Days With ≥ 0.1" Precipitation	1	1	2	2	4	4	6	7	4	3	2	1	37
Days With ≥ 1.0" Precipitation	0	0	0	0	0	0	1	1	1	0	0	0	3
Mean Snowfall (in.)	4.3	4.2	5.0	2.6	0.8	trace	0.0	0.0	trace	2.0	3.2	5.2	27.3
Days With ≥ 1.0" Snow Depth	5	3	1	1	0	0	0	0	0	0	0	2	5	17

Stanley 1 NNE *Santa Fe County*   Elevation: 6,377 ft.   Latitude: 35° 10' N   Longitude: 105° 58' W

	JAN	FEB	MAR	APR	MAY	JUN	JUL	AUG	SEP	OCT	NOV	DEC	YEAR
Mean Maximum Temp. (°F)	42.6	49.2	56.8	64.5	74.0	83.9	86.6	83.8	77.7	67.6	54.1	44.6	65.5
Mean Temp. (°F)	29.3	34.6	40.9	47.5	56.7	66.0	70.1	68.1	61.3	50.4	38.9	30.3	49.5
Mean Minimum Temp. (°F)	15.8	20.0	24.9	30.4	39.4	48.1	53.5	52.4	44.7	33.2	23.7	15.9	33.5
Extreme Maximum Temp. (°F)	65	70	79	85	92	101	100	98	92	86	75	67	101
Extreme Minimum Temp. (°F)	-30	-15	0	7	12	31	40	38	22	3	-18	-18	-30
Days Maximum Temp. ≥ 90°F	0	0	0	0	0	7	10	4	0	0	0	0	21
Days Maximum Temp. ≤ 32°F	4	2	0	0	0	0	0	0	0	0	1	4	11
Days Minimum Temp. ≤ 32°F	31	27	27	18	5	0	0	0	1	14	26	31	180
Days Minimum Temp. ≤ 0°F	2	1	0	0	0	0	0	0	0	0	0	2	5
Heating Degree Days (base 65°F)	1,102	852	740	520	257	50	4	13	130	446	775	1,069	5,958
Cooling Degree Days (base 65°F)	0	0	0	0	9	86	166	120	23	0	0	0	404
Mean Precipitation (in.)	0.50	0.36	0.59	0.59	1.12	1.41	2.30	2.71	1.57	1.32	0.68	0.49	13.64
Days With ≥ 0.1" Precipitation	2	2	2	2	3	3	6	7	4	3	2	2	38
Days With ≥ 1.0" Precipitation	0	0	0	0	0	0	0	0	0	0	0	0	0
Mean Snowfall (in.)	4.4	4.0	2.7	1.5	0.1	0.0	0.0	0.0	trace	0.8	2.7	4.4	20.6
Days With ≥ 1.0" Snow Depth	10	4	2	1	0	0	0	0	0	0	2	7	26

Star Lake *McKinley County*   Elevation: 6,633 ft.   Latitude: 35° 56' N   Longitude: 107° 28' W

	JAN	FEB	MAR	APR	MAY	JUN	JUL	AUG	SEP	OCT	NOV	DEC	YEAR
Mean Maximum Temp. (°F)	40.0	46.4	55.2	63.7	73.1	83.7	86.9	84.2	77.5	66.2	52.1	42.3	64.3
Mean Temp. (°F)	25.2	32.0	39.0	45.6	54.8	64.4	69.8	68.0	60.5	48.6	36.3	27.0	47.6
Mean Minimum Temp. (°F)	10.3	17.7	22.8	27.4	36.3	45.0	52.7	51.8	43.4	30.9	20.5	11.5	30.9
Extreme Maximum Temp. (°F)	64	69	76	83	94	97	98	99	96	89	75	70	99
Extreme Minimum Temp. (°F)	-38	-24	-15	6	13	25	37	33	22	6	-28	-36	-38
Days Maximum Temp. ≥ 90°F	0	0	0	0	0	6	9	4	0	0	0	0	19
Days Maximum Temp. ≤ 32°F	6	2	0	0	0	0	0	0	0	0	1	4	13
Days Minimum Temp. ≤ 32°F	31	27	28	22	9	1	0	0	2	18	28	30	196
Days Minimum Temp. ≤ 0°F	6	1	0	0	0	0	0	0	0	0	1	4	12
Heating Degree Days (base 65°F)	1,229	924	799	576	313	75	3	12	146	502	854	1,173	6,606
Cooling Degree Days (base 65°F)	0	0	0	0	2	60	150	114	16	0	0	0	342
Mean Precipitation (in.)	0.51	0.36	0.52	0.53	0.63	0.63	1.43	1.80	1.28	0.94	0.73	0.54	9.90
Days With ≥ 0.1" Precipitation	2	1	2	2	2	2	4	5	3	3	2	2	30
Days With ≥ 1.0" Precipitation	0	0	0	0	0	0	0	0	0	0	0	0	0
Mean Snowfall (in.)	5.9	3.5	2.7	1.0	0.7	0.0	0.0	0.0	trace	0.8	2.1	4.5	21.2
Days With ≥ 1.0" Snow Depth	14	7	1	0	0	0	0	0	0	0	1	7	30

State University *Dona Ana County*   Elevation: 3,877 ft.   Latitude: 32° 17' N   Longitude: 106° 46' W

	JAN	FEB	MAR	APR	MAY	JUN	JUL	AUG	SEP	OCT	NOV	DEC	YEAR
Mean Maximum Temp. (°F)	57.9	63.5	70.0	77.0	85.4	94.4	94.7	91.7	86.9	78.1	66.8	57.9	77.0
Mean Temp. (°F)	43.1	47.6	53.6	60.1	68.6	77.8	80.9	78.4	72.7	62.0	50.6	43.2	61.5
Mean Minimum Temp. (°F)	28.2	31.8	37.1	43.1	51.8	61.0	67.0	65.1	58.4	45.9	34.2	28.4	46.0
Extreme Maximum Temp. (°F)	78	84	90	96	101	110	107	104	100	93	87	77	110
Extreme Minimum Temp. (°F)	7	12	13	24	32	43	55	51	42	22	-4	5	-4
Days Maximum Temp. ≥ 90°F	0	0	0	1	8	24	26	22	12	1	0	0	94
Days Maximum Temp. ≤ 32°F	0	0	0	0	0	0	0	0	0	0	0	0	0
Days Minimum Temp. ≤ 32°F	24	16	7	2	0	0	0	0	0	1	12	23	85
Days Minimum Temp. ≤ 0°F	0	0	0	0	0	0	0	0	0	0	0	0	0
Heating Degree Days (base 65°F)	673	483	349	165	27	0	0	0	9	128	426	669	2,929
Cooling Degree Days (base 65°F)	0	0	1	28	166	403	510	441	261	45	0	0	1,855
Mean Precipitation (in.)	0.55	0.33	0.22	0.23	0.37	0.55	1.43	2.37	1.34	1.02	0.45	0.79	9.65
Days With ≥ 0.1" Precipitation	2	1	1	1	1	1	3	5	3	3	1	2	24
Days With ≥ 1.0" Precipitation	0	0	0	0	0	0	0	1	0	0	0	0	1
Mean Snowfall (in.)	1.4	0.4	trace	0.2	0.0	0.0	0.0	0.0	0.0	trace	0.5	1.5	4.0
Days With ≥ 1.0" Snow Depth	1	0	0	0	0	0	0	0	0	0	0	1	2

Sumner Lake *Debaca County*   Elevation: 4,304 ft.   Latitude: 34° 36' N   Longitude: 104° 23' W

	JAN	FEB	MAR	APR	MAY	JUN	JUL	AUG	SEP	OCT	NOV	DEC	YEAR
Mean Maximum Temp. (°F)	51.4	57.0	64.3	72.4	81.0	90.4	92.5	90.1	83.4	73.7	61.6	52.9	72.6
Mean Temp. (°F)	36.8	41.9	48.5	56.3	65.5	74.6	78.0	76.0	69.0	57.9	46.5	38.2	57.4
Mean Minimum Temp. (°F)	22.1	26.8	32.6	40.2	49.9	58.8	63.5	61.9	54.6	42.1	31.4	23.5	42.3
Extreme Maximum Temp. (°F)	78	81	92	95	102	111	108	105	101	93	84	78	111
Extreme Minimum Temp. (°F)	-26	-2	10	21	30	42	53	45	31	12	-3	-12	-26
Days Maximum Temp. ≥ 90°F	0	0	0	1	5	18	23	19	7	1	0	0	74
Days Maximum Temp. ≤ 32°F	2	2	0	0	0	0	0	0	0	0	0	2	6
Days Minimum Temp. ≤ 32°F	28	22	15	4	0	0	0	0	0	3	17	26	115
Days Minimum Temp. ≤ 0°F	0	0	0	0	0	0	0	0	0	0	0	1	1
Heating Degree Days (base 65°F)	867	646	507	265	73	6	0	1	36	229	547	824	4,001
Cooling Degree Days (base 65°F)	0	0	1	12	105	307	419	355	168	16	0	0	1,383
Mean Precipitation (in.)	0.39	0.42	0.54	0.80	1.75	1.81	2.24	2.85	1.77	1.18	0.65	0.59	14.99
Days With ≥ 0.1" Precipitation	1	2	1	2	3	3	4	6	4	2	1	2	31
Days With ≥ 1.0" Precipitation	0	0	0	0	0	0	0	1	0	0	0	0	1
Mean Snowfall (in.)	na	na	0.2	0.2	0.0	0.0	0.0	0.0	0.0	trace	trace	1.7	na
Days With ≥ 1.0" Snow Depth	na	na	0	0	0	0	0	0	0	0	0	na	na

Taos *Taos County*   Elevation: 6,961 ft.   Latitude: 36° 23' N   Longitude: 105° 35' W

	JAN	FEB	MAR	APR	MAY	JUN	JUL	AUG	SEP	OCT	NOV	DEC	YEAR
Mean Maximum Temp. (°F)	40.2	45.4	52.8	61.4	70.6	81.2	85.0	82.4	76.0	64.9	50.8	41.9	62.7
Mean Temp. (°F)	24.7	30.8	38.2	45.2	54.0	63.5	68.0	66.2	59.4	48.3	35.9	26.7	46.8
Mean Minimum Temp. (°F)	9.2	16.3	23.6	28.9	37.4	45.7	51.0	50.1	42.7	31.7	21.0	11.4	30.7
Extreme Maximum Temp. (°F)	63	68	76	81	88	97	97	92	93	85	72	65	97
Extreme Minimum Temp. (°F)	-27	-21	-5	4	18	29	37	38	23	0	-21	-27	-27
Days Maximum Temp. ≥ 90°F	0	0	0	0	0	3	5	2	0	0	0	0	10
Days Maximum Temp. ≤ 32°F	5	2	0	0	0	0	0	0	0	0	1	4	12
Days Minimum Temp. ≤ 32°F	31	28	28	21	7	0	0	0	1	17	28	31	192
Days Minimum Temp. ≤ 0°F	7	2	0	0	0	0	0	0	0	0	0	4	13
Heating Degree Days (base 65°F)	1,243	957	824	588	336	86	10	25	171	510	866	1,181	6,797
Cooling Degree Days (base 65°F)	0	0	0	0	2	49	113	76	11	0	0	0	251
Mean Precipitation (in.)	0.58	0.55	0.86	0.78	1.18	0.92	1.40	1.89	1.40	1.19	0.92	0.64	12.31
Days With ≥ 0.1" Precipitation	2	2	3	2	4	2	4	5	3	3	3	2	35
Days With ≥ 1.0" Precipitation	0	0	0	0	0	0	0	0	0	0	0	0	0
Mean Snowfall (in.)	8.4	6.0	5.8	2.4	0.5	0.0	0.0	0.0	trace	0.9	4.3	7.8	36.1
Days With ≥ 1.0" Snow Depth	16	8	3	1	0	0	0	0	0	1	3	9	41

Tatum *Lea County*   Elevation: 4,097 ft.   Latitude: 33° 16' N   Longitude: 103° 19' W

	JAN	FEB	MAR	APR	MAY	JUN	JUL	AUG	SEP	OCT	NOV	DEC	YEAR
Mean Maximum Temp. (°F)	54.5	60.2	67.6	75.0	83.0	90.9	91.7	89.8	83.6	75.1	63.6	55.5	74.2
Mean Temp. (°F)	38.6	43.1	49.6	57.1	66.1	74.4	76.7	74.9	68.6	58.4	47.1	39.5	57.8
Mean Minimum Temp. (°F)	22.6	25.9	31.5	39.1	49.1	57.8	61.7	60.0	53.5	41.7	30.4	23.5	41.4
Extreme Maximum Temp. (°F)	81	86	92	97	103	115	110	104	103	98	85	78	115
Extreme Minimum Temp. (°F)	-11	-1	3	10	27	39	49	46	28	11	1	-8	-11
Days Maximum Temp. ≥ 90°F	0	0	0	1	7	18	21	18	8	1	0	0	74
Days Maximum Temp. ≤ 32°F	2	1	0	0	0	0	0	0	0	0	0	2	5
Days Minimum Temp. ≤ 32°F	28	22	17	6	0	0	0	0	0	4	18	27	122
Days Minimum Temp. ≤ 0°F	0	0	0	0	0	0	0	0	0	0	0	0	0
Heating Degree Days (base 65°F)	811	613	475	249	63	5	0	1	44	215	533	784	3,793
Cooling Degree Days (base 65°F)	0	0	1	15	107	302	393	343	172	19	0	0	1,352
Mean Precipitation (in.)	0.36	0.38	0.53	0.52	2.07	2.14	2.45	2.87	2.78	1.39	0.65	0.53	16.67
Days With ≥ 0.1" Precipitation	1	1	1	1	4	4	4	5	4	2	1	1	29
Days With ≥ 1.0" Precipitation	0	0	0	0	1	1	1	1	1	0	0	0	5
Mean Snowfall (in.)	0.8	1.4	0.5	0.6	0.0	0.0	0.0	0.0	0.0	trace	0.3	na	na
Days With ≥ 1.0" Snow Depth	0	na	0	0	0	0	0	0	0	0	0	na	na

Tierra Amarilla 4 N *Rio Arriba County*   Elevation: 7,463 ft.   Latitude: 36° 46' N   Longitude: 106° 33' W

	JAN	FEB	MAR	APR	MAY	JUN	JUL	AUG	SEP	OCT	NOV	DEC	YEAR
Mean Maximum Temp. (°F)	38.4	43.4	50.2	58.3	67.6	77.8	82.0	79.7	73.2	63.2	48.7	39.8	60.2
Mean Temp. (°F)	21.1	26.5	34.1	41.0	49.4	57.6	63.6	62.4	54.9	45.0	32.5	23.4	42.6
Mean Minimum Temp. (°F)	3.8	9.6	18.0	23.8	31.1	37.4	45.2	44.9	36.6	26.7	16.3	6.9	25.0
Extreme Maximum Temp. (°F)	60	64	74	78	84	95	95	91	89	85	72	66	95
Extreme Minimum Temp. (°F)	-39	-28	-10	-9	12	21	31	31	19	5	-19	-31	-39
Days Maximum Temp. ≥ 90°F	0	0	0	0	0	1	1	1	0	0	0	0	3
Days Maximum Temp. ≤ 32°F	6	2	1	0	0	0	0	0	0	0	2	5	16
Days Minimum Temp. ≤ 32°F	30	28	30	26	18	6	0	0	8	24	27	30	227
Days Minimum Temp. ≤ 0°F	11	5	1	0	0	0	0	0	0	0	2	8	27
Heating Degree Days (base 65°F)	1,353	1,082	950	713	478	218	59	87	297	614	973	1,283	8,107
Cooling Degree Days (base 65°F)	0	0	0	0	0	3	21	13	0	0	0	0	37
Mean Precipitation (in.)	1.16	1.09	1.29	1.00	1.34	0.83	1.93	2.65	1.90	1.39	1.25	0.89	16.72
Days With ≥ 0.1" Precipitation	3	3	4	3	4	3	5	7	5	4	3	2	46
Days With ≥ 1.0" Precipitation	0	0	0	0	0	0	0	0	0	0	0	0	0
Mean Snowfall (in.)	12.1	11.6	10.8	4.6	0.3	0.0	0.0	0.0	trace	2.4	10.8	11.8	64.4
Days With ≥ 1.0" Snow Depth	20	14	9	1	0	0	0	0	0	1	5	12	62

Torreon Navajo Mission *Sandoval County*   Elevation: 6,699 ft.   Latitude: 35° 48' N   Longitude: 107° 11' W

	JAN	FEB	MAR	APR	MAY	JUN	JUL	AUG	SEP	OCT	NOV	DEC	YEAR
Mean Maximum Temp. (°F)	41.7	47.8	56.9	65.6	75.1	86.2	88.8	85.8	78.8	67.5	52.8	43.3	65.9
Mean Temp. (°F)	28.5	34.3	41.2	48.4	57.5	67.6	72.2	70.1	62.8	51.2	38.4	29.8	50.2
Mean Minimum Temp. (°F)	15.2	20.7	25.5	31.0	39.9	48.8	55.6	54.5	46.8	34.8	23.8	16.1	34.4
Extreme Maximum Temp. (°F)	68	70	79	86	93	101	101	99	93	86	79	67	101
Extreme Minimum Temp. (°F)	-33	-14	-2	9	20	29	41	37	26	11	-21	-18	-33
Days Maximum Temp. ≥ 90°F	0	0	0	0	0	11	15	7	1	0	0	0	34
Days Maximum Temp. ≤ 32°F	5	2	0	0	0	0	0	0	0	0	1	3	11
Days Minimum Temp. ≤ 32°F	30	27	25	17	5	0	0	0	1	11	26	30	172
Days Minimum Temp. ≤ 0°F	3	1	0	0	0	0	0	0	0	0	0	1	5
Heating Degree Days (base 65°F)	1,124	861	731	493	232	37	1	6	98	421	794	1,088	5,886
Cooling Degree Days (base 65°F)	0	0	0	0	9	120	233	184	41	0	0	0	587
Mean Precipitation (in.)	0.59	0.43	0.64	0.62	0.80	0.58	1.64	1.88	1.29	1.03	0.76	0.46	10.72
Days With ≥ 0.1" Precipitation	2	2	2	2	2	2	5	5	4	3	2	2	33
Days With ≥ 1.0" Precipitation	0	0	0	0	0	0	0	0	0	0	0	0	0
Mean Snowfall (in.)	5.9	3.7	2.4	1.3	0.4	0.0	0.0	0.0	0.0	0.6	2.1	4.2	20.6
Days With ≥ 1.0" Snow Depth	8	3	1	0	0	0	0	0	0	0	1	5	18

Tucumcari 4 NE *Quay County*   Elevation: 4,084 ft.   Latitude: 35° 12' N   Longitude: 103° 41' W

	JAN	FEB	MAR	APR	MAY	JUN	JUL	AUG	SEP	OCT	NOV	DEC	YEAR
Mean Maximum Temp. (°F)	53.1	58.3	65.7	73.1	81.5	90.5	93.3	90.9	84.3	74.7	62.5	54.1	73.5
Mean Temp. (°F)	38.4	43.1	50.0	57.3	66.4	75.3	78.9	76.9	69.9	59.4	48.0	39.7	58.6
Mean Minimum Temp. (°F)	23.6	28.0	34.2	41.6	51.2	60.1	64.5	62.8	55.5	44.1	33.3	25.2	43.7
Extreme Maximum Temp. (°F)	80	83	92	97	100	109	107	107	104	95	87	82	109
Extreme Minimum Temp. (°F)	-10	-4	6	14	31	43	52	49	30	12	-2	-12	-12
Days Maximum Temp. ≥ 90°F	0	0	0	1	5	17	24	20	9	1	0	0	77
Days Maximum Temp. ≤ 32°F	2	1	0	0	0	0	0	0	0	0	0	2	5
Days Minimum Temp. ≤ 32°F	27	20	13	4	0	0	0	0	0	2	14	25	105
Days Minimum Temp. ≤ 0°F	0	0	0	0	0	0	0	0	0	0	0	0	0
Heating Degree Days (base 65°F)	818	610	461	245	64	6	0	1	38	197	506	779	3,725
Cooling Degree Days (base 65°F)	0	0	2	21	106	313	440	375	190	28	1	0	1,476
Mean Precipitation (in.)	0.41	0.44	0.79	1.16	1.82	2.19	2.66	2.82	1.77	1.37	0.74	0.50	16.67
Days With ≥ 0.1" Precipitation	1	1	2	3	4	5	5	5	3	3	2	1	35
Days With ≥ 1.0" Precipitation	0	0	0	0	0	1	1	1	0	0	0	0	3
Mean Snowfall (in.)	na	3.6	1.9	1.6	0.0	0.0	0.0	0.0	0.0	0.5	1.1	3.9	na
Days With ≥ 1.0" Snow Depth	na	2	1	1	0	0	0	0	0	0	1	3	na

Tularosa *Otero County*   Elevation: 4,429 ft.   Latitude: 33° 04' N   Longitude: 106° 02' W

	JAN	FEB	MAR	APR	MAY	JUN	JUL	AUG	SEP	OCT	NOV	DEC	YEAR
Mean Maximum Temp. (°F)	56.6	61.5	68.8	75.9	84.0	93.0	92.8	90.7	85.2	75.7	64.0	55.7	75.3
Mean Temp. (°F)	42.4	46.9	53.0	59.6	67.9	76.4	78.2	76.5	70.8	60.9	49.6	42.1	60.4
Mean Minimum Temp. (°F)	28.0	32.2	37.1	43.1	51.9	59.8	63.5	62.3	56.5	45.9	35.3	28.7	45.4
Extreme Maximum Temp. (°F)	87	81	90	95	101	110	107	102	100	90	84	74	110
Extreme Minimum Temp. (°F)	1	5	14	21	27	44	49	50	39	21	0	4	0
Days Maximum Temp. ≥ 90°F	0	0	0	1	6	22	24	21	8	0	0	0	82
Days Maximum Temp. ≤ 32°F	0	0	0	0	0	0	0	0	0	0	0	0	0
Days Minimum Temp. ≤ 32°F	23	15	9	3	0	0	0	0	0	1	10	22	83
Days Minimum Temp. ≤ 0°F	0	0	0	0	0	0	0	0	0	0	0	0	0
Heating Degree Days (base 65°F)	694	505	368	177	34	1	0	0	14	144	445	702	3,084
Cooling Degree Days (base 65°F)	0	0	2	24	139	350	421	369	198	28	0	0	1,531
Mean Precipitation (in.)	0.54	0.50	0.41	0.28	0.61	0.71	1.90	2.02	1.39	1.25	0.68	0.93	11.22
Days With ≥ 0.1" Precipitation	2	2	1	1	2	2	5	5	4	2	2	3	31
Days With ≥ 1.0" Precipitation	0	0	0	0	0	0	0	0	0	0	0	0	0
Mean Snowfall (in.)	0.3	0.4	trace	trace	0.0	0.0	0.0	0.0	0.0	0.0	0.4	0.3	1.4
Days With ≥ 1.0" Snow Depth	0	0	0	0	0	0	0	0	0	0	0	0	0

Valmora *Mora County*   Elevation: 6,309 ft.   Latitude: 35° 49' N   Longitude: 104° 56' W

	JAN	FEB	MAR	APR	MAY	JUN	JUL	AUG	SEP	OCT	NOV	DEC	YEAR
Mean Maximum Temp. (°F)	48.2	52.4	57.6	64.0	72.6	82.0	85.2	82.9	77.1	68.7	57.7	50.0	66.5
Mean Temp. (°F)	31.1	35.0	40.5	46.7	55.4	64.3	68.7	66.9	60.3	50.3	40.1	32.5	49.3
Mean Minimum Temp. (°F)	13.9	17.6	23.3	29.3	38.2	46.6	52.3	51.0	43.5	31.7	22.4	14.9	32.0
Extreme Maximum Temp. (°F)	75	79	82	86	92	101	98	96	94	87	79	77	101
Extreme Minimum Temp. (°F)	-30	-26	-10	6	12	31	41	36	19	3	-13	-25	-30
Days Maximum Temp. ≥ 90°F	0	0	0	0	0	5	7	3	1	0	0	0	16
Days Maximum Temp. ≤ 32°F	3	1	1	0	0	0	0	0	0	0	1	2	8
Days Minimum Temp. ≤ 32°F	30	27	28	20	6	0	0	0	2	18	27	30	188
Days Minimum Temp. ≤ 0°F	3	1	0	0	0	0	0	0	0	0	0	2	6
Heating Degree Days (base 65°F)	1,045	837	753	543	294	72	8	19	149	450	741	1,001	5,912
Cooling Degree Days (base 65°F)	0	0	0	0	0	5	60	137	94	16	0	0	312
Mean Precipitation (in.)	0.44	0.45	0.78	1.01	2.08	1.88	3.46	3.24	2.17	1.05	0.75	0.56	17.87
Days With ≥ 0.1" Precipitation	1	1	2	2	4	4	7	7	4	3	2	2	39
Days With ≥ 1.0" Precipitation	0	0	0	0	0	0	1	1	1	0	0	0	3
Mean Snowfall (in.)	5.7	4.8	5.5	3.8	trace	0.0	0.0	0.0	0.0	2.2	2.7	6.4	31.1
Days With ≥ 1.0" Snow Depth	4	2	2	1	0	0	0	0	0	0	1	4	14

White Sands Nat'l Monument *Otero County*   Elevation: 3,992 ft.   Latitude: 32° 47' N   Longitude: 106° 11' W

	JAN	FEB	MAR	APR	MAY	JUN	JUL	AUG	SEP	OCT	NOV	DEC	YEAR
Mean Maximum Temp. (°F)	57.1	63.3	70.9	79.0	87.8	96.6	96.9	93.9	88.5	78.6	65.8	56.7	77.9
Mean Temp. (°F)	39.9	44.8	51.2	58.7	68.0	77.3	80.2	77.5	71.3	59.6	47.2	39.3	59.6
Mean Minimum Temp. (°F)	22.7	26.3	31.4	38.4	48.2	57.8	63.4	61.1	54.0	40.5	28.2	21.9	41.2
Extreme Maximum Temp. (°F)	78	83	89	96	103	111	110	106	103	94	84	75	111
Extreme Minimum Temp. (°F)	-5	4	0	16	24	36	49	49	34	13	-12	-5	-12
Days Maximum Temp. ≥ 90°F	0	0	0	1	13	27	28	25	14	2	0	0	110
Days Maximum Temp. ≤ 32°F	0	0	0	0	0	0	0	0	0	0	0	0	0
Days Minimum Temp. ≤ 32°F	27	21	17	9	1	0	0	0	0	6	21	27	129
Days Minimum Temp. ≤ 0°F	0	0	0	0	0	0	0	0	0	0	0	0	0
Heating Degree Days (base 65°F)	770	563	423	204	36	1	0	0	14	184	528	789	3,512
Cooling Degree Days (base 65°F)	0	0	1	25	140	377	474	402	209	23	0	0	1,651
Mean Precipitation (in.)	0.59	0.38	0.28	0.29	0.49	0.82	1.41	2.09	1.40	1.05	0.56	0.84	10.20
Days With ≥ 0.1" Precipitation	2	1	1	1	2	2	4	5	3	3	2	2	28
Days With ≥ 1.0" Precipitation	0	0	0	0	0	0	0	1	0	0	0	0	1
Mean Snowfall (in.)	1.3	0.3	trace	0.0	0.0	0.0	0.0	0.0	0.0	trace	0.3	1.4	3.3
Days With ≥ 1.0" Snow Depth	*0*	0	0	0	0	0	0	0	0	0	0	1	*1*

White Signal *Grant County*   Elevation: 6,066 ft.   Latitude: 32° 33' N   Longitude: 108° 22' W

	JAN	FEB	MAR	APR	MAY	JUN	JUL	AUG	SEP	OCT	NOV	DEC	YEAR
Mean Maximum Temp. (°F)	51.2	55.2	60.9	68.8	77.6	87.1	86.4	83.4	78.9	70.1	59.0	51.5	69.2
Mean Temp. (°F)	37.4	41.0	45.3	51.9	60.7	70.2	72.5	70.0	64.4	54.5	43.8	37.9	54.1
Mean Minimum Temp. (°F)	23.7	26.7	30.0	34.8	43.6	53.3	58.6	56.5	49.8	38.9	28.8	24.1	39.1
Extreme Maximum Temp. (°F)	73	75	81	86	94	103	102	98	98	91	79	72	103
Extreme Minimum Temp. (°F)	-9	5	5	17	17	35	44	45	32	13	9	-7	-9
Days Maximum Temp. ≥ 90°F	0	0	0	0	1	11	10	3	1	0	0	0	26
Days Maximum Temp. ≤ 32°F	0	0	0	0	0	0	0	0	0	0	0	1	1
Days Minimum Temp. ≤ 32°F	28	22	20	13	2	0	0	0	0	6	21	26	138
Days Minimum Temp. ≤ 0°F	0	0	0	0	0	0	0	0	0	0	0	0	0
Heating Degree Days (base 65°F)	847	672	603	390	153	15	2	6	70	322	627	834	4,541
Cooling Degree Days (base 65°F)	0	0	0	3	29	176	225	161	51	2	0	0	647
Mean Precipitation (in.)	1.31	1.14	0.87	0.32	0.52	0.60	3.07	2.83	1.79	1.48	1.05	1.58	16.56
Days With ≥ 0.1" Precipitation	3	3	3	1	1	2	7	6	4	3	2	3	38
Days With ≥ 1.0" Precipitation	0	0	0	0	0	0	1	1	0	0	0	0	2
Mean Snowfall (in.)	4.1	*3.6*	2.3	0.4	trace	0.0	0.0	0.0	0.0	0.5	1.2	3.3	*15.4*
Days With ≥ 1.0" Snow Depth	na	na	*0*	0	0	0	0	0	0	0	0	*1*	na

Winston *Sierra County*   Elevation: 6,194 ft.   Latitude: 33° 21' N   Longitude: 107° 39' W

	JAN	FEB	MAR	APR	MAY	JUN	JUL	AUG	SEP	OCT	NOV	DEC	YEAR
Mean Maximum Temp. (°F)	52.7	57.0	62.1	69.5	77.5	87.1	86.7	83.4	79.1	71.3	60.9	52.5	70.0
Mean Temp. (°F)	35.8	40.2	44.4	50.6	58.4	67.8	70.5	67.9	62.3	52.8	42.7	35.5	52.4
Mean Minimum Temp. (°F)	18.8	23.3	26.6	31.5	39.2	48.5	54.3	52.5	45.4	34.2	24.3	18.2	34.7
Extreme Maximum Temp. (°F)	74	77	82	88	94	102	102	96	92	86	78	72	102
Extreme Minimum Temp. (°F)	-23	-8	4	12	17	32	41	*40*	25	12	-12	-8	*-23*
Days Maximum Temp. ≥ 90°F	0	0	0	0	1	*11*	10	3	1	0	0	0	*26*
Days Maximum Temp. ≤ 32°F	1	0	0	0	0	0	0	0	0	0	0	0	1
Days Minimum Temp. ≤ 32°F	30	24	25	*15*	*4*	0	0	0	1	*11*	27	30	*167*
Days Minimum Temp. ≤ 0°F	1	0	0	0	0	0	0	0	0	0	0	0	1
Heating Degree Days (base 65°F)	902	695	633	429	209	30	1	7	101	373	666	909	4,955
Cooling Degree Days (base 65°F)	0	0	0	0	12	127	173	105	23	0	0	0	440
Mean Precipitation (in.)	0.51	0.48	0.26	0.19	0.79	0.81	2.87	3.33	2.15	1.22	0.52	0.67	13.80
Days With ≥ 0.1" Precipitation	*2*	1	1	1	2	2	7	7	4	2	1	2	*32*
Days With ≥ 1.0" Precipitation	0	0	0	0	0	0	0	1	0	0	0	0	1
Mean Snowfall (in.)	4.3	2.5	1.2	trace	0.0	0.0	0.0	0.0	0.0	1.2	1.0	4.5	14.7
Days With ≥ 1.0" Snow Depth	na	*0*	*0*	0	0	0	0	0	0	0	0	*1*	na

Wolf Canyon *Sandoval County*   Elevation: 8,218 ft.   Latitude: 35° 57' N   Longitude: 106° 45' W

	JAN	FEB	MAR	APR	MAY	JUN	JUL	AUG	SEP	OCT	NOV	DEC	YEAR
Mean Maximum Temp. (°F)	37.5	40.4	45.6	53.6	62.7	73.1	75.7	72.8	67.3	57.5	45.2	38.5	55.8
Mean Temp. (°F)	22.5	25.8	31.4	38.1	45.8	54.0	58.7	57.2	51.2	41.4	30.8	23.9	40.1
Mean Minimum Temp. (°F)	7.5	11.2	17.2	22.5	28.8	34.9	41.7	41.6	34.9	25.3	16.4	9.2	24.3
Extreme Maximum Temp. (°F)	62	62	67	76	80	89	88	86	85	75	71	64	89
Extreme Minimum Temp. (°F)	-36	-24	-12	-6	11	14	18	28	14	3	-24	-26	-36
Days Maximum Temp. ≥ 90°F	0	0	0	0	0	0	0	0	0	0	0	0	0
Days Maximum Temp. ≤ 32°F	9	5	2	0	0	0	0	0	0	0	3	7	26
Days Minimum Temp. ≤ 32°F	31	28	31	29	24	10	1	1	10	27	29	30	251
Days Minimum Temp. ≤ 0°F	8	4	1	0	0	0	0	0	0	0	2	6	21
Heating Degree Days (base 65°F)	1,311	1,101	1,035	802	589	324	189	234	409	723	1,018	1,266	9,001
Cooling Degree Days (base 65°F)	0	0	0	0	0	0	1	0	0	0	0	0	1
Mean Precipitation (in.)	1.98	1.57	2.08	1.38	1.42	1.25	3.25	3.95	2.16	1.95	1.78	1.56	24.33
Days With ≥ 0.1" Precipitation	5	5	6	4	4	3	8	9	5	5	5	4	63
Days With ≥ 1.0" Precipitation	0	0	0	0	0	0	1	0	0	0	0	0	1
Mean Snowfall (in.)	26.2	21.8	25.1	13.2	3.3	trace	0.0	0.0	0.2	5.0	14.3	19.3	128.4
Days With ≥ 1.0" Snow Depth	24	20	16	6	1	0	0	0	0	2	9	20	98

Zuni *McKinley County*   Elevation: 6,309 ft.   Latitude: 35° 04' N   Longitude: 108° 50' W

	JAN	FEB	MAR	APR	MAY	JUN	JUL	AUG	SEP	OCT	NOV	DEC	YEAR
Mean Maximum Temp. (°F)	46.8	51.8	57.7	65.8	74.7	85.2	88.5	85.4	79.5	69.4	56.6	48.2	67.5
Mean Temp. (°F)	*31.5*	36.2	41.5	47.9	56.0	65.3	70.9	69.4	62.6	51.8	*40.2*	*32.6*	*50.5*
Mean Minimum Temp. (°F)	*16.4*	20.7	25.2	29.7	37.2	45.3	53.3	53.3	45.6	34.1	*23.9*	*17.0*	*33.5*
Extreme Maximum Temp. (°F)	70	74	81	86	93	102	105	99	93	93	79	73	105
Extreme Minimum Temp. (°F)	*-26*	-9	-1	3	9	27	36	35	24	9	*-2*	-20	*-26*
Days Maximum Temp. ≥ 90°F	0	0	0	0	0	8	14	7	1	0	0	0	30
Days Maximum Temp. ≤ 32°F	2	0	0	0	0	0	0	0	0	0	0	1	3
Days Minimum Temp. ≤ 32°F	*30*	27	26	21	7	0	0	0	1	13	26	*30*	*181*
Days Minimum Temp. ≤ 0°F	*2*	0	0	0	0	0	0	0	0	0	0	1	*3*
Heating Degree Days (base 65°F)	*1,030*	807	722	513	277	58	2	8	100	404	*738*	997	*5,656*
Cooling Degree Days (base 65°F)	0	0	0	0	3	71	190	162	34	1	0	0	461
Mean Precipitation (in.)	0.95	0.77	0.98	0.64	0.58	0.42	2.00	2.38	1.34	1.20	0.89	0.88	13.03
Days With ≥ 0.1" Precipitation	3	3	3	2	2	1	5	6	3	3	2	2	35
Days With ≥ 1.0" Precipitation	0	0	0	0	0	0	0	0	0	0	0	0	0
Mean Snowfall (in.)	*3.0*	*1.6*	*0.9*	0.4	trace	0.0	0.0	0.0	0.0	0.2	*0.9*	3.0	*10.0*
Days With ≥ 1.0" Snow Depth	*1*	na	*0*	0	0	0	0	0	0	0	0	*0*	2	na

Note: See Appendix D for explanation of data.

NEW YORK

PHYSICAL FEATURES. New York State contains 49,576 square miles, inclusive of 1,637 square miles of inland water, but exclusive of the boundary-water areas of Long Island Sound, New York Harbor, Lake Ontario, and Lake Erie. The major portion of the State lies generally between latitudes 42° and 45° N. and between longitudes 73° 30' and 79° 45' W. However, in the extreme southeast, a triangular portion extends southward to about latitude 40° 30' N., while Long Island lies eastward to about longitude 72° W.

The principal highland regions of the State are the Adirondacks in the northeast and the Appalachian Plateau (Southern Plateau) in the south. A minor highland region occurs in southeastern New York where the Hudson River has cut a valley between the Palisades on the west, near the New Jersey border, and the Taconic Mountains on the east, along the Connecticut and Massachusetts border. Just west of the Adirondacks and the upper Black River Valley in Lewis County is another minor highland known as Tug Hill. Much of the eastern border of the State consists of a long, narrow lowland region which is occupied by Lake Champlain, Lake George, and the middle and lower portions of the Hudson Valley.

Approximately 40 percent of New York State has an elevation of more than 1,000 feet above sea level. In northwestern Essex County are a number of peaks with an elevation of between 4,000 to 5,000 feet. The highest point, Mount Marcy, reaches a height of 5,344 feet above sea level. The Appalachian Plateau merges variously into the Great Lakes Plain of western New York with gradual- to steep-sloping terrain. This Plateau is penetrated by the valleys of the Finger Lakes which extend southward from the Great Lakes Plain. Other prominent lakes plus innumerable smaller lakes and ponds dot the landscape, with more than 1,500 in the Adirondack region alone.

GENERAL CLIMATE. The climate of New York State is broadly representative of the humid continental type which prevails in the Northeastern United States, but its diversity is not usually encountered within an area of comparable size. The geographical position of the State and the usual course of air masses, governed by the large-scale patterns of atmospheric circulation, provide general climatic controls. Differences in latitude, character of the topography, and proximity to large bodies of water have pronounced effects on the climate.

Lengthy periods of either abnormally cold or warm weather result from the movement of great high pressure (anticyclonic) systems into and through the Eastern United States. Cold winter temperatures prevail over New York whenever Arctic air masses, under high barometric pressure, flow southward from central Canada or from Hudson Bay. High pressure systems often move just off the Atlantic coast, become more or less stagnant for several days, and then a persistent air flow from the southwest or south affects the State. This circulation brings the very warm, often humid weather of the summer season and the mild, more pleasant temperatures during the fall, winter, and spring seasons.

TEMPERATURE. Many atmospheric and physiographic controls on the climate result in a considerable variation of temperature conditions over New York State. The average annual mean temperature ranges from about 40°F. in the Adirondacks to near 55°F. in the New York City area. The winters are long and cold in the Plateau Divisions of the State. Winter temperatures are moderated considerably in the Great Lakes Plain of western New York. The moderating influence of Lakes Erie and Ontario is comparable to that produced by the Atlantic Ocean in the southern portion of the Hudson Valley.

The summer climate is cool in the Adirondacks, Catskills, and higher elevations of the Southern Plateau. The New York City area and lower portions of the Hudson Valley have rather warm summers by comparison, with some periods of high, uncomfortable humidity. The remainder of New York State enjoys pleasantly warm summers, marred by only occasional, brief intervals of sultry conditions. Summer daytime temperatures usually range from the upper 70s to mid-80s over much of the State. The moderating effect of Lakes Erie and Ontario on temperatures assumes practical importance during the spring and fall seasons. The lake waters warm slowly in the spring, the effect of which is to reduce the warming of the atmosphere over adjacent land areas. In the fall season, the lake waters cool more slowly than the land areas and thus serve as a heat source.

PRECIPITATION. Moisture for precipitation in New York State is transported primarily from the Gulf of Mexico and Atlantic Ocean through circulation patterns and storm systems of the atmosphere. Distribution of precipitation within the State is greatly influenced by topography and proximity to the Great Lakes or Atlantic Ocean. Average annual amounts in excess of 50 inches occur in the western Adirondacks, Tug Hill area, and the Catskills, while slightly less than that amount is noted in the higher elevations of the Western Plateau southeast of Lake Erie. Areas of least rainfall, with average accumulations of about 30 inches, occur near Lake Ontario in the extreme western counties, in the lower half of the Genesee River Valley, and in the vicinity of Lake Champlain.

New York State has a fairly uniform distribution of precipitation during the year. There are no distinctly dry or wet seasons which are regularly repeated on an annual basis. Minimum precipitation occurs in the winter season. Maximum amounts are noted in the summer season throughout the State except along the Great Lakes where slight peaks of similar magnitude occur in both the spring and fall seasons.

SNOWFALL. The climate of New York State is marked by abundant snowfall. With the exception of the Coastal Division, the State receives an average seasonal amount of 40 inches or more. The average snowfall is greater than 70 inches over some 60 percent of New York's area. The moderating influence of the Atlantic Ocean reduces the snow accumulation to 25 to 35 inches in the New York City area and on Long Island. About one-third of the winter season precipitation in the Coastal Division occurs from storms which also yield at least one inch of snow. The great bulk of the winter precipitation in upstate New York comes as snow.

A durable snow cover generally begins to develop in the Adirondacks and northern lowlands by late November and remains on the ground until various times in April, depending upon late winter snowfall and early spring temperatures. The Southern Plateau, Great Lakes Plain in southern portions of western upstate New York, and the Hudson Valley experience a continuous snow cover from about mid-December to mid-March, with maximum depths usually occurring in February. Bare ground may occur briefly in the lower elevations of these regions during some winters. From late December or early January through February, the Atlantic coastal region of the State experiences alternating periods of measurable snow cover and bare ground.

FLOODS. Although major floods are relatively infrequent, the greatest potential and frequency for floods occur in the early spring when substantial rains combine with rapid snowmelting to produce a heavy runoff. Damaging floods are caused at other times of the year by prolonged periods of heavy rainfall.

WINDS AND STORMS. The prevailing wind is generally from the west in New York State. A southwest component becomes evident in winds during the warmer months while a northwest component is characteristic of the colder one-half of the year. Thunderstorms occur on an average of about 30 days in a year throughout the State. Destructive winds and lightning strikes in local areas are common with the more vigorous warm-season thunderstorms. Locally, hail occurs with more severe thunderstorms. Tornadoes are not common. About 3 or 4 of these storms strike limited, localized areas of New York State in most years. Tornadoes occur generally between late May and late August. Storms of freezing rain occur on one or more occasions during the winter season and often affect a wide area of the State in any one incident. Such storms are usually limited to a thin but dangerous coating of ice on exposed surfaces. Hurricanes and tropical storms periodically cause serious and heavy losses in the vicinity of Long Island and southeastern upstate New York. The greatest storm hazard in terms of area affected is heavy snow. Coastal northeaster storms occur with some frequency in most winters. Blizzard conditions of heavy snow, high winds, and rapidly falling temperature occur occasionally, but are much less characteristic of New York's climate than in the plains of Midwestern United States.

OTHER CLIMATIC ELEMENTS. The climate of the State features much cloudy weather during the months of November, December, and January in upstate New York. From June through September, however, about 60 to 70 percent of the possible sunshine hours is received. In the Atlantic coastal region, the sunshine hours increases from 50 percent of possible in the winter to about 65 percent of possible in the summer. The occurrence of heavy dense fog is variable over the State. The valleys and ridges of the Southern Plateau are most subject to periods of fog, with occurrences averaging about 50 days in a year. In the Great Lakes Plain and northern valleys, the frequency decreases to only 10 to 20 days annually. In those portions of the State with greater maritime influence, the frequency of dense fog in a year ranges from about 35 days on the south shore of Long Island to 25 days in the Hudson Valley.

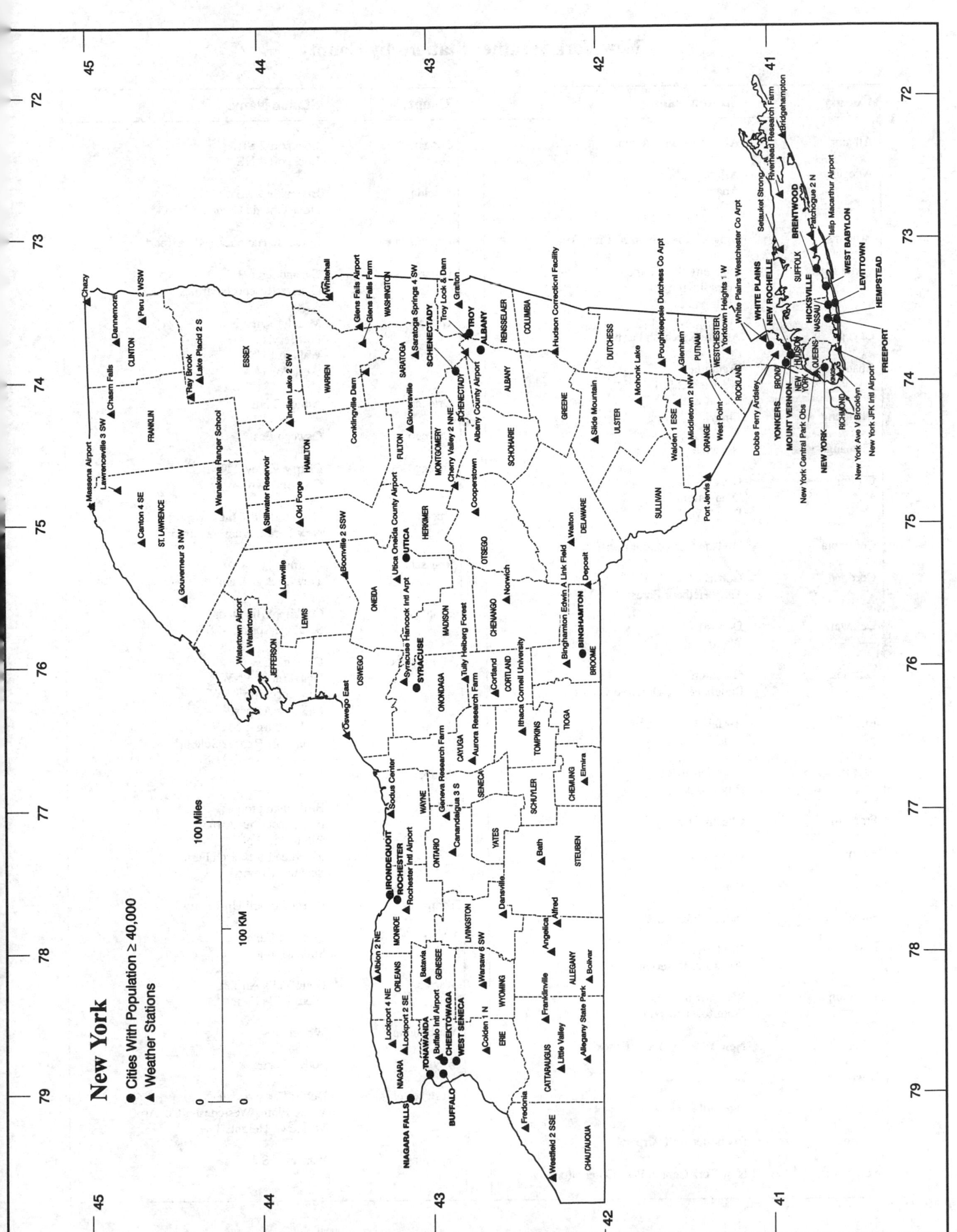

New York

● Cities With Population ≥ 40,000
▲ Weather Stations

New York Weather Stations by County

County	Station Name
Albany	Albany County Airport
Allegany	Alfred
	Angelica
	Bolivar
Broome	Binghamton Edwin A. Link Field
Cattaraugus	Allegany State Park
	Franklinville
	Little Valley
Cayuga	Aurora Research Farm
Chautauqua	Fredonia
	Westfield 2 SSE
Chemung	Elmira
Chenango	Norwich
Clinton	Chazy
	Dannemora
	Peru 2 WSW
Columbia	Hudson Correctionl Facility
Cortland	Cortland
	Tully Heiberg Forest
Delaware	Deposit
	Walton
Dutchess	Glenham
	Poughkeepsie Dutchess Co. Arpt.
Erie	Buffalo Int'l Airport
	Colden 1 N
Essex	Lake Placid 2 S
	Ray Brook
Franklin	Chasm Falls
Fulton	Gloversville
Genesee	Batavia
Hamilton	Indian Lake 2 SW
Herkimer	Old Forge
	Stillwater Reservoir
Jefferson	Watertown
	Watertown Airport
Kings	New York Avenue V Brooklyn
Lewis	Lowville
Livingston	Dansville
Monroe	Rochester Int'l Airport
New York	New York Central Park Observatory

County	Station Name
Niagara	Lockport 2 SE
	Lockport 4 NE
Oneida	Boonville 2 SSW
	Utica Oneida County Airport
Onondaga	Syracuse Hancock Int'l Airport
Ontario	Canandaigua 3 S
	Geneva Research Farm
Orange	Middletown 2 NW
	Port Jervis
	Walden 1 ESE
	West Point
Orleans	Albion 2 NE
Oswego	Oswego East
Otsego	Cherry Valley 2 NNE
	Cooperstown
Queens	New York JFK Int'l Airport
	New York Laguardia Airport
Rensselaer	Grafton
	Troy Lock & Dam
Saratoga	Conklingville Dam
	Saratoga Springs 4 SW
St. Lawrence	Canton 4 SE
	Gouverneur 3 NW
	Lawrenceville 3 SW
	Massena Airport
	Ogdensburg 4 NE
	Wanakena Ranger School
Steuben	Bath
Suffolk	Bridgehampton
	Islip Macarthur Airport
	Patchogue 2 N
	Riverhead Research Farm
	Setauket Strong
Tompkins	Ithaca Cornell University
Ulster	Mohonk Lake
	Slide Mountain
Warren	Glens Falls Airport
	Glens Falls Farm
Washington	Whitehall
Wayne	Sodus Center
Westchester	Dobbs Ferry Ardsley
	White Plains Westchester Co. Arpt.
	Yorktown Heights 1 W
Wyoming	Warsaw 6 SW

New York Weather Stations by City

City	Station Name	Miles
Albany	Albany County Airport	6
	Grafton	18
	Troy Lock & Dam	8
Binghamton	Binghamton Edwin A. Link Field	8
	Montrose, PA	17
Brentwood	Patchogue 2 N	13
	Setauket Strong	15
	Islip Macarthur Airport	8
Buffalo	Buffalo Int'l Airport	6
	Colden 1 N	19
	Lockport 2 SE	17
Cheektowaga	Buffalo Int'l Airport	2
	Colden 1 N	17
	Lockport 2 SE	16
Freeport	New York JFK Int'l Airport	11
	New York Laguardia Airport	18
Hempstead	New York Central Park Observatory	19
	New York JFK Int'l Airport	10
	New York Laguardia Airport	15
Hicksville	New York JFK Int'l Airport	16
	New York Laguardia Airport	19
Irondequoit	Rochester Int'l Airport	8
Levittown	New York JFK Int'l Airport	16
	New York Laguardia Airport	20
Mount Vernon	Dobbs Ferry Ardsley	6
	New York Central Park Observatory	11
	New York JFK Int'l Airport	18
	New York Laguardia Airport	9
	White Plains Westchester Co. Arpt.	12
New Rochelle	Stamford 5 N, CT	18
	Dobbs Ferry Ardsley	6
	New York Central Park Observatory	13
	New York JFK Int'l Airport	19
	New York Laguardia Airport	11
	White Plains Westchester Co. Arpt.	11
New York	Little Falls, NJ	20
	Newark Int'l Airport, NJ	14
	Dobbs Ferry Ardsley	20
	New York Avenue V Brooklyn	9
	New York Central Park Observatory	5
	New York JFK Int'l Airport	8
	New York Laguardia Airport	4
Niagara Falls	Buffalo Int'l Airport	18
	Lockport 2 SE	17
Rochester	Rochester Int'l Airport	5
Schenectady	Albany County Airport	8
	Saratoga Springs 4 SW	17
	Troy Lock & Dam	13

City	Station Name	Miles
Syracuse (cont.)	Syracuse Hancock Int'l Airport	6
	Tully Heiberg Forest	19
Tonawanda	Buffalo Int'l Airport	7
	Lockport 2 SE	13
	Lockport 4 NE	19
Troy	Albany County Airport	6
	Grafton	11
	Troy Lock & Dam	1
Utica	Utica Oneida County Airport	8
West Babylon	Patchogue 2 N	20
	Islip Macarthur Airport	14
West Seneca	Buffalo Int'l Airport	7
	Colden 1 N	12
White Plains	Stamford 5 N, CT	13
	Dobbs Ferry Ardsley	4
	New York Central Park Observatory	20
	New York Laguardia Airport	18
	White Plains Westchester Co. Arpt.	4
	Yorktown Heights 1 W	17
Yonkers	Little Falls, NJ	19
	Dobbs Ferry Ardsley	5
	New York Central Park Observatory	12
	New York Laguardia Airport	11
	White Plains Westchester Co. Arpt.	12

Note: Miles is the distance between the geographic center of the city and the weather station.

New York Weather Stations by Elevation

Feet	Station Name
2,647	Slide Mountain
1,938	Lake Placid 2 S
1,896	Tully Heiberg Forest
1,817	Warsaw 6 SW
1,768	Alfred
1,719	Old Forge
1,689	Stillwater Reservoir
1,660	Indian Lake 2 SW
1,624	Little Valley
1,617	Ray Brook
1,597	Binghamton Edwin A. Link Field
1,578	Bolivar
1,578	Boonville 2 SSW
1,558	Grafton
1,548	Franklinville
1,509	Wanakena Ranger School
1,499	Allegany State Park
1,443	Angelica
1,358	Cherry Valley 2 NNE
1,338	Dannemora
1,243	Mohonk Lake
1,240	Walton
1,197	Cooperstown
1,128	Cortland
1,118	Bath
1,059	Chasm Falls
1,023	Colden 1 N
1,017	Norwich
997	Deposit
958	Ithaca Cornell University
898	Batavia
898	Gloversville
859	Lowville
843	Elmira
830	Aurora Research Farm
807	Conklingville Dam
757	Fredonia
718	Canandaigua 3 S
715	Geneva Research Farm
711	Utica Oneida County Airport
705	Westfield 2 SSE
702	Buffalo Int'l Airport
698	Middletown 2 NW
669	Yorktown Heights 1 W
659	Dansville
603	Lockport 2 SE
597	Rochester Int'l Airport
508	Peru 2 WSW
501	Glens Falls Farm
498	Lawrenceville 3 SW
495	Watertown
469	Port Jervis
439	Albion 2 NE
439	Lockport 4 NE
419	Gouverneur 3 NW

Feet	Station Name
419	Sodus Center
410	Syracuse Hancock Int'l Airport
396	Canton 4 SE
396	White Plains Westchester Co. Arpt.
377	Walden 1 ESE
347	Oswego East
318	Glens Falls Airport
318	West Point
314	Watertown Airport
308	Saratoga Springs 4 SW
278	Ogdensburg 4 NE
272	Albany County Airport
272	Glenham
213	Massena Airport
200	Dobbs Ferry Ardsley
167	Chazy
154	Poughkeepsie Dutchess Co. Arpt.
131	New York Central Park Observatory
118	Whitehall
98	Riverhead Research Farm
82	Islip Macarthur Airport
59	Bridgehampton
59	Hudson Correctionl Facility
52	Patchogue 2 N
39	Setauket Strong
22	Troy Lock & Dam
19	New York Avenue V Brooklyn
13	New York JFK Int'l Airport
9	New York Laguardia Airport

Albany County Airport

Albany is located on the west bank of the Hudson River some 150 miles north of New York City, and 8 miles south of the confluence of the Mohawk and Hudson Rivers. The river-front portion of the city is only a few feet above sea level, and there is a tidal effect upstream to Troy. Eleven miles west of Albany the Helderberg hill range rises to 1,800 feet. Between it and the Hudson River the valley floor is gently rolling, ranging some 200 to 500 feet above sea level. East of the city there is more rugged terrain 5 or 6 miles wide with elevations of 300 to 600 feet. Farther to the east the terrain rises more sharply. It reaches a north-south range of hills 12 miles east of Albany with elevations ranging to 2,000 feet.

The climate at Albany is primarily continental in character, but is subjected to some modification by the Atlantic Ocean. The moderating effect on temperatures is more pronounced during the warmer months than in winter when outbursts of cold air sweep down from Canada. In the warmer seasons, temperatures rise rapidly in the daytime. However, temperatures also fall rapidly after sunset so that the nights are relatively cool. Occasionally there are extended periods of oppressive heat up to a week or more in duration.

Winters are usually cold and sometimes fairly severe. Maximum temperatures during the colder winters are often below freezing and nighttime lows are frequently below 10 degrees. Sub-zero readings occur about 12 times a year. Snowfall throughout the area is quite variable and snow flurries are quite frequent during the winter. Precipitation is sufficient to serve the economy of the region in most years, and only occasionally do periods of drought exist. Most of the rainfall in the summer is from thunderstorms. Tornadoes are quite rare and hail is not usually of any consequence.

Wind velocities are moderate. The north-south Hudson River Valley has a marked effect on the lighter winds and in the warm months, average wind direction is usually southerly. Destructive winds rarely occur.

The area enjoys one of the highest percentages of sunshine in the entire state. Seldom does the area experience long periods of cloudy days and long periods of smog are rare.

Based on the 1951-1980 period, the average first occurrence of 32 degrees Fahrenheit in the fall is September 29 and the average last occurrence in the spring is May 7.

Albany County Airport *Albany County*   Elevation: 272 ft.   Latitude: 42° 45' N   Longitude: 73° 48' W

	JAN	FEB	MAR	APR	MAY	JUN	JUL	AUG	SEP	OCT	NOV	DEC	YEAR
Mean Maximum Temp. (°F)	30.7	34.2	44.3	57.7	70.0	77.7	82.7	80.3	72.0	60.3	48.0	36.0	57.8
Mean Temp. (°F)	21.7	24.8	34.7	46.8	58.2	66.3	71.4	69.3	61.0	49.6	39.4	28.0	47.6
Mean Minimum Temp. (°F)	12.7	15.3	25.0	35.8	46.5	54.9	60.0	58.2	50.0	38.8	30.8	19.9	37.3
Extreme Maximum Temp. (°F)	65	68	89	92	94	96	99	97	93	86	81	71	99
Extreme Minimum Temp. (°F)	-28	-21	-6	13	28	36	40	34	28	17	5	-20	-28
Days Maximum Temp. ≥ 90°F	0	0	0	0	0	1	4	2	0	0	0	0	7
Days Maximum Temp. ≤ 32°F	17	12	4	0	0	0	0	0	0	0	1	10	44
Days Minimum Temp. ≤ 32°F	29	26	24	12	1	0	0	0	1	8	18	27	146
Days Minimum Temp. ≤ 0°F	6	4	0	0	0	0	0	0	0	0	0	2	12
Heating Degree Days (base 65°F)	1,336	1,130	933	544	231	60	8	24	161	474	762	1,141	6,804
Cooling Degree Days (base 65°F)	0	0	1	3	28	108	220	169	49	3	0	0	581
Mean Precipitation (in.)	2.63	2.24	3.14	3.21	3.56	3.62	3.42	3.63	3.33	3.23	3.29	2.75	38.05
Maximum Precipitation (in.)	6.4	5.0	5.9	7.9	9.0	7.4	7.0	7.3	7.9	8.8	8.1	6.7	47.2
Minimum Precipitation (in.)	0.4	0.2	0.3	1.1	1.0	0.6	0.5	0.7	0.4	0.2	0.6	0.6	21.5
Maximum 24-hr. Precipitation (in.)	1.8	1.6	2.0	2.0	2.2	3.5	2.7	4.1	3.5	2.8	2.2	3.2	4.1
Days With ≥ 0.1" Precipitation	6	5	6	7	8	7	6	7	7	6	7	7	79
Days With ≥ 1.0" Precipitation	0	0	1	1	1	1	1	1	1	1	1	0	9
Mean Snowfall (in.)	17.2	12.5	11.1	2.5	trace	trace	trace	0.0	trace	0.2	5.0	13.6	62.1
Maximum Snowfall (in.)	48	35	35	18	2	0	0	0	0	7	25	58	107
Maximum 24-hr. Snowfall (in.)	13	17	22	17	2	0	0	0	0	7	22	14	22
Days With ≥ 1.0" Snow Depth	20	17	8	1	0	0	0	0	0	0	3	13	62
Thunderstorm Days	< 1	< 1	1	1	3	5	6	5	2	1	< 1	< 1	24
Foggy Days	10	9	11	9	12	13	14	17	17	15	13	12	152
Predominant Sky Cover	OVR	OVR	OVR	OVR	OVR	OVR	OVR	OVR	OVR	OVR	OVR	OVR	OVR
Mean Relative Humidity 7am (%)	77	77	76	72	74	77	80	85	88	86	82	80	80
Mean Relative Humidity 4pm (%)	64	59	54	48	50	53	53	55	57	56	64	67	57
Mean Dewpoint (°F)	14	15	23	33	45	55	60	59	52	41	31	20	38
Prevailing Wind Direction	WNW	WNW	WNW	WNW	S	S	S	S	S	S	WNW	WNW	S
Prevailing Wind Speed (mph)	15	15	15	15	10	9	8	8	9	9	14	14	12
Maximum Wind Gust (mph)	62	67	61	58	67	59	77	62	64	60	67	63	77

Binghamton Edwin A. Link Field

Binghamton, in south central New York lies in a comparatively narrow valley at the confluence of the Susquehanna and Chenango Rivers. Within a radius of 5 miles, hills rise to elevations of 1,400-1,600 feet above mean sea level. In the spring, melting snow, sometimes supplemented by rainfall, occasionally causes flooding in the city and along the streams.

The climate of Binghamton is representative of the humid area of the north-eastern United States and is primarily continental in type. The area, being adjacent to the so-called St. Lawrence Valley storm track, and also subject to cold air masses approaching from the west and north, has a variable climate, characterized by frequent and rapid changes. Furthermore, diurnal and seasonal changes assist in the production of an invigorating climate. As a rule, the temperature rises rapidly to moderate daytime levels with readings of 90 degrees or above only a few days in any month summer nights provide favorable sleeping conditions.

Winters are usually cold, but not commonly severe. Highest daytime temperatures average in the high 20s to low 30s, while the lowest nighttime readings average from the mid-teens to low 20s. Ordinarily a few sub-zero readings may be expected in January and February, with a lesser number in November, December, and March. The transitional seasons, spring and autumn, are the most variable of the year.

Most of the precipitation in the Binghamton area derives from moisture laden air transported from the Gulf of Mexico and cyclonic systems moving northward along the Atlantic coast. The annual rainfall is rather evenly distributed over the year. However, the greatest average monthly amounts occur during the growing season, April through September. As a rule, rainfall is ample for good crop growth and comes mostly in the form of thunderstorms. Annual snowfall is around 50 inches in Binghamton and above 85 inches at Edwin A. Link Field, some 10 miles to the NNW, and about 700 feet higher in elevation. Most of the snow falls during the normal winter months. However, heavy snows can occur as early as November and as late as April. Being adjacent to the track of storms that move through the St. Lawrence Valley, and being under the influence of winds that sweep across Lakes Erie and Ontario to the interior of the state, the area is subject to much cloudiness and winter snow flurries.

For the most part, the winds at Binghamton have northerly and westerly components. Tornadoes, although rare, have struck in the Binghamton area.

Based on the 1951-1980 period, the growing season averages 150 to 160 days. Usually the last spring frost occurs during early May, and the first frost in autumn during early October.

Binghamton Edwin A. Link Field *Broome County*   Elevation: 1,597 ft.   Latitude: 42° 12' N   Longitude: 75° 59' W

	JAN	FEB	MAR	APR	MAY	JUN	JUL	AUG	SEP	OCT	NOV	DEC	YEAR
Mean Maximum Temp. (°F)	28.8	31.5	40.8	53.7	66.1	73.9	78.8	76.6	68.4	57.1	44.8	33.9	54.5
Mean Temp. (°F)	21.9	24.1	32.8	44.6	56.4	64.4	69.4	67.3	59.5	48.6	38.0	27.5	46.2
Mean Minimum Temp. (°F)	15.0	16.6	24.6	35.4	46.6	54.8	59.9	58.0	50.5	40.1	31.2	21.1	37.8
Extreme Maximum Temp. (°F)	63	63	82	88	89	92	98	94	91	81	77	65	98
Extreme Minimum Temp. (°F)	-15	-15	-7	9	25	33	43	38	25	17	3	-18	-18
Days Maximum Temp. ≥ 90°F	0	0	0	0	0	0	1	0	0	0	0	0	1
Days Maximum Temp. ≤ 32°F	20	15	8	1	0	0	0	0	0	0	4	14	62
Days Minimum Temp. ≤ 32°F	29	26	24	12	1	0	0	0	0	6	18	27	143
Days Minimum Temp. ≤ 0°F	4	2	0	0	0	0	0	0	0	0	0	1	7
Heating Degree Days (base 65°F)	1,329	1,148	994	610	284	87	20	40	194	504	804	1,155	7,169
Cooling Degree Days (base 65°F)	0	0	1	3	23	79	164	122	37	2	0	0	431
Mean Precipitation (in.)	2.51	2.42	2.94	3.39	3.42	3.68	3.52	3.40	3.64	2.95	3.34	3.08	38.29
Maximum Precipitation (in.)	6.4	4.4	6.0	8.6	6.5	9.5	7.4	7.5	9.7	9.4	7.5	6.1	48.0
Minimum Precipitation (in.)	0.8	0.4	0.7	1.0	0.8	1.0	0.8	0.6	0.6	0.3	1.0	0.9	29.9
Maximum 24-hr. Precipitation (in.)	1.5	2.2	1.6	2.9	2.9	3.1	3.2	2.6	3.5	3.5	2.6	2.7	3.5
Days With ≥ 0.1" Precipitation	6	6	7	7	8	8	7	7	7	7	8	7	85
Days With ≥ 1.0" Precipitation	0	0	0	1	0	1	1	1	1	1	0	0	6
Mean Snowfall (in.)	19.8	15.7	14.5	4.5	0.2	trace	0.0	0.0	trace	0.8	7.8	17.5	80.8
Maximum Snowfall (in.)	44	44	38	23	3	0	0	0	trace	12	29	60	138
Maximum 24-hr. Snowfall (in.)	18	21	19	12	3	0	0	0	trace	7	11	14	21
Days With ≥ 1.0" Snow Depth	24	21	14	2	0	0	0	0	0	0	6	16	83
Thunderstorm Days	< 1	< 1	1	2	4	6	7	5	3	1	< 1	< 1	29
Foggy Days	11	10	13	12	14	15	16	19	17	15	14	13	169
Predominant Sky Cover	OVR	OVR	OVR	OVR	OVR	OVR	OVR	OVR	OVR	OVR	OVR	OVR	OVR
Mean Relative Humidity 7am (%)	80	79	79	76	78	83	85	89	90	85	82	82	82
Mean Relative Humidity 4pm (%)	69	65	60	54	54	57	57	59	62	60	68	72	61
Mean Dewpoint (°F)	15	16	23	32	44	54	59	58	51	40	31	20	37
Prevailing Wind Direction	WNW	NW	NW	NW	NW	SW	SW	SW	SW	S	SW	WNW	NW
Prevailing Wind Speed (mph)	14	14	14	13	12	9	8	8	9	9	10	14	12
Maximum Wind Gust (mph)	61	56	58	64	54	60	74	63	48	51	58	54	74

Buffalo Int'l Airport

The country surrounding Buffalo is comparatively low and level to the west. To the east and south the land is gently rolling, rising to pronounced hills within 12 to 18 miles, and to 1,000 feet above the level of Lake Erie about 35 miles south-southeast of the city. A steep slope of 50 to 100 feet lies east-west one and a half miles to the north. The eastern end of Lake Erie is nine miles to the west-southwest, while Lake Ontario lies 25 miles to the north, the two being connected by the Niagara River, which flows north-northwestward from the end of Lake Erie.

Buffalo is located near the mean position of the polar front. Its weather is varied and changeable, characteristic of the latitude. Wide seasonal swings of temperature from hot to cold are tempered appreciably by the proximity of Lakes Erie and Ontario. Lake Erie lies to the southwest, the direction of the prevailing wind. Wind flow throughout the year is somewhat higher due to this exposure. The vigorous interplay of warm and cold air masses during the winter and early spring months causes one or more windstorms. Precipitation is moderate and fairly evenly divided throughout the twelve months.

The spring season is more cloudy and cooler than points not affected by the cold lake. Spring growth of vegetation is retarded, protecting it from late spring frosts. With heavy winter ice accumulations in the lake, typical spring conditions are delayed until late May or early June.

Summer comes suddenly in mid-June. Lake breezes temper the extreme heat of the summer season. Temperatures of 90 degrees and above are infrequent. There is more summer sunshine here than in any other section of the state. Due to the stabilizing effects of Lake Erie, thunderstorms are relatively infrequent. Most of them are caused by frontal action. To the north and south of the city thunderstorms occur more often.

Autumn has long, dry periods and is frost free usually until mid-October. Cloudiness increases in November, continuing mostly cloudy throughout the winter and early spring. Snow flurries off the lake begin in mid-November or early December. Outbreaks of Arctic air in December and throughout the winter months produce locally heavy snowfalls from the lake. At the same time, temperatures of well below zero over Canada and the midwest are raised 10 to 30 degrees in crossing the lakes. Only on rare occasions do polar air masses drop southward from eastern Hudson Bay across Lake Ontario without appreciable warming.

Buffalo Int'l Airport *Erie County*   Elevation: 702 ft.   Latitude: 42° 56' N   Longitude: 78° 44' W

	JAN	FEB	MAR	APR	MAY	JUN	JUL	AUG	SEP	OCT	NOV	DEC	YEAR
Mean Maximum Temp. (°F)	30.9	32.8	41.9	54.4	66.8	75.4	80.3	78.4	70.6	59.3	47.1	36.4	56.2
Mean Temp. (°F)	24.3	25.6	33.9	45.4	57.3	66.2	71.3	69.5	61.8	51.0	40.5	30.1	48.1
Mean Minimum Temp. (°F)	17.6	18.4	25.8	36.4	47.6	56.9	62.2	60.5	53.0	42.7	33.9	23.8	39.9
Extreme Maximum Temp. (°F)	67	70	79	94	90	96	97	96	90	82	73	74	97
Extreme Minimum Temp. (°F)	-16	-18	-7	12	28	36	47	38	32	22	9	-10	-18
Days Maximum Temp. ≥ 90°F	0	0	0	0	0	0	2	1	0	0	0	0	3
Days Maximum Temp. ≤ 32°F	17	14	7	1	0	0	0	0	0	0	2	11	52
Days Minimum Temp. ≤ 32°F	28	25	24	10	0	0	0	0	0	3	14	25	129
Days Minimum Temp. ≤ 0°F	2	1	0	0	0	0	0	0	0	0	0	1	4
Heating Degree Days (base 65°F)	1,256	1,105	957	585	262	62	7	19	142	431	729	1,076	6,631
Cooling Degree Days (base 65°F)	0	0	0	4	28	105	218	169	54	4	0	0	582
Mean Precipitation (in.)	3.14	2.42	2.98	2.99	3.30	3.69	3.18	3.83	3.86	3.29	3.83	3.79	40.30
Maximum Precipitation (in.)	6.9	5.9	6.0	5.9	7.2	8.4	8.9	10.7	9.0	9.1	9.8	8.7	53.5
Minimum Precipitation (in.)	1.0	0.8	1.2	1.3	1.2	0.1	0.9	1.1	0.8	0.3	1.5	1.7	28.5
Maximum 24-hr. Precipitation (in.)	1.8	2.1	2.0	1.7	3.4	5.0	3.4	3.9	4.9	2.5	2.1	1.7	5.0
Days With ≥ 0.1" Precipitation	9	7	8	8	7	7	6	7	7	8	9	10	93
Days With ≥ 1.0" Precipitation	0	0	0	0	1	1	1	1	1	0	1	0	6
Mean Snowfall (in.)	26.7	18.0	12.5	3.5	0.3	trace	trace	trace	trace	0.3	9.6	24.8	95.7
Maximum Snowfall (in.)	68	54	29	15	8	0	0	0	trace	3	31	68	176
Maximum 24-hr. Snowfall (in.)	18	18	15	6	8	0	0	0	trace	3	19	34	34
Days With ≥ 1.0" Snow Depth	21	20	10	2	0	0	0	0	0	0	4	15	72
Thunderstorm Days	< 1	< 1	1	2	3	5	6	6	4	2	1	< 1	30
Foggy Days	12	12	14	13	14	13	13	15	13	13	13	13	158
Predominant Sky Cover	OVR	OVR	OVR	OVR	OVR	OVR	SCT	OVR	OVR	OVR	OVR	OVR	OVR
Mean Relative Humidity 7am (%)	79	80	80	77	76	77	79	83	83	81	80	80	79
Mean Relative Humidity 4pm (%)	73	70	65	57	55	54	54	56	59	60	69	73	62
Mean Dewpoint (°F)	18	18	25	34	44	54	59	59	52	42	33	23	39
Prevailing Wind Direction	WSW	WSW	SW	SW	SW	SW	SW	SW	SW	SW	W	W	SW
Prevailing Wind Speed (mph)	18	17	16	15	14	14	13	13	13	15	15	15	15
Maximum Wind Gust (mph)	71	82	73	74	64	79	59	81	62	63	73	69	82

Islip Macarthur Airport

Long Island is the terminal moraine marking the southernmost advance of the ice sheet along the Atlantic Coast during the last ice age. The terrain is generally flat, with only a gradual rise in elevation from Long Island Sound on the northern shore and from the Atlantic Ocean on the southern shore toward the middle of the island. Islip is located about half-way out Long Island on the southern coast. The airport is located about seven miles to the northeast of the city. Islip is protected from flooding during periods of high tides by Fire Island, a natural barrier located about three miles offshore. Most of the air masses affecting Islip are continental in origin, however the ocean has a pronounced influence on the climate of the area.

A cool sea breeze blowing off the ocean during the summer months helps to alleviate the afternoon heat. There are an average of 7 days between June and September when the afternoon temperature exceeds 90 degrees, while farther inland there are 10 to 15 such days.

It is uncommon for the eye of a tropical storm to pass directly over Long Island. Tropical weather systems moving along the Atlantic Coast, however, are capable of producing episodes of heavy rain and strong winds in the late summer or fall.

The winter season is relatively mild. Below zero temperatures are reported on only one or two days in about half the winters. Temperatures of 10 degrees below zero or colder are extremely rare. The seasonal snowfall averages about 29 inches. Almost all of this snow falls between December and March. Coastal low pressure systems, Northeasters, are the principle source of this snow. These weather systems will occasionally produce a heavy snowfall. There are usually extended periods during the winter when the ground is bare of snow.

Based on the 1951-1980 period, the average date of the last spring temperature of 32 degrees is April 27 and the average first fall occurrence is October 21. Inland locations would expect a shorter freeze-free season.

Islip Macarthur Airport *Suffolk County*   Elevation: 82 ft.   Latitude: 40° 47' N   Longitude: 73° 06' W

	JAN	FEB	MAR	APR	MAY	JUN	JUL	AUG	SEP	OCT	NOV	DEC	YEAR
Mean Maximum Temp. (°F)	na	na	na	na	na	na	na	na	na	na	na	na	na
Mean Temp. (°F)	na	na	na	na	na	na	na	na	na	na	na	na	na
Mean Minimum Temp. (°F)	na	na	na	na	na	na	na	na	na	na	na	na	na
Extreme Maximum Temp. (°F)	na	na	na	na	na	na	na	na	na	na	na	na	na
Extreme Minimum Temp. (°F)	na	na	na	na	na	na	na	na	na	na	na	na	na
Days Maximum Temp. ≥ 90°F	na	na	na	na	na	na	na	na	na	na	na	na	na
Days Maximum Temp. ≤ 32°F	na	na	na	na	na	na	na	na	na	na	na	na	na
Days Minimum Temp. ≤ 32°F	na	na	na	na	na	na	na	na	na	na	na	na	na
Days Minimum Temp. ≤ 0°F	na	na	na	na	na	na	na	na	na	na	na	na	na
Heating Degree Days (base 65°F)	na	na	na	na	na	na	na	na	na	na	na	na	na
Cooling Degree Days (base 65°F)	na	na	na	na	na	na	na	na	na	*11*	na	na	na
Mean Precipitation (in.)	na	na	na	na	na	na	na	na	na	na	na	na	na
Maximum Precipitation (in.)	6.3	5.5	5.5	5.1	10.1	7.9	8.4	13.8	5.1	8.7	8.0	6.1	65.3
Minimum Precipitation (in.)	1.3	1.1	1.3	1.3	0.7	0.6	1.2	0.5	0.8	0.3	1.3	0.9	34.4
Maximum 24-hr. Precipitation (in.)	1.6	2.3	2.5	1.8	4.0	3.5	2.7	6.7	2.2	3.9	2.6	2.6	6.7
Days With ≥ 0.1" Precipitation	na	na	na	na	na	na	na	na	na	na	na	na	na
Days With ≥ 1.0" Precipitation	na	na	na	na	na	na	na	na	na	na	na	na	na
Mean Snowfall (in.)	na	na	na	na	na	na	na	na	na	na	na	na	na
Maximum Snowfall (in.)	14	20	13	3	0	0	0	0	0	0	8	10	34
Maximum 24-hr. Snowfall (in.)	6	7	8	3	0	0	0	0	0	0	8	9	9
Days With ≥ 1.0" Snow Depth	na	na	na	na	na	na	na	na	na	na	na	na	na
Thunderstorm Days	< 1	< 1	1	2	3	5	6	4	2	1	1	< 1	25
Foggy Days	15	14	16	16	18	16	22	19	17	15	14	14	196
Predominant Sky Cover	OVR	OVR	OVR	OVR	OVR	SCT	OVR	SCT	OVR	CLR	OVR	OVR	OVR
Mean Relative Humidity 7am (%)	76	76	77	76	76	77	81	84	85	85	80	76	79
Mean Relative Humidity 4pm (%)	62	59	57	58	59	59	63	63	63	62	62	60	61
Mean Dewpoint (°F)	22	22	28	38	48	58	65	64	57	46	36	26	43
Prevailing Wind Direction	WNW	NW	NW	SW	SW	SW	SW	SW	SW	SW	SW	WNW	SW
Prevailing Wind Speed (mph)	13	13	13	10	10	10	10	9	10	10	10	12	12
Maximum Wind Gust (mph)	na	na	na	na	na	na	na	na	na	na	na	na	na

New York Central Park Observatory

New York City, in area exceeding 300 square miles, is located on the Atlantic coastal plain at the mouth of the Hudson River. The terrain is laced with numerous waterways, all but one of the five boroughs in the city are situated on islands. Elevations range from less than 50 feet over most of Manhattan, Brooklyn, and Queens to almost 300 feet in northern Manhattan and the Bronx, and over 400 feet in Staten Island.

The New York Metropolitan area is close to the path of most storm and frontal systems which move across the North American continent. Therefore, weather conditions affecting the city most often approach from a westerly direction, resulting in higher temperatures in summer and lower ones in winter than would otherwise be expected in a coastal area. However, the frequent passage of weather systems often helps reduce the length of extremes.

Although continental influence predominates, oceanic influence is by no means absent. During the summer local sea breezes, winds blowing onshore from the cool water surface, often moderate the afternoon heat. The effect of the sea breeze diminishes inland. On winter mornings, ocean temperatures which are warm relative to the land reinforce the effect of the city heat island and low temperatures are often 10-20 degrees lower in the inland suburbs than in the central city. The relatively warm water temperatures also delay the advent of winter snows. Conversely, the lag in warming of water temperatures keeps spring temperatures relatively cool.

Precipitation is moderate and distributed fairly evenly throughout the year. Most of the rainfall from May through October comes from thunderstorms, usually of brief duration and sometimes intense. Heavy rains of long duration associated with tropical storms occur infrequently in late summer or fall. For the other seasons precipitation is associated with widespread storm areas, producing day-long rain or snow. Coastal storms, occurring most often in the fall and winter months, produce on occasion considerable amounts of precipitation, record rains, snows, and high winds.

The average annual precipitation is reasonably uniform within the city but higher in the suburbs and less on eastern Long Island. Annual snowfall totals also show a consistent increase to the north and west of the city with lesser amounts along the south shores and the eastern end of Long Island.

Local Climatological Data is published for three locations in New York City, Central Park, La Guardia Airport, and John°F. Kennedy International Airport.

Based on the 1951-1980 period, the average first occurrence of 32 degrees Fahrenheit in the fall is November 11 and the average last occurrence in the spring is April 1.

New York Central Park Observatory *New York County*   Elevation: 131 ft.   Latitude: 40° 47' N   Longitude: 73° 58' W

	JAN	FEB	MAR	APR	MAY	JUN	JUL	AUG	SEP	OCT	NOV	DEC	YEAR
Mean Maximum Temp. (°F)	38.5	41.3	50.2	61.6	71.8	79.9	85.5	83.9	76.1	64.7	54.1	43.7	62.6
Mean Temp. (°F)	32.2	34.6	42.6	52.9	63.0	71.6	77.2	75.8	68.3	57.2	47.7	37.8	55.1
Mean Minimum Temp. (°F)	26.0	27.7	34.9	44.2	54.1	63.2	68.9	67.8	60.5	49.6	41.1	31.8	47.5
Extreme Maximum Temp. (°F)	66	75	86	96	97	98	104	99	99	88	81	75	104
Extreme Minimum Temp. (°F)	-2	0	10	21	36	46	53	50	43	29	17	-1	-2
Days Maximum Temp. ≥ 90°F	0	0	0	0	1	3	8	5	1	0	0	0	18
Days Maximum Temp. ≤ 32°F	9	5	1	0	0	0	0	0	0	0	0	4	19
Days Minimum Temp. ≤ 32°F	22	19	11	1	0	0	0	0	0	0	4	15	72
Days Minimum Temp. ≤ 0°F	0	0	0	0	0	0	0	0	0	0	0	0	0
Heating Degree Days (base 65°F)	1,009	853	691	367	121	14	1	1	40	253	516	836	4,702
Cooling Degree Days (base 65°F)	0	0	3	8	68	228	393	341	144	19	2	0	1,206
Mean Precipitation (in.)	4.07	3.30	4.27	4.06	4.62	3.75	4.52	4.22	4.15	3.91	4.35	3.94	49.16
Maximum Precipitation (in.)	10.5	6.0	10.4	8.3	10.2	9.3	11.8	12.4	9.3	7.8	12.4	10.0	67.0
Minimum Precipitation (in.)	0.6	0.5	0.9	1.3	0.6	1.2	1.3	0.2	1.3	0.1	0.3	0.6	26.1
Maximum 24-hr. Precipitation (in.)	3.4	3.0	3.4	3.4	4.0	3.1	3.5	4.6	5.5	4.1	7.4	2.5	7.4
Days With ≥ 0.1" Precipitation	7	6	7	7	8	7	7	6	6	6	6	7	80
Days With ≥ 1.0" Precipitation	1	1	1	1	1	1	1	1	1	1	1	1	12
Mean Snowfall (in.)	7.3	7.5	3.4	0.4	trace	0.0	trace	0.0	0.0	trace	0.4	2.2	21.2
Maximum Snowfall (in.)	20	26	17	10	trace	0	0	0	0	trace	5	12	53
Maximum 24-hr. Snowfall (in.)	12	16	10	10	trace	0	0	0	0	trace	4	7	16
Days With ≥ 1.0" Snow Depth	9	8	2	0	0	0	0	0	0	0	0	2	21
Thunderstorm Days	< 1	< 1	1	1	3	4	5	4	1	1	< 1	< 1	20
Foggy Days	0	0	0	0	0	0	0	0	0	0	0	< 1	1
Predominant Sky Cover	OVR	OVR	OVR	OVR	OVR	SCT	SCT	SCT	OVR	CLR	OVR	OVR	OVR
Mean Relative Humidity 7am (%)	67	67	66	64	72	74	74	76	78	75	72	69	71
Mean Relative Humidity 4pm (%)	55	53	50	45	52	55	53	54	56	55	58	59	54
Mean Dewpoint (°F)	18	19	26	34	47	57	62	62	56	44	34	25	40
Prevailing Wind Direction	NW	NW	NW	NW	NE	SW	SW	SW	SW	W	W	NW	NW
Prevailing Wind Speed (mph)	12	12	13	12	10	8	8	8	8	9	9	12	10
Maximum Wind Gust (mph)	52	51	63	46	44	41	46	43	52	46	58	64	64

New York JFK Int'l Airport

New York City, in area exceeding 300 square miles, is located on the Atlantic coastal plain at the mouth of the Hudson River. The terrain is laced with numerous waterways, all but one of the five boroughs in the city are situated on islands. Elevations range from less than 50 feet over most of Manhattan, Brooklyn, and Queens to almost 300 feet in northern Manhattan and the Bronx, and over 400 feet in Staten Island.

The New York Metropolitan area is close to the path of most storm and frontal systems which move across the North American continent. Therefore, weather conditions affecting the city most often approach from a westerly direction, resulting in higher temperatures in summer and lower ones in winter than would otherwise be expected in a coastal area. However, the frequent passage of weather systems often helps reduce the length of extremes.

Although continental influence predominates, oceanic influence is by no means absent. During the summer local sea breezes, winds blowing onshore from the cool water surface, often moderate the afternoon heat. The effect of the sea breeze diminishes inland. On winter mornings, ocean temperatures which are warm relative to the land reinforce the effect of the city heat island and low temperatures are often 10-20 degrees lower in the inland suburbs than in the central city. The relatively warm water temperatures also delay the advent of winter snows. Conversely, the lag in warming of water temperatures keeps spring temperatures relatively cool.

Precipitation is moderate and distributed fairly evenly throughout the year. Most of the rainfall from May through October comes from thunderstorms, usually of brief duration and sometimes intense. Heavy rains of long duration associated with tropical storms occur infrequently in late summer or fall. For the other seasons precipitation is associated with widespread storm areas, producing day-long rain or snow. Coastal storms, occurring most often in the fall and winter months, produce on occasion considerable amounts of precipitation, record rains, snows, and high winds.

The average annual precipitation is reasonably uniform within the city but higher in the suburbs and less on eastern Long Island. Annual snowfall totals also show a consistent increase to the north and west of the city with lesser amounts along the south shores and the eastern end of Long Island.

Local Climatological Data is published for three locations in New York City, Central Park, La Guardia Airport, and John°F. Kennedy International Airport.

Based on the 1951-1980 period, the average first occurrence of 32 degrees Fahrenheit in the fall is November 11 and the average last occurrence in the spring is April 1.

New York JFK Int'l Airport *Queens County*   Elevation: 13 ft.   Latitude: 40° 39' N   Longitude: 73° 48' W

	JAN	FEB	MAR	APR	MAY	JUN	JUL	AUG	SEP	OCT	NOV	DEC	YEAR
Mean Maximum Temp. (°F)	38.7	40.9	48.6	58.7	68.3	77.3	83.0	82.1	75.1	64.3	54.0	44.1	61.2
Mean Temp. (°F)	32.4	34.3	41.6	51.0	60.7	69.8	75.8	74.9	67.9	57.0	47.4	37.9	54.2
Mean Minimum Temp. (°F)	26.0	27.6	34.5	43.4	53.0	62.3	68.6	67.7	60.6	49.6	40.7	31.7	47.1
Extreme Maximum Temp. (°F)	65	71	85	90	95	98	102	100	98	88	77	75	102
Extreme Minimum Temp. (°F)	-2	2	8	20	37	48	55	50	41	30	19	2	-2
Days Maximum Temp. ≥ 90°F	0	0	0	0	0	2	4	3	1	0	0	0	10
Days Maximum Temp. ≤ 32°F	8	5	1	0	0	0	0	0	0	0	0	3	17
Days Minimum Temp. ≤ 32°F	23	19	11	1	0	0	0	0	0	0	4	16	74
Days Minimum Temp. ≤ 0°F	0	0	0	0	0	0	0	0	0	0	0	0	0
Heating Degree Days (base 65°F)	1,005	862	720	414	160	17	0	2	39	256	524	834	4,833
Cooling Degree Days (base 65°F)	0	0	0	1	36	178	351	313	133	15	0	0	1,027
Mean Precipitation (in.)	3.55	2.75	3.78	3.72	4.07	3.57	3.76	3.62	3.41	3.08	3.46	3.30	42.07
Maximum Precipitation (in.)	8.3	4.9	8.2	9.5	10.7	8.1	8.5	8.3	9.6	6.6	9.5	6.7	59.1
Minimum Precipitation (in.)	0.5	1.0	0.9	1.4	0.6	trace	0.5	0.2	1.0	0.9	0.3	0.6	25.4
Maximum 24-hr. Precipitation (in.)	2.6	2.5	2.4	3.1	2.9	2.8	3.2	3.8	4.5	3.2	3.9	2.5	4.5
Days With ≥ 0.1" Precipitation	7	6	7	6	7	6	6	6	6	5	6	6	74
Days With ≥ 1.0" Precipitation	1	1	1	1	1	1	1	1	1	1	1	1	12
Mean Snowfall (in.)	6.8	7.1	3.4	0.6	trace	0.0	trace	0.0	0.0	trace	0.3	2.3	20.5
Maximum Snowfall (in.)	20	25	16	8	0	0	0	0	0	trace	4	22	49
Maximum 24-hr. Snowfall (in.)	13	20	9	8	0	0	0	0	0	trace	3	18	20
Days With ≥ 1.0" Snow Depth	6	5	2	0	0	0	0	0	0	0	0	2	15
Thunderstorm Days	< 1	< 1	1	2	3	4	5	5	2	1	1	< 1	24
Foggy Days	10	9	11	11	13	12	13	12	11	10	11	10	133
Predominant Sky Cover	OVR	OVR	OVR	OVR	OVR	OVR	SCT	SCT	OVR	CLR	OVR	OVR	OVR
Mean Relative Humidity 7am (%)	71	71	71	70	73	74	75	78	79	78	76	73	74
Mean Relative Humidity 4pm (%)	61	59	57	58	61	63	63	63	62	60	61	62	61
Mean Dewpoint (°F)	21	22	28	37	48	58	64	63	57	46	36	26	42
Prevailing Wind Direction	NW	NW	NW	S	S	S	S	S	S	WSW	NW	NW	S
Prevailing Wind Speed (mph)	16	17	17	13	13	12	12	12	12	10	15	16	14
Maximum Wind Gust (mph)	59	60	68	61	71	56	54	68	60	62	67	61	71

New York Laguardia Airport

New York City, in area exceeding 300 square miles, is located on the Atlantic coastal plain at the mouth of the Hudson River. The terrain is laced with numerous waterways, all but one of the five boroughs in the city are situated on islands. Elevations range from less than 50 feet over most of Manhattan, Brooklyn, and Queens to almost 300 feet in northern Manhattan and the Bronx, and over 400 feet in Staten Island.

The New York Metropolitan area is close to the path of most storm and frontal systems which move across the North American continent. Therefore, weather conditions affecting the city most often approach from a westerly direction, resulting in higher temperatures in summer and lower ones in winter than would otherwise be expected in a coastal area. However, the frequent passage of weather systems often helps reduce the length of extremes.

Although continental influence predominates, oceanic influence is by no means absent. During the summer local sea breezes, winds blowing onshore from the cool water surface, often moderate the afternoon heat. The effect of the sea breeze diminishes inland. On winter mornings, ocean temperatures which are warm relative to the land reinforce the effect of the city heat island and low temperatures are often 10-20 degrees lower in the inland suburbs than in the central city. The relatively warm water temperatures also delay the advent of winter snows. Conversely, the lag in warming of water temperatures keeps spring temperatures relatively cool.

Precipitation is moderate and distributed fairly evenly throughout the year. Most of the rainfall from May through October comes from thunderstorms, usually of brief duration and sometimes intense. Heavy rains of long duration associated with tropical storms occur infrequently in late summer or fall. For the other seasons precipitation is associated with widespread storm areas, producing day-long rain or snow. Coastal storms, occurring most often in the fall and winter months, produce on occasion considerable amounts of precipitation, record rains, snows, and high winds.

The average annual precipitation is reasonably uniform within the city but higher in the suburbs and less on eastern Long Island. Annual snowfall totals also show a consistent increase to the north and west of the city with lesser amounts along the south shores and the eastern end of Long Island.

Local Climatological Data is published for three locations in New York City, Central Park, La Guardia Airport, and John°F. Kennedy International Airport.

Based on the 1951-1980 period, the average first occurrence of 32 degrees Fahrenheit in the fall is November 11 and the average last occurrence in the spring is April 1.

New York Laguardia Airport *Queens County*   Elevation: 9 ft.   Latitude: 40° 47' N   Longitude: 73° 53' W

	JAN	FEB	MAR	APR	MAY	JUN	JUL	AUG	SEP	OCT	NOV	DEC	YEAR
Mean Maximum Temp. (°F)	38.2	40.8	49.0	59.9	70.5	79.2	84.7	82.9	75.3	64.3	53.7	43.7	61.8
Mean Temp. (°F)	32.3	34.5	41.9	52.1	62.4	71.5	77.2	75.9	68.5	57.6	47.7	38.0	55.0
Mean Minimum Temp. (°F)	26.3	28.1	34.8	44.4	54.3	63.7	69.6	68.8	61.6	50.9	41.7	32.2	48.0
Extreme Maximum Temp. (°F)	66	73	83	91	97	99	103	99	96	87	80	75	103
Extreme Minimum Temp. (°F)	-3	0	8	22	38	46	56	51	44	32	18	-1	-3
Days Maximum Temp. ≥ 90°F	0	0	0	0	1	3	6	4	1	0	0	0	15
Days Maximum Temp. ≤ 32°F	9	6	1	0	0	0	0	0	0	0	0	4	20
Days Minimum Temp. ≤ 32°F	22	18	10	1	0	0	0	0	0	0	3	14	68
Days Minimum Temp. ≤ 0°F	0	0	0	0	0	0	0	0	0	0	0	0	0
Heating Degree Days (base 65°F)	1,007	855	710	386	130	14	1	1	37	241	514	830	4,726
Cooling Degree Days (base 65°F)	0	0	1	4	63	231	399	352	156	21	1	0	1,228
Mean Precipitation (in.)	3.49	2.81	3.93	3.64	4.08	3.50	4.24	4.04	3.67	3.29	3.72	3.45	43.86
Maximum Precipitation (in.)	8.7	5.7	8.7	11.5	9.3	8.1	12.3	16.0	9.6	7.3	9.9	7.7	60.8
Minimum Precipitation (in.)	0.5	0.7	0.9	1.0	0.4	trace	0.7	0.1	1.0	0.1	0.3	0.3	22.2
Maximum 24-hr. Precipitation (in.)	3.1	2.2	3.1	2.8	2.8	4.0	3.5	6.4	3.6	3.4	4.4	2.7	6.4
Days With ≥ 0.1" Precipitation	7	6	7	6	7	6	6	6	6	5	6	7	75
Days With ≥ 1.0" Precipitation	1	1	1	1	1	1	1	1	1	1	1	1	12
Mean Snowfall (in.)	7.4	7.9	3.8	0.4	trace	0.0	trace	0.0	0.0	trace	0.4	2.7	22.6
Maximum Snowfall (in.)	18	26	19	8	trace	0	0	0	0	1	6	22	60
Maximum 24-hr. Snowfall (in.)	11	17	14	8	trace	0	0	0	0	0	6	16	17
Days With ≥ 1.0" Snow Depth	8	6	2	0	0	0	0	0	0	0	0	2	18
Thunderstorm Days	< 1	< 1	1	2	3	4	5	5	2	1	< 1	< 1	23
Foggy Days	10	9	10	10	11	9	8	8	8	8	9	10	110
Predominant Sky Cover	OVR	OVR	OVR	OVR	OVR	OVR	SCT	SCT	OVR	OVR	OVR	OVR	OVR
Mean Relative Humidity 7am (%)	67	67	67	67	71	71	73	75	76	74	71	68	71
Mean Relative Humidity 4pm (%)	57	55	52	51	53	53	54	56	56	56	55	57	55
Mean Dewpoint (°F)	20	21	27	36	48	57	63	62	56	45	35	25	41
Prevailing Wind Direction	NW	WNW	NW	NW	S	S	S	S	S	SW	WNW	WNW	NW
Prevailing Wind Speed (mph)	17	17	17	16	12	12	12	12	10	12	15	16	14
Maximum Wind Gust (mph)	61	67	71	63	56	56	59	73	64	71	76	77	77

Rochester Int'l Airport

Rochester is located at the mouth of the Genesee River at about the mid point of the south shore of Lake Ontario. The river flows northward from northwest Pennsylvania and empties into Lake Ontario. The land slopes from a lakeshore elevation of 246 feet to over 1,000 feet some 20 miles south. The airport is located just south of the city.

Lake Ontario plays a major role in the Rochester weather. In the summer its cooling effect inhibits the temperature from rising much above the low to mid 90s. In the winter the modifying temperature effect prevents temperatures from falling below -15 degrees most of the time, although temperatures at locations more than 15 miles inland do drop below -30 degrees.

The lake plays a major role in winter snowfall distribution. Well inland from the lake and toward the airport, the seasonal snowfall is usually less than in the area north of the airport and toward the lakeshore where wide variations occur. This is due to what is called the lake effect. Snowfalls of one to two feet or more in 24 hours are common near the lake in winter due the lake effect alone. The lake rarely freezes over because of its depth. The area is also prone to other heavy snowstorms and blizzards because of its proximity to the paths of low pressure systems coming up the east coast, out of the Ohio Valley.

Precipitation is rather evenly distributed throughout the year. Excessive rains occur infrequently but may be caused by slowly moving thunderstorms, slowly moving or stalled major low pressure systems, or by hurricanes and tropical storms that move inland. Hail occurs occasionally and heavy fog is rare.

The growing season averages 150 to 180 days. The years first frost usually occurs in late September and the last frost typically occurs in mid-May.

Rochester Int'l Airport *Monroe County*   Elevation: 597 ft.   Latitude: 43° 07' N   Longitude: 77° 41' W

	JAN	FEB	MAR	APR	MAY	JUN	JUL	AUG	SEP	OCT	NOV	DEC	YEAR
Mean Maximum Temp. (°F)	31.3	33.3	42.6	55.8	68.4	77.3	82.1	79.7	71.7	60.2	47.7	36.6	57.2
Mean Temp. (°F)	24.1	25.4	34.0	45.9	57.6	66.5	71.5	69.5	61.7	50.9	40.4	29.9	48.1
Mean Minimum Temp. (°F)	16.8	17.5	25.4	36.0	46.7	55.7	60.9	59.2	51.7	41.5	33.0	23.1	39.0
Extreme Maximum Temp. (°F)	68	73	83	93	94	95	98	95	95	86	79	72	98
Extreme Minimum Temp. (°F)	-17	-19	-7	13	26	36	45	38	30	20	5	-12	-19
Days Maximum Temp. ≥ 90°F	0	0	0	0	0	1	4	2	0	0	0	0	7
Days Maximum Temp. ≤ 32°F	17	14	6	1	0	0	0	0	0	0	2	10	50
Days Minimum Temp. ≤ 32°F	28	25	23	11	1	0	0	0	0	4	15	25	132
Days Minimum Temp. ≤ 0°F	3	2	0	0	0	0	0	0	0	0	0	1	6
Heating Degree Days (base 65°F)	1,263	1,111	954	572	258	62	9	22	148	437	732	1,081	6,649
Cooling Degree Days (base 65°F)	0	0	1	4	31	106	211	164	52	4	0	0	573
Mean Precipitation (in.)	2.30	2.05	2.56	2.69	2.77	3.34	2.97	3.53	3.41	2.69	2.88	2.79	33.98
Maximum Precipitation (in.)	5.8	5.1	5.0	4.1	6.6	6.8	6.0	6.0	6.3	7.8	7.0	4.6	40.5
Minimum Precipitation (in.)	0.7	0.7	0.5	1.2	0.4	0.2	0.6	0.8	0.3	0.2	0.4	0.6	22.4
Maximum 24-hr. Precipitation (in.)	1.3	1.8	1.5	1.8	3.4	2.6	3.3	2.3	3.5	2.9	2.0	1.5	3.5
Days With ≥ 0.1" Precipitation	7	6	7	7	7	7	6	7	7	6	7	8	82
Days With ≥ 1.0" Precipitation	0	0	0	0	0	1	1	1	1	0	0	0	4
Mean Snowfall (in.)	25.7	22.1	16.3	4.9	0.5	trace	trace	0.0	trace	0.1	8.0	21.9	99.5
Maximum Snowfall (in.)	60	65	40	20	11	0	0	0	trace	3	23	46	152
Maximum 24-hr. Snowfall (in.)	18	18	18	10	11	0	0	0	trace	3	12	18	18
Days With ≥ 1.0" Snow Depth	22	21	13	2	0	0	0	0	0	0	4	15	77
Thunderstorm Days	< 1	< 1	1	2	3	5	6	6	3	1	< 1	< 1	27
Foggy Days	8	9	10	10	10	10	11	13	12	11	11	10	125
Predominant Sky Cover	OVR	OVR	OVR	OVR	OVR	OVR	SCT	OVR	OVR	OVR	OVR	OVR	OVR
Mean Relative Humidity 7am (%)	79	80	80	78	77	79	82	86	88	85	82	81	81
Mean Relative Humidity 4pm (%)	71	69	63	56	53	53	52	55	59	60	69	73	61
Mean Dewpoint (°F)	18	18	25	35	45	55	60	59	53	42	33	23	39
Prevailing Wind Direction	WSW	WSW	WSW	WSW	WSW	WSW	SW	SW	SW	WSW	WSW	WSW	WSW
Prevailing Wind Speed (mph)	16	15	15	14	13	12	8	8	8	12	14	14	13
Maximum Wind Gust (mph)	63	70	68	71	64	52	56	62	51	60	67	55	71

Syracuse Hancock Int'l Airport

Syracuse is located approximately at the geographical center of the state. Gently rolling terrain stretches northward for about 30 miles to the eastern end of Lake Ontario. Oneida Lake is about 8 miles northeast of Syracuse. Approximately five miles south of the city, hills rise to 1,500 feet. Immediately to the west, the terrain is gently rolling with elevations 500 to 800 feet above sea level.

The climate of Syracuse is primarily continental in character and comparatively humid. Nearly all cyclonic systems moving from the interior of the country through the St. Lawrence Valley will affect the Syracuse area. Seasonal and diurnal changes are marked and produce an invigorating climate.

In the summer and in portions of the transitional seasons, temperatures usually rise rapidly during the daytime to moderate levels and as a rule fall rapidly after sunset. The nights are relatively cool and comfortable. There are only a few days in a year when atmospheric humidity causes great personal discomfort.

Winters are usually cold and are sometimes severe in part. Daytime temperatures average in the low 30s with nighttime lows in the teens. Low winter temperatures below -25 degrees have been recorded. The autumn, winter, and spring seasons display marked variability.

Based on the 1951-1980 period, the average first occurrence of 32 degrees Fahrenheit in the fall is October 16 and the average last occurrence in the spring is April 28.

Precipitation in the Syracuse area is derived principally from cyclonic storms which pass from the interior of the country through the St. Lawrence Valley. Lake Ontario provides the source of significant winter precipitation. The lake is quite deep and never freezes so cold air flowing over the lake is quickly saturated and produces the cloudiness and snow squalls which are a well-known feature of winter weather in the Syracuse area.

The precipitation is uncommonly well distributed, averaging about 3 inches per month throughout the year. Snowfall is moderately heavy with an average just over 100 inches. There are about 30 days per year with thunderstorms.

Wind velocities are moderate, but during the winter months there are numerous days with sufficient winds to cause blowing and drifting snow.

During December, January, and February there is much cloudiness. Syracuse receives only about one-third of possible sunshine during winter months. Approximately two-thirds of possible sunshine is received during the warm months.

Syracuse Hancock Int'l Airport *Onondaga County*   Elevation: 410 ft.   Latitude: 43° 07' N   Longitude: 76° 06' W

	JAN	FEB	MAR	APR	MAY	JUN	JUL	AUG	SEP	OCT	NOV	DEC	YEAR
Mean Maximum Temp. (°F)	31.1	33.4	42.9	56.3	68.9	77.2	81.9	79.6	71.3	59.8	47.6	36.4	57.2
Mean Temp. (°F)	23.1	25.0	34.0	46.1	57.8	66.2	71.2	69.3	61.4	50.4	40.2	29.2	47.8
Mean Minimum Temp. (°F)	15.0	16.4	25.1	35.9	46.5	55.1	60.5	58.9	51.3	40.9	32.7	21.9	38.4
Extreme Maximum Temp. (°F)	69	69	87	92	96	97	97	97	93	84	76	70	97
Extreme Minimum Temp. (°F)	-25	-26	-15	9	27	36	45	42	28	19	5	-22	-26
Days Maximum Temp. ≥ 90°F	0	0	0	0	0	2	4	2	0	0	0	0	8
Days Maximum Temp. ≤ 32°F	17	13	6	0	0	0	0	0	0	0	2	10	48
Days Minimum Temp. ≤ 32°F	28	25	24	11	1	0	0	0	0	5	15	26	135
Days Minimum Temp. ≤ 0°F	4	3	1	0	0	0	0	0	0	0	0	1	9
Heating Degree Days (base 65°F)	1,294	1,124	954	564	248	65	8	23	153	450	739	1,104	6,726
Cooling Degree Days (base 65°F)	0	0	1	4	29	109	215	167	50	3	0	0	578
Mean Precipitation (in.)	2.54	2.10	3.02	3.37	3.33	3.66	4.07	3.61	4.19	3.26	3.79	3.15	40.09
Maximum Precipitation (in.)	5.8	5.4	6.8	8.1	7.4	12.3	9.5	8.4	8.8	8.3	6.8	5.5	57.9
Minimum Precipitation (in.)	1.0	0.6	1.0	1.2	0.8	1.0	0.9	1.3	0.8	0.2	1.3	0.8	27.1
Maximum 24-hr. Precipitation (in.)	1.4	1.9	1.3	2.4	2.4	3.6	3.9	3.0	2.5	3.5	2.1	1.8	3.9
Days With ≥ 0.1" Precipitation	7	6	8	8	8	8	7	7	8	8	9	9	93
Days With ≥ 1.0" Precipitation	0	0	0	1	0	1	1	1	1	1	0	0	6
Mean Snowfall (in.)	33.0	24.0	19.0	4.8	0.2	trace	trace	0.0	trace	0.5	10.7	28.0	120.2
Maximum Snowfall (in.)	72	73	54	16	2	0	0	trace	trace	6	34	65	208
Maximum 24-hr. Snowfall (in.)	22	21	22	7	2	0	0	trace	trace	3	12	16	22
Days With ≥ 1.0" Snow Depth	24	21	14	2	0	0	0	0	0	0	5	16	82
Thunderstorm Days	< 1	< 1	1	2	3	5	6	5	3	1	1	< 1	27
Foggy Days	10	9	11	10	11	11	12	13	14	12	12	11	136
Predominant Sky Cover	OVR	OVR	OVR	OVR	OVR	OVR	OVR	OVR	OVR	OVR	OVR	OVR	OVR
Mean Relative Humidity 7am (%)	77	78	78	76	76	77	79	85	86	84	80	79	80
Mean Relative Humidity 4pm (%)	69	67	60	52	53	54	54	57	60	60	68	72	60
Mean Dewpoint (°F)	16	17	24	34	45	55	60	59	53	42	32	22	38
Prevailing Wind Direction	WSW	WSW	WNW	WNW	WNW	WNW	WSW	WSW	WSW	WSW	WSW	WSW	WSW
Prevailing Wind Speed (mph)	15	14	14	14	12	12	9	9	9	10	13	14	12
Maximum Wind Gust (mph)	58	56	61	63	76	67	66	49	48	60	58	63	76

Albion 2 NE *Orleans County*   Elevation: 439 ft.   Latitude: 43° 17' N   Longitude: 78° 10' W

	JAN	FEB	MAR	APR	MAY	JUN	JUL	AUG	SEP	OCT	NOV	DEC	YEAR
Mean Maximum Temp. (°F)	31.2	33.6	42.9	56.0	68.8	77.9	82.5	80.3	72.6	60.8	47.8	37.0	57.6
Mean Temp. (°F)	24.2	25.9	34.3	46.1	57.7	67.0	71.8	70.0	62.8	51.5	40.5	30.3	48.5
Mean Minimum Temp. (°F)	17.0	18.2	25.6	36.0	46.6	55.9	61.1	59.6	52.9	42.0	33.2	23.6	39.3
Extreme Maximum Temp. (°F)	67	74	80	90	91	96	101	97	92	84	74	75	101
Extreme Minimum Temp. (°F)	-15	-20	-5	9	28	35	45	39	32	22	8	-10	-20
Days Maximum Temp. ≥ 90°F	0	0	0	0	0	1	4	2	0	0	0	0	7
Days Maximum Temp. ≤ 32°F	17	13	6	1	0	0	0	0	0	0	2	9	48
Days Minimum Temp. ≤ 32°F	29	25	24	11	1	0	0	0	0	4	15	25	134
Days Minimum Temp. ≤ 0°F	2	2	0	0	0	0	0	0	0	0	0	0	4
Heating Degree Days (base 65°F)	1,260	1,097	945	567	252	57	7	18	126	418	730	1,069	6,546
Cooling Degree Days (base 65°F)	0	0	1	4	34	126	236	187	68	5	0	0	661
Mean Precipitation (in.)	2.63	2.07	2.78	3.06	2.94	3.54	2.59	3.08	3.75	2.88	3.23	3.16	35.71
Days With ≥ 0.1" Precipitation	7	6	7	8	7	7	6	7	7	7	9	9	87
Days With ≥ 1.0" Precipitation	0	0	0	0	0	1	0	1	1	0	0	0	3
Mean Snowfall (in.)	19.1	14.9	10.2	2.2	0.3	0.0	0.0	0.0	0.0	trace	5.8	15.1	67.6
Days With ≥ 1.0" Snow Depth	16	13	7	1	0	0	0	0	0	0	4	11	52

Alfred *Allegany County*   Elevation: 1,768 ft.   Latitude: 42° 16' N   Longitude: 77° 47' W

	JAN	FEB	MAR	APR	MAY	JUN	JUL	AUG	SEP	OCT	NOV	DEC	YEAR
Mean Maximum Temp. (°F)	30.6	33.9	43.5	55.8	68.0	75.7	79.6	77.8	70.3	59.4	46.4	36.1	56.4
Mean Temp. (°F)	21.2	23.4	32.2	43.5	54.7	62.9	67.1	65.5	58.5	47.7	37.3	27.5	45.1
Mean Minimum Temp. (°F)	11.8	12.9	21.1	31.1	41.4	50.0	54.6	53.1	46.6	35.9	28.2	19.0	33.8
Extreme Maximum Temp. (°F)	63	66	83	91	93	93	96	93	91	81	75	68	96
Extreme Minimum Temp. (°F)	-25	-26	-16	5	18	28	37	27	20	15	2	-21	-26
Days Maximum Temp. ≥ 90°F	0	0	0	0	0	0	1	1	0	0	0	0	2
Days Maximum Temp. ≤ 32°F	17	13	5	1	0	0	0	0	0	0	2	11	49
Days Minimum Temp. ≤ 32°F	29	27	26	17	6	0	0	0	2	11	21	28	167
Days Minimum Temp. ≤ 0°F	6	6	2	0	0	0	0	0	0	0	0	2	16
Heating Degree Days (base 65°F)	1,351	1,169	1,009	642	327	113	38	59	215	531	823	1,155	7,432
Cooling Degree Days (base 65°F)	0	0	0	1	14	57	110	76	23	0	0	0	281
Mean Precipitation (in.)	2.14	1.97	2.66	2.98	3.42	4.46	3.71	3.28	3.98	3.33	3.30	2.79	38.02
Days With ≥ 0.1" Precipitation	6	6	7	8	8	8	8	7	8	7	8	8	89
Days With ≥ 1.0" Precipitation	0	0	0	0	0	1	1	1	1	1	0	0	5
Mean Snowfall (in.)	20.2	16.7	14.5	4.2	0.4	0.0	0.0	0.0	0.0	0.5	8.6	18.3	83.4
Days With ≥ 1.0" Snow Depth	25	22	15	2	0	0	0	0	0	0	5	17	86

Allegany State Park *Cattaraugus County*   Elevation: 1,499 ft.   Latitude: 42° 06' N   Longitude: 78° 45' W

	JAN	FEB	MAR	APR	MAY	JUN	JUL	AUG	SEP	OCT	NOV	DEC	YEAR
Mean Maximum Temp. (°F)	30.1	32.7	41.7	54.5	66.6	74.8	78.5	76.7	69.0	58.1	45.6	34.9	55.3
Mean Temp. (°F)	21.3	22.8	31.1	42.8	53.5	62.0	66.1	64.7	57.6	47.1	37.3	27.2	44.5
Mean Minimum Temp. (°F)	12.4	12.9	20.4	31.0	40.4	49.2	53.7	52.7	46.1	36.0	28.9	19.5	33.6
Extreme Maximum Temp. (°F)	63	68	80	89	90	92	97	93	89	82	74	70	97
Extreme Minimum Temp. (°F)	-22	-25	-17	9	19	24	29	31	23	14	-1	-16	-25
Days Maximum Temp. ≥ 90°F	0	0	0	0	0	0	1	0	0	0	0	0	1
Days Maximum Temp. ≤ 32°F	18	15	7	1	0	0	0	0	0	0	3	12	56
Days Minimum Temp. ≤ 32°F	30	27	27	19	7	1	0	0	2	11	21	28	173
Days Minimum Temp. ≤ 0°F	5	5	2	0	0	0	0	0	0	0	0	2	14
Heating Degree Days (base 65°F)	1,349	1,185	1,045	662	360	131	53	72	238	548	825	1,165	7,633
Cooling Degree Days (base 65°F)	0	0	0	1	12	48	96	70	21	1	0	0	249
Mean Precipitation (in.)	3.03	2.48	3.29	3.47	3.88	4.88	4.31	4.13	4.50	3.81	4.06	3.67	45.51
Days With ≥ 0.1" Precipitation	9	8	9	9	9	10	8	8	9	10	10	11	110
Days With ≥ 1.0" Precipitation	0	0	0	0	1	1	1	1	1	1	0	0	6
Mean Snowfall (in.)	na	na	na	na	trace	0.0	0.0	0.0	0.0	0.1	na	na	na
Days With ≥ 1.0" Snow Depth	27	25	18	2	0	0	0	0	0	0	7	19	98

Angelica *Allegany County*   Elevation: 1,443 ft.   Latitude: 42° 18' N   Longitude: 77° 59' W

	JAN	FEB	MAR	APR	MAY	JUN	JUL	AUG	SEP	OCT	NOV	DEC	YEAR
Mean Maximum Temp. (°F)	31.2	33.8	43.1	55.8	68.0	75.5	79.6	77.5	70.5	59.7	46.8	36.2	56.5
Mean Temp. (°F)	22.0	23.3	32.0	43.3	54.3	62.4	66.8	65.2	58.4	47.8	37.9	27.8	45.1
Mean Minimum Temp. (°F)	12.7	12.8	20.7	30.8	40.5	49.3	54.0	52.8	46.3	35.9	29.0	19.4	33.7
Extreme Maximum Temp. (°F)	63	67	82	89	91	93	97	94	90	82	77	70	97
Extreme Minimum Temp. (°F)	-33	-30	-20	9	19	28	36	30	21	14	0	-20	-33
Days Maximum Temp. ≥ 90°F	0	0	0	0	0	0	1	1	0	0	0	0	2
Days Maximum Temp. ≤ 32°F	17	13	6	1	0	0	0	0	0	0	2	11	50
Days Minimum Temp. ≤ 32°F	29	26	26	18	8	1	0	0	2	12	20	28	170
Days Minimum Temp. ≤ 0°F	6	6	2	0	0	0	0	0	0	0	0	2	16
Heating Degree Days (base 65°F)	1,329	1,171	1,019	647	337	125	44	64	216	528	808	1,147	7,435
Cooling Degree Days (base 65°F)	0	0	0	1	10	48	98	69	22	1	0	0	249
Mean Precipitation (in.)	2.01	2.00	2.43	2.90	3.18	4.60	3.73	3.82	3.76	3.16	3.00	2.49	37.08
Days With ≥ 0.1" Precipitation	6	6	7	7	8	9	8	8	8	8	8	7	90
Days With ≥ 1.0" Precipitation	0	0	0	0	0	1	1	1	1	1	0	0	5
Mean Snowfall (in.)	15.1	11.3	10.1	3.0	0.2	0.0	0.0	0.0	0.0	0.3	5.7	13.4	59.1
Days With ≥ 1.0" Snow Depth	24	21	13	2	0	0	0	0	0	0	5	16	81

Aurora Research Farm *Cayuga County*   Elevation: 830 ft.   Latitude: 42° 44' N   Longitude: 76° 39' W

	JAN	FEB	MAR	APR	MAY	JUN	JUL	AUG	SEP	OCT	NOV	DEC	YEAR
Mean Maximum Temp. (°F)	31.0	33.0	41.9	54.9	67.5	76.2	81.2	79.5	71.7	59.8	47.5	36.7	56.7
Mean Temp. (°F)	23.3	24.9	33.3	45.3	57.0	65.9	70.7	69.0	61.6	50.4	40.1	29.6	47.6
Mean Minimum Temp. (°F)	15.6	16.6	24.8	35.6	46.4	55.6	60.1	58.5	51.4	40.9	32.6	22.5	38.4
Extreme Maximum Temp. (°F)	67	67	85	93	94	96	101	97	98	85	81	69	101
Extreme Minimum Temp. (°F)	-21	-19	-11	10	25	34	43	40	27	20	5	-15	-21
Days Maximum Temp. ≥ 90°F	0	0	0	0	1	1	4	2	1	0	0	0	9
Days Maximum Temp. ≤ 32°F	17	13	7	1	0	0	0	0	0	0	2	10	50
Days Minimum Temp. ≤ 32°F	29	26	24	12	1	0	0	0	0	5	15	26	138
Days Minimum Temp. ≤ 0°F	3	2	0	0	0	0	0	0	0	0	0	1	6
Heating Degree Days (base 65°F)	1,285	1,128	975	591	277	76	18	30	152	451	740	1,090	6,813
Cooling Degree Days (base 65°F)	0	0	1	6	35	115	210	168	61	5	0	0	601
Mean Precipitation (in.)	1.87	1.87	2.50	3.22	3.20	4.16	3.40	3.65	4.25	3.26	3.43	2.52	37.33
Days With ≥ 0.1" Precipitation	5	5	7	8	8	8	8	7	8	7	8	6	85
Days With ≥ 1.0" Precipitation	0	0	0	0	0	1	0	1	1	1	0	0	4
Mean Snowfall (in.)	14.0	12.1	11.3	4.3	0.4	0.0	0.0	0.0	0.0	0.4	5.9	13.4	61.8
Days With ≥ 1.0" Snow Depth	23	21	13	3	0	0	0	0	0	0	5	15	80

Batavia *Genesee County*   Elevation: 898 ft.   Latitude: 43° 00' N   Longitude: 78° 11' W

	JAN	FEB	MAR	APR	MAY	JUN	JUL	AUG	SEP	OCT	NOV	DEC	YEAR
Mean Maximum Temp. (°F)	31.7	34.0	43.7	56.6	68.9	77.7	81.7	79.5	72.2	61.2	48.2	36.8	57.7
Mean Temp. (°F)	23.9	25.3	34.3	46.1	57.8	66.7	71.1	69.1	62.0	51.2	40.3	29.5	48.1
Mean Minimum Temp. (°F)	16.0	16.5	24.8	35.5	46.6	55.7	60.5	58.6	51.8	41.1	32.5	22.2	38.5
Extreme Maximum Temp. (°F)	64	72	81	92	92	95	96	95	93	83	76	73	96
Extreme Minimum Temp. (°F)	-22	-25	-15	6	24	32	45	33	29	20	2	-18	-25
Days Maximum Temp. ≥ 90°F	0	0	0	0	0	1	2	1	0	0	0	0	4
Days Maximum Temp. ≤ 32°F	16	13	6	0	0	0	0	0	0	0	2	10	47
Days Minimum Temp. ≤ 32°F	29	26	24	12	1	0	0	0	0	5	16	26	139
Days Minimum Temp. ≤ 0°F	3	3	1	0	0	0	0	0	0	0	0	1	8
Heating Degree Days (base 65°F)	1,270	1,115	946	566	250	59	9	25	140	427	733	1,092	6,632
Cooling Degree Days (base 65°F)	0	0	1	5	32	118	211	158	56	5	0	0	586
Mean Precipitation (in.)	1.92	1.88	2.30	3.01	3.31	3.90	3.31	3.60	4.01	3.10	2.80	2.41	35.55
Days With ≥ 0.1" Precipitation	5	5	6	7	8	8	6	7	8	8	7	7	82
Days With ≥ 1.0" Precipitation	0	0	0	0	0	1	1	1	1	1	0	0	5
Mean Snowfall (in.)	21.3	17.1	12.6	3.9	0.4	0.0	0.0	0.0	0.0	0.2	6.8	20.0	82.3
Days With ≥ 1.0" Snow Depth	20	17	9	2	0	0	0	0	0	0	3	15	66

Bath *Steuben County*   Elevation: 1,118 ft.   Latitude: 42° 21' N   Longitude: 77° 21' W

	JAN	FEB	MAR	APR	MAY	JUN	JUL	AUG	SEP	OCT	NOV	DEC	YEAR
Mean Maximum Temp. (°F)	32.1	34.0	42.7	55.9	68.1	76.5	81.0	79.2	71.8	60.1	46.8	36.4	57.0
Mean Temp. (°F)	22.7	23.6	32.0	44.0	54.9	63.5	68.1	66.3	59.1	48.1	38.0	28.0	45.7
Mean Minimum Temp. (°F)	12.9	13.1	21.2	32.1	41.7	50.5	55.2	53.4	46.5	35.9	29.0	19.5	34.2
Extreme Maximum Temp. (°F)	64	69	84	90	94	93	101	96	92	85	77	70	101
Extreme Minimum Temp. (°F)	-24	-25	-18	8	23	28	39	28	24	15	1	-16	-25
Days Maximum Temp. ≥ 90°F	0	0	0	0	0	1	3	1	0	0	0	0	5
Days Maximum Temp. ≤ 32°F	16	13	6	0	0	0	0	0	0	0	2	10	47
Days Minimum Temp. ≤ 32°F	29	27	26	17	5	0	0	0	2	12	20	28	166
Days Minimum Temp. ≤ 0°F	5	5	1	0	0	0	0	0	0	0	0	2	13
Heating Degree Days (base 65°F)	1,297	1,163	1,016	624	318	105	33	52	203	518	805	1,142	7,276
Cooling Degree Days (base 65°F)	0	0	0	2	14	68	137	95	29	1	0	0	346
Mean Precipitation (in.)	1.77	1.67	2.22	2.72	2.80	3.78	3.24	2.68	3.44	2.64	2.84	2.16	31.96
Days With ≥ 0.1" Precipitation	4	4	6	7	7	7	7	6	7	6	7	5	73
Days With ≥ 1.0" Precipitation	0	0	0	0	0	1	1	1	1	1	0	0	5
Mean Snowfall (in.)	11.3	10.9	9.2	1.7	trace	trace	0.0	0.0	0.0	trace	3.8	9.8	46.7
Days With ≥ 1.0" Snow Depth	21	21	12	2	0	0	0	0	0	0	4	14	74

Bolivar *Allegany County*   Elevation: 1,578 ft.   Latitude: 42° 05' N   Longitude: 78° 11' W

	JAN	FEB	MAR	APR	MAY	JUN	JUL	AUG	SEP	OCT	NOV	DEC	YEAR
Mean Maximum Temp. (°F)	30.4	33.4	42.5	55.0	66.9	74.6	78.6	77.0	69.4	58.8	46.0	35.3	55.7
Mean Temp. (°F)	20.6	22.5	31.6	43.0	53.7	61.8	66.2	64.8	57.5	46.7	37.0	26.7	44.3
Mean Minimum Temp. (°F)	10.7	11.6	20.7	31.0	40.5	48.9	53.7	52.6	45.7	34.5	28.0	18.0	33.0
Extreme Maximum Temp. (°F)	62	65	82	88	92	91	97	93	88	82	76	68	97
Extreme Minimum Temp. (°F)	-34	-32	-20	8	19	26	35	31	23	12	0	-25	-34
Days Maximum Temp. ≥ 90°F	0	0	0	0	0	0	1	1	0	0	0	0	2
Days Maximum Temp. ≤ 32°F	18	14	6	1	0	0	0	0	0	0	3	12	54
Days Minimum Temp. ≤ 32°F	30	27	27	18	8	1	0	0	2	14	22	28	177
Days Minimum Temp. ≤ 0°F	7	6	2	0	0	0	0	0	0	0	0	3	18
Heating Degree Days (base 65°F)	1,370	1,193	1,029	654	356	138	55	70	237	562	833	1,181	7,678
Cooling Degree Days (base 65°F)	0	0	0	1	12	52	104	75	18	1	0	0	263
Mean Precipitation (in.)	2.27	1.87	2.73	3.07	3.37	4.95	4.41	3.77	4.15	3.20	3.23	2.82	39.84
Days With ≥ 0.1" Precipitation	6	6	8	8	8	9	9	8	8	8	8	8	94
Days With ≥ 1.0" Precipitation	0	0	0	0	1	1	1	1	1	1	0	0	6
Mean Snowfall (in.)	19.3	14.7	12.4	2.9	0.2	trace	0.0	0.0	0.0	0.5	7.5	18.9	76.4
Days With ≥ 1.0" Snow Depth	26	24	16	3	0	0	0	0	0	0	7	20	96

Boonville 2 SSW *Oneida County*   Elevation: 1,578 ft.   Latitude: 43° 27' N   Longitude: 75° 21' W

	JAN	FEB	MAR	APR	MAY	JUN	JUL	AUG	SEP	OCT	NOV	DEC	YEAR
Mean Maximum Temp. (°F)	24.4	27.3	36.1	49.8	63.6	71.5	75.9	74.1	65.6	54.2	41.1	29.7	51.1
Mean Temp. (°F)	16.0	18.5	27.7	40.6	53.5	61.6	66.2	64.5	56.4	45.4	34.1	22.3	42.2
Mean Minimum Temp. (°F)	7.6	9.7	19.2	31.4	43.3	51.5	56.4	55.0	47.2	36.6	27.1	14.9	33.3
Extreme Maximum Temp. (°F)	57	55	77	85	87	89	94	93	89	79	69	62	94
Extreme Minimum Temp. (°F)	-31	-24	-18	-1	22	29	33	35	25	14	1	-33	-33
Days Maximum Temp. ≥ 90°F	0	0	0	0	0	0	0	0	0	0	0	0	0
Days Maximum Temp. ≤ 32°F	24	19	12	2	0	0	0	0	0	0	6	19	82
Days Minimum Temp. ≤ 32°F	30	27	28	18	3	0	0	0	1	11	22	29	169
Days Minimum Temp. ≤ 0°F	10	8	2	0	0	0	0	0	0	0	0	4	24
Heating Degree Days (base 65°F)	1,513	1,307	1,151	725	362	141	50	76	269	601	919	1,318	8,432
Cooling Degree Days (base 65°F)	0	0	0	1	10	43	93	67	15	0	0	0	229
Mean Precipitation (in.)	5.68	4.37	5.00	4.56	4.38	4.77	4.06	4.58	5.98	4.78	5.82	5.85	59.83
Days With ≥ 0.1" Precipitation	13	10	11	9	9	9	8	8	9	10	12	13	121
Days With ≥ 1.0" Precipitation	1	1	1	1	1	1	1	1	2	1	1	1	13
Mean Snowfall (in.)	59.3	42.8	34.7	10.2	0.9	trace	0.0	0.0	trace	2.2	21.2	47.3	218.6
Days With ≥ 1.0" Snow Depth	30	28	30	14	1	0	0	0	0	1	13	27	144

Bridgehampton *Suffolk County*   Elevation: 59 ft.   Latitude: 40° 57' N   Longitude: 72° 18' W

	JAN	FEB	MAR	APR	MAY	JUN	JUL	AUG	SEP	OCT	NOV	DEC	YEAR
Mean Maximum Temp. (°F)	38.4	39.4	46.4	55.6	65.4	74.4	80.7	79.7	72.9	62.9	53.1	43.7	59.4
Mean Temp. (°F)	30.6	31.9	38.5	47.1	56.7	65.8	72.1	71.2	64.1	53.7	44.9	35.9	51.1
Mean Minimum Temp. (°F)	22.9	24.4	30.5	38.6	47.8	57.2	63.5	62.7	55.3	44.5	36.7	28.1	42.7
Extreme Maximum Temp. (°F)	62	63	79	85	93	95	102	98	93	83	73	70	102
Extreme Minimum Temp. (°F)	-11	-5	6	14	29	39	48	41	35	24	10	-5	-11
Days Maximum Temp. ≥ 90°F	0	0	0	0	0	0	2	1	0	0	0	0	3
Days Maximum Temp. ≤ 32°F	8	6	1	0	0	0	0	0	0	0	0	3	18
Days Minimum Temp. ≤ 32°F	26	22	19	6	0	0	0	0	0	3	11	21	108
Days Minimum Temp. ≤ 0°F	0	0	0	0	0	0	0	0	0	0	0	0	0
Heating Degree Days (base 65°F)	1,058	928	816	530	262	53	4	8	87	348	597	895	5,586
Cooling Degree Days (base 65°F)	0	0	0	0	11	91	237	198	65	6	0	0	608
Mean Precipitation (in.)	4.56	3.82	4.50	4.27	3.76	3.61	3.07	3.93	3.87	3.73	4.45	4.31	47.88
Days With ≥ 0.1" Precipitation	7	6	8	7	7	6	5	5	5	6	7	8	77
Days With ≥ 1.0" Precipitation	1	1	1	1	1	1	1	1	1	1	1	1	12
Mean Snowfall (in.)	8.0	7.8	4.4	0.8	trace	0.0	0.0	0.0	0.0	trace	0.8	2.4	24.2
Days With ≥ 1.0" Snow Depth	9	7	3	0	0	0	0	0	0	0	0	2	21

Canandaigua 3 S *Ontario County*   Elevation: 718 ft.   Latitude: 42° 51' N   Longitude: 77° 17' W

	JAN	FEB	MAR	APR	MAY	JUN	JUL	AUG	SEP	OCT	NOV	DEC	YEAR
Mean Maximum Temp. (°F)	32.4	34.3	42.5	55.0	67.7	76.7	81.7	79.6	71.9	60.6	48.6	37.9	57.4
Mean Temp. (°F)	24.5	25.8	33.8	45.2	57.0	66.3	71.5	69.7	62.4	51.3	41.1	30.8	48.3
Mean Minimum Temp. (°F)	16.5	17.2	25.0	35.4	46.3	55.9	61.3	59.8	52.8	42.0	33.6	23.6	39.1
Extreme Maximum Temp. (°F)	66	67	85	88	93	94	98	96	95	85	80	71	98
Extreme Minimum Temp. (°F)	-14	-17	-4	12	27	37	45	42	33	23	9	-12	-17
Days Maximum Temp. ≥ 90°F	0	0	0	0	0	1	3	2	0	0	0	0	6
Days Maximum Temp. ≤ 32°F	16	13	6	1	0	0	0	0	0	0	2	9	47
Days Minimum Temp. ≤ 32°F	28	26	24	11	1	0	0	0	0	3	14	25	132
Days Minimum Temp. ≤ 0°F	2	2	0	0	0	0	0	0	0	0	0	0	4
Heating Degree Days (base 65°F)	1,250	1,100	961	589	270	65	10	23	134	422	710	1,055	6,589
Cooling Degree Days (base 65°F)	0	0	0	2	30	113	227	175	63	6	0	0	616
Mean Precipitation (in.)	1.76	1.65	2.37	3.01	2.87	3.92	3.15	3.18	3.56	2.96	2.90	2.24	33.57
Days With ≥ 0.1" Precipitation	5	5	6	7	8	8	7	7	7	7	7	6	80
Days With ≥ 1.0" Precipitation	0	0	0	0	0	1	0	1	1	0	0	0	3
Mean Snowfall (in.)	na	na	na	na	0.0	0.0	0.0	0.0	0.0	trace	na	na	na
Days With ≥ 1.0" Snow Depth	na	na	na	na	0	0	0	0	0	0	na	na	na

Canton 4 SE *St. Lawrence County*   Elevation: 396 ft.   Latitude: 44° 35' N   Longitude: 75° 07' W

	JAN	FEB	MAR	APR	MAY	JUN	JUL	AUG	SEP	OCT	NOV	DEC	YEAR
Mean Maximum Temp. (°F)	25.6	28.3	38.4	52.4	66.0	74.3	79.3	77.1	68.6	56.8	44.3	31.6	53.6
Mean Temp. (°F)	14.8	17.3	28.3	42.1	55.1	63.6	68.6	66.3	58.0	46.4	35.9	22.1	43.2
Mean Minimum Temp. (°F)	3.9	6.3	18.1	31.8	44.1	52.9	57.8	55.5	47.3	35.9	27.4	12.7	32.8
Extreme Maximum Temp. (°F)	66	65	92	89	90	92	93	97	91	82	77	68	97
Extreme Minimum Temp. (°F)	-40	-40	-26	-8	21	29	35	32	22	13	-4	-37	-40
Days Maximum Temp. ≥ 90°F	0	0	0	0	0	0	1	0	0	0	0	0	1
Days Maximum Temp. ≤ 32°F	21	17	10	1	0	0	0	0	0	0	4	15	68
Days Minimum Temp. ≤ 32°F	30	27	27	17	3	0	0	0	2	12	21	29	168
Days Minimum Temp. ≤ 0°F	13	11	3	0	0	0	0	0	0	0	0	7	34
Heating Degree Days (base 65°F)	1,552	1,342	1,131	682	321	109	36	67	236	572	868	1,323	8,239
Cooling Degree Days (base 65°F)	0	0	0	2	18	75	155	112	30	2	0	0	394
Mean Precipitation (in.)	2.34	2.01	2.40	2.89	2.98	3.28	3.56	3.99	4.19	3.35	3.43	2.73	37.15
Days With ≥ 0.1" Precipitation	6	5	6	7	8	7	7	8	9	8	8	7	86
Days With ≥ 1.0" Precipitation	0	0	0	0	0	1	1	1	1	1	1	0	6
Mean Snowfall (in.)	23.8	19.7	15.4	4.5	0.2	0.0	0.0	0.0	trace	0.4	6.9	20.0	90.9
Days With ≥ 1.0" Snow Depth	27	24	19	4	0	0	0	0	0	0	7	20	101

Chasm Falls *Franklin County* Elevation: 1,059 ft.   Latitude: 44° 45' N   Longitude: 74° 13' W

	JAN	FEB	MAR	APR	MAY	JUN	JUL	AUG	SEP	OCT	NOV	DEC	YEAR
Mean Maximum Temp. (°F)	25.7	28.5	38.9	52.3	66.9	74.6	78.8	75.9	67.2	56.2	43.2	30.4	53.2
Mean Temp. (°F)	15.3	17.4	28.2	41.2	54.2	62.4	67.0	64.6	56.5	45.9	34.9	21.1	42.4
Mean Minimum Temp. (°F)	4.7	6.3	17.5	30.1	41.5	50.2	55.2	53.3	45.8	35.6	26.4	11.9	31.5
Extreme Maximum Temp. (°F)	61	64	75	87	90	93	95	95	88	81	72	64	95
Extreme Minimum Temp. (°F)	-36	-42	-24	-5	20	27	35	31	23	12	-5	-30	-42
Days Maximum Temp. ≥ 90°F	0	0	0	0	0	0	1	0	0	0	0	0	1
Days Maximum Temp. ≤ 32°F	21	18	9	1	0	0	0	0	0	0	5	17	71
Days Minimum Temp. ≤ 32°F	30	27	28	19	5	0	0	0	2	13	23	29	176
Days Minimum Temp. ≤ 0°F	12	11	4	0	0	0	0	0	0	0	0	7	34
Heating Degree Days (base 65°F)	1,536	1,338	1,134	710	342	127	45	83	266	585	898	1,352	8,416
Cooling Degree Days (base 65°F)	0	0	0	0	10	48	108	70	14	0	na	0	na
Mean Precipitation (in.)	2.69	2.54	2.85	2.97	3.32	4.04	4.28	5.55	4.38	3.55	3.79	3.47	43.43
Days With ≥ 0.1" Precipitation	9	7	9	9	9	9	9	10	9	9	10	9	108
Days With ≥ 1.0" Precipitation	0	0	0	0	0	1	1	1	1	1	1	0	6
Mean Snowfall (in.)	27.3	26.1	20.3	8.3	0.4	trace	0.0	0.0	0.0	0.8	11.9	26.1	121.2
Days With ≥ 1.0" Snow Depth	30	28	29	12	0	0	0	0	0	1	11	25	136

Chazy *Clinton County* Elevation: 167 ft.   Latitude: 44° 53' N   Longitude: 73° 26' W

	JAN	FEB	MAR	APR	MAY	JUN	JUL	AUG	SEP	OCT	NOV	DEC	YEAR
Mean Maximum Temp. (°F)	26.7	29.6	39.6	54.5	68.2	76.3	80.7	78.4	68.9	57.0	44.5	32.3	54.7
Mean Temp. (°F)	16.4	19.1	29.7	43.8	56.3	64.9	69.5	67.2	58.3	47.2	36.3	23.3	44.3
Mean Minimum Temp. (°F)	6.0	8.6	19.7	33.0	44.4	53.5	58.3	56.0	47.7	37.5	28.1	14.4	33.9
Extreme Maximum Temp. (°F)	61	60	79	90	94	97	97	100	93	85	74	66	100
Extreme Minimum Temp. (°F)	-44	-41	-22	6	25	30	38	32	22	14	-2	-28	-44
Days Maximum Temp. ≥ 90°F	0	0	0	0	0	1	2	1	0	0	0	0	4
Days Maximum Temp. ≤ 32°F	20	16	8	0	0	0	0	0	0	0	3	15	62
Days Minimum Temp. ≤ 32°F	30	27	26	15	2	0	0	0	1	10	20	28	159
Days Minimum Temp. ≤ 0°F	12	9	3	0	0	0	0	0	0	0	0	6	30
Heating Degree Days (base 65°F)	1,502	1,290	1,088	631	280	75	18	44	219	545	854	1,286	7,832
Cooling Degree Days (base 65°F)	0	0	0	2	14	80	165	117	26	1	0	0	405
Mean Precipitation (in.)	1.15	na	1.37	2.38	2.92	3.15	3.56	3.90	3.46	3.04	2.58	1.51	na
Days With ≥ 0.1" Precipitation	na	na	na	na	7	7	8	7	7	7	na	na	na
Days With ≥ 1.0" Precipitation	0	na	0	0	0	0	1	1	1	1	0	na	na
Mean Snowfall (in.)	14.0	11.0	9.1	2.9	0.1	0.0	0.0	0.0	0.0	0.3	5.8	12.8	56.0
Days With ≥ 1.0" Snow Depth	24	22	15	2	0	0	0	0	0	0	4	19	86

Cherry Valley 2 NNE *Otsego County* Elevation: 1,358 ft.   Latitude: 42° 49' N   Longitude: 74° 44' W

	JAN	FEB	MAR	APR	MAY	JUN	JUL	AUG	SEP	OCT	NOV	DEC	YEAR
Mean Maximum Temp. (°F)	27.7	30.4	39.9	53.3	66.3	74.0	78.2	76.1	68.1	57.0	44.6	32.9	54.0
Mean Temp. (°F)	19.3	21.7	30.8	43.1	55.2	63.4	68.0	66.1	58.6	47.7	37.0	25.3	44.7
Mean Minimum Temp. (°F)	10.9	12.8	21.7	33.0	44.2	52.7	57.6	56.1	49.0	38.3	29.4	17.7	35.3
Extreme Maximum Temp. (°F)	65	62	80	85	87	89	93	92	87	81	76	66	93
Extreme Minimum Temp. (°F)	-23	-26	-14	7	20	32	38	35	25	15	3	-25	-26
Days Maximum Temp. ≥ 90°F	0	0	0	0	0	0	0	0	0	0	0	0	0
Days Maximum Temp. ≤ 32°F	20	16	8	1	0	0	0	0	0	0	4	15	64
Days Minimum Temp. ≤ 32°F	30	27	27	16	2	0	0	0	1	9	19	29	160
Days Minimum Temp. ≤ 0°F	7	5	1	0	0	0	0	0	0	0	0	3	16
Heating Degree Days (base 65°F)	1,410	1,218	1,053	651	312	104	30	55	215	532	833	1,223	7,636
Cooling Degree Days (base 65°F)	0	0	0	1	14	60	129	93	28	1	0	0	326
Mean Precipitation (in.)	2.97	2.59	3.64	3.82	4.20	4.37	4.37	3.82	4.15	3.56	3.90	3.28	44.67
Days With ≥ 0.1" Precipitation	8	6	8	8	9	9	8	7	8	8	9	8	96
Days With ≥ 1.0" Precipitation	0	1	1	1	1	1	1	1	1	1	1	1	10
Mean Snowfall (in.)	29.9	19.0	21.7	6.6	0.9	0.0	0.0	0.0	trace	0.8	12.0	25.2	116.1
Days With ≥ 1.0" Snow Depth	22	21	15	4	0	0	0	0	0	0	6	17	85

Colden 1 N *Erie County* Elevation: 1,023 ft.   Latitude: 42° 40' N   Longitude: 78° 41' W

	JAN	FEB	MAR	APR	MAY	JUN	JUL	AUG	SEP	OCT	NOV	DEC	YEAR
Mean Maximum Temp. (°F)	30.0	32.5	41.4	54.3	66.9	75.1	79.1	77.3	69.9	58.9	46.4	35.4	55.6
Mean Temp. (°F)	21.5	22.8	31.3	43.3	54.6	63.2	67.5	66.1	58.9	48.3	38.3	28.0	45.3
Mean Minimum Temp. (°F)	13.0	13.1	21.1	32.2	42.2	51.3	56.0	54.7	47.9	37.6	30.1	20.6	35.0
Extreme Maximum Temp. (°F)	64	70	80	91	88	91	96	95	92	84	75	72	96
Extreme Minimum Temp. (°F)	-24	-30	-18	4	21	28	39	30	27	15	-3	-25	-30
Days Maximum Temp. ≥ 90°F	0	0	0	0	0	0	1	0	0	0	0	0	1
Days Maximum Temp. ≤ 32°F	18	14	8	1	0	0	0	0	0	0	3	12	56
Days Minimum Temp. ≤ 32°F	30	27	26	17	5	0	0	0	1	9	20	28	163
Days Minimum Temp. ≤ 0°F	6	5	2	0	0	0	0	0	0	0	0	2	15
Heating Degree Days (base 65°F)	1,342	1,185	1,038	648	333	112	35	54	208	513	794	1,141	7,403
Cooling Degree Days (base 65°F)	0	0	0	2	15	62	119	91	29	1	0	0	319
Mean Precipitation (in.)	3.73	2.80	3.55	3.73	3.60	4.22	4.13	4.20	4.92	4.00	4.81	4.51	48.20
Days With ≥ 0.1" Precipitation	11	9	10	9	9	8	8	8	9	10	11	12	114
Days With ≥ 1.0" Precipitation	0	0	0	1	0	1	1	1	1	1	1	1	8
Mean Snowfall (in.)	47.2	28.6	18.7	6.3	0.3	0.0	0.0	0.0	0.0	0.7	17.8	37.9	157.5
Days With ≥ 1.0" Snow Depth	28	25	19	3	0	0	0	0	0	0	7	21	103

Conklingville Dam *Saratoga County* Elevation: 807 ft. Latitude: 43° 19' N Longitude: 73° 56' W

	JAN	FEB	MAR	APR	MAY	JUN	JUL	AUG	SEP	OCT	NOV	DEC	YEAR
Mean Maximum Temp. (°F)	29.0	32.7	41.6	54.3	66.9	74.5	79.0	76.8	68.8	57.6	45.8	33.6	55.0
Mean Temp. (°F)	18.7	21.6	31.3	43.6	55.7	63.9	68.6	66.8	58.8	47.6	37.5	25.1	44.9
Mean Minimum Temp. (°F)	8.3	10.4	20.9	32.9	44.4	53.2	58.2	56.7	48.7	37.6	29.3	16.5	34.8
Extreme Maximum Temp. (°F)	60	61	80	86	90	92	95	90	87	82	75	67	95
Extreme Minimum Temp. (°F)	-29	-30	-13	7	27	30	43	35	28	17	4	-22	-30
Days Maximum Temp. ≥ 90°F	0	0	0	0	0	0	1	0	0	0	0	0	1
Days Maximum Temp. ≤ 32°F	19	13	5	0	0	0	0	0	0	0	1	12	50
Days Minimum Temp. ≤ 32°F	30	27	27	15	2	0	0	0	0	8	20	29	158
Days Minimum Temp. ≤ 0°F	9	7	2	0	0	0	0	0	0	0	0	3	21
Heating Degree Days (base 65°F)	1,431	1,221	1,039	635	299	91	20	42	202	533	817	1,232	7,562
Cooling Degree Days (base 65°F)	0	0	0	0	14	64	141	105	23	1	0	0	348
Mean Precipitation (in.)	3.75	2.87	4.05	3.84	4.11	4.00	3.89	3.95	4.08	3.63	4.08	3.70	45.95
Days With ≥ 0.1" Precipitation	7	6	8	8	8	8	7	7	7	7	8	8	89
Days With ≥ 1.0" Precipitation	1	1	1	1	1	1	1	1	1	1	1	1	12
Mean Snowfall (in.)	21.5	14.5	14.8	3.0	0.1	0.0	0.0	0.0	0.0	trace	4.9	17.5	76.3
Days With ≥ 1.0" Snow Depth	26	26	22	3	0	0	0	0	0	0	4	20	101

Cooperstown *Otsego County* Elevation: 1,197 ft. Latitude: 42° 42' N Longitude: 74° 55' W

	JAN	FEB	MAR	APR	MAY	JUN	JUL	AUG	SEP	OCT	NOV	DEC	YEAR
Mean Maximum Temp. (°F)	30.4	33.5	42.7	55.7	68.3	75.6	79.8	77.8	69.9	59.2	46.6	35.3	56.2
Mean Temp. (°F)	20.9	23.0	32.2	43.8	55.4	63.5	67.9	66.4	58.8	48.2	37.8	26.8	45.4
Mean Minimum Temp. (°F)	11.5	12.5	21.6	31.8	42.5	51.3	56.0	55.0	47.7	37.1	29.0	18.3	34.5
Extreme Maximum Temp. (°F)	64	64	87	90	90	92	97	92	90	83	79	66	97
Extreme Minimum Temp. (°F)	-29	-30	-18	6	22	30	37	33	25	12	2	-24	-30
Days Maximum Temp. ≥ 90°F	0	0	0	0	0	0	1	0	0	0	0	0	1
Days Maximum Temp. ≤ 32°F	18	13	5	0	0	0	0	0	0	0	3	12	51
Days Minimum Temp. ≤ 32°F	30	27	26	17	5	0	0	0	2	10	20	28	165
Days Minimum Temp. ≤ 0°F	7	6	2	0	0	0	0	0	0	0	0	3	18
Heating Degree Days (base 65°F)	1,360	1,179	1,011	631	303	100	30	47	208	516	810	1,178	7,373
Cooling Degree Days (base 65°F)	0	0	0	1	11	61	128	97	27	1	0	0	326
Mean Precipitation (in.)	2.89	2.27	3.29	3.53	3.59	4.24	3.84	3.69	4.00	3.22	3.43	3.03	41.02
Days With ≥ 0.1" Precipitation	7	6	8	8	8	8	7	7	8	8	8	8	91
Days With ≥ 1.0" Precipitation	0	0	1	1	1	1	1	1	1	1	1	0	9
Mean Snowfall (in.)	23.0	16.5	16.0	5.6	0.8	0.0	0.0	0.0	trace	0.2	7.2	18.2	87.5
Days With ≥ 1.0" Snow Depth	27	26	19	4	0	0	0	0	0	0	6	20	102

Cortland *Cortland County* Elevation: 1,128 ft. Latitude: 42° 36' N Longitude: 76° 11' W

	JAN	FEB	MAR	APR	MAY	JUN	JUL	AUG	SEP	OCT	NOV	DEC	YEAR
Mean Maximum Temp. (°F)	30.2	32.5	41.3	54.1	67.4	76.0	80.7	79.1	70.3	58.9	46.0	35.2	56.0
Mean Temp. (°F)	22.6	24.0	32.6	44.3	56.4	65.1	69.8	68.0	59.8	49.2	38.8	28.5	46.6
Mean Minimum Temp. (°F)	15.0	15.5	23.8	34.4	45.3	54.1	58.9	56.9	49.2	39.5	31.6	21.7	37.2
Extreme Maximum Temp. (°F)	64	65	85	90	93	96	100	98	92	85	79	68	100
Extreme Minimum Temp. (°F)	-18	-18	-13	11	24	33	45	39	28	18	7	-17	-18
Days Maximum Temp. ≥ 90°F	0	0	0	0	1	1	3	2	0	0	0	0	7
Days Maximum Temp. ≤ 32°F	18	14	8	1	0	0	0	0	0	0	3	12	56
Days Minimum Temp. ≤ 32°F	29	25	24	14	2	0	0	0	0	7	16	26	143
Days Minimum Temp. ≤ 0°F	4	4	1	0	0	0	0	0	0	0	0	1	10
Heating Degree Days (base 65°F)	1,306	1,151	998	619	287	85	20	38	188	484	779	1,125	7,080
Cooling Degree Days (base 65°F)	0	0	1	3	26	103	190	144	40	2	0	0	509
Mean Precipitation (in.)	2.66	2.53	3.11	3.23	3.18	4.03	3.51	3.03	3.97	3.22	3.49	3.50	39.46
Days With ≥ 0.1" Precipitation	7	6	7	7	8	8	7	6	7	8	8	9	88
Days With ≥ 1.0" Precipitation	0	0	0	0	0	1	1	1	1	1	0	0	5
Mean Snowfall (in.)	22.4	19.1	15.1	4.0	trace	0.0	0.0	0.0	0.0	0.4	8.3	22.0	91.3
Days With ≥ 1.0" Snow Depth	26	24	16	3	0	0	0	0	0	0	6	18	93

Dannemora *Clinton County* Elevation: 1,338 ft. Latitude: 44° 43' N Longitude: 73° 43' W

	JAN	FEB	MAR	APR	MAY	JUN	JUL	AUG	SEP	OCT	NOV	DEC	YEAR
Mean Maximum Temp. (°F)	25.8	29.1	38.7	52.0	66.3	74.5	79.0	76.4	67.7	56.0	42.1	30.8	53.2
Mean Temp. (°F)	16.6	19.8	29.5	42.4	55.5	64.0	68.8	66.4	57.8	46.8	34.7	22.6	43.7
Mean Minimum Temp. (°F)	7.4	10.5	20.3	32.8	44.6	53.5	58.5	56.3	47.9	37.6	27.4	14.3	34.3
Extreme Maximum Temp. (°F)	64	62	77	86	90	94	98	97	90	82	72	63	98
Extreme Minimum Temp. (°F)	-34	-25	-22	2	18	32	42	33	25	15	0	-28	-34
Days Maximum Temp. ≥ 90°F	0	0	0	0	0	1	1	0	0	0	0	0	2
Days Maximum Temp. ≤ 32°F	22	17	9	1	0	0	0	0	0	0	6	17	72
Days Minimum Temp. ≤ 32°F	30	27	27	15	2	0	0	0	1	10	21	29	162
Days Minimum Temp. ≤ 0°F	10	7	2	0	0	0	0	0	0	0	0	5	24
Heating Degree Days (base 65°F)	1,496	1,271	1,094	674	309	95	23	52	233	558	901	1,309	8,015
Cooling Degree Days (base 65°F)	0	0	0	2	16	71	140	93	22	1	0	0	345
Mean Precipitation (in.)	2.33	1.95	2.31	2.91	3.17	3.62	3.82	4.37	3.95	3.36	3.33	2.84	37.96
Days With ≥ 0.1" Precipitation	6	5	6	7	8	8	8	8	8	8	8	7	87
Days With ≥ 1.0" Precipitation	0	0	0	0	0	1	1	1	1	1	1	0	6
Mean Snowfall (in.)	na	na	na	3.6	trace	0.0	0.0	0.0	trace	0.2	na	na	na
Days With ≥ 1.0" Snow Depth	na	na	na	na	0	0	0	0	0	0	na	na	na

Dansville *Livingston County*   Elevation: 659 ft.   Latitude: 42° 34' N   Longitude: 77° 43' W

	JAN	FEB	MAR	APR	MAY	JUN	JUL	AUG	SEP	OCT	NOV	DEC	YEAR
Mean Maximum Temp. (°F)	32.8	35.3	44.3	56.7	69.5	78.3	82.7	80.8	73.0	61.7	48.9	38.2	58.5
Mean Temp. (°F)	24.2	25.9	34.1	45.4	57.0	65.9	70.5	68.7	61.3	50.4	40.3	30.3	47.8
Mean Minimum Temp. (°F)	15.6	16.4	24.0	34.1	44.5	53.4	58.3	56.5	49.4	39.1	31.7	22.4	37.1
Extreme Maximum Temp. (°F)	68	71	85	91	94	95	100	96	94	85	80	73	100
Extreme Minimum Temp. (°F)	-22	-18	-8	12	22	30	41	33	28	16	7	-17	-22
Days Maximum Temp. ≥ 90°F	0	0	0	0	1	2	5	3	1	0	0	0	12
Days Maximum Temp. ≤ 32°F	16	12	5	1	0	0	0	0	0	0	1	9	44
Days Minimum Temp. ≤ 32°F	29	26	24	15	3	0	0	0	1	7	17	26	148
Days Minimum Temp. ≤ 0°F	4	3	1	0	0	0	0	0	0	0	0	1	9
Heating Degree Days (base 65°F)	1,257	1,097	950	587	272	76	17	33	161	449	733	1,067	6,699
Cooling Degree Days (base 65°F)	0	0	1	4	28	110	198	151	54	3	0	0	549
Mean Precipitation (in.)	1.50	1.34	1.85	2.57	2.91	3.66	3.21	3.36	3.56	2.78	2.62	2.04	31.40
Days With ≥ 0.1" Precipitation	4	4	5	7	8	8	7	7	7	7	6	6	76
Days With ≥ 1.0" Precipitation	0	0	0	0	0	1	1	1	1	1	0	0	5
Mean Snowfall (in.)	12.6	10.4	7.4	2.5	0.2	0.0	0.0	0.0	0.0	trace	3.6	10.5	47.2
Days With ≥ 1.0" Snow Depth	16	14	5	1	0	0	0	0	0	0	2	8	46

Deposit *Delaware County*   Elevation: 997 ft.   Latitude: 42° 04' N   Longitude: 75° 26' W

	JAN	FEB	MAR	APR	MAY	JUN	JUL	AUG	SEP	OCT	NOV	DEC	YEAR
Mean Maximum Temp. (°F)	31.5	35.2	44.8	58.3	70.3	77.0	80.7	79.2	71.1	60.5	47.7	36.0	57.7
Mean Temp. (°F)	22.2	24.8	33.9	45.7	56.8	64.7	68.9	67.7	60.2	49.2	38.9	27.8	46.7
Mean Minimum Temp. (°F)	12.9	14.3	23.0	33.0	43.3	52.3	57.1	56.1	49.3	37.9	30.0	19.6	35.7
Extreme Maximum Temp. (°F)	63	67	85	90	92	92	98	92	92	84	80	68	98
Extreme Minimum Temp. (°F)	-31	-25	-14	11	22	29	37	34	27	14	2	-19	-31
Days Maximum Temp. ≥ 90°F	0	0	0	0	0	1	2	1	0	0	0	0	4
Days Maximum Temp. ≤ 32°F	16	11	4	0	0	0	0	0	0	0	1	10	42
Days Minimum Temp. ≤ 32°F	29	26	25	15	4	0	0	0	1	10	19	28	157
Days Minimum Temp. ≤ 0°F	6	5	1	0	0	0	0	0	0	0	0	2	14
Heating Degree Days (base 65°F)	1,322	1,130	958	574	265	78	22	33	174	484	778	1,147	6,965
Cooling Degree Days (base 65°F)	0	0	0	1	15	72	151	117	35	2	0	0	393
Mean Precipitation (in.)	2.88	2.65	3.36	3.82	3.91	3.93	3.99	4.06	3.78	3.56	4.04	3.35	43.33
Days With ≥ 0.1" Precipitation	7	7	8	8	9	9	8	7	7	7	8	7	92
Days With ≥ 1.0" Precipitation	0	0	0	1	1	1	1	1	1	1	1	1	9
Mean Snowfall (in.)	17.0	11.4	na	3.2	trace	0.0	0.0	0.0	0.0	trace	4.2	na	na
Days With ≥ 1.0" Snow Depth	18	na	na	1	0	0	0	0	0	0	3	na	na

Dobbs Ferry Ardsley *Westchester County*   Elevation: 200 ft.   Latitude: 41° 00' N   Longitude: 73° 50' W

	JAN	FEB	MAR	APR	MAY	JUN	JUL	AUG	SEP	OCT	NOV	DEC	YEAR
Mean Maximum Temp. (°F)	37.9	41.2	50.1	61.9	72.6	80.4	85.6	83.6	75.8	64.6	53.7	42.8	62.5
Mean Temp. (°F)	30.4	32.9	40.9	51.2	61.5	69.9	75.3	73.8	66.2	55.1	45.5	35.6	53.2
Mean Minimum Temp. (°F)	22.9	24.4	31.5	40.5	50.5	59.3	64.9	63.8	56.5	45.6	37.3	28.3	43.8
Extreme Maximum Temp. (°F)	65	75	86	96	97	98	104	97	98	85	80	77	104
Extreme Minimum Temp. (°F)	-10	3	4	17	29	40	49	44	34	27	12	-4	-10
Days Maximum Temp. ≥ 90°F	0	0	0	0	1	3	7	5	1	0	0	0	17
Days Maximum Temp. ≤ 32°F	10	6	1	0	0	0	0	0	0	0	0	4	21
Days Minimum Temp. ≤ 32°F	26	22	17	4	0	0	0	0	0	2	9	21	101
Days Minimum Temp. ≤ 0°F	1	0	0	0	0	0	0	0	0	0	0	0	1
Heating Degree Days (base 65°F)	1,066	901	742	413	149	22	1	3	66	310	580	906	5,159
Cooling Degree Days (base 65°F)	0	0	1	4	47	174	324	271	106	11	1	0	939
Mean Precipitation (in.)	4.30	3.45	4.55	4.50	4.85	3.81	4.38	4.25	4.68	4.16	4.58	4.23	51.74
Days With ≥ 0.1" Precipitation	7	6	7	7	8	7	7	6	6	6	7	8	82
Days With ≥ 1.0" Precipitation	1	1	1	1	1	1	1	1	1	1	1	1	12
Mean Snowfall (in.)	9.7	9.2	6.1	0.9	trace	0.0	0.0	0.0	0.0	trace	0.8	4.5	31.2
Days With ≥ 1.0" Snow Depth	14	12	4	0	0	0	0	0	0	0	1	5	36

Elmira *Chemung County*   Elevation: 843 ft.   Latitude: 42° 06' N   Longitude: 76° 48' W

	JAN	FEB	MAR	APR	MAY	JUN	JUL	AUG	SEP	OCT	NOV	DEC	YEAR
Mean Maximum Temp. (°F)	32.5	35.2	44.0	57.0	69.6	78.1	82.6	80.7	72.7	60.9	48.5	37.5	58.3
Mean Temp. (°F)	23.7	25.4	33.6	45.3	56.7	65.3	70.1	68.3	60.7	49.2	39.6	29.5	47.3
Mean Minimum Temp. (°F)	14.8	15.5	23.3	33.6	43.6	52.6	57.7	55.9	48.6	37.6	30.6	21.5	36.3
Extreme Maximum Temp. (°F)	66	69	86	92	96	97	102	97	95	87	78	69	102
Extreme Minimum Temp. (°F)	-19	-21	-9	9	24	32	40	31	28	15	3	-16	-21
Days Maximum Temp. ≥ 90°F	0	0	0	0	1	2	4	3	1	0	0	0	11
Days Maximum Temp. ≤ 32°F	15	12	5	0	0	0	0	0	0	0	1	9	42
Days Minimum Temp. ≤ 32°F	29	26	25	15	3	0	0	0	1	9	18	27	153
Days Minimum Temp. ≤ 0°F	4	3	0	0	0	0	0	0	0	0	0	1	8
Heating Degree Days (base 65°F)	1,275	1,112	966	587	277	79	17	33	168	483	756	1,094	6,847
Cooling Degree Days (base 65°F)	0	0	0	3	27	108	200	152	49	2	0	0	541
Mean Precipitation (in.)	1.88	1.99	2.64	2.86	2.96	3.82	3.50	3.33	3.52	2.86	3.06	2.38	34.80
Days With ≥ 0.1" Precipitation	5	5	6	7	8	8	7	6	7	6	7	6	78
Days With ≥ 1.0" Precipitation	0	0	1	0	0	1	1	1	1	1	1	0	7
Mean Snowfall (in.)	10.2	9.9	8.8	1.7	0.1	0.0	0.0	0.0	0.0	0.2	2.9	8.9	42.7
Days With ≥ 1.0" Snow Depth	18	16	8	1	0	0	0	0	0	0	2	10	55

Franklinville *Cattaraugus County*   Elevation: 1,548 ft.   Latitude: 42° 20' N   Longitude: 78° 28' W

	JAN	FEB	MAR	APR	MAY	JUN	JUL	AUG	SEP	OCT	NOV	DEC	YEAR
Mean Maximum Temp. (°F)	29.0	31.5	40.4	52.9	65.7	73.9	78.1	76.1	68.8	57.8	45.0	34.3	54.5
Mean Temp. (°F)	19.7	21.1	29.5	41.5	52.6	61.5	65.7	64.0	57.1	46.4	36.5	26.2	43.5
Mean Minimum Temp. (°F)	10.3	10.7	18.6	30.0	39.5	48.8	53.3	51.9	45.4	35.0	27.9	18.1	32.4
Extreme Maximum Temp. (°F)	62	67	80	87	90	92	97	95	89	80	74	71	97
Extreme Minimum Temp. (°F)	-28	-36	-23	2	20	26	35	28	23	14	-3	-28	-36
Days Maximum Temp. ≥ 90°F	0	0	0	0	0	0	1	0	0	0	0	0	1
Days Maximum Temp. ≤ 32°F	19	15	8	1	0	0	0	0	0	0	4	13	60
Days Minimum Temp. ≤ 32°F	30	27	28	19	9	0	0	0	2	13	21	28	177
Days Minimum Temp. ≤ 0°F	8	7	3	0	0	0	0	0	0	0	0	3	21
Heating Degree Days (base 65°F)	1,400	1,233	1,094	699	387	143	60	83	249	569	848	1,196	7,961
Cooling Degree Days (base 65°F)	0	0	0	1	10	46	90	61	18	0	0	0	226
Mean Precipitation (in.)	2.51	2.01	2.81	3.16	3.60	4.33	3.99	3.81	4.30	3.66	3.56	3.07	40.81
Days With ≥ 0.1" Precipitation	8	6	8	8	8	9	8	8	9	9	9	9	99
Days With ≥ 1.0" Precipitation	0	0	0	0	0	1	1	1	1	1	0	0	5
Mean Snowfall (in.)	*28.0*	16.5	14.6	4.2	0.2	0.0	0.0	0.0	0.0	0.6	*11.5*	*25.5*	*101.1*
Days With ≥ 1.0" Snow Depth	25	22	15	3	0	0	0	0	0	0	7	20	92

Fredonia *Chautauqua County*   Elevation: 757 ft.   Latitude: 42° 27' N   Longitude: 79° 14' W

	JAN	FEB	MAR	APR	MAY	JUN	JUL	AUG	SEP	OCT	NOV	DEC	YEAR
Mean Maximum Temp. (°F)	32.4	34.7	44.0	56.1	68.0	76.5	80.4	78.7	72.4	61.4	49.1	38.1	57.6
Mean Temp. (°F)	25.7	26.9	35.3	46.5	57.9	66.8	71.2	69.7	63.4	52.8	42.3	31.9	49.2
Mean Minimum Temp. (°F)	18.9	19.0	26.6	36.9	47.7	57.1	61.9	60.6	54.3	44.2	35.5	25.7	40.7
Extreme Maximum Temp. (°F)	66	71	82	91	90	93	95	93	90	83	75	74	95
Extreme Minimum Temp. (°F)	-17	-17	-10	10	27	35	47	37	34	22	8	-8	-17
Days Maximum Temp. ≥ 90°F	0	0	0	0	0	0	1	1	0	0	0	0	2
Days Maximum Temp. ≤ 32°F	15	13	6	0	0	0	0	0	0	0	1	9	44
Days Minimum Temp. ≤ 32°F	28	25	23	10	1	0	0	0	0	2	12	24	125
Days Minimum Temp. ≤ 0°F	2	2	0	0	0	0	0	0	0	0	0	0	4
Heating Degree Days (base 65°F)	1,212	1,070	914	554	247	60	8	17	112	377	674	1,019	6,264
Cooling Degree Days (base 65°F)	0	0	2	5	33	122	208	173	72	7	0	0	622
Mean Precipitation (in.)	2.59	2.13	2.73	3.22	3.28	3.94	3.85	3.82	4.98	4.12	4.20	3.38	42.24
Days With ≥ 0.1" Precipitation	8	7	7	8	7	7	7	7	9	9	10	10	96
Days With ≥ 1.0" Precipitation	0	0	0	0	0	1	1	1	1	1	1	0	6
Mean Snowfall (in.)	27.0	16.6	10.5	2.5	0.3	0.0	0.0	0.0	0.0	0.3	7.6	21.2	86.0
Days With ≥ 1.0" Snow Depth	24	20	10	1	0	0	0	0	0	0	4	15	74

Geneva Research Farm *Ontario County*   Elevation: 715 ft.   Latitude: 42° 53' N   Longitude: 77° 02' W

	JAN	FEB	MAR	APR	MAY	JUN	JUL	AUG	SEP	OCT	NOV	DEC	YEAR
Mean Maximum Temp. (°F)	29.8	32.0	40.7	53.8	66.6	75.4	80.1	78.3	70.4	58.6	46.6	35.8	55.7
Mean Temp. (°F)	22.3	24.1	32.7	44.8	56.7	65.7	70.5	68.7	61.1	49.8	39.5	28.9	47.0
Mean Minimum Temp. (°F)	14.7	16.2	24.6	35.8	46.7	55.9	60.8	59.1	51.6	40.9	32.3	22.0	38.4
Extreme Maximum Temp. (°F)	67	69	84	85	92	95	97	95	92	83	77	70	97
Extreme Minimum Temp. (°F)	-15	-16	-7	10	27	36	46	40	30	22	6	-12	-16
Days Maximum Temp. ≥ 90°F	0	0	0	0	0	1	2	1	0	0	0	0	4
Days Maximum Temp. ≤ 32°F	18	15	8	1	0	0	0	0	0	0	2	11	55
Days Minimum Temp. ≤ 32°F	29	26	25	11	1	0	0	0	0	4	16	27	139
Days Minimum Temp. ≤ 0°F	3	3	0	0	0	0	0	0	0	0	0	1	7
Heating Degree Days (base 65°F)	1,318	1,149	996	603	280	74	14	30	159	468	761	1,112	6,964
Cooling Degree Days (base 65°F)	0	0	1	4	27	103	196	149	46	3	0	0	529
Mean Precipitation (in.)	1.76	1.63	2.24	2.81	2.97	3.67	3.15	3.18	3.59	3.09	3.00	2.34	33.43
Days With ≥ 0.1" Precipitation	5	5	6	7	8	8	7	7	7	7	7	6	80
Days With ≥ 1.0" Precipitation	0	0	0	0	0	1	1	1	1	1	0	0	5
Mean Snowfall (in.)	15.0	14.6	11.5	3.3	0.1	0.0	0.0	0.0	0.0	0.2	4.5	13.1	62.3
Days With ≥ 1.0" Snow Depth	22	20	12	2	0	0	0	0	0	0	4	14	74

Glenham *Dutchess County*   Elevation: 272 ft.   Latitude: 41° 31' N   Longitude: 73° 56' W

	JAN	FEB	MAR	APR	MAY	JUN	JUL	AUG	SEP	OCT	NOV	DEC	YEAR
Mean Maximum Temp. (°F)	35.7	38.9	48.4	60.2	72.3	80.6	85.7	84.2	76.1	64.5	*52.5*	*40.4*	*61.6*
Mean Temp. (°F)	25.9	28.7	38.3	49.7	60.8	69.5	74.6	73.0	64.8	53.2	*43.0*	*31.6*	*51.1*
Mean Minimum Temp. (°F)	16.2	18.5	28.1	39.0	49.4	58.2	63.4	61.7	53.4	41.9	*33.4*	*22.8*	*40.5*
Extreme Maximum Temp. (°F)	66	75	84	96	98	*100*	103	99	*100*	90	82	73	*103*
Extreme Minimum Temp. (°F)	-16	-11	-2	16	30	*38*	45	39	*31*	20	11	-10	*-16*
Days Maximum Temp. ≥ 90°F	0	0	0	0	2	3	8	6	2	0	*0*	*0*	*21*
Days Maximum Temp. ≤ 32°F	12	8	2	0	0	0	0	0	0	0	*0*	6	*28*
Days Minimum Temp. ≤ 32°F	29	25	21	7	0	0	0	0	0	5	*15*	26	*128*
Days Minimum Temp. ≤ 0°F	3	1	0	0	0	0	0	0	0	0	*0*	*0*	*4*
Heating Degree Days (base 65°F)	1,204	1,019	823	463	176	32	3	9	95	367	*653*	*1,028*	*5,872*
Cooling Degree Days (base 65°F)	*0*	0	1	7	56	*178*	320	267	*97*	*10*	*1*	*0*	*937*
Mean Precipitation (in.)	3.28	2.91	3.41	3.97	4.44	4.09	4.76	4.00	3.99	3.74	*3.82*	*3.33*	*45.74*
Days With ≥ 0.1" Precipitation	6	6	7	7	8	7	7	6	6	6	*6*	*6*	*78*
Days With ≥ 1.0" Precipitation	1	1	1	1	1	1	1	1	1	1	*1*	*1*	*12*
Mean Snowfall (in.)	11.7	9.5	5.8	1.1	trace	0.0	0.0	0.0	0.0	0.1	*1.9*	*6.6*	*36.7*
Days With ≥ 1.0" Snow Depth	15	12	5	1	0	0	0	0	0	0	*1*	*7*	*41*

Glens Falls Airport *Warren County*   Elevation: 318 ft.   Latitude: 43° 21' N   Longitude: 73° 37' W

	JAN	FEB	MAR	APR	MAY	JUN	JUL	AUG	SEP	OCT	NOV	DEC	YEAR
Mean Maximum Temp. (°F)	28.0	31.9	42.1	56.1	68.4	76.9	81.6	79.1	70.2	58.2	45.8	33.8	56.0
Mean Temp. (°F)	17.8	21.3	32.1	44.9	56.5	65.0	70.0	67.8	58.9	47.3	37.1	25.2	45.3
Mean Minimum Temp. (°F)	7.4	10.6	22.1	33.7	44.5	53.1	58.3	56.4	47.6	36.4	28.4	16.6	34.6
Extreme Maximum Temp. (°F)	64	65	86	90	93	97	100	96	95	82	78	69	100
Extreme Minimum Temp. (°F)	-35	-30	-16	9	24	34	40	31	25	16	1	-29	-35
Days Maximum Temp. ≥ 90°F	0	0	0	0	0	1	3	1	0	0	0	0	5
Days Maximum Temp. ≤ 32°F	19	14	5	0	0	0	0	0	0	0	2	13	53
Days Minimum Temp. ≤ 32°F	29	27	26	14	2	0	0	0	1	11	21	28	159
Days Minimum Temp. ≤ 0°F	10	7	1	0	0	0	0	0	0	0	0	4	22
Heating Degree Days (base 65°F)	1,459	1,228	1,013	597	275	74	15	37	207	542	830	1,227	7,504
Cooling Degree Days (base 65°F)	0	0	0	1	16	81	179	130	30	1	0	0	438
Mean Precipitation (in.)	2.95	2.16	3.10	3.01	3.72	3.39	3.50	3.70	3.40	3.09	3.19	2.87	38.08
Days With ≥ 0.1" Precipitation	6	5	7	7	8	7	7	7	7	6	7	6	80
Days With ≥ 1.0" Precipitation	1	0	1	1	1	0	1	1	1	1	0	1	9
Mean Snowfall (in.)	19.7	12.8	12.7	2.3	trace	0.0	trace	0.0	0.0	trace	4.2	14.2	65.9
Days With ≥ 1.0" Snow Depth	25	23	14	1	0	0	0	0	0	0	3	17	83

Glens Falls Farm *Warren County*   Elevation: 501 ft.   Latitude: 43° 20' N   Longitude: 73° 44' W

	JAN	FEB	MAR	APR	MAY	JUN	JUL	AUG	SEP	OCT	NOV	DEC	YEAR
Mean Maximum Temp. (°F)	30.3	34.4	44.1	58.1	70.8	78.8	83.0	80.5	72.0	60.7	46.9	35.0	57.9
Mean Temp. (°F)	19.6	22.9	32.8	45.6	57.5	65.7	70.4	68.1	60.0	48.7	37.7	25.7	46.2
Mean Minimum Temp. (°F)	8.8	11.4	21.5	33.0	44.2	52.5	57.6	55.7	47.8	36.8	28.5	16.5	34.5
Extreme Maximum Temp. (°F)	63	65	86	90	92	97	98	96	92	83	75	65	98
Extreme Minimum Temp. (°F)	-34	-26	-13	0	19	31	40	32	23	9	-2	-25	-34
Days Maximum Temp. ≥ 90°F	0	0	0	0	0	2	4	2	0	0	0	0	8
Days Maximum Temp. ≤ 32°F	17	11	3	0	0	0	0	0	0	0	1	11	43
Days Minimum Temp. ≤ 32°F	30	27	27	15	2	0	0	0	1	11	20	29	162
Days Minimum Temp. ≤ 0°F	9	7	1	0	0	0	0	0	0	0	0	4	21
Heating Degree Days (base 65°F)	1,402	1,182	991	580	247	65	11	31	181	499	812	1,211	7,212
Cooling Degree Days (base 65°F)	0	0	0	2	22	101	197	147	40	2	0	0	511
Mean Precipitation (in.)	3.35	2.56	3.68	3.66	4.38	4.12	4.07	4.31	4.12	3.61	4.07	3.40	45.33
Days With ≥ 0.1" Precipitation	7	5	7	7	8	8	7	7	7	7	8	7	85
Days With ≥ 1.0" Precipitation	1	0	1	1	1	1	1	1	1	1	1	1	11
Mean Snowfall (in.)	20.6	12.0	12.6	2.3	trace	0.0	0.0	0.0	0.0	trace	4.2	14.5	66.2
Days With ≥ 1.0" Snow Depth	28	26	19	3	0	0	0	0	0	0	4	20	100

Gloversville *Fulton County*   Elevation: 898 ft.   Latitude: 43° 04' N   Longitude: 74° 20' W

	JAN	FEB	MAR	APR	MAY	JUN	JUL	AUG	SEP	OCT	NOV	DEC	YEAR
Mean Maximum Temp. (°F)	28.1	31.5	41.3	55.5	68.5	76.1	80.5	78.5	70.1	58.5	45.2	33.2	55.6
Mean Temp. (°F)	19.2	21.7	31.5	44.4	56.6	65.0	69.6	67.6	59.6	47.9	37.3	25.3	45.5
Mean Minimum Temp. (°F)	10.2	11.8	21.6	33.2	44.8	53.7	58.6	56.6	49.0	37.2	29.3	17.5	35.3
Extreme Maximum Temp. (°F)	60	62	83	89	90	94	94	95	91	83	76	60	95
Extreme Minimum Temp. (°F)	-29	-26	-14	9	27	36	44	38	27	17	5	-23	-29
Days Maximum Temp. ≥ 90°F	0	0	0	0	0	1	2	1	0	0	0	0	4
Days Maximum Temp. ≤ 32°F	20	15	6	0	0	0	0	0	0	0	2	13	56
Days Minimum Temp. ≤ 32°F	30	27	27	15	2	0	0	0	1	10	19	29	160
Days Minimum Temp. ≤ 0°F	8	6	1	0	0	0	0	0	0	0	0	3	18
Heating Degree Days (base 65°F)	1,414	1,217	1,032	612	272	75	17	35	187	524	826	1,222	7,433
Cooling Degree Days (base 65°F)	0	0	0	1	17	83	164	116	30	1	0	0	412
Mean Precipitation (in.)	3.07	2.74	3.53	3.69	4.01	4.23	3.98	4.05	4.13	3.60	3.77	3.48	44.28
Days With ≥ 0.1" Precipitation	7	6	7	7	8	8	7	7	8	7	8	8	88
Days With ≥ 1.0" Precipitation	1	0	1	1	1	1	1	1	1	1	1	0	10
Mean Snowfall (in.)	20.9	15.6	14.1	3.0	trace	0.0	0.0	0.0	0.0	trace	5.1	17.5	76.2
Days With ≥ 1.0" Snow Depth	27	27	23	4	0	0	0	0	0	0	5	22	108

Gouverneur 3 NW *St. Lawrence County*   Elevation: 419 ft.   Latitude: 44° 21' N   Longitude: 75° 31' W

	JAN	FEB	MAR	APR	MAY	JUN	JUL	AUG	SEP	OCT	NOV	DEC	YEAR
Mean Maximum Temp. (°F)	27.0	30.1	40.3	54.6	68.0	76.1	80.9	78.8	70.2	58.3	44.9	32.6	55.1
Mean Temp. (°F)	16.3	19.2	29.6	43.3	55.4	64.0	68.7	66.6	58.4	47.3	36.4	23.4	44.0
Mean Minimum Temp. (°F)	5.5	8.3	18.8	31.9	42.7	51.8	56.4	54.4	46.6	36.3	28.0	14.1	32.9
Extreme Maximum Temp. (°F)	65	64	81	87	90	96	95	98	94	81	78	69	98
Extreme Minimum Temp. (°F)	-45	-37	-27	-2	20	29	36	32	22	14	-3	-37	-45
Days Maximum Temp. ≥ 90°F	0	0	0	0	0	0	2	1	0	0	0	0	3
Days Maximum Temp. ≤ 32°F	20	16	8	0	0	0	0	0	0	0	3	14	61
Days Minimum Temp. ≤ 32°F	30	27	26	17	3	0	0	0	2	11	20	28	164
Days Minimum Temp. ≤ 0°F	12	9	4	0	0	0	0	0	0	0	0	6	31
Heating Degree Days (base 65°F)	1,506	1,287	1,091	648	305	95	26	54	219	543	851	1,285	7,910
Cooling Degree Days (base 65°F)	0	0	0	2	10	68	144	106	26	1	0	0	357
Mean Precipitation (in.)	2.49	2.04	2.52	3.02	3.09	3.19	3.14	3.73	4.20	3.45	3.66	2.93	37.46
Days With ≥ 0.1" Precipitation	7	5	7	7	8	7	7	7	8	8	9	7	87
Days With ≥ 1.0" Precipitation	0	0	0	0	0	0	1	1	1	1	1	0	5
Mean Snowfall (in.)	23.5	17.0	14.7	3.8	0.1	trace	0.0	0.0	trace	0.4	8.1	19.9	87.5
Days With ≥ 1.0" Snow Depth	28	25	19	3	0	0	0	0	0	0	6	21	102

Grafton *Rensselaer County*   Elevation: 1,558 ft.   Latitude: 42° 47' N   Longitude: 73° 28' W

	JAN	FEB	MAR	APR	MAY	JUN	JUL	AUG	SEP	OCT	NOV	DEC	YEAR
Mean Maximum Temp. (°F)	28.5	31.5	40.8	54.0	66.7	73.8	78.4	75.8	67.7	57.0	44.5	33.4	54.3
Mean Temp. (°F)	20.1	22.7	31.7	43.9	56.0	63.7	68.3	66.3	58.6	48.1	37.0	25.8	45.2
Mean Minimum Temp. (°F)	11.6	13.9	22.5	33.7	45.2	53.5	58.2	56.7	49.4	39.2	29.5	18.2	36.0
Extreme Maximum Temp. (°F)	61	62	83	87	88	90	93	91	89	81	76	62	93
Extreme Minimum Temp. (°F)	-26	-23	-11	5	23	32	41	32	27	15	3	-23	-26
Days Maximum Temp. ≥ 90°F	0	0	0	0	0	0	0	0	0	0	0	0	0
Days Maximum Temp. ≤ 32°F	20	15	7	1	0	0	0	0	0	0	4	15	62
Days Minimum Temp. ≤ 32°F	30	27	26	15	2	0	0	0	1	8	19	28	156
Days Minimum Temp. ≤ 0°F	6	5	1	0	0	0	0	0	0	0	0	3	15
Heating Degree Days (base 65°F)	1,387	1,189	1,027	629	290	97	24	50	214	518	833	1,208	7,466
Cooling Degree Days (base 65°F)	0	0	0	2	14	62	135	95	26	1	0	0	335
Mean Precipitation (in.)	3.00	2.43	3.38	3.81	4.57	4.66	4.34	4.72	4.28	4.07	3.97	2.94	46.17
Days With ≥ 0.1" Precipitation	7	6	8	9	9	9	8	8	8	8	9	8	97
Days With ≥ 1.0" Precipitation	1	0	1	1	1	1	1	1	1	1	1	0	10
Mean Snowfall (in.)	20.0	15.1	14.2	6.9	0.7	0.0	0.0	0.0	trace	0.9	7.9	15.8	81.5
Days With ≥ 1.0" Snow Depth	25	24	18	4	0	0	0	0	0	0	5	19	95

Hudson Correctionl Facility *Columbia County*   Elevation: 59 ft.   Latitude: 42° 15' N   Longitude: 73° 48' W

	JAN	FEB	MAR	APR	MAY	JUN	JUL	AUG	SEP	OCT	NOV	DEC	YEAR
Mean Maximum Temp. (°F)	33.6	37.1	47.3	61.3	73.0	80.5	84.8	82.3	73.7	62.6	50.2	38.4	60.4
Mean Temp. (°F)	24.2	27.1	36.6	48.6	59.9	68.1	72.6	70.7	62.7	51.5	41.2	30.4	49.5
Mean Minimum Temp. (°F)	14.8	17.1	25.9	35.8	46.7	55.7	60.5	59.1	51.7	40.5	32.1	22.3	38.5
Extreme Maximum Temp. (°F)	66	72	91	94	95	100	101	100	96	85	82	71	101
Extreme Minimum Temp. (°F)	-26	-18	-8	12	24	34	40	37	28	18	5	-15	-26
Days Maximum Temp. ≥ 90°F	0	0	0	0	1	3	6	3	1	0	0	0	14
Days Maximum Temp. ≤ 32°F	13	9	2	0	0	0	0	0	0	0	1	7	32
Days Minimum Temp. ≤ 32°F	29	25	23	12	1	0	0	0	0	6	17	27	140
Days Minimum Temp. ≤ 0°F	5	3	0	0	0	0	0	0	0	0	0	1	9
Heating Degree Days (base 65°F)	1,259	1,062	874	491	188	36	4	13	124	414	708	1,066	6,239
Cooling Degree Days (base 65°F)	0	0	1	3	35	138	244	196	62	4	0	0	683
Mean Precipitation (in.)	3.00	2.48	3.24	3.58	4.32	3.63	3.79	3.81	3.87	3.53	3.35	2.95	41.55
Days With ≥ 0.1" Precipitation	6	5	6	7	8	7	6	6	7	6	6	6	76
Days With ≥ 1.0" Precipitation	1	0	1	1	1	1	1	1	1	1	1	1	11
Mean Snowfall (in.)	na	na	*4.4*	*1.5*	0.0	0.0	0.0	0.0	0.0	0.1	*1.1*	na	na
Days With ≥ 1.0" Snow Depth	*17*	14	6	0	0	0	0	0	0	0	*1*	9	*47*

Indian Lake 2 SW *Hamilton County*   Elevation: 1,660 ft.   Latitude: 43° 45' N   Longitude: 74° 17' W

	JAN	FEB	MAR	APR	MAY	JUN	JUL	AUG	SEP	OCT	NOV	DEC	YEAR
Mean Maximum Temp. (°F)	25.4	28.2	36.8	49.2	63.2	71.1	75.3	73.4	65.1	54.0	41.4	30.3	51.1
Mean Temp. (°F)	14.2	16.3	25.6	38.3	50.9	59.4	63.9	62.2	54.3	43.3	33.0	20.9	40.2
Mean Minimum Temp. (°F)	3.1	4.3	14.3	27.2	38.5	47.6	52.5	51.0	43.5	32.6	24.6	11.4	29.2
Extreme Maximum Temp. (°F)	55	56	74	85	87	90	93	94	88	77	68	64	94
Extreme Minimum Temp. (°F)	-35	-36	-25	-2	20	27	34	29	23	9	-9	-29	-36
Days Maximum Temp. ≥ 90°F	0	0	0	0	0	0	0	0	0	0	0	0	0
Days Maximum Temp. ≤ 32°F	23	18	10	1	0	0	0	0	0	0	6	18	76
Days Minimum Temp. ≤ 32°F	30	28	29	22	9	1	0	0	3	17	24	30	193
Days Minimum Temp. ≤ 0°F	14	12	5	0	0	0	0	0	0	0	0	6	37
Heating Degree Days (base 65°F)	1,569	1,372	1,215	795	436	187	87	119	321	666	954	1,361	9,082
Cooling Degree Days (base 65°F)	0	0	0	0	4	24	60	38	8	0	0	0	134
Mean Precipitation (in.)	3.05	2.29	3.08	2.79	3.49	3.71	3.54	3.86	4.28	3.75	3.51	2.70	40.05
Days With ≥ 0.1" Precipitation	7	5	7	7	8	9	8	8	8	8	7	7	89
Days With ≥ 1.0" Precipitation	0	0	1	0	0	1	1	1	1	1	1	0	7
Mean Snowfall (in.)	na	na	na	na	0.0	0.0	0.0	0.0	0.0	0.2	na	na	na
Days With ≥ 1.0" Snow Depth	na	na	na	na	0	0	0	0	0	0	na	na	na

Ithaca Cornell University *Tompkins County*   Elevation: 958 ft.   Latitude: 42° 27' N   Longitude: 76° 27' W

	JAN	FEB	MAR	APR	MAY	JUN	JUL	AUG	SEP	OCT	NOV	DEC	YEAR
Mean Maximum Temp. (°F)	30.5	32.5	41.2	54.0	66.6	74.8	79.6	78.1	70.3	58.7	46.6	35.8	55.7
Mean Temp. (°F)	22.1	23.4	32.3	43.9	55.3	63.9	68.5	67.2	59.7	48.6	38.9	28.4	46.0
Mean Minimum Temp. (°F)	13.6	14.4	23.2	33.7	43.9	52.9	57.5	56.2	49.0	38.5	31.2	21.0	36.3
Extreme Maximum Temp. (°F)	66	67	85	89	93	93	98	93	92	84	78	69	98
Extreme Minimum Temp. (°F)	-24	-23	-17	11	22	31	40	34	24	17	-4	-19	-24
Days Maximum Temp. ≥ 90°F	0	0	0	0	0	0	2	1	0	0	0	0	3
Days Maximum Temp. ≤ 32°F	18	14	7	1	0	0	0	0	0	0	2	11	53
Days Minimum Temp. ≤ 32°F	29	26	25	15	3	0	0	0	1	9	17	27	152
Days Minimum Temp. ≤ 0°F	5	5	1	0	0	0	0	0	0	0	0	2	13
Heating Degree Days (base 65°F)	1,325	1,167	1,009	631	315	105	34	49	193	504	776	1,127	7,235
Cooling Degree Days (base 65°F)	0	0	1	2	20	77	153	126	41	2	0	0	422
Mean Precipitation (in.)	2.05	2.04	2.54	3.19	3.22	3.82	3.67	3.48	3.88	3.26	3.17	2.53	36.85
Days With ≥ 0.1" Precipitation	6	5	6	8	8	8	8	7	7	7	7	6	83
Days With ≥ 1.0" Precipitation	0	0	0	0	0	1	1	1	1	1	0	0	5
Mean Snowfall (in.)	17.6	14.1	12.2	3.7	0.1	0.0	0.0	0.0	0.0	0.6	5.8	13.8	67.9
Days With ≥ 1.0" Snow Depth	22	21	12	2	0	0	0	0	0	0	5	14	76

Lake Placid 2 S *Essex County*   Elevation: 1,938 ft.   Latitude: 44° 15' N   Longitude: 73° 59' W

	JAN	FEB	MAR	APR	MAY	JUN	JUL	AUG	SEP	OCT	NOV	DEC	YEAR
Mean Maximum Temp. (°F)	25.8	29.4	38.5	50.9	64.6	72.6	76.6	74.1	66.0	55.1	42.2	30.9	52.2
Mean Temp. (°F)	14.9	18.0	27.1	39.3	51.7	60.0	64.5	62.4	54.8	44.3	33.1	20.9	40.9
Mean Minimum Temp. (°F)	4.1	6.2	15.6	27.6	38.7	47.5	52.4	50.6	43.3	33.4	24.0	10.9	29.5
Extreme Maximum Temp. (°F)	60	62	78	86	87	92	94	92	92	79	68	62	94
Extreme Minimum Temp. (°F)	-32	-37	-30	-5	19	25	31	27	20	11	-8	-31	-37
Days Maximum Temp. ≥ 90°F	0	0	0	0	0	0	0	0	0	0	0	0	0
Days Maximum Temp. ≤ 32°F	22	18	10	1	0	0	0	0	0	0	6	17	74
Days Minimum Temp. ≤ 32°F	30	27	29	21	9	1	0	0	4	16	25	30	192
Days Minimum Temp. ≤ 0°F	13	10	5	0	0	0	0	0	0	0	1	8	37
Heating Degree Days (base 65°F)	1,549	1,325	1,168	765	413	176	77	117	311	636	949	1,362	8,848
Cooling Degree Days (base 65°F)	0	0	0	0	5	32	70	45	9	0	0	0	161
Mean Precipitation (in.)	2.62	1.98	2.70	2.70	3.19	3.96	4.00	4.29	4.32	3.58	3.35	2.62	39.31
Days With ≥ 0.1" Precipitation	7	5	7	7	9	9	9	9	9	8	8	7	94
Days With ≥ 1.0" Precipitation	0	0	0	0	0	1	1	1	1	1	1	0	6
Mean Snowfall (in.)	na	na	na	na	*0.3*	*0.0*	*0.0*	0.0	trace	*1.1*	na	na	na
Days With ≥ 1.0" Snow Depth	na	na	na	na	*0*	*0*	*0*	0	0	*1*	na	na	na

Lawrenceville 3 SW *St. Lawrence County*   Elevation: 498 ft.   Latitude: 44° 43' N   Longitude: 74° 45' W

	JAN	FEB	MAR	APR	MAY	JUN	JUL	AUG	SEP	OCT	NOV	DEC	YEAR
Mean Maximum Temp. (°F)	25.5	29.0	39.3	53.8	67.9	75.9	80.2	77.8	69.2	57.5	44.1	31.2	54.3
Mean Temp. (°F)	16.0	19.1	29.4	43.5	56.3	64.9	69.7	67.5	59.2	47.9	36.2	22.6	44.4
Mean Minimum Temp. (°F)	6.4	9.2	19.4	32.8	44.7	54.0	59.2	57.1	49.1	38.2	28.3	14.0	34.4
Extreme Maximum Temp. (°F)	67	64	80	86	90	94	93	97	92	82	75	68	97
Extreme Minimum Temp. (°F)	-34	-31	-21	3	22	30	35	36	24	17	0	-29	-34
Days Maximum Temp. ≥ 90°F	0	0	0	0	0	1	1	0	0	0	0	0	2
Days Maximum Temp. ≤ 32°F	21	17	9	1	0	0	0	0	0	0	5	17	70
Days Minimum Temp. ≤ 32°F	30	27	27	16	3	0	0	0	1	9	21	29	163
Days Minimum Temp. ≤ 0°F	11	8	3	0	0	0	0	0	0	0	0	6	28
Heating Degree Days (base 65°F)	1,515	1,290	1,096	642	287	87	20	46	203	526	858	1,310	7,880
Cooling Degree Days (base 65°F)	0	0	0	2	22	95	179	133	35	3	0	0	469
Mean Precipitation (in.)	2.14	1.92	2.22	2.73	2.83	3.69	3.75	4.16	3.95	3.23	3.20	2.58	36.40
Days With ≥ 0.1" Precipitation	7	6	7	8	7	8	8	8	8	7	9	8	91
Days With ≥ 1.0" Precipitation	0	0	0	0	0	1	1	1	1	0	0	0	4
Mean Snowfall (in.)	17.1	14.2	13.3	4.9	0.4	0.0	0.0	0.0	0.0	0.7	7.2	14.9	72.7
Days With ≥ 1.0" Snow Depth	27	24	19	4	0	0	0	0	0	0	7	20	101

Little Valley *Cattaraugus County*   Elevation: 1,624 ft.   Latitude: 42° 15' N   Longitude: 78° 49' W

	JAN	FEB	MAR	APR	MAY	JUN	JUL	AUG	SEP	OCT	NOV	DEC	YEAR
Mean Maximum Temp. (°F)	29.7	32.1	41.0	53.6	66.2	74.5	78.8	76.9	69.2	58.0	45.6	34.7	55.0
Mean Temp. (°F)	21.1	22.4	30.7	42.4	53.6	62.3	66.8	65.3	58.2	47.5	37.5	27.3	44.6
Mean Minimum Temp. (°F)	12.4	12.7	20.4	31.3	40.9	50.1	54.7	53.6	47.1	37.0	29.5	19.8	34.1
Extreme Maximum Temp. (°F)	62	67	80	88	89	92	96	94	90	81	75	71	96
Extreme Minimum Temp. (°F)	-26	-28	-16	6	20	29	36	31	26	15	-5	-22	-28
Days Maximum Temp. ≥ 90°F	0	0	0	0	0	0	1	0	0	0	0	0	1
Days Maximum Temp. ≤ 32°F	19	15	8	1	0	0	0	0	0	0	4	13	60
Days Minimum Temp. ≤ 32°F	30	27	26	18	7	0	0	0	1	10	20	28	167
Days Minimum Temp. ≤ 0°F	6	6	2	0	0	0	0	0	0	0	0	2	16
Heating Degree Days (base 65°F)	1,356	1,195	1,056	671	362	127	46	63	224	536	817	1,161	7,614
Cooling Degree Days (base 65°F)	0	0	0	1	12	52	110	78	24	1	0	0	278
Mean Precipitation (in.)	3.69	3.01	3.57	3.63	3.83	4.75	4.29	4.37	4.85	4.15	4.78	4.33	49.25
Days With ≥ 0.1" Precipitation	12	9	10	10	9	10	9	9	10	10	12	13	123
Days With ≥ 1.0" Precipitation	0	0	0	0	0	1	1	1	1	1	1	0	6
Mean Snowfall (in.)	31.5	22.3	18.1	6.3	0.4	0.0	0.0	0.0	0.0	1.0	14.9	33.4	127.9
Days With ≥ 1.0" Snow Depth	26	23	15	3	0	0	0	0	0	0	8	19	94

Lockport 2 SE *Niagara County*   Elevation: 603 ft.   Latitude: 43° 08' N   Longitude: 78° 41' W

	JAN	FEB	MAR	APR	MAY	JUN	JUL	AUG	SEP	OCT	NOV	DEC	YEAR
Mean Maximum Temp. (°F)	31.6	33.9	43.2	56.5	69.2	77.2	81.5	79.4	71.4	60.0	47.5	36.6	57.3
Mean Temp. (°F)	24.1	25.8	34.0	46.0	58.1	66.4	71.3	69.5	61.8	51.0	40.0	29.6	48.1
Mean Minimum Temp. (°F)	16.6	17.6	24.8	35.5	46.8	55.4	61.0	59.6	52.1	41.9	32.5	22.6	38.9
Extreme Maximum Temp. (°F)	66	65	81	89	91	93	100	95	94	84	76	73	100
Extreme Minimum Temp. (°F)	-15	-19	-7	7	26	33	46	38	30	19	6	-12	-19
Days Maximum Temp. ≥ 90°F	0	0	0	0	0	1	2	1	0	0	0	0	4
Days Maximum Temp. ≤ 32°F	16	13	5	0	0	0	0	0	0	0	2	10	46
Days Minimum Temp. ≤ 32°F	29	26	25	12	1	0	0	0	0	4	16	27	140
Days Minimum Temp. ≤ 0°F	2	2	0	0	0	0	0	0	0	0	0	1	5
Heating Degree Days (base 65°F)	1,261	1,102	953	566	241	61	8	20	144	431	742	1,090	6,619
Cooling Degree Days (base 65°F)	0	0	0	4	32	109	217	171	56	4	0	0	593
Mean Precipitation (in.)	2.53	2.24	2.77	3.12	3.03	3.56	3.05	3.42	3.72	3.06	3.47	3.25	37.22
Days With ≥ 0.1" Precipitation	8	7	7	8	6	7	5	6	7	7	9	9	86
Days With ≥ 1.0" Precipitation	0	0	0	0	1	1	1	1	1	0	0	0	5
Mean Snowfall (in.)	24.3	18.5	12.1	4.2	0.4	trace	0.0	0.0	trace	trace	7.5	19.1	86.1
Days With ≥ 1.0" Snow Depth	23	21	12	0	0	0	0	0	0	0	4	16	77

Lockport 4 NE *Niagara County*   Elevation: 439 ft.   Latitude: 43° 12' N   Longitude: 78° 38' W

	JAN	FEB	MAR	APR	MAY	JUN	JUL	AUG	SEP	OCT	NOV	DEC	YEAR
Mean Maximum Temp. (°F)	30.7	32.3	41.5	54.4	67.2	75.9	80.9	79.1	71.4	59.6	47.8	36.1	56.4
Mean Temp. (°F)	23.6	24.7	33.3	45.2	56.7	65.5	70.7	69.0	61.4	50.3	40.5	29.4	47.5
Mean Minimum Temp. (°F)	16.4	17.1	25.0	35.9	46.2	55.1	60.4	58.8	51.4	41.0	33.1	22.6	38.6
Extreme Maximum Temp. (°F)	61	62	80	86	90	93	99	96	94	85	75	74	99
Extreme Minimum Temp. (°F)	-14	-16	-7	11	28	36	46	40	31	22	9	-12	-16
Days Maximum Temp. ≥ 90°F	0	0	0	0	0	0	2	1	0	0	0	0	3
Days Maximum Temp. ≤ 32°F	17	15	7	1	0	0	0	0	0	0	2	10	52
Days Minimum Temp. ≤ 32°F	29	26	24	12	1	0	0	0	0	4	15	26	137
Days Minimum Temp. ≤ 0°F	2	1	0	0	0	0	0	0	0	0	0	0	3
Heating Degree Days (base 65°F)	1,279	1,131	978	592	281	77	13	27	155	453	730	1,097	6,813
Cooling Degree Days (base 65°F)	0	0	0	5	29	97	208	163	56	4	na	0	na
Mean Precipitation (in.)	2.08	2.24	2.75	3.24	2.92	3.56	3.09	3.59	3.86	2.94	3.23	3.34	36.84
Days With ≥ 0.1" Precipitation	7	6	7	8	7	8	6	7	7	8	9	8	88
Days With ≥ 1.0" Precipitation	0	0	0	0	0	1	1	1	1	0	0	0	4
Mean Snowfall (in.)	15.2	15.6	8.8	2.9	0.3	0.0	0.0	0.0	0.0	trace	4.0	16.1	62.9
Days With ≥ 1.0" Snow Depth	22	22	12	2	0	0	0	0	0	0	4	16	78

Lowville *Lewis County*   Elevation: 859 ft.   Latitude: 43° 48' N   Longitude: 75° 29' W

	JAN	FEB	MAR	APR	MAY	JUN	JUL	AUG	SEP	OCT	NOV	DEC	YEAR
Mean Maximum Temp. (°F)	26.1	29.0	38.1	52.2	65.9	74.4	79.0	76.9	68.0	56.2	43.6	31.6	53.4
Mean Temp. (°F)	16.4	19.0	28.8	42.2	54.5	63.1	67.7	65.7	57.2	46.3	35.8	23.2	43.3
Mean Minimum Temp. (°F)	6.6	8.9	19.5	32.2	43.1	51.8	56.3	54.5	46.3	36.4	28.0	14.8	33.2
Extreme Maximum Temp. (°F)	58	59	80	87	89	97	94	94	92	81	70	65	97
Extreme Minimum Temp. (°F)	-35	-32	-25	5	23	28	39	32	24	17	0	-29	-35
Days Maximum Temp. ≥ 90°F	0	0	0	0	0	0	1	1	0	0	0	0	2
Days Maximum Temp. ≤ 32°F	21	17	9	1	0	0	0	0	0	0	4	15	67
Days Minimum Temp. ≤ 32°F	30	27	27	17	3	0	0	0	2	11	21	29	167
Days Minimum Temp. ≤ 0°F	11	9	3	0	0	0	0	0	0	0	0	5	28
Heating Degree Days (base 65°F)	1,502	1,292	1,115	679	333	114	36	64	250	573	870	1,289	8,117
Cooling Degree Days (base 65°F)	0	0	0	1	11	58	121	89	22	1	0	0	303
Mean Precipitation (in.)	3.57	2.50	3.03	3.12	3.08	3.39	3.58	3.52	4.11	3.53	4.11	3.62	41.16
Days With ≥ 0.1" Precipitation	9	6	7	7	8	7	7	7	8	8	9	9	92
Days With ≥ 1.0" Precipitation	0	0	0	0	0	0	1	1	1	1	1	1	6
Mean Snowfall (in.)	37.9	22.7	17.5	5.0	0.3	0.0	0.0	0.0	trace	0.7	10.3	30.7	125.1
Days With ≥ 1.0" Snow Depth	29	26	21	5	0	0	0	0	0	0	8	24	113

Massena Airport *St. Lawrence County*   Elevation: 213 ft.   Latitude: 44° 56' N   Longitude: 74° 51' W

	JAN	FEB	MAR	APR	MAY	JUN	JUL	AUG	SEP	OCT	NOV	DEC	YEAR
Mean Maximum Temp. (°F)	24.2	27.4	38.0	53.4	68.0	76.3	81.2	78.5	69.1	56.9	43.3	30.2	53.9
Mean Temp. (°F)	14.2	17.4	28.6	43.3	56.5	64.9	69.9	67.4	58.5	47.0	35.6	21.6	43.7
Mean Minimum Temp. (°F)	4.0	7.4	19.1	33.1	45.0	53.5	58.6	56.2	47.8	37.0	27.8	13.0	33.5
Extreme Maximum Temp. (°F)	66	63	84	89	95	97	96	100	95	85	74	65	100
Extreme Minimum Temp. (°F)	-38	-38	-26	7	20	31	38	36	26	15	-5	-33	-38
Days Maximum Temp. ≥ 90°F	0	0	0	0	0	1	3	1	0	0	0	0	5
Days Maximum Temp. ≤ 32°F	22	18	10	1	0	0	0	0	0	0	5	17	73
Days Minimum Temp. ≤ 32°F	30	27	27	15	2	0	0	0	1	11	20	29	162
Days Minimum Temp. ≤ 0°F	12	10	3	0	0	0	0	0	0	0	0	7	32
Heating Degree Days (base 65°F)	1,572	1,338	1,123	647	279	82	18	46	219	555	875	1,338	8,092
Cooling Degree Days (base 65°F)	0	0	0	1	20	88	181	123	29	2	0	0	444
Mean Precipitation (in.)	2.54	2.11	2.43	2.84	2.68	3.27	3.39	3.55	3.86	2.99	3.05	3.00	35.71
Days With ≥ 0.1" Precipitation	8	6	7	7	7	7	7	7	7	7	8	8	86
Days With ≥ 1.0" Precipitation	0	0	0	0	0	1	1	1	1	0	0	0	4
Mean Snowfall (in.)	17.6	15.7	11.3	4.4	0.1	trace	trace	0.0	trace	0.9	6.3	17.5	73.8
Days With ≥ 1.0" Snow Depth	27	24	18	3	0	0	0	0	0	0	5	20	97

Middletown 2 NW *Orange County*   Elevation: 698 ft.   Latitude: 41° 28' N   Longitude: 74° 27' W

	JAN	FEB	MAR	APR	MAY	JUN	JUL	AUG	SEP	OCT	NOV	DEC	YEAR
Mean Maximum Temp. (°F)	34.8	38.6	48.2	60.8	72.0	79.4	83.9	82.2	74.6	63.7	51.1	39.6	60.7
Mean Temp. (°F)	26.4	29.2	38.2	49.8	60.7	68.7	73.5	71.8	64.4	53.5	42.8	32.1	50.9
Mean Minimum Temp. (°F)	17.9	19.8	28.1	38.9	49.4	58.0	63.0	61.4	54.2	43.2	34.6	24.4	41.1
Extreme Maximum Temp. (°F)	64	71	85	92	92	93	101	96	94	87	78	71	101
Extreme Minimum Temp. (°F)	-23	-13	-3	18	32	40	45	41	27	23	12	-10	-23
Days Maximum Temp. ≥ 90°F	0	0	0	0	0	2	4	2	1	0	0	0	9
Days Maximum Temp. ≤ 32°F	13	8	2	0	0	0	0	0	0	0	0	7	30
Days Minimum Temp. ≤ 32°F	28	25	21	6	0	0	0	0	0	3	13	25	121
Days Minimum Temp. ≤ 0°F	2	1	0	0	0	0	0	0	0	0	0	0	3
Heating Degree Days (base 65°F)	1,191	1,003	825	454	167	27	2	7	93	356	659	1,014	5,798
Cooling Degree Days (base 65°F)	0	0	1	5	42	152	279	225	83	7	0	0	794
Mean Precipitation (in.)	3.02	2.52	3.29	3.94	4.56	4.18	4.04	3.79	4.18	3.63	3.68	3.11	43.94
Days With ≥ 0.1" Precipitation	6	5	7	7	8	8	7	6	6	6	6	6	78
Days With ≥ 1.0" Precipitation	1	0	1	1	1	1	1	1	1	1	1	1	11
Mean Snowfall (in.)	na	na	na	na	trace	0.0	0.0	0.0	0.0	trace	na	na	na
Days With ≥ 1.0" Snow Depth	na	na	na	na	0	0	0	0	0	0	na	na	na

Mohonk Lake *Ulster County*   Elevation: 1,243 ft.   Latitude: 41° 46' N   Longitude: 74° 09' W

	JAN	FEB	MAR	APR	MAY	JUN	JUL	AUG	SEP	OCT	NOV	DEC	YEAR
Mean Maximum Temp. (°F)	31.5	35.0	44.3	57.3	68.3	75.4	80.0	77.9	70.1	59.3	47.3	36.2	56.9
Mean Temp. (°F)	24.2	26.9	35.5	47.4	58.7	66.6	71.5	69.8	62.2	51.5	40.5	29.7	48.7
Mean Minimum Temp. (°F)	16.9	18.7	26.6	37.5	49.0	57.7	63.0	61.7	54.2	43.7	33.7	23.1	40.5
Extreme Maximum Temp. (°F)	59	70	84	91	90	94	98	96	92	82	76	67	98
Extreme Minimum Temp. (°F)	-19	-13	-3	10	28	37	46	43	33	21	9	-9	-19
Days Maximum Temp. ≥ 90°F	0	0	0	0	0	1	2	1	0	0	0	0	4
Days Maximum Temp. ≤ 32°F	17	12	4	0	0	0	0	0	0	0	2	11	46
Days Minimum Temp. ≤ 32°F	29	25	23	9	0	0	0	0	0	3	14	26	129
Days Minimum Temp. ≤ 0°F	3	1	0	0	0	0	0	0	0	0	0	0	4
Heating Degree Days (base 65°F)	1,257	1,071	909	525	221	52	7	16	131	414	728	1,088	6,419
Cooling Degree Days (base 65°F)	0	0	1	3	33	120	230	178	58	4	0	0	627
Mean Precipitation (in.)	3.76	3.15	4.27	4.20	5.20	4.18	4.56	4.32	4.72	4.17	4.14	3.84	50.51
Days With ≥ 0.1" Precipitation	7	6	8	7	8	7	7	7	7	6	7	7	84
Days With ≥ 1.0" Precipitation	1	1	1	1	1	1	1	1	2	1	1	1	13
Mean Snowfall (in.)	15.9	13.4	12.5	3.7	0.5	0.0	0.0	0.0	0.0	0.2	4.0	12.9	63.1
Days With ≥ 1.0" Snow Depth	24	22	16	2	0	0	0	0	0	0	3	14	81

New York Avenue V Brooklyn *Kings County*   Elevation: 19 ft.   Latitude: 40° 36' N   Longitude: 73° 59' W

	JAN	FEB	MAR	APR	MAY	JUN	JUL	AUG	SEP	OCT	NOV	DEC	YEAR
Mean Maximum Temp. (°F)	38.8	41.8	49.6	60.2	70.7	79.3	84.8	83.3	76.1	65.0	54.2	43.6	62.3
Mean Temp. (°F)	32.5	34.9	42.2	52.2	62.5	71.5	77.2	76.0	68.7	57.6	47.7	37.6	55.1
Mean Minimum Temp. (°F)	26.1	28.0	34.8	44.0	54.2	63.6	69.6	68.5	61.3	50.2	41.1	31.6	47.8
Extreme Maximum Temp. (°F)	65	73	83	89	96	97	103	101	98	86	80	75	103
Extreme Minimum Temp. (°F)	-4	1	10	19	38	46	54	51	44	30	17	-1	-4
Days Maximum Temp. ≥ 90°F	0	0	0	0	1	3	6	4	1	0	0	0	15
Days Maximum Temp. ≤ 32°F	8	5	1	0	0	0	0	0	0	0	0	4	18
Days Minimum Temp. ≤ 32°F	22	18	11	1	0	0	0	0	0	0	4	15	71
Days Minimum Temp. ≤ 0°F	0	0	0	0	0	0	0	0	0	0	0	0	0
Heating Degree Days (base 65°F)	1,000	843	699	384	127	12	0	1	32	239	514	842	4,693
Cooling Degree Days (base 65°F)	0	0	0	4	57	218	391	342	150	17	1	0	1,180
Mean Precipitation (in.)	3.85	3.02	4.06	3.94	4.32	3.51	4.29	4.14	3.92	3.43	3.90	3.55	45.93
Days With ≥ 0.1" Precipitation	7	6	7	6	7	7	6	6	6	5	6	6	75
Days With ≥ 1.0" Precipitation	1	1	1	1	1	1	1	1	1	1	1	1	12
Mean Snowfall (in.)	7.2	7.8	3.6	0.4	trace	0.0	0.0	0.0	0.0	trace	0.4	2.1	21.5
Days With ≥ 1.0" Snow Depth	8	7	3	0	0	0	0	0	0	0	0	1	19

Norwich *Chenango County*   Elevation: 1,017 ft.   Latitude: 42° 32' N   Longitude: 75° 32' W

	JAN	FEB	MAR	APR	MAY	JUN	JUL	AUG	SEP	OCT	NOV	DEC	YEAR
Mean Maximum Temp. (°F)	31.2	34.0	43.6	56.3	68.9	76.5	80.8	79.0	71.0	59.9	47.0	35.6	57.0
Mean Temp. (°F)	21.5	23.2	32.6	44.3	55.8	64.0	68.5	66.9	59.2	48.2	37.9	27.4	45.8
Mean Minimum Temp. (°F)	11.7	12.5	21.6	32.3	42.7	51.4	56.1	54.7	47.3	36.4	28.7	19.1	34.5
Extreme Maximum Temp. (°F)	62	65	86	89	91	93	96	96	93	84	79	66	96
Extreme Minimum Temp. (°F)	-27	-25	-15	9	20	30	38	32	22	11	3	-22	-27
Days Maximum Temp. ≥ 90°F	0	0	0	0	0	1	2	1	0	0	0	0	4
Days Maximum Temp. ≤ 32°F	17	13	5	0	0	0	0	0	0	0	2	11	48
Days Minimum Temp. ≤ 32°F	30	26	26	16	4	0	0	0	2	11	21	28	164
Days Minimum Temp. ≤ 0°F	7	6	1	0	0	0	0	0	0	0	0	2	16
Heating Degree Days (base 65°F)	1,342	1,173	997	615	295	95	26	44	201	515	807	1,159	7,269
Cooling Degree Days (base 65°F)	0	0	0	2	16	76	153	117	34	1	0	0	399
Mean Precipitation (in.)	2.77	2.35	3.02	3.40	3.72	4.09	3.57	3.45	4.22	3.27	3.73	3.34	40.93
Days With ≥ 0.1" Precipitation	7	6	7	8	9	8	7	7	8	7	8	8	90
Days With ≥ 1.0" Precipitation	0	0	0	0	1	1	1	1	1	1	1	0	7
Mean Snowfall (in.)	18.0	14.0	11.4	3.3	0.1	0.0	0.0	0.0	0.0	0.3	6.0	15.8	68.9
Days With ≥ 1.0" Snow Depth	26	25	16	2	0	0	0	0	0	0	5	16	90

Ogdensburg 4 NE *St. Lawrence County*   Elevation: 278 ft.   Latitude: 44° 44' N   Longitude: 75° 27' W

	JAN	FEB	MAR	APR	MAY	JUN	JUL	AUG	SEP	OCT	NOV	DEC	YEAR
Mean Maximum Temp. (°F)	*26.0*	29.4	40.0	53.9	67.7	76.7	81.6	79.6	70.2	58.1	*45.1*	31.8	*55.0*
Mean Temp. (°F)	*16.8*	19.7	30.6	43.8	56.6	65.5	70.8	68.4	59.5	48.6	*37.6*	23.7	*45.1*
Mean Minimum Temp. (°F)	*7.4*	10.1	21.0	33.7	45.5	54.2	59.9	57.3	49.0	39.0	29.8	15.6	*35.2*
Extreme Maximum Temp. (°F)	66	60	81	83	89	96	94	99	92	82	75	65	99
Extreme Minimum Temp. (°F)	-31	-31	-22	3	20	33	42	35	25	14	-1	-26	-31
Days Maximum Temp. ≥ 90°F	0	0	0	0	0	1	2	1	0	0	0	0	4
Days Maximum Temp. ≤ 32°F	20	16	7	0	0	0	0	0	0	0	3	14	60
Days Minimum Temp. ≤ 32°F	28	26	26	14	1	0	0	0	1	7	18	26	147
Days Minimum Temp. ≤ 0°F	11	7	2	0	0	0	0	0	0	0	0	5	25
Heating Degree Days (base 65°F)	*1,491*	1,272	1,061	630	272	70	9	30	185	505	*817*	1,272	*7,614*
Cooling Degree Days (base 65°F)	*0*	0	0	1	19	95	207	148	23	2	*0*	*0*	495
Mean Precipitation (in.)	2.48	2.02	2.17	2.63	2.75	3.10	3.23	3.67	3.88	2.99	3.14	2.74	34.80
Days With ≥ 0.1" Precipitation	6	6	6	7	7	7	7	7	7	7	7	6	80
Days With ≥ 1.0" Precipitation	0	0	0	0	0	0	1	1	1	0	0	0	3
Mean Snowfall (in.)	na	*11.2*	*9.4*	*2.4*	0.0	0.0	0.0	0.0	0.0	0.2	*3.9*	na	na
Days With ≥ 1.0" Snow Depth	25	24	20	2	0	0	0	0	0	0	*4*	18	*93*

Old Forge *Herkimer County*   Elevation: 1,719 ft.   Latitude: 43° 42' N   Longitude: 74° 59' W

	JAN	FEB	MAR	APR	MAY	JUN	JUL	AUG	SEP	OCT	NOV	DEC	YEAR
Mean Maximum Temp. (°F)	24.5	28.3	37.1	49.8	64.2	71.8	75.9	73.7	65.3	54.2	41.0	29.8	51.3
Mean Temp. (°F)	13.1	15.9	25.4	37.9	51.2	59.5	63.8	62.1	54.2	43.3	32.2	20.0	39.9
Mean Minimum Temp. (°F)	1.4	3.4	13.6	26.0	38.1	47.2	51.7	50.4	43.1	32.3	23.4	10.0	28.4
Extreme Maximum Temp. (°F)	59	58	76	86	87	89	90	91	87	78	69	60	91
Extreme Minimum Temp. (°F)	-43	-52	-36	-10	16	24	30	23	19	3	-10	-38	-52
Days Maximum Temp. ≥ 90°F	0	0	0	0	0	0	0	0	0	0	0	0	0
Days Maximum Temp. ≤ 32°F	24	18	11	2	0	0	0	0	0	0	7	19	81
Days Minimum Temp. ≤ 32°F	31	28	29	23	9	1	0	0	4	17	25	30	197
Days Minimum Temp. ≤ 0°F	15	12	6	0	0	0	0	0	0	0	1	8	42
Heating Degree Days (base 65°F)	1,607	1,381	1,223	807	426	184	85	119	325	667	976	1,391	9,191
Cooling Degree Days (base 65°F)	0	0	0	1	5	30	61	39	8	0	0	0	144
Mean Precipitation (in.)	4.15	2.90	3.73	3.65	4.04	4.23	4.45	4.43	5.28	4.46	4.85	4.30	50.47
Days With ≥ 0.1" Precipitation	12	8	9	9	9	9	9	9	9	10	11	11	115
Days With ≥ 1.0" Precipitation	0	0	0	1	0	1	1	1	1	1	1	1	8
Mean Snowfall (in.)	58.9	39.1	38.1	13.4	2.2	trace	0.0	0.0	trace	3.4	24.5	47.1	226.7
Days With ≥ 1.0" Snow Depth	*30*	*26*	*27*	13	1	0	0	0	0	1	14	27	*139*

Oswego East *Oswego County*   Elevation: 347 ft.   Latitude: 43° 28' N   Longitude: 76° 30' W

	JAN	FEB	MAR	APR	MAY	JUN	JUL	AUG	SEP	OCT	NOV	DEC	YEAR
Mean Maximum Temp. (°F)	30.2	32.3	41.0	53.3	65.7	75.2	80.2	78.4	70.5	58.9	46.9	35.8	55.7
Mean Temp. (°F)	23.3	25.2	33.6	44.9	56.0	65.4	71.0	69.6	62.1	51.2	40.8	29.8	47.7
Mean Minimum Temp. (°F)	16.4	18.0	26.2	36.4	46.3	55.5	61.7	60.7	53.7	43.4	34.7	23.7	39.7
Extreme Maximum Temp. (°F)	65	63	83	90	91	94	94	95	90	85	74	69	95
Extreme Minimum Temp. (°F)	-15	-20	-7	13	28	36	47	43	30	21	11	-16	-20
Days Maximum Temp. ≥ 90°F	0	0	0	0	0	0	2	1	0	0	0	0	3
Days Maximum Temp. ≤ 32°F	18	15	7	0	0	0	0	0	0	0	1	11	52
Days Minimum Temp. ≤ 32°F	29	25	24	10	1	0	0	0	0	3	12	25	129
Days Minimum Temp. ≤ 0°F	3	2	0	0	0	0	0	0	0	0	0	1	6
Heating Degree Days (base 65°F)	1,285	1,118	967	600	292	77	8	15	132	425	720	1,086	6,725
Cooling Degree Days (base 65°F)	0	0	1	2	19	95	205	169	52	4	0	0	547
Mean Precipitation (in.)	3.78	2.87	3.36	3.25	3.14	3.40	3.01	3.64	4.20	3.80	4.44	3.81	42.70
Days With ≥ 0.1" Precipitation	10	8	9	8	8	8	6	7	8	8	11	10	101
Days With ≥ 1.0" Precipitation	0	0	0	0	0	0	0	1	1	1	1	0	4
Mean Snowfall (in.)	51.1	35.6	19.5	4.1	trace	0.0	0.0	0.0	trace	0.4	9.1	33.5	153.3
Days With ≥ 1.0" Snow Depth	27	25	17	2	0	0	0	0	0	0	5	18	94

Patchogue 2 N *Suffolk County*   Elevation: 52 ft.   Latitude: 40° 48' N   Longitude: 73° 00' W

	JAN	FEB	MAR	APR	MAY	JUN	JUL	AUG	SEP	OCT	NOV	DEC	YEAR
Mean Maximum Temp. (°F)	39.1	41.2	49.2	59.4	69.5	78.3	83.4	82.4	75.4	64.8	54.3	44.2	61.8
Mean Temp. (°F)	30.3	32.2	39.6	48.8	58.8	68.0	73.7	72.7	65.5	54.6	45.3	35.9	52.1
Mean Minimum Temp. (°F)	21.5	23.1	30.0	38.1	48.0	57.6	63.9	62.9	55.6	44.3	36.2	27.5	42.4
Extreme Maximum Temp. (°F)	62	68	83	90	97	96	98	102	97	84	77	68	102
Extreme Minimum Temp. (°F)	-13	-6	5	12	28	36	46	40	34	20	10	0	-13
Days Maximum Temp. ≥ 90°F	0	0	0	0	0	1	4	3	1	0	0	0	9
Days Maximum Temp. ≤ 32°F	8	5	1	0	0	0	0	0	0	0	0	3	17
Days Minimum Temp. ≤ 32°F	26	23	19	7	1	0	0	0	0	3	12	22	113
Days Minimum Temp. ≤ 0°F	1	1	0	0	0	0	0	0	0	0	0	0	2
Heating Degree Days (base 65°F)	1,068	921	780	481	209	33	2	5	71	324	585	896	5,375
Cooling Degree Days (base 65°F)	0	0	0	1	25	144	291	248	93	10	0	0	812
Mean Precipitation (in.)	4.25	3.66	4.39	4.44	4.06	4.20	3.44	4.54	3.74	3.98	4.61	4.59	49.90
Days With ≥ 0.1" Precipitation	8	7	8	8	8	7	6	6	6	6	8	9	87
Days With ≥ 1.0" Precipitation	1	1	1	1	1	1	1	1	1	1	1	1	12
Mean Snowfall (in.)	9.7	9.5	5.1	1.3	trace	0.0	0.0	0.0	0.0	trace	0.8	4.1	30.5
Days With ≥ 1.0" Snow Depth	10	7	2	0	0	0	0	0	0	0	0	3	22

Peru 2 WSW *Clinton County*   Elevation: 508 ft.   Latitude: 44° 34' N   Longitude: 73° 34' W

	JAN	FEB	MAR	APR	MAY	JUN	JUL	AUG	SEP	OCT	NOV	DEC	YEAR
Mean Maximum Temp. (°F)	27.7	31.0	41.1	54.5	68.6	76.9	81.8	78.9	69.8	58.0	45.0	32.9	55.5
Mean Temp. (°F)	17.8	20.9	31.1	43.7	56.4	65.3	70.2	67.5	58.9	47.7	36.8	24.3	45.0
Mean Minimum Temp. (°F)	7.9	10.8	21.0	32.8	44.2	53.5	58.6	56.0	47.9	37.3	28.5	15.6	34.5
Extreme Maximum Temp. (°F)	64	63	83	90	93	98	100	100	90	84	74	69	100
Extreme Minimum Temp. (°F)	-34	-30	-17	5	24	29	40	36	24	16	1	-26	-34
Days Maximum Temp. ≥ 90°F	0	0	0	0	0	1	3	2	0	0	0	0	6
Days Maximum Temp. ≤ 32°F	20	15	7	0	0	0	0	0	0	0	3	14	59
Days Minimum Temp. ≤ 32°F	30	27	26	16	2	0	0	0	1	10	20	28	160
Days Minimum Temp. ≤ 0°F	10	7	2	0	0	0	0	0	0	0	0	4	23
Heating Degree Days (base 65°F)	1,457	1,239	1,045	635	282	74	14	42	206	532	840	1,256	7,622
Cooling Degree Days (base 65°F)	0	0	0	2	22	92	190	126	30	2	0	0	464
Mean Precipitation (in.)	1.58	1.54	1.84	2.58	2.61	3.34	3.38	3.42	3.10	2.76	2.67	2.02	30.84
Days With ≥ 0.1" Precipitation	4	*4*	5	6	7	7	7	7	6	6	6	4	*69*
Days With ≥ 1.0" Precipitation	0	0	0	0	0	1	1	1	1	1	1	0	6
Mean Snowfall (in.)	*13.5*	12.1	11.1	4.0	0.0	0.0	0.0	0.0	0.0	0.5	4.3	12.9	*58.4*
Days With ≥ 1.0" Snow Depth	na	na	na	1	0	0	0	0	0	0	*1*	na	na

Port Jervis *Orange County*   Elevation: 469 ft.   Latitude: 41° 23' N   Longitude: 74° 41' W

	JAN	FEB	MAR	APR	MAY	JUN	JUL	AUG	SEP	OCT	NOV	DEC	YEAR
Mean Maximum Temp. (°F)	34.7	38.8	48.9	62.1	73.1	80.1	84.5	82.0	73.5	62.1	50.6	39.2	60.8
Mean Temp. (°F)	25.9	28.9	38.0	49.4	60.2	68.0	72.8	70.9	63.0	51.3	41.5	31.1	50.1
Mean Minimum Temp. (°F)	17.1	19.0	26.9	36.6	47.2	55.9	61.0	59.7	52.4	40.4	32.4	23.0	39.3
Extreme Maximum Temp. (°F)	66	74	87	96	96	96	100	97	94	84	79	73	100
Extreme Minimum Temp. (°F)	-19	-14	-3	11	26	35	40	38	28	18	9	-13	-19
Days Maximum Temp. ≥ 90°F	0	0	0	0	1	2	6	3	1	0	0	0	13
Days Maximum Temp. ≤ 32°F	12	7	2	0	0	0	0	0	0	0	1	7	29
Days Minimum Temp. ≤ 32°F	28	25	23	11	1	0	0	0	0	7	17	27	139
Days Minimum Temp. ≤ 0°F	3	2	0	0	0	0	0	0	0	0	0	1	6
Heating Degree Days (base 65°F)	1,206	1,011	832	467	181	36	3	11	121	421	699	1,043	6,031
Cooling Degree Days (base 65°F)	0	0	1	5	39	137	264	206	70	4	0	0	726
Mean Precipitation (in.)	3.41	2.98	3.85	4.01	4.42	4.12	4.10	3.64	4.44	3.47	3.79	3.44	45.67
Days With ≥ 0.1" Precipitation	7	6	7	8	8	7	7	6	6	6	6	7	81
Days With ≥ 1.0" Precipitation	1	1	1	1	1	1	1	1	1	1	1	1	12
Mean Snowfall (in.)	12.7	9.6	7.9	1.6	trace	0.0	0.0	0.0	0.0	trace	2.7	7.5	42.0
Days With ≥ 1.0" Snow Depth	21	17	9	0	0	0	0	0	0	0	0	2	10	59

Poughkeepsie Dutchess Co. Arpt. *Dutchess County*   Elevation: 154 ft.   Latitude: 41° 38' N   Longitude: 73° 53' W

	JAN	FEB	MAR	APR	MAY	JUN	JUL	AUG	SEP	OCT	NOV	DEC	YEAR
Mean Maximum Temp. (°F)	34.1	38.1	47.5	59.5	70.5	78.8	83.8	82.0	74.0	62.4	50.8	39.3	60.1
Mean Temp. (°F)	24.7	28.1	37.1	47.9	58.7	67.2	72.4	70.8	62.6	50.8	41.1	30.6	49.3
Mean Minimum Temp. (°F)	15.2	17.9	26.6	36.2	46.8	55.6	60.9	59.6	51.1	39.2	31.3	21.9	38.5
Extreme Maximum Temp. (°F)	64	73	86	94	95	96	103	98	97	85	80	72	103
Extreme Minimum Temp. (°F)	-20	-15	-3	16	28	35	43	38	30	18	3	-14	-20
Days Maximum Temp. ≥ 90°F	0	0	0	0	0	2	6	3	1	0	0	0	12
Days Maximum Temp. ≤ 32°F	13	8	2	0	0	0	0	0	0	0	1	7	31
Days Minimum Temp. ≤ 32°F	29	25	23	11	1	0	0	0	0	8	18	27	142
Days Minimum Temp. ≤ 0°F	4	2	0	0	0	0	0	0	0	0	0	1	7
Heating Degree Days (base 65°F)	1,241	1,037	858	510	218	46	6	14	130	436	712	1,059	6,267
Cooling Degree Days (base 65°F)	0	0	0	3	29	111	240	195	64	3	0	0	645
Mean Precipitation (in.)	3.02	2.61	3.48	3.80	4.80	3.65	4.79	3.87	3.55	3.56	3.54	3.14	43.81
Days With ≥ 0.1" Precipitation	6	6	7	6	8	7	7	6	6	6	6	7	78
Days With ≥ 1.0" Precipitation	0	0	1	1	1	1	1	1	1	1	1	1	10
Mean Snowfall (in.)	10.6	8.2	5.5	1.6	0.0	0.0	0.0	0.0	0.0	trace	2.2	6.4	34.5
Days With ≥ 1.0" Snow Depth	17	12	5	1	0	0	0	0	0	0	1	8	44

Ray Brook *Essex County*   Elevation: 1,617 ft.   Latitude: 44° 18' N   Longitude: 74° 06' W

	JAN	FEB	MAR	APR	MAY	JUN	JUL	AUG	SEP	OCT	NOV	DEC	YEAR
Mean Maximum Temp. (°F)	25.6	28.9	37.8	50.3	64.4	72.5	77.0	75.1	66.6	54.6	41.4	30.2	52.0
Mean Temp. (°F)	14.8	16.9	25.9	38.9	51.5	60.2	64.7	62.8	54.7	43.7	32.8	20.8	40.7
Mean Minimum Temp. (°F)	4.0	4.8	13.9	27.4	38.6	47.8	52.4	50.4	42.8	32.9	24.2	11.4	29.2
Extreme Maximum Temp. (°F)	61	60	79	89	89	93	93	96	93	79	69	61	96
Extreme Minimum Temp. (°F)	-35	-34	-25	-5	18	26	33	28	22	9	-5	-31	-35
Days Maximum Temp. ≥ 90°F	0	0	0	0	0	0	1	0	0	0	0	0	1
Days Maximum Temp. ≤ 32°F	22	18	10	2	0	0	0	0	0	0	7	18	77
Days Minimum Temp. ≤ 32°F	30	27	29	22	9	1	0	0	5	16	25	30	194
Days Minimum Temp. ≤ 0°F	13	13	6	0	0	0	0	0	0	0	0	7	39
Heating Degree Days (base 65°F)	1,552	1,355	1,206	777	418	174	78	115	314	653	959	1,365	8,966
Cooling Degree Days (base 65°F)	0	0	0	1	6	37	80	56	12	0	0	0	192
Mean Precipitation (in.)	2.67	2.08	2.73	2.87	3.16	3.89	3.91	4.18	4.17	3.47	3.57	2.97	39.67
Days With ≥ 0.1" Precipitation	8	6	7	8	9	8	8	9	8	8	9	8	96
Days With ≥ 1.0" Precipitation	0	0	0	0	0	1	1	1	1	1	0	0	5
Mean Snowfall (in.)	27.7	21.6	21.3	11.0	1.2	trace	0.0	trace	trace	2.0	14.8	24.9	124.5
Days With ≥ 1.0" Snow Depth	na	na	na	na	0	0	0	0	0	0	na	na	na

Riverhead Research Farm *Suffolk County*   Elevation: 98 ft.   Latitude: 40° 58' N   Longitude: 72° 43' W

	JAN	FEB	MAR	APR	MAY	JUN	JUL	AUG	SEP	OCT	NOV	DEC	YEAR
Mean Maximum Temp. (°F)	39.1	40.6	48.4	59.2	70.6	79.1	84.2	82.5	75.5	64.7	54.1	44.3	61.9
Mean Temp. (°F)	31.7	33.1	40.3	49.6	60.2	69.1	74.6	73.3	66.6	55.9	46.4	37.1	53.2
Mean Minimum Temp. (°F)	24.2	25.6	32.1	39.9	49.8	59.1	64.9	64.0	57.6	47.1	38.7	29.9	44.4
Extreme Maximum Temp. (°F)	68	68	80	92	96	97	100	96	97	84	78	76	100
Extreme Minimum Temp. (°F)	-8	-1	9	18	32	40	47	45	37	28	17	0	-8
Days Maximum Temp. ≥ 90°F	0	0	0	0	1	2	5	3	1	0	0	0	12
Days Maximum Temp. ≤ 32°F	8	5	1	0	0	0	0	0	0	0	0	3	17
Days Minimum Temp. ≤ 32°F	25	22	17	3	0	0	0	0	0	1	7	19	94
Days Minimum Temp. ≤ 0°F	0	0	0	0	0	0	0	0	0	0	0	0	0
Heating Degree Days (base 65°F)	1,026	894	760	459	174	24	1	2	51	283	551	857	5,082
Cooling Degree Days (base 65°F)	0	0	0	1	35	167	319	265	106	10	0	0	903
Mean Precipitation (in.)	4.30	3.50	4.22	4.10	3.76	3.64	3.16	4.10	3.61	3.87	4.32	4.04	46.62
Days With ≥ 0.1" Precipitation	7	6	7	7	7	6	5	6	5	6	7	7	76
Days With ≥ 1.0" Precipitation	1	1	1	1	1	1	1	1	1	1	1	1	12
Mean Snowfall (in.)	8.8	8.6	4.1	0.7	trace	0.0	0.0	0.0	0.0	trace	0.5	3.0	25.7
Days With ≥ 1.0" Snow Depth	9	7	2	0	0	0	0	0	0	0	0	2	20

Saratoga Springs 4 SW *Saratoga County*   Elevation: 308 ft.   Latitude: 43° 02' N   Longitude: 73° 49' W

	JAN	FEB	MAR	APR	MAY	JUN	JUL	AUG	SEP	OCT	NOV	DEC	YEAR
Mean Maximum Temp. (°F)	30.7	34.3	44.8	58.9	71.9	79.4	84.0	81.5	72.9	61.1	47.9	35.8	58.6
Mean Temp. (°F)	20.5	23.4	33.9	46.5	58.6	66.7	71.5	69.3	60.7	49.3	38.7	26.9	47.2
Mean Minimum Temp. (°F)	10.3	12.5	23.0	34.0	45.2	53.9	59.0	57.0	48.6	37.5	29.6	18.0	35.7
Extreme Maximum Temp. (°F)	63	64	88	92	92	96	97	96	94	85	82	67	97
Extreme Minimum Temp. (°F)	-33	-29	-13	10	25	33	40	37	24	15	5	-22	-33
Days Maximum Temp. ≥ 90°F	0	0	0	0	1	2	5	2	1	0	0	0	11
Days Maximum Temp. ≤ 32°F	17	11	3	0	0	0	0	0	0	0	1	10	42
Days Minimum Temp. ≤ 32°F	30	26	25	14	2	0	0	0	1	11	19	28	156
Days Minimum Temp. ≤ 0°F	8	6	1	0	0	0	0	0	0	0	0	3	18
Heating Degree Days (base 65°F)	1,373	1,169	957	552	223	54	7	23	169	483	783	1,174	6,967
Cooling Degree Days (base 65°F)	0	0	0	3	30	118	227	171	50	3	0	0	602
Mean Precipitation (in.)	3.28	2.49	3.53	3.52	3.97	3.93	3.69	3.98	3.70	3.54	3.73	3.33	42.69
Days With ≥ 0.1" Precipitation	7	5	7	7	8	7	6	6	7	7	7	7	81
Days With ≥ 1.0" Precipitation	1	0	1	1	1	1	1	1	1	1	1	1	11
Mean Snowfall (in.)	19.3	12.2	11.5	2.5	trace	0.0	0.0	0.0	trace	trace	4.2	13.5	63.2
Days With ≥ 1.0" Snow Depth	26	25	16	2	0	0	0	0	0	0	3	19	91

Setauket Strong *Suffolk County*   Elevation: 39 ft.   Latitude: 40° 58' N   Longitude: 73° 06' W

	JAN	FEB	MAR	APR	MAY	JUN	JUL	AUG	SEP	OCT	NOV	DEC	YEAR
Mean Maximum Temp. (°F)	39.0	41.0	49.3	60.2	70.1	78.3	83.3	81.7	74.8	64.6	54.6	44.3	61.8
Mean Temp. (°F)	31.7	33.1	40.4	50.3	60.0	68.8	74.2	73.0	66.4	56.1	46.8	37.1	53.2
Mean Minimum Temp. (°F)	24.4	25.2	31.8	40.4	49.8	59.1	65.1	64.1	58.0	47.5	38.9	29.8	44.5
Extreme Maximum Temp. (°F)	67	69	81	92	95	96	99	95	96	83	77	75	99
Extreme Minimum Temp. (°F)	-4	-1	7	17	30	41	48	45	39	29	17	-2	-4
Days Maximum Temp. ≥ 90°F	0	0	0	0	0	2	4	2	1	0	0	0	9
Days Maximum Temp. ≤ 32°F	8	4	1	0	0	0	0	0	0	0	0	3	16
Days Minimum Temp. ≤ 32°F	25	22	16	4	0	0	0	0	0	0	6	19	92
Days Minimum Temp. ≤ 0°F	0	0	0	0	0	0	0	0	0	0	0	0	0
Heating Degree Days (base 65°F)	1,026	893	755	436	182	28	1	3	53	278	541	858	5,054
Cooling Degree Days (base 65°F)	0	0	0	2	39	154	301	250	101	9	0	0	856
Mean Precipitation (in.)	3.85	3.04	4.11	4.18	3.86	3.71	3.55	3.92	3.61	3.91	3.91	3.95	45.60
Days With ≥ 0.1" Precipitation	*6*	6	*6*	7	7	6	6	5	6	6	6	7	*74*
Days With ≥ 1.0" Precipitation	1	1	1	1	1	1	1	1	1	1	1	1	12
Mean Snowfall (in.)	4.1	3.8	2.0	0.2	0.0	0.0	0.0	0.0	0.0	0.0	0.1	*1.4*	*11.6*
Days With ≥ 1.0" Snow Depth	na	na	*1*	0	0	0	0	0	0	0	0	*0*	na

Slide Mountain *Ulster County*   Elevation: 2,647 ft.   Latitude: 42° 01' N   Longitude: 74° 25' W

	JAN	FEB	MAR	APR	MAY	JUN	JUL	AUG	SEP	OCT	NOV	DEC	YEAR
Mean Maximum Temp. (°F)	26.4	28.8	36.7	48.4	60.9	67.6	71.8	70.4	63.1	53.4	41.6	30.4	50.0
Mean Temp. (°F)	17.9	19.6	27.5	38.9	50.7	58.1	62.6	61.3	54.3	44.1	34.0	23.0	41.0
Mean Minimum Temp. (°F)	9.4	10.4	18.3	29.3	40.5	48.6	53.3	52.2	45.3	34.7	26.3	15.6	32.0
Extreme Maximum Temp. (°F)	57	57	76	85	85	85	88	85	83	77	72	58	88
Extreme Minimum Temp. (°F)	-23	-20	-13	2	21	30	39	35	26	14	0	-22	-23
Days Maximum Temp. ≥ 90°F	0	0	0	0	0	0	0	0	0	0	0	0	0
Days Maximum Temp. ≤ 32°F	22	17	11	2	0	0	0	0	0	0	7	18	77
Days Minimum Temp. ≤ 32°F	30	27	28	20	6	0	0	0	2	13	23	30	179
Days Minimum Temp. ≤ 0°F	8	6	2	0	0	0	0	0	0	0	0	3	19
Heating Degree Days (base 65°F)	1,454	1,276	1,155	777	439	213	106	131	323	642	924	1,295	8,735
Cooling Degree Days (base 65°F)	0	0	0	0	4	15	42	26	7	0	0	0	94
Mean Precipitation (in.)	5.21	4.32	5.52	5.25	5.96	5.33	5.08	4.84	5.40	5.49	6.08	5.13	63.61
Days With ≥ 0.1" Precipitation	8	7	9	8	10	9	9	8	8	8	9	9	101
Days With ≥ 1.0" Precipitation	1	1	1	2	1	1	1	1	1	2	2	1	15
Mean Snowfall (in.)	23.9	20.1	19.7	7.3	1.4	0.0	0.0	0.0	0.0	0.5	8.6	20.3	101.8
Days With ≥ 1.0" Snow Depth	28	27	25	9	0	0	0	0	0	0	9	23	121

Sodus Center *Wayne County*   Elevation: 419 ft.   Latitude: 43° 12' N   Longitude: 77° 01' W

	JAN	FEB	MAR	APR	MAY	JUN	JUL	AUG	SEP	OCT	NOV	DEC	YEAR
Mean Maximum Temp. (°F)	32.0	34.3	43.3	55.8	68.7	77.6	81.9	80.0	72.4	60.7	48.5	37.0	57.7
Mean Temp. (°F)	24.5	26.0	34.5	46.1	57.5	66.4	71.3	69.6	62.4	51.2	41.1	30.2	48.4
Mean Minimum Temp. (°F)	16.9	17.6	25.7	36.3	46.3	55.2	60.5	59.1	52.4	41.7	33.5	23.3	39.1
Extreme Maximum Temp. (°F)	68	67	85	92	92	95	99	97	94	85	76	70	99
Extreme Minimum Temp. (°F)	-15	-24	-6	13	26	35	45	40	28	21	10	-9	-24
Days Maximum Temp. ≥ 90°F	0	0	0	0	0	2	4	2	1	0	0	0	9
Days Maximum Temp. ≤ 32°F	16	13	5	0	0	0	0	0	0	0	1	9	44
Days Minimum Temp. ≤ 32°F	28	25	24	10	1	0	0	0	0	4	14	26	132
Days Minimum Temp. ≤ 0°F	3	2	0	0	0	0	0	0	0	0	0	1	6
Heating Degree Days (base 65°F)	1,249	1,096	939	569	254	63	9	21	132	425	713	1,073	6,543
Cooling Degree Days (base 65°F)	0	0	1	4	27	109	209	167	57	4	0	0	578
Mean Precipitation (in.)	2.48	2.04	2.57	3.13	3.11	3.65	3.18	3.37	4.00	3.87	3.96	2.89	38.25
Days With ≥ 0.1" Precipitation	7	6	7	8	7	7	7	7	8	9	10	8	91
Days With ≥ 1.0" Precipitation	0	0	0	0	0	1	1	1	1	1	0	0	5
Mean Snowfall (in.)	26.7	17.5	12.6	3.1	trace	0.0	0.0	0.0	0.0	trace	6.7	22.7	89.3
Days With ≥ 1.0" Snow Depth	24	23	13	1	0	0	0	0	0	0	4	16	81

Stillwater Reservoir *Herkimer County*   Elevation: 1,689 ft.   Latitude: 43° 53' N   Longitude: 75° 02' W

	JAN	FEB	MAR	APR	MAY	JUN	JUL	AUG	SEP	OCT	NOV	DEC	YEAR
Mean Maximum Temp. (°F)	24.5	27.5	36.4	48.9	63.3	70.6	75.1	73.2	65.1	54.3	41.1	29.6	50.8
Mean Temp. (°F)	13.1	15.3	25.0	38.5	52.2	60.5	65.1	63.6	55.7	44.6	33.5	20.4	40.6
Mean Minimum Temp. (°F)	1.5	3.0	13.5	28.1	41.0	50.3	55.1	53.9	46.1	34.9	25.8	11.2	30.4
Extreme Maximum Temp. (°F)	59	58	75	84	88	88	89	90	88	80	71	61	90
Extreme Minimum Temp. (°F)	-40	-44	-34	-12	19	30	38	31	26	12	-6	-33	-44
Days Maximum Temp. ≥ 90°F	0	0	0	0	0	0	0	0	0	0	0	0	0
Days Maximum Temp. ≤ 32°F	24	19	11	2	0	0	0	0	0	0	7	19	82
Days Minimum Temp. ≤ 32°F	30	27	29	21	5	0	0	0	1	14	23	29	179
Days Minimum Temp. ≤ 0°F	15	13	7	0	0	0	0	0	0	0	0	7	42
Heating Degree Days (base 65°F)	1,607	1,399	1,234	789	398	163	66	91	286	625	938	1,376	8,972
Cooling Degree Days (base 65°F)	0	0	0	0	6	33	75	53	11	0	0	0	178
Mean Precipitation (in.)	3.65	2.70	3.31	3.61	3.92	4.28	4.62	4.79	5.08	4.20	4.64	4.21	49.01
Days With ≥ 0.1" Precipitation	11	8	10	9	9	9	9	9	9	10	11	11	115
Days With ≥ 1.0" Precipitation	0	0	0	0	0	1	1	1	1	1	1	0	6
Mean Snowfall (in.)	51.7	35.4	29.8	10.4	1.1	0.0	0.0	0.0	trace	2.2	19.1	41.1	190.8
Days With ≥ 1.0" Snow Depth	*31*	28	29	9	0	0	0	0	0	1	13	*28*	*139*

Troy Lock & Dam *Rensselaer County*   Elevation: 22 ft.   Latitude: 42° 45' N   Longitude: 73° 41' W

	JAN	FEB	MAR	APR	MAY	JUN	JUL	AUG	SEP	OCT	NOV	DEC	YEAR
Mean Maximum Temp. (°F)	31.4	34.4	44.1	57.4	70.5	78.7	83.9	82.0	73.5	61.4	49.0	36.9	58.6
Mean Temp. (°F)	22.4	24.9	34.8	47.2	59.4	68.1	73.3	71.3	62.7	50.9	40.8	29.2	48.8
Mean Minimum Temp. (°F)	13.3	15.4	25.4	37.0	48.3	57.5	62.6	60.5	52.0	40.4	32.4	21.5	38.9
Extreme Maximum Temp. (°F)	65	67	86	89	92	96	101	96	96	86	83	69	101
Extreme Minimum Temp. (°F)	-23	-17	-3	15	30	39	47	40	30	21	10	-15	-23
Days Maximum Temp. ≥ 90°F	0	0	0	0	1	2	6	3	1	0	0	0	13
Days Maximum Temp. ≤ 32°F	16	11	4	0	0	0	0	0	0	0	1	9	41
Days Minimum Temp. ≤ 32°F	29	26	24	9	0	0	0	0	0	5	16	26	135
Days Minimum Temp. ≤ 0°F	5	3	0	0	0	0	0	0	0	0	0	1	9
Heating Degree Days (base 65°F)	1,314	1,125	929	531	200	41	4	13	126	432	721	1,102	6,538
Cooling Degree Days (base 65°F)	0	0	0	3	32	140	270	217	67	3	1	0	733
Mean Precipitation (in.)	2.21	1.93	2.71	3.22	3.68	3.75	3.97	4.02	3.30	3.35	3.08	2.36	37.58
Days With ≥ 0.1" Precipitation	5	5	6	7	8	7	7	7	7	6	7	6	78
Days With ≥ 1.0" Precipitation	0	0	1	1	1	1	1	1	1	1	0	0	8
Mean Snowfall (in.)	*12.1*	9.4	7.2	1.6	trace	0.0	0.0	0.0	0.0	trace	3.4	*7.4*	*41.1*
Days With ≥ 1.0" Snow Depth	21	17	8	1	0	0	0	0	0	0	2	11	60

Tully Heiberg Forest *Cortland County*   Elevation: 1,896 ft.   Latitude: 42° 46' N   Longitude: 76° 05' W

	JAN	FEB	MAR	APR	MAY	JUN	JUL	AUG	SEP	OCT	NOV	DEC	YEAR
Mean Maximum Temp. (°F)	26.5	28.8	37.3	50.3	63.2	71.3	76.0	74.3	66.2	55.0	42.7	31.5	51.9
Mean Temp. (°F)	18.7	20.6	29.0	41.1	53.2	61.6	66.3	64.8	57.1	46.2	35.5	24.6	43.2
Mean Minimum Temp. (°F)	10.9	12.3	20.6	31.9	43.1	51.9	56.6	55.3	47.8	37.4	28.3	17.6	34.5
Extreme Maximum Temp. (°F)	61	58	80	85	88	89	93	90	89	80	74	65	93
Extreme Minimum Temp. (°F)	-20	-22	-11	5	17	30	37	33	22	14	1	-29	-29
Days Maximum Temp. ≥ 90°F	0	0	0	0	0	0	0	0	0	0	0	0	0
Days Maximum Temp. ≤ 32°F	22	18	11	2	0	0	0	0	0	0	6	17	76
Days Minimum Temp. ≤ 32°F	30	27	27	16	4	0	0	0	1	10	21	29	165
Days Minimum Temp. ≤ 0°F	7	5	1	0	0	0	0	0	0	0	0	2	15
Heating Degree Days (base 65°F)	1,429	1,249	1,111	713	371	141	52	74	253	576	877	1,247	8,093
Cooling Degree Days (base 65°F)	0	0	0	2	10	49	102	74	21	1	0	0	259
Mean Precipitation (in.)	2.91	2.87	3.40	3.84	3.95	4.61	4.02	3.79	4.91	3.78	3.86	3.63	45.57
Days With ≥ 0.1" Precipitation	9	8	9	9	9	9	7	8	9	9	9	10	105
Days With ≥ 1.0" Precipitation	0	0	0	1	1	1	1	1	1	1	1	0	8
Mean Snowfall (in.)	27.5	24.4	22.8	8.7	0.7	trace	0.0	0.0	trace	1.6	12.5	27.0	125.2
Days With ≥ 1.0" Snow Depth	28	27	26	9	0	0	0	0	0	1	11	24	126

Utica Oneida County Airport *Oneida County*   Elevation: 711 ft.   Latitude: 43° 09' N   Longitude: 75° 23' W

	JAN	FEB	MAR	APR	MAY	JUN	JUL	AUG	SEP	OCT	NOV	DEC	YEAR
Mean Maximum Temp. (°F)	28.7	31.2	40.6	54.3	67.5	75.9	80.5	78.4	69.9	57.9	45.4	34.0	55.4
Mean Temp. (°F)	21.1	23.3	32.5	44.9	57.0	65.5	70.4	68.6	60.4	49.1	38.5	27.2	46.5
Mean Minimum Temp. (°F)	13.6	15.4	24.3	35.5	46.4	55.1	60.2	58.7	50.8	40.2	31.5	20.3	37.7
Extreme Maximum Temp. (°F)	65	64	85	91	91	95	96	95	94	83	79	69	96
Extreme Minimum Temp. (°F)	-27	-21	-12	9	25	33	44	40	25	19	6	-23	-27
Days Maximum Temp. ≥ 90°F	0	0	0	0	0	1	3	1	0	0	0	0	5
Days Maximum Temp. ≤ 32°F	19	15	7	0	0	0	0	0	0	0	3	13	57
Days Minimum Temp. ≤ 32°F	28	26	24	11	1	0	0	0	0	6	16	27	139
Days Minimum Temp. ≤ 0°F	5	4	1	0	0	0	0	0	0	0	0	2	12
Heating Degree Days (base 65°F)	1,351	1,171	1,002	598	265	76	13	30	176	489	789	1,165	7,125
Cooling Degree Days (base 65°F)	0	0	1	2	23	94	188	142	43	2	0	0	495
Mean Precipitation (in.)	3.47	2.99	3.66	3.55	3.73	4.08	3.69	3.57	4.48	3.36	4.04	4.03	44.65
Days With ≥ 0.1" Precipitation	10	8	9	8	9	8	6	7	8	8	10	10	101
Days With ≥ 1.0" Precipitation	0	0	1	1	0	1	1	1	1	1	0	1	8
Mean Snowfall (in.)	26.4	19.0	17.1	3.7	trace	0.0	trace	trace	trace	0.6	9.8	21.9	98.5
Days With ≥ 1.0" Snow Depth	26	23	16	3	0	0	0	0	0	0	6	18	92

Walden 1 ESE *Orange County*   Elevation: 377 ft.   Latitude: 41° 33' N   Longitude: 74° 10' W

	JAN	FEB	MAR	APR	MAY	JUN	JUL	AUG	SEP	OCT	NOV	DEC	YEAR
Mean Maximum Temp. (°F)	34.4	37.6	46.9	58.9	70.2	78.4	83.2	81.4	73.4	62.3	51.0	38.9	59.7
Mean Temp. (°F)	24.2	26.5	36.2	47.5	58.0	66.5	71.4	69.6	61.1	49.5	40.4	29.7	48.4
Mean Minimum Temp. (°F)	13.9	15.4	25.5	36.0	45.7	54.6	59.5	57.7	48.7	36.6	29.8	20.4	37.0
Extreme Maximum Temp. (°F)	69	70	86	95	94	94	100	96	96	89	80	73	100
Extreme Minimum Temp. (°F)	-27	-18	-7	12	27	33	41	35	27	16	4	-14	-27
Days Maximum Temp. ≥ 90°F	0	0	0	0	0	2	5	3	1	0	0	0	11
Days Maximum Temp. ≤ 32°F	13	9	3	0	0	0	0	0	0	0	1	7	33
Days Minimum Temp. ≤ 32°F	29	26	24	11	2	0	0	0	1	11	20	28	152
Days Minimum Temp. ≤ 0°F	5	3	0	0	0	0	0	0	0	0	0	1	9
Heating Degree Days (base 65°F)	1,259	1,080	886	524	239	60	10	22	159	476	731	1,089	6,535
Cooling Degree Days (base 65°F)	0	0	1	4	27	110	218	170	48	3	0	0	581
Mean Precipitation (in.)	3.37	2.41	3.59	3.86	4.49	4.11	4.22	3.56	3.99	3.39	3.75	3.28	44.02
Days With ≥ 0.1" Precipitation	7	6	7	7	8	7	7	6	7	6	6	7	81
Days With ≥ 1.0" Precipitation	1	0	1	1	1	1	1	1	1	1	1	1	11
Mean Snowfall (in.)	12.2	8.2	7.4	1.4	trace	0.0	0.0	0.0	0.0	trace	1.8	7.0	38.0
Days With ≥ 1.0" Snow Depth	20	16	8	1	0	0	0	0	0	0	1	10	56

Walton *Delaware County*   Elevation: 1,240 ft.   Latitude: 42° 10' N   Longitude: 75° 08' W

	JAN	FEB	MAR	APR	MAY	JUN	JUL	AUG	SEP	OCT	NOV	DEC	YEAR
Mean Maximum Temp. (°F)	31.1	34.3	43.9	56.9	69.5	76.8	81.3	79.3	70.8	60.1	47.0	35.4	57.2
Mean Temp. (°F)	21.5	23.8	33.4	44.8	56.1	64.0	68.5	67.1	59.4	48.6	38.1	27.1	46.0
Mean Minimum Temp. (°F)	11.8	13.3	22.7	32.7	42.6	51.0	55.7	54.8	47.9	37.1	29.2	18.8	34.8
Extreme Maximum Temp. (°F)	61	67	83	89	92	92	98	94	92	85	80	66	98
Extreme Minimum Temp. (°F)	-33	-26	-17	7	21	29	36	31	24	11	0	-22	-33
Days Maximum Temp. ≥ 90°F	0	0	0	0	0	1	2	1	0	0	0	0	4
Days Maximum Temp. ≤ 32°F	17	13	5	0	0	0	0	0	0	0	3	12	50
Days Minimum Temp. ≤ 32°F	29	26	25	15	5	0	0	0	2	11	20	28	161
Days Minimum Temp. ≤ 0°F	7	6	2	0	0	0	0	0	0	0	0	3	18
Heating Degree Days (base 65°F)	1,343	1,157	974	600	287	92	26	41	196	504	800	1,168	7,188
Cooling Degree Days (base 65°F)	0	0	0	1	14	67	144	108	32	2	0	0	368
Mean Precipitation (in.)	3.02	2.82	3.58	3.96	4.25	4.16	4.45	4.12	3.98	4.02	4.32	3.67	46.35
Days With ≥ 0.1" Precipitation	7	7	8	9	9	9	9	7	8	7	8	8	96
Days With ≥ 1.0" Precipitation	0	0	1	1	1	1	1	1	1	1	1	1	10
Mean Snowfall (in.)	23.4	19.0	16.9	6.4	0.4	trace	0.0	0.0	trace	0.5	9.0	20.3	95.9
Days With ≥ 1.0" Snow Depth	26	24	17	4	0	0	0	0	0	0	7	20	98

Wanakena Ranger School *St. Lawrence County*   Elevation: 1,509 ft.   Latitude: 44° 09' N   Longitude: 74° 54' W

	JAN	FEB	MAR	APR	MAY	JUN	JUL	AUG	SEP	OCT	NOV	DEC	YEAR
Mean Maximum Temp. (°F)	26.2	29.1	38.6	51.3	66.0	73.6	77.7	75.4	66.8	55.3	42.0	31.1	52.8
Mean Temp. (°F)	14.7	16.7	26.7	40.0	53.3	61.5	65.9	63.9	55.7	44.8	33.5	21.5	41.5
Mean Minimum Temp. (°F)	3.2	4.3	14.8	28.5	40.6	49.5	54.1	52.3	44.6	34.3	25.0	11.8	30.3
Extreme Maximum Temp. (°F)	62	59	74	83	88	93	94	95	90	79	71	62	95
Extreme Minimum Temp. (°F)	-41	-41	-31	-10	19	27	35	30	22	10	-12	-35	-41
Days Maximum Temp. ≥ 90°F	0	0	0	0	0	0	0	0	0	0	0	0	0
Days Maximum Temp. ≤ 32°F	22	17	9	1	0	0	0	0	0	0	6	16	71
Days Minimum Temp. ≤ 32°F	30	27	28	21	7	1	0	0	3	15	24	29	185
Days Minimum Temp. ≤ 0°F	13	12	5	0	0	0	0	0	0	0	1	7	38
Heating Degree Days (base 65°F)	1,553	1,360	1,180	745	366	143	57	90	285	621	937	1,337	8,674
Cooling Degree Days (base 65°F)	0	0	0	1	9	47	94	63	13	0	0	0	227
Mean Precipitation (in.)	3.03	2.38	2.91	3.03	3.73	3.93	4.59	4.25	4.60	3.83	3.96	3.25	43.49
Days With ≥ 0.1" Precipitation	10	7	8	8	9	9	9	8	9	8	10	9	104
Days With ≥ 1.0" Precipitation	0	0	0	0	1	1	1	1	1	1	0	0	6
Mean Snowfall (in.)	32.8	24.8	21.2	7.4	1.0	0.0	0.0	0.0	trace	1.2	12.9	26.7	128.0
Days With ≥ 1.0" Snow Depth	30	28	28	9	0	0	0	0	0	1	11	25	132

Warsaw 6 SW *Wyoming County*   Elevation: 1,817 ft.   Latitude: 42° 41' N   Longitude: 78° 13' W

	JAN	FEB	MAR	APR	MAY	JUN	JUL	AUG	SEP	OCT	NOV	DEC	YEAR
Mean Maximum Temp. (°F)	27.4	30.0	38.8	51.9	64.4	73.0	*77.4*	75.2	68.0	56.9	43.8	32.9	*53.3*
Mean Temp. (°F)	19.6	21.4	29.8	42.2	53.7	62.7	*67.0*	65.1	58.0	47.5	36.3	25.8	*44.1*
Mean Minimum Temp. (°F)	11.6	12.8	20.5	32.4	43.1	52.3	*56.5*	54.9	48.1	38.0	28.8	18.6	*34.8*
Extreme Maximum Temp. (°F)	61	66	80	86	88	88	99	91	91	82	72	70	99
Extreme Minimum Temp. (°F)	-22	-28	-15	*8*	22	30	40	32	26	16	-4	-23	*-28*
Days Maximum Temp. ≥ 90°F	0	0	0	0	0	0	1	0	0	0	0	0	1
Days Maximum Temp. ≤ 32°F	21	17	11	1	0	0	0	0	0	0	5	15	70
Days Minimum Temp. ≤ 32°F	30	27	27	17	4	0	0	0	1	9	21	28	164
Days Minimum Temp. ≤ 0°F	6	5	1	0	0	0	0	0	0	0	0	2	14
Heating Degree Days (base 65°F)	1,403	1,224	1,084	679	357	122	*44*	70	230	537	854	1,211	*7,815*
Cooling Degree Days (base 65°F)	0	0	1	2	16	56	113	78	22	1	0	0	289
Mean Precipitation (in.)	2.99	2.30	3.07	3.32	3.65	4.41	4.18	3.81	4.60	3.79	3.82	3.47	43.41
Days With ≥ 0.1" Precipitation	10	8	9	9	9	9	8	8	10	9	10	11	110
Days With ≥ 1.0" Precipitation	0	0	0	1	1	1	1	1	1	0	0	0	6
Mean Snowfall (in.)	*29.8*	21.2	*17.3*	4.9	0.3	0.0	0.0	0.0	0.0	0.6	*12.8*	*23.0*	*109.9*
Days With ≥ 1.0" Snow Depth	*27*	23	18	4	0	0	0	0	0	0	8	*21*	*101*

Watertown *Jefferson County*   Elevation: 495 ft.   Latitude: 43° 59' N   Longitude: 75° 53' W

	JAN	FEB	MAR	APR	MAY	JUN	JUL	AUG	SEP	OCT	NOV	DEC	YEAR
Mean Maximum Temp. (°F)	28.3	30.6	39.8	53.3	66.3	75.2	79.8	78.1	69.8	57.9	45.8	34.1	54.9
Mean Temp. (°F)	18.6	20.7	30.8	44.0	56.5	65.6	70.5	68.8	60.5	48.8	38.2	25.8	45.7
Mean Minimum Temp. (°F)	9.0	10.8	21.7	34.7	46.7	56.0	61.2	59.4	51.1	39.6	30.6	17.4	36.5
Extreme Maximum Temp. (°F)	65	61	82	92	89	94	94	97	93	83	74	68	97
Extreme Minimum Temp. (°F)	-34	-30	-19	2	25	33	42	39	29	18	3	-30	-34
Days Maximum Temp. ≥ 90°F	0	0	0	0	0	0	1	1	0	0	0	0	2
Days Maximum Temp. ≤ 32°F	18	15	8	1	0	0	0	0	0	0	3	12	57
Days Minimum Temp. ≤ 32°F	29	26	25	13	1	0	0	0	0	8	17	28	147
Days Minimum Temp. ≤ 0°F	10	8	2	0	0	0	0	0	0	0	0	4	24
Heating Degree Days (base 65°F)	1,431	1,245	1,054	626	283	76	17	32	174	499	797	1,210	7,444
Cooling Degree Days (base 65°F)	0	0	0	4	25	103	195	158	47	3	0	0	535
Mean Precipitation (in.)	3.55	2.49	2.83	2.98	3.25	3.48	3.21	3.81	4.55	3.84	4.45	3.74	42.18
Days With ≥ 0.1" Precipitation	10	7	7	7	8	7	7	7	8	9	10	10	97
Days With ≥ 1.0" Precipitation	0	0	0	0	0	1	1	1	1	1	1	0	6
Mean Snowfall (in.)	35.0	22.4	14.5	3.3	trace	0.0	0.0	0.0	0.0	0.3	7.8	27.5	110.8
Days With ≥ 1.0" Snow Depth	25	23	16	2	0	0	0	0	0	0	5	18	89

Watertown Airport *Jefferson County*   Elevation: 314 ft.   Latitude: 44° 00' N   Longitude: 76° 01' W

	JAN	FEB	MAR	APR	MAY	JUN	JUL	AUG	SEP	OCT	NOV	DEC	YEAR
Mean Maximum Temp. (°F)	28.8	30.9	40.2	53.6	65.7	74.3	79.4	77.8	69.6	58.1	45.8	34.4	54.9
Mean Temp. (°F)	19.2	20.9	30.5	43.3	54.9	63.5	68.8	67.0	58.9	48.1	37.7	25.7	44.9
Mean Minimum Temp. (°F)	9.3	10.9	20.8	33.0	44.0	52.6	58.2	56.2	48.2	38.0	29.6	17.0	34.8
Extreme Maximum Temp. (°F)	66	63	83	89	86	94	94	95	93	84	77	68	95
Extreme Minimum Temp. (°F)	-43	-34	-24	9	21	30	39	34	22	12	-3	-37	-43
Days Maximum Temp. ≥ 90°F	0	0	0	0	0	0	1	1	0	0	0	0	2
Days Maximum Temp. ≤ 32°F	17	15	8	0	0	0	0	0	0	0	2	12	54
Days Minimum Temp. ≤ 32°F	28	26	26	15	2	0	0	0	2	10	18	27	154
Days Minimum Temp. ≤ 0°F	9	8	2	0	0	0	0	0	0	0	0	4	23
Heating Degree Days (base 65°F)	1,415	1,239	1,062	645	320	107	24	48	212	521	812	1,211	7,616
Cooling Degree Days (base 65°F)	0	0	0	1	12	60	145	111	34	3	0	0	366
Mean Precipitation (in.)	2.71	2.28	2.36	2.76	2.75	2.88	2.45	2.97	3.80	3.10	3.39	2.80	34.25
Days With ≥ 0.1" Precipitation	7	6	6	7	7	6	5	6	7	8	8	8	81
Days With ≥ 1.0" Precipitation	0	0	0	0	0	0	0	1	1	0	0	0	2
Mean Snowfall (in.)	27.8	19.3	12.1	2.5	trace	trace	trace	trace	trace	0.2	6.5	22.7	91.1
Days With ≥ 1.0" Snow Depth	24	21	14	2	0	0	0	0	0	0	4	17	82

West Point *Orange County*   Elevation: 318 ft.   Latitude: 41° 23' N   Longitude: 73° 58' W

	JAN	FEB	MAR	APR	MAY	JUN	JUL	AUG	SEP	OCT	NOV	DEC	YEAR
Mean Maximum Temp. (°F)	35.8	39.4	49.0	61.7	72.9	81.1	86.1	83.8	75.2	63.5	51.7	40.4	61.7
Mean Temp. (°F)	28.0	30.6	39.4	50.8	61.4	69.9	74.9	73.2	65.1	54.0	43.9	33.3	52.0
Mean Minimum Temp. (°F)	20.0	21.8	29.8	39.7	49.9	58.6	63.7	62.5	55.0	44.5	36.1	26.2	42.3
Extreme Maximum Temp. (°F)	63	71	85	96	95	98	102	98	98	86	81	72	102
Extreme Minimum Temp. (°F)	-15	-7	2	15	27	40	46	41	32	22	10	-7	-15
Days Maximum Temp. ≥ 90°F	0	0	0	0	1	3	9	5	1	0	0	0	19
Days Maximum Temp. ≤ 32°F	11	7	1	0	0	0	0	0	0	0	0	6	25
Days Minimum Temp. ≤ 32°F	27	24	19	5	0	0	0	0	0	2	11	24	112
Days Minimum Temp. ≤ 0°F	1	0	0	0	0	0	0	0	0	0	0	0	1
Heating Degree Days (base 65°F)	1,142	965	787	428	153	21	1	5	79	341	625	976	5,523
Cooling Degree Days (base 65°F)	0	0	1	6	47	175	315	260	86	5	0	0	895
Mean Precipitation (in.)	4.01	3.15	4.08	4.20	4.89	4.09	4.30	4.24	4.45	4.22	4.51	3.89	50.03
Days With ≥ 0.1" Precipitation	7	6	7	7	8	7	7	7	7	6	7	7	83
Days With ≥ 1.0" Precipitation	1	1	1	1	1	1	1	1	1	1	1	1	12
Mean Snowfall (in.)	10.0	8.9	5.7	0.3	0.0	0.0	0.0	0.0	0.0	trace	0.9	4.6	30.4
Days With ≥ 1.0" Snow Depth	12	12	3	0	0	0	0	0	0	0	0	5	32

Westfield 2 SSE *Chautauqua County*   Elevation: 705 ft.   Latitude: 42° 18' N   Longitude: 79° 35' W

	JAN	FEB	MAR	APR	MAY	JUN	JUL	AUG	SEP	OCT	NOV	DEC	YEAR
Mean Maximum Temp. (°F)	31.7	33.9	42.6	54.6	66.7	75.3	79.6	77.5	70.4	59.3	47.8	37.3	56.4
Mean Temp. (°F)	25.1	26.5	34.6	45.9	57.8	66.6	71.3	69.6	62.8	52.0	41.5	31.3	48.7
Mean Minimum Temp. (°F)	18.4	19.0	26.6	37.2	48.8	57.8	63.0	61.6	55.1	44.6	35.2	25.4	41.1
Extreme Maximum Temp. (°F)	66	68	82	90	91	97	99	99	89	81	74	72	99
Extreme Minimum Temp. (°F)	-16	-19	-13	14	28	35	47	41	36	27	6	-8	-19
Days Maximum Temp. ≥ 90°F	0	0	0	0	0	1	2	1	0	0	0	0	4
Days Maximum Temp. ≤ 32°F	16	13	7	1	0	0	0	0	0	0	2	10	49
Days Minimum Temp. ≤ 32°F	28	25	23	10	0	0	0	0	0	1	12	24	123
Days Minimum Temp. ≤ 0°F	2	2	0	0	0	0	0	0	0	0	0	0	4
Heating Degree Days (base 65°F)	1,231	1,083	936	572	255	65	9	17	123	403	699	1,037	6,430
Cooling Degree Days (base 65°F)	0	0	2	5	39	123	225	172	65	6	0	0	637
Mean Precipitation (in.)	2.47	2.24	2.97	3.37	3.70	4.28	4.23	4.55	5.57	4.81	4.53	3.51	46.23
Days With ≥ 0.1" Precipitation	7	6	8	8	8	8	7	7	9	10	10	9	97
Days With ≥ 1.0" Precipitation	0	0	0	1	1	1	1	1	1	1	1	0	8
Mean Snowfall (in.)	22.5	16.0	11.1	2.9	0.3	0.0	0.0	0.0	trace	0.6	8.7	24.0	86.1
Days With ≥ 1.0" Snow Depth	25	21	12	2	0	0	0	0	0	0	5	17	82

White Plains Westchester Co. Arpt. *Westchester County*   Elevation: 396 ft.   Latitude: 41° 04' N   Longitude: 73° 43' W

	JAN	FEB	MAR	APR	MAY	JUN	JUL	AUG	SEP	OCT	NOV	DEC	YEAR
Mean Maximum Temp. (°F)	35.5	38.5	47.2	58.3	68.8	77.0	82.4	80.2	72.1	61.3	51.4	40.3	59.4
Mean Temp. (°F)	28.3	30.7	38.7	49.1	59.3	67.8	73.4	71.8	63.6	52.7	43.8	33.4	51.0
Mean Minimum Temp. (°F)	21.0	22.9	30.1	39.9	49.8	58.4	64.5	63.3	55.1	44.0	36.1	26.5	42.6
Extreme Maximum Temp. (°F)	65	75	82	90	95	97	100	98	98	82	78	72	100
Extreme Minimum Temp. (°F)	-9	-10	6	16	33	39	46	41	33	24	15	-5	-10
Days Maximum Temp. ≥ 90°F	0	0	0	0	0	2	4	2	1	0	0	0	9
Days Maximum Temp. ≤ 32°F	12	8	2	0	0	0	0	0	0	0	0	6	28
Days Minimum Temp. ≤ 32°F	27	23	19	4	0	0	0	0	0	2	10	23	108
Days Minimum Temp. ≤ 0°F	1	0	0	0	0	0	0	0	0	0	0	0	1
Heating Degree Days (base 65°F)	1,132	961	810	474	201	42	3	8	105	381	630	972	5,719
Cooling Degree Days (base 65°F)	0	0	1	3	32	141	285	229	78	7	0	0	776
Mean Precipitation (in.)	4.50	3.12	4.78	4.43	4.48	3.66	3.60	3.97	4.79	4.24	4.30	4.08	49.95
Days With ≥ 0.1" Precipitation	8	6	7	7	7	6	6	6	6	6	6	7	78
Days With ≥ 1.0" Precipitation	1	1	1	1	1	1	1	1	2	1	1	1	13
Mean Snowfall (in.)	9.4	8.4	5.4	1.0	trace	0.0	0.0	0.0	0.0	trace	0.4	4.7	29.3
Days With ≥ 1.0" Snow Depth	9	7	3	0	0	0	0	0	0	0	0	3	22

Whitehall *Washington County*   Elevation: 118 ft.   Latitude: 43° 33' N   Longitude: 73° 24' W

	JAN	FEB	MAR	APR	MAY	JUN	JUL	AUG	SEP	OCT	NOV	DEC	YEAR
Mean Maximum Temp. (°F)	29.4	33.3	43.3	57.7	71.7	80.1	84.7	81.5	72.3	60.0	46.9	34.9	58.0
Mean Temp. (°F)	19.7	22.8	33.3	46.7	59.5	68.1	72.6	70.1	61.7	50.1	39.2	26.9	47.6
Mean Minimum Temp. (°F)	9.9	12.3	23.3	35.6	47.4	56.0	60.5	58.7	51.0	40.2	31.5	18.8	37.1
Extreme Maximum Temp. (°F)	64	60	84	92	94	98	100	98	94	83	75	68	100
Extreme Minimum Temp. (°F)	-36	-38	-14	9	28	34	43	37	29	17	4	-25	-38
Days Maximum Temp. ≥ 90°F	0	0	0	0	1	3	6	2	0	0	0	0	12
Days Maximum Temp. ≤ 32°F	18	13	4	0	0	0	0	0	0	0	1	12	48
Days Minimum Temp. ≤ 32°F	30	26	25	12	1	0	0	0	0	6	17	28	145
Days Minimum Temp. ≤ 0°F	8	6	1	0	0	0	0	0	0	0	0	3	18
Heating Degree Days (base 65°F)	1,400	1,185	976	546	197	38	4	17	145	456	767	1,174	6,905
Cooling Degree Days (base 65°F)	0	0	0	2	30	136	247	185	58	3	0	0	661
Mean Precipitation (in.)	3.23	2.39	3.06	2.99	3.80	3.25	3.91	4.27	3.86	3.48	3.57	2.83	40.64
Days With ≥ 0.1" Precipitation	7	5	7	7	8	7	7	7	7	6	7	6	81
Days With ≥ 1.0" Precipitation	1	0	1	1	1	1	1	1	1	1	1	0	10
Mean Snowfall (in.)	18.2	12.0	13.1	2.2	trace	0.0	0.0	0.0	0.0	trace	4.3	14.2	64.0
Days With ≥ 1.0" Snow Depth	na	na	na	0	0	0	0	0	0	0	na	na	na

Yorktown Heights 1 W *Westchester County*   Elevation: 669 ft.   Latitude: 41° 16' N   Longitude: 73° 48' W

	JAN	FEB	MAR	APR	MAY	JUN	JUL	AUG	SEP	OCT	NOV	DEC	YEAR
Mean Maximum Temp. (°F)	34.2	37.4	46.4	58.4	69.5	77.2	82.2	80.5	73.0	62.1	50.6	39.2	59.2
Mean Temp. (°F)	26.1	28.7	37.3	48.4	59.1	67.4	72.5	70.9	63.3	52.3	42.5	31.8	50.0
Mean Minimum Temp. (°F)	18.0	19.9	28.1	38.5	48.7	57.5	62.7	61.1	53.6	42.5	34.3	24.3	40.8
Extreme Maximum Temp. (°F)	63	73	85	93	94	94	100	95	95	85	79	73	100
Extreme Minimum Temp. (°F)	-15	-10	0	14	30	38	46	39	33	20	11	-9	-15
Days Maximum Temp. ≥ 90°F	0	0	0	0	0	1	3	2	1	0	0	0	7
Days Maximum Temp. ≤ 32°F	13	10	2	0	0	0	0	0	0	0	1	7	33
Days Minimum Temp. ≤ 32°F	29	25	21	6	0	0	0	0	0	3	14	26	124
Days Minimum Temp. ≤ 0°F	2	1	0	0	0	0	0	0	0	0	0	0	3
Heating Degree Days (base 65°F)	1,198	1,018	853	496	208	45	5	13	111	392	670	1,024	6,033
Cooling Degree Days (base 65°F)	0	0	1	4	34	130	254	202	66	5	0	0	696
Mean Precipitation (in.)	3.97	3.17	4.20	4.38	4.76	4.13	4.62	4.48	4.75	4.17	4.57	3.76	50.96
Days With ≥ 0.1" Precipitation	7	6	7	8	8	7	7	7	6	6	7	7	83
Days With ≥ 1.0" Precipitation	1	1	1	1	2	1	1	1	2	1	2	1	15
Mean Snowfall (in.)	10.4	10.0	7.5	2.2	trace	0.0	0.0	0.0	0.0	0.3	1.5	6.1	38.0
Days With ≥ 1.0" Snow Depth	17	16	8	1	0	0	0	0	0	0	1	9	52

Note: See Appendix D for explanation of data.

NORTH CAROLINA

PHYSICAL FEATURES. North Carolina lies between 33.5° and 37° N. latitude and between 75° and 84.5° W. longitude. The span of longitude is greater than that of any other state east of the Mississippi River. The greatest length from east to west is 503 miles. The greatest breadth from north to south is 187 miles. The total area is 52,712 square miles: 49,142 square miles of land and 3,570 square miles of water.

The range of altitude is also the greatest of any eastern state. North Carolina rises from sea level along the Atlantic coast to 6,684 feet at the summit of Mount Mitchell, the highest peak in the eastern United States. Mount Mitchell is in the heart of the Blue Ridge Range. This Range, along with the Great Smokies, lies partly in North Carolina and partly in Tennessee and forms the highest part of the Appalachian Mountains.

The three principal physiographic divisions of the eastern United States are particularly well developed in North Carolina. Beginning in the east, they are: the Coastal Plain, the Piedmont, and the Mountains. The land and water areas of the Coastal Plain Division comprise nearly half the area of the State. The tidewater portion is generally flat and swampy, while the interior is gently sloping and, for the most part, naturally well drained. The Piedmont Division rises gently from about 200 feet at the fall line to near 1,500 feet at the base of the mountains; its area is about one-third of the State. The land is mostly gently rolling. There are several ranges of steeper hills. The Mountain Division is the smallest of the three, little more than one-fifth of the State's area. In elevation it ranges downward from Mount Mitchell's peak to about 1,000 feet above mean sea level in the lowest valleys. There are more than 40 peaks higher than 6,000 feet and about 80 others over 5,000 feet high.

North Carolina rivers fall into two groups: those that flow into the Atlantic Ocean and those that drain westward into the Mississippi River system. The two are separated by a ridge averaging 2,200 feet above mean sea level. A second chain of mountains ranging up to 6,000 feet marks the western boundary of the State. Most of the State, including the Coastal Plain, the Piedmont, and the eastern and southern slopes, drains into the Atlantic Ocean. The principal rivers involved are the Roanoke, Tar, Neuse, Cape Fear, Yadkin, and Catawba. The main stream draining the extreme western part of North Carolina is the French Broad River. The northern mountains are drained by streams flowing into the Ohio River system. All eventually reach the Mississippi.

GENERAL CLIMATE. North Carolina has the most varied climate of any eastern state. This is due mainly to its wide range in elevation and distance from the ocean. In all seasons of the year the average temperature varies more than 20 from the lower coast to the highest mountain elevations. Altitude also has an important effect on rainfall. The rainiest part of the eastern United States, with an annual average of more than 80 inches, is in southwestern North Carolina where moist southerly winds are forced upward in passing over the mountain barrier.

In winter the greater part of North Carolina is partially protected by the mountain ranges from the frequent outbreaks of cold which move southeastward across the Central States. Such outbreaks often spread southward all the way to the Gulf of Mexico without attaining strength and depth to cross the Appalachian Range. When cold waves do break across they are usually modified by the crossing and the descent on the eastern slopes. The temperature drops to around 10 over central North Carolina once or twice during an average winter. Near the coast a comparable figure is some 10 degrees higher, and in the upper mountains 10 degrees lower. Temperatures as low as 0 are rare outside the mountains, but have occurred at one time or another throughout the western part of the State.

Winter temperatures in the eastern Coastal Plain are modified by the proximity of the Atlantic Ocean. This effect raises the average winter temperature and reduces the average day-to-night range. The Gulf Stream, contrary to popular opinion, has little direct effect on North Carolina temperatures, even on the immediate coast. The Stream lies some 50 miles offshore at its nearest point. The southern reaches of the cold Labrador Current pass between the Gulf Stream and the North Carolina coast. This offsets any warming effect the Stream might otherwise have on coastal temperatures. The meeting of the two opposing currents does provide a breeding ground for rough weather. Not infrequently low pressure storms having their origin there develop major proportions, causing rain on the North Carolina coast and over states to the north.

In spring the storm systems that bring cold weather southward reach North Carolina less forcefully than in winter, and temperatures begin to modify. Day-to-day variations in temperature are less pronounced, and warm weather is more likely to occur in conjunction with fair weather. During the summer, when the drying of the air is sufficient to keep cloudiness at a minimum for several days, temperatures may occasionally reach 100°F. or a little higher in interior sections at elevations below 1,500 feet. Ordinarily, however, summer cloudiness develops to limit the sun's heating while temperatures are still in the 90°F. range. Autumn is the season of most rapidly changing temperature, the daily downward trend being greater than the corresponding rise in spring. The dropoff is most rapid in October and continues almost as fast in November.

PRECIPITATION.　There are no distinct wet and dry seasons in North Carolina. There is some seasonal variation in average precipitation. Summer rainfall is normally the greatest, and July the wettest month. Since the rain at this time of year comes mostly with thunderstorms and convective showers, it is also more variable than at other seasons. Daily showers are not uncommon, nor are periods of one or two weeks without rain. Autumn is the driest season, and October the driest month. Precipitation in winter and spring occurs mostly with migratory low pressure storms. It appears with greater regularity and more even distribution than summer showers.

Winter precipitation usually occurs with southerly through easterly winds, and is seldom associated with very cold weather. Snow and sleet occur on an average of once or twice a year near the coast, and not much more often over the southeastern half of the State. Over the Mountains and western Piedmont frozen precipitation sometimes occurs with interior low pressure storms. In the extreme west it can happen with a cold front passage from northwest. Average winter snowfall ranges from about one inch per year on the Outer Banks and the lower coast, to about nine inches in the northern Piedmont and southern Mountains. Some of the higher mountain peaks and upper slopes receive an average of nearly 50 inches a year.

OTHER CLIMATIC ELEMENTS.　Relative humidity may vary greatly from day to day and even from hour to hour, especially in winter. The average relative humidity, however, does not vary greatly from season to season, there being a slight tendency for highest averages in winter and lowest in spring. The lowest relative humidities are found over the southern Piedmont; the highest are along the immediate coast.

Sunshine is abundant, the average annual percentage of possible ranging from 60 to 65 percent at most recording points. Measurable rain falls on about 120 days. Prevailing winds blow from southwest 10 months of the year, and from northeast during September and October. The average wind speed for interior locations is about eight m.p.h., for coastal points about 12 m.p.h.

STORMS AND FLOODS.　Intense rainstorms occur in the precipitous mountain terrain, especially in the southern portion. Streams here rise quickly to flood, and almost as quickly subside when rain ends. Floods occur frequently, affecting some part of North Carolina each year. Floods may occur at any season, but are most frequent in early spring, summer, and early fall. Rains associated with West Indian hurricanes are the main cause of summer and fall floods. The greatest economic loss entailed in North Carolina because of stormy weather is that due to summer thunderstorms. These usually affect only limited areas. In any given locality, 40 to 50 days with thunderstorms may be expected in a year.

North Carolina is outside the principal tornado area of the United States, experiencing an average of less than 4 per year. Tropical hurricanes come close enough to influence North Carolina weather about twice in an average year. Only about once in 10 years, on the average, does this type storm strike the State with sufficient force to do much damage.

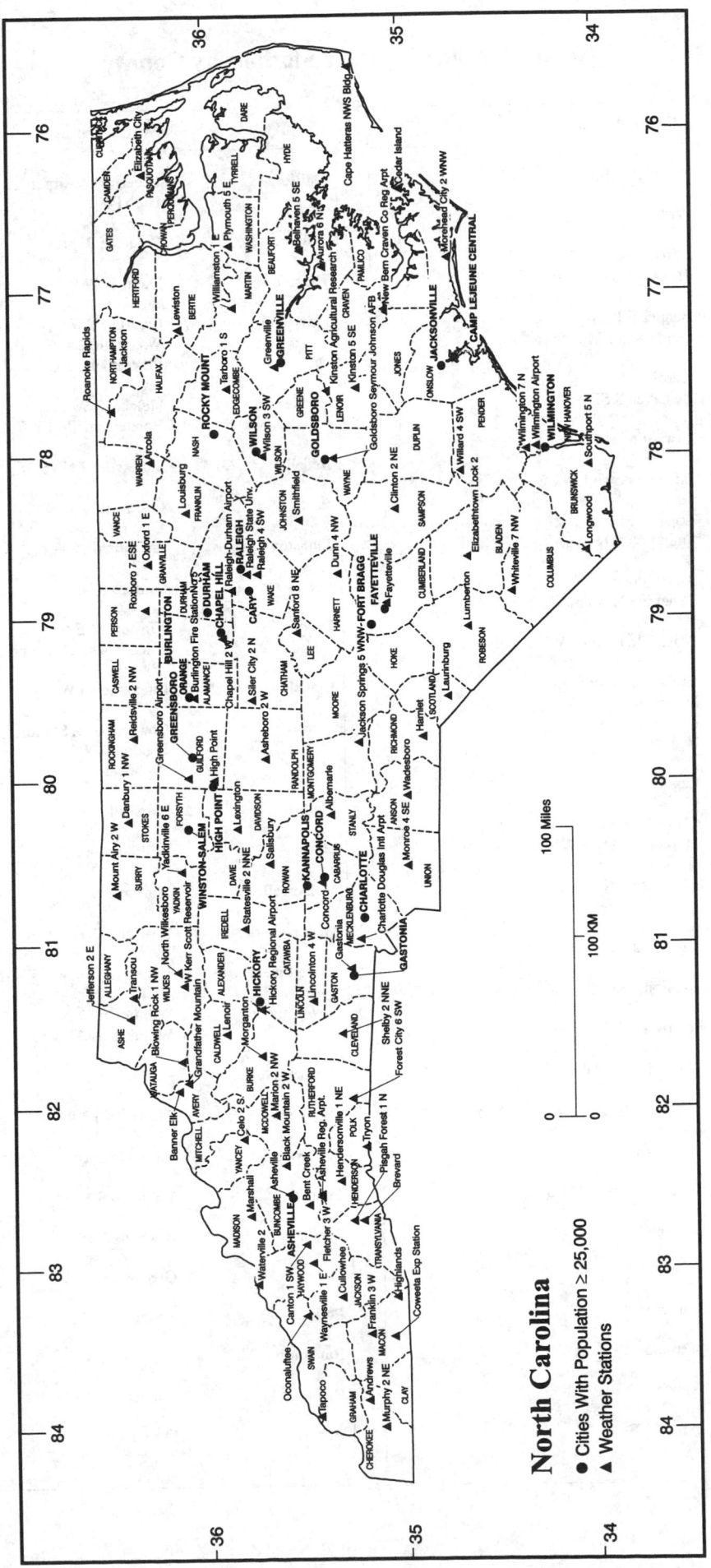

North Carolina

● Cities With Population ≥ 25,000
▲ Weather Stations

North Carolina Weather Stations by County

County	Station Name
Alamance	Burlington Fire Station 5
Anson	Wadesboro
Ashe	Jefferson 2 E
	Transou
Avery	Banner Elk
	Grandfather Mountain
Beaufort	Aurora 6 N
	Belhaven 5 SE
Bertie	Lewiston
Bladen	Elizabethtown Lock 2
Brunswick	Longwood
	Southport 5 N
Buncombe	Asheville
	Asheville Regional Airport
	Bent Creek
	Black Mountain 2 W
Burke	Hickory Regional Airport
	Morganton
Cabarrus	Concord
Caldwell	Lenoir
Carteret	Cedar Island
	Morehead City 2 WNW
Chatham	Siler City 2 N
Cherokee	Andrews
	Murphy 2 NE
Chowan	Edenton
Cleveland	Shelby 2 NNE
Columbus	Whiteville 7 NW
Craven	New Bern Craven Co. Reg. Airport
Cumberland	Fayetteville
Dare	Cape Hatteras NWS Bldg
Davidson	Lexington
Edgecombe	Tarboro 1 S
Franklin	Louisburg
Gaston	Gastonia
Graham	Tapoco
Granville	Oxford 1 E

County	Station Name
Guilford	Greensboro Airport
	High Point
Halifax	Roanoke Rapids
Harnett	Dunn 4 NW
Haywood	Canton 1 SW
	Waterville 2
	Waynesville 1 E
Henderson	Fletcher 3 W
	Hendersonville 1 NE
Iredell	Statesville 2 NNE
Jackson	Cullowhee
Johnston	Smithfield
Lee	Sanford 8 NE
Lenoir	Kinston 5 SE
	Kinston Agr. Research Center
Lincoln	Lincolnton 4 W
Macon	Coweeta Exp. Station
	Franklin 3 W
	Highlands
Madison	Marshall
Martin	Williamston 1 E
McDowell	Marion 2 NW
Mecklenburg	Charlotte Douglas Int'l Airport
Montgomery	Jackson Springs 5 WNW
New Hanover	Wilmington 7 N
	Wilmington Airport
Northampton	Jackson
Orange	Chapel Hill 2 W
Pasquotank	Elizabeth City
Pender	Willard 4 SW
Person	Roxboro 7 ESE
Pitt	Greenville
Polk	Tryon
Randolph	Asheboro 2 W
Richmond	Hamlet
Robeson	Lumberton

County	Station Name
Rockingham	Reidsville 2 NW
Rowan	Salisbury
Rutherford	Forest City 6 SW
Sampson	Clinton 2 NE
Scotland	Laurinburg
Stanly	Albemarle
Stokcs	Danbury 1 NW
Surry	Mount Airy 2 W
Swain	Oconaluftee
Transylvania	Brevard Pisgah Forest 1 N
Union	Monroe 4 SE
Wake	Raleigh 4 SW Raleigh State University Raleigh-Durham Airport
Warren	Arcola
Washington	Plymouth 5 E
Watauga	Blowing Rock 1 NW
Wayne	Goldsboro Seymour Johnson AFB
Wilkes	North Wilkesboro W Kerr Scott Reservoir
Wilson	Wilson 3 SW
Yadkin	Yadkinville 6 E
Yancey	Celo 2 S

North Carolina Weather Stations by City

City	Station Name	Miles
Asheville	Asheville Regional Airport	10
	Asheville	2
	Bent Creek	6
	Black Mountain 2 W	12
	Canton 1 SW	17
	Fletcher 3 W	10
	Hendersonville 1 NE	18
	Marshall	16
Burlington	Burlington Fire Station 5	2
Cary	Chapel Hill 2 W	19
	Raleigh-Durham Airport	6
	Raleigh 4 SW	6
	Raleigh State University	5
Chapel Hill	Chapel Hill 2 W	2
	Raleigh-Durham Airport	15
Charlotte	Charlotte Douglas Int'l Airport	8
	Concord	20
	Gastonia	18
Concord	Concord	1
	Salisbury	20
Durham	Chapel Hill 2 W	11
	Raleigh-Durham Airport	11
	Raleigh State University	18
Fayetteville	Fayetteville	2
Fort Bragg	Fayetteville	9
Gastonia	Charlotte Douglas Int'l Airport	13
	Gastonia	3
	Lincolnton 4 W	17
Goldsboro	Goldsboro Seymour Johnson AFB	3
Greensboro	Greensboro Airport	8
	High Point	11
Greenville	Greenville	3
	Kinston Agr. Research Center	19
Hickory	Hickory Regional Airport	3
	Lenoir	17
	Lincolnton 4 W	19
	Morganton	19
High Point	Greensboro Airport	9
	High Point	2
	Lexington	17
Kannapolis	Concord	5
	Salisbury	15
Raleigh	Raleigh-Durham Airport	8
	Raleigh 4 SW	6
	Raleigh State University	3
Rocky Mount	Tarboro 1 S	16
	Wilson 3 SW	19

City	Station Name	Miles
Wilmington	Southport 5 N	16
	Wilmington Airport	3
	Wilmington 7 N	7
Wilson	Wilson 3 SW	3
Winston-Salem	Greensboro Airport	18
	High Point	19
	Lexington	17
	Yadkinville 6 E	16

Note: Miles is the distance between the geographic center of the city and the weather station.

North Carolina Weather Stations by Elevation

Feet	Station Name
5,298	Grandfather Mountain
3,848	Blowing Rock 1 NW
3,838	Highlands
3,746	Banner Elk
2,874	Transou
2,769	Jefferson 2 E
2,677	Celo 2 S
2,660	Canton 1 SW
2,657	Waynesville 1 E
2,290	Black Mountain 2 W
2,247	Coweeta Exp. Station
2,237	Asheville
2,211	Brevard
2,191	Cullowhee
2,168	Franklin 3 W
2,158	Hendersonville 1 NE
2,139	Asheville Regional Airport
2,109	Bent Creek
2,109	Pisgah Forest 1 N
2,066	Fletcher 3 W
2,037	Oconaluftee
1,998	Marshall
1,748	Andrews
1,637	Murphy 2 NE
1,463	Marion 2 NW
1,437	Waterville 2
1,197	Lenoir
1,158	Morganton
1,141	Hickory Regional Airport
1,118	North Wilkesboro
1,108	Tapoco
1,079	Tryon
1,069	W Kerr Scott Reservoir
1,040	Mount Airy 2 W
987	Forest City 6 SW
948	Statesville 2 NNE
918	Shelby 2 NNE
898	High Point
898	Lincolnton 4 W
895	Greensboro Airport
889	Reidsville 2 NW
872	Yadkinville 6 E
869	Asheboro 2 W
839	Danbury 1 NW
757	Lexington
728	Jackson Springs 5 WNW
725	Charlotte Douglas Int'l Airport
708	Roxboro 7 ESE
698	Gastonia
698	Salisbury
688	Concord
659	Burlington Fire Station 5
606	Albemarle
606	Siler City 2 N
577	Monroe 4 SE

Feet	Station Name
498	Chapel Hill 2 W
498	Oxford 1 E
479	Wadesboro
419	Raleigh 4 SW
413	Raleigh-Durham Airport
396	Raleigh State University
347	Hamlet
328	Arcola
259	Louisburg
259	Sanford 8 NE
209	Laurinburg
209	Roanoke Rapids
200	Dunn 4 NW
157	Clinton 2 NE
147	Smithfield
127	Jackson
111	Lumberton
108	Goldsboro Seymour Johnson AFB
108	Wilson 3 SW
95	Fayetteville
88	Whiteville 7 NW
59	Elizabethtown Lock 2
59	Kinston Agr. Research Center
52	Kinston 5 SE
52	Willard 4 SW
49	Lewiston
39	Longwood
39	Wilmington 7 N
32	Tarboro 1 S
29	Greenville
29	Wilmington Airport
19	Aurora 6 N
19	Edenton
19	Plymouth 5 E
19	Southport 5 N
19	Williamston 1 E
13	New Bern Craven Co. Reg. Airport
9	Cape Hatteras NWS Bldg
9	Morehead City 2 WNW
6	Belhaven 5 SE
6	Cedar Island
6	Elizabeth City

Asheville Regional Airport

The city of Asheville is located on both banks of the French Broad River, near the center of the French Broad Basin. Upstream from Asheville, the valley runs south for 18 miles and then curves toward the south-southwest. Downstream from the city, the valley is oriented toward the north-northwest. Two miles upstream from the principal section of Asheville, the Swannanoa River joins the French Broad from the east. The entire valley is known as the Asheville Plateau, having an average elevation near 2,200 feet above sea level, and is flanked by mountain ridges to the east and west, whose peaks range from 2,000 to 4,400 feet above the valley floor. At the Carolina-Tennessee border, about 25 miles north-northwest of Asheville, a relatively high ridge of mountains blocks the northern end of the valley. Thirty miles south, the Blue Ridge Mountains form a steep slope, having a general elevation of about 2,700 feet above sea level.

Asheville has a temperate, but invigorating, climate. Considerable variation in temperature often occurs from day to day in summer, as well as during the other seasons.

The growing season in this area is of sufficient length for commercial crops, the average length of freeze-free period being about 195 days. The average last occurrence in spring of a temperature 32 degrees or lower is mid-April and the average first occurrence in fall of 32 degrees is late October.

The orientation of the French Broad Valley appears to have a pronounced influence on the wind direction. Prevailing winds are from the northwest during all months of the year. Also, the shielding effect of the nearby mountain barriers apparently has a direct bearing on the annual amount of precipitation received in this vicinity. In an area northwest of Asheville, the average annual precipitation is the lowest in North Carolina. Precipitation increases sharply in all other directions, especially to the south and southwest.

Destructive events caused directly by meteorological conditions are infrequent. The most frequent, occurring at approximately 12-year intervals, are floods on the French Broad River. These floods are usually associated with heavy rains caused by storms moving out of the Gulf of Mexico. Snowstorms which have seriously disrupted normal life in this community are infrequent. Hailstorms that cause property damage are extremely rare.

Asheville Regional Airport *Buncombe County*   Elevation: 2,139 ft.   Latitude: 35° 26' N   Longitude: 82° 32' W

	JAN	FEB	MAR	APR	MAY	JUN	JUL	AUG	SEP	OCT	NOV	DEC	YEAR
Mean Maximum Temp. (°F)	47.1	51.3	59.0	68.0	74.7	81.1	84.5	83.0	77.6	68.4	58.8	51.0	67.0
Mean Temp. (°F)	36.7	39.9	47.3	55.2	62.8	70.0	74.0	72.8	66.9	56.2	47.3	40.3	55.8
Mean Minimum Temp. (°F)	26.2	28.6	35.5	42.4	50.9	58.9	63.5	62.5	56.2	44.0	35.8	29.5	44.5
Extreme Maximum Temp. (°F)	80	78	83	89	93	95	96	100	92	86	81	78	100
Extreme Minimum Temp. (°F)	-16	-1	2	22	28	37	44	42	35	21	8	-7	-16
Days Maximum Temp. ≥ 90°F	0	0	0	0	0	2	5	3	0	0	0	0	10
Days Maximum Temp. ≤ 32°F	3	1	0	0	0	0	0	0	0	0	0	1	5
Days Minimum Temp. ≤ 32°F	23	19	12	4	0	0	0	0	0	4	13	20	95
Days Minimum Temp. ≤ 0°F	1	0	0	0	0	0	0	0	0	0	0	0	1
Heating Degree Days (base 65°F)	870	701	543	293	110	14	1	2	49	275	525	759	4,142
Cooling Degree Days (base 65°F)	0	0	1	7	54	181	299	251	104	9	0	0	906
Mean Precipitation (in.)	4.02	3.83	4.55	3.43	4.43	4.38	3.94	4.24	3.65	3.36	3.74	3.41	46.98
Maximum Precipitation (in.)	7.5	7.0	9.9	7.3	8.8	10.7	10.4	11.3	9.1	9.1	9.9	8.5	64.9
Minimum Precipitation (in.)	0.4	0.2	0.8	0.3	0.5	0.9	0.5	0.5	0.2	0.2	0.8	0.2	26.6
Maximum 24-hr. Precipitation (in.)	3.9	3.4	4.2	2.8	4.4	3.9	4.0	4.3	4.4	5.2	2.9	3.3	5.2
Days With ≥ 0.1" Precipitation	7	6	8	6	8	8	7	7	6	5	6	6	80
Days With ≥ 1.0" Precipitation	1	1	1	1	1	1	1	1	1	1	1	1	12
Mean Snowfall (in.)	4.7	3.2	2.5	0.6	trace	trace	trace	trace	0.0	trace	0.4	1.8	13.2
Maximum Snowfall (in.)	18	26	18	12	trace	0	0	0	0	trace	10	16	50
Maximum 24-hr. Snowfall (in.)	14	9	14	12	trace	0	0	0	0	trace	5	16	16
Days With ≥ 1.0" Snow Depth	4	2	1	0	0	0	0	0	0	0	0	1	8
Thunderstorm Days	< 1	1	2	3	7	9	10	9	3	1	1	< 1	46
Foggy Days	14	11	12	10	19	23	26	29	26	20	14	14	218
Predominant Sky Cover	OVR	OVR	OVR	OVR	OVR	OVR	BRK	OVR	OVR	CLR	OVR	OVR	OVR
Mean Relative Humidity 7am (%)	84	83	83	84	90	92	94	96	96	93	87	85	89
Mean Relative Humidity 4pm (%)	57	53	50	47	56	60	63	64	62	54	54	56	56
Mean Dewpoint (°F)	27	28	34	42	53	61	65	64	58	46	36	29	45
Prevailing Wind Direction	NNW	NNW	NNW	NNW	NNW	NNW	NNW	NNW	NNW	NNW	NNW	NNW	NNW
Prevailing Wind Speed (mph)	14	14	14	13	10	9	8	8	9	10	13	13	12
Maximum Wind Gust (mph)	58	54	64	58	49	52	61	43	51	58	55	53	64

Cape Hatteras NWS Bldg

Hatteras Island is the largest and easternmost island in North Carolina. The average elevation of the island is less than 10 feet above mean sea level. It is separated from the mainland by the Pamlico Sound and is part of a chain of islands known as the Outer Banks. The Island is narrow, ranging from a few hundred yards wide to a few miles wide and is about 54 miles long. Much of the island is a National Park and waterfowl reserve.

The Weather Office is located in the village of Buxton about one mile west-northwest of the famous Cape Hatteras Lighthouse. Weather observations have been taken continuously since 1874 from locations all within 10 miles of the present stations location.

With its maritime climate, Cape Hatteras is very humid, with cooler summers and warmer winters than mainland North Carolina. Ninety degree temperatures are rare in summer, as are the teens in winter. The average first occurrence of freezing temperatures is early December, and the average last occurrence is late February.

Average rainfall is greater than any other coastal station in the state. Rainfall is rather evenly distributed throughout the year, with the maximum during July, August, and September. Snowfall is rare and generally light, usually melting as it falls.

Winter storms frequently breed offshore where the warm waters of the Gulf Stream and the southermost penetration of the Labrador Current meet some 20 to 50 miles off the coast. Late summer and fall tracks of tropical cyclones occasionally threaten the island. These storms produce strong winds, heavy rains and tidal flooding from both the ocean and Pamlico Sound. Many ships have been lost near, or wrecked on, the beaches of the island.

More than a million tourists visit the island each year. The proximity of the gulfstream, natural beaches, excellent surf, and offshore fishing make Cape Hatteras a preferred place for vacationers, sportsmen, and campers. The surfing conditions are said to be the best on the east coast.

Cape Hatteras NWS Bldg *Dare County*   Elevation: 9 ft.   Latitude: 35° 16' N   Longitude: 75° 33' W

	JAN	FEB	MAR	APR	MAY	JUN	JUL	AUG	SEP	OCT	NOV	DEC	YEAR
Mean Maximum Temp. (°F)	53.4	54.4	60.0	67.7	74.9	81.5	85.4	84.9	81.2	72.7	64.9	57.6	69.9
Mean Temp. (°F)	45.8	46.7	52.2	59.7	67.5	74.8	79.2	78.6	74.9	65.8	57.6	50.1	62.8
Mean Minimum Temp. (°F)	38.3	38.9	44.3	51.7	60.1	68.1	72.8	72.4	68.5	58.9	50.2	42.6	55.6
Extreme Maximum Temp. (°F)	75	76	81	89	91	95	96	93	92	89	81	78	96
Extreme Minimum Temp. (°F)	6	15	22	26	39	45	54	56	45	32	26	12	6
Days Maximum Temp. ≥ 90°F	0	0	0	0	0	1	3	2	1	0	0	0	7
Days Maximum Temp. ≤ 32°F	1	0	0	0	0	0	0	0	0	0	0	0	1
Days Minimum Temp. ≤ 32°F	9	7	3	0	0	0	0	0	0	0	1	5	25
Days Minimum Temp. ≤ 0°F	0	0	0	0	0	0	0	0	0	0	0	0	0
Heating Degree Days (base 65°F)	588	513	396	181	42	3	0	0	2	68	240	459	2,492
Cooling Degree Days (base 65°F)	1	1	6	33	131	314	464	432	299	105	27	4	1,817
Mean Precipitation (in.)	5.83	4.01	5.03	3.26	3.93	3.81	4.95	6.46	5.51	5.35	5.05	4.53	57.72
Maximum Precipitation (in.)	12.4	8.4	11.2	9.6	11.4	10.8	10.0	16.1	20.0	15.0	16.2	9.6	90.8
Minimum Precipitation (in.)	1.8	1.1	1.0	0.4	0.3	0.4	0.4	1.0	0.1	0.5	1.1	0.6	41.5
Maximum 24-hr. Precipitation (in.)	5.9	2.9	4.6	5.1	3.3	6.1	5.3	7.5	5.5	8.3	7.7	3.6	8.3
Days With ≥ 0.1" Precipitation	8	6	8	5	6	7	8	8	6	6	6	7	81
Days With ≥ 1.0" Precipitation	2	1	1	1	1	1	1	2	2	2	1	1	16
Mean Snowfall (in.)	0.4	0.5	0.3	trace	0.0	0.0	0.0	0.0	0.0	0.0	trace	0.8	2.0
Maximum Snowfall (in.)	4	4	9	trace	0	0	0	0	0	0	trace	14	14
Maximum 24-hr. Snowfall (in.)	4	4	7	trace	0	0	0	0	0	0	trace	8	8
Days With ≥ 1.0" Snow Depth	0	0	0	0	0	0	0	0	0	0	0	0	0
Thunderstorm Days	1	2	2	3	5	5	8	8	3	2	1	1	41
Foggy Days	13	11	12	8	10	9	8	9	7	10	10	11	118
Predominant Sky Cover	OVR	OVR	OVR	OVR	OVR	OVR	OVR	OVR	OVR	OVR	OVR	OVR	OVR
Mean Relative Humidity 7am (%)	80	80	80	78	81	82	85	86	83	82	81	80	82
Mean Relative Humidity 4pm (%)	69	66	65	62	67	70	72	72	69	68	69	69	68
Mean Dewpoint (°F)	37	37	43	50	59	67	72	72	67	57	49	41	54
Prevailing Wind Direction	N	NNE	NNE	SW	SW	SW	SW	SW	NE	NNE	NNE	N	NNE
Prevailing Wind Speed (mph)	13	14	14	13	12	12	12	12	12	13	13	12	13
Maximum Wind Gust (mph)	60	69	69	83	55	64	62	98	94	66	78	64	98

Charlotte Douglas Int'l Airport

Charlotte is located in the Piedmont of the Carolinas, a transitional area of rolling country between the mountains to the west and the Coastal Plain to the east. The mountains are to the northwest about 80 miles from Charlotte. The general elevation of the area around Charlotte is about 730 feet. The Atlantic ocean is about 160 miles southeast.

The mountains have a moderating effect on winter temperatures, causing appreciable warming of cold air from the northwest winds. The ocean is too far away to have any immediate effect on summer temperatures but in winter an occasional general and sustained flow of air from the warm ocean waters results in considerable warming.

Charlotte enjoys a moderate climate, characterized by cool winters and quite warm summers. Temperatures fall as low as the freezing point on a little over one-half of the days in the winter months. Winter weather is changeable, with occasional cold periods, but extreme cold is rare. Snow is infrequent, and the first snowfall of the season usually comes in late November or December. Heavy snowfalls have occurred, but any appreciable accumulation of snow on the ground for more than a day or two is rare.

Summers are long and quite warm, with afternoon temperatures frequently in the low 90s. The growing season is also long, the average length of the freeze-free period being 216 days. On the average, the last occurrence in spring with a temperature of 32 degrees is early April. In the fall the average first occurrence of 32 degrees is early November.

Rainfall is generally rather evenly distributed throughout the year, the driest weather usually coming in the fall. Summer rainfall comes principally from thunderstorms with occasional dry spells of one to three weeks duration.

Hurricanes which strike the Carolina coast may produce heavy rain but seldom cause dangerous winds.

Charlotte Douglas Int'l Airport *Mecklenburg County*   Elevation: 725 ft.   Latitude: 35° 13' N   Longitude: 80° 57' W

	JAN	FEB	MAR	APR	MAY	JUN	JUL	AUG	SEP	OCT	NOV	DEC	YEAR
Mean Maximum Temp. (°F)	50.2	54.8	63.0	72.2	78.9	85.5	89.2	87.4	81.6	71.8	62.1	53.5	70.8
Mean Temp. (°F)	40.7	44.2	52.0	60.4	68.2	75.7	79.6	78.1	72.1	61.2	51.7	44.0	60.6
Mean Minimum Temp. (°F)	31.2	33.6	40.8	48.6	57.5	65.7	69.9	68.8	62.6	50.5	41.2	34.4	50.4
Extreme Maximum Temp. (°F)	77	81	87	91	94	100	103	103	96	93	83	78	103
Extreme Minimum Temp. (°F)	-5	7	4	25	34	45	55	54	39	27	13	4	-5
Days Maximum Temp. ≥ 90°F	0	0	0	0	1	8	16	11	4	0	0	0	40
Days Maximum Temp. ≤ 32°F	1	0	0	0	0	0	0	0	0	0	0	0	1
Days Minimum Temp. ≤ 32°F	17	13	6	1	0	0	0	0	0	0	6	14	57
Days Minimum Temp. ≤ 0°F	0	0	0	0	0	0	0	0	0	0	0	0	0
Heating Degree Days (base 65°F)	746	581	405	174	41	3	0	0	15	158	399	646	3,168
Cooling Degree Days (base 65°F)	0	1	9	46	161	354	484	420	235	52	4	1	1,767
Mean Precipitation (in.)	3.92	3.59	4.37	2.84	3.71	3.39	3.93	3.75	3.65	3.83	3.33	3.25	43.56
Maximum Precipitation (in.)	7.4	7.6	8.8	7.6	12.5	8.3	8.3	10.0	9.7	14.7	8.7	7.5	62.1
Minimum Precipitation (in.)	0.4	0.2	0.6	0.3	0.3	0.1	0.5	0.6	trace	trace	0.5	0.4	26.9
Maximum 24-hr. Precipitation (in.)	3.4	2.9	3.0	3.2	3.7	3.8	2.8	5.2	3.6	4.2	3.3	2.5	5.2
Days With ≥ 0.1" Precipitation	7	7	8	5	6	6	7	6	5	5	6	6	74
Days With ≥ 1.0" Precipitation	1	1	1	1	1	1	1	1	1	1	1	1	12
Mean Snowfall (in.)	1.6	1.6	1.2	trace	trace	trace	0.0	0.0	0.0	trace	trace	0.7	5.1
Maximum Snowfall (in.)	12	15	19	trace	0	0	0	0	0	0	3	8	23
Maximum 24-hr. Snowfall (in.)	12	10	10	trace	0	0	0	0	0	0	2	8	12
Days With ≥ 1.0" Snow Depth	1	1	0	0	0	0	0	0	0	0	0	0	2
Thunderstorm Days	1	1	2	3	6	7	9	7	3	1	1	< 1	41
Foggy Days	13	11	12	9	13	13	16	18	16	13	13	13	160
Predominant Sky Cover	OVR	OVR	OVR	OVR	OVR	OVR	OVR	OVR	OVR	CLR	CLR	OVR	OVR
Mean Relative Humidity 7am (%)	78	77	78	78	82	83	86	88	88	86	83	79	82
Mean Relative Humidity 4pm (%)	53	48	46	43	49	51	54	55	54	50	50	53	51
Mean Dewpoint (°F)	29	30	36	44	55	63	67	67	61	50	39	32	48
Prevailing Wind Direction	SW	SW	SW	SW	SW	SW	SW	NE	NE	NNE	NNE	SW	SW
Prevailing Wind Speed (mph)	10	12	12	12	9	8	8	8	8	9	9	9	9
Maximum Wind Gust (mph)	64	53	60	56	48	60	55	77	87	40	51	52	87

Greensboro Airport

The Greensboro-High Point-Winston-Salem Regional Airport is located in the west-central part of Guilford County, in the northern Piedmont section of North Carolina. The location is near the headwaters of the Haw and Deep Rivers, both branches of the Cape Fear River system. A few miles west is a ridge beyond which lies the Yadkin River Basin. To the north, across a similar ridge, the waters of the Dan River flow northeastward into the Roanoke. West, beyond the Yadkin River Basin, the land gradually rises into the Brushy Mountains. To the northwest, other outcroppings southeast of the Blue Ridge rise into peaks occasionally exceeding 2,500 feet. Winter temperatures and rainfall are both modified by the mountain barrier, but to a lesser extent than in areas closer to the Appalachian Range. Shallow cold air masses from the west tend to be stopped by the mountains, while deeper masses are lifted over the range, losing moisture and warming during the passage. For this reason the lowest temperatures recorded in Forsyth and Guilford Counties usually occur when clear, cold air drifts southward, east of the Appalachian Range. The summer temperatures vary, but are generally mild.

Northwesterly winds seldom bring heavy or prolonged winter rain or snow. Flurries of light snow may fall when cold air blows across the mountains, but the heavier winter precipitation comes with winds blowing from northeast through east and south to southwest. When moist winds blowing from an easterly or southerly direction meet cold air moving out of the north or northwest in the vicinity of North Carolina, snow, sleet, or glaze may occur.

Seasonal snowfall has a wide range and there have been a few winters with only a trace of snow. Snow seldom stays on the ground more than a few days.

Summer precipitation is largely from thunderstorms, mostly local in character. The frequency of these showers and the amount of rain received varies greatly from year to year and from place to place. Sizeable areas are sometimes without significant rain in late spring or early summer for two or more weeks, while other areas in the vicinity may be well watered.

Damaging storms are infrequent in the Northern Piedmont area. The highest winds to occur have been associated with thunderstorms, and were of brief duration. Hail is reported within Guilford and Forsyth Counties each year. The occurrence of tornadoes is rare. Hurricanes have produced heavy rainfall here, but no winds of destructive force.

Based on the 1951-1980 period, the average first occurrence of 32 degrees Fahrenheit in the fall is October 27 and the average last occurrence in the spring is April 11.

Greensboro Airport *Guilford County*   Elevation: 895 ft.   Latitude: 36° 06' N   Longitude: 79° 57' W

	JAN	FEB	MAR	APR	MAY	JUN	JUL	AUG	SEP	OCT	NOV	DEC	YEAR
Mean Maximum Temp. (°F)	47.1	51.5	60.1	69.9	76.8	83.8	87.8	85.7	79.7	69.5	59.9	50.9	68.6
Mean Temp. (°F)	37.4	41.0	48.9	57.8	65.8	73.6	77.9	76.1	69.8	58.4	49.1	41.1	58.1
Mean Minimum Temp. (°F)	27.7	30.3	37.7	45.7	54.7	63.4	68.0	66.5	59.8	47.1	38.1	31.2	47.5
Extreme Maximum Temp. (°F)	78	81	86	91	93	98	102	103	98	92	85	78	103
Extreme Minimum Temp. (°F)	-8	1	8	23	32	42	49	45	37	25	10	1	-8
Days Maximum Temp. ≥ 90°F	0	0	0	0	1	6	12	8	2	0	0	0	29
Days Maximum Temp. ≤ 32°F	3	1	0	0	0	0	0	0	0	0	0	1	5
Days Minimum Temp. ≤ 32°F	21	18	9	2	0	0	0	0	0	1	9	18	78
Days Minimum Temp. ≤ 0°F	0	0	0	0	0	0	0	0	0	0	0	0	0
Heating Degree Days (base 65°F)	847	673	495	236	72	7	0	1	29	224	474	734	3,792
Cooling Degree Days (base 65°F)	0	0	4	27	108	284	422	353	176	28	1	1	1,404
Mean Precipitation (in.)	3.46	3.16	3.87	3.43	3.97	3.51	4.45	3.88	3.99	3.46	2.99	3.10	43.27
Maximum Precipitation (in.)	7.7	5.8	8.8	8.0	8.3	9.5	12.7	11.7	13.1	12.6	8.3	6.4	56.5
Minimum Precipitation (in.)	0.7	0.4	0.7	0.4	0.4	trace	1.0	0.7	trace	0.3	0.3	0.3	29.7
Maximum 24-hr. Precipitation (in.)	2.5	2.2	3.6	4.0	3.2	4.2	3.6	4.5	5.1	6.2	3.3	3.1	6.2
Days With ≥ 0.1" Precipitation	7	6	7	6	6	6	7	6	5	5	6	6	73
Days With ≥ 1.0" Precipitation	1	1	1	1	1	1	1	1	1	1	1	1	12
Mean Snowfall (in.)	2.7	2.8	1.4	trace	trace	0.0	trace	0.0	0.0	0.0	trace	1.0	7.9
Maximum Snowfall (in.)	23	16	21	trace	0	0	0	0	0	0	6	8	32
Maximum 24-hr. Snowfall (in.)	10	9	11	trace	0	0	0	0	0	0	3	5	11
Days With ≥ 1.0" Snow Depth	3	2	1	0	0	0	0	0	0	0	0	1	7
Thunderstorm Days	< 1	1	2	3	6	8	10	8	3	1	1	< 1	43
Foggy Days	13	12	12	10	14	16	18	21	18	13	12	12	171
Predominant Sky Cover	OVR	OVR	OVR	OVR	OVR	OVR	OVR	OVR	OVR	CLR	OVR	OVR	OVR
Mean Relative Humidity 7am (%)	79	77	78	77	82	84	87	90	90	88	83	79	83
Mean Relative Humidity 4pm (%)	54	49	46	44	52	54	57	58	56	51	51	53	52
Mean Dewpoint (°F)	27	28	34	43	54	63	67	66	60	48	37	29	46
Prevailing Wind Direction	SW	SW	SW	SW	SW	SW	SW	SW	NE	NE	SW	SW	SW
Prevailing Wind Speed (mph)	9	9	9	9	8	8	7	7	9	9	8	8	8
Maximum Wind Gust (mph)	63	62	53	55	59	51	98	81	54	60	48	47	98

Raleigh-Durham Airport

The Raleigh-Durham Airport is located in the zone of transition between the Coastal Plain and the Piedmont Plateau. The surrounding terrain is rolling, with an average elevation of around 400 feet, the range over a 10-mile radius is roughly between 200 and 550 feet. Being centrally located between the mountains on the west and the coast on the south and east, the Raleigh-Durham area enjoys a favorable climate. The mountains form a partial barrier to cold air masses moving eastward from the interior of the nation. As a result, there are few days in the heart of the winter season when the temperature falls below 20 degrees. Tropical air is present over the eastern and central sections of North Carolina during much of the summer season, bringing warm temperatures and rather high humidities to the Raleigh-Durham area. Afternoon temperatures reach 90 degrees or higher on about one-fourth of the days in the middle of summer, but reach 100 degrees less than once per year. Even in the hottest weather, early morning temperatures almost always drop into the lower 70s.

Rainfall is well distributed throughout the year as a whole. July and August have the greatest amount of rainfall, and October and November the least. There are times in spring and summer when soil moisture is scanty. This usually results from too many days between rains rather than from a shortage of total rainfall, but occasionally the accumulated total during the growing season falls short of plant needs. Most summer rain is produced by thunderstorms, which may occasionally be accompanied by strong winds, intense rains, and hail. The Raleigh-Durham area is far enough from the coast so that the bad weather effects of coastal storms are reduced.

From September 1887 to December 1950, the office was located in the downtown areas of Raleigh. The various buildings occupied were within an area of three blocks. All thermometers were exposed on the roof, and this, plus the smoke over the city, had an effect on the temperature record of that period. Lowest temperatures at the city office were frequently from two to five degrees higher than those recorded in surrounding rural areas. Maximum temperatures in the city were generally a degree or two lower.

From September 1946 to May 1954, simultaneous records were kept at a surface location on the North Carolina State College campus in Raleigh, and at the Raleigh-Durham Airport 10 and a half air miles to the northwest.

Based on the 1951-1980 period, the average first occurrence of 32 degrees Fahrenheit in the fall is October 27 and the average last occurrence in the spring is April 11.

Raleigh-Durham Airport *Wake County*   Elevation: 413 ft.   Latitude: 35° 52' N   Longitude: 78° 47' W

	JAN	FEB	MAR	APR	MAY	JUN	JUL	AUG	SEP	OCT	NOV	DEC	YEAR
Mean Maximum Temp. (°F)	49.7	53.8	62.2	71.9	78.5	85.4	89.0	87.1	81.5	71.7	62.5	53.5	70.6
Mean Temp. (°F)	39.5	42.7	50.5	59.2	66.9	74.6	78.8	77.2	71.3	60.1	51.0	43.2	59.6
Mean Minimum Temp. (°F)	29.4	31.6	38.7	46.4	55.2	63.6	68.5	67.2	61.1	48.4	39.5	32.8	48.5
Extreme Maximum Temp. (°F)	77	84	90	95	95	100	104	105	98	93	86	80	105
Extreme Minimum Temp. (°F)	-9	0	11	23	31	38	48	49	37	25	11	4	-9
Days Maximum Temp. ≥ 90°F	0	0	0	0	2	8	14	11	3	0	0	0	38
Days Maximum Temp. ≤ 32°F	2	1	0	0	0	0	0	0	0	0	0	1	4
Days Minimum Temp. ≤ 32°F	19	16	9	2	0	0	0	0	0	1	9	17	73
Days Minimum Temp. ≤ 0°F	0	0	0	0	0	0	0	0	0	0	0	0	0
Heating Degree Days (base 65°F)	782	623	454	208	59	5	0	1	19	187	419	671	3,428
Cooling Degree Days (base 65°F)	1	1	9	41	132	318	459	391	213	46	4	2	1,617
Mean Precipitation (in.)	3.89	3.51	4.11	2.72	3.86	3.36	4.27	3.71	4.17	3.33	2.93	3.08	42.94
Maximum Precipitation (in.)	7.5	6.4	7.8	6.1	7.7	9.4	10.3	12.2	6.8	9.1	8.2	6.6	54.1
Minimum Precipitation (in.)	0.9	0.3	1.0	0.2	0.9	0.3	0.8	0.8	0.2	0.4	0.6	0.3	33.7
Maximum 24-hr. Precipitation (in.)	3.0	3.2	3.2	3.4	4.3	3.3	2.8	4.2	2.8	4.0	4.5	3.0	4.5
Days With ≥ 0.1" Precipitation	7	6	7	6	7	6	7	6	5	5	5	6	73
Days With ≥ 1.0" Precipitation	1	1	1	1	1	1	1	1	1	1	1	1	12
Mean Snowfall (in.)	1.4	2.6	1.2	trace	trace	trace	trace	0.0	0.0	0.0	0.1	0.6	5.9
Maximum Snowfall (in.)	14	17	14	2	0	0	0	0	0	0	3	11	21
Maximum 24-hr. Snowfall (in.)	9	10	9	2	0	0	0	0	0	0	3	9	10
Days With ≥ 1.0" Snow Depth	1	2	0	0	0	0	0	0	0	0	0	0	3
Thunderstorm Days	< 1	1	2	3	6	7	11	8	3	1	1	< 1	43
Foggy Days	12	12	12	11	16	18	20	22	19	16	13	13	184
Predominant Sky Cover	OVR	OVR	OVR	OVR	OVR	OVR	OVR	OVR	OVR	CLR	CLR	OVR	OVR
Mean Relative Humidity 7am (%)	79	78	80	80	84	86	89	91	92	90	84	80	84
Mean Relative Humidity 4pm (%)	53	48	46	42	51	54	57	58	57	52	51	53	52
Mean Dewpoint (°F)	28	29	35	44	56	64	68	68	61	50	39	31	48
Prevailing Wind Direction	SW	SW	SW	SW	SW	SW	SW	SSW	NE	NNE	SW	SW	SW
Prevailing Wind Speed (mph)	9	10	10	10	9	8	8	7	8	9	9	9	9
Maximum Wind Gust (mph)	55	62	60	56	55	51	48	61	46	44	41	55	62

Wilmington Airport

Wilmington is located in the tidewater section of southeastern North Carolina, near the Atlantic Ocean. The city proper is built adjacent to the east bank of the Cape Fear River. Because of the curvature of the coastline in this area, the ocean lies about five miles east and about 20 miles south. The surrounding terrain is typical of coastal Carolina. It is low-lying with an average elevation of less than 40 feet, and is characterized by level to gently rolling land with rivers, creeks, and lakes.

The maritime location makes the climate of Wilmington unusually mild for its latitude. All wind directions from the east-northeast through southwest have some moderating effects on temperatures throughout the year, because the ocean is relatively warm in winter and cool in summer. The daily range in temperatures is moderate compared to a continental type of climate. As a rule, summers are quite warm and humid, but excessive heat is rare. Sea breezes, arriving early in the afternoon, tend to alleviate the heat further inland. Long-term averages show afternoon temperatures reach 90 degrees or higher on one-third of the days in midsummer, but several years may pass without 100 degree weather. During the colder part of the year, numerous outbreaks of polar air masses reach the Atlantic Coast, causing sharp drops in temperatures. However, these cold outbreaks are significantly moderated by the long trajectories from the source regions, the effects of passing over the Appalachian Range, and the warming effects of the ocean air. As a result, most winters are short and quite mild.

Rainfall in this area is usually ample and well-distributed throughout the year, the greatest amount occurring in the summer. Summer rainfall comes principally from thunderstorms, and is therefore usually of short duration, but often heavy and unevenly distributed. Thunderstorms occur about one out of three days from June through August. Winter rain is more likely to be of the slow, steady type, lasting one or two days. Generally, the winter rain is evenly distributed and associated with slow-moving, low-pressure systems. Seldom is there a winter without a few flakes of snow, but several years may pass without a measurable amount. Hail occurs less than once a year. Sunshine is abundant, with the area receiving about two-thirds of the sunshine hours possible at its latitude.

Because of these many factors, the growing season is long, averaging 244 days, but records show the range is from 180 days to as long as 302 days.

In common with most Atlantic Coastal localities, the area is subject to the effects of coastal storms and occasional hurricanes which produce high winds, above normal tides, and heavy rains.

Wilmington Airport *New Hanover County*   Elevation: 29 ft.   Latitude: 34° 16' N   Longitude: 77° 54' W

	JAN	FEB	MAR	APR	MAY	JUN	JUL	AUG	SEP	OCT	NOV	DEC	YEAR
Mean Maximum Temp. (°F)	56.1	59.3	66.0	74.2	80.5	86.4	89.9	88.3	84.3	75.7	67.9	60.0	74.1
Mean Temp. (°F)	45.9	48.3	54.8	62.8	70.2	77.0	81.2	79.7	75.1	64.9	56.6	49.2	63.8
Mean Minimum Temp. (°F)	35.6	37.3	43.6	51.3	59.7	67.5	72.3	71.1	65.9	54.1	45.2	38.3	53.5
Extreme Maximum Temp. (°F)	82	83	89	94	96	101	102	103	98	95	87	82	103
Extreme Minimum Temp. (°F)	5	11	9	30	38	48	55	55	44	30	20	0	0
Days Maximum Temp. ≥ 90°F	0	0	0	1	2	9	17	12	5	0	0	0	46
Days Maximum Temp. ≤ 32°F	0	0	0	0	0	0	0	0	0	0	0	0	0
Days Minimum Temp. ≤ 32°F	13	10	4	0	0	0	0	0	0	0	3	10	40
Days Minimum Temp. ≤ 0°F	0	0	0	0	0	0	0	0	0	0	0	0	0
Heating Degree Days (base 65°F)	589	470	325	129	26	1	0	0	3	90	272	489	2,394
Cooling Degree Days (base 65°F)	2	5	15	65	193	378	520	458	303	96	25	5	2,065
Mean Precipitation (in.)	4.43	3.70	4.38	2.83	4.40	5.30	7.55	7.49	6.61	3.33	3.18	3.83	57.03
Maximum Precipitation (in.)	10.2	8.7	8.3	8.2	9.1	12.9	18.0	14.1	18.9	9.8	7.9	7.1	66.6
Minimum Precipitation (in.)	0.7	0.6	0.9	0.2	0.9	0.9	1.6	1.7	0.7	0.2	0.5	0.5	36.9
Maximum 24-hr. Precipitation (in.)	2.6	2.7	4.4	3.5	4.3	4.8	6.5	4.8	7.5	5.5	4.1	3.8	7.5
Days With ≥ 0.1" Precipitation	8	6	7	5	6	7	9	9	7	5	5	6	80
Days With ≥ 1.0" Precipitation	1	1	1	1	1	2	2	2	2	1	1	1	16
Mean Snowfall (in.)	0.4	0.5	0.4	trace	trace	trace	trace	0.0	0.0	0.0	trace	0.7	2.0
Maximum Snowfall (in.)	5	13	7	trace	0	0	0	0	0	0	trace	15	16
Maximum 24-hr. Snowfall (in.)	5	7	5	trace	0	0	0	0	0	0	trace	10	10
Days With ≥ 1.0" Snow Depth	0	0	0	0	0	0	0	0	0	0	0	0	0
Thunderstorm Days	< 1	1	2	3	6	8	12	9	4	1	1	< 1	47
Foggy Days	15	12	14	12	15	16	14	17	17	16	15	14	177
Predominant Sky Cover	OVR	OVR	OVR	CLR	OVR	OVR	SCT	OVR	OVR	CLR	CLR	OVR	OVR
Mean Relative Humidity 7am (%)	82	80	82	81	84	85	87	90	90	89	86	82	85
Mean Relative Humidity 4pm (%)	58	55	54	51	58	62	66	67	66	60	58	58	59
Mean Dewpoint (°F)	36	37	43	50	60	68	72	71	66	56	46	38	54
Prevailing Wind Direction	N	SW	SW	SW	SW	SW	SW	SW	NNE	N	N	N	SW
Prevailing Wind Speed (mph)	9	12	12	12	10	9	9	8	9	10	10	9	10
Maximum Wind Gust (mph)	64	63	77	59	55	64	78	64	74	52	54	55	78

Albemarle *Stanly County*   Elevation: 606 ft.   Latitude: 35° 22' N   Longitude: 80° 11' W

	JAN	FEB	MAR	APR	MAY	JUN	JUL	AUG	SEP	OCT	NOV	DEC	YEAR
Mean Maximum Temp. (°F)	51.7	56.2	64.5	73.1	79.3	85.8	89.0	87.6	82.2	72.9	63.5	54.9	71.7
Mean Temp. (°F)	40.9	44.2	51.8	59.3	67.0	74.5	78.4	77.0	71.1	60.3	51.2	43.7	60.0
Mean Minimum Temp. (°F)	30.0	32.2	39.1	45.4	54.6	63.2	67.6	66.3	60.1	47.6	38.9	32.6	48.1
Extreme Maximum Temp. (°F)	79	81	87	92	95	99	103	107	99	94	85	80	107
Extreme Minimum Temp. (°F)	-6	2	5	23	29	42	50	47	35	25	11	2	-6
Days Maximum Temp. ≥ 90°F	0	0	0	0	1	8	15	11	4	0	0	0	39
Days Maximum Temp. ≤ 32°F	1	0	0	0	0	0	0	0	0	0	0	0	1
Days Minimum Temp. ≤ 32°F	18	15	9	3	0	0	0	0	0	2	9	16	72
Days Minimum Temp. ≤ 0°F	0	0	0	0	0	0	0	0	0	0	0	0	0
Heating Degree Days (base 65°F)	740	581	409	199	54	5	0	0	19	178	411	654	3,250
Cooling Degree Days (base 65°F)	0	1	7	36	139	323	455	393	212	43	3	1	1,613
Mean Precipitation (in.)	4.15	3.95	4.91	3.27	4.48	4.37	5.44	4.14	3.99	3.66	3.29	3.45	49.10
Days With ≥ 0.1" Precipitation	7	6	7	5	7	6	8	6	5	5	5	6	73
Days With ≥ 1.0" Precipitation	1	1	2	1	2	1	1	1	1	1	1	1	14
Mean Snowfall (in.)	1.3	*2.0*	1.1	trace	0.0	0.0	0.0	0.0	0.0	0.0	trace	0.7	*5.1*
Days With ≥ 1.0" Snow Depth	*0*	*1*	*0*	0	0	0	0	0	0	0	0	0	*1*

Andrews *Cherokee County*   Elevation: 1,748 ft.   Latitude: 35° 12' N   Longitude: 83° 50' W

	JAN	FEB	MAR	APR	MAY	JUN	JUL	AUG	SEP	OCT	NOV	DEC	YEAR
Mean Maximum Temp. (°F)	48.3	52.7	60.8	69.4	76.3	82.4	85.5	84.7	80.0	70.5	60.9	52.4	68.7
Mean Temp. (°F)	36.1	39.5	47.0	54.5	62.6	69.7	73.5	72.6	67.1	56.0	47.2	39.9	55.5
Mean Minimum Temp. (°F)	23.8	26.1	33.2	39.5	48.8	57.0	61.5	60.3	54.3	41.5	33.5	27.3	42.2
Extreme Maximum Temp. (°F)	74	81	83	90	92	94	99	98	95	86	82	76	99
Extreme Minimum Temp. (°F)	-19	-3	-4	18	27	36	48	48	30	22	7	-4	-19
Days Maximum Temp. ≥ 90°F	0	0	0	0	0	2	7	4	2	0	0	0	15
Days Maximum Temp. ≤ 32°F	2	1	0	0	0	0	0	0	0	0	0	1	4
Days Minimum Temp. ≤ 32°F	23	21	16	8	1	0	0	0	0	6	16	22	113
Days Minimum Temp. ≤ 0°F	1	0	0	0	0	0	0	0	0	0	0	0	1
Heating Degree Days (base 65°F)	888	716	553	317	119	17	1	1	45	282	528	771	4,238
Cooling Degree Days (base 65°F)	0	0	1	7	53	176	286	245	110	11	1	0	890
Mean Precipitation (in.)	7.00	6.10	6.96	5.12	5.38	5.69	5.03	5.30	4.36	3.68	5.23	6.11	65.96
Days With ≥ 0.1" Precipitation	10	8	10	8	10	10	9	9	7	6	8	9	104
Days With ≥ 1.0" Precipitation	2	2	2	1	2	2	1	2	1	1	2	2	20
Mean Snowfall (in.)	2.8	3.1	1.7	0.4	0.0	0.0	0.0	0.0	0.0	trace	trace	0.3	8.3
Days With ≥ 1.0" Snow Depth	*1*	1	0	0	0	0	0	0	0	0	0	0	*2*

Arcola *Warren County*   Elevation: 328 ft.   Latitude: 36° 17' N   Longitude: 77° 59' W

	JAN	FEB	MAR	APR	MAY	JUN	JUL	AUG	SEP	OCT	NOV	DEC	YEAR
Mean Maximum Temp. (°F)	49.2	53.2	61.6	71.8	78.5	86.0	89.6	87.8	82.5	72.1	63.8	53.9	70.8
Mean Temp. (°F)	38.1	41.5	49.0	58.0	65.9	73.5	77.8	76.0	70.2	58.9	50.6	42.6	58.5
Mean Minimum Temp. (°F)	27.1	29.6	36.3	44.2	53.1	61.1	65.9	64.2	57.9	45.4	37.4	31.2	46.1
Extreme Maximum Temp. (°F)	76	82	89	95	96	100	102	103	100	93	85	79	103
Extreme Minimum Temp. (°F)	-7	-3	11	19	30	40	47	43	36	20	13	3	-7
Days Maximum Temp. ≥ 90°F	0	0	0	0	2	9	17	12	4	0	0	0	44
Days Maximum Temp. ≤ 32°F	2	1	0	0	0	0	0	0	0	0	0	1	4
Days Minimum Temp. ≤ 32°F	22	19	11	3	0	0	0	0	0	2	11	18	86
Days Minimum Temp. ≤ 0°F	0	0	0	0	0	0	0	0	0	0	0	0	0
Heating Degree Days (base 65°F)	829	660	495	233	70	7	0	1	26	212	430	687	3,650
Cooling Degree Days (base 65°F)	0	0	4	28	106	277	416	337	172	29	3	1	1,373
Mean Precipitation (in.)	3.90	3.62	4.49	3.16	3.91	4.01	4.81	4.82	4.12	3.85	3.29	3.23	47.21
Days With ≥ 0.1" Precipitation	7	6	7	6	7	6	7	7	5	5	5	6	74
Days With ≥ 1.0" Precipitation	1	1	1	1	1	1	2	1	1	1	1	1	13
Mean Snowfall (in.)	1.5	2.7	1.3	trace	0.0	0.0	0.0	0.0	0.0	0.0	trace	0.5	6.0
Days With ≥ 1.0" Snow Depth	2	2	1	0	0	0	0	0	0	0	0	0	5

Asheboro 2 W *Randolph County*   Elevation: 869 ft.   Latitude: 35° 42' N   Longitude: 79° 50' W

	JAN	FEB	MAR	APR	MAY	JUN	JUL	AUG	SEP	OCT	NOV	DEC	YEAR
Mean Maximum Temp. (°F)	49.7	54.5	63.2	72.7	78.3	84.6	88.6	86.8	81.4	71.7	62.5	53.6	70.6
Mean Temp. (°F)	40.0	43.8	51.7	60.2	67.2	74.3	78.5	76.9	71.4	60.6	51.7	43.8	60.0
Mean Minimum Temp. (°F)	30.4	33.0	40.1	47.7	55.9	64.0	68.5	67.0	61.3	49.4	40.8	33.9	49.3
Extreme Maximum Temp. (°F)	78	82	90	93	94	97	102	105	100	93	87	79	105
Extreme Minimum Temp. (°F)	-8	2	8	24	33	39	51	49	39	27	12	-1	-8
Days Maximum Temp. ≥ 90°F	0	0	0	0	1	6	14	11	4	0	0	0	36
Days Maximum Temp. ≤ 32°F	1	1	0	0	0	0	0	0	0	0	0	1	3
Days Minimum Temp. ≤ 32°F	19	14	7	1	0	0	0	0	0	1	7	15	64
Days Minimum Temp. ≤ 0°F	0	0	0	0	0	0	0	0	0	0	0	0	0
Heating Degree Days (base 65°F)	768	593	416	182	50	5	0	0	18	171	398	652	3,253
Cooling Degree Days (base 65°F)	0	1	9	42	129	304	442	375	207	43	4	2	1,558
Mean Precipitation (in.)	4.28	3.76	4.31	3.47	4.25	3.94	4.15	4.44	4.16	3.75	3.18	3.29	46.98
Days With ≥ 0.1" Precipitation	8	6	8	6	7	6	7	7	5	5	6	7	78
Days With ≥ 1.0" Precipitation	1	1	1	1	1	1	1	1	1	1	1	1	12
Mean Snowfall (in.)	1.8	2.0	1.0	trace	0.0	0.0	0.0	0.0	0.0	0.0	trace	0.6	5.4
Days With ≥ 1.0" Snow Depth	1	1	0	0	0	0	0	0	0	0	0	0	2

Asheville *Buncombe County*   Elevation: 2,237 ft.   Latitude: 35° 36' N   Longitude: 82° 32' W

	JAN	FEB	MAR	APR	MAY	JUN	JUL	AUG	SEP	OCT	NOV	DEC	YEAR
Mean Maximum Temp. (°F)	46.3	50.5	58.3	67.5	74.6	81.2	84.8	83.3	77.6	67.9	58.1	50.3	66.7
Mean Temp. (°F)	36.9	40.4	47.7	56.2	63.6	70.7	74.6	73.4	67.5	56.9	48.0	40.8	56.4
Mean Minimum Temp. (°F)	27.6	30.2	37.2	44.8	52.7	60.3	64.3	63.3	57.4	46.0	37.8	31.2	46.1
Extreme Maximum Temp. (°F)	78	78	87	89	93	95	98	99	92	86	81	75	99
Extreme Minimum Temp. (°F)	-17	-5	4	22	30	42	51	46	36	24	7	-8	-17
Days Maximum Temp. ≥ 90°F	0	0	0	0	0	1	6	3	1	0	0	0	11
Days Maximum Temp. ≤ 32°F	3	2	0	0	0	0	0	0	0	0	0	2	7
Days Minimum Temp. ≤ 32°F	21	17	10	3	0	0	0	0	0	2	10	18	81
Days Minimum Temp. ≤ 0°F	1	0	0	0	0	0	0	0	0	0	0	0	1
Heating Degree Days (base 65°F)	863	689	530	272	98	11	1	1	44	255	506	745	4,015
Cooling Degree Days (base 65°F)	0	0	3	14	67	201	320	266	116	14	1	0	1,002
Mean Precipitation (in.)	3.03	3.20	3.82	3.11	3.50	3.28	2.99	3.37	3.04	2.51	2.89	2.63	37.37
Days With ≥ 0.1" Precipitation	7	6	7	6	7	7	7	7	6	5	5	6	76
Days With ≥ 1.0" Precipitation	0	1	1	1	1	1	0	1	1	1	1	1	10
Mean Snowfall (in.)	4.4	3.2	2.5	0.8	trace	trace	0.0	0.0	0.0	trace	0.4	2.0	13.3
Days With ≥ 1.0" Snow Depth	3	2	1	0	0	0	0	0	0	0	0	1	7

Aurora 6 N *Beaufort County*   Elevation: 19 ft.   Latitude: 35° 23' N   Longitude: 76° 47' W

	JAN	FEB	MAR	APR	MAY	JUN	JUL	AUG	SEP	OCT	NOV	DEC	YEAR
Mean Maximum Temp. (°F)	52.5	55.2	62.9	71.8	78.7	85.3	89.1	87.1	83.0	73.0	65.2	56.0	71.7
Mean Temp. (°F)	43.1	45.6	52.9	61.4	69.0	76.3	80.2	78.6	74.2	63.5	55.5	46.6	62.3
Mean Minimum Temp. (°F)	33.7	35.9	42.8	51.0	59.2	67.2	71.3	70.0	65.4	54.0	45.8	37.0	52.8
Extreme Maximum Temp. (°F)	78	84	90	93	96	100	100	103	100	92	86	82	103
Extreme Minimum Temp. (°F)	-1	8	11	28	42	51	58	55	46	29	20	10	-1
Days Maximum Temp. ≥ 90°F	0	0	0	1	2	8	15	10	3	0	0	0	39
Days Maximum Temp. ≤ 32°F	1	0	0	0	0	0	0	0	0	0	0	0	1
Days Minimum Temp. ≤ 32°F	14	10	4	0	0	0	0	0	0	0	2	10	40
Days Minimum Temp. ≤ 0°F	0	0	0	0	0	0	0	0	0	0	0	0	0
Heating Degree Days (base 65°F)	673	543	381	155	33	2	0	1	4	109	293	567	2,761
Cooling Degree Days (base 65°F)	1	2	11	50	168	357	494	426	283	79	15	4	1,890
Mean Precipitation (in.)	4.33	3.04	4.24	3.18	4.21	4.79	5.83	6.32	4.55	3.18	2.86	3.41	49.94
Days With ≥ 0.1" Precipitation	8	6	7	6	7	7	8	8	6	5	5	6	79
Days With ≥ 1.0" Precipitation	1	1	1	1	1	1	2	2	1	1	1	1	14
Mean Snowfall (in.)	0.3	0.6	0.0	0.0	0.0	0.0	0.0	0.0	0.0	0.0	0.0	trace	0.9
Days With ≥ 1.0" Snow Depth	0	0	0	0	0	0	0	0	0	0	0	0	0

Banner Elk *Avery County*   Elevation: 3,746 ft.   Latitude: 36° 10' N   Longitude: 81° 53' W

	JAN	FEB	MAR	APR	MAY	JUN	JUL	AUG	SEP	OCT	NOV	DEC	YEAR
Mean Maximum Temp. (°F)	41.7	44.7	52.4	60.9	68.0	74.0	77.5	76.3	71.5	62.9	53.8	46.1	60.8
Mean Temp. (°F)	31.3	33.9	41.2	48.9	56.7	63.3	67.0	66.0	61.0	51.3	42.7	35.6	49.9
Mean Minimum Temp. (°F)	20.9	23.2	30.0	37.0	45.4	52.6	56.5	55.6	50.3	39.6	31.5	25.1	39.0
Extreme Maximum Temp. (°F)	69	74	81	86	84	86	90	92	87	79	76	69	92
Extreme Minimum Temp. (°F)	-31	-13	-9	11	24	27	38	34	27	12	-4	-20	-31
Days Maximum Temp. ≥ 90°F	0	0	0	0	0	0	0	0	0	0	0	0	0
Days Maximum Temp. ≤ 32°F	6	4	1	0	0	0	0	0	0	0	1	4	16
Days Minimum Temp. ≤ 32°F	25	22	18	10	2	0	0	0	1	8	16	22	124
Days Minimum Temp. ≤ 0°F	2	1	0	0	0	0	0	0	0	0	0	1	4
Heating Degree Days (base 65°F)	1,038	872	730	475	255	77	19	28	136	419	663	904	5,616
Cooling Degree Days (base 65°F)	0	0	0	0	7	42	106	71	23	1	0	0	250
Mean Precipitation (in.)	4.19	3.86	4.80	4.15	4.77	4.64	4.45	4.44	4.09	3.73	3.82	3.20	50.14
Days With ≥ 0.1" Precipitation	9	8	9	8	10	9	9	8	7	6	7	7	97
Days With ≥ 1.0" Precipitation	1	1	1	1	1	1	1	1	1	1	1	0	11
Mean Snowfall (in.)	10.5	12.4	8.1	2.8	0.2	0.0	0.0	0.0	0.0	0.4	2.5	5.7	42.6
Days With ≥ 1.0" Snow Depth	7	7	3	1	0	0	0	0	0	0	1	4	23

Belhaven 5 SE *Beaufort County*   Elevation: 6 ft.   Latitude: 35° 30' N   Longitude: 76° 41' W

	JAN	FEB	MAR	APR	MAY	JUN	JUL	AUG	SEP	OCT	NOV	DEC	YEAR
Mean Maximum Temp. (°F)	52.0	54.9	62.5	71.5	78.4	85.0	88.6	86.9	82.5	73.0	64.9	55.8	71.3
Mean Temp. (°F)	42.3	44.6	51.8	60.5	68.4	75.8	79.9	78.2	73.2	62.5	54.5	45.9	61.5
Mean Minimum Temp. (°F)	32.5	34.3	41.1	49.4	58.4	66.5	71.1	69.5	63.9	51.9	43.8	36.0	51.5
Extreme Maximum Temp. (°F)	78	82	89	94	96	100	101	101	97	94	85	81	101
Extreme Minimum Temp. (°F)	-10	4	15	28	40	44	54	51	44	28	19	8	-10
Days Maximum Temp. ≥ 90°F	0	0	0	0	2	7	13	9	2	0	0	0	33
Days Maximum Temp. ≤ 32°F	1	1	0	0	0	0	0	0	0	0	0	0	2
Days Minimum Temp. ≤ 32°F	16	13	6	0	0	0	0	0	0	0	4	12	51
Days Minimum Temp. ≤ 0°F	0	0	0	0	0	0	0	0	0	0	0	0	0
Heating Degree Days (base 65°F)	698	570	411	176	40	3	0	0	7	131	320	588	2,944
Cooling Degree Days (base 65°F)	0	1	9	44	156	342	485	410	253	66	12	2	1,780
Mean Precipitation (in.)	4.19	3.10	4.16	3.04	4.51	4.65	5.61	5.58	4.97	3.35	2.93	3.21	49.30
Days With ≥ 0.1" Precipitation	9	6	7	6	7	7	8	8	6	5	5	6	80
Days With ≥ 1.0" Precipitation	1	1	1	1	1	1	2	1	2	1	1	1	14
Mean Snowfall (in.)	0.7	1.6	1.0	0.2	0.0	0.0	0.0	0.0	0.0	0.0	0.0	0.4	3.9
Days With ≥ 1.0" Snow Depth	0	1	0	0	0	0	0	0	0	0	0	0	1

Bent Creek *Buncombe County*   Elevation: 2,109 ft.   Latitude: 35° 30' N   Longitude: 82° 36' W

	JAN	FEB	MAR	APR	MAY	JUN	JUL	AUG	SEP	OCT	NOV	DEC	YEAR
Mean Maximum Temp. (°F)	47.8	52.1	59.9	69.3	75.4	81.2	84.5	83.2	78.1	69.0	59.4	51.4	67.6
Mean Temp. (°F)	37.0	40.1	47.3	55.1	62.6	69.3	73.3	72.2	66.7	56.3	47.4	40.3	55.6
Mean Minimum Temp. (°F)	26.1	28.0	34.6	41.0	49.7	57.4	61.9	61.2	55.3	43.6	35.4	29.2	43.6
Extreme Maximum Temp. (°F)	81	81	84	90	91	95	97	100	95	88	80	76	100
Extreme Minimum Temp. (°F)	-16	-5	-1	20	26	36	42	41	31	18	4	-5	-16
Days Maximum Temp. ≥ 90°F	0	0	0	0	0	1	5	3	1	0	0	0	10
Days Maximum Temp. ≤ 32°F	2	1	0	0	0	0	0	0	0	0	0	1	4
Days Minimum Temp. ≤ 32°F	22	19	13	6	1	0	0	0	0	5	13	20	99
Days Minimum Temp. ≤ 0°F	1	0	0	0	0	0	0	0	0	0	0	0	1
Heating Degree Days (base 65°F)	862	699	544	296	114	17	1	2	49	272	523	759	4,138
Cooling Degree Days (base 65°F)	0	0	1	8	51	166	280	239	103	11	1	0	860
Mean Precipitation (in.)	3.97	3.93	5.07	3.77	4.39	3.69	3.87	3.91	4.02	3.49	4.02	3.33	47.46
Days With ≥ 0.1" Precipitation	7	6	8	6	8	8	7	7	6	5	6	6	80
Days With ≥ 1.0" Precipitation	1	1	1	1	1	1	1	1	1	1	1	1	12
Mean Snowfall (in.)	2.8	2.4	1.4	0.5	0.0	0.0	0.0	0.0	0.0	0.0	0.0	1.1	8.2
Days With ≥ 1.0" Snow Depth	2	1	1	0	0	0	0	0	0	0	0	1	5

Black Mountain 2 W *Buncombe County*   Elevation: 2,290 ft.   Latitude: 35° 37' N   Longitude: 82° 21' W

	JAN	FEB	MAR	APR	MAY	JUN	JUL	AUG	SEP	OCT	NOV	DEC	YEAR
Mean Maximum Temp. (°F)	48.8	52.6	60.4	69.2	75.3	81.1	84.7	83.1	78.0	69.8	60.3	52.8	68.0
Mean Temp. (°F)	37.3	40.6	47.5	55.4	62.2	69.1	72.9	71.8	66.3	56.5	47.6	40.9	55.7
Mean Minimum Temp. (°F)	25.8	28.4	34.6	41.6	49.2	57.1	61.1	60.4	54.5	43.1	35.0	29.0	43.3
Extreme Maximum Temp. (°F)	74	78	86	90	90	94	99	97	93	85	80	76	99
Extreme Minimum Temp. (°F)	-14	-7	7	18	26	32	44	43	28	19	7	-13	-14
Days Maximum Temp. ≥ 90°F	0	0	0	0	0	2	4	3	0	0	0	0	9
Days Maximum Temp. ≤ 32°F	2	1	0	0	0	0	0	0	0	0	0	1	4
Days Minimum Temp. ≤ 32°F	22	19	14	5	1	0	0	0	0	5	13	20	99
Days Minimum Temp. ≤ 0°F	0	0	0	0	0	0	0	0	0	0	0	0	0
Heating Degree Days (base 65°F)	847	677	536	287	117	18	2	3	54	268	515	742	4,066
Cooling Degree Days (base 65°F)	0	0	1	7	43	148	258	215	90	11	0	0	773
Mean Precipitation (in.)	4.07	3.78	4.82	3.89	4.91	4.28	3.89	4.09	3.78	3.74	4.14	3.40	48.79
Days With ≥ 0.1" Precipitation	7	6	8	7	8	7	8	7	6	5	7	6	82
Days With ≥ 1.0" Precipitation	1	1	1	1	1	1	1	1	1	1	1	1	12
Mean Snowfall (in.)	3.4	2.3	1.4	0.3	0.0	0.0	0.0	0.0	0.0	trace	0.2	1.5	9.1
Days With ≥ 1.0" Snow Depth	1	1	0	0	0	0	0	0	0	0	0	0	2

Blowing Rock 1 NW *Watauga County*   Elevation: 3,848 ft.   Latitude: 36° 09' N   Longitude: 81° 42' W

	JAN	FEB	MAR	APR	MAY	JUN	JUL	AUG	SEP	OCT	NOV	DEC	YEAR
Mean Maximum Temp. (°F)	38.4	42.0	49.8	59.0	66.3	72.5	76.5	75.0	69.5	60.1	51.1	42.9	58.6
Mean Temp. (°F)	29.5	32.5	40.0	48.7	56.7	63.4	67.6	66.2	60.7	50.4	42.0	34.0	49.3
Mean Minimum Temp. (°F)	20.7	23.0	30.3	38.4	47.0	54.3	58.6	57.3	51.8	40.7	32.8	25.1	40.0
Extreme Maximum Temp. (°F)	66	74	74	82	87	89	92	90	88	80	72	68	92
Extreme Minimum Temp. (°F)	-24	-9	-5	13	26	33	44	39	31	17	-1	-14	-24
Days Maximum Temp. ≥ 90°F	0	0	0	0	0	0	0	0	0	0	0	0	0
Days Maximum Temp. ≤ 32°F	9	6	2	0	0	0	0	0	0	0	1	6	24
Days Minimum Temp. ≤ 32°F	25	22	17	9	1	0	0	0	0	6	15	23	118
Days Minimum Temp. ≤ 0°F	2	1	0	0	0	0	0	0	0	0	0	1	4
Heating Degree Days (base 65°F)	1,093	911	767	484	259	83	20	33	146	446	686	953	5,881
Cooling Degree Days (base 65°F)	0	0	0	1	9	49	118	78	24	1	0	0	280
Mean Precipitation (in.)	5.46	4.75	6.65	5.78	6.52	6.47	5.96	6.11	5.57	5.12	5.85	4.46	68.70
Days With ≥ 0.1" Precipitation	8	8	9	8	10	9	10	9	7	6	7	8	99
Days With ≥ 1.0" Precipitation	2	1	2	2	2	2	2	1	2	1	2	1	20
Mean Snowfall (in.)	8.9	8.0	5.4	1.1	trace	0.0	0.0	0.0	0.0	0.1	1.3	5.2	30.0
Days With ≥ 1.0" Snow Depth	8	6	3	1	0	0	0	0	0	0	1	4	23

Brevard *Transylvania County*   Elevation: 2,211 ft.   Latitude: 35° 13' N   Longitude: 82° 42' W

	JAN	FEB	MAR	APR	MAY	JUN	JUL	AUG	SEP	OCT	NOV	DEC	YEAR
Mean Maximum Temp. (°F)	48.8	52.9	61.0	69.7	75.7	81.3	83.9	83.0	78.3	69.9	60.7	52.5	68.1
Mean Temp. (°F)	37.2	40.2	47.6	55.4	62.4	69.3	72.9	72.1	66.8	56.3	47.8	40.5	55.7
Mean Minimum Temp. (°F)	25.4	27.4	34.1	40.9	49.0	57.2	61.7	61.1	55.3	42.7	34.9	28.5	43.2
Extreme Maximum Temp. (°F)	75	78	84	90	91	97	97	96	91	87	82	76	97
Extreme Minimum Temp. (°F)	-15	-2	6	20	25	36	43	44	30	18	6	-4	-15
Days Maximum Temp. ≥ 90°F	0	0	0	0	0	1	3	2	0	0	0	0	6
Days Maximum Temp. ≤ 32°F	2	0	0	0	0	0	0	0	0	0	0	1	3
Days Minimum Temp. ≤ 32°F	23	19	13	6	1	0	0	0	0	5	14	20	101
Days Minimum Temp. ≤ 0°F	1	0	0	0	0	0	0	0	0	0	0	0	1
Heating Degree Days (base 65°F)	856	695	534	290	115	16	1	2	46	271	510	752	4,088
Cooling Degree Days (base 65°F)	0	0	1	7	43	156	262	225	94	10	0	0	798
Mean Precipitation (in.)	5.88	5.01	6.33	4.46	5.94	6.06	5.17	5.40	5.22	5.36	5.43	5.78	66.04
Days With ≥ 0.1" Precipitation	7	7	8	6	9	9	9	8	7	6	7	8	91
Days With ≥ 1.0" Precipitation	2	2	2	2	2	2	2	2	2	2	2	2	24
Mean Snowfall (in.)	3.7	2.3	1.6	0.5	0.0	0.0	0.0	0.0	0.0	trace	0.2	1.0	9.3
Days With ≥ 1.0" Snow Depth	2	1	1	0	0	0	0	0	0	0	0	0	4

Burlington Fire Station 5 *Alamance County*   Elevation: 659 ft.   Latitude: 36° 04' N   Longitude: 79° 27' W

	JAN	FEB	MAR	APR	MAY	JUN	JUL	AUG	SEP	OCT	NOV	DEC	YEAR
Mean Maximum Temp. (°F)	49.1	53.3	62.0	72.3	78.8	86.3	90.2	88.5	82.0	71.9	62.7	53.3	70.9
Mean Temp. (°F)	38.4	41.6	49.6	58.8	66.4	74.8	79.0	77.3	70.6	59.2	50.3	42.0	59.0
Mean Minimum Temp. (°F)	27.6	29.9	37.2	45.3	54.1	63.3	67.7	66.0	59.2	46.4	37.9	30.7	47.1
Extreme Maximum Temp. (°F)	84	83	89	95	98	101	105	104	100	93	86	79	105
Extreme Minimum Temp. (°F)	-6	4	8	22	29	43	48	41	36	25	15	-4	-6
Days Maximum Temp. ≥ 90°F	0	0	0	1	2	10	19	14	5	0	0	0	51
Days Maximum Temp. ≤ 32°F	2	1	0	0	0	0	0	0	0	0	0	1	4
Days Minimum Temp. ≤ 32°F	22	18	10	2	0	0	0	0	0	1	9	18	80
Days Minimum Temp. ≤ 0°F	0	0	0	0	0	0	0	0	0	0	0	0	0
Heating Degree Days (base 65°F)	819	654	476	214	65	5	0	1	24	205	438	707	3,608
Cooling Degree Days (base 65°F)	0	0	5	31	117	315	454	387	188	32	2	0	1,531
Mean Precipitation (in.)	3.82	3.40	4.24	3.24	4.22	4.12	4.51	4.02	4.09	3.50	3.05	3.18	45.39
Days With ≥ 0.1" Precipitation	7	6	7	6	7	7	7	6	5	5	6	6	75
Days With ≥ 1.0" Precipitation	1	1	1	1	1	1	1	1	1	1	1	1	12
Mean Snowfall (in.)	0.8	0.8	0.2	trace	0.0	0.0	0.0	0.0	0.0	0.0	trace	0.4	2.2
Days With ≥ 1.0" Snow Depth	1	0	0	0	0	0	0	0	0	0	0	0	1

Canton 1 SW *Haywood County*   Elevation: 2,660 ft.   Latitude: 35° 31' N   Longitude: 82° 51' W

	JAN	FEB	MAR	APR	MAY	JUN	JUL	AUG	SEP	OCT	NOV	DEC	YEAR
Mean Maximum Temp. (°F)	46.2	50.1	58.1	66.8	73.2	79.8	82.7	81.6	76.1	66.9	58.1	50.1	65.8
Mean Temp. (°F)	34.7	37.8	45.5	53.1	60.5	67.4	71.0	70.1	64.6	53.8	45.3	38.4	53.5
Mean Minimum Temp. (°F)	23.2	25.5	32.9	39.3	47.6	54.9	59.3	58.5	53.0	40.7	32.5	26.6	41.2
Extreme Maximum Temp. (°F)	71	79	85	87	87	92	95	96	93	84	79	72	96
Extreme Minimum Temp. (°F)	-20	-2	-4	18	27	36	43	42	31	19	4	-5	-20
Days Maximum Temp. ≥ 90°F	0	0	0	0	0	1	2	1	0	0	0	0	4
Days Maximum Temp. ≤ 32°F	4	2	1	0	0	0	0	0	0	0	0	2	9
Days Minimum Temp. ≤ 32°F	24	22	16	7	1	0	0	0	0	7	16	23	116
Days Minimum Temp. ≤ 0°F	1	0	0	0	0	0	0	0	0	0	0	0	1
Heating Degree Days (base 65°F)	932	762	599	355	155	26	3	5	75	343	584	819	4,658
Cooling Degree Days (base 65°F)	0	0	1	3	na	na	na	na	na	na	na	na	na
Mean Precipitation (in.)	3.03	3.53	4.46	3.36	4.50	3.09	4.27	3.82	3.36	2.66	3.18	3.12	42.38
Days With ≥ 0.1" Precipitation	7	7	8	6	9	7	8	7	6	5	6	6	82
Days With ≥ 1.0" Precipitation	0	1	1	1	1	0	1	1	1	1	1	1	10
Mean Snowfall (in.)	na	na	0.9	0.6	0.0	0.0	0.0	0.0	0.0	trace	trace	na	na
Days With ≥ 1.0" Snow Depth	3	na	1	0	0	0	0	0	0	0	0	na	na

Cedar Island *Carteret County*   Elevation: 6 ft.   Latitude: 34° 59' N   Longitude: 76° 18' W

	JAN	FEB	MAR	APR	MAY	JUN	JUL	AUG	SEP	OCT	NOV	DEC	YEAR
Mean Maximum Temp. (°F)	53.0	55.7	63.1	72.3	79.5	85.7	89.3	87.2	82.2	72.8	64.3	56.5	71.8
Mean Temp. (°F)	44.8	46.9	53.7	62.1	69.9	76.7	80.5	79.2	74.7	65.0	56.2	48.4	63.2
Mean Minimum Temp. (°F)	36.4	38.0	44.3	51.8	60.2	67.7	71.7	71.1	67.2	57.1	48.0	40.2	54.5
Extreme Maximum Temp. (°F)	76	79	87	93	98	101	102	102	98	95	84	77	102
Extreme Minimum Temp. (°F)	2	15	10	28	39	46	51	57	44	33	25	8	2
Days Maximum Temp. ≥ 90°F	0	0	0	0	2	8	15	10	3	0	0	0	38
Days Maximum Temp. ≤ 32°F	1	0	0	0	0	0	0	0	0	0	0	0	1
Days Minimum Temp. ≤ 32°F	11	9	3	0	0	0	0	0	0	0	2	7	32
Days Minimum Temp. ≤ 0°F	0	0	0	0	0	0	0	0	0	0	0	0	0
Heating Degree Days (base 65°F)	621	507	353	136	23	1	0	0	1	80	275	512	2,509
Cooling Degree Days (base 65°F)	1	2	10	56	185	371	508	448	295	90	17	3	1,986
Mean Precipitation (in.)	5.27	3.65	4.72	3.11	4.16	4.19	6.18	7.05	6.48	4.51	3.90	4.48	57.70
Days With ≥ 0.1" Precipitation	9	7	7	5	7	6	9	9	8	6	6	7	86
Days With ≥ 1.0" Precipitation	2	1	1	1	1	1	2	2	2	1	1	1	16
Mean Snowfall (in.)	0.8	0.6	0.6	trace	0.0	0.0	0.0	0.0	0.0	0.0	trace	0.6	2.6
Days With ≥ 1.0" Snow Depth	0	0	0	0	0	0	0	0	0	0	0	0	0

Celo 2 S *Yancey County*   Elevation: 2,677 ft.   Latitude: 35° 50' N   Longitude: 82° 11' W

	JAN	FEB	MAR	APR	MAY	JUN	JUL	AUG	SEP	OCT	NOV	DEC	YEAR
Mean Maximum Temp. (°F)	45.7	49.1	56.5	65.3	71.9	77.5	81.0	79.5	74.6	66.2	57.5	49.7	64.5
Mean Temp. (°F)	33.6	36.3	43.7	51.5	58.8	65.4	69.4	68.2	62.6	52.2	44.1	37.0	51.9
Mean Minimum Temp. (°F)	21.5	23.5	30.7	37.6	45.7	53.3	57.8	56.8	50.5	38.1	30.6	24.1	39.2
Extreme Maximum Temp. (°F)	79	81	84	86	90	90	92	95	94	84	78	77	95
Extreme Minimum Temp. (°F)	-16	-9	-4	13	25	29	36	35	27	14	0	-10	-16
Days Maximum Temp. ≥ 90°F	0	0	0	0	0	0	1	1	0	0	0	0	2
Days Maximum Temp. ≤ 32°F	4	3	1	0	0	0	0	0	0	0	0	2	10
Days Minimum Temp. ≤ 32°F	26	23	18	9	2	0	0	0	1	10	18	24	131
Days Minimum Temp. ≤ 0°F	1	1	0	0	0	0	0	0	0	0	0	0	2
Heating Degree Days (base 65°F)	966	804	655	401	202	54	11	14	108	393	622	862	5,092
Cooling Degree Days (base 65°F)	0	0	1	3	20	84	174	126	45	2	0	0	455
Mean Precipitation (in.)	5.49	5.08	6.26	4.59	5.33	4.54	4.44	5.06	4.52	4.69	5.01	4.21	59.22
Days With ≥ 0.1" Precipitation	8	8	10	8	8	9	8	8	7	6	7	7	94
Days With ≥ 1.0" Precipitation	2	2	2	1	1	1	1	1	1	2	2	1	17
Mean Snowfall (in.)	5.7	4.6	3.0	0.8	trace	0.0	0.0	0.0	0.0	trace	0.4	2.2	16.7
Days With ≥ 1.0" Snow Depth	5	4	2	0	0	0	0	0	0	0	0	2	13

Chapel Hill 2 W *Orange County*   Elevation: 498 ft.   Latitude: 35° 55' N   Longitude: 79° 05' W

	JAN	FEB	MAR	APR	MAY	JUN	JUL	AUG	SEP	OCT	NOV	DEC	YEAR
Mean Maximum Temp. (°F)	49.4	53.3	61.5	71.4	78.2	85.2	89.3	87.5	81.8	71.5	62.7	53.4	70.4
Mean Temp. (°F)	38.3	41.3	49.1	58.1	65.9	73.6	77.8	76.2	70.1	58.4	50.0	42.0	58.4
Mean Minimum Temp. (°F)	27.2	29.2	36.7	44.8	53.6	61.9	66.1	64.8	58.4	45.2	37.2	30.5	46.3
Extreme Maximum Temp. (°F)	76	83	89	94	95	100	105	106	100	94	86	80	106
Extreme Minimum Temp. (°F)	-8	3	9	23	29	40	48	40	36	21	13	0	-8
Days Maximum Temp. ≥ 90°F	0	0	0	0	2	8	15	11	4	0	0	0	40
Days Maximum Temp. ≤ 32°F	2	1	0	0	0	0	0	0	0	0	0	1	4
Days Minimum Temp. ≤ 32°F	22	19	11	3	0	0	0	0	0	3	11	19	88
Days Minimum Temp. ≤ 0°F	0	0	0	0	0	0	0	0	0	0	0	0	0
Heating Degree Days (base 65°F)	822	663	490	232	73	8	1	1	28	224	449	708	3,699
Cooling Degree Days (base 65°F)	0	0	7	33	119	289	425	367	188	29	2	1	1,461
Mean Precipitation (in.)	4.33	3.68	4.57	3.14	4.47	4.03	3.84	4.47	4.37	3.85	3.64	3.27	47.66
Days With ≥ 0.1" Precipitation	8	6	8	6	7	6	7	7	5	5	5	6	76
Days With ≥ 1.0" Precipitation	1	1	1	1	1	1	1	1	1	1	1	1	12
Mean Snowfall (in.)	1.3	2.3	0.9	trace	0.0	0.0	0.0	0.0	0.0	0.0	trace	0.6	5.1
Days With ≥ 1.0" Snow Depth	1	0	0	0	0	0	0	0	0	0	0	0	1

Clinton 2 NE *Sampson County*   Elevation: 157 ft.   Latitude: 35° 01' N   Longitude: 78° 17' W

	JAN	FEB	MAR	APR	MAY	JUN	JUL	AUG	SEP	OCT	NOV	DEC	YEAR
Mean Maximum Temp. (°F)	53.0	56.6	64.4	73.7	80.4	86.7	90.1	88.4	83.6	74.1	65.6	56.3	72.8
Mean Temp. (°F)	42.4	45.2	52.7	60.9	68.7	75.9	79.8	78.3	72.9	61.8	53.7	45.4	61.5
Mean Minimum Temp. (°F)	31.7	33.7	40.8	48.0	57.0	64.9	69.5	68.1	62.3	49.4	41.7	34.4	50.1
Extreme Maximum Temp. (°F)	78	83	89	94	96	100	102	104	100	96	85	81	104
Extreme Minimum Temp. (°F)	-2	3	8	26	35	42	52	46	40	24	18	5	-2
Days Maximum Temp. ≥ 90°F	0	0	0	1	3	10	18	14	5	0	0	0	51
Days Maximum Temp. ≤ 32°F	1	0	0	0	0	0	0	0	0	0	0	1	1
Days Minimum Temp. ≤ 32°F	18	14	7	1	0	0	0	0	0	1	7	15	63
Days Minimum Temp. ≤ 0°F	0	0	0	0	0	0	0	0	0	0	0	0	0
Heating Degree Days (base 65°F)	696	554	389	169	41	3	0	0	12	150	348	605	2,967
Cooling Degree Days (base 65°F)	1	2	11	50	165	348	485	420	248	59	11	3	1,803
Mean Precipitation (in.)	4.29	3.28	4.51	3.12	3.69	4.42	6.07	5.42	4.99	3.31	2.89	3.29	49.28
Days With ≥ 0.1" Precipitation	8	6	8	5	7	7	9	7	6	5	5	6	79
Days With ≥ 1.0" Precipitation	1	1	1	1	1	1	2	2	1	1	1	1	14
Mean Snowfall (in.)	0.5	0.9	0.8	trace	0.0	0.0	0.0	0.0	0.0	0.0	trace	0.5	2.7
Days With ≥ 1.0" Snow Depth	1	1	0	0	0	0	0	0	0	0	0	0	2

Concord *Cabarrus County*   Elevation: 688 ft.   Latitude: 35° 25' N   Longitude: 80° 36' W

	JAN	FEB	MAR	APR	MAY	JUN	JUL	AUG	SEP	OCT	NOV	DEC	YEAR
Mean Maximum Temp. (°F)	50.7	55.3	63.5	73.2	79.8	86.7	90.5	88.9	83.4	73.3	63.7	54.5	72.0
Mean Temp. (°F)	39.4	42.7	50.5	59.3	67.3	75.2	79.4	78.0	71.8	60.2	50.9	42.8	59.8
Mean Minimum Temp. (°F)	28.0	30.0	37.4	45.3	54.6	63.6	68.3	67.0	60.2	47.1	38.0	31.1	47.6
Extreme Maximum Temp. (°F)	79	82	89	95	98	100	105	107	100	94	88	80	107
Extreme Minimum Temp. (°F)	-5	6	1	24	32	43	53	50	40	25	13	4	-5
Days Maximum Temp. ≥ 90°F	0	0	0	1	3	11	19	15	7	0	0	0	56
Days Maximum Temp. ≤ 32°F	1	0	0	0	0	0	0	0	0	0	0	1	2
Days Minimum Temp. ≤ 32°F	21	18	10	2	0	0	0	0	0	1	10	19	81
Days Minimum Temp. ≤ 0°F	0	0	0	0	0	0	0	0	0	0	0	0	0
Heating Degree Days (base 65°F)	788	625	449	203	57	5	0	0	18	181	423	681	3,430
Cooling Degree Days (base 65°F)	0	0	6	37	137	331	472	408	218	41	3	1	1,654
Mean Precipitation (in.)	4.17	3.51	4.44	3.39	3.98	4.46	4.75	3.65	4.05	4.16	3.41	3.35	47.32
Days With ≥ 0.1" Precipitation	8	6	8	6	7	7	7	6	5	5	6	7	78
Days With ≥ 1.0" Precipitation	1	1	1	1	1	1	1	1	1	2	1	1	13
Mean Snowfall (in.)	1.4	1.6	0.9	trace	0.0	0.0	0.0	0.0	0.0	0.0	trace	0.6	4.5
Days With ≥ 1.0" Snow Depth	2	1	0	0	0	0	0	0	0	0	0	0	3

Coweeta Exp. Station *Macon County*   Elevation: 2,247 ft.   Latitude: 35° 04' N   Longitude: 83° 26' W

	JAN	FEB	MAR	APR	MAY	JUN	JUL	AUG	SEP	OCT	NOV	DEC	YEAR
Mean Maximum Temp. (°F)	48.5	52.7	60.0	68.4	74.7	80.5	83.8	82.5	77.6	69.2	60.2	52.1	67.5
Mean Temp. (°F)	36.4	39.6	46.8	54.4	61.6	68.0	71.7	70.7	65.5	55.3	46.7	39.6	54.7
Mean Minimum Temp. (°F)	24.2	26.4	33.5	40.5	48.5	55.5	59.5	58.9	53.4	41.4	33.2	27.1	41.8
Extreme Maximum Temp. (°F)	78	79	81	88	92	93	97	97	93	86	78	74	97
Extreme Minimum Temp. (°F)	-18	-3	-1	16	27	34	44	44	30	20	6	-5	-18
Days Maximum Temp. ≥ 90°F	0	0	0	0	0	1	4	2	0	0	0	0	7
Days Maximum Temp. ≤ 32°F	2	1	0	0	0	0	0	0	0	0	0	1	4
Days Minimum Temp. ≤ 32°F	24	21	15	7	1	0	0	0	0	7	17	23	115
Days Minimum Temp. ≤ 0°F	1	0	0	0	0	0	0	0	0	0	0	0	1
Heating Degree Days (base 65°F)	881	711	558	317	131	23	3	3	59	298	542	780	4,306
Cooling Degree Days (base 65°F)	0	0	1	7	39	135	233	192	78	6	0	0	691
Mean Precipitation (in.)	7.38	7.00	8.06	5.63	6.22	5.54	4.54	5.00	5.36	4.91	6.25	6.54	72.43
Days With ≥ 0.1" Precipitation	9	8	9	8	9	9	8	8	7	6	8	8	97
Days With ≥ 1.0" Precipitation	3	2	3	2	2	2	1	1	2	2	2	2	24
Mean Snowfall (in.)	*2.3*	*2.2*	1.2	0.3	0.0	0.0	0.0	0.0	0.0	0.0	trace	0.2	*6.2*
Days With ≥ 1.0" Snow Depth	2	*1*	1	0	0	0	0	0	0	0	0	0	*4*

Cullowhee *Jackson County*   Elevation: 2,191 ft.   Latitude: 35° 20' N   Longitude: 83° 11' W

	JAN	FEB	MAR	APR	MAY	JUN	JUL	AUG	SEP	OCT	NOV	DEC	YEAR
Mean Maximum Temp. (°F)	48.7	53.4	61.7	70.3	76.7	82.0	85.0	83.7	78.7	70.1	60.3	52.0	68.6
Mean Temp. (°F)	37.6	41.1	48.3	55.7	63.2	69.7	73.4	72.4	67.2	56.9	47.7	40.7	56.2
Mean Minimum Temp. (°F)	26.4	28.7	34.9	41.0	49.8	57.3	61.7	61.0	55.7	43.7	35.1	29.3	43.7
Extreme Maximum Temp. (°F)	74	78	86	89	92	95	97	98	93	87	78	73	98
Extreme Minimum Temp. (°F)	-19	-1	-1	18	26	34	45	45	32	21	6	-5	-19
Days Maximum Temp. ≥ 90°F	0	0	0	0	0	1	5	3	1	0	0	0	10
Days Maximum Temp. ≤ 32°F	2	1	0	0	0	0	0	0	0	0	0	1	4
Days Minimum Temp. ≤ 32°F	21	18	13	6	1	0	0	0	0	5	14	20	98
Days Minimum Temp. ≤ 0°F	1	0	0	0	0	0	0	0	0	0	0	0	1
Heating Degree Days (base 65°F)	842	669	510	281	97	14	1	1	40	254	513	747	3,969
Cooling Degree Days (base 65°F)	0	0	0	9	57	175	285	247	111	12	0	0	896
Mean Precipitation (in.)	4.84	4.72	5.41	3.83	4.78	4.43	4.32	3.92	3.58	3.33	4.10	4.37	51.63
Days With ≥ 0.1" Precipitation	9	8	9	7	9	9	8	8	7	5	7	8	94
Days With ≥ 1.0" Precipitation	1	1	1	1	1	1	1	1	1	1	1	1	12
Mean Snowfall (in.)	3.5	2.1	2.0	trace	0.0	0.0	0.0	0.0	0.0	trace	0.2	1.5	9.3
Days With ≥ 1.0" Snow Depth	2	1	0	0	0	0	0	0	0	0	0	0	3

Danbury 1 NW *Stokes County*   Elevation: 839 ft.   Latitude: 36° 25' N   Longitude: 80° 13' W

	JAN	FEB	MAR	APR	MAY	JUN	JUL	AUG	SEP	OCT	NOV	DEC	YEAR
Mean Maximum Temp. (°F)	46.9	51.0	59.1	69.2	76.0	83.0	86.9	85.6	80.0	70.1	60.4	51.1	68.3
Mean Temp. (°F)	36.2	39.3	46.9	55.9	63.5	71.6	75.9	74.6	68.3	56.6	47.8	39.9	56.4
Mean Minimum Temp. (°F)	25.5	27.6	34.7	42.5	50.9	60.2	64.9	63.5	56.6	43.1	35.2	28.6	44.4
Extreme Maximum Temp. (°F)	75	81	86	91	91	97	102	103	100	90	85	80	103
Extreme Minimum Temp. (°F)	-10	-8	10	23	28	42	47	42	33	23	8	-1	-10
Days Maximum Temp. ≥ 90°F	0	0	0	0	0	4	10	7	3	0	0	0	24
Days Maximum Temp. ≤ 32°F	3	1	0	0	0	0	0	0	0	0	0	1	5
Days Minimum Temp. ≤ 32°F	24	20	13	3	0	0	0	0	0	4	13	21	98
Days Minimum Temp. ≤ 0°F	0	0	0	0	0	0	0	0	0	0	0	0	0
Heating Degree Days (base 65°F)	886	720	556	285	107	12	1	2	43	269	510	773	4,164
Cooling Degree Days (base 65°F)	0	0	2	16	69	229	360	303	142	16	1	0	1,138
Mean Precipitation (in.)	3.79	3.30	4.61	3.76	4.70	3.97	4.92	4.06	4.25	4.21	3.26	3.53	48.36
Days With ≥ 0.1" Precipitation	6	6	7	6	7	7	8	6	6	6	6	6	77
Days With ≥ 1.0" Precipitation	1	1	1	1	1	1	1	1	1	1	1	1	12
Mean Snowfall (in.)	2.0	3.8	1.8	trace	0.0	0.0	0.0	0.0	0.0	trace	0.8	8.4	
Days With ≥ 1.0" Snow Depth	3	2	0	0	0	0	0	0	0	0	0	1	6

Dunn 4 NW *Harnett County*   Elevation: 200 ft.   Latitude: 35° 19' N   Longitude: 78° 41' W

	JAN	FEB	MAR	APR	MAY	JUN	JUL	AUG	SEP	OCT	NOV	DEC	YEAR
Mean Maximum Temp. (°F)	51.7	56.4	64.4	73.7	80.0	86.4	89.7	87.8	82.8	73.3	64.4	55.7	72.2
Mean Temp. (°F)	40.8	44.4	52.1	60.5	67.9	75.3	79.1	77.6	71.9	60.7	51.9	44.3	60.5
Mean Minimum Temp. (°F)	29.7	32.4	39.7	47.1	55.8	64.1	68.5	67.2	60.9	48.0	39.3	32.7	48.8
Extreme Maximum Temp. (°F)	80	83	89	93	97	100	102	108	100	94	86	80	108
Extreme Minimum Temp. (°F)	-4	4	10	25	35	43	52	47	37	21	12	1	-4
Days Maximum Temp. ≥ 90°F	0	0	0	1	3	9	16	12	4	0	0	0	45
Days Maximum Temp. ≤ 32°F	1	0	0	0	0	0	0	0	0	0	0	0	1
Days Minimum Temp. ≤ 32°F	19	15	8	1	0	0	0	0	0	1	9	17	70
Days Minimum Temp. ≤ 0°F	0	0	0	0	0	0	0	0	0	0	0	0	0
Heating Degree Days (base 65°F)	746	574	402	175	46	3	0	0	15	173	394	638	3,166
Cooling Degree Days (base 65°F)	0	1	9	44	141	331	465	398	224	48	7	2	1,670
Mean Precipitation (in.)	4.02	3.67	4.78	3.26	3.81	4.30	5.70	4.86	4.30	3.32	3.05	3.64	48.71
Days With ≥ 0.1" Precipitation	7	7	7	5	6	6	8	8	6	4	5	7	76
Days With ≥ 1.0" Precipitation	1	1	1	1	1	1	2	1	1	1	1	1	13
Mean Snowfall (in.)	0.7	1.0	0.4	0.0	0.0	0.0	0.0	0.0	0.0	0.0	0.0	0.2	2.3
Days With ≥ 1.0" Snow Depth	0	0	0	0	0	0	0	0	0	0	0	0	0

Edenton *Chowan County*   Elevation: 19 ft.   Latitude: 36° 03' N   Longitude: 76° 37' W

	JAN	FEB	MAR	APR	MAY	JUN	JUL	AUG	SEP	OCT	NOV	DEC	YEAR
Mean Maximum Temp. (°F)	52.2	55.5	63.4	72.1	78.8	85.4	88.7	86.6	81.9	72.6	64.6	56.2	71.5
Mean Temp. (°F)	42.9	45.3	52.4	60.6	68.5	75.8	79.9	78.1	73.0	62.7	54.6	46.7	61.7
Mean Minimum Temp. (°F)	33.5	34.9	41.4	49.1	58.1	66.3	71.0	69.5	64.1	52.7	44.5	37.1	51.9
Extreme Maximum Temp. (°F)	78	83	89	94	98	99	98	99	95	93	84	80	99
Extreme Minimum Temp. (°F)	-4	5	17	28	37	44	52	50	44	31	21	6	-4
Days Maximum Temp. ≥ 90°F	0	0	0	0	1	7	14	9	2	0	0	0	33
Days Maximum Temp. ≤ 32°F	1	0	0	0	0	0	0	0	0	0	0	0	1
Days Minimum Temp. ≤ 32°F	14	12	5	0	0	0	0	0	0	0	3	10	44
Days Minimum Temp. ≤ 0°F	0	0	0	0	0	0	0	0	0	0	0	0	0
Heating Degree Days (base 65°F)	680	552	392	171	38	3	0	0	8	124	318	563	2,849
Cooling Degree Days (base 65°F)	0	0	9	40	156	345	486	402	240	60	10	1	1,749
Mean Precipitation (in.)	4.11	3.44	4.43	3.38	4.18	4.31	5.44	5.12	4.63	3.68	2.77	3.09	48.58
Days With ≥ 0.1" Precipitation	8	7	7	6	7	6	8	7	6	5	5	6	78
Days With ≥ 1.0" Precipitation	1	1	1	1	1	1	2	2	1	1	1	1	14
Mean Snowfall (in.)	0.8	1.8	0.9	0.1	0.0	0.0	0.0	0.0	0.0	0.0	0.0	0.2	3.8
Days With ≥ 1.0" Snow Depth	0	0	0	0	0	0	0	0	0	0	0	0	0

Elizabeth City *Pasquotank County* Elevation: 6 ft.   Latitude: 36° 19' N   Longitude: 76° 12' W

	JAN	FEB	MAR	APR	MAY	JUN	JUL	AUG	SEP	OCT	NOV	DEC	YEAR
Mean Maximum Temp. (°F)	52.0	54.9	62.8	71.8	78.5	85.3	89.0	87.5	83.1	73.3	65.0	56.3	71.6
Mean Temp. (°F)	42.0	44.2	51.6	59.8	67.8	75.4	79.6	78.1	73.3	62.5	54.3	46.1	61.2
Mean Minimum Temp. (°F)	31.9	33.8	40.4	48.0	57.0	65.5	70.2	68.7	63.4	51.6	43.4	35.9	50.8
Extreme Maximum Temp. (°F)	77	82	90	95	98	100	102	103	98	94	85	82	103
Extreme Minimum Temp. (°F)	-2	5	14	26	32	43	49	50	42	25	21	5	-2
Days Maximum Temp. ≥ 90°F	0	0	0	1	2	8	14	11	4	0	0	0	40
Days Maximum Temp. ≤ 32°F	1	0	0	0	0	0	0	0	0	0	0	0	1
Days Minimum Temp. ≤ 32°F	16	13	7	1	0	0	0	0	0	1	5	13	56
Days Minimum Temp. ≤ 0°F	0	0	0	0	0	0	0	0	0	0	0	0	0
Heating Degree Days (base 65°F)	707	581	417	191	50	3	0	0	6	132	330	581	2,998
Cooling Degree Days (base 65°F)	0	1	9	40	150	339	486	413	258	65	11	2	1,774
Mean Precipitation (in.)	4.34	3.37	4.11	3.10	3.88	4.17	5.70	5.23	4.41	3.40	2.96	3.13	47.80
Days With ≥ 0.1" Precipitation	8	6	8	6	7	7	8	7	6	5	5	6	79
Days With ≥ 1.0" Precipitation	1	1	1	1	1	1	2	2	1	1	1	1	14
Mean Snowfall (in.)	trace	*trace*	trace	0.0	0.0	0.0	0.0	0.0	0.0	0.0	0.0	0.0	*trace*
Days With ≥ 1.0" Snow Depth	0	0	0	0	0	0	0	0	0	0	0	0	0

Elizabethtown Lock 2 *Bladen County* Elevation: 59 ft.   Latitude: 34° 38' N   Longitude: 78° 35' W

	JAN	FEB	MAR	APR	MAY	JUN	JUL	AUG	SEP	OCT	NOV	DEC	YEAR
Mean Maximum Temp. (°F)	55.0	*59.4*	na	75.1	*80.9*	*86.3*	89.5	*88.3*	*84.2*	75.1	67.3	59.2	na
Mean Temp. (°F)	*43.5*	*46.8*	na	61.8	na	*75.4*	79.3	78.4	73.6	62.9	na	na	na
Mean Minimum Temp. (°F)	*32.3*	*34.3*	*41.5*	48.5	*57.3*	64.7	69.3	68.3	63.0	50.8	na	*35.0*	na
Extreme Maximum Temp. (°F)	81	85	90	94	96	101	100	104	99	95	89	82	104
Extreme Minimum Temp. (°F)	-3	8	13	24	35	45	53	50	41	24	16	-3	-3
Days Maximum Temp. ≥ 90°F	0	0	0	1	2	7	16	12	5	0	0	0	43
Days Maximum Temp. ≤ 32°F	1	0	0	0	0	0	0	0	0	0	0	0	1
Days Minimum Temp. ≤ 32°F	15	12	6	1	0	0	0	0	0	1	6	12	53
Days Minimum Temp. ≤ 0°F	0	0	0	0	0	0	0	0	0	0	0	0	0
Heating Degree Days (base 65°F)	*660*	*506*	na	*149*	na	*1*	*0*	*0*	7	*129*	na	na	na
Cooling Degree Days (base 65°F)	na	*2*	na	47	na	na	*466*	na	na	na	na	na	na
Mean Precipitation (in.)	4.24	3.38	4.48	3.06	3.44	4.73	5.80	6.06	5.08	3.27	2.66	3.36	49.56
Days With ≥ 0.1" Precipitation	7	5	6	5	6	6	8	7	5	4	4	5	68
Days With ≥ 1.0" Precipitation	1	1	1	1	1	1	2	2	1	1	1	1	14
Mean Snowfall (in.)	*0.3*	0.6	trace	0.0	0.0	0.0	0.0	0.0	0.0	0.0	0.0	0.1	*1.0*
Days With ≥ 1.0" Snow Depth	*0*	0	0	0	0	0	0	0	0	0	0	0	*0*

Fayetteville *Cumberland County* Elevation: 95 ft.   Latitude: 35° 04' N   Longitude: 78° 52' W

	JAN	FEB	MAR	APR	MAY	JUN	JUL	AUG	SEP	OCT	NOV	DEC	YEAR
Mean Maximum Temp. (°F)	52.3	56.1	64.2	73.7	80.3	87.2	90.6	88.5	83.5	73.9	65.1	56.0	72.6
Mean Temp. (°F)	41.4	44.3	51.8	60.6	68.4	76.1	80.4	78.4	72.9	61.5	52.7	44.7	61.1
Mean Minimum Temp. (°F)	30.4	32.3	39.4	47.4	56.3	64.9	70.0	68.4	62.2	49.1	40.2	33.3	49.5
Extreme Maximum Temp. (°F)	79	83	89	95	97	102	103	105	98	96	88	81	105
Extreme Minimum Temp. (°F)	-1	5	14	22	34	44	53	49	41	26	17	4	-1
Days Maximum Temp. ≥ 90°F	0	0	0	1	3	12	19	15	6	0	0	0	56
Days Maximum Temp. ≤ 32°F	1	0	0	0	0	0	0	0	0	0	0	0	1
Days Minimum Temp. ≤ 32°F	19	16	8	1	0	0	0	0	0	1	8	16	69
Days Minimum Temp. ≤ 0°F	0	0	0	0	0	0	0	0	0	0	0	0	0
Heating Degree Days (base 65°F)	726	580	411	176	45	4	0	0	13	156	373	626	3,110
Cooling Degree Days (base 65°F)	1	1	9	47	155	353	498	421	245	57	7	3	1,797
Mean Precipitation (in.)	4.04	3.49	4.42	3.08	3.31	4.16	5.15	5.19	4.64	3.15	2.88	3.20	46.71
Days With ≥ 0.1" Precipitation	7	6	8	5	7	6	8	8	6	5	5	6	77
Days With ≥ 1.0" Precipitation	1	1	1	1	1	1	2	2	1	1	1	1	14
Mean Snowfall (in.)	0.2	0.4	0.3	0.0	0.0	0.0	0.0	0.0	0.0	0.0	trace	0.3	1.2
Days With ≥ 1.0" Snow Depth	0	0	0	0	0	0	0	0	0	0	0	0	0

Fletcher 3 W *Henderson County* Elevation: 2,066 ft.   Latitude: 35° 26' N   Longitude: 82° 33' W

	JAN	FEB	MAR	APR	MAY	JUN	JUL	AUG	SEP	OCT	NOV	DEC	YEAR
Mean Maximum Temp. (°F)	46.4	50.6	58.4	67.5	74.3	80.6	84.3	82.8	77.6	68.3	58.6	50.4	66.6
Mean Temp. (°F)	35.6	38.7	46.1	53.9	61.7	68.9	72.9	71.7	66.0	55.0	46.3	39.0	54.6
Mean Minimum Temp. (°F)	24.7	26.8	33.7	40.2	49.1	57.0	61.4	60.6	54.3	41.6	34.0	27.6	42.6
Extreme Maximum Temp. (°F)	80	80	83	88	95	94	98	99	93	87	84	77	99
Extreme Minimum Temp. (°F)	-16	-7	-1	21	25	35	42	41	32	18	6	-8	-16
Days Maximum Temp. ≥ 90°F	0	0	0	0	0	2	5	3	0	0	0	0	10
Days Maximum Temp. ≤ 32°F	3	2	0	0	0	0	0	0	0	0	0	2	7
Days Minimum Temp. ≤ 32°F	24	21	15	6	1	0	0	0	0	6	15	22	110
Days Minimum Temp. ≤ 0°F	1	0	0	0	0	0	0	0	0	0	0	0	1
Heating Degree Days (base 65°F)	906	736	579	332	134	21	2	3	59	310	555	799	4,436
Cooling Degree Days (base 65°F)	0	0	1	4	41	149	263	217	85	5	0	0	765
Mean Precipitation (in.)	4.51	4.10	5.09	3.67	4.80	4.82	4.39	4.93	3.95	3.69	4.02	3.87	51.84
Days With ≥ 0.1" Precipitation	7	7	8	6	8	8	8	8	7	6	7	7	87
Days With ≥ 1.0" Precipitation	1	1	2	1	1	1	1	1	1	1	1	1	13
Mean Snowfall (in.)	3.7	2.5	1.9	0.5	trace	0.0	0.0	0.0	0.0	trace	0.3	1.3	10.2
Days With ≥ 1.0" Snow Depth	2	*1*	1	0	0	0	0	0	0	0	0	0	*4*

Forest City 6 SW *Rutherford County*   Elevation: 987 ft.   Latitude: 35° 16' N   Longitude: 81° 56' W

	JAN	FEB	MAR	APR	MAY	JUN	JUL	AUG	SEP	OCT	NOV	DEC	YEAR
Mean Maximum Temp. (°F)	49.6	54.8	62.2	71.6	78.7	85.6	89.6	87.7	81.4	71.9	62.5	53.3	70.7
Mean Temp. (°F)	37.8	41.9	48.8	57.3	65.3	72.9	76.9	75.4	69.1	58.3	49.4	41.0	57.8
Mean Minimum Temp. (°F)	26.0	29.0	35.3	43.0	51.8	60.2	64.2	63.1	56.7	44.6	36.3	28.6	44.9
Extreme Maximum Temp. (°F)	78	82	87	93	97	101	106	107	97	91	82	78	107
Extreme Minimum Temp. (°F)	-8	2	5	23	27	39	50	45	35	25	15	-3	-8
Days Maximum Temp. ≥ 90°F	0	0	0	0	1	9	16	12	4	0	0	0	42
Days Maximum Temp. ≤ 32°F	1	0	0	0	0	0	0	0	0	0	0	1	2
Days Minimum Temp. ≤ 32°F	23	19	12	3	0	0	0	0	0	2	12	21	92
Days Minimum Temp. ≤ 0°F	0	0	0	0	0	0	0	0	0	0	0	0	0
Heating Degree Days (base 65°F)	837	645	498	245	77	6	1	1	30	224	461	738	3,763
Cooling Degree Days (base 65°F)	0	0	3	20	91	257	389	330	159	25	1	1	1,276
Mean Precipitation (in.)	4.94	4.19	5.37	3.59	4.42	4.07	3.92	4.44	4.00	4.71	4.01	3.67	51.33
Days With ≥ 0.1" Precipitation	7	7	8	6	8	7	8	6	6	5	6	7	81
Days With ≥ 1.0" Precipitation	2	1	1	1	1	1	1	1	1	2	1	1	14
Mean Snowfall (in.)	2.6	1.5	1.0	trace	0.0	0.0	0.0	0.0	0.0	0.0	trace	0.2	5.3
Days With ≥ 1.0" Snow Depth	2	1	1	0	0	0	0	0	0	0	0	0	4

Franklin 3 W *Macon County*   Elevation: 2,168 ft.   Latitude: 35° 11' N   Longitude: 83° 25' W

	JAN	FEB	MAR	APR	MAY	JUN	JUL	AUG	SEP	OCT	NOV	DEC	YEAR
Mean Maximum Temp. (°F)	49.2	53.7	61.4	70.1	76.6	82.4	85.8	84.5	79.5	70.8	61.0	52.5	69.0
Mean Temp. (°F)	37.4	40.7	48.0	55.2	63.0	69.9	74.0	73.1	67.7	56.8	47.6	40.3	56.1
Mean Minimum Temp. (°F)	25.5	27.7	34.5	40.3	49.3	57.4	62.2	61.7	55.8	42.8	34.1	28.1	43.3
Extreme Maximum Temp. (°F)	75	78	84	91	91	96	98	99	98	88	82	73	99
Extreme Minimum Temp. (°F)	-15	-2	-5	17	25	34	49	47	32	20	6	-5	-15
Days Maximum Temp. ≥ 90°F	0	0	0	0	0	2	7	4	1	0	0	0	14
Days Maximum Temp. ≤ 32°F	1	1	0	0	0	0	0	0	0	0	0	1	3
Days Minimum Temp. ≤ 32°F	22	19	14	7	1	0	0	0	0	6	15	21	105
Days Minimum Temp. ≤ 0°F	1	0	0	0	0	0	0	0	0	0	0	0	1
Heating Degree Days (base 65°F)	848	679	521	294	104	14	0	1	39	257	517	758	4,032
Cooling Degree Days (base 65°F)	0	0	0	8	49	174	297	255	112	11	0	0	906
Mean Precipitation (in.)	5.30	4.92	5.76	4.01	4.92	4.56	4.12	4.50	3.93	3.48	4.47	4.54	54.51
Days With ≥ 0.1" Precipitation	9	7	9	7	9	9	9	8	7	6	7	8	95
Days With ≥ 1.0" Precipitation	2	1	2	1	1	1	1	1	1	1	1	1	14
Mean Snowfall (in.)	2.4	2.0	0.8	0.5	0.0	0.0	0.0	0.0	0.0	0.0	0.1	0.6	6.4
Days With ≥ 1.0" Snow Depth	2	1	0	0	0	0	0	0	0	0	0	0	3

Gastonia *Gaston County*   Elevation: 698 ft.   Latitude: 35° 16' N   Longitude: 81° 08' W

	JAN	FEB	MAR	APR	MAY	JUN	JUL	AUG	SEP	OCT	NOV	DEC	YEAR
Mean Maximum Temp. (°F)	51.3	56.3	64.4	73.2	79.9	86.1	89.7	88.2	82.7	72.9	63.2	54.5	71.9
Mean Temp. (°F)	41.0	44.7	52.3	60.3	68.1	75.3	79.3	78.0	72.2	61.1	51.6	43.9	60.7
Mean Minimum Temp. (°F)	30.6	32.9	40.1	47.4	56.3	64.5	68.8	67.8	61.6	49.3	40.1	33.4	49.4
Extreme Maximum Temp. (°F)	79	80	87	92	94	100	102	104	98	91	85	80	104
Extreme Minimum Temp. (°F)	-5	10	-1	25	32	43	54	49	39	26	11	3	-5
Days Maximum Temp. ≥ 90°F	0	0	0	0	2	8	17	13	5	0	0	0	45
Days Maximum Temp. ≤ 32°F	1	0	0	0	0	0	0	0	0	0	0	0	1
Days Minimum Temp. ≤ 32°F	17	14	8	1	0	0	0	0	0	1	8	16	65
Days Minimum Temp. ≤ 0°F	0	0	0	0	0	0	0	0	0	0	0	0	0
Heating Degree Days (base 65°F)	737	569	394	173	40	3	0	0	15	158	399	646	3,134
Cooling Degree Days (base 65°F)	0	1	7	39	153	340	473	424	235	47	3	1	1,723
Mean Precipitation (in.)	4.24	3.80	4.29	2.86	3.82	3.66	3.73	4.48	3.94	3.90	3.12	3.59	45.43
Days With ≥ 0.1" Precipitation	7	6	7	5	6	6	7	6	5	5	6	6	72
Days With ≥ 1.0" Precipitation	1	1	1	1	1	1	1	1	1	1	1	1	12
Mean Snowfall (in.)	0.2	0.2	0.0	0.0	0.0	0.0	0.0	0.0	0.0	0.0	0.0	trace	0.4
Days With ≥ 1.0" Snow Depth	0	0	0	0	0	0	0	0	0	0	0	0	0

Goldsboro Seymour Johnson AFB *Wayne County*   Elevation: 108 ft.   Latitude: 35° 20' N   Longitude: 77° 58' W

	JAN	FEB	MAR	APR	MAY	JUN	JUL	AUG	SEP	OCT	NOV	DEC	YEAR
Mean Maximum Temp. (°F)	52.5	55.9	64.0	73.6	80.7	87.2	90.7	88.8	83.8	74.0	65.3	56.4	72.7
Mean Temp. (°F)	42.6	45.2	52.8	61.7	69.6	76.8	80.9	79.3	73.8	62.4	53.5	45.9	62.0
Mean Minimum Temp. (°F)	32.7	34.4	41.6	49.7	58.5	66.4	71.1	69.8	63.7	50.7	41.8	35.4	51.3
Extreme Maximum Temp. (°F)	80	86	90	95	99	102	106	106	100	95	87	86	106
Extreme Minimum Temp. (°F)	5	5	10	29	38	45	51	51	42	26	16	1	1
Days Maximum Temp. ≥ 90°F	0	0	0	1	4	12	19	15	7	0	0	0	58
Days Maximum Temp. ≤ 32°F	2	0	0	0	0	0	0	0	0	0	0	0	2
Days Minimum Temp. ≤ 32°F	15	13	5	0	0	0	0	0	0	1	6	13	53
Days Minimum Temp. ≤ 0°F	0	0	0	0	0	0	0	0	0	0	0	0	0
Heating Degree Days (base 65°F)	690	555	385	156	33	2	0	0	10	138	352	588	2,909
Cooling Degree Days (base 65°F)	2	4	15	65	197	380	524	456	276	67	11	4	2,001
Mean Precipitation (in.)	4.51	3.75	4.59	3.42	3.83	3.87	5.52	5.51	5.46	3.25	2.94	3.42	50.07
Days With ≥ 0.1" Precipitation	8	7	7	6	7	6	8	8	6	5	5	6	79
Days With ≥ 1.0" Precipitation	1	1	1	1	1	1	2	1	2	1	1	1	14
Mean Snowfall (in.)	0.8	1.4	0.9	trace	0.0	0.0	0.0	0.0	0.0	0.0	trace	0.5	3.6
Days With ≥ 1.0" Snow Depth	1	1	0	0	0	0	0	0	0	0	0	0	2

Grandfather Mountain *Avery County*   Elevation: 5,298 ft.   Latitude: 36° 07' N   Longitude: 81° 50' W

	JAN	FEB	MAR	APR	MAY	JUN	JUL	AUG	SEP	OCT	NOV	DEC	YEAR
Mean Maximum Temp. (°F)	35.6	38.2	44.9	53.8	60.5	66.1	69.8	68.3	63.3	54.9	46.4	39.9	53.5
Mean Temp. (°F)	27.8	30.2	36.7	45.2	53.1	59.5	63.4	62.2	57.0	47.8	39.1	32.2	46.2
Mean Minimum Temp. (°F)	19.9	22.0	28.5	36.6	45.5	52.7	56.9	56.1	50.8	40.7	31.8	24.5	38.8
Extreme Maximum Temp. (°F)	62	64	72	74	78	78	82	83	78	75	68	62	83
Extreme Minimum Temp. (°F)	-32	-14	-9	5	21	32	42	36	27	16	-8	-21	-32
Days Maximum Temp. ≥ 90°F	0	0	0	0	0	0	0	0	0	0	0	0	0
Days Maximum Temp. ≤ 32°F	11	8	4	1	0	0	0	0	0	0	3	7	34
Days Minimum Temp. ≤ 32°F	25	22	18	10	2	0	0	0	0	7	15	23	122
Days Minimum Temp. ≤ 0°F	3	2	0	0	0	0	0	0	0	0	0	1	6
Heating Degree Days (base 65°F)	1,145	976	869	587	364	167	74	98	235	527	769	1,010	6,821
Cooling Degree Days (base 65°F)	0	0	0	0	1	8	34	21	3	0	0	0	67
Mean Precipitation (in.)	4.67	4.83	5.76	4.97	6.13	6.61	5.41	5.72	5.69	4.96	4.66	4.05	63.46
Days With ≥ 0.1" Precipitation	10	9	10	8	11	10	10	9	8	6	7	8	106
Days With ≥ 1.0" Precipitation	1	1	1	1	2	2	1	1	2	2	1	1	16
Mean Snowfall (in.)	15.2	14.6	9.9	4.4	0.5	0.0	0.0	0.0	trace	0.5	3.1	9.6	57.8
Days With ≥ 1.0" Snow Depth	10	12	6	2	0	0	0	0	0	0	2	7	39

Greenville *Pitt County*   Elevation: 29 ft.   Latitude: 35° 38' N   Longitude: 77° 24' W

	JAN	FEB	MAR	APR	MAY	JUN	JUL	AUG	SEP	OCT	NOV	DEC	YEAR
Mean Maximum Temp. (°F)	51.9	55.6	63.7	73.1	79.9	86.3	90.0	88.2	83.1	73.5	64.9	56.0	72.2
Mean Temp. (°F)	41.4	44.3	51.9	60.6	68.3	75.4	79.7	78.0	72.5	61.3	52.7	44.8	60.9
Mean Minimum Temp. (°F)	30.8	33.0	40.0	48.0	56.7	64.5	69.4	67.8	61.9	49.0	40.4	33.7	49.6
Extreme Maximum Temp. (°F)	80	84	91	96	97	101	104	104	100	95	87	82	104
Extreme Minimum Temp. (°F)	-4	4	15	27	37	44	51	49	40	25	14	1	-4
Days Maximum Temp. ≥ 90°F	0	0	0	1	3	10	17	13	5	0	0	0	49
Days Maximum Temp. ≤ 32°F	1	0	0	0	0	0	0	0	0	0	0	0	1
Days Minimum Temp. ≤ 32°F	18	15	8	1	0	0	0	0	0	1	7	15	65
Days Minimum Temp. ≤ 0°F	0	0	0	0	0	0	0	0	0	0	0	0	0
Heating Degree Days (base 65°F)	727	580	413	179	45	3	0	0	12	159	375	620	3,113
Cooling Degree Days (base 65°F)	1	3	12	51	159	339	487	411	242	57	10	3	1,775
Mean Precipitation (in.)	4.33	3.54	4.05	3.20	4.04	4.34	5.22	5.80	5.23	3.36	2.80	3.25	49.16
Days With ≥ 0.1" Precipitation	8	6	7	6	7	7	7	7	6	5	5	7	78
Days With ≥ 1.0" Precipitation	1	1	1	1	1	1	2	2	2	1	0	1	14
Mean Snowfall (in.)	0.7	1.5	0.8	trace	0.0	0.0	0.0	0.0	0.0	0.0	0.0	0.2	3.2
Days With ≥ 1.0" Snow Depth	0	1	0	0	0	0	0	0	0	0	0	0	1

Hamlet *Richmond County*   Elevation: 347 ft.   Latitude: 34° 53' N   Longitude: 79° 42' W

	JAN	FEB	MAR	APR	MAY	JUN	JUL	AUG	SEP	OCT	NOV	DEC	YEAR
Mean Maximum Temp. (°F)	52.6	57.6	65.9	75.2	81.9	88.2	91.4	89.2	84.1	74.4	65.1	56.3	73.5
Mean Temp. (°F)	40.7	44.3	52.0	60.7	68.6	75.7	79.7	77.9	72.3	61.1	51.5	43.8	60.7
Mean Minimum Temp. (°F)	28.8	31.1	38.2	46.1	55.3	63.3	67.9	66.5	60.3	47.6	38.0	31.3	47.8
Extreme Maximum Temp. (°F)	80	84	94	95	99	102	106	107	100	96	86	81	107
Extreme Minimum Temp. (°F)	-6	4	7	17	27	32	50	41	35	24	11	3	-6
Days Maximum Temp. ≥ 90°F	0	0	0	1	4	13	21	16	7	1	0	0	63
Days Maximum Temp. ≤ 32°F	1	0	0	0	0	0	0	0	0	0	0	0	1
Days Minimum Temp. ≤ 32°F	20	17	10	2	0	0	0	0	0	2	11	18	80
Days Minimum Temp. ≤ 0°F	0	0	0	0	0	0	0	0	0	0	0	0	0
Heating Degree Days (base 65°F)	748	578	404	173	38	4	0	0	15	166	403	651	3,180
Cooling Degree Days (base 65°F)	0	1	9	47	153	338	474	396	221	50	5	1	1,695
Mean Precipitation (in.)	4.26	3.64	4.46	2.96	3.77	4.35	6.32	4.32	4.32	3.89	3.30	3.29	48.88
Days With ≥ 0.1" Precipitation	8	7	8	5	7	7	9	7	6	5	6	7	82
Days With ≥ 1.0" Precipitation	1	1	1	1	1	1	2	1	1	1	1	1	13
Mean Snowfall (in.)	0.2	0.4	0.6	0.0	0.0	0.0	0.0	0.0	0.0	0.0	0.0	0.2	1.4
Days With ≥ 1.0" Snow Depth	0	0	0	0	0	0	0	0	0	0	0	0	0

Hendersonville 1 NE *Henderson County*   Elevation: 2,158 ft.   Latitude: 35° 20' N   Longitude: 82° 27' W

	JAN	FEB	MAR	APR	MAY	JUN	JUL	AUG	SEP	OCT	NOV	DEC	YEAR
Mean Maximum Temp. (°F)	48.0	52.0	60.1	69.1	75.4	81.4	84.9	83.2	77.9	68.7	59.3	51.5	67.6
Mean Temp. (°F)	37.5	40.7	48.1	55.9	63.5	70.3	74.4	73.0	67.2	56.7	47.7	40.7	56.3
Mean Minimum Temp. (°F)	27.0	29.2	36.0	42.7	51.6	59.3	63.7	62.7	56.5	44.6	36.2	30.0	45.0
Extreme Maximum Temp. (°F)	76	79	84	91	91	96	98	101	94	87	81	77	101
Extreme Minimum Temp. (°F)	-14	0	-2	22	24	39	48	44	33	21	4	-4	-14
Days Maximum Temp. ≥ 90°F	0	0	0	0	0	2	6	3	1	0	0	0	12
Days Maximum Temp. ≤ 32°F	2	1	0	0	0	0	0	0	0	0	0	1	4
Days Minimum Temp. ≤ 32°F	21	18	12	4	0	0	0	0	0	3	12	20	90
Days Minimum Temp. ≤ 0°F	0	0	0	0	0	0	0	0	0	0	0	0	0
Heating Degree Days (base 65°F)	846	681	518	275	93	13	1	2	43	263	512	746	3,993
Cooling Degree Days (base 65°F)	0	0	0	1	11	60	199	326	272	118	15	0	1,002
Mean Precipitation (in.)	5.13	4.55	5.89	4.06	4.92	4.76	4.52	5.50	4.19	4.27	4.56	4.25	56.60
Days With ≥ 0.1" Precipitation	7	7	8	6	8	8	8	8	6	6	6	7	85
Days With ≥ 1.0" Precipitation	2	1	2	2	1	1	1	1	1	1	2	1	16
Mean Snowfall (in.)	3.4	2.3	2.0	0.3	0.0	0.0	0.0	0.0	0.0	0.0	0.3	0.7	9.0
Days With ≥ 1.0" Snow Depth	1	1	0	0	0	0	0	0	0	0	0	0	2

Hickory Regional Airport *Burke County*   Elevation: 1,141 ft.   Latitude: 35° 44' N   Longitude: 81° 23' W

	JAN	FEB	MAR	APR	MAY	JUN	JUL	AUG	SEP	OCT	NOV	DEC	YEAR
Mean Maximum Temp. (°F)	48.0	52.5	60.7	70.2	77.1	83.8	87.6	85.8	79.8	70.2	60.5	51.8	69.0
Mean Temp. (°F)	38.3	41.8	49.7	58.3	66.0	73.6	77.6	76.1	69.9	59.1	49.8	41.9	58.5
Mean Minimum Temp. (°F)	28.6	31.1	38.6	46.4	54.9	63.3	67.6	66.4	60.0	47.8	39.1	31.9	48.0
Extreme Maximum Temp. (°F)	78	83	86	92	96	100	102	102	95	91	84	78	102
Extreme Minimum Temp. (°F)	-8	2	9	20	30	41	52	45	40	27	10	2	-8
Days Maximum Temp. ≥ 90°F	0	0	0	0	1	5	12	8	2	0	0	0	28
Days Maximum Temp. ≤ 32°F	2	1	0	0	0	0	0	0	0	0	0	1	4
Days Minimum Temp. ≤ 32°F	20	17	8	2	0	0	0	0	0	1	8	17	73
Days Minimum Temp. ≤ 0°F	0	0	0	0	0	0	0	0	0	0	0	0	0
Heating Degree Days (base 65°F)	820	648	471	221	64	5	0	1	25	205	451	709	3,620
Cooling Degree Days (base 65°F)	0	0	4	28	106	288	427	360	176	32	2	0	1,423
Mean Precipitation (in.)	4.05	3.94	5.02	3.55	4.48	4.80	4.23	4.14	4.15	3.84	3.71	3.59	49.50
Days With ≥ 0.1" Precipitation	7	6	8	6	8	7	7	7	6	5	6	6	79
Days With ≥ 1.0" Precipitation	1	1	2	1	2	1	1	1	1	1	1	1	14
Mean Snowfall (in.)	3.7	2.2	1.6	0.2	trace	0.0	0.0	0.0	0.0	0.0	trace	0.7	8.4
Days With ≥ 1.0" Snow Depth	3	2	1	0	0	0	0	0	0	0	0	0	6

High Point *Guilford County*   Elevation: 898 ft.   Latitude: 35° 58' N   Longitude: 79° 58' W

	JAN	FEB	MAR	APR	MAY	JUN	JUL	AUG	SEP	OCT	NOV	DEC	YEAR
Mean Maximum Temp. (°F)	49.7	54.5	62.8	72.5	79.1	85.5	89.1	87.4	81.8	71.9	62.0	53.1	70.8
Mean Temp. (°F)	39.6	43.3	50.9	59.6	67.1	74.3	78.3	76.8	70.9	60.1	50.9	43.0	59.6
Mean Minimum Temp. (°F)	29.5	31.9	38.9	46.7	55.1	63.1	67.5	66.2	60.0	48.2	39.9	32.8	48.3
Extreme Maximum Temp. (°F)	78	85	88	91	95	99	102	104	98	92	89	80	104
Extreme Minimum Temp. (°F)	-7	2	7	22	33	39	49	46	38	24	14	0	-7
Days Maximum Temp. ≥ 90°F	0	0	0	0	1	7	15	11	3	0	0	0	37
Days Maximum Temp. ≤ 32°F	1	0	0	0	0	0	0	0	0	0	0	1	2
Days Minimum Temp. ≤ 32°F	19	16	8	2	0	0	0	0	0	1	8	16	70
Days Minimum Temp. ≤ 0°F	0	0	0	0	0	0	0	0	0	0	0	0	0
Heating Degree Days (base 65°F)	780	608	437	192	51	5	0	0	22	182	420	676	3,373
Cooling Degree Days (base 65°F)	0	1	6	36	126	302	431	370	196	38	2	0	1,508
Mean Precipitation (in.)	4.02	3.51	4.27	3.65	4.26	3.87	4.13	4.52	3.79	3.65	3.25	3.42	46.34
Days With ≥ 0.1" Precipitation	7	6	7	6	8	7	7	6	5	5	6	7	77
Days With ≥ 1.0" Precipitation	1	1	1	1	1	1	1	1	1	1	1	1	12
Mean Snowfall (in.)	1.8	1.7	0.8	trace	0.0	0.0	0.0	0.0	0.0	0.0	trace	0.7	5.0
Days With ≥ 1.0" Snow Depth	1	1	0	0	0	0	0	0	0	0	0	0	2

Highlands *Macon County*   Elevation: 3,838 ft.   Latitude: 35° 03' N   Longitude: 83° 11' W

	JAN	FEB	MAR	APR	MAY	JUN	JUL	AUG	SEP	OCT	NOV	DEC	YEAR
Mean Maximum Temp. (°F)	42.5	46.1	54.3	62.6	69.2	74.7	77.9	76.4	71.4	62.1	52.7	45.3	61.3
Mean Temp. (°F)	33.3	35.9	43.3	50.8	58.3	64.6	68.2	67.1	61.9	51.7	42.9	36.4	51.2
Mean Minimum Temp. (°F)	24.0	25.6	32.4	38.9	47.3	54.4	58.5	57.7	52.2	41.2	33.0	27.4	41.0
Extreme Maximum Temp. (°F)	68	73	77	83	86	88	91	90	87	80	72	67	91
Extreme Minimum Temp. (°F)	-19	-6	0	13	28	35	43	44	30	20	3	-11	-19
Days Maximum Temp. ≥ 90°F	0	0	0	0	0	0	0	0	0	0	0	0	0
Days Maximum Temp. ≤ 32°F	4	2	1	0	0	0	0	0	0	0	0	3	10
Days Minimum Temp. ≤ 32°F	23	21	16	8	1	0	0	0	0	6	15	22	112
Days Minimum Temp. ≤ 0°F	1	0	0	0	0	0	0	0	0	0	0	0	1
Heating Degree Days (base 65°F)	976	816	665	422	210	56	12	18	113	408	657	881	5,234
Cooling Degree Days (base 65°F)	0	0	0	0	9	51	122	80	21	1	0	0	284
Mean Precipitation (in.)	7.97	7.05	8.93	6.38	7.93	7.23	6.69	6.64	6.78	6.51	8.08	7.66	87.85
Days With ≥ 0.1" Precipitation	9	8	10	8	10	10	11	10	8	7	8	9	108
Days With ≥ 1.0" Precipitation	3	2	3	2	2	2	2	2	2	2	3	2	27
Mean Snowfall (in.)	5.7	4.3	2.8	0.9	0.2	0.0	0.0	0.0	0.0	trace	0.4	1.9	16.2
Days With ≥ 1.0" Snow Depth	6	3	1	0	0	0	0	0	0	0	0	2	12

Jackson *Northampton County*   Elevation: 127 ft.   Latitude: 36° 24' N   Longitude: 77° 25' W

	JAN	FEB	MAR	APR	MAY	JUN	JUL	AUG	SEP	OCT	NOV	DEC	YEAR
Mean Maximum Temp. (°F)	50.0	54.2	62.3	72.4	79.2	86.4	90.1	88.5	83.2	72.4	63.3	54.0	71.3
Mean Temp. (°F)	39.6	42.4	50.1	58.9	66.9	74.8	79.1	77.4	71.7	60.0	51.3	43.1	59.6
Mean Minimum Temp. (°F)	29.1	30.7	37.9	45.3	54.6	63.2	68.0	66.3	60.1	47.6	39.2	32.1	47.8
Extreme Maximum Temp. (°F)	79	84	92	97	97	100	104	105	104	90	86	81	105
Extreme Minimum Temp. (°F)	-8	-4	12	19	34	44	50	44	40	24	15	-1	-8
Days Maximum Temp. ≥ 90°F	0	0	0	1	2	11	18	14	5	0	0	0	51
Days Maximum Temp. ≤ 32°F	2	1	0	0	0	0	0	0	0	0	0	0	4
Days Minimum Temp. ≤ 32°F	20	17	10	2	0	0	0	0	0	1	9	17	76
Days Minimum Temp. ≤ 0°F	0	0	0	0	0	0	0	0	0	0	0	0	0
Heating Degree Days (base 65°F)	781	632	464	216	60	5	0	1	16	189	413	674	3,451
Cooling Degree Days (base 65°F)	0	0	7	38	128	320	464	392	216	41	5	1	1,612
Mean Precipitation (in.)	4.16	3.30	4.30	3.16	4.15	3.68	4.96	3.95	4.29	3.43	3.03	3.25	45.66
Days With ≥ 0.1" Precipitation	8	7	8	6	7	7	7	6	5	4	5	6	76
Days With ≥ 1.0" Precipitation	1	1	1	1	1	1	2	1	1	1	1	1	13
Mean Snowfall (in.)	1.7	2.6	1.5	0.2	0.0	0.0	0.0	0.0	0.0	0.0	0.0	0.5	6.5
Days With ≥ 1.0" Snow Depth	1	2	0	0	0	0	0	0	0	0	0	1	4

Jackson Springs 5 WNW *Montgomery County*   Elevation: 728 ft.   Latitude: 35° 13' N   Longitude: 79° 44' W

	JAN	FEB	MAR	APR	MAY	JUN	JUL	AUG	SEP	OCT	NOV	DEC	YEAR
Mean Maximum Temp. (°F)	50.2	54.4	62.7	72.4	79.0	86.0	89.6	87.6	82.6	72.5	63.1	54.0	71.2
Mean Temp. (°F)	40.1	43.2	51.0	59.9	67.5	74.9	78.8	77.1	71.7	60.8	52.1	43.7	60.1
Mean Minimum Temp. (°F)	29.9	32.0	39.1	47.4	55.8	63.7	67.9	66.6	60.8	49.0	41.0	33.4	48.9
Extreme Maximum Temp. (°F)	77	81	88	93	96	103	103	107	99	93	86	79	107
Extreme Minimum Temp. (°F)	-5	3	10	22	34	45	52	50	39	28	15	3	-5
Days Maximum Temp. ≥ 90°F	0	0	0	1	2	9	16	12	5	0	0	0	45
Days Maximum Temp. ≤ 32°F	2	1	0	0	0	0	0	0	0	0	0	1	4
Days Minimum Temp. ≤ 32°F	19	15	8	1	0	0	0	0	0	1	6	15	65
Days Minimum Temp. ≤ 0°F	0	0	0	0	0	0	0	0	0	0	0	0	0
Heating Degree Days (base 65°F)	766	610	435	191	52	5	0	0	17	166	388	654	3,284
Cooling Degree Days (base 65°F)	0	1	7	42	143	321	451	385	215	47	5	1	1,618
Mean Precipitation (in.)	4.47	3.65	4.66	3.13	3.61	4.02	5.18	4.40	4.14	3.99	3.26	3.35	47.86
Days With ≥ 0.1" Precipitation	8	6	8	6	6	6	8	7	5	5	5	7	77
Days With ≥ 1.0" Precipitation	1	1	1	1	1	1	2	1	1	2	1	1	14
Mean Snowfall (in.)	*0.7*	1.0	0.7	0.0	0.0	0.0	0.0	0.0	0.0	0.0	0.0	0.5	*2.9*
Days With ≥ 1.0" Snow Depth	*0*	0	0	0	0	0	0	0	0	0	0	0	*0*

Jefferson 2 E *Ashe County*   Elevation: 2,769 ft.   Latitude: 36° 25' N   Longitude: 81° 26' W

	JAN	FEB	MAR	APR	MAY	JUN	JUL	AUG	SEP	OCT	NOV	DEC	YEAR
Mean Maximum Temp. (°F)	42.9	46.2	54.4	63.6	70.8	77.1	80.9	79.6	73.8	64.3	55.2	47.2	63.0
Mean Temp. (°F)	32.7	35.4	42.9	50.9	58.6	65.8	69.9	68.5	62.5	51.7	43.4	36.2	51.6
Mean Minimum Temp. (°F)	22.6	24.6	31.4	38.1	46.4	54.3	58.8	57.4	51.1	39.1	31.6	25.2	40.1
Extreme Maximum Temp. (°F)	70	74	81	84	90	90	94	96	94	82	77	74	96
Extreme Minimum Temp. (°F)	-15	-13	2	13	22	28	36	33	26	16	-5	-9	-15
Days Maximum Temp. ≥ 90°F	0	0	0	0	0	0	1	1	0	0	0	0	2
Days Maximum Temp. ≤ 32°F	5	4	1	0	0	0	0	0	0	0	0	3	13
Days Minimum Temp. ≤ 32°F	25	22	17	9	2	0	0	0	1	9	17	24	126
Days Minimum Temp. ≤ 0°F	1	0	0	0	0	0	0	0	0	0	0	0	1
Heating Degree Days (base 65°F)	992	828	678	419	205	48	9	14	114	407	641	884	5,239
Cooling Degree Days (base 65°F)	0	0	0	2	15	82	179	133	44	2	0	0	457
Mean Precipitation (in.)	3.98	3.77	4.61	3.87	4.92	4.28	4.47	4.31	3.86	3.56	3.80	3.26	48.69
Days With ≥ 0.1" Precipitation	7	6	8	7	8	7	8	7	6	5	6	6	81
Days With ≥ 1.0" Precipitation	1	1	1	1	1	1	1	1	1	1	1	1	12
Mean Snowfall (in.)	5.2	5.6	3.1	0.5	0.0	0.0	0.0	0.0	0.0	0.1	0.8	2.8	18.1
Days With ≥ 1.0" Snow Depth	5	5	1	0	0	0	0	0	0	0	1	3	15

Kinston 5 SE *Lenoir County*   Elevation: 52 ft.   Latitude: 35° 13' N   Longitude: 77° 32' W

	JAN	FEB	MAR	APR	MAY	JUN	JUL	AUG	SEP	OCT	NOV	DEC	YEAR
Mean Maximum Temp. (°F)	52.2	55.9	63.8	73.1	79.7	86.2	89.6	87.9	83.2	73.8	65.4	56.1	72.2
Mean Temp. (°F)	41.5	44.1	51.5	59.7	67.3	74.6	78.6	76.9	71.8	60.9	52.9	44.7	60.4
Mean Minimum Temp. (°F)	30.7	32.2	39.2	46.4	54.9	62.9	67.6	65.8	60.2	47.9	40.3	33.1	48.4
Extreme Maximum Temp. (°F)	80	84	90	95	96	100	104	104	100	95	86	82	104
Extreme Minimum Temp. (°F)	-2	4	15	22	34	42	47	42	35	23	17	1	-2
Days Maximum Temp. ≥ 90°F	0	0	0	1	3	9	17	13	5	0	0	0	48
Days Maximum Temp. ≤ 32°F	2	0	0	0	0	0	0	0	0	0	0	0	2
Days Minimum Temp. ≤ 32°F	18	16	8	2	0	0	0	0	0	1	8	16	69
Days Minimum Temp. ≤ 0°F	0	0	0	0	0	0	0	0	0	0	0	0	0
Heating Degree Days (base 65°F)	723	587	422	195	57	5	0	0	16	168	369	627	3,169
Cooling Degree Days (base 65°F)	1	2	10	43	142	316	449	376	220	50	9	3	1,621
Mean Precipitation (in.)	4.37	3.47	4.22	3.38	4.06	4.64	5.85	5.55	5.35	3.64	2.78	3.56	50.87
Days With ≥ 0.1" Precipitation	8	6	7	6	7	7	8	8	6	5	5	6	79
Days With ≥ 1.0" Precipitation	1	1	1	1	1	1	2	2	1	1	1	1	14
Mean Snowfall (in.)	0.3	0.6	0.8	0.0	0.0	0.0	0.0	0.0	0.0	0.0	trace	0.4	2.1
Days With ≥ 1.0" Snow Depth	0	0	0	0	0	0	0	0	0	0	0	0	0

Kinston Agr. Research Center *Lenoir County*   Elevation: 59 ft.   Latitude: 35° 22' N   Longitude: 77° 33' W

	JAN	FEB	MAR	APR	MAY	JUN	JUL	AUG	SEP	OCT	NOV	DEC	YEAR
Mean Maximum Temp. (°F)	54.7	58.7	66.5	75.0	82.0	87.6	90.7	89.3	84.5	75.8	67.7	58.6	74.3
Mean Temp. (°F)	43.8	46.6	53.7	61.4	69.3	75.9	80.1	78.4	73.3	63.1	55.2	47.4	62.4
Mean Minimum Temp. (°F)	32.8	34.4	40.7	47.8	56.6	64.2	69.4	67.5	62.0	50.5	42.7	36.2	50.4
Extreme Maximum Temp. (°F)	78	84	89	95	100	101	103	103	102	96	87	83	103
Extreme Minimum Temp. (°F)	-2	3	8	24	35	42	52	47	38	24	17	6	-2
Days Maximum Temp. ≥ 90°F	0	0	0	1	4	12	19	16	6	0	0	0	58
Days Maximum Temp. ≤ 32°F	1	0	0	0	0	0	0	0	0	0	0	0	1
Days Minimum Temp. ≤ 32°F	15	13	7	1	0	0	0	0	0	1	6	13	56
Days Minimum Temp. ≤ 0°F	0	0	0	0	0	0	0	0	0	0	0	0	0
Heating Degree Days (base 65°F)	652	516	355	156	31	3	0	0	8	121	304	542	2,688
Cooling Degree Days (base 65°F)	1	2	13	58	185	363	499	428	261	79	17	5	1,911
Mean Precipitation (in.)	4.28	3.56	4.27	3.07	3.82	4.44	5.47	5.31	5.42	3.42	2.88	3.32	49.26
Days With ≥ 0.1" Precipatation	8	6	7	5	7	7	9	7	5	5	5	6	77
Days With ≥ 1.0" Precipitation	1	1	1	1	1	2	2	2	2	1	1	1	16
Mean Snowfall (in.)	0.2	0.3	0.3	0.0	0.0	0.0	0.0	0.0	0.0	0.0	0.0	0.3	1.1
Days With ≥ 1.0" Snow Depth	0	*0*	0	0	0	0	0	0	0	0	0	0	*0*

Laurinburg *Scotland County*   Elevation: 209 ft.   Latitude: 34° 45' N   Longitude: 79° 27' W

	JAN	FEB	MAR	APR	MAY	JUN	JUL	AUG	SEP	OCT	NOV	DEC	YEAR
Mean Maximum Temp. (°F)	54.2	59.0	67.0	76.3	82.9	88.9	91.7	89.7	84.9	75.6	66.4	57.4	74.5
Mean Temp. (°F)	43.2	46.7	54.2	62.4	70.1	77.0	80.6	79.0	73.7	62.9	54.1	46.2	62.5
Mean Minimum Temp. (°F)	32.1	34.3	41.3	48.4	57.3	65.1	69.5	68.3	62.5	50.2	41.8	35.0	50.5
Extreme Maximum Temp. (°F)	79	84	91	96	98	104	105	107	100	97	87	81	107
Extreme Minimum Temp. (°F)	-3	6	8	26	34	46	55	50	41	26	15	6	-3
Days Maximum Temp. ≥ 90°F	0	0	0	1	5	15	22	17	8	1	0	0	69
Days Maximum Temp. ≤ 32°F	1	0	0	0	0	0	0	0	0	0	0	0	1
Days Minimum Temp. ≤ 32°F	16	13	6	1	0	0	0	0	0	1	7	14	58
Days Minimum Temp. ≤ 0°F	0	0	0	0	0	0	0	0	0	0	0	0	0
Heating Degree Days (base 65°F)	671	513	342	138	27	2	0	0	9	125	333	578	2,738
Cooling Degree Days (base 65°F)	1	2	14	59	193	378	506	438	262	69	11	3	1,936
Mean Precipitation (in.)	4.17	3.64	4.51	2.74	3.34	4.90	5.47	4.86	4.65	3.51	2.97	3.31	48.07
Days With ≥ 0.1" Precipitation	7	6	7	5	6	7	8	7	6	5	5	6	75
Days With ≥ 1.0" Precipitation	1	1	1	1	1	1	1	2	1	1	1	1	13
Mean Snowfall (in.)	0.5	0.9	0.6	trace	0.0	0.0	0.0	0.0	0.0	0.0	trace	0.3	2.3
Days With ≥ 1.0" Snow Depth	1	0	0	0	0	0	0	0	0	0	0	0	1

Lenoir *Caldwell County*   Elevation: 1,197 ft.   Latitude: 35° 55' N   Longitude: 81° 32' W

	JAN	FEB	MAR	APR	MAY	JUN	JUL	AUG	SEP	OCT	NOV	DEC	YEAR
Mean Maximum Temp. (°F)	49.7	54.3	62.6	72.1	78.7	84.7	88.4	86.7	81.2	72.0	61.9	53.4	70.5
Mean Temp. (°F)	38.5	42.0	49.7	58.1	65.7	73.0	77.0	75.5	69.6	59.0	49.4	41.7	58.3
Mean Minimum Temp. (°F)	27.2	29.7	36.7	44.0	52.8	61.2	65.5	64.4	58.0	45.9	36.9	30.0	46.0
Extreme Maximum Temp. (°F)	80	83	88	92	96	99	101	105	95	90	85	78	105
Extreme Minimum Temp. (°F)	-7	-2	6	20	29	37	48	46	37	24	8	0	-7
Days Maximum Temp. ≥ 90°F	0	0	0	0	1	6	14	9	3	0	0	0	33
Days Maximum Temp. ≤ 32°F	1	0	0	0	0	0	0	0	0	0	0	0	1
Days Minimum Temp. ≤ 32°F	22	19	11	3	0	0	0	0	0	2	11	20	88
Days Minimum Temp. ≤ 0°F	0	0	0	0	0	0	0	0	0	0	0	0	0
Heating Degree Days (base 65°F)	815	644	472	224	67	6	0	0	27	205	462	715	3,637
Cooling Degree Days (base 65°F)	0	0	4	22	106	275	407	353	174	29	1	0	1,371
Mean Precipitation (in.)	3.86	3.79	4.72	3.97	4.70	4.51	4.44	4.13	4.23	3.83	3.58	3.51	49.27
Days With ≥ 0.1" Precipitation	7	6	8	6	8	7	8	7	6	5	6	6	80
Days With ≥ 1.0" Precipitation	1	1	1	1	2	1	1	1	1	1	1	1	13
Mean Snowfall (in.)	3.2	2.2	1.8	0.1	0.0	0.0	0.0	0.0	0.0	0.0	trace	0.9	8.2
Days With ≥ 1.0" Snow Depth	1	1	0	0	0	0	0	0	0	0	0	0	2

Lewiston *Bertie County*   Elevation: 49 ft.   Latitude: 36° 08' N   Longitude: 77° 10' W

	JAN	FEB	MAR	APR	MAY	JUN	JUL	AUG	SEP	OCT	NOV	DEC	YEAR
Mean Maximum Temp. (°F)	51.7	55.3	63.5	73.0	79.8	86.2	90.1	88.5	83.1	74.0	64.7	56.5	72.2
Mean Temp. (°F)	41.0	43.7	51.0	59.6	67.4	74.5	78.9	77.2	71.5	61.5	52.5	45.4	60.4
Mean Minimum Temp. (°F)	30.3	32.0	38.5	46.2	55.0	62.7	67.7	65.8	59.9	48.9	40.2	34.3	48.5
Extreme Maximum Temp. (°F)	81	85	92	100	100	100	104	105	101	93	86	82	105
Extreme Minimum Temp. (°F)	-5	2	15	24	30	38	45	40	37	18	13	8	-5
Days Maximum Temp. ≥ 90°F	0	0	0	1	3	9	18	14	5	0	0	0	50
Days Maximum Temp. ≤ 32°F	1	0	0	0	0	0	0	0	0	0	0	0	1
Days Minimum Temp. ≤ 32°F	18	15	9	2	0	0	0	0	0	1	9	14	68
Days Minimum Temp. ≤ 0°F	0	0	0	0	0	0	0	0	0	0	0	0	0
Heating Degree Days (base 65°F)	736	597	437	197	55	5	0	1	17	156	381	604	3,186
Cooling Degree Days (base 65°F)	1	2	11	47	155	325	479	402	221	62	11	3	1,719
Mean Precipitation (in.)	4.01	3.49	4.03	3.02	3.96	3.86	5.55	4.79	4.98	3.40	2.72	3.34	47.15
Days With ≥ 0.1" Precipitation	7	6	7	6	7	6	8	7	6	4	5	6	75
Days With ≥ 1.0" Precipitation	1	1	1	1	1	1	2	1	2	1	0	1	13
Mean Snowfall (in.)	0.7	2.0	1.0	0.0	0.0	0.0	0.0	0.0	0.0	0.0	trace	trace	3.7
Days With ≥ 1.0" Snow Depth	1	1	0	0	0	0	0	0	0	0	0	0	2

Lexington *Davidson County*   Elevation: 757 ft.   Latitude: 35° 51' N   Longitude: 80° 16' W

	JAN	FEB	MAR	APR	MAY	JUN	JUL	AUG	SEP	OCT	NOV	DEC	YEAR
Mean Maximum Temp. (°F)	49.8	54.6	63.5	73.1	79.8	86.1	89.8	88.1	82.4	72.3	62.1	53.3	71.3
Mean Temp. (°F)	39.1	42.8	50.7	59.3	67.2	74.5	78.5	76.9	70.8	59.7	50.1	42.4	59.3
Mean Minimum Temp. (°F)	28.4	30.9	37.9	45.5	54.5	62.8	67.1	65.6	59.1	47.0	38.1	31.4	47.4
Extreme Maximum Temp. (°F)	78	83	88	94	95	98	105	104	98	91	86	78	105
Extreme Minimum Temp. (°F)	-6	2	5	21	30	39	47	45	35	26	14	1	-6
Days Maximum Temp. ≥ 90°F	0	0	0	0	2	8	17	13	5	0	0	0	45
Days Maximum Temp. ≤ 32°F	1	0	0	0	0	0	0	0	0	0	0	0	1
Days Minimum Temp. ≤ 32°F	20	17	10	2	0	0	0	0	0	2	10	18	79
Days Minimum Temp. ≤ 0°F	0	0	0	0	0	0	0	0	0	0	0	0	0
Heating Degree Days (base 65°F)	795	622	441	198	52	4	0	1	24	193	443	696	3,469
Cooling Degree Days (base 65°F)	0	0	4	27	117	291	423	359	185	33	2	1	1,442
Mean Precipitation (in.)	3.97	3.82	4.32	3.55	3.91	4.15	3.87	3.85	3.68	3.66	3.45	3.42	45.65
Days With ≥ 0.1" Precipitation	7	6	8	6	7	6	7	6	5	5	6	6	75
Days With ≥ 1.0" Precipitation	1	1	1	1	1	1	1	1	1	1	1	1	12
Mean Snowfall (in.)	2.3	2.1	1.0	trace	0.0	0.0	0.0	0.0	0.0	0.0	trace	0.5	5.9
Days With ≥ 1.0" Snow Depth	1	1	0	0	0	0	0	0	0	0	0	0	2

Lincolnton 4 W *Lincoln County*   Elevation: 898 ft.   Latitude: 35° 28' N   Longitude: 81° 20' W

	JAN	FEB	MAR	APR	MAY	JUN	JUL	AUG	SEP	OCT	NOV	DEC	YEAR
Mean Maximum Temp. (°F)	49.7	54.5	62.8	71.8	78.3	84.7	88.4	86.6	81.2	71.6	61.5	53.0	70.3
Mean Temp. (°F)	39.4	43.1	50.7	58.9	66.5	73.8	77.7	76.2	70.3	59.6	50.1	42.5	59.1
Mean Minimum Temp. (°F)	29.1	31.5	38.7	45.9	54.7	62.8	67.0	65.7	59.4	47.5	38.7	32.1	47.8
Extreme Maximum Temp. (°F)	77	80	86	91	94	100	102	105	95	91	85	78	105
Extreme Minimum Temp. (°F)	-6	2	6	23	28	41	50	47	36	24	11	1	-6
Days Maximum Temp. ≥ 90°F	0	0	0	0	1	6	13	8	3	0	0	0	31
Days Maximum Temp. ≤ 32°F	1	0	0	0	0	0	0	0	0	0	0	0	1
Days Minimum Temp. ≤ 32°F	19	16	8	2	0	0	0	0	0	2	9	17	73
Days Minimum Temp. ≤ 0°F	0	0	0	0	0	0	0	0	0	0	0	0	0
Heating Degree Days (base 65°F)	786	613	439	205	55	4	0	0	23	195	443	690	3,453
Cooling Degree Days (base 65°F)	0	0	4	28	114	290	418	357	181	35	2	1	1,430
Mean Precipitation (in.)	4.23	3.88	4.79	3.37	4.63	4.00	4.03	4.07	3.79	4.35	3.59	3.80	48.53
Days With ≥ 0.1" Precipitation	7	6	8	6	7	7	7	6	5	5	6	7	77
Days With ≥ 1.0" Precipitation	1	1	1	1	1	1	1	1	1	2	1	1	13
Mean Snowfall (in.)	2.8	1.8	1.4	trace	0.0	0.0	0.0	0.0	0.0	0.0	trace	0.7	6.7
Days With ≥ 1.0" Snow Depth	2	1	1	0	0	0	0	0	0	0	0	0	4

Longwood *Brunswick County*   Elevation: 39 ft.   Latitude: 34° 01' N   Longitude: 78° 33' W

	JAN	FEB	MAR	APR	MAY	JUN	JUL	AUG	SEP	OCT	NOV	DEC	YEAR
Mean Maximum Temp. (°F)	56.1	59.4	66.5	74.1	80.7	86.1	89.8	88.5	84.2	76.0	68.5	59.2	74.1
Mean Temp. (°F)	44.2	46.5	53.4	60.6	68.3	75.1	79.3	77.8	72.8	62.6	55.2	46.6	61.9
Mean Minimum Temp. (°F)	32.2	33.6	40.2	47.1	55.7	64.1	68.7	67.0	61.4	49.1	41.7	34.0	49.6
Extreme Maximum Temp. (°F)	80	83	88	94	96	101	101	103	98	95	87	82	103
Extreme Minimum Temp. (°F)	0	5	5	21	32	44	47	46	35	18	20	-4	-4
Days Maximum Temp. ≥ 90°F	0	0	0	1	2	7	17	13	5	0	0	0	45
Days Maximum Temp. ≤ 32°F	0	0	0	0	0	0	0	0	0	0	0	0	0
Days Minimum Temp. ≤ 32°F	16	14	8	2	0	0	0	0	0	2	8	15	65
Days Minimum Temp. ≤ 0°F	0	0	0	0	0	0	0	0	0	0	0	0	0
Heating Degree Days (base 65°F)	640	516	363	167	42	3	0	0	10	136	306	567	2,750
Cooling Degree Days (base 65°F)	1	2	9	42	150	329	472	411	250	77	18	4	1,765
Mean Precipitation (in.)	4.59	3.61	4.12	3.11	4.09	5.23	5.62	7.28	6.52	3.36	3.01	3.93	54.47
Days With ≥ 0.1" Precipitation	8	6	6	5	7	7	8	9	7	4	5	7	79
Days With ≥ 1.0" Precipitation	1	1	1	1	1	2	2	2	2	1	1	1	16
Mean Snowfall (in.)	*0.3*	*trace*	0.7	0.0	0.0	0.0	0.0	0.0	0.0	0.0	0.0	0.7	*1.7*
Days With ≥ 1.0" Snow Depth	*0*	*0*	0	0	0	0	0	0	0	0	0	0	*0*

Louisburg *Franklin County*   Elevation: 259 ft.   Latitude: 36° 06' N   Longitude: 78° 18' W

	JAN	FEB	MAR	APR	MAY	JUN	JUL	AUG	SEP	OCT	NOV	DEC	YEAR
Mean Maximum Temp. (°F)	50.2	53.7	62.5	72.4	79.1	86.4	89.7	88.2	82.5	72.5	63.0	53.9	71.2
Mean Temp. (°F)	37.6	39.7	48.3	56.9	64.8	73.2	77.5	75.7	69.5	57.9	48.3	40.6	57.5
Mean Minimum Temp. (°F)	24.7	26.0	33.9	41.5	50.6	59.9	65.2	63.0	56.4	43.0	34.0	27.2	43.8
Extreme Maximum Temp. (°F)	78	83	91	95	96	101	102	103	100	91	85	80	103
Extreme Minimum Temp. (°F)	-10	-5	8	20	30	36	43	40	33	20	11	3	-10
Days Maximum Temp. ≥ 90°F	0	0	0	1	3	11	18	13	5	0	0	0	51
Days Maximum Temp. ≤ 32°F	2	1	0	0	0	0	0	0	0	0	0	1	4
Days Minimum Temp. ≤ 32°F	24	21	15	5	1	0	0	0	0	5	15	22	108
Days Minimum Temp. ≤ 0°F	0	0	0	0	0	0	0	0	0	0	0	0	0
Heating Degree Days (base 65°F)	844	710	517	261	88	11	1	2	34	237	498	749	3,952
Cooling Degree Days (base 65°F)	0	1	6	27	90	276	411	331	170	25	2	1	1,340
Mean Precipitation (in.)	4.14	3.64	4.44	3.18	4.34	3.54	4.35	5.16	4.32	3.71	3.23	3.09	47.14
Days With ≥ 0.1" Precipitation	7	6	8	5	7	5	7	6	6	5	5	6	73
Days With ≥ 1.0" Precipitation	1	1	1	1	1	1	1	2	1	2	1	1	14
Mean Snowfall (in.)	1.0	1.0	0.5	trace	0.0	0.0	0.0	0.0	0.0	0.0	trace	0.4	2.9
Days With ≥ 1.0" Snow Depth	1	0	0	0	0	0	0	0	0	0	0	0	1

Lumberton *Robeson County*   Elevation: 111 ft.   Latitude: 34° 38' N   Longitude: 79° 01' W

	JAN	FEB	MAR	APR	MAY	JUN	JUL	AUG	SEP	OCT	NOV	DEC	YEAR
Mean Maximum Temp. (°F)	52.8	56.7	64.9	74.2	80.9	86.9	90.1	88.4	83.8	74.5	66.0	*57.2*	*73.0*
Mean Temp. (°F)	41.3	44.2	52.0	60.4	68.0	75.3	79.2	77.4	72.1	60.9	52.7	*45.2*	*60.7*
Mean Minimum Temp. (°F)	29.7	31.7	39.0	46.6	55.0	63.6	68.2	66.4	60.5	47.3	39.4	32.9	48.3
Extreme Maximum Temp. (°F)	78	84	89	94	96	102	103	104	98	96	87	81	104
Extreme Minimum Temp. (°F)	-1	3	9	23	29	40	50	48	35	23	13	-2	-2
Days Maximum Temp. ≥ 90°F	0	0	0	1	3	10	17	14	6	0	0	0	51
Days Maximum Temp. ≤ 32°F	1	0	0	0	0	0	0	0	0	0	0	0	1
Days Minimum Temp. ≤ 32°F	19	15	8	2	0	0	0	0	0	2	9	16	71
Days Minimum Temp. ≤ 0°F	0	0	0	0	0	0	0	0	0	0	0	0	0
Heating Degree Days (base 65°F)	727	582	403	179	47	5	0	0	15	166	374	*611*	*3,109*
Cooling Degree Days (base 65°F)	*1*	1	7	42	147	335	*466*	389	227	*49*	*10*	*2*	*1,676*
Mean Precipitation (in.)	4.17	3.50	4.33	2.83	3.96	4.65	5.62	5.15	4.64	3.34	2.70	3.36	48.25
Days With ≥ 0.1" Precipitation	7	6	7	5	6	7	8	7	5	5	5	6	74
Days With ≥ 1.0" Precipitation	1	1	1	1	1	1	2	1	1	1	1	1	13
Mean Snowfall (in.)	0.2	0.8	0.8	0.0	0.0	0.0	0.0	0.0	0.0	0.0	0.0	0.2	2.0
Days With ≥ 1.0" Snow Depth	0	0	0	0	0	0	0	0	0	0	0	0	0

Marion 2 NW *McDowell County*   Elevation: 1,463 ft.   Latitude: 35° 40' N   Longitude: 82° 02' W

	JAN	FEB	MAR	APR	MAY	JUN	JUL	AUG	SEP	OCT	NOV	DEC	YEAR
Mean Maximum Temp. (°F)	49.1	54.1	62.7	71.7	78.3	84.3	87.7	85.7	79.9	70.5	60.8	52.9	69.8
Mean Temp. (°F)	38.3	42.2	50.0	58.2	65.6	72.7	76.5	74.9	69.1	58.4	49.1	41.8	58.1
Mean Minimum Temp. (°F)	27.5	30.3	37.2	44.6	52.8	61.0	65.2	64.0	58.2	46.2	37.3	30.6	46.2
Extreme Maximum Temp. (°F)	77	79	86	91	92	98	102	101	95	88	82	80	102
Extreme Minimum Temp. (°F)	-11	6	7	24	30	41	50	42	26	18	13	0	-11
Days Maximum Temp. ≥ 90°F	0	0	0	0	1	5	11	6	1	0	0	0	24
Days Maximum Temp. ≤ 32°F	1	0	0	0	0	0	0	0	0	0	0	0	1
Days Minimum Temp. ≤ 32°F	20	17	9	2	0	0	0	0	0	2	10	18	78
Days Minimum Temp. ≤ 0°F	0	0	0	0	0	0	0	0	0	0	0	0	0
Heating Degree Days (base 65°F)	820	635	461	220	60	7	1	1	29	218	473	713	3,638
Cooling Degree Days (base 65°F)	0	0	3	20	88	258	383	316	148	23	0	0	1,239
Mean Precipitation (in.)	4.17	4.29	5.37	4.32	5.38	4.65	4.28	4.37	4.42	4.29	4.38	4.00	53.92
Days With ≥ 0.1" Precipitation	7	6	8	6	8	7	8	8	7	5	6	6	82
Days With ≥ 1.0" Precipitation	1	1	2	1	1	1	1	1	1	2	1	1	14
Mean Snowfall (in.)	3.5	2.2	2.1	0.3	0.0	0.0	0.0	0.0	0.0	0.0	0.2	1.3	9.6
Days With ≥ 1.0" Snow Depth	na	1	0	0	0	0	0	0	0	0	0	0	na

Marshall *Madison County*   Elevation: 1,998 ft.   Latitude: 35° 48' N   Longitude: 82° 40' W

	JAN	FEB	MAR	APR	MAY	JUN	JUL	AUG	SEP	OCT	NOV	DEC	YEAR
Mean Maximum Temp. (°F)	46.0	50.8	59.3	68.3	75.1	81.2	84.7	83.6	78.8	69.1	58.9	50.9	67.2
Mean Temp. (°F)	35.4	38.9	46.5	54.3	62.0	69.2	73.2	72.2	66.7	55.7	46.5	39.8	55.0
Mean Minimum Temp. (°F)	24.7	27.0	33.7	40.3	48.9	57.1	61.7	60.7	54.6	42.2	34.2	28.5	42.8
Extreme Maximum Temp. (°F)	74	80	90	89	91	95	96	100	95	86	81	77	100
Extreme Minimum Temp. (°F)	-18	-11	-3	19	27	31	45	42	31	20	5	-7	-18
Days Maximum Temp. ≥ 90°F	0	0	0	0	0	1	5	3	1	0	0	0	10
Days Maximum Temp. ≤ 32°F	4	2	1	0	0	0	0	0	0	0	0	2	9
Days Minimum Temp. ≤ 32°F	23	20	15	7	1	0	0	0	0	6	14	20	106
Days Minimum Temp. ≤ 0°F	1	0	0	0	0	0	0	0	0	0	0	0	1
Heating Degree Days (base 65°F)	912	730	567	320	128	19	1	2	51	293	548	776	4,347
Cooling Degree Days (base 65°F)	0	0	1	5	46	159	275	235	104	11	0	0	836
Mean Precipitation (in.)	3.36	3.28	3.95	3.37	3.92	3.55	3.77	3.79	2.86	2.45	2.96	2.88	40.14
Days With ≥ 0.1" Precipitation	8	7	9	7	8	8	8	8	6	5	7	7	88
Days With ≥ 1.0" Precipitation	0	0	1	1	1	0	1	1	1	0	1	1	8
Mean Snowfall (in.)	4.6	4.0	3.5	0.9	0.0	0.0	0.0	0.0	0.0	trace	0.4	2.3	15.7
Days With ≥ 1.0" Snow Depth	4	3	1	0	0	0	0	0	0	0	0	1	9

Monroe 4 SE *Union County*   Elevation: 577 ft.   Latitude: 34° 58' N   Longitude: 80° 30' W

	JAN	FEB	MAR	APR	MAY	JUN	JUL	AUG	SEP	OCT	NOV	DEC	YEAR
Mean Maximum Temp. (°F)	51.9	56.6	64.7	73.7	80.0	86.5	89.7	87.9	82.8	73.3	63.6	55.2	72.2
Mean Temp. (°F)	41.6	45.0	52.6	60.6	68.1	75.3	79.1	77.4	71.9	61.0	51.9	44.6	60.8
Mean Minimum Temp. (°F)	31.2	33.4	40.4	47.5	56.2	64.1	68.4	67.0	61.0	48.6	40.2	33.9	49.3
Extreme Maximum Temp. (°F)	78	81	86	92	95	100	103	107	98	93	86	78	107
Extreme Minimum Temp. (°F)	-5	6	5	24	32	43	53	47	38	24	11	5	-5
Days Maximum Temp. ≥ 90°F	0	0	0	0	1	9	16	12	4	0	0	0	42
Days Maximum Temp. ≤ 32°F	1	0	0	0	0	0	0	0	0	0	0	0	1
Days Minimum Temp. ≤ 32°F	17	14	8	2	0	0	0	0	0	2	8	15	66
Days Minimum Temp. ≤ 0°F	0	0	0	0	0	0	0	0	0	0	0	0	0
Heating Degree Days (base 65°F)	719	558	388	170	41	3	0	0	17	164	392	627	3,079
Cooling Degree Days (base 65°F)	0	1	9	43	147	333	459	392	218	48	4	2	1,656
Mean Precipitation (in.)	4.58	3.83	4.91	2.95	3.64	4.23	4.66	4.67	4.15	4.30	3.28	3.61	48.81
Days With ≥ 0.1" Precipitation	8	7	8	5	7	7	7	6	5	5	5	7	77
Days With ≥ 1.0" Precipitation	1	1	1	1	1	1	1	1	1	1	1	1	12
Mean Snowfall (in.)	0.9	1.1	0.7	trace	0.0	0.0	0.0	0.0	0.0	0.0	trace	0.6	3.3
Days With ≥ 1.0" Snow Depth	1	1	0	0	0	0	0	0	0	0	0	0	2

Morehead City 2 WNW *Carteret County*   Elevation: 9 ft.   Latitude: 34° 44' N   Longitude: 76° 44' W

	JAN	FEB	MAR	APR	MAY	JUN	JUL	AUG	SEP	OCT	NOV	DEC	YEAR
Mean Maximum Temp. (°F)	56.1	58.2	64.1	71.3	78.1	84.1	87.6	87.0	83.8	75.8	67.9	60.0	72.8
Mean Temp. (°F)	45.7	47.4	53.5	61.0	69.0	76.0	80.0	79.0	75.0	65.6	57.1	49.5	63.2
Mean Minimum Temp. (°F)	35.3	36.6	42.8	50.6	59.8	67.8	72.3	71.0	66.1	55.3	46.4	39.0	53.6
Extreme Maximum Temp. (°F)	78	77	86	92	96	99	100	98	93	95	84	79	100
Extreme Minimum Temp. (°F)	1	8	12	27	35	44	54	55	44	27	19	3	1
Days Maximum Temp. ≥ 90°F	0	0	0	0	0	2	8	5	1	0	0	0	16
Days Maximum Temp. ≤ 32°F	0	0	0	0	0	0	0	0	0	0	0	0	0
Days Minimum Temp. ≤ 32°F	13	11	5	1	0	0	0	0	0	0	3	10	43
Days Minimum Temp. ≤ 0°F	0	0	0	0	0	0	0	0	0	0	0	0	0
Heating Degree Days (base 65°F)	591	491	354	151	27	1	0	0	2	76	253	475	2,421
Cooling Degree Days (base 65°F)	0	0	3	37	157	345	488	441	298	103	22	2	1,896
Mean Precipitation (in.)	5.33	4.10	4.39	2.75	4.61	3.88	5.87	7.41	6.22	4.46	3.96	4.52	57.50
Days With ≥ 0.1" Precipitation	8	6	7	5	7	6	9	9	7	5	6	7	82
Days With ≥ 1.0" Precipitation	1	1	1	1	1	1	2	2	2	1	1	1	15
Mean Snowfall (in.)	0.2	0.7	0.7	0.0	0.0	0.0	0.0	0.0	0.0	0.0	trace	trace	1.6
Days With ≥ 1.0" Snow Depth	0	0	0	0	0	0	0	0	0	0	0	0	0

Morganton *Burke County*   Elevation: 1,158 ft.   Latitude: 35° 44' N   Longitude: 81° 40' W

	JAN	FEB	MAR	APR	MAY	JUN	JUL	AUG	SEP	OCT	NOV	DEC	YEAR
Mean Maximum Temp. (°F)	50.6	55.4	63.8	72.9	79.6	85.9	89.5	87.7	81.9	72.3	62.2	53.7	71.3
Mean Temp. (°F)	38.8	42.5	50.0	58.3	65.9	73.1	77.1	75.8	69.6	58.7	49.2	41.7	58.4
Mean Minimum Temp. (°F)	27.0	29.5	36.2	43.6	52.1	60.3	64.7	63.8	57.3	45.0	36.2	29.6	45.4
Extreme Maximum Temp. (°F)	79	81	86	93	96	99	102	104	97	90	86	78	104
Extreme Minimum Temp. (°F)	-9	-1	0	20	30	40	46	42	34	20	9	-1	-9
Days Maximum Temp. ≥ 90°F	0	0	0	0	1	8	16	11	4	0	0	0	40
Days Maximum Temp. ≤ 32°F	1	0	0	0	0	0	0	0	0	0	0	0	1
Days Minimum Temp. ≤ 32°F	22	18	11	4	0	0	0	0	0	3	12	20	90
Days Minimum Temp. ≤ 0°F	0	0	0	0	0	0	0	0	0	0	0	0	0
Heating Degree Days (base 65°F)	804	630	461	218	64	6	0	1	29	213	470	717	3,613
Cooling Degree Days (base 65°F)	0	0	3	20	98	259	392	333	158	22	1	0	1,286
Mean Precipitation (in.)	4.39	4.16	4.81	3.70	4.52	4.86	3.96	3.98	3.98	4.04	3.77	3.71	49.88
Days With ≥ 0.1" Precipitation	7	6	8	6	7	7	7	7	6	5	6	7	79
Days With ≥ 1.0" Precipitation	1	1	1	1	1	2	1	1	1	1	1	1	13
Mean Snowfall (in.)	2.1	1.4	1.4	trace	0.0	0.0	0.0	0.0	0.0	0.0	trace	0.6	5.5
Days With ≥ 1.0" Snow Depth	3	1	1	0	0	0	0	0	0	0	0	0	5

Mount Airy 2 W *Surry County*   Elevation: 1,040 ft.   Latitude: 36° 29' N   Longitude: 80° 40' W

	JAN	FEB	MAR	APR	MAY	JUN	JUL	AUG	SEP	OCT	NOV	DEC	YEAR
Mean Maximum Temp. (°F)	47.1	51.9	60.8	70.7	77.7	84.2	87.8	86.4	80.7	70.8	60.3	51.0	69.1
Mean Temp. (°F)	36.5	39.9	47.8	56.3	64.5	72.1	76.1	74.7	68.6	57.4	47.9	39.8	56.8
Mean Minimum Temp. (°F)	25.9	27.9	34.8	41.9	51.3	59.9	64.3	62.9	56.6	43.9	35.4	28.6	44.4
Extreme Maximum Temp. (°F)	75	80	87	90	94	98	101	101	97	91	82	76	101
Extreme Minimum Temp. (°F)	-10	-3	2	20	29	39	46	42	32	22	10	-1	-10
Days Maximum Temp. ≥ 90°F	0	0	0	0	1	5	12	9	3	0	0	0	30
Days Maximum Temp. ≤ 32°F	2	1	0	0	0	0	0	0	0	0	0	1	4
Days Minimum Temp. ≤ 32°F	23	21	13	5	1	0	0	0	0	4	13	21	101
Days Minimum Temp. ≤ 0°F	0	0	0	0	0	0	0	0	0	0	0	0	0
Heating Degree Days (base 65°F)	877	701	528	267	87	10	1	1	36	247	509	774	4,038
Cooling Degree Days (base 65°F)	0	0	2	13	80	238	365	306	145	19	1	0	1,169
Mean Precipitation (in.)	3.93	3.40	4.42	3.80	4.70	4.05	4.46	3.92	4.22	3.49	3.46	3.30	47.15
Days With ≥ 0.1" Precipitation	7	7	8	7	8	7	8	7	6	5	6	6	82
Days With ≥ 1.0" Precipitation	1	1	1	1	1	1	1	1	1	1	1	1	12
Mean Snowfall (in.)	3.6	3.6	1.2	trace	0.0	0.0	0.0	0.0	0.0	0.0	0.1	1.3	9.8
Days With ≥ 1.0" Snow Depth	2	2	0	0	0	0	0	0	0	0	0	0	4

Murphy 2 NE *Cherokee County*   Elevation: 1,637 ft.   Latitude: 35° 07' N   Longitude: 84° 00' W

	JAN	FEB	MAR	APR	MAY	JUN	JUL	AUG	SEP	OCT	NOV	DEC	YEAR
Mean Maximum Temp. (°F)	48.4	52.8	60.9	69.7	76.4	82.8	86.1	85.5	80.4	71.0	61.0	52.2	68.9
Mean Temp. (°F)	36.9	40.1	47.2	54.8	62.8	70.2	74.2	73.5	68.0	56.7	47.6	40.1	56.0
Mean Minimum Temp. (°F)	25.4	27.3	33.4	39.9	49.0	57.6	62.2	61.5	55.4	42.3	34.1	27.9	43.0
Extreme Maximum Temp. (°F)	76	81	85	92	90	97	98	99	96	87	84	75	99
Extreme Minimum Temp. (°F)	-16	-4	-3	18	25	33	46	48	33	21	6	-4	-16
Days Maximum Temp. ≥ 90°F	0	0	0	0	0	3	8	5	2	0	0	0	18
Days Maximum Temp. ≤ 32°F	2	1	0	0	0	0	0	0	0	0	0	1	4
Days Minimum Temp. ≤ 32°F	22	20	15	8	1	0	0	0	0	7	16	21	110
Days Minimum Temp. ≤ 0°F	1	0	0	0	0	0	0	0	0	0	0	0	1
Heating Degree Days (base 65°F)	864	699	548	307	117	15	1	1	37	266	518	765	4,138
Cooling Degree Days (base 65°F)	0	0	1	9	55	186	308	272	128	16	1	0	976
Mean Precipitation (in.)	5.63	5.08	5.85	4.47	4.86	4.76	4.98	4.64	3.78	3.24	4.44	4.70	56.43
Days With ≥ 0.1" Precipitation	9	8	9	8	8	9	9	8	7	5	8	8	96
Days With ≥ 1.0" Precipitation	2	2	2	1	1	1	1	1	1	1	1	1	15
Mean Snowfall (in.)	na	*1.6*	*0.9*	trace	0.0	0.0	*0.0*	0.0	0.0	*trace*	trace	na	na
Days With ≥ 1.0" Snow Depth	na	na	*0*	0	0	0	*0*	0	0	*0*	*0*	na	na

New Bern Craven Co. Reg. Airport *Craven County*   Elevation: 13 ft.   Latitude: 35° 04' N   Longitude: 77° 03' W

	JAN	FEB	MAR	APR	MAY	JUN	JUL	AUG	SEP	OCT	NOV	DEC	YEAR
Mean Maximum Temp. (°F)	*54.1*	*57.7*	65.0	73.9	80.1	86.0	89.3	87.8	83.6	*75.0*	67.2	*58.5*	73.2
Mean Temp. (°F)	44.2	46.8	53.8	62.2	69.7	76.4	80.4	79.1	74.5	64.3	56.1	47.8	62.9
Mean Minimum Temp. (°F)	34.2	35.8	42.6	50.4	59.2	66.8	71.5	70.4	65.3	53.6	44.9	37.1	52.6
Extreme Maximum Temp. (°F)	*80*	*83*	90	95	96	101	102	101	98	*95*	87	*83*	*102*
Extreme Minimum Temp. (°F)	*1*	*6*	17	30	38	49	55	57	43	*29*	23	*-4*	*-4*
Days Maximum Temp. ≥ 90°F	*0*	*0*	0	1	3	8	15	12	4	*0*	*0*	*0*	*43*
Days Maximum Temp. ≤ 32°F	*1*	*0*	0	0	0	0	0	0	0	*0*	*0*	*0*	*1*
Days Minimum Temp. ≤ 32°F	*14*	*11*	4	0	0	0	0	0	0	*0*	*3*	*12*	*44*
Days Minimum Temp. ≤ 0°F	*0*	*0*	0	0	0	0	0	0	0	*0*	*0*	*0*	*0*
Heating Degree Days (base 65°F)	*641*	*510*	353	139	27	1	0	0	4	*99*	283	531	2,588
Cooling Degree Days (base 65°F)	*1*	*4*	*13*	*60*	*186*	*373*	*518*	*454*	*289*	*87*	*20*	*4*	*2,009*
Mean Precipitation (in.)	*4.70*	*3.86*	4.52	3.15	4.29	4.69	6.24	6.87	5.40	*3.46*	*3.18*	*3.77*	54.13
Days With ≥ 0.1" Precipitation	*8*	*6*	8	6	7	7	9	9	6	*5*	*5*	*6*	82
Days With ≥ 1.0" Precipitation	*1*	*1*	1	1	1	2	2	2	2	*1*	*1*	*1*	*16*
Mean Snowfall (in.)	*0.4*	*0.9*	*0.5*	*trace*	*trace*	0.0	0.0	0.0	0.0	*0.0*	*trace*	0.6	2.4
Days With ≥ 1.0" Snow Depth	*0*	*0*	0	*0*	*0*	0	*0*	*0*	*0*	*0*	*0*	*0*	*0*

North Wilkesboro *Wilkes County*   Elevation: 1,118 ft.   Latitude: 36° 10' N   Longitude: 81° 09' W

	JAN	FEB	MAR	APR	MAY	JUN	JUL	AUG	SEP	OCT	NOV	DEC	YEAR
Mean Maximum Temp. (°F)	47.4	51.8	60.2	70.3	77.3	84.1	87.7	86.1	80.0	70.4	60.5	51.3	68.9
Mean Temp. (°F)	35.5	38.7	46.7	55.6	63.7	71.6	75.5	74.0	67.6	56.0	46.9	38.9	55.9
Mean Minimum Temp. (°F)	23.6	25.7	33.1	40.9	50.0	59.1	63.3	61.9	55.1	41.5	33.3	26.4	42.8
Extreme Maximum Temp. (°F)	76	83	88	94	93	102	101	102	95	90	85	81	102
Extreme Minimum Temp. (°F)	-9	1	2	18	29	38	46	42	33	21	7	-2	-9
Days Maximum Temp. ≥ 90°F	0	0	0	0	1	6	12	9	3	0	0	0	31
Days Maximum Temp. ≤ 32°F	2	1	0	0	0	0	0	0	0	0	0	1	4
Days Minimum Temp. ≤ 32°F	26	22	16	6	1	0	0	0	0	6	16	23	116
Days Minimum Temp. ≤ 0°F	0	0	0	0	0	0	0	0	0	0	0	0	0
Heating Degree Days (base 65°F)	908	735	562	291	107	13	1	2	48	284	536	804	4,291
Cooling Degree Days (base 65°F)	0	0	3	16	80	239	360	298	135	14	1	0	1,146
Mean Precipitation (in.)	4.30	3.98	4.83	4.28	4.69	4.45	4.34	4.49	4.32	4.03	3.50	3.62	50.83
Days With ≥ 0.1" Precipitation	7	7	8	7	9	7	8	7	6	5	7	7	85
Days With ≥ 1.0" Precipitation	1	1	1	1	1	1	1	1	1	1	1	1	12
Mean Snowfall (in.)	3.4	2.8	2.0	trace	0.0	0.0	0.0	0.0	0.0	0.0	trace	1.4	9.6
Days With ≥ 1.0" Snow Depth	3	2	1	0	0	0	0	0	0	0	0	1	7

Oconaluftee *Swain County*   Elevation: 2,037 ft.   Latitude: 35° 31' N   Longitude: 83° 18' W

	JAN	FEB	MAR	APR	MAY	JUN	JUL	AUG	SEP	OCT	NOV	DEC	YEAR
Mean Maximum Temp. (°F)	47.7	52.3	60.4	69.0	76.2	82.4	85.6	85.1	80.3	70.9	60.8	51.7	68.5
Mean Temp. (°F)	34.3	37.9	45.1	52.9	60.8	68.0	71.7	70.8	65.2	54.3	45.3	37.8	53.7
Mean Minimum Temp. (°F)	21.0	23.5	29.8	36.7	45.3	53.5	57.8	56.5	50.0	37.6	29.9	23.8	38.8
Extreme Maximum Temp. (°F)	73	80	85	91	94	94	98	100	96	86	84	73	100
Extreme Minimum Temp. (°F)	-23	-3	-4	14	20	32	40	39	23	17	7	-8	-23
Days Maximum Temp. ≥ 90°F	0	0	0	0	0	2	6	5	1	0	0	0	14
Days Maximum Temp. ≤ 32°F	2	1	0	0	0	0	0	0	0	0	0	1	4
Days Minimum Temp. ≤ 32°F	26	23	20	11	2	0	0	0	1	11	19	24	137
Days Minimum Temp. ≤ 0°F	1	0	0	0	0	0	0	0	0	0	0	0	1
Heating Degree Days (base 65°F)	943	759	607	359	155	25	2	3	69	332	584	836	4,674
Cooling Degree Days (base 65°F)	0	0	0	3	37	130	231	197	80	6	0	0	684
Mean Precipitation (in.)	5.86	4.83	6.14	4.54	5.38	4.87	4.74	4.31	3.97	3.47	4.68	5.18	57.97
Days With ≥ 0.1" Precipitation	9	8	9	8	9	9	9	8	7	6	7	8	97
Days With ≥ 1.0" Precipitation	2	1	2	1	1	1	1	1	1	1	1	2	15
Mean Snowfall (in.)	3.8	na	0.9	1.0	0.0	0.0	0.0	0.0	0.0	0.0	trace	0.6	na
Days With ≥ 1.0" Snow Depth	na	na	0	0	0	0	0	0	0	0	0	0	na

Oxford 1 E *Granville County*   Elevation: 498 ft.   Latitude: 36° 18' N   Longitude: 78° 37' W

	JAN	FEB	MAR	APR	MAY	JUN	JUL	AUG	SEP	OCT	NOV	DEC	YEAR
Mean Maximum Temp. (°F)	49.0	53.6	62.4	72.2	79.2	85.8	89.7	87.6	82.4	71.8	62.5	53.2	70.8
Mean Temp. (°F)	39.0	42.3	50.4	59.1	67.2	74.3	78.5	76.9	71.2	59.8	51.0	42.7	59.4
Mean Minimum Temp. (°F)	28.9	30.9	38.4	45.9	55.1	62.8	67.3	66.1	60.1	47.7	39.5	32.2	47.9
Extreme Maximum Temp. (°F)	77	84	88	97	96	100	103	104	100	93	86	79	104
Extreme Minimum Temp. (°F)	-8	2	12	24	34	42	48	45	37	25	15	2	-8
Days Maximum Temp. ≥ 90°F	0	0	0	0	2	8	16	12	4	0	0	0	42
Days Maximum Temp. ≤ 32°F	2	1	0	0	0	0	0	0	0	0	0	1	4
Days Minimum Temp. ≤ 32°F	20	17	10	2	0	0	0	0	0	2	8	17	76
Days Minimum Temp. ≤ 0°F	0	0	0	0	0	0	0	0	0	0	0	0	0
Heating Degree Days (base 65°F)	798	636	453	205	53	4	0	1	20	195	418	684	3,467
Cooling Degree Days (base 65°F)	0	1	8	35	138	308	na	na	na	43	4	1	na
Mean Precipitation (in.)	3.73	3.47	4.43	3.15	4.32	3.30	4.47	4.61	3.77	3.67	3.30	3.23	45.45
Days With ≥ 0.1" Precipitation	7	6	8	6	7	6	6	7	5	5	6	7	76
Days With ≥ 1.0" Precipitation	1	1	1	1	1	1	1	1	1	1	1	1	12
Mean Snowfall (in.)	2.0	2.5	1.3	trace	0.0	0.0	0.0	0.0	0.0	0.0	trace	0.7	6.5
Days With ≥ 1.0" Snow Depth	1	1	0	0	0	0	0	0	0	0	0	0	2

Pisgah Forest 1 N *Transylvania County*   Elevation: 2,109 ft.   Latitude: 35° 16' N   Longitude: 82° 42' W

	JAN	FEB	MAR	APR	MAY	JUN	JUL	AUG	SEP	OCT	NOV	DEC	YEAR
Mean Maximum Temp. (°F)	47.9	51.8	59.0	68.1	74.5	80.7	84.1	82.7	77.7	69.1	60.0	51.7	67.3
Mean Temp. (°F)	35.6	38.6	45.2	53.4	60.9	68.1	72.0	70.9	65.6	55.0	46.1	38.9	54.2
Mean Minimum Temp. (°F)	23.3	25.4	31.4	38.7	47.2	55.4	59.9	59.1	53.4	40.8	32.2	26.1	41.1
Extreme Maximum Temp. (°F)	74	78	82	89	93	94	96	97	91	88	80	76	97
Extreme Minimum Temp. (°F)	-15	-2	-2	19	26	35	40	43	29	21	7	-3	-15
Days Maximum Temp. ≥ 90°F	0	0	0	0	0	2	5	2	1	0	0	1	10
Days Maximum Temp. ≤ 32°F	2	1	0	0	0	0	0	0	0	0	0	1	4
Days Minimum Temp. ≤ 32°F	25	22	18	8	1	0	0	0	0	7	17	24	122
Days Minimum Temp. ≤ 0°F	1	0	0	0	0	0	0	0	0	0	0	0	1
Heating Degree Days (base 65°F)	904	740	607	345	151	25	3	4	61	310	560	802	4,512
Cooling Degree Days (base 65°F)	0	0	0	3	31	131	239	192	77	7	0	0	680
Mean Precipitation (in.)	6.19	5.33	6.49	4.51	5.87	5.16	5.34	5.54	4.98	4.97	5.34	5.19	64.91
Days With ≥ 0.1" Precipitation	8	7	9	7	10	9	8	9	7	6	7	8	95
Days With ≥ 1.0" Precipitation	2	2	2	1	2	1	2	2	2	2	2	2	22
Mean Snowfall (in.)	3.8	2.2	1.5	0.4	0.0	0.0	0.0	0.0	0.0	0.0	0.2	1.2	9.3
Days With ≥ 1.0" Snow Depth	3	1	0	0	0	0	0	0	0	0	0	0	4

Plymouth 5 E *Washington County*   Elevation: 19 ft.   Latitude: 35° 52' N   Longitude: 76° 39' W

	JAN	FEB	MAR	APR	MAY	JUN	JUL	AUG	SEP	OCT	NOV	DEC	YEAR
Mean Maximum Temp. (°F)	53.6	57.1	64.7	73.9	80.5	86.9	90.2	88.4	83.8	74.5	66.0	57.6	73.1
Mean Temp. (°F)	42.7	45.1	52.0	60.3	68.1	75.3	79.3	77.7	72.7	62.4	53.9	46.4	61.3
Mean Minimum Temp. (°F)	31.8	33.1	39.3	46.6	55.6	63.7	68.3	66.9	61.6	50.3	41.8	35.0	49.5
Extreme Maximum Temp. (°F)	79	84	90	94	97	102	99	103	99	93	87	82	103
Extreme Minimum Temp. (°F)	-5	4	16	25	34	43	47	46	38	23	17	2	-5
Days Maximum Temp. ≥ 90°F	0	0	0	1	3	10	17	13	5	0	0	0	49
Days Maximum Temp. ≤ 32°F	1	0	0	0	0	0	0	0	0	0	0	0	1
Days Minimum Temp. ≤ 32°F	17	14	9	2	0	0	0	0	0	1	7	13	63
Days Minimum Temp. ≤ 0°F	0	0	0	0	0	0	0	0	0	0	0	0	0
Heating Degree Days (base 65°F)	685	558	406	179	44	3	0	0	7	131	339	574	2,926
Cooling Degree Days (base 65°F)	1	2	10	47	159	337	476	405	245	64	11	3	1,760
Mean Precipitation (in.)	4.47	3.54	4.71	3.42	4.38	4.85	5.37	5.55	4.94	3.90	3.15	3.25	51.53
Days With ≥ 0.1" Precipitation	8	7	8	6	8	7	9	7	6	5	5	6	82
Days With ≥ 1.0" Precipitation	1	1	1	1	1	1	2	2	2	1	1	1	15
Mean Snowfall (in.)	0.7	1.6	0.8	0.0	0.0	0.0	0.0	0.0	0.0	0.0	0.0	0.3	3.4
Days With ≥ 1.0" Snow Depth	0	1	0	0	0	0	0	0	0	0	0	0	1

Raleigh 4 SW *Wake County*   Elevation: 419 ft.   Latitude: 35° 44' N   Longitude: 78° 41' W

	JAN	FEB	MAR	APR	MAY	JUN	JUL	AUG	SEP	OCT	NOV	DEC	YEAR
Mean Maximum Temp. (°F)	51.5	55.7	63.7	72.9	79.4	85.9	89.2	87.7	82.8	72.7	63.6	54.9	71.7
Mean Temp. (°F)	41.3	44.4	51.9	60.2	67.7	74.9	78.7	77.4	72.0	60.9	52.2	44.6	60.5
Mean Minimum Temp. (°F)	31.0	33.1	40.0	47.5	56.0	63.8	68.1	67.0	61.1	49.1	40.7	34.1	49.3
Extreme Maximum Temp. (°F)	77	82	87	93	93	99	104	103	99	89	85	78	104
Extreme Minimum Temp. (°F)	-6	8	14	24	33	41	48	48	37	24	15	5	-6
Days Maximum Temp. ≥ 90°F	0	0	0	1	1	8	15	11	4	0	0	0	40
Days Maximum Temp. ≤ 32°F	1	0	0	0	0	0	0	0	0	0	0	0	1
Days Minimum Temp. ≤ 32°F	18	14	8	2	0	0	0	0	0	1	7	15	65
Days Minimum Temp. ≤ 0°F	0	0	0	0	0	0	0	0	0	0	0	0	0
Heating Degree Days (base 65°F)	729	576	409	182	45	4	0	0	16	165	387	629	3,142
Cooling Degree Days (base 65°F)	0	1	8	45	145	324	452	392	225	49	6	2	1,649
Mean Precipitation (in.)	4.29	3.65	4.45	2.97	4.06	3.89	4.48	4.17	4.14	3.74	3.19	3.24	46.27
Days With ≥ 0.1" Precipitation	7	7	8	5	7	6	7	6	5	5	6	6	75
Days With ≥ 1.0" Precipitation	1	1	1	1	1	1	1	1	1	1	1	1	12
Mean Snowfall (in.)	1.0	1.7	0.8	trace	0.0	0.0	0.0	0.0	0.0	0.0	0.0	0.3	3.8
Days With ≥ 1.0" Snow Depth	0	0	0	0	0	0	0	0	0	0	0	0	0

Raleigh State University *Wake County*   Elevation: 396 ft.   Latitude: 35° 48' N   Longitude: 78° 42' W

	JAN	FEB	MAR	APR	MAY	JUN	JUL	AUG	SEP	OCT	NOV	DEC	YEAR
Mean Maximum Temp. (°F)	49.3	53.4	61.5	71.2	77.9	85.0	88.7	86.9	81.4	71.0	62.3	52.9	70.1
Mean Temp. (°F)	39.6	42.9	50.6	59.6	67.3	75.0	79.1	77.6	71.7	60.3	52.0	43.2	59.9
Mean Minimum Temp. (°F)	29.9	32.2	39.6	47.9	56.7	64.9	69.4	68.1	62.0	49.5	41.6	33.6	49.6
Extreme Maximum Temp. (°F)	77	83	88	94	94	99	103	104	100	92	87	78	104
Extreme Minimum Temp. (°F)	-6	2	12	24	36	43	54	49	42	28	13	4	-6
Days Maximum Temp. ≥ 90°F	0	0	0	0	1	7	14	11	4	0	0	0	37
Days Maximum Temp. ≤ 32°F	2	1	0	0	0	0	0	0	0	0	0	1	4
Days Minimum Temp. ≤ 32°F	19	15	7	1	0	0	0	0	0	1	6	15	64
Days Minimum Temp. ≤ 0°F	0	0	0	0	0	0	0	0	0	0	0	0	0
Heating Degree Days (base 65°F)	780	620	448	197	54	5	0	0	17	179	392	669	3,361
Cooling Degree Days (base 65°F)	0	1	9	43	139	324	458	390	217	42	5	2	1,630
Mean Precipitation (in.)	4.34	3.60	4.51	2.95	4.09	4.07	4.34	4.27	4.00	3.97	3.05	3.30	46.49
Days With ≥ 0.1" Precipitation	8	7	8	6	7	6	8	6	5	5	5	6	77
Days With ≥ 1.0" Precipitation	1	1	1	1	1	1	1	1	1	1	1	1	12
Mean Snowfall (in.)	1.0	1.7	0.9	trace	0.0	0.0	0.0	0.0	0.0	0.0	trace	0.5	4.1
Days With ≥ 1.0" Snow Depth	1	1	0	0	0	0	0	0	0	0	0	0	2

Reidsville 2 NW *Rockingham County*   Elevation: 889 ft.   Latitude: 36° 23' N   Longitude: 79° 42' W

	JAN	FEB	MAR	APR	MAY	JUN	JUL	AUG	SEP	OCT	NOV	DEC	YEAR
Mean Maximum Temp. (°F)	46.3	50.4	58.9	69.1	76.3	83.5	87.5	85.9	80.2	69.6	60.0	50.7	68.2
Mean Temp. (°F)	36.6	39.9	47.8	57.4	65.2	73.0	77.0	75.2	69.1	57.7	49.1	40.8	57.4
Mean Minimum Temp. (°F)	26.9	29.3	36.6	45.6	54.1	62.3	66.4	64.4	57.9	45.7	38.1	30.7	46.5
Extreme Maximum Temp. (°F)	76	82	87	91	95	99	101	103	98	90	85	80	103
Extreme Minimum Temp. (°F)	-9	0	10	21	32	41	50	45	35	23	10	-1	-9
Days Maximum Temp. ≥ 90°F	0	0	0	0	1	6	12	9	3	0	0	0	31
Days Maximum Temp. ≤ 32°F	3	2	0	0	0	0	0	0	0	0	0	1	6
Days Minimum Temp. ≤ 32°F	22	18	11	2	0	0	0	0	0	0	2	9	19	83
Days Minimum Temp. ≤ 0°F	0	0	0	0	0	0	0	0	0	0	0	0	0
Heating Degree Days (base 65°F)	872	703	532	249	83	10	1	2	37	243	474	745	3,951
Cooling Degree Days (base 65°F)	0	0	5	28	104	276	402	332	167	27	2	1	1,344
Mean Precipitation (in.)	4.14	3.51	4.42	3.73	4.18	3.98	4.74	3.73	4.23	3.87	3.24	3.21	46.98
Days With ≥ 0.1" Precipitation	7	7	8	6	7	6	7	6	5	5	6	6	76
Days With ≥ 1.0" Precipitation	1	1	1	1	1	1	2	1	1	1	1	1	13
Mean Snowfall (in.)	3.1	3.7	1.6	trace	0.0	0.0	0.0	0.0	0.0	0.0	trace	0.9	9.3
Days With ≥ 1.0" Snow Depth	4	3	1	0	0	0	0	0	0	0	0	1	9

Roanoke Rapids *Halifax County*   Elevation: 209 ft.   Latitude: 36° 29' N   Longitude: 77° 40' W

	JAN	FEB	MAR	APR	MAY	JUN	JUL	AUG	SEP	OCT	NOV	DEC	YEAR
Mean Maximum Temp. (°F)	48.9	51.5	60.0	70.0	77.5	85.1	89.5	87.9	81.6	71.2	62.3	52.3	69.8
Mean Temp. (°F)	38.6	40.8	48.6	57.7	66.0	74.1	78.9	77.1	70.6	59.1	50.7	41.8	58.6
Mean Minimum Temp. (°F)	28.1	30.0	37.0	45.3	54.4	63.0	68.1	66.3	59.6	46.9	39.1	31.5	47.4
Extreme Maximum Temp. (°F)	79	83	87	94	95	101	103	103	99	93	85	83	103
Extreme Minimum Temp. (°F)	-3	0	10	23	34	44	50	47	39	26	18	4	-3
Days Maximum Temp. ≥ 90°F	0	0	0	0	2	8	15	12	4	0	0	0	41
Days Maximum Temp. ≤ 32°F	2	1	0	0	0	0	0	0	0	0	0	1	4
Days Minimum Temp. ≤ 32°F	21	18	10	2	0	0	0	0	0	1	8	18	78
Days Minimum Temp. ≤ 0°F	0	0	0	0	0	0	0	0	0	0	0	0	0
Heating Degree Days (base 65°F)	812	679	508	241	74	6	0	1	24	208	429	714	3,696
Cooling Degree Days (base 65°F)	0	0	5	26	116	299	457	382	199	35	4	2	1,525
Mean Precipitation (in.)	4.12	3.34	4.25	3.31	3.91	3.65	4.37	4.27	4.61	3.47	3.41	3.33	46.04
Days With ≥ 0.1" Precipitation	7	6	7	6	7	6	7	7	5	5	6	7	76
Days With ≥ 1.0" Precipitation	1	1	1	1	1	1	1	1	1	1	1	1	12
Mean Snowfall (in.)	0.2	0.8	0.0	0.0	0.0	0.0	0.0	0.0	0.0	0.0	0.0	0.0	1.0
Days With ≥ 1.0" Snow Depth	0	0	0	0	0	0	0	0	0	0	0	0	0

Roxboro 7 ESE *Person County*   Elevation: 708 ft.   Latitude: 36° 19' N   Longitude: 78° 54' W

	JAN	FEB	MAR	APR	MAY	JUN	JUL	AUG	SEP	OCT	NOV	DEC	YEAR
Mean Maximum Temp. (°F)	47.7	52.0	60.4	70.6	77.2	84.2	88.1	86.6	80.7	70.4	61.3	51.5	69.2
Mean Temp. (°F)	37.0	40.4	48.1	57.4	65.0	72.7	76.8	75.2	68.7	57.7	49.0	40.4	57.4
Mean Minimum Temp. (°F)	26.3	28.7	35.7	44.2	53.1	61.1	65.4	63.7	56.8	44.7	36.7	29.2	45.5
Extreme Maximum Temp. (°F)	76	81	87	96	93	98	103	102	99	91	84	79	103
Extreme Minimum Temp. (°F)	-9	-8	7	22	32	39	49	41	33	22	13	-1	-9
Days Maximum Temp. ≥ 90°F	0	0	0	0	1	6	12	10	3	0	0	0	32
Days Maximum Temp. ≤ 32°F	3	1	0	0	0	0	0	0	0	0	0	1	5
Days Minimum Temp. ≤ 32°F	23	20	12	3	0	0	0	0	0	3	11	20	92
Days Minimum Temp. ≤ 0°F	0	0	0	0	0	0	0	0	0	0	0	0	0
Heating Degree Days (base 65°F)	861	689	522	251	85	11	1	2	42	244	477	757	3,942
Cooling Degree Days (base 65°F)	0	0	5	25	92	250	382	324	154	23	2	1	1,258
Mean Precipitation (in.)	4.12	3.45	4.37	3.18	3.74	3.51	4.82	3.94	4.34	4.05	3.47	3.39	46.38
Days With ≥ 0.1" Precipitation	7	6	8	6	7	6	7	6	5	5	6	6	75
Days With ≥ 1.0" Precipitation	1	1	1	1	1	1	2	1	1	1	1	1	13
Mean Snowfall (in.)	2.4	3.3	1.5	trace	0.0	0.0	0.0	0.0	0.0	trace	0.2	1.1	8.5
Days With ≥ 1.0" Snow Depth	3	2	0	0	0	0	0	0	0	0	0	1	6

Salisbury *Rowan County*   Elevation: 698 ft.   Latitude: 35° 41' N   Longitude: 80° 29' W

	JAN	FEB	MAR	APR	MAY	JUN	JUL	AUG	SEP	OCT	NOV	DEC	YEAR
Mean Maximum Temp. (°F)	50.6	55.4	63.8	73.2	79.7	86.1	89.7	88.2	82.1	72.4	62.8	53.5	71.5
Mean Temp. (°F)	40.0	43.6	51.5	59.9	67.4	74.8	78.7	77.4	71.0	59.8	50.9	42.7	59.8
Mean Minimum Temp. (°F)	29.3	31.7	39.1	46.5	55.1	63.3	67.7	66.6	59.9	47.3	39.0	31.9	48.1
Extreme Maximum Temp. (°F)	77	81	89	93	98	100	104	105	99	92	85	79	105
Extreme Minimum Temp. (°F)	-4	4	2	21	29	41	50	48	35	23	13	3	-4
Days Maximum Temp. ≥ 90°F	0	0	0	0	2	9	16	13	4	0	0	0	44
Days Maximum Temp. ≤ 32°F	1	0	0	0	0	0	0	0	0	0	0	0	1
Days Minimum Temp. ≤ 32°F	20	16	8	2	0	0	0	0	0	2	9	17	74
Days Minimum Temp. ≤ 0°F	0	0	0	0	0	0	0	0	0	0	0	0	0
Heating Degree Days (base 65°F)	768	599	419	185	48	4	0	0	21	188	421	684	3,337
Cooling Degree Days (base 65°F)	0	1	6	37	136	320	453	399	205	38	2	1	1,598
Mean Precipitation (in.)	3.49	3.66	4.17	3.27	3.75	3.97	3.92	3.34	3.55	3.82	3.07	3.18	43.19
Days With ≥ 0.1" Precipitation	6	6	7	6	6	6	6	5	4	5	5	6	68
Days With ≥ 1.0" Precipitation	1	1	1	1	1	1	1	1	1	1	1	1	12
Mean Snowfall (in.)	2.0	1.8	0.6	trace	0.0	0.0	0.0	0.0	0.0	0.0	trace	0.5	4.9
Days With ≥ 1.0" Snow Depth	0	0	0	0	0	0	0	0	0	0	0	0	0

Sanford 8 NE *Lee County*   Elevation: 259 ft.   Latitude: 35° 32' N   Longitude: 79° 03' W

	JAN	FEB	MAR	APR	MAY	JUN	JUL	AUG	SEP	OCT	NOV	DEC	YEAR
Mean Maximum Temp. (°F)	52.3	57.0	65.7	75.0	81.4	87.5	91.1	88.9	83.6	73.9	64.4	55.3	73.0
Mean Temp. (°F)	40.5	43.9	51.7	59.9	67.6	74.8	79.0	77.1	71.3	59.8	51.1	43.0	60.0
Mean Minimum Temp. (°F)	28.6	30.7	37.6	44.8	53.8	62.0	66.8	65.3	58.9	45.6	37.8	30.8	46.9
Extreme Maximum Temp. (°F)	79	83	89	93	96	101	105	107	100	93	88	80	107
Extreme Minimum Temp. (°F)	-3	0	11	19	29	35	41	42	34	19	11	2	-3
Days Maximum Temp. ≥ 90°F	0	0	0	1	3	12	20	14	5	0	0	0	55
Days Maximum Temp. ≤ 32°F	1	0	0	0	0	0	0	0	0	0	0	0	1
Days Minimum Temp. ≤ 32°F	20	17	11	4	0	0	0	0	0	4	12	19	87
Days Minimum Temp. ≤ 0°F	0	0	0	0	0	0	0	0	0	0	0	0	0
Heating Degree Days (base 65°F)	754	591	418	190	54	6	0	1	21	196	416	675	3,322
Cooling Degree Days (base 65°F)	0	1	9	43	143	315	451	380	210	44	4	2	1,602
Mean Precipitation (in.)	4.37	3.68	4.29	2.87	4.03	4.47	4.76	4.11	4.46	3.71	3.34	3.33	47.42
Days With ≥ 0.1" Precipitation	7	7	7	5	7	6	8	6	6	5	5	6	75
Days With ≥ 1.0" Precipitation	1	1	1	1	1	2	1	1	1	1	1	1	13
Mean Snowfall (in.)	1.1	1.7	0.6	trace	0.0	0.0	0.0	0.0	0.0	0.0	trace	0.2	3.6
Days With ≥ 1.0" Snow Depth	0	0	0	0	0	0	0	0	0	0	0	0	0

Shelby 2 NNE *Cleveland County* Elevation: 918 ft. Latitude: 35° 19' N Longitude: 81° 32' W

	JAN	FEB	MAR	APR	MAY	JUN	JUL	AUG	SEP	OCT	NOV	DEC	YEAR
Mean Maximum Temp. (°F)	50.9	55.7	63.7	72.4	78.8	85.4	89.0	87.3	81.7	72.1	62.5	53.7	71.1
Mean Temp. (°F)	40.1	43.7	51.2	59.0	66.4	73.7	77.6	76.3	70.2	59.2	50.3	42.8	59.2
Mean Minimum Temp. (°F)	29.2	31.8	38.6	45.6	54.0	62.0	66.1	65.2	58.6	46.3	38.1	31.9	47.3
Extreme Maximum Temp. (°F)	77	80	85	92	97	100	104	105	96	92	86	78	105
Extreme Minimum Temp. (°F)	-7	3	6	24	29	39	52	48	36	25	11	0	-7
Days Maximum Temp. ≥ 90°F	0	0	0	0	1	7	15	10	4	0	0	0	37
Days Maximum Temp. ≤ 32°F	1	0	0	0	0	0	0	0	0	0	0	0	1
Days Minimum Temp. ≤ 32°F	19	16	9	3	0	0	0	0	0	0	2	10	17	76
Days Minimum Temp. ≤ 0°F	0	0	0	0	0	0	0	0	0	0	0	0	0
Heating Degree Days (base 65°F)	765	594	426	201	58	5	0	0	25	201	436	682	3,393
Cooling Degree Days (base 65°F)	0	0	5	28	113	285	415	362	179	28	1	1	1,417
Mean Precipitation (in.)	4.30	3.97	4.91	3.28	4.83	4.19	4.12	4.68	3.67	4.24	3.66	3.81	49.66
Days With ≥ 0.1" Precipitation	6	6	7	6	7	6	7	6	5	5	6	7	74
Days With ≥ 1.0" Precipitation	1	1	1	1	1	1	1	2	1	1	1	1	13
Mean Snowfall (in.)	2.5	1.7	1.1	trace	0.0	0.0	0.0	0.0	0.0	0.0	trace	0.6	5.9
Days With ≥ 1.0" Snow Depth	*0*	0	0	0	0	0	0	0	0	0	0	*0*	*0*

Siler City 2 N *Chatham County* Elevation: 606 ft. Latitude: 35° 46' N Longitude: 79° 28' W

	JAN	FEB	MAR	APR	MAY	JUN	JUL	AUG	SEP	OCT	NOV	DEC	YEAR
Mean Maximum Temp. (°F)	49.3	53.4	61.7	71.0	77.8	84.7	88.6	87.0	81.5	71.4	62.3	53.3	70.2
Mean Temp. (°F)	38.0	41.0	49.1	57.5	65.5	73.2	77.3	75.7	69.7	58.2	49.6	41.6	58.0
Mean Minimum Temp. (°F)	26.6	28.5	36.4	43.9	53.1	61.7	66.0	64.3	57.9	44.9	36.8	30.0	45.8
Extreme Maximum Temp. (°F)	76	82	88	92	96	99	104	105	99	92	86	79	105
Extreme Minimum Temp. (°F)	-11	-3	0	19	28	36	46	46	34	19	8	1	-11
Days Maximum Temp. ≥ 90°F	0	0	0	0	1	6	14	11	4	0	0	0	36
Days Maximum Temp. ≤ 32°F	2	1	0	0	0	0	0	0	0	0	0	1	4
Days Minimum Temp. ≤ 32°F	22	19	11	4	0	0	0	0	0	3	12	19	90
Days Minimum Temp. ≤ 0°F	0	0	0	0	0	0	0	0	0	0	0	0	0
Heating Degree Days (base 65°F)	830	672	492	246	79	10	1	1	31	231	459	718	3,770
Cooling Degree Days (base 65°F)	0	1	7	32	116	290	427	360	185	31	2	1	1,452
Mean Precipitation (in.)	4.47	3.73	4.70	3.29	4.65	3.97	4.73	4.19	4.10	3.98	3.34	3.27	48.42
Days With ≥ 0.1" Precipitation	7	6	8	6	7	6	7	6	5	5	6	6	75
Days With ≥ 1.0" Precipitation	1	1	1	1	1	1	2	1	1	1	1	1	13
Mean Snowfall (in.)	1.6	2.0	0.6	trace	0.0	0.0	0.0	0.0	0.0	0.0	trace	0.4	4.6
Days With ≥ 1.0" Snow Depth	0	1	0	0	0	0	0	0	0	0	0	0	1

Smithfield *Johnston County* Elevation: 147 ft. Latitude: 35° 31' N Longitude: 78° 21' W

	JAN	FEB	MAR	APR	MAY	JUN	JUL	AUG	SEP	OCT	NOV	DEC	YEAR
Mean Maximum Temp. (°F)	52.1	56.3	64.4	74.1	80.8	87.3	90.6	88.7	83.5	73.3	64.5	55.8	72.6
Mean Temp. (°F)	41.3	44.4	52.0	60.3	67.9	75.0	78.9	77.3	71.6	60.3	51.7	44.3	60.4
Mean Minimum Temp. (°F)	30.5	32.5	39.5	46.5	54.9	62.6	67.2	65.8	59.6	47.1	38.8	32.7	48.1
Extreme Maximum Temp. (°F)	78	83	89	95	98	101	103	105	100	93	86	81	105
Extreme Minimum Temp. (°F)	-4	5	10	25	33	41	48	45	37	23	14	-1	-4
Days Maximum Temp. ≥ 90°F	0	0	0	1	3	11	19	14	6	0	0	0	54
Days Maximum Temp. ≤ 32°F	1	0	0	0	0	0	0	0	0	0	0	0	1
Days Minimum Temp. ≤ 32°F	19	16	8	1	0	0	0	0	0	2	10	17	73
Days Minimum Temp. ≤ 0°F	0	0	0	0	0	0	0	0	0	0	0	0	0
Heating Degree Days (base 65°F)	728	577	407	179	44	3	0	0	17	182	401	637	3,175
Cooling Degree Days (base 65°F)	1	1	9	43	142	324	457	387	215	42	5	2	1,628
Mean Precipitation (in.)	4.17	3.71	4.62	3.20	4.16	3.95	5.20	4.43	4.47	3.30	2.96	3.04	47.21
Days With ≥ 0.1" Precipitation	8	6	8	6	7	6	8	7	6	5	5	6	78
Days With ≥ 1.0" Precipitation	1	1	1	1	1	1	2	1	1	1	1	1	13
Mean Snowfall (in.)	0.7	1.5	0.7	0.0	0.0	0.0	0.0	0.0	0.0	0.0	0.0	trace	2.9
Days With ≥ 1.0" Snow Depth	0	0	0	0	0	0	0	0	0	0	0	0	0

Southport 5 N *Brunswick County* Elevation: 19 ft. Latitude: 34° 00' N Longitude: 78° 01' W

	JAN	FEB	MAR	APR	MAY	JUN	JUL	AUG	SEP	OCT	NOV	DEC	YEAR
Mean Maximum Temp. (°F)	56.2	58.7	65.4	72.9	*79.4*	85.5	88.9	*87.9*	83.7	75.8	68.6	59.8	*73.6*
Mean Temp. (°F)	44.3	46.6	53.6	60.9	*68.4*	75.9	80.0	*78.5*	73.4	63.3	*55.5*	47.6	*62.3*
Mean Minimum Temp. (°F)	32.1	34.4	41.4	49.0	*57.3*	66.3	71.0	*69.0*	63.1	50.9	*42.5*	35.3	*51.0*
Extreme Maximum Temp. (°F)	79	81	90	94	97	101	102	102	96	94	88	83	102
Extreme Minimum Temp. (°F)	0	9	8	25	36	45	52	53	35	24	16	-3	-3
Days Maximum Temp. ≥ 90°F	0	0	0	0	1	5	13	10	2	0	0	0	31
Days Maximum Temp. ≤ 32°F	1	0	0	0	0	0	0	0	0	0	0	0	1
Days Minimum Temp. ≤ 32°F	16	13	6	1	0	0	0	0	0	1	7	13	57
Days Minimum Temp. ≤ 0°F	0	0	0	0	0	0	0	0	0	0	0	0	0
Heating Degree Days (base 65°F)	636	515	355	158	*34*	2	0	*0*	6	118	*298*	538	*2,660*
Cooling Degree Days (base 65°F)	1	2	7	39	142	347	484	*422*	252	76	17	4	*1,793*
Mean Precipitation (in.)	5.14	4.26	4.57	2.98	4.21	5.06	6.49	7.66	8.90	3.99	3.45	4.26	60.97
Days With ≥ 0.1" Precipitation	8	6	6	4	7	6	8	9	8	5	5	7	79
Days With ≥ 1.0" Precipitation	1	1	2	1	1	2	2	3	3	1	1	1	19
Mean Snowfall (in.)	trace	0.2	0.3	0.0	0.0	0.0	0.0	0.0	0.0	0.0	0.0	0.5	1.0
Days With ≥ 1.0" Snow Depth	0	0	0	0	0	0	0	0	0	0	0	0	0

Statesville 2 NNE *Iredell County*   Elevation: 948 ft.   Latitude: 35° 49' N   Longitude: 80° 53' W

	JAN	FEB	MAR	APR	MAY	JUN	JUL	AUG	SEP	OCT	NOV	DEC	YEAR
Mean Maximum Temp. (°F)	50.0	54.7	63.3	73.0	79.4	85.7	89.1	87.3	81.7	72.1	62.0	52.9	70.9
Mean Temp. (°F)	38.3	41.7	49.6	58.0	66.2	73.4	77.4	75.9	69.7	58.6	49.0	41.1	58.2
Mean Minimum Temp. (°F)	26.6	28.6	35.9	42.9	52.8	61.0	65.6	64.4	57.6	45.0	36.0	29.4	45.5
Extreme Maximum Temp. (°F)	77	82	88	94	97	101	103	106	99	91	85	79	106
Extreme Minimum Temp. (°F)	-7	2	7	17	29	38	44	44	33	20	6	1	-7
Days Maximum Temp. ≥ 90°F	0	0	0	1	2	8	15	11	4	0	0	0	41
Days Maximum Temp. ≤ 32°F	1	0	0	0	0	0	0	0	0	0	0	0	1
Days Minimum Temp. ≤ 32°F	22	19	12	5	0	0	0	0	0	4	13	20	95
Days Minimum Temp. ≤ 0°F	0	0	0	0	0	0	0	0	0	0	0	0	0
Heating Degree Days (base 65°F)	820	650	474	229	63	7	0	1	29	220	475	736	3,704
Cooling Degree Days (base 65°F)	0	0	4	28	119	285	417	353	177	32	2	1	1,418
Mean Precipitation (in.)	3.76	3.60	4.43	3.37	4.17	4.52	3.89	3.96	3.92	3.61	3.26	3.65	46.14
Days With ≥ 0.1" Precipitation	7	6	8	6	7	7	7	6	5	5	6	7	77
Days With ≥ 1.0" Precipitation	1	1	1	1	1	1	1	1	1	1	1	1	12
Mean Snowfall (in.)	2.2	1.6	1.2	0.0	0.0	0.0	0.0	0.0	0.0	0.0	0.0	0.4	5.4
Days With ≥ 1.0" Snow Depth	1	1	0	0	0	0	0	0	0	0	0	0	2

Tapoco *Graham County*   Elevation: 1,108 ft.   Latitude: 35° 27' N   Longitude: 83° 56' W

	JAN	FEB	MAR	APR	MAY	JUN	JUL	AUG	SEP	OCT	NOV	DEC	YEAR
Mean Maximum Temp. (°F)	49.9	54.4	63.1	72.4	78.6	84.4	87.3	86.3	80.9	71.4	61.8	53.6	70.3
Mean Temp. (°F)	39.5	42.8	50.5	58.4	65.3	71.8	75.0	74.2	69.3	58.9	50.0	43.0	58.2
Mean Minimum Temp. (°F)	29.0	31.2	38.0	44.3	52.0	59.1	62.6	62.0	57.7	46.3	38.2	32.4	46.1
Extreme Maximum Temp. (°F)	75	85	87	92	92	100	101	99	95	88	82	79	101
Extreme Minimum Temp. (°F)	-14	-3	-1	20	30	38	49	46	34	24	10	-4	-14
Days Maximum Temp. ≥ 90°F	0	0	0	0	1	5	11	8	2	0	0	0	27
Days Maximum Temp. ≤ 32°F	2	1	0	0	0	0	0	0	0	0	0	1	4
Days Minimum Temp. ≤ 32°F	20	16	10	3	0	0	0	0	0	2	10	17	78
Days Minimum Temp. ≤ 0°F	0	0	0	0	0	0	0	0	0	0	0	0	0
Heating Degree Days (base 65°F)	784	620	446	214	67	6	0	0	24	207	446	676	3,490
Cooling Degree Days (base 65°F)	0	0	3	22	89	228	334	296	155	24	2	1	1,154
Mean Precipitation (in.)	5.74	5.19	6.25	4.76	5.56	5.53	5.58	4.21	4.15	3.40	4.50	5.17	60.04
Days With ≥ 0.1" Precipitation	9	9	10	8	9	9	9	7	7	6	7	9	99
Days With ≥ 1.0" Precipitation	2	1	2	1	1	2	2	1	1	1	1	2	17
Mean Snowfall (in.)	*1.3*	2.2	0.5	0.3	0.0	0.0	0.0	0.0	0.0	0.0	trace	0.2	*4.5*
Days With ≥ 1.0" Snow Depth	*0*	*0*	0	0	0	0	0	0	0	0	0	0	*0*

Tarboro 1 S *Edgecombe County*   Elevation: 32 ft.   Latitude: 35° 53' N   Longitude: 77° 32' W

	JAN	FEB	MAR	APR	MAY	JUN	JUL	AUG	SEP	OCT	NOV	DEC	YEAR
Mean Maximum Temp. (°F)	52.4	55.7	64.0	73.5	80.6	87.2	90.7	88.9	84.0	74.0	64.7	55.8	72.6
Mean Temp. (°F)	41.0	43.5	51.1	59.7	67.8	75.2	79.4	77.7	72.2	61.2	51.9	44.0	60.4
Mean Minimum Temp. (°F)	29.5	31.3	38.2	45.9	55.0	63.2	68.1	66.5	60.5	48.0	39.0	32.3	48.1
Extreme Maximum Temp. (°F)	80	84	91	96	98	101	103	105	100	94	85	83	105
Extreme Minimum Temp. (°F)	-5	2	8	25	34	41	49	45	37	20	14	0	-5
Days Maximum Temp. ≥ 90°F	0	0	0	1	4	11	19	15	5	0	0	0	55
Days Maximum Temp. ≤ 32°F	1	0	0	0	0	0	0	0	0	0	0	0	1
Days Minimum Temp. ≤ 32°F	20	16	9	2	0	0	0	0	0	2	9	17	75
Days Minimum Temp. ≤ 0°F	0	0	0	0	0	0	0	0	0	0	0	0	0
Heating Degree Days (base 65°F)	738	601	430	195	49	4	0	0	13	162	396	645	3,233
Cooling Degree Days (base 65°F)	1	1	8	40	142	327	469	396	227	49	6	2	1,668
Mean Precipitation (in.)	4.16	3.69	4.22	3.07	3.67	3.77	4.53	4.78	4.28	3.14	2.62	3.09	45.02
Days With ≥ 0.1" Precipitation	7	7	7	6	7	6	7	7	5	5	5	6	75
Days With ≥ 1.0" Precipitation	1	1	1	1	1	1	1	1	1	1	1	1	12
Mean Snowfall (in.)	1.0	2.7	1.3	trace	0.0	0.0	0.0	0.0	0.0	0.0	trace	0.2	5.2
Days With ≥ 1.0" Snow Depth	0	*0*	0	0	0	0	0	0	0	0	0	0	*0*

Transou *Ashe County*   Elevation: 2,874 ft.   Latitude: 36° 24' N   Longitude: 81° 18' W

	JAN	FEB	MAR	APR	MAY	JUN	JUL	AUG	SEP	OCT	NOV	DEC	YEAR
Mean Maximum Temp. (°F)	42.3	45.8	54.0	63.3	70.2	76.6	80.6	79.1	73.4	64.0	54.3	46.3	62.5
Mean Temp. (°F)	31.7	34.6	42.1	50.0	57.6	64.7	68.8	67.3	61.4	50.9	42.3	35.0	50.5
Mean Minimum Temp. (°F)	21.1	23.3	30.2	36.7	45.0	52.8	56.9	55.4	49.4	37.8	30.3	23.7	38.5
Extreme Maximum Temp. (°F)	72	75	78	83	89	90	92	93	89	82	75	73	93
Extreme Minimum Temp. (°F)	-24	-15	-1	13	19	30	35	32	23	16	2	-12	-24
Days Maximum Temp. ≥ 90°F	0	0	0	0	0	0	0	0	0	0	0	0	0
Days Maximum Temp. ≤ 32°F	6	3	1	0	0	0	0	0	0	0	0	3	13
Days Minimum Temp. ≤ 32°F	26	23	19	11	3	0	0	0	1	11	19	24	137
Days Minimum Temp. ≤ 0°F	2	0	0	0	0	0	0	0	0	0	0	1	3
Heating Degree Days (base 65°F)	1,025	853	703	444	233	64	13	22	133	431	674	922	5,517
Cooling Degree Days (base 65°F)	0	0	0	1	13	67	149	102	31	1	0	0	364
Mean Precipitation (in.)	4.35	4.04	5.56	4.71	5.63	5.00	4.79	4.88	4.72	4.74	4.85	3.65	56.92
Days With ≥ 0.1" Precipitation	7	7	8	7	9	8	9	7	7	6	7	7	89
Days With ≥ 1.0" Precipitation	1	1	2	1	2	1	1	1	1	1	1	1	14
Mean Snowfall (in.)	8.2	6.7	3.8	1.4	trace	0.0	0.0	0.0	0.0	0.1	1.0	3.5	24.7
Days With ≥ 1.0" Snow Depth	6	5	2	0	0	0	0	0	0	0	0	3	16

Tryon *Polk County*   Elevation: 1,079 ft.   Latitude: 35° 12' N   Longitude: 82° 14' W

	JAN	FEB	MAR	APR	MAY	JUN	JUL	AUG	SEP	OCT	NOV	DEC	YEAR
Mean Maximum Temp. (°F)	51.9	56.8	65.1	74.0	80.3	85.9	89.1	87.3	81.8	72.8	62.9	55.0	71.9
Mean Temp. (°F)	41.5	44.9	52.5	60.2	67.5	74.1	78.0	76.5	70.9	60.7	51.6	44.3	60.2
Mean Minimum Temp. (°F)	31.0	33.1	39.8	46.3	54.7	62.3	66.9	65.8	60.0	48.5	40.2	33.6	48.5
Extreme Maximum Temp. (°F)	80	82	89	94	97	98	102	103	97	91	85	81	103
Extreme Minimum Temp. (°F)	-8	8	14	26	30	43	51	49	40	26	14	3	-8
Days Maximum Temp. ≥ 90°F	0	0	0	1	1	8	15	10	3	0	0	0	38
Days Maximum Temp. ≤ 32°F	1	0	0	0	0	0	0	0	0	0	0	0	1
Days Minimum Temp. ≤ 32°F	17	14	7	1	0	0	0	0	0	1	7	15	62
Days Minimum Temp. ≤ 0°F	0	0	0	0	0	0	0	0	0	0	0	0	0
Heating Degree Days (base 65°F)	723	561	388	171	39	3	0	0	15	162	398	635	3,095
Cooling Degree Days (base 65°F)	0	1	6	34	130	299	432	375	196	37	2	1	1,513
Mean Precipitation (in.)	5.75	5.15	6.57	4.63	5.82	5.60	5.29	6.36	5.46	5.28	4.84	4.83	65.58
Days With ≥ 0.1" Precipitation	8	7	9	7	8	8	8	8	6	6	7	7	89
Days With ≥ 1.0" Precipitation	2	2	2	2	2	2	2	2	2	2	1	2	23
Mean Snowfall (in.)	3.2	2.0	1.4	trace	trace	0.0	0.0	0.0	0.0	0.0	trace	1.0	7.6
Days With ≥ 1.0" Snow Depth	3	1	1	0	0	0	0	0	0	0	0	0	5

W Kerr Scott Reservoir *Wilkes County*   Elevation: 1,069 ft.   Latitude: 36° 08' N   Longitude: 81° 14' W

	JAN	FEB	MAR	APR	MAY	JUN	JUL	AUG	SEP	OCT	NOV	DEC	YEAR
Mean Maximum Temp. (°F)	47.5	51.9	60.1	69.9	77.2	84.1	87.9	86.3	80.4	70.7	60.8	51.7	69.0
Mean Temp. (°F)	35.8	39.1	46.9	55.5	63.9	71.8	75.9	74.5	68.3	56.8	47.6	39.4	56.3
Mean Minimum Temp. (°F)	24.0	26.1	33.6	41.0	50.6	59.5	63.9	62.6	56.1	42.8	34.4	27.0	43.5
Extreme Maximum Temp. (°F)	76	82	87	94	96	98	100	102	97	91	84	80	102
Extreme Minimum Temp. (°F)	-10	-6	1	20	29	38	46	44	33	23	7	-3	-10
Days Maximum Temp. ≥ 90°F	0	0	0	0	1	6	13	9	3	0	0	0	32
Days Maximum Temp. ≤ 32°F	2	1	0	0	0	0	0	0	0	0	0	1	4
Days Minimum Temp. ≤ 32°F	25	22	15	5	0	0	0	0	0	4	14	23	108
Days Minimum Temp. ≤ 0°F	1	0	0	0	0	0	0	0	0	0	0	0	1
Heating Degree Days (base 65°F)	899	726	557	294	102	12	1	1	41	262	516	787	4,198
Cooling Degree Days (base 65°F)	0	0	3	15	81	240	366	304	142	16	0	0	1,167
Mean Precipitation (in.)	4.48	3.91	5.09	4.44	4.91	4.73	4.60	5.16	4.80	4.01	3.64	3.76	53.53
Days With ≥ 0.1" Precipitation	7	7	8	7	8	7	8	7	7	5	6	7	84
Days With ≥ 1.0" Precipitation	1	1	2	1	2	1	1	2	2	1	1	1	16
Mean Snowfall (in.)	3.8	3.5	1.8	0.0	0.0	0.0	0.0	0.0	0.0	0.0	trace	1.1	10.2
Days With ≥ 1.0" Snow Depth	3	3	1	0	0	0	0	0	0	0	0	1	8

Wadesboro *Anson County*   Elevation: 479 ft.   Latitude: 34° 58' N   Longitude: 80° 04' W

	JAN	FEB	MAR	APR	MAY	JUN	JUL	AUG	SEP	OCT	NOV	DEC	YEAR
Mean Maximum Temp. (°F)	51.5	55.9	64.1	73.5	80.1	86.8	90.4	88.5	83.3	73.6	64.4	55.2	72.3
Mean Temp. (°F)	41.3	44.7	52.5	61.3	68.8	76.2	80.1	78.5	72.9	61.7	53.1	44.8	61.3
Mean Minimum Temp. (°F)	31.1	33.5	41.0	49.0	57.5	65.5	69.8	68.5	62.5	49.8	41.9	34.4	50.4
Extreme Maximum Temp. (°F)	78	82	89	94	98	103	104	107	100	94	86	80	107
Extreme Minimum Temp. (°F)	-4	6	8	26	33	46	55	54	43	29	16	5	-4
Days Maximum Temp. ≥ 90°F	0	0	0	1	3	10	19	14	5	0	0	0	52
Days Maximum Temp. ≤ 32°F	1	0	0	0	0	0	0	0	0	0	0	0	1
Days Minimum Temp. ≤ 32°F	18	14	6	1	0	0	0	0	0	1	6	14	60
Days Minimum Temp. ≤ 0°F	0	0	0	0	0	0	0	0	0	0	0	0	0
Heating Degree Days (base 65°F)	728	567	389	161	37	3	0	0	13	147	358	622	3,025
Cooling Degree Days (base 65°F)	0	2	11	54	169	362	497	430	250	57	7	2	1,841
Mean Precipitation (in.)	4.50	3.67	4.66	2.89	3.53	4.56	5.24	4.53	4.09	3.88	3.02	3.30	47.87
Days With ≥ 0.1" Precipitation	8	6	8	5	6	7	8	7	5	5	5	6	76
Days With ≥ 1.0" Precipitation	1	1	1	1	1	1	1	2	1	1	1	1	13
Mean Snowfall (in.)	0.9	1.3	0.6	0.0	0.0	0.0	0.0	0.0	0.0	0.0	trace	0.7	3.5
Days With ≥ 1.0" Snow Depth	1	0	0	0	0	0	0	0	0	0	0	0	1

Waterville 2 *Haywood County*   Elevation: 1,437 ft.   Latitude: 35° 46' N   Longitude: 83° 06' W

	JAN	FEB	MAR	APR	MAY	JUN	JUL	AUG	SEP	OCT	NOV	DEC	YEAR
Mean Maximum Temp. (°F)	47.5	51.7	60.3	69.7	76.4	83.2	86.3	84.4	78.5	68.5	59.0	50.6	68.0
Mean Temp. (°F)	37.7	41.0	48.8	57.1	64.6	71.8	75.4	74.1	68.4	57.6	48.3	41.0	57.1
Mean Minimum Temp. (°F)	27.8	30.2	37.3	44.4	52.7	60.4	64.4	63.7	58.3	46.6	37.6	31.3	46.2
Extreme Maximum Temp. (°F)	74	84	88	90	93	98	100	98	99	87	80	76	100
Extreme Minimum Temp. (°F)	-17	-5	5	21	31	40	50	47	39	26	11	-2	-17
Days Maximum Temp. ≥ 90°F	0	0	0	0	0	4	9	4	1	0	0	0	18
Days Maximum Temp. ≤ 32°F	3	2	0	0	0	0	0	0	0	0	0	2	7
Days Minimum Temp. ≤ 32°F	21	17	10	3	0	0	0	0	0	1	10	18	80
Days Minimum Temp. ≤ 0°F	0	0	0	0	0	0	0	0	0	0	0	0	0
Heating Degree Days (base 65°F)	840	673	498	249	85	7	0	1	33	239	496	737	3,858
Cooling Degree Days (base 65°F)	0	0	2	17	83	228	345	298	139	17	1	0	1,130
Mean Precipitation (in.)	3.86	3.81	4.74	4.01	4.87	5.35	5.18	4.20	3.85	2.48	3.15	3.67	49.17
Days With ≥ 0.1" Precipitation	8	8	10	8	10	9	10	8	7	5	7	8	98
Days With ≥ 1.0" Precipitation	1	1	1	1	1	1	1	1	1	1	1	1	12
Mean Snowfall (in.)	na	na	*1.4*	0.9	0.0	0.0	0.0	0.0	0.0	0.0	0.0	*0.3*	na
Days With ≥ 1.0" Snow Depth	na	na	*0*	0	0	0	0	0	0	0	0	*0*	na

Waynesville 1 E *Haywood County*   Elevation: 2,657 ft.   Latitude: 35° 29' N   Longitude: 82° 58' W

	JAN	FEB	MAR	APR	MAY	JUN	JUL	AUG	SEP	OCT	NOV	DEC	YEAR
Mean Maximum Temp. (°F)	48.4	52.1	59.9	68.0	74.5	80.4	83.5	82.1	77.1	68.5	59.2	51.8	67.1
Mean Temp. (°F)	36.2	39.1	46.4	53.5	60.8	67.6	71.2	70.2	64.8	54.4	45.8	39.4	54.1
Mean Minimum Temp. (°F)	24.0	26.1	32.8	39.0	47.0	54.7	58.9	58.2	52.3	40.3	32.4	26.9	41.1
Extreme Maximum Temp. (°F)	75	79	84	87	92	92	95	94	92	85	79	72	95
Extreme Minimum Temp. (°F)	-22	-13	-8	15	24	34	40	41	28	17	3	-6	-22
Days Maximum Temp. ≥ 90°F	0	0	0	0	0	1	2	1	0	0	0	0	4
Days Maximum Temp. ≤ 32°F	2	2	0	0	0	0	0	0	0	0	0	1	5
Days Minimum Temp. ≤ 32°F	23	20	16	8	2	0	0	0	0	8	16	22	115
Days Minimum Temp. ≤ 0°F	1	0	0	0	0	0	0	0	0	0	0	0	1
Heating Degree Days (base 65°F)	886	725	571	342	152	26	2	4	69	326	570	787	4,460
Cooling Degree Days (base 65°F)	0	0	1	4	32	121	218	180	69	5	0	0	630
Mean Precipitation (in.)	4.54	4.52	5.19	3.75	4.37	4.05	3.57	4.10	3.64	3.01	3.72	4.07	48.53
Days With ≥ 0.1" Precipitation	8	7	9	7	8	8	8	8	7	5	6	8	89
Days With ≥ 1.0" Precipitation	1	1	1	1	1	1	1	1	1	1	1	1	12
Mean Snowfall (in.)	4.6	4.0	2.4	1.0	0.2	0.0	0.0	0.0	0.0	trace	0.4	1.9	14.5
Days With ≥ 1.0" Snow Depth	3	2	1	0	0	0	0	0	0	0	0	1	7

Whiteville 7 NW *Columbus County*   Elevation: 88 ft.   Latitude: 34° 24' N   Longitude: 78° 48' W

	JAN	FEB	MAR	APR	MAY	JUN	JUL	AUG	SEP	OCT	NOV	DEC	YEAR
Mean Maximum Temp. (°F)	54.8	58.6	66.6	75.0	81.6	87.2	90.6	89.0	84.5	75.3	67.4	58.2	74.1
Mean Temp. (°F)	43.7	46.4	53.8	61.4	69.1	76.0	79.9	78.3	73.3	62.5	54.5	46.5	62.1
Mean Minimum Temp. (°F)	32.4	34.1	40.9	47.8	56.7	64.6	69.0	67.6	62.0	49.7	41.5	34.8	50.1
Extreme Maximum Temp. (°F)	80	86	89	92	98	102	101	104	98	95	85	85	104
Extreme Minimum Temp. (°F)	8	5	10	27	35	45	53	52	40	24	18	-2	-2
Days Maximum Temp. ≥ 90°F	0	0	0	1	3	11	20	16	7	0	0	0	58
Days Maximum Temp. ≤ 32°F	1	0	0	0	0	0	0	0	0	0	0	0	1
Days Minimum Temp. ≤ 32°F	17	14	7	1	0	0	0	0	0	1	7	15	62
Days Minimum Temp. ≤ 0°F	0	0	0	0	0	0	0	0	0	0	0	0	0
Heating Degree Days (base 65°F)	656	521	355	154	33	2	0	0	9	135	325	570	2,760
Cooling Degree Days (base 65°F)	1	2	13	49	169	350	485	417	254	66	13	4	1,823
Mean Precipitation (in.)	4.27	3.54	4.53	2.89	4.51	4.46	5.69	5.58	5.41	3.13	2.76	3.27	50.04
Days With ≥ 0.1" Precipitation	8	6	8	5	7	7	9	8	6	5	5	6	80
Days With ≥ 1.0" Precipitation	1	1	1	1	1	1	2	2	2	1	1	1	15
Mean Snowfall (in.)	0.4	1.1	0.5	trace	0.0	0.0	0.0	0.0	0.0	0.0	0.0	0.6	2.6
Days With ≥ 1.0" Snow Depth	0	0	0	0	0	0	0	0	0	0	0	0	0

Willard 4 SW *Pender County*   Elevation: 52 ft.   Latitude: 34° 40' N   Longitude: 78° 03' W

	JAN	FEB	MAR	APR	MAY	JUN	JUL	AUG	SEP	OCT	NOV	DEC	YEAR
Mean Maximum Temp. (°F)	56.2	60.4	68.3	76.6	82.3	87.4	90.3	88.5	84.0	75.1	67.6	59.6	74.7
Mean Temp. (°F)	44.8	47.8	54.9	62.5	69.8	76.1	79.7	78.3	73.4	63.3	55.3	47.7	62.8
Mean Minimum Temp. (°F)	33.3	35.2	41.4	48.4	57.3	64.7	69.0	68.0	62.7	51.4	42.9	35.8	50.8
Extreme Maximum Temp. (°F)	80	84	92	97	97	100	103	103	101	93	85	82	103
Extreme Minimum Temp. (°F)	-2	2	2	24	35	44	52	52	40	26	15	-8	-8
Days Maximum Temp. ≥ 90°F	0	0	0	1	4	11	19	13	5	0	0	0	53
Days Maximum Temp. ≤ 32°F	1	0	0	0	0	0	0	0	0	0	0	0	1
Days Minimum Temp. ≤ 32°F	15	12	7	1	0	0	0	0	0	1	6	13	55
Days Minimum Temp. ≤ 0°F	0	0	0	0	0	0	0	0	0	0	0	0	0
Heating Degree Days (base 65°F)	621	483	323	133	25	1	0	0	7	116	304	532	2,545
Cooling Degree Days (base 65°F)	1	3	16	63	187	353	476	416	256	75	17	4	1,867
Mean Precipitation (in.)	4.39	3.60	4.45	3.04	4.03	4.96	6.97	6.60	6.13	3.29	2.93	3.42	53.81
Days With ≥ 0.1" Precipitation	8	6	8	5	7	7	9	8	7	5	5	6	81
Days With ≥ 1.0" Precipitation	1	1	1	1	1	2	2	2	2	1	1	1	16
Mean Snowfall (in.)	0.5	1.0	0.6	trace	0.0	0.0	0.0	0.0	0.0	0.0	0.0	0.8	2.9
Days With ≥ 1.0" Snow Depth	0	0	0	0	0	0	0	0	0	0	0	0	0

Williamston 1 E *Martin County*   Elevation: 19 ft.   Latitude: 35° 51' N   Longitude: 77° 02' W

	JAN	FEB	MAR	APR	MAY	JUN	JUL	AUG	SEP	OCT	NOV	DEC	YEAR
Mean Maximum Temp. (°F)	52.5	55.4	63.2	72.6	79.1	85.7	89.2	87.5	83.0	73.4	65.1	55.6	71.9
Mean Temp. (°F)	42.3	44.5	51.9	60.3	67.9	75.3	79.4	77.8	72.8	61.6	53.6	45.0	61.0
Mean Minimum Temp. (°F)	32.0	33.5	40.6	47.9	56.7	64.8	69.6	68.1	62.5	49.8	42.1	34.4	50.2
Extreme Maximum Temp. (°F)	80	83	89	95	96	99	101	101	98	93	86	82	101
Extreme Minimum Temp. (°F)	6	8	7	28	35	45	51	51	40	25	20	4	4
Days Maximum Temp. ≥ 90°F	0	0	0	1	2	8	16	11	4	0	0	0	42
Days Maximum Temp. ≤ 32°F	1	0	0	0	0	0	0	0	0	0	0	0	1
Days Minimum Temp. ≤ 32°F	16	14	6	1	0	0	0	0	0	1	6	15	59
Days Minimum Temp. ≤ 0°F	0	0	0	0	0	0	0	0	0	0	0	0	0
Heating Degree Days (base 65°F)	698	574	409	181	46	4	0	0	10	152	348	614	3,036
Cooling Degree Days (base 65°F)	1	2	9	40	140	323	464	*386*	230	50	10	2	*1,657*
Mean Precipitation (in.)	4.40	3.22	4.29	3.15	3.98	4.45	5.49	5.11	5.37	3.96	2.84	3.13	49.39
Days With ≥ 0.1" Precipitation	8	6	7	6	7	7	8	7	6	5	5	7	79
Days With ≥ 1.0" Precipitation	1	1	1	1	1	1	2	2	2	1	1	1	15
Mean Snowfall (in.)	0.6	1.6	1.1	0.0	0.0	0.0	0.0	0.0	0.0	0.0	0.0	0.3	3.6
Days With ≥ 1.0" Snow Depth	0	1	0	0	0	0	0	0	0	0	0	0	1

Wilmington 7 N *New Hanover County*   Elevation: 39 ft.   Latitude: 34° 19' N   Longitude: 77° 55' W

	JAN	FEB	MAR	APR	MAY	JUN	JUL	AUG	SEP	OCT	NOV	DEC	YEAR
Mean Maximum Temp. (°F)	56.0	59.1	66.3	74.6	81.0	86.8	90.0	88.3	83.9	75.0	67.8	59.6	74.0
Mean Temp. (°F)	44.7	47.2	54.2	61.9	69.5	76.4	80.2	78.6	73.7	63.3	55.6	47.9	62.8
Mean Minimum Temp. (°F)	33.3	35.2	42.1	49.1	57.9	65.9	70.3	68.8	63.5	51.6	43.3	36.2	51.4
Extreme Maximum Temp. (°F)	80	84	90	94	97	102	103	104	96	96	87	83	104
Extreme Minimum Temp. (°F)	0	10	9	26	32	45	47	52	39	26	18	0	0
Days Maximum Temp. ≥ 90°F	0	0	0	1	3	9	18	13	5	0	0	0	49
Days Maximum Temp. ≤ 32°F	1	0	0	0	0	0	0	0	0	0	0	0	1
Days Minimum Temp. ≤ 32°F	15	12	6	1	0	0	0	0	0	1	6	12	53
Days Minimum Temp. ≤ 0°F	0	0	0	0	0	0	0	0	0	0	0	0	0
Heating Degree Days (base 65°F)	625	500	343	147	33	2	0	0	8	119	297	528	2,602
Cooling Degree Days (base 65°F)	1	3	13	56	178	363	491	427	263	74	18	5	1,892
Mean Precipitation (in.)	4.67	3.90	4.52	2.99	4.67	5.07	7.86	7.49	6.73	3.23	3.12	4.03	58.28
Days With ≥ 0.1" Precipitation	8	6	7	5	7	7	9	9	7	5	5	6	81
Days With ≥ 1.0" Precipitation	1	1	1	1	1	2	2	2	2	1	1	1	16
Mean Snowfall (in.)	0.4	0.6	0.6	0.0	0.0	0.0	0.0	0.0	0.0	0.0	0.0	0.7	2.3
Days With ≥ 1.0" Snow Depth	0	0	0	0	0	0	0	0	0	0	0	0	0

Wilson 3 SW *Wilson County*   Elevation: 108 ft.   Latitude: 35° 42' N   Longitude: 77° 57' W

	JAN	FEB	MAR	APR	MAY	JUN	JUL	AUG	SEP	OCT	NOV	DEC	YEAR
Mean Maximum Temp. (°F)	51.1	54.9	62.8	72.7	79.6	87.0	90.4	88.7	83.5	73.4	64.6	55.1	72.0
Mean Temp. (°F)	40.2	43.2	50.6	59.7	67.6	75.3	79.3	77.7	71.9	60.6	52.1	43.8	60.2
Mean Minimum Temp. (°F)	29.4	31.6	38.4	46.6	55.4	63.6	68.2	66.6	60.3	47.8	39.5	32.5	48.3
Extreme Maximum Temp. (°F)	79	84	91	96	96	102	104	105	101	94	87	81	105
Extreme Minimum Temp. (°F)	-5	5	7	26	36	43	49	47	38	23	17	3	-5
Days Maximum Temp. ≥ 90°F	0	0	0	1	3	11	19	15	6	0	0	0	55
Days Maximum Temp. ≤ 32°F	2	0	0	0	0	0	0	0	0	0	0	1	3
Days Minimum Temp. ≤ 32°F	20	16	8	1	0	0	0	0	0	2	8	17	72
Days Minimum Temp. ≤ 0°F	0	0	0	0	0	0	0	0	0	0	0	0	0
Heating Degree Days (base 65°F)	762	610	448	196	52	4	0	1	17	175	390	652	3,307
Cooling Degree Days (base 65°F)	1	2	8	39	139	329	465	395	219	45	6	2	1,650
Mean Precipitation (in.)	4.20	3.48	4.42	3.16	4.09	3.83	5.22	4.44	4.77	3.15	3.04	3.37	47.17
Days With ≥ 0.1" Precipitation	8	7	7	6	7	6	8	6	6	5	5	6	77
Days With ≥ 1.0" Precipitation	1	1	1	1	1	1	2	1	2	1	1	1	14
Mean Snowfall (in.)	0.4	1.3	0.9	trace	0.0	0.0	0.0	0.0	0.0	0.0	trace	0.3	2.9
Days With ≥ 1.0" Snow Depth	0	1	0	0	0	0	0	0	0	0	0	0	1

Yadkinville 6 E *Yadkin County*   Elevation: 872 ft.   Latitude: 36° 08' N   Longitude: 80° 33' W

	JAN	FEB	MAR	APR	MAY	JUN	JUL	AUG	SEP	OCT	NOV	DEC	YEAR
Mean Maximum Temp. (°F)	48.9	53.9	62.6	72.5	79.0	85.4	89.2	87.6	81.9	72.1	61.6	52.3	70.6
Mean Temp. (°F)	37.9	41.5	49.5	57.9	65.7	73.0	77.0	75.6	69.6	58.5	49.0	41.1	58.0
Mean Minimum Temp. (°F)	26.9	29.1	36.2	43.4	52.5	60.7	64.8	63.5	57.3	44.9	36.4	29.8	45.5
Extreme Maximum Temp. (°F)	77	82	89	92	96	102	105	104	99	94	87	80	105
Extreme Minimum Temp. (°F)	-8	-1	6	22	30	39	47	44	34	23	8	0	-8
Days Maximum Temp. ≥ 90°F	0	0	0	1	2	8	16	12	5	0	0	0	44
Days Maximum Temp. ≤ 32°F	2	0	0	0	0	0	0	0	0	0	0	1	3
Days Minimum Temp. ≤ 32°F	22	19	12	4	0	0	0	0	0	3	12	19	91
Days Minimum Temp. ≤ 0°F	0	0	0	0	0	0	0	0	0	0	0	0	0
Heating Degree Days (base 65°F)	832	656	479	230	70	7	1	1	29	221	475	735	3,736
Cooling Degree Days (base 65°F)	0	0	4	24	103	270	396	339	171	29	2	0	1,338
Mean Precipitation (in.)	3.84	3.53	4.64	3.43	4.35	3.89	4.15	3.62	3.86	3.86	3.09	3.55	45.81
Days With ≥ 0.1" Precipitation	7	6	8	7	8	7	7	6	6	5	6	6	79
Days With ≥ 1.0" Precipitation	1	1	1	1	1	1	1	1	1	1	1	1	12
Mean Snowfall (in.)	3.7	3.0	1.2	trace	0.0	0.0	0.0	0.0	0.0	0.0	trace	1.1	9.0
Days With ≥ 1.0" Snow Depth	4	2	1	0	0	0	0	0	0	0	0	0	7

Note: See Appendix D for explanation of data.

NORTH DAKOTA

PHYSICAL FEATURES. North Dakota is typically plains country located near the center of the North American Continent. The eastern part of the State is flat, with an elevation in the Red River Valley of 780 feet at Pembina in the north to 962 feet above sea level at Wahpeton in the south. To the westward there is a gradual rise of terrain until an elevation of 3,468 feet is reached at Black Butte in the southwestern part of the State. The Turtle Mountains in the north-central part of the State are only about 500 feet higher than the surrounding area, with the highest elevation about 2,300 feet above sea level.

GENERAL CLIMATE. Summers are usually very pleasant, but hot winds and periods of prolonged high temperatures occur occasionally. However, minimum temperatures are seldom above 70°F., so it is unusual to have uncomfortable nights. Winters are usually cold with occasional mild ones.

TEMPERATURE. The annual mean temperature for North Dakota ranges from about 36°F. in the northeast to 43°F. in the extreme south. Temperatures above 100°F. are occasionally recorded, and zero readings are common in winter. The average number of days a year when the temperature reaches 90°F. or higher is 14, and the average number with zero or lower is 53. The average growing season is about 121 days, ranging from 110 days in the northeast and north-central to 135 in the extreme south. For the State, the average date of the last freeze in spring is May 19, and the first in fall is September 18. Freezing temperatures have occurred, however, as late as the first part of June and as early in the fall as the first few days of September.

PRECIPITATION. Precipitation in the eastern third of the State averages about 19 inches, in the middle third about 16 inches, and in the western third about 15 inches. On an average, about 77 percent of the annual precipitation occurs during the crop-growing freeze-free season, April to September, and almost 50 percent falls during May, June, and July. The normal precipitation for the driest months, November to February, is about one-half inch a month. The greatest amount falls between 5 p.m. and 8 p.m. and again about midnight. In North Dakota, precipitation is considered the most important climatic factor.

Most of the rain in the summer months occurs in storms accompanied by thunder and lightning, often with heavy falls for a short time. The average number of thunderstorm days in 30, mostly in June, July, and August. In most years at least some part of the State is visited by a storm that brings a rainfall of two or three inches in 24 hours, and occasionally five or six inches falls in one day. On an average, rain falls about one day in four during the summer months. The annual number of days with measurable precipitation averages 66, ranging from about 50 in the west to 90 in the east.

The first light snow in autumn occasionally falls in September, but usually very little occurs until after October. The average number of days with 0.1 inch or more of snow is 23. The average annual snowfall is 32 inches with the greatest amount in the northeast and least in the southwest. Occasionally there is heavy snowfall in winter, and the amount of snow on the ground accumulates to a considerable depth.

RIVERS AND FLOODS. The streams of North Dakota fall into two main groups — those in the west and south-central portions draining into the Missouri Basin, and those in the east and north-central portions draining into the Red River of the North.

Some of the important tributaries which drain into the Missouri in North Dakota are: the Cannonball, Grand, Heart, Knife, Little Missouri, and James. Local floods occur occasionally on all the tributaries, mainly associated with ice breakup, notably on the Heart River where serious floods have occurred from ice jams. Floods along the main stem of the Missouri in the past have been caused primarily by snowmelt in the high plains. The resulting flooding has been almost invariably aggravated by ice jams.

The streams draining the east and north-central portions of North Dakota flow into the Red River of the North, which flows in a northerly direction between Minnesota and North Dakota into Canada. The most important tributaries in the eastern portion of North Dakota are the Sheyenne and the Pembina. The latter rises in the province of Manitoba, Canada. In the north-central portion the Souris River originates in the province of Saskatchewan, Canada, flows southeastward into North Dakota, and then curves back into Canada and flows in a northerly direction into the Assiniboine River which empties into the Red River of the North above the International Boundary.

Floods in the Red River of the North Basin occur primarily during the spring season (April and May) and are caused chiefly by melting snow. Ice conditions, particularly on the northward flowing streams, increase flood crests and occasionally cause extremely high flood stages due to jams. Early freeze-up in the fall before snow occurs is also a contributing factor in producing flood conditions in the spring. Considerably higher crests result along the tributaries and the main stem of the river if the snowmelt is accompanied by a period of prolonged heavy rains. Major rainstorms causing more than local flooding (without snowmelt) are extremely rare.

OTHER CLIMATIC ELEMENTS. The prevailing direction of the wind in all months of the year is from the northwest, unless it is influenced by local conditions. More southerly winds are observed during the summer than during the winter. The average annual wind speed is about 11 m.p.h. The highest speeds are in spring and the lowest in late summer. High winds frequently accompany severe thunderstorms. Tornadoes are reported in North Dakota.

The average relative humidity is about 68 percent, slightly higher in the east than in the west. Humidity is frequently low during the afternoon in summer, sometimes below 20 percent. Dense fogs are experienced, on an average, on only eight days of the year.

The average number of clear days is 160, partly cloudy 100, and cloudy 105. On a clear day the sun shines for more than 15 hours from the middle of May to the end of July. The yearly average amount of sunshine is 59 percent of the possible amount, with 74 percent in July and 72 percent in August.

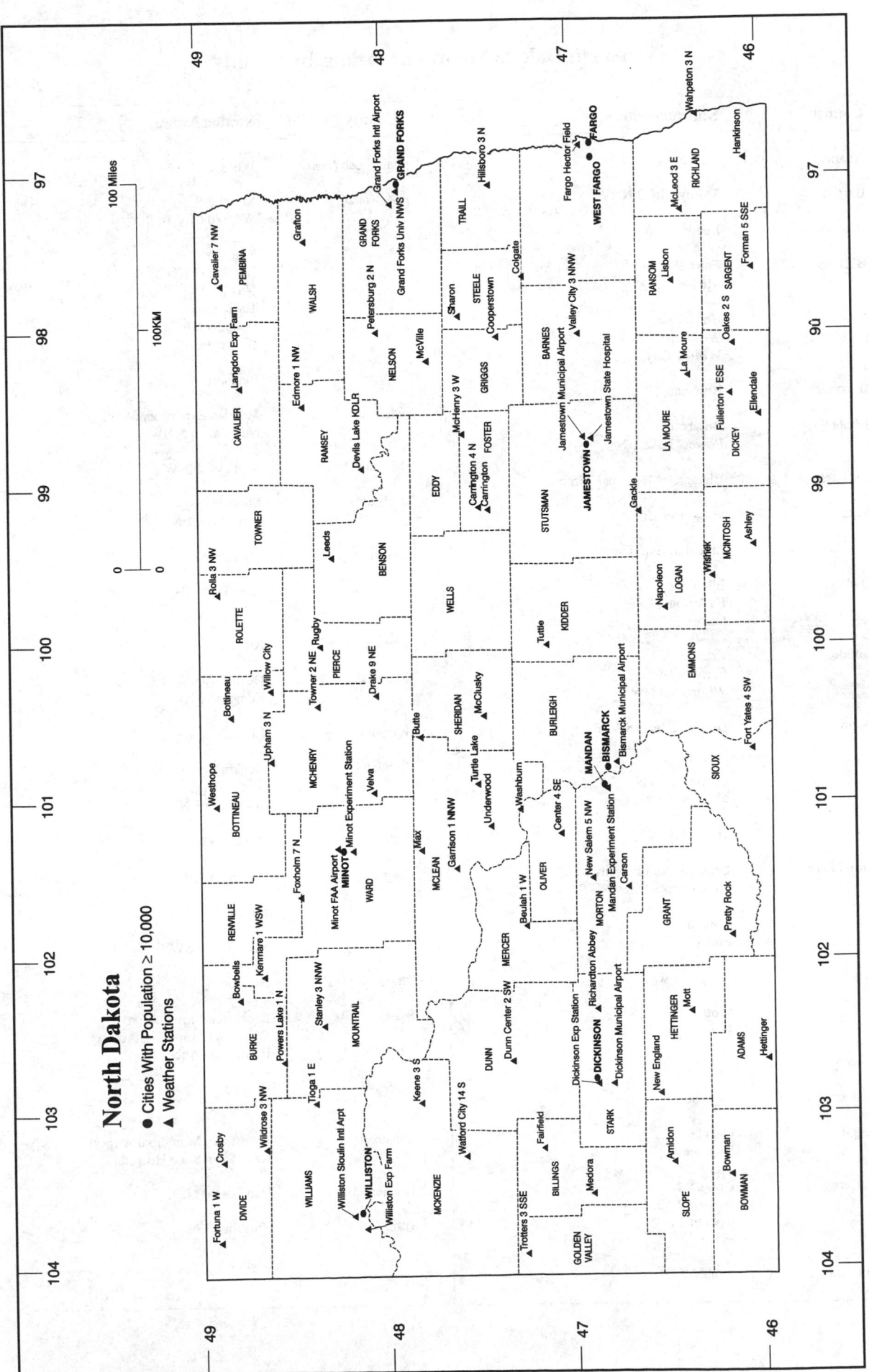

North Dakota

● Cities With Population ≥ 10,000
▲ Weather Stations

North Dakota Weather Stations by County

County	Station Name
Adams	Hettinger
Barnes	Valley City 3 NNW
Benson	Leeds
Billings	Fairfield
	Medora
Bottineau	Bottineau
	Westhope
	Willow City
Bowman	Bowman
Burke	Bowbells
	Powers Lake 1 N
Burleigh	Bismarck Municipal Airport
Cass	Fargo Hector Field
Cavalier	Langdon Exp. Farm
Dickey	Ellendale
	Fullerton 1 ESE
	Oakes 2 S
Divide	Crosby
	Fortuna 1 W
	Wildrose 3 NW
Dunn	Dunn Center 2 SW
Foster	Carrington
	Carrington 4 N
	McHenry 3 W
Golden Valley	Trotters 3 SSE
Grand Forks	Grand Forks Int'l Airport
	Grand Forks Univ. NWS
Grant	Carson
	Pretty Rock
Griggs	Cooperstown
Hettinger	Mott
	New England
Kidder	Tuttle
Lamoure	La Moure
Logan	Gackle
	Napoleon
McHenry	Drake 9 NE
	Towner 2 NE
	Upham 3 N
	Velva
McIntosh	Ashley

County	Station Name
McIntosh *(cont.)*	Wishek
McKenzie	Keene 3 S
	Watford City 14 S
McLean	Butte
	Garrison 1 NNW
	Max
	Turtle Lake
	Underwood
	Washburn
Mercer	Beulah 1 W
Morton	Mandan Experiment Station
	New Salem 5 NW
Mountrail	Stanley 3 NNW
Nelson	McVille
	Petersburg 2 N
Oliver	Center 4 SE
Pembina	Cavalier 7 NW
	Pembina
Pierce	Rugby
Ramsey	Devils Lake KDLR
	Edmore 1 NW
Ransom	Lisbon
Richland	Hankinson
	McLeod 3 E
	Wahpeton 3 N
Rolette	Rolla 3 NW
Sargent	Forman 5 SSE
Sheridan	McClusky
Sioux	Fort Yates 4 SW
Slope	Amidon
Stark	Dickinson Exp. Station
	Dickinson Municipal Airport
	Richardton Abbey
Steele	Colgate
	Sharon
Stutsman	Jamestown Municipal Airport
	Jamestown State Hospital
Towner	Hansboro 4 NNE
Traill	Hillsboro 3 N
Walsh	Grafton

County	Station Name
Ward	Foxholm 7 N
	Kenmare 1 WSW
	Minot Experiment Station
	Minot FAA Airport
Williams	Tioga 1 E
	Williston Exp. Farm
	Williston Sloulin Int'l Airport

North Dakota Weather Stations by City

City	Station Name	Miles
Bismarck	Bismarck Municipal Airport	3
	Mandan Experiment Station	6
Dickinson	Dickinson Municipal Airport	6
	Dickinson Exp. Station	1
Fargo	Fargo Hector Field	4
Grand Forks	Grand Forks Int'l Airport	7
	Grand Forks Univ. NWS	2
Jamestown	Jamestown Municipal Airport	1
	Jamestown State Hospital	2
Mandan	Bismarck Municipal Airport	8
	Mandan Experiment Station	1
Minot	Minot FAA Airport	2
	Minot Experiment Station	4
West Fargo	Fargo Hector Field	6
Williston	Williston Exp. Farm	5
	Williston Sloulin Int'l Airport	3

Note: Miles is the distance between the geographic center of the city and the weather station.

North Dakota Weather Stations by Elevation

Feet	Station Name	Feet	Station Name
2,959	Bowman	1,532	Edmore 1 NW
2,910	Amidon	1,528	Drake 9 NE
2,749	Fairfield	1,528	Leeds
2,677	Hettinger	1,528	Petersburg 2 N
2,637	New England	1,522	Sharon
2,582	Dickinson Municipal Airport	1,509	Velva
2,522	Mott	1,499	Westhope
2,477	Pretty Rock	1,489	Jamestown Municipal Airport
2,467	Keene 3 S	1,479	Towner 2 NE
2,467	Richardton Abbey	1,466	Jamestown State Hospital
2,457	Dickinson Exp. Station	1,466	McVille
2,417	Trotters 3 SSE	1,463	Devils Lake KDLR
2,349	Fortuna 1 W	1,459	Willow City
2,309	Carson	1,453	Ellendale
2,290	Medora	1,433	Fullerton 1 ESE
2,276	Stanley 3 NNW	1,423	Upham 3 N
2,257	Wildrose 3 NW	1,377	Cooperstown
2,244	Tioga 1 E	1,358	La Moure
2,230	Dunn Center 2 SW	1,309	Oakes 2 S
2,204	Powers Lake 1 N	1,250	Forman 5 SSE
2,148	New Salem 5 NW	1,207	Valley City 3 NNW
2,119	Wishek	1,177	Colgate
2,109	Max	1,102	Lisbon
2,103	Williston Exp. Farm	1,072	McLeod 3 E
2,017	Underwood	1,069	Hankinson
1,998	Ashley	954	Wahpeton 3 N
1,988	Center 4 SE	908	Hillsboro 3 N
1,978	Napoleon	898	Fargo Hector Field
1,955	Bowbells	889	Cavalier 7 NW
1,952	Crosby	846	Grand Forks Int'l Airport
1,948	Gackle	830	Grand Forks Univ. NWS
1,948	Rolla 3 NW	826	Grafton
1,942	Watford City 14 S	787	Pembina
1,938	Garrison 1 NNW		
1,922	McClusky		
1,896	Williston Sloulin Int'l Airport		
1,889	Turtle Lake		
1,876	Tuttle		
1,807	Kenmare 1 WSW		
1,784	Beulah 1 W		
1,768	Minot Experiment Station		
1,748	Mandan Experiment Station		
1,732	Washburn		
1,712	Minot FAA Airport		
1,673	Fort Yates 4 SW		
1,673	Foxholm 7 N		
1,660	Butte		
1,646	Bismarck Municipal Airport		
1,637	Bottineau		
1,614	Langdon Exp. Farm		
1,584	Carrington		
1,558	Carrington 4 N		
1,555	McHenry 3 W		
1,548	Rugby		
1,538	Hansboro 4 NNE		

Bismarck Municipal Airport

Bismarck, the State Capital and County Seat of Burleigh County, is located in south-central North Dakota, near the center of North America. It is on the east bank of the Missouri River in a shallow basin seven miles wide and 11 miles long.

The Weather Service Forecast Office is located at the Municipal Airport approximately two miles southeast of city center. It is almost entirely surrounded by low-lying hills. The closest hills, three miles to the north, and other hills five miles to the southeast, are about 200 to 300 feet high. West across the Missouri River the land is more hilly and 300 to 600 feet higher.

The climate is semi-arid, typically continental in character, and invigorating. Summers are warm, but there are not many hot days, and very few hot and humid days. Winters tend to be long and quite cold, but there are plenty of mild days to make winter weather pleasant much of the time. Sunshine is abundant, averaging 2,700 hours out of a possible 4,470 hours.

More than 75 percent of annual precipitation falls during the six month period from April through September, and nearly 50 percent during May, June, and July. Snow has been reported in all months except July and August. Three inches or more can be expected on about three days each year.

Most summer precipitation occurs during thunderstorms in the late afternoon and evening. Thunderstorms occur on about 34 days each year, accompanied by hail on two or three of the days. A damaging hailstorm is experienced about once every ten years. Tornadoes are rare, but damaging winds occasionally occur with the heavier thunderstorms.

The winter season usually begins in late November and continues until late March. Winter precipitation is nearly all in the form of snow and is often associated with strong winds and low temperatures. This combination produces winter storms and occasional blizzards that must never be taken lightly. A severe blizzard lasting two or three days may be expected every few years. But several times each winter storms lasting a few hours occur in which drifting snow can make travel difficult and even block roads. A stalled motorist can be in serious trouble if he is not prepared with adequate winter clothing and some kind of emergency provisions.

The temperature range from summer to winter is very large and typical of the Northern Great Plains. The average freeze-free period is 134 days, from mid-May to late September.

Bismarck Municipal Airport *Burleigh County*   Elevation: 1,646 ft.   Latitude: 46° 46' N   Longitude: 100° 45' W

	JAN	FEB	MAR	APR	MAY	JUN	JUL	AUG	SEP	OCT	NOV	DEC	YEAR
Mean Maximum Temp. (°F)	20.2	27.8	39.1	55.2	68.6	77.6	84.2	83.1	71.3	57.7	37.9	25.5	54.0
Mean Temp. (°F)	9.6	17.7	28.9	43.0	55.7	64.7	70.3	68.8	57.5	44.9	27.9	15.2	42.0
Mean Minimum Temp. (°F)	-1.0	7.5	18.7	30.7	42.8	51.7	56.3	54.6	43.7	32.0	17.9	4.9	30.0
Extreme Maximum Temp. (°F)	62	69	78	93	96	107	109	107	104	94	79	65	109
Extreme Minimum Temp. (°F)	-42	-43	-28	-12	17	32	35	33	11	-10	-30	-40	-43
Days Maximum Temp. ≥ 90°F	0	0	0	0	1	3	8	8	2	0	0	0	22
Days Maximum Temp. ≤ 32°F	23	16	9	1	0	0	0	0	0	1	10	20	80
Days Minimum Temp. ≤ 32°F	31	28	28	18	4	0	0	0	3	16	28	31	187
Days Minimum Temp. ≤ 0°F	16	9	3	0	0	0	0	0	0	0	2	11	41
Heating Degree Days (base 65°F)	1,714	1,332	1,113	656	299	87	17	41	250	617	1,105	1,538	8,769
Cooling Degree Days (base 65°F)	0	0	0	2	20	89	191	173	31	1	0	0	507
Mean Precipitation (in.)	0.45	0.46	0.82	1.54	2.20	2.54	2.50	2.13	1.63	1.22	0.70	0.44	16.63
Maximum Precipitation (in.)	1.3	1.6	3.2	5.5	5.2	6.5	13.8	5.0	6.9	4.3	2.1	0.9	27.0
Minimum Precipitation (in.)	0	trace	0.1	trace	0.3	0.5	0.2	trace	trace	trace	trace	trace	9.3
Maximum 24-hr. Precipitation (in.)	0.7	0.6	1.2	1.5	1.9	3.1	4.3	2.6	4.3	1.3	0.7	0.6	4.3
Days With ≥ 0.1" Precipitation	1	2	2	4	5	6	5	4	3	2	2	1	37
Days With ≥ 1.0" Precipitation	0	0	0	0	0	0	0	0	0	0	0	0	0
Mean Snowfall (in.)	8.9	7.9	9.1	4.6	0.3	trace	trace	trace	0.2	2.3	9.2	8.0	50.5
Maximum Snowfall (in.)	25	26	31	19	10	0	0	0	5	24	30	17	97
Maximum 24-hr. Snowfall (in.)	8	9	16	12	7	0	0	0	4	9	11	10	16
Days With ≥ 1.0" Snow Depth	26	20	13	3	0	0	0	0	0	1	10	22	95
Thunderstorm Days	0	< 1	< 1	1	4	9	9	8	3	1	< 1	0	35
Foggy Days	5	6	7	5	4	4	3	4	4	5	5	7	59
Predominant Sky Cover	OVR	OVR	OVR	OVR	OVR	OVR	SCT	CLR	CLR	OVR	OVR	OVR	OVR
Mean Relative Humidity 6am (%)	76	78	82	80	79	84	84	84	82	80	81	79	81
Mean Relative Humidity 3pm (%)	67	66	59	45	43	47	42	40	42	44	58	67	52
Mean Dewpoint (°F)	2	8	19	29	40	51	55	53	43	32	20	9	30
Prevailing Wind Direction	WNW	WNW	NW	NNW	SSE	SSE	SSE	SSE	WNW	WNW	WNW	WNW	WNW
Prevailing Wind Speed (mph)	14	13	16	15	14	13	12	13	13	13	14	14	14
Maximum Wind Gust (mph)	67	73	64	71	66	59	74	69	84	60	56	63	84

Fargo Hector Field

Moorhead, Minnesota, and Fargo are twin cities in the Red River Valley of the north. The Red River of the north flows northward between the two cities and is a part of the Hudson Bay drainage area. The Red River is approximately two miles east of the airport at its nearest point and has no significant effect on the weather. In recent years, spring floods due to melting snow have been common. Summer floods caused by heavy rains are infrequent.

The surrounding terrain is flat and open. Northerly winds blowing up the valley occasionally causing low cloudiness and fog. However, this upslope cloudiness is very infrequent. Aside from this, there are no pronounced climatic differences due to geographical features in the immediate area.

The summers are generally comfortable with very few days of hot and humid weather. Nights, with few exceptions, are comfortably cool. The winter months are cold and dry with temperatures rising above freezing only on an average of six days each month, and nighttime lows dropping below zero approximately half of the time.

Precipitation is the most important climatic factor in the area. The Red River Valley lies in an area where lighter amounts fall to the west and heavier amounts to the east. Seventy-five percent of the precipitation occurs during the growing season (April to September) and is often accompanied by electrical storms and heavy falls in a short time. Winter precipitation is light, indicating that heavy snowfall is the exception rather than the rule. The first light snow in the fall occasionally falls in September, but usually very little, if any, occurs until October or November. The latest fall is generally in April.

With the flat terrain, surface friction has little effect on the wind in the area and this fact has led to the legendary Dakota blizzards. Strong winds with even light snowfall cause much drifting and blowing snow, reducing visibility to near zero. Fortunately, these conditions occur only several times during the winter months.

Fargo Hector Field *Cass County*   Elevation: 898 ft.   Latitude: 46° 56' N   Longitude: 96° 49' W

	JAN	FEB	MAR	APR	MAY	JUN	JUL	AUG	SEP	OCT	NOV	DEC	YEAR
Mean Maximum Temp. (°F)	15.6	22.5	34.7	54.2	69.3	77.6	82.3	81.0	69.9	56.1	35.2	21.1	51.6
Mean Temp. (°F)	6.5	13.7	26.6	43.3	57.1	66.1	70.7	69.1	58.2	45.3	27.2	12.9	41.4
Mean Minimum Temp. (°F)	-2.6	4.9	18.4	32.2	45.0	54.6	59.1	57.1	46.4	34.6	19.1	4.8	31.1
Extreme Maximum Temp. (°F)	52	55	76	100	95	100	106	106	99	90	74	56	106
Extreme Minimum Temp. (°F)	-35	-39	-23	-7	21	33	39	33	23	7	-24	-31	-39
Days Maximum Temp. ≥ 90°F	0	0	0	0	1	2	5	5	1	0	0	0	14
Days Maximum Temp. ≤ 32°F	27	20	12	1	0	0	0	0	0	1	12	24	97
Days Minimum Temp. ≤ 32°F	31	28	27	16	3	0	0	0	2	13	27	31	178
Days Minimum Temp. ≤ 0°F	18	11	4	0	0	0	0	0	0	0	2	12	47
Heating Degree Days (base 65°F)	1,812	1,444	1,185	649	270	69	16	34	240	604	1,129	1,610	9,062
Cooling Degree Days (base 65°F)	0	0	0	4	36	112	198	173	38	2	0	0	563
Mean Precipitation (in.)	0.76	0.56	1.17	1.40	2.61	3.20	2.82	2.46	2.18	1.96	0.91	0.56	20.59
Maximum Precipitation (in.)	1.8	1.7	2.6	5.3	7.3	9.4	8.4	6.5	6.1	7.0	4.6	2.2	32.3
Minimum Precipitation (in.)	0.1	trace	trace	trace	0.5	0.6	0.4	0.2	0.1	0	trace	trace	8.8
Maximum 24-hr. Precipitation (in.)	0.8	0.7	1.1	1.8	4.0	2.8	4.4	2.8	3.4	3.1	1.6	0.7	4.4
Days With ≥ 0.1" Precipitation	2	2	3	4	5	6	5	4	4	4	3	2	44
Days With ≥ 1.0" Precipitation	0	0	0	0	1	1	1	1	1	0	0	0	5
Mean Snowfall (in.)	12.3	6.7	8.8	2.5	trace	trace	trace	trace	trace	0.6	7.5	7.8	46.2
Maximum Snowfall (in.)	32	20	19	13	1	0	0	0	trace	8	24	20	68
Maximum 24-hr. Snowfall (in.)	16	11	11	9	1	0	0	0	trace	7	12	9	16
Days With ≥ 1.0" Snow Depth	28	24	18	2	0	0	0	0	0	0	9	22	103
Thunderstorm Days	< 1	< 1	< 1	1	4	7	8	7	3	1	< 1	< 1	31
Foggy Days	7	7	9	6	6	5	4	5	6	6	7	9	77
Predominant Sky Cover	OVR	OVR	OVR	OVR	OVR	OVR	SCT	SCT	OVR	OVR	OVR	OVR	OVR
Mean Relative Humidity 6am (%)	75	77	82	79	77	82	86	86	85	80	81	78	81
Mean Relative Humidity 3pm (%)	70	71	67	51	45	50	50	47	49	51	65	73	57
Mean Dewpoint (°F)	0	6	19	30	41	53	59	56	46	35	21	7	31
Prevailing Wind Direction	NNW	N	N	N	SSE	SSE	SSE	SSE	SSE	SSE	SSE	S	SSE
Prevailing Wind Speed (mph)	16	14	15	16	15	14	13	14	14	15	15	12	14
Maximum Wind Gust (mph)	60	59	58	63	62	81	71	66	62	58	61	59	81

Williston Sloulin Int'l Airport

Williston lies in a flat valley at the junction of the Missouri River and Little Muddy Creek. The surrounding country is rolling. Hills to the east are highest, ranging from 250 to 300 feet in height at a distance of five to seven miles. Across the Missouri River to the south, the bluffs are about 225 feet high at four miles distance.

Great extremes of temperatures are encountered, winters being cold, while summer days are usually warm. In winter, temperatures below zero are common and lows of -50 degrees have been recorded. When temperatures are lowest, however, the air is generally dry, with little or no wind and the weather is fine and invigorating. At the other extreme, temperatures above 100 degrees have been reached in all months from May to September. The low humidity that generally prevails on the hottest summer days keeps them from becoming oppressive.

The climate of Williston and vicinity is continental, semi-arid, characterized by marked season changes. Winter is the relatively dry season, with only about half an inch of monthly precipitation occurring from November to February. There is considerably less than the average amount of snowfall for similar locations in the United States. Ice crystals, which rarely yield more than a trace of precipitation, are common in the cold months. Summer precipitation is variable from year to year. The amount of rain occurring during the growing period is the most important element of climate for agricultural interests in the vicinity of Williston. Generally, considerably more precipitation occurs in the spring and summer months than in winter.

The growing season averages 131 days. It has ranged from 94 to 172 days during the period of record.

Clear and partly cloudy skies, nearly equally distributed, occur about 70 percent of the time. Heavy fog occurs on the average about ten times a year. Because of the northern latitude of Williston, it enjoys long hours of daylight in the spring and summer. Relatively little cloudiness occurs then, so that the duration of sunshine averages about two-thirds of the possible amount.

Summer storms are generally in the form of thunderstorms or rain showers, occasionally accompanied by hail and squally winds. Tornadoes are rare in this area. In the winter, cold waves and occasionally blizzard conditions occur. Cold waves result when extremely cold air advances southward from northwestern Canada. In blizzard conditions the advancing cold wave is accompanied by winds of gale force and the air is filled with fine, wind-driven snow. In extreme instances in the country, it becomes impossible for persons to ascertain their bearings or to remain alive many hours without shelter in such storms.

Williston Sloulin Int'l Airport *Williams County*   Elevation: 1,896 ft.   Latitude: 48° 12' N   Longitude: 103° 39' W

	JAN	FEB	MAR	APR	MAY	JUN	JUL	AUG	SEP	OCT	NOV	DEC	YEAR
Mean Maximum Temp. (°F)	19.5	28.0	39.9	56.1	68.6	78.2	84.0	83.4	70.4	57.2	36.9	24.6	53.9
Mean Temp. (°F)	8.9	17.7	29.1	43.3	55.4	64.9	70.1	69.0	56.7	44.2	26.8	14.3	41.7
Mean Minimum Temp. (°F)	-1.7	7.4	18.3	30.5	42.2	51.5	56.1	54.6	42.9	31.1	16.5	4.0	29.5
Extreme Maximum Temp. (°F)	53	66	78	92	106	106	109	107	104	92	76	58	109
Extreme Minimum Temp. (°F)	-36	-37	-28	-15	17	26	38	34	17	-3	-27	-50	-50
Days Maximum Temp. ≥ 90°F	0	0	0	0	1	3	8	9	2	0	0	0	23
Days Maximum Temp. ≤ 32°F	23	15	8	1	0	0	0	0	0	1	11	20	79
Days Minimum Temp. ≤ 32°F	31	28	29	18	4	0	0	0	3	17	28	31	189
Days Minimum Temp. ≤ 0°F	16	10	4	0	0	0	0	0	0	0	3	12	45
Heating Degree Days (base 65°F)	1,736	1,331	1,105	644	311	84	20	40	269	640	1,141	1,567	8,888
Cooling Degree Days (base 65°F)	0	0	0	1	23	91	187	185	27	1	0	0	515
Mean Precipitation (in.)	0.54	0.38	0.74	1.10	1.90	2.34	2.26	1.46	1.37	0.87	0.56	0.57	14.09
Maximum Precipitation (in.)	1.4	1.5	2.3	3.3	7.4	6.2	6.3	4.7	3.1	3.6	1.1	1.4	21.8
Minimum Precipitation (in.)	trace	trace	trace	trace	0.1	0.7	0.3	0.1	0.1	trace	trace	0.1	9.2
Maximum 24-hr. Precipitation (in.)	0.6	0.3	0.7	1.9	1.5	2.2	4.9	3.0	1.6	1.8	0.4	0.9	4.9
Days With ≥ 0.1" Precipitation	2	1	3	3	5	5	5	3	3	2	2	1	35
Days With ≥ 1.0" Precipitation	0	0	0	0	0	0	0	0	0	0	0	0	0
Mean Snowfall (in.)	8.8	5.5	7.5	4.1	0.9	trace	trace	trace	0.3	1.7	6.2	8.2	43.2
Maximum Snowfall (in.)	24	22	31	22	16	0	0	0	4	14	16	16	79
Maximum 24-hr. Snowfall (in.)	10	7	7	15	12	0	0	0	3	11	7	8	15
Days With ≥ 1.0" Snow Depth	26	18	12	3	0	0	0	0	0	1	10	21	91
Thunderstorm Days	0	< 1	< 1	1	3	8	9	6	2	< 1	0	0	29
Foggy Days	6	5	6	5	3	3	3	2	3	4	6	7	52
Predominant Sky Cover	OVR	OVR	OVR	OVR	OVR	OVR	SCT	SCT	CLR	OVR	OVR	OVR	OVR
Mean Relative Humidity 6am (%)	78	80	83	80	79	81	81	78	80	79	82	80	80
Mean Relative Humidity 3pm (%)	69	66	57	44	42	44	39	36	42	44	60	68	51
Mean Dewpoint (°F)	3	10	20	29	39	49	53	50	41	31	19	8	29
Prevailing Wind Direction	SW	SSW	N	N	N	SE	N	SE	N	SSW	SSW	SSW	N
Prevailing Wind Speed (mph)	8	8	12	13	13	12	9	12	12	8	8	7	10
Maximum Wind Gust (mph)	62	53	62	70	76	75	70	55	60	62	64	63	76

Amidon *Slope County*   Elevation: 2,910 ft.   Latitude: 46° 29' N   Longitude: 103° 19' W

	JAN	FEB	MAR	APR	MAY	JUN	JUL	AUG	SEP	OCT	NOV	DEC	YEAR
Mean Maximum Temp. (°F)	24.9	31.8	41.1	54.0	66.4	76.2	83.3	83.5	71.3	57.6	39.9	29.8	55.0
Mean Temp. (°F)	14.5	21.5	30.3	42.3	54.0	63.6	69.7	69.0	57.6	45.1	29.6	19.2	43.0
Mean Minimum Temp. (°F)	4.0	11.2	19.5	30.5	41.7	50.9	56.0	54.4	43.9	32.4	19.3	8.6	31.0
Extreme Maximum Temp. (°F)	64	68	81	90	98	107	107	105	105	94	81	64	107
Extreme Minimum Temp. (°F)	-34	-35	-21	-5	20	31	40	35	17	-8	-26	-40	-40
Days Maximum Temp. ≥ 90°F	0	0	0	0	1	2	8	10	2	0	0	0	23
Days Maximum Temp. ≤ 32°F	19	12	8	2	0	0	0	0	0	1	9	16	67
Days Minimum Temp. ≤ 32°F	30	27	28	18	4	0	0	0	3	15	27	31	183
Days Minimum Temp. ≤ 0°F	12	7	3	0	0	0	0	0	0	0	2	8	32
Heating Degree Days (base 65°F)	1,564	1,220	1,070	676	348	109	30	41	256	614	1,057	1,416	8,401
Cooling Degree Days (base 65°F)	0	0	0	2	17	79	189	185	43	2	0	0	517
Mean Precipitation (in.)	0.37	0.33	0.56	1.21	2.45	3.05	2.19	1.43	1.41	1.18	0.53	0.33	15.04
Days With ≥ 0.1" Precipitation	1	1	2	4	6	6	5	4	4	3	2	1	39
Days With ≥ 1.0" Precipitation	0	0	0	0	0	1	0	0	0	0	0	0	1
Mean Snowfall (in.)	*4.8*	*4.5*	na	2.3	0.5	0.0	0.0	0.0	0.2	1.1	na	na	na
Days With ≥ 1.0" Snow Depth	na	8	na	2	0	0	0	0	0	0	na	na	na

Ashley *McIntosh County*   Elevation: 1,998 ft.   Latitude: 46° 02' N   Longitude: 99° 22' W

	JAN	FEB	MAR	APR	MAY	JUN	JUL	AUG	SEP	OCT	NOV	DEC	YEAR
Mean Maximum Temp. (°F)	19.4	26.5	37.6	54.7	68.3	77.1	83.4	82.4	71.8	57.9	37.4	24.7	53.4
Mean Temp. (°F)	9.1	16.4	27.3	42.4	55.6	64.8	70.2	68.5	57.9	45.0	27.6	14.9	41.6
Mean Minimum Temp. (°F)	-1.2	6.1	17.0	30.1	42.8	52.4	57.0	54.5	44.0	32.1	17.7	5.1	29.8
Extreme Maximum Temp. (°F)	60	60	76	97	97	103	107	105	102	92	78	59	107
Extreme Minimum Temp. (°F)	-35	-40	-26	-10	18	33	35	33	13	-2	-21	-36	-40
Days Maximum Temp. ≥ 90°F	0	0	0	0	1	2	7	6	2	0	0	0	18
Days Maximum Temp. ≤ 32°F	24	17	10	1	0	0	0	0	0	1	11	21	85
Days Minimum Temp. ≤ 32°F	31	28	29	19	4	0	0	0	3	15	28	31	188
Days Minimum Temp. ≤ 0°F	17	10	4	0	0	0	0	0	0	0	2	11	44
Heating Degree Days (base 65°F)	1,730	1,369	1,162	672	304	84	23	42	247	616	1,117	1,548	8,914
Cooling Degree Days (base 65°F)	0	0	0	2	20	86	191	155	35	2	0	0	491
Mean Precipitation (in.)	0.41	0.35	0.92	1.51	2.73	3.47	2.45	2.23	1.58	1.58	0.61	0.27	18.11
Days With ≥ 0.1" Precipitation	1	1	2	4	6	6	5	4	4	3	2	1	39
Days With ≥ 1.0" Precipitation	0	0	0	0	1	1	0	1	0	0	0	0	3
Mean Snowfall (in.)	6.6	4.3	5.7	3.4	trace	0.0	0.0	0.0	trace	0.7	5.4	3.7	29.8
Days With ≥ 1.0" Snow Depth	24	19	15	2	0	0	0	0	0	0	11	18	89

Beulah 1 W *Mercer County*   Elevation: 1,784 ft.   Latitude: 47° 16' N   Longitude: 101° 47' W

	JAN	FEB	MAR	APR	MAY	JUN	JUL	AUG	SEP	OCT	NOV	DEC	YEAR
Mean Maximum Temp. (°F)	20.3	28.1	39.7	56.2	69.6	78.3	84.3	83.9	72.2	59.0	38.1	25.5	54.6
Mean Temp. (°F)	9.5	17.5	28.4	42.5	55.3	64.3	69.4	68.3	57.1	44.8	27.5	15.1	41.7
Mean Minimum Temp. (°F)	-1.3	6.9	17.1	28.8	40.9	50.4	54.4	52.7	41.9	30.6	16.9	4.6	28.7
Extreme Maximum Temp. (°F)	59	65	80	97	99	105	107	105	108	96	82	65	108
Extreme Minimum Temp. (°F)	-41	-42	-32	-11	19	27	36	30	13	-12	-25	-46	-46
Days Maximum Temp. ≥ 90°F	0	0	0	0	1	4	8	9	2	0	0	0	24
Days Maximum Temp. ≤ 32°F	22	16	10	1	0	0	0	0	0	1	10	19	79
Days Minimum Temp. ≤ 32°F	31	28	29	20	6	0	0	0	4	18	28	31	195
Days Minimum Temp. ≤ 0°F	15	9	4	0	0	0	0	0	0	0	2	11	41
Heating Degree Days (base 65°F)	1,717	1,337	1,128	670	316	98	26	49	264	620	1,118	1,543	8,886
Cooling Degree Days (base 65°F)	0	0	0	3	24	92	174	169	32	2	0	0	496
Mean Precipitation (in.)	0.32	0.39	0.73	1.75	2.30	3.24	2.39	1.52	1.63	1.30	0.65	0.37	16.59
Days With ≥ 0.1" Precipitation	1	1	2	4	5	6	6	4	4	3	3	1	40
Days With ≥ 1.0" Precipitation	0	0	0	0	0	1	0	0	0	0	0	0	1
Mean Snowfall (in.)	*5.6*	*4.9*	*5.1*	3.0	0.1	0.0	0.0	0.0	0.1	*1.7*	6.1	*4.7*	*31.3*
Days With ≥ 1.0" Snow Depth	*28*	*21*	*14*	3	0	0	0	0	0	*1*	10	*23*	*100*

Bottineau *Bottineau County*   Elevation: 1,637 ft.   Latitude: 48° 50' N   Longitude: 100° 27' W

	JAN	FEB	MAR	APR	MAY	JUN	JUL	AUG	SEP	OCT	NOV	DEC	YEAR
Mean Maximum Temp. (°F)	13.1	20.9	32.2	51.8	67.1	75.3	79.6	79.2	67.4	53.6	32.8	18.3	49.3
Mean Temp. (°F)	3.0	10.9	22.9	40.4	54.5	63.2	67.1	65.9	54.6	41.6	23.5	8.7	38.0
Mean Minimum Temp. (°F)	-7.1	0.9	13.4	28.9	41.8	51.1	54.6	52.6	41.9	29.5	14.3	-1.0	26.7
Extreme Maximum Temp. (°F)	47	63	66	95	98	99	100	100	101	89	73	49	101
Extreme Minimum Temp. (°F)	-41	-39	-37	-16	16	31	37	34	17	-6	-28	-40	-41
Days Maximum Temp. ≥ 90°F	0	0	0	0	1	2	3	4	1	0	0	0	11
Days Maximum Temp. ≤ 32°F	28	22	14	2	0	0	0	0	0	1	15	27	109
Days Minimum Temp. ≤ 32°F	31	28	30	20	5	0	0	0	3	20	29	31	197
Days Minimum Temp. ≤ 0°F	20	13	7	0	0	0	0	0	0	0	5	16	61
Heating Degree Days (base 65°F)	1,920	1,524	1,301	733	339	116	44	72	321	720	1,239	1,744	10,073
Cooling Degree Days (base 65°F)	0	0	0	1	19	69	113	109	17	0	0	0	328
Mean Precipitation (in.)	0.50	0.41	0.75	1.23	2.16	3.28	3.12	2.57	2.00	1.30	0.61	0.52	18.45
Days With ≥ 0.1" Precipitation	2	1	2	3	6	8	6	5	4	3	2	2	44
Days With ≥ 1.0" Precipitation	0	0	0	0	0	0	1	1	0	0	0	0	2
Mean Snowfall (in.)	8.4	6.0	6.9	3.1	0.3	trace	0.0	0.0	0.2	2.0	6.9	7.7	41.5
Days With ≥ 1.0" Snow Depth	30	25	21	4	0	0	0	0	0	2	13	27	122

Bowbells *Burke County*   Elevation: 1,955 ft.   Latitude: 48° 48' N   Longitude: 102° 15' W

	JAN	FEB	MAR	APR	MAY	JUN	JUL	AUG	SEP	OCT	NOV	DEC	YEAR
Mean Maximum Temp. (°F)	15.8	22.9	33.7	52.3	66.8	75.9	80.5	80.1	67.8	54.6	33.4	21.1	50.4
Mean Temp. (°F)	5.8	13.1	23.8	40.0	53.2	62.6	67.0	65.4	54.3	41.9	24.2	11.4	38.5
Mean Minimum Temp. (°F)	-4.2	3.3	13.9	27.7	39.6	49.2	53.4	50.7	40.6	29.2	14.8	1.6	26.6
Extreme Maximum Temp. (°F)	52	62	71	93	102	102	103	104	101	93	73	56	104
Extreme Minimum Temp. (°F)	-36	-41	-31	-15	17	30	39	26	17	-7	-27	-40	-41
Days Maximum Temp. ≥ 90°F	0	0	0	0	1	2	5	5	1	0	0	0	14
Days Maximum Temp. ≤ 32°F	25	19	13	2	0	0	0	0	0	1	14	23	97
Days Minimum Temp. ≤ 32°F	31	28	30	21	6	0	0	0	4	20	29	30	199
Days Minimum Temp. ≤ 0°F	19	12	6	0	0	0	0	0	0	0	4	13	54
Heating Degree Days (base 65°F)	1,834	1,462	1,272	743	372	123	47	80	337	708	1,220	1,662	9,860
Cooling Degree Days (base 65°F)	0	0	0	1	15	57	111	102	18	0	0	0	304
Mean Precipitation (in.)	0.47	0.44	0.68	1.41	2.24	3.00	2.95	1.92	1.99	1.15	0.44	0.31	17.00
Days With ≥ 0.1" Precipitation	2	1	2	3	5	6	6	4	4	3	2	1	39
Days With ≥ 1.0" Precipitation	0	0	0	0	0	1	1	0	1	0	0	0	3
Mean Snowfall (in.)	9.0	*5.9*	5.8	3.4	0.3	trace	0.0	0.0	0.1	2.0	*5.4*	*5.9*	*37.8*
Days With ≥ 1.0" Snow Depth	na	na	na	*2*	0	0	0	0	0	0	*0*	na	na	na

Bowman *Bowman County*   Elevation: 2,959 ft.   Latitude: 46° 11' N   Longitude: 103° 24' W

	JAN	FEB	MAR	APR	MAY	JUN	JUL	AUG	SEP	OCT	NOV	DEC	YEAR
Mean Maximum Temp. (°F)	25.0	31.7	41.0	53.9	65.8	75.6	82.8	82.6	70.6	57.7	40.2	29.7	54.7
Mean Temp. (°F)	14.6	21.1	30.0	41.9	53.6	63.2	69.3	68.3	56.6	44.5	29.3	18.8	42.6
Mean Minimum Temp. (°F)	4.1	10.4	19.0	29.9	41.4	50.8	55.8	53.8	42.6	31.4	18.5	7.9	30.5
Extreme Maximum Temp. (°F)	66	69	78	90	95	102	106	103	102	94	80	65	106
Extreme Minimum Temp. (°F)	-34	-31	-28	-11	21	32	35	33	17	-6	-24	-36	-36
Days Maximum Temp. ≥ 90°F	0	0	0	0	0	2	7	8	2	0	0	0	19
Days Maximum Temp. ≤ 32°F	19	13	8	2	0	0	0	0	0	1	9	16	68
Days Minimum Temp. ≤ 32°F	31	28	29	19	4	0	0	0	4	16	28	31	190
Days Minimum Temp. ≤ 0°F	13	7	3	0	0	0	0	0	0	0	3	8	34
Heating Degree Days (base 65°F)	1,559	1,235	1,078	686	358	113	31	45	276	628	1,063	1,426	8,498
Cooling Degree Days (base 65°F)	0	0	0	1	13	66	171	157	32	1	0	0	441
Mean Precipitation (in.)	0.49	0.47	0.72	1.38	2.61	3.11	1.93	1.29	1.35	1.31	0.53	0.41	15.60
Days With ≥ 0.1" Precipitation	2	2	2	4	6	7	4	4	3	3	2	2	41
Days With ≥ 1.0" Precipitation	0	0	0	0	0	1	0	0	0	0	0	0	1
Mean Snowfall (in.)	9.4	8.4	9.4	7.0	0.9	0.0	0.0	0.0	0.7	2.7	9.0	9.0	56.5
Days With ≥ 1.0" Snow Depth	27	20	18	8	1	0	0	0	0	2	12	23	111

Butte *McLean County*   Elevation: 1,660 ft.   Latitude: 47° 49' N   Longitude: 100° 35' W

	JAN	FEB	MAR	APR	MAY	JUN	JUL	AUG	SEP	OCT	NOV	DEC	YEAR
Mean Maximum Temp. (°F)	17.8	25.8	37.1	55.6	70.2	79.0	84.1	83.8	71.2	57.3	36.5	23.5	53.5
Mean Temp. (°F)	8.8	16.7	27.5	43.3	56.8	66.0	70.7	69.7	58.7	45.6	28.0	14.7	42.2
Mean Minimum Temp. (°F)	-0.4	7.6	17.9	30.8	43.4	53.0	57.2	55.6	45.6	33.7	19.4	5.9	30.8
Extreme Maximum Temp. (°F)	53	64	71	93	98	103	104	103	103	94	76	57	104
Extreme Minimum Temp. (°F)	-33	-38	-26	-8	16	34	42	33	22	-1	-22	-36	-38
Days Maximum Temp. ≥ 90°F	0	0	0	0	1	4	7	9	2	0	0	0	23
Days Maximum Temp. ≤ 32°F	23	17	10	1	0	0	0	0	0	1	11	21	84
Days Minimum Temp. ≤ 32°F	30	28	29	18	4	0	0	0	2	14	26	30	181
Days Minimum Temp. ≤ 0°F	15	9	3	0	0	0	0	0	0	0	2	11	40
Heating Degree Days (base 65°F)	1,742	1,360	1,156	649	276	69	15	34	227	598	1,105	1,554	8,785
Cooling Degree Days (base 65°F)	0	0	0	3	30	105	196	194	43	2	0	0	573
Mean Precipitation (in.)	0.47	0.41	0.72	1.53	2.36	2.74	2.73	1.52	1.63	1.36	0.65	0.40	16.52
Days With ≥ 0.1" Precipitation	2	1	2	4	5	6	5	4	4	2	2	1	38
Days With ≥ 1.0" Precipitation	0	0	0	0	0	0	1	0	0	0	0	0	1
Mean Snowfall (in.)	6.4	*4.9*	*4.6*	3.4	trace	0.0	0.0	0.0	trace	1.9	6.2	5.1	*32.5*
Days With ≥ 1.0" Snow Depth	*17*	12	10	2	0	0	0	0	0	1	7	12	*61*

Carrington *Foster County*   Elevation: 1,584 ft.   Latitude: 47° 27' N   Longitude: 99° 08' W

	JAN	FEB	MAR	APR	MAY	JUN	JUL	AUG	SEP	OCT	NOV	DEC	YEAR
Mean Maximum Temp. (°F)	15.9	22.8	33.8	51.7	66.8	75.1	80.2	79.4	68.4	55.0	34.3	21.2	50.4
Mean Temp. (°F)	6.5	13.4	24.7	40.7	54.6	63.7	68.4	66.8	56.0	43.5	25.5	12.3	39.7
Mean Minimum Temp. (°F)	-3.0	4.1	15.6	29.5	42.2	52.1	56.6	54.1	43.6	32.0	16.7	3.4	28.9
Extreme Maximum Temp. (°F)	53	59	70	97	95	100	107	102	101	90	75	53	107
Extreme Minimum Temp. (°F)	-32	-36	-26	-8	21	33	42	35	23	0	-22	-34	-36
Days Maximum Temp. ≥ 90°F	0	0	0	0	0	2	4	4	1	0	0	0	11
Days Maximum Temp. ≤ 32°F	25	20	13	2	0	0	0	0	0	1	13	24	98
Days Minimum Temp. ≤ 32°F	31	28	30	20	5	0	0	0	2	16	28	31	191
Days Minimum Temp. ≤ 0°F	18	12	5	0	0	0	0	0	0	0	3	13	51
Heating Degree Days (base 65°F)	1,814	1,452	1,242	726	334	104	30	57	287	660	1,179	1,628	9,513
Cooling Degree Days (base 65°F)	0	0	0	3	19	73	145	122	23	1	0	0	386
Mean Precipitation (in.)	0.68	0.53	0.89	1.44	2.14	3.28	3.07	2.03	1.61	1.33	0.85	0.51	18.36
Days With ≥ 0.1" Precipitation	2	2	3	4	5	7	6	5	4	3	3	2	46
Days With ≥ 1.0" Precipitation	0	0	0	0	0	1	1	0	0	0	0	0	1
Mean Snowfall (in.)	9.6	7.0	7.6	3.5	0.4	0.0	0.0	0.0	trace	1.4	8.5	7.4	45.4
Days With ≥ 1.0" Snow Depth	na	*22*	*16*	3	0	0	0	0	0	1	*10*	*19*	na

Carrington 4 N *Foster County*   Elevation: 1,558 ft.   Latitude: 47° 30' N   Longitude: 99° 07' W

	JAN	FEB	MAR	APR	MAY	JUN	JUL	AUG	SEP	OCT	NOV	DEC	YEAR
Mean Maximum Temp. (°F)	16.8	24.1	35.3	54.0	69.7	77.6	82.1	81.7	71.1	57.0	35.1	22.4	52.2
Mean Temp. (°F)	6.9	14.1	25.7	41.8	55.7	64.5	68.5	67.3	57.1	44.4	25.9	12.8	40.4
Mean Minimum Temp. (°F)	-3.1	4.0	16.1	29.6	41.7	51.3	54.8	52.9	42.9	31.8	16.7	3.1	28.5
Extreme Maximum Temp. (°F)	55	58	70	99	97	99	107	107	105	92	78	52	107
Extreme Minimum Temp. (°F)	-35	-39	-26	-12	17	32	34	28	15	-3	-27	-36	-39
Days Maximum Temp. ≥ 90°F	0	0	0	0	1	2	5	6	2	0	0	0	16
Days Maximum Temp. ≤ 32°F	25	19	11	2	0	0	0	0	0	1	12	23	93
Days Minimum Temp. ≤ 32°F	31	28	29	20	5	0	0	0	3	16	28	31	191
Days Minimum Temp. ≤ 0°F	18	12	5	0	0	0	0	0	0	0	0	3	13	51
Heating Degree Days (base 65°F)	1,801	1,436	1,213	692	307	89	27	53	262	635	1,170	1,612	9,297
Cooling Degree Days (base 65°F)	0	0	0	3	23	83	147	137	28	1	0	0	422
Mean Precipitation (in.)	0.51	0.38	0.74	1.51	2.53	3.70	3.08	2.35	1.84	1.72	0.80	0.41	19.57
Days With ≥ 0.1" Precipitation	2	1	2	3	6	7	6	5	4	3	2	1	42
Days With ≥ 1.0" Precipitation	0	0	0	0	0	1	1	0	0	0	0	0	2
Mean Snowfall (in.)	na	na	5.2	1.7	trace	0.0	0.0	0.0	0.0	1.0	na	na	na
Days With ≥ 1.0" Snow Depth	na	na	na	0	0	0	0	0	0	0	na	na	na

Carson *Grant County*   Elevation: 2,309 ft.   Latitude: 46° 25' N   Longitude: 101° 34' W

	JAN	FEB	MAR	APR	MAY	JUN	JUL	AUG	SEP	OCT	NOV	DEC	YEAR
Mean Maximum Temp. (°F)	20.7	27.6	37.6	53.2	66.8	75.4	81.4	81.0	69.6	57.1	37.4	25.2	52.8
Mean Temp. (°F)	10.4	17.4	27.4	41.4	54.3	63.5	68.8	67.7	56.5	44.2	27.3	15.1	41.2
Mean Minimum Temp. (°F)	0.1	7.1	17.0	29.5	41.9	51.5	56.1	54.2	43.2	31.4	17.2	5.0	29.5
Extreme Maximum Temp. (°F)	65	66	78	94	94	101	105	101	102	94	75	63	105
Extreme Minimum Temp. (°F)	-37	-35	-26	-12	21	30	36	33	15	-6	-25	-39	-39
Days Maximum Temp. ≥ 90°F	0	0	0	0	0	2	5	6	1	0	0	0	14
Days Maximum Temp. ≤ 32°F	22	16	11	2	0	0	0	0	0	1	11	20	83
Days Minimum Temp. ≤ 32°F	31	28	29	20	4	0	0	0	3	17	28	31	191
Days Minimum Temp. ≤ 0°F	15	10	4	0	0	0	0	0	0	0	3	10	42
Heating Degree Days (base 65°F)	1,689	1,340	1,158	703	340	109	35	53	281	638	1,125	1,541	9,012
Cooling Degree Days (base 65°F)	0	0	0	3	17	72	158	149	29	2	0	0	430
Mean Precipitation (in.)	0.31	0.40	0.89	1.75	2.42	2.97	2.47	1.70	1.41	1.34	0.62	0.36	16.64
Days With ≥ 0.1" Precipitation	1	2	3	4	5	6	5	4	4	3	2	1	40
Days With ≥ 1.0" Precipitation	0	0	0	0	0	1	1	0	0	0	0	0	2
Mean Snowfall (in.)	5.7	5.4	7.9	5.3	0.3	0.0	0.0	0.0	0.2	2.3	5.9	5.7	38.7
Days With ≥ 1.0" Snow Depth	16	11	9	3	0	0	0	0	0	1	5	na	na

Cavalier 7 NW *Pembina County*   Elevation: 889 ft.   Latitude: 48° 52' N   Longitude: 97° 42' W

	JAN	FEB	MAR	APR	MAY	JUN	JUL	AUG	SEP	OCT	NOV	DEC	YEAR
Mean Maximum Temp. (°F)	12.3	19.6	31.3	50.9	67.6	75.4	78.8	78.6	67.8	53.5	32.8	18.3	48.9
Mean Temp. (°F)	2.7	9.8	22.5	39.9	54.6	63.5	67.2	65.7	55.4	42.6	24.3	9.4	38.1
Mean Minimum Temp. (°F)	-6.9	-0.0	13.6	28.8	41.5	51.5	55.5	52.8	43.0	31.5	15.7	0.5	27.3
Extreme Maximum Temp. (°F)	48	53	69	96	97	98	101	103	103	93	75	51	103
Extreme Minimum Temp. (°F)	-39	-40	-26	-10	18	31	35	30	24	-2	-33	-32	-40
Days Maximum Temp. ≥ 90°F	0	0	0	0	1	2	2	3	1	0	0	0	9
Days Maximum Temp. ≤ 32°F	28	22	15	3	0	0	0	0	0	1	15	25	109
Days Minimum Temp. ≤ 32°F	31	28	30	20	5	0	0	0	3	16	29	31	193
Days Minimum Temp. ≤ 0°F	21	15	6	1	0	0	0	0	0	0	4	15	62
Heating Degree Days (base 65°F)	1,932	1,555	1,312	749	340	111	38	70	300	689	1,216	1,721	10,033
Cooling Degree Days (base 65°F)	0	0	0	2	24	66	104	95	16	1	0	0	308
Mean Precipitation (in.)	0.40	0.38	0.69	1.22	2.23	3.09	3.29	2.55	1.79	1.55	0.61	0.39	18.19
Days With ≥ 0.1" Precipitation	1	1	2	3	5	6	7	5	4	3	2	1	40
Days With ≥ 1.0" Precipitation	0	0	0	0	0	1	1	1	0	0	0	0	3
Mean Snowfall (in.)	7.0	5.2	5.7	2.8	0.4	0.0	trace	0.0	trace	2.2	7.6	6.3	37.2
Days With ≥ 1.0" Snow Depth	31	27	25	6	0	0	0	0	0	2	17	26	134

Center 4 SE *Oliver County*   Elevation: 1,988 ft.   Latitude: 47° 04' N   Longitude: 101° 12' W

	JAN	FEB	MAR	APR	MAY	JUN	JUL	AUG	SEP	OCT	NOV	DEC	YEAR
Mean Maximum Temp. (°F)	21.2	27.8	38.9	54.9	68.3	76.9	82.7	82.4	70.9	57.7	38.1	26.2	53.8
Mean Temp. (°F)	10.4	17.3	27.9	42.1	54.7	63.7	68.9	67.7	56.8	44.5	27.5	15.8	41.4
Mean Minimum Temp. (°F)	-0.5	7.0	16.9	29.2	41.2	50.5	55.0	53.0	42.6	31.3	16.8	5.3	29.0
Extreme Maximum Temp. (°F)	60	66	76	94	96	105	104	106	104	93	79	65	106
Extreme Minimum Temp. (°F)	-38	-39	-27	-6	14	26	35	32	11	-3	-19	-37	-39
Days Maximum Temp. ≥ 90°F	0	0	0	0	0	2	6	7	2	0	0	0	17
Days Maximum Temp. ≤ 32°F	22	16	10	1	0	0	0	0	0	1	10	19	79
Days Minimum Temp. ≤ 32°F	31	28	29	20	6	0	0	0	4	17	28	31	194
Days Minimum Temp. ≤ 0°F	17	10	4	0	0	0	0	0	0	0	3	11	45
Heating Degree Days (base 65°F)	1,691	1,340	1,144	683	327	100	28	50	268	630	1,122	1,521	8,904
Cooling Degree Days (base 65°F)	0	0	0	2	16	66	154	143	25	1	0	0	407
Mean Precipitation (in.)	0.42	0.41	0.69	1.70	2.32	2.90	2.65	1.76	1.87	1.51	0.65	0.40	17.28
Days With ≥ 0.1" Precipitation	1	1	2	4	5	7	5	4	4	3	2	1	39
Days With ≥ 1.0" Precipitation	0	0	0	0	0	0	1	0	0	0	0	0	1
Mean Snowfall (in.)	5.9	4.5	6.1	3.1	trace	0.0	0.0	0.0	trace	1.5	5.4	5.2	31.7
Days With ≥ 1.0" Snow Depth	24	19	12	3	0	0	0	0	0	1	8	18	85

Colgate *Steele County*   Elevation: 1,177 ft.   Latitude: 47° 15' N   Longitude: 97° 39' W

	JAN	FEB	MAR	APR	MAY	JUN	JUL	AUG	SEP	OCT	NOV	DEC	YEAR
Mean Maximum Temp. (°F)	15.6	23.0	35.0	55.2	70.7	78.7	83.2	82.7	71.6	56.9	35.0	21.2	52.4
Mean Temp. (°F)	5.9	12.9	25.7	42.7	56.7	65.4	69.6	68.4	57.9	44.7	26.0	12.3	40.7
Mean Minimum Temp. (°F)	-3.9	2.8	16.3	30.2	42.7	52.0	55.8	54.0	44.1	32.6	16.9	3.2	28.9
Extreme Maximum Temp. (°F)	52	56	74	100	100	99	107	107	104	92	77	53	107
Extreme Minimum Temp. (°F)	-38	-40	-31	-10	17	30	37	28	17	0	-31	-34	-40
Days Maximum Temp. ≥ 90°F	0	0	0	0	1	3	6	7	2	0	0	0	19
Days Maximum Temp. ≤ 32°F	27	19	11	1	0	0	0	0	0	1	13	24	96
Days Minimum Temp. ≤ 32°F	31	28	29	19	5	0	0	0	3	15	29	31	190
Days Minimum Temp. ≤ 0°F	19	12	5	0	0	0	0	0	0	0	3	13	52
Heating Degree Days (base 65°F)	1,832	1,465	1,217	664	277	75	19	41	243	624	1,165	1,629	9,251
Cooling Degree Days (base 65°F)	0	0	0	3	29	93	167	154	32	1	0	0	479
Mean Precipitation (in.)	0.47	0.32	0.82	1.23	2.53	3.00	2.64	2.39	2.07	1.64	0.70	0.38	18.19
Days With ≥ 0.1" Precipitation	2	1	2	3	6	6	5	5	4	3	2	1	40
Days With ≥ 1.0" Precipitation	0	0	0	0	0	1	1	0	0	0	0	0	2
Mean Snowfall (in.)	7.6	4.4	5.2	1.9	0.2	0.0	0.0	0.0	0.0	0.6	7.3	5.0	32.2
Days With ≥ 1.0" Snow Depth	24	21	16	2	0	0	0	0	0	0	9	21	93

Cooperstown *Griggs County*   Elevation: 1,377 ft.   Latitude: 47° 24' N   Longitude: 98° 02' W

	JAN	FEB	MAR	APR	MAY	JUN	JUL	AUG	SEP	OCT	NOV	DEC	YEAR
Mean Maximum Temp. (°F)	16.0	23.9	35.3	54.5	69.7	77.9	82.5	81.6	70.8	56.8	34.8	21.3	52.1
Mean Temp. (°F)	6.1	13.9	25.7	42.4	56.4	65.3	69.6	68.0	57.6	44.7	25.8	12.0	40.6
Mean Minimum Temp. (°F)	-3.8	3.8	16.0	30.2	43.0	52.6	56.7	54.4	44.2	32.5	16.7	2.7	29.1
Extreme Maximum Temp. (°F)	53	56	73	98	96	96	104	104	103	91	76	53	104
Extreme Minimum Temp. (°F)	-34	-38	-27	-9	19	29	39	31	20	-1	-31	-35	-38
Days Maximum Temp. ≥ 90°F	0	0	0	0	1	3	6	5	2	0	0	0	17
Days Maximum Temp. ≤ 32°F	26	19	11	2	0	0	0	0	0	1	13	24	96
Days Minimum Temp. ≤ 32°F	31	28	29	19	4	0	0	0	3	15	29	31	189
Days Minimum Temp. ≤ 0°F	19	12	5	0	0	0	0	0	0	0	3	13	52
Heating Degree Days (base 65°F)	1,824	1,440	1,213	673	287	78	20	42	251	624	1,172	1,639	9,263
Cooling Degree Days (base 65°F)	0	0	0	3	27	87	160	137	29	0	0	0	443
Mean Precipitation (in.)	0.66	0.50	1.03	1.35	2.58	3.29	3.34	2.67	2.05	1.55	0.86	0.50	20.38
Days With ≥ 0.1" Precipitation	2	2	3	3	6	6	6	5	4	3	3	2	45
Days With ≥ 1.0" Precipitation	0	0	0	0	0	1	1	1	0	0	0	0	3
Mean Snowfall (in.)	8.8	5.1	6.5	2.0	trace	0.0	0.0	0.0	trace	0.7	8.0	6.1	37.2
Days With ≥ 1.0" Snow Depth	26	22	17	3	0	0	0	0	0	1	12	21	102

Crosby *Divide County*   Elevation: 1,952 ft.   Latitude: 48° 54' N   Longitude: 103° 18' W

	JAN	FEB	MAR	APR	MAY	JUN	JUL	AUG	SEP	OCT	NOV	DEC	YEAR
Mean Maximum Temp. (°F)	17.5	25.6	37.6	55.8	69.4	78.2	83.1	82.4	70.0	56.1	35.2	22.5	52.8
Mean Temp. (°F)	7.7	15.9	27.3	42.9	55.7	64.8	69.1	67.7	56.5	44.0	26.0	13.1	40.9
Mean Minimum Temp. (°F)	-2.1	6.1	17.0	29.9	41.9	51.2	55.1	53.0	42.9	31.9	16.9	3.7	28.9
Extreme Maximum Temp. (°F)	50	64	75	92	103	105	105	107	103	89	70	53	107
Extreme Minimum Temp. (°F)	-36	-40	-28	-13	21	30	40	33	18	-4	-25	-40	-40
Days Maximum Temp. ≥ 90°F	0	0	0	0	1	3	7	6	1	0	0	0	18
Days Maximum Temp. ≤ 32°F	24	17	10	1	0	0	0	0	0	1	12	22	87
Days Minimum Temp. ≤ 32°F	31	28	29	19	4	0	0	0	3	15	28	31	188
Days Minimum Temp. ≤ 0°F	17	10	4	0	0	0	0	0	0	0	3	12	46
Heating Degree Days (base 65°F)	1,774	1,383	1,163	660	304	84	25	47	271	644	1,163	1,604	9,122
Cooling Degree Days (base 65°F)	0	0	0	2	23	87	159	148	22	1	0	0	442
Mean Precipitation (in.)	0.48	0.33	0.59	1.12	1.99	2.67	2.74	1.50	1.65	0.94	0.43	0.46	14.90
Days With ≥ 0.1" Precipitation	2	1	2	3	5	6	5	4	4	3	1	2	38
Days With ≥ 1.0" Precipitation	0	0	0	0	0	1	1	0	0	0	0	0	1
Mean Snowfall (in.)	8.1	5.0	5.9	4.4	0.4	0.0	0.0	0.0	trace	2.1	6.0	7.7	39.6
Days With ≥ 1.0" Snow Depth	24	19	14	4	0	0	0	0	0	1	9	20	91

Devils Lake KDLR *Ramsey County*   Elevation: 1,463 ft.   Latitude: 48° 07' N   Longitude: 98° 52' W

	JAN	FEB	MAR	APR	MAY	JUN	JUL	AUG	SEP	OCT	NOV	DEC	YEAR
Mean Maximum Temp. (°F)	15.1	22.4	32.9	51.8	67.0	75.2	80.1	79.1	67.5	53.8	33.4	20.2	49.9
Mean Temp. (°F)	5.8	13.4	24.2	41.1	55.4	64.4	69.0	67.4	56.4	43.8	25.8	12.0	39.9
Mean Minimum Temp. (°F)	-3.2	4.3	15.5	30.4	43.7	53.6	57.8	55.6	45.2	33.7	18.2	3.8	29.9
Extreme Maximum Temp. (°F)	53	55	67	97	96	98	103	102	100	93	77	51	103
Extreme Minimum Temp. (°F)	-35	-37	-28	-12	20	34	41	33	22	-2	-25	-37	-37
Days Maximum Temp. ≥ 90°F	0	0	0	0	1	2	3	3	1	0	0	0	10
Days Maximum Temp. ≤ 32°F	26	20	13	2	0	0	0	0	0	1	14	24	100
Days Minimum Temp. ≤ 32°F	31	28	30	18	4	0	0	0	2	13	28	31	185
Days Minimum Temp. ≤ 0°F	18	12	5	0	0	0	0	0	0	0	2	13	50
Heating Degree Days (base 65°F)	1,835	1,455	1,258	711	315	94	26	52	276	651	1,168	1,641	9,482
Cooling Degree Days (base 65°F)	0	0	0	2	25	81	151	136	25	1	0	0	421
Mean Precipitation (in.)	0.58	0.50	0.83	0.93	2.20	3.92	3.19	2.18	1.73	1.47	0.87	0.57	18.97
Days With ≥ 0.1" Precipitation	2	2	3	3	5	7	6	5	4	3	2	2	44
Days With ≥ 1.0" Precipitation	0	0	0	0	0	1	1	0	0	0	0	0	2
Mean Snowfall (in.)	na	na	na	1.7	0.2	0.0	0.0	0.0	trace	1.6	5.1	na	na
Days With ≥ 1.0" Snow Depth	na	24	18	3	0	0	0	0	0	1	10	21	na

Dickinson Exp. Station *Stark County*   Elevation: 2,457 ft.   Latitude: 46° 53' N   Longitude: 102° 48' W

	JAN	FEB	MAR	APR	MAY	JUN	JUL	AUG	SEP	OCT	NOV	DEC	YEAR
Mean Maximum Temp. (°F)	23.3	30.5	40.1	54.0	66.9	76.2	82.6	82.8	71.0	57.8	39.4	28.6	54.4
Mean Temp. (°F)	11.6	18.7	28.1	41.1	53.4	62.6	68.0	67.2	55.4	43.2	27.4	16.6	41.1
Mean Minimum Temp. (°F)	-0.2	6.8	16.1	28.0	39.8	49.0	53.4	51.5	39.8	28.6	15.4	4.5	27.7
Extreme Maximum Temp. (°F)	60	67	76	93	98	105	110	105	104	93	81	67	110
Extreme Minimum Temp. (°F)	-38	-36	-33	-16	17	26	33	30	14	-9	-29	-41	-41
Days Maximum Temp. ≥ 90°F	0	0	0	0	1	2	7	8	2	0	0	0	20
Days Maximum Temp. ≤ 32°F	20	14	9	2	0	0	0	0	0	1	9	17	72
Days Minimum Temp. ≤ 32°F	31	28	30	21	6	0	0	0	6	21	29	31	203
Days Minimum Temp. ≤ 0°F	15	10	4	0	0	0	0	0	0	0	0	4	11	44
Heating Degree Days (base 65°F)	1,653	1,303	1,136	712	365	126	42	60	306	669	1,121	1,495	8,988
Cooling Degree Days (base 65°F)	0	0	0	1	13	65	143	141	23	1	0	0	387
Mean Precipitation (in.)	0.36	0.35	0.68	1.70	2.40	3.49	2.21	1.65	1.63	1.30	0.57	0.37	16.71
Days With ≥ 0.1" Precipitation	1	1	2	4	5	7	5	4	4	3	2	1	39
Days With ≥ 1.0" Precipitation	0	0	0	0	0	1	0	0	0	0	0	0	1
Mean Snowfall (in.)	5.3	5.9	6.4	4.8	0.4	0.0	0.0	0.0	0.4	2.1	5.4	5.7	36.4
Days With ≥ 1.0" Snow Depth	na	na	8	2	0	0	0	0	0	1	4	na	na

Dickinson Municipal Airport *Stark County*   Elevation: 2,582 ft.   Latitude: 46° 48' N   Longitude: 102° 48' W

	JAN	FEB	MAR	APR	MAY	JUN	JUL	AUG	SEP	OCT	NOV	DEC	YEAR
Mean Maximum Temp. (°F)	23.2	30.2	40.3	54.5	67.0	76.3	83.3	82.7	70.5	57.4	38.8	28.1	54.4
Mean Temp. (°F)	13.7	20.7	29.9	42.6	54.5	63.6	69.5	68.6	57.1	45.1	29.2	18.3	42.7
Mean Minimum Temp. (°F)	4.2	11.1	19.5	30.6	41.9	50.9	55.6	54.5	43.7	32.8	19.4	8.6	31.1
Extreme Maximum Temp. (°F)	63	68	78	94	99	104	109	104	104	92	80	67	109
Extreme Minimum Temp. (°F)	-34	-31	-26	-10	22	30	37	34	17	-7	-18	-34	-34
Days Maximum Temp. ≥ 90°F	0	0	0	0	0	2	7	8	2	0	0	0	19
Days Maximum Temp. ≤ 32°F	20	14	9	2	0	0	0	0	0	1	10	17	73
Days Minimum Temp. ≤ 32°F	30	27	28	17	4	0	0	0	3	15	27	30	181
Days Minimum Temp. ≤ 0°F	13	7	3	0	0	0	0	0	0	0	3	9	35
Heating Degree Days (base 65°F)	1,586	1,247	1,080	668	335	101	29	44	264	611	1,069	1,442	8,476
Cooling Degree Days (base 65°F)	0	0	0	1	18	73	183	173	34	2	0	0	484
Mean Precipitation (in.)	0.38	0.41	0.69	1.82	2.40	3.29	2.09	1.51	1.65	1.32	0.53	0.33	16.42
Days With ≥ 0.1" Precipitation	1	1	2	4	6	7	5	3	4	3	2	1	39
Days With ≥ 1.0" Precipitation	0	0	0	0	0	1	0	0	0	0	0	0	1
Mean Snowfall (in.)	5.6	4.9	6.5	5.4	0.5	trace	trace	trace	0.4	2.1	5.4	4.6	35.4
Days With ≥ 1.0" Snow Depth	22	16	12	5	0	0	0	0	0	1	10	18	84

Drake 9 NE *McHenry County*   Elevation: 1,528 ft.   Latitude: 48° 03' N   Longitude: 100° 19' W

	JAN	FEB	MAR	APR	MAY	JUN	JUL	AUG	SEP	OCT	NOV	DEC	YEAR
Mean Maximum Temp. (°F)	16.5	24.1	35.6	54.3	69.1	77.8	82.4	82.1	70.5	56.4	35.2	22.0	52.2
Mean Temp. (°F)	6.4	14.1	25.6	42.0	56.1	65.1	69.4	68.3	57.1	44.2	26.0	12.3	40.5
Mean Minimum Temp. (°F)	-3.9	4.1	15.6	29.6	43.0	52.4	56.4	54.4	43.7	31.9	16.7	2.5	28.9
Extreme Maximum Temp. (°F)	52	63	71	99	100	105	108	106	107	93	78	55	108
Extreme Minimum Temp. (°F)	-37	-43	-33	-12	19	34	39	28	19	-8	-32	-41	-43
Days Maximum Temp. ≥ 90°F	0	0	0	0	1	3	5	6	2	0	0	0	17
Days Maximum Temp. ≤ 32°F	25	18	11	2	0	0	0	0	0	1	12	23	92
Days Minimum Temp. ≤ 32°F	31	28	29	19	4	0	0	0	3	16	28	31	189
Days Minimum Temp. ≤ 0°F	18	12	5	0	0	0	0	0	0	0	4	14	53
Heating Degree Days (base 65°F)	1,816	1,432	1,216	686	298	79	22	43	260	639	1,165	1,631	9,287
Cooling Degree Days (base 65°F)	0	0	0	3	29	89	172	155	28	1	0	0	477
Mean Precipitation (in.)	0.37	0.37	0.59	1.30	2.23	2.99	2.79	1.79	1.52	1.21	0.60	0.34	16.10
Days With ≥ 0.1" Precipitation	1	1	2	3	5	6	5	4	4	2	2	1	36
Days With ≥ 1.0" Precipitation	0	0	0	0	0	1	1	0	0	0	0	0	2
Mean Snowfall (in.)	6.6	5.0	6.4	3.7	0.2	0.0	0.0	0.0	0.1	1.7	6.5	5.2	35.4
Days With ≥ 1.0" Snow Depth	28	24	21	5	0	0	0	0	0	1	13	24	116

Dunn Center 2 SW *Dunn County*   Elevation: 2,230 ft.   Latitude: 47° 21' N   Longitude: 102° 39' W

	JAN	FEB	MAR	APR	MAY	JUN	JUL	AUG	SEP	OCT	NOV	DEC	YEAR
Mean Maximum Temp. (°F)	22.2	29.5	39.8	55.1	68.1	76.9	83.6	83.8	71.9	57.7	37.8	26.7	54.4
Mean Temp. (°F)	11.5	19.0	28.7	42.6	55.3	64.3	69.7	68.9	57.8	45.0	27.9	16.3	42.3
Mean Minimum Temp. (°F)	0.8	8.3	17.5	30.2	42.5	51.5	55.7	54.0	43.5	32.3	18.0	5.9	30.0
Extreme Maximum Temp. (°F)	56	61	80	92	98	107	108	104	105	94	77	61	108
Extreme Minimum Temp. (°F)	-37	-35	-28	-14	21	31	39	33	14	-5	-21	-38	-38
Days Maximum Temp. ≥ 90°F	0	0	0	0	1	3	8	9	2	0	0	0	23
Days Maximum Temp. ≤ 32°F	21	14	9	1	0	0	0	0	0	1	9	18	73
Days Minimum Temp. ≤ 32°F	31	28	29	18	4	0	0	0	3	15	27	30	185
Days Minimum Temp. ≤ 0°F	15	9	4	0	0	0	0	0	0	0	3	10	41
Heating Degree Days (base 65°F)	1,656	1,295	1,119	665	313	89	24	39	245	614	1,105	1,503	8,667
Cooling Degree Days (base 65°F)	0	0	0	0	1	24	89	183	179	39	1	0	0	516
Mean Precipitation (in.)	0.41	0.39	0.67	1.64	2.40	3.35	2.24	1.71	1.62	1.24	0.66	0.39	16.72
Days With ≥ 0.1" Precipitation	1	1	2	4	5	7	5	4	4	3	2	1	39
Days With ≥ 1.0" Precipitation	0	0	0	0	0	1	0	0	0	0	0	0	1
Mean Snowfall (in.)	6.4	5.7	7.2	5.3	0.5	0.0	0.0	0.0	0.4	2.1	6.8	5.6	40.0
Days With ≥ 1.0" Snow Depth	24	19	14	4	0	0	0	0	0	1	10	18	90

Edmore 1 NW *Ramsey County*　Elevation: 1,532 ft.　Latitude: 48° 26' N　Longitude: 98° 28' W

	JAN	FEB	MAR	APR	MAY	JUN	JUL	AUG	SEP	OCT	NOV	DEC	YEAR
Mean Maximum Temp. (°F)	12.4	20.0	31.4	51.8	67.6	75.8	79.9	79.4	67.9	53.6	32.3	18.0	49.2
Mean Temp. (°F)	2.4	9.9	21.8	40.0	54.1	63.0	67.0	65.4	54.8	41.7	23.2	8.6	37.7
Mean Minimum Temp. (°F)	-7.6	-0.2	12.1	28.1	40.6	50.0	54.0	51.4	41.6	29.8	14.0	-0.9	26.1
Extreme Maximum Temp. (°F)	48	55	68	97	96	98	107	101	101	91	75	49	107
Extreme Minimum Temp. (°F)	-42	-46	-35	-13	14	28	33	25	18	-4	-30	-38	-46
Days Maximum Temp. ≥ 90°F	0	0	0	0	0	2	3	3	1	0	0	0	9
Days Maximum Temp. ≤ 32°F	28	22	15	3	0	0	0	0	0	1	15	26	110
Days Minimum Temp. ≤ 32°F	31	28	30	21	6	0	0	0	4	19	29	31	199
Days Minimum Temp. ≤ 0°F	21	14	7	1	0	0	0	0	0	0	5	16	64
Heating Degree Days (base 65°F)	1,940	1,553	1,335	745	348	116	44	73	318	715	1,248	1,746	10,181
Cooling Degree Days (base 65°F)	0	0	0	2	19	64	114	97	16	0	0	0	312
Mean Precipitation (in.)	0.50	0.37	0.66	1.10	2.22	3.17	3.37	2.47	1.68	1.36	0.67	0.45	18.02
Days With ≥ 0.1" Precipitation	2	1	2	3	5	7	7	5	4	3	2	1	42
Days With ≥ 1.0" Precipitation	0	0	0	0	0	1	1	1	0	0	0	0	3
Mean Snowfall (in.)	6.1	4.5	5.1	2.6	0.4	0.0	0.0	0.0	trace	1.7	6.3	5.4	32.1
Days With ≥ 1.0" Snow Depth	29	24	19	4	0	0	0	0	0	1	12	23	112

Ellendale *Dickey County*　Elevation: 1,453 ft.　Latitude: 46° 00' N　Longitude: 98° 32' W

	JAN	FEB	MAR	APR	MAY	JUN	JUL	AUG	SEP	OCT	NOV	DEC	YEAR
Mean Maximum Temp. (°F)	20.1	27.3	38.6	57.0	71.0	79.4	85.2	84.2	73.7	59.3	37.4	25.0	54.8
Mean Temp. (°F)	10.1	17.3	29.0	44.4	57.3	66.2	71.6	70.1	59.7	46.6	28.2	15.4	43.0
Mean Minimum Temp. (°F)	0.0	7.4	19.3	31.9	43.6	53.0	58.0	56.0	45.6	33.9	18.9	5.8	31.1
Extreme Maximum Temp. (°F)	63	63	78	98	96	99	108	105	104	92	75	57	108
Extreme Minimum Temp. (°F)	-37	-37	-23	-11	16	34	40	35	16	5	-23	-34	-37
Days Maximum Temp. ≥ 90°F	0	0	0	0	1	3	9	8	2	0	0	0	23
Days Maximum Temp. ≤ 32°F	23	16	9	1	0	0	0	0	0	0	11	21	81
Days Minimum Temp. ≤ 32°F	31	28	28	16	3	0	0	0	2	13	28	31	180
Days Minimum Temp. ≤ 0°F	16	9	3	0	0	0	0	0	0	0	2	11	41
Heating Degree Days (base 65°F)	1,700	1,340	1,111	613	258	62	12	27	203	565	1,098	1,533	8,522
Cooling Degree Days (base 65°F)	0	0	0	3	30	107	227	196	47	2	0	0	612
Mean Precipitation (in.)	0.49	0.48	1.08	2.03	3.01	3.70	2.84	2.48	2.23	2.01	0.75	0.31	21.41
Days With ≥ 0.1" Precipitation	2	2	3	4	6	7	6	5	4	4	3	1	47
Days With ≥ 1.0" Precipitation	0	0	0	0	1	1	1	1	1	1	0	0	6
Mean Snowfall (in.)	8.1	5.7	7.4	4.3	trace	0.0	0.0	0.0	trace	1.0	7.9	5.5	39.9
Days With ≥ 1.0" Snow Depth	*20*	na	*8*	1	0	0	0	0	0	0	6	*13*	na

Fairfield *Billings County*　Elevation: 2,749 ft.　Latitude: 47° 11' N　Longitude: 103° 13' W

	JAN	FEB	MAR	APR	MAY	JUN	JUL	AUG	SEP	OCT	NOV	DEC	YEAR
Mean Maximum Temp. (°F)	21.5	28.8	38.5	53.5	66.1	75.4	81.7	81.5	68.9	55.9	37.1	26.0	52.9
Mean Temp. (°F)	12.0	19.0	28.3	41.7	53.7	63.0	68.6	67.7	56.2	44.1	27.8	16.3	41.5
Mean Minimum Temp. (°F)	2.4	9.2	18.0	29.8	41.2	50.6	55.3	54.0	43.4	32.3	18.4	6.6	30.1
Extreme Maximum Temp. (°F)	57	62	75	90	98	104	109	103	101	91	78	62	109
Extreme Minimum Temp. (°F)	-36	-36	-20	-7	18	30	39	33	19	-5	-21	-38	-38
Days Maximum Temp. ≥ 90°F	0	0	0	0	0	2	6	7	2	0	0	0	17
Days Maximum Temp. ≤ 32°F	22	14	10	2	0	0	0	0	0	1	11	19	79
Days Minimum Temp. ≤ 32°F	31	28	29	19	4	0	0	0	3	15	27	30	186
Days Minimum Temp. ≤ 0°F	14	8	3	0	0	0	0	0	0	0	3	10	38
Heating Degree Days (base 65°F)	1,642	1,295	1,132	694	357	113	34	51	285	642	1,111	1,505	8,861
Cooling Degree Days (base 65°F)	0	0	0	1	15	64	152	149	27	1	0	0	409
Mean Precipitation (in.)	0.31	0.31	0.57	1.51	2.18	3.06	2.14	1.62	1.58	1.13	0.45	0.30	15.16
Days With ≥ 0.1" Precipitation	1	1	2	4	5	6	5	4	3	3	2	1	37
Days With ≥ 1.0" Precipitation	0	0	0	0	0	1	0	0	0	0	0	0	1
Mean Snowfall (in.)	5.6	4.8	5.3	4.7	0.7	0.0	0.0	0.0	0.3	2.0	4.9	4.3	32.6
Days With ≥ 1.0" Snow Depth	*20*	*14*	11	4	0	0	0	0	0	1	8	*16*	*74*

Forman 5 SSE *Sargent County*　Elevation: 1,250 ft.　Latitude: 46° 02' N　Longitude: 97° 36' W

	JAN	FEB	MAR	APR	MAY	JUN	JUL	AUG	SEP	OCT	NOV	DEC	YEAR
Mean Maximum Temp. (°F)	17.5	24.8	36.6	54.8	69.2	78.1	83.8	82.7	71.6	57.6	37.2	24.0	53.2
Mean Temp. (°F)	7.3	14.6	27.1	43.4	57.0	66.1	71.2	69.4	58.3	45.3	27.9	14.4	41.8
Mean Minimum Temp. (°F)	-3.0	4.4	17.5	32.0	44.7	54.1	58.6	56.1	45.0	32.9	18.4	4.8	30.5
Extreme Maximum Temp. (°F)	65	60	80	98	97	105	105	106	102	92	78	60	106
Extreme Minimum Temp. (°F)	-37	-40	-27	-2	19	35	40	32	19	6	-22	-36	-40
Days Maximum Temp. ≥ 90°F	0	0	0	0	1	3	7	6	2	0	0	0	19
Days Maximum Temp. ≤ 32°F	25	18	10	1	0	0	0	0	0	0	11	22	87
Days Minimum Temp. ≤ 32°F	31	28	28	16	3	0	0	0	3	16	28	31	184
Days Minimum Temp. ≤ 0°F	18	12	4	0	0	0	0	0	0	0	2	12	48
Heating Degree Days (base 65°F)	1,770	1,417	1,169	644	275	72	16	36	237	607	1,108	1,564	8,915
Cooling Degree Days (base 65°F)	0	0	0	3	35	111	215	180	41	2	0	0	587
Mean Precipitation (in.)	0.64	0.51	1.25	1.68	2.60	3.56	2.89	2.20	1.94	1.71	0.98	0.41	20.37
Days With ≥ 0.1" Precipitation	2	2	3	4	5	6	5	5	4	4	2	1	43
Days With ≥ 1.0" Precipitation	0	0	0	0	1	1	1	1	0	0	0	0	4
Mean Snowfall (in.)	8.3	5.2	6.2	2.0	trace	0.0	0.0	0.0	trace	0.5	7.0	4.6	33.8
Days With ≥ 1.0" Snow Depth	*19*	na	*10*	2	0	0	0	0	0	0	5	*12*	na

Fort Yates 4 SW *Sioux County*   Elevation: 1,673 ft.   Latitude: 46° 03' N   Longitude: 100° 40' W

	JAN	FEB	MAR	APR	MAY	JUN	JUL	AUG	SEP	OCT	NOV	DEC	YEAR
Mean Maximum Temp. (°F)	24.2	31.1	41.5	57.6	70.4	79.6	85.8	85.1	74.6	61.1	41.1	28.5	56.7
Mean Temp. (°F)	13.8	21.0	30.9	45.3	58.2	67.6	73.1	71.9	61.0	48.4	31.3	18.7	45.1
Mean Minimum Temp. (°F)	3.5	10.8	20.2	32.9	46.0	55.5	60.4	58.6	47.4	35.7	21.5	8.9	33.5
Extreme Maximum Temp. (°F)	60	72	75	99	96	107	110	103	103	95	80	63	110
Extreme Minimum Temp. (°F)	-39	-45	-27	-7	23	29	36	32	18	-4	-20	-32	-45
Days Maximum Temp. ≥ 90°F	0	0	0	0	1	4	9	10	2	0	0	0	26
Days Maximum Temp. ≤ 32°F	20	15	7	1	0	0	0	0	0	0	7	17	67
Days Minimum Temp. ≤ 32°F	30	27	27	14	2	0	0	0	2	11	26	31	170
Days Minimum Temp. ≤ 0°F	14	7	3	0	0	0	0	0	0	0	2	9	35
Heating Degree Days (base 65°F)	1,582	1,236	1,051	589	238	48	8	15	171	511	1,003	1,430	7,882
Cooling Degree Days (base 65°F)	0	0	0	7	41	136	269	241	57	3	0	0	754
Mean Precipitation (in.)	0.25	0.29	0.64	1.38	2.14	2.61	2.03	1.60	1.32	1.24	0.37	0.24	14.11
Days With ≥ 0.1" Precipitation	1	1	2	3	5	6	4	3	3	3	1	1	33
Days With ≥ 1.0" Precipitation	0	0	0	0	0	0	1	0	0	0	0	0	1
Mean Snowfall (in.)	5.0	4.5	5.6	1.9	0.3	0.0	0.0	0.0	trace	0.4	4.7	5.3	27.7
Days With ≥ 1.0" Snow Depth	19	13	8	2	0	0	0	0	0	0	7	15	64

Fortuna 1 W *Divide County*   Elevation: 2,349 ft.   Latitude: 48° 55' N   Longitude: 103° 49' W

	JAN	FEB	MAR	APR	MAY	JUN	JUL	AUG	SEP	OCT	NOV	DEC	YEAR
Mean Maximum Temp. (°F)	15.2	22.3	34.3	52.0	65.2	74.2	79.7	79.5	66.9	53.9	33.7	21.1	49.8
Mean Temp. (°F)	5.4	12.6	24.5	40.1	52.8	61.9	66.6	65.5	53.7	41.4	24.3	11.4	38.4
Mean Minimum Temp. (°F)	-4.5	3.4	14.6	28.2	40.3	49.6	53.5	51.6	40.4	28.8	14.8	1.7	26.9
Extreme Maximum Temp. (°F)	45	64	74	90	100	103	102	105	102	91	73	53	105
Extreme Minimum Temp. (°F)	-44	-39	-24	-11	18	30	38	31	19	-5	-26	-45	-45
Days Maximum Temp. ≥ 90°F	0	0	0	0	0	2	4	5	1	0	0	0	12
Days Maximum Temp. ≤ 32°F	26	19	13	2	0	0	0	0	0	2	14	23	99
Days Minimum Temp. ≤ 32°F	31	28	30	21	6	0	0	0	5	21	29	31	202
Days Minimum Temp. ≤ 0°F	18	11	5	0	0	0	0	0	0	0	4	13	51
Heating Degree Days (base 65°F)	1,849	1,476	1,250	740	383	139	52	81	348	725	1,216	1,658	9,917
Cooling Degree Days (base 65°F)	0	0	0	0	12	60	110	111	16	0	0	0	309
Mean Precipitation (in.)	0.36	*0.42*	0.77	0.99	1.99	2.78	2.67	1.62	1.36	0.85	0.31	0.39	*14.51*
Days With ≥ 0.1" Precipitation	1	na	*2*	2	6	7	5	4	3	2	1	1	na
Days With ≥ 1.0" Precipitation	0	na	*0*	0	0	0	1	0	0	0	0	0	na
Mean Snowfall (in.)	*4.8*	na	na	2.0	0.7	0.0	0.0	0.0	trace	*1.4*	*3.4*	na	na
Days With ≥ 1.0" Snow Depth	na	na	na	na	0	0	0	0	0	*0*	na	na	na

Foxholm 7 N *Ward County*   Elevation: 1,673 ft.   Latitude: 48° 28' N   Longitude: 101° 34' W

	JAN	FEB	MAR	APR	MAY	JUN	JUL	AUG	SEP	OCT	NOV	DEC	YEAR
Mean Maximum Temp. (°F)	*18.2*	*24.7*	37.4	54.7	69.0	*78.2*	83.5	82.8	70.2	56.9	*36.1*	na	na
Mean Temp. (°F)	*7.6*	*14.5*	26.5	41.9	55.6	64.9	69.1	67.7	56.2	44.3	26.1	na	na
Mean Minimum Temp. (°F)	*-3.1*	4.7	15.6	28.8	*41.9*	51.4	54.7	52.5	42.0	31.7	16.0	na	na
Extreme Maximum Temp. (°F)	53	63	73	94	101	104	109	106	103	94	79	58	109
Extreme Minimum Temp. (°F)	-40	-37	-27	-11	17	32	35	28	21	-1	-27	-37	-40
Days Maximum Temp. ≥ 90°F	0	0	0	0	1	3	6	7	1	0	0	0	18
Days Maximum Temp. ≤ 32°F	21	16	10	1	0	0	0	0	0	1	10	18	77
Days Minimum Temp. ≤ 32°F	28	26	29	19	4	0	0	0	3	15	25	26	175
Days Minimum Temp. ≤ 0°F	16	11	5	0	0	0	0	0	0	0	3	11	46
Heating Degree Days (base 65°F)	*1,778*	*1,422*	1,188	689	*305*	82	23	*51*	281	634	*1,163*	na	na
Cooling Degree Days (base 65°F)	*0*	*0*	*0*	2	28	99	162	145	na	na	na	na	na
Mean Precipitation (in.)	0.53	0.43	0.80	1.40	1.94	2.95	2.62	1.81	1.68	1.36	0.63	0.47	16.62
Days With ≥ 0.1" Precipitation	2	1	3	3	4	6	5	4	3	2	2	1	36
Days With ≥ 1.0" Precipitation	0	0	0	0	0	1	1	0	0	0	0	0	2
Mean Snowfall (in.)	8.7	5.9	6.8	3.6	0.3	trace	0.0	0.0	trace	2.1	6.6	7.3	41.3
Days With ≥ 1.0" Snow Depth	23	16	14	3	0	0	0	0	0	1	8	19	84

Fullerton 1 ESE *Dickey County*   Elevation: 1,433 ft.   Latitude: 46° 09' N   Longitude: 98° 24' W

	JAN	FEB	MAR	APR	MAY	JUN	JUL	AUG	SEP	OCT	NOV	DEC	YEAR
Mean Maximum Temp. (°F)	19.3	27.0	38.7	57.3	71.2	79.4	85.1	83.8	73.4	58.9	37.2	24.5	54.7
Mean Temp. (°F)	9.1	16.7	28.6	44.4	57.4	66.2	71.3	69.6	59.3	46.1	28.0	14.8	42.6
Mean Minimum Temp. (°F)	-1.1	6.3	18.4	31.5	43.6	53.1	57.5	55.3	45.0	33.3	18.8	5.1	30.6
Extreme Maximum Temp. (°F)	60	60	80	98	97	105	108	107	105	91	76	59	108
Extreme Minimum Temp. (°F)	-40	-44	-25	-8	18	33	39	30	18	5	-23	-35	-44
Days Maximum Temp. ≥ 90°F	0	0	0	0	1	3	9	7	2	0	0	0	22
Days Maximum Temp. ≤ 32°F	24	17	9	1	0	0	0	0	0	0	11	21	83
Days Minimum Temp. ≤ 32°F	31	28	29	17	4	0	0	0	3	14	28	31	185
Days Minimum Temp. ≤ 0°F	16	11	4	0	0	0	0	0	0	0	2	11	44
Heating Degree Days (base 65°F)	1,729	1,360	1,122	614	255	63	13	32	211	581	1,104	1,552	8,636
Cooling Degree Days (base 65°F)	0	0	0	3	29	103	203	166	39	1	0	0	544
Mean Precipitation (in.)	0.76	0.60	1.40	1.99	2.90	3.14	2.85	2.18	2.02	1.81	1.03	0.39	21.07
Days With ≥ 0.1" Precipitation	3	2	4	5	5	6	5	4	4	4	3	2	47
Days With ≥ 1.0" Precipitation	0	0	0	0	1	1	1	0	1	1	0	0	5
Mean Snowfall (in.)	8.3	6.3	8.2	2.7	trace	0.0	0.0	0.0	trace	0.6	7.6	*4.1*	*37.8*
Days With ≥ 1.0" Snow Depth	*19*	na	11	1	0	0	0	0	0	0	7	na	na

Gackle *Logan County*   Elevation: 1,948 ft.   Latitude: 46° 38' N   Longitude: 99° 09' W

	JAN	FEB	MAR	APR	MAY	JUN	JUL	AUG	SEP	OCT	NOV	DEC	YEAR
Mean Maximum Temp. (°F)	18.2	25.5	36.8	55.3	69.5	78.1	83.6	82.7	71.7	57.7	36.1	23.2	53.2
Mean Temp. (°F)	8.7	16.0	27.3	43.3	56.7	65.9	71.0	69.6	58.8	45.8	27.4	14.2	42.1
Mean Minimum Temp. (°F)	-0.7	6.5	17.7	31.3	44.0	53.7	58.5	56.5	45.8	34.0	18.6	5.3	30.9
Extreme Maximum Temp. (°F)	57	61	76	97	95	99	109	105	104	93	76	54	109
Extreme Minimum Temp. (°F)	-35	-35	-25	-7	19	34	39	36	18	-2	-22	-37	-37
Days Maximum Temp. ≥ 90°F	0	0	0	0	0	2	7	7	2	0	0	0	18
Days Maximum Temp. ≤ 32°F	25	17	10	1	0	0	0	0	0	1	13	23	90
Days Minimum Temp. ≤ 32°F	31	28	29	17	3	0	0	0	2	13	28	31	182
Days Minimum Temp. ≤ 0°F	16	10	4	0	0	0	0	0	0	0	2	11	43
Heating Degree Days (base 65°F)	1,742	1,378	1,162	647	275	67	16	31	223	589	1,123	1,570	8,823
Cooling Degree Days (base 65°F)	0	0	0	4	27	95	199	175	40	2	0	0	542
Mean Precipitation (in.)	0.44	0.35	0.92	1.51	2.61	3.33	2.99	1.98	1.91	1.48	0.75	0.34	18.61
Days With ≥ 0.1" Precipitation	1	1	2	4	6	7	5	5	4	3	2	1	41
Days With ≥ 1.0" Precipitation	0	0	0	0	0	1	1	0	0	0	0	0	2
Mean Snowfall (in.)	7.8	5.1	7.4	2.8	0.2	0.0	trace	0.0	0.1	1.2	7.1	5.5	37.2
Days With ≥ 1.0" Snow Depth	21	19	13	3	0	0	0	0	0	0	8	15	79

Garrison 1 NNW *McLean County*   Elevation: 1,938 ft.   Latitude: 47° 38' N   Longitude: 101° 25' W

	JAN	FEB	MAR	APR	MAY	JUN	JUL	AUG	SEP	OCT	NOV	DEC	YEAR
Mean Maximum Temp. (°F)	17.8	25.2	36.4	53.4	66.9	75.8	81.3	81.3	69.3	56.0	36.0	24.0	51.9
Mean Temp. (°F)	7.3	14.7	25.9	41.1	54.2	63.4	68.1	67.3	55.7	43.2	26.2	14.2	40.1
Mean Minimum Temp. (°F)	-3.2	4.2	15.5	28.7	41.4	51.0	54.9	53.1	42.1	30.3	16.4	4.3	28.2
Extreme Maximum Temp. (°F)	53	62	75	93	95	101	105	104	104	92	75	61	105
Extreme Minimum Temp. (°F)	-38	-37	-29	-12	17	31	36	29	17	-3	-19	-42	-42
Days Maximum Temp. ≥ 90°F	0	0	0	0	0	2	5	6	1	0	0	0	14
Days Maximum Temp. ≤ 32°F	24	18	11	2	0	0	0	0	0	1	11	20	87
Days Minimum Temp. ≤ 32°F	31	28	30	19	5	0	0	0	4	18	28	30	193
Days Minimum Temp. ≤ 0°F	17	11	4	0	0	0	0	0	0	0	3	11	46
Heating Degree Days (base 65°F)	1,787	1,416	1,204	713	343	106	34	54	293	670	1,159	1,571	9,350
Cooling Degree Days (base 65°F)	0	0	0	2	16	67	133	136	22	1	0	0	377
Mean Precipitation (in.)	0.41	0.36	0.65	1.25	2.02	3.10	2.64	1.81	1.44	1.18	0.53	0.39	15.78
Days With ≥ 0.1" Precipitation	1	1	2	3	5	6	5	4	3	3	2	2	37
Days With ≥ 1.0" Precipitation	0	0	0	0	0	1	1	0	0	0	0	0	2
Mean Snowfall (in.)	na	na	na	2.8	0.2	0.0	0.0	0.0	0.1	1.6	6.1	na	na
Days With ≥ 1.0" Snow Depth	na	na	na	2	0	0	0	0	0	1	na	na	na

Grafton *Walsh County*   Elevation: 826 ft.   Latitude: 48° 25' N   Longitude: 97° 25' W

	JAN	FEB	MAR	APR	MAY	JUN	JUL	AUG	SEP	OCT	NOV	DEC	YEAR
Mean Maximum Temp. (°F)	13.8	21.9	34.1	54.1	70.9	78.9	82.7	81.8	70.7	55.8	34.0	19.5	51.5
Mean Temp. (°F)	5.0	12.7	25.2	42.8	57.9	66.6	70.5	68.8	58.4	45.1	26.2	11.3	40.9
Mean Minimum Temp. (°F)	-4.0	3.4	16.3	31.5	44.9	54.3	58.3	55.7	46.1	34.5	18.4	3.0	30.2
Extreme Maximum Temp. (°F)	50	55	70	100	100	101	102	102	104	90	78	54	104
Extreme Minimum Temp. (°F)	-36	-40	-35	-11	20	33	36	32	21	3	-31	-32	-40
Days Maximum Temp. ≥ 90°F	0	0	0	0	2	3	5	5	1	0	0	0	16
Days Maximum Temp. ≤ 32°F	27	20	13	2	0	0	0	0	0	1	13	25	101
Days Minimum Temp. ≤ 32°F	31	27	28	16	4	0	0	0	2	12	27	31	178
Days Minimum Temp. ≤ 0°F	19	13	5	0	0	0	0	0	0	0	3	14	54
Heating Degree Days (base 65°F)	1,860	1,474	1,227	661	259	65	15	38	231	610	1,157	1,662	9,259
Cooling Degree Days (base 65°F)	0	0	0	5	48	128	196	177	40	1	0	0	595
Mean Precipitation (in.)	0.53	0.48	0.87	1.21	2.44	3.11	2.80	2.30	1.76	1.43	0.79	0.44	18.16
Days With ≥ 0.1" Precipitation	2	2	3	3	6	6	6	5	4	3	2	2	44
Days With ≥ 1.0" Precipitation	0	0	0	0	1	1	1	0	0	0	0	0	3
Mean Snowfall (in.)	na	na	na	0.6	0.0	0.0	0.0	0.0	trace	na	na	na
Days With ≥ 1.0" Snow Depth	na	na	na	0	0	0	0	0	0	na	na	na

Grand Forks Int'l Airport *Grand Forks County*   Elevation: 846 ft.   Latitude: 47° 57' N   Longitude: 97° 11' W

	JAN	FEB	MAR	APR	MAY	JUN	JUL	AUG	SEP	OCT	NOV	DEC	YEAR
Mean Maximum Temp. (°F)	14.3	21.3	33.2	52.7	69.0	77.2	81.2	80.3	69.0	54.8	33.8	19.6	50.5
Mean Temp. (°F)	4.6	12.1	24.9	41.9	56.3	65.1	69.0	67.4	56.8	43.9	25.7	11.0	39.9
Mean Minimum Temp. (°F)	-4.8	2.9	16.4	31.1	43.6	53.0	56.8	54.5	44.5	33.0	17.5	2.3	29.2
Extreme Maximum Temp. (°F)	52	54	69	100	98	100	104	104	103	92	75	56	104
Extreme Minimum Temp. (°F)	-35	-40	-26	-8	18	33	30	31	20	6	-31	-31	-40
Days Maximum Temp. ≥ 90°F	0	0	0	0	1	2	4	4	1	0	0	0	12
Days Maximum Temp. ≤ 32°F	27	21	13	2	0	0	0	0	0	1	14	25	103
Days Minimum Temp. ≤ 32°F	30	28	27	17	3	0	0	0	2	15	28	31	181
Days Minimum Temp. ≤ 0°F	19	13	6	0	0	0	0	0	0	0	3	15	56
Heating Degree Days (base 65°F)	1,871	1,491	1,238	687	292	82	25	50	270	646	1,174	1,672	9,498
Cooling Degree Days (base 65°F)	0	0	0	2	33	93	159	141	28	1	0	0	457
Mean Precipitation (in.)	0.70	0.53	0.90	1.23	2.31	2.87	3.06	2.68	2.02	1.61	0.90	0.59	19.40
Days With ≥ 0.1" Precipitation	2	2	3	3	5	6	6	6	4	4	3	2	46
Days With ≥ 1.0" Precipitation	0	0	0	0	0	1	1	0	0	0	0	0	2
Mean Snowfall (in.)	11.0	6.1	7.0	2.6	trace	0.0	trace	trace	trace	1.1	8.0	8.0	43.8
Days With ≥ 1.0" Snow Depth	29	24	18	3	0	0	0	0	0	1	11	23	108

Grand Forks Univ. NWS *Grand Forks County*   Elevation: 830 ft.   Latitude: 47° 55' N   Longitude: 97° 06' W

	JAN	FEB	MAR	APR	MAY	JUN	JUL	AUG	SEP	OCT	NOV	DEC	YEAR
Mean Maximum Temp. (°F)	14.6	22.3	34.4	54.5	70.3	78.2	82.0	81.3	70.2	55.9	34.4	20.4	51.5
Mean Temp. (°F)	5.8	13.4	26.0	43.2	57.5	66.3	70.1	68.8	58.2	45.4	26.7	12.3	41.1
Mean Minimum Temp. (°F)	-3.0	4.4	17.5	31.9	44.6	54.3	58.2	56.2	46.1	34.9	19.0	4.1	30.7
Extreme Maximum Temp. (°F)	54	54	73	98	97	97	105	104	102	93	73	56	105
Extreme Minimum Temp. (°F)	-34	-39	-24	-4	19	33	41	34	21	5	-24	-30	-39
Days Maximum Temp. ≥ 90°F	0	0	0	0	1	2	4	5	1	0	0	0	13
Days Maximum Temp. ≤ 32°F	27	20	12	1	0	0	0	0	0	1	13	25	99
Days Minimum Temp. ≤ 32°F	31	28	28	16	4	0	0	0	2	12	27	31	179
Days Minimum Temp. ≤ 0°F	19	12	4	0	0	0	0	0	0	0	2	13	50
Heating Degree Days (base 65°F)	1,833	1,454	1,204	650	264	64	19	37	235	602	1,142	1,632	9,136
Cooling Degree Days (base 65°F)	0	0	0	4	42	108	190	168	34	1	0	0	547
Mean Precipitation (in.)	0.78	0.57	0.95	1.22	2.14	3.06	2.95	2.89	2.00	1.60	0.83	0.59	19.58
Days With ≥ 0.1" Precipitation	2	2	3	3	5	6	6	5	4	4	2	2	44
Days With ≥ 1.0" Precipitation	0	0	0	0	0	1	1	1	0	0	0	0	3
Mean Snowfall (in.)	10.4	5.9	6.7	1.3	trace	0.0	0.0	0.0	trace	0.8	5.5	8.4	39.0
Days With ≥ 1.0" Snow Depth	28	23	15	2	0	0	0	0	0	0	9	21	98

Hankinson *Richland County*   Elevation: 1,069 ft.   Latitude: 46° 04' N   Longitude: 96° 54' W

	JAN	FEB	MAR	APR	MAY	JUN	JUL	AUG	SEP	OCT	NOV	DEC	YEAR
Mean Maximum Temp. (°F)	19.8	25.5	36.9	55.2	69.9	78.6	84.5	82.3	71.1	58.3	38.4	24.2	53.7
Mean Temp. (°F)	8.8	14.6	27.0	43.6	57.2	66.3	71.8	69.1	58.1	45.7	28.6	13.9	42.1
Mean Minimum Temp. (°F)	-2.2	3.7	17.1	32.0	44.5	54.0	58.9	55.8	45.0	33.1	18.7	3.5	30.4
Extreme Maximum Temp. (°F)	60	63	79	98	94	104	107	104	99	92	78	60	107
Extreme Minimum Temp. (°F)	-34	-31	-22	0	19	28	42	38	21	8	-17	-32	-34
Days Maximum Temp. ≥ 90°F	0	0	0	0	1	3	8	6	2	0	0	0	20
Days Maximum Temp. ≤ 32°F	24	18	10	1	0	0	0	0	0	0	na	22	na
Days Minimum Temp. ≤ 32°F	31	28	29	16	3	0	0	0	2	15	na	31	na
Days Minimum Temp. ≤ 0°F	18	12	4	0	0	0	0	0	0	0	2	13	49
Heating Degree Days (base 65°F)	1,742	1,419	1,171	637	266	65	13	35	239	593	1,086	1,581	8,847
Cooling Degree Days (base 65°F)	0	0	0	5	39	108	221	170	32	na	na	na	na
Mean Precipitation (in.)	0.74	0.65	1.25	1.81	2.73	3.51	3.10	2.65	2.23	1.61	1.08	0.44	21.80
Days With ≥ 0.1" Precipitation	2	3	3	5	6	7	6	5	4	4	3	2	50
Days With ≥ 1.0" Precipitation	0	0	0	0	0	1	1	1	1	0	0	0	4
Mean Snowfall (in.)	na	na	na	na	trace	0.0	0.0	0.0	0.0	na	na	na	na
Days With ≥ 1.0" Snow Depth	na	na	na	na	0	0	0	0	0	na	na	na	na

Hansboro 4 NNE *Towner County*   Elevation: 1,538 ft.   Latitude: 49° 00' N   Longitude: 99° 21' W

	JAN	FEB	MAR	APR	MAY	JUN	JUL	AUG	SEP	OCT	NOV	DEC	YEAR
Mean Maximum Temp. (°F)	14.3	21.3	32.4	51.9	67.8	75.9	79.8	79.6	68.8	54.6	33.0	19.6	49.9
Mean Temp. (°F)	3.9	11.3	22.7	40.2	54.3	62.8	66.7	65.4	55.1	42.4	23.4	10.1	38.2
Mean Minimum Temp. (°F)	-6.5	1.1	12.9	28.4	40.7	49.7	53.6	51.1	41.4	30.2	13.8	0.4	26.4
Extreme Maximum Temp. (°F)	48	60	64	96	98	99	102	101	100	93	72	54	102
Extreme Minimum Temp. (°F)	-41	-45	-31	-18	15	28	33	27	20	-10	-31	-39	-45
Days Maximum Temp. ≥ 90°F	0	0	0	0	1	2	3	4	1	0	0	0	11
Days Maximum Temp. ≤ 32°F	26	21	13	2	0	0	0	0	0	1	14	25	102
Days Minimum Temp. ≤ 32°F	31	28	30	21	6	0	0	0	4	18	29	31	198
Days Minimum Temp. ≤ 0°F	20	14	7	0	0	0	0	0	0	0	5	15	61
Heating Degree Days (base 65°F)	1,892	1,515	1,307	741	345	117	44	77	308	693	1,242	1,703	9,984
Cooling Degree Days (base 65°F)	0	0	0	2	20	59	100	101	16	1	0	0	299
Mean Precipitation (in.)	0.66	0.59	0.88	1.18	2.43	3.13	2.98	2.54	1.64	1.20	0.76	0.56	18.55
Days With ≥ 0.1" Precipitation	2	1	2	3	6	7	6	5	4	3	2	2	43
Days With ≥ 1.0" Precipitation	0	0	0	0	0	1	1	1	0	0	0	0	3
Mean Snowfall (in.)	7.3	6.1	7.6	2.4	0.2	0.0	0.0	0.0	0.2	2.6	6.6	6.9	39.9
Days With ≥ 1.0" Snow Depth	26	23	20	4	0	0	0	0	0	1	13	23	110

Hettinger *Adams County*   Elevation: 2,677 ft.   Latitude: 45° 59' N   Longitude: 102° 39' W

	JAN	FEB	MAR	APR	MAY	JUN	JUL	AUG	SEP	OCT	NOV	DEC	YEAR
Mean Maximum Temp. (°F)	24.6	31.3	40.5	54.7	66.8	76.6	83.7	83.5	72.0	58.3	39.4	28.8	55.0
Mean Temp. (°F)	14.0	20.9	29.5	42.3	54.0	63.3	69.3	68.4	57.1	44.7	28.6	17.9	42.5
Mean Minimum Temp. (°F)	3.4	10.5	18.5	29.9	41.0	50.6	54.9	53.2	42.2	30.9	17.7	6.9	30.0
Extreme Maximum Temp. (°F)	68	68	78	92	95	104	111	103	104	94	78	69	111
Extreme Minimum Temp. (°F)	-34	-39	-36	-8	19	28	36	31	16	-7	-24	-37	-39
Days Maximum Temp. ≥ 90°F	0	0	0	0	0	2	7	8	2	0	0	0	19
Days Maximum Temp. ≤ 32°F	19	14	9	2	0	0	0	0	0	1	9	18	72
Days Minimum Temp. ≤ 32°F	31	28	29	18	5	0	0	0	4	18	28	31	192
Days Minimum Temp. ≤ 0°F	13	7	3	0	0	0	0	0	0	0	3	9	35
Heating Degree Days (base 65°F)	1,577	1,239	1,095	675	349	106	32	45	264	625	1,087	1,456	8,550
Cooling Degree Days (base 65°F)	0	0	0	1	14	70	171	158	34	1	0	0	449
Mean Precipitation (in.)	0.29	0.30	0.60	1.60	2.61	3.01	2.14	1.47	1.40	1.38	0.53	0.32	15.65
Days With ≥ 0.1" Precipitation	1	1	2	4	6	6	5	3	3	3	2	1	37
Days With ≥ 1.0" Precipitation	0	0	0	0	1	1	0	0	0	0	0	0	2
Mean Snowfall (in.)	5.0	5.5	6.9	3.9	0.6	0.0	0.0	0.0	0.5	2.0	5.4	5.2	35.0
Days With ≥ 1.0" Snow Depth	24	17	13	4	0	0	0	0	0	1	9	19	87

Hillsboro 3 N *Traill County*   Elevation: 908 ft.   Latitude: 47° 26' N   Longitude: 97° 04' W

	JAN	FEB	MAR	APR	MAY	JUN	JUL	AUG	SEP	OCT	NOV	DEC	YEAR
Mean Maximum Temp. (°F)	15.3	22.8	34.4	53.8	69.9	78.4	82.7	81.8	70.6	56.2	35.0	21.1	51.8
Mean Temp. (°F)	5.9	13.2	25.5	42.7	57.0	66.1	70.2	68.7	57.9	45.0	26.6	12.6	41.0
Mean Minimum Temp. (°F)	-3.5	3.7	16.6	31.5	44.0	53.7	57.7	55.6	45.2	33.8	18.1	4.1	30.0
Extreme Maximum Temp. (°F)	48	55	75	99	97	99	106	106	102	94	78	55	106
Extreme Minimum Temp. (°F)	-35	-37	-23	-5	24	35	41	35	21	8	-26	-29	-37
Days Maximum Temp. ≥ 90°F	0	0	0	0	1	3	6	5	2	0	0	0	17
Days Maximum Temp. ≤ 32°F	27	20	12	1	0	0	0	0	0	1	13	24	98
Days Minimum Temp. ≤ 32°F	31	28	29	16	3	0	0	0	2	14	28	31	182
Days Minimum Temp. ≤ 0°F	19	12	5	0	0	0	0	0	0	0	3	13	52
Heating Degree Days (base 65°F)	1,832	1,458	1,218	667	273	66	18	33	240	615	1,148	1,620	9,188
Cooling Degree Days (base 65°F)	0	0	0	4	33	96	167	148	29	1	0	0	478
Mean Precipitation (in.)	0.49	0.50	0.96	1.56	2.37	3.34	3.20	2.68	2.05	1.84	0.77	0.45	20.21
Days With ≥ 0.1" Precipitation	2	2	3	4	6	7	6	5	5	3	2	1	46
Days With ≥ 1.0" Precipitation	0	0	0	0	0	1	1	1	1	0	0	0	4
Mean Snowfall (in.)	na	na	na	na	0.0	0.0	0.0	0.0	0.0	0.4	3.6	na	na
Days With ≥ 1.0" Snow Depth	na	na	12	1	0	0	0	0	0	0	5	na	na

Jamestown Municipal Airport *Stutsman County*   Elevation: 1,489 ft.   Latitude: 46° 55' N   Longitude: 98° 41' W

	JAN	FEB	MAR	APR	MAY	JUN	JUL	AUG	SEP	OCT	NOV	DEC	YEAR
Mean Maximum Temp. (°F)	17.5	24.8	36.2	54.1	68.9	77.5	83.1	82.1	70.3	56.3	35.7	22.7	52.4
Mean Temp. (°F)	8.2	15.7	27.4	42.8	56.6	65.6	70.7	69.1	57.9	45.1	27.2	14.1	41.7
Mean Minimum Temp. (°F)	-1.0	6.5	18.6	31.6	44.2	53.7	58.3	56.1	45.4	33.8	18.6	5.4	30.9
Extreme Maximum Temp. (°F)	54	63	76	97	97	100	108	106	105	94	77	54	108
Extreme Minimum Temp. (°F)	-32	-35	-23	-6	21	34	39	32	21	-1	-19	-37	-37
Days Maximum Temp. ≥ 90°F	0	0	0	0	1	3	7	7	2	0	0	0	20
Days Maximum Temp. ≤ 32°F	25	18	11	1	0	0	0	0	0	1	12	23	91
Days Minimum Temp. ≤ 32°F	30	28	28	17	3	0	0	0	2	13	28	31	180
Days Minimum Temp. ≤ 0°F	16	11	4	0	0	0	0	0	0	0	2	12	45
Heating Degree Days (base 65°F)	1,760	1,388	1,159	661	282	75	15	35	244	612	1,128	1,575	8,934
Cooling Degree Days (base 65°F)	0	0	0	4	31	102	202	173	35	1	0	0	548
Mean Precipitation (in.)	0.62	0.47	0.88	1.37	2.23	3.04	3.18	2.24	1.71	1.33	0.70	0.44	18.21
Days With ≥ 0.1" Precipitation	2	2	3	3	5	6	5	5	4	3	2	1	41
Days With ≥ 1.0" Precipitation	0	0	0	0	0	1	1	0	0	0	0	0	2
Mean Snowfall (in.)	9.8	5.7	7.4	3.4	0.3	trace	trace	trace	trace	0.7	6.8	6.4	40.5
Days With ≥ 1.0" Snow Depth	27	22	16	3	0	0	0	0	0	1	11	22	102

Jamestown State Hospital *Stutsman County*   Elevation: 1,466 ft.   Latitude: 46° 53' N   Longitude: 98° 41' W

	JAN	FEB	MAR	APR	MAY	JUN	JUL	AUG	SEP	OCT	NOV	DEC	YEAR
Mean Maximum Temp. (°F)	17.1	25.0	36.6	55.1	70.3	78.9	84.1	83.1	71.6	57.2	35.9	22.8	53.1
Mean Temp. (°F)	8.1	16.1	27.7	43.4	57.3	66.3	71.2	69.6	58.6	45.7	27.3	14.3	42.1
Mean Minimum Temp. (°F)	-0.9	7.2	18.9	31.7	44.2	53.6	58.2	56.0	45.5	34.1	18.8	5.7	31.1
Extreme Maximum Temp. (°F)	52	63	74	99	97	100	109	104	104	94	78	54	109
Extreme Minimum Temp. (°F)	-34	-39	-27	-7	21	32	40	36	20	0	-23	-32	-39
Days Maximum Temp. ≥ 90°F	0	0	0	0	1	4	8	7	2	0	0	0	22
Days Maximum Temp. ≤ 32°F	25	18	10	1	0	0	0	0	0	1	12	23	90
Days Minimum Temp. ≤ 32°F	31	28	28	16	3	0	0	0	2	13	28	31	180
Days Minimum Temp. ≤ 0°F	17	10	3	0	0	0	0	0	0	0	2	11	43
Heating Degree Days (base 65°F)	1,761	1,376	1,148	642	263	65	13	32	229	593	1,123	1,568	8,813
Cooling Degree Days (base 65°F)	0	0	0	3	30	107	205	181	38	1	0	0	565
Mean Precipitation (in.)	0.51	0.30	0.69	1.25	2.29	3.22	3.19	2.34	2.00	1.42	0.61	0.33	18.15
Days With ≥ 0.1" Precipitation	2	1	2	3	5	6	6	5	4	3	2	1	40
Days With ≥ 1.0" Precipitation	0	0	0	0	0	1	1	1	1	0	0	0	4
Mean Snowfall (in.)	9.8	5.6	7.8	1.6	0.3	0.0	0.0	0.0	0.0	0.3	7.4	4.8	37.6
Days With ≥ 1.0" Snow Depth	na	na	na	1	0	0	0	0	0	0	7	na	na

Keene 3 S *McKenzie County*   Elevation: 2,467 ft.   Latitude: 47° 50' N   Longitude: 102° 55' W

	JAN	FEB	MAR	APR	MAY	JUN	JUL	AUG	SEP	OCT	NOV	DEC	YEAR
Mean Maximum Temp. (°F)	20.8	28.9	40.6	57.0	69.6	77.9	83.7	83.6	72.1	58.6	37.5	25.6	54.7
Mean Temp. (°F)	10.4	18.6	29.4	43.4	55.3	64.1	69.1	68.5	57.6	45.2	27.6	15.5	42.1
Mean Minimum Temp. (°F)	0.0	8.2	18.1	29.8	41.1	50.2	54.4	53.4	43.0	31.8	17.6	5.4	29.4
Extreme Maximum Temp. (°F)	55	65	80	96	101	105	106	102	102	92	80	58	106
Extreme Minimum Temp. (°F)	-41	-34	-26	-14	12	29	37	30	13	-7	-24	-43	-43
Days Maximum Temp. ≥ 90°F	0	0	0	0	1	3	7	8	2	0	0	0	21
Days Maximum Temp. ≤ 32°F	21	15	8	1	0	0	0	0	0	1	11	19	76
Days Minimum Temp. ≤ 32°F	31	28	29	18	6	0	0	0	3	16	27	31	189
Days Minimum Temp. ≤ 0°F	15	9	4	0	0	0	0	0	0	0	3	11	42
Heating Degree Days (base 65°F)	1,689	1,308	1,098	643	314	99	31	46	252	608	1,117	1,530	8,735
Cooling Degree Days (base 65°F)	0	0	0	2	23	86	165	170	38	2	0	0	486
Mean Precipitation (in.)	0.39	0.37	0.61	1.26	2.35	3.17	2.53	1.54	1.68	1.07	0.55	0.39	15.91
Days With ≥ 0.1" Precipitation	1	1	2	3	6	7	5	4	4	3	2	1	39
Days With ≥ 1.0" Precipitation	0	0	0	0	0	1	0	0	0	0	0	0	1
Mean Snowfall (in.)	na	na	na	1.5	0.1	0.0	0.0	0.0	0.2	1.2	na	na	na
Days With ≥ 1.0" Snow Depth	18	na	10	2	0	0	0	0	0	0	1	6	na

Kenmare 1 WSW *Ward County*   Elevation: 1,807 ft.   Latitude: 48° 40' N   Longitude: 102° 06' W

	JAN	FEB	MAR	APR	MAY	JUN	JUL	AUG	SEP	OCT	NOV	DEC	YEAR
Mean Maximum Temp. (°F)	17.1	24.5	35.5	52.6	66.6	75.6	80.6	80.4	68.5	55.1	35.5	22.6	51.2
Mean Temp. (°F)	6.8	14.0	25.2	40.4	53.6	62.9	67.3	65.8	54.7	42.7	25.7	12.9	39.3
Mean Minimum Temp. (°F)	-3.5	3.9	14.9	28.1	40.7	50.2	53.8	51.2	40.8	30.1	15.8	3.1	27.4
Extreme Maximum Temp. (°F)	51	63	73	91	100	103	105	104	101	93	76	56	105
Extreme Minimum Temp. (°F)	-39	-40	-33	-12	11	32	38	27	19	-2	-27	-40	-40
Days Maximum Temp. ≥ 90°F	0	0	0	0	1	2	4	5	1	0	0	0	13
Days Maximum Temp. ≤ 32°F	24	18	11	2	0	0	0	0	0	1	12	21	89
Days Minimum Temp. ≤ 32°F	31	28	30	21	6	0	0	0	4	18	28	30	196
Days Minimum Temp. ≤ 0°F	18	12	5	0	0	0	0	0	0	0	4	13	52
Heating Degree Days (base 65°F)	1,801	1,433	1,225	731	360	119	44	76	321	685	1,174	1,614	9,583
Cooling Degree Days (base 65°F)	0	0	0	1	16	66	117	116	21	1	0	0	338
Mean Precipitation (in.)	0.83	0.65	0.92	1.32	2.02	2.69	2.73	1.71	1.95	1.15	0.62	0.56	17.15
Days With ≥ 0.1" Precipitation	3	2	3	3	5	6	6	4	4	3	2	2	43
Days With ≥ 1.0" Precipitation	0	0	0	0	0	0	0	0	1	0	0	0	1
Mean Snowfall (in.)	10.1	6.3	7.2	4.1	0.6	trace	0.0	0.0	0.2	2.4	5.2	5.9	42.0
Days With ≥ 1.0" Snow Depth	na	na	na	na	0	0	0	0	0	1	na	na	na

La Moure *Lamoure County*   Elevation: 1,358 ft.   Latitude: 46° 22' N   Longitude: 98° 17' W

	JAN	FEB	MAR	APR	MAY	JUN	JUL	AUG	SEP	OCT	NOV	DEC	YEAR
Mean Maximum Temp. (°F)	18.2	25.5	37.6	54.7	69.2	77.8	83.4	82.2	71.3	57.9	37.3	24.3	53.3
Mean Temp. (°F)	7.6	14.7	27.3	42.5	55.9	65.1	70.0	67.8	57.0	44.4	27.0	13.9	41.1
Mean Minimum Temp. (°F)	-3.6	3.6	16.9	30.2	42.3	52.4	56.6	53.5	42.6	30.8	16.7	3.5	28.8
Extreme Maximum Temp. (°F)	60	60	80	91	95	101	108	104	101	94	76	64	108
Extreme Minimum Temp. (°F)	-39	-39	-22	-10	20	30	38	25	18	2	-24	-33	-39
Days Maximum Temp. ≥ 90°F	0	0	0	0	0	3	7	6	1	0	0	0	17
Days Maximum Temp. ≤ 32°F	24	17	9	1	0	0	0	0	0	0	11	22	84
Days Minimum Temp. ≤ 32°F	31	28	29	18	4	0	0	0	4	18	29	31	192
Days Minimum Temp. ≤ 0°F	18	11	4	0	0	0	0	0	0	0	3	13	49
Heating Degree Days (base 65°F)	1,787	1,417	1,162	671	300	85	21	49	264	636	1,146	1,578	9,116
Cooling Degree Days (base 65°F)	0	0	0	3	25	94	181	142	28	1	0	0	474
Mean Precipitation (in.)	0.76	0.60	1.36	1.91	2.68	3.65	3.34	2.21	2.00	1.69	0.88	0.43	21.51
Days With ≥ 0.1" Precipitation	2	2	3	4	5	7	6	5	4	3	3	2	46
Days With ≥ 1.0" Precipitation	0	0	0	0	1	1	1	0	0	0	0	0	3
Mean Snowfall (in.)	*10.5*	*6.3*	7.9	3.1	trace	0.0	0.0	0.0	trace	*0.6*	8.2	5.4	*42.0*
Days With ≥ 1.0" Snow Depth	*27*	*21*	*14*	3	0	0	0	0	0	0	*10*	18	*93*

Langdon Exp. Farm *Cavalier County*   Elevation: 1,614 ft.   Latitude: 48° 46' N   Longitude: 98° 21' W

	JAN	FEB	MAR	APR	MAY	JUN	JUL	AUG	SEP	OCT	NOV	DEC	YEAR
Mean Maximum Temp. (°F)	10.6	18.0	29.7	49.1	65.6	73.7	77.4	77.1	66.3	51.8	30.9	16.4	47.2
Mean Temp. (°F)	1.1	8.3	20.4	38.3	52.9	61.9	65.7	64.4	53.8	40.7	22.2	7.5	36.4
Mean Minimum Temp. (°F)	-8.4	-1.6	11.1	27.5	40.1	50.1	53.9	51.6	41.3	29.5	13.5	-1.5	25.6
Extreme Maximum Temp. (°F)	45	49	66	97	98	96	102	100	103	90	74	47	103
Extreme Minimum Temp. (°F)	-39	-41	-33	-15	17	31	36	28	19	-3	-28	-37	-41
Days Maximum Temp. ≥ 90°F	0	0	0	0	0	1	1	2	1	0	0	0	5
Days Maximum Temp. ≤ 32°F	29	23	16	3	0	0	0	0	0	2	16	28	117
Days Minimum Temp. ≤ 32°F	31	28	31	22	7	0	0	0	5	20	29	31	204
Days Minimum Temp. ≤ 0°F	22	16	8	1	0	0	0	0	0	0	6	17	70
Heating Degree Days (base 65°F)	1,981	1,599	1,378	796	384	139	61	90	345	748	1,278	1,781	10,580
Cooling Degree Days (base 65°F)	0	0	0	1	17	52	85	79	14	0	0	0	248
Mean Precipitation (in.)	0.43	0.37	0.61	1.07	2.41	3.29	3.22	2.62	1.75	1.36	0.59	0.39	18.11
Days With ≥ 0.1" Precipitation	1	1	2	3	5	7	7	5	4	3	2	1	41
Days With ≥ 1.0" Precipitation	0	0	0	0	0	1	1	1	0	0	0	0	3
Mean Snowfall (in.)	6.9	5.4	6.2	3.6	0.4	0.0	0.0	0.0	trace	1.9	7.2	5.9	37.5
Days With ≥ 1.0" Snow Depth	30	27	25	7	0	0	0	0	0	1	16	27	133

Leeds *Benson County*   Elevation: 1,528 ft.   Latitude: 48° 17' N   Longitude: 99° 26' W

	JAN	FEB	MAR	APR	MAY	JUN	JUL	AUG	SEP	OCT	NOV	DEC	YEAR
Mean Maximum Temp. (°F)	14.1	21.3	32.5	51.4	67.3	75.7	80.3	80.2	68.1	54.5	33.9	20.1	50.0
Mean Temp. (°F)	4.0	11.1	22.7	39.9	54.2	63.4	67.5	66.0	54.9	42.4	24.7	10.5	38.4
Mean Minimum Temp. (°F)	-6.1	0.9	12.8	28.2	41.0	51.1	54.7	51.7	41.6	30.2	15.3	0.8	26.9
Extreme Maximum Temp. (°F)	52	60	66	97	97	105	105	102	103	95	74	52	105
Extreme Minimum Temp. (°F)	-39	-42	-36	-12	17	32	38	32	17	-11	-31	-39	-42
Days Maximum Temp. ≥ 90°F	0	0	0	0	1	2	3	5	1	0	0	0	12
Days Maximum Temp. ≤ 32°F	27	20	13	2	0	0	0	0	0	1	14	25	102
Days Minimum Temp. ≤ 32°F	31	28	30	21	6	0	0	0	4	19	29	31	199
Days Minimum Temp. ≤ 0°F	20	14	7	0	0	0	0	0	0	0	4	15	60
Heating Degree Days (base 65°F)	1,891	1,520	1,306	748	347	111	38	70	316	696	1,205	1,687	9,935
Cooling Degree Days (base 65°F)	0	0	0	1	18	68	123	110	18	1	0	0	339
Mean Precipitation (in.)	0.56	0.50	0.85	1.35	2.24	2.95	3.10	2.04	1.65	1.50	0.74	0.47	17.95
Days With ≥ 0.1" Precipitation	2	2	2	3	5	6	6	5	4	3	2	2	42
Days With ≥ 1.0" Precipitation	0	0	0	0	0	1	1	0	0	0	0	0	2
Mean Snowfall (in.)	8.0	5.3	*6.3*	2.7	0.4	0.0	0.0	0.0	0.2	1.8	6.5	5.9	*37.1*
Days With ≥ 1.0" Snow Depth	na	na	na	*1*	0	0	0	0	0	*0*	na	na	na

Lisbon *Ransom County*   Elevation: 1,102 ft.   Latitude: 46° 27' N   Longitude: 97° 41' W

	JAN	FEB	MAR	APR	MAY	JUN	JUL	AUG	SEP	OCT	NOV	DEC	YEAR
Mean Maximum Temp. (°F)	18.1	25.3	37.1	56.1	70.1	78.7	83.8	82.5	71.9	58.3	37.1	24.5	53.6
Mean Temp. (°F)	7.9	14.9	27.4	43.7	56.7	65.5	70.6	68.8	58.2	45.5	27.6	14.8	41.8
Mean Minimum Temp. (°F)	-2.4	4.5	17.6	31.2	43.5	52.4	57.3	55.1	44.3	32.6	18.3	5.0	30.0
Extreme Maximum Temp. (°F)	60	58	77	99	95	101	105	105	104	92	75	61	105
Extreme Minimum Temp. (°F)	-41	-39	-28	0	18	33	34	32	20	4	-23	-36	-41
Days Maximum Temp. ≥ 90°F	0	0	0	0	1	3	7	6	2	0	0	0	19
Days Maximum Temp. ≤ 32°F	24	18	10	1	0	0	0	0	0	0	10	22	85
Days Minimum Temp. ≤ 32°F	30	27	28	17	4	0	0	0	3	15	28	31	183
Days Minimum Temp. ≤ 0°F	17	11	4	0	0	0	0	0	0	0	2	12	46
Heating Degree Days (base 65°F)	1,768	1,411	1,160	634	279	76	17	37	240	599	1,114	1,552	8,887
Cooling Degree Days (base 65°F)	0	0	0	2	29	100	193	165	37	1	0	0	527
Mean Precipitation (in.)	0.62	0.46	1.07	1.44	2.68	3.36	2.86	2.28	2.19	1.84	0.88	0.44	20.12
Days With ≥ 0.1" Precipitation	2	2	3	4	6	6	5	4	4	4	2	2	44
Days With ≥ 1.0" Precipitation	0	0	0	0	0	1	1	0	0	0	0	0	2
Mean Snowfall (in.)	na	4.8	na	1.7	0.1	0.0	0.0	0.0	trace	0.4	8.3	5.9	na
Days With ≥ 1.0" Snow Depth	na	na	na	1	0	0	0	0	0	0	8	na	na

Mandan Experiment Station *Morton County*   Elevation: 1,748 ft.   Latitude: 46° 49' N   Longitude: 100° 55' W

	JAN	FEB	MAR	APR	MAY	JUN	JUL	AUG	SEP	OCT	NOV	DEC	YEAR
Mean Maximum Temp. (°F)	19.9	26.9	37.9	54.1	67.8	76.7	82.9	82.0	70.5	57.2	37.8	25.3	53.2
Mean Temp. (°F)	9.5	17.0	27.9	42.6	55.5	64.8	70.2	68.6	57.3	44.6	28.0	15.3	41.8
Mean Minimum Temp. (°F)	-0.9	6.9	17.9	31.0	43.2	52.7	57.5	55.3	44.1	31.9	18.2	5.3	30.3
Extreme Maximum Temp. (°F)	63	64	78	94	95	105	107	104	103	95	80	66	107
Extreme Minimum Temp. (°F)	-36	-38	-24	-8	19	32	36	35	14	-5	-26	-38	-38
Days Maximum Temp. ≥ 90°F	0	0	0	0	1	2	7	7	2	0	0	0	19
Days Maximum Temp. ≤ 32°F	23	17	10	1	0	0	0	0	0	1	11	20	83
Days Minimum Temp. ≤ 32°F	31	28	29	17	4	0	0	0	3	16	28	31	187
Days Minimum Temp. ≤ 0°F	16	10	4	0	0	0	0	0	0	0	2	11	43
Heating Degree Days (base 65°F)	1,719	1,352	1,143	669	308	89	22	45	260	628	1,103	1,537	8,875
Cooling Degree Days (base 65°F)	0	0	0	2	24	92	191	166	35	2	0	0	512
Mean Precipitation (in.)	0.37	0.32	0.56	1.62	2.42	2.82	2.87	1.98	1.58	1.38	0.60	0.34	16.86
Days With ≥ 0.1" Precipitation	1	1	2	4	5	6	5	4	4	3	2	1	38
Days With ≥ 1.0" Precipitation	0	0	0	0	0	1	1	0	0	0	0	0	2
Mean Snowfall (in.)	7.8	5.4	6.8	3.0	0.2	0.0	0.0	0.0	0.1	1.1	7.5	5.4	37.3
Days With ≥ 1.0" Snow Depth	na	na	9	2	0	0	0	0	0	1	4	na	na

Max *McLean County*   Elevation: 2,109 ft.   Latitude: 47° 49' N   Longitude: 101° 18' W

	JAN	FEB	MAR	APR	MAY	JUN	JUL	AUG	SEP	OCT	NOV	DEC	YEAR
Mean Maximum Temp. (°F)	16.2	23.7	34.8	52.0	66.5	75.6	81.4	80.7	68.4	54.7	34.5	21.8	50.9
Mean Temp. (°F)	6.5	13.8	25.0	40.5	54.1	63.4	68.4	66.7	55.2	42.4	25.1	12.3	39.5
Mean Minimum Temp. (°F)	-3.3	3.9	15.1	29.0	41.6	51.0	55.1	52.7	42.0	30.1	15.7	2.7	28.0
Extreme Maximum Temp. (°F)	50	60	73	94	98	101	105	103	105	91	74	59	105
Extreme Minimum Temp. (°F)	-37	-36	-31	-8	18	31	38	33	16	-4	-22	-38	-38
Days Maximum Temp. ≥ 90°F	0	0	0	0	1	2	5	5	1	0	0	0	14
Days Maximum Temp. ≤ 32°F	26	19	12	2	0	0	0	0	0	1	13	23	96
Days Minimum Temp. ≤ 32°F	31	28	30	20	5	0	0	0	3	18	29	31	195
Days Minimum Temp. ≤ 0°F	18	12	5	0	0	0	0	0	0	0	4	13	52
Heating Degree Days (base 65°F)	1,812	1,441	1,236	730	349	111	32	60	311	694	1,190	1,630	9,596
Cooling Degree Days (base 65°F)	0	0	0	2	19	75	144	130	21	1	0	0	392
Mean Precipitation (in.)	0.55	0.41	0.74	1.56	2.16	3.15	2.84	1.70	1.72	1.37	0.59	0.44	17.23
Days With ≥ 0.1" Precipitation	2	1	3	3	5	7	6	4	4	3	2	2	42
Days With ≥ 1.0" Precipitation	0	0	0	0	0	1	1	0	0	0	0	0	2
Mean Snowfall (in.)	8.6	5.9	7.7	4.0	0.4	trace	0.0	0.0	0.3	3.7	8.1	6.2	44.9
Days With ≥ 1.0" Snow Depth	29	24	20	5	0	0	0	0	0	2	12	26	118

McClusky *Sheridan County*   Elevation: 1,922 ft.   Latitude: 47° 29' N   Longitude: 100° 27' W

	JAN	FEB	MAR	APR	MAY	JUN	JUL	AUG	SEP	OCT	NOV	DEC	YEAR
Mean Maximum Temp. (°F)	17.7	25.1	36.9	54.4	69.6	78.6	83.4	83.0	71.6	57.2	35.5	23.7	53.1
Mean Temp. (°F)	8.6	15.9	27.4	42.5	56.7	66.0	70.5	69.3	58.6	45.3	27.0	14.9	41.9
Mean Minimum Temp. (°F)	-0.6	6.7	17.9	30.6	43.7	53.3	57.6	55.6	45.6	33.4	18.4	6.2	30.7
Extreme Maximum Temp. (°F)	52	61	73	95	97	104	107	105	106	91	75	57	107
Extreme Minimum Temp. (°F)	-34	-33	-23	-10	19	34	40	35	18	-3	-19	-31	-34
Days Maximum Temp. ≥ 90°F	0	0	0	0	1	3	7	8	2	0	0	0	21
Days Maximum Temp. ≤ 32°F	25	18	11	2	0	0	0	0	0	1	12	22	91
Days Minimum Temp. ≤ 32°F	31	28	28	17	3	0	0	0	2	13	28	31	181
Days Minimum Temp. ≤ 0°F	16	10	4	0	0	0	0	0	0	0	3	11	44
Heating Degree Days (base 65°F)	1,746	1,381	1,160	670	278	69	15	35	225	604	1,134	1,547	8,864
Cooling Degree Days (base 65°F)	0	0	0	3	27	105	188	178	38	1	0	0	540
Mean Precipitation (in.)	0.59	0.46	0.71	1.62	2.11	3.31	2.78	1.86	1.67	1.36	0.69	0.50	17.66
Days With ≥ 0.1" Precipitation	2	1	2	4	5	7	6	4	4	3	2	2	42
Days With ≥ 1.0" Precipitation	0	0	0	0	0	1	0	0	0	0	0	0	1
Mean Snowfall (in.)	9.2	6.3	6.6	4.2	0.2	0.0	0.0	0.0	trace	2.6	7.6	6.5	43.2
Days With ≥ 1.0" Snow Depth	27	22	15	3	0	0	0	0	0	1	12	22	102

McHenry 3 W *Foster County*   Elevation: 1,555 ft.   Latitude: 47° 35' N   Longitude: 98° 39' W

	JAN	FEB	MAR	APR	MAY	JUN	JUL	AUG	SEP	OCT	NOV	DEC	YEAR
Mean Maximum Temp. (°F)	13.9	21.3	32.8	51.3	67.4	75.7	80.7	79.9	68.6	54.9	33.8	19.9	50.0
Mean Temp. (°F)	3.7	11.0	23.4	40.1	54.6	63.6	68.2	66.6	55.7	42.7	24.4	10.4	38.7
Mean Minimum Temp. (°F)	-6.6	0.7	13.8	28.8	41.8	51.4	55.6	53.2	42.7	30.5	15.0	0.9	27.3
Extreme Maximum Temp. (°F)	53	56	72	98	97	96	103	107	104	92	76	50	107
Extreme Minimum Temp. (°F)	-38	-41	-32	-13	19	33	38	28	19	-5	-29	-39	-41
Days Maximum Temp. ≥ 90°F	0	0	0	0	0	2	4	4	1	0	0	0	11
Days Maximum Temp. ≤ 32°F	27	21	13	2	0	0	0	0	0	1	14	25	103
Days Minimum Temp. ≤ 32°F	31	28	30	20	5	0	0	0	3	18	29	31	195
Days Minimum Temp. ≤ 0°F	20	14	6	0	0	0	0	0	0	0	4	15	59
Heating Degree Days (base 65°F)	1,901	1,522	1,284	744	333	107	31	61	298	684	1,211	1,689	9,865
Cooling Degree Days (base 65°F)	0	0	0	2	19	71	135	120	23	1	0	0	371
Mean Precipitation (in.)	0.61	0.43	0.85	1.37	2.27	3.49	3.08	2.66	1.98	1.40	0.97	0.56	19.67
Days With ≥ 0.1" Precipitation	2	1	3	4	5	7	6	6	4	3	3	2	46
Days With ≥ 1.0" Precipitation	0	0	0	0	0	1	1	0	0	0	0	0	2
Mean Snowfall (in.)	9.5	6.1	7.6	3.6	0.5	0.0	0.0	0.0	0.2	2.2	10.3	7.4	47.4
Days With ≥ 1.0" Snow Depth	29	26	20	4	0	0	0	0	0	1	14	25	119

McLeod 3 E *Richland County*   Elevation: 1,072 ft.   Latitude: 46° 24' N   Longitude: 97° 14' W

	JAN	FEB	MAR	APR	MAY	JUN	JUL	AUG	SEP	OCT	NOV	DEC	YEAR
Mean Maximum Temp. (°F)	18.2	25.7	37.7	57.2	71.8	79.9	84.3	83.1	72.8	59.0	37.6	23.9	54.3
Mean Temp. (°F)	7.8	15.3	27.8	44.5	58.2	67.1	71.6	69.8	59.6	46.8	28.2	14.4	42.6
Mean Minimum Temp. (°F)	-2.6	5.0	17.8	31.7	44.7	54.3	58.8	56.5	46.3	34.4	18.9	4.7	30.9
Extreme Maximum Temp. (°F)	55	59	76	99	95	99	106	106	102	91	78	57	106
Extreme Minimum Temp. (°F)	-40	-41	-26	-7	20	32	41	35	19	6	-28	-36	-41
Days Maximum Temp. ≥ 90°F	0	0	0	0	1	3	7	6	2	0	0	0	19
Days Maximum Temp. ≤ 32°F	25	18	9	1	0	0	0	0	0	0	10	22	85
Days Minimum Temp. ≤ 32°F	31	28	28	16	4	0	0	0	2	13	28	31	181
Days Minimum Temp. ≤ 0°F	18	11	4	0	0	0	0	0	0	0	2	12	47
Heating Degree Days (base 65°F)	1,771	1,398	1,148	613	239	54	11	27	205	562	1,097	1,565	8,690
Cooling Degree Days (base 65°F)	0	0	0	4	39	124	218	186	46	3	0	0	620
Mean Precipitation (in.)	0.65	0.46	0.98	1.27	2.62	3.44	3.41	2.30	2.06	1.78	0.87	0.40	20.24
Days With ≥ 0.1" Precipitation	2	1	3	3	5	6	6	4	4	3	2	1	40
Days With ≥ 1.0" Precipitation	0	0	0	0	1	1	1	0	0	0	0	0	3
Mean Snowfall (in.)	*6.1*	*4.1*	*3.6*	1.4	trace	0.0	0.0	0.0	trace	0.5	4.9	*4.5*	*25.1*
Days With ≥ 1.0" Snow Depth	28	22	15	2	0	0	0	0	0	1	10	19	97

McVille *Nelson County*   Elevation: 1,466 ft.   Latitude: 47° 46' N   Longitude: 98° 11' W

	JAN	FEB	MAR	APR	MAY	JUN	JUL	AUG	SEP	OCT	NOV	DEC	YEAR
Mean Maximum Temp. (°F)	14.4	21.5	34.1	53.4	69.8	77.8	82.9	81.3	69.8	55.5	33.3	18.9	51.1
Mean Temp. (°F)	4.9	11.8	24.8	41.7	56.5	65.3	*69.6*	*67.5*	56.8	43.7	25.0	10.2	*39.8*
Mean Minimum Temp. (°F)	-4.7	1.9	15.5	30.0	43.1	52.7	*56.5*	*53.9*	43.8	31.9	16.5	1.4	*28.5*
Extreme Maximum Temp. (°F)	53	55	66	99	96	99	104	104	104	88	75	49	104
Extreme Minimum Temp. (°F)	-41	-41	-25	-11	18	33	*39*	31	18	-4	-24	-37	*-41*
Days Maximum Temp. ≥ 90°F	0	0	0	0	1	3	*6*	6	2	0	0	0	*18*
Days Maximum Temp. ≤ 32°F	27	21	13	2	0	0	0	0	0	1	*15*	26	*105*
Days Minimum Temp. ≤ 32°F	31	28	29	19	5	0	*0*	0	4	16	28	31	*191*
Days Minimum Temp. ≤ 0°F	19	13	5	0	0	0	*0*	0	0	0	3	*15*	*55*
Heating Degree Days (base 65°F)	1,862	1,500	1,239	695	287	78	*24*	*55*	271	653	1,194	1,695	*9,553*
Cooling Degree Days (base 65°F)	0	0	0	3	*32*	87	*171*	*147*	27	*0*	*0*	*0*	*467*
Mean Precipitation (in.)	*0.52*	*0.34*	*0.88*	1.14	2.30	3.32	3.24	2.53	2.12	1.31	*0.83*	*0.46*	*18.99*
Days With ≥ 0.1" Precipitation	na	na	na	3	5	6	6	5	4	*3*	na	na	na
Days With ≥ 1.0" Precipitation	na	na	*0*	0	0	1	1	1	0	*0*	*0*	na	na
Mean Snowfall (in.)	na	na	na	na	*0.2*	0.0	0.0	0.0	*trace*	*1.3*	na	na	na
Days With ≥ 1.0" Snow Depth	na	na	na	*1*	*0*	0	0	0	*0*	*0*	na	na	na

Medora *Billings County*   Elevation: 2,290 ft.   Latitude: 46° 55' N   Longitude: 103° 31' W

	JAN	FEB	MAR	APR	MAY	JUN	JUL	AUG	SEP	OCT	NOV	DEC	YEAR
Mean Maximum Temp. (°F)	28.0	35.8	45.3	59.1	71.0	80.5	87.3	87.2	75.3	61.4	42.6	31.9	58.8
Mean Temp. (°F)	15.9	23.6	32.5	44.8	56.3	65.6	71.4	70.4	58.7	46.4	30.7	19.9	44.7
Mean Minimum Temp. (°F)	3.7	11.3	19.7	30.5	41.6	50.7	55.5	53.6	42.1	31.3	18.8	7.8	30.5
Extreme Maximum Temp. (°F)	66	70	80	95	101	107	110	105	106	94	83	66	110
Extreme Minimum Temp. (°F)	-40	-40	-34	-13	18	29	34	30	17	-13	-31	-44	-44
Days Maximum Temp. ≥ 90°F	0	0	0	0	1	5	12	13	4	0	0	0	35
Days Maximum Temp. ≤ 32°F	17	10	6	1	0	0	0	0	0	0	7	13	54
Days Minimum Temp. ≤ 32°F	30	27	28	17	4	0	0	0	4	17	27	30	184
Days Minimum Temp. ≤ 0°F	13	7	2	0	0	0	0	0	0	0	2	9	33
Heating Degree Days (base 65°F)	1,519	1,162	1,000	602	286	76	16	28	225	575	1,022	1,392	7,903
Cooling Degree Days (base 65°F)	0	0	0	2	26	108	227	216	42	1	0	0	622
Mean Precipitation (in.)	0.36	0.35	0.65	1.44	2.38	3.01	2.14	1.37	1.48	1.11	0.50	0.37	15.16
Days With ≥ 0.1" Precipitation	1	1	2	4	5	6	4	3	3	3	2	1	35
Days With ≥ 1.0" Precipitation	0	0	0	0	0	0	1	0	0	0	0	0	1
Mean Snowfall (in.)	5.6	5.2	5.4	3.6	0.5	0.0	0.0	0.0	0.3	1.4	4.5	5.4	31.9
Days With ≥ 1.0" Snow Depth	22	15	9	2	0	0	0	0	0	1	8	17	74

Minot Experiment Station *Ward County*   Elevation: 1,768 ft.   Latitude: 48° 11' N   Longitude: 101° 18' W

	JAN	FEB	MAR	APR	MAY	JUN	JUL	AUG	SEP	OCT	NOV	DEC	YEAR
Mean Maximum Temp. (°F)	16.6	23.7	34.7	52.3	67.0	75.9	80.7	80.3	68.1	54.6	34.7	22.2	50.9
Mean Temp. (°F)	7.1	14.5	25.3	40.8	54.6	63.9	68.2	66.9	55.6	43.1	25.9	13.0	39.9
Mean Minimum Temp. (°F)	-2.4	5.2	15.9	29.3	42.1	51.9	55.7	53.4	43.1	31.5	17.0	3.7	28.9
Extreme Maximum Temp. (°F)	52	62	71	94	98	100	103	101	102	91	77	59	103
Extreme Minimum Temp. (°F)	-37	-37	-26	-12	19	32	42	31	19	-3	-22	-39	-39
Days Maximum Temp. ≥ 90°F	0	0	0	0	1	2	4	5	1	0	0	0	13
Days Maximum Temp. ≤ 32°F	25	19	12	2	0	0	0	0	0	1	13	22	94
Days Minimum Temp. ≤ 32°F	31	28	30	19	5	0	0	0	3	17	28	31	192
Days Minimum Temp. ≤ 0°F	18	11	5	0	0	0	0	0	0	0	3	13	50
Heating Degree Days (base 65°F)	1,793	1,423	1,224	721	336	100	32	60	297	673	1,167	1,609	9,435
Cooling Degree Days (base 65°F)	0	0	0	2	20	77	135	132	22	1	0	0	389
Mean Precipitation (in.)	0.78	0.60	1.02	1.71	2.29	2.93	2.68	1.96	1.80	1.39	0.95	0.64	18.75
Days With ≥ 0.1" Precipitation	3	2	3	4	5	7	5	5	4	3	3	2	46
Days With ≥ 1.0" Precipitation	0	0	0	0	1	1	1	0	0	0	0	0	3
Mean Snowfall (in.)	10.0	7.1	9.1	4.5	0.3	0.0	0.0	0.0	0.3	3.0	8.6	8.0	50.9
Days With ≥ 1.0" Snow Depth	29	22	17	5	0	0	0	0	0	2	12	24	111

Minot FAA Airport *Ward County*   Elevation: 1,712 ft.   Latitude: 48° 16' N   Longitude: 101° 17' W

	JAN	FEB	MAR	APR	MAY	JUN	JUL	AUG	SEP	OCT	NOV	DEC	YEAR
Mean Maximum Temp. (°F)	17.3	24.4	35.7	53.2	67.1	75.8	81.3	80.6	68.2	55.0	34.9	23.4	51.4
Mean Temp. (°F)	8.8	16.5	27.2	42.5	55.5	64.6	69.6	68.1	56.8	44.6	27.2	15.4	41.4
Mean Minimum Temp. (°F)	0.5	8.4	18.8	31.8	43.9	53.3	57.8	55.6	45.4	34.2	19.4	7.4	31.4
Extreme Maximum Temp. (°F)	56	65	71	94	99	102	105	103	106	92	79	58	106
Extreme Minimum Temp. (°F)	-34	-34	-20	-5	22	34	42	34	22	6	-17	-36	-36
Days Maximum Temp. ≥ 90°F	0	0	0	0	1	2	4	5	1	0	0	0	13
Days Maximum Temp. ≤ 32°F	24	19	12	2	0	0	0	0	0	1	13	21	92
Days Minimum Temp. ≤ 32°F	30	27	28	15	3	0	0	0	2	12	27	30	174
Days Minimum Temp. ≤ 0°F	15	9	3	0	0	0	0	0	0	0	2	10	39
Heating Degree Days (base 65°F)	1,740	1,367	1,164	669	309	88	19	48	268	626	1,128	1,532	8,958
Cooling Degree Days (base 65°F)	0	0	0	2	24	83	168	159	29	2	0	0	467
Mean Precipitation (in.)	0.69	0.55	1.05	1.73	2.32	3.07	2.83	1.92	1.79	1.33	0.84	0.63	18.75
Days With ≥ 0.1" Precipitation	2	2	3	4	5	7	5	4	4	3	2	2	43
Days With ≥ 1.0" Precipitation	0	0	0	0	0	1	1	0	0	0	0	0	2
Mean Snowfall (in.)	9.3	6.0	8.4	6.1	0.7	trace	trace	trace	0.2	3.0	7.6	7.3	48.6
Days With ≥ 1.0" Snow Depth	27	21	16	4	0	0	0	0	0	1	11	23	103

Mott *Hettinger County*   Elevation: 2,522 ft.   Latitude: 46° 23' N   Longitude: 102° 20' W

	JAN	FEB	MAR	APR	MAY	JUN	JUL	AUG	SEP	OCT	NOV	DEC	YEAR
Mean Maximum Temp. (°F)	24.0	31.4	40.8	55.1	67.7	77.0	83.6	83.5	72.0	58.7	39.8	28.9	55.2
Mean Temp. (°F)	12.6	20.2	29.4	42.3	54.6	64.0	69.6	68.5	57.0	44.6	28.5	17.4	42.4
Mean Minimum Temp. (°F)	1.2	8.9	18.0	29.4	41.4	50.8	55.4	53.4	41.9	30.5	17.2	5.8	29.5
Extreme Maximum Temp. (°F)	67	71	79	95	96	103	108	104	102	95	84	67	108
Extreme Minimum Temp. (°F)	-38	-35	-33	-13	19	29	37	33	17	-8	-25	-39	-39
Days Maximum Temp. ≥ 90°F	0	0	0	0	0	3	8	9	2	0	0	0	22
Days Maximum Temp. ≤ 32°F	19	13	8	2	0	0	0	0	0	1	9	17	69
Days Minimum Temp. ≤ 32°F	31	28	29	19	5	0	0	0	4	18	28	31	193
Days Minimum Temp. ≤ 0°F	14	8	3	0	0	0	0	0	0	0	3	10	38
Heating Degree Days (base 65°F)	1,619	1,261	1,096	677	330	97	28	44	266	627	1,089	1,472	8,606
Cooling Degree Days (base 65°F)	0	0	0	1	16	77	184	169	34	1	0	0	482
Mean Precipitation (in.)	0.40	0.49	0.80	1.92	2.67	3.13	2.09	1.71	1.29	1.18	0.61	0.39	16.68
Days With ≥ 0.1" Precipitation	2	1	2	4	6	7	5	4	3	3	2	1	40
Days With ≥ 1.0" Precipitation	0	0	0	0	0	1	0	0	0	0	0	0	1
Mean Snowfall (in.)	6.3	5.1	6.0	3.5	0.6	trace	0.0	0.0	0.3	2.1	6.3	5.5	35.7
Days With ≥ 1.0" Snow Depth	18	12	8	3	0	0	0	0	0	1	7	16	65

Napoleon *Logan County*   Elevation: 1,978 ft.   Latitude: 46° 30' N   Longitude: 99° 46' W

	JAN	FEB	MAR	APR	MAY	JUN	JUL	AUG	SEP	OCT	NOV	DEC	YEAR
Mean Maximum Temp. (°F)	17.7	25.0	36.1	53.0	67.2	76.4	82.8	81.6	70.2	56.5	36.8	23.3	52.2
Mean Temp. (°F)	7.8	14.9	26.2	41.5	54.9	64.4	69.8	68.2	56.8	44.0	27.3	13.7	40.8
Mean Minimum Temp. (°F)	-2.2	4.7	16.2	29.9	42.5	52.4	57.0	54.6	43.5	31.5	17.7	4.1	29.3
Extreme Maximum Temp. (°F)	57	57	76	94	94	102	108	104	102	90	75	59	108
Extreme Minimum Temp. (°F)	-40	-40	-25	-11	18	30	33	33	13	-6	-23	-39	-40
Days Maximum Temp. ≥ 90°F	0	0	0	0	0	2	6	6	1	0	0	0	15
Days Maximum Temp. ≤ 32°F	25	18	11	2	0	0	0	0	0	1	12	22	91
Days Minimum Temp. ≤ 32°F	31	28	29	19	4	0	0	0	3	17	28	31	190
Days Minimum Temp. ≤ 0°F	17	11	5	0	0	0	0	0	0	0	2	12	47
Heating Degree Days (base 65°F)	1,771	1,411	1,196	701	326	94	24	48	271	644	1,126	1,587	9,199
Cooling Degree Days (base 65°F)	0	0	0	2	21	82	176	153	32	1	0	0	467
Mean Precipitation (in.)	0.59	0.48	0.95	1.69	2.47	3.14	2.78	2.14	1.80	1.55	0.80	0.42	18.81
Days With ≥ 0.1" Precipitation	2	2	3	4	6	6	5	4	3	4	3	1	43
Days With ≥ 1.0" Precipitation	0	0	0	0	0	1	0	0	0	0	0	0	1
Mean Snowfall (in.)	9.6	7.0	8.1	3.7	0.5	0.0	0.0	0.0	0.2	1.3	8.6	7.1	46.1
Days With ≥ 1.0" Snow Depth	27	25	18	3	0	0	0	0	0	1	12	23	109

New England *Hettinger County*   Elevation: 2,637 ft.   Latitude: 46° 33' N   Longitude: 102° 52' W

	JAN	FEB	MAR	APR	MAY	JUN	JUL	AUG	SEP	OCT	NOV	DEC	YEAR
Mean Maximum Temp. (°F)	24.5	31.4	41.5	55.2	68.2	77.3	83.8	83.2	71.2	58.2	39.8	29.9	55.3
Mean Temp. (°F)	13.9	20.9	30.2	42.6	55.0	64.2	69.8	68.8	57.4	45.1	29.3	19.2	43.0
Mean Minimum Temp. (°F)	3.3	10.3	18.8	29.9	41.7	51.0	55.6	54.4	43.5	32.0	18.7	8.4	30.6
Extreme Maximum Temp. (°F)	64	71	78	94	97	103	107	103	104	91	80	65	107
Extreme Minimum Temp. (°F)	-37	-35	-31	-11	21	30	38	34	18	-10	-25	-36	-37
Days Maximum Temp. ≥ 90°F	0	0	0	0	1	3	8	8	2	0	0	0	22
Days Maximum Temp. ≤ 32°F	19	14	8	1	0	0	0	0	0	1	9	16	68
Days Minimum Temp. ≤ 32°F	31	28	29	19	4	0	0	0	3	16	28	31	189
Days Minimum Temp. ≤ 0°F	13	8	3	0	0	0	0	0	0	0	2	9	35
Heating Degree Days (base 65°F)	1,579	1,240	1,073	667	318	93	23	34	253	609	1,066	1,415	8,370
Cooling Degree Days (base 65°F)	0	0	0	1	16	78	177	166	31	1	0	0	470
Mean Precipitation (in.)	0.41	0.38	0.70	1.69	2.56	3.44	1.83	1.80	1.48	1.32	0.50	0.37	16.48
Days With ≥ 0.1" Precipitation	2	1	2	4	6	7	5	4	3	3	2	2	41
Days With ≥ 1.0" Precipitation	0	0	0	0	1	1	0	1	0	0	0	0	3
Mean Snowfall (in.)	*8.6*	6.3	7.5	5.6	0.4	0.0	0.0	0.0	trace	2.2	5.9	7.0	*43.5*
Days With ≥ 1.0" Snow Depth	na	na	na	3	0	0	0	0	0	1	na	na	na

New Salem 5 NW *Morton County*   Elevation: 2,148 ft.   Latitude: 46° 54' N   Longitude: 101° 29' W

	JAN	FEB	MAR	APR	MAY	JUN	JUL	AUG	SEP	OCT	NOV	DEC	YEAR
Mean Maximum Temp. (°F)	20.5	28.0	38.9	55.2	68.8	77.5	83.8	83.1	71.9	57.7	37.3	25.3	54.0
Mean Temp. (°F)	10.4	17.9	28.2	42.5	55.4	64.2	69.7	68.6	57.8	44.8	27.6	15.4	41.9
Mean Minimum Temp. (°F)	0.3	7.7	17.5	29.7	41.9	50.9	55.6	54.0	43.6	31.8	17.8	5.5	29.7
Extreme Maximum Temp. (°F)	62	68	77	92	95	104	105	104	106	93	82	65	106
Extreme Minimum Temp. (°F)	-40	-35	-26	-14	18	28	32	33	10	-5	-26	-38	-40
Days Maximum Temp. ≥ 90°F	0	0	0	0	1	3	8	8	2	0	0	0	22
Days Maximum Temp. ≤ 32°F	22	16	10	2	0	0	0	0	0	1	11	20	82
Days Minimum Temp. ≤ 32°F	31	28	29	19	4	0	0	0	3	16	28	31	189
Days Minimum Temp. ≤ 0°F	15	9	4	0	0	0	0	0	0	0	3	11	42
Heating Degree Days (base 65°F)	1,690	1,325	1,135	671	311	94	23	43	246	621	1,115	1,534	8,808
Cooling Degree Days (base 65°F)	0	0	0	3	21	82	182	168	35	1	0	0	492
Mean Precipitation (in.)	0.48	0.45	0.81	1.90	2.49	3.05	2.75	2.05	1.53	1.36	0.73	0.49	18.09
Days With ≥ 0.1" Precipitation	2	2	2	4	6	7	6	4	4	3	2	2	44
Days With ≥ 1.0" Precipitation	0	0	0	0	0	1	1	0	0	0	0	0	2
Mean Snowfall (in.)	6.8	5.9	7.9	5.0	0.4	0.0	0.0	0.0	0.3	2.7	8.3	6.3	43.6
Days With ≥ 1.0" Snow Depth	19	16	12	4	0	0	0	0	0	1	10	15	77

Oakes 2 S *Dickey County*   Elevation: 1,309 ft.   Latitude: 46° 08' N   Longitude: 98° 05' W

	JAN	FEB	MAR	APR	MAY	JUN	JUL	AUG	SEP	OCT	NOV	DEC	YEAR
Mean Maximum Temp. (°F)	17.6	25.2	37.3	55.9	70.4	79.3	84.4	83.6	72.6	58.1	37.2	24.2	53.8
Mean Temp. (°F)	6.7	14.4	27.2	43.3	56.8	66.1	71.0	69.3	58.5	44.8	27.1	13.8	41.6
Mean Minimum Temp. (°F)	-4.3	3.4	17.0	30.6	43.2	52.9	57.4	55.0	44.2	31.6	16.9	3.3	29.3
Extreme Maximum Temp. (°F)	61	60	79	101	98	107	109	107	103	92	75	60	109
Extreme Minimum Temp. (°F)	-39	-45	-28	3	21	34	41	35	21	1	-24	-35	-45
Days Maximum Temp. ≥ 90°F	0	0	0	0	1	4	8	7	2	0	0	0	22
Days Maximum Temp. ≤ 32°F	25	18	10	1	0	0	0	0	0	0	11	22	87
Days Minimum Temp. ≤ 32°F	31	28	29	18	3	0	0	0	2	17	28	31	187
Days Minimum Temp. ≤ 0°F	18	12	4	0	0	0	0	0	0	0	3	13	50
Heating Degree Days (base 65°F)	1,805	1,427	1,167	646	276	68	15	34	234	620	1,130	1,584	9,006
Cooling Degree Days (base 65°F)	0	0	0	3	30	106	203	169	37	1	0	0	549
Mean Precipitation (in.)	*0.50*	*0.45*	1.07	1.76	2.50	3.20	2.68	2.00	2.28	1.85	*0.81*	*0.39*	*19.49*
Days With ≥ 0.1" Precipitation	na	na	*2*	3	5	6	5	4	4	3	*2*	na	na
Days With ≥ 1.0" Precipitation	*0*	*0*	0	0	1	1	1	0	1	1	*0*	*0*	*5*
Mean Snowfall (in.)	*11.1*	na	na	*3.3*	trace	0.0	0.0	0.0	0.0	0.6	*9.5*	na	na
Days With ≥ 1.0" Snow Depth	na	na	na	*0*	0	0	0	0	0	0	na	na	na

Pembina *Pembina County*   Elevation: 787 ft.   Latitude: 48° 58' N   Longitude: 97° 14' W

	JAN	FEB	MAR	APR	MAY	JUN	JUL	AUG	SEP	OCT	NOV	DEC	YEAR
Mean Maximum Temp. (°F)	11.2	18.7	31.1	51.0	67.5	75.9	79.7	79.2	67.8	53.4	32.4	17.7	48.8
Mean Temp. (°F)	0.9	8.0	21.4	39.3	54.1	63.2	66.9	65.0	54.3	41.7	23.4	8.1	37.2
Mean Minimum Temp. (°F)	-9.4	-2.7	11.6	27.5	40.8	50.5	54.0	50.9	40.8	29.8	14.3	-1.5	25.6
Extreme Maximum Temp. (°F)	48	51	66	96	98	100	101	104	101	93	78	53	104
Extreme Minimum Temp. (°F)	-42	-40	-33	-12	12	27	34	29	18	0	-39	-36	-42
Days Maximum Temp. ≥ 90°F	0	0	0	0	1	2	3	3	1	0	0	0	10
Days Maximum Temp. ≤ 32°F	28	23	15	2	0	0	0	0	0	1	15	26	110
Days Minimum Temp. ≤ 32°F	31	28	30	21	6	0	0	0	5	19	29	31	200
Days Minimum Temp. ≤ 0°F	23	17	8	1	0	0	0	0	0	0	5	16	70
Heating Degree Days (base 65°F)	1,991	1,606	1,345	765	356	117	45	83	330	718	1,243	1,762	10,361
Cooling Degree Days (base 65°F)	0	0	0	1	26	69	106	93	13	0	0	0	308
Mean Precipitation (in.)	0.45	0.39	0.74	1.09	2.18	3.37	2.99	2.47	2.17	1.45	0.75	0.45	18.50
Days With ≥ 0.1" Precipitation	2	2	2	3	5	7	6	5	5	4	2	2	45
Days With ≥ 1.0" Precipitation	0	0	0	0	1	1	1	1	1	0	0	0	4
Mean Snowfall (in.)	*6.5*	4.3	*3.8*	*1.9*	trace	0.0	0.0	0.0	trace	1.1	*7.2*	*5.9*	*30.7*
Days With ≥ 1.0" Snow Depth	*31*	27	na	*4*	0	0	0	0	0	1	*13*	24	na

Petersburg 2 N *Nelson County*   Elevation: 1,528 ft.   Latitude: 48° 02' N   Longitude: 98° 00' W

	JAN	FEB	MAR	APR	MAY	JUN	JUL	AUG	SEP	OCT	NOV	DEC	YEAR
Mean Maximum Temp. (°F)	12.6	19.8	31.0	50.1	66.1	74.9	79.1	78.6	67.7	53.5	32.3	18.4	48.7
Mean Temp. (°F)	2.4	9.6	21.6	39.2	53.6	62.9	66.9	65.3	54.6	41.6	23.4	8.9	37.5
Mean Minimum Temp. (°F)	-7.8	-0.7	12.3	28.3	41.1	50.9	54.5	52.0	41.5	29.7	14.5	-0.7	26.3
Extreme Maximum Temp. (°F)	50	54	67	98	95	95	100	101	102	91	75	50	102
Extreme Minimum Temp. (°F)	-42	-44	-30	-12	16	32	30	25	18	-1	-25	-39	-44
Days Maximum Temp. ≥ 90°F	0	0	0	0	0	1	2	3	1	0	0	0	7
Days Maximum Temp. ≤ 32°F	28	23	15	3	0	0	0	0	0	1	16	26	112
Days Minimum Temp. ≤ 32°F	31	28	31	21	6	0	0	0	4	19	29	31	200
Days Minimum Temp. ≤ 0°F	21	15	7	0	0	0	0	0	0	0	4	16	63
Heating Degree Days (base 65°F)	1,940	1,564	1,338	768	364	118	44	79	323	718	1,242	1,736	10,234
Cooling Degree Days (base 65°F)	0	0	0	2	20	65	109	103	18	1	0	0	318
Mean Precipitation (in.)	0.69	0.42	0.95	1.24	2.33	3.48	3.29	2.66	2.05	1.51	0.87	0.52	20.01
Days With ≥ 0.1" Precipitation	3	1	2	3	6	7	6	6	4	4	3	2	47
Days With ≥ 1.0" Precipitation	0	0	0	0	0	1	1	0	0	0	0	0	2
Mean Snowfall (in.)	9.4	na	7.9	2.2	0.4	0.0	0.0	0.0	0.2	2.2	7.9	6.8	na
Days With ≥ 1.0" Snow Depth	na	na	na	na	0	0	0	0	0	0	na	na	na

Powers Lake 1 N *Burke County*   Elevation: 2,204 ft.   Latitude: 48° 34' N   Longitude: 102° 39' W

	JAN	FEB	MAR	APR	MAY	JUN	JUL	AUG	SEP	OCT	NOV	DEC	YEAR
Mean Maximum Temp. (°F)	15.7	23.2	34.1	52.0	66.2	74.5	79.8	79.5	67.4	54.4	34.4	21.6	50.2
Mean Temp. (°F)	5.0	12.9	23.8	39.7	52.8	61.8	66.7	65.4	53.8	41.2	24.2	11.0	38.2
Mean Minimum Temp. (°F)	-5.8	2.4	13.5	27.4	39.5	49.2	53.3	51.2	40.2	27.9	13.9	0.4	26.1
Extreme Maximum Temp. (°F)	48	60	75	94	102	103	103	103	101	91	76	51	103
Extreme Minimum Temp. (°F)	-44	-43	-30	-24	14	29	36	30	15	-9	-30	-48	-48
Days Maximum Temp. ≥ 90°F	0	0	0	0	1	2	4	4	1	0	0	0	12
Days Maximum Temp. ≤ 32°F	25	19	13	2	0	0	0	0	0	2	13	23	97
Days Minimum Temp. ≤ 32°F	31	28	30	22	7	0	0	0	5	22	29	31	205
Days Minimum Temp. ≤ 0°F	19	12	7	0	0	0	0	0	0	0	4	14	56
Heating Degree Days (base 65°F)	1,859	1,468	1,270	752	384	142	52	82	346	733	1,218	1,667	9,973
Cooling Degree Days (base 65°F)	0	0	0	1	15	59	108	109	17	1	0	0	310
Mean Precipitation (in.)	0.39	0.37	0.72	1.32	2.10	2.71	2.96	1.90	1.77	1.06	0.50	0.32	16.12
Days With ≥ 0.1" Precipitation	2	1	3	3	5	6	6	4	4	3	2	1	40
Days With ≥ 1.0" Precipitation	0	0	0	0	0	1	1	0	0	0	0	0	2
Mean Snowfall (in.)	6.3	5.1	7.8	5.3	0.6	trace	0.0	0.0	0.4	3.0	5.7	5.0	39.2
Days With ≥ 1.0" Snow Depth	27	21	16	5	1	0	0	0	0	2	11	21	104

Pretty Rock *Grant County*   Elevation: 2,477 ft.   Latitude: 46° 10' N   Longitude: 101° 51' W

	JAN	FEB	MAR	APR	MAY	JUN	JUL	AUG	SEP	OCT	NOV	DEC	YEAR
Mean Maximum Temp. (°F)	23.4	30.6	40.5	55.7	68.9	77.9	84.9	84.2	72.8	58.6	39.1	28.3	55.4
Mean Temp. (°F)	13.1	20.3	29.7	42.9	55.4	64.6	70.4	69.3	58.2	45.5	28.8	17.9	43.0
Mean Minimum Temp. (°F)	2.7	10.0	18.9	30.1	41.9	51.4	55.8	54.4	43.5	32.4	18.6	7.6	30.6
Extreme Maximum Temp. (°F)	67	71	78	93	97	103	108	104	106	94	80	67	108
Extreme Minimum Temp. (°F)	-34	-39	-32	-6	16	28	35	32	13	-8	-23	-36	-39
Days Maximum Temp. ≥ 90°F	0	0	0	0	1	3	9	9	2	0	0	0	24
Days Maximum Temp. ≤ 32°F	20	14	9	1	0	0	0	0	0	1	10	18	73
Days Minimum Temp. ≤ 32°F	31	27	28	18	5	0	0	0	3	15	28	31	186
Days Minimum Temp. ≤ 0°F	13	8	3	0	0	0	0	0	0	0	2	9	35
Heating Degree Days (base 65°F)	1,606	1,257	1,088	658	307	87	21	35	238	598	1,078	1,454	8,427
Cooling Degree Days (base 65°F)	0	0	0	2	17	85	196	178	38	1	0	0	517
Mean Precipitation (in.)	0.33	0.37	0.82	1.91	2.76	3.04	2.29	1.77	1.43	1.33	0.53	0.32	16.90
Days With ≥ 0.1" Precipitation	1	1	2	5	5	7	4	4	3	3	2	1	38
Days With ≥ 1.0" Precipitation	0	0	0	0	1	1	0	0	0	0	0	0	2
Mean Snowfall (in.)	7.1	7.2	9.9	7.1	0.6	0.0	0.0	0.0	0.5	3.1	8.2	6.0	49.7
Days With ≥ 1.0" Snow Depth	24	18	15	5	0	0	0	0	0	1	10	17	90

Richardton Abbey *Stark County*   Elevation: 2,467 ft.   Latitude: 46° 53' N   Longitude: 102° 19' W

	JAN	FEB	MAR	APR	MAY	JUN	JUL	AUG	SEP	OCT	NOV	DEC	YEAR
Mean Maximum Temp. (°F)	22.2	29.4	39.9	54.8	68.0	76.8	82.8	81.9	70.2	56.6	37.7	26.7	53.9
Mean Temp. (°F)	13.2	20.3	29.9	43.2	55.7	64.7	70.2	69.2	58.1	45.5	29.0	17.8	43.1
Mean Minimum Temp. (°F)	4.1	11.1	19.8	31.6	43.4	52.6	57.4	56.3	45.8	34.4	20.2	8.9	32.1
Extreme Maximum Temp. (°F)	61	65	74	93	95	103	104	103	102	89	78	64	104
Extreme Minimum Temp. (°F)	-33	-33	-23	-8	19	33	38	36	18	-4	-20	-33	-33
Days Maximum Temp. ≥ 90°F	0	0	0	0	0	2	7	6	1	0	0	0	16
Days Maximum Temp. ≤ 32°F	21	15	9	1	0	0	0	0	0	1	10	18	75
Days Minimum Temp. ≤ 32°F	30	27	28	16	3	0	0	0	2	12	26	30	174
Days Minimum Temp. ≤ 0°F	12	8	3	0	0	0	0	0	0	0	2	9	34
Heating Degree Days (base 65°F)	1,603	1,257	1,083	648	300	86	21	34	239	598	1,074	1,458	8,401
Cooling Degree Days (base 65°F)	0	0	0	2	21	89	193	174	37	1	0	0	517
Mean Precipitation (in.)	0.47	0.44	0.87	1.85	2.62	3.33	2.27	1.87	1.62	1.38	0.70	0.45	17.87
Days With ≥ 0.1" Precipitation	1	1	3	4	5	7	5	4	4	3	2	1	40
Days With ≥ 1.0" Precipitation	0	0	0	0	1	1	1	0	0	0	0	0	3
Mean Snowfall (in.)	6.3	5.4	8.5	6.5	0.5	0.0	0.0	0.0	0.7	3.0	7.2	5.9	44.0
Days With ≥ 1.0" Snow Depth	24	18	14	6	0	0	0	0	0	0	2	12	19	95

Rolla 3 NW *Rolette County* Elevation: 1,948 ft. Latitude: 48° 54' N Longitude: 99° 40' W

	JAN	FEB	MAR	APR	MAY	JUN	JUL	AUG	SEP	OCT	NOV	DEC	YEAR
Mean Maximum Temp. (°F)	13.5	20.2	30.1	47.5	63.7	71.7	75.8	75.3	63.8	50.8	31.1	18.3	46.8
Mean Temp. (°F)	4.3	10.9	21.5	37.2	52.2	61.2	65.7	64.3	53.3	41.0	23.2	9.7	37.0
Mean Minimum Temp. (°F)	-5.0	1.5	12.9	26.9	40.6	50.6	55.5	53.4	42.8	31.1	15.2	1.2	27.2
Extreme Maximum Temp. (°F)	53	57	64	94	94	97	100	100	98	89	71	51	100
Extreme Minimum Temp. (°F)	-37	-43	-29	-20	18	32	31	34	24	-1	-34	-37	-43
Days Maximum Temp. ≥ 90°F	0	0	0	0	0	1	1	1	0	0	0	0	3
Days Maximum Temp. ≤ 32°F	27	22	17	4	0	0	0	0	0	2	17	26	115
Days Minimum Temp. ≤ 32°F	31	28	30	21	6	0	0	0	3	17	28	31	195
Days Minimum Temp. ≤ 0°F	19	13	6	1	0	0	0	0	0	0	4	15	58
Heating Degree Days (base 65°F)	1,885	1,526	1,342	828	403	154	59	93	356	739	1,249	1,710	10,344
Cooling Degree Days (base 65°F)	0	0	0	1	13	46	82	79	11	1	0	0	233
Mean Precipitation (in.)	0.51	0.50	0.74	1.20	2.31	3.40	2.89	2.49	1.97	1.24	0.70	0.53	18.48
Days With ≥ 0.1" Precipitation	2	2	2	3	5	7	6	5	5	3	2	2	44
Days With ≥ 1.0" Precipitation	0	0	0	0	0	1	1	0	0	0	0	0	2
Mean Snowfall (in.)	na	na	na	na	0.7	0.0	0.0	0.0	trace	1.2	na	na	na
Days With ≥ 1.0" Snow Depth	na	na	na	5	0	0	0	0	0	0	0	na	na

Rugby *Pierce County* Elevation: 1,548 ft. Latitude: 48° 21' N Longitude: 100° 00' W

	JAN	FEB	MAR	APR	MAY	JUN	JUL	AUG	SEP	OCT	NOV	DEC	YEAR
Mean Maximum Temp. (°F)	14.9	22.9	34.5	54.0	69.1	77.8	81.9	81.4	69.3	55.8	34.1	20.6	51.4
Mean Temp. (°F)	5.1	13.3	25.1	42.3	56.2	65.3	69.2	68.0	56.6	43.9	25.3	11.1	40.1
Mean Minimum Temp. (°F)	-4.8	3.6	15.6	30.4	43.3	52.6	56.4	54.5	43.9	32.0	16.5	1.5	28.8
Extreme Maximum Temp. (°F)	52	62	70	96	100	104	107	105	99	91	75	55	107
Extreme Minimum Temp. (°F)	-45	-47	-33	-8	18	31	38	30	20	-6	-27	-40	-47
Days Maximum Temp. ≥ 90°F	0	0	0	0	1	3	4	5	1	0	0	0	14
Days Maximum Temp. ≤ 32°F	26	20	12	2	0	0	0	0	0	1	13	24	98
Days Minimum Temp. ≤ 32°F	31	28	29	18	4	0	0	0	3	16	28	31	188
Days Minimum Temp. ≤ 0°F	19	12	5	0	0	0	0	0	0	0	3	14	53
Heating Degree Days (base 65°F)	1,856	1,457	1,232	678	291	83	24	45	270	646	1,184	1,668	9,434
Cooling Degree Days (base 65°F)	0	0	0	3	25	90	146	141	22	1	0	0	428
Mean Precipitation (in.)	0.50	0.45	0.80	1.33	2.30	2.96	3.23	2.24	1.95	1.31	0.63	0.51	18.21
Days With ≥ 0.1" Precipitation	2	1	2	3	6	7	6	5	4	3	2	2	43
Days With ≥ 1.0" Precipitation	0	0	0	0	0	1	1	1	1	0	0	0	4
Mean Snowfall (in.)	na	na	na	3.7	0.3	0.0	0.0	0.0	trace	1.5	na	na	na
Days With ≥ 1.0" Snow Depth	na	na	na	1	0	0	0	0	0	0	0	na	na

Sharon *Steele County* Elevation: 1,522 ft. Latitude: 47° 36' N Longitude: 97° 54' W

	JAN	FEB	MAR	APR	MAY	JUN	JUL	AUG	SEP	OCT	NOV	DEC	YEAR
Mean Maximum Temp. (°F)	13.4	21.3	33.0	52.6	67.9	75.3	79.4	79.2	68.6	54.8	33.2	19.0	49.8
Mean Temp. (°F)	4.5	12.2	24.3	41.4	55.5	63.9	68.0	66.9	56.5	43.9	24.9	10.7	39.4
Mean Minimum Temp. (°F)	-4.4	3.1	15.6	30.2	43.2	52.4	56.5	54.5	44.3	33.0	16.6	2.3	28.9
Extreme Maximum Temp. (°F)	52	53	73	96	94	94	100	101	100	88	74	49	101
Extreme Minimum Temp. (°F)	-38	-39	-25	-10	20	33	36	28	20	1	-26	-36	-39
Days Maximum Temp. ≥ 90°F	0	0	0	0	0	1	2	3	1	0	0	0	7
Days Maximum Temp. ≤ 32°F	28	21	13	2	0	0	0	0	0	1	15	26	106
Days Minimum Temp. ≤ 32°F	31	28	29	19	4	0	0	0	2	15	28	31	187
Days Minimum Temp. ≤ 0°F	19	13	5	0	0	0	0	0	0	0	3	14	54
Heating Degree Days (base 65°F)	1,874	1,488	1,256	702	308	96	31	55	275	647	1,197	1,679	9,608
Cooling Degree Days (base 65°F)	0	0	0	2	23	70	130	120	23	0	0	0	368
Mean Precipitation (in.)	0.69	0.51	1.16	1.40	2.72	3.54	3.42	2.61	2.14	1.63	0.93	0.53	21.28
Days With ≥ 0.1" Precipitation	2	2	3	3	6	7	7	6	4	4	3	2	49
Days With ≥ 1.0" Precipitation	0	0	0	0	0	1	1	1	0	0	0	0	3
Mean Snowfall (in.)	8.9	5.9	7.8	2.8	0.2	0.0	0.0	0.0	trace	1.4	8.1	6.8	41.9
Days With ≥ 1.0" Snow Depth	30	25	19	4	0	0	0	0	0	1	14	24	117

Stanley 3 NNW *Mountrail County* Elevation: 2,276 ft. Latitude: 48° 21' N Longitude: 102° 25' W

	JAN	FEB	MAR	APR	MAY	JUN	JUL	AUG	SEP	OCT	NOV	DEC	YEAR
Mean Maximum Temp. (°F)	15.2	23.4	34.4	51.5	65.7	74.5	79.9	80.1	67.2	54.0	33.8	20.8	50.1
Mean Temp. (°F)	5.5	13.6	24.0	39.1	52.4	61.6	66.3	65.1	53.3	41.1	24.2	11.2	38.1
Mean Minimum Temp. (°F)	-4.3	3.8	13.6	26.7	39.0	48.7	52.5	50.0	39.3	28.2	14.5	1.5	26.1
Extreme Maximum Temp. (°F)	48	60	71	94	98	102	105	104	100	92	74	52	105
Extreme Minimum Temp. (°F)	-41	-42	-24	-15	16	31	39	31	16	-3	-25	-47	-47
Days Maximum Temp. ≥ 90°F	0	0	0	0	0	2	4	5	1	0	0	0	12
Days Maximum Temp. ≤ 32°F	26	19	13	2	0	0	0	0	0	1	14	23	98
Days Minimum Temp. ≤ 32°F	31	28	30	23	7	0	0	0	5	21	29	31	205
Days Minimum Temp. ≤ 0°F	18	12	6	0	0	0	0	0	0	0	4	14	54
Heating Degree Days (base 65°F)	1,845	1,446	1,265	769	395	143	54	86	358	734	1,219	1,665	9,979
Cooling Degree Days (base 65°F)	0	0	0	0	11	54	100	102	15	1	0	0	283
Mean Precipitation (in.)	0.56	0.45	0.89	1.66	2.64	3.89	3.05	2.12	2.21	1.24	0.74	0.55	20.00
Days With ≥ 0.1" Precipitation	2	1	3	4	6	8	7	5	6	3	3	2	50
Days With ≥ 1.0" Precipitation	0	0	0	0	0	1	1	0	0	0	0	0	2
Mean Snowfall (in.)	8.2	5.7	9.4	6.2	1.0	trace	0.0	0.0	0.4	3.2	7.5	7.1	48.7
Days With ≥ 1.0" Snow Depth	29	24	20	6	0	0	0	0	0	2	13	27	121

Tioga 1 E *Williams County*   Elevation: 2,244 ft.   Latitude: 48° 24' N   Longitude: 102° 55' W

	JAN	FEB	MAR	APR	MAY	JUN	JUL	AUG	SEP	OCT	NOV	DEC	YEAR
Mean Maximum Temp. (°F)	15.7	23.5	35.1	52.4	66.0	75.2	80.9	80.8	68.0	54.6	34.1	21.5	50.7
Mean Temp. (°F)	5.4	13.2	24.5	40.0	53.0	62.4	67.1	65.9	53.9	41.3	24.1	11.3	38.5
Mean Minimum Temp. (°F)	-5.0	3.0	13.9	27.5	39.9	49.5	53.2	51.0	39.8	28.0	14.1	1.0	26.3
Extreme Maximum Temp. (°F)	51	63	75	93	101	102	108	104	101	92	76	55	108
Extreme Minimum Temp. (°F)	-41	-40	-30	-17	16	28	34	27	12	-6	-27	-50	-50
Days Maximum Temp. ≥ 90°F	0	0	0	0	0	2	5	6	1	0	0	0	14
Days Maximum Temp. ≤ 32°F	25	19	13	2	0	0	0	0	0	2	14	22	97
Days Minimum Temp. ≤ 32°F	31	28	30	21	7	0	0	0	6	21	29	31	204
Days Minimum Temp. ≤ 0°F	19	12	6	0	0	0	0	0	0	0	5	14	56
Heating Degree Days (base 65°F)	1,847	1,457	1,249	744	379	131	50	80	344	728	1,222	1,661	9,892
Cooling Degree Days (base 65°F)	0	0	0	1	15	63	121	124	20	1	0	0	345
Mean Precipitation (in.)	0.47	0.36	0.58	1.22	2.00	2.52	2.25	1.73	1.63	0.90	0.53	0.38	14.57
Days With ≥ 0.1" Precipitation	2	1	2	3	6	6	5	4	4	2	2	1	38
Days With ≥ 1.0" Precipitation	0	0	0	0	0	0	1	0	0	0	0	0	1
Mean Snowfall (in.)	6.6	4.8	6.0	4.4	1.1	trace	0.0	0.0	0.5	2.3	6.0	5.3	37.0
Days With ≥ 1.0" Snow Depth	29	23	17	4	0	0	0	0	0	2	13	24	112

Towner 2 NE *McHenry County*   Elevation: 1,479 ft.   Latitude: 48° 22' N   Longitude: 100° 23' W

	JAN	FEB	MAR	APR	MAY	JUN	JUL	AUG	SEP	OCT	NOV	DEC	YEAR
Mean Maximum Temp. (°F)	14.7	22.6	33.8	52.8	67.9	77.3	82.0	81.8	69.3	55.8	34.3	20.8	51.1
Mean Temp. (°F)	3.9	11.7	23.4	40.4	54.4	64.0	68.1	66.9	55.2	42.4	24.5	10.4	38.8
Mean Minimum Temp. (°F)	-6.9	0.7	12.7	27.8	40.8	50.6	54.0	51.4	40.8	29.1	14.6	-0.0	26.3
Extreme Maximum Temp. (°F)	51	63	69	95	98	101	105	103	99	93	76	56	105
Extreme Minimum Temp. (°F)	-49	-46	-34	-16	18	30	35	22	12	-15	-34	-44	-49
Days Maximum Temp. ≥ 90°F	0	0	0	0	1	3	4	6	1	0	0	0	15
Days Maximum Temp. ≤ 32°F	26	20	13	2	0	0	0	0	0	1	13	24	99
Days Minimum Temp. ≤ 32°F	31	28	30	22	6	0	0	0	5	20	29	31	202
Days Minimum Temp. ≤ 0°F	19	13	7	0	0	0	0	0	0	0	4	15	58
Heating Degree Days (base 65°F)	1,895	1,503	1,283	733	340	102	34	62	308	694	1,211	1,690	9,855
Cooling Degree Days (base 65°F)	0	0	0	1	17	72	130	126	18	0	0	0	364
Mean Precipitation (in.)	0.57	0.52	0.71	1.32	1.91	2.60	2.75	2.05	1.94	1.32	0.61	0.53	16.83
Days With ≥ 0.1" Precipitation	2	1	2	3	4	6	5	4	4	3	2	2	38
Days With ≥ 1.0" Precipitation	0	0	0	0	0	0	1	0	0	0	0	0	1
Mean Snowfall (in.)	8.1	5.9	5.3	*3.4*	0.3	0.0	0.0	0.0	0.1	1.8	6.8	6.5	*38.2*
Days With ≥ 1.0" Snow Depth	29	25	19	4	0	0	0	0	0	1	10	22	110

Trotters 3 SSE *Golden Valley County*   Elevation: 2,417 ft.   Latitude: 47° 17' N   Longitude: 103° 54' W

	JAN	FEB	MAR	APR	MAY	JUN	JUL	AUG	SEP	OCT	NOV	DEC	YEAR
Mean Maximum Temp. (°F)	23.0	30.3	41.0	55.8	67.6	76.9	83.7	83.4	70.8	57.2	38.2	27.3	54.6
Mean Temp. (°F)	13.4	20.7	30.4	43.3	54.8	64.0	69.7	68.9	57.3	45.0	28.7	17.8	42.8
Mean Minimum Temp. (°F)	3.7	11.0	19.7	30.7	41.9	51.0	55.6	54.4	43.8	32.9	19.1	8.2	31.0
Extreme Maximum Temp. (°F)	58	66	79	92	101	106	110	105	103	93	81	61	110
Extreme Minimum Temp. (°F)	-37	-34	-25	-7	18	29	39	33	17	-3	-22	-37	-37
Days Maximum Temp. ≥ 90°F	0	0	0	0	1	2	8	9	2	0	0	0	22
Days Maximum Temp. ≤ 32°F	20	13	8	1	0	0	0	0	0	1	10	18	71
Days Minimum Temp. ≤ 32°F	30	27	28	18	4	0	0	0	3	14	27	30	181
Days Minimum Temp. ≤ 0°F	13	8	3	0	0	0	0	0	0	0	3	9	36
Heating Degree Days (base 65°F)	1,597	1,246	1,066	646	326	97	25	41	256	614	1,084	1,459	8,457
Cooling Degree Days (base 65°F)	0	0	0	1	19	77	186	180	35	1	0	0	499
Mean Precipitation (in.)	0.36	0.37	0.58	1.26	2.20	2.93	1.89	1.49	1.67	1.17	0.55	0.39	14.86
Days With ≥ 0.1" Precipitation	1	1	2	4	6	6	4	4	4	2	2	1	37
Days With ≥ 1.0" Precipitation	0	0	0	0	0	1	0	0	0	0	0	0	1
Mean Snowfall (in.)	5.1	5.0	5.4	4.1	1.2	trace	trace	0.0	0.4	2.1	5.4	5.1	33.8
Days With ≥ 1.0" Snow Depth	26	19	13	3	0	0	0	0	0	2	11	22	96

Turtle Lake *McLean County*   Elevation: 1,889 ft.   Latitude: 47° 31' N   Longitude: 100° 53' W

	JAN	FEB	MAR	APR	MAY	JUN	JUL	AUG	SEP	OCT	NOV	DEC	YEAR
Mean Maximum Temp. (°F)	18.4	25.8	37.3	54.4	68.4	76.8	82.3	81.9	70.2	56.5	36.0	23.3	52.6
Mean Temp. (°F)	8.3	15.6	26.8	41.7	55.0	64.1	68.9	67.7	56.6	43.7	26.1	13.5	40.7
Mean Minimum Temp. (°F)	-2.3	5.3	16.3	28.9	41.5	51.3	55.5	53.5	43.0	30.9	16.2	3.7	28.6
Extreme Maximum Temp. (°F)	53	64	74	95	97	103	105	106	106	93	78	58	106
Extreme Minimum Temp. (°F)	-37	-38	-28	-8	18	32	40	31	18	-9	-25	-38	-38
Days Maximum Temp. ≥ 90°F	0	0	0	0	1	2	6	7	2	0	0	0	18
Days Maximum Temp. ≤ 32°F	25	17	10	2	0	0	0	0	0	1	12	22	89
Days Minimum Temp. ≤ 32°F	31	28	30	20	4	0	0	0	3	17	28	31	192
Days Minimum Temp. ≤ 0°F	17	11	4	0	0	0	0	0	0	0	3	12	47
Heating Degree Days (base 65°F)	1,753	1,390	1,179	693	323	97	27	48	274	653	1,159	1,593	9,189
Cooling Degree Days (base 65°F)	0	0	0	2	17	68	140	128	23	1	0	0	379
Mean Precipitation (in.)	0.64	0.48	0.84	1.52	2.19	3.23	2.76	1.74	1.52	1.29	0.71	0.53	17.45
Days With ≥ 0.1" Precipitation	2	2	2	4	5	7	6	4	4	2	2	2	42
Days With ≥ 1.0" Precipitation	0	0	0	0	0	1	0	0	0	0	0	0	1
Mean Snowfall (in.)	8.4	*5.7*	4.8	0.8	trace	0.0	0.0	0.0	0.1	1.3	*7.6*	5.6	*34.3*
Days With ≥ 1.0" Snow Depth	na	na	*11*	2	0	0	0	0	0	1	*6*	15	na

Tuttle *Kidder County*   Elevation: 1,876 ft.   Latitude: 47° 08' N   Longitude: 100° 00' W

	JAN	FEB	MAR	APR	MAY	JUN	JUL	AUG	SEP	OCT	NOV	DEC	YEAR
Mean Maximum Temp. (°F)	17.5	23.3	35.9	53.0	67.7	76.5	82.3	81.6	69.6	56.0	36.2	22.3	51.8
Mean Temp. (°F)	7.2	13.1	26.0	41.4	55.0	64.0	68.9	67.2	55.8	43.1	26.1	12.0	40.0
Mean Minimum Temp. (°F)	-3.0	2.8	16.0	29.7	42.2	51.4	55.5	52.8	41.9	30.2	15.8	1.7	28.1
Extreme Maximum Temp. (°F)	52	56	75	94	95	105	107	105	104	90	74	55	107
Extreme Minimum Temp. (°F)	-35	-42	-28	-9	18	30	39	33	11	-8	-30	-39	-42
Days Maximum Temp. ≥ 90°F	0	0	0	0	0	2	6	7	1	0	0	0	16
Days Maximum Temp. ≤ 32°F	25	19	11	2	0	0	0	0	0	1	12	23	93
Days Minimum Temp. ≤ 32°F	31	28	30	19	5	0	0	0	4	19	29	31	196
Days Minimum Temp. ≤ 0°F	17	13	5	0	0	0	0	0	0	0	3	14	52
Heating Degree Days (base 65°F)	1,788	1,463	1,204	703	324	101	29	60	296	673	1,163	1,639	9,443
Cooling Degree Days (base 65°F)	0	0	0	0	23	78	158	140	26	1	0	0	428
Mean Precipitation (in.)	0.40	0.35	0.65	1.53	2.22	3.17	2.73	1.71	1.78	1.22	0.54	0.36	16.66
Days With ≥ 0.1" Precipitation	1	1	2	4	6	6	6	4	3	3	2	1	39
Days With ≥ 1.0" Precipitation	0	0	0	0	0	1	1	0	0	0	0	0	2
Mean Snowfall (in.)	6.7	5.6	6.8	4.1	0.5	0.0	0.0	0.0	0.2	2.4	6.6	5.8	38.7
Days With ≥ 1.0" Snow Depth	27	22	17	3	0	0	0	0	0	1	9	22	101

Underwood *McLean County*   Elevation: 2,017 ft.   Latitude: 47° 27' N   Longitude: 101° 09' W

	JAN	FEB	MAR	APR	MAY	JUN	JUL	AUG	SEP	OCT	NOV	DEC	YEAR
Mean Maximum Temp. (°F)	18.9	26.1	38.7	55.2	69.4	78.3	83.2	82.9	71.5	57.4	35.9	23.2	53.4
Mean Temp. (°F)	9.6	16.6	28.4	42.9	56.2	65.5	70.0	68.9	58.2	45.2	27.3	14.3	41.9
Mean Minimum Temp. (°F)	0.4	7.0	17.9	30.6	43.0	52.6	56.7	54.9	44.9	32.9	18.6	5.2	30.4
Extreme Maximum Temp. (°F)	54	63	74	94	95	102	105	104	102	93	78	59	105
Extreme Minimum Temp. (°F)	-33	-35	-24	-9	18	35	38	35	18	-6	-18	-34	-35
Days Maximum Temp. ≥ 90°F	0	0	0	0	1	3	7	7	2	0	0	0	20
Days Maximum Temp. ≤ 32°F	23	17	9	1	0	0	0	0	0	1	11	22	84
Days Minimum Temp. ≤ 32°F	31	28	29	18	4	0	0	0	2	15	27	31	185
Days Minimum Temp. ≤ 0°F	16	10	4	0	0	0	0	0	0	0	3	11	44
Heating Degree Days (base 65°F)	1,714	1,363	1,130	657	289	74	19	37	234	610	1,124	1,571	8,822
Cooling Degree Days (base 65°F)	0	0	0	4	26	100	181	174	37	2	0	0	524
Mean Precipitation (in.)	0.53	0.40	0.75	1.82	2.25	3.38	2.61	1.67	1.62	1.32	0.73	0.54	17.62
Days With ≥ 0.1" Precipitation	2	1	2	4	5	7	5	4	4	3	2	2	41
Days With ≥ 1.0" Precipitation	0	0	0	0	0	1	0	0	0	0	0	0	1
Mean Snowfall (in.)	na	na	na	2.2	0.3	0.0	0.0	0.0	trace	1.9	5.7	na	na
Days With ≥ 1.0" Snow Depth	na	na	na	3	0	0	0	0	0	1	6	na	na

Upham 3 N *McHenry County*   Elevation: 1,423 ft.   Latitude: 48° 37' N   Longitude: 100° 44' W

	JAN	FEB	MAR	APR	MAY	JUN	JUL	AUG	SEP	OCT	NOV	DEC	YEAR
Mean Maximum Temp. (°F)	14.2	22.6	34.1	53.4	68.1	76.5	81.2	81.0	69.3	55.5	34.5	20.3	50.9
Mean Temp. (°F)	2.6	10.6	22.9	40.4	54.5	63.5	67.4	66.1	54.7	41.3	23.9	9.2	38.1
Mean Minimum Temp. (°F)	-9.1	-1.4	11.6	27.5	40.8	50.4	53.5	51.2	40.0	27.2	13.1	-1.9	25.2
Extreme Maximum Temp. (°F)	49	66	72	98	100	103	105	105	102	93	74	55	105
Extreme Minimum Temp. (°F)	-45	-48	-38	-17	17	29	36	28	14	-10	-29	-42	-48
Days Maximum Temp. ≥ 90°F	0	0	0	0	1	2	4	5	1	0	0	0	13
Days Maximum Temp. ≤ 32°F	27	20	13	2	0	0	0	0	0	1	13	24	100
Days Minimum Temp. ≤ 32°F	31	28	30	22	6	0	0	0	6	23	29	31	206
Days Minimum Temp. ≤ 0°F	21	14	8	0	0	0	0	0	0	0	5	16	64
Heating Degree Days (base 65°F)	1,935	1,532	1,300	731	338	109	41	70	321	728	1,228	1,728	10,061
Cooling Degree Days (base 65°F)	0	0	0	2	21	73	122	121	16	0	0	0	355
Mean Precipitation (in.)	0.58	0.45	0.76	1.39	2.05	3.17	2.69	1.90	1.79	1.28	0.76	0.56	17.38
Days With ≥ 0.1" Precipitation	2	1	2	3	5	7	5	4	4	3	2	2	40
Days With ≥ 1.0" Precipitation	0	0	0	0	0	1	1	0	0	0	0	0	2
Mean Snowfall (in.)	9.8	6.6	7.8	4.8	0.3	trace	0.0	0.0	0.2	2.8	8.0	8.6	48.9
Days With ≥ 1.0" Snow Depth	30	26	22	4	0	0	0	0	0	2	13	26	123

Valley City 3 NNW *Barnes County*   Elevation: 1,207 ft.   Latitude: 46° 57' N   Longitude: 98° 01' W

	JAN	FEB	MAR	APR	MAY	JUN	JUL	AUG	SEP	OCT	NOV	DEC	YEAR
Mean Maximum Temp. (°F)	16.4	23.3	34.9	53.2	68.0	76.1	81.2	80.0	69.7	56.4	35.6	22.0	51.4
Mean Temp. (°F)	5.9	12.7	24.9	40.9	54.8	63.8	68.6	66.5	56.0	43.5	25.8	12.2	39.6
Mean Minimum Temp. (°F)	-4.6	2.1	14.9	28.5	41.6	51.4	55.9	53.0	42.3	30.6	16.0	2.3	27.8
Extreme Maximum Temp. (°F)	52	57	75	96	95	100	104	102	102	93	75	56	104
Extreme Minimum Temp. (°F)	-42	-44	-32	-13	20	33	40	33	21	3	-25	-37	-44
Days Maximum Temp. ≥ 90°F	0	0	0	0	0	2	4	4	1	0	0	0	11
Days Maximum Temp. ≤ 32°F	26	19	12	2	0	0	0	0	0	1	12	23	95
Days Minimum Temp. ≤ 32°F	31	28	29	20	5	0	0	0	4	18	29	31	195
Days Minimum Temp. ≤ 0°F	19	13	6	0	0	0	0	0	0	0	3	13	54
Heating Degree Days (base 65°F)	1,831	1,473	1,237	718	327	103	26	61	290	660	1,170	1,634	9,530
Cooling Degree Days (base 65°F)	0	0	0	2	20	75	140	121	24	1	0	0	383
Mean Precipitation (in.)	0.53	0.43	0.80	1.27	2.61	3.27	2.74	2.34	2.14	1.53	0.77	0.40	18.83
Days With ≥ 0.1" Precipitation	2	2	3	3	6	7	5	5	4	3	2	1	43
Days With ≥ 1.0" Precipitation	0	0	0	0	1	1	1	1	0	0	0	0	4
Mean Snowfall (in.)	8.8	5.7	5.9	2.6	0.1	0.0	0.0	0.0	0.0	0.5	6.2	5.6	35.4
Days With ≥ 1.0" Snow Depth	na	20	14	2	0	0	0	0	0	0	6	18	na

Velva McHenry County   Elevation: 1,509 ft.   Latitude: 48° 04' N   Longitude: 100° 56' W

	JAN	FEB	MAR	APR	MAY	JUN	JUL	AUG	SEP	OCT	NOV	DEC	YEAR
Mean Maximum Temp. (°F)	18.4	26.0	37.9	54.9	69.7	78.2	83.1	82.7	70.8	57.5	36.6	23.6	53.3
Mean Temp. (°F)	8.0	15.7	27.2	42.2	56.2	65.4	69.7	68.4	57.0	44.7	27.0	13.5	41.2
Mean Minimum Temp. (°F)	-2.6	5.3	16.5	29.6	42.6	52.4	56.3	54.1	43.2	31.9	17.4	3.3	29.2
Extreme Maximum Temp. (°F)	55	60	73	98	100	101	105	105	108	94	82	60	108
Extreme Minimum Temp. (°F)	-41	-37	-30	-12	19	31	38	29	18	-3	-25	-38	-41
Days Maximum Temp. ≥ 90°F	0	0	0	0	1	3	7	7	2	0	0	0	20
Days Maximum Temp. ≤ 32°F	23	17	10	1	0	0	0	0	0	1	11	22	85
Days Minimum Temp. ≤ 32°F	31	28	28	19	5	0	0	0	3	16	28	31	189
Days Minimum Temp. ≤ 0°F	17	11	4	0	0	0	0	0	0	0	3	13	48
Heating Degree Days (base 65°F)	1,764	1,385	1,165	680	294	78	23	40	264	624	1,134	1,593	9,044
Cooling Degree Days (base 65°F)	0	0	0	3	26	96	171	155	30	1	0	0	482
Mean Precipitation (in.)	0.70	0.46	0.76	1.56	2.20	3.18	2.94	1.77	1.64	1.68	0.81	0.52	18.22
Days With ≥ 0.1" Precipitation	2	2	3	3	4	6	5	4	4	3	2	2	40
Days With ≥ 1.0" Precipitation	0	0	0	0	0	1	1	0	0	0	0	0	2
Mean Snowfall (in.)	9.0	6.1	6.9	4.6	trace	0.0	0.0	0.0	0.3	2.5	6.9	6.5	42.8
Days With ≥ 1.0" Snow Depth	na	na	na	1	0	0	0	0	0	1	na	na	na

Wahpeton 3 N Richland County   Elevation: 954 ft.   Latitude: 46° 19' N   Longitude: 96° 37' W

	JAN	FEB	MAR	APR	MAY	JUN	JUL	AUG	SEP	OCT	NOV	DEC	YEAR
Mean Maximum Temp. (°F)	17.4	24.6	36.6	56.6	71.7	80.1	84.4	82.6	72.1	57.7	36.3	23.2	53.6
Mean Temp. (°F)	8.3	15.6	28.2	45.0	59.0	67.8	72.1	70.2	60.1	47.0	28.5	14.8	43.1
Mean Minimum Temp. (°F)	-0.9	6.5	19.6	33.5	46.2	55.5	59.8	57.8	47.9	36.3	20.6	6.2	32.4
Extreme Maximum Temp. (°F)	57	58	76	99	97	101	105	107	98	91	73	54	107
Extreme Minimum Temp. (°F)	-35	-36	-21	-3	25	35	43	38	24	9	-20	-31	-36
Days Maximum Temp. ≥ 90°F	0	0	0	0	1	4	7	5	2	0	0	0	19
Days Maximum Temp. ≤ 32°F	26	19	10	1	0	0	0	0	0	0	12	23	91
Days Minimum Temp. ≤ 32°F	31	28	27	14	2	0	0	0	1	11	27	31	172
Days Minimum Temp. ≤ 0°F	17	10	3	0	0	0	0	0	0	0	2	11	43
Heating Degree Days (base 65°F)	1,756	1,391	1,135	596	222	44	9	23	194	552	1,088	1,552	8,562
Cooling Degree Days (base 65°F)	0	0	0	4	46	136	233	195	50	2	0	0	666
Mean Precipitation (in.)	0.63	0.38	1.03	1.79	2.90	3.42	3.43	2.63	2.43	2.04	0.76	0.37	21.81
Days With ≥ 0.1" Precipitation	2	1	3	4	6	7	6	5	5	4	2	1	46
Days With ≥ 1.0" Precipitation	0	0	0	0	1	1	1	1	1	0	0	0	5
Mean Snowfall (in.)	8.1	3.9	5.6	2.1	trace	0.0	0.0	0.0	trace	0.5	5.1	3.9	29.2
Days With ≥ 1.0" Snow Depth	27	22	17	3	0	0	0	0	0	0	9	18	96

Washburn McLean County   Elevation: 1,732 ft.   Latitude: 47° 17' N   Longitude: 101° 02' W

	JAN	FEB	MAR	APR	MAY	JUN	JUL	AUG	SEP	OCT	NOV	DEC	YEAR
Mean Maximum Temp. (°F)	21.5	29.4	40.1	56.9	70.2	78.8	84.5	84.0	72.7	59.0	38.3	25.5	55.1
Mean Temp. (°F)	11.3	19.1	29.6	44.3	56.8	65.7	70.8	69.7	58.8	46.3	29.1	16.1	43.1
Mean Minimum Temp. (°F)	1.1	8.9	19.0	31.6	43.4	52.5	57.0	55.4	44.9	33.5	19.9	6.6	31.1
Extreme Maximum Temp. (°F)	57	66	78	98	99	107	106	108	104	94	77	61	108
Extreme Minimum Temp. (°F)	-34	-30	-21	-5	21	34	40	34	18	0	-17	-34	-34
Days Maximum Temp. ≥ 90°F	0	0	0	0	1	4	8	9	2	0	0	0	24
Days Maximum Temp. ≤ 32°F	22	15	9	1	0	0	0	0	0	1	9	19	76
Days Minimum Temp. ≤ 32°F	31	28	28	17	3	0	0	0	2	14	26	31	180
Days Minimum Temp. ≤ 0°F	15	9	3	0	0	0	0	0	0	0	2	10	39
Heating Degree Days (base 65°F)	1,663	1,288	1,092	618	273	73	15	33	220	574	1,067	1,513	8,429
Cooling Degree Days (base 65°F)	0	0	0	4	28	92	197	177	37	2	0	0	537
Mean Precipitation (in.)	0.45	0.43	0.75	1.84	2.22	3.19	2.69	1.94	1.71	1.36	0.65	0.41	17.64
Days With ≥ 0.1" Precipitation	2	1	2	4	5	6	5	4	4	2	2	1	38
Days With ≥ 1.0" Precipitation	0	0	0	0	0	1	1	0	0	0	0	0	2
Mean Snowfall (in.)	6.7	6.0	8.4	4.5	0.2	0.0	0.0	0.0	0.3	2.3	7.2	6.5	42.1
Days With ≥ 1.0" Snow Depth	26	20	13	2	0	0	0	0	0	1	11	21	94

Watford City 14 S McKenzie County   Elevation: 1,942 ft.   Latitude: 47° 36' N   Longitude: 103° 16' W

	JAN	FEB	MAR	APR	MAY	JUN	JUL	AUG	SEP	OCT	NOV	DEC	YEAR
Mean Maximum Temp. (°F)	24.7	33.0	43.8	58.7	71.2	80.0	86.8	86.9	74.6	61.2	41.0	30.4	57.7
Mean Temp. (°F)	13.1	21.5	31.7	44.8	56.8	65.7	71.3	70.5	58.9	46.7	29.8	18.9	44.1
Mean Minimum Temp. (°F)	1.4	10.0	19.5	30.8	42.4	51.3	55.6	54.1	43.0	32.1	18.5	7.5	30.5
Extreme Maximum Temp. (°F)	61	67	78	94	102	109	110	110	107	94	80	65	110
Extreme Minimum Temp. (°F)	-40	-42	-32	-11	19	24	34	31	18	-10	-27	-45	-45
Days Maximum Temp. ≥ 90°F	0	0	0	0	1	4	12	13	3	0	0	0	33
Days Maximum Temp. ≤ 32°F	19	12	7	1	0	0	0	0	0	0	8	15	62
Days Minimum Temp. ≤ 32°F	30	27	28	17	4	0	0	0	4	15	27	30	182
Days Minimum Temp. ≤ 0°F	14	8	3	0	0	0	0	0	0	0	3	9	37
Heating Degree Days (base 65°F)	1,608	1,221	1,027	603	274	74	18	29	222	563	1,051	1,422	8,112
Cooling Degree Days (base 65°F)	0	0	0	3	29	103	217	214	44	2	0	0	612
Mean Precipitation (in.)	0.36	0.36	0.62	1.36	2.23	2.81	2.27	1.65	1.71	1.27	0.48	0.37	15.49
Days With ≥ 0.1" Precipitation	1	1	2	3	5	7	5	4	4	2	2	1	37
Days With ≥ 1.0" Precipitation	0	0	0	0	0	1	1	0	0	0	0	0	2
Mean Snowfall (in.)	6.0	5.4	5.3	3.7	0.5	0.0	0.0	0.0	trace	1.7	4.9	6.2	33.7
Days With ≥ 1.0" Snow Depth	22	16	8	3	0	0	0	0	0	1	7	16	73

Westhope *Bottineau County* Elevation: 1,499 ft. Latitude: 48° 55' N Longitude: 101° 01' W

	JAN	FEB	MAR	APR	MAY	JUN	JUL	AUG	SEP	OCT	NOV	DEC	YEAR
Mean Maximum Temp. (°F)	13.6	22.4	34.3	54.6	69.5	77.2	81.1	81.4	70.4	56.1	33.9	19.4	51.2
Mean Temp. (°F)	3.7	12.7	24.8	42.1	55.8	64.3	67.9	67.0	56.5	43.5	24.9	10.1	39.4
Mean Minimum Temp. (°F)	-6.2	2.9	15.3	29.5	42.1	51.3	54.6	52.6	42.6	30.8	15.8	0.7	27.7
Extreme Maximum Temp. (°F)	46	63	68	95	100	101	102	103	99	93	74	55	103
Extreme Minimum Temp. (°F)	-41	-44	-37	-13	17	32	34	29	17	-9	-27	-41	-44
Days Maximum Temp. ≥ 90°F	0	0	0	0	1	2	4	5	1	0	0	0	13
Days Maximum Temp. ≤ 32°F	26	20	12	2	0	0	0	0	0	1	13	25	99
Days Minimum Temp. ≤ 32°F	31	28	29	19	5	0	0	0	3	17	29	31	192
Days Minimum Temp. ≤ 0°F	19	12	6	0	0	0	0	0	0	0	4	15	56
Heating Degree Days (base 65°F)	1,900	1,475	1,239	683	301	91	33	57	271	661	1,197	1,700	9,608
Cooling Degree Days (base 65°F)	0	0	0	0	2	26	82	134	139	23	0	0	406
Mean Precipitation (in.)	0.47	0.44	0.71	1.23	2.02	2.97	2.87	1.96	1.79	1.21	0.54	0.48	16.69
Days With ≥ 0.1" Precipitation	2	1	2	3	5	6	5	4	3	3	2	1	37
Days With ≥ 1.0" Precipitation	0	0	0	0	0	1	1	1	0	0	0	0	3
Mean Snowfall (in.)	7.7	5.7	6.3	3.3	0.3	0.0	0.0	0.0	trace	2.7	5.8	6.7	*38.5*
Days With ≥ 1.0" Snow Depth	28	26	22	5	0	0	0	0	0	2	12	25	120

Wildrose 3 NW *Divide County* Elevation: 2,257 ft. Latitude: 48° 40' N Longitude: 103° 13' W

	JAN	FEB	MAR	APR	MAY	JUN	JUL	AUG	SEP	OCT	NOV	DEC	YEAR
Mean Maximum Temp. (°F)	16.1	23.8	35.3	52.7	66.2	75.4	80.4	80.3	67.6	54.2	34.3	21.9	50.7
Mean Temp. (°F)	6.4	14.1	25.3	40.7	53.5	62.9	67.2	65.9	54.3	42.0	25.1	12.4	39.1
Mean Minimum Temp. (°F)	-3.4	4.3	15.3	28.6	40.7	50.2	54.0	51.4	41.0	29.6	15.9	2.9	27.6
Extreme Maximum Temp. (°F)	48	63	73	91	99	103	104	103	100	91	73	54	104
Extreme Minimum Temp. (°F)	-38	-41	-28	-16	20	31	39	32	17	-3	-24	-42	-42
Days Maximum Temp. ≥ 90°F	0	0	0	0	0	2	5	5	1	0	0	0	13
Days Maximum Temp. ≤ 32°F	25	18	12	2	0	0	0	0	0	1	14	23	95
Days Minimum Temp. ≤ 32°F	31	28	30	20	5	0	0	0	4	19	29	31	197
Days Minimum Temp. ≤ 0°F	18	11	5	0	0	0	0	0	0	0	4	13	51
Heating Degree Days (base 65°F)	1,816	1,434	1,224	722	364	121	44	76	330	707	1,191	1,627	9,656
Cooling Degree Days (base 65°F)	0	0	0	0	15	64	116	120	18	0	0	0	333
Mean Precipitation (in.)	0.42	0.34	0.60	1.08	2.02	2.45	2.81	1.51	1.54	0.84	0.44	0.44	14.49
Days With ≥ 0.1" Precipitation	1	1	2	3	5	6	5	4	4	2	1	1	35
Days With ≥ 1.0" Precipitation	0	0	0	0	0	0	1	0	0	0	0	0	1
Mean Snowfall (in.)	7.1	5.1	6.3	3.3	0.4	0.0	0.0	0.0	trace	1.8	4.9	6.2	35.1
Days With ≥ 1.0" Snow Depth	22	17	12	3	0	0	0	0	0	2	9	19	84

Williston Exp. Farm *Williams County* Elevation: 2,103 ft. Latitude: 48° 08' N Longitude: 103° 44' W

	JAN	FEB	MAR	APR	MAY	JUN	JUL	AUG	SEP	OCT	NOV	DEC	YEAR
Mean Maximum Temp. (°F)	20.5	29.3	41.5	57.5	70.2	79.0	84.9	84.9	72.7	59.3	37.9	25.5	55.3
Mean Temp. (°F)	10.7	19.3	30.4	44.3	56.6	65.6	70.8	70.0	58.6	46.3	28.4	15.9	43.1
Mean Minimum Temp. (°F)	0.9	9.2	19.2	31.1	43.0	52.1	56.6	55.1	44.4	33.1	18.8	6.3	30.8
Extreme Maximum Temp. (°F)	52	65	78	92	102	105	108	106	105	92	76	59	108
Extreme Minimum Temp. (°F)	-37	-36	-25	-14	21	32	41	35	19	-3	-22	-40	-40
Days Maximum Temp. ≥ 90°F	0	0	0	0	1	4	9	10	2	0	0	0	26
Days Maximum Temp. ≤ 32°F	22	14	8	1	0	0	0	0	0	1	10	19	75
Days Minimum Temp. ≤ 32°F	31	28	28	17	4	0	0	0	2	14	27	31	182
Days Minimum Temp. ≤ 0°F	15	9	3	0	0	0	0	0	0	0	3	11	41
Heating Degree Days (base 65°F)	1,681	1,286	1,068	615	279	73	17	33	228	575	1,093	1,517	8,465
Cooling Degree Days (base 65°F)	0	0	0	0	2	28	105	206	207	44	2	0	0	594
Mean Precipitation (in.)	0.48	0.33	0.63	1.16	2.14	2.70	2.44	1.64	1.57	0.94	0.50	0.45	14.98
Days With ≥ 0.1" Precipitation	1	1	2	3	5	6	5	4	3	2	2	1	35
Days With ≥ 1.0" Precipitation	0	0	0	0	0	1	0	0	0	0	0	0	1
Mean Snowfall (in.)	6.0	4.3	5.4	3.0	0.6	0.0	0.0	0.0	0.2	1.6	4.7	5.9	31.7
Days With ≥ 1.0" Snow Depth	21	14	9	2	0	0	0	0	0	1	8	18	73

Willow City *Bottineau County* Elevation: 1,459 ft. Latitude: 48° 37' N Longitude: 100° 17' W

	JAN	FEB	MAR	APR	MAY	JUN	JUL	AUG	SEP	OCT	NOV	DEC	YEAR
Mean Maximum Temp. (°F)	12.6	20.6	32.2	51.8	67.0	75.5	80.0	79.8	67.9	54.6	33.5	18.8	49.5
Mean Temp. (°F)	1.8	9.5	21.7	39.8	53.9	63.0	67.1	65.4	54.0	41.3	23.5	8.4	37.5
Mean Minimum Temp. (°F)	-9.1	-1.7	11.1	27.7	40.8	50.5	54.1	51.0	40.0	27.9	13.4	-2.0	25.3
Extreme Maximum Temp. (°F)	50	63	68	97	99	100	101	105	102	91	74	53	105
Extreme Minimum Temp. (°F)	-49	-47	-40	-22	18	31	36	28	17	-13	-33	-44	-49
Days Maximum Temp. ≥ 90°F	0	0	0	0	1	2	3	5	1	0	0	0	12
Days Maximum Temp. ≤ 32°F	27	21	14	2	0	0	0	0	0	1	14	25	104
Days Minimum Temp. ≤ 32°F	31	28	30	21	6	0	0	0	5	22	30	31	204
Days Minimum Temp. ≤ 0°F	21	15	8	0	0	0	0	0	0	0	5	17	66
Heating Degree Days (base 65°F)	1,959	1,565	1,338	751	353	117	44	78	336	730	1,240	1,751	10,262
Cooling Degree Days (base 65°F)	0	0	0	0	1	19	68	116	109	13	0	0	326
Mean Precipitation (in.)	0.52	0.39	0.79	1.23	1.95	3.04	2.84	2.24	1.74	1.18	0.55	0.44	16.91
Days With ≥ 0.1" Precipitation	2	2	2	3	5	7	6	4	4	3	2	1	41
Days With ≥ 1.0" Precipitation	0	0	0	0	0	1	1	0	0	0	0	0	2
Mean Snowfall (in.)	9.5	5.2	6.7	2.8	trace	0.0	0.0	0.0	0.1	1.1	6.2	7.2	38.8
Days With ≥ 1.0" Snow Depth	na	na	na	3	0	0	0	0	0	0	0	*4*	na	na

Wishek *McIntosh County*   Elevation: 2,119 ft.   Latitude: 46° 15' N   Longitude: 99° 34' W

	JAN	FEB	MAR	APR	MAY	JUN	JUL	AUG	SEP	OCT	NOV	DEC	YEAR
Mean Maximum Temp. (°F)	18.4	25.3	36.7	53.2	67.1	75.8	82.2	81.2	70.2	56.5	36.7	23.9	52.3
Mean Temp. (°F)	8.0	14.9	26.4	41.1	54.2	63.3	68.6	66.9	56.1	43.5	26.5	13.9	40.3
Mean Minimum Temp. (°F)	-2.5	4.6	16.1	29.0	41.2	50.6	54.9	52.5	41.9	30.4	16.2	3.9	28.2
Extreme Maximum Temp. (°F)	56	56	78	93	93	101	107	103	103	93	75	60	107
Extreme Minimum Temp. (°F)	-41	-39	-25	-13	17	30	28	30	9	2	-27	-36	-41
Days Maximum Temp. ≥ 90°F	0	0	0	0	0	2	6	5	2	0	0	0	15
Days Maximum Temp. ≤ 32°F	25	17	11	1	0	0	0	0	0	1	12	22	89
Days Minimum Temp. ≤ 32°F	31	28	29	20	5	0	0	0	4	18	29	31	195
Days Minimum Temp. ≤ 0°F	17	11	5	0	0	0	0	0	0	0	3	12	48
Heating Degree Days (base 65°F)	1,769	1,401	1,192	712	344	108	33	61	289	662	1,150	1,579	9,300
Cooling Degree Days (base 65°F)	0	0	0	1	15	63	144	124	25	1	0	0	373
Mean Precipitation (in.)	0.40	0.43	0.85	1.68	2.40	3.76	2.66	2.19	1.60	1.45	0.52	0.31	18.25
Days With ≥ 0.1" Precipitation	1	2	3	4	6	7	5	4	4	4	2	1	43
Days With ≥ 1.0" Precipitation	0	0	0	0	0	1	1	1	0	0	0	0	3
Mean Snowfall (in.)	8.4	8.0	7.5	3.3	0.4	0.0	0.0	0.0	trace	1.2	8.6	5.2	42.6
Days With ≥ 1.0" Snow Depth	na	na	na	2	0	0	0	0	0	0	6	na	na

Note: See Appendix D for explanation of data.

OHIO

PHYSICAL FEATURES AND GENERAL CLIMATE. The climate of Ohio is remarkably varied. Less than one-half of its area is occupied by typical plains, while most of eastern and much of southern Ohio is hilly. Topography ranges in elevation from 430 feet above sea level at the junction of the Great Miami and Ohio Rivers up to 1,550 feet on a summit near Bellefontaine. In addition to this high point there are innumerable other hills which rise above 1,400 feet (mean sea level). These are located mainly along the dividing line between the Ohio River and Lake Erie drainage basins. Large areas in the State have elevations above 1,000 feet. An extensive area in northwestern Ohio is occupied by a flat lake plain — once the bottom of glacial Lake Maumee which was much larger than the present Lake Erie. The greater part of eastern Ohio is within the Allegheny Plateau, an unglaciated area consisting of picturesque hills, many of which rise above 1,300 feet and comprise many winding rivers and streams.

The Ohio River, which forms the southern and southeastern boundaries of Ohio, and its tributaries drain the greater portion of the State. A number of streams drain northward into Lake Erie. Although this area comprises nearly a third of the State, the divide between the two drainages is only 20 to 40 miles from the lake shore for a distance of more than 100 miles until it dips south of the arrowhead-shaped Maumee Basin. The largest streams in this region are the Maumee, Sandusky, and Cuyahoga Rivers. Principal tributaries flowing southward into the Ohio River include the Muskingum in the east, the Scioto in the central section, and the Great Miami in the west. A small portion in the west-central region drains westward into the Wabash River basin of Indiana.

Located west of the Appalachian Mountains, Ohio has a climate essentially continental in nature, characterized by moderate extremes of heat and cold, and wetness and dryness. Summers are moderately warm and humid, with occasional days when temperatures exceed 100°F.; winters are reasonably cold, with an average of about two days of subzero weather; and autumns are predominately cool, dry, and invigorating. Spring is the wettest season and vegetation is lush and profuse.

PRECIPITATION. Annual precipitation is slightly in excess of the national average and is well distributed, though with peaks in early spring and summer. In spite of the relatively small range in latitude and the compact shape of Ohio, rainfall varies considerably in amount and seasonal distribution. This is accounted for not only by the presence of Lake Erie on the north, but also by its topography and proximity to rain producing storm paths. Annual precipitation averages about 38 inches, being most generous in spring (about four inches in April) and least in the fall (about 2.5 inches in October). Greatest amounts are measured in the southwest where Wilmington has an average of 44.36 inches; the lake shore is driest, with Gilbralter Island having a normal of only 29.06 inches.

The southern half of the State is visited more frequently by productive rainstorms which, together with the general roughness of terrain, accounts for the larger total precipitation. The lifting of moist air masses over the hills tends to increase the yield of rainfall, especially in winter and spring. There is a marked tendency during the cold season for northeastern counties to receive snowfall amounts substantially in excess of those measured elsewhere. Northerly winds have a long fetch across Lake Huron and the widest part of Lake Erie, thus picking up moisture and heat from the lakes. This moisture is then forced to condense as the air is lifted abruptly over the divide a short distance from the lake. Average snowfall ranges from 60 inches in parts of Lake and adjoining counties down to 16 inches or less along the Ohio River.

TEMPERATURE. The normal annual temperature for the State ranges from 49.6°F. at Hiram in Portage County up to 56.9°F. at Portsmouth on the Ohio River. Variations over the State are due mainly to differences in latitude and topography, but the immediate lake shore area experiences a moderating effect due to its proximity to a large body of water. Widest temperature ranges are found generally among the eastern hills. In an average year, 90°F. heat may be expected about 20 times in summer with 100°F. or more once or twice. Readings of zero or lower are generally to be expected on two to four days each winter, and these are just as likely to occur in the south as the north. However, one winter out of six or eight will pass without experiencing zero readings anywhere in the State.

OTHER CLIMATIC ELEMENTS. The growing season, as defined by the period 32°F. or higher, ranges widely because of latitude and proximity to Lake Erie. The longest is about 200 days on the lake shore and the shortest is in the northeastern valleys within the Ohio River drainage. Dates of the average last freezing temperature in spring range from April 15 to May 18 and the mean first freeze date in fall varies from September 30 to November 6, the latter being on the western lake shore.

Damaging windstorms are mostly associated with heavy thunderstorms or line squalls. Three or four tornadoes may be expected to strike in Ohio each year. Most tornadoes, however, are of limited effect having paths that are short and narrow.

Most floods in Ohio are caused by unusual precipitation. The storms causing floods may bring rainfall of unusual intensity or of unusual duration and extent. Some floods may be caused by a series of ordinary storms which follow one another in rapid succession. Others may result from rain falling at relatively high temperatures on snow-covered areas. At times, though infrequent, flood conditions are caused or aggravated by ice gorges, especially in the tributary streams. Severe thunderstorms frequently cause local flash flooding. General flooding occurs most frequently during January to March and rarely occurs during August to October.

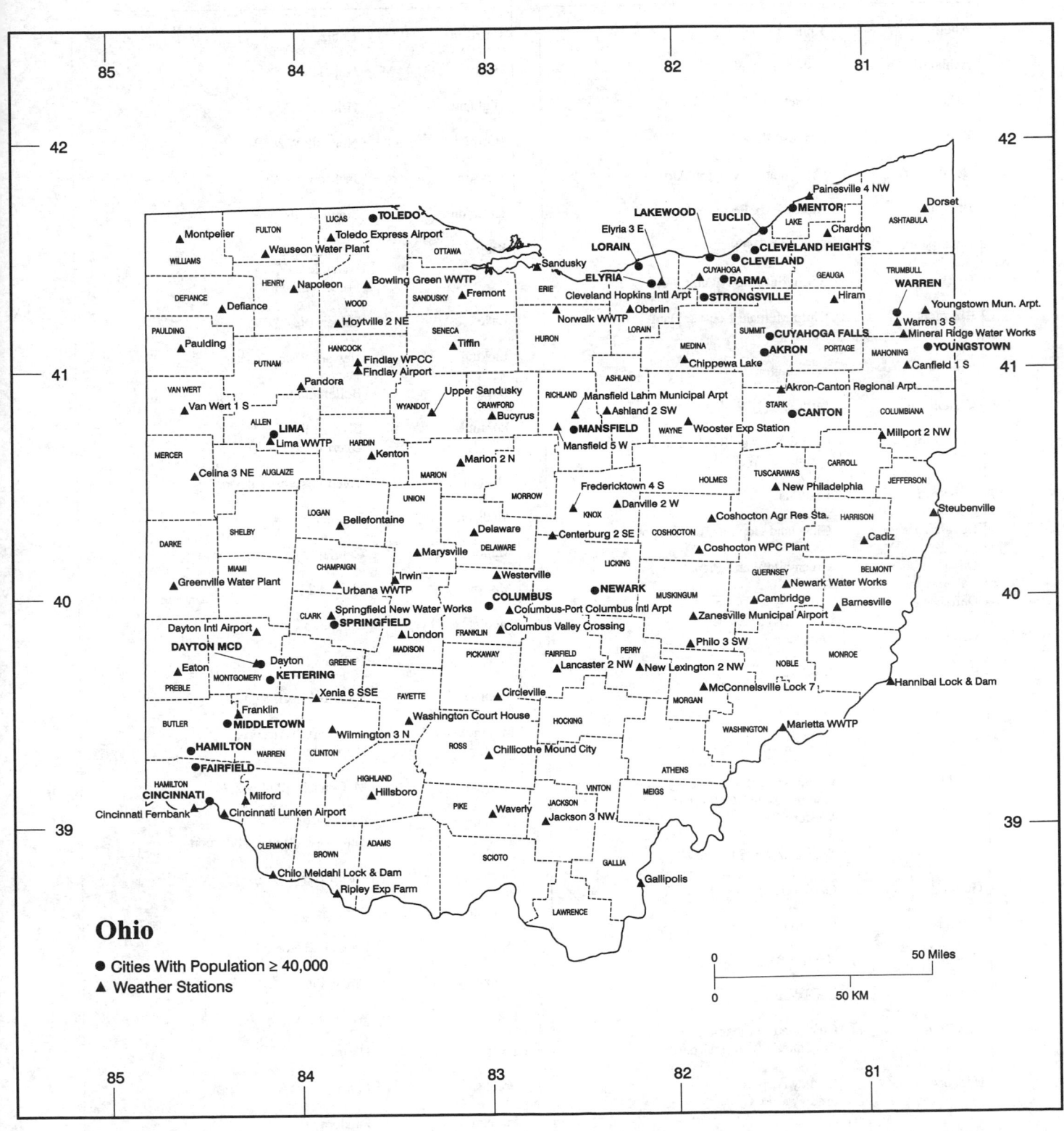

Ohio

- ● Cities With Population ≥ 40,000
- ▲ Weather Stations

Ohio Weather Stations by County

County	Station Name
Allen	Lima WWTP
Ashland	Ashland 2 SW
Ashtabula	Dorset
Belmont	Barnesville
Boone	Cincinnati Covington Airport
Brown	Ripley Exp. Farm
Champaign	Urbana WWTP
Clark	Springfield New Water Works
Clermont	Chilo Meldahl Lock & Dam Milford
Clinton	Wilmington 3 N
Columbiana	Millport 2 NW
Coshocton	Coshocton Agr. Res. Station Coshocton WPC Plant
Crawford	Bucyrus
Cuyahoga	Cleveland Hopkins Int'l Airport
Darke	Greenville Water Plant
Defiance	Defiance
Delaware	Delaware
Erie	Sandusky
Fairfield	Lancaster 2 NW
Fayette	Washington Court House
Franklin	Columbus Valley Crossing Columbus-Port Columbus Int'l Westerville
Fulton	Wauseon Water Plant
Gallia	Gallipolis
Geauga	Chardon
Greene	Xenia 6 SSE
Guernsey	Cambridge
Hamilton	Cincinnati Fernbank Cincinnati Lunken Airport
Hancock	Findlay Airport Findlay WPCC
Hardin	Kenton

County	Station Name
Harrison	Cadiz
Henry	Napoleon
Highland	Hillsboro
Huron	Norwalk WWTP
Jackson	Jackson 3 NW
Jefferson	Steubenville
Knox	Centerburg 2 SE Danville 2 W Fredericktown 4 S
Lake	Painesville 4 NW
Licking	Newark Water Works
Logan	Bellefontaine
Lorain	Elyria 3 E Oberlin
Lucas	Toledo Express Airport
Madison	London
Mahoning	Canfield 1 S
Marion	Marion 2 N
Medina	Chippewa Lake
Mercer	Celina 3 NE
Monroe	Hannibal Lock & Dam
Montgomery	Dayton Int'l Airport Dayton MCD
Morgan	McConnelsville Lock 7
Muskingum	Philo 3 SW Zanesville Municipal Airport
Ottawa	Put-In-Bay
Paulding	Paulding
Perry	New Lexington 2 NW
Pickaway	Circleville
Pike	Waverly
Portage	Hiram
Preble	Eaton
Putnam	Pandora
Richland	Mansfield 5 W

County	Station Name
Richland (cont.)	Mansfield Lahm Municipal Airport
Ross	Chillicothe Mound City
Sandusky	Fremont
Scioto	Portsmouth Sciotoville
Seneca	Tiffin
Summit	Akron-Canton Regional Airport
Trumbull	Mineral Ridge Water Works Warren 3 S Youngstown Municipal Airport
Tuscarawas	New Philadelphia
Union	Irwin Marysville
Van Wert	Van Wert 1 S
Warren	Franklin
Washington	Marietta WWTP
Wayne	Wooster Exp. Station
Williams	Montpelier
Wood	Bowling Green WWTP Hoytville 2 NE
Wyandot	Upper Sandusky

Ohio Weather Stations by City

City	Station Name	Miles
Akron	Akron-Canton Regional Airport	12
Canton	Akron-Canton Regional Airport	8
Cincinnati	Cincinnati Covington Airport	11
	Cincinnati Fernbank	10
	Cincinnati Lunken Airport	5
	Milford	12
Cleveland	Cleveland Hopkins Int'l Airport	11
Cleveland Heights	Cleveland Hopkins Int'l Airport	17
Columbus	Columbus Valley Crossing	8
	Columbus-Port Columbus Int'l	6
	Westerville	9
Cuyahoga Falls	Akron-Canton Regional Airport	16
Dayton	Dayton MCD	1
	Dayton Int'l Airport	10
	Franklin	16
	Xenia 6 SSE	19
Elyria	Cleveland Hopkins Int'l Airport	13
	Elyria 3 E	3
	Oberlin	10
Euclid	Chardon	17
	Painesville 4 NW	16
Fairfield	Cincinnati Fernbank	17
	Cincinnati Lunken Airport	17
	Franklin	20
	Milford	17
Hamilton	Franklin	17
Kettering	Dayton MCD	5
	Dayton Int'l Airport	15
	Franklin	13
	Xenia 6 SSE	14
Lakewood	Cleveland Hopkins Int'l Airport	6
	Elyria 3 E	15
Lima	Lima WWTP	2
	Pandora	16
Lorain	Cleveland Hopkins Int'l Airport	17
	Elyria 3 E	8
	Oberlin	13
Mansfield	Ashland 2 SW	11
	Mansfield Lahm Municipal Airport	4
	Mansfield 5 W	5
Mentor	Chardon	11
	Painesville 4 NW	5
Middletown	Franklin	4
Parma	Cleveland Hopkins Int'l Airport	6
	Elyria 3 E	17

City	Station Name	Miles
Springfield	London	19
	Springfield New Water Works	3
	Urbana WWTP	12
Strongsville	Chippewa Lake	19
	Cleveland Hopkins Int'l Airport	6
	Elyria 3 E	12
Toledo	Monroe, MI	20
	Bowling Green WWTP	19
	Toledo Express Airport	13
Warren	Canfield 1 S	16
	Hiram	18
	Mineral Ridge Water Works	6
	Warren 3 S	3
	Youngstown Municipal Airport	8
Youngstown	Canfield 1 S	8
	Mineral Ridge Water Works	8
	Warren 3 S	11
	Youngstown Municipal Airport	11
	New Castle 1 N, PA	16

Note: Miles is the distance between the geographic center of the city and the weather station.

Ohio Weather Stations by Elevation

Feet	Station Name	Feet	Station Name
1,348	Mansfield 5 W	797	Jackson 3 NW
1,292	Mansfield Lahm Municipal Airport	787	Van Wert 1 S
1,263	Ashland 2 SW	767	Cleveland Hopkins Int'l Airport
1,259	Cadiz	767	Findlay WPCC
1,240	Barnesville	767	Pandora
1,227	Hiram	757	Coshocton WPC Plant
1,207	Akron-Canton Regional Airport	757	McConnelsville Lock 7
1,204	Centerburg 2 SE	748	Wauseon Water Plant
1,184	Bellefontaine	744	Dayton MCD
1,177	Chippewa Lake	738	Tiffin
1,177	Youngstown Municipal Airport	734	Columbus Valley Crossing
1,148	Millport 2 NW	728	Elyria 3 E
1,138	Canfield 1 S	725	Paulding
1,138	Coshocton Agr. Res. Station	698	Defiance
1,128	Chardon	698	Hoytville 2 NE
1,099	Hillsboro	679	Napoleon
1,049	Fredericktown 4 S	672	Bowling Green WWTP
1,026	Wilmington 3 N	672	Circleville
1,023	Greenville Water Plant	669	Franklin
1,017	London	669	Norwalk WWTP
1,017	Philo 3 SW	666	Toledo Express Airport
1,017	Wooster Exp. Station	649	Chillicothe Mound City
1,007	Irwin	620	Hannibal Lock & Dam
1,000	Eaton	597	Fremont
997	Dayton Int'l Airport	597	Painesville 4 NW
997	Marysville	583	Sandusky
997	Urbana WWTP	577	Marietta WWTP
994	Kenton	577	Put-In-Bay
990	Steubenville	567	Gallipolis
977	Dorset	557	Waverly
967	Danville 2 W	538	Portsmouth Sciotoville
967	Xenia 6 SSE	518	Milford
964	Marion 2 N	498	Chilo Meldahl Lock & Dam
958	Washington Court House	498	Cincinnati Fernbank
954	Bucyrus	488	Cincinnati Lunken Airport
928	Springfield New Water Works		
918	Delaware		
898	Warren 3 S		
892	New Philadelphia		
889	Mineral Ridge Water Works		
889	New Lexington 2 NW		
879	Ripley Exp. Farm		
879	Zanesville Municipal Airport		
866	Cincinnati Covington Airport		
859	Celina 3 NE		
859	Lancaster 2 NW		
859	Montpelier		
853	Upper Sandusky		
849	Lima WWTP		
833	Newark Water Works		
813	Oberlin		
807	Columbus-Port Columbus Int'l		
807	Westerville		
797	Cambridge		
797	Findlay Airport		

Akron-Canton Regional Airport

The station at the Akron-Canton Airport is located about midway between Akron and Canton, a few miles south of the crest separating the Lake Erie and Muskingum River drainage areas. Precipitation at the station and southward drains through the Muskingum River into the Ohio, while northward of the crest the Cuyahoga and other streams flow into Lake Erie. The terrain is rolling with highest elevations near 1,300 feet above sea level and many small lakes provide water for local industry as well as recreational facilities for the densely populated region. The area is mainly industrial, agricultural operations having diminished rapidly in recent years.

Lake Erie has considerable influence on the area weather, tempering cold air masses during the late fall and winter, as well as contributing to the formation of brief, but heavy snow squalls until the lake freezes over.

The arrival of spring is late in this area, allowing growing of normally frost-susceptible fruits. Summers are moderately warm, but quite humid, while the months of September, October, and sometimes November are usually pleasant although with considerable morning fog. The average last occurrence of freezing temperatures in spring is the end of April, and the first occurrence in fall is late October. In past years, growing seasons for most vegetation has varied from 120 to 211 days. Temperatures and occurences of frost vary widely over the area because of the hilly terrain. Due to the influence of Lake Erie, snowfall is usually much heavier north of the station.

Akron-Canton Regional Airport *Summit County*   Elevation: 1,207 ft.   Latitude: 40° 55' N   Longitude: 81° 26' W

	JAN	FEB	MAR	APR	MAY	JUN	JUL	AUG	SEP	OCT	NOV	DEC	YEAR
Mean Maximum Temp. (°F)	33.5	36.8	46.9	59.1	69.7	78.4	82.4	80.7	73.3	61.6	49.2	38.4	59.2
Mean Temp. (°F)	26.0	28.7	37.7	48.5	59.1	68.0	72.2	70.6	63.4	52.1	41.5	31.5	49.9
Mean Minimum Temp. (°F)	18.4	20.5	28.4	37.9	48.6	57.6	61.9	60.5	53.5	42.5	33.8	24.5	40.7
Extreme Maximum Temp. (°F)	65	70	81	88	93	100	101	97	93	81	75	76	101
Extreme Minimum Temp. (°F)	-25	-13	-3	14	27	32	43	41	35	22	2	-16	-25
Days Maximum Temp. ≥ 90°F	0	0	0	0	0	1	4	2	0	0	0	0	7
Days Maximum Temp. ≤ 32°F	14	11	4	0	0	0	0	0	0	0	2	9	40
Days Minimum Temp. ≤ 32°F	28	23	21	9	1	0	0	0	0	3	14	25	124
Days Minimum Temp. ≤ 0°F	3	2	0	0	0	0	0	0	0	0	0	1	6
Heating Degree Days (base 65°F)	1,204	1,020	841	494	216	46	7	14	116	398	697	1,031	6,084
Cooling Degree Days (base 65°F)	0	0	1	7	43	142	249	197	72	5	0	0	716
Mean Precipitation (in.)	2.50	2.30	3.13	3.34	3.94	3.63	3.90	3.52	3.40	2.61	3.08	2.96	38.31
Maximum Precipitation (in.)	8.7	5.2	8.8	6.5	9.6	8.4	11.4	8.2	9.0	8.4	9.4	6.7	65.7
Minimum Precipitation (in.)	0.7	0.3	1.0	0.9	1.0	0.4	0.7	0.5	0.2	0.4	0.6	0.3	23.8
Maximum 24-hr. Precipitation (in.)	2.8	2.0	3.2	2.0	2.6	2.8	3.3	3.7	3.7	2.6	1.9	1.6	3.7
Days With ≥ 0.1" Precipitation	7	6	8	8	8	7	7	7	6	6	7	7	84
Days With ≥ 1.0" Precipitation	0	0	0	1	1	1	1	1	1	0	0	1	7
Mean Snowfall (in.)	12.9	9.5	9.0	2.6	trace	trace	0.0	0.0	trace	0.6	3.2	9.1	46.9
Maximum Snowfall (in.)	38	20	21	21	3	0	0	0	0	7	22	29	72
Maximum 24-hr. Snowfall (in.)	9	10	8	20	3	0	0	0	0	4	7	16	20
Days With ≥ 1.0" Snow Depth	16	12	6	1	0	0	0	0	0	0	1	9	45
Thunderstorm Days	< 1	< 1	2	4	6	7	8	6	3	1	1	< 1	38
Foggy Days	13	12	13	13	14	15	17	19	17	15	13	14	175
Predominant Sky Cover	OVR	OVR	OVR	OVR	OVR	OVR	OVR	OVR	OVR	OVR	OVR	OVR	OVR
Mean Relative Humidity 7am (%)	80	80	79	77	77	80	84	87	88	84	80	81	82
Mean Relative Humidity 4pm (%)	69	65	59	53	52	54	54	55	56	56	64	70	59
Mean Dewpoint (°F)	19	20	27	36	47	56	61	60	53	42	32	24	40
Prevailing Wind Direction	SW	WSW	W	SW	SW	SW	SW	SW	S	S	S	WSW	SW
Prevailing Wind Speed (mph)	13	12	13	12	10	9	8	8	8	9	12	13	10
Maximum Wind Gust (mph)	76	58	64	60	56	63	68	62	52	51	58	61	76

Cincinnati Covington Airport

Greater Cincinnati Airport is located on a gently rolling plateau about 12 miles southwest of downtown Cincinnati and two miles south of the Ohio River at its nearest point. The river valley is rather narrow and steep-sided varying from one to three miles in width and the river bed is 500 feet below the level of the airport.

The climate is continental with a rather wide range of temperatures from winter to summer. A precipitation maximum occurs during winter and spring with a late summer and fall minimum. On the average, the maximum snowfall occurs during January, although the heaviest 24-hour amounts have been recorded during late November and February.

The heaviest precipitation, as well as the precipitation of the longest duration, is normally associated with low pressure disturbances moving in a general southwest to northeast direction through the Ohio valley and south of the Cincinnati area.

Summers are warm and rather humid. The temperature will reach 100 degrees or more in one year out of three. However, the temperature will reach 90 degrees or higher on about 19 days each year. Winters are moderately cold with frequent periods of extensive cloudiness.

The freeze free period lasts on the average 187 days from mid-April to the latter part of October.

Cincinnati Covington Airport *Boone County*   Elevation: 866 ft.   Latitude: 39° 03' N   Longitude: 84° 40' W

	JAN	FEB	MAR	APR	MAY	JUN	JUL	AUG	SEP	OCT	NOV	DEC	YEAR
Mean Maximum Temp. (°F)	37.4	42.0	52.7	64.1	73.8	81.7	85.8	84.2	77.7	65.8	53.1	42.4	63.4
Mean Temp. (°F)	29.1	33.1	42.9	53.2	63.0	71.4	75.8	74.0	67.2	55.2	44.2	34.5	53.6
Mean Minimum Temp. (°F)	20.7	24.2	33.0	42.2	52.2	61.0	65.6	63.8	56.6	44.5	35.3	26.4	43.8
Extreme Maximum Temp. (°F)	70	74	84	89	92	102	103	101	95	87	81	75	103
Extreme Minimum Temp. (°F)	-25	-11	-11	15	30	39	48	43	31	19	1	-20	-25
Days Maximum Temp. ≥ 90°F	0	0	0	0	0	4	8	5	2	0	0	0	19
Days Maximum Temp. ≤ 32°F	11	7	1	0	0	0	0	0	0	0	1	6	26
Days Minimum Temp. ≤ 32°F	26	21	16	5	0	0	0	0	0	3	13	21	105
Days Minimum Temp. ≤ 0°F	3	1	0	0	0	0	0	0	0	0	0	1	5
Heating Degree Days (base 65°F)	1,108	894	681	363	132	17	1	2	64	315	618	941	5,136
Cooling Degree Days (base 65°F)	0	0	3	13	77	225	352	294	132	19	1	1	1,117
Mean Precipitation (in.)	2.81	2.61	3.95	4.06	4.48	4.46	3.75	3.79	2.79	3.00	3.46	3.29	42.45
Maximum Precipitation (in.)	9.4	6.7	12.2	7.2	9.5	7.4	8.4	7.7	8.6	8.6	7.5	7.9	57.6
Minimum Precipitation (in.)	0.6	0.3	1.1	1.0	1.1	0.9	1.2	0.3	0.2	0.3	0.4	0.5	28.0
Maximum 24-hr. Precipitation (in.)	4.0	2.8	5.2	2.1	3.0	3.3	3.9	3.5	3.2	4.3	3.3	2.5	5.2
Days With ≥ 0.1" Precipitation	6	6	9	8	8	7	7	7	5	6	7	7	83
Days With ≥ 1.0" Precipitation	0	1	1	1	1	1	1	1	1	1	1	1	11
Mean Snowfall (in.)	7.7	6.1	4.2	0.6	trace	trace	trace	0.0	0.0	0.4	1.3	3.3	23.6
Maximum Snowfall (in.)	32	20	13	4	trace	0	0	0	0	6	12	13	54
Maximum 24-hr. Snowfall (in.)	8	9	10	3	trace	0	0	0	0	6	9	8	10
Days With ≥ 1.0" Snow Depth	8	7	3	0	0	0	0	0	0	0	0	3	21
Thunderstorm Days	1	1	3	4	6	7	8	6	3	1	1	< 1	41
Foggy Days	13	12	12	9	12	13	16	19	16	14	12	14	162
Predominant Sky Cover	OVR	OVR	OVR	OVR	OVR	OVR	OVR	OVR	OVR	OVR	OVR	OVR	OVR
Mean Relative Humidity 7am (%)	80	79	77	76	80	82	85	88	87	83	79	80	81
Mean Relative Humidity 4pm (%)	65	60	55	50	52	53	54	53	52	51	59	65	56
Mean Dewpoint (°F)	22	24	31	40	51	60	64	63	56	44	34	26	43
Prevailing Wind Direction	SSW	SSW	SSW	SSW	SSW	SSW	SW	SSW	SSW	SSW	SSW	SSW	SSW
Prevailing Wind Speed (mph)	12	12	13	12	9	9	8	7	8	9	12	12	10
Maximum Wind Gust (mph)	71	55	64	71	59	67	83	62	54	59	56	61	83

Cleveland Hopkins Int'l Airport

Cleveland is on the south shore of Lake Erie in northeast Ohio. The metropolitan area has a lake frontage of 31 miles. The surrounding terrain is generally level except for an abrupt ridge on the eastern edge of the city which rises some 500 feet above the shore terrain. The Cuyahoga River, which flows through a rather deep but narrow north-south valley, bisects the city.

Local climate is continental in character but with strong modifying influences by Lake Erie. West to northerly winds blowing off Lake Erie tend to lower daily high temperatures in summer and raise temperatures in winter. Temperatures at Hopkins Airport which is 5 miles south of the lakeshore average from two to four degrees higher than the lakeshore in summer, while overnight low temperatures average from two to four degrees lower than the lakefront during all seasons.

In this area, summers are moderately warm and humid with occasional days when temperatures exceed 90 degrees. Winters are relatively cold and cloudy with an average of five days with sub-zero temperatures. Weather changes occur every few days from the passing of cold fronts.

The daily range in temperature is usually greatest in late summer and least in winter. Annual extremes in temperature normally occur soon after late June and December. Maximum temperatures below freezing occur most often in December, January, and February. Temperatures of 100 degrees or higher are rare. On the average, freezing temperatures in fall are first recorded in October while the last freezing temperature in spring normally occurs in April.

As is characteristic of continental climates, precipitation varies widely from year to year. However, it is normally abundant and well distributed throughout the year with spring being the wettest season. Showers and thunderstorms account for most of the rainfall during the growing season. Thunderstorms are most frequent from April through August. Snowfall may fluctuate widely. Mean annual snowfall increases from west to east in Cuyahoga County ranging from about 45 inches in the west to more than 90 inches in the extreme east.

Damaging winds of 50 mph or greater are usually associated with thunderstorms. Tornadoes, one of the most destructive of all atmospheric storms, occasionally occur in Cuyahoga County.

Cleveland Hopkins Int'l Airport *Cuyahoga County*   Elevation: 767 ft.   Latitude: 41° 24' N   Longitude: 81° 51' W

	JAN	FEB	MAR	APR	MAY	JUN	JUL	AUG	SEP	OCT	NOV	DEC	YEAR
Mean Maximum Temp. (°F)	33.1	36.4	46.3	58.0	69.2	78.0	82.4	80.4	73.6	62.0	49.9	38.7	59.0
Mean Temp. (°F)	25.9	28.7	37.6	48.1	58.9	68.0	72.5	70.9	64.1	52.9	42.5	32.0	50.2
Mean Minimum Temp. (°F)	18.7	20.9	28.9	38.2	48.5	57.9	62.5	61.3	54.5	43.7	35.0	25.3	41.3
Extreme Maximum Temp. (°F)	67	71	82	88	91	104	100	99	95	84	77	77	104
Extreme Minimum Temp. (°F)	-20	-10	-5	11	27	31	45	38	34	19	3	-15	-20
Days Maximum Temp. ≥ 90°F	0	0	0	0	0	2	4	2	1	0	0	0	9
Days Maximum Temp. ≤ 32°F	15	12	4	0	0	0	0	0	0	0	0	0	9
Days Minimum Temp. ≤ 32°F	28	23	21	9	1	0	0	0	0	0	1	9	41
Days Minimum Temp. ≤ 0°F	3	2	0	0	0	0	0	0	0	0	2	13	24	121
Days Minimum Temp. ≤ 0°F	3	2	0	0	0	0	0	0	0	0	0	1	6
Heating Degree Days (base 65°F)	1,205	1,019	844	508	227	51	6	12	106	376	670	1,016	6,040
Cooling Degree Days (base 65°F)	0	0	2	7	45	148	257	203	82	8	1	0	753
Mean Precipitation (in.)	2.43	2.27	2.96	3.34	3.42	3.87	3.57	3.56	3.77	2.75	3.42	3.12	38.48
Maximum Precipitation (in.)	7.0	4.7	6.1	6.6	9.1	9.1	9.1	9.0	7.3	9.5	8.8	8.6	53.8
Minimum Precipitation (in.)	0.4	0.5	0.8	1.2	1.0	0.6	1.2	0.5	0.7	0.6	0.8	0.7	18.8
Maximum 24-hr. Precipitation (in.)	2.5	2.0	2.8	2.1	3.4	3.0	2.7	3.5	2.3	3.4	2.2	2.4	3.5
Days With ≥ 0.1" Precipitation	7	6	8	8	8	7	6	7	7	7	8	8	87
Days With ≥ 1.0" Precipitation	0	0	0	0	1	1	1	1	1	0	1	0	6
Mean Snowfall (in.)	16.4	13.4	10.8	2.5	trace	trace	trace	0.0	trace	0.4	4.9	12.6	61.0
Maximum Snowfall (in.)	43	39	26	13	2	0	0	0	0	8	22	30	97
Maximum 24-hr. Snowfall (in.)	10	14	11	9	2	0	0	0	0	7	13	12	14
Days With ≥ 1.0" Snow Depth	17	14	7	1	0	0	0	0	0	0	3	10	52
Thunderstorm Days	< 1	< 1	2	3	5	6	6	5	3	2	1	< 1	33
Foggy Days	13	12	13	12	13	11	12	14	12	11	12	13	148
Predominant Sky Cover	OVR	OVR	OVR	OVR	OVR	OVR	OVR	OVR	OVR	OVR	OVR	OVR	OVR
Mean Relative Humidity 7am (%)	79	79	79	76	77	79	81	85	84	81	78	78	80
Mean Relative Humidity 4pm (%)	70	67	62	56	54	55	55	58	58	58	65	70	61
Mean Dewpoint (°F)	19	21	27	37	47	57	61	61	54	43	33	24	40
Prevailing Wind Direction	SW	SW	SW	S	N	SSW	SW	SW	S	SSW	SW	SW	SW
Prevailing Wind Speed (mph)	13	13	14	13	9	10	9	8	9	10	13	13	12
Maximum Wind Gust (mph)	82	64	63	78	55	77	67	51	58	54	59	71	82

Columbus-Port Columbus Int'l

Columbus is located in the center of the state and in the drainage area of the Ohio River. The airport is located at the eastern boundary of the city approximately seven miles from the center of the business district.

Four nearly parallel streams run through or adjacent to the city. The Scioto River is the principal stream and flows from the northwest into the center of the city and then flows straight south toward the Ohio River. The Olentangy River runs almost due south and empties into the Scioto just west of the business district. Alum Creek empties into the Big Walnut southeast of the city and the Big Walnut Creek empties into the Scioto a few miles downstream.

The narrow valleys associated with the streams flowing through the city supply the only variation in the micro-climate of the area. The city proper shows the typical metropolitan effect with shrubs and flowers blossoming earlier than in the immediate surroundings and in retarding light frost on clear quiet nights. Many small areas to the southeast and to the north and northeast show marked effects of air drainage as evidenced by the frequent formation of shallow ground fog at daybreak during the summer and fall months and the higher frequency of frost in the spring and fall.

The average occurrence of the last freezing temperature in the spring within the city proper is mid-April, and the first freeze in the fall is very late October, but in the immediate surroundings there is much variation. For example, at Valley Crossing located at the southeastern outskirts of the city, the average occurrence of the last 32 degree temperature in the spring is very early May, while the first 32 degree temperature in the fall is mid-October.

The records show a high frequency of calm or very low wind speeds during the late evening and early morning hours, from June through September. The rolling landscape is conducive to calm winds from the Weather Service location at the airport these are toward the northwest with the wind direction indicated as southeast, at speeds generally 4 mph or less.

Columbus is located in the area of changeable weather. Air masses from central and northwest Canada frequently invade this region. Air from the Gulf of Mexico often reaches central Ohio during the summer and to a much lesser extent in the fall and winter. There are also occasional weather changes brought about by cool outbreaks from the Hudson Bay region of Canada, especially during the spring months. At infrequent intervals the general circulation will bring showers or snow to Columbus from the Atlantic.

Columbus-Port Columbus Int'l *Franklin County*   Elevation: 807 ft.   Latitude: 39° 59' N   Longitude: 82° 53' W

	JAN	FEB	MAR	APR	MAY	JUN	JUL	AUG	SEP	OCT	NOV	DEC	YEAR
Mean Maximum Temp. (°F)	35.2	39.4	50.6	62.4	72.7	81.0	84.7	83.1	76.5	64.5	51.6	40.6	61.9
Mean Temp. (°F)	27.6	31.2	41.0	51.4	61.8	70.4	74.5	72.9	66.0	54.0	43.2	33.4	52.3
Mean Minimum Temp. (°F)	19.9	22.8	31.4	40.3	50.8	59.7	64.2	62.6	55.4	43.5	34.7	26.1	42.6
Extreme Maximum Temp. (°F)	70	74	83	88	93	101	100	101	97	86	80	76	101
Extreme Minimum Temp. (°F)	-22	-13	-6	14	30	35	43	40	33	21	5	-17	-22
Days Maximum Temp. ≥ 90°F	0	0	0	0	1	3	6	4	1	0	0	0	15
Days Maximum Temp. ≤ 32°F	12	9	2	0	0	0	0	0	0	0	1	7	31
Days Minimum Temp. ≤ 32°F	27	22	18	6	0	0	0	0	0	3	13	23	112
Days Minimum Temp. ≤ 0°F	3	1	0	0	0	0	0	0	0	0	0	1	5
Heating Degree Days (base 65°F)	1,154	950	738	412	159	25	3	6	77	345	649	973	5,491
Cooling Degree Days (base 65°F)	0	0	2	9	66	201	319	267	114	12	1	0	991
Mean Precipitation (in.)	2.46	2.16	2.90	3.30	3.88	4.15	4.60	3.72	2.91	2.29	3.21	2.89	38.47
Maximum Precipitation (in.)	8.3	5.1	9.6	6.4	9.1	9.8	12.4	8.6	6.8	5.2	10.7	7.0	53.2
Minimum Precipitation (in.)	0.6	0.3	1.0	0.7	0.9	0.7	1.0	0.6	0.5	0.1	0.6	0.5	24.5
Maximum 24-hr. Precipitation (in.)	4.8	2.1	3.4	2.0	2.1	2.5	5.1	3.2	2.7	1.7	2.4	1.7	5.1
Days With ≥ 0.1" Precipitation	6	6	8	7	8	7	7	7	5	5	7	7	80
Days With ≥ 1.0" Precipitation	0	0	0	1	1	1	1	1	1	0	1	0	7
Mean Snowfall (in.)	10.5	6.1	4.3	1.2	trace	trace	trace	0.0	trace	0.2	1.6	4.5	28.4
Maximum Snowfall (in.)	34	16	14	13	1	0	0	0	trace	5	15	17	48
Maximum 24-hr. Snowfall (in.)	7	9	9	12	1	0	0	0	trace	4	8	8	12
Days With ≥ 1.0" Snow Depth	12	8	3	0	0	0	0	0	0	0	0	4	27
Thunderstorm Days	< 1	1	2	4	6	8	8	6	3	1	1	< 1	40
Foggy Days	13	11	12	10	13	14	16	19	15	14	12	14	163
Predominant Sky Cover	OVR	OVR	OVR	OVR	OVR	OVR	OVR	SCT	OVR	OVR	OVR	OVR	OVR
Mean Relative Humidity 7am (%)	78	78	76	76	79	81	84	87	87	83	80	80	81
Mean Relative Humidity 4pm (%)	67	62	55	51	52	53	54	53	53	52	61	67	57
Mean Dewpoint (°F)	20	22	29	38	49	59	63	62	55	43	34	25	42
Prevailing Wind Direction	S	S	WNW	S	S	S	S	S	S	S	S	S	S
Prevailing Wind Speed (mph)	9	9	12	9	8	8	7	7	8	8	9	9	9
Maximum Wind Gust (mph)	69	58	62	78	76	68	67	66	62	53	53	61	78

Dayton Int'l Airport

Dayton is located near the center of the Miami River Valley, which is a nearly flat plain, 50 to 200 feet below the general elevation of the adjacent rolling country. Three Miami River tributaries, the Mad River, the Stillwater River, and Wolf Creek converge, fanwise, from the north to join the master stream within the city limits of Dayton. Heavy rains in March 1913 caused the worst flood disaster in the history of the Miami Valley. During the flood more than 400 people lost their lives and property damage amounted to $100 million. After the 1913 flood, dams were built on the streams north of Dayton, forming retarding basins. No floods have occurred at Dayton since the construction of these dams.

The elevation of the city of Dayton is about 750 feet. Terrain north of the city slopes gradually upward to about 1,100 feet at Indian Lake. Ten miles southeast of Indian Lake, near Bellefontaine, is the highest point in the state, with an elevation of about 1,550 feet. South of the city, the terrain slopes gradually downward to about 450 feet where the Miami River empties into the Ohio River.

Precipitation, which is rather evenly distributed throughout the year, and moderate temperatures help to make the Miami Valley a rich agricultural region. High relative humidities during much of the year cause some discomfort to people with allergies. Temperatures of zero or below will be experienced in about four years out of five, while 100 degrees or higher will be recorded in about one year out of five. Extreme temperatures are usually of short duration. The downward slope of about 700 feet in the 163 miles of the Miami River may have some moderating influence on the winter temperatures in the Miami Valley.

Based on the 1951-1980 period, the average last occurrence in the spring of freezing temperatures is mid-April, and the average first occurrence in the autumn is late October.

Cold, polar air, flowing across the Great Lakes, causes much cloudiness during the winter, and is accompanied by frequent snow flurries. These add little to the total snowfall.

Dayton Int'l Airport *Montgomery County*   Elevation: 997 ft.   Latitude: 39° 54' N   Longitude: 84° 13' W

	JAN	FEB	MAR	APR	MAY	JUN	JUL	AUG	SEP	OCT	NOV	DEC	YEAR
Mean Maximum Temp. (°F)	34.3	38.9	49.9	61.9	72.3	81.1	85.1	83.1	76.4	64.2	51.0	39.8	61.5
Mean Temp. (°F)	26.6	30.5	40.5	51.2	61.8	70.7	74.8	72.8	65.7	53.9	42.8	32.4	52.0
Mean Minimum Temp. (°F)	18.9	22.1	31.0	40.5	51.2	60.3	64.5	62.4	54.9	43.6	34.4	24.9	42.4
Extreme Maximum Temp. (°F)	66	73	82	88	92	102	102	102	96	86	79	72	102
Extreme Minimum Temp. (°F)	-25	-12	-7	15	28	40	44	41	32	23	5	-20	-25
Days Maximum Temp. ≥ 90°F	0	0	0	0	0	3	7	4	1	0	0	0	15
Days Maximum Temp. ≤ 32°F	13	9	3	0	0	0	0	0	0	0	1	8	34
Days Minimum Temp. ≤ 32°F	27	22	18	6	0	0	0	0	0	3	14	24	114
Days Minimum Temp. ≤ 0°F	3	2	0	0	0	0	0	0	0	0	0	1	6
Heating Degree Days (base 65°F)	1,184	967	755	417	161	22	2	6	85	349	662	1,006	5,616
Cooling Degree Days (base 65°F)	0	0	2	9	63	201	319	258	109	12	1	0	974
Mean Precipitation (in.)	2.53	2.26	3.29	4.07	4.16	4.21	3.73	3.44	2.59	2.70	3.28	3.06	39.32
Maximum Precipitation (in.)	9.9	5.8	7.6	6.8	9.0	10.9	8.5	8.0	5.7	6.3	8.1	10.0	59.8
Minimum Precipitation (in.)	0.3	0.2	1.1	0.6	1.5	0.3	0.5	0.3	0.3	0.2	0.5	0.4	24.2
Maximum 24-hr. Precipitation (in.)	4.2	2.6	2.9	3.1	3.2	3.8	3.2	3.4	2.6	3.5	2.8	2.8	4.2
Days With ≥ 0.1" Precipitation	6	5	8	8	8	7	7	6	5	6	7	7	80
Days With ≥ 1.0" Precipitation	0	0	0	1	1	1	1	1	1	0	1	1	8
Mean Snowfall (in.)	9.7	6.6	4.7	0.8	trace	0.0	trace	0.0	0.0	0.4	1.5	4.4	28.1
Maximum Snowfall (in.)	40	18	14	5	trace	0	0	0	0	6	13	16	53
Maximum 24-hr. Snowfall (in.)	12	7	11	5	trace	0	0	0	0	5	8	6	12
Days With ≥ 1.0" Snow Depth	12	9	3	0	0	0	0	0	0	0	1	5	30
Thunderstorm Days	< 1	1	2	4	6	7	8	6	3	2	1	< 1	40
Foggy Days	15	12	14	12	13	13	15	18	15	14	14	15	170
Predominant Sky Cover	OVR	OVR	OVR	OVR	OVR	OVR	OVR	OVR	OVR	OVR	OVR	OVR	OVR
Mean Relative Humidity 7am (%)	80	79	79	77	78	80	83	86	87	83	81	81	81
Mean Relative Humidity 4pm (%)	68	64	59	53	52	52	53	53	52	52	63	69	57
Mean Dewpoint (°F)	20	22	30	39	49	58	63	62	54	43	33	25	42
Prevailing Wind Direction	W	WNW	WNW	SSW	SSW	SSW	SW	SW	SSW	SSW	SSW	SSW	SSW
Prevailing Wind Speed (mph)	13	13	13	13	12	10	9	9	9	10	13	13	12
Maximum Wind Gust (mph)	69	52	67	63	60	60	71	61	48	46	54	62	71

Mansfield Lahm Municipal Airport

Mansfield is in the north central highlands at the geographical and climatological junction of central Ohio, northwest Ohio, and northeast Ohio. The station is on a plateau 3 miles north of the city of Mansfield and surrounded by rolling open farmland. The general elevation ranges from around 1,300 to 1,400 feet above sea level with the 1,000-foot contour east to west some 15 miles to the north. The climate is continental, with the modifying effects of Lake Erie most pronounced in winter. Lake Erie is just 38 miles due north.

The lake influence, plus the elevation, produce cloudy skies and considerable snow shower activity from late November into April with any wind flow from northwest through northeast. Because of this, any windshift with a cold frontal passage in winter does not bring the clearing skies, indeed, more snow is often measured from the flurry activity behind the front than from the pre-frontal conditions. A frozen Lake Erie will allow clearing skies, but an open lake dictates overcast and snow flurries. Usually the lake is open enough to set off the flurries and cloudy conditions. The major snow producer will be an intense storm moving out of the southwest with the Gulf of Mexico moisture available. Snow cover is almost constant from December through March due to almost daily snow flurries, but the depth of cover is rarely more than 8 inches. Daytime winter temperatures are not above the freezing mark too often.

Spring is a short period of rapid transition from hard winter to summer conditions. April usually brings abundant shower activity and the crops and vegetation get a quick start.

Summer is a pleasant season with low humidities and no extremely high temperatures. Rarely does the temperature climb above the 90 degree point. Thunderstorms average about once every three days during the season from June through September. Highest winds are associated with the heavier thunderstorms, and while hail does not occur often, it is of major concern to the applegrowers in the area. Flooding problems are confined to the flash-flood type on the small streams in the area.

The growing season is normally about 153 days. Autumn usually produces many clear warm days and cool invigorating nights. Ground fog is at a maximum incidence during the autumn. Little rainfall occurs to interfere with harvest time and county fair time.

Mansfield Lahm Municipal Airport *Richland County*   Elevation: 1,292 ft.   Latitude: 40° 49' N   Longitude: 82° 31' W

	JAN	FEB	MAR	APR	MAY	JUN	JUL	AUG	SEP	OCT	NOV	DEC	YEAR
Mean Maximum Temp. (°F)	32.4	35.8	46.4	58.6	69.5	78.0	82.1	80.0	73.4	61.8	48.9	37.6	58.7
Mean Temp. (°F)	25.0	28.0	37.5	48.4	59.1	67.9	72.2	70.4	63.6	52.3	41.3	30.7	49.7
Mean Minimum Temp. (°F)	17.6	20.1	28.4	38.1	48.7	57.7	62.2	60.7	53.7	42.7	33.6	23.8	40.6
Extreme Maximum Temp. (°F)	65	68	82	86	90	101	100	97	92	84	76	73	101
Extreme Minimum Temp. (°F)	-22	-11	-6	8	26	37	43	42	33	20	2	-17	-22
Days Maximum Temp. ≥ 90°F	0	0	0	0	0	1	3	1	1	0	0	0	6
Days Maximum Temp. ≤ 32°F	16	12	4	0	0	0	0	0	0	0	2	10	44
Days Minimum Temp. ≤ 32°F	28	24	21	9	1	0	0	0	0	4	15	25	127
Days Minimum Temp. ≤ 0°F	4	2	0	0	0	0	0	0	0	0	0	1	7
Heating Degree Days (base 65°F)	1,234	1,038	848	499	219	50	7	17	115	396	706	1,056	6,185
Cooling Degree Days (base 65°F)	0	0	2	7	43	143	238	185	73	7	0	0	698
Mean Precipitation (in.)	2.57	2.11	3.33	4.20	4.42	4.42	4.30	4.45	3.51	2.70	3.80	3.24	43.05
Maximum Precipitation (in.)	11.5	5.4	7.0	7.0	8.8	10.0	13.2	8.6	7.8	6.4	12.8	11.2	67.2
Minimum Precipitation (in.)	0.4	0.3	1.2	0.8	1.1	0.6	0.9	0.6	0.7	0.4	0.7	0.7	21.8
Maximum 24-hr. Precipitation (in.)	2.7	2.8	2.4	2.3	2.6	3.7	3.4	3.8	2.3	3.3	3.1	2.6	3.8
Days With ≥ 0.1" Precipitation	6	5	8	9	9	7	7	7	6	6	7	7	84
Days With ≥ 1.0" Precipitation	0	0	1	1	1	1	1	1	1	0	1	1	9
Mean Snowfall (in.)	12.9	9.8	6.9	2.0	trace	trace	0.0	0.0	trace	0.6	2.5	8.6	43.3
Maximum Snowfall (in.)	42	18	17	13	1	0	0	0	0	10	12	23	59
Maximum 24-hr. Snowfall (in.)	10	9	8	12	1	0	0	0	0	8	5	12	12
Days With ≥ 1.0" Snow Depth	17	14	6	1	0	0	0	0	0	0	2	10	50
Thunderstorm Days	< 1	< 1	2	3	5	6	7	6	3	1	1	< 1	34
Foggy Days	13	12	14	13	14	13	14	17	15	13	13	15	166
Predominant Sky Cover	OVR	OVR	OVR	OVR	OVR	OVR	SCT	SCT	OVR	OVR	OVR	OVR	OVR
Mean Relative Humidity 7am (%)	82	81	81	78	78	81	83	87	87	83	82	83	82
Mean Relative Humidity 4pm (%)	72	69	64	56	55	56	56	57	58	56	67	74	62
Mean Dewpoint (°F)	20	21	28	37	47	58	62	61	54	42	33	24	40
Prevailing Wind Direction	WSW	WSW	WSW	WSW	SSW	SSW	SW	SSW	S	S	SW	WSW	WSW
Prevailing Wind Speed (mph)	15	14	15	14	13	12	10	10	9	10	14	14	13
Maximum Wind Gust (mph)	62	59	62	68	60	68	81	69	61	53	69	69	81

Toledo Express Airport

Toledo is located on the western end of Lake Erie at the mouth of the Maumee River. Except for a bank up from the river about 30 feet, the terrain is generally level with only a slight slope toward the river and Lake Erie. The city has quite a diversified industrial section and excellent harbor facilities, making it a large transportation center for rail, water, and motor freight. Generally rich agricultural land is found in the surrounding area, especially up the Maumee Valley toward the Indiana state line.

Rainfall is usually sufficient for general agriculture. The terrain is level and drainage rather poor, therefore, a little less than the normal precipitation during the growing season is better than excessive amounts. Snowfall is generally light in this area, distributed throughout the winter from November to March with frequent thaws.

The nearness of Lake Erie and the other Great Lakes has a moderating effect on the temperature, and extremes are seldom recorded. On average, only fifteen days a year experience temperatures of 90 degrees or higher, and only eight days when it drops to zero or lower. The growing season averages 160 days, but has ranged from over 220 to less than 125 days.

Humidity is rather high throughout the year in this area, and there is an excessive amount of cloudiness. In the winter months the sun shines during only about 30 percent of the daylight hours. December and January, the cloudiest months, sometimes have as little as 16 percent of the possible hours of sunshine.

Severe windstorms, causing more than minor damage, occur infrequently. There are on the average twenty-three days per year having a sustained wind velocity of 32 mph or more.

Flooding in the Toledo area is produced by several factors. Heavy rains of one inch or more will cause a sudden rise in creeks and drainage ditches to the point of overflow. The western shores of Lake Erie are subject to flooding when the lake level is high and prolonged periods of east to northeast winds prevail.

Toledo Express Airport *Lucas County*   Elevation: 666 ft.   Latitude: 41° 35' N   Longitude: 83° 48' W

	JAN	FEB	MAR	APR	MAY	JUN	JUL	AUG	SEP	OCT	NOV	DEC	YEAR
Mean Maximum Temp. (°F)	30.9	34.5	45.8	58.9	70.9	79.9	84.0	81.7	74.6	62.3	48.4	36.4	59.0
Mean Temp. (°F)	23.5	26.5	36.6	48.0	59.3	68.4	72.8	70.6	63.2	51.4	40.2	29.3	49.1
Mean Minimum Temp. (°F)	16.0	18.4	27.3	37.1	47.6	56.9	61.5	59.4	51.8	40.5	31.9	22.2	39.2
Extreme Maximum Temp. (°F)	65	71	81	88	94	104	104	99	98	87	78	69	104
Extreme Minimum Temp. (°F)	-20	-14	-6	8	25	32	40	34	26	15	5	-19	-20
Days Maximum Temp. ≥ 90°F	0	0	0	0	1	3	6	3	1	0	0	0	14
Days Maximum Temp. ≤ 32°F	17	12	4	0	0	0	0	0	0	0	2	10	45
Days Minimum Temp. ≤ 32°F	29	25	22	10	1	0	0	0	0	6	17	26	136
Days Minimum Temp. ≤ 0°F	5	3	0	0	0	0	0	0	0	0	0	1	9
Heating Degree Days (base 65°F)	1,282	1,081	875	510	216	44	6	16	125	421	738	1,099	6,413
Cooling Degree Days (base 65°F)	0	0	1	6	47	161	270	206	77	6	0	0	774
Mean Precipitation (in.)	1.93	1.88	2.65	3.27	3.05	3.77	2.93	3.15	2.87	2.32	2.80	2.61	33.23
Maximum Precipitation (in.)	4.6	5.4	5.7	6.1	5.1	8.5	6.8	8.5	8.1	5.5	6.9	6.8	40.8
Minimum Precipitation (in.)	0.3	0.3	0.6	0.9	1.0	0.3	0.3	0.4	0.6	0.3	0.5	0.5	22.0
Maximum 24-hr. Precipitation (in.)	1.5	2.6	2.6	2.9	1.7	3.1	4.3	2.4	3.3	2.9	2.7	3.5	4.3
Days With ≥ 0.1" Precipitation	5	5	7	8	7	7	6	6	6	6	6	7	76
Days With ≥ 1.0" Precipitation	0	0	0	0	1	1	1	1	1	0	0	0	5
Mean Snowfall (in.)	10.9	8.2	5.7	1.4	trace	trace	trace	trace	trace	0.2	2.7	8.1	37.2
Maximum Snowfall (in.)	31	17	18	12	1	0	0	0	trace	2	18	24	72
Maximum 24-hr. Snowfall (in.)	10	8	9	7	1	0	0	0	trace	2	7	14	14
Days With ≥ 1.0" Snow Depth	17	14	5	1	0	0	0	0	0	0	1	10	48
Thunderstorm Days	< 1	1	2	4	5	7	7	6	4	1	1	< 1	38
Foggy Days	13	11	14	12	12	11	14	18	15	13	14	15	162
Predominant Sky Cover	OVR	OVR	OVR	OVR	OVR	OVR	SCT	SCT	OVR	OVR	OVR	OVR	OVR
Mean Relative Humidity 7am (%)	80	80	81	80	80	82	86	91	91	86	83	83	84
Mean Relative Humidity 4pm (%)	68	65	59	53	51	52	53	56	54	55	65	72	58
Mean Dewpoint (°F)	17	19	27	36	47	57	62	61	54	42	32	23	40
Prevailing Wind Direction	WSW	WSW	ENE	WSW	WSW	SW	SW	SW	SW	SW	WSW	WSW	WSW
Prevailing Wind Speed (mph)	13	13	12	13	12	9	8	8	9	10	13	13	12
Maximum Wind Gust (mph)	62	52	64	63	58	59	66	75	54	49	55	56	75

Youngstown Municipal Airport

The Youngstown Municipal Airport is located in northeastern Ohio approximately eight miles north of the city of Youngstown in Trumbull County. Airport elevation is 1,178 feet, about 200 feet higher than most communities in the Mahoning and Shenango River Valleys. There are numerous natural and man-made lakes in the region, including Lake Erie, 45 miles to the north. Drainage from the area flows southward through the Mahoning and Shenango Rivers which join to form the Beaver River at New Castle, Pennsylvania. The Beaver empties into the Ohio River at Rochester, Pennsylvania.

This entire area experiences frequent outbreaks of cold Canadian air masses which may be modified by passage over Lake Erie. This effect produces widespread cloudiness especially during the cool months of the year. The winter months are characterized by persistent cloudiness and intermittent snow flurries. The daily temperature range during most winter days is quite small. During most winters, the bulk of the snow falls as flurries of 2 inches or less per occurrence, although several snowstorms per year will produce amounts in the four to 10 inch range.

Destructive storms seldom occur, and tornadoes are not common. During recent years flood control projects have all but eliminated the threat of serious river flooding. Flash flooding of small streams and creeks rarely affects residential areas. Certain communities have well known areas of urban flooding during periods of prolonged heavy thunderstorms.

The climate of the Youngstown district has had an important role in the growth and development of this industrial area. Temperatures seldom reach extreme values especially during the summer months. However, high humidity during most days of the year tends to accentuate the temperature. Rainfall, reasonably well distributed throughout the year, provides a more than adequate supply of water for agriculture, industrial, and residential use.

Based on the 1951-1980 period, the average first occurrence of 32 degrees Fahrenheit in the fall is October 14 and the average last occurrence in the spring is May 6.

Youngstown Municipal Airport *Trumbull County*   Elevation: 1,177 ft.   Latitude: 41° 15' N   Longitude: 80° 40' W

	JAN	FEB	MAR	APR	MAY	JUN	JUL	AUG	SEP	OCT	NOV	DEC	YEAR
Mean Maximum Temp. (°F)	31.9	35.5	45.7	58.3	69.4	77.6	81.9	80.1	72.5	60.9	48.3	37.3	58.3
Mean Temp. (°F)	24.7	27.5	36.5	47.7	58.1	66.4	70.7	69.1	62.0	51.1	40.9	30.7	48.8
Mean Minimum Temp. (°F)	17.5	19.5	27.3	37.0	46.7	55.2	59.5	58.1	51.4	41.4	33.5	24.0	39.3
Extreme Maximum Temp. (°F)	67	71	82	88	90	99	100	97	92	83	78	76	100
Extreme Minimum Temp. (°F)	-22	-14	-10	14	24	30	42	32	29	20	1	-12	-22
Days Maximum Temp. ≥ 90°F	0	0	0	0	0	1	3	2	0	0	0	0	6
Days Maximum Temp. ≤ 32°F	16	12	5	0	0	0	0	0	0	0	2	10	45
Days Minimum Temp. ≤ 32°F	28	24	22	11	1	0	0	0	0	5	15	25	131
Days Minimum Temp. ≤ 0°F	3	2	0	0	0	0	0	0	0	0	0	1	6
Heating Degree Days (base 65°F)	1,242	1,052	877	522	244	67	13	25	144	427	716	1,057	6,386
Cooling Degree Days (base 65°F)	0	0	2	7	35	118	208	163	59	6	1	0	599
Mean Precipitation (in.)	2.30	2.03	3.06	3.27	3.42	3.91	4.12	3.38	3.87	2.50	3.17	2.95	37.98
Maximum Precipitation (in.)	7.6	5.3	6.2	6.4	6.2	10.7	9.7	7.9	6.1	8.6	9.1	6.5	48.6
Minimum Precipitation (in.)	0.7	0.5	1.1	1.0	0.8	0.7	1.6	0.5	0.3	0.4	0.9	0.9	23.8
Maximum 24-hr. Precipitation (in.)	2.6	1.9	2.0	1.6	1.9	3.6	3.8	3.5	3.0	4.3	2.7	1.9	4.3
Days With ≥ 0.1" Precipitation	6	6	8	8	8	8	7	6	7	6	7	7	84
Days With ≥ 1.0" Precipitation	0	0	0	1	1	1	1	1	1	0	0	0	6
Mean Snowfall (in.)	14.1	10.5	10.7	2.2	trace	trace	trace	0.0	trace	0.6	4.5	12.1	54.7
Maximum Snowfall (in.)	36	23	31	12	5	0	0	0	trace	8	31	30	91
Maximum 24-hr. Snowfall (in.)	17	9	15	12	5	0	0	0	trace	5	17	12	17
Days With ≥ 1.0" Snow Depth	18	14	7	1	0	0	0	0	0	0	2	11	53
Thunderstorm Days	< 1	< 1	2	3	4	7	7	5	3	1	1	< 1	33
Foggy Days	13	12	14	13	15	16	17	20	17	15	13	14	179
Predominant Sky Cover	OVR	OVR	OVR	OVR	OVR	OVR	OVR	OVR	OVR	OVR	OVR	OVR	OVR
Mean Relative Humidity 7am (%)	81	80	80	77	79	82	85	88	89	85	81	82	82
Mean Relative Humidity 4pm (%)	70	66	60	54	52	54	55	55	57	57	66	72	60
Mean Dewpoint (°F)	18	19	26	36	46	56	60	60	53	42	32	23	39
Prevailing Wind Direction	WSW	WSW	W	SW	SW	SW	SW	SW	SW	SW	SW	WSW	SW
Prevailing Wind Speed (mph)	14	13	13	13	12	9	9	8	9	10	12	14	12
Maximum Wind Gust (mph)	67	54	78	75	70	58	66	58	62	51	53	62	78

Ashland 2 SW *Ashland County*   Elevation: 1,263 ft.   Latitude: 40° 50' N   Longitude: 82° 21' W

	JAN	FEB	MAR	APR	MAY	JUN	JUL	AUG	SEP	OCT	NOV	DEC	YEAR
Mean Maximum Temp. (°F)	32.3	36.1	46.5	59.2	70.2	78.9	83.1	81.0	74.4	62.3	48.8	37.7	59.2
Mean Temp. (°F)	23.9	27.1	36.3	47.5	58.5	67.4	71.5	69.3	62.7	51.2	40.0	29.8	48.8
Mean Minimum Temp. (°F)	15.5	18.0	26.1	35.7	46.6	55.8	59.8	57.6	50.9	40.0	31.2	21.8	38.3
Extreme Maximum Temp. (°F)	65	69	80	87	90	100	99	96	94	85	76	74	100
Extreme Minimum Temp. (°F)	-23	-16	-15	6	25	31	39	37	29	20	0	-18	-23
Days Maximum Temp. ≥ 90°F	0	0	0	0	0	2	5	2	1	0	0	0	10
Days Maximum Temp. ≤ 32°F	16	11	4	0	0	0	0	0	0	0	2	10	43
Days Minimum Temp. ≤ 32°F	29	25	23	12	1	0	0	0	1	7	18	27	143
Days Minimum Temp. ≤ 0°F	5	3	1	0	0	0	0	0	0	0	0	1	10
Heating Degree Days (base 65°F)	1,268	1,064	883	525	235	57	12	23	133	427	744	1,086	6,457
Cooling Degree Days (base 65°F)	0	0	1	5	35	133	221	159	63	5	0	0	622
Mean Precipitation (in.)	2.36	2.10	2.80	3.55	4.05	3.96	4.22	4.09	3.40	2.57	3.17	2.66	38.93
Days With ≥ 0.1" Precipitation	6	5	7	8	9	8	7	6	6	6	7	7	82
Days With ≥ 1.0" Precipitation	0	0	0	1	1	1	1	1	1	0	1	0	7
Mean Snowfall (in.)	10.0	7.9	5.4	1.5	trace	0.0	0.0	0.0	0.0	trace	2.1	7.1	34.0
Days With ≥ 1.0" Snow Depth	16	13	5	1	0	0	0	0	0	0	2	9	46

Barnesville *Belmont County*   Elevation: 1,240 ft.   Latitude: 39° 59' N   Longitude: 81° 09' W

	JAN	FEB	MAR	APR	MAY	JUN	JUL	AUG	SEP	OCT	NOV	DEC	YEAR
Mean Maximum Temp. (°F)	34.5	38.2	48.8	60.4	70.3	78.3	82.1	80.8	74.5	62.8	50.8	40.0	60.1
Mean Temp. (°F)	25.8	28.8	38.3	48.7	58.8	67.2	71.4	69.8	63.2	51.5	41.5	31.8	49.7
Mean Minimum Temp. (°F)	17.0	19.2	27.8	36.9	47.2	56.1	60.6	58.8	51.8	40.0	32.2	23.6	39.3
Extreme Maximum Temp. (°F)	71	72	82	87	90	96	100	96	94	83	77	75	100
Extreme Minimum Temp. (°F)	-23	-20	-5	13	22	31	42	38	28	16	0	-17	-23
Days Maximum Temp. ≥ 90°F	0	0	0	0	0	1	2	2	1	0	0	0	6
Days Maximum Temp. ≤ 32°F	14	10	3	0	0	0	0	0	0	0	1	8	36
Days Minimum Temp. ≤ 32°F	28	24	22	11	2	0	0	0	0	6	16	25	134
Days Minimum Temp. ≤ 0°F	4	2	0	0	0	0	0	0	0	0	0	1	7
Heating Degree Days (base 65°F)	1,208	1,015	821	491	221	51	9	18	118	417	698	1,022	6,089
Cooling Degree Days (base 65°F)	0	0	2	8	37	136	237	185	69	5	0	0	679
Mean Precipitation (in.)	3.01	2.69	3.53	3.85	4.35	4.88	4.73	3.90	3.54	2.97	3.69	3.20	44.34
Days With ≥ 0.1" Precipitation	7	6	8	9	9	8	8	7	6	6	8	8	90
Days With ≥ 1.0" Precipitation	0	0	1	1	1	1	1	1	1	1	1	0	9
Mean Snowfall (in.)	11.6	7.6	5.1	1.2	trace	0.0	0.0	trace	0.0	trace	1.7	5.7	32.9
Days With ≥ 1.0" Snow Depth	14	12	5	0	0	0	0	0	0	0	2	7	40

Bellefontaine *Logan County*   Elevation: 1,184 ft.   Latitude: 40° 21' N   Longitude: 83° 46' W

	JAN	FEB	MAR	APR	MAY	JUN	JUL	AUG	SEP	OCT	NOV	DEC	YEAR
Mean Maximum Temp. (°F)	32.3	37.1	48.1	60.6	71.5	79.6	83.3	81.5	75.9	63.5	49.7	38.2	60.1
Mean Temp. (°F)	24.6	28.6	38.5	49.8	60.8	69.2	73.0	71.3	64.9	53.2	41.3	30.8	50.5
Mean Minimum Temp. (°F)	16.9	20.0	29.0	39.0	50.0	58.7	62.6	61.0	53.9	42.8	33.0	23.2	40.8
Extreme Maximum Temp. (°F)	64	71	82	87	90	101	99	101	95	85	77	71	101
Extreme Minimum Temp. (°F)	-27	-13	-12	9	25	37	45	39	30	17	5	-22	-27
Days Maximum Temp. ≥ 90°F	0	0	0	0	0	2	4	2	1	0	0	0	9
Days Maximum Temp. ≤ 32°F	15	11	3	0	0	0	0	0	0	0	2	9	40
Days Minimum Temp. ≤ 32°F	28	24	21	8	1	0	0	0	0	5	16	25	128
Days Minimum Temp. ≤ 0°F	4	2	0	0	0	0	0	0	0	0	0	1	7
Heating Degree Days (base 65°F)	1,245	1,022	814	457	180	35	4	11	94	370	704	1,054	5,990
Cooling Degree Days (base 65°F)	0	0	1	6	54	169	265	217	94	11	0	0	817
Mean Precipitation (in.)	2.25	1.98	2.75	3.56	3.95	3.97	3.92	3.42	2.67	2.44	3.06	2.95	36.92
Days With ≥ 0.1" Precipitation	6	5	7	8	8	7	7	6	5	6	7	7	79
Days With ≥ 1.0" Precipitation	0	0	0	1	1	1	1	1	1	0	0	1	7
Mean Snowfall (in.)	*6.9*	4.1	1.7	0.4	trace	0.0	0.0	0.0	0.0	0.2	0.8	*3.7*	*17.8*
Days With ≥ 1.0" Snow Depth	11	6	2	0	0	0	0	0	0	0	0	4	23

Bowling Green WWTP *Wood County*   Elevation: 672 ft.   Latitude: 41° 23' N   Longitude: 83° 37' W

	JAN	FEB	MAR	APR	MAY	JUN	JUL	AUG	SEP	OCT	NOV	DEC	YEAR
Mean Maximum Temp. (°F)	31.3	35.4	46.5	59.6	71.7	81.1	84.6	82.2	76.0	63.5	49.2	37.2	59.8
Mean Temp. (°F)	23.8	27.4	37.0	48.4	60.0	69.6	73.3	70.8	64.1	52.4	40.7	29.9	49.8
Mean Minimum Temp. (°F)	16.2	19.3	27.5	37.2	48.3	58.2	61.9	59.4	52.2	41.3	32.2	22.6	39.7
Extreme Maximum Temp. (°F)	64	71	80	88	92	104	101	98	96	88	78	70	104
Extreme Minimum Temp. (°F)	-20	-13	-7	8	25	36	41	38	30	21	6	-19	-20
Days Maximum Temp. ≥ 90°F	0	0	0	0	1	4	6	3	1	0	0	0	15
Days Maximum Temp. ≤ 32°F	16	12	4	0	0	0	0	0	0	0	1	9	42
Days Minimum Temp. ≤ 32°F	29	25	23	10	1	0	0	0	0	5	17	26	136
Days Minimum Temp. ≤ 0°F	4	2	0	0	0	0	0	0	0	0	0	1	7
Heating Degree Days (base 65°F)	1,272	1,056	860	498	200	33	4	14	107	393	722	1,080	6,239
Cooling Degree Days (base 65°F)	0	0	1	7	49	177	269	197	80	9	0	0	789
Mean Precipitation (in.)	1.73	1.59	2.40	3.27	3.53	3.52	3.70	3.28	2.60	2.50	2.69	2.33	33.14
Days With ≥ 0.1" Precipitation	5	4	6	8	7	7	7	6	5	6	6	6	73
Days With ≥ 1.0" Precipitation	0	0	0	0	1	1	1	1	1	0	0	0	5
Mean Snowfall (in.)	7.2	5.4	3.1	0.7	trace	0.0	0.0	0.0	0.0	trace	0.7	4.8	21.9
Days With ≥ 1.0" Snow Depth	14	12	4	0	0	0	0	0	0	0	1	6	37

Bucyrus *Crawford County*   Elevation: 954 ft.   Latitude: 40° 49' N   Longitude: 82° 58' W

	JAN	FEB	MAR	APR	MAY	JUN	JUL	AUG	SEP	OCT	NOV	DEC	YEAR
Mean Maximum Temp. (°F)	31.5	35.1	45.8	58.7	70.2	79.1	83.1	81.0	74.5	62.0	48.6	37.1	58.9
Mean Temp. (°F)	23.8	26.7	36.3	47.7	58.7	68.0	72.0	69.9	63.0	51.3	40.2	29.8	48.9
Mean Minimum Temp. (°F)	16.0	18.2	26.7	36.6	47.2	56.8	61.0	58.8	51.4	40.4	31.8	22.5	38.9
Extreme Maximum Temp. (°F)	64	69	81	88	91	102	100	99	93	85	76	72	102
Extreme Minimum Temp. (°F)	-26	-18	-11	10	26	37	43	39	27	18	3	-18	-26
Days Maximum Temp. ≥ 90°F	0	0	0	0	0	2	5	2	1	0	0	0	10
Days Maximum Temp. ≤ 32°F	16	12	4	0	0	0	0	0	0	0	2	10	44
Days Minimum Temp. ≤ 32°F	29	25	23	11	1	0	0	0	0	6	17	26	138
Days Minimum Temp. ≤ 0°F	4	3	0	0	0	0	0	0	0	0	0	1	8
Heating Degree Days (base 65°F)	1,271	1,077	885	520	230	49	9	20	128	425	736	1,085	6,435
Cooling Degree Days (base 65°F)	0	0	1	6	41	149	245	185	72	7	0	0	706
Mean Precipitation (in.)	2.24	1.90	2.67	3.52	3.95	4.40	4.48	3.83	3.16	2.37	3.10	2.76	38.38
Days With ≥ 0.1" Precipitation	6	5	7	8	8	7	7	6	6	6	7	7	80
Days With ≥ 1.0" Precipitation	0	0	0	1	1	1	1	1	1	0	1	0	7
Mean Snowfall (in.)	7.9	5.9	3.6	0.8	trace	0.0	0.0	0.0	0.0	trace	1.0	4.0	23.2
Days With ≥ 1.0" Snow Depth	15	10	4	0	0	0	0	0	0	0	1	6	36

Cadiz *Harrison County*   Elevation: 1,259 ft.   Latitude: 40° 16' N   Longitude: 81° 00' W

	JAN	FEB	MAR	APR	MAY	JUN	JUL	AUG	SEP	OCT	NOV	DEC	YEAR
Mean Maximum Temp. (°F)	34.9	39.3	49.9	61.8	71.3	79.0	82.7	81.5	75.6	64.0	51.0	40.4	61.0
Mean Temp. (°F)	27.0	30.4	39.9	50.6	60.6	68.6	72.6	71.3	65.0	53.4	42.4	32.6	51.2
Mean Minimum Temp. (°F)	19.1	21.5	29.7	39.3	49.8	58.1	62.5	61.1	54.5	42.8	33.8	24.8	41.4
Extreme Maximum Temp. (°F)	69	72	81	89	89	97	101	96	94	84	79	75	101
Extreme Minimum Temp. (°F)	-24	-10	-6	14	23	33	42	40	33	21	1	-17	-24
Days Maximum Temp. ≥ 90°F	0	0	0	0	0	1	3	2	1	0	0	0	7
Days Maximum Temp. ≤ 32°F	13	9	3	0	0	0	0	0	0	0	1	8	34
Days Minimum Temp. ≤ 32°F	28	23	20	8	1	0	0	0	0	4	14	25	123
Days Minimum Temp. ≤ 0°F	3	2	0	0	0	0	0	0	0	0	0	1	6
Heating Degree Days (base 65°F)	1,171	970	775	439	180	36	5	9	87	361	670	997	5,700
Cooling Degree Days (base 65°F)	0	0	2	11	47	150	258	211	91	10	1	0	781
Mean Precipitation (in.)	2.79	2.38	3.18	3.39	4.09	4.37	4.43	4.13	3.23	2.59	3.28	3.00	40.86
Days With ≥ 0.1" Precipitation	7	6	8	9	9	8	8	7	6	6	7	7	88
Days With ≥ 1.0" Precipitation	0	0	0	0	1	1	1	1	1	0	0	0	5
Mean Snowfall (in.)	11.5	6.5	5.1	1.2	0.0	0.0	0.0	0.0	0.0	trace	1.7	*6.3*	*32.3*
Days With ≥ 1.0" Snow Depth	na	na	na	0	0	0	0	0	0	0	*1*	na	na

Cambridge *Guernsey County*   Elevation: 797 ft.   Latitude: 40° 01' N   Longitude: 81° 35' W

	JAN	FEB	MAR	APR	MAY	JUN	JUL	AUG	SEP	OCT	NOV	DEC	YEAR
Mean Maximum Temp. (°F)	37.4	41.9	52.9	65.0	74.3	81.7	85.1	83.6	77.4	65.9	53.2	42.4	63.4
Mean Temp. (°F)	28.7	32.2	41.7	52.2	61.6	69.6	73.6	72.2	65.8	53.9	43.6	34.1	52.4
Mean Minimum Temp. (°F)	20.1	22.5	30.5	39.3	48.8	57.5	62.1	60.8	54.0	41.9	33.9	25.7	41.4
Extreme Maximum Temp. (°F)	71	73	83	90	92	99	102	99	96	85	79	77	102
Extreme Minimum Temp. (°F)	-32	-16	-3	14	25	30	42	37	32	19	0	-17	-32
Days Maximum Temp. ≥ 90°F	0	0	0	0	0	3	6	4	1	0	0	0	14
Days Maximum Temp. ≤ 32°F	10	7	1	0	0	0	0	0	0	0	0	6	24
Days Minimum Temp. ≤ 32°F	27	22	19	8	1	0	0	0	0	5	14	23	119
Days Minimum Temp. ≤ 0°F	3	2	0	0	0	0	0	0	0	0	0	1	6
Heating Degree Days (base 65°F)	1,118	920	717	389	154	26	3	7	77	347	638	952	5,348
Cooling Degree Days (base 65°F)	0	0	2	12	56	183	301	247	108	10	0	0	919
Mean Precipitation (in.)	2.67	2.25	2.99	3.39	3.96	4.07	4.32	3.87	2.97	2.61	3.25	2.84	39.19
Days With ≥ 0.1" Precipitation	7	6	8	7	8	8	8	7	6	6	7	7	85
Days With ≥ 1.0" Precipitation	0	0	0	1	1	1	1	1	1	0	1	0	7
Mean Snowfall (in.)	7.4	4.1	2.9	0.6	trace	0.0	0.0	0.0	0.0	trace	0.8	2.6	18.4
Days With ≥ 1.0" Snow Depth	11	7	2	0	0	0	0	0	0	0	0	4	24

Canfield 1 S *Mahoning County*   Elevation: 1,138 ft.   Latitude: 41° 01' N   Longitude: 80° 46' W

	JAN	FEB	MAR	APR	MAY	JUN	JUL	AUG	SEP	OCT	NOV	DEC	YEAR
Mean Maximum Temp. (°F)	34.1	36.9	48.6	60.1	70.9	79.1	82.9	81.7	74.5	62.8	49.7	38.8	60.0
Mean Temp. (°F)	25.2	27.0	37.4	47.3	57.8	66.4	70.4	68.9	61.8	50.6	40.4	30.4	48.6
Mean Minimum Temp. (°F)	16.3	17.1	26.1	34.4	44.7	53.7	57.9	56.0	49.1	38.4	31.0	21.9	37.2
Extreme Maximum Temp. (°F)	65	70	84	94	89	96	101	98	92	*84*	75	74	*101*
Extreme Minimum Temp. (°F)	-24	-23	-15	12	20	29	38	27	26	15	-3	-16	-24
Days Maximum Temp. ≥ 90°F	0	0	0	0	0	1	4	2	0	0	0	0	7
Days Maximum Temp. ≤ 32°F	14	11	3	0	0	0	0	0	0	0	1	9	38
Days Minimum Temp. ≤ 32°F	28	25	23	14	4	0	0	0	1	9	18	27	149
Days Minimum Temp. ≤ 0°F	4	3	1	0	0	0	0	0	0	0	0	1	9
Heating Degree Days (base 65°F)	1,227	1,065	851	528	246	63	15	27	147	442	733	1,066	6,410
Cooling Degree Days (base 65°F)	0	0	1	*4*	28	112	200	153	51	3	0	0	*552*
Mean Precipitation (in.)	1.97	1.80	2.89	3.03	3.87	4.19	4.37	3.57	3.78	2.77	3.07	2.66	37.97
Days With ≥ 0.1" Precipitation	*5*	6	7	7	9	8	8	7	7	6	7	6	*83*
Days With ≥ 1.0" Precipitation	0	0	0	0	1	1	1	1	1	0	0	0	5
Mean Snowfall (in.)	na	na	*3.3*	0.7	0.0	0.0	0.0	0.0	0.0	0.3	*1.1*	na	na
Days With ≥ 1.0" Snow Depth	na	na	*3*	1	0	0	0	0	0	0	1	na	na

Celina 3 NE *Mercer County* Elevation: 859 ft. Latitude: 40° 34' N Longitude: 84° 32' W

	JAN	FEB	MAR	APR	MAY	JUN	JUL	AUG	SEP	OCT	NOV	DEC	YEAR
Mean Maximum Temp. (°F)	32.5	37.2	48.8	61.9	73.0	81.3	84.6	82.4	76.9	64.6	50.0	38.1	60.9
Mean Temp. (°F)	25.1	29.0	39.4	50.9	61.8	70.7	74.1	71.8	65.8	54.2	42.1	31.2	51.3
Mean Minimum Temp. (°F)	17.7	20.8	29.9	39.8	50.6	59.9	63.6	61.2	54.5	43.7	34.2	24.2	41.7
Extreme Maximum Temp. (°F)	62	69	82	86	94	103	101	101	96	88	76	70	103
Extreme Minimum Temp. (°F)	-23	-16	-9	9	28	40	43	39	30	20	6	-20	-23
Days Maximum Temp. ≥ 90°F	0	0	0	0	0	3	6	3	1	0	0	0	13
Days Maximum Temp. ≤ 32°F	15	10	3	0	0	0	0	0	0	0	1	9	38
Days Minimum Temp. ≤ 32°F	28	24	20	7	1	0	0	0	0	3	14	25	122
Days Minimum Temp. ≤ 0°F	4	2	0	0	0	0	0	0	0	0	0	1	7
Heating Degree Days (base 65°F)	1,230	1,009	788	426	159	25	3	10	83	342	680	1,042	5,797
Cooling Degree Days (base 65°F)	0	0	1	9	67	205	298	232	110	15	0	0	937
Mean Precipitation (in.)	2.13	2.06	2.79	3.52	3.63	3.80	4.51	3.53	2.66	2.33	2.97	2.63	36.56
Days With ≥ 0.1" Precipitation	6	5	7	8	8	7	7	6	6	6	6	7	79
Days With ≥ 1.0" Precipitation	0	0	0	1	1	1	1	1	1	0	0	0	6
Mean Snowfall (in.)	11.4	7.7	4.7	1.1	0.0	0.0	0.0	0.0	0.0	0.3	1.6	6.3	33.1
Days With ≥ 1.0" Snow Depth	14	9	3	0	0	0	0	0	0	0	1	6	33

Centerburg 2 SE *Knox County* Elevation: 1,204 ft. Latitude: 40° 18' N Longitude: 82° 39' W

	JAN	FEB	MAR	APR	MAY	JUN	JUL	AUG	SEP	OCT	NOV	DEC	YEAR
Mean Maximum Temp. (°F)	32.2	36.3	47.1	59.6	69.8	78.6	82.3	80.8	74.4	62.2	49.2	37.4	59.2
Mean Temp. (°F)	24.1	27.5	37.5	48.7	59.0	68.0	71.8	70.3	63.4	51.3	40.6	29.8	49.3
Mean Minimum Temp. (°F)	15.6	18.5	27.7	37.5	48.1	57.4	61.3	59.5	52.2	40.4	31.9	22.4	39.4
Extreme Maximum Temp. (°F)	66	72	82	86	89	99	99	97	94	87	78	70	99
Extreme Minimum Temp. (°F)	-29	-16	-6	11	25	32	43	38	31	20	0	-23	-29
Days Maximum Temp. ≥ 90°F	0	0	0	0	0	1	3	2	1	0	0	0	7
Days Maximum Temp. ≤ 32°F	15	11	4	0	0	0	0	0	0	0	2	10	42
Days Minimum Temp. ≤ 32°F	29	25	22	10	1	0	0	0	0	7	17	26	137
Days Minimum Temp. ≤ 0°F	4	3	0	0	0	0	0	0	0	0	0	1	8
Heating Degree Days (base 65°F)	1,262	1,053	848	491	219	44	8	17	118	424	727	1,086	6,297
Cooling Degree Days (base 65°F)	0	0	2	7	42	146	242	195	71	6	0	0	711
Mean Precipitation (in.)	2.45	2.13	2.98	3.66	4.03	4.59	4.56	3.85	3.21	2.80	3.61	3.02	40.89
Days With ≥ 0.1" Precipitation	6	6	7	8	8	8	8	6	5	6	7	7	82
Days With ≥ 1.0" Precipitation	0	0	0	1	1	1	1	1	1	1	1	1	9
Mean Snowfall (in.)	na	3.2	na	0.3	trace	0.0	0.0	0.0	0.0	trace	0.9	na	na
Days With ≥ 1.0" Snow Depth	9	6	3	1	0	0	0	0	0	0	1	5	25

Chardon *Geauga County* Elevation: 1,128 ft. Latitude: 41° 35' N Longitude: 81° 11' W

	JAN	FEB	MAR	APR	MAY	JUN	JUL	AUG	SEP	OCT	NOV	DEC	YEAR
Mean Maximum Temp. (°F)	31.4	34.5	43.9	56.1	67.7	76.3	80.1	78.7	71.9	60.4	48.0	37.0	57.2
Mean Temp. (°F)	22.8	24.8	33.9	44.9	55.9	64.7	69.0	67.5	60.7	49.8	39.8	29.5	46.9
Mean Minimum Temp. (°F)	14.1	15.1	23.8	33.7	44.1	53.1	57.8	56.2	49.3	39.2	31.6	21.9	36.7
Extreme Maximum Temp. (°F)	65	69	82	88	89	100	98	96	91	83	76	73	100
Extreme Minimum Temp. (°F)	-23	-26	-17	5	22	30	38	33	25	15	-2	-21	-26
Days Maximum Temp. ≥ 90°F	0	0	0	0	0	1	2	1	0	0	0	0	4
Days Maximum Temp. ≤ 32°F	17	13	6	1	0	0	0	0	0	0	2	10	49
Days Minimum Temp. ≤ 32°F	29	26	25	15	3	0	0	0	1	7	18	27	151
Days Minimum Temp. ≤ 0°F	5	4	1	0	0	0	0	0	0	0	0	1	11
Heating Degree Days (base 65°F)	1,303	1,130	959	600	296	94	30	40	173	466	748	1,095	6,934
Cooling Degree Days (base 65°F)	0	0	0	4	22	96	169	126	48	3	0	0	468
Mean Precipitation (in.)	3.22	2.70	3.44	3.77	4.08	4.42	4.00	4.58	4.49	3.88	4.29	4.14	47.01
Days With ≥ 0.1" Precipitation	10	8	9	9	9	8	8	7	9	9	10	11	107
Days With ≥ 1.0" Precipitation	0	0	0	1	1	1	1	1	1	1	1	0	8
Mean Snowfall (in.)	26.2	18.9	14.4	2.9	trace	0.0	0.0	0.0	0.0	0.9	10.1	23.6	97.0
Days With ≥ 1.0" Snow Depth	24	20	12	2	0	0	0	0	0	0	6	17	81

Chillicothe Mound City *Ross County* Elevation: 649 ft. Latitude: 39° 22' N Longitude: 83° 00' W

	JAN	FEB	MAR	APR	MAY	JUN	JUL	AUG	SEP	OCT	NOV	DEC	YEAR
Mean Maximum Temp. (°F)	37.6	41.9	52.7	64.0	74.0	82.0	86.2	85.1	78.6	66.5	53.9	42.7	63.8
Mean Temp. (°F)	28.4	31.8	41.5	51.7	61.7	70.2	74.5	72.9	65.8	53.8	43.6	33.7	52.5
Mean Minimum Temp. (°F)	19.1	21.6	30.2	39.3	49.4	58.4	62.8	60.8	52.9	40.7	33.2	24.5	41.1
Extreme Maximum Temp. (°F)	73	76	83	90	93	103	103	105	100	88	82	80	105
Extreme Minimum Temp. (°F)	-29	-14	-10	13	29	35	41	39	31	17	-2	-21	-29
Days Maximum Temp. ≥ 90°F	0	0	0	0	1	4	9	7	2	0	0	0	23
Days Maximum Temp. ≤ 32°F	10	7	2	0	0	0	0	0	0	0	0	6	25
Days Minimum Temp. ≤ 32°F	27	23	20	8	1	0	0	0	0	6	16	24	125
Days Minimum Temp. ≤ 0°F	3	2	0	0	0	0	0	0	0	0	0	1	6
Heating Degree Days (base 65°F)	1,128	932	723	405	159	27	2	7	83	354	637	965	5,422
Cooling Degree Days (base 65°F)	0	0	3	12	62	200	317	265	114	14	1	0	988
Mean Precipitation (in.)	2.49	2.34	3.38	3.52	4.37	3.45	3.91	3.59	2.80	2.55	2.93	2.63	37.96
Days With ≥ 0.1" Precipitation	6	5	7	8	8	7	7	6	5	5	6	6	76
Days With ≥ 1.0" Precipitation	0	1	1	1	1	1	1	1	1	1	0	1	10
Mean Snowfall (in.)	7.1	4.6	3.1	0.4	trace	0.0	0.0	0.0	0.0	0.1	0.4	2.2	17.9
Days With ≥ 1.0" Snow Depth	10	6	2	0	0	0	0	0	0	0	0	3	21

Chilo Meldahl Lock & Dam *Clermont County*   Elevation: 498 ft.   Latitude: 38° 48' N   Longitude: 84° 10' W

	JAN	FEB	MAR	APR	MAY	JUN	JUL	AUG	SEP	OCT	NOV	DEC	YEAR
Mean Maximum Temp. (°F)	38.5	43.2	53.0	64.9	73.8	82.0	86.2	85.3	79.3	67.6	54.8	43.8	64.4
Mean Temp. (°F)	29.6	33.4	42.1	52.6	62.0	70.8	75.4	74.3	67.7	55.9	45.0	35.1	53.6
Mean Minimum Temp. (°F)	20.4	23.1	31.3	40.3	50.1	59.5	64.3	63.2	56.1	44.1	35.2	26.3	42.8
Extreme Maximum Temp. (°F)	71	73	82	89	91	98	101	107	98	90	82	73	107
Extreme Minimum Temp. (°F)	-22	-8	-4	20	29	39	47	44	33	21	5	-15	-22
Days Maximum Temp. ≥ 90°F	0	0	0	0	0	3	9	7	3	0	0	0	22
Days Maximum Temp. ≤ 32°F	9	6	1	0	0	0	0	0	0	0	0	5	21
Days Minimum Temp. ≤ 32°F	26	23	18	6	0	0	0	0	0	2	12	22	109
Days Minimum Temp. ≤ 0°F	2	1	0	0	0	0	0	0	0	0	0	1	4
Heating Degree Days (base 65°F)	1,091	888	704	373	145	20	1	2	54	289	595	921	5,083
Cooling Degree Days (base 65°F)	0	0	1	9	54	208	344	307	139	17	0	0	1,079
Mean Precipitation (in.)	3.04	2.97	4.17	3.81	4.48	4.29	3.79	3.94	3.11	2.88	3.28	3.29	43.05
Days With ≥ 0.1" Precipitation	7	5	8	8	7	7	6	6	5	5	6	6	76
Days With ≥ 1.0" Precipitation	1	1	1	1	1	1	1	1	1	1	1	1	12
Mean Snowfall (in.)	na	na	1.0	0.0	0.0	0.0	0.0	0.0	0.0	0.0	trace	1.5	na
Days With ≥ 1.0" Snow Depth	4	5	1	0	0	0	0	0	0	0	0	1	11

Chippewa Lake *Medina County*   Elevation: 1,177 ft.   Latitude: 41° 03' N   Longitude: 81° 56' W

	JAN	FEB	MAR	APR	MAY	JUN	JUL	AUG	SEP	OCT	NOV	DEC	YEAR
Mean Maximum Temp. (°F)	32.7	36.7	47.0	59.7	70.7	79.1	83.0	81.3	74.5	62.8	49.6	38.0	59.6
Mean Temp. (°F)	24.6	27.6	36.9	47.9	58.7	67.4	71.5	69.9	63.0	51.9	41.0	30.5	49.2
Mean Minimum Temp. (°F)	16.7	18.3	26.7	36.0	46.5	55.7	59.9	58.3	51.5	40.9	32.3	22.9	38.8
Extreme Maximum Temp. (°F)	64	70	83	88	90	102	102	99	94	84	77	75	102
Extreme Minimum Temp. (°F)	-26	-17	-14	8	23	28	39	34	28	16	-2	-18	-26
Days Maximum Temp. ≥ 90°F	0	0	0	0	0	1	4	2	1	0	0	0	8
Days Maximum Temp. ≤ 32°F	15	11	4	0	0	0	0	0	0	0	2	9	41
Days Minimum Temp. ≤ 32°F	29	25	23	12	2	0	0	0	0	5	17	26	139
Days Minimum Temp. ≤ 0°F	4	3	0	0	0	0	0	0	0	0	0	1	8
Heating Degree Days (base 65°F)	1,244	1,051	864	511	226	52	10	18	123	406	715	1,064	6,284
Cooling Degree Days (base 65°F)	0	0	1	5	36	136	230	183	69	6	0	0	666
Mean Precipitation (in.)	2.28	2.11	2.98	3.37	3.64	3.81	3.88	3.58	3.67	2.51	3.39	3.00	38.22
Days With ≥ 0.1" Precipitation	7	6	8	9	8	8	7	7	6	7	8	8	89
Days With ≥ 1.0" Precipitation	0	0	0	0	1	1	1	1	1	0	1	0	6
Mean Snowfall (in.)	10.7	8.6	6.7	2.1	trace	0.0	0.0	0.0	0.0	0.2	3.3	8.2	39.8
Days With ≥ 1.0" Snow Depth	17	14	6	1	0	0	0	0	0	0	2	9	49

Cincinnati Fernbank *Hamilton County*   Elevation: 498 ft.   Latitude: 39° 07' N   Longitude: 84° 42' W

	JAN	FEB	MAR	APR	MAY	JUN	JUL	AUG	SEP	OCT	NOV	DEC	YEAR
Mean Maximum Temp. (°F)	38.1	43.6	53.8	65.1	74.7	82.4	86.6	85.3	78.5	67.2	55.4	43.7	64.6
Mean Temp. (°F)	29.2	33.3	42.6	52.7	62.5	71.0	75.5	74.1	66.7	55.2	45.3	34.8	53.6
Mean Minimum Temp. (°F)	20.2	23.0	31.3	40.1	50.3	59.5	64.4	62.8	54.8	43.1	35.1	25.8	42.5
Extreme Maximum Temp. (°F)	70	77	84	90	93	106	107	105	96	87	88	78	107
Extreme Minimum Temp. (°F)	-25	-10	-10	17	29	41	46	42	33	18	1	-18	-25
Days Maximum Temp. ≥ 90°F	0	0	0	0	1	5	9	7	2	0	0	0	24
Days Maximum Temp. ≤ 32°F	10	6	1	0	0	0	0	0	0	0	0	5	22
Days Minimum Temp. ≤ 32°F	26	22	18	7	0	0	0	0	0	3	13	23	112
Days Minimum Temp. ≤ 0°F	3	1	0	0	0	0	0	0	0	0	0	1	5
Heating Degree Days (base 65°F)	1,104	888	691	377	142	20	1	3	69	315	586	930	5,126
Cooling Degree Days (base 65°F)	0	0	3	12	66	209	342	293	129	21	1	0	1,076
Mean Precipitation (in.)	3.46	2.91	4.35	4.42	5.51	4.62	4.52	4.08	2.88	3.30	3.74	3.64	47.43
Days With ≥ 0.1" Precipitation	7	6	9	10	9	8	7	7	5	6	8	7	89
Days With ≥ 1.0" Precipitation	1	1	1	1	2	1	2	1	1	1	1	1	14
Mean Snowfall (in.)	6.7	na	2.6	0.1	trace	0.0	0.0	0.0	0.0	trace	0.4	2.2	na
Days With ≥ 1.0" Snow Depth	7	6	2	0	0	0	0	0	0	0	0	3	18

Cincinnati Lunken Airport *Hamilton County*   Elevation: 488 ft.   Latitude: 39° 06' N   Longitude: 84° 26' W

	JAN	FEB	MAR	APR	MAY	JUN	JUL	AUG	SEP	OCT	NOV	DEC	YEAR
Mean Maximum Temp. (°F)	38.5	43.5	54.2	65.4	74.7	82.8	86.8	85.2	78.6	67.1	54.6	43.9	64.6
Mean Temp. (°F)	30.4	34.4	44.2	54.3	63.8	72.4	76.8	75.1	68.1	56.0	45.4	35.8	54.7
Mean Minimum Temp. (°F)	22.2	25.4	34.2	43.1	52.9	62.0	66.7	64.9	57.4	44.9	36.1	27.7	44.8
Extreme Maximum Temp. (°F)	70	76	85	90	93	101	105	103	97	87	82	75	105
Extreme Minimum Temp. (°F)	-22	-9	-6	21	32	41	47	43	35	20	7	-14	-22
Days Maximum Temp. ≥ 90°F	0	0	0	0	1	5	11	7	3	0	0	0	27
Days Maximum Temp. ≤ 32°F	10	6	1	0	0	0	0	0	0	0	0	5	22
Days Minimum Temp. ≤ 32°F	25	21	14	3	0	0	0	0	0	2	12	21	98
Days Minimum Temp. ≤ 0°F	1	0	0	0	0	0	0	0	0	0	0	0	1
Heating Degree Days (base 65°F)	1,066	857	639	330	114	11	0	2	52	287	582	899	4,839
Cooling Degree Days (base 65°F)	0	0	2	14	82	243	387	327	142	17	1	0	1,215
Mean Precipitation (in.)	2.70	2.43	3.88	3.74	4.61	4.00	3.83	4.07	3.12	2.95	3.39	3.17	41.89
Days With ≥ 0.1" Precipitation	6	5	9	8	8	8	7	6	5	5	7	7	81
Days With ≥ 1.0" Precipitation	1	0	1	1	1	1	1	1	1	1	1	0	10
Mean Snowfall (in.)	4.6	3.7	2.6	0.2	trace	trace	trace	0.0	0.0	0.1	0.4	1.6	13.2
Days With ≥ 1.0" Snow Depth	7	6	2	0	0	0	0	0	0	0	0	2	17

Circleville *Pickaway County*   Elevation: 672 ft.   Latitude: 39° 37' N   Longitude: 82° 57' W

	JAN	FEB	MAR	APR	MAY	JUN	JUL	AUG	SEP	OCT	NOV	DEC	YEAR
Mean Maximum Temp. (°F)	37.0	41.2	52.4	64.3	73.9	82.0	85.5	84.2	78.3	66.6	53.3	42.2	63.4
Mean Temp. (°F)	28.9	32.1	41.9	52.3	62.3	70.8	74.6	72.9	66.4	54.8	44.0	34.3	52.9
Mean Minimum Temp. (°F)	20.8	23.0	31.3	40.2	50.5	59.6	63.6	61.5	54.5	42.9	34.6	26.4	42.4
Extreme Maximum Temp. (°F)	70	75	83	90	91	100	100	101	97	87	81	79	101
Extreme Minimum Temp. (°F)	-22	-15	-5	17	30	35	42	40	31	19	5	-19	-22
Days Maximum Temp. ≥ 90°F	0	0	0	0	1	4	7	5	1	0	0	0	18
Days Maximum Temp. ≤ 32°F	11	7	2	0	0	0	0	0	0	0	1	6	27
Days Minimum Temp. ≤ 32°F	26	22	18	7	0	0	0	0	0	4	14	22	113
Days Minimum Temp. ≤ 0°F	2	2	0	0	0	0	0	0	0	0	0	1	5
Heating Degree Days (base 65°F)	1,111	921	713	388	148	21	2	6	71	325	625	944	5,275
Cooling Degree Days (base 65°F)	0	0	2	11	61	200	309	255	110	16	1	0	965
Mean Precipitation (in.)	2.35	2.14	2.77	3.48	4.62	3.88	3.87	3.85	3.11	2.64	3.07	2.67	38.45
Days With ≥ 0.1" Precipitation	6	5	7	8	8	7	7	6	5	6	7	6	78
Days With ≥ 1.0" Precipitation	0	0	0	1	1	1	1	1	1	0	1	0	7
Mean Snowfall (in.)	5.9	4.0	2.0	0.4	0.0	0.0	0.0	0.0	0.0	0.1	0.7	1.8	14.9
Days With ≥ 1.0" Snow Depth	9	6	2	0	0	0	0	0	0	0	0	4	21

Columbus Valley Crossing *Franklin County*   Elevation: 734 ft.   Latitude: 39° 54' N   Longitude: 82° 56' W

	JAN	FEB	MAR	APR	MAY	JUN	JUL	AUG	SEP	OCT	NOV	DEC	YEAR
Mean Maximum Temp. (°F)	36.2	41.0	52.1	64.3	74.0	82.0	85.3	83.5	77.9	66.3	52.9	41.6	63.1
Mean Temp. (°F)	28.1	32.0	41.9	52.4	62.3	71.0	74.6	72.6	66.3	54.7	43.7	33.7	52.8
Mean Minimum Temp. (°F)	20.0	23.1	31.6	40.5	50.7	59.8	63.7	61.6	54.6	43.0	34.4	25.7	42.4
Extreme Maximum Temp. (°F)	70	74	83	90	93	100	100	100	95	87	79	76	100
Extreme Minimum Temp. (°F)	-28	-14	-2	17	30	37	45	38	28	19	2	-21	-28
Days Maximum Temp. ≥ 90°F	0	0	0	0	1	4	7	4	1	0	0	0	17
Days Maximum Temp. ≤ 32°F	11	7	2	0	0	0	0	0	0	0	1	6	27
Days Minimum Temp. ≤ 32°F	27	22	18	7	0	0	0	0	0	4	14	23	115
Days Minimum Temp. ≤ 0°F	3	1	0	0	0	0	0	0	0	0	0	1	5
Heating Degree Days (base 65°F)	1,138	924	712	381	141	18	1	5	72	326	635	965	5,318
Cooling Degree Days (base 65°F)	0	0	1	9	61	203	311	246	110	12	1	0	954
Mean Precipitation (in.)	2.51	2.03	3.00	3.72	4.34	4.08	4.39	4.26	2.88	2.52	3.34	2.89	39.96
Days With ≥ 0.1" Precipitation	6	5	7	7	8	7	7	7	5	6	7	6	78
Days With ≥ 1.0" Precipitation	0	0	0	1	1	1	1	1	1	0	1	0	7
Mean Snowfall (in.)	8.4	5.0	1.9	0.6	trace	0.0	0.0	0.0	0.0	trace	0.6	2.8	19.3
Days With ≥ 1.0" Snow Depth	9	na	1	0	0	0	0	0	0	0	0	3	na

Coshocton Agr. Res. Station *Coshocton County*   Elevation: 1,138 ft.   Latitude: 40° 22' N   Longitude: 81° 48' W

	JAN	FEB	MAR	APR	MAY	JUN	JUL	AUG	SEP	OCT	NOV	DEC	YEAR
Mean Maximum Temp. (°F)	33.3	36.9	47.4	59.2	69.6	78.1	82.0	80.5	74.1	62.4	50.1	38.9	59.4
Mean Temp. (°F)	25.5	28.6	38.2	49.5	60.1	68.6	72.7	71.3	64.7	52.9	41.9	31.6	50.5
Mean Minimum Temp. (°F)	17.7	20.2	29.0	39.7	50.6	59.1	63.3	62.0	55.2	43.3	33.8	24.1	41.5
Extreme Maximum Temp. (°F)	68	71	82	85	91	98	101	97	94	83	78	74	101
Extreme Minimum Temp. (°F)	-26	-15	1	14	28	38	47	39	32	21	1	-17	-26
Days Maximum Temp. ≥ 90°F	0	0	0	0	0	1	3	2	1	0	0	0	7
Days Maximum Temp. ≤ 32°F	15	11	4	0	0	0	0	0	0	0	1	9	40
Days Minimum Temp. ≤ 32°F	28	24	21	7	0	0	0	0	0	3	15	25	123
Days Minimum Temp. ≤ 0°F	3	2	0	0	0	0	0	0	0	0	0	1	6
Heating Degree Days (base 65°F)	1,216	1,022	824	469	196	38	5	11	94	379	687	1,030	5,971
Cooling Degree Days (base 65°F)	0	0	2	9	48	163	270	225	92	10	1	0	820
Mean Precipitation (in.)	2.28	2.04	2.91	3.34	3.79	4.01	4.04	3.53	2.95	2.40	3.10	2.65	37.04
Days With ≥ 0.1" Precipitation	5	5	7	7	7	7	7	6	6	6	6	6	75
Days With ≥ 1.0" Precipitation	0	0	0	1	1	1	1	1	1	0	1	0	7
Mean Snowfall (in.)	na	na	na	trace	0.0	0.0	0.0	0.0	0.0	trace	0.2	na	na
Days With ≥ 1.0" Snow Depth	na	na	na	0	0	0	0	0	0	0	0	na	na

Coshocton WPC Plant *Coshocton County*   Elevation: 757 ft.   Latitude: 40° 14' N   Longitude: 81° 52' W

	JAN	FEB	MAR	APR	MAY	JUN	JUL	AUG	SEP	OCT	NOV	DEC	YEAR
Mean Maximum Temp. (°F)	36.1	40.4	51.2	62.6	72.6	80.4	84.2	82.6	76.1	64.7	52.3	41.2	62.0
Mean Temp. (°F)	27.3	30.6	40.3	50.3	60.4	68.7	72.7	71.2	64.3	52.6	42.3	32.7	51.1
Mean Minimum Temp. (°F)	18.4	20.9	29.4	38.0	48.2	57.0	61.3	59.7	52.4	40.4	32.3	24.1	40.2
Extreme Maximum Temp. (°F)	69	72	84	89	92	101	101	99	96	86	80	77	101
Extreme Minimum Temp. (°F)	-24	-14	-6	12	20	31	41	39	29	19	1	-19	-24
Days Maximum Temp. ≥ 90°F	0	0	0	0	0	2	5	3	1	0	0	0	11
Days Maximum Temp. ≤ 32°F	12	8	2	0	0	0	0	0	0	0	1	6	29
Days Minimum Temp. ≤ 32°F	28	24	21	9	1	0	0	0	0	6	17	25	131
Days Minimum Temp. ≤ 0°F	3	2	0	0	0	0	0	0	0	0	0	1	6
Heating Degree Days (base 65°F)	1,163	964	759	440	182	34	5	11	98	384	673	996	5,709
Cooling Degree Days (base 65°F)	0	0	1	7	47	159	271	219	80	6	1	0	791
Mean Precipitation (in.)	2.54	2.36	3.16	3.79	4.11	4.03	4.45	4.15	3.21	2.69	3.47	3.00	40.96
Days With ≥ 0.1" Precipitation	7	6	8	8	8	8	8	7	6	6	8	7	87
Days With ≥ 1.0" Precipitation	0	0	0	1	1	1	1	1	1	0	1	0	7
Mean Snowfall (in.)	8.8	5.6	3.0	0.8	trace	0.0	0.0	0.0	0.0	trace	0.9	3.6	22.7
Days With ≥ 1.0" Snow Depth	13	8	3	0	0	0	0	0	0	0	1	5	30

Danville 2 W *Knox County*   Elevation: 967 ft.   Latitude: 40° 26' N   Longitude: 82° 18' W

	JAN	FEB	MAR	APR	MAY	JUN	JUL	AUG	SEP	OCT	NOV	DEC	YEAR
Mean Maximum Temp. (°F)	34.0	38.5	49.6	61.6	72.0	80.3	84.3	82.7	76.2	64.2	51.0	39.6	61.2
Mean Temp. (°F)	25.0	28.4	38.1	48.2	58.4	67.3	71.4	69.7	62.8	50.9	40.7	30.9	49.3
Mean Minimum Temp. (°F)	16.0	18.3	26.7	34.7	44.8	54.2	58.5	56.7	49.3	37.5	30.3	22.1	37.4
Extreme Maximum Temp. (°F)	67	72	83	89	94	102	102	98	96	84	78	74	102
Extreme Minimum Temp. (°F)	-35	-22	-18	9	21	27	35	32	26	15	-2	-22	-35
Days Maximum Temp. ≥ 90°F	0	0	0	0	0	2	5	3	1	0	0	0	11
Days Maximum Temp. ≤ 32°F	14	9	3	0	0	0	0	0	0	0	1	8	35
Days Minimum Temp. ≤ 32°F	28	25	22	14	3	0	0	0	1	11	19	26	149
Days Minimum Temp. ≤ 0°F	5	3	0	0	0	0	0	0	0	0	0	2	10
Heating Degree Days (base 65°F)	1,234	1,026	827	502	230	51	10	21	130	434	724	1,051	6,240
Cooling Degree Days (base 65°F)	0	0	0	3	31	124	220	169	62	4	0	0	613
Mean Precipitation (in.)	2.62	2.38	3.12	3.67	4.22	4.68	4.32	3.75	3.33	2.65	3.37	3.10	41.21
Days With ≥ 0.1" Precipitation	6	6	8	8	9	8	7	6	6	6	7	7	84
Days With ≥ 1.0" Precipitation	0	0	0	1	1	1	1	1	1	0	1	1	8
Mean Snowfall (in.)	12.4	8.4	4.6	1.3	trace	0.0	0.0	0.0	0.0	trace	1.8	7.0	35.5
Days With ≥ 1.0" Snow Depth	16	11	4	1	0	0	0	0	0	0	2	8	42

Dayton MCD *Montgomery County*   Elevation: 744 ft.   Latitude: 39° 46' N   Longitude: 84° 11' W

	JAN	FEB	MAR	APR	MAY	JUN	JUL	AUG	SEP	OCT	NOV	DEC	YEAR
Mean Maximum Temp. (°F)	34.9	39.8	50.5	63.0	74.1	83.1	87.3	85.4	78.8	65.8	52.2	41.0	63.0
Mean Temp. (°F)	27.7	31.5	41.3	52.6	63.7	72.9	77.1	75.0	68.1	55.6	44.2	33.9	53.6
Mean Minimum Temp. (°F)	20.4	23.2	32.0	42.3	53.2	62.6	66.9	64.6	57.3	45.3	36.1	26.7	44.2
Extreme Maximum Temp. (°F)	69	75	84	90	95	103	104	103	97	89	81	75	104
Extreme Minimum Temp. (°F)	-21	-6	2	18	33	42	51	45	35	24	8	-16	-21
Days Maximum Temp. ≥ 90°F	0	0	0	0	2	7	12	8	3	0	0	0	32
Days Maximum Temp. ≤ 32°F	13	8	2	0	0	0	0	0	0	0	1	7	31
Days Minimum Temp. ≤ 32°F	26	22	17	4	0	0	0	0	0	2	11	22	104
Days Minimum Temp. ≤ 0°F	2	1	0	0	0	0	0	0	0	0	0	1	4
Heating Degree Days (base 65°F)	1,152	939	732	382	129	15	1	2	57	306	619	958	5,292
Cooling Degree Days (base 65°F)	0	0	4	16	92	264	397	330	156	23	1	0	1,283
Mean Precipitation (in.)	2.57	2.32	3.07	4.07	4.38	4.11	3.90	3.28	2.57	2.68	3.25	2.93	39.13
Days With ≥ 0.1" Precipitation	6	6	7	8	8	7	7	6	5	5	6	6	77
Days With ≥ 1.0" Precipitation	0	0	0	1	1	1	1	1	1	1	1	1	9
Mean Snowfall (in.)	6.3	3.6	2.4	0.2	0.0	0.0	0.0	0.0	0.0	trace	0.4	2.8	15.7
Days With ≥ 1.0" Snow Depth	*11*	7	2	0	0	0	0	0	0	0	0	3	*23*

Defiance *Defiance County*   Elevation: 698 ft.   Latitude: 41° 17' N   Longitude: 84° 23' W

	JAN	FEB	MAR	APR	MAY	JUN	JUL	AUG	SEP	OCT	NOV	DEC	YEAR
Mean Maximum Temp. (°F)	31.1	35.0	45.7	59.1	71.3	80.7	84.6	82.4	75.6	63.1	48.7	36.9	59.5
Mean Temp. (°F)	22.9	26.1	35.9	47.8	59.3	69.0	73.0	70.9	63.8	51.9	40.1	29.3	49.2
Mean Minimum Temp. (°F)	14.7	17.1	26.1	36.4	47.4	57.2	61.5	59.4	51.9	40.6	31.4	21.6	38.8
Extreme Maximum Temp. (°F)	64	71	80	89	92	104	104	99	95	88	77	70	104
Extreme Minimum Temp. (°F)	-22	-19	-6	4	26	38	45	43	29	18	6	-19	-22
Days Maximum Temp. ≥ 90°F	0	0	0	0	1	4	7	4	1	0	0	0	17
Days Maximum Temp. ≤ 32°F	16	12	4	0	0	0	0	0	0	0	1	10	43
Days Minimum Temp. ≤ 32°F	29	25	24	10	1	0	0	0	0	5	18	27	139
Days Minimum Temp. ≤ 0°F	5	4	0	0	0	0	0	0	0	0	0	2	11
Heating Degree Days (base 65°F)	1,298	1,094	895	519	215	41	6	13	114	409	741	1,099	6,444
Cooling Degree Days (base 65°F)	0	0	1	7	48	174	280	216	85	9	0	0	820
Mean Precipitation (in.)	1.90	1.79	2.68	3.45	3.59	3.72	4.03	3.13	3.16	2.62	3.00	2.57	35.64
Days With ≥ 0.1" Precipitation	5	5	7	8	8	7	7	6	6	6	6	6	77
Days With ≥ 1.0" Precipitation	0	0	0	1	1	1	1	1	1	0	1	0	7
Mean Snowfall (in.)	6.8	5.3	2.4	0.6	trace	0.0	0.0	0.0	0.0	trace	1.2	4.5	20.8
Days With ≥ 1.0" Snow Depth	16	12	4	0	0	0	0	0	0	0	1	8	41

Delaware *Delaware County*   Elevation: 918 ft.   Latitude: 40° 19' N   Longitude: 83° 04' W

	JAN	FEB	MAR	APR	MAY	JUN	JUL	AUG	SEP	OCT	NOV	DEC	YEAR
Mean Maximum Temp. (°F)	33.3	37.2	47.9	60.5	71.3	80.0	83.9	82.4	76.2	63.9	49.9	38.9	60.5
Mean Temp. (°F)	24.7	27.8	37.7	48.9	59.5	68.6	72.6	70.7	63.8	51.9	40.6	30.8	49.8
Mean Minimum Temp. (°F)	16.2	18.5	27.5	37.1	47.6	57.1	61.2	59.0	51.4	39.9	31.3	22.6	39.1
Extreme Maximum Temp. (°F)	68	72	82	87	90	101	100	100	96	87	78	74	101
Extreme Minimum Temp. (°F)	-28	-16	-9	14	27	35	41	37	31	16	2	-27	-28
Days Maximum Temp. ≥ 90°F	0	0	0	0	0	3	6	3	1	0	0	0	13
Days Maximum Temp. ≤ 32°F	14	10	3	0	0	0	0	0	0	0	1	8	36
Days Minimum Temp. ≤ 32°F	28	24	22	10	1	0	0	0	0	7	18	25	135
Days Minimum Temp. ≤ 0°F	4	3	0	0	0	0	0	0	0	0	0	1	8
Heating Degree Days (base 65°F)	1,243	1,044	839	484	210	41	6	15	111	407	725	1,054	6,179
Cooling Degree Days (base 65°F)	0	0	1	6	46	161	266	206	81	9	0	0	776
Mean Precipitation (in.)	2.29	1.88	2.47	3.44	3.96	4.20	4.12	3.54	2.78	2.45	3.47	2.73	37.33
Days With ≥ 0.1" Precipitation	6	5	7	7	8	8	7	6	5	5	7	7	78
Days With ≥ 1.0" Precipitation	0	0	0	1	1	1	1	1	1	0	1	0	7
Mean Snowfall (in.)	8.1	4.3	2.9	0.9	0.0	0.0	0.0	0.0	0.0	trace	0.8	3.7	20.7
Days With ≥ 1.0" Snow Depth	13	9	3	0	0	0	0	0	0	0	1	5	31

Dorset *Ashtabula County*   Elevation: 977 ft.   Latitude: 41° 41' N   Longitude: 80° 40' W

	JAN	FEB	MAR	APR	MAY	JUN	JUL	AUG	SEP	OCT	NOV	DEC	YEAR
Mean Maximum Temp. (°F)	31.4	34.7	44.3	56.6	68.3	76.9	81.2	79.7	73.1	61.3	48.4	37.0	57.8
Mean Temp. (°F)	23.1	25.3	34.5	45.5	56.3	65.1	69.4	67.9	61.4	50.4	40.3	29.6	47.4
Mean Minimum Temp. (°F)	14.6	15.8	24.7	34.3	44.2	53.2	57.4	56.0	49.6	39.5	32.1	22.2	37.0
Extreme Maximum Temp. (°F)	67	69	83	88	89	99	100	98	95	85	83	74	100
Extreme Minimum Temp. (°F)	-28	-28	-20	-4	22	30	37	30	26	17	2	-22	-28
Days Maximum Temp. ≥ 90°F	0	0	0	0	0	1	2	1	0	0	0	0	4
Days Maximum Temp. ≤ 32°F	17	12	6	1	0	0	0	0	0	0	2	10	48
Days Minimum Temp. ≤ 32°F	29	26	24	14	4	0	0	0	1	6	17	26	147
Days Minimum Temp. ≤ 0°F	5	4	1	0	0	0	0	0	0	0	0	1	11
Heating Degree Days (base 65°F)	1,294	1,116	938	583	290	88	28	36	162	448	736	1,090	6,809
Cooling Degree Days (base 65°F)	0	0	0	5	28	100	180	136	62	3	0	0	514
Mean Precipitation (in.)	2.60	2.26	3.16	3.55	3.69	4.53	4.20	4.06	4.31	3.79	3.88	3.27	43.30
Days With ≥ 0.1" Precipitation	7	7	9	9	9	8	7	7	8	9	10	9	99
Days With ≥ 1.0" Precipitation	0	0	0	0	1	1	1	1	1	1	0	0	6
Mean Snowfall (in.)	17.5	12.9	12.1	2.9	trace	0.0	0.0	0.0	0.0	0.6	8.7	18.4	73.1
Days With ≥ 1.0" Snow Depth	21	18	10	2	0	0	0	0	0	0	5	15	71

Eaton *Preble County*   Elevation: 1,000 ft.   Latitude: 39° 44' N   Longitude: 84° 38' W

	JAN	FEB	MAR	APR	MAY	JUN	JUL	AUG	SEP	OCT	NOV	DEC	YEAR
Mean Maximum Temp. (°F)	33.4	38.4	49.3	61.4	72.3	80.8	84.7	83.3	77.2	64.7	50.9	39.2	61.3
Mean Temp. (°F)	24.4	28.3	38.5	48.9	60.2	68.9	72.8	71.2	64.4	52.1	41.0	30.8	50.1
Mean Minimum Temp. (°F)	15.4	18.2	27.6	36.8	48.0	56.9	60.8	59.0	51.5	39.3	31.1	22.1	38.9
Extreme Maximum Temp. (°F)	65	72	82	87	91	100	102	101	96	90	79	72	102
Extreme Minimum Temp. (°F)	-33	-20	-11	14	25	36	42	38	26	12	-3	-30	-33
Days Maximum Temp. ≥ 90°F	0	0	0	0	0	3	6	4	2	0	0	0	15
Days Maximum Temp. ≤ 32°F	14	10	3	0	0	0	0	0	0	0	1	8	36
Days Minimum Temp. ≤ 32°F	28	25	22	10	1	0	0	0	0	7	18	26	137
Days Minimum Temp. ≤ 0°F	5	3	0	0	0	0	0	0	0	0	0	2	10
Heating Degree Days (base 65°F)	1,251	1,029	816	481	189	36	6	9	103	401	714	1,054	6,089
Cooling Degree Days (base 65°F)	0	0	1	4	47	167	265	220	91	9	0	0	804
Mean Precipitation (in.)	2.46	2.24	3.25	4.11	4.64	3.81	3.65	3.38	2.57	2.72	3.41	3.02	39.26
Days With ≥ 0.1" Precipitation	6	6	7	8	8	7	6	6	5	5	7	6	77
Days With ≥ 1.0" Precipitation	0	0	1	1	1	1	1	1	1	1	1	1	10
Mean Snowfall (in.)	na	na	na	0.5	0.0	0.0	0.0	0.0	0.0	0.0	*trace*	na	na
Days With ≥ 1.0" Snow Depth	12	9	4	0	0	0	0	0	0	0	1	5	31

Elyria 3 E *Lorain County*   Elevation: 728 ft.   Latitude: 41° 23' N   Longitude: 82° 03' W

	JAN	FEB	MAR	APR	MAY	JUN	JUL	AUG	SEP	OCT	NOV	DEC	YEAR
Mean Maximum Temp. (°F)	34.0	37.6	47.8	60.4	71.7	80.5	84.6	82.5	75.9	64.0	51.0	39.4	60.8
Mean Temp. (°F)	26.5	29.2	38.3	49.4	60.1	69.3	73.6	71.8	65.3	53.9	43.0	32.4	51.1
Mean Minimum Temp. (°F)	18.9	20.7	28.8	38.4	48.5	57.9	62.5	61.0	54.6	43.8	35.0	25.3	41.3
Extreme Maximum Temp. (°F)	66	72	84	89	93	104	102	100	95	86	78	76	104
Extreme Minimum Temp. (°F)	-22	-15	-10	11	27	33	44	40	32	18	7	-14	-22
Days Maximum Temp. ≥ 90°F	0	0	0	0	1	4	8	4	1	0	0	0	18
Days Maximum Temp. ≤ 32°F	14	10	3	0	0	0	0	0	0	0	1	7	35
Days Minimum Temp. ≤ 32°F	28	24	21	9	1	0	0	0	0	2	13	24	122
Days Minimum Temp. ≤ 0°F	3	2	0	0	0	0	0	0	0	0	0	1	6
Heating Degree Days (base 65°F)	1,187	1,005	822	470	196	35	4	9	85	346	653	1,003	5,815
Cooling Degree Days (base 65°F)	0	0	2	9	53	173	289	229	98	11	0	0	864
Mean Precipitation (in.)	2.37	2.17	2.74	3.19	3.42	3.98	3.65	3.76	3.54	2.69	3.18	3.07	37.76
Days With ≥ 0.1" Precipitation	7	6	7	8	8	7	7	7	7	7	8	8	87
Days With ≥ 1.0" Precipitation	0	0	0	0	0	1	1	1	1	0	0	0	4
Mean Snowfall (in.)	12.0	10.2	7.2	1.7	trace	trace	0.0	0.0	0.0	0.1	3.2	9.2	43.6
Days With ≥ 1.0" Snow Depth	16	13	5	0	0	0	0	0	0	0	1	9	44

Findlay Airport *Hancock County*   Elevation: 797 ft.   Latitude: 41° 01' N   Longitude: 83° 40' W

	JAN	FEB	MAR	APR	MAY	JUN	JUL	AUG	SEP	OCT	NOV	DEC	YEAR
Mean Maximum Temp. (°F)	31.1	34.7	46.0	58.5	70.2	78.9	82.8	80.5	74.3	62.0	48.4	36.7	58.7
Mean Temp. (°F)	24.3	27.5	37.6	48.7	60.0	69.0	73.0	70.8	64.0	52.4	41.0	30.3	49.9
Mean Minimum Temp. (°F)	17.5	20.3	29.1	38.8	49.8	59.1	63.1	60.9	53.7	42.7	33.6	23.8	41.0
Extreme Maximum Temp. (°F)	66	72	80	86	94	104	102	99	94	86	79	70	104
Extreme Minimum Temp. (°F)	-20	-14	-12	10	28	39	44	40	30	21	7	-18	-20
Days Maximum Temp. ≥ 90°F	0	0	0	0	1	2	5	2	1	0	0	0	11
Days Maximum Temp. ≤ 32°F	16	12	4	0	0	0	0	0	0	0	2	11	45
Days Minimum Temp. ≤ 32°F	28	23	20	8	0	0	0	0	0	4	15	25	123
Days Minimum Temp. ≤ 0°F	4	2	0	0	0	0	0	0	0	0	0	1	7
Heating Degree Days (base 65°F)	1,252	1,051	844	490	200	36	4	13	108	392	712	1,068	6,170
Cooling Degree Days (base 65°F)	0	0	1	6	51	165	265	200	82	9	0	0	779
Mean Precipitation (in.)	1.80	1.65	2.52	3.24	3.74	4.07	3.88	3.66	2.83	2.17	2.73	2.39	34.68
Days With ≥ 0.1" Precipitation	5	4	7	8	7	7	6	6	6	5	6	6	73
Days With ≥ 1.0" Precipitation	0	0	0	0	1	1	1	1	1	0	0	0	5
Mean Snowfall (in.)	8.2	5.3	3.2	0.7	trace	trace	0.0	0.0	trace	0.1	1.2	5.5	24.2
Days With ≥ 1.0" Snow Depth	15	11	4	0	0	0	0	0	0	0	1	7	38

Findlay WPCC *Hancock County* Elevation: 767 ft. Latitude: 41° 03' N Longitude: 83° 40' W

	JAN	FEB	MAR	APR	MAY	JUN	JUL	AUG	SEP	OCT	NOV	DEC	YEAR
Mean Maximum Temp. (°F)	31.3	35.2	46.5	59.2	71.1	79.8	83.6	81.2	74.6	62.2	48.2	36.5	59.1
Mean Temp. (°F)	24.3	27.7	37.7	49.0	60.6	69.7	73.6	71.4	64.5	52.6	40.7	29.9	50.1
Mean Minimum Temp. (°F)	17.2	20.1	28.8	38.8	50.1	59.5	63.6	61.5	54.2	42.9	33.1	23.4	41.1
Extreme Maximum Temp. (°F)	66	71	81	86	93	104	101	99	96	88	78	70	104
Extreme Minimum Temp. (°F)	-20	-12	-11	8	26	40	47	42	31	19	6	-18	-20
Days Maximum Temp. ≥ 90°F	0	0	0	0	1	3	5	3	1	0	0	0	13
Days Maximum Temp. ≤ 32°F	16	12	4	0	0	0	0	0	0	0	2	11	45
Days Minimum Temp. ≤ 32°F	28	24	21	7	1	0	0	0	0	3	16	25	125
Days Minimum Temp. ≤ 0°F	4	2	0	0	0	0	0	0	0	0	0	1	7
Heating Degree Days (base 65°F)	1,256	1,047	841	480	186	32	3	11	100	387	724	1,080	6,147
Cooling Degree Days (base 65°F)	0	0	2	7	58	187	294	230	97	10	0	0	885
Mean Precipitation (in.)	2.15	1.98	2.72	3.28	3.92	4.13	3.91	4.05	2.95	2.35	2.78	2.73	36.95
Days With ≥ 0.1" Precipitation	6	5	7	8	8	8	6	6	6	6	7	6	79
Days With ≥ 1.0" Precipitation	0	0	0	1	1	1	1	1	1	0	0	0	6
Mean Snowfall (in.)	10.2	6.2	4.3	1.2	trace	0.0	0.0	0.0	0.0	0.2	1.4	6.0	29.5
Days With ≥ 1.0" Snow Depth	16	12	4	0	0	0	0	0	0	0	1	8	41

Franklin *Warren County* Elevation: 669 ft. Latitude: 39° 33' N Longitude: 84° 19' W

	JAN	FEB	MAR	APR	MAY	JUN	JUL	AUG	SEP	OCT	NOV	DEC	YEAR
Mean Maximum Temp. (°F)	36.0	40.5	51.1	62.8	73.2	81.6	85.5	84.2	78.0	65.6	52.8	41.7	62.7
Mean Temp. (°F)	27.2	30.8	40.5	51.1	61.3	70.1	74.1	72.3	65.3	53.0	42.9	33.1	51.8
Mean Minimum Temp. (°F)	18.4	21.0	29.9	39.3	49.3	58.6	62.7	60.4	52.5	40.2	32.9	24.4	40.8
Extreme Maximum Temp. (°F)	68	74	86	88	96	100	101	100	95	90	79	74	101
Extreme Minimum Temp. (°F)	-24	-12	-7	18	29	38	42	39	32	18	5	-21	-24
Days Maximum Temp. ≥ 90°F	0	0	0	0	0	4	7	5	2	0	0	0	18
Days Maximum Temp. ≤ 32°F	11	8	2	0	0	0	0	0	0	0	1	6	28
Days Minimum Temp. ≤ 32°F	27	23	20	8	1	0	0	0	0	7	16	24	126
Days Minimum Temp. ≤ 0°F	3	2	0	0	0	0	0	0	0	0	0	1	6
Heating Degree Days (base 65°F)	1,164	959	753	420	167	26	3	7	90	376	657	982	5,604
Cooling Degree Days (base 65°F)	0	0	2	7	55	188	298	245	99	9	0	0	903
Mean Precipitation (in.)	2.48	2.30	3.20	3.93	4.40	3.67	4.15	3.27	2.65	2.96	3.34	2.99	39.34
Days With ≥ 0.1" Precipitation	6	6	7	8	8	7	7	6	5	6	7	6	79
Days With ≥ 1.0" Precipitation	0	0	0	1	1	1	1	1	1	1	1	0	8
Mean Snowfall (in.)	na	2.4	1.6	trace	0.0	0.0	0.0	0.0	0.0	0.0	0.5	1.4	na
Days With ≥ 1.0" Snow Depth	8	7	2	0	0	0	0	0	0	0	0	2	19

Fredericktown 4 S *Knox County* Elevation: 1,049 ft. Latitude: 40° 25' N Longitude: 82° 32' W

	JAN	FEB	MAR	APR	MAY	JUN	JUL	AUG	SEP	OCT	NOV	DEC	YEAR
Mean Maximum Temp. (°F)	32.2	36.6	47.4	59.6	70.5	79.3	83.1	81.5	75.1	63.1	49.8	38.8	59.7
Mean Temp. (°F)	22.9	26.5	36.6	47.4	58.0	67.0	70.7	68.7	61.9	50.3	39.9	30.3	48.3
Mean Minimum Temp. (°F)	13.5	16.4	25.7	35.2	45.4	54.6	58.2	55.8	48.6	37.5	30.0	21.7	36.9
Extreme Maximum Temp. (°F)	66	70	82	88	91	100	98	98	94	87	78	75	100
Extreme Minimum Temp. (°F)	-30	-26	-21	12	21	34	38	32	26	15	0	-16	-30
Days Maximum Temp. ≥ 90°F	0	0	0	0	0	2	4	2	1	0	0	0	9
Days Maximum Temp. ≤ 32°F	15	11	4	0	0	0	0	0	0	0	1	8	39
Days Minimum Temp. ≤ 32°F	29	26	24	13	2	0	0	0	1	10	19	26	150
Days Minimum Temp. ≤ 0°F	6	4	1	0	0	0	0	0	0	0	0	2	13
Heating Degree Days (base 65°F)	1,300	1,081	876	526	246	56	14	29	147	452	745	1,070	6,542
Cooling Degree Days (base 65°F)	0	0	1	4	32	123	207	147	54	3	0	0	571
Mean Precipitation (in.)	2.58	2.14	2.97	3.56	4.26	4.37	4.15	3.73	3.29	2.61	3.30	2.94	39.90
Days With ≥ 0.1" Precipitation	6	5	7	8	8	8	7	6	6	6	7	7	81
Days With ≥ 1.0" Precipitation	0	0	0	1	1	1	1	1	1	1	1	1	9
Mean Snowfall (in.)	7.8	5.3	3.1	0.7	trace	0.0	0.0	0.0	0.0	0.0	1.0	3.5	21.4
Days With ≥ 1.0" Snow Depth	na	7	2	0	0	0	0	0	0	0	1	3	na

Fremont *Sandusky County* Elevation: 597 ft. Latitude: 41° 20' N Longitude: 83° 07' W

	JAN	FEB	MAR	APR	MAY	JUN	JUL	AUG	SEP	OCT	NOV	DEC	YEAR
Mean Maximum Temp. (°F)	31.3	34.5	44.9	58.1	70.3	79.1	83.5	81.2	74.7	62.2	49.2	36.8	58.8
Mean Temp. (°F)	23.7	26.4	36.2	48.0	59.6	68.8	73.1	70.6	63.7	51.5	41.0	29.6	49.3
Mean Minimum Temp. (°F)	16.0	18.3	27.5	37.9	48.8	58.4	62.5	60.0	52.6	40.7	32.8	22.3	39.8
Extreme Maximum Temp. (°F)	62	72	81	87	92	104	100	99	95	86	77	71	104
Extreme Minimum Temp. (°F)	-20	-11	-5	8	29	38	46	41	31	19	9	-17	-20
Days Maximum Temp. ≥ 90°F	0	0	0	0	1	3	6	2	1	0	0	0	13
Days Maximum Temp. ≤ 32°F	16	12	5	0	0	0	0	0	0	0	1	10	44
Days Minimum Temp. ≤ 32°F	29	25	23	8	0	0	0	0	0	5	15	26	131
Days Minimum Temp. ≤ 0°F	5	3	0	0	0	0	0	0	0	0	0	1	9
Heating Degree Days (base 65°F)	1,275	1,082	887	510	211	43	5	16	116	421	713	1,092	6,371
Cooling Degree Days (base 65°F)	0	0	2	7	53	165	275	201	82	9	0	0	794
Mean Precipitation (in.)	2.09	1.89	2.71	3.31	3.72	4.26	3.44	3.33	3.07	2.56	2.93	2.73	36.04
Days With ≥ 0.1" Precipitation	6	5	7	8	8	7	6	6	6	6	7	7	79
Days With ≥ 1.0" Precipitation	0	0	0	1	1	1	1	1	1	0	0	0	6
Mean Snowfall (in.)	6.7	5.2	3.6	0.3	trace	0.0	0.0	0.0	0.0	trace	0.6	na	na
Days With ≥ 1.0" Snow Depth	8	6	3	0	0	0	0	0	0	0	0	na	na

Gallipolis *Gallia County*   Elevation: 567 ft.   Latitude: 38° 49' N   Longitude: 82° 11' W

	JAN	FEB	MAR	APR	MAY	JUN	JUL	AUG	SEP	OCT	NOV	DEC	YEAR
Mean Maximum Temp. (°F)	41.9	46.8	57.5	68.2	76.7	83.9	87.4	86.1	80.2	69.3	57.4	46.8	66.8
Mean Temp. (°F)	32.2	35.7	44.9	54.3	63.5	71.6	75.8	74.4	68.1	56.3	46.1	37.0	55.0
Mean Minimum Temp. (°F)	22.4	24.5	32.2	40.4	50.2	59.3	64.1	62.5	55.8	43.2	34.8	27.1	43.0
Extreme Maximum Temp. (°F)	76	77	86	91	96	102	105	105	98	87	82	80	105
Extreme Minimum Temp. (°F)	-28	-14	-8	16	26	34	44	40	31	17	6	-13	-28
Days Maximum Temp. ≥ 90°F	0	0	0	0	1	5	11	8	3	0	0	0	28
Days Maximum Temp. ≤ 32°F	7	4	1	0	0	0	0	0	0	0	0	3	15
Days Minimum Temp. ≤ 32°F	25	21	17	7	1	0	0	0	0	4	14	22	111
Days Minimum Temp. ≤ 0°F	2	1	0	0	0	0	0	0	0	0	0	0	3
Heating Degree Days (base 65°F)	1,012	821	621	329	119	14	1	3	49	281	562	861	4,673
Cooling Degree Days (base 65°F)	0	0	3	16	81	228	359	306	142	19	2	0	1,156
Mean Precipitation (in.)	2.90	2.90	3.60	3.29	3.98	3.88	4.32	3.66	2.98	2.79	3.09	3.27	40.66
Days With ≥ 0.1" Precipitation	7	7	8	8	8	8	7	7	6	6	7	7	86
Days With ≥ 1.0" Precipitation	0	0	0	0	1	1	1	1	1	1	1	1	8
Mean Snowfall (in.)	6.1	4.6	2.2	trace	0.0	0.0	0.0	0.0	0.0	trace	0.3	1.0	14.2
Days With ≥ 1.0" Snow Depth	7	6	1	0	0	0	0	0	0	0	0	1	15

Greenville Water Plant *Darke County*   Elevation: 1,023 ft.   Latitude: 40° 06' N   Longitude: 84° 39' W

	JAN	FEB	MAR	APR	MAY	JUN	JUL	AUG	SEP	OCT	NOV	DEC	YEAR
Mean Maximum Temp. (°F)	32.2	36.7	47.7	60.4	71.5	80.2	84.1	82.4	76.6	64.1	50.0	38.3	60.3
Mean Temp. (°F)	23.6	27.2	37.6	49.0	59.8	68.9	72.7	70.3	63.5	51.6	40.6	29.9	49.6
Mean Minimum Temp. (°F)	15.0	17.7	27.5	37.6	48.1	57.6	61.1	58.2	50.4	39.0	31.1	21.5	38.7
Extreme Maximum Temp. (°F)	63	72	82	89	92	101	104	101	94	87	78	72	104
Extreme Minimum Temp. (°F)	-33	-23	-14	10	26	37	43	36	28	14	1	-21	-33
Days Maximum Temp. ≥ 90°F	0	0	0	0	0	3	5	3	2	0	0	0	13
Days Maximum Temp. ≤ 32°F	15	11	4	0	0	0	0	0	0	0	1	9	40
Days Minimum Temp. ≤ 32°F	29	25	23	9	1	0	0	0	0	8	18	26	139
Days Minimum Temp. ≤ 0°F	5	4	0	0	0	0	0	0	0	0	0	2	11
Heating Degree Days (base 65°F)	1,277	1,060	843	481	202	39	6	17	121	417	727	1,081	6,271
Cooling Degree Days (base 65°F)	0	0	1	6	48	168	260	193	80	8	0	0	764
Mean Precipitation (in.)	2.16	2.05	2.91	3.56	4.04	3.98	4.24	3.18	2.47	2.73	3.11	2.69	37.12
Days With ≥ 0.1" Precipitation	5	5	7	8	8	7	6	6	5	6	7	6	76
Days With ≥ 1.0" Precipitation	0	0	0	1	1	1	1	1	1	1	1	0	8
Mean Snowfall (in.)	8.3	5.6	3.0	0.5	trace	0.0	0.0	0.0	0.0	0.2	0.8	3.3	21.7
Days With ≥ 1.0" Snow Depth	na	na	2	0	0	0	0	0	0	0	na	na	na

Hannibal Lock & Dam *Monroe County*   Elevation: 620 ft.   Latitude: 39° 40' N   Longitude: 80° 52' W

	JAN	FEB	MAR	APR	MAY	JUN	JUL	AUG	SEP	OCT	NOV	DEC	YEAR
Mean Maximum Temp. (°F)	37.1	41.5	51.4	63.0	72.6	80.6	84.1	82.7	76.4	65.0	53.6	42.2	62.5
Mean Temp. (°F)	28.4	31.6	40.3	50.3	60.3	68.6	73.3	72.1	65.4	53.5	43.6	33.6	51.8
Mean Minimum Temp. (°F)	19.6	21.7	29.0	37.6	47.8	56.6	62.4	61.4	54.4	41.9	33.4	25.1	40.9
Extreme Maximum Temp. (°F)	71	73	83	90	91	96	99	100	95	85	80	74	100
Extreme Minimum Temp. (°F)	-24	-11	-8	18	26	38	42	42	34	22	6	-14	-24
Days Maximum Temp. ≥ 90°F	0	0	0	0	0	2	6	4	1	0	0	0	13
Days Maximum Temp. ≤ 32°F	11	6	2	0	0	0	0	0	0	0	0	6	25
Days Minimum Temp. ≤ 32°F	27	23	21	9	1	0	0	0	0	3	15	24	123
Days Minimum Temp. ≤ 0°F	2	1	0	0	0	0	0	0	0	0	0	0	3
Heating Degree Days (base 65°F)	1,129	936	758	439	181	32	3	7	76	357	637	965	5,520
Cooling Degree Days (base 65°F)	0	0	0	5	37	147	272	235	91	8	0	0	795
Mean Precipitation (in.)	3.08	2.57	3.57	3.25	4.12	3.65	4.63	3.41	3.01	2.63	3.33	3.09	40.34
Days With ≥ 0.1" Precipitation	7	7	8	8	9	7	7	6	5	6	7	7	84
Days With ≥ 1.0" Precipitation	1	0	1	0	1	1	1	1	1	1	0	0	8
Mean Snowfall (in.)	na	na	na	trace	0.0	0.0	0.0	0.0	0.0	0.0	trace	na	na
Days With ≥ 1.0" Snow Depth	na	na	1	0	0	0	0	0	0	0	0	0	na

Hillsboro *Highland County*   Elevation: 1,099 ft.   Latitude: 39° 12' N   Longitude: 83° 37' W

	JAN	FEB	MAR	APR	MAY	JUN	JUL	AUG	SEP	OCT	NOV	DEC	YEAR
Mean Maximum Temp. (°F)	35.6	40.5	51.1	62.7	71.7	79.3	83.3	81.9	76.3	64.9	52.3	41.3	61.7
Mean Temp. (°F)	27.8	31.6	41.4	52.0	61.6	69.7	73.9	72.1	65.9	54.6	43.6	33.5	52.3
Mean Minimum Temp. (°F)	19.9	22.8	31.5	41.4	51.4	60.0	64.3	62.3	55.5	44.1	34.9	25.7	42.8
Extreme Maximum Temp. (°F)	72	73	81	87	89	98	100	99	96	87	80	76	100
Extreme Minimum Temp. (°F)	-23	-9	-1	16	32	37	46	40	25	20	4	-21	-23
Days Maximum Temp. ≥ 90°F	0	0	0	0	0	1	4	2	1	0	0	0	8
Days Maximum Temp. ≤ 32°F	12	8	2	0	0	0	0	0	0	0	1	6	29
Days Minimum Temp. ≤ 32°F	27	22	18	5	0	0	0	0	0	3	14	23	112
Days Minimum Temp. ≤ 0°F	2	1	0	0	0	0	0	0	0	0	0	1	4
Heating Degree Days (base 65°F)	1,148	935	729	396	157	25	2	7	76	332	637	970	5,414
Cooling Degree Days (base 65°F)	0	0	2	14	54	176	289	238	105	16	1	0	895
Mean Precipitation (in.)	2.94	2.68	3.79	4.11	4.70	4.21	4.03	4.27	3.36	2.90	3.22	3.12	43.33
Days With ≥ 0.1" Precipitation	7	6	8	8	9	8	7	6	5	6	7	6	83
Days With ≥ 1.0" Precipitation	0	0	1	1	1	1	1	1	1	1	1	1	10
Mean Snowfall (in.)	7.3	5.0	3.8	0.6	trace	0.0	0.0	0.0	0.0	0.2	0.8	2.8	20.5
Days With ≥ 1.0" Snow Depth	9	8	3	0	0	0	0	0	0	0	0	4	24

Hiram *Portage County*   Elevation: 1,227 ft.   Latitude: 41° 18' N   Longitude: 81° 09' W

	JAN	FEB	MAR	APR	MAY	JUN	JUL	AUG	SEP	OCT	NOV	DEC	YEAR
Mean Maximum Temp. (°F)	31.7	35.8	45.8	58.5	69.6	77.3	81.6	79.9	72.8	61.0	48.5	36.9	58.3
Mean Temp. (°F)	24.1	27.4	36.3	47.9	58.8	66.7	71.4	69.8	62.8	51.5	40.7	29.9	48.9
Mean Minimum Temp. (°F)	16.5	18.8	27.1	37.2	47.9	56.1	61.0	59.7	52.9	41.9	33.0	22.8	39.6
Extreme Maximum Temp. (°F)	65	69	81	87	90	100	99	95	91	81	75	73	100
Extreme Minimum Temp. (°F)	-25	-10	-6	12	25	34	44	38	32	21	1	-15	-25
Days Maximum Temp. ≥ 90°F	0	0	0	0	0	1	2	1	0	0	0	0	4
Days Maximum Temp. ≤ 32°F	16	12	4	0	0	0	0	0	0	0	1	10	43
Days Minimum Temp. ≤ 32°F	29	25	23	10	1	0	0	0	0	4	16	27	135
Days Minimum Temp. ≤ 0°F	3	2	0	0	0	0	0	0	0	0	0	1	6
Heating Degree Days (base 65°F)	1,261	1,056	883	514	225	61	9	18	123	418	722	1,082	6,372
Cooling Degree Days (base 65°F)	0	0	1	7	36	121	223	178	63	4	0	0	633
Mean Precipitation (in.)	2.67	2.30	3.38	3.55	3.75	4.08	3.89	3.79	4.15	3.23	3.65	3.47	41.91
Days With ≥ 0.1" Precipitation	8	7	9	9	8	8	7	7	8	8	9	9	97
Days With ≥ 1.0" Precipitation	0	0	0	0	0	1	1	1	1	1	0	0	5
Mean Snowfall (in.)	16.1	12.4	10.2	1.5	trace	0.0	0.0	0.0	0.0	0.2	6.0	15.2	61.6
Days With ≥ 1.0" Snow Depth	20	17	8	1	0	0	0	0	0	0	4	14	64

Hoytville 2 NE *Wood County*   Elevation: 698 ft.   Latitude: 41° 13' N   Longitude: 83° 46' W

	JAN	FEB	MAR	APR	MAY	JUN	JUL	AUG	SEP	OCT	NOV	DEC	YEAR
Mean Maximum Temp. (°F)	31.1	34.8	46.0	59.1	71.2	80.1	83.8	81.4	75.5	63.1	48.8	36.8	59.3
Mean Temp. (°F)	23.1	26.3	36.3	47.7	59.4	68.8	72.5	69.9	63.3	51.5	40.3	29.3	49.0
Mean Minimum Temp. (°F)	15.0	17.7	26.6	36.3	47.5	57.4	61.1	58.3	51.0	39.8	31.7	21.7	38.7
Extreme Maximum Temp. (°F)	65	71	82	88	93	105	101	98	95	87	78	69	105
Extreme Minimum Temp. (°F)	-22	-15	-9	1	25	36	41	37	27	17	8	-19	-22
Days Maximum Temp. ≥ 90°F	0	0	0	0	1	4	5	3	1	0	0	0	14
Days Maximum Temp. ≤ 32°F	16	12	4	0	0	0	0	0	0	0	1	10	43
Days Minimum Temp. ≤ 32°F	29	25	23	11	1	0	0	0	0	7	18	27	141
Days Minimum Temp. ≤ 0°F	5	3	0	0	0	0	0	0	0	0	0	2	10
Heating Degree Days (base 65°F)	1,293	1,087	884	520	218	43	8	22	125	420	735	1,101	6,456
Cooling Degree Days (base 65°F)	0	0	1	7	48	162	255	183	76	8	0	0	740
Mean Precipitation (in.)	1.78	1.70	2.51	3.26	3.41	3.60	3.86	3.54	2.64	2.40	2.79	2.40	33.89
Days With ≥ 0.1" Precipitation	5	4	6	8	7	7	7	6	5	5	7	6	73
Days With ≥ 1.0" Precipitation	0	0	0	1	1	1	1	1	0	0	0	0	5
Mean Snowfall (in.)	7.5	5.5	3.4	1.0	trace	0.0	0.0	0.0	0.0	trace	1.3	5.2	23.9
Days With ≥ 1.0" Snow Depth	15	11	4	1	0	0	0	0	0	0	1	8	40

Irwin *Union County*   Elevation: 1,007 ft.   Latitude: 40° 07' N   Longitude: 83° 29' W

	JAN	FEB	MAR	APR	MAY	JUN	JUL	AUG	SEP	OCT	NOV	DEC	YEAR
Mean Maximum Temp. (°F)	34.5	39.6	51.5	64.0	74.3	82.5	85.6	84.2	78.3	66.7	51.8	*39.6*	62.7
Mean Temp. (°F)	25.8	29.9	40.4	51.1	61.5	70.0	73.3	71.5	65.0	53.8	42.2	*31.3*	*51.3*
Mean Minimum Temp. (°F)	17.1	20.2	29.3	38.2	48.6	57.5	61.0	58.8	51.7	40.8	32.5	23.2	39.9
Extreme Maximum Temp. (°F)	66	72	82	88	93	101	101	101	95	88	79	72	101
Extreme Minimum Temp. (°F)	-28	-21	-17	11	27	34	41	35	28	15	2	-19	-28
Days Maximum Temp. ≥ 90°F	0	0	0	0	1	4	7	4	1	0	0	0	17
Days Maximum Temp. ≤ 32°F	13	9	2	0	0	0	0	0	0	0	1	*7*	*32*
Days Minimum Temp. ≤ 32°F	28	24	20	10	1	0	0	0	1	7	16	25	132
Days Minimum Temp. ≤ 0°F	5	3	0	0	0	0	0	0	0	0	0	1	9
Heating Degree Days (base 65°F)	1,208	984	759	419	163	24	4	11	90	352	678	*1,037*	*5,729*
Cooling Degree Days (base 65°F)	0	0	1	8	58	183	281	230	93	11	0	*0*	*865*
Mean Precipitation (in.)	2.25	1.93	2.62	3.52	4.14	4.28	4.67	3.67	2.92	2.57	3.13	2.68	38.38
Days With ≥ 0.1" Precipitation	*5*	*4*	6	7	8	7	7	6	5	5	6	*6*	*72*
Days With ≥ 1.0" Precipitation	0	0	0	1	1	1	1	1	1	0	1	*1*	*8*
Mean Snowfall (in.)	*6.8*	*4.5*	2.5	0.8	trace	0.0	0.0	0.0	0.0	trace	1.0	na	na
Days With ≥ 1.0" Snow Depth	*10*	*7*	*2*	0	0	0	0	0	0	0	1	na	na

Jackson 3 NW *Jackson County*   Elevation: 797 ft.   Latitude: 39° 05' N   Longitude: 82° 42' W

	JAN	FEB	MAR	APR	MAY	JUN	JUL	AUG	SEP	OCT	NOV	DEC	YEAR
Mean Maximum Temp. (°F)	*38.3*	*42.9*	53.1	64.8	73.9	81.0	84.6	*83.3*	*77.3*	65.8	54.0	43.3	*63.5*
Mean Temp. (°F)	*28.6*	*32.4*	41.4	51.5	61.1	69.0	73.3	*71.9*	*65.3*	53.2	43.1	33.8	*52.1*
Mean Minimum Temp. (°F)	*19.1*	*21.9*	29.6	38.1	48.2	57.0	61.9	*60.5*	*53.3*	40.5	32.2	24.2	*40.5*
Extreme Maximum Temp. (°F)	*74*	*76*	85	91	91	100	101	*102*	*96*	86	*81*	79	*102*
Extreme Minimum Temp. (°F)	*-28*	*-14*	*-15*	16	26	31	40	*36*	*30*	17	*-5*	-20	*-28*
Days Maximum Temp. ≥ 90°F	0	0	0	0	0	2	6	*4*	*1*	0	0	0	*13*
Days Maximum Temp. ≤ 32°F	*10*	*6*	2	0	0	0	0	*0*	*0*	0	0	6	*24*
Days Minimum Temp. ≤ 32°F	*27*	23	*19*	9	2	0	0	*0*	*0*	7	16	24	*127*
Days Minimum Temp. ≤ 0°F	*2*	*2*	0	0	0	0	0	*0*	*0*	0	0	1	*5*
Heating Degree Days (base 65°F)	*1,120*	*914*	728	407	169	33	4	*9*	*85*	370	651	961	*5,451*
Cooling Degree Days (base 65°F)	*0*	*0*	*3*	10	*57*	*171*	288	*240*	*103*	12	1	*0*	*885*
Mean Precipitation (in.)	2.76	2.76	3.75	3.43	3.96	4.14	4.03	*3.92*	*3.17*	2.82	3.12	3.27	*41.13*
Days With ≥ 0.1" Precipitation	*6*	*7*	8	8	8	8	7	*7*	*6*	6	6	8	*85*
Days With ≥ 1.0" Precipitation	*0*	0	1	0	1	1	1	*1*	*1*	0	1	1	*8*
Mean Snowfall (in.)	na	na	na	*0.7*	0.0	0.0	0.0	*0.0*	*0.0*	0.0	na	na	na
Days With ≥ 1.0" Snow Depth	na	na	na	*0*	0	0	0	*0*	*0*	0	na	na	na

Kenton *Hardin County*   Elevation: 994 ft.   Latitude: 40° 39' N   Longitude: 83° 36' W

	JAN	FEB	MAR	APR	MAY	JUN	JUL	AUG	SEP	OCT	NOV	DEC	YEAR
Mean Maximum Temp. (°F)	32.4	37.0	47.3	60.2	72.0	80.9	85.1	82.9	76.3	63.9	49.7	37.7	60.5
Mean Temp. (°F)	24.3	28.2	37.7	49.1	60.5	69.5	73.9	71.4	64.5	52.6	40.9	30.0	50.2
Mean Minimum Temp. (°F)	15.9	19.0	28.0	37.9	49.0	58.2	62.4	59.9	52.7	41.1	32.1	22.2	39.8
Extreme Maximum Temp. (°F)	64	71	82	89	93	104	103	103	96	87	78	71	104
Extreme Minimum Temp. (°F)	-22	-17	-5	10	26	36	42	39	27	16	3	-18	-22
Days Maximum Temp. ≥ 90°F	0	0	0	0	1	4	8	4	2	0	0	0	19
Days Maximum Temp. ≤ 32°F	15	10	4	0	0	0	0	0	0	0	2	9	40
Days Minimum Temp. ≤ 32°F	29	25	22	9	1	0	0	0	0	5	16	27	134
Days Minimum Temp. ≤ 0°F	4	3	0	0	0	0	0	0	0	0	0	1	8
Heating Degree Days (base 65°F)	1,256	1,032	841	478	189	37	4	14	103	389	715	1,080	6,138
Cooling Degree Days (base 65°F)	0	0	1	10	60	190	303	237	99	11	0	0	911
Mean Precipitation (in.)	2.23	2.02	2.75	3.48	3.84	3.53	4.01	3.30	2.61	2.14	2.84	2.72	35.47
Days With ≥ 0.1" Precipitation	6	6	7	8	7	7	7	6	5	5	7	7	78
Days With ≥ 1.0" Precipitation	0	0	0	1	1	1	1	1	1	0	0	0	6
Mean Snowfall (in.)	*10.0*	*6.4*	4.2	0.6	0.0	0.0	0.0	0.0	0.0	trace	*1.2*	*5.4*	27.8
Days With ≥ 1.0" Snow Depth	na	na	*4*	0	0	0	0	0	0	0	*1*	*6*	na

Lancaster 2 NW *Fairfield County*   Elevation: 859 ft.   Latitude: 39° 44' N   Longitude: 82° 38' W

	JAN	FEB	MAR	APR	MAY	JUN	JUL	AUG	SEP	OCT	NOV	DEC	YEAR
Mean Maximum Temp. (°F)	34.5	*38.7*	*49.6*	61.6	*71.8*	80.4	*84.2*	82.9	76.9	65.1	51.8	*40.5*	61.5
Mean Temp. (°F)	25.8	*29.1*	*38.9*	49.5	*59.7*	68.9	*72.8*	71.4	64.6	52.8	42.1	*32.0*	50.6
Mean Minimum Temp. (°F)	17.0	*19.4*	*28.2*	37.4	47.6	57.3	61.6	59.8	52.4	40.4	32.4	*23.4*	39.7
Extreme Maximum Temp. (°F)	68	71	*82*	89	92	101	99	101	96	86	80	78	*101*
Extreme Minimum Temp. (°F)	-24	-15	*-7*	8	27	34	41	35	30	19	3	-20	*-24*
Days Maximum Temp. ≥ 90°F	0	0	*0*	0	0	2	6	4	1	0	0	0	*13*
Days Maximum Temp. ≤ 32°F	14	9	*3*	0	0	0	0	0	0	0	1	7	*34*
Days Minimum Temp. ≤ 32°F	28	23	*22*	10	1	0	0	0	0	7	16	24	*131*
Days Minimum Temp. ≤ 0°F	4	*2*	*0*	0	0	0	0	0	0	0	0	1	7
Heating Degree Days (base 65°F)	1,209	*1,008*	803	468	206	37	*6*	14	104	381	681	*1,017*	5,934
Cooling Degree Days (base 65°F)	0	*0*	2	*11*	*48*	170	*273*	233	99	11	1	*0*	848
Mean Precipitation (in.)	2.28	*2.17*	2.65	*3.22*	*4.18*	3.82	4.37	3.64	2.76	2.46	3.09	2.91	37.55
Days With ≥ 0.1" Precipitation	5	*5*	6	*6*	7	6	7	6	5	5	7	6	*71*
Days With ≥ 1.0" Precipitation	0	0	*1*	*1*	1	1	1	1	1	0	1	0	8
Mean Snowfall (in.)	na	na	na	0.7	0.0	0.0	0.0	0.0	0.0	trace	*0.3*	na	na
Days With ≥ 1.0" Snow Depth	na	na	na	0	0	0	0	0	0	0	na	na	na

Lima WWTP *Allen County*   Elevation: 849 ft.   Latitude: 40° 43' N   Longitude: 84° 08' W

	JAN	FEB	MAR	APR	MAY	JUN	JUL	AUG	SEP	OCT	NOV	DEC	YEAR
Mean Maximum Temp. (°F)	33.1	37.6	48.3	60.9	72.5	80.9	84.7	82.5	76.6	64.3	50.4	38.7	60.9
Mean Temp. (°F)	25.6	29.4	39.1	50.3	61.6	70.5	74.4	72.4	66.0	54.1	42.5	31.7	51.5
Mean Minimum Temp. (°F)	18.0	21.1	29.9	39.7	50.7	60.0	64.1	62.2	55.3	43.9	34.4	24.5	42.0
Extreme Maximum Temp. (°F)	64	71	81	89	93	97	100	99	95	94	77	70	100
Extreme Minimum Temp. (°F)	-21	-15	-3	8	27	40	46	42	30	19	6	-17	-21
Days Maximum Temp. ≥ 90°F	0	0	0	0	1	3	6	3	1	0	0	0	14
Days Maximum Temp. ≤ 32°F	14	10	3	0	0	0	0	0	0	0	2	8	37
Days Minimum Temp. ≤ 32°F	28	23	20	7	1	0	0	0	0	3	14	24	120
Days Minimum Temp. ≤ 0°F	3	1	0	0	0	0	0	0	0	0	0	1	5
Heating Degree Days (base 65°F)	1,217	996	797	443	166	26	2	8	79	344	668	1,027	5,773
Cooling Degree Days (base 65°F)	0	0	2	10	66	201	310	251	113	15	0	0	968
Mean Precipitation (in.)	2.20	1.94	2.70	3.48	3.91	4.04	4.36	3.28	3.08	2.38	3.13	2.65	37.15
Days With ≥ 0.1" Precipitation	6	5	6	8	8	7	7	6	6	6	7	6	78
Days With ≥ 1.0" Precipitation	0	0	0	1	1	1	1	1	1	0	0	0	6
Mean Snowfall (in.)	na	na	na	0.1	0.0	0.0	0.0	0.0	0.0	trace	*trace*	na	na
Days With ≥ 1.0" Snow Depth	na	na	na	0	0	0	0	0	0	0	*0*	na	na

London *Madison County*   Elevation: 1,017 ft.   Latitude: 39° 53' N   Longitude: 83° 27' W

	JAN	FEB	MAR	APR	MAY	JUN	JUL	AUG	SEP	OCT	NOV	DEC	YEAR
Mean Maximum Temp. (°F)	34.4	39.1	50.4	62.6	73.2	81.5	85.1	83.0	77.1	65.3	51.3	40.0	61.9
Mean Temp. (°F)	26.3	30.0	39.9	50.4	61.0	69.8	73.5	71.4	64.7	53.2	42.1	32.1	51.2
Mean Minimum Temp. (°F)	18.1	20.8	29.3	38.2	48.7	58.0	61.8	59.7	52.4	41.0	32.8	24.2	40.4
Extreme Maximum Temp. (°F)	67	71	82	88	92	102	100	101	95	88	79	74	102
Extreme Minimum Temp. (°F)	-24	-19	-14	12	26	35	42	38	30	16	0	-18	-24
Days Maximum Temp. ≥ 90°F	0	0	0	0	0	4	7	4	1	0	0	0	16
Days Maximum Temp. ≤ 32°F	13	9	2	0	0	0	0	0	0	0	1	7	32
Days Minimum Temp. ≤ 32°F	27	23	20	9	1	0	0	0	0	6	16	24	126
Days Minimum Temp. ≤ 0°F	4	2	0	0	0	0	0	0	0	0	0	1	7
Heating Degree Days (base 65°F)	1,194	982	774	440	174	30	4	12	99	370	681	1,014	5,774
Cooling Degree Days (base 65°F)	0	0	1	7	55	184	286	222	93	10	0	0	858
Mean Precipitation (in.)	2.38	2.16	2.80	3.59	4.07	4.30	3.99	3.34	2.82	2.58	3.28	2.96	38.27
Days With ≥ 0.1" Precipitation	5	5	7	8	8	7	7	6	5	5	7	7	77
Days With ≥ 1.0" Precipitation	0	0	0	1	1	1	1	1	1	0	1	0	7
Mean Snowfall (in.)	*6.9*	na	na	0.4	0.0	0.0	0.0	0.0	0.0	0.2	*0.5*	na	na
Days With ≥ 1.0" Snow Depth	na	na	*2*	0	0	0	0	0	0	0	*0*	na	na

Mansfield 5 W *Richland County* Elevation: 1,348 ft. Latitude: 40° 46' N Longitude: 82° 37' W

	JAN	FEB	MAR	APR	MAY	JUN	JUL	AUG	SEP	OCT	NOV	DEC	YEAR
Mean Maximum Temp. (°F)	31.9	35.9	46.6	59.2	69.9	78.2	81.9	80.2	73.5	61.8	48.7	37.5	58.8
Mean Temp. (°F)	23.7	27.1	36.7	47.8	58.5	66.9	70.8	69.2	62.7	51.3	40.2	29.7	48.7
Mean Minimum Temp. (°F)	15.4	18.3	26.7	36.3	47.0	55.5	59.7	58.2	51.7	40.7	31.6	21.9	38.6
Extreme Maximum Temp. (°F)	66	69	81	87	89	100	99	97	94	84	76	69	100
Extreme Minimum Temp. (°F)	-25	-22	-11	5	18	28	38	37	25	15	3	-19	-25
Days Maximum Temp. ≥ 90°F	0	0	0	0	0	1	3	1	0	0	0	0	5
Days Maximum Temp. ≤ 32°F	15	12	5	0	0	0	0	0	0	0	2	10	44
Days Minimum Temp. ≤ 32°F	29	25	23	12	2	0	0	0	1	6	17	26	141
Days Minimum Temp. ≤ 0°F	5	3	1	0	0	0	0	0	0	0	0	1	10
Heating Degree Days (base 65°F)	1,276	1,063	871	518	232	59	14	22	133	426	739	1,087	6,440
Cooling Degree Days (base 65°F)	0	0	1	6	36	127	212	164	66	7	0	0	619
Mean Precipitation (in.)	2.08	1.69	2.65	3.54	4.14	4.16	3.92	3.63	3.27	2.51	2.91	2.55	37.05
Days With ≥ 0.1" Precipitation	5	5	7	8	9	7	7	7	6	6	6	6	79
Days With ≥ 1.0" Precipitation	0	0	0	1	1	1	1	1	1	0	1	0	7
Mean Snowfall (in.)	na	na	na	0.3	trace	0.0	0.0	0.0	0.0	trace	*1.0*	na	na
Days With ≥ 1.0" Snow Depth	na	na	*3*	0	0	0	0	0	0	0	*1*	na	na

Marietta WWTP *Washington County* Elevation: 577 ft. Latitude: 39° 25' N Longitude: 81° 26' W

	JAN	FEB	MAR	APR	MAY	JUN	JUL	AUG	SEP	OCT	NOV	DEC	YEAR
Mean Maximum Temp. (°F)	39.5	43.8	54.2	65.5	74.7	82.2	85.8	84.5	78.2	66.9	54.9	44.7	64.6
Mean Temp. (°F)	30.8	33.9	43.1	53.1	62.6	70.8	74.9	73.5	66.9	55.1	44.8	36.0	53.8
Mean Minimum Temp. (°F)	22.1	24.0	31.9	40.6	50.5	59.4	64.0	62.5	55.5	43.2	34.8	27.2	43.0
Extreme Maximum Temp. (°F)	73	75	85	91	93	99	102	100	96	86	81	78	102
Extreme Minimum Temp. (°F)	-23	-10	0	19	29	37	44	38	33	20	10	-11	-23
Days Maximum Temp. ≥ 90°F	0	0	0	0	1	3	8	6	2	0	0	0	20
Days Maximum Temp. ≤ 32°F	9	5	1	0	0	0	0	0	0	0	0	4	19
Days Minimum Temp. ≤ 32°F	25	22	17	6	1	0	0	0	0	3	14	22	110
Days Minimum Temp. ≤ 0°F	1	1	0	0	0	0	0	0	0	0	0	0	2
Heating Degree Days (base 65°F)	1,053	872	674	362	134	19	1	4	61	313	599	892	4,984
Cooling Degree Days (base 65°F)	0	0	2	11	64	205	332	274	116	13	1	0	1,018
Mean Precipitation (in.)	3.12	2.75	3.69	3.10	4.04	4.40	4.22	4.16	3.31	2.87	3.17	3.37	42.20
Days With ≥ 0.1" Precipitation	8	7	8	8	9	8	7	7	6	6	7	8	89
Days With ≥ 1.0" Precipitation	0	0	1	0	1	1	1	1	1	1	0	0	7
Mean Snowfall (in.)	*7.2*	na	3.4	0.5	0.0	0.0	0.0	0.0	0.0	trace	*0.6*	*2.6*	na
Days With ≥ 1.0" Snow Depth	*9*	na	1	0	0	0	0	0	0	0	*0*	*2*	na

Marion 2 N *Marion County* Elevation: 964 ft. Latitude: 40° 37' N Longitude: 83° 08' W

	JAN	FEB	MAR	APR	MAY	JUN	JUL	AUG	SEP	OCT	NOV	DEC	YEAR
Mean Maximum Temp. (°F)	32.3	36.7	47.3	60.2	71.1	80.3	84.0	82.2	75.7	63.5	49.8	38.0	60.1
Mean Temp. (°F)	24.1	27.7	37.5	48.8	59.7	69.2	73.0	70.8	63.8	52.1	41.0	30.4	49.8
Mean Minimum Temp. (°F)	15.8	18.7	27.6	37.4	48.3	58.0	61.9	59.3	51.9	40.7	32.1	22.8	39.6
Extreme Maximum Temp. (°F)	67	72	81	87	91	103	100	99	97	90	79	73	103
Extreme Minimum Temp. (°F)	-23	-20	-5	8	25	36	43	35	24	17	4	-19	-23
Days Maximum Temp. ≥ 90°F	0	0	0	0	1	4	6	4	2	0	0	0	17
Days Maximum Temp. ≤ 32°F	15	11	4	0	0	0	0	0	0	0	1	9	40
Days Minimum Temp. ≤ 32°F	29	25	22	10	1	0	0	0	0	6	17	26	136
Days Minimum Temp. ≤ 0°F	4	3	0	0	0	0	0	0	0	0	0	1	8
Heating Degree Days (base 65°F)	1,262	1,047	848	488	210	39	6	18	116	401	714	1,064	6,213
Cooling Degree Days (base 65°F)	0	0	2	8	51	172	270	206	83	10	0	0	802
Mean Precipitation (in.)	2.35	1.72	2.31	3.69	4.17	4.24	4.38	3.69	3.03	2.73	3.01	2.84	38.16
Days With ≥ 0.1" Precipitation	5	5	6	9	8	7	7	6	6	6	7	7	79
Days With ≥ 1.0" Precipitation	0	0	0	1	1	1	1	1	1	1	1	1	8
Mean Snowfall (in.)	9.7	5.3	3.2	0.6	0.0	0.0	0.0	0.0	0.0	trace	0.8	4.4	24.0
Days With ≥ 1.0" Snow Depth	*14*	*10*	*3*	0	0	0	0	0	0	0	1	5	*33*

Marysville *Union County* Elevation: 997 ft. Latitude: 40° 14' N Longitude: 83° 22' W

	JAN	FEB	MAR	APR	MAY	JUN	JUL	AUG	SEP	OCT	NOV	DEC	YEAR
Mean Maximum Temp. (°F)	33.5	37.8	49.0	61.2	72.2	80.4	84.2	82.3	75.7	63.5	50.0	38.7	60.7
Mean Temp. (°F)	25.8	29.2	39.2	50.2	61.1	69.7	73.7	71.7	64.8	53.0	41.7	31.5	51.0
Mean Minimum Temp. (°F)	17.9	20.7	29.4	39.1	50.0	58.8	63.1	61.0	53.8	42.4	33.3	24.1	41.1
Extreme Maximum Temp. (°F)	66	72	82	88	92	101	100	99	96	86	78	72	101
Extreme Minimum Temp. (°F)	-23	-18	-11	12	29	36	44	41	31	18	4	-20	-23
Days Maximum Temp. ≥ 90°F	0	0	0	0	0	3	6	3	1	0	0	0	13
Days Maximum Temp. ≤ 32°F	14	10	3	0	0	0	0	0	0	0	1	8	36
Days Minimum Temp. ≤ 32°F	28	24	21	7	0	0	0	0	0	4	15	25	124
Days Minimum Temp. ≤ 0°F	4	2	0	0	0	0	0	0	0	0	0	1	7
Heating Degree Days (base 65°F)	1,210	1,004	794	445	173	29	3	9	95	374	694	1,033	5,863
Cooling Degree Days (base 65°F)	0	0	2	7	58	180	292	232	95	9	0	0	875
Mean Precipitation (in.)	2.26	1.93	2.59	3.38	3.88	4.32	4.05	3.27	2.64	2.44	2.95	2.66	36.37
Days With ≥ 0.1" Precipitation	6	5	7	7	8	7	7	7	5	6	7	6	78
Days With ≥ 1.0" Precipitation	0	0	0	1	1	1	1	1	1	0	1	0	7
Mean Snowfall (in.)	6.5	4.8	3.3	0.9	0.0	0.0	0.0	0.0	0.0	trace	1.1	3.6	20.2
Days With ≥ 1.0" Snow Depth	13	8	0	0	0	0	0	0	0	0	1	5	30

McConnelsville Lock 7 *Morgan County*   Elevation: 757 ft.   Latitude: 39° 39' N   Longitude: 81° 51' W

	JAN	FEB	MAR	APR	MAY	JUN	JUL	AUG	SEP	OCT	NOV	DEC	YEAR
Mean Maximum Temp. (°F)	37.9	41.9	52.6	64.5	74.0	81.4	85.0	83.7	77.6	66.2	54.1	43.3	63.5
Mean Temp. (°F)	27.8	30.7	40.2	50.6	60.5	68.8	73.1	71.7	64.9	52.8	42.8	33.4	51.5
Mean Minimum Temp. (°F)	17.6	19.5	27.8	36.7	46.9	56.2	61.2	59.7	52.2	39.4	31.5	23.5	39.3
Extreme Maximum Temp. (°F)	74	75	84	91	94	99	102	99	97	87	81	77	102
Extreme Minimum Temp. (°F)	-32	-15	-11	15	26	32	40	39	31	18	1	-16	-32
Days Maximum Temp. ≥ 90°F	0	0	0	0	1	3	7	5	2	0	0	0	18
Days Maximum Temp. ≤ 32°F	11	6	1	0	0	0	0	0	0	0	0	5	23
Days Minimum Temp. ≤ 32°F	28	24	22	11	2	0	0	0	0	7	18	25	137
Days Minimum Temp. ≤ 0°F	3	3	0	0	0	0	0	0	0	0	0	1	7
Heating Degree Days (base 65°F)	1,145	962	761	433	180	32	4	9	91	377	659	973	5,626
Cooling Degree Days (base 65°F)	0	0	1	7	39	150	265	218	86	7	0	0	773
Mean Precipitation (in.)	3.03	2.49	3.48	3.64	4.37	4.14	4.85	4.35	3.22	2.79	3.38	3.22	42.96
Days With ≥ 0.1" Precipitation	8	7	8	8	9	7	8	7	6	6	7	8	89
Days With ≥ 1.0" Precipitation	0	0	1	1	1	1	1	1	1	1	1	0	9
Mean Snowfall (in.)	7.9	5.7	3.4	0.9	0.0	0.0	0.0	0.0	0.0	0.0	0.7	2.6	21.2
Days With ≥ 1.0" Snow Depth	na	5	2	0	0	0	0	0	0	0	0	2	na

Milford *Clermont County*   Elevation: 518 ft.   Latitude: 39° 11' N   Longitude: 84° 17' W

	JAN	FEB	MAR	APR	MAY	JUN	JUL	AUG	SEP	OCT	NOV	DEC	YEAR
Mean Maximum Temp. (°F)	37.0	41.3	52.4	64.3	74.6	82.4	86.8	85.2	78.5	66.9	53.7	42.5	63.8
Mean Temp. (°F)	27.8	31.1	41.0	51.3	61.7	70.2	74.7	73.1	65.9	53.7	43.0	33.4	52.3
Mean Minimum Temp. (°F)	18.6	20.9	29.6	38.5	48.6	57.9	62.6	61.0	53.2	40.5	32.1	24.3	40.6
Extreme Maximum Temp. (°F)	72	76	84	89	93	97	104	101	98	88	81	75	104
Extreme Minimum Temp. (°F)	-25	-13	-10	18	27	36	40	41	26	12	-3	-22	-25
Days Maximum Temp. ≥ 90°F	0	0	0	0	1	4	10	8	2	0	0	0	25
Days Maximum Temp. ≤ 32°F	11	7	1	0	0	0	0	0	0	0	1	6	26
Days Minimum Temp. ≤ 32°F	27	23	20	9	1	0	0	0	0	6	16	24	126
Days Minimum Temp. ≤ 0°F	3	2	0	0	0	0	0	0	0	0	0	1	6
Heating Degree Days (base 65°F)	1,146	951	739	412	157	23	2	5	80	355	652	973	5,495
Cooling Degree Days (base 65°F)	0	0	2	8	65	202	335	279	112	13	0	0	1,016
Mean Precipitation (in.)	3.14	2.57	3.78	4.18	4.98	4.51	4.03	4.22	3.15	3.14	3.67	3.35	44.72
Days With ≥ 0.1" Precipitation	7	6	8	9	9	8	7	7	6	7	8	7	89
Days With ≥ 1.0" Precipitation	0	0	1	1	1	1	1	1	1	1	1	1	10
Mean Snowfall (in.)	5.8	4.9	2.1	0.4	trace	0.0	0.0	trace	0.0	0.1	0.4	2.2	15.9
Days With ≥ 1.0" Snow Depth	8	7	2	0	0	0	0	0	0	0	0	3	20

Millport 2 NW *Columbiana County*   Elevation: 1,148 ft.   Latitude: 40° 43' N   Longitude: 80° 54' W

	JAN	FEB	MAR	APR	MAY	JUN	JUL	AUG	SEP	OCT	NOV	DEC	YEAR
Mean Maximum Temp. (°F)	34.7	39.1	49.5	61.5	71.3	79.6	83.3	82.0	75.1	63.4	50.7	39.8	60.8
Mean Temp. (°F)	25.6	28.9	38.3	48.5	58.4	66.8	70.8	69.2	62.5	51.1	40.9	31.3	49.4
Mean Minimum Temp. (°F)	16.5	18.7	26.9	35.5	45.4	54.0	58.3	56.5	49.8	38.7	31.1	22.7	37.8
Extreme Maximum Temp. (°F)	67	72	82	90	91	98	103	99	94	82	77	74	103
Extreme Minimum Temp. (°F)	-34	-21	-17	10	20	28	38	27	26	14	-5	-20	-34
Days Maximum Temp. ≥ 90°F	0	0	0	0	0	2	5	3	1	0	0	0	11
Days Maximum Temp. ≤ 32°F	13	8	3	0	0	0	0	0	0	0	1	8	33
Days Minimum Temp. ≤ 32°F	28	24	22	13	3	0	0	0	1	9	18	25	143
Days Minimum Temp. ≤ 0°F	5	3	1	0	0	0	0	0	0	0	0	1	10
Heating Degree Days (base 65°F)	1,214	1,012	823	492	229	54	11	22	131	428	716	1,038	6,170
Cooling Degree Days (base 65°F)	0	0	1	4	29	120	214	164	59	4	0	0	595
Mean Precipitation (in.)	2.47	2.31	3.11	3.24	4.09	3.83	4.15	3.12	3.27	2.53	3.25	3.12	38.49
Days With ≥ 0.1" Precipitation	7	7	8	8	9	8	8	6	7	6	8	8	90
Days With ≥ 1.0" Precipitation	0	0	0	0	1	1	1	1	1	0	0	0	5
Mean Snowfall (in.)	7.8	6.7	6.1	1.3	trace	0.0	0.0	0.0	0.0	trace	2.2	6.1	30.2
Days With ≥ 1.0" Snow Depth	na	na	na	0	0	0	0	0	0	0	1	na	na

Mineral Ridge Water Works *Trumbull County*   Elevation: 889 ft.   Latitude: 41° 09' N   Longitude: 80° 47' W

	JAN	FEB	MAR	APR	MAY	JUN	JUL	AUG	SEP	OCT	NOV	DEC	YEAR
Mean Maximum Temp. (°F)	35.2	39.5	50.1	62.5	73.6	81.5	85.7	83.7	76.9	65.1	51.7	40.9	62.2
Mean Temp. (°F)	26.8	29.9	39.0	49.8	60.3	68.7	73.2	71.5	64.8	53.4	42.7	33.2	51.1
Mean Minimum Temp. (°F)	18.3	20.3	27.8	37.0	47.1	55.9	60.6	59.2	52.7	41.6	33.6	25.4	40.0
Extreme Maximum Temp. (°F)	67	73	82	90	92	98	102	100	94	91	79	74	102
Extreme Minimum Temp. (°F)	-24	-16	-6	13	24	29	41	34	26	14	4	-11	-24
Days Maximum Temp. ≥ 90°F	0	0	0	0	0	4	8	5	1	0	0	0	18
Days Maximum Temp. ≤ 32°F	12	8	2	0	0	0	0	0	0	0	1	7	30
Days Minimum Temp. ≤ 32°F	28	24	22	10	2	0	0	0	0	5	15	25	131
Days Minimum Temp. ≤ 0°F	3	2	0	0	0	0	0	0	0	0	0	0	5
Heating Degree Days (base 65°F)	1,178	984	801	457	188	38	5	12	93	361	664	980	5,761
Cooling Degree Days (base 65°F)	0	0	1	6	50	158	279	223	93	7	0	0	817
Mean Precipitation (in.)	2.16	1.82	2.67	3.11	3.41	4.32	4.19	3.34	3.97	2.55	2.99	2.68	37.21
Days With ≥ 0.1" Precipitation	6	6	7	7	8	8	7	6	7	6	7	7	82
Days With ≥ 1.0" Precipitation	0	0	0	0	0	1	1	1	1	0	0	0	4
Mean Snowfall (in.)	9.8	6.9	7.1	1.1	trace	0.0	0.0	0.0	0.0	trace	1.8	7.8	34.5
Days With ≥ 1.0" Snow Depth	16	13	7	0	0	0	0	0	0	0	1	7	41

Montpelier *Williams County*   Elevation: 859 ft.   Latitude: 41° 35' N   Longitude: 84° 36' W

	JAN	FEB	MAR	APR	MAY	JUN	JUL	AUG	SEP	OCT	NOV	DEC	YEAR
Mean Maximum Temp. (°F)	30.3	34.4	45.0	58.3	70.7	80.2	84.1	81.9	74.9	62.1	48.0	36.1	58.8
Mean Temp. (°F)	21.8	25.1	35.1	46.8	58.3	67.8	71.9	69.7	62.2	50.1	39.0	28.3	48.0
Mean Minimum Temp. (°F)	13.3	15.7	25.1	35.2	45.8	55.5	59.7	57.4	49.5	38.1	29.9	20.4	37.1
Extreme Maximum Temp. (°F)	62	71	80	88	92	104	104	102	95	89	76	69	104
Extreme Minimum Temp. (°F)	-25	-22	-7	8	26	36	43	36	28	18	5	-19	-25
Days Maximum Temp. ≥ 90°F	0	0	0	0	1	4	6	3	1	0	0	0	15
Days Maximum Temp. ≤ 32°F	17	12	4	0	0	0	0	0	0	0	2	10	45
Days Minimum Temp. ≤ 32°F	30	27	25	12	2	0	0	0	1	9	20	28	154
Days Minimum Temp. ≤ 0°F	6	4	0	0	0	0	0	0	0	0	0	2	12
Heating Degree Days (base 65°F)	1,332	1,121	922	544	239	50	9	22	140	459	774	1,133	6,745
Cooling Degree Days (base 65°F)	0	0	1	5	39	152	248	187	64	4	0	0	700
Mean Precipitation (in.)	1.92	1.89	2.86	3.60	3.54	3.53	3.47	3.57	3.22	2.55	3.13	2.54	35.82
Days With ≥ 0.1" Precipitation	5	5	7	8	7	7	7	7	6	6	7	7	79
Days With ≥ 1.0" Precipitation	0	0	0	1	1	1	1	1	1	0	0	0	6
Mean Snowfall (in.)	9.9	8.5	4.5	0.8	0.0	0.0	0.0	0.0	0.0	0.2	1.9	8.1	33.9
Days With ≥ 1.0" Snow Depth	17	14	5	0	0	0	0	0	0	0	2	8	46

Napoleon *Henry County*   Elevation: 679 ft.   Latitude: 41° 22' N   Longitude: 84° 00' W

	JAN	FEB	MAR	APR	MAY	JUN	JUL	AUG	SEP	OCT	NOV	DEC	YEAR
Mean Maximum Temp. (°F)	31.1	35.1	47.3	60.2	72.3	81.5	85.0	83.0	75.9	63.9	49.8	37.1	60.2
Mean Temp. (°F)	23.2	26.5	37.4	48.6	60.1	69.5	73.5	71.3	64.1	52.7	41.2	29.6	49.8
Mean Minimum Temp. (°F)	15.2	17.7	27.4	37.0	47.8	57.4	62.0	59.5	52.3	41.4	32.6	22.0	39.4
Extreme Maximum Temp. (°F)	62	69	80	88	93	105	104	99	95	88	77	70	105
Extreme Minimum Temp. (°F)	-24	-13	-7	5	28	39	40	38	27	22	6	-18	-24
Days Maximum Temp. ≥ 90°F	0	0	0	0	1	4	7	4	1	0	0	0	17
Days Maximum Temp. ≤ 32°F	16	11	3	0	0	0	0	0	0	0	1	9	40
Days Minimum Temp. ≤ 32°F	29	25	22	10	1	0	0	0	1	5	16	26	135
Days Minimum Temp. ≤ 0°F	4	3	0	0	0	0	0	0	0	0	0	2	9
Heating Degree Days (base 65°F)	1,290	1,083	850	493	200	33	4	14	110	383	708	1,091	6,259
Cooling Degree Days (base 65°F)	0	0	1	8	48	160	272	208	79	6	0	0	782
Mean Precipitation (in.)	1.96	1.65	2.68	3.62	3.52	3.40	3.94	3.42	2.72	2.52	2.91	2.47	34.81
Days With ≥ 0.1" Precipitation	5	5	6	8	7	7	7	6	6	6	6	7	76
Days With ≥ 1.0" Precipitation	0	0	0	1	1	1	1	1	0	0	0	0	5
Mean Snowfall (in.)	8.7	5.8	2.8	1.1	0.0	0.0	0.0	0.0	0.0	0.1	0.9	5.2	24.6
Days With ≥ 1.0" Snow Depth	15	12	3	0	0	0	0	0	0	0	1	7	38

New Lexington 2 NW *Perry County*   Elevation: 889 ft.   Latitude: 39° 44' N   Longitude: 82° 13' W

	JAN	FEB	MAR	APR	MAY	JUN	JUL	AUG	SEP	OCT	NOV	DEC	YEAR
Mean Maximum Temp. (°F)	36.7	41.4	52.4	64.2	73.8	81.2	84.7	83.1	77.1	65.7	52.9	42.0	62.9
Mean Temp. (°F)	27.2	30.6	40.3	50.4	60.3	68.6	72.6	71.1	64.6	52.7	42.1	32.8	51.1
Mean Minimum Temp. (°F)	17.6	19.8	28.1	36.6	46.9	56.0	60.5	59.1	52.0	39.6	31.2	23.5	39.2
Extreme Maximum Temp. (°F)	72	74	84	91	92	100	101	100	95	85	80	77	101
Extreme Minimum Temp. (°F)	-35	-20	-11	14	27	32	40	37	30	17	-4	-24	-35
Days Maximum Temp. ≥ 90°F	0	0	0	0	1	3	6	4	1	0	0	0	15
Days Maximum Temp. ≤ 32°F	11	7	2	0	0	0	0	0	0	0	1	6	27
Days Minimum Temp. ≤ 32°F	28	24	21	12	2	0	0	0	0	8	17	25	137
Days Minimum Temp. ≤ 0°F	4	2	0	0	0	0	0	0	0	0	0	1	7
Heating Degree Days (base 65°F)	1,167	964	761	438	183	33	4	11	94	382	683	992	5,712
Cooling Degree Days (base 65°F)	0	0	1	6	39	144	251	203	81	6	0	0	731
Mean Precipitation (in.)	2.87	2.64	3.38	3.76	4.29	4.25	4.68	3.94	2.82	2.65	3.38	3.08	41.74
Days With ≥ 0.1" Precipitation	8	6	8	9	9	8	8	7	6	6	8	7	90
Days With ≥ 1.0" Precipitation	0	0	0	1	1	1	1	1	1	0	1	0	7
Mean Snowfall (in.)	9.2	5.9	3.6	0.5	trace	0.0	0.0	0.0	0.0	trace	0.7	3.0	22.9
Days With ≥ 1.0" Snow Depth	14	9	4	0	0	0	0	0	0	0	1	5	33

New Philadelphia *Tuscarawas County*   Elevation: 892 ft.   Latitude: 40° 30' N   Longitude: 81° 28' W

	JAN	FEB	MAR	APR	MAY	JUN	JUL	AUG	SEP	OCT	NOV	DEC	YEAR
Mean Maximum Temp. (°F)	34.7	38.7	49.1	61.0	71.9	80.3	84.1	82.9	76.1	64.1	51.2	40.1	61.2
Mean Temp. (°F)	26.2	29.1	38.2	48.7	59.1	68.1	72.2	70.9	63.9	52.0	41.7	32.0	50.2
Mean Minimum Temp. (°F)	17.6	19.4	27.3	36.3	46.3	55.8	60.2	58.8	51.6	39.8	32.2	23.8	39.1
Extreme Maximum Temp. (°F)	69	73	84	90	91	99	102	99	96	87	79	76	102
Extreme Minimum Temp. (°F)	-22	-12	-5	13	25	30	42	36	30	18	4	-16	-22
Days Maximum Temp. ≥ 90°F	0	0	0	0	0	3	6	4	1	0	0	0	14
Days Maximum Temp. ≤ 32°F	13	9	3	0	0	0	0	0	0	0	1	7	33
Days Minimum Temp. ≤ 32°F	28	24	22	12	2	0	0	0	0	7	17	25	137
Days Minimum Temp. ≤ 0°F	3	3	0	0	0	0	0	0	0	0	0	1	7
Heating Degree Days (base 65°F)	1,197	1,008	824	491	218	46	8	16	112	402	692	1,017	6,031
Cooling Degree Days (base 65°F)	0	0	1	7	41	147	253	211	83	7	1	0	751
Mean Precipitation (in.)	2.74	2.40	3.22	3.54	4.08	4.43	4.10	4.21	3.22	2.62	3.28	3.04	40.88
Days With ≥ 0.1" Precipitation	6	6	8	8	8	8	7	7	6	6	7	7	84
Days With ≥ 1.0" Precipitation	0	0	0	1	1	1	1	1	1	0	1	0	7
Mean Snowfall (in.)	9.9	6.6	5.1	1.5	trace	0.0	0.0	0.0	0.0	trace	1.4	5.2	29.7
Days With ≥ 1.0" Snow Depth	15	11	5	0	0	0	0	0	0	0	1	6	38

Newark Water Works *Licking County*   Elevation: 833 ft.   Latitude: 40° 05' N   Longitude: 81° 25' W

	JAN	FEB	MAR	APR	MAY	JUN	JUL	AUG	SEP	OCT	NOV	DEC	YEAR
Mean Maximum Temp. (°F)	35.4	39.9	51.0	63.1	73.3	81.3	84.9	83.0	76.5	64.6	51.8	40.6	62.1
Mean Temp. (°F)	27.3	30.8	40.6	51.1	61.0	69.5	73.4	71.7	64.9	53.0	42.5	32.7	51.5
Mean Minimum Temp. (°F)	19.1	21.6	30.2	39.0	48.7	57.7	61.9	60.3	53.2	41.4	33.1	24.8	40.9
Extreme Maximum Temp. (°F)	69	73	82	89	91	100	100	100	96	87	78	76	100
Extreme Minimum Temp. (°F)	-24	-14	-7	15	29	32	41	38	31	19	3	-17	-24
Days Maximum Temp. ≥ 90°F	0	0	0	0	0	3	6	4	1	0	0	0	14
Days Maximum Temp. ≤ 32°F	12	8	2	0	0	0	0	0	0	0	1	7	30
Days Minimum Temp. ≤ 32°F	27	23	19	9	1	0	0	0	0	5	15	24	123
Days Minimum Temp. ≤ 0°F	3	2	0	0	0	0	0	0	0	0	0	1	6
Heating Degree Days (base 65°F)	1,163	960	751	421	170	29	4	9	93	373	670	994	5,637
Cooling Degree Days (base 65°F)	0	0	1	7	49	170	280	224	90	8	1	0	830
Mean Precipitation (in.)	2.84	2.45	3.16	3.89	4.26	4.40	4.53	4.17	2.96	2.66	3.37	3.17	41.86
Days With ≥ 0.1" Precipitation	7	6	8	8	8	8	8	7	6	6	7	7	86
Days With ≥ 1.0" Precipitation	0	0	0	1	1	1	1	1	1	0	1	0	7
Mean Snowfall (in.)	8.4	5.3	2.8	0.9	trace	0.0	0.0	0.0	0.0	trace	0.5	2.7	20.6
Days With ≥ 1.0" Snow Depth	12	8	3	0	0	0	0	0	0	0	0	4	27

Norwalk WWTP *Huron County*   Elevation: 669 ft.   Latitude: 41° 16' N   Longitude: 82° 37' W

	JAN	FEB	MAR	APR	MAY	JUN	JUL	AUG	SEP	OCT	NOV	DEC	YEAR
Mean Maximum Temp. (°F)	32.3	35.4	45.3	57.9	69.5	78.5	82.6	80.7	74.3	62.4	49.3	37.8	58.8
Mean Temp. (°F)	24.4	27.0	36.3	47.4	58.6	67.9	72.1	70.2	63.3	51.9	41.2	30.5	49.2
Mean Minimum Temp. (°F)	16.5	18.6	27.2	37.0	47.7	57.2	61.6	59.6	52.3	41.3	33.1	23.2	39.6
Extreme Maximum Temp. (°F)	65	70	81	87	91	103	98	98	94	85	77	73	103
Extreme Minimum Temp. (°F)	-21	-11	-7	7	26	33	41	41	30	17	6	-17	-21
Days Maximum Temp. ≥ 90°F	0	0	0	0	0	3	5	2	1	0	0	0	11
Days Maximum Temp. ≤ 32°F	16	12	4	0	0	0	0	0	0	0	1	9	42
Days Minimum Temp. ≤ 32°F	29	25	22	10	1	0	0	0	0	5	16	26	134
Days Minimum Temp. ≤ 0°F	4	3	0	0	0	0	0	0	0	0	0	1	8
Heating Degree Days (base 65°F)	1,253	1,065	885	529	237	56	12	20	124	408	708	1,062	6,359
Cooling Degree Days (base 65°F)	0	0	2	8	46	152	250	192	81	9	0	0	740
Mean Precipitation (in.)	2.16	1.79	2.72	3.32	3.50	4.22	3.72	3.81	3.24	2.41	2.98	2.75	36.62
Days With ≥ 0.1" Precipitation	6	5	7	8	8	7	7	6	7	6	7	7	81
Days With ≥ 1.0" Precipitation	0	0	0	0	1	1	1	1	1	0	0	0	5
Mean Snowfall (in.)	8.6	6.2	4.8	0.8	trace	0.0	0.0	trace	0.0	trace	0.9	5.4	26.7
Days With ≥ 1.0" Snow Depth	15	13	5	1	0	0	0	0	0	0	1	8	43

Oberlin *Lorain County*   Elevation: 813 ft.   Latitude: 41° 16' N   Longitude: 82° 13' W

	JAN	FEB	MAR	APR	MAY	JUN	JUL	AUG	SEP	OCT	NOV	DEC	YEAR
Mean Maximum Temp. (°F)	33.0	36.8	46.9	59.6	71.2	79.9	83.9	82.0	75.3	63.3	50.0	38.3	60.0
Mean Temp. (°F)	24.6	27.6	36.9	48.0	59.0	67.9	72.2	70.1	63.2	51.8	41.0	30.3	49.4
Mean Minimum Temp. (°F)	16.1	18.4	26.7	36.4	46.8	56.0	60.5	58.2	51.0	40.3	32.1	22.3	38.7
Extreme Maximum Temp. (°F)	65	71	82	87	92	104	100	100	96	85	76	75	104
Extreme Minimum Temp. (°F)	-23	-18	-15	11	24	30	38	32	25	16	4	-18	-23
Days Maximum Temp. ≥ 90°F	0	0	0	0	0	3	6	3	1	0	0	0	13
Days Maximum Temp. ≤ 32°F	15	11	4	0	0	0	0	0	0	0	1	8	39
Days Minimum Temp. ≤ 32°F	29	25	23	11	2	0	0	0	0	5	17	26	138
Days Minimum Temp. ≤ 0°F	4	3	0	0	0	0	0	0	0	0	0	1	8
Heating Degree Days (base 65°F)	1,247	1,049	867	510	222	52	10	17	123	409	712	1,069	6,287
Cooling Degree Days (base 65°F)	0	0	2	6	44	146	246	184	71	6	0	0	705
Mean Precipitation (in.)	2.19	1.96	2.66	3.20	3.55	3.91	3.70	3.41	3.34	2.46	3.18	2.76	36.32
Days With ≥ 0.1" Precipitation	6	6	7	8	8	8	7	6	6	6	8	7	83
Days With ≥ 1.0" Precipitation	0	0	0	0	1	1	1	1	1	0	0	0	5
Mean Snowfall (in.)	11.9	*9.7*	7.1	1.6	trace	0.0	0.0	0.0	0.0	trace	2.5	8.6	*41.4*
Days With ≥ 1.0" Snow Depth	na	na	na	1	0	0	0	0	0	0	*1*	na	na

Painesville 4 NW *Lake County*   Elevation: 597 ft.   Latitude: 41° 45' N   Longitude: 81° 18' W

	JAN	FEB	MAR	APR	MAY	JUN	JUL	AUG	SEP	OCT	NOV	DEC	YEAR
Mean Maximum Temp. (°F)	34.3	36.6	45.6	56.3	67.7	76.7	81.4	79.8	74.2	63.2	51.2	40.3	58.9
Mean Temp. (°F)	27.2	29.0	37.1	47.6	58.6	67.8	72.6	71.3	65.4	54.7	44.1	33.7	50.8
Mean Minimum Temp. (°F)	20.1	21.4	28.7	38.8	49.5	58.9	63.8	62.8	56.6	46.1	36.9	27.1	42.6
Extreme Maximum Temp. (°F)	67	74	82	91	92	98	96	93	91	86	78	75	98
Extreme Minimum Temp. (°F)	-19	-8	0	17	29	39	45	39	33	24	5	-11	-19
Days Maximum Temp. ≥ 90°F	0	0	0	0	0	1	2	1	0	0	0	0	4
Days Maximum Temp. ≤ 32°F	13	11	4	0	0	0	0	0	0	0	0	6	34
Days Minimum Temp. ≤ 32°F	27	24	21	7	0	0	0	0	0	1	9	22	111
Days Minimum Temp. ≤ 0°F	2	1	0	0	0	0	0	0	0	0	0	0	3
Heating Degree Days (base 65°F)	1,166	1,009	858	522	229	45	3	7	74	324	624	962	5,823
Cooling Degree Days (base 65°F)	0	0	1	5	38	135	257	213	94	11	0	0	754
Mean Precipitation (in.)	2.28	1.78	2.76	3.15	3.02	3.80	3.13	3.72	4.12	3.28	3.54	2.94	37.52
Days With ≥ 0.1" Precipitation	7	5	7	8	7	7	6	7	7	8	9	8	86
Days With ≥ 1.0" Precipitation	0	0	0	0	0	1	1	1	1	0	1	0	5
Mean Snowfall (in.)	10.2	*7.3*	5.2	1.2	trace	0.0	0.0	0.0	0.0	trace	*2.1*	*8.8*	*34.8*
Days With ≥ 1.0" Snow Depth	17	11	4	0	0	0	0	0	0	0	1	9	42

Pandora *Putnam County* Elevation: 767 ft. Latitude: 40° 57' N Longitude: 83° 58' W

	JAN	FEB	MAR	APR	MAY	JUN	JUL	AUG	SEP	OCT	NOV	DEC	YEAR
Mean Maximum Temp. (°F)	31.6	35.7	47.1	59.9	71.7	80.5	84.0	81.7	75.4	62.9	48.9	37.1	59.7
Mean Temp. (°F)	24.2	27.6	37.8	49.1	60.6	69.6	73.2	70.8	64.1	52.5	41.0	30.2	50.1
Mean Minimum Temp. (°F)	16.7	19.6	28.5	38.2	49.4	58.7	62.3	59.9	52.8	42.0	33.1	23.2	40.4
Extreme Maximum Temp. (°F)	65	71	82	89	94	103	101	100	96	87	78	71	103
Extreme Minimum Temp. (°F)	-21	-17	-13	6	25	37	44	40	28	19	8	-19	-21
Days Maximum Temp. ≥ 90°F	0	0	0	0	1	3	6	3	1	0	0	0	14
Days Maximum Temp. ≤ 32°F	16	12	4	0	0	0	0	0	0	0	2	10	44
Days Minimum Temp. ≤ 32°F	28	24	21	9	1	0	0	0	0	5	16	26	130
Days Minimum Temp. ≤ 0°F	5	3	0	0	0	0	0	0	0	0	0	1	9
Heating Degree Days (base 65°F)	1,260	1,048	838	481	190	32	4	14	107	390	714	1,073	6,151
Cooling Degree Days (base 65°F)	0	0	2	8	59	179	278	210	87	10	0	0	833
Mean Precipitation (in.)	2.04	1.86	2.74	3.32	3.65	3.97	3.86	3.35	3.01	2.31	2.86	2.66	35.63
Days With ≥ 0.1" Precipitation	6	5	7	8	7	7	7	6	6	5	7	6	77
Days With ≥ 1.0" Precipitation	0	0	0	0	1	1	1	1	1	0	0	0	5
Mean Snowfall (in.)	9.5	7.1	4.2	1.2	trace	0.0	0.0	0.0	trace	0.1	2.0	6.6	30.7
Days With ≥ 1.0" Snow Depth	16	12	5	1	0	0	0	0	0	0	1	8	43

Paulding *Paulding County* Elevation: 725 ft. Latitude: 41° 07' N Longitude: 84° 36' W

	JAN	FEB	MAR	APR	MAY	JUN	JUL	AUG	SEP	OCT	NOV	DEC	YEAR
Mean Maximum Temp. (°F)	30.4	34.5	45.8	58.9	70.9	80.3	84.2	81.9	75.4	62.5	48.7	36.6	59.2
Mean Temp. (°F)	22.0	25.6	36.0	47.6	59.1	68.7	72.4	69.8	62.9	50.7	39.6	28.7	48.6
Mean Minimum Temp. (°F)	13.7	16.6	26.2	36.2	47.2	57.1	60.5	57.7	50.2	38.8	30.4	20.8	37.9
Extreme Maximum Temp. (°F)	62	71	80	87	92	104	100	99	95	85	79	70	104
Extreme Minimum Temp. (°F)	-25	-20	-11	7	25	36	45	39	27	17	5	-20	-25
Days Maximum Temp. ≥ 90°F	0	0	0	0	0	3	6	3	1	0	0	0	13
Days Maximum Temp. ≤ 32°F	17	12	4	0	0	0	0	0	0	0	2	10	45
Days Minimum Temp. ≤ 32°F	30	26	24	10	1	0	0	0	1	7	19	27	145
Days Minimum Temp. ≤ 0°F	6	3	0	0	0	0	0	0	0	0	0	2	11
Heating Degree Days (base 65°F)	1,327	1,106	892	520	221	41	7	20	127	443	755	1,117	6,576
Cooling Degree Days (base 65°F)	0	0	0	4	45	159	251	179	74	5	0	0	717
Mean Precipitation (in.)	1.90	1.73	2.68	3.38	3.78	3.43	3.41	2.95	3.00	2.50	2.95	2.58	34.29
Days With ≥ 0.1" Precipitation	5	4	6	7	7	6	6	5	6	6	6	6	70
Days With ≥ 1.0" Precipitation	0	0	0	1	1	1	1	1	0	0	1	0	6
Mean Snowfall (in.)	5.5	5.3	3.2	0.4	0.0	0.0	0.0	0.0	0.0	trace	1.2	4.1	19.7
Days With ≥ 1.0" Snow Depth	na	na	na	0	0	0	0	0	0	0	1	na	na

Philo 3 SW *Muskingum County* Elevation: 1,017 ft. Latitude: 39° 50' N Longitude: 81° 55' W

	JAN	FEB	MAR	APR	MAY	JUN	JUL	AUG	SEP	OCT	NOV	DEC	YEAR
Mean Maximum Temp. (°F)	34.9	39.6	50.4	62.0	71.0	78.0	81.7	80.6	74.4	63.5	51.0	40.1	60.6
Mean Temp. (°F)	27.3	30.9	40.5	51.0	60.1	67.7	71.5	70.3	63.9	52.9	42.5	32.6	50.9
Mean Minimum Temp. (°F)	19.6	22.2	30.5	39.9	49.3	57.3	61.3	59.8	53.2	42.3	34.0	25.0	41.2
Extreme Maximum Temp. (°F)	67	73	83	89	89	98	102	99	97	85	80	76	102
Extreme Minimum Temp. (°F)	-27	-10	-2	12	25	33	43	39	28	19	2	-18	-27
Days Maximum Temp. ≥ 90°F	0	0	0	0	0	0	3	1	1	0	0	0	5
Days Maximum Temp. ≤ 32°F	13	9	3	0	0	0	0	0	0	0	2	8	35
Days Minimum Temp. ≤ 32°F	27	23	19	7	1	0	0	0	0	5	15	24	121
Days Minimum Temp. ≤ 0°F	2	1	0	0	0	0	0	0	0	0	0	1	4
Heating Degree Days (base 65°F)	1,164	958	759	428	192	42	9	16	109	377	669	998	5,721
Cooling Degree Days (base 65°F)	0	0	3	11	42	126	222	182	75	9	1	0	671
Mean Precipitation (in.)	2.09	2.07	2.70	3.11	4.08	4.18	4.19	3.77	2.83	2.50	2.97	2.54	37.03
Days With ≥ 0.1" Precipitation	6	5	7	7	8	8	7	6	6	6	7	6	79
Days With ≥ 1.0" Precipitation	0	0	0	1	1	1	1	1	1	0	0	0	6
Mean Snowfall (in.)	9.4	5.3	4.3	1.1	trace	0.0	0.0	0.0	0.0	trace	1.1	3.6	24.8
Days With ≥ 1.0" Snow Depth	13	9	3	0	0	0	0	0	0	0	1	5	31

Portsmouth Sciotoville *Scioto County* Elevation: 538 ft. Latitude: 38° 45' N Longitude: 82° 53' W

	JAN	FEB	MAR	APR	MAY	JUN	JUL	AUG	SEP	OCT	NOV	DEC	YEAR
Mean Maximum Temp. (°F)	39.7	44.4	55.1	66.4	75.5	82.8	86.7	85.4	79.3	67.9	55.9	45.2	65.3
Mean Temp. (°F)	30.9	34.6	44.2	54.1	63.5	71.5	75.5	73.8	67.2	55.4	45.4	36.2	54.4
Mean Minimum Temp. (°F)	22.1	24.8	33.4	42.0	51.5	60.0	64.2	62.2	55.0	42.9	34.8	27.1	43.3
Extreme Maximum Temp. (°F)	74	76	84	92	93	101	104	104	100	88	82	76	104
Extreme Minimum Temp. (°F)	-29	-8	0	12	28	38	40	35	31	22	7	-18	-29
Days Maximum Temp. ≥ 90°F	0	0	0	0	1	5	10	7	2	0	0	0	25
Days Maximum Temp. ≤ 32°F	8	5	1	0	0	0	0	0	0	0	0	4	18
Days Minimum Temp. ≤ 32°F	26	22	15	5	0	0	0	0	0	4	13	21	106
Days Minimum Temp. ≤ 0°F	1	1	0	0	0	0	0	0	0	0	0	1	3
Heating Degree Days (base 65°F)	1,049	851	640	337	120	17	1	5	63	306	584	887	4,860
Cooling Degree Days (base 65°F)	0	0	2	13	74	213	330	269	114	14	1	0	1,030
Mean Precipitation (in.)	3.16	2.82	3.65	3.44	4.37	3.86	4.06	4.00	3.05	2.63	3.02	3.33	41.39
Days With ≥ 0.1" Precipitation	7	7	8	8	9	7	8	6	5	6	7	7	85
Days With ≥ 1.0" Precipitation	1	1	1	1	1	1	1	1	1	0	1	1	11
Mean Snowfall (in.)	5.5	3.7	2.3	0.3	trace	0.0	0.0	0.0	0.0	trace	0.3	1.2	13.3
Days With ≥ 1.0" Snow Depth	7	6	2	0	0	0	0	0	0	0	0	1	16

Put-In-Bay *Ottawa County*   Elevation: 577 ft.   Latitude: 41° 39' N   Longitude: 82° 48' W

	JAN	FEB	MAR	APR	MAY	JUN	JUL	AUG	SEP	OCT	NOV	DEC	YEAR
Mean Maximum Temp. (°F)	31.2	33.9	43.1	55.3	67.1	77.3	82.3	80.6	73.7	61.3	48.4	36.9	57.6
Mean Temp. (°F)	24.8	26.7	35.9	47.2	59.2	69.4	74.6	73.5	66.6	54.5	42.6	31.2	50.5
Mean Minimum Temp. (°F)	18.4	19.7	28.6	39.1	51.2	61.5	66.9	66.3	59.4	47.6	36.6	25.5	43.4
Extreme Maximum Temp. (°F)	60	63	78	87	91	99	100	95	97	84	79	68	100
Extreme Minimum Temp. (°F)	-18	-10	-2	13	33	41	51	50	37	30	11	-14	-18
Days Maximum Temp. ≥ 90°F	0	0	0	0	0	1	4	2	1	0	0	0	8
Days Maximum Temp. ≤ 32°F	16	13	4	0	0	0	0	0	0	0	1	8	42
Days Minimum Temp. ≤ 32°F	28	25	21	5	0	0	0	0	0	0	9	23	111
Days Minimum Temp. ≤ 0°F	2	1	0	0	0	0	0	0	0	0	0	1	4
Heating Degree Days (base 65°F)	1,239	1,075	896	532	211	27	1	3	61	329	667	1,040	6,081
Cooling Degree Days (base 65°F)	0	0	0	6	35	162	307	269	105	8	0	0	892
Mean Precipitation (in.)	1.58	1.44	5.21	2.91	3.33	3.41	3.06	3.31	3.16	2.55	2.68	2.15	34.79
Days With ≥ 0.1" Precipitation	5	4	5	7	7	6	6	6	6	6	6	5	69
Days With ≥ 1.0" Precipitation	0	0	0	0	1	1	1	1	1	0	0	0	5
Mean Snowfall (in.)	7.3	5.3	2.8	0.4	trace	0.0	0.0	0.0	0.0	trace	0.2	3.7	19.7
Days With ≥ 1.0" Snow Depth	17	12	5	0	0	0	0	0	0	0	0	7	41

Ripley Exp. Farm *Brown County*   Elevation: 879 ft.   Latitude: 38° 47' N   Longitude: 83° 48' W

	JAN	FEB	MAR	APR	MAY	JUN	JUL	AUG	SEP	OCT	NOV	DEC	YEAR
Mean Maximum Temp. (°F)	38.0	42.8	53.1	64.3	73.4	81.5	85.2	84.0	78.1	66.3	53.6	43.4	63.6
Mean Temp. (°F)	29.1	32.9	42.3	52.7	62.2	70.5	74.4	72.8	66.2	54.3	43.9	34.4	53.0
Mean Minimum Temp. (°F)	20.2	22.9	31.5	41.0	50.9	59.6	63.5	61.6	54.3	42.2	34.1	25.4	42.3
Extreme Maximum Temp. (°F)	73	74	81	88	90	102	103	103	96	87	81	76	103
Extreme Minimum Temp. (°F)	-28	-11	-5	15	30	37	43	39	30	18	2	-22	-28
Days Maximum Temp. ≥ 90°F	0	0	0	0	0	3	7	5	2	0	0	0	17
Days Maximum Temp. ≤ 32°F	10	7	2	0	0	0	0	0	0	0	1	5	25
Days Minimum Temp. ≤ 32°F	27	22	18	6	0	0	0	0	0	5	14	23	115
Days Minimum Temp. ≤ 0°F	3	1	0	0	0	0	0	0	0	0	0	1	5
Heating Degree Days (base 65°F)	1,106	901	699	377	147	22	2	6	76	339	628	942	5,245
Cooling Degree Days (base 65°F)	0	0	2	11	66	200	314	262	111	14	1	0	981
Mean Precipitation (in.)	2.84	2.77	4.14	4.17	4.97	4.49	4.56	4.09	3.25	3.05	3.43	3.57	45.33
Days With ≥ 0.1" Precipitation	6	6	8	9	9	8	7	7	6	6	7	8	87
Days With ≥ 1.0" Precipitation	0	1	1	1	1	1	2	1	1	1	1	1	12
Mean Snowfall (in.)	7.5	5.6	4.1	0.5	trace	0.0	0.0	0.0	0.0	trace	0.9	2.9	21.5
Days With ≥ 1.0" Snow Depth	10	8	3	0	0	0	0	0	0	0	0	4	25

Sandusky *Erie County*   Elevation: 583 ft.   Latitude: 41° 27' N   Longitude: 82° 43' W

	JAN	FEB	MAR	APR	MAY	JUN	JUL	AUG	SEP	OCT	NOV	DEC	YEAR
Mean Maximum Temp. (°F)	32.2	35.0	44.1	56.3	68.0	77.5	82.3	80.3	73.7	62.0	49.3	37.9	58.2
Mean Temp. (°F)	25.1	27.6	36.5	47.8	59.5	69.1	73.7	71.9	64.8	53.3	42.2	31.3	50.2
Mean Minimum Temp. (°F)	18.0	20.2	28.8	39.2	50.9	60.6	65.1	63.4	55.9	44.6	35.0	24.7	42.2
Extreme Maximum Temp. (°F)	65	71	81	88	93	103	99	98	94	86	77	73	103
Extreme Minimum Temp. (°F)	-20	-7	-7	16	32	43	41	45	36	24	9	-16	-20
Days Maximum Temp. ≥ 90°F	0	0	0	0	0	2	4	2	1	0	0	0	9
Days Maximum Temp. ≤ 32°F	16	12	5	0	0	0	0	0	0	0	1	9	43
Days Minimum Temp. ≤ 32°F	28	24	21	5	0	0	0	0	0	2	13	25	118
Days Minimum Temp. ≤ 0°F	3	2	0	0	0	0	0	0	0	0	0	1	6
Heating Degree Days (base 65°F)	1,230	1,049	878	518	212	36	3	7	92	365	678	1,039	6,107
Cooling Degree Days (base 65°F)	0	0	2	7	46	165	285	231	91	10	0	0	837
Mean Precipitation (in.)	1.86	1.71	2.48	3.06	3.29	4.10	3.38	3.58	3.13	2.32	2.75	2.53	34.19
Days With ≥ 0.1" Precipitation	5	4	6	7	7	7	6	6	6	6	6	6	72
Days With ≥ 1.0" Precipitation	0	0	0	0	1	1	1	1	1	0	0	0	5
Mean Snowfall (in.)	8.7	6.0	3.0	0.6	trace	0.0	0.0	0.0	0.0	trace	0.3	4.3	22.9
Days With ≥ 1.0" Snow Depth	14	8	3	0	0	0	0	0	0	0	0	6	31

Springfield New Water Works *Clark County*   Elevation: 928 ft.   Latitude: 39° 58' N   Longitude: 83° 49' W

	JAN	FEB	MAR	APR	MAY	JUN	JUL	AUG	SEP	OCT	NOV	DEC	YEAR
Mean Maximum Temp. (°F)	33.7	37.9	48.6	60.5	71.4	80.0	83.8	82.4	76.3	63.9	50.7	39.6	60.7
Mean Temp. (°F)	25.2	28.5	38.5	49.2	59.9	69.2	72.8	70.9	64.0	52.0	41.5	31.5	50.3
Mean Minimum Temp. (°F)	16.5	19.1	28.4	37.8	48.4	58.2	61.8	59.3	51.7	40.1	32.2	23.3	39.7
Extreme Maximum Temp. (°F)	68	73	81	93	91	98	98	100	95	86	79	72	100
Extreme Minimum Temp. (°F)	-26	-18	-13	14	26	34	43	39	29	15	3	-26	-26
Days Maximum Temp. ≥ 90°F	0	0	0	0	0	2	5	3	1	0	0	0	11
Days Maximum Temp. ≤ 32°F	14	10	3	0	0	0	0	0	0	0	1	8	36
Days Minimum Temp. ≤ 32°F	28	24	21	10	1	0	0	0	0	7	17	25	133
Days Minimum Temp. ≤ 0°F	4	3	0	0	0	0	0	0	0	0	0	1	8
Heating Degree Days (base 65°F)	1,229	1,025	815	476	199	37	6	15	111	405	701	1,032	6,051
Cooling Degree Days (base 65°F)	0	0	2	6	49	176	270	213	86	9	0	0	811
Mean Precipitation (in.)	2.27	1.81	2.51	3.40	4.34	4.45	4.15	3.62	2.90	2.57	2.96	2.71	37.69
Days With ≥ 0.1" Precipitation	5	5	6	7	8	8	7	6	5	5	6	7	75
Days With ≥ 1.0" Precipitation	0	0	0	1	1	1	1	1	1	1	1	0	8
Mean Snowfall (in.)	na	na	na	trace	0.0	0.0	0.0	0.0	0.0	trace	0.1	na	na
Days With ≥ 1.0" Snow Depth	na	na	na	0	0	0	0	0	0	0	0	na	na

Steubenville *Jefferson County*   Elevation: 990 ft.   Latitude: 40° 23' N   Longitude: 80° 38' W

	JAN	FEB	MAR	APR	MAY	JUN	JUL	AUG	SEP	OCT	NOV	DEC	YEAR
Mean Maximum Temp. (°F)	36.5	40.4	50.8	62.4	72.0	79.9	83.3	82.0	75.6	64.1	52.1	41.6	61.7
Mean Temp. (°F)	28.4	31.6	40.6	50.8	60.8	69.2	73.3	72.0	65.5	53.8	43.5	33.8	51.9
Mean Minimum Temp. (°F)	20.3	22.7	30.3	39.2	49.5	58.4	63.2	62.0	55.4	43.5	34.8	26.0	42.1
Extreme Maximum Temp. (°F)	72	74	83	89	90	98	102	96	95	84	80	77	102
Extreme Minimum Temp. (°F)	-22	-8	-1	16	27	34	45	42	34	22	5	-14	-22
Days Maximum Temp. ≥ 90°F	0	0	0	0	0	2	4	2	1	0	0	0	9
Days Maximum Temp. ≤ 32°F	12	8	2	0	0	0	0	0	0	0	1	7	30
Days Minimum Temp. ≤ 32°F	27	22	19	8	1	0	0	0	0	2	13	23	115
Days Minimum Temp. ≤ 0°F	2	1	0	0	0	0	0	0	0	0	0	0	3
Heating Degree Days (base 65°F)	1,128	937	753	427	172	30	3	7	78	348	640	961	5,484
Cooling Degree Days (base 65°F)	0	0	2	8	47	165	280	233	96	9	1	0	841
Mean Precipitation (in.)	2.80	2.43	3.31	3.20	3.98	4.45	4.20	3.72	3.25	2.61	3.42	3.00	40.37
Days With ≥ 0.1" Precipitation	7	6	8	8	9	8	8	7	6	6	8	7	88
Days With ≥ 1.0" Precipitation	0	0	0	0	1	1	1	1	1	0	1	0	6
Mean Snowfall (in.)	na	na	na	trace	0.0	0.0	0.0	0.0	0.0	0.2	*0.3*	na	na
Days With ≥ 1.0" Snow Depth	na	na	na	0	0	0	0	0	0	0	*0*	na	na

Tiffin *Seneca County*   Elevation: 738 ft.   Latitude: 41° 07' N   Longitude: 83° 10' W

	JAN	FEB	MAR	APR	MAY	JUN	JUL	AUG	SEP	OCT	NOV	DEC	YEAR
Mean Maximum Temp. (°F)	32.1	36.1	47.6	60.2	71.9	80.3	84.4	82.2	76.0	63.3	49.5	37.8	60.1
Mean Temp. (°F)	24.8	28.2	38.4	49.5	60.7	69.5	73.7	71.4	64.8	52.7	41.6	30.8	50.5
Mean Minimum Temp. (°F)	17.5	20.2	29.2	38.7	49.5	58.6	63.0	60.6	53.6	42.0	33.6	23.8	40.9
Extreme Maximum Temp. (°F)	67	72	82	88	93	105	101	98	95	86	79	72	105
Extreme Minimum Temp. (°F)	-21	-15	-2	8	28	38	44	39	31	19	7	-18	-21
Days Maximum Temp. ≥ 90°F	0	0	0	0	1	3	6	3	1	0	0	0	14
Days Maximum Temp. ≤ 32°F	15	11	3	0	0	0	0	0	0	0	1	9	39
Days Minimum Temp. ≤ 32°F	28	24	20	8	0	0	0	0	0	4	15	25	124
Days Minimum Temp. ≤ 0°F	3	2	0	0	0	0	0	0	0	0	0	1	6
Heating Degree Days (base 65°F)	1,239	1,033	818	469	185	37	4	12	96	384	696	1,054	6,027
Cooling Degree Days (base 65°F)	0	0	2	9	59	178	290	220	93	9	0	0	860
Mean Precipitation (in.)	2.26	1.97	2.69	3.39	3.68	4.19	3.34	3.77	3.14	2.39	3.00	2.93	36.75
Days With ≥ 0.1" Precipitation	6	5	7	8	8	8	7	6	6	6	7	7	81
Days With ≥ 1.0" Precipitation	0	0	0	1	1	1	1	1	1	0	0	0	6
Mean Snowfall (in.)	8.8	6.2	3.7	1.2	trace	0.0	0.0	0.0	0.0	trace	1.2	6.7	27.8
Days With ≥ 1.0" Snow Depth	16	13	4	1	0	0	0	0	0	0	1	8	43

Upper Sandusky *Wyandot County*   Elevation: 853 ft.   Latitude: 40° 50' N   Longitude: 83° 17' W

	JAN	FEB	MAR	APR	MAY	JUN	JUL	AUG	SEP	OCT	NOV	DEC	YEAR
Mean Maximum Temp. (°F)	32.4	36.6	47.6	60.4	71.7	80.6	84.4	82.7	76.4	63.9	49.8	38.1	60.4
Mean Temp. (°F)	24.8	28.2	38.2	49.3	60.3	69.5	73.4	71.5	64.7	52.8	41.4	30.8	50.4
Mean Minimum Temp. (°F)	17.2	19.8	28.7	38.1	48.9	58.3	62.2	60.1	53.0	41.8	32.9	23.5	40.4
Extreme Maximum Temp. (°F)	67	72	82	87	92	104	102	99	95	88	79	72	104
Extreme Minimum Temp. (°F)	-23	-16	-8	9	26	37	43	40	28	18	6	-20	-23
Days Maximum Temp. ≥ 90°F	0	0	0	0	1	3	6	4	1	0	0	0	15
Days Maximum Temp. ≤ 32°F	15	11	3	0	0	0	0	0	0	0	1	9	39
Days Minimum Temp. ≤ 32°F	28	24	20	9	1	0	0	0	0	5	16	25	128
Days Minimum Temp. ≤ 0°F	4	2	0	0	0	0	0	0	0	0	0	1	7
Heating Degree Days (base 65°F)	1,239	1,033	826	474	195	35	5	12	98	383	701	1,052	6,053
Cooling Degree Days (base 65°F)	0	0	2	7	52	174	275	219	90	11	0	0	830
Mean Precipitation (in.)	2.11	1.77	2.63	3.50	3.98	3.72	4.17	3.22	3.03	2.22	3.05	2.63	36.03
Days With ≥ 0.1" Precipitation	6	5	6	8	8	7	7	6	6	6	7	7	79
Days With ≥ 1.0" Precipitation	0	0	0	1	1	1	1	1	1	0	1	0	7
Mean Snowfall (in.)	8.3	5.8	3.6	1.2	trace	0.0	0.0	0.0	0.0	trace	1.4	6.3	26.6
Days With ≥ 1.0" Snow Depth	14	11	4	0	0	0	0	0	0	0	1	6	36

Urbana WWTP *Champaign County*   Elevation: 997 ft.   Latitude: 40° 06' N   Longitude: 83° 47' W

	JAN	FEB	MAR	APR	MAY	JUN	JUL	AUG	SEP	OCT	NOV	DEC	YEAR
Mean Maximum Temp. (°F)	33.4	37.5	48.1	60.5	71.5	80.3	84.4	82.7	76.4	63.7	50.4	39.1	60.7
Mean Temp. (°F)	25.1	28.5	38.3	49.3	60.1	69.2	72.9	70.8	64.0	52.1	41.4	31.1	50.2
Mean Minimum Temp. (°F)	16.8	19.4	28.5	38.1	48.7	58.0	61.5	58.9	51.5	40.5	32.4	23.1	39.8
Extreme Maximum Temp. (°F)	66	68	80	87	93	99	100	101	96	87	76	72	101
Extreme Minimum Temp. (°F)	-26	-18	-8	14	28	36	42	39	28	18	1	-22	-26
Days Maximum Temp. ≥ 90°F	0	0	0	0	0	3	6	3	1	0	0	0	13
Days Maximum Temp. ≤ 32°F	14	10	3	0	0	0	0	0	0	0	1	8	36
Days Minimum Temp. ≤ 32°F	28	24	21	9	1	0	0	0	0	6	16	25	130
Days Minimum Temp. ≤ 0°F	4	3	0	0	0	0	0	0	0	0	0	1	8
Heating Degree Days (base 65°F)	1,230	1,025	820	470	194	35	5	14	108	400	700	1,043	6,044
Cooling Degree Days (base 65°F)	0	0	0	5	46	167	266	205	81	7	0	0	777
Mean Precipitation (in.)	2.33	2.09	2.85	3.52	4.37	4.46	4.97	3.61	2.87	2.78	3.05	2.90	39.80
Days With ≥ 0.1" Precipitation	6	5	7	8	8	8	7	6	5	6	6	6	79
Days With ≥ 1.0" Precipitation	1	0	0	1	1	1	2	1	1	1	1	1	11
Mean Snowfall (in.)	na	na	na	0.5	0.0	0.0	0.0	0.0	0.0	0.1	*0.3*	na	na
Days With ≥ 1.0" Snow Depth	na	na	na	0	0	0	0	0	0	0	*0*	na	na

Van Wert 1 S *Van Wert County*   Elevation: 787 ft.   Latitude: 40° 51' N   Longitude: 84° 35' W

	JAN	FEB	MAR	APR	MAY	JUN	JUL	AUG	SEP	OCT	NOV	DEC	YEAR
Mean Maximum Temp. (°F)	32.2	36.3	47.6	60.7	72.6	81.5	85.2	82.9	76.6	64.1	49.6	37.6	60.6
Mean Temp. (°F)	24.4	27.8	38.0	49.6	61.1	70.4	74.1	71.8	64.9	52.9	41.2	30.3	50.5
Mean Minimum Temp. (°F)	16.6	19.1	28.3	38.4	49.6	59.2	63.0	60.6	53.1	41.6	32.8	23.0	40.5
Extreme Maximum Temp. (°F)	64	72	81	88	94	104	103	99	97	89	77	71	104
Extreme Minimum Temp. (°F)	-22	-14	-9	9	28	39	44	41	30	20	7	-18	-22
Days Maximum Temp. ≥ 90°F	0	0	0	0	1	4	7	4	2	0	0	0	18
Days Maximum Temp. ≤ 32°F	15	10	3	0	0	0	0	0	0	0	1	9	38
Days Minimum Temp. ≤ 32°F	29	25	21	8	1	0	0	0	0	4	16	26	130
Days Minimum Temp. ≤ 0°F	4	3	0	0	0	0	0	0	0	0	0	1	8
Heating Degree Days (base 65°F)	1,253	1,045	831	464	176	28	3	11	97	380	708	1,068	6,064
Cooling Degree Days (base 65°F)	0	0	1	8	62	198	301	232	97	11	0	0	910
Mean Precipitation (in.)	2.00	1.83	2.66	3.57	3.81	4.16	3.93	3.28	2.90	2.63	3.07	2.68	36.52
Days With ≥ 0.1" Precipitation	5	5	7	8	8	7	7	6	6	6	7	6	78
Days With ≥ 1.0" Precipitation	0	0	0	1	1	1	1	1	1	1	1	0	8
Mean Snowfall (in.)	*9.3*	6.8	2.8	1.2	0.0	0.0	0.0	0.0	0.0	0.2	1.8	7.7	*29.8*
Days With ≥ 1.0" Snow Depth	12	11	4	0	0	0	0	0	0	0	1	6	34

Warren 3 S *Trumbull County*   Elevation: 898 ft.   Latitude: 41° 12' N   Longitude: 80° 49' W

	JAN	FEB	MAR	APR	MAY	JUN	JUL	AUG	SEP	OCT	NOV	DEC	YEAR
Mean Maximum Temp. (°F)	33.9	37.6	47.9	60.1	71.0	79.1	83.1	81.4	74.2	62.7	50.2	39.3	60.1
Mean Temp. (°F)	25.0	27.6	36.8	47.3	57.8	66.4	70.5	69.0	62.0	50.8	40.7	31.0	48.7
Mean Minimum Temp. (°F)	15.9	17.6	25.5	34.4	44.5	53.5	57.9	56.6	49.7	38.8	31.2	22.6	37.3
Extreme Maximum Temp. (°F)	67	73	82	90	91	99	101	99	93	83	78	76	101
Extreme Minimum Temp. (°F)	-26	-20	-11	10	20	28	38	30	27	16	-7	-17	-26
Days Maximum Temp. ≥ 90°F	0	0	0	0	0	2	4	2	1	0	0	0	9
Days Maximum Temp. ≤ 32°F	14	10	4	0	0	0	0	0	0	0	1	8	37
Days Minimum Temp. ≤ 32°F	29	25	24	14	4	0	0	0	1	9	18	26	150
Days Minimum Temp. ≤ 0°F	4	3	0	0	0	0	0	0	0	0	0	1	8
Heating Degree Days (base 65°F)	1,236	1,049	871	529	246	62	14	24	144	437	722	1,048	6,382
Cooling Degree Days (base 65°F)	0	0	1	5	30	114	208	162	58	3	0	0	581
Mean Precipitation (in.)	2.24	1.67	2.95	3.25	3.59	4.01	4.22	3.32	3.93	2.69	3.10	2.80	37.77
Days With ≥ 0.1" Precipitation	6	5	8	8	8	8	7	7	8	7	7	7	86
Days With ≥ 1.0" Precipitation	0	0	0	1	1	1	1	1	1	0	0	0	6
Mean Snowfall (in.)	11.1	8.2	5.5	0.5	trace	0.0	0.0	0.0	0.0	trace	1.3	7.3	33.9
Days With ≥ 1.0" Snow Depth	16	11	4	0	0	0	0	0	0	0	1	8	40

Washington Court House *Fayette County*   Elevation: 958 ft.   Latitude: 39° 31' N   Longitude: 83° 25' W

	JAN	FEB	MAR	APR	MAY	JUN	JUL	AUG	SEP	OCT	NOV	DEC	YEAR
Mean Maximum Temp. (°F)	35.6	40.4	51.3	63.4	72.4	79.5	82.6	81.8	76.5	65.8	52.4	40.9	61.9
Mean Temp. (°F)	28.0	31.8	41.6	52.2	62.1	70.1	73.6	72.3	66.2	54.9	43.5	33.4	52.5
Mean Minimum Temp. (°F)	20.3	23.2	31.8	40.9	51.7	60.6	64.5	62.8	55.9	44.0	34.6	25.8	43.0
Extreme Maximum Temp. (°F)	69	73	83	89	91	93	97	97	95	86	80	77	97
Extreme Minimum Temp. (°F)	-27	-11	-4	16	30	39	47	42	33	19	1	-20	-27
Days Maximum Temp. ≥ 90°F	0	0	0	0	0	1	3	3	1	0	0	0	8
Days Maximum Temp. ≤ 32°F	12	8	2	0	0	0	0	0	0	0	1	7	30
Days Minimum Temp. ≤ 32°F	27	22	18	6	0	0	0	0	0	3	14	23	113
Days Minimum Temp. ≤ 0°F	2	1	0	0	0	0	0	0	0	0	0	1	4
Heating Degree Days (base 65°F)	1,140	930	722	388	148	22	2	6	71	319	640	974	5,362
Cooling Degree Days (base 65°F)	0	0	2	9	63	186	284	243	113	14	1	0	915
Mean Precipitation (in.)	2.43	2.35	3.32	3.60	4.70	3.79	3.95	3.85	2.64	2.65	3.01	2.81	39.10
Days With ≥ 0.1" Precipitation	6	6	8	8	8	7	7	6	5	6	6	7	80
Days With ≥ 1.0" Precipitation	0	0	1	0	1	1	1	1	1	1	1	0	8
Mean Snowfall (in.)	8.7	6.1	4.1	0.7	trace	0.0	0.0	0.0	0.0	0.2	1.0	3.5	24.3
Days With ≥ 1.0" Snow Depth	11	8	3	0	0	0	0	0	0	0	1	4	27

Wauseon Water Plant *Fulton County*   Elevation: 748 ft.   Latitude: 41° 31' N   Longitude: 84° 09' W

	JAN	FEB	MAR	APR	MAY	JUN	JUL	AUG	SEP	OCT	NOV	DEC	YEAR
Mean Maximum Temp. (°F)	30.8	35.0	46.4	59.8	71.8	80.9	84.3	81.9	75.7	63.2	48.8	36.5	59.6
Mean Temp. (°F)	23.0	26.6	36.9	48.5	59.8	69.1	72.6	70.3	63.6	51.9	40.3	29.2	49.3
Mean Minimum Temp. (°F)	15.3	18.0	27.3	37.2	47.7	57.3	60.8	58.6	51.4	40.6	31.7	22.0	39.0
Extreme Maximum Temp. (°F)	62	69	79	88	93	103	101	98	95	88	76	68	103
Extreme Minimum Temp. (°F)	-24	-16	-7	2	26	37	40	37	28	17	5	-21	-24
Days Maximum Temp. ≥ 90°F	0	0	0	0	0	3	6	3	1	0	0	0	13
Days Maximum Temp. ≤ 32°F	16	11	3	0	0	0	0	0	0	0	2	10	42
Days Minimum Temp. ≤ 32°F	29	26	23	10	1	0	0	0	0	6	18	27	140
Days Minimum Temp. ≤ 0°F	5	3	0	0	0	0	0	0	0	0	0	1	9
Heating Degree Days (base 65°F)	1,295	1,080	867	493	203	34	5	15	112	404	736	1,102	6,346
Cooling Degree Days (base 65°F)	0	0	0	6	51	172	266	197	80	6	0	0	778
Mean Precipitation (in.)	1.85	1.61	2.53	3.37	3.39	3.69	3.44	3.65	3.09	2.60	2.95	2.42	34.59
Days With ≥ 0.1" Precipitation	5	4	6	8	7	7	6	7	6	6	7	6	75
Days With ≥ 1.0" Precipitation	0	0	0	0	1	1	1	1	1	0	0	0	5
Mean Snowfall (in.)	8.7	7.0	4.4	0.9	trace	0.0	0.0	0.0	0.0	trace	2.2	5.8	29.0
Days With ≥ 1.0" Snow Depth	14	12	4	0	0	0	0	0	0	0	2	7	39

Waverly *Pike County*   Elevation: 557 ft.   Latitude: 39° 07' N   Longitude: 82° 59' W

	JAN	FEB	MAR	APR	MAY	JUN	JUL	AUG	SEP	OCT	NOV	DEC	YEAR
Mean Maximum Temp. (°F)	39.0	44.0	55.0	66.8	75.4	82.9	86.5	85.2	79.2	68.0	55.6	44.7	65.2
Mean Temp. (°F)	29.1	32.8	42.5	52.6	62.1	70.5	74.6	72.8	66.2	54.1	43.9	34.5	53.0
Mean Minimum Temp. (°F)	19.2	21.7	29.9	38.3	48.8	58.1	62.7	60.5	53.1	40.1	32.2	24.3	40.7
Extreme Maximum Temp. (°F)	75	77	88	92	96	101	102	102	99	87	81	79	102
Extreme Minimum Temp. (°F)	-31	-17	-12	15	27	31	41	38	28	17	7	-21	-31
Days Maximum Temp. ≥ 90°F	0	0	0	0	1	5	9	7	2	0	0	0	24
Days Maximum Temp. ≤ 32°F	8	5	1	0	0	0	0	0	0	0	0	4	18
Days Minimum Temp. ≤ 32°F	27	23	20	9	1	0	0	0	0	7	17	23	127
Days Minimum Temp. ≤ 0°F	2	1	0	0	0	0	0	0	0	0	0	1	4
Heating Degree Days (base 65°F)	1,106	902	696	376	146	21	2	6	74	343	627	939	5,238
Cooling Degree Days (base 65°F)	0	0	1	9	59	194	313	251	104	12	0	0	943
Mean Precipitation (in.)	2.69	2.27	3.62	3.56	4.18	3.86	3.99	4.40	2.63	2.56	3.08	3.02	39.86
Days With ≥ 0.1" Precipitation	5	5	8	8	8	7	7	6	5	5	7	7	78
Days With ≥ 1.0" Precipitation	0	0	1	1	1	1	1	1	1	1	0	1	9
Mean Snowfall (in.)	*4.7*	na	3.0	0.1	0.0	0.0	0.0	0.0	0.0	trace	0.1	*1.5*	na
Days With ≥ 1.0" Snow Depth	na	na	*1*	0	0	0	0	0	0	0	0	na	na

Westerville *Franklin County*   Elevation: 807 ft.   Latitude: 40° 08' N   Longitude: 82° 57' W

	JAN	FEB	MAR	APR	MAY	JUN	JUL	AUG	SEP	OCT	NOV	DEC	YEAR
Mean Maximum Temp. (°F)	35.6	40.6	51.8	64.1	74.2	82.1	85.3	84.0	77.9	66.1	52.4	41.0	62.9
Mean Temp. (°F)	27.0	30.8	41.0	51.6	61.8	70.3	73.8	72.3	65.7	54.0	43.1	33.0	52.0
Mean Minimum Temp. (°F)	18.4	21.0	30.1	39.1	49.3	58.3	62.2	60.6	53.5	41.9	33.7	25.0	41.1
Extreme Maximum Temp. (°F)	68	73	82	88	92	100	101	101	97	86	79	76	101
Extreme Minimum Temp. (°F)	-27	-25	-8	14	27	33	41	36	29	17	3	-25	-27
Days Maximum Temp. ≥ 90°F	0	0	0	0	0	3	7	5	2	0	0	0	17
Days Maximum Temp. ≤ 32°F	12	8	2	0	0	0	0	0	0	0	1	7	30
Days Minimum Temp. ≤ 32°F	27	23	19	9	1	0	0	0	0	5	15	24	123
Days Minimum Temp. ≤ 0°F	4	3	0	0	0	0	0	0	0	0	0	1	8
Heating Degree Days (base 65°F)	1,171	959	739	404	155	24	3	8	82	346	652	985	5,528
Cooling Degree Days (base 65°F)	0	0	2	10	65	200	306	257	116	14	1	0	971
Mean Precipitation (in.)	2.52	2.23	2.79	3.61	4.03	4.64	4.04	3.51	2.90	2.62	3.36	2.91	39.16
Days With ≥ 0.1" Precipitation	6	5	7	8	8	8	7	6	5	6	7	7	80
Days With ≥ 1.0" Precipitation	0	0	0	1	1	1	1	1	1	0	1	0	7
Mean Snowfall (in.)	7.7	5.1	2.3	0.7	trace	0.0	0.0	0.0	0.0	trace	0.5	3.3	19.6
Days With ≥ 1.0" Snow Depth	12	7	2	0	0	0	0	0	0	0	0	4	25

Wilmington 3 N *Clinton County*   Elevation: 1,026 ft.   Latitude: 39° 29' N   Longitude: 83° 49' W

	JAN	FEB	MAR	APR	MAY	JUN	JUL	AUG	SEP	OCT	NOV	DEC	YEAR
Mean Maximum Temp. (°F)	35.0	39.1	50.0	61.6	71.8	80.2	83.9	82.6	76.9	64.8	51.6	40.5	61.5
Mean Temp. (°F)	26.7	30.0	39.9	50.3	60.6	69.3	73.0	71.1	64.8	53.1	42.3	32.5	51.1
Mean Minimum Temp. (°F)	18.4	20.9	29.6	38.9	49.3	58.3	62.1	59.5	52.6	41.3	33.0	24.4	40.7
Extreme Maximum Temp. (°F)	69	72	82	87	90	99	99	99	95	86	78	73	99
Extreme Minimum Temp. (°F)	-25	-20	-10	12	27	37	40	37	30	12	2	-24	-25
Days Maximum Temp. ≥ 90°F	0	0	0	0	0	2	5	4	1	0	0	0	12
Days Maximum Temp. ≤ 32°F	13	9	3	0	0	0	0	0	0	0	1	7	33
Days Minimum Temp. ≤ 32°F	27	23	20	8	1	0	0	0	0	6	15	24	124
Days Minimum Temp. ≤ 0°F	3	3	0	0	0	0	0	0	0	0	0	1	7
Heating Degree Days (base 65°F)	1,181	981	774	444	181	32	4	14	98	373	675	1,002	5,759
Cooling Degree Days (base 65°F)	0	0	2	9	48	174	274	215	94	12	1	0	829
Mean Precipitation (in.)	2.57	2.38	3.40	4.06	4.81	4.25	4.35	3.33	2.81	2.89	3.36	2.91	41.12
Days With ≥ 0.1" Precipitation	6	6	8	9	9	8	8	6	5	6	7	6	84
Days With ≥ 1.0" Precipitation	1	0	1	1	1	1	1	1	1	1	1	0	10
Mean Snowfall (in.)	8.2	6.3	3.9	0.7	trace	0.0	0.0	0.0	0.0	0.2	1.4	3.0	23.7
Days With ≥ 1.0" Snow Depth	11	9	3	0	0	0	0	0	0	0	1	4	28

Wooster Exp. Station *Wayne County*   Elevation: 1,017 ft.   Latitude: 40° 47' N   Longitude: 81° 55' W

	JAN	FEB	MAR	APR	MAY	JUN	JUL	AUG	SEP	OCT	NOV	DEC	YEAR
Mean Maximum Temp. (°F)	32.4	36.1	46.9	58.8	69.5	78.0	81.8	80.0	73.0	61.2	48.8	37.7	58.7
Mean Temp. (°F)	25.0	28.0	37.6	48.2	58.6	67.3	71.2	69.4	62.5	51.1	40.9	30.8	49.2
Mean Minimum Temp. (°F)	17.6	19.9	28.4	37.5	47.8	56.6	60.6	58.9	51.8	40.9	32.9	23.8	39.7
Extreme Maximum Temp. (°F)	64	70	80	86	90	100	101	95	92	83	75	74	101
Extreme Minimum Temp. (°F)	-24	-13	-6	14	25	31	41	36	30	17	5	-17	-24
Days Maximum Temp. ≥ 90°F	0	0	0	0	0	1	2	1	0	0	0	0	4
Days Maximum Temp. ≤ 32°F	16	11	4	0	0	0	0	0	0	0	2	10	43
Days Minimum Temp. ≤ 32°F	28	24	21	10	1	0	0	0	0	6	16	25	131
Days Minimum Temp. ≤ 0°F	4	2	0	0	0	0	0	0	0	0	0	1	7
Heating Degree Days (base 65°F)	1,233	1,038	842	503	226	53	10	21	134	429	717	1,055	6,261
Cooling Degree Days (base 65°F)	0	0	1	5	36	133	225	170	60	5	0	0	635
Mean Precipitation (in.)	2.22	1.94	2.76	3.44	3.92	4.02	4.00	3.91	3.43	2.61	3.07	2.65	37.97
Days With ≥ 0.1" Precipitation	6	5	7	8	8	8	7	7	6	6	7	6	81
Days With ≥ 1.0" Precipitation	0	0	0	1	1	1	1	1	1	0	0	0	6
Mean Snowfall (in.)	10.0	7.2	5.1	1.2	trace	0.0	0.0	trace	0.0	trace	1.9	6.3	31.7
Days With ≥ 1.0" Snow Depth	16	13	6	1	0	0	0	0	0	0	1	9	46

Xenia 6 SSE *Greene County*   Elevation: 967 ft.   Latitude: 39° 37' N   Longitude: 83° 54' W

	JAN	FEB	MAR	APR	MAY	JUN	JUL	AUG	SEP	OCT	NOV	DEC	YEAR
Mean Maximum Temp. (°F)	35.8	40.7	52.0	63.4	73.0	80.4	83.7	82.1	76.3	65.1	52.3	41.2	62.2
Mean Temp. (°F)	27.6	31.6	41.9	51.9	61.8	69.8	73.2	71.2	64.9	53.8	43.1	33.1	52.0
Mean Minimum Temp. (°F)	19.3	22.5	31.8	40.4	50.6	59.2	62.7	60.2	53.5	42.4	33.8	24.9	41.8
Extreme Maximum Temp. (°F)	68	74	83	88	91	102	100	98	95	89	80	74	102
Extreme Minimum Temp. (°F)	-28	-20	-5	14	28	37	42	38	25	16	3	-24	-28
Days Maximum Temp. ≥ 90°F	0	0	0	0	0	2	4	2	1	0	0	0	9
Days Maximum Temp. ≤ 32°F	12	8	2	0	0	0	0	0	0	0	1	6	29
Days Minimum Temp. ≤ 32°F	26	22	18	7	1	0	0	0	0	5	15	24	118
Days Minimum Temp. ≤ 0°F	3	2	0	0	0	0	0	0	0	0	0	1	6
Heating Degree Days (base 65°F)	1,154	936	712	395	151	25	3	10	90	353	652	983	5,464
Cooling Degree Days (base 65°F)	0	0	2	10	61	185	279	216	96	12	1	0	862
Mean Precipitation (in.)	2.51	2.23	3.16	3.91	4.42	3.87	4.09	3.66	2.73	2.84	3.23	3.02	39.67
Days With ≥ 0.1" Precipitation	6	6	7	8	8	7	8	7	5	6	7	7	82
Days With ≥ 1.0" Precipitation	0	0	0	1	1	1	1	1	1	1	1	1	9
Mean Snowfall (in.)	8.8	5.6	3.5	0.4	trace	0.0	0.0	0.0	0.0	0.2	0.9	*3.3*	*22.7*
Days With ≥ 1.0" Snow Depth	na	na	*1*	0	0	0	0	0	0	0	*0*	na	na

Zanesville Municipal Airport *Muskingum County*   Elevation: 879 ft.   Latitude: 39° 57' N   Longitude: 81° 54' W

	JAN	FEB	MAR	APR	MAY	JUN	JUL	AUG	SEP	OCT	NOV	DEC	YEAR
Mean Maximum Temp. (°F)	36.0	40.6	51.3	62.4	72.2	80.1	83.9	82.2	75.6	64.0	52.2	40.9	61.8
Mean Temp. (°F)	28.1	31.7	41.2	51.2	61.1	69.3	73.4	71.8	64.8	53.1	43.2	33.2	51.8
Mean Minimum Temp. (°F)	20.1	22.6	31.1	39.9	49.9	58.5	62.9	61.4	53.9	42.1	34.2	25.5	41.8
Extreme Maximum Temp. (°F)	70	72	83	88	90	101	103	98	96	84	79	76	103
Extreme Minimum Temp. (°F)	-25	-13	-2	16	26	37	42	37	30	18	2	-17	-25
Days Maximum Temp. ≥ 90°F	0	0	0	0	0	2	5	3	1	0	0	0	11
Days Maximum Temp. ≤ 32°F	12	8	2	0	0	0	0	0	0	0	1	7	30
Days Minimum Temp. ≤ 32°F	27	22	18	7	1	0	0	0	0	5	15	23	118
Days Minimum Temp. ≤ 0°F	2	2	0	0	0	0	0	0	0	0	0	1	5
Heating Degree Days (base 65°F)	1,137	934	733	418	170	30	3	9	93	371	648	979	5,525
Cooling Degree Days (base 65°F)	0	0	2	8	52	171	286	230	94	10	1	0	854
Mean Precipitation (in.)	2.53	2.31	3.09	3.54	4.11	4.39	4.19	3.96	2.94	2.56	3.10	2.75	39.47
Days With ≥ 0.1" Precipitation	7	6	8	8	8	7	7	7	6	6	7	7	84
Days With ≥ 1.0" Precipitation	0	0	0	1	1	1	1	1	1	0	0	0	6
Mean Snowfall (in.)	8.6	4.3	3.5	1.4	trace	trace	trace	0.0	trace	trace	1.2	3.5	22.5
Days With ≥ 1.0" Snow Depth	12	8	3	0	0	0	0	0	0	0	1	4	28

Note: See Appendix D for explanation of data.

OKLAHOMA

PHYSICAL FEATURES. Oklahoma is located in the southern Great Plains. Of the 50 states, it ranks 18th in size with an area of approximately 70,000 square miles, only 935 of which are covered by lakes and ponds. Its northern boundary is about 465 miles in length and its southern boundary 315 miles in length. Greatest depth is 222 miles.

The terrain is mostly rolling plains, sloping downward from west to east. The plains are broken by scattered hilly areas where most points are 600 feet or less above the adjacent countryside, and by a mountainous area in the southeast where some peaks rise more than 2,000 feet above their base. The hilly areas consist of the Wichita Mountains with some isolated peaks in the southwest the Arbuckle Mountains in the south-central and an extension of the Ozarks in the northeast. The Ouachita Mountains occupy much of the southeast. Elevations in the State range from 4,976 feet above sea level on Black Mesa in the northwestern corner of the Panhandle, to about 305 feet above sea level in the bed of the Red River where it leaves Oklahoma at the southeastern corner of the State.

Oklahoma lies entirely within the drainage basin of the Mississippi River. The two main rivers in the State are the Arkansas which drains the northern two-thirds of Oklahoma and the Red River which drains the southern third and forms the State's southern boundary. Principal tributaries of the Arkansas are the Verdigris, Grand (Neosho), Illinois, Cimarron, North Canadian, and Canadian Rivers. The Red draws largely from the North Fork of the Red, Washita, Boggy, and Little Rivers.

In western Oklahoma, rivers tend to be broad, shallow, sand choked, and dry or nearly dry much of the time. Basins are mostly long and narrow. In the east, rivers are fairly swift and clear and basins more oval in form. Most lakes are manmade and were built for flood control, irrigation, municipal water storage, recreational, and hydroelectric power purposes.

GENERAL CLIMATE. The climate of Oklahoma is mostly continental in type, as in all of the central Great Plains. Warm, moist air moving northward from the Gulf of Mexico exerts much influence at times, particularly over the southern and more eastern sections of the State where, as a result, humidities and cloudiness are generally greater and precipitation considerably heavier than in the western and northern sections. Summers are long and occasionally very hot. Winters are shorter and less rigorous than those of the more northern Plains States. Periods of extreme cold are infrequent.

The mean annual temperature over the State ranges from 64°F. along the southern border to about 60°F. along the northern border. It then decreases westward across the Panhandle to about 57°F. in Cimarron County. Temperatures of 90°F. or higher occur, on an average, about 85 days per year in the western Panhandle and in the northeast corner of the State. In the southwest, the average is about 120 days, and in the southeast from 95 to 100 days. Temperatures of 100°F. or higher are common over the State from May well into September. In the southwest part of the State the average number of 100°F. days is 20 to 25 per year. Other sections of the State will average somewhat less, but very seldom will any location in the State not reach a 100°F. temperature sometime during the summer months.

Low humidities and good southerly breezes usually accompany the high summer temperatures and somewhat lessen their discomforting effect. Occasionally strong, hot winds accompany the high daytime temperatures; this combination produces rapid evaporation and often injures crops. When these conditions persist for long periods of time, droughts develop and occasionally become severe. Nights are generally comfortable because the clear skies and dry air allows for rapid cooling after sunset.

Temperatures of 32°F. or less occur on an average of 55 to 65 days per year along the southern tier of counties and from 90 to 100 days per year along the Kansas border in the north-central and northeastern sections of the State. In the Panhandle, days with 32°F. or less occur, on an average, 125 to 140 days per year.

The average length of the growing season, or freeze-free period, ranges from 168 days in the northwestern corner of the Panhandle, to about 225 days along the Red River in the south-central and southeastern sections of Oklahoma. Freezing temperatures have occurred as late as April 20 along the southern border and as late as May 15 in the extreme northwest and in the Panhandle. Fall freezes have occurred as early as September 20 in the Panhandle and as early as October 9 along the southern border. Frozen soil is not a major problem, nor much of a deterrent to seasonal activities. The average maximum depth that frost penetrates the soil ranges from less than three inches in the southeastern corner of the State to more than 10 inches in the extreme northwestern portion.

PRECIPITATION. The geographical distribution of rainfall decreases sharply from east to west. Average annual precipitation ranges from about 56 inches in the southeastern corner of the State, to 15 inches in the extreme western Panhandle. Frequency of rainfall, as determined from the average number of days with 0.01 inch or more, varies from 95 to 100 days a year in the extreme east to from 70 to 80 days a year over the western third of the State.

Excessively heavy rains occur at times. Amounts of 10 inches or more within a 24-hour period have been recorded. Floods may occur during any season. They occur with greater frequency, however, from May to July and in September and October, representing periods when storms are of greater magnitude and rains of greatest intensities. In general, floods in other seasons are the result of more abnormal and persistent buildup of soil moisture plus a concurrent increase in stream-flow due to prolonged rains.

SNOWFALL. The geographical distribution of annual snowfall is usually almost the reverse of the annual precipitation pattern and ranges, on an average, from approximately two inches in the southeastern corner of the State to approximately 20 inches in the western sections of the Panhandle. Snow rarely remains on the ground more than a few days. At times, strong winds with heavy snowfalls cause bad drifting and occasionally produce blizzard conditions.

OTHER CLIMATIC ELEMENTS. Relative humidity averages about 10 percent higher in the eastern portion of the State because of lower elevations and more frequent inflow of Gulf moisture. Summer afternoon and early evening relative humidities are considerably lower than those of winter.

Oklahoma, along with other states in the southern Great Plains, has at times been subject to droughts of varying degree and duration, although drought years have been far less frequent than dry summers and falls. Average annual lake evaporation varies from about 48 inches in the extreme eastern sections of the State to as high as 65 inches in the southwestern corner. In the western Panhandle approximately 58 inches of water is evaporated each year.

Prevailing winds are southerly although northerly winds predominate during the winter months. Average yearly wind speeds vary from nine m.p.h. in the east to approximately 14 m.p.h. in the west. March and April are the windiest months, and July and August the calmest.

Thunderstorms occur, on an average, on 50 to 60 days per year in the eastern half of the State and from 40 to 50 days per year in the western half. Some of the more severe thunderstorms are accompanied by tornadoes and damaging hail, and approximately 75 percent of these occur during the spring season.

Skies are preponderantly clear in western and central sections and about equally clear and cloudy in eastern sections. Sunshine records show an annual average of 68 percent of the possible amount at Oklahoma City and 63 percent at Tulsa. Summer is the period of greatest possible sunshine and winter the least.

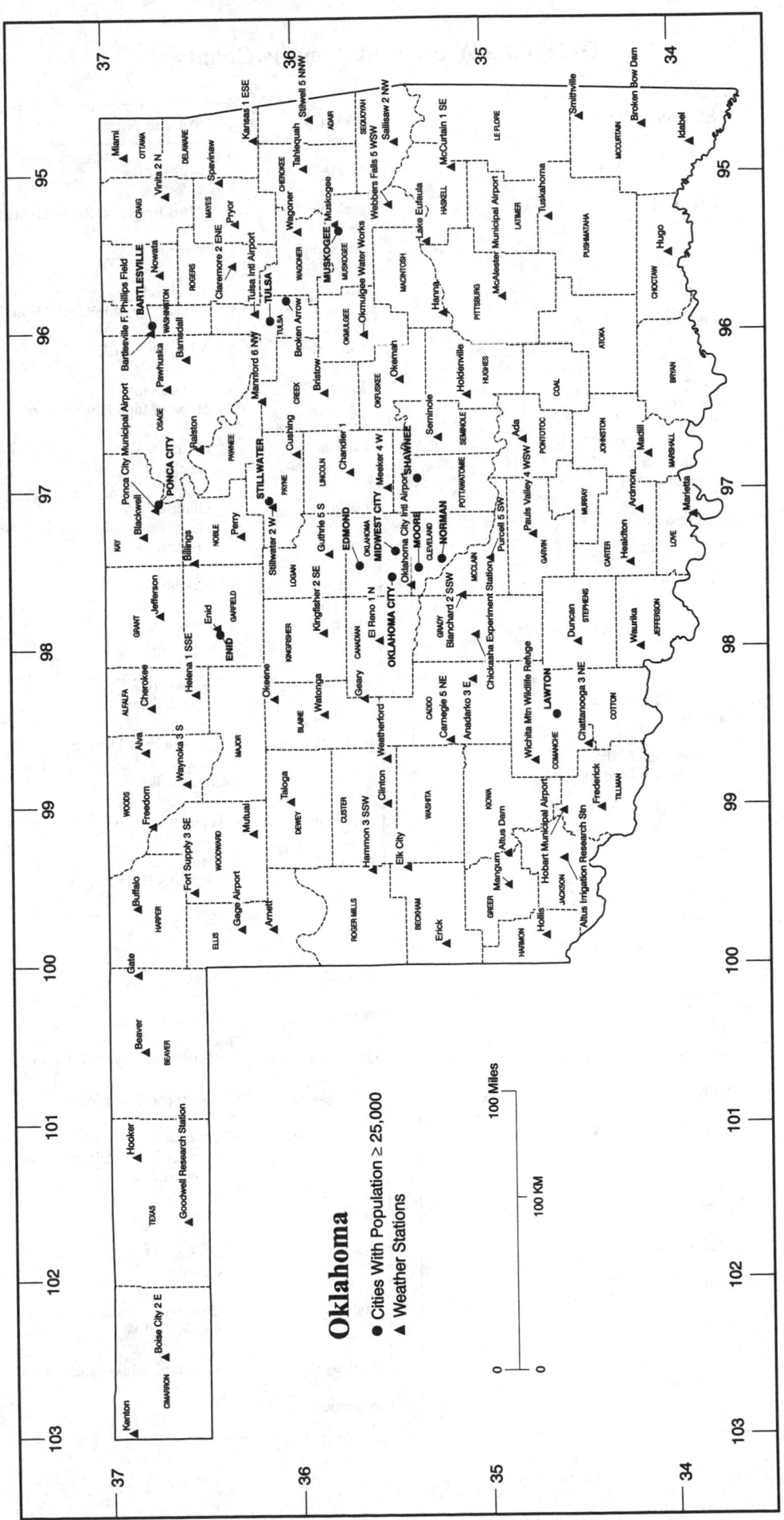

Oklahoma

- ● Cities With Population ≥ 25,000
- ▲ Weather Stations

Oklahoma Weather Stations by County

County	Station Name
Adair	Stilwell 5 NNW
Alfalfa	Cherokee Helena 1 SSE
Beaver	Beaver Gate
Beckham	Elk City Erick
Blaine	Geary Okeene Watonga
Caddo	Anadarko 3 E Carnegie 5 NE
Canadian	El Reno 1 N
Carter	Ardmore Healdton
Cherokee	Tahlequah
Choctaw	Hugo
Cimarron	Boise City 2 E Kenton
Comanche	Chattanooga 3 NE Wichita Mtn Wildlife Refuge
Craig	Vinita 2 N
Creek	Bristow
Custer	Clinton Weatherford
Delaware	Kansas 1 ESE
Dewey	Taloga
Ellis	Arnett Gage Airport
Garfield	Enid
Garvin	Pauls Valley 4 WSW
Grady	Chickasha Experiment Station
Grant	Jefferson
Greer	Mangum
Harmon	Hollis
Harper	Buffalo
Haskell	Lake Eufaula McCurtain 1 SE

County	Station Name
Hughes	Holdenville
Jackson	Altus Irrigation Research Station
Jefferson	Waurika
Kay	Blackwell Ponca City Municipal Airport
Kingfisher	Kingfisher 2 SE
Kiowa	Altus Dam Hobart Municipal Airport
Lincoln	Chandler 1 Meeker 4 W
Logan	Guthrie 5 S
Love	Marietta
Marshall	Madill
Mayes	Pryor Spavinaw
McClain	Blanchard 2 SSW Purcell 5 SW
McCurtain	Broken Bow Dam Idabel Smithville
McIntosh	Hanna
Muskogee	Muskogee Webbers Falls 5 WSW
Noble	Billings Perry
Nowata	Nowata
Okfuskee	Okemah
Oklahoma	Oklahoma City Int'l Airport
Okmulgee	Okmulgee Water Works
Osage	Barnsdall Bartlesville°F. Phillips Field Pawhuska
Ottawa	Miami
Pawnee	Mannford 6 NW Ralston
Payne	Cushing Stillwater 2 W
Pittsburg	McAlester Municipal Airport
Pontotoc	Ada

County	Station Name
Pushmataha	Tuskahoma
Roger Mills	Hammon 3 SSW
Rogers	Claremore 2 ENE
Seminole	Seminole
Sequoyah	Sallisaw 2 NW
Stephens	Duncan
Texas	Goodwell Research Station Hooker
Tillman	Frederick
Tulsa	Tulsa Int'l Airport
Wagoner	Wagoner
Woods	Alva Freedom Waynoka 3 S
Woodward	Fort Supply 3 SE Mutual

Oklahoma Weather Stations by City

City	Station Name	Miles
Bartlesville	Barnsdall	17
	Bartlesville°F. Phillips Field	3
	Nowata	18
Broken Arrow	Tulsa Int'l Airport	13
Edmond	Guthrie 5 S	12
	Oklahoma City Int'l Airport	20
Enid	Enid	2
Lawton	Chattanooga 3 NE	16
	Wichita Mtn Wildlife Refuge	18
Midwest City	Oklahoma City Int'l Airport	13
Moore	Blanchard 2 SSW	18
	Oklahoma City Int'l Airport	7
Muskogee	Muskogee	2
	Wagoner	15
Norman	Blanchard 2 SSW	15
	Oklahoma City Int'l Airport	15
	Purcell 5 SW	17
Oklahoma City	Oklahoma City Int'l Airport	7
Ponca City	Blackwell	13
	Ponca City Municipal Airport	2
Shawnee	Meeker 4 W	11
	Seminole	16
Stillwater	Cushing	19
	Perry	16
	Stillwater 2 W	2
Tulsa	Tulsa Int'l Airport	6

Note: Miles is the distance between the geographic center of the city and the weather station.

Oklahoma Weather Stations by Elevation

Feet	Station Name
4,347	Kenton
4,143	Boise City 2 E
3,307	Goodwell Research Station
2,992	Hooker
2,463	Arnett
2,463	Beaver
2,247	Gate
2,188	Gage Airport
2,057	Erick
2,027	Fort Supply 3 SE
1,961	Elk City
1,863	Mutual
1,817	Hammon 3 SSW
1,794	Buffalo
1,702	Taloga
1,663	Wichita Mtn Wildlife Refuge
1,640	Weatherford
1,620	Hollis
1,607	Clinton
1,594	Geary
1,594	Mangum
1,568	Hobart Municipal Airport
1,548	Watonga
1,528	Freedom
1,528	Waynoka 3 S
1,522	Altus Dam
1,479	Carnegie 5 NE
1,404	Alva
1,377	Altus Irrigation Research Station
1,348	Helena 1 SSE
1,312	El Reno 1 N
1,302	Oklahoma City Int'l Airport
1,282	Frederick
1,272	Blanchard 2 SSW
1,243	Enid
1,207	Okeene
1,177	Cherokee
1,177	Kansas 1 ESE
1,167	Anadarko 3 E
1,151	Chattanooga 3 NE
1,122	Duncan
1,108	Guthrie 5 S
1,099	Kingfisher 2 SE
1,082	Chickasha Experiment Station
1,043	Jefferson
1,040	Purcell 5 SW
1,023	Perry
1,013	Ada
997	Billings
997	Blackwell
997	Ponca City Municipal Airport
997	Stilwell 5 NNW
948	Cushing
938	Pauls Valley 4 WSW
935	Okemah

Feet	Station Name
921	Chandler 1
921	Meeker 4 W
892	Stillwater 2 W
879	Ardmore
872	Waurika
869	Marietta
862	Seminole
859	Holdenville
849	Lake Eufaula
849	Tahlequah
833	Pawhuska
830	Mannford 6 NW
830	Smithville
823	Ralston
820	Bristow
803	Miami
767	Barnsdall
767	Madill
757	McAlester Municipal Airport
738	Nowata
734	Vinita 2 N
731	Healdton
711	Bartlesville°F. Phillips Field
682	Spavinaw
679	Hanna
659	Sallisaw 2 NW
656	McCurtain 1 SE
649	Tulsa Int'l Airport
646	Okmulgee Water Works
623	Pryor
597	Tuskahoma
587	Claremore 2 ENE
587	Wagoner
580	Muskogee
567	Hugo
547	Webbers Falls 5 WSW
459	Idabel
442	Broken Bow Dam

Oklahoma City Int'l Airport

Oklahoma City is located along the North Canadian River, a frequently nearly-dry stream, at the geographic center of the state. The surrounding country is gently rolling with the nearest hills or low mountains, the Arbuckles, 80 miles south. The elevation ranges around 1,250 feet above sea level.

Although some influence is exerted at times by warm, moist air currents from the Gulf of Mexico, the climate of Oklahoma City falls mainly under continental controls characteristic of the Great Plains Region. The continental effect produces pronounced daily and seasonal temperature changes and considerable variation in seasonal and annual precipitation. Summers are long and usually hot. Winters are comparatively mild and short.

During the year, temperatures of 100 degrees or more occur on an average of 10 days, but have occurred on as many as 50 days or more. While summers are usually hot, the discomforting effect of extreme heat is considerably mitigated by low humidity and the prevalence of a moderate southerly breeze.

The length of the growing season varies from 180 to 251 days. Average date of last freeze is early April and average date of first freeze is early November. Freezes have occurred in early October.

During an average year, skies are clear approximately 40 percent of the time, partly cloudy 25 percent, and cloudy 35 percent of the time. The city is almost smoke-free as a result of favorable atmospheric conditions and the almost exclusive use of natural gas for heating.

Summer rainfall comes mainly from showers and thunderstorms. Winter precipitation is generally associated with frontal passages. Measurable precipitation has occurred on as many as 122 days and as few as 55 days during the year. The seasonal distribution of precipitation is normally 12 percent in winter, 34 percent in spring, 30 percent in summer, and 24 percent in fall. The The period with the least number of days with precipitation is November through January, and the month with the most rainy days is May. Thunderstorms occur most often in late spring and early summer. Large hail and/or destructive winds on occasion accompany these thunderstorms.

Snowfall averages less than 10 inches per year and seldom remains on the ground very long. Occasional brief periods of freezing rain and sleet storms occur.

Heavy fogs are infrequent. Prevailing winds are southerly except in January and February when northerly breezes predominate.

Oklahoma City Int'l Airport *Oklahoma County*   Elevation: 1,302 ft.   Latitude: 35° 23' N   Longitude: 97° 36' W

	JAN	FEB	MAR	APR	MAY	JUN	JUL	AUG	SEP	OCT	NOV	DEC	YEAR
Mean Maximum Temp. (°F)	46.8	53.3	62.2	71.3	78.8	87.4	93.2	92.4	83.9	73.2	59.7	50.4	71.0
Mean Temp. (°F)	36.4	42.1	50.7	59.8	68.3	76.9	82.0	81.1	73.1	61.8	49.0	39.9	60.1
Mean Minimum Temp. (°F)	25.9	30.9	39.1	48.2	57.8	66.4	70.8	69.8	62.3	50.4	38.2	29.4	49.1
Extreme Maximum Temp. (°F)	80	92	92	100	104	105	110	110	107	96	87	77	110
Extreme Minimum Temp. (°F)	-4	-3	8	21	37	48	53	53	36	16	11	-8	-8
Days Maximum Temp. ≥ 90°F	0	0	0	0	2	12	22	23	9	1	0	0	69
Days Maximum Temp. ≤ 32°F	5	2	0	0	0	0	0	0	0	0	0	2	9
Days Minimum Temp. ≤ 32°F	23	15	8	1	0	0	0	0	0	1	8	19	75
Days Minimum Temp. ≤ 0°F	0	0	0	0	0	0	0	0	0	0	0	0	0
Heating Degree Days (base 65°F)	881	640	445	191	40	1	0	0	28	153	478	770	3,627
Cooling Degree Days (base 65°F)	0	1	7	39	158	372	545	518	278	56	4	0	1,978
Mean Precipitation (in.)	1.27	1.52	2.86	3.00	5.62	4.53	2.80	2.51	4.25	3.56	2.05	1.77	35.74
Maximum Precipitation (in.)	5.7	4.6	7.8	7.3	12.1	14.7	8.4	6.8	11.8	13.2	5.7	8.1	46.5
Minimum Precipitation (in.)	0	trace	0.1	0.2	0.9	0.6	trace	0.3	trace	trace	trace	trace	17.8
Maximum 24-hr. Precipitation (in.)	1.8	2.2	2.8	3.4	6.6	4.6	5.6	2.9	7.5	5.4	2.2	2.5	7.5
Days With ≥ 0.1" Precipitation	2	3	5	5	7	6	4	4	5	4	3	3	51
Days With ≥ 1.0" Precipitation	0	0	1	1	2	2	1	1	1	1	1	1	12
Mean Snowfall (in.)	2.8	2.1	0.8	trace	trace	trace	trace	trace	trace	trace	0.6	1.8	8.1
Maximum Snowfall (in.)	17	12	14	1	0	0	0	0	0	trace	8	8	25
Maximum 24-hr. Snowfall (in.)	8	7	8	1	0	0	0	0	0	trace	8	8	8
Days With ≥ 1.0" Snow Depth	3	2	0	0	0	0	0	0	0	0	6	2	7
Thunderstorm Days	1	1	3	5	9	9	6	6	5	3	1	1	50
Foggy Days	11	10	10	8	9	5	4	5	8	7	8	10	95
Predominant Sky Cover	OVR	OVR	OVR	OVR	OVR	SCT	CLR	CLR	CLR	CLR	CLR	OVR	CLR
Mean Relative Humidity 6am (%)	79	78	76	78	84	85	82	81	83	79	78	78	80
Mean Relative Humidity 3pm (%)	53	52	47	46	53	52	45	44	48	46	48	52	49
Mean Dewpoint (°F)	25	29	35	45	56	64	66	65	59	48	36	28	46
Prevailing Wind Direction	N	N	SSE	SSE	SSE	SSE	SSE	SSE	SSE	SSE	S	S	SSE
Prevailing Wind Speed (mph)	15	15	15	15	14	13	10	10	12	13	14	14	14
Maximum Wind Gust (mph)	55	62	64	92	74	74	93	59	69	55	63	54	93

Tulsa Int'l Airport

The city of Tulsa lies along the Arkansas River at an elevation of 700 feet above sea level. The surrounding terrain is gently rolling.

At latitude 36 degrees, Tulsa is far enough north to escape the long periods of heat in summer, yet far enough south to miss the extreme cold of winter. The influence of warm moist air from the Gulf of Mexico is often noted, due to the high humidity, but the climate is essentially continental characterized by rapid changes in temperature. Generally the winter months are mild. Temperatures occasionally fall below zero but only last a very short time. Temperatures of 100 degrees or higher are often experienced from late July to early September, but are usually accompanied by low relative humidity and a good southerly breeze. The fall season is long with a great number of pleasant, sunny days and cool, bracing nights.

Rainfall is ample for most agricultural pursuits and is distributed favorably throughout the year. Spring is the wettest season, having an abundance of rain in the form of showers and thunderstorms. The steady rains of fall are a contrast to the spring and summer showers and provide a good supply of moisture and more ideal conditions for the growth of winter grains and pastures. The greatest amounts of snow are received in January and early March. The snow is usually light and only remains on the ground for brief periods.

The average date of the last 32 degree temperature occurrence is late March and the average date of the first 32 degree occurrence is early November. The average growing season is 216 days.

The Tulsa area is occasionally subjected to large hail and violent windstorms which occur mostly during spring and early summer, although occurrences have been noted throughout the year.

Prevailing surface winds are southerly during most of the year. Heavy fogs are infrequent. Sunshine is abundant. The prevalence of good flying weather throughout the year has contributed to the development of Tulsa as an aviation center.

Tulsa Int'l Airport *Tulsa County*   Elevation: 649 ft.   Latitude: 36° 12' N   Longitude: 95° 53' W

	JAN	FEB	MAR	APR	MAY	JUN	JUL	AUG	SEP	OCT	NOV	DEC	YEAR
Mean Maximum Temp. (°F)	45.7	52.5	62.0	71.9	79.2	87.7	93.6	92.9	83.7	73.3	59.6	49.7	71.0
Mean Temp. (°F)	35.9	41.7	51.0	60.7	69.1	77.8	83.3	82.0	73.4	62.1	49.5	39.9	60.5
Mean Minimum Temp. (°F)	26.0	31.0	40.0	49.5	59.0	67.9	73.0	71.1	63.0	50.9	39.3	30.1	50.1
Extreme Maximum Temp. (°F)	77	90	96	102	96	102	111	110	107	98	85	77	111
Extreme Minimum Temp. (°F)	-6	-11	7	23	36	50	51	52	35	18	10	-8	-11
Days Maximum Temp. ≥ 90°F	0	0	0	0	2	13	24	22	9	1	0	0	71
Days Maximum Temp. ≤ 32°F	5	3	0	0	0	0	0	0	0	0	0	3	11
Days Minimum Temp. ≤ 32°F	23	15	7	1	0	0	0	0	0	0	7	18	71
Days Minimum Temp. ≤ 0°F	0	0	0	0	0	0	0	0	0	0	0	0	0
Heating Degree Days (base 65°F)	896	651	436	174	36	1	0	0	27	150	465	772	3,608
Cooling Degree Days (base 65°F)	0	1	10	50	175	398	583	546	285	65	7	1	2,121
Mean Precipitation (in.)	1.54	1.93	3.51	4.04	6.02	4.67	2.75	2.91	4.95	4.11	3.38	2.36	42.17
Maximum Precipitation (in.)	6.6	5.7	11.9	8.7	11.3	11.2	11.4	6.7	18.8	9.3	7.3	8.7	69.9
Minimum Precipitation (in.)	0	0.4	0.1	0.3	1.2	0.5	trace	0.3	trace	trace	trace	0.2	23.2
Maximum 24-hr. Precipitation (in.)	2.1	3.0	2.5	4.4	6.9	4.9	7.5	5.4	5.8	5.4	4.6	3.3	7.5
Days With ≥ 0.1" Precipitation	3	4	5	6	7	6	4	4	6	4	5	4	58
Days With ≥ 1.0" Precipitation	0	0	1	1	2	1	1	1	2	1	1	1	12
Mean Snowfall (in.)	3.0	2.3	1.6	trace	trace	trace	trace	0.0	trace	trace	0.6	1.3	8.8
Maximum Snowfall (in.)	13	10	14	2	0	0	0	0	0	trace	6	10	29
Maximum 24-hr. Snowfall (in.)	9	4	13	2	0	0	0	0	0	trace	4	8	13
Days With ≥ 1.0" Snow Depth	4	2	1	0	0	0	0	0	0	0	0	1	8
Thunderstorm Days	1	1	3	6	9	8	6	6	5	3	2	1	51
Foggy Days	11	10	9	7	8	6	5	6	9	8	8	10	97
Predominant Sky Cover	OVR	OVR	OVR	OVR	OVR	SCT	CLR	CLR	CLR	CLR	CLR	OVR	CLR
Mean Relative Humidity 6am (%)	79	78	76	78	86	86	82	84	85	82	78	79	81
Mean Relative Humidity 3pm (%)	54	51	47	47	54	54	48	46	49	46	49	53	50
Mean Dewpoint (°F)	25	29	35	46	58	66	68	66	60	49	36	29	47
Prevailing Wind Direction	S	S	S	S	S	S	S	S	S	S	S	S	S
Prevailing Wind Speed (mph)	12	12	14	14	13	13	10	10	12	12	13	12	12
Maximum Wind Gust (mph)	52	53	66	73	69	70	58	52	55	66	62	67	73

Ada *Pontotoc County*   Elevation: 1,013 ft.   Latitude: 34° 47' N   Longitude: 96° 41' W

	JAN	FEB	MAR	APR	MAY	JUN	JUL	AUG	SEP	OCT	NOV	DEC	YEAR
Mean Maximum Temp. (°F)	50.9	56.8	65.1	73.7	80.5	87.6	93.1	93.0	85.2	75.4	62.6	53.6	73.1
Mean Temp. (°F)	39.4	44.6	52.6	61.0	69.1	76.7	81.8	81.1	73.3	63.0	50.9	42.3	61.3
Mean Minimum Temp. (°F)	27.9	32.4	40.2	48.3	57.6	65.8	70.4	69.1	61.2	50.5	39.1	30.9	49.5
Extreme Maximum Temp. (°F)	79	91	95	98	98	105	107	107	108	95	84	78	108
Extreme Minimum Temp. (°F)	-3	-1	5	22	38	47	52	51	36	18	10	-8	-8
Days Maximum Temp. ≥ 90°F	0	0	0	0	2	11	24	24	9	1	0	0	71
Days Maximum Temp. ≤ 32°F	3	1	0	0	0	0	0	0	0	0	0	1	5
Days Minimum Temp. ≤ 32°F	21	14	6	1	0	0	0	0	0	1	7	17	67
Days Minimum Temp. ≤ 0°F	0	0	0	0	0	0	0	0	0	0	0	0	0
Heating Degree Days (base 65°F)	788	571	386	154	27	1	0	0	22	127	421	698	3,195
Cooling Degree Days (base 65°F)	0	1	8	39	165	367	545	522	286	64	5	0	2,002
Mean Precipitation (in.)	1.78	2.23	3.62	3.89	5.52	4.51	2.75	3.10	5.11	4.21	2.98	2.41	42.11
Days With ≥ 0.1" Precipitation	3	4	5	6	7	6	4	4	6	5	4	4	58
Days With ≥ 1.0" Precipitation	0	1	1	1	2	2	1	1	2	1	1	1	14
Mean Snowfall (in.)	*1.6*	*1.2*	0.8	0.0	0.0	0.0	0.0	0.0	0.0	0.0	0.3	0.6	*4.5*
Days With ≥ 1.0" Snow Depth	*1*	na	0	0	0	0	0	0	0	0	0	0	na

Altus Dam *Kiowa County*   Elevation: 1,522 ft.   Latitude: 34° 53' N   Longitude: 99° 18' W

	JAN	FEB	MAR	APR	MAY	JUN	JUL	AUG	SEP	OCT	NOV	DEC	YEAR
Mean Maximum Temp. (°F)	48.5	54.7	63.6	73.3	81.6	90.6	96.2	94.1	85.4	74.9	61.2	52.0	73.0
Mean Temp. (°F)	36.8	42.5	51.0	60.8	69.9	79.1	84.3	82.4	73.9	62.4	49.3	40.2	61.0
Mean Minimum Temp. (°F)	25.1	30.2	38.3	48.2	58.2	67.5	72.3	70.6	62.2	49.9	37.4	28.3	49.0
Extreme Maximum Temp. (°F)	83	91	99	103	105	114	110	108	109	103	88	82	114
Extreme Minimum Temp. (°F)	-5	-5	1	22	33	47	55	54	30	12	6	-10	-10
Days Maximum Temp. ≥ 90°F	0	0	0	2	6	18	26	24	12	2	0	0	90
Days Maximum Temp. ≤ 32°F	4	2	0	0	0	0	0	0	0	0	0	2	8
Days Minimum Temp. ≤ 32°F	24	16	8	1	0	0	0	0	0	1	10	22	82
Days Minimum Temp. ≤ 0°F	0	0	0	0	0	0	0	0	0	0	0	0	0
Heating Degree Days (base 65°F)	866	629	436	178	36	2	0	1	28	148	469	763	3,556
Cooling Degree Days (base 65°F)	0	1	11	55	196	430	616	562	307	75	5	0	2,258
Mean Precipitation (in.)	1.01	1.18	1.98	2.49	4.65	4.03	2.06	2.77	3.31	2.72	1.57	1.17	28.94
Days With ≥ 0.1" Precipitation	2	3	4	4	6	5	3	4	5	4	3	2	45
Days With ≥ 1.0" Precipitation	0	0	0	1	1	1	1	1	1	1	0	0	7
Mean Snowfall (in.)	*1.9*	*1.8*	0.2	0.0	0.0	0.0	0.0	0.0	0.0	0.0	0.1	1.0	*5.0*
Days With ≥ 1.0" Snow Depth	na	na	0	0	0	0	0	0	0	0	0	0	na

Altus Irrigation Research Station *Jackson County*   Elevation: 1,377 ft.   Latitude: 34° 35' N   Longitude: 99° 20' W

	JAN	FEB	MAR	APR	MAY	JUN	JUL	AUG	SEP	OCT	NOV	DEC	YEAR
Mean Maximum Temp. (°F)	52.6	59.0	68.3	77.1	84.5	93.1	97.7	95.6	87.7	78.1	64.3	54.8	76.1
Mean Temp. (°F)	39.4	44.8	53.5	62.1	71.1	79.8	84.2	82.4	74.8	64.0	51.2	41.9	62.4
Mean Minimum Temp. (°F)	26.1	30.7	38.7	47.1	57.7	66.5	70.7	69.1	61.9	49.9	38.0	29.0	48.8
Extreme Maximum Temp. (°F)	85	93	103	105	107	115	112	109	108	104	90	83	115
Extreme Minimum Temp. (°F)	-7	-7	9	23	34	48	54	54	28	17	12	-10	-10
Days Maximum Temp. ≥ 90°F	0	0	1	3	9	21	28	26	15	3	0	0	106
Days Maximum Temp. ≤ 32°F	3	1	0	0	0	0	0	0	0	0	0	1	5
Days Minimum Temp. ≤ 32°F	24	16	8	2	0	0	0	0	0	1	9	21	81
Days Minimum Temp. ≤ 0°F	0	0	0	0	0	0	0	0	0	0	0	0	0
Heating Degree Days (base 65°F)	788	564	364	142	22	0	0	0	20	110	415	709	3,134
Cooling Degree Days (base 65°F)	0	1	14	59	220	445	608	565	330	85	7	0	2,334
Mean Precipitation (in.)	0.95	1.16	1.70	2.38	4.73	4.13	1.99	2.90	3.43	2.45	1.43	1.16	28.41
Days With ≥ 0.1" Precipitation	2	3	3	4	6	5	3	4	4	4	3	2	43
Days With ≥ 1.0" Precipitation	0	0	0	1	2	1	0	1	1	1	0	0	7
Mean Snowfall (in.)	*1.3*	na	0.1	0.0	0.0	0.0	0.0	0.0	0.0	0.0	0.2	0.4	na
Days With ≥ 1.0" Snow Depth	*1*	*1*	0	0	0	0	0	0	0	0	0	0	*2*

Alva *Woods County*   Elevation: 1,404 ft.   Latitude: 36° 48' N   Longitude: 98° 39' W

	JAN	FEB	MAR	APR	MAY	JUN	JUL	AUG	SEP	OCT	NOV	DEC	YEAR
Mean Maximum Temp. (°F)	*46.1*	*53.0*	*62.2*	*72.7*	*80.5*	*91.3*	*96.9*	*94.6*	*85.9*	*75.4*	*59.1*	*49.4*	*72.3*
Mean Temp. (°F)	*34.5*	*40.3*	*49.1*	*59.2*	*68.1*	*78.2*	*83.6*	*81.5*	*73.1*	*61.6*	*47.1*	*37.9*	*59.5*
Mean Minimum Temp. (°F)	*22.9*	*27.5*	*35.9*	*45.7*	*55.7*	*65.1*	*70.2*	*68.4*	*60.3*	*47.8*	*35.0*	*26.4*	*46.7*
Extreme Maximum Temp. (°F)	*79*	*93*	*95*	*100*	*107*	*110*	*113*	*112*	*108*	*97*	*91*	*78*	*113*
Extreme Minimum Temp. (°F)	*-8*	*-6*	*5*	*19*	*36*	*47*	*52*	*51*	na	*14*	*8*	*-15*	na
Days Maximum Temp. ≥ 90°F	*0*	*0*	*0*	*1*	*5*	na	na	*23*	*13*	*3*	*0*	*0*	na
Days Maximum Temp. ≤ 32°F	*6*	*3*	*1*	*0*	*0*	*0*	*0*	*0*	*0*	*0*	*0*	*2*	*12*
Days Minimum Temp. ≤ 32°F	*26*	*19*	*12*	*2*	*0*	*0*	*0*	*0*	*0*	*1*	*11*	*24*	*95*
Days Minimum Temp. ≤ 0°F	*1*	*0*	*0*	*0*	*0*	*0*	*0*	*0*	*0*	*0*	*0*	*0*	*1*
Heating Degree Days (base 65°F)	*939*	*692*	*494*	*209*	*53*	*2*	*0*	*0*	*29*	*168*	*535*	*831*	*3,952*
Cooling Degree Days (base 65°F)	na	na	na	na	na	na	na	na	na	na	na	na	na
Mean Precipitation (in.)	*0.83*	*0.82*	*2.17*	*2.76*	*4.47*	*3.19*	*2.53*	*3.42*	*2.37*	*1.66*	*1.75*	*0.96*	*26.93*
Days With ≥ 0.1" Precipitation	*2*	*2*	na	*4*	*6*	*5*	*4*	*5*	*4*	*3*	*3*	*2*	na
Days With ≥ 1.0" Precipitation	*0*	*0*	*1*	*1*	*2*	*1*	*1*	*1*	*1*	*0*	*0*	*0*	*8*
Mean Snowfall (in.)	na	na	na	*0.7*	*0.0*	*0.0*	*0.0*	*0.0*	*0.0*	*0.0*	*1.0*	na	na
Days With ≥ 1.0" Snow Depth	na	na	na	*0*	*0*	*0*	*0*	*0*	*0*	*0*	*1*	na	na

Anadarko 3 E *Caddo County*   Elevation: 1,167 ft.   Latitude: 35° 04' N   Longitude: 98° 12' W

	JAN	FEB	MAR	APR	MAY	JUN	JUL	AUG	SEP	OCT	NOV	DEC	YEAR
Mean Maximum Temp. (°F)	49.0	55.6	64.7	73.5	81.4	89.5	95.0	93.6	86.2	75.3	61.8	51.9	73.1
Mean Temp. (°F)	36.6	42.5	51.3	60.1	69.2	77.4	82.5	81.0	73.8	62.0	49.2	39.7	60.4
Mean Minimum Temp. (°F)	24.1	29.3	37.9	46.7	56.9	65.3	70.0	68.4	61.3	48.7	36.6	27.3	47.7
Extreme Maximum Temp. (°F)	80	89	95	101	104	110	109	107	106	98	86	76	110
Extreme Minimum Temp. (°F)	-13	-6	5	19	34	42	51	45	29	16	9	-17	-17
Days Maximum Temp. ≥ 90°F	0	0	0	1	4	15	25	24	11	2	0	0	82
Days Maximum Temp. ≤ 32°F	4	2	0	0	0	0	0	0	0	0	0	2	8
Days Minimum Temp. ≤ 32°F	25	17	10	2	0	0	0	0	0	2	10	22	88
Days Minimum Temp. ≤ 0°F	0	0	0	0	0	0	0	0	0	0	0	0	0
Heating Degree Days (base 65°F)	874	628	430	187	36	2	0	0	25	153	469	779	3,583
Cooling Degree Days (base 65°F)	0	0	9	37	166	374	547	505	289	61	4	0	1,992
Mean Precipitation (in.)	1.08	1.53	2.41	2.57	4.87	3.87	2.32	2.79	3.35	2.92	1.74	1.69	31.14
Days With ≥ 0.1" Precipitation	2	3	4	4	6	4	3	4	5	4	3	3	45
Days With ≥ 1.0" Precipitation	0	0	1	1	2	1	1	1	1	1	1	0	10
Mean Snowfall (in.)	na	1.7	0.2	0.0	0.0	0.0	0.0	0.0	0.0	0.0	trace	0.5	na
Days With ≥ 1.0" Snow Depth	1	0	0	0	0	0	0	0	0	0	0	0	1

Ardmore *Carter County*   Elevation: 879 ft.   Latitude: 34° 10' N   Longitude: 97° 08' W

	JAN	FEB	MAR	APR	MAY	JUN	JUL	AUG	SEP	OCT	NOV	DEC	YEAR
Mean Maximum Temp. (°F)	52.7	58.8	67.4	75.4	82.4	89.8	94.7	94.5	87.2	77.4	64.4	55.8	75.0
Mean Temp. (°F)	41.8	47.1	55.4	63.6	71.7	79.3	83.8	83.3	76.3	65.7	53.6	44.9	63.9
Mean Minimum Temp. (°F)	30.7	35.4	43.4	51.9	61.0	68.8	72.9	72.0	65.2	54.0	42.8	34.0	52.7
Extreme Maximum Temp. (°F)	83	93	98	98	100	112	110	108	106	99	88	80	112
Extreme Minimum Temp. (°F)	0	-1	13	27	41	50	58	55	39	20	17	-8	-8
Days Maximum Temp. ≥ 90°F	0	0	0	0	4	16	26	25	12	2	0	0	85
Days Maximum Temp. ≤ 32°F	2	1	0	0	0	0	0	0	0	0	0	1	4
Days Minimum Temp. ≤ 32°F	18	10	4	0	0	0	0	0	0	0	5	13	50
Days Minimum Temp. ≤ 0°F	0	0	0	0	0	0	0	0	0	0	0	0	0
Heating Degree Days (base 65°F)	714	501	311	109	14	1	0	0	13	86	350	616	2,715
Cooling Degree Days (base 65°F)	0	3	18	64	220	425	582	579	347	106	13	1	2,358
Mean Precipitation (in.)	1.76	2.17	3.13	3.30	5.06	3.99	2.37	2.52	4.39	4.27	2.55	2.08	37.59
Days With ≥ 0.1" Precipitation	3	3	5	5	6	5	3	4	5	5	4	3	51
Days With ≥ 1.0" Precipitation	0	1	1	1	2	1	1	1	2	1	1	1	13
Mean Snowfall (in.)	1.5	0.6	0.3	trace	0.0	0.0	0.0	0.0	0.0	trace	0.2	0.3	2.9
Days With ≥ 1.0" Snow Depth	0	0	0	0	0	0	0	0	0	0	0	1	1

Arnett *Ellis County*   Elevation: 2,463 ft.   Latitude: 36° 08' N   Longitude: 99° 46' W

	JAN	FEB	MAR	APR	MAY	JUN	JUL	AUG	SEP	OCT	NOV	DEC	YEAR
Mean Maximum Temp. (°F)	44.9	51.0	59.1	69.3	77.2	86.4	92.4	90.9	82.2	71.7	57.4	47.8	69.2
Mean Temp. (°F)	32.5	38.0	46.0	55.9	65.1	74.5	79.7	78.3	69.8	58.3	44.9	35.7	56.6
Mean Minimum Temp. (°F)	20.2	25.0	33.0	42.5	52.9	62.4	67.1	65.6	57.3	44.8	32.3	23.5	43.9
Extreme Maximum Temp. (°F)	85	88	93	98	101	110	109	105	103	99	88	78	110
Extreme Minimum Temp. (°F)	-11	-9	1	18	31	44	52	51	30	14	5	-11	-11
Days Maximum Temp. ≥ 90°F	0	0	0	1	3	11	22	20	8	1	0	0	66
Days Maximum Temp. ≤ 32°F	6	4	1	0	0	0	0	0	0	0	1	4	16
Days Minimum Temp. ≤ 32°F	29	22	15	4	0	0	0	0	0	2	15	27	114
Days Minimum Temp. ≤ 0°F	1	1	0	0	0	0	0	0	0	0	0	1	3
Heating Degree Days (base 65°F)	1,000	755	583	291	91	10	1	1	56	234	598	902	4,522
Cooling Degree Days (base 65°F)	0	0	3	22	98	293	462	425	206	29	1	0	1,539
Mean Precipitation (in.)	0.61	0.92	1.83	2.23	4.44	3.33	2.11	2.48	2.60	1.79	1.47	0.99	24.80
Days With ≥ 0.1" Precipitation	2	2	4	4	6	5	4	4	4	3	3	2	43
Days With ≥ 1.0" Precipitation	0	0	1	1	2	1	1	1	1	0	0	0	8
Mean Snowfall (in.)	1.0	2.7	1.4	0.5	0.0	0.0	0.0	0.0	0.0	trace	2.1	1.4	9.1
Days With ≥ 1.0" Snow Depth	4	4	1	0	0	0	0	0	0	0	1	3	13

Barnsdall *Osage County*   Elevation: 767 ft.   Latitude: 36° 34' N   Longitude: 96° 10' W

	JAN	FEB	MAR	APR	MAY	JUN	JUL	AUG	SEP	OCT	NOV	DEC	YEAR
Mean Maximum Temp. (°F)	46.4	53.2	63.0	73.1	79.9	87.9	94.0	93.8	84.9	74.0	60.2	50.1	71.7
Mean Temp. (°F)	34.9	40.8	50.4	60.3	68.3	76.7	82.1	81.0	72.8	61.1	48.6	38.8	59.7
Mean Minimum Temp. (°F)	23.3	28.4	37.7	47.5	56.7	65.4	70.1	68.2	60.6	48.2	37.0	27.4	47.5
Extreme Maximum Temp. (°F)	78	90	95	101	95	105	112	111	109	99	88	77	112
Extreme Minimum Temp. (°F)	-17	-17	2	19	34	45	49	46	30	14	6	-13	-17
Days Maximum Temp. ≥ 90°F	0	0	0	0	2	12	24	23	10	1	0	0	72
Days Maximum Temp. ≤ 32°F	5	2	0	0	0	0	0	0	0	0	0	2	9
Days Minimum Temp. ≤ 32°F	25	19	11	2	0	0	0	0	0	2	10	22	91
Days Minimum Temp. ≤ 0°F	1	1	0	0	0	0	0	0	0	0	0	1	3
Heating Degree Days (base 65°F)	927	678	458	187	42	2	0	0	30	171	489	806	3,790
Cooling Degree Days (base 65°F)	0	1	10	47	145	348	531	502	263	50	6	0	1,903
Mean Precipitation (in.)	1.51	1.93	3.56	4.08	5.38	4.97	3.22	3.33	5.29	3.48	3.39	2.16	42.30
Days With ≥ 0.1" Precipitation	3	4	5	6	8	6	4	5	6	5	4	4	60
Days With ≥ 1.0" Precipitation	0	1	1	2	2	2	1	1	2	1	1	1	15
Mean Snowfall (in.)	3.4	2.6	1.2	trace	0.0	0.0	0.0	0.0	0.0	trace	0.4	1.5	9.1
Days With ≥ 1.0" Snow Depth	na	na	1	0	0	0	0	0	0	0	0	1	na

Bartlesville°F. Phillips Field *Osage County*   Elevation: 711 ft.   Latitude: 36° 45' N   Longitude: 96° 00' W

	JAN	FEB	MAR	APR	MAY	JUN	JUL	AUG	SEP	OCT	NOV	DEC	YEAR
Mean Maximum Temp. (°F)	46.5	53.2	63.2	73.2	80.2	88.4	94.3	93.7	84.9	74.2	60.3	49.9	71.8
Mean Temp. (°F)	34.9	40.8	50.5	60.4	68.6	77.0	82.1	80.8	72.7	61.1	48.7	38.8	59.7
Mean Minimum Temp. (°F)	23.3	28.4	37.7	47.5	56.8	65.5	69.9	67.8	60.3	48.0	37.1	27.7	47.5
Extreme Maximum Temp. (°F)	78	91	94	104	96	104	112	111	106	96	86	78	112
Extreme Minimum Temp. (°F)	-13	-15	4	18	32	44	48	46	29	16	3	-13	-15
Days Maximum Temp. ≥ 90°F	0	0	0	1	2	15	25	24	10	1	0	0	78
Days Maximum Temp. ≤ 32°F	5	3	0	0	0	0	0	0	0	0	0	2	10
Days Minimum Temp. ≤ 32°F	24	19	11	2	0	0	0	0	0	2	11	21	90
Days Minimum Temp. ≤ 0°F	1	0	0	0	0	0	0	0	0	0	0	0	1
Heating Degree Days (base 65°F)	926	677	454	183	40	2	0	0	30	169	486	806	3,773
Cooling Degree Days (base 65°F)	0	1	11	49	159	373	544	502	268	53	6	1	1,967
Mean Precipitation (in.)	1.42	1.89	3.41	3.97	4.52	4.44	2.97	2.86	4.59	3.43	3.17	2.04	38.71
Days With ≥ 0.1" Precipitation	3	3	6	6	7	6	5	4	6	5	4	4	59
Days With ≥ 1.0" Precipitation	0	0	1	1	1	1	1	1	1	1	1	1	10
Mean Snowfall (in.)	3.6	2.6	2.1	0.0	0.0	0.0	0.0	0.0	0.0	trace	0.6	1.1	10.0
Days With ≥ 1.0" Snow Depth	4	3	1	0	0	0	0	0	0	0	0	2	10

Beaver *Beaver County*   Elevation: 2,463 ft.   Latitude: 36° 49' N   Longitude: 100° 32' W

	JAN	FEB	MAR	APR	MAY	JUN	JUL	AUG	SEP	OCT	NOV	DEC	YEAR
Mean Maximum Temp. (°F)	45.2	51.9	59.8	70.3	78.8	89.0	95.0	92.9	84.5	73.7	58.7	48.6	70.7
Mean Temp. (°F)	31.2	36.9	44.9	55.0	64.8	74.9	80.6	78.9	70.0	57.6	43.6	34.3	56.1
Mean Minimum Temp. (°F)	17.1	21.8	30.0	39.8	50.9	60.8	66.3	64.8	55.4	41.6	28.5	19.9	41.4
Extreme Maximum Temp. (°F)	80	89	93	102	107	113	109	109	107	100	89	79	113
Extreme Minimum Temp. (°F)	-18	-17	1	16	26	42	46	45	27	13	-6	-13	-18
Days Maximum Temp. ≥ 90°F	0	0	0	1	4	15	25	22	11	2	0	0	80
Days Maximum Temp. ≤ 32°F	7	4	1	0	0	0	0	0	0	0	1	4	17
Days Minimum Temp. ≤ 32°F	30	25	19	6	0	0	0	0	0	5	21	29	135
Days Minimum Temp. ≤ 0°F	2	1	0	0	0	0	0	0	0	0	0	1	4
Heating Degree Days (base 65°F)	1,041	787	618	316	102	12	1	1	56	254	634	946	4,768
Cooling Degree Days (base 65°F)	0	0	2	21	102	309	491	445	217	32	1	0	1,620
Mean Precipitation (in.)	0.54	0.74	1.76	1.89	3.06	3.17	2.77	2.46	1.80	1.23	1.10	0.77	21.29
Days With ≥ 0.1" Precipitation	1	2	4	4	5	5	4	4	4	2	2	2	39
Days With ≥ 1.0" Precipitation	0	0	0	0	1	1	1	1	0	0	0	0	4
Mean Snowfall (in.)	*1.2*	*3.0*	*1.1*	0.2	0.0	0.0	0.0	0.0	0.0	0.2	*1.1*	*1.3*	*8.1*
Days With ≥ 1.0" Snow Depth	*1*	na	*1*	0	0	0	0	0	0	0	*1*	*1*	na

Billings *Noble County*   Elevation: 997 ft.   Latitude: 36° 32' N   Longitude: 97° 27' W

	JAN	FEB	MAR	APR	MAY	JUN	JUL	AUG	SEP	OCT	NOV	DEC	YEAR
Mean Maximum Temp. (°F)	44.0	50.2	59.7	69.7	78.3	88.5	94.6	92.9	84.0	73.3	57.9	47.1	70.0
Mean Temp. (°F)	33.4	38.7	47.9	57.0	66.7	77.0	82.7	80.9	72.3	60.7	46.6	36.8	58.4
Mean Minimum Temp. (°F)	22.7	27.2	35.7	44.3	55.3	65.5	70.7	68.8	60.6	47.9	35.3	26.5	46.7
Extreme Maximum Temp. (°F)	79	90	91	101	104	106	113	110	107	94	87	78	113
Extreme Minimum Temp. (°F)	-15	-12	4	20	34	42	52	45	29	11	9	-13	-15
Days Maximum Temp. ≥ 90°F	0	0	0	0	1	14	25	23	10	1	0	0	74
Days Maximum Temp. ≤ 32°F	6	4	1	0	0	0	0	0	0	0	0	3	14
Days Minimum Temp. ≤ 32°F	26	19	11	3	0	0	0	0	0	1	12	23	95
Days Minimum Temp. ≤ 0°F	1	1	0	0	0	0	0	0	0	0	0	1	3
Heating Degree Days (base 65°F)	974	737	526	257	64	3	0	0	34	175	547	870	4,187
Cooling Degree Days (base 65°F)	0	0	3	22	123	357	545	500	265	44	3	0	1,862
Mean Precipitation (in.)	1.16	1.49	3.07	3.70	4.70	4.26	3.11	3.18	4.00	2.86	2.51	1.58	35.62
Days With ≥ 0.1" Precipitation	3	3	5	5	6	6	4	4	5	3	3	3	50
Days With ≥ 1.0" Precipitation	0	0	1	1	1	1	1	1	1	1	1	0	9
Mean Snowfall (in.)	2.5	3.0	1.9	trace	trace	0.0	0.0	0.0	0.0	trace	0.5	1.2	9.1
Days With ≥ 1.0" Snow Depth	*1*	*1*	1	0	0	0	0	0	0	0	0	1	*4*

Blackwell *Kay County*   Elevation: 997 ft.   Latitude: 36° 48' N   Longitude: 97° 17' W

	JAN	FEB	MAR	APR	MAY	JUN	JUL	AUG	SEP	OCT	NOV	DEC	YEAR
Mean Maximum Temp. (°F)	*44.3*	*50.7*	*60.2*	*70.2*	*78.6*	*89.1*	*95.0*	*93.9*	*85.0*	*73.3*	*58.4*	*47.7*	*70.5*
Mean Temp. (°F)	*34.0*	*39.5*	*48.4*	*58.1*	*67.3*	*77.2*	*82.6*	*81.4*	*73.2*	*61.1*	*47.6*	*37.5*	*59.0*
Mean Minimum Temp. (°F)	*23.7*	*28.3*	*36.6*	*45.9*	*55.9*	*65.2*	*70.1*	*68.9*	*61.3*	*48.9*	*36.6*	*27.3*	*47.4*
Extreme Maximum Temp. (°F)	*75*	*92*	*89*	*93*	*101*	*108*	*114*	*111*	*107*	*94*	*87*	*76*	*114*
Extreme Minimum Temp. (°F)	*-10*	*-8*	*8*	*19*	*33*	*46*	*49*	*46*	*29*	*15*	*8*	*-12*	*-12*
Days Maximum Temp. ≥ 90°F	*0*	*0*	*0*	*0*	*2*	*15*	*25*	*23*	*11*	*1*	*0*	*0*	*77*
Days Maximum Temp. ≤ 32°F	*6*	*4*	*0*	*0*	*0*	*0*	*0*	*0*	*0*	*0*	*0*	*3*	*13*
Days Minimum Temp. ≤ 32°F	26	18	11	2	0	0	0	0	0	1	11	22	91
Days Minimum Temp. ≤ 0°F	*1*	*1*	*0*	*0*	*0*	*0*	*0*	*0*	*0*	*0*	*0*	*1*	*3*
Heating Degree Days (base 65°F)	*953*	*714*	*512*	*229*	*56*	*2*	*0*	*0*	*28*	*169*	*519*	*845*	*4,027*
Cooling Degree Days (base 65°F)	0	0	4	27	136	376	550	517	282	52	2	0	1,946
Mean Precipitation (in.)	*1.01*	*1.19*	*2.80*	*3.75*	*5.40*	*4.49*	*3.45*	*3.62*	*3.58*	*2.66*	*2.56*	*1.37*	*35.88*
Days With ≥ 0.1" Precipitation	*2*	*2*	*5*	*6*	*7*	*6*	*5*	*5*	*5*	*4*	*4*	*3*	*54*
Days With ≥ 1.0" Precipitation	*0*	*0*	*1*	*1*	*2*	*2*	*1*	*1*	*1*	*1*	*1*	*0*	*11*
Mean Snowfall (in.)	2.8	2.9	1.0	trace	0.0	0.0	0.0	0.0	0.0	trace	0.4	1.7	8.8
Days With ≥ 1.0" Snow Depth	*4*	*4*	*0*	*0*	*0*	*0*	*0*	*0*	*0*	*0*	*0*	*2*	*10*

Blanchard 2 SSW *McClain County* Elevation: 1,272 ft. Latitude: 35° 07' N Longitude: 97° 40' W

	JAN	FEB	MAR	APR	MAY	JUN	JUL	AUG	SEP	OCT	NOV	DEC	YEAR
Mean Maximum Temp. (°F)	49.0	55.4	64.0	73.4	80.4	87.9	94.2	93.3	85.5	75.0	61.2	52.0	72.6
Mean Temp. (°F)	38.2	43.6	51.9	61.2	69.5	76.9	82.3	81.5	73.9	62.7	50.0	41.1	61.1
Mean Minimum Temp. (°F)	27.3	31.8	39.6	49.0	58.6	66.0	70.5	69.5	62.2	50.4	38.8	30.3	49.5
Extreme Maximum Temp. (°F)	80	91	94	100	97	107	110	107	109	100	86	79	110
Extreme Minimum Temp. (°F)	-6	-2	7	19	35	45	53	52	36	18	10	-11	-11
Days Maximum Temp. ≥ 90°F	0	0	0	1	2	12	24	24	10	1	0	0	74
Days Maximum Temp. ≤ 32°F	4	2	0	0	0	0	0	0	0	0	0	2	8
Days Minimum Temp. ≤ 32°F	21	14	8	1	0	0	0	0	0	1	8	18	71
Days Minimum Temp. ≤ 0°F	0	0	0	0	0	0	0	0	0	0	0	0	0
Heating Degree Days (base 65°F)	826	599	413	164	29	2	0	0	24	135	449	732	3,373
Cooling Degree Days (base 65°F)	0	1	12	48	178	366	556	528	300	70	7	0	2,066
Mean Precipitation (in.)	1.17	1.67	2.68	3.32	5.33	3.65	2.51	2.63	4.09	3.41	2.07	1.90	34.43
Days With ≥ 0.1" Precipitation	2	3	5	5	7	5	4	4	5	4	3	3	50
Days With ≥ 1.0" Precipitation	0	1	1	1	2	1	1	1	1	1	0	0	10
Mean Snowfall (in.)	2.3	1.2	0.7	trace	0.0	0.0	0.0	0.0	0.0	trace	0.7	0.8	5.7
Days With ≥ 1.0" Snow Depth	1	1	0	0	0	0	0	0	0	0	0	1	3

Boise City 2 E *Cimarron County* Elevation: 4,143 ft. Latitude: 36° 44' N Longitude: 102° 29' W

	JAN	FEB	MAR	APR	MAY	JUN	JUL	AUG	SEP	OCT	NOV	DEC	YEAR
Mean Maximum Temp. (°F)	49.4	54.4	62.1	70.4	78.4	88.5	92.7	90.1	83.1	73.1	59.5	50.8	71.0
Mean Temp. (°F)	34.2	38.7	45.8	54.2	63.0	72.9	77.5	75.5	67.9	56.8	44.2	36.1	55.6
Mean Minimum Temp. (°F)	19.0	22.9	29.4	37.9	47.5	57.2	62.3	60.8	52.7	40.5	28.9	21.3	40.1
Extreme Maximum Temp. (°F)	80	84	88	95	101	109	106	103	105	92	87	80	109
Extreme Minimum Temp. (°F)	-16	-15	1	12	20	39	49	45	25	9	-7	-13	-16
Days Maximum Temp. ≥ 90°F	0	0	0	1	3	15	23	19	8	0	0	0	69
Days Maximum Temp. ≤ 32°F	4	2	1	0	0	0	0	0	0	0	1	3	11
Days Minimum Temp. ≤ 32°F	30	25	19	7	1	0	0	0	0	5	20	28	135
Days Minimum Temp. ≤ 0°F	1	1	0	0	0	0	0	0	0	0	0	1	3
Heating Degree Days (base 65°F)	947	739	588	326	117	14	1	2	57	261	616	890	4,558
Cooling Degree Days (base 65°F)	0	0	0	10	64	254	401	345	161	16	0	0	1,251
Mean Precipitation (in.)	0.37	0.43	1.05	1.49	2.58	2.98	2.62	2.88	1.54	1.02	0.73	0.50	18.19
Days With ≥ 0.1" Precipitation	1	1	3	3	5	5	5	5	4	2	2	1	37
Days With ≥ 1.0" Precipitation	0	0	0	0	1	1	0	1	0	0	0	0	3
Mean Snowfall (in.)	6.6	4.6	6.6	2.7	0.4	0.0	0.0	0.0	0.1	1.3	3.4	5.9	31.6
Days With ≥ 1.0" Snow Depth	5	2	1	1	0	0	0	0	0	0	1	2	12

Bristow *Creek County* Elevation: 820 ft. Latitude: 35° 50' N Longitude: 96° 23' W

	JAN	FEB	MAR	APR	MAY	JUN	JUL	AUG	SEP	OCT	NOV	DEC	YEAR
Mean Maximum Temp. (°F)	49.1	56.5	65.2	74.6	81.0	88.4	94.5	94.4	85.8	75.8	62.0	52.6	73.3
Mean Temp. (°F)	37.2	43.4	52.1	61.5	69.1	76.9	82.0	81.2	73.0	62.3	50.2	40.8	60.8
Mean Minimum Temp. (°F)	25.3	30.1	38.9	48.4	57.2	65.4	69.5	67.9	60.2	48.9	38.3	28.9	48.2
Extreme Maximum Temp. (°F)	78	92	94	102	98	103	111	109	110	98	87	77	111
Extreme Minimum Temp. (°F)	-10	-12	4	25	34	45	49	50	28	16	6	-14	-14
Days Maximum Temp. ≥ 90°F	0	0	0	1	2	14	26	24	11	1	0	0	79
Days Maximum Temp. ≤ 32°F	4	1	0	0	0	0	0	0	0	0	0	2	7
Days Minimum Temp. ≤ 32°F	23	17	9	1	0	0	0	0	0	2	9	20	81
Days Minimum Temp. ≤ 0°F	0	0	0	0	0	0	0	0	0	0	0	0	0
Heating Degree Days (base 65°F)	855	606	407	158	36	1	0	0	27	145	446	745	3,426
Cooling Degree Days (base 65°F)	0	1	13	56	171	370	542	519	280	64	9	1	2,026
Mean Precipitation (in.)	1.41	2.07	3.47	3.66	5.68	4.25	2.42	2.59	4.98	3.81	3.29	2.52	40.15
Days With ≥ 0.1" Precipitation	3	4	5	6	7	6	4	4	6	5	5	4	59
Days With ≥ 1.0" Precipitation	0	0	1	1	2	1	1	1	2	1	1	1	12
Mean Snowfall (in.)	3.2	2.4	1.1	0.0	0.0	0.0	0.0	0.0	0.0	trace	0.5	1.5	8.7
Days With ≥ 1.0" Snow Depth	4	2	0	0	0	0	0	0	0	0	0	2	8

Broken Bow Dam *McCurtain County* Elevation: 442 ft. Latitude: 34° 08' N Longitude: 94° 42' W

	JAN	FEB	MAR	APR	MAY	JUN	JUL	AUG	SEP	OCT	NOV	DEC	YEAR
Mean Maximum Temp. (°F)	51.8	57.6	66.1	74.5	81.3	88.9	93.5	93.5	86.2	76.5	63.9	55.5	74.1
Mean Temp. (°F)	39.7	44.5	52.6	60.7	69.0	76.6	80.7	80.3	73.7	62.7	51.5	43.4	61.3
Mean Minimum Temp. (°F)	27.5	31.3	39.2	46.8	56.7	64.2	67.7	67.0	61.0	48.9	39.0	31.4	48.4
Extreme Maximum Temp. (°F)	78	89	89	95	95	102	107	108	108	95	87	79	108
Extreme Minimum Temp. (°F)	2	0	8	24	34	46	54	53	38	25	11	2	0
Days Maximum Temp. ≥ 90°F	0	0	0	1	2	15	25	24	12	2	0	0	81
Days Maximum Temp. ≤ 32°F	1	1	0	0	0	0	0	0	0	0	0	1	3
Days Minimum Temp. ≤ 32°F	23	16	8	1	0	0	0	0	0	1	9	19	77
Days Minimum Temp. ≤ 0°F	0	0	0	0	0	0	0	0	0	0	0	0	0
Heating Degree Days (base 65°F)	779	575	384	161	29	1	0	0	16	127	405	662	3,139
Cooling Degree Days (base 65°F)	0	0	8	37	161	356	493	488	279	61	7	1	1,891
Mean Precipitation (in.)	3.16	3.58	5.12	4.66	6.46	4.44	4.41	2.89	4.65	5.36	5.17	4.74	54.64
Days With ≥ 0.1" Precipitation	5	6	6	6	8	6	5	4	6	6	6	6	70
Days With ≥ 1.0" Precipitation	1	1	2	2	2	1	1	1	1	2	2	2	18
Mean Snowfall (in.)	na	na	trace	0.0	0.0	0.0	0.0	0.0	0.0	0.0	0.0	trace	na
Days With ≥ 1.0" Snow Depth	na	na	0	0	0	0	0	0	0	0	0	0	na

Buffalo *Harper County*   Elevation: 1,794 ft.   Latitude: 36° 51' N   Longitude: 99° 38' W

	JAN	FEB	MAR	APR	MAY	JUN	JUL	AUG	SEP	OCT	NOV	DEC	YEAR
Mean Maximum Temp. (°F)	48.8	56.4	64.9	74.6	82.3	92.2	97.9	96.4	87.9	76.9	60.8	51.1	74.2
Mean Temp. (°F)	34.8	41.1	49.3	58.9	67.9	77.7	83.2	81.7	73.3	61.2	46.6	37.4	59.4
Mean Minimum Temp. (°F)	20.7	25.7	33.7	43.1	53.4	63.2	68.4	66.9	58.6	45.5	32.4	23.6	44.6
Extreme Maximum Temp. (°F)	87	91	96	105	108	111	115	111	108	100	93	79	115
Extreme Minimum Temp. (°F)	-14	-13	-3	15	30	42	45	45	26	13	5	-10	-14
Days Maximum Temp. ≥ 90°F	0	0	1	2	7	19	28	25	14	3	0	0	99
Days Maximum Temp. ≤ 32°F	5	2	0	0	0	0	0	0	0	0	0	2	9
Days Minimum Temp. ≤ 32°F	28	21	14	4	0	0	0	0	0	3	15	26	111
Days Minimum Temp. ≤ 0°F	1	1	0	0	0	0	0	0	0	0	0	1	3
Heating Degree Days (base 65°F)	930	670	488	222	57	4	0	0	30	173	546	849	3,969
Cooling Degree Days (base 65°F)	0	0	7	44	156	388	576	534	296	59	2	0	2,062
Mean Precipitation (in.)	0.54	0.92	2.02	2.49	4.21	3.60	2.58	2.80	2.67	1.84	1.61	0.85	26.13
Days With ≥ 0.1" Precipitation	2	2	5	5	6	6	5	5	4	3	3	2	48
Days With ≥ 1.0" Precipitation	0	0	1	1	2	1	1	1	1	0	0	0	8
Mean Snowfall (in.)	*2.0*	4.9	*2.1*	0.2	0.0	0.0	0.0	0.0	0.0	trace	1.5	2.4	*13.1*
Days With ≥ 1.0" Snow Depth	na	*0*	*0*	0	0	0	0	0	0	0	0	na	na

Carnegie 5 NE *Caddo County*   Elevation: 1,479 ft.   Latitude: 35° 11' N   Longitude: 98° 35' W

	JAN	FEB	MAR	APR	MAY	JUN	JUL	AUG	SEP	OCT	NOV	DEC	YEAR
Mean Maximum Temp. (°F)	49.4	55.8	64.8	74.2	82.0	91.1	96.0	94.5	86.6	76.1	61.8	52.3	73.7
Mean Temp. (°F)	37.2	43.1	51.6	60.8	69.9	78.8	83.4	81.7	74.1	62.9	49.7	40.4	61.1
Mean Minimum Temp. (°F)	25.0	30.2	38.4	47.4	57.7	66.5	70.7	68.9	61.6	49.6	37.6	28.4	48.5
Extreme Maximum Temp. (°F)	82	89	94	103	108	113	111	109	107	98	88	80	113
Extreme Minimum Temp. (°F)	-13	-4	5	19	34	47	51	51	26	12	7	-14	-14
Days Maximum Temp. ≥ 90°F	0	0	0	1	5	18	26	24	13	2	0	0	89
Days Maximum Temp. ≤ 32°F	4	2	0	0	0	0	0	0	0	0	0	2	8
Days Minimum Temp. ≤ 32°F	25	16	9	2	0	0	0	0	0	1	10	21	84
Days Minimum Temp. ≤ 0°F	0	0	0	0	0	0	0	0	0	0	0	0	0
Heating Degree Days (base 65°F)	855	613	419	172	31	1	0	0	25	136	456	757	3,465
Cooling Degree Days (base 65°F)	0	1	9	48	192	419	579	534	308	72	5	0	2,167
Mean Precipitation (in.)	1.09	1.25	2.27	2.76	5.69	4.09	2.33	2.62	3.17	2.58	1.61	1.35	30.81
Days With ≥ 0.1" Precipitation	2	3	4	4	6	5	3	4	4	4	3	3	45
Days With ≥ 1.0" Precipitation	0	0	1	1	2	2	1	1	1	1	0	0	10
Mean Snowfall (in.)	3.2	2.3	0.4	0.0	0.0	0.0	0.0	0.0	0.0	0.0	0.3	1.2	7.4
Days With ≥ 1.0" Snow Depth	3	2	0	0	0	0	0	0	0	0	0	1	6

Chandler 1 *Lincoln County*   Elevation: 921 ft.   Latitude: 35° 42' N   Longitude: 96° 53' W

	JAN	FEB	MAR	APR	MAY	JUN	JUL	AUG	SEP	OCT	NOV	DEC	YEAR
Mean Maximum Temp. (°F)	48.2	54.6	64.0	73.1	80.2	88.0	93.8	93.3	84.7	74.6	61.5	52.4	72.4
Mean Temp. (°F)	37.4	42.9	52.0	61.0	69.1	77.3	82.5	81.4	73.5	62.6	50.4	41.4	61.0
Mean Minimum Temp. (°F)	26.5	31.2	40.0	48.8	58.0	66.6	71.1	69.5	62.2	50.6	39.2	30.3	49.5
Extreme Maximum Temp. (°F)	80	92	94	102	95	103	111	108	110	98	86	77	111
Extreme Minimum Temp. (°F)	-6	-7	7	23	38	49	52	52	*37*	24	9	-13	*-13*
Days Maximum Temp. ≥ 90°F	0	0	0	0	2	13	24	23	9	1	0	0	72
Days Maximum Temp. ≤ 32°F	4	2	0	0	0	0	0	0	0	0	0	2	8
Days Minimum Temp. ≤ 32°F	22	15	7	1	0	0	0	0	0	1	8	*17*	*71*
Days Minimum Temp. ≤ 0°F	0	0	0	0	0	0	0	0	0	0	0	0	0
Heating Degree Days (base 65°F)	848	617	408	167	34	1	0	0	24	136	438	724	3,397
Cooling Degree Days (base 65°F)	0	1	12	46	171	378	552	518	280	57	7	1	2,023
Mean Precipitation (in.)	1.41	1.93	3.12	3.37	5.25	4.08	2.50	2.59	4.43	3.55	2.87	1.76	36.86
Days With ≥ 0.1" Precipitation	2	3	5	5	7	5	3	4	5	4	4	3	50
Days With ≥ 1.0" Precipitation	0	1	1	1	2	1	1	1	1	1	1	1	12
Mean Snowfall (in.)	3.2	*2.4*	0.5	0.0	0.0	0.0	0.0	0.0	0.0	trace	0.4	0.8	*7.3*
Days With ≥ 1.0" Snow Depth	3	2	0	0	0	0	0	0	0	0	0	0	5

Chattanooga 3 NE *Comanche County*   Elevation: 1,151 ft.   Latitude: 34° 27' N   Longitude: 98° 37' W

	JAN	FEB	MAR	APR	MAY	JUN	JUL	AUG	SEP	OCT	NOV	DEC	YEAR
Mean Maximum Temp. (°F)	51.8	58.4	67.1	76.1	84.3	93.3	98.6	97.0	88.8	78.6	64.1	54.7	76.1
Mean Temp. (°F)	39.1	44.7	53.0	61.8	70.9	79.8	84.5	83.2	75.6	64.6	51.2	42.0	62.5
Mean Minimum Temp. (°F)	26.3	31.0	38.8	47.3	57.5	66.2	70.4	69.3	62.4	50.5	38.3	29.3	48.9
Extreme Maximum Temp. (°F)	82	92	99	100	107	116	113	111	110	105	88	81	116
Extreme Minimum Temp. (°F)	-9	-4	9	20	36	47	53	53	34	16	12	-13	-13
Days Maximum Temp. ≥ 90°F	0	0	0	2	8	22	29	27	16	4	0	0	108
Days Maximum Temp. ≤ 32°F	3	1	0	0	0	0	0	0	0	0	0	1	5
Days Minimum Temp. ≤ 32°F	24	15	8	2	0	0	0	0	0	1	9	20	79
Days Minimum Temp. ≤ 0°F	0	0	0	0	0	0	0	0	0	0	0	0	0
Heating Degree Days (base 65°F)	796	566	377	147	22	1	0	0	17	104	413	706	3,149
Cooling Degree Days (base 65°F)	0	0	9	49	217	451	621	590	351	96	6	0	2,390
Mean Precipitation (in.)	1.03	1.48	2.53	2.66	4.89	3.89	2.22	2.60	3.44	2.74	1.63	1.56	30.67
Days With ≥ 0.1" Precipitation	2	3	4	4	6	5	3	4	5	3	3	3	45
Days With ≥ 1.0" Precipitation	0	0	1	1	2	1	1	1	1	1	0	0	9
Mean Snowfall (in.)	*1.0*	*0.6*	0.2	0.0	0.0	0.0	0.0	0.0	0.0	trace	trace	*0.3*	*2.1*
Days With ≥ 1.0" Snow Depth	*0*	na	0	0	0	0	0	0	0	0	0	0	na

Cherokee *Alfalfa County*   Elevation: 1,177 ft.   Latitude: 36° 46' N   Longitude: 98° 22' W

	JAN	FEB	MAR	APR	MAY	JUN	JUL	AUG	SEP	OCT	NOV	DEC	YEAR
Mean Maximum Temp. (°F)	46.5	53.6	62.9	73.0	81.7	91.9	97.1	95.7	86.6	75.3	59.5	49.5	72.8
Mean Temp. (°F)	34.4	40.4	49.3	59.1	68.6	78.7	84.0	82.6	73.8	61.6	47.3	37.7	59.8
Mean Minimum Temp. (°F)	22.2	27.1	35.7	45.1	55.6	65.6	70.8	69.5	61.0	48.1	35.1	25.8	46.8
Extreme Maximum Temp. (°F)	77	91	93	100	105	111	111	111	107	97	90	76	111
Extreme Minimum Temp. (°F)	-15	-15	3	18	33	45	50	51	30	14	6	-12	-15
Days Maximum Temp. ≥ 90°F	0	0	0	1	5	19	27	24	13	2	0	0	91
Days Maximum Temp. ≤ 32°F	6	2	0	0	0	0	0	0	0	0	0	3	11
Days Minimum Temp. ≤ 32°F	27	20	12	3	0	0	0	0	0	1	12	25	100
Days Minimum Temp. ≤ 0°F	1	1	0	0	0	0	0	0	0	0	0	1	3
Heating Degree Days (base 65°F)	943	694	486	214	48	1	0	0	27	164	527	839	3,943
Cooling Degree Days (base 65°F)	0	0	5	38	171	424	599	566	306	61	2	0	2,172
Mean Precipitation (in.)	0.97	1.13	2.83	2.83	4.43	4.00	3.18	3.49	3.00	2.17	1.78	1.26	31.07
Days With ≥ 0.1" Precipitation	2	2	4	4	6	5	4	4	4	3	3	3	44
Days With ≥ 1.0" Precipitation	0	0	1	1	2	1	1	1	1	1	0	0	9
Mean Snowfall (in.)	*2.6*	*4.1*	*2.8*	0.2	0.0	0.0	0.0	0.0	0.0	0.0	0.8	2.4	*12.9*
Days With ≥ 1.0" Snow Depth	*1*	*1*	*0*	0	0	0	0	0	0	0	0	*1*	*3*

Chickasha Experiment Station *Grady County*   Elevation: 1,082 ft.   Latitude: 35° 03' N   Longitude: 97° 55' W

	JAN	FEB	MAR	APR	MAY	JUN	JUL	AUG	SEP	OCT	NOV	DEC	YEAR
Mean Maximum Temp. (°F)	49.8	57.0	65.5	75.3	82.4	90.4	95.6	94.0	86.8	76.8	63.0	53.3	74.2
Mean Temp. (°F)	37.7	43.8	52.4	61.9	70.4	78.8	83.2	81.6	74.1	63.2	50.4	41.3	61.6
Mean Minimum Temp. (°F)	25.6	30.5	39.1	48.3	58.4	67.1	70.8	69.1	61.4	49.5	37.8	29.1	48.9
Extreme Maximum Temp. (°F)	78	90	93	102	107	112	111	107	109	103	89	77	112
Extreme Minimum Temp. (°F)	-11	-3	6	19	35	47	52	49	33	14	5	-12	-12
Days Maximum Temp. ≥ 90°F	0	0	0	1	5	18	27	25	12	2	0	0	90
Days Maximum Temp. ≤ 32°F	3	2	0	0	0	0	0	0	0	0	0	2	7
Days Minimum Temp. ≤ 32°F	24	17	8	1	0	0	0	0	0	1	10	20	81
Days Minimum Temp. ≤ 0°F	0	0	0	0	0	0	0	0	0	0	0	0	0
Heating Degree Days (base 65°F)	839	594	398	149	26	1	0	0	22	130	438	729	3,326
Cooling Degree Days (base 65°F)	0	1	10	54	201	418	578	539	307	76	5	0	2,189
Mean Precipitation (in.)	1.29	1.76	2.78	3.61	5.25	3.91	2.09	2.78	3.69	3.57	2.04	1.84	34.61
Days With ≥ 0.1" Precipitation	2	3	5	5	7	6	3	5	5	5	4	3	53
Days With ≥ 1.0" Precipitation	0	0	1	1	2	1	1	1	1	1	1	1	11
Mean Snowfall (in.)	1.4	na	0.2	trace	0.0	0.0	0.0	0.0	0.0	trace	trace	0.6	na
Days With ≥ 1.0" Snow Depth	*0*	*0*	0	0	0	0	0	0	0	0	0	0	*0*

Claremore 2 ENE *Rogers County*   Elevation: 587 ft.   Latitude: 36° 19' N   Longitude: 95° 35' W

	JAN	FEB	MAR	APR	MAY	JUN	JUL	AUG	SEP	OCT	NOV	DEC	YEAR
Mean Maximum Temp. (°F)	44.6	51.4	60.5	70.3	77.8	86.3	92.4	92.1	83.3	72.8	59.0	49.3	70.0
Mean Temp. (°F)	33.4	39.2	48.4	58.1	66.7	75.7	81.0	79.8	71.9	60.1	47.6	38.2	58.4
Mean Minimum Temp. (°F)	22.1	27.0	36.3	45.8	55.6	65.1	69.6	67.6	60.5	47.3	36.2	27.1	46.7
Extreme Maximum Temp. (°F)	76	90	93	102	93	102	109	109	107	96	85	76	109
Extreme Minimum Temp. (°F)	-20	-16	4	23	33	45	48	50	32	17	4	-12	-20
Days Maximum Temp. ≥ 90°F	0	0	0	0	1	10	22	21	9	1	0	0	64
Days Maximum Temp. ≤ 32°F	6	3	1	0	0	0	0	0	0	0	0	3	13
Days Minimum Temp. ≤ 32°F	27	20	11	2	0	0	0	0	0	2	12	22	96
Days Minimum Temp. ≤ 0°F	1	0	0	0	0	0	0	0	0	0	0	0	1
Heating Degree Days (base 65°F)	974	721	513	236	64	3	0	0	39	193	520	823	4,086
Cooling Degree Days (base 65°F)	0	0	6	30	126	339	510	481	256	45	6	1	1,800
Mean Precipitation (in.)	1.74	2.14	3.68	4.17	5.27	4.70	3.47	3.04	5.07	3.88	3.96	2.58	43.70
Days With ≥ 0.1" Precipitation	4	4	6	6	8	7	4	5	6	5	5	4	64
Days With ≥ 1.0" Precipitation	0	0	1	1	2	1	1	1	2	1	1	1	12
Mean Snowfall (in.)	3.1	2.9	1.7	0.0	0.0	0.0	0.0	0.0	0.0	trace	0.3	1.2	9.2
Days With ≥ 1.0" Snow Depth	4	2	1	0	0	0	0	0	0	0	0	1	8

Clinton *Custer County*   Elevation: 1,607 ft.   Latitude: 35° 31' N   Longitude: 98° 59' W

	JAN	FEB	MAR	APR	MAY	JUN	JUL	AUG	SEP	OCT	NOV	DEC	YEAR
Mean Maximum Temp. (°F)	48.8	55.1	64.5	73.8	81.6	90.9	96.9	95.3	86.5	75.3	61.1	51.6	73.5
Mean Temp. (°F)	36.9	42.4	51.2	60.2	69.3	78.5	83.8	82.3	74.1	62.2	49.0	39.8	60.8
Mean Minimum Temp. (°F)	24.8	29.6	37.8	46.5	56.9	66.1	70.6	69.1	61.5	49.1	36.8	27.9	48.1
Extreme Maximum Temp. (°F)	82	89	96	102	106	112	115	111	106	101	88	79	115
Extreme Minimum Temp. (°F)	-9	-7	4	21	30	47	50	51	33	15	9	-11	-11
Days Maximum Temp. ≥ 90°F	0	0	0	1	5	18	27	25	12	1	0	0	89
Days Maximum Temp. ≤ 32°F	4	2	0	0	0	0	0	0	0	0	0	2	8
Days Minimum Temp. ≤ 32°F	25	17	9	2	0	0	0	0	0	1	10	22	86
Days Minimum Temp. ≤ 0°F	0	0	0	0	0	0	0	0	0	0	0	0	0
Heating Degree Days (base 65°F)	866	633	430	183	37	2	0	0	24	144	476	776	3,571
Cooling Degree Days (base 65°F)	0	0	7	43	182	417	595	553	312	62	3	0	2,174
Mean Precipitation (in.)	1.05	1.14	2.37	2.40	5.09	3.85	2.32	3.10	3.72	2.80	1.83	1.30	30.97
Days With ≥ 0.1" Precipitation	2	3	4	4	6	6	4	5	5	4	3	3	49
Days With ≥ 1.0" Precipitation	0	0	1	1	2	1	1	1	1	1	0	0	9
Mean Snowfall (in.)	3.0	2.7	*0.7*	trace	0.0	0.0	0.0	0.0	0.0	trace	0.6	1.8	*8.8*
Days With ≥ 1.0" Snow Depth	*0*	na	0	0	0	0	0	0	0	0	0	na	na

Cushing *Payne County* Elevation: 948 ft. Latitude: 35° 59' N Longitude: 96° 46' W

	JAN	FEB	MAR	APR	MAY	JUN	JUL	AUG	SEP	OCT	NOV	DEC	YEAR
Mean Maximum Temp. (°F)	45.5	52.0	60.9	71.0	78.3	86.7	92.8	92.4	83.6	73.2	59.4	49.6	70.5
Mean Temp. (°F)	34.7	40.5	49.3	59.3	67.8	76.4	81.8	80.9	72.6	61.3	48.7	39.0	59.4
Mean Minimum Temp. (°F)	23.8	29.0	37.6	47.5	57.4	66.1	70.7	69.4	61.5	49.4	37.9	28.4	48.2
Extreme Maximum Temp. (°F)	79	91	93	101	97	103	110	107	107	95	84	78	110
Extreme Minimum Temp. (°F)	-5	-6	6	22	39	49	53	52	35	20	11	-9	-9
Days Maximum Temp. ≥ 90°F	0	0	0	0	2	11	23	22	9	1	0	0	68
Days Maximum Temp. ≤ 32°F	5	3	0	0	0	0	0	0	0	0	1	3	12
Days Minimum Temp. ≤ 32°F	25	17	9	1	0	0	0	0	0	1	9	20	82
Days Minimum Temp. ≤ 0°F	1	0	0	0	0	0	0	0	0	0	0	0	1
Heating Degree Days (base 65°F)	933	685	489	206	48	2	0	0	32	163	488	799	3,845
Cooling Degree Days (base 65°F)	0	0	8	36	144	357	533	510	272	52	6	0	1,918
Mean Precipitation (in.)	1.21	1.86	3.13	3.89	5.54	4.27	2.90	2.65	4.31	3.42	2.87	1.86	37.91
Days With ≥ 0.1" Precipitation	2	3	5	5	7	6	4	4	6	4	4	3	53
Days With ≥ 1.0" Precipitation	0	0	1	1	2	1	1	1	1	1	1	1	11
Mean Snowfall (in.)	*1.9*	*1.4*	0.7	trace	0.0	0.0	0.0	0.0	0.0	0.0	0.2	1.1	*5.3*
Days With ≥ 1.0" Snow Depth	*2*	na	0	0	0	0	0	0	0	0	0	0	na

Duncan *Stephens County* Elevation: 1,122 ft. Latitude: 34° 30' N Longitude: 97° 58' W

	JAN	FEB	MAR	APR	MAY	JUN	JUL	AUG	SEP	OCT	NOV	DEC	YEAR
Mean Maximum Temp. (°F)	49.9	56.3	64.8	73.6	80.9	89.1	94.7	93.7	85.8	75.9	62.7	53.6	73.4
Mean Temp. (°F)	38.6	44.3	52.7	61.7	69.8	78.2	83.2	82.1	74.4	63.7	51.3	42.1	61.8
Mean Minimum Temp. (°F)	27.2	32.2	40.5	49.7	58.7	67.2	71.6	70.4	63.0	51.4	39.7	30.6	50.2
Extreme Maximum Temp. (°F)	81	90	95	100	103	111	*110*	111	106	102	87	78	*111*
Extreme Minimum Temp. (°F)	-4	-2	10	26	39	49	55	55	38	19	14	-7	-7
Days Maximum Temp. ≥ 90°F	0	0	0	0	3	15	26	*25*	12	2	0	0	*83*
Days Maximum Temp. ≤ 32°F	3	2	0	0	0	0	0	0	0	0	0	*2*	*7*
Days Minimum Temp. ≤ 32°F	22	13	*6*	1	0	0	0	0	0	1	7	*18*	68
Days Minimum Temp. ≤ 0°F	0	0	0	0	0	0	0	0	0	0	0	0	0
Heating Degree Days (base 65°F)	811	580	387	149	29	1	0	0	24	120	413	701	3,215
Cooling Degree Days (base 65°F)	0	1	11	49	178	397	572	541	310	81	6	0	2,146
Mean Precipitation (in.)	1.32	1.82	2.71	3.43	5.13	4.27	2.53	2.49	4.20	3.60	2.12	1.94	35.56
Days With ≥ 0.1" Precipitation	3	3	4	5	6	5	3	4	6	5	4	3	51
Days With ≥ 1.0" Precipitation	0	0	1	1	2	2	1	1	1	1	1	1	12
Mean Snowfall (in.)	1.3	*1.0*	0.2	0.0	0.0	0.0	0.0	0.0	0.0	trace	0.2	*0.3*	*3.0*
Days With ≥ 1.0" Snow Depth	*0*	*0*	0	0	0	0	0	0	0	0	0	*0*	*0*

El Reno 1 N *Canadian County* Elevation: 1,312 ft. Latitude: 35° 33' N Longitude: 97° 57' W

	JAN	FEB	MAR	APR	MAY	JUN	JUL	AUG	SEP	OCT	NOV	DEC	YEAR
Mean Maximum Temp. (°F)	47.5	54.1	63.4	72.8	80.4	88.8	94.4	93.3	85.3	74.4	60.0	50.7	72.1
Mean Temp. (°F)	36.3	42.1	51.0	60.1	68.8	77.2	82.4	81.2	73.2	62.1	48.8	39.7	60.3
Mean Minimum Temp. (°F)	25.0	30.1	38.4	47.4	57.1	65.6	70.4	69.0	61.2	49.8	37.6	28.7	48.4
Extreme Maximum Temp. (°F)	80	90	97	103	105	108	110	107	106	98	85	77	110
Extreme Minimum Temp. (°F)	-10	-5	4	18	36	45	51	50	35	17	10	-11	-11
Days Maximum Temp. ≥ 90°F	0	0	0	1	3	14	25	24	10	1	0	0	78
Days Maximum Temp. ≤ 32°F	4	2	0	0	0	0	0	0	0	0	0	2	8
Days Minimum Temp. ≤ 32°F	24	17	9	2	0	0	0	0	0	1	9	21	83
Days Minimum Temp. ≤ 0°F	0	0	0	0	0	0	0	0	0	0	0	0	0
Heating Degree Days (base 65°F)	883	640	441	186	38	2	0	0	26	150	484	779	3,629
Cooling Degree Days (base 65°F)	0	1	11	43	165	375	551	520	272	63	3	0	2,004
Mean Precipitation (in.)	1.07	1.32	2.67	3.02	5.78	4.86	2.66	2.82	3.63	2.86	2.11	1.31	34.11
Days With ≥ 0.1" Precipitation	2	3	5	4	7	6	4	4	5	4	3	3	50
Days With ≥ 1.0" Precipitation	0	0	1	1	2	2	1	1	1	1	1	0	11
Mean Snowfall (in.)	2.5	1.8	0.3	trace	0.0	0.0	0.0	0.0	0.0	0.0	0.4	0.7	5.7
Days With ≥ 1.0" Snow Depth	*0*	*0*	0	0	0	0	0	0	0	0	0	0	*0*

Elk City *Beckham County* Elevation: 1,961 ft. Latitude: 35° 25' N Longitude: 99° 23' W

	JAN	FEB	MAR	APR	MAY	JUN	JUL	AUG	SEP	OCT	NOV	DEC	YEAR
Mean Maximum Temp. (°F)	48.3	54.7	63.7	73.0	80.8	89.4	94.7	92.6	85.6	74.4	60.0	50.8	72.3
Mean Temp. (°F)	36.3	41.9	50.3	59.4	68.3	77.0	81.9	80.0	73.0	61.3	48.0	39.2	59.7
Mean Minimum Temp. (°F)	24.4	29.1	36.9	45.7	55.9	64.5	69.0	67.3	60.3	48.1	35.9	27.5	47.1
Extreme Maximum Temp. (°F)	80	90	97	100	101	111	109	106	106	97	87	81	111
Extreme Minimum Temp. (°F)	-12	-4	1	21	33	44	52	51	28	17	11	-9	-12
Days Maximum Temp. ≥ 90°F	0	0	0	1	4	16	25	23	11	1	0	0	81
Days Maximum Temp. ≤ 32°F	4	2	0	0	0	0	0	0	0	0	0	2	8
Days Minimum Temp. ≤ 32°F	25	17	10	2	0	0	0	0	0	1	11	22	88
Days Minimum Temp. ≤ 0°F	0	0	0	0	0	0	0	0	0	0	0	0	0
Heating Degree Days (base 65°F)	882	644	454	197	42	2	0	1	25	162	505	794	3,708
Cooling Degree Days (base 65°F)	0	0	5	32	145	357	521	480	258	51	1	0	1,850
Mean Precipitation (in.)	0.87	1.19	2.30	2.44	4.90	3.66	2.24	3.09	3.05	2.14	1.60	1.00	28.48
Days With ≥ 0.1" Precipitation	2	2	4	4	7	5	3	4	4	3	3	2	43
Days With ≥ 1.0" Precipitation	0	0	1	1	2	1	1	1	1	1	0	0	9
Mean Snowfall (in.)	na	na	0.2	0.1	0.0	0.0	0.0	0.0	0.0	trace	0.2	*2.1*	na
Days With ≥ 1.0" Snow Depth	na	na	0	0	0	0	0	0	0	0	0	*1*	na

Enid *Garfield County*   Elevation: 1,243 ft.   Latitude: 36° 25' N   Longitude: 97° 52' W

	JAN	FEB	MAR	APR	MAY	JUN	JUL	AUG	SEP	OCT	NOV	DEC	YEAR
Mean Maximum Temp. (°F)	45.3	52.4	61.5	71.4	79.9	89.7	95.1	93.4	85.0	73.8	58.5	49.0	71.3
Mean Temp. (°F)	35.2	41.3	49.8	59.6	68.8	78.2	83.3	81.8	73.7	62.1	48.2	39.1	60.1
Mean Minimum Temp. (°F)	25.0	30.1	38.0	47.7	57.6	66.6	71.5	70.0	62.4	50.3	37.8	29.2	48.8
Extreme Maximum Temp. (°F)	79	90	94	101	104	109	110	108	106	96	89	76	110
Extreme Minimum Temp. (°F)	-6	-7	5	21	37	48	53	51	33	17	10	-10	-10
Days Maximum Temp. ≥ 90°F	0	0	0	0	3	17	25	23	11	1	0	0	80
Days Maximum Temp. ≤ 32°F	6	3	1	0	0	0	0	0	0	0	0	2	12
Days Minimum Temp. ≤ 32°F	23	16	9	1	0	0	0	0	0	1	9	20	79
Days Minimum Temp. ≤ 0°F	0	0	0	0	0	0	0	0	0	0	0	0	0
Heating Degree Days (base 65°F)	918	663	473	200	41	2	0	0	28	152	502	795	3,774
Cooling Degree Days (base 65°F)	0	1	6	40	164	399	578	531	300	60	3	0	2,082
Mean Precipitation (in.)	1.11	1.59	2.57	3.41	4.78	4.32	2.75	3.49	3.26	3.20	2.18	1.40	34.06
Days With ≥ 0.1" Precipitation	2	3	5	5	7	6	4	4	5	4	3	3	51
Days With ≥ 1.0" Precipitation	0	1	1	1	1	2	1	1	1	1	1	0	11
Mean Snowfall (in.)	2.2	na	1.6	trace	0.0	0.0	0.0	0.0	0.0	trace	*0.3*	1.0	na
Days With ≥ 1.0" Snow Depth	*2*	na	1	0	0	0	0	0	0	0	*0*	1	na

Erick *Beckham County*   Elevation: 2,057 ft.   Latitude: 35° 13' N   Longitude: 99° 52' W

	JAN	FEB	MAR	APR	MAY	JUN	JUL	AUG	SEP	OCT	NOV	DEC	YEAR
Mean Maximum Temp. (°F)	50.1	56.3	64.8	74.1	81.4	89.8	95.5	93.7	86.0	75.4	61.8	52.4	73.5
Mean Temp. (°F)	36.7	42.3	50.3	59.4	68.1	76.7	81.7	80.0	72.5	61.1	48.4	39.3	59.7
Mean Minimum Temp. (°F)	23.3	28.3	35.8	44.5	54.7	63.5	67.9	66.3	59.0	46.8	34.9	26.1	45.9
Extreme Maximum Temp. (°F)	83	93	99	100	106	111	109	109	105	99	90	80	111
Extreme Minimum Temp. (°F)	-9	-4	-2	19	32	43	50	50	27	13	8	-9	-9
Days Maximum Temp. ≥ 90°F	0	0	0	2	6	16	26	24	12	2	0	0	88
Days Maximum Temp. ≤ 32°F	4	2	0	0	0	0	0	0	0	0	0	2	8
Days Minimum Temp. ≤ 32°F	27	18	11	2	0	0	0	0	0	2	12	24	96
Days Minimum Temp. ≤ 0°F	0	0	0	0	0	0	0	0	0	0	0	0	0
Heating Degree Days (base 65°F)	869	634	453	199	46	2	0	0	29	162	494	790	3,678
Cooling Degree Days (base 65°F)	0	0	4	35	153	356	530	481	261	47	2	0	1,869
Mean Precipitation (in.)	0.64	0.88	1.93	2.19	4.57	3.33	1.83	2.67	3.13	2.29	1.34	0.88	25.68
Days With ≥ 0.1" Precipitation	2	2	4	4	6	5	4	4	4	3	3	2	43
Days With ≥ 1.0" Precipitation	0	0	1	1	1	1	0	1	1	1	0	0	7
Mean Snowfall (in.)	3.0	2.6	1.1	0.2	trace	0.0	0.0	0.0	0.0	trace	1.3	2.1	10.3
Days With ≥ 1.0" Snow Depth	3	2	1	0	0	0	0	0	0	0	1	2	9

Fort Supply 3 SE *Woodward County*   Elevation: 2,027 ft.   Latitude: 36° 33' N   Longitude: 99° 32' W

	JAN	FEB	MAR	APR	MAY	JUN	JUL	AUG	SEP	OCT	NOV	DEC	YEAR
Mean Maximum Temp. (°F)	*45.8*	51.9	60.7	70.3	77.8	87.3	93.1	91.7	83.4	72.6	58.8	48.5	*70.2*
Mean Temp. (°F)	*32.9*	38.0	47.1	56.9	65.9	75.4	80.7	79.1	70.6	58.6	45.2	35.6	*57.2*
Mean Minimum Temp. (°F)	19.7	24.2	33.5	43.2	53.8	63.4	68.2	66.5	57.7	44.7	31.8	22.6	44.1
Extreme Maximum Temp. (°F)	86	90	95	98	105	110	110	108	105	98	89	78	110
Extreme Minimum Temp. (°F)	-14	-9	1	18	34	36	50	47	31	15	4	-13	-14
Days Maximum Temp. ≥ 90°F	0	0	0	1	3	12	23	21	10	1	0	0	71
Days Maximum Temp. ≤ 32°F	6	3	1	0	0	0	0	0	0	0	1	4	15
Days Minimum Temp. ≤ 32°F	*28*	21	14	4	0	0	0	0	0	3	16	27	*113*
Days Minimum Temp. ≤ 0°F	1	1	0	0	0	0	0	0	0	0	0	1	3
Heating Degree Days (base 65°F)	*991*	749	559	271	81	8	0	2	46	230	588	906	*4,431*
Cooling Degree Days (base 65°F)	0	0	3	27	108	314	487	449	218	31	2	0	1,639
Mean Precipitation (in.)	0.61	0.87	1.98	2.22	3.97	3.12	2.41	2.60	2.35	1.64	1.41	0.85	24.03
Days With ≥ 0.1" Precipitation	2	2	4	4	6	5	4	5	4	3	3	2	44
Days With ≥ 1.0" Precipitation	0	0	1	0	1	1	1	1	1	0	0	0	6
Mean Snowfall (in.)	3.0	3.7	2.6	0.9	trace	0.0	0.0	0.0	0.0	0.2	1.1	2.5	14.0
Days With ≥ 1.0" Snow Depth	*3*	3	2	0	0	0	0	0	0	0	1	2	*11*

Frederick *Tillman County*   Elevation: 1,282 ft.   Latitude: 34° 23' N   Longitude: 99° 01' W

	JAN	FEB	MAR	APR	MAY	JUN	JUL	AUG	SEP	OCT	NOV	DEC	YEAR
Mean Maximum Temp. (°F)	51.1	57.2	66.2	75.2	83.0	91.9	97.4	95.5	87.2	76.8	63.2	54.5	74.9
Mean Temp. (°F)	38.9	44.3	52.9	61.9	70.3	79.4	84.5	82.6	74.8	63.7	50.9	42.3	62.2
Mean Minimum Temp. (°F)	26.6	31.3	39.6	48.5	57.6	66.8	71.6	69.9	62.5	50.6	38.7	29.6	49.4
Extreme Maximum Temp. (°F)	83	87	104	103	106	115	114	114	106	104	90	82	115
Extreme Minimum Temp. (°F)	1	0	7	25	34	40	55	56	38	21	13	-11	-11
Days Maximum Temp. ≥ 90°F	0	0	1	2	8	20	27	25	14	3	0	0	100
Days Maximum Temp. ≤ 32°F	3	2	0	0	0	0	0	0	0	0	0	1	6
Days Minimum Temp. ≤ 32°F	23	15	7	1	0	0	0	0	0	0	8	19	73
Days Minimum Temp. ≤ 0°F	0	0	0	0	0	0	0	0	0	0	0	0	0
Heating Degree Days (base 65°F)	803	578	380	148	28	1	0	0	19	116	421	698	3,192
Cooling Degree Days (base 65°F)	0	0	10	53	187	424	610	555	318	74	6	0	2,237
Mean Precipitation (in.)	1.12	1.43	2.42	2.51	4.85	3.74	2.11	2.91	3.48	2.77	1.71	1.41	30.46
Days With ≥ 0.1" Precipitation	2	3	4	4	6	4	3	4	4	4	3	3	44
Days With ≥ 1.0" Precipitation	0	0	1	1	2	1	1	1	1	1	1	0	10
Mean Snowfall (in.)	*1.1*	1.5	0.2	trace	0.0	0.0	0.0	0.0	0.0	0.0	0.2	*0.6*	*3.6*
Days With ≥ 1.0" Snow Depth	*1*	0	0	0	0	0	0	0	0	0	0	1	*1*

Freedom *Woods County*   Elevation: 1,528 ft.   Latitude: 36° 46' N   Longitude: 99° 07' W

	JAN	FEB	MAR	APR	MAY	JUN	JUL	AUG	SEP	OCT	NOV	DEC	YEAR
Mean Maximum Temp. (°F)	47.0	53.9	62.8	72.6	81.2	90.8	96.3	94.5	86.1	75.0	59.9	49.9	72.5
Mean Temp. (°F)	33.2	39.2	47.9	58.0	67.7	77.3	82.4	80.7	72.2	59.8	45.7	36.2	58.4
Mean Minimum Temp. (°F)	19.4	24.5	33.3	43.3	54.2	63.7	68.5	66.8	58.3	44.6	31.5	22.4	44.2
Extreme Maximum Temp. (°F)	86	92	97	103	104	112	111	110	107	99	88	80	112
Extreme Minimum Temp. (°F)	-15	-15	2	14	27	43	49	47	28	10	3	-17	-17
Days Maximum Temp. ≥ 90°F	0	0	0	1	5	17	26	24	12	2	0	0	87
Days Maximum Temp. ≤ 32°F	5	3	1	0	0	0	0	0	0	0	1	3	13
Days Minimum Temp. ≤ 32°F	29	22	15	5	0	0	0	0	0	4	17	27	119
Days Minimum Temp. ≤ 0°F	1	1	0	0	0	0	0	0	0	0	0	1	3
Heating Degree Days (base 65°F)	979	722	530	244	59	4	0	1	37	204	575	887	4,242
Cooling Degree Days (base 65°F)	0	0	4	35	144	365	539	486	252	43	2	0	1,870
Mean Precipitation (in.)	0.74	0.87	2.04	2.48	4.17	3.01	2.48	2.63	2.63	1.79	1.64	1.04	25.52
Days With ≥ 0.1" Precipitation	2	2	4	4	6	5	4	4	4	3	3	2	43
Days With ≥ 1.0" Precipitation	0	0	0	1	1	1	1	1	1	0	0	0	6
Mean Snowfall (in.)	1.4	1.3	1.0	trace	0.0	0.0	0.0	0.0	0.0	trace	0.9	1.6	6.2
Days With ≥ 1.0" Snow Depth	1	1	0	0	0	0	0	0	0	0	0	1	3

Gage Airport *Ellis County*   Elevation: 2,188 ft.   Latitude: 36° 18' N   Longitude: 99° 46' W

	JAN	FEB	MAR	APR	MAY	JUN	JUL	AUG	SEP	OCT	NOV	DEC	YEAR
Mean Maximum Temp. (°F)	46.4	52.7	61.2	71.2	78.6	88.1	93.9	92.3	83.4	73.2	58.8	49.2	70.8
Mean Temp. (°F)	33.1	38.7	47.2	57.0	65.9	75.6	80.8	79.4	70.5	58.9	45.3	35.9	57.4
Mean Minimum Temp. (°F)	19.7	24.6	33.2	42.7	53.2	63.0	67.6	66.4	57.5	44.5	31.7	22.6	43.9
Extreme Maximum Temp. (°F)	86	90	94	99	105	111	111	107	104	99	89	80	111
Extreme Minimum Temp. (°F)	-15	-10	1	15	31	43	47	45	29	10	3	-13	-15
Days Maximum Temp. ≥ 90°F	0	0	0	1	3	14	24	22	10	1	0	0	75
Days Maximum Temp. ≤ 32°F	6	3	1	0	0	0	0	0	0	0	1	4	15
Days Minimum Temp. ≤ 32°F	29	22	15	4	0	0	0	0	0	3	17	27	117
Days Minimum Temp. ≤ 0°F	2	0	0	0	0	0	0	0	0	0	0	1	3
Heating Degree Days (base 65°F)	982	737	548	265	80	6	0	1	50	225	587	895	4,376
Cooling Degree Days (base 65°F)	0	0	4	31	117	323	497	462	225	39	2	0	1,700
Mean Precipitation (in.)	0.48	0.74	1.75	2.07	3.77	2.87	1.89	2.49	2.05	1.38	1.14	0.85	21.48
Days With ≥ 0.1" Precipitation	2	2	3	4	6	5	4	4	4	2	2	2	40
Days With ≥ 1.0" Precipitation	0	0	0	0	1	1	0	1	1	0	0	0	4
Mean Snowfall (in.)	3.6	4.5	2.1	0.7	trace	trace	0.0	trace	trace	0.3	1.7	3.1	16.0
Days With ≥ 1.0" Snow Depth	5	3	1	0	0	0	0	0	0	0	1	3	13

Gate *Beaver County*   Elevation: 2,247 ft.   Latitude: 36° 51' N   Longitude: 100° 03' W

	JAN	FEB	MAR	APR	MAY	JUN	JUL	AUG	SEP	OCT	NOV	DEC	YEAR
Mean Maximum Temp. (°F)	46.7	53.0	61.3	71.2	79.6	89.8	95.4	93.7	85.3	74.2	59.5	49.4	71.6
Mean Temp. (°F)	34.0	39.3	47.5	57.2	66.6	76.5	81.9	80.2	71.8	59.9	46.2	36.8	58.2
Mean Minimum Temp. (°F)	21.2	25.6	33.7	43.2	53.7	63.2	68.3	66.7	58.3	45.4	32.8	24.1	44.7
Extreme Maximum Temp. (°F)	85	89	95	102	105	113	112	109	107	100	90	77	113
Extreme Minimum Temp. (°F)	-25	-11	1	16	32	44	50	48	31	16	5	-12	-25
Days Maximum Temp. ≥ 90°F	0	0	0	1	4	16	25	23	11	3	0	0	83
Days Maximum Temp. ≤ 32°F	6	3	1	0	0	0	0	0	0	0	1	3	14
Days Minimum Temp. ≤ 32°F	28	21	14	3	0	0	0	0	0	2	14	27	109
Days Minimum Temp. ≤ 0°F	1	1	0	0	0	0	0	0	0	0	0	1	3
Heating Degree Days (base 65°F)	955	719	541	261	74	7	0	1	39	204	558	869	4,228
Cooling Degree Days (base 65°F)	0	0	4	32	127	338	522	476	249	43	3	0	1,794
Mean Precipitation (in.)	0.69	0.73	1.95	1.94	3.16	2.81	2.62	2.79	2.12	1.40	1.27	0.89	22.37
Days With ≥ 0.1" Precipitation	2	2	4	4	5	5	4	4	4	3	2	2	41
Days With ≥ 1.0" Precipitation	0	0	0	0	1	1	1	1	1	0	0	0	5
Mean Snowfall (in.)	4.0	3.6	5.3	1.0	0.1	trace	0.0	0.0	trace	0.4	2.9	4.6	21.9
Days With ≥ 1.0" Snow Depth	6	2	2	0	0	0	0	0	0	0	0	4	15

Geary *Blaine County*   Elevation: 1,594 ft.   Latitude: 35° 38' N   Longitude: 98° 19' W

	JAN	FEB	MAR	APR	MAY	JUN	JUL	AUG	SEP	OCT	NOV	DEC	YEAR
Mean Maximum Temp. (°F)	47.0	53.0	62.2	71.6	79.5	88.2	93.6	92.7	84.2	73.2	59.4	50.1	71.2
Mean Temp. (°F)	36.4	41.7	50.2	59.4	68.2	77.0	82.0	80.9	72.7	61.6	48.4	39.6	59.8
Mean Minimum Temp. (°F)	25.7	30.3	38.1	47.1	56.9	65.7	70.3	69.0	61.3	49.8	37.4	29.0	48.4
Extreme Maximum Temp. (°F)	79	90	91	100	103	109	107	107	107	98	89	79	109
Extreme Minimum Temp. (°F)	-10	-3	6	24	34	47	51	51	33	21	9	-12	-12
Days Maximum Temp. ≥ 90°F	0	0	0	0	3	13	23	23	9	1	0	0	72
Days Maximum Temp. ≤ 32°F	5	3	0	0	0	0	0	0	0	0	0	2	10
Days Minimum Temp. ≤ 32°F	23	16	8	1	0	0	0	0	0	1	9	20	78
Days Minimum Temp. ≤ 0°F	0	0	0	0	0	0	0	0	0	0	0	0	0
Heating Degree Days (base 65°F)	880	652	459	200	44	2	0	0	28	159	493	780	3,697
Cooling Degree Days (base 65°F)	0	1	6	33	151	367	532	504	265	50	2	0	1,911
Mean Precipitation (in.)	0.80	1.18	2.25	2.76	4.78	3.96	1.98	2.32	3.24	2.34	1.92	1.27	28.80
Days With ≥ 0.1" Precipitation	1	2	4	4	6	5	3	3	4	4	3	2	41
Days With ≥ 1.0" Precipitation	0	0	1	1	2	1	1	1	1	1	1	0	10
Mean Snowfall (in.)	1.9	1.3	0.2	0.0	0.0	0.0	0.0	0.0	0.0	trace	0.6	0.6	4.6
Days With ≥ 1.0" Snow Depth	0	0	0	0	0	0	0	0	0	0	0	0	0

Goodwell Research Station *Texas County*   Elevation: 3,307 ft.   Latitude: 36° 36' N   Longitude: 101° 37' W

	JAN	FEB	MAR	APR	MAY	JUN	JUL	AUG	SEP	OCT	NOV	DEC	YEAR
Mean Maximum Temp. (°F)	46.6	52.4	60.3	69.2	77.4	87.9	93.1	91.0	83.5	72.2	58.3	48.8	70.1
Mean Temp. (°F)	32.5	37.5	45.0	54.0	63.1	73.4	78.6	76.7	68.7	56.7	43.6	34.6	55.4
Mean Minimum Temp. (°F)	18.2	22.5	29.6	38.7	48.8	58.8	63.9	62.3	53.7	41.0	28.9	20.7	40.6
Extreme Maximum Temp. (°F)	81	87	94	100	103	111	107	106	109	96	89	80	111
Extreme Minimum Temp. (°F)	-14	-11	-2	9	28	40	47	46	28	11	-5	-13	-14
Days Maximum Temp. ≥ 90°F	0	0	0	1	3	14	23	20	10	1	0	0	72
Days Maximum Temp. ≤ 32°F	6	3	1	0	0	0	0	0	0	0	1	4	15
Days Minimum Temp. ≤ 32°F	30	24	20	7	1	0	0	0	0	5	20	29	136
Days Minimum Temp. ≤ 0°F	2	1	0	0	0	0	0	0	0	0	0	1	4
Heating Degree Days (base 65°F)	1,001	770	615	336	123	14	1	2	61	274	634	936	4,767
Cooling Degree Days (base 65°F)	0	0	1	13	66	274	435	388	188	24	0	0	1,389
Mean Precipitation (in.)	0.29	0.36	0.98	1.43	3.11	2.43	2.42	2.21	1.54	1.08	0.62	0.34	16.81
Days With ≥ 0.1" Precipitation	1	1	3	3	5	5	4	4	3	2	2	1	34
Days With ≥ 1.0" Precipitation	0	0	0	0	1	1	1	1	0	0	0	0	4
Mean Snowfall (in.)	3.8	2.3	2.4	1.3	0.1	0.0	0.0	0.0	trace	0.3	1.5	2.5	14.2
Days With ≥ 1.0" Snow Depth	4	3	1	0	0	0	0	0	0	0	1	2	11

Guthrie 5 S *Logan County*   Elevation: 1,108 ft.   Latitude: 35° 49' N   Longitude: 97° 24' W

	JAN	FEB	MAR	APR	MAY	JUN	JUL	AUG	SEP	OCT	NOV	DEC	YEAR
Mean Maximum Temp. (°F)	48.2	55.0	64.3	74.2	81.5	89.4	95.5	95.2	86.3	75.5	61.4	51.8	73.2
Mean Temp. (°F)	36.8	42.8	51.6	61.3	69.7	78.0	83.3	82.5	74.3	62.9	49.9	40.7	61.1
Mean Minimum Temp. (°F)	25.3	30.5	38.9	48.3	57.8	66.5	71.1	69.9	62.2	50.2	38.3	29.5	49.0
Extreme Maximum Temp. (°F)	82	93	93	101	104	107	113	111	112	97	89	79	113
Extreme Minimum Temp. (°F)	-12	-14	7	20	33	43	51	51	32	17	7	-13	-14
Days Maximum Temp. ≥ 90°F	0	0	0	1	4	15	27	25	12	1	0	0	85
Days Maximum Temp. ≤ 32°F	4	2	0	0	0	0	0	0	0	0	0	2	8
Days Minimum Temp. ≤ 32°F	24	17	9	2	0	0	0	0	0	1	9	19	81
Days Minimum Temp. ≤ 0°F	1	0	0	0	0	0	0	0	0	0	0	0	1
Heating Degree Days (base 65°F)	867	621	423	169	33	2	0	0	24	137	453	746	3,475
Cooling Degree Days (base 65°F)	0	1	15	61	193	404	586	565	314	74	7	0	2,220
Mean Precipitation (in.)	1.31	1.82	3.28	3.30	5.07	4.31	2.27	2.44	3.90	3.10	2.71	1.99	35.50
Days With ≥ 0.1" Precipitation	3	3	5	5	6	6	4	4	5	4	4	3	52
Days With ≥ 1.0" Precipitation	0	0	1	1	2	1	1	1	1	1	1	1	11
Mean Snowfall (in.)	*2.7*	*1.8*	0.6	0.0	0.0	0.0	0.0	0.0	0.0	trace	0.2	*1.5*	*6.8*
Days With ≥ 1.0" Snow Depth	*1*	na	0	0	0	0	0	0	0	0	0	*1*	na

Hammon 3 SSW *Roger Mills County*   Elevation: 1,817 ft.   Latitude: 35° 36' N   Longitude: 99° 24' W

	JAN	FEB	MAR	APR	MAY	JUN	JUL	AUG	SEP	OCT	NOV	DEC	YEAR
Mean Maximum Temp. (°F)	47.4	53.9	62.0	71.7	79.3	88.9	94.9	92.9	84.4	73.8	59.6	50.0	71.6
Mean Temp. (°F)	34.0	39.8	47.7	57.3	66.2	76.1	81.6	79.9	71.3	59.3	46.0	36.6	58.0
Mean Minimum Temp. (°F)	20.6	25.7	33.3	42.7	53.1	63.2	68.2	66.9	58.1	44.8	32.4	23.1	44.3
Extreme Maximum Temp. (°F)	82	91	96	101	106	115	110	110	104	99	89	80	115
Extreme Minimum Temp. (°F)	-15	-16	-5	17	30	44	50	46	29	12	5	-9	-16
Days Maximum Temp. ≥ 90°F	0	0	0	1	4	15	25	23	10	1	0	0	79
Days Maximum Temp. ≤ 32°F	6	3	1	0	0	0	0	0	0	0	1	3	14
Days Minimum Temp. ≤ 32°F	29	22	15	4	0	0	0	0	0	3	15	27	115
Days Minimum Temp. ≤ 0°F	1	1	0	0	0	0	0	0	0	0	0	0	2
Heating Degree Days (base 65°F)	954	704	536	255	75	5	0	1	44	210	564	874	4,222
Cooling Degree Days (base 65°F)	0	0	2	23	114	328	507	466	234	33	1	0	1,708
Mean Precipitation (in.)	0.83	0.94	2.15	2.43	4.62	3.59	2.04	2.92	3.17	2.12	1.66	1.02	27.49
Days With ≥ 0.1" Precipitation	2	2	4	4	6	5	3	4	5	3	3	2	43
Days With ≥ 1.0" Precipitation	0	0	1	1	2	1	1	1	1	1	0	0	9
Mean Snowfall (in.)	1.5	2.0	0.8	0.3	0.0	0.0	0.0	0.0	0.0	0.0	0.3	1.8	6.7
Days With ≥ 1.0" Snow Depth	*1*	*1*	0	0	0	0	0	0	0	0	*0*	1	*3*

Hanna *McIntosh County*   Elevation: 679 ft.   Latitude: 35° 12' N   Longitude: 95° 53' W

	JAN	FEB	MAR	APR	MAY	JUN	JUL	AUG	SEP	OCT	NOV	DEC	YEAR
Mean Maximum Temp. (°F)	49.3	55.6	64.8	73.9	80.3	87.9	93.5	93.5	85.4	75.4	62.1	52.8	72.9
Mean Temp. (°F)	38.4	44.0	52.9	61.7	69.3	77.2	81.8	81.0	73.5	62.6	51.1	42.1	61.3
Mean Minimum Temp. (°F)	27.5	32.2	40.8	49.4	58.3	66.4	70.0	68.5	61.7	49.9	40.0	31.5	49.7
Extreme Maximum Temp. (°F)	77	91	96	95	94	103	109	108	109	95	85	78	109
Extreme Minimum Temp. (°F)	-15	-3	4	23	38	46	50	51	35	19	10	-9	-15
Days Maximum Temp. ≥ 90°F	0	0	0	0	1	12	25	24	10	1	0	0	73
Days Maximum Temp. ≤ 32°F	3	1	0	0	0	0	0	0	0	0	0	2	6
Days Minimum Temp. ≤ 32°F	22	15	7	1	0	0	0	0	0	1	8	17	71
Days Minimum Temp. ≤ 0°F	0	0	0	0	0	0	0	0	0	0	0	0	0
Heating Degree Days (base 65°F)	818	589	383	149	29	1	0	0	23	134	420	702	3,248
Cooling Degree Days (base 65°F)	0	1	12	52	173	380	532	513	286	65	9	1	2,024
Mean Precipitation (in.)	1.98	2.38	4.20	4.22	6.12	4.14	2.78	2.79	5.36	4.45	4.04	2.87	45.33
Days With ≥ 0.1" Precipitation	4	4	6	6	7	6	4	4	6	5	5	4	61
Days With ≥ 1.0" Precipitation	0	1	2	1	2	1	1	1	2	2	1	1	15
Mean Snowfall (in.)	*1.7*	2.0	0.9	0.0	0.0	0.0	0.0	0.0	0.0	trace	0.5	0.9	*6.0*
Days With ≥ 1.0" Snow Depth	*1*	*1*	0	0	0	0	0	0	0	0	0	1	*3*

Healdton *Carter County*   Elevation: 731 ft.   Latitude: 34° 13' N   Longitude: 97° 28' W

	JAN	FEB	MAR	APR	MAY	JUN	JUL	AUG	SEP	OCT	NOV	DEC	YEAR
Mean Maximum Temp. (°F)	51.9	58.3	66.8	75.3	82.1	89.8	96.0	*96.0*	87.0	77.1	63.9	55.0	*74.9*
Mean Temp. (°F)	39.6	45.4	53.6	62.2	70.0	78.1	83.0	*82.4*	74.5	63.8	51.6	43.0	*62.3*
Mean Minimum Temp. (°F)	27.3	32.4	40.5	49.0	57.9	66.2	70.1	*68.7*	61.9	50.5	39.3	30.9	*49.6*
Extreme Maximum Temp. (°F)	82	91	97	98	100	114	112	110	110	101	86	80	114
Extreme Minimum Temp. (°F)	-10	1	1	20	32	43	50	51	35	18	8	-10	-10
Days Maximum Temp. ≥ 90°F	0	0	0	1	4	16	27	24	12	2	0	0	86
Days Maximum Temp. ≤ 32°F	2	1	0	0	0	0	0	0	0	0	0	1	4
Days Minimum Temp. ≤ 32°F	22	14	8	2	0	0	0	0	0	1	9	18	74
Days Minimum Temp. ≤ 0°F	0	0	0	0	0	0	0	0	0	0	0	0	0
Heating Degree Days (base 65°F)	779	551	362	141	27	1	0	*0*	20	118	403	677	*3,079*
Cooling Degree Days (base 65°F)	0	1	14	56	192	400	573	*565*	309	84	9	1	*2,204*
Mean Precipitation (in.)	1.63	2.09	3.20	3.37	5.21	4.28	2.24	2.24	4.68	3.64	2.35	2.15	37.08
Days With ≥ 0.1" Precipitation	3	4	5	5	6	5	3	3	5	5	4	3	51
Days With ≥ 1.0" Precipitation	0	1	1	1	2	2	1	1	2	1	1	1	14
Mean Snowfall (in.)	*1.2*	1.2	0.5	0.0	0.0	0.0	0.0	0.0	0.0	0.0	0.2	0.5	*3.6*
Days With ≥ 1.0" Snow Depth	*2*	*0*	0	0	0	0	0	0	0	0	0	0	*2*

Helena 1 SSE *Alfalfa County*   Elevation: 1,348 ft.   Latitude: 36° 32' N   Longitude: 98° 17' W

	JAN	FEB	MAR	APR	MAY	JUN	JUL	AUG	SEP	OCT	NOV	DEC	YEAR
Mean Maximum Temp. (°F)	43.8	50.1	59.4	69.6	78.8	89.1	94.9	93.4	84.3	72.7	57.5	47.3	70.1
Mean Temp. (°F)	32.3	37.8	46.9	56.6	66.5	76.6	82.0	80.4	71.8	59.6	45.6	35.9	57.7
Mean Minimum Temp. (°F)	20.8	25.4	34.2	43.5	54.1	64.0	68.9	67.4	59.3	46.5	33.7	24.5	45.2
Extreme Maximum Temp. (°F)	79	90	90	99	105	112	113	108	107	98	88	77	113
Extreme Minimum Temp. (°F)	-14	-15	4	18	33	47	50	48	31	12	5	-15	-15
Days Maximum Temp. ≥ 90°F	0	0	0	0	3	15	25	23	11	1	0	0	78
Days Maximum Temp. ≤ 32°F	7	4	1	0	0	0	0	0	0	0	1	4	17
Days Minimum Temp. ≤ 32°F	29	21	13	3	0	0	0	0	0	2	14	26	108
Days Minimum Temp. ≤ 0°F	1	1	0	0	0	0	0	0	0	0	0	1	3
Heating Degree Days (base 65°F)	1,005	762	559	272	73	4	0	1	41	206	577	894	4,394
Cooling Degree Days (base 65°F)	0	0	3	27	129	362	542	499	261	42	2	0	1,867
Mean Precipitation (in.)	0.93	1.23	2.74	2.96	4.45	3.77	3.09	3.12	3.15	2.50	2.00	1.27	31.21
Days With ≥ 0.1" Precipitation	2	3	4	5	6	6	5	5	5	4	3	3	51
Days With ≥ 1.0" Precipitation	0	0	1	1	1	1	1	1	1	1	1	0	9
Mean Snowfall (in.)	3.9	4.7	3.3	0.7	0.0	0.0	0.0	0.0	0.0	trace	1.4	4.2	18.2
Days With ≥ 1.0" Snow Depth	7	5	2	0	0	0	0	0	0	0	1	4	19

Hobart Municipal Airport *Kiowa County*   Elevation: 1,568 ft.   Latitude: 34° 35' N   Longitude: 99° 02' W

	JAN	FEB	MAR	APR	MAY	JUN	JUL	AUG	SEP	OCT	NOV	DEC	YEAR
Mean Maximum Temp. (°F)	47.6	53.9	63.3	73.1	80.8	90.3	95.3	93.7	84.5	74.2	60.3	50.7	72.3
Mean Temp. (°F)	36.2	41.7	50.6	60.0	69.0	78.3	83.2	81.8	73.3	62.0	48.9	39.5	60.4
Mean Minimum Temp. (°F)	24.8	29.5	37.9	46.9	57.1	66.3	71.0	69.8	62.0	49.7	37.4	28.3	48.4
Extreme Maximum Temp. (°F)	82	89	95	102	107	116	111	107	106	99	88	78	116
Extreme Minimum Temp. (°F)	-9	-2	3	22	33	48	54	51	31	18	9	-9	-9
Days Maximum Temp. ≥ 90°F	0	0	0	1	5	17	26	23	11	1	0	0	84
Days Maximum Temp. ≤ 32°F	5	3	0	0	0	0	0	0	0	0	0	2	10
Days Minimum Temp. ≤ 32°F	25	17	8	2	0	0	0	0	0	1	10	22	85
Days Minimum Temp. ≤ 0°F	0	0	0	0	0	0	0	0	0	0	0	0	0
Heating Degree Days (base 65°F)	886	652	446	188	42	2	0	0	30	151	480	782	3,659
Cooling Degree Days (base 65°F)	0	*1*	7	45	179	408	581	547	294	65	4	0	*2,131*
Mean Precipitation (in.)	0.91	0.97	1.90	2.35	4.79	3.17	2.44	2.57	3.56	2.60	1.52	1.23	28.01
Days With ≥ 0.1" Precipitation	2	3	3	4	7	5	4	4	4	4	3	2	45
Days With ≥ 1.0" Precipitation	0	0	1	1	1	1	1	1	1	1	0	0	8
Mean Snowfall (in.)	2.3	*2.3*	0.2	trace	trace	trace	trace	trace	trace	trace	0.3	1.6	*6.7*
Days With ≥ 1.0" Snow Depth	3	2	0	0	0	0	0	0	0	0	0	1	6

Holdenville *Hughes County*   Elevation: 859 ft.   Latitude: 35° 05' N   Longitude: 96° 24' W

	JAN	FEB	MAR	APR	MAY	JUN	JUL	AUG	SEP	OCT	NOV	DEC	YEAR
Mean Maximum Temp. (°F)	49.4	55.7	65.0	73.6	80.1	*87.6*	93.4	93.8	85.3	75.4	61.9	52.8	*72.8*
Mean Temp. (°F)	38.3	44.0	52.9	61.4	69.2	*76.8*	81.7	81.3	73.6	63.1	50.9	42.1	*61.3*
Mean Minimum Temp. (°F)	27.3	32.2	40.7	49.2	58.3	*66.0*	69.9	68.7	61.8	50.7	39.8	31.4	*49.7*
Extreme Maximum Temp. (°F)	79	93	95	98	96	103	110	106	104	95	85	77	110
Extreme Minimum Temp. (°F)	-13	-6	9	26	36	45	53	51	35	18	10	-8	-13
Days Maximum Temp. ≥ 90°F	0	0	0	0	1	11	24	24	10	1	0	0	71
Days Maximum Temp. ≤ 32°F	3	1	0	0	0	0	0	0	0	0	0	2	6
Days Minimum Temp. ≤ 32°F	21	15	7	1	0	0	0	0	0	1	8	18	71
Days Minimum Temp. ≤ 0°F	0	0	0	0	0	0	0	0	0	0	0	0	0
Heating Degree Days (base 65°F)	821	588	380	152	30	*1*	0	0	22	125	425	703	*3,247*
Cooling Degree Days (base 65°F)	0	1	11	50	168	*371*	525	519	283	65	7	1	*2,001*
Mean Precipitation (in.)	1.51	2.04	3.43	4.15	5.56	4.37	2.69	2.94	4.65	4.23	3.38	2.36	41.31
Days With ≥ 0.1" Precipitation	3	4	5	6	7	6	4	4	6	5	5	4	59
Days With ≥ 1.0" Precipitation	0	1	1	1	2	2	1	1	1	1	1	1	13
Mean Snowfall (in.)	*1.7*	*2.2*	0.5	0.0	0.0	0.0	0.0	0.0	0.0	0.0	0.4	0.7	*5.5*
Days With ≥ 1.0" Snow Depth	na	*0*	0	0	0	0	0	0	0	0	0	0	na

Hollis *Harmon County* Elevation: 1,620 ft.   Latitude: 34° 41' N   Longitude: 99° 49' W

	JAN	FEB	MAR	APR	MAY	JUN	JUL	AUG	SEP	OCT	NOV	DEC	YEAR
Mean Maximum Temp. (°F)	52.6	58.9	68.3	77.2	84.5	93.2	97.5	95.8	87.7	77.7	63.8	54.8	76.0
Mean Temp. (°F)	38.6	44.3	52.8	61.7	70.6	79.5	83.3	81.8	74.1	63.0	50.0	41.1	61.7
Mean Minimum Temp. (°F)	24.5	29.6	37.3	46.1	56.6	65.6	69.5	68.0	60.7	48.4	36.2	27.4	47.5
Extreme Maximum Temp. (°F)	85	92	102	103	106	116	110	111	108	100	89	82	116
Extreme Minimum Temp. (°F)	-6	-10	2	20	34	44	56	52	31	17	10	-9	-10
Days Maximum Temp. ≥ 90°F	0	0	1	3	9	22	28	26	14	3	0	0	106
Days Maximum Temp. ≤ 32°F	3	1	0	0	0	0	0	0	0	0	0	2	6
Days Minimum Temp. ≤ 32°F	26	18	9	2	0	0	0	0	0	1	10	23	89
Days Minimum Temp. ≤ 0°F	0	0	0	0	0	0	0	0	0	0	0	0	0
Heating Degree Days (base 65°F)	812	579	382	150	25	1	0	0	20	125	447	734	3,275
Cooling Degree Days (base 65°F)	0	1	8	50	199	431	563	528	294	62	3	0	2,139
Mean Precipitation (in.)	0.70	1.15	1.49	2.55	3.85	3.91	1.71	2.57	3.16	2.33	1.19	0.91	25.52
Days With ≥ 0.1" Precipitation	2	3	3	4	5	5	3	4	4	3	3	2	41
Days With ≥ 1.0" Precipitation	0	0	0	1	1	1	0	1	1	1	0	0	6
Mean Snowfall (in.)	1.7	2.0	0.2	0.1	0.0	0.0	0.0	0.0	0.0	trace	0.2	0.9	5.1
Days With ≥ 1.0" Snow Depth	*1*	*0*	0	0	0	0	0	0	0	0	0	0	*1*

Hooker *Texas County* Elevation: 2,992 ft.   Latitude: 36° 52' N   Longitude: 101° 12' W

	JAN	FEB	MAR	APR	MAY	JUN	JUL	AUG	SEP	OCT	NOV	DEC	YEAR
Mean Maximum Temp. (°F)	46.5	52.7	61.5	70.5	79.0	89.5	94.1	92.1	84.1	73.3	58.2	48.7	70.9
Mean Temp. (°F)	32.7	38.1	46.2	55.3	64.7	74.9	79.5	77.8	69.6	57.8	44.0	35.1	56.3
Mean Minimum Temp. (°F)	18.9	23.5	30.8	40.0	50.3	60.2	64.9	63.4	55.0	42.3	29.8	21.5	41.7
Extreme Maximum Temp. (°F)	82	88	92	101	105	112	110	108	108	97	91	78	112
Extreme Minimum Temp. (°F)	-21	-16	1	7	27	41	48	45	29	13	-6	-14	-21
Days Maximum Temp. ≥ 90°F	0	0	0	1	4	16	24	21	10	2	0	0	78
Days Maximum Temp. ≤ 32°F	6	3	1	0	0	0	0	0	0	0	1	4	15
Days Minimum Temp. ≤ 32°F	30	24	17	5	0	0	0	0	0	4	19	29	128
Days Minimum Temp. ≤ 0°F	1	1	0	0	0	0	0	0	0	0	0	1	3
Heating Degree Days (base 65°F)	994	751	579	303	95	8	1	1	50	245	625	920	4,572
Cooling Degree Days (base 65°F)	0	0	1	18	91	302	459	421	204	29	1	0	1,526
Mean Precipitation (in.)	0.48	0.49	1.16	1.52	2.99	2.35	2.50	2.25	1.83	1.11	0.79	0.54	18.01
Days With ≥ 0.1" Precipitation	1	1	3	3	5	5	5	4	3	2	2	2	36
Days With ≥ 1.0" Precipitation	0	0	0	0	1	0	1	0	1	0	0	0	3
Mean Snowfall (in.)	4.2	3.7	4.2	0.9	trace	0.0	0.0	0.0	trace	0.3	1.6	3.7	18.6
Days With ≥ 1.0" Snow Depth	6	3	2	1	0	0	0	0	0	0	1	*4*	*17*

Hugo *Choctaw County* Elevation: 567 ft.   Latitude: 34° 00' N   Longitude: 95° 31' W

	JAN	FEB	MAR	APR	MAY	JUN	JUL	AUG	SEP	OCT	NOV	DEC	YEAR
Mean Maximum Temp. (°F)	52.8	59.0	67.4	75.6	82.0	89.1	94.2	94.3	87.7	77.2	64.2	55.7	74.9
Mean Temp. (°F)	42.1	47.4	55.6	63.6	71.0	78.2	82.4	81.9	75.5	64.6	53.3	45.1	63.4
Mean Minimum Temp. (°F)	31.4	35.9	43.6	51.5	59.9	67.3	70.5	69.3	63.2	52.0	42.2	34.5	51.8
Extreme Maximum Temp. (°F)	79	90	92	94	96	103	114	110	108	98	86	80	114
Extreme Minimum Temp. (°F)	1	3	12	27	41	50	54	53	38	22	13	-4	-4
Days Maximum Temp. ≥ 90°F	0	0	0	0	2	14	26	25	13	1	0	0	81
Days Maximum Temp. ≤ 32°F	2	0	0	0	0	0	0	0	0	0	0	1	3
Days Minimum Temp. ≤ 32°F	18	11	4	0	0	0	0	0	0	0	5	13	51
Days Minimum Temp. ≤ 0°F	0	0	0	0	0	0	0	0	0	0	0	0	0
Heating Degree Days (base 65°F)	703	492	306	105	15	0	0	0	13	99	358	612	2,703
Cooling Degree Days (base 65°F)	0	3	19	67	208	405	548	539	326	89	12	2	2,218
Mean Precipitation (in.)	2.56	3.39	4.13	3.93	5.55	4.66	3.01	2.60	4.12	5.08	4.61	3.85	47.49
Days With ≥ 0.1" Precipitation	5	5	6	6	7	6	4	4	5	6	5	6	65
Days With ≥ 1.0" Precipitation	1	1	2	2	2	2	1	1	1	2	2	1	18
Mean Snowfall (in.)	*0.4*	1.0	0.3	0.0	0.0	0.0	0.0	0.0	0.0	0.0	0.2	0.5	*2.4*
Days With ≥ 1.0" Snow Depth	na	1	0	0	0	0	0	0	0	0	0	1	na

Idabel *McCurtain County* Elevation: 459 ft.   Latitude: 33° 53' N   Longitude: 94° 49' W

	JAN	FEB	MAR	APR	MAY	JUN	JUL	AUG	SEP	OCT	NOV	DEC	YEAR
Mean Maximum Temp. (°F)	52.7	58.7	66.7	74.4	81.4	88.8	93.0	93.3	86.5	76.8	64.4	56.0	74.4
Mean Temp. (°F)	40.8	46.0	53.9	61.2	69.5	77.3	81.2	80.9	74.1	63.3	52.0	44.1	62.0
Mean Minimum Temp. (°F)	28.9	33.3	40.9	48.0	57.7	65.8	69.4	68.4	61.7	49.8	39.6	32.2	49.6
Extreme Maximum Temp. (°F)	79	89	92	93	96	102	108	110	109	98	86	81	110
Extreme Minimum Temp. (°F)	2	2	10	21	35	48	53	52	36	23	8	-2	-2
Days Maximum Temp. ≥ 90°F	0	0	0	0	2	15	24	24	11	2	0	0	78
Days Maximum Temp. ≤ 32°F	1	1	0	0	0	0	0	0	0	0	0	1	3
Days Minimum Temp. ≤ 32°F	21	13	6	1	0	0	0	0	0	1	8	17	67
Days Minimum Temp. ≤ 0°F	0	0	0	0	0	0	0	0	0	0	0	0	0
Heating Degree Days (base 65°F)	743	531	351	153	27	1	0	0	15	121	392	642	2,976
Cooling Degree Days (base 65°F)	0	2	13	43	171	379	517	510	296	76	9	2	2,018
Mean Precipitation (in.)	3.11	3.54	4.57	4.40	5.68	4.23	3.58	2.49	4.14	5.05	4.73	4.53	50.05
Days With ≥ 0.1" Precipitation	5	5	6	6	7	6	5	4	6	5	5	6	66
Days With ≥ 1.0" Precipitation	1	1	2	2	2	1	1	1	1	2	2	1	17
Mean Snowfall (in.)	*0.2*	*1.0*	0.1	0.0	0.0	0.0	0.0	0.0	0.0	0.0	trace	0.3	*1.6*
Days With ≥ 1.0" Snow Depth	na	na	0	0	0	0	0	0	0	0	0	0	na

Jefferson *Grant County*   Elevation: 1,043 ft.   Latitude: 36° 43' N   Longitude: 97° 47' W

	JAN	FEB	MAR	APR	MAY	JUN	JUL	AUG	SEP	OCT	NOV	DEC	YEAR
Mean Maximum Temp. (°F)	46.1	52.9	62.4	72.4	81.0	91.2	96.3	95.0	86.2	74.9	59.5	49.2	72.3
Mean Temp. (°F)	34.4	40.3	49.3	59.1	68.5	78.3	83.2	81.7	73.2	61.6	47.6	37.9	59.6
Mean Minimum Temp. (°F)	22.7	27.6	36.3	45.8	56.0	65.3	70.1	68.4	60.3	48.2	35.8	26.4	46.9
Extreme Maximum Temp. (°F)	79	92	90	102	104	109	113	110	108	98	89	77	113
Extreme Minimum Temp. (°F)	-16	-15	3	19	32	45	45	49	27	11	6	-16	-16
Days Maximum Temp. ≥ 90°F	0	0	0	1	4	19	27	25	12	2	0	0	90
Days Maximum Temp. ≤ 32°F	5	3	0	0	0	0	0	0	0	0	0	3	11
Days Minimum Temp. ≤ 32°F	26	19	12	3	0	0	0	0	0	2	12	24	98
Days Minimum Temp. ≤ 0°F	1	1	0	0	0	0	0	0	0	0	0	1	3
Heating Degree Days (base 65°F)	941	691	486	212	46	1	0	0	28	161	518	834	3,918
Cooling Degree Days (base 65°F)	0	0	6	40	163	403	572	530	284	57	3	0	2,058
Mean Precipitation (in.)	1.01	1.30	2.87	3.32	4.86	4.29	3.45	3.09	3.54	3.09	2.24	1.38	34.44
Days With ≥ 0.1" Precipitation	2	3	5	6	7	6	5	5	5	4	3	3	54
Days With ≥ 1.0" Precipitation	0	0	1	1	1	1	1	1	1	1	1	0	9
Mean Snowfall (in.)	*1.6*	2.4	0.9	0.2	0.0	0.0	0.0	0.0	0.0	trace	0.5	*1.2*	*6.8*
Days With ≥ 1.0" Snow Depth	*3*	3	0	0	0	0	0	0	0	0	0	*1*	*7*

Kansas 1 ESE *Delaware County*   Elevation: 1,177 ft.   Latitude: 36° 12' N   Longitude: 94° 47' W

	JAN	FEB	MAR	APR	MAY	JUN	JUL	AUG	SEP	OCT	NOV	DEC	YEAR
Mean Maximum Temp. (°F)	46.4	52.9	62.1	71.4	77.6	85.0	90.9	90.6	82.5	72.5	59.4	50.1	70.1
Mean Temp. (°F)	36.2	41.9	50.6	59.6	67.0	74.8	79.8	79.0	71.5	61.0	49.2	40.1	59.2
Mean Minimum Temp. (°F)	26.0	30.9	39.1	47.8	56.3	64.5	68.7	67.4	60.5	49.5	38.9	30.1	48.3
Extreme Maximum Temp. (°F)	75	88	89	93	91	100	108	106	105	93	84	76	108
Extreme Minimum Temp. (°F)	-11	-8	5	21	35	45	48	49	33	16	6	-13	-13
Days Maximum Temp. ≥ 90°F	0	0	0	0	0	5	18	18	6	0	0	0	47
Days Maximum Temp. ≤ 32°F	4	2	0	0	0	0	0	0	0	0	0	2	8
Days Minimum Temp. ≤ 32°F	22	16	9	1	0	0	0	0	0	1	8	18	75
Days Minimum Temp. ≤ 0°F	1	0	0	0	0	0	0	0	0	0	0	0	1
Heating Degree Days (base 65°F)	886	645	447	194	50	3	0	0	33	165	470	763	3,656
Cooling Degree Days (base 65°F)	0	1	8	34	116	306	476	455	234	46	3	0	1,679
Mean Precipitation (in.)	2.31	2.40	4.33	4.51	5.37	5.01	2.93	3.43	5.81	4.28	4.63	3.58	48.59
Days With ≥ 0.1" Precipitation	5	5	7	7	8	7	5	5	7	5	5	5	71
Days With ≥ 1.0" Precipitation	1	1	2	1	2	2	1	1	2	1	2	1	17
Mean Snowfall (in.)	4.6	3.2	3.0	trace	0.0	0.0	0.0	0.0	0.0	trace	1.1	1.9	13.8
Days With ≥ 1.0" Snow Depth	6	3	1	0	0	0	0	0	0	0	1	1	12

Kenton *Cimarron County*   Elevation: 4,347 ft.   Latitude: 36° 54' N   Longitude: 102° 58' W

	JAN	FEB	MAR	APR	MAY	JUN	JUL	AUG	SEP	OCT	NOV	DEC	YEAR
Mean Maximum Temp. (°F)	49.9	53.9	61.1	68.6	77.9	87.8	91.9	89.1	82.4	72.4	59.3	50.7	70.4
Mean Temp. (°F)	34.1	38.1	45.3	53.4	63.0	72.6	77.4	75.2	67.7	56.0	43.6	35.3	55.1
Mean Minimum Temp. (°F)	18.4	22.1	29.4	38.1	48.1	57.4	62.9	61.4	52.9	39.5	27.9	19.9	39.8
Extreme Maximum Temp. (°F)	80	82	89	94	102	107	108	103	104	94	89	82	108
Extreme Minimum Temp. (°F)	-22	-19	-4	13	27	39	48	44	27	6	-15	-17	-22
Days Maximum Temp. ≥ 90°F	0	0	0	0	3	13	21	17	8	0	0	0	62
Days Maximum Temp. ≤ 32°F	*4*	3	1	0	0	0	0	0	0	0	1	3	*12*
Days Minimum Temp. ≤ 32°F	30	25	20	8	1	0	0	0	0	6	22	29	141
Days Minimum Temp. ≤ 0°F	1	1	0	0	0	0	0	0	0	0	0	1	3
Heating Degree Days (base 65°F)	949	754	604	352	118	14	1	2	64	288	635	912	4,693
Cooling Degree Days (base 65°F)	0	0	1	9	61	238	387	324	151	12	0	0	1,183
Mean Precipitation (in.)	0.38	0.42	0.84	1.55	2.33	2.08	3.12	2.68	1.67	0.96	0.70	0.33	17.06
Days With ≥ 0.1" Precipitation	1	1	2	3	5	5	6	5	3	2	2	1	36
Days With ≥ 1.0" Precipitation	0	0	0	0	1	0	1	1	0	0	0	0	3
Mean Snowfall (in.)	4.2	*3.7*	*5.7*	*1.5*	0.2	0.0	0.0	0.0	0.2	1.0	*2.5*	*3.8*	*22.8*
Days With ≥ 1.0" Snow Depth	na	*2*	na	1	0	0	0	0	0	0	*2*	*4*	na

Kingfisher 2 SE *Kingfisher County*   Elevation: 1,099 ft.   Latitude: 35° 51' N   Longitude: 97° 54' W

	JAN	FEB	MAR	APR	MAY	JUN	JUL	AUG	SEP	OCT	NOV	DEC	YEAR
Mean Maximum Temp. (°F)	47.2	53.7	63.1	72.6	80.6	89.8	95.4	94.3	85.7	74.7	60.2	50.6	72.3
Mean Temp. (°F)	35.8	41.5	50.4	59.7	68.7	77.8	83.0	81.8	73.6	62.2	48.7	39.4	60.2
Mean Minimum Temp. (°F)	24.4	29.4	37.6	46.8	56.8	65.9	70.5	69.1	61.5	49.6	37.2	28.1	48.1
Extreme Maximum Temp. (°F)	81	92	95	103	105	111	111	111	109	101	89	79	111
Extreme Minimum Temp. (°F)	-12	-15	6	20	35	46	51	49	31	16	6	-14	-15
Days Maximum Temp. ≥ 90°F	0	0	0	1	4	17	26	24	11	1	0	0	84
Days Maximum Temp. ≤ 32°F	5	2	0	0	0	0	0	0	0	0	0	2	9
Days Minimum Temp. ≤ 32°F	25	17	10	2	0	0	0	0	0	1	10	21	86
Days Minimum Temp. ≤ 0°F	1	0	0	0	0	0	0	0	0	0	0	0	1
Heating Degree Days (base 65°F)	898	656	456	199	44	2	0	0	26	151	486	788	3,706
Cooling Degree Days (base 65°F)	0	0	8	41	159	385	561	525	288	62	4	0	2,033
Mean Precipitation (in.)	1.08	1.47	2.59	3.25	4.87	4.02	2.16	2.86	3.73	2.43	2.33	1.58	32.37
Days With ≥ 0.1" Precipitation	2	3	4	5	6	6	4	4	5	3	4	3	49
Days With ≥ 1.0" Precipitation	0	0	1	1	2	1	1	1	1	1	1	1	10
Mean Snowfall (in.)	1.7	*0.8*	0.4	trace	0.0	0.0	0.0	0.0	0.0	trace	0.2	1.0	*4.1*
Days With ≥ 1.0" Snow Depth	1	*0*	0	0	0	0	0	0	0	0	0	0	*1*

Lake Eufaula *Haskell County*   Elevation: 849 ft.   Latitude: 35° 17' N   Longitude: 95° 26' W

	JAN	FEB	MAR	APR	MAY	JUN	JUL	AUG	SEP	OCT	NOV	DEC	YEAR
Mean Maximum Temp. (°F)	47.1	53.2	62.4	71.9	78.5	86.5	*93.1*	92.6	84.3	74.1	60.9	51.5	*71.3*
Mean Temp. (°F)	36.9	42.3	51.7	60.6	68.4	76.6	*82.2*	81.0	73.3	62.4	50.7	41.2	*60.6*
Mean Minimum Temp. (°F)	26.6	31.4	40.7	49.3	58.1	66.6	*71.1*	69.2	62.2	50.7	40.5	30.9	*49.8*
Extreme Maximum Temp. (°F)	80	91	92	95	95	101	109	107	107	95	86	80	109
Extreme Minimum Temp. (°F)	-4	-4	8	25	38	51	54	54	38	20	14	-8	-8
Days Maximum Temp. ≥ 90°F	0	0	0	0	1	10	21	22	9	1	0	0	64
Days Maximum Temp. ≤ 32°F	5	2	0	0	0	0	0	0	0	0	0	2	9
Days Minimum Temp. ≤ 32°F	22	14	6	0	0	0	0	0	0	0	6	17	65
Days Minimum Temp. ≤ 0°F	0	0	0	0	0	0	0	0	0	0	0	0	0
Heating Degree Days (base 65°F)	866	635	417	176	40	1	*0*	0	26	142	430	731	*3,464*
Cooling Degree Days (base 65°F)	0	1	13	49	152	362	*552*	522	287	68	9	1	*2,016*
Mean Precipitation (in.)	2.24	2.45	4.12	4.34	5.94	4.48	2.62	2.68	5.29	4.65	3.95	3.00	45.76
Days With ≥ 0.1" Precipitation	4	4	6	7	8	6	4	4	6	5	5	4	63
Days With ≥ 1.0" Precipitation	1	1	1	1	2	1	1	1	2	1	1	1	14
Mean Snowfall (in.)	*2.3*	*0.3*	0.3	trace	0.0	0.0	0.0	0.0	0.0	0.0	trace	*0.4*	*3.3*
Days With ≥ 1.0" Snow Depth	na	*1*	0	0	0	0	0	0	0	0	0	1	na

Madill *Marshall County*   Elevation: 767 ft.   Latitude: 34° 07' N   Longitude: 96° 47' W

	JAN	FEB	MAR	APR	MAY	JUN	JUL	AUG	SEP	OCT	NOV	DEC	YEAR
Mean Maximum Temp. (°F)	51.6	57.6	66.2	74.8	81.4	89.1	94.7	94.5	86.6	76.7	64.0	54.8	74.3
Mean Temp. (°F)	40.7	46.2	54.5	63.1	70.7	78.5	83.4	82.6	75.3	64.8	53.2	44.3	63.1
Mean Minimum Temp. (°F)	29.9	34.8	42.8	51.3	60.0	67.8	72.1	70.7	63.9	52.8	42.3	33.6	51.8
Extreme Maximum Temp. (°F)	81	93	97	96	99	109	110	109	110	98	87	79	110
Extreme Minimum Temp. (°F)	1	1	12	26	40	49	53	53	37	22	14	-8	-8
Days Maximum Temp. ≥ 90°F	0	0	0	1	3	15	26	25	12	2	0	0	84
Days Maximum Temp. ≤ 32°F	2	1	0	0	0	0	0	0	0	0	0	1	4
Days Minimum Temp. ≤ 32°F	19	11	5	1	0	0	0	0	0	0	5	14	55
Days Minimum Temp. ≤ 0°F	0	0	0	0	0	0	0	0	0	0	0	0	0
Heating Degree Days (base 65°F)	746	525	327	118	20	1	0	0	17	100	361	638	2,853
Cooling Degree Days (base 65°F)	0	2	16	65	205	412	580	561	333	94	14	1	2,283
Mean Precipitation (in.)	2.08	2.52	3.66	3.62	5.50	5.00	2.25	2.82	4.90	4.62	2.94	2.52	42.43
Days With ≥ 0.1" Precipitation	4	4	5	5	7	6	3	4	5	5	4	4	56
Days With ≥ 1.0" Precipitation	0	1	1	1	2	2	1	1	2	1	1	1	14
Mean Snowfall (in.)	*1.2*	1.3	trace	0.0	0.0	0.0	0.0	0.0	0.0	0.0	0.1	0.7	*3.3*
Days With ≥ 1.0" Snow Depth	*1*	*0*	0	0	0	0	0	0	0	0	0	0	*1*

Mangum *Greer County*   Elevation: 1,594 ft.   Latitude: 34° 53' N   Longitude: 99° 30' W

	JAN	FEB	MAR	APR	MAY	JUN	JUL	AUG	SEP	OCT	NOV	DEC	YEAR
Mean Maximum Temp. (°F)	51.5	58.5	68.0	77.5	84.8	93.4	98.5	96.6	88.4	78.1	63.7	54.0	76.1
Mean Temp. (°F)	38.3	44.3	53.0	61.9	70.9	79.4	83.9	82.3	74.6	63.5	50.4	41.1	62.0
Mean Minimum Temp. (°F)	25.1	30.0	37.8	46.3	56.9	65.4	69.2	67.8	60.8	48.9	37.0	28.1	47.8
Extreme Maximum Temp. (°F)	84	94	100	106	109	117	117	112	108	101	90	82	117
Extreme Minimum Temp. (°F)	-8	-3	3	24	33	45	54	53	31	14	8	-11	-11
Days Maximum Temp. ≥ 90°F	0	0	1	3	9	21	29	26	16	3	0	0	108
Days Maximum Temp. ≤ 32°F	3	1	0	0	0	0	0	0	0	0	0	1	5
Days Minimum Temp. ≤ 32°F	26	17	8	2	0	0	0	0	0	1	9	22	85
Days Minimum Temp. ≤ 0°F	0	0	0	0	0	0	0	0	0	0	0	0	0
Heating Degree Days (base 65°F)	821	579	379	148	24	1	0	0	20	119	436	735	3,262
Cooling Degree Days (base 65°F)	0	1	12	56	207	429	588	546	313	73	3	0	2,228
Mean Precipitation (in.)	0.89	1.13	1.69	2.20	4.61	4.11	2.14	2.79	3.37	2.58	1.35	1.04	27.90
Days With ≥ 0.1" Precipitation	2	2	3	4	6	5	3	4	4	4	3	2	42
Days With ≥ 1.0" Precipitation	0	0	0	1	2	1	1	1	1	1	0	0	8
Mean Snowfall (in.)	1.3	*0.9*	trace	trace	0.0	0.0	0.0	0.0	0.0	0.0	trace	0.9	*3.1*
Days With ≥ 1.0" Snow Depth	*1*	0	0	0	0	0	0	0	0	0	0	0	*1*

Mannford 6 NW *Pawnee County*   Elevation: 830 ft.   Latitude: 36° 10' N   Longitude: 96° 26' W

	JAN	FEB	MAR	APR	MAY	JUN	JUL	AUG	SEP	OCT	NOV	DEC	YEAR
Mean Maximum Temp. (°F)	48.0	54.8	64.1	74.2	79.9	87.8	94.6	94.3	85.1	74.8	61.3	51.3	72.5
Mean Temp. (°F)	36.1	42.1	51.5	61.3	68.3	76.6	82.0	80.7	72.6	61.9	49.6	40.0	60.2
Mean Minimum Temp. (°F)	24.2	29.4	38.8	48.3	56.7	65.3	69.3	67.4	60.1	48.9	37.8	28.6	47.9
Extreme Maximum Temp. (°F)	80	92	96	102	96	103	113	112	107	98	88	79	113
Extreme Minimum Temp. (°F)	-10	-14	3	24	33	42	47	49	31	13	3	-16	-16
Days Maximum Temp. ≥ 90°F	0	0	0	1	2	12	25	24	10	1	0	0	75
Days Maximum Temp. ≤ 32°F	4	2	0	0	0	0	0	0	0	0	0	2	8
Days Minimum Temp. ≤ 32°F	24	17	9	1	0	0	0	0	0	2	10	20	83
Days Minimum Temp. ≤ 0°F	1	1	0	0	0	0	0	0	0	0	0	1	3
Heating Degree Days (base 65°F)	889	640	429	167	41	2	0	0	32	154	463	770	3,587
Cooling Degree Days (base 65°F)	0	2	17	61	157	362	541	504	274	64	9	1	1,992
Mean Precipitation (in.)	1.52	2.07	3.51	3.76	5.20	4.16	2.69	3.46	4.43	3.55	3.31	2.14	39.80
Days With ≥ 0.1" Precipitation	3	4	5	6	8	6	4	4	6	5	5	4	60
Days With ≥ 1.0" Precipitation	0	0	1	1	2	1	1	1	1	1	1	0	10
Mean Snowfall (in.)	2.8	*2.4*	1.5	0.0	0.0	0.0	0.0	0.0	0.0	trace	0.2	1.3	*8.2*
Days With ≥ 1.0" Snow Depth	*2*	*1*	0	0	0	0	0	0	0	0	0	*0*	*3*

Marietta *Love County*   Elevation: 869 ft.   Latitude: 33° 53' N   Longitude: 97° 10' W

	JAN	FEB	MAR	APR	MAY	JUN	JUL	AUG	SEP	OCT	NOV	DEC	YEAR
Mean Maximum Temp. (°F)	52.3	58.5	67.2	75.1	81.3	88.9	94.5	94.5	86.7	77.0	64.2	55.5	74.6
Mean Temp. (°F)	41.2	46.6	55.0	63.1	70.6	78.3	83.1	82.6	75.4	65.2	53.1	44.4	63.2
Mean Minimum Temp. (°F)	30.1	34.7	42.7	51.1	59.8	67.7	71.6	70.5	64.0	53.3	42.0	33.3	51.7
Extreme Maximum Temp. (°F)	83	96	97	97	101	111	110	107	107	100	87	80	111
Extreme Minimum Temp. (°F)	-1	0	7	24	38	50	55	54	36	20	13	-8	-8
Days Maximum Temp. ≥ 90°F	0	0	0	0	2	14	26	26	12	2	0	0	82
Days Maximum Temp. ≤ 32°F	2	1	0	0	0	0	0	0	0	0	0	1	4
Days Minimum Temp. ≤ 32°F	19	11	5	1	0	0	0	0	0	0	6	15	57
Days Minimum Temp. ≤ 0°F	0	0	0	0	0	0	0	0	0	0	0	0	0
Heating Degree Days (base 65°F)	731	515	322	117	20	0	0	0	16	96	364	634	2,815
Cooling Degree Days (base 65°F)	0	3	18	71	209	416	577	577	343	108	14	2	2,338
Mean Precipitation (in.)	1.68	2.20	3.34	3.45	5.18	4.04	2.14	2.78	4.31	4.24	2.56	2.28	38.20
Days With ≥ 0.1" Precipitation	4	4	5	5	7	6	4	4	5	5	4	4	57
Days With ≥ 1.0" Precipitation	0	0	1	1	2	1	1	1	1	1	1	1	11
Mean Snowfall (in.)	*1.6*	*1.3*	0.5	0.0	0.0	0.0	0.0	0.0	0.0	0.0	0.3	0.8	*4.5*
Days With ≥ 1.0" Snow Depth	*1*	*1*	0	0	0	0	0	0	0	0	0	1	*3*

McAlester Municipal Airport *Pittsburg County*   Elevation: 757 ft.   Latitude: 34° 53' N   Longitude: 95° 47' W

	JAN	FEB	MAR	APR	MAY	JUN	JUL	AUG	SEP	OCT	NOV	DEC	YEAR
Mean Maximum Temp. (°F)	48.4	54.5	63.9	72.9	79.1	87.2	92.6	93.1	84.5	74.8	62.3	52.4	72.1
Mean Temp. (°F)	37.9	43.4	52.7	61.5	68.8	77.2	81.9	81.6	73.7	62.9	51.5	42.1	61.3
Mean Minimum Temp. (°F)	27.4	32.2	41.4	50.0	58.5	67.3	71.1	70.1	62.8	51.0	40.7	31.8	50.3
Extreme Maximum Temp. (°F)	77	92	94	94	92	103	110	107	103	95	85	80	110
Extreme Minimum Temp. (°F)	-14	-6	9	25	38	45	51	51	34	19	9	-5	-14
Days Maximum Temp. ≥ 90°F	0	0	0	0	1	11	22	23	9	1	0	0	67
Days Maximum Temp. ≤ 32°F	4	2	0	0	0	0	0	0	0	0	0	2	8
Days Minimum Temp. ≤ 32°F	22	14	7	1	0	0	0	0	0	1	8	17	70
Days Minimum Temp. ≤ 0°F	0	0	0	0	0	0	0	0	0	0	0	0	0
Heating Degree Days (base 65°F)	833	605	389	156	38	1	0	0	25	137	409	704	3,297
Cooling Degree Days (base 65°F)	0	2	15	57	170	387	540	544	298	81	13	2	2,109
Mean Precipitation (in.)	2.16	2.63	3.95	4.36	6.04	4.56	2.65	2.74	4.87	4.91	3.76	2.93	45.56
Days With ≥ 0.1" Precipitation	4	4	6	6	7	6	4	4	6	6	5	5	63
Days With ≥ 1.0" Precipitation	0	1	1	2	2	1	1	2	2	1	1	15
Mean Snowfall (in.)	3.2	2.1	0.7	trace	trace	trace	trace	trace	0.0	trace	0.3	0.8	7.1
Days With ≥ 1.0" Snow Depth	3	2	0	0	0	0	0	0	0	0	0	1	6

McCurtain 1 SE *Haskell County*   Elevation: 656 ft.   Latitude: 35° 09' N   Longitude: 94° 58' W

	JAN	FEB	MAR	APR	MAY	JUN	JUL	AUG	SEP	OCT	NOV	DEC	YEAR
Mean Maximum Temp. (°F)	50.6	56.8	65.6	74.6	80.8	88.2	94.2	93.8	85.8	76.1	63.5	54.1	73.7
Mean Temp. (°F)	39.8	45.3	53.9	62.6	69.9	77.6	82.8	81.8	74.2	63.6	52.4	43.4	62.3
Mean Minimum Temp. (°F)	29.1	33.8	42.2	50.6	58.9	67.0	71.4	69.7	62.5	51.2	41.2	32.5	50.8
Extreme Maximum Temp. (°F)	79	93	93	94	95	103	110	109	111	95	88	79	111
Extreme Minimum Temp. (°F)	-8	-4	6	22	36	46	52	50	33	20	9	-9	-9
Days Maximum Temp. ≥ 90°F	0	0	0	0	2	13	25	24	11	1	0	0	76
Days Maximum Temp. ≤ 32°F	3	1	0	0	0	0	0	0	0	0	0	2	6
Days Minimum Temp. ≤ 32°F	19	13	6	1	0	0	0	0	0	1	7	16	63
Days Minimum Temp. ≤ 0°F	0	0	0	0	0	0	0	0	0	0	0	0	0
Heating Degree Days (base 65°F)	773	553	358	135	28	1	0	0	21	121	384	666	3,040
Cooling Degree Days (base 65°F)	1	3	22	68	189	393	567	538	302	83	12	2	2,180
Mean Precipitation (in.)	2.60	2.84	4.30	4.74	5.67	5.01	3.17	2.85	5.22	4.22	5.09	3.31	49.02
Days With ≥ 0.1" Precipitation	5	5	7	7	7	7	4	5	6	5	5	5	68
Days With ≥ 1.0" Precipitation	1	1	1	1	2	2	1	1	2	1	2	1	16
Mean Snowfall (in.)	3.4	2.5	0.8	0.0	0.0	0.0	0.0	0.0	0.0	trace	0.2	0.5	7.4
Days With ≥ 1.0" Snow Depth	3	2	0	0	0	0	0	0	0	0	0	0	5

Meeker 4 W *Lincoln County*   Elevation: 921 ft.   Latitude: 35° 30' N   Longitude: 96° 59' W

	JAN	FEB	MAR	APR	MAY	JUN	JUL	AUG	SEP	OCT	NOV	DEC	YEAR
Mean Maximum Temp. (°F)	47.7	54.5	63.2	72.7	79.1	87.0	92.7	92.8	84.2	74.3	60.8	51.5	71.7
Mean Temp. (°F)	36.7	42.4	50.9	60.4	68.2	76.4	81.5	80.7	72.6	62.0	49.4	40.5	60.2
Mean Minimum Temp. (°F)	25.6	30.3	38.6	48.0	57.4	65.9	70.1	68.6	61.1	49.7	38.0	29.5	48.6
Extreme Maximum Temp. (°F)	80	91	91	103	96	104	110	110	107	96	87	79	110
Extreme Minimum Temp. (°F)	-6	-4	6	22	33	46	50	50	33	18	8	-15	-15
Days Maximum Temp. ≥ 90°F	0	0	0	0	1	11	22	22	9	1	0	0	66
Days Maximum Temp. ≤ 32°F	4	2	0	0	0	0	0	0	0	0	0	2	8
Days Minimum Temp. ≤ 32°F	23	16	9	2	0	0	0	0	0	1	9	19	79
Days Minimum Temp. ≤ 0°F	0	0	0	0	0	0	0	0	0	0	0	0	0
Heating Degree Days (base 65°F)	871	632	438	182	44	2	0	0	31	149	465	752	3,566
Cooling Degree Days (base 65°F)	0	1	12	48	154	355	526	499	266	59	6	1	1,927
Mean Precipitation (in.)	1.16	1.95	3.30	3.48	5.53	4.57	2.55	2.17	4.65	4.15	2.78	1.87	38.16
Days With ≥ 0.1" Precipitation	2	3	5	5	7	6	4	4	5	4	4	3	52
Days With ≥ 1.0" Precipitation	0	0	1	1	2	2	1	1	1	1	1	1	12
Mean Snowfall (in.)	*1.4*	*1.1*	0.3	trace	0.0	0.0	0.0	0.0	0.0	trace	0.2	0.5	*3.5*
Days With ≥ 1.0" Snow Depth	*1*	*1*	0	0	0	0	0	0	0	0	0	*0*	*2*

Miami *Ottawa County* Elevation: 803 ft. Latitude: 36° 53' N Longitude: 94° 53' W

	JAN	FEB	MAR	APR	MAY	JUN	JUL	AUG	SEP	OCT	NOV	DEC	YEAR
Mean Maximum Temp. (°F)	44.4	50.4	60.5	70.8	78.0	86.0	91.6	91.4	82.9	72.1	58.1	48.1	69.5
Mean Temp. (°F)	33.1	38.5	48.3	58.1	66.3	74.9	79.7	78.6	70.6	59.1	46.8	37.2	57.6
Mean Minimum Temp. (°F)	21.6	26.6	35.9	45.3	54.5	63.7	67.7	65.9	58.3	46.1	35.5	26.2	45.6
Extreme Maximum Temp. (°F)	75	85	91	98	93	102	110	108	102	95	85	75	110
Extreme Minimum Temp. (°F)	-15	-12	4	20	32	44	47	47	29	13	7	-15	-15
Days Maximum Temp. ≥ 90°F	0	0	0	0	1	10	21	20	8	0	0	0	60
Days Maximum Temp. ≤ 32°F	6	3	1	0	0	0	0	0	0	0	0	3	13
Days Minimum Temp. ≤ 32°F	26	20	12	2	0	0	0	0	0	2	12	22	96
Days Minimum Temp. ≤ 0°F	1	1	0	0	0	0	0	0	0	0	0	1	3
Heating Degree Days (base 65°F)	983	741	516	233	65	4	0	1	44	213	543	847	4,190
Cooling Degree Days (base 65°F)	0	0	5	29	109	313	462	438	212	33	2	0	1,603
Mean Precipitation (in.)	1.60	2.10	3.87	4.09	5.22	3.94	3.62	3.48	5.25	3.78	4.34	2.72	44.01
Days With ≥ 0.1" Precipitation	4	3	6	6	7	6	5	5	6	5	5	4	62
Days With ≥ 1.0" Precipitation	0	0	1	1	2	1	1	1	2	1	2	1	13
Mean Snowfall (in.)	na	na	0.8	trace	0.0	0.0	0.0	0.0	0.0	trace	0.3	1.2	na
Days With ≥ 1.0" Snow Depth	na	na	0	0	0	0	0	0	0	0	0	2	na

Muskogee *Muskogee County* Elevation: 580 ft. Latitude: 35° 46' N Longitude: 95° 20' W

	JAN	FEB	MAR	APR	MAY	JUN	JUL	AUG	SEP	OCT	NOV	DEC	YEAR
Mean Maximum Temp. (°F)	47.6	54.0	64.1	73.2	79.9	87.4	93.4	93.0	84.8	74.0	60.5	50.8	71.9
Mean Temp. (°F)	37.4	43.1	52.6	61.5	69.3	77.1	82.2	81.3	73.5	62.5	50.3	40.9	61.0
Mean Minimum Temp. (°F)	27.2	32.3	41.1	49.8	58.6	66.7	70.9	69.6	62.4	50.9	39.9	31.2	50.1
Extreme Maximum Temp. (°F)	76	90	93	92	94	101	112	108	107	92	84	78	112
Extreme Minimum Temp. (°F)	-9	-4	8	23	34	47	49	52	34	26	10	-7	-9
Days Maximum Temp. ≥ 90°F	0	0	0	0	1	12	24	22	9	0	0	0	68
Days Maximum Temp. ≤ 32°F	4	2	0	0	0	0	0	0	0	0	0	2	8
Days Minimum Temp. ≤ 32°F	22	15	7	1	0	0	0	0	0	1	7	17	70
Days Minimum Temp. ≤ 0°F	0	0	0	0	0	0	0	0	0	0	0	0	0
Heating Degree Days (base 65°F)	849	612	391	155	30	1	0	0	25	135	440	739	3,377
Cooling Degree Days (base 65°F)	0	0	16	57	177	377	544	521	294	67	6	1	2,060
Mean Precipitation (in.)	1.91	2.26	3.77	4.05	5.24	4.81	2.81	2.54	5.33	4.38	4.05	3.02	44.17
Days With ≥ 0.1" Precipitation	4	5	6	6	7	6	4	4	6	5	5	4	62
Days With ≥ 1.0" Precipitation	0	1	1	1	2	2	1	1	2	1	1	1	14
Mean Snowfall (in.)	2.3	2.3	0.8	0.0	0.0	0.0	0.0	0.0	0.0	trace	0.1	1.1	6.6
Days With ≥ 1.0" Snow Depth	na	0	0	0	0	0	0	0	0	0	0	0	na

Mutual *Woodward County* Elevation: 1,863 ft. Latitude: 36° 14' N Longitude: 99° 10' W

	JAN	FEB	MAR	APR	MAY	JUN	JUL	AUG	SEP	OCT	NOV	DEC	YEAR
Mean Maximum Temp. (°F)	45.0	51.0	59.9	69.8	78.1	88.5	95.1	93.4	84.1	72.6	57.8	48.1	70.3
Mean Temp. (°F)	33.1	38.3	46.8	56.4	65.7	75.9	81.6	80.0	71.1	59.1	45.6	36.3	57.5
Mean Minimum Temp. (°F)	21.1	25.6	33.7	42.9	53.3	63.2	68.1	66.5	58.1	45.5	33.3	24.5	44.7
Extreme Maximum Temp. (°F)	81	91	92	100	104	110	115	111	108	99	88	78	115
Extreme Minimum Temp. (°F)	-10	-11	4	19	31	44	48	47	31	13	7	-12	-12
Days Maximum Temp. ≥ 90°F	0	0	0	1	3	15	25	22	11	2	0	0	79
Days Maximum Temp. ≤ 32°F	6	4	1	0	0	0	0	0	0	0	1	4	16
Days Minimum Temp. ≤ 32°F	28	21	14	4	0	0	0	0	0	2	14	26	109
Days Minimum Temp. ≤ 0°F	1	1	0	0	0	0	0	0	0	0	0	1	3
Heating Degree Days (base 65°F)	983	747	561	280	84	7	0	1	48	219	576	883	4,389
Cooling Degree Days (base 65°F)	0	0	3	23	105	327	516	472	236	37	1	0	1,720
Mean Precipitation (in.)	0.75	0.95	2.16	2.64	4.42	3.13	2.56	2.31	2.47	1.84	1.54	0.96	25.73
Days With ≥ 0.1" Precipitation	2	2	4	5	6	5	4	4	4	3	3	2	44
Days With ≥ 1.0" Precipitation	0	0	0	1	2	1	1	1	1	0	0	0	7
Mean Snowfall (in.)	3.2	3.4	2.2	0.6	0.0	0.0	0.0	0.0	0.0	trace	1.2	3.3	13.9
Days With ≥ 1.0" Snow Depth	5	3	1	0	0	0	0	0	0	0	1	4	14

Nowata *Nowata County* Elevation: 738 ft. Latitude: 36° 42' N Longitude: 95° 38' W

	JAN	FEB	MAR	APR	MAY	JUN	JUL	AUG	SEP	OCT	NOV	DEC	YEAR
Mean Maximum Temp. (°F)	44.7	51.5	62.0	71.7	78.7	87.2	93.3	93.0	83.8	73.5	59.8	49.2	70.7
Mean Temp. (°F)	34.0	39.9	50.1	59.4	67.6	76.3	81.6	80.7	72.1	60.8	48.7	38.5	59.1
Mean Minimum Temp. (°F)	23.4	28.2	38.0	47.0	56.6	65.4	69.8	68.5	60.3	48.4	37.5	27.8	47.6
Extreme Maximum Temp. (°F)	75	87	93	101	94	103	112	112	107	97	86	75	112
Extreme Minimum Temp. (°F)	-11	-9	5	18	29	47	50	50	33	17	5	-13	-13
Days Maximum Temp. ≥ 90°F	0	0	0	0	1	11	23	23	8	1	0	0	67
Days Maximum Temp. ≤ 32°F	5	3	0	0	0	0	0	0	0	0	0	3	11
Days Minimum Temp. ≤ 32°F	25	18	9	2	0	0	0	0	0	1	10	21	86
Days Minimum Temp. ≤ 0°F	1	0	0	0	0	0	0	0	0	0	0	0	1
Heating Degree Days (base 65°F)	953	704	464	201	47	1	0	0	33	168	487	816	3,874
Cooling Degree Days (base 65°F)	0	1	8	38	132	350	523	499	248	45	6	0	1,850
Mean Precipitation (in.)	1.61	1.97	3.68	3.96	4.80	4.68	2.75	2.92	5.32	3.35	3.78	2.37	41.19
Days With ≥ 0.1" Precipitation	4	4	6	6	7	6	4	4	6	4	5	4	60
Days With ≥ 1.0" Precipitation	0	1	1	1	1	2	1	1	2	1	1	1	13
Mean Snowfall (in.)	2.9	3.0	1.5	trace	0.0	0.0	0.0	0.0	0.0	0.0	0.5	1.2	9.1
Days With ≥ 1.0" Snow Depth	na	na	0	0	0	0	0	0	0	0	0	0	na

Okeene *Blaine County* Elevation: 1,207 ft. Latitude: 36° 07' N Longitude: 98° 19' W

	JAN	FEB	MAR	APR	MAY	JUN	JUL	AUG	SEP	OCT	NOV	DEC	YEAR
Mean Maximum Temp. (°F)	48.4	55.3	63.8	73.5	81.7	91.1	96.3	95.0	86.6	75.9	60.8	50.9	73.3
Mean Temp. (°F)	36.2	42.1	50.3	59.8	68.9	78.2	83.3	81.8	73.7	62.4	48.7	39.3	60.4
Mean Minimum Temp. (°F)	23.9	28.9	36.8	46.0	56.2	65.3	70.2	68.6	60.8	48.8	36.5	27.5	47.5
Extreme Maximum Temp. (°F)	81	91	93	101	105	109	110	109	106	100	89	79	110
Extreme Minimum Temp. (°F)	-11	-13	7	20	35	45	51	50	33	13	8	-13	-13
Days Maximum Temp. ≥ 90°F	0	0	0	1	5	19	27	25	12	2	0	0	91
Days Maximum Temp. ≤ 32°F	5	2	0	0	0	0	0	0	0	0	0	2	9
Days Minimum Temp. ≤ 32°F	26	18	10	2	0	0	0	0	0	1	10	23	90
Days Minimum Temp. ≤ 0°F	0	0	0	0	0	0	0	0	0	0	0	1	1
Heating Degree Days (base 65°F)	887	639	456	195	41	1	0	0	25	145	486	792	3,667
Cooling Degree Days (base 65°F)	0	0	6	41	168	401	577	534	297	60	3	0	2,087
Mean Precipitation (in.)	0.89	1.33	2.56	2.83	4.72	3.99	2.45	2.88	3.54	2.63	2.02	1.34	31.18
Days With ≥ 0.1" Precipitation	2	3	4	5	6	5	4	4	4	3	3	3	46
Days With ≥ 1.0" Precipitation	0	0	1	1	2	1	1	1	1	1	1	0	10
Mean Snowfall (in.)	*3.1*	na	1.3	0.3	0.0	0.0	0.0	0.0	0.0	0.2	0.4	*2.5*	na
Days With ≥ 1.0" Snow Depth	na	na	0	0	0	0	0	0	0	0	0	*1*	na

Okemah *Okfuskee County* Elevation: 935 ft. Latitude: 35° 26' N Longitude: 96° 18' W

	JAN	FEB	MAR	APR	MAY	JUN	JUL	AUG	SEP	OCT	NOV	DEC	YEAR
Mean Maximum Temp. (°F)	48.3	54.9	64.0	73.4	80.2	87.9	93.8	93.8	85.2	74.6	61.3	51.8	72.4
Mean Temp. (°F)	38.3	44.0	52.7	61.7	69.6	77.4	82.3	81.7	74.0	63.3	51.0	42.0	61.5
Mean Minimum Temp. (°F)	28.2	33.1	41.3	50.1	58.8	66.8	70.7	69.5	62.8	51.9	40.8	32.1	50.5
Extreme Maximum Temp. (°F)	77	93	93	99	97	102	109	108	109	97	85	77	109
Extreme Minimum Temp. (°F)	-5	-1	9	23	37	45	53	53	35	20	11	-9	-9
Days Maximum Temp. ≥ 90°F	0	0	0	0	2	13	24	24	10	1	0	0	74
Days Maximum Temp. ≤ 32°F	4	2	0	0	0	0	0	0	0	0	0	2	8
Days Minimum Temp. ≤ 32°F	20	13	6	1	0	0	0	0	0	0	6	16	62
Days Minimum Temp. ≤ 0°F	0	0	0	0	0	0	0	0	0	0	0	0	0
Heating Degree Days (base 65°F)	822	587	387	144	27	1	0	0	21	122	419	707	3,237
Cooling Degree Days (base 65°F)	0	2	12	54	184	393	557	539	304	74	8	1	2,128
Mean Precipitation (in.)	1.66	2.08	3.48	4.10	5.50	4.85	2.90	2.46	5.24	3.98	3.44	2.41	42.10
Days With ≥ 0.1" Precipitation	3	4	6	6	7	6	4	4	6	5	4	4	59
Days With ≥ 1.0" Precipitation	0	1	1	1	2	2	1	1	2	1	1	1	14
Mean Snowfall (in.)	*2.1*	*1.1*	0.8	0.0	0.0	0.0	0.0	0.0	0.0	trace	0.4	*0.6*	*5.0*
Days With ≥ 1.0" Snow Depth	2	2	0	0	0	0	0	0	0	0	0	0	4

Okmulgee Water Works *Okmulgee County* Elevation: 646 ft. Latitude: 35° 37' N Longitude: 96° 01' W

	JAN	FEB	MAR	APR	MAY	JUN	JUL	AUG	SEP	OCT	NOV	DEC	YEAR
Mean Maximum Temp. (°F)	48.5	55.5	64.4	73.4	79.8	87.5	93.4	93.3	85.1	75.5	62.1	53.0	72.6
Mean Temp. (°F)	36.5	42.5	51.6	60.5	68.4	76.4	80.8	80.0	72.4	61.7	50.0	41.0	60.1
Mean Minimum Temp. (°F)	24.5	29.7	38.7	47.5	56.8	65.1	68.4	66.8	59.7	47.8	37.7	28.9	47.6
Extreme Maximum Temp. (°F)	79	91	96	101	95	102	108	109	109	96	86	79	109
Extreme Minimum Temp. (°F)	-10	-8	3	24	26	43	47	48	33	17	9	-14	-14
Days Maximum Temp. ≥ 90°F	0	0	0	0	2	12	24	23	11	1	0	0	73
Days Maximum Temp. ≤ 32°F	4	2	0	0	0	0	0	0	0	0	0	2	8
Days Minimum Temp. ≤ 32°F	24	17	9	1	0	0	0	0	0	2	10	20	83
Days Minimum Temp. ≤ 0°F	0	0	0	0	0	0	0	0	0	0	0	0	0
Heating Degree Days (base 65°F)	876	629	421	179	42	2	0	0	30	158	451	738	3,526
Cooling Degree Days (base 65°F)	0	1	9	40	147	345	492	474	252	52	6	1	1,819
Mean Precipitation (in.)	1.59	2.29	3.82	4.24	5.61	4.58	3.04	2.65	4.81	4.33	3.84	2.65	43.45
Days With ≥ 0.1" Precipitation	3	4	6	6	7	6	4	4	6	4	5	4	59
Days With ≥ 1.0" Precipitation	0	1	1	1	2	2	1	1	2	1	1	1	14
Mean Snowfall (in.)	*2.3*	na	0.9	0.0	0.0	0.0	0.0	0.0	0.0	trace	trace	0.3	na
Days With ≥ 1.0" Snow Depth	na	na	*0*	0	0	0	0	0	0	0	0	0	na

Pauls Valley 4 WSW *Garvin County* Elevation: 938 ft. Latitude: 34° 44' N Longitude: 97° 17' W

	JAN	FEB	MAR	APR	MAY	JUN	JUL	AUG	SEP	OCT	NOV	DEC	YEAR
Mean Maximum Temp. (°F)	51.5	57.8	66.1	75.1	81.8	89.3	95.0	94.7	86.6	76.8	63.5	54.4	74.4
Mean Temp. (°F)	39.6	45.1	53.2	62.2	70.0	77.9	82.9	82.0	74.5	63.6	51.4	42.6	62.1
Mean Minimum Temp. (°F)	27.7	32.4	40.4	49.3	58.2	66.5	70.7	69.2	62.3	50.3	39.3	30.8	49.8
Extreme Maximum Temp. (°F)	80	92	96	100	100	108	110	108	109	97	86	79	110
Extreme Minimum Temp. (°F)	-10	-1	0	24	36	46	53	50	34	17	10	-10	-10
Days Maximum Temp. ≥ 90°F	0	0	0	1	3	16	26	25	12	2	0	0	85
Days Maximum Temp. ≤ 32°F	2	1	0	0	0	0	0	0	0	0	0	1	4
Days Minimum Temp. ≤ 32°F	22	14	7	1	0	0	0	0	0	1	9	18	72
Days Minimum Temp. ≤ 0°F	0	0	0	0	0	0	0	0	0	0	0	0	0
Heating Degree Days (base 65°F)	779	556	375	141	26	1	0	0	22	118	410	688	3,116
Cooling Degree Days (base 65°F)	0	1	15	57	178	386	554	534	306	75	9	1	2,116
Mean Precipitation (in.)	1.64	2.00	3.06	3.50	5.96	4.37	2.36	2.06	4.61	3.98	2.76	2.08	38.38
Days With ≥ 0.1" Precipitation	3	4	5	5	7	6	3	4	6	4	4	4	55
Days With ≥ 1.0" Precipitation	0	0	1	1	2	1	1	1	2	1	1	0	11
Mean Snowfall (in.)	2.4	*1.6*	0.8	0.0	0.0	0.0	0.0	0.0	0.0	0.0	0.2	1.4	*6.4*
Days With ≥ 1.0" Snow Depth	*2*	*1*	0	0	0	0	0	0	0	0	0	*0*	*3*

Pawhuska *Osage County*   Elevation: 833 ft.   Latitude: 36° 40' N   Longitude: 96° 21' W

	JAN	FEB	MAR	APR	MAY	JUN	JUL	AUG	SEP	OCT	NOV	DEC	YEAR
Mean Maximum Temp. (°F)	46.0	53.0	62.8	72.7	79.3	87.1	93.0	92.7	84.3	73.9	59.8	49.6	71.2
Mean Temp. (°F)	34.5	40.6	50.1	59.9	67.8	76.2	81.5	80.3	72.4	61.0	48.3	38.4	59.3
Mean Minimum Temp. (°F)	22.9	28.0	37.4	47.1	56.3	65.2	70.0	68.0	60.5	48.1	36.9	27.2	47.3
Extreme Maximum Temp. (°F)	77	90	94	101	95	104	111	109	107	95	85	77	111
Extreme Minimum Temp. (°F)	-13	-15	4	18	33	44	49	46	29	15	5	-14	-15
Days Maximum Temp. ≥ 90°F	0	0	0	1	1	11	24	22	9	1	0	0	69
Days Maximum Temp. ≤ 32°F	5	3	0	0	0	0	0	0	0	0	0	2	10
Days Minimum Temp. ≤ 32°F	25	19	11	2	0	0	0	0	0	2	11	22	92
Days Minimum Temp. ≤ 0°F	1	1	0	0	0	0	0	0	0	0	0	1	3
Heating Degree Days (base 65°F)	940	685	464	197	48	2	0	0	32	172	498	818	3,856
Cooling Degree Days (base 65°F)	0	1	10	47	144	346	523	489	263	53	6	1	1,883
Mean Precipitation (in.)	1.45	2.05	3.43	4.56	5.31	5.09	3.81	3.62	5.20	3.51	3.23	2.05	43.31
Days With ≥ 0.1" Precipitation	3	4	5	6	8	7	5	5	6	5	4	4	62
Days With ≥ 1.0" Precipitation	0	0	1	1	2	2	1	1	2	1	1	1	13
Mean Snowfall (in.)	3.5	2.7	1.2	trace	0.0	0.0	0.0	0.0	0.0	0.0	0.5	1.8	9.7
Days With ≥ 1.0" Snow Depth	4	3	1	0	0	0	0	0	0	0	0	1	9

Perry *Noble County*   Elevation: 1,023 ft.   Latitude: 36° 17' N   Longitude: 97° 17' W

	JAN	FEB	MAR	APR	MAY	JUN	JUL	AUG	SEP	OCT	NOV	DEC	YEAR
Mean Maximum Temp. (°F)	47.3	54.1	63.4	73.7	81.2	89.4	94.9	94.3	85.9	75.4	60.9	50.7	72.6
Mean Temp. (°F)	35.9	41.9	50.8	60.8	69.4	77.9	82.9	81.9	73.9	62.6	49.5	39.6	60.6
Mean Minimum Temp. (°F)	24.6	29.7	38.2	47.8	57.6	66.3	70.8	69.5	61.8	49.8	37.8	28.5	48.5
Extreme Maximum Temp. (°F)	81	91	94	102	103	109	114	110	108	98	88	79	114
Extreme Minimum Temp. (°F)	-8	-12	5	18	35	46	52	48	30	17	11	-18	-18
Days Maximum Temp. ≥ 90°F	0	0	0	1	4	16	26	25	12	1	0	0	85
Days Maximum Temp. ≤ 32°F	5	3	0	0	0	0	0	0	0	0	0	2	10
Days Minimum Temp. ≤ 32°F	24	17	10	1	0	0	0	0	0	1	9	20	82
Days Minimum Temp. ≤ 0°F	0	0	0	0	0	0	0	0	0	0	0	1	1
Heating Degree Days (base 65°F)	894	644	446	176	37	3	0	0	25	138	464	781	3,608
Cooling Degree Days (base 65°F)	0	1	13	54	185	400	565	541	303	66	7	0	2,135
Mean Precipitation (in.)	1.09	1.62	2.82	3.48	5.25	4.06	2.90	3.25	4.43	2.97	2.40	1.65	35.92
Days With ≥ 0.1" Precipitation	2	3	5	5	7	6	4	5	5	4	4	3	53
Days With ≥ 1.0" Precipitation	0	0	1	1	2	1	1	1	2	1	1	0	11
Mean Snowfall (in.)	1.7	1.8	1.5	0.0	0.0	0.0	0.0	0.0	0.0	0.0	0.3	*0.8*	*6.1*
Days With ≥ 1.0" Snow Depth	*1*	na	0	0	0	0	0	0	0	0	0	*0*	na

Ponca City Municipal Airport *Kay County*   Elevation: 997 ft.   Latitude: 36° 44' N   Longitude: 97° 06' W

	JAN	FEB	MAR	APR	MAY	JUN	JUL	AUG	SEP	OCT	NOV	DEC	YEAR
Mean Maximum Temp. (°F)	43.4	50.6	60.3	70.7	79.0	88.2	94.2	93.0	83.6	72.4	57.9	47.5	70.1
Mean Temp. (°F)	33.5	39.5	48.8	58.9	68.2	77.5	82.9	81.7	72.8	61.0	47.5	37.6	59.2
Mean Minimum Temp. (°F)	23.5	28.4	37.3	47.0	57.3	66.8	71.6	70.3	62.0	49.5	37.2	27.6	48.2
Extreme Maximum Temp. (°F)	79	92	90	101	100	106	116	109	108	95	87	76	116
Extreme Minimum Temp. (°F)	-12	-8	5	19	33	45	50	49	28	15	8	-10	-12
Days Maximum Temp. ≥ 90°F	0	0	0	1	2	14	24	23	9	1	0	0	74
Days Maximum Temp. ≤ 32°F	7	4	1	0	0	0	0	0	0	0	1	3	16
Days Minimum Temp. ≤ 32°F	26	18	11	2	0	0	0	0	0	1	11	22	91
Days Minimum Temp. ≤ 0°F	1	1	0	0	0	0	0	0	0	0	0	0	2
Heating Degree Days (base 65°F)	970	713	503	222	53	2	0	0	33	178	521	844	4,039
Cooling Degree Days (base 65°F)	0	1	9	46	167	397	580	547	294	62	5	0	2,108
Mean Precipitation (in.)	1.16	1.38	2.85	3.54	4.78	4.42	3.38	3.45	3.88	3.15	2.50	1.70	36.19
Days With ≥ 0.1" Precipitation	2	3	5	5	7	6	5	4	5	4	3	3	52
Days With ≥ 1.0" Precipitation	0	0	1	1	2	1	1	1	1	1	1	1	11
Mean Snowfall (in.)	2.3	2.8	1.6	trace	trace	trace	trace	0.0	trace	trace	0.3	1.7	8.7
Days With ≥ 1.0" Snow Depth	4	3	1	0	0	0	0	0	0	0	0	2	10

Pryor *Mayes County*   Elevation: 623 ft.   Latitude: 36° 18' N   Longitude: 95° 19' W

	JAN	FEB	MAR	APR	MAY	JUN	JUL	AUG	SEP	OCT	NOV	DEC	YEAR
Mean Maximum Temp. (°F)	45.4	51.5	61.2	71.3	78.4	86.3	92.3	91.9	83.3	73.1	59.7	49.4	70.3
Mean Temp. (°F)	34.1	39.7	48.8	58.4	66.9	75.3	80.5	79.4	71.3	59.8	48.0	38.2	58.4
Mean Minimum Temp. (°F)	22.4	27.3	36.3	45.7	55.4	64.3	68.9	67.2	59.4	46.4	36.1	27.0	46.4
Extreme Maximum Temp. (°F)	74	88	93	97	93	101	108	108	105	98	84	76	108
Extreme Minimum Temp. (°F)	-20	-14	3	24	34	45	49	48	31	17	6	-14	-20
Days Maximum Temp. ≥ 90°F	0	0	0	0	1	9	22	20	8	1	0	0	61
Days Maximum Temp. ≤ 32°F	5	3	0	0	0	0	0	0	0	0	0	3	11
Days Minimum Temp. ≤ 32°F	26	*19*	12	2	0	0	0	0	0	2	12	22	*95*
Days Minimum Temp. ≤ 0°F	1	1	1	0	0	0	0	0	0	0	0	1	3
Heating Degree Days (base 65°F)	953	710	501	226	58	3	0	1	41	199	509	826	4,027
Cooling Degree Days (base 65°F)	0	0	6	24	118	323	481	455	225	34	4	0	1,670
Mean Precipitation (in.)	1.96	2.05	3.85	4.13	4.98	4.48	3.14	3.26	5.40	4.09	4.02	2.50	43.86
Days With ≥ 0.1" Precipitation	3	4	5	6	7	6	4	5	6	5	5	4	60
Days With ≥ 1.0" Precipitation	1	1	1	1	1	1	1	1	2	2	2	1	14
Mean Snowfall (in.)	*2.6*	na	1.7	trace	0.0	0.0	0.0	0.0	0.0	trace	*0.5*	*1.3*	na
Days With ≥ 1.0" Snow Depth	*4*	na	1	0	0	0	0	0	0	0	*0*	*2*	na

Purcell 5 SW *McClain County*   Elevation: 1,040 ft.   Latitude: 34° 58' N   Longitude: 97° 26' W

	JAN	FEB	MAR	APR	MAY	JUN	JUL	AUG	SEP	OCT	NOV	DEC	YEAR
Mean Maximum Temp. (°F)	49.6	56.3	65.4	74.3	81.3	89.0	95.0	94.5	86.5	76.0	62.0	52.8	73.6
Mean Temp. (°F)	37.6	43.6	52.4	61.3	69.5	77.6	82.7	81.7	74.3	63.0	50.0	41.1	61.2
Mean Minimum Temp. (°F)	25.6	30.8	39.4	48.3	57.7	66.1	70.3	68.9	62.0	49.9	38.0	29.3	48.9
Extreme Maximum Temp. (°F)	80	90	93	100	102	107	109	108	111	100	86	77	111
Extreme Minimum Temp. (°F)	-12	-4	3	21	35	46	46	49	33	12	9	-13	-13
Days Maximum Temp. ≥ 90°F	0	0	0	0	3	15	25	25	11	1	0	0	80
Days Maximum Temp. ≤ 32°F	3	2	0	0	0	0	0	0	0	0	0	2	7
Days Minimum Temp. ≤ 32°F	24	16	9	2	0	0	0	0	0	1	9	20	81
Days Minimum Temp. ≤ 0°F	0	0	0	0	0	0	0	0	0	0	0	0	0
Heating Degree Days (base 65°F)	842	600	397	159	31	1	0	0	22	133	449	736	3,370
Cooling Degree Days (base 65°F)	0	1	11	49	172	374	549	521	299	69	6	0	2,051
Mean Precipitation (in.)	1.58	2.20	3.49	3.87	5.98	4.61	2.75	2.90	4.60	4.20	2.78	2.46	41.42
Days With ≥ 0.1" Precipitation	3	4	5	5	8	7	4	5	6	5	5	4	61
Days With ≥ 1.0" Precipitation	0	1	1	1	2	2	1	1	2	1	1	1	14
Mean Snowfall (in.)	3.0	1.7	0.8	0.0	0.0	0.0	0.0	0.0	0.0	trace	0.4	1.3	7.2
Days With ≥ 1.0" Snow Depth	4	2	0	0	0	0	0	0	0	0	0	1	7

Ralston *Pawnee County*   Elevation: 823 ft.   Latitude: 36° 30' N   Longitude: 96° 44' W

	JAN	FEB	MAR	APR	MAY	JUN	JUL	AUG	SEP	OCT	NOV	DEC	YEAR
Mean Maximum Temp. (°F)	47.0	53.8	63.2	73.3	80.5	88.4	94.2	93.6	85.2	74.9	60.6	50.5	72.1
Mean Temp. (°F)	35.2	41.2	50.4	60.1	68.6	76.9	81.8	80.7	72.7	61.3	48.6	38.8	59.7
Mean Minimum Temp. (°F)	23.4	28.5	37.6	46.9	56.6	65.3	69.3	67.7	60.1	47.7	36.5	27.1	47.2
Extreme Maximum Temp. (°F)	78	92	93	100	97	105	112	110	108	98	88	76	112
Extreme Minimum Temp. (°F)	-11	-15	3	18	33	44	49	43	30	13	6	-13	-15
Days Maximum Temp. ≥ 90°F	0	0	0	1	3	14	26	23	11	1	0	0	79
Days Maximum Temp. ≤ 32°F	5	2	0	0	0	0	0	0	0	0	0	2	9
Days Minimum Temp. ≤ 32°F	25	18	11	2	0	0	0	0	0	2	11	22	91
Days Minimum Temp. ≤ 0°F	1	1	0	0	0	0	0	0	0	0	0	0	2
Heating Degree Days (base 65°F)	916	667	456	190	41	2	0	0	30	165	489	805	3,761
Cooling Degree Days (base 65°F)	0	1	9	48	165	372	537	504	274	58	5	0	1,973
Mean Precipitation (in.)	1.29	1.74	3.33	3.80	5.23	4.24	3.08	3.62	4.48	3.09	2.67	1.86	38.43
Days With ≥ 0.1" Precipitation	3	3	5	6	7	6	5	5	6	4	4	3	57
Days With ≥ 1.0" Precipitation	0	0	1	1	2	1	1	1	1	1	1	1	11
Mean Snowfall (in.)	3.0	3.2	1.5	0.1	0.0	0.0	0.0	0.0	0.0	trace	0.6	1.5	9.9
Days With ≥ 1.0" Snow Depth	4	4	1	0	0	0	0	0	0	0	0	2	11

Sallisaw 2 NW *Sequoyah County*   Elevation: 659 ft.   Latitude: 35° 27' N   Longitude: 94° 48' W

	JAN	FEB	MAR	APR	MAY	JUN	JUL	AUG	SEP	OCT	NOV	DEC	YEAR
Mean Maximum Temp. (°F)	48.8	55.3	64.0	73.6	80.1	87.7	93.3	92.7	85.2	75.0	61.6	52.1	72.5
Mean Temp. (°F)	38.0	43.6	52.1	61.2	69.1	76.8	81.7	80.9	73.7	62.7	50.6	41.5	61.0
Mean Minimum Temp. (°F)	26.8	31.8	40.1	48.9	57.9	66.0	70.0	69.1	62.2	50.4	39.4	30.8	49.4
Extreme Maximum Temp. (°F)	77	84	94	93	94	102	108	107	107	93	89	79	108
Extreme Minimum Temp. (°F)	-9	-8	8	24	36	45	50	50	33	18	9	-9	-9
Days Maximum Temp. ≥ 90°F	0	0	0	0	1	12	23	23	9	1	0	0	69
Days Maximum Temp. ≤ 32°F	3	1	0	0	0	0	0	0	0	0	0	2	6
Days Minimum Temp. ≤ 32°F	23	14	7	1	0	0	0	0	0	1	8	18	72
Days Minimum Temp. ≤ 0°F	0	0	0	0	0	0	0	0	0	0	0	0	0
Heating Degree Days (base 65°F)	832	600	403	159	31	2	0	0	21	131	432	724	3,335
Cooling Degree Days (base 65°F)	0	1	9	44	157	360	519	503	281	62	5	1	1,942
Mean Precipitation (in.)	2.12	2.77	4.23	4.52	5.55	4.37	2.79	3.25	4.91	4.52	4.68	2.97	46.68
Days With ≥ 0.1" Precipitation	3	4	6	6	7	6	4	4	6	5	5	4	60
Days With ≥ 1.0" Precipitation	1	1	1	2	2	1	1	1	2	2	2	1	17
Mean Snowfall (in.)	2.3	1.7	0.6	trace	0.0	0.0	0.0	0.0	0.0	trace	0.4	0.8	5.8
Days With ≥ 1.0" Snow Depth	*2*	*1*	0	0	0	0	0	0	0	0	0	1	*4*

Seminole *Seminole County*   Elevation: 862 ft.   Latitude: 35° 14' N   Longitude: 96° 40' W

	JAN	FEB	MAR	APR	MAY	JUN	JUL	AUG	SEP	OCT	NOV	DEC	YEAR
Mean Maximum Temp. (°F)	50.1	57.1	65.9	75.3	81.8	89.4	95.2	95.0	86.7	76.6	62.6	53.6	74.1
Mean Temp. (°F)	39.0	44.9	53.5	62.7	70.4	78.3	83.3	82.5	74.6	64.0	51.5	42.5	62.3
Mean Minimum Temp. (°F)	27.7	32.7	41.0	50.0	59.0	67.1	71.5	70.0	62.6	51.3	40.3	31.3	50.4
Extreme Maximum Temp. (°F)	80	90	95	99	100	104	109	108	108	98	85	77	109
Extreme Minimum Temp. (°F)	-8	-1	7	25	39	46	52	53	36	18	10	-9	-9
Days Maximum Temp. ≥ 90°F	0	0	0	1	4	16	27	26	12	2	0	0	88
Days Maximum Temp. ≤ 32°F	3	1	0	0	0	0	0	0	0	0	0	2	6
Days Minimum Temp. ≤ 32°F	22	14	7	1	0	0	0	0	0	0	7	17	68
Days Minimum Temp. ≤ 0°F	0	0	0	0	0	0	0	0	0	0	0	0	0
Heating Degree Days (base 65°F)	800	561	366	132	24	1	0	0	19	112	408	691	3,114
Cooling Degree Days (base 65°F)	0	2	16	62	198	405	580	557	308	78	9	1	2,216
Mean Precipitation (in.)	1.71	2.13	3.39	4.12	5.47	4.64	2.54	2.67	4.83	4.03	3.17	2.28	40.98
Days With ≥ 0.1" Precipitation	3	4	5	6	7	6	3	4	6	5	4	4	57
Days With ≥ 1.0" Precipitation	1	1	1	1	2	2	1	1	2	1	1	1	15
Mean Snowfall (in.)	*1.4*	*1.2*	0.5	0.0	0.0	0.0	0.0	0.0	0.0	0.0	0.2	0.4	*3.7*
Days With ≥ 1.0" Snow Depth	na	*0*	0	0	0	0	0	0	0	0	0	0	na

Smithville *McCurtain County*   Elevation: 830 ft.   Latitude: 34° 28' N   Longitude: 94° 39' W

	JAN	FEB	MAR	APR	MAY	JUN	JUL	AUG	SEP	OCT	NOV	DEC	YEAR
Mean Maximum Temp. (°F)	50.9	56.3	64.7	72.7	*78.7*	86.4	91.9	91.2	*84.4*	74.4	61.9	53.5	*72.2*
Mean Temp. (°F)	39.0	43.5	51.8	59.5	*67.1*	74.7	79.1	78.3	*71.7*	60.7	49.9	42.1	*59.8*
Mean Minimum Temp. (°F)	26.8	30.8	38.9	46.4	55.5	62.9	66.6	65.3	*59.0*	47.1	37.9	30.5	*47.3*
Extreme Maximum Temp. (°F)	76	84	91	92	93	100	110	110	105	95	85	78	110
Extreme Minimum Temp. (°F)	-2	0	4	18	32	43	46	45	29	16	8	-6	-6
Days Maximum Temp. ≥ 90°F	0	0	0	0	0	7	21	19	8	1	0	0	56
Days Maximum Temp. ≤ 32°F	1	1	0	0	0	0	0	0	0	0	0	1	3
Days Minimum Temp. ≤ 32°F	22	17	9	3	0	0	0	0	0	3	11	18	83
Days Minimum Temp. ≤ 0°F	0	0	0	0	0	0	0	0	0	0	0	0	0
Heating Degree Days (base 65°F)	800	600	409	192	*49*	2	0	0	*27*	170	451	704	*3,404*
Cooling Degree Days (base 65°F)	0	0	6	28	*117*	298	436	*418*	227	46	5	1	*1,582*
Mean Precipitation (in.)	3.33	3.48	5.23	5.01	6.56	4.33	4.10	3.07	4.81	6.32	4.96	4.98	56.18
Days With ≥ 0.1" Precipitation	5	5	6	7	8	6	5	5	5	5	6	5	68
Days With ≥ 1.0" Precipitation	1	1	2	2	2	1	1	1	2	2	2	2	19
Mean Snowfall (in.)	*1.1*	*1.7*	trace	trace	0.0	0.0	0.0	0.0	0.0	0.0	0.1	0.3	*3.2*
Days With ≥ 1.0" Snow Depth	na	*0*	0	0	0	0	0	0	0	0	0	0	na

Spavinaw *Mayes County*   Elevation: 682 ft.   Latitude: 36° 23' N   Longitude: 95° 03' W

	JAN	FEB	MAR	APR	MAY	JUN	JUL	AUG	SEP	OCT	NOV	DEC	YEAR
Mean Maximum Temp. (°F)	48.5	54.7	63.5	72.7	79.4	86.7	92.5	92.4	84.1	73.9	61.3	51.6	71.8
Mean Temp. (°F)	37.8	43.2	51.9	60.9	68.9	76.8	82.1	81.3	73.5	62.9	51.0	41.4	61.0
Mean Minimum Temp. (°F)	27.0	31.6	40.2	49.0	58.2	66.8	71.6	70.1	62.8	51.9	40.7	31.0	50.1
Extreme Maximum Temp. (°F)	76	85	92	92	96	103	109	109	105	92	82	76	109
Extreme Minimum Temp. (°F)	-21	-10	7	21	37	47	50	52	35	19	8	-11	-21
Days Maximum Temp. ≥ 90°F	0	0	0	0	1	10	23	22	8	0	0	0	64
Days Maximum Temp. ≤ 32°F	3	2	0	0	0	0	0	0	0	0	0	2	7
Days Minimum Temp. ≤ 32°F	22	15	8	1	0	0	0	0	0	1	7	18	72
Days Minimum Temp. ≤ 0°F	1	0	0	0	0	0	0	0	0	0	0	0	1
Heating Degree Days (base 65°F)	838	611	410	172	35	1	0	0	24	131	421	728	3,371
Cooling Degree Days (base 65°F)	0	1	12	51	162	370	549	523	293	73	9	1	2,044
Mean Precipitation (in.)	1.96	2.05	3.83	4.36	4.85	4.51	2.97	3.50	5.19	3.82	4.34	2.87	44.25
Days With ≥ 0.1" Precipitation	4	4	6	6	7	6	4	5	6	5	5	4	62
Days With ≥ 1.0" Precipitation	0	0	1	1	2	1	1	1	1	1	2	1	12
Mean Snowfall (in.)	2.5	1.7	2.1	trace	0.0	0.0	0.0	0.0	0.0	0.0	trace	1.2	7.5
Days With ≥ 1.0" Snow Depth	4	2	1	0	0	0	0	0	0	0	0	1	8

Stillwater 2 W *Payne County*   Elevation: 892 ft.   Latitude: 36° 07' N   Longitude: 97° 06' W

	JAN	FEB	MAR	APR	MAY	JUN	JUL	AUG	SEP	OCT	NOV	DEC	YEAR
Mean Maximum Temp. (°F)	45.8	52.1	61.0	71.0	78.7	87.2	93.1	92.7	83.9	73.6	59.9	50.0	70.7
Mean Temp. (°F)	34.3	40.0	49.0	58.7	67.8	76.5	81.8	80.7	72.3	60.7	48.3	38.7	59.1
Mean Minimum Temp. (°F)	22.7	27.8	37.1	46.4	56.8	65.8	70.5	68.8	60.6	47.7	36.8	27.3	47.3
Extreme Maximum Temp. (°F)	81	92	93	104	101	105	112	109	108	97	87	78	112
Extreme Minimum Temp. (°F)	-11	-18	0	21	36	46	52	50	31	15	7	-15	-18
Days Maximum Temp. ≥ 90°F	0	0	0	1	2	12	23	22	9	1	0	0	70
Days Maximum Temp. ≤ 32°F	5	3	0	0	0	0	0	0	0	0	0	3	11
Days Minimum Temp. ≤ 32°F	27	19	11	2	0	0	0	0	0	2	11	23	95
Days Minimum Temp. ≤ 0°F	1	0	0	0	0	0	0	0	0	0	0	1	2
Heating Degree Days (base 65°F)	945	701	495	220	54	2	0	0	37	180	497	810	3,941
Cooling Degree Days (base 65°F)	0	1	7	39	148	359	532	505	269	50	5	1	1,916
Mean Precipitation (in.)	1.27	1.58	3.16	3.59	5.21	4.13	2.68	3.10	4.34	3.14	2.52	1.71	36.43
Days With ≥ 0.1" Precipitation	3	3	5	5	7	6	4	4	5	4	4	3	53
Days With ≥ 1.0" Precipitation	0	0	1	1	1	1	1	1	1	1	1	0	9
Mean Snowfall (in.)	2.8	2.1	1.6	trace	0.0	0.0	0.0	0.0	0.0	trace	0.3	1.9	8.7
Days With ≥ 1.0" Snow Depth	3	3	0	0	0	0	0	0	0	0	0	1	7

Stilwell 5 NNW *Adair County*   Elevation: 997 ft.   Latitude: 35° 54' N   Longitude: 94° 39' W

	JAN	FEB	MAR	APR	MAY	JUN	JUL	AUG	SEP	OCT	NOV	DEC	YEAR
Mean Maximum Temp. (°F)	47.0	53.2	61.9	71.1	77.6	85.1	90.9	90.1	82.4	72.5	59.9	50.5	70.2
Mean Temp. (°F)	36.7	42.2	50.6	59.4	66.9	74.7	79.7	78.6	71.6	61.1	49.7	40.5	59.3
Mean Minimum Temp. (°F)	26.3	31.1	39.3	47.7	56.2	64.2	68.5	67.1	60.7	49.6	39.4	30.4	48.4
Extreme Maximum Temp. (°F)	75	85	90	89	92	100	108	106	104	91	87	79	108
Extreme Minimum Temp. (°F)	-12	-9	3	22	34	41	47	47	31	24	5	-12	-12
Days Maximum Temp. ≥ 90°F	0	0	0	0	0	6	19	17	6	0	0	0	48
Days Maximum Temp. ≤ 32°F	4	2	0	0	0	0	0	0	0	0	0	2	8
Days Minimum Temp. ≤ 32°F	22	16	9	2	0	0	0	0	0	1	8	18	76
Days Minimum Temp. ≤ 0°F	1	0	0	0	0	0	0	0	0	0	0	0	1
Heating Degree Days (base 65°F)	872	638	447	199	53	3	0	0	32	164	457	754	3,619
Cooling Degree Days (base 65°F)	0	0	7	34	117	300	464	433	232	48	5	0	1,640
Mean Precipitation (in.)	2.37	2.74	4.54	4.88	5.94	4.80	3.14	3.59	5.19	4.32	4.83	3.60	49.94
Days With ≥ 0.1" Precipitation	4	5	7	7	8	7	5	5	7	5	6	5	71
Days With ≥ 1.0" Precipitation	1	1	1	1	2	2	1	1	2	1	2	1	16
Mean Snowfall (in.)	4.4	3.2	1.8	trace	0.0	0.0	0.0	0.0	0.0	trace	1.1	1.4	11.9
Days With ≥ 1.0" Snow Depth	6	4	1	0	0	0	0	0	0	0	1	2	14

Tahlequah *Cherokee County*   Elevation: 849 ft.   Latitude: 35° 56' N   Longitude: 94° 58' W

	JAN	FEB	MAR	APR	MAY	JUN	JUL	AUG	SEP	OCT	NOV	DEC	YEAR
Mean Maximum Temp. (°F)	48.0	53.9	63.4	72.7	79.3	86.5	92.2	92.3	84.2	73.8	61.0	51.3	71.5
Mean Temp. (°F)	37.1	41.9	51.3	60.4	68.1	75.5	80.3	79.9	72.5	62.0	50.2	40.7	60.0
Mean Minimum Temp. (°F)	26.1	30.4	39.3	48.0	56.8	64.6	68.6	67.5	60.9	49.9	39.3	30.0	48.5
Extreme Maximum Temp. (°F)	76	88	92	93	97	100	110	106	107	94	86	80	110
Extreme Minimum Temp. (°F)	-13	-11	5	21	33	42	45	48	28	20	9	-14	-14
Days Maximum Temp. ≥ 90°F	0	0	0	0	0	9	22	22	8	0	0	0	61
Days Maximum Temp. ≤ 32°F	3	2	0	0	0	0	0	0	0	0	0	2	7
Days Minimum Temp. ≤ 32°F	23	16	9	2	0	0	0	0	0	1	9	18	78
Days Minimum Temp. ≤ 0°F	1	0	0	0	0	0	0	0	0	0	0	0	1
Heating Degree Days (base 65°F)	859	645	426	180	44	2	0	0	29	149	444	748	3,526
Cooling Degree Days (base 65°F)	0	0	9	41	138	326	491	474	250	52	5	1	1,787
Mean Precipitation (in.)	2.28	2.36	4.15	4.20	5.57	4.89	3.38	3.31	5.66	4.64	4.53	3.16	48.13
Days With ≥ 0.1" Precipitation	4	4	6	6	8	7	4	5	7	5	6	5	67
Days With ≥ 1.0" Precipitation	1	1	1	1	2	1	1	1	2	1	1	1	14
Mean Snowfall (in.)	2.4	1.6	0.7	0.0	0.0	0.0	0.0	0.0	0.0	trace	0.6	1.0	6.3
Days With ≥ 1.0" Snow Depth	3	1	0	0	0	0	0	0	0	0	0	1	5

Taloga *Dewey County*   Elevation: 1,702 ft.   Latitude: 36° 02' N   Longitude: 98° 58' W

	JAN	FEB	MAR	APR	MAY	JUN	JUL	AUG	SEP	OCT	NOV	DEC	YEAR
Mean Maximum Temp. (°F)	47.9	54.3	62.9	72.2	80.4	89.9	95.8	93.9	85.3	74.4	59.9	50.5	72.3
Mean Temp. (°F)	34.9	40.6	49.0	58.1	67.1	76.9	82.0	80.3	72.2	60.3	46.8	37.7	58.8
Mean Minimum Temp. (°F)	21.8	26.8	35.0	43.9	53.9	63.9	68.1	66.7	59.0	46.2	33.6	24.8	45.3
Extreme Maximum Temp. (°F)	81	91	93	99	103	110	111	108	105	98	89	79	111
Extreme Minimum Temp. (°F)	-15	-17	3	17	30	44	49	47	30	9	4	-16	-17
Days Maximum Temp. ≥ 90°F	0	0	0	1	4	17	27	24	12	1	0	0	86
Days Maximum Temp. ≤ 32°F	5	2	0	0	0	0	0	0	0	0	0	2	9
Days Minimum Temp. ≤ 32°F	27	20	12	3	0	0	0	0	0	3	15	25	105
Days Minimum Temp. ≤ 0°F	1	0	0	0	0	0	0	0	0	0	0	1	2
Heating Degree Days (base 65°F)	925	683	495	230	61	3	0	0	33	186	541	841	3,998
Cooling Degree Days (base 65°F)	0	0	4	28	129	364	535	491	256	43	1	0	1,851
Mean Precipitation (in.)	0.80	1.02	2.13	2.91	4.95	3.59	2.27	2.61	2.91	2.37	1.94	0.98	28.48
Days With ≥ 0.1" Precipitation	2	2	4	5	6	6	3	4	4	3	3	2	44
Days With ≥ 1.0" Precipitation	0	0	1	1	2	1	1	1	1	1	0	0	9
Mean Snowfall (in.)	4.1	4.0	1.8	0.6	0.0	0.0	0.0	0.0	0.0	trace	1.6	3.7	15.8
Days With ≥ 1.0" Snow Depth	4	4	1	0	0	0	0	0	0	0	1	3	13

Tuskahoma *Pushmataha County*   Elevation: 597 ft.   Latitude: 34° 38' N   Longitude: 95° 17' W

	JAN	FEB	MAR	APR	MAY	JUN	JUL	AUG	SEP	OCT	NOV	DEC	YEAR
Mean Maximum Temp. (°F)	52.5	58.6	67.2	75.4	81.4	88.4	94.4	94.4	86.7	77.0	64.1	55.5	74.6
Mean Temp. (°F)	40.6	45.8	54.1	62.2	69.7	77.2	82.1	81.4	74.5	63.7	52.4	43.8	62.3
Mean Minimum Temp. (°F)	28.7	32.9	41.1	49.0	58.0	66.0	69.7	68.2	62.1	50.4	40.5	32.2	49.9
Extreme Maximum Temp. (°F)	78	87	93	95	96	103	112	110	112	97	86	80	112
Extreme Minimum Temp. (°F)	-13	-4	5	21	35	40	47	47	32	18	7	-10	-13
Days Maximum Temp. ≥ 90°F	0	0	0	0	1	13	25	25	12	2	0	0	78
Days Maximum Temp. ≤ 32°F	2	1	0	0	0	0	0	0	0	0	0	1	4
Days Minimum Temp. ≤ 32°F	20	15	8	2	0	0	0	0	0	2	9	17	73
Days Minimum Temp. ≤ 0°F	0	0	0	0	0	0	0	0	0	0	0	0	0
Heating Degree Days (base 65°F)	749	540	349	142	30	1	0	0	21	124	386	651	2,993
Cooling Degree Days (base 65°F)	1	3	19	60	183	379	543	527	312	89	14	2	2,132
Mean Precipitation (in.)	2.41	2.84	4.19	4.86	6.72	5.08	3.70	2.80	5.18	4.97	4.54	3.23	50.52
Days With ≥ 0.1" Precipitation	4	4	6	7	8	7	5	4	6	6	6	5	68
Days With ≥ 1.0" Precipitation	1	1	1	2	2	2	1	1	2	2	2	1	18
Mean Snowfall (in.)	1.9	1.5	0.2	0.0	0.0	0.0	0.0	0.0	0.0	trace	0.2	0.3	4.1
Days With ≥ 1.0" Snow Depth	2	1	0	0	0	0	0	0	0	0	0	0	3

Vinita 2 N *Craig County*   Elevation: 734 ft.   Latitude: 36° 40' N   Longitude: 95° 08' W

	JAN	FEB	MAR	APR	MAY	JUN	JUL	AUG	SEP	OCT	NOV	DEC	YEAR
Mean Maximum Temp. (°F)	44.6	51.5	61.4	71.1	77.9	86.1	91.8	91.6	83.3	72.6	59.2	48.9	70.0
Mean Temp. (°F)	34.1	40.1	49.4	58.9	66.8	75.4	80.3	79.3	71.6	60.3	48.3	38.4	58.6
Mean Minimum Temp. (°F)	23.6	28.5	37.3	46.6	55.6	64.6	68.8	66.8	59.9	47.9	37.4	27.7	47.1
Extreme Maximum Temp. (°F)	75	86	90	98	93	101	107	111	105	94	84	75	111
Extreme Minimum Temp. (°F)	-17	-19	1	20	32	41	45	46	30	15	3	-14	-19
Days Maximum Temp. ≥ 90°F	0	0	0	0	0	8	20	20	8	0	0	0	56
Days Maximum Temp. ≤ 32°F	5	3	0	0	0	0	0	0	0	0	0	3	11
Days Minimum Temp. ≤ 32°F	24	18	11	2	0	0	0	0	0	2	11	21	89
Days Minimum Temp. ≤ 0°F	1	0	0	0	0	0	0	0	0	0	0	1	2
Heating Degree Days (base 65°F)	952	699	484	212	54	2	0	0	34	184	498	819	3,938
Cooling Degree Days (base 65°F)	0	1	6	34	119	336	500	466	247	43	6	0	1,758
Mean Precipitation (in.)	1.84	2.00	3.94	4.06	5.42	4.44	3.15	3.28	5.58	4.06	4.42	2.84	45.03
Days With ≥ 0.1" Precipitation	4	4	6	6	8	6	4	4	6	5	5	4	62
Days With ≥ 1.0" Precipitation	0	0	1	1	2	1	1	1	2	1	1	1	12
Mean Snowfall (in.)	4.6	2.8	2.4	trace	0.0	0.0	0.0	0.0	0.0	trace	0.6	1.8	12.2
Days With ≥ 1.0" Snow Depth	5	3	1	0	0	0	0	0	0	0	0	2	11

Wagoner *Wagoner County* Elevation: 587 ft. Latitude: 35° 58' N Longitude: 95° 22' W

	JAN	FEB	MAR	APR	MAY	JUN	JUL	AUG	SEP	OCT	NOV	DEC	YEAR
Mean Maximum Temp. (°F)	47.5	54.0	63.7	73.0	79.3	86.9	92.8	92.3	84.0	73.8	61.0	51.8	71.7
Mean Temp. (°F)	37.1	42.9	52.0	61.1	68.9	76.8	81.9	81.0	73.3	62.5	50.7	41.7	60.8
Mean Minimum Temp. (°F)	26.8	31.7	40.3	49.3	58.4	66.7	71.0	69.6	62.6	51.2	40.3	31.1	49.9
Extreme Maximum Temp. (°F)	76	87	94	95	93	100	109	108	108	94	84	78	109
Extreme Minimum Temp. (°F)	-9	-8	6	19	36	49	50	51	33	20	8	-11	-11
Days Maximum Temp. ≥ 90°F	0	0	0	0	1	10	23	22	8	1	0	0	65
Days Maximum Temp. ≤ 32°F	4	2	0	0	0	0	0	0	0	0	0	2	8
Days Minimum Temp. ≤ 32°F	22	15	8	1	0	0	0	0	0	1	7	17	71
Days Minimum Temp. ≤ 0°F	1	0	0	0	0	0	0	0	0	0	0	0	1
Heating Degree Days (base 65°F)	857	620	408	162	34	1	0	0	24	138	431	717	3,392
Cooling Degree Days (base 65°F)	0	1	12	50	165	373	543	518	285	66	9	1	2,023
Mean Precipitation (in.)	1.94	2.17	3.60	4.40	5.39	5.19	2.86	2.94	5.15	4.41	4.12	2.86	45.03
Days With ≥ 0.1" Precipitation	4	4	6	6	7	7	4	4	6	5	5	4	62
Days With ≥ 1.0" Precipitation	0	1	1	1	1	2	1	1	1	1	1	1	12
Mean Snowfall (in.)	3.1	2.0	1.3	trace	0.0	0.0	0.0	0.0	0.0	trace	0.3	0.7	7.4
Days With ≥ 1.0" Snow Depth	4	2	1	0	0	0	0	0	0	0	0	1	8

Watonga *Blaine County* Elevation: 1,548 ft. Latitude: 35° 51' N Longitude: 98° 25' W

	JAN	FEB	MAR	APR	MAY	JUN	JUL	AUG	SEP	OCT	NOV	DEC	YEAR
Mean Maximum Temp. (°F)	47.0	53.3	62.1	71.8	79.9	89.0	94.4	93.0	84.7	73.7	59.3	49.8	71.5
Mean Temp. (°F)	35.9	41.4	49.9	59.3	68.3	77.4	82.5	81.1	73.0	61.6	48.0	38.8	59.8
Mean Minimum Temp. (°F)	24.6	29.4	37.5	46.8	56.6	65.7	70.5	69.1	61.2	49.4	36.7	27.8	47.9
Extreme Maximum Temp. (°F)	81	91	90	99	103	108	109	109	105	99	88	77	109
Extreme Minimum Temp. (°F)	-10	-15	5	19	35	46	50	52	33	13	7	-14	-15
Days Maximum Temp. ≥ 90°F	0	0	0	1	3	15	25	23	10	1	0	0	78
Days Maximum Temp. ≤ 32°F	5	2	0	0	0	0	0	0	0	0	0	2	9
Days Minimum Temp. ≤ 32°F	25	17	10	2	0	0	0	0	0	1	11	21	87
Days Minimum Temp. ≤ 0°F	1	0	0	0	0	0	0	0	0	0	0	0	1
Heating Degree Days (base 65°F)	896	660	470	207	47	2	0	0	29	160	506	804	3,781
Cooling Degree Days (base 65°F)	0	0	7	41	158	383	558	517	283	59	3	0	2,009
Mean Precipitation (in.)	1.08	1.35	2.65	2.87	4.86	3.60	2.51	2.82	3.10	2.49	2.06	1.43	30.82
Days With ≥ 0.1" Precipitation	2	3	4	4	7	6	4	4	4	3	3	3	47
Days With ≥ 1.0" Precipitation	0	0	1	1	1	1	1	1	1	1	0	0	8
Mean Snowfall (in.)	3.2	3.3	1.1	0.5	0.0	0.0	0.0	0.0	0.0	trace	1.0	2.9	12.0
Days With ≥ 1.0" Snow Depth	3	3	1	0	0	0	0	0	0	0	0	2	9

Waurika *Jefferson County* Elevation: 872 ft. Latitude: 34° 10' N Longitude: 98° 00' W

	JAN	FEB	MAR	APR	MAY	JUN	JUL	AUG	SEP	OCT	NOV	DEC	YEAR
Mean Maximum Temp. (°F)	53.5	59.8	68.6	76.4	83.7	91.5	96.9	95.8	88.1	78.3	65.1	56.8	76.2
Mean Temp. (°F)	41.0	46.7	55.0	63.2	71.6	79.5	84.3	83.1	75.7	65.2	52.8	44.5	63.5
Mean Minimum Temp. (°F)	28.4	33.4	41.3	50.0	59.4	67.5	71.6	70.3	63.4	52.2	40.3	32.0	50.8
Extreme Maximum Temp. (°F)	83	93	97	99	108	115	112	110	109	100	87	81	115
Extreme Minimum Temp. (°F)	-6	-8	5	21	33	48	51	53	36	19	10	-10	-10
Days Maximum Temp. ≥ 90°F	0	0	0	1	6	19	28	27	14	3	0	0	98
Days Maximum Temp. ≤ 32°F	2	1	0	0	0	0	0	0	0	0	0	1	4
Days Minimum Temp. ≤ 32°F	20	13	6	1	0	0	0	0	0	1	7	17	65
Days Minimum Temp. ≤ 0°F	0	0	0	0	0	0	0	0	0	0	0	0	0
Heating Degree Days (base 65°F)	739	513	325	120	17	0	0	0	15	95	371	632	2,827
Cooling Degree Days (base 65°F)	1	2	18	71	237	444	615	587	358	108	11	1	2,453
Mean Precipitation (in.)	1.24	1.72	2.68	2.89	4.71	3.62	1.79	2.43	3.44	2.98	1.75	1.80	31.05
Days With ≥ 0.1" Precipitation	2	3	4	4	5	4	3	4	5	4	3	3	44
Days With ≥ 1.0" Precipitation	0	0	1	1	2	1	1	1	1	1	1	1	11
Mean Snowfall (in.)	*1.3*	*0.9*	0.5	trace	0.0	0.0	0.0	0.0	0.0	trace	0.1	0.4	*3.2*
Days With ≥ 1.0" Snow Depth	*0*	na	0	0	0	0	0	0	0	0	0	*0*	na

Waynoka 3 S *Woods County* Elevation: 1,528 ft. Latitude: 36° 35' N Longitude: 98° 51' W

	JAN	FEB	MAR	APR	MAY	JUN	JUL	AUG	SEP	OCT	NOV	DEC	YEAR
Mean Maximum Temp. (°F)	47.2	54.0	63.1	73.3	81.2	90.4	96.0	94.1	86.0	75.1	60.4	50.0	72.5
Mean Temp. (°F)	34.6	40.4	49.3	59.0	68.3	77.6	80.9	72.9	59.9	61.0	47.2	37.8	59.3
Mean Minimum Temp. (°F)	22.0	26.8	35.4	44.6	55.4	64.8	69.7	67.9	59.9	46.8	33.9	24.8	46.0
Extreme Maximum Temp. (°F)	83	90	93	99	104	111	112	109	108	100	91	81	112
Extreme Minimum Temp. (°F)	-14	-11	4	20	31	44	48	45	30	8	5	-14	-14
Days Maximum Temp. ≥ 90°F	0	0	0	1	5	17	26	23	12	2	0	0	86
Days Maximum Temp. ≤ 32°F	5	3	0	0	0	0	0	0	0	0	0	3	11
Days Minimum Temp. ≤ 32°F	27	20	12	3	0	0	0	0	0	2	13	25	102
Days Minimum Temp. ≤ 0°F	1	0	0	0	0	0	0	0	0	0	0	1	2
Heating Degree Days (base 65°F)	935	687	488	217	49	2	0	0	30	178	531	856	3,973
Cooling Degree Days (base 65°F)	0	1	5	37	157	376	558	498	275	51	2	0	1,960
Mean Precipitation (in.)	0.72	1.02	2.11	2.43	4.63	3.02	2.55	2.83	2.74	2.05	1.58	0.95	26.63
Days With ≥ 0.1" Precipitation	2	2	4	4	6	5	4	4	4	3	3	2	43
Days With ≥ 1.0" Precipitation	0	0	1	1	2	1	1	1	1	0	0	0	8
Mean Snowfall (in.)	2.6	*3.7*	2.3	0.2	0.0	0.0	0.0	0.0	0.0	0.0	0.9	2.3	*12.0*
Days With ≥ 1.0" Snow Depth	*2*	*2*	1	0	0	0	0	0	0	0	0	1	*6*

Weatherford *Custer County*   Elevation: 1,640 ft.   Latitude: 35° 31' N   Longitude: 98° 42' W

	JAN	FEB	MAR	APR	MAY	JUN	JUL	AUG	SEP	OCT	NOV	DEC	YEAR
Mean Maximum Temp. (°F)	47.1	53.9	62.7	72.2	80.9	90.0	95.7	94.1	85.3	74.6	59.9	50.0	72.2
Mean Temp. (°F)	35.8	41.7	50.1	59.3	68.7	77.8	82.9	81.4	73.1	61.7	48.4	38.8	60.0
Mean Minimum Temp. (°F)	24.5	29.5	37.3	46.3	56.5	65.5	70.1	68.7	60.8	48.9	36.8	27.5	47.7
Extreme Maximum Temp. (°F)	81	89	93	100	108	112	110	109	109	99	89	79	112
Extreme Minimum Temp. (°F)	-7	-4	11	22	36	48	54	51	33	18	9	-10	-10
Days Maximum Temp. ≥ 90°F	0	0	0	1	5	17	27	24	11	1	0	0	86
Days Maximum Temp. ≤ 32°F	5	2	0	0	0	0	0	0	0	0	0	3	10
Days Minimum Temp. ≤ 32°F	25	17	9	1	0	0	0	0	0	1	10	22	85
Days Minimum Temp. ≤ 0°F	0	0	0	0	0	0	0	0	0	0	0	1	1
Heating Degree Days (base 65°F)	899	651	462	204	43	3	0	1	32	156	494	806	3,751
Cooling Degree Days (base 65°F)	0	0	5	33	157	381	560	519	277	53	3	0	1,988
Mean Precipitation (in.)	0.97	1.12	2.18	2.50	5.02	3.88	2.07	2.75	3.41	2.60	1.73	1.22	29.45
Days With ≥ 0.1" Precipitation	2	3	4	5	6	5	3	4	4	3	3	3	45
Days With ≥ 1.0" Precipitation	0	0	1	1	2	1	1	1	1	1	0	0	9
Mean Snowfall (in.)	*2.3*	*1.8*	0.4	0.1	0.0	0.0	0.0	0.0	0.0	0.1	0.4	*1.7*	*6.8*
Days With ≥ 1.0" Snow Depth	*2*	*1*	0	0	0	0	0	0	0	0	0	*2*	*5*

Webbers Falls 5 WSW *Muskogee County*   Elevation: 547 ft.   Latitude: 35° 29' N   Longitude: 95° 12' W

	JAN	FEB	MAR	APR	MAY	JUN	JUL	AUG	SEP	OCT	NOV	DEC	YEAR
Mean Maximum Temp. (°F)	46.7	53.4	62.5	72.2	79.2	87.5	93.2	92.4	84.7	74.5	61.3	51.9	71.6
Mean Temp. (°F)	35.6	41.5	50.5	59.7	68.0	76.6	81.4	80.3	73.0	61.4	49.7	40.7	59.8
Mean Minimum Temp. (°F)	24.5	29.6	38.2	47.0	56.8	65.5	69.5	68.0	61.2	48.4	38.0	29.3	48.0
Extreme Maximum Temp. (°F)	76	92	91	95	95	101	109	109	112	95	85	80	112
Extreme Minimum Temp. (°F)	-15	-4	2	25	37	45	50	50	35	19	9	-11	-15
Days Maximum Temp. ≥ 90°F	0	0	0	0	1	13	24	21	9	1	0	0	69
Days Maximum Temp. ≤ 32°F	4	2	0	0	0	0	0	0	0	0	0	1	7
Days Minimum Temp. ≤ 32°F	25	17	9	2	0	0	0	0	0	1	9	20	83
Days Minimum Temp. ≤ 0°F	1	0	0	0	0	0	0	0	0	0	0	0	1
Heating Degree Days (base 65°F)	901	658	448	193	46	1	0	0	28	159	458	747	3,639
Cooling Degree Days (base 65°F)	0	1	7	35	147	359	518	492	279	54	5	0	1,897
Mean Precipitation (in.)	2.23	2.54	4.26	4.39	5.44	4.32	2.68	2.99	5.58	4.62	4.25	3.13	46.43
Days With ≥ 0.1" Precipitation	4	4	6	7	7	6	4	4	7	5	5	5	64
Days With ≥ 1.0" Precipitation	1	1	1	1	2	1	1	1	2	1	2	1	15
Mean Snowfall (in.)	*3.4*	*1.6*	1.2	0.0	0.0	0.0	0.0	0.0	0.0	trace	0.3	*0.4*	*6.9*
Days With ≥ 1.0" Snow Depth	na	na	0	0	0	0	0	0	0	0	0	0	na

Wichita Mtn Wildlife Refuge *Comanche County*   Elevation: 1,663 ft.   Latitude: 34° 44' N   Longitude: 98° 43' W

	JAN	FEB	MAR	APR	MAY	JUN	JUL	AUG	SEP	OCT	NOV	DEC	YEAR
Mean Maximum Temp. (°F)	49.2	55.5	64.1	73.1	80.8	89.2	95.1	93.7	85.4	75.5	61.5	52.3	73.0
Mean Temp. (°F)	36.6	42.6	50.8	59.6	68.4	77.0	82.3	80.7	72.6	61.8	48.8	39.8	60.1
Mean Minimum Temp. (°F)	24.0	29.6	37.5	46.0	56.0	64.6	69.3	67.6	59.8	48.2	36.0	27.3	47.2
Extreme Maximum Temp. (°F)	80	88	97	99	104	111	110	109	106	101	90	80	111
Extreme Minimum Temp. (°F)	-6	-4	1	19	33	42	46	48	34	17	10	-2	-6
Days Maximum Temp. ≥ 90°F	0	0	0	1	4	15	26	24	11	1	0	0	82
Days Maximum Temp. ≤ 32°F	4	2	0	0	0	0	0	0	0	0	0	2	8
Days Minimum Temp. ≤ 32°F	26	18	9	2	0	0	0	0	0	1	11	22	89
Days Minimum Temp. ≤ 0°F	0	0	0	0	0	0	0	0	0	0	0	0	0
Heating Degree Days (base 65°F)	873	626	441	198	43	2	0	1	33	153	486	777	3,633
Cooling Degree Days (base 65°F)	0	0	7	36	149	353	541	500	261	53	3	0	1,903
Mean Precipitation (in.)	1.40	1.57	2.76	2.87	5.14	3.83	2.42	2.51	4.17	3.02	2.24	1.55	33.48
Days With ≥ 0.1" Precipitation	2	3	4	4	6	5	4	4	4	4	3	3	46
Days With ≥ 1.0" Precipitation	0	0	1	1	2	1	1	1	1	1	1	1	11
Mean Snowfall (in.)	*0.9*	*0.9*	0.2	0.0	0.0	0.0	0.0	0.0	0.0	trace	trace	0.4	*2.4*
Days With ≥ 1.0" Snow Depth	*1*	*1*	0	0	0	0	0	0	0	0	0	*0*	*2*

Note: See Appendix D for explanation of data.

OREGON

PHYSICAL FEATURES AND GENERAL CLIMATE. Oregon enjoys a mild though varied climate with only a rare occurrence of devastating weather elements. The single most important geographic feature of the climate of Oregon is the Pacific Ocean whose coastline makes up the western border. Because of the normal movement of air masses from west to east, most of the systems moving across Oregon have been modified extensively in traveling over the Pacific. As a result, winter minimum and summer maximum temperatures in the west, and to a lesser extent in the eastern portion, are greatly moderated. The occurrence of extreme low or high temperatures is generally associated with the occasional invasion of the continental air masses. The unlimited supply of moisture available to those air masses that move across the Pacific is largely responsible for the abundant rainfall over western Oregon and the higher elevations of the eastern portion.

Beginning near and following the coast the full length of the State, the Coast Range is the farthest west of the three mountain ranges that exert an important influence on Oregon's climate. This range, disrupts the path of the moisture laden marine air moving in from the Pacific, forcing it to rise as it moves eastward. The resultant cooling and condensation produces some of the heaviest annual rainfalls in the United States along the higher western slopes, and materially reduces the available moisture in the air.

The Cascade Mountains parallel the Coast Range about 75 miles to the east. The Cascades rise from the broad valley of the Willamette eastward to an average height of about 5,000 feet, with a few peaks over 10,000 feet. One of these, Mount Hood, at an elevation of 11,245 feet, is the highest point in the State. Once again, the air masses from the west are forced to ascend causing them to give up additional moisture. The rain potential of the marine air, however, was greatly reduced by passage over the Coast Range; therefore, the rainfall on the west slopes of the Cascades at a corresponding elevation is only about one-half to two-thirds as great as on the Coast Range. Precipitation amounts decrease rapidly once the crest is crossed and descent down the eastward side begins.

Cutting through both the Cascade and the Coast Ranges, the Columbia River Gorge offers ready passage of marine air from the Pacific. Temperatures are moderated to the east in both summer and winter. Continental air occasionally passes in reverse and produces the more extreme low temperatures in the western valleys. Winding through the rugged terrain that makes up much of Oregon are the Columbia and Snake River Basins, the valleys of the many streams that head in the mountains and several very wide plateau regions. The Columbia Plateau covers about two-thirds of the State's total area and extends from the eastern border westward to the eastern slopes of the Cascade Mountains and from the southern border north to the Columbia River. Its elevation ranges from 4,000 to 6,000 feet and because of its arid nature and scant vegetation, summer heating and winter cooling often become extreme.

TEMPERATURE. Few states have greater temperature extremes than Oregon. The most extreme temperatures generally occur east of the Cascades. In the coastal sections they never drop as low as zero and on very few occasions pass the 100°F. mark. Here the mean of the coldest month, January, is 45°F., only 15 less than that of July, the warmest month. In the Willamette Valley, mean temperatures average 38°F. in January and 66°F. in July. In the inland valleys of the southwest the average summer temperatures are about 5 higher than in the northwest and maximums of 90°F. or more occur 40 to 50 days a year. In south-central Oregon the median annual maximum temperatures over a period of years have been between 95 and 100°F.; in most other areas east of the Cascades this variance is between 100 and 105°F. Median annual minimum temperatures for eastern Oregon vary from near zero in the more protected areas of the Columbia Basin to -26°F. in the high mountain and plateau regions.

PRECIPITATION. The average annual rainfall in Oregon varies from less than 8 inches in drier Plateau Regions to as much as 200 inches at points along the upper west slopes of the Coast Range. The State as a whole has a very definite winter rainfall climate. West of the Cascades about one-half of the annual total precipitation falls from December through February, about one-fourth in the spring and fall, and very little during the summer months. East of the Cascades the differences are not as pronounced, with slightly more precipitation in winter than in spring and fall, while only about 10 percent falls during the summer. Along the coast the normal annual total is from 75 to 90 inches, and increases up the west slopes of the Coast Range to almost 200 inches near the crest. Amounts decrease on the eastern slopes and in the Willamette Valley. On the western slopes of the Cascades there is again a marked increase in precipitation with elevation as annual averages range up to 75 inches. Amounts decrease rapidly on the east side. The annual average precipitation for the great plateau of the State is often less than 8 inches. In the Columbia River Basin and the Blue Mountains, totals are about 15 to 20 inches; however, some of the mountain regions receive as much as 35 inches.

SNOWFALL. In the high Cascades, where the State's heaviest snowfalls occur, it appears that annual average totals can range from 300 to 550 inches. Winter precipitation along the Coast Range, due to its lower elevations, occurs largely in the form of rain, although it too is occasionally subject to very heavy snows. In the Blue Mountains, seasonal totals range between 150 to 300 inches and depths on the ground may occasionally exceed 120 inches. The periods of continuous snow cover vary with elevation. On the peaks of the Cascades higher than 7,000 feet above sea level, it persists in glacial form the year around. In most mountain areas above 4,500 feet, snow cover lasts from early December until the latter part of April. Along the coast the average annual snowfall is only one to three inches, with many years in which there is no measurable amount.

STORMS. Hailstorms occur each year, but are generally light and cover very small areas. Practically all of these storms occur east of the Cascades. In the western part of the State thunderstorms occur in the valleys an average of 4 or 5 days a year and are not usually severe. In the eastern part, they occur on 12 to 15 days with heavier precipitation and greater wind damage. It is in the mountain areas that these storms occur most frequently and each year many forest fires are started by the accompanying lightning.

Several times each year winds of hurricane force (74 m.p.h. and over) strike the Oregon coast. They sometimes move inland to the western valleys and up the Columbia Gorge. The few tornadoes reported have been short lived. The prevailing wind direction is influenced by the surrounding terrain. In the Columbia Gorge the prevailing direction of the wind follows the orientation of the gorge at that point. Similarly, in the Willamette Valley prevailing directions are aligned north-south with the valley. The very strong winds, of course, are determined by the direction of the major storm movements.

FLOODS. Most of the State is drained into the Pacific Ocean through the Columbia River. The Snake River makes up more than half of Oregon's eastern border and drains practically all of the State east of the Blue Mountains. The west slope of the Coast Range and all areas south of the Willamette Basin and west of the summit of the Cascades are drained directly into the Pacific Ocean by three large river systems — the Umpqua, Rogue and Smith Rivers. The only major river draining south central Oregon is the Klamath. The remainder of the area lying south of the Deschutes and John Day Basins and between the Cascades and the Blue Mountains has only internal drainage into brackish lakes. Many of these lakes become dry during the summer months.

Major flooding in the Willamette Basin and the coastal streams may result from several days of moderate to heavy rain extending over the entire Basin. When combined with sharply rising air temperatures and a warm southerly wind, the melting of a heavy snowpack on the middle and upper slopes of the Coast Range and/or the Cascades greatly increases the flood potential. Flooding in the main channel of the Columbia River usually occurs during late spring and early summer when snow melt in the mountains is most rapid. Simultaneous occurrences of heavy, warm rain over large parts of the Columbia Basin have, on occasion, produced some very damaging floods.

During the early morning hours the relative humidity is greatest and there is little variation at this time between winter and summer readings in eastern and western Oregon. In contrast, the afternoon averages, when the relative humidities are least, show a very marked difference between summer and winter and also between the areas east and west of the Cascades.

SUNSHINE. The north coastal area has the least sunshine, while the southeast corner of the State has the most. The sun shines about 20 percent of the time possible in the coastal area and 45 percent of the time possible in the southeast. These values increase in April to values of 50 to 70 percent in July to 55 percent in the northwest and 90 percent in the southeast. By October they have declined to 40 and 65 percent respectively.

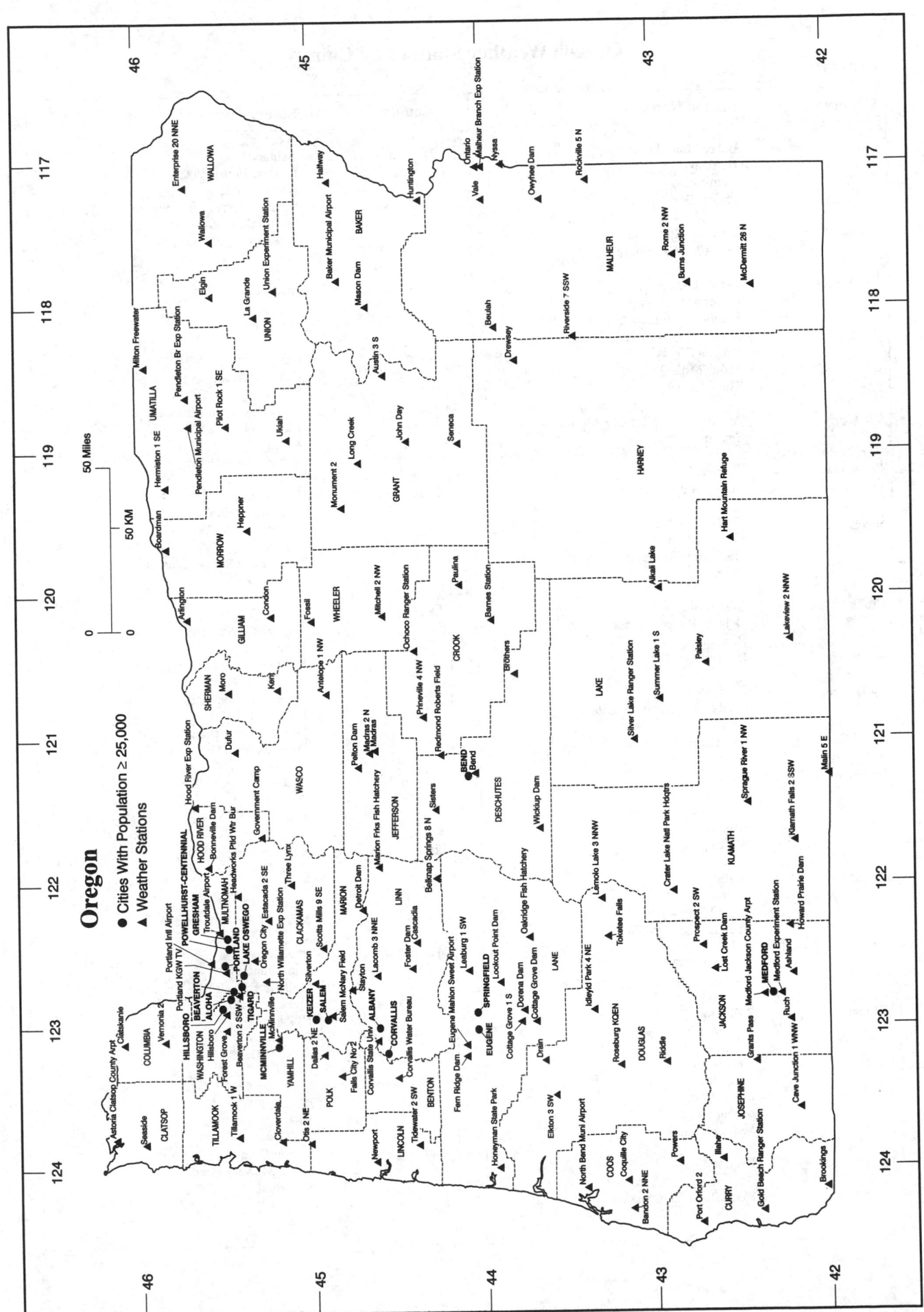

Oregon

● Cities With Population ≥ 25,000
▲ Weather Stations

Oregon Weather Stations by County

County	Station Name
Baker	Baker Municipal Airport
	Halfway
	Huntington
	Mason Dam
Benton	Corvallis State Univ
	Corvallis Water Bureau
Clackamas	Estacada 2 SE
	Government Camp
	Headworks Ptld. Wtr. Bur.
	North Willamette Exp. Station
	Oregon City
	Scotts Mills 9 SE
	Three Lynx
Clatsop	Astoria Clatsop County Airport
	Seaside
Columbia	Clatskanie
	Vernonia 2
Coos	Bandon 2 NNE
	Coquille City
	North Bend Municipal Airport
	Powers
Crook	Barnes Station
	Ochoco Ranger Station
	Paulina
	Prineville 4 NW
Curry	Brookings
	Gold Beach Ranger Station
	Illahe
	Port Orford 2
Deschutes	Bend
	Brothers
	Redmond Roberts Field
	Sisters
	Wickiup Dam
Douglas	Drain
	Elkton 3 SW
	Idleyld Park 4 NE
	Lemolo Lake 3 NNW
	Riddle
	Roseburg KQEN
	Toketee Falls
Gilliam	Arlington
	Condon
Grant	Austin 3 S
	John Day
	Long Creek
	Monument 2
	Seneca
Harney	Drewsey
Hood River	Hood River Exp. Station

County	Station Name
Jackson	Ashland
	Howard Prairie Dam
	Lost Creek Dam
	Medford Experiment Station
	Medford Jackson County Airport
	Prospect 2 SW
	Ruch
Jefferson	Madras
	Madras 2 N
	Pelton Dam
Josephine	Cave Junction 1 WNW
	Grants Pass
Klamath	Crater Lake Nat'l Park Hdqtrs.
	Klamath Falls 2 SSW
	Malin 5 E
	Sprague River 1 NW
Lake	Alkali Lake
	Hart Mountain Refuge
	Lakeview 2 NNW
	Paisley
	Silver Lake Ranger Station
	Summer Lake 1 S
Lane	Cottage Grove 1 S
	Cottage Grove Dam
	Dorena Dam
	Eugene Mahlon Sweet Airport
	Fern Ridge Dam
	Honeyman State Park
	Leaburg 1 SW
	Lookout Point Dam
	Oakridge Fish Hatchery
Lincoln	Newport
	Otis 2 NE
	Tidewater 2 SW
Linn	Belknap Springs 8 N
	Cascadia
	Foster Dam
	Lacomb 3 NNE
	Marion Frks. Fish Hatchery
Malheur	Beulah
	Burns Junction
	Malheur Branch Exp. Station
	McDermitt 26 N
	Nyssa
	Ontario
	Owyhee Dam
	Riverside 7 SSW
	Rockville 5 N
	Rome 2 NW
	Vale
Marion	Detroit Dam
	Salem McNary Field
	Silverton
	Stayton

County	Station Name
Morrow	Boardman
	Heppner
Multnomah	Bonneville Dam
	Portland Int'l Airport
	Portland KGW TV
	Troutdale Airport
Polk	Dallas 2 NE
	Falls City 2
Sherman	Kent
	Moro
Tillamook	Cloverdale
	Tillamook 1 W
Umatilla	Hermiston 1 SE
	Milton Freewater
	Pendleton Br. Exp. Station
	Pendleton Municipal Airport
	Pilot Rock 1 SE
	Ukiah
Union	Elgin
	La Grande
	Union Experiment Station
Wallowa	Enterprise 20 NNE
	Wallowa
Wasco	Antelope 1 NW
	Dufur
Washington	Beaverton 2 SSW
	Forest Grove
	Hillsboro
Wheeler	Fossil
	Mitchell 2 NW
Yamhill	McMinnville

Oregon Weather Stations by City

City	Station Name	Miles
Albany	Corvallis State Univ	5
	Corvallis Water Bureau	19
	Lacomb 3 NNE	18
	Salem McNary Field	20
	Stayton	17
Aloha	Beaverton 2 SSW	4
	Forest Grove	11
	Hillsboro	6
	North Willamette Exp. Station	15
	Oregon City	16
	Portland KGW TV	9
	Portland Int'l Airport	14
	Vancouver 4 NNE, WA	17
Beaverton	Beaverton 2 SSW	2
	Forest Grove	14
	Hillsboro	9
	North Willamette Exp. Station	13
	Oregon City	13
	Portland KGW TV	7
	Portland Int'l Airport	13
	Vancouver 4 NNE, WA	17
Bend	Bend	1
	Redmond Roberts Field	15
	Sisters	20
Corvallis	Corvallis State Univ	6
	Corvallis Water Bureau	9
Eugene	Cottage Grove 1 S	18
	Dorena Dam	20
	Eugene Mahlon Sweet Airport	7
	Fern Ridge Dam	11
	Lookout Point Dam	19
Gresham	Beaverton 2 SSW	18
	Estacada 2 SE	18
	Headworks Ptld. Wtr. Bur.	15
	Oregon City	13
	Portland KGW TV	12
	Portland Int'l Airport	11
	Troutdale Airport	4
	Battle Ground, WA	20
	Skamania Fish Hatchery, WA	13
	Vancouver 4 NNE, WA	16
Hillsboro	Beaverton 2 SSW	9
	Forest Grove	7
	Hillsboro	1
	North Willamette Exp. Station	19
	Portland KGW TV	13
	Portland Int'l Airport	18
	Vancouver 4 NNE, WA	19
Keizer	Dallas 2 NE	13
	McMinnville	17
	Salem McNary Field	7
	Silverton	13
	Stayton	18
Lake Oswego	Beaverton 2 SSW	6
	Hillsboro	15

City	Station Name	Miles
Lake Oswego (cont.)	North Willamette Exp. Station	9
	Oregon City	7
	Portland KGW TV	7
	Portland Int'l Airport	13
	Troutdale Airport	17
	Vancouver 4 NNE, WA	19
McMinnville	Dallas 2 NE	19
	McMinnville	2
Medford	Ashland	11
	Medford Experiment Station	2
	Medford Jackson County Airport	3
	Ruch	12
Portland	Beaverton 2 SSW	10
	Hillsboro	17
	North Willamette Exp. Station	17
	Oregon City	12
	Portland KGW TV	2
	Portland Int'l Airport	6
	Troutdale Airport	12
	Battle Ground, WA	19
	Vancouver 4 NNE, WA	11
Powellhurst-Centennial	Beaverton 2 SSW	15
	Estacada 2 SE	19
	Headworks Ptld. Wtr. Bur.	18
	North Willamette Exp. Station	19
	Oregon City	11
	Portland KGW TV	8
	Portland Int'l Airport	9
	Troutdale Airport	7
	Battle Ground, WA	20
	Skamania Fish Hatchery, WA	17
	Vancouver 4 NNE, WA	14
Salem	Dallas 2 NE	13
	Salem McNary Field	2
	Silverton	14
	Stayton	14
Springfield	Cottage Grove 1 S	18
	Dorena Dam	19
	Eugene Mahlon Sweet Airport	12
	Fern Ridge Dam	16
	Leaburg 1 SW	15
	Lookout Point Dam	14
Tigard	Beaverton 2 SSW	2
	Forest Grove	17
	Hillsboro	12
	North Willamette Exp. Station	10
	Oregon City	10
	Portland KGW TV	8
	Portland Int'l Airport	14
	Vancouver 4 NNE, WA	19

Note: Miles is the distance between the geographic center of the city and the weather station.

Oregon Weather Stations by Elevation

Feet	Station Name
6,473	Crater Lake Nat'l Park Hdqtrs.
5,613	Hart Mountain Refuge
4,776	Lakeview 2 NNW
4,658	Seneca
4,639	Brothers
4,625	Malin 5 E
4,566	Howard Prairie Dam
4,461	McDermitt 26 N
4,379	Silver Lake Ranger Station
4,356	Paisley
4,356	Wickiup Dam
4,330	Alkali Lake
4,304	Sprague River 1 NW
4,212	Austin 3 S
4,189	Summer Lake 1 S
4,097	Klamath Falls 2 SSW
4,074	Lemolo Lake 3 NNW
3,979	Government Camp
3,973	Ochoco Ranger Station
3,969	Barnes Station
3,927	Burns Junction
3,897	Mason Dam
3,717	Long Creek
3,681	Paulina
3,667	Rockville 5 N
3,595	Bend
3,513	Drewsey
3,402	Rome 2 NW
3,379	Riverside 7 SSW
3,366	Baker Municipal Airport
3,346	Ukiah
3,277	Enterprise 20 NNE
3,267	Beulah
3,179	Sisters
3,061	John Day
3,057	Redmond Roberts Field
2,919	Wallowa
2,837	Antelope 1 NW
2,837	Condon
2,837	Prineville 4 NW
2,762	Union Experiment Station
2,752	La Grande
2,709	Kent
2,664	Halfway
2,654	Elgin
2,647	Fossil
2,644	Mitchell 2 NW
2,480	Prospect 2 SW
2,473	Marion Frks. Fish Hatchery
2,437	Madras 2 N
2,398	Owyhee Dam
2,312	Scotts Mills 9 SE
2,257	Malheur Branch Exp. Station
2,237	Vale
2,227	Madras

Feet	Station Name
2,191	Ontario
2,171	Nyssa
2,148	Belknap Springs 8 N
2,109	Huntington
2,057	Toketee Falls
1,994	Monument 2
1,883	Heppner
1,870	Moro
1,722	Ashland
1,719	Pilot Rock 1 SE
1,578	Lost Creek Dam
1,509	Ruch
1,486	Pendleton Br. Exp. Station
1,479	Pendleton Municipal Airport
1,456	Medford Experiment Station
1,407	Pelton Dam
1,328	Dufur
1,299	Medford Jackson County Airport
1,279	Cave Junction 1 WNW
1,272	Oakridge Fish Hatchery
1,217	Detroit Dam
1,118	Three Lynx
1,079	Idleyld Park 4 NE
967	Milton Freewater
921	Grants Pass
859	Cascadia
830	Cottage Grove Dam
816	Dorena Dam
748	Headworks Ptld. Wtr. Bur.
711	Lookout Point Dam
679	Riddle
672	Leaburg 1 SW
639	Hermiston 1 SE
623	Vernonia 2
593	Cottage Grove 1 S
590	Corvallis Water Bureau
547	Foster Dam
518	Lacomb 3 NNE
498	Hood River Exp. Station
482	Fern Ridge Dam
449	Estacada 2 SE
423	Roseburg KQEN
423	Stayton
419	Falls City 2
406	Silverton
354	Eugene Mahlon Sweet Airport
347	Illahe
298	Boardman
291	Drain
288	Dallas 2 NE
275	Arlington
269	Beaverton 2 SSW
229	Powers
223	Corvallis State Univ
193	Salem McNary Field

Feet	Station Name
177	Forest Grove
164	Oregon City
157	Hillsboro
157	Portland KGW TV
154	McMinnville
147	North Willamette Exp. Station
147	Otis 2 NE
121	Newport
118	Elkton 3 SW
114	Honeyman State Park
59	Bonneville Dam
49	Gold Beach Ranger Station
45	Brookings
39	Port Orford 2
32	Tidewater 2 SW
26	Troutdale Airport
22	Coquille City
19	Bandon 2 NNE
19	Clatskanie
16	Portland Int'l Airport
9	Cloverdale
9	Seaside
9	Tillamook 1 W
6	Astoria Clatsop County Airport
3	North Bend Municipal Airport

Astoria Clatsop County Airport

Astoria is ringed by low mountains on the north, east, and south. On the west, the area is open to the Pacific Ocean at the mouth of the Columbia River. North of the station, eight to 12 miles distant, the Washington hills rise to 1,000 to 1,200 feet. Maximum visibility is 19 miles north-northeastward to the Willapa Hills. East-northeastward two to four miles, the Astoria hills rise to 600 feet. East-southeastward four to 14 miles, consecutively, rise other ridges of the Coast Ranges, and southeastward is the most prominent landmark, Saddle Mountain, 3,283 feet high. Forests cover most of the uplands. From Seaside northward to the south bank of the Columbia are 18 miles of sandy beaches, and a two to three mile wide stretch of dune lands.

The airport sits by the south bank of the Columbia estuary, west of Youngs Bay, on the flood plain or tidal flats. Low dikes prevent flooding and increase the bog-like characteristics of the area. When air temperature falls below water temperature, fog forms easily, or rolls in from the ocean, river, or bay. This usually begins from late afternoon to early morning, and may persist well into the following day. During the summer months, sea breezes commonly blow up the river by noon and stop the diurnal rise in temperature. In winter, cold air may funnel down the Columbia from the interior.

Weather hazards occasionally occur. Flying hazards, the greatest are fog and gales. Even with moderate surface velocities, wind and turbulence at 800 feet may be severe enough to upset a heavy plane. Heavy rains inundate lowlands, and high tides aggravated by gales may push seawater across highways or up beaches. Rains may cause earthslides, mostly in highway cuts. Lightning strikes are rare. Showers of ice pellets may briefly whiten the ground during many of the months. Occasionally in winter there may be rather brief periods of freezing temperatures, with snow or ice.

The climate is generally healthful, except for dampness and a lack of sunshine in winter. Heat waves are uncommon and usually brief. Soil leaching necessitates supplementary mineral diets for both animals and plants.

Astoria Clatsop County Airport *Clatsop County*   Elevation: 6 ft.   Latitude: 46° 09' N   Longitude: 123° 53' W

	JAN	FEB	MAR	APR	MAY	JUN	JUL	AUG	SEP	OCT	NOV	DEC	YEAR
Mean Maximum Temp. (°F)	48.5	51.3	53.6	56.3	60.5	64.1	67.7	68.9	67.8	61.1	53.5	48.6	58.5
Mean Temp. (°F)	42.6	44.4	46.1	48.5	52.9	57.0	60.3	61.0	58.6	52.6	47.0	42.8	51.1
Mean Minimum Temp. (°F)	36.7	37.5	38.5	40.6	45.3	49.8	52.8	53.1	49.3	43.9	40.4	36.9	43.7
Extreme Maximum Temp. (°F)	67	72	73	83	87	92	93	96	95	85	71	64	96
Extreme Minimum Temp. (°F)	11	9	22	30	31	37	39	39	33	26	19	6	6
Days Maximum Temp. ≥ 90°F	0	0	0	0	0	0	0	0	0	0	0	0	0
Days Maximum Temp. ≤ 32°F	0	0	0	0	0	0	0	0	0	0	0	1	1
Days Minimum Temp. ≤ 32°F	9	6	5	1	0	0	0	0	0	1	4	8	34
Days Minimum Temp. ≤ 0°F	0	0	0	0	0	0	0	0	0	0	0	0	0
Heating Degree Days (base 65°F)	688	573	579	488	369	237	145	124	192	380	534	682	4,991
Cooling Degree Days (base 65°F)	0	0	0	0	0	1	3	3	7	6	1	0	21
Mean Precipitation (in.)	9.71	7.88	7.33	5.06	3.20	2.47	1.16	1.19	2.66	5.65	10.70	10.74	67.75
Maximum Precipitation (in.)	18.9	21.9	13.5	9.5	6.6	5.5	4.4	5.2	6.9	12.6	17.5	16.6	87.4
Minimum Precipitation (in.)	0.7	1.3	0.9	1.3	0.4	0.5	trace	0.1	trace	0.5	1.4	2.7	41.6
Maximum 24-hr. Precipitation (in.)	4.5	2.8	2.5	2.7	1.7	2.1	1.7	1.6	2.4	3.5	3.7	3.6	4.5
Days With ≥ 0.1" Precipitation	16	14	15	12	9	6	3	3	6	10	17	16	127
Days With ≥ 1.0" Precipitation	2	2	2	1	0	0	0	0	0	1	3	4	15
Mean Snowfall (in.)	1.1	0.4	0.1	trace	trace	trace	0.0	0.0	trace	trace	0.2	0.6	2.4
Maximum Snowfall (in.)	26	4	7	1	trace	0	0	0	0	trace	5	19	27
Maximum 24-hr. Snowfall (in.)	11	4	5	1	trace	0	0	0	0	trace	4	6	11
Days With ≥ 1.0" Snow Depth	1	0	0	0	0	0	0	0	0	0	0	1	2
Thunderstorm Days	1	< 1	< 1	1	< 1	< 1	< 1	< 1	1	1	1	1	6
Foggy Days	18	16	15	14	12	13	13	17	18	20	17	18	191
Predominant Sky Cover	OVR	OVR	OVR	OVR	OVR	OVR	OVR	OVR	OVR	OVR	OVR	OVR	OVR
Mean Relative Humidity 7am (%)	87	88	89	88	86	86	87	90	90	91	88	87	88
Mean Relative Humidity 4pm (%)	78	75	71	70	70	71	70	71	70	73	78	81	73
Mean Dewpoint (°F)	37	39	39	42	46	50	53	54	52	47	42	38	45
Prevailing Wind Direction	E	E	SE	SW	NW	NW	NW	NW	SW	ESE	E	E	ESE
Prevailing Wind Speed (mph)	8	8	6	10	13	13	12	12	9	6	7	8	9
Maximum Wind Gust (mph)	79	76	70	63	61	45	45	46	56	67	68	79	79

Eugene Mahlon Sweet Airport

Eugene is located at the upper or southern end of the fertile Willamette Valley. Mahlon Sweet Field, location of the National Weather Service Office, is nine miles northwest of the city center. The Cascade Mountains to the east and the Coast Range to the west bound the valley, and low hills to the south nearly close it, but northward the level valley floor broadens rapidly. Hills of the rolling, wooded Coast Range begin about five miles west of the airport and rise to elevations of 1,500 to 2,500 feet midway between Eugene and the Pacific Ocean lying 50 miles to the west. About 10 miles east, the Coburg Hills, rising to an elevation of 2,500 feet, obscure the snow-covered peaks of the Cascade Range, which reach elevations of 10,000 feet about 75 miles away.

The Willamette River passes about five miles east of the airport. The Fern Ridge flood control reservoir, with a normal area of 9,360 acres, begins about two miles southwest. These two water areas are the main sources of local fog, but numerous small creeks and low places, which fill with water in the wet season, also produce considerable fog. The Coast Range acts as a barrier to coastal fog, but active storms cross these ridges with little hindrance. The Cascade Range blocks westward passage of all but the strongest continental air masses, but when air does flow into the valley from the east, dry, hot weather develops in summer causing an extreme fire hazard. In winter this situation causes clear, sunny days and cool, frosty nights.

The centers of low barometric pressure, result in southwest winds with speeds of 10 to 20 mph that usually accompany rainfall. Heavier storms bring winds of 30 to 40 mph. Fair weather in both summer and winter is most often accompanied by calm nights and daytime northerly winds increasing to speeds of five to 15 mph in the afternoon.

The first fall rains usually arrive during the second or third week of September, July and August are normally very dry. When snow occurs, it frequently melts on contact with the ground or within a few hours, but occasionally an accumulation of a few inches will persist as a ground covering for several days. Snowfall for a winter season exceeds five inches in about one-third of the years.

Temperatures are so largely controlled by maritime air from the Pacific that long periods of extremely hot or severely cold weather never occur. Temperatures of 95 degrees or higher have occurred only in the months of June, July, August, and September, and average three days a year.

Based on the 1951-1980 period, the average first occurrence of 32 degrees Fahrenheit in the fall is October 25 and the average last occurrence in the spring is April 24.

Eugene Mahlon Sweet Airport *Lane County*   Elevation: 354 ft.   Latitude: 44° 07' N   Longitude: 123° 13' W

	JAN	FEB	MAR	APR	MAY	JUN	JUL	AUG	SEP	OCT	NOV	DEC	YEAR
Mean Maximum Temp. (°F)	46.8	51.1	56.2	60.7	67.2	73.7	82.1	82.3	76.8	64.8	52.4	45.9	63.3
Mean Temp. (°F)	40.3	43.3	46.9	50.2	55.3	60.8	66.9	67.1	62.2	53.1	45.3	39.9	52.6
Mean Minimum Temp. (°F)	33.8	35.4	37.4	39.5	43.4	47.9	51.7	51.8	47.5	41.4	38.0	33.9	41.8
Extreme Maximum Temp. (°F)	67	72	77	81	93	102	105	108	103	94	76	68	108
Extreme Minimum Temp. (°F)	7	4	21	27	29	32	39	39	31	19	12	-12	-12
Days Maximum Temp. ≥ 90°F	0	0	0	0	0	1	6	6	3	0	0	0	16
Days Maximum Temp. ≤ 32°F	1	0	0	0	0	0	0	0	0	0	0	1	2
Days Minimum Temp. ≤ 32°F	14	9	6	3	0	0	0	0	0	2	7	12	53
Days Minimum Temp. ≤ 0°F	0	0	0	0	0	0	0	0	0	0	0	0	0
Heating Degree Days (base 65°F)	759	606	556	438	300	144	36	27	111	363	585	772	4,697
Cooling Degree Days (base 65°F)	0	0	0	0	7	22	94	97	34	2	0	0	256
Mean Precipitation (in.)	7.81	6.26	5.80	3.69	2.59	1.53	0.62	0.99	1.55	3.39	8.66	8.54	51.43
Maximum Precipitation (in.)	15.4	14.2	12.5	7.8	6.9	4.8	3.0	5.8	4.6	12.7	20.5	21.0	65.6
Minimum Precipitation (in.)	0.3	0.7	0.8	0.5	0.1	trace	0	0	trace	0.1	1.2	1.2	29.3
Maximum 24-hr. Precipitation (in.)	4.7	3.9	2.2	2.0	1.9	1.6	2.4	1.9	1.3	3.7	4.2	4.9	4.9
Days With ≥ 0.1" Precipitation	12	11	12	9	7	4	1	2	4	7	13	13	95
Days With ≥ 1.0" Precipitation	2	1	1	1	0	0	0	0	0	1	3	2	11
Mean Snowfall (in.)	1.4	1.6	0.1	trace	trace	trace	0.0	0.0	trace	trace	0.2	1.4	4.7
Maximum Snowfall (in.)	47	9	11	trace	trace	0	0	0	0	trace	6	10	47
Maximum 24-hr. Snowfall (in.)	14	6	5	trace	trace	0	0	0	0	trace	4	5	14
Days With ≥ 1.0" Snow Depth	1	1	0	0	0	0	0	0	0	0	0	1	3
Thunderstorm Days	< 1	< 1	< 1	< 1	1	1	1	1	< 1	< 1	< 1	< 1	4
Foggy Days	18	15	11	7	6	4	2	5	10	20	20	20	138
Predominant Sky Cover	OVR	OVR	OVR	OVR	OVR	OVR	CLR	CLR	CLR	OVR	OVR	OVR	OVR
Mean Relative Humidity 7am (%)	91	92	91	88	84	81	78	82	89	94	93	92	88
Mean Relative Humidity 4pm (%)	80	72	64	58	54	49	38	39	44	61	79	84	60
Mean Dewpoint (°F)	36	38	39	42	46	50	38	52	49	46	41	37	44
Prevailing Wind Direction	S	S	S	S	N	N	N	N	N	S	S	S	N
Prevailing Wind Speed (mph)	10	10	10	9	9	10	10	10	10	8	10	10	10
Maximum Wind Gust (mph)	66	53	60	58	51	41	51	39	36	43	58	61	66

Medford Jackson County Airport

Medford is located in a mountain valley formed by the famous Rogue River and one of its tributaries, Bear Creek. The major portion of the valley ranges in elevation from 1,300 to 1,400 feet above sea level. Mountains surround the valley on all sides, to the east the Cascades, ranging up to 9,500 feet, to the south the Siskiyous, ranging up to 7,600 feet, and to the west and north, the Coast Range and Umpqua Divide, ranging up to 5,500 feet above sea level. The valley exits to the ocean 80 miles westward through the narrow canyon of the Rogue River.

Medford has a moderate climate of marked seasonal characteristics. Late fall, winter, and early spring months are damp, cloudy, and cool under the influence of marine air. Late spring, summer, and early fall are warm, dry, and sunny.

Most of the light annual rainfall falls during the winter season. Summertime rainfall is brought by thunderstorm activity. Snowfall is quite heavy in the surrounding mountains during the winter. The mountains provide irrigation water storage which is necessary for production of most commercial crops during the dry summer. Snowfall is light.

High temperatures in the summer months average slightly below 90 degrees, and are always accompanied by low humidity. Hot days give way to cool nights as cool air drains down the mountain slopes into the valley. The length of the growing season is 170 days, from late April to mid-October. The last date of 32 degrees in the spring normally occurs in mid-June and the first date of 32 degrees in the fall occurs in mid- September.

Valley winds are usually very light, prevailing from the north or northwest much of the year. Winds exceeding 10 mph during the winter months nearly always come from the southerly quadrant. Summer thunderstorms produce gusty winds to 40 or 50 mph which may come from any direction.

Fog often fills the lower portion of the valley during the winter and early spring months. Duration of the fog is seldom more than three days. Geographical and meteorological conditions contribute to a smoke problem, which occasionally reduces visibility to one to three miles.

Medford Jackson County Airport *Jackson County*   Elevation: 1,299 ft.   Latitude: 42° 23' N   Longitude: 122° 52' W

	JAN	FEB	MAR	APR	MAY	JUN	JUL	AUG	SEP	OCT	NOV	DEC	YEAR
Mean Maximum Temp. (°F)	47.2	53.9	58.6	64.4	72.7	81.5	90.6	90.2	83.4	69.9	52.8	44.9	67.5
Mean Temp. (°F)	39.2	43.5	47.3	51.5	58.3	65.8	73.0	72.6	65.8	55.0	44.1	38.0	54.5
Mean Minimum Temp. (°F)	31.2	32.9	35.8	38.6	43.8	50.1	55.3	54.9	48.2	40.1	35.3	31.1	41.5
Extreme Maximum Temp. (°F)	71	79	83	93	103	111	110	114	110	99	77	69	114
Extreme Minimum Temp. (°F)	10	9	22	24	28	33	38	41	32	18	10	-6	-6
Days Maximum Temp. ≥ 90°F	0	0	0	0	2	7	18	18	9	1	0	0	55
Days Maximum Temp. ≤ 32°F	0	0	0	0	0	0	0	0	0	0	0	2	2
Days Minimum Temp. ≤ 32°F	18	13	10	5	1	0	0	0	0	3	11	17	78
Days Minimum Temp. ≤ 0°F	0	0	0	0	0	0	0	0	0	0	0	0	0
Heating Degree Days (base 65°F)	793	602	543	400	227	65	8	6	67	311	621	829	4,472
Cooling Degree Days (base 65°F)	0	0	0	2	30	97	260	257	107	9	0	0	762
Mean Precipitation (in.)	2.51	2.06	1.84	1.24	1.19	0.68	0.29	0.53	0.77	1.30	3.11	2.98	18.50
Maximum Precipitation (in.)	6.2	5.7	5.5	3.1	4.2	2.9	1.6	2.8	4.2	9.2	7.0	12.7	30.1
Minimum Precipitation (in.)	0.2	0.2	0.3	0.2	trace	0	0	0	0	trace	0.2	0.4	10.4
Maximum 24-hr. Precipitation (in.)	2.3	1.9	1.4	1.0	1.7	1.0	1.1	0.9	2.8	2.6	2.9	3.3	3.3
Days With ≥ 0.1" Precipitation	6	6	5	4	4	2	1	1	2	4	8	7	50
Days With ≥ 1.0" Precipitation	0	0	0	0	0	0	0	0	0	0	1	0	1
Mean Snowfall (in.)	1.6	0.7	0.6	trace	trace	trace	trace	trace	0.0	trace	0.4	1.7	5.0
Maximum Snowfall (in.)	20	12	8	4	trace	0	0	0	0	1	11	12	23
Maximum 24-hr. Snowfall (in.)	7	4	5	4	trace	0	0	0	0	1	11	12	23
Days With ≥ 1.0" Snow Depth	0	0	0	0	0	0	0	0	0	0	0	1	1
Thunderstorm Days	0	< 1	< 1	1	2	2	2	1	1	< 1	< 1	< 1	9
Foggy Days	20	13	6	2	2	1	< 1	1	2	11	20	22	100
Predominant Sky Cover	OVR	OVR	OVR	OVR	OVR	CLR	CLR	CLR	CLR	OVR	OVR	OVR	OVR
Mean Relative Humidity 7am (%)	91	90	88	83	76	70	64	69	78	89	92	92	82
Mean Relative Humidity 4pm (%)	71	59	50	44	39	34	26	27	31	45	67	77	47
Mean Dewpoint (°F)	32	35	35	38	42	46	49	49	45	42	37	34	40
Prevailing Wind Direction	N	N	NW	NW	NW	NW	WNW	WNW	WNW	S	N	N	NW
Prevailing Wind Speed (mph)	5	6	7	8	8	8	9	8	8	6	6	6	7
Maximum Wind Gust (mph)	56	47	53	47	39	53	46	46	55	40	62	59	62

Pendleton Municipal Airport

Pendleton is located in the southeastern part of the Columbia Basin, that low country of northern Oregon and central and eastern Washington which is almost entirely surrounded by mountains; these have important influences on the general climate of Pendleton and the surrounding territory.

The Weather Service Office at Pendleton Airport is located in rolling country which slopes generally upward toward the Blue Mountains about 15 miles to the east and southeast. The Columbia River approaches the area from the northwest to its junction with the Walla Walla River at an elevation of 351 feet and some 25 miles north of Pendleton, then turns southwestward to be joined a few miles below by the Umatilla River. The observation station is at an elevation of nearly 1,500 feet, about three miles northwest of downtown Pendleton.

Precipitation in the Pendleton area is definitely seasonal in occurrence with an average of only 10 percent of the annual total occurring in the three-month period, July-September. Most precipitation reaching this area accompanies cyclonic storms moving in from the Pacific Ocean. These storms reach their greatest intensity and frequency from October through April. This influence is felt, particularly, in the desert area of the central part of the Basin. A gradual rise in elevation from the Columbia River to the foothills of the Blue Mountains again results in increased precipitation.

The lighter summertime precipitation usually accompanies thunderstorms which often move into the area from the south or southwest. These storms can bee quite intense, causing flash flooding.

The last occurrence in spring of temperatures as low as 32 degrees is mid-April, and the average last occurrence in the fall of 32 degrees is late October. At the city station, where cool air settles in the valley on still nights, temperatures of 32 degrees have been recorded later in the spring and earlier in the fall. Under usual atmospheric conditions, air from the Pacific, with moderate temperature characteristics, moves across the Cascades or through the Columbia Gorge resulting in mild temperatures in the Pendleton area. When this flow of air from the west is impeded by slow-moving high pressure systems over the interior of the continent, temperature conditions sometimes become rather severe, hot in summer and cold in winter. During winter, coldest temperatures occur when air from a cold high pressure system in central Canada moves southwestward across the Rockies and flows down into the Columbia Basin. Extreme winter temperatures are not particularly common in the Pendleton area. Below zero readings are recorded in approximately 60 percent of winters. Maximum temperatures usually reach 100 degrees or slightly higher on a few days during the summer.

Pendleton Municipal Airport *Umatilla County*   Elevation: 1,479 ft.   Latitude: 45° 42' N   Longitude: 118° 50' W

	JAN	FEB	MAR	APR	MAY	JUN	JUL	AUG	SEP	OCT	NOV	DEC	YEAR
Mean Maximum Temp. (°F)	40.0	46.2	54.3	61.4	69.7	78.3	87.3	86.2	76.5	63.5	48.7	40.3	62.7
Mean Temp. (°F)	33.7	38.6	44.9	50.5	57.8	65.2	72.5	71.8	63.1	52.1	41.3	34.1	52.1
Mean Minimum Temp. (°F)	27.3	30.9	35.3	39.5	45.8	52.1	57.6	57.4	49.6	40.6	33.9	27.8	41.5
Extreme Maximum Temp. (°F)	70	75	74	91	100	103	108	111	100	92	80	67	111
Extreme Minimum Temp. (°F)	-12	-13	1	24	29	35	42	40	30	18	-12	-19	-19
Days Maximum Temp. ≥ 90°F	0	0	0	0	1	4	14	11	3	0	0	0	33
Days Maximum Temp. ≤ 32°F	8	4	0	0	0	0	0	0	0	0	2	9	23
Days Minimum Temp. ≤ 32°F	20	15	9	3	0	0	0	0	0	4	11	21	83
Days Minimum Temp. ≤ 0°F	1	1	0	0	0	0	0	0	0	0	0	1	3
Heating Degree Days (base 65°F)	964	739	617	430	240	79	12	13	115	397	704	953	5,263
Cooling Degree Days (base 65°F)	0	0	0	2	23	78	229	218	67	3	0	0	620
Mean Precipitation (in.)	1.52	1.17	1.21	1.13	1.18	0.77	0.41	0.56	0.59	0.94	1.65	1.49	12.62
Maximum Precipitation (in.)	3.9	2.6	2.8	2.8	3.2	2.3	1.4	2.6	2.1	2.7	3.8	4.7	17.8
Minimum Precipitation (in.)	0.2	0.1	0.3	trace	trace	trace	trace	0	0	trace	0.2	0.2	6.8
Maximum 24-hr. Precipitation (in.)	1.2	1.1	1.0	1.2	1.3	1.1	1.2	2.2	1.1	1.4	1.3	1.3	2.2
Days With ≥ 0.1" Precipitation	5	4	4	4	4	3	1	1	2	3	5	5	41
Days With ≥ 1.0" Precipitation	0	0	0	0	0	0	0	0	0	0	0	0	0
Mean Snowfall (in.)	5.0	3.5	1.0	0.1	trace	trace	trace	0.0	0.0	0.3	2.2	5.0	17.1
Maximum Snowfall (in.)	42	17	5	2	trace	0	0	0	0	3	15	27	53
Maximum 24-hr. Snowfall (in.)	11	16	4	2	trace	0	0	0	0	3	8	10	16
Days With ≥ 1.0" Snow Depth	8	3	1	0	0	0	0	0	0	0	2	6	20
Thunderstorm Days	0	< 1	< 1	1	2	2	2	2	1	< 1	< 1	< 1	10
Foggy Days	14	9	4	1	1	1	< 1	< 1	1	2	11	15	59
Predominant Sky Cover	OVR	OVR	OVR	OVR	OVR	CLR	CLR	CLR	CLR	OVR	OVR	OVR	OVR
Mean Relative Humidity 7am (%)	80	78	74	68	62	56	47	50	60	72	80	81	67
Mean Relative Humidity 4pm (%)	74	65	50	42	37	32	23	26	32	46	69	77	48
Mean Dewpoint (°F)	26	30	31	34	39	43	43	43	40	37	32	28	36
Prevailing Wind Direction	SSE	SSE	W	W	W	W	W	W	SE	SE	SSE	SSE	W
Prevailing Wind Speed (mph)	7	7	16	16	15	15	13	14	7	6	6	7	10
Maximum Wind Gust (mph)	76	69	74	64	60	62	62	55	56	51	58	63	76

Portland Int'l Airport

The Portland Weather Service Office is located 6 miles north-northeast of downtown Portland. Portland is situated about 65 miles inland from the Pacific Coast and midway between the northerly oriented low coast range on the west and the higher Cascade range on the east, each about 30 miles distant. The airport lies on the south bank of the Columbia River. The coast range provides limited shielding from the Pacific Ocean. The Cascade range provides a steep slope for orographic lift of moisture-laden westerly winds and consequent moderate rainfall, and also forms a barrier from continental air masses originating over the interior Columbia Basin. Airflow is usually northwesterly in Portland in spring and summer and southeasterly in fall and winter. The Portland Airport location is drier than most surrounding localities.

Portland has a very definite winter rainfall climate. Approximately 88 percent of the annual total occurs in the months of October through May, nine percent in June and September, while only three percent comes in July and August. Precipitation is mostly rain, as on the average there are only five days each year with measurable snow. Snowfalls are seldom more than a couple of inches, and generally last only a few days.

The winter season is marked by relatively mild temperatures, cloudy skies and rain with southeasterly surface winds predominating. Summer produces pleasantly mild temperatures, northwesterly winds and very little precipitation. Fall and spring are transitional in nature. Fall and early winter are times with most frequent fog.

At all times, incursions of marine air are a frequent moderating influence. Outbreaks of continental high pressure from east of the Cascade Mountains produce strong easterly flow through the Columbia Gorge into the Portland area. In winter this brings the coldest weather with the extremes of low temperature registered in the cold air mass. Freezing rain and ice glaze are sometimes transitional effects. Temperatures below zero are very infrequent. In summer, hot, dry continental air brings the highest temperatures. Temperatures above 100 degrees are infrequent, but 90 degrees or higher are reached every year, but seldom persist for more than two or three days.

Destructive storms are infrequent in the Portland area. Surface winds seldom exceed gale force and rarely in the period of record have winds reached higher than 75 mph. Thunderstorms occur about once a month through the spring and summer months. Heavy downpours are infrequent but gentle rains occur almost daily during winter months.

Based on the 1951-1980 period, the average first occurrence of 32 degrees Fahrenheit in the fall is November 7 and the average last occurrence in the spring is April 3.

Portland Int'l Airport *Multnomah County*   Elevation: 16 ft.   Latitude: 45° 36' N   Longitude: 122° 37' W

	JAN	FEB	MAR	APR	MAY	JUN	JUL	AUG	SEP	OCT	NOV	DEC	YEAR
Mean Maximum Temp. (°F)	46.0	50.9	56.5	61.2	67.8	73.6	80.2	80.7	75.5	64.3	52.7	46.0	63.0
Mean Temp. (°F)	40.4	43.7	47.9	51.9	57.9	63.4	68.8	69.2	64.1	54.8	46.5	40.6	54.1
Mean Minimum Temp. (°F)	34.6	36.4	39.3	42.4	48.0	53.2	57.3	57.6	52.6	45.3	40.2	35.2	45.2
Extreme Maximum Temp. (°F)	63	71	77	90	100	100	104	107	105	92	73	65	107
Extreme Minimum Temp. (°F)	12	9	19	30	35	41	45	44	36	26	13	8	8
Days Maximum Temp. ≥ 90°F	0	0	0	0	0	1	5	5	2	0	0	0	13
Days Maximum Temp. ≤ 32°F	1	0	0	0	0	0	0	0	0	0	0	1	2
Days Minimum Temp. ≤ 32°F	12	7	3	1	0	0	0	0	0	1	4	10	38
Days Minimum Temp. ≤ 0°F	0	0	0	0	0	0	0	0	0	0	0	0	0
Heating Degree Days (base 65°F)	758	596	522	389	228	89	19	13	76	312	550	749	4,301
Cooling Degree Days (base 65°F)	0	0	0	1	17	47	143	156	62	3	0	0	429
Mean Precipitation (in.)	5.27	4.18	3.69	2.68	2.34	1.57	0.72	0.92	1.64	2.87	5.72	5.85	37.45
Maximum Precipitation (in.)	12.8	11.4	8.1	6.2	4.4	4.1	2.7	4.5	5.5	8.4	14.4	17.4	55.5
Minimum Precipitation (in.)	0.1	0.6	0.8	0.5	0.1	trace	0	trace	trace	0.2	0.4	1.4	22.5
Maximum 24-hr. Precipitation (in.)	2.5	1.9	2.1	1.8	1.5	2.0	1.1	1.5	2.2	2.4	2.4	4.0	4.0
Days With ≥ 0.1" Precipitation	12	10	10	8	7	4	2	2	4	7	13	12	91
Days With ≥ 1.0" Precipitation	1	1	0	0	0	0	0	0	0	1	1	1	4
Mean Snowfall (in.)	1.1	1.3	trace	trace	trace	trace	0.0	trace	0.0	trace	0.6	1.3	4.3
Maximum Snowfall (in.)	41	13	13	trace	trace	0	0	0	0	0	8	16	44
Maximum 24-hr. Snowfall (in.)	9	6	8	trace	trace	0	0	0	0	0	7	8	9
Days With ≥ 1.0" Snow Depth	1	1	0	0	0	0	0	0	0	0	0	1	3
Thunderstorm Days	< 1	< 1	1	1	1	1	1	1	1	< 1	< 1	< 1	7
Foggy Days	15	12	9	7	5	4	3	5	12	18	17	16	123
Predominant Sky Cover	OVR	OVR	OVR	OVR	OVR	OVR	CLR	CLR	CLR	OVR	OVR	OVR	OVR
Mean Relative Humidity 7am (%)	85	86	86	84	80	78	77	81	87	90	88	87	84
Mean Relative Humidity 4pm (%)	75	67	60	55	53	51	45	45	48	61	74	78	59
Mean Dewpoint (°F)	33	36	38	41	46	50	53	54	51	47	40	36	44
Prevailing Wind Direction	ESE	ESE	ESE	NW	NW	NW	NW	NW	NW	ESE	ESE	ESE	ESE
Prevailing Wind Speed (mph)	13	12	10	8	8	8	9	8	8	9	12	13	10
Maximum Wind Gust (mph)	63	68	71	63	48	40	35	38	51	78	71	61	78

Salem McNary Field

Salem is located in the middle Willamette Valley some 60 airline miles east of the Pacific Ocean. The valley here is approximately 50 miles wide with the city about equidistant from the valley walls formed by the Coast Range on the west and the Cascade Range on the east.

The usual movement of very moist maritime air masses from the Pacific Ocean inland over the Coast Range produces, near its crest, some of the heaviest yearly rainfall in the United States. Annual totals of nearly 170 inches have been recorded in the mountains. From the ridge crest of the Coast Range, approximately 3,000 feet above sea level, there is a gradual decrease of rainfall downslope to the valley floor where annual totals are between 35 and 45 inches. As these marine conditioned air masses continue to move farther inland they are forced to ascend the west slopes of the Cascades to approximately 5,000 feet above sea level and again rainfall amounts substantially increase with elevation.

Most of this precipitation in both the valley and its bordering mountain ranges occurs during the winter. At Salem, 70 percent of the annual total occurs during the five months of November through March while only 6 percent occurs during the three summer months, with practically all of it falling in the form of rain. In the immediate area, there are only three or four days a year with measurable amounts of snow.

The seasonal difference in temperatures is much less marked than that of precipitation. There is a range of about 28 degrees between the temperature for January, the coldest month, and July, the warmest. Highs of 100 degrees or more seldom occur, and only in a few years since records began in 1892, have 0 degree or lower temperatures been observed. There is an average growing season of six and a half months.

The mild temperatures, long growing season, and plentiful supply of moisture are ideal for a wide variety of crops. In dollar value of agricultural returns, this is the most productive area in Oregon. Large orchards of sweet cherries are grown and processed here for maraschino cherries. Hops, filberts, walnuts, cane, and strawberries each contribute many millions of dollars to the annual farm income. A wide variety of vegetables is raised for both the fresh market and to support a large number of processing plants located in Salem. This climate is also suitable for the production of a number of specialty crops including mint, several seed crops, and nursery stock, particularly roses and ornamental shrubs.

Based on the 1951-1980 period, the average first occurrence of 32 degrees Fahrenheit in the fall is October 22 and the average last occurrence in the spring is May 5.

Salem McNary Field *Marion County*   Elevation: 193 ft.   Latitude: 44° 54' N   Longitude: 123° 00' W

	JAN	FEB	MAR	APR	MAY	JUN	JUL	AUG	SEP	OCT	NOV	DEC	YEAR
Mean Maximum Temp. (°F)	47.2	51.4	56.3	60.9	67.6	74.1	81.7	82.0	76.6	64.5	52.6	46.3	63.4
Mean Temp. (°F)	40.5	43.0	46.5	49.8	55.5	61.3	66.8	67.0	62.1	52.9	45.3	40.1	52.6
Mean Minimum Temp. (°F)	33.8	34.6	36.6	38.7	43.3	48.4	51.9	51.9	47.5	41.2	37.9	33.9	41.6
Extreme Maximum Temp. (°F)	65	71	77	85	100	105	103	108	104	93	72	68	108
Extreme Minimum Temp. (°F)	6	-1	12	26	29	32	38	36	26	23	15	-12	-12
Days Maximum Temp. ≥ 90°F	0	0	0	0	0	2	6	6	2	0	0	0	16
Days Maximum Temp. ≤ 32°F	1	0	0	0	0	0	0	0	0	0	0	1	2
Days Minimum Temp. ≤ 32°F	13	11	8	5	1	0	0	0	0	3	7	13	61
Days Minimum Temp. ≤ 0°F	0	0	0	0	0	0	0	0	0	0	0	0	0
Heating Degree Days (base 65°F)	753	614	567	449	295	134	36	32	114	371	586	764	4,715
Cooling Degree Days (base 65°F)	0	0	0	0	10	28	99	104	36	2	0	0	279
Mean Precipitation (in.)	6.24	5.01	4.13	2.80	2.12	1.45	0.57	0.68	1.47	3.06	6.54	6.67	40.74
Maximum Precipitation (in.)	15.4	12.3	8.6	5.6	4.5	4.2	2.6	4.2	4.0	10.7	15.3	12.4	56.5
Minimum Precipitation (in.)	0.2	0.5	0.9	0.6	0	trace	0	0	0	0.1	1.0	1.3	23.7
Maximum 24-hr. Precipitation (in.)	3.1	2.9	2.0	1.6	1.8	1.6	1.8	1.1	1.8	2.7	2.7	2.5	3.1
Days With ≥ 0.1" Precipitation	13	11	11	8	6	4	2	2	4	7	13	13	94
Days With ≥ 1.0" Precipitation	1	1	0	0	0	0	0	0	0	0	1	2	5
Mean Snowfall (in.)	1.3	2.1	0.1	trace	trace	0.0	0.0	0.0	trace	trace	0.4	1.9	5.8
Maximum Snowfall (in.)	33	14	11	trace	trace	0	0	0	0	trace	6	15	34
Maximum 24-hr. Snowfall (in.)	6	12	7	trace	trace	0	0	0	0	trace	6	8	12
Days With ≥ 1.0" Snow Depth	1	1	0	0	0	0	0	0	0	0	0	1	3
Thunderstorm Days	< 1	< 1	< 1	< 1	1	1	1	1	1	< 1	< 1	< 1	5
Foggy Days	16	11	8	5	3	2	1	3	8	16	17	17	107
Predominant Sky Cover	OVR	OVR	OVR	OVR	OVR	OVR	CLR	CLR	CLR	OVR	OVR	OVR	OVR
Mean Relative Humidity 7am (%)	87	89	88	85	80	77	75	79	87	91	90	89	85
Mean Relative Humidity 4pm (%)	76	69	62	56	53	49	40	40	45	61	76	81	59
Mean Dewpoint (°F)	34	37	38	40	45	49	52	52	49	45	40	36	43
Prevailing Wind Direction	S	S	S	S	S	S	N	N	S	S	S	S	S
Prevailing Wind Speed (mph)	13	12	12	9	8	7	8	8	8	9	12	13	10
Maximum Wind Gust (mph)	61	53	61	60	46	38	36	37	39	47	71	59	71

Alkali Lake *Lake County*   Elevation: 4,330 ft.   Latitude: 42° 58' N   Longitude: 120° 00' W

	JAN	FEB	MAR	APR	MAY	JUN	JUL	AUG	SEP	OCT	NOV	DEC	YEAR
Mean Maximum Temp. (°F)	41.8	46.3	51.8	59.2	68.8	78.2	87.3	86.4	77.8	65.3	49.5	41.7	62.8
Mean Temp. (°F)	30.5	34.5	38.8	44.0	51.9	60.3	67.3	66.0	57.4	47.3	36.7	30.0	47.1
Mean Minimum Temp. (°F)	19.0	22.7	25.8	28.8	35.0	42.3	47.2	45.6	36.9	29.2	24.0	18.3	31.2
Extreme Maximum Temp. (°F)	63	72	76	88	97	100	103	105	101	90	75	69	105
Extreme Minimum Temp. (°F)	-17	-26	-11	8	15	23	30	26	14	3	-10	-33	-33
Days Maximum Temp. ≥ 90°F	0	0	0	0	1	5	14	13	3	0	0	0	36
Days Maximum Temp. ≤ 32°F	5	2	0	0	0	0	0	0	0	0	1	4	12
Days Minimum Temp. ≤ 32°F	26	23	24	21	11	2	0	1	7	20	22	27	184
Days Minimum Temp. ≤ 0°F	3	1	0	0	0	0	0	0	0	0	0	2	6
Heating Degree Days (base 65°F)	1,063	855	805	622	400	178	53	62	236	544	839	1,078	6,735
Cooling Degree Days (base 65°F)	0	0	0	0	7	42	120	100	15	0	0	0	284
Mean Precipitation (in.)	0.55	0.49	0.77	0.88	1.11	0.86	0.62	0.69	0.47	0.65	0.72	0.63	8.44
Days With ≥ 0.1" Precipitation	2	2	3	3	3	3	1	2	1	2	3	2	27
Days With ≥ 1.0" Precipitation	0	0	0	0	0	0	0	0	0	0	0	0	0
Mean Snowfall (in.)	2.6	1.9	1.9	1.4	0.7	trace	0.0	0.0	trace	0.3	2.2	4.4	15.4
Days With ≥ 1.0" Snow Depth	6	3	1	0	0	0	0	0	0	0	2	5	17

Antelope 1 NW *Wasco County*   Elevation: 2,837 ft.   Latitude: 44° 55' N   Longitude: 120° 44' W

	JAN	FEB	MAR	APR	MAY	JUN	JUL	AUG	SEP	OCT	NOV	DEC	YEAR
Mean Maximum Temp. (°F)	40.1	45.1	51.9	58.2	66.5	74.9	84.0	84.0	74.9	62.9	47.9	39.6	60.8
Mean Temp. (°F)	32.4	36.2	41.2	45.8	52.6	60.0	67.1	67.1	59.2	49.5	39.0	32.0	48.5
Mean Minimum Temp. (°F)	24.6	27.3	30.5	33.3	38.7	45.1	50.2	50.1	43.6	36.0	30.2	24.4	36.2
Extreme Maximum Temp. (°F)	63	68	74	87	98	100	102	107	100	89	73	65	107
Extreme Minimum Temp. (°F)	-15	-13	10	16	21	27	33	31	26	9	-7	-17	-17
Days Maximum Temp. ≥ 90°F	0	0	0	0	0	2	9	9	2	0	0	0	22
Days Maximum Temp. ≤ 32°F	6	3	0	0	0	0	0	0	0	0	1	6	16
Days Minimum Temp. ≤ 32°F	25	21	19	14	6	1	0	0	1	10	18	25	140
Days Minimum Temp. ≤ 0°F	1	1	0	0	0	0	0	0	0	0	0	1	3
Heating Degree Days (base 65°F)	1,005	807	730	569	385	187	63	59	199	476	771	1,017	6,268
Cooling Degree Days (base 65°F)	0	0	0	0	8	32	108	111	32	1	0	0	292
Mean Precipitation (in.)	1.68	1.22	1.25	1.15	1.37	1.07	0.45	0.60	0.75	0.89	1.92	1.63	13.98
Days With ≥ 0.1" Precipitation	6	4	5	4	4	3	2	2	2	3	6	5	46
Days With ≥ 1.0" Precipitation	0	0	0	0	0	0	0	0	0	0	0	0	0
Mean Snowfall (in.)	4.8	3.3	1.8	1.0	0.3	0.0	0.0	0.0	0.0	0.3	2.9	4.8	19.2
Days With ≥ 1.0" Snow Depth	4	2	0	0	0	0	0	0	0	0	1	2	9

Arlington *Gilliam County*   Elevation: 275 ft.   Latitude: 45° 43' N   Longitude: 120° 12' W

	JAN	FEB	MAR	APR	MAY	JUN	JUL	AUG	SEP	OCT	NOV	DEC	YEAR
Mean Maximum Temp. (°F)	40.9	46.8	56.7	65.5	74.8	82.7	90.9	89.8	80.0	65.5	50.2	41.2	65.4
Mean Temp. (°F)	35.2	39.4	46.8	54.0	62.0	69.3	76.2	75.4	66.0	53.8	43.2	35.6	54.7
Mean Minimum Temp. (°F)	29.4	31.8	36.9	42.4	49.1	56.0	61.5	60.9	52.0	42.1	36.1	29.9	44.0
Extreme Maximum Temp. (°F)	65	70	77	94	107	110	111	110	102	89	73	65	111
Extreme Minimum Temp. (°F)	-10	-11	16	23	32	37	42	40	31	17	-3	-7	-11
Days Maximum Temp. ≥ 90°F	0	0	0	0	2	8	18	16	4	0	0	0	48
Days Maximum Temp. ≤ 32°F	5	2	0	0	0	0	0	0	0	0	1	5	13
Days Minimum Temp. ≤ 32°F	17	14	8	2	0	0	0	0	0	3	8	17	69
Days Minimum Temp. ≤ 0°F	1	0	0	0	0	0	0	0	0	0	0	0	1
Heating Degree Days (base 65°F)	917	719	557	329	140	27	3	3	66	345	648	905	4,659
Cooling Degree Days (base 65°F)	0	0	0	6	58	156	348	326	111	5	0	0	1,010
Mean Precipitation (in.)	1.48	0.96	0.76	0.69	0.67	0.35	0.19	0.30	0.43	0.63	1.29	1.47	9.22
Days With ≥ 0.1" Precipitation	5	3	3	2	2	1	1	1	1	2	4	5	30
Days With ≥ 1.0" Precipitation	0	0	0	0	0	0	0	0	0	0	0	0	0
Mean Snowfall (in.)	2.7	1.7	0.2	0.0	0.0	0.0	0.0	0.0	0.0	trace	0.9	2.1	7.6
Days With ≥ 1.0" Snow Depth	3	1	0	0	0	0	0	0	0	0	1	3	8

Ashland *Jackson County*   Elevation: 1,722 ft.   Latitude: 42° 13' N   Longitude: 122° 43' W

	JAN	FEB	MAR	APR	MAY	JUN	JUL	AUG	SEP	OCT	NOV	DEC	YEAR
Mean Maximum Temp. (°F)	47.7	53.1	57.0	62.4	70.3	78.6	87.0	86.2	79.5	67.6	52.7	46.3	65.7
Mean Temp. (°F)	39.1	42.7	45.6	49.5	56.1	63.1	69.5	68.7	62.4	53.0	43.4	38.1	52.6
Mean Minimum Temp. (°F)	30.4	32.1	34.1	36.6	41.9	47.7	51.9	51.1	45.2	38.4	33.9	29.9	39.4
Extreme Maximum Temp. (°F)	70	78	82	87	97	105	106	108	103	97	77	70	108
Extreme Minimum Temp. (°F)	9	8	20	21	27	33	37	37	30	19	13	-4	-4
Days Maximum Temp. ≥ 90°F	0	0	0	0	1	4	13	11	4	0	0	0	33
Days Maximum Temp. ≤ 32°F	0	0	0	0	0	0	0	0	0	0	0	1	1
Days Minimum Temp. ≤ 32°F	19	16	13	8	2	0	0	0	0	6	13	20	97
Days Minimum Temp. ≤ 0°F	0	0	0	0	0	0	0	0	0	0	0	0	0
Heating Degree Days (base 65°F)	796	624	595	458	282	109	24	25	117	367	643	826	4,866
Cooling Degree Days (base 65°F)	0	0	0	1	14	54	155	138	44	3	0	0	409
Mean Precipitation (in.)	2.53	1.91	2.06	1.69	1.54	0.96	0.46	0.61	0.88	1.45	2.98	2.88	19.95
Days With ≥ 0.1" Precipitation	6	5	6	6	5	3	1	1	3	4	8	7	55
Days With ≥ 1.0" Precipitation	0	0	0	0	0	0	0	0	0	0	0	0	0
Mean Snowfall (in.)	1.3	0.8	0.4	trace	0.0	0.0	0.0	0.0	0.0	0.0	trace	1.3	3.8
Days With ≥ 1.0" Snow Depth	1	0	0	0	0	0	0	0	0	0	0	1	2

Austin 3 S *Grant County*   Elevation: 4,212 ft.   Latitude: 44° 34' N   Longitude: 118° 29' W

	JAN	FEB	MAR	APR	MAY	JUN	JUL	AUG	SEP	OCT	NOV	DEC	YEAR
Mean Maximum Temp. (°F)	35.1	40.8	47.1	54.5	63.0	71.7	81.4	82.3	72.7	60.7	43.0	35.0	57.3
Mean Temp. (°F)	23.2	27.9	33.8	40.2	47.2	54.2	60.6	60.3	51.9	42.9	32.0	23.7	41.5
Mean Minimum Temp. (°F)	11.2	14.8	20.4	25.8	31.5	36.7	39.7	38.3	31.2	25.0	21.0	12.4	25.7
Extreme Maximum Temp. (°F)	55	65	72	85	92	97	100	101	99	89	72	57	101
Extreme Minimum Temp. (°F)	-29	-35	-10	4	15	21	25	22	14	-5	-23	-37	-37
Days Maximum Temp. ≥ 90°F	0	0	0	0	0	1	6	7	1	0	0	0	15
Days Maximum Temp. ≤ 32°F	11	3	1	0	0	0	0	0	0	0	3	10	28
Days Minimum Temp. ≤ 32°F	31	28	30	25	18	8	3	5	18	26	28	31	251
Days Minimum Temp. ≤ 0°F	8	3	1	0	0	0	0	0	0	0	1	5	18
Heating Degree Days (base 65°F)	1,290	1,042	960	738	544	324	156	163	391	679	986	1,273	8,546
Cooling Degree Days (base 65°F)	0	0	0	0	1	4	21	24	4	0	0	0	54
Mean Precipitation (in.)	2.85	1.96	2.02	1.51	1.63	1.50	0.90	0.96	1.03	1.14	2.87	3.03	21.40
Days With ≥ 0.1" Precipitation	9	7	7	5	5	5	3	3	3	4	8	10	69
Days With ≥ 1.0" Precipitation	0	0	0	0	0	0	0	0	0	0	0	0	0
Mean Snowfall (in.)	22.3	14.6	10.3	4.9	0.4	trace	0.0	0.0	trace	1.3	14.8	23.4	92.0
Days With ≥ 1.0" Snow Depth	30	27	22	5	0	0	0	0	0	1	12	28	125

Baker Municipal Airport *Baker County*   Elevation: 3,366 ft.   Latitude: 44° 50' N   Longitude: 117° 49' W

	JAN	FEB	MAR	APR	MAY	JUN	JUL	AUG	SEP	OCT	NOV	DEC	YEAR
Mean Maximum Temp. (°F)	34.3	41.4	50.8	58.8	67.1	75.3	84.5	84.8	75.2	62.5	45.0	35.1	59.6
Mean Temp. (°F)	25.8	31.7	39.0	45.1	52.7	60.0	66.5	66.3	57.1	46.4	35.0	26.3	46.0
Mean Minimum Temp. (°F)	17.2	22.0	27.2	31.3	38.3	44.6	48.6	47.6	39.0	30.3	24.9	17.5	32.4
Extreme Maximum Temp. (°F)	57	66	78	89	94	99	102	104	101	89	72	60	104
Extreme Minimum Temp. (°F)	-27	-28	1	15	17	27	31	27	19	9	-15	-39	-39
Days Maximum Temp. ≥ 90°F	0	0	0	0	0	2	10	11	2	0	0	0	25
Days Maximum Temp. ≤ 32°F	12	4	0	0	0	0	0	0	0	0	2	10	28
Days Minimum Temp. ≤ 32°F	28	25	24	18	6	1	0	0	5	19	24	29	179
Days Minimum Temp. ≤ 0°F	4	1	0	0	0	0	0	0	0	0	0	3	8
Heating Degree Days (base 65°F)	1,209	933	799	591	377	177	54	55	242	569	894	1,193	7,093
Cooling Degree Days (base 65°F)	0	0	0	0	5	29	97	98	15	0	0	0	244
Mean Precipitation (in.)	0.95	0.61	0.83	0.84	1.40	1.27	0.74	0.87	0.70	0.54	0.98	0.97	10.70
Days With ≥ 0.1" Precipitation	3	2	3	3	4	4	2	2	2	2	3	3	33
Days With ≥ 1.0" Precipitation	0	0	0	0	0	0	0	0	0	0	0	0	0
Mean Snowfall (in.)	6.1	4.1	2.7	1.1	0.5	trace	trace	trace	trace	0.3	3.9	7.4	26.1
Days With ≥ 1.0" Snow Depth	17	9	3	0	0	0	0	0	0	0	4	13	46

Bandon 2 NNE *Coos County*   Elevation: 19 ft.   Latitude: 43° 09' N   Longitude: 124° 24' W

	JAN	FEB	MAR	APR	MAY	JUN	JUL	AUG	SEP	OCT	NOV	DEC	YEAR
Mean Maximum Temp. (°F)	54.3	55.7	56.3	58.0	61.1	64.2	66.8	67.7	67.6	63.6	57.4	53.9	60.6
Mean Temp. (°F)	46.5	47.7	48.3	49.7	52.9	56.3	58.9	59.3	57.8	53.9	49.6	46.2	52.3
Mean Minimum Temp. (°F)	38.7	39.8	40.2	41.3	44.6	48.4	50.9	50.9	48.1	44.2	41.8	38.5	43.9
Extreme Maximum Temp. (°F)	75	79	78	86	90	85	85	84	100	97	78	77	100
Extreme Minimum Temp. (°F)	16	14	26	29	30	35	38	35	32	27	21	8	8
Days Maximum Temp. ≥ 90°F	0	0	0	0	0	0	0	0	0	0	0	0	0
Days Maximum Temp. ≤ 32°F	0	0	0	0	0	0	0	0	0	0	0	0	0
Days Minimum Temp. ≤ 32°F	7	5	3	1	0	0	0	0	0	1	3	6	26
Days Minimum Temp. ≤ 0°F	0	0	0	0	0	0	0	0	0	0	0	0	0
Heating Degree Days (base 65°F)	566	481	512	454	370	254	183	169	209	338	455	575	4,566
Cooling Degree Days (base 65°F)	0	0	0	0	0	0	1	1	1	2	0	0	5
Mean Precipitation (in.)	9.38	7.44	7.40	4.73	3.12	1.63	0.42	0.89	1.67	3.83	9.28	9.91	59.70
Days With ≥ 0.1" Precipitation	15	13	15	11	7	4	1	2	4	7	15	15	109
Days With ≥ 1.0" Precipitation	3	2	1	1	1	0	0	0	0	1	2	3	14
Mean Snowfall (in.)	0.2	0.2	trace	trace	0.0	0.0	0.0	0.0	0.0	0.0	trace	0.1	0.5
Days With ≥ 1.0" Snow Depth	0	0	0	0	0	0	0	0	0	0	0	0	0

Barnes Station *Crook County*   Elevation: 3,969 ft.   Latitude: 43° 57' N   Longitude: 120° 13' W

	JAN	FEB	MAR	APR	MAY	JUN	JUL	AUG	SEP	OCT	NOV	DEC	YEAR
Mean Maximum Temp. (°F)	39.1	44.3	50.6	57.7	66.1	75.0	84.4	83.9	75.6	63.9	46.8	39.1	60.6
Mean Temp. (°F)	29.1	33.7	38.5	43.4	50.6	58.1	65.2	64.4	56.3	47.1	36.2	29.0	46.0
Mean Minimum Temp. (°F)	19.1	23.0	26.4	29.1	35.0	41.1	45.9	44.8	37.0	30.2	25.5	19.0	31.3
Extreme Maximum Temp. (°F)	60	70	75	86	94	97	100	102	100	91	72	62	102
Extreme Minimum Temp. (°F)	-23	-26	-1	10	16	23	27	26	17	-1	-18	-30	-30
Days Maximum Temp. ≥ 90°F	0	0	0	0	0	2	10	9	2	0	0	0	23
Days Maximum Temp. ≤ 32°F	6	2	0	0	0	0	0	0	0	0	1	6	15
Days Minimum Temp. ≤ 32°F	28	24	25	20	12	3	1	1	8	19	23	28	192
Days Minimum Temp. ≤ 0°F	3	1	0	0	0	0	0	0	0	0	1	2	7
Heating Degree Days (base 65°F)	1,106	877	814	640	442	223	76	86	263	549	858	1,108	7,042
Cooling Degree Days (base 65°F)	0	0	0	0	4	21	84	74	13	0	0	0	196
Mean Precipitation (in.)	1.49	1.04	1.22	1.04	1.43	1.06	0.82	0.87	0.66	0.84	1.70	1.61	13.78
Days With ≥ 0.1" Precipitation	5	4	4	3	5	3	2	2	2	3	6	5	44
Days With ≥ 1.0" Precipitation	0	0	0	0	0	0	0	0	0	0	0	0	0
Mean Snowfall (in.)	9.7	8.1	4.0	1.7	0.6	trace	trace	0.0	0.1	1.1	7.9	12.3	45.5
Days With ≥ 1.0" Snow Depth	18	9	2	0	0	0	0	0	0	0	5	14	48

Beaverton 2 SSW *Washington County*   Elevation: 269 ft.   Latitude: 45° 27' N   Longitude: 122° 49' W

	JAN	FEB	MAR	APR	MAY	JUN	JUL	AUG	SEP	OCT	NOV	DEC	YEAR
Mean Maximum Temp. (°F)	46.5	50.9	56.5	61.4	67.2	72.8	79.2	79.7	75.1	64.2	52.5	46.3	62.7
Mean Temp. (°F)	40.0	43.1	47.0	50.9	56.2	61.5	66.5	66.5	62.3	53.4	45.2	40.1	52.7
Mean Minimum Temp. (°F)	33.4	35.1	37.4	40.4	45.2	50.1	53.7	53.3	49.4	42.5	37.9	33.9	42.7
Extreme Maximum Temp. (°F)	64	73	79	*94*	*100*	*99*	102	105	*101*	91	72	64	*105*
Extreme Minimum Temp. (°F)	10	8	19	*27*	*31*	*34*	41	36	*34*	26	9	0	*0*
Days Maximum Temp. ≥ 90°F	0	0	0	0	0	1	4	4	2	0	0	0	11
Days Maximum Temp. ≤ 32°F	1	0	0	0	0	0	0	0	0	0	0	1	2
Days Minimum Temp. ≤ 32°F	14	10	6	3	0	0	0	0	0	1	7	12	53
Days Minimum Temp. ≤ 0°F	0	0	0	0	0	0	0	0	0	0	0	0	0
Heating Degree Days (base 65°F)	767	613	551	419	279	135	46	44	115	357	588	765	4,679
Cooling Degree Days (base 65°F)	0	0	0	2	16	35	100	103	39	3	0	0	298
Mean Precipitation (in.)	5.66	4.84	3.99	2.77	2.34	1.65	0.72	0.88	1.54	2.88	6.17	6.39	39.83
Days With ≥ 0.1" Precipitation	12	11	11	9	7	5	2	2	4	7	14	12	96
Days With ≥ 1.0" Precipitation	1	1	0	0	0	0	0	0	0	0	1	1	4
Mean Snowfall (in.)	*0.6*	0.7	trace	0.0	0.0	0.0	0.0	0.0	0.0	0.0	0.4	0.5	*2.2*
Days With ≥ 1.0" Snow Depth	*0*	0	0	0	0	0	0	0	0	0	0	1	*1*

Belknap Springs 8 N *Linn County*   Elevation: 2,148 ft.   Latitude: 44° 17' N   Longitude: 122° 02' W

	JAN	FEB	MAR	APR	MAY	JUN	JUL	AUG	SEP	OCT	NOV	DEC	YEAR
Mean Maximum Temp. (°F)	39.5	44.5	50.5	56.6	65.2	72.7	81.4	81.6	75.4	62.8	46.6	38.5	59.6
Mean Temp. (°F)	33.7	36.8	40.8	45.3	52.2	58.7	65.1	65.0	59.5	50.3	39.7	33.5	48.4
Mean Minimum Temp. (°F)	27.8	29.1	31.1	34.0	39.1	44.8	48.8	48.4	43.6	37.8	32.8	28.5	37.2
Extreme Maximum Temp. (°F)	69	72	76	93	100	102	103	106	105	92	69	58	106
Extreme Minimum Temp. (°F)	4	-2	6	22	27	32	34	35	28	19	8	-4	-4
Days Maximum Temp. ≥ 90°F	0	0	0	0	1	2	8	7	3	0	0	0	21
Days Maximum Temp. ≤ 32°F	2	1	0	0	0	0	0	0	0	0	0	2	5
Days Minimum Temp. ≤ 32°F	25	22	21	13	3	0	0	0	1	5	15	25	130
Days Minimum Temp. ≤ 0°F	0	0	0	0	0	0	0	0	0	0	0	0	0
Heating Degree Days (base 65°F)	965	790	743	584	398	208	77	72	185	450	751	969	6,192
Cooling Degree Days (base 65°F)	0	0	0	0	9	27	88	83	32	1	0	0	240
Mean Precipitation (in.)	11.54	9.49	7.88	5.87	3.91	2.64	1.01	1.13	2.41	5.53	12.57	12.90	76.88
Days With ≥ 0.1" Precipitation	15	13	15	13	9	7	3	3	5	9	17	16	125
Days With ≥ 1.0" Precipitation	4	3	2	1	0	0	0	0	0	2	4	4	20
Mean Snowfall (in.)	16.3	15.0	9.2	1.8	trace	0.0	0.0	0.0	0.0	0.3	5.8	16.5	64.9
Days With ≥ 1.0" Snow Depth	17	14	10	2	0	0	0	0	0	0	4	17	64

Bend *Deschutes County*   Elevation: 3,595 ft.   Latitude: 44° 04' N   Longitude: 121° 19' W

	JAN	FEB	MAR	APR	MAY	JUN	JUL	AUG	SEP	OCT	NOV	DEC	YEAR
Mean Maximum Temp. (°F)	41.5	45.6	51.4	57.3	65.0	73.0	81.2	81.3	73.3	63.0	48.0	41.1	60.1
Mean Temp. (°F)	32.1	35.1	39.2	43.6	50.2	57.2	63.7	63.4	55.7	47.5	37.8	31.9	46.4
Mean Minimum Temp. (°F)	22.7	24.5	27.0	29.8	35.3	41.2	46.1	45.4	38.1	31.9	27.6	22.6	32.7
Extreme Maximum Temp. (°F)	67	73	76	86	92	95	98	102	100	90	74	66	102
Extreme Minimum Temp. (°F)	-16	-17	-5	9	16	23	27	29	16	3	-10	-24	-24
Days Maximum Temp. ≥ 90°F	0	0	0	0	0	1	6	6	1	0	0	0	14
Days Maximum Temp. ≤ 32°F	5	3	0	0	0	0	0	0	0	0	1	4	13
Days Minimum Temp. ≤ 32°F	25	23	24	20	12	3	1	0	7	17	21	26	179
Days Minimum Temp. ≤ 0°F	1	1	0	0	0	0	0	0	0	0	0	1	3
Heating Degree Days (base 65°F)	1,012	839	793	636	457	250	105	107	282	538	809	1,021	6,849
Cooling Degree Days (base 65°F)	0	0	0	0	5	20	70	65	16	0	0	0	176
Mean Precipitation (in.)	1.81	1.09	0.96	0.71	0.89	0.79	0.63	0.60	0.48	0.63	1.54	1.79	11.92
Days With ≥ 0.1" Precipitation	5	4	3	2	2	3	2	2	2	2	4	5	36
Days With ≥ 1.0" Precipitation	0	0	0	0	0	0	0	0	0	0	0	0	0
Mean Snowfall (in.)	8.6	5.9	3.1	0.9	0.2	0.0	0.0	0.0	trace	0.3	5.0	8.2	32.2
Days With ≥ 1.0" Snow Depth	9	5	2	0	0	0	0	0	0	0	3	9	28

Beulah *Malheur County*   Elevation: 3,267 ft.   Latitude: 43° 55' N   Longitude: 118° 09' W

	JAN	FEB	MAR	APR	MAY	JUN	JUL	AUG	SEP	OCT	NOV	DEC	YEAR
Mean Maximum Temp. (°F)	36.9	44.5	53.5	61.6	71.0	79.8	89.4	88.9	79.8	*68.3*	na	38.1	na
Mean Temp. (°F)	26.7	33.1	40.5	46.9	55.6	63.3	71.0	69.9	60.5	*49.7*	na	27.2	na
Mean Minimum Temp. (°F)	16.4	21.9	27.4	32.1	40.1	46.7	52.5	50.9	41.0	*31.0*	na	16.2	na
Extreme Maximum Temp. (°F)	59	67	78	90	99	101	105	105	100	92	74	62	105
Extreme Minimum Temp. (°F)	-21	-21	-5	15	22	28	32	30	22	2	-5	-29	-29
Days Maximum Temp. ≥ 90°F	0	0	0	0	1	6	18	17	5	0	0	0	47
Days Maximum Temp. ≤ 32°F	8	2	0	0	0	0	0	0	0	0	1	6	17
Days Minimum Temp. ≤ 32°F	29	26	24	16	5	0	0	0	4	17	*24*	28	*173*
Days Minimum Temp. ≤ 0°F	4	1	0	0	0	0	0	0	0	0	0	3	8
Heating Degree Days (base 65°F)	1,181	894	754	538	300	117	24	25	165	*469*	na	1,167	na
Cooling Degree Days (base 65°F)	0	0	0	0	15	60	192	169	37	*0*	*0*	0	*473*
Mean Precipitation (in.)	1.50	1.04	1.24	0.91	1.20	0.86	0.42	0.54	0.50	0.65	1.49	1.67	12.02
Days With ≥ 0.1" Precipitation	4	3	4	3	4	3	1	2	1	2	*4*	4	*35*
Days With ≥ 1.0" Precipitation	0	0	0	0	0	0	0	0	0	0	0	0	0
Mean Snowfall (in.)	7.5	3.8	1.4	0.2	trace	0.0	0.0	0.0	0.0	0.1	3.8	10.0	26.8
Days With ≥ 1.0" Snow Depth	13	5	0	0	0	0	0	0	0	0	2	11	31

Boardman *Morrow County*   Elevation: 298 ft.   Latitude: 45° 50' N   Longitude: 119° 42' W

	JAN	FEB	MAR	APR	MAY	JUN	JUL	AUG	SEP	OCT	NOV	DEC	YEAR
Mean Maximum Temp. (°F)	41.0	47.8	57.8	65.9	74.1	81.6	89.5	88.2	79.1	66.2	51.3	42.1	65.4
Mean Temp. (°F)	33.7	38.8	46.2	53.1	60.6	67.7	74.0	72.9	63.9	52.3	42.5	35.0	53.4
Mean Minimum Temp. (°F)	26.5	29.7	34.5	40.3	47.1	53.9	58.5	57.6	48.6	38.5	33.6	27.8	41.4
Extreme Maximum Temp. (°F)	70	74	80	92	102	104	106	107	99	88	76	68	107
Extreme Minimum Temp. (°F)	-12	-13	10	22	30	35	39	39	25	14	-9	-15	-15
Days Maximum Temp. ≥ 90°F	0	0	0	0	2	6	16	14	2	0	0	0	40
Days Maximum Temp. ≤ 32°F	6	2	0	0	0	0	0	0	0	0	1	5	14
Days Minimum Temp. ≤ 32°F	22	17	11	3	0	0	0	0	0	6	11	21	91
Days Minimum Temp. ≤ 0°F	1	1	0	0	0	0	0	0	0	0	0	1	3
Heating Degree Days (base 65°F)	962	735	576	353	165	38	5	6	91	386	669	925	4,911
Cooling Degree Days (base 65°F)	0	0	0	3	39	120	284	258	68	1	0	0	773
Mean Precipitation (in.)	1.18	0.93	0.71	0.76	0.63	0.45	0.29	0.33	0.42	0.56	1.23	1.22	8.71
Days With ≥ 0.1" Precipitation	4	3	3	2	2	2	1	1	1	2	5	4	30
Days With ≥ 1.0" Precipitation	0	0	0	0	0	0	0	0	0	0	0	0	0
Mean Snowfall (in.)	2.2	1.9	0.2	trace	0.0	0.0	0.0	0.0	0.0	trace	0.7	3.2	8.2
Days With ≥ 1.0" Snow Depth	5	2	0	0	0	0	0	0	0	0	1	3	11

Bonneville Dam *Multnomah County*   Elevation: 59 ft.   Latitude: 45° 38' N   Longitude: 121° 57' W

	JAN	FEB	MAR	APR	MAY	JUN	JUL	AUG	SEP	OCT	NOV	DEC	YEAR
Mean Maximum Temp. (°F)	43.1	47.4	54.3	59.6	66.7	72.1	78.6	79.4	74.1	63.6	51.1	43.8	61.1
Mean Temp. (°F)	38.3	41.6	46.5	50.9	57.1	62.3	67.7	68.1	63.6	55.2	45.8	39.4	53.0
Mean Minimum Temp. (°F)	33.6	35.8	38.6	42.2	47.4	52.5	56.9	56.8	52.9	46.8	40.5	34.9	44.9
Extreme Maximum Temp. (°F)	64	67	74	88	97	102	102	107	100	86	71	65	107
Extreme Minimum Temp. (°F)	7	7	20	29	32	39	45	46	34	29	9	6	6
Days Maximum Temp. ≥ 90°F	0	0	0	0	0	1	3	3	1	0	0	0	8
Days Maximum Temp. ≤ 32°F	3	1	0	0	0	0	0	0	0	0	1	2	7
Days Minimum Temp. ≤ 32°F	11	7	3	1	0	0	0	0	0	0	2	8	32
Days Minimum Temp. ≤ 0°F	0	0	0	0	0	0	0	0	0	0	0	0	0
Heating Degree Days (base 65°F)	819	655	568	417	254	117	30	23	93	302	568	787	4,633
Cooling Degree Days (base 65°F)	0	0	0	1	17	43	126	136	62	6	0	0	391
Mean Precipitation (in.)	11.41	9.66	7.78	6.14	3.81	2.93	1.04	1.34	3.11	5.69	12.35	13.00	78.26
Days With ≥ 0.1" Precipitation	16	14	15	13	9	7	3	3	6	10	17	16	129
Days With ≥ 1.0" Precipitation	4	3	2	1	0	0	0	0	1	1	4	4	20
Mean Snowfall (in.)	7.2	3.7	0.9	trace	0.0	0.0	0.0	0.0	0.0	0.0	1.3	3.6	16.7
Days With ≥ 1.0" Snow Depth	4	1	0	0	0	0	0	0	0	0	1	1	7

Brookings *Curry County*   Elevation: 45 ft.   Latitude: 42° 02' N   Longitude: 124° 15' W

	JAN	FEB	MAR	APR	MAY	JUN	JUL	AUG	SEP	OCT	NOV	DEC	YEAR
Mean Maximum Temp. (°F)	55.3	56.6	57.8	59.8	63.5	66.6	68.1	67.6	68.2	64.6	58.2	54.9	61.8
Mean Temp. (°F)	48.7	49.6	50.1	51.6	55.1	58.2	60.0	60.1	59.8	56.3	51.4	48.2	54.1
Mean Minimum Temp. (°F)	41.8	42.5	42.5	43.4	46.7	49.7	51.9	52.6	51.4	48.0	44.6	41.4	46.4
Extreme Maximum Temp. (°F)	73	83	80	85	94	101	102	101	103	94	79	79	103
Extreme Minimum Temp. (°F)	25	24	30	31	36	37	44	43	40	34	29	18	18
Days Maximum Temp. ≥ 90°F	0	0	0	0	0	0	0	0	1	0	0	0	1
Days Maximum Temp. ≤ 32°F	0	0	0	0	0	0	0	0	0	0	0	0	0
Days Minimum Temp. ≤ 32°F	2	1	0	0	0	0	0	0	0	0	0	2	5
Days Minimum Temp. ≤ 0°F	0	0	0	0	0	0	0	0	0	0	0	0	0
Heating Degree Days (base 65°F)	501	430	453	396	303	206	157	152	165	268	400	515	3,946
Cooling Degree Days (base 65°F)	0	0	0	2	2	9	11	9	13	8	0	0	54
Mean Precipitation (in.)	11.37	9.90	9.77	5.80	3.63	1.77	0.51	1.07	1.98	5.33	10.90	12.70	74.73
Days With ≥ 0.1" Precipitation	14	14	15	11	6	3	1	2	3	7	14	15	105
Days With ≥ 1.0" Precipitation	4	3	3	1	1	0	0	0	1	2	4	4	23
Mean Snowfall (in.)	0.2	0.3	trace	trace	0.0	0.0	0.0	0.0	0.0	0.0	0.0	trace	0.5
Days With ≥ 1.0" Snow Depth	0	0	0	0	0	0	0	0	0	0	0	0	0

Brothers *Deschutes County*   Elevation: 4,639 ft.   Latitude: 43° 49' N   Longitude: 120° 36' W

	JAN	FEB	MAR	APR	MAY	JUN	JUL	AUG	SEP	OCT	NOV	DEC	YEAR
Mean Maximum Temp. (°F)	37.7	42.2	48.3	55.9	64.1	72.5	81.6	81.2	72.9	62.0	45.3	37.8	58.5
Mean Temp. (°F)	27.8	31.5	35.8	41.0	48.0	55.3	62.3	61.5	53.8	45.2	34.2	27.5	43.7
Mean Minimum Temp. (°F)	17.7	20.7	23.3	26.0	31.9	38.0	42.9	41.8	34.6	28.3	23.0	17.2	28.8
Extreme Maximum Temp. (°F)	61	67	72	85	92	94	98	99	97	87	72	60	99
Extreme Minimum Temp. (°F)	-22	-19	-10	7	8	12	19	22	10	2	-16	-30	-30
Days Maximum Temp. ≥ 90°F	0	0	0	0	0	1	6	5	1	0	0	0	13
Days Maximum Temp. ≤ 32°F	8	4	0	0	0	0	0	0	0	0	2	7	21
Days Minimum Temp. ≤ 32°F	28	26	27	23	17	7	3	4	11	22	25	29	222
Days Minimum Temp. ≤ 0°F	3	1	0	0	0	0	0	0	0	0	1	2	7
Heating Degree Days (base 65°F)	1,147	940	899	713	521	298	133	145	336	608	918	1,154	7,812
Cooling Degree Days (base 65°F)	0	0	0	0	3	13	55	41	8	0	0	0	120
Mean Precipitation (in.)	0.90	0.43	0.70	0.68	1.18	0.84	0.63	0.66	0.52	0.66	1.14	1.02	9.36
Days With ≥ 0.1" Precipitation	3	1	3	2	3	3	2	2	2	2	3	3	29
Days With ≥ 1.0" Precipitation	0	0	0	0	0	0	0	0	0	0	0	0	0
Mean Snowfall (in.)	4.3	3.0	2.0	1.1	0.7	trace	0.0	0.0	trace	0.6	3.3	5.9	20.9
Days With ≥ 1.0" Snow Depth	13	5	1	0	0	0	0	0	0	0	3	10	32

Burns Junction _Malheur County_ Elevation: 3,927 ft. Latitude: 42° 47' N Longitude: 117° 51' W

	JAN	FEB	MAR	APR	MAY	JUN	JUL	AUG	SEP	OCT	NOV	DEC	YEAR
Mean Maximum Temp. (°F)	40.5	47.6	55.4	_63.3_	72.1	82.4	91.9	90.5	81.3	68.4	50.7	41.1	_65.4_
Mean Temp. (°F)	29.4	35.6	41.9	_48.2_	56.4	65.3	73.0	71.1	62.0	50.6	37.8	29.9	_50.1_
Mean Minimum Temp. (°F)	18.4	23.6	28.3	_33.1_	40.6	48.2	54.1	51.7	42.6	32.7	24.7	18.4	_34.7_
Extreme Maximum Temp. (°F)	65	71	79	_91_	98	105	108	107	102	92	74	69	_108_
Extreme Minimum Temp. (°F)	-25	-19	-9	_12_	20	28	32	31	18	7	-6	-32	_-32_
Days Maximum Temp. ≥ 90°F	0	0	0	_0_	1	8	21	20	7	0	0	0	_57_
Days Maximum Temp. ≤ 32°F	6	2	0	_0_	0	0	0	0	0	0	1	5	_14_
Days Minimum Temp. ≤ 32°F	28	23	22	_15_	5	1	0	0	3	_15_	23	27	_162_
Days Minimum Temp. ≤ 0°F	3	1	0	_0_	0	0	0	0	0	0	0	3	_7_
Heating Degree Days (base 65°F)	1,096	824	710	_499_	281	92	14	22	138	442	810	1,083	_6,011_
Cooling Degree Days (base 65°F)	0	0	0	_2_	25	110	270	239	60	1	0	0	_707_
Mean Precipitation (in.)	0.80	0.84	0.88	_1.04_	1.05	0.82	0.49	0.43	0.46	0.46	0.80	0.80	_8.87_
Days With ≥ 0.1" Precipitation	3	3	3	_4_	4	3	2	1	1	2	3	3	_32_
Days With ≥ 1.0" Precipitation	0	0	0	_0_	0	0	0	0	0	0	0	0	_0_
Mean Snowfall (in.)	_3.3_	_1.4_	0.8	_0.2_	0.1	0.0	0.0	0.0	0.0	0.2	1.5	_3.8_	_11.3_
Days With ≥ 1.0" Snow Depth	9	3	_0_	_0_	0	0	0	0	0	0	1	6	_19_

Cascadia _Linn County_ Elevation: 859 ft. Latitude: 44° 24' N Longitude: 122° 29' W

	JAN	FEB	MAR	APR	MAY	JUN	JUL	AUG	SEP	OCT	NOV	DEC	YEAR
Mean Maximum Temp. (°F)	45.9	50.8	55.0	59.1	65.2	70.8	78.2	79.5	74.4	64.0	51.2	44.4	61.5
Mean Temp. (°F)	38.8	41.9	45.0	48.3	53.5	58.7	63.7	63.9	58.9	51.3	43.6	38.3	50.5
Mean Minimum Temp. (°F)	31.7	33.0	34.9	37.4	41.7	46.5	49.2	48.3	43.7	38.5	36.0	32.2	39.4
Extreme Maximum Temp. (°F)	69	75	78	86	95	99	100	104	101	93	76	61	104
Extreme Minimum Temp. (°F)	3	2	18	24	29	31	37	31	27	23	11	-2	-2
Days Maximum Temp. ≥ 90°F	0	0	0	0	0	1	3	4	2	0	0	0	10
Days Maximum Temp. ≤ 32°F	0	1	0	0	0	0	0	0	0	0	0	1	2
Days Minimum Temp. ≤ 32°F	17	14	12	5	1	0	0	0	1	6	10	16	82
Days Minimum Temp. ≤ 0°F	0	0	0	0	0	0	0	0	0	0	0	0	0
Heating Degree Days (base 65°F)	804	646	614	496	354	197	85	76	188	418	635	820	5,333
Cooling Degree Days (base 65°F)	0	0	0	0	5	15	48	47	13	1	0	0	129
Mean Precipitation (in.)	8.26	6.83	6.88	5.90	4.58	2.98	0.99	1.31	2.53	4.81	10.16	9.42	64.65
Days With ≥ 0.1" Precipitation	15	14	15	13	10	7	3	3	5	9	16	16	126
Days With ≥ 1.0" Precipitation	2	1	1	1	0	0	0	0	0	1	3	3	12
Mean Snowfall (in.)	2.0	2.5	0.5	trace	trace	0.0	0.0	0.0	0.0	0.0	trace	0.9	5.9
Days With ≥ 1.0" Snow Depth	2	2	0	0	0	0	0	0	0	0	1	1	6

Cave Junction 1 WNW _Josephine County_ Elevation: 1,279 ft. Latitude: 42° 11' N Longitude: 123° 41' W

	JAN	FEB	MAR	APR	MAY	JUN	JUL	AUG	SEP	OCT	NOV	DEC	YEAR
Mean Maximum Temp. (°F)	47.7	53.3	58.2	64.1	72.7	80.5	89.2	89.0	82.8	70.3	53.4	46.3	67.3
Mean Temp. (°F)	40.2	43.6	46.7	50.4	56.9	63.6	69.9	69.1	63.7	54.7	45.1	39.5	53.6
Mean Minimum Temp. (°F)	32.6	33.9	35.2	36.6	41.1	46.5	50.5	49.2	44.6	39.1	36.7	32.7	39.9
Extreme Maximum Temp. (°F)	66	76	82	90	97	109	108	109	110	97	78	69	110
Extreme Minimum Temp. (°F)	11	4	20	22	28	31	36	35	25	19	11	-6	-6
Days Maximum Temp. ≥ 90°F	0	0	0	0	2	6	16	16	8	1	0	0	49
Days Maximum Temp. ≤ 32°F	0	0	0	0	0	0	0	0	0	0	0	0	0
Days Minimum Temp. ≤ 32°F	16	13	12	8	2	0	0	0	1	5	8	16	81
Days Minimum Temp. ≤ 0°F	0	0	0	0	0	0	0	0	0	0	0	0	0
Heating Degree Days (base 65°F)	763	597	560	432	257	97	21	19	86	315	591	783	4,521
Cooling Degree Days (base 65°F)	0	0	0	1	15	58	183	162	61	4	0	0	484
Mean Precipitation (in.)	10.98	9.40	8.15	4.08	2.23	0.72	0.25	0.54	1.30	3.65	10.51	11.28	63.09
Days With ≥ 0.1" Precipitation	12	12	12	8	4	2	1	1	3	6	12	12	85
Days With ≥ 1.0" Precipitation	4	4	3	1	1	0	0	0	0	1	4	4	22
Mean Snowfall (in.)	3.1	4.6	2.1	1.0	trace	0.0	0.0	0.0	0.0	trace	0.8	2.9	14.5
Days With ≥ 1.0" Snow Depth	2	1	0	0	0	0	0	0	0	0	0	1	4

Clatskanie _Columbia County_ Elevation: 19 ft. Latitude: 46° 06' N Longitude: 123° 12' W

	JAN	FEB	MAR	APR	MAY	JUN	JUL	AUG	SEP	OCT	NOV	DEC	YEAR
Mean Maximum Temp. (°F)	45.3	49.9	54.6	58.6	64.3	68.4	73.6	74.7	71.5	61.6	50.7	44.8	59.8
Mean Temp. (°F)	39.6	42.5	45.9	49.1	54.4	58.8	63.2	63.9	60.2	52.0	44.3	39.4	51.1
Mean Minimum Temp. (°F)	33.8	34.9	37.2	39.4	44.5	49.2	52.7	53.1	48.8	42.3	37.9	34.0	42.3
Extreme Maximum Temp. (°F)	60	72	78	86	92	99	98	103	100	88	66	64	103
Extreme Minimum Temp. (°F)	9	1	20	26	30	35	41	40	32	25	9	1	1
Days Maximum Temp. ≥ 90°F	0	0	0	0	0	0	1	1	0	0	0	0	2
Days Maximum Temp. ≤ 32°F	1	0	0	0	0	0	0	0	0	0	0	1	2
Days Minimum Temp. ≤ 32°F	13	10	7	3	0	0	0	0	0	2	7	12	54
Days Minimum Temp. ≤ 0°F	0	0	0	0	0	0	0	0	0	0	0	0	0
Heating Degree Days (base 65°F)	782	630	583	471	325	191	88	69	151	396	613	787	5,086
Cooling Degree Days (base 65°F)	0	0	0	0	5	12	39	45	15	1	0	0	117
Mean Precipitation (in.)	8.47	6.76	5.91	4.18	2.64	1.79	0.84	0.97	2.25	4.14	8.97	9.59	56.51
Days With ≥ 0.1" Precipitation	14	13	13	10	8	6	2	3	5	9	15	16	114
Days With ≥ 1.0" Precipitation	2	1	1	0	0	0	0	0	0	1	2	3	10
Mean Snowfall (in.)	2.4	1.3	0.3	trace	0.0	0.0	0.0	0.0	0.0	0.0	0.4	1.5	5.9
Days With ≥ 1.0" Snow Depth	2	1	0	0	0	0	0	0	0	0	1	2	6

Cloverdale *Tillamook County*   Elevation: 9 ft.   Latitude: 45° 12' N   Longitude: 123° 54' W

	JAN	FEB	MAR	APR	MAY	JUN	JUL	AUG	SEP	OCT	NOV	DEC	YEAR
Mean Maximum Temp. (°F)	50.9	53.6	55.4	58.0	62.4	65.9	70.0	71.2	70.0	63.9	55.2	50.6	60.6
Mean Temp. (°F)	44.3	46.1	47.2	49.1	53.2	56.7	59.9	60.7	59.2	54.0	48.1	44.0	51.9
Mean Minimum Temp. (°F)	37.6	38.5	38.9	40.2	43.9	47.5	49.7	50.2	48.3	44.0	40.9	37.4	43.1
Extreme Maximum Temp. (°F)	67	76	76	85	91	97	99	106	96	94	74	71	106
Extreme Minimum Temp. (°F)	14	11	25	29	30	33	36	37	33	28	17	9	9
Days Maximum Temp. ≥ 90°F	0	0	0	0	0	0	0	0	1	0	0	0	1
Days Maximum Temp. ≤ 32°F	0	0	0	0	0	0	0	0	0	0	0	1	1
Days Minimum Temp. ≤ 32°F	8	5	4	2	0	0	0	0	0	0	3	7	29
Days Minimum Temp. ≤ 0°F	0	0	0	0	0	0	0	0	0	0	0	0	0
Heating Degree Days (base 65°F)	635	528	545	470	361	245	155	132	176	337	501	644	4,729
Cooling Degree Days (base 65°F)	0	0	0	0	2	4	2	6	7	3	0	0	24
Mean Precipitation (in.)	12.01	9.60	9.16	6.07	4.54	3.12	1.51	1.42	3.77	6.26	12.75	13.19	83.40
Days With ≥ 0.1" Precipitation	16	15	17	13	10	7	3	3	6	10	18	17	135
Days With ≥ 1.0" Precipitation	4	3	2	1	1	0	0	0	1	2	4	5	23
Mean Snowfall (in.)	0.4	trace	0.2	trace	0.0	0.0	0.0	0.0	0.0	trace	0.1	0.3	1.0
Days With ≥ 1.0" Snow Depth	0	0	0	0	0	0	0	0	0	0	0	0	0

Condon *Gilliam County*   Elevation: 2,837 ft.   Latitude: 45° 14' N   Longitude: 120° 11' W

	JAN	FEB	MAR	APR	MAY	JUN	JUL	AUG	SEP	OCT	NOV	DEC	YEAR
Mean Maximum Temp. (°F)	38.4	43.2	50.3	56.7	65.1	73.0	81.9	81.3	72.2	60.8	46.0	38.8	59.0
Mean Temp. (°F)	31.2	35.0	40.4	45.3	52.2	59.0	66.1	65.8	57.8	48.3	37.8	31.3	47.5
Mean Minimum Temp. (°F)	23.9	26.9	30.3	33.8	39.3	45.0	50.2	50.3	43.4	35.7	29.6	23.9	36.0
Extreme Maximum Temp. (°F)	62	71	72	83	95	98	100	103	99	88	74	63	103
Extreme Minimum Temp. (°F)	-12	-19	11	20	24	28	35	33	22	6	-14	-22	-22
Days Maximum Temp. ≥ 90°F	0	0	0	0	0	1	6	5	1	0	0	0	13
Days Maximum Temp. ≤ 32°F	9	4	0	0	0	0	0	0	0	0	2	8	23
Days Minimum Temp. ≤ 32°F	25	21	20	14	6	0	0	0	1	10	19	26	142
Days Minimum Temp. ≤ 0°F	1	1	0	0	0	0	0	0	0	0	0	1	3
Heating Degree Days (base 65°F)	1,042	840	758	585	395	202	69	67	226	512	810	1,036	6,542
Cooling Degree Days (base 65°F)	0	0	0	0	8	25	100	96	20	1	0	0	250
Mean Precipitation (in.)	1.65	1.34	1.36	1.40	1.41	1.03	0.55	0.60	0.67	1.03	1.93	1.59	14.56
Days With ≥ 0.1" Precipitation	5	5	5	4	4	3	1	2	2	3	7	5	46
Days With ≥ 1.0" Precipitation	0	0	0	0	0	0	0	0	0	0	0	0	0
Mean Snowfall (in.)	5.0	4.9	2.2	1.0	0.1	0.0	0.0	0.0	0.0	0.5	4.7	5.2	23.6
Days With ≥ 1.0" Snow Depth	8	4	1	0	0	0	0	0	0	0	3	6	22

Coquille City *Coos County*   Elevation: 22 ft.   Latitude: 43° 11' N   Longitude: 124° 12' W

	JAN	FEB	MAR	APR	MAY	JUN	JUL	AUG	SEP	OCT	NOV	DEC	YEAR
Mean Maximum Temp. (°F)	54.2	56.3	57.9	60.2	64.2	68.0	71.9	73.1	72.7	67.5	58.1	53.5	63.1
Mean Temp. (°F)	45.1	47.1	48.4	50.2	53.9	57.7	61.1	61.8	60.0	55.1	48.9	44.8	52.8
Mean Minimum Temp. (°F)	35.9	37.7	38.9	40.1	43.4	47.3	50.2	50.5	47.2	42.7	39.6	36.0	42.5
Extreme Maximum Temp. (°F)	74	85	81	88	95	96	98	94	101	102	79	72	102
Extreme Minimum Temp. (°F)	12	11	25	29	31	34	39	37	31	26	18	8	8
Days Maximum Temp. ≥ 90°F	0	0	0	0	0	0	0	0	1	0	0	0	1
Days Maximum Temp. ≤ 32°F	0	0	0	0	0	0	0	0	0	0	0	0	0
Days Minimum Temp. ≤ 32°F	11	7	4	2	0	0	0	0	0	1	5	11	41
Days Minimum Temp. ≤ 0°F	0	0	0	0	0	0	0	0	0	0	0	0	0
Heating Degree Days (base 65°F)	611	500	506	439	340	215	121	98	149	300	476	620	4,375
Cooling Degree Days (base 65°F)	0	0	0	0	2	2	5	6	6	2	0	0	23
Mean Precipitation (in.)	8.28	7.26	6.93	4.54	2.97	1.37	0.43	0.71	1.49	3.47	9.01	8.97	55.43
Days With ≥ 0.1" Precipitation	14	13	13	11	7	4	1	2	3	7	15	15	105
Days With ≥ 1.0" Precipitation	2	2	1	1	0	0	0	0	0	1	3	2	12
Mean Snowfall (in.)	0.3	trace	trace	trace	0.0	0.0	0.0	0.0	0.0	0.0	trace	0.2	0.5
Days With ≥ 1.0" Snow Depth	0	0	0	0	0	0	0	0	0	0	0	0	0

Corvallis State Univ *Benton County*   Elevation: 223 ft.   Latitude: 44° 38' N   Longitude: 123° 11' W

	JAN	FEB	MAR	APR	MAY	JUN	JUL	AUG	SEP	OCT	NOV	DEC	YEAR
Mean Maximum Temp. (°F)	46.2	50.5	55.6	59.9	66.6	72.9	80.7	81.7	76.3	64.7	52.4	45.7	62.8
Mean Temp. (°F)	40.0	42.9	46.7	49.9	55.3	60.8	66.2	66.7	62.2	53.3	45.3	39.8	52.4
Mean Minimum Temp. (°F)	33.7	35.3	37.7	39.8	43.9	48.6	51.8	51.5	48.1	41.8	38.2	33.9	42.0
Extreme Maximum Temp. (°F)	64	68	76	83	96	102	103	108	103	92	72	66	108
Extreme Minimum Temp. (°F)	9	7	12	27	28	33	38	37	32	25	15	-7	-7
Days Maximum Temp. ≥ 90°F	0	0	0	0	0	1	5	5	2	0	0	0	13
Days Maximum Temp. ≤ 32°F	1	0	0	0	0	0	0	0	0	0	0	1	2
Days Minimum Temp. ≤ 32°F	14	10	6	3	0	0	0	0	0	2	6	13	54
Days Minimum Temp. ≤ 0°F	0	0	0	0	0	0	0	0	0	0	0	0	0
Heating Degree Days (base 65°F)	768	617	561	447	302	149	47	37	113	358	583	775	4,757
Cooling Degree Days (base 65°F)	0	0	0	0	9	27	93	97	40	2	0	0	268
Mean Precipitation (in.)	6.70	5.69	4.54	3.01	2.24	1.44	0.57	0.73	1.49	3.06	7.09	7.70	44.26
Days With ≥ 0.1" Precipitation	13	12	12	9	6	4	2	2	4	7	14	13	98
Days With ≥ 1.0" Precipitation	2	1	0	0	0	0	0	0	0	0	1	2	6
Mean Snowfall (in.)	1.1	2.1	0.1	trace	0.0	0.0	0.0	0.0	0.0	trace	0.2	1.3	4.8
Days With ≥ 1.0" Snow Depth	1	1	0	0	0	0	0	0	0	0	0	1	3

Corvallis Water Bureau *Benton County*   Elevation: 590 ft.   Latitude: 44° 31' N   Longitude: 123° 27' W

	JAN	FEB	MAR	APR	MAY	JUN	JUL	AUG	SEP	OCT	NOV	DEC	YEAR
Mean Maximum Temp. (°F)	45.2	49.2	54.1	58.9	65.5	71.3	78.3	78.9	73.7	63.1	50.9	44.4	61.1
Mean Temp. (°F)	38.8	41.5	44.9	48.4	54.1	59.3	64.4	64.7	60.5	51.9	43.7	38.4	50.9
Mean Minimum Temp. (°F)	32.3	33.8	35.7	37.9	42.6	47.3	50.4	50.5	47.3	40.8	36.4	32.5	40.6
Extreme Maximum Temp. (°F)	60	67	74	83	93	100	100	107	98	88	69	60	107
Extreme Minimum Temp. (°F)	4	2	20	28	30	33	39	35	32	23	11	2	2
Days Maximum Temp. ≥ 90°F	0	0	0	0	0	1	4	3	1	0	0	0	9
Days Maximum Temp. ≤ 32°F	1	0	0	0	0	0	0	0	0	0	0	1	2
Days Minimum Temp. ≤ 32°F	16	13	9	5	0	0	0	0	0	1	9	16	69
Days Minimum Temp. ≤ 0°F	0	0	0	0	0	0	0	0	0	0	0	0	0
Heating Degree Days (base 65°F)	807	656	616	491	337	185	75	63	151	400	634	817	5,232
Cooling Degree Days (base 65°F)	0	0	0	0	6	18	59	58	22	1	0	0	164
Mean Precipitation (in.)	11.67	9.54	7.57	4.69	2.79	1.49	0.49	0.66	1.80	4.23	10.99	12.85	68.77
Days With ≥ 0.1" Precipitation	15	14	14	10	7	4	1	2	4	7	16	16	110
Days With ≥ 1.0" Precipitation	4	3	2	1	0	0	0	0	0	1	4	4	19
Mean Snowfall (in.)	1.8	3.5	0.3	trace	0.0	0.0	0.0	0.0	0.0	0.0	0.3	1.5	7.4
Days With ≥ 1.0" Snow Depth	1	2	0	0	0	0	0	0	0	0	0	2	5

Cottage Grove 1 S *Lane County*   Elevation: 593 ft.   Latitude: 43° 48' N   Longitude: 123° 03' W

	JAN	FEB	MAR	APR	MAY	JUN	JUL	AUG	SEP	OCT	NOV	DEC	YEAR
Mean Maximum Temp. (°F)	48.6	53.3	57.6	61.9	68.3	74.3	81.6	82.1	77.2	66.2	53.8	47.6	64.4
Mean Temp. (°F)	40.9	43.9	46.8	49.7	54.8	60.0	64.9	65.0	60.5	53.1	45.7	40.6	52.1
Mean Minimum Temp. (°F)	33.1	34.4	35.9	37.5	41.3	45.7	48.1	47.8	43.7	39.9	37.5	33.5	39.9
Extreme Maximum Temp. (°F)	67	75	78	87	97	101	101	105	104	96	76	72	105
Extreme Minimum Temp. (°F)	0	0	19	24	25	29	34	32	25	18	9	-5	-5
Days Maximum Temp. ≥ 90°F	0	0	0	0	0	1	5	5	3	0	0	0	14
Days Maximum Temp. ≤ 32°F	0	0	0	0	0	0	0	0	0	0	0	1	1
Days Minimum Temp. ≤ 32°F	14	11	10	6	3	0	0	0	1	4	7	14	70
Days Minimum Temp. ≤ 0°F	0	0	0	0	0	0	0	0	0	0	0	0	0
Heating Degree Days (base 65°F)	742	591	558	452	313	161	60	56	146	363	573	751	4,766
Cooling Degree Days (base 65°F)	0	0	0	0	6	19	61	63	22	1	0	0	172
Mean Precipitation (in.)	6.38	5.34	5.14	4.01	2.58	1.52	0.61	0.92	1.45	3.09	7.47	6.83	45.34
Days With ≥ 0.1" Precipitation	12	11	12	10	7	4	2	2	4	7	14	13	98
Days With ≥ 1.0" Precipitation	2	1	1	0	0	0	0	0	0	0	1	1	6
Mean Snowfall (in.)	1.0	1.5	0.2	trace	0.0	0.0	0.0	0.0	0.0	0.0	0.2	0.9	3.8
Days With ≥ 1.0" Snow Depth	1	1	0	0	0	0	0	0	0	0	0	1	3

Cottage Grove Dam *Lane County*   Elevation: 830 ft.   Latitude: 43° 43' N   Longitude: 123° 03' W

	JAN	FEB	MAR	APR	MAY	JUN	JUL	AUG	SEP	OCT	NOV	DEC	YEAR
Mean Maximum Temp. (°F)	46.7	51.3	55.2	59.2	65.4	71.4	79.0	80.0	75.0	64.4	52.2	46.0	62.2
Mean Temp. (°F)	39.6	42.6	45.5	48.7	54.1	59.5	65.0	65.4	60.9	52.8	44.4	39.3	51.5
Mean Minimum Temp. (°F)	32.4	33.9	35.8	38.2	42.7	47.5	50.9	50.7	46.8	41.1	36.6	32.5	40.8
Extreme Maximum Temp. (°F)	65	74	77	88	95	99	101	105	100	94	76	70	105
Extreme Minimum Temp. (°F)	7	1	21	28	32	36	39	39	32	24	16	-2	-2
Days Maximum Temp. ≥ 90°F	0	0	0	0	0	1	3	4	2	0	0	0	10
Days Maximum Temp. ≤ 32°F	1	0	0	0	0	0	0	0	0	0	0	1	2
Days Minimum Temp. ≤ 32°F	16	12	9	3	0	0	0	0	0	1	8	16	65
Days Minimum Temp. ≤ 0°F	0	0	0	0	0	0	0	0	0	0	0	0	0
Heating Degree Days (base 65°F)	782	626	597	482	336	179	66	54	142	373	610	791	5,038
Cooling Degree Days (base 65°F)	0	0	0	0	7	16	65	67	26	3	0	0	184
Mean Precipitation (in.)	6.92	5.72	5.47	4.31	3.08	1.67	0.68	0.97	1.71	3.69	7.97	7.58	49.77
Days With ≥ 0.1" Precipitation	12	12	13	12	8	5	2	2	4	8	14	14	106
Days With ≥ 1.0" Precipitation	2	1	1	0	0	0	0	0	0	1	2	2	9
Mean Snowfall (in.)	0.9	2.1	0.2	trace	0.0	0.0	0.0	0.0	0.0	0.0	0.1	0.3	3.6
Days With ≥ 1.0" Snow Depth	0	0	0	0	0	0	0	0	0	0	0	1	1

Crater Lake Nat'l Park Hdqtrs. *Klamath County*   Elevation: 6,473 ft.   Latitude: 42° 54' N   Longitude: 122° 08' W

	JAN	FEB	MAR	APR	MAY	JUN	JUL	AUG	SEP	OCT	NOV	DEC	YEAR
Mean Maximum Temp. (°F)	34.4	34.9	36.9	41.6	49.2	57.6	67.5	68.8	62.2	52.5	38.0	34.4	48.2
Mean Temp. (°F)	26.2	26.7	28.1	31.7	38.4	45.5	53.7	54.6	49.1	41.4	30.2	26.4	37.7
Mean Minimum Temp. (°F)	18.0	18.5	19.2	21.8	27.5	33.4	39.8	40.4	35.9	30.2	22.4	18.3	27.1
Extreme Maximum Temp. (°F)	57	60	62	68	76	83	86	90	87	78	68	64	90
Extreme Minimum Temp. (°F)	-9	-13	-7	0	7	15	24	24	11	8	-4	-13	-13
Days Maximum Temp. ≥ 90°F	0	0	0	0	0	0	0	0	0	0	0	0	0
Days Maximum Temp. ≤ 32°F	14	12	10	6	1	0	0	0	0	2	9	14	68
Days Minimum Temp. ≤ 32°F	31	28	31	27	23	14	4	3	9	19	27	31	247
Days Minimum Temp. ≤ 0°F	1	1	0	0	0	0	0	0	0	0	0	1	3
Heating Degree Days (base 65°F)	1,196	1,075	1,138	992	819	579	347	321	472	724	1,038	1,191	9,892
Cooling Degree Days (base 65°F)	0	0	0	0	0	0	2	4	1	0	0	0	7
Mean Precipitation (in.)	9.98	8.26	7.87	5.39	3.50	2.05	0.94	1.06	2.24	4.55	10.88	10.65	67.37
Days With ≥ 0.1" Precipitation	14	14	15	11	8	5	2	3	4	7	15	15	113
Days With ≥ 1.0" Precipitation	3	2	2	1	0	0	0	0	1	1	4	4	18
Mean Snowfall (in.)	84.0	80.4	75.4	45.9	19.1	4.4	0.3	0.2	3.9	19.9	72.3	82.3	488.1
Days With ≥ 1.0" Snow Depth	31	28	31	30	30	19	4	0	1	8	25	31	238

Dallas 2 NE *Polk County*   Elevation: 288 ft.   Latitude: 44° 57' N   Longitude: 123° 17' W

	JAN	FEB	MAR	APR	MAY	JUN	JUL	AUG	SEP	OCT	NOV	DEC	YEAR
Mean Maximum Temp. (°F)	46.2	50.8	56.2	61.2	68.2	74.4	82.2	82.7	77.5	65.6	51.6	45.1	63.5
Mean Temp. (°F)	40.0	43.0	46.7	50.2	55.9	60.9	66.2	66.2	62.3	53.6	44.8	39.4	52.4
Mean Minimum Temp. (°F)	33.8	35.3	37.1	39.1	43.3	47.4	50.1	49.7	47.1	41.7	37.9	33.8	41.4
Extreme Maximum Temp. (°F)	65	67	76	85	98	102	103	105	103	91	72	65	105
Extreme Minimum Temp. (°F)	7	7	10	26	30	31	36	34	30	22	12	-2	-2
Days Maximum Temp. ≥ 90°F	0	0	0	0	0	2	6	6	3	0	0	0	17
Days Maximum Temp. ≤ 32°F	1	0	0	0	0	0	0	0	0	0	0	1	2
Days Minimum Temp. ≤ 32°F	13	10	8	4	1	0	0	0	0	2	7	13	58
Days Minimum Temp. ≤ 0°F	0	0	0	0	0	0	0	0	0	0	0	0	0
Heating Degree Days (base 65°F)	768	614	563	439	285	146	44	40	114	348	600	786	4,747
Cooling Degree Days (base 65°F)	0	0	0	0	12	29	87	89	45	3	0	0	265
Mean Precipitation (in.)	8.07	6.57	5.33	3.20	2.19	1.39	0.50	0.67	1.45	3.32	7.97	9.01	49.67
Days With ≥ 0.1" Precipitation	12	10	11	8	6	4	1	2	4	6	13	13	90
Days With ≥ 1.0" Precipitation	2	1	1	0	0	0	0	0	0	1	2	2	9
Mean Snowfall (in.)	0.6	1.9	0.1	trace	0.0	0.0	0.0	0.0	0.0	0.0	0.3	1.8	4.7
Days With ≥ 1.0" Snow Depth	0	1	0	0	0	0	0	0	0	0	0	1	2

Detroit Dam *Marion County*   Elevation: 1,217 ft.   Latitude: 44° 43' N   Longitude: 122° 15' W

	JAN	FEB	MAR	APR	MAY	JUN	JUL	AUG	SEP	OCT	NOV	DEC	YEAR
Mean Maximum Temp. (°F)	43.8	47.3	52.3	57.0	64.0	70.1	77.7	78.6	73.2	62.2	49.4	43.7	59.9
Mean Temp. (°F)	38.7	41.0	44.4	48.0	54.0	59.6	65.5	66.3	61.8	53.4	44.1	39.0	51.3
Mean Minimum Temp. (°F)	33.6	34.6	36.4	39.0	43.9	49.0	53.2	53.8	50.3	44.7	38.8	34.3	42.6
Extreme Maximum Temp. (°F)	63	71	73	87	104	101	103	105	107	92	70	64	107
Extreme Minimum Temp. (°F)	10	5	19	30	34	36	42	40	35	26	15	5	5
Days Maximum Temp. ≥ 90°F	0	0	0	0	0	1	3	4	1	0	0	0	9
Days Maximum Temp. ≤ 32°F	1	0	0	0	0	0	0	0	0	0	0	1	2
Days Minimum Temp. ≤ 32°F	11	7	4	1	0	0	0	0	0	0	3	8	34
Days Minimum Temp. ≤ 0°F	0	0	0	0	0	0	0	0	0	0	0	0	0
Heating Degree Days (base 65°F)	809	672	632	503	344	186	70	52	133	355	621	799	5,176
Cooling Degree Days (base 65°F)	0	0	0	1	11	27	90	100	48	3	0	0	280
Mean Precipitation (in.)	12.70	10.88	9.48	7.54	5.40	3.48	1.03	1.36	3.40	6.37	14.54	14.43	90.61
Days With ≥ 0.1" Precipitation	16	15	16	14	11	7	3	3	6	10	17	17	135
Days With ≥ 1.0" Precipitation	4	3	2	1	1	1	0	0	1	2	5	5	25
Mean Snowfall (in.)	3.1	4.4	0.7	0.2	0.0	0.0	0.0	0.0	0.0	0.0	0.8	1.5	10.7
Days With ≥ 1.0" Snow Depth	3	3	1	0	0	0	0	0	0	0	1	2	10

Dorena Dam *Lane County*   Elevation: 816 ft.   Latitude: 43° 47' N   Longitude: 122° 58' W

	JAN	FEB	MAR	APR	MAY	JUN	JUL	AUG	SEP	OCT	NOV	DEC	YEAR
Mean Maximum Temp. (°F)	47.4	52.1	56.0	60.1	66.3	72.3	80.0	81.0	75.7	65.0	52.8	46.5	62.9
Mean Temp. (°F)	39.9	42.8	45.7	49.1	54.4	59.7	65.1	65.3	60.7	52.8	44.8	39.7	51.7
Mean Minimum Temp. (°F)	32.4	33.5	35.4	38.1	42.5	47.1	50.2	49.5	45.5	40.6	36.8	32.8	40.4
Extreme Maximum Temp. (°F)	67	75	79	89	96	100	106	105	101	94	76	73	106
Extreme Minimum Temp. (°F)	4	0	18	26	30	33	38	38	31	22	13	-4	-4
Days Maximum Temp. ≥ 90°F	0	0	0	0	0	1	4	5	2	0	0	0	12
Days Maximum Temp. ≤ 32°F	1	0	0	0	0	0	0	0	0	0	0	1	2
Days Minimum Temp. ≤ 32°F	16	12	10	4	1	0	0	0	0	2	8	14	67
Days Minimum Temp. ≤ 0°F	0	0	0	0	0	0	0	0	0	0	0	0	0
Heating Degree Days (base 65°F)	771	620	592	471	329	172	64	57	147	373	599	778	4,973
Cooling Degree Days (base 65°F)	0	0	0	1	9	20	77	77	27	2	0	0	213
Mean Precipitation (in.)	6.21	5.29	5.28	4.33	3.18	1.76	0.74	1.03	1.84	3.46	7.59	6.85	47.56
Days With ≥ 0.1" Precipitation	13	11	13	12	8	5	2	2	5	8	14	13	106
Days With ≥ 1.0" Precipitation	1	1	1	0	0	0	0	0	0	1	2	1	7
Mean Snowfall (in.)	1.0	2.0	0.3	0.1	trace	0.0	0.0	0.0	0.0	trace	0.1	0.7	4.2
Days With ≥ 1.0" Snow Depth	1	0	0	0	0	0	0	0	0	0	0	1	2

Drain *Douglas County*   Elevation: 291 ft.   Latitude: 43° 40' N   Longitude: 123° 20' W

	JAN	FEB	MAR	APR	MAY	JUN	JUL	AUG	SEP	OCT	NOV	DEC	YEAR
Mean Maximum Temp. (°F)	48.6	53.5	58.2	62.5	69.2	75.0	82.7	83.1	78.4	67.2	54.2	47.7	65.0
Mean Temp. (°F)	41.5	44.7	47.9	51.1	56.6	61.8	67.1	67.1	62.5	54.6	46.8	41.3	53.6
Mean Minimum Temp. (°F)	34.4	35.9	37.5	39.7	43.9	48.5	51.4	51.0	46.5	42.1	39.4	34.9	42.1
Extreme Maximum Temp. (°F)	67	78	83	91	99	104	106	107	106	96	75	70	107
Extreme Minimum Temp. (°F)	9	4	24	27	31	34	37	37	26	22	16	1	1
Days Maximum Temp. ≥ 90°F	0	0	0	0	1	2	7	7	4	0	0	0	21
Days Maximum Temp. ≤ 32°F	0	0	0	0	0	0	0	0	0	0	0	1	1
Days Minimum Temp. ≤ 32°F	11	8	6	3	0	0	0	0	0	2	4	10	44
Days Minimum Temp. ≤ 0°F	0	0	0	0	0	0	0	0	0	0	0	0	0
Heating Degree Days (base 65°F)	720	567	524	410	267	127	37	32	106	317	539	728	4,374
Cooling Degree Days (base 65°F)	0	0	0	1	15	34	107	106	43	4	0	0	310
Mean Precipitation (in.)	7.19	5.96	5.30	3.83	2.48	1.31	0.46	0.87	1.33	3.29	7.97	7.99	47.98
Days With ≥ 0.1" Precipitation	13	12	12	10	7	4	1	2	3	7	14	14	99
Days With ≥ 1.0" Precipitation	2	1	1	0	0	0	0	0	0	1	2	2	9
Mean Snowfall (in.)	trace	1.2	trace	0.0	0.0	0.0	0.0	0.0	0.0	0.0	0.2	0.7	2.1
Days With ≥ 1.0" Snow Depth	0	0	0	0	0	0	0	0	0	0	0	0	0

Drewsey *Harney County*   Elevation: 3,513 ft.   Latitude: 43° 48' N   Longitude: 118° 23' W

	JAN	FEB	MAR	APR	MAY	JUN	JUL	AUG	SEP	OCT	NOV	DEC	YEAR
Mean Maximum Temp. (°F)	35.2	42.8	52.8	61.5	70.7	79.6	88.9	87.8	78.5	65.4	46.7	36.1	62.2
Mean Temp. (°F)	25.0	31.7	39.3	45.6	53.9	61.7	68.8	66.7	57.2	46.3	34.6	25.9	46.4
Mean Minimum Temp. (°F)	14.7	20.6	25.6	29.7	37.2	43.8	48.6	45.6	35.8	27.1	22.3	15.6	30.6
Extreme Maximum Temp. (°F)	64	67	78	89	100	101	104	104	100	90	70	60	104
Extreme Minimum Temp. (°F)	-27	-33	-19	9	13	25	29	26	11	-1	-17	-36	-36
Days Maximum Temp. ≥ 90°F	0	0	0	0	1	5	17	14	4	0	0	0	41
Days Maximum Temp. ≤ 32°F	10	3	0	0	0	0	0	0	0	0	2	9	24
Days Minimum Temp. ≤ 32°F	29	25	25	19	8	2	0	1	11	22	26	29	197
Days Minimum Temp. ≤ 0°F	5	1	0	0	0	0	0	0	0	0	1	3	10
Heating Degree Days (base 65°F)	1,234	933	790	574	342	142	30	48	239	574	906	1,208	7,020
Cooling Degree Days (base 65°F)	0	0	0	0	6	43	144	104	13	0	0	0	310
Mean Precipitation (in.)	1.32	1.01	1.12	0.80	0.97	0.74	0.39	0.45	0.46	0.56	1.32	1.36	10.50
Days With ≥ 0.1" Precipitation	5	4	4	3	4	2	1	1	2	2	5	5	38
Days With ≥ 1.0" Precipitation	0	0	0	0	0	0	0	0	0	0	0	0	0
Mean Snowfall (in.)	7.7	5.2	1.6	0.3	trace	0.0	0.0	0.0	0.0	trace	2.9	*8.3*	*26.0*
Days With ≥ 1.0" Snow Depth	na	*6*	1	0	0	0	0	0	0	0	2	na	na

Dufur *Wasco County*   Elevation: 1,328 ft.   Latitude: 45° 27' N   Longitude: 121° 08' W

	JAN	FEB	MAR	APR	MAY	JUN	JUL	AUG	SEP	OCT	NOV	DEC	YEAR
Mean Maximum Temp. (°F)	40.6	46.9	55.5	62.6	71.2	78.2	86.3	86.0	77.9	64.6	48.7	40.4	63.2
Mean Temp. (°F)	32.7	37.5	43.3	48.4	55.3	61.5	67.6	67.4	60.5	50.1	39.7	33.0	49.8
Mean Minimum Temp. (°F)	24.8	28.0	31.1	34.2	39.3	44.6	48.9	48.8	43.1	35.6	30.6	25.5	36.2
Extreme Maximum Temp. (°F)	69	73	80	89	103	104	109	108	103	87	75	67	109
Extreme Minimum Temp. (°F)	-15	-14	5	18	23	26	34	33	24	14	-12	-19	-19
Days Maximum Temp. ≥ 90°F	0	0	0	0	1	4	12	11	3	0	0	0	31
Days Maximum Temp. ≤ 32°F	6	2	0	0	0	0	0	0	0	0	1	6	15
Days Minimum Temp. ≤ 32°F	25	20	19	13	6	1	0	0	1	11	18	25	139
Days Minimum Temp. ≤ 0°F	1	0	0	0	0	0	0	0	0	0	0	1	2
Heating Degree Days (base 65°F)	993	771	665	493	307	142	45	43	156	455	753	984	5,807
Cooling Degree Days (base 65°F)	0	0	0	1	17	44	143	138	38	0	0	0	381
Mean Precipitation (in.)	2.13	1.43	1.26	0.96	0.83	0.62	0.33	0.45	0.52	0.91	1.87	2.06	13.37
Days With ≥ 0.1" Precipitation	6	5	5	3	3	2	1	1	1	3	5	6	41
Days With ≥ 1.0" Precipitation	0	0	0	0	0	0	0	0	0	0	0	0	0
Mean Snowfall (in.)	7.5	3.6	0.9	trace	0.0	0.0	0.0	0.0	0.0	0.2	3.1	6.3	21.6
Days With ≥ 1.0" Snow Depth	8	3	0	0	0	0	0	0	0	0	2	6	19

Elgin *Union County*   Elevation: 2,654 ft.   Latitude: 45° 34' N   Longitude: 117° 55' W

	JAN	FEB	MAR	APR	MAY	JUN	JUL	AUG	SEP	OCT	NOV	DEC	YEAR
Mean Maximum Temp. (°F)	38.1	44.6	52.7	60.7	69.4	77.4	86.5	87.4	78.1	64.9	47.3	38.5	62.1
Mean Temp. (°F)	29.9	34.7	40.7	46.6	53.8	60.6	66.4	66.2	57.8	47.8	37.8	30.4	47.7
Mean Minimum Temp. (°F)	21.7	24.7	28.6	32.4	38.1	43.7	46.2	45.0	37.6	30.7	28.4	22.3	33.3
Extreme Maximum Temp. (°F)	65	68	78	91	98	98	103	104	102	92	73	61	104
Extreme Minimum Temp. (°F)	-23	-22	0	16	20	26	29	25	19	11	-23	-31	-31
Days Maximum Temp. ≥ 90°F	0	0	0	0	1	4	13	14	4	0	0	0	36
Days Maximum Temp. ≤ 32°F	7	2	0	0	0	0	0	0	0	0	1	6	16
Days Minimum Temp. ≤ 32°F	26	22	22	15	6	1	0	1	8	19	20	26	166
Days Minimum Temp. ≤ 0°F	3	1	0	0	0	0	0	0	0	0	0	2	6
Heating Degree Days (base 65°F)	1,080	848	746	545	347	160	50	54	221	526	808	1,065	6,450
Cooling Degree Days (base 65°F)	0	0	0	0	7	30	88	95	15	0	0	0	235
Mean Precipitation (in.)	3.34	2.55	2.16	2.01	1.96	1.61	0.87	0.72	1.00	1.66	3.33	3.42	24.63
Days With ≥ 0.1" Precipitation	8	7	7	6	6	5	3	2	3	5	9	9	70
Days With ≥ 1.0" Precipitation	0	0	0	0	0	0	0	0	0	0	0	0	0
Mean Snowfall (in.)	15.7	8.0	3.1	0.9	trace	0.0	0.0	0.0	0.0	0.1	6.5	16.0	50.3
Days With ≥ 1.0" Snow Depth	*15*	6	1	0	0	0	0	0	0	0	3	10	*35*

Elkton 3 SW *Douglas County*   Elevation: 118 ft.   Latitude: 43° 36' N   Longitude: 123° 35' W

	JAN	FEB	MAR	APR	MAY	JUN	JUL	AUG	SEP	OCT	NOV	DEC	YEAR
Mean Maximum Temp. (°F)	49.5	54.3	59.1	63.9	70.5	76.4	83.6	84.5	80.3	*67.9*	*54.6*	48.0	*66.0*
Mean Temp. (°F)	43.2	46.3	49.5	52.7	58.0	62.8	68.0	68.4	64.5	*56.3*	*48.2*	42.5	*55.0*
Mean Minimum Temp. (°F)	36.9	38.3	39.8	41.5	45.4	49.1	52.3	52.3	48.6	*44.7*	41.7	36.9	*44.0*
Extreme Maximum Temp. (°F)	65	76	79	91	96	102	106	107	102	96	74	68	107
Extreme Minimum Temp. (°F)	10	4	26	30	34	35	38	40	30	25	16	0	0
Days Maximum Temp. ≥ 90°F	0	0	0	0	1	3	8	8	4	0	0	0	24
Days Maximum Temp. ≤ 32°F	0	0	0	0	0	0	0	0	0	0	0	1	1
Days Minimum Temp. ≤ 32°F	7	5	2	1	0	0	0	0	0	0	1	7	25
Days Minimum Temp. ≤ 0°F	0	0	0	0	0	0	0	0	0	0	0	0	0
Heating Degree Days (base 65°F)	669	521	475	363	228	101	23	14	68	*268*	*497*	691	*3,918*
Cooling Degree Days (base 65°F)	0	0	0	2	18	38	118	121	59	5	0	0	361
Mean Precipitation (in.)	8.34	6.88	6.05	3.95	2.36	1.09	0.34	0.67	1.42	3.34	9.08	9.50	53.02
Days With ≥ 0.1" Precipitation	13	*11*	12	*9*	6	3	1	2	3	na	*14*	*14*	na
Days With ≥ 1.0" Precipitation	2	*2*	1	0	0	0	0	0	0	1	*2*	3	*12*
Mean Snowfall (in.)	0.5	0.2	0.1	trace	0.0	0.0	0.0	0.0	0.0	trace	0.1	0.3	1.2
Days With ≥ 1.0" Snow Depth	0	0	0	0	0	0	0	0	0	0	0	0	0

Enterprise 20 NNE *Wallowa County*   Elevation: 3,277 ft.   Latitude: 45° 43' N   Longitude: 117° 09' W

	JAN	FEB	MAR	APR	MAY	JUN	JUL	AUG	SEP	OCT	NOV	DEC	YEAR
Mean Maximum Temp. (°F)	37.2	44.0	51.6	59.4	67.3	75.1	84.2	85.0	75.9	63.2	45.8	36.8	60.5
Mean Temp. (°F)	27.0	32.3	38.4	44.5	51.3	58.0	63.9	63.7	55.5	45.8	35.2	26.9	45.2
Mean Minimum Temp. (°F)	16.8	20.6	25.0	29.5	35.2	40.8	43.5	42.2	35.1	28.4	24.5	17.0	29.9
Extreme Maximum Temp. (°F)	62	71	80	93	96	99	106	106	105	97	74	61	106
Extreme Minimum Temp. (°F)	-28	-30	-6	11	15	23	27	24	16	2	-21	-33	-33
Days Maximum Temp. ≥ 90°F	0	0	0	0	1	3	10	11	3	0	0	0	28
Days Maximum Temp. ≤ 32°F	8	2	0	0	0	0	0	0	0	0	2	7	19
Days Minimum Temp. ≤ 32°F	30	27	27	20	11	3	1	1	11	23	26	30	210
Days Minimum Temp. ≤ 0°F	4	2	0	0	0	0	0	0	0	0	1	3	10
Heating Degree Days (base 65°F)	1,172	917	819	608	420	220	86	89	285	588	888	1,175	7,267
Cooling Degree Days (base 65°F)	0	0	0	0	3	14	58	59	10	0	0	0	144
Mean Precipitation (in.)	1.73	1.44	1.61	1.98	2.22	1.98	1.36	1.15	1.14	1.13	2.15	1.91	19.80
Days With ≥ 0.1" Precipitation	6	5	6	7	7	6	4	3	3	4	7	6	64
Days With ≥ 1.0" Precipitation	0	0	0	0	0	0	0	0	0	0	0	0	0
Mean Snowfall (in.)	9.7	5.5	2.5	0.2	trace	0.0	0.0	0.0	0.0	trace	4.4	7.2	29.5
Days With ≥ 1.0" Snow Depth	15	9	3	0	0	0	0	0	0	0	4	10	41

Estacada 2 SE *Clackamas County*   Elevation: 449 ft.   Latitude: 45° 16' N   Longitude: 122° 19' W

	JAN	FEB	MAR	APR	MAY	JUN	JUL	AUG	SEP	OCT	NOV	DEC	YEAR
Mean Maximum Temp. (°F)	45.9	50.0	55.2	60.2	66.6	72.0	78.6	78.6	73.1	61.2	51.0	45.4	61.5
Mean Temp. (°F)	40.2	43.0	46.5	50.3	55.8	60.7	65.8	65.7	61.1	52.3	45.0	39.9	52.2
Mean Minimum Temp. (°F)	34.5	36.0	37.9	40.4	45.0	49.5	53.0	52.8	49.1	43.4	38.9	34.4	42.9
Extreme Maximum Temp. (°F)	67	71	76	90	105	100	103	105	105	89	69	68	105
Extreme Minimum Temp. (°F)	13	8	22	28	32	35	39	41	33	25	13	6	6
Days Maximum Temp. ≥ 90°F	0	0	0	0	0	1	4	3	2	0	0	0	10
Days Maximum Temp. ≤ 32°F	1	0	0	0	0	0	0	0	0	0	0	1	2
Days Minimum Temp. ≤ 32°F	12	8	4	2	0	0	0	0	0	1	4	11	42
Days Minimum Temp. ≤ 0°F	0	0	0	0	0	0	0	0	0	0	0	0	0
Heating Degree Days (base 65°F)	762	614	566	435	287	146	46	44	138	389	592	771	4,790
Cooling Degree Days (base 65°F)	0	0	0	1	10	23	76	78	28	2	0	0	218
Mean Precipitation (in.)	8.30	6.85	6.17	5.22	3.93	2.63	1.06	1.28	2.54	4.74	8.68	8.64	60.04
Days With ≥ 0.1" Precipitation	14	13	14	12	10	6	3	3	5	9	15	15	119
Days With ≥ 1.0" Precipitation	2	2	1	1	0	0	0	0	0	1	2	2	11
Mean Snowfall (in.)	0.8	0.9	0.1	0.0	0.0	0.0	0.0	0.0	0.0	0.0	0.3	0.6	2.7
Days With ≥ 1.0" Snow Depth	1	0	0	0	0	0	0	0	0	0	0	0	1

Falls City 2 *Polk County*   Elevation: 419 ft.   Latitude: 44° 51' N   Longitude: 123° 26' W

	JAN	FEB	MAR	APR	MAY	JUN	JUL	AUG	SEP	OCT	NOV	DEC	YEAR
Mean Maximum Temp. (°F)	46.4	50.7	55.5	60.0	66.7	72.6	80.3	81.5	76.2	65.0	52.4	46.0	62.8
Mean Temp. (°F)	39.3	42.2	45.5	48.9	54.3	59.5	65.0	65.6	61.4	52.8	44.5	39.2	51.5
Mean Minimum Temp. (°F)	32.1	33.7	35.5	37.7	41.8	46.4	49.6	49.6	46.5	40.6	36.5	32.4	40.2
Extreme Maximum Temp. (°F)	64	70	78	85	98	101	104	104	105	92	71	63	105
Extreme Minimum Temp. (°F)	6	7	19	27	29	32	35	35	30	24	10	2	2
Days Maximum Temp. ≥ 90°F	0	0	0	0	0	1	5	5	3	0	0	0	14
Days Maximum Temp. ≤ 32°F	1	0	0	0	0	0	0	0	0	0	0	1	2
Days Minimum Temp. ≤ 32°F	18	13	10	5	1	0	0	0	0	2	9	16	74
Days Minimum Temp. ≤ 0°F	0	0	0	0	0	0	0	0	0	0	0	0	0
Heating Degree Days (base 65°F)	791	637	596	477	332	180	67	53	136	372	608	792	5,041
Cooling Degree Days (base 65°F)	0	0	0	0	9	23	77	85	39	2	0	0	235
Mean Precipitation (in.)	11.39	9.58	7.67	4.59	2.48	1.41	0.51	0.74	1.73	4.35	11.22	13.00	68.67
Days With ≥ 0.1" Precipitation	14	13	13	10	6	4	1	2	4	8	16	15	106
Days With ≥ 1.0" Precipitation	4	3	2	1	0	0	0	0	0	1	3	5	19
Mean Snowfall (in.)	2.5	2.8	0.6	0.2	0.0	0.0	0.0	0.0	0.0	trace	0.5	2.8	9.4
Days With ≥ 1.0" Snow Depth	2	2	0	0	0	0	0	0	0	0	0	2	6

Fern Ridge Dam *Lane County*   Elevation: 482 ft.   Latitude: 44° 07' N   Longitude: 123° 18' W

	JAN	FEB	MAR	APR	MAY	JUN	JUL	AUG	SEP	OCT	NOV	DEC	YEAR
Mean Maximum Temp. (°F)	na	50.8	56.6	60.4	66.6	73.9	81.6	81.9	77.0	na	na	na	na
Mean Temp. (°F)	na	42.6	47.0	49.8	55.0	61.4	66.8	67.1	62.7	na	na	na	na
Mean Minimum Temp. (°F)	na	34.6	37.2	39.2	43.4	48.8	51.9	52.3	48.4	na	na	na	na
Extreme Maximum Temp. (°F)	65	73	77	83	95	104	104	107	102	92	74	66	107
Extreme Minimum Temp. (°F)	9	6	24	29	31	35	39	38	32	25	16	-3	-3
Days Maximum Temp. ≥ 90°F	0	0	0	0	0	1	5	6	3	0	0	0	15
Days Maximum Temp. ≤ 32°F	1	0	0	0	0	0	0	0	0	0	0	1	2
Days Minimum Temp. ≤ 32°F	12	9	6	2	0	0	0	0	0	1	6	11	47
Days Minimum Temp. ≤ 0°F	0	0	0	0	0	0	0	0	0	0	0	0	0
Heating Degree Days (base 65°F)	na	626	553	450	309	135	43	31	105	na	na	na	na
Cooling Degree Days (base 65°F)	na	na	0	0	na	35	112	110	54	na	na	na	na
Mean Precipitation (in.)	6.49	5.38	4.72	3.13	2.10	1.39	0.52	0.70	1.31	2.82	7.35	7.77	43.68
Days With ≥ 0.1" Precipitation	10	10	10	8	5	3	1	2	3	6	11	11	80
Days With ≥ 1.0" Precipitation	1	1	0	0	0	0	0	0	0	0	1	2	5
Mean Snowfall (in.)	0.1	0.5	trace	trace	0.0	0.0	0.0	0.0	0.0	0.0	0.1	1.0	1.7
Days With ≥ 1.0" Snow Depth	0	0	0	0	0	0	0	0	0	0	0	0	0

Forest Grove *Washington County*   Elevation: 177 ft.   Latitude: 45° 31' N   Longitude: 123° 06' W

	JAN	FEB	MAR	APR	MAY	JUN	JUL	AUG	SEP	OCT	NOV	DEC	YEAR
Mean Maximum Temp. (°F)	46.0	50.9	56.6	61.6	68.9	74.8	82.3	83.1	77.1	65.2	52.4	45.6	63.7
Mean Temp. (°F)	39.4	42.5	46.8	50.6	56.8	62.2	67.9	68.1	62.7	53.1	44.9	39.4	52.9
Mean Minimum Temp. (°F)	32.8	34.3	37.1	39.6	44.7	49.5	53.5	53.0	48.3	41.0	37.4	33.2	42.0
Extreme Maximum Temp. (°F)	63	72	78	89	98	105	108	108	104	93	72	64	108
Extreme Minimum Temp. (°F)	-1	5	13	27	30	32	39	39	32	23	6	-4	-4
Days Maximum Temp. ≥ 90°F	0	0	0	0	1	2	7	8	4	0	0	0	22
Days Maximum Temp. ≤ 32°F	1	0	0	0	0	0	0	0	0	0	0	1	2
Days Minimum Temp. ≤ 32°F	15	11	7	4	0	0	0	0	0	3	8	13	61
Days Minimum Temp. ≤ 0°F	0	0	0	0	0	0	0	0	0	0	0	0	0
Heating Degree Days (base 65°F)	786	630	556	425	265	126	38	32	113	365	596	787	4,719
Cooling Degree Days (base 65°F)	0	0	0	1	23	46	136	140	57	3	0	0	406
Mean Precipitation (in.)	7.19	6.08	4.83	3.08	2.01	1.42	0.53	0.75	1.52	3.22	7.59	8.12	46.34
Days With ≥ 0.1" Precipitation	13	13	12	8	6	4	2	2	4	7	14	14	99
Days With ≥ 1.0" Precipitation	2	1	1	0	0	0	0	0	0	1	1	2	8
Mean Snowfall (in.)	1.2	1.3	0.2	trace	0.0	0.0	0.0	0.0	0.0	0.2	0.7	1.4	5.0
Days With ≥ 1.0" Snow Depth	1	0	0	0	0	0	0	0	0	0	0	1	2

Fossil *Wheeler County*   Elevation: 2,647 ft.   Latitude: 45° 00' N   Longitude: 120° 13' W

	JAN	FEB	MAR	APR	MAY	JUN	JUL	AUG	SEP	OCT	NOV	DEC	YEAR
Mean Maximum Temp. (°F)	41.4	46.4	52.5	58.6	66.9	74.5	83.7	84.0	75.8	64.5	48.7	41.6	61.6
Mean Temp. (°F)	33.1	36.6	41.0	45.3	51.9	58.5	64.7	64.9	57.9	49.3	39.4	33.7	48.0
Mean Minimum Temp. (°F)	24.8	26.9	29.6	32.1	36.8	42.4	45.6	45.8	40.0	34.0	29.9	25.7	34.5
Extreme Maximum Temp. (°F)	67	72	78	87	97	101	101	103	97	92	74	67	103
Extreme Minimum Temp. (°F)	-19	-22	4	14	20	25	25	31	20	3	-16	-24	-24
Days Maximum Temp. ≥ 90°F	0	0	0	0	0	1	8	9	2	0	0	0	20
Days Maximum Temp. ≤ 32°F	6	2	0	0	0	0	0	0	0	0	2	5	15
Days Minimum Temp. ≤ 32°F	23	20	20	16	9	2	0	0	5	12	17	23	147
Days Minimum Temp. ≤ 0°F	1	1	0	0	0	0	0	0	0	0	0	1	3
Heating Degree Days (base 65°F)	981	795	737	583	405	212	84	73	219	482	763	964	6,298
Cooling Degree Days (base 65°F)	0	0	0	0	5	19	74	77	14	1	0	0	190
Mean Precipitation (in.)	1.56	1.24	1.50	1.46	1.57	1.12	0.56	0.72	0.78	1.31	1.82	1.59	15.23
Days With ≥ 0.1" Precipitation	5	4	5	5	4	3	2	2	3	4	6	4	47
Days With ≥ 1.0" Precipitation	0	0	0	0	0	0	0	0	0	0	0	0	0
Mean Snowfall (in.)	*2.4*	1.9	0.7	0.3	0.2	0.0	0.0	0.0	0.0	0.5	2.2	*2.9*	*11.1*
Days With ≥ 1.0" Snow Depth	*5*	2	0	0	0	0	0	0	0	0	1	4	*12*

Foster Dam *Linn County*   Elevation: 547 ft.   Latitude: 44° 25' N   Longitude: 122° 40' W

	JAN	FEB	MAR	APR	MAY	JUN	JUL	AUG	SEP	OCT	NOV	DEC	YEAR
Mean Maximum Temp. (°F)	47.7	51.9	56.2	60.2	66.6	72.3	79.8	80.5	75.3	64.8	53.2	47.0	63.0
Mean Temp. (°F)	40.7	43.7	46.8	50.0	55.1	60.3	65.4	65.4	61.0	53.2	45.8	40.7	52.3
Mean Minimum Temp. (°F)	33.6	35.4	37.3	39.8	43.7	48.2	50.9	50.3	46.5	41.6	38.4	34.4	41.7
Extreme Maximum Temp. (°F)	67	71	77	85	96	102	102	105	102	93	75	69	105
Extreme Minimum Temp. (°F)	0	2	22	27	1	35	40	36	32	24	16	0	0
Days Maximum Temp. ≥ 90°F	0	0	0	0	0	1	4	4	2	0	0	0	11
Days Maximum Temp. ≤ 32°F	1	0	0	0	0	0	0	0	0	0	0	1	2
Days Minimum Temp. ≤ 32°F	13	9	5	2	0	0	0	0	0	2	6	11	48
Days Minimum Temp. ≤ 0°F	0	0	0	0	0	0	0	0	0	0	0	0	0
Heating Degree Days (base 65°F)	748	596	558	443	307	160	57	51	139	360	569	747	4,735
Cooling Degree Days (base 65°F)	0	0	0	1	10	24	73	73	28	2	0	0	211
Mean Precipitation (in.)	7.14	6.19	5.72	4.70	3.93	2.56	0.86	1.15	1.99	3.92	8.64	7.97	54.77
Days With ≥ 0.1" Precipitation	14	13	14	12	9	6	2	3	5	9	16	15	118
Days With ≥ 1.0" Precipitation	2	1	1	0	0	0	0	0	0	2	2	8
Mean Snowfall (in.)	0.5	0.8	trace	trace	0.0	0.0	0.0	0.0	0.0	0.0	trace	0.3	1.6
Days With ≥ 1.0" Snow Depth	0	0	0	0	0	0	0	0	0	0	0	1	1

Gold Beach Ranger Station *Curry County*   Elevation: 49 ft.   Latitude: 42° 24' N   Longitude: 124° 25' W

	JAN	FEB	MAR	APR	MAY	JUN	JUL	AUG	SEP	OCT	NOV	DEC	YEAR
Mean Maximum Temp. (°F)	*55.1*	*55.8*	56.7	58.3	61.5	65.0	67.9	68.4	67.9	64.2	*57.3*	*54.4*	*61.0*
Mean Temp. (°F)	*48.0*	*48.7*	49.2	50.6	53.5	57.1	59.6	60.3	59.3	55.8	*50.4*	*47.5*	*53.3*
Mean Minimum Temp. (°F)	*41.0*	*41.4*	41.7	42.8	45.5	49.3	51.3	52.1	50.7	47.3	43.4	*40.5*	*45.6*
Extreme Maximum Temp. (°F)	73	77	73	80	81	85	83	88	102	91	76	72	102
Extreme Minimum Temp. (°F)	23	21	28	28	31	35	40	41	40	31	28	16	16
Days Maximum Temp. ≥ 90°F	0	0	0	0	0	0	0	0	0	0	0	0	0
Days Maximum Temp. ≤ 32°F	0	0	0	0	0	0	0	0	0	0	0	0	0
Days Minimum Temp. ≤ 32°F	3	2	1	0	0	0	0	0	0	0	1	2	9
Days Minimum Temp. ≤ 0°F	0	0	0	0	0	0	0	0	0	0	0	0	0
Heating Degree Days (base 65°F)	*519*	*455*	483	426	350	230	161	141	169	283	*432*	*536*	*4,185*
Cooling Degree Days (base 65°F)	*0*	*0*	0	0	0	1	2	1	3	4	0	0	*0*
Mean Precipitation (in.)	12.19	10.69	10.59	6.58	3.78	1.83	0.45	1.09	2.20	4.97	12.05	13.73	80.15
Days With ≥ 0.1" Precipitation	na	na	na	*8*	*6*	*3*	1	2	2	*5*	na	na	na
Days With ≥ 1.0" Precipitation	na	na	na	*2*	1	0	0	0	0	*2*	na	na	na
Mean Snowfall (in.)	0.2	trace	trace	trace	0.0	0.0	0.0	0.0	0.0	0.0	0.0	trace	0.2
Days With ≥ 1.0" Snow Depth	0	0	0	0	0	0	0	0	0	0	0	0	0

Government Camp *Clackamas County*   Elevation: 3,979 ft.   Latitude: 45° 18' N   Longitude: 121° 44' W

	JAN	FEB	MAR	APR	MAY	JUN	JUL	AUG	SEP	OCT	NOV	DEC	YEAR
Mean Maximum Temp. (°F)	35.6	38.1	40.9	45.0	52.4	59.4	67.6	68.5	62.5	53.3	40.2	35.8	49.9
Mean Temp. (°F)	29.9	31.9	34.5	37.7	43.9	50.1	57.1	57.7	52.7	44.8	34.9	30.3	42.1
Mean Minimum Temp. (°F)	24.1	25.7	27.9	30.4	35.3	40.9	46.5	46.9	42.8	36.4	29.5	24.7	34.2
Extreme Maximum Temp. (°F)	62	67	66	80	93	91	91	105	94	83	70	62	105
Extreme Minimum Temp. (°F)	-5	-13	1	14	21	27	32	32	23	10	-3	-12	-13
Days Maximum Temp. ≥ 90°F	0	0	0	0	0	0	0	0	0	0	0	0	0
Days Maximum Temp. ≤ 32°F	11	7	5	2	0	0	0	0	0	0	5	10	40
Days Minimum Temp. ≤ 32°F	27	24	25	21	12	2	0	0	2	9	21	27	170
Days Minimum Temp. ≤ 0°F	1	0	0	0	0	0	0	0	0	0	0	1	2
Heating Degree Days (base 65°F)	1,082	928	939	812	649	444	264	244	370	619	898	1,071	8,320
Cooling Degree Days (base 65°F)	0	0	0	0	2	4	24	25	10	1	0	0	66
Mean Precipitation (in.)	13.02	10.14	8.52	7.77	5.08	3.78	1.34	1.60	3.72	6.39	13.53	14.56	89.45
Days With ≥ 0.1" Precipitation	16	15	16	14	12	8	4	4	6	10	17	17	139
Days With ≥ 1.0" Precipitation	5	3	2	2	1	1	0	0	1	2	4	6	27
Mean Snowfall (in.)	52.8	41.4	37.1	27.4	7.3	0.6	trace	0.0	0.3	5.7	37.3	46.8	256.7
Days With ≥ 1.0" Snow Depth	30	26	28	21	7	0	0	0	0	3	17	29	161

Grants Pass *Josephine County*   Elevation: 921 ft.   Latitude: 42° 26' N   Longitude: 123° 21' W

	JAN	FEB	MAR	APR	MAY	JUN	JUL	AUG	SEP	OCT	NOV	DEC	YEAR
Mean Maximum Temp. (°F)	48.3	54.8	60.5	66.3	74.2	81.5	89.7	89.6	83.5	70.5	54.2	46.3	68.3
Mean Temp. (°F)	40.8	44.7	48.4	52.4	58.7	65.1	71.1	70.6	64.6	55.3	45.8	39.8	54.8
Mean Minimum Temp. (°F)	33.3	34.5	36.2	38.4	43.3	48.6	52.6	51.5	45.6	40.0	37.4	33.4	41.2
Extreme Maximum Temp. (°F)	69	76	81	93	102	106	109	108	108	98	77	67	109
Extreme Minimum Temp. (°F)	13	12	22	24	26	33	39	36	29	20	12	-1	-1
Days Maximum Temp. ≥ 90°F	0	0	0	0	3	7	17	16	9	1	0	0	53
Days Maximum Temp. ≤ 32°F	0	0	0	0	0	0	0	0	0	0	0	1	1
Days Minimum Temp. ≤ 32°F	14	11	9	6	1	0	0	0	1	4	6	13	65
Days Minimum Temp. ≤ 0°F	0	0	0	0	0	0	0	0	0	0	0	0	0
Heating Degree Days (base 65°F)	742	568	509	375	213	77	13	13	74	300	569	773	4,226
Cooling Degree Days (base 65°F)	0	0	0	3	26	78	200	188	72	6	0	0	573
Mean Precipitation (in.)	5.00	4.25	3.68	1.98	1.20	0.55	0.33	0.43	0.84	2.16	5.40	5.61	31.43
Days With ≥ 0.1" Precipitation	9	9	8	5	4	2	1	1	2	5	10	10	66
Days With ≥ 1.0" Precipitation	1	1	1	0	0	0	0	0	0	0	1	1	5
Mean Snowfall (in.)	0.7	0.3	0.2	trace	trace	0.0	0.0	0.0	0.0	trace	trace	1.0	2.2
Days With ≥ 1.0" Snow Depth	0	0	0	0	0	0	0	0	0	0	0	1	1

Halfway *Baker County*   Elevation: 2,664 ft.   Latitude: 44° 53' N   Longitude: 117° 07' W

	JAN	FEB	MAR	APR	MAY	JUN	JUL	AUG	SEP	OCT	NOV	DEC	YEAR
Mean Maximum Temp. (°F)	32.9	40.2	51.7	62.0	70.9	78.9	87.6	87.3	77.7	64.7	45.8	34.0	61.1
Mean Temp. (°F)	24.2	30.0	39.3	46.7	54.3	61.4	67.8	66.9	58.2	47.6	35.6	25.2	46.4
Mean Minimum Temp. (°F)	15.4	19.7	26.9	31.5	37.5	43.9	47.9	46.5	38.6	30.5	25.3	16.4	31.7
Extreme Maximum Temp. (°F)	54	66	78	90	95	100	104	103	101	87	69	61	104
Extreme Minimum Temp. (°F)	-29	-31	-6	14	18	26	32	28	19	7	-23	-28	-31
Days Maximum Temp. ≥ 90°F	0	0	0	0	1	4	14	14	3	0	0	0	36
Days Maximum Temp. ≤ 32°F	13	5	0	0	0	0	0	0	0	0	2	11	31
Days Minimum Temp. ≤ 32°F	30	26	24	17	8	1	0	0	6	19	24	30	185
Days Minimum Temp. ≤ 0°F	5	2	0	0	0	0	0	0	0	0	0	4	11
Heating Degree Days (base 65°F)	1,259	983	789	540	332	140	37	43	211	532	875	1,226	6,967
Cooling Degree Days (base 65°F)	0	0	0	0	6	35	122	109	16	0	0	0	288
Mean Precipitation (in.)	3.47	2.34	1.99	1.58	1.71	1.29	0.65	0.62	0.86	1.21	3.14	3.67	22.53
Days With ≥ 0.1" Precipitation	9	7	7	5	5	4	2	2	3	3	8	8	63
Days With ≥ 1.0" Precipitation	0	0	0	0	0	0	0	0	0	0	0	1	1
Mean Snowfall (in.)	23.5	11.0	3.8	0.4	trace	trace	0.0	0.0	0.0	0.4	11.4	22.6	73.1
Days With ≥ 1.0" Snow Depth	28	24	10	0	0	0	0	0	0	0	6	23	91

Hart Mountain Refuge *Lake County*   Elevation: 5,613 ft.   Latitude: 42° 33' N   Longitude: 119° 39' W

	JAN	FEB	MAR	APR	MAY	JUN	JUL	AUG	SEP	OCT	NOV	DEC	YEAR
Mean Maximum Temp. (°F)	39.7	42.5	46.5	53.7	62.7	72.0	81.2	80.4	71.9	60.7	46.0	*39.5*	*58.1*
Mean Temp. (°F)	29.5	31.7	35.0	40.2	47.8	55.3	62.3	61.9	54.3	45.6	34.7	*28.7*	*43.9*
Mean Minimum Temp. (°F)	19.2	21.0	23.5	26.8	32.7	38.5	43.3	43.2	36.7	30.5	23.5	*17.9*	*29.7*
Extreme Maximum Temp. (°F)	63	67	70	81	88	93	97	98	94	89	72	63	98
Extreme Minimum Temp. (°F)	-17	-26	-8	-4	12	18	23	22	12	4	-17	-32	-32
Days Maximum Temp. ≥ 90°F	0	0	0	0	0	0	4	3	0	0	0	0	7
Days Maximum Temp. ≤ 32°F	6	4	1	0	0	0	0	0	0	0	2	6	19
Days Minimum Temp. ≤ 32°F	28	25	26	22	15	6	2	2	8	18	23	28	203
Days Minimum Temp. ≤ 0°F	2	1	0	0	0	0	0	0	0	0	1	2	6
Heating Degree Days (base 65°F)	1,095	933	925	736	528	294	119	130	317	593	901	*1,120*	*7,691*
Cooling Degree Days (base 65°F)	0	0	0	0	1	9	41	40	4	0	0	*0*	*95*
Mean Precipitation (in.)	0.94	0.90	1.40	1.53	1.68	1.23	0.46	0.50	0.77	0.99	1.22	1.15	12.77
Days With ≥ 0.1" Precipitation	3	3	4	4	5	3	1	1	2	3	4	3	36
Days With ≥ 1.0" Precipitation	0	0	0	0	0	0	0	0	0	0	0	0	0
Mean Snowfall (in.)	*6.2*	7.6	8.3	3.9	2.3	0.6	trace	0.0	0.6	1.8	6.1	*7.7*	*45.1*
Days With ≥ 1.0" Snow Depth	9	8	6	2	1	0	0	0	0	1	5	*10*	*42*

Headworks Ptld. Wtr. Bur. *Clackamas County* Elevation: 748 ft. Latitude: 45° 27' N Longitude: 122° 09' W

	JAN	FEB	MAR	APR	MAY	JUN	JUL	AUG	SEP	OCT	NOV	DEC	YEAR
Mean Maximum Temp. (°F)	45.8	49.9	54.5	59.8	66.8	72.2	79.0	79.6	74.3	63.8	51.4	45.4	61.9
Mean Temp. (°F)	40.2	42.9	46.1	50.0	55.7	60.6	65.9	66.4	62.2	54.3	45.3	40.1	52.5
Mean Minimum Temp. (°F)	34.5	35.9	37.6	40.1	44.5	49.0	52.7	53.2	50.1	44.7	39.2	34.8	43.0
Extreme Maximum Temp. (°F)	63	72	82	88	99	102	102	105	104	94	73	63	105
Extreme Minimum Temp. (°F)	9	5	19	29	32	38	43	40	34	28	16	5	5
Days Maximum Temp. ≥ 90°F	0	0	0	0	1	1	4	4	2	0	0	0	12
Days Maximum Temp. ≤ 32°F	1	0	0	0	0	0	0	0	0	0	0	1	2
Days Minimum Temp. ≤ 32°F	11	7	4	1	0	0	0	0	0	0	4	9	36
Days Minimum Temp. ≤ 0°F	0	0	0	0	0	0	0	0	0	0	0	0	0
Heating Degree Days (base 65°F)	764	617	580	444	291	150	51	40	117	332	584	765	4,735
Cooling Degree Days (base 65°F)	0	0	0	1	13	28	91	103	44	7	0	0	287
Mean Precipitation (in.)	10.70	8.84	8.21	7.27	5.42	3.98	1.58	1.84	4.08	6.20	11.14	11.51	80.77
Days With ≥ 0.1" Precipitation	17	15	16	15	11	8	4	4	6	11	17	17	141
Days With ≥ 1.0" Precipitation	3	2	2	2	1	1	0	0	1	1	3	3	19
Mean Snowfall (in.)	3.1	2.0	0.7	0.2	trace	0.0	0.0	0.0	0.0	trace	1.4	1.7	9.1
Days With ≥ 1.0" Snow Depth	2	1	0	0	0	0	0	0	0	0	1	1	5

Heppner *Morrow County* Elevation: 1,883 ft. Latitude: 45° 22' N Longitude: 119° 34' W

	JAN	FEB	MAR	APR	MAY	JUN	JUL	AUG	SEP	OCT	NOV	DEC	YEAR
Mean Maximum Temp. (°F)	42.3	47.1	54.2	60.7	69.1	77.1	85.7	85.2	75.8	64.2	50.1	42.2	62.8
Mean Temp. (°F)	34.3	38.3	44.0	48.9	56.0	63.0	69.5	69.2	61.0	51.4	41.3	34.5	50.9
Mean Minimum Temp. (°F)	26.2	29.4	33.6	36.9	42.9	48.7	53.2	53.1	46.1	38.5	32.5	26.7	39.0
Extreme Maximum Temp. (°F)	69	75	74	88	98	102	105	108	98	92	79	70	108
Extreme Minimum Temp. (°F)	-12	-15	10	20	28	33	35	37	25	14	-9	-15	-15
Days Maximum Temp. ≥ 90°F	0	0	0	0	1	3	11	10	2	0	0	0	27
Days Maximum Temp. ≤ 32°F	7	3	0	0	0	0	0	0	0	0	1	6	17
Days Minimum Temp. ≤ 32°F	22	17	14	7	1	0	0	0	1	6	14	23	105
Days Minimum Temp. ≤ 0°F	1	1	0	0	0	0	0	0	0	0	0	1	3
Heating Degree Days (base 65°F)	946	748	646	479	288	119	32	28	154	418	703	939	5,500
Cooling Degree Days (base 65°F)	0	0	0	1	20	58	171	162	47	2	0	0	461
Mean Precipitation (in.)	1.48	1.19	1.57	1.43	1.64	1.08	0.36	0.54	0.69	1.07	1.80	1.34	14.19
Days With ≥ 0.1" Precipitation	5	4	5	5	5	3	1	2	2	3	6	5	46
Days With ≥ 1.0" Precipitation	0	0	0	0	0	0	0	0	0	0	0	0	0
Mean Snowfall (in.)	5.3	2.8	0.5	0.2	trace	0.0	0.0	0.0	0.0	0.3	2.3	3.5	14.9
Days With ≥ 1.0" Snow Depth	7	4	1	0	0	0	0	0	0	0	2	6	20

Hermiston 1 SE *Umatilla County* Elevation: 639 ft. Latitude: 45° 50' N Longitude: 119° 16' W

	JAN	FEB	MAR	APR	MAY	JUN	JUL	AUG	SEP	OCT	NOV	DEC	YEAR
Mean Maximum Temp. (°F)	40.3	47.4	57.3	64.9	73.7	80.6	88.0	87.4	78.3	65.9	50.3	40.8	64.6
Mean Temp. (°F)	33.1	38.2	45.8	52.2	60.2	66.9	72.9	72.1	62.9	51.9	41.3	33.7	52.6
Mean Minimum Temp. (°F)	25.7	28.9	34.2	39.4	46.6	53.1	57.7	56.7	47.6	37.8	32.4	26.5	40.6
Extreme Maximum Temp. (°F)	69	75	80	88	102	102	107	108	98	87	77	68	108
Extreme Minimum Temp. (°F)	-15	-14	10	19	29	34	39	38	25	11	-11	-17	-17
Days Maximum Temp. ≥ 90°F	0	0	0	0	2	6	14	12	3	0	0	0	37
Days Maximum Temp. ≤ 32°F	7	3	0	0	0	0	0	0	0	0	1	7	18
Days Minimum Temp. ≤ 32°F	23	18	12	5	0	0	0	0	1	7	14	23	103
Days Minimum Temp. ≤ 0°F	1	1	0	0	0	0	0	0	0	0	0	1	3
Heating Degree Days (base 65°F)	984	752	588	382	182	56	11	11	114	402	703	963	5,148
Cooling Degree Days (base 65°F)	0	0	0	4	47	113	246	227	66	2	0	0	705
Mean Precipitation (in.)	1.65	1.02	0.98	0.89	0.82	0.56	0.25	0.38	0.51	0.66	1.52	1.33	10.57
Days With ≥ 0.1" Precipitation	5	3	3	2	2	2	1	1	1	2	4	5	31
Days With ≥ 1.0" Precipitation	0	0	0	0	0	0	0	0	0	0	0	0	0
Mean Snowfall (in.)	3.7	2.2	0.3	0.0	0.0	0.0	0.0	0.0	0.0	0.0	1.4	2.6	10.2
Days With ≥ 1.0" Snow Depth	7	3	0	0	0	0	0	0	0	0	1	4	15

Hillsboro *Washington County* Elevation: 157 ft. Latitude: 45° 31' N Longitude: 122° 59' W

	JAN	FEB	MAR	APR	MAY	JUN	JUL	AUG	SEP	OCT	NOV	DEC	YEAR
Mean Maximum Temp. (°F)	46.2	50.9	56.4	61.3	68.0	73.4	80.3	80.9	75.8	64.6	52.4	45.9	63.0
Mean Temp. (°F)	40.0	43.1	47.0	50.7	56.4	61.7	66.8	66.6	61.8	53.0	45.3	40.0	52.7
Mean Minimum Temp. (°F)	33.8	35.2	37.6	40.0	44.8	49.9	53.2	52.3	47.9	41.4	38.1	34.0	42.3
Extreme Maximum Temp. (°F)	62	70	78	90	100	102	105	106	103	92	71	64	106
Extreme Minimum Temp. (°F)	9	8	20	28	29	37	39	38	31	21	9	-2	-2
Days Maximum Temp. ≥ 90°F	0	0	0	0	1	1	5	5	2	0	0	0	14
Days Maximum Temp. ≤ 32°F	1	0	0	0	0	0	0	0	0	0	0	1	2
Days Minimum Temp. ≤ 32°F	14	10	6	2	0	0	0	0	0	0	6	12	52
Days Minimum Temp. ≤ 0°F	0	0	0	0	0	0	0	0	0	2	12	0	0
Heating Degree Days (base 65°F)	769	612	550	423	272	130	43	42	122	366	585	769	4,683
Cooling Degree Days (base 65°F)	0	0	0	2	16	38	105	102	39	2	0	0	304
Mean Precipitation (in.)	5.92	4.73	3.90	2.49	1.87	1.43	0.59	0.90	1.59	2.68	5.99	6.52	38.61
Days With ≥ 0.1" Precipitation	12	11	11	8	6	4	2	2	4	7	13	13	93
Days With ≥ 1.0" Precipitation	1	1	0	0	0	0	0	0	0	0	1	1	4
Mean Snowfall (in.)	0.9	0.9	0.1	trace	0.0	0.0	0.0	0.0	0.0	0.0	0.3	0.9	3.1
Days With ≥ 1.0" Snow Depth	1	0	0	0	0	0	0	0	0	0	0	1	2

Honeyman State Park *Lane County* Elevation: 114 ft. Latitude: 43° 56' N Longitude: 124° 06' W

	JAN	FEB	MAR	APR	MAY	JUN	JUL	AUG	SEP	OCT	NOV	DEC	YEAR
Mean Maximum Temp. (°F)	50.7	53.7	56.1	59.1	*63.5*	66.3	69.3	*69.7*	69.9	63.3	54.4	50.0	*60.5*
Mean Temp. (°F)	44.2	46.4	47.8	50.1	*53.8*	*57.0*	59.8	*60.4*	59.6	54.4	48.0	43.8	*52.1*
Mean Minimum Temp. (°F)	37.6	39.1	39.5	41.0	*44.3*	47.8	50.2	*51.1*	49.3	45.3	41.5	37.7	*43.7*
Extreme Maximum Temp. (°F)	65	75	78	86	92	97	95	91	99	92	69	65	99
Extreme Minimum Temp. (°F)	14	13	23	29	31	36	40	39	32	24	20	9	9
Days Maximum Temp. ≥ 90°F	0	0	0	0	0	0	0	0	0	0	0	0	0
Days Maximum Temp. ≤ 32°F	0	0	0	0	0	0	0	0	0	0	0	0	0
Days Minimum Temp. ≤ 32°F	7	5	3	1	0	0	0	0	0	0	2	6	24
Days Minimum Temp. ≤ 0°F	0	0	0	0	0	0	0	0	0	0	0	0	0
Heating Degree Days (base 65°F)	640	519	525	442	*343*	*233*	158	*138*	164	325	505	649	*4,641*
Cooling Degree Days (base 65°F)	0	0	0	0	1	2	2	2	7	2	0	0	*16*
Mean Precipitation (in.)	10.40	9.27	8.97	5.34	3.81	2.45	0.95	1.16	2.29	5.33	10.99	12.13	73.09
Days With ≥ 0.1" Precipitation	14	14	14	11	7	5	2	3	4	8	14	15	111
Days With ≥ 1.0" Precipitation	3	3	2	1	0	0	0	0	0	1	3	3	16
Mean Snowfall (in.)	0.1	0.5	trace	trace	0.0	0.0	0.0	0.0	0.0	0.0	trace	0.3	0.9
Days With ≥ 1.0" Snow Depth	0	0	0	0	0	0	0	0	0	0	0	0	0

Hood River Exp. Station *Hood River County* Elevation: 498 ft. Latitude: 45° 41' N Longitude: 121° 31' W

	JAN	FEB	MAR	APR	MAY	JUN	JUL	AUG	SEP	OCT	NOV	DEC	YEAR
Mean Maximum Temp. (°F)	40.9	46.3	54.1	60.3	68.1	73.8	80.7	81.3	75.0	63.7	49.2	41.2	61.2
Mean Temp. (°F)	34.7	38.6	44.4	49.5	56.3	61.9	67.4	67.2	60.3	50.8	41.8	35.5	50.7
Mean Minimum Temp. (°F)	28.5	30.8	34.6	38.7	44.4	50.0	54.0	53.0	45.6	37.9	34.5	29.6	40.1
Extreme Maximum Temp. (°F)	63	66	78	88	102	105	104	108	100	88	69	66	108
Extreme Minimum Temp. (°F)	-6	-9	13	25	29	32	37	36	26	19	-5	-10	-10
Days Maximum Temp. ≥ 90°F	0	0	0	0	1	2	6	6	2	0	0	0	17
Days Maximum Temp. ≤ 32°F	5	2	0	0	0	0	0	0	0	0	1	4	12
Days Minimum Temp. ≤ 32°F	20	16	11	5	1	0	0	0	1	7	11	20	92
Days Minimum Temp. ≤ 0°F	0	0	0	0	0	0	0	0	0	0	0	0	0
Heating Degree Days (base 65°F)	932	740	632	459	280	134	45	44	162	433	688	908	5,457
Cooling Degree Days (base 65°F)	0	0	0	2	19	46	127	121	32	1	0	0	348
Mean Precipitation (in.)	5.60	4.28	2.85	1.86	1.06	0.77	0.31	0.49	1.16	2.23	5.48	6.02	32.11
Days With ≥ 0.1" Precipitation	11	9	8	6	4	2	1	1	3	5	12	11	73
Days With ≥ 1.0" Precipitation	1	1	0	0	0	0	0	0	0	0	1	1	4
Mean Snowfall (in.)	12.6	7.2	0.9	trace	0.0	0.0	0.0	0.0	0.0	trace	3.9	8.2	32.8
Days With ≥ 1.0" Snow Depth	11	5	1	0	0	0	0	0	0	0	2	7	26

Howard Prairie Dam *Jackson County* Elevation: 4,566 ft. Latitude: 42° 14' N Longitude: 122° 23' W

	JAN	FEB	MAR	APR	MAY	JUN	JUL	AUG	SEP	OCT	NOV	DEC	YEAR
Mean Maximum Temp. (°F)	37.1	41.8	46.4	52.3	61.3	70.0	79.0	79.1	72.5	60.8	42.9	36.0	56.6
Mean Temp. (°F)	28.8	32.0	35.8	40.4	47.7	54.9	61.7	61.4	55.3	46.6	34.8	28.7	44.0
Mean Minimum Temp. (°F)	20.4	22.2	25.2	28.5	33.9	39.9	44.4	43.6	38.0	32.4	26.6	21.3	31.4
Extreme Maximum Temp. (°F)	55	67	73	82	92	95	97	100	97	86	68	55	100
Extreme Minimum Temp. (°F)	-10	-20	-1	7	21	26	29	29	22	8	1	-20	-20
Days Maximum Temp. ≥ 90°F	0	0	0	0	0	0	3	3	1	0	0	0	7
Days Maximum Temp. ≤ 32°F	7	2	1	0	0	0	0	0	0	0	2	9	21
Days Minimum Temp. ≤ 32°F	29	27	29	24	14	4	0	0	5	16	26	29	203
Days Minimum Temp. ≤ 0°F	1	1	0	0	0	0	0	0	0	0	0	1	3
Heating Degree Days (base 65°F)	1,115	924	898	730	533	304	135	140	290	563	900	1,119	7,651
Cooling Degree Days (base 65°F)	0	0	0	0	0	1	9	42	36	7	0	0	95
Mean Precipitation (in.)	4.87	3.74	3.73	2.36	2.06	1.36	0.57	0.72	1.08	2.06	5.04	5.40	32.99
Days With ≥ 0.1" Precipitation	10	9	10	8	6	4	1	2	3	5	11	11	80
Days With ≥ 1.0" Precipitation	1	1	0	0	0	0	0	0	0	0	1	1	4
Mean Snowfall (in.)	24.4	23.3	19.6	9.6	2.9	0.3	0.0	0.0	0.2	1.8	19.5	27.2	128.8
Days With ≥ 1.0" Snow Depth	30	27	23	9	2	0	0	0	0	1	12	27	131

Huntington *Baker County* Elevation: 2,109 ft. Latitude: 44° 21' N Longitude: 117° 15' W

	JAN	FEB	MAR	APR	MAY	JUN	JUL	AUG	SEP	OCT	NOV	DEC	YEAR
Mean Maximum Temp. (°F)	36.1	44.1	55.1	63.9	73.5	82.8	92.3	91.2	80.4	66.7	48.2	37.4	64.3
Mean Temp. (°F)	28.0	34.6	43.6	51.2	60.3	69.0	77.7	75.5	64.9	52.1	38.1	29.1	52.0
Mean Minimum Temp. (°F)	19.9	25.0	32.0	38.4	47.1	55.1	63.1	60.1	49.4	37.4	28.0	20.8	39.7
Extreme Maximum Temp. (°F)	58	68	78	91	98	104	107	108	101	94	71	60	108
Extreme Minimum Temp. (°F)	-19	-19	10	20	26	32	41	41	28	18	-8	-15	-19
Days Maximum Temp. ≥ 90°F	0	0	0	0	2	8	21	20	7	0	0	0	58
Days Maximum Temp. ≤ 32°F	10	3	0	0	0	0	0	0	0	0	1	6	20
Days Minimum Temp. ≤ 32°F	28	23	16	6	1	0	0	0	1	9	22	28	134
Days Minimum Temp. ≤ 0°F	2	1	0	0	0	0	0	0	0	0	0	1	4
Heating Degree Days (base 65°F)	1,140	851	658	412	188	51	4	9	98	398	801	1,106	5,716
Cooling Degree Days (base 65°F)	0	0	0	5	51	160	389	332	102	5	0	0	1,044
Mean Precipitation (in.)	1.90	1.46	1.41	0.94	1.23	0.91	0.56	0.53	0.56	0.78	1.77	2.02	14.07
Days With ≥ 0.1" Precipitation	6	5	5	3	4	3	1	2	2	3	6	6	46
Days With ≥ 1.0" Precipitation	0	0	0	0	0	0	0	0	0	0	0	0	0
Mean Snowfall (in.)	8.0	2.9	0.5	trace	trace	0.0	0.0	0.0	0.0	trace	3.0	7.6	22.0
Days With ≥ 1.0" Snow Depth	13	5	0	0	0	0	0	0	0	0	2	10	*30*

Idleyld Park 4 NE *Douglas County* Elevation: 1,079 ft. Latitude: 43° 22' N Longitude: 122° 58' W

	JAN	FEB	MAR	APR	MAY	JUN	JUL	AUG	SEP	OCT	NOV	DEC	YEAR
Mean Maximum Temp. (°F)	46.9	52.2	56.9	62.0	69.3	75.5	83.0	82.8	77.3	65.5	51.7	45.2	64.0
Mean Temp. (°F)	39.8	43.2	46.4	49.9	55.5	60.9	66.0	65.7	60.9	52.6	44.4	39.0	52.0
Mean Minimum Temp. (°F)	32.8	34.1	35.8	37.8	41.7	46.3	49.0	48.5	44.5	39.7	37.1	32.7	40.0
Extreme Maximum Temp. (°F)	70	75	79	90	95	100	102	104	102	96	73	63	104
Extreme Minimum Temp. (°F)	11	6	16	24	26	31	34	34	28	21	13	-1	-1
Days Maximum Temp. ≥ 90°F	0	0	0	0	1	1	6	6	3	0	0	0	17
Days Maximum Temp. ≤ 32°F	0	0	0	0	0	0	0	0	0	0	0	1	1
Days Minimum Temp. ≤ 32°F	16	13	11	6	2	0	0	0	1	4	8	16	77
Days Minimum Temp. ≤ 0°F	0	0	0	0	0	0	0	0	0	0	0	0	0
Heating Degree Days (base 65°F)	774	611	571	447	296	140	43	43	138	378	611	801	4,853
Cooling Degree Days (base 65°F)	0	0	0	1	8	22	78	70	24	1	0	0	204
Mean Precipitation (in.)	9.13	7.40	6.94	5.40	3.46	1.88	0.78	1.08	2.07	4.67	10.67	10.43	63.91
Days With ≥ 0.1" Precipitation	14	13	14	12	8	5	2	2	4	8	15	15	112
Days With ≥ 1.0" Precipitation	3	2	1	1	0	0	0	0	1	1	3	3	15
Mean Snowfall (in.)	4.3	4.4	1.7	0.5	trace	0.0	0.0	0.0	0.0	trace	0.9	3.6	15.4
Days With ≥ 1.0" Snow Depth	3	2	1	0	0	0	0	0	0	0	0	3	9

Illahe *Curry County* Elevation: 347 ft. Latitude: 42° 38' N Longitude: 124° 03' W

	JAN	FEB	MAR	APR	MAY	JUN	JUL	AUG	SEP	OCT	NOV	DEC	YEAR
Mean Maximum Temp. (°F)	50.2	54.1	58.7	64.0	71.6	78.8	87.5	87.5	83.8	69.2	55.1	49.1	67.5
Mean Temp. (°F)	43.4	46.0	48.8	52.1	57.8	63.9	70.1	70.0	66.3	56.6	48.0	42.6	55.5
Mean Minimum Temp. (°F)	36.5	37.8	38.9	40.2	44.0	48.9	52.6	52.4	48.8	44.1	40.5	36.0	43.4
Extreme Maximum Temp. (°F)	67	75	81	92	98	105	106	110	*108*	*99*	*71*	68	*110*
Extreme Minimum Temp. (°F)	15	13	27	28	31	36	37	32	*31*	25	*17*	6	*6*
Days Maximum Temp. ≥ 90°F	0	0	0	0	2	4	13	14	9	1	0	0	43
Days Maximum Temp. ≤ 32°F	0	0	0	0	0	0	0	0	0	0	0	0	0
Days Minimum Temp. ≤ 32°F	9	5	3	1	0	0	0	0	0	1	2	9	30
Days Minimum Temp. ≤ 0°F	0	0	0	0	0	0	0	0	0	0	0	0	0
Heating Degree Days (base 65°F)	664	530	495	381	234	81	15	14	47	258	504	687	3,910
Cooling Degree Days (base 65°F)	0	0	0	1	21	52	195	193	102	6	0	0	*570*
Mean Precipitation (in.)	14.14	11.54	10.43	5.55	3.21	1.28	0.29	0.82	2.23	5.11	13.49	14.19	82.28
Days With ≥ 0.1" Precipitation	13	13	14	9	5	3	1	2	3	6	13	14	96
Days With ≥ 1.0" Precipitation	6	4	4	2	1	0	0	0	1	2	5	6	31
Mean Snowfall (in.)	2.1	2.0	1.0	0.3	trace	0.0	0.0	0.0	0.0	0.0	0.1	1.9	7.4
Days With ≥ 1.0" Snow Depth	0	0	0	0	0	0	0	0	0	0	0	1	1

John Day *Grant County* Elevation: 3,061 ft. Latitude: 44° 26' N Longitude: 118° 57' W

	JAN	FEB	MAR	APR	MAY	JUN	JUL	AUG	SEP	OCT	NOV	DEC	YEAR
Mean Maximum Temp. (°F)	41.2	47.5	53.7	60.1	68.8	77.9	87.7	88.0	78.2	66.1	49.6	42.0	63.4
Mean Temp. (°F)	31.4	36.3	41.3	46.4	54.0	61.5	68.4	68.0	59.3	49.5	38.9	32.1	48.9
Mean Minimum Temp. (°F)	21.6	24.9	28.9	32.8	39.1	45.1	49.0	48.0	40.3	33.0	28.1	22.1	34.4
Extreme Maximum Temp. (°F)	66	73	80	91	98	103	107	106	105	95	79	66	107
Extreme Minimum Temp. (°F)	-16	-20	9	15	22	30	35	30	21	5	-9	-23	-23
Days Maximum Temp. ≥ 90°F	0	0	0	0	1	5	15	15	5	0	0	0	41
Days Maximum Temp. ≤ 32°F	5	2	0	0	0	0	0	0	0	0	1	4	12
Days Minimum Temp. ≤ 32°F	27	24	22	15	5	0	0	0	4	15	21	27	160
Days Minimum Temp. ≤ 0°F	1	1	0	0	0	0	0	0	0	0	0	1	3
Heating Degree Days (base 65°F)	1,033	805	727	550	345	151	42	41	195	474	776	1,013	6,152
Cooling Degree Days (base 65°F)	0	0	0	1	13	48	145	141	33	1	0	0	382
Mean Precipitation (in.)	1.18	0.78	1.28	1.33	1.75	1.27	0.65	0.85	0.80	0.87	1.45	1.39	13.60
Days With ≥ 0.1" Precipitation	4	3	4	4	5	4	2	2	3	3	5	5	44
Days With ≥ 1.0" Precipitation	0	0	0	0	0	0	0	0	0	0	0	0	0
Mean Snowfall (in.)	5.1	3.2	2.5	0.8	trace	0.0	0.0	0.0	0.0	0.4	2.4	6.3	20.7
Days With ≥ 1.0" Snow Depth	11	4	2	1	0	0	0	0	0	0	3	8	29

Kent *Sherman County* Elevation: 2,709 ft. Latitude: 45° 12' N Longitude: 120° 42' W

	JAN	FEB	MAR	APR	MAY	JUN	JUL	AUG	SEP	OCT	NOV	DEC	YEAR
Mean Maximum Temp. (°F)	38.8	43.8	51.4	57.8	66.6	*74.7*	84.2	84.3	75.2	63.3	47.4	39.5	*60.6*
Mean Temp. (°F)	31.2	35.2	40.9	45.7	52.8	*60.1*	67.8	68.0	60.2	50.1	38.5	31.7	*48.5*
Mean Minimum Temp. (°F)	23.5	26.6	30.4	33.5	38.9	*45.4*	51.3	51.7	45.1	36.9	29.5	23.8	*36.4*
Extreme Maximum Temp. (°F)	63	69	75	86	94	103	107	108	102	92	77	64	108
Extreme Minimum Temp. (°F)	-14	-14	12	17	24	28	32	37	24	10	-10	-18	-18
Days Maximum Temp. ≥ 90°F	0	0	0	0	0	2	10	10	2	0	0	0	24
Days Maximum Temp. ≤ 32°F	8	4	0	0	0	0	0	0	0	0	2	7	21
Days Minimum Temp. ≤ 32°F	25	22	20	14	6	1	0	0	1	8	19	26	142
Days Minimum Temp. ≤ 0°F	1	1	0	0	0	0	0	0	0	0	0	1	3
Heating Degree Days (base 65°F)	1,042	835	740	574	383	*186*	59	49	182	458	790	1,031	*6,329*
Cooling Degree Days (base 65°F)	0	0	0	0	13	45	147	153	54	4	0	0	416
Mean Precipitation (in.)	1.52	1.18	1.16	1.12	1.14	0.86	0.50	0.47	0.56	0.85	1.71	1.54	12.61
Days With ≥ 0.1" Precipitation	5	4	4	4	3	3	1	1	2	2	5	4	38
Days With ≥ 1.0" Precipitation	0	0	0	0	0	0	0	0	0	0	0	0	0
Mean Snowfall (in.)	na	3.8	1.6	0.6	0.0	0.0	0.0	0.0	0.0	0.3	3.3	3.8	na
Days With ≥ 1.0" Snow Depth	9	5	1	0	0	0	0	0	0	0	4	**3.8**	26

Klamath Falls 2 SSW *Klamath County*   Elevation: 4,097 ft.   Latitude: 42° 12' N   Longitude: 121° 47' W

	JAN	FEB	MAR	APR	MAY	JUN	JUL	AUG	SEP	OCT	NOV	DEC	YEAR
Mean Maximum Temp. (°F)	39.9	45.9	51.9	59.1	68.3	77.0	85.9	85.2	76.7	64.6	47.5	39.2	61.8
Mean Temp. (°F)	30.9	35.7	40.4	45.6	53.7	61.5	69.0	67.8	60.1	49.8	37.6	30.7	48.6
Mean Minimum Temp. (°F)	21.9	25.4	28.8	32.0	39.1	45.9	52.0	50.2	43.4	35.0	27.6	22.1	35.3
Extreme Maximum Temp. (°F)	58	69	73	87	98	100	102	104	100	88	71	59	104
Extreme Minimum Temp. (°F)	-9	-10	4	15	20	24	30	32	20	11	1	-17	-17
Days Maximum Temp. ≥ 90°F	0	0	0	0	1	3	11	10	2	0	0	0	27
Days Maximum Temp. ≤ 32°F	5	1	0	0	0	0	0	0	0	0	1	5	12
Days Minimum Temp. ≤ 32°F	26	23	22	16	6	1	0	0	2	12	22	27	157
Days Minimum Temp. ≤ 0°F	1	0	0	0	0	0	0	0	0	0	0	1	2
Heating Degree Days (base 65°F)	1,049	821	756	576	356	151	38	45	173	465	816	1,058	6,304
Cooling Degree Days (base 65°F)	0	0	0	0	15	52	171	140	32	1	0	0	411
Mean Precipitation (in.)	2.03	1.38	1.54	0.86	1.10	0.69	0.36	0.50	0.57	0.87	2.05	2.03	13.98
Days With ≥ 0.1" Precipitation	6	4	5	3	3	2	1	1	2	3	6	6	42
Days With ≥ 1.0" Precipitation	0	0	0	0	0	0	0	0	0	0	0	0	0
Mean Snowfall (in.)	8.7	5.2	3.0	0.5	trace	0.0	0.0	0.0	0.0	0.4	4.4	9.5	31.7
Days With ≥ 1.0" Snow Depth	11	5	1	0	0	0	0	0	0	0	3	9	29

La Grande *Union County*   Elevation: 2,752 ft.   Latitude: 45° 19' N   Longitude: 118° 04' W

	JAN	FEB	MAR	APR	MAY	JUN	JUL	AUG	SEP	OCT	NOV	DEC	YEAR
Mean Maximum Temp. (°F)	37.9	43.3	51.2	58.5	67.2	75.8	85.5	86.0	76.3	63.2	46.4	38.4	60.8
Mean Temp. (°F)	30.9	35.0	41.0	46.8	54.4	62.1	69.2	68.9	59.8	49.3	38.4	31.5	48.9
Mean Minimum Temp. (°F)	23.8	26.7	30.8	35.1	41.6	48.3	52.9	51.8	43.2	35.4	30.5	24.5	37.1
Extreme Maximum Temp. (°F)	61	66	75	88	95	100	103	104	100	88	71	59	104
Extreme Minimum Temp. (°F)	-17	-14	9	20	25	29	32	32	23	13	-14	-18	-18
Days Maximum Temp. ≥ 90°F	0	0	0	0	0	3	11	12	3	0	0	0	29
Days Maximum Temp. ≤ 32°F	8	2	0	0	0	0	0	0	0	0	1	6	17
Days Minimum Temp. ≤ 32°F	25	20	18	11	2	0	0	0	2	11	17	25	131
Days Minimum Temp. ≤ 0°F	1	1	0	0	0	0	0	0	0	0	0	1	3
Heating Degree Days (base 65°F)	1,051	840	736	539	331	138	35	36	184	480	791	1,032	6,193
Cooling Degree Days (base 65°F)	0	0	0	0	12	53	163	165	37	0	0	0	430
Mean Precipitation (in.)	1.88	1.34	1.49	1.62	1.87	1.55	0.73	0.86	0.85	1.24	2.24	1.95	17.62
Days With ≥ 0.1" Precipitation	6	4	5	5	5	5	2	2	3	4	6	6	53
Days With ≥ 1.0" Precipitation	0	0	0	0	0	0	0	0	0	0	0	0	0
Mean Snowfall (in.)	7.5	3.1	1.3	0.5	trace	0.0	0.0	0.0	0.0	0.2	3.0	6.3	21.9
Days With ≥ 1.0" Snow Depth	11	4	1	0	0	0	0	0	0	0	2	9	27

Lacomb 3 NNE *Linn County*   Elevation: 518 ft.   Latitude: 44° 38' N   Longitude: 122° 43' W

	JAN	FEB	MAR	APR	MAY	JUN	JUL	AUG	SEP	OCT	NOV	DEC	YEAR
Mean Maximum Temp. (°F)	46.7	50.9	55.7	60.0	66.0	71.7	78.6	79.6	75.5	64.1	51.9	46.0	62.2
Mean Temp. (°F)	39.7	42.5	45.9	49.4	54.5	59.6	64.4	64.7	60.7	52.4	44.5	39.8	51.5
Mean Minimum Temp. (°F)	32.6	34.0	36.0	38.7	42.9	47.5	50.3	49.7	45.9	40.6	37.1	33.5	40.7
Extreme Maximum Temp. (°F)	67	73	75	85	95	100	101	104	101	94	73	70	104
Extreme Minimum Temp. (°F)	1	5	21	27	29	32	38	36	31	25	15	2	1
Days Maximum Temp. ≥ 90°F	0	0	0	0	0	1	3	4	2	0	0	1	2
Days Maximum Temp. ≤ 32°F	1	0	0	0	0	0	0	0	0	0	0	0	1
Days Minimum Temp. ≤ 32°F	16	12	9	5	1	0	0	0	0	2	8	14	67
Days Minimum Temp. ≤ 0°F	0	0	0	0	0	0	0	0	0	0	0	0	0
Heating Degree Days (base 65°F)	779	629	586	461	325	174	71	64	145	385	607	775	5,001
Cooling Degree Days (base 65°F)	0	0	0	0	7	18	62	65	24	1	0	0	177
Mean Precipitation (in.)	7.05	6.31	6.01	4.92	4.06	2.85	1.12	1.26	2.06	4.44	9.01	8.31	57.40
Days With ≥ 0.1" Precipitation	14	13	14	12	10	7	3	3	5	9	16	15	121
Days With ≥ 1.0" Precipitation	2	1	1	0	1	0	0	0	0	1	2	2	10
Mean Snowfall (in.)	0.8	1.2	trace	trace	0.0	0.0	0.0	0.0	0.0	0.0	0.2	0.6	2.8
Days With ≥ 1.0" Snow Depth	1	0	0	0	0	0	0	0	0	0	0	0	na

Lakeview 2 NNW *Lake County*   Elevation: 4,776 ft.   Latitude: 42° 13' N   Longitude: 120° 22' W

	JAN	FEB	MAR	APR	MAY	JUN	JUL	AUG	SEP	OCT	NOV	DEC	YEAR
Mean Maximum Temp. (°F)	38.2	42.6	48.4	55.7	65.2	73.9	84.0	83.1	75.4	62.9	45.7	38.7	59.5
Mean Temp. (°F)	29.2	33.0	37.9	43.4	51.4	59.0	67.2	65.7	58.5	47.9	35.9	29.5	46.6
Mean Minimum Temp. (°F)	20.3	23.4	27.4	31.0	37.6	44.0	50.3	48.2	41.5	32.9	26.0	20.3	33.6
Extreme Maximum Temp. (°F)	59	69	72	87	96	101	100	102	98	89	72	62	102
Extreme Minimum Temp. (°F)	-14	-9	-4	12	17	26	30	26	20	9	-5	-20	-20
Days Maximum Temp. ≥ 90°F	0	0	0	0	0	1	8	6	1	0	0	0	16
Days Maximum Temp. ≤ 32°F	7	3	1	0	0	0	0	0	0	0	1	6	18
Days Minimum Temp. ≤ 32°F	27	24	24	18	8	2	0	0	3	15	24	28	173
Days Minimum Temp. ≤ 0°F	2	1	0	0	0	0	0	0	0	0	0	2	5
Heating Degree Days (base 65°F)	1,102	896	833	642	420	202	50	70	212	522	867	1,093	6,909
Cooling Degree Days (base 65°F)	0	0	0	0	5	24	123	97	26	1	0	0	276
Mean Precipitation (in.)	1.95	1.63	1.67	1.29	1.42	1.05	0.46	0.42	0.69	0.98	1.98	1.91	15.45
Days With ≥ 0.1" Precipitation	6	5	5	4	5	3	1	1	2	3	6	6	47
Days With ≥ 1.0" Precipitation	0	0	0	0	0	0	0	0	0	0	0	0	0
Mean Snowfall (in.)	10.8	10.6	6.2	4.5	1.3	trace	0.0	0.0	0.2	1.3	8.5	12.2	55.6
Days With ≥ 1.0" Snow Depth	14	11	3	1	0	0	0	0	0	0	4	11	44

Leaburg 1 SW *Lane County*   Elevation: 672 ft.   Latitude: 44° 06' N   Longitude: 122° 41' W

	JAN	FEB	MAR	APR	MAY	JUN	JUL	AUG	SEP	OCT	NOV	DEC	YEAR
Mean Maximum Temp. (°F)	47.7	52.1	56.7	60.9	67.4	73.6	81.6	82.4	76.6	65.6	52.8	46.4	63.6
Mean Temp. (°F)	40.7	43.6	46.7	50.1	55.5	60.8	66.2	66.4	61.8	53.8	45.5	40.1	52.6
Mean Minimum Temp. (°F)	33.6	34.9	36.7	39.3	43.5	48.0	50.7	50.4	46.9	42.1	38.2	33.8	41.5
Extreme Maximum Temp. (°F)	65	74	79	85	94	102	104	106	101	97	74	66	106
Extreme Minimum Temp. (°F)	9	4	20	28	30	35	40	38	32	26	20	2	2
Days Maximum Temp. ≥ 90°F	0	0	0	0	0	2	6	6	3	0	0	0	17
Days Maximum Temp. ≤ 32°F	0	0	0	0	0	0	0	0	0	0	0	1	1
Days Minimum Temp. ≤ 32°F	13	9	6	2	0	0	0	0	0	0	1	12	48
Days Minimum Temp. ≤ 0°F	0	0	0	0	0	0	0	0	0	0	0	0	0
Heating Degree Days (base 65°F)	747	599	560	441	298	150	50	41	123	341	578	765	4,693
Cooling Degree Days (base 65°F)	0	0	0	1	10	27	90	89	34	3	0	0	254
Mean Precipitation (in.)	8.90	7.64	7.27	5.90	4.18	2.62	0.86	1.14	2.59	5.02	10.74	10.05	66.91
Days With ≥ 0.1" Precipitation	15	14	15	13	9	6	2	3	5	9	16	16	123
Days With ≥ 1.0" Precipitation	2	2	1	1	1	0	0	0	1	1	3	3	15
Mean Snowfall (in.)	1.4	1.9	0.2	trace	trace	0.0	0.0	0.0	0.0	0.0	0.3	1.1	4.9
Days With ≥ 1.0" Snow Depth	1	1	0	0	0	0	0	0	0	0	0	1	3

Lemolo Lake 3 NNW *Douglas County*   Elevation: 4,074 ft.   Latitude: 43° 19' N   Longitude: 122° 11' W

	JAN	FEB	MAR	APR	MAY	JUN	JUL	AUG	SEP	OCT	NOV	DEC	YEAR
Mean Maximum Temp. (°F)	41.1	43.3	48.0	52.7	61.4	70.2	79.4	79.8	na	61.3	44.7	40.0	na
Mean Temp. (°F)	33.1	34.7	38.2	42.0	48.7	56.0	62.8	62.7	na	48.4	36.8	32.2	na
Mean Minimum Temp. (°F)	25.1	26.1	28.4	31.3	36.0	41.7	46.2	45.6	41.0	35.4	28.8	24.4	34.2
Extreme Maximum Temp. (°F)	60	71	72	86	93	98	98	100	101	91	71	67	101
Extreme Minimum Temp. (°F)	-1	-10	6	17	20	27	30	29	23	17	5	-17	-17
Days Maximum Temp. ≥ 90°F	0	0	0	0	0	1	4	4	2	0	0	0	11
Days Maximum Temp. ≤ 32°F	3	2	0	0	0	0	0	0	0	0	1	4	10
Days Minimum Temp. ≤ 32°F	28	24	25	18	10	2	0	0	3	10	23	29	172
Days Minimum Temp. ≤ 0°F	0	0	0	0	0	0	0	0	0	0	0	0	0
Heating Degree Days (base 65°F)	981	848	823	682	501	278	119	119	na	510	840	1,010	na
Cooling Degree Days (base 65°F)	0	0	0	0	4	15	58	55	21	2	0	0	155
Mean Precipitation (in.)	9.23	8.21	6.33	5.57	3.87	2.84	1.31	1.26	2.25	4.82	10.17	10.44	66.30
Days With ≥ 0.1" Precipitation	13	13	14	11	9	7	3	3	5	8	15	14	115
Days With ≥ 1.0" Precipitation	3	2	1	1	0	0	0	0	0	1	3	4	15
Mean Snowfall (in.)	39.6	43.1	28.0	21.5	4.3	0.1	0.0	0.0	0.6	4.4	34.6	45.2	221.4
Days With ≥ 1.0" Snow Depth	29	27	27	19	4	0	0	0	0	2	15	28	151

Long Creek *Grant County*   Elevation: 3,717 ft.   Latitude: 44° 43' N   Longitude: 119° 06' W

	JAN	FEB	MAR	APR	MAY	JUN	JUL	AUG	SEP	OCT	NOV	DEC	YEAR
Mean Maximum Temp. (°F)	39.2	44.7	50.3	56.3	64.5	73.0	81.9	82.2	72.8	61.9	47.0	39.4	59.4
Mean Temp. (°F)	30.6	34.7	39.0	43.5	50.3	57.1	63.7	63.8	55.9	47.5	37.4	30.5	46.2
Mean Minimum Temp. (°F)	22.0	24.8	27.7	30.7	36.1	41.2	45.4	45.4	38.9	33.2	27.6	21.5	32.9
Extreme Maximum Temp. (°F)	61	69	74	85	92	95	100	102	97	88	75	65	102
Extreme Minimum Temp. (°F)	-16	-21	2	11	21	26	31	29	19	2	-10	-25	-25
Days Maximum Temp. ≥ 90°F	0	0	0	0	0	1	6	6	1	0	0	0	14
Days Maximum Temp. ≤ 32°F	7	2	0	0	0	0	0	0	0	0	2	6	17
Days Minimum Temp. ≤ 32°F	26	23	22	19	9	2	0	0	5	14	21	27	168
Days Minimum Temp. ≤ 0°F	2	1	0	0	0	0	0	0	0	0	0	1	4
Heating Degree Days (base 65°F)	1,062	847	799	638	450	246	94	92	275	535	822	1,062	6,922
Cooling Degree Days (base 65°F)	0	0	0	0	4	13	57	63	12	1	0	0	150
Mean Precipitation (in.)	1.73	1.26	1.65	1.71	1.88	1.37	0.80	0.90	0.83	1.20	1.80	1.64	16.77
Days With ≥ 0.1" Precipitation	6	4	5	6	6	4	2	2	3	4	6	5	53
Days With ≥ 1.0" Precipitation	0	0	0	0	0	0	0	0	0	0	0	0	0
Mean Snowfall (in.)	8.2	6.0	5.0	3.1	0.5	trace	trace	0.0	trace	0.8	4.5	7.8	35.9
Days With ≥ 1.0" Snow Depth	9	4	1	0	0	0	0	0	0	0	2	7	23

Lookout Point Dam *Lane County*   Elevation: 711 ft.   Latitude: 43° 55' N   Longitude: 122° 46' W

	JAN	FEB	MAR	APR	MAY	JUN	JUL	AUG	SEP	OCT	NOV	DEC	YEAR
Mean Maximum Temp. (°F)	47.6	51.8	55.6	59.5	65.9	71.9	79.8	80.4	75.0	64.5	53.1	47.0	62.7
Mean Temp. (°F)	41.2	44.2	47.3	50.5	55.6	60.8	66.7	66.9	62.7	54.9	46.7	41.2	53.2
Mean Minimum Temp. (°F)	34.8	36.7	38.9	41.3	45.2	49.6	53.5	53.4	50.3	45.3	40.2	35.4	43.7
Extreme Maximum Temp. (°F)	68	73	77	84	90	101	100	106	101	89	71	72	106
Extreme Minimum Temp. (°F)	6	7	23	28	30	36	42	42	33	28	17	3	3
Days Maximum Temp. ≥ 90°F	0	0	0	0	0	1	4	4	1	0	0	0	10
Days Maximum Temp. ≤ 32°F	1	0	0	0	0	0	0	0	0	0	0	1	2
Days Minimum Temp. ≤ 32°F	11	6	2	1	0	0	0	0	0	0	3	9	32
Days Minimum Temp. ≤ 0°F	0	0	0	0	0	0	0	0	0	0	0	0	0
Heating Degree Days (base 65°F)	730	580	542	430	295	147	45	34	105	309	543	730	4,490
Cooling Degree Days (base 65°F)	0	0	0	1	10	25	99	100	45	5	0	0	285
Mean Precipitation (in.)	6.01	5.05	5.03	4.22	3.42	2.10	0.79	1.11	1.79	3.31	7.23	6.69	46.75
Days With ≥ 0.1" Precipitation	13	12	13	12	9	6	2	3	5	8	14	14	111
Days With ≥ 1.0" Precipitation	1	1	1	0	0	0	0	0	0	0	2	1	6
Mean Snowfall (in.)	0.6	0.6	0.0	0.0	trace	0.0	0.0	0.0	0.0	0.0	trace	0.7	1.9
Days With ≥ 1.0" Snow Depth	1	1	0	0	0	0	0	0	0	0	0	1	3

Lost Creek Dam *Jackson County*   Elevation: 1,578 ft.   Latitude: 42° 40' N   Longitude: 122° 41' W

	JAN	FEB	MAR	APR	MAY	JUN	JUL	AUG	SEP	OCT	NOV	DEC	YEAR
Mean Maximum Temp. (°F)	47.7	53.1	57.7	63.1	71.2	79.6	88.7	89.0	82.6	70.7	53.2	46.2	66.9
Mean Temp. (°F)	38.3	41.8	45.4	49.7	56.1	62.8	69.4	69.3	63.0	53.7	43.3	37.8	52.6
Mean Minimum Temp. (°F)	28.7	30.5	33.0	36.2	40.9	46.1	50.1	49.6	43.4	36.7	33.4	29.4	38.2
Extreme Maximum Temp. (°F)	70	78	83	92	101	103	108	112	108	104	79	64	112
Extreme Minimum Temp. (°F)	7	2	15	21	27	29	36	37	26	16	11	-10	-10
Days Maximum Temp. ≥ 90°F	0	0	0	0	2	5	16	16	9	2	0	0	50
Days Maximum Temp. ≤ 32°F	0	0	0	0	0	0	0	0	0	0	0	0	0
Days Minimum Temp. ≤ 32°F	22	17	15	9	2	0	0	0	1	7	14	20	107
Days Minimum Temp. ≤ 0°F	0	0	0	0	0	0	0	0	0	0	0	0	0
Heating Degree Days (base 65°F)	822	649	601	455	287	120	29	23	111	348	644	835	4,924
Cooling Degree Days (base 65°F)	0	0	0	1	18	55	161	163	63	5	0	0	466
Mean Precipitation (in.)	4.83	3.97	3.83	2.43	2.06	1.02	0.49	0.68	1.09	2.43	5.59	5.63	34.05
Days With ≥ 0.1" Precipitation	10	9	10	8	5	3	1	2	3	5	12	12	80
Days With ≥ 1.0" Precipitation	1	1	1	0	0	0	0	0	0	0	1	1	5
Mean Snowfall (in.)	1.4	0.8	0.3	trace	trace	trace	0.0	0.0	trace	0.0	0.3	1.9	4.7
Days With ≥ 1.0" Snow Depth	1	1	0	0	0	0	0	0	0	0	0	1	3

Madras *Jefferson County*   Elevation: 2,227 ft.   Latitude: 44° 38' N   Longitude: 121° 08' W

	JAN	FEB	MAR	APR	MAY	JUN	JUL	AUG	SEP	OCT	NOV	DEC	YEAR
Mean Maximum Temp. (°F)	43.2	49.0	56.4	62.6	71.2	79.0	87.6	87.4	78.9	66.2	51.1	43.1	64.6
Mean Temp. (°F)	33.5	37.8	42.8	47.5	54.4	61.4	67.6	67.1	59.3	49.4	40.1	33.5	49.5
Mean Minimum Temp. (°F)	23.7	26.7	29.1	32.0	37.5	43.4	47.5	46.6	39.8	32.6	29.0	23.8	34.3
Extreme Maximum Temp. (°F)	68	74	80	88	101	104	107	109	104	93	77	68	109
Extreme Minimum Temp. (°F)	-24	-18	6	11	20	26	32	31	20	9	-13	-29	-29
Days Maximum Temp. ≥ 90°F	0	0	0	0	1	4	14	13	4	0	0	0	36
Days Maximum Temp. ≤ 32°F	5	2	0	0	0	0	0	0	0	0	1	4	12
Days Minimum Temp. ≤ 32°F	24	20	20	16	8	1	0	0	5	16	18	25	153
Days Minimum Temp. ≤ 0°F	1	1	0	0	0	0	0	0	0	0	0	1	3
Heating Degree Days (base 65°F)	970	761	684	520	332	145	43	45	184	479	742	970	5,875
Cooling Degree Days (base 65°F)	0	0	0	1	13	41	128	115	27	0	0	0	325
Mean Precipitation (in.)	1.26	0.87	0.88	0.85	0.95	0.61	0.53	0.48	0.47	0.73	1.46	1.24	10.33
Days With ≥ 0.1" Precipitation	4	3	3	3	3	2	1	2	1	2	4	4	32
Days With ≥ 1.0" Precipitation	0	0	0	0	0	0	0	0	0	0	0	0	0
Mean Snowfall (in.)	3.4	1.9	0.2	trace	0.0	0.0	0.0	0.0	0.0	0.0	2.0	2.4	9.9
Days With ≥ 1.0" Snow Depth	5	2	0	0	0	0	0	0	0	0	2	4	13

Madras 2 N *Jefferson County*   Elevation: 2,437 ft.   Latitude: 44° 40' N   Longitude: 121° 09' W

	JAN	FEB	MAR	APR	MAY	JUN	JUL	AUG	SEP	OCT	NOV	DEC	YEAR
Mean Maximum Temp. (°F)	40.9	45.5	53.4	60.1	67.8	76.0	84.2	84.2	76.1	63.3	48.5	40.9	61.8
Mean Temp. (°F)	32.7	36.1	41.6	46.9	53.3	60.5	67.0	66.9	59.7	49.4	39.1	32.7	48.8
Mean Minimum Temp. (°F)	24.3	26.7	29.8	33.5	38.8	45.0	49.8	49.5	43.2	35.4	29.6	24.5	35.9
Extreme Maximum Temp. (°F)	66	73	77	89	101	101	105	106	101	90	75	65	106
Extreme Minimum Temp. (°F)	-14	-14	11	18	23	29	34	36	26	11	-7	-16	-16
Days Maximum Temp. ≥ 90°F	0	0	0	0	0	3	10	10	2	0	0	0	25
Days Maximum Temp. ≤ 32°F	6	3	0	0	0	0	0	0	0	0	2	6	17
Days Minimum Temp. ≤ 32°F	25	21	21	14	6	1	0	0	1	10	19	25	143
Days Minimum Temp. ≤ 0°F	1	1	0	0	0	0	0	0	0	0	0	1	3
Heating Degree Days (base 65°F)	995	809	718	539	365	169	58	54	185	478	770	993	6,133
Cooling Degree Days (base 65°F)	0	0	0	1	13	41	130	126	36	1	0	0	348
Mean Precipitation (in.)	1.64	1.20	1.03	1.08	1.16	0.78	0.63	0.57	0.46	0.78	1.60	1.39	12.32
Days With ≥ 0.1" Precipitation	5	4	4	3	4	2	2	2	2	3	5	5	41
Days With ≥ 1.0" Precipitation	0	0	0	0	0	0	0	0	0	0	0	0	0
Mean Snowfall (in.)	4.9	3.6	1.2	trace	trace	0.0	0.0	0.0	0.0	trace	2.3	3.9	15.9
Days With ≥ 1.0" Snow Depth	5	3	0	0	0	0	0	0	0	0	2	4	14

Malheur Branch Exp. Station *Malheur County*   Elevation: 2,257 ft.   Latitude: 43° 59' N   Longitude: 117° 01' W

	JAN	FEB	MAR	APR	MAY	JUN	JUL	AUG	SEP	OCT	NOV	DEC	YEAR
Mean Maximum Temp. (°F)	34.2	42.8	54.8	63.8	73.2	82.1	90.6	90.1	79.3	65.6	47.6	35.8	63.3
Mean Temp. (°F)	26.6	33.7	43.2	50.5	59.2	67.2	74.1	72.7	62.5	50.5	37.7	28.0	50.5
Mean Minimum Temp. (°F)	19.1	24.5	31.4	37.1	45.2	52.2	57.6	55.3	45.6	35.4	27.8	20.1	37.6
Extreme Maximum Temp. (°F)	58	65	79	91	100	103	106	106	98	94	77	65	106
Extreme Minimum Temp. (°F)	-24	-24	5	19	26	34	36	37	25	18	-5	-21	-24
Days Maximum Temp. ≥ 90°F	0	0	0	0	2	7	19	18	5	0	0	0	51
Days Maximum Temp. ≤ 32°F	12	3	0	0	0	0	0	0	0	0	1	9	25
Days Minimum Temp. ≤ 32°F	28	24	19	8	1	0	0	0	1	10	22	29	142
Days Minimum Temp. ≤ 0°F	3	1	0	0	0	0	0	0	0	0	0	2	6
Heating Degree Days (base 65°F)	1,182	877	671	431	208	62	10	13	128	443	810	1,140	5,975
Cooling Degree Days (base 65°F)	0	0	0	3	38	120	284	255	64	1	0	0	765
Mean Precipitation (in.)	1.35	0.98	1.08	0.82	0.99	0.79	0.36	0.38	0.50	0.64	1.24	1.41	10.54
Days With ≥ 0.1" Precipitation	4	3	4	3	3	2	1	1	2	2	4	5	34
Days With ≥ 1.0" Precipitation	0	0	0	0	0	0	0	0	0	0	0	0	0
Mean Snowfall (in.)	6.5	3.0	0.7	trace	trace	0.0	0.0	0.0	0.0	0.1	2.4	6.6	19.3
Days With ≥ 1.0" Snow Depth	18	10	1	0	0	0	0	0	0	0	2	12	43

Malin 5 E *Klamath County*   Elevation: 4,625 ft.   Latitude: 42° 00' N   Longitude: 121° 19' W

	JAN	FEB	MAR	APR	MAY	JUN	JUL	AUG	SEP	OCT	NOV	DEC	YEAR
Mean Maximum Temp. (°F)	40.9	45.4	49.2	56.4	65.9	74.6	82.9	82.1	74.4	63.0	46.7	40.2	60.1
Mean Temp. (°F)	31.5	35.4	38.4	43.6	51.4	59.1	65.8	65.0	58.1	49.0	36.8	31.0	47.1
Mean Minimum Temp. (°F)	22.1	25.4	27.4	30.8	36.8	43.5	48.6	47.9	41.7	35.0	26.9	21.7	34.0
Extreme Maximum Temp. (°F)	60	76	72	83	93	96	98	102	98	88	74	62	102
Extreme Minimum Temp. (°F)	-5	-18	1	9	18	25	29	29	23	8	-3	-20	-20
Days Maximum Temp. ≥ 90°F	0	0	0	0	0	1	6	5	1	0	0	0	13
Days Maximum Temp. ≤ 32°F	3	1	0	0	0	0	0	0	0	0	1	4	9
Days Minimum Temp. ≤ 32°F	24	20	21	16	9	2	0	0	3	11	20	25	151
Days Minimum Temp. ≤ 0°F	0	0	0	0	0	0	0	0	0	0	0	1	1
Heating Degree Days (base 65°F)	1,032	829	820	634	420	202	67	75	218	490	840	1,048	6,675
Cooling Degree Days (base 65°F)	0	0	0	0	7	27	90	75	19	1	0	0	219
Mean Precipitation (in.)	1.60	1.25	1.57	1.07	1.40	1.01	0.44	0.59	0.72	1.01	1.53	1.45	13.64
Days With ≥ 0.1" Precipitation	4	3	4	3	3	2	1	1	2	3	4	4	34
Days With ≥ 1.0" Precipitation	0	0	0	0	0	0	0	0	0	0	0	0	0
Mean Snowfall (in.)	6.5	5.7	3.7	1.9	0.8	trace	trace	0.0	trace	0.6	4.6	8.3	32.1
Days With ≥ 1.0" Snow Depth	12	8	3	1	0	0	0	0	0	0	4	11	39

Marion Frks. Fish Hatchery *Linn County*   Elevation: 2,473 ft.   Latitude: 44° 37' N   Longitude: 121° 57' W

	JAN	FEB	MAR	APR	MAY	JUN	JUL	AUG	SEP	OCT	NOV	DEC	YEAR
Mean Maximum Temp. (°F)	39.1	43.9	49.3	54.9	63.5	71.5	80.0	80.1	72.7	61.1	45.4	38.2	58.3
Mean Temp. (°F)	32.7	35.8	39.6	43.9	50.6	57.3	63.2	62.7	56.2	47.8	38.2	32.6	46.7
Mean Minimum Temp. (°F)	26.3	27.6	29.8	32.8	37.5	43.1	46.4	45.2	39.7	34.5	31.0	26.8	35.1
Extreme Maximum Temp. (°F)	58	69	77	89	101	100	102	105	99	92	67	54	105
Extreme Minimum Temp. (°F)	-2	-8	8	19	27	29	33	33	26	17	2	-8	-8
Days Maximum Temp. ≥ 90°F	0	0	0	0	1	2	6	6	2	0	0	0	17
Days Maximum Temp. ≤ 32°F	2	1	0	0	0	0	0	0	0	0	0	2	5
Days Minimum Temp. ≤ 32°F	27	24	24	17	6	1	0	0	3	12	19	28	161
Days Minimum Temp. ≤ 0°F	0	0	0	0	0	0	0	0	0	0	0	0	0
Heating Degree Days (base 65°F)	994	818	781	626	445	244	107	113	264	525	797	999	6,713
Cooling Degree Days (base 65°F)	0	0	0	0	5	17	55	46	9	0	0	0	132
Mean Precipitation (in.)	10.79	8.76	7.30	5.47	3.88	2.60	1.09	1.11	2.37	4.94	11.50	11.69	71.50
Days With ≥ 0.1" Precipitation	14	13	14	12	10	7	3	3	5	9	16	15	121
Days With ≥ 1.0" Precipitation	4	3	1	1	1	0	0	0	0	1	3	4	18
Mean Snowfall (in.)	18.0	19.3	13.9	7.1	0.5	0.0	0.0	0.0	0.0	0.4	9.8	19.7	88.7
Days With ≥ 1.0" Snow Depth	23	18	14	5	0	0	0	0	0	0	7	19	86

Mason Dam *Baker County*   Elevation: 3,897 ft.   Latitude: 44° 40' N   Longitude: 118° 00' W

	JAN	FEB	MAR	APR	MAY	JUN	JUL	AUG	SEP	OCT	NOV	DEC	YEAR
Mean Maximum Temp. (°F)	34.0	40.5	48.1	56.1	65.1	73.0	81.9	81.6	72.4	60.5	43.3	33.6	57.5
Mean Temp. (°F)	23.4	28.1	35.5	42.4	50.1	56.8	63.2	62.9	54.9	45.2	33.7	24.1	43.4
Mean Minimum Temp. (°F)	12.7	15.7	22.8	28.6	35.0	40.5	44.4	44.3	37.4	29.9	24.1	14.6	29.2
Extreme Maximum Temp. (°F)	59	64	73	85	91	95	98	98	95	85	65	54	98
Extreme Minimum Temp. (°F)	-28	-40	-9	6	20	22	27	26	20	5	-10	-28	-40
Days Maximum Temp. ≥ 90°F	0	0	0	0	0	1	5	5	1	0	0	0	12
Days Maximum Temp. ≤ 32°F	11	3	1	0	0	0	0	0	0	0	2	12	29
Days Minimum Temp. ≤ 32°F	30	27	29	23	11	3	0	0	7	20	27	30	207
Days Minimum Temp. ≤ 0°F	6	4	0	0	0	0	0	0	0	0	1	3	14
Heating Degree Days (base 65°F)	1,284	1,034	908	671	457	254	99	105	301	606	932	1,260	7,911
Cooling Degree Days (base 65°F)	0	0	0	0	2	11	47	50	7	0	0	0	117
Mean Precipitation (in.)	1.90	1.34	1.56	1.25	1.80	1.66	0.89	0.95	0.83	0.91	1.93	2.02	17.04
Days With ≥ 0.1" Precipitation	6	5	6	4	5	4	3	3	2	3	6	6	53
Days With ≥ 1.0" Precipitation	0	0	0	0	0	0	0	0	0	0	0	0	0
Mean Snowfall (in.)	11.4	5.9	2.4	0.2	trace	0.0	0.0	0.0	0.0	trace	5.3	12.8	38.0
Days With ≥ 1.0" Snow Depth	na	na	3	0	0	0	0	0	0	0	na	na	na

McDermitt 26 N *Malheur County*   Elevation: 4,461 ft.   Latitude: 42° 25' N   Longitude: 117° 52' W

	JAN	FEB	MAR	APR	MAY	JUN	JUL	AUG	SEP	OCT	NOV	DEC	YEAR
Mean Maximum Temp. (°F)	41.0	47.0	53.8	61.3	70.8	81.1	91.1	89.8	79.8	67.6	50.4	41.4	64.6
Mean Temp. (°F)	30.0	34.7	40.0	45.5	53.8	62.3	70.1	68.6	59.6	49.6	37.7	29.9	48.5
Mean Minimum Temp. (°F)	19.0	22.3	26.1	29.6	36.7	43.5	49.0	47.3	39.4	31.6	25.1	18.4	32.3
Extreme Maximum Temp. (°F)	64	70	75	87	97	105	107	105	100	92	75	65	107
Extreme Minimum Temp. (°F)	-18	-24	-3	8	15	22	28	20	16	4	-8	-30	-30
Days Maximum Temp. ≥ 90°F	0	0	0	0	1	7	20	18	5	0	0	0	51
Days Maximum Temp. ≤ 32°F	6	2	0	0	0	0	0	0	0	0	1	5	14
Days Minimum Temp. ≤ 32°F	27	24	24	19	10	2	0	1	6	17	23	28	181
Days Minimum Temp. ≤ 0°F	3	1	0	0	0	0	0	0	0	0	0	2	6
Heating Degree Days (base 65°F)	1,077	850	769	579	351	138	24	36	189	472	813	1,081	6,379
Cooling Degree Days (base 65°F)	0	0	0	1	13	57	184	158	36	1	0	0	450
Mean Precipitation (in.)	0.79	0.62	1.05	1.09	1.36	1.02	0.44	0.47	0.52	0.64	0.91	0.91	9.82
Days With ≥ 0.1" Precipitation	2	2	3	4	4	3	1	1	2	2	3	3	30
Days With ≥ 1.0" Precipitation	0	0	0	0	0	0	0	0	0	0	0	0	0
Mean Snowfall (in.)	2.5	2.6	3.5	1.4	0.3	0.0	0.0	0.0	trace	0.1	1.3	3.0	14.7
Days With ≥ 1.0" Snow Depth	3	1	1	0	0	0	0	0	0	0	0	na	na

McMinnville *Yamhill County*   Elevation: 154 ft.   Latitude: 45° 13' N   Longitude: 123° 10' W

	JAN	FEB	MAR	APR	MAY	JUN	JUL	AUG	SEP	OCT	NOV	DEC	YEAR
Mean Maximum Temp. (°F)	46.7	51.2	56.7	61.8	69.0	74.9	82.4	82.8	77.0	65.2	53.0	46.2	63.9
Mean Temp. (°F)	40.4	43.6	47.1	50.7	56.3	61.3	66.7	66.9	62.2	53.6	45.8	40.2	52.9
Mean Minimum Temp. (°F)	34.0	35.9	37.4	39.5	43.8	47.6	51.0	51.0	47.4	42.0	38.5	34.1	41.8
Extreme Maximum Temp. (°F)	62	69	75	85	100	103	104	106	105	95	71	64	106
Extreme Minimum Temp. (°F)	8	8	18	25	29	31	34	31	28	23	15	-5	-5
Days Maximum Temp. ≥ 90°F	0	0	0	0	0	2	6	6	3	0	0	0	17
Days Maximum Temp. ≤ 32°F	1	0	0	0	0	0	0	0	0	0	0	1	2
Days Minimum Temp. ≤ 32°F	13	9	7	4	0	0	0	0	0	0	2	6	12	53
Days Minimum Temp. ≤ 0°F	0	0	0	0	0	0	0	0	0	0	0	0	0
Heating Degree Days (base 65°F)	756	600	549	423	274	136	40	36	117	349	569	738	4,587
Cooling Degree Days (base 65°F)	0	0	0	0	15	35	104	109	44	3	0	0	310
Mean Precipitation (in.)	6.73	5.57	4.73	2.88	1.93	1.07	0.43	0.53	1.65	2.87	6.26	7.72	42.37
Days With ≥ 0.1" Precipitation	11	10	11	7	5	3	1	1	4	6	12	12	83
Days With ≥ 1.0" Precipitation	2	1	1	0	0	0	0	0	0	0	1	2	7
Mean Snowfall (in.)	1.1	0.6	trace	trace	0.0	0.0	0.0	0.0	0.0	0.0	0.1	1.2	3.0
Days With ≥ 1.0" Snow Depth	0	0	0	0	0	0	0	0	0	0	0	0	0

Medford Experiment Station *Jackson County*   Elevation: 1,456 ft.   Latitude: 42° 18' N   Longitude: 122° 52' W

	JAN	FEB	MAR	APR	MAY	JUN	JUL	AUG	SEP	OCT	NOV	DEC	YEAR
Mean Maximum Temp. (°F)	46.8	53.4	58.3	64.3	72.6	80.3	87.8	87.4	80.6	67.9	51.8	45.0	66.4
Mean Temp. (°F)	38.6	42.7	46.6	50.8	57.3	64.1	69.6	69.0	62.5	52.8	42.9	37.8	52.9
Mean Minimum Temp. (°F)	30.4	32.0	34.8	37.2	41.9	47.8	51.2	50.6	44.3	37.5	34.0	30.5	39.4
Extreme Maximum Temp. (°F)	69	77	79	93	96	104	105	109	102	95	73	68	109
Extreme Minimum Temp. (°F)	9	0	20	25	29	30	35	37	27	17	9	-8	-8
Days Maximum Temp. ≥ 90°F	0	0	0	0	2	5	14	12	5	0	0	0	38
Days Maximum Temp. ≤ 32°F	0	0	0	0	0	0	0	0	0	0	0	1	1
Days Minimum Temp. ≤ 32°F	18	15	12	7	2	0	0	0	1	8	12	17	92
Days Minimum Temp. ≤ 0°F	0	0	0	0	0	0	0	0	0	0	0	0	0
Heating Degree Days (base 65°F)	810	622	565	421	249	95	24	20	115	374	655	838	4,788
Cooling Degree Days (base 65°F)	0	0	0	2	18	64	148	135	44	2	0	0	413
Mean Precipitation (in.)	2.81	2.27	2.22	1.56	1.40	0.78	0.48	0.58	0.96	1.46	3.43	3.37	21.32
Days With ≥ 0.1" Precipitation	5	5	5	4	4	2	1	1	2	3	6	6	44
Days With ≥ 1.0" Precipitation	0	0	0	0	0	0	0	0	0	0	1	1	1
Mean Snowfall (in.)	1.0	0.3	0.2	trace	0.0	0.0	0.0	0.0	0.0	0.0	trace	0.9	2.4
Days With ≥ 1.0" Snow Depth	0	0	0	0	0	0	0	0	0	0	0	1	1

Milton Freewater *Umatilla County*   Elevation: 967 ft.   Latitude: 45° 57' N   Longitude: 118° 25' W

	JAN	FEB	MAR	APR	MAY	JUN	JUL	AUG	SEP	OCT	NOV	DEC	YEAR
Mean Maximum Temp. (°F)	41.7	47.6	56.3	63.7	71.7	79.6	88.1	87.4	77.6	65.0	50.7	42.4	64.3
Mean Temp. (°F)	34.7	39.9	47.0	53.1	60.1	67.1	74.0	73.1	64.2	53.3	42.6	35.4	53.7
Mean Minimum Temp. (°F)	27.8	32.1	37.7	42.4	48.5	54.5	59.9	58.9	50.7	41.5	34.5	28.4	43.1
Extreme Maximum Temp. (°F)	70	78	80	88	98	104	108	109	100	92	82	71	109
Extreme Minimum Temp. (°F)	-14	-17	6	24	29	38	39	42	28	17	-12	-16	-17
Days Maximum Temp. ≥ 90°F	0	0	0	0	1	5	14	13	2	0	0	0	35
Days Maximum Temp. ≤ 32°F	7	3	0	0	0	0	0	0	0	0	2	7	19
Days Minimum Temp. ≤ 32°F	20	13	6	1	0	0	0	0	0	1	4	12	21	78
Days Minimum Temp. ≤ 0°F	1	0	0	0	0	0	0	0	0	0	0	1	2
Heating Degree Days (base 65°F)	931	704	551	356	184	55	8	9	99	361	666	910	4,834
Cooling Degree Days (base 65°F)	0	0	0	5	45	118	289	269	92	5	1	0	824
Mean Precipitation (in.)	1.78	1.30	1.69	1.49	1.54	1.06	0.55	0.69	0.75	1.13	2.09	1.76	15.83
Days With ≥ 0.1" Precipitation	6	5	5	5	4	3	2	2	2	3	6	6	49
Days With ≥ 1.0" Precipitation	0	0	0	0	0	0	0	0	0	0	0	0	0
Mean Snowfall (in.)	3.5	2.4	0.4	trace	0.0	0.0	0.0	0.0	0.0	trace	0.8	3.4	10.5
Days With ≥ 1.0" Snow Depth	5	2	0	0	0	0	0	0	0	0	0	1	4	12

Mitchell 2 NW *Wheeler County*   Elevation: 2,644 ft.   Latitude: 44° 35' N   Longitude: 120° 11' W

	JAN	FEB	MAR	APR	MAY	JUN	JUL	AUG	SEP	OCT	NOV	DEC	YEAR
Mean Maximum Temp. (°F)	41.2	47.0	53.5	59.9	68.8	77.3	85.6	85.7	76.1	64.7	48.6	41.6	62.5
Mean Temp. (°F)	32.4	36.9	42.1	46.8	54.2	61.9	68.4	68.3	59.6	50.3	38.9	32.9	49.4
Mean Minimum Temp. (°F)	23.6	26.8	30.6	33.7	39.5	46.4	51.1	50.9	43.0	35.8	29.2	24.2	36.2
Extreme Maximum Temp. (°F)	68	72	77	91	100	102	103	107	102	92	76	69	107
Extreme Minimum Temp. (°F)	-15	-16	12	10	24	25	35	33	24	11	-11	-27	-27
Days Maximum Temp. ≥ 90°F	0	0	0	0	1	5	12	12	3	0	0	0	33
Days Maximum Temp. ≤ 32°F	6	2	0	0	0	0	0	0	0	0	2	5	15
Days Minimum Temp. ≤ 32°F	25	21	20	14	4	0	0	0	1	10	19	25	139
Days Minimum Temp. ≤ 0°F	1	1	0	0	0	0	0	0	0	0	0	1	3
Heating Degree Days (base 65°F)	1,004	787	704	540	345	152	45	46	188	453	777	989	6,030
Cooling Degree Days (base 65°F)	0	0	0	1	23	71	157	na	47	4	0	0	na
Mean Precipitation (in.)	0.85	0.59	1.04	1.20	1.49	1.22	0.68	0.75	0.70	0.77	1.16	1.00	11.45
Days With ≥ 0.1" Precipitation	3	2	4	4	4	4	2	2	2	3	4	4	38
Days With ≥ 1.0" Precipitation	0	0	0	0	0	0	0	0	0	0	0	0	0
Mean Snowfall (in.)	3.4	2.3	1.6	0.4	trace	0.0	0.0	0.0	0.0	0.8	3.0	na	na
Days With ≥ 1.0" Snow Depth	8	4	1	0	0	0	0	0	0	0	3	6	22

Monument 2 *Grant County* Elevation: 1,994 ft. Latitude: 44° 49' N Longitude: 119° 25' W

	JAN	FEB	MAR	APR	MAY	JUN	JUL	AUG	SEP	OCT	NOV	DEC	YEAR
Mean Maximum Temp. (°F)	*42.1*	na	56.9	*64.2*	*71.5*	80.9	*90.8*	90.3	*80.7*	68.5	na	na	na
Mean Temp. (°F)	na	na	43.5	*49.1*	na	63.7	na	69.3	*60.7*	50.3	na	na	na
Mean Minimum Temp. (°F)	*21.7*	*25.2*	30.1	34.0	na	46.2	na	48.5	40.6	*32.0*	na	na	na
Extreme Maximum Temp. (°F)	69	74	80	95	101	104	108	110	105	96	78	67	110
Extreme Minimum Temp. (°F)	-19	-21	13	18	24	31	35	31	23	10	-15	-25	-25
Days Maximum Temp. ≥ 90°F	0	0	0	0	2	7	17	18	7	1	0	0	52
Days Maximum Temp. ≤ 32°F	4	1	0	0	0	0	0	0	0	0	1	3	9
Days Minimum Temp. ≤ 32°F	24	21	19	11	3	0	0	0	3	15	18	24	138
Days Minimum Temp. ≤ 0°F	1	1	0	0	0	0	0	0	0	0	0	1	3
Heating Degree Days (base 65°F)	na	na	*667*	*481*	na	*107*	na	25	*164*	*452*	na	na	na
Cooling Degree Days (base 65°F)	na	na	na	na	na	na	na	*164*	na	*1*	na	na	na
Mean Precipitation (in.)	1.48	1.13	1.50	1.41	1.54	1.23	0.56	0.77	0.61	0.90	1.60	1.41	14.14
Days With ≥ 0.1" Precipitation	5	4	5	4	5	4	2	2	2	3	5	4	45
Days With ≥ 1.0" Precipitation	0	0	0	0	0	0	0	0	0	0	0	0	0
Mean Snowfall (in.)	5.0	3.0	1.5	0.1	0.0	0.0	0.0	0.0	0.0	0.1	2.0	5.2	16.9
Days With ≥ 1.0" Snow Depth	8	2	1	0	0	0	0	0	0	0	1	6	18

Moro *Sherman County* Elevation: 1,870 ft. Latitude: 45° 29' N Longitude: 120° 43' W

	JAN	FEB	MAR	APR	MAY	JUN	JUL	AUG	SEP	OCT	NOV	DEC	YEAR
Mean Maximum Temp. (°F)	38.3	43.5	51.2	57.7	65.7	73.5	81.7	81.9	73.6	61.9	46.9	38.6	59.5
Mean Temp. (°F)	31.5	35.7	41.8	47.0	53.9	61.0	67.9	67.7	59.6	49.4	39.0	32.1	48.9
Mean Minimum Temp. (°F)	24.7	27.9	32.3	36.2	42.1	48.3	53.9	53.5	45.6	36.9	31.1	25.5	38.2
Extreme Maximum Temp. (°F)	63	67	73	87	100	102	106	106	100	88	71	63	106
Extreme Minimum Temp. (°F)	-14	-15	3	20	26	27	35	31	23	12	-15	-16	-16
Days Maximum Temp. ≥ 90°F	0	0	0	0	0	2	8	7	1	0	0	0	18
Days Maximum Temp. ≤ 32°F	8	4	0	0	0	0	0	0	0	0	2	8	22
Days Minimum Temp. ≤ 32°F	25	20	16	8	2	0	0	0	1	8	17	24	121
Days Minimum Temp. ≤ 0°F	1	1	0	0	0	0	0	0	0	0	0	1	3
Heating Degree Days (base 65°F)	1,032	821	713	535	349	168	60	56	191	478	775	1,014	6,192
Cooling Degree Days (base 65°F)	0	0	0	1	15	48	147	143	42	2	0	0	398
Mean Precipitation (in.)	1.65	1.10	1.09	0.90	0.88	0.60	0.32	0.38	0.52	0.82	1.70	1.57	11.53
Days With ≥ 0.1" Precipitation	5	4	4	3	3	2	1	1	2	3	5	5	38
Days With ≥ 1.0" Precipitation	0	0	0	0	0	0	0	0	0	0	0	0	0
Mean Snowfall (in.)	6.0	3.4	1.0	trace	trace	0.0	0.0	0.0	0.0	0.3	2.4	5.1	18.2
Days With ≥ 1.0" Snow Depth	10	4	1	0	0	0	0	0	0	0	3	8	26

Newport *Lincoln County* Elevation: 121 ft. Latitude: 44° 39' N Longitude: 124° 03' W

	JAN	FEB	MAR	APR	MAY	JUN	JUL	AUG	SEP	OCT	NOV	DEC	YEAR
Mean Maximum Temp. (°F)	51.0	53.1	54.2	55.9	59.2	62.1	64.8	65.7	65.5	61.2	54.8	50.9	58.2
Mean Temp. (°F)	44.8	46.2	47.0	48.4	51.9	55.3	57.7	58.3	57.1	53.1	48.4	44.8	51.1
Mean Minimum Temp. (°F)	38.6	39.2	39.7	40.8	44.6	48.4	50.5	50.8	48.8	44.9	41.9	38.7	43.9
Extreme Maximum Temp. (°F)	69	76	74	83	89	94	92	91	96	94	72	69	96
Extreme Minimum Temp. (°F)	4	12	26	23	32	34	33	37	32	25	18	1	1
Days Maximum Temp. ≥ 90°F	0	0	0	0	0	0	0	0	0	0	0	0	0
Days Maximum Temp. ≤ 32°F	0	0	0	0	0	0	0	0	0	0	0	1	1
Days Minimum Temp. ≤ 32°F	6	4	3	2	0	0	0	0	0	0	0	1	1
Days Minimum Temp. ≤ 0°F	0	0	0	0	0	0	0	0	0	0	2	5	22
Heating Degree Days (base 65°F)	619	525	552	491	399	286	220	203	234	364	492	619	5,004
Cooling Degree Days (base 65°F)	0	0	0	0	1	1	0	0	4	2	0	0	9
Mean Precipitation (in.)	10.46	8.60	7.72	5.01	3.65	2.65	1.04	1.03	2.48	5.15	10.82	11.66	70.27
Days With ≥ 0.1" Precipitation	16	14	15	12	9	6	2	3	5	9	17	16	124
Days With ≥ 1.0" Precipitation	3	2	2	1	1	0	0	0	0	1	3	4	17
Mean Snowfall (in.)	0.3	0.2	trace	trace	trace	0.0	0.0	0.0	0.0	0.0	trace	0.5	1.0
Days With ≥ 1.0" Snow Depth	0	0	0	0	0	0	0	0	0	0	0	1	1

North Bend Municipal Airport *Coos County* Elevation: 3 ft. Latitude: 43° 25' N Longitude: 124° 15' W

	JAN	FEB	MAR	APR	MAY	JUN	JUL	AUG	SEP	OCT	NOV	DEC	YEAR
Mean Maximum Temp. (°F)	52.8	54.7	55.5	57.2	60.8	63.8	66.5	67.5	67.1	63.0	56.8	52.6	59.9
Mean Temp. (°F)	46.3	47.9	48.6	50.1	53.9	57.2	59.7	60.3	58.8	54.6	49.9	46.1	52.8
Mean Minimum Temp. (°F)	39.8	41.0	41.7	43.0	46.9	50.5	52.8	53.1	50.4	46.1	43.0	39.6	45.7
Extreme Maximum Temp. (°F)	69	82	78	87	84	92	88	84	95	95	73	70	95
Extreme Minimum Temp. (°F)	19	14	27	30	35	39	43	44	34	28	22	10	10
Days Maximum Temp. ≥ 90°F	0	0	0	0	0	0	0	0	0	0	0	0	0
Days Maximum Temp. ≤ 32°F	0	0	0	0	0	0	0	0	0	0	0	0	0
Days Minimum Temp. ≤ 32°F	5	3	1	0	0	0	0	0	0	0	0	0	0
Days Minimum Temp. ≤ 0°F	0	0	0	0	0	0	0	0	0	0	2	4	15
Heating Degree Days (base 65°F)	572	477	501	439	338	229	158	139	183	318	446	578	4,378
Cooling Degree Days (base 65°F)	0	0	0	0	0	0	0	2	2	1	0	0	5
Mean Precipitation (in.)	10.07	8.03	7.92	5.29	3.40	1.69	0.50	0.86	1.76	4.60	10.51	10.83	65.46
Days With ≥ 0.1" Precipitation	16	14	14	12	8	5	2	2	4	8	16	15	116
Days With ≥ 1.0" Precipitation	3	2	2	1	0	0	0	0	0	1	3	3	15
Mean Snowfall (in.)	0.6	0.2	trace	trace	trace	trace	0.0	0.0	trace	trace	trace	0.3	1.1
Days With ≥ 1.0" Snow Depth	0	0	0	0	0	0	0	0	0	0	0	0	0

North Willamette Exp. Station *Clackamas County* Elevation: 147 ft. Latitude: 45° 17' N Longitude: 122° 45' W

	JAN	FEB	MAR	APR	MAY	JUN	JUL	AUG	SEP	OCT	NOV	DEC	YEAR
Mean Maximum Temp. (°F)	47.0	51.3	56.1	60.3	67.1	73.3	80.5	80.9	75.6	64.4	52.7	45.7	62.9
Mean Temp. (°F)	40.2	43.1	46.7	50.2	56.0	61.6	66.9	66.9	62.2	53.1	45.3	39.2	52.6
Mean Minimum Temp. (°F)	33.5	34.8	37.2	40.1	44.9	49.9	53.2	52.9	48.7	41.7	37.8	32.6	42.3
Extreme Maximum Temp. (°F)	63	71	78	86	101	104	103	105	105	95	71	67	105
Extreme Minimum Temp. (°F)	8	8	20	27	29	35	41	38	30	25	14	-15	-15
Days Maximum Temp. ≥ 90°F	0	0	0	0	1	1	5	5	3	0	0	0	15
Days Maximum Temp. ≤ 32°F	1	0	0	0	0	0	0	0	0	0	0	2	3
Days Minimum Temp. ≤ 32°F	14	10	7	3	0	0	0	0	0	2	7	14	57
Days Minimum Temp. ≤ 0°F	0	0	0	0	0	0	0	0	0	0	0	0	0
Heating Degree Days (base 65°F)	761	613	561	438	284	132	40	37	119	365	586	795	4,731
Cooling Degree Days (base 65°F)	0	0	0	1	15	39	103	109	44	2	0	0	313
Mean Precipitation (in.)	6.12	5.07	4.24	3.14	2.47	1.72	0.73	0.83	1.77	3.36	6.61	6.63	42.69
Days With ≥ 0.1" Precipitation	13	12	12	10	7	5	2	2	5	8	14	13	103
Days With ≥ 1.0" Precipitation	1	1	0	0	0	0	0	0	0	0	1	2	5
Mean Snowfall (in.)	0.5	0.3	trace	0.0	trace	0.0	0.0	0.0	0.0	0.0	trace	0.6	1.4
Days With ≥ 1.0" Snow Depth	0	0	0	0	0	0	0	0	0	0	0	1	1

Nyssa *Malheur County* Elevation: 2,171 ft. Latitude: 43° 52' N Longitude: 117° 00' W

	JAN	FEB	MAR	APR	MAY	JUN	JUL	AUG	SEP	OCT	NOV	DEC	YEAR
Mean Maximum Temp. (°F)	34.6	43.7	55.6	64.4	73.1	81.8	90.5	89.6	78.8	65.7	48.1	36.0	63.5
Mean Temp. (°F)	27.9	34.8	44.1	51.5	59.7	67.9	74.9	73.4	63.0	51.4	38.7	29.0	51.4
Mean Minimum Temp. (°F)	21.0	25.9	32.5	38.5	46.3	53.8	59.3	57.2	47.1	37.0	29.3	22.0	39.2
Extreme Maximum Temp. (°F)	63	67	81	92	100	102	104	106	97	92	70	67	106
Extreme Minimum Temp. (°F)	-18	-18	10	22	24	35	35	42	29	21	-1	-18	-18
Days Maximum Temp. ≥ 90°F	0	0	0	0	1	7	19	18	4	0	0	0	49
Days Maximum Temp. ≤ 32°F	12	3	0	0	0	0	0	0	0	0	1	10	26
Days Minimum Temp. ≤ 32°F	27	22	15	5	0	0	0	0	1	8	20	27	125
Days Minimum Temp. ≤ 0°F	2	1	0	0	0	0	0	0	0	0	0	1	4
Heating Degree Days (base 65°F)	1,145	848	642	403	195	53	7	9	115	417	782	1,109	5,725
Cooling Degree Days (base 65°F)	0	0	0	4	45	141	320	286	69	1	0	0	866
Mean Precipitation (in.)	1.37	1.05	0.99	0.83	1.04	0.84	0.36	0.35	0.58	0.61	1.26	1.42	10.70
Days With ≥ 0.1" Precipitation	5	4	4	3	4	3	1	1	2	2	4	5	38
Days With ≥ 1.0" Precipitation	0	0	0	0	0	0	0	0	0	0	0	0	0
Mean Snowfall (in.)	5.8	2.0	0.3	0.0	0.0	trace	0.0	0.0	0.0	trace	1.6	7.2	16.9
Days With ≥ 1.0" Snow Depth	14	4	0	0	0	0	0	0	0	0	2	9	29

Oakridge Fish Hatchery *Lane County* Elevation: 1,272 ft. Latitude: 43° 45' N Longitude: 122° 27' W

	JAN	FEB	MAR	APR	MAY	JUN	JUL	AUG	SEP	OCT	NOV	DEC	YEAR
Mean Maximum Temp. (°F)	46.1	51.6	56.2	60.9	67.6	74.1	81.4	82.0	76.9	66.5	51.2	44.6	63.3
Mean Temp. (°F)	38.3	41.7	45.2	49.1	54.9	60.6	65.8	65.8	60.8	52.6	43.1	37.7	51.3
Mean Minimum Temp. (°F)	30.4	31.8	34.2	37.3	42.1	47.0	50.1	49.6	44.6	38.6	34.9	30.8	39.3
Extreme Maximum Temp. (°F)	70	76	81	91	106	103	103	108	106	98	73	65	108
Extreme Minimum Temp. (°F)	8	2	18	25	29	33	37	36	28	22	14	-1	-1
Days Maximum Temp. ≥ 90°F	0	0	0	0	1	2	5	5	4	0	0	0	17
Days Maximum Temp. ≤ 32°F	0	0	0	0	0	0	0	0	0	0	0	1	1
Days Minimum Temp. ≤ 32°F	19	15	13	5	1	0	0	0	1	4	10	18	86
Days Minimum Temp. ≤ 0°F	0	0	0	0	0	0	0	0	0	0	0	0	0
Heating Degree Days (base 65°F)	822	651	606	472	318	156	54	50	147	380	651	839	5,146
Cooling Degree Days (base 65°F)	0	0	0	1	11	25	74	76	28	2	0	0	217
Mean Precipitation (in.)	6.29	4.97	4.82	4.10	2.94	1.79	0.61	1.11	1.63	3.24	7.35	6.98	45.83
Days With ≥ 0.1" Precipitation	12	11	12	11	8	5	2	3	4	7	14	13	102
Days With ≥ 1.0" Precipitation	1	1	0	0	0	0	0	0	0	0	2	2	6
Mean Snowfall (in.)	1.6	1.8	0.5	0.1	trace	0.0	0.0	0.0	0.0	trace	0.6	1.5	6.1
Days With ≥ 1.0" Snow Depth	0	0	0	0	0	0	0	0	0	0	0	1	1

Ochoco Ranger Station *Crook County* Elevation: 3,973 ft. Latitude: 44° 24' N Longitude: 120° 26' W

	JAN	FEB	MAR	APR	MAY	JUN	JUL	AUG	SEP	OCT	NOV	DEC	YEAR
Mean Maximum Temp. (°F)	35.9	41.4	48.5	55.5	63.7	72.8	81.9	83.0	74.0	61.8	43.6	35.2	58.1
Mean Temp. (°F)	26.4	30.9	36.3	41.4	47.9	55.0	61.6	62.0	54.0	45.0	33.9	26.4	43.4
Mean Minimum Temp. (°F)	17.1	20.3	24.0	27.3	32.0	37.2	41.3	40.9	33.9	28.1	24.1	17.7	28.6
Extreme Maximum Temp. (°F)	61	69	74	85	95	98	100	101	100	93	71	54	101
Extreme Minimum Temp. (°F)	-22	-26	-4	10	17	21	18	27	19	0	-10	-24	-26
Days Maximum Temp. ≥ 90°F	0	0	0	0	0	1	7	7	2	0	0	0	17
Days Maximum Temp. ≤ 32°F	9	4	1	0	0	0	0	0	0	0	2	10	26
Days Minimum Temp. ≤ 32°F	29	27	29	25	18	7	2	2	13	24	27	30	233
Days Minimum Temp. ≤ 0°F	2	1	0	0	0	0	0	0	0	0	0	2	5
Heating Degree Days (base 65°F)	1,190	957	883	696	526	302	137	129	329	614	927	1,191	7,881
Cooling Degree Days (base 65°F)	0	0	0	0	2	8	40	43	6	0	0	0	99
Mean Precipitation (in.)	2.20	1.54	1.35	1.11	1.29	1.08	0.82	0.82	0.84	1.14	2.28	2.07	16.54
Days With ≥ 0.1" Precipitation	5	4	4	4	4	3	2	3	3	3	7	5	47
Days With ≥ 1.0" Precipitation	0	0	0	0	0	0	0	0	0	0	0	0	0
Mean Snowfall (in.)	10.2	7.7	4.0	2.0	0.6	0.0	0.0	0.0	trace	0.8	6.9	11.1	43.3
Days With ≥ 1.0" Snow Depth	14	11	6	1	0	0	0	0	0	0	4	10	46

Ontario *Malheur County*   Elevation: 2,191 ft.   Latitude: 44° 01' N   Longitude: 117° 01' W

	JAN	FEB	MAR	APR	MAY	JUN	JUL	AUG	SEP	OCT	NOV	DEC	YEAR
Mean Maximum Temp. (°F)	35.5	44.2	56.4	65.7	75.5	84.8	94.1	92.9	81.5	67.1	48.4	36.5	65.2
Mean Temp. (°F)	27.5	34.4	43.8	51.0	60.0	68.2	75.8	73.7	62.9	50.7	38.0	28.2	51.2
Mean Minimum Temp. (°F)	19.4	24.6	31.1	36.3	44.4	51.5	57.5	54.4	44.3	34.2	27.6	20.0	37.1
Extreme Maximum Temp. (°F)	58	66	79	94	103	108	110	110	101	91	68	65	110
Extreme Minimum Temp. (°F)	-19	-24	10	19	25	31	34	36	24	15	-6	-23	-24
Days Maximum Temp. ≥ 90°F	0	0	0	0	3	10	24	22	7	0	0	0	66
Days Maximum Temp. ≤ 32°F	10	3	0	0	0	0	0	0	0	0	0	8	22
Days Minimum Temp. ≤ 32°F	28	24	19	9	2	0	0	0	1	13	22	28	146
Days Minimum Temp. ≤ 0°F	2	1	0	0	0	0	0	0	0	0	0	2	5
Heating Degree Days (base 65°F)	1,155	858	650	415	187	51	5	9	116	438	804	1,133	5,821
Cooling Degree Days (base 65°F)	0	0	0	2	41	140	335	282	63	1	0	0	864
Mean Precipitation (in.)	1.35	0.88	0.85	0.68	0.94	0.68	0.30	0.28	0.49	0.54	1.26	1.44	9.69
Days With ≥ 0.1" Precipitation	4	3	3	2	3	2	1	1	2	2	5	5	33
Days With ≥ 1.0" Precipitation	0	0	0	0	0	0	0	0	0	0	0	0	0
Mean Snowfall (in.)	6.2	2.1	0.3	trace	0.0	0.0	0.0	0.0	0.0	trace	2.5	6.2	17.3
Days With ≥ 1.0" Snow Depth	12	6	0	0	0	0	0	0	0	0	1	8	27

Oregon City *Clackamas County*   Elevation: 164 ft.   Latitude: 45° 21' N   Longitude: 122° 36' W

	JAN	FEB	MAR	APR	MAY	JUN	JUL	AUG	SEP	OCT	NOV	DEC	YEAR
Mean Maximum Temp. (°F)	47.6	52.5	57.6	62.7	69.9	75.7	82.3	82.4	77.5	65.6	53.1	46.7	64.5
Mean Temp. (°F)	41.6	44.9	48.6	52.5	58.6	63.8	69.0	69.1	64.7	55.4	46.6	41.2	54.7
Mean Minimum Temp. (°F)	35.6	37.2	39.6	42.3	47.3	52.0	55.7	55.6	51.8	45.2	40.0	35.6	44.8
Extreme Maximum Temp. (°F)	66	75	81	92	104	102	104	107	105	96	73	68	107
Extreme Minimum Temp. (°F)	12	10	22	28	33	37	41	42	34	24	15	6	6
Days Maximum Temp. ≥ 90°F	0	0	0	0	1	2	6	5	3	0	0	0	17
Days Maximum Temp. ≤ 32°F	1	0	0	0	0	0	0	0	0	0	0	1	2
Days Minimum Temp. ≤ 32°F	10	7	3	1	0	0	0	0	0	0	4	9	34
Days Minimum Temp. ≤ 0°F	0	0	0	0	0	0	0	0	0	0	0	0	0
Heating Degree Days (base 65°F)	718	562	502	370	216	88	19	16	72	296	545	731	4,135
Cooling Degree Days (base 65°F)	0	0	0	3	27	58	149	153	76	6	0	0	472
Mean Precipitation (in.)	6.90	5.50	4.68	3.51	2.65	1.78	0.81	1.03	1.91	3.47	6.95	7.53	46.72
Days With ≥ 0.1" Precipitation	13	12	12	9	7	5	2	3	5	7	13	13	101
Days With ≥ 1.0" Precipitation	2	1	0	0	0	0	0	0	0	0	1	2	6
Mean Snowfall (in.)	0.6	0.8	trace	trace	0.0	0.0	0.0	0.0	0.0	0.0	0.1	0.6	2.1
Days With ≥ 1.0" Snow Depth	1	0	0	0	0	0	0	0	0	0	0	0	1

Otis 2 NE *Lincoln County*   Elevation: 147 ft.   Latitude: 45° 02' N   Longitude: 123° 55' W

	JAN	FEB	MAR	APR	MAY	JUN	JUL	AUG	SEP	OCT	NOV	DEC	YEAR
Mean Maximum Temp. (°F)	47.4	51.2	54.5	57.5	62.0	65.5	69.7	71.0	69.5	61.3	52.1	46.8	59.0
Mean Temp. (°F)	42.1	44.5	46.6	48.7	52.9	56.6	59.8	60.8	58.9	52.9	46.3	41.6	51.0
Mean Minimum Temp. (°F)	36.7	37.7	38.7	39.9	43.8	47.6	49.9	50.4	48.3	44.4	40.4	36.5	42.9
Extreme Maximum Temp. (°F)	62	69	78	83	90	99	96	98	92	82	70	64	99
Extreme Minimum Temp. (°F)	15	11	23	29	31	35	40	39	32	27	15	4	4
Days Maximum Temp. ≥ 90°F	0	0	0	0	0	0	0	0	0	0	0	0	0
Days Maximum Temp. ≤ 32°F	0	0	0	0	0	0	0	0	0	0	0	0	0
Days Minimum Temp. ≤ 32°F	9	6	4	2	0	0	0	0	0	0	1	9	35
Days Minimum Temp. ≤ 0°F	0	0	0	0	0	0	0	0	0	0	0	0	0
Heating Degree Days (base 65°F)	704	574	562	481	368	250	159	132	181	369	556	717	5,053
Cooling Degree Days (base 65°F)	0	0	0	0	1	4	4	8	6	1	0	0	24
Mean Precipitation (in.)	14.43	11.74	10.82	7.37	5.20	3.61	1.73	1.65	3.90	7.52	14.81	16.25	99.03
Days With ≥ 0.1" Precipitation	18	15	17	13	11	7	4	3	6	11	19	18	142
Days With ≥ 1.0" Precipitation	5	4	3	2	1	1	0	0	1	3	5	6	31
Mean Snowfall (in.)	0.6	trace	0.2	trace	trace	0.0	0.0	0.0	0.0	0.0	0.1	0.5	1.4
Days With ≥ 1.0" Snow Depth	1	0	0	0	0	0	0	0	0	0	0	1	2

Owyhee Dam *Malheur County*   Elevation: 2,398 ft.   Latitude: 43° 39' N   Longitude: 117° 15' W

	JAN	FEB	MAR	APR	MAY	JUN	JUL	AUG	SEP	OCT	NOV	DEC	YEAR
Mean Maximum Temp. (°F)	38.5	45.7	55.6	63.8	73.5	82.8	91.8	91.1	80.2	67.4	50.1	39.4	65.0
Mean Temp. (°F)	30.2	36.2	44.1	50.6	58.7	66.4	73.0	72.2	63.1	52.5	39.8	30.8	51.5
Mean Minimum Temp. (°F)	21.9	26.7	32.5	37.3	43.9	49.9	54.2	53.2	45.9	37.6	29.4	22.1	37.9
Extreme Maximum Temp. (°F)	67	70	79	92	100	104	107	108	102	93	75	66	108
Extreme Minimum Temp. (°F)	-15	-13	14	14	24	34	35	36	27	14	0	-16	-16
Days Maximum Temp. ≥ 90°F	0	0	0	0	2	8	21	20	6	0	0	0	57
Days Maximum Temp. ≤ 32°F	8	3	0	0	0	0	0	0	0	0	1	6	18
Days Minimum Temp. ≤ 32°F	26	21	15	7	1	0	0	0	1	7	19	28	125
Days Minimum Temp. ≤ 0°F	1	0	0	0	0	0	0	0	0	0	0	1	2
Heating Degree Days (base 65°F)	1,071	806	642	428	219	68	11	13	119	384	749	1,055	5,565
Cooling Degree Days (base 65°F)	0	0	0	3	38	123	277	261	79	6	0	0	787
Mean Precipitation (in.)	1.03	0.80	0.97	0.91	1.13	1.00	0.51	0.46	0.53	0.59	0.94	1.11	9.98
Days With ≥ 0.1" Precipitation	4	3	4	3	4	3	1	1	2	2	3	4	34
Days With ≥ 1.0" Precipitation	0	0	0	0	0	0	0	0	0	0	0	0	0
Mean Snowfall (in.)	2.7	0.6	0.3	trace	0.0	0.0	0.0	0.0	0.0	trace	0.6	3.0	7.2
Days With ≥ 1.0" Snow Depth	5	2	0	0	0	0	0	0	0	0	1	4	12

Paisley *Lake County*   Elevation: 4,356 ft.   Latitude: 42° 42' N   Longitude: 120° 32' W

	JAN	FEB	MAR	APR	MAY	JUN	JUL	AUG	SEP	OCT	NOV	DEC	YEAR
Mean Maximum Temp. (°F)	42.3	46.7	52.1	59.2	68.3	76.2	84.9	84.4	76.7	65.4	49.4	41.3	62.2
Mean Temp. (°F)	32.5	36.0	40.4	45.7	53.7	60.5	66.9	66.3	58.7	49.3	38.1	31.4	48.3
Mean Minimum Temp. (°F)	22.8	25.2	28.5	32.1	39.0	44.8	48.9	48.1	40.6	33.1	26.7	21.5	34.3
Extreme Maximum Temp. (°F)	62	72	76	85	92	98	99	100	98	90	74	67	100
Extreme Minimum Temp. (°F)	-15	-25	-6	11	10	22	29	27	18	9	-7	-28	-28
Days Maximum Temp. ≥ 90°F	0	0	0	0	0	2	9	9	1	0	0	0	21
Days Maximum Temp. ≤ 32°F	5	2	0	0	0	0	0	0	0	0	1	4	12
Days Minimum Temp. ≤ 32°F	24	22	21	16	7	1	0	0	5	14	21	24	155
Days Minimum Temp. ≤ 0°F	1	0	0	0	0	0	0	0	0	0	0	1	2
Heating Degree Days (base 65°F)	1,000	813	756	574	353	166	49	57	205	481	802	1,031	6,287
Cooling Degree Days (base 65°F)	0	0	0	1	10	34	107	104	24	1	0	0	281
Mean Precipitation (in.)	1.42	0.95	1.08	0.82	0.99	0.93	0.51	0.60	0.55	0.60	1.22	1.17	10.84
Days With ≥ 0.1" Precipitation	3	3	4	3	3	3	2	1	2	2	3	3	32
Days With ≥ 1.0" Precipitation	0	0	0	0	0	0	0	0	0	0	0	0	0
Mean Snowfall (in.)	2.3	3.0	2.4	1.1	0.5	trace	0.0	0.0	trace	0.3	2.1	4.3	16.0
Days With ≥ 1.0" Snow Depth	4	3	2	0	0	0	0	0	0	0	1	5	15

Paulina *Crook County*   Elevation: 3,681 ft.   Latitude: 44° 08' N   Longitude: 119° 58' W

	JAN	FEB	MAR	APR	MAY	JUN	JUL	AUG	SEP	OCT	NOV	DEC	YEAR
Mean Maximum Temp. (°F)	38.8	45.2	52.2	59.7	68.1	77.0	86.6	86.3	78.2	65.9	47.5	39.0	62.0
Mean Temp. (°F)	27.9	33.4	38.9	43.8	51.0	58.4	65.0	64.0	55.8	46.1	35.6	28.0	45.7
Mean Minimum Temp. (°F)	17.0	21.6	25.5	27.8	33.7	39.8	43.5	41.7	33.3	26.3	23.5	16.9	29.2
Extreme Maximum Temp. (°F)	59	71	75	87	98	99	103	105	101	92	74	59	105
Extreme Minimum Temp. (°F)	-28	-33	1	8	8	18	26	21	11	-8	-20	-38	-38
Days Maximum Temp. ≥ 90°F	0	0	0	0	0	3	14	12	4	0	0	0	33
Days Maximum Temp. ≤ 32°F	7	2	0	0	0	0	0	0	0	0	1	6	16
Days Minimum Temp. ≤ 32°F	28	25	25	22	14	5	1	2	14	23	23	27	209
Days Minimum Temp. ≤ 0°F	4	1	0	0	0	0	0	0	0	0	1	3	9
Heating Degree Days (base 65°F)	1,143	885	803	629	431	212	69	84	275	579	877	1,141	7,128
Cooling Degree Days (base 65°F)	0	0	0	0	2	18	65	54	6	0	0	0	145
Mean Precipitation (in.)	1.43	0.81	1.13	0.94	1.26	0.91	0.64	0.64	0.46	0.80	1.29	1.12	11.43
Days With ≥ 0.1" Precipitation	4	3	4	3	4	3	2	2	2	3	4	4	38
Days With ≥ 1.0" Precipitation	0	0	0	0	0	0	0	0	0	0	0	0	0
Mean Snowfall (in.)	6.8	3.9	1.8	0.5	trace	0.0	0.0	0.0	0.0	0.3	3.0	7.4	23.7
Days With ≥ 1.0" Snow Depth	12	5	1	0	0	0	0	0	0	0	2	8	28

Pelton Dam *Jefferson County*   Elevation: 1,407 ft.   Latitude: 44° 44' N   Longitude: 121° 15' W

	JAN	FEB	MAR	APR	MAY	JUN	JUL	AUG	SEP	OCT	NOV	DEC	YEAR
Mean Maximum Temp. (°F)	45.6	52.3	60.5	67.7	76.9	84.7	93.8	93.3	84.0	70.8	53.6	45.3	69.1
Mean Temp. (°F)	35.8	40.5	45.9	51.2	58.7	65.6	72.2	71.8	63.7	53.4	42.6	35.8	53.1
Mean Minimum Temp. (°F)	25.9	28.6	31.2	34.7	40.4	46.5	50.6	50.2	43.2	36.0	31.6	26.4	37.1
Extreme Maximum Temp. (°F)	71	78	86	95	108	107	114	117	108	103	81	69	117
Extreme Minimum Temp. (°F)	-10	-11	10	17	24	29	36	36	25	14	-2	-15	-15
Days Maximum Temp. ≥ 90°F	0	0	0	0	4	10	21	21	10	1	0	0	67
Days Maximum Temp. ≤ 32°F	3	1	0	0	0	0	0	0	0	0	1	3	8
Days Minimum Temp. ≤ 32°F	24	19	19	12	4	0	0	0	1	10	16	24	129
Days Minimum Temp. ≤ 0°F	0	0	0	0	0	0	0	0	0	0	0	1	1
Heating Degree Days (base 65°F)	898	685	586	409	218	72	13	11	98	358	666	897	4,911
Cooling Degree Days (base 65°F)	0	0	0	4	34	92	243	238	76	5	0	0	692
Mean Precipitation (in.)	1.70	1.03	0.95	0.82	0.85	0.57	0.36	0.44	0.42	0.64	1.57	1.49	10.84
Days With ≥ 0.1" Precipitation	5	3	3	2	3	2	1	1	1	2	4	5	32
Days With ≥ 1.0" Precipitation	0	0	0	0	0	0	0	0	0	0	0	0	0
Mean Snowfall (in.)	1.0	trace	0.0	0.0	0.0	0.0	0.0	0.0	0.0	0.0	0.8	1.1	2.9
Days With ≥ 1.0" Snow Depth	1	0	0	0	0	0	0	0	0	0	0	0	1

Pendleton Br. Exp. Station *Umatilla County*   Elevation: 1,486 ft.   Latitude: 45° 43' N   Longitude: 118° 38' W

	JAN	FEB	MAR	APR	MAY	JUN	JUL	AUG	SEP	OCT	NOV	DEC	YEAR
Mean Maximum Temp. (°F)	40.6	46.4	54.3	61.6	69.6	78.2	88.1	87.6	77.7	65.1	49.4	41.0	63.3
Mean Temp. (°F)	32.9	37.7	43.6	49.0	55.8	62.9	70.0	69.4	60.3	49.8	40.6	33.4	50.4
Mean Minimum Temp. (°F)	25.2	28.8	32.8	36.3	42.0	47.5	51.9	51.1	42.9	34.4	31.6	25.8	37.5
Extreme Maximum Temp. (°F)	67	74	75	86	96	104	108	111	103	90	78	67	111
Extreme Minimum Temp. (°F)	-21	-20	-3	20	23	30	33	33	20	11	-21	-26	-26
Days Maximum Temp. ≥ 90°F	0	0	0	0	1	4	15	13	3	0	0	0	36
Days Maximum Temp. ≤ 32°F	8	3	0	0	0	0	0	0	0	0	2	8	21
Days Minimum Temp. ≤ 32°F	23	19	16	8	2	0	0	0	2	13	16	23	122
Days Minimum Temp. ≤ 0°F	2	1	0	0	0	0	0	0	0	0	0	1	4
Heating Degree Days (base 65°F)	988	766	656	475	290	120	28	29	170	466	727	972	5,687
Cooling Degree Days (base 65°F)	0	0	0	0	1	15	59	187	171	41	2	0	476
Mean Precipitation (in.)	2.03	1.57	1.85	1.69	1.63	1.04	0.39	0.72	0.80	1.24	2.34	2.00	17.30
Days With ≥ 0.1" Precipitation	6	6	6	5	5	3	1	2	3	3	7	7	54
Days With ≥ 1.0" Precipitation	0	0	0	0	0	0	0	0	0	0	0	0	0
Mean Snowfall (in.)	5.8	3.3	0.7	trace	trace	0.0	0.0	0.0	0.0	0.2	2.3	5.6	17.9
Days With ≥ 1.0" Snow Depth	10	5	0	0	0	0	0	0	0	0	0	2	7	24

Pilot Rock 1 SE *Umatilla County*   Elevation: 1,719 ft.   Latitude: 45° 29' N   Longitude: 118° 50' W

	JAN	FEB	MAR	APR	MAY	JUN	JUL	AUG	SEP	OCT	NOV	DEC	YEAR
Mean Maximum Temp. (°F)	42.7	47.9	55.3	62.0	70.1	78.8	88.3	87.9	78.2	65.8	51.1	42.8	64.2
Mean Temp. (°F)	34.2	38.4	44.1	49.2	56.2	63.4	70.3	70.1	61.5	51.4	41.4	34.3	51.2
Mean Minimum Temp. (°F)	25.7	28.8	32.8	36.3	42.2	48.0	52.2	52.2	44.7	37.0	31.5	25.9	38.1
Extreme Maximum Temp. (°F)	71	77	76	89	98	103	108	111	102	92	81	69	111
Extreme Minimum Temp. (°F)	-16	-16	3	8	26	31	34	33	25	12	-11	-21	-21
Days Maximum Temp. ≥ 90°F	0	0	0	0	1	5	15	14	4	0	0	0	39
Days Maximum Temp. ≤ 32°F	7	3	0	0	0	0	0	0	0	0	2	7	19
Days Minimum Temp. ≤ 32°F	22	18	15	8	2	0	0	0	1	8	16	23	113
Days Minimum Temp. ≤ 0°F	2	1	0	0	0	0	0	0	0	0	0	1	4
Heating Degree Days (base 65°F)	948	746	641	469	282	111	26	24	146	418	703	944	5,458
Cooling Degree Days (base 65°F)	0	0	0	2	17	64	189	186	53	3	0	0	514
Mean Precipitation (in.)	1.42	1.13	1.51	1.46	1.61	1.26	0.39	0.67	0.71	0.93	1.72	1.38	14.19
Days With ≥ 0.1" Precipitation	5	4	5	5	5	4	1	2	2	3	6	5	47
Days With ≥ 1.0" Precipitation	0	0	0	0	0	0	0	0	0	0	0	0	0
Mean Snowfall (in.)	5.7	3.9	1.3	0.3	0.0	0.0	0.0	0.0	0.0	0.2	3.1	5.0	19.5
Days With ≥ 1.0" Snow Depth	6	4	1	0	0	0	0	0	0	0	2	5	18

Port Orford 2 *Curry County*   Elevation: 39 ft.   Latitude: 42° 45' N   Longitude: 124° 30' W

	JAN	FEB	MAR	APR	MAY	JUN	JUL	AUG	SEP	OCT	NOV	DEC	YEAR
Mean Maximum Temp. (°F)	54.3	55.2	55.8	57.9	61.4	64.8	68.0	69.0	68.6	63.9	57.1	53.9	60.8
Mean Temp. (°F)	47.2	48.0	48.5	50.1	53.7	57.2	60.2	60.7	59.6	55.3	50.1	47.1	53.1
Mean Minimum Temp. (°F)	39.9	40.8	41.2	42.2	45.8	49.5	52.2	52.4	50.6	46.6	43.1	40.2	45.4
Extreme Maximum Temp. (°F)	73	75	77	84	91	88	87	86	93	89	76	80	93
Extreme Minimum Temp. (°F)	21	19	27	28	31	28	39	39	25	28	24	13	13
Days Maximum Temp. ≥ 90°F	0	0	0	0	0	0	0	0	0	0	0	0	0
Days Maximum Temp. ≤ 32°F	0	0	0	0	0	0	0	0	0	0	0	0	0
Days Minimum Temp. ≤ 32°F	5	3	1	0	0	0	0	0	0	0	2	5	16
Days Minimum Temp. ≤ 0°F	0	0	0	0	0	0	0	0	0	0	0	0	0
Heating Degree Days (base 65°F)	546	474	505	442	345	229	144	128	161	297	441	549	4,261
Cooling Degree Days (base 65°F)	0	0	0	0	0	1	1	3	4	2	0	0	11
Mean Precipitation (in.)	11.51	9.31	9.66	5.80	3.85	2.06	0.63	1.20	2.03	4.84	11.13	12.51	74.53
Days With ≥ 0.1" Precipitation	15	13	15	11	8	5	1	2	3	8	15	15	111
Days With ≥ 1.0" Precipitation	4	3	3	1	1	0	0	0	0	2	3	4	21
Mean Snowfall (in.)	trace	trace	trace	trace	0.0	0.0	0.0	0.0	0.0	trace	0.0	0.2	0.2
Days With ≥ 1.0" Snow Depth	0	0	0	0	0	0	0	0	0	0	0	0	0

Portland KGW TV *Multnomah County*   Elevation: 157 ft.   Latitude: 45° 31' N   Longitude: 122° 41' W

	JAN	FEB	MAR	APR	MAY	JUN	JUL	AUG	SEP	OCT	NOV	DEC	YEAR
Mean Maximum Temp. (°F)	46.3	*50.6*	56.3	61.3	*67.3*	73.1	79.2	79.4	75.0	63.6	52.3	46.1	*62.5*
Mean Temp. (°F)	41.4	*44.5*	48.6	52.6	*58.0*	63.1	68.1	68.5	64.7	55.7	46.9	41.5	*54.5*
Mean Minimum Temp. (°F)	36.4	*38.4*	40.8	43.9	*48.6*	53.2	57.0	57.5	54.3	47.6	41.5	36.8	*46.3*
Extreme Maximum Temp. (°F)	62	*71*	79	*88*	*103*	101	104	106	103	92	71	67	*106*
Extreme Minimum Temp. (°F)	12	*8*	24	31	*36*	41	47	46	41	31	23	10	*8*
Days Maximum Temp. ≥ 90°F	0	*0*	0	0	*1*	1	4	4	2	0	0	0	*12*
Days Maximum Temp. ≤ 32°F	1	*0*	0	0	*0*	0	0	0	0	0	0	1	*2*
Days Minimum Temp. ≤ 32°F	8	*4*	1	0	*0*	0	0	0	0	0	2	7	*22*
Days Minimum Temp. ≤ 0°F	0	*0*	0	0	*0*	0	0	0	0	0	0	0	*0*
Heating Degree Days (base 65°F)	726	*572*	502	368	*234*	101	28	21	73	288	535	721	*4,169*
Cooling Degree Days (base 65°F)	0	0	0	3	25	46	128	143	68	5	0	0	418
Mean Precipitation (in.)	6.00	*5.30*	4.48	3.15	*2.58*	1.62	0.80	1.05	1.76	3.49	6.74	6.70	*43.67*
Days With ≥ 0.1" Precipitation	*12*	*12*	12	9	*8*	4	2	3	*4*	7	*14*	13	*100*
Days With ≥ 1.0" Precipitation	*1*	*1*	0	0	*0*	0	0	0	0	1	1	1	*5*
Mean Snowfall (in.)	*1.2*	*0.9*	0.1	0.0	*0.0*	0.0	0.0	0.0	0.0	0.0	0.4	0.9	*3.5*
Days With ≥ 1.0" Snow Depth	*0*	*0*	0	0	*0*	0	0	0	0	0	0	1	*1*

Powers *Coos County*   Elevation: 229 ft.   Latitude: 42° 53' N   Longitude: 124° 04' W

	JAN	FEB	MAR	APR	MAY	JUN	JUL	AUG	SEP	OCT	NOV	DEC	YEAR
Mean Maximum Temp. (°F)	53.5	56.7	58.8	62.3	67.5	72.5	78.4	79.4	77.5	69.5	58.0	52.5	65.6
Mean Temp. (°F)	44.2	46.5	48.4	51.1	55.8	60.4	64.8	65.0	62.1	55.8	48.4	43.7	53.9
Mean Minimum Temp. (°F)	34.9	36.3	37.9	39.9	44.0	48.2	51.2	50.6	46.6	42.1	38.7	34.9	42.1
Extreme Maximum Temp. (°F)	74	83	82	90	98	95	101	104	103	103	77	73	104
Extreme Minimum Temp. (°F)	12	7	24	28	30	35	39	37	29	25	17	5	5
Days Maximum Temp. ≥ 90°F	0	0	0	0	0	1	2	2	3	1	0	0	9
Days Maximum Temp. ≤ 32°F	0	0	0	0	0	0	0	0	0	0	0	0	0
Days Minimum Temp. ≤ 32°F	12	8	5	2	0	0	0	0	0	0	0	0	0
Days Minimum Temp. ≤ 0°F	0	0	0	0	0	0	0	0	0	1	6	12	46
Heating Degree Days (base 65°F)	638	515	507	410	284	147	51	46	107	282	491	652	4,130
Cooling Degree Days (base 65°F)	0	0	0	1	7	14	53	57	32	6	0	0	170
Mean Precipitation (in.)	9.56	8.06	7.63	5.23	2.86	1.14	0.31	0.68	1.61	3.53	9.09	10.16	59.86
Days With ≥ 0.1" Precipitation	13	12	13	11	7	4	1	1	3	7	14	14	100
Days With ≥ 1.0" Precipitation	3	3	2	1	0	0	0	0	1	3	3	16	
Mean Snowfall (in.)	0.8	0.6	trace	trace	0.0	0.0	0.0	0.0	0.0	0.0	trace	0.5	1.9
Days With ≥ 1.0" Snow Depth	0	0	0	0	0	0	0	0	0	0	0	0	0

Prineville 4 NW *Crook County*   Elevation: 2,837 ft.   Latitude: 44° 21' N   Longitude: 120° 54' W

	JAN	FEB	MAR	APR	MAY	JUN	JUL	AUG	SEP	OCT	NOV	DEC	YEAR
Mean Maximum Temp. (°F)	43.1	48.8	55.1	61.4	69.5	77.8	86.8	86.4	78.1	66.1	50.5	42.7	63.9
Mean Temp. (°F)	32.7	36.7	40.8	45.1	52.3	59.2	65.2	64.4	56.9	47.9	38.6	32.2	47.7
Mean Minimum Temp. (°F)	22.3	24.7	26.4	28.9	35.1	40.6	43.6	42.4	35.6	29.6	26.7	21.7	31.5
Extreme Maximum Temp. (°F)	67	75	79	90	99	102	105	105	107	93	77	67	107
Extreme Minimum Temp. (°F)	-21	-18	6	9	14	25	29	28	18	6	-11	-34	-34
Days Maximum Temp. ≥ 90°F	0	0	0	0	1	4	13	12	4	0	0	0	34
Days Maximum Temp. ≤ 32°F	4	1	0	0	0	0	0	0	0	0	1	3	9
Days Minimum Temp. ≤ 32°F	26	23	24	20	12	3	1	1	10	21	22	27	190
Days Minimum Temp. ≤ 0°F	1	1	0	0	0	0	0	0	0	0	0	1	3
Heating Degree Days (base 65°F)	994	792	743	589	390	190	67	78	245	523	784	1,009	6,404
Cooling Degree Days (base 65°F)	0	0	0	0	5	21	74	66	11	0	0	0	177
Mean Precipitation (in.)	1.18	0.96	0.94	0.82	1.05	0.88	0.58	0.46	0.43	0.80	1.34	1.20	10.64
Days With ≥ 0.1" Precipitation	4	3	3	3	3	3	1	1	2	3	4	4	34
Days With ≥ 1.0" Precipitation	0	0	0	0	0	0	0	0	0	0	0	0	0
Mean Snowfall (in.)	3.0	2.0	0.5	0.2	0.0	0.0	0.0	0.0	0.0	0.1	1.8	2.3	9.9
Days With ≥ 1.0" Snow Depth	3	0	0	0	0	0	0	0	0	0	1	1	5

Prospect 2 SW *Jackson County*   Elevation: 2,480 ft.   Latitude: 42° 44' N   Longitude: 122° 31' W

	JAN	FEB	MAR	APR	MAY	JUN	JUL	AUG	SEP	OCT	NOV	DEC	YEAR
Mean Maximum Temp. (°F)	47.6	52.1	56.1	61.6	69.7	77.6	86.6	86.9	81.0	69.3	52.1	45.9	65.5
Mean Temp. (°F)	38.3	41.2	44.1	47.9	54.4	61.1	67.6	67.3	61.8	53.1	42.6	37.4	51.4
Mean Minimum Temp. (°F)	28.9	30.3	32.0	34.2	39.1	44.4	48.5	47.7	42.5	36.8	33.1	29.0	37.2
Extreme Maximum Temp. (°F)	66	76	79	89	102	103	106	110	106	98	75	71	110
Extreme Minimum Temp. (°F)	5	0	5	20	26	28	33	33	25	14	8	-8	-8
Days Maximum Temp. ≥ 90°F	0	0	0	0	1	4	12	12	7	1	0	0	37
Days Maximum Temp. ≤ 32°F	0	0	0	0	0	0	0	0	0	0	0	1	1
Days Minimum Temp. ≤ 32°F	22	19	18	13	6	1	0	0	2	8	15	22	126
Days Minimum Temp. ≤ 0°F	0	0	0	0	0	0	0	0	0	0	0	0	0
Heating Degree Days (base 65°F)	821	665	642	506	332	153	43	40	129	367	666	848	5,212
Cooling Degree Days (base 65°F)	0	0	0	1	10	39	122	116	47	5	0	0	340
Mean Precipitation (in.)	6.14	4.93	4.71	3.08	2.57	1.16	0.62	0.87	1.43	3.04	6.97	6.89	42.41
Days With ≥ 0.1" Precipitation	12	11	11	8	6	3	2	2	3	6	13	12	89
Days With ≥ 1.0" Precipitation	1	1	1	0	0	0	0	0	0	1	1	2	7
Mean Snowfall (in.)	8.2	6.9	4.7	1.9	trace	0.0	0.0	0.0	trace	0.3	2.6	8.7	33.3
Days With ≥ 1.0" Snow Depth	8	4	2	0	0	0	0	0	0	0	2	7	23

Redmond Roberts Field *Deschutes County*   Elevation: 3,057 ft.   Latitude: 44° 15' N   Longitude: 121° 10' W

	JAN	FEB	MAR	APR	MAY	JUN	JUL	AUG	SEP	OCT	NOV	DEC	YEAR
Mean Maximum Temp. (°F)	41.6	47.0	53.1	59.3	67.4	76.3	84.9	84.4	75.7	64.5	49.0	41.7	62.1
Mean Temp. (°F)	32.1	36.1	40.1	44.7	51.5	59.3	66.0	65.6	57.6	48.5	37.9	31.8	47.6
Mean Minimum Temp. (°F)	22.6	25.2	27.0	30.0	35.6	42.2	47.0	46.6	39.4	32.4	27.1	22.0	33.1
Extreme Maximum Temp. (°F)	67	73	77	88	99	100	103	108	105	95	76	66	108
Extreme Minimum Temp. (°F)	-16	-19	0	10	17	24	30	31	17	4	-11	-28	-28
Days Maximum Temp. ≥ 90°F	0	0	0	0	1	3	11	10	3	0	0	0	28
Days Maximum Temp. ≤ 32°F	6	3	0	0	0	0	0	0	0	0	2	5	16
Days Minimum Temp. ≤ 32°F	26	22	24	19	11	3	0	0	5	16	22	26	174
Days Minimum Temp. ≤ 0°F	2	1	0	0	0	0	0	0	0	0	0	1	4
Heating Degree Days (base 65°F)	1,012	810	767	603	416	198	71	72	235	505	807	1,022	6,518
Cooling Degree Days (base 65°F)	0	0	0	0	8	31	98	96	25	1	0	0	259
Mean Precipitation (in.)	0.99	0.65	0.76	0.65	0.93	0.65	0.57	0.54	0.38	0.53	1.01	0.86	8.52
Days With ≥ 0.1" Precipitation	3	2	3	2	2	2	2	2	1	2	3	3	27
Days With ≥ 1.0" Precipitation	0	0	0	0	0	0	0	0	0	0	0	0	0
Mean Snowfall (in.)	4.6	3.3	1.6	0.7	trace	trace	trace	trace	trace	0.2	3.1	4.6	18.1
Days With ≥ 1.0" Snow Depth	7	4	1	0	0	0	0	0	0	0	2	6	20

Riddle *Douglas County*   Elevation: 679 ft.   Latitude: 42° 57' N   Longitude: 123° 21' W

	JAN	FEB	MAR	APR	MAY	JUN	JUL	AUG	SEP	OCT	NOV	DEC	YEAR
Mean Maximum Temp. (°F)	49.8	55.2	59.1	63.3	69.8	76.5	83.8	84.2	79.5	69.0	55.2	48.4	66.2
Mean Temp. (°F)	42.3	45.6	48.4	51.5	57.1	62.9	68.5	68.3	63.2	55.4	47.3	41.7	54.3
Mean Minimum Temp. (°F)	34.7	36.0	37.7	39.6	44.3	49.3	53.2	52.3	46.7	41.8	39.4	35.0	42.5
Extreme Maximum Temp. (°F)	69	80	85	94	99	101	105	110	108	102	77	74	110
Extreme Minimum Temp. (°F)	11	8	25	9	31	36	37	40	31	22	13	3	3
Days Maximum Temp. ≥ 90°F	0	0	0	0	1	2	8	8	5	1	0	0	25
Days Maximum Temp. ≤ 32°F	0	0	0	0	0	0	0	0	0	0	0	0	0
Days Minimum Temp. ≤ 32°F	10	7	6	2	0	0	0	0	0	0	2	4	40
Days Minimum Temp. ≤ 0°F	0	0	0	0	0	0	0	0	0	0	0	0	0
Heating Degree Days (base 65°F)	698	541	508	400	255	104	24	21	98	295	525	716	4,185
Cooling Degree Days (base 65°F)	0	0	0	2	19	49	143	134	54	6	0	0	407
Mean Precipitation (in.)	4.72	3.77	3.53	2.37	1.52	0.85	0.33	0.62	1.04	2.13	5.34	5.41	31.63
Days With ≥ 0.1" Precipitation	10	8	9	7	5	3	1	2	3	5	12	11	76
Days With ≥ 1.0" Precipitation	1	0	0	0	0	0	0	0	0	0	1	1	3
Mean Snowfall (in.)	0.6	0.9	0.2	trace	0.0	0.0	0.0	0.0	0.0	0.0	0.3	0.8	2.8
Days With ≥ 1.0" Snow Depth	0	0	0	0	0	0	0	0	0	0	0	0	0

Riverside 7 SSW *Malheur County*   Elevation: 3,379 ft.   Latitude: 43° 27' N   Longitude: 118° 13' W

	JAN	FEB	MAR	APR	MAY	JUN	JUL	AUG	SEP	OCT	NOV	DEC	YEAR
Mean Maximum Temp. (°F)	37.4	45.1	54.2	62.3	71.4	80.6	89.6	87.8	78.4	66.0	48.8	37.6	63.3
Mean Temp. (°F)	28.5	34.4	41.1	47.0	55.1	63.3	70.4	68.7	59.2	48.7	37.2	28.3	48.5
Mean Minimum Temp. (°F)	19.6	23.7	27.9	31.6	38.7	45.9	51.2	49.5	39.9	31.4	25.6	19.0	33.7
Extreme Maximum Temp. (°F)	64	71	78	90	97	103	106	108	100	93	75	65	108
Extreme Minimum Temp. (°F)	-25	-24	-10	8	14	22	31	28	16	2	-8	-32	-32
Days Maximum Temp. ≥ 90°F	0	0	0	0	1	6	18	14	3	0	0	0	42
Days Maximum Temp. ≤ 32°F	9	2	0	0	0	0	0	0	0	0	1	8	20
Days Minimum Temp. ≤ 32°F	27	23	22	17	6	1	0	1	5	17	23	27	169
Days Minimum Temp. ≤ 0°F	2	1	0	0	0	0	0	0	0	0	0	3	6
Heating Degree Days (base 65°F)	1,124	856	735	534	310	117	23	33	193	499	826	1,131	6,381
Cooling Degree Days (base 65°F)	0	0	0	0	9	65	189	146	24	0	0	0	433
Mean Precipitation (in.)	1.15	0.87	1.08	0.81	1.09	0.90	0.52	0.51	0.45	0.59	1.02	1.17	10.16
Days With ≥ 0.1" Precipitation	4	3	4	3	3	3	2	2	1	2	4	4	35
Days With ≥ 1.0" Precipitation	0	0	0	0	0	0	0	0	0	0	0	0	0
Mean Snowfall (in.)	4.1	2.0	1.0	0.3	trace	trace	0.0	0.0	0.0	trace	1.9	5.4	14.7
Days With ≥ 1.0" Snow Depth	11	2	1	0	0	0	0	0	0	0	2	9	25

Rockville 5 N *Malheur County*   Elevation: 3,667 ft.   Latitude: 43° 22' N   Longitude: 117° 07' W

	JAN	FEB	MAR	APR	MAY	JUN	JUL	AUG	SEP	OCT	NOV	DEC	YEAR
Mean Maximum Temp. (°F)	37.8	44.1	53.2	61.7	70.4	79.3	88.1	87.1	76.8	63.9	48.0	38.2	62.4
Mean Temp. (°F)	28.2	33.2	39.6	45.7	53.3	60.8	67.3	66.2	56.7	46.3	35.8	28.2	46.8
Mean Minimum Temp. (°F)	18.6	22.2	26.0	29.6	36.2	42.2	46.5	45.2	36.5	28.6	23.6	18.0	31.1
Extreme Maximum Temp. (°F)	62	69	79	88	94	100	103	102	96	90	73	64	103
Extreme Minimum Temp. (°F)	-24	-28	-5	8	18	25	28	26	17	3	-14	-33	-33
Days Maximum Temp. ≥ 90°F	0	0	0	0	0	4	15	13	2	0	0	0	34
Days Maximum Temp. ≤ 32°F	9	3	0	0	0	0	0	0	0	0	1	8	21
Days Minimum Temp. ≤ 32°F	28	25	25	20	10	2	0	1	9	21	24	28	193
Days Minimum Temp. ≤ 0°F	3	1	0	0	0	0	0	0	0	0	1	3	8
Heating Degree Days (base 65°F)	1,133	891	781	572	359	157	40	50	254	575	869	1,136	6,817
Cooling Degree Days (base 65°F)	0	0	0	0	5	37	116	101	15	1	0	0	275
Mean Precipitation (in.)	1.06	0.94	1.40	1.36	1.64	1.16	0.55	0.53	0.65	0.79	1.19	1.10	12.37
Days With ≥ 0.1" Precipitation	5	4	6	5	5	4	2	2	2	3	5	5	48
Days With ≥ 1.0" Precipitation	0	0	0	0	0	0	0	0	0	0	0	0	0
Mean Snowfall (in.)	4.3	3.8	1.9	0.3	0.2	0.0	0.0	0.0	trace	0.2	2.0	5.6	18.3
Days With ≥ 1.0" Snow Depth	7	3	1	0	0	0	0	0	0	0	2	7	20

Rome 2 NW *Malheur County*   Elevation: 3,402 ft.   Latitude: 42° 52' N   Longitude: 117° 39' W

	JAN	FEB	MAR	APR	MAY	JUN	JUL	AUG	SEP	OCT	NOV	DEC	YEAR
Mean Maximum Temp. (°F)	39.9	47.5	55.4	63.2	72.6	82.3	91.4	90.5	80.6	67.8	51.0	40.0	65.2
Mean Temp. (°F)	29.1	35.5	41.0	47.0	55.8	64.2	71.4	69.5	59.9	49.1	37.6	29.3	49.1
Mean Minimum Temp. (°F)	18.3	23.3	26.6	30.8	38.9	46.1	51.4	48.5	39.2	30.3	24.1	18.5	33.0
Extreme Maximum Temp. (°F)	67	70	80	91	100	105	107	107	102	92	75	65	107
Extreme Minimum Temp. (°F)	-27	-17	-4	9	18	24	28	30	20	6	-9	-26	-27
Days Maximum Temp. ≥ 90°F	0	0	0	0	2	8	20	19	6	0	0	0	55
Days Maximum Temp. ≤ 32°F	7	2	0	0	0	0	0	0	0	0	1	6	16
Days Minimum Temp. ≤ 32°F	28	24	23	17	6	1	0	0	5	19	24	28	175
Days Minimum Temp. ≤ 0°F	3	1	0	0	0	0	0	0	0	0	0	2	6
Heating Degree Days (base 65°F)	1,107	829	737	533	291	98	15	22	173	487	814	1,098	6,204
Cooling Degree Days (base 65°F)	0	0	0	1	15	74	204	167	31	0	0	0	492
Mean Precipitation (in.)	0.77	0.57	0.78	0.82	1.19	0.88	0.47	0.28	0.55	0.47	0.76	0.78	8.32
Days With ≥ 0.1" Precipitation	2	2	3	3	4	3	1	1	1	2	3	3	28
Days With ≥ 1.0" Precipitation	0	0	0	0	0	0	0	0	0	0	0	0	0
Mean Snowfall (in.)	3.4	0.6	1.2	0.3	0.2	0.0	0.0	0.0	trace	0.2	1.6	3.6	11.1
Days With ≥ 1.0" Snow Depth	8	2	1	0	0	0	0	0	0	0	1	6	18

Roseburg KQEN *Douglas County*   Elevation: 423 ft.   Latitude: 43° 13' N   Longitude: 123° 22' W

	JAN	FEB	MAR	APR	MAY	JUN	JUL	AUG	SEP	OCT	NOV	DEC	YEAR
Mean Maximum Temp. (°F)	49.4	54.0	58.7	63.5	70.1	76.7	84.6	85.0	79.4	67.9	55.0	48.1	66.0
Mean Temp. (°F)	42.3	45.3	48.6	51.9	57.7	63.6	69.6	69.8	64.5	55.8	47.5	41.7	54.9
Mean Minimum Temp. (°F)	35.2	36.6	38.3	40.4	45.2	50.3	54.5	54.5	49.6	43.6	39.8	35.3	43.6
Extreme Maximum Temp. (°F)	71	78	82	95	98	106	109	108	105	101	78	73	109
Extreme Minimum Temp. (°F)	9	3	24	27	29	36	41	41	34	23	12	3	3
Days Maximum Temp. ≥ 90°F	0	0	0	0	1	3	9	9	5	1	0	0	28
Days Maximum Temp. ≤ 32°F	0	0	0	0	0	0	0	0	0	0	0	1	1
Days Minimum Temp. ≤ 32°F	10	7	4	2	0	0	0	0	0	0	3	9	36
Days Minimum Temp. ≤ 0°F	0	0	0	0	0	0	0	0	0	0	0	0	0
Heating Degree Days (base 65°F)	696	549	504	387	239	93	20	12	78	287	520	714	4,099
Cooling Degree Days (base 65°F)	0	0	0	2	22	58	173	173	78	9	0	0	515
Mean Precipitation (in.)	5.00	4.01	3.85	2.65	1.79	0.91	0.44	0.67	1.07	2.26	5.56	5.51	33.72
Days With ≥ 0.1" Precipitation	11	10	10	8	6	3	1	2	3	6	12	12	84
Days With ≥ 1.0" Precipitation	1	0	0	0	0	0	0	0	0	0	1	1	3
Mean Snowfall (in.)	0.4	0.5	trace	trace	0.0	0.0	0.0	0.0	0.0	trace	trace	0.4	1.3
Days With ≥ 1.0" Snow Depth	0	0	0	0	0	0	0	0	0	0	0	0	0

Ruch *Jackson County*   Elevation: 1,509 ft.   Latitude: 42° 14' N   Longitude: 123° 03' W

	JAN	FEB	MAR	APR	MAY	JUN	JUL	AUG	SEP	OCT	NOV	DEC	YEAR
Mean Maximum Temp. (°F)	49.6	55.8	60.3	66.1	74.3	82.1	90.0	89.5	83.0	70.9	54.8	47.5	68.7
Mean Temp. (°F)	39.9	43.8	47.0	51.2	57.7	64.4	70.1	69.6	63.6	54.7	44.4	39.0	53.8
Mean Minimum Temp. (°F)	30.2	31.7	33.7	36.3	41.0	46.6	50.1	49.6	44.2	38.4	33.9	30.4	38.9
Extreme Maximum Temp. (°F)	69	81	84	91	99	103	109	111	106	102	77	71	111
Extreme Minimum Temp. (°F)	8	2	20	20	26	30	34	35	27	19	13	-3	-3
Days Maximum Temp. ≥ 90°F	0	0	0	0	2	8	17	16	9	1	0	0	53
Days Maximum Temp. ≤ 32°F	0	0	0	0	0	0	0	0	0	0	0	0	0
Days Minimum Temp. ≤ 32°F	20	16	14	9	3	0	0	0	1	5	12	19	99
Days Minimum Temp. ≤ 0°F	0	0	0	0	0	0	0	0	0	0	0	0	0
Heating Degree Days (base 65°F)	770	594	550	408	237	85	18	15	95	319	611	801	4,503
Cooling Degree Days (base 65°F)	0	0	0	2	20	71	175	165	63	7	0	0	503
Mean Precipitation (in.)	3.90	2.86	3.05	1.83	1.20	0.79	0.47	0.55	1.01	1.72	4.01	4.41	25.80
Days With ≥ 0.1" Precipitation	8	7	8	6	4	3	1	2	2	4	9	9	63
Days With ≥ 1.0" Precipitation	1	0	0	0	0	0	0	0	0	0	1	1	3
Mean Snowfall (in.)	3.2	4.0	2.0	0.2	trace	0.0	0.0	0.0	0.0	trace	1.0	3.7	14.1
Days With ≥ 1.0" Snow Depth	1	1	0	0	0	0	0	0	0	0	0	1	3

Scotts Mills 9 SE *Clackamas County*   Elevation: 2,312 ft.   Latitude: 44° 57' N   Longitude: 122° 31' W

	JAN	FEB	MAR	APR	MAY	JUN	JUL	AUG	SEP	OCT	NOV	DEC	YEAR
Mean Maximum Temp. (°F)	44.0	46.6	48.8	52.9	59.2	64.8	71.9	72.5	68.0	58.6	47.5	43.1	56.5
Mean Temp. (°F)	38.0	39.9	41.3	44.3	49.8	54.9	60.5	61.1	57.7	50.0	41.5	37.6	48.1
Mean Minimum Temp. (°F)	32.0	33.1	33.8	35.7	40.3	45.0	49.1	49.7	47.3	41.5	35.5	32.0	39.6
Extreme Maximum Temp. (°F)	69	68	71	82	97	94	98	99	98	87	74	65	99
Extreme Minimum Temp. (°F)	7	0	10	18	27	32	35	36	28	17	11	-6	-6
Days Maximum Temp. ≥ 90°F	0	0	0	0	0	0	1	1	0	0	0	0	2
Days Maximum Temp. ≤ 32°F	2	1	0	0	0	0	0	0	0	0	1	2	6
Days Minimum Temp. ≤ 32°F	16	13	14	10	2	0	0	0	0	2	10	16	83
Days Minimum Temp. ≤ 0°F	0	0	0	0	0	0	0	0	0	0	0	0	0
Heating Degree Days (base 65°F)	829	703	727	614	469	305	165	151	238	459	698	843	6,201
Cooling Degree Days (base 65°F)	0	0	0	0	5	10	34	40	25	3	0	0	117
Mean Precipitation (in.)	11.94	9.71	9.05	7.00	5.26	3.46	1.35	1.54	3.42	6.16	12.48	12.76	84.13
Days With ≥ 0.1" Precipitation	16	14	16	14	11	7	3	4	6	10	17	17	135
Days With ≥ 1.0" Precipitation	4	3	2	2	1	1	0	0	1	1	4	4	23
Mean Snowfall (in.)	12.9	14.3	12.7	6.3	0.5	trace	0.0	0.0	0.0	0.4	6.5	12.7	66.3
Days With ≥ 1.0" Snow Depth	9	7	7	2	0	0	0	0	0	0	4	9	38

Seaside *Clatsop County*   Elevation: 9 ft.   Latitude: 45° 59' N   Longitude: 123° 55' W

	JAN	FEB	MAR	APR	MAY	JUN	JUL	AUG	SEP	OCT	NOV	DEC	YEAR
Mean Maximum Temp. (°F)	51.5	53.9	55.6	57.9	61.7	64.6	67.6	68.7	69.3	63.4	55.3	51.4	60.1
Mean Temp. (°F)	44.6	46.1	47.3	49.5	53.5	56.9	59.7	60.5	59.2	54.0	48.1	44.4	52.0
Mean Minimum Temp. (°F)	37.5	38.2	39.0	41.1	45.2	49.1	51.8	52.2	49.0	44.5	40.8	37.4	43.8
Extreme Maximum Temp. (°F)	69	77	77	85	95	95	101	104	96	92	76	68	104
Extreme Minimum Temp. (°F)	11	9	24	24	30	36	39	40	31	25	15	5	5
Days Maximum Temp. ≥ 90°F	0	0	0	0	0	0	0	0	1	0	0	0	1
Days Maximum Temp. ≤ 32°F	0	0	0	0	0	0	0	0	0	0	0	1	1
Days Minimum Temp. ≤ 32°F	8	6	5	2	0	0	0	0	0	1	4	8	34
Days Minimum Temp. ≤ 0°F	0	0	0	0	0	0	0	0	0	0	0	0	0
Heating Degree Days (base 65°F)	627	528	540	459	351	239	160	139	182	338	501	631	4,695
Cooling Degree Days (base 65°F)	0	0	0	0	1	3	3	6	8	1	0	0	22
Mean Precipitation (in.)	10.56	9.54	8.41	5.87	3.89	2.83	1.62	1.33	3.06	6.13	11.57	11.80	76.61
Days With ≥ 0.1" Precipitation	16	15	16	12	9	6	4	3	5	9	18	17	130
Days With ≥ 1.0" Precipitation	3	3	2	1	1	0	0	0	1	2	3	3	19
Mean Snowfall (in.)	0.4	trace	trace	trace	0.0	0.0	0.0	0.0	0.0	0.0	0.0	trace	0.4
Days With ≥ 1.0" Snow Depth	0	0	0	0	0	0	0	0	0	0	0	0	0

Seneca *Grant County*   Elevation: 4,658 ft.   Latitude: 44° 08' N   Longitude: 118° 58' W

	JAN	FEB	MAR	APR	MAY	JUN	JUL	AUG	SEP	OCT	NOV	DEC	YEAR
Mean Maximum Temp. (°F)	33.9	39.3	45.3	52.4	60.9	69.7	79.8	80.5	70.9	59.6	43.0	34.4	55.8
Mean Temp. (°F)	21.9	26.7	33.3	39.2	46.5	53.2	59.1	58.1	49.4	40.3	31.4	22.9	40.2
Mean Minimum Temp. (°F)	9.9	14.0	21.2	25.9	32.1	36.5	38.4	35.7	27.7	21.0	19.7	11.3	24.4
Extreme Maximum Temp. (°F)	54	64	70	81	88	94	96	98	96	86	69	55	98
Extreme Minimum Temp. (°F)	-40	-48	-15	10	15	18	21	14	6	-9	-31	-48	-48
Days Maximum Temp. ≥ 90°F	0	0	0	0	0	0	4	4	1	0	0	0	9
Days Maximum Temp. ≤ 32°F	11	5	1	0	0	0	0	0	0	0	3	11	31
Days Minimum Temp. ≤ 32°F	30	27	29	24	17	7	5	9	22	28	28	30	256
Days Minimum Temp. ≤ 0°F	8	4	1	0	0	0	0	0	0	0	2	6	21
Heating Degree Days (base 65°F)	1,329	1,076	976	768	565	355	191	217	461	759	1,002	1,299	8,998
Cooling Degree Days (base 65°F)	0	0	0	0	0	4	14	11	1	0	0	0	30
Mean Precipitation (in.)	1.44	1.04	1.30	1.06	1.57	1.17	0.70	0.72	0.67	0.81	1.52	1.66	13.66
Days With ≥ 0.1" Precipitation	5	4	4	4	5	4	2	2	2	3	6	5	46
Days With ≥ 1.0" Precipitation	0	0	0	0	0	0	0	0	0	0	0	0	0
Mean Snowfall (in.)	na	9.1	5.0	2.0	0.7	trace	0.0	0.0	trace	1.0	5.9	na	na
Days With ≥ 1.0" Snow Depth	21	15	6	1	0	0	0	0	0	0	5	18	66

Silver Lake Ranger Station *Lake County*   Elevation: 4,379 ft.   Latitude: 43° 07' N   Longitude: 121° 04' W

	JAN	FEB	MAR	APR	MAY	JUN	JUL	AUG	SEP	OCT	NOV	DEC	YEAR
Mean Maximum Temp. (°F)	40.0	43.7	50.0	57.4	66.4	74.7	83.4	83.6	75.7	64.0	46.6	*38.4*	*60.3*
Mean Temp. (°F)	30.7	33.3	37.7	42.6	50.0	57.2	63.6	63.7	56.1	46.7	36.3	*28.8*	*45.6*
Mean Minimum Temp. (°F)	21.3	22.7	25.2	27.8	33.5	39.6	43.8	43.8	36.3	29.4	25.9	*19.1*	*30.7*
Extreme Maximum Temp. (°F)	62	74	76	84	92	96	105	102	99	88	72	62	105
Extreme Minimum Temp. (°F)	-16	-30	-9	6	14	19	23	22	12	6	-12	-33	-33
Days Maximum Temp. ≥ 90°F	0	0	0	0	0	1	8	8	1	0	0	0	18
Days Maximum Temp. ≤ 32°F	6	3	0	0	0	0	0	0	0	0	2	7	18
Days Minimum Temp. ≤ 32°F	26	24	25	21	14	5	2	1	9	20	22	25	194
Days Minimum Temp. ≤ 0°F	2	1	0	0	0	0	0	0	0	0	0	1	6
Heating Degree Days (base 65°F)	1,058	887	839	664	461	245	102	99	269	560	855	*1,116*	*7,155*
Cooling Degree Days (base 65°F)	0	0	0	0	3	15	57	62	8	0	0	0	145
Mean Precipitation (in.)	1.01	0.73	0.81	0.67	1.09	0.82	0.57	0.59	0.58	0.57	1.16	1.15	9.75
Days With ≥ 0.1" Precipitation	*3*	2	3	2	3	2	2	2	2	2	3	3	*29*
Days With ≥ 1.0" Precipitation	0	0	0	0	0	0	0	0	0	0	0	0	0
Mean Snowfall (in.)	*4.8*	4.0	2.8	1.3	0.5	0.0	0.0	0.0	0.0	0.2	1.9	*5.6*	*21.1*
Days With ≥ 1.0" Snow Depth	*5*	2	1	0	0	0	0	0	0	0	1	*4*	13

Silverton *Marion County*   Elevation: 406 ft.   Latitude: 45° 00' N   Longitude: 122° 46' W

	JAN	FEB	MAR	APR	MAY	JUN	JUL	AUG	SEP	OCT	NOV	DEC	YEAR
Mean Maximum Temp. (°F)	46.2	50.6	55.2	59.4	66.1	71.7	78.7	79.3	74.2	63.3	52.1	45.6	61.9
Mean Temp. (°F)	39.9	43.1	46.8	50.2	56.0	61.1	66.5	66.8	62.4	53.6	45.4	39.6	52.6
Mean Minimum Temp. (°F)	33.6	35.6	38.4	40.9	45.8	50.5	54.2	54.3	50.4	43.8	38.6	33.6	43.3
Extreme Maximum Temp. (°F)	65	70	74	86	102	100	101	104	103	91	72	66	104
Extreme Minimum Temp. (°F)	4	6	19	28	32	38	42	40	35	23	13	0	0
Days Maximum Temp. ≥ 90°F	0	0	0	0	0	1	4	3	2	0	0	0	10
Days Maximum Temp. ≤ 32°F	1	0	0	0	0	0	0	0	0	0	0	1	2
Days Minimum Temp. ≤ 32°F	14	9	4	2	0	0	0	0	0	1	6	14	50
Days Minimum Temp. ≤ 0°F	0	0	0	0	0	0	0	0	0	0	0	0	0
Heating Degree Days (base 65°F)	772	612	557	438	286	145	46	38	115	350	581	780	4,720
Cooling Degree Days (base 65°F)	0	0	0	1	15	34	96	105	45	3	0	0	299
Mean Precipitation (in.)	6.64	5.64	5.06	3.81	2.91	2.06	0.86	0.99	1.96	3.57	7.27	7.30	48.07
Days With ≥ 0.1" Precipitation	14	12	13	11	8	6	2	3	5	8	15	14	111
Days With ≥ 1.0" Precipitation	1	1	0	0	0	0	0	0	0	0	2	2	6
Mean Snowfall (in.)	0.9	1.3	trace	trace	0.0	0.0	0.0	0.0	0.0	0.0	0.3	1.3	3.8
Days With ≥ 1.0" Snow Depth	1	0	0	0	0	0	0	0	0	0	0	1	2

Sisters *Deschutes County*   Elevation: 3,179 ft.   Latitude: 44° 17' N   Longitude: 121° 33' W

	JAN	FEB	MAR	APR	MAY	JUN	JUL	AUG	SEP	OCT	NOV	DEC	YEAR
Mean Maximum Temp. (°F)	*40.8*	44.8	51.6	57.9	*66.3*	75.1	84.2	84.2	75.4	63.3	47.1	40.4	*60.9*
Mean Temp. (°F)	*30.9*	*34.0*	39.0	42.9	*49.9*	56.9	63.1	62.7	55.2	46.1	36.3	30.4	*45.6*
Mean Minimum Temp. (°F)	*20.9*	22.9	26.2	28.4	*33.4*	38.6	41.9	41.1	34.7	28.8	25.5	20.4	*30.2*
Extreme Maximum Temp. (°F)	65	72	77	87	98	103	109	106	103	92	73	64	109
Extreme Minimum Temp. (°F)	-22	-22	-1	11	11	20	24	25	15	1	-16	-28	-28
Days Maximum Temp. ≥ 90°F	0	0	0	0	0	2	10	9	2	0	0	0	23
Days Maximum Temp. ≤ 32°F	5	2	0	0	0	0	0	0	0	0	1	5	13
Days Minimum Temp. ≤ 32°F	27	23	25	21	14	7	3	3	12	21	23	27	206
Days Minimum Temp. ≤ 0°F	1	1	0	0	0	0	0	0	0	0	1	2	5
Heating Degree Days (base 65°F)	*1,052*	*869*	801	657	*464*	255	112	118	296	579	854	1,070	*7,127*
Cooling Degree Days (base 65°F)	0	*0*	0	0	*2*	14	55	55	8	0	0	0	*134*
Mean Precipitation (in.)	2.42	1.71	1.19	0.91	0.81	0.61	0.47	0.50	0.48	0.98	2.23	2.15	14.46
Days With ≥ 0.1" Precipitation	5	*4*	4	2	2	2	1	2	1	3	5	5	*36*
Days With ≥ 1.0" Precipitation	0	0	0	0	0	0	0	0	0	0	0	0	0
Mean Snowfall (in.)	na	*9.1*	*3.5*	0.3	trace	0.0	0.0	0.0	0.0	0.2	4.8	*6.8*	na
Days With ≥ 1.0" Snow Depth	10	7	2	0	0	0	0	0	0	0	3	7	29

Sprague River 1 NW *Klamath County*   Elevation: 4,304 ft.   Latitude: 42° 28' N   Longitude: 121° 31' W

	JAN	FEB	MAR	APR	MAY	JUN	JUL	AUG	SEP	OCT	NOV	DEC	YEAR
Mean Maximum Temp. (°F)	39.3	45.4	50.5	57.7	67.1	75.9	85.1	84.8	77.2	65.3	47.4	39.2	61.2
Mean Temp. (°F)	28.2	33.1	37.4	41.6	49.2	56.4	62.9	*62.1*	54.6	45.4	35.3	28.2	*44.5*
Mean Minimum Temp. (°F)	17.1	20.9	24.4	25.6	31.3	36.9	40.7	*39.3*	31.9	25.4	23.0	17.0	*27.8*
Extreme Maximum Temp. (°F)	59	67	73	83	94	99	102	104	101	90	71	65	104
Extreme Minimum Temp. (°F)	-16	-24	-13	7	12	12	20	18	10	4	-10	-32	-32
Days Maximum Temp. ≥ 90°F	0	0	0	0	0	2	9	8	2	0	0	0	21
Days Maximum Temp. ≤ 32°F	6	2	0	0	0	0	0	0	0	0	1	5	14
Days Minimum Temp. ≤ 32°F	27	25	27	24	18	8	3	5	16	25	24	27	229
Days Minimum Temp. ≤ 0°F	3	1	0	0	0	0	0	0	0	0	1	3	8
Heating Degree Days (base 65°F)	1,132	893	847	697	485	265	113	*127*	310	601	886	1,136	*7,492*
Cooling Degree Days (base 65°F)	0	0	0	0	2	10	44	*35*	5	0	*0*	*0*	*96*
Mean Precipitation (in.)	2.55	1.76	2.00	1.01	1.13	0.72	0.45	0.54	0.64	1.10	2.27	2.43	16.60
Days With ≥ 0.1" Precipitation	7	5	5	3	3	2	1	2	2	3	6	7	46
Days With ≥ 1.0" Precipitation	0	0	0	0	0	0	0	0	0	0	0	0	0
Mean Snowfall (in.)	*10.0*	6.9	*5.6*	1.6	0.5	trace	0.0	0.0	trace	0.2	5.7	10.7	*41.2*
Days With ≥ 1.0" Snow Depth	14	7	3	1	0	0	0	0	0	0	3	9	37

Stayton *Marion County*   Elevation: 423 ft.   Latitude: 44° 47' N   Longitude: 122° 49' W

	JAN	FEB	MAR	APR	MAY	JUN	JUL	AUG	SEP	OCT	NOV	DEC	YEAR
Mean Maximum Temp. (°F)	47.0	51.2	55.8	60.1	66.8	72.8	79.7	80.4	75.1	64.2	52.6	46.3	62.7
Mean Temp. (°F)	40.2	43.3	47.0	50.3	55.8	61.1	66.1	66.3	61.6	53.4	45.5	40.1	52.6
Mean Minimum Temp. (°F)	33.2	35.4	38.1	40.4	44.8	49.3	52.4	52.2	48.2	42.5	38.4	33.8	42.4
Extreme Maximum Temp. (°F)	66	70	74	84	98	100	101	106	101	91	76	66	106
Extreme Minimum Temp. (°F)	4	7	20	25	31	33	39	38	31	23	11	-7	-7
Days Maximum Temp. ≥ 90°F	0	0	0	0	0	1	4	4	2	0	0	0	11
Days Maximum Temp. ≤ 32°F	1	0	0	0	0	0	0	0	0	0	0	1	2
Days Minimum Temp. ≤ 32°F	14	10	5	2	0	0	0	0	0	1	6	13	51
Days Minimum Temp. ≤ 0°F	0	0	0	0	0	0	0	0	0	0	0	0	0
Heating Degree Days (base 65°F)	763	607	552	436	288	140	48	41	125	353	577	766	4,696
Cooling Degree Days (base 65°F)	0	0	0	0	11	28	85	87	35	2	0	0	248
Mean Precipitation (in.)	7.39	6.35	5.37	4.29	3.24	2.41	0.85	1.14	2.27	4.02	8.32	8.19	53.84
Days With ≥ 0.1" Precipitation	14	13	14	11	8	6	2	3	5	9	15	14	114
Days With ≥ 1.0" Precipitation	2	1	1	0	0	0	0	0	0	1	2	2	9
Mean Snowfall (in.)	0.6	0.9	trace	trace	trace	0.0	0.0	0.0	0.0	0.0	trace	0.6	2.1
Days With ≥ 1.0" Snow Depth	0	0	0	0	0	0	0	0	0	0	0	0	0

Summer Lake 1 S *Lake County*   Elevation: 4,189 ft.   Latitude: 42° 58' N   Longitude: 120° 47' W

	JAN	FEB	MAR	APR	MAY	JUN	JUL	AUG	SEP	OCT	NOV	DEC	YEAR
Mean Maximum Temp. (°F)	41.7	46.3	51.6	58.6	67.9	76.7	86.1	85.5	77.1	65.0	48.9	41.3	62.2
Mean Temp. (°F)	32.8	36.6	40.9	46.1	54.0	61.6	68.8	67.8	59.9	49.9	39.0	32.4	49.2
Mean Minimum Temp. (°F)	23.9	26.9	30.2	33.5	40.0	46.6	51.7	50.1	42.7	34.8	29.1	23.5	36.1
Extreme Maximum Temp. (°F)	61	70	75	86	96	99	103	103	102	90	73	64	103
Extreme Minimum Temp. (°F)	-10	-16	1	17	23	29	33	23	21	10	-1	-16	-16
Days Maximum Temp. ≥ 90°F	0	0	0	0	0	2	11	11	3	0	0	0	27
Days Maximum Temp. ≤ 32°F	5	2	0	0	0	0	0	0	0	0	1	4	12
Days Minimum Temp. ≤ 32°F	24	22	20	15	5	0	0	0	2	12	20	26	146
Days Minimum Temp. ≤ 0°F	1	0	0	0	0	0	0	0	0	0	0	1	2
Heating Degree Days (base 65°F)	990	795	740	562	345	146	34	39	176	461	773	1,003	6,064
Cooling Degree Days (base 65°F)	0	0	0	1	13	54	159	140	37	1	0	0	405
Mean Precipitation (in.)	1.58	1.20	1.14	0.93	1.14	0.88	0.52	0.53	0.58	0.75	1.76	1.68	12.69
Days With ≥ 0.1" Precipitation	4	4	4	3	4	3	2	2	2	3	5	5	41
Days With ≥ 1.0" Precipitation	0	0	0	0	0	0	0	0	0	0	0	0	0
Mean Snowfall (in.)	4.7	4.4	2.4	0.9	0.2	trace	0.0	0.0	trace	trace	2.5	5.0	20.1
Days With ≥ 1.0" Snow Depth	5	3	1	0	0	0	0	0	0	0	2	5	16

Three Lynx *Clackamas County*   Elevation: 1,118 ft.   Latitude: 45° 08' N   Longitude: 122° 04' W

	JAN	FEB	MAR	APR	MAY	JUN	JUL	AUG	SEP	OCT	NOV	DEC	YEAR
Mean Maximum Temp. (°F)	41.8	46.2	52.1	57.5	64.3	69.9	77.2	78.4	73.4	62.0	47.9	41.6	59.4
Mean Temp. (°F)	36.3	39.2	43.4	47.5	53.3	58.6	64.0	64.4	59.8	51.2	41.9	36.6	49.7
Mean Minimum Temp. (°F)	30.8	32.2	34.6	37.4	42.3	47.2	50.8	50.4	46.2	40.4	35.9	31.5	40.0
Extreme Maximum Temp. (°F)	63	69	76	87	101	101	104	106	104	92	66	58	106
Extreme Minimum Temp. (°F)	9	1	10	27	30	34	40	39	30	25	7	3	1
Days Maximum Temp. ≥ 90°F	0	0	0	0	1	1	3	3	2	0	0	0	10
Days Maximum Temp. ≤ 32°F	2	1	0	0	0	0	0	0	0	0	0	1	4
Days Minimum Temp. ≤ 32°F	18	14	10	4	0	0	0	0	0	2	8	17	73
Days Minimum Temp. ≤ 0°F	0	0	0	0	0	0	0	0	0	0	0	0	0
Heating Degree Days (base 65°F)	883	722	663	519	363	205	86	75	172	422	687	875	5,672
Cooling Degree Days (base 65°F)	0	0	0	0	9	19	57	63	24	1	0	0	173
Mean Precipitation (in.)	10.83	8.73	7.63	6.10	4.24	2.99	0.99	1.08	2.89	5.15	11.14	11.16	72.93
Days With ≥ 0.1" Precipitation	16	14	16	14	11	7	3	3	6	10	16	15	131
Days With ≥ 1.0" Precipitation	3	2	1	1	0	0	0	0	1	1	3	3	15
Mean Snowfall (in.)	5.6	2.9	1.0	0.4	trace	0.0	0.0	0.0	0.0	trace	2.3	3.7	15.9
Days With ≥ 1.0" Snow Depth	5	2	1	0	0	0	0	0	0	0	1	2	11

Tidewater 2 SW *Lincoln County*   Elevation: 32 ft.   Latitude: 44° 24' N   Longitude: 123° 56' W

	JAN	FEB	MAR	APR	MAY	JUN	JUL	AUG	SEP	OCT	NOV	DEC	YEAR
Mean Maximum Temp. (°F)	51.2	55.5	58.4	61.4	66.3	70.3	74.8	76.3	75.4	67.6	55.7	50.0	63.6
Mean Temp. (°F)	43.9	46.8	48.8	50.9	55.4	59.5	63.6	64.4	62.6	56.5	48.1	43.4	53.7
Mean Minimum Temp. (°F)	36.6	37.9	39.1	40.2	44.4	48.7	52.3	52.5	49.8	45.4	40.5	36.7	43.7
Extreme Maximum Temp. (°F)	68	79	81	89	95	99	101	104	99	93	75	67	104
Extreme Minimum Temp. (°F)	11	10	26	26	30	35	38	40	29	26	18	5	5
Days Maximum Temp. ≥ 90°F	0	0	0	0	0	1	1	1	1	0	0	0	4
Days Maximum Temp. ≤ 32°F	0	0	0	0	0	0	0	0	0	0	0	0	0
Days Minimum Temp. ≤ 32°F	10	6	4	2	0	0	0	0	0	0	3	8	33
Days Minimum Temp. ≤ 0°F	0	0	0	0	0	0	0	0	0	0	0	0	0
Heating Degree Days (base 65°F)	647	509	496	417	294	170	66	46	91	259	500	663	4,158
Cooling Degree Days (base 65°F)	0	0	0	0	6	11	34	38	30	2	0	0	121
Mean Precipitation (in.)	14.01	11.43	10.68	7.07	4.38	2.66	0.85	1.16	2.70	5.62	14.21	15.56	90.33
Days With ≥ 0.1" Precipitation	16	15	16	14	9	7	2	3	5	9	17	17	130
Days With ≥ 1.0" Precipitation	5	4	3	2	0	0	0	0	1	2	4	5	26
Mean Snowfall (in.)	0.2	0.7	0.0	trace	0.0	0.0	0.0	0.0	0.0	0.0	0.0	0.5	1.4
Days With ≥ 1.0" Snow Depth	0	0	0	0	0	0	0	0	0	0	0	0	0

Tillamook 1 W *Tillamook County*   Elevation: 9 ft.   Latitude: 45° 27' N   Longitude: 123° 52' W

	JAN	FEB	MAR	APR	MAY	JUN	JUL	AUG	SEP	OCT	NOV	DEC	YEAR
Mean Maximum Temp. (°F)	50.4	53.1	54.8	57.3	61.3	64.5	67.5	68.9	68.9	62.6	54.6	50.0	59.5
Mean Temp. (°F)	43.4	45.2	46.2	48.3	52.2	55.8	58.7	59.4	57.7	52.2	47.0	43.2	50.8
Mean Minimum Temp. (°F)	36.4	37.1	37.5	39.2	43.1	47.0	49.8	49.8	46.4	41.8	39.4	36.3	42.0
Extreme Maximum Temp. (°F)	69	73	73	84	86	92	93	102	97	92	73	66	102
Extreme Minimum Temp. (°F)	11	8	21	23	25	31	36	34	27	22	14	4	4
Days Maximum Temp. ≥ 90°F	0	0	0	0	0	0	0	0	0	0	0	0	0
Days Maximum Temp. ≤ 32°F	0	0	0	0	0	0	0	0	0	0	0	1	1
Days Minimum Temp. ≤ 32°F	10	8	8	5	1	0	0	0	1	3	6	9	51
Days Minimum Temp. ≤ 0°F	0	0	0	0	0	0	0	0	0	0	0	0	0
Heating Degree Days (base 65°F)	663	554	576	496	390	272	192	172	218	390	532	670	5,125
Cooling Degree Days (base 65°F)	0	0	0	0	1	1	2	5	4	1	0	0	14
Mean Precipitation (in.)	13.33	10.71	9.92	7.00	4.73	3.33	1.65	1.40	3.77	7.21	13.96	14.45	91.46
Days With ≥ 0.1" Precipitation	17	16	17	14	11	8	4	4	7	11	18	18	145
Days With ≥ 1.0" Precipitation	4	3	2	1	1	1	0	0	1	2	4	5	24
Mean Snowfall (in.)	0.6	0.3	0.1	trace	0.0	0.0	0.0	0.0	0.0	0.0	0.2	0.2	1.4
Days With ≥ 1.0" Snow Depth	0	0	0	0	0	0	0	0	0	0	0	0	0

Toketee Falls *Douglas County*   Elevation: 2,057 ft.   Latitude: 43° 17' N   Longitude: 122° 27' W

	JAN	FEB	MAR	APR	MAY	JUN	JUL	AUG	SEP	OCT	NOV	DEC	YEAR
Mean Maximum Temp. (°F)	42.5	47.7	53.6	60.4	69.3	77.1	85.2	85.0	76.8	62.3	47.3	41.0	62.4
Mean Temp. (°F)	36.2	39.4	43.5	48.4	55.4	62.0	67.9	67.4	60.6	50.3	40.7	35.5	50.6
Mean Minimum Temp. (°F)	29.9	31.2	33.4	36.3	41.5	46.9	50.6	49.7	44.4	38.2	34.0	30.0	38.8
Extreme Maximum Temp. (°F)	63	70	75	90	105	104	108	109	105	93	72	57	109
Extreme Minimum Temp. (°F)	7	4	14	23	28	31	35	34	26	18	12	-5	-5
Days Maximum Temp. ≥ 90°F	0	0	0	0	2	4	11	10	3	0	0	0	30
Days Maximum Temp. ≤ 32°F	1	0	0	0	0	0	0	0	0	0	0	1	2
Days Minimum Temp. ≤ 32°F	22	17	15	8	1	0	0	0	1	5	13	21	103
Days Minimum Temp. ≤ 0°F	0	0	0	0	0	0	0	0	0	0	0	0	0
Heating Degree Days (base 65°F)	885	715	658	493	304	130	33	36	152	450	723	906	5,485
Cooling Degree Days (base 65°F)	0	0	0	1	16	41	121	111	28	0	0	0	318
Mean Precipitation (in.)	6.72	5.43	5.40	4.26	3.09	1.76	0.86	1.12	1.64	3.62	7.90	7.54	49.34
Days With ≥ 0.1" Precipitation	13	12	13	11	8	5	2	3	4	7	14	13	105
Days With ≥ 1.0" Precipitation	2	1	1	0	0	0	0	0	0	1	2	2	9
Mean Snowfall (in.)	8.2	8.1	4.1	0.2	trace	0.0	0.0	0.0	0.0	0.2	3.8	8.1	32.7
Days With ≥ 1.0" Snow Depth	10	7	2	0	0	0	0	0	0	0	3	8	30

Troutdale Airport *Multnomah County*   Elevation: 26 ft.   Latitude: 45° 33' N   Longitude: 122° 24' W

	JAN	FEB	MAR	APR	MAY	JUN	JUL	AUG	SEP	OCT	NOV	DEC	YEAR
Mean Maximum Temp. (°F)	45.6	*50.4*	*57.0*	62.2	*69.2*	75.0	*81.4*	82.0	*76.2*	65.2	53.1	46.2	*63.6*
Mean Temp. (°F)	39.8	*43.4*	*47.9*	52.0	*58.0*	63.4	*68.1*	68.3	*63.2*	54.8	46.5	40.5	*53.8*
Mean Minimum Temp. (°F)	33.9	*36.4*	*38.9*	41.8	*46.7*	51.7	*54.8*	54.7	*50.1*	44.3	39.8	34.7	*44.0*
Extreme Maximum Temp. (°F)	65	70	79	89	98	104	105	108	103	88	75	68	108
Extreme Minimum Temp. (°F)	8	0	15	29	33	39	38	43	28	26	12	9	0
Days Maximum Temp. ≥ 90°F	0	0	0	0	1	2	6	6	2	0	0	0	17
Days Maximum Temp. ≤ 32°F	2	0	0	0	0	0	0	0	0	0	0	1	3
Days Minimum Temp. ≤ 32°F	12	6	3	1	0	0	0	0	0	0	4	9	35
Days Minimum Temp. ≤ 0°F	0	0	0	0	0	0	0	0	0	0	0	0	0
Heating Degree Days (base 65°F)	774	*603*	*522*	384	*227*	99	*28*	24	*98*	312	548	755	*4,374*
Cooling Degree Days (base 65°F)	*0*	*0*	*0*	2	*21*	56	*129*	na	*52*	2	0	*0*	na
Mean Precipitation (in.)	6.32	5.11	4.29	3.68	2.78	2.17	0.94	1.10	2.06	3.31	6.63	6.76	45.15
Days With ≥ 0.1" Precipitation	12	10	10	10	7	5	2	2	4	7	13	12	94
Days With ≥ 1.0" Precipitation	1	1	0	0	0	0	0	0	0	0	1	1	4
Mean Snowfall (in.)	0.8	0.6	0.5	trace	0.0	0.0	0.0	0.0	0.0	0.0	0.5	0.7	3.1
Days With ≥ 1.0" Snow Depth	1	0	0	0	0	0	0	0	0	0	0	0	1

Ukiah *Umatilla County*   Elevation: 3,346 ft.   Latitude: 45° 08' N   Longitude: 118° 56' W

	JAN	FEB	MAR	APR	MAY	JUN	JUL	AUG	SEP	OCT	NOV	DEC	YEAR
Mean Maximum Temp. (°F)	37.0	42.9	49.4	56.0	64.0	72.6	81.5	82.7	73.6	62.9	46.4	37.4	58.9
Mean Temp. (°F)	26.0	31.0	36.6	42.0	48.5	55.5	60.9	60.8	52.6	44.1	34.8	27.0	43.3
Mean Minimum Temp. (°F)	15.1	19.0	23.8	27.9	32.9	38.4	40.2	38.9	31.4	25.3	23.2	16.5	27.7
Extreme Maximum Temp. (°F)	60	70	74	87	92	97	101	102	102	92	76	65	102
Extreme Minimum Temp. (°F)	-32	-36	-9	11	14	20	23	21	12	-2	-32	-38	-38
Days Maximum Temp. ≥ 90°F	0	0	0	0	0	1	6	8	2	0	0	0	17
Days Maximum Temp. ≤ 32°F	8	3	1	0	0	0	0	0	0	0	2	7	21
Days Minimum Temp. ≤ 32°F	29	26	27	24	15	7	3	5	18	26	26	29	235
Days Minimum Temp. ≤ 0°F	4	2	0	0	0	0	0	0	0	0	1	4	11
Heating Degree Days (base 65°F)	1,201	956	873	685	507	288	152	152	370	641	900	1,172	7,897
Cooling Degree Days (base 65°F)	0	0	0	0	1	7	24	26	4	0	0	0	62
Mean Precipitation (in.)	1.88	1.38	1.39	1.45	1.75	1.32	0.76	0.85	0.81	1.24	1.97	2.02	16.82
Days With ≥ 0.1" Precipitation	6	5	5	5	5	4	2	2	3	4	*6*	6	*53*
Days With ≥ 1.0" Precipitation	0	0	0	0	0	0	0	0	0	0	0	0	0
Mean Snowfall (in.)	8.9	5.1	3.5	1.1	0.2	trace	0.0	0.0	trace	0.3	5.3	7.8	32.2
Days With ≥ 1.0" Snow Depth	16	7	3	1	0	0	0	0	0	0	3	11	41

Union Experiment Station *Union County* Elevation: 2,762 ft. Latitude: 45° 12' N Longitude: 117° 53' W

	JAN	FEB	MAR	APR	MAY	JUN	JUL	AUG	SEP	OCT	NOV	DEC	YEAR
Mean Maximum Temp. (°F)	37.1	43.3	51.1	58.1	65.9	73.9	83.1	84.3	74.5	62.6	46.6	38.0	59.9
Mean Temp. (°F)	30.7	35.3	40.8	46.2	53.0	59.9	66.4	66.6	57.7	48.2	38.7	31.4	47.9
Mean Minimum Temp. (°F)	24.2	27.3	30.4	34.4	40.1	46.0	49.6	48.9	40.8	33.7	30.7	24.9	35.9
Extreme Maximum Temp. (°F)	61	66	76	90	94	97	104	102	98	89	74	59	104
Extreme Minimum Temp. (°F)	-19	-16	8	19	25	30	34	29	21	12	-11	-22	-22
Days Maximum Temp. ≥ 90°F	0	0	0	0	0	2	9	10	2	0	0	0	23
Days Maximum Temp. ≤ 32°F	9	3	0	0	0	0	0	0	0	0	2	6	20
Days Minimum Temp. ≤ 32°F	24	20	19	12	3	0	0	0	3	13	17	24	135
Days Minimum Temp. ≤ 0°F	1	1	0	0	0	0	0	0	0	0	0	1	3
Heating Degree Days (base 65°F)	1,058	832	744	557	371	182	62	58	230	515	783	1,034	6,426
Cooling Degree Days (base 65°F)	0	0	0	1	9	35	105	118	20	0	0	0	288
Mean Precipitation (in.)	1.19	0.95	1.20	1.55	2.04	1.54	0.73	0.86	0.90	0.97	1.57	1.20	14.70
Days With ≥ 0.1" Precipitation	4	3	4	5	6	5	2	2	3	3	5	4	46
Days With ≥ 1.0" Precipitation	0	0	0	0	0	0	0	0	0	0	0	0	0
Mean Snowfall (in.)	6.7	3.1	1.8	0.6	trace	trace	trace	0.0	trace	0.2	2.8	5.3	20.5
Days With ≥ 1.0" Snow Depth	13	6	1	0	0	0	0	0	0	0	0	4	10	34

Vale *Malheur County* Elevation: 2,237 ft. Latitude: 43° 59' N Longitude: 117° 15' W

	JAN	FEB	MAR	APR	MAY	JUN	JUL	AUG	SEP	OCT	NOV	DEC	YEAR
Mean Maximum Temp. (°F)	35.3	44.5	56.7	65.5	75.1	84.4	93.3	91.6	80.3	66.2	48.0	36.2	64.8
Mean Temp. (°F)	27.0	34.5	43.8	50.7	59.6	67.9	75.1	72.9	62.3	50.2	37.7	27.7	50.8
Mean Minimum Temp. (°F)	18.7	24.5	30.8	35.7	44.1	51.3	56.8	54.2	44.3	34.1	27.3	19.3	36.8
Extreme Maximum Temp. (°F)	59	67	81	92	102	106	107	107	98	91	68	66	107
Extreme Minimum Temp. (°F)	-22	-23	7	14	21	30	36	30	20	12	-14	-27	-27
Days Maximum Temp. ≥ 90°F	0	0	0	0	3	10	23	20	6	0	0	0	62
Days Maximum Temp. ≤ 32°F	11	3	0	0	0	0	0	0	0	0	1	9	24
Days Minimum Temp. ≤ 32°F	28	23	19	11	2	0	0	0	2	13	22	29	149
Days Minimum Temp. ≤ 0°F	3	1	0	0	0	0	0	0	0	0	0	2	6
Heating Degree Days (base 65°F)	1,171	854	651	428	204	57	7	13	133	454	813	1,151	5,936
Cooling Degree Days (base 65°F)	0	0	0	3	45	138	310	256	61	1	0	0	814
Mean Precipitation (in.)	1.22	0.90	0.98	0.83	1.05	0.80	0.48	0.38	0.54	0.62	1.15	1.37	10.32
Days With ≥ 0.1" Precipitation	4	3	4	3	3	3	1	1	2	2	4	5	35
Days With ≥ 1.0" Precipitation	0	0	0	0	0	0	0	0	0	0	0	0	0
Mean Snowfall (in.)	4.7	1.1	0.2	0.0	0.0	0.0	0.0	0.0	0.0	trace	1.7	4.5	12.2
Days With ≥ 1.0" Snow Depth	8	3	0	0	0	0	0	0	0	0	1	6	18

Vernonia 2 *Columbia County* Elevation: 623 ft. Latitude: 45° 52' N Longitude: 123° 11' W

	JAN	FEB	MAR	APR	MAY	JUN	JUL	AUG	SEP	OCT	NOV	DEC	YEAR
Mean Maximum Temp. (°F)	44.6	49.2	53.7	58.0	64.0	69.1	75.4	76.6	72.6	62.4	50.4	44.0	60.0
Mean Temp. (°F)	37.3	40.1	43.6	46.9	52.0	56.8	61.4	61.8	57.5	49.7	42.2	37.3	48.9
Mean Minimum Temp. (°F)	29.9	31.0	33.4	35.7	40.0	44.5	47.2	46.9	42.5	37.0	33.9	30.4	37.7
Extreme Maximum Temp. (°F)	62	71	79	87	99	98	100	102	103	93	73	63	103
Extreme Minimum Temp. (°F)	-2	-6	13	22	28	30	36	32	25	20	2	-12	-12
Days Maximum Temp. ≥ 90°F	0	0	0	0	0	1	3	3	1	0	0	0	8
Days Maximum Temp. ≤ 32°F	1	0	0	0	0	0	0	0	0	0	0	1	2
Days Minimum Temp. ≤ 32°F	19	17	15	10	2	0	0	0	2	8	12	18	103
Days Minimum Temp. ≤ 0°F	0	0	0	0	0	0	0	0	0	0	0	0	0
Heating Degree Days (base 65°F)	853	696	657	537	399	247	137	124	225	467	677	853	5,872
Cooling Degree Days (base 65°F)	0	0	0	0	3	7	29	29	8	0	0	0	76
Mean Precipitation (in.)	7.62	5.95	5.26	3.76	2.32	1.61	0.63	0.80	2.03	3.73	7.67	8.39	49.77
Days With ≥ 0.1" Precipitation	15	13	14	10	7	5	2	2	5	8	16	15	112
Days With ≥ 1.0" Precipitation	2	1	1	0	0	0	0	0	0	1	2	2	9
Mean Snowfall (in.)	2.8	3.1	0.4	trace	trace	0.0	0.0	0.0	0.0	0.0	1.1	2.2	9.6
Days With ≥ 1.0" Snow Depth	2	1	0	0	0	0	0	0	0	0	1	2	6

Wallowa *Wallowa County* Elevation: 2,919 ft. Latitude: 45° 34' N Longitude: 117° 32' W

	JAN	FEB	MAR	APR	MAY	JUN	JUL	AUG	SEP	OCT	NOV	DEC	YEAR
Mean Maximum Temp. (°F)	34.7	42.1	51.5	59.4	67.9	76.1	84.7	84.9	76.0	62.8	44.8	35.4	60.0
Mean Temp. (°F)	26.7	32.1	39.4	45.5	52.6	59.6	65.2	64.8	56.5	46.4	35.5	27.3	46.0
Mean Minimum Temp. (°F)	18.6	22.1	27.1	31.6	37.3	43.0	45.8	44.6	37.0	30.1	26.2	19.1	31.9
Extreme Maximum Temp. (°F)	64	67	79	90	95	101	106	104	100	89	74	62	106
Extreme Minimum Temp. (°F)	-24	-27	-5	16	19	26	29	25	17	6	-22	-28	-28
Days Maximum Temp. ≥ 90°F	0	0	0	0	0	3	10	11	3	0	0	0	27
Days Maximum Temp. ≤ 32°F	11	4	0	0	0	0	0	0	0	0	2	10	27
Days Minimum Temp. ≤ 32°F	28	25	24	16	7	2	0	1	9	20	23	28	183
Days Minimum Temp. ≤ 0°F	3	1	0	0	0	0	0	0	0	0	0	3	7
Heating Degree Days (base 65°F)	1,182	922	788	577	380	180	61	70	256	569	879	1,163	7,027
Cooling Degree Days (base 65°F)	0	0	0	0	4	23	74	77	11	0	0	0	189
Mean Precipitation (in.)	1.87	1.44	1.28	1.41	1.72	1.48	0.98	0.94	1.09	1.30	2.12	1.89	17.52
Days With ≥ 0.1" Precipitation	6	4	5	4	6	5	3	3	3	4	7	6	56
Days With ≥ 1.0" Precipitation	0	0	0	0	0	0	0	0	0	0	0	0	0
Mean Snowfall (in.)	11.8	7.2	3.3	1.0	0.1	trace	0.0	0.0	0.0	0.3	6.6	10.3	40.6
Days With ≥ 1.0" Snow Depth	19	12	3	0	0	0	0	0	0	0	5	14	53

Wickiup Dam *Deschutes County*   Elevation: 4,356 ft.   Latitude: 43° 41' N   Longitude: 121° 41' W

	JAN	FEB	MAR	APR	MAY	JUN	JUL	AUG	SEP	OCT	NOV	DEC	YEAR
Mean Maximum Temp. (°F)	38.1	42.2	47.0	53.3	62.3	70.8	80.0	80.2	72.5	61.3	44.7	37.7	57.5
Mean Temp. (°F)	28.0	31.3	35.7	40.8	48.2	55.5	62.2	61.7	54.3	45.5	35.1	28.3	43.9
Mean Minimum Temp. (°F)	17.9	20.3	24.3	28.3	34.1	40.2	44.4	43.1	36.1	29.6	25.5	18.8	30.2
Extreme Maximum Temp. (°F)	62	70	73	82	95	98	99	101	100	87	72	57	101
Extreme Minimum Temp. (°F)	-20	-20	-8	9	19	23	24	27	19	0	-10	-22	-22
Days Maximum Temp. ≥ 90°F	0	0	0	0	0	1	5	4	1	0	0	0	11
Days Maximum Temp. ≤ 32°F	7	3	1	0	0	0	0	0	0	0	1	6	18
Days Minimum Temp. ≤ 32°F	29	27	29	24	14	3	1	1	9	23	26	30	216
Days Minimum Temp. ≤ 0°F	2	1	0	0	0	0	0	0	0	0	0	2	5
Heating Degree Days (base 65°F)	1,140	946	902	718	515	288	127	134	318	599	891	1,131	7,709
Cooling Degree Days (base 65°F)	0	0	0	0	2	11	49	37	7	0	0	0	106
Mean Precipitation (in.)	3.51	2.54	2.05	1.34	1.15	1.04	0.80	0.83	0.81	1.35	3.28	3.42	22.12
Days With ≥ 0.1" Precipitation	8	7	6	4	4	3	2	2	2	3	8	9	58
Days With ≥ 1.0" Precipitation	1	0	0	0	0	0	0	0	0	0	0	0	1
Mean Snowfall (in.)	18.2	16.3	10.5	4.3	0.5	trace	trace	0.0	trace	1.8	12.3	18.9	82.8
Days With ≥ 1.0" Snow Depth	26	21	15	4	0	0	0	0	0	1	10	21	98

Note: See Appendix D for explanation of data.

PENNSYLVANIA

PHYSICAL FEATURES. The erratic course of the Delaware River is the only natural boundary of Pennsylvania. All others are arbitrary boundaries that do not conform to physical features. Notable contrasts in topography, climate, and soils exist. Within this 45,126-square-mile area lies a great variety of physical land forms of which the most notable is the Appalachian Mountain system composed of two ranges, the Blue Ridge and the Allegheny. These mountains divide the Commonwealth into three major topographical sections. In addition, two plain areas of relatively small size also exist, one in the southeast and the other in the northwest.

In the extreme southeast is the Coastal Plain situated along the Delaware River and covering an area 50 miles long and 10 miles wide. The land is low, flat, and poorly drained. Bordering the Coastal Plain and extending 60 to 80 miles northwest to the Blue Ridge is the Piedmont Plateau, with elevations ranging from 100 to 500 feet and including rolling or undulating uplands, low hills, fertile valleys, and well-drained soils. Just northwest of the Piedmont and between the Blue Ridge and Allegheny Mountains is the Ridge and Valley Region, 80 to 100 miles wide and characterized by parallel ridges and valleys oriented northeast-southwest. The mountain ridges vary from 1,300 to 1,600 feet above sea level. North and west of the Ridge and Valley Region and extending to the New York and Ohio borders is the area known as the Allegheny Plateau. This is the largest natural division of the State and occupies more than half its area. It is crossed by many deep narrow valleys and drained by the Delaware, Susquehanna, Allegheny, and Monongahela River systems. Elevations are generally 1,000 to 2,000 feet above sea level. Bordering Lake Erie is a narrow 40-mile strip of flat, rich land three to four miles wide called the Lake Erie Plain.

GENERAL CLIMATE. Pennsylvania is generally considered to have a humid continental type of climate, but the varied physiographic features have a marked effect on the weather and climate of the various sections within the State. The prevailing westerly winds carry most of the weather disturbances that affect Pennsylvania from the interior of the continent, so that the Atlantic Ocean has only limited influence upon the climate of the State.

TEMPERATURE. Throughout the State temperatures generally remain between 0 and 100°F. and average from near 47°F. annually in the north-central mountains to 57°F. annually in the extreme southeast. Summers are generally warm, averaging about 68°F. along Lake Erie to 74°F. in southeastern counties. High temperatures, 90°F. or above, occur on the average of 10 to 20 days per year in most sections. During the coldest months temperatures average near the freezing point with daily minimum readings sometimes near 0°F. or below. Freezing temperatures occur on the average of 100 or more days annually with the greatest number of occurrences in mountainous regions.

PRECIPITATION. Precipitation is fairly evenly distributed throughout the year. Annual amounts generally range between 34 to 52 inches, while the majority of places receive 38 to 46 inches. Greatest amounts usually occur in spring and summer months, while February is the driest month. Precipitation tends to be somewhat greater in eastern sections due primarily to coastal storms which occasionally frequent the area. During the warm season these storms bring heavy rain, while in winter heavy snow or a mixture of rain and snow may be produced. Thunderstorms, which average between 30 and 35 per year, are concentrated in the warm months and are responsible for most of the summertime rainfall. Winter precipitation is usually three to four inches less than summer rainfall and is produced most frequently from northeastward-moving storms. When temperatures are low enough these storms sometimes cause heavy snow which may accumulate to 20 inches or more. Annual snowfall ranges between wide limits from year to year and place to place. Some years are quite lean as snowfall may total less than 10 inches while other years may produce upwards to 100 inches mostly in northern and mountainous areas. Measurable snow generally occurs between November 20 and March 15 although snow has been observed as early as the beginning of October and as late as May, especially in northern counties. Greatest monthly amounts usually fall in December and January, however, greatest amounts from individual storms generally occur in March as the moisture supply increases with the annual march of temperature.

STORMS. Hurricanes or low pressure systems with a tropical origin seldom affect the State. However, tornadoes do occur in Pennsylvania. At least one tornado has been noted in almost all counties. On the average, five or six tornadoes are observed annually in Pennsylvania, and the State ranks 27th nationally. June is the month of highest frequency, followed closely by July and August. Principal areas of tornado concentration are in the extreme northwest, the Southwest Plateau, and the Southeastern Piedmont.

CLIMATIC AREAS. The topographic features of Pennsylvania divide the State into four rather distinct climatic areas: (1) the Southeastern Coastal Plain and Piedmont Plateau; (2) the Ridge and Valley Province; (3) the Allegheny Plateau; and (4) the Lake Erie Plain.

In the Southeastern Coastal Plain and Piedmont Plateau summers are long and at times uncomfortably hot. Daily temperatures reach 90°F. or above on the average of 25 days during the summer season. From about July 1 to the in length, during which light wind movement and high relative humidity make conditions oppressive. In general, the winters are comparatively mild, with an average of less than 100 days with minimum temperatures below the freezing point. Average annual precipitation in the area ranges from about 30 inches in the lower Susquehanna Valley to about 46 in Chester County. Under the influence of an occasional severe coastal storm, a normal month's rainfall, or more, may occur within a period of 48 hours. The average seasonal snowfall is about 30 inches, and fields are ordinarily snow covered about one-third of the time during the winter season.

The Ridge and Valley Province is not rugged enough for a true mountain type of climate, but it does have many of the characteristics of such a climate. The mountain-and-valley influence on the air movements causes somewhat greater temperature extremes than are experienced in the southeastern part of the State where the modifying coastal and Chesapeake Bay influence hold them relatively constant, and the daily range of temperature increases somewhat under the valley influences. The effects of nocturnal radiation in the valleys and the tendency for cool airmasses to flow down them at night result in a shortening of the growing season by causing freezes later in spring and earlier in fall than would otherwise occur. The annual precipitation in this area has a mean value of three or four inches more than in the southeastern part of the State, but its geographic distribution is less uniform. The mountain ridges are high enough to have some deflecting influence on general storm winds, while summer showers and thunderstorms are often shunted up the valleys. Seasonal snowfall of the Ridge and Valley Province varies considerably within short distances.

The Allegheny Plateau is fairly typical of a continental type of climate, with changeable temperatures and more frequent precipitation than other parts of the State. In the more northerly sections the influence of latitude, together with higher elevation and radiation conditions, serve to make this the coldest area in the State. Occasionally, winter minimum temperatures are severe. The daily temperature range is fairly large. Annual precipitation has a mean of about 41 inches, ranging from less than 35 inches to more than 45 inches. The seasonal snowfall averages 54 inches in northern areas, while southern sections receive several inches less. Fields are normally snow covered three-fourths of the time during the winter season. Although average annual precipitation is about equal to that for the State as a whole, it usually occurs in smaller amounts at more frequent intervals.

Although the Lake Erie Plain is of relatively small size, it has a unique and agriculturally advantageous climate typical of the coastal areas surrounding much of the Great Lakes. Both in spring and autumn the lake water exerts a retarding influence on the temperature regime and the freeze-free season is extended about 45 days. In the autumn this prevents early freezing temperatures. Annual precipitation totals about 34.5 inches, which is fairly evenly distributed throughout the year. Snowfall exceeds 54 inches per year, with heavy snows sometimes experienced late in April.

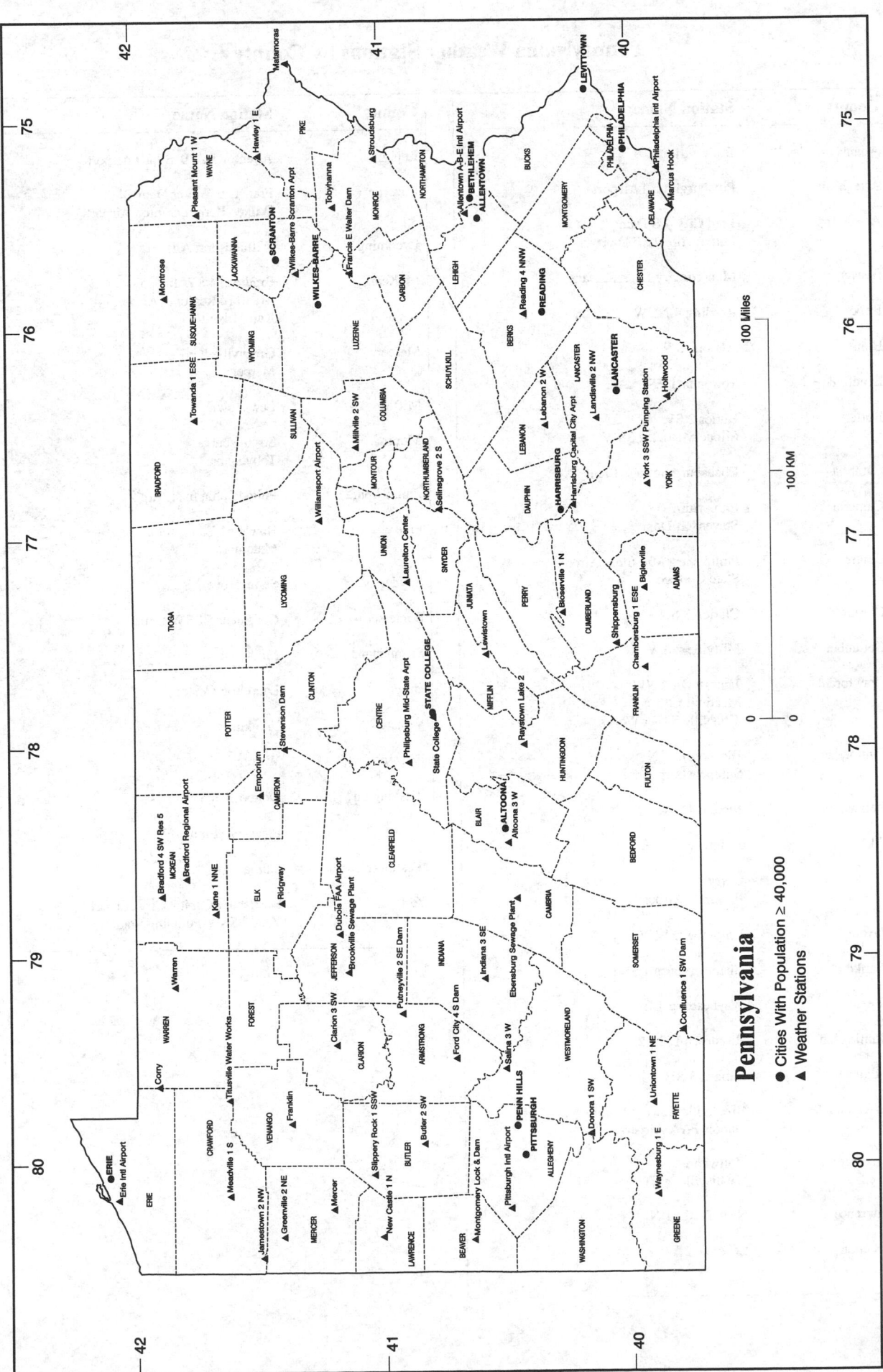

Pennsylvania

- ● Cities With Population ≥ 40,000
- ▲ Weather Stations

100 Miles

100 KM

Pennsylvania Weather Stations by County

County	Station Name
Adams	Biglerville
Allegheny	Pittsburgh Int'l Airport
Armstrong	Ford City 4 S Dam
	Putneyville 2 SE Dam
Beaver	Montgomery Lock & Dam
Berks	Reading 4 NNW
Blair	Altoona 3 W
Bradford	Towanda 1 ESE
Butler	Butler 2 SW
	Slippery Rock 1 SSW
Cambria	Ebensburg Sewage Plant
Cameron	Emporium
	Stevenson Dam
Centre	Philipsburg Mid-State Airport
	State College
Clarion	Clarion 3 SW
Columbia	Millville 2 SW
Crawford	Jamestown 2 NW
	Meadville 1 S
	Titusville Water Works
Cumberland	Bloserville 1 N
	Shippensburg
Delaware	Marcus Hook
Elk	Ridgway
Erie	Corry
	Erie Int'l Airport
Fayette	Uniontown 1 NE
Franklin	Chambersburg 1 ESE
Greene	Waynesburg 1 E
Huntingdon	Raystown Lake 2
Indiana	Indiana 3 SE
Jefferson	Brookville Sewage Plant
	Dubois FAA Airport
Lancaster	Holtwood
	Landisville 2 NW
Lawrence	New Castle 1 N
Lebanon	Lebanon 2 W

County	Station Name
Lehigh	Allentown A-B-E Int'l Airport
Luzerne	Francis E Walter Dam
	Wilkes-Barre Scranton Airport
Lycoming	Williamsport Airport
McKean	Bradford 4 SW Res. 5
	Bradford Regional Airport
	Kane 1 NNE
Mercer	Greenville 2 NE
	Mercer
Mifflin	Lewistown
Monroe	Stroudsburg
	Tobyhanna
Philadelphia	Philadelphia Int'l Airport
Pike	Hawley 1 E
	Matamoras
Snyder	Selinsgrove 2 S
Somerset	Confluence 1 SW Dam
Susquehanna	Montrose
Union	Laurelton Center
Venango	Franklin
Warren	Warren
Washington	Donora 1 SW
Wayne	Pleasant Mount 1 W
Westmoreland	Salina 3 W
York	Harrisburg Capital City Airport
	York 3 SSW Pumping Station

Pennsylvania Weather Stations by City

City	Station Name	Miles
Allentown	Allentown A-B-E Int'l Airport	4
Altoona	Altoona 3 W	4
	Ebensburg Sewage Plant	18
Bethlehem	Allentown A-B-E Int'l Airport	4
Erie	Erie Int'l Airport	6
Harrisburg	Harrisburg Capital City Airport	4
Lancaster	Holtwood	14
	Landisville 2 NW	9
Levittown	Hightstown 2 W, NJ	17
	Lambertville, NJ	16
	Pemberton, NJ	16
Penn Hills	Salina 3 W	15
Philadelphia	Glassboro 2 W, NJ	19
	Marcus Hook	19
	Philadelphia Int'l Airport	11
Pittsburgh	Donora 1 SW	20
	Pittsburgh Int'l Airport	14
Reading	Reading 4 NNW	5
Scranton	Wilkes-Barre Scranton Airport	7
State College	Philipsburg Mid-State Airport	14
	State College	1
Wilkes-Barre	Francis E Walter Dam	12
	Wilkes-Barre Scranton Airport	10

Note: Miles is the distance between the geographic center of the city and the weather station.

Pennsylvania Weather Stations by Elevation

Feet	Station Name
2,116	Bradford Regional Airport
1,948	Tobyhanna
1,938	Ebensburg Sewage Plant
1,922	Philipsburg Mid-State Airport
1,811	Dubois FAA Airport
1,797	Pleasant Mount 1 W
1,748	Kane 1 NNE
1,689	Bradford 4 SW Res. 5
1,505	Francis E Walter Dam
1,489	Confluence 1 SW Dam
1,437	Corry
1,417	Montrose
1,358	Ridgway
1,318	Altoona 3 W
1,279	Putneyville 2 SE Dam
1,250	Slippery Rock 1 SSW
1,217	Mercer
1,217	Titusville Water Works
1,207	Brookville Sewage Plant
1,207	Warren
1,167	State College
1,148	Pittsburgh Int'l Airport
1,128	Greenville 2 NE
1,108	Salina 3 W
1,099	Indiana 3 SE
1,062	Meadville 1 S
1,040	Clarion 3 SW
1,040	Emporium
1,040	Jamestown 2 NW
997	Butler 2 SW
987	Franklin
954	Uniontown 1 NE
938	Waynesburg 1 E
931	Stevenson Dam
928	Ford City 4 S Dam
928	Wilkes-Barre Scranton Airport
889	Hawley 1 E
859	Millville 2 SW
839	Raystown Lake 2
823	New Castle 1 N
797	Laurelton Center
761	Donora 1 SW
748	Towanda 1 ESE
728	Erie Int'l Airport
718	Biglerville
698	Bloserville 1 N
688	Montgomery Lock & Dam
679	Shippensburg
639	Chambersburg 1 ESE
518	Williamsport Airport
459	Lewistown
459	Stroudsburg
449	Lebanon 2 W
419	Matamoras
419	Selinsgrove 2 S

Feet	Station Name
387	Allentown A-B-E Int'l Airport
387	York 3 SSW Pumping Station
357	Landisville 2 NW
357	Reading 4 NNW
337	Harrisburg Capital City Airport
187	Holtwood
9	Marcus Hook
3	Philadelphia Int'l Airport

Allentown A-B-E Int'l Airport

Allentown is located in the east central section of the state and in the Lehigh River valley. Twelve miles to the north is Blue Mountain, a ridge from 1,000 to 1,800 feet in height. The South Mountain, 500 to 1,000 feet high, fringes the southern edge of the city. Otherwise the country is generally rolling with numerous small streams. A modified climate prevails. Temperatures are usually moderate and precipitation generally ample with the largest amounts occurring during the summer months when precipitation is generally showery. General climatological features of the area are slightly modified by the mountain ranges so that at times during the winter there is a temperature difference of 10 to 15 degrees between Allentown and Philadelphia, only 50 miles to the south.

The growing season averages 177 days, and generally ranges from 170 to 185 days. It begins late in April and ends late in October. The average occurrence of the last temperature of 32 degrees in the spring is late April, and the average first fall minimum of 32 degrees is mid-October.

Maximum temperatures during most years are not excessively high and temperatures above 100 degrees are seldom recorded. However, the average humidity in the valley is quite high, and combined with the normal summer temperatures, causes periods of discomfort.

Winters in the valley are comparatively mild. Minimum temperatures during December, January, and February are usually below freezing, but below zero temperatures are seldom recorded.

Seasonal snowfall is quite variable. Freezing rain is a common problem throughout the Lehigh Valley. Snowstorms producing 10 inches or more occur an average of once in two years. The accumulation of snowfall over the drainage area of the Lehigh River to the north of Allentown, combined with spring rains, frequently presents a flood threat to the city and surrounding area. The valley is also subject to torrential rains that cause quick rises in the river and feeder creeks.

The area is seldom subject to destructive storms of large extent. Heavy thunderstorms and tornadoes occasionally cause damage over limited areas. An exception to the usual weather was the storm that battered the east coast on November 25, 1950, when gusts of 88 mph were observed at the station.

Allentown A-B-E Int'l Airport *Lehigh County*   Elevation: 387 ft.   Latitude: 40° 39' N   Longitude: 75° 27' W

	JAN	FEB	MAR	APR	MAY	JUN	JUL	AUG	SEP	OCT	NOV	DEC	YEAR
Mean Maximum Temp. (°F)	35.4	39.2	49.0	60.9	71.6	79.9	84.6	82.5	74.9	63.7	52.0	40.8	61.2
Mean Temp. (°F)	27.7	30.7	39.6	50.1	60.8	69.6	74.4	72.4	64.7	53.3	43.2	33.2	51.6
Mean Minimum Temp. (°F)	20.1	22.2	30.1	39.3	49.9	59.2	64.1	62.2	54.5	42.8	34.3	25.6	42.0
Extreme Maximum Temp. (°F)	69	76	87	93	94	97	101	97	99	86	79	72	101
Extreme Minimum Temp. (°F)	-15	-8	4	16	29	39	48	41	32	21	11	-5	-15
Days Maximum Temp. ≥ 90°F	0	0	0	0	1	3	7	4	1	0	0	0	16
Days Maximum Temp. ≤ 32°F	12	8	1	0	0	0	0	0	0	0	0	6	27
Days Minimum Temp. ≤ 32°F	28	23	19	6	0	0	0	0	0	3	13	24	116
Days Minimum Temp. ≤ 0°F	1	0	0	0	0	0	0	0	0	0	0	0	1
Heating Degree Days (base 65°F)	1,148	961	781	444	171	25	2	7	90	364	649	980	5,622
Cooling Degree Days (base 65°F)	0	0	1	5	49	173	310	241	89	8	0	0	876
Mean Precipitation (in.)	3.45	2.77	3.52	3.53	4.39	3.88	4.33	4.24	4.35	3.46	3.83	3.34	45.09
Maximum Precipitation (in.)	8.4	5.4	7.2	10.1	10.6	8.6	10.4	12.1	8.9	7.5	9.7	7.9	67.7
Minimum Precipitation (in.)	0.7	0.9	1.0	0.6	0.1	0.3	0.4	0.8	0.9	0.1	0.7	0.4	29.8
Maximum 24-hr. Precipitation (in.)	2.4	2.0	3.0	2.5	3.2	3.5	4.1	4.2	5.8	2.8	3.3	2.7	5.8
Days With ≥ 0.1" Precipitation	6	6	7	7	8	7	7	6	6	6	7	7	80
Days With ≥ 1.0" Precipitation	1	0	1	1	1	1	1	1	1	1	1	1	11
Mean Snowfall (in.)	10.2	9.1	5.5	0.8	trace	trace	0.0	0.0	0.0	trace	1.1	3.9	30.6
Maximum Snowfall (in.)	34	30	31	13	trace	0	0	0	0	1	8	28	74
Maximum 24-hr. Snowfall (in.)	12	24	17	11	trace	0	0	0	0	1	6	13	24
Days With ≥ 1.0" Snow Depth	13	11	4	0	0	0	0	0	0	0	1	5	34
Thunderstorm Days	< 1	< 1	1	2	4	6	7	6	3	1	1	< 1	31
Foggy Days	14	12	13	12	16	16	18	20	19	17	15	14	186
Predominant Sky Cover	OVR	OVR	OVR	OVR	OVR	OVR	OVR	OVR	OVR	OVR	OVR	OVR	OVR
Mean Relative Humidity 7am (%)	77	76	76	75	78	79	82	86	88	87	82	79	80
Mean Relative Humidity 4pm (%)	62	57	52	48	51	52	52	55	57	55	60	64	55
Mean Dewpoint (°F)	19	20	26	36	48	57	62	62	55	44	33	23	41
Prevailing Wind Direction	W	W	WNW	WSW	WSW	WSW	WSW	WSW	WSW	WSW	W	W	WSW
Prevailing Wind Speed (mph)	14	15	16	10	9	9	8	8	8	9	13	13	12
Maximum Wind Gust (mph)	68	64	60	68	54	77	66	92	60	63	78	62	92

Erie Int'l Airport

Erie is located on the southeast shore of Lake Erie and observations are made at Erie International Airport, which is six miles southwest of the center of the city and about one mile from the lake shore. The terrain rises gradually in a series of ridges paralleling the shoreline to 500 feet above the lake level three to four miles inland and to 1,000 feet about 15 miles inland. Snowfall from instability showers moving southward off the lake usually increases due to the upslope terrain. Snowfall is somewhat higher south of the city than along the lake shore.

During the winter months, the many cold air masses moving south from Canada are modified by the relatively warm waters of Lake Erie. However, the temperature difference between air and water produces an excess of cloudiness and frequent snow from November through March.

Spring weather is quite variable in Erie, but generally cloudy and cool. Proximity to the lake frequently prevents killing frosts that occur inland. This has led to the establishment of numerous vineyards and orchards in a narrow belt along the shore. Summer heat waves are tempered by cool lake breezes that may reach several miles inland, and days with temperatures above 90 degrees are infrequent. Summer thunderstorms are usually less destructive in Erie than inland areas because of the stabilizing effects of Lake Erie.

Autumn, with long dry periods and an abundance of sunshine, is usually the most pleasant period of the year in Erie. The growing season is extended by the influence of the warmer waters of the lake. Precipitation is well distributed throughout the year, although the number of days with measurable amounts varies considerably from a low average of about one day in three for the period June through September to about one-half of the days from November through March, when snow flurries and squalls move in from the lake.

Erie Int'l Airport *Erie County*   Elevation: 728 ft.   Latitude: 42° 05' N   Longitude: 80° 11' W

	JAN	FEB	MAR	APR	MAY	JUN	JUL	AUG	SEP	OCT	NOV	DEC	YEAR
Mean Maximum Temp. (°F)	32.3	34.1	43.0	54.4	66.0	74.7	79.3	78.0	71.1	60.1	48.6	38.0	56.6
Mean Temp. (°F)	25.7	26.9	35.0	45.7	56.8	65.9	70.9	69.8	63.0	52.4	42.2	32.2	48.9
Mean Minimum Temp. (°F)	19.1	19.6	26.9	36.9	47.5	57.1	62.5	61.5	54.9	44.6	35.8	26.3	41.1
Extreme Maximum Temp. (°F)	68	70	82	89	90	100	99	93	91	84	78	75	100
Extreme Minimum Temp. (°F)	-18	-17	-9	12	26	32	46	37	33	24	7	-6	-18
Days Maximum Temp. ≥ 90°F	0	0	0	0	0	1	1	1	0	0	0	0	3
Days Maximum Temp. ≤ 32°F	16	13	7	0	0	0	0	0	0	0	1	9	46
Days Minimum Temp. ≤ 32°F	28	25	23	11	1	0	0	0	0	1	11	23	123
Days Minimum Temp. ≤ 0°F	2	2	0	0	0	0	0	0	0	0	0	0	4
Heating Degree Days (base 65°F)	1,211	1,071	925	579	280	73	12	16	118	390	678	1,010	6,363
Cooling Degree Days (base 65°F)	0	0	2	6	36	122	230	191	74	8	1	0	670
Mean Precipitation (in.)	2.50	2.28	3.11	3.29	3.31	4.18	3.37	4.09	4.88	3.92	3.94	3.66	42.53
Maximum Precipitation (in.)	5.5	5.7	6.8	7.1	7.8	7.7	7.7	11.1	10.6	9.9	10.4	6.9	61.7
Minimum Precipitation (in.)	0.9	0.6	0.6	1.6	1.0	0.8	0.6	1.0	1.3	0.4	1.5	1.4	28.1
Maximum 24-hr. Precipitation (in.)	1.3	2.1	1.9	2.0	2.2	2.7	2.8	3.3	4.7	4.3	2.3	2.1	4.7
Days With ≥ 0.1" Precipitation	7	6	8	8	8	7	6	7	9	9	10	9	94
Days With ≥ 1.0" Precipitation	0	0	0	0	0	1	1	1	1	1	0	0	5
Mean Snowfall (in.)	26.4	17.0	11.2	2.3	trace	trace	trace	trace	trace	0.3	8.2	24.2	89.6
Maximum Snowfall (in.)	62	32	27	10	trace	0	0	0	0	4	36	67	147
Maximum 24-hr. Snowfall (in.)	13	12	12	7	trace	0	0	0	0	3	17	14	17
Days With ≥ 1.0" Snow Depth	21	17	8	1	0	0	0	0	0	0	3	12	62
Thunderstorm Days	< 1	< 1	2	3	4	6	7	7	4	2	1	< 1	36
Foggy Days	12	12	14	12	12	11	10	11	11	10	12	13	140
Predominant Sky Cover	OVR	OVR	OVR	OVR	OVR	OVR	SCT	OVR	OVR	OVR	OVR	OVR	OVR
Mean Relative Humidity 7am (%)	78	79	78	75	75	78	79	82	81	77	76	77	78
Mean Relative Humidity 4pm (%)	73	72	67	60	58	60	61	62	63	64	69	73	65
Mean Dewpoint (°F)	19	20	26	35	45	56	61	60	54	43	33	24	40
Prevailing Wind Direction	SSW	WSW	WSW	WSW	S	S	S	S	S	S	S	SSW	S
Prevailing Wind Speed (mph)	14	14	14	14	9	9	8	8	9	10	13	14	12
Maximum Wind Gust (mph)	78	74	67	71	54	62	69	54	69	62	69	60	78

Harrisburg Capital City Airport

Harrisburg, the capital of Pennsylvania, is situated on the east bank of the Susquehanna River. It is in the Great Valley formed by the eastern foothills of the Appalachian Chain, and about 60 miles southeast of the Commonwealths geographic center. It is nestled in a saucer-like bowl, 10 miles south of Blue Mountain, which serves as a barrier to the severe winter climate experienced 50 to 100 miles to the north and west. Although the severity of the winter climate is lessened, the city lies a little too far inland to derive the full benefits of the coastal climate.

Air masses change with some regularity, and any one condition does not persist for many days in succession. The mountain barrier occasionally prevents cold waves from reaching the Great Valley. The city is favorably located to receive precipitation produced when warm, maritime air from the Atlantic Ocean is forced upslope to cross the Blue Ridge Mountains.

The growing season in the Harrisburg area is about 192 days. Prolonged dry spells occur on occasion. Flood stage on the Susquehanna River occurs on the average of about every three years in Harrisburg, but serious flooding is much less frequent. About one-third of all floods have occurred during the month of March. Tropical hurricanes rarely reach Harrisburg with destructive winds, but have produced rainfalls in excess of 15 inches.

Harrisburg Capital City Airport *York County*   Elevation: 337 ft.   Latitude: 40° 13' N   Longitude: 76° 51' W

	JAN	FEB	MAR	APR	MAY	JUN	JUL	AUG	SEP	OCT	NOV	DEC	YEAR
Mean Maximum Temp. (°F)	36.3	40.0	50.4	61.9	72.6	80.5	85.5	83.8	76.0	na	na	na	na
Mean Temp. (°F)	29.2	32.1	41.4	51.7	62.3	70.6	75.6	74.3	66.4	na	na	na	na
Mean Minimum Temp. (°F)	22.0	24.2	32.4	41.4	51.9	60.6	65.8	64.7	56.8	na	na	na	na
Extreme Maximum Temp. (°F)	71	75	84	93	94	97	104	100	97	na	na	na	na
Extreme Minimum Temp. (°F)	-9	-5	5	19	35	40	50	45	35	na	na	na	na
Days Maximum Temp. ≥ 90°F	0	0	0	0	1	3	8	5	2	na	na	na	na
Days Maximum Temp. ≤ 32°F	11	7	1	0	0	0	0	0	0	na	na	na	na
Days Minimum Temp. ≤ 32°F	27	23	16	4	0	0	0	0	0	na	na	na	na
Days Minimum Temp. ≤ 0°F	1	0	0	0	0	0	0	0	0	na	na	na	na
Heating Degree Days (base 65°F)	1,105	922	725	404	143	20	2	4	67	na	na	na	na
Cooling Degree Days (base 65°F)	na	na	na	na	na	na	na	na	na	na	na	na	na
Mean Precipitation (in.)	2.95	2.97	3.27	3.34	4.87	4.31	3.47	3.37	3.62	na	na	na	59.3
Maximum Precipitation (in.)	8.0	5.9	6.1	8.0	9.7	18.5	9.7	9.1	15.0	9.9	7.2	7.6	29.0
Minimum Precipitation (in.)	0.4	0.2	1.0	0.4	0.5	0.1	0.8	0.9	0.6	trace	0.8	0.2	29.0
Maximum 24-hr. Precipitation (in.)	2.1	2.0	2.0	2.2	2.6	9.1	4.0	2.8	4.6	3.9	2.3	2.7	9.1
Days With ≥ 0.1" Precipitation	6	6	7	7	8	7	6	6	6	na	na	na	na
Days With ≥ 1.0" Precipitation	1	1	1	1	1	1	1	1	1	na	na	na	na
Mean Snowfall (in.)	9.9	9.6	4.8	0.8	trace	0.0	0.0	0.0	0.0	na	na	na	na
Maximum Snowfall (in.)	34	30	23	10	trace	0	0	0	0	1	15	28	82
Maximum 24-hr. Snowfall (in.)	14	24	11	6	trace	0	0	0	0	1	9	10	24
Days With ≥ 1.0" Snow Depth	14	10	3	0	0	0	0	0	0	na	na	na	na
Thunderstorm Days	< 1	< 1	1	2	5	6	7	5	3	1	1	< 1	31
Foggy Days	12	11	11	10	13	12	13	16	15	15	13	12	153
Predominant Sky Cover	OVR	OVR	OVR	OVR	OVR	OVR	OVR	OVR	OVR	OVR	OVR	OVR	OVR
Mean Relative Humidity 7am (%)	71	71	70	71	75	77	79	83	85	82	77	72	76
Mean Relative Humidity 4pm (%)	56	53	49	47	51	51	52	54	55	53	56	58	53
Mean Dewpoint (°F)	18	20	26	36	48	58	63	62	56	44	33	23	41
Prevailing Wind Direction	WNW	WNW	WNW	WNW	W	W	W	W	W	W	WNW	WNW	WNW
Prevailing Wind Speed (mph)	13	14	14	13	8	8	7	7	7	8	13	13	10
Maximum Wind Gust (mph)	na	na	na	na	na	na	na	na	na	30	na	na	30

Philadelphia Int'l Airport

The Appalachian Mountains to the west and the Atlantic Ocean to the east have a moderating effect on climate. Periods of very high or very low temperatures seldom last for more than three or four days. Temperatures below zero or above 100 degrees are a rarity. On occasion, the area becomes engulfed with maritime air during the summer months, and high humidity adds to the discomfort of seasonably warm temperatures.

Precipitation is fairly evenly distributed throughout the year with maximum amounts during the late summer months. Much of the summer rainfall is from local thunderstorms and amounts vary in different areas of the city. This is due, in part, to the higher elevations to the west and north. Snowfall amounts are often considerably larger in the northern suburbs than in the central and southern parts of the city. In many cases, the precipitation will change from snow to rain within the city. Single storms of 10 inches or more occur about every five years.

The prevailing wind direction for the summer months is from the southwest, while northwesterly winds prevail during the winter. The annual prevailing direction is from the west-southwest. Destructive velocities are comparatively rare and occur mostly in gustiness during summer thunderstorms. High winds occurring in the winter months, as a rule, come with the advance of cold air after the passage of a deep low pressure system. Only rarely have hurricanes in the vicinity caused widespread damage, primarily because of flooding.

Flood stages in the Schuylkill River normally occur about twice a year. Flood stages seldom last over 12 hours and usually occur after excessive thunderstorms. Flooding rarely occurs on the Delaware River.

Philadelphia Int'l Airport *Philadelphia County* Elevation: 3 ft.   Latitude: 39° 52' N   Longitude: 75° 14' W

	JAN	FEB	MAR	APR	MAY	JUN	JUL	AUG	SEP	OCT	NOV	DEC	YEAR
Mean Maximum Temp. (°F)	39.3	42.7	52.0	63.4	73.7	82.1	86.9	85.2	77.9	66.4	55.5	44.8	64.2
Mean Temp. (°F)	31.9	34.6	43.0	53.2	63.7	72.4	77.7	76.3	68.9	57.1	47.0	37.3	55.3
Mean Minimum Temp. (°F)	24.4	26.4	33.9	43.0	53.6	62.7	68.5	67.4	59.9	47.7	38.5	29.8	46.3
Extreme Maximum Temp. (°F)	70	74	86	94	97	100	103	99	98	88	81	73	103
Extreme Minimum Temp. (°F)	-7	-2	7	19	34	44	52	44	40	27	15	1	-7
Days Maximum Temp. ≥ 90°F	0	0	0	0	1	5	11	7	2	0	0	0	26
Days Maximum Temp. ≤ 32°F	8	5	1	0	0	0	0	0	0	0	0	3	17
Days Minimum Temp. ≤ 32°F	25	21	13	2	0	0	0	0	0	1	7	19	88
Days Minimum Temp. ≤ 0°F	0	0	0	0	0	0	0	0	0	0	0	0	0
Heating Degree Days (base 65°F)	1,020	852	678	356	108	11	0	1	36	260	536	851	4,709
Cooling Degree Days (base 65°F)	0	0	2	9	77	250	417	355	157	22	1	0	1,290
Mean Precipitation (in.)	3.44	2.74	3.72	3.60	3.87	3.32	4.30	3.86	3.63	2.82	3.24	3.32	41.86
Maximum Precipitation (in.)	8.9	6.4	7.0	8.1	7.4	7.9	10.4	9.7	8.8	6.0	9.1	7.4	54.4
Minimum Precipitation (in.)	0.4	0.7	0.7	0.5	0.5	0.1	0.6	0.5	0.4	0.1	0.3	0.3	29.3
Maximum 24-hr. Precipitation (in.)	2.3	1.9	2.3	2.4	2.5	4.6	4.4	4.8	4.7	3.8	4.0	2.3	4.8
Days With ≥ 0.1" Precipitation	7	6	7	7	7	6	6	6	6	5	6	6	75
Days With ≥ 1.0" Precipitation	1	1	1	1	1	1	1	1	1	1	1	1	12
Mean Snowfall (in.)	6.2	6.3	3.3	0.5	0.0	trace	0.0	0.0	0.0	trace	0.4	1.6	18.3
Maximum Snowfall (in.)	23	28	13	4	trace	0	0	0	0	2	9	19	57
Maximum 24-hr. Snowfall (in.)	9	21	12	4	trace	0	0	0	0	2	5	12	21
Days With ≥ 1.0" Snow Depth	6	5	1	0	0	0	0	0	0	0	0	1	13
Thunderstorm Days	< 1	< 1	1	2	4	5	6	5	2	1	1	< 1	27
Foggy Days	13	11	12	11	14	15	16	16	15	15	13	13	164
Predominant Sky Cover	OVR	OVR	OVR	OVR	OVR	OVR	OVR	OVR	OVR	OVR	OVR	OVR	OVR
Mean Relative Humidity 7am (%)	74	73	73	72	75	77	79	82	83	83	79	75	77
Mean Relative Humidity 4pm (%)	59	55	51	48	51	52	54	55	55	54	57	60	54
Mean Dewpoint (°F)	22	22	29	38	50	59	65	64	57	46	36	26	43
Prevailing Wind Direction	WNW	WNW	WNW	WNW	SW	SW	SW	SW	SW	WSW	WNW	WNW	SW
Prevailing Wind Speed (mph)	13	14	14	13	10	9	9	8	9	8	12	13	12
Maximum Wind Gust (mph)	59	60	69	64	67	54	61	56	53	63	61	63	69

Pittsburgh Int'l Airport

Pittsburgh lies at the foothills of the Allegheny Mountains at the confluence of the Allegheny and Monongahela Rivers which form the Ohio. The city is a little over 100 miles southeast of Lake Erie. It has a humid continental type of climate modified only slightly by its nearness to the Atlantic Seaboard and the Great Lakes.

The predominant winter air masses influencing the climate of Pittsburgh have a polar continental source in Canada and move in from the Hudson Bay region or the Canadian Rockies. During the summer, frequent invasions of air from the Gulf of Mexico bring warm humid weather. Occasionally, Gulf air reaches as far north as Pittsburgh during the winter and produces intermittent periods of thawing. The last spring temperature of 32 degrees usually occurs in late April and the first in late October. The average growing season is about 180 days. There is a wide variation in the time of the first and last frosts over a radius of 25 miles from the center of Pittsburgh due to terrain differences.

Precipitation is distributed well throughout the year. During the winter months about a fourth of the precipitation occurs as snow and there is about a 50 percent chance of measurable precipitation on any day. Thunderstorms occur normally during all months, except midwinter, and have a maximum frequency in midsummer. The first appreciable snowfall generally occurs in late November and usually the last occurs early in April. Snow lies on the ground in the suburbs on an average of about 33 days during the year.

Seven months of the year, April through October, have sunshine more than 50 percent of the possible time. During the remaining five months cloudiness is heavier because the track of migratory storms from west to east is closer to the area and because of the frequent periods of cloudy, showery weather associated with northwest winds from across the Great Lakes. Cold air drainage induced by the many hills leads to the frequent formation of early morning fog which may be quite persistent in the river valleys during the colder months.

The Allegheny River flowing south and the Monongahela River flowing north meet to form the Ohio River at Pittsburgh. Heavier rainfall and steeper topography cause the Monongahela River to flood more frequently than the Allegheny River.

Both rivers combine to cause the Ohio River at Pittsburgh to reach the 25 foot flood stage approximately once every four years. The serious flood level of 30 feet is reached much less frequently.

Pittsburgh Int'l Airport *Allegheny County*   Elevation: 1,148 ft.   Latitude: 40° 30' N   Longitude: 80° 14' W

	JAN	FEB	MAR	APR	MAY	JUN	JUL	AUG	SEP	OCT	NOV	DEC	YEAR
Mean Maximum Temp. (°F)	34.8	38.5	49.1	60.8	70.9	79.1	82.8	81.3	74.4	62.4	50.5	40.0	60.4
Mean Temp. (°F)	27.3	30.3	39.5	50.0	60.1	68.4	72.7	71.2	64.3	52.5	42.5	32.9	51.0
Mean Minimum Temp. (°F)	19.7	22.0	29.9	39.1	49.2	57.7	62.5	61.0	54.0	42.6	34.3	25.6	41.5
Extreme Maximum Temp. (°F)	69	73	82	89	91	98	103	100	93	83	77	74	103
Extreme Minimum Temp. (°F)	-22	-12	-1	14	26	34	44	39	33	20	0	-12	-22
Days Maximum Temp. ≥ 90°F	0	0	0	0	0	2	4	2	1	0	0	0	9
Days Maximum Temp. ≤ 32°F	13	9	3	0	0	0	0	0	0	0	1	8	34
Days Minimum Temp. ≤ 32°F	27	23	19	8	1	0	0	0	0	4	14	24	120
Days Minimum Temp. ≤ 0°F	2	1	0	0	0	0	0	0	0	0	0	1	4
Heating Degree Days (base 65°F)	1,163	974	784	453	192	40	5	11	101	387	671	990	5,771
Cooling Degree Days (base 65°F)	0	0	2	9	46	157	267	217	85	7	0	0	790
Mean Precipitation (in.)	2.69	2.35	3.20	3.01	3.76	4.09	3.88	3.30	3.20	2.34	3.06	2.88	37.76
Maximum Precipitation (in.)	6.3	6.0	6.1	7.6	6.6	10.3	8.7	7.9	6.0	8.2	11.0	8.5	52.2
Minimum Precipitation (in.)	0.8	0.5	1.1	0.5	1.2	0.6	1.6	0.5	0.3	0.2	0.9	0.4	26.8
Maximum 24-hr. Precipitation (in.)	1.5	2.3	1.8	1.6	2.3	3.0	3.0	3.1	2.1	3.6	1.8	2.8	3.6
Days With ≥ 0.1" Precipitation	7	6	8	8	8	8	7	6	7	6	7	7	85
Days With ≥ 1.0" Precipitation	0	0	0	0	1	1	1	1	1	0	0	0	5
Mean Snowfall (in.)	12.3	8.6	8.5	1.5	trace	trace	trace	trace	trace	0.4	3.0	7.2	41.5
Maximum Snowfall (in.)	40	24	34	8	3	0	0	0	0	9	30	21	77
Maximum 24-hr. Snowfall (in.)	12	10	24	5	3	0	0	0	0	7	12	9	24
Days With ≥ 1.0" Snow Depth	14	11	6	1	0	0	0	0	0	0	2	7	41
Thunderstorm Days	< 1	< 1	2	3	5	7	7	6	3	1	1	< 1	35
Foggy Days	14	12	13	11	15	16	18	21	18	15	13	14	180
Predominant Sky Cover	OVR	OVR	OVR	OVR	OVR	OVR	OVR	OVR	OVR	OVR	OVR	OVR	OVR
Mean Relative Humidity 7am (%)	76	75	76	73	76	79	82	85	85	81	78	77	79
Mean Relative Humidity 4pm (%)	64	60	54	49	50	51	53	54	54	53	60	65	55
Mean Dewpoint (°F)	18	20	27	36	46	56	60	60	53	41	32	23	40
Prevailing Wind Direction	WSW	WSW	WSW	WSW	WSW	WSW	WSW	WSW	WSW	WSW	WSW	WSW	WSW
Prevailing Wind Speed (mph)	14	13	14	14	12	10	9	9	10	12	13	14	12
Maximum Wind Gust (mph)	68	78	76	74	61	71	83	89	62	77	71	62	89

Wilkes-Barre Scranton Airport

The Wilkes-Barre Scranton National Weather Service Office is located about midway between the two cities, at the southwest end of the crescent-shaped Lackawanna River Valley. The river flows through this valley and empties into the Susquehanna River and the Wyoming Valley a few miles west of the airport. The surrounding mountains protect both cities and the airport from high winds. They influence the temperature and precipitation during both summer and winter, causing wide departures in both within a few miles of the station. Because of the proximity of the mountains, the climate is relatively cool in summer with frequent shower and thunderstorm activity, usually of brief duration. The winter temperatures in the valley are not severe.

Although severe snowstorms are infrequent, when they do occur they approach blizzard conditions.

While the incidence of tornadoes is very low, Wilkes-Barre has occasionally been hit with these storms which caused loss of life and great property damage.

The area has felt the effects of tropical storms. Considerable wind damage has occasionally occurred, but the most devastating damage has come from flooding caused by the large amounts of precipitation deposited by the storms.

Wilkes-Barre Scranton Airport *Luzerne County*   Elevation: 928 ft.   Latitude: 41° 20' N   Longitude: 75° 44' W

	JAN	FEB	MAR	APR	MAY	JUN	JUL	AUG	SEP	OCT	NOV	DEC	YEAR
Mean Maximum Temp. (°F)	32.8	36.0	45.7	58.1	69.8	77.3	81.9	80.0	72.0	60.7	48.8	37.8	58.4
Mean Temp. (°F)	25.6	28.1	36.9	48.2	59.1	67.0	71.8	70.0	62.4	51.3	41.4	31.1	49.4
Mean Minimum Temp. (°F)	18.3	20.2	28.2	38.1	48.5	56.6	61.6	60.1	52.7	41.9	33.9	24.4	40.4
Extreme Maximum Temp. (°F)	66	71	85	92	91	94	101	95	95	83	80	69	101
Extreme Minimum Temp. (°F)	-21	-16	-3	14	27	34	43	38	30	19	9	-9	-21
Days Maximum Temp. ≥ 90°F	0	0	0	0	0	1	4	2	0	0	0	0	7
Days Maximum Temp. ≤ 32°F	15	11	4	0	0	0	0	0	0	0	1	9	40
Days Minimum Temp. ≤ 32°F	28	24	21	8	1	0	0	0	0	4	14	25	125
Days Minimum Temp. ≤ 0°F	2	1	0	0	0	0	0	0	0	0	0	0	3
Heating Degree Days (base 65°F)	1,214	1,035	864	504	211	51	8	16	132	422	703	1,043	6,203
Cooling Degree Days (base 65°F)	0	0	1	5	37	123	238	183	62	5	0	0	654
Mean Precipitation (in.)	2.41	2.08	2.67	3.29	3.68	3.85	3.71	3.13	3.86	3.05	3.17	2.52	37.42
Maximum Precipitation (in.)	6.5	8.1	4.8	9.6	8.0	7.6	7.3	11.8	8.1	8.1	7.7	6.6	50.8
Minimum Precipitation (in.)	0.4	0.2	0.5	1.0	0.8	0.3	1.0	0.7	0.8	trace	0.8	0.3	26.2
Maximum 24-hr. Precipitation (in.)	1.6	2.9	2.2	2.8	2.9	2.8	3.0	4.4	6.0	4.0	4.3	3.6	6.0
Days With ≥ 0.1" Precipitation	6	5	7	7	8	8	7	7	7	5	6	6	79
Days With ≥ 1.0" Precipitation	0	0	0	1	1	1	1	1	1	1	1	0	8
Mean Snowfall (in.)	13.4	10.1	9.1	2.7	0.1	0.0	trace	trace	trace	0.2	4.2	7.4	47.2
Maximum Snowfall (in.)	42	22	32	27	2	0	0	0	trace	4	23	34	82
Maximum 24-hr. Snowfall (in.)	18	13	19	9	2	0	0	0	trace	4	19	12	19
Days With ≥ 1.0" Snow Depth	17	15	6	1	0	0	0	0	0	0	2	8	49
Thunderstorm Days	< 1	< 1	1	2	4	6	7	5	3	1	< 1	< 1	29
Foggy Days	12	9	11	9	11	12	14	15	15	12	11	12	143
Predominant Sky Cover	OVR	OVR	OVR	OVR	OVR	OVR	OVR	OVR	OVR	OVR	OVR	OVR	OVR
Mean Relative Humidity 7am (%)	76	75	74	72	76	81	83	86	87	84	79	78	79
Mean Relative Humidity 4pm (%)	64	60	55	50	50	53	54	56	58	56	63	66	57
Mean Dewpoint (°F)	17	18	25	34	45	56	60	60	53	42	32	22	39
Prevailing Wind Direction	SW	SW	NW	SW	SW	SW	SW	SW	SW	SW	SW	SW	SW
Prevailing Wind Speed (mph)	10	10	12	10	10	9	9	8	9	9	9	9	9
Maximum Wind Gust (mph)	74	59	56	64	64	58	58	51	52	58	61	64	74

Williamsport Airport

The climate of the Lycoming valley is favorably influenced by the lower elevation of the area compared to the surrounding terrain. Since the prevailing winds reach the area from the southwest to the north, there is a slight moderating effect on winter extremes of cold. Radiation cooling on clear nights is somewhat more frequent than in adjacent areas. Deep valley fogs occasionally persist until nearly midday. Cold air drainage from the surrounding hills is experienced during several nights but the cool temperatures are often modified by the proximity of the river and adjacent damp areas. The winters are milder than those experienced to the west and cold spells are frequently interrupted by incursions of warmer coastal weather. In summer the air frequently becomes trapped in the valley and higher temperatures and humidities result, generally benefitting the local agriculture.

The long irregular range south of the river forms an effective barrier to free air movement. Moderate or strong south to southwest winds are deflected to southeast or south winds in crossing the range and the air becomes quite turbulent with distinct wave effects. Banner clouds with one to three rolls are frequently observed with low overcasts.

An average growing season of 168 days extends from April 29 to October 14. Snowfall in the valley is generally uniform but varies considerably with the rise in terrain. Snow depth on the ridge two miles south of the observation point is frequently double the amount at the station.

Williamsport Airport *Lycoming County*   Elevation: 518 ft.   Latitude: 41° 15' N   Longitude: 76° 55' W

	JAN	FEB	MAR	APR	MAY	JUN	JUL	AUG	SEP	OCT	NOV	DEC	YEAR
Mean Maximum Temp. (°F)	33.9	37.8	48.0	60.6	71.7	79.4	83.7	81.9	73.7	62.0	49.7	38.8	60.1
Mean Temp. (°F)	26.0	29.1	38.3	49.6	60.0	68.3	73.0	71.3	63.6	51.9	41.6	31.7	50.4
Mean Minimum Temp. (°F)	18.2	20.2	28.6	38.5	48.3	57.1	62.2	60.8	53.4	41.6	33.4	24.6	40.6
Extreme Maximum Temp. (°F)	65	71	87	92	96	97	103	97	94	84	81	69	103
Extreme Minimum Temp. (°F)	-20	-13	-2	15	28	36	47	39	32	20	8	-13	-20
Days Maximum Temp. ≥ 90°F	0	0	0	0	1	2	5	3	1	0	0	0	12
Days Maximum Temp. ≤ 32°F	13	8	2	0	0	0	0	0	0	0	1	7	31
Days Minimum Temp. ≤ 32°F	28	24	21	8	1	0	0	0	0	5	15	24	126
Days Minimum Temp. ≤ 0°F	2	1	0	0	0	0	0	0	0	0	0	1	4
Heating Degree Days (base 65°F)	1,201	1,009	820	463	188	35	4	10	109	405	697	1,025	5,966
Cooling Degree Days (base 65°F)	0	0	1	5	42	145	271	213	70	5	0	0	752
Mean Precipitation (in.)	2.81	2.66	3.19	3.42	3.74	4.40	4.05	3.40	3.93	3.29	3.71	2.99	41.59
Maximum Precipitation (in.)	8.3	8.4	6.0	7.5	7.3	16.8	9.6	7.7	10.0	9.6	8.1	7.4	61.3
Minimum Precipitation (in.)	0.5	0.3	0.8	0.7	0.8	0.7	1.0	0.9	0.5	0.2	0.8	0.7	31.1
Maximum 24-hr. Precipitation (in.)	2.5	2.7	2.4	2.3	2.7	8.7	2.8	4.3	4.0	4.4	3.4	3.3	8.7
Days With ≥ 0.1" Precipitation	6	5	7	7	8	8	8	6	7	6	6	6	80
Days With ≥ 1.0" Precipitation	1	0	1	1	1	1	1	1	1	1	1	1	11
Mean Snowfall (in.)	12.3	9.5	7.8	1.2	trace	trace	trace	trace	0.0	trace	2.9	6.7	40.4
Maximum Snowfall (in.)	40	34	30	14	trace	0	0	0	0	1	14	36	77
Maximum 24-hr. Snowfall (in.)	20	20	15	9	trace	0	0	0	0	1	11	15	20
Days With ≥ 1.0" Snow Depth	16	14	6	0	0	0	0	0	0	0	2	7	45
Thunderstorm Days	< 1	< 1	1	2	5	7	8	6	3	1	1	< 1	34
Foggy Days	14	12	14	13	16	19	21	24	23	20	16	15	207
Predominant Sky Cover	OVR	OVR	OVR	OVR	OVR	OVR	OVR	OVR	OVR	OVR	OVR	OVR	OVR
Mean Relative Humidity 7am (%)	76	76	76	75	80	84	87	90	92	88	81	78	82
Mean Relative Humidity 4pm (%)	60	56	51	47	49	52	53	55	57	55	61	63	55
Mean Dewpoint (°F)	18	19	25	35	47	57	62	61	55	43	33	22	40
Prevailing Wind Direction	W	WNW	WNW	W	W	W	W	W	W	W	W	W	W
Prevailing Wind Speed (mph)	13	13	13	12	9	9	8	8	8	9	12	12	10
Maximum Wind Gust (mph)	59	55	60	60	55	79	58	61	54	47	63	64	79

Altoona 3 W *Blair County*   Elevation: 1,318 ft.   Latitude: 40° 30' N   Longitude: 78° 28' W

	JAN	FEB	MAR	APR	MAY	JUN	JUL	AUG	SEP	OCT	NOV	DEC	YEAR
Mean Maximum Temp. (°F)	32.2	35.5	45.1	57.6	68.2	76.6	80.7	79.4	72.1	60.6	48.6	37.4	57.8
Mean Temp. (°F)	24.3	27.1	36.1	47.4	57.5	65.8	70.2	68.7	61.9	50.4	40.5	30.1	48.3
Mean Minimum Temp. (°F)	16.5	18.7	27.0	37.0	46.8	55.0	59.6	57.9	51.6	40.1	32.3	22.7	38.8
Extreme Maximum Temp. (°F)	65	71	83	90	90	95	99	98	94	85	78	69	99
Extreme Minimum Temp. (°F)	-20	-12	-3	11	25	34	43	34	26	18	6	-11	-20
Days Maximum Temp. ≥ 90°F	0	0	0	0	0	0	2	1	0	0	0	0	3
Days Maximum Temp. ≤ 32°F	15	11	4	0	0	0	0	0	0	0	2	9	41
Days Minimum Temp. ≤ 32°F	29	25	22	10	1	0	0	0	0	6	16	27	136
Days Minimum Temp. ≤ 0°F	3	2	0	0	0	0	0	0	0	0	0	1	6
Heating Degree Days (base 65°F)	1,254	1,065	891	528	252	64	15	25	142	450	730	1,075	6,491
Cooling Degree Days (base 65°F)	0	0	1	5	28	100	196	152	51	3	0	0	536
Mean Precipitation (in.)	2.72	2.61	3.66	3.73	4.44	4.30	4.18	3.43	4.10	3.41	3.89	3.07	43.54
Days With ≥ 0.1" Precipitation	7	6	8	8	9	8	8	6	7	6	8	7	88
Days With ≥ 1.0" Precipitation	0	0	1	1	1	1	1	1	1	1	1	1	10
Mean Snowfall (in.)	12.1	9.5	7.5	0.8	trace	0.0	0.0	0.0	0.0	trace	1.6	5.3	36.8
Days With ≥ 1.0" Snow Depth	16	14	8	1	0	0	0	0	0	0	1	7	47

Biglerville *Adams County*   Elevation: 718 ft.   Latitude: 39° 56' N   Longitude: 77° 15' W

	JAN	FEB	MAR	APR	MAY	JUN	JUL	AUG	SEP	OCT	NOV	DEC	YEAR
Mean Maximum Temp. (°F)	36.9	40.2	49.3	61.1	71.2	79.8	84.5	82.9	75.4	63.7	52.4	41.5	61.6
Mean Temp. (°F)	27.9	30.5	39.2	49.9	60.0	68.6	73.5	71.8	64.1	52.2	42.6	32.7	51.1
Mean Minimum Temp. (°F)	19.0	20.8	29.0	38.7	48.8	57.5	62.5	60.6	52.9	40.6	32.8	24.0	40.6
Extreme Maximum Temp. (°F)	68	78	86	92	95	96	102	100	96	90	81	75	102
Extreme Minimum Temp. (°F)	-18	-9	0	13	28	36	47	38	32	20	8	-8	-18
Days Maximum Temp. ≥ 90°F	0	0	0	0	1	3	7	5	1	0	0	0	17
Days Maximum Temp. ≤ 32°F	10	7	2	0	0	0	0	0	0	0	0	5	24
Days Minimum Temp. ≤ 32°F	29	25	20	7	0	0	0	0	0	5	15	26	127
Days Minimum Temp. ≤ 0°F	1	1	0	0	0	0	0	0	0	0	0	0	2
Heating Degree Days (base 65°F)	1,142	968	794	454	193	37	5	11	101	398	666	993	5,762
Cooling Degree Days (base 65°F)	0	0	2	6	45	159	291	223	82	8	0	0	816
Mean Precipitation (in.)	3.58	2.85	3.75	3.69	4.37	3.95	3.78	3.24	4.45	3.48	3.64	3.24	44.02
Days With ≥ 0.1" Precipitation	7	6	7	7	8	7	6	6	6	6	6	6	78
Days With ≥ 1.0" Precipitation	1	1	1	1	1	1	1	1	1	1	1	1	12
Mean Snowfall (in.)	9.9	7.6	4.1	0.5	0.0	0.0	0.0	0.0	0.0	trace	0.6	2.8	25.5
Days With ≥ 1.0" Snow Depth	13	10	5	0	0	0	0	0	0	0	1	3	32

Bloserville 1 N *Cumberland County*   Elevation: 698 ft.   Latitude: 40° 16' N   Longitude: 77° 22' W

	JAN	FEB	MAR	APR	MAY	JUN	JUL	AUG	SEP	OCT	NOV	DEC	YEAR
Mean Maximum Temp. (°F)	36.2	39.7	48.6	60.6	71.1	79.1	84.1	82.6	75.2	63.6	51.8	41.1	61.1
Mean Temp. (°F)	28.2	30.8	39.2	50.0	60.1	68.3	73.4	71.8	64.4	52.9	43.0	33.2	51.3
Mean Minimum Temp. (°F)	19.9	21.7	29.7	39.4	49.0	57.4	62.7	60.9	53.5	42.1	34.1	25.2	41.3
Extreme Maximum Temp. (°F)	67	77	85	93	95	97	101	100	98	89	82	77	101
Extreme Minimum Temp. (°F)	-19	-6	2	13	26	37	44	42	31	20	6	-1	-19
Days Maximum Temp. ≥ 90°F	0	0	0	0	0	2	7	4	1	0	0	0	14
Days Maximum Temp. ≤ 32°F	11	7	2	0	0	0	0	0	0	0	0	6	26
Days Minimum Temp. ≤ 32°F	28	24	19	6	1	0	0	0	0	3	14	26	121
Days Minimum Temp. ≤ 0°F	1	1	0	0	0	0	0	0	0	0	0	0	2
Heating Degree Days (base 65°F)	1,133	967	795	452	191	37	6	8	95	377	656	979	5,696
Cooling Degree Days (base 65°F)	0	0	2	5	43	154	292	223	78	8	0	0	805
Mean Precipitation (in.)	3.12	2.63	3.35	3.41	4.05	4.12	3.94	3.46	4.29	3.29	3.41	2.99	42.06
Days With ≥ 0.1" Precipitation	6	5	7	7	8	7	7	6	7	7	6	6	77
Days With ≥ 1.0" Precipitation	1	0	1	1	1	1	1	1	1	1	1	1	11
Mean Snowfall (in.)	6.6	6.2	4.4	0.3	0.0	0.0	0.0	0.0	0.0	trace	1.1	2.6	21.2
Days With ≥ 1.0" Snow Depth	4	2	1	0	0	0	0	0	0	0	0	1	8

Bradford 4 SW Res. 5 *McKean County*   Elevation: 1,689 ft.   Latitude: 41° 54' N   Longitude: 78° 43' W

	JAN	FEB	MAR	APR	MAY	JUN	JUL	AUG	SEP	OCT	NOV	DEC	YEAR
Mean Maximum Temp. (°F)	29.8	33.0	42.2	55.0	67.2	74.9	78.5	76.6	69.5	58.6	45.8	34.8	55.5
Mean Temp. (°F)	20.4	22.7	31.5	43.3	54.1	62.2	66.3	64.6	57.7	47.0	37.1	26.8	44.5
Mean Minimum Temp. (°F)	11.0	12.3	20.8	31.5	41.0	49.5	54.0	52.4	45.9	35.3	28.4	18.6	33.4
Extreme Maximum Temp. (°F)	64	66	83	87	93	95	98	93	89	80	73	68	98
Extreme Minimum Temp. (°F)	-36	-29	-22	8	21	27	34	28	23	14	0	-22	-36
Days Maximum Temp. ≥ 90°F	0	0	0	0	0	0	1	0	0	0	0	0	1
Days Maximum Temp. ≤ 32°F	18	14	7	1	0	0	0	0	0	0	3	13	56
Days Minimum Temp. ≤ 32°F	30	27	27	18	7	1	0	0	2	12	22	29	175
Days Minimum Temp. ≤ 0°F	7	5	2	0	0	0	0	0	0	0	0	3	17
Heating Degree Days (base 65°F)	1,378	1,191	1,030	647	343	125	50	70	232	552	830	1,180	7,628
Cooling Degree Days (base 65°F)	0	0	0	1	12	49	99	64	18	0	0	0	243
Mean Precipitation (in.)	2.88	2.50	3.35	3.54	4.01	5.42	4.59	4.19	4.86	3.82	3.93	3.78	46.87
Days With ≥ 0.1" Precipitation	9	7	8	9	9	9	9	8	9	9	10	11	107
Days With ≥ 1.0" Precipitation	0	0	0	1	1	2	1	1	1	1	1	0	9
Mean Snowfall (in.)	20.5	16.7	12.2	2.6	0.1	0.0	0.0	0.0	0.0	0.3	8.0	22.2	82.6
Days With ≥ 1.0" Snow Depth	26	24	17	2	0	0	0	0	0	0	6	19	94

Bradford Regional Airport *McKean County*   Elevation: 2,116 ft.   Latitude: 41° 48' N   Longitude: 78° 38' W

	JAN	FEB	MAR	APR	MAY	JUN	JUL	AUG	SEP	OCT	NOV	DEC	YEAR
Mean Maximum Temp. (°F)	26.7	30.1	40.2	53.2	65.1	72.5	77.0	75.0	67.4	55.9	43.6	32.2	53.2
Mean Temp. (°F)	19.4	21.7	31.0	42.9	53.3	60.9	65.8	64.0	56.9	46.2	36.3	25.3	43.6
Mean Minimum Temp. (°F)	12.2	13.2	21.8	32.5	41.4	49.3	54.6	52.9	46.4	36.5	28.9	18.3	34.0
Extreme Maximum Temp. (°F)	59	63	78	85	86	89	97	93	86	79	73	69	97
Extreme Minimum Temp. (°F)	-27	-30	-21	6	18	25	33	25	24	11	-2	-20	-30
Days Maximum Temp. ≥ 90°F	0	0	0	0	0	0	1	0	0	0	0	0	1
Days Maximum Temp. ≤ 32°F	21	16	9	1	0	0	0	0	0	0	6	16	69
Days Minimum Temp. ≤ 32°F	30	26	26	16	6	1	0	0	2	11	21	29	168
Days Minimum Temp. ≤ 0°F	6	5	1	0	0	0	0	0	0	0	0	3	15
Heating Degree Days (base 65°F)	1,404	1,216	1,047	659	368	156	60	86	257	577	856	1,224	7,910
Cooling Degree Days (base 65°F)	0	0	0	3	10	40	99	61	20	0	0	0	233
Mean Precipitation (in.)	3.21	3.07	3.83	3.50	4.04	5.48	4.44	4.17	4.37	3.24	3.96	4.14	47.45
Days With ≥ 0.1" Precipitation	9	8	9	8	9	9	9	8	9	8	10	11	107
Days With ≥ 1.0" Precipitation	0	0	1	1	1	1	1	1	1	0	1	1	9
Mean Snowfall (in.)	19.6	18.5	15.8	4.0	0.5	trace	trace	trace	trace	1.6	7.5	21.8	89.3
Days With ≥ 1.0" Snow Depth	26	24	16	3	0	0	0	0	0	0	8	21	98

Brookville Sewage Plant *Jefferson County*   Elevation: 1,207 ft.   Latitude: 41° 09' N   Longitude: 79° 05' W

	JAN	FEB	MAR	APR	MAY	JUN	JUL	AUG	SEP	OCT	NOV	DEC	YEAR
Mean Maximum Temp. (°F)	33.3	37.0	47.3	60.1	70.5	77.7	81.4	80.0	73.1	62.4	49.9	38.2	59.2
Mean Temp. (°F)	24.4	26.6	35.9	46.8	56.9	64.8	69.0	67.6	60.8	49.9	40.4	30.0	47.8
Mean Minimum Temp. (°F)	15.5	16.2	24.5	33.6	43.3	51.7	56.6	55.2	48.5	37.5	30.9	21.7	36.3
Extreme Maximum Temp. (°F)	68	69	82	89	89	93	99	93	91	84	78	74	99
Extreme Minimum Temp. (°F)	-32	-21	-10	6	21	29	35	31	26	16	3	-18	-32
Days Maximum Temp. ≥ 90°F	0	0	0	0	0	0	1	1	0	0	0	0	2
Days Maximum Temp. ≤ 32°F	14	10	3	0	0	0	0	0	0	0	1	8	36
Days Minimum Temp. ≤ 32°F	29	26	24	15	5	0	0	0	1	10	18	26	154
Days Minimum Temp. ≤ 0°F	4	4	1	0	0	0	0	0	0	0	0	2	11
Heating Degree Days (base 65°F)	1,251	1,079	895	541	265	75	20	33	162	462	732	1,079	6,594
Cooling Degree Days (base 65°F)	0	0	0	2	19	73	157	118	37	2	0	0	408
Mean Precipitation (in.)	2.81	2.58	3.50	3.50	4.13	5.45	5.16	4.18	4.16	3.27	3.66	3.55	45.95
Days With ≥ 0.1" Precipitation	7	7	8	8	9	9	9	7	8	7	8	9	96
Days With ≥ 1.0" Precipitation	0	0	1	1	0	2	1	1	1	1	1	0	9
Mean Snowfall (in.)	14.8	11.0	7.6	1.3	trace	0.0	0.0	0.0	0.0	trace	2.0	10.6	47.3
Days With ≥ 1.0" Snow Depth	20	19	8	1	0	0	0	0	0	0	3	13	64

Butler 2 SW *Butler County*   Elevation: 997 ft.   Latitude: 40° 51' N   Longitude: 79° 55' W

	JAN	FEB	MAR	APR	MAY	JUN	JUL	AUG	SEP	OCT	NOV	DEC	YEAR
Mean Maximum Temp. (°F)	34.5	38.0	47.6	60.0	70.6	79.0	82.9	81.6	74.7	62.8	50.6	39.7	60.2
Mean Temp. (°F)	25.6	28.0	36.5	47.2	57.3	66.1	70.4	69.1	62.1	50.6	40.9	31.3	48.7
Mean Minimum Temp. (°F)	16.6	17.9	25.4	34.4	43.9	53.1	57.8	56.5	49.5	38.3	31.2	22.9	37.3
Extreme Maximum Temp. (°F)	68	72	84	90	91	97	102	100	94	87	79	74	102
Extreme Minimum Temp. (°F)	-20	-19	-7	9	22	31	39	32	28	17	0	-14	-20
Days Maximum Temp. ≥ 90°F	0	0	0	0	0	1	4	2	1	0	0	0	8
Days Maximum Temp. ≤ 32°F	13	9	4	0	0	0	0	0	0	0	1	7	34
Days Minimum Temp. ≤ 32°F	28	25	24	14	3	0	0	0	0	8	18	26	146
Days Minimum Temp. ≤ 0°F	4	3	0	0	0	0	0	0	0	0	0	1	8
Heating Degree Days (base 65°F)	1,216	1,039	877	532	258	65	15	23	138	443	716	1,038	6,360
Cooling Degree Days (base 65°F)	0	0	0	3	25	110	201	163	58	3	0	0	563
Mean Precipitation (in.)	2.77	2.48	3.43	3.49	4.21	4.26	4.52	3.97	4.07	2.76	3.62	3.19	42.77
Days With ≥ 0.1" Precipitation	7	6	8	8	9	8	8	7	7	7	8	8	91
Days With ≥ 1.0" Precipitation	0	0	0	1	1	1	1	1	1	0	1	0	7
Mean Snowfall (in.)	11.7	8.4	5.4	0.9	0.0	0.0	0.0	0.0	0.0	0.1	1.7	6.7	34.9
Days With ≥ 1.0" Snow Depth	16	13	6	1	0	0	0	0	0	0	2	8	46

Chambersburg 1 ESE *Franklin County*   Elevation: 639 ft.   Latitude: 39° 56' N   Longitude: 77° 38' W

	JAN	FEB	MAR	APR	MAY	JUN	JUL	AUG	SEP	OCT	NOV	DEC	YEAR
Mean Maximum Temp. (°F)	36.4	40.8	50.6	63.0	72.7	80.7	85.0	83.4	76.1	64.3	52.5	41.8	62.3
Mean Temp. (°F)	28.4	31.8	40.5	51.4	61.3	69.6	73.9	72.3	65.0	53.0	43.2	33.8	52.0
Mean Minimum Temp. (°F)	20.3	22.7	30.4	39.7	49.9	58.5	62.8	61.1	53.7	41.7	33.8	25.8	41.7
Extreme Maximum Temp. (°F)	68	79	88	92	96	98	103	102	98	87	81	75	103
Extreme Minimum Temp. (°F)	-21	-10	-2	18	29	38	43	37	30	17	10	-5	-21
Days Maximum Temp. ≥ 90°F	0	0	0	0	1	3	7	4	1	0	0	0	16
Days Maximum Temp. ≤ 32°F	11	6	1	0	0	0	0	0	0	0	0	5	23
Days Minimum Temp. ≤ 32°F	28	23	19	7	1	0	0	0	0	5	14	24	121
Days Minimum Temp. ≤ 0°F	1	0	0	0	0	0	0	0	0	0	0	0	1
Heating Degree Days (base 65°F)	1,129	932	753	411	161	26	3	8	87	373	648	961	5,492
Cooling Degree Days (base 65°F)	0	0	2	8	55	182	305	244	92	10	0	0	898
Mean Precipitation (in.)	3.20	2.68	3.54	3.56	4.08	3.94	3.65	3.44	3.56	3.22	3.49	3.21	41.57
Days With ≥ 0.1" Precipitation	6	6	7	7	8	7	7	6	6	6	7	6	79
Days With ≥ 1.0" Precipitation	1	0	1	1	1	1	1	1	1	1	1	1	11
Mean Snowfall (in.)	10.9	8.1	5.7	0.6	0.0	0.0	0.0	0.0	0.0	trace	1.9	4.2	31.4
Days With ≥ 1.0" Snow Depth	14	10	4	0	0	0	0	0	0	0	1	5	34

Clarion 3 SW *Clarion County*   Elevation: 1,040 ft.   Latitude: 41° 12' N   Longitude: 79° 26' W

	JAN	FEB	MAR	APR	MAY	JUN	JUL	AUG	SEP	OCT	NOV	DEC	YEAR
Mean Maximum Temp. (°F)	33.1	36.9	47.4	60.5	72.7	79.6	83.3	81.4	74.0	62.2	48.6	37.7	59.8
Mean Temp. (°F)	24.6	26.9	35.8	47.1	58.4	66.1	70.3	68.9	61.9	50.4	39.8	30.0	48.4
Mean Minimum Temp. (°F)	16.0	16.9	24.5	33.8	44.0	52.6	57.3	56.5	49.8	38.6	30.9	22.3	36.9
Extreme Maximum Temp. (°F)	64	72	84	92	93	99	100	98	93	85	78	70	100
Extreme Minimum Temp. (°F)	-23	-21	-12	10	17	25	37	31	26	16	-1	-14	-23
Days Maximum Temp. ≥ 90°F	0	0	0	0	1	2	5	3	1	0	0	0	12
Days Maximum Temp. ≤ 32°F	14	10	4	0	0	0	0	0	0	0	2	9	39
Days Minimum Temp. ≤ 32°F	29	26	25	15	4	0	0	0	1	9	19	26	154
Days Minimum Temp. ≤ 0°F	4	3	1	0	0	0	0	0	0	0	0	1	9
Heating Degree Days (base 65°F)	1,245	1,070	900	534	231	65	15	22	139	448	751	1,079	6,499
Cooling Degree Days (base 65°F)	0	0	0	1	29	109	199	156	55	2	0	0	551
Mean Precipitation (in.)	2.88	2.50	3.24	3.73	4.08	5.42	4.99	4.43	4.67	3.39	4.09	3.38	46.80
Days With ≥ 0.1" Precipitation	8	7	8	8	9	9	8	8	8	8	8	8	97
Days With ≥ 1.0" Precipitation	0	0	0	1	1	1	1	1	1	1	1	0	8
Mean Snowfall (in.)	11.3	8.1	5.6	1.1	0.0	0.0	0.0	0.0	0.0	trace	1.6	8.7	36.4
Days With ≥ 1.0" Snow Depth	20	18	8	1	0	0	0	0	0	0	2	11	60

Confluence 1 SW Dam *Somerset County*   Elevation: 1,489 ft.   Latitude: 39° 48' N   Longitude: 79° 22' W

	JAN	FEB	MAR	APR	MAY	JUN	JUL	AUG	SEP	OCT	NOV	DEC	YEAR
Mean Maximum Temp. (°F)	36.1	40.0	49.5	61.5	71.8	80.2	84.0	82.9	76.1	64.5	52.0	41.0	61.6
Mean Temp. (°F)	26.0	28.6	37.2	47.7	57.8	66.3	70.6	69.5	62.7	50.8	40.6	31.2	49.1
Mean Minimum Temp. (°F)	15.8	17.1	24.8	33.9	43.7	52.4	57.1	56.1	49.3	37.1	29.2	21.4	36.5
Extreme Maximum Temp. (°F)	69	74	85	92	93	98	104	101	96	85	79	79	104
Extreme Minimum Temp. (°F)	-30	-20	-8	12	23	32	36	33	29	16	5	-18	-30
Days Maximum Temp. ≥ 90°F	0	0	0	0	1	3	6	4	1	0	0	0	15
Days Maximum Temp. ≤ 32°F	12	7	3	0	0	0	0	0	0	0	1	7	30
Days Minimum Temp. ≤ 32°F	29	25	24	14	3	0	0	0	1	10	20	27	153
Days Minimum Temp. ≤ 0°F	4	3	0	0	0	0	0	0	0	0	0	1	8
Heating Degree Days (base 65°F)	1,204	1,022	855	515	243	57	12	20	123	436	725	1,040	6,252
Cooling Degree Days (base 65°F)	0	0	0	2	27	110	207	168	58	3	0	0	575
Mean Precipitation (in.)	3.53	2.88	3.92	4.02	4.44	3.93	4.81	3.74	4.02	3.05	3.63	3.58	45.55
Days With ≥ 0.1" Precipitation	9	7	9	9	10	8	9	8	8	7	8	8	100
Days With ≥ 1.0" Precipitation	0	0	1	1	1	1	1	1	1	1	1	1	10
Mean Snowfall (in.)	19.1	12.7	10.3	1.7	trace	0.0	0.0	0.0	0.0	trace	4.4	11.0	59.2
Days With ≥ 1.0" Snow Depth	21	17	9	1	0	0	0	0	0	0	3	12	63

Corry *Erie County*   Elevation: 1,437 ft.   Latitude: 41° 55' N   Longitude: 79° 38' W

	JAN	FEB	MAR	APR	MAY	JUN	JUL	AUG	SEP	OCT	NOV	DEC	YEAR
Mean Maximum Temp. (°F)	31.2	34.5	45.1	57.6	68.8	76.4	80.0	78.2	70.9	60.2	47.2	36.2	57.2
Mean Temp. (°F)	23.3	25.2	34.9	46.0	56.3	64.7	68.7	67.3	60.5	50.1	39.6	29.3	47.2
Mean Minimum Temp. (°F)	15.4	15.7	24.6	34.3	43.8	53.0	57.4	56.3	50.1	39.9	32.0	22.3	37.1
Extreme Maximum Temp. (°F)	64	69	81	87	88	92	95	94	90	83	76	70	95
Extreme Minimum Temp. (°F)	-30	-24	-19	5	19	28	38	30	27	16	0	-12	-30
Days Maximum Temp. ≥ 90°F	0	0	0	0	0	0	1	0	0	0	0	0	1
Days Maximum Temp. ≤ 32°F	17	13	5	0	0	0	0	0	0	0	2	10	47
Days Minimum Temp. ≤ 32°F	29	26	24	14	4	0	0	0	0	7	18	26	148
Days Minimum Temp. ≤ 0°F	4	4	1	0	0	0	0	0	0	0	0	1	10
Heating Degree Days (base 65°F)	1,286	1,119	927	568	285	84	25	37	169	458	756	1,102	6,816
Cooling Degree Days (base 65°F)	0	0	0	3	22	83	153	118	40	2	0	0	421
Mean Precipitation (in.)	2.92	2.80	3.49	3.46	3.72	4.94	4.68	4.49	4.71	3.98	4.25	4.24	47.68
Days With ≥ 0.1" Precipitation	9	8	9	9	9	9	8	8	9	9	11	12	110
Days With ≥ 1.0" Precipitation	0	0	0	0	1	1	1	1	1	1	1	1	7
Mean Snowfall (in.)	30.0	21.8	16.1	5.3	0.2	0.0	0.0	0.0	trace	1.0	13.7	33.5	121.6
Days With ≥ 1.0" Snow Depth	25	22	12	1	0	0	0	0	0	0	6	19	85

Donora 1 SW *Washington County*   Elevation: 761 ft.   Latitude: 40° 10' N   Longitude: 79° 52' W

	JAN	FEB	MAR	APR	MAY	JUN	JUL	AUG	SEP	OCT	NOV	DEC	YEAR
Mean Maximum Temp. (°F)	39.6	43.1	53.3	64.8	74.6	81.9	85.6	84.3	78.3	67.1	54.9	44.4	64.3
Mean Temp. (°F)	30.4	32.9	41.9	51.8	61.8	69.8	74.0	72.9	66.6	55.0	44.7	35.3	53.1
Mean Minimum Temp. (°F)	21.2	22.7	30.4	38.7	48.9	57.6	62.3	61.4	54.9	42.8	34.5	26.1	41.8
Extreme Maximum Temp. (°F)	74	74	85	92	93	99	102	99	96	87	82	74	102
Extreme Minimum Temp. (°F)	-19	-11	0	11	25	37	40	40	33	20	4	-11	-19
Days Maximum Temp. ≥ 90°F	0	0	0	0	1	3	7	5	1	0	0	0	17
Days Maximum Temp. ≤ 32°F	9	5	1	0	0	0	0	0	0	0	0	5	20
Days Minimum Temp. ≤ 32°F	26	22	18	8	1	0	0	0	0	3	14	23	115
Days Minimum Temp. ≤ 0°F	1	1	0	0	0	0	0	0	0	0	0	1	3
Heating Degree Days (base 65°F)	1,065	900	711	398	154	26	2	5	63	315	603	916	5,158
Cooling Degree Days (base 65°F)	0	0	1	8	57	181	305	255	116	12	0	0	935
Mean Precipitation (in.)	2.51	2.15	3.36	3.16	3.76	3.81	3.80	3.74	3.06	2.43	2.94	2.72	37.44
Days With ≥ 0.1" Precipitation	6	6	8	8	9	8	7	6	6	6	7	7	84
Days With ≥ 1.0" Precipitation	0	0	1	1	1	1	1	1	1	0	1	0	8
Mean Snowfall (in.)	na	na	*4.4*	0.2	0.0	0.0	0.0	0.0	0.0	trace	*0.5*	*3.5*	na
Days With ≥ 1.0" Snow Depth	na	na	*2*	0	0	0	0	0	0	0	*1*	na	na

Dubois FAA Airport *Jefferson County*   Elevation: 1,811 ft.   Latitude: 41° 11' N   Longitude: 78° 54' W

	JAN	FEB	MAR	APR	MAY	JUN	JUL	AUG	SEP	OCT	NOV	DEC	YEAR
Mean Maximum Temp. (°F)	29.8	33.3	43.6	56.2	67.3	75.1	78.9	77.4	69.6	58.1	45.9	35.0	55.8
Mean Temp. (°F)	23.0	25.6	34.8	46.3	57.0	64.9	69.2	67.8	60.4	49.3	39.0	28.5	47.1
Mean Minimum Temp. (°F)	16.2	17.8	26.0	36.3	46.7	54.8	59.4	58.1	51.1	40.4	32.0	21.9	38.4
Extreme Maximum Temp. (°F)	65	67	79	88	89	90	98	95	89	80	76	72	98
Extreme Minimum Temp. (°F)	-26	-11	-6	8	24	33	41	34	29	17	2	-14	-26
Days Maximum Temp. ≥ 90°F	0	0	0	0	0	0	1	1	0	0	0	0	2
Days Maximum Temp. ≤ 32°F	18	14	6	0	0	0	0	0	0	0	4	13	55
Days Minimum Temp. ≤ 32°F	29	25	23	11	1	0	0	0	0	6	17	27	139
Days Minimum Temp. ≤ 0°F	3	3	0	0	0	0	0	0	0	0	0	1	7
Heating Degree Days (base 65°F)	1,292	1,107	929	561	269	76	19	32	172	481	774	1,126	6,838
Cooling Degree Days (base 65°F)	0	*0*	*0*	6	25	79	162	*124*	*36*	1	0	*0*	*433*
Mean Precipitation (in.)	2.82	2.75	3.68	3.37	3.95	5.17	4.23	4.00	3.95	3.11	3.37	3.50	43.90
Days With ≥ 0.1" Precipitation	8	7	8	8	9	9	8	7	8	7	8	9	96
Days With ≥ 1.0" Precipitation	0	0	1	1	1	1	1	1	1	1	0	0	8
Mean Snowfall (in.)	14.5	13.3	*10.6*	2.6	0.1	0.0	trace	0.0	0.0	0.7	4.6	12.5	*58.9*
Days With ≥ 1.0" Snow Depth	22	20	10	2	0	0	0	0	0	0	4	15	73

Ebensburg Sewage Plant *Cambria County*   Elevation: 1,938 ft.   Latitude: 40° 28' N   Longitude: 78° 44' W

	JAN	FEB	MAR	APR	MAY	JUN	JUL	AUG	SEP	OCT	NOV	DEC	YEAR
Mean Maximum Temp. (°F)	34.6	38.4	47.7	60.1	70.1	77.6	81.3	79.8	73.1	62.5	50.1	39.3	59.6
Mean Temp. (°F)	25.1	27.5	35.9	46.7	56.4	64.2	68.5	67.0	60.7	49.7	39.9	30.2	47.6
Mean Minimum Temp. (°F)	15.6	16.5	24.1	33.2	42.6	50.8	55.6	54.2	48.1	36.8	29.7	21.1	35.7
Extreme Maximum Temp. (°F)	67	71	83	89	90	91	98	94	90	82	78	70	98
Extreme Minimum Temp. (°F)	-28	-22	-11	10	21	28	36	30	23	12	0	-20	-28
Days Maximum Temp. ≥ 90°F	0	0	0	0	0	0	1	1	0	0	0	0	2
Days Maximum Temp. ≤ 32°F	13	9	3	0	0	0	0	0	0	0	2	8	35
Days Minimum Temp. ≤ 32°F	29	26	25	15	5	1	0	0	2	11	20	27	161
Days Minimum Temp. ≤ 0°F	5	3	1	0	0	0	0	0	0	0	0	2	11
Heating Degree Days (base 65°F)	1,230	1,053	894	544	275	86	26	40	165	469	746	1,073	6,601
Cooling Degree Days (base 65°F)	0	0	0	1	17	76	153	113	41	2	0	0	403
Mean Precipitation (in.)	3.94	3.26	4.42	4.34	4.70	4.58	5.08	4.06	4.30	3.29	4.22	3.83	50.02
Days With ≥ 0.1" Precipitation	11	9	10	10	10	9	9	7	8	7	9	10	109
Days With ≥ 1.0" Precipitation	0	0	1	1	1	1	1	1	1	1	1	1	10
Mean Snowfall (in.)	27.4	22.5	18.6	5.2	trace	0.0	0.0	0.0	trace	0.3	7.2	18.0	99.2
Days With ≥ 1.0" Snow Depth	24	21	14	2	0	0	0	0	0	0	5	15	81

Emporium *Cameron County*   Elevation: 1,040 ft.   Latitude: 41° 30' N   Longitude: 78° 14' W

	JAN	FEB	MAR	APR	MAY	JUN	JUL	AUG	SEP	OCT	NOV	DEC	YEAR
Mean Maximum Temp. (°F)	32.6	36.5	46.2	59.5	70.7	78.3	82.3	80.7	73.2	62.0	48.7	37.3	59.0
Mean Temp. (°F)	23.5	25.8	34.8	46.3	56.7	65.0	69.8	68.4	61.2	49.7	39.3	29.0	47.5
Mean Minimum Temp. (°F)	14.3	15.0	23.3	33.1	42.7	51.6	57.2	56.1	49.1	37.3	30.0	20.7	35.9
Extreme Maximum Temp. (°F)	64	70	84	92	93	97	101	98	91	86	80	70	101
Extreme Minimum Temp. (°F)	-28	-22	-9	10	22	32	37	34	27	12	3	-15	-28
Days Maximum Temp. ≥ 90°F	0	0	0	0	0	1	4	2	0	0	0	0	7
Days Maximum Temp. ≤ 32°F	15	10	3	0	0	0	0	0	0	0	1	8	37
Days Minimum Temp. ≤ 32°F	29	26	26	16	4	0	0	0	0	9	20	27	157
Days Minimum Temp. ≤ 0°F	5	4	1	0	0	0	0	0	0	0	0	2	12
Heating Degree Days (base 65°F)	1,279	1,101	931	556	273	79	16	26	156	470	766	1,109	6,762
Cooling Degree Days (base 65°F)	0	0	0	3	22	87	179	138	45	2	0	0	476
Mean Precipitation (in.)	2.63	2.22	3.14	3.33	3.86	4.83	4.21	3.82	4.11	3.18	3.58	2.98	41.89
Days With ≥ 0.1" Precipitation	7	6	8	9	9	9	8	7	8	7	7	7	92
Days With ≥ 1.0" Precipitation	0	0	0	0	1	1	1	1	1	1	1	0	7
Mean Snowfall (in.)	10.4	9.2	*8.7*	0.6	trace	0.0	0.0	0.0	0.0	trace	2.1	*7.3*	*38.3*
Days With ≥ 1.0" Snow Depth	21	19	10	1	0	0	0	0	0	0	3	12	66

Ford City 4 S Dam *Armstrong County*   Elevation: 928 ft.   Latitude: 40° 43' N   Longitude: 79° 30' W

	JAN	FEB	MAR	APR	MAY	JUN	JUL	AUG	SEP	OCT	NOV	DEC	YEAR
Mean Maximum Temp. (°F)	35.2	38.8	48.7	61.2	71.7	79.5	83.6	82.3	75.6	63.9	51.7	40.7	61.1
Mean Temp. (°F)	26.1	28.5	37.5	48.4	58.6	67.0	71.5	70.2	63.3	51.3	41.8	31.9	49.7
Mean Minimum Temp. (°F)	17.0	18.2	26.3	35.6	45.3	54.4	59.3	57.9	50.8	38.7	31.8	23.1	38.2
Extreme Maximum Temp. (°F)	70	74	87	90	92	99	101	98	95	86	79	75	101
Extreme Minimum Temp. (°F)	-29	-20	-6	15	22	33	40	37	29	19	4	-14	-29
Days Maximum Temp. ≥ 90°F	0	0	0	0	0	2	5	4	1	0	0	0	12
Days Maximum Temp. ≤ 32°F	13	8	3	0	0	0	0	0	0	0	1	7	32
Days Minimum Temp. ≤ 32°F	28	24	23	12	2	0	0	0	0	8	17	26	140
Days Minimum Temp. ≤ 0°F	4	3	0	0	0	0	0	0	0	0	0	1	8
Heating Degree Days (base 65°F)	1,199	1,024	846	499	227	55	10	17	118	423	692	1,018	6,128
Cooling Degree Days (base 65°F)	0	0	1	6	36	134	245	197	75	5	0	0	699
Mean Precipitation (in.)	2.73	2.32	3.20	3.12	4.00	4.62	4.09	4.02	3.82	2.69	3.46	2.83	40.90
Days With ≥ 0.1" Precipitation	7	6	8	7	9	8	8	7	7	6	7	7	87
Days With ≥ 1.0" Precipitation	0	0	1	0	1	1	1	1	1	0	0	0	7
Mean Snowfall (in.)	10.7	7.7	5.4	0.9	trace	0.0	0.0	0.0	0.0	trace	1.5	5.7	31.9
Days With ≥ 1.0" Snow Depth	15	12	5	0	0	0	0	0	0	0	0	1	41

Francis E Walter Dam *Luzerne County*   Elevation: 1,505 ft.   Latitude: 41° 07' N   Longitude: 75° 44' W

	JAN	FEB	MAR	APR	MAY	JUN	JUL	AUG	SEP	OCT	NOV	DEC	YEAR
Mean Maximum Temp. (°F)	31.1	34.1	43.3	55.4	67.4	74.4	78.9	77.8	69.7	59.0	46.6	35.9	56.1
Mean Temp. (°F)	21.2	23.5	32.7	43.6	54.9	62.4	66.9	65.7	57.9	47.1	37.1	26.7	45.0
Mean Minimum Temp. (°F)	11.4	12.9	22.0	31.8	42.4	50.3	54.9	53.6	46.0	35.1	27.5	17.8	33.8
Extreme Maximum Temp. (°F)	62	69	84	90	91	92	95	96	91	83	77	66	96
Extreme Minimum Temp. (°F)	-26	-28	-8	4	21	27	35	32	23	12	2	-22	-28
Days Maximum Temp. ≥ 90°F	0	0	0	0	0	0	1	0	0	0	0	0	1
Days Maximum Temp. ≤ 32°F	16	13	5	0	0	0	0	0	0	0	2	11	47
Days Minimum Temp. ≤ 32°F	29	26	26	17	4	1	0	0	2	14	21	28	168
Days Minimum Temp. ≤ 0°F	5	4	1	0	0	0	0	0	0	0	0	2	12
Heating Degree Days (base 65°F)	1,353	1,159	998	638	317	121	43	60	231	550	828	1,179	7,477
Cooling Degree Days (base 65°F)	0	0	0	1	11	48	110	86	22	1	0	0	279
Mean Precipitation (in.)	3.13	2.56	3.26	3.77	4.48	4.67	4.70	4.28	4.76	3.78	3.88	3.14	46.41
Days With ≥ 0.1" Precipitation	5	5	7	7	8	8	8	7	7	6	6	6	80
Days With ≥ 1.0" Precipitation	0	0	1	1	1	1	1	1	1	1	1	1	10
Mean Snowfall (in.)	13.4	10.6	9.3	3.2	0.2	0.0	0.0	0.0	0.0	0.1	3.2	8.1	48.1
Days With ≥ 1.0" Snow Depth	22	19	12	2	0	0	0	0	0	0	3	12	70

Franklin *Venango County*   Elevation: 987 ft.   Latitude: 41° 23' N   Longitude: 79° 49' W

	JAN	FEB	MAR	APR	MAY	JUN	JUL	AUG	SEP	OCT	NOV	DEC	YEAR
Mean Maximum Temp. (°F)	33.3	36.0	45.8	58.7	70.2	78.6	82.7	81.0	73.3	61.4	49.1	38.3	59.0
Mean Temp. (°F)	24.9	26.7	35.3	46.6	57.2	66.1	70.4	69.1	62.0	50.5	40.7	30.8	48.4
Mean Minimum Temp. (°F)	16.6	17.4	24.7	34.4	44.1	53.4	58.1	57.1	50.6	39.6	32.2	23.2	37.6
Extreme Maximum Temp. (°F)	68	72	81	90	91	95	99	97	92	87	78	74	99
Extreme Minimum Temp. (°F)	-22	-16	-9	11	26	33	36	37	31	19	4	-10	-22
Days Maximum Temp. ≥ 90°F	0	0	0	0	0	2	4	2	0	0	0	0	8
Days Maximum Temp. ≤ 32°F	14	11	4	0	0	0	0	0	0	0	1	8	38
Days Minimum Temp. ≤ 32°F	29	25	25	14	3	0	0	0	0	6	16	26	144
Days Minimum Temp. ≤ 0°F	3	3	1	0	0	0	0	0	0	0	0	1	8
Heating Degree Days (base 65°F)	1,235	1,075	914	549	261	64	14	22	139	444	725	1,054	6,496
Cooling Degree Days (base 65°F)	0	0	0	3	25	107	202	162	55	2	0	0	556
Mean Precipitation (in.)	2.59	2.36	3.30	3.55	3.74	4.81	5.02	4.08	4.35	3.16	3.67	3.22	43.85
Days With ≥ 0.1" Precipitation	7	7	8	9	9	8	8	8	8	7	8	8	95
Days With ≥ 1.0" Precipitation	0	0	0	1	1	1	1	1	1	0	1	0	7
Mean Snowfall (in.)	16.4	11.5	10.1	1.4	trace	0.0	0.0	0.0	0.0	trace	2.5	12.5	54.4
Days With ≥ 1.0" Snow Depth	21	16	8	1	0	0	0	0	0	0	2	11	59

Greenville 2 NE *Mercer County*   Elevation: 1,128 ft.   Latitude: 41° 25' N   Longitude: 80° 22' W

	JAN	FEB	MAR	APR	MAY	JUN	JUL	AUG	SEP	OCT	NOV	DEC	YEAR
Mean Maximum Temp. (°F)	33.1	36.4	46.9	59.5	70.6	78.7	82.6	81.5	74.3	62.8	49.8	38.3	59.5
Mean Temp. (°F)	24.1	26.3	36.0	47.1	57.9	66.4	70.4	69.0	61.9	50.7	40.6	30.0	48.4
Mean Minimum Temp. (°F)	15.0	16.2	25.1	34.7	45.0	54.1	58.1	56.5	49.4	38.5	31.4	21.7	37.1
Extreme Maximum Temp. (°F)	67	68	82	89	90	98	101	95	93	87	77	72	101
Extreme Minimum Temp. (°F)	-26	-18	-11	10	23	30	39	32	28	17	-1	-14	-26
Days Maximum Temp. ≥ 90°F	0	0	0	0	0	1	4	2	1	0	0	0	8
Days Maximum Temp. ≤ 32°F	15	11	4	0	0	0	0	0	0	0	1	9	40
Days Minimum Temp. ≤ 32°F	29	26	24	14	3	0	0	0	1	8	18	27	150
Days Minimum Temp. ≤ 0°F	4	4	1	0	0	0	0	0	0	0	0	1	10
Heating Degree Days (base 65°F)	1,262	1,087	892	536	249	64	17	26	146	440	726	1,077	6,522
Cooling Degree Days (base 65°F)	0	0	0	6	32	113	197	152	49	2	0	0	551
Mean Precipitation (in.)	1.90	1.83	2.83	3.34	3.76	4.42	4.21	3.74	4.29	3.07	3.37	2.85	39.61
Days With ≥ 0.1" Precipitation	6	5	8	9	9	8	8	7	8	8	8	8	91
Days With ≥ 1.0" Precipitation	0	0	0	0	1	1	1	1	1	0	0	0	5
Mean Snowfall (in.)	13.8	11.2	9.7	2.2	trace	0.0	0.0	0.0	0.0	0.2	4.4	12.3	53.8
Days With ≥ 1.0" Snow Depth	16	13	6	1	0	0	0	0	0	0	2	12	50

Hawley 1 E *Pike County*   Elevation: 889 ft.   Latitude: 41° 29' N   Longitude: 75° 10' W

	JAN	FEB	MAR	APR	MAY	JUN	JUL	AUG	SEP	OCT	NOV	DEC	YEAR
Mean Maximum Temp. (°F)	33.3	36.3	44.8	56.9	68.4	75.5	80.0	78.5	71.0	61.2	49.7	37.8	57.8
Mean Temp. (°F)	22.9	25.0	33.8	45.0	55.8	63.8	68.4	66.9	59.5	48.5	39.4	28.6	46.5
Mean Minimum Temp. (°F)	12.5	13.8	22.8	33.0	43.1	52.0	56.8	55.3	47.9	36.0	29.1	19.4	35.2
Extreme Maximum Temp. (°F)	64	70	85	91	94	94	98	94	92	86	82	69	98
Extreme Minimum Temp. (°F)	-31	-19	-11	12	26	32	41	37	27	17	6	-19	-31
Days Maximum Temp. ≥ 90°F	0	0	0	0	0	1	2	1	0	0	0	0	4
Days Maximum Temp. ≤ 32°F	14	10	4	0	0	0	0	0	0	0	0	9	38
Days Minimum Temp. ≤ 32°F	30	27	27	15	3	0	0	0	1	12	21	28	164
Days Minimum Temp. ≤ 0°F	5	4	1	0	0	0	0	0	0	0	0	2	12
Heating Degree Days (base 65°F)	1,298	1,122	961	597	294	96	27	41	192	506	761	1,121	7,016
Cooling Degree Days (base 65°F)	0	0	0	1	15	72	152	113	35	2	0	0	390
Mean Precipitation (in.)	3.08	2.68	3.10	3.66	4.00	4.03	3.65	3.43	3.79	3.26	3.56	3.02	41.26
Days With ≥ 0.1" Precipitation	6	6	6	7	8	8	7	6	7	6	6	6	79
Days With ≥ 1.0" Precipitation	1	0	1	1	1	1	1	1	1	1	1	0	10
Mean Snowfall (in.)	11.1	9.6	8.8	2.6	trace	0.0	0.0	0.0	0.0	trace	2.9	8.7	43.7
Days With ≥ 1.0" Snow Depth	22	19	11	1	0	0	0	0	0	0	2	13	68

Holtwood *Lancaster County*   Elevation: 187 ft.   Latitude: 39° 50' N   Longitude: 76° 20' W

	JAN	FEB	MAR	APR	MAY	JUN	JUL	AUG	SEP	OCT	NOV	DEC	YEAR
Mean Maximum Temp. (°F)	37.1	40.4	49.2	60.8	71.6	80.0	84.6	83.1	76.0	64.3	53.0	42.2	61.9
Mean Temp. (°F)	29.8	32.6	40.8	51.4	61.9	70.7	75.6	74.3	66.9	55.1	44.7	35.0	53.2
Mean Minimum Temp. (°F)	22.4	24.7	32.4	41.8	52.2	61.5	66.6	65.3	57.8	45.9	36.4	27.7	44.6
Extreme Maximum Temp. (°F)	66	73	82	90	98	95	99	99	99	87	82	74	99
Extreme Minimum Temp. (°F)	-8	-9	7	21	32	43	51	45	37	26	14	0	-9
Days Maximum Temp. ≥ 90°F	0	0	0	0	0	2	6	4	1	0	0	0	13
Days Maximum Temp. ≤ 32°F	9	6	1	0	0	0	0	0	0	0	0	3	19
Days Minimum Temp. ≤ 32°F	28	23	16	3	0	0	0	0	0	1	9	23	103
Days Minimum Temp. ≤ 0°F	1	0	0	0	0	0	0	0	0	0	0	0	1
Heating Degree Days (base 65°F)	1,085	909	743	409	143	16	1	2	56	310	602	923	5,199
Cooling Degree Days (base 65°F)	0	0	0	4	56	200	346	286	116	13	0	0	1,021
Mean Precipitation (in.)	3.04	2.26	2.97	3.10	3.84	3.38	3.61	3.07	3.25	3.05	3.23	3.00	37.80
Days With ≥ 0.1" Precipitation	6	5	6	6	8	7	7	5	5	5	6	6	72
Days With ≥ 1.0" Precipitation	1	0	1	1	1	1	1	1	1	1	1	1	11
Mean Snowfall (in.)	na	na	na	trace	0.0	0.0	0.0	0.0	0.0	0.0	0.1	na	na
Days With ≥ 1.0" Snow Depth	na	na	na	0	0	0	0	0	0	0	0	0	na

Indiana 3 SE *Indiana County*   Elevation: 1,099 ft.   Latitude: 40° 36' N   Longitude: 79° 07' W

	JAN	FEB	MAR	APR	MAY	JUN	JUL	AUG	SEP	OCT	NOV	DEC	YEAR
Mean Maximum Temp. (°F)	35.6	39.3	49.5	61.5	71.5	78.7	82.2	80.7	73.8	63.1	51.4	40.8	60.7
Mean Temp. (°F)	26.9	29.5	38.5	48.9	58.8	66.6	70.8	69.5	63.0	52.0	42.0	32.5	49.9
Mean Minimum Temp. (°F)	18.2	19.6	27.5	36.2	46.1	54.5	59.3	58.3	52.0	40.7	32.6	24.2	39.1
Extreme Maximum Temp. (°F)	71	74	86	91	90	93	98	99	95	82	80	75	99
Extreme Minimum Temp. (°F)	-24	-20	-6	12	22	31	35	36	30	17	2	-14	-24
Days Maximum Temp. ≥ 90°F	0	0	0	0	0	1	3	2	0	0	0	0	6
Days Maximum Temp. ≤ 32°F	12	8	3	0	0	0	0	0	0	0	1	7	31
Days Minimum Temp. ≤ 32°F	28	25	22	12	2	0	0	0	0	6	16	25	136
Days Minimum Temp. ≤ 0°F	3	2	0	0	0	0	0	0	0	0	0	1	6
Heating Degree Days (base 65°F)	1,174	998	815	481	213	52	9	16	117	401	683	999	5,958
Cooling Degree Days (base 65°F)	0	0	0	3	25	111	203	163	60	4	0	0	569
Mean Precipitation (in.)	3.48	2.96	3.92	3.73	4.47	4.96	4.98	4.17	4.28	3.05	4.02	3.36	47.38
Days With ≥ 0.1" Precipitation	9	7	9	9	9	9	8	7	8	7	8	8	98
Days With ≥ 1.0" Precipitation	0	0	1	1	1	1	1	1	1	1	1	0	9
Mean Snowfall (in.)	17.5	12.7	9.5	1.8	trace	0.0	0.0	0.0	0.0	trace	3.3	8.7	53.5
Days With ≥ 1.0" Snow Depth	18	15	7	1	0	0	0	0	0	0	2	9	52

Jamestown 2 NW *Crawford County*   Elevation: 1,040 ft.   Latitude: 41° 30' N   Longitude: 80° 28' W

	JAN	FEB	MAR	APR	MAY	JUN	JUL	AUG	SEP	OCT	NOV	DEC	YEAR
Mean Maximum Temp. (°F)	32.4	35.3	45.1	57.3	69.0	77.6	81.7	80.0	73.2	61.5	48.9	37.8	58.3
Mean Temp. (°F)	23.4	25.6	34.8	45.9	56.8	65.7	69.8	68.2	61.4	50.3	40.2	29.8	47.7
Mean Minimum Temp. (°F)	14.3	15.8	24.4	34.4	44.6	53.7	57.7	56.4	49.6	38.9	31.5	21.9	36.9
Extreme Maximum Temp. (°F)	67	70	84	89	90	98	101	97	93	85	78	73	101
Extreme Minimum Temp. (°F)	-27	-24	-12	7	22	29	40	32	30	17	0	-19	-27
Days Maximum Temp. ≥ 90°F	0	0	0	0	0	1	3	2	0	0	0	0	6
Days Maximum Temp. ≤ 32°F	16	12	5	1	0	0	0	0	0	0	1	9	44
Days Minimum Temp. ≤ 32°F	29	26	24	14	3	0	0	0	0	7	18	27	148
Days Minimum Temp. ≤ 0°F	5	4	1	0	0	0	0	0	0	0	0	1	11
Heating Degree Days (base 65°F)	1,283	1,107	930	572	274	75	21	32	154	452	737	1,083	6,720
Cooling Degree Days (base 65°F)	0	0	1	5	26	108	187	145	52	3	0	0	527
Mean Precipitation (in.)	2.45	2.31	2.99	3.48	3.64	4.14	4.26	4.06	4.03	3.15	3.57	3.21	41.29
Days With ≥ 0.1" Precipitation	7	6	9	9	8	8	7	7	8	7	8	9	93
Days With ≥ 1.0" Precipitation	0	0	0	1	0	1	1	1	1	0	0	0	5
Mean Snowfall (in.)	18.2	13.1	11.6	2.5	trace	0.0	0.0	0.0	0.0	0.5	6.0	16.3	68.2
Days With ≥ 1.0" Snow Depth	21	17	10	1	0	0	0	0	0	0	4	14	67

Kane 1 NNE *McKean County*   Elevation: 1,748 ft.   Latitude: 41° 41' N   Longitude: 78° 48' W

	JAN	FEB	MAR	APR	MAY	JUN	JUL	AUG	SEP	OCT	NOV	DEC	YEAR
Mean Maximum Temp. (°F)	29.5	32.8	42.1	54.7	66.7	74.5	78.5	76.8	69.4	58.1	45.1	34.3	55.2
Mean Temp. (°F)	20.3	22.2	30.9	42.4	52.8	61.2	65.4	63.9	56.8	46.2	36.4	26.3	43.7
Mean Minimum Temp. (°F)	11.2	11.5	19.7	30.1	38.9	47.8	52.3	50.8	44.1	34.1	27.7	18.3	32.2
Extreme Maximum Temp. (°F)	63	66	81	87	90	92	96	92	92	82	75	70	96
Extreme Minimum Temp. (°F)	-35	-30	-23	0	16	25	32	25	23	12	-6	-22	-35
Days Maximum Temp. ≥ 90°F	0	0	0	0	0	0	1	0	0	0	0	0	1
Days Maximum Temp. ≤ 32°F	19	14	7	1	0	0	0	0	0	0	4	13	58
Days Minimum Temp. ≤ 32°F	30	27	27	19	10	1	0	0	4	15	23	28	184
Days Minimum Temp. ≤ 0°F	7	6	2	0	0	0	0	0	0	0	0	3	18
Heating Degree Days (base 65°F)	1,378	1,205	1,050	673	379	147	62	87	258	578	851	1,192	7,860
Cooling Degree Days (base 65°F)	0	0	0	1	8	40	83	58	15	0	0	0	205
Mean Precipitation (in.)	3.29	2.64	3.61	3.78	4.10	5.05	4.29	4.35	4.34	3.49	4.04	3.81	46.79
Days With ≥ 0.1" Precipitation	8	8	9	9	9	9	8	8	9	9	10	10	106
Days With ≥ 1.0" Precipitation	0	0	1	0	1	1	1	1	1	1	1	1	8
Mean Snowfall (in.)	23.5	18.2	14.7	3.0	0.2	0.0	0.0	0.0	trace	0.5	8.3	21.4	89.8
Days With ≥ 1.0" Snow Depth	27	25	17	2	0	0	0	0	0	0	8	21	100

Landisville 2 NW *Lancaster County*   Elevation: 357 ft.   Latitude: 40° 07' N   Longitude: 76° 26' W

	JAN	FEB	MAR	APR	MAY	JUN	JUL	AUG	SEP	OCT	NOV	DEC	YEAR
Mean Maximum Temp. (°F)	37.7	41.7	51.7	63.8	74.1	82.0	86.0	84.6	77.8	66.5	53.9	42.8	63.6
Mean Temp. (°F)	29.1	32.1	41.1	51.4	61.8	70.3	74.2	72.5	65.5	54.1	43.9	34.4	52.5
Mean Minimum Temp. (°F)	20.4	22.3	30.4	38.9	49.4	58.4	62.3	60.3	53.1	41.7	33.8	26.0	41.4
Extreme Maximum Temp. (°F)	68	77	86	92	94	98	102	100	97	89	81	76	102
Extreme Minimum Temp. (°F)	-24	-20	-2	18	22	34	42	35	29	20	12	-3	-24
Days Maximum Temp. ≥ 90°F	0	0	0	0	1	4	8	5	2	0	0	0	20
Days Maximum Temp. ≤ 32°F	9	5	1	0	0	0	0	0	0	0	0	4	19
Days Minimum Temp. ≤ 32°F	27	23	19	8	0	0	0	0	0	6	15	23	121
Days Minimum Temp. ≤ 0°F	2	1	0	0	0	0	0	0	0	0	0	0	3
Heating Degree Days (base 65°F)	1,106	924	736	410	146	19	3	8	81	342	627	940	5,342
Cooling Degree Days (base 65°F)	0	0	1	7	59	195	312	251	100	13	0	0	938
Mean Precipitation (in.)	3.20	2.39	3.27	3.54	4.25	4.46	4.94	3.30	3.91	3.40	3.71	3.06	43.43
Days With ≥ 0.1" Precipitation	6	5	7	7	9	7	7	6	6	6	6	6	78
Days With ≥ 1.0" Precipitation	1	0	1	1	1	1	1	1	1	1	1	1	11
Mean Snowfall (in.)	8.4	7.5	3.8	0.4	0.0	0.0	0.0	0.0	0.0	trace	0.8	2.7	23.6
Days With ≥ 1.0" Snow Depth	12	8	3	0	0	0	0	0	0	0	0	3	26

Laurelton Center *Union County*   Elevation: 797 ft.   Latitude: 40° 54' N   Longitude: 77° 13' W

	JAN	FEB	MAR	APR	MAY	JUN	JUL	AUG	SEP	OCT	NOV	DEC	YEAR
Mean Maximum Temp. (°F)	36.9	41.6	51.7	65.4	76.0	83.0	86.9	85.1	76.9	65.8	52.5	41.1	63.6
Mean Temp. (°F)	27.1	30.6	39.3	50.9	61.2	68.9	73.3	71.6	63.9	52.7	41.9	31.8	51.1
Mean Minimum Temp. (°F)	17.3	19.5	26.8	36.4	46.4	54.8	59.6	58.0	50.9	39.6	31.3	22.4	38.6
Extreme Maximum Temp. (°F)	66	76	89	95	98	100	105	100	97	88	82	72	105
Extreme Minimum Temp. (°F)	-22	-15	-8	15	24	32	42	33	29	14	1	-11	-22
Days Maximum Temp. ≥ 90°F	0	0	0	0	2	4	10	6	2	0	0	0	24
Days Maximum Temp. ≤ 32°F	10	5	1	0	0	0	0	0	0	0	0	5	21
Days Minimum Temp. ≤ 32°F	30	25	23	11	2	0	0	0	0	7	18	27	143
Days Minimum Temp. ≤ 0°F	2	2	0	0	0	0	0	0	0	0	0	1	5
Heating Degree Days (base 65°F)	1,168	966	792	425	162	28	4	9	102	381	687	1,022	5,746
Cooling Degree Days (base 65°F)	0	0	1	7	51	155	281	219	75	7	0	0	796
Mean Precipitation (in.)	3.17	2.95	3.55	3.49	4.16	4.71	4.28	3.70	4.53	3.44	3.89	3.19	45.06
Days With ≥ 0.1" Precipitation	6	6	7	8	8	8	8	6	7	6	7	6	83
Days With ≥ 1.0" Precipitation	1	1	1	1	1	1	1	1	1	1	1	1	12
Mean Snowfall (in.)	*10.3*	*7.6*	*5.1*	0.6	0.0	0.0	0.0	0.0	0.0	0.0	1.1	na	na
Days With ≥ 1.0" Snow Depth	*14*	11	6	0	0	0	0	0	0	0	1	6	*38*

Lebanon 2 W *Lebanon County*   Elevation: 449 ft.   Latitude: 40° 20' N   Longitude: 76° 28' W

	JAN	FEB	MAR	APR	MAY	JUN	JUL	AUG	SEP	OCT	NOV	DEC	YEAR
Mean Maximum Temp. (°F)	36.8	40.3	49.8	62.0	72.3	80.4	84.9	83.0	75.6	64.8	53.0	42.1	62.1
Mean Temp. (°F)	28.2	31.0	39.6	50.3	60.5	68.8	73.6	71.5	*64.4*	53.0	43.1	33.7	*51.5*
Mean Minimum Temp. (°F)	19.8	21.7	29.4	38.7	48.6	57.4	62.2	60.2	*53.4*	41.4	33.1	25.4	*40.9*
Extreme Maximum Temp. (°F)	66	75	84	90	94	98	102	98	98	89	82	75	102
Extreme Minimum Temp. (°F)	-22	-12	-4	18	28	37	44	38	30	18	9	-2	-22
Days Maximum Temp. ≥ 90°F	0	0	0	0	1	3	7	4	1	0	0	0	16
Days Maximum Temp. ≤ 32°F	10	7	1	0	0	0	0	0	0	0	0	4	22
Days Minimum Temp. ≤ 32°F	28	24	20	*8*	1	0	0	0	0	5	15	24	*125*
Days Minimum Temp. ≤ 0°F	1	1	0	0	0	0	0	0	0	0	0	0	2
Heating Degree Days (base 65°F)	1,131	954	780	441	177	30	3	10	*97*	372	653	964	*5,612*
Cooling Degree Days (base 65°F)	0	0	0	4	41	154	283	215	79	9	0	0	785
Mean Precipitation (in.)	3.32	2.56	3.23	3.78	4.54	3.96	4.67	3.51	4.02	3.37	3.75	3.15	43.86
Days With ≥ 0.1" Precipitation	6	6	7	7	9	7	7	6	6	6	6	*6*	79
Days With ≥ 1.0" Precipitation	1	0	1	1	1	1	1	1	1	1	1	1	11
Mean Snowfall (in.)	*7.6*	*7.0*	*3.5*	trace	trace	0.0	0.0	0.0	0.0	trace	0.7	na	na
Days With ≥ 1.0" Snow Depth	na	na	*2*	0	0	0	0	0	0	0	0	na	na

Lewistown *Mifflin County*   Elevation: 459 ft.   Latitude: 40° 35' N   Longitude: 77° 34' W

	JAN	FEB	MAR	APR	MAY	JUN	JUL	AUG	SEP	OCT	NOV	DEC	YEAR
Mean Maximum Temp. (°F)	36.0	39.9	49.6	62.3	72.8	80.3	84.8	83.3	75.4	64.3	51.9	40.5	61.7
Mean Temp. (°F)	27.7	30.5	39.2	50.3	60.2	68.3	73.1	71.6	64.2	52.6	42.6	32.9	51.1
Mean Minimum Temp. (°F)	19.5	21.1	28.7	38.3	47.7	56.3	61.4	59.8	52.6	40.8	33.3	25.2	40.4
Extreme Maximum Temp. (°F)	68	76	87	92	96	95	102	97	98	85	82	75	102
Extreme Minimum Temp. (°F)	-17	-8	3	15	28	38	41	35	30	21	11	-6	-17
Days Maximum Temp. ≥ 90°F	0	0	0	0	1	2	7	4	1	0	0	0	15
Days Maximum Temp. ≤ 32°F	11	7	1	0	0	0	0	0	0	0	0	5	24
Days Minimum Temp. ≤ 32°F	28	25	21	7	1	0	0	0	0	5	14	25	126
Days Minimum Temp. ≤ 0°F	2	1	0	0	0	0	0	0	0	0	0	0	
Heating Degree Days (base 65°F)	1,149	968	795	442	182	33	4	9	97	385	667	990	5,721
Cooling Degree Days (base 65°F)	0	0	1	5	39	138	264	211	71	6	0	0	735
Mean Precipitation (in.)	2.69	2.46	3.39	3.23	4.15	4.61	4.26	3.24	3.64	3.12	3.60	2.93	41.32
Days With ≥ 0.1" Precipitation	6	6	7	7	8	8	7	6	7	5	7	6	80
Days With ≥ 1.0" Precipitation	1	1	1	0	1	1	1	1	1	1	1	1	10
Mean Snowfall (in.)	*8.8*	*6.4*	*6.0*	0.2	0.0	0.0	0.0	0.0	0.0	0.0	*0.9*	na	na
Days With ≥ 1.0" Snow Depth	na	na	4	0	0	0	0	0	0	0	*0*	na	na

Marcus Hook *Delaware County*   Elevation: 9 ft.   Latitude: 39° 49' N   Longitude: 75° 25' W

	JAN	FEB	MAR	APR	MAY	JUN	JUL	AUG	SEP	OCT	NOV	DEC	YEAR
Mean Maximum Temp. (°F)	39.1	42.7	51.3	63.3	73.9	82.8	87.4	85.2	77.3	65.2	54.3	44.2	63.9
Mean Temp. (°F)	33.3	36.2	43.9	54.5	64.7	73.7	78.6	76.8	69.4	57.7	47.8	38.5	56.3
Mean Minimum Temp. (°F)	27.4	29.6	36.4	45.6	55.4	64.4	69.7	68.4	61.5	50.2	41.3	32.8	48.6
Extreme Maximum Temp. (°F)	66	70	83	95	97	100	103	101	100	87	80	74	103
Extreme Minimum Temp. (°F)	-4	1	10	20	39	46	54	50	40	31	19	3	-4
Days Maximum Temp. ≥ 90°F	0	0	0	0	2	6	12	8	2	0	0	0	30
Days Maximum Temp. ≤ 32°F	8	4	1	0	0	0	0	0	0	0	0	3	16
Days Minimum Temp. ≤ 32°F	21	18	9	1	0	0	0	0	0	0	4	14	67
Days Minimum Temp. ≤ 0°F	0	0	0	0	0	0	0	0	0	0	0	0	0
Heating Degree Days (base 65°F)	978	807	650	323	96	7	1	1	31	240	511	815	4,460
Cooling Degree Days (base 65°F)	0	0	1	10	94	276	434	358	165	21	1	0	1,360
Mean Precipitation (in.)	2.74	2.56	3.29	3.50	4.04	3.23	4.01	3.42	4.09	2.94	3.34	2.99	40.15
Days With ≥ 0.1" Precipitation	5	5	5	6	7	6	5	5	5	5	5	5	64
Days With ≥ 1.0" Precipitation	1	1	1	1	1	1	1	1	1	1	1	1	12
Mean Snowfall (in.)	na	*4.7*	*1.0*	trace	0.0	0.0	0.0	0.0	0.0	trace	0.1	*1.0*	na
Days With ≥ 1.0" Snow Depth	na	*2*	*0*	0	0	0	0	0	0	0	0	*0*	na

Matamoras *Pike County*   Elevation: 419 ft.   Latitude: 41° 22' N   Longitude: 74° 42' W

	JAN	FEB	MAR	APR	MAY	JUN	JUL	AUG	SEP	OCT	NOV	DEC	YEAR
Mean Maximum Temp. (°F)	34.8	39.0	48.2	*60.8*	*72.6*	79.2	*84.2*	82.3	74.6	63.6	50.9	39.3	*60.8*
Mean Temp. (°F)	25.7	28.9	37.5	*48.5*	*59.7*	67.0	*71.9*	70.5	63.0	51.6	41.3	31.1	*49.7*
Mean Minimum Temp. (°F)	16.6	18.8	26.7	*36.0*	*46.8*	54.7	*59.6*	58.7	51.4	39.7	31.6	22.8	*38.6*
Extreme Maximum Temp. (°F)	66	74	88	*95*	*93*	95	*100*	97	96	88	*81*	*73*	*100*
Extreme Minimum Temp. (°F)	-18	-12	-1	*11*	*27*	35	*42*	36	26	19	*10*	*-10*	*-18*
Days Maximum Temp. ≥ 90°F	0	0	0	*0*	*1*	2	*7*	3	1	0	0	0	*14*
Days Maximum Temp. ≤ 32°F	12	7	2	*0*	*0*	0	*0*	0	0	0	1	7	*29*
Days Minimum Temp. ≤ 32°F	29	25	23	*11*	*1*	0	*0*	0	0	8	17	26	*140*
Days Minimum Temp. ≤ 0°F	3	1	0	*0*	*0*	0	*0*	0	0	0	0	1	*5*
Heating Degree Days (base 65°F)	1,211	1,011	846	*496*	*193*	48	*6*	14	119	412	706	1,045	*6,107*
Cooling Degree Days (base 65°F)	0	0	*0*	*4*	*31*	100	*217*	174	61	5	*0*	*0*	*592*
Mean Precipitation (in.)	3.20	2.88	3.58	*3.81*	*4.38*	4.30	*4.14*	3.71	4.52	3.42	3.67	3.33	*44.94*
Days With ≥ 0.1" Precipitation	7	6	7	*7*	*8*	7	*7*	7	6	6	6	7	*81*
Days With ≥ 1.0" Precipitation	1	1	1	*1*	*1*	1	*1*	1	1	1	1	1	*12*
Mean Snowfall (in.)	*10.2*	7.4	*5.9*	*1.4*	*trace*	0.0	*0.0*	0.0	0.0	trace	*1.4*	*5.7*	*32.0*
Days With ≥ 1.0" Snow Depth	19	14	6	*1*	*0*	0	*0*	0	0	0	0	1	*50*

Meadville 1 S *Crawford County*   Elevation: 1,062 ft.   Latitude: 41° 38' N   Longitude: 80° 10' W

	JAN	FEB	MAR	APR	MAY	JUN	JUL	AUG	SEP	OCT	NOV	DEC	YEAR
Mean Maximum Temp. (°F)	32.2	35.1	44.8	57.2	68.8	77.1	81.1	79.4	72.4	61.0	48.3	37.5	57.9
Mean Temp. (°F)	23.7	25.6	34.2	45.3	56.1	64.9	69.1	67.8	61.0	50.2	39.9	30.0	47.3
Mean Minimum Temp. (°F)	15.2	16.0	23.7	33.5	43.4	52.6	57.1	56.1	49.5	39.3	31.5	22.3	36.7
Extreme Maximum Temp. (°F)	66	71	82	89	90	96	100	98	92	85	77	72	100
Extreme Minimum Temp. (°F)	-22	-19	-12	10	24	29	39	33	30	17	3	-13	-22
Days Maximum Temp. ≥ 90°F	0	0	0	0	0	1	2	1	0	0	0	0	4
Days Maximum Temp. ≤ 32°F	16	12	6	0	0	0	0	0	0	0	2	9	45
Days Minimum Temp. ≤ 32°F	29	26	25	15	4	0	0	0	0	6	18	27	150
Days Minimum Temp. ≤ 0°F	4	4	1	0	0	0	0	0	0	0	0	1	10
Heating Degree Days (base 65°F)	1,273	1,106	947	587	291	85	24	34	160	456	746	1,080	6,789
Cooling Degree Days (base 65°F)	0	0	0	3	21	91	168	134	45	2	0	0	464
Mean Precipitation (in.)	2.81	2.60	3.24	3.35	3.63	4.46	4.29	4.44	4.40	3.64	3.99	3.71	44.56
Days With ≥ 0.1" Precipitation	8	7	9	8	8	8	7	8	8	8	9	10	98
Days With ≥ 1.0" Precipitation	0	0	0	1	1	1	1	1	1	1	0	0	7
Mean Snowfall (in.)	29.4	20.8	17.8	5.3	trace	trace	0.0	0.0	0.0	0.8	11.7	25.4	111.2
Days With ≥ 1.0" Snow Depth	23	20	12	2	0	0	0	0	0	0	5	17	79

Mercer *Mercer County*   Elevation: 1,217 ft.   Latitude: 41° 13' N   Longitude: 80° 14' W

	JAN	FEB	MAR	APR	MAY	JUN	JUL	AUG	SEP	OCT	NOV	DEC	YEAR
Mean Maximum Temp. (°F)	33.7	37.6	47.8	59.9	70.1	77.6	81.6	80.3	73.8	62.3	49.6	38.7	59.4
Mean Temp. (°F)	25.0	28.0	37.0	47.7	57.9	65.8	69.8	68.3	62.0	50.9	40.7	30.6	48.6
Mean Minimum Temp. (°F)	16.3	18.3	26.2	35.5	45.5	53.9	57.9	56.5	50.2	39.4	31.7	22.5	37.8
Extreme Maximum Temp. (°F)	65	70	82	88	90	94	99	96	93	83	78	73	99
Extreme Minimum Temp. (°F)	-32	-18	-13	11	22	30	39	31	26	17	0	-18	-32
Days Maximum Temp. ≥ 90°F	0	0	0	0	0	1	3	1	0	0	0	0	5
Days Maximum Temp. ≤ 32°F	14	10	3	0	0	0	0	0	0	0	1	9	37
Days Minimum Temp. ≤ 32°F	29	25	22	13	3	0	0	0	1	8	17	26	144
Days Minimum Temp. ≤ 0°F	4	2	1	0	0	0	0	0	0	0	0	1	8
Heating Degree Days (base 65°F)	1,235	1,037	861	518	244	67	17	28	139	435	724	1,060	6,365
Cooling Degree Days (base 65°F)	0	0	1	5	26	97	173	131	52	3	0	0	488
Mean Precipitation (in.)	2.72	2.55	3.30	3.58	3.67	4.61	4.33	3.83	4.33	2.85	3.76	3.37	42.90
Days With ≥ 0.1" Precipitation	7	7	8	8	8	8	7	7	8	6	8	9	91
Days With ≥ 1.0" Precipitation	0	0	1	1	1	1	1	1	1	0	0	0	7
Mean Snowfall (in.)	13.3	10.6	8.9	2.0	trace	0.0	0.0	0.0	0.0	trace	4.5	10.8	50.1
Days With ≥ 1.0" Snow Depth	20	16	9	1	0	0	0	0	0	0	3	12	61

Millville 2 SW *Columbia County*   Elevation: 859 ft.   Latitude: 41° 06' N   Longitude: 76° 34' W

	JAN	FEB	MAR	APR	MAY	JUN	JUL	AUG	SEP	OCT	NOV	DEC	YEAR
Mean Maximum Temp. (°F)	32.4	36.3	46.3	58.5	70.0	77.5	82.2	80.6	73.1	na	49.4	37.5	na
Mean Temp. (°F)	23.4	26.5	35.7	46.8	57.5	65.2	70.2	68.7	61.1	na	40.1	29.4	na
Mean Minimum Temp. (°F)	14.4	16.8	25.1	35.2	45.0	53.0	58.1	56.7	49.1	na	30.7	21.2	na
Extreme Maximum Temp. (°F)	67	71	85	91	91	94	103	95	94	85	79	66	103
Extreme Minimum Temp. (°F)	-17	-16	-1	12	27	33	44	37	28	19	6	-11	-17
Days Maximum Temp. ≥ 90°F	0	0	0	0	0	1	4	2	1	0	0	0	8
Days Maximum Temp. ≤ 32°F	14	10	3	0	0	0	0	0	0	0	1	8	36
Days Minimum Temp. ≤ 32°F	30	25	24	12	2	0	0	0	1	8	19	27	148
Days Minimum Temp. ≤ 0°F	4	2	0	0	0	0	0	0	0	0	0	1	7
Heating Degree Days (base 65°F)	1,282	1,081	901	544	250	70	14	26	157	na	740	1,097	na
Cooling Degree Days (base 65°F)	na	na	na	na	na	na	na	na	na	na	na	na	na
Mean Precipitation (in.)	2.48	2.52	3.04	3.23	4.04	4.96	4.17	3.44	4.14	na	3.42	3.07	na
Days With ≥ 0.1" Precipitation	6	6	7	7	8	9	8	7	7	6	6	7	84
Days With ≥ 1.0" Precipitation	0	0	0	1	1	1	1	1	1	1	1	0	8
Mean Snowfall (in.)	10.1	7.3	5.6	1.0	trace	0.0	0.0	0.0	0.0	na	2.1	4.6	na
Days With ≥ 1.0" Snow Depth	19	16	7	1	0	0	0	0	0	0	1	8	52

Montgomery Lock & Dam *Beaver County*   Elevation: 688 ft.   Latitude: 40° 39' N   Longitude: 80° 23' W

	JAN	FEB	MAR	APR	MAY	JUN	JUL	AUG	SEP	OCT	NOV	DEC	YEAR
Mean Maximum Temp. (°F)	36.6	40.6	50.9	63.4	73.4	80.7	84.2	82.2	75.6	64.2	52.2	41.5	62.1
Mean Temp. (°F)	28.7	31.6	40.3	51.0	60.9	69.1	73.1	71.6	65.1	53.8	43.6	34.0	51.9
Mean Minimum Temp. (°F)	20.7	22.6	29.6	38.6	48.4	57.4	62.0	60.9	54.6	43.3	34.9	26.4	41.6
Extreme Maximum Temp. (°F)	70	73	82	90	90	98	105	100	92	86	82	74	105
Extreme Minimum Temp. (°F)	-18	-10	-4	14	26	34	44	39	30	20	-5	-9	-18
Days Maximum Temp. ≥ 90°F	0	0	0	0	0	2	5	2	0	0	0	0	9
Days Maximum Temp. ≤ 32°F	11	7	2	0	0	0	0	0	0	0	0	5	25
Days Minimum Temp. ≤ 32°F	26	22	19	9	1	0	0	0	0	0	5	23	115
Days Minimum Temp. ≤ 0°F	2	1	0	0	0	0	0	0	0	0	0	1	4
Heating Degree Days (base 65°F)	1,119	936	760	421	166	30	3	7	83	347	637	956	5,465
Cooling Degree Days (base 65°F)	0	0	1	7	43	163	280	225	96	7	1	0	823
Mean Precipitation (in.)	2.46	2.10	3.07	3.05	3.77	3.78	4.07	3.29	3.43	2.32	3.07	2.88	37.29
Days With ≥ 0.1" Precipitation	7	6	8	8	9	8	8	6	6	6	8	7	87
Days With ≥ 1.0" Precipitation	0	0	0	0	1	1	1	1	1	0	0	0	5
Mean Snowfall (in.)	6.0	3.2	3.3	0.2	0.0	0.0	0.0	0.0	0.0	trace	0.4	3.2	16.3
Days With ≥ 1.0" Snow Depth	12	9	4	0	0	0	0	0	0	0	1	5	31

Montrose *Susquehanna County*   Elevation: 1,417 ft.   Latitude: 41° 52' N   Longitude: 75° 51' W

	JAN	FEB	MAR	APR	MAY	JUN	JUL	AUG	SEP	OCT	NOV	DEC	YEAR
Mean Maximum Temp. (°F)	29.6	32.5	41.5	53.7	66.1	74.2	78.7	77.0	69.2	58.1	45.5	34.4	55.0
Mean Temp. (°F)	21.0	23.1	31.9	43.3	54.8	63.3	67.8	66.1	58.3	47.4	37.1	26.6	45.1
Mean Minimum Temp. (°F)	12.3	13.5	22.3	32.8	43.5	52.2	56.8	55.1	47.4	36.8	28.7	18.7	35.0
Extreme Maximum Temp. (°F)	62	65	83	88	89	95	97	94	91	82	78	66	97
Extreme Minimum Temp. (°F)	-29	-18	-8	8	24	30	38	35	26	13	0	-17	-29
Days Maximum Temp. ≥ 90°F	0	0	0	0	0	0	1	0	0	0	0	0	1
Days Maximum Temp. ≤ 32°F	19	14	7	1	0	0	0	0	0	0	0	13	57
Days Minimum Temp. ≤ 32°F	30	27	26	16	3	0	0	0	1	10	20	29	162
Days Minimum Temp. ≤ 0°F	5	5	1	0	0	0	0	0	0	0	0	2	13
Heating Degree Days (base 65°F)	1,361	1,181	1,022	651	326	108	34	54	223	541	832	1,188	7,521
Cooling Degree Days (base 65°F)	0	0	0	2	15	65	135	95	28	1	0	0	341
Mean Precipitation (in.)	3.18	2.81	3.38	3.91	3.89	4.29	4.19	3.65	4.01	3.49	3.91	3.38	44.09
Days With ≥ 0.1" Precipitation	8	7	8	8	8	9	8	7	7	7	8	8	93
Days With ≥ 1.0" Precipitation	0	0	0	1	1	1	1	1	1	1	1	0	8
Mean Snowfall (in.)	21.6	17.5	16.6	6.4	0.4	0.0	0.0	0.0	trace	0.8	9.1	16.7	89.1
Days With ≥ 1.0" Snow Depth	24	22	15	3	0	0	0	0	0	0	5	15	84

New Castle 1 N *Lawrence County*   Elevation: 823 ft.   Latitude: 41° 01' N   Longitude: 80° 22' W

	JAN	FEB	MAR	APR	MAY	JUN	JUL	AUG	SEP	OCT	NOV	DEC	YEAR
Mean Maximum Temp. (°F)	35.0	38.9	49.1	61.5	72.2	80.1	83.9	82.3	75.8	64.3	51.6	40.4	61.3
Mean Temp. (°F)	26.3	29.0	37.7	48.2	58.7	67.2	71.4	70.1	63.5	52.1	42.1	32.2	49.9
Mean Minimum Temp. (°F)	17.6	19.1	26.1	34.9	45.1	54.2	58.9	57.7	51.2	39.8	32.5	23.9	38.4
Extreme Maximum Temp. (°F)	69	73	83	89	91	97	100	98	93	87	79	76	100
Extreme Minimum Temp. (°F)	-27	-15	-8	11	22	30	40	32	30	17	2	-14	-27
Days Maximum Temp. ≥ 90°F	0	0	0	0	0	2	5	2	1	0	0	0	10
Days Maximum Temp. ≤ 32°F	13	8	3	0	0	0	0	0	0	0	0	7	32
Days Minimum Temp. ≤ 32°F	28	25	23	14	3	0	0	0	0	1	7	25	142
Days Minimum Temp. ≤ 0°F	3	2	0	0	0	0	0	0	0	0	0	1	6
Heating Degree Days (base 65°F)	1,192	1,009	842	502	224	53	10	18	113	399	681	1,011	6,054
Cooling Degree Days (base 65°F)	0	0	0	4	28	120	216	177	69	5	0	0	619
Mean Precipitation (in.)	2.27	2.08	2.96	3.22	3.43	4.33	4.21	3.68	3.70	2.71	3.23	2.82	38.64
Days With ≥ 0.1" Precipitation	6	6	7	8	8	8	8	7	7	6	7	7	85
Days With ≥ 1.0" Precipitation	0	0	0	0	1	1	1	1	1	0	0	0	5
Mean Snowfall (in.)	9.1	6.1	4.1	0.7	0.0	0.0	0.0	0.0	0.0	trace	1.8	4.6	26.4
Days With ≥ 1.0" Snow Depth	12	10	3	0	0	0	0	0	0	0	1	5	31

Philipsburg Mid-State Airport *Centre County*   Elevation: 1,922 ft.   Latitude: 40° 54' N   Longitude: 78° 05' W

	JAN	FEB	MAR	APR	MAY	JUN	JUL	AUG	SEP	OCT	NOV	DEC	YEAR
Mean Maximum Temp. (°F)	29.7	33.7	43.5	56.5	67.0	74.2	78.2	76.3	68.8	57.5	46.1	34.8	55.5
Mean Temp. (°F)	22.3	25.1	34.2	45.6	55.6	63.3	67.6	65.9	58.6	48.0	38.6	27.8	46.1
Mean Minimum Temp. (°F)	14.9	16.5	24.9	34.6	44.1	52.2	56.9	55.4	48.4	38.6	31.1	20.5	36.5
Extreme Maximum Temp. (°F)	62	65	81	86	89	96	97	94	89	81	78	64	97
Extreme Minimum Temp. (°F)	-25	-20	-9	9	20	28	34	27	22	8	3	-16	-25
Days Maximum Temp. ≥ 90°F	0	0	0	0	0	0	1	0	0	0	0	0	1
Days Maximum Temp. ≤ 32°F	19	14	6	0	0	0	0	0	0	0	3	12	54
Days Minimum Temp. ≤ 32°F	29	25	24	14	4	0	0	0	2	8	18	27	151
Days Minimum Temp. ≤ 0°F	4	3	1	0	0	0	0	0	0	0	0	2	10
Heating Degree Days (base 65°F)	1,315	1,121	947	580	302	105	38	60	212	520	785	1,145	7,130
Cooling Degree Days (base 65°F)	0	0	0	3	16	56	130	92	27	1	0	0	325
Mean Precipitation (in.)	2.51	2.52	3.25	3.29	3.96	4.86	4.39	3.71	4.11	3.26	3.68	2.87	42.41
Days With ≥ 0.1" Precipitation	7	6	8	8	9	8	8	7	7	6	7	7	88
Days With ≥ 1.0" Precipitation	0	0	0	1	1	1	1	1	1	1	1	0	8
Mean Snowfall (in.)	11.5	14.4	10.6	1.4	trace	0.0	0.0	0.0	0.0	0.4	3.3	8.4	50.0
Days With ≥ 1.0" Snow Depth	21	18	11	1	0	0	0	0	0	0	3	12	66

Pleasant Mount 1 W *Wayne County*   Elevation: 1,797 ft.   Latitude: 41° 44' N   Longitude: 75° 27' W

	JAN	FEB	MAR	APR	MAY	JUN	JUL	AUG	SEP	OCT	NOV	DEC	YEAR
Mean Maximum Temp. (°F)	28.5	31.4	39.6	52.2	64.3	72.0	76.8	75.3	67.4	56.8	44.3	33.2	53.5
Mean Temp. (°F)	19.4	21.5	29.6	41.6	53.0	61.2	65.7	64.2	56.5	45.9	35.8	25.0	43.3
Mean Minimum Temp. (°F)	10.2	11.5	19.6	30.9	41.6	50.2	54.6	53.1	45.6	35.0	27.1	16.8	33.0
Extreme Maximum Temp. (°F)	60	67	79	86	89	90	95	90	88	82	75	65	95
Extreme Minimum Temp. (°F)	-25	-20	-12	4	19	30	33	33	22	12	0	-24	-25
Days Maximum Temp. ≥ 90°F	0	0	0	0	0	0	0	0	0	0	0	0	0
Days Maximum Temp. ≤ 32°F	20	15	9	1	0	0	0	0	0	0	4	15	64
Days Minimum Temp. ≤ 32°F	30	27	28	18	4	0	0	0	2	13	23	29	174
Days Minimum Temp. ≤ 0°F	7	5	1	0	0	0	0	0	0	0	0	3	16
Heating Degree Days (base 65°F)	1,408	1,222	1,090	696	373	145	56	79	265	586	871	1,232	8,023
Cooling Degree Days (base 65°F)	0	0	0	0	8	39	92	66	17	1	0	0	223
Mean Precipitation (in.)	3.34	2.85	3.42	4.11	4.84	4.81	4.33	4.20	4.49	4.18	4.36	3.64	48.57
Days With ≥ 0.1" Precipitation	7	6	7	8	9	9	8	8	8	7	8	8	93
Days With ≥ 1.0" Precipitation	1	0	1	1	1	1	1	1	1	1	1	1	11
Mean Snowfall (in.)	18.2	14.9	13.6	4.0	0.3	0.0	0.0	0.0	0.0	0.4	7.2	13.8	72.4
Days With ≥ 1.0" Snow Depth	27	25	21	5	0	0	0	0	0	0	6	18	102

Putneyville 2 SE Dam *Armstrong County*   Elevation: 1,279 ft.   Latitude: 40° 56' N   Longitude: 79° 17' W

	JAN	FEB	MAR	APR	MAY	JUN	JUL	AUG	SEP	OCT	NOV	DEC	YEAR
Mean Maximum Temp. (°F)	33.4	36.5	46.3	59.1	70.1	78.0	82.0	80.5	73.3	61.5	49.1	38.4	59.0
Mean Temp. (°F)	24.3	26.5	35.2	46.4	56.9	65.2	69.6	68.1	61.1	49.7	39.8	30.1	47.7
Mean Minimum Temp. (°F)	15.1	16.5	24.0	33.6	43.6	52.5	57.1	55.7	48.9	37.8	30.5	21.7	36.4
Extreme Maximum Temp. (°F)	68	73	84	90	90	98	103	99	94	86	80	73	103
Extreme Minimum Temp. (°F)	-28	-18	-8	11	23	30	36	33	28	15	3	-17	-28
Days Maximum Temp. ≥ 90°F	0	0	0	0	0	1	4	2	1	0	0	0	8
Days Maximum Temp. ≤ 32°F	15	11	4	0	0	0	0	0	0	0	2	9	41
Days Minimum Temp. ≤ 32°F	29	25	25	15	4	0	0	0	1	10	20	27	156
Days Minimum Temp. ≤ 0°F	5	4	1	0	0	0	0	0	0	0	0	1	11
Heating Degree Days (base 65°F)	1,255	1,080	920	557	271	76	21	32	160	471	749	1,076	6,668
Cooling Degree Days (base 65°F)	0	0	0	1	4	26	94	183	141	49	3	0	501
Mean Precipitation (in.)	3.11	2.72	3.71	3.58	4.01	4.52	4.65	4.15	4.01	3.06	3.75	3.40	44.67
Days With ≥ 0.1" Precipitation	8	7	9	8	9	9	8	7	8	7	8	8	96
Days With ≥ 1.0" Precipitation	0	0	1	1	1	1	1	1	1	1	1	1	10
Mean Snowfall (in.)	11.4	8.8	7.2	0.7	0.0	0.0	0.0	0.0	0.0	trace	1.9	6.7	36.7
Days With ≥ 1.0" Snow Depth	19	16	8	1	0	0	0	0	0	0	2	10	56

Raystown Lake 2 *Huntingdon County*   Elevation: 839 ft.   Latitude: 40° 26' N   Longitude: 78° 00' W

	JAN	FEB	MAR	APR	MAY	JUN	JUL	AUG	SEP	OCT	NOV	DEC	YEAR
Mean Maximum Temp. (°F)	34.8	39.1	47.9	60.4	71.0	79.2	83.5	82.3	74.6	63.3	51.2	40.0	60.6
Mean Temp. (°F)	26.4	29.6	37.4	48.8	58.9	67.2	71.9	70.5	63.0	51.6	41.8	32.0	49.9
Mean Minimum Temp. (°F)	17.9	20.0	26.8	37.0	46.6	55.1	60.3	58.7	51.4	39.9	32.4	23.9	39.2
Extreme Maximum Temp. (°F)	66	79	84	91	93	94	104	99	96	89	81	72	104
Extreme Minimum Temp. (°F)	-15	-12	0	15	25	33	42	37	29	20	10	-7	-15
Days Maximum Temp. ≥ 90°F	0	0	0	0	0	2	6	4	1	0	0	0	13
Days Maximum Temp. ≤ 32°F	12	8	3	0	0	0	0	0	0	0	1	6	30
Days Minimum Temp. ≤ 32°F	28	24	23	10	1	0	0	0	0	6	16	26	134
Days Minimum Temp. ≤ 0°F	2	1	0	0	0	0	0	0	0	0	0	0	3
Heating Degree Days (base 65°F)	1,190	994	850	487	217	48	7	14	118	412	689	1,018	6,044
Cooling Degree Days (base 65°F)	0	0	1	4	30	124	238	190	69	6	0	0	662
Mean Precipitation (in.)	2.70	2.10	3.32	3.17	3.98	3.67	3.38	3.18	3.35	3.24	3.28	2.54	37.91
Days With ≥ 0.1" Precipitation	6	5	7	7	8	7	7	6	7	5	6	5	76
Days With ≥ 1.0" Precipitation	0	0	1	0	1	1	1	1	1	1	1	0	8
Mean Snowfall (in.)	na	na	na	0.6	0.0	0.0	0.0	0.0	0.0	trace	1.0	na	na
Days With ≥ 1.0" Snow Depth	na	na	na	0	0	0	0	0	0	0	0	na	na

Reading 4 NNW *Berks County*   Elevation: 357 ft.   Latitude: 40° 25' N   Longitude: 75° 56' W

	JAN	FEB	MAR	APR	MAY	JUN	JUL	AUG	SEP	OCT	NOV	DEC	YEAR
Mean Maximum Temp. (°F)	37.1	40.7	50.2	61.9	72.6	80.7	85.3	83.7	76.1	65.0	53.6	41.8	62.4
Mean Temp. (°F)	28.3	30.9	39.9	50.5	61.0	69.8	74.6	72.9	64.9	53.2	43.8	33.4	52.0
Mean Minimum Temp. (°F)	19.5	21.1	29.5	39.1	49.5	58.8	63.8	62.1	53.7	41.4	34.0	24.9	41.4
Extreme Maximum Temp. (°F)	69	77	88	97	96	97	102	102	100	92	82	77	102
Extreme Minimum Temp. (°F)	-20	-8	-2	16	26	39	46	42	30	20	8	-4	-20
Days Maximum Temp. ≥ 90°F	0	0	0	0	1	3	9	5	1	0	0	0	19
Days Maximum Temp. ≤ 32°F	10	6	1	0	0	0	0	0	0	0	0	5	22
Days Minimum Temp. ≤ 32°F	28	24	20	6	0	0	0	0	0	5	14	25	122
Days Minimum Temp. ≤ 0°F	2	1	0	0	0	0	0	0	0	0	0	0	3
Heating Degree Days (base 65°F)	1,131	956	772	436	168	28	4	8	88	368	629	973	5,561
Cooling Degree Days (base 65°F)	0	0	2	7	56	183	321	257	98	12	1	0	937
Mean Precipitation (in.)	3.83	2.65	3.65	3.78	4.45	4.19	4.13	3.67	4.39	3.29	3.39	3.29	44.71
Days With ≥ 0.1" Precipitation	6	6	7	7	9	8	7	6	6	6	6	6	80
Days With ≥ 1.0" Precipitation	1	0	1	1	1	1	1	1	1	1	1	1	11
Mean Snowfall (in.)	na	na	na	trace	0.0	0.0	0.0	0.0	0.0	trace	0.5	na	na
Days With ≥ 1.0" Snow Depth	na	na	na	0	0	0	0	0	0	0	0	na	na

Ridgway *Elk County*   Elevation: 1,358 ft.   Latitude: 41° 25' N   Longitude: 78° 45' W

	JAN	FEB	MAR	APR	MAY	JUN	JUL	AUG	SEP	OCT	NOV	DEC	YEAR
Mean Maximum Temp. (°F)	31.9	35.1	44.4	57.0	68.5	75.9	79.8	78.4	71.4	60.4	47.6	36.8	57.3
Mean Temp. (°F)	22.5	24.5	32.9	43.9	54.4	62.6	66.9	65.7	58.9	47.9	38.2	28.4	45.6
Mean Minimum Temp. (°F)	13.0	13.9	21.4	30.8	40.2	49.1	53.9	52.8	46.3	35.5	28.7	19.9	33.8
Extreme Maximum Temp. (°F)	67	69	80	88	94	92	95	94	89	83	77	73	95
Extreme Minimum Temp. (°F)	-31	-25	-14	3	20	27	34	26	26	13	3	-16	-31
Days Maximum Temp. ≥ 90°F	0	0	0	0	0	0	1	1	0	0	0	0	2
Days Maximum Temp. ≤ 32°F	16	12	5	0	0	0	0	0	0	0	2	10	45
Days Minimum Temp. ≤ 32°F	29	26	26	19	7	1	0	0	2	13	21	27	171
Days Minimum Temp. ≤ 0°F	6	5	1	0	0	0	0	0	0	0	0	2	14
Heating Degree Days (base 65°F)	1,311	1,137	987	627	335	118	42	56	205	522	797	1,128	7,265
Cooling Degree Days (base 65°F)	0	0	0	1	11	50	108	80	23	1	0	0	274
Mean Precipitation (in.)	2.77	2.34	3.27	3.54	4.18	4.98	4.72	4.06	3.91	3.25	3.68	3.07	43.77
Days With ≥ 0.1" Precipitation	7	6	8	9	9	9	8	8	8	8	8	8	96
Days With ≥ 1.0" Precipitation	0	0	1	1	1	1	1	1	1	1	1	0	9
Mean Snowfall (in.)	15.0	13.0	8.6	1.6	trace	0.0	0.0	0.0	0.0	trace	3.6	11.4	53.2
Days With ≥ 1.0" Snow Depth	22	20	10	1	0	0	0	0	0	0	4	14	71

Salina 3 W *Westmoreland County*   Elevation: 1,108 ft.   Latitude: 40° 31' N   Longitude: 79° 33' W

	JAN	FEB	MAR	APR	MAY	JUN	JUL	AUG	SEP	OCT	NOV	DEC	YEAR
Mean Maximum Temp. (°F)	36.2	39.8	49.7	62.0	72.1	79.9	83.6	82.0	75.5	64.0	51.8	41.5	61.5
Mean Temp. (°F)	26.7	29.2	37.9	48.6	58.5	66.7	70.9	69.2	62.9	51.5	41.8	32.3	49.7
Mean Minimum Temp. (°F)	17.2	18.7	26.3	35.2	45.0	53.5	58.4	56.5	50.3	39.0	31.7	23.1	37.9
Extreme Maximum Temp. (°F)	71	73	83	90	92	96	101	100	93	83	80	74	101
Extreme Minimum Temp. (°F)	-30	-21	-14	12	21	29	36	32	28	17	4	-20	-30
Days Maximum Temp. ≥ 90°F	0	0	0	0	0	2	5	3	1	0	0	0	11
Days Maximum Temp. ≤ 32°F	12	8	2	0	0	0	0	0	0	0	1	6	29
Days Minimum Temp. ≤ 32°F	28	25	23	13	3	0	0	0	1	9	17	25	144
Days Minimum Temp. ≤ 0°F	4	3	0	0	0	0	0	0	0	0	0	1	8
Heating Degree Days (base 65°F)	1,180	1,004	833	490	226	56	10	22	124	417	690	1,007	6,059
Cooling Degree Days (base 65°F)	0	0	0	4	26	111	199	145	57	4	0	0	546
Mean Precipitation (in.)	2.57	2.41	3.28	3.33	4.16	4.27	4.53	3.84	3.69	2.65	3.55	2.96	41.24
Days With ≥ 0.1" Precipitation	7	7	8	8	9	8	8	7	7	7	8	8	92
Days With ≥ 1.0" Precipitation	0	0	1	1	1	1	1	1	1	0	1	0	8
Mean Snowfall (in.)	10.3	7.6	4.6	0.5	trace	0.0	0.0	0.0	0.0	0.0	1.7	4.8	29.5
Days With ≥ 1.0" Snow Depth	15	12	5	0	0	0	0	0	0	0	1	7	40

Selinsgrove 2 S *Snyder County*   Elevation: 419 ft.   Latitude: 40° 46' N   Longitude: 76° 52' W

	JAN	FEB	MAR	APR	MAY	JUN	JUL	AUG	SEP	OCT	NOV	DEC	YEAR
Mean Maximum Temp. (°F)	34.4	38.3	47.8	60.5	71.4	79.8	84.1	81.9	74.4	62.7	50.7	39.5	60.4
Mean Temp. (°F)	26.0	28.8	37.4	48.9	59.3	68.1	72.7	70.6	63.1	51.2	41.3	31.4	49.9
Mean Minimum Temp. (°F)	17.4	19.2	27.1	37.3	47.1	56.4	61.3	59.2	51.7	39.7	31.8	23.3	39.3
Extreme Maximum Temp. (°F)	65	77	87	91	96	97	105	97	96	88	80	73	105
Extreme Minimum Temp. (°F)	-26	-14	-3	15	25	36	42	35	31	16	4	-10	-26
Days Maximum Temp. ≥ 90°F	0	0	0	0	1	2	7	3	1	0	0	0	14
Days Maximum Temp. ≤ 32°F	12	8	2	0	0	0	0	0	0	0	0	7	29
Days Minimum Temp. ≤ 32°F	29	25	23	9	1	0	0	0	0	7	17	25	136
Days Minimum Temp. ≤ 0°F	2	2	0	0	0	0	0	0	0	0	0	1	5
Heating Degree Days (base 65°F)	1,203	1,016	848	481	209	40	7	16	118	426	705	1,034	6,103
Cooling Degree Days (base 65°F)	0	0	1	4	36	143	264	196	68	6	0	0	718
Mean Precipitation (in.)	3.16	2.40	3.21	3.70	3.82	4.17	3.76	3.87	3.79	3.38	3.56	2.79	41.61
Days With ≥ 0.1" Precipitation	7	6	7	8	8	7	7	6	6	6	6	6	80
Days With ≥ 1.0" Precipitation	1	0	1	1	1	1	1	1	1	1	1	1	11
Mean Snowfall (in.)	11.8	7.7	6.1	0.7	trace	0.0	0.0	0.0	0.0	trace	1.7	3.9	31.9
Days With ≥ 1.0" Snow Depth	14	12	6	0	0	0	0	0	0	0	1	5	38

Shippensburg *Cumberland County*   Elevation: 679 ft.   Latitude: 40° 03' N   Longitude: 77° 31' W

	JAN	FEB	MAR	APR	MAY	JUN	JUL	AUG	SEP	OCT	NOV	DEC	YEAR
Mean Maximum Temp. (°F)	36.0	40.2	50.1	62.4	72.8	80.8	85.3	83.5	76.1	64.7	51.9	41.0	62.1
Mean Temp. (°F)	28.5	31.7	40.3	51.3	61.6	70.0	74.5	72.7	65.5	54.0	43.3	33.7	52.3
Mean Minimum Temp. (°F)	21.0	23.2	30.6	40.3	50.4	59.1	63.6	61.8	54.8	43.3	34.7	26.4	42.4
Extreme Maximum Temp. (°F)	69	79	87	94	97	99	104	102	98	88	80	75	104
Extreme Minimum Temp. (°F)	-16	-9	3	15	28	39	47	38	29	20	9	-6	-16
Days Maximum Temp. ≥ 90°F	0	0	0	0	1	3	8	5	1	0	0	0	18
Days Maximum Temp. ≤ 32°F	12	7	2	0	0	0	0	0	0	0	1	6	28
Days Minimum Temp. ≤ 32°F	27	23	19	5	0	0	0	0	0	3	13	24	114
Days Minimum Temp. ≤ 0°F	1	0	0	0	0	0	0	0	0	0	0	0	1
Heating Degree Days (base 65°F)	1,124	933	759	413	156	26	3	7	80	345	645	963	5,454
Cooling Degree Days (base 65°F)	0	0	2	9	61	192	329	258	98	12	0	0	961
Mean Precipitation (in.)	3.11	2.65	3.62	3.38	3.77	3.77	3.64	3.00	3.65	2.95	3.39	3.03	39.96
Days With ≥ 0.1" Precipitation	7	6	7	7	7	7	7	6	6	5	6	6	77
Days With ≥ 1.0" Precipitation	1	0	1	1	1	1	1	1	1	1	1	1	11
Mean Snowfall (in.)	11.3	9.2	7.3	0.8	0.0	0.0	0.0	0.0	0.0	trace	2.3	4.7	35.6
Days With ≥ 1.0" Snow Depth	15	11	5	0	0	0	0	0	0	0	1	5	37

Slippery Rock 1 SSW *Butler County*   Elevation: 1,250 ft.   Latitude: 41° 03' N   Longitude: 80° 04' W

	JAN	FEB	MAR	APR	MAY	JUN	JUL	AUG	SEP	OCT	NOV	DEC	YEAR
Mean Maximum Temp. (°F)	33.5	37.2	46.9	59.0	70.2	78.1	82.1	80.9	74.2	62.5	49.9	38.9	59.5
Mean Temp. (°F)	23.8	26.6	35.3	45.8	56.4	64.7	68.8	67.3	60.9	49.5	39.6	29.8	47.4
Mean Minimum Temp. (°F)	13.9	16.0	23.6	32.6	42.5	51.2	55.4	53.8	47.6	36.5	29.3	20.7	35.2
Extreme Maximum Temp. (°F)	68	70	82	88	92	97	102	97	92	84	78	74	102
Extreme Minimum Temp. (°F)	-28	-21	-10	9	22	30	37	28	27	12	3	-20	-28
Days Maximum Temp. ≥ 90°F	0	0	0	0	0	1	3	2	0	0	0	0	6
Days Maximum Temp. ≤ 32°F	15	10	4	0	0	0	0	0	0	0	2	8	39
Days Minimum Temp. ≤ 32°F	29	25	25	16	5	0	0	0	1	11	20	27	159
Days Minimum Temp. ≤ 0°F	6	4	1	0	0	0	0	0	0	0	0	2	13
Heating Degree Days (base 65°F)	1,272	1,078	915	571	281	85	25	38	163	475	755	1,084	6,742
Cooling Degree Days (base 65°F)	0	0	1	2	19	84	161	124	47	2	0	0	440
Mean Precipitation (in.)	2.70	2.31	3.44	3.41	3.86	4.70	4.48	4.01	3.88	3.02	3.54	3.12	42.47
Days With ≥ 0.1" Precipitation	7	7	8	8	9	9	8	7	7	7	8	8	93
Days With ≥ 1.0" Precipitation	0	0	1	1	0	1	1	1	1	0	1	1	8
Mean Snowfall (in.)	12.6	8.9	7.1	1.1	trace	0.0	0.0	0.0	0.0	trace	2.7	8.7	41.1
Days With ≥ 1.0" Snow Depth	19	14	7	1	0	0	0	0	0	0	2	10	53

State College *Centre County*   Elevation: 1,167 ft.   Latitude: 40° 48' N   Longitude: 77° 52' W

	JAN	FEB	MAR	APR	MAY	JUN	JUL	AUG	SEP	OCT	NOV	DEC	YEAR
Mean Maximum Temp. (°F)	32.7	36.7	45.9	58.8	69.8	77.6	81.7	80.2	72.7	60.9	48.9	38.2	58.7
Mean Temp. (°F)	25.1	28.1	36.3	48.1	58.9	67.1	71.3	69.7	62.4	50.7	40.7	31.0	49.1
Mean Minimum Temp. (°F)	17.4	19.4	26.7	37.3	47.8	56.5	60.9	59.1	52.0	40.3	32.3	23.7	39.5
Extreme Maximum Temp. (°F)	66	73	84	94	93	94	102	97	93	86	80	71	102
Extreme Minimum Temp. (°F)	-18	-10	-1	11	29	35	44	36	30	16	10	-11	-18
Days Maximum Temp. ≥ 90°F	0	0	0	0	0	1	3	2	0	0	0	0	6
Days Maximum Temp. ≤ 32°F	15	10	4	0	0	0	0	0	0	0	1	8	38
Days Minimum Temp. ≤ 32°F	28	25	23	9	0	0	0	0	0	5	16	26	132
Days Minimum Temp. ≤ 0°F	2	1	0	0	0	0	0	0	0	0	0	1	4
Heating Degree Days (base 65°F)	1,230	1,037	883	512	225	53	10	20	133	443	726	1,047	6,319
Cooling Degree Days (base 65°F)	0	0	1	6	35	122	220	166	55	5	0	0	610
Mean Precipitation (in.)	2.85	2.61	3.39	3.17	3.61	4.26	3.66	3.35	3.56	2.97	3.50	2.87	39.80
Days With ≥ 0.1" Precipitation	7	6	7	7	8	8	8	6	7	6	7	6	83
Days With ≥ 1.0" Precipitation	1	0	1	0	1	1	1	1	1	1	1	0	9
Mean Snowfall (in.)	14.0	11.7	11.0	1.4	trace	0.0	0.0	0.0	0.0	0.1	3.2	7.4	48.8
Days With ≥ 1.0" Snow Depth	19	15	8	1	0	0	0	0	0	0	2	8	53

Stevenson Dam *Cameron County*   Elevation: 931 ft.   Latitude: 41° 24' N   Longitude: 78° 01' W

	JAN	FEB	MAR	APR	MAY	JUN	JUL	AUG	SEP	OCT	NOV	DEC	YEAR
Mean Maximum Temp. (°F)	33.1	36.8	46.2	58.8	70.5	78.5	82.3	81.2	73.4	62.1	49.2	37.9	59.2
Mean Temp. (°F)	24.1	26.3	35.0	46.1	56.9	65.6	70.0	69.2	61.8	50.3	39.9	29.8	47.9
Mean Minimum Temp. (°F)	15.2	15.8	23.8	33.3	43.2	52.7	57.7	57.2	50.2	38.4	30.5	21.7	36.7
Extreme Maximum Temp. (°F)	67	69	83	90	93	95	101	99	95	87	79	71	101
Extreme Minimum Temp. (°F)	-22	-18	-9	13	25	33	39	39	31	18	4	-13	-22
Days Maximum Temp. ≥ 90°F	0	0	0	0	0	1	4	2	0	0	0	0	7
Days Maximum Temp. ≤ 32°F	14	10	3	0	0	0	0	0	0	0	1	8	36
Days Minimum Temp. ≤ 32°F	30	26	25	15	3	0	0	0	0	8	19	27	153
Days Minimum Temp. ≤ 0°F	4	4	1	0	0	0	0	0	0	0	0	1	10
Heating Degree Days (base 65°F)	1,261	1,085	922	565	269	67	14	19	141	452	746	1,084	6,625
Cooling Degree Days (base 65°F)	0	0	0	3	23	97	185	160	52	3	0	0	523
Mean Precipitation (in.)	2.54	2.46	3.31	3.26	3.78	4.60	4.31	3.95	4.02	3.31	3.79	2.97	42.30
Days With ≥ 0.1" Precipitation	7	6	8	8	9	9	9	7	8	7	7	7	92
Days With ≥ 1.0" Precipitation	0	0	1	1	0	1	1	1	1	1	1	0	8
Mean Snowfall (in.)	10.5	9.2	7.2	1.1	trace	0.0	0.0	0.0	0.0	trace	1.7	6.6	36.3
Days With ≥ 1.0" Snow Depth	21	17	9	1	0	0	0	0	0	0	2	10	60

Stroudsburg *Monroe County* Elevation: 459 ft. Latitude: 41° 01' N Longitude: 75° 11' W

	JAN	FEB	MAR	APR	MAY	JUN	JUL	AUG	SEP	OCT	NOV	DEC	YEAR
Mean Maximum Temp. (°F)	36.1	40.2	50.1	63.0	74.5	82.2	86.7	84.4	76.3	64.5	51.7	40.6	62.5
Mean Temp. (°F)	27.2	30.1	39.1	50.0	60.7	68.8	73.7	71.7	64.1	52.3	42.2	32.2	51.0
Mean Minimum Temp. (°F)	18.2	19.9	28.0	37.0	46.9	55.3	60.5	59.0	51.9	40.1	32.5	23.7	39.4
Extreme Maximum Temp. (°F)	65	71	87	96	97	97	102	98	99	86	80	72	102
Extreme Minimum Temp. (°F)	-19	-14	-4	13	27	34	41	36	28	17	6	-11	-19
Days Maximum Temp. ≥ 90°F	0	0	0	0	1	4	9	6	1	0	0	0	21
Days Maximum Temp. ≤ 32°F	11	6	1	0	0	0	0	0	0	0	0	6	24
Days Minimum Temp. ≤ 32°F	28	24	21	10	1	0	0	0	0	8	16	25	133
Days Minimum Temp. ≤ 0°F	2	1	0	0	0	0	0	0	0	0	0	1	4
Heating Degree Days (base 65°F)	1,166	981	797	450	169	29	3	9	103	392	678	1,010	5,787
Cooling Degree Days (base 65°F)	0	0	1	5	43	155	295	226	87	7	0	0	819
Mean Precipitation (in.)	3.81	2.99	3.79	3.97	4.92	4.28	4.53	4.34	4.99	4.07	4.33	3.88	49.90
Days With ≥ 0.1" Precipitation	7	6	7	7	9	8	7	7	7	6	7	7	85
Days With ≥ 1.0" Precipitation	1	1	1	1	1	1	1	1	2	1	1	1	13
Mean Snowfall (in.)	10.4	9.5	6.7	1.3	trace	0.0	0.0	0.0	0.0	trace	2.0	5.3	35.2
Days With ≥ 1.0" Snow Depth	19	14	5	0	0	0	0	0	0	0	1	7	46

Titusville Water Works *Crawford County* Elevation: 1,217 ft. Latitude: 41° 38' N Longitude: 79° 42' W

	JAN	FEB	MAR	APR	MAY	JUN	JUL	AUG	SEP	OCT	NOV	DEC	YEAR
Mean Maximum Temp. (°F)	31.8	34.9	44.2	56.6	68.7	76.9	80.9	79.2	72.0	60.9	47.7	36.6	57.5
Mean Temp. (°F)	22.5	24.4	33.1	44.1	55.3	64.0	68.2	66.4	59.6	48.6	38.5	28.3	46.1
Mean Minimum Temp. (°F)	13.1	14.0	21.9	31.6	41.8	51.1	55.3	53.6	47.1	36.3	29.2	19.9	34.6
Extreme Maximum Temp. (°F)	66	69	81	88	91	94	100	96	90	87	78	72	100
Extreme Minimum Temp. (°F)	-31	-20	-18	4	19	30	36	32	23	14	0	-16	-31
Days Maximum Temp. ≥ 90°F	0	0	0	0	0	0	2	1	0	0	0	0	3
Days Maximum Temp. ≤ 32°F	16	13	6	1	0	0	0	0	0	0	2	10	48
Days Minimum Temp. ≤ 32°F	30	26	26	18	5	0	0	0	1	11	21	27	165
Days Minimum Temp. ≤ 0°F	5	5	1	0	0	0	0	0	0	0	0	2	13
Heating Degree Days (base 65°F)	1,311	1,140	983	623	311	98	33	49	193	501	790	1,132	7,164
Cooling Degree Days (base 65°F)	0	0	0	2	19	79	149	104	36	1	0	0	390
Mean Precipitation (in.)	2.51	2.38	3.17	3.74	4.01	4.74	4.42	4.28	4.65	3.62	3.90	3.22	44.64
Days With ≥ 0.1" Precipitation	7	7	8	9	9	9	8	8	8	8	9	9	99
Days With ≥ 1.0" Precipitation	0	0	0	0	1	1	1	1	1	1	0	0	6
Mean Snowfall (in.)	18.3	14.3	12.0	3.0	trace	0.0	0.0	0.0	0.0	0.5	7.8	18.1	74.0
Days With ≥ 1.0" Snow Depth	24	21	11	2	0	0	0	0	0	0	5	17	80

Tobyhanna *Monroe County* Elevation: 1,948 ft. Latitude: 41° 11' N Longitude: 75° 25' W

	JAN	FEB	MAR	APR	MAY	JUN	JUL	AUG	SEP	OCT	NOV	DEC	YEAR
Mean Maximum Temp. (°F)	30.8	34.0	42.6	54.7	66.7	73.7	78.2	76.7	68.9	58.1	46.4	36.1	55.6
Mean Temp. (°F)	22.1	24.4	32.7	43.8	54.7	62.3	67.0	65.7	58.3	47.5	37.8	28.1	45.4
Mean Minimum Temp. (°F)	13.3	14.8	22.8	32.7	42.8	50.7	55.8	54.7	47.6	37.0	29.2	20.0	35.1
Extreme Maximum Temp. (°F)	61	65	81	88	87	88	94	92	89	81	77	66	94
Extreme Minimum Temp. (°F)	-26	-20	-14	8	22	29	35	31	23	16	2	-20	-26
Days Maximum Temp. ≥ 90°F	0	0	0	0	0	0	1	0	0	0	0	0	1
Days Maximum Temp. ≤ 32°F	16	13	6	0	0	0	0	0	0	0	2	12	49
Days Minimum Temp. ≤ 32°F	28	26	26	16	4	0	0	0	2	11	20	27	160
Days Minimum Temp. ≤ 0°F	4	3	1	0	0	0	0	0	0	0	0	2	10
Heating Degree Days (base 65°F)	1,324	1,142	997	632	321	121	39	56	220	535	809	1,138	7,334
Cooling Degree Days (base 65°F)	0	0	0	1	9	45	113	80	22	1	0	0	271
Mean Precipitation (in.)	3.99	3.48	4.16	4.48	4.76	4.43	4.03	4.01	4.88	3.90	4.35	3.57	50.04
Days With ≥ 0.1" Precipitation	6	6	7	8	8	8	7	6	7	6	6	6	81
Days With ≥ 1.0" Precipitation	1	1	1	1	1	1	1	1	1	1	1	1	12
Mean Snowfall (in.)	15.9	14.8	13.6	5.0	0.4	0.0	0.0	0.0	trace	0.4	4.3	12.0	66.4
Days With ≥ 1.0" Snow Depth	21	19	13	3	0	0	0	0	0	0	3	14	73

Towanda 1 ESE *Bradford County* Elevation: 748 ft. Latitude: 41° 45' N Longitude: 76° 26' W

	JAN	FEB	MAR	APR	MAY	JUN	JUL	AUG	SEP	OCT	NOV	DEC	YEAR
Mean Maximum Temp. (°F)	33.7	36.8	46.1	59.0	70.5	78.3	82.6	80.9	73.1	62.0	49.4	38.6	59.2
Mean Temp. (°F)	24.7	27.0	35.9	47.2	58.0	66.3	70.9	69.2	61.7	50.6	40.5	30.7	48.6
Mean Minimum Temp. (°F)	15.7	17.1	25.6	35.3	45.4	54.4	59.1	57.5	50.3	39.2	31.5	22.7	37.8
Extreme Maximum Temp. (°F)	67	68	85	90	96	99	102	98	95	88	81	70	102
Extreme Minimum Temp. (°F)	-27	-23	-5	13	26	34	43	35	29	18	5	-17	-27
Days Maximum Temp. ≥ 90°F	0	0	0	0	0	1	4	2	1	0	0	0	8
Days Maximum Temp. ≤ 32°F	14	10	3	0	0	0	0	0	0	0	1	7	35
Days Minimum Temp. ≤ 32°F	29	25	23	13	2	0	0	0	0	8	17	26	143
Days Minimum Temp. ≤ 0°F	4	3	1	0	0	0	0	0	0	0	0	1	9
Heating Degree Days (base 65°F)	1,242	1,067	897	533	239	59	12	22	145	441	729	1,058	6,444
Cooling Degree Days (base 65°F)	0	0	0	3	26	109	208	157	53	3	0	0	559
Mean Precipitation (in.)	2.08	2.10	2.59	3.07	3.18	3.67	3.26	2.95	3.40	2.75	2.93	2.38	34.36
Days With ≥ 0.1" Precipitation	5	5	6	7	7	8	7	6	6	5	6	6	74
Days With ≥ 1.0" Precipitation	0	0	1	1	1	1	1	1	1	1	1	0	8
Mean Snowfall (in.)	11.0	9.6	8.2	1.6	trace	0.0	0.0	0.0	0.0	0.2	2.8	6.8	40.2
Days With ≥ 1.0" Snow Depth	18	17	9	1	0	0	0	0	0	0	2	9	56

Uniontown 1 NE *Fayette County*   Elevation: 954 ft.   Latitude: 39° 55' N   Longitude: 79° 43' W

	JAN	FEB	MAR	APR	MAY	JUN	JUL	AUG	SEP	OCT	NOV	DEC	YEAR
Mean Maximum Temp. (°F)	38.7	41.5	51.6	62.3	72.5	80.4	84.2	82.7	76.5	64.8	53.6	43.4	62.7
Mean Temp. (°F)	29.3	31.2	39.8	49.3	59.5	67.9	72.2	70.6	64.0	52.0	42.7	34.1	51.1
Mean Minimum Temp. (°F)	19.7	20.8	27.9	36.3	46.5	55.4	60.2	58.4	51.4	39.2	31.8	24.7	39.4
Extreme Maximum Temp. (°F)	73	75	84	93	92	96	102	99	96	87	80	77	102
Extreme Minimum Temp. (°F)	-22	-16	-3	15	23	33	37	34	29	16	8	-14	-22
Days Maximum Temp. ≥ 90°F	0	0	0	0	0	2	6	4	1	0	0	0	13
Days Maximum Temp. ≤ 32°F	10	7	2	0	0	0	0	0	0	0	1	6	26
Days Minimum Temp. ≤ 32°F	26	23	21	12	2	0	0	0	0	8	17	24	133
Days Minimum Temp. ≤ 0°F	2	2	0	0	0	0	0	0	0	0	0	1	5
Heating Degree Days (base 65°F)	1,100	948	775	471	204	47	7	16	107	401	663	952	5,691
Cooling Degree Days (base 65°F)	0	0	1	6	37	134	244	190	76	7	0	0	695
Mean Precipitation (in.)	2.98	2.71	3.69	3.68	4.36	4.29	4.63	3.88	3.70	2.92	3.43	3.16	43.43
Days With ≥ 0.1" Precipitation	8	7	8	9	10	9	8	7	8	7	8	8	97
Days With ≥ 1.0" Precipitation	0	0	0	1	1	1	1	1	1	1	1	0	8
Mean Snowfall (in.)	na	na	na	0.4	trace	0.0	0.0	0.0	0.0	trace	*0.9*	na	na
Days With ≥ 1.0" Snow Depth	na	na	na	0	0	0	0	0	0	0	*1*	na	na

Warren *Warren County*   Elevation: 1,207 ft.   Latitude: 41° 51' N   Longitude: 79° 09' W

	JAN	FEB	MAR	APR	MAY	JUN	JUL	AUG	SEP	OCT	NOV	DEC	YEAR
Mean Maximum Temp. (°F)	32.2	35.7	45.0	58.1	70.0	78.2	82.1	80.2	72.7	61.0	48.0	37.1	58.4
Mean Temp. (°F)	24.2	26.2	34.4	45.9	57.0	65.6	70.0	68.6	61.5	50.3	39.8	29.8	47.8
Mean Minimum Temp. (°F)	16.1	16.6	23.7	33.7	43.9	53.0	57.9	56.9	50.2	39.4	31.6	22.5	37.1
Extreme Maximum Temp. (°F)	64	73	82	92	92	94	99	100	93	83	79	74	100
Extreme Minimum Temp. (°F)	-20	-34	-18	10	22	29	38	36	28	17	3	-12	-34
Days Maximum Temp. ≥ 90°F	0	0	0	0	0	2	4	2	0	0	0	0	8
Days Maximum Temp. ≤ 32°F	15	12	5	0	0	0	0	0	0	0	2	9	43
Days Minimum Temp. ≤ 32°F	29	26	25	15	3	0	0	0	0	7	17	26	148
Days Minimum Temp. ≤ 0°F	4	3	1	0	0	0	0	0	0	0	0	1	9
Heating Degree Days (base 65°F)	1,258	1,091	942	571	271	72	17	27	149	453	748	1,085	6,684
Cooling Degree Days (base 65°F)	0	0	0	4	27	100	188	150	50	3	0	0	522
Mean Precipitation (in.)	2.97	2.42	3.37	3.65	3.94	5.09	4.15	4.38	4.38	3.46	3.99	3.64	45.44
Days With ≥ 0.1" Precipitation	8	7	9	9	9	9	8	7	8	9	10	10	103
Days With ≥ 1.0" Precipitation	0	0	0	1	1	1	1	1	1	1	0	0	7
Mean Snowfall (in.)	17.3	12.1	9.9	1.9	trace	0.0	0.0	0.0	0.0	0.2	6.9	15.4	63.7
Days With ≥ 1.0" Snow Depth	22	20	10	1	0	0	0	0	0	0	4	15	72

Waynesburg 1 E *Greene County*   Elevation: 938 ft.   Latitude: 39° 54' N   Longitude: 80° 10' W

	JAN	FEB	MAR	APR	MAY	JUN	JUL	AUG	SEP	OCT	NOV	DEC	YEAR
Mean Maximum Temp. (°F)	37.8	41.3	51.3	62.4	72.2	80.0	83.7	82.3	76.3	65.1	53.5	42.8	62.4
Mean Temp. (°F)	27.8	30.3	39.0	48.8	58.7	67.1	71.3	69.9	63.2	51.4	42.0	33.1	50.2
Mean Minimum Temp. (°F)	17.8	19.3	26.7	35.1	45.1	54.2	58.8	57.5	50.2	37.7	30.4	23.4	38.0
Extreme Maximum Temp. (°F)	75	74	85	90	90	96	102	98	94	86	83	77	102
Extreme Minimum Temp. (°F)	-25	-15	-6	15	24	31	38	34	30	16	2	-16	-25
Days Maximum Temp. ≥ 90°F	0	0	0	0	0	1	5	3	1	0	0	0	10
Days Maximum Temp. ≤ 32°F	11	7	2	0	0	0	0	0	0	0	1	6	27
Days Minimum Temp. ≤ 32°F	28	24	23	13	2	0	0	0	0	10	19	25	144
Days Minimum Temp. ≤ 0°F	3	2	0	0	0	0	0	0	0	0	0	1	6
Heating Degree Days (base 65°F)	1,147	974	800	484	221	51	9	18	116	419	684	981	5,904
Cooling Degree Days (base 65°F)	0	0	1	5	31	126	226	177	67	5	0	0	638
Mean Precipitation (in.)	2.95	2.44	3.51	3.26	4.14	3.74	3.93	4.03	3.21	2.64	3.29	2.85	39.99
Days With ≥ 0.1" Precipitation	7	6	8	8	9	8	7	7	7	6	7	7	87
Days With ≥ 1.0" Precipitation	1	0	0	0	1	1	1	1	1	0	1	0	7
Mean Snowfall (in.)	11.2	6.4	6.1	1.0	trace	0.0	0.0	0.0	0.0	trace	1.7	4.2	30.6
Days With ≥ 1.0" Snow Depth	12	8	4	0	0	0	0	0	0	0	1	5	30

York 3 SSW Pumping Station *York County*   Elevation: 387 ft.   Latitude: 39° 55' N   Longitude: 76° 45' W

	JAN	FEB	MAR	APR	MAY	JUN	JUL	AUG	SEP	OCT	NOV	DEC	YEAR
Mean Maximum Temp. (°F)	39.3	43.7	53.5	65.3	75.2	82.8	86.9	85.2	78.3	67.4	54.9	44.0	64.7
Mean Temp. (°F)	30.0	33.2	41.9	52.0	62.1	70.4	74.9	73.1	66.3	54.8	44.4	35.1	53.2
Mean Minimum Temp. (°F)	20.6	22.6	30.4	38.7	48.9	57.9	62.7	61.0	54.2	42.1	33.8	26.1	41.6
Extreme Maximum Temp. (°F)	71	77	88	93	95	98	102	101	98	90	83	76	102
Extreme Minimum Temp. (°F)	-21	-16	-3	17	25	35	43	35	30	19	9	-3	-21
Days Maximum Temp. ≥ 90°F	0	0	0	0	1	5	10	6	2	0	0	0	24
Days Maximum Temp. ≤ 32°F	8	4	1	0	0	0	0	0	0	0	0	4	17
Days Minimum Temp. ≤ 32°F	27	23	19	8	1	0	0	0	0	6	15	23	122
Days Minimum Temp. ≤ 0°F	2	1	0	0	0	0	0	0	0	0	0	0	3
Heating Degree Days (base 65°F)	1,079	892	710	391	143	21	2	6	71	323	613	921	5,172
Cooling Degree Days (base 65°F)	0	0	2	8	60	198	331	263	114	15	0	0	991
Mean Precipitation (in.)	3.37	2.74	3.59	3.58	4.18	4.39	3.99	3.39	3.88	3.25	3.56	3.26	43.18
Days With ≥ 0.1" Precipitation	6	6	7	7	8	7	7	6	6	5	6	6	77
Days With ≥ 1.0" Precipitation	1	1	1	1	1	1	1	1	1	1	1	1	12
Mean Snowfall (in.)	8.9	8.3	3.8	0.4	0.0	0.0	0.0	0.0	0.0	trace	0.9	2.5	24.8
Days With ≥ 1.0" Snow Depth	10	*7*	1	0	0	0	0	0	0	0	0	1	2	*21*

Note: See Appendix D for explanation of data.

RHODE ISLAND

PHYSICAL FEATURES. Rhode Island, the smallest of the states, shares the southeastern corner of New England with a portion of Massachusetts. The State extends for 50 miles in a north-south direction and has an average width of about 30 miles. The total area, including Block Island some 10 miles offshore, is 1,497 square miles of which Narragansett Bay occupies about 25 percent. There are three topographical divisions of the State. A narrow coastal plain with an elevation of less than 100 feet occurs along the south shore and around Narragansett Bay. A second division with gently rolling uplands of up to 200 feet elevation lies to the north and east of the Bay. The western two-thirds of Rhode Island consists of predominantly hilly uplands of mostly 200 to 600 feet elevation, rising to a maximum of 800 feet above sea level in the northwest corner of the State.

Narragansett Bay has a very irregular shoreline, indented by numerous small bays or coves and the mouths of the Taunton and Blackstone Rivers. The Bay contains several islands of which the one known as Aquidneck, or Rhode Island, is the largest. The shore line facing Long Island Sound is about 20 miles long. No point in the State is more than 25 miles from the ocean. The Blackstone River in northeastern Rhode Island is the principal river. A number of smaller rivers or brooks originating in the western uplands of the State or in southeastern Massachusetts empty into Narragansett Bay or Long Island Sound.

GENERAL CLIMATE. The chief characteristics of Rhode Island's climate may be summarized as follows: (1) equable distribution of precipitation among the four seasons; (2) large ranges of temperature both daily and annual; (3) great differences in the same season of different years; and (4) considerable diversity of the weather over short periods of time. These characteristics are modified by nearness to the Bay or ocean, elevation, and nature of the terrain.

Rhode Island lies in the "prevailing westerlies," the belt of generally eastward air movement which encircles the globe in middle latitudes. Embedded in this circulation are extensive masses of air originating in higher and lower latitudes and interacting to produce storm systems. A large number of these systems and air-mass fronts pass near or over Rhode Island in a year.

Air masses affecting the State belong to three types: (1) cold, dry air pouring down from subarctic North America; (2) warm, moist air streaming up on a long overland journey from the Gulf of Mexico and adjacent waters; and (3) cool, damp air moving from the North Atlantic. Because the atmospheric flow is usually from continental areas, Rhode Island is more influenced by the first two types than it is by the third. The ocean constitutes an important modifying factor, particularly in southeast sections of the State, but does not dominate the climate as it would if the prevailing circulation was onshore.

The procession of contrasting air masses and the relatively frequent passage of low-pressure systems bring about a roughly twice-weekly alternation from fair to cloudy or stormy weather, usually attended by abrupt changes in temperature, moisture, sunshine, wind direction, and speed. There is no regular or persistent rhythm to this sequence, and it is sometimes interrupted by periods of several days, or infrequently of a few weeks, with the same weather pattern.

TEMPERATURE. The mean annual temperature ranges from 48 to 49°F., except near the south shore, Narragansett Bay, and in the area around Providence, where it is 50 to 51°F. Southwestern Rhode Island, from four to 10 miles inland, exhibits a coolness not suggested by the nearness to the ocean or the general elevation of 50 to 150 feet. Here the annual mean temperature is not more than 48°F., making the section as cool as the cooler areas of the northwest interior.

The average daily minimum temperature in January and February is 19 to 20°F. over about two-thirds of the State, increasing to near 25°F. in immediate coastal sections. The number of days with minimum temperatures of zero or below averages one or less per year in the Bay and coastal areas, increasing to about five per year in most of the interior. A maximum temperature of 32°F. or lower occurs on an average of 20 to 25 days per year along the shoreline and 30 to 40 days in the remainder of the State. Summer temperatures are considerably influenced by proximity to the coastal waters and the frequent onshore flow of air during the warmer months. The average July maximum temperature is about 80°F., except in the northwestern interior where it is a few degrees higher. The greatest number of hot days occurs in the metropolitan areas and in parts of the northern interior. Here, about eight to 10 days of temperatures 90°F. or higher may be expected per year. Near the immediate coast the occurrence of 90°F. temperatures is limited to one day in the average summer, if it occurs at all. The length of the freeze-free season, as limited by the occurrence of temperatures of 32°F. or lower, averages from 155 to 180 days in most of the State. Climatic differences of temperature in this small State are very striking in the fall season. Autumnal coloration of foliage will be past its peak of brilliance in the northwestern interior before leaves have begun to noticeably turn color in the Newport area of the southeast.

PRECIPITATION. The climate of Rhode Island is characterized by the rather even distribution of precipitation throughout the year. Storm centers and their accompanying fronts are the principal year-round producers of precipitation. Storms moving up the Atlantic coast generally yield the heaviest amounts of rain and snow. Bands and patches of thunderstorms or convective showers contribute considerable precipitation in the summer and make up the difference resulting from decreased activity of the storm centers. In comparison with the general storms, these are of brief duration, but they yield the heaviest local rainfall.

Annual precipitation averages 42 to 46 inches over most of the State, with a tendency for decreasing amounts from west to east. It varies from about 40 inches in the immediate southeastern Bay area and on Block Island to 48 inches in the western uplands. Total precipitation in the freeze-free season of April through October shows similar differences over the State with an average of 22 to 24 inches near the Bay and 26 to 29 inches in the western interior. While there are no pronounced wet and dry months as in other climates, the months of May through July are relatively dry in proximity of the Bay. Measurable precipitation falls on an average of one day in three or on approximately 120 days per year. Periods of five days or more of successive daily precipitation occur a few times during most years. Extended periods of little or no precipitation are observed nearly every summer or early fall. Such a period may last from 10 to 20 days.

SNOWFALL. The average annual snowfall in Rhode Island increases from about 20 inches on Block Island and along the southeast shores of Narragansett Bay to from 40 to 55 inches in the western third of the State. Most of the snow falls in January and February; however, there are occasional winters when in coastal sections particularly, heavier monthly amounts will occur in December or March. In the western and northern portions of the State the first snowfall of one inch or more usually occurs in mid or late November. The southeastern Bay area does not observe measurable snow before December in the great majority of years. The last measurable snowfall usually occurs by late March in the populous areas of the State, although an April snowstorm is by no means rare. The average number of days with one inch or more of snow on the ground also increases from the shore areas to the western interior. In the latter, a snowcover prevails most of the time from mid or late December to about mid-March. Near the Bay a snow cover does not last more than a few days unless a heavy snowstorm is followed by prolonged cold temperatures.

WINDS AND STORMS. The prevailing wind in Rhode Island is northwesterly from December through March, and southwesterly in the remaining months. An important feature of the climate is the sea breeze which affects a considerable portion of the State's area. From approximately late spring to mid autumn this cool onshore wind blows during the afternoon hours and penetrates from five to 10 miles inland. The fact that much of Rhode Island is within 10 miles of the Sound or Bay, accounts for the relatively cool summer maximum temperatures. Aside from hurricanes, coastal storms or "northeasters" are the most serious weather hazard in Rhode Island. They generate very strong winds and heavy rains, and produce the greatest snowfalls in the winter. Hurricanes or storms of tropical origin occasionally affect the State during the summer or fall months. Localized thunderstorms with heavy and intense rainfall on occasions cause damaging flash floods in the small as well as the larger streams of the State.

OTHER CLIMATIC ELEMENTS. The percentage of possible sunshine averages 55 to 60 percent, ranging from about 50 percent in the winter months to a little over 60 percent during the summer. The average number of clear and cloudy days per year are about equal. The highest number of clear days per month usually occurs in September or October, while the maximum number of cloudy days are noted in December and January. Heavy fog is observed on an average of about 50 days per year in the southeastern areas of the Bay. This number decreases to 30 or 35 along the western and northern shores of the Bay, and to about 25 days in the western interior.

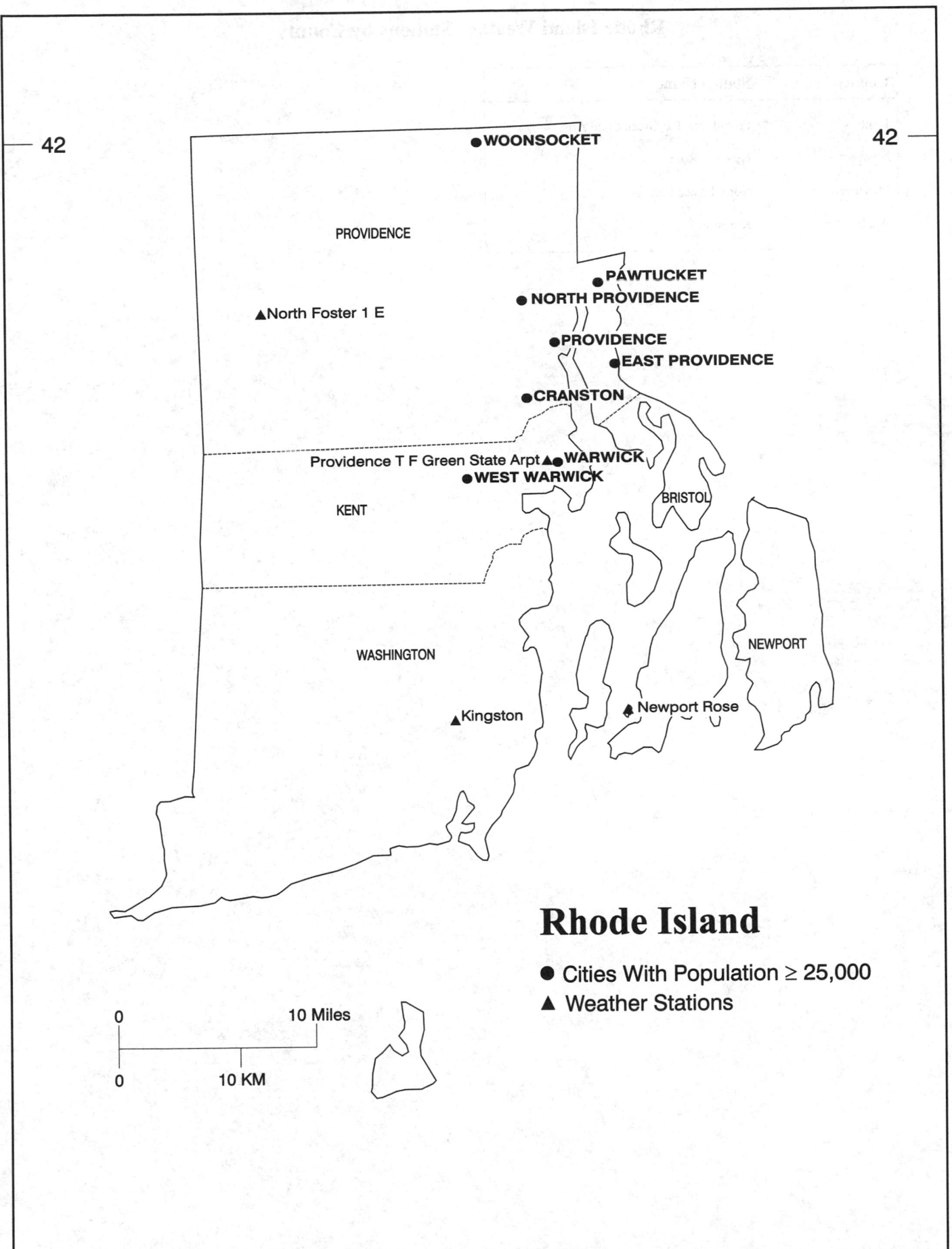

Rhode Island

● Cities With Population ≥ 25,000
▲ Weather Stations

Rhode Island Weather Stations by County

County	Station Name
Kent	Providence T F Green State Arpt.
Newport	Newport Rose
Providence	North Foster 1 E
Washington	Kingston

Rhode Island Weather Stations by City

City	Station Name	Miles
Cranston	Newport Rose	20
	North Foster 1 E	15
	Providence T F Green State Arpt.	4
East Providence	Taunton, MA	17
	North Foster 1 E	19
	Providence T F Green State Arpt.	7
North Providence	West Medway, MA	19
	North Foster 1 E	14
	Providence T F Green State Arpt.	10
Pawtucket	Taunton, MA	16
	West Medway, MA	18
	North Foster 1 E	18
	Providence T F Green State Arpt.	11
Providence	Taunton, MA	19
	North Foster 1 E	16
	Providence T F Green State Arpt.	7
Warwick	Kingston	17
	Newport Rose	15
	North Foster 1 E	19
	Providence T F Green State Arpt.	1
West Warwick	Kingston	15
	Newport Rose	16
	North Foster 1 E	15
	Providence T F Green State Arpt.	4
Woonsocket	Walpole 2, MA	17
	West Medway, MA	10
	North Foster 1 E	16

Note: Miles is the distance between the geographic center of the city and the weather station.

Rhode Island Weather Stations by Elevation

Feet	Station Name
629	North Foster 1 E
98	Kingston
49	Providence T F Green State Arpt.
13	Newport Rose

Providence T F Green State Arpt.

The proximity to Narragansett Bay and the Atlantic Ocean plays an important part in determining the climate for Providence and vicinity. In winter, the temperatures are modified considerably, and many major snowstorms change to rain before reaching the area. In summer, many days that could be uncomfortably warm are cooled by refreshing sea breezes. At other times of the year, sea fog may be advected in over land by onshore winds. In fact, most cases of dense fog are produced this way, but the number of such days is few, averaging two or three days per month. In early fall, severe coastal storms of tropical origin sometimes bring destructive winds to this area. Even at other times of the year, it is usually coastal storms which produce the severest weather.

The temperature for the entire year averages around 50 degrees with 70 degree temperatures common from near the end of May to the latter part of September. During this period, there may be several days reaching 90 degrees or more. Temperatures of 100 degrees and more are rare.

Freezing temperatures occur on the average about 125 days per year. They become a common daily occurrence in the latter part of November, and become less frequent near the end of March. The average date for the last freeze in spring is mid-April, while the average date for the first freeze in fall is late October, making the growing season about 195 days in length. Sub-zero weather in winter seldom occurs, averaging less than one day for December and one or two days each for January and February.

Measurable precipitation occurs on about one day out of every three, and is fairly evenly distributed throughout the year. There is usually no definite dry season, but occasionally droughts do occur.

Thunderstorms are responsible for much of the rainfall from May through August. They usually produce heavy, and sometimes even excessive amounts of rainfall. However, since their duration is relatively short, damage is ordinarily light. The thunderstorms of summer are frequently accompanied by extremely gusty winds.

The first measurable snowfall of winter usually comes toward the end of November, and the last in spring is about the middle of March. Winters with over 50 inches of snow are not common. The area normally receives less than 25 inches. The month of greatest snowfall is usually February, but January and March are close seconds. It is unusual for the ground to remain well covered with snow for any long period of time.

Providence T F Green State Arpt. *Kent County*   Elevation: 49 ft.   Latitude: 41° 43' N   Longitude: 71° 26' W

	JAN	FEB	MAR	APR	MAY	JUN	JUL	AUG	SEP	OCT	NOV	DEC	YEAR
Mean Maximum Temp. (°F)	36.8	39.2	47.3	58.2	68.5	77.2	82.7	81.1	73.5	63.0	52.5	42.1	60.2
Mean Temp. (°F)	28.4	30.8	38.6	48.6	58.7	67.6	73.5	72.0	64.0	53.1	43.8	33.8	51.1
Mean Minimum Temp. (°F)	20.0	22.3	29.8	39.1	48.8	57.9	64.2	62.8	54.6	43.1	35.1	25.6	41.9
Extreme Maximum Temp. (°F)	69	72	85	98	95	97	102	104	100	86	78	77	104
Extreme Minimum Temp. (°F)	-13	-7	4	18	30	41	48	41	33	20	6	-10	-13
Days Maximum Temp. ≥ 90°F	0	0	0	0	1	2	4	3	1	0	0	0	11
Days Maximum Temp. ≤ 32°F	11	7	1	0	0	0	0	0	0	0	0	5	24
Days Minimum Temp. ≤ 32°F	27	24	19	5	0	0	0	0	0	3	13	24	115
Days Minimum Temp. ≤ 0°F	1	1	0	0	0	0	0	0	0	0	0	0	2
Heating Degree Days (base 65°F)	1,127	960	813	487	215	42	3	8	97	369	628	958	5,707
Cooling Degree Days (base 65°F)	0	0	0	2	26	131	279	231	77	7	0	0	753
Mean Precipitation (in.)	4.24	3.53	4.41	4.12	3.64	3.36	3.08	4.04	3.64	3.80	4.42	4.15	46.43
Maximum Precipitation (in.)	11.7	7.2	8.8	12.7	10.6	11.1	8.1	11.1	7.9	11.9	11.0	10.8	67.5
Minimum Precipitation (in.)	0.5	0.4	0.6	1.5	0.7	0	0.3	0.7	0.8	0.4	0.8	0.6	25.4
Maximum 24-hr. Precipitation (in.)	2.9	2.6	3.1	4.3	5.1	3.0	4.8	6.3	4.7	5.4	3.5	3.5	6.3
Days With ≥ 0.1" Precipitation	7	6	8	7	7	6	5	6	6	6	7	8	79
Days With ≥ 1.0" Precipitation	1	1	1	1	1	1	1	1	1	1	1	1	12
Mean Snowfall (in.)	9.7	9.3	5.7	0.7	0.3	0.0	0.0	0.0	0.0	0.1	1.3	5.8	32.9
Maximum Snowfall (in.)	32	31	32	8	trace	0	0	0	0	3	8	20	71
Maximum 24-hr. Snowfall (in.)	10	18	15	7	trace	0	0	0	0	3	8	11	18
Days With ≥ 1.0" Snow Depth	11	9	3	0	0	0	0	0	0	0	1	5	29
Thunderstorm Days	< 1	< 1	1	1	3	4	4	4	2	1	1	< 1	21
Foggy Days	11	10	13	13	15	16	17	17	15	14	13	12	166
Predominant Sky Cover	OVR	OVR	OVR	OVR	OVR	OVR	OVR	OVR	OVR	OVR	OVR	OVR	OVR
Mean Relative Humidity 7am (%)	71	71	71	70	73	76	78	81	83	81	78	74	76
Mean Relative Humidity 4pm (%)	58	55	54	51	55	58	58	60	60	58	60	60	57
Mean Dewpoint (°F)	18	18	25	34	45	56	62	61	54	43	34	23	39
Prevailing Wind Direction	NW	NW	NW	NW	S	S	SW	SW	SW	N	NW	NW	WNW
Prevailing Wind Speed (mph)	13	13	13	13	10	9	10	9	10	10	12	13	12
Maximum Wind Gust (mph)	73	68	71	61	54	54	54	105	81	59	71	68	105

Kingston *Washington County*   Elevation: 98 ft.   Latitude: 41° 29' N   Longitude: 71° 32' W

	JAN	FEB	MAR	APR	MAY	JUN	JUL	AUG	SEP	OCT	NOV	DEC	YEAR
Mean Maximum Temp. (°F)	38.5	40.5	48.0	58.1	68.4	76.6	81.9	80.6	73.8	63.9	53.3	43.3	60.6
Mean Temp. (°F)	28.6	30.5	37.9	47.0	56.8	65.5	71.1	69.9	62.7	52.1	43.2	33.9	49.9
Mean Minimum Temp. (°F)	18.6	20.4	27.7	35.8	45.3	54.3	60.3	59.2	51.6	40.3	33.0	24.4	39.2
Extreme Maximum Temp. (°F)	64	67	79	89	95	94	98	100	92	85	78	73	100
Extreme Minimum Temp. (°F)	-21	-15	-1	15	26	34	41	34	28	16	-4	-12	-21
Days Maximum Temp. ≥ 90°F	0	0	0	0	0	1	3	1	0	0	0	0	5
Days Maximum Temp. ≤ 32°F	9	6	1	0	0	0	0	0	0	0	0	4	20
Days Minimum Temp. ≤ 32°F	27	24	22	11	2	0	0	0	1	8	16	24	135
Days Minimum Temp. ≤ 0°F	2	1	0	0	0	0	0	0	0	0	0	0	3
Heating Degree Days (base 65°F)	1,123	968	834	535	260	63	8	18	122	398	648	959	5,936
Cooling Degree Days (base 65°F)	0	0	0	0	13	89	212	178	60	5	0	0	557
Mean Precipitation (in.)	4.62	3.90	4.89	4.65	4.17	3.91	3.22	4.38	4.11	4.04	5.19	4.59	51.67
Days With ≥ 0.1" Precipitation	7	6	7	7	8	6	5	6	6	6	7	8	79
Days With ≥ 1.0" Precipitation	1	1	1	1	1	1	1	1	1	1	2	1	13
Mean Snowfall (in.)	9.3	8.5	4.4	1.1	trace	0.0	0.0	0.0	0.0	trace	0.8	4.9	29.0
Days With ≥ 1.0" Snow Depth	11	9	3	0	0	0	0	0	0	0	0	4	27

Newport Rose *Newport County*   Elevation: 13 ft.   Latitude: 41° 30' N   Longitude: 71° 21' W

	JAN	FEB	MAR	APR	MAY	JUN	JUL	AUG	SEP	OCT	NOV	DEC	YEAR
Mean Maximum Temp. (°F)	38.5	39.7	46.3	55.2	64.6	72.8	78.6	78.2	72.0	62.6	53.0	43.6	58.8
Mean Temp. (°F)	30.8	32.0	38.5	46.8	56.2	65.0	71.1	70.9	64.6	55.0	45.7	36.2	51.1
Mean Minimum Temp. (°F)	23.0	24.3	30.6	38.4	47.8	57.0	63.5	63.7	57.2	47.3	38.4	28.7	43.3
Extreme Maximum Temp. (°F)	60	65	78	86	88	93	96	98	93	80	75	69	98
Extreme Minimum Temp. (°F)	-9	-3	3	10	25	37	41	42	39	28	11	-5	-9
Days Maximum Temp. ≥ 90°F	0	0	0	0	0	0	1	0	0	0	0	0	1
Days Maximum Temp. ≤ 32°F	8	6	1	0	0	0	0	0	0	0	0	4	19
Days Minimum Temp. ≤ 32°F	25	22	18	5	0	0	0	0	0	0	7	20	97
Days Minimum Temp. ≤ 0°F	1	0	0	0	0	0	0	0	0	0	0	0	1
Heating Degree Days (base 65°F)	1,053	926	816	539	273	55	4	6	69	308	573	887	5,509
Cooling Degree Days (base 65°F)	0	0	0	0	7	65	203	197	66	5	0	0	543
Mean Precipitation (in.)	4.14	3.63	4.53	4.33	3.59	3.12	2.92	3.77	3.57	3.77	4.50	4.22	46.09
Days With ≥ 0.1" Precipitation	7	6	8	7	7	6	5	6	6	6	7	7	78
Days With ≥ 1.0" Precipitation	1	1	1	1	1	1	1	1	1	1	1	1	12
Mean Snowfall (in.)	7.0	na	3.6	0.8	0.0	0.0	0.0	0.0	0.0	0.0	0.6	2.8	na
Days With ≥ 1.0" Snow Depth	na	na	na	0	0	0	0	0	0	0	0	na	na

North Foster 1 E *Providence County*   Elevation: 629 ft.   Latitude: 41° 51' N   Longitude: 71° 44' W

	JAN	FEB	MAR	APR	MAY	JUN	JUL	AUG	SEP	OCT	NOV	DEC	YEAR
Mean Maximum Temp. (°F)	34.5	37.5	46.2	57.3	68.8	75.8	80.7	78.7	71.3	60.9	50.2	39.0	58.4
Mean Temp. (°F)	25.5	28.2	36.2	46.6	57.3	65.1	70.5	68.9	61.1	50.4	41.1	30.5	48.5
Mean Minimum Temp. (°F)	16.6	18.9	26.3	35.8	45.8	54.3	60.3	58.9	50.8	40.0	32.0	22.0	38.5
Extreme Maximum Temp. (°F)	64	68	88	93	93	94	97	97	94	84	78	75	97
Extreme Minimum Temp. (°F)	-13	-11	-1	14	27	38	42	39	33	21	4	-15	-15
Days Maximum Temp. ≥ 90°F	0	0	0	0	0	1	2	1	0	0	0	0	4
Days Maximum Temp. ≤ 32°F	14	9	3	0	0	0	0	0	0	0	1	8	35
Days Minimum Temp. ≤ 32°F	29	25	24	10	1	0	0	0	0	6	18	27	140
Days Minimum Temp. ≤ 0°F	2	1	0	0	0	0	0	0	0	0	0	1	4
Heating Degree Days (base 65°F)	1,217	1,032	886	549	252	74	11	25	154	447	710	1,065	6,422
Cooling Degree Days (base 65°F)	0	0	0	1	19	85	195	153	48	3	0	0	505
Mean Precipitation (in.)	5.25	3.87	5.12	4.43	3.80	3.86	3.79	4.64	4.01	4.79	4.95	4.39	52.90
Days With ≥ 0.1" Precipitation	8	6	8	7	7	7	6	6	6	7	7	8	83
Days With ≥ 1.0" Precipitation	2	1	1	1	1	1	1	2	1	2	1	1	15
Mean Snowfall (in.)	14.4	12.2	10.6	3.6	0.5	0.0	0.0	0.0	0.0	0.2	3.0	11.0	55.5
Days With ≥ 1.0" Snow Depth	17	15	9	1	0	0	0	0	0	0	2	11	55

Note: See Appendix D for explanation of data.

SOUTH CAROLINA

PHYSICAL FEATURES. South Carolina is located on the southeastern coast of the United States between the southern part of the Appalachian Mountains and the Atlantic Ocean. Its north-south extent is 220 miles, from 32° to 35.2° N. latitude. The mountains in the extreme northwestern part of the State are 240 miles from the coastline. The coastline is 185 miles long and oriented southwest to northeast.

South Carolina shares some common topographic features with several eastern seaboard states. All of these features have a southwest to northeast orientation and extend across the whole State. The Blue Ridge Range of the Appalachian Mountains lies in the extreme northwestern part of the State. Elevations range from 1,000 to 2,000 feet with several peaks going over 3,000 feet. Sassafras Mountain, at 3,554 feet elevation, is the highest point in the State. The Mountain Region covers less than 10 percent of the State's area and to its southeast lies the Piedmont Plateau. The Plateau extends nearly to the center of the State with elevations decreasing northwest to southeast from 1,000 to 500 feet. There is a narrow hilly region where the Plateau descends to the Coastal Plain. In South Carolina this "fall line" region is known as the "Sand Hills;" where elevations range from 500 to 200 feet. The width of the Sand Hills area is about 30 to 40 miles. Between the Sand Hills and the Atlantic Ocean lies the Coastal Plain. The Plain is broad and nearly level with elevations mostly between 50 and 200 feet. About 40 percent of the area of the State lies in the Coastal Plain.

All of the State's rivers drain southeast from the Mountain Region or Piedmont Plateau toward the ocean. There are three major and one minor river-basin systems. The Santee is the largest and drains the entire center portion of the State. The Savannah drains the western part of the State. The third major system is the Pee Dee, located in the northeastern section. The Edisto is a lesser river system lying between the Santee and Savannah.

There are many low sea islands separated from the mainland by shallow straits, sounds, and coastal streams. The Intracoastal Waterway can be found along much of the coastline.

GENERAL CLIMATE. Several major factors combine to give South Carolina a pleasant, mild, and humid climate. It is located at a relatively low latitude (32 to 35° N.) and most of the State is under 1,000 feet in elevation. It has a long coastline along which moves the warm Gulf Stream current. The mountains to the north and west block or delay many cold air masses approaching from those directions. Even the deep cold air masses which cross the mountains rapidly are warmed somewhat as the air is heated by compression when it descends on the southeastern side. This effect can be seen on the maps of minimum temperature in January and to a lesser degree in July, where a fairly large area of relatively higher temperature appears just southeast of the mountains.

It is convenient for climatic discussion to divide the State into areas coinciding closely with the topographic features already discussed. Six areas can be defined: (1) the Outer Coastal Plain; (2) the Inner Coastal Plain; (3) the Sand Hills; (4) the Lower Piedmont Plateau; (5) the Upper Piedmont Plateau; and (6) the Mountain Region.

TEMPERATURE. Lower temperatures can be expected in the Upper Piedmont and Mountain Region, where latitude, elevation and distance inland all have large values. Higher temperatures will result from smaller values of the three factors, as are found along the southern coast. There is a gradual decrease in annual average temperature northwestward from 68°F. at the coast to 58°F. at the edge of the mountains. Within the Mountain Region, variations in temperature are due almost entirely to elevation differences. The ocean waters have very small daily and annual changes in temperature when compared with the land surface. The air over the coastal water is cooler than the air over the land in summer and warmer than the air over land in winter, and this has a controlling effect on the temperatures of locations on and very near the coast. The highest temperatures are found in the central part of the State with the coast being four to five degrees cooler. Clouds and rainfall have a minor effect on temperature. Maximum temperatures in summer are reduced slightly in areas where afternoon cloudiness and rain are persistent. Such an area is found along the Outer Coastal Plain where sea breezes produce clouds and rain nearly every summer day and dissipate at night.

Summers are rather hot and air conditioning is desirable at elevations below 500 feet. Fall and spring are mild and winters are rather cool at elevations above 500 feet.

PRECIPITATION. Rainfall is adequate in all parts of the State. Annual rainfall averages up to 80 inches in the highest part of the Mountain Region and less than 42 inches in parts of the Inner Coastal Plain and the Sand Hills. The Mountain Region is wet with amounts of 56 inches or more, the Upper Piedmont is relatively wet with amounts of 48 to 55 inches, the Lower Piedmont is relatively dry with amounts of 43 to 47 inches, the Outer Coastal Plain is relatively wet with amounts of 48 to 53 inches, and the Inner Coastal Plain is relatively dry with amounts of 38 to 47 inches. The Sand Hills area is less clear cut but is in general a relatively wet strip with a small dry area imbedded in it a few miles south of Columbia. The immediate south coast is also on the dry side. The driest period is in October and November when there is little cyclonic storm activity. Rainfall increases gradually and reaches a peak in March when cyclone and cold front activity are at a maximum. There is a general decrease again to a dry period from late April through early June. From the latter part of June through early September is a wet period primarily due to thunderstorm and shower activity which reaches its peak in July, the wettest summer month. The summer maximum stretches a little into the fall along the coast due to occasional tropical storm activity.

Solid forms of precipitation include snow, sleet, and hail. Hail is not frequent but does occur with spring thunderstorms from March through early May. Snow and sleet may occur separately, combined or mixed with rain during the winter months of December through February. Snow may occur from one to three times in winter. Seldom do accumulations remain very long on the ground except in the mountains. Statewide snows of notable amounts can occur when a cyclonic storm moves northeastward along or just off the coast. Freezing rain also occurs from one to three times per winter in the northern half of the State. Severe drought occurs about once in 15 years with less severe and less widespread droughts about once in seven or eight years.

OTHER CLIMATIC ELEMENTS. The percent of possible sunshine received varies over the State, similar to the variation in cloudiness and precipitation. Values in winter range from 50 to 60 percent, in summer from 60 to 70, with the dry periods in spring and fall receiving 70 to 75 percent. The variation in relative humidity with time of day is considerably greater than day to day and month to month variations. Highest values of 80 to 90 percent or more are reached at about sunrise and the lowest values of 45 to 50 percent occur an hour or two after local noon. There is about a 10 percent difference between winter and summer, with summer being the higher of the two seasons. The prevailing surface winds tend to be either from northeast or southwest due to the presence and orientation of the Appalachian Mountains. Winds of all directions occur throughout the State during the year, but the prevailing directions by seasons are: spring—southwest; summer—south and southwest; autumn—northeast; and winter—northeast and southwest.

STORMS. Severe weather comes to South Carolina occasionally in the form of violent thunderstorms, tornadoes and hurricanes. Although thunderstorms are common in the summer months, the more violent ones generally accompany the squall lines and active cold fronts of spring. Generally, they bring high winds, hail, and considerable lightning, and sometimes spawn a tornado (average of seven or eight a year). Sixty percent of the tornadoes occur from March through June with April being the peak month with 25 percent. Tropical storms or hurricanes affect the State about one year out of two. Most of the occurrences are tropical storms which do little damage, frequently bringing rains at a time when they are needed. Most of the hurricanes affect only the Outer Coastal Plain. If they do come far inland, they decrease in intensity quite rapidly. Considerable flooding accompanies hurricanes which come very far inland and high tides occur along the coast to the north and east of the storm centers.

There is minor flooding somewhere in the State every year. It can occur on any of the many streams and rivers. There is a major flood about once every seven or eight years.

There have been many earth tremors in South Carolina over the years. The southern part of the Coastal Plain is indicated as earthquake prone.

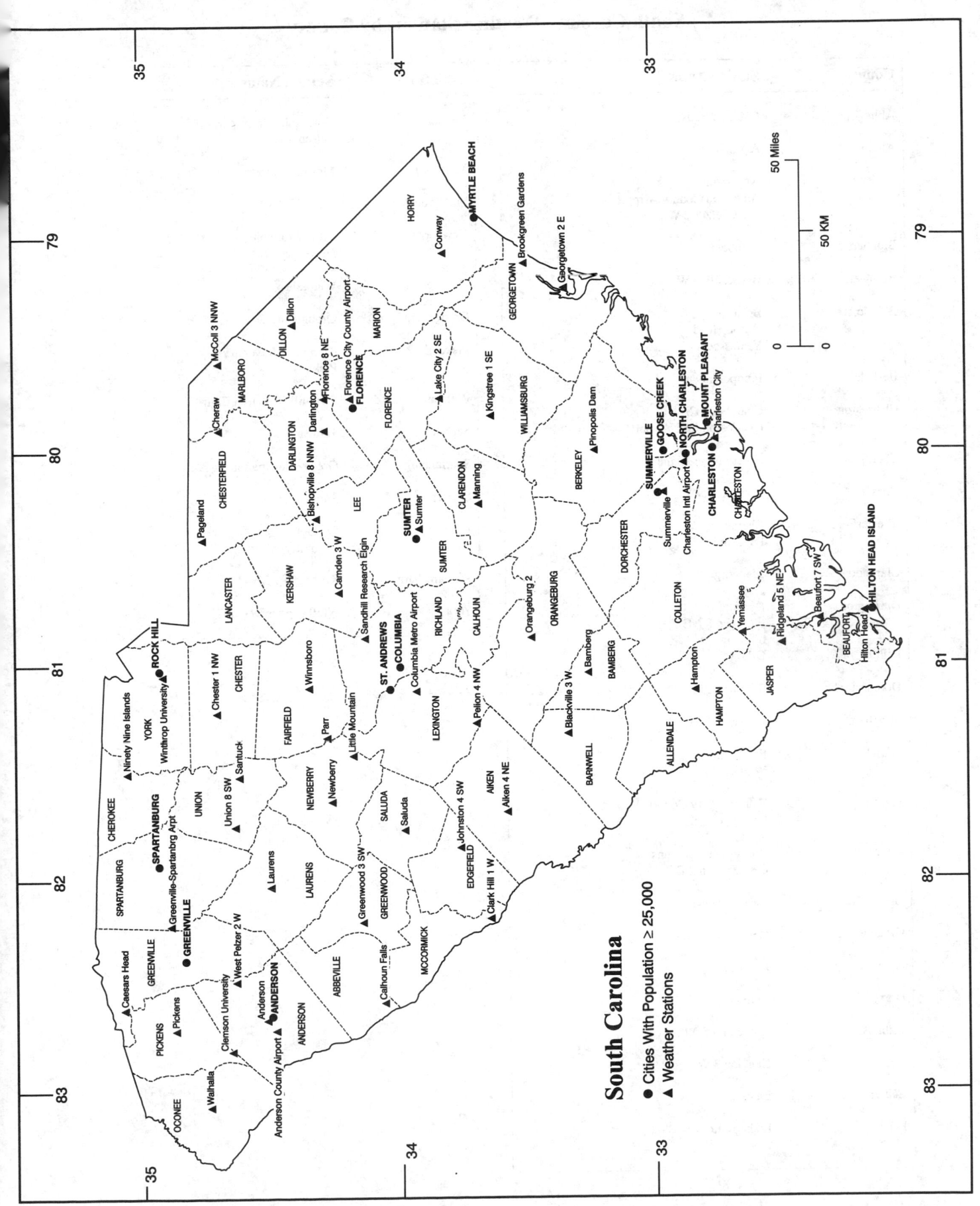

South Carolina

- ● Cities With Population ≥ 25,000
- ▲ Weather Stations

South Carolina Weather Stations by County

County	Station Name
Abbeville	Calhoun Falls
Aiken	Aiken 4 NE
Anderson	Anderson Anderson County Airport West Pelzer 2 W
Bamberg	Bamberg
Barnwell	Blackville 3 W
Beaufort	Beaufort 7 SW Hilton Head Yemassee
Berkeley	Pinopolis Dam
Charleston	Charleston City Charleston Int'l Airport
Cherokee	Ninety Nine Islands
Chester	Chester 1 NW
Chesterfield	Cheraw Pageland
Clarendon	Manning
Darlington	Darlington Florence 8 NE
Dillon	Dillon
Dorchester	Summerville
Edgefield	Johnston 4 SW
Fairfield	Parr Winnsboro
Florence	Florence City County Airport Lake City 2 SE
Georgetown	Brookgreen Gardens Georgetown 2 E
Greenville	Caesars Head
Greenwood	Greenwood 3 SW
Hampton	Hampton
Horry	Conway
Jasper	Ridgeland 5 NE
Kershaw	Camden 3 W
Laurens	Laurens
Lee	Bishopville 8 NNW

County	Station Name
Lexington	Columbia Metro Airport Pelion 4 NW
Marlboro	McColl 3 NNW
McCormick	Clark Hill 1 W
Newberry	Little Mountain Newberry
Oconee	Walhalla
Orangeburg	Orangeburg 2
Pickens	Clemson University Pickens
Richland	Sandhill Research Elgin
Saluda	Saluda
Spartanburg	Greenville-Spartanbrg Airport
Sumter	Sumter
Union	Santuck Union 8 SW
Williamsburg	Kingstree 1 SE
York	Winthrop University

South Carolina Weather Stations by City

City	Station Name	Miles
Anderson	Hartwell, GA	20
	Anderson	2
	Anderson County Airport	4
	Clemson University	14
	West Pelzer 2 W	13
Charleston	Charleston Int'l Airport	8
	Charleston City	3
	Summerville	18
Columbia	Columbia Metro Airport	8
	Sandhill Research Elgin	12
Florence	Darlington	10
	Florence City County Airport	3
	Florence 8 NE	8
Goose Creek	Charleston Int'l Airport	6
	Charleston City	14
	Pinopolis Dam	19
	Summerville	11
Greenville	Greenville-Spartanbrg Airport	10
	Pickens	19
	West Pelzer 2 W	15
Hilton Head Island	Beaufort 7 SW	14
	Hilton Head	2
Mount Pleasant	Charleston Int'l Airport	12
	Charleston City	5
Myrtle Beach	Brookgreen Gardens	18
	Conway	13
North Charleston	Charleston Int'l Airport	1
	Charleston City	9
	Summerville	11
Rock Hill	Charlotte Douglas Int'l Airport, NC	20
	Chester 1 NW	19
	Winthrop University	0
Spartanburg	Greenville-Spartanbrg Airport	16
St. Andrews	Columbia Metro Airport	7
	Sandhill Research Elgin	15
Summerville	Charleston Int'l Airport	11
	Summerville	1
Sumter	Manning	19
	Sumter	3

Note: Miles is the distance between the geographic center of the city and the weather station.

South Carolina Weather Stations by Elevation

Feet	Station Name
3,198	Caesars Head
1,161	Pickens
977	Walhalla
954	Greenville-Spartanbrg Airport
859	West Pelzer 2 W
823	Clemson University
797	Anderson
757	Anderson County Airport
708	Little Mountain
688	Winthrop University
620	Johnston 4 SW
620	Pageland
613	Greenwood 3 SW
587	Laurens
557	Union 8 SW
557	Winnsboro
528	Calhoun Falls
518	Chester 1 NW
518	Santuck
498	Ninety Nine Islands
479	Saluda
475	Newberry
449	Pelion 4 NW
439	Sandhill Research Elgin
396	Aiken 4 NE
377	Clark Hill 1 W
321	Blackville 3 W
255	Parr
246	Bishopville 8 NNW
209	Columbia Metro Airport
187	McColl 3 NNW
177	Orangeburg 2
173	Sumter
164	Bamberg
147	Darlington
144	Florence City County Airport
137	Camden 3 W
137	Cheraw
118	Florence 8 NE
114	Dillon
98	Manning
95	Hampton
72	Lake City 2 SE
59	Kingstree 1 SE
49	Pinopolis Dam
39	Charleston Int'l Airport
32	Summerville
22	Yemassee
19	Beaufort 7 SW
19	Brookgreen Gardens
19	Conway
19	Ridgeland 5 NE
13	Hilton Head
9	Charleston City
9	Georgetown 2 E

Charleston Int'l Airport

Charleston is a peninsula city bounded on the west and south by the Ashley River, on the east by the Cooper River, and on the southeast by a spacious harbor. Weather records for the airport are from a site some 10 miles inland. The terrain is generally level, ranging in elevation from sea level to 20 feet on the peninsula, with gradual increases in elevation toward inland areas.

The climate is temperate, modified considerably by the nearness to the ocean. The marine influence is noticeable during winter when the low temperatures are sometimes 10-15 degrees higher on the peninsula than at the airport. By the same token, high temperatures are generally a few degrees lower on the peninsula. The prevailing winds are northerly in the fall and winter, southerly in the spring and summer.

Summer is warm and humid. Temperatures of 100 degrees or more are infrequent. High temperatures are generally several degrees lower along the coast than inland due to the cooling effect of the sea breeze. Summer is the rainiest season with 41 percent of the annual total. The rain, except during occasional tropical storms, generally occurs as showers or thunderstorms.

The fall season passes through the warm Indian Summer period to the pre-winter cold spells which begin late in November. From late September to early November the weather is mostly sunny and temperature extremes are rare. Late summer and early fall is the period of maximum threat to the South Carolina coast from hurricanes.

The winter months, December through February, are mild with periods of rain. However, the winter rainfall is generally of a more uniform type. There is some chance of a snow flurry, with the best probability of its occurrence in January, but a significant amount is rarely measured. An average winter would experience less than one cold wave and severe freeze. Temperatures of 20 degrees or less on the peninsula and along the coast are very unusual.

The most spectacular time of the year, weatherwise, is spring with its rapid changes from windy and cold in March to warm and pleasant in May. Severe local storms are more likely to occur in spring than in summer.

The average occurrence of the first freeze in the fall is early December, and the average last freeze is late February, giving an average growing season of about 294 days.

Charleston Int'l Airport *Charleston County*   Elevation: 39 ft.   Latitude: 32° 54' N   Longitude: 80° 02' W

	JAN	FEB	MAR	APR	MAY	JUN	JUL	AUG	SEP	OCT	NOV	DEC	YEAR
Mean Maximum Temp. (°F)	58.6	62.1	69.1	76.2	82.9	87.8	91.0	89.4	85.2	77.1	69.6	62.0	75.9
Mean Temp. (°F)	48.4	51.2	58.1	64.8	72.5	78.6	82.2	80.9	76.6	66.8	58.6	51.5	65.9
Mean Minimum Temp. (°F)	38.1	40.3	47.1	53.3	62.1	69.3	73.4	72.4	67.9	56.5	47.6	40.9	55.8
Extreme Maximum Temp. (°F)	81	87	90	94	98	101	104	105	98	94	87	83	105
Extreme Minimum Temp. (°F)	6	12	15	30	42	50	59	56	46	27	16	11	6
Days Maximum Temp. ≥ 90°F	0	0	0	1	4	11	20	16	6	0	0	0	58
Days Maximum Temp. ≤ 32°F	0	0	0	0	0	0	0	0	0	0	0	0	0
Days Minimum Temp. ≤ 32°F	10	7	2	0	0	0	0	0	0	0	2	7	28
Days Minimum Temp. ≤ 0°F	0	0	0	0	0	0	0	0	0	0	0	0	0
Heating Degree Days (base 65°F)	511	389	237	91	10	0	0	0	2	64	220	422	1,946
Cooling Degree Days (base 65°F)	2	9	30	94	253	429	559	511	352	132	37	9	2,417
Mean Precipitation (in.)	4.03	3.11	4.13	2.75	3.77	5.81	5.97	7.12	5.76	3.23	2.59	3.25	51.52
Maximum Precipitation (in.)	8.9	6.3	11.1	9.5	9.3	27.2	18.5	17.0	17.3	12.1	7.3	7.1	73.0
Minimum Precipitation (in.)	0.6	0.3	0.7	trace	0.7	1.0	1.8	0.7	0.2	0.2	0.5	0.7	30.3
Maximum 24-hr. Precipitation (in.)	3.9	2.3	4.5	4.1	6.2	9.4	5.4	4.7	6.2	4.5	5.2	3.4	9.4
Days With ≥ 0.1" Precipitation	7	6	6	5	6	8	9	9	7	4	4	6	77
Days With ≥ 1.0" Precipitation	1	1	1	1	1	2	2	2	2	1	1	1	16
Mean Snowfall (in.)	trace	0.4	trace	trace	0.0	trace	trace	0.0	0.0	0.0	trace	0.5	0.9
Maximum Snowfall (in.)	1	7	2	0	0	0	0	0	0	0	trace	8	9
Maximum 24-hr. Snowfall (in.)	1	5	2	0	0	0	0	0	0	0	trace	6	6
Days With ≥ 1.0" Snow Depth	0	0	0	0	0	0	0	0	0	0	0	0	0
Thunderstorm Days	1	1	2	3	7	10	14	12	5	2	1	1	59
Foggy Days	14	11	13	12	14	13	11	14	16	14	14	14	160
Predominant Sky Cover	OVR	OVR	OVR	CLR	OVR	BRK	BRK	BRK	OVR	CLR	CLR	OVR	OVR
Mean Relative Humidity 7am (%)	83	81	83	84	85	86	88	90	91	89	86	83	86
Mean Relative Humidity 4pm (%)	55	52	51	51	56	62	66	66	65	58	56	55	58
Mean Dewpoint (°F)	38	39	45	52	61	68	72	72	67	57	47	40	55
Prevailing Wind Direction	NNE	SSW	SSW	SSW	S	S	SSW	S	NNE	NNE	NNE	NNE	NNE
Prevailing Wind Speed (mph)	9	12	12	12	9	8	9	8	9	9	9	9	9
Maximum Wind Gust (mph)	67	62	69	71	60	64	61	69	98	54	55	55	98

Columbia Metro Airport

Columbia is centrally located within the state of South Carolina and lies on the Congaree River near the confluence of the Broad and Saluda Rivers. The surrounding terrain is rolling, sloping from about 350 feet above sea level in northern Columbia to about 200 feet in the southeastern part of the city.

The climate in the Columbia area is relatively temperate. The Appalachian Mountain chain, some 150 miles to the northwest, frequently retards the approach of unseasonable cold weather in the winter. The terrain offers little moderating effect on the summer heat.

Long summers are prevalent with warm weather usually lasting from sometime in May into September. In summer the Bermuda high is the greatest single weather factor influencing the area. This permanent high more or less blocks the entry of cold fronts so that many stall before reaching central South Carolina. Also, the southwestern flow around the offshore Bermuda high pressure supplies moisture for the many summer thunderstorms. There are relatively few breaks in the heat during midsummer. The typical summer has about six days with 100 degrees or more. Thunderstorm activity usually shows a decided increase during June, decreasing about the first of September. About once or twice a year, passing tropical storms produce strong winds and heavy rains. The incidence of these storms is greatest in September, although they represent a possible threat from midsummer to late fall. Damage from tropical storms is usually minor in the Columbia area.

Fall is the most pleasant time of the year. Rainfall during the late fall is at an annual minimum, while the sunshine is at a relative maximum. Winters are mild with the cold weather usually lasting from late November to mid-March. The winter weather at Columbia is largely made up of polar air outbreaks that reach this area in a much modified form. On rare occasions in winter, Arctic air masses push southward as far as central South Carolina and cause some of the coldest temperatures. Disruption of activities from snowfall is unusual, in fact, more than three days of sustained snow cover is rare.

Spring is the most changeable season of the year. The temperature varies from an occasional cold snap in March to generally warm and pleasant in May. While tornadoes are infrequent, they occur most often in the spring. Hailstorms are not frequent, with the annual incidence at a maximum in spring and early summer. The average occurrence of the last spring freeze is very late March, and the first fall freeze is early November, for a growing period of about 218 days.

Columbia Metro Airport *Lexington County* Elevation: 209 ft.   Latitude: 33° 57' N   Longitude: 81° 07' W

	JAN	FEB	MAR	APR	MAY	JUN	JUL	AUG	SEP	OCT	NOV	DEC	YEAR
Mean Maximum Temp. (°F)	55.9	60.4	68.3	76.7	83.5	89.3	92.5	90.4	85.6	76.3	67.4	59.2	75.5
Mean Temp. (°F)	44.6	48.0	55.4	63.1	71.0	78.0	81.7	80.1	74.8	63.6	54.6	47.5	63.5
Mean Minimum Temp. (°F)	33.3	35.5	42.4	49.5	58.5	66.5	70.9	69.8	63.9	50.8	41.7	35.7	51.6
Extreme Maximum Temp. (°F)	84	84	91	94	98	106	106	107	99	95	89	83	107
Extreme Minimum Temp. (°F)	-1	5	4	26	35	44	55	56	41	25	12	6	-1
Days Maximum Temp. ≥ 90°F	0	0	0	2	6	16	23	18	9	1	0	0	75
Days Maximum Temp. ≤ 32°F	1	0	0	0	0	0	0	0	0	0	0	0	1
Days Minimum Temp. ≤ 32°F	16	12	6	1	0	0	0	0	0	1	7	13	56
Days Minimum Temp. ≤ 0°F	0	0	0	0	0	0	0	0	0	0	0	0	0
Heating Degree Days (base 65°F)	627	478	312	125	21	1	0	0	7	116	321	542	2,550
Cooling Degree Days (base 65°F)	1	5	19	71	216	413	545	481	295	81	13	4	2,144
Mean Precipitation (in.)	4.47	3.89	4.74	2.96	3.29	4.97	5.60	5.52	3.86	3.16	2.82	3.50	48.78
Maximum Precipitation (in.)	9.3	8.7	10.9	6.8	8.8	14.8	17.5	16.7	8.8	12.1	7.2	8.5	70.5
Minimum Precipitation (in.)	0.8	0.3	0.6	0.3	0.3	0.7	0.6	1.0	0.1	trace	0.4	0.3	27.4
Maximum 24-hr. Precipitation (in.)	2.8	3.7	3.2	3.0	4.7	5.4	5.8	5.0	5.1	4.1	2.6	3.2	5.8
Days With ≥ 0.1" Precipitation	8	6	7	5	6	7	8	7	5	4	5	6	74
Days With ≥ 1.0" Precipitation	1	1	1	1	1	1	2	2	1	1	1	1	14
Mean Snowfall (in.)	0.5	1.1	0.3	trace	0.0	0.0	0.0	trace	0.0	0.0	trace	0.1	2.0
Maximum Snowfall (in.)	4	16	4	0	0	0	0	0	0	0	trace	9	18
Maximum 24-hr. Snowfall (in.)	4	12	4	0	0	0	0	0	0	0	trace	9	12
Days With ≥ 1.0" Snow Depth	0	0	0	0	0	0	0	0	0	0	0	0	0
Thunderstorm Days	1	2	3	4	6	9	13	10	4	1	1	< 1	54
Foggy Days	13	12	13	10	14	15	15	20	18	15	13	13	171
Predominant Sky Cover	OVR	OVR	OVR	CLR	OVR	SCT	SCT	SCT	OVR	CLR	CLR	OVR	OVR
Mean Relative Humidity 7am (%)	83	83	84	83	84	85	88	91	91	90	88	84	86
Mean Relative Humidity 4pm (%)	51	47	44	41	46	50	54	56	54	49	48	51	49
Mean Dewpoint (°F)	34	35	41	48	58	65	69	69	64	52	43	36	51
Prevailing Wind Direction	WSW	WSW	SW	SW	SW	SW	SW	SW	NE	NE	SW	WSW	SW
Prevailing Wind Speed (mph)	8	9	9	9	8	8	7	7	9	9	8	8	8
Maximum Wind Gust (mph)	54	69	69	61	61	78	64	56	70	54	51	49	78

Greenville-Spartanbrg Airport

This station, three miles south of Greer, South Carolina, is located in the Piedmont section, on the eastern slope of the Southern Appalachian Mountains. It is rolling country with the first ridge of the mountains about 20 miles to the northwest and the main ridge about 55 miles to the northwest. These mountains usually protect this area from the full force of the cold air masses which move southeastward from central Canada during the winter months.

At present, the National Weather Service Office is located at the Greenville-Spartanburg Jet Age Airport, on a level with, or slightly higher than, most of the surrounding countryside. No bodies of water are nearby. Temperatures are quite consistent with those in Greer, Greenville, and Spartanburg.

The elevation of the area, ranging from 800 to 1,100 feet is conducive to cool nights, especially during the summer months. Winters are quite pleasant, with the temperature remaining below freezing throughout the daylight hours only a few times during a normal year. There are usually two freezing rainstorms each winter and two or three small snowstorms.

Rainfall in this section is usually abundant and spread quite evenly through the months. Droughts have been experienced, but are usually of short duration.

The mountain ridges, which lie in a northeast-southwest direction, appear to have a definite overall influence on the direction of the wind. The prevailing directions are northeast and southwest, divided almost evenly, with fall and winter favoring northeast and spring and summer favoring southwest. Destructive winds occur occasionally, while tornadoes are infrequent in this vicinity.

In the southern two-thirds of Greenville and Spartanburg Counties, including the cities of the same names, the average occurrence of the last temperature of 32 degrees in spring is late March and the average occurrence of the first in fall is early November, giving an average growing season of 225 days. In a normal year some flowering shrubs bloom through the winter. In the higher elevations in the northern thirds of these counties, the growing season begins about one month later and ends about one month earlier.

Greenville-Spartanbrg Airport *Spartanburg County*   Elevation: 954 ft.   Latitude: 34° 54' N   Longitude: 82° 13' W

	JAN	FEB	MAR	APR	MAY	JUN	JUL	AUG	SEP	OCT	NOV	DEC	YEAR
Mean Maximum Temp. (°F)	50.6	55.2	63.2	72.0	79.0	85.7	89.1	87.1	81.5	71.7	62.0	53.7	70.9
Mean Temp. (°F)	40.7	44.3	51.6	59.6	67.6	75.1	78.9	77.4	71.4	60.5	51.2	44.0	60.2
Mean Minimum Temp. (°F)	30.7	33.3	40.1	47.1	56.3	64.4	68.7	67.6	61.4	49.2	40.3	34.1	49.4
Extreme Maximum Temp. (°F)	79	81	89	93	94	100	104	103	96	92	85	76	104
Extreme Minimum Temp. (°F)	-4	8	11	25	31	40	54	53	39	25	12	5	-4
Days Maximum Temp. ≥ 90°F	0	0	0	0	1	8	15	10	3	0	0	0	37
Days Maximum Temp. ≤ 32°F	1	0	0	0	0	0	0	0	0	0	0	0	1
Days Minimum Temp. ≤ 32°F	18	14	7	1	0	0	0	0	0	1	7	15	63
Days Minimum Temp. ≤ 0°F	0	0	0	0	0	0	0	0	0	0	0	0	0
Heating Degree Days (base 65°F)	748	579	413	188	44	2	0	0	17	171	412	646	3,220
Cooling Degree Days (base 65°F)	0	0	6	33	136	327	457	396	207	40	2	1	1,605
Mean Precipitation (in.)	4.35	4.30	5.28	3.48	4.62	4.00	4.55	4.16	3.87	4.11	3.72	3.89	50.33
Maximum Precipitation (in.)	7.2	7.4	11.4	11.3	8.9	10.1	13.6	17.4	11.6	10.2	7.8	8.4	70.4
Minimum Precipitation (in.)	0.3	0.3	1.1	0.7	1.1	0.2	0.8	0.9	0.3	0.2	1.3	0.4	35.5
Maximum 24-hr. Precipitation (in.)	3.0	3.4	3.8	3.3	3.3	4.2	3.6	9.3	4.4	4.5	2.8	2.7	9.3
Days With ≥ 0.1" Precipitation	7	7	8	6	7	7	7	6	6	5	6	7	79
Days With ≥ 1.0" Precipitation	1	1	2	1	1	1	1	1	1	1	1	1	13
Mean Snowfall (in.)	2.3	1.5	1.2	trace	trace	trace	trace	0.0	0.0	0.0	trace	0.7	5.7
Maximum Snowfall (in.)	12	12	10	trace	0	0	0	0	0	0	2	11	19
Maximum 24-hr. Snowfall (in.)	12	8	9	trace	0	0	0	0	0	0	2	11	12
Days With ≥ 1.0" Snow Depth	1	1	0	0	0	0	0	0	0	0	0	0	2
Thunderstorm Days	1	1	2	3	6	7	10	7	3	1	1	< 1	42
Foggy Days	13	11	11	9	12	14	16	19	15	11	11	12	154
Predominant Sky Cover	OVR	OVR	OVR	CLR	OVR	OVR	OVR	OVR	OVR	CLR	CLR	OVR	OVR
Mean Relative Humidity 7am (%)	77	75	77	78	83	85	88	90	90	85	81	78	82
Mean Relative Humidity 4pm (%)	52	47	46	44	51	54	57	58	57	51	51	53	52
Mean Dewpoint (°F)	28	29	37	44	55	63	68	67	61	49	39	32	48
Prevailing Wind Direction	SW	NE	SW	SW	SW	SW	SW	NNE	NE	NNE	NNE	SW	NE
Prevailing Wind Speed (mph)	9	9	10	10	9	8	8	7	8	8	8	9	9
Maximum Wind Gust (mph)	63	66	61	71	53	60	66	58	45	48	53	51	71

Aiken 4 NE *Aiken County*   Elevation: 396 ft.   Latitude: 33° 36' N   Longitude: 81° 41' W

	JAN	FEB	MAR	APR	MAY	JUN	JUL	AUG	SEP	OCT	NOV	DEC	YEAR
Mean Maximum Temp. (°F)	58.2	62.9	70.4	78.4	84.9	90.5	93.5	91.6	87.1	78.2	69.1	60.9	77.1
Mean Temp. (°F)	45.8	49.6	56.6	63.6	*71.2*	78.1	81.5	80.0	74.8	64.4	55.1	48.1	*64.1*
Mean Minimum Temp. (°F)	33.5	36.2	42.5	48.6	*57.3*	65.6	69.5	68.4	62.3	50.5	41.0	35.1	*50.9*
Extreme Maximum Temp. (°F)	82	88	88	99	100	107	108	109	100	*97*	86	82	*109*
Extreme Minimum Temp. (°F)	-4	9	14	*21*	34	42	51	52	37	*25*	16	4	*-4*
Days Maximum Temp. ≥ 90°F	0	0	0	2	7	18	25	21	11	1	0	0	85
Days Maximum Temp. ≤ 32°F	0	0	0	0	0	0	0	0	0	0	0	0	0
Days Minimum Temp. ≤ 32°F	15	11	6	2	0	0	0	0	0	0	1	7	56
Days Minimum Temp. ≤ 0°F	0	0	0	0	0	0	0	0	0	0	0	0	0
Heating Degree Days (base 65°F)	587	433	275	112	*18*	0	0	0	5	100	305	515	*2,350*
Cooling Degree Days (base 65°F)	1	4	22	82	231	421	546	481	295	87	13	2	2,185
Mean Precipitation (in.)	5.20	4.57	5.47	3.28	4.26	5.57	5.31	5.19	4.19	3.52	3.20	3.88	53.64
Days With ≥ 0.1" Precipitation	8	7	7	6	6	7	9	8	6	5	5	7	81
Days With ≥ 1.0" Precipitation	1	2	2	1	1	2	2	2	1	1	1	1	17
Mean Snowfall (in.)	*0.3*	0.7	trace	0.0	0.0	0.0	0.0	0.0	0.0	0.0	0.0	0.0	*1.0*
Days With ≥ 1.0" Snow Depth	*0*	0	0	0	0	0	0	0	0	0	0	0	*0*

Anderson *Anderson County*   Elevation: 797 ft.   Latitude: 34° 32' N   Longitude: 82° 40' W

	JAN	FEB	MAR	APR	MAY	JUN	JUL	AUG	SEP	OCT	NOV	DEC	YEAR
Mean Maximum Temp. (°F)	54.4	59.1	66.7	75.4	81.6	88.2	91.2	89.5	84.4	75.0	65.3	56.8	74.0
Mean Temp. (°F)	42.6	46.1	52.9	60.9	68.5	75.8	79.4	78.2	72.5	61.7	52.6	44.9	61.3
Mean Minimum Temp. (°F)	30.8	33.0	39.2	46.3	55.3	63.3	67.5	66.8	60.6	48.5	39.9	33.0	48.7
Extreme Maximum Temp. (°F)	80	80	88	94	100	106	106	104	100	91	86	80	106
Extreme Minimum Temp. (°F)	-5	10	5	24	33	42	53	52	40	27	13	4	-5
Days Maximum Temp. ≥ 90°F	0	0	0	0	2	13	20	16	6	0	0	0	57
Days Maximum Temp. ≤ 32°F	1	0	0	0	0	0	0	0	0	0	0	0	1
Days Minimum Temp. ≤ 32°F	18	14	8	2	0	0	0	0	0	1	8	16	67
Days Minimum Temp. ≤ 0°F	0	0	0	0	0	0	0	0	0	0	0	0	0
Heating Degree Days (base 65°F)	687	528	373	158	31	2	0	0	11	139	368	616	2,913
Cooling Degree Days (base 65°F)	0	0	5	44	150	346	471	424	236	49	4	1	1,730
Mean Precipitation (in.)	5.17	4.36	5.26	3.48	4.21	3.39	4.33	4.06	4.03	4.06	4.14	4.54	51.03
Days With ≥ 0.1" Precipitation	8	6	7	6	6	6	7	7	6	5	7	7	78
Days With ≥ 1.0" Precipitation	2	1	2	1	1	1	1	1	1	1	1	1	14
Mean Snowfall (in.)	*0.6*	0.5	0.3	0.0	0.0	0.0	0.0	0.0	0.0	0.0	0.0	trace	*1.4*
Days With ≥ 1.0" Snow Depth	0	0	0	0	0	0	0	0	0	0	0	0	0

Anderson County Airport *Anderson County*   Elevation: 757 ft.   Latitude: 34° 30' N   Longitude: 82° 43' W

	JAN	FEB	MAR	APR	MAY	JUN	JUL	AUG	SEP	OCT	NOV	DEC	YEAR
Mean Maximum Temp. (°F)	51.9	56.8	64.9	73.6	80.6	87.5	90.5	88.6	83.1	73.4	63.8	55.3	72.5
Mean Temp. (°F)	42.1	46.0	53.5	61.3	69.2	76.8	80.2	78.8	73.0	62.1	52.8	45.4	61.8
Mean Minimum Temp. (°F)	32.3	35.1	42.1	49.0	57.8	66.0	69.8	69.0	62.9	50.7	41.7	35.4	51.0
Extreme Maximum Temp. (°F)	79	80	87	93	95	102	106	104	97	93	86	77	106
Extreme Minimum Temp. (°F)	-6	9	5	24	34	45	57	57	41	26	16	-3	-6
Days Maximum Temp. ≥ 90°F	0	0	0	0	3	11	19	14	5	0	0	0	52
Days Maximum Temp. ≤ 32°F	1	0	0	0	0	0	0	0	0	0	0	0	1
Days Minimum Temp. ≤ 32°F	16	12	5	1	0	0	0	0	0	1	6	12	53
Days Minimum Temp. ≤ 0°F	0	0	0	0	0	0	0	0	0	0	0	0	0
Heating Degree Days (base 65°F)	702	531	358	150	29	1	0	0	10	138	368	603	2,890
Cooling Degree Days (base 65°F)	0	0	8	42	163	362	488	436	243	54	4	2	1,802
Mean Precipitation (in.)	4.49	4.20	4.96	3.31	4.03	3.30	3.68	3.96	4.04	3.38	3.62	3.84	46.81
Days With ≥ 0.1" Precipitation	8	7	8	6	6	6	7	6	5	5	6	6	76
Days With ≥ 1.0" Precipitation	1	1	2	1	1	1	1	1	1	1	1	1	13
Mean Snowfall (in.)	0.9	0.8	0.6	0.0	trace	0.0	0.0	0.0	0.0	0.0	trace	0.4	2.7
Days With ≥ 1.0" Snow Depth	1	0	0	0	0	0	0	0	0	0	0	0	1

Bamberg *Bamberg County*   Elevation: 164 ft.   Latitude: 33° 17' N   Longitude: 81° 02' W

	JAN	FEB	MAR	APR	MAY	JUN	JUL	AUG	SEP	OCT	NOV	DEC	YEAR
Mean Maximum Temp. (°F)	57.2	62.1	70.4	77.6	83.7	88.7	91.4	89.4	84.7	75.7	67.2	59.8	75.7
Mean Temp. (°F)	46.7	50.2	57.5	64.2	71.4	77.6	81.0	79.5	74.8	64.6	56.1	49.3	64.4
Mean Minimum Temp. (°F)	36.1	38.2	44.6	50.8	59.1	66.5	70.5	69.6	64.8	53.4	44.9	38.7	53.1
Extreme Maximum Temp. (°F)	81	85	90	94	97	103	106	107	101	98	84	81	107
Extreme Minimum Temp. (°F)	2	8	10	28	37	48	56	56	43	28	17	7	2
Days Maximum Temp. ≥ 90°F	0	0	0	1	5	13	21	15	6	0	0	0	61
Days Maximum Temp. ≤ 32°F	0	0	0	0	0	0	0	0	0	0	0	0	0
Days Minimum Temp. ≤ 32°F	12	9	4	0	0	0	0	0	0	0	0	0	0
Days Minimum Temp. ≤ 0°F	0	0	0	0	0	0	0	0	0	0	5	10	40
Heating Degree Days (base 65°F)	563	418	250	95	13	0	0	0	4	95	281	488	2,207
Cooling Degree Days (base 65°F)	2	6	26	78	226	398	520	465	297	91	18	5	2,132
Mean Precipitation (in.)	4.46	3.90	4.38	3.01	3.57	5.42	4.99	5.60	3.86	2.95	2.79	3.62	48.55
Days With ≥ 0.1" Precipitation	8	6	7	5	6	7	8	8	6	5	5	6	77
Days With ≥ 1.0" Precipitation	1	1	1	1	1	2	1	2	1	1	1	1	14
Mean Snowfall (in.)	0.3	0.9	trace	0.0	0.0	0.0	0.0	0.0	0.0	0.0	0.0	0.1	1.3
Days With ≥ 1.0" Snow Depth	0	0	0	0	0	0	0	0	0	0	0	0	0

Beaufort 7 SW *Beaufort County*   Elevation: 19 ft.   Latitude: 32° 23' N   Longitude: 80° 46' W

	JAN	FEB	MAR	APR	MAY	JUN	JUL	AUG	SEP	OCT	NOV	DEC	YEAR
Mean Maximum Temp. (°F)	59.4	63.0	69.9	76.7	83.1	87.9	90.5	89.0	85.0	77.4	69.3	62.1	76.1
Mean Temp. (°F)	49.8	52.7	59.4	66.1	73.3	79.1	82.1	81.0	77.0	68.2	59.8	52.9	66.8
Mean Minimum Temp. (°F)	40.2	42.3	48.9	55.5	63.4	70.3	73.6	72.9	68.9	59.0	50.2	43.6	57.4
Extreme Maximum Temp. (°F)	83	84	93	92	96	101	103	104	99	92	87	85	104
Extreme Minimum Temp. (°F)	5	17	21	33	38	53	60	56	47	34	17	10	5
Days Maximum Temp. ≥ 90°F	0	0	0	0	3	10	20	15	5	0	0	0	53
Days Maximum Temp. ≤ 32°F	0	0	0	0	0	0	0	0	0	0	0	0	0
Days Minimum Temp. ≤ 32°F	7	5	1	0	0	0	0	0	0	0	1	4	18
Days Minimum Temp. ≤ 0°F	0	0	0	0	0	0	0	0	0	0	0	0	0
Heating Degree Days (base 65°F)	466	347	196	61	5	0	0	0	1	45	188	378	1,687
Cooling Degree Days (base 65°F)	2	6	28	101	270	444	553	511	362	155	37	9	2,478
Mean Precipitation (in.)	4.08	3.10	3.87	3.02	3.21	5.45	5.64	7.52	5.03	3.24	2.56	3.20	49.92
Days With ≥ 0.1" Precipitation	7	6	6	5	5	8	8	9	7	4	4	6	75
Days With ≥ 1.0" Precipitation	1	1	1	1	1	2	2	2	2	1	1	1	16
Mean Snowfall (in.)	trace	0.2	trace	0.0	0.0	0.0	0.0	0.0	0.0	0.0	0.0	0.2	0.4
Days With ≥ 1.0" Snow Depth	0	0	0	0	0	0	0	0	0	0	0	0	0

Bishopville 8 NNW *Lee County*   Elevation: 246 ft.   Latitude: 34° 20' N   Longitude: 80° 18' W

	JAN	FEB	MAR	APR	MAY	JUN	JUL	AUG	SEP	OCT	NOV	DEC	YEAR
Mean Maximum Temp. (°F)	53.1	58.0	66.0	74.8	81.7	88.0	90.7	88.9	84.1	75.0	66.1	57.8	73.7
Mean Temp. (°F)	42.1	45.7	53.3	61.4	69.4	76.6	79.8	78.3	73.1	62.6	53.5	46.1	61.8
Mean Minimum Temp. (°F)	31.2	33.4	40.5	47.9	57.0	65.2	68.9	67.7	62.0	50.0	40.7	34.4	49.9
Extreme Maximum Temp. (°F)	78	85	88	93	98	104	105	106	98	96	86	82	106
Extreme Minimum Temp. (°F)	-2	9	8	24	31	47	54	53	41	23	14	5	-2
Days Maximum Temp. ≥ 90°F	0	0	0	1	4	12	19	15	6	0	0	0	57
Days Maximum Temp. ≤ 32°F	1	0	0	0	0	0	0	0	0	0	0	0	1
Days Minimum Temp. ≤ 32°F	17	14	7	1	0	0	0	0	0	1	7	15	62
Days Minimum Temp. ≤ 0°F	0	0	0	0	0	0	0	0	0	0	0	0	0
Heating Degree Days (base 65°F)	702	539	368	158	33	2	0	0	11	133	352	582	2,880
Cooling Degree Days (base 65°F)	1	3	12	52	178	376	486	431	254	71	9	3	1,876
Mean Precipitation (in.)	4.28	3.42	4.17	2.91	3.53	4.21	4.87	4.51	3.77	3.35	2.99	3.28	45.29
Days With ≥ 0.1" Precipitation	8	6	7	5	6	7	7	7	5	5	5	6	74
Days With ≥ 1.0" Precipitation	1	1	1	1	1	1	1	1	1	1	1	1	12
Mean Snowfall (in.)	0.4	0.9	0.4	0.0	0.0	0.0	0.0	0.0	0.0	0.0	0.0	0.2	1.9
Days With ≥ 1.0" Snow Depth	1	1	0	0	0	0	0	0	0	0	0	0	2

Blackville 3 W *Barnwell County*   Elevation: 321 ft.   Latitude: 33° 22' N   Longitude: 81° 19' W

	JAN	FEB	MAR	APR	MAY	JUN	JUL	AUG	SEP	OCT	NOV	DEC	YEAR
Mean Maximum Temp. (°F)	58.6	63.1	70.8	78.3	84.5	89.8	92.4	90.6	86.6	78.0	69.6	61.7	77.0
Mean Temp. (°F)	46.8	50.2	57.4	64.2	71.3	77.5	80.5	79.1	74.6	64.8	56.5	49.5	64.4
Mean Minimum Temp. (°F)	35.0	37.3	43.9	50.0	58.1	65.1	68.6	67.6	62.7	51.6	43.3	37.3	51.7
Extreme Maximum Temp. (°F)	81	86	91	95	100	104	105	108	103	97	87	83	108
Extreme Minimum Temp. (°F)	-1	7	9	25	36	46	55	50	38	25	15	7	-1
Days Maximum Temp. ≥ 90°F	0	0	0	1	6	16	24	19	10	1	0	0	77
Days Maximum Temp. ≤ 32°F	0	0	0	0	0	0	0	0	0	0	0	0	0
Days Minimum Temp. ≤ 32°F	13	10	4	1	0	0	0	0	0	1	6	11	46
Days Minimum Temp. ≤ 0°F	0	0	0	0	0	0	0	0	0	0	0	0	0
Heating Degree Days (base 65°F)	559	415	254	98	14	0	0	0	5	92	268	479	2,184
Cooling Degree Days (base 65°F)	1	6	26	79	222	395	507	451	296	96	18	5	2,102
Mean Precipitation (in.)	4.45	3.94	4.51	2.95	3.63	5.42	4.60	5.07	3.42	3.25	2.62	3.49	47.35
Days With ≥ 0.1" Precipitation	7	6	7	5	6	8	8	8	5	4	5	6	75
Days With ≥ 1.0" Precipitation	1	1	1	1	1	2	1	2	1	1	1	1	14
Mean Snowfall (in.)	0.1	0.8	trace	0.0	0.0	0.0	0.0	0.0	0.0	0.0	0.0	trace	0.9
Days With ≥ 1.0" Snow Depth	0	0	0	0	0	0	0	0	0	0	0	0	0

Brookgreen Gardens *Georgetown County*   Elevation: 19 ft.   Latitude: 33° 31' N   Longitude: 79° 06' W

	JAN	FEB	MAR	APR	MAY	JUN	JUL	AUG	SEP	OCT	NOV	DEC	YEAR
Mean Maximum Temp. (°F)	57.6	61.1	68.0	75.4	82.0	87.1	90.5	88.7	84.7	76.7	68.7	61.0	75.1
Mean Temp. (°F)	46.9	49.5	56.3	63.2	70.7	76.9	80.8	79.4	75.0	65.5	57.3	50.0	64.3
Mean Minimum Temp. (°F)	36.1	37.9	44.6	51.0	59.4	66.7	71.2	70.0	65.3	54.3	45.8	38.9	53.4
Extreme Maximum Temp. (°F)	84	85	90	94	95	102	103	101	98	96	86	83	103
Extreme Minimum Temp. (°F)	4	13	14	27	30	46	55	55	43	26	17	4	4
Days Maximum Temp. ≥ 90°F	0	0	0	1	3	9	18	12	4	0	0	0	47
Days Maximum Temp. ≤ 32°F	0	0	0	0	0	0	0	0	0	0	0	0	0
Days Minimum Temp. ≤ 32°F	12	9	4	1	0	0	0	0	0	0	4	10	40
Days Minimum Temp. ≤ 0°F	0	0	0	0	0	0	0	0	0	0	0	0	0
Heating Degree Days (base 65°F)	557	435	283	114	18	1	0	0	3	81	252	465	2,209
Cooling Degree Days (base 65°F)	1	5	18	62	203	378	516	457	298	106	26	6	2,076
Mean Precipitation (in.)	4.60	3.58	4.29	3.03	4.04	5.00	5.80	6.49	6.05	4.30	3.12	4.17	54.47
Days With ≥ 0.1" Precipitation	8	6	7	5	6	7	9	9	6	5	5	7	80
Days With ≥ 1.0" Precipitation	1	1	1	1	1	2	2	2	2	2	1	1	17
Mean Snowfall (in.)	0.2	0.4	0.2	0.0	0.0	0.0	0.0	0.0	0.0	0.0	0.0	0.4	1.2
Days With ≥ 1.0" Snow Depth	0	0	0	0	0	0	0	0	0	0	0	0	0

Caesars Head *Greenville County*   Elevation: 3,198 ft.   Latitude: 35° 05' N   Longitude: 82° 37' W

	JAN	FEB	MAR	APR	MAY	JUN	JUL	AUG	SEP	OCT	NOV	DEC	YEAR
Mean Maximum Temp. (°F)	44.4	48.3	56.4	65.7	71.4	76.7	79.7	78.1	73.2	63.7	54.6	47.6	63.3
Mean Temp. (°F)	35.7	39.1	46.5	55.1	61.8	68.2	71.8	70.3	65.2	55.1	46.4	39.3	54.5
Mean Minimum Temp. (°F)	27.1	29.9	36.5	44.4	52.2	59.6	63.8	62.4	57.1	46.6	38.2	30.9	45.7
Extreme Maximum Temp. (°F)	71	73	79	86	89	89	97	99	89	79	79	70	99
Extreme Minimum Temp. (°F)	-20	-2	4	20	31	40	50	45	37	24	7	-5	-20
Days Maximum Temp. ≥ 90°F	0	0	0	0	0	0	1	0	0	0	0	0	1
Days Maximum Temp. ≤ 32°F	3	2	0	0	0	0	0	0	0	0	0	2	7
Days Minimum Temp. ≤ 32°F	20	16	11	3	0	0	0	0	0	1	9	17	77
Days Minimum Temp. ≤ 0°F	1	0	0	0	0	0	0	0	0	0	0	0	1
Heating Degree Days (base 65°F)	905	725	568	303	126	24	4	7	66	304	550	791	4,373
Cooling Degree Days (base 65°F)	0	0	1	11	34	132	228	177	76	5	0	0	664
Mean Precipitation (in.)	6.34	5.68	7.45	5.45	6.98	6.62	6.52	5.80	6.03	6.10	6.44	6.12	75.53
Days With ≥ 0.1" Precipitation	8	7	8	7	9	9	10	9	8	6	7	8	96
Days With ≥ 1.0" Precipitation	2	2	2	2	2	2	2	2	2	2	2	2	24
Mean Snowfall (in.)	3.8	1.9	1.7	trace	trace	0.0	0.0	0.0	0.0	0.0	0.1	1.2	8.7
Days With ≥ 1.0" Snow Depth	2	0	1	0	0	0	0	0	0	0	0	0	3

Calhoun Falls *Abbeville County*   Elevation: 528 ft.   Latitude: 34° 05' N   Longitude: 82° 35' W

	JAN	FEB	MAR	APR	MAY	JUN	JUL	AUG	SEP	OCT	NOV	DEC	YEAR
Mean Maximum Temp. (°F)	52.7	57.6	66.0	74.4	81.4	87.8	91.4	89.7	84.4	74.5	65.0	55.8	73.4
Mean Temp. (°F)	42.0	45.4	53.1	60.7	68.9	76.3	80.3	78.9	73.0	61.8	52.5	44.7	61.5
Mean Minimum Temp. (°F)	31.3	33.1	40.1	46.9	56.3	64.7	69.1	68.0	61.6	49.1	40.0	33.8	49.5
Extreme Maximum Temp. (°F)	85	81	89	93	96	103	106	105	100	95	87	82	106
Extreme Minimum Temp. (°F)	-2	10	10	27	34	45	51	53	42	25	15	5	-2
Days Maximum Temp. ≥ 90°F	0	0	0	0	3	12	21	16	7	0	0	0	59
Days Maximum Temp. ≤ 32°F	1	0	0	0	0	0	0	0	0	0	0	0	1
Days Minimum Temp. ≤ 32°F	18	14	7	1	0	0	0	0	0	1	8	15	64
Days Minimum Temp. ≤ 0°F	0	0	0	0	0	0	0	0	0	0	0	0	0
Heating Degree Days (base 65°F)	707	548	371	165	34	2	0	0	12	145	375	623	2,982
Cooling Degree Days (base 65°F)	0	1	8	41	168	360	508	451	253	57	7	1	1,855
Mean Precipitation (in.)	4.86	4.45	5.14	3.27	3.84	3.96	4.55	3.70	3.39	3.30	3.58	3.78	47.82
Days With ≥ 0.1" Precipitation	8	7	7	6	6	6	6	6	5	4	6	7	74
Days With ≥ 1.0" Precipitation	1	1	2	1	1	1	1	1	1	1	1	1	13
Mean Snowfall (in.)	0.2	0.4	0.5	0.0	0.0	0.0	0.0	0.0	0.0	0.0	trace	0.1	1.2
Days With ≥ 1.0" Snow Depth	0	0	0	0	0	0	0	0	0	0	0	0	0

Camden 3 W *Kershaw County*   Elevation: 137 ft.   Latitude: 34° 15' N   Longitude: 80° 39' W

	JAN	FEB	MAR	APR	MAY	JUN	JUL	AUG	SEP	OCT	NOV	DEC	YEAR
Mean Maximum Temp. (°F)	53.4	58.0	66.0	73.9	80.0	86.1	89.4	87.3	82.5	73.2	64.6	56.6	72.6
Mean Temp. (°F)	41.3	44.4	51.9	59.6	67.4	74.8	78.9	77.3	71.8	60.6	51.5	44.1	60.3
Mean Minimum Temp. (°F)	29.1	30.7	37.7	45.2	54.7	63.6	68.3	67.3	61.1	48.0	38.4	31.5	48.0
Extreme Maximum Temp. (°F)	79	83	88	91	94	101	102	104	97	92	85	81	104
Extreme Minimum Temp. (°F)	-3	7	7	25	33	44	52	53	40	26	11	5	-3
Days Maximum Temp. ≥ 90°F	0	0	0	0	1	8	16	11	3	0	0	0	39
Days Maximum Temp. ≤ 32°F	1	0	0	0	0	0	0	0	0	0	0	0	1
Days Minimum Temp. ≤ 32°F	20	17	10	3	0	0	0	0	0	1	11	18	80
Days Minimum Temp. ≤ 0°F	0	0	0	0	0	0	0	0	0	0	0	0	0
Heating Degree Days (base 65°F)	729	576	408	192	47	3	0	0	15	172	403	644	3,189
Cooling Degree Days (base 65°F)	0	2	8	33	134	320	458	399	222	47	5	2	1,630
Mean Precipitation (in.)	4.40	3.52	4.40	2.89	3.27	4.33	4.87	5.01	4.00	3.48	3.01	3.43	46.61
Days With ≥ 0.1" Precipitation	8	6	7	5	6	7	7	7	6	5	5	6	75
Days With ≥ 1.0" Precipitation	1	1	1	1	1	1	1	2	1	1	1	1	13
Mean Snowfall (in.)	0.2	0.7	0.2	0.0	0.0	0.0	0.0	0.0	0.0	0.0	trace	trace	1.1
Days With ≥ 1.0" Snow Depth	0	0	0	0	0	0	0	0	0	0	0	0	0

Charleston City *Charleston County*   Elevation: 9 ft.   Latitude: 32° 47' N   Longitude: 79° 56' W

	JAN	FEB	MAR	APR	MAY	JUN	JUL	AUG	SEP	OCT	NOV	DEC	YEAR
Mean Maximum Temp. (°F)	56.8	59.7	65.6	73.0	79.6	85.1	88.5	87.1	83.1	75.1	67.5	60.3	73.4
Mean Temp. (°F)	49.5	52.1	58.3	65.7	73.1	79.0	82.4	81.2	77.3	68.2	60.2	53.0	66.7
Mean Minimum Temp. (°F)	42.1	44.5	51.0	58.3	66.5	72.9	76.3	75.4	71.5	61.4	52.8	45.6	59.9
Extreme Maximum Temp. (°F)	80	80	88	94	96	104	103	103	98	93	85	81	104
Extreme Minimum Temp. (°F)	10	19	22	36	49	58	65	59	55	40	24	18	10
Days Maximum Temp. ≥ 90°F	0	0	0	0	1	6	12	10	3	0	0	0	32
Days Maximum Temp. ≤ 32°F	0	0	0	0	0	0	0	0	0	0	0	0	0
Days Minimum Temp. ≤ 32°F	5	2	0	0	0	0	0	0	0	0	0	2	9
Days Minimum Temp. ≤ 0°F	0	0	0	0	0	0	0	0	0	0	0	0	0
Heating Degree Days (base 65°F)	477	362	222	68	6	0	0	0	1	41	177	374	1,728
Cooling Degree Days (base 65°F)	1	5	21	90	265	433	558	513	370	152	39	8	2,455
Mean Precipitation (in.)	3.47	2.66	3.92	2.45	2.90	4.99	5.36	6.82	6.00	3.13	2.12	2.81	46.63
Days With ≥ 0.1" Precipitation	6	5	6	5	5	7	7	8	6	4	4	5	68
Days With ≥ 1.0" Precipitation	1	1	1	1	1	1	2	2	1	1	1	1	14
Mean Snowfall (in.)	na	na	na	na	na	na	na	na	na	na	na	na	na
Days With ≥ 1.0" Snow Depth	na	na	na	na	na	na	na	na	na	na	na	na	na

Cheraw *Chesterfield County* Elevation: 137 ft. Latitude: 34° 42' N Longitude: 79° 53' W

	JAN	FEB	MAR	APR	MAY	JUN	JUL	AUG	SEP	OCT	NOV	DEC	YEAR
Mean Maximum Temp. (°F)	52.7	56.9	65.0	74.4	80.9	87.4	90.7	88.4	83.5	73.9	65.1	56.3	72.9
Mean Temp. (°F)	41.0	44.4	51.8	60.5	68.3	75.9	79.9	78.2	72.8	61.5	52.3	44.6	60.9
Mean Minimum Temp. (°F)	29.7	31.7	38.8	46.6	55.6	64.2	69.0	67.9	62.0	48.9	39.6	32.7	48.9
Extreme Maximum Temp. (°F)	77	85	90	94	99	106	107	106	99	96	85	81	107
Extreme Minimum Temp. (°F)	0	10	9	27	35	45	55	50	42	23	17	10	0
Days Maximum Temp. ≥ 90°F	0	0	0	1	3	11	19	14	5	0	0	0	53
Days Maximum Temp. ≤ 32°F	1	0	0	0	0	0	0	0	0	0	0	0	1
Days Minimum Temp. ≤ 32°F	19	16	8	1	0	0	0	0	0	1	9	16	70
Days Minimum Temp. ≤ 0°F	0	0	0	0	0	0	0	0	0	0	0	0	0
Heating Degree Days (base 65°F)	737	577	411	173	41	3	0	0	12	154	384	628	3,120
Cooling Degree Days (base 65°F)	0	2	10	45	157	353	493	428	246	56	7	2	1,799
Mean Precipitation (in.)	4.33	3.54	4.47	2.86	3.50	4.62	5.40	5.12	3.96	3.85	2.82	3.25	47.72
Days With ≥ 0.1" Precipitation	7	6	7	5	7	7	8	7	5	5	5	6	75
Days With ≥ 1.0" Precipitation	1	1	1	1	1	2	2	2	1	1	1	1	15
Mean Snowfall (in.)	0.4	1.1	0.5	0.0	0.0	0.0	0.0	0.0	0.0	0.0	trace	0.3	2.3
Days With ≥ 1.0" Snow Depth	0	1	0	0	0	0	0	0	0	0	0	0	1

Chester 1 NW *Chester County* Elevation: 518 ft. Latitude: 34° 43' N Longitude: 81° 13' W

	JAN	FEB	MAR	APR	MAY	JUN	JUL	AUG	SEP	OCT	NOV	DEC	YEAR
Mean Maximum Temp. (°F)	52.2	57.4	65.6	74.3	80.5	86.9	90.6	88.6	83.6	74.1	64.8	55.7	72.8
Mean Temp. (°F)	41.3	45.0	52.7	60.5	68.0	75.5	79.6	78.1	72.4	61.3	52.2	44.4	60.9
Mean Minimum Temp. (°F)	30.3	32.6	39.7	46.6	55.5	64.2	68.5	67.6	61.3	48.4	39.7	33.0	48.9
Extreme Maximum Temp. (°F)	80	83	88	92	96	101	105	106	98	93	88	79	106
Extreme Minimum Temp. (°F)	-3	5	4	21	31	43	53	50	37	22	12	4	-3
Days Maximum Temp. ≥ 90°F	0	0	0	0	2	10	19	14	6	0	0	0	51
Days Maximum Temp. ≤ 32°F	1	0	0	0	0	0	0	0	0	0	0	0	1
Days Minimum Temp. ≤ 32°F	18	15	9	2	0	0	0	0	0	2	9	17	72
Days Minimum Temp. ≤ 0°F	0	0	0	0	0	0	0	0	0	0	0	0	0
Heating Degree Days (base 65°F)	730	559	385	175	44	3	0	0	14	161	384	634	3,089
Cooling Degree Days (base 65°F)	0	0	8	38	136	330	467	406	222	48	5	1	1,661
Mean Precipitation (in.)	4.60	3.80	4.84	3.32	3.42	4.48	3.99	4.62	3.87	3.78	3.53	3.51	47.76
Days With ≥ 0.1" Precipitation	8	6	7	5	6	7	7	6	5	4	5	7	73
Days With ≥ 1.0" Precipitation	1	1	2	1	1	1	1	2	1	1	1	1	14
Mean Snowfall (in.)	0.6	1.1	0.7	0.0	0.0	0.0	0.0	0.0	0.0	0.0	trace	0.4	2.8
Days With ≥ 1.0" Snow Depth	1	1	0	0	0	0	0	0	0	0	0	0	2

Clark Hill 1 W *McCormick County* Elevation: 377 ft. Latitude: 33° 40' N Longitude: 82° 11' W

	JAN	FEB	MAR	APR	MAY	JUN	JUL	AUG	SEP	OCT	NOV	DEC	YEAR
Mean Maximum Temp. (°F)	54.5	59.7	67.7	76.0	83.3	89.7	93.0	91.4	86.6	76.9	67.2	57.9	75.3
Mean Temp. (°F)	42.5	46.4	53.9	61.7	69.6	76.6	80.3	78.9	73.6	62.7	53.6	45.6	62.1
Mean Minimum Temp. (°F)	30.5	33.1	40.2	47.4	55.8	63.5	67.5	66.4	60.6	48.4	40.0	33.3	48.9
Extreme Maximum Temp. (°F)	79	84	90	92	97	104	109	108	103	94	87	81	109
Extreme Minimum Temp. (°F)	-2	5	12	23	32	45	56	49	38	26	17	9	-2
Days Maximum Temp. ≥ 90°F	0	0	0	1	6	16	24	21	11	1	0	0	80
Days Maximum Temp. ≤ 32°F	0	0	0	0	0	0	0	0	0	0	0	0	0
Days Minimum Temp. ≤ 32°F	18	14	7	1	0	0	0	0	0	1	8	15	64
Days Minimum Temp. ≤ 0°F	0	0	0	0	0	0	0	0	0	0	0	0	0
Heating Degree Days (base 65°F)	691	520	347	147	28	2	0	0	9	130	344	596	2,814
Cooling Degree Days (base 65°F)	0	2	12	51	182	367	503	445	264	66	9	1	1,902
Mean Precipitation (in.)	4.80	4.14	5.12	3.10	3.40	3.66	4.51	4.06	3.21	3.88	3.08	3.82	46.78
Days With ≥ 0.1" Precipitation	7	6	7	5	6	6	7	7	5	5	5	6	72
Days With ≥ 1.0" Precipitation	1	1	2	1	1	1	1	1	1	1	1	1	13
Mean Snowfall (in.)	0.0	0.4	0.0	0.0	0.0	0.0	0.0	0.0	0.0	0.0	0.0	0.0	0.4
Days With ≥ 1.0" Snow Depth	0	0	0	0	0	0	0	0	0	0	0	0	0

Clemson University *Pickens County* Elevation: 823 ft. Latitude: 34° 40' N Longitude: 82° 49' W

	JAN	FEB	MAR	APR	MAY	JUN	JUL	AUG	SEP	OCT	NOV	DEC	YEAR
Mean Maximum Temp. (°F)	51.8	56.4	63.9	72.6	79.2	86.0	89.8	88.0	82.9	73.2	63.8	55.1	71.9
Mean Temp. (°F)	40.8	44.4	51.7	59.7	67.5	74.9	78.8	77.5	71.9	60.9	51.8	44.0	60.3
Mean Minimum Temp. (°F)	29.8	32.4	39.5	46.7	55.7	63.7	67.8	67.0	61.0	48.5	39.8	32.9	48.7
Extreme Maximum Temp. (°F)	78	81	89	92	93	100	104	104	96	91	85	79	104
Extreme Minimum Temp. (°F)	-3	8	4	24	32	42	56	54	38	26	14	5	-3
Days Maximum Temp. ≥ 90°F	0	0	0	0	1	9	17	12	5	0	0	0	44
Days Maximum Temp. ≤ 32°F	1	0	0	0	0	0	0	0	0	0	0	0	1
Days Minimum Temp. ≤ 32°F	19	15	8	1	0	0	0	0	0	1	8	17	69
Days Minimum Temp. ≤ 0°F	0	0	0	0	0	0	0	0	0	0	0	0	0
Heating Degree Days (base 65°F)	743	575	409	186	45	2	0	0	15	161	392	643	3,171
Cooling Degree Days (base 65°F)	0	0	4	34	133	317	451	404	220	42	2	1	1,608
Mean Precipitation (in.)	5.50	4.89	5.78	3.89	4.45	3.66	4.25	4.76	4.02	4.21	4.09	4.58	54.08
Days With ≥ 0.1" Precipitation	8	7	8	6	8	6	7	7	6	5	7	8	83
Days With ≥ 1.0" Precipitation	2	1	2	1	2	1	1	1	1	1	1	1	15
Mean Snowfall (in.)	1.2	1.1	0.8	0.0	0.0	0.0	0.0	0.0	0.0	0.0	trace	0.4	3.5
Days With ≥ 1.0" Snow Depth	1	0	0	0	0	0	0	0	0	0	0	0	1

Conway *Horry County* Elevation: 19 ft. Latitude: 33° 50' N Longitude: 79° 03' W

	JAN	FEB	MAR	APR	MAY	JUN	JUL	AUG	SEP	OCT	NOV	DEC	YEAR
Mean Maximum Temp. (°F)	56.9	60.4	67.7	75.5	82.2	87.6	90.9	89.2	84.9	76.6	68.9	60.3	75.1
Mean Temp. (°F)	45.7	48.5	55.7	63.2	70.9	77.4	81.2	79.8	75.0	64.9	56.7	48.8	64.0
Mean Minimum Temp. (°F)	34.4	36.5	43.6	50.9	59.5	67.1	71.4	70.4	65.1	53.1	44.4	37.3	52.8
Extreme Maximum Temp. (°F)	82	83	90	94	98	103	103	105	100	96	87	82	105
Extreme Minimum Temp. (°F)	4	12	12	22	41	42	58	55	45	27	20	8	4
Days Maximum Temp. ≥ 90°F	0	0	0	1	4	12	20	16	7	0	0	0	60
Days Maximum Temp. ≤ 32°F	0	0	0	0	0	0	0	0	0	0	0	0	0
Days Minimum Temp. ≤ 32°F	14	10	3	0	0	0	0	0	0	0	4	11	42
Days Minimum Temp. ≤ 0°F	0	0	0	0	0	0	0	0	0	0	0	0	0
Heating Degree Days (base 65°F)	593	464	300	119	20	2	0	0	4	93	267	501	2,363
Cooling Degree Days (base 65°F)	1	5	16	65	215	396	529	476	306	103	22	5	2,139
Mean Precipitation (in.)	4.61	3.52	4.15	3.07	4.37	4.66	6.76	6.72	5.79	3.41	2.66	3.68	53.40
Days With ≥ 0.1" Precipitation	8	6	7	5	7	7	9	8	7	4	4	7	79
Days With ≥ 1.0" Precipitation	1	1	2	1	1	1	2	2	2	1	1	1	16
Mean Snowfall (in.)	trace	0.5	0.0	0.0	0.0	0.0	0.0	0.0	0.0	0.0	0.0	0.5	1.0
Days With ≥ 1.0" Snow Depth	0	0	0	0	0	0	0	0	0	0	0	0	0

Darlington *Darlington County* Elevation: 147 ft. Latitude: 34° 18' N Longitude: 79° 53' W

	JAN	FEB	MAR	APR	MAY	JUN	JUL	AUG	SEP	OCT	NOV	DEC	YEAR
Mean Maximum Temp. (°F)	56.2	61.1	68.9	77.4	83.7	89.1	92.1	89.8	85.4	76.5	67.7	59.3	75.6
Mean Temp. (°F)	45.2	48.7	56.0	63.7	71.1	77.7	81.3	79.4	74.5	64.0	55.2	48.1	63.7
Mean Minimum Temp. (°F)	34.1	36.2	43.1	50.0	58.4	66.3	70.4	69.1	63.6	51.4	42.7	36.8	51.8
Extreme Maximum Temp. (°F)	82	84	89	96	98	104	108	106	104	95	90	84	108
Extreme Minimum Temp. (°F)	-4	4	14	26	34	46	54	50	36	25	15	7	-4
Days Maximum Temp. ≥ 90°F	0	0	0	1	5	15	23	17	8	1	0	0	70
Days Maximum Temp. ≤ 32°F	0	0	0	0	0	0	0	0	0	0	0	0	0
Days Minimum Temp. ≤ 32°F	15	11	5	1	0	0	0	0	0	1	6	11	50
Days Minimum Temp. ≤ 0°F	0	0	0	0	0	0	0	0	0	0	0	0	0
Heating Degree Days (base 65°F)	609	460	291	111	18	1	0	0	8	105	304	522	2,429
Cooling Degree Days (base 65°F)	1	6	22	79	220	406	527	453	289	81	14	5	2,103
Mean Precipitation (in.)	4.36	3.46	4.56	2.79	3.38	4.35	4.79	5.46	3.87	3.34	2.64	3.68	46.68
Days With ≥ 0.1" Precipitation	7	6	8	5	7	7	8	7	5	5	5	7	77
Days With ≥ 1.0" Precipitation	1	1	1	1	1	1	2	2	1	1	1	1	14
Mean Snowfall (in.)	0.3	0.6	0.2	0.0	0.0	0.0	0.0	0.0	0.0	0.0	0.0	trace	1.1
Days With ≥ 1.0" Snow Depth	0	0	0	0	0	0	0	0	0	0	0	0	0

Dillon *Dillon County* Elevation: 114 ft. Latitude: 34° 25' N Longitude: 79° 23' W

	JAN	FEB	MAR	APR	MAY	JUN	JUL	AUG	SEP	OCT	NOV	DEC	YEAR
Mean Maximum Temp. (°F)	54.0	57.9	66.1	74.6	81.9	87.8	91.1	89.3	84.5	75.1	66.4	57.5	73.9
Mean Temp. (°F)	42.8	45.9	53.2	61.3	69.3	76.4	80.5	78.9	73.5	62.3	53.6	46.0	62.0
Mean Minimum Temp. (°F)	31.6	33.6	40.3	47.9	56.7	65.0	69.9	68.4	62.5	49.5	40.7	34.3	50.0
Extreme Maximum Temp. (°F)	80	83	91	94	96	104	104	106	101	97	87	82	106
Extreme Minimum Temp. (°F)	-1	5	11	25	35	42	55	49	39	22	12	2	-1
Days Maximum Temp. ≥ 90°F	0	0	0	1	4	13	20	16	8	1	0	0	63
Days Maximum Temp. ≤ 32°F	1	0	0	0	0	0	0	0	0	0	0	0	1
Days Minimum Temp. ≤ 32°F	17	14	7	1	0	0	0	0	0	1	8	14	62
Days Minimum Temp. ≤ 0°F	0	0	0	0	0	0	0	0	0	0	0	0	0
Heating Degree Days (base 65°F)	682	539	371	162	35	3	0	0	11	140	352	588	2,883
Cooling Degree Days (base 65°F)	1	3	12	53	184	368	510	442	263	69	13	4	1,922
Mean Precipitation (in.)	4.05	3.34	4.46	3.13	3.32	4.37	5.49	5.30	3.96	3.08	2.79	3.58	46.87
Days With ≥ 0.1" Precipitation	8	6	7	5	7	6	8	8	5	5	5	6	76
Days With ≥ 1.0" Precipitation	1	1	1	1	1	1	2	2	1	1	1	1	14
Mean Snowfall (in.)	0.4	0.4	0.5	0.0	0.0	0.0	0.0	0.0	0.0	0.0	0.0	0.4	1.7
Days With ≥ 1.0" Snow Depth	0	0	0	0	0	0	0	0	0	0	0	0	0

Florence 8 NE *Darlington County* Elevation: 118 ft. Latitude: 34° 18' N Longitude: 79° 44' W

	JAN	FEB	MAR	APR	MAY	JUN	JUL	AUG	SEP	OCT	NOV	DEC	YEAR
Mean Maximum Temp. (°F)	54.3	58.3	66.2	75.0	82.0	88.0	91.2	89.3	84.7	75.4	67.0	58.1	74.1
Mean Temp. (°F)	43.5	46.7	54.4	62.7	70.5	77.4	81.0	79.2	74.0	63.0	54.6	46.8	62.8
Mean Minimum Temp. (°F)	32.7	35.0	42.6	50.2	58.9	66.7	70.8	69.1	63.2	50.6	42.3	35.4	51.5
Extreme Maximum Temp. (°F)	81	85	88	93	98	105	103	105	99	97	87	85	105
Extreme Minimum Temp. (°F)	1	4	16	27	35	49	56	53	42	27	16	9	1
Days Maximum Temp. ≥ 90°F	0	0	0	1	5	13	21	16	8	1	0	0	65
Days Maximum Temp. ≤ 32°F	1	0	0	0	0	0	0	0	0	0	0	0	1
Days Minimum Temp. ≤ 32°F	16	12	5	1	0	0	0	0	0	1	6	13	54
Days Minimum Temp. ≤ 0°F	0	0	0	0	0	0	0	0	0	0	0	0	0
Heating Degree Days (base 65°F)	660	514	337	133	26	2	0	0	9	127	321	563	2,692
Cooling Degree Days (base 65°F)	1	3	15	68	208	397	527	456	278	77	15	5	2,050
Mean Precipitation (in.)	4.47	3.37	4.43	2.76	3.53	4.20	5.46	5.34	3.92	3.35	2.69	3.67	47.19
Days With ≥ 0.1" Precipitation	8	6	7	5	6	7	8	8	5	5	4	6	75
Days With ≥ 1.0" Precipitation	1	1	1	1	1	1	2	2	1	1	1	1	14
Mean Snowfall (in.)	0.1	0.5	0.4	0.0	0.0	0.0	0.0	0.0	0.0	0.0	0.0	0.2	1.2
Days With ≥ 1.0" Snow Depth	0	0	0	0	0	0	0	0	0	0	0	0	0

Florence City County Airport *Florence County*   Elevation: 144 ft.   Latitude: 34° 12' N   Longitude: 79° 44' W

	JAN	FEB	MAR	APR	MAY	JUN	JUL	AUG	SEP	OCT	NOV	DEC	YEAR
Mean Maximum Temp. (°F)	55.8	59.5	67.6	76.0	82.7	88.3	91.3	89.4	84.8	75.8	67.4	58.9	74.8
Mean Temp. (°F)	45.6	48.6	56.0	63.6	71.3	78.0	81.5	80.0	75.0	64.5	55.9	48.3	64.0
Mean Minimum Temp. (°F)	35.4	37.6	44.3	51.1	59.8	67.6	71.7	70.5	65.1	53.1	44.3	37.7	53.2
Extreme Maximum Temp. (°F)	85	85	92	97	97	105	104	106	100	97	89	86	106
Extreme Minimum Temp. (°F)	0	11	11	27	36	49	57	54	43	29	18	8	0
Days Maximum Temp. ≥ 90°F	0	0	0	2	5	13	21	16	8	0	0	0	65
Days Maximum Temp. ≤ 32°F	1	0	0	0	0	0	0	0	0	0	0	0	1
Days Minimum Temp. ≤ 32°F	13	9	4	0	0	0	0	0	0	0	4	10	40
Days Minimum Temp. ≤ 0°F	0	0	0	0	0	0	0	0	0	0	0	0	0
Heating Degree Days (base 65°F)	598	462	297	116	19	1	0	0	6	100	289	517	2,405
Cooling Degree Days (base 65°F)	2	6	22	78	224	410	536	474	300	91	19	6	2,168
Mean Precipitation (in.)	4.05	3.15	4.08	2.77	3.30	4.29	5.28	5.25	3.68	3.04	2.52	3.54	44.95
Days With ≥ 0.1" Precipitation	7	6	7	5	7	7	8	7	6	4	5	6	75
Days With ≥ 1.0" Precipitation	1	1	1	1	1	1	1	2	1	1	1	1	13
Mean Snowfall (in.)	0.7	1.3	0.4	0.0	0.0	0.0	0.0	0.0	0.0	trace	trace	0.3	2.7
Days With ≥ 1.0" Snow Depth	1	0	0	0	0	0	0	0	0	0	0	0	1

Georgetown 2 E *Georgetown County*   Elevation: 9 ft.   Latitude: 33° 22' N   Longitude: 79° 13' W

	JAN	FEB	MAR	APR	MAY	JUN	JUL	AUG	SEP	OCT	NOV	DEC	YEAR
Mean Maximum Temp. (°F)	59.6	62.7	69.7	76.6	82.9	87.6	90.7	89.2	85.4	77.2	70.1	63.2	76.2
Mean Temp. (°F)	48.5	50.8	57.4	64.1	71.4	77.5	81.1	79.8	75.9	66.4	58.5	52.0	65.3
Mean Minimum Temp. (°F)	37.5	38.9	45.1	51.6	59.9	67.2	71.4	70.3	66.4	55.5	46.8	40.7	54.3
Extreme Maximum Temp. (°F)	83	84	90	94	96	106	105	103	98	96	87	83	106
Extreme Minimum Temp. (°F)	6	13	11	28	38	49	56	46	45	16	21	11	6
Days Maximum Temp. ≥ 90°F	0	0	0	1	3	11	18	14	5	0	0	0	52
Days Maximum Temp. ≤ 32°F	0	0	0	0	0	0	0	0	0	0	0	0	0
Days Minimum Temp. ≤ 32°F	10	7	3	0	0	0	0	0	0	0	2	7	29
Days Minimum Temp. ≤ 0°F	0	0	0	0	0	0	0	0	0	0	0	0	0
Heating Degree Days (base 65°F)	506	399	252	94	12	1	0	0	2	64	218	404	1,952
Cooling Degree Days (base 65°F)	2	5	21	77	220	396	522	465	*330*	116	26	*7*	*2,187*
Mean Precipitation (in.)	4.63	3.45	4.08	2.60	4.20	5.63	6.20	7.45	6.24	4.70	3.13	3.92	56.23
Days With ≥ 0.1" Precipitation	7	6	5	4	5	7	8	9	6	5	5	6	73
Days With ≥ 1.0" Precipitation	1	1	1	1	1	2	2	2	2	1	1	1	16
Mean Snowfall (in.)	0.2	trace	0.1	0.0	0.0	0.0	0.0	0.0	0.0	0.0	0.0	trace	0.3
Days With ≥ 1.0" Snow Depth	0	0	0	0	0	0	0	0	0	0	0	0	0

Greenwood 3 SW *Greenwood County*   Elevation: 613 ft.   Latitude: 34° 10' N   Longitude: 82° 12' W

	JAN	FEB	MAR	APR	MAY	JUN	JUL	AUG	SEP	OCT	NOV	DEC	YEAR
Mean Maximum Temp. (°F)	52.0	57.0	65.2	73.8	80.8	87.2	90.8	88.9	83.6	73.3	64.0	55.2	72.7
Mean Temp. (°F)	40.8	44.2	51.6	59.6	67.5	75.1	79.0	77.7	71.9	60.3	51.2	43.7	60.2
Mean Minimum Temp. (°F)	29.5	31.3	38.1	45.3	54.3	62.9	67.2	66.4	60.2	47.3	38.3	32.2	47.7
Extreme Maximum Temp. (°F)	79	80	89	92	95	102	106	105	97	91	85	78	106
Extreme Minimum Temp. (°F)	-2	2	3	24	32	41	55	52	41	25	13	5	-2
Days Maximum Temp. ≥ 90°F	0	0	0	0	2	10	19	14	6	0	0	0	51
Days Maximum Temp. ≤ 32°F	1	0	0	0	0	0	0	0	0	0	0	0	1
Days Minimum Temp. ≤ 32°F	20	16	10	2	0	0	0	0	0	1	10	17	76
Days Minimum Temp. ≤ 0°F	0	0	0	0	0	0	0	0	0	0	0	0	0
Heating Degree Days (base 65°F)	746	582	412	193	46	3	0	0	16	177	413	655	3,243
Cooling Degree Days (base 65°F)	0	0	4	33	132	321	459	405	224	42	4	1	1,625
Mean Precipitation (in.)	4.85	4.30	4.95	3.19	3.77	3.62	4.00	3.60	3.22	3.64	3.60	3.78	46.52
Days With ≥ 0.1" Precipitation	8	7	7	6	6	6	7	6	5	4	6	7	75
Days With ≥ 1.0" Precipitation	1	1	2	1	1	1	1	1	1	1	1	1	13
Mean Snowfall (in.)	0.9	0.9	0.5	0.0	0.0	0.0	0.0	0.0	0.0	0.0	trace	0.1	2.4
Days With ≥ 1.0" Snow Depth	1	1	0	0	0	0	0	0	0	0	0	0	2

Hampton *Hampton County*   Elevation: 95 ft.   Latitude: 32° 52' N   Longitude: 81° 07' W

	JAN	FEB	MAR	APR	MAY	JUN	JUL	AUG	SEP	OCT	NOV	DEC	YEAR
Mean Maximum Temp. (°F)	60.0	64.3	71.7	78.6	84.8	89.9	92.5	90.7	86.6	78.3	70.3	62.7	77.5
Mean Temp. (°F)	48.7	52.0	59.1	65.4	72.5	78.7	81.9	80.5	76.1	66.3	58.0	51.3	65.9
Mean Minimum Temp. (°F)	37.3	39.7	46.3	52.2	60.3	67.4	71.2	70.2	65.5	54.2	45.7	39.8	54.2
Extreme Maximum Temp. (°F)	83	84	93	94	97	104	107	104	102	94	85	82	107
Extreme Minimum Temp. (°F)	1	13	16	29	39	47	54	56	40	23	11	8	1
Days Maximum Temp. ≥ 90°F	0	0	0	1	6	17	24	19	10	1	0	0	78
Days Maximum Temp. ≤ 32°F	0	0	0	0	0	0	0	0	0	0	0	0	0
Days Minimum Temp. ≤ 32°F	11	8	3	0	0	0	0	0	0	0	4	9	35
Days Minimum Temp. ≤ 0°F	0	0	0	0	0	0	0	0	0	0	0	0	0
Heating Degree Days (base 65°F)	503	369	212	76	8	0	0	0	2	69	231	428	1,898
Cooling Degree Days (base 65°F)	3	10	33	96	256	435	549	497	341	125	31	8	2,384
Mean Precipitation (in.)	4.40	3.49	4.29	3.05	3.46	5.65	5.02	6.05	3.84	2.99	2.68	3.40	48.32
Days With ≥ 0.1" Precipitation	7	6	7	5	6	8	8	9	5	4	4	6	75
Days With ≥ 1.0" Precipitation	1	1	1	1	2	1	2	1	1	1	1	1	14
Mean Snowfall (in.)	0.2	0.5	trace	0.0	0.0	0.0	0.0	0.0	0.0	0.0	trace	0.1	0.8
Days With ≥ 1.0" Snow Depth	0	0	0	0	0	0	0	0	0	0	0	0	0

Hilton Head *Beaufort County*   Elevation: 13 ft.   Latitude: 32° 13' N   Longitude: 80° 45' W

	JAN	FEB	MAR	APR	MAY	JUN	JUL	AUG	SEP	OCT	NOV	DEC	YEAR
Mean Maximum Temp. (°F)	59.7	63.0	69.6	75.9	81.9	86.8	89.5	88.2	84.5	77.3	69.7	62.5	75.7
Mean Temp. (°F)	49.4	52.1	59.0	64.9	72.1	77.8	*81.1*	80.1	76.5	67.6	59.4	52.2	*66.0*
Mean Minimum Temp. (°F)	39.1	41.2	48.3	53.9	62.3	68.8	*72.6*	71.9	68.4	57.9	49.0	41.9	*56.3*
Extreme Maximum Temp. (°F)	85	84	89	95	99	101	107	99	98	97	86	83	107
Extreme Minimum Temp. (°F)	4	16	21	32	43	45	60	53	50	32	24	10	4
Days Maximum Temp. ≥ 90°F	0	0	0	1	2	7	14	11	4	0	0	0	39
Days Maximum Temp. ≤ 32°F	0	0	0	0	0	0	0	0	0	0	0	0	0
Days Minimum Temp. ≤ 32°F	9	5	2	0	0	0	0	0	0	0	1	6	23
Days Minimum Temp. ≤ 0°F	0	0	0	0	0	0	0	0	0	0	0	0	0
Heating Degree Days (base 65°F)	479	363	207	76	6	2	*0*	0	0	50	196	397	*1,776*
Cooling Degree Days (base 65°F)	2	7	28	81	*239*	*407*	*524*	484	350	148	36	7	*2,313*
Mean Precipitation (in.)	4.33	3.39	3.94	3.05	3.23	5.04	5.85	8.59	6.09	4.05	2.74	3.24	53.54
Days With ≥ 0.1" Precipitation	7	6	6	4	5	7	8	9	7	4	4	6	73
Days With ≥ 1.0" Precipitation	1	1	1	1	1	1	2	3	2	1	1	1	16
Mean Snowfall (in.)	trace	trace	trace	0.0	0.0	0.0	0.0	0.0	0.0	0.0	0.0	0.0	trace
Days With ≥ 1.0" Snow Depth	0	0	0	0	0	0	0	0	0	0	0	0	0

Johnston 4 SW *Edgefield County*   Elevation: 620 ft.   Latitude: 33° 47' N   Longitude: 81° 51' W

	JAN	FEB	MAR	APR	MAY	JUN	JUL	AUG	SEP	OCT	NOV	DEC	YEAR
Mean Maximum Temp. (°F)	53.5	58.0	66.0	74.6	81.8	88.3	91.8	89.6	84.5	75.0	66.0	57.1	73.8
Mean Temp. (°F)	42.6	45.9	53.4	61.2	69.1	76.3	80.0	78.3	72.9	62.3	53.6	45.7	61.8
Mean Minimum Temp. (°F)	31.6	33.7	40.8	47.8	56.4	64.2	68.1	66.8	61.3	49.4	41.1	34.3	49.6
Extreme Maximum Temp. (°F)	79	83	88	93	99	104	107	107	105	93	88	81	107
Extreme Minimum Temp. (°F)	-2	9	1	26	36	46	53	53	42	28	15	5	-2
Days Maximum Temp. ≥ 90°F	0	0	0	1	5	13	21	17	8	0	0	0	65
Days Maximum Temp. ≤ 32°F	1	0	0	0	0	0	0	0	0	0	0	0	1
Days Minimum Temp. ≤ 32°F	17	13	7	1	0	0	0	0	0	1	7	15	61
Days Minimum Temp. ≤ 0°F	0	0	0	0	0	0	0	0	0	0	0	0	0
Heating Degree Days (base 65°F)	688	535	362	158	32	2	0	0	12	137	347	593	2,866
Cooling Degree Days (base 65°F)	0	2	10	49	177	364	498	430	256	62	9	2	1,859
Mean Precipitation (in.)	4.90	4.15	5.08	3.40	3.59	4.43	4.38	4.81	3.78	3.45	3.07	3.59	48.63
Days With ≥ 0.1" Precipitation	7	7	7	6	6	6	7	7	5	4	5	6	73
Days With ≥ 1.0" Precipitation	2	1	2	1	1	1	1	1	1	1	1	1	14
Mean Snowfall (in.)	0.4	1.1	0.2	0.0	0.0	0.0	0.0	0.0	0.0	0.0	0.0	0.1	1.8
Days With ≥ 1.0" Snow Depth	0	0	0	0	0	0	0	0	0	0	0	0	0

Kingstree 1 SE *Williamsburg County*   Elevation: 59 ft.   Latitude: 33° 39' N   Longitude: 79° 49' W

	JAN	FEB	MAR	APR	MAY	JUN	JUL	AUG	SEP	OCT	NOV	DEC	YEAR
Mean Maximum Temp. (°F)	56.6	60.4	68.3	76.2	83.2	88.7	92.1	90.2	85.5	76.7	68.5	59.9	75.5
Mean Temp. (°F)	44.2	47.0	54.6	61.9	69.6	76.4	80.3	78.8	73.6	62.9	54.4	47.0	62.6
Mean Minimum Temp. (°F)	31.7	33.5	40.8	47.6	56.0	64.0	68.4	67.4	61.6	49.2	40.3	34.0	49.5
Extreme Maximum Temp. (°F)	81	86	89	93	97	103	108	107	98	98	87	84	108
Extreme Minimum Temp. (°F)	0	0	12	25	34	45	53	53	36	25	14	4	0
Days Maximum Temp. ≥ 90°F	0	0	0	1	6	15	23	18	9	1	0	0	73
Days Maximum Temp. ≤ 32°F	1	0	0	0	0	0	0	0	0	0	0	0	1
Days Minimum Temp. ≤ 32°F	18	14	7	2	0	0	0	0	0	1	9	16	67
Days Minimum Temp. ≤ 0°F	0	0	0	0	0	0	0	0	0	0	0	0	0
Heating Degree Days (base 65°F)	642	506	332	143	30	2	0	0	9	127	328	556	2,675
Cooling Degree Days (base 65°F)	1	4	15	57	185	369	501	445	270	76	16	5	1,944
Mean Precipitation (in.)	4.64	3.65	4.44	3.18	3.63	4.95	5.04	5.73	4.59	3.54	2.61	4.01	50.01
Days With ≥ 0.1" Precipitation	9	6	7	5	6	8	8	8	6	5	5	7	80
Days With ≥ 1.0" Precipitation	1	1	1	1	1	2	2	2	1	1	1	1	15
Mean Snowfall (in.)	0.3	1.0	0.2	0.0	0.0	0.0	0.0	0.0	0.0	0.0	0.0	0.3	1.8
Days With ≥ 1.0" Snow Depth	0	0	0	0	0	0	0	0	0	0	0	0	0

Lake City 2 SE *Florence County*   Elevation: 72 ft.   Latitude: 33° 51' N   Longitude: 79° 44' W

	JAN	FEB	MAR	APR	MAY	JUN	JUL	AUG	SEP	OCT	NOV	DEC	YEAR
Mean Maximum Temp. (°F)	56.2	59.8	67.6	75.9	82.6	88.3	91.8	89.9	85.3	76.2	68.2	58.9	75.1
Mean Temp. (°F)	44.6	47.5	54.8	62.2	69.9	76.9	80.8	79.5	74.2	63.5	55.0	46.9	63.0
Mean Minimum Temp. (°F)	33.0	34.9	41.8	48.2	57.1	65.4	69.9	69.0	63.0	50.8	41.8	34.8	50.8
Extreme Maximum Temp. (°F)	81	84	89	93	97	104	105	103	99	97	87	*82*	*105*
Extreme Minimum Temp. (°F)	2	5	10	*26*	35	46	53	55	42	26	19	6	*2*
Days Maximum Temp. ≥ 90°F	0	0	0	1	4	13	22	18	7	0	0	0	65
Days Maximum Temp. ≤ 32°F	1	0	0	0	0	0	0	0	0	0	0	0	1
Days Minimum Temp. ≤ 32°F	16	13	6	1	0	0	0	0	0	1	6	13	56
Days Minimum Temp. ≤ 0°F	0	0	0	0	0	0	0	0	0	0	0	0	0
Heating Degree Days (base 65°F)	629	492	327	139	28	1	0	0	6	117	311	558	2,608
Cooling Degree Days (base 65°F)	1	4	15	53	185	*379*	511	458	275	79	19	3	*1,982*
Mean Precipitation (in.)	4.41	3.60	4.79	2.97	3.32	4.17	5.57	6.19	4.87	3.14	2.57	3.93	49.53
Days With ≥ 0.1" Precipitation	8	6	6	5	6	6	8	8	5	4	4	6	72
Days With ≥ 1.0" Precipitation	1	1	1	1	1	1	2	2	2	1	1	1	15
Mean Snowfall (in.)	0.5	1.1	0.3	0.0	0.0	0.0	0.0	0.0	0.0	0.0	0.0	0.3	2.2
Days With ≥ 1.0" Snow Depth	0	0	0	0	0	0	0	0	0	0	0	0	0

Laurens *Laurens County*   Elevation: 587 ft.   Latitude: 34° 31' N   Longitude: 82° 02' W

	JAN	FEB	MAR	APR	MAY	JUN	JUL	AUG	SEP	OCT	NOV	DEC	YEAR
Mean Maximum Temp. (°F)	52.5	57.0	65.2	73.9	81.1	87.9	91.5	89.5	84.1	73.9	64.5	55.7	73.1
Mean Temp. (°F)	40.5	43.4	51.6	59.5	67.6	75.5	79.4	77.5	71.4	59.7	50.4	43.1	60.0
Mean Minimum Temp. (°F)	28.4	30.0	37.9	45.1	54.1	63.0	67.2	65.5	58.7	45.5	36.3	30.5	46.8
Extreme Maximum Temp. (°F)	78	82	89	93	97	107	107	105	99	93	85	79	107
Extreme Minimum Temp. (°F)	-2	5	6	23	31	42	54	49	37	25	13	5	-2
Days Maximum Temp. ≥ 90°F	0	0	0	0	3	13	21	16	7	0	0	0	60
Days Maximum Temp. ≤ 32°F	1	0	0	0	0	0	0	0	0	0	0	0	1
Days Minimum Temp. ≤ 32°F	21	18	9	3	0	0	0	0	0	3	11	19	84
Days Minimum Temp. ≤ 0°F	0	0	0	0	0	0	0	0	0	0	0	0	0
Heating Degree Days (base 65°F)	754	605	415	193	46	2	0	0	18	188	437	673	3,331
Cooling Degree Days (base 65°F)	0	0	6	34	141	335	465	402	210	33	3	1	1,630
Mean Precipitation (in.)	4.87	4.28	5.10	3.36	3.81	3.54	3.45	3.93	3.53	3.93	3.82	3.88	47.50
Days With ≥ 0.1" Precipitation	8	7	7	6	6	6	6	6	6	5	6	7	76
Days With ≥ 1.0" Precipitation	1	1	1	1	1	1	1	1	1	1	1	1	12
Mean Snowfall (in.)	0.8	0.6	0.5	0.0	0.0	0.0	0.0	0.0	0.0	0.0	trace	0.4	2.3
Days With ≥ 1.0" Snow Depth	0	0	0	0	0	0	0	0	0	0	0	0	0

Little Mountain *Newberry County*   Elevation: 708 ft.   Latitude: 34° 12' N   Longitude: 81° 25' W

	JAN	FEB	MAR	APR	MAY	JUN	JUL	AUG	SEP	OCT	NOV	DEC	YEAR
Mean Maximum Temp. (°F)	53.6	58.4	66.2	74.5	81.1	87.3	90.5	88.4	83.4	74.0	65.1	56.8	73.3
Mean Temp. (°F)	43.9	47.5	54.8	62.5	69.8	76.6	80.1	78.5	73.3	62.9	54.3	46.8	62.6
Mean Minimum Temp. (°F)	34.2	36.7	43.5	50.5	58.5	65.9	69.6	68.5	63.1	51.7	43.4	36.8	51.9
Extreme Maximum Temp. (°F)	79	80	88	92	96	101	106	104	98	96	87	79	106
Extreme Minimum Temp. (°F)	-2	7	9	26	38	43	58	52	41	27	15	4	-2
Days Maximum Temp. ≥ 90°F	0	0	0	0	2	10	19	13	5	0	0	0	49
Days Maximum Temp. ≤ 32°F	1	0	0	0	0	0	0	0	0	0	0	0	1
Days Minimum Temp. ≤ 32°F	14	10	5	1	0	0	0	0	0	0	5	11	46
Days Minimum Temp. ≤ 0°F	0	0	0	0	0	0	0	0	0	0	0	0	0
Heating Degree Days (base 65°F)	648	489	323	132	26	2	0	0	11	125	327	560	2,643
Cooling Degree Days (base 65°F)	0	2	15	58	182	361	484	422	251	67	10	3	1,855
Mean Precipitation (in.)	4.71	4.00	4.97	3.01	3.40	4.04	4.86	4.92	4.16	3.62	3.14	3.66	48.49
Days With ≥ 0.1" Precipitation	7	7	7	5	6	6	7	7	5	4	5	6	72
Days With ≥ 1.0" Precipitation	1	1	2	1	1	1	2	1	1	1	1	1	14
Mean Snowfall (in.)	0.5	1.0	0.7	0.0	0.0	0.0	0.0	0.0	0.0	trace	trace	0.2	2.4
Days With ≥ 1.0" Snow Depth	1	0	0	0	0	0	0	0	0	0	0	0	1

Manning *Clarendon County*   Elevation: 98 ft.   Latitude: 33° 42' N   Longitude: 80° 14' W

	JAN	FEB	MAR	APR	MAY	JUN	JUL	AUG	SEP	OCT	NOV	DEC	YEAR
Mean Maximum Temp. (°F)	56.2	61.1	69.2	77.3	84.3	89.7	93.2	91.4	86.3	77.3	69.2	59.5	76.2
Mean Temp. (°F)	44.4	48.2	55.8	63.2	70.7	77.2	81.0	79.6	74.2	63.4	55.7	47.4	63.4
Mean Minimum Temp. (°F)	32.5	35.2	42.4	49.0	57.1	64.6	68.8	67.7	61.9	49.5	42.1	35.1	50.5
Extreme Maximum Temp. (°F)	81	84	90	95	99	104	108	108	101	99	88	83	108
Extreme Minimum Temp. (°F)	0	12	7	24	34	40	48	49	37	22	19	7	0
Days Maximum Temp. ≥ 90°F	0	0	0	2	7	17	24	21	10	1	0	0	82
Days Maximum Temp. ≤ 32°F	0	0	0	0	0	0	0	0	0	0	0	0	0
Days Minimum Temp. ≤ 32°F	16	12	6	1	0	0	0	0	0	0	1	7	14	57
Days Minimum Temp. ≤ 0°F	0	0	0	0	0	0	0	0	0	0	0	0	0
Heating Degree Days (base 65°F)	634	473	298	120	24	2	0	0	7	119	293	545	2,515
Cooling Degree Days (base 65°F)	1	4	19	72	216	392	512	468	291	85	18	5	2,083
Mean Precipitation (in.)	4.64	3.79	4.27	3.14	3.68	5.27	4.86	5.58	4.41	2.85	2.73	3.80	49.02
Days With ≥ 0.1" Precipitation	8	7	7	5	7	8	8	8	6	5	5	6	80
Days With ≥ 1.0" Precipitation	1	1	1	1	1	2	1	2	1	1	1	1	14
Mean Snowfall (in.)	0.4	1.1	0.2	0.0	0.0	0.0	0.0	0.0	0.0	0.0	0.0	trace	1.7
Days With ≥ 1.0" Snow Depth	0	0	0	0	0	0	0	0	0	0	0	0	0

McColl 3 NNW *Marlboro County*   Elevation: 187 ft.   Latitude: 34° 42' N   Longitude: 79° 34' W

	JAN	FEB	MAR	APR	MAY	JUN	JUL	AUG	SEP	OCT	NOV	DEC	YEAR
Mean Maximum Temp. (°F)	54.7	59.1	66.9	76.0	82.5	89.1	91.7	89.5	84.3	74.9	66.1	57.5	74.4
Mean Temp. (°F)	44.0	47.3	54.5	62.7	70.5	77.7	80.7	78.9	73.7	62.8	54.2	46.5	62.8
Mean Minimum Temp. (°F)	32.8	35.4	42.0	49.3	58.3	66.1	69.6	68.3	63.0	50.6	42.2	35.3	51.1
Extreme Maximum Temp. (°F)	82	85	91	95	98	104	106	107	100	94	88	81	107
Extreme Minimum Temp. (°F)	-5	7	8	25	34	46	48	52	40	24	15	5	-5
Days Maximum Temp. ≥ 90°F	0	0	0	2	5	17	23	17	6	0	0	0	70
Days Maximum Temp. ≤ 32°F	1	0	0	0	0	0	0	0	0	0	0	0	1
Days Minimum Temp. ≤ 32°F	16	12	6	1	0	0	0	0	0	0	1	6	13	55
Days Minimum Temp. ≤ 0°F	0	0	0	0	0	0	0	0	0	0	0	0	0
Heating Degree Days (base 65°F)	648	494	335	130	23	2	0	0	8	129	332	571	2,672
Cooling Degree Days (base 65°F)	1	1	12	65	195	390	501	436	250	67	10	3	1,931
Mean Precipitation (in.)	3.57	3.31	3.78	2.23	2.92	3.48	4.28	3.49	3.30	2.58	2.65	2.82	38.41
Days With ≥ 0.1" Precipitation	6	6	7	4	6	5	7	6	5	4	5	5	66
Days With ≥ 1.0" Precipitation	1	1	1	1	1	1	1	1	1	1	1	1	12
Mean Snowfall (in.)	0.4	0.7	0.4	0.0	0.0	0.0	0.0	0.0	0.0	0.0	trace	0.3	1.8
Days With ≥ 1.0" Snow Depth	1	0	0	0	0	0	0	0	0	0	0	0	1

Newberry *Newberry County*   Elevation: 475 ft.   Latitude: 34° 17' N   Longitude: 81° 38' W

	JAN	FEB	MAR	APR	MAY	JUN	JUL	AUG	SEP	OCT	NOV	DEC	YEAR
Mean Maximum Temp. (°F)	54.9	60.2	68.3	76.6	83.2	89.3	92.5	90.5	85.3	75.7	66.4	58.0	75.1
Mean Temp. (°F)	43.6	47.4	54.8	62.3	69.9	77.1	80.7	79.1	73.6	62.8	53.8	46.3	62.6
Mean Minimum Temp. (°F)	32.3	34.5	41.0	47.9	56.6	64.7	68.9	67.7	61.8	49.8	41.1	34.6	50.1
Extreme Maximum Temp. (°F)	81	82	89	94	97	102	107	108	100	95	87	80	108
Extreme Minimum Temp. (°F)	-1	10	-1	25	34	45	55	51	39	26	16	1	-1
Days Maximum Temp. ≥ 90°F	0	0	0	1	5	15	23	18	8	0	0	0	70
Days Maximum Temp. ≤ 32°F	0	0	0	0	0	0	0	0	0	0	0	0	0
Days Minimum Temp. ≤ 32°F	17	13	7	1	0	0	0	0	0	0	0	0	0
Days Minimum Temp. ≤ 0°F	0	0	0	0	0	0	0	0	0	1	7	14	60
Heating Degree Days (base 65°F)	657	492	322	133	25	2	0	0	9	125	340	574	2,679
Cooling Degree Days (base 65°F)	1	1	11	59	190	387	518	457	270	68	9	2	1,973
Mean Precipitation (in.)	4.70	4.17	4.93	3.10	3.49	4.43	4.23	4.87	4.47	3.87	3.36	3.65	49.27
Days With ≥ 0.1" Precipitation	8	6	7	5	6	6	7	6	5	4	5	6	71
Days With ≥ 1.0" Precipitation	1	1	2	1	1	1	1	1	2	1	1	1	14
Mean Snowfall (in.)	0.5	0.6	0.5	0.0	0.0	0.0	0.0	0.0	0.0	0.0	0.0	0.2	1.8
Days With ≥ 1.0" Snow Depth	0	0	0	0	0	0	0	0	0	0	0	0	0

Ninety Nine Islands *Cherokee County*   Elevation: 498 ft.   Latitude: 35° 04' N   Longitude: 81° 30' W

	JAN	FEB	MAR	APR	MAY	JUN	JUL	AUG	SEP	OCT	NOV	DEC	YEAR
Mean Maximum Temp. (°F)	51.4	55.9	63.8	72.7	79.1	85.5	89.3	87.6	82.1	72.8	63.1	54.6	71.5
Mean Temp. (°F)	39.3	42.6	49.9	57.9	65.8	73.4	77.7	76.5	70.4	59.2	49.5	42.2	58.7
Mean Minimum Temp. (°F)	27.2	29.3	36.0	43.0	52.5	61.3	66.1	65.3	58.6	45.4	35.8	29.7	45.8
Extreme Maximum Temp. (°F)	79	80	87	92	93	99	104	106	98	91	87	80	106
Extreme Minimum Temp. (°F)	-4	3	8	18	28	38	51	47	35	22	9	-1	-4
Days Maximum Temp. ≥ 90°F	0	0	0	0	1	7	16	12	5	0	0	0	41
Days Maximum Temp. ≤ 32°F	1	0	0	0	0	0	0	0	0	0	0	0	1
Days Minimum Temp. ≤ 32°F	21	18	12	5	0	0	0	0	0	3	13	20	92
Days Minimum Temp. ≤ 0°F	0	0	0	0	0	0	0	0	0	0	0	0	0
Heating Degree Days (base 65°F)	789	625	463	227	65	5	0	0	23	206	462	702	3,567
Cooling Degree Days (base 65°F)	0	0	2	19	96	268	410	359	176	30	2	1	1,363
Mean Precipitation (in.)	4.42	4.11	4.89	3.03	4.25	3.80	3.87	5.03	3.92	3.96	3.63	3.72	48.63
Days With ≥ 0.1" Precipitation	7	7	8	6	7	6	7	6	5	5	6	7	77
Days With ≥ 1.0" Precipitation	1	1	1	1	1	1	1	1	1	1	1	1	12
Mean Snowfall (in.)	1.0	0.8	0.7	0.0	0.0	0.0	0.0	0.0	0.0	0.0	trace	0.6	3.1
Days With ≥ 1.0" Snow Depth	1	0	0	0	0	0	0	0	0	0	0	0	1

Orangeburg 2 *Orangeburg County*   Elevation: 177 ft.   Latitude: 33° 30' N   Longitude: 80° 52' W

	JAN	FEB	MAR	APR	MAY	JUN	JUL	AUG	SEP	OCT	NOV	DEC	YEAR
Mean Maximum Temp. (°F)	56.4	60.7	68.6	76.7	83.3	88.9	91.9	90.3	85.5	76.3	68.1	59.8	75.6
Mean Temp. (°F)	45.3	48.6	56.2	63.6	71.0	77.6	81.1	79.7	74.0	64.0	55.5	48.2	63.8
Mean Minimum Temp. (°F)	34.1	36.5	43.7	50.3	58.6	66.2	70.1	69.1	63.8	51.6	42.9	36.6	52.0
Extreme Maximum Temp. (°F)	82	85	89	95	99	104	105	106	100	96	87	85	106
Extreme Minimum Temp. (°F)	2	9	6	27	37	47	54	53	43	27	18	8	2
Days Maximum Temp. ≥ 90°F	0	0	0	1	5	15	22	19	9	1	0	0	72
Days Maximum Temp. ≤ 32°F	1	0	0	0	0	0	0	0	0	0	0	0	1
Days Minimum Temp. ≤ 32°F	14	10	4	0	0	0	0	0	0	0	0	0	0
Days Minimum Temp. ≤ 0°F	0	0	0	0	0	0	0	0	0	0	5	12	45
Heating Degree Days (base 65°F)	607	460	287	112	18	1	0	0	7	107	294	518	2,411
Cooling Degree Days (base 65°F)	2	5	21	73	219	399	522	474	305	92	18	6	2,136
Mean Precipitation (in.)	4.66	3.71	4.25	2.70	3.74	4.80	4.97	5.46	3.95	3.20	2.69	3.43	47.56
Days With ≥ 0.1" Precipitation	8	6	6	5	6	7	8	7	5	5	4	6	73
Days With ≥ 1.0" Precipitation	1	1	1	1	1	1	2	2	1	1	1	1	14
Mean Snowfall (in.)	trace	0.5	trace	0.0	0.0	0.0	0.0	0.0	0.0	0.0	0.0	trace	0.5
Days With ≥ 1.0" Snow Depth	0	0	0	0	0	0	0	0	0	0	0	0	0

Pageland *Chesterfield County*   Elevation: 620 ft.   Latitude: 34° 46' N   Longitude: 80° 24' W

	JAN	FEB	MAR	APR	MAY	JUN	JUL	AUG	SEP	OCT	NOV	DEC	YEAR
Mean Maximum Temp. (°F)	53.5	58.7	66.7	75.2	81.6	87.7	90.8	88.8	83.9	74.8	65.4	57.2	73.7
Mean Temp. (°F)	42.9	46.9	54.1	62.2	69.6	76.5	80.1	78.3	73.2	62.8	53.9	46.5	62.3
Mean Minimum Temp. (°F)	32.2	35.2	41.5	49.2	57.6	65.2	69.4	67.8	62.5	50.6	42.3	35.7	50.8
Extreme Maximum Temp. (°F)	79	82	87	92	98	101	103	106	97	93	86	79	106
Extreme Minimum Temp. (°F)	3	5	6	23	32	46	54	46	40	24	15	4	3
Days Maximum Temp. ≥ 90°F	0	0	0	1	3	12	19	14	5	0	0	0	54
Days Maximum Temp. ≤ 32°F	1	0	0	0	0	0	0	0	0	0	0	0	1
Days Minimum Temp. ≤ 32°F	16	12	6	1	0	0	0	0	0	1	6	13	55
Days Minimum Temp. ≤ 0°F	0	0	0	0	0	0	0	0	0	0	0	0	0
Heating Degree Days (base 65°F)	680	506	339	139	28	2	0	0	9	126	338	570	2,737
Cooling Degree Days (base 65°F)	0	3	14	63	186	372	500	429	259	69	9	2	1,906
Mean Precipitation (in.)	4.52	3.93	4.73	2.99	3.33	4.13	5.92	4.64	3.83	3.96	3.45	3.60	49.03
Days With ≥ 0.1" Precipitation	7	6	8	5	7	6	8	7	6	5	5	6	76
Days With ≥ 1.0" Precipitation	1	1	1	1	1	1	2	2	1	1	1	1	14
Mean Snowfall (in.)	0.4	trace	0.6	0.0	0.0	0.0	0.0	0.0	0.0	0.0	trace	0.3	1.3
Days With ≥ 1.0" Snow Depth	0	0	0	0	0	0	0	0	0	0	0	0	0

Parr *Fairfield County*   Elevation: 255 ft.   Latitude: 34° 18' N   Longitude: 81° 20' W

	JAN	FEB	MAR	APR	MAY	JUN	JUL	AUG	SEP	OCT	NOV	DEC	YEAR
Mean Maximum Temp. (°F)	54.8	59.7	67.6	76.1	83.0	89.4	92.7	90.8	85.4	76.3	66.8	57.8	75.0
Mean Temp. (°F)	42.7	46.1	53.5	61.3	69.2	76.6	80.7	79.1	73.5	62.3	53.1	45.2	61.9
Mean Minimum Temp. (°F)	30.6	32.4	39.3	46.4	55.3	63.8	68.5	67.4	61.5	48.3	39.3	32.6	48.8
Extreme Maximum Temp. (°F)	79	82	88	94	99	103	107	107	99	94	88	81	107
Extreme Minimum Temp. (°F)	0	9	2	22	30	43	53	52	35	25	8	5	0
Days Maximum Temp. ≥ 90°F	0	0	0	1	5	16	24	18	9	0	0	0	73
Days Maximum Temp. ≤ 32°F	0	0	0	0	0	0	0	0	0	0	0	0	0
Days Minimum Temp. ≤ 32°F	19	16	9	2	0	0	0	0	0	1	9	16	72
Days Minimum Temp. ≤ 0°F	0	0	0	0	0	0	0	0	0	0	0	0	0
Heating Degree Days (base 65°F)	684	528	361	154	31	2	0	0	11	135	360	608	2,874
Cooling Degree Days (base 65°F)	1	1	7	45	166	369	510	447	256	58	7	1	1,868
Mean Precipitation (in.)	4.63	3.93	4.79	2.82	3.41	3.96	4.20	4.31	3.81	3.52	2.92	3.42	45.72
Days With ≥ 0.1" Precipitation	8	6	7	5	6	6	6	6	4	4	5	6	69
Days With ≥ 1.0" Precipitation	1	1	1	1	1	1	1	2	1	1	1	1	13
Mean Snowfall (in.)	0.3	0.3	0.2	0.0	0.0	0.0	0.0	0.0	0.0	0.0	0.0	0.1	0.9
Days With ≥ 1.0" Snow Depth	0	0	0	0	0	0	0	0	0	0	0	0	0

Pelion 4 NW *Lexington County*   Elevation: 449 ft.   Latitude: 33° 43' N   Longitude: 81° 16' W

	JAN	FEB	MAR	APR	MAY	JUN	JUL	AUG	SEP	OCT	NOV	DEC	YEAR
Mean Maximum Temp. (°F)	55.8	60.5	68.5	76.7	83.4	89.0	91.5	89.6	85.1	76.1	67.1	59.0	75.2
Mean Temp. (°F)	44.5	47.9	55.3	62.6	70.4	77.1	80.6	79.0	73.8	63.2	54.3	47.2	63.0
Mean Minimum Temp. (°F)	33.1	35.2	42.0	48.5	57.3	65.2	69.5	68.3	62.5	50.1	41.4	35.3	50.7
Extreme Maximum Temp. (°F)	79	84	89	94	98	103	107	107	99	98	85	83	107
Extreme Minimum Temp. (°F)	-2	2	-1	22	32	42	51	52	38	22	10	5	-2
Days Maximum Temp. ≥ 90°F	0	0	0	1	5	15	21	16	8	0	0	0	66
Days Maximum Temp. ≤ 32°F	0	0	0	0	0	0	0	0	0	0	0	0	0
Days Minimum Temp. ≤ 32°F	15	12	7	2	0	0	0	0	0	1	8	13	58
Days Minimum Temp. ≤ 0°F	0	0	0	0	0	0	0	0	0	0	0	0	0
Heating Degree Days (base 65°F)	630	480	311	129	21	1	0	0	7	121	328	548	2,576
Cooling Degree Days (base 65°F)	1	4	17	64	203	385	507	444	273	75	12	3	1,988
Mean Precipitation (in.)	4.70	4.12	4.90	3.04	3.41	5.20	5.69	5.66	4.38	3.31	3.05	3.72	51.18
Days With ≥ 0.1" Precipitation	8	7	7	5	6	8	9	8	6	4	5	6	79
Days With ≥ 1.0" Precipitation	1	1	2	1	1	2	2	2	1	1	1	1	16
Mean Snowfall (in.)	0.3	0.8	trace	0.0	0.0	0.0	0.0	0.0	0.0	0.0	0.0	trace	1.1
Days With ≥ 1.0" Snow Depth	0	0	0	0	0	0	0	0	0	0	0	0	0

Pickens *Pickens County*   Elevation: 1,161 ft.   Latitude: 34° 53' N   Longitude: 82° 43' W

	JAN	FEB	MAR	APR	MAY	JUN	JUL	AUG	SEP	OCT	NOV	DEC	YEAR
Mean Maximum Temp. (°F)	51.4	56.3	64.8	73.3	79.6	85.9	89.1	87.6	82.4	72.6	62.7	54.1	71.7
Mean Temp. (°F)	41.1	45.1	52.9	60.6	67.7	74.6	78.2	76.9	71.7	61.2	51.8	44.1	60.5
Mean Minimum Temp. (°F)	30.9	33.9	40.8	47.8	55.8	63.3	67.2	66.2	61.0	49.8	40.9	34.0	49.3
Extreme Maximum Temp. (°F)	78	81	88	93	98	100	104	105	100	89	85	77	105
Extreme Minimum Temp. (°F)	-6	1	8	24	34	43	52	52	39	27	10	2	-6
Days Maximum Temp. ≥ 90°F	0	0	0	0	2	8	15	11	4	0	0	0	40
Days Maximum Temp. ≤ 32°F	1	0	0	0	0	0	0	0	0	0	0	0	1
Days Minimum Temp. ≤ 32°F	17	13	7	1	0	0	0	0	0	1	7	15	61
Days Minimum Temp. ≤ 0°F	0	0	0	0	0	0	0	0	0	0	0	0	0
Heating Degree Days (base 65°F)	733	555	374	166	39	2	0	0	13	153	392	641	3,068
Cooling Degree Days (base 65°F)	0	0	5	40	134	310	433	383	211	45	2	0	1,563
Mean Precipitation (in.)	5.74	4.88	5.70	3.88	4.94	4.27	4.61	4.93	3.80	4.53	4.28	4.66	56.22
Days With ≥ 0.1" Precipitation	8	7	8	6	7	7	7	7	6	5	6	8	82
Days With ≥ 1.0" Precipitation	2	1	2	1	2	1	1	2	1	2	1	1	17
Mean Snowfall (in.)	1.1	1.1	0.3	trace	0.0	0.0	0.0	0.0	0.0	0.0	trace	0.5	3.0
Days With ≥ 1.0" Snow Depth	0	0	0	0	0	0	0	0	0	0	0	0	0

Pinopolis Dam *Berkeley County*   Elevation: 49 ft.   Latitude: 33° 15' N   Longitude: 79° 59' W

	JAN	FEB	MAR	APR	MAY	JUN	JUL	AUG	SEP	OCT	NOV	DEC	YEAR
Mean Maximum Temp. (°F)	56.3	60.0	67.9	75.7	82.6	88.6	91.8	89.9	85.6	76.6	68.6	60.3	75.3
Mean Temp. (°F)	45.6	48.4	55.9	63.0	70.7	77.4	81.1	79.8	75.2	64.7	56.6	49.1	63.9
Mean Minimum Temp. (°F)	34.8	36.8	43.8	50.2	58.7	66.2	70.4	69.6	64.6	52.9	44.6	37.8	52.5
Extreme Maximum Temp. (°F)	81	84	89	92	96	102	104	102	98	95	86	84	104
Extreme Minimum Temp. (°F)	8	12	18	29	37	47	55	54	44	27	18	14	8
Days Maximum Temp. ≥ 90°F	0	0	0	1	4	14	22	18	9	1	0	0	69
Days Maximum Temp. ≤ 32°F	0	0	0	0	0	0	0	0	0	0	0	0	0
Days Minimum Temp. ≤ 32°F	14	10	3	0	0	0	0	0	0	0	4	11	42
Days Minimum Temp. ≤ 0°F	0	0	0	0	0	0	0	0	0	0	0	0	0
Heating Degree Days (base 65°F)	597	466	294	119	19	1	0	0	5	95	266	494	2,356
Cooling Degree Days (base 65°F)	0	5	17	63	205	402	532	na	306	95	20	7	na
Mean Precipitation (in.)	4.38	3.25	4.42	2.77	4.19	5.40	5.73	6.53	4.76	3.09	2.57	3.48	50.57
Days With ≥ 0.1" Precipitation	8	6	7	5	7	7	8	9	6	4	4	6	77
Days With ≥ 1.0" Precipitation	1	1	1	1	1	2	2	2	1	1	1	1	15
Mean Snowfall (in.)	trace	0.0	0.0	0.0	0.0	0.0	0.0	0.0	0.0	0.0	0.0	trace	trace
Days With ≥ 1.0" Snow Depth	0	0	0	0	0	0	0	0	0	0	0	0	0

Ridgeland 5 NE *Jasper County* Elevation: 19 ft. Latitude: 32° 32' N Longitude: 80° 54' W

	JAN	FEB	MAR	APR	MAY	JUN	JUL	AUG	SEP	OCT	NOV	DEC	YEAR
Mean Maximum Temp. (°F)	59.5	63.8	71.0	77.9	83.7	88.7	91.8	89.5	85.5	77.5	69.6	62.4	76.7
Mean Temp. (°F)	48.4	51.6	58.7	65.2	72.2	77.9	81.2	79.7	75.6	66.2	57.9	51.4	65.5
Mean Minimum Temp. (°F)	37.2	39.5	46.3	52.5	60.5	67.1	70.7	69.8	65.6	54.9	46.2	40.1	54.2
Extreme Maximum Temp. (°F)	83	86	91	95	99	104	105	102	102	93	86	84	105
Extreme Minimum Temp. (°F)	2	15	16	29	38	46	58	56	45	25	14	7	2
Days Maximum Temp. ≥ 90°F	0	0	0	2	5	13	22	17	7	1	0	0	67
Days Maximum Temp. ≤ 32°F	0	0	0	0	0	0	0	0	0	0	0	0	0
Days Minimum Temp. ≤ 32°F	11	8	2	0	0	0	0	0	0	0	4	8	33
Days Minimum Temp. ≤ 0°F	0	0	0	0	0	0	0	0	0	0	0	0	0
Heating Degree Days (base 65°F)	511	377	219	79	8	0	0	0	2	71	234	424	1,925
Cooling Degree Days (base 65°F)	1	8	30	87	241	410	522	468	321	120	27	7	2,242
Mean Precipitation (in.)	4.31	3.47	4.02	3.34	3.83	5.33	5.40	6.97	4.89	3.29	2.75	3.54	51.14
Days With ≥ 0.1" Precipitation	8	6	6	5	6	8	8	9	7	4	5	6	78
Days With ≥ 1.0" Precipitation	1	1	1	1	1	2	2	2	1	1	1	1	15
Mean Snowfall (in.)	trace	0.3	trace	0.0	0.0	0.0	0.0	0.0	0.0	0.0	0.0	0.2	0.5
Days With ≥ 1.0" Snow Depth	0	0	0	0	0	0	0	0	0	0	0	0	0

Saluda *Saluda County* Elevation: 479 ft. Latitude: 34° 00' N Longitude: 81° 46' W

	JAN	FEB	MAR	APR	MAY	JUN	JUL	AUG	SEP	OCT	NOV	DEC	YEAR
Mean Maximum Temp. (°F)	53.5	58.6	66.5	75.5	82.5	89.1	92.7	90.8	85.5	75.4	65.5	56.6	74.3
Mean Temp. (°F)	41.9	45.4	53.0	61.2	69.1	76.6	80.3	78.8	73.0	61.5	52.1	44.8	61.5
Mean Minimum Temp. (°F)	29.9	32.2	39.5	46.8	55.5	64.0	68.0	66.8	60.5	47.5	38.6	33.0	48.5
Extreme Maximum Temp. (°F)	78	82	87	94	101	103	109	107	102	95	87	80	109
Extreme Minimum Temp. (°F)	-2	10	5	23	32	43	52	48	35	22	14	6	-2
Days Maximum Temp. ≥ 90°F	0	0	0	1	5	14	23	20	10	0	0	0	73
Days Maximum Temp. ≤ 32°F	1	0	0	0	0	0	0	0	0	0	0	0	1
Days Minimum Temp. ≤ 32°F	19	15	8	2	0	0	0	0	0	2	9	17	72
Days Minimum Temp. ≤ 0°F	0	0	0	0	0	0	0	0	0	0	0	0	0
Heating Degree Days (base 65°F)	712	551	373	160	36	2	0	0	13	154	390	621	3,012
Cooling Degree Days (base 65°F)	0	2	11	55	182	381	519	452	259	57	7	2	1,927
Mean Precipitation (in.)	4.82	4.11	5.00	3.08	3.63	4.14	4.83	4.47	3.40	3.62	3.17	3.75	48.02
Days With ≥ 0.1" Precipitation	8	6	7	5	6	6	7	6	5	4	5	7	72
Days With ≥ 1.0" Precipitation	1	1	2	1	1	1	1	1	1	1	1	1	13
Mean Snowfall (in.)	0.4	0.5	0.3	0.0	0.0	0.0	0.0	0.0	0.0	0.0	0.0	0.2	1.4
Days With ≥ 1.0" Snow Depth	0	0	0	0	0	0	0	0	0	0	0	0	0

Sandhill Research Elgin *Richland County* Elevation: 439 ft. Latitude: 34° 09' N Longitude: 80° 52' W

	JAN	FEB	MAR	APR	MAY	JUN	JUL	AUG	SEP	OCT	NOV	DEC	YEAR
Mean Maximum Temp. (°F)	53.6	58.1	66.0	74.8	81.5	87.7	91.1	89.0	84.1	74.6	66.0	57.4	73.7
Mean Temp. (°F)	42.9	46.4	54.0	62.3	69.9	76.8	80.5	78.8	73.5	62.8	54.3	46.3	62.4
Mean Minimum Temp. (°F)	32.2	34.6	41.9	49.8	58.2	65.7	69.9	68.6	62.9	51.0	42.5	35.2	51.1
Extreme Maximum Temp. (°F)	78	84	88	92	98	104	106	105	99	95	88	80	106
Extreme Minimum Temp. (°F)	-2	9	6	24	38	47	57	52	42	23	15	8	-2
Days Maximum Temp. ≥ 90°F	0	0	0	1	4	12	20	15	7	0	0	0	59
Days Maximum Temp. ≤ 32°F	1	0	0	0	0	0	0	0	0	0	0	0	1
Days Minimum Temp. ≤ 32°F	16	12	6	1	0	0	0	0	0	0	5	13	53
Days Minimum Temp. ≤ 0°F	0	0	0	0	0	0	0	0	0	0	0	0	0
Heating Degree Days (base 65°F)	679	521	348	138	28	2	0	0	10	126	329	574	2,755
Cooling Degree Days (base 65°F)	0	3	13	61	196	379	509	440	262	69	10	2	1,944
Mean Precipitation (in.)	4.60	3.60	4.70	3.06	3.40	3.91	5.08	4.92	3.79	3.34	3.09	3.49	46.98
Days With ≥ 0.1" Precipitation	8	6	7	5	6	6	8	7	5	5	5	7	75
Days With ≥ 1.0" Precipitation	1	1	2	1	1	1	1	1	1	1	1	1	13
Mean Snowfall (in.)	0.2	0.0	0.2	0.0	0.0	0.0	0.0	0.0	0.0	0.0	0.0	trace	0.4
Days With ≥ 1.0" Snow Depth	0	0	0	0	0	0	0	0	0	0	0	0	0

Santuck *Union County* Elevation: 518 ft. Latitude: 34° 38' N Longitude: 81° 31' W

	JAN	FEB	MAR	APR	MAY	JUN	JUL	AUG	SEP	OCT	NOV	DEC	YEAR
Mean Maximum Temp. (°F)	52.8	57.9	66.0	74.8	81.0	87.2	90.6	88.3	82.3	72.4	63.6	55.5	72.7
Mean Temp. (°F)	42.5	46.3	53.7	61.8	69.1	76.1	79.9	78.2	72.3	61.3	52.6	45.3	61.6
Mean Minimum Temp. (°F)	32.2	34.6	41.4	48.7	57.1	64.8	69.2	68.0	62.1	50.2	41.6	34.9	50.4
Extreme Maximum Temp. (°F)	79	82	87	93	95	103	105	104	97	91	85	78	105
Extreme Minimum Temp. (°F)	-4	7	7	26	32	45	56	52	40	26	13	4	-4
Days Maximum Temp. ≥ 90°F	0	0	0	0	3	11	19	13	4	0	0	0	50
Days Maximum Temp. ≤ 32°F	1	0	0	0	0	0	0	0	0	0	0	0	1
Days Minimum Temp. ≤ 32°F	16	13	7	1	0	0	0	0	0	0	0	0	59
Days Minimum Temp. ≤ 0°F	0	0	0	0	0	0	0	0	0	1	7	14	0
Heating Degree Days (base 65°F)	691	523	353	145	30	1	0	0	14	157	372	607	2,893
Cooling Degree Days (base 65°F)	0	2	11	53	167	355	487	420	228	51	5	2	1,781
Mean Precipitation (in.)	4.45	4.12	4.94	3.07	3.32	3.87	4.03	3.99	3.95	3.79	3.39	3.54	46.46
Days With ≥ 0.1" Precipitation	7	7	8	6	6	6	7	6	6	5	6	7	77
Days With ≥ 1.0" Precipitation	1	1	2	1	1	1	1	1	1	1	1	1	13
Mean Snowfall (in.)	1.0	1.3	0.6	0.0	trace	0.0	0.0	0.0	0.0	0.0	trace	0.6	3.5
Days With ≥ 1.0" Snow Depth	1	1	0	0	0	0	0	0	0	0	0	0	2

Summerville *Dorchester County* Elevation: 32 ft. Latitude: 32° 59' N Longitude: 80° 11' W

	JAN	FEB	MAR	APR	MAY	JUN	JUL	AUG	SEP	OCT	NOV	DEC	YEAR
Mean Maximum Temp. (°F)	57.7	61.6	69.2	76.2	82.7	87.9	90.8	89.2	85.1	76.6	69.2	61.3	75.6
Mean Temp. (°F)	46.2	49.1	56.5	62.8	70.7	77.2	80.6	79.5	75.0	64.7	56.5	49.2	64.0
Mean Minimum Temp. (°F)	34.6	36.6	43.7	49.3	58.6	66.5	70.4	69.7	64.8	52.8	43.7	37.1	52.3
Extreme Maximum Temp. (°F)	82	87	89	96	97	103	104	101	97	94	86	83	104
Extreme Minimum Temp. (°F)	5	4	19	28	36	48	51	55	43	26	12	9	4
Days Maximum Temp. ≥ 90°F	0	0	0	1	4	12	20	16	7	1	0	0	61
Days Maximum Temp. ≤ 32°F	0	0	0	0	0	0	0	0	0	0	0	0	0
Days Minimum Temp. ≤ 32°F	15	10	5	1	0	0	0	0	0	0	5	11	47
Days Minimum Temp. ≤ 0°F	0	0	0	0	0	0	0	0	0	0	0	0	0
Heating Degree Days (base 65°F)	579	447	279	123	20	1	0	0	4	96	274	487	2,310
Cooling Degree Days (base 65°F)	1	5	20	62	210	392	510	465	302	98	26	5	2,096
Mean Precipitation (in.)	4.63	3.48	4.56	3.09	3.86	5.82	5.97	6.80	5.45	3.39	2.81	3.54	53.40
Days With ≥ 0.1" Precipitation	8	6	6	5	6	8	9	9	6	5	5	7	80
Days With ≥ 1.0" Precipitation	1	1	1	1	1	2	2	2	2	1	1	1	16
Mean Snowfall (in.)	trace	0.6	0.0	0.0	0.0	0.0	0.0	0.0	0.0	0.0	0.0	0.3	0.9
Days With ≥ 1.0" Snow Depth	0	0	0	0	0	0	0	0	0	0	0	0	0

Sumter *Sumter County* Elevation: 173 ft. Latitude: 33° 56' N Longitude: 80° 21' W

	JAN	FEB	MAR	APR	MAY	JUN	JUL	AUG	SEP	OCT	NOV	DEC	YEAR
Mean Maximum Temp. (°F)	56.1	60.6	68.4	76.7	83.3	88.9	91.9	89.9	85.4	76.1	67.8	59.4	75.4
Mean Temp. (°F)	44.8	48.1	55.4	63.1	70.4	77.0	80.7	78.9	74.1	63.4	55.0	47.7	63.2
Mean Minimum Temp. (°F)	33.4	35.6	42.3	49.4	57.5	65.0	69.5	68.0	62.6	50.5	42.0	35.9	51.0
Extreme Maximum Temp. (°F)	82	85	90	93	100	103	105	105	99	96	87	83	105
Extreme Minimum Temp. (°F)	2	4	11	26	37	46	56	50	40	24	16	9	2
Days Maximum Temp. ≥ 90°F	0	0	0	1	5	14	23	17	8	0	0	0	68
Days Maximum Temp. ≤ 32°F	0	0	0	0	0	0	0	0	0	0	0	0	0
Days Minimum Temp. ≤ 32°F	15	12	6	1	0	0	0	0	0	1	7	13	55
Days Minimum Temp. ≤ 0°F	0	0	0	0	0	0	0	0	0	0	0	0	0
Heating Degree Days (base 65°F)	622	475	312	122	23	1	0	0	8	116	311	536	2,526
Cooling Degree Days (base 65°F)	1	4	14	60	188	374	507	437	273	70	11	3	1,942
Mean Precipitation (in.)	4.56	3.64	4.49	2.89	3.50	5.56	5.51	5.06	4.05	3.22	2.79	3.64	48.91
Days With ≥ 0.1" Precipitation	8	6	7	5	6	7	8	7	6	4	5	6	75
Days With ≥ 1.0" Precipitation	1	1	1	1	1	2	2	2	1	1	1	1	15
Mean Snowfall (in.)	0.0	0.2	trace	0.0	0.0	0.0	0.0	0.0	0.0	0.0	0.0	0.0	0.2
Days With ≥ 1.0" Snow Depth	0	0	0	0	0	0	0	0	0	0	0	0	0

Union 8 SW *Union County* Elevation: 557 ft. Latitude: 34° 39' N Longitude: 81° 45' W

	JAN	FEB	MAR	APR	MAY	JUN	JUL	AUG	SEP	OCT	NOV	DEC	YEAR
Mean Maximum Temp. (°F)	51.8	56.7	64.8	74.0	80.7	87.1	90.7	88.8	83.3	73.5	63.9	55.3	72.5
Mean Temp. (°F)	39.6	43.0	50.4	58.7	66.5	74.2	78.3	76.9	70.8	59.3	50.2	42.7	59.2
Mean Minimum Temp. (°F)	27.3	29.1	35.9	43.3	52.4	61.3	65.9	64.9	58.2	45.1	36.4	30.1	45.8
Extreme Maximum Temp. (°F)	78	83	90	95	96	102	105	104	99	92	87	80	105
Extreme Minimum Temp. (°F)	-1	5	12	23	29	40	51	50	37	25	10	3	-1
Days Maximum Temp. ≥ 90°F	0	0	0	1	3	11	20	14	7	0	0	0	56
Days Maximum Temp. ≤ 32°F	1	0	0	0	0	0	0	0	0	0	0	0	1
Days Minimum Temp. ≤ 32°F	21	19	12	4	0	0	0	0	0	3	12	20	91
Days Minimum Temp. ≤ 0°F	0	0	0	0	0	0	0	0	0	0	0	0	0
Heating Degree Days (base 65°F)	781	616	454	214	61	5	0	0	23	201	443	685	3,483
Cooling Degree Days (base 65°F)	0	0	5	31	119	302	441	384	198	34	3	1	1,518
Mean Precipitation (in.)	5.07	4.32	5.37	3.32	3.63	3.93	3.94	4.17	3.72	4.32	3.76	3.88	49.43
Days With ≥ 0.1" Precipitation	8	7	8	5	6	6	7	5	5	5	6	7	75
Days With ≥ 1.0" Precipitation	2	1	2	1	1	1	1	1	1	2	1	1	15
Mean Snowfall (in.)	0.8	0.8	0.2	0.0	0.0	0.0	0.0	0.0	0.0	0.0	0.0	0.4	2.2
Days With ≥ 1.0" Snow Depth	0	0	0	0	0	0	0	0	0	0	0	0	0

Walhalla *Oconee County* Elevation: 977 ft. Latitude: 34° 45' N Longitude: 83° 05' W

	JAN	FEB	MAR	APR	MAY	JUN	JUL	AUG	SEP	OCT	NOV	DEC	YEAR
Mean Maximum Temp. (°F)	52.0	56.8	64.6	73.0	79.1	85.2	88.7	87.0	82.0	72.8	62.9	54.9	71.6
Mean Temp. (°F)	40.9	44.3	51.4	58.6	66.1	73.2	76.9	75.8	70.5	60.0	50.7	43.6	59.3
Mean Minimum Temp. (°F)	29.8	31.7	38.1	44.3	53.0	61.1	65.1	64.5	58.9	47.2	38.4	32.3	47.0
Extreme Maximum Temp. (°F)	79	82	86	93	93	98	105	103	100	91	83	79	105
Extreme Minimum Temp. (°F)	-5	4	3	22	28	39	50	50	36	23	11	2	-5
Days Maximum Temp. ≥ 90°F	0	0	0	0	1	6	14	9	3	0	0	0	33
Days Maximum Temp. ≤ 32°F	1	0	0	0	0	0	0	0	0	0	0	0	1
Days Minimum Temp. ≤ 32°F	18	16	10	4	0	0	0	0	0	2	10	17	77
Days Minimum Temp. ≤ 0°F	0	0	0	0	0	0	0	0	0	0	0	0	0
Heating Degree Days (base 65°F)	739	578	418	205	56	3	0	0	18	180	426	657	3,280
Cooling Degree Days (base 65°F)	0	0	3	21	98	264	389	347	182	33	1	1	1,339
Mean Precipitation (in.)	5.82	5.23	6.21	4.29	5.55	4.43	4.72	5.40	4.59	4.58	4.80	4.91	60.53
Days With ≥ 0.1" Precipitation	8	7	8	6	8	7	8	8	6	5	7	8	86
Days With ≥ 1.0" Precipitation	2	2	2	1	2	1	1	2	1	2	1	2	19
Mean Snowfall (in.)	2.1	1.2	0.8	trace	0.0	0.0	0.0	0.0	0.0	0.0	trace	0.4	4.5
Days With ≥ 1.0" Snow Depth	1	0	0	0	0	0	0	0	0	0	0	0	1

West Pelzer 2 W *Anderson County*   Elevation: 859 ft.   Latitude: 34° 39' N   Longitude: 82° 29' W

	JAN	FEB	MAR	APR	MAY	JUN	JUL	AUG	SEP	OCT	NOV	DEC	YEAR
Mean Maximum Temp. (°F)	52.0	57.0	64.9	73.4	80.2	86.7	90.4	88.5	83.0	73.2	63.5	55.0	72.3
Mean Temp. (°F)	41.3	45.1	52.5	60.3	68.1	75.4	79.3	77.9	72.1	61.1	51.9	44.2	60.8
Mean Minimum Temp. (°F)	30.7	33.0	40.1	47.1	55.9	64.0	68.1	67.2	61.2	48.9	40.1	33.4	49.2
Extreme Maximum Temp. (°F)	78	81	88	93	94	100	104	104	97	92	85	79	104
Extreme Minimum Temp. (°F)	-4	7	7	24	32	41	55	54	39	25	12	1	-4
Days Maximum Temp. ≥ 90°F	0	0	0	0	2	9	18	13	5	0	0	0	47
Days Maximum Temp. ≤ 32°F	1	0	0	0	0	0	0	0	0	0	0	0	1
Days Minimum Temp. ≤ 32°F	18	14	8	1	0	0	0	0	0	1	8	16	66
Days Minimum Temp. ≤ 0°F	0	0	0	0	0	0	0	0	0	0	0	0	0
Heating Degree Days (base 65°F)	727	557	387	173	38	2	0	0	14	159	390	639	3,086
Cooling Degree Days (base 65°F)	0	0	6	37	144	334	473	420	227	46	3	1	1,691
Mean Precipitation (in.)	5.17	4.42	5.45	3.57	4.34	3.75	4.05	4.00	4.41	4.00	3.88	4.21	51.25
Days With ≥ 0.1" Precipitation	8	7	8	6	7	6	7	6	6	5	6	7	79
Days With ≥ 1.0" Precipitation	1	1	2	1	1	1	1	1	1	1	1	1	13
Mean Snowfall (in.)	1.0	1.2	0.9	0.0	0.0	0.0	0.0	0.0	0.0	0.0	trace	0.3	3.4
Days With ≥ 1.0" Snow Depth	1	1	0	0	0	0	0	0	0	0	0	0	2

Winnsboro *Fairfield County*   Elevation: 557 ft.   Latitude: 34° 22' N   Longitude: 81° 06' W

	JAN	FEB	MAR	APR	MAY	JUN	JUL	AUG	SEP	OCT	NOV	DEC	YEAR
Mean Maximum Temp. (°F)	53.0	57.7	65.9	74.6	81.2	87.6	91.2	88.8	83.5	74.2	65.1	56.3	73.3
Mean Temp. (°F)	41.9	45.5	53.3	61.4	69.2	76.3	80.4	78.6	72.8	61.9	52.9	45.2	61.6
Mean Minimum Temp. (°F)	30.9	33.1	40.6	48.4	57.1	64.9	69.6	68.3	62.1	49.6	40.7	33.9	49.9
Extreme Maximum Temp. (°F)	82	82	88	92	97	102	106	105	98	93	87	81	106
Extreme Minimum Temp. (°F)	-1	8	5	26	32	41	56	52	41	25	13	7	-1
Days Maximum Temp. ≥ 90°F	0	0	0	1	3	12	20	15	6	0	0	0	57
Days Maximum Temp. ≤ 32°F	1	0	0	0	0	0	0	0	0	0	0	0	1
Days Minimum Temp. ≤ 32°F	18	14	7	1	0	0	0	0	0	1	7	15	63
Days Minimum Temp. ≤ 0°F	0	0	0	0	0	0	0	0	0	0	0	0	0
Heating Degree Days (base 65°F)	709	548	368	156	34	3	0	0	12	143	367	610	2,950
Cooling Degree Days (base 65°F)	0	2	12	55	179	368	512	437	246	59	6	2	1,878
Mean Precipitation (in.)	4.68	3.84	4.76	2.97	3.52	4.04	4.03	4.25	3.59	3.65	3.09	3.40	45.82
Days With ≥ 0.1" Precipitation	8	6	7	5	6	6	7	6	5	4	5	6	71
Days With ≥ 1.0" Precipitation	1	1	2	1	1	1	1	1	1	1	1	1	13
Mean Snowfall (in.)	0.6	0.6	0.1	0.0	0.0	0.0	0.0	0.0	0.0	0.0	trace	0.2	1.5
Days With ≥ 1.0" Snow Depth	0	0	0	0	0	0	0	0	0	0	0	0	0

Winthrop University *York County*   Elevation: 688 ft.   Latitude: 34° 56' N   Longitude: 81° 02' W

	JAN	FEB	MAR	APR	MAY	JUN	JUL	AUG	SEP	OCT	NOV	DEC	YEAR
Mean Maximum Temp. (°F)	51.1	56.2	64.4	73.2	79.9	86.5	90.0	88.0	82.5	72.6	63.2	54.5	71.8
Mean Temp. (°F)	41.7	45.5	53.1	61.3	69.0	76.3	80.0	78.5	72.8	62.0	52.8	45.0	61.5
Mean Minimum Temp. (°F)	32.2	34.8	41.7	49.4	58.0	66.0	70.0	68.9	63.0	51.4	42.3	35.4	51.1
Extreme Maximum Temp. (°F)	79	83	87	93	95	99	104	106	96	92	82	78	106
Extreme Minimum Temp. (°F)	-4	7	4	25	37	46	56	54	41	28	15	3	-4
Days Maximum Temp. ≥ 90°F	0	0	0	0	2	9	17	12	4	0	0	0	44
Days Maximum Temp. ≤ 32°F	1	0	0	0	0	0	0	0	0	0	0	0	1
Days Minimum Temp. ≤ 32°F	16	12	6	1	0	0	0	0	0	0	6	13	54
Days Minimum Temp. ≤ 0°F	0	0	0	0	0	0	0	0	0	0	0	0	0
Heating Degree Days (base 65°F)	716	546	372	152	31	1	0	0	11	138	366	616	2,949
Cooling Degree Days (base 65°F)	0	1	9	48	167	364	495	432	246	57	4	2	1,825
Mean Precipitation (in.)	4.59	3.96	5.02	3.22	3.56	4.28	4.09	4.24	4.29	4.02	3.53	3.58	48.38
Days With ≥ 0.1" Precipitation	8	6	8	6	6	7	7	6	5	5	6	7	77
Days With ≥ 1.0" Precipitation	1	1	1	1	1	1	1	1	2	1	1	1	13
Mean Snowfall (in.)	1.4	0.9	0.7	trace	0.0	0.0	0.0	0.0	0.0	0.0	trace	0.5	3.5
Days With ≥ 1.0" Snow Depth	1	1	1	0	0	0	0	0	0	0	0	0	3

Yemassee *Beaufort County*   Elevation: 22 ft.   Latitude: 32° 41' N   Longitude: 80° 51' W

	JAN	FEB	MAR	APR	MAY	JUN	JUL	AUG	SEP	OCT	NOV	DEC	YEAR
Mean Maximum Temp. (°F)	60.4	64.3	71.7	78.7	85.4	90.3	92.9	90.8	86.7	78.3	70.4	63.3	77.8
Mean Temp. (°F)	47.9	51.0	57.9	64.3	71.4	77.8	81.1	79.6	75.0	65.2	56.8	50.4	64.9
Mean Minimum Temp. (°F)	35.4	37.5	44.0	49.8	57.4	65.2	69.2	68.3	63.3	52.0	43.2	37.5	51.9
Extreme Maximum Temp. (°F)	83	86	92	99	98	108	106	104	99	95	86	86	108
Extreme Minimum Temp. (°F)	0	8	16	27	33	45	56	53	39	26	10	10	0
Days Maximum Temp. ≥ 90°F	0	0	0	2	8	18	25	20	10	1	0	0	84
Days Maximum Temp. ≤ 32°F	0	0	0	0	0	0	0	0	0	0	0	0	0
Days Minimum Temp. ≤ 32°F	12	9	4	1	0	0	0	0	0	1	6	11	44
Days Minimum Temp. ≤ 0°F	0	0	0	0	0	0	0	0	0	0	0	0	0
Heating Degree Days (base 65°F)	526	396	242	94	12	0	0	0	3	86	262	451	2,072
Cooling Degree Days (base 65°F)	2	7	25	79	227	404	518	461	308	105	24	6	2,166
Mean Precipitation (in.)	4.21	3.69	4.44	3.43	3.72	6.12	5.44	6.91	5.03	3.47	2.42	3.54	52.42
Days With ≥ 0.1" Precipitation	7	6	6	5	5	8	8	8	6	4	5	5	73
Days With ≥ 1.0" Precipitation	1	1	1	1	1	2	2	2	1	1	1	1	15
Mean Snowfall (in.)	0.0	trace	trace	0.0	0.0	0.0	0.0	0.0	0.0	0.0	0.0	0.1	0.1
Days With ≥ 1.0" Snow Depth	0	0	0	0	0	0	0	0	0	0	0	0	0

Note: See Appendix D for explanation of data.

SOUTH DAKOTA

PHYSICAL FEATURES. Rolling plains are the main feature of South Dakota, varying from nearly level land to hilly ridges, and increasing in elevation from the eastern border to the western edge of the State. The general elevation above sea level in the extreme eastern portion is about 1,500 feet, and in the extreme west is about 3,000 feet, except in the Black Hills area. The Black Hills, an isolated group of forest-covered mountains, have a climate of their own.

The soil covering the State was laid down in past ages by glaciers, water, and wind. There are occasional outcroppings of bedrock. The Missouri River and its tributaries drain all of South Dakota except for a small portion of the northeastern part of the State. Some of this small drainage area is in the headwaters of the Red River of the North in the Hudson Bay Drainage, and the remainder is in the headwater area of the Minnesota River which forms a part of the upper Mississippi River Basin.

South Dakota is bisected by the Missouri River which flows in a southerly direction to Pierre and then turns to the south-southeast where it forms the South Dakota-Nebraska State line. West of the Missouri lies a country of canyons, broad upland flats, and buttes. The principal tributaries which drain this region are the Grand, the Moreau and Cheyenne which drain the Black Hills, and the White. To the east of the Missouri is mostly prairie land with numerous small ponds and lakes, some of which dry up in periods of droughts. The principal rivers in this area are the James and the Big Sioux. The larger of the two, the James River, has an extremely low slope and consequently is sluggish and meanders. Water falling on much of the eastern area does not reach the stream valleys at all, but lies in depressions until it evaporates or soaks into the ground.

GENERAL CLIMATE. Since South Dakota is situated in the heart of the North American Continent, it is near the paths of many cyclones and anticyclones, and has the extremes of summer heat and winter cold that are characteristic of continental climates. Rapid fluctuations in temperature are common. Partly because of the great distance from any large body of water, the ranges of daily, monthly, and annual temperatures are very large. Temperatures of 100°F. or higher are experienced in some part of the State each summer, and on rare occasions such readings have been noted as early as April and as late as October. These high temperatures are usually attended by low humidity, which greatly reduces the oppressiveness of the heat. Below-zero temperatures occur frequently on midwinter mornings, but it is not often that the temperature stays below zero during the entire day. In the north, subzero temperatures can occur in October and April.

Warm "chinook" winds and frequent sunny skies make the Black Hills area the warmest part of the State in winter. Also, because of the tendency for very cold air masses to stay at low elevations, some of the Arctic air outbreaks that blanket the eastern counties do not reach the higher counties in the west. During summer, the higher elevation of the Black Hills results in that section having cooler temperatures than the rest of the State. At this season, the central and southeastern counties are warmest. The freeze-free season is shortest high in the Black Hills where brief freezing has been known to occur at any time of summer. Elsewhere, the first autumn freeze generally occurs in mid-September in the northwest, in late September in the central and east, and in the first week of October in the extreme southeastern corner. The average time of the last freeze in spring ranges from early May in the southeast to late May in the northwest.

PRECIPITATION. The annual precipitation decreases northwestward from about 25 inches in the extreme southeast to less than 13 inches in part of the northwest. The Black Hills are again an exception, varying from 16 inches in their southern portion to almost 25 inches in the northern, where rain and snow are often formed when the prevailing winds are abruptly forced up the mountainsides. Most of the State's precipitation occurs from April through September. On the average, it reaches a maximum during June, and decreases sharply in early July. The least precipitation is received during winter.

SNOWFALL. Occasionally there is heavy snowfall in winter and the amount of snow on the ground accumulates to a considerable depth, but as a rule the snow cover is not great. Wind usually accompanies the snow, causing a large proportion of it to collect in gullies and behind windbreaks. In the worst storms, isolated drifts many feet deep may block roads, while windswept fields nearby are nearly bare of snow. Snow that falls early in the season seldom stays on the ground very long. Snow that falls after the ground has frozen deeply and the days become very short remains longer. Once a snow cover is present, there is a tendency for it to continue, since the temperature falls to much lower levels over snow than over bare ground. Snowfall reaches a maximum in February and early March, and decreases markedly near the end of March. Violent, cold winds carrying snow picked up from the ground, commonly called "blizzards," are occasional occurances.

STORMS. Rainstorms occur most frequently in early summer, hailstorms are most frequent in midsummer, and lightning does its worst damage in late summer. In dry seasons, and particularly in the west in late summer, thunderstorm bases may be as high as two miles above the ground; consequently, the rain showers may evaporate before reaching ground. When the thundershowers do reach the ground during summer, there is a high incidence of hail. Tornadoes are not as frequent as in states farther south and east. Much more damage is caused by straight-line thunderstorm winds. Such winds are not impeded by trees or other obstacles on the open prairie, and speeds near the ground become very high.

The most serious flooding has been caused by rapid melting of a heavy snow pack and aggravated by ice jams. Heavy rainfall alone causes severe floods on tributary streams, especially in the eastern part of the State. Intense local storms result in flash flooding along minor tributaries.

OTHER CLIMATIC ELEMENTS. South Dakota has considerable fair weather. The air is generally clear with excellent visibility, since much of it arrives by way of the Rocky Mountains and Canada. The wind is most frequently from the south and southeast during the summer, and from the north and northwest during the winter. Wind speeds are often moderate to brisk at midday and almost calm at night, averaging 11 or 12 m.p.h. on a year-round basis.

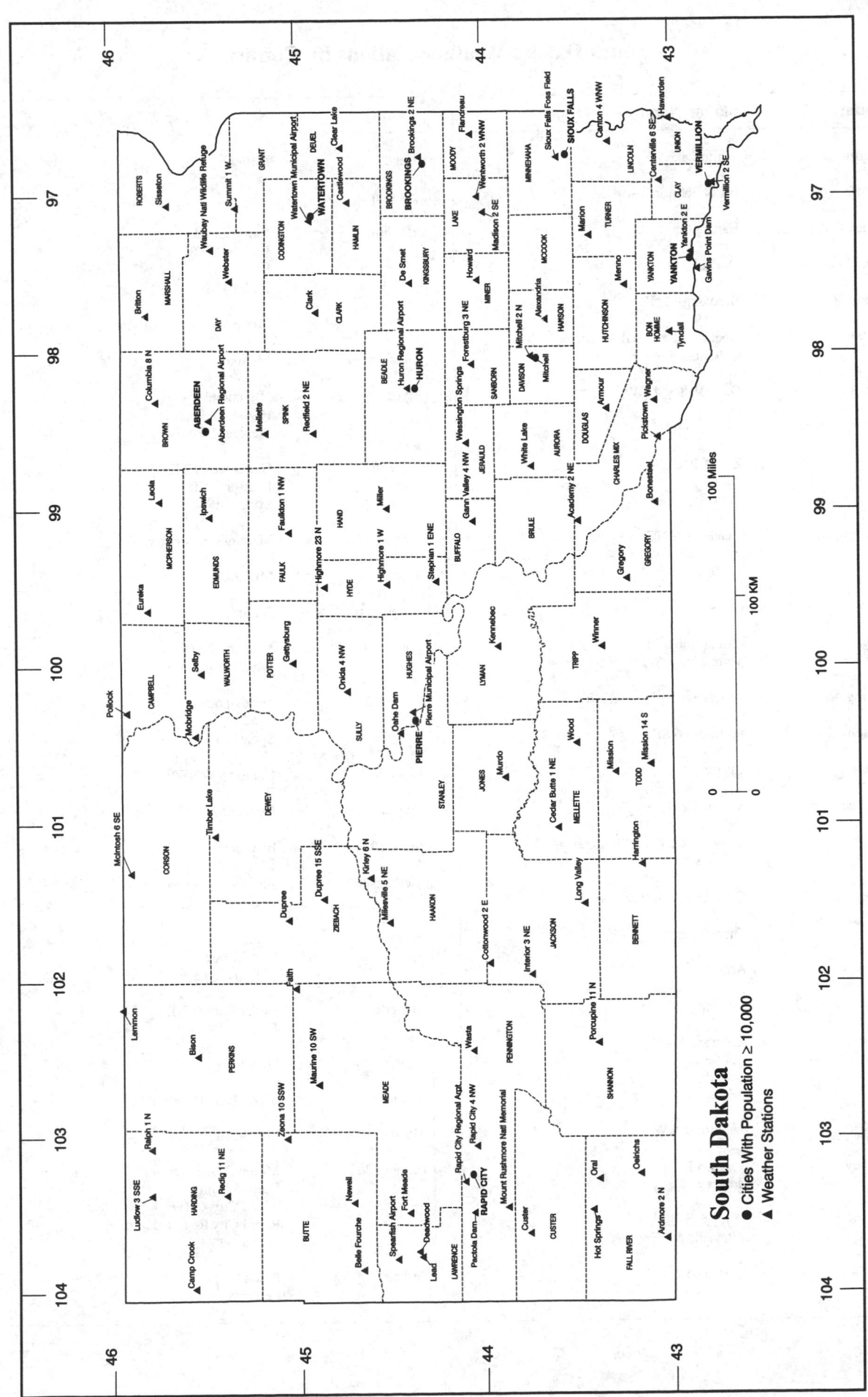

South Dakota

● Cities With Population ≥ 10,000
▲ Weather Stations

South Dakota Weather Stations by County

County	Station Name
Aurora	White Lake
Beadle	Huron Regional Airport
Bennett	Harrington
Bon Homme	Tyndall
Brookings	Brookings 2 NE
Brown	Aberdeen Regional Airport
	Columbia 8 N
Buffalo	Gann Valley 4 NW
Butte	Belle Fourche
	Newell
	Zeona 10 SSW
Campbell	Pollock
Charles Mix	Academy 2 NE
	Pickstown
	Wagner
Clark	Clark
Clay	Centerville 6 SE
	Vermillion 2 SE
Codington	Watertown Municipal Airport
Corson	McIntosh 6 SE
Custer	Custer
Davison	Mitchell 2 N
Day	Waubay Nat'l Wildlife Refuge
	Webster
Deuel	Clear Lake
Dewey	Timber Lake
Douglas	Armour
Edmunds	Ipswich
Fall River	Ardmore 2 N
	Hot Springs
	Oelrichs
	Oral
Faulk	Faulkton 1 NW
Gregory	Bonesteel
	Gregory
Haakon	Kirley 6 N
	Milesville 5 NE
Hamlin	Castlewood

County	Station Name
Hand	Miller
Hanson	Alexandria
Harding	Camp Crook
	Ludlow 3 SSE
	Ralph 1 N
	Redig 11 NE
Hughes	Pierre Municipal Airport
Hutchinson	Menno
Hyde	Highmore 1 W
	Highmore 23 N
	Stephan 1 ENE
Jackson	Cottonwood 2 E
	Interior 3 NE
	Long Valley
Jerauld	Wessington Springs
Jones	Murdo
Kingsbury	De Smet
Lake	Madison 2 SE
	Wentworth 2 WNW
Lawrence	Deadwood
	Lead
	Spearfish Airport
Lincoln	Canton 4 WNW
Lyman	Kennebec
Marshall	Britton
McPherson	Eureka
	Leola
Meade	Faith
	Fort Meade
	Maurine 10 SW
Mellette	Cedar Butte 1 NE
	Wood
Miner	Howard
Minnehaha	Sioux Falls Foss Field
Moody	Flandreau
Pennington	Mount Rushmore Nat'l Memorial
	Pactola Dam
	Rapid City 4 NW
	Rapid City Regional Airport
	Wasta
Perkins	Bison
	Lemmon

County	Station Name
Potter	Gettysburg
Roberts	Sisseton
	Summit 1 W
Sanborn	Forestburg 3 NE
Shannon	Porcupine 11 N
Spink	Mellette
	Redfield 2 NE
Stanley	Oahe Dam
Sully	Onida 4 NW
Todd	Mission
	Mission 14 S
Tripp	Winner
Turner	Marion
Walworth	Mobridge
	Selby
Yankton	Yankton 2 E
Ziebach	Dupree
	Dupree 15 SSE

South Dakota Weather Stations by City

City	Station Name	Miles
Aberdeen	Aberdeen Regional Airport	3
Brookings	Brookings 2 NE	1
Huron	Huron Regional Airport	3
Mitchell	Alexandria	13
	Mitchell 2 N	1
Pierre	Oahe Dam	7
	Pierre Municipal Airport	3
Rapid City	Mount Rushmore Nat'l Memorial	17
	Pactola Dam	12
	Rapid City 4 NW	4
	Rapid City Regional Airport	9
Sioux Falls	Canton 4 WNW	16
	Sioux Falls Foss Field	4
Vermillion	Centerville 6 SE	19
	Vermillion 2 SE	1
Watertown	Castlewood	14
	Watertown Municipal Airport	2
Yankton	Gavins Point Dam, NE	4
	Hartington, NE	19
	Yankton 2 E	1

Note: Miles is the distance between the geographic center of the city and the weather station.

South Dakota Weather Stations by Elevation

Feet	Station Name
5,479	Custer
5,347	Lead
5,249	Mount Rushmore Nat'l Memorial
4,717	Pactola Dam
4,668	Deadwood
3,910	Spearfish Airport
3,556	Hot Springs
3,549	Ardmore 2 N
3,448	Rapid City 4 NW
3,339	Oelrichs
3,297	Fort Meade
3,159	Rapid City Regional Airport
3,120	Camp Crook
3,067	Redig 11 NE
3,018	Belle Fourche
2,988	Ludlow 3 SSE
2,979	Harrington
2,959	Oral
2,857	Newell
2,818	Porcupine 11 N
2,808	Mission 14 S
2,788	Ralph 1 N
2,778	Bison
2,729	Zeona 10 SSW
2,709	Maurine 10 SW
2,591	Faith
2,585	Mission
2,565	Lemmon
2,467	Long Valley
2,437	Interior 3 NE
2,411	Cottonwood 2 E
2,372	Dupree
2,319	Murdo
2,319	Wasta
2,247	Cedar Butte 1 NE
2,234	Milesville 5 NE
2,178	Wood
2,171	McIntosh 6 SE
2,158	Gregory
2,158	Kirley 6 N
2,148	Timber Lake
2,099	Dupree 15 SSE
2,066	Gettysburg
2,007	Winner
1,984	Bonesteel
1,948	Summit 1 W
1,889	Highmore 1 W
1,870	Highmore 23 N
1,870	Selby
1,863	Stephan 1 ENE
1,856	Eureka
1,853	Webster
1,847	Onida 4 NW
1,827	Waubay Nat'l Wildlife Refuge
1,797	Clear Lake

Feet	Station Name
1,778	Clark
1,748	Watertown Municipal Airport
1,725	Pierre Municipal Airport
1,719	De Smet
1,719	Gann Valley 4 NW
1,699	Kennebec
1,689	Wentworth 2 WNW
1,683	Castlewood
1,679	Academy 2 NE
1,669	Mobridge
1,660	Madison 2 SE
1,660	Oahe Dam
1,646	Wessington Springs
1,637	Brookings 2 NE
1,633	Pollock
1,627	White Lake
1,587	Miller
1,578	Leola
1,568	Faulkton 1 NW
1,558	Flandreau
1,558	Howard
1,528	Ipswich
1,509	Armour
1,489	Pickstown
1,450	Marion
1,427	Sioux Falls Foss Field
1,427	Wagner
1,420	Tyndall
1,351	Alexandria
1,345	Canton 4 WNW
1,338	Britton
1,322	Menno
1,299	Columbia 8 N
1,295	Aberdeen Regional Airport
1,289	Mellette
1,289	Redfield 2 NE
1,279	Huron Regional Airport
1,259	Centerville 6 SE
1,250	Mitchell 2 N
1,227	Forestburg 3 NE
1,217	Sisseton
1,187	Vermillion 2 SE
1,177	Yankton 2 E

Aberdeen Regional Airport

Aberdeen is located in the northeast quarter of South Dakota, approximately 200 miles south of the geographical center of the North American continent. The surrounding area, extensively cultivated, is the bed of glacial Lake Dakota, which is by far the largest flat area in South Dakota. The lake bed slopes gently to the south. The elevation of Aberdeen at the northern end of the lake bed is 1,300 feet. The elevation at the southern end, some 30 miles distant is 1,280 feet. Low hills rim the area on the east and west. These hills effect ceilings, visibility, and precipitation. Located near the center of the North American land mass, the climate is continental with distinct seasons. Frequent and rapid weather changes occur during all seasons of the year as migratory storms sweep through the area. The winters are cold and dry. Sub-zero minimum temperatures may set in as early as late November, although temperatures of zero and below are generally not recorded until mid-December. Lowest temperatures of the winter generally occur in the period from mid-January to mid-February. During the coldest periods the days are generally sunny with light winds, and these conditions partially moderate the discomfort experienced at such low temperatures. Some days of the winter will be extremely unpleasant with temperatures near or below zero and brisk winds. Heavy snowfalls rarely occur during the first two-thirds of the winter season, with heaviest snowfalls developing during late February and early March as temperatures moderate. Blizzards are infrequent, and many winters will pass without a single occurrence of this type of weather phenomenon. However, difficult driving conditions occur several times during most winters during periods of weather termed ground blizzards by state residents.

Spring is a very short and transitional period, the shortest season of the four distinct seasons, and one marked by very rapid weather changes. Cool to quite cold nights prevail into mid-May, although afternoon temperatures may be quite warm, as high as the mid-80s. By mid-May temperatures below the freezing point rarely occur and frost is rarely experienced after the end of May.

Summers are pleasant with a maximum of sunshine, warm days, and generally cool and comfortable nights. Temperatures of 100 degrees or above may occur several times during the summer season, but low humidities, brisk winds during the heat of the day, and rapid cooling during the evening hours, which generally occur during the periods of elevated temperatures, markedly moderate the physical discomfort normally experienced at these high temperatures. Thunderstorms occur frequently.

Autumn is most pleasant with mild days, cool nights, ample sunshine, and declining occurrences and amounts of precipitation. The first frost may be expected by late September, although it may occur as early as late August.

Aberdeen Regional Airport *Brown County*   Elevation: 1,295 ft.   Latitude: 45° 27' N   Longitude: 98° 25' W

	JAN	FEB	MAR	APR	MAY	JUN	JUL	AUG	SEP	OCT	NOV	DEC	YEAR
Mean Maximum Temp. (°F)	21.2	27.9	39.5	57.0	69.9	78.7	84.8	83.8	73.1	59.2	39.2	26.4	55.1
Mean Temp. (°F)	10.9	18.1	30.1	45.1	57.6	66.8	72.2	70.7	59.9	46.8	29.6	16.5	43.7
Mean Minimum Temp. (°F)	0.5	8.3	20.6	33.2	45.3	54.9	59.6	57.5	46.6	34.3	20.0	6.7	32.3
Extreme Maximum Temp. (°F)	60	62	80	98	96	108	109	107	103	93	78	59	109
Extreme Minimum Temp. (°F)	-35	-45	-32	-2	20	36	39	32	20	8	-24	-34	-45
Days Maximum Temp. ≥ 90°F	0	0	0	0	0	3	8	7	2	0	0	0	20
Days Maximum Temp. ≤ 32°F	23	16	9	1	0	0	0	0	0	0	9	20	78
Days Minimum Temp. ≤ 32°F	31	27	27	15	2	0	0	0	2	13	27	31	175
Days Minimum Temp. ≤ 0°F	15	9	3	0	0	0	0	0	0	0	2	10	39
Heating Degree Days (base 65°F)	1,675	1,319	1,076	594	252	56	10	24	201	559	1,055	1,497	8,318
Cooling Degree Days (base 65°F)	0	0	0	4	32	111	233	192	48	2	0	0	622
Mean Precipitation (in.)	0.49	0.45	1.25	1.85	2.63	3.38	2.80	2.38	1.76	1.64	0.67	0.36	19.66
Maximum Precipitation (in.)	1.6	2.1	3.4	7.9	7.4	8.4	7.7	5.9	5.3	5.1	2.4	1.6	28.1
Minimum Precipitation (in.)	0	0.1	trace	0.1	0.3	0.4	0.3	0.3	0	trace	trace	trace	7.9
Maximum 24-hr. Precipitation (in.)	0.6	0.9	2.5	1.9	3.8	3.8	2.5	3.3	2.5	1.9	1.3	0.9	3.8
Days With ≥ 0.1" Precipitation	2	2	3	4	6	6	6	4	3	3	2	1	42
Days With ≥ 1.0" Precipitation	0	0	0	0	0	1	1	1	0	0	0	0	3
Mean Snowfall (in.)	7.4	6.2	7.9	3.5	trace	trace	trace	trace	trace	1.0	6.5	5.4	37.9
Maximum Snowfall (in.)	16	25	28	24	2	0	0	0	trace	6	30	16	63
Maximum 24-hr. Snowfall (in.)	8	14	12	13	2	0	0	0	trace	3	12	9	14
Days With ≥ 1.0" Snow Depth	22	17	12	2	0	0	0	0	0	0	7	15	75
Thunderstorm Days	0	0	< 1	2	5	10	10	8	3	1	0	0	39
Foggy Days	8	8	11	9	7	6	6	7	8	7	8	10	95
Predominant Sky Cover	OVR	OVR	OVR	OVR	OVR	OVR	SCT	CLR	CLR	OVR	OVR	OVR	OVR
Mean Relative Humidity 6am (%)	76	79	83	81	81	85	86	87	85	81	82	80	82
Mean Relative Humidity 3pm (%)	69	68	63	48	46	52	47	45	46	47	60	69	55
Mean Dewpoint (°F)	3	11	21	32	43	55	59	57	46	35	22	10	33
Prevailing Wind Direction	S	S	N	N	SSE	S	SSE	SSE	S	S	S	S	S
Prevailing Wind Speed (mph)	10	10	16	15	15	12	12	13	13	12	10	10	13
Maximum Wind Gust (mph)	63	56	56	66	62	61	68	69	58	52	58	59	69

Huron Regional Airport

Located on the west bank of the James River at about the middle of the river valley, Huron has a climate that can be classified as continental with frequent daily temperature fluctuations and distinct seasons. The seasons have varied quite markedly from year to year.

Winter is characteristically cold and dry with storms of short duration. Normal temperatures for the season are in the middle teens and precipitation is mainly in the form of snow. Seasonal snowfall has varied from under nine inches to over 75 inches. Wintertime storms of blizzard proportions are infrequent, but they do occur. These blizzards are characterized by strong winds, low temperatures, snow, and very poor visibility. Many mild days can be expected during the winter since about 39 percent of the daily maximum temperatures are above the freezing mark.

Spring is characterized by marked upward trends in both precipitation and temperature with the moisture amounts increasing some three to four fold over winter. Nearly one-third, over five inches, of the annual total precipitation usually falls during the spring months. In early spring some of the precipitation falls as snow. As a consequence, the month of March has a slightly higher snowfall average than any of the winter months.

Based on the 1951-1980 period, the average first occurrence of 32 degrees Fahrenheit in the fall is September 29 and the average last occurrence in the spring is May 11.

Summers are hot but not extreme. Temperatures of 100 degrees or higher usually occur three or four times a year, but nights are normally cool and comfortable. Summertime precipitation is mainly in the form of showers and thunderstorms. Hail occurs about three times a year in the summertime thunderstorms. Sunshine also reaches its maximum during the summer months, when the sun shines during more than 70 percent of the daylight hours.

Autumn, with a relatively slow drop in temperature and steadily lessening amounts of rainfall, is a delightful season with mildly warm days, cool nights, and plentiful sunshine.

The terrain around Huron is exceptionally level and flat. Even the James River has a slope of only 4 to 6 inches per mile. Heavy rains from summertime thunderstorms may, at times, cause some local flooding problems in the city. Moderate to fresh winds occur quite frequently during the daytime in all seasons of the year. Winds are normally from the north in the winter and from the south in the summer. The unusually level terrain helps to accentuate this tendency toward windy days.

Huron Regional Airport *Beadle County*   Elevation: 1,279 ft.   Latitude: 44° 24' N   Longitude: 98° 13' W

	JAN	FEB	MAR	APR	MAY	JUN	JUL	AUG	SEP	OCT	NOV	DEC	YEAR
Mean Maximum Temp. (°F)	24.4	30.9	42.4	58.2	70.4	80.4	86.2	84.5	74.6	60.7	41.7	29.1	57.0
Mean Temp. (°F)	14.1	21.1	32.5	46.2	58.2	68.0	73.6	71.7	61.3	48.0	31.9	19.2	45.5
Mean Minimum Temp. (°F)	3.7	11.2	22.5	34.2	45.8	55.5	61.0	58.9	47.9	35.3	22.0	9.2	33.9
Extreme Maximum Temp. (°F)	62	66	81	97	94	109	109	107	106	94	86	66	109
Extreme Minimum Temp. (°F)	-37	-41	-18	-2	17	34	37	37	19	9	-19	-30	-41
Days Maximum Temp. ≥ 90°F	0	0	0	0	0	4	11	9	3	0	0	0	27
Days Maximum Temp. ≤ 32°F	20	14	6	1	0	0	0	0	0	0	7	17	65
Days Minimum Temp. ≤ 32°F	31	27	25	13	2	0	0	0	2	12	26	31	169
Days Minimum Temp. ≤ 0°F	13	7	2	0	0	0	0	0	0	0	1	8	31
Heating Degree Days (base 65°F)	1,575	1,235	1,002	562	235	46	8	19	176	523	987	1,415	7,783
Cooling Degree Days (base 65°F)	0	0	0	6	33	143	272	232	71	4	0	0	761
Mean Precipitation (in.)	0.49	0.56	1.72	2.36	2.94	3.30	2.87	2.05	1.84	1.59	0.87	0.40	20.99
Maximum Precipitation (in.)	2.2	3.9	5.9	5.8	7.7	11.6	6.7	6.7	6.8	6.4	3.0	2.1	31.7
Minimum Precipitation (in.)	trace	trace	0.1	trace	0.3	0.7	0.1	0.1	0.1	trace	trace	trace	9.7
Maximum 24-hr. Precipitation (in.)	1.6	1.9	2.8	2.3	3.4	5.3	4.3	4.1	2.3	2.9	1.3	1.3	5.3
Days With ≥ 0.1" Precipitation	2	2	4	5	6	6	6	4	4	3	2	1	45
Days With ≥ 1.0" Precipitation	0	0	0	0	1	1	1	0	0	0	0	0	3
Mean Snowfall (in.)	8.1	7.5	9.5	3.1	trace	trace	trace	trace	trace	1.4	6.3	6.4	42.3
Maximum Snowfall (in.)	28	40	34	26	4	0	0	0	1	11	33	26	81
Maximum 24-hr. Snowfall (in.)	12	16	18	12	3	0	0	0	1	9	10	10	18
Days With ≥ 1.0" Snow Depth	22	18	10	1	0	0	0	0	0	1	6	15	73
Thunderstorm Days	< 1	< 1	< 1	2	5	9	9	8	4	1	< 1	< 1	38
Foggy Days	5	6	6	5	4	4	4	5	5	5	5	6	60
Predominant Sky Cover	OVR	OVR	OVR	OVR	OVR	OVR	SCT	CLR	CLR	CLR	OVR	OVR	OVR
Mean Relative Humidity 6am (%)	77	81	84	83	84	86	87	88	86	82	82	81	83
Mean Relative Humidity 3pm (%)	66	66	61	49	49	51	46	46	46	46	58	66	54
Mean Dewpoint (°F)	6	13	23	33	45	56	60	59	48	36	23	13	35
Prevailing Wind Direction	NW	NNW	NNW	SSE	SSE	SSE	SSE	SSE	SSE	SSE	NW	SSE	SSE
Prevailing Wind Speed (mph)	14	14	15	16	15	14	14	14	14	14	15	13	14
Maximum Wind Gust (mph)	61	52	62	68	60	71	82	76	75	58	58	60	82

Rapid City Regional Airport

Rapid City, which is not far from the geographical center of North America, experiences the large temperature ranges, both daily and seasonal, that are typical of semi-arid continental climates.

The city is surrounded by contrasting landforms, with the forested Black Hills rising immediately west of the city, and rolling prairie extending out in the other directions. From 40 to 70 miles southeast lie the eroded Badlands. The Black Hills, many of which are more than 5,000 feet above sea level, with a number of peaks above 7,000 feet, exert a pronounced influence on the climate of this area. The rolling land to the east of the city is cut by the valleys of the Box Elder and Rapid Creeks, which flow generally east-southeastward. The station is located on the north slope of the irrigated Rapid Valley. An east-west ridge 200 to 300 feet higher than the airport separates the station from the Box Elder Creek Valley.

Although the annual precipitation is light at lower elevations, the distribution is beneficial to agriculture with the greatest amounts occurring during the growing season. The heaviest snows are expected in the spring, which helps to furnish moisture for the early maturing crops such as wheat, while heavy winter snows at the higher elevations provide irrigation water for the fertile valleys.

Summer days are normally warm with cool, comfortable nights. Nearly all of the summer precipitation occurs as thunderstorms. Hail is often associated with the more severe thunderstorms, with resultant damage to vegetation as well as other fragile material in the path of the storms. Autumn, which begins soon after the first of September, is characterized by mild, balmy days, and cool, invigorating mornings and evenings. Autumn weather usually extends into November and often into December.

Temperatures for the winter months of December, January, and February are among the warmest in South Dakota due to the protection of the Black Hills, the frequent occurrence of Chinook winds, and the fact that the winter tracks of arctic air masses usually pass east of Rapid City.

Snowfall is normally light with the greatest monthly average of about eight inches occurring in March. Cold waves can be expected occasionally, and one or more blizzards may occur each winter.

Spring is characterized by unsettled conditions. Wide variations usually occur in temperatures, and snows may fall as late as May.

Based on the 1951-1980 period, the average first occurrence of 32 degrees Fahrenheit in the fall is September 29 and the average last occurrence in the spring is May 7.

Rapid City Regional Airport *Pennington County*   Elevation: 3,159 ft.   Latitude: 44° 03' N   Longitude: 103° 03' W

	JAN	FEB	MAR	APR	MAY	JUN	JUL	AUG	SEP	OCT	NOV	DEC	YEAR
Mean Maximum Temp. (°F)	33.8	39.2	46.9	57.8	68.0	78.0	85.8	85.7	75.2	61.8	45.4	36.8	59.5
Mean Temp. (°F)	22.5	27.6	35.0	45.1	55.4	65.0	71.8	71.2	60.6	48.2	33.9	25.1	46.8
Mean Minimum Temp. (°F)	11.1	15.8	22.9	32.3	42.7	51.9	57.9	56.6	45.9	34.6	22.3	13.4	34.0
Extreme Maximum Temp. (°F)	76	75	82	93	93	106	110	106	104	94	83	71	110
Extreme Minimum Temp. (°F)	-24	-31	-21	1	22	32	39	38	18	-2	-15	-30	-31
Days Maximum Temp. ≥ 90°F	0	0	0	0	0	3	11	11	4	0	0	0	29
Days Maximum Temp. ≤ 32°F	13	9	5	1	0	0	0	0	0	0	6	11	45
Days Minimum Temp. ≤ 32°F	30	27	26	16	3	0	0	0	2	11	26	30	171
Days Minimum Temp. ≤ 0°F	8	4	1	0	0	0	0	0	0	0	1	5	19
Heating Degree Days (base 65°F)	1,313	1,051	925	594	306	84	15	18	188	516	926	1,230	7,166
Cooling Degree Days (base 65°F)	0	0	0	3	16	88	235	223	62	3	0	0	630
Mean Precipitation (in.)	0.38	0.48	1.03	1.88	2.96	2.85	1.99	1.61	1.13	1.36	0.62	0.42	16.71
Maximum Precipitation (in.)	1.7	2.5	2.7	5.2	7.0	7.0	6.1	4.8	3.1	3.8	2.2	1.6	26.0
Minimum Precipitation (in.)	trace	0.1	0.1	trace	0.3	0.6	0.4	0.3	trace	trace	0.1	trace	9.1
Maximum 24-hr. Precipitation (in.)	0.6	0.9	1.4	2.1	3.2	3.8	1.9	2.6	2.1	2.5	0.7	1.0	3.8
Days With ≥ 0.1" Precipitation	1	2	3	4	6	6	4	4	3	3	2	1	39
Days With ≥ 1.0" Precipitation	0	0	0	0	1	1	0	0	0	0	0	0	2
Mean Snowfall (in.)	5.3	6.5	9.4	6.6	0.5	trace	trace	trace	0.2	2.0	6.4	5.5	42.4
Maximum Snowfall (in.)	24	24	31	31	12	4	0	0	2	10	34	18	79
Maximum 24-hr. Snowfall (in.)	9	9	15	16	7	4	0	0	2	7	9	10	16
Days With ≥ 1.0" Snow Depth	15	12	8	3	0	0	0	0	0	1	7	13	59
Thunderstorm Days	0	0	< 1	1	6	10	12	8	3	< 1	< 1	< 1	40
Foggy Days	3	5	5	5	4	3	2	2	2	2	4	4	41
Predominant Sky Cover	OVR	OVR	OVR	OVR	OVR	SCT	SCT	SCT	CLR	CLR	OVR	OVR	OVR
Mean Relative Humidity 6am (%)	69	73	76	72	73	74	70	69	69	68	71	70	71
Mean Relative Humidity 3pm (%)	54	53	49	42	45	47	38	33	35	38	49	56	45
Mean Dewpoint (°F)	13	15	22	29	41	51	53	50	40	31	21	14	32
Prevailing Wind Direction	NNW	NNW	NNW	NNW	NNW	NNW	NNW	NNW	NNW	NNW	NNW	NNW	NNW
Prevailing Wind Speed (mph)	18	18	20	20	17	15	14	14	16	17	18	18	17
Maximum Wind Gust (mph)	68	69	73	69	83	68	73	69	75	73	75	66	83

Sioux Falls Foss Field

Sioux Falls is located in the Big Sioux River Valley in southeast South Dakota. The surrounding terrain is gently rolling. The land slopes upward for about 100 miles north and northwest to an elevation about 400 feet higher than the city. To the southeast, the land slopes downward 200 to 300 feet over the same distance. The climate is of the continental type. There are frequent weather changes from day to day or week to week as the locality is visited by differing air masses. Cold air masses arrive from the interior of Canada, cool, dry air from the northern Pacific, warm, moist air from the Gulf of Mexico, or hot, dry air from the southwest.

Temperatures fluctuate frequently as cold air masses move in very rapidly. During the late fall and winter, cold fronts accompanied by strong, gusty winds drop temperatures by 20 to 30 degrees in a 24-hour period. Severe cold spells usually last only a few days. The winter months of December through February have experienced cold spells with average temperatures under 8 degrees and more than 60 consecutive days below 32 degrees.

Temperatures of 100 degrees and above occur about one in every three years. Summer nights are usually comfortable with temperatures below 70 degrees.

Rainfall is heavier during the spring and summer with lighter amounts in winter. Nearly 64 percent of the normal yearly precipitation falls during the growing season of April through August.

One or two very heavy snows usually fall each winter. Eight to 12 inches of snow may fall in 24 hours. There have been a few snows in excess of 15 inches and almost 30 inches have fallen during a severe winter storm. Strong winds often cause drifting snow, and blizzard conditions may block highways for a day or so.

Southerly winds prevail from late spring to early fall with northwest winds the remainder of the year. Strong winds of 70 mph with gusts to 90 mph have occurred.

Thunderstorms are frequent during the late spring and summer with June and July the most active months. The thunderstorms usually occur during the late afternoon and evening with a secondary peak of activity between 2 and 5 in the morning.

There is occasional flooding in the lower areas of Sioux Falls along the Big Sioux River and Skunk Creek. A diversion canal around Sioux Falls has reduced the threat of damaging floods.

Based on the 1951-1980 period, the average first occurrence of 32 degrees Fahrenheit in the fall is October 1 and the average last occurrence in the spring is May 10.

Sioux Falls Foss Field *Minnehaha County*   Elevation: 1,427 ft.   Latitude: 43° 35' N   Longitude: 96° 45' W

	JAN	FEB	MAR	APR	MAY	JUN	JUL	AUG	SEP	OCT	NOV	DEC	YEAR
Mean Maximum Temp. (°F)	24.2	30.7	42.7	58.4	70.8	80.4	85.3	82.8	73.7	60.5	41.8	28.6	56.7
Mean Temp. (°F)	14.3	21.2	32.9	46.6	58.8	68.5	73.7	71.4	61.4	48.3	32.2	19.2	45.7
Mean Minimum Temp. (°F)	4.3	11.6	23.1	34.7	46.8	56.7	62.1	59.9	49.1	36.1	22.5	9.7	34.7
Extreme Maximum Temp. (°F)	66	70	84	93	93	110	108	108	104	89	81	63	110
Extreme Minimum Temp. (°F)	-36	-29	-15	5	21	36	38	39	22	9	-13	-28	-36
Days Maximum Temp. ≥ 90°F	0	0	0	0	1	4	9	6	2	0	0	0	22
Days Maximum Temp. ≤ 32°F	21	15	7	1	0	0	0	0	0	0	7	18	69
Days Minimum Temp. ≤ 32°F	31	27	25	13	2	0	0	0	1	11	26	31	167
Days Minimum Temp. ≤ 0°F	13	7	1	0	0	0	0	0	0	0	1	8	30
Heating Degree Days (base 65°F)	1,568	1,231	987	553	224	44	7	18	171	514	978	1,415	7,710
Cooling Degree Days (base 65°F)	0	0	0	7	40	156	274	219	69	4	0	0	769
Mean Precipitation (in.)	0.50	0.47	1.84	2.69	3.37	3.51	2.92	2.92	2.64	1.97	1.35	0.52	24.70
Maximum Precipitation (in.)	1.8	4.0	4.1	6.0	9.0	8.4	8.4	9.3	9.3	5.7	2.9	3.0	36.1
Minimum Precipitation (in.)	trace	trace	0.1	0.2	0.1	0.9	0.3	0.5	0.3	trace	trace	trace	11.4
Maximum 24-hr. Precipitation (in.)	1.6	1.6	2.4	2.6	4.0	4.3	3.3	4.6	4.0	4.5	1.5	1.4	4.6
Days With ≥ 0.1" Precipitation	1	2	4	6	7	6	5	5	5	3	3	2	49
Days With ≥ 1.0" Precipitation	0	0	0	1	1	1	1	1	1	0	0	0	6
Mean Snowfall (in.)	7.4	5.9	8.6	3.4	trace	trace	trace	0.0	trace	1.2	7.0	6.9	40.4
Maximum Snowfall (in.)	21	48	32	18	3	0	0	0	1	10	22	41	78
Maximum 24-hr. Snowfall (in.)	11	18	18	11	3	0	0	0	1	9	10	12	18
Days With ≥ 1.0" Snow Depth	24	18	10	2	0	0	0	0	0	0	6	17	77
Thunderstorm Days	< 1	< 1	1	3	5	8	8	7	5	2	< 1	< 1	39
Foggy Days	8	8	9	7	6	5	5	7	6	6	8	10	85
Predominant Sky Cover	OVR	OVR	OVR	OVR	OVR	OVR	SCT	CLR	CLR	CLR	OVR	OVR	OVR
Mean Relative Humidity 6am (%)	75	78	81	79	80	82	84	86	84	80	80	79	81
Mean Relative Humidity 3pm (%)	65	64	60	47	47	50	48	49	49	47	58	66	54
Mean Dewpoint (°F)	6	13	23	33	45	55	60	59	49	36	24	13	35
Prevailing Wind Direction	NW	NW	NNW	N	S	S	S	S	S	S	NW	NW	S
Prevailing Wind Speed (mph)	15	15	15	14	14	13	13	13	13	13	16	15	14
Maximum Wind Gust (mph)	69	67	61	66	69	73	82	74	53	62	74	55	82

Academy 2 NE *Charles Mix County*   Elevation: 1,679 ft.   Latitude: 43° 29' N   Longitude: 99° 04' W

	JAN	FEB	MAR	APR	MAY	JUN	JUL	AUG	SEP	OCT	NOV	DEC	YEAR
Mean Maximum Temp. (°F)	29.9	36.8	46.9	60.4	72.1	81.9	88.2	87.0	77.9	63.8	44.7	34.0	60.3
Mean Temp. (°F)	18.7	25.3	34.9	47.3	59.0	68.7	74.4	72.7	63.1	50.0	33.9	23.1	47.6
Mean Minimum Temp. (°F)	7.4	13.8	22.9	34.2	45.8	55.6	60.6	58.4	48.3	36.1	23.0	12.0	34.8
Extreme Maximum Temp. (°F)	69	75	89	98	101	107	112	110	106	98	87	74	112
Extreme Minimum Temp. (°F)	-32	-32	-17	0	21	34	39	35	21	10	-12	-30	-32
Days Maximum Temp. ≥ 90°F	0	0	0	0	1	5	14	12	5	1	0	0	38
Days Maximum Temp. ≤ 32°F	16	11	5	1	0	0	0	0	0	0	5	13	51
Days Minimum Temp. ≤ 32°F	31	27	26	14	2	0	0	0	1	11	25	31	168
Days Minimum Temp. ≤ 0°F	11	5	1	0	0	0	0	0	0	0	1	6	24
Heating Degree Days (base 65°F)	1,431	1,115	926	530	215	40	9	15	145	465	927	1,295	7,113
Cooling Degree Days (base 65°F)	0	0	0	8	35	147	287	240	86	6	0	0	809
Mean Precipitation (in.)	0.48	0.61	1.56	2.77	3.75	3.38	2.95	2.17	2.28	1.84	0.97	0.42	23.18
Days With ≥ 0.1" Precipitation	2	1	4	6	7	6	6	4	4	4	3	2	49
Days With ≥ 1.0" Precipitation	0	0	0	1	1	1	1	1	1	0	0	0	6
Mean Snowfall (in.)	6.9	6.7	9.2	5.2	trace	0.0	0.0	0.0	0.3	1.9	7.5	6.5	44.2
Days With ≥ 1.0" Snow Depth	20	12	9	2	0	0	0	0	0	1	6	14	64

Alexandria *Hanson County*   Elevation: 1,351 ft.   Latitude: 43° 39' N   Longitude: 97° 47' W

	JAN	FEB	MAR	APR	MAY	JUN	JUL	AUG	SEP	OCT	NOV	DEC	YEAR
Mean Maximum Temp. (°F)	26.3	33.4	45.3	60.8	72.7	82.1	87.0	85.1	76.5	63.2	43.5	30.6	58.9
Mean Temp. (°F)	16.8	23.8	35.1	48.8	60.8	70.2	75.1	73.2	63.9	51.0	34.3	21.5	47.9
Mean Minimum Temp. (°F)	7.2	14.2	24.9	36.7	48.8	58.2	63.1	61.2	51.2	38.9	25.0	12.4	36.8
Extreme Maximum Temp. (°F)	66	68	85	96	94	107	107	105	105	94	80	67	107
Extreme Minimum Temp. (°F)	-29	-34	-17	6	24	36	41	41	21	11	-13	-31	-34
Days Maximum Temp. ≥ 90°F	0	0	0	0	0	5	11	8	3	0	0	0	27
Days Maximum Temp. ≤ 32°F	19	13	5	0	0	0	0	0	0	0	6	16	59
Days Minimum Temp. ≤ 32°F	31	27	23	10	1	0	0	0	1	8	24	30	155
Days Minimum Temp. ≤ 0°F	10	6	1	0	0	0	0	0	0	0	1	6	24
Heating Degree Days (base 65°F)	1,491	1,158	921	489	175	26	4	10	124	434	915	1,342	7,089
Cooling Degree Days (base 65°F)	0	0	0	10	52	189	316	268	98	8	0	0	941
Mean Precipitation (in.)	0.43	0.52	1.51	2.64	3.18	3.44	2.87	2.64	2.31	1.75	1.09	0.39	22.77
Days With ≥ 0.1" Precipitation	1	2	4	6	6	6	6	4	4	3	3	1	46
Days With ≥ 1.0" Precipitation	0	0	0	0	1	1	1	1	0	1	0	0	5
Mean Snowfall (in.)	5.4	5.2	6.3	2.7	trace	trace	trace	trace	trace	1.0	4.3	5.7	30.6
Days With ≥ 1.0" Snow Depth	19	15	6	1	0	0	0	0	0	0	5	14	60

Ardmore 2 N *Fall River County*   Elevation: 3,549 ft.   Latitude: 43° 03' N   Longitude: 103° 39' W

	JAN	FEB	MAR	APR	MAY	JUN	JUL	AUG	SEP	OCT	NOV	DEC	YEAR
Mean Maximum Temp. (°F)	34.5	41.0	50.3	60.6	70.6	81.8	89.0	88.2	77.6	64.1	47.1	36.4	61.8
Mean Temp. (°F)	20.5	26.4	35.5	45.3	55.6	65.8	72.3	70.9	59.8	47.0	32.6	21.8	46.1
Mean Minimum Temp. (°F)	6.4	11.9	20.7	29.9	40.5	49.7	55.6	53.4	41.9	29.7	18.1	7.4	30.4
Extreme Maximum Temp. (°F)	69	74	83	93	95	109	109	107	104	92	83	70	109
Extreme Minimum Temp. (°F)	-30	-36	-29	-8	19	31	36	32	16	-14	-22	-43	-43
Days Maximum Temp. ≥ 90°F	0	0	0	0	1	7	15	15	5	0	0	0	43
Days Maximum Temp. ≤ 32°F	12	7	3	1	0	0	0	0	0	0	4	11	38
Days Minimum Temp. ≤ 32°F	31	28	28	19	4	0	0	0	5	19	27	31	192
Days Minimum Temp. ≤ 0°F	10	5	1	0	0	0	0	0	0	0	2	8	26
Heating Degree Days (base 65°F)	1,373	1,084	907	584	297	72	10	15	194	555	965	1,332	7,388
Cooling Degree Days (base 65°F)	0	0	0	1	12	96	240	210	47	1	0	0	607
Mean Precipitation (in.)	0.37	0.50	0.99	1.79	2.86	2.84	2.28	1.61	1.37	1.33	0.60	0.43	16.97
Days With ≥ 0.1" Precipitation	1	2	3	5	6	6	5	4	4	3	2	1	42
Days With ≥ 1.0" Precipitation	0	0	0	0	0	1	0	0	0	0	0	0	1
Mean Snowfall (in.)	6.5	6.3	8.3	5.2	0.7	trace	trace	0.0	0.6	3.3	6.1	7.9	44.9
Days With ≥ 1.0" Snow Depth	20	11	7	2	0	0	0	0	0	1	7	16	64

Armour *Douglas County*   Elevation: 1,509 ft.   Latitude: 43° 20' N   Longitude: 98° 21' W

	JAN	FEB	MAR	APR	MAY	JUN	JUL	AUG	SEP	OCT	NOV	DEC	YEAR
Mean Maximum Temp. (°F)	28.9	36.4	47.8	61.3	73.2	83.1	88.7	87.0	77.8	64.1	44.8	32.9	60.5
Mean Temp. (°F)	18.4	25.5	36.4	48.7	60.5	70.3	75.6	73.8	64.0	50.9	34.5	22.7	48.4
Mean Minimum Temp. (°F)	7.9	14.6	24.7	36.0	47.7	57.5	62.4	60.5	50.2	37.6	24.2	12.5	36.3
Extreme Maximum Temp. (°F)	70	73	83	95	95	107	109	108	104	95	81	70	109
Extreme Minimum Temp. (°F)	-32	-30	-17	5	21	37	39	37	23	11	-11	-31	-32
Days Maximum Temp. ≥ 90°F	0	0	0	0	1	7	14	12	5	0	0	0	39
Days Maximum Temp. ≤ 32°F	17	11	4	0	0	0	0	0	0	0	5	14	51
Days Minimum Temp. ≤ 32°F	30	27	24	11	1	0	0	0	1	10	24	31	159
Days Minimum Temp. ≤ 0°F	10	5	1	0	0	0	0	0	0	0	1	6	23
Heating Degree Days (base 65°F)	1,438	1,109	880	491	180	26	4	9	125	438	908	1,304	6,912
Cooling Degree Days (base 65°F)	0	0	0	11	51	191	332	288	104	8	0	0	985
Mean Precipitation (in.)	0.57	0.66	1.77	2.75	3.65	3.35	3.15	2.19	2.30	1.74	1.07	0.62	23.82
Days With ≥ 0.1" Precipitation	2	2	4	6	6	6	6	4	4	3	3	2	48
Days With ≥ 1.0" Precipitation	0	0	0	0	1	1	1	0	1	0	0	0	4
Mean Snowfall (in.)	6.1	5.5	6.5	2.5	trace	0.0	0.0	0.0	trace	0.9	5.8	6.9	34.2
Days With ≥ 1.0" Snow Depth	20	13	6	1	0	0	0	0	0	0	6	15	61

Belle Fourche *Butte County*   Elevation: 3,018 ft.   Latitude: 44° 40' N   Longitude: 103° 51' W

	JAN	FEB	MAR	APR	MAY	JUN	JUL	AUG	SEP	OCT	NOV	DEC	YEAR
Mean Maximum Temp. (°F)	34.8	41.4	48.5	60.5	70.9	81.2	88.0	87.8	77.1	64.3	47.2	37.8	61.6
Mean Temp. (°F)	22.4	28.3	35.1	46.5	56.9	66.7	72.6	71.4	60.5	48.6	34.6	25.2	47.4
Mean Minimum Temp. (°F)	10.0	15.1	21.7	32.4	42.8	52.1	57.1	55.0	43.9	32.8	22.0	12.7	33.1
Extreme Maximum Temp. (°F)	69	72	82	93	97	106	110	108	107	91	83	74	110
Extreme Minimum Temp. (°F)	-31	-32	-29	-1	21	33	38	36	18	-12	-14	-44	-44
Days Maximum Temp. ≥ 90°F	0	0	0	0	1	5	14	14	4	0	0	0	38
Days Maximum Temp. ≤ 32°F	12	7	4	0	0	0	0	0	0	0	4	9	36
Days Minimum Temp. ≤ 32°F	29	26	27	15	3	0	0	0	2	15	26	30	173
Days Minimum Temp. ≤ 0°F	9	5	2	0	0	0	0	0	0	0	1	6	23
Heating Degree Days (base 65°F)	1,314	1,031	919	551	262	56	10	12	178	504	905	1,226	6,968
Cooling Degree Days (base 65°F)	0	0	0	3	17	107	240	219	48	2	0	0	636
Mean Precipitation (in.)	0.47	0.53	1.12	2.00	3.15	2.99	2.08	1.37	1.32	1.73	0.69	0.63	18.08
Days With ≥ 0.1" Precipitation	2	2	3	5	7	6	5	3	3	4	2	2	44
Days With ≥ 1.0" Precipitation	0	0	0	0	1	1	0	0	0	0	0	0	2
Mean Snowfall (in.)	7.1	4.4	8.9	4.7	0.2	0.0	0.0	0.0	trace	1.6	5.1	6.9	38.9
Days With ≥ 1.0" Snow Depth	na	7	4	1	0	0	0	0	0	0	4	na	na

Bison *Perkins County*   Elevation: 2,778 ft.   Latitude: 45° 32' N   Longitude: 102° 28' W

	JAN	FEB	MAR	APR	MAY	JUN	JUL	AUG	SEP	OCT	NOV	DEC	YEAR
Mean Maximum Temp. (°F)	26.3	33.1	42.6	56.4	68.7	78.5	85.4	85.5	74.1	60.1	41.1	30.5	56.8
Mean Temp. (°F)	16.3	22.8	31.7	44.1	55.8	65.4	71.5	70.7	59.8	47.1	31.0	20.4	44.7
Mean Minimum Temp. (°F)	6.2	12.6	20.8	31.7	42.9	52.3	57.5	55.8	45.3	34.2	20.8	10.3	32.5
Extreme Maximum Temp. (°F)	67	71	78	92	93	104	107	106	103	92	81	69	107
Extreme Minimum Temp. (°F)	-29	-31	-28	-1	21	28	39	37	20	-7	-17	-34	-34
Days Maximum Temp. ≥ 90°F	0	0	0	0	0	3	11	10	3	0	0	0	27
Days Maximum Temp. ≤ 32°F	18	12	7	1	0	0	0	0	0	1	8	16	63
Days Minimum Temp. ≤ 32°F	30	27	27	17	3	0	0	0	2	13	26	30	175
Days Minimum Temp. ≤ 0°F	12	6	2	0	0	0	0	0	0	0	2	7	29
Heating Degree Days (base 65°F)	1,507	1,184	1,026	624	296	76	15	23	202	550	1,015	1,377	7,895
Cooling Degree Days (base 65°F)	0	0	0	2	20	95	225	206	56	4	0	0	608
Mean Precipitation (in.)	0.45	0.48	1.20	2.22	2.82	2.86	2.27	1.54	1.25	1.47	0.61	0.50	17.67
Days With ≥ 0.1" Precipitation	2	2	3	5	6	6	5	4	3	3	2	2	43
Days With ≥ 1.0" Precipitation	0	0	0	0	1	1	0	0	0	0	0	0	2
Mean Snowfall (in.)	5.4	5.6	6.9	4.4	0.3	0.0	0.0	0.0	trace	1.2	4.4	5.2	33.4
Days With ≥ 1.0" Snow Depth	na	na	na	0	0	0	0	0	0	0	1	na	na

Bonesteel *Gregory County*   Elevation: 1,984 ft.   Latitude: 43° 05' N   Longitude: 98° 57' W

	JAN	FEB	MAR	APR	MAY	JUN	JUL	AUG	SEP	OCT	NOV	DEC	YEAR
Mean Maximum Temp. (°F)	29.5	36.1	46.7	59.1	70.9	80.9	86.8	85.6	76.4	63.1	44.5	34.3	59.5
Mean Temp. (°F)	18.8	25.2	35.2	47.0	58.6	68.5	74.5	72.8	63.0	49.8	34.0	23.8	47.6
Mean Minimum Temp. (°F)	8.0	14.3	23.6	34.8	46.3	56.1	62.3	59.9	49.5	36.7	23.5	13.4	35.7
Extreme Maximum Temp. (°F)	72	75	87	95	96	104	106	105	103	94	82	73	106
Extreme Minimum Temp. (°F)	-30	-29	-19	2	20	36	40	41	22	10	-11	-28	-30
Days Maximum Temp. ≥ 90°F	0	0	0	0	1	5	12	10	4	0	0	0	32
Days Maximum Temp. ≤ 32°F	16	11	5	1	0	0	0	0	0	0	6	13	52
Days Minimum Temp. ≤ 32°F	30	26	24	12	2	0	0	0	1	9	25	30	159
Days Minimum Temp. ≤ 0°F	10	6	1	0	0	0	0	0	0	0	1	5	23
Heating Degree Days (base 65°F)	1,429	1,116	924	539	224	41	8	14	146	470	923	1,271	7,105
Cooling Degree Days (base 65°F)	0	0	0	5	30	134	289	246	87	5	0	0	796
Mean Precipitation (in.)	0.32	0.60	1.86	3.10	4.38	3.70	3.51	2.91	3.01	1.94	0.99	0.44	26.76
Days With ≥ 0.1" Precipitation	1	2	4	6	7	6	6	4	4	3	3	2	48
Days With ≥ 1.0" Precipitation	0	0	1	1	1	1	1	1	1	1	0	0	8
Mean Snowfall (in.)	6.2	5.8	8.2	5.8	trace	trace	0.0	0.0	0.1	1.8	7.1	6.5	41.5
Days With ≥ 1.0" Snow Depth	18	13	9	3	0	0	0	0	0	1	7	14	65

Britton *Marshall County*   Elevation: 1,338 ft.   Latitude: 45° 47' N   Longitude: 97° 45' W

	JAN	FEB	MAR	APR	MAY	JUN	JUL	AUG	SEP	OCT	NOV	DEC	YEAR
Mean Maximum Temp. (°F)	20.0	27.4	39.6	57.7	71.6	80.1	85.7	84.1	74.1	60.2	38.7	25.7	55.4
Mean Temp. (°F)	9.6	17.3	29.7	45.4	58.5	67.3	72.6	71.0	60.7	47.7	29.3	16.0	43.8
Mean Minimum Temp. (°F)	-0.8	7.2	19.8	32.9	45.3	54.6	59.4	57.7	47.2	35.1	19.9	6.3	32.1
Extreme Maximum Temp. (°F)	66	62	80	100	95	108	105	105	101	91	76	59	108
Extreme Minimum Temp. (°F)	-36	-40	-26	-2	19	33	37	32	16	3	-24	-39	-40
Days Maximum Temp. ≥ 90°F	0	0	0	0	1	3	10	8	2	0	0	0	24
Days Maximum Temp. ≤ 32°F	24	16	8	1	0	0	0	0	0	0	10	20	79
Days Minimum Temp. ≤ 32°F	31	28	27	15	3	0	0	0	2	12	27	31	176
Days Minimum Temp. ≤ 0°F	16	10	3	0	0	0	0	0	0	0	2	10	41
Heating Degree Days (base 65°F)	1,713	1,342	1,087	588	234	55	13	25	188	534	1,064	1,513	8,356
Cooling Degree Days (base 65°F)	0	0	0	0	6	40	129	248	211	60	4	0	698
Mean Precipitation (in.)	0.62	0.51	1.00	1.71	2.84	3.46	3.22	2.25	2.11	1.62	0.78	0.35	20.47
Days With ≥ 0.1" Precipitation	2	2	3	4	6	6	5	5	4	4	2	1	44
Days With ≥ 1.0" Precipitation	0	0	0	0	1	1	1	0	0	0	0	0	3
Mean Snowfall (in.)	na	na	na	2.1	trace	0.0	0.0	0.0	0.0	0.3	7.4	6.7	na
Days With ≥ 1.0" Snow Depth	25	23	15	2	0	0	0	0	0	0	8	15	88

Brookings 2 NE *Brookings County*   Elevation: 1,637 ft.   Latitude: 44° 19' N   Longitude: 96° 46' W

	JAN	FEB	MAR	APR	MAY	JUN	JUL	AUG	SEP	OCT	NOV	DEC	YEAR
Mean Maximum Temp. (°F)	20.4	26.9	38.2	54.4	67.9	77.2	81.9	79.7	70.8	57.9	39.0	25.8	53.3
Mean Temp. (°F)	10.2	16.9	29.0	43.3	56.0	65.6	70.1	67.9	58.2	45.5	29.5	16.3	42.4
Mean Minimum Temp. (°F)	-0.1	6.8	19.7	32.0	44.1	54.1	58.4	55.9	45.5	33.1	20.0	6.7	31.4
Extreme Maximum Temp. (°F)	65	63	78	93	92	103	100	103	100	90	77	63	103
Extreme Minimum Temp. (°F)	-36	-37	-19	-2	21	35	37	36	20	9	-22	-32	-37
Days Maximum Temp. ≥ 90°F	0	0	0	0	0	2	5	3	1	0	0	0	11
Days Maximum Temp. ≤ 32°F	24	17	10	1	0	0	0	0	0	0	10	21	83
Days Minimum Temp. ≤ 32°F	31	28	27	17	3	0	0	0	3	15	27	31	182
Days Minimum Temp. ≤ 0°F	16	10	3	0	0	0	0	0	0	0	2	10	41
Heating Degree Days (base 65°F)	1,698	1,354	1,110	647	295	77	21	45	238	599	1,057	1,505	8,646
Cooling Degree Days (base 65°F)	0	0	0	2	24	102	180	138	38	2	0	0	486
Mean Precipitation (in.)	0.35	0.37	1.29	2.08	2.92	4.26	3.13	2.93	2.49	1.83	0.96	0.25	22.86
Days With ≥ 0.1" Precipitation	1	1	3	6	6	7	6	5	5	4	2	1	47
Days With ≥ 1.0" Precipitation	0	0	0	0	1	1	1	1	1	0	0	0	5
Mean Snowfall (in.)	6.4	5.2	7.4	2.7	trace	0.0	0.0	0.0	trace	1.0	5.7	6.1	34.5
Days With ≥ 1.0" Snow Depth	22	17	10	3	0	0	0	0	0	1	7	16	76

Camp Crook *Harding County*   Elevation: 3,120 ft.   Latitude: 45° 33' N   Longitude: 103° 58' W

	JAN	FEB	MAR	APR	MAY	JUN	JUL	AUG	SEP	OCT	NOV	DEC	YEAR
Mean Maximum Temp. (°F)	29.5	36.3	45.4	57.6	68.7	78.8	86.7	87.1	75.7	61.7	43.3	33.5	58.7
Mean Temp. (°F)	17.8	24.3	32.7	44.0	54.6	64.4	70.5	69.8	58.7	46.3	31.2	21.5	44.7
Mean Minimum Temp. (°F)	6.0	12.2	19.9	30.2	40.5	50.0	54.3	52.5	41.5	30.9	19.1	9.4	30.6
Extreme Maximum Temp. (°F)	69	72	77	91	99	103	110	105	104	91	84	67	110
Extreme Minimum Temp. (°F)	-38	-38	-32	-9	17	30	34	28	14	-12	-28	-46	-46
Days Maximum Temp. ≥ 90°F	0	0	0	0	1	3	12	13	3	0	0	0	32
Days Maximum Temp. ≤ 32°F	15	10	5	1	0	0	0	0	0	1	6	13	51
Days Minimum Temp. ≤ 32°F	30	27	28	18	5	0	0	0	5	17	28	30	188
Days Minimum Temp. ≤ 0°F	11	6	2	0	0	0	0	0	0	0	2	7	28
Heating Degree Days (base 65°F)	1,459	1,145	996	625	327	90	22	28	224	573	1,007	1,342	7,838
Cooling Degree Days (base 65°F)	0	0	0	1	15	82	204	195	41	1	0	0	539
Mean Precipitation (in.)	0.32	0.29	0.61	1.46	2.82	2.59	2.03	1.22	1.14	1.23	0.45	0.32	14.48
Days With ≥ 0.1" Precipitation	1	1	2	4	6	6	4	3	3	3	1	1	35
Days With ≥ 1.0" Precipitation	0	0	0	0	1	0	0	0	0	0	0	0	1
Mean Snowfall (in.)	6.0	5.5	6.8	4.2	1.0	trace	0.0	0.0	0.5	1.7	5.7	5.2	36.6
Days With ≥ 1.0" Snow Depth	19	12	9	3	0	0	0	0	0	1	7	16	67

Canton 4 WNW *Lincoln County*   Elevation: 1,345 ft.   Latitude: 43° 19' N   Longitude: 96° 39' W

	JAN	FEB	MAR	APR	MAY	JUN	JUL	AUG	SEP	OCT	NOV	DEC	YEAR
Mean Maximum Temp. (°F)	25.4	32.6	44.9	60.9	73.3	82.3	85.7	82.9	75.6	63.1	43.0	29.8	58.3
Mean Temp. (°F)	15.1	22.5	34.2	48.1	60.5	69.8	73.6	71.0	62.4	50.1	33.3	20.2	46.7
Mean Minimum Temp. (°F)	4.7	12.3	23.5	35.3	47.6	57.2	61.4	59.0	49.2	37.1	23.5	10.5	35.1
Extreme Maximum Temp. (°F)	66	69	84	95	97	105	107	104	104	91	82	65	107
Extreme Minimum Temp. (°F)	-35	-35	-18	5	20	35	39	37	21	11	-15	-30	-35
Days Maximum Temp. ≥ 90°F	0	0	0	0	1	5	9	5	2	0	0	0	22
Days Maximum Temp. ≤ 32°F	20	13	5	1	0	0	0	0	0	0	6	17	62
Days Minimum Temp. ≤ 32°F	31	27	25	12	2	0	0	0	1	10	24	31	163
Days Minimum Temp. ≤ 0°F	12	6	2	0	0	0	0	0	0	0	1	7	28
Heating Degree Days (base 65°F)	1,542	1,194	948	509	185	29	5	16	144	460	946	1,384	7,362
Cooling Degree Days (base 65°F)	0	0	0	11	53	175	263	201	76	7	0	0	786
Mean Precipitation (in.)	0.37	0.37	1.57	2.48	2.99	3.74	3.10	3.16	2.22	1.85	1.20	0.47	23.52
Days With ≥ 0.1" Precipitation	1	1	3	6	7	6	5	5	4	4	3	1	46
Days With ≥ 1.0" Precipitation	0	0	0	0	0	1	1	1	1	1	0	0	5
Mean Snowfall (in.)	5.9	4.2	5.3	1.8	trace	0.0	0.0	0.0	0.0	0.6	4.6	5.9	28.3
Days With ≥ 1.0" Snow Depth	22	17	8	1	0	0	0	0	0	0	6	17	71

Castlewood *Hamlin County*   Elevation: 1,683 ft.   Latitude: 44° 43' N   Longitude: 97° 02' W

	JAN	FEB	MAR	APR	MAY	JUN	JUL	AUG	SEP	OCT	NOV	DEC	YEAR
Mean Maximum Temp. (°F)	21.5	28.9	40.0	57.0	70.3	79.2	84.3	82.4	73.1	59.8	39.6	26.5	55.2
Mean Temp. (°F)	10.6	18.1	29.7	44.3	57.1	66.6	71.3	69.3	59.4	46.5	29.6	16.5	43.3
Mean Minimum Temp. (°F)	-0.4	7.2	19.3	31.6	43.8	53.9	58.4	56.2	45.7	33.2	19.5	6.4	31.2
Extreme Maximum Temp. (°F)	66	62	76	97	91	104	105	104	101	90	79	58	105
Extreme Minimum Temp. (°F)	-37	-44	-22	-4	18	32	34	31	20	8	-22	-33	-44
Days Maximum Temp. ≥ 90°F	0	0	0	0	0	3	9	6	2	0	0	0	20
Days Maximum Temp. ≤ 32°F	24	16	8	1	0	0	0	0	0	0	9	21	79
Days Minimum Temp. ≤ 32°F	31	27	28	17	4	0	0	0	2	15	26	31	181
Days Minimum Temp. ≤ 0°F	16	9	3	0	0	0	0	0	0	0	2	10	40
Heating Degree Days (base 65°F)	1,684	1,319	1,087	616	264	61	17	31	211	567	1,055	1,497	8,409
Cooling Degree Days (base 65°F)	0	0	0	4	24	104	203	156	42	1	0	0	534
Mean Precipitation (in.)	0.70	0.55	1.36	1.99	2.91	4.18	3.30	2.87	2.33	1.95	1.03	0.49	23.66
Days With ≥ 0.1" Precipitation	2	2	4	5	6	7	6	5	4	4	3	2	50
Days With ≥ 1.0" Precipitation	0	0	0	0	1	1	1	1	1	0	0	0	5
Mean Snowfall (in.)	6.8	4.1	5.2	1.3	trace	0.0	0.0	0.0	trace	0.4	5.0	4.2	27.0
Days With ≥ 1.0" Snow Depth	24	19	11	1	0	0	0	0	0	0	6	18	79

Cedar Butte 1 NE *Mellette County*   Elevation: 2,247 ft.   Latitude: 43° 36' N   Longitude: 101° 01' W

	JAN	FEB	MAR	APR	MAY	JUN	JUL	AUG	SEP	OCT	NOV	DEC	YEAR
Mean Maximum Temp. (°F)	33.9	39.9	49.7	61.1	72.6	83.4	90.7	89.8	79.5	65.0	47.4	37.2	62.5
Mean Temp. (°F)	21.6	27.9	36.8	47.7	59.3	69.2	75.7	74.7	64.3	51.1	35.9	25.8	49.2
Mean Minimum Temp. (°F)	9.7	15.8	24.0	34.5	45.9	55.2	60.7	59.6	49.1	37.1	24.2	14.3	35.8
Extreme Maximum Temp. (°F)	73	77	86	96	98	112	112	110	106	97	87	73	112
Extreme Minimum Temp. (°F)	-26	-29	-15	4	23	35	39	39	22	1	-12	-30	-30
Days Maximum Temp. ≥ 90°F	0	0	0	0	2	7	17	16	7	1	0	0	50
Days Maximum Temp. ≤ 32°F	13	9	4	0	0	0	0	0	0	0	4	10	40
Days Minimum Temp. ≤ 32°F	29	25	25	13	2	0	0	0	1	9	23	29	156
Days Minimum Temp. ≤ 0°F	8	5	1	0	0	0	0	0	0	0	1	5	20
Heating Degree Days (base 65°F)	1,344	1,043	862	523	214	36	5	8	125	435	866	1,214	6,675
Cooling Degree Days (base 65°F)	0	0	0	10	45	158	327	307	113	10	1	0	971
Mean Precipitation (in.)	0.36	0.41	1.27	2.17	3.24	3.46	2.83	1.79	1.40	1.47	0.58	0.35	19.33
Days With ≥ 0.1" Precipitation	1	1	3	5	7	6	6	4	3	3	2	1	42
Days With ≥ 1.0" Precipitation	0	0	0	0	1	1	1	0	0	0	0	0	3
Mean Snowfall (in.)	4.7	5.9	7.1	5.1	trace	0.0	0.0	0.0	trace	1.8	5.7	5.1	35.4
Days With ≥ 1.0" Snow Depth	17	12	7	2	0	0	0	0	0	1	6	14	59

Centerville 6 SE *Clay County*   Elevation: 1,259 ft.   Latitude: 43° 03' N   Longitude: 96° 54' W

	JAN	FEB	MAR	APR	MAY	JUN	JUL	AUG	SEP	OCT	NOV	DEC	YEAR
Mean Maximum Temp. (°F)	25.1	32.0	43.5	59.1	71.3	81.0	85.2	83.1	75.2	62.4	43.2	29.5	57.5
Mean Temp. (°F)	14.5	21.6	33.0	46.9	59.1	68.9	73.1	70.8	61.5	48.8	32.9	19.6	45.9
Mean Minimum Temp. (°F)	4.0	11.0	22.5	34.6	46.9	56.9	60.9	58.5	47.7	35.2	22.6	9.7	34.2
Extreme Maximum Temp. (°F)	70	72	84	95	98	107	105	106	106	94	82	67	107
Extreme Minimum Temp. (°F)	-32	-30	-19	1	21	36	38	32	19	10	-20	-33	-33
Days Maximum Temp. ≥ 90°F	0	0	0	0	1	4	9	6	3	0	0	0	23
Days Maximum Temp. ≤ 32°F	20	14	7	1	0	0	0	0	0	0	6	17	65
Days Minimum Temp. ≤ 32°F	31	28	26	13	2	0	0	0	2	12	26	31	171
Days Minimum Temp. ≤ 0°F	13	7	2	0	0	0	0	0	0	0	1	7	30
Heating Degree Days (base 65°F)	1,560	1,221	985	546	220	41	8	21	171	501	955	1,401	7,630
Cooling Degree Days (base 65°F)	0	0	0	10	46	166	259	201	71	5	0	0	758
Mean Precipitation (in.)	0.43	0.48	1.64	2.52	3.69	3.91	3.30	2.76	2.35	1.84	1.32	0.55	24.79
Days With ≥ 0.1" Precipitation	1	1	4	5	8	7	5	5	5	4	3	2	50
Days With ≥ 1.0" Precipitation	0	0	0	0	1	1	1	1	1	0	0	0	5
Mean Snowfall (in.)	5.3	4.5	5.9	2.2	0.0	0.0	0.0	0.0	trace	0.8	5.4	5.6	29.7
Days With ≥ 1.0" Snow Depth	na	na	7	1	0	0	0	0	0	0	3	na	na

Clark *Clark County*   Elevation: 1,778 ft.   Latitude: 44° 53' N   Longitude: 97° 44' W

	JAN	FEB	MAR	APR	MAY	JUN	JUL	AUG	SEP	OCT	NOV	DEC	YEAR
Mean Maximum Temp. (°F)	20.8	27.8	39.1	55.9	69.1	77.7	83.4	81.7	72.1	58.6	38.5	25.9	54.2
Mean Temp. (°F)	11.0	18.0	29.4	44.4	57.4	66.5	71.8	70.0	60.0	46.9	29.5	16.7	43.5
Mean Minimum Temp. (°F)	1.1	8.2	19.6	32.7	45.6	55.3	60.2	58.2	47.8	35.2	20.4	7.4	32.7
Extreme Maximum Temp. (°F)	66	63	74	95	92	106	105	105	100	88	78	61	106
Extreme Minimum Temp. (°F)	-35	-36	-17	-8	22	36	43	41	20	5	-17	-33	-36
Days Maximum Temp. ≥ 90°F	0	0	0	0	0	2	7	5	2	0	0	0	16
Days Maximum Temp. ≤ 32°F	24	16	9	1	0	0	0	0	0	0	10	20	80
Days Minimum Temp. ≤ 32°F	31	28	28	16	2	0	0	0	1	12	27	31	176
Days Minimum Temp. ≤ 0°F	15	9	3	0	0	0	0	0	0	0	2	9	38
Heating Degree Days (base 65°F)	1,671	1,321	1,098	617	257	60	13	27	198	557	1,059	1,493	8,371
Cooling Degree Days (base 65°F)	0	0	0	4	27	105	219	174	48	2	0	0	579
Mean Precipitation (in.)	0.66	0.60	1.35	2.05	2.81	3.82	3.11	2.85	2.01	1.79	1.01	0.47	22.53
Days With ≥ 0.1" Precipitation	2	2	4	5	6	6	6	5	4	4	3	2	49
Days With ≥ 1.0" Precipitation	0	0	0	0	0	1	1	1	0	0	0	0	3
Mean Snowfall (in.)	8.0	6.3	5.5	1.6	0.0	0.0	0.0	0.0	trace	0.9	5.5	5.4	33.2
Days With ≥ 1.0" Snow Depth	27	20	15	2	0	0	0	0	0	0	7	16	87

Clear Lake *Deuel County*   Elevation: 1,797 ft.   Latitude: 44° 45' N   Longitude: 96° 41' W

	JAN	FEB	MAR	APR	MAY	JUN	JUL	AUG	SEP	OCT	NOV	DEC	YEAR
Mean Maximum Temp. (°F)	21.0	27.5	39.0	56.3	69.7	78.3	82.7	80.2	71.3	58.6	38.7	25.8	54.1
Mean Temp. (°F)	11.8	18.3	29.7	44.8	57.8	67.0	71.5	69.4	60.1	47.6	30.2	17.1	43.8
Mean Minimum Temp. (°F)	2.4	9.0	20.4	33.3	45.7	55.6	60.3	58.5	48.8	36.6	21.7	8.4	33.4
Extreme Maximum Temp. (°F)	66	61	75	94	89	102	103	101	96	87	78	60	103
Extreme Minimum Temp. (°F)	-31	-33	-17	0	22	34	42	37	23	9	-15	-30	-33
Days Maximum Temp. ≥ 90°F	0	0	0	0	0	2	5	3	1	0	0	0	11
Days Maximum Temp. ≤ 32°F	24	16	8	1	0	0	0	0	0	0	10	21	80
Days Minimum Temp. ≤ 32°F	31	27	26	15	3	0	0	0	1	11	26	31	171
Days Minimum Temp. ≤ 0°F	15	8	2	0	0	0	0	0	0	0	1	9	35
Heating Degree Days (base 65°F)	1,647	1,315	1,087	602	248	55	13	28	193	535	1,037	1,479	8,239
Cooling Degree Days (base 65°F)	0	0	0	4	31	115	210	167	50	2	0	0	579
Mean Precipitation (in.)	0.78	0.63	1.81	2.34	3.14	4.32	3.50	3.13	2.47	2.15	1.30	0.51	26.08
Days With ≥ 0.1" Precipitation	2	2	4	5	6	7	6	6	5	4	3	2	52
Days With ≥ 1.0" Precipitation	0	0	0	0	1	1	1	1	1	1	0	0	6
Mean Snowfall (in.)	10.4	7.1	10.8	4.3	trace	0.0	0.0	0.0	trace	1.2	9.3	7.0	50.1
Days With ≥ 1.0" Snow Depth	25	21	14	3	0	0	0	0	0	1	10	18	92

Columbia 8 N *Brown County*   Elevation: 1,299 ft.   Latitude: 45° 44' N   Longitude: 98° 18' W

	JAN	FEB	MAR	APR	MAY	JUN	JUL	AUG	SEP	OCT	NOV	DEC	YEAR
Mean Maximum Temp. (°F)	19.6	27.1	38.2	56.1	69.2	78.3	84.3	82.7	72.6	58.6	37.8	25.0	54.1
Mean Temp. (°F)	8.9	16.8	28.3	44.2	57.3	66.5	71.7	69.7	59.1	45.9	28.5	15.1	42.7
Mean Minimum Temp. (°F)	-1.8	6.4	18.3	32.3	45.3	54.7	59.0	56.6	45.6	33.2	19.1	5.1	31.2
Extreme Maximum Temp. (°F)	60	63	79	94	93	105	106	104	99	92	75	60	106
Extreme Minimum Temp. (°F)	-36	-45	-28	-9	22	35	38	37	17	5	-26	-37	-45
Days Maximum Temp. ≥ 90°F	0	0	0	0	0	2	7	5	2	0	0	0	16
Days Maximum Temp. ≤ 32°F	24	17	9	1	0	0	0	0	0	0	10	21	82
Days Minimum Temp. ≤ 32°F	31	28	28	16	3	0	0	0	2	15	28	31	182
Days Minimum Temp. ≤ 0°F	17	10	3	0	0	0	0	0	0	0	2	11	43
Heating Degree Days (base 65°F)	1,735	1,357	1,132	619	258	60	13	29	216	584	1,090	1,543	8,636
Cooling Degree Days (base 65°F)	0	0	0	3	27	102	210	166	34	1	0	0	543
Mean Precipitation (in.)	0.59	0.46	1.34	1.87	2.77	3.16	2.80	2.26	2.00	1.73	0.75	0.37	20.10
Days With ≥ 0.1" Precipitation	2	2	3	4	6	6	5	4	3	3	2	1	41
Days With ≥ 1.0" Precipitation	0	0	0	0	1	1	1	0	0	1	0	0	4
Mean Snowfall (in.)	8.0	6.4	8.6	3.3	trace	0.0	0.0	0.0	trace	0.9	7.6	5.3	40.1
Days With ≥ 1.0" Snow Depth	26	22	15	2	0	0	0	0	0	0	10	20	95

Cottonwood 2 E *Jackson County*   Elevation: 2,411 ft.   Latitude: 43° 58' N   Longitude: 101° 52' W

	JAN	FEB	MAR	APR	MAY	JUN	JUL	AUG	SEP	OCT	NOV	DEC	YEAR
Mean Maximum Temp. (°F)	32.2	38.7	46.9	59.7	70.8	81.2	88.8	88.8	78.7	63.4	45.8	35.7	60.9
Mean Temp. (°F)	19.2	25.3	33.6	45.4	56.8	66.9	73.4	72.4	61.5	47.3	32.3	22.1	46.3
Mean Minimum Temp. (°F)	6.2	11.8	20.2	31.0	42.8	52.6	57.9	55.9	44.3	31.1	18.7	8.5	31.8
Extreme Maximum Temp. (°F)	70	75	85	95	99	109	111	110	106	94	85	71	111
Extreme Minimum Temp. (°F)	-34	-34	-33	5	16	31	34	34	16	-7	-24	-33	-34
Days Maximum Temp. ≥ 90°F	0	0	0	0	1	6	15	16	6	1	0	0	45
Days Maximum Temp. ≤ 32°F	14	9	5	1	0	0	0	0	0	0	5	11	45
Days Minimum Temp. ≤ 32°F	31	28	28	17	4	0	0	0	3	17	28	31	187
Days Minimum Temp. ≤ 0°F	10	6	2	0	0	0	0	0	0	0	2	7	27
Heating Degree Days (base 65°F)	1,414	1,117	966	585	273	62	12	19	174	544	976	1,323	7,465
Cooling Degree Days (base 65°F)	0	0	0	4	27	115	272	249	66	2	0	0	735
Mean Precipitation (in.)	0.39	0.53	1.15	1.71	3.02	3.10	2.34	1.66	1.15	1.35	0.66	0.37	17.43
Days With ≥ 0.1" Precipitation	1	2	3	4	6	7	4	3	3	3	2	1	39
Days With ≥ 1.0" Precipitation	0	0	0	0	1	1	1	1	0	0	0	0	4
Mean Snowfall (in.)	5.7	7.0	8.9	4.6	trace	0.0	0.0	0.0	trace	1.5	6.1	5.6	39.4
Days With ≥ 1.0" Snow Depth	19	13	10	2	0	0	0	0	0	1	8	15	68

Custer *Custer County*   Elevation: 5,479 ft.   Latitude: 43° 46' N   Longitude: 103° 37' W

	JAN	FEB	MAR	APR	MAY	JUN	JUL	AUG	SEP	OCT	NOV	DEC	YEAR
Mean Maximum Temp. (°F)	34.4	38.9	44.3	52.2	62.3	72.3	79.3	78.4	69.5	58.0	43.7	36.8	55.8
Mean Temp. (°F)	22.4	26.6	32.0	40.0	50.0	59.3	65.7	64.3	55.1	44.2	32.1	24.9	43.1
Mean Minimum Temp. (°F)	10.4	14.3	19.7	27.7	37.7	46.2	52.0	50.0	40.6	30.5	20.4	13.0	30.2
Extreme Maximum Temp. (°F)	68	66	71	84	88	96	99	96	97	85	76	68	99
Extreme Minimum Temp. (°F)	-26	-31	-18	-8	18	27	30	30	11	-5	-15	-34	-34
Days Maximum Temp. ≥ 90°F	0	0	0	0	0	1	3	1	0	0	0	0	5
Days Maximum Temp. ≤ 32°F	13	8	5	2	0	0	0	0	0	1	5	10	44
Days Minimum Temp. ≤ 32°F	30	27	28	22	8	1	0	0	6	17	26	29	194
Days Minimum Temp. ≤ 0°F	7	4	2	0	0	0	0	0	0	0	2	5	20
Heating Degree Days (base 65°F)	1,314	1,078	1,015	745	460	195	68	82	308	637	981	1,236	8,119
Cooling Degree Days (base 65°F)	0	0	0	0	2	33	106	74	19	0	0	0	234
Mean Precipitation (in.)	0.39	0.64	1.05	2.01	3.31	3.26	3.01	2.43	1.52	1.42	0.67	0.52	20.23
Days With ≥ 0.1" Precipitation	1	2	3	5	7	7	7	5	4	3	2	2	48
Days With ≥ 1.0" Precipitation	0	0	0	0	1	0	1	0	0	0	0	0	2
Mean Snowfall (in.)	6.2	*8.4*	*13.0*	*10.4*	0.8	0.2	0.0	0.0	0.6	3.7	na	*7.9*	na
Days With ≥ 1.0" Snow Depth	na	na	na	na	0	0	0	0	0	1	na	na	na

De Smet *Kingsbury County*   Elevation: 1,719 ft.   Latitude: 44° 23' N   Longitude: 97° 33' W

	JAN	FEB	MAR	APR	MAY	JUN	JUL	AUG	SEP	OCT	NOV	DEC	YEAR
Mean Maximum Temp. (°F)	22.9	30.1	41.0	57.9	70.5	79.7	84.7	82.9	73.5	60.0	39.9	27.4	55.9
Mean Temp. (°F)	13.2	20.4	31.2	46.1	58.5	67.9	72.9	71.0	61.4	48.2	31.0	18.1	45.0
Mean Minimum Temp. (°F)	3.0	10.3	21.3	34.3	46.3	56.0	61.0	59.0	49.1	36.3	21.9	8.8	33.9
Extreme Maximum Temp. (°F)	65	67	78	96	91	105	104	106	102	89	78	63	106
Extreme Minimum Temp. (°F)	-32	-36	-18	-3	22	38	43	41	22	8	-16	-30	-36
Days Maximum Temp. ≥ 90°F	0	0	0	0	0	3	9	6	2	0	0	0	20
Days Maximum Temp. ≤ 32°F	22	15	8	1	0	0	0	0	0	0	9	20	75
Days Minimum Temp. ≤ 32°F	31	28	27	13	1	0	0	0	1	11	26	31	169
Days Minimum Temp. ≤ 0°F	14	7	2	0	0	0	0	0	0	0	1	9	33
Heating Degree Days (base 65°F)	1,604	1,253	1,038	565	227	43	9	17	169	518	1,016	1,449	7,908
Cooling Degree Days (base 65°F)	0	0	0	6	32	129	243	198	60	3	0	0	671
Mean Precipitation (in.)	0.63	0.60	1.57	2.28	2.99	3.94	3.57	2.73	2.38	1.72	0.99	0.46	23.86
Days With ≥ 0.1" Precipitation	2	2	4	5	6	7	6	5	4	3	3	2	49
Days With ≥ 1.0" Precipitation	0	0	0	0	1	1	1	1	1	0	0	0	5
Mean Snowfall (in.)	7.1	6.2	7.7	2.5	trace	0.0	0.0	0.0	trace	1.3	6.8	5.7	37.3
Days With ≥ 1.0" Snow Depth	*23*	*19*	13	1	0	0	0	0	0	0	*6*	*17*	*79*

Deadwood *Lawrence County*   Elevation: 4,668 ft.   Latitude: 44° 22' N   Longitude: 103° 44' W

	JAN	FEB	MAR	APR	MAY	JUN	JUL	AUG	SEP	OCT	NOV	DEC	YEAR
Mean Maximum Temp. (°F)	33.4	37.6	44.1	53.2	63.7	74.0	81.0	80.3	70.1	57.1	42.6	36.5	56.1
Mean Temp. (°F)	22.3	26.4	32.3	41.1	51.3	61.0	67.3	66.2	56.2	44.4	31.8	25.3	43.8
Mean Minimum Temp. (°F)	11.1	15.2	20.4	29.0	38.8	47.9	53.6	52.0	42.2	31.7	20.9	14.1	31.4
Extreme Maximum Temp. (°F)	65	67	74	91	90	99	101	98	98	86	75	64	101
Extreme Minimum Temp. (°F)	-24	-29	-16	-2	14	23	35	34	17	-7	-19	-30	-30
Days Maximum Temp. ≥ 90°F	0	0	0	0	0	1	5	4	1	0	0	0	11
Days Maximum Temp. ≤ 32°F	13	9	6	2	0	0	0	0	0	1	7	11	49
Days Minimum Temp. ≤ 32°F	31	27	28	20	7	1	0	0	4	16	27	30	191
Days Minimum Temp. ≤ 0°F	7	4	2	0	0	0	0	0	0	0	1	4	18
Heating Degree Days (base 65°F)	1,318	1,082	1,007	711	423	160	48	58	280	632	989	1,223	7,931
Cooling Degree Days (base 65°F)	0	0	0	1	5	50	133	108	24	0	0	0	321
Mean Precipitation (in.)	1.34	1.16	2.37	3.55	4.70	3.96	2.70	2.13	1.74	2.24	1.39	1.37	28.65
Days With ≥ 0.1" Precipitation	4	4	5	7	8	8	6	4	4	4	4	5	63
Days With ≥ 1.0" Precipitation	0	0	0	1	1	1	0	0	0	0	0	0	3
Mean Snowfall (in.)	13.9	14.5	21.7	12.2	2.0	0.0	0.0	0.0	0.3	7.5	13.5	16.2	101.8
Days With ≥ 1.0" Snow Depth	na	na	na	na	0	0	0	0	0	na	na	na	na

Dupree *Ziebach County*   Elevation: 2,372 ft.   Latitude: 45° 03' N   Longitude: 101° 36' W

	JAN	FEB	MAR	APR	MAY	JUN	JUL	AUG	SEP	OCT	NOV	DEC	YEAR
Mean Maximum Temp. (°F)	27.4	34.4	43.3	58.4	70.8	80.5	87.8	87.4	76.3	62.0	42.3	30.6	58.4
Mean Temp. (°F)	16.8	23.6	32.2	45.4	57.4	66.8	73.1	72.0	61.2	48.3	31.6	20.2	45.7
Mean Minimum Temp. (°F)	6.0	12.9	21.0	32.4	44.0	53.1	58.4	56.6	46.1	34.5	20.9	9.8	33.0
Extreme Maximum Temp. (°F)	68	71	78	96	99	105	108	109	105	93	78	67	109
Extreme Minimum Temp. (°F)	-31	-34	-31	-1	19	35	39	35	18	-6	-22	-34	-34
Days Maximum Temp. ≥ 90°F	0	0	0	0	1	5	13	13	4	0	0	0	36
Days Maximum Temp. ≤ 32°F	17	12	7	1	0	0	0	0	0	0	7	15	59
Days Minimum Temp. ≤ 32°F	30	27	27	16	3	0	0	0	2	12	27	30	174
Days Minimum Temp. ≤ 0°F	11	6	2	0	0	0	0	0	0	0	2	7	28
Heating Degree Days (base 65°F)	1,491	1,163	1,011	587	257	57	10	17	177	515	993	1,383	7,661
Cooling Degree Days (base 65°F)	0	0	0	5	30	109	260	238	65	4	0	0	711
Mean Precipitation (in.)	0.32	0.48	1.10	1.81	3.04	3.29	2.26	1.73	1.24	1.55	0.53	0.37	17.72
Days With ≥ 0.1" Precipitation	1	2	3	4	7	6	5	4	3	3	2	1	41
Days With ≥ 1.0" Precipitation	0	0	0	0	0	1	0	0	0	0	0	0	1
Mean Snowfall (in.)	5.1	6.1	8.1	4.7	0.3	0.0	0.0	0.0	trace	1.2	4.8	5.9	36.2
Days With ≥ 1.0" Snow Depth	20	14	11	3	0	0	0	0	0	1	7	16	72

Dupree 15 SSE *Ziebach County*   Elevation: 2,099 ft.   Latitude: 44° 52' N   Longitude: 101° 28' W

	JAN	FEB	MAR	APR	MAY	JUN	JUL	AUG	SEP	OCT	NOV	DEC	YEAR
Mean Maximum Temp. (°F)	26.8	33.9	43.1	57.6	69.5	80.4	87.5	87.3	76.1	61.7	42.8	31.0	58.1
Mean Temp. (°F)	16.2	23.1	32.3	45.3	56.9	67.2	73.3	72.4	61.0	47.8	31.5	20.4	45.6
Mean Minimum Temp. (°F)	5.5	12.2	21.3	32.9	44.1	54.0	59.1	57.5	45.9	33.8	20.2	9.8	33.0
Extreme Maximum Temp. (°F)	67	73	81	97	101	110	110	111	106	95	83	69	111
Extreme Minimum Temp. (°F)	-35	-32	-30	1	19	31	35	35	13	-5	-13	-31	-35
Days Maximum Temp. ≥ 90°F	0	0	0	0	1	5	13	13	4	0	0	0	36
Days Maximum Temp. ≤ 32°F	18	12	7	1	0	0	0	0	0	0	7	15	60
Days Minimum Temp. ≤ 32°F	30	27	26	14	3	0	0	0	2	13	27	31	173
Days Minimum Temp. ≤ 0°F	12	6	2	0	0	0	0	0	0	0	1	7	28
Heating Degree Days (base 65°F)	1,508	1,177	1,009	587	271	55	11	16	181	530	1,000	1,377	7,722
Cooling Degree Days (base 65°F)	0	0	0	4	27	124	272	257	69	4	0	0	757
Mean Precipitation (in.)	0.33	0.47	1.00	1.61	3.02	2.98	2.56	1.58	1.36	1.56	0.57	0.36	17.40
Days With ≥ 0.1" Precipitation	1	2	3	4	6	6	5	3	3	3	2	1	39
Days With ≥ 1.0" Precipitation	0	0	0	0	1	1	1	0	0	0	0	0	3
Mean Snowfall (in.)	5.7	6.1	7.3	6.1	0.3	trace	0.0	0.0	trace	1.6	5.4	6.2	38.7
Days With ≥ 1.0" Snow Depth	18	13	10	3	0	0	0	0	0	1	8	15	68

Eureka *McPherson County*   Elevation: 1,856 ft.   Latitude: 45° 47' N   Longitude: 99° 38' W

	JAN	FEB	MAR	APR	MAY	JUN	JUL	AUG	SEP	OCT	NOV	DEC	YEAR
Mean Maximum Temp. (°F)	20.0	27.6	39.3	56.7	69.7	78.4	84.8	83.9	73.3	59.0	37.8	25.0	54.6
Mean Temp. (°F)	10.0	17.7	28.8	44.0	56.6	65.6	71.2	69.9	59.2	46.1	28.1	15.6	42.7
Mean Minimum Temp. (°F)	-0.1	7.7	18.3	31.2	43.5	52.8	57.5	55.7	45.1	33.2	18.4	6.0	30.8
Extreme Maximum Temp. (°F)	58	64	77	96	98	107	108	109	103	92	74	57	109
Extreme Minimum Temp. (°F)	-37	-41	-24	-7	20	34	38	34	15	0	-20	-39	-41
Days Maximum Temp. ≥ 90°F	0	0	0	0	1	3	9	8	3	0	0	0	24
Days Maximum Temp. ≤ 32°F	23	16	9	1	0	0	0	0	0	0	11	21	81
Days Minimum Temp. ≤ 32°F	31	28	29	18	3	0	0	0	2	15	28	31	185
Days Minimum Temp. ≤ 0°F	16	9	3	0	0	0	0	0	0	0	2	10	40
Heating Degree Days (base 65°F)	1,702	1,331	1,115	626	275	69	15	29	216	581	1,101	1,529	8,589
Cooling Degree Days (base 65°F)	0	0	0	3	23	92	208	183	45	2	0	0	556
Mean Precipitation (in.)	0.36	0.38	0.89	1.81	2.62	3.15	2.77	2.27	1.46	1.66	0.68	0.33	18.38
Days With ≥ 0.1" Precipitation	1	1	3	4	6	6	5	4	3	3	2	1	39
Days With ≥ 1.0" Precipitation	0	0	0	0	1	1	1	1	0	0	0	0	4
Mean Snowfall (in.)	7.1	6.3	7.2	4.2	trace	0.0	0.0	0.0	trace	1.1	7.8	5.9	39.6
Days With ≥ 1.0" Snow Depth	25	22	17	4	0	0	0	0	0	0	10	16	94

Faith *Meade County*   Elevation: 2,591 ft.   Latitude: 45° 01' N   Longitude: 102° 02' W

	JAN	FEB	MAR	APR	MAY	JUN	JUL	AUG	SEP	OCT	NOV	DEC	YEAR
Mean Maximum Temp. (°F)	27.0	33.6	43.2	57.8	70.0	79.9	87.3	86.6	75.9	61.0	42.3	31.1	58.0
Mean Temp. (°F)	17.0	23.4	32.4	45.5	57.2	66.7	73.3	72.1	61.6	48.1	31.9	21.1	45.9
Mean Minimum Temp. (°F)	6.9	13.2	21.6	33.1	44.2	53.5	59.1	57.7	47.3	35.1	21.5	11.1	33.7
Extreme Maximum Temp. (°F)	67	72	79	98	98	105	108	109	105	93	80	68	109
Extreme Minimum Temp. (°F)	-34	-32	-20	1	23	35	43	39	22	-3	-19	-34	-34
Days Maximum Temp. ≥ 90°F	0	0	0	0	1	4	12	12	3	0	0	0	32
Days Maximum Temp. ≤ 32°F	18	12	7	1	0	0	0	0	0	0	7	15	60
Days Minimum Temp. ≤ 32°F	30	27	27	14	3	0	0	0	0	1	15	30	170
Days Minimum Temp. ≤ 0°F	11	6	2	0	0	0	0	0	0	0	2	7	28
Heating Degree Days (base 65°F)	1,484	1,168	1,004	583	261	60	9	16	167	519	986	1,354	7,611
Cooling Degree Days (base 65°F)	0	0	0	3	26	114	269	248	69	4	0	0	733
Mean Precipitation (in.)	0.41	0.60	1.10	1.88	2.99	2.75	2.59	1.40	1.22	1.56	0.59	0.41	17.50
Days With ≥ 0.1" Precipitation	1	2	3	4	6	6	5	3	3	3	2	1	39
Days With ≥ 1.0" Precipitation	0	0	0	0	1	1	1	0	0	0	0	0	3
Mean Snowfall (in.)	7.1	7.5	10.4	6.4	0.3	0.0	0.0	0.0	0.1	1.6	6.0	7.0	46.4
Days With ≥ 1.0" Snow Depth	20	14	10	3	0	0	0	0	0	1	7	16	71

Faulkton 1 NW *Faulk County*   Elevation: 1,568 ft.   Latitude: 45° 02' N   Longitude: 99° 08' W

	JAN	FEB	MAR	APR	MAY	JUN	JUL	AUG	SEP	OCT	NOV	DEC	YEAR
Mean Maximum Temp. (°F)	23.5	30.4	41.6	58.3	71.0	80.2	86.7	85.7	75.5	61.4	40.7	28.2	56.9
Mean Temp. (°F)	13.2	20.3	31.3	45.6	57.9	67.2	72.8	71.4	61.1	48.1	30.7	18.3	44.8
Mean Minimum Temp. (°F)	2.9	10.1	21.0	32.9	44.7	54.2	58.9	57.0	46.7	34.8	20.6	8.3	32.7
Extreme Maximum Temp. (°F)	66	66	78	98	98	111	110	109	106	93	82	66	111
Extreme Minimum Temp. (°F)	-37	-35	-21	9	14	34	35	36	16	2	-17	-35	-37
Days Maximum Temp. ≥ 90°F	0	0	0	0	1	4	11	10	4	0	0	0	30
Days Maximum Temp. ≤ 32°F	21	15	7	1	0	0	0	0	0	0	8	18	70
Days Minimum Temp. ≤ 32°F	31	27	26	15	3	0	0	0	2	12	27	30	173
Days Minimum Temp. ≤ 0°F	14	8	2	0	0	0	0	0	0	0	1	9	34
Heating Degree Days (base 65°F)	1,602	1,256	1,037	578	244	53	11	21	180	521	1,025	1,443	7,971
Cooling Degree Days (base 65°F)	0	0	0	5	32	117	247	215	65	4	0	0	685
Mean Precipitation (in.)	0.49	0.56	1.46	2.00	2.98	2.90	2.56	2.48	1.75	1.65	0.78	0.39	20.00
Days With ≥ 0.1" Precipitation	2	2	3	4	6	6	5	4	3	3	2	1	41
Days With ≥ 1.0" Precipitation	0	0	0	0	1	1	1	1	0	0	0	0	4
Mean Snowfall (in.)	6.1	6.8	*6.1*	3.9	trace	0.0	0.0	0.0	0.0	1.2	*6.6*	4.5	*35.2*
Days With ≥ 1.0" Snow Depth	na	na	*6*	1	0	0	0	0	0	0	*4*	na	na

Flandreau *Moody County*   Elevation: 1,558 ft.   Latitude: 44° 03' N   Longitude: 96° 36' W

	JAN	FEB	MAR	APR	MAY	JUN	JUL	AUG	SEP	OCT	NOV	DEC	YEAR
Mean Maximum Temp. (°F)	21.6	28.1	39.2	55.3	68.8	78.0	82.8	80.6	71.9	59.1	40.1	26.9	54.4
Mean Temp. (°F)	10.7	17.6	29.6	44.2	57.0	66.7	71.3	68.7	59.2	46.4	30.4	17.0	43.2
Mean Minimum Temp. (°F)	-0.2	7.0	20.0	32.9	45.1	55.4	59.7	56.8	46.4	33.6	20.7	7.1	32.0
Extreme Maximum Temp. (°F)	64	65	85	93	92	105	103	105	101	91	78	63	105
Extreme Minimum Temp. (°F)	-40	-38	-22	-2	20	35	37	35	21	10	-16	-34	-40
Days Maximum Temp. ≥ 90°F	0	0	0	0	0	2	6	4	1	0	0	0	13
Days Maximum Temp. ≤ 32°F	23	16	9	1	0	0	0	0	0	0	9	20	78
Days Minimum Temp. ≤ 32°F	31	28	27	14	2	0	0	0	2	14	27	31	176
Days Minimum Temp. ≤ 0°F	16	10	3	0	0	0	0	0	0	0	1	10	40
Heating Degree Days (base 65°F)	1,678	1,334	1,090	622	269	62	16	37	214	573	1,031	1,482	8,408
Cooling Degree Days (base 65°F)	0	0	0	4	27	117	210	154	43	2	0	0	557
Mean Precipitation (in.)	0.41	0.36	1.33	2.22	2.92	3.86	3.36	3.04	2.56	2.11	1.07	0.39	23.63
Days With ≥ 0.1" Precipitation	1	1	3	5	6	7	6	5	5	4	3	1	47
Days With ≥ 1.0" Precipitation	0	0	0	0	1	1	1	1	1	1	0	0	6
Mean Snowfall (in.)	6.2	4.3	6.5	2.2	trace	0.0	0.0	0.0	0.0	1.2	5.9	6.1	32.4
Days With ≥ 1.0" Snow Depth	*23*	*20*	*11*	1	0	0	0	0	0	0	*2*	*14*	*71*

Forestburg 3 NE *Sanborn County*   Elevation: 1,227 ft.   Latitude: 44° 03' N   Longitude: 98° 04' W

	JAN	FEB	MAR	APR	MAY	JUN	JUL	AUG	SEP	OCT	NOV	DEC	YEAR
Mean Maximum Temp. (°F)	25.2	32.4	44.2	60.2	71.9	81.4	87.0	85.6	76.5	62.3	42.8	29.9	58.3
Mean Temp. (°F)	14.6	21.8	33.4	47.5	59.3	68.9	74.1	72.4	62.7	49.5	32.8	19.8	46.4
Mean Minimum Temp. (°F)	3.9	11.2	22.6	34.7	46.6	56.3	61.2	59.2	48.9	36.6	22.7	9.7	34.5
Extreme Maximum Temp. (°F)	65	66	86	99	93	112	107	109	106	95	83	69	112
Extreme Minimum Temp. (°F)	-36	-40	-21	3	22	36	40	38	20	8	-18	-33	-40
Days Maximum Temp. ≥ 90°F	0	0	0	0	0	5	11	10	4	0	0	0	30
Days Maximum Temp. ≤ 32°F	20	13	5	0	0	0	0	0	0	0	6	17	61
Days Minimum Temp. ≤ 32°F	31	27	25	13	2	0	0	0	1	11	26	31	167
Days Minimum Temp. ≤ 0°F	12	7	2	0	0	0	0	0	0	0	1	8	30
Heating Degree Days (base 65°F)	1,559	1,214	972	524	205	35	5	14	147	479	961	1,394	7,509
Cooling Degree Days (base 65°F)	0	0	0	7	37	156	288	246	84	5	0	0	823
Mean Precipitation (in.)	0.47	0.55	1.64	2.63	3.29	3.26	2.82	2.11	1.97	1.79	1.12	0.45	22.10
Days With ≥ 0.1" Precipitation	2	2	4	6	6	6	6	4	4	4	3	2	49
Days With ≥ 1.0" Precipitation	0	0	0	0	1	1	1	1	0	0	0	0	4
Mean Snowfall (in.)	5.8	5.3	7.0	2.9	trace	0.0	0.0	0.0	trace	1.3	5.5	5.8	33.6
Days With ≥ 1.0" Snow Depth	22	18	10	1	0	0	0	0	0	1	6	17	75

Fort Meade *Meade County*   Elevation: 3,297 ft.   Latitude: 44° 25' N   Longitude: 103° 29' W

	JAN	FEB	MAR	APR	MAY	JUN	JUL	AUG	SEP	OCT	NOV	DEC	YEAR
Mean Maximum Temp. (°F)	35.5	40.6	47.4	58.3	69.0	79.1	86.4	86.1	75.8	62.5	45.8	38.4	60.4
Mean Temp. (°F)	24.1	29.0	35.5	46.0	56.5	66.1	72.7	71.8	61.7	49.2	34.8	26.9	47.9
Mean Minimum Temp. (°F)	12.7	17.4	23.6	33.6	43.9	53.0	58.9	57.4	47.6	35.9	23.8	15.3	35.3
Extreme Maximum Temp. (°F)	72	75	82	90	93	105	107	105	104	90	83	74	107
Extreme Minimum Temp. (°F)	-24	-26	-20	0	23	34	42	39	20	-1	-16	-30	-30
Days Maximum Temp. ≥ 90°F	0	0	0	0	0	4	12	11	4	0	0	0	31
Days Maximum Temp. ≤ 32°F	12	8	5	1	0	0	0	0	0	0	6	9	41
Days Minimum Temp. ≤ 32°F	29	25	25	14	2	0	0	0	2	10	24	29	160
Days Minimum Temp. ≤ 0°F	8	4	1	0	0	0	0	0	0	0	1	4	18
Heating Degree Days (base 65°F)	1,263	1,010	908	568	278	70	11	15	165	486	900	1,177	6,851
Cooling Degree Days (base 65°F)	0	0	0	6	23	104	254	236	73	4	0	0	700
Mean Precipitation (in.)	0.56	0.67	1.50	2.72	3.78	3.68	2.19	1.46	1.31	1.89	0.94	0.61	21.31
Days With ≥ 0.1" Precipitation	2	2	4	5	7	6	5	4	3	4	3	2	47
Days With ≥ 1.0" Precipitation	0	0	0	1	1	1	0	0	0	0	0	0	3
Mean Snowfall (in.)	5.0	5.5	6.9	5.7	0.5	0.0	0.0	0.0	trace	0.9	4.4	na	na
Days With ≥ 1.0" Snow Depth	14	12	9	3	0	0	0	0	0	1	6	13	58

Gann Valley 4 NW *Buffalo County*   Elevation: 1,719 ft.   Latitude: 44° 03' N   Longitude: 99° 04' W

	JAN	FEB	MAR	APR	MAY	JUN	JUL	AUG	SEP	OCT	NOV	DEC	YEAR
Mean Maximum Temp. (°F)	25.4	32.8	44.1	59.3	71.2	81.0	87.6	86.6	77.1	62.4	42.5	30.4	58.4
Mean Temp. (°F)	14.5	21.8	32.7	46.1	58.2	68.0	73.9	72.5	62.3	48.7	31.8	19.6	45.8
Mean Minimum Temp. (°F)	3.6	10.7	21.2	32.8	45.1	55.0	60.2	58.3	47.4	34.9	21.0	8.9	33.2
Extreme Maximum Temp. (°F)	64	69	86	98	95	106	112	111	105	96	84	73	112
Extreme Minimum Temp. (°F)	-35	-44	-21	-1	17	33	37	38	16	7	-15	-36	-44
Days Maximum Temp. ≥ 90°F	0	0	0	0	1	5	13	12	5	0	0	0	36
Days Maximum Temp. ≤ 32°F	20	13	6	1	0	0	0	0	0	0	7	16	63
Days Minimum Temp. ≤ 32°F	31	28	27	15	2	0	0	0	2	12	27	31	175
Days Minimum Temp. ≤ 0°F	12	7	2	0	0	0	0	0	0	0	1	8	30
Heating Degree Days (base 65°F)	1,562	1,216	995	565	236	48	11	17	161	503	990	1,400	7,704
Cooling Degree Days (base 65°F)	0	0	0	6	30	132	272	237	77	3	0	0	757
Mean Precipitation (in.)	0.26	0.40	1.20	2.05	3.01	3.19	2.58	2.21	1.79	1.67	0.69	0.40	19.45
Days With ≥ 0.1" Precipitation	1	1	3	5	6	6	6	4	4	3	2	1	42
Days With ≥ 1.0" Precipitation	0	0	0	0	1	1	1	1	0	0	0	0	4
Mean Snowfall (in.)	4.0	5.3	5.1	3.5	trace	0.0	0.0	0.0	trace	0.6	4.3	4.5	27.3
Days With ≥ 1.0" Snow Depth	18	15	7	1	0	0	0	0	0	0	5	12	58

Gettysburg *Potter County*   Elevation: 2,066 ft.   Latitude: 45° 01' N   Longitude: 99° 58' W

	JAN	FEB	MAR	APR	MAY	JUN	JUL	AUG	SEP	OCT	NOV	DEC	YEAR
Mean Maximum Temp. (°F)	22.4	29.1	39.8	55.8	68.2	77.8	84.7	83.9	73.2	59.2	39.5	27.4	55.1
Mean Temp. (°F)	12.4	19.2	29.6	44.0	56.1	65.8	71.8	70.2	59.6	46.5	29.8	17.7	43.6
Mean Minimum Temp. (°F)	2.3	9.2	19.3	32.2	44.0	53.8	58.7	56.5	45.9	33.7	20.2	7.9	32.0
Extreme Maximum Temp. (°F)	63	65	81	97	100	108	107	107	105	93	80	65	108
Extreme Minimum Temp. (°F)	-32	-34	-23	0	20	35	38	38	20	1	-13	-31	-34
Days Maximum Temp. ≥ 90°F	0	0	0	0	1	3	9	8	3	0	0	0	24
Days Maximum Temp. ≤ 32°F	22	15	9	1	0	0	0	0	0	1	9	18	75
Days Minimum Temp. ≤ 32°F	31	28	28	16	3	0	0	0	2	13	27	31	179
Days Minimum Temp. ≤ 0°F	14	8	3	0	0	0	0	0	0	0	2	9	36
Heating Degree Days (base 65°F)	1,627	1,288	1,091	625	291	73	16	28	211	569	1,049	1,462	8,330
Cooling Degree Days (base 65°F)	0	0	0	4	25	102	227	198	54	3	0	0	613
Mean Precipitation (in.)	0.41	0.56	1.16	2.01	2.84	3.03	2.63	2.17	1.45	1.54	0.72	0.45	18.97
Days With ≥ 0.1" Precipitation	1	2	3	4	6	6	5	4	3	3	2	1	40
Days With ≥ 1.0" Precipitation	0	0	0	0	1	1	0	1	0	0	0	0	3
Mean Snowfall (in.)	na	na	na	2.8	trace	0.0	0.0	0.0	trace	1.0	na	na	na
Days With ≥ 1.0" Snow Depth	na	na	na	1	0	0	0	0	0	0	na	na	na

Gregory *Gregory County*   Elevation: 2,158 ft.   Latitude: 43° 14' N   Longitude: 99° 26' W

	JAN	FEB	MAR	APR	MAY	JUN	JUL	AUG	SEP	OCT	NOV	DEC	YEAR
Mean Maximum Temp. (°F)	31.8	38.6	48.4	61.2	72.7	82.6	88.5	87.3	78.3	65.4	46.5	35.8	61.4
Mean Temp. (°F)	19.9	26.3	35.6	47.6	58.8	68.8	74.4	72.9	63.4	50.6	34.7	24.1	48.1
Mean Minimum Temp. (°F)	7.9	13.9	22.7	33.9	44.9	54.9	60.3	58.4	48.5	35.7	22.7	12.4	34.7
Extreme Maximum Temp. (°F)	71	76	89	98	98	105	110	109	104	94	85	73	110
Extreme Minimum Temp. (°F)	-28	-28	-24	7	21	34	38	39	20	7	-10	-36	-36
Days Maximum Temp. ≥ 90°F	0	0	0	0	1	6	15	13	5	1	0	0	41
Days Maximum Temp. ≤ 32°F	15	10	4	1	0	0	0	0	0	0	5	12	47
Days Minimum Temp. ≤ 32°F	30	27	26	14	3	0	0	0	1	11	25	30	167
Days Minimum Temp. ≤ 0°F	10	5	2	0	0	0	0	0	0	0	1	7	25
Heating Degree Days (base 65°F)	1,394	1,087	905	524	219	39	7	11	137	448	905	1,262	6,938
Cooling Degree Days (base 65°F)	0	0	0	10	36	156	297	257	90	7	0	0	853
Mean Precipitation (in.)	0.51	0.59	1.93	2.99	3.86	3.76	3.40	2.43	2.67	2.13	1.17	0.63	26.07
Days With ≥ 0.1" Precipitation	1	2	4	7	8	7	7	5	4	4	3	2	54
Days With ≥ 1.0" Precipitation	0	0	0	1	1	1	1	1	1	1	0	0	7
Mean Snowfall (in.)	7.7	5.8	9.3	4.3	0.0	0.0	0.0	0.0	0.0	0.4	2.3	6.8	7.8	44.4
Days With ≥ 1.0" Snow Depth	na	na	na	0	0	0	0	0	0	0	na	na	na

Harrington *Bennett County*   Elevation: 2,979 ft.   Latitude: 43° 10' N   Longitude: 101° 15' W

	JAN	FEB	MAR	APR	MAY	JUN	JUL	AUG	SEP	OCT	NOV	DEC	YEAR
Mean Maximum Temp. (°F)	32.6	38.6	47.1	59.3	70.6	80.6	86.9	86.0	77.0	63.2	45.6	36.0	60.3
Mean Temp. (°F)	20.2	26.3	34.5	45.5	56.8	66.6	72.6	71.2	61.5	48.4	33.1	23.6	46.7
Mean Minimum Temp. (°F)	7.8	13.9	21.8	31.8	42.9	52.7	58.2	56.4	45.9	33.5	20.6	11.2	33.0
Extreme Maximum Temp. (°F)	71	73	83	96	94	106	109	106	102	95	84	71	109
Extreme Minimum Temp. (°F)	-30	-35	-28	-1	19	30	36	36	20	-2	-19	-38	-38
Days Maximum Temp. ≥ 90°F	0	0	0	0	1	5	13	12	5	0	0	0	36
Days Maximum Temp. ≤ 32°F	14	9	5	1	0	0	0	0	0	0	6	11	46
Days Minimum Temp. ≤ 32°F	31	27	27	16	4	0	0	0	3	14	27	30	179
Days Minimum Temp. ≤ 0°F	9	5	2	0	0	0	0	0	0	0	2	6	24
Heating Degree Days (base 65°F)	1,384	1,088	939	581	270	63	13	19	173	511	949	1,277	7,267
Cooling Degree Days (base 65°F)	0	0	0	4	24	112	247	216	72	3	0	0	678
Mean Precipitation (in.)	0.47	0.57	1.36	2.28	3.35	3.14	2.79	1.85	1.47	1.46	0.78	0.45	19.97
Days With ≥ 0.1" Precipitation	1	2	4	5	6	6	6	4	4	3	3	2	46
Days With ≥ 1.0" Precipitation	0	0	0	0	1	1	1	0	0	0	0	0	3
Mean Snowfall (in.)	6.7	6.8	10.5	6.9	0.5	0.0	0.0	0.0	0.2	3.4	8.0	6.3	49.3
Days With ≥ 1.0" Snow Depth	17	13	8	2	0	0	0	0	0	1	8	15	64

Highmore 1 W *Hyde County*   Elevation: 1,889 ft.   Latitude: 44° 31' N   Longitude: 99° 28' W

	JAN	FEB	MAR	APR	MAY	JUN	JUL	AUG	SEP	OCT	NOV	DEC	YEAR
Mean Maximum Temp. (°F)	25.0	32.5	43.1	59.2	71.5	81.4	87.9	87.0	76.8	62.2	42.1	29.9	58.2
Mean Temp. (°F)	14.3	22.0	32.0	46.0	57.9	67.8	73.6	72.5	62.2	48.7	31.9	19.6	45.7
Mean Minimum Temp. (°F)	3.6	11.3	20.8	32.7	44.3	54.1	59.3	57.8	47.5	35.2	21.6	9.3	33.1
Extreme Maximum Temp. (°F)	64	67	84	98	96	110	110	111	108	96	81	66	111
Extreme Minimum Temp. (°F)	-33	-40	-25	-1	19	35	36	35	17	0	-15	-36	-40
Days Maximum Temp. ≥ 90°F	0	0	0	0	1	6	13	12	4	0	0	0	36
Days Maximum Temp. ≤ 32°F	20	13	7	1	0	0	0	0	0	0	7	16	64
Days Minimum Temp. ≤ 32°F	31	27	27	15	3	0	0	0	2	12	26	31	174
Days Minimum Temp. ≤ 0°F	13	7	2	0	0	0	0	0	0	0	1	8	31
Heating Degree Days (base 65°F)	1,567	1,211	1,019	567	243	49	11	18	162	503	989	1,401	7,740
Cooling Degree Days (base 65°F)	0	0	0	5	31	124	262	238	75	4	0	0	739
Mean Precipitation (in.)	0.41	0.53	1.38	2.61	3.01	3.20	3.23	2.25	1.67	1.83	0.74	0.38	21.24
Days With ≥ 0.1" Precipitation	2	2	3	6	7	7	6	5	4	4	3	1	50
Days With ≥ 1.0" Precipitation	0	0	0	1	1	1	1	1	0	1	0	0	6
Mean Snowfall (in.)	7.0	8.0	9.0	5.4	trace	0.0	0.0	0.0	trace	1.8	5.9	6.6	43.7
Days With ≥ 1.0" Snow Depth	18	12	6	1	0	0	0	0	0	0	5	13	55

Highmore 23 N *Hyde County*   Elevation: 1,870 ft.   Latitude: 44° 51' N   Longitude: 99° 29' W

	JAN	FEB	MAR	APR	MAY	JUN	JUL	AUG	SEP	OCT	NOV	DEC	YEAR
Mean Maximum Temp. (°F)	24.4	31.1	42.5	59.2	71.2	80.6	87.0	86.2	76.2	62.1	41.5	28.5	57.5
Mean Temp. (°F)	13.3	20.2	31.3	45.6	57.2	66.7	72.4	71.1	60.9	47.9	30.7	18.0	44.6
Mean Minimum Temp. (°F)	2.2	9.7	20.1	31.9	43.1	52.9	57.7	55.9	45.6	33.6	19.8	7.5	31.7
Extreme Maximum Temp. (°F)	65	68	82	96	98	110	111	109	105	94	81	66	111
Extreme Minimum Temp. (°F)	-38	-38	-22	-5	15	31	32	34	11	-1	-19	-38	-38
Days Maximum Temp. ≥ 90°F	0	0	0	0	1	4	12	11	4	0	0	0	32
Days Maximum Temp. ≤ 32°F	20	14	7	1	0	0	0	0	0	0	7	17	66
Days Minimum Temp. ≤ 32°F	30	28	28	17	4	0	0	0	3	14	27	30	181
Days Minimum Temp. ≤ 0°F	14	8	3	0	0	0	0	0	0	0	2	9	36
Heating Degree Days (base 65°F)	1,599	1,260	1,037	579	259	58	12	23	185	524	1,024	1,453	8,013
Cooling Degree Days (base 65°F)	0	0	0	4	25	112	238	212	64	4	0	0	659
Mean Precipitation (in.)	0.43	0.58	1.21	1.96	2.53	2.84	2.84	1.95	1.62	1.49	0.72	0.50	18.67
Days With ≥ 0.1" Precipitation	2	2	3	4	5	5	5	4	3	3	2	2	40
Days With ≥ 1.0" Precipitation	0	0	0	0	1	1	1	0	0	0	0	0	2
Mean Snowfall (in.)	4.2	6.6	8.1	3.0	trace	0.0	0.0	0.0	trace	1.1	5.8	5.5	34.3
Days With ≥ 1.0" Snow Depth	19	15	9	1	0	0	0	0	0	0	5	12	61

Hot Springs *Fall River County*   Elevation: 3,556 ft.   Latitude: 43° 26' N   Longitude: 103° 28' W

	JAN	FEB	MAR	APR	MAY	JUN	JUL	AUG	SEP	OCT	NOV	DEC	YEAR
Mean Maximum Temp. (°F)	38.2	44.1	51.8	61.1	71.1	81.6	88.7	87.9	78.5	65.8	48.5	40.1	63.1
Mean Temp. (°F)	24.9	30.0	37.3	46.4	56.5	66.1	72.6	71.2	61.3	49.5	35.4	27.0	48.2
Mean Minimum Temp. (°F)	11.6	16.0	22.8	31.7	41.8	50.6	56.4	54.6	44.0	33.1	22.2	13.9	33.2
Extreme Maximum Temp. (°F)	69	72	80	91	93	106	111	106	102	91	80	69	111
Extreme Minimum Temp. (°F)	-25	-34	-21	-5	21	30	37	36	18	-5	-15	-37	-37
Days Maximum Temp. ≥ 90°F	0	0	0	0	0	6	14	14	5	0	0	0	39
Days Maximum Temp. ≤ 32°F	9	5	3	0	0	0	0	0	0	0	4	7	28
Days Minimum Temp. ≤ 32°F	30	27	27	16	4	0	0	0	3	14	26	30	177
Days Minimum Temp. ≤ 0°F	8	4	1	0	0	0	0	0	0	0	1	4	18
Heating Degree Days (base 65°F)	1,235	982	851	552	272	67	10	15	164	476	883	1,172	6,679
Cooling Degree Days (base 65°F)	0	0	0	2	16	103	248	227	61	2	0	0	659
Mean Precipitation (in.)	0.34	0.45	0.91	1.81	3.02	2.85	2.64	1.78	1.35	1.26	0.52	0.35	17.28
Days With ≥ 0.1" Precipitation	1	2	3	4	6	6	5	4	3	3	2	1	40
Days With ≥ 1.0" Precipitation	0	0	0	0	1	1	1	0	0	0	0	0	3
Mean Snowfall (in.)	5.5	5.1	7.0	3.6	trace	0.0	0.0	0.0	0.1	1.6	4.3	6.2	33.4
Days With ≥ 1.0" Snow Depth	15	9	5	2	0	0	0	0	0	1	6	13	51

Howard *Miner County*   Elevation: 1,558 ft.   Latitude: 44° 01' N   Longitude: 97° 32' W

	JAN	FEB	MAR	APR	MAY	JUN	JUL	AUG	SEP	OCT	NOV	DEC	YEAR
Mean Maximum Temp. (°F)	23.0	30.4	42.5	58.6	71.4	80.6	86.1	83.8	74.4	60.5	40.9	28.0	56.7
Mean Temp. (°F)	13.3	20.6	32.4	46.7	59.2	68.5	73.7	71.4	61.6	48.5	31.7	18.6	45.5
Mean Minimum Temp. (°F)	3.4	10.7	22.2	34.8	46.9	56.4	61.1	58.9	48.8	36.4	22.4	9.2	34.3
Extreme Maximum Temp. (°F)	61	64	82	96	93	108	106	104	104	90	78	65	108
Extreme Minimum Temp. (°F)	-34	-36	-18	3	22	37	38	39	19	8	-15	-31	-36
Days Maximum Temp. ≥ 90°F	0	0	0	0	0	4	10	7	2	0	0	0	23
Days Maximum Temp. ≤ 32°F	22	14	6	1	0	0	0	0	0	0	8	19	70
Days Minimum Temp. ≤ 32°F	31	27	26	13	1	0	0	0	1	11	25	30	165
Days Minimum Temp. ≤ 0°F	13	7	2	0	0	0	0	0	0	0	1	8	31
Heating Degree Days (base 65°F)	1,601	1,250	1,006	547	213	41	8	18	168	509	993	1,434	7,788
Cooling Degree Days (base 65°F)	0	0	0	7	39	147	265	205	65	4	0	0	732
Mean Precipitation (in.)	0.54	0.60	1.60	2.49	2.93	3.66	3.13	2.88	2.26	1.89	1.22	0.49	23.69
Days With ≥ 0.1" Precipitation	2	2	4	6	6	7	6	5	4	4	3	2	51
Days With ≥ 1.0" Precipitation	0	0	0	0	0	1	1	1	0	0	0	0	3
Mean Snowfall (in.)	*6.9*	6.2	*7.4*	2.9	0.0	0.0	0.0	0.0	trace	1.0	*5.8*	*6.6*	*36.8*
Days With ≥ 1.0" Snow Depth	na	na	na	*0*	0	0	0	0	0	0	*1*	na	na

Interior 3 NE *Jackson County*   Elevation: 2,437 ft.   Latitude: 43° 45' N   Longitude: 101° 57' W

	JAN	FEB	MAR	APR	MAY	JUN	JUL	AUG	SEP	OCT	NOV	DEC	YEAR
Mean Maximum Temp. (°F)	35.0	41.4	50.3	62.3	72.9	83.3	90.8	90.6	80.4	66.2	47.1	38.3	63.2
Mean Temp. (°F)	23.8	29.4	37.9	48.9	59.9	69.7	76.3	75.6	65.5	52.1	36.1	27.1	50.2
Mean Minimum Temp. (°F)	12.4	17.4	25.4	35.7	46.9	56.0	62.0	60.7	50.6	37.9	25.0	15.8	37.1
Extreme Maximum Temp. (°F)	69	74	85	94	98	109	111	110	105	96	84	71	111
Extreme Minimum Temp. (°F)	-26	-31	-21	3	25	32	42	35	25	2	-15	-31	-31
Days Maximum Temp. ≥ 90°F	0	0	0	0	2	8	17	19	7	1	0	0	54
Days Maximum Temp. ≤ 32°F	12	8	4	0	0	0	0	0	0	0	4	9	37
Days Minimum Temp. ≤ 32°F	28	25	23	11	1	0	0	0	1	8	23	27	147
Days Minimum Temp. ≤ 0°F	8	4	1	0	0	0	0	0	0	0	1	5	19
Heating Degree Days (base 65°F)	1,271	999	836	482	198	33	4	7	107	403	860	1,168	6,368
Cooling Degree Days (base 65°F)	0	0	0	11	53	179	360	350	131	13	0	0	1,097
Mean Precipitation (in.)	0.38	0.51	1.08	2.07	3.20	2.94	2.32	1.76	1.31	1.46	0.60	0.32	17.95
Days With ≥ 0.1" Precipitation	1	1	3	5	6	6	5	4	3	3	2	1	40
Days With ≥ 1.0" Precipitation	0	0	0	0	1	1	0	0	0	0	0	0	2
Mean Snowfall (in.)	3.6	4.8	*5.5*	*3.6*	0.0	trace	0.0	0.0	trace	0.6	*3.4*	3.6	*25.1*
Days With ≥ 1.0" Snow Depth	na	na	*5*	1	0	0	0	0	0	*0*	na	*9*	na

Ipswich *Edmunds County*   Elevation: 1,528 ft.   Latitude: 45° 27' N   Longitude: 99° 02' W

	JAN	FEB	MAR	APR	MAY	JUN	JUL	AUG	SEP	OCT	NOV	DEC	YEAR
Mean Maximum Temp. (°F)	22.2	29.0	41.0	58.1	71.0	79.6	85.7	84.8	74.4	60.6	39.7	27.0	56.1
Mean Temp. (°F)	11.0	18.0	29.7	44.7	57.1	66.2	71.6	70.1	59.5	46.5	28.9	16.4	43.3
Mean Minimum Temp. (°F)	-0.1	6.9	18.4	31.2	43.2	52.8	57.5	55.2	44.5	32.4	18.1	5.6	30.5
Extreme Maximum Temp. (°F)	65	66	79	97	98	106	108	106	105	92	77	65	108
Extreme Minimum Temp. (°F)	-35	-38	-22	-8	18	28	36	35	16	-4	-20	-40	-40
Days Maximum Temp. ≥ 90°F	0	0	0	0	0	3	10	9	3	0	0	0	25
Days Maximum Temp. ≤ 32°F	21	16	8	1	0	0	0	0	0	0	9	19	74
Days Minimum Temp. ≤ 32°F	31	28	29	17	4	0	0	0	3	16	28	31	187
Days Minimum Temp. ≤ 0°F	16	10	3	0	0	0	0	0	0	0	2	10	41
Heating Degree Days (base 65°F)	1,670	1,323	1,087	606	260	63	12	25	208	568	1,076	1,502	8,400
Cooling Degree Days (base 65°F)	0	0	0	3	22	98	212	177	41	1	0	0	554
Mean Precipitation (in.)	0.42	0.41	1.16	1.94	2.70	3.47	2.94	2.15	1.67	1.42	0.69	0.30	19.27
Days With ≥ 0.1" Precipitation	1	1	3	4	6	7	6	4	3	3	2	1	41
Days With ≥ 1.0" Precipitation	0	0	0	0	1	1	1	1	0	0	0	0	4
Mean Snowfall (in.)	6.1	5.6	6.5	3.0	trace	0.0	0.0	0.0	0.0	0.6	5.9	5.2	32.9
Days With ≥ 1.0" Snow Depth	24	18	12	2	0	0	0	0	0	0	8	15	79

Kennebec *Lyman County*   Elevation: 1,699 ft.   Latitude: 43° 55' N   Longitude: 99° 52' W

	JAN	FEB	MAR	APR	MAY	JUN	JUL	AUG	SEP	OCT	NOV	DEC	YEAR
Mean Maximum Temp. (°F)	29.7	36.7	47.4	61.8	73.6	83.6	90.7	89.3	79.5	65.0	44.8	33.5	61.3
Mean Temp. (°F)	18.2	25.0	35.2	47.9	59.8	69.9	76.0	74.6	64.2	50.6	33.5	22.2	48.1
Mean Minimum Temp. (°F)	6.7	13.3	22.9	33.9	46.0	56.2	61.4	59.8	48.8	36.2	22.2	10.9	34.9
Extreme Maximum Temp. (°F)	70	75	89	99	96	111	112	112	108	96	89	74	112
Extreme Minimum Temp. (°F)	-37	-38	-25	-5	15	33	35	35	20	5	-18	-31	-38
Days Maximum Temp. ≥ 90°F	0	0	0	0	2	7	17	16	6	1	0	0	49
Days Maximum Temp. ≤ 32°F	16	10	5	1	0	0	0	0	0	0	5	13	50
Days Minimum Temp. ≤ 32°F	30	27	25	14	2	0	0	0	2	11	26	31	168
Days Minimum Temp. ≤ 0°F	11	6	2	0	0	0	0	0	0	0	1	7	27
Heating Degree Days (base 65°F)	1,446	1,122	917	515	200	33	5	10	131	447	937	1,320	7,083
Cooling Degree Days (base 65°F)	0	0	0	10	49	174	341	306	104	7	0	0	991
Mean Precipitation (in.)	0.32	0.42	1.24	2.11	3.10	2.99	2.73	2.07	1.47	1.50	0.60	0.32	18.87
Days With ≥ 0.1" Precipitation	1	1	3	5	6	6	6	4	4	3	2	1	42
Days With ≥ 1.0" Precipitation	0	0	0	0	1	1	1	1	0	0	0	0	4
Mean Snowfall (in.)	5.0	6.1	8.0	3.5	trace	trace	0.0	0.0	trace	1.1	4.3	5.4	33.4
Days With ≥ 1.0" Snow Depth	13	10	6	1	0	0	0	0	0	0	4	10	44

Kirley 6 N *Haakon County*   Elevation: 2,158 ft.   Latitude: 44° 37' N   Longitude: 101° 20' W

	JAN	FEB	MAR	APR	MAY	JUN	JUL	AUG	SEP	OCT	NOV	DEC	YEAR
Mean Maximum Temp. (°F)	27.4	34.0	43.8	58.4	69.9	79.9	87.4	87.0	76.1	61.7	43.1	31.5	58.4
Mean Temp. (°F)	17.2	23.7	33.1	46.2	57.8	67.7	74.0	72.9	62.1	48.9	32.7	21.3	46.5
Mean Minimum Temp. (°F)	6.9	13.3	22.4	34.1	45.7	55.3	60.6	58.9	48.1	36.0	22.3	11.1	34.6
Extreme Maximum Temp. (°F)	69	72	83	98	101	110	110	110	108	97	84	70	110
Extreme Minimum Temp. (°F)	-27	-34	-24	0	24	36	41	38	22	-3	-15	-33	-34
Days Maximum Temp. ≥ 90°F	0	0	0	0	1	4	13	13	5	1	0	0	37
Days Maximum Temp. ≤ 32°F	17	12	6	1	0	0	0	0	0	0	7	15	58
Days Minimum Temp. ≤ 32°F	30	27	26	13	2	0	0	0	0	1	26	30	165
Days Minimum Temp. ≤ 0°F	11	6	2	0	0	0	0	0	0	0	1	6	26
Heating Degree Days (base 65°F)	1,478	1,161	981	561	251	54	9	16	166	498	962	1,345	7,482
Cooling Degree Days (base 65°F)	0	0	0	7	38	135	292	272	83	6	0	0	833
Mean Precipitation (in.)	0.43	0.62	1.35	1.77	3.10	2.88	2.67	1.77	1.42	1.64	0.70	0.51	18.86
Days With ≥ 0.1" Precipitation	1	2	3	4	6	6	5	4	3	3	2	2	41
Days With ≥ 1.0" Precipitation	0	0	0	0	1	0	1	0	0	0	0	0	2
Mean Snowfall (in.)	5.8	7.7	9.5	5.0	0.4	trace	0.0	0.0	trace	1.6	5.8	6.8	42.6
Days With ≥ 1.0" Snow Depth	22	16	11	3	0	0	0	0	0	1	7	17	77

Lead *Lawrence County*   Elevation: 5,347 ft.   Latitude: 44° 21' N   Longitude: 103° 46' W

	JAN	FEB	MAR	APR	MAY	JUN	JUL	AUG	SEP	OCT	NOV	DEC	YEAR
Mean Maximum Temp. (°F)	33.9	37.4	42.6	51.0	61.8	72.1	79.0	78.5	68.6	56.1	42.3	35.8	54.9
Mean Temp. (°F)	24.1	27.5	32.5	40.7	50.9	60.6	67.0	66.3	56.7	45.3	32.9	26.2	44.2
Mean Minimum Temp. (°F)	14.3	17.6	22.4	30.3	40.0	49.1	55.0	54.2	44.8	34.4	23.5	16.6	33.5
Extreme Maximum Temp. (°F)	69	66	74	84	87	95	98	96	96	83	74	65	98
Extreme Minimum Temp. (°F)	-23	-32	-15	-1	18	29	36	35	15	-5	-14	-33	-33
Days Maximum Temp. ≥ 90°F	0	0	0	0	0	1	2	1	0	0	0	0	4
Days Maximum Temp. ≤ 32°F	13	9	7	2	0	0	0	0	0	1	7	11	50
Days Minimum Temp. ≤ 32°F	28	26	26	19	5	0	0	0	3	13	23	28	171
Days Minimum Temp. ≤ 0°F	6	3	1	0	0	0	0	0	0	0	1	4	15
Heating Degree Days (base 65°F)	1,262	1,052	1,000	724	435	172	53	60	274	604	957	1,196	7,789
Cooling Degree Days (base 65°F)	0	0	0	1	6	45	121	106	29	0	0	0	308
Mean Precipitation (in.)	1.36	1.41	2.62	3.78	4.33	3.82	2.72	2.13	1.67	2.79	1.81	1.54	29.98
Days With ≥ 0.1" Precipitation	5	4	7	8	8	8	6	5	4	5	5	5	70
Days With ≥ 1.0" Precipitation	0	0	0	1	1	1	0	0	0	1	0	0	4
Mean Snowfall (in.)	23.3	21.2	35.9	34.1	6.6	1.1	0.0	trace	2.4	18.5	24.0	25.9	193.0
Days With ≥ 1.0" Snow Depth	26	21	16	9	1	0	0	0	0	5	14	21	113

Lemmon *Perkins County*   Elevation: 2,565 ft.   Latitude: 45° 56' N   Longitude: 102° 10' W

	JAN	FEB	MAR	APR	MAY	JUN	JUL	AUG	SEP	OCT	NOV	DEC	YEAR
Mean Maximum Temp. (°F)	24.6	31.7	41.4	55.8	68.3	77.5	84.1	83.6	72.5	58.9	40.2	28.9	55.6
Mean Temp. (°F)	14.6	21.5	30.5	43.5	55.6	64.8	70.7	69.7	58.7	46.3	30.3	19.0	43.8
Mean Minimum Temp. (°F)	4.5	11.3	19.6	31.2	42.8	52.0	57.3	55.8	45.0	33.7	20.3	9.1	31.9
Extreme Maximum Temp. (°F)	69	70	77	93	95	102	107	104	105	92	82	67	107
Extreme Minimum Temp. (°F)	-31	-30	-23	-4	23	32	40	38	19	-4	-17	-33	-33
Days Maximum Temp. ≥ 90°F	0	0	0	0	0	3	8	8	2	0	0	0	21
Days Maximum Temp. ≤ 32°F	19	14	8	1	0	0	0	0	0	1	9	17	69
Days Minimum Temp. ≤ 32°F	30	27	28	17	3	0	0	0	2	13	27	30	177
Days Minimum Temp. ≤ 0°F	13	7	2	0	0	0	0	0	0	0	2	8	32
Heating Degree Days (base 65°F)	1,559	1,223	1,062	639	302	84	18	31	225	574	1,035	1,420	8,172
Cooling Degree Days (base 65°F)	0	0	0	2	19	89	212	196	47	3	0	0	568
Mean Precipitation (in.)	0.45	0.50	0.97	1.92	2.76	3.08	2.65	1.92	1.38	1.41	0.71	0.53	18.28
Days With ≥ 0.1" Precipitation	2	2	3	5	6	6	5	4	3	3	2	2	43
Days With ≥ 1.0" Precipitation	0	0	0	0	1	1	1	0	0	0	0	0	3
Mean Snowfall (in.)	5.1	5.7	7.3	5.0	0.4	0.0	0.0	0.0	0.3	1.5	6.6	6.2	38.1
Days With ≥ 1.0" Snow Depth	23	18	13	4	0	0	0	0	0	1	10	17	86

Leola *McPherson County*   Elevation: 1,578 ft.   Latitude: 45° 43' N   Longitude: 98° 56' W

	JAN	FEB	MAR	APR	MAY	JUN	JUL	AUG	SEP	OCT	NOV	DEC	YEAR
Mean Maximum Temp. (°F)	20.8	28.0	39.2	56.8	70.2	79.0	85.0	83.9	73.4	59.3	38.5	25.7	55.0
Mean Temp. (°F)	10.9	18.2	29.2	44.4	57.1	66.2	71.6	70.1	59.6	46.6	28.9	16.3	43.3
Mean Minimum Temp. (°F)	0.9	8.3	19.2	31.9	44.0	53.4	58.2	56.2	45.7	33.9	19.4	6.8	31.5
Extreme Maximum Temp. (°F)	62	64	79	97	99	107	109	107	105	93	75	62	109
Extreme Minimum Temp. (°F)	-33	-31	-20	-4	22	35	42	37	19	-1	-19	-32	-33
Days Maximum Temp. ≥ 90°F	0	0	0	0	1	3	9	8	2	0	0	0	23
Days Maximum Temp. ≤ 32°F	23	16	9	1	0	0	0	0	0	0	11	21	81
Days Minimum Temp. ≤ 32°F	31	28	28	16	3	0	0	0	2	14	27	31	180
Days Minimum Temp. ≤ 0°F	15	9	3	0	0	0	0	0	0	0	2	10	39
Heating Degree Days (base 65°F)	1,676	1,317	1,103	614	260	60	11	25	203	565	1,076	1,505	8,415
Cooling Degree Days (base 65°F)	0	0	0	3	24	101	217	185	44	2	0	0	576
Mean Precipitation (in.)	0.54	0.51	1.33	1.97	2.77	3.13	2.63	2.09	1.73	1.48	0.86	0.38	19.42
Days With ≥ 0.1" Precipitation	2	2	4	4	6	6	6	4	4	3	2	1	44
Days With ≥ 1.0" Precipitation	0	0	0	0	1	1	0	0	0	0	0	0	2
Mean Snowfall (in.)	7.6	8.0	9.1	4.6	0.1	0.0	0.0	0.0	trace	0.6	9.0	5.9	44.9
Days With ≥ 1.0" Snow Depth	na	na	12	1	0	0	0	0	0	0	7	15	na

Long Valley *Jackson County*   Elevation: 2,467 ft.   Latitude: 43° 28' N   Longitude: 101° 30' W

	JAN	FEB	MAR	APR	MAY	JUN	JUL	AUG	SEP	OCT	NOV	DEC	YEAR
Mean Maximum Temp. (°F)	35.1	40.8	48.4	59.9	71.2	81.6	88.5	88.1	77.8	64.4	47.0	38.4	61.8
Mean Temp. (°F)	23.0	28.4	35.8	46.6	57.8	67.8	74.0	72.9	62.7	50.1	35.0	26.3	48.4
Mean Minimum Temp. (°F)	10.8	15.9	23.1	33.3	44.3	54.0	59.5	57.7	47.5	35.8	23.0	14.1	34.9
Extreme Maximum Temp. (°F)	73	75	84	95	96	107	110	110	105	95	85	71	110
Extreme Minimum Temp. (°F)	-27	-30	-26	6	19	32	37	34	17	0	-19	-35	-35
Days Maximum Temp. ≥ 90°F	0	0	0	0	1	6	14	15	5	1	0	0	42
Days Maximum Temp. ≤ 32°F	12	8	4	1	0	0	0	0	0	0	5	10	40
Days Minimum Temp. ≤ 32°F	29	26	25	14	2	0	0	0	2	11	25	29	163
Days Minimum Temp. ≤ 0°F	9	4	1	0	0	0	0	0	0	0	1	5	20
Heating Degree Days (base 65°F)	1,297	1,028	900	550	245	53	8	13	155	462	893	1,195	6,799
Cooling Degree Days (base 65°F)	0	0	0	6	29	132	275	256	88	8	0	0	794
Mean Precipitation (in.)	0.33	0.49	1.37	2.22	3.07	3.08	2.72	1.68	1.44	1.37	0.63	0.36	18.76
Days With ≥ 0.1" Precipitation	1	2	4	5	7	6	5	4	3	3	2	1	43
Days With ≥ 1.0" Precipitation	0	0	0	0	1	1	1	0	0	0	0	0	3
Mean Snowfall (in.)	4.7	5.7	10.7	6.3	0.1	0.0	0.0	0.0	trace	2.0	6.7	5.2	41.4
Days With ≥ 1.0" Snow Depth	18	13	10	3	0	0	0	0	0	1	9	15	69

Ludlow 3 SSE *Harding County*   Elevation: 2,988 ft.   Latitude: 45° 47' N   Longitude: 103° 22' W

	JAN	FEB	MAR	APR	MAY	JUN	JUL	AUG	SEP	OCT	NOV	DEC	YEAR
Mean Maximum Temp. (°F)	26.8	33.6	42.4	56.0	67.8	77.3	84.7	84.8	73.1	59.2	41.0	31.0	56.5
Mean Temp. (°F)	16.3	23.0	31.2	43.5	54.6	64.0	70.2	69.3	58.4	45.8	30.3	20.2	43.9
Mean Minimum Temp. (°F)	5.7	12.4	19.9	30.9	41.3	50.5	55.7	53.8	43.6	32.4	19.6	9.4	31.3
Extreme Maximum Temp. (°F)	70	69	78	91	98	106	115	106	105	91	79	65	115
Extreme Minimum Temp. (°F)	-38	-32	-29	-6	18	28	34	30	15	-9	-20	-38	-38
Days Maximum Temp. ≥ 90°F	0	0	0	0	0	3	9	10	3	0	0	0	25
Days Maximum Temp. ≤ 32°F	17	12	7	2	0	0	0	0	0	1	8	15	62
Days Minimum Temp. ≤ 32°F	30	27	28	18	4	0	0	0	3	15	27	30	182
Days Minimum Temp. ≤ 0°F	12	6	3	0	0	0	0	0	0	0	2	8	31
Heating Degree Days (base 65°F)	1,505	1,181	1,042	638	328	97	22	33	234	589	1,035	1,383	8,087
Cooling Degree Days (base 65°F)	0	0	0	1	13	72	192	175	40	2	0	0	495
Mean Precipitation (in.)	0.44	0.34	0.73	2.00	3.01	3.14	2.15	1.36	1.28	1.46	0.54	0.42	16.87
Days With ≥ 0.1" Precipitation	2	1	2	4	6	6	5	3	3	3	2	1	38
Days With ≥ 1.0" Precipitation	0	0	0	0	1	1	0	0	0	0	0	0	2
Mean Snowfall (in.)	na	na	na	na	0.4	0.0	0.0	0.0	0.2	1.7	na	na	na
Days With ≥ 1.0" Snow Depth	na	na	na	na	0	0	0	0	0	1	4	na	na

Madison 2 SE *Lake County*   Elevation: 1,660 ft.   Latitude: 43° 59' N   Longitude: 97° 06' W

	JAN	FEB	MAR	APR	MAY	JUN	JUL	AUG	SEP	OCT	NOV	DEC	YEAR
Mean Maximum Temp. (°F)	21.8	28.3	40.2	56.6	69.5	78.9	83.4	81.7	72.9	59.6	40.0	27.1	55.0
Mean Temp. (°F)	12.2	18.9	30.9	45.4	57.9	67.3	71.9	70.0	60.6	47.7	30.9	17.9	44.3
Mean Minimum Temp. (°F)	2.5	9.4	21.5	34.1	46.2	55.7	60.4	58.2	48.4	35.7	21.8	8.7	33.6
Extreme Maximum Temp. (°F)	66	64	81	94	92	105	103	104	102	89	78	64	105
Extreme Minimum Temp. (°F)	-33	-31	-15	1	24	35	39	39	22	9	-14	-28	-33
Days Maximum Temp. ≥ 90°F	0	0	0	0	0	3	7	5	2	0	0	0	17
Days Maximum Temp. ≤ 32°F	23	16	8	1	0	0	0	0	0	0	9	20	77
Days Minimum Temp. ≤ 32°F	31	28	26	13	2	0	0	0	1	11	26	31	169
Days Minimum Temp. ≤ 0°F	14	8	2	0	0	0	0	0	0	0	1	9	34
Heating Degree Days (base 65°F)	1,634	1,297	1,050	585	245	53	12	26	182	533	1,017	1,455	8,089
Cooling Degree Days (base 65°F)	0	0	0	5	29	122	216	174	51	2	0	0	599
Mean Precipitation (in.)	0.52	0.64	1.73	2.60	3.19	3.76	3.12	3.16	2.53	2.00	1.28	0.56	25.09
Days With ≥ 0.1" Precipitation	2	2	4	6	6	7	5	5	5	4	3	2	51
Days With ≥ 1.0" Precipitation	0	0	0	0	1	1	1	1	1	0	0	0	6
Mean Snowfall (in.)	6.5	6.4	7.6	3.0	trace	0.0	0.0	0.0	trace	1.0	6.4	6.5	37.4
Days With ≥ 1.0" Snow Depth	24	20	10	1	0	0	0	0	0	0	5	16	76

Marion *Turner County*   Elevation: 1,450 ft.   Latitude: 43° 25' N   Longitude: 97° 15' W

	JAN	FEB	MAR	APR	MAY	JUN	JUL	AUG	SEP	OCT	NOV	DEC	YEAR
Mean Maximum Temp. (°F)	24.0	30.5	42.6	58.0	70.8	80.3	85.2	83.0	74.3	61.0	42.0	28.5	56.7
Mean Temp. (°F)	13.9	20.4	32.4	46.3	58.9	68.6	73.4	71.0	61.4	48.4	32.1	18.9	45.5
Mean Minimum Temp. (°F)	3.8	10.3	22.0	34.4	46.9	56.8	61.5	59.0	48.5	35.7	22.2	9.3	34.2
Extreme Maximum Temp. (°F)	68	72	84	93	93	107	108	106	104	92	81	68	108
Extreme Minimum Temp. (°F)	-31	-30	-19	6	25	37	39	39	22	11	-20	-30	-31
Days Maximum Temp. ≥ 90°F	0	0	0	0	1	4	9	6	2	0	0	0	22
Days Maximum Temp. ≤ 32°F	21	15	7	1	0	0	0	0	0	0	7	18	69
Days Minimum Temp. ≤ 32°F	30	27	26	13	1	0	0	0	1	11	26	31	166
Days Minimum Temp. ≤ 0°F	13	7	2	0	0	0	0	0	0	0	1	8	31
Heating Degree Days (base 65°F)	1,580	1,253	1,005	561	221	41	7	17	169	511	979	1,423	7,767
Cooling Degree Days (base 65°F)	0	0	0	6	39	154	268	204	66	3	0	0	740
Mean Precipitation (in.)	0.53	0.51	1.92	2.84	3.40	3.55	2.88	2.83	2.62	1.94	1.42	0.54	24.98
Days With ≥ 0.1" Precipitation	2	2	4	6	7	6	6	5	5	4	3	2	52
Days With ≥ 1.0" Precipitation	0	0	1	1	1	1	1	1	1	1	0	0	8
Mean Snowfall (in.)	6.7	5.8	7.5	3.2	0.0	0.0	0.0	0.0	0.0	0.6	6.8	6.2	36.8
Days With ≥ 1.0" Snow Depth	na	na	na	1	0	0	0	0	0	0	2	11	na

Maurine 10 SW *Meade County*   Elevation: 2,709 ft.   Latitude: 44° 54' N   Longitude: 102° 39' W

	JAN	FEB	MAR	APR	MAY	JUN	JUL	AUG	SEP	OCT	NOV	DEC	YEAR
Mean Maximum Temp. (°F)	27.9	34.2	43.4	57.7	69.0	79.1	86.9	86.4	76.0	61.4	42.8	32.2	58.1
Mean Temp. (°F)	16.8	22.8	31.6	44.2	55.7	65.4	72.3	71.1	60.3	46.8	30.8	20.5	44.9
Mean Minimum Temp. (°F)	5.6	11.4	19.8	30.7	42.4	51.7	57.7	55.7	44.6	32.3	18.8	8.8	31.6
Extreme Maximum Temp. (°F)	67	72	80	93	96	106	114	110	106	95	82	69	114
Extreme Minimum Temp. (°F)	-32	-36	-26	-2	21	30	39	35	20	-10	-24	-36	-36
Days Maximum Temp. ≥ 90°F	0	0	0	0	1	4	12	12	4	0	0	0	33
Days Maximum Temp. ≤ 32°F	17	12	7	1	0	0	0	0	0	0	0	0	33
Days Minimum Temp. ≤ 32°F	30	27	28	17	4	0	0	0	0	8	14	59
Days Minimum Temp. ≤ 0°F	11	7	2	0	0	0	0	0	0	0	2	7	29
Heating Degree Days (base 65°F)	1,488	1,188	1,026	617	300	79	15	21	195	559	1,017	1,374	7,879
Cooling Degree Days (base 65°F)	0	0	0	2	21	93	245	226	56	3	0	0	646
Mean Precipitation (in.)	0.59	0.66	1.43	1.83	2.75	3.00	2.31	1.51	0.98	1.38	0.74	0.79	17.97
Days With ≥ 0.1" Precipitation	3	2	4	5	6	6	5	3	2	3	3	3	45
Days With ≥ 1.0" Precipitation	0	0	0	0	0	1	0	0	0	0	0	0	1
Mean Snowfall (in.)	5.3	6.0	na	5.3	0.2	0.0	0.0	0.0	trace	0.9	4.8	6.4	na
Days With ≥ 1.0" Snow Depth	23	14	12	3	0	0	0	0	0	1	9	na	na

McIntosh 6 SE *Corson County*   Elevation: 2,171 ft.   Latitude: 45° 53' N   Longitude: 101° 18' W

	JAN	FEB	MAR	APR	MAY	JUN	JUL	AUG	SEP	OCT	NOV	DEC	YEAR
Mean Maximum Temp. (°F)	23.9	31.2	41.1	56.9	69.8	79.2	86.1	85.1	73.4	59.6	39.3	27.4	56.1
Mean Temp. (°F)	13.8	21.1	30.6	44.5	56.9	66.3	72.2	70.9	59.5	46.8	29.6	17.7	44.2
Mean Minimum Temp. (°F)	3.6	11.0	20.0	32.1	44.0	53.4	58.3	56.6	45.6	34.1	19.7	7.9	32.2
Extreme Maximum Temp. (°F)	68	71	80	96	96	106	109	104	103	94	80	65	109
Extreme Minimum Temp. (°F)	-37	-35	-25	-1	21	31	42	39	19	-8	-19	-34	-37
Days Maximum Temp. ≥ 90°F	0	0	0	0	1	4	11	10	3	0	0	0	29
Days Maximum Temp. ≤ 32°F	20	14	8	1	0	0	0	0	0	0	0	0	29
Days Minimum Temp. ≤ 32°F	31	27	28	16	3	0	0	0	0	0	10	18	71
Days Minimum Temp. ≤ 0°F	13	7	2	0	0	0	0	0	0	0	2	9	33
Heating Degree Days (base 65°F)	1,583	1,233	1,060	610	267	63	11	21	207	559	1,054	1,462	8,130
Cooling Degree Days (base 65°F)	0	0	0	3	25	107	233	206	52	3	0	0	629
Mean Precipitation (in.)	0.37	0.41	0.79	1.79	2.56	2.99	2.23	1.73	1.37	1.43	0.54	0.38	16.59
Days With ≥ 0.1" Precipitation	1	1	2	4	6	6	5	4	3	3	2	1	38
Days With ≥ 1.0" Precipitation	0	0	0	0	1	1	0	0	0	0	0	0	2
Mean Snowfall (in.)	5.8	5.2	8.1	5.2	0.3	0.0	0.0	0.0	0.2	1.3	6.4	5.3	37.8
Days With ≥ 1.0" Snow Depth	24	18	16	4	0	0	0	0	0	1	11	19	93

Mellette *Spink County*   Elevation: 1,289 ft.   Latitude: 45° 09' N   Longitude: 98° 30' W

	JAN	FEB	MAR	APR	MAY	JUN	JUL	AUG	SEP	OCT	NOV	DEC	YEAR
Mean Maximum Temp. (°F)	20.8	28.5	39.8	57.4	70.6	79.7	85.6	84.2	73.9	59.9	40.0	26.5	55.6
Mean Temp. (°F)	9.6	17.4	29.2	44.6	57.4	66.8	72.1	70.0	59.3	45.8	29.1	15.6	43.1
Mean Minimum Temp. (°F)	-1.6	6.2	18.6	31.8	44.1	54.0	58.6	55.8	44.5	31.7	18.1	4.9	30.6
Extreme Maximum Temp. (°F)	63	65	79	99	98	110	110	108	105	95	79	64	110
Extreme Minimum Temp. (°F)	-39	-45	-26	-7	15	33	35	33	17	6	-24	-38	-45
Days Maximum Temp. ≥ 90°F	0	0	0	0	1	4	9	8	3	0	0	0	25
Days Maximum Temp. ≤ 32°F	23	16	8	1	0	0	0	0	0	0	0	0	25
Days Minimum Temp. ≤ 32°F	31	28	28	17	4	0	0	0	0	0	9	19	76
Days Minimum Temp. ≤ 0°F	17	10	3	0	0	0	0	0	3	17	28	31	187
Heating Degree Days (base 65°F)	1,715	1,338	1,103	609	259	64	14	30	219	591	1,070	1,527	8,539
Cooling Degree Days (base 65°F)	0	0	0	3	33	119	228	189	46	2	0	0	620
Mean Precipitation (in.)	0.55	0.56	1.41	2.28	2.82	3.50	2.86	2.96	2.04	1.65	0.84	0.41	21.88
Days With ≥ 0.1" Precipitation	2	2	4	5	6	7	5	5	4	3	2	1	46
Days With ≥ 1.0" Precipitation	0	0	0	1	1	1	1	1	1	0	0	0	5
Mean Snowfall (in.)	8.3	6.6	6.0	3.6	trace	0.0	0.0	0.0	0.0	0.5	7.0	6.2	38.2
Days With ≥ 1.0" Snow Depth	na	17	12	1	0	0	0	0	0	0	8	15	na

Menno *Hutchinson County*   Elevation: 1,322 ft.   Latitude: 43° 14' N   Longitude: 97° 34' W

	JAN	FEB	MAR	APR	MAY	JUN	JUL	AUG	SEP	OCT	NOV	DEC	YEAR
Mean Maximum Temp. (°F)	27.6	34.9	46.4	61.7	73.7	83.6	87.7	85.6	77.6	64.1	44.1	31.1	59.8
Mean Temp. (°F)	17.0	24.4	35.5	48.9	61.0	70.6	75.0	72.9	63.8	51.0	34.0	21.2	47.9
Mean Minimum Temp. (°F)	6.5	13.8	24.5	35.9	48.1	57.5	62.2	60.1	49.9	37.9	23.9	11.5	36.0
Extreme Maximum Temp. (°F)	68	75	87	96	96	107	108	107	105	96	82	68	108
Extreme Minimum Temp. (°F)	-33	-32	-20	8	20	36	41	37	20	12	-16	-29	-33
Days Maximum Temp. ≥ 90°F	0	0	0	0	1	7	12	9	4	0	0	0	33
Days Maximum Temp. ≤ 32°F	18	12	5	0	0	0	0	0	0	0	0	0	33
Days Minimum Temp. ≤ 32°F	31	27	24	11	1	0	0	0	0	1	9	24	56
Days Minimum Temp. ≤ 0°F	11	6	1	0	0	0	0	0	0	0	1	7	26
Heating Degree Days (base 65°F)	1,483	1,139	906	486	172	24	4	11	127	435	922	1,352	7,061
Cooling Degree Days (base 65°F)	0	0	0	11	56	196	304	251	95	8	0	0	921
Mean Precipitation (in.)	0.41	0.48	1.71	2.51	3.48	3.43	3.19	2.31	2.39	1.72	1.23	0.47	23.33
Days With ≥ 0.1" Precipitation	1	2	4	6	7	6	6	5	4	4	3	2	50
Days With ≥ 1.0" Precipitation	0	0	0	0	1	1	1	1	1	0	0	0	5
Mean Snowfall (in.)	6.2	5.8	6.9	2.9	trace	trace	0.0	trace	trace	1.1	5.9	7.1	35.9
Days With ≥ 1.0" Snow Depth	22	16	7	1	0	0	0	0	0	0	5	18	69

Milesville 5 NE *Haakon County*   Elevation: 2,234 ft.   Latitude: 44° 31' N   Longitude: 101° 37' W

	JAN	FEB	MAR	APR	MAY	JUN	JUL	AUG	SEP	OCT	NOV	DEC	YEAR
Mean Maximum Temp. (°F)	28.9	35.8	45.3	59.3	70.8	80.9	88.2	87.6	77.1	62.8	43.9	32.4	59.4
Mean Temp. (°F)	18.0	24.7	33.8	46.6	57.9	67.9	74.2	73.1	62.4	49.3	32.9	21.7	46.9
Mean Minimum Temp. (°F)	7.2	13.5	22.3	33.9	44.9	54.7	60.2	58.6	47.6	35.7	21.9	10.9	34.3
Extreme Maximum Temp. (°F)	69	73	82	96	103	107	110	110	106	96	85	70	110
Extreme Minimum Temp. (°F)	-31	-37	-29	2	23	35	40	38	21	-5	-19	-33	-37
Days Maximum Temp. ≥ 90°F	0	0	0	0	1	5	14	13	5	0	0	0	38
Days Maximum Temp. ≤ 32°F	16	11	6	1	0	0	0	0	0	0	6	14	54
Days Minimum Temp. ≤ 32°F	30	27	27	13	2	0	0	0	1	11	26	30	167
Days Minimum Temp. ≤ 0°F	10	6	2	0	0	0	0	0	0	0	1	7	26
Heating Degree Days (base 65°F)	1,450	1,132	959	548	243	47	8	13	156	486	955	1,337	7,334
Cooling Degree Days (base 65°F)	0	0	0	5	30	127	289	266	79	4	0	0	800
Mean Precipitation (in.)	0.41	0.56	1.17	1.87	3.43	3.04	2.90	2.03	1.37	1.70	0.61	0.45	19.54
Days With ≥ 0.1" Precipitation	1	1	3	5	6	6	5	4	3	3	2	1	40
Days With ≥ 1.0" Precipitation	0	0	0	0	1	0	1	0	0	0	0	0	2
Mean Snowfall (in.)	7.4	8.9	10.5	6.2	0.4	0.0	0.0	0.0	trace	2.0	6.8	8.1	50.3
Days With ≥ 1.0" Snow Depth	20	13	10	2	0	0	0	0	0	1	7	16	69

Miller *Hand County*   Elevation: 1,587 ft.   Latitude: 44° 31' N   Longitude: 98° 59' W

	JAN	FEB	MAR	APR	MAY	JUN	JUL	AUG	SEP	OCT	NOV	DEC	YEAR
Mean Maximum Temp. (°F)	25.5	32.9	43.3	58.9	71.2	80.5	86.9	85.7	75.6	61.9	41.9	30.0	57.8
Mean Temp. (°F)	15.4	22.6	32.6	46.3	58.6	68.2	74.0	72.3	62.2	49.2	32.2	20.2	46.2
Mean Minimum Temp. (°F)	5.3	12.2	21.8	33.7	46.1	55.9	61.0	58.9	48.7	36.5	22.4	10.4	34.4
Extreme Maximum Temp. (°F)	65	68	79	98	92	109	105	109	105	93	80	68	109
Extreme Minimum Temp. (°F)	-30	-37	-16	0	21	36	40	40	22	6	-15	-32	-37
Days Maximum Temp. ≥ 90°F	0	0	0	0	1	4	12	10	4	0	0	0	31
Days Maximum Temp. ≤ 32°F	19	13	6	1	0	0	0	0	0	0	7	16	62
Days Minimum Temp. ≤ 32°F	31	27	26	14	2	0	0	0	1	10	25	31	167
Days Minimum Temp. ≤ 0°F	12	7	2	0	0	0	0	0	0	0	1	7	29
Heating Degree Days (base 65°F)	1,531	1,193	998	560	226	43	9	15	160	488	979	1,383	7,585
Cooling Degree Days (base 65°F)	0	0	0	6	35	131	275	232	75	4	0	0	758
Mean Precipitation (in.)	0.42	0.55	1.32	2.13	3.08	2.98	2.60	1.99	1.81	1.72	0.76	0.46	19.82
Days With ≥ 0.1" Precipitation	1	2	3	5	6	6	5	5	3	3	2	1	42
Days With ≥ 1.0" Precipitation	0	0	0	0	1	1	1	0	0	0	0	0	3
Mean Snowfall (in.)	6.1	7.4	6.6	2.3	trace	0.0	0.0	0.0	trace	1.6	5.2	5.4	34.6
Days With ≥ 1.0" Snow Depth	na	na	4	1	0	0	0	0	0	0	3	na	na

Mission *Todd County*   Elevation: 2,585 ft.   Latitude: 43° 18' N   Longitude: 100° 40' W

	JAN	FEB	MAR	APR	MAY	JUN	JUL	AUG	SEP	OCT	NOV	DEC	YEAR
Mean Maximum Temp. (°F)	31.4	36.9	45.0	57.0	68.8	79.3	86.5	85.3	75.6	62.1	44.6	35.3	59.0
Mean Temp. (°F)	20.0	25.3	33.3	44.9	56.3	66.6	72.9	71.3	60.9	48.0	33.1	23.6	46.3
Mean Minimum Temp. (°F)	8.1	13.6	21.6	32.7	43.8	53.9	59.2	57.3	46.1	33.8	21.6	11.8	33.6
Extreme Maximum Temp. (°F)	75	74	85	95	95	107	109	108	104	94	85	71	109
Extreme Minimum Temp. (°F)	-28	-30	-27	6	18	32	35	36	18	1	-16	-32	-32
Days Maximum Temp. ≥ 90°F	0	0	0	0	0	4	12	11	4	0	0	0	31
Days Maximum Temp. ≤ 32°F	15	11	7	1	0	0	0	0	0	0	6	12	52
Days Minimum Temp. ≤ 32°F	30	27	27	15	3	0	0	0	2	13	26	30	173
Days Minimum Temp. ≤ 0°F	10	6	2	0	0	0	0	0	0	0	1	6	25
Heating Degree Days (base 65°F)	1,390	1,116	975	601	288	71	15	23	190	525	950	1,276	7,420
Cooling Degree Days (base 65°F)	0	0	0	5	27	121	256	224	72	4	0	0	709
Mean Precipitation (in.)	0.32	0.43	1.18	2.13	3.47	3.12	2.90	1.92	1.59	1.54	0.68	0.48	19.76
Days With ≥ 0.1" Precipitation	1	1	3	5	7	6	6	4	4	4	2	2	45
Days With ≥ 1.0" Precipitation	0	0	0	0	1	1	1	0	0	0	0	0	3
Mean Snowfall (in.)	5.4	5.0	8.3	5.2	trace	0.0	0.0	0.0	0.1	1.7	5.5	5.7	36.9
Days With ≥ 1.0" Snow Depth	17	12	8	3	0	0	0	0	0	1	8	14	63

Mission 14 S *Todd County*   Elevation: 2,808 ft.   Latitude: 43° 07' N   Longitude: 100° 37' W

	JAN	FEB	MAR	APR	MAY	JUN	JUL	AUG	SEP	OCT	NOV	DEC	YEAR
Mean Maximum Temp. (°F)	31.6	37.9	46.8	58.8	70.2	80.7	86.9	85.8	76.5	62.9	44.9	35.9	59.9
Mean Temp. (°F)	20.1	26.1	34.3	45.5	56.9	67.2	73.0	71.3	61.7	48.9	33.5	24.5	46.9
Mean Minimum Temp. (°F)	8.5	14.3	21.8	32.1	43.6	53.7	59.0	56.8	46.9	34.8	22.1	13.1	33.9
Extreme Maximum Temp. (°F)	71	75	84	95	98	109	110	106	103	95	85	72	110
Extreme Minimum Temp. (°F)	-25	-30	-21	6	19	33	39	40	20	0	-16	-31	-31
Days Maximum Temp. ≥ 90°F	0	0	0	0	0	5	13	10	4	0	0	0	32
Days Maximum Temp. ≤ 32°F	15	11	6	1	0	0	0	0	0	0	7	12	52
Days Minimum Temp. ≤ 32°F	30	27	27	16	3	0	0	0	2	12	26	30	173
Days Minimum Temp. ≤ 0°F	9	5	2	0	0	0	0	0	0	0	1	5	22
Heating Degree Days (base 65°F)	1,387	1,092	944	582	266	57	11	19	168	496	938	1,250	7,210
Cooling Degree Days (base 65°F)	0	0	0	5	25	125	262	218	78	5	0	0	718
Mean Precipitation (in.)	0.39	0.55	1.33	2.17	3.54	3.06	3.18	2.15	1.68	1.41	0.76	0.46	20.68
Days With ≥ 0.1" Precipitation	1	2	3	5	7	6	6	5	4	3	2	2	46
Days With ≥ 1.0" Precipitation	0	0	0	0	1	1	1	1	0	0	0	0	4
Mean Snowfall (in.)	5.5	6.4	9.2	6.0	trace	0.0	0.0	0.0	0.3	2.0	6.6	5.1	41.1
Days With ≥ 1.0" Snow Depth	17	14	9	3	0	0	0	0	0	1	7	13	64

Mitchell 2 N *Davison County*   Elevation: 1,250 ft.   Latitude: 43° 44' N   Longitude: 98° 01' W

	JAN	FEB	MAR	APR	MAY	JUN	JUL	AUG	SEP	OCT	NOV	DEC	YEAR
Mean Maximum Temp. (°F)	25.3	32.3	43.8	58.6	71.2	81.0	86.7	85.0	75.9	61.9	43.1	30.5	58.0
Mean Temp. (°F)	15.1	22.2	33.4	47.1	59.4	69.4	74.7	72.7	62.7	49.2	33.2	20.5	46.6
Mean Minimum Temp. (°F)	4.9	11.9	22.9	35.4	47.6	57.7	62.6	60.3	49.5	36.5	23.1	10.5	35.2
Extreme Maximum Temp. (°F)	67	68	89	97	96	107	108	109	104	96	81	70	109
Extreme Minimum Temp. (°F)	-38	-40	-16	7	25	35	39	39	21	12	-12	-30	-40
Days Maximum Temp. ≥ 90°F	0	0	0	0	1	5	11	9	4	0	0	0	30
Days Maximum Temp. ≤ 32°F	20	14	6	1	0	0	0	0	0	0	6	16	63
Days Minimum Temp. ≤ 32°F	31	27	25	11	1	0	0	0	0	1	10	25	162
Days Minimum Temp. ≤ 0°F	12	7	2	0	0	0	0	0	0	0	1	7	29
Heating Degree Days (base 65°F)	1,543	1,205	973	539	208	37	6	13	148	489	949	1,373	7,483
Cooling Degree Days (base 65°F)	0	0	0	8	43	170	300	250	81	4	0	0	856
Mean Precipitation (in.)	0.45	0.62	1.67	2.78	3.26	3.55	2.63	2.15	2.31	1.57	1.14	0.54	22.67
Days With ≥ 0.1" Precipitation	1	2	4	6	6	6	5	4	4	4	2	2	46
Days With ≥ 1.0" Precipitation	0	0	0	1	1	1	1	1	1	0	0	0	6
Mean Snowfall (in.)	5.7	6.2	*5.0*	2.1	0.0	0.0	0.0	0.0	0.0	0.4	4.0	na	na
Days With ≥ 1.0" Snow Depth	na	na	7	1	0	0	0	0	0	0	2	na	na

Mobridge *Walworth County*   Elevation: 1,669 ft.   Latitude: 45° 32' N   Longitude: 100° 26' W

	JAN	FEB	MAR	APR	MAY	JUN	JUL	AUG	SEP	OCT	NOV	DEC	YEAR
Mean Maximum Temp. (°F)	23.1	30.2	41.2	56.4	69.2	78.6	84.5	83.3	72.5	58.9	39.5	26.7	55.3
Mean Temp. (°F)	13.0	19.8	30.8	44.7	57.3	67.1	72.7	71.3	60.6	47.6	30.5	17.5	44.4
Mean Minimum Temp. (°F)	2.8	9.5	20.4	32.9	45.5	55.6	60.9	59.3	48.6	36.2	21.5	8.3	33.5
Extreme Maximum Temp. (°F)	62	70	78	96	101	105	105	106	102	92	76	60	106
Extreme Minimum Temp. (°F)	-30	-38	-21	-1	26	35	45	42	24	1	-20	-33	-38
Days Maximum Temp. ≥ 90°F	0	0	0	0	1	3	8	8	2	0	0	0	22
Days Maximum Temp. ≤ 32°F	21	15	8	1	0	0	0	0	0	0	9	19	73
Days Minimum Temp. ≤ 32°F	31	28	28	15	2	0	0	0	0	1	9	27	172
Days Minimum Temp. ≤ 0°F	14	8	2	0	0	0	0	0	0	0	1	9	34
Heating Degree Days (base 65°F)	1,609	1,270	1,054	605	256	49	9	19	183	536	1,028	1,466	8,084
Cooling Degree Days (base 65°F)	0	0	0	4	28	121	248	224	53	2	0	0	680
Mean Precipitation (in.)	0.33	0.39	0.99	1.77	2.60	2.93	2.25	1.88	1.41	1.53	0.60	0.39	17.07
Days With ≥ 0.1" Precipitation	1	1	2	4	6	6	5	4	3	3	2	1	38
Days With ≥ 1.0" Precipitation	0	0	0	0	1	1	0	0	0	0	0	0	2
Mean Snowfall (in.)	5.3	5.4	7.6	4.1	0.2	0.0	0.0	0.0	trace	0.7	5.7	5.5	34.5
Days With ≥ 1.0" Snow Depth	24	17	13	3	0	0	0	0	0	0	7	18	82

Mt. Rushmore Nat'l Memorial *Pennington County*   Elevation: 5,249 ft.   Latitude: 43° 53' N   Longitude: 103° 27' W

	JAN	FEB	MAR	APR	MAY	JUN	JUL	AUG	SEP	OCT	NOV	DEC	YEAR
Mean Maximum Temp. (°F)	35.2	38.7	44.0	52.0	62.8	73.5	80.6	79.6	69.7	57.2	43.3	36.9	56.1
Mean Temp. (°F)	25.7	29.1	34.1	42.1	52.3	62.7	69.5	68.6	59.0	47.2	34.4	27.9	46.1
Mean Minimum Temp. (°F)	16.3	19.5	24.2	32.1	41.9	51.8	58.3	57.6	48.2	37.1	25.5	18.7	35.9
Extreme Maximum Temp. (°F)	68	68	76	85	90	99	100	99	97	84	75	67	100
Extreme Minimum Temp. (°F)	-23	-29	-11	1	18	27	35	37	19	1	-12	-31	-31
Days Maximum Temp. ≥ 90°F	0	0	0	0	0	2	5	3	1	0	0	0	11
Days Maximum Temp. ≤ 32°F	11	8	6	2	0	0	0	0	0	1	6	10	44
Days Minimum Temp. ≤ 32°F	27	24	24	16	4	0	0	0	2	11	22	27	157
Days Minimum Temp. ≤ 0°F	6	3	1	0	0	0	0	0	0	0	1	3	14
Heating Degree Days (base 65°F)	1,210	1,006	950	683	396	137	39	40	228	549	912	1,145	7,295
Cooling Degree Days (base 65°F)	0	0	0	2	11	70	176	155	51	4	0	0	469
Mean Precipitation (in.)	0.38	0.55	1.18	2.19	4.05	3.80	3.13	2.09	1.59	1.54	0.62	0.46	21.58
Days With ≥ 0.1" Precipitation	1	2	3	5	8	8	7	5	4	4	2	2	51
Days With ≥ 1.0" Precipitation	0	0	0	0	1	1	1	0	0	0	0	0	3
Mean Snowfall (in.)	6.0	7.5	10.6	12.2	1.2	0.1	0.0	0.0	0.7	3.8	7.5	6.6	56.2
Days With ≥ 1.0" Snow Depth	12	11	10	6	1	0	0	0	0	2	9	12	63

Murdo *Jones County*   Elevation: 2,319 ft.   Latitude: 43° 53' N   Longitude: 100° 42' W

	JAN	FEB	MAR	APR	MAY	JUN	JUL	AUG	SEP	OCT	NOV	DEC	YEAR
Mean Maximum Temp. (°F)	30.3	37.2	46.2	59.5	71.0	81.3	88.6	87.6	77.5	63.2	44.5	34.0	60.1
Mean Temp. (°F)	19.4	25.8	34.4	46.6	58.1	68.2	74.6	73.3	63.0	49.9	33.7	23.1	47.5
Mean Minimum Temp. (°F)	8.4	14.3	22.5	33.7	45.2	55.0	60.6	58.9	48.5	36.5	22.9	12.2	34.9
Extreme Maximum Temp. (°F)	75	74	87	98	98	108	109	109	106	97	85	71	109
Extreme Minimum Temp. (°F)	-26	-28	-17	5	23	32	41	42	22	0	-14	-29	-29
Days Maximum Temp. ≥ 90°F	0	0	0	0	1	6	15	14	6	1	0	0	43
Days Maximum Temp. ≤ 32°F	15	10	6	1	0	0	0	0	0	0	6	13	51
Days Minimum Temp. ≤ 32°F	30	27	26	14	2	0	0	0	1	10	25	30	165
Days Minimum Temp. ≤ 0°F	10	5	2	0	0	0	0	0	0	0	1	6	24
Heating Degree Days (base 65°F)	1,409	1,101	942	549	239	46	7	11	150	470	932	1,293	7,149
Cooling Degree Days (base 65°F)	0	0	0	5	36	141	300	276	97	6	0	0	861
Mean Precipitation (in.)	0.46	0.51	1.64	2.25	2.96	3.31	2.77	1.71	1.27	1.63	0.75	0.47	19.73
Days With ≥ 0.1" Precipitation	1	2	4	5	6	6	6	4	3	3	2	2	44
Days With ≥ 1.0" Precipitation	0	0	0	0	1	1	1	0	0	0	0	0	3
Mean Snowfall (in.)	5.7	5.4	8.9	5.0	0.2	trace	0.0	0.0	trace	1.4	6.7	5.9	39.2
Days With ≥ 1.0" Snow Depth	na	7	7	2	0	0	0	0	0	1	*4*	na	na

Newell *Butte County*   Elevation: 2,857 ft.   Latitude: 44° 43' N   Longitude: 103° 25' W

	JAN	FEB	MAR	APR	MAY	JUN	JUL	AUG	SEP	OCT	NOV	DEC	YEAR
Mean Maximum Temp. (°F)	29.7	36.1	44.5	57.0	67.5	78.0	85.9	85.3	74.6	61.1	43.8	33.5	58.1
Mean Temp. (°F)	18.3	24.5	32.8	44.6	55.3	65.4	72.1	70.8	59.8	46.9	32.0	21.5	45.3
Mean Minimum Temp. (°F)	6.9	12.9	21.2	32.1	43.0	52.8	58.2	56.3	45.0	32.6	20.3	9.5	32.6
Extreme Maximum Temp. (°F)	69	75	81	92	96	103	110	108	106	94	81	69	110
Extreme Minimum Temp. (°F)	-35	-35	-24	2	22	34	40	38	19	-10	-22	-38	-38
Days Maximum Temp. ≥ 90°F	0	0	0	0	0	3	11	10	4	0	0	0	28
Days Maximum Temp. ≤ 32°F	16	11	6	1	0	0	0	0	0	1	7	13	55
Days Minimum Temp. ≤ 32°F	31	27	28	15	3	0	0	0	2	14	27	30	177
Days Minimum Temp. ≤ 0°F	10	6	2	0	0	0	0	0	0	0	2	7	27
Heating Degree Days (base 65°F)	1,440	1,137	991	608	310	80	16	21	203	557	982	1,343	7,688
Cooling Degree Days (base 65°F)	0	0	0	2	18	99	239	215	54	2	0	0	629
Mean Precipitation (in.)	0.38	0.43	0.93	1.72	2.78	2.76	1.90	1.34	1.01	1.38	0.56	0.36	15.55
Days With ≥ 0.1" Precipitation	1	2	3	4	6	6	5	3	2	3	2	1	38
Days With ≥ 1.0" Precipitation	0	0	0	0	1	1	0	0	0	0	0	0	2
Mean Snowfall (in.)	6.1	4.5	na	2.8	0.5	0.0	0.0	0.0	trace	1.2	4.6	5.2	na
Days With ≥ 1.0" Snow Depth	na	10	8	2	0	0	0	0	0	0	1	4	10	na

Oahe Dam *Stanley County*   Elevation: 1,660 ft.   Latitude: 44° 27' N   Longitude: 100° 25' W

	JAN	FEB	MAR	APR	MAY	JUN	JUL	AUG	SEP	OCT	NOV	DEC	YEAR
Mean Maximum Temp. (°F)	27.3	32.5	43.2	57.2	69.3	80.5	88.5	87.2	75.8	61.9	43.4	31.8	58.2
Mean Temp. (°F)	17.4	22.7	32.5	45.6	57.5	68.2	75.2	73.7	62.6	49.7	33.6	22.1	46.7
Mean Minimum Temp. (°F)	7.5	12.7	21.8	34.0	45.7	55.9	61.9	59.8	49.2	37.4	23.9	12.4	35.2
Extreme Maximum Temp. (°F)	65	71	87	98	103	114	111	112	108	98	86	69	114
Extreme Minimum Temp. (°F)	-27	-34	-17	6	24	34	45	42	22	6	-9	-31	-34
Days Maximum Temp. ≥ 90°F	0	0	0	0	1	5	13	12	4	0	0	0	35
Days Maximum Temp. ≤ 32°F	17	13	6	1	0	0	0	0	0	0	6	14	57
Days Minimum Temp. ≤ 32°F	29	26	26	13	1	0	0	0	1	8	23	29	156
Days Minimum Temp. ≤ 0°F	10	5	1	0	0	0	0	0	0	0	1	5	22
Heating Degree Days (base 65°F)	1,470	1,192	1,000	578	250	46	6	10	152	473	934	1,324	7,435
Cooling Degree Days (base 65°F)	0	0	0	4	37	145	325	294	83	6	0	0	894
Mean Precipitation (in.)	0.27	0.35	0.76	1.52	2.55	2.71	2.28	1.54	1.23	1.04	0.42	0.28	14.95
Days With ≥ 0.1" Precipitation	0	1	2	3	4	5	4	3	2	2	1	1	28
Days With ≥ 1.0" Precipitation	0	0	0	0	0	1	0	0	0	0	0	0	1
Mean Snowfall (in.)	na	na	na	trace	0.0	0.0	0.0	0.0	0.0	trace	na	na	na
Days With ≥ 1.0" Snow Depth	na	na	na	0	0	0	0	0	0	0	na	na	na

Oelrichs *Fall River County*   Elevation: 3,339 ft.   Latitude: 43° 11' N   Longitude: 103° 14' W

	JAN	FEB	MAR	APR	MAY	JUN	JUL	AUG	SEP	OCT	NOV	DEC	YEAR
Mean Maximum Temp. (°F)	34.0	40.9	49.8	60.7	71.0	81.9	90.0	89.3	78.9	64.6	46.5	36.7	62.0
Mean Temp. (°F)	22.4	28.5	36.3	46.4	56.7	66.6	73.8	72.8	62.2	49.1	34.1	24.8	47.8
Mean Minimum Temp. (°F)	10.8	16.0	22.7	32.0	42.3	51.3	57.6	56.2	45.5	33.6	21.7	12.9	33.5
Extreme Maximum Temp. (°F)	69	73	81	92	93	108	114	109	104	95	83	71	114
Extreme Minimum Temp. (°F)	-26	-34	-24	-1	22	32	36	36	16	-11	-18	-37	-37
Days Maximum Temp. ≥ 90°F	0	0	0	0	1	6	17	16	6	0	0	0	46
Days Maximum Temp. ≤ 32°F	12	7	4	0	0	0	0	0	0	0	5	10	38
Days Minimum Temp. ≤ 32°F	30	27	26	16	3	0	0	0	2	13	26	30	173
Days Minimum Temp. ≤ 0°F	8	4	1	0	0	0	0	0	0	0	1	5	19
Heating Degree Days (base 65°F)	1,315	1,025	883	554	266	63	8	10	155	488	919	1,239	6,925
Cooling Degree Days (base 65°F)	0	0	0	1	17	107	277	257	75	2	0	0	736
Mean Precipitation (in.)	0.40	0.47	0.94	1.93	3.09	2.85	2.14	1.64	1.30	1.29	0.64	0.41	17.10
Days With ≥ 0.1" Precipitation	1	2	3	5	7	6	5	4	3	3	2	1	42
Days With ≥ 1.0" Precipitation	0	0	0	0	0	1	0	0	0	0	0	0	1
Mean Snowfall (in.)	6.6	6.1	8.9	5.7	0.6	0.0	0.0	0.0	0.2	3.0	6.8	7.5	45.4
Days With ≥ 1.0" Snow Depth	15	8	5	1	0	0	0	0	0	1	5	12	47

Onida 4 NW *Sully County*   Elevation: 1,847 ft.   Latitude: 44° 44' N   Longitude: 100° 09' W

	JAN	FEB	MAR	APR	MAY	JUN	JUL	AUG	SEP	OCT	NOV	DEC	YEAR
Mean Maximum Temp. (°F)	25.0	32.8	43.2	59.7	71.8	81.2	88.4	87.3	77.1	62.3	41.5	29.3	58.3
Mean Temp. (°F)	14.8	22.4	32.4	46.5	58.7	68.0	74.2	72.9	62.6	49.1	31.7	19.6	46.1
Mean Minimum Temp. (°F)	4.6	11.9	21.6	33.4	45.5	54.7	59.9	58.5	48.0	35.9	21.8	9.7	33.8
Extreme Maximum Temp. (°F)	62	68	83	98	98	110	110	109	108	94	81	69	110
Extreme Minimum Temp. (°F)	-31	-38	-24	-1	19	36	38	38	18	-1	-16	-32	-38
Days Maximum Temp. ≥ 90°F	0	0	0	0	1	5	14	12	4	0	0	0	36
Days Maximum Temp. ≤ 32°F	20	13	7	1	0	0	0	0	0	0	7	17	65
Days Minimum Temp. ≤ 32°F	31	28	27	14	2	0	0	0	1	11	26	31	171
Days Minimum Temp. ≤ 0°F	12	6	2	0	0	0	0	0	0	0	1	7	28
Heating Degree Days (base 65°F)	1,552	1,198	1,004	553	225	47	9	13	152	491	993	1,404	7,641
Cooling Degree Days (base 65°F)	0	0	0	6	36	134	286	256	80	4	0	0	802
Mean Precipitation (in.)	0.61	0.65	1.37	1.91	2.73	3.12	2.74	2.09	1.59	1.57	0.83	0.57	19.78
Days With ≥ 0.1" Precipitation	2	2	4	5	6	6	5	4	3	3	3	2	45
Days With ≥ 1.0" Precipitation	0	0	0	0	0	1	1	0	0	0	0	0	2
Mean Snowfall (in.)	6.3	7.0	9.7	4.1	trace	0.0	0.0	0.0	trace	1.8	6.9	6.7	42.5
Days With ≥ 1.0" Snow Depth	23	17	11	2	0	0	0	0	0	1	9	19	82

Oral *Fall River County*   Elevation: 2,959 ft.   Latitude: 43° 24' N   Longitude: 103° 16' W

	JAN	FEB	MAR	APR	MAY	JUN	JUL	AUG	SEP	OCT	NOV	DEC	YEAR
Mean Maximum Temp. (°F)	36.6	42.1	50.9	61.2	71.1	81.8	89.6	88.4	78.5	65.4	47.8	39.3	62.7
Mean Temp. (°F)	23.2	28.0	36.4	46.3	56.5	66.4	72.9	71.1	60.6	48.5	33.9	25.6	47.4
Mean Minimum Temp. (°F)	9.9	14.1	21.9	31.3	41.9	50.9	56.1	53.8	42.6	31.6	20.3	11.8	32.2
Extreme Maximum Temp. (°F)	71	73	83	94	97	109	112	108	104	94	83	71	112
Extreme Minimum Temp. (°F)	-33	-38	-32	-5	22	32	36	31	17	-8	-21	-43	-43
Days Maximum Temp. ≥ 90°F	0	0	0	0	1	7	17	15	6	1	0	0	47
Days Maximum Temp. ≤ 32°F	10	7	4	1	0	0	0	0	0	0	4	8	34
Days Minimum Temp. ≤ 32°F	30	26	27	17	4	0	0	0	0	4	16	27	180
Days Minimum Temp. ≤ 0°F	8	4	1	0	0	0	0	0	0	0	2	5	20
Heating Degree Days (base 65°F)	1,291	1,042	878	557	279	69	13	19	182	505	925	1,216	6,976
Cooling Degree Days (base 65°F)	0	0	0	2	22	111	258	220	52	2	0	0	667
Mean Precipitation (in.)	0.37	0.45	0.86	1.65	2.89	2.95	2.28	1.86	1.23	1.16	0.62	0.39	16.71
Days With ≥ 0.1" Precipitation	1	2	3	4	6	7	5	4	3	3	2	1	41
Days With ≥ 1.0" Precipitation	0	0	0	0	1	1	0	0	0	0	0	0	2
Mean Snowfall (in.)	4.7	4.6	6.2	3.4	0.1	0.0	0.0	0.0	trace	1.2	3.8	5.7	29.7
Days With ≥ 1.0" Snow Depth	13	9	5	2	0	0	0	0	0	0	6	12	47

Pactola Dam *Pennington County*   Elevation: 4,717 ft.   Latitude: 44° 04' N   Longitude: 103° 29' W

	JAN	FEB	MAR	APR	MAY	JUN	JUL	AUG	SEP	OCT	NOV	DEC	YEAR
Mean Maximum Temp. (°F)	35.0	38.8	43.1	50.9	61.2	71.5	78.5	78.3	68.4	56.8	43.2	36.9	55.2
Mean Temp. (°F)	21.8	25.3	30.1	38.0	48.0	57.6	63.7	62.7	52.7	42.1	30.7	23.7	41.4
Mean Minimum Temp. (°F)	8.6	11.6	17.0	25.1	34.7	43.6	48.7	47.1	37.0	27.4	18.2	10.4	27.5
Extreme Maximum Temp. (°F)	68	68	78	85	86	98	100	98	97	85	75	65	100
Extreme Minimum Temp. (°F)	-28	-34	-22	-8	15	27	29	29	15	-8	-19	-35	-35
Days Maximum Temp. ≥ 90°F	0	0	0	0	0	1	3	2	1	0	0	0	7
Days Maximum Temp. ≤ 32°F	12	8	6	2	0	0	0	0	0	1	6	11	46
Days Minimum Temp. ≤ 32°F	30	28	30	25	11	2	0	0	8	23	28	31	216
Days Minimum Temp. ≤ 0°F	8	5	3	0	0	0	0	0	0	0	2	6	24
Heating Degree Days (base 65°F)	1,333	1,115	1,076	808	520	234	95	107	370	702	1,014	1,275	8,649
Cooling Degree Days (base 65°F)	0	0	0	0	1	19	64	43	6	0	0	0	133
Mean Precipitation (in.)	0.30	0.44	1.03	2.36	3.70	3.89	3.18	2.24	1.44	1.57	0.62	0.40	21.17
Days With ≥ 0.1" Precipitation	1	1	3	5	7	8	7	5	3	3	2	1	46
Days With ≥ 1.0" Precipitation	0	0	0	0	1	1	1	0	0	0	0	0	3
Mean Snowfall (in.)	4.4	5.0	10.6	11.7	1.5	0.2	0.0	0.0	0.4	3.5	6.1	5.5	48.9
Days With ≥ 1.0" Snow Depth	17	12	12	8	1	0	0	0	0	2	9	15	76

Pickstown *Charles Mix County*   Elevation: 1,489 ft.   Latitude: 43° 04' N   Longitude: 98° 32' W

	JAN	FEB	MAR	APR	MAY	JUN	JUL	AUG	SEP	OCT	NOV	DEC	YEAR
Mean Maximum Temp. (°F)	30.2	36.9	47.0	60.1	71.9	82.0	87.6	86.1	76.7	63.5	45.3	34.2	60.1
Mean Temp. (°F)	19.7	26.3	35.9	48.3	59.9	69.9	75.4	74.0	64.1	51.3	35.6	24.3	48.7
Mean Minimum Temp. (°F)	9.1	15.7	24.7	36.4	47.8	57.8	63.2	61.8	51.4	39.1	25.8	14.2	37.3
Extreme Maximum Temp. (°F)	70	78	89	96	96	108	109	106	103	95	84	73	109
Extreme Minimum Temp. (°F)	-25	-25	-13	5	25	37	43	41	27	13	-8	-26	-26
Days Maximum Temp. ≥ 90°F	0	0	0	0	1	6	13	11	4	0	0	0	35
Days Maximum Temp. ≤ 32°F	17	11	5	0	0	0	0	0	0	0	5	13	51
Days Minimum Temp. ≤ 32°F	30	26	24	10	1	0	0	0	1	7	23	30	152
Days Minimum Temp. ≤ 0°F	9	5	1	0	0	0	0	0	0	0	1	5	21
Heating Degree Days (base 65°F)	1,400	1,086	896	504	196	31	4	9	126	424	876	1,257	6,809
Cooling Degree Days (base 65°F)	0	0	0	11	44	180	326	290	103	7	0	0	961
Mean Precipitation (in.)	0.42	0.52	1.63	2.90	3.65	3.53	2.82	2.44	2.33	1.75	0.96	0.49	23.44
Days With ≥ 0.1" Precipitation	1	1	4	6	7	7	6	4	4	3	2	1	46
Days With ≥ 1.0" Precipitation	0	0	0	1	1	1	1	1	0	0	0	0	5
Mean Snowfall (in.)	4.2	3.9	4.5	1.6	0.0	0.0	0.0	0.0	trace	0.5	3.6	4.4	22.7
Days With ≥ 1.0" Snow Depth	21	13	8	1	0	0	0	0	0	0	4	15	62

Pierre Municipal Airport *Hughes County*   Elevation: 1,725 ft.   Latitude: 44° 23' N   Longitude: 100° 17' W

	JAN	FEB	MAR	APR	MAY	JUN	JUL	AUG	SEP	OCT	NOV	DEC	YEAR
Mean Maximum Temp. (°F)	27.4	34.5	44.9	59.4	71.3	81.4	89.2	87.8	77.0	62.2	43.5	31.9	59.2
Mean Temp. (°F)	17.4	24.2	34.2	47.1	58.8	68.7	75.5	74.0	63.0	49.5	33.5	22.1	47.3
Mean Minimum Temp. (°F)	7.3	13.9	23.4	34.7	46.2	56.0	61.7	60.1	49.0	36.7	23.5	12.2	35.4
Extreme Maximum Temp. (°F)	68	75	87	98	102	112	113	114	108	98	87	77	114
Extreme Minimum Temp. (°F)	-32	-35	-19	4	23	34	42	39	21	4	-11	-31	-35
Days Maximum Temp. ≥ 90°F	0	0	0	0	1	6	15	14	5	0	0	0	41
Days Maximum Temp. ≤ 32°F	18	12	6	1	0	0	0	0	0	0	6	15	58
Days Minimum Temp. ≤ 32°F	30	27	25	12	1	0	0	0	1	9	25	30	160
Days Minimum Temp. ≤ 0°F	11	5	1	0	0	0	0	0	0	0	1	6	24
Heating Degree Days (base 65°F)	1,468	1,146	949	536	220	40	5	11	147	479	939	1,325	7,265
Cooling Degree Days (base 65°F)	0	0	0	6	38	154	338	301	95	6	0	0	938
Mean Precipitation (in.)	0.52	0.55	1.19	2.06	3.09	3.53	2.77	2.02	1.63	1.64	0.71	0.50	20.21
Days With ≥ 0.1" Precipitation	2	2	3	5	6	6	5	4	3	3	2	2	43
Days With ≥ 1.0" Precipitation	0	0	0	0	1	1	1	0	0	0	0	0	3
Mean Snowfall (in.)	5.4	5.4	6.8	3.7	trace	trace	trace	trace	trace	1.4	5.1	5.1	32.9
Days With ≥ 1.0" Snow Depth	19	12	8	2	0	0	0	0	0	0	6	13	60

Pollock *Campbell County*   Elevation: 1,633 ft.   Latitude: 45° 54' N   Longitude: 100° 17' W

	JAN	FEB	MAR	APR	MAY	JUN	JUL	AUG	SEP	OCT	NOV	DEC	YEAR
Mean Maximum Temp. (°F)	22.5	30.5	41.3	58.2	71.6	80.3	86.6	85.4	74.6	60.2	39.6	26.6	56.5
Mean Temp. (°F)	11.3	19.3	30.2	45.1	57.9	67.1	72.8	71.2	60.4	46.9	29.6	16.1	44.0
Mean Minimum Temp. (°F)	0.0	8.0	19.1	31.9	44.3	54.0	59.0	56.9	46.2	33.6	19.5	5.5	31.5
Extreme Maximum Temp. (°F)	61	71	79	97	98	106	109	104	105	95	79	62	109
Extreme Minimum Temp. (°F)	-40	-47	-31	2	20	33	40	37	15	-5	-27	-39	-47
Days Maximum Temp. ≥ 90°F	0	0	0	0	1	4	12	10	3	0	0	0	30
Days Maximum Temp. ≤ 32°F	21	15	7	1	0	0	0	0	0	0	8	19	71
Days Minimum Temp. ≤ 32°F	30	28	28	16	2	0	0	0	2	14	28	31	179
Days Minimum Temp. ≤ 0°F	16	9	3	0	0	0	0	0	0	0	2	11	41
Heating Degree Days (base 65°F)	1,662	1,287	1,072	594	240	49	8	17	184	554	1,057	1,512	8,236
Cooling Degree Days (base 65°F)	0	0	0	3	31	120	252	222	52	2	0	0	682
Mean Precipitation (in.)	0.40	0.44	0.98	1.78	2.55	2.98	2.37	2.14	1.46	1.47	0.68	0.35	17.60
Days With ≥ 0.1" Precipitation	1	1	3	4	6	6	5	4	3	3	2	1	39
Days With ≥ 1.0" Precipitation	0	0	0	0	1	1	1	0	0	0	0	0	3
Mean Snowfall (in.)	*7.5*	7.4	*7.6*	3.5	0.2	0.0	0.0	0.0	trace	0.6	6.7	*6.3*	*39.8*
Days With ≥ 1.0" Snow Depth	na	na	na	*2*	0	0	0	0	0	0	*8*	na	na

Porcupine 11 N *Shannon County*   Elevation: 2,818 ft.   Latitude: 43° 24' N   Longitude: 102° 23' W

	JAN	FEB	MAR	APR	MAY	JUN	JUL	AUG	SEP	OCT	NOV	DEC	YEAR
Mean Maximum Temp. (°F)	33.9	41.2	49.5	60.3	71.0	81.6	89.2	88.9	78.5	64.6	46.7	37.3	61.9
Mean Temp. (°F)	21.1	27.8	35.8	45.9	56.9	67.0	73.6	72.6	61.4	48.0	33.2	23.7	47.3
Mean Minimum Temp. (°F)	8.3	14.3	22.1	31.5	42.8	52.4	57.9	56.3	44.2	31.5	19.7	10.0	32.6
Extreme Maximum Temp. (°F)	69	73	87	95	96	109	112	114	106	97	84	70	114
Extreme Minimum Temp. (°F)	-33	-44	-32	0	15	31	35	33	12	-11	-22	-45	-45
Days Maximum Temp. ≥ 90°F	0	0	0	0	1	7	15	15	6	0	0	0	44
Days Maximum Temp. ≤ 32°F	13	8	4	1	0	0	0	0	0	0	5	10	41
Days Minimum Temp. ≤ 32°F	30	27	26	16	4	0	0	0	4	16	27	30	180
Days Minimum Temp. ≤ 0°F	9	5	1	0	0	0	0	0	0	0	2	7	24
Heating Degree Days (base 65°F)	1,356	1,046	897	569	268	65	15	13	178	521	947	1,275	7,150
Cooling Degree Days (base 65°F)	0	0	0	4	27	123	269	249	68	2	0	0	742
Mean Precipitation (in.)	0.37	0.44	0.96	1.82	2.77	2.96	2.66	1.57	1.40	1.46	0.59	0.38	17.38
Days With ≥ 0.1" Precipitation	1	2	3	4	6	6	5	4	3	3	2	1	40
Days With ≥ 1.0" Precipitation	0	0	0	0	1	1	1	0	0	0	0	0	3
Mean Snowfall (in.)	4.4	5.6	*4.6*	4.3	0.1	0.0	0.0	0.0	trace	2.0	*6.3*	*5.2*	*32.5*
Days With ≥ 1.0" Snow Depth	17	11	7	2	0	0	0	0	0	1	8	14	60

Ralph 1 N *Harding County*   Elevation: 2,788 ft.   Latitude: 45° 47' N   Longitude: 103° 04' W

	JAN	FEB	MAR	APR	MAY	JUN	JUL	AUG	SEP	OCT	NOV	DEC	YEAR
Mean Maximum Temp. (°F)	27.7	34.8	44.1	57.5	69.1	78.3	85.4	85.9	74.3	60.7	42.3	31.7	57.6
Mean Temp. (°F)	15.9	22.7	31.5	43.6	54.9	63.9	69.8	69.3	57.8	45.5	29.9	19.6	43.7
Mean Minimum Temp. (°F)	4.1	10.6	18.8	29.6	40.6	49.5	54.2	52.6	41.2	30.2	17.5	7.5	29.7
Extreme Maximum Temp. (°F)	69	72	79	95	95	104	112	104	105	92	82	66	112
Extreme Minimum Temp. (°F)	-40	-37	-34	-8	13	29	32	30	14	-12	-20	-37	-40
Days Maximum Temp. ≥ 90°F	0	0	0	0	0	3	10	11	3	0	0	0	27
Days Maximum Temp. ≤ 32°F	17	11	6	1	0	0	0	0	0	0	8	15	58
Days Minimum Temp. ≤ 32°F	31	28	29	19	5	0	0	0	5	18	28	31	194
Days Minimum Temp. ≤ 0°F	13	6	3	0	0	0	0	0	0	0	2	9	33
Heating Degree Days (base 65°F)	1,520	1,178	1,033	636	321	93	23	30	243	601	1,044	1,401	8,123
Cooling Degree Days (base 65°F)	0	0	0	1	13	71	191	178	36	1	0	0	491
Mean Precipitation (in.)	0.43	0.39	0.69	1.77	2.89	2.99	2.03	1.42	1.25	1.34	0.56	0.39	16.15
Days With ≥ 0.1" Precipitation	1	1	2	4	6	6	5	3	3	3	2	2	38
Days With ≥ 1.0" Precipitation	0	0	0	0	1	1	0	0	0	0	0	0	2
Mean Snowfall (in.)	na	na	na	*5.3*	0.7	0.0	0.0	0.0	0.5	1.7	na	na	na
Days With ≥ 1.0" Snow Depth	na	*10*	na	*3*	0	0	0	0	0	1	8	*13*	na

Rapid City 4 NW *Pennington County*   Elevation: 3,448 ft.   Latitude: 44° 07' N   Longitude: 103° 17' W

	JAN	FEB	MAR	APR	MAY	JUN	JUL	AUG	SEP	OCT	NOV	DEC	YEAR
Mean Maximum Temp. (°F)	36.1	41.3	47.8	57.9	67.7	78.2	85.3	84.9	75.2	62.5	46.7	40.0	60.3
Mean Temp. (°F)	23.8	29.0	35.5	45.2	55.1	65.3	71.6	70.6	60.7	48.9	35.0	27.5	47.4
Mean Minimum Temp. (°F)	11.6	16.6	23.1	32.5	42.6	52.3	58.0	56.3	46.2	35.3	23.3	15.1	34.4
Extreme Maximum Temp. (°F)	73	78	81	90	92	105	107	104	101	92	83	74	107
Extreme Minimum Temp. (°F)	-25	-28	-19	0	23	32	41	38	21	-3	-17	-29	-29
Days Maximum Temp. ≥ 90°F	0	0	0	0	0	3	10	9	3	0	0	0	25
Days Maximum Temp. ≤ 32°F	11	7	5	1	0	0	0	0	0	0	5	8	37
Days Minimum Temp. ≤ 32°F	29	26	26	15	3	0	0	0	2	10	24	29	164
Days Minimum Temp. ≤ 0°F	8	4	1	0	0	0	0	0	0	0	1	4	18
Heating Degree Days (base 65°F)	1,269	1,011	909	590	312	82	16	18	179	494	893	1,156	6,929
Cooling Degree Days (base 65°F)	0	0	0	4	16	89	219	192	52	3	0	0	575
Mean Precipitation (in.)	0.32	0.37	0.91	1.90	3.52	3.03	2.69	2.11	1.26	1.57	0.49	0.30	18.47
Days With ≥ 0.1" Precipitation	1	1	3	4	7	6	6	4	3	3	2	1	41
Days With ≥ 1.0" Precipitation	0	0	0	0	1	1	0	0	0	0	0	0	2
Mean Snowfall (in.)	5.0	4.9	8.6	6.6	0.5	0.0	0.0	0.0	trace	1.5	5.0	4.4	36.5
Days With ≥ 1.0" Snow Depth	*9*	6	4	2	0	0	0	0	0	1	5	*7*	*34*

Redfield 2 NE *Spink County*   Elevation: 1,289 ft.   Latitude: 44° 54' N   Longitude: 98° 30' W

	JAN	FEB	MAR	APR	MAY	JUN	JUL	AUG	SEP	OCT	NOV	DEC	YEAR
Mean Maximum Temp. (°F)	20.8	28.7	40.2	57.4	70.3	79.6	86.2	84.7	74.5	60.3	39.9	27.7	55.9
Mean Temp. (°F)	10.1	18.4	30.1	45.0	57.4	67.0	72.8	70.9	60.2	46.8	29.7	17.2	43.8
Mean Minimum Temp. (°F)	-0.7	8.0	20.0	32.4	44.4	54.4	59.4	57.0	45.8	32.9	19.6	6.7	31.7
Extreme Maximum Temp. (°F)	63	64	79	98	96	110	109	106	106	93	79	65	110
Extreme Minimum Temp. (°F)	-38	-47	-22	-8	17	33	36	35	16	7	-20	-34	-47
Days Maximum Temp. ≥ 90°F	0	0	0	0	1	3	10	9	3	0	0	0	26
Days Maximum Temp. ≤ 32°F	23	16	8	1	0	0	0	0	0	0	8	19	75
Days Minimum Temp. ≤ 32°F	31	28	27	16	4	0	0	0	2	15	27	31	181
Days Minimum Temp. ≤ 0°F	16	9	2	0	0	0	0	0	0	0	2	9	38
Heating Degree Days (base 65°F)	1,700	1,313	1,078	597	260	58	11	24	200	561	1,053	1,479	8,334
Cooling Degree Days (base 65°F)	0	0	0	3	31	117	245	203	55	2	0	0	656
Mean Precipitation (in.)	0.38	0.50	1.22	2.05	2.98	3.24	3.03	2.37	1.84	1.65	0.62	0.32	20.20
Days With ≥ 0.1" Precipitation	1	2	3	4	6	6	5	4	3	3	2	1	40
Days With ≥ 1.0" Precipitation	0	0	0	0	1	1	1	1	0	0	0	0	5
Mean Snowfall (in.)	*5.8*	*5.8*	6.6	2.8	trace	0.0	0.0	0.0	trace	0.6	*5.3*	*5.7*	*32.6*
Days With ≥ 1.0" Snow Depth	21	*17*	11	2	0	0	0	0	0	0	6	12	69

Redig 11 NE *Harding County*   Elevation: 3,067 ft.   Latitude: 45° 23' N   Longitude: 103° 22' W

	JAN	FEB	MAR	APR	MAY	JUN	JUL	AUG	SEP	OCT	NOV	DEC	YEAR
Mean Maximum Temp. (°F)	28.0	34.4	43.2	55.9	67.3	77.0	84.8	84.7	73.5	60.0	42.4	32.1	56.9
Mean Temp. (°F)	16.9	23.2	31.5	43.2	54.2	63.6	70.1	69.2	58.4	46.0	30.9	20.8	44.0
Mean Minimum Temp. (°F)	5.8	12.0	19.6	30.4	41.0	50.2	55.4	53.6	43.1	32.0	19.3	9.4	31.0
Extreme Maximum Temp. (°F)	70	72	77	92	96	104	110	106	103	92	82	66	110
Extreme Minimum Temp. (°F)	-35	-36	-29	-10	19	32	37	33	16	-11	-22	-38	-38
Days Maximum Temp. ≥ 90°F	0	0	0	0	0	2	9	10	3	0	0	0	24
Days Maximum Temp. ≤ 32°F	17	11	7	1	0	0	0	0	0	1	8	14	59
Days Minimum Temp. ≤ 32°F	31	28	29	19	4	0	0	0	3	15	28	31	188
Days Minimum Temp. ≤ 0°F	11	6	3	0	0	0	0	0	0	0	2	8	30
Heating Degree Days (base 65°F)	1,488	1,174	1,034	648	338	102	21	32	230	583	1,016	1,367	8,033
Cooling Degree Days (base 65°F)	0	0	0	1	11	68	189	175	39	2	0	0	485
Mean Precipitation (in.)	0.32	0.39	0.75	1.61	2.97	3.06	2.07	1.46	1.00	1.30	0.47	0.33	15.73
Days With ≥ 0.1" Precipitation	1	2	2	4	6	6	5	3	3	3	2	1	38
Days With ≥ 1.0" Precipitation	0	0	0	0	1	1	0	0	0	0	0	0	2
Mean Snowfall (in.)	7.8	8.1	9.3	7.7	1.2	0.0	0.0	0.0	0.3	2.3	7.7	7.4	51.8
Days With ≥ 1.0" Snow Depth	21	14	12	4	0	0	0	0	0	1	9	17	78

Selby *Walworth County*   Elevation: 1,870 ft.   Latitude: 45° 30' N   Longitude: 100° 02' W

	JAN	FEB	MAR	APR	MAY	JUN	JUL	AUG	SEP	OCT	NOV	DEC	YEAR
Mean Maximum Temp. (°F)	21.7	28.6	39.3	55.4	68.8	78.1	84.6	83.5	72.6	58.6	38.7	26.6	54.7
Mean Temp. (°F)	11.3	18.4	29.0	43.5	56.4	65.9	71.5	69.9	58.9	45.7	28.9	16.7	43.0
Mean Minimum Temp. (°F)	0.9	8.1	18.6	31.5	43.9	53.5	58.4	56.4	45.1	32.8	19.0	6.9	31.3
Extreme Maximum Temp. (°F)	63	65	78	97	98	109	110	108	104	93	75	63	110
Extreme Minimum Temp. (°F)	-35	-36	-29	-3	20	34	38	36	17	-2	-20	-36	-36
Days Maximum Temp. ≥ 90°F	0	0	0	0	1	3	8	8	2	0	0	0	22
Days Maximum Temp. ≤ 32°F	23	16	9	1	0	0	0	0	0	1	10	19	79
Days Minimum Temp. ≤ 32°F	31	28	28	17	3	0	0	0	3	15	28	31	184
Days Minimum Temp. ≤ 0°F	15	9	3	0	0	0	0	0	0	0	2	10	39
Heating Degree Days (base 65°F)	1,661	1,312	1,109	643	286	72	17	30	226	592	1,078	1,491	8,517
Cooling Degree Days (base 65°F)	0	0	0	4	26	98	214	186	45	2	0	0	575
Mean Precipitation (in.)	0.37	0.44	1.02	1.90	2.54	2.99	2.50	2.06	1.36	1.48	0.71	0.37	17.74
Days With ≥ 0.1" Precipitation	1	1	3	4	5	6	5	4	3	3	2	1	38
Days With ≥ 1.0" Precipitation	0	0	0	0	1	1	1	0	0	0	0	0	3
Mean Snowfall (in.)	4.7	5.5	6.5	4.8	trace	0.0	0.0	0.0	trace	0.9	5.7	4.9	33.0
Days With ≥ 1.0" Snow Depth	27	23	18	5	0	0	0	0	0	1	12	22	108

Sisseton *Roberts County*   Elevation: 1,217 ft.   Latitude: 45° 40' N   Longitude: 97° 03' W

	JAN	FEB	MAR	APR	MAY	JUN	JUL	AUG	SEP	OCT	NOV	DEC	YEAR
Mean Maximum Temp. (°F)	21.2	28.1	39.5	57.1	71.0	79.4	84.5	82.7	72.9	59.6	39.3	26.8	55.2
Mean Temp. (°F)	11.5	18.8	30.4	45.5	58.6	67.3	72.6	70.6	60.8	48.2	30.6	17.6	44.4
Mean Minimum Temp. (°F)	1.8	9.3	21.3	33.8	46.2	55.2	60.6	58.5	48.6	36.7	21.8	8.3	33.5
Extreme Maximum Temp. (°F)	65	62	80	99	92	104	107	105	99	94	78	59	107
Extreme Minimum Temp. (°F)	-33	-33	-16	0	22	35	43	39	23	9	-16	-30	-33
Days Maximum Temp. ≥ 90°F	0	0	0	0	1	3	8	6	2	0	0	0	20
Days Maximum Temp. ≤ 32°F	23	16	8	1	0	0	0	0	0	0	9	19	76
Days Minimum Temp. ≤ 32°F	31	27	26	14	2	0	0	0	1	10	26	30	167
Days Minimum Temp. ≤ 0°F	15	9	2	0	0	0	0	0	0	0	1	10	37
Heating Degree Days (base 65°F)	1,655	1,301	1,065	584	227	50	9	22	182	520	1,026	1,465	8,106
Cooling Degree Days (base 65°F)	0	0	0	5	38	116	236	194	55	4	0	0	648
Mean Precipitation (in.)	0.72	0.59	1.50	2.02	2.78	3.31	3.05	2.56	1.98	1.87	1.11	0.43	21.92
Days With ≥ 0.1" Precipitation	2	2	4	5	6	6	6	5	4	4	3	2	49
Days With ≥ 1.0" Precipitation	0	0	0	0	1	1	1	1	0	0	0	0	4
Mean Snowfall (in.)	9.8	6.7	8.3	3.3	trace	0.0	0.0	0.0	trace	0.7	7.7	5.3	41.8
Days With ≥ 1.0" Snow Depth	*22*	*17*	*7*	1	0	0	0	0	0	0	6	14	*67*

Spearfish Airport *Lawrence County*   Elevation: 3,910 ft.   Latitude: 44° 29' N   Longitude: 103° 47' W

	JAN	FEB	MAR	APR	MAY	JUN	JUL	AUG	SEP	OCT	NOV	DEC	YEAR
Mean Maximum Temp. (°F)	35.0	38.7	45.0	55.8	66.4	76.5	84.3	83.5	72.9	59.9	44.6	37.7	58.4
Mean Temp. (°F)	24.1	27.9	34.3	44.5	54.8	64.3	71.3	70.1	59.7	48.0	34.3	27.0	46.7
Mean Minimum Temp. (°F)	13.2	17.1	23.5	33.2	43.2	52.0	58.3	56.6	46.4	36.0	24.0	16.2	35.0
Extreme Maximum Temp. (°F)	69	75	80	91	93	101	105	104	105	91	78	70	105
Extreme Minimum Temp. (°F)	-30	-25	-16	4	19	33	40	32	20	9	-17	-31	-31
Days Maximum Temp. ≥ 90°F	0	0	0	0	0	2	9	8	2	0	0	0	21
Days Maximum Temp. ≤ 32°F	12	9	6	1	0	0	0	0	0	1	6	10	45
Days Minimum Temp. ≤ 32°F	28	25	25	14	2	0	0	0	1	10	23	27	155
Days Minimum Temp. ≤ 0°F	8	4	1	0	0	0	0	0	0	0	1	5	19
Heating Degree Days (base 65°F)	1,260	1,041	945	612	325	96	17	26	204	524	913	1,172	7,135
Cooling Degree Days (base 65°F)	0	0	0	3	16	80	228	198	50	3	0	0	578
Mean Precipitation (in.)	0.59	0.71	1.43	2.49	3.59	3.96	2.24	1.80	1.47	2.02	0.91	0.78	21.99
Days With ≥ 0.1" Precipitation	2	2	4	5	7	7	5	4	4	4	3	2	49
Days With ≥ 1.0" Precipitation	0	0	0	1	1	1	0	0	0	0	0	0	3
Mean Snowfall (in.)	10.7	9.7	14.5	8.2	0.8	0.0	0.0	0.0	trace	4.1	7.6	9.7	65.3
Days With ≥ 1.0" Snow Depth	19	12	9	4	0	0	0	0	0	2	9	15	70

Stephan 1 ENE *Hyde County*   Elevation: 1,863 ft.   Latitude: 44° 15' N   Longitude: 99° 27' W

	JAN	FEB	MAR	APR	MAY	JUN	JUL	AUG	SEP	OCT	NOV	DEC	YEAR
Mean Maximum Temp. (°F)	26.1	32.8	44.3	59.8	71.9	81.5	88.2	87.2	77.2	62.5	42.8	30.7	58.7
Mean Temp. (°F)	14.5	21.4	32.2	45.7	57.6	67.4	73.3	71.9	61.7	48.2	31.2	19.4	45.4
Mean Minimum Temp. (°F)	2.9	10.0	20.1	31.6	43.3	53.1	58.3	56.6	46.2	33.8	19.5	8.0	32.0
Extreme Maximum Temp. (°F)	65	71	85	99	97	110	111	111	107	95	82	70	111
Extreme Minimum Temp. (°F)	-36	-40	-24	-1	17	31	37	31	17	2	-17	-32	-40
Days Maximum Temp. ≥ 90°F	0	0	0	0	1	5	14	12	4	0	0	0	36
Days Maximum Temp. ≤ 32°F	19	13	6	1	0	0	0	0	0	0	7	16	62
Days Minimum Temp. ≤ 32°F	31	28	28	17	3	0	0	0	2	14	28	31	182
Days Minimum Temp. ≤ 0°F	14	8	3	0	0	0	0	0	0	0	2	9	36
Heating Degree Days (base 65°F)	1,561	1,225	1,011	576	247	51	8	19	166	517	1,008	1,409	7,798
Cooling Degree Days (base 65°F)	0	0	0	3	27	120	258	231	73	3	0	0	715
Mean Precipitation (in.)	0.41	0.49	1.30	2.03	2.91	2.97	2.65	2.04	1.73	1.79	0.61	0.40	19.33
Days With ≥ 0.1" Precipitation	1	2	3	5	6	6	5	4	3	3	2	1	41
Days With ≥ 1.0" Precipitation	0	0	0	0	1	1	1	0	0	0	0	0	3
Mean Snowfall (in.)	6.0	8.1	8.1	3.8	trace	0.0	0.0	0.0	trace	1.2	4.1	6.2	37.5
Days With ≥ 1.0" Snow Depth	na	na	na	0	0	0	0	0	0	0	na	na	na

Summit 1 W *Roberts County*   Elevation: 1,948 ft.   Latitude: 45° 18' N   Longitude: 97° 04' W

	JAN	FEB	MAR	APR	MAY	JUN	JUL	AUG	SEP	OCT	NOV	DEC	YEAR
Mean Maximum Temp. (°F)	18.8	25.3	36.6	54.5	68.3	77.1	82.0	80.3	71.0	57.7	36.5	23.8	52.7
Mean Temp. (°F)	9.1	15.8	27.2	42.6	55.7	65.0	69.5	67.9	58.2	45.6	27.4	14.5	41.5
Mean Minimum Temp. (°F)	-0.6	6.2	17.8	30.7	43.0	52.7	57.1	55.5	45.5	33.4	18.3	5.1	30.4
Extreme Maximum Temp. (°F)	64	57	73	94	89	103	101	100	96	88	75	57	103
Extreme Minimum Temp. (°F)	-36	-40	-25	-5	18	30	38	32	15	5	-25	-34	-40
Days Maximum Temp. ≥ 90°F	0	0	0	0	0	1	5	4	1	0	0	0	11
Days Maximum Temp. ≤ 32°F	25	19	11	1	0	0	0	0	0	0	12	23	91
Days Minimum Temp. ≤ 32°F	31	28	28	18	5	0	0	0	3	14	27	31	185
Days Minimum Temp. ≤ 0°F	16	10	3	0	0	0	0	0	0	0	2	12	43
Heating Degree Days (base 65°F)	1,730	1,386	1,163	667	301	83	25	45	237	598	1,122	1,562	8,919
Cooling Degree Days (base 65°F)	0	0	0	3	21	85	165	136	37	2	0	0	449
Mean Precipitation (in.)	0.53	0.51	1.46	2.06	2.82	3.77	3.59	3.26	2.12	1.86	0.87	0.33	23.18
Days With ≥ 0.1" Precipitation	2	2	4	5	6	7	6	6	4	4	3	1	50
Days With ≥ 1.0" Precipitation	0	0	0	0	1	1	1	1	0	0	0	0	4
Mean Snowfall (in.)	9.3	8.3	10.3	4.7	trace	trace	0.0	0.0	trace	1.3	7.9	5.6	47.4
Days With ≥ 1.0" Snow Depth	26	23	16	3	0	0	0	0	0	1	10	19	98

Timber Lake *Dewey County*   Elevation: 2,148 ft.   Latitude: 45° 26' N   Longitude: 101° 04' W

	JAN	FEB	MAR	APR	MAY	JUN	JUL	AUG	SEP	OCT	NOV	DEC	YEAR
Mean Maximum Temp. (°F)	24.5	31.6	41.5	57.0	69.6	78.8	85.0	84.1	73.5	59.5	40.1	28.5	56.2
Mean Temp. (°F)	14.6	21.7	31.2	45.0	57.2	66.5	72.2	71.0	60.2	47.3	30.5	19.0	44.7
Mean Minimum Temp. (°F)	4.5	11.7	20.9	32.9	44.7	54.1	59.3	57.7	46.9	35.1	20.9	9.4	33.2
Extreme Maximum Temp. (°F)	66	70	78	95	98	105	109	107	102	92	77	64	109
Extreme Minimum Temp. (°F)	-32	-35	-24	-1	24	34	40	37	19	-6	-20	-34	-35
Days Maximum Temp. ≥ 90°F	0	0	0	0	0	3	9	8	2	0	0	0	22
Days Maximum Temp. ≤ 32°F	20	14	7	1	0	0	0	0	0	0	8	17	67
Days Minimum Temp. ≤ 32°F	31	27	27	15	2	0	0	0	2	12	27	31	174
Days Minimum Temp. ≤ 0°F	13	7	2	0	0	0	0	0	0	0	2	8	32
Heating Degree Days (base 65°F)	1,560	1,218	1,042	597	261	61	14	20	193	543	1,027	1,422	7,958
Cooling Degree Days (base 65°F)	0	0	0	4	27	105	237	213	55	3	0	0	644
Mean Precipitation (in.)	0.41	0.53	1.10	2.04	2.88	3.19	2.45	1.93	1.32	1.61	0.70	0.52	18.68
Days With ≥ 0.1" Precipitation	2	2	3	5	6	6	5	4	3	3	2	2	43
Days With ≥ 1.0" Precipitation	0	0	0	0	1	1	0	0	0	1	0	0	3
Mean Snowfall (in.)	5.5	6.4	7.9	6.1	0.2	0.0	0.0	0.0	trace	1.2	6.4	6.6	40.3
Days With ≥ 1.0" Snow Depth	24	16	14	3	0	0	0	0	0	1	9	18	85

Tyndall *Bon Homme County*   Elevation: 1,420 ft.   Latitude: 43° 00' N   Longitude: 97° 52' W

	JAN	FEB	MAR	APR	MAY	JUN	JUL	AUG	SEP	OCT	NOV	DEC	YEAR
Mean Maximum Temp. (°F)	28.5	35.6	46.5	60.9	72.6	82.8	87.6	85.4	77.1	63.6	44.4	32.5	59.8
Mean Temp. (°F)	18.2	25.0	35.8	48.8	60.8	70.6	75.3	73.3	64.1	51.0	34.5	22.7	48.3
Mean Minimum Temp. (°F)	7.8	14.4	25.1	36.6	48.9	58.4	63.0	61.3	51.0	38.3	24.6	12.8	36.9
Extreme Maximum Temp. (°F)	70	74	85	96	96	108	109	108	103	94	82	68	109
Extreme Minimum Temp. (°F)	-30	-29	-16	6	25	37	42	40	24	12	-11	-31	-31
Days Maximum Temp. ≥ 90°F	0	0	0	0	1	7	13	10	4	0	0	0	35
Days Maximum Temp. ≤ 32°F	17	11	5	0	0	0	0	0	0	0	5	14	52
Days Minimum Temp. ≤ 32°F	31	27	24	10	1	0	0	0	0	1	24	30	156
Days Minimum Temp. ≤ 0°F	10	5	1	0	0	0	0	0	0	0	1	6	23
Heating Degree Days (base 65°F)	1,446	1,124	898	489	178	27	4	8	125	436	907	1,306	6,948
Cooling Degree Days (base 65°F)	0	0	0	12	54	199	327	273	104	7	0	0	976
Mean Precipitation (in.)	0.46	0.66	1.69	2.60	3.59	3.09	3.65	2.51	2.33	1.64	1.31	0.60	24.13
Days With ≥ 0.1" Precipitation	2	2	4	6	7	6	6	5	5	4	3	2	52
Days With ≥ 1.0" Precipitation	0	0	0	0	1	1	1	1	1	0	0	0	5
Mean Snowfall (in.)	5.8	5.7	5.3	2.6	trace	0.0	0.0	0.0	trace	0.6	5.9	6.8	32.7
Days With ≥ 1.0" Snow Depth	19	12	5	0	0	0	0	0	0	0	4	13	53

Vermillion 2 SE *Clay County*   Elevation: 1,187 ft.   Latitude: 42° 46' N   Longitude: 96° 55' W

	JAN	FEB	MAR	APR	MAY	JUN	JUL	AUG	SEP	OCT	NOV	DEC	YEAR
Mean Maximum Temp. (°F)	29.9	37.1	49.1	63.9	75.3	84.7	88.7	86.4	79.2	66.3	46.7	33.8	61.8
Mean Temp. (°F)	18.9	25.8	37.0	50.3	61.8	71.6	76.2	74.0	65.2	52.4	35.8	23.3	49.4
Mean Minimum Temp. (°F)	7.9	14.4	25.0	36.5	48.6	58.4	63.6	61.6	51.1	38.3	25.0	12.9	36.9
Extreme Maximum Temp. (°F)	71	74	86	96	100	108	108	106	103	93	83	68	108
Extreme Minimum Temp. (°F)	-28	-33	-16	7	23	37	37	40	23	10	-18	-30	-33
Days Maximum Temp. ≥ 90°F	0	0	0	1	2	8	14	10	5	0	0	0	40
Days Maximum Temp. ≤ 32°F	16	11	4	0	0	0	0	0	0	0	4	13	48
Days Minimum Temp. ≤ 32°F	31	27	24	11	1	0	0	0	1	9	23	30	157
Days Minimum Temp. ≤ 0°F	10	5	1	0	0	0	0	0	0	0	1	6	23
Heating Degree Days (base 65°F)	1,423	1,100	861	450	158	20	3	7	106	397	868	1,286	6,679
Cooling Degree Days (base 65°F)	0	0	0	16	67	233	347	294	121	13	0	0	1,091
Mean Precipitation (in.)	0.39	0.41	1.89	2.84	3.75	3.57	3.50	2.75	2.49	2.01	1.48	0.51	25.59
Days With ≥ 0.1" Precipitation	1	1	4	5	7	6	5	5	4	4	3	2	47
Days With ≥ 1.0" Precipitation	0	0	0	1	1	1	1	1	1	0	0	0	6
Mean Snowfall (in.)	5.6	5.1	5.2	2.6	trace	0.0	0.0	trace	trace	0.8	6.4	6.2	31.9
Days With ≥ 1.0" Snow Depth	18	12	6	1	0	0	0	0	0	0	4	15	56

Wagner *Charles Mix County*   Elevation: 1,427 ft.   Latitude: 43° 05' N   Longitude: 98° 18' W

	JAN	FEB	MAR	APR	MAY	JUN	JUL	AUG	SEP	OCT	NOV	DEC	YEAR
Mean Maximum Temp. (°F)	30.2	36.9	48.0	62.5	74.3	84.5	89.9	87.8	78.4	64.5	45.4	33.6	61.3
Mean Temp. (°F)	19.9	26.4	36.7	49.8	61.8	71.6	76.9	75.0	65.1	52.0	35.4	24.0	49.6
Mean Minimum Temp. (°F)	9.6	15.9	25.4	37.0	49.1	58.6	64.0	62.2	51.9	39.4	25.4	14.2	37.7
Extreme Maximum Temp. (°F)	70	74	88	99	95	108	110	106	104	94	81	71	110
Extreme Minimum Temp. (°F)	-27	-26	-15	5	24	38	41	41	25	10	-11	-29	-29
Days Maximum Temp. ≥ 90°F	0	0	0	1	1	9	17	13	5	0	0	0	46
Days Maximum Temp. ≤ 32°F	16	11	4	0	0	0	0	0	0	0	5	13	49
Days Minimum Temp. ≤ 32°F	30	26	24	10	1	0	0	0	0	7	23	30	152
Days Minimum Temp. ≤ 0°F	9	5	1	0	0	0	0	0	0	0	1	5	21
Heating Degree Days (base 65°F)	1,393	1,083	869	463	155	19	2	6	109	405	880	1,266	6,650
Cooling Degree Days (base 65°F)	0	0	0	14	60	212	362	309	116	10	0	0	1,083
Mean Precipitation (in.)	0.58	0.77	1.82	2.92	3.93	3.33	3.08	2.71	2.65	1.92	1.28	0.65	25.64
Days With ≥ 0.1" Precipitation	2	2	4	6	7	6	6	5	4	4	3	2	51
Days With ≥ 1.0" Precipitation	0	0	0	1	1	1	1	1	1	0	0	0	6
Mean Snowfall (in.)	6.7	6.9	6.5	3.7	trace	0.0	0.0	0.0	trace	1.0	6.6	8.3	39.7
Days With ≥ 1.0" Snow Depth	17	10	6	1	0	0	0	0	0	0	5	13	52

Wasta *Pennington County*   Elevation: 2,319 ft.   Latitude: 44° 04' N   Longitude: 102° 26' W

	JAN	FEB	MAR	APR	MAY	JUN	JUL	AUG	SEP	OCT	NOV	DEC	YEAR
Mean Maximum Temp. (°F)	33.3	40.2	48.9	61.1	71.8	81.8	89.0	88.0	77.5	63.7	46.4	36.6	61.5
Mean Temp. (°F)	20.8	27.3	35.9	47.2	58.2	67.9	74.3	73.0	61.9	48.9	33.9	23.9	47.8
Mean Minimum Temp. (°F)	8.3	14.3	22.8	33.2	44.5	54.0	59.7	57.9	46.4	34.1	21.4	11.2	34.0
Extreme Maximum Temp. (°F)	73	77	84	97	98	108	110	109	106	94	86	72	110
Extreme Minimum Temp. (°F)	-30	-38	-29	5	23	32	38	35	19	-4	-19	-33	-38
Days Maximum Temp. ≥ 90°F	0	0	0	0	1	6	15	14	5	0	0	0	41
Days Maximum Temp. ≤ 32°F	13	8	4	0	0	0	0	0	0	0	5	10	40
Days Minimum Temp. ≤ 32°F	31	27	26	14	2	0	0	0	2	12	27	31	172
Days Minimum Temp. ≤ 0°F	9	5	1	0	0	0	0	0	0	0	1	6	22
Heating Degree Days (base 65°F)	1,364	1,058	896	532	232	47	7	11	157	493	925	1,269	6,991
Cooling Degree Days (base 65°F)	0	0	0	4	29	137	298	269	71	3	0	0	811
Mean Precipitation (in.)	0.37	0.46	1.10	1.92	3.02	2.67	2.11	1.67	1.17	1.51	0.71	0.41	17.12
Days With ≥ 0.1" Precipitation	1	2	3	4	6	6	4	4	3	3	2	2	40
Days With ≥ 1.0" Precipitation	0	0	0	1	1	1	0	0	0	0	0	0	3
Mean Snowfall (in.)	5.0	5.4	7.6	4.1	trace	0.0	0.0	0.0	trace	1.1	4.9	5.0	33.1
Days With ≥ 1.0" Snow Depth	17	11	7	2	0	0	0	0	0	0	6	13	56

Watertown Municipal Airport *Codington County*   Elevation: 1,748 ft.   Latitude: 44° 55' N   Longitude: 97° 09' W

	JAN	FEB	MAR	APR	MAY	JUN	JUL	AUG	SEP	OCT	NOV	DEC	YEAR
Mean Maximum Temp. (°F)	20.7	26.5	39.0	55.5	69.1	78.2	83.7	81.4	71.0	57.4	38.7	25.2	53.9
Mean Temp. (°F)	10.5	16.8	29.4	44.1	57.1	66.5	71.7	69.5	59.0	46.1	29.6	16.0	43.0
Mean Minimum Temp. (°F)	0.3	7.1	19.8	32.5	45.0	54.8	59.7	57.5	46.9	34.8	20.5	6.7	32.1
Extreme Maximum Temp. (°F)	65	60	74	95	91	105	104	101	100	89	77	57	105
Extreme Minimum Temp. (°F)	-35	-35	-19	-2	17	32	37	38	21	8	-19	-30	-35
Days Maximum Temp. ≥ 90°F	0	0	0	0	0	2	7	5	2	0	0	0	16
Days Maximum Temp. ≤ 32°F	23	18	9	1	0	0	0	0	0	0	10	21	82
Days Minimum Temp. ≤ 32°F	31	28	27	16	3	0	0	0	2	13	27	31	178
Days Minimum Temp. ≤ 0°F	15	10	3	0	0	0	0	0	0	0	1	10	39
Heating Degree Days (base 65°F)	1,688	1,356	1,095	624	266	63	14	33	220	579	1,055	1,516	8,509
Cooling Degree Days (base 65°F)	*0*	0	0	3	30	113	*226*	*178*	42	1	0	0	*593*
Mean Precipitation (in.)	0.54	0.47	1.34	2.04	2.67	4.14	2.82	2.80	2.15	1.80	0.92	0.39	22.08
Days With ≥ 0.1" Precipitation	2	1	4	5	6	7	6	5	4	3	2	1	46
Days With ≥ 1.0" Precipitation	0	0	0	0	1	1	1	1	0	0	0	0	4
Mean Snowfall (in.)	6.2	5.4	6.5	1.9	trace	trace	*trace*	*0.0*	trace	1.4	5.4	4.4	*31.2*
Days With ≥ 1.0" Snow Depth	26	21	13	2	0	0	*0*	0	*0*	1	7	20	*90*

Waubay Nat'l Wildlife Refuge *Day County*   Elevation: 1,827 ft.   Latitude: 45° 26' N   Longitude: 97° 20' W

	JAN	FEB	MAR	APR	MAY	JUN	JUL	AUG	SEP	OCT	NOV	DEC	YEAR
Mean Maximum Temp. (°F)	20.7	26.9	38.2	55.9	69.4	78.0	83.5	81.9	72.5	59.0	38.0	25.4	54.1
Mean Temp. (°F)	10.6	16.9	28.2	44.0	57.4	66.5	71.7	70.0	60.3	47.5	29.2	16.1	43.2
Mean Minimum Temp. (°F)	0.5	6.7	18.1	32.2	45.3	55.0	59.9	58.1	48.0	36.0	20.3	6.6	32.2
Extreme Maximum Temp. (°F)	62	57	74	94	89	102	104	104	97	91	75	57	104
Extreme Minimum Temp. (°F)	-35	-43	-24	-3	22	33	41	38	23	8	-23	-34	-43
Days Maximum Temp. ≥ 90°F	0	0	0	0	0	1	6	5	1	0	0	0	13
Days Maximum Temp. ≤ 32°F	24	17	9	1	0	0	0	0	0	0	10	21	82
Days Minimum Temp. ≤ 32°F	31	28	28	16	2	0	0	0	1	11	26	30	173
Days Minimum Temp. ≤ 0°F	15	10	3	0	0	0	0	0	0	0	2	10	40
Heating Degree Days (base 65°F)	1,684	1,353	1,135	625	253	56	12	26	189	538	1,074	1,509	8,454
Cooling Degree Days (base 65°F)	0	0	0	3	25	105	218	186	52	2	0	0	591
Mean Precipitation (in.)	0.55	0.48	1.09	1.76	2.63	3.48	3.30	2.84	1.88	1.80	0.78	0.36	20.95
Days With ≥ 0.1" Precipitation	2	1	3	4	6	6	5	5	4	4	2	1	43
Days With ≥ 1.0" Precipitation	0	0	0	0	1	1	1	1	0	0	0	0	4
Mean Snowfall (in.)	8.4	6.4	6.2	3.0	trace	0.0	0.0	0.0	trace	0.9	6.1	5.1	36.1
Days With ≥ 1.0" Snow Depth	27	23	16	3	0	0	0	0	0	0	10	19	98

Webster *Day County*   Elevation: 1,853 ft.   Latitude: 45° 20' N   Longitude: 97° 32' W

	JAN	FEB	MAR	APR	MAY	JUN	JUL	AUG	SEP	OCT	NOV	DEC	YEAR
Mean Maximum Temp. (°F)	19.4	26.5	38.2	55.6	69.5	78.1	83.6	81.6	71.3	57.3	37.4	24.4	53.6
Mean Temp. (°F)	9.8	17.1	28.7	44.1	57.4	66.6	71.7	69.7	59.1	46.2	28.7	15.6	42.9
Mean Minimum Temp. (°F)	0.1	7.6	19.2	32.7	45.3	55.0	59.6	57.8	46.9	35.0	19.9	6.7	32.2
Extreme Maximum Temp. (°F)	64	59	75	96	90	105	107	102	98	89	75	55	107
Extreme Minimum Temp. (°F)	-36	-34	-21	-6	19	33	39	38	17	5	-20	-32	-36
Days Maximum Temp. ≥ 90°F	0	0	0	0	0	2	7	5	2	0	0	0	16
Days Maximum Temp. ≤ 32°F	24	17	9	1	0	0	0	0	0	1	11	22	85
Days Minimum Temp. ≤ 32°F	31	28	28	15	2	0	0	0	1	13	27	31	176
Days Minimum Temp. ≤ 0°F	16	9	3	0	0	0	0	0	0	0	2	10	40
Heating Degree Days (base 65°F)	1,710	1,348	1,117	623	256	61	14	28	217	577	1,083	1,529	8,563
Cooling Degree Days (base 65°F)	0	0	0	5	31	112	223	181	45	2	0	0	599
Mean Precipitation (in.)	0.74	0.56	1.10	1.84	2.66	3.49	3.64	3.02	1.89	1.71	0.82	0.47	21.94
Days With ≥ 0.1" Precipitation	2	2	3	4	5	7	6	5	4	4	3	2	47
Days With ≥ 1.0" Precipitation	0	0	0	0	0	1	1	1	0	0	0	0	3
Mean Snowfall (in.)	na	na	na	*2.3*	trace	0.0	0.0	0.0	trace	0.6	*4.9*	na	na
Days With ≥ 1.0" Snow Depth	na	na	*8*	1	0	0	0	0	0	0	*4*	*12*	na

Wentworth 2 WNW *Lake County*   Elevation: 1,689 ft.   Latitude: 44° 01' N   Longitude: 97° 00' W

	JAN	FEB	MAR	APR	MAY	JUN	JUL	AUG	SEP	OCT	NOV	DEC	YEAR
Mean Maximum Temp. (°F)	23.9	30.6	42.1	58.7	71.3	79.9	84.4	82.2	73.7	60.6	41.1	28.2	56.4
Mean Temp. (°F)	13.9	20.7	32.2	46.6	59.1	68.2	72.7	70.7	61.5	48.8	32.0	19.0	45.5
Mean Minimum Temp. (°F)	3.8	10.8	22.2	34.5	46.9	56.4	61.0	59.1	49.2	36.9	22.9	9.8	34.5
Extreme Maximum Temp. (°F)	66	65	82	95	92	104	107	105	103	92	80	64	107
Extreme Minimum Temp. (°F)	-34	-34	-17	0	23	38	37	38	23	9	-14	-29	-34
Days Maximum Temp. ≥ 90°F	0	0	0	0	0	3	8	5	2	0	0	0	18
Days Maximum Temp. ≤ 32°F	21	14	7	1	0	0	0	0	0	0	8	19	70
Days Minimum Temp. ≤ 32°F	31	27	26	13	2	0	0	0	1	11	25	31	167
Days Minimum Temp. ≤ 0°F	13	7	2	0	0	0	0	0	0	0	1	8	31
Heating Degree Days (base 65°F)	1,581	1,244	1,010	550	214	41	8	21	164	499	983	1,419	7,734
Cooling Degree Days (base 65°F)	0	0	0	6	38	140	242	195	61	3	0	0	685
Mean Precipitation (in.)	0.49	0.66	1.65	2.33	3.14	3.96	3.22	3.10	2.57	1.83	1.29	0.53	24.77
Days With ≥ 0.1" Precipitation	2	2	4	6	6	7	6	5	5	4	3	2	52
Days With ≥ 1.0" Precipitation	0	0	0	0	1	1	1	1	1	0	0	0	5
Mean Snowfall (in.)	6.9	6.6	8.3	3.5	trace	0.0	0.0	0.0	trace	1.4	7.3	6.5	40.5
Days With ≥ 1.0" Snow Depth	25	20	12	0	0	0	0	0	0	0	1	9	19	88

Wessington Springs *Jerauld County*　Elevation: 1,646 ft.　Latitude: 44° 05' N　Longitude: 98° 34' W

	JAN	FEB	MAR	APR	MAY	JUN	JUL	AUG	SEP	OCT	NOV	DEC	YEAR
Mean Maximum Temp. (°F)	26.0	32.6	43.5	58.8	71.1	80.9	86.6	85.5	75.8	61.3	42.0	30.3	57.9
Mean Temp. (°F)	16.8	23.3	33.7	47.4	59.6	69.5	74.8	73.4	63.7	50.3	33.4	21.5	47.3
Mean Minimum Temp. (°F)	7.5	14.0	23.9	36.0	48.1	57.9	63.0	61.2	51.5	39.2	24.8	12.8	36.7
Extreme Maximum Temp. (°F)	63	70	85	98	94	109	108	109	105	93	84	68	109
Extreme Minimum Temp. (°F)	-28	-32	-13	5	25	35	43	43	27	10	-10	-27	-32
Days Maximum Temp. ≥ 90°F	0	0	0	0	0	4	11	10	3	0	0	0	28
Days Maximum Temp. ≤ 32°F	19	13	6	1	0	0	0	0	0	0	7	17	63
Days Minimum Temp. ≤ 32°F	30	26	24	11	1	0	0	0	0	7	24	30	153
Days Minimum Temp. ≤ 0°F	11	6	1	0	0	0	0	0	0	0	1	6	25
Heating Degree Days (base 65°F)	1,492	1,172	963	530	201	30	4	10	127	458	943	1,342	7,272
Cooling Degree Days (base 65°F)	0	0	0	8	46	168	308	279	95	8	0	0	912
Mean Precipitation (in.)	0.47	0.53	1.94	2.71	3.74	3.18	2.76	2.19	2.20	1.86	1.04	0.43	23.05
Days With ≥ 0.1" Precipitation	1	1	4	6	6	6	6	4	4	4	3	1	46
Days With ≥ 1.0" Precipitation	0	0	0	0	1	1	1	1	1	1	0	0	6
Mean Snowfall (in.)	5.5	5.8	7.8	4.7	trace	trace	0.0	0.0	0.0	1.7	5.5	5.5	36.5
Days With ≥ 1.0" Snow Depth	21	16	10	2	0	0	0	0	0	1	6	14	70

White Lake *Aurora County*　Elevation: 1,627 ft.　Latitude: 43° 44' N　Longitude: 98° 43' W

	JAN	FEB	MAR	APR	MAY	JUN	JUL	AUG	SEP	OCT	NOV	DEC	YEAR
Mean Maximum Temp. (°F)	27.8	34.6	45.6	60.6	72.4	82.0	88.1	86.8	77.8	63.1	43.6	31.8	59.5
Mean Temp. (°F)	17.1	24.0	34.5	47.8	59.6	69.1	74.8	73.2	63.7	50.1	33.4	21.5	47.4
Mean Minimum Temp. (°F)	6.3	13.3	23.3	34.8	46.7	56.2	61.5	59.6	49.5	37.1	23.0	11.3	35.2
Extreme Maximum Temp. (°F)	67	73	86	97	96	110	110	111	105	94	81	72	111
Extreme Minimum Temp. (°F)	-32	-32	-18	3	16	32	37	38	23	8	-11	-32	-32
Days Maximum Temp. ≥ 90°F	0	0	0	0	0	5	13	12	4	0	0	0	34
Days Maximum Temp. ≤ 32°F	18	12	5	1	0	0	0	0	0	0	6	15	57
Days Minimum Temp. ≤ 32°F	31	27	25	13	2	0	0	0	1	0	25	31	165
Days Minimum Temp. ≤ 0°F	11	6	1	0	0	0	0	0	0	0	1	7	26
Heating Degree Days (base 65°F)	1,481	1,152	939	517	202	36	5	11	128	461	943	1,341	7,216
Cooling Degree Days (base 65°F)	0	0	0	7	42	158	301	261	92	6	0	0	867
Mean Precipitation (in.)	0.27	0.55	1.51	2.58	3.54	3.24	2.85	2.21	2.12	1.63	0.91	0.36	21.77
Days With ≥ 0.1" Precipitation	1	2	3	5	6	6	5	4	3	3	2	1	41
Days With ≥ 1.0" Precipitation	0	0	0	0	1	1	1	1	0	0	0	0	4
Mean Snowfall (in.)	4.2	6.3	5.9	2.4	trace	0.0	0.0	0.0	trace	1.3	4.3	4.2	28.6
Days With ≥ 1.0" Snow Depth	17	13	7	1	0	0	0	0	0	0	4	12	54

Winner *Tripp County*　Elevation: 2,007 ft.　Latitude: 43° 22' N　Longitude: 99° 52' W

	JAN	FEB	MAR	APR	MAY	JUN	JUL	AUG	SEP	OCT	NOV	DEC	YEAR
Mean Maximum Temp. (°F)	32.6	39.6	49.3	62.1	73.7	83.6	90.1	88.6	79.6	65.5	46.2	36.3	62.3
Mean Temp. (°F)	21.9	28.4	37.2	49.0	60.6	70.5	76.3	74.8	65.3	52.4	35.9	25.9	49.9
Mean Minimum Temp. (°F)	11.1	17.2	25.2	36.0	47.5	57.3	62.5	61.0	50.9	39.1	25.6	15.4	37.4
Extreme Maximum Temp. (°F)	73	75	88	99	96	109	110	110	105	96	86	74	110
Extreme Minimum Temp. (°F)	-26	-27	-18	7	20	34	40	40	25	6	-11	-29	-29
Days Maximum Temp. ≥ 90°F	0	0	0	1	2	8	17	15	7	1	0	0	51
Days Maximum Temp. ≤ 32°F	14	9	4	0	0	0	0	0	0	0	5	11	43
Days Minimum Temp. ≤ 32°F	29	25	23	11	1	0	0	0	1	7	22	29	148
Days Minimum Temp. ≤ 0°F	9	4	1	0	0	0	0	0	0	0	1	5	20
Heating Degree Days (base 65°F)	1,332	1,026	854	484	184	29	4	8	112	398	866	1,208	6,505
Cooling Degree Days (base 65°F)	0	0	0	14	59	190	352	315	128	13	0	0	1,071
Mean Precipitation (in.)	0.53	0.62	1.78	2.73	3.79	3.36	3.28	2.18	2.10	1.92	0.95	0.54	23.78
Days With ≥ 0.1" Precipitation	2	2	5	6	7	6	7	5	4	3	3	2	52
Days With ≥ 1.0" Precipitation	0	0	0	0	1	1	1	1	0	0	0	0	4
Mean Snowfall (in.)	7.6	7.5	9.0	5.5	trace	0.0	0.0	0.0	0.2	2.2	7.8	7.0	46.8
Days With ≥ 1.0" Snow Depth	16	8	6	1	0	0	0	0	0	0	4	10	45

Wood *Mellette County*　Elevation: 2,178 ft.　Latitude: 43° 30' N　Longitude: 100° 29' W

	JAN	FEB	MAR	APR	MAY	JUN	JUL	AUG	SEP	OCT	NOV	DEC	YEAR
Mean Maximum Temp. (°F)	32.7	39.5	48.2	60.0	71.4	82.0	89.3	88.5	79.1	64.6	46.8	36.7	61.6
Mean Temp. (°F)	21.1	27.6	35.7	47.2	58.6	68.9	75.2	74.1	64.2	50.8	35.6	25.3	48.7
Mean Minimum Temp. (°F)	9.4	15.5	23.3	34.3	45.6	55.7	61.1	59.7	49.2	36.8	24.4	13.8	35.7
Extreme Maximum Temp. (°F)	76	78	87	97	99	109	110	109	106	97	88	73	110
Extreme Minimum Temp. (°F)	-28	-32	-29	7	19	35	37	36	20	3	-11	-31	-32
Days Maximum Temp. ≥ 90°F	0	0	0	0	1	7	16	15	7	1	0	0	47
Days Maximum Temp. ≤ 32°F	14	9	5	1	0	0	0	0	0	0	5	11	45
Days Minimum Temp. ≤ 32°F	30	26	25	13	2	0	0	0	1	10	24	30	161
Days Minimum Temp. ≤ 0°F	9	5	1	0	0	0	0	0	0	0	1	5	21
Heating Degree Days (base 65°F)	1,357	1,051	900	536	230	44	8	10	133	444	874	1,225	6,812
Cooling Degree Days (base 65°F)	0	0	0	8	35	147	302	287	110	8	1	0	898
Mean Precipitation (in.)	0.37	0.51	1.29	2.09	3.46	2.83	2.86	1.57	1.61	1.56	0.72	0.47	19.34
Days With ≥ 0.1" Precipitation	1	1	3	5	7	6	6	4	3	3	2	2	43
Days With ≥ 1.0" Precipitation	0	0	0	0	1	1	1	0	1	0	0	0	4
Mean Snowfall (in.)	na	6.9	8.7	5.4	0.2	0.0	0.0	0.0	0.0	1.9	6.0	6.6	na
Days With ≥ 1.0" Snow Depth	13	11	8	2	0	0	0	0	0	1	6	13	54

Yankton 2 E *Yankton County*   Elevation: 1,177 ft.   Latitude: 42° 53' N   Longitude: 97° 22' W

	JAN	FEB	MAR	APR	MAY	JUN	JUL	AUG	SEP	OCT	NOV	DEC	YEAR
Mean Maximum Temp. (°F)	27.9	34.6	45.5	60.2	72.4	82.3	87.4	85.1	76.6	63.7	45.0	33.1	59.5
Mean Temp. (°F)	17.5	23.9	34.5	47.8	59.9	70.0	74.9	72.7	63.3	50.7	34.7	23.0	47.7
Mean Minimum Temp. (°F)	7.0	13.3	23.4	35.3	47.3	57.6	62.4	60.2	49.9	37.6	24.4	12.9	35.9
Extreme Maximum Temp. (°F)	74	78	86	95	96	110	108	107	102	96	83	70	110
Extreme Minimum Temp. (°F)	-29	-25	-14	2	24	41	41	39	23	14	-13	-31	-31
Days Maximum Temp. ≥ 90°F	0	0	0	1	2	6	12	9	4	0	0	0	34
Days Maximum Temp. ≤ 32°F	18	13	6	0	0	0	0	0	0	0	5	14	56
Days Minimum Temp. ≤ 32°F	31	27	25	11	1	0	0	0	1	8	25	31	160
Days Minimum Temp. ≤ 0°F	11	6	1	0	0	0	0	0	0	0	1	5	24
Heating Degree Days (base 65°F)	1,469	1,155	939	519	201	32	5	11	140	445	903	1,295	7,114
Cooling Degree Days (base 65°F)	0	0	0	11	49	192	316	263	98	7	0	0	936
Mean Precipitation (in.)	0.42	0.47	1.79	2.52	3.95	3.67	3.27	2.72	2.25	1.88	1.25	0.51	24.70
Days With ≥ 0.1" Precipitation	1	1	4	6	7	6	5	5	5	4	3	1	48
Days With ≥ 1.0" Precipitation	0	0	0	0	1	1	1	1	0	0	0	0	4
Mean Snowfall (in.)	5.4	4.8	5.8	2.4	trace	0.0	0.0	0.0	trace	0.5	5.9	5.7	30.5
Days With ≥ 1.0" Snow Depth	19	12	8	1	0	0	0	0	0	0	5	13	58

Zeona 10 SSW *Butte County*   Elevation: 2,729 ft.   Latitude: 45° 04' N   Longitude: 103° 00' W

	JAN	FEB	MAR	APR	MAY	JUN	JUL	AUG	SEP	OCT	NOV	DEC	YEAR
Mean Maximum Temp. (°F)	27.2	34.1	43.3	56.4	67.9	78.5	86.5	86.5	75.3	60.9	43.0	32.4	57.7
Mean Temp. (°F)	15.9	22.8	31.6	43.7	55.2	65.4	71.9	70.8	59.4	46.0	30.9	20.3	44.5
Mean Minimum Temp. (°F)	4.5	11.4	19.9	30.9	42.5	52.1	57.2	55.1	43.3	31.1	18.8	8.2	31.2
Extreme Maximum Temp. (°F)	68	73	80	91	96	106	110	108	106	96	83	70	110
Extreme Minimum Temp. (°F)	-36	-43	-25	0	17	33	37	33	18	-14	-24	-40	-43
Days Maximum Temp. ≥ 90°F	0	0	0	0	1	4	12	12	4	0	0	0	33
Days Maximum Temp. ≤ 32°F	17	12	7	1	0	0	0	0	0	1	7	14	59
Days Minimum Temp. ≤ 32°F	31	28	28	17	4	0	0	0	4	17	28	31	188
Days Minimum Temp. ≤ 0°F	12	7	3	0	0	0	0	0	0	0	2	8	32
Heating Degree Days (base 65°F)	1,519	1,187	1,028	634	316	81	17	24	215	585	1,017	1,380	8,003
Cooling Degree Days (base 65°F)	0	0	0	2	20	99	244	216	54	2	0	0	637
Mean Precipitation (in.)	0.36	0.45	0.82	1.53	2.80	2.89	1.93	1.58	0.93	1.29	0.53	0.41	15.52
Days With ≥ 0.1" Precipitation	1	2	2	4	6	6	4	4	3	3	2	1	38
Days With ≥ 1.0" Precipitation	0	0	0	0	1	1	0	0	0	0	0	0	2
Mean Snowfall (in.)	5.6	5.7	7.5	5.0	0.8	0.0	0.0	0.0	trace	1.0	5.2	5.8	36.6
Days With ≥ 1.0" Snow Depth	na	7	7	3	0	0	0	0	0	0	3	8	na

Note: See Appendix D for explanation of data.

TENNESSEE

PHYSICAL FEATURES. The topography of Tennessee is quite varied, stretching from the lowlands of the Mississippi Valley to the mountain peaks in the east. The westernmost part of the State, between the bluffs overlooking the Mississippi River and the western valley of the Tennessee River, is a region of gently rolling plains sloping gradually from 200 to 250 feet in the west to about 600 feet above sea level in the hills overlooking the Tennessee River. The hilly Highland Rim, in a wide circle touching the Tennessee River Valley on the west and the Cumberland Plateau on the east, together with the enclosed Central Basin makes up the whole of Middle Tennessee. The Highland Rim ranges from about 600 feet in elevation along the Tennessee River to 1,000 feet in the east and rises 300 to 400 feet above the Central Basin. The Cumberland Plateau, with an average elevation of 2,000 feet above sea level, extends roughly northeast-southwest across the State in a belt 30 to 50 miles wide, being bounded on the west by the Highland Rim and overlooking the Great Valley of East Tennessee on the east. The Great Valley, paralleling the Plateau to the west and the Great Smoky Mountains to the east, is a funnel-shaped valley varying in width from about 30 miles in the south to about 90 miles in the north. Within the valley, which slopes from 1,500 feet in the north to 700 feet above sea level in the south, are a series of northeast-southwest ridges. Along the Tennessee-North Carolina border lie the Great Smoky Mountains, the most rugged and elevated portion of Tennessee, with numerous peaks from 4,000 to 6,000 feet above sea level.

Tennessee, except for a small area east of Chattanooga, lies entirely within the drainage of the Mississippi River system. The extreme western section of the State is drained through several relatively small rivers directly into the Mississippi River. Otherwise drainage is into either the Cumberland or Tennessee Rivers, both of which flow northward near the end of their courses to join the Ohio River along the Kentucky-Illinois border.

TEMPERATURE. Most aspects of the State's climate are related to the widely varying topography within its borders. The decrease of temperature with elevation is quite apparent, averaging 3°F. per 1,000 feet increase in elevation. Thus higher portions of the State, such as the Cumberland Plateau and the mountains of the east, have lower average temperatures than the Great Valley of East Tennessee, which they flank, and other lower parts of the State. In the Great Valley temperature increases from north to south. Across the State, the average annual temperature varies from over 62°F. in the extreme southwest to near 45°F. atop the highest peaks of the east. While most of the State can be described as having a warm, humid summer and a mild winter, this must be qualified to include variations with elevation. Thus with increasing elevations, summers become cooler and more pleasant while winters become colder and more blustery.

Length of growing season (freeze-free period) is linked to topography in a way similar to temperature, varying from 237 days at low-lying Memphis to near 130 days on the highest mountains in the east. Most of the State is included in the range.

PRECIPITATION. Since the principal source of moist air for this area is the Gulf region, there exists a gradual decrease of average precipitation from south to north. This effect is largely obscured, however, by the overruling influence of topography. Air forced to ascend cools and condenses out a portion of its moisture charge; thus average precipitation is generally greater at higher elevations. This is apparent in all parts of the State. In West Tennessee average annual precipitation ranges from 46 to 54 inches, increasing from Mississippi bottomlands to the slight hills farther east. In Middle Tennessee the variation is from a minimum of 45 inches in the Central Basin to 50 to 55 inches in the surrounding hilly Highland Rim. Over the elevated Cumberland Plateau average annual precipitation is generally from 50 to 55 inches. In contrast, average annual precipitation in the Great Valley of East Tennessee increases from near 40 inches in northern portions to over 50 inches in the south. The northern minimum, lowest for the entire State, results from the shielding influence of the Great Smoky Mountains to the southeast and the Cumberland Plateau to the northwest. The mountainous eastern border of the State is its wettest part, having average annual precipitation ranging up to about 80 inches on the higher, well-exposed peaks of the Smokies.

Over most of the State greatest precipitation occurs during the winter and early spring due to the more frequent passage of large scale storms over and near the State during those months. A secondary maximum of precipitation occurs in midsummer in response to shower and thundershower activity. This is especially pronounced in the mountains of the east where July rainfall exceeds the precipitation of any other month. Lightest precipitation, observed in the fall, is brought about by the maximum occurrence of slow moving, rain suppressing high pressure areas during that season. Although all parts of Tennessee are generally well supplied with precipitation, there occurs on the average one or more prolonged dry spells each year during summer and fall.

The most important flood season is during the winter and early spring (December through March) when the frequent migratory storms bring general rains of high intensity. During this period both widespread flooding and local flash floods can occur. During summer, heavy thunderstorm rains frequently result in local flash flooding. In the fall, while flood producing rains are rare, hurricanes on occasion cause serious floods in the east.

Average snowfall varies from four to six inches in southern and western parts of the State and in most of the Great Valley of East Tennessee, to more than 10 inches over the northern Cumberland Plateau and the mountains of the east. Over most of the State, due to relatively mild winter temperatures, a snow cover rarely persists for more than a few days.

STORMS. Severe storms are relatively infrequent in Tennessee, being east of the center of tornado activity, south of most blizzard conditions, and too far inland to be often affected by hurricanes. On the average four or five tornadoes are observed in the State each year, with greatest frequency in March, when one or two usually occur. Tornado occurrence is not evenly distributed throughout the State, being largely confined to areas west of the Cumberland Plateau. Damage from tropical storms is rare, occurring only about once every 18 years. Hailstorms are observed two or three times a year and damaging glaze storms occur in the State every five or six years. Thunderstorms are frequent and severe thunderstorms with damaging winds are experienced at scattered locations throughout the State each year during the warm season.

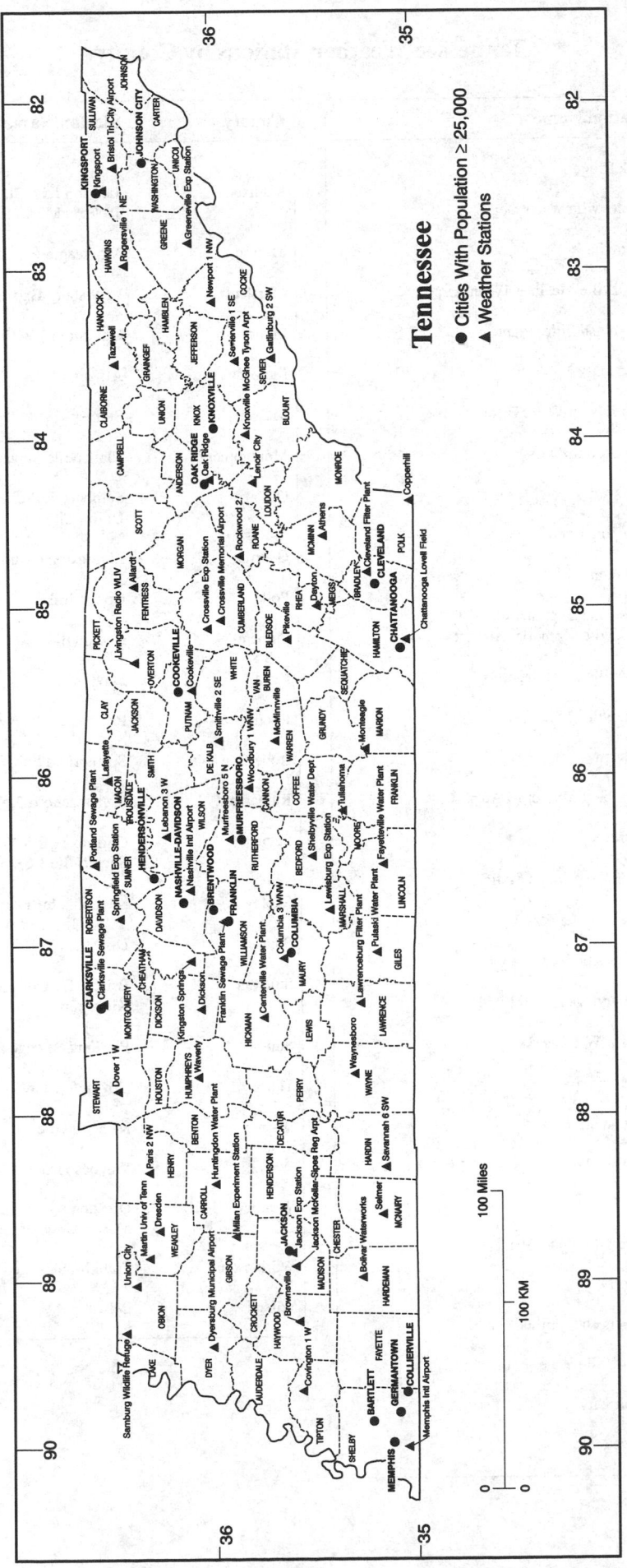

Tennessee

- Cities With Population ≥ 25,000
- ▲ Weather Stations

Tennessee Weather Stations by County

County	Station Name
Anderson	Oak Ridge
Bedford	Shelbyville Water Dept.
Bledsoe	Pikeville
Blount	Knoxville McGhee Tyson Airport
Bradley	Cleveland Filter Plant
Cannon	Woodbury 1 WNW
Carroll	Huntingdon Water Plant
Cheatham	Kingston Springs
Claiborne	Tazewell
Cocke	Newport 1 NW
Coffee	Tullahoma
Cumberland	Crossville Exp. Station Crossville Memorial Airport
Davidson	Nashville Int'l Airport
De Kalb	Smithville 2 SE
Dickson	Dickson
Dyer	Dyersburg Municipal Airport
Fentress	Allardt
Gibson	Milan Experiment Station
Giles	Pulaski Water Plant
Greene	Greeneville Exp. Station
Hamilton	Chattanooga Lovell Field
Hardeman	Bolivar Waterworks
Hardin	Savannah 6 SW
Hawkins	Rogersville 1 NE
Haywood	Brownsville
Henry	Paris 2 NW
Hickman	Centerville Water Plant
Humphreys	Waverly
Lawrence	Lawrenceburg Filter Plant
Lincoln	Fayetteville Water Plant
Loudon	Lenoir City
Macon	Lafayette

County	Station Name
Madison	Jackson Exp. Station Jackson McKellar-Sipes Reg. Arpt.
Marion	Monteagle
Marshall	Lewisburg Exp. Station
Maury	Columbia 3 WNW
McMinn	Athens
McNairy	Selmer
Montgomery	Clarksville Sewage Plant
Obion	Samburg Wildlife Refuge Union City
Overton	Livingston Radio WLIV
Polk	Copperhill
Putnam	Cookeville
Rhea	Dayton
Roane	Rockwood 2
Robertson	Springfield Exp. Station
Rutherford	Murfreesboro 5 N
Sevier	Gatlinburg 2 SW Sevierville 1 SE
Shelby	Memphis Int'l Airport
Stewart	Dover 1 W
Sullivan	Bristol Tri-City Airport Kingsport
Sumner	Portland Sewage Plant
Tipton	Covington 1 W
Warren	McMinnville
Wayne	Waynesboro
Weakley	Dresden Martin Univ. of Tennessee
Williamson	Franklin Sewage Plant
Wilson	Lebanon 3 W

Tennessee Weather Stations by City

City	Station Name	Miles
Bartlett	Memphis Int'l Airport	14
Brentwood	Franklin Sewage Plant	5
	Kingston Springs	19
	Nashville Int'l Airport	10
Chattanooga	Chattanooga Lovell Field	3
Clarksville	Clarksville Sewage Plant	1
Cleveland	Cleveland Filter Plant	5
Collierville	Memphis Int'l Airport	18
Columbia	Columbia 3 WNW	3
	Lewisburg Exp. Station	19
Cookeville	Cookeville	5
	Livingston Radio WLIV	18
Franklin	Franklin Sewage Plant	2
	Kingston Springs	19
	Nashville Int'l Airport	17
Germantown	Memphis Int'l Airport	12
Hendersonville	Lebanon 3 W	14
	Nashville Int'l Airport	13
	Springfield Exp. Station	18
Jackson	Jackson McKellar-Sipes Reg. Arpt.	6
	Jackson Exp. Station	1
	Milan Experiment Station	19
Johnson City	Bristol Tri-City Airport	10
	Kingsport	16
Kingsport	Bristol Tri-City Airport	10
	Kingsport	2
Knoxville	Knoxville McGhee Tyson Airport	11
	Oak Ridge	17
Memphis	West Memphis, AR	12
	Memphis Int'l Airport	5
Murfreesboro	Murfreesboro 5 N	4
	Woodbury 1 WNW	17
Nashville-Davidson	Franklin Sewage Plant	15
	Kingston Springs	19
	Nashville Int'l Airport	5
Oak Ridge	Lenoir City	16
	Oak Ridge	1

Note: Miles is the distance between the geographic center of the city and the weather station.

Tennessee Weather Stations by Elevation

Feet	Station Name
1,866	Crossville Memorial Airport
1,847	Monteagle
1,807	Crossville Exp. Station
1,673	Allardt
1,499	Bristol Tri-City Airport
1,453	Gatlinburg 2 SW
1,450	Copperhill
1,364	Tazewell
1,354	Rogersville 1 NE
1,318	Greeneville Exp. Station
1,282	Kingsport
1,089	Cookeville
1,033	Newport 1 NW
1,020	Tullahoma
974	Lafayette
974	Livingston Radio WLIV
961	Knoxville McGhee Tyson Airport
938	Athens
938	McMinnville
928	Sevierville 1 SE
902	Oak Ridge
889	Smithville 2 SE
875	Pikeville
869	Lawrenceburg Filter Plant
862	Dayton
859	Rockwood 2
797	Cleveland Filter Plant
793	Portland Sewage Plant
784	Lenoir City
784	Lewisburg Exp. Station
777	Dickson
757	Shelbyville Water Dept.
748	Waynesboro
748	Woodbury 1 WNW
744	Springfield Exp. Station
725	Fayetteville Water Plant
669	Chattanooga Lovell Field
659	Centerville Water Plant
652	Franklin Sewage Plant
649	Columbia 3 WNW
633	Pulaski Water Plant
577	Nashville Int'l Airport
577	Paris 2 NW
567	Waverly
547	Murfreesboro 5 N
534	Lebanon 3 W
524	Kingston Springs
472	Dover 1 W
469	Selmer
452	Bolivar Waterworks
449	Dresden
439	Huntingdon Water Plant
433	Jackson McKellar-Sipes Reg. Arpt.
423	Milan Experiment Station
419	Savannah 6 SW

Feet	Station Name
396	Jackson Exp. Station
380	Clarksville Sewage Plant
347	Union City
337	Martin Univ. of Tennessee
334	Dyersburg Municipal Airport
328	Brownsville
308	Covington 1 W
308	Samburg Wildlife Refuge
262	Memphis Int'l Airport

Bristol Tri-City Airport

The Weather Service Office is located an almost equal distance of 15 miles in the middle of a geographical triangle between the cities of Bristol, Tennessee-Virginia, Kingsport and Johnson City, Tennessee, and is more commonly known as the Tri-City Area. This location is situated in the extreme upper East Tennessee Valley. The terrain immediately surrounding the station ranges from gently rolling on the east and south to very hilly on the west and north. Mountain ranges begin about 10 miles to the southeast and about 15 miles to the west and north, with many peaks and ridges rising to 4,000 feet, and some to 6,000 feet toward the southeast.

This section does not lie directly within any of the principal storm tracks that cross the country, but comes under the influence of storm centers that pass along the Gulf Coast and then up the Atlantic Coast toward the northeast. Being quite varied, the topography has considerable influence on the weather. Moist air from the east is forced up the slopes of the mountains causing much of the moisture to be precipitated before the air mass reaches the Bristol area. The same process occurs to a lesser extent when air masses move over the smaller mountain ranges to the west and north. The maximum monthly precipitation occurs in July, usually from afternoon and early evening thunderstorms. A second maximum of precipitation occurs in the late winter months, due mainly to moist air associated with storm centers to the south or northeast. Annual precipitation amounts recorded in mountainous sections to the east and southeast are almost double what they are in the immediate vicinity.

Lowest temperatures normally occur during the early morning hours, but rise rapidly during the morning hours. Periods of cold weather are generally associated with air flow from winter storm centers near the northeast coast. Periods of unusually high temperatures occur most frequently when Gulf air associated with the Bermuda high pressure system dominates the area.

Snowfall seldom occurs before November and rarely remains on the ground for more than a few days. However, mountains to the east and south of the station are frequently well blanketed with snow for much longer periods of time.

Agricultural activies within this area include such staple crops as tobacco, beans, and hay. The last freezing temperature in spring normally occurs in late April, and the first in autumn around mid-October. The growing season of 180 days, usually coupled with ample sunshine and rainfall, permits a second planting and harvesting of some staple crops.

Bristol Tri-City Airport *Sullivan County*   Elevation: 1,499 ft.   Latitude: 36° 28' N   Longitude: 82° 24' W

	JAN	FEB	MAR	APR	MAY	JUN	JUL	AUG	SEP	OCT	NOV	DEC	YEAR
Mean Maximum Temp. (°F)	44.6	49.2	58.7	67.8	75.3	82.2	85.4	84.5	79.3	68.9	58.2	48.9	66.9
Mean Temp. (°F)	35.1	38.6	47.1	55.4	63.6	71.4	75.0	73.9	68.0	56.6	47.0	39.0	55.9
Mean Minimum Temp. (°F)	25.6	28.0	35.5	43.0	51.9	60.4	64.6	63.1	56.6	44.2	35.8	29.0	44.8
Extreme Maximum Temp. (°F)	78	80	82	89	89	96	100	101	97	85	81	77	101
Extreme Minimum Temp. (°F)	-21	-15	-2	21	30	41	48	43	34	24	10	-6	-21
Days Maximum Temp. ≥ 90°F	0	0	0	0	0	2	6	4	2	0	0	0	14
Days Maximum Temp. ≤ 32°F	5	3	0	0	0	0	0	0	0	0	0	2	10
Days Minimum Temp. ≤ 32°F	22	19	13	4	0	0	0	0	0	3	13	20	94
Days Minimum Temp. ≤ 0°F	1	0	0	0	0	0	0	0	0	0	0	0	1
Heating Degree Days (base 65°F)	920	738	548	294	103	10	0	1	41	268	534	800	4,257
Cooling Degree Days (base 65°F)	0	0	1	11	67	217	330	282	126	12	0	0	1,046
Mean Precipitation (in.)	3.50	3.43	3.84	3.31	4.27	3.82	4.12	3.02	3.07	2.41	3.04	3.44	41.27
Maximum Precipitation (in.)	9.2	7.8	9.6	5.8	9.7	7.0	9.7	7.1	7.1	5.6	5.9	6.8	54.5
Minimum Precipitation (in.)	1.4	0.3	1.3	0.2	1.3	0.8	0.7	0.5	0.5	0.1	1.1	0.2	30.7
Maximum 24-hr. Precipitation (in.)	2.3	2.5	2.9	2.5	2.3	3.1	2.8	2.4	3.1	3.6	2.3	2.7	3.6
Days With ≥ 0.1" Precipitation	8	8	9	7	9	8	8	6	6	5	7	8	89
Days With ≥ 1.0" Precipitation	1	1	1	0	1	1	1	1	1	1	0	1	10
Mean Snowfall (in.)	5.6	4.3	1.9	0.8	trace	trace	0.0	0.0	trace	trace	0.3	2.2	15.1
Maximum Snowfall (in.)	22	20	28	15	trace	0	0	0	0	1	18	13	48
Maximum 24-hr. Snowfall (in.)	9	10	13	10	trace	0	0	0	0	1	16	9	16
Days With ≥ 1.0" Snow Depth	5	3	1	0	0	0	0	0	0	0	0	1	10
Thunderstorm Days	< 1	1	2	4	7	8	9	7	3	1	< 1	< 1	42
Foggy Days	13	10	9	8	15	17	20	22	18	15	13	12	172
Predominant Sky Cover	OVR	OVR	OVR	OVR	OVR	OVR	OVR	SCT	OVR	CLR	OVR	OVR	OVR
Mean Relative Humidity 7am (%)	82	81	80	80	87	89	91	93	92	89	84	82	86
Mean Relative Humidity 4pm (%)	59	54	49	46	52	54	57	57	54	50	53	59	54
Mean Dewpoint (°F)	27	28	34	41	53	61	65	64	58	46	36	29	45
Prevailing Wind Direction	WSW	WSW	WSW	WSW	WSW	WSW	WSW	NE	NE	NE	WSW	WSW	WSW
Prevailing Wind Speed (mph)	10	12	12	12	9	8	8	5	5	5	10	10	9
Maximum Wind Gust (mph)	60	53	58	68	60	59	87	54	54	43	53	52	87

Chattanooga Lovell Field

Chattanooga is located in the southern portion of the Great Valley of Tennessee, an area of the Tennessee River between the Cumberland Mountains to the west and the Appalachian Mountains to the east. The Tennessee River approaches Chattanooga from the northeast and forms a loop southwest to west to northwest of the city at an elevation of about 630 feet above mean sea level. Most of the city lies on the south side of the river. On the north and southwest sides, the terrain rises abruptly to about 1,200 feet above the river. This complex topography results in marked variations in air drainage, wind, and minimum temperatures within short distances. In winter the Cumberland Mountains have a moderating influence on the local climate by retarding the flow of cold air from the north and west.

Chattanooga enjoys a moderate climate, characterized by cool winters and quite warm summers. Because of the sheltering effect of the mountains, winter temperatures average about 3.0 degrees warmer than at stations on the southern Cumberland Plateau section of the state. Winter weather is changeable and alternates between cool spells with an occasional cold period, but extreme cold is rare. Temperatures fall as low as the freezing point on a little over one-half of the winter days, but temperatures below zero rarely occur. Snowfall from year to year is highly variable with some winters having little or none. Heavy snowfalls have occurred, but any accumulation of snow seldom remains on the ground more than a few days. Ice storms of freezing rain or glaze are not uncommon, occasionally midwinter icing becomes severe enough to do some damage in the area.

Summer temperatures are either in the high 80s or low 90s and temperatures over 100 degrees are unusual. Most afternoon temperatures are modified by thunderstorms. Temperatures frequently plunge 10 to 15 degrees in a matter of minutes during one of these showers.

Precipitation in the Chattanooga area is well distributed throughout the year with the greater amounts in wintertime when cyclonic storms from the Gulf of Mexico reach the area with greater intensity and frequency. A second peak rainfall period generally occurs in July, principally from thunderstorms that move into the area from the south and southwest. During any year there are usually a few of these storms that can be classified as severe, with hail and damaging winds.

Based on the 1951-1980 period, the growing season averages 228 days. The average occurrence of last freezing temperature in spring is early April and the average first freezing temperature in the fall is early November.

Chattanooga Lovell Field *Hamilton County* Elevation: 669 ft. Latitude: 35° 02' N Longitude: 85° 12' W

	JAN	FEB	MAR	APR	MAY	JUN	JUL	AUG	SEP	OCT	NOV	DEC	YEAR
Mean Maximum Temp. (°F)	48.5	53.8	62.5	72.2	79.0	86.1	89.8	88.6	82.6	72.2	61.1	52.4	70.7
Mean Temp. (°F)	39.1	43.0	51.1	59.6	67.5	75.4	79.5	78.5	72.2	60.4	50.3	42.6	59.9
Mean Minimum Temp. (°F)	29.6	32.3	39.7	47.0	56.0	64.5	69.2	68.3	61.8	48.6	39.3	32.9	49.1
Extreme Maximum Temp. (°F)	75	79	86	92	94	101	105	104	101	90	82	77	105
Extreme Minimum Temp. (°F)	-10	2	9	25	34	41	51	53	40	26	13	-2	-10
Days Maximum Temp. ≥ 90°F	0	0	0	0	1	9	17	14	5	0	0	0	46
Days Maximum Temp. ≤ 32°F	3	1	0	0	0	0	0	0	0	0	0	1	5
Days Minimum Temp. ≤ 32°F	19	15	7	1	0	0	0	0	0	1	9	16	68
Days Minimum Temp. ≤ 0°F	0	0	0	0	0	0	0	0	0	0	0	0	0
Heating Degree Days (base 65°F)	797	615	429	190	46	2	0	0	15	173	438	688	3,393
Cooling Degree Days (base 65°F)	0	0	6	35	141	336	479	437	232	40	2	1	1,709
Mean Precipitation (in.)	5.31	4.83	6.17	4.19	4.33	3.99	4.74	3.53	4.29	3.42	4.71	4.89	54.40
Maximum Precipitation (in.)	11.0	9.7	16.3	11.9	9.2	9.4	11.9	7.5	14.2	9.9	13.6	13.7	73.7
Minimum Precipitation (in.)	0.9	0.7	1.2	1.0	1.1	0.6	0.2	0.6	0.5	0.2	0.9	0.9	34.9
Maximum 24-hr. Precipitation (in.)	3.7	3.3	6.2	3.4	3.4	4.8	4.6	3.0	6.4	3.5	4.5	4.6	6.4
Days With ≥ 0.1" Precipitation	8	7	9	7	8	7	7	6	6	5	7	8	85
Days With ≥ 1.0" Precipitation	2	2	2	1	1	1	1	1	1	1	2	1	16
Mean Snowfall (in.)	1.9	1.1	1.2	0.2	0.0	trace	0.0	0.0	0.0	trace	trace	0.3	4.7
Maximum Snowfall (in.)	10	10	20	3	0	0	0	0	0	trace	3	9	23
Maximum 24-hr. Snowfall (in.)	10	9	19	3	0	0	0	0	0	trace	3	6	19
Days With ≥ 1.0" Snow Depth	2	1	0	0	0	0	0	0	0	0	0	0	3
Thunderstorm Days	1	2	4	5	7	9	11	9	4	1	1	1	55
Foggy Days	13	11	11	8	13	14	16	19	17	16	14	13	165
Predominant Sky Cover	OVR	OVR	OVR	OVR	OVR	SCT	SCT	SCT	OVR	CLR	OVR	OVR	OVR
Mean Relative Humidity 7am (%)	82	82	82	83	89	89	90	92	92	91	86	83	87
Mean Relative Humidity 4pm (%)	58	52	48	44	51	53	55	55	55	50	52	57	53
Mean Dewpoint (°F)	30	32	38	46	57	65	68	68	62	50	39	33	49
Prevailing Wind Direction	S	S	S	S	S	S	S	S	S	S	S	S	S
Prevailing Wind Speed (mph)	8	9	9	9	8	7	6	6	7	7	8	8	8
Maximum Wind Gust (mph)	60	53	60	53	54	68	67	75	52	39	47	45	75

Knoxville McGhee Tyson Airport

Knoxville is located in a broad valley between the Cumberland Mountains, which lie northwest of the city, and the Great Smoky Mountains, which lie southeast of the city. These two mountain ranges exercise a marked influence upon the climate of the valley. The Cumberland Mountains, to the northwest, serve to retard and weaken the force of the cold winter air which frequently penetrates far south of the latitude of Knoxville over the plains areas to the west of the mountains.

The mountains also serve to modify the hot summer winds which are common to the plains to the west. In addition, they serve as a fixed incline plane which lifts the warm, moist air flowing northward from the Gulf of Mexico and thereby increases the frequency of afternoon thunderstorms. Relief from extremely high temperatures which such thunderstorms produce serves to reduce the number of extremely warm days in the valley.

July is usually the warmest month of the year. The coldest weather usually occurs during the month of January. Sudden great temperature changes occur infrequently. This again is due mainly to the retarding effect of the mountains. Summer nights are nearly always comfortable.

Rainfall is ample for agricultural purposes and is favorably distributed during the year for most crops. Precipitation is greatest in the wintertime. Another peak period occurs during the late spring and summer months. The period of lowest rainfall occurs during the fall. A cumulative total of approximately 12 inches of snow falls annually. However, this usually comes in amounts of less than 4 inches at one time. It is unusual for snow to remain on the ground in measurable amounts longer than one week.

The topography also has a pronounced effect upon the prevailing wind direction. Daytime winds usually have a southwesterly component, while nighttime winds usually move from the northeast. The winds are relatively light and tornadoes are extremely rare.

Knoxville McGhee Tyson Airport *Blount County*   Elevation: 961 ft.   Latitude: 35° 49' N   Longitude: 83° 59' W

	JAN	FEB	MAR	APR	MAY	JUN	JUL	AUG	SEP	OCT	NOV	DEC	YEAR
Mean Maximum Temp. (°F)	46.6	52.1	61.1	70.4	77.5	84.7	88.0	87.2	81.6	70.7	59.8	50.8	69.2
Mean Temp. (°F)	37.7	41.9	50.1	58.6	66.6	74.3	78.2	77.3	71.3	59.3	49.4	41.5	58.8
Mean Minimum Temp. (°F)	28.7	31.6	39.0	46.7	55.5	63.8	68.4	67.3	60.9	47.9	38.9	32.2	48.4
Extreme Maximum Temp. (°F)	74	83	85	91	92	102	102	101	97	89	83	80	102
Extreme Minimum Temp. (°F)	-24	-8	1	22	32	44	49	53	37	25	13	-6	-24
Days Maximum Temp. ≥ 90°F	0	0	0	0	0	5	13	10	3	0	0	0	31
Days Maximum Temp. ≤ 32°F	3	1	0	0	0	0	0	0	0	0	0	1	5
Days Minimum Temp. ≤ 32°F	20	15	8	2	0	0	0	0	0	1	8	17	71
Days Minimum Temp. ≤ 0°F	0	0	0	0	0	0	0	0	0	0	0	0	0
Heating Degree Days (base 65°F)	841	647	460	215	61	3	0	0	20	200	464	722	3,633
Cooling Degree Days (base 65°F)	0	0	5	26	118	296	432	395	205	32	2	1	1,512
Mean Precipitation (in.)	4.50	3.99	5.13	4.00	4.51	4.07	4.61	3.00	3.00	2.83	3.88	4.56	48.08
Maximum Precipitation (in.)	11.7	8.8	11.8	7.9	11.0	8.2	10.1	6.7	9.2	6.7	10.4	11.6	63.3
Minimum Precipitation (in.)	0.9	0.3	1.7	0.4	0.7	0.5	0.3	0.8	0.4	trace	1.2	0.4	32.5
Maximum 24-hr. Precipitation (in.)	3.8	2.7	5.8	3.2	3.4	2.9	4.3	3.3	3.3	2.4	4.0	4.7	5.8
Days With ≥ 0.1" Precipitation	8	7	9	7	8	7	7	6	5	5	7	8	84
Days With ≥ 1.0" Precipitation	1	1	1	1	1	1	1	1	1	1	1	1	12
Mean Snowfall (in.)	3.9	3.0	1.6	0.7	trace	trace	0.0	trace	0.0	trace	trace	0.8	10.0
Maximum Snowfall (in.)	15	23	20	11	0	0	0	0	0	trace	18	13	54
Maximum 24-hr. Snowfall (in.)	10	18	11	11	0	0	0	0	0	trace	16	7	18
Days With ≥ 1.0" Snow Depth	3	2	0	0	0	0	0	0	0	0	0	0	5
Thunderstorm Days	1	1	3	4	7	8	10	7	3	1	1	1	47
Foggy Days	14	12	11	9	14	15	17	20	18	17	14	14	175
Predominant Sky Cover	OVR	OVR	OVR	OVR	OVR	OVR	SCT	SCT	OVR	CLR	OVR	OVR	OVR
Mean Relative Humidity 7am (%)	81	80	80	80	85	87	89	91	91	89	84	83	85
Mean Relative Humidity 4pm (%)	60	54	50	47	52	55	56	56	54	51	54	60	54
Mean Dewpoint (°F)	29	31	37	45	56	64	67	67	61	49	38	32	48
Prevailing Wind Direction	NE	NE	SW	SW	SW	SW	SW	NE	NE	NE	NE	NE	NE
Prevailing Wind Speed (mph)	7	8	12	12	9	9	8	7	7	7	7	7	8
Maximum Wind Gust (mph)	60	60	56	59	53	58	69	86	43	51	64	59	86

Memphis Int'l Airport

Topography varies from the level alluvial area in east-central Arkansas to the slightly rolling area in northwestern Mississippi and southwestern Tennessee.

Agricultural interests are varied, with major crops being cotton, corn, hay, soybeans, peaches, apples, and a considerable number of vegetables. The climate is quite favorable for dairy interests, and for the raising of cattle and hogs.

The growing season is about 230 days in length. The average date for the last occurrence of temperatures as low as 32 degrees is late March. The average date of the first temperature of 32 degrees or below is early November.

Precipitation of nearly 50 inches per year is fairly well distributed. Crops and pastures receive, on the average, an adequate supply of moisture during the growing season, with lesser amounts during the fall harvesting period.

Sunshine averages slightly over 70 percent of the possible amount during the growing season. Relative humidity averages about 70 percent for the year.

Memphis, although not in the normal paths of storms coming from the Gulf or from western Canada, is affected by both, and thereby has comparatively frequent changes in weather. Extremely high or low temperatures, however, are relatively rare.

Memphis Int'l Airport *Shelby County*   Elevation: 262 ft.   Latitude: 35° 03' N   Longitude: 90° 00' W

	JAN	FEB	MAR	APR	MAY	JUN	JUL	AUG	SEP	OCT	NOV	DEC	YEAR
Mean Maximum Temp. (°F)	48.4	54.2	63.3	72.9	80.7	88.5	91.6	90.3	84.6	74.4	61.9	52.7	72.0
Mean Temp. (°F)	40.1	44.9	53.5	62.7	71.2	79.2	82.8	81.3	74.9	63.8	52.6	44.2	62.6
Mean Minimum Temp. (°F)	31.6	35.6	43.8	52.5	61.6	69.9	73.9	72.1	65.2	53.1	43.3	35.6	53.2
Extreme Maximum Temp. (°F)	78	80	85	94	99	101	108	102	102	93	84	81	108
Extreme Minimum Temp. (°F)	-4	4	16	29	40	50	57	53	42	30	15	-4	-4
Days Maximum Temp. ≥ 90°F	0	0	0	0	3	14	22	19	9	0	0	0	67
Days Maximum Temp. ≤ 32°F	3	1	0	0	0	0	0	0	0	0	0	1	5
Days Minimum Temp. ≤ 32°F	17	11	4	0	0	0	0	0	0	0	4	12	48
Days Minimum Temp. ≤ 0°F	0	0	0	0	0	0	0	0	0	0	0	0	0
Heating Degree Days (base 65°F)	767	561	364	138	20	0	0	0	12	118	377	640	2,997
Cooling Degree Days (base 65°F)	1	2	16	73	224	443	571	526	319	88	12	4	2,279
Mean Precipitation (in.)	4.24	4.26	5.61	5.87	5.14	4.36	4.31	3.04	3.40	3.50	5.62	5.72	55.07
Maximum Precipitation (in.)	15.9	10.5	12.1	17.1	11.6	7.5	8.8	9.6	7.6	7.8	10.5	13.8	76.8
Minimum Precipitation (in.)	0.6	1.1	1.5	1.4	0.8	trace	0.4	0.4	0.2	trace	0.5	1.0	38.5
Maximum 24-hr. Precipitation (in.)	3.9	4.1	4.9	4.9	4.1	4.1	3.5	3.2	3.6	3.5	5.6	5.4	5.6
Days With ≥ 0.1" Precipitation	7	6	8	7	7	6	6	5	5	5	7	7	76
Days With ≥ 1.0" Precipitation	1	1	2	2	2	1	1	1	1	1	2	2	17
Mean Snowfall (in.)	2.2	1.3	0.3	trace	trace	trace	0.0	0.0	0.0	trace	0.1	0.1	4.0
Maximum Snowfall (in.)	12	8	17	trace	0	0	0	0	0	trace	2	14	22
Maximum 24-hr. Snowfall (in.)	8	5	9	trace	0	0	0	0	0	trace	1	14	14
Days With ≥ 1.0" Snow Depth	2	1	0	0	0	0	0	0	0	0	0	0	3
Thunderstorm Days	2	2	4	6	7	8	8	6	3	2	2	2	52
Foggy Days	13	10	9	7	8	6	7	9	10	9	10	11	109
Predominant Sky Cover	OVR	OVR	OVR	OVR	OVR	SCT	SCT	SCT	CLR	CLR	OVR	OVR	OVR
Mean Relative Humidity 7am (%)	79	78	75	74	77	77	80	81	82	81	79	78	78
Mean Relative Humidity 4pm (%)	60	56	52	49	53	53	55	54	53	49	54	60	54
Mean Dewpoint (°F)	30	34	40	48	59	66	70	69	62	50	40	33	50
Prevailing Wind Direction	S	S	S	S	S	S	S	S	NNE	S	S	S	S
Prevailing Wind Speed (mph)	12	10	12	12	9	8	8	7	9	8	10	10	9
Maximum Wind Gust (mph)	58	53	61	81	66	71	60	55	43	59	55	64	81

Nashville Int'l Airport

The city of Nashville is located on the Cumberland River, in the northwestern corner of the Central Basin of middle Tennessee near the escarpment of the Highland Rim. The Rim, as it is called, rises to the height of 300 to 400 feet above the mean elevation of the basin, forming an amphitheater about the city from the southwest to the southeast, with the south being more or less open but undulating.

Temperatures are moderate, with great extremes of either heat or cold rarely occurring, yet there are changes of sufficient amplitude and frequency to give variety.

Based on the 1951-1980 period, the average first occurrence of 32 degrees Fahrenheit in the fall is October 29 and the average last occurrence in the spring is April 5.

The average relative humidity is moderate as compared with the general conditions east of the Mississippi River and south of the Ohio.

Nashville is in the zone of moderate frequency of thunderstorms. The thunderstorm season usually begins in the latter part of March and continues through September.

Nashville Int'l Airport *Davidson County*   Elevation: 577 ft.   Latitude: 36° 07' N   Longitude: 86° 41' W

	JAN	FEB	MAR	APR	MAY	JUN	JUL	AUG	SEP	OCT	NOV	DEC	YEAR
Mean Maximum Temp. (°F)	46.4	51.7	61.2	70.9	78.5	86.1	89.6	88.7	82.6	72.0	60.1	50.9	69.9
Mean Temp. (°F)	37.2	41.5	50.3	59.1	67.6	75.6	79.6	78.5	72.1	60.4	49.9	41.6	59.4
Mean Minimum Temp. (°F)	27.9	31.1	39.4	47.3	56.6	65.1	69.6	68.2	61.4	48.8	39.7	32.2	48.9
Extreme Maximum Temp. (°F)	78	83	86	91	93	103	105	103	102	91	84	79	105
Extreme Minimum Temp. (°F)	-17	-5	2	23	34	43	54	49	36	26	9	-10	-17
Days Maximum Temp. ≥ 90°F	0	0	0	0	1	9	17	13	6	0	0	0	46
Days Maximum Temp. ≤ 32°F	5	2	0	0	0	0	0	0	0	0	0	2	9
Days Minimum Temp. ≤ 32°F	21	16	9	2	0	0	0	0	0	1	8	17	74
Days Minimum Temp. ≤ 0°F	1	0	0	0	0	0	0	0	0	0	0	0	1
Heating Degree Days (base 65°F)	856	659	458	210	54	1	0	0	22	183	452	721	3,616
Cooling Degree Days (base 65°F)	0	1	10	38	145	339	481	435	234	48	5	1	1,737
Mean Precipitation (in.)	3.89	3.61	4.89	3.95	5.01	4.25	3.81	3.32	3.62	2.96	4.31	4.54	48.16
Maximum Precipitation (in.)	13.9	10.3	12.3	8.4	11.0	9.4	7.8	8.0	11.4	6.1	7.8	13.6	70.1
Minimum Precipitation (in.)	0.2	0.6	1.2	0.5	0.8	0.4	0.7	0.7	0.3	trace	0.5	1.0	30.2
Maximum 24-hr. Precipitation (in.)	3.8	4.7	4.7	2.4	3.9	3.4	3.3	4.1	6.6	2.9	3.2	4.5	6.6
Days With ≥ 0.1" Precipitation	7	7	9	7	7	7	7	6	5	5	7	8	82
Days With ≥ 1.0" Precipitation	1	1	1	1	2	1	1	1	1	1	1	1	13
Mean Snowfall (in.)	3.7	3.4	1.0	trace	0.0	trace	0.0	trace	0.0	trace	trace	0.5	8.6
Maximum Snowfall (in.)	19	19	16	1	0	0	0	0	0	trace	9	13	39
Maximum 24-hr. Snowfall (in.)	8	7	8	1	0	0	0	0	0	trace	7	6	8
Days With ≥ 1.0" Snow Depth	3	3	0	0	0	0	0	0	0	0	0	0	6
Thunderstorm Days	1	2	4	5	7	8	10	8	4	2	2	1	54
Foggy Days	14	13	11	9	12	11	14	16	15	14	12	13	154
Predominant Sky Cover	OVR	OVR	OVR	OVR	OVR	SCT	SCT	SCT	CLR	CLR	OVR	OVR	OVR
Mean Relative Humidity 6am (%)	81	81	80	81	86	86	88	90	90	87	82	82	85
Mean Relative Humidity 3pm (%)	61	56	51	48	52	53	54	53	52	49	55	60	54
Mean Dewpoint (°F)	29	31	37	46	57	64	68	67	61	49	39	32	48
Prevailing Wind Direction	S	S	S	S	S	S	S	S	S	S	S	S	S
Prevailing Wind Speed (mph)	10	9	10	9	8	7	7	7	7	8	9	9	8
Maximum Wind Gust (mph)	66	53	56	94	55	59	58	70	51	48	60	54	94

Oak Ridge

Oak Ridge is located in a broad valley between the Cumberland Mountains, which lie to the northwest of the area, and the Great Smoky Mountains, to the southeast. These mountain ranges are oriented northeast-southwest and the valley between is corrugated by broken ridges 300 to 500 feet high and oriented parallel to the main valley. During periods of light winds, daytime winds are usually southwesterly, nighttime winds northeasterly. Wind velocities are somewhat decreased by the ridges. Tornadoes rarely occur in the valley between the Cumberlands and the Great Smokies. In winter the Cumberland Mountains have a moderating influence on the local climate by retarding the flow of cold air from the north and west.

Temperatures of 100 degrees or more have occurred during less than one-half of the years of the period of record, and temperatures of zero or below are rare. Summer nights are seldom oppressively hot and humid.

Precipitation is more than adequate for agriculture and is normally well distributed through the year for agricultural purposes.

Occasionally there is sufficient dry weather in late summer or early fall to cause small damage to crops and pastures and to create conditions favorable for destructive forest fires. Winter and early spring are the seasons of heaviest precipitation. A few of the larger monthly precipitation amounts recorded have occurred in the normally drier fall months.

Light snow usually occurs in all of the months from November through March, but the total monthly snowfall is often only a trace. Snowfalls sufficiently heavy to interfere with traffic and outdoor activities occur infrequently.

Based on the 1951-1980 period, the average first occurrence of 32 degrees Fahrenheit in the fall is October 27 and the average last occurrence in the spring is April 11.

Oak Ridge *Anderson County*   Elevation: 902 ft.   Latitude: 36° 00' N   Longitude: 84° 15' W

	JAN	FEB	MAR	APR	MAY	JUN	JUL	AUG	SEP	OCT	NOV	DEC	YEAR
Mean Maximum Temp. (°F)	45.4	51.2	60.8	70.5	77.8	84.8	88.2	87.1	81.3	70.9	59.0	49.3	68.9
Mean Temp. (°F)	36.1	40.2	48.7	57.2	65.5	73.2	77.3	76.2	70.1	58.4	47.7	39.6	57.5
Mean Minimum Temp. (°F)	26.7	29.2	36.6	43.7	53.2	61.6	66.3	65.2	59.0	45.9	36.4	29.9	46.2
Extreme Maximum Temp. (°F)	72	79	86	92	93	101	103	103	101	89	81	78	103
Extreme Minimum Temp. (°F)	-17	-13	1	20	30	39	49	50	36	24	10	-7	-17
Days Maximum Temp. ≥ 90°F	0	0	0	0	1	6	14	10	4	0	0	0	35
Days Maximum Temp. ≤ 32°F	4	1	0	0	0	0	0	0	0	0	0	2	7
Days Minimum Temp. ≤ 32°F	22	18	12	3	0	0	0	0	0	2	12	20	89
Days Minimum Temp. ≤ 0°F	0	0	0	0	0	0	0	0	0	0	0	0	0
Heating Degree Days (base 65°F)	889	695	501	249	78	5	0	0	28	221	512	780	3,958
Cooling Degree Days (base 65°F)	0	0	4	22	113	279	415	371	191	28	1	0	1,424
Mean Precipitation (in.)	4.93	4.48	5.68	4.40	4.92	4.60	5.11	3.62	3.74	3.22	4.77	5.38	54.85
Maximum Precipitation (in.)	9.6	9.8	12.2	9.8	10.7	11.1	19.3	9.1	8.9	6.9	10.8	12.6	76.3
Minimum Precipitation (in.)	0.9	0.7	2.2	0.9	0.8	0.5	1.2	1.3	1.4	trace	1.8	0.7	38.8
Maximum 24-hr. Precipitation (in.)	3.1	2.9	3.8	5.4	4.4	3.5	4.7	4.9	3.3	2.2	5.0	4.9	5.4
Days With ≥ 0.1" Precipitation	8	8	9	7	8	8	8	7	6	6	7	9	91
Days With ≥ 1.0" Precipitation	1	1	2	1	1	1	1	1	1	1	1	2	14
Mean Snowfall (in.)	3.4	3.1	1.3	0.2	trace	trace	trace	trace	0.0	trace	trace	1.2	9.2
Maximum Snowfall (in.)	10	17	12	6	0	0	0	0	0	trace	1	15	25
Maximum 24-hr. Snowfall (in.)	7	5	7	3	0	0	0	0	0	trace	1	8	8
Days With ≥ 1.0" Snow Depth	3	2	0	0	0	0	0	0	0	0	0	0	5
Thunderstorm Days	0	1	0	0	0	0	0	0	0	0	0	0	1
Foggy Days	1	2	0	0	0	0	0	0	0	0	2	0	5
Predominant Sky Cover	na	na	na	na	na	na	na	na	na	na	na	na	na
Mean Relative Humidity 7am (%)	na	na	na	na	na	na	na	na	na	na	na	na	na
Mean Relative Humidity 4pm (%)	na	na	na	na	na	na	na	na	na	na	na	na	na
Mean Dewpoint (°F)	na	na	na	na	na	na	na	na	na	na	na	na	na
Prevailing Wind Direction	na	na	na	na	na	na	na	na	na	na	na	na	na
Prevailing Wind Speed (mph)	na	na	na	na	na	na	na	na	na	na	na	na	na
Maximum Wind Gust (mph)	na	na	na	na	na	na	na	na	na	na	na	na	na

Allardt *Fentress County*   Elevation: 1,673 ft.   Latitude: 36° 23' N   Longitude: 84° 53' W

	JAN	FEB	MAR	APR	MAY	JUN	JUL	AUG	SEP	OCT	NOV	DEC	YEAR
Mean Maximum Temp. (°F)	44.2	48.6	57.5	67.3	73.8	80.7	83.7	82.9	77.4	67.6	56.7	47.9	65.7
Mean Temp. (°F)	35.1	38.6	46.8	55.6	62.8	70.3	73.8	72.7	67.1	56.5	46.8	38.8	55.4
Mean Minimum Temp. (°F)	26.0	28.7	36.0	43.8	51.7	59.8	63.9	62.5	56.7	45.2	36.9	29.7	45.1
Extreme Maximum Temp. (°F)	70	76	81	87	88	98	103	100	94	85	79	73	103
Extreme Minimum Temp. (°F)	-27	-11	-4	19	31	40	47	42	33	19	4	-12	-27
Days Maximum Temp. ≥ 90°F	0	0	0	0	0	1	3	2	1	0	0	0	7
Days Maximum Temp. ≤ 32°F	5	3	1	0	0	0	0	0	0	0	0	3	12
Days Minimum Temp. ≤ 32°F	22	18	13	4	0	0	0	0	0	3	11	19	90
Days Minimum Temp. ≤ 0°F	1	1	0	0	0	0	0	0	0	0	0	0	2
Heating Degree Days (base 65°F)	920	738	560	291	116	13	1	2	53	271	538	805	4,308
Cooling Degree Days (base 65°F)	0	0	2	14	56	184	294	251	120	14	1	0	936
Mean Precipitation (in.)	4.90	4.19	5.43	3.95	5.55	5.15	5.14	4.67	3.65	3.30	4.63	4.89	55.45
Days With ≥ 0.1" Precipitation	9	8	9	8	9	8	8	7	6	6	8	9	95
Days With ≥ 1.0" Precipitation	1	1	1	1	2	2	1	1	1	1	1	1	14
Mean Snowfall (in.)	5.0	5.4	2.7	0.3	0.0	0.0	0.0	0.0	0.0	trace	0.4	2.0	15.8
Days With ≥ 1.0" Snow Depth	6	5	1	0	0	0	0	0	0	0	0	2	14

Athens *McMinn County*   Elevation: 938 ft.   Latitude: 35° 26' N   Longitude: 84° 35' W

	JAN	FEB	MAR	APR	MAY	JUN	JUL	AUG	SEP	OCT	NOV	DEC	YEAR
Mean Maximum Temp. (°F)	46.8	51.9	61.0	70.6	77.9	85.2	88.6	87.6	81.9	71.4	60.3	51.0	69.5
Mean Temp. (°F)	36.4	40.3	48.6	57.1	65.3	73.3	77.3	76.2	70.1	58.2	48.4	40.3	57.6
Mean Minimum Temp. (°F)	26.0	28.5	36.2	43.6	52.6	61.3	65.9	64.8	58.3	44.9	36.4	29.6	45.7
Extreme Maximum Temp. (°F)	73	79	85	90	94	101	105	102	99	89	82	76	105
Extreme Minimum Temp. (°F)	-16	-4	2	22	29	39	49	52	37	24	9	-3	-16
Days Maximum Temp. ≥ 90°F	0	0	0	0	1	6	15	11	4	0	0	0	37
Days Maximum Temp. ≤ 32°F	3	1	0	0	0	0	0	0	0	0	0	1	5
Days Minimum Temp. ≤ 32°F	23	19	12	4	0	0	0	0	0	3	12	20	93
Days Minimum Temp. ≤ 0°F	1	0	0	0	0	0	0	0	0	0	0	0	1
Heating Degree Days (base 65°F)	879	693	505	252	80	6	0	0	27	228	493	758	3,921
Cooling Degree Days (base 65°F)	0	0	4	22	99	269	399	358	184	26	1	1	1,363
Mean Precipitation (in.)	6.02	4.92	6.32	4.84	4.82	4.16	4.70	3.69	4.83	3.80	4.85	5.43	58.38
Days With ≥ 0.1" Precipitation	9	8	9	8	8	7	8	6	7	6	7	8	91
Days With ≥ 1.0" Precipitation	2	2	2	1	1	1	1	1	2	1	1	2	17
Mean Snowfall (in.)	2.8	2.2	0.9	0.4	0.0	0.0	0.0	0.0	0.0	0.0	trace	0.3	6.6
Days With ≥ 1.0" Snow Depth	2	1	0	0	0	0	0	0	0	0	0	0	3

Bolivar Waterworks *Hardeman County*   Elevation: 452 ft.   Latitude: 35° 16' N   Longitude: 88° 59' W

	JAN	FEB	MAR	APR	MAY	JUN	JUL	AUG	SEP	OCT	NOV	DEC	YEAR
Mean Maximum Temp. (°F)	47.3	52.7	61.9	71.6	78.8	86.3	89.9	88.9	83.1	73.1	61.4	51.6	70.5
Mean Temp. (°F)	37.5	42.0	50.7	59.7	67.7	75.7	79.5	77.9	71.5	60.1	50.0	41.7	59.5
Mean Minimum Temp. (°F)	27.7	31.2	39.4	47.9	56.5	65.0	69.0	66.8	59.7	47.0	38.7	31.7	48.4
Extreme Maximum Temp. (°F)	79	83	86	92	95	101	105	101	101	92	85	77	105
Extreme Minimum Temp. (°F)	-11	1	11	26	34	44	52	47	37	26	11	-7	-11
Days Maximum Temp. ≥ 90°F	0	0	0	0	1	10	18	15	6	0	0	0	50
Days Maximum Temp. ≤ 32°F	4	2	0	0	0	0	0	0	0	0	0	2	8
Days Minimum Temp. ≤ 32°F	22	16	9	2	0	0	0	0	0	2	10	17	78
Days Minimum Temp. ≤ 0°F	0	0	0	0	0	0	0	0	0	0	0	0	0
Heating Degree Days (base 65°F)	846	645	446	197	51	2	0	0	28	193	448	717	3,573
Cooling Degree Days (base 65°F)	0	1	10	44	147	342	470	423	231	48	6	2	1,724
Mean Precipitation (in.)	4.29	4.31	5.80	5.25	5.63	4.46	4.07	3.18	4.16	3.55	5.12	5.51	55.33
Days With ≥ 0.1" Precipitation	7	7	8	7	8	6	6	5	6	5	6	8	79
Days With ≥ 1.0" Precipitation	1	1	2	1	2	1	1	1	1	1	1	2	16
Mean Snowfall (in.)	0.9	1.0	trace	trace	0.0	0.0	0.0	0.0	0.0	trace	trace	trace	1.9
Days With ≥ 1.0" Snow Depth	0	0	0	0	0	0	0	0	0	0	0	0	0

Brownsville *Haywood County*   Elevation: 328 ft.   Latitude: 35° 35' N   Longitude: 89° 15' W

	JAN	FEB	MAR	APR	MAY	JUN	JUL	AUG	SEP	OCT	NOV	DEC	YEAR
Mean Maximum Temp. (°F)	46.1	52.0	61.2	71.6	79.3	87.0	90.4	89.3	83.6	73.3	60.8	50.9	70.5
Mean Temp. (°F)	37.2	42.1	51.0	60.7	69.0	77.0	80.5	78.8	72.3	60.9	50.5	41.7	60.2
Mean Minimum Temp. (°F)	28.2	32.2	40.8	49.6	58.7	66.9	70.6	68.4	61.0	48.5	40.3	32.4	49.8
Extreme Maximum Temp. (°F)	79	81	87	92	95	100	105	101	100	92	86	80	105
Extreme Minimum Temp. (°F)	-10	1	12	27	38	48	52	49	38	27	12	-8	-10
Days Maximum Temp. ≥ 90°F	0	0	0	0	2	12	19	16	7	1	0	0	57
Days Maximum Temp. ≤ 32°F	5	2	0	0	0	0	0	0	0	0	0	2	9
Days Minimum Temp. ≤ 32°F	21	15	7	1	0	0	0	0	0	1	8	16	69
Days Minimum Temp. ≤ 0°F	0	0	0	0	0	0	0	0	0	0	0	0	0
Heating Degree Days (base 65°F)	856	641	437	181	38	1	0	0	24	175	435	717	3,505
Cooling Degree Days (base 65°F)	0	1	10	52	170	371	498	442	243	53	7	1	1,848
Mean Precipitation (in.)	4.23	4.31	5.39	4.97	5.62	4.37	4.34	2.92	3.59	3.25	4.84	5.81	53.64
Days With ≥ 0.1" Precipitation	7	7	8	7	8	6	6	4	5	5	6	7	77
Days With ≥ 1.0" Precipitation	1	1	2	1	2	1	1	1	1	1	1	2	15
Mean Snowfall (in.)	2.8	2.0	0.4	trace	0.0	0.0	0.0	0.0	0.0	trace	trace	0.2	5.4
Days With ≥ 1.0" Snow Depth	4	2	0	0	0	0	0	0	0	0	0	0	6

Centerville Water Plant *Hickman County*   Elevation: 659 ft.   Latitude: 35° 45' N   Longitude: 87° 26' W

	JAN	FEB	MAR	APR	MAY	JUN	JUL	AUG	SEP	OCT	NOV	DEC	YEAR
Mean Maximum Temp. (°F)	48.5	55.1	64.6	74.6	80.4	86.3	89.7	89.1	83.6	73.6	61.7	52.4	71.6
Mean Temp. (°F)	36.7	41.5	50.0	58.7	66.2	73.3	77.1	76.0	70.0	58.6	48.4	40.8	58.1
Mean Minimum Temp. (°F)	24.9	27.7	35.4	42.8	51.9	60.2	64.5	62.9	56.3	43.6	35.1	29.1	44.5
Extreme Maximum Temp. (°F)	79	84	87	91	93	100	103	101	101	90	89	76	103
Extreme Minimum Temp. (°F)	-26	-17	0	18	27	35	44	42	27	18	1	-10	-26
Days Maximum Temp. ≥ 90°F	0	0	0	0	1	9	17	15	6	0	0	0	48
Days Maximum Temp. ≤ 32°F	3	1	0	0	0	0	0	0	0	0	0	2	6
Days Minimum Temp. ≤ 32°F	22	19	13	6	1	0	0	0	0	0	0	0	98
Days Minimum Temp. ≤ 0°F	1	0	0	0	0	0	0	0	0	5	13	19	1
Heating Degree Days (base 65°F)	869	658	464	212	65	5	0	1	33	221	494	745	3,767
Cooling Degree Days (base 65°F)	0	0	7	32	115	273	402	363	187	32	3	1	1,415
Mean Precipitation (in.)	4.23	4.32	5.75	4.73	5.57	4.35	4.65	2.98	3.97	3.45	5.05	5.47	54.52
Days With ≥ 0.1" Precipitation	7	7	9	8	8	7	7	5	6	5	7	8	84
Days With ≥ 1.0" Precipitation	1	1	1	2	1	1	1	1	1	1	2	2	15
Mean Snowfall (in.)	0.9	1.2	0.3	trace	0.0	0.0	0.0	0.0	0.0	0.0	trace	0.2	2.6
Days With ≥ 1.0" Snow Depth	0	0	0	0	0	0	0	0	0	0	0	0	0

Clarksville Sewage Plant *Montgomery County*   Elevation: 380 ft.   Latitude: 36° 33' N   Longitude: 87° 21' W

	JAN	FEB	MAR	APR	MAY	JUN	JUL	AUG	SEP	OCT	NOV	DEC	YEAR
Mean Maximum Temp. (°F)	45.0	50.5	60.6	71.0	78.4	86.1	90.4	89.1	83.2	72.1	60.1	50.0	69.7
Mean Temp. (°F)	34.7	39.0	48.4	57.9	66.1	74.5	79.0	77.3	70.7	58.7	48.3	39.3	57.8
Mean Minimum Temp. (°F)	24.3	27.6	36.2	44.7	53.7	62.8	67.5	65.5	58.3	45.3	36.4	28.8	45.9
Extreme Maximum Temp. (°F)	80	82	87	92	94	103	105	103	101	93	86	78	105
Extreme Minimum Temp. (°F)	-15	-10	0	22	32	43	48	44	32	20	11	-12	-15
Days Maximum Temp. ≥ 90°F	0	0	0	0	2	10	19	15	7	0	0	0	53
Days Maximum Temp. ≤ 32°F	5	2	0	0	0	0	0	0	0	0	0	2	9
Days Minimum Temp. ≤ 32°F	24	19	12	4	0	0	0	0	0	0	0	0	94
Days Minimum Temp. ≤ 0°F	1	1	0	0	0	0	0	0	0	3	12	20	2
Heating Degree Days (base 65°F)	935	726	512	241	74	5	0	0	31	223	499	790	4,036
Cooling Degree Days (base 65°F)	0	0	6	34	119	311	462	406	207	36	3	0	1,584
Mean Precipitation (in.)	4.07	4.23	5.45	4.30	4.87	4.63	4.25	3.36	3.65	3.47	4.55	5.27	52.10
Days With ≥ 0.1" Precipitation	7	7	8	8	8	8	7	6	6	6	7	7	85
Days With ≥ 1.0" Precipitation	1	1	1	1	1	1	1	1	1	1	1	2	13
Mean Snowfall (in.)	2.3	2.4	0.2	0.0	0.0	0.0	0.0	0.0	0.0	0.0	trace	0.4	5.3
Days With ≥ 1.0" Snow Depth	2	1	0	0	0	0	0	0	0	0	0	0	3

Cleveland Filter Plant *Bradley County*   Elevation: 797 ft.   Latitude: 35° 13' N   Longitude: 84° 48' W

	JAN	FEB	MAR	APR	MAY	JUN	JUL	AUG	SEP	OCT	NOV	DEC	YEAR
Mean Maximum Temp. (°F)	48.1	53.3	61.9	71.2	78.0	84.8	88.5	87.5	81.8	71.6	60.6	51.7	69.9
Mean Temp. (°F)	37.7	41.9	49.6	57.8	65.6	73.4	77.5	76.4	70.3	58.8	48.6	41.2	58.2
Mean Minimum Temp. (°F)	27.4	30.3	37.3	44.3	53.2	61.9	66.3	65.2	58.7	46.0	36.5	30.7	46.5
Extreme Maximum Temp. (°F)	73	78	86	91	92	98	105	104	98	89	82	76	105
Extreme Minimum Temp. (°F)	-16	-2	0	20	30	39	50	51	36	21	9	-4	-16
Days Maximum Temp. ≥ 90°F	0	0	0	0	0	5	14	10	4	0	0	0	33
Days Maximum Temp. ≤ 32°F	3	1	0	0	0	0	0	0	0	0	0	1	5
Days Minimum Temp. ≤ 32°F	21	17	10	3	0	0	0	0	0	0	0	19	84
Days Minimum Temp. ≤ 0°F	0	0	0	0	0	0	0	0	0	2	12	0	0
Heating Degree Days (base 65°F)	839	648	474	233	71	4	0	0	25	211	488	731	3,724
Cooling Degree Days (base 65°F)	0	0	5	24	104	280	415	369	185	29	1	0	1,412
Mean Precipitation (in.)	5.28	4.57	6.27	4.44	5.04	4.70	4.36	3.35	4.45	3.61	4.67	5.04	55.78
Days With ≥ 0.1" Precipitation	8	8	9	7	8	8	7	6	6	6	7	8	88
Days With ≥ 1.0" Precipitation	1	2	2	1	1	1	1	1	1	1	1	1	14
Mean Snowfall (in.)	0.9	0.4	0.1	0.2	0.0	0.0	0.0	0.0	0.0	0.0	trace	trace	1.6
Days With ≥ 1.0" Snow Depth	1	0	0	0	0	0	0	0	0	0	0	0	1

Columbia 3 WNW *Maury County*   Elevation: 649 ft.   Latitude: 35° 39' N   Longitude: 87° 05' W

	JAN	FEB	MAR	APR	MAY	JUN	JUL	AUG	SEP	OCT	NOV	DEC	YEAR
Mean Maximum Temp. (°F)	46.4	51.6	60.7	70.3	77.6	85.0	88.8	88.0	82.2	71.5	60.4	51.1	69.5
Mean Temp. (°F)	35.9	40.1	48.4	56.9	65.3	73.4	77.6	76.4	69.9	57.9	48.2	40.4	57.5
Mean Minimum Temp. (°F)	25.4	28.6	36.0	43.7	53.1	61.8	66.4	64.7	57.6	44.3	36.0	29.5	45.6
Extreme Maximum Temp. (°F)	75	81	87	90	92	100	105	101	100	90	88	78	105
Extreme Minimum Temp. (°F)	-20	-7	4	20	31	40	51	49	34	23	11	-10	-20
Days Maximum Temp. ≥ 90°F	0	0	0	0	1	7	15	12	5	0	0	0	40
Days Maximum Temp. ≤ 32°F	4	2	0	0	0	0	0	0	0	0	0	2	8
Days Minimum Temp. ≤ 32°F	23	19	13	4	0	0	0	0	0	0	0	20	96
Days Minimum Temp. ≤ 0°F	1	0	0	0	0	0	0	0	0	4	13	0	1
Heating Degree Days (base 65°F)	894	696	514	262	80	6	0	1	36	239	499	757	3,984
Cooling Degree Days (base 65°F)	0	0	5	18	97	264	405	360	175	25	2	1	1,352
Mean Precipitation (in.)	4.59	4.34	6.21	4.98	5.56	4.23	5.03	3.47	3.95	3.48	4.70	5.39	55.93
Days With ≥ 0.1" Precipitation	8	7	8	7	7	7	7	5	6	6	7	8	83
Days With ≥ 1.0" Precipitation	1	1	2	1	2	1	1	1	1	1	1	2	15
Mean Snowfall (in.)	1.4	1.0	0.2	trace	0.0	0.0	0.0	0.0	0.0	0.0	trace	0.2	2.8
Days With ≥ 1.0" Snow Depth	1	0	0	0	0	0	0	0	0	0	0	0	1

Cookeville *Putnam County*   Elevation: 1,089 ft.   Latitude: 36° 06' N   Longitude: 85° 30' W

	JAN	FEB	MAR	APR	MAY	JUN	JUL	AUG	SEP	OCT	NOV	DEC	YEAR
Mean Maximum Temp. (°F)	45.2	49.7	59.1	68.8	76.4	83.8	87.4	86.7	81.2	70.8	59.5	50.0	68.2
Mean Temp. (°F)	35.1	38.4	47.1	55.9	64.2	72.3	76.3	75.1	68.9	57.5	47.7	39.6	56.5
Mean Minimum Temp. (°F)	25.0	27.1	35.1	42.9	51.9	60.8	65.2	63.4	56.5	44.0	35.9	29.1	44.7
Extreme Maximum Temp. (°F)	74	80	85	90	91	98	104	101	97	90	85	76	104
Extreme Minimum Temp. (°F)	-22	-13	-1	20	30	41	46	46	36	23	7	-8	-22
Days Maximum Temp. ≥ 90°F	0	0	0	0	0	4	11	9	4	0	0	0	28
Days Maximum Temp. ≤ 32°F	6	3	0	0	0	0	0	0	0	0	0	3	12
Days Minimum Temp. ≤ 32°F	23	20	14	4	0	0	0	0	0	4	13	20	98
Days Minimum Temp. ≤ 0°F	1	0	0	0	0	0	0	0	0	0	0	0	1
Heating Degree Days (base 65°F)	920	744	552	287	102	11	0	1	42	253	515	782	4,209
Cooling Degree Days (base 65°F)	0	0	4	15	84	240	373	321	153	24	2	0	1,216
Mean Precipitation (in.)	5.25	4.48	5.75	4.49	5.56	4.51	5.10	4.35	4.18	3.61	4.84	5.65	57.77
Days With ≥ 0.1" Precipitation	9	8	9	8	9	8	8	7	6	6	8	9	95
Days With ≥ 1.0" Precipitation	1	1	2	1	2	1	2	1	1	1	1	2	16
Mean Snowfall (in.)	3.3	2.6	0.9	trace	0.0	0.0	0.0	0.0	0.0	0.0	0.3	0.8	7.9
Days With ≥ 1.0" Snow Depth	4	2	0	0	0	0	0	0	0	0	0	0	6

Copperhill *Polk County*   Elevation: 1,450 ft.   Latitude: 35° 00' N   Longitude: 84° 23' W

	JAN	FEB	MAR	APR	MAY	JUN	JUL	AUG	SEP	OCT	NOV	DEC	YEAR
Mean Maximum Temp. (°F)	48.1	52.6	60.9	70.8	77.9	84.0	87.9	86.6	81.2	71.7	61.1	52.2	69.6
Mean Temp. (°F)	37.2	40.3	47.7	56.1	64.1	71.2	75.7	74.7	68.6	57.6	48.3	40.6	56.9
Mean Minimum Temp. (°F)	26.3	28.0	34.6	41.2	50.4	58.3	63.5	62.7	56.0	43.5	35.5	29.0	44.1
Extreme Maximum Temp. (°F)	74	78	85	90	92	98	102	101	98	90	82	76	102
Extreme Minimum Temp. (°F)	-16	-5	2	19	30	39	48	46	32	25	9	-8	-16
Days Maximum Temp. ≥ 90°F	0	0	0	0	0	4	11	8	2	0	0	0	25
Days Maximum Temp. ≤ 32°F	3	1	0	0	0	0	0	0	0	0	0	1	5
Days Minimum Temp. ≤ 32°F	21	19	13	6	0	0	0	0	0	4	13	19	95
Days Minimum Temp. ≤ 0°F	1	0	0	0	0	0	0	0	0	0	0	0	1
Heating Degree Days (base 65°F)	855	694	529	275	92	10	1	1	36	239	495	748	3,975
Cooling Degree Days (base 65°F)	0	0	2	12	77	206	358	300	135	18	1	0	1,109
Mean Precipitation (in.)	5.82	5.60	6.49	4.88	5.13	4.60	5.43	4.87	4.39	3.63	4.86	5.05	60.75
Days With ≥ 0.1" Precipitation	9	7	9	7	8	8	8	8	6	5	7	7	89
Days With ≥ 1.0" Precipitation	2	2	2	1	1	1	2	1	1	1	1	1	16
Mean Snowfall (in.)	0.9	1.0	1.3	trace	0.0	0.0	0.0	0.0	0.0	trace	trace	0.2	3.4
Days With ≥ 1.0" Snow Depth	1	1	0	0	0	0	0	0	0	0	0	0	2

Covington 1 W *Tipton County*   Elevation: 308 ft.   Latitude: 35° 34' N   Longitude: 89° 40' W

	JAN	FEB	MAR	APR	MAY	JUN	JUL	AUG	SEP	OCT	NOV	DEC	YEAR
Mean Maximum Temp. (°F)	45.2	50.9	60.6	71.1	79.7	87.8	91.2	89.5	83.7	73.3	60.3	50.3	70.3
Mean Temp. (°F)	36.4	41.1	50.3	59.9	68.7	76.9	80.4	78.4	72.0	60.9	50.1	41.2	59.7
Mean Minimum Temp. (°F)	27.5	31.2	39.9	48.8	57.6	66.0	69.7	67.3	60.3	48.3	39.8	31.9	49.0
Extreme Maximum Temp. (°F)	77	80	85	92	98	100	106	103	100	92	87	79	106
Extreme Minimum Temp. (°F)	-10	0	12	28	36	47	52	48	39	28	13	-7	-10
Days Maximum Temp. ≥ 90°F	0	0	0	0	3	13	21	17	8	0	0	0	62
Days Maximum Temp. ≤ 32°F	5	3	0	0	0	0	0	0	0	0	0	2	10
Days Minimum Temp. ≤ 32°F	21	16	8	1	0	0	0	0	0	0	8	17	71
Days Minimum Temp. ≤ 0°F	0	0	0	0	0	0	0	0	0	0	0	0	0
Heating Degree Days (base 65°F)	880	670	458	197	44	1	0	0	25	177	449	733	3,634
Cooling Degree Days (base 65°F)	0	1	10	50	171	376	503	438	243	57	8	1	1,858
Mean Precipitation (in.)	4.21	4.27	5.46	5.41	5.15	4.26	4.16	2.84	3.63	3.47	5.18	5.68	53.72
Days With ≥ 0.1" Precipitation	7	7	8	8	8	6	6	4	5	5	7	7	78
Days With ≥ 1.0" Precipitation	1	1	2	2	2	1	1	1	1	1	2	2	17
Mean Snowfall (in.)	3.1	2.3	0.6	trace	0.0	0.0	0.0	0.0	0.0	trace	0.1	0.2	6.3
Days With ≥ 1.0" Snow Depth	4	2	0	0	0	0	0	0	0	0	0	0	6

Crossville Exp. Station *Cumberland County*   Elevation: 1,807 ft.   Latitude: 36° 01' N   Longitude: 85° 08' W

	JAN	FEB	MAR	APR	MAY	JUN	JUL	AUG	SEP	OCT	NOV	DEC	YEAR
Mean Maximum Temp. (°F)	42.3	47.0	55.8	65.4	73.3	80.3	84.1	83.2	77.5	67.3	56.3	47.1	65.0
Mean Temp. (°F)	32.1	36.0	44.9	53.8	61.8	69.2	73.0	71.8	65.9	54.9	45.5	37.0	53.8
Mean Minimum Temp. (°F)	22.1	25.2	33.9	42.1	50.4	58.0	62.0	60.4	54.2	42.3	34.7	26.8	42.7
Extreme Maximum Temp. (°F)	69	74	80	85	90	101	101	96	95	89	79	72	101
Extreme Minimum Temp. (°F)	-25	-15	-6	18	28	39	46	41	30	21	4	-15	-25
Days Maximum Temp. ≥ 90°F	0	0	0	0	0	1	5	3	1	0	0	0	10
Days Maximum Temp. ≤ 32°F	7	5	1	0	0	0	0	0	0	0	0	4	17
Days Minimum Temp. ≤ 32°F	24	20	15	5	0	0	0	0	0	5	14	21	104
Days Minimum Temp. ≤ 0°F	2	1	0	0	0	0	0	0	0	0	0	1	4
Heating Degree Days (base 65°F)	1,013	812	618	339	139	22	2	4	68	317	579	863	4,776
Cooling Degree Days (base 65°F)	0	0	1	9	54	167	280	232	101	11	0	0	855
Mean Precipitation (in.)	5.73	4.82	6.38	4.91	5.79	4.86	5.05	3.96	3.86	3.83	5.22	6.18	60.59
Days With ≥ 0.1" Precipitation	10	8	10	9	9	8	8	7	6	6	8	9	98
Days With ≥ 1.0" Precipitation	1	1	2	1	2	1	2	1	1	1	2	2	17
Mean Snowfall (in.)	5.1	5.0	2.8	0.3	0.0	0.0	0.0	0.0	0.0	trace	0.4	1.7	15.3
Days With ≥ 1.0" Snow Depth	6	5	2	0	0	0	0	0	0	0	0	2	15

Crossville Memorial Airport *Cumberland County*   Elevation: 1,866 ft.   Latitude: 35° 57' N   Longitude: 85° 05' W

	JAN	FEB	MAR	APR	MAY	JUN	JUL	AUG	SEP	OCT	NOV	DEC	YEAR
Mean Maximum Temp. (°F)	43.6	48.4	57.2	66.6	73.8	80.6	84.0	83.2	77.4	67.4	56.6	47.9	65.6
Mean Temp. (°F)	34.8	38.8	46.9	55.3	63.0	70.3	74.3	73.2	67.2	56.1	46.8	39.1	55.5
Mean Minimum Temp. (°F)	25.9	29.1	36.5	44.0	52.1	60.0	64.5	63.2	57.0	44.8	37.0	30.3	45.4
Extreme Maximum Temp. (°F)	70	76	81	88	89	99	101	99	95	86	79	72	101
Extreme Minimum Temp. (°F)	-21	-16	-2	22	27	39	47	44	33	20	6	-8	-21
Days Maximum Temp. ≥ 90°F	0	0	0	0	0	1	4	3	1	0	0	0	9
Days Maximum Temp. ≤ 32°F	6	4	1	0	0	0	0	0	0	0	0	3	14
Days Minimum Temp. ≤ 32°F	22	18	13	4	0	0	0	0	0	3	11	19	90
Days Minimum Temp. ≤ 0°F	1	0	0	0	0	0	0	0	0	0	0	0	1
Heating Degree Days (base 65°F)	929	733	556	297	119	15	1	2	54	281	540	794	4,321
Cooling Degree Days (base 65°F)	0	0	2	13	65	190	311	267	121	14	1	0	984
Mean Precipitation (in.)	5.07	4.36	6.07	4.75	5.38	4.76	5.09	4.26	3.96	3.37	5.15	5.28	57.50
Days With ≥ 0.1" Precipitation	9	8	10	8	9	8	9	6	6	6	8	9	96
Days With ≥ 1.0" Precipitation	1	1	2	1	1	1	2	1	1	1	2	1	15
Mean Snowfall (in.)	4.2	3.9	2.0	0.4	trace	0.0	0.0	trace	0.0	trace	0.3	1.2	12.0
Days With ≥ 1.0" Snow Depth	6	3	1	0	0	0	0	0	0	0	0	1	11

Dayton *Rhea County*   Elevation: 862 ft.   Latitude: 35° 28' N   Longitude: 85° 00' W

	JAN	FEB	MAR	APR	MAY	JUN	JUL	AUG	SEP	OCT	NOV	DEC	YEAR
Mean Maximum Temp. (°F)	46.9	52.8	62.3	72.6	78.9	85.6	88.5	87.6	81.6	71.2	59.9	50.7	69.9
Mean Temp. (°F)	37.6	41.8	50.2	58.9	66.3	73.7	77.3	76.4	70.5	59.1	49.2	41.2	58.5
Mean Minimum Temp. (°F)	28.2	30.7	38.1	45.2	53.8	61.6	66.1	65.1	59.2	47.0	38.5	31.6	47.1
Extreme Maximum Temp. (°F)	75	79	85	92	94	100	107	104	97	90	82	76	107
Extreme Minimum Temp. (°F)	-15	-4	3	22	33	41	49	52	36	24	9	-5	-15
Days Maximum Temp. ≥ 90°F	0	0	0	0	1	6	14	10	4	0	0	0	35
Days Maximum Temp. ≤ 32°F	2	1	0	0	0	0	0	0	0	0	0	1	4
Days Minimum Temp. ≤ 32°F	20	16	10	3	0	0	0	0	0	2	10	17	78
Days Minimum Temp. ≤ 0°F	0	0	0	0	0	0	0	0	0	0	0	0	0
Heating Degree Days (base 65°F)	843	650	454	202	54	3	0	0	22	203	469	733	3,633
Cooling Degree Days (base 65°F)	0	0	3	27	104	277	399	364	179	27	1	1	1,382
Mean Precipitation (in.)	5.41	4.73	6.26	4.42	5.37	3.97	4.77	4.24	4.55	3.78	5.16	5.76	58.42
Days With ≥ 0.1" Precipitation	9	7	9	7	8	7	9	7	7	6	7	8	91
Days With ≥ 1.0" Precipitation	2	1	2	1	2	1	1	1	1	1	2	2	17
Mean Snowfall (in.)	1.9	1.6	0.7	trace	0.0	0.0	0.0	0.0	0.0	0.0	trace	0.2	4.4
Days With ≥ 1.0" Snow Depth	2	1	0	0	0	0	0	0	0	0	0	0	3

Dickson *Dickson County*   Elevation: 777 ft.   Latitude: 36° 04' N   Longitude: 87° 23' W

	JAN	FEB	MAR	APR	MAY	JUN	JUL	AUG	SEP	OCT	NOV	DEC	YEAR
Mean Maximum Temp. (°F)	45.9	51.7	61.5	71.6	78.3	85.2	88.8	88.0	81.9	71.1	59.7	50.5	69.5
Mean Temp. (°F)	36.0	40.5	49.3	58.4	66.3	73.9	77.8	76.7	70.5	58.8	48.6	40.4	58.1
Mean Minimum Temp. (°F)	26.1	29.3	37.1	45.2	54.3	62.5	66.9	65.3	59.0	46.4	37.5	30.1	46.6
Extreme Maximum Temp. (°F)	76	82	88	91	92	101	105	101	100	91	84	76	105
Extreme Minimum Temp. (°F)	-23	-7	-1	20	33	42	50	46	34	23	10	-13	-23
Days Maximum Temp. ≥ 90°F	0	0	0	0	1	7	15	12	4	0	0	0	39
Days Maximum Temp. ≤ 32°F	5	2	0	0	0	0	0	0	0	0	0	2	9
Days Minimum Temp. ≤ 32°F	22	18	12	3	0	0	0	0	0	3	10	19	87
Days Minimum Temp. ≤ 0°F	1	0	0	0	0	0	0	0	0	0	0	0	1
Heating Degree Days (base 65°F)	893	684	485	223	63	3	0	0	29	217	488	758	3,843
Cooling Degree Days (base 65°F)	0	0	6	27	109	278	414	373	193	32	2	0	1,434
Mean Precipitation (in.)	4.26	4.50	5.79	4.67	5.79	4.80	4.63	3.14	4.19	3.58	5.19	5.42	55.96
Days With ≥ 0.1" Precipitation	7	7	8	7	8	7	7	6	5	5	7	7	81
Days With ≥ 1.0" Precipitation	1	1	2	1	2	1	1	1	1	1	2	2	16
Mean Snowfall (in.)	2.0	2.2	0.6	trace	0.0	0.0	0.0	0.0	0.0	trace	0.1	0.6	5.5
Days With ≥ 1.0" Snow Depth	2	1	0	0	0	0	0	0	0	0	0	0	3

Dover 1 W *Stewart County*   Elevation: 472 ft.   Latitude: 36° 29' N   Longitude: 87° 52' W

	JAN	FEB	MAR	APR	MAY	JUN	JUL	AUG	SEP	OCT	NOV	DEC	YEAR
Mean Maximum Temp. (°F)	43.7	49.4	59.8	70.2	77.2	84.5	88.4	87.4	81.5	70.9	58.7	48.9	68.4
Mean Temp. (°F)	33.9	38.4	48.3	57.9	65.6	73.7	77.7	75.9	69.5	57.9	47.9	38.8	57.1
Mean Minimum Temp. (°F)	24.0	27.4	36.7	45.6	54.0	62.8	66.9	64.7	57.5	44.9	36.9	28.7	45.8
Extreme Maximum Temp. (°F)	75	82	88	91	92	101	104	103	100	92	84	77	104
Extreme Minimum Temp. (°F)	-15	-4	0	22	30	42	48	46	29	21	7	-13	-15
Days Maximum Temp. ≥ 90°F	0	0	0	0	0	6	14	11	5	0	0	0	36
Days Maximum Temp. ≤ 32°F	6	3	0	0	0	0	0	0	0	0	0	3	12
Days Minimum Temp. ≤ 32°F	24	19	12	3	0	0	0	0	0	3	11	19	91
Days Minimum Temp. ≤ 0°F	1	1	0	0	0	0	0	0	0	0	0	0	2
Heating Degree Days (base 65°F)	958	746	519	244	80	6	0	1	43	244	511	806	4,158
Cooling Degree Days (base 65°F)	0	0	9	39	109	277	419	356	183	31	3	1	1,427
Mean Precipitation (in.)	4.11	4.54	5.38	4.52	4.71	4.49	4.52	3.62	3.82	3.71	4.74	5.20	53.36
Days With ≥ 0.1" Precipitation	7	7	8	8	7	7	7	5	6	6	7	7	82
Days With ≥ 1.0" Precipitation	1	1	2	1	1	1	1	1	1	1	1	2	14
Mean Snowfall (in.)	2.9	3.3	0.5	trace	0.0	0.0	0.0	0.0	0.0	trace	0.2	0.3	7.2
Days With ≥ 1.0" Snow Depth	3	2	0	0	0	0	0	0	0	0	0	0	5

Dresden *Weakley County*   Elevation: 449 ft.   Latitude: 36° 17' N   Longitude: 88° 42' W

	JAN	FEB	MAR	APR	MAY	JUN	JUL	AUG	SEP	OCT	NOV	DEC	YEAR
Mean Maximum Temp. (°F)	43.2	49.1	59.3	69.8	78.0	85.9	89.3	88.2	82.7	71.9	59.1	48.8	68.8
Mean Temp. (°F)	33.9	38.6	48.5	58.2	66.9	75.0	78.6	77.0	70.9	59.3	48.5	39.2	57.9
Mean Minimum Temp. (°F)	24.5	28.4	37.7	46.5	55.7	64.1	67.9	65.6	58.9	46.6	37.8	29.5	46.9
Extreme Maximum Temp. (°F)	75	80	87	90	94	100	102	101	99	91	87	78	102
Extreme Minimum Temp. (°F)	-17	-3	7	23	34	43	48	47	36	23	10	-11	-17
Days Maximum Temp. ≥ 90°F	0	0	0	0	1	9	17	13	6	0	0	0	46
Days Maximum Temp. ≤ 32°F	6	4	0	0	0	0	0	0	0	0	0	3	13
Days Minimum Temp. ≤ 32°F	23	18	11	2	0	0	0	0	0	2	10	20	86
Days Minimum Temp. ≤ 0°F	1	0	0	0	0	0	0	0	0	0	0	0	1
Heating Degree Days (base 65°F)	958	739	511	236	62	4	0	0	32	212	494	795	4,043
Cooling Degree Days (base 65°F)	0	0	8	35	129	320	448	395	212	41	4	1	1,593
Mean Precipitation (in.)	4.08	4.28	5.17	5.07	5.39	5.08	4.95	3.52	3.81	3.40	4.72	5.19	54.66
Days With ≥ 0.1" Precipitation	7	6	9	8	8	7	6	5	5	5	7	7	80
Days With ≥ 1.0" Precipitation	1	1	1	2	2	2	1	1	1	1	2	2	17
Mean Snowfall (in.)	2.6	2.1	0.3	trace	0.0	0.0	0.0	0.0	0.0	0.0	0.2	0.2	5.4
Days With ≥ 1.0" Snow Depth	3	2	0	0	0	0	0	0	0	0	0	0	5

Dyersburg Municipal Airport *Dyer County*   Elevation: 334 ft.   Latitude: 36° 01' N   Longitude: 89° 24' W

	JAN	FEB	MAR	APR	MAY	JUN	JUL	AUG	SEP	OCT	NOV	DEC	YEAR
Mean Maximum Temp. (°F)	45.0	51.2	61.1	70.9	79.3	87.3	90.6	89.0	82.7	72.3	59.7	49.6	69.9
Mean Temp. (°F)	37.1	42.6	51.9	61.0	69.5	77.8	81.1	79.2	72.4	61.6	50.9	41.9	60.6
Mean Minimum Temp. (°F)	29.3	34.0	42.6	51.0	59.8	67.9	71.5	69.4	62.2	50.9	42.0	34.1	51.2
Extreme Maximum Temp. (°F)	76	79	83	93	95	102	104	100	100	90	82	77	104
Extreme Minimum Temp. (°F)	-12	0	12	26	40	46	55	49	32	28	14	-7	-12
Days Maximum Temp. ≥ 90°F	0	0	0	0	2	11	19	14	5	0	0	0	51
Days Maximum Temp. ≤ 32°F	5	2	0	0	0	0	0	0	0	0	0	2	9
Days Minimum Temp. ≤ 32°F	18	13	5	1	0	0	0	0	0	1	6	14	58
Days Minimum Temp. ≤ 0°F	0	0	0	0	0	0	0	0	0	0	0	0	0
Heating Degree Days (base 65°F)	858	626	410	170	31	0	0	0	20	155	425	709	3,404
Cooling Degree Days (base 65°F)	0	1	12	55	178	398	519	459	244	57	7	1	1,931
Mean Precipitation (in.)	3.76	4.29	4.56	4.80	4.71	4.58	4.20	3.21	3.13	3.58	4.88	5.24	50.94
Days With ≥ 0.1" Precipitation	6	6	7	7	7	6	6	4	5	5	7	7	73
Days With ≥ 1.0" Precipitation	1	1	1	1	1	1	1	1	1	1	1	1	12
Mean Snowfall (in.)	2.7	2.7	0.7	trace	trace	0.0	0.0	0.0	0.0	trace	trace	0.5	6.6
Days With ≥ 1.0" Snow Depth	4	3	0	0	0	0	0	0	0	0	0	0	7

Fayetteville Water Plant *Lincoln County*   Elevation: 725 ft.   Latitude: 35° 09' N   Longitude: 86° 32' W

	JAN	FEB	MAR	APR	MAY	JUN	JUL	AUG	SEP	OCT	NOV	DEC	YEAR
Mean Maximum Temp. (°F)	47.5	52.4	61.4	70.8	78.6	85.7	89.3	88.9	83.2	72.6	61.2	51.8	70.3
Mean Temp. (°F)	37.1	41.0	49.4	57.5	66.1	73.5	77.5	76.6	70.6	58.8	49.0	41.0	58.2
Mean Minimum Temp. (°F)	26.7	29.5	37.4	44.1	53.5	61.3	65.7	64.2	57.9	44.9	36.7	30.2	46.0
Extreme Maximum Temp. (°F)	75	82	85	90	93	100	103	102	100	92	86	77	103
Extreme Minimum Temp. (°F)	-20	-2	1	19	28	38	47	48	33	20	8	-8	-20
Days Maximum Temp. ≥ 90°F	0	0	0	0	1	8	17	14	6	0	0	0	46
Days Maximum Temp. ≤ 32°F	4	2	0	0	0	0	0	0	0	0	0	1	7
Days Minimum Temp. ≤ 32°F	22	18	11	5	0	0	0	0	0	4	11	19	90
Days Minimum Temp. ≤ 0°F	1	0	0	0	0	0	0	0	0	0	0	0	1
Heating Degree Days (base 65°F)	857	672	482	245	71	6	0	1	32	221	478	737	3,802
Cooling Degree Days (base 65°F)	0	0	7	25	121	282	416	384	205	38	3	1	1,482
Mean Precipitation (in.)	5.15	4.52	6.38	4.48	4.95	4.56	4.17	3.11	4.11	3.78	5.14	5.76	56.11
Days With ≥ 0.1" Precipitation	8	7	9	7	8	7	8	6	6	5	8	8	87
Days With ≥ 1.0" Precipitation	1	1	2	1	1	1	1	1	1	1	2	2	15
Mean Snowfall (in.)	1.4	1.1	0.3	trace	0.0	0.0	0.0	0.0	0.0	0.0	trace	0.3	3.1
Days With ≥ 1.0" Snow Depth	2	1	0	0	0	0	0	0	0	0	0	0	3

Franklin Sewage Plant *Williamson County*   Elevation: 652 ft.   Latitude: 35° 57' N   Longitude: 86° 52' W

	JAN	FEB	MAR	APR	MAY	JUN	JUL	AUG	SEP	OCT	NOV	DEC	YEAR
Mean Maximum Temp. (°F)	46.8	52.6	61.7	71.2	78.5	85.9	89.8	88.6	83.1	72.5	60.6	51.4	70.2
Mean Temp. (°F)	36.5	40.7	49.3	57.9	66.0	73.9	78.0	76.4	70.3	58.6	48.8	40.8	58.1
Mean Minimum Temp. (°F)	26.2	28.8	37.0	44.5	53.5	62.0	66.2	64.2	57.6	44.8	37.0	30.2	46.0
Extreme Maximum Temp. (°F)	76	81	87	90	94	101	105	101	99	91	83	76	105
Extreme Minimum Temp. (°F)	-21	-6	0	22	30	39	43	47	32	21	7	-11	-21
Days Maximum Temp. ≥ 90°F	0	0	0	0	1	9	18	14	6	0	0	0	48
Days Maximum Temp. ≤ 32°F	4	1	0	0	0	0	0	0	0	0	0	2	7
Days Minimum Temp. ≤ 32°F	22	18	12	4	0	0	0	0	0	4	11	19	90
Days Minimum Temp. ≤ 0°F	1	0	0	0	0	0	0	0	0	0	0	0	1
Heating Degree Days (base 65°F)	876	680	487	237	72	5	0	1	31	225	481	743	3,838
Cooling Degree Days (base 65°F)	0	0	7	24	108	281	419	361	187	34	2	1	1,424
Mean Precipitation (in.)	4.35	4.21	5.79	4.34	5.59	4.28	4.70	3.62	3.90	3.23	4.81	5.44	54.26
Days With ≥ 0.1" Precipitation	8	7	9	7	8	7	7	6	6	5	7	8	85
Days With ≥ 1.0" Precipitation	1	1	2	1	2	1	1	1	1	1	2	2	16
Mean Snowfall (in.)	1.7	1.1	0.4	0.0	0.0	0.0	0.0	0.0	0.0	trace	0.1	0.2	3.5
Days With ≥ 1.0" Snow Depth	1	1	0	0	0	0	0	0	0	0	0	0	2

Gatlinburg 2 SW *Sevier County*   Elevation: 1,453 ft.   Latitude: 35° 41' N   Longitude: 83° 32' W

	JAN	FEB	MAR	APR	MAY	JUN	JUL	AUG	SEP	OCT	NOV	DEC	YEAR
Mean Maximum Temp. (°F)	47.6	51.8	60.7	69.8	76.0	82.1	84.8	83.6	78.8	69.3	60.3	51.6	68.0
Mean Temp. (°F)	36.2	39.2	47.0	55.0	62.4	69.6	73.1	72.0	66.8	55.5	46.9	39.7	55.3
Mean Minimum Temp. (°F)	24.7	26.5	33.2	40.1	48.7	57.1	61.6	60.4	54.6	41.6	33.5	27.6	42.5
Extreme Maximum Temp. (°F)	76	85	86	92	90	93	97	98	97	87	82	78	98
Extreme Minimum Temp. (°F)	-18	-10	-6	20	29	37	48	44	35	23	7	-4	-18
Days Maximum Temp. ≥ 90°F	0	0	0	0	0	2	5	3	1	0	0	0	11
Days Maximum Temp. ≤ 32°F	4	2	1	0	0	0	0	0	0	0	0	2	9
Days Minimum Temp. ≤ 32°F	23	21	16	8	1	0	0	0	0	0	5	15	22	111
Days Minimum Temp. ≤ 0°F	1	0	0	0	0	0	0	0	0	0	0	0	1
Heating Degree Days (base 65°F)	887	724	554	307	125	18	1	1	48	298	536	779	4,278
Cooling Degree Days (base 65°F)	0	0	2	12	56	176	276	231	104	11	1	0	869
Mean Precipitation (in.)	4.82	4.26	5.50	4.41	5.44	5.72	6.07	4.59	4.68	3.03	3.98	4.53	57.03
Days With ≥ 0.1" Precipitation	9	8	10	8	10	10	10	8	7	5	7	9	101
Days With ≥ 1.0" Precipitation	1	1	1	1	1	2	2	1	2	1	1	1	15
Mean Snowfall (in.)	3.8	1.7	2.3	0.7	0.0	0.0	0.0	0.0	0.0	trace	0.1	1.1	9.7
Days With ≥ 1.0" Snow Depth	2	2	0	0	0	0	0	0	0	0	0	0	4

Greeneville Exp. Station *Greene County*   Elevation: 1,318 ft.   Latitude: 36° 06' N   Longitude: 82° 51' W

	JAN	FEB	MAR	APR	MAY	JUN	JUL	AUG	SEP	OCT	NOV	DEC	YEAR
Mean Maximum Temp. (°F)	46.4	51.1	59.9	69.1	76.8	83.6	87.2	86.3	81.2	70.6	60.1	50.9	68.6
Mean Temp. (°F)	35.2	38.6	46.6	54.6	63.3	71.3	75.3	74.1	68.2	56.3	46.7	38.8	55.8
Mean Minimum Temp. (°F)	23.9	26.1	33.2	40.1	49.7	58.8	63.4	61.8	55.2	41.9	33.3	26.8	42.9
Extreme Maximum Temp. (°F)	75	82	86	90	91	100	100	100	97	89	84	80	100
Extreme Minimum Temp. (°F)	-29	-23	-9	18	26	36	45	43	28	21	10	-5	-29
Days Maximum Temp. ≥ 90°F	0	0	0	0	0	4	11	8	3	0	0	0	26
Days Maximum Temp. ≤ 32°F	4	2	0	0	0	0	0	0	0	0	0	2	8
Days Minimum Temp. ≤ 32°F	24	21	16	7	1	0	0	0	0	0	6	16	22	113
Days Minimum Temp. ≤ 0°F	1	1	0	0	0	0	0	0	0	0	0	0	2
Heating Degree Days (base 65°F)	918	738	565	316	114	12	1	2	43	279	543	805	4,336
Cooling Degree Days (base 65°F)	0	0	1	10	64	205	327	278	129	15	1	1	1,031
Mean Precipitation (in.)	3.48	3.44	4.09	3.62	4.28	4.17	4.63	3.83	3.19	2.41	2.97	3.46	43.57
Days With ≥ 0.1" Precipitation	8	7	9	7	8	8	8	7	6	5	7	7	87
Days With ≥ 1.0" Precipitation	0	1	1	1	1	1	1	1	1	0	1	1	10
Mean Snowfall (in.)	4.2	2.8	1.6	0.8	0.0	0.0	0.0	0.0	0.0	trace	trace	1.0	10.4
Days With ≥ 1.0" Snow Depth	1	1	1	0	0	0	0	0	0	0	0	1	4

Huntingdon Water Plant *Carroll County*   Elevation: 439 ft.   Latitude: 36° 00' N   Longitude: 88° 25' W

	JAN	FEB	MAR	APR	MAY	JUN	JUL	AUG	SEP	OCT	NOV	DEC	YEAR
Mean Maximum Temp. (°F)	45.1	50.9	60.5	70.8	78.7	86.2	89.7	88.9	83.1	72.1	59.6	49.8	69.6
Mean Temp. (°F)	35.2	39.6	48.8	58.3	66.7	74.8	78.7	77.1	70.6	58.6	48.3	39.7	58.0
Mean Minimum Temp. (°F)	25.4	28.3	37.1	45.7	54.6	63.4	67.6	65.3	58.0	45.1	37.0	29.5	46.4
Extreme Maximum Temp. (°F)	77	83	86	91	94	101	103	103	100	91	85	77	103
Extreme Minimum Temp. (°F)	-14	-2	7	25	33	45	51	47	32	24	10	-10	-14
Days Maximum Temp. ≥ 90°F	0	0	0	0	1	10	18	14	7	0	0	0	50
Days Maximum Temp. ≤ 32°F	5	3	0	0	0	0	0	0	0	0	0	2	10
Days Minimum Temp. ≤ 32°F	23	19	12	3	0	0	0	0	0	0	3	12	19	91
Days Minimum Temp. ≤ 0°F	1	0	0	0	0	0	0	0	0	0	0	0	1
Heating Degree Days (base 65°F)	916	712	502	233	66	4	0	0	34	227	498	780	3,972
Cooling Degree Days (base 65°F)	0	0	7	34	124	311	440	385	197	33	3	1	1,535
Mean Precipitation (in.)	4.38	4.41	5.43	4.64	5.07	4.61	4.88	3.37	4.54	3.82	4.92	5.49	55.56
Days With ≥ 0.1" Precipitation	7	7	8	7	8	7	7	5	6	5	7	7	81
Days With ≥ 1.0" Precipitation	1	1	2	1	2	1	2	1	1	1	1	1	15
Mean Snowfall (in.)	2.1	2.0	0.3	trace	0.0	0.0	0.0	0.0	0.0	trace	trace	0.4	4.8
Days With ≥ 1.0" Snow Depth	2	2	0	0	0	0	0	0	0	0	0	0	4

Jackson Exp. Station *Madison County*   Elevation: 396 ft.   Latitude: 35° 37' N   Longitude: 88° 50' W

	JAN	FEB	MAR	APR	MAY	JUN	JUL	AUG	SEP	OCT	NOV	DEC	YEAR
Mean Maximum Temp. (°F)	45.5	51.0	60.6	70.6	78.1	85.6	89.1	88.4	82.8	72.4	60.2	50.5	69.6
Mean Temp. (°F)	36.7	41.1	50.3	59.5	67.9	75.7	79.5	78.1	71.9	60.3	50.0	41.3	59.3
Mean Minimum Temp. (°F)	27.8	31.2	40.0	48.3	57.6	65.7	69.7	67.8	60.9	48.2	39.7	32.0	49.1
Extreme Maximum Temp. (°F)	78	81	85	90	95	100	103	102	100	92	85	78	103
Extreme Minimum Temp. (°F)	-10	-1	11	26	34	45	51	50	35	26	13	-7	-10
Days Maximum Temp. ≥ 90°F	0	0	0	0	1	8	17	14	6	0	0	0	46
Days Maximum Temp. ≤ 32°F	5	3	0	0	0	0	0	0	0	0	0	2	10
Days Minimum Temp. ≤ 32°F	21	16	8	2	0	0	0	0	0	0	2	8	17	74
Days Minimum Temp. ≤ 0°F	0	0	0	0	0	0	0	0	0	0	0	0	0
Heating Degree Days (base 65°F)	872	670	458	208	53	3	0	0	27	190	451	730	3,662
Cooling Degree Days (base 65°F)	0	1	10	48	152	339	469	426	237	51	6	1	1,740
Mean Precipitation (in.)	4.31	4.15	5.38	4.87	5.76	5.03	4.75	2.92	3.93	3.52	5.07	5.38	55.07
Days With ≥ 0.1" Precipitation	7	7	8	7	8	7	6	5	6	5	7	7	80
Days With ≥ 1.0" Precipitation	1	1	2	1	2	1	1	1	1	1	2	2	17
Mean Snowfall (in.)	1.6	1.8	0.3	trace	0.0	0.0	0.0	0.0	0.0	trace	trace	0.1	3.8
Days With ≥ 1.0" Snow Depth	3	1	0	0	0	0	0	0	0	0	0	0	4

Jackson McKellar-Sipes Reg. Arpt. *Madison County*   Elevation: 433 ft.   Latitude: 35° 36' N   Longitude: 88° 55' W

	JAN	FEB	MAR	APR	MAY	JUN	JUL	AUG	SEP	OCT	NOV	DEC	YEAR
Mean Maximum Temp. (°F)	46.4	52.5	62.3	72.2	79.7	87.5	90.9	90.1	83.6	73.3	60.9	51.4	70.9
Mean Temp. (°F)	37.2	42.2	51.4	60.6	68.7	76.7	80.3	78.9	72.2	61.0	50.4	42.0	60.1
Mean Minimum Temp. (°F)	27.9	31.9	40.5	48.9	57.6	65.9	69.6	67.6	60.7	48.6	40.0	32.5	49.3
Extreme Maximum Temp. (°F)	78	81	87	95	97	103	105	104	101	92	84	77	105
Extreme Minimum Temp. (°F)	-10	0	9	25	37	46	52	48	36	27	11	-7	-10
Days Maximum Temp. ≥ 90°F	0	0	0	0	2	12	20	18	7	0	0	0	59
Days Maximum Temp. ≤ 32°F	4	2	0	0	0	0	0	0	0	0	0	2	8
Days Minimum Temp. ≤ 32°F	21	15	8	1	0	0	0	0	0	1	9	16	71
Days Minimum Temp. ≤ 0°F	0	0	0	0	0	0	0	0	0	0	0	0	0
Heating Degree Days (base 65°F)	856	638	424	181	39	0	0	0	24	171	437	708	3,478
Cooling Degree Days (base 65°F)	0	1	10	53	161	365	493	447	238	52	7	2	1,829
Mean Precipitation (in.)	4.10	4.27	5.19	5.14	5.71	4.91	4.68	2.87	3.82	3.50	5.22	5.43	54.84
Days With ≥ 0.1" Precipitation	6	6	8	7	8	7	6	5	6	5	7	7	78
Days With ≥ 1.0" Precipitation	1	1	1	2	2	2	2	1	1	1	2	2	18
Mean Snowfall (in.)	2.6	2.1	0.6	trace	trace	trace	0.0	trace	0.0	trace	0.1	0.2	5.6
Days With ≥ 1.0" Snow Depth	3	2	0	0	0	0	0	0	0	0	0	0	5

Kingsport *Sullivan County*   Elevation: 1,282 ft.   Latitude: 36° 31' N   Longitude: 82° 32' W

	JAN	FEB	MAR	APR	MAY	JUN	JUL	AUG	SEP	OCT	NOV	DEC	YEAR
Mean Maximum Temp. (°F)	46.2	51.5	61.4	71.3	78.1	84.3	87.6	86.5	81.1	71.0	59.7	50.2	69.1
Mean Temp. (°F)	37.1	40.8	49.3	57.9	65.7	72.8	76.6	75.5	69.7	58.6	48.8	40.7	57.8
Mean Minimum Temp. (°F)	27.9	30.0	37.2	44.5	53.2	61.2	65.5	64.4	58.4	46.3	37.8	31.1	46.4
Extreme Maximum Temp. (°F)	76	82	86	91	90	97	98	101	97	87	82	77	101
Extreme Minimum Temp. (°F)	-18	-11	-2	24	30	42	49	45	36	24	9	-3	-18
Days Maximum Temp. ≥ 90°F	0	0	0	0	0	3	11	7	2	0	0	0	23
Days Maximum Temp. ≤ 32°F	4	2	0	0	0	0	0	0	0	0	0	2	8
Days Minimum Temp. ≤ 32°F	20	16	10	3	0	0	0	0	0	2	10	18	79
Days Minimum Temp. ≤ 0°F	1	0	0	0	0	0	0	0	0	0	0	0	1
Heating Degree Days (base 65°F)	860	679	482	231	67	6	0	1	26	214	480	747	3,793
Cooling Degree Days (base 65°F)	0	0	3	24	98	255	381	335	167	24	1	0	1,288
Mean Precipitation (in.)	3.87	3.68	4.14	3.44	4.46	3.97	4.57	3.74	3.10	2.73	3.20	3.61	44.51
Days With ≥ 0.1" Precipitation	8	7	9	8	9	8	9	7	6	6	7	7	91
Days With ≥ 1.0" Precipitation	1	1	1	1	1	1	1	1	1	1	1	1	12
Mean Snowfall (in.)	4.8	3.6	1.4	0.4	trace	0.0	0.0	0.0	0.0	trace	0.2	1.7	12.1
Days With ≥ 1.0" Snow Depth	4	3	1	0	0	0	0	0	0	0	0	1	9

Kingston Springs *Cheatham County*   Elevation: 524 ft.   Latitude: 36° 07' N   Longitude: 87° 06' W

	JAN	FEB	MAR	APR	MAY	JUN	JUL	AUG	SEP	OCT	NOV	DEC	YEAR
Mean Maximum Temp. (°F)	45.1	50.4	60.5	70.3	77.5	84.8	88.6	88.4	82.4	72.3	60.4	50.3	69.3
Mean Temp. (°F)	34.2	38.1	47.6	56.3	64.6	72.9	77.1	76.1	69.5	57.7	47.7	39.0	56.7
Mean Minimum Temp. (°F)	23.3	25.6	34.6	42.1	51.7	60.8	65.4	63.7	56.0	42.7	34.5	27.4	44.0
Extreme Maximum Temp. (°F)	75	84	88	90	92	100	102	103	101	90	85	78	103
Extreme Minimum Temp. (°F)	-23	-9	2	21	29	39	47	43	32	20	5	-11	-23
Days Maximum Temp. ≥ 90°F	0	0	0	0	1	6	16	13	6	0	0	0	42
Days Maximum Temp. ≤ 32°F	6	3	0	0	0	0	0	0	0	0	0	2	11
Days Minimum Temp. ≤ 32°F	24	21	15	6	0	0	0	0	0	5	14	21	106
Days Minimum Temp. ≤ 0°F	1	0	0	0	0	0	0	0	0	0	0	0	1
Heating Degree Days (base 65°F)	948	752	540	279	96	8	0	1	41	248	516	799	4,228
Cooling Degree Days (base 65°F)	0	0	7	23	96	259	401	367	173	28	2	0	1,356
Mean Precipitation (in.)	3.85	4.46	5.44	4.29	5.23	4.58	4.05	3.30	4.05	3.77	4.58	5.08	52.68
Days With ≥ 0.1" Precipitation	7	7	9	7	8	7	6	5	6	5	7	7	81
Days With ≥ 1.0" Precipitation	1	1	2	1	2	1	1	1	1	1	1	2	15
Mean Snowfall (in.)	*1.5*	1.1	0.4	trace	0.0	0.0	0.0	0.0	0.0	trace	trace	0.2	*3.2*
Days With ≥ 1.0" Snow Depth	*1*	*0*	0	0	0	0	0	0	0	0	0	0	*1*

Lafayette *Macon County*   Elevation: 974 ft.   Latitude: 36° 31' N   Longitude: 86° 02' W

	JAN	FEB	MAR	APR	MAY	JUN	JUL	AUG	SEP	OCT	NOV	DEC	YEAR
Mean Maximum Temp. (°F)	45.3	50.9	61.0	70.8	78.0	84.9	88.5	87.6	81.8	71.5	59.9	50.2	69.2
Mean Temp. (°F)	36.2	40.9	49.8	58.9	66.6	74.1	77.9	76.6	70.5	59.5	49.7	40.9	58.5
Mean Minimum Temp. (°F)	27.1	30.7	38.7	46.9	55.1	63.3	67.2	65.5	59.1	47.5	39.3	31.5	47.7
Extreme Maximum Temp. (°F)	73	78	85	90	94	103	104	102	100	90	82	77	104
Extreme Minimum Temp. (°F)	-19	-2	-1	22	31	40	50	46	36	24	6	-13	-19
Days Maximum Temp. ≥ 90°F	0	0	0	0	1	6	13	11	4	0	0	0	35
Days Maximum Temp. ≤ 32°F	5	2	0	0	0	0	0	0	0	0	0	2	9
Days Minimum Temp. ≤ 32°F	21	16	10	2	0	0	0	0	0	1	8	17	75
Days Minimum Temp. ≤ 0°F	1	0	0	0	0	0	0	0	0	0	0	0	1
Heating Degree Days (base 65°F)	885	676	473	215	64	4	0	0	28	199	457	742	3,743
Cooling Degree Days (base 65°F)	0	0	9	38	130	302	436	390	201	39	3	1	1,549
Mean Precipitation (in.)	4.56	4.41	5.68	4.39	5.62	4.58	4.81	3.87	4.49	3.71	4.83	5.60	56.55
Days With ≥ 0.1" Precipitation	7	7	9	7	7	7	7	6	5	5	7	7	81
Days With ≥ 1.0" Precipitation	1	1	2	1	2	1	1	2	1	1	2	2	18
Mean Snowfall (in.)	3.9	*3.3*	1.2	trace	0.0	0.0	0.0	0.0	0.0	trace	0.1	0.8	*9.3*
Days With ≥ 1.0" Snow Depth	na	*0*	0	0	0	0	0	0	0	0	0	0	na

Lawrenceburg Filter Plant *Lawrence County*　Elevation: 869 ft.　Latitude: 35° 16' N　Longitude: 87° 21' W

	JAN	FEB	MAR	APR	MAY	JUN	JUL	AUG	SEP	OCT	NOV	DEC	YEAR
Mean Maximum Temp. (°F)	48.3	53.7	62.9	72.0	78.3	85.0	88.3	87.6	82.3	72.3	61.2	52.1	70.3
Mean Temp. (°F)	37.9	42.3	50.7	58.8	66.2	73.5	77.1	76.1	70.4	59.2	49.7	41.8	58.6
Mean Minimum Temp. (°F)	27.6	30.8	38.6	45.5	54.1	61.9	65.9	64.5	58.4	46.1	38.1	31.5	46.9
Extreme Maximum Temp. (°F)	76	81	84	89	94	99	103	101	99	89	83	75	103
Extreme Minimum Temp. (°F)	-14	-4	4	22	30	39	48	47	36	24	8	-10	-14
Days Maximum Temp. ≥ 90°F	0	0	0	0	1	6	13	11	4	0	0	0	35
Days Maximum Temp. ≤ 32°F	3	1	0	0	0	0	0	0	0	0	0	1	5
Days Minimum Temp. ≤ 32°F	21	16	10	3	0	0	0	0	0	0	0	0	81
Days Minimum Temp. ≤ 0°F	1	0	0	0	0	0	0	0	0	3	11	17	1
Heating Degree Days (base 65°F)	832	636	442	210	63	4	0	1	29	205	456	714	3,592
Cooling Degree Days (base 65°F)	0	0	6	27	112	270	391	356	189	33	2	2	1,388
Mean Precipitation (in.)	5.50	4.70	6.58	4.88	5.82	4.09	5.02	3.72	4.79	3.73	5.47	6.02	60.32
Days With ≥ 0.1" Precipitation	8	6	8	7	8	7	8	6	6	5	7	8	84
Days With ≥ 1.0" Precipitation	2	2	2	2	2	1	1	1	1	1	2	2	19
Mean Snowfall (in.)	1.8	1.8	0.4	trace	0.0	0.0	0.0	0.0	0.0	trace	trace	0.6	4.6
Days With ≥ 1.0" Snow Depth	1	1	0	0	0	0	0	0	0	0	0	0	2

Lebanon 3 W *Wilson County*　Elevation: 534 ft.　Latitude: 36° 14' N　Longitude: 86° 22' W

	JAN	FEB	MAR	APR	MAY	JUN	JUL	AUG	SEP	OCT	NOV	DEC	YEAR
Mean Maximum Temp. (°F)	45.6	50.9	60.3	70.4	78.3	86.1	89.9	89.0	83.0	72.0	60.1	50.4	69.7
Mean Temp. (°F)	34.8	38.9	47.9	57.0	65.6	74.1	78.2	76.6	69.9	57.8	47.9	39.3	57.3
Mean Minimum Temp. (°F)	24.0	26.9	35.5	43.6	52.8	62.0	66.3	64.1	56.8	43.6	35.6	28.2	44.9
Extreme Maximum Temp. (°F)	75	80	87	90	94	102	105	103	102	94	84	79	105
Extreme Minimum Temp. (°F)	-20	-9	-2	20	29	40	50	43	33	21	6	-11	-20
Days Maximum Temp. ≥ 90°F	0	0	0	0	1	10	18	15	7	0	0	0	51
Days Maximum Temp. ≤ 32°F	5	2	0	0	0	0	0	0	0	0	0	2	9
Days Minimum Temp. ≤ 32°F	24	20	13	5	0	0	0	0	0	0	0	0	100
Days Minimum Temp. ≤ 0°F	1	0	0	0	0	0	0	0	0	5	13	20	1
Heating Degree Days (base 65°F)	929	731	529	264	86	7	0	1	39	249	511	789	4,135
Cooling Degree Days (base 65°F)	0	0	8	29	116	290	431	375	185	34	3	1	1,472
Mean Precipitation (in.)	4.44	4.23	5.54	4.42	5.22	4.65	4.66	4.03	3.97	3.50	4.51	5.18	54.35
Days With ≥ 0.1" Precipitation	8	7	9	7	7	7	7	6	6	5	7	8	84
Days With ≥ 1.0" Precipitation	1	1	2	2	1	1	1	1	1	1	1	2	15
Mean Snowfall (in.)	2.0	2.4	0.3	trace	0.0	0.0	0.0	0.0	0.0	0.0	trace	0.2	4.9
Days With ≥ 1.0" Snow Depth	4	2	0	0	0	0	0	0	0	0	0	1	7

Lenoir City *Loudon County*　Elevation: 784 ft.　Latitude: 35° 47' N　Longitude: 84° 16' W

	JAN	FEB	MAR	APR	MAY	JUN	JUL	AUG	SEP	OCT	NOV	DEC	YEAR
Mean Maximum Temp. (°F)	46.6	51.6	60.8	70.4	77.7	85.0	88.5	87.7	82.3	71.5	60.4	51.0	69.5
Mean Temp. (°F)	36.6	40.3	48.8	57.4	65.8	74.0	77.9	76.9	70.8	58.7	48.8	40.6	58.1
Mean Minimum Temp. (°F)	26.7	28.9	36.8	44.4	53.8	62.9	67.3	65.9	59.4	45.9	37.1	30.2	46.6
Extreme Maximum Temp. (°F)	75	80	84	91	91	101	104	102	98	91	81	77	104
Extreme Minimum Temp. (°F)	-14	-7	1	24	32	41	50	53	37	25	11	-5	-14
Days Maximum Temp. ≥ 90°F	0	0	0	0	0	6	14	11	4	0	0	0	35
Days Maximum Temp. ≤ 32°F	3	1	0	0	0	0	0	0	0	0	0	1	5
Days Minimum Temp. ≤ 32°F	22	18	11	3	0	0	0	0	0	0	0	1	87
Days Minimum Temp. ≤ 0°F	1	0	0	0	0	0	0	0	0	2	11	20	1
Heating Degree Days (base 65°F)	873	692	498	243	73	5	0	0	23	215	482	749	3,853
Cooling Degree Days (base 65°F)	0	0	4	24	116	303	436	394	210	31	1	0	1,519
Mean Precipitation (in.)	5.04	4.57	5.74	4.50	4.93	4.15	4.38	3.65	3.28	3.23	4.20	5.18	52.85
Days With ≥ 0.1" Precipitation	9	8	9	8	8	7	8	7	6	5	7	9	91
Days With ≥ 1.0" Precipitation	1	1	2	1	1	1	1	1	1	1	1	1	13
Mean Snowfall (in.)	2.9	3.0	1.1	0.4	0.0	0.0	0.0	0.0	0.0	trace	trace	0.8	8.2
Days With ≥ 1.0" Snow Depth	2	2	0	0	0	0	0	0	0	0	0	0	4

Lewisburg Exp. Station *Marshall County*　Elevation: 784 ft.　Latitude: 35° 25' N　Longitude: 86° 48' W

	JAN	FEB	MAR	APR	MAY	JUN	JUL	AUG	SEP	OCT	NOV	DEC	YEAR
Mean Maximum Temp. (°F)	46.2	51.0	60.0	70.0	77.8	85.2	88.9	88.6	82.7	71.9	60.2	50.8	69.4
Mean Temp. (°F)	35.8	39.6	47.9	56.6	65.1	73.3	77.3	76.1	69.7	58.0	48.1	39.9	57.3
Mean Minimum Temp. (°F)	25.4	28.0	35.8	43.1	52.4	61.3	65.8	63.6	56.7	44.0	36.1	28.9	45.1
Extreme Maximum Temp. (°F)	74	81	84	90	96	102	102	103	102	92	84	78	103
Extreme Minimum Temp. (°F)	-20	-5	2	19	29	39	49	44	32	20	10	-12	-20
Days Maximum Temp. ≥ 90°F	0	0	0	0	1	8	15	14	6	0	0	0	44
Days Maximum Temp. ≤ 32°F	5	2	0	0	0	0	0	0	0	0	0	2	9
Days Minimum Temp. ≤ 32°F	22	19	13	5	0	0	0	0	0	0	0	0	96
Days Minimum Temp. ≤ 0°F	1	0	0	0	0	0	0	0	0	5	13	19	1
Heating Degree Days (base 65°F)	897	713	527	270	89	8	0	1	40	243	502	773	4,063
Cooling Degree Days (base 65°F)	0	0	4	22	104	273	405	361	183	33	2	0	1,387
Mean Precipitation (in.)	4.94	4.08	6.13	4.48	5.39	4.45	4.60	3.12	4.43	3.96	5.02	5.33	55.93
Days With ≥ 0.1" Precipitation	8	7	9	7	7	7	7	5	6	5	7	8	83
Days With ≥ 1.0" Precipitation	1	1	2	1	2	1	1	1	1	1	2	1	15
Mean Snowfall (in.)	*1.9*	*0.5*	0.3	trace	0.0	0.0	0.0	0.0	0.0	0.0	0.1	0.3	*3.1*
Days With ≥ 1.0" Snow Depth	2	1	0	0	0	0	0	0	0	0	0	0	3

Livingston Radio WLIV *Overton County*   Elevation: 974 ft.   Latitude: 36° 23' N   Longitude: 85° 20' W

	JAN	FEB	MAR	APR	MAY	JUN	JUL	AUG	SEP	OCT	NOV	DEC	YEAR
Mean Maximum Temp. (°F)	46.3	51.8	61.2	70.9	77.5	84.6	87.9	87.0	81.3	71.0	60.0	51.0	69.2
Mean Temp. (°F)	36.7	40.7	49.4	57.7	65.1	72.8	76.5	75.2	69.1	58.0	48.7	41.1	57.6
Mean Minimum Temp. (°F)	26.9	29.6	37.5	44.5	52.6	61.0	65.1	63.3	56.9	44.9	37.3	31.1	45.9
Extreme Maximum Temp. (°F)	73	82	86	91	94	100	108	104	97	88	84	77	108
Extreme Minimum Temp. (°F)	-25	-14	4	20	27	35	45	43	27	21	2	-8	-25
Days Maximum Temp. ≥ 90°F	0	0	0	0	1	5	13	8	3	0	0	0	30
Days Maximum Temp. ≤ 32°F	4	2	0	0	0	0	0	0	0	0	0	2	8
Days Minimum Temp. ≤ 32°F	21	17	12	4	0	0	0	0	0	3	11	18	86
Days Minimum Temp. ≤ 0°F	1	0	0	0	0	0	0	0	0	0	0	0	1
Heating Degree Days (base 65°F)	872	679	485	238	85	6	0	1	35	236	486	736	3,859
Cooling Degree Days (base 65°F)	0	0	8	30	105	265	400	352	172	30	3	1	1,366
Mean Precipitation (in.)	4.45	3.96	5.41	4.01	5.15	4.44	5.00	4.28	3.52	3.04	4.39	4.90	52.55
Days With ≥ 0.1" Precipitation	8	7	8	7	8	7	7	6	6	5	7	7	83
Days With ≥ 1.0" Precipitation	1	1	1	1	1	1	2	1	1	1	1	1	13
Mean Snowfall (in.)	3.1	3.3	0.9	0.2	0.0	0.0	0.0	0.0	0.0	trace	0.2	0.9	8.6
Days With ≥ 1.0" Snow Depth	2	1	0	0	0	0	0	0	0	0	0	0	3

Martin Univ. of Tennessee *Weakley County*   Elevation: 337 ft.   Latitude: 36° 20' N   Longitude: 88° 52' W

	JAN	FEB	MAR	APR	MAY	JUN	JUL	AUG	SEP	OCT	NOV	DEC	YEAR
Mean Maximum Temp. (°F)	43.7	49.6	59.7	69.8	78.3	86.5	90.1	89.1	83.2	72.3	59.8	49.1	69.3
Mean Temp. (°F)	34.1	39.0	48.6	58.1	67.0	75.3	79.1	77.3	70.7	59.1	48.7	39.3	58.0
Mean Minimum Temp. (°F)	24.5	28.2	37.4	46.4	55.7	64.2	68.1	65.5	58.2	45.9	37.5	29.5	46.8
Extreme Maximum Temp. (°F)	76	78	85	90	98	102	102	102	101	92	84	78	102
Extreme Minimum Temp. (°F)	-15	-5	9	23	33	44	52	44	33	22	11	-13	-15
Days Maximum Temp. ≥ 90°F	0	0	0	0	2	11	19	15	7	0	0	0	54
Days Maximum Temp. ≤ 32°F	6	4	0	0	0	0	0	0	0	0	0	3	13
Days Minimum Temp. ≤ 32°F	24	18	11	3	0	0	0	0	0	3	10	19	88
Days Minimum Temp. ≤ 0°F	1	0	0	0	0	0	0	0	0	0	0	0	1
Heating Degree Days (base 65°F)	951	729	510	237	62	3	0	1	36	216	487	790	4,022
Cooling Degree Days (base 65°F)	0	0	6	32	128	321	455	395	200	39	4	1	1,581
Mean Precipitation (in.)	3.73	4.21	4.93	5.16	5.06	4.72	4.81	3.23	3.74	3.74	4.93	5.24	53.50
Days With ≥ 0.1" Precipitation	6	7	8	8	8	7	6	5	5	6	7	7	80
Days With ≥ 1.0" Precipitation	1	1	1	2	2	1	2	1	1	1	2	2	17
Mean Snowfall (in.)	2.3	1.7	0.4	trace	0.0	0.0	0.0	0.0	0.0	0.0	trace	0.2	4.6
Days With ≥ 1.0" Snow Depth	1	0	0	0	0	0	0	0	0	0	0	0	1

McMinnville *Warren County*   Elevation: 938 ft.   Latitude: 35° 41' N   Longitude: 85° 48' W

	JAN	FEB	MAR	APR	MAY	JUN	JUL	AUG	SEP	OCT	NOV	DEC	YEAR
Mean Maximum Temp. (°F)	48.0	52.9	62.0	71.3	78.1	85.1	88.2	87.3	81.6	71.7	60.9	52.4	70.0
Mean Temp. (°F)	38.5	42.4	50.6	58.8	66.3	73.8	77.4	76.3	70.5	59.4	49.9	42.6	58.9
Mean Minimum Temp. (°F)	29.0	31.7	39.1	46.1	54.4	62.5	66.5	65.3	59.4	47.1	39.0	32.8	47.7
Extreme Maximum Temp. (°F)	75	80	86	90	94	100	104	102	98	89	82	76	104
Extreme Minimum Temp. (°F)	-19	-17	1	22	32	39	51	49	33	22	9	-6	-19
Days Maximum Temp. ≥ 90°F	0	0	0	0	0	6	13	9	3	0	0	0	31
Days Maximum Temp. ≤ 32°F	4	2	0	0	0	0	0	0	0	0	0	2	8
Days Minimum Temp. ≤ 32°F	19	16	10	3	0	0	0	0	0	2	9	16	75
Days Minimum Temp. ≤ 0°F	1	0	0	0	0	0	0	0	0	0	0	0	1
Heating Degree Days (base 65°F)	815	635	449	214	66	4	0	0	26	203	449	688	3,549
Cooling Degree Days (base 65°F)	0	1	9	33	118	284	409	365	194	38	4	1	1,456
Mean Precipitation (in.)	4.53	4.15	5.82	4.27	5.02	4.64	4.55	3.50	3.97	3.41	4.79	5.21	53.86
Days With ≥ 0.1" Precipitation	8	8	9	7	8	7	8	6	6	5	8	9	89
Days With ≥ 1.0" Precipitation	1	1	2	1	1	1	1	1	1	1	2	1	14
Mean Snowfall (in.)	2.7	2.4	0.7	trace	0.0	0.0	0.0	0.0	0.0	trace	trace	0.7	6.5
Days With ≥ 1.0" Snow Depth	2	1	0	0	0	0	0	0	0	0	0	0	3

Milan Experiment Station *Gibson County*   Elevation: 423 ft.   Latitude: 35° 54' N   Longitude: 88° 44' W

	JAN	FEB	MAR	APR	MAY	JUN	JUL	AUG	SEP	OCT	NOV	DEC	YEAR
Mean Maximum Temp. (°F)	44.7	50.3	59.9	70.3	78.5	86.0	89.4	88.9	83.3	72.4	59.6	49.8	69.4
Mean Temp. (°F)	34.8	39.4	48.5	58.1	66.8	74.6	78.3	76.9	70.4	58.6	48.1	39.3	57.8
Mean Minimum Temp. (°F)	24.8	28.4	37.1	45.9	55.1	63.2	67.2	64.8	57.4	44.8	36.7	28.8	46.2
Extreme Maximum Temp. (°F)	77	81	85	92	94	98	101	101	100	93	85	78	101
Extreme Minimum Temp. (°F)	-20	-5	7	23	33	43	49	43	33	22	11	-10	-20
Days Maximum Temp. ≥ 90°F	0	0	0	0	2	10	17	15	7	0	0	0	51
Days Maximum Temp. ≤ 32°F	6	3	0	0	0	0	0	0	0	0	0	2	11
Days Minimum Temp. ≤ 32°F	24	18	12	3	0	0	0	0	0	4	12	20	93
Days Minimum Temp. ≤ 0°F	1	0	0	0	0	0	0	0	0	0	0	0	1
Heating Degree Days (base 65°F)	929	719	512	239	67	4	0	1	38	230	504	789	4,032
Cooling Degree Days (base 65°F)	0	1	8	36	136	310	438	396	208	40	4	1	1,578
Mean Precipitation (in.)	4.26	4.45	5.33	4.84	5.51	4.82	4.69	3.23	4.42	3.60	4.73	5.87	55.75
Days With ≥ 0.1" Precipitation	7	7	9	8	8	7	7	4	5	5	7	7	81
Days With ≥ 1.0" Precipitation	1	1	1	1	2	2	1	1	1	1	1	2	15
Mean Snowfall (in.)	3.3	3.5	1.1	trace	0.0	0.0	0.0	0.0	0.0	trace	0.3	0.5	8.7
Days With ≥ 1.0" Snow Depth	5	3	0	0	0	0	0	0	0	0	0	1	9

Monteagle *Marion County*   Elevation: 1,847 ft.   Latitude: 35° 14' N   Longitude: 85° 51' W

	JAN	FEB	MAR	APR	MAY	JUN	JUL	AUG	SEP	OCT	NOV	DEC	YEAR
Mean Maximum Temp. (°F)	44.0	49.2	57.3	66.8	73.7	80.5	83.7	83.1	78.0	67.9	57.0	48.3	65.8
Mean Temp. (°F)	35.4	40.0	47.5	56.3	63.9	71.2	74.7	73.7	68.5	57.9	47.8	39.7	56.4
Mean Minimum Temp. (°F)	26.9	30.6	37.8	45.9	54.1	61.8	65.6	64.2	59.0	47.8	38.6	31.1	47.0
Extreme Maximum Temp. (°F)	70	77	81	87	89	93	97	95	94	84	80	71	97
Extreme Minimum Temp. (°F)	-20	-5	5	20	30	40	49	49	37	26	5	-9	-20
Days Maximum Temp. ≥ 90°F	0	0	0	0	0	1	3	2	1	0	0	0	7
Days Maximum Temp. ≤ 32°F	6	3	1	0	0	0	0	0	0	0	0	2	12
Days Minimum Temp. ≤ 32°F	20	16	11	3	0	0	0	0	0	0	1	9	18	78
Days Minimum Temp. ≤ 0°F	1	0	0	0	0	0	0	0	0	0	0	0	1
Heating Degree Days (base 65°F)	909	700	537	274	96	10	0	1	38	233	510	776	4,084
Cooling Degree Days (base 65°F)	0	0	3	18	72	204	318	282	148	19	1	0	1,065
Mean Precipitation (in.)	5.81	5.19	6.66	5.04	5.51	4.77	5.45	4.17	4.88	4.44	5.68	6.01	63.61
Days With ≥ 0.1" Precipitation	9	8	10	8	8	8	9	7	7	6	8	9	97
Days With ≥ 1.0" Precipitation	2	2	2	1	1	1	2	1	1	1	2	2	18
Mean Snowfall (in.)	2.1	1.3	1.5	trace	0.0	0.0	0.0	0.0	0.0	trace	0.2	0.8	5.9
Days With ≥ 1.0" Snow Depth	3	1	0	0	0	0	0	0	0	0	0	0	4

Murfreesboro 5 N *Rutherford County*   Elevation: 547 ft.   Latitude: 35° 55' N   Longitude: 86° 23' W

	JAN	FEB	MAR	APR	MAY	JUN	JUL	AUG	SEP	OCT	NOV	DEC	YEAR
Mean Maximum Temp. (°F)	46.0	51.1	60.5	70.3	77.9	85.6	89.3	88.7	82.8	72.1	60.5	50.8	69.6
Mean Temp. (°F)	35.8	39.5	48.5	57.3	65.9	74.0	78.2	76.9	70.4	58.4	48.7	40.2	57.8
Mean Minimum Temp. (°F)	25.5	27.9	36.4	44.3	53.8	62.5	67.0	65.0	57.9	44.7	36.9	29.6	46.0
Extreme Maximum Temp. (°F)	75	81	86	89	93	102	106	105	101	91	86	76	106
Extreme Minimum Temp. (°F)	-13	-10	2	21	32	41	52	44	35	23	9	-9	-13
Days Maximum Temp. ≥ 90°F	0	0	0	0	1	8	16	14	6	0	0	0	45
Days Maximum Temp. ≤ 32°F	5	2	0	0	0	0	0	0	0	0	0	2	9
Days Minimum Temp. ≤ 32°F	23	19	13	4	0	0	0	0	0	3	11	20	93
Days Minimum Temp. ≤ 0°F	1	0	0	0	0	0	0	0	0	0	0	0	1
Heating Degree Days (base 65°F)	899	714	511	252	77	5	0	1	34	230	485	761	3,969
Cooling Degree Days (base 65°F)	0	0	6	27	115	290	432	384	195	35	3	0	1,487
Mean Precipitation (in.)	4.54	4.00	5.78	4.26	5.24	4.71	4.89	3.69	4.49	3.53	4.70	5.21	55.04
Days With ≥ 0.1" Precipitation	7	7	9	7	7	7	7	6	6	5	7	8	83
Days With ≥ 1.0" Precipitation	1	1	2	1	2	1	1	1	1	1	1	2	15
Mean Snowfall (in.)	1.6	1.0	0.4	trace	0.0	0.0	0.0	0.0	0.0	trace	trace	0.3	3.3
Days With ≥ 1.0" Snow Depth	2	1	0	0	0	0	0	0	0	0	0	0	3

Newport 1 NW *Cocke County*   Elevation: 1,033 ft.   Latitude: 35° 59' N   Longitude: 83° 12' W

	JAN	FEB	MAR	APR	MAY	JUN	JUL	AUG	SEP	OCT	NOV	DEC	YEAR
Mean Maximum Temp. (°F)	46.5	51.7	60.6	70.0	77.0	84.1	87.6	86.5	81.3	70.8	60.4	50.8	68.9
Mean Temp. (°F)	36.2	39.8	48.0	56.5	64.6	72.6	76.5	75.3	69.3	57.3	47.8	39.6	57.0
Mean Minimum Temp. (°F)	25.7	27.8	35.3	43.0	52.2	61.1	65.4	64.1	57.2	43.8	35.3	28.4	44.9
Extreme Maximum Temp. (°F)	78	84	84	91	91	98	100	100	97	89	85	80	100
Extreme Minimum Temp. (°F)	-23	-15	-4	20	29	40	47	47	34	22	9	-4	-23
Days Maximum Temp. ≥ 90°F	0	0	0	0	0	4	12	9	3	0	0	0	28
Days Maximum Temp. ≤ 32°F	4	2	0	0	0	0	0	0	0	0	0	2	8
Days Minimum Temp. ≤ 32°F	22	19	13	4	0	0	0	0	0	4	13	21	96
Days Minimum Temp. ≤ 0°F	1	0	0	0	0	0	0	0	0	0	0	0	1
Heating Degree Days (base 65°F)	887	706	523	264	88	7	0	1	31	249	510	780	4,046
Cooling Degree Days (base 65°F)	0	0	2	16	88	256	379	331	157	19	1	0	1,249
Mean Precipitation (in.)	3.69	3.59	4.43	3.70	4.76	3.81	4.45	3.83	3.17	2.37	3.22	3.79	44.81
Days With ≥ 0.1" Precipitation	8	7	9	8	9	8	8	7	6	5	7	8	90
Days With ≥ 1.0" Precipitation	1	1	1	1	1	1	1	1	1	0	1	1	11
Mean Snowfall (in.)	4.6	2.5	1.4	trace	0.0	0.0	0.0	0.0	0.0	trace	trace	1.2	9.7
Days With ≥ 1.0" Snow Depth	4	2	1	0	0	0	0	0	0	0	0	1	8

Paris 2 NW *Henry County*   Elevation: 577 ft.   Latitude: 36° 20' N   Longitude: 88° 21' W

	JAN	FEB	MAR	APR	MAY	JUN	JUL	AUG	SEP	OCT	NOV	DEC	YEAR
Mean Maximum Temp. (°F)	42.9	48.7	58.9	69.3	76.9	84.4	88.1	87.2	81.1	69.7	58.0	48.2	67.8
Mean Temp. (°F)	33.7	38.3	47.8	57.3	65.6	73.6	77.6	76.2	69.8	57.9	47.7	38.8	57.0
Mean Minimum Temp. (°F)	24.6	27.8	36.6	45.2	54.1	62.8	67.0	65.2	58.5	46.0	37.4	29.3	46.2
Extreme Maximum Temp. (°F)	76	81	89	89	92	100	105	102	100	90	83	78	105
Extreme Minimum Temp. (°F)	-16	-5	3	23	31	43	49	42	35	25	10	-12	-16
Days Maximum Temp. ≥ 90°F	0	0	0	0	1	6	13	10	4	0	0	0	34
Days Maximum Temp. ≤ 32°F	7	4	0	0	0	0	0	0	0	0	0	3	14
Days Minimum Temp. ≤ 32°F	24	19	12	3	0	0	0	0	0	2	11	19	90
Days Minimum Temp. ≤ 0°F	1	0	0	0	0	0	0	0	0	0	0	0	1
Heating Degree Days (base 65°F)	963	749	532	256	78	6	0	1	39	242	515	807	4,188
Cooling Degree Days (base 65°F)	0	0	6	28	103	275	405	359	181	28	3	1	1,389
Mean Precipitation (in.)	4.22	4.43	5.30	4.74	4.91	4.85	4.51	3.75	3.97	3.57	4.81	5.22	54.28
Days With ≥ 0.1" Precipitation	7	7	8	7	9	7	7	5	6	5	7	7	82
Days With ≥ 1.0" Precipitation	1	1	1	1	1	1	1	1	1	1	2	2	14
Mean Snowfall (in.)	3.2	2.8	0.7	trace	0.0	0.0	0.0	0.0	0.0	trace	0.2	0.4	7.3
Days With ≥ 1.0" Snow Depth	4	2	1	0	0	0	0	0	0	0	0	0	6

Pikeville *Bledsoe County* Elevation: 875 ft.   Latitude: 35° 37' N   Longitude: 85° 12' W

	JAN	FEB	MAR	APR	MAY	JUN	JUL	AUG	SEP	OCT	NOV	DEC	YEAR
Mean Maximum Temp. (°F)	48.6	54.2	62.6	72.1	78.7	85.3	88.6	87.9	82.7	72.6	61.0	52.2	70.5
Mean Temp. (°F)	38.4	42.4	50.1	58.2	65.8	73.3	77.2	76.1	70.5	58.9	48.9	41.5	58.4
Mean Minimum Temp. (°F)	28.0	30.6	37.4	44.3	52.9	61.3	65.7	64.2	58.2	45.2	36.8	30.7	46.3
Extreme Maximum Temp. (°F)	74	79	84	91	93	100	107	103	98	89	83	78	107
Extreme Minimum Temp. (°F)	-20	-11	1	18	30	39	47	48	35	21	9	-6	-20
Days Maximum Temp. ≥ 90°F	0	0	0	0	1	6	13	10	4	0	0	0	34
Days Maximum Temp. ≤ 32°F	2	1	0	0	0	0	0	0	0	0	0	1	4
Days Minimum Temp. ≤ 32°F	20	16	10	4	0	0	0	0	0	4	12	18	84
Days Minimum Temp. ≤ 0°F	0	0	0	0	0	0	0	0	0	0	0	0	0
Heating Degree Days (base 65°F)	819	632	461	223	68	5	0	0	25	211	479	722	3,645
Cooling Degree Days (base 65°F)	0	0	3	23	100	268	398	353	185	29	1	1	1,361
Mean Precipitation (in.)	5.13	4.63	5.69	4.49	5.09	4.38	4.25	3.65	4.13	3.43	4.65	5.27	54.79
Days With ≥ 0.1" Precipitation	8	7	9	7	8	8	8	7	6	5	7	8	88
Days With ≥ 1.0" Precipitation	2	1	1	1	2	1	1	1	1	1	1	1	14
Mean Snowfall (in.)	2.4	1.7	0.8	trace	0.0	0.0	0.0	0.0	0.0	trace	trace	0.5	5.4
Days With ≥ 1.0" Snow Depth	1	1	0	0	0	0	0	0	0	0	0	0	2

Portland Sewage Plant *Sumner County* Elevation: 793 ft.   Latitude: 36° 35' N   Longitude: 86° 32' W

	JAN	FEB	MAR	APR	MAY	JUN	JUL	AUG	SEP	OCT	NOV	DEC	YEAR
Mean Maximum Temp. (°F)	43.4	48.6	58.9	69.0	76.7	84.2	88.3	86.9	81.3	70.2	58.4	48.3	67.8
Mean Temp. (°F)	34.3	38.7	48.1	57.6	66.0	74.0	78.0	76.4	70.2	58.4	48.3	38.9	57.4
Mean Minimum Temp. (°F)	25.1	28.8	37.2	46.0	55.2	63.7	67.7	65.8	59.0	46.6	38.2	29.5	46.9
Extreme Maximum Temp. (°F)	72	81	85	89	92	100	102	101	100	89	84	76	102
Extreme Minimum Temp. (°F)	-17	-6	8	23	30	42	48	45	34	24	9	-14	-17
Days Maximum Temp. ≥ 90°F	0	0	0	0	0	6	14	11	4	0	0	0	35
Days Maximum Temp. ≤ 32°F	6	3	0	0	0	0	0	0	0	0	0	3	12
Days Minimum Temp. ≤ 32°F	23	18	11	3	0	0	0	0	0	2	10	19	86
Days Minimum Temp. ≤ 0°F	1	0	0	0	0	0	0	0	0	0	0	0	1
Heating Degree Days (base 65°F)	945	731	523	250	78	6	0	1	34	230	496	802	4,096
Cooling Degree Days (base 65°F)	0	0	8	34	127	297	441	383	199	34	2	0	1,525
Mean Precipitation (in.)	4.18	4.12	5.61	4.16	5.20	4.64	4.37	3.66	3.84	3.54	4.58	5.06	52.96
Days With ≥ 0.1" Precipitation	7	6	8	8	8	7	7	6	6	6	7	7	83
Days With ≥ 1.0" Precipitation	1	1	2	1	1	1	1	1	1	1	1	1	13
Mean Snowfall (in.)	2.4	1.7	0.1	trace	0.0	0.0	0.0	0.0	0.0	0.0	0.1	0.3	4.6
Days With ≥ 1.0" Snow Depth	3	2	0	0	0	0	0	0	0	0	0	0	5

Pulaski Water Plant *Giles County* Elevation: 633 ft.   Latitude: 35° 11' N   Longitude: 87° 03' W

	JAN	FEB	MAR	APR	MAY	JUN	JUL	AUG	SEP	OCT	NOV	DEC	YEAR
Mean Maximum Temp. (°F)	49.5	55.1	64.1	73.5	80.2	86.9	90.1	89.6	84.6	74.4	62.9	53.7	72.0
Mean Temp. (°F)	39.1	43.4	51.8	60.1	67.6	75.1	78.9	77.7	72.0	60.7	50.9	43.1	60.0
Mean Minimum Temp. (°F)	28.6	31.7	39.4	46.7	55.0	63.3	67.6	65.8	59.4	47.0	39.0	32.4	48.0
Extreme Maximum Temp. (°F)	75	80	85	91	96	100	105	101	100	92	86	78	105
Extreme Minimum Temp. (°F)	-16	2	3	22	30	41	51	50	35	25	10	-8	-16
Days Maximum Temp. ≥ 90°F	0	0	0	0	2	10	18	16	8	0	0	0	54
Days Maximum Temp. ≤ 32°F	3	1	0	0	0	0	0	0	0	0	0	1	5
Days Minimum Temp. ≤ 32°F	20	16	9	2	0	0	0	0	0	2	10	16	75
Days Minimum Temp. ≤ 0°F	0	0	0	0	0	0	0	0	0	0	0	0	0
Heating Degree Days (base 65°F)	797	605	414	182	48	2	0	0	19	174	419	674	3,334
Cooling Degree Days (base 65°F)	0	0	1	37	135	319	448	405	229	48	4	1	1,636
Mean Precipitation (in.)	5.07	4.66	6.18	4.37	5.07	4.55	4.50	3.24	4.31	3.71	5.10	5.76	56.52
Days With ≥ 0.1" Precipitation	7	7	9	7	7	7	7	5	6	5	7	8	82
Days With ≥ 1.0" Precipitation	1	1	2	1	2	2	1	1	1	1	2	2	17
Mean Snowfall (in.)	1.2	0.9	0.2	trace	0.0	0.0	0.0	0.0	0.0	0.0	trace	0.3	2.6
Days With ≥ 1.0" Snow Depth	1	1	0	0	0	0	0	0	0	0	0	0	2

Rockwood 2 *Roane County* Elevation: 859 ft.   Latitude: 35° 51' N   Longitude: 84° 42' W

	JAN	FEB	MAR	APR	MAY	JUN	JUL	AUG	SEP	OCT	NOV	DEC	YEAR
Mean Maximum Temp. (°F)	45.6	50.6	59.9	70.0	77.1	84.1	87.5	86.6	81.3	70.6	59.4	49.9	68.6
Mean Temp. (°F)	35.4	38.9	47.2	56.2	64.1	72.1	76.0	74.9	69.0	57.2	47.1	39.1	56.4
Mean Minimum Temp. (°F)	25.1	27.2	34.4	42.4	51.1	60.0	64.4	63.1	56.6	43.6	34.8	28.4	44.3
Extreme Maximum Temp. (°F)	74	78	86	91	91	100	107	101	97	89	81	77	107
Extreme Minimum Temp. (°F)	-8	-10	1	21	30	40	47	49	31	23	9	-6	-10
Days Maximum Temp. ≥ 90°F	0	0	0	0	0	4	12	9	4	0	0	0	29
Days Maximum Temp. ≤ 32°F	3	2	0	0	0	0	0	0	0	0	0	1	6
Days Minimum Temp. ≤ 32°F	23	20	14	4	0	0	0	0	0	4	14	21	100
Days Minimum Temp. ≤ 0°F	1	0	0	0	0	0	0	0	0	0	0	0	1
Heating Degree Days (base 65°F)	913	730	547	273	94	9	0	1	35	253	529	796	4,180
Cooling Degree Days (base 65°F)	0	0	1	14	76	238	362	317	155	18	1	0	1,182
Mean Precipitation (in.)	5.68	4.88	6.12	4.63	5.60	5.20	5.49	4.36	3.94	3.81	5.10	5.75	60.56
Days With ≥ 0.1" Precipitation	9	8	9	8	8	7	9	7	6	5	7	8	91
Days With ≥ 1.0" Precipitation	2	1	2	1	2	2	2	1	1	1	2	2	19
Mean Snowfall (in.)	1.4	1.0	0.6	0.2	0.0	0.0	0.0	0.0	0.0	0.0	trace	0.3	3.5
Days With ≥ 1.0" Snow Depth	0	0	0	0	0	0	0	0	0	0	0	0	0

Rogersville 1 NE *Hawkins County*   Elevation: 1,354 ft.   Latitude: 36° 25' N   Longitude: 82° 59' W

	JAN	FEB	MAR	APR	MAY	JUN	JUL	AUG	SEP	OCT	NOV	DEC	YEAR
Mean Maximum Temp. (°F)	45.9	51.3	61.0	70.3	77.2	83.7	87.1	86.1	80.7	70.4	59.2	49.9	68.6
Mean Temp. (°F)	36.1	40.1	48.6	56.8	64.4	71.6	75.4	74.3	68.7	57.4	47.7	39.7	56.7
Mean Minimum Temp. (°F)	26.3	28.8	36.1	43.2	51.7	59.5	63.7	62.5	56.7	44.2	36.3	29.4	44.9
Extreme Maximum Temp. (°F)	76	81	84	89	91	97	98	99	96	87	82	77	99
Extreme Minimum Temp. (°F)	-23	-11	-4	20	29	37	44	44	32	21	8	-8	-23
Days Maximum Temp. ≥ 90°F	0	0	0	0	0	3	10	6	2	0	0	0	21
Days Maximum Temp. ≤ 32°F	3	1	0	0	0	0	0	0	0	0	0	2	6
Days Minimum Temp. ≤ 32°F	22	18	12	4	0	0	0	0	0	0	4	11	20	91
Days Minimum Temp. ≤ 0°F	1	0	0	0	0	0	0	0	0	0	0	0	1
Heating Degree Days (base 65°F)	889	697	504	256	85	8	1	1	33	246	512	778	4,010
Cooling Degree Days (base 65°F)	0	0	2	16	80	229	351	305	149	19	0	0	1,151
Mean Precipitation (in.)	3.91	3.55	4.23	3.88	4.68	3.53	3.98	3.67	3.22	2.75	3.63	4.20	45.23
Days With ≥ 0.1" Precipitation	7	6	8	6	6	7	6	6	5	5	6	6	74
Days With ≥ 1.0" Precipitation	1	1	1	1	1	1	1	1	1	1	1	1	12
Mean Snowfall (in.)	3.4	1.8	0.8	0.5	0.0	0.0	0.0	0.0	0.0	0.0	trace	0.5	7.0
Days With ≥ 1.0" Snow Depth	2	1	0	0	0	0	0	0	0	0	0	0	3

Samburg Wildlife Refuge *Obion County*   Elevation: 308 ft.   Latitude: 36° 27' N   Longitude: 89° 19' W

	JAN	FEB	MAR	APR	MAY	JUN	JUL	AUG	SEP	OCT	NOV	DEC	YEAR
Mean Maximum Temp. (°F)	42.9	49.1	58.9	69.7	78.4	86.4	90.3	88.7	82.6	72.2	59.5	48.4	68.9
Mean Temp. (°F)	33.9	39.1	48.8	58.4	67.3	75.4	79.3	77.3	70.7	59.4	49.1	39.2	58.2
Mean Minimum Temp. (°F)	24.9	29.1	38.6	47.1	56.2	64.3	68.3	65.8	58.8	46.4	38.8	29.9	47.3
Extreme Maximum Temp. (°F)	74	76	84	91	93	100	105	100	98	90	82	79	105
Extreme Minimum Temp. (°F)	-15	-3	9	23	34	43	50	46	36	26	14	-10	-15
Days Maximum Temp. ≥ 90°F	0	0	0	0	1	10	18	13	5	0	0	0	47
Days Maximum Temp. ≤ 32°F	7	3	0	0	0	0	0	0	0	0	0	2	12
Days Minimum Temp. ≤ 32°F	23	18	10	2	0	0	0	0	0	0	2	8	17	80
Days Minimum Temp. ≤ 0°F	1	0	0	0	0	0	0	0	0	0	0	0	1
Heating Degree Days (base 65°F)	957	724	504	231	56	3	0	1	31	208	473	795	3,983
Cooling Degree Days (base 65°F)	0	0	7	33	129	319	na	394	198	37	3	na	na
Mean Precipitation (in.)	3.45	4.02	4.76	5.08	5.29	4.57	3.92	3.29	3.37	3.81	4.70	5.29	51.55
Days With ≥ 0.1" Precipitation	6	5	8	7	6	6	5	4	5	5	6	6	69
Days With ≥ 1.0" Precipitation	1	1	1	2	1	1	1	1	1	1	1	2	14
Mean Snowfall (in.)	3.0	2.3	0.6	trace	0.0	0.0	0.0	0.0	0.0	0.0	0.3	0.2	6.4
Days With ≥ 1.0" Snow Depth	2	1	0	0	0	0	0	0	0	0	0	0	3

Savannah 6 SW *Hardin County*   Elevation: 419 ft.   Latitude: 35° 09' N   Longitude: 88° 19' W

	JAN	FEB	MAR	APR	MAY	JUN	JUL	AUG	SEP	OCT	NOV	DEC	YEAR
Mean Maximum Temp. (°F)	49.8	56.2	65.7	75.1	80.9	87.6	91.1	90.5	84.9	75.1	63.1	53.8	72.8
Mean Temp. (°F)	39.3	44.0	53.1	61.5	68.6	75.9	79.6	78.5	72.6	61.7	51.5	43.4	60.8
Mean Minimum Temp. (°F)	28.8	32.1	40.3	47.8	56.3	64.2	67.9	66.4	60.2	48.3	40.0	33.0	48.8
Extreme Maximum Temp. (°F)	78	84	87	92	95	103	107	105	104	94	85	79	107
Extreme Minimum Temp. (°F)	-13	-5	10	24	32	43	51	47	38	24	11	-10	-13
Days Maximum Temp. ≥ 90°F	0	0	0	0	2	12	20	18	8	0	0	0	60
Days Maximum Temp. ≤ 32°F	3	1	0	0	0	0	0	0	0	0	0	1	5
Days Minimum Temp. ≤ 32°F	20	15	8	2	0	0	0	0	0	0	2	9	16	72
Days Minimum Temp. ≤ 0°F	0	0	0	0	0	0	0	0	0	0	0	0	0
Heating Degree Days (base 65°F)	790	587	377	156	35	1	0	0	18	154	404	663	3,185
Cooling Degree Days (base 65°F)	0	1	14	56	162	347	474	439	255	64	7	2	1,821
Mean Precipitation (in.)	4.99	4.54	6.13	5.33	6.56	4.57	4.46	3.35	4.16	3.76	5.57	5.90	59.32
Days With ≥ 0.1" Precipitation	7	7	8	7	8	6	6	5	6	5	7	8	80
Days With ≥ 1.0" Precipitation	1	1	2	2	2	2	1	1	1	1	2	2	18
Mean Snowfall (in.)	1.6	0.8	trace	trace	0.0	0.0	0.0	0.0	0.0	0.0	trace	0.2	2.6
Days With ≥ 1.0" Snow Depth	1	0	0	0	0	0	0	0	0	0	0	0	1

Selmer *McNairy County*   Elevation: 469 ft.   Latitude: 35° 10' N   Longitude: 88° 36' W

	JAN	FEB	MAR	APR	MAY	JUN	JUL	AUG	SEP	OCT	NOV	DEC	YEAR
Mean Maximum Temp. (°F)	47.2	52.8	62.2	72.3	79.3	86.5	90.2	89.4	83.6	73.3	61.5	51.9	70.8
Mean Temp. (°F)	37.0	41.5	50.4	59.3	67.2	74.9	78.6	77.4	71.2	59.8	49.9	41.6	59.1
Mean Minimum Temp. (°F)	26.9	30.1	38.5	46.2	55.0	63.2	67.1	65.4	58.8	46.2	38.2	31.2	47.2
Extreme Maximum Temp. (°F)	78	81	85	92	94	101	105	104	100	93	86	77	105
Extreme Minimum Temp. (°F)	-14	-11	7	23	29	39	47	47	34	24	5	-7	-14
Days Maximum Temp. ≥ 90°F	0	0	0	0	2	10	18	17	7	0	0	0	54
Days Maximum Temp. ≤ 32°F	4	2	0	0	0	0	0	0	0	0	0	2	8
Days Minimum Temp. ≤ 32°F	22	17	10	3	0	0	0	0	0	3	11	18	84
Days Minimum Temp. ≤ 0°F	0	0	0	0	0	0	0	0	0	0	0	0	0
Heating Degree Days (base 65°F)	860	658	454	210	60	4	1	0	29	198	453	721	3,648
Cooling Degree Days (base 65°F)	0	1	11	47	146	328	452	413	230	47	5	2	1,682
Mean Precipitation (in.)	5.01	4.48	6.01	5.31	6.10	4.31	4.64	2.89	4.39	3.54	5.52	5.85	58.05
Days With ≥ 0.1" Precipitation	8	7	8	7	8	7	7	5	5	5	7	8	82
Days With ≥ 1.0" Precipitation	2	1	2	2	2	1	1	1	1	1	2	2	18
Mean Snowfall (in.)	1.1	1.1	0.1	trace	0.0	0.0	0.0	0.0	0.0	trace	trace	0.2	2.5
Days With ≥ 1.0" Snow Depth	1	0	0	0	0	0	0	0	0	0	0	0	1

Sevierville 1 SE *Sevier County*   Elevation: 928 ft.   Latitude: 35° 52' N   Longitude: 83° 33' W

	JAN	FEB	MAR	APR	MAY	JUN	JUL	AUG	SEP	OCT	NOV	DEC	YEAR
Mean Maximum Temp. (°F)	47.0	52.3	61.8	71.0	78.1	84.6	87.7	86.9	81.6	71.2	60.0	51.2	69.5
Mean Temp. (°F)	36.3	40.0	48.2	56.5	64.7	72.2	75.9	75.0	69.0	57.3	47.2	39.7	56.8
Mean Minimum Temp. (°F)	25.5	27.7	34.5	41.9	51.2	59.7	64.1	63.0	56.4	43.4	34.3	28.2	44.2
Extreme Maximum Temp. (°F)	78	85	87	90	91	98	101	102	101	90	83	80	102
Extreme Minimum Temp. (°F)	-24	-16	-4	18	27	37	46	47	33	19	7	-7	-24
Days Maximum Temp. ≥ 90°F	0	0	0	0	0	5	13	9	4	0	0	0	31
Days Maximum Temp. ≤ 32°F	3	2	0	0	0	0	0	0	0	0	0	1	6
Days Minimum Temp. ≤ 32°F	22	19	14	5	0	0	0	0	0	4	13	20	97
Days Minimum Temp. ≤ 0°F	1	0	0	0	0	0	0	0	0	0	0	0	1
Heating Degree Days (base 65°F)	884	699	518	262	83	7	0	0	31	252	529	778	4,043
Cooling Degree Days (base 65°F)	0	0	4	17	89	260	379	347	170	26	1	0	1,293
Mean Precipitation (in.)	3.78	3.54	4.26	3.67	4.53	3.98	4.00	3.13	3.27	2.64	3.23	3.74	43.77
Days With ≥ 0.1" Precipitation	7	7	8	7	8	7	8	6	5	5	6	7	81
Days With ≥ 1.0" Precipitation	1	1	1	1	1	1	1	1	1	1	1	1	12
Mean Snowfall (in.)	*3.0*	1.4	1.2	0.6	0.0	0.0	0.0	0.0	0.0	0.0	trace	0.3	*6.5*
Days With ≥ 1.0" Snow Depth	2	1	0	0	0	0	0	0	0	0	0	0	3

Shelbyville Water Dept. *Bedford County*   Elevation: 757 ft.   Latitude: 35° 30' N   Longitude: 86° 29' W

	JAN	FEB	MAR	APR	MAY	JUN	JUL	AUG	SEP	OCT	NOV	DEC	YEAR
Mean Maximum Temp. (°F)	48.3	53.7	62.6	72.2	79.4	86.4	89.6	89.1	83.5	73.0	61.3	52.4	71.0
Mean Temp. (°F)	38.4	42.6	50.9	59.1	67.2	74.6	78.4	77.5	71.4	60.1	50.1	42.3	59.4
Mean Minimum Temp. (°F)	28.4	31.3	39.1	46.0	55.0	62.8	67.1	65.8	59.3	47.1	38.9	32.2	47.7
Extreme Maximum Temp. (°F)	75	79	85	92	95	101	104	102	101	92	83	77	104
Extreme Minimum Temp. (°F)	-20	-6	3	21	30	40	51	49	35	24	9	-9	-20
Days Maximum Temp. ≥ 90°F	0	0	0	0	1	9	17	15	6	0	0	0	48
Days Maximum Temp. ≤ 32°F	3	1	0	0	0	0	0	0	0	0	0	2	6
Days Minimum Temp. ≤ 32°F	20	16	9	3	0	0	0	0	0	2	10	17	77
Days Minimum Temp. ≤ 0°F	1	0	0	0	0	0	0	0	0	0	0	0	1
Heating Degree Days (base 65°F)	818	628	436	206	53	3	0	0	24	189	444	698	3,499
Cooling Degree Days (base 65°F)	0	1	8	32	134	304	438	399	218	46	3	1	1,584
Mean Precipitation (in.)	5.00	4.35	6.06	4.24	5.31	4.68	5.09	3.35	4.27	4.05	5.31	5.43	57.14
Days With ≥ 0.1" Precipitation	8	8	9	7	8	7	7	5	6	5	7	9	86
Days With ≥ 1.0" Precipitation	1	1	2	1	2	1	1	1	1	1	2	2	16
Mean Snowfall (in.)	2.3	1.7	0.4	trace	0.0	0.0	0.0	0.0	0.0	trace	trace	0.4	4.8
Days With ≥ 1.0" Snow Depth	2	2	0	0	0	0	0	0	0	0	0	0	4

Smithville 2 SE *De Kalb County*   Elevation: 889 ft.   Latitude: 35° 58' N   Longitude: 85° 48' W

	JAN	FEB	MAR	APR	MAY	JUN	JUL	AUG	SEP	OCT	NOV	DEC	YEAR
Mean Maximum Temp. (°F)	45.7	50.2	60.0	69.3	77.2	84.2	87.8	86.9	80.9	71.0	60.0	50.3	68.6
Mean Temp. (°F)	35.3	38.7	47.5	55.7	64.4	72.1	76.2	74.8	68.2	57.0	47.4	39.2	56.4
Mean Minimum Temp. (°F)	24.9	27.1	35.0	42.1	51.4	60.0	64.6	62.6	55.5	42.9	34.7	28.2	44.1
Extreme Maximum Temp. (°F)	74	78	85	90	91	100	104	102	99	89	81	76	104
Extreme Minimum Temp. (°F)	-24	-14	0	20	29	38	49	44	29	21	9	-7	-24
Days Maximum Temp. ≥ 90°F	0	0	0	0	0	5	13	8	3	0	0	0	29
Days Maximum Temp. ≤ 32°F	5	3	0	0	0	0	0	0	0	0	0	2	10
Days Minimum Temp. ≤ 32°F	23	20	14	5	0	0	0	0	0	4	14	21	101
Days Minimum Temp. ≤ 0°F	1	0	0	0	0	0	0	0	0	0	0	0	1
Heating Degree Days (base 65°F)	913	735	538	287	96	10	0	2	47	262	524	791	4,205
Cooling Degree Days (base 65°F)	0	0	3	14	84	238	367	315	148	19	1	1	1,190
Mean Precipitation (in.)	4.99	4.33	6.07	3.93	5.29	4.58	4.77	4.12	4.24	3.62	4.80	5.58	56.32
Days With ≥ 0.1" Precipitation	9	8	9	7	9	8	8	6	6	6	8	9	93
Days With ≥ 1.0" Precipitation	1	1	2	1	1	1	1	1	1	1	1	1	13
Mean Snowfall (in.)	na	na	0.2	0.1	0.0	0.0	0.0	0.0	0.0	0.0	trace	0.3	na
Days With ≥ 1.0" Snow Depth	na	na	0	0	0	0	0	0	0	0	0	0	na

Springfield Exp. Station *Robertson County*   Elevation: 744 ft.   Latitude: 36° 28' N   Longitude: 86° 51' W

	JAN	FEB	MAR	APR	MAY	JUN	JUL	AUG	SEP	OCT	NOV	DEC	YEAR
Mean Maximum Temp. (°F)	43.0	48.3	58.1	68.3	76.4	84.3	88.4	87.5	81.5	70.1	57.9	48.3	67.7
Mean Temp. (°F)	33.4	37.5	46.8	56.2	64.8	73.1	77.1	75.6	69.3	57.5	47.3	38.4	56.4
Mean Minimum Temp. (°F)	23.8	26.7	35.4	44.0	53.2	61.9	65.8	63.6	57.0	44.9	36.7	28.5	45.1
Extreme Maximum Temp. (°F)	75	82	85	88	92	101	103	103	101	89	83	76	103
Extreme Minimum Temp. (°F)	-17	-6	1	21	30	42	47	44	34	22	8	-16	-17
Days Maximum Temp. ≥ 90°F	0	0	0	0	0	6	15	12	5	0	0	0	38
Days Maximum Temp. ≤ 32°F	7	4	1	0	0	0	0	0	0	0	0	3	15
Days Minimum Temp. ≤ 32°F	24	19	13	4	0	0	0	0	0	4	12	20	96
Days Minimum Temp. ≤ 0°F	1	0	0	0	0	0	0	0	0	0	0	0	1
Heating Degree Days (base 65°F)	973	769	564	287	98	9	1	2	47	256	527	819	4,352
Cooling Degree Days (base 65°F)	0	0	6	27	102	263	395	345	177	31	3	0	1,349
Mean Precipitation (in.)	3.98	3.99	5.16	4.21	5.40	4.62	4.11	3.23	3.71	3.49	4.37	4.95	51.22
Days With ≥ 0.1" Precipitation	7	6	8	8	8	8	6	6	5	5	7	7	81
Days With ≥ 1.0" Precipitation	1	1	1	1	2	1	1	1	1	1	1	2	14
Mean Snowfall (in.)	3.8	4.3	1.0	trace	0.0	0.0	0.0	0.0	0.0	trace	0.1	0.7	9.9
Days With ≥ 1.0" Snow Depth	5	3	0	0	0	0	0	0	0	0	0	1	9

Tazewell *Claiborne County*　Elevation: 1,364 ft.　Latitude: 36° 28' N　Longitude: 83° 34' W

	JAN	FEB	MAR	APR	MAY	JUN	JUL	AUG	SEP	OCT	NOV	DEC	YEAR
Mean Maximum Temp. (°F)	43.9	48.8	58.1	67.8	75.2	82.6	86.1	85.2	79.8	69.3	57.9	48.4	66.9
Mean Temp. (°F)	32.8	36.2	44.5	53.2	61.8	70.0	74.2	73.2	67.0	54.7	44.7	36.7	54.1
Mean Minimum Temp. (°F)	21.7	23.6	30.9	38.5	48.3	57.4	62.2	61.1	54.0	40.1	31.4	24.9	41.2
Extreme Maximum Temp. (°F)	75	79	83	90	90	97	99	102	96	88	81	78	102
Extreme Minimum Temp. (°F)	-24	-22	-10	18	25	28	41	42	29	18	6	-8	-24
Days Maximum Temp. ≥ 90°F	0	0	0	0	0	2	8	5	2	0	0	0	17
Days Maximum Temp. ≤ 32°F	5	3	0	0	0	0	0	0	0	0	0	2	10
Days Minimum Temp. ≤ 32°F	25	22	18	9	2	0	0	0	0	8	17	24	125
Days Minimum Temp. ≤ 0°F	2	1	0	0	0	0	0	0	0	0	0	0	3
Heating Degree Days (base 65°F)	992	807	629	355	145	19	1	2	57	322	603	871	4,803
Cooling Degree Days (base 65°F)	0	0	1	6	60	193	321	275	122	11	0	0	989
Mean Precipitation (in.)	4.91	4.36	5.21	4.50	5.24	4.25	4.45	4.01	3.31	3.20	4.19	4.82	52.45
Days With ≥ 0.1" Precipitation	9	8	9	8	8	8	8	7	6	6	8	9	94
Days With ≥ 1.0" Precipitation	1	1	1	1	2	1	1	1	1	1	1	1	13
Mean Snowfall (in.)	5.7	4.8	2.5	0.5	0.0	0.0	0.0	0.0	0.0	trace	0.6	2.6	16.7
Days With ≥ 1.0" Snow Depth	5	3	1	0	0	0	0	0	0	0	0	1	10

Tullahoma *Coffee County*　Elevation: 1,020 ft.　Latitude: 35° 21' N　Longitude: 86° 13' W

	JAN	FEB	MAR	APR	MAY	JUN	JUL	AUG	SEP	OCT	NOV	DEC	YEAR
Mean Maximum Temp. (°F)	47.4	52.3	61.5	71.0	77.7	84.5	87.6	87.2	81.7	71.6	60.3	51.3	69.5
Mean Temp. (°F)	37.9	41.8	50.1	58.6	66.2	73.6	77.3	76.4	70.6	59.3	49.5	41.6	58.6
Mean Minimum Temp. (°F)	28.4	31.2	38.7	46.1	54.7	62.6	67.0	65.5	59.3	47.0	38.6	31.8	47.6
Extreme Maximum Temp. (°F)	75	78	84	90	92	96	101	100	99	88	81	75	101
Extreme Minimum Temp. (°F)	-20	-4	3	20	33	41	47	50	35	23	9	-8	-20
Days Maximum Temp. ≥ 90°F	0	0	0	0	0	5	12	10	4	0	0	0	31
Days Maximum Temp. ≤ 32°F	3	2	0	0	0	0	0	0	0	0	0	2	7
Days Minimum Temp. ≤ 32°F	20	16	10	3	0	0	0	0	0	2	9	17	77
Days Minimum Temp. ≤ 0°F	1	0	0	0	0	0	0	0	0	0	0	0	1
Heating Degree Days (base 65°F)	833	650	459	214	62	4	0	0	27	200	461	719	3,629
Cooling Degree Days (base 65°F)	0	0	4	24	105	270	397	359	190	32	2	1	1,384
Mean Precipitation (in.)	5.66	4.92	6.68	4.99	5.03	4.73	4.90	3.59	4.27	4.05	5.37	5.76	59.95
Days With ≥ 0.1" Precipitation	9	8	9	7	8	7	8	6	7	6	8	9	92
Days With ≥ 1.0" Precipitation	1	1	2	2	1	1	1	1	1	2	2	1	16
Mean Snowfall (in.)	*1.4*	1.9	0.8	trace	0.0	0.0	0.0	0.0	0.0	trace	trace	0.5	*4.6*
Days With ≥ 1.0" Snow Depth	*2*	1	0	0	0	0	0	0	0	0	0	0	*3*

Union City *Obion County*　Elevation: 347 ft.　Latitude: 36° 24' N　Longitude: 89° 02' W

	JAN	FEB	MAR	APR	MAY	JUN	JUL	AUG	SEP	OCT	NOV	DEC	YEAR
Mean Maximum Temp. (°F)	42.4	48.3	58.2	68.8	77.5	85.8	89.3	88.1	82.1	71.3	58.4	48.0	68.2
Mean Temp. (°F)	33.5	38.3	47.8	57.6	66.7	75.2	78.8	76.6	69.9	58.2	47.8	38.8	57.4
Mean Minimum Temp. (°F)	24.6	28.3	37.3	46.3	55.9	64.5	68.1	65.1	57.6	45.1	37.1	29.5	46.6
Extreme Maximum Temp. (°F)	76	77	84	89	93	100	103	101	99	92	83	78	103
Extreme Minimum Temp. (°F)	-14	-6	11	25	34	44	49	47	33	26	13	-10	-14
Days Maximum Temp. ≥ 90°F	0	0	0	0	1	9	17	13	5	0	0	0	45
Days Maximum Temp. ≤ 32°F	7	4	0	0	0	0	0	0	0	0	0	3	14
Days Minimum Temp. ≤ 32°F	24	19	11	2	0	0	0	0	0	3	11	20	90
Days Minimum Temp. ≤ 0°F	1	0	0	0	0	0	0	0	0	0	0	0	1
Heating Degree Days (base 65°F)	969	747	531	248	65	3	0	1	39	236	513	807	4,159
Cooling Degree Days (base 65°F)	0	0	5	29	128	324	447	380	187	34	3	1	1,538
Mean Precipitation (in.)	3.75	3.96	4.95	4.87	4.93	5.10	4.15	3.38	3.31	4.04	4.95	5.05	52.44
Days With ≥ 0.1" Precipitation	7	6	8	8	8	7	6	5	5	5	7	7	79
Days With ≥ 1.0" Precipitation	1	1	1	2	1	1	1	1	1	1	1	1	13
Mean Snowfall (in.)	3.6	3.4	1.2	trace	0.0	0.0	0.0	0.0	0.0	trace	0.3	0.8	9.3
Days With ≥ 1.0" Snow Depth	4	3	0	0	0	0	0	0	0	0	0	1	8

Waverly *Humphreys County*　Elevation: 567 ft.　Latitude: 36° 05' N　Longitude: 87° 47' W

	JAN	FEB	MAR	APR	MAY	JUN	JUL	AUG	SEP	OCT	NOV	DEC	YEAR
Mean Maximum Temp. (°F)	46.1	51.5	61.1	71.1	*79.1*	85.5	*89.5*	*88.9*	82.9	72.1	*60.1*	50.3	*69.9*
Mean Temp. (°F)	34.6	38.9	48.0	*57.2*	*66.4*	73.6	*77.8*	76.5	*69.8*	*57.7*	47.4	*38.6*	*57.2*
Mean Minimum Temp. (°F)	23.1	26.3	34.8	*43.3*	*53.5*	61.7	*66.0*	*64.0*	56.6	*43.2*	*34.6*	27.1	*44.5*
Extreme Maximum Temp. (°F)	76	82	87	91	94	102	104	101	102	91	86	78	104
Extreme Minimum Temp. (°F)	-24	-7	-1	19	29	40	46	42	32	19	8	-11	-24
Days Maximum Temp. ≥ 90°F	0	0	0	0	1	7	15	13	5	0	0	0	41
Days Maximum Temp. ≤ 32°F	4	2	0	0	0	0	0	0	0	0	0	2	8
Days Minimum Temp. ≤ 32°F	23	19	13	4	0	0	0	0	0	5	13	20	97
Days Minimum Temp. ≤ 0°F	1	1	0	0	0	0	0	0	0	0	0	0	2
Heating Degree Days (base 65°F)	935	731	527	*256*	*71*	7	*0*	*1*	38	251	524	811	4,152
Cooling Degree Days (base 65°F)	0	0	6	*27*	*132*	289	*441*	*392*	192	*36*	*3*	*1*	*1,519*
Mean Precipitation (in.)	4.39	4.66	5.81	4.72	5.43	4.99	4.58	3.87	4.16	3.43	4.95	5.27	56.26
Days With ≥ 0.1" Precipitation	6	7	8	7	7	7	6	4	5	5	6	7	75
Days With ≥ 1.0" Precipitation	1	1	2	1	1	2	1	1	1	1	2	2	17
Mean Snowfall (in.)	na	*0.6*	0.2	trace	0.0	0.0	0.0	0.0	0.0	0.0	trace	0.2	na
Days With ≥ 1.0" Snow Depth	na	*0*	0	0	0	0	0	0	0	0.0	trace	0	na

Waynesboro *Wayne County*   Elevation: 748 ft.   Latitude: 35° 18' N   Longitude: 87° 46' W

	JAN	FEB	MAR	APR	MAY	JUN	JUL	AUG	SEP	OCT	NOV	DEC	YEAR
Mean Maximum Temp. (°F)	46.9	52.3	61.5	71.5	78.1	85.4	89.0	88.3	83.0	72.4	61.0	51.2	70.1
Mean Temp. (°F)	35.6	39.5	48.0	56.9	64.6	72.9	76.9	75.5	69.5	57.5	47.7	39.8	57.0
Mean Minimum Temp. (°F)	24.3	26.7	34.6	42.2	51.1	60.3	64.8	62.6	55.9	42.6	34.4	28.2	44.0
Extreme Maximum Temp. (°F)	77	82	87	91	96	99	105	102	100	90	86	76	105
Extreme Minimum Temp. (°F)	-17	-8	3	19	27	35	45	44	32	21	3	-9	-17
Days Maximum Temp. ≥ 90°F	0	0	0	0	1	8	17	13	6	0	0	0	45
Days Maximum Temp. ≤ 32°F	4	2	0	0	0	0	0	0	0	0	0	2	8
Days Minimum Temp. ≤ 32°F	23	20	15	6	0	0	0	0	0	0	6	15	20	105
Days Minimum Temp. ≤ 0°F	1	0	0	0	0	0	0	0	0	0	0	0	1
Heating Degree Days (base 65°F)	903	713	523	262	94	8	0	2	40	251	514	776	4,086
Cooling Degree Days (base 65°F)	0	0	5	22	89	261	390	341	177	27	2	1	1,315
Mean Precipitation (in.)	5.06	4.71	6.43	5.24	6.32	4.81	5.26	3.74	4.19	3.70	5.44	5.93	60.83
Days With ≥ 0.1" Precipitation	7	7	9	8	8	6	7	6	6	6	7	8	85
Days With ≥ 1.0" Precipitation	1	1	2	2	2	2	2	1	1	1	2	2	19
Mean Snowfall (in.)	1.2	0.3	0.2	trace	0.0	0.0	0.0	0.0	0.0	trace	trace	0.2	1.9
Days With ≥ 1.0" Snow Depth	2	0	0	0	0	0	0	0	0	0	0	0	2

Woodbury 1 WNW *Cannon County*   Elevation: 748 ft.   Latitude: 35° 50' N   Longitude: 86° 05' W

	JAN	FEB	MAR	APR	MAY	JUN	JUL	AUG	SEP	OCT	NOV	DEC	YEAR
Mean Maximum Temp. (°F)	48.5	53.8	62.8	72.3	79.2	86.4	89.5	89.1	83.5	73.5	61.9	52.9	71.1
Mean Temp. (°F)	37.4	41.4	49.7	57.8	65.8	73.5	76.9	76.3	70.0	58.7	48.9	41.3	58.2
Mean Minimum Temp. (°F)	26.2	28.9	36.6	43.2	52.2	60.6	65.2	63.5	56.5	43.9	35.8	29.6	45.2
Extreme Maximum Temp. (°F)	75	83	87	91	97	103	106	105	102	90	84	77	106
Extreme Minimum Temp. (°F)	-28	-14	0	18	28	37	50	44	31	20	7	-9	-28
Days Maximum Temp. ≥ 90°F	0	0	0	0	1	9	16	14	6	0	0	0	5
Days Maximum Temp. ≤ 32°F	3	1	0	0	0	0	0	0	0	0	0	1	5
Days Minimum Temp. ≤ 32°F	22	18	13	5	0	0	0	0	0	5	13	19	95
Days Minimum Temp. ≤ 0°F	1	0	0	0	0	0	0	0	0	0	0	0	1
Heating Degree Days (base 65°F)	849	660	473	233	71	5	0	0	31	220	480	729	3,751
Cooling Degree Days (base 65°F)	0	0	6	23	108	282	415	371	183	32	2	1	1,423
Mean Precipitation (in.)	5.03	4.47	6.13	4.36	5.32	4.63	4.82	4.03	4.46	3.92	4.60	5.59	57.36
Days With ≥ 0.1" Precipitation	9	8	9	8	8	8	8	7	6	6	7	8	92
Days With ≥ 1.0" Precipitation	1	1	2	1	2	1	1	1	1	1	1	1	14
Mean Snowfall (in.)	na	*0.6*	0.4	trace	0.0	0.0	0.0	0.0	0.0	trace	trace	*0.2*	na
Days With ≥ 1.0" Snow Depth	na	1	0	0	0	0	0	0	0	0	0	0	na

Note: See Appendix D for explanation of data.

TEXAS

PHYSICAL FEATURES. Texas has been called "the crossroads of North American geology." Within the State's boundaries four great physiographic subdivisions of the North American Continent come together. These are: the Gulf Coastal Forested Plain; Great Western Lower Plains; Great Western High Plains; and the Rocky Mountain Region. Texas may be described as a vast amphitheater, sloping upward from sea level along the coast of the Gulf of Mexico to more than 4,000 feet general elevation along the Texas-New Mexico line. While much of the State is relatively flat, there are 90 mountains a mile or more high, all of them in the Trans-Pecos region. Guadalupe Peak, at 8,751 feet, is the State's highest.

Texas contains 267,339 square miles or 7.4 percent of the Nation's total area. In straight-line distance, Texas extends 801 miles from north to south and 773 miles from east to west. The boundary of Texas extends 4,137 miles. The Rio Grande forms the longest segment of the boundary, 1,569 miles. The second longest segment, 726 miles, is formed by the Red River. The tidewater coastline extends 624 miles. Texas ranks second only to Alaska among the 50 states in volume of inland water with nearly 6,000 square miles of lakes and streams. Most Texas rivers parallel each other and flow directly into the Gulf, but the Canadian, Red, and Sulphur Rivers are part of the Mississippi River system. The Brazos is the largest river between the Rio Grande and the Red and third in size of all rivers flowing either partly or wholly in Texas. Other principal rivers are the Colorado, Trinity, Sabine, Nueces, Neches, and Guadalupe.

GENERAL CLIMATE. Wedged between the warm waters of the Gulf of Mexico and the high plateaus and mountain ranges of the North American Continent, Texas has diverse meteorological and climatological conditions. Continental, marine, and mountain types of climates are all found in Texas, the marine climate modified by surges of continental air. The High Plains, separated from the Lower Plains by the Cap Rock Escarpment, lies in a cool-temperature climatic zone. Most of the remainder of the State lies in a warm-temperature subtropical zone.

The proximity to the Gulf of Mexico, the persistent southerly and southeasterly flow of warm tropical maritime air into Texas from around the westward extension of the Azores High, and adequate rainfall combine to produce a humid subtropical climate with hot summers across the eastern third of the State. The Gulf moisture supply gradually decreases westward and is cut off more frequently during the colder months by intrusions of drier polar air from the north and west; as a result, most of Central Texas, as far north as the High Plains, has a subtropical climate with dry winters and humid summers. This region is semi-arid. As the distance from the Gulf increases westward, the summer moisture supply continues to decrease gradually, producing a subtropical steppe climate across a broad section along the middle Rio Grande Valley that extends as far west as the Pecos Valley. The area west of the Pecos is mostly arid subtropical. The mountain climates in the Trans-Pecos are cooler throughout the year than those of the adjacent lowlands.

Stretching over the largest level plain of its kind in the United States, the High Plains rise gradually from about 2,700 feet on the east to more than 4,000 feet in spots along the New Mexico border. The combination of high elevation, remoteness from moisture source regions, and frequent intrusions of dry polar airmasses, results in a dry steppe climate with relatively mild winters.

While the changes in climate across Texas are considerable, they are nevertheless gradual; no natural boundary separates the moist East from the dry West or the cool North from the warm South.

PRECIPITATION. Rainfall in Texas is not evenly distributed over the State and varies greatly from year to year. Average annual rainfall along the Louisiana border exceeds 56 inches, and in the western extremity of the State, is less than 8 inches. Except along the upper Texas coast, it is possible for one or two thunderstorms to account for the entire month's rainfall. Torrential rains of 10 to 20 inches or more may accompany a tropical storm as it moves inland across the Texas coast. Rains occur most frequently in late spring as a result of squall-line thunderstorms; consequently, most areas of the State show a peak in May. Rainfall in the Pecos Valley, most of southern Texas, the lower Rio Grande Valley, and in the coastal section, shows a peak in September, with a secondary peak in May. On the High Plains a significant percentage of the total annual precipitation occurs during the summer months (following the May peak). Throughout the central part of the State, July and August are relatively dry months. In the mountainous Trans-Pecos area of West Texas, afternoon thundershowers during July, August, and September account for most of the annual rainfall. Throughout most of East Texas, rainfall is fairly evenly distributed throughout the year. East of about 96° W. longitude, annual rainfall exceeds average potential evapotranspiration. West of this meridian, average potential evapotranspiration exceeds annual average rainfall.

FLOOD AND DROUGHT. In most of Texas a large portion of the annual rainfall occurs within short periods of time, resulting in excessive run-off and frequently producing damaging floods. Flood stage is reached on some Texas streams nearly every year. From the early days of Texas history recorded by Spaniards exploring the Southwest, drought has been a re-occurring problem. A drought in Central Texas dried up the San Gabriel River in 1756, forcing the abandonment of a settlement of missionaries and Indians. Stephen F. Austin's first colonists also were hurt by drought. Their initial corn crop was snuffed out in 1822, forcing the once ambitious farmers into desperate hunters. In most years, some sections of the State receive less than normal rainfall, while other sections receive a greater than normal supply. Severe drought or excessively wet conditions rarely exist over the entire State at the same time.

TEMPERATURE. The vast land area of Texas experiences a wide range of temperatures. The High Plains experiences rather low temperatures in winter, while there are several separate areas within the State that experience very high temperatures in summer. Extended periods of subfreezing temperatures are rare, even on the High Plains. In South Texas, subfreezing temperatures associated with Arctic airmasses ordinarily are confined to several hours prior to sunrise, and seasons may pass with no subfreezing temperatures at all. In summer, the temperature contrast is much less pronounced from north to south with daily highs generally in the 90s. August is the hottest month.

OTHER CLIMATIC ELEMENTS. Relative humidity is highest in the coastal region, and decreases gradually inland, as the distance from the Gulf of Mexico increases. Mean annual relative humidity at noon varies from slightly more than 60 percent near the coast to around 35 percent in the El Paso area. As temperatures increase, relative humidities generally decrease.

Sunshine is abundant in the extreme southwestern section of the State, decreasing gradually eastward. On an average, the western Trans-Pecos receives 80 percent of the total possible sunshine annually, while the Upper Coast receives only 60 percent.

Significant amounts of snowfall are confined almost entirely to the mountainous Trans-Pecos region and the High Plains. Measurable snow falls south of the High Plains but usually melts almost as fast as it falls. Blizzards, characterized by subfreezing temperatures, very strong winds, and considerable blowing or drifting of snow, may occur in extreme West Texas or Northwest Texas during the winter or early spring months, but are rare.

STORMS. Tropical cyclones are a threat to all sections of the Texas coast during the summer and fall. Those tropical cyclones with sustained wind speeds of 64 knots (74 m.p.h.) or greater are known as hurricanes. Virtually all tropical cyclones which have affected the Texas coast originated in the Gulf of Mexico, the Caribbean Sea, or the southern part of the North Atlantic Ocean. The season extends from June to October; storms are most frequent in August and September, and rarely affect the Texas coast after the first days of October. The average storm frequency for the entire Texas coast is approximately one per year.

Tornadoes have occurred in Texas during all seasons; however, they have occurred with greatest frequency during April, May, and June. Approximately one-fourth of the total annual number of tornadoes occur in the month of May alone. Hailstorms occur in all parts of the State. The most frequent and most damaging of these occur in spring and early summer. Thunderstorms, from which most damaging local weather develops (tornadoes, hail, windstorms, and high intensity showers) occur on about 60 days each year in the extreme eastern section of the State. The mean annual number of thunderstorm days decreases to about 40 in extreme West Texas, and to 30 in the lower Rio Grande Valley.

Blowing dust and sand may occur occasionally in West Texas where strong winds are more frequent and vegetation is sparse.

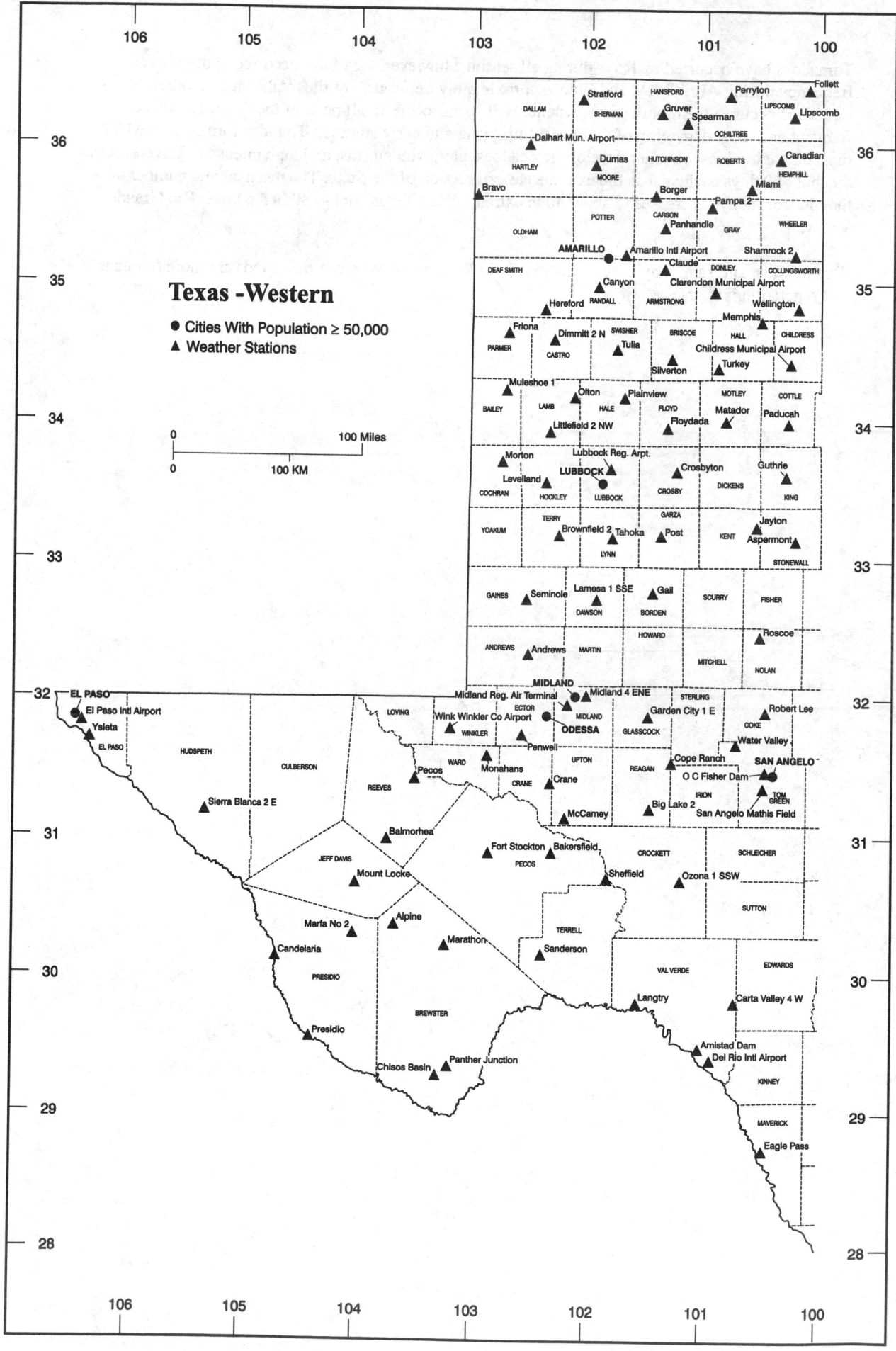

Texas -Western

● Cities With Population ≥ 50,000
▲ Weather Stations

0 _____ 100 Miles

0 _____ 100 KM

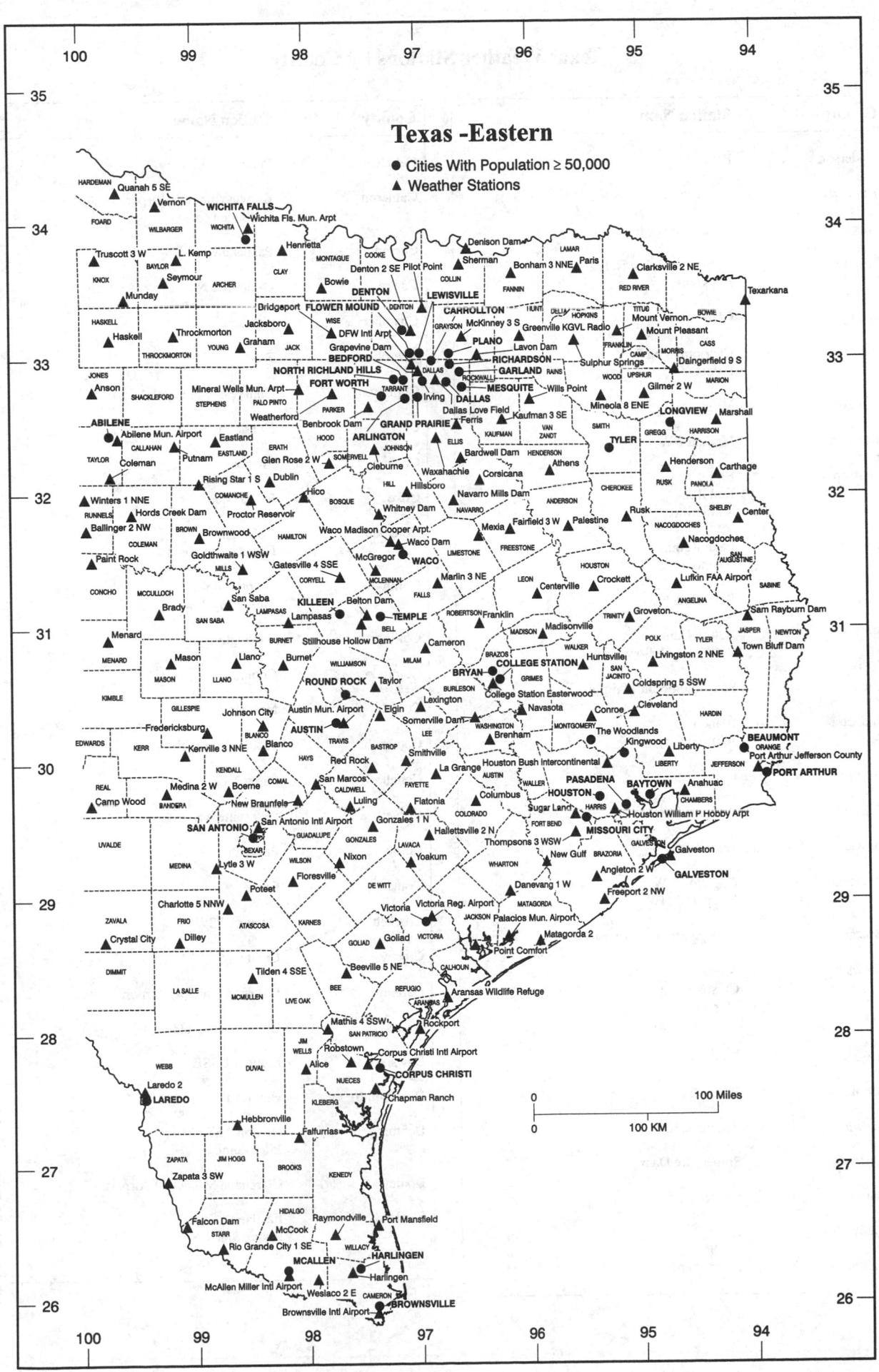

Texas -Eastern

● Cities With Population ≥ 50,000
▲ Weather Stations

Texas Weather Stations by County

County	Station Name
Anderson	Palestine
Andrews	Andrews
Angelina	Lufkin FAA Airport
Aransas	Aransas Wildlife Refuge Rockport
Armstrong	Claude
Atascosa	Charlotte 5 NNW Poteet
Bailey	Muleshoe 1
Bandera	Medina 2 W
Bastrop	Elgin Red Rock Smithville
Baylor	Lake Kemp Seymour
Bee	Beeville 5 NE
Bell	Belton Dam Stillhouse Hollow Dam
Bexar	San Antonio Int'l Airport
Blanco	Blanco Johnson City
Borden	Gail
Bosque	Whitney Dam
Bowie	Texarkana
Brazoria	Angleton 2 W Freeport 2 NW
Brazos	College Station Easterwood
Brewster	Alpine Chisos Basin Marathon Panther Junction
Briscoe	Silverton
Brooks	Falfurrias
Brown	Brownwood
Burleson	Somerville Dam
Burnet	Burnet
Caldwell	Luling
Calhoun	Point Comfort

County	Station Name
Callahan	Putnam
Cameron	Brownsville Int'l Airport Harlingen
Carson	Panhandle
Castro	Dimmitt 2 N
Chambers	Anahuac
Cherokee	Rusk
Childress	Childress Municipal Airport
Clay	Henrietta
Cochran	Morton
Coke	Robert Lee
Coleman	Coleman Hords Creek Dam
Collin	Lavon Dam McKinney 3 S
Collingsworth	Wellington
Colorado	Columbus
Comal	New Braunfels
Comanche	Proctor Reservoir
Concho	Paint Rock
Coryell	Gatesville 4 SSE
Cottle	Paducah
Crane	Crane
Crockett	Ozona 1 SSW
Crosby	Crosbyton
Dallam	Dalhart Municipal Airport
Dallas	Dallas Love Field
Dawson	Lamesa 1 SSE
Deaf Smith	Hereford
Denton	Denton 2 SE Pilot Point
Donley	Clarendon Municipal Airport
Eastland	Eastland Rising Star 1 S

County	Station Name
Ector	Penwell
El Paso	El Paso Int'l Airport
	Ysleta
Ellis	Bardwell Dam
	Ferris
	Waxahachie
Erath	Dublin
Falls	Marlin 3 NE
Fannin	Bonham 3 NNE
Fayette	Flatonia
	La Grange
Floyd	Floydada
Fort Bend	Sugar Land
	Thompsons 3 WSW
Franklin	Mount Vernon
Freestone	Fairfield 3 W
Frio	Dilley
Gaines	Seminole
Galveston	Galveston
Garza	Post
Gillespie	Fredericksburg
Glasscock	Garden City 1 E
Goliad	Goliad
Gonzales	Gonzales 1 N
	Nixon
Gray	Pampa 2
Grayson	Denison Dam
	Sherman
Grimes	Navasota
Hale	Plainview
Hall	Memphis
	Turkey
Hamilton	Hico
Hansford	Gruver
	Spearman
Hardeman	Quanah 5 SE
Harris	Houston Bush Intercontinental
	Houston William P. Hobby Airport

County	Station Name
Harrison	Marshall
Hartley	Bravo
Haskell	Haskell
Hays	San Marcos
Hemphill	Canadian
Henderson	Athens
Hidalgo	McAllen Miller Int'l Airport
	McCook
	Weslaco 2 E
Hill	Hillsboro
Hockley	Levelland
Hopkins	Sulphur Springs
Houston	Crockett
Hudspeth	Sierra Blanca 2 E
Hunt	Greenville KGVL Radio
Hutchinson	Borger
Jack	Jacksboro
Jasper	Sam Rayburn Dam
Jeff Davis	Mount Locke
Jefferson	Port Arthur Jefferson County
Jim Hogg	Hebbronville
Jim Wells	Alice
	Mathis 4 SSW
Johnson	Cleburne
Jones	Anson
Kaufman	Kaufman 3 SE
Kendall	Boerne
Kent	Jayton
Kerr	Kerrville 3 NNE
King	Guthrie
Knox	Munday
	Truscott 3 W
Lamar	Paris
Lamb	Littlefield 2 NW
	Olton
Lampasas	Lampasas

County	Station Name
Lavaca	Hallettsville 2 N
	Yoakum
Lee	Lexington
Leon	Centerville
Liberty	Cleveland
	Liberty
Limestone	Mexia
Lipscomb	Follett
	Lipscomb
Llano	Llano
Lubbock	Lubbock Regional Airport
Lynn	Tahoka
Madison	Madisonville
Mason	Mason
Matagorda	Matagorda 2
	Palacios Municipal Airport
Maverick	Eagle Pass
McCulloch	Brady
McLennan	McGregor
	Waco Dam
	Waco Madison Cooper Airport
McMullen	Tilden 4 SSE
Medina	Lytle 3 W
Menard	Menard
Midland	Midland 4 ENE
	Midland Regional Air Terminal
Milam	Cameron
Mills	Goldthwaite 1 WSW
Montague	Bowie
Montgomery	Conroe
Moore	Dumas
Morris	Daingerfield 9 S
Motley	Matador
Nacogdoches	Nacogdoches
Navarro	Corsicana
	Navarro Mills Dam
Newton	Toledo Bend Dam
Nolan	Roscoe

County	Station Name
Nueces	Chapman Ranch
	Corpus Christi Int'l Airport
	Robstown
Ochiltree	Perryton
Palo Pinto	Mineral Wells Municipal Airport
Panola	Carthage
Parker	Weatherford
Parmer	Friona
Pecos	Bakersfield
	Fort Stockton
	Sheffield
Polk	Livingston 2 NNE
Potter	Amarillo Int'l Airport
Presidio	Candelaria
	Marfa 2
	Presidio
Randall	Canyon
Reagan	Big Lake 2
	Cope Ranch
Real	Camp Wood
Red River	Clarksville 2 NE
Reeves	Balmorhea
	Pecos
Roberts	Miami
Robertson	Franklin
Runnels	Ballinger 2 NW
	Winters 1 NNE
Rusk	Henderson
San Jacinto	Coldspring 5 SSW
San Saba	San Saba
Shelby	Center
Sherman	Stratford
Somervell	Glen Rose 2 W
Starr	Falcon Dam
	Rio Grande City 1 SE
Stonewall	Aspermont
Swisher	Tulia
Tarrant	Benbrook Dam
	Dallas-Fort Worth Int'l Airport
	Grapevine Dam

County	Station Name
Taylor	Abilene Municipal Airport
Terrell	Sanderson
Terry	Brownfield 2
Throckmorton	Throckmorton
Titus	Mount Pleasant
Tom Green	O C Fisher Dam San Angelo Mathis Field Water Valley
Travis	Austin Municipal Airport
Trinity	Groveton
Tyler	Town Bluff Dam
Upshur	Gilmer 2 W
Upton	McCamey
Val Verde	Amistad Dam Carta Valley 4 W Del Rio Int'l Airport Langtry
Van Zandt	Wills Point
Victoria	Victoria Regional Airport
Walker	Huntsville
Ward	Monahans
Washington	Brenham
Webb	Laredo 2
Wharton	Danevang 1 W New Gulf
Wheeler	Shamrock 2
Wichita	Wichita Falls Municipal Airport
Wilbarger	Vernon
Willacy	Port Mansfield Raymondville
Williamson	Taylor
Wilson	Floresville
Winkler	Wink Winkler Co. Airport
Wise	Bridgeport
Wood	Mineola 8 ENE
Young	Graham
Zapata	Zapata 3 SW
Zavala	Crystal City

Texas Weather Stations by City

City	Station Name	Miles
Abilene	Abilene Municipal Airport	5
Amarillo	Amarillo Int'l Airport	9
	Canyon	15
Arlington	Benbrook Dam	19
	Dallas-Fort Worth Int'l Airport	15
	Dallas Love Field	19
	Grapevine Dam	17
Austin	Austin Municipal Airport	3
Baytown	Anahuac	18
	Houston William P. Hobby Airport	20
Beaumont	Port Arthur Jefferson County	12
Bedford	Dallas-Fort Worth Int'l Airport	8
	Dallas Love Field	17
	Grapevine Dam	9
Brownsville	Brownsville Int'l Airport	3
Bryan	College Station Easterwood	6
Carrollton	Dallas-Fort Worth Int'l Airport	10
	Dallas Love Field	10
	Denton 2 SE	19
	Grapevine Dam	10
	McKinney 3 S	20
College Station	College Station Easterwood	3
	Navasota	20
Corpus Christi	Chapman Ranch	11
	Corpus Christi Int'l Airport	7
	Robstown	16
Dallas	Dallas-Fort Worth Int'l Airport	15
	Dallas Love Field	5
	Grapevine Dam	18
Denton	Denton 2 SE	2
	Grapevine Dam	19
	Pilot Point	15
El Paso	El Paso Int'l Airport	4
	Ysleta	13
Flower Mound	Dallas-Fort Worth Int'l Airport	10
	Dallas Love Field	18
	Denton 2 SE	11
	Grapevine Dam	6
Fort Worth	Benbrook Dam	9
Galveston	Galveston	1
Garland	Dallas Love Field	13
	Lavon Dam	13
	McKinney 3 S	18
Grand Prairie	Dallas-Fort Worth Int'l Airport	12
	Dallas Love Field	13

City	Station Name	Miles
Grand Prairie (cont.)	Grapevine Dam	16
Harlingen	Harlingen	2
	Weslaco 2 E	17
Houston	Houston Bush Intercontinental	18
	Houston William P. Hobby Airport	10
	Sugar Land	16
Irving	Dallas-Fort Worth Int'l Airport	5
	Dallas Love Field	7
	Grapevine Dam	9
Killeen	Belton Dam	14
	Gatesville 4 SSE	19
	Stillhouse Hollow Dam	12
Kingwood	Houston Bush Intercontinental	11
Laredo	Laredo 2	3
Lewisville	Dallas-Fort Worth Int'l Airport	9
	Dallas Love Field	16
	Denton 2 SE	12
	Grapevine Dam	6
Lubbock	Lubbock Regional Airport	8
McAllen	McAllen Miller Int'l Airport	2
	Weslaco 2 E	17
Mesquite	Dallas Love Field	14
	Ferris	19
	Lavon Dam	19
Midland	Midland Regional Air Terminal	6
	Midland 4 ENE	6
Missouri City	Houston William P. Hobby Airport	16
	Sugar Land	6
	Thompsons 3 WSW	9
North Richland Hills	Benbrook Dam	19
	Dallas-Fort Worth Int'l Airport	12
	Grapevine Dam	12
Odessa	Midland Regional Air Terminal	12
	Penwell	16
Pasadena	Houston William P. Hobby Airport	6
Plano	Dallas-Fort Worth Int'l Airport	19
	Dallas Love Field	15
	Grapevine Dam	20
	Lavon Dam	14
	McKinney 3 S	11
Port Arthur	Port Arthur Jefferson County	5
Richardson	Dallas-Fort Worth Int'l Airport	17
	Dallas Love Field	11
	Grapevine Dam	19
	Lavon Dam	15
	McKinney 3 S	16

City	Station Name	Miles
Round Rock	Austin Municipal Airport	15
	Taylor	16
San Angelo	O C Fisher Dam	2
	San Angelo Mathis Field	7
San Antonio	San Antonio Int'l Airport	6
Temple	Belton Dam	7
	Stillhouse Hollow Dam	11
The Woodlands	Conroe	12
	Houston Bush Intercontinental	13
Victoria	Victoria Regional Airport	4
Waco	McGregor	16
	Waco Dam	5
	Waco Madison Cooper Airport	6
Wichita Falls	Henrietta	19
	Wichita Falls Municipal Airport	6

Note: Miles is the distance between the geographic center of the city and the weather station.

Texas Weather Stations by Elevation

Feet	Station Name
6,788	Mount Locke
5,298	Chisos Basin
4,757	Marfa 2
4,534	Sierra Blanca 2 E
4,527	Alpine
4,160	Bravo
4,087	Marathon
4,009	Friona
3,989	Dalhart Municipal Airport
3,917	El Paso Int'l Airport
3,848	Dimmitt 2 N
3,822	Muleshoe 1
3,818	Hereford
3,759	Morton
3,740	Panther Junction
3,690	Stratford
3,667	Ysleta
3,654	Dumas
3,608	Olton
3,589	Canyon
3,585	Amarillo Int'l Airport
3,549	Levelland
3,530	Panhandle
3,503	Littlefield 2 NW
3,467	Tulia
3,395	Claude
3,369	Plainview
3,339	Seminole
3,297	Brownfield 2
3,277	Silverton
3,251	Lubbock Regional Airport
3,218	Balmorhea
3,218	Floydada
3,169	Andrews
3,169	Gruver
3,149	Pampa 2
3,139	Borger
3,120	Tahoka
3,093	Spearman
3,008	Crosbyton
2,979	Fort Stockton
2,962	Lamesa 1 SSE
2,939	Penwell
2,939	Perryton
2,874	Candelaria
2,870	Clarendon Municipal Airport
2,860	Midland Regional Air Terminal
2,837	Sanderson
2,805	Wink Winkler Co. Airport
2,769	Follett
2,752	Miami
2,739	Midland 4 ENE
2,687	Big Lake 2
2,657	Monahans
2,637	Garden City 1 E

Feet	Station Name
2,627	Crane
2,618	Post
2,608	Pecos
2,582	Presidio
2,568	Cope Ranch
2,539	Bakersfield
2,526	Gail
2,447	Lipscomb
2,447	McCamey
2,378	Roscoe
2,358	Shamrock 2
2,349	Canadian
2,339	Ozona 1 SSW
2,329	Turkey
2,290	Matador
2,168	Sheffield
2,119	Water Valley
2,089	Memphis
2,037	Wellington
2,007	Jayton
1,961	O C Fisher Dam
1,948	Childress Municipal Airport
1,948	Menard
1,938	Hords Creek Dam
1,916	San Angelo Mathis Field
1,899	Paducah
1,860	Winters 1 NNE
1,788	Abilene Municipal Airport
1,781	Kerrville 3 NNE
1,778	Carta Valley 4 W
1,778	Robert Lee
1,751	Ballinger 2 NW
1,738	Guthrie
1,725	Coleman
1,719	Brady
1,709	Anson
1,702	Medina 2 W
1,683	Fredericksburg
1,669	Aspermont
1,630	Rising Star 1 S
1,624	Paint Rock
1,597	Haskell
1,587	Putnam
1,568	Truscott 3 W
1,499	Dublin
1,499	Goldthwaite 1 WSW
1,492	Quanah 5 SE
1,479	Munday
1,469	Camp Wood
1,443	Boerne
1,430	Eastland
1,427	Mason
1,384	Brownwood
1,368	Blanco
1,368	Throckmorton

Feet	Station Name
1,289	Langtry
1,282	Seymour
1,272	Burnet
1,230	Johnson City
1,227	Vernon
1,220	Proctor Reservoir
1,194	San Saba
1,164	Lake Kemp
1,154	Amistad Dam
1,099	Jacksboro
1,079	Bowie
1,049	Graham
1,026	Wichita Falls Municipal Airport
1,023	Hico
1,023	Lampasas
1,017	Llano
997	Del Rio Int'l Airport
954	Weatherford
928	Henrietta
928	Mineral Wells Municipal Airport
807	Eagle Pass
807	San Antonio Int'l Airport
787	Benbrook Dam
780	Cleburne
757	Gatesville 4 SSE
757	Sherman
744	Bridgeport
721	Lytle 3 W
721	McGregor
718	Rusk
708	New Braunfels
705	Stillhouse Hollow Dam
688	Pilot Point
662	Belton Dam
652	Glen Rose 2 W
629	Denton 2 SE
629	Waxahachie
620	Austin Municipal Airport
610	Denison Dam
610	San Marcos
597	Bonham 3 NNE
593	McKinney 3 S
583	Grapevine Dam
577	Crystal City
577	Elgin
577	Hebbronville
574	Whitney Dam
564	Taylor
557	Dallas-Fort Worth Int'l Airport
547	Dilley
547	Hillsboro
544	Greenville KGVL Radio
541	Paris
534	Mexia
521	Wills Point

Feet	Station Name
518	Flatonia
518	Red Rock
508	Lavon Dam
501	Sulphur Springs
498	Waco Madison Cooper Airport
492	Huntsville
492	Waco Dam
479	Mount Vernon
479	Palestine
479	Poteet
469	Ferris
469	Franklin
462	Lexington
459	Bardwell Dam
452	Navarro Mills Dam
446	Athens
439	Charlotte 5 NNW
439	Dallas Love Field
433	Clarksville 2 NE
433	Nacogdoches
429	Fairfield 3 W
429	Laredo 2
423	Mount Pleasant
419	Henderson
419	Kaufman 3 SE
410	Corsicana
396	Floresville
396	Luling
396	Nixon
387	Gilmer 2 W
387	Marlin 3 NE
387	Texarkana
383	Mineola 8 ENE
377	Gonzales 1 N
360	Cameron
354	Coldspring 5 SSW
354	La Grange
351	Marshall
347	Groveton
344	Crockett
344	Tilden 4 SSE
337	Carthage
337	Smithville
324	Center
324	Yoakum
318	Centerville
318	Falcon Dam
318	Zapata 3 SW
311	Brenham
311	College Station Easterwood
298	Daingerfield 9 S
275	Lufkin FAA Airport
272	Hallettsville 2 N
262	Somerville Dam
252	Beeville 5 NE

Feet	Station Name
249	Madisonville
242	Conroe
219	McCook
219	Navasota
213	Town Bluff Dam
200	Alice
196	Columbus
193	Cleveland
187	Sam Rayburn Dam
187	Toledo Bend Dam
177	Livingston 2 NNE
170	Rio Grande City 1 SE
141	Goliad
137	Mathis 4 SSW
118	Falfurrias
114	Victoria Regional Airport
98	McAllen Miller Int'l Airport
95	Houston Bush Intercontinental
82	Robstown
82	Sugar Land
72	Weslaco 2 E
68	Danevang 1 W
68	New Gulf
68	Thompsons 3 WSW
49	Houston William P. Hobby Airport
42	Corpus Christi Int'l Airport
36	Harlingen
32	Liberty
29	Raymondville
26	Angleton 2 W
22	Anahuac
22	Chapman Ranch
19	Point Comfort
16	Brownsville Int'l Airport
13	Aransas Wildlife Refuge
13	Galveston
13	Palacios Municipal Airport
13	Port Arthur Jefferson County
9	Matagorda 2
6	Freeport 2 NW
6	Port Mansfield
6	Rockport

Abilene Municipal Airport

Abilene is located in north central Texas. The station elevation is 1,750 feet above sea level. Topography of the area includes rolling plains, treeless except for mesquite, broken by low hills to the south and west. The land rises gently to the east and southeast. Regional agricultural products are mainly cattle, dry-land cotton, and feed crops.

Abilene is on the boundary between the humid east Texas climate and the semi-arid west and north Texas climate. The rainfall pattern is typical of the Great Plains. Most precipitation occurs from April to October and is usually associated with thunderstorms. Severe storms are infrequent, occurring mostly in the spring.

The large range of high and low temperatures, characteristic of the Great Plains, extends south to the Abilene area. High daytime temperatures prevail in the summer, but are normally broken by thunderstorms about five times a month. Rapid cooling after sunset results in pleasant nights with low summertime temperatures in the upper 60s and low 70s. High summer temperatures are usually associated with fair skies, southwesterly winds, and low humidities.

Rapid wintertime temperature changes occur when cold, dry, arctic air replaces warm moist tropical air. Drops in temperature of 20 to 30 degrees in one hour are not unusual. However, cold weather periods are short lived. Fair, mild weather is typical.

South is the prevailing wind direction, and southerly winds are frequently high and persist for several days. Strong northerly winds often occur during the passage of cold fronts. Dusty conditions are infrequent, occurring mostly with westerly winds. Dust storm frequency and intensity depend on soil conditions in eastern New Mexico, west Texas, and the Texas Panhandle.

Based on the 1951-1980 period, the average first occurrence of 32 degrees Fahrenheit in the fall is November 13 and the average last occurrence in the spring is March 25.

Abilene Municipal Airport *Taylor County*   Elevation: 1,788 ft.   Latitude: 32° 25' N   Longitude: 99° 41' W

	JAN	FEB	MAR	APR	MAY	JUN	JUL	AUG	SEP	OCT	NOV	DEC	YEAR
Mean Maximum Temp. (°F)	54.8	60.3	68.7	77.0	84.1	90.9	94.5	93.4	86.3	77.3	65.1	57.2	75.8
Mean Temp. (°F)	43.1	48.3	56.1	64.4	72.5	79.7	83.4	82.4	75.4	65.8	53.7	45.6	64.2
Mean Minimum Temp. (°F)	31.4	36.2	43.5	51.8	60.8	68.5	72.2	71.3	64.5	54.2	42.2	34.0	52.5
Extreme Maximum Temp. (°F)	84	93	97	98	106	109	110	105	105	103	92	82	110
Extreme Minimum Temp. (°F)	-1	-7	10	25	36	51	57	50	38	23	14	-7	-7
Days Maximum Temp. ≥ 90°F	0	0	1	2	8	19	26	25	12	2	0	0	95
Days Maximum Temp. ≤ 32°F	2	1	0	0	0	0	0	0	0	0	0	1	4
Days Minimum Temp. ≤ 32°F	17	10	4	1	0	0	0	0	0	0	5	14	51
Days Minimum Temp. ≤ 0°F	0	0	0	0	0	0	0	0	0	0	0	0	0
Heating Degree Days (base 65°F)	673	470	297	108	20	0	0	0	17	91	349	595	2,620
Cooling Degree Days (base 65°F)	1	5	28	98	265	446	584	563	343	126	17	2	2,478
Mean Precipitation (in.)	0.97	1.18	1.46	1.73	2.87	2.94	1.69	2.68	2.96	2.70	1.21	1.25	23.64
Maximum Precipitation (in.)	4.3	3.6	5.2	6.8	13.2	9.6	7.1	8.2	11.0	10.7	4.6	6.3	36.8
Minimum Precipitation (in.)	trace	trace	trace	trace	0.1	trace	trace	trace	trace	0	0	trace	9.8
Maximum 24-hr. Precipitation (in.)	1.9	1.8	2.1	2.4	4.7	3.6	3.7	6.3	4.5	5.0	2.4	2.2	6.3
Days With ≥ 0.1" Precipitation	2	3	3	3	4	4	3	4	4	4	2	3	39
Days With ≥ 1.0" Precipitation	0	0	0	0	1	1	0	1	1	1	0	0	5
Mean Snowfall (in.)	2.5	1.0	0.5	0.3	trace	trace	trace	trace	0.0	trace	0.5	0.8	5.6
Maximum Snowfall (in.)	14	8	7	0	0	0	0	0	0	trace	8	8	19
Maximum 24-hr. Snowfall (in.)	7	5	6	0	0	0	0	0	0	trace	4	4	7
Days With ≥ 1.0" Snow Depth	1	1	0	0	0	0	0	0	0	0	0	1	3
Thunderstorm Days	1	1	3	5	8	6	5	5	4	3	1	1	43
Foggy Days	7	7	4	4	4	2	1	1	5	5	5	7	52
Predominant Sky Cover	OVR	OVR	CLR	CLR	CLR	CLR	CLR	CLR	CLR	CLR	CLR	CLR	CLR
Mean Relative Humidity 6am (%)	73	73	69	72	80	79	73	73	78	76	74	72	74
Mean Relative Humidity 3pm (%)	45	44	37	38	43	41	38	38	44	42	42	44	41
Mean Dewpoint (°F)	28	32	36	45	56	62	63	62	59	49	38	30	47
Prevailing Wind Direction	S	S	S	SSE	SSE	S	SSE	SSE	SSE	S	S	S	S
Prevailing Wind Speed (mph)	13	13	15	15	14	14	12	10	10	12	13	13	13
Maximum Wind Gust (mph)	51	56	74	61	71	73	78	55	59	58	62	59	78

Amarillo Int'l Airport

The station is located 7 statute miles east northeast of the downtown post office in a region of rather flat topography. The Canadian River flows eastward 18 miles north of the station, with its bed about 800 feet below the plains. The Prairie Dog Town Fork of the Red River flows southeastward about 15 miles south of the station where it enters the Palo Duro Canyon, which is about 1,000 feet deep. There are numerous shallow Playa lakes, often dry, over the area, and the nearly treeless grasslands slope downward to the east. The terrain gradually rises to the west and northwest.

Three-fourths of the total annual precipitation falls from April through September, occurring from thunderstorm activity. Snow usually melts within a few days after it falls. Heavier snowfalls of 10 inches or more, usually with near blizzard conditions, average once every five years and last two to three days.

The Amarillo area is subject to rapid and large temperature changes, especially during the winter months when cold fronts from the northern Rocky Mountain and Plains states sweep across the area. Temperature drops of 50 to 60 degrees within a 12-hour period are not uncommon. Temperature drops of 40 degrees have occurred within a few minutes.

Humidity averages are low, occasionally dropping below 20 percent in the spring. Low humidity moderates the effect of high summer afternoon temperatures, permits evaporative cooling systems to be very effective, and provides many pleasant evenings and nights.

Severe local storms are infrequent, although a few thunderstorms with damaging hail, lightning, and wind in a very localized area occur most years, usually in spring and summer. These storms are often accompanied by very heavy rain, which produces local flooding, particularly of roads and streets. Tornadoes are rare.

Based on the 1951-1980 period, the average first occurrence of 32 degrees Fahrenheit in the fall is October 29 and the average last occurrence in the spring is April 14.

Amarillo Int'l Airport *Potter County*   Elevation: 3,585 ft.   Latitude: 35° 13' N   Longitude: 101° 42' W

	JAN	FEB	MAR	APR	MAY	JUN	JUL	AUG	SEP	OCT	NOV	DEC	YEAR
Mean Maximum Temp. (°F)	48.6	53.8	61.9	70.6	78.5	87.6	91.0	88.6	81.6	71.7	58.7	50.3	70.2
Mean Temp. (°F)	35.3	40.1	47.4	55.9	65.0	74.3	78.2	76.2	69.0	58.0	45.3	37.1	56.8
Mean Minimum Temp. (°F)	21.8	26.4	32.9	41.2	51.4	60.9	65.3	63.8	56.4	44.3	31.8	23.9	43.3
Extreme Maximum Temp. (°F)	80	86	94	98	103	108	105	104	103	94	87	80	108
Extreme Minimum Temp. (°F)	-11	-12	4	17	30	41	51	51	30	12	0	-8	-12
Days Maximum Temp. ≥ 90°F	0	0	0	1	4	13	20	16	7	1	0	0	62
Days Maximum Temp. ≤ 32°F	5	3	1	0	0	0	0	0	0	0	1	3	13
Days Minimum Temp. ≤ 32°F	28	21	15	4	0	0	0	0	0	2	16	27	113
Days Minimum Temp. ≤ 0°F	0	1	0	0	0	0	0	0	0	0	0	1	2
Heating Degree Days (base 65°F)	915	696	540	284	89	8	1	1	54	238	585	857	4,268
Cooling Degree Days (base 65°F)	0	0	2	17	96	291	420	365	182	26	0	0	1,399
Mean Precipitation (in.)	0.62	0.55	1.06	1.36	2.59	3.15	2.72	2.97	1.89	1.40	0.66	0.56	19.53
Maximum Precipitation (in.)	2.3	1.8	4.0	2.8	9.8	10.7	7.6	7.5	5.0	4.8	2.3	4.5	36.6
Minimum Precipitation (in.)	0	trace	trace	trace	trace	trace	0.1	0.3	trace	0	0	trace	9.6
Maximum 24-hr. Precipitation (in.)	1.5	1.3	1.4	2.0	3.9	4.9	3.1	3.6	2.3	2.3	2.0	1.6	4.9
Days With ≥ 0.1" Precipitation	2	1	3	3	5	5	5	5	4	3	2	2	40
Days With ≥ 1.0" Precipitation	0	0	0	0	1	1	1	1	0	0	0	0	4
Mean Snowfall (in.)	4.7	3.8	2.4	0.8	trace	trace	trace	trace	trace	0.5	2.2	3.0	17.4
Maximum Snowfall (in.)	15	17	15	6	1	0	0	0	trace	4	14	15	47
Maximum 24-hr. Snowfall (in.)	9	11	8	4	1	0	0	0	trace	3	8	8	11
Days With ≥ 1.0" Snow Depth	5	3	1	0	0	0	0	0	0	0	1	3	13
Thunderstorm Days	< 1	< 1	2	3	8	10	9	9	4	2	1	< 1	48
Foggy Days	7	8	8	6	8	4	3	4	6	6	6	7	73
Predominant Sky Cover	CLR	CLR	CLR	CLR	CLR	CLR	SCT	SCT	CLR	CLR	CLR	CLR	CLR
Mean Relative Humidity 6am (%)	71	72	68	69	76	77	75	78	78	73	71	70	73
Mean Relative Humidity 3pm (%)	42	41	34	31	37	37	36	39	40	36	38	40	38
Mean Dewpoint (°F)	19	22	25	33	45	55	58	58	51	39	28	21	38
Prevailing Wind Direction	SW	SW	SW	S	S	S	S	S	S	SSW	SW	SW	S
Prevailing Wind Speed (mph)	14	14	15	16	16	16	14	13	14	14	14	13	14
Maximum Wind Gust (mph)	64	67	76	81	70	69	69	66	60	74	73	63	81

Austin Municipal Airport

Austin, capital of Texas, is located on the Colorado River where the stream crosses the Balcones steep slope separating the Texas Hill Country from the Blackland Prairies to the east. Elevations within the city vary from 400 feet to nearly 1,000 feet above sea level. Native trees include cedar, oak, walnut, mesquite, and pecan.

The climate of Austin is humid subtropical with hot summers. Winters are mild, with below freezing temperatures occurring on an average of about 25 days each year. Rather strong northerly winds, accompanied by sharp drops in temperature, frequently occur during the winter months in connection with cold fronts, but cold spells are usually of short duration, seldom lasting more than two days. Daytime temperatures in summer are hot, but summer nights are usually pleasant.

Precipitation is fairly evenly distributed throughout the year, with heaviest amounts occurring in late spring. A secondary rainfall peak occurs in September, primarily because of tropical cyclones that migrate out of the Gulf of Mexico. Precipitation from April through September usually results from thunderstorms, with fairly large amounts of rain falling within short periods of time. While thunderstorms and heavy rains may occur in all months of the year, most of the winter precipitation consists of light rain. Snow is insignificant as a source of moisture, and usually melts as rapidly as it falls. The city may experience several seasons in succession with no measurable snowfall.

Prevailing winds are southerly, however in winter, northerly winds are about as frequent as those from the south. Destructive winds and damaging hailstorms are infrequent. On rare occasions dissipating tropical storms produce strong winds and heavy rains in the area. Blowing dust occurs occasionally in spring, but visibility rarely drops substantially, and then only for a few hours.

The average length of the warm season (freeze-free period) is 273 days. The average occurrence of the last temperature of 32 degrees in spring is early March and the average occurrence of the first temperature of 32 degrees is late November.

Austin Municipal Airport *Travis County*   Elevation: 620 ft.   Latitude: 30° 18' N   Longitude: 97° 42' W

	JAN	FEB	MAR	APR	MAY	JUN	JUL	AUG	SEP	OCT	NOV	DEC	YEAR
Mean Maximum Temp. (°F)	59.7	64.7	72.1	79.0	84.8	91.0	94.7	95.3	89.6	81.1	70.2	62.7	78.7
Mean Temp. (°F)	49.7	54.3	61.5	68.5	75.3	81.5	84.4	84.7	79.6	70.6	59.8	52.6	68.5
Mean Minimum Temp. (°F)	39.7	43.9	50.8	58.0	65.7	71.9	74.2	74.1	69.5	60.0	49.5	42.4	58.3
Extreme Maximum Temp. (°F)	90	99	98	98	102	108	105	106	104	98	89	86	108
Extreme Minimum Temp. (°F)	11	14	19	35	47	53	64	62	48	30	20	4	4
Days Maximum Temp. ≥ 90°F	0	0	1	2	7	21	28	28	18	4	0	0	109
Days Maximum Temp. ≤ 32°F	0	0	0	0	0	0	0	0	0	0	0	0	0
Days Minimum Temp. ≤ 32°F	7	4	1	0	0	0	0	0	0	0	1	5	18
Days Minimum Temp. ≤ 0°F	0	0	0	0	0	0	0	0	0	0	0	0	0
Heating Degree Days (base 65°F)	474	314	163	42	2	0	0	0	2	32	201	393	1,623
Cooling Degree Days (base 65°F)	8	20	59	158	345	511	624	639	459	222	58	16	3,119
Mean Precipitation (in.)	1.85	2.12	2.18	2.48	5.20	3.64	1.96	2.34	2.98	3.94	2.42	2.34	33.45
Maximum Precipitation (in.)	9.2	6.6	6.0	9.9	10.0	15.0	10.5	8.9	7.4	12.3	7.3	14.2	52.2
Minimum Precipitation (in.)	trace	0.3	trace	0.1	0.8	trace	0	0	0.1	trace	trace	trace	11.4
Maximum 24-hr. Precipitation (in.)	4.4	3.0	2.7	3.6	5.5	5.7	4.8	5.7	4.7	4.6	4.6	4.2	5.7
Days With ≥ 0.1" Precipitation	4	4	4	4	6	5	3	3	5	5	4	4	51
Days With ≥ 1.0" Precipitation	0	0	1	1	2	1	0	1	1	1	1	1	10
Mean Snowfall (in.)	0.4	0.1	trace	trace	trace	0.0	0.0	0.0	0.0	0.0	trace	trace	0.5
Maximum Snowfall (in.)	8	6	2	0	0	0	0	0	0	0	2	trace	9
Maximum 24-hr. Snowfall (in.)	7	5	2	0	0	0	0	0	0	0	1	trace	7
Days With ≥ 1.0" Snow Depth	0	0	0	0	0	0	0	0	0	0	0	0	0
Thunderstorm Days	1	2	3	5	7	5	4	5	4	3	2	1	42
Foggy Days	13	11	12	12	12	7	4	4	9	11	11	12	118
Predominant Sky Cover	OVR	OVR	OVR	OVR	OVR	SCT	SCT	SCT	CLR	CLR	OVR	OVR	OVR
Mean Relative Humidity 6am (%)	80	80	80	83	89	89	89	87	86	84	81	80	84
Mean Relative Humidity 3pm (%)	53	51	47	50	54	50	43	42	47	47	49	52	49
Mean Dewpoint (°F)	38	41	46	55	64	69	69	68	65	56	47	40	55
Prevailing Wind Direction	N	S	S	S	SSE	S	S	S	S	S	S	S	S
Prevailing Wind Speed (mph)	14	9	12	10	10	10	9	8	8	8	9	9	10
Maximum Wind Gust (mph)	54	55	56	58	63	54	69	47	81	46	58	63	81

Brownsville Int'l Airport

Brownsville is located at the southern tip of Texas. It is the largest city in the four county area referred to as the Lower Rio Grande Valley or just the Valley.

The Gulf of Mexico, located about 18 miles east, is the dominant influence on local weather. Prevailing southeast breezes off the Gulf provide a humid but generally mild climate. Winds are frequently strong and gusty in the spring.

Brownsville weather is generally favorable for outdoor activities and the Valley is a popular tourist area, especially for Winter Texans who come to enjoy the mild winters. High temperatures range mostly in the 70s and 80s from October through April, with lows in the 50s and 60s during the same period. For the remainder of the year highs are frequently in the 90s with lows in the 70s.

Temperature extremes are rare but do occur. Temperatures in the 90s have occurred in every month of the year, with 100 degree readings noted as early as March and as late as September. Very hot temperatures are often moderated by a cooling sea breeze from the Gulf during the afternoon hours.

Located about 150 miles north of the tropics, cold weather in Brownsville is infrequent and of short duration. Some winters pass without a single day with freezing temperatures. This climate permits year around gardening and cultivation of citrus and other cold sensitive tropical and sub-tropical plants. Damaging cold comes from frigid air masses, called northers or arctic outbreaks, plunging south from Canada or the Arctic. The worst of these can drop temperatures well below freezing for several hours, and a few have produced readings in the teens. Fortunately such events are very rare since they are disasterous to the local economy.

Rainfall is not well distributed. Heaviest rains occur in May through June and mid August through mid October. Extended periods of cool rainy weather, called overrunning, can occur in winter. Torrential rains of 10 to 20 inches or more may accompany tropical storms or hurricanes that occasionally move over the area in summer or fall. Rainy spells may be followed by long dry periods. Irrigation is required to ensure production of corps such as cotton, grains, and vegetables. Snow and freezing rain or drizzle are so rare that years may pass between occurrences.

Damaging hail or winds from heavy thunderstorms are generally limited to the spring and many years elapse between occurrences. Tornadoes are even more rare. Tropical storms and hurricanes from the Gulf are a threat each summer and fall, but damaging storms are quite rare.

Brownsville Int'l Airport *Cameron County*   Elevation: 16 ft.   Latitude: 25° 54' N   Longitude: 97° 26' W

	JAN	FEB	MAR	APR	MAY	JUN	JUL	AUG	SEP	OCT	NOV	DEC	YEAR
Mean Maximum Temp. (°F)	69.7	73.2	78.9	83.3	87.8	91.5	93.4	93.7	90.3	85.1	78.1	72.0	83.1
Mean Temp. (°F)	60.2	63.4	69.3	74.6	79.8	83.4	84.6	84.7	81.6	75.7	68.5	62.4	74.0
Mean Minimum Temp. (°F)	50.7	53.5	59.6	65.7	71.8	75.2	75.7	75.6	72.9	66.3	58.8	52.8	64.9
Extreme Maximum Temp. (°F)	93	94	106	102	102	102	101	101	99	96	97	94	106
Extreme Minimum Temp. (°F)	24	26	32	38	52	60	68	69	55	35	31	16	16
Days Maximum Temp. ≥ 90°F	0	0	2	3	11	24	28	28	20	6	0	0	122
Days Maximum Temp. ≤ 32°F	0	0	0	0	0	0	0	0	0	0	0	0	0
Days Minimum Temp. ≤ 32°F	1	0	0	0	0	0	0	0	0	0	0	1	2
Days Minimum Temp. ≤ 0°F	0	0	0	0	0	0	0	0	0	0	0	0	0
Heating Degree Days (base 65°F)	203	117	44	8	0	0	0	0	0	6	63	162	603
Cooling Degree Days (base 65°F)	59	83	174	293	478	576	630	630	512	351	182	91	4,059
Mean Precipitation (in.)	1.47	1.18	0.84	2.02	2.53	2.95	1.84	2.91	5.52	3.80	1.74	1.07	27.87
Maximum Precipitation (in.)	4.8	10.3	3.5	10.3	9.1	8.5	9.4	9.6	20.2	17.1	7.7	4.0	47.5
Minimum Precipitation (in.)	trace	trace	trace	trace	trace	trace	trace	trace	0.1	0.3	trace	trace	11.6
Maximum 24-hr. Precipitation (in.)	2.3	4.3	2.6	9.2	3.4	7.5	3.7	5.5	12.+	6.7	4.1	2.5	12.+
Days With ≥ 0.1" Precipitation	3	2	2	2	3	4	3	4	6	5	3	3	40
Days With ≥ 1.0" Precipitation	0	0	0	1	1	1	1	1	2	1	1	0	9
Mean Snowfall (in.)	trace	trace	trace	0.0	0.0	0.0	0.0	trace	0.0	0.0	trace	trace	trace
Maximum Snowfall (in.)	trace	trace	0	0	0	0	0	0	0	0	trace	trace	trace
Maximum 24-hr. Snowfall (in.)	trace	trace	0	0	0	0	0	0	0	0	trace	trace	trace
Days With ≥ 1.0" Snow Depth	0	0	0	0	0	0	0	0	0	0	0	0	0
Thunderstorm Days	< 1	1	1	2	3	3	3	5	5	2	1	< 1	26
Foggy Days	17	14	13	12	9	4	3	3	5	7	11	15	113
Predominant Sky Cover	OVR	OVR	OVR	OVR	BRK	SCT	SCT	SCT	SCT	SCT	OVR	OVR	OVR
Mean Relative Humidity 6am (%)	88	89	88	89	90	91	92	92	91	89	87	87	90
Mean Relative Humidity 3pm (%)	63	60	57	58	60	59	54	55	60	58	59	62	59
Mean Dewpoint (°F)	52	55	59	65	70	73	73	73	72	66	59	54	64
Prevailing Wind Direction	NNW	SSE	SSE	SSE	SE	SE	SSE	SE	SE	SE	SSE	NNW	SSE
Prevailing Wind Speed (mph)	13	15	16	17	14	13	13	12	10	10	13	12	13
Maximum Wind Gust (mph)	53	68	59	66	81	62	51	78	109	55	53	53	109

Corpus Christi Int'l Airport

Corpus Christi is located on Corpus Christi Bay, an inlet of the Gulf of Mexico, in south Texas. The climatic conditions vary between the humid subtropical region to the northeast along the Texas coast and the semi-arid region to the west and southwest. Temperatures at the International Airport, which is about 7 miles west of downtown Corpus Christi, may be substantially different than those in the city during calm winter mornings and during summer afternoon sea breezes.

Peak rainfall months are May and September. Winter months have the least amounts of rainfall. The hurricane season from June to November can greatly effect the rainfall totals. Dry periods frequently occur. Several months during the years of record have had no rainfall, or only a trace. Snow falls on an average of about one day every two years.

There is little change in the day-to-day weather of the summer months, except for an occasional rainshower or a tropical storm in the area. High temperatures range in the high 80s to mid 90s, except for brief periods in the high 90s. The sea breeze during the afternoon and evening hours moderates the summer heat. Low temperatures are usually in the mid 70s. Summertime temperatures rarely reach 100 degrees near the bay, but occasionally do in most other parts of the city. In the summer season the region receives nearly 80 percent of the possible sunshine.

September and October are an extension of summer. November is a transition to the conditions of the coming winter months, with greater temperature extremes, stronger winds, and the first occurrences of northers. The winter months are relatively mild, but with temperatures sufficiently low to be stimulating. January is the coldest month with a prevailing northerly wind. Daytime highs that do not exceed 32 degrees, do not occur more than once every three or four years. The earliest occurrence of a temperature below 32 degrees is in early November and the latest occurrence in the spring is mid to late March.

Relative humidity, because of the nearness of the Gulf of Mexico, is high throughout the year. However, during the afternoons the humidity usually drops to between 50 and 60 percent.

Severe tropical storms average about one every ten years. Lesser strength storms average about one every five years. The city of Corpus Christi has a bluff that rises 30 to 40 feet above the level of the lowlands area near the bay. This serves as a natural protection from high water.

Chief hurricane months are August and September, although tropical storms have occurred as early as June and as late as October. The majority of the storms pass either to the south or east of the city.

Corpus Christi Int'l Airport *Nueces County* Elevation: 42 ft. Latitude: 27° 46' N Longitude: 97° 31' W

	JAN	FEB	MAR	APR	MAY	JUN	JUL	AUG	SEP	OCT	NOV	DEC	YEAR
Mean Maximum Temp. (°F)	66.1	70.0	76.2	81.4	86.1	90.6	93.4	93.5	90.0	84.0	75.4	69.0	81.3
Mean Temp. (°F)	56.2	59.8	66.3	72.1	77.9	82.3	84.1	84.3	81.2	74.3	65.6	59.0	71.9
Mean Minimum Temp. (°F)	46.4	49.4	56.3	62.7	69.7	73.9	74.8	75.1	72.3	64.5	55.8	49.1	62.5
Extreme Maximum Temp. (°F)	91	97	102	102	103	106	100	102	103	97	98	91	106
Extreme Minimum Temp. (°F)	18	23	24	33	47	58	67	65	52	28	28	13	13
Days Maximum Temp. ≥ 90°F	0	0	1	2	5	20	28	28	19	6	0	0	109
Days Maximum Temp. ≤ 32°F	0	0	0	0	0	0	0	0	0	0	0	0	0
Days Minimum Temp. ≤ 32°F	3	1	0	0	0	0	0	0	0	0	0	2	6
Days Minimum Temp. ≤ 0°F	0	0	0	0	0	0	0	0	0	0	0	0	0
Heating Degree Days (base 65°F)	297	186	77	18	0	0	0	0	0	11	100	235	924
Cooling Degree Days (base 65°F)	29	46	112	224	406	528	599	608	490	306	128	55	3,531
Mean Precipitation (in.)	1.66	1.86	1.66	2.02	3.45	3.75	2.06	3.75	5.25	3.98	1.69	1.71	32.84
Maximum Precipitation (in.)	10.8	8.1	4.9	8.0	9.4	13.3	11.9	14.8	20.3	11.0	5.2	9.8	48.1
Minimum Precipitation (in.)	trace	trace	trace	trace	trace	trace	0	0.1	0.5	0	trace	trace	14.7
Maximum 24-hr. Precipitation (in.)	4.5	4.7	2.8	7.2	4.0	4.9	3.8	6.9	7.6	7.9	2.8	6.8	7.9
Days With ≥ 0.1" Precipitation	4	3	2	3	5	5	3	4	7	4	3	3	46
Days With ≥ 1.0" Precipitation	0	1	1	1	1	1	1	1	2	1	0	0	10
Mean Snowfall (in.)	trace	trace	trace	trace	trace	0.0	0.0	0.0	0.0	trace	trace	trace	trace
Maximum Snowfall (in.)	1	1	trace	0	0	0	0	0	0	0	trace	trace	1
Maximum 24-hr. Snowfall (in.)	1	1	trace	0	0	0	0	0	0	0	trace	trace	1
Days With ≥ 1.0" Snow Depth	0	0	0	0	0	0	0	0	0	0	0	0	0
Thunderstorm Days	1	1	1	2	4	3	2	4	5	2	1	1	27
Foggy Days	16	14	14	12	9	4	2	3	5	7	10	14	110
Predominant Sky Cover	OVR	OVR	OVR	OVR	BRK	SCT	SCT	SCT	SCT	CLR	OVR	OVR	OVR
Mean Relative Humidity 6am (%)	87	88	87	89	92	92	93	92	90	89	86	86	89
Mean Relative Humidity 3pm (%)	62	60	58	61	64	62	56	56	60	57	58	60	59
Mean Dewpoint (°F)	48	51	56	63	70	73	74	74	71	64	58	50	62
Prevailing Wind Direction	SSE	SSE	SSE	SE	SE	SE	SE	SE	SE	SE	SSE	SSE	SE
Prevailing Wind Speed (mph)	15	16	17	15	14	13	13	13	12	12	15	15	14
Maximum Wind Gust (mph)	53	61	54	67	62	61	58	161	70	53	60	54	161

Dallas-Fort Worth Int'l Airport

The Dallas-Fort Worth Metroplex is located in North Central Texas, approximately 250 miles north of the Gulf of Mexico. It is near the headwaters of the Trinity River, which lie in the upper margins of the Coastal Plain. The rolling hills in the area range from 500 to 800 feet in elevation.

The Dallas-Fort Worth climate is humid subtropical with hot summers. It is also continental, characterized by a wide annual temperature range. Precipitation also varies considerably, ranging from less than 20 to more than 50 inches.

Winters are mild, but northers occur about three times each month, and often are accompanied by sudden drops in temperature. Periods of extreme cold that occasionally occur are short-lived, so that even in January mild weather occurs frequently.

The highest temperatures of summer are associated with fair skies, westerly winds and low humidities. Characteristically, hot spells in summer are broken into three-to-five day periods by thunderstorm activity. There are only a few nights each summer when the low temperature exceeds 80 degrees. Summer daytime temperatures frequently exceed 100 degrees. Air conditioners are recommended for maximum comfort indoors and while traveling via automobile.

Throughout the year, rainfall occurs more frequently during the night. Usually, periods of rainy weather last for only a day or two, and are followed by several days with fair skies. A large part of the annual precipitation results from thunderstorm activity, with occasional heavy rainfall over brief periods of time. Thunderstorms occur throughout the year, but are most frequent in the spring. Hail falls on about two or three days a year, ordinarily with only slight and scattered damage. Windstorms occurring during thunderstorm activity are sometimes destructive. Snowfall is rare.

The average length of the warm season (freeze-free period) in the Dallas-Fort Worth Metroplex is about 249 days. The average last occurrence of 32 degrees or below is mid March and the average first occurrence of 32 degrees or below is in late November.

Dallas-Fort Worth Int'l Airport *Tarrant County* Elevation: 557 ft. Latitude: 32° 54' N Longitude: 97° 01' W

	JAN	FEB	MAR	APR	MAY	JUN	JUL	AUG	SEP	OCT	NOV	DEC	YEAR
Mean Maximum Temp. (°F)	54.2	59.9	67.9	76.0	83.2	91.6	96.3	95.7	88.4	78.5	66.0	57.2	76.2
Mean Temp. (°F)	44.1	49.3	57.1	65.0	73.3	81.2	85.5	85.0	77.7	67.3	55.6	47.1	65.7
Mean Minimum Temp. (°F)	33.9	38.7	46.2	54.0	63.2	70.7	74.7	74.1	66.9	56.0	45.2	36.9	55.0
Extreme Maximum Temp. (°F)	83	95	96	95	103	113	110	107	108	102	89	83	113
Extreme Minimum Temp. (°F)	7	7	15	29	41	54	62	59	43	29	22	-1	-1
Days Maximum Temp. ≥ 90°F	0	0	0	1	5	20	28	27	16	3	0	0	100
Days Maximum Temp. ≤ 32°F	2	1	0	0	0	0	0	0	0	0	0	1	4
Days Minimum Temp. ≤ 32°F	14	7	2	0	0	0	0	0	0	0	3	10	36
Days Minimum Temp. ≤ 0°F	0	0	0	0	0	0	0	0	0	0	0	0	0
Heating Degree Days (base 65°F)	642	441	268	84	11	0	0	0	7	68	298	552	2,371
Cooling Degree Days (base 65°F)	1	4	28	91	275	493	644	634	402	143	24	5	2,744
Mean Precipitation (in.)	1.94	2.44	3.12	3.15	5.43	3.18	2.09	2.10	2.42	4.01	2.43	2.50	34.81
Maximum Precipitation (in.)	5.4	6.2	6.7	12.2	13.7	8.8	11.1	6.8	9.5	14.2	6.2	8.8	53.5
Minimum Precipitation (in.)	trace	0.1	0.1	0.1	1.0	trace	0	trace	0.1	trace	trace	trace	18.5
Maximum 24-hr. Precipitation (in.)	2.4	3.1	3.9	4.5	4.7	3.1	3.0	4.0	4.2	4.8	2.5	4.2	4.8
Days With ≥ 0.1" Precipitation	4	4	5	5	7	5	3	3	4	4	4	4	52
Days With ≥ 1.0" Precipitation	0	1	1	1	2	1	1	1	1	1	1	1	12
Mean Snowfall (in.)	*0.7*	*1.2*	*trace*	*trace*	*trace*	*0.0*	*0.0*	*0.0*	*0.0*	*trace*	*0.2*	*0.2*	*2.3*
Maximum Snowfall (in.)	12	14	3	0	0	0	0	0	0	trace	5	3	18
Maximum 24-hr. Snowfall (in.)	8	8	3	0	0	0	0	0	0	trace	5	2	8
Days With ≥ 1.0" Snow Depth	*1*	*1*	*0*	*0*	*0*	*0*	*0*	*0*	*0*	*0*	*0*	*0*	*2*
Thunderstorm Days	1	2	4	6	8	6	5	5	4	3	2	1	47
Foggy Days	11	9	9	8	8	3	2	2	5	7	8	10	82
Predominant Sky Cover	OVR	OVR	OVR	OVR	OVR	SCT	CLR	CLR	CLR	CLR	CLR	OVR	CLR
Mean Relative Humidity 6am (%)	80	79	79	82	87	85	80	80	84	82	81	80	82
Mean Relative Humidity 3pm (%)	53	51	48	50	53	48	42	41	47	47	49	52	48
Mean Dewpoint (°F)	32	36	42	52	61	67	68	67	63	53	43	35	52
Prevailing Wind Direction	S	S	S	S	S	S	S	S	S	S	S	S	S
Prevailing Wind Speed (mph)	13	13	15	15	14	13	12	10	12	12	13	12	13
Maximum Wind Gust (mph)	69	64	79	76	71	69	71	83	64	63	68	60	83

Del Rio Int'l Airport

Del Rio is located on the Rio Grande River, on the western tip of the Balcones escarpment, in southwest Texas. Elevation is near 1,000 feet and varies little within the city but rises to 2,300 feet in the northern part of the county. Regional agriculture is chiefly wool and mohair production to the north and west of Del Rio and garden crops to the southeast. Lake Amistad, a reservoir of 65,000 surface acres, lies 10 miles west of Del Rio.

The climate of Del Rio is semi-arid continental. Annual precipitation is insufficient for dry farming. However, San Felipe Springs and the Rio Grande provide adequate water for irrigation farming. Over 80 percent of the average annual precipitation occurs from April through October. During this period, rainfall is chiefly in the form of showers and thunderstorms, often as heavy downpours, resulting in flash flooding. The small amount of precipitation for November through March usually falls as steady light rain.

Hail occurs in the vicinity of Del Rio about once per year and reaches severe proportions about once every five years. Sleet or snow falls on an average of once a year, but frequently melts as it falls. A snowfall heavy enough to blanket the ground only occurs about once every four or five years, and seldom remains more than 24 hours.

Temperature averages indicate mild winters and quite warm summers. Cold periods in winter are ushered in by strong, dry, dusty north, and northwest winds known as northers, and temperature drops of as much as 25 degrees in a few hours are not uncommon. Cold weather periods usually do not last more than two or three days. Temperatures as low as 32 degrees have occurred as early as October and as late as March. Normal occurrences of the earliest freezing temperature in autumn and the latest in spring are early December and mid February, which results in an average growing season of 300 days. Hot weather is rather persistent from late May to mid September and temperatures above 100 degrees have been recorded as early as March and as late as October. Low humidity and fresh breezes tend to alleviate uncomfortable conditions usually associated with high temperatures. The mean early morning humidity is about 79 percent, and the mean afternoon humidity is near 44 percent.

Clear to partly cloudy skies predominate, and even in the more cloudy winter months, the mean number of cloudy days are less than the number of clear days.

Del Rio Int'l Airport *Val Verde County*   Elevation: 997 ft.   Latitude: 29° 23' N   Longitude: 100° 56' W

	JAN	FEB	MAR	APR	MAY	JUN	JUL	AUG	SEP	OCT	NOV	DEC	YEAR
Mean Maximum Temp. (°F)	63.0	68.5	76.3	83.2	88.8	94.0	96.2	96.1	90.6	82.0	71.5	64.4	81.2
Mean Temp. (°F)	51.3	56.3	64.0	71.0	77.8	83.1	85.3	85.1	80.0	71.1	60.2	52.9	69.9
Mean Minimum Temp. (°F)	39.6	44.1	51.6	58.8	66.7	72.2	74.4	74.0	69.3	60.2	48.9	41.4	58.4
Extreme Maximum Temp. (°F)	89	99	101	106	106	112	108	106	105	106	96	90	112
Extreme Minimum Temp. (°F)	15	14	21	33	45	55	64	65	48	28	22	10	10
Days Maximum Temp. ≥ 90°F	0	0	2	6	15	25	28	28	20	5	0	0	129
Days Maximum Temp. ≤ 32°F	0	0	0	0	0	0	0	0	0	0	0	0	0
Days Minimum Temp. ≤ 32°F	6	3	1	0	0	0	0	0	0	0	0	0	0
Days Minimum Temp. ≤ 0°F	0	0	0	0	0	0	0	0	0	0	1	4	15
Heating Degree Days (base 65°F)	420	257	112	26	1	0	0	0	3	24	179	371	1,393
Cooling Degree Days (base 65°F)	3	20	84	217	422	569	659	655	471	232	46	4	3,382
Mean Precipitation (in.)	0.58	0.98	0.97	1.69	2.37	2.24	2.00	2.03	2.34	1.83	0.86	0.74	18.63
Maximum Precipitation (in.)	1.9	3.8	3.2	7.5	10.2	5.7	13.2	6.1	15.8	11.3	3.4	3.1	33.2
Minimum Precipitation (in.)	trace	0	trace	trace	trace	trace	trace	0	trace	0	trace	trace	4.3
Maximum 24-hr. Precipitation (in.)	1.0	2.6	1.7	2.9	3.6	2.9	4.8	2.8	5.2	7.6	2.1	1.4	7.6
Days With ≥ 0.1" Precipitation	2	2	2	3	4	3	3	2	3	3	2	2	31
Days With ≥ 1.0" Precipitation	0	0	0	1	1	1	1	1	1	0	0	0	6
Mean Snowfall (in.)	0.7	0.1	trace	trace	trace	0.0	0.0	0.0	0.0	trace	trace	trace	0.8
Maximum Snowfall (in.)	10	3	3	0	0	0	0	0	0	1	trace	trace	10
Maximum 24-hr. Snowfall (in.)	8	3	3	0	0	0	0	0	0	1	trace	trace	8
Days With ≥ 1.0" Snow Depth	0	0	0	0	0	0	0	0	0	0	0	0	0
Thunderstorm Days	< 1	1	2	4	8	4	3	4	3	2	1	< 1	32
Foggy Days	10	7	6	6	6	2	1	1	3	5	8	9	64
Predominant Sky Cover	OVR	CLR	CLR	OVR	OVR	CLR	CLR	CLR	CLR	CLR	CLR	CLR	CLR
Mean Relative Humidity 6am (%)	76	73	70	76	82	82	78	78	81	80	78	75	77
Mean Relative Humidity 3pm (%)	44	40	35	40	45	42	37	38	43	43	43	42	41
Mean Dewpoint (°F)	35	36	42	52	61	65	65	65	63	55	44	36	52
Prevailing Wind Direction	SE	SE	SE	SE	SE	SE	SE	ESE	SE	SE	SE	SE	SE
Prevailing Wind Speed (mph)	9	10	13	13	13	13	12	10	10	10	10	9	12
Maximum Wind Gust (mph)	59	54	56	59	71	52	46	52	54	53	44	56	71

El Paso Int'l Airport

The city of El Paso is located in the extreme west point of Texas at an elevation of about 3,700 feet . The National Weather Service station is located on a mesa about 200 feet higher than the city. The climate of the region is characterized by an abundance of sunshine throughout the year, high daytime summer temperatures, very low humidity, scanty rainfall, and a relatively mild winter season. The Franklin Mountains begin within the city limits and extend northward for about 16 miles. Peaks of these mountains range from 4,687 to 7,152 feet above sea level.

Rainfall throughout the year is light, insufficient for any growth except desert vegetation. Irrigation is necessary for crops, gardens, and lawns. Dry periods lasting several months are not unusual. Almost half of the precipitation occurs in the three-month period, July through September, from brief but often heavy thunderstorms. Small amounts of snow fall nearly every winter, but snow cover rarely amounts to more than an inch and seldom remains on the ground for more than a few hours.

Daytime summer temperatures are high, frequently above 90 degrees and occasionally above 100 degrees. Summer nights are usually comfortable, with temperatures in the 60s. When temperatures are high the relative humidity is generally quite low. With temperatures above 90 degrees in April, May, and June the humidity averaged from 10 to 14 percent, while in July, August, and September it averaged 22 to 24 percent.

Winter daytime temperatures are mild. At night they drop below freezing about half the time in December and January. The flat, irrigated land of the Rio Grande Valley in the vicinity of El Paso is noticeably cooler, particularly at night, than the airport or the city proper, both in summer and winter. This results in more comfortable temperatures in summer but increases the severity of freezes in winter. The cooler air in the Valley also causes marked short-period fluctuations of temperature and dewpoint at the airport with changes in wind direction, especially during the early morning hours.

Dust and sandstorms are the most unpleasant features of the weather in El Paso. While wind velocities are not excessively high, the soil surface is dry and loose and natural vegetation is sparse, so moderately strong winds raise considerable dust and sand. Duststorms are most frequent in March and April, and comparatively rare in the period July through December. prevailing winds are from the north in winter and the south in summer.

El Paso Int'l Airport *El Paso County*   Elevation: 3,917 ft.   Latitude: 31° 49' N   Longitude: 106° 23' W

	JAN	FEB	MAR	APR	MAY	JUN	JUL	AUG	SEP	OCT	NOV	DEC	YEAR
Mean Maximum Temp. (°F)	57.9	64.1	70.9	78.8	87.4	96.3	95.5	93.0	87.7	78.5	66.5	58.4	77.9
Mean Temp. (°F)	44.4	49.7	56.1	63.5	72.3	81.0	82.3	80.3	74.5	64.0	52.1	44.9	63.8
Mean Minimum Temp. (°F)	30.9	35.3	41.2	48.1	57.2	65.6	69.1	67.6	61.2	49.4	37.7	31.4	49.6
Extreme Maximum Temp. (°F)	80	83	89	98	103	114	112	108	104	96	87	80	114
Extreme Minimum Temp. (°F)	3	8	14	23	35	46	57	56	42	25	1	6	1
Days Maximum Temp. ≥ 90°F	0	0	0	2	13	26	27	24	14	2	0	0	108
Days Maximum Temp. ≤ 32°F	0	0	0	0	0	0	0	0	0	0	0	0	0
Days Minimum Temp. ≤ 32°F	18	10	4	1	0	0	0	0	0	1	8	18	60
Days Minimum Temp. ≤ 0°F	0	0	0	0	0	0	0	0	0	0	0	0	0
Heating Degree Days (base 65°F)	631	425	278	108	11	0	0	0	9	96	381	615	2,554
Cooling Degree Days (base 65°F)	0	1	7	73	260	498	554	498	314	80	2	0	2,287
Mean Precipitation (in.)	0.46	0.40	0.28	0.22	0.40	0.81	1.48	1.74	1.64	0.80	0.39	0.76	9.38
Maximum Precipitation (in.)	1.8	1.7	2.3	1.4	4.2	3.2	5.5	5.6	6.7	3.1	1.6	3.3	17.2
Minimum Precipitation (in.)	0	0	0	0	0	trace	trace	trace	trace	0	0	0	4.3
Maximum 24-hr. Precipitation (in.)	0.5	0.8	0.8	1.0	1.3	1.2	1.8	2.0	2.3	1.3	0.8	1.5	2.3
Days With ≥ 0.1" Precipitation	2	1	1	1	1	2	4	4	3	2	1	2	24
Days With ≥ 1.0" Precipitation	0	0	0	0	0	0	0	0	0	0	0	0	0
Mean Snowfall (in.)	1.4	0.8	0.3	0.7	trace	trace	trace	0.0	trace	trace	0.8	2.3	6.3
Maximum Snowfall (in.)	8	9	7	17	0	0	0	0	0	1	13	26	33
Maximum 24-hr. Snowfall (in.)	5	7	6	7	0	0	0	0	0	1	7	15	15
Days With ≥ 1.0" Snow Depth	1	0	0	0	0	0	0	0	0	0	0	1	2
Thunderstorm Days	< 1	< 1	1	1	3	4	10	10	4	2	< 1	< 1	35
Foggy Days	2	1	1	< 1	< 1	< 1	< 1	< 1	1	1	1	2	9
Predominant Sky Cover	CLR	CLR	CLR	CLR	CLR	CLR	SCT	SCT	CLR	CLR	CLR	CLR	CLR
Mean Relative Humidity 6am (%)	68	60	50	43	44	46	63	69	72	66	63	68	59
Mean Relative Humidity 3pm (%)	34	27	21	17	17	17	28	30	32	29	30	36	26
Mean Dewpoint (°F)	24	24	24	26	34	42	54	56	52	40	29	26	36
Prevailing Wind Direction	NNE	WSW	W	WSW	WSW	SE	SE	SE	SE	N	NNE	N	WSW
Prevailing Wind Speed (mph)	7	12	15	14	13	8	8	7	7	7	7	7	9
Maximum Wind Gust (mph)	61	73	84	74	55	69	73	67	63	59	59	74	84

Galveston

The city of Galveston is located on Galveston Island off the southeast coast of Texas. The island is about two and three fourths miles across at the widest point and 29 miles long. It is bounded on the southeast by the Gulf of Mexico and on the northwest by Galveston Bay, which is about three miles wide at this point. The climate of the Galveston area is predominantly marine, with periods of modified continental influence during the colder months, when cold fronts from the northwest sometimes reach the coast.

Because of its coastal location and relatively low latitude, cold fronts which do reach the area are very seldom severe and temperatures below 32 degrees are recorded on an average only four times a year. Normal monthly high temperatures range from about 60 degrees in January to nearly 88 degrees in August. Lows range from about 48 degrees in January to the upper 70s during the summer season.

High humidities prevail throughout the year. Annual precipitation averages about 42 inches. Rainfall during the summer months may vary greatly on different parts of the island, as most of the rain in this season is from local thunderstorm activity. Hail is rare because the necessary strong vertical lifting is usually absent. There have been several instances when a monthly rainfall total amounted to only a trace, but these have been offset in the means by many monthly totals in excess of 15 inches. Winter precipitation comes mainly from frontal activity and from low stratus clouds, which produce slow, steady rains.

The island has been subject at infrequent intervals to major tropical storms of hurricane force.

Galveston *Galveston County*   Elevation: 13 ft.   Latitude: 29° 18' N   Longitude: 94° 48' W

	JAN	FEB	MAR	APR	MAY	JUN	JUL	AUG	SEP	OCT	NOV	DEC	YEAR
Mean Maximum Temp. (°F)	59.4	62.1	67.8	73.9	80.4	85.8	88.2	88.7	85.5	78.2	69.4	63.0	75.2
Mean Temp. (°F)	53.7	56.5	62.5	69.2	76.1	81.7	83.9	84.1	80.5	73.1	63.8	57.1	70.2
Mean Minimum Temp. (°F)	48.0	50.9	57.2	64.5	71.9	77.5	79.6	79.4	75.5	68.0	58.1	51.3	65.2
Extreme Maximum Temp. (°F)	78	80	82	90	94	96	97	102	98	92	85	81	102
Extreme Minimum Temp. (°F)	20	24	26	42	56	64	69	69	56	39	31	14	14
Days Maximum Temp. ≥ 90°F	0	0	0	0	0	2	8	10	5	0	0	0	25
Days Maximum Temp. ≤ 32°F	0	0	0	0	0	0	0	0	0	0	0	0	0
Days Minimum Temp. ≤ 32°F	2	1	0	0	0	0	0	0	0	0	0	1	4
Days Minimum Temp. ≤ 0°F	0	0	0	0	0	0	0	0	0	0	0	0	0
Heating Degree Days (base 65°F)	347	240	110	21	0	0	0	0	0	15	117	258	1,108
Cooling Degree Days (base 65°F)	4	8	42	156	364	517	609	613	488	282	90	23	3,196
Mean Precipitation (in.)	4.08	2.64	2.88	2.63	3.74	4.10	3.53	4.26	6.08	3.64	3.55	3.50	44.63
Maximum Precipitation (in.)	10.8	8.3	9.5	10.4	11.0	13.0	17.5	13.4	14.3	9.0	9.5	9.0	60.5
Minimum Precipitation (in.)	0.2	0.2	0.1	trace	trace	0.4	0.1	0.2	0.3	0	0.6	0.5	29.3
Maximum 24-hr. Precipitation (in.)	4.1	4.5	8.0	5.1	7.1	4.9	11.+	11.+	6.3	3.9	4.3	4.7	11.+
Days With ≥ 0.1" Precipitation	6	4	4	3	4	5	5	6	6	5	5	5	58
Days With ≥ 1.0" Precipitation	1	1	1	1	1	1	1	1	2	1	1	1	13
Mean Snowfall (in.)	trace	trace	trace	trace	trace	0.0	0.0	0.0	0.0	0.0	0.0	trace	trace
Maximum Snowfall (in.)	3	2	trace	0	0	0	0	0	0	0	0	1	4
Maximum 24-hr. Snowfall (in.)	3	2	trace	0	0	0	0	0	0	0	0	1	3
Days With ≥ 1.0" Snow Depth	0	0	0	0	0	0	0	0	0	0	0	0	0
Thunderstorm Days	1	< 1	1	3	4	2	2	4	3	2	1	< 1	23
Foggy Days	9	6	10	10	3	3	1	2	2	6	5	8	65
Predominant Sky Cover	na	na	na	na	na	na	na	na	na	na	na	na	na
Mean Relative Humidity 7am (%)	na	na	na	na	na	na	na	na	na	na	na	na	na
Mean Relative Humidity 4pm (%)	na	na	na	na	na	na	na	na	na	na	na	na	na
Mean Dewpoint (°F)	na	na	na	na	na	na	na	na	na	na	na	na	na
Prevailing Wind Direction	na	na	na	na	na	na	na	na	na	na	na	na	na
Prevailing Wind Speed (mph)	na	na	na	na	na	na	na	na	na	na	na	na	na
Maximum Wind Gust (mph)	na	na	na	na	na	na	na	na	na	na	na	na	na

Houston Bush Intercontinental

Houston, the largest city in Texas, is located in the flat Coastal Plains, about 50 miles from the Gulf of Mexico and about 25 miles from Galveston Bay. The climate is predominantly marine. The terrain includes numerous small streams and bayous which, together with the nearness to Galveston Bay, favor the development of both ground and advective fogs. Prevailing winds are from the southeast and south, except in January, when frequent passages of high pressure areas bring invasions of polar air and prevailing northerly winds.

Temperatures are moderated by the influence of winds from the Gulf, which result in mild winters. Another effect of the nearness of the Gulf is abundant rainfall, except for rare extended dry periods. Polar air penetrates the area frequently enough to provide variability in the weather.

Records of sky cover for daylight hours indicate about one-fourth of the days per year as clear, with a high number of clear days in October and November. Cloudy days are relatively frequent from December to May and partly cloudy days are the more frequent for June through September. Sunshine averages nearly 60 percent of the possible amount for the year ranging from 42 percent in January to 67 percent in June.

Heavy fog occurs on an average of 16 days a year and light fog occurs about 62 days a year in the city. The frequency of heavy fog is considerably higher at William P. Hobby Airport and at Intercontinental Airport.

Destructive windstorms are fairly infrequent, but both thundersqualls and tropical storms occasionally pass through the area.

Houston Bush Intercontinental *Harris County*   Elevation: 95 ft.   Latitude: 30° 00' N   Longitude: 95° 22' W

	JAN	FEB	MAR	APR	MAY	JUN	JUL	AUG	SEP	OCT	NOV	DEC	YEAR
Mean Maximum Temp. (°F)	61.8	66.0	72.7	79.0	85.3	90.8	93.7	93.5	89.0	81.4	71.7	64.8	79.1
Mean Temp. (°F)	51.6	55.2	61.9	68.4	75.4	81.1	83.5	83.2	78.8	70.0	60.8	54.2	68.7
Mean Minimum Temp. (°F)	41.3	44.3	51.0	57.7	65.5	71.3	73.2	72.8	68.5	58.6	49.8	43.5	58.1
Extreme Maximum Temp. (°F)	84	91	91	95	99	103	104	107	102	96	89	85	107
Extreme Minimum Temp. (°F)	12	20	22	31	44	52	62	60	48	29	19	7	7
Days Maximum Temp. ≥ 90°F	0	0	0	1	6	20	27	26	16	3	0	0	99
Days Maximum Temp. ≤ 32°F	0	0	0	0	0	0	0	0	0	0	0	0	0
Days Minimum Temp. ≤ 32°F	7	4	1	0	0	0	0	0	0	0	1	5	18
Days Minimum Temp. ≤ 0°F	0	0	0	0	0	0	0	0	0	0	0	0	0
Heating Degree Days (base 65°F)	426	293	155	45	2	0	0	0	1	36	188	356	1,502
Cooling Degree Days (base 65°F)	12	26	67	161	354	509	598	596	438	213	70	29	3,073
Mean Precipitation (in.)	3.70	2.99	3.48	3.49	5.22	5.25	3.23	3.83	4.40	4.70	3.95	3.62	47.86
Maximum Precipitation (in.)	9.8	6.0	8.5	10.9	14.4	16.3	8.1	9.4	11.3	16.0	8.9	9.3	70.2
Minimum Precipitation (in.)	0.4	0.4	0.9	0.4	0.8	0.3	0.5	0.3	0.8	0	0.4	0.6	22.9
Maximum 24-hr. Precipitation (in.)	2.6	2.2	7.5	8.2	6.2	10.+	3.6	6.7	7.7	9.3	3.8	3.4	10.+
Days With ≥ 0.1" Precipitation	6	5	5	4	6	6	5	6	6	5	5	5	64
Days With ≥ 1.0" Precipitation	1	1	1	1	2	2	1	1	1	2	1	1	15
Mean Snowfall (in.)	0.1	0.2	trace	trace	trace	trace	0.0	0.0	0.0	0.0	trace	trace	0.3
Maximum Snowfall (in.)	2	3	0	0	0	0	0	0	0	0	trace	2	5
Maximum 24-hr. Snowfall (in.)	2	1	0	0	0	0	0	0	0	0	trace	2	2
Days With ≥ 1.0" Snow Depth	0	0	0	0	0	0	0	0	0	0	0	0	0
Thunderstorm Days	2	2	4	4	7	8	10	11	8	4	3	2	65
Foggy Days	18	15	18	17	19	13	11	14	16	16	15	17	189
Predominant Sky Cover	OVR	OVR	OVR	OVR	OVR	SCT	SCT	SCT	SCT	CLR	OVR	OVR	OVR
Mean Relative Humidity 6am (%)	86	87	88	89	92	92	93	93	93	91	89	87	90
Mean Relative Humidity 3pm (%)	58	55	54	55	57	57	54	55	56	52	55	57	55
Mean Dewpoint (°F)	42	45	51	58	66	71	72	72	68	60	51	46	59
Prevailing Wind Direction	N	N	SE	SE	SE	SE	S	S	ENE	SE	N	N	SE
Prevailing Wind Speed (mph)	9	9	12	12	10	10	8	8	7	9	8	9	9
Maximum Wind Gust (mph)	44	61	54	59	69	68	68	98	56	58	49	56	98

Lubbock Regional Airport

Lubbock is located on a plateau area of Northwestern Texas that is referred to locally as the South Plains Region. The general elevation of the area is about 3,250 feet. The Region is a major part of the Llano Estacado (staked plains). The latter, which includes a large portion of Northwest Texas, is bounded on the east and southeast by an erosional escarpment that is usually referred to as the Cap Rock. The Llano Estacado extends southwestward into the upper Pecos Valley and westward into eastern New Mexico.

The South Plains are predominately flat, but contain numerous small playas (or clay lined depressions) and small stream valleys. During the rainy months the playas collect run-off water and form small lakes or ponds. The stream valleys drain into the major rivers of West Texas, but throughout most of the year these streams carry only very light flows.

Cap Rock causes a noticeable distortion of the smooth wind flow patterns across the South Plains, the most noticeable on southeasterly winds as they are deflected upward along its face.

The Lubbock area is the heart of the largest cotton-producing section of Texas. Irrigation from underground sources is often used as a supplement to natural rainfall to improve crop yields. The soils of the region are sandy clay loams.

The area is semi-arid, transitional between the desert conditions on the west and the humid climates to the east and southeast. The greatest monthly rainfall totals occur from May through September when warm moist tropical air may be carried into the area from the Gulf of Mexico. This air mass often brings moderate to heavy afternoon and evening thunderstorms, accompanied by hail. Precipitation across the area is characterized by its variability. The monthly precipitation extremes range from trace amounts in several isolated months to 14 inches.

Snow may occur from late October until April. Each snowfall is generally light and seldom remains on the ground for more than two or three days at any one period.

High winds are associated primarily with intense thunderstorms and at times may cause significant damage to structures. Winds in excess of 25 mph occasionally occur for periods of 12 hours or longer. These prolonged winds are generally associated with late winter and springtime low-pressure centers. Spring winds often bring widespread dust.

The summer heat is moderated by a variable, but usually gentle, wind. Dry air from the west often reduce any discomfort from the summer heat and lower temperatures into the 60s.

The average first occurrence of temperatures below 32 degrees Fahrenheit in the fall is the first of November and the average last occurrence in the spring is in mid April.

Lubbock Regional Airport *Lubbock County* Elevation: 3,251 ft. Latitude: 33° 40' N Longitude: 101° 49' W

	JAN	FEB	MAR	APR	MAY	JUN	JUL	AUG	SEP	OCT	NOV	DEC	YEAR
Mean Maximum Temp. (°F)	52.7	58.6	66.7	75.2	83.2	90.6	92.3	90.1	83.4	74.8	62.7	54.5	73.7
Mean Temp. (°F)	39.2	44.3	51.9	60.6	69.6	77.6	80.3	78.4	71.4	61.4	49.3	41.2	60.4
Mean Minimum Temp. (°F)	25.6	29.9	37.0	46.0	56.0	64.6	68.2	66.5	59.4	47.9	35.9	27.7	47.0
Extreme Maximum Temp. (°F)	83	87	95	100	105	114	108	103	102	98	88	81	114
Extreme Minimum Temp. (°F)	-4	-2	8	22	32	46	55	54	33	18	1	-2	-4
Days Maximum Temp. ≥ 90°F	0	0	0	2	8	18	22	19	9	1	0	0	79
Days Maximum Temp. ≤ 32°F	3	1	0	0	0	0	0	0	0	0	0	2	6
Days Minimum Temp. ≤ 32°F	25	17	9	2	0	0	0	0	0	1	10	22	86
Days Minimum Temp. ≤ 0°F	0	0	0	0	0	0	0	0	0	0	0	0	0
Heating Degree Days (base 65°F)	794	579	407	174	37	2	0	0	32	157	465	732	3,379
Cooling Degree Days (base 65°F)	0	1	7	48	190	387	498	443	237	54	2	0	1,867
Mean Precipitation (in.)	0.50	0.71	0.73	1.24	2.43	2.75	2.06	2.39	2.63	1.63	0.67	0.64	18.38
Maximum Precipitation (in.)	4.0	2.5	3.2	3.5	7.8	7.9	7.2	8.8	8.2	10.8	2.7	2.2	29.4
Minimum Precipitation (in.)	0	trace	trace	trace	0.1	trace	trace	0	trace	0	0	trace	10.8
Maximum 24-hr. Precipitation (in.)	1.1	2.1	1.4	2.2	3.7	5.7	2.6	3.1	4.7	5.4	1.6	0.7	5.7
Days With ≥ 0.1" Precipitation	1	2	2	3	4	5	4	4	4	3	2	2	36
Days With ≥ 1.0" Precipitation	0	0	0	0	1	1	1	1	1	0	0	0	5
Mean Snowfall (in.)	3.0	2.4	0.7	0.2	trace	trace	trace	0.0	0.0	0.3	1.4	2.1	10.1
Maximum Snowfall (in.)	25	17	14	5	0	0	0	0	0	8	21	10	36
Maximum 24-hr. Snowfall (in.)	11	12	8	4	0	0	0	0	0	8	11	6	12
Days With ≥ 1.0" Snow Depth	2	2	0	0	0	0	0	0	0	0	1	1	6
Thunderstorm Days	< 1	1	2	4	8	9	8	7	5	3	1	< 1	48
Foggy Days	7	7	5	4	6	3	2	3	6	6	6	6	61
Predominant Sky Cover	CLR	CLR	CLR	CLR	CLR	CLR	SCT	SCT	CLR	CLR	CLR	CLR	CLR
Mean Relative Humidity 6am (%)	73	72	68	68	76	78	73	78	82	77	74	73	74
Mean Relative Humidity 3pm (%)	41	39	32	29	34	36	38	42	45	38	38	41	38
Mean Dewpoint (°F)	22	25	29	36	47	57	60	60	56	43	32	24	41
Prevailing Wind Direction	WSW	WSW	S	S	S	S	S	S	S	S	SW	WSW	S
Prevailing Wind Speed (mph)	12	13	14	15	15	14	13	12	12	12	12	10	13
Maximum Wind Gust (mph)	59	66	77	71	70	85	85	59	58	64	66	64	85

Midland Regional Air Terminal

The Midland-Odessa region is on the southern extension of the South Plains of Texas. The terrain is level with only slight occasional undulations.

The climate is typical of a semi-arid region. The vegetation of the area consists mostly of native grasses and a few trees, mostly of the mesquite variety.

Most of the annual precipitation in the area comes as a result of very violent spring and early summer thunderstorms. These are usually accompanied by excessive rainfall, over limited areas, and sometimes hail. Due to the flat nature of the countryside, local flooding occurs, but is of short duration. Tornadoes are occasionally sighted.

During the late winter and early spring months, blowing dust occurs frequently. The flat plains of the area with only grass as vegetation offer little resistance to the strong winds. The sky is occasionally obscured by dust but in most storms visibilities range from one to three miles.

Daytime temperatures are quite hot in the summer, but there is a large diurnal range of temperature and most nights are comfortable. The temperature drops below 32 degrees in the fall about mid- November and the last temperature below 32 degrees in spring comes early in April.

Winters are characterized by frequent cold periods followed by rapid warming. Cold frontal passages are followed by chilly weather for two or three days. Cloudiness is at a minimum. Summers are hot and dry with numerous small convective showers.

The prevailing wind direction in this area is from the southeast. This, together with the upslope of the terrain from the same direction, causes occasional low cloudiness and drizzle during winter and spring months. Snow is infrequent. Maximum temperatures during the summer months frequently are from two to six degrees cooler than those at places 100 miles southeast, due to the cooling effect of the upslope winds.

Very low humidities are conducive to personal comfort, because even though summer afternoon temperatures are frequently above 90 degrees, the low humidity with resultant rapid evaporation, has a cooling effect. The climate of the area is generally quite pleasant with the most disagreeable weather concentrated in the late winter and spring months.

Midland Regional Air Terminal *Midland County*   Elevation: 2,860 ft.   Latitude: 31° 57' N   Longitude: 102° 11' W

	JAN	FEB	MAR	APR	MAY	JUN	JUL	AUG	SEP	OCT	NOV	DEC	YEAR
Mean Maximum Temp. (°F)	56.6	62.7	70.5	78.6	86.6	92.8	94.2	92.7	85.9	77.5	66.2	58.8	76.9
Mean Temp. (°F)	43.1	48.3	55.6	63.5	72.5	79.5	81.6	80.3	73.7	64.3	52.5	45.1	63.3
Mean Minimum Temp. (°F)	29.4	33.9	40.6	48.4	58.4	66.2	68.9	67.8	61.5	51.1	38.7	31.4	49.7
Extreme Maximum Temp. (°F)	84	90	95	101	108	116	112	106	105	100	90	84	116
Extreme Minimum Temp. (°F)	0	-11	9	20	34	47	53	54	36	24	13	-1	-11
Days Maximum Temp. ≥ 90°F	0	0	1	3	12	21	26	23	12	2	0	0	100
Days Maximum Temp. ≤ 32°F	2	1	0	0	0	0	0	0	0	0	0	1	4
Days Minimum Temp. ≤ 32°F	20	12	5	1	0	0	0	0	0	0	7	18	63
Days Minimum Temp. ≤ 0°F	0	0	0	0	0	0	0	0	0	0	0	0	0
Heating Degree Days (base 65°F)	673	466	301	117	18	1	0	0	19	100	373	609	2,677
Cooling Degree Days (base 65°F)	0	2	14	81	266	452	538	501	298	92	5	0	2,249
Mean Precipitation (in.)	0.51	0.63	0.49	0.74	1.76	1.64	1.89	1.80	2.38	1.72	0.62	0.64	14.82
Maximum Precipitation (in.)	3.7	2.5	2.9	2.8	7.6	4.0	8.5	4.4	9.7	7.4	2.3	3.3	32.1
Minimum Precipitation (in.)	0	trace	trace	0	0.1	trace	trace	0.2	0.1	0	0	0	4.6
Maximum 24-hr. Precipitation (in.)	1.1	1.2	2.2	1.6	4.8	3.1	4.1	2.4	3.3	3.6	1.8	1.2	4.8
Days With ≥ 0.1" Precipitation	1	2	1	2	3	3	3	3	4	3	1	2	28
Days With ≥ 1.0" Precipitation	0	0	0	0	0	1	0	0	1	0	0	0	2
Mean Snowfall (in.)	2.2	0.8	0.4	trace	trace	trace	trace	trace	0.0	trace	0.5	1.5	5.4
Maximum Snowfall (in.)	9	4	6	1	0	0	0	0	0	1	7	9	12
Maximum 24-hr. Snowfall (in.)	6	3	5	1	0	0	0	0	0	1	6	4	6
Days With ≥ 1.0" Snow Depth	1	0	0	0	0	0	0	0	0	0	0	0	1
Thunderstorm Days	< 1	1	1	3	7	6	6	6	4	3	1	< 1	38
Foggy Days	7	7	4	3	3	1	1	1	4	5	6	7	49
Predominant Sky Cover	CLR	CLR	CLR	CLR	CLR	CLR	CLR	CLR	CLR	CLR	CLR	CLR	CLR
Mean Relative Humidity 6am (%)	72	72	65	67	75	76	73	74	79	78	74	71	73
Mean Relative Humidity 3pm (%)	38	35	27	27	31	32	34	34	40	37	35	37	34
Mean Dewpoint (°F)	25	28	30	38	48	57	59	59	56	46	34	27	43
Prevailing Wind Direction	S	S	S	S	SSE	SSE	SSE	SSE	SSE	S	S	S	S
Prevailing Wind Speed (mph)	9	10	13	13	14	13	12	10	10	12	10	10	12
Maximum Wind Gust (mph)	59	63	74	76	83	71	82	66	82	69	60	69	83

Port Arthur Jefferson County

Port Arthur is located on the flat Coastal Plain in the extreme southeast corner of Texas. The climate is a mixture of tropical and temperate zone conditions.

Sea breezes prevent extremely high temperatures in the summer, except on rare occasions. The area lies far enough south so that cold air masses modify in severity but still provide freezing temperatures up to six times a year.

High humidity is the result of fairly evenly distributed high normal rainfall and prevailing southerly winds from the Gulf of Mexico.

Cloudy, rainy weather is most common in the winter. Only slightly more than half the winters record even a trace of sleet or snow. Heavy rainfall in summer occurs in short duration thunderstorms and in infrequent tropical storms.

Slow moving systems in the spring and fall often result in three to five days of stormy weather and heavy rain. The lightest precipitation usually occurs in March and October. Funnel clouds and waterspouts are common near the coast. The area enjoys approximately 60 percent of possible sunshine.

Fog, most frequent in midwinter and early spring, is rare in summer. It usually dissipates before noon, but occasionally under stagnant conditions lasts a day or two. Along the immediate coast, fog usually does not form until daybreak, but inland it may form before midnight.

The average wind movement is near 11 mph. Except for severe storms and tropical disturbances, wind seldom exceeds 45 mph. It exceeds 30 mph on only about 40 days in any one year.

The climate is favorable for outdoor activities throughout the year. The abundant rainfall, moderate temperatures, and the short period of temperatures below freezing are particularly favorable for farming and livestock production. Heaviest rain usually falls in the summer when needed for rice. The comparatively dry harvest season simplifies the gathering of rice and feed crops. Cattle on the open range of the coastal marshes need little supplemental feeding or protection. Improved pastures are easily provided because of the moderate temperatures and abundant rainfall.

Port Arthur Jefferson County *Jefferson County* Elevation: 13 ft. Latitude: 29° 57' N Longitude: 94° 01' W

	JAN	FEB	MAR	APR	MAY	JUN	JUL	AUG	SEP	OCT	NOV	DEC	YEAR
Mean Maximum Temp. (°F)	61.1	65.1	71.8	77.8	84.2	89.5	91.6	91.7	88.0	80.5	70.9	64.3	78.0
Mean Temp. (°F)	52.0	55.4	62.1	68.4	75.4	81.0	82.9	82.7	79.0	70.2	61.0	54.8	68.8
Mean Minimum Temp. (°F)	42.7	45.7	52.4	59.0	66.6	72.5	74.2	73.7	70.0	59.9	51.1	45.2	59.4
Extreme Maximum Temp. (°F)	81	85	87	94	97	99	103	101	100	95	88	84	103
Extreme Minimum Temp. (°F)	15	20	23	32	47	56	61	60	50	30	22	12	12
Days Maximum Temp. ≥ 90°F	0	0	0	0	2	17	24	24	13	2	0	0	82
Days Maximum Temp. ≤ 32°F	0	0	0	0	0	0	0	0	0	0	0	0	0
Days Minimum Temp. ≤ 32°F	5	3	1	0	0	0	0	0	0	0	1	4	14
Days Minimum Temp. ≤ 0°F	0	0	0	0	0	0	0	0	0	0	0	0	0
Heating Degree Days (base 65°F)	409	280	140	38	1	0	0	0	0	32	178	337	1,415
Cooling Degree Days (base 65°F)	10	18	57	146	338	492	571	568	430	205	66	27	2,928
Mean Precipitation (in.)	5.69	3.42	3.80	3.64	5.82	6.52	5.20	4.93	6.24	5.14	4.46	5.25	60.11
Maximum Precipitation (in.)	14.9	13.1	10.2	8.7	13.2	18.9	18.7	17.3	22.0	15.1	10.8	18.0	81.5
Minimum Precipitation (in.)	0.6	0.2	0.1	0.3	0.1	0.8	0.6	1.0	0.5	0	0.1	1.3	33.1
Maximum 24-hr. Precipitation (in.)	4.3	9.4	4.2	4.3	9.9	8.7	8.6	8.3	12.+	8.0	5.8	8.0	12.+
Days With ≥ 0.1" Precipitation	7	5	5	4	5	7	7	7	7	5	6	6	71
Days With ≥ 1.0" Precipitation	2	1	1	1	2	2	1	1	2	2	2	2	19
Mean Snowfall (in.)	0.1	trace	trace	trace	trace	0.0	trace	0.0	0.0	0.0	trace	trace	0.1
Maximum Snowfall (in.)	3	4	1	0	0	0	0	0	0	0	trace	trace	4
Maximum 24-hr. Snowfall (in.)	3	4	1	0	0	0	0	0	0	0	trace	1	4
Days With ≥ 1.0" Snow Depth	0	0	0	0	0	0	0	0	0	0	trace	0	0
Thunderstorm Days	3	3	4	4	6	8	14	12	7	3	3	2	69
Foggy Days	18	16	17	15	14	10	8	11	14	16	15	17	171
Predominant Sky Cover	OVR	OVR	OVR	OVR	SCT	SCT	SCT	SCT	SCT	CLR	OVR	OVR	OVR
Mean Relative Humidity 6am (%)	88	88	88	90	92	93	94	94	92	91	89	89	91
Mean Relative Humidity 3pm (%)	64	61	59	61	62	62	64	62	60	55	59	64	61
Mean Dewpoint (°F)	45	47	52	60	67	72	74	74	70	61	52	47	60
Prevailing Wind Direction	N	S	S	SSE	S	S	S	S	NE	N	N	N	S
Prevailing Wind Speed (mph)	12	12	13	14	12	10	8	8	9	9	10	12	10
Maximum Wind Gust (mph)	56	54	60	59	62	76	69	59	58	48	61	61	76

San Angelo Mathis Field

San Angelo is located near the center of Texas at the northern edge of the Edwards Plateau. Ground elevation ranges from about 1,700 to 2,700 feet above sea level. Topography varies from level and slightly rolling to broken. The climate is generally classified as semi-arid or steppe, but has some humid temperate characteristics. Warm, dry weather predominates, although changes may be rapid and frequent with the passage of cold fronts or northers.

High temperatures of summer are associated with fair skies, south to southwest winds and dry air. Low humidities, however, are conducive to personal comfort because of rapid evaporation. Rapid temperature drops occur after sunset, and most nights are pleasant with lows in the upper 60s and lower 70s. Rapid temperature drops occur in the winter as cold polar air invades the region. Temperature drops of 20 to 30 degrees in a short time are not uncommon. Cold polar outbreaks have produced record low temperatures of zero or below throughout the area.

The rainfall is typical of the Great Plains. Much of the rainfall occurs from thunderstorm activity, and wide variations in annual precipitation occur from year to year. Heavy rainfall occurs in April, May, June, September and October. Also, in the late summer months, heavy precipitation may occur when tropical disturbances move inland over south Texas and pass near the San Angelo area.

The prevailing wind direction is from the south, and winds are frequently high and persistent for several days. Dusty conditions are infrequent and occur in early spring when west or northwest winds predominate. The frequency and intensity of the dust storms are dependent on soil conditions in the Texas Panhandle and in New Mexico.

Agriculture in the region consists of cattle, sheep, and goat raising. Cotton, from dry-land and irrigated fields, maize, corn, melons, truck farming, and pecan production are also important crops.

San Angelo Mathis Field *Tom Green County*   Elevation: 1,916 ft.   Latitude: 31° 21' N   Longitude: 100° 30' W

	JAN	FEB	MAR	APR	MAY	JUN	JUL	AUG	SEP	OCT	NOV	DEC	YEAR
Mean Maximum Temp. (°F)	58.1	63.7	71.4	79.6	86.1	91.6	95.0	93.8	87.2	78.7	67.6	60.4	77.8
Mean Temp. (°F)	45.1	50.1	57.5	65.6	73.5	79.9	82.9	81.9	75.4	66.0	54.7	47.3	65.0
Mean Minimum Temp. (°F)	32.0	36.4	43.6	51.5	60.9	68.0	70.8	69.9	63.6	53.2	41.8	34.2	52.2
Extreme Maximum Temp. (°F)	86	97	97	103	107	110	109	109	106	99	93	85	110
Extreme Minimum Temp. (°F)	5	-1	8	25	37	49	56	54	37	26	13	-4	-4
Days Maximum Temp. ≥ 90°F	0	0	1	5	11	20	27	25	13	3	0	0	105
Days Maximum Temp. ≤ 32°F	1	0	0	0	0	0	0	0	0	0	0	1	2
Days Minimum Temp. ≤ 32°F	17	10	4	1	0	0	0	0	0	0	6	14	52
Days Minimum Temp. ≤ 0°F	0	0	0	0	0	0	0	0	0	0	0	0	0
Heating Degree Days (base 65°F)	611	419	256	88	13	0	0	0	12	80	319	543	2,341
Cooling Degree Days (base 65°F)	1	4	28	107	288	449	568	544	333	120	18	1	2,461
Mean Precipitation (in.)	0.82	1.22	1.04	1.62	3.08	2.42	1.10	2.07	3.07	2.48	1.00	0.92	20.84
Maximum Precipitation (in.)	3.6	4.4	5.0	5.1	11.2	6.0	7.2	8.1	11.0	8.7	3.5	4.0	33.9
Minimum Precipitation (in.)	0	trace	trace	0.1	0.3	0	trace	trace	trace	0	0	trace	7.4
Maximum 24-hr. Precipitation (in.)	2.2	3.2	3.9	3.1	2.6	2.6	2.3	2.8	6.2	5.0	2.2	1.5	6.2
Days With ≥ 0.1" Precipitation	2	2	2	3	5	4	2	3	4	4	2	2	35
Days With ≥ 1.0" Precipitation	0	0	0	0	1	1	0	1	1	1	0	0	5
Mean Snowfall (in.)	2.0	0.5	0.2	trace	trace	trace	trace	0.0	trace	trace	0.3	0.2	3.2
Maximum Snowfall (in.)	9	6	3	trace	0	0	0	0	0	trace	9	4	14
Maximum 24-hr. Snowfall (in.)	7	3	3	trace	0	0	0	0	0	trace	6	3	7
Days With ≥ 1.0" Snow Depth	1	0	0	0	0	0	0	0	0	0	0	0	1
Thunderstorm Days	1	1	2	4	7	5	4	5	4	3	1	1	38
Foggy Days	7	6	4	3	4	1	1	1	4	4	5	6	46
Predominant Sky Cover	OVR	CLR	CLR	CLR	CLR	CLR	CLR	CLR	CLR	CLR	CLR	CLR	CLR
Mean Relative Humidity 6am (%)	76	76	71	74	81	80	77	77	82	81	78	76	77
Mean Relative Humidity 3pm (%)	44	41	35	35	40	40	36	36	44	43	41	43	40
Mean Dewpoint (°F)	30	33	37	46	56	62	62	62	60	51	40	32	48
Prevailing Wind Direction	SSW	SSW	S	S	S	S	S	S	S	S	SSW	SSW	S
Prevailing Wind Speed (mph)	13	13	14	14	13	13	12	10	10	12	12	13	13
Maximum Wind Gust (mph)	61	59	63	76	93	71	68	67	76	68	74	60	93

San Antonio Int'l Airport

The city of San Antonio is located in the south-central portion of Texas on the Balcones escarpment. Northwest of the city, the terrain slopes upward to the Edwards Plateau and to the southeast it slopes downward to the Gulf Coastal Plains. Soils are blackland clay and silty loam on the Plains and thin limestone soils on the Edwards Plateau.

The location of San Antonio on the edge of the Gulf Coastal Plains is influenced by a modified subtropical climate, predominantly continental during the winter months and marine during the summer months. Temperatures range from 50 degrees in January to the middle 80s in July and August. While the summer is hot, with daily temperatures above 90 degrees over 80 percent of the time, extremely high temperatures are rare. Mild weather prevails during much of the winter months, with below-freezing temperatures occurring on an average of about 20 days each year.

San Antonio is situated between a semi-arid area to the west and the coastal area of heavy precipitation to the east. Precipitation is fairly well distributed throughout the year with the heaviest amounts occurring during May and September. The precipitation from April through September usually occurs from thunderstorms. Most of the winter precipitation occurs as light rain or drizzle. Thunderstorms and heavy rains have occurred in all months of the year. Hail of damaging intensity seldom occurs but light hail is frequent with the springtime thunderstorms. Measurable snow occurs only once in three or four years.

Northerly winds prevail during most of the winter, and strong northerly winds occasionally occur during storms called northers. Southeasterly winds from the Gulf of Mexico also occur frequently during winter and are predominant in summer.

Since San Antonio is located only 140 miles from the Gulf of Mexico, tropical storms occasionally affect the city with strong winds and heavy rains. One of the fastest winds recorded, 74 mph, occurred as a tropical storm moved inland east of the city in August 1942.

Relative humidity is above 80 percent during the early morning hours most of the year, dropping to near 50 percent in the late afternoon.

San Antonio has about 50 percent of the possible amount of sunshine during the winter months and more than 70 percent during the summer months. Skies are clear to partly cloudy more than 60 percent of the time and cloudy less than 40 percent.

The first occurrence of 32 degrees Fahrenheit is in late November and the average last occurrence is in early March.

San Antonio Int'l Airport *Bexar County*   Elevation: 807 ft.   Latitude: 29° 32' N   Longitude: 98° 28' W

	JAN	FEB	MAR	APR	MAY	JUN	JUL	AUG	SEP	OCT	NOV	DEC	YEAR
Mean Maximum Temp. (°F)	61.8	66.9	74.0	80.3	85.9	91.4	94.5	94.7	89.9	82.1	71.7	64.5	79.8
Mean Temp. (°F)	50.4	55.0	62.2	69.0	76.0	81.8	84.6	84.5	79.7	70.8	60.3	53.2	69.0
Mean Minimum Temp. (°F)	39.1	43.0	50.4	57.7	66.0	72.2	74.7	74.2	69.4	59.5	48.8	41.7	58.1
Extreme Maximum Temp. (°F)	89	100	100	101	103	107	106	108	103	99	94	88	108
Extreme Minimum Temp. (°F)	13	14	19	31	43	55	64	61	46	27	21	6	6
Days Maximum Temp. ≥ 90°F	0	0	1	2	8	21	28	28	18	5	0	0	111
Days Maximum Temp. ≤ 32°F	0	0	0	0	0	0	0	0	0	0	0	0	0
Days Minimum Temp. ≤ 32°F	8	5	1	0	0	0	0	0	0	0	2	6	22
Days Minimum Temp. ≤ 0°F	0	0	0	0	0	0	0	0	0	0	0	0	0
Heating Degree Days (base 65°F)	453	296	148	41	1	0	0	0	2	32	195	377	1,545
Cooling Degree Days (base 65°F)	7	20	64	168	368	527	632	638	462	228	61	17	3,192
Mean Precipitation (in.)	1.65	1.77	1.93	2.59	4.85	4.07	2.05	2.60	3.06	3.72	2.30	1.91	32.50
Maximum Precipitation (in.)	8.5	6.4	6.1	9.3	12.8	11.9	8.3	11.1	13.1	9.8	6.0	14.0	52.3
Minimum Precipitation (in.)	trace	trace	trace	0.1	0.2	trace	trace	0	0.5	trace	trace	trace	13.7
Maximum 24-hr. Precipitation (in.)	2.7	2.4	2.5	3.6	6.3	6.2	4.4	5.6	6.5	4.5	4.9	6.0	6.5
Days With ≥ 0.1" Precipitation	4	3	4	4	5	5	3	4	4	5	4	3	48
Days With ≥ 1.0" Precipitation	0	0	1	1	2	1	1	1	1	1	1	0	10
Mean Snowfall (in.)	0.7	trace	trace	trace	trace	trace	0.0	0.0	0.0	trace	trace	trace	0.7
Maximum Snowfall (in.)	16	4	trace	0	0	0	0	0	0	trace	trace	trace	16
Maximum 24-hr. Snowfall (in.)	13	3	trace	0	0	0	0	0	0	trace	trace	trace	13
Days With ≥ 1.0" Snow Depth	0	0	0	0	0	0	0	0	0	trace	trace	trace	0
Thunderstorm Days	1	1	3	4	6	5	3	4	4	3	2	1	37
Foggy Days	14	12	13	13	12	6	4	4	7	10	12	13	120
Predominant Sky Cover	OVR	OVR	OVR	OVR	OVR	SCT	SCT	SCT	SCT	CLR	OVR	OVR	OVR
Mean Relative Humidity 6am (%)	80	80	79	82	87	88	87	86	85	83	81	80	83
Mean Relative Humidity 3pm (%)	51	48	45	48	52	49	43	42	46	46	48	50	47
Mean Dewpoint (°F)	38	41	46	55	64	68	69	68	65	57	47	41	55
Prevailing Wind Direction	N	N	SSE	SE	SE	SSE	SSE	SSE	SE	SSE	N	N	SSE
Prevailing Wind Speed (mph)	10	12	12	12	12	12	10	9	9	9	10	10	10
Maximum Wind Gust (mph)	54	56	64	74	63	58	77	49	61	54	54	48	77

Victoria Regional Airport

The city of Victoria is located in the south-central Texas Coastal Plain. The climate is classified as humid subtropical. Summers are hot with about 100 days with temperatures of 90 degrees or above. However, pleasant sea breezes from the nearby Gulf of Mexico make the high temperatures bearable.

Spring is characterized by mild days, brisk winds, and occasional showers and thunderstorms. Strong southeast winds begin in March, diminish in April and May, and become pleasant sea breezes in the first half of June. Thunderstorm activity increases through March and April, reaching a peak in May. Considerable cloudiness is the rule, with almost 50 percent of the days in the spring having overcast or nearly overcast skies.

The sea breeze diminishes during the summer, and at times fails altogether, and some hot nights are experienced in late June, July, and early August. High summer humidity gives way to clear, drier air in late August. Nighttime temperatures drop to pleasant levels. Thunderstorms continue, and lawns and fields remain green.

The first norther usually arrives near the beginning of fall, in late September. October and November are ideal fall months with long periods of clear days with mild temperatures and cool nights. The amount of rainfall decreases.

The winter season weather conditions alternate between clear, cold, dry periods and cloudy, mild, drizzly days as fronts move down from the north. The temperature drops below 32 degrees on an average of about a dozen mornings per year.

The normal rainfall of about 36 inches is well distributed throughout the year, with the heaviest falls coming during the growing season. Some of the smaller streams dry up in the late summer, and during occasional periods of general drought some of the larger streams may reach pool stage.

The area is subject to occasional tropical disturbances during summer and fall. Destructive winds and torrential rains may occur in these storms. Approximately 50 days per year have thunderstorms, but hail is infrequent. Destructive storms with tornados are rare.

Victoria Regional Airport *Victoria County*   Elevation: 114 ft.   Latitude: 28° 52' N   Longitude: 96° 56' W

	JAN	FEB	MAR	APR	MAY	JUN	JUL	AUG	SEP	OCT	NOV	DEC	YEAR
Mean Maximum Temp. (°F)	63.5	67.7	74.3	80.1	85.6	90.8	93.7	93.9	89.7	83.0	73.5	66.4	80.2
Mean Temp. (°F)	53.5	57.1	63.9	70.2	76.8	82.1	84.4	84.3	80.1	72.2	62.8	56.1	70.3
Mean Minimum Temp. (°F)	43.3	46.5	53.5	60.2	67.9	73.3	75.0	74.6	70.5	61.4	52.2	45.7	60.3
Extreme Maximum Temp. (°F)	88	95	97	95	99	106	103	105	102	99	93	85	106
Extreme Minimum Temp. (°F)	14	19	21	33	49	59	67	62	49	31	24	9	9
Days Maximum Temp. ≥ 90°F	0	0	0	1	6	20	28	28	18	5	0	0	106
Days Maximum Temp. ≤ 32°F	0	0	0	0	0	0	0	0	0	0	0	0	0
Days Minimum Temp. ≤ 32°F	4	2	1	0	0	0	0	0	0	0	1	3	11
Days Minimum Temp. ≤ 0°F	0	0	0	0	0	0	0	0	0	0	0	0	0
Heating Degree Days (base 65°F)	370	242	112	27	1	0	0	0	1	21	143	303	1,220
Cooling Degree Days (base 65°F)	16	29	78	184	379	528	617	617	469	258	87	35	3,297
Mean Precipitation (in.)	2.41	2.07	2.33	2.95	5.19	4.91	2.99	3.07	5.20	4.20	2.47	2.43	40.22
Maximum Precipitation (in.)	7.8	9.1	6.9	11.1	14.7	12.7	13.6	7.7	19.0	10.5	8.7	7.0	56.7
Minimum Precipitation (in.)	trace	0.2	trace	trace	0.7	trace	0.1	0.3	0.8	0.3	trace	0.4	14.3
Maximum 24-hr. Precipitation (in.)	3.1	2.7	2.6	9.9	7.6	9.3	7.6	4.6	7.8	6.5	6.6	6.1	9.9
Days With ≥ 0.1" Precipitation	4	4	4	3	5	6	4	5	6	4	4	4	53
Days With ≥ 1.0" Precipitation	1	1	1	1	2	2	1	1	2	1	1	1	15
Mean Snowfall (in.)	0.1	trace	trace	0.0	trace	0.0	0.0	trace	0.0	0.0	trace	trace	0.1
Maximum Snowfall (in.)	2	3	trace	0	0	0	0	0	0	0	trace	trace	3
Maximum 24-hr. Snowfall (in.)	2	3	trace	0	0	0	0	0	0	0	trace	trace	0
Days With ≥ 1.0" Snow Depth	0	0	0	0	0	0	0	0	0	0	0	0	0
Thunderstorm Days	1	2	3	4	6	6	7	9	8	4	2	1	53
Foggy Days	18	17	19	18	19	12	10	12	15	16	16	17	189
Predominant Sky Cover	OVR	OVR	OVR	OVR	OVR	SCT	SCT	SCT	SCT	CLR	OVR	OVR	OVR
Mean Relative Humidity 6am (%)	87	87	86	88	91	92	92	92	91	89	87	86	89
Mean Relative Humidity 3pm (%)	59	56	54	56	59	58	53	53	56	52	54	58	56
Mean Dewpoint (°F)	44	47	53	61	67	72	73	73	70	61	53	47	60
Prevailing Wind Direction	N	N	SSE	SSE	SSE	SSE	S	S	SE	N	N	N	SSE
Prevailing Wind Speed (mph)	14	14	13	14	13	12	10	10	9	10	13	13	12
Maximum Wind Gust (mph)	59	63	59	62	68	81	99	67	54	75	55	54	99

Waco Madison Cooper Airport

One of the major cities of Texas, Waco is located in the rich agricultural region of the Brazos River Valley in North Central Texas. The city lies on the edge of the gently rolling Blackland Prairies. To the west lies the rolling to hilly Grand Prairie. Waco is a commercial hub with an economy based on industry, education and agriculture. Baylor University, founded in 1845, is located here. Regional agriculture includes chiefly cattle, poultry, sorghum, cotton and corn. Soils are black waxy, loam and sandy types. Lake Waco, a reservoir of 7,260 surface acres, lies within the Waco city limits, with the north shoreline approximately 0.8 mile south of the Municipal Airport.

The climate of Waco is humid subtropical with hot summers. It is a continental type climate characterized by extreme variations in temperature. Tropical maritime air masses predominate throughout the late spring, summer and early fall months, while Polar air masses frequent the area in winter. In an average year, April and May are the wettest months, while the July-August period is the driest. Most warm season rainfall occurs from thunderstorm activity. Consequently, considerable spatial variation in amounts occur.

Winters are mild. Cold fronts moving down from the High Plains often are accompanied by strong, gusty, northerly winds and sharp drops in temperature. Cold spells are of short duration, rarely lasting longer than two or three days before a rapid warming occurs. Winter precipitation is closely associated with frontal activity, and may fall as rain, freezing rain, sleet or snow. During most years, snowfall is of little or no consequence.

Daytime temperatures are hot in summer, particularly in July and August. The highest temperatures are associated with fair skies, light winds, and comparatively low humidities. There is little variety in the day-to-day weather during July and August. Air conditioning is recommended for maximum comfort indoors or while traveling.

The spring and fall seasons are very pleasant at Waco. Temperatures are comfortable. Cloudiness and showers are more frequent in the spring than in the fall. The average first occurrence of 32 degrees Fahrenheit is late November and the average last occurrence is in mid March.

Waco Madison Cooper Airport *McLennan County*   Elevation: 498 ft.   Latitude: 31° 37' N   Longitude: 97° 14' W

	JAN	FEB	MAR	APR	MAY	JUN	JUL	AUG	SEP	OCT	NOV	DEC	YEAR
Mean Maximum Temp. (°F)	56.6	61.9	69.8	77.6	84.7	92.1	96.7	97.0	89.9	80.2	68.0	59.6	77.9
Mean Temp. (°F)	45.9	50.8	58.5	66.2	74.2	81.6	85.6	85.4	78.7	68.6	57.1	49.0	66.8
Mean Minimum Temp. (°F)	35.3	39.6	47.1	54.8	63.6	70.9	74.5	73.9	67.5	56.8	46.1	38.2	55.7
Extreme Maximum Temp. (°F)	88	96	100	97	102	109	109	109	106	101	92	85	109
Extreme Minimum Temp. (°F)	4	4	16	27	37	54	60	53	40	25	17	-4	-4
Days Maximum Temp. ≥ 90°F	0	0	0	1	7	22	29	28	18	4	0	0	109
Days Maximum Temp. ≤ 32°F	1	0	0	0	0	0	0	0	0	0	0	1	2
Days Minimum Temp. ≤ 32°F	13	7	2	0	0	0	0	0	0	0	3	9	34
Days Minimum Temp. ≤ 0°F	0	0	0	0	0	0	0	0	0	0	0	0	0
Heating Degree Days (base 65°F)	585	403	234	73	7	0	0	0	5	57	266	498	2,128
Cooling Degree Days (base 65°F)	2	8	36	114	307	509	655	651	423	172	37	7	2,921
Mean Precipitation (in.)	1.85	2.41	2.57	2.96	4.37	2.85	2.20	1.89	3.08	3.63	2.36	2.70	32.87
Maximum Precipitation (in.)	5.8	6.3	5.6	13.4	15.0	12.1	8.6	8.9	7.3	10.5	6.2	8.4	48.9
Minimum Precipitation (in.)	trace	0.2	trace	0.1	0.6	0.3	0	trace	0	0	0.1	trace	14.9
Maximum 24-hr. Precipitation (in.)	1.9	4.0	3.1	3.4	4.6	3.0	4.5	4.1	3.8	3.7	3.8	3.7	4.6
Days With ≥ 0.1" Precipitation	4	4	4	4	6	5	3	3	4	5	4	4	50
Days With ≥ 1.0" Precipitation	0	1	1	1	1	1	1	1	1	1	1	1	11
Mean Snowfall (in.)	0.5	0.3	trace	trace	trace	0.0	0.0	trace	0.0	trace	0.2	trace	1.0
Maximum Snowfall (in.)	7	5	1	0	0	0	0	0	0	trace	2	1	7
Maximum 24-hr. Snowfall (in.)	7	4	1	0	0	0	0	0	0	trace	2	1	7
Days With ≥ 1.0" Snow Depth	0	0	0	0	0	0	0	0	0	0	0	0	0
Thunderstorm Days	1	2	4	6	8	6	4	4	4	3	2	1	45
Foggy Days	12	11	11	11	11	5	3	4	8	10	11	12	109
Predominant Sky Cover	OVR	OVR	OVR	OVR	OVR	CLR	CLR	SCT	CLR	CLR	CLR	OVR	CLR
Mean Relative Humidity 6am (%)	83	83	81	84	88	86	83	82	85	84	83	82	83
Mean Relative Humidity 3pm (%)	56	53	49	52	54	49	42	40	46	47	50	54	49
Mean Dewpoint (°F)	36	39	45	54	63	68	69	68	64	55	45	38	54
Prevailing Wind Direction	S	S	S	S	S	S	S	S	S	S	S	S	S
Prevailing Wind Speed (mph)	13	13	15	15	14	14	13	12	13	12	13	13	13
Maximum Wind Gust (mph)	54	60	75	87	61	61	49	54	60	64	58	66	87

Wichita Falls Municipal Airport

Wichita Falls is located in the West Cross Timbers subdivision of the North Central Plains of Texas, about 10 miles south of the Red River and 400 miles northwest of the nearest portion of the Gulf of Mexico. The topography is gently rolling mesquite plain, and the elevation of the area is about 1,000 feet.

This region lies between the humid subtropical climate of east Texas and a continental climate to the north and west. The climate of Wichita Falls is classified as continental. It is characterized by rapid changes in temperature, large daily and annual temperature extremes, and by rather erratic rainfall.

The area lies in the path of polar air masses which move down from the north during the winter season. With the passage of cold fronts or northers in the fall and winter, abrupt drops in temperature of as much as 20 to 30 degrees within an hour sometimes occur. January, the coldest month, has an average temperature around 40 degrees.

The summers in Wichita Falls are generally of the continental climate type, characterized by low humidity and windy conditions. Temperatures over 100 degrees are frequent during the common periods of hot weather. July and August, the hottest months, have average temperatures in the middle 80s.

The normal rainfall is nearly 27 inches per year, but the distribution is erratic. Several lakes in the area provide water for domestic, industrial, and irrigation purposes. The greater part of the rainfall comes in the form of showers rather than general rains. Over 75 percent of the annual moisture occurs during the period from late March to mid November, but dry periods of three to four weeks are to be expected during this time almost every year. Moderate flooding along Holliday Creek and the Wichita River, which run through the city, occur about once in each ten-year period. Snowfall, measuring an inch or more, occurs on average only two days a year.

Wind speeds average over 11 mph, and southerly winds prevail. Rather strong winds are observed in all months.

Wichita Falls Municipal Airport *Wichita County*　Elevation: 1,026 ft.　Latitude: 33° 59' N　Longitude: 98° 30' W

	JAN	FEB	MAR	APR	MAY	JUN	JUL	AUG	SEP	OCT	NOV	DEC	YEAR
Mean Maximum Temp. (°F)	52.0	58.0	67.0	75.8	83.5	92.2	97.6	96.1	87.7	77.2	64.1	55.2	75.5
Mean Temp. (°F)	40.3	45.6	54.0	62.6	71.4	80.0	85.0	83.6	75.7	64.7	52.1	43.4	63.2
Mean Minimum Temp. (°F)	28.6	33.2	40.9	49.3	59.2	67.7	72.2	71.1	63.7	52.1	39.9	31.5	50.8
Extreme Maximum Temp. (°F)	85	93	100	102	108	117	114	112	108	102	89	83	117
Extreme Minimum Temp. (°F)	-1	-8	8	24	36	51	54	53	38	21	15	-7	-8
Days Maximum Temp. ≥ 90°F	0	0	1	2	8	20	28	26	15	3	0	0	103
Days Maximum Temp. ≤ 32°F	3	2	0	0	0	0	0	0	0	0	0	2	7
Days Minimum Temp. ≤ 32°F	21	13	6	1	0	0	0	0	0	0	7	17	65
Days Minimum Temp. ≤ 0°F	0	0	0	0	0	0	0	0	0	0	0	0	0
Heating Degree Days (base 65°F)	759	542	354	136	22	0	0	0	17	105	392	664	2,991
Cooling Degree Days (base 65°F)	0	2	17	66	227	452	628	598	352	100	10	1	2,453
Mean Precipitation (in.)	1.10	1.57	2.29	2.62	3.90	3.62	1.56	2.40	3.33	2.94	1.52	1.65	28.50
Maximum Precipitation (in.)	4.5	4.5	5.4	8.5	13.2	8.6	11.9	7.6	10.2	7.9	5.7	6.9	41.6
Minimum Precipitation (in.)	0	trace	trace	0.3	trace	0.3	trace	trace	trace	trace	0	trace	16.1
Maximum 24-hr. Precipitation (in.)	2.0	1.9	3.6	3.9	5.1	5.4	3.0	4.5	6.2	3.9	2.6	2.3	6.2
Days With ≥ 0.1" Precipitation	2	3	4	4	6	4	3	4	4	4	3	3	44
Days With ≥ 1.0" Precipitation	0	0	1	1	1	1	0	1	1	1	0	0	7
Mean Snowfall (in.)	2.2	1.3	0.6	trace	*trace*	*trace*	0.0	0.0	0.0	trace	0.4	0.9	*5.4*
Maximum Snowfall (in.)	12	12	11	1	0	0	0	0	0	1	4	7	17
Maximum 24-hr. Snowfall (in.)	8	4	10	1	0	0	0	0	0	1	4	6	10
Days With ≥ 1.0" Snow Depth	2	1	0	0	*0*	0	0	0	0	0	0	0	*3*
Thunderstorm Days	1	1	3	5	9	7	5	5	4	3	2	1	46
Foggy Days	9	9	8	7	7	4	2	3	6	6	7	9	77
Predominant Sky Cover	OVR	OVR	CLR	CLR	OVR	CLR	CLR	CLR	CLR	CLR	CLR	CLR	CLR
Mean Relative Humidity 6am (%)	79	78	76	78	85	83	78	78	83	81	79	78	80
Mean Relative Humidity 3pm (%)	48	47	42	42	47	44	38	38	44	43	44	47	44
Mean Dewpoint (°F)	28	32	37	47	58	64	65	64	60	50	38	30	48
Prevailing Wind Direction	N	N	S	S	SSE	SSE	S	S	SSE	S	S	S	S
Prevailing Wind Speed (mph)	14	14	15	15	14	14	13	12	12	13	13	12	13
Maximum Wind Gust (mph)	62	75	69	69	90	79	74	81	69	68	62	61	90

Alice *Jim Wells County*   Elevation: 200 ft.   Latitude: 27° 44' N   Longitude: 98° 04' W

	JAN	FEB	MAR	APR	MAY	JUN	JUL	AUG	SEP	OCT	NOV	DEC	YEAR
Mean Maximum Temp. (°F)	67.1	71.1	78.5	84.0	88.2	93.3	96.1	96.3	91.9	85.3	76.9	69.8	83.2
Mean Temp. (°F)	55.6	59.2	66.6	72.4	78.1	82.9	84.9	85.1	81.1	73.8	65.2	58.3	71.9
Mean Minimum Temp. (°F)	44.1	47.3	54.6	60.8	67.9	72.4	73.6	73.8	70.3	62.2	53.5	46.8	60.6
Extreme Maximum Temp. (°F)	93	100	102	107	*108*	111	*105*	105	103	101	*97*	94	*111*
Extreme Minimum Temp. (°F)	19	25	23	37	49	57	65	*65*	52	28	26	12	*12*
Days Maximum Temp. ≥ 90°F	0	1	3	7	13	25	29	29	22	10	1	0	140
Days Maximum Temp. ≤ 32°F	0	0	0	0	0	0	0	0	0	0	0	0	0
Days Minimum Temp. ≤ 32°F	3	2	0	0	0	0	0	0	0	0	0	0	8
Days Minimum Temp. ≤ 0°F	0	0	0	0	0	0	0	0	0	0	1	2	0
Heating Degree Days (base 65°F)	312	203	78	19	1	0	0	0	1	14	110	250	988
Cooling Degree Days (base 65°F)	25	50	128	247	428	558	637	644	502	303	129	51	3,702
Mean Precipitation (in.)	1.25	1.45	1.36	1.66	3.13	3.45	1.78	2.92	4.59	3.47	1.40	1.16	27.62
Days With ≥ 0.1" Precipitation	3	3	2	3	4	5	3	4	5	3	2	2	39
Days With ≥ 1.0" Precipitation	0	0	0	1	1	1	1	1	1	1	0	0	7
Mean Snowfall (in.)	trace	0.0	0.0	0.0	0.0	0.0	0.0	0.0	0.0	0.0	trace	0.0	trace
Days With ≥ 1.0" Snow Depth	0	0	0	0	0	0	0	0	0	0	0	0	0

Alpine *Brewster County*   Elevation: 4,527 ft.   Latitude: 30° 22' N   Longitude: 103° 40' W

	JAN	FEB	MAR	APR	MAY	JUN	JUL	AUG	SEP	OCT	NOV	DEC	YEAR
Mean Maximum Temp. (°F)	61.1	65.7	72.1	79.0	*85.6*	90.8	89.2	87.5	83.2	78.0	69.0	62.2	*76.9*
Mean Temp. (°F)	46.1	49.9	55.6	62.3	*69.9*	76.2	76.3	74.7	70.1	62.8	53.6	47.3	*62.1*
Mean Minimum Temp. (°F)	31.0	33.9	39.1	45.5	*54.1*	61.5	63.4	61.8	57.0	47.6	38.2	32.4	*47.1*
Extreme Maximum Temp. (°F)	80	85	91	96	101	107	103	100	100	95	87	82	107
Extreme Minimum Temp. (°F)	0	-1	10	20	30	41	52	51	36	21	-2	-3	-3
Days Maximum Temp. ≥ 90°F	0	0	0	1	8	18	16	12	5	1	0	0	61
Days Maximum Temp. ≤ 32°F	0	0	0	0	0	0	0	0	0	0	0	0	0
Days Minimum Temp. ≤ 32°F	18	12	7	2	0	0	0	0	0	0	0	0	0
Days Minimum Temp. ≤ 0°F	0	0	0	0	0	0	0	0	0	1	8	16	64
Heating Degree Days (base 65°F)	581	422	292	127	*22*	1	0	0	25	112	336	542	*2,460*
Cooling Degree Days (base 65°F)	0	1	7	48	na	351	367	317	191	55	3	0	na
Mean Precipitation (in.)	0.45	0.54	0.39	0.59	1.32	2.11	3.03	2.89	3.41	1.52	0.44	0.66	17.35
Days With ≥ 0.1" Precipitation	1	1	1	1	3	4	6	6	6	3	1	1	34
Days With ≥ 1.0" Precipitation	0	0	0	0	0	0	1	0	1	0	0	0	2
Mean Snowfall (in.)	*0.3*	*trace*	trace	trace	0.0	0.0	0.0	0.0	0.0	trace	trace	0.2	*0.5*
Days With ≥ 1.0" Snow Depth	*0*	*0*	0	0	0	0	0	0	0	0	0	0	*0*

Amistad Dam *Val Verde County*   Elevation: 1,154 ft.   Latitude: 29° 28' N   Longitude: 101° 02' W

	JAN	FEB	MAR	APR	MAY	JUN	JUL	AUG	SEP	OCT	NOV	DEC	YEAR
Mean Maximum Temp. (°F)	62.1	67.3	75.8	83.1	89.0	94.2	96.6	96.6	90.9	81.9	71.3	63.7	81.1
Mean Temp. (°F)	50.3	55.0	63.0	70.4	77.2	82.8	85.0	84.8	79.6	70.4	59.8	52.3	69.2
Mean Minimum Temp. (°F)	38.4	42.6	50.1	57.6	65.4	71.3	73.4	73.0	68.3	58.7	48.3	40.8	57.3
Extreme Maximum Temp. (°F)	88	98	100	105	108	113	114	110	108	102	95	90	114
Extreme Minimum Temp. (°F)	14	17	24	34	42	57	63	64	47	30	24	9	9
Days Maximum Temp. ≥ 90°F	0	0	2	7	16	25	28	28	21	5	0	0	132
Days Maximum Temp. ≤ 32°F	0	0	0	0	0	0	0	0	0	0	0	0	0
Days Minimum Temp. ≤ 32°F	7	4	1	0	0	0	0	0	0	0	0	0	0
Days Minimum Temp. ≤ 0°F	0	0	0	0	0	0	0	0	0	0	1	4	17
Heating Degree Days (base 65°F)	450	288	126	30	2	0	0	0	3	29	186	390	1,504
Cooling Degree Days (base 65°F)	1	14	72	202	410	562	655	652	464	216	44	3	3,295
Mean Precipitation (in.)	0.58	0.82	0.95	1.29	2.28	2.36	1.96	2.24	3.11	1.66	0.98	0.74	18.97
Days With ≥ 0.1" Precipitation	1	2	2	3	4	3	3	3	4	3	2	2	32
Days With ≥ 1.0" Precipitation	0	0	0	0	1	1	1	1	1	0	0	0	5
Mean Snowfall (in.)	0.1	0.0	0.0	0.0	0.0	0.0	0.0	0.0	0.0	0.0	0.0	0.0	0.1
Days With ≥ 1.0" Snow Depth	0	0	0	0	0	0	0	0	0	0	0	0	0

Anahuac *Chambers County*   Elevation: 22 ft.   Latitude: 29° 47' N   Longitude: 94° 40' W

	JAN	FEB	MAR	APR	MAY	JUN	JUL	AUG	SEP	OCT	NOV	DEC	YEAR
Mean Maximum Temp. (°F)	60.9	64.5	71.3	77.4	84.0	89.6	91.9	92.1	88.6	81.1	71.5	64.1	78.1
Mean Temp. (°F)	51.3	54.5	61.5	67.9	75.1	81.1	83.1	82.9	78.8	69.9	61.0	54.2	68.4
Mean Minimum Temp. (°F)	41.4	44.5	51.6	58.3	66.2	72.4	74.4	73.6	68.9	58.8	50.4	44.2	58.7
Extreme Maximum Temp. (°F)	82	82	93	93	97	102	103	103	100	100	89	87	103
Extreme Minimum Temp. (°F)	16	21	24	36	48	56	64	60	50	33	25	8	8
Days Maximum Temp. ≥ 90°F	0	0	0	0	3	16	24	25	15	2	0	0	85
Days Maximum Temp. ≤ 32°F	0	0	0	0	0	0	0	0	0	0	0	0	0
Days Minimum Temp. ≤ 32°F	6	3	1	0	0	0	0	0	0	0	0	0	0
Days Minimum Temp. ≤ 0°F	0	0	0	0	0	0	0	0	0	0	1	3	14
Heating Degree Days (base 65°F)	427	302	149	41	1	0	0	0	1	33	173	349	1,476
Cooling Degree Days (base 65°F)	7	13	46	131	327	495	577	571	425	202	64	21	2,879
Mean Precipitation (in.)	4.87	2.83	3.47	3.41	5.20	5.94	4.71	4.83	6.59	4.43	4.10	4.34	54.72
Days With ≥ 0.1" Precipitation	7	5	5	4	5	7	7	7	7	5	6	6	71
Days With ≥ 1.0" Precipitation	1	1	1	1	2	2	1	1	2	2	1	1	16
Mean Snowfall (in.)	trace	trace	0.0	0.0	0.0	0.0	0.0	0.0	0.0	0.0	trace	trace	trace
Days With ≥ 1.0" Snow Depth	0	0	0	0	0	0	0	0	0	0	0	0	0

Andrews *Andrews County*   Elevation: 3,169 ft.   Latitude: 32° 19' N   Longitude: 102° 32' W

	JAN	FEB	MAR	APR	MAY	JUN	JUL	AUG	SEP	OCT	NOV	DEC	YEAR
Mean Maximum Temp. (°F)	57.6	63.8	71.7	80.1	87.3	93.5	94.2	92.6	86.5	78.7	66.5	59.5	77.6
Mean Temp. (°F)	43.9	49.2	56.3	64.3	72.6	79.5	81.1	79.9	73.8	64.9	52.8	45.8	63.7
Mean Minimum Temp. (°F)	30.2	34.6	40.8	48.4	57.9	65.3	68.1	67.1	61.1	51.1	39.1	32.2	49.7
Extreme Maximum Temp. (°F)	85	89	97	99	104	113	111	105	101	98	93	81	113
Extreme Minimum Temp. (°F)	1	-1	8	23	33	41	57	54	39	22	11	1	-1
Days Maximum Temp. ≥ 90°F	0	0	0	3	13	23	26	23	12	3	0	0	103
Days Maximum Temp. ≤ 32°F	1	0	0	0	0	0	0	0	0	0	0	1	2
Days Minimum Temp. ≤ 32°F	19	12	6	1	0	0	0	0	0	0	7	16	61
Days Minimum Temp. ≤ 0°F	0	0	0	0	0	0	0	0	0	0	0	0	0
Heating Degree Days (base 65°F)	647	441	282	101	14	0	0	0	18	90	364	588	2,545
Cooling Degree Days (base 65°F)	0	3	17	89	273	457	528	490	302	103	6	0	2,268
Mean Precipitation (in.)	0.47	0.53	0.58	0.86	1.77	1.94	2.24	1.77	2.29	1.39	0.61	0.59	15.04
Days With ≥ 0.1" Precipitation	2	2	1	2	3	3	3	4	4	3	1	2	30
Days With ≥ 1.0" Precipitation	0	0	0	0	0	1	1	0	1	0	0	0	3
Mean Snowfall (in.)	1.7	0.6	trace	trace	0.0	0.0	0.0	0.0	0.0	trace	0.9	1.0	4.2
Days With ≥ 1.0" Snow Depth	0	0	0	0	0	0	0	0	0	0	0	0	0

Angleton 2 W *Brazoria County*   Elevation: 26 ft.   Latitude: 29° 09' N   Longitude: 95° 27' W

	JAN	FEB	MAR	APR	MAY	JUN	JUL	AUG	SEP	OCT	NOV	DEC	YEAR
Mean Maximum Temp. (°F)	62.4	65.7	72.0	77.5	83.5	89.1	91.8	91.8	88.0	81.2	72.4	65.5	78.4
Mean Temp. (°F)	52.4	55.6	62.1	68.1	74.7	80.2	82.4	82.1	78.5	70.3	61.8	55.1	68.6
Mean Minimum Temp. (°F)	42.3	45.4	52.2	58.6	65.7	71.2	72.9	72.4	68.9	59.3	51.2	44.6	58.7
Extreme Maximum Temp. (°F)	81	86	89	93	98	98	100	101	101	95	89	84	101
Extreme Minimum Temp. (°F)	14	20	22	32	43	55	62	60	49	30	21	7	7
Days Maximum Temp. ≥ 90°F	0	0	0	0	2	15	25	24	13	2	0	0	81
Days Maximum Temp. ≤ 32°F	0	0	0	0	0	0	0	0	0	0	0	0	0
Days Minimum Temp. ≤ 32°F	6	3	1	0	0	0	0	0	0	0	1	3	14
Days Minimum Temp. ≤ 0°F	0	0	0	0	0	0	0	0	0	0	0	0	0
Heating Degree Days (base 65°F)	397	280	138	40	2	0	0	0	1	30	159	324	1,371
Cooling Degree Days (base 65°F)	11	22	59	141	323	481	561	558	425	216	75	27	2,899
Mean Precipitation (in.)	4.78	3.53	4.01	3.78	5.40	6.51	4.34	5.04	7.80	4.48	4.62	4.08	58.37
Days With ≥ 0.1" Precipitation	7	6	5	4	6	6	5	7	7	5	6	6	70
Days With ≥ 1.0" Precipitation	1	1	1	1	2	2	1	2	2	1	1	1	16
Mean Snowfall (in.)	trace	trace	0.0	0.0	0.0	0.0	0.0	0.0	0.0	0.0	0.0	trace	trace
Days With ≥ 1.0" Snow Depth	0	0	0	0	0	0	0	0	0	0	0	0	0

Anson *Jones County*   Elevation: 1,709 ft.   Latitude: 32° 46' N   Longitude: 99° 54' W

	JAN	FEB	MAR	APR	MAY	JUN	JUL	AUG	SEP	OCT	NOV	DEC	YEAR
Mean Maximum Temp. (°F)	56.6	62.3	70.9	79.4	86.3	92.8	96.2	94.7	87.6	79.0	66.7	59.1	77.6
Mean Temp. (°F)	44.1	49.4	57.1	65.6	73.6	80.7	84.2	82.8	75.8	66.4	54.4	46.8	65.1
Mean Minimum Temp. (°F)	31.6	36.4	43.3	51.8	60.8	68.5	72.1	70.9	64.1	53.7	42.0	34.4	52.4
Extreme Maximum Temp. (°F)	86	95	100	99	109	114	110	107	107	103	92	84	114
Extreme Minimum Temp. (°F)	3	-4	9	26	38	51	58	50	32	24	14	-12	-12
Days Maximum Temp. ≥ 90°F	0	0	1	4	11	22	28	26	14	3	0	1	109
Days Maximum Temp. ≤ 32°F	2	1	0	0	0	0	0	0	0	0	0	1	4
Days Minimum Temp. ≤ 32°F	16	10	4	1	0	0	0	0	0	0	5	13	49
Days Minimum Temp. ≤ 0°F	0	0	0	0	0	0	0	0	0	0	0	0	0
Heating Degree Days (base 65°F)	641	441	272	90	14	0	0	0	15	80	330	560	2,443
Cooling Degree Days (base 65°F)	1	7	27	104	285	466	597	568	337	121	16	1	2,530
Mean Precipitation (in.)	1.05	1.60	1.29	2.12	3.21	3.03	2.09	3.08	4.18	2.35	1.10	1.36	26.46
Days With ≥ 0.1" Precipitation	2	3	3	3	5	4	3	4	5	4	2	3	41
Days With ≥ 1.0" Precipitation	0	0	0	1	1	1	1	1	1	1	0	0	7
Mean Snowfall (in.)	1.2	na	0.3	0.4	0.0	0.0	0.0	0.0	0.0	0.0	0.3	0.7	na
Days With ≥ 1.0" Snow Depth	0	0	0	0	0	0	0	0	0	0	0	0	0

Aransas Wildlife Refuge *Aransas County*   Elevation: 13 ft.   Latitude: 28° 16' N   Longitude: 96° 48' W

	JAN	FEB	MAR	APR	MAY	JUN	JUL	AUG	SEP	OCT	NOV	DEC	YEAR
Mean Maximum Temp. (°F)	64.1	67.4	73.7	78.1	83.4	88.2	90.2	90.4	87.8	81.7	73.8	66.3	78.8
Mean Temp. (°F)	55.0	58.2	64.8	70.5	77.0	81.7	83.3	83.3	80.1	73.2	65.1	57.2	70.8
Mean Minimum Temp. (°F)	45.6	48.9	56.0	62.9	70.5	75.3	76.4	76.2	72.2	64.4	55.7	48.0	62.7
Extreme Maximum Temp. (°F)	82	87	93	94	102	98	98	99	97	97	96	83	102
Extreme Minimum Temp. (°F)	17	20	22	33	46	60	54	64	48	28	26	9	9
Days Maximum Temp. ≥ 90°F	0	0	0	0	1	9	19	21	11	1	0	0	62
Days Maximum Temp. ≤ 32°F	0	0	0	0	0	0	0	0	0	0	0	0	0
Days Minimum Temp. ≤ 32°F	4	2	0	0	0	0	0	0	0	0	1	2	9
Days Minimum Temp. ≤ 0°F	0	0	0	0	0	0	0	0	0	0	0	0	0
Heating Degree Days (base 65°F)	318	209	86	20	0	0	0	0	0	14	102	267	1,016
Cooling Degree Days (base 65°F)	16	25	81	191	390	520	588	591	471	287	117	37	3,314
Mean Precipitation (in.)	2.82	2.76	2.38	2.17	4.28	3.80	2.93	3.62	5.60	4.17	3.45	2.39	40.37
Days With ≥ 0.1" Precipitation	4	4	3	3	4	4	4	4	6	4	4	4	47
Days With ≥ 1.0" Precipitation	1	1	1	1	2	1	1	1	1	1	1	1	13
Mean Snowfall (in.)	trace	trace	trace	0.0	0.0	0.0	0.0	0.0	0.0	0.0	trace	0.0	trace
Days With ≥ 1.0" Snow Depth	0	0	0	0	0	0	0	0	0	0	0	0	0

Aspermont *Stonewall County*   Elevation: 1,669 ft.   Latitude: 33° 09' N   Longitude: 100° 14' W

	JAN	FEB	MAR	APR	MAY	JUN	JUL	AUG	SEP	OCT	NOV	DEC	YEAR
Mean Maximum Temp. (°F)	53.6	59.7	68.8	77.9	85.8	93.6	97.5	95.5	87.2	77.8	64.8	56.7	76.6
Mean Temp. (°F)	40.6	45.9	53.9	62.7	71.6	79.9	83.6	82.1	74.4	64.1	51.3	43.2	62.8
Mean Minimum Temp. (°F)	27.5	32.0	38.9	47.5	57.3	66.2	69.8	68.7	61.5	50.3	37.7	29.8	48.9
Extreme Maximum Temp. (°F)	85	92	101	103	107	117	114	108	107	108	91	85	117
Extreme Minimum Temp. (°F)	2	-4	12	23	34	45	56	52	34	19	11	-1	-4
Days Maximum Temp. ≥ 90°F	0	0	1	4	12	22	28	25	14	3	0	0	109
Days Maximum Temp. ≤ 32°F	3	1	0	0	0	0	0	0	0	0	0	1	5
Days Minimum Temp. ≤ 32°F	22	15	7	1	0	0	0	0	0	1	8	19	73
Days Minimum Temp. ≤ 0°F	0	0	0	0	0	0	0	0	0	0	0	0	0
Heating Degree Days (base 65°F)	749	535	354	140	27	1	0	0	22	114	411	670	3,023
Cooling Degree Days (base 65°F)	0	3	15	79	247	457	599	561	320	92	6	0	2,379
Mean Precipitation (in.)	0.90	1.37	1.22	1.68	3.48	2.77	1.31	2.79	3.17	2.38	1.13	1.01	23.21
Days With ≥ 0.1" Precipitation	2	3	2	3	5	4	3	4	4	4	2	2	38
Days With ≥ 1.0" Precipitation	0	0	0	0	1	1	0	1	1	1	0	0	5
Mean Snowfall (in.)	1.8	*0.6*	0.2	0.0	0.0	0.0	0.0	0.0	0.0	0.0	0.3	0.4	*3.3*
Days With ≥ 1.0" Snow Depth	*0*	*0*	0	0	0	0	0	0	0	0	0	0	*0*

Athens *Henderson County*   Elevation: 446 ft.   Latitude: 32° 10' N   Longitude: 95° 50' W

	JAN	FEB	MAR	APR	MAY	JUN	JUL	AUG	SEP	OCT	NOV	DEC	YEAR
Mean Maximum Temp. (°F)	57.3	63.0	70.4	77.2	83.4	90.0	94.4	95.0	88.8	79.1	68.0	60.1	77.2
Mean Temp. (°F)	46.1	50.9	57.9	64.9	72.3	79.3	82.7	82.7	76.9	66.6	56.2	48.7	65.4
Mean Minimum Temp. (°F)	34.8	38.8	45.3	52.6	61.1	68.5	71.1	70.3	65.0	54.1	44.3	37.2	53.6
Extreme Maximum Temp. (°F)	85	93	95	92	97	103	109	108	108	97	88	84	109
Extreme Minimum Temp. (°F)	-5	-6	15	25	39	41	53	55	38	26	10	-2	-6
Days Maximum Temp. ≥ 90°F	0	0	0	0	4	17	27	27	16	2	0	0	93
Days Maximum Temp. ≤ 32°F	1	0	0	0	0	0	0	0	0	0	0	1	2
Days Minimum Temp. ≤ 32°F	14	8	3	0	0	0	0	0	0	0	4	11	40
Days Minimum Temp. ≤ 0°F	0	0	0	0	0	0	0	0	0	0	0	0	0
Heating Degree Days (base 65°F)	583	399	242	80	8	0	0	0	5	71	284	508	2,180
Cooling Degree Days (base 65°F)	3	9	27	82	243	434	552	563	370	131	24	8	2,446
Mean Precipitation (in.)	2.92	3.48	3.68	3.43	4.67	3.78	1.80	2.45	3.24	4.96	3.60	3.61	41.62
Days With ≥ 0.1" Precipitation	5	5	5	5	5	5	3	3	4	5	4	5	54
Days With ≥ 1.0" Precipitation	1	1	1	1	2	1	1	1	1	2	1	1	14
Mean Snowfall (in.)	0.6	0.2	trace	0.0	0.0	0.0	0.0	0.0	0.0	0.0	0.0	trace	0.8
Days With ≥ 1.0" Snow Depth	0	0	0	0	0	0	0	0	0	0	0	0	0

Bakersfield *Pecos County*   Elevation: 2,539 ft.   Latitude: 30° 53' N   Longitude: 102° 19' W

	JAN	FEB	MAR	APR	MAY	JUN	JUL	AUG	SEP	OCT	NOV	DEC	YEAR
Mean Maximum Temp. (°F)	60.0	65.2	73.2	81.6	88.5	93.7	95.2	94.2	88.0	79.3	68.8	61.6	79.1
Mean Temp. (°F)	46.3	51.2	58.8	67.1	75.0	81.2	83.3	82.4	76.2	66.9	55.7	48.1	66.0
Mean Minimum Temp. (°F)	32.6	37.1	44.3	52.6	61.6	68.8	71.5	70.5	64.4	54.3	42.6	34.6	52.9
Extreme Maximum Temp. (°F)	87	91	97	101	109	114	110	107	105	104	91	86	114
Extreme Minimum Temp. (°F)	7	3	12	24	35	46	59	57	39	24	11	5	3
Days Maximum Temp. ≥ 90°F	0	0	1	6	14	23	27	26	16	3	0	0	116
Days Maximum Temp. ≤ 32°F	1	0	0	0	0	0	0	0	0	0	0	1	2
Days Minimum Temp. ≤ 32°F	15	8	4	0	0	0	0	0	0	0	4	13	44
Days Minimum Temp. ≤ 0°F	0	0	0	0	0	0	0	0	0	0	0	0	0
Heating Degree Days (base 65°F)	572	386	221	71	10	1	0	0	14	71	286	516	2,148
Cooling Degree Days (base 65°F)	0	6	37	143	341	507	594	562	370	146	17	0	2,723
Mean Precipitation (in.)	0.49	0.64	0.43	0.92	1.87	1.74	1.08	1.75	3.36	2.02	0.66	0.62	15.58
Days With ≥ 0.1" Precipitation	2	2	1	2	3	3	3	4	3	2	2	29	
Days With ≥ 1.0" Precipitation	0	0	0	0	1	0	0	1	1	0	0	0	3
Mean Snowfall (in.)	0.6	0.2	trace	0.0	0.0	0.0	0.0	0.0	0.0	trace	0.3	0.3	1.4
Days With ≥ 1.0" Snow Depth	0	0	0	0	0	0	0	0	0	0	0	0	0

Ballinger 2 NW *Runnels County*   Elevation: 1,751 ft.   Latitude: 31° 44' N   Longitude: 99° 59' W

	JAN	FEB	MAR	APR	MAY	JUN	JUL	AUG	SEP	OCT	NOV	DEC	YEAR
Mean Maximum Temp. (°F)	59.2	65.6	73.5	81.6	87.0	92.3	95.1	94.0	88.0	80.3	68.6	61.2	78.9
Mean Temp. (°F)	45.2	50.8	58.5	66.7	73.9	80.0	82.7	81.8	75.6	66.4	55.0	47.1	65.3
Mean Minimum Temp. (°F)	31.2	36.0	43.4	51.7	60.7	67.7	70.2	69.4	63.1	52.5	41.5	33.3	51.7
Extreme Maximum Temp. (°F)	87	98	98	101	106	110	110	107	107	101	91	85	110
Extreme Minimum Temp. (°F)	-5	-3	8	24	36	47	56	51	38	22	8	-3	-5
Days Maximum Temp. ≥ 90°F	0	0	1	6	12	22	27	25	14	4	0	0	111
Days Maximum Temp. ≤ 32°F	1	0	0	0	0	0	0	0	0	0	0	1	2
Days Minimum Temp. ≤ 32°F	17	10	5	1	0	0	0	0	0	1	6	15	55
Days Minimum Temp. ≤ 0°F	0	0	0	0	0	0	0	0	0	0	0	0	0
Heating Degree Days (base 65°F)	607	399	234	72	10	0	0	0	12	73	312	549	2,268
Cooling Degree Days (base 65°F)	1	6	35	129	305	466	572	554	346	133	20	1	2,568
Mean Precipitation (in.)	0.97	1.42	1.38	1.88	3.40	2.98	1.39	2.42	3.15	2.37	1.14	1.20	23.70
Days With ≥ 0.1" Precipitation	3	3	3	3	5	4	3	3	4	4	2	2	39
Days With ≥ 1.0" Precipitation	0	0	0	1	1	1	0	1	1	1	0	0	6
Mean Snowfall (in.)	*0.9*	*0.4*	trace	0.0	0.0	0.0	0.0	0.0	0.0	0.0	0.1	trace	*1.4*
Days With ≥ 1.0" Snow Depth	*0*	*0*	0	0	0	0	0	0	0	0	0	0	*0*

Balmorhea *Reeves County*   Elevation: 3,218 ft.   Latitude: 30° 59' N   Longitude: 103° 44' W

	JAN	FEB	MAR	APR	MAY	JUN	JUL	AUG	SEP	OCT	NOV	DEC	YEAR
Mean Maximum Temp. (°F)	61.2	66.4	73.8	81.5	89.0	95.2	95.5	93.3	87.3	79.8	70.6	62.1	79.6
Mean Temp. (°F)	45.6	50.0	56.6	64.3	72.4	79.5	80.9	79.1	73.2	64.1	54.1	46.3	63.8
Mean Minimum Temp. (°F)	29.9	33.5	39.4	47.1	55.7	63.7	66.2	64.9	59.0	48.4	37.4	30.5	48.0
Extreme Maximum Temp. (°F)	88	90	96	99	106	111	108	106	105	98	90	87	111
Extreme Minimum Temp. (°F)	5	2	13	27	38	45	57	50	40	26	10	2	2
Days Maximum Temp. ≥ 90°F	0	0	1	6	16	24	26	24	14	4	0	0	115
Days Maximum Temp. ≤ 32°F	1	0	0	0	0	0	0	0	0	0	0	1	2
Days Minimum Temp. ≤ 32°F	20	13	6	1	0	0	0	0	0	1	8	19	68
Days Minimum Temp. ≤ 0°F	0	0	0	0	0	0	0	0	0	0	0	0	0
Heating Degree Days (base 65°F)	596	420	270	101	15	1	0	0	20	99	328	573	2,423
Cooling Degree Days (base 65°F)	0	3	17	81	254	436	500	449	274	80	7	0	2,101
Mean Precipitation (in.)	0.59	0.60	0.30	0.63	1.45	1.20	1.75	2.37	3.23	1.18	0.52	0.60	14.42
Days With ≥ 0.1" Precipitation	2	1	1	1	3	3	4	4	5	2	1	1	28
Days With ≥ 1.0" Precipitation	0	0	0	0	0	0	0	1	1	0	0	0	2
Mean Snowfall (in.)	1.7	0.4	trace	trace	0.0	0.0	0.0	0.0	0.0	0.0	0.2	0.3	2.6
Days With ≥ 1.0" Snow Depth	1	0	0	0	0	0	0	0	0	0	0	0	1

Bardwell Dam *Ellis County*   Elevation: 459 ft.   Latitude: 32° 16' N   Longitude: 96° 38' W

	JAN	FEB	MAR	APR	MAY	JUN	JUL	AUG	SEP	OCT	NOV	DEC	YEAR
Mean Maximum Temp. (°F)	54.7	60.1	67.8	75.3	82.7	90.3	95.0	95.1	88.4	78.9	66.6	58.2	76.1
Mean Temp. (°F)	43.2	48.4	56.4	64.0	72.1	79.5	83.6	83.2	76.4	66.1	55.0	46.7	64.5
Mean Minimum Temp. (°F)	31.7	36.7	44.9	52.8	61.6	68.7	72.1	71.2	64.5	53.3	43.3	35.1	53.0
Extreme Maximum Temp. (°F)	81	95	91	93	100	108	108	108	106	99	89	82	108
Extreme Minimum Temp. (°F)	2	8	15	25	43	49	57	53	37	26	20	-7	-7
Days Maximum Temp. ≥ 90°F	0	0	0	0	4	18	27	27	16	3	0	0	95
Days Maximum Temp. ≤ 32°F	2	1	0	0	0	0	0	0	0	0	0	1	4
Days Minimum Temp. ≤ 32°F	17	9	3	0	0	0	0	0	0	0	4	12	45
Days Minimum Temp. ≤ 0°F	0	0	0	0	0	0	0	0	0	0	0	0	0
Heating Degree Days (base 65°F)	668	466	282	99	13	0	0	0	10	80	313	564	2,495
Cooling Degree Days (base 65°F)	1	4	21	71	244	440	586	582	363	117	20	4	2,453
Mean Precipitation (in.)	2.50	2.82	2.95	3.09	4.72	3.47	2.16	2.13	3.30	4.16	3.05	2.95	37.30
Days With ≥ 0.1" Precipitation	5	5	5	4	6	5	3	4	4	4	5	4	54
Days With ≥ 1.0" Precipitation	0	1	1	1	2	1	1	0	1	1	1	1	11
Mean Snowfall (in.)	0.2	trace	trace	0.0	0.0	0.0	0.0	0.0	0.0	0.0	trace	0.0	0.2
Days With ≥ 1.0" Snow Depth	0	0	0	0	0	0	0	0	0	0	0	0	0

Beeville 5 NE *Bee County*   Elevation: 252 ft.   Latitude: 28° 27' N   Longitude: 97° 42' W

	JAN	FEB	MAR	APR	MAY	JUN	JUL	AUG	SEP	OCT	NOV	DEC	YEAR
Mean Maximum Temp. (°F)	64.1	67.9	74.8	80.6	85.9	91.2	94.4	94.5	90.5	83.5	74.0	67.1	80.7
Mean Temp. (°F)	53.0	56.6	63.7	69.9	76.3	81.3	83.5	83.5	79.7	71.7	62.8	55.9	69.8
Mean Minimum Temp. (°F)	41.9	45.1	52.5	59.2	66.5	71.3	72.6	72.4	68.7	60.0	51.6	44.7	58.9
Extreme Maximum Temp. (°F)	91	98	98	104	101	110	104	105	107	99	95	88	110
Extreme Minimum Temp. (°F)	14	20	19	30	46	53	63	60	46	29	24	8	8
Days Maximum Temp. ≥ 90°F	0	0	1	2	8	21	27	27	19	6	0	0	111
Days Maximum Temp. ≤ 32°F	0	0	0	0	0	0	0	0	0	0	0	0	0
Days Minimum Temp. ≤ 32°F	5	3	1	0	0	0	0	0	0	0	1	4	14
Days Minimum Temp. ≤ 0°F	0	0	0	0	0	0	0	0	0	0	0	0	0
Heating Degree Days (base 65°F)	381	258	119	33	2	0	0	0	1	24	146	307	1,271
Cooling Degree Days (base 65°F)	15	29	79	185	374	517	601	601	465	250	93	36	3,245
Mean Precipitation (in.)	1.98	1.88	1.88	2.71	3.58	4.11	2.74	3.08	4.37	3.51	1.84	1.79	33.47
Days With ≥ 0.1" Precipitation	4	3	3	4	5	5	4	4	5	4	3	3	47
Days With ≥ 1.0" Precipitation	0	0	1	1	1	2	1	1	1	1	0	0	9
Mean Snowfall (in.)	0.0	trace	0.0	0.0	0.0	0.0	0.0	0.0	0.0	0.0	trace	0.0	trace
Days With ≥ 1.0" Snow Depth	0	0	0	0	0	0	0	0	0	0	0	0	0

Belton Dam *Bell County*   Elevation: 662 ft.   Latitude: 31° 06' N   Longitude: 97° 29' W

	JAN	FEB	MAR	APR	MAY	JUN	JUL	AUG	SEP	OCT	NOV	DEC	YEAR
Mean Maximum Temp. (°F)	56.4	61.5	70.2	77.5	83.2	89.9	94.3	94.9	88.6	79.8	68.4	60.4	77.1
Mean Temp. (°F)	45.1	49.9	58.6	66.2	72.9	79.5	82.9	83.0	77.4	67.7	56.9	48.8	65.8
Mean Minimum Temp. (°F)	33.7	38.2	46.9	55.0	62.6	69.0	71.5	71.1	66.2	55.6	45.4	37.2	54.4
Extreme Maximum Temp. (°F)	88	95	97	95	99	106	107	104	104	100	92	86	107
Extreme Minimum Temp. (°F)	8	6	17	31	42	50	62	58	42	29	20	-1	-1
Days Maximum Temp. ≥ 90°F	0	0	0	1	4	19	27	na	16	4	0	0	na
Days Maximum Temp. ≤ 32°F	1	0	0	0	0	0	0	0	0	0	0	1	2
Days Minimum Temp. ≤ 32°F	14	7	2	0	0	0	0	0	0	0	3	9	35
Days Minimum Temp. ≤ 0°F	0	0	0	0	0	0	0	0	0	0	0	0	0
Heating Degree Days (base 65°F)	613	426	227	68	7	0	0	0	5	58	266	500	2,170
Cooling Degree Days (base 65°F)	na	na	na	na	na	na	na	na	na	na	na	na	na
Mean Precipitation (in.)	1.81	2.74	2.65	2.57	4.92	3.97	1.99	2.49	3.56	3.87	2.73	2.45	35.75
Days With ≥ 0.1" Precipitation	4	5	5	4	6	5	3	3	5	5	4	4	53
Days With ≥ 1.0" Precipitation	0	1	1	1	1	1	1	1	1	1	1	1	11
Mean Snowfall (in.)	na	na	0.0	0.0	0.0	0.0	0.0	0.0	0.0	0.0	0.0	trace	na
Days With ≥ 1.0" Snow Depth	na	0	0	0	0	0	0	0	0	0	0	0	na

Benbrook Dam *Tarrant County*   Elevation: 787 ft.   Latitude: 32° 39' N   Longitude: 97° 27' W

	JAN	FEB	MAR	APR	MAY	JUN	JUL	AUG	SEP	OCT	NOV	DEC	YEAR
Mean Maximum Temp. (°F)	54.2	59.7	67.4	75.4	82.5	90.4	95.6	95.3	88.0	78.3	66.1	57.7	75.9
Mean Temp. (°F)	42.7	47.9	55.7	63.9	71.7	79.6	83.9	83.5	76.6	66.3	54.8	46.3	64.4
Mean Minimum Temp. (°F)	31.1	36.1	43.8	52.3	60.8	68.7	72.2	71.6	65.1	54.3	43.5	34.9	52.9
Extreme Maximum Temp. (°F)	83	94	91	95	99	110	109	107	108	99	89	82	110
Extreme Minimum Temp. (°F)	4	5	12	28	41	52	59	54	40	22	18	-6	-6
Days Maximum Temp. ≥ 90°F	0	0	0	1	4	18	28	27	15	3	0	0	96
Days Maximum Temp. ≤ 32°F	2	1	0	0	0	0	0	0	0	0	0	1	4
Days Minimum Temp. ≤ 32°F	17	10	3	0	0	0	0	0	0	0	4	12	46
Days Minimum Temp. ≤ 0°F	0	0	0	0	0	0	0	0	0	0	0	0	0
Heating Degree Days (base 65°F)	685	480	303	105	16	1	0	0	11	81	318	574	2,574
Cooling Degree Days (base 65°F)	0	4	19	77	236	450	603	599	373	127	21	1	2,510
Mean Precipitation (in.)	1.65	2.30	2.70	3.27	4.59	3.27	2.31	2.08	3.07	4.03	2.15	2.43	33.85
Days With ≥ 0.1" Precipitation	4	4	5	5	6	5	3	3	4	5	4	4	52
Days With ≥ 1.0" Precipitation	0	1	1	1	1	1	1	1	1	1	1	0	10
Mean Snowfall (in.)	trace	trace	trace	0.0	0.0	0.0	0.0	0.0	0.0	0.0	0.1	trace	0.1
Days With ≥ 1.0" Snow Depth	0	0	0	0	0	0	0	0	0	0	0	0	0

Big Lake 2 *Reagan County*   Elevation: 2,687 ft.   Latitude: 31° 12' N   Longitude: 101° 28' W

	JAN	FEB	MAR	APR	MAY	JUN	JUL	AUG	SEP	OCT	NOV	DEC	YEAR
Mean Maximum Temp. (°F)	57.2	62.6	70.3	78.8	86.0	91.6	94.0	93.0	86.5	77.5	66.5	59.0	76.9
Mean Temp. (°F)	43.2	47.9	55.8	64.1	72.2	78.5	80.9	79.7	73.5	63.9	52.7	44.9	63.1
Mean Minimum Temp. (°F)	29.1	33.3	41.2	49.3	58.3	65.4	67.8	66.4	60.4	50.2	38.9	30.8	49.3
Extreme Maximum Temp. (°F)	85	88	94	100	106	110	109	107	104	100	90	84	110
Extreme Minimum Temp. (°F)	2	8	5	24	34	45	52	53	32	24	11	1	1
Days Maximum Temp. ≥ 90°F	0	0	0	4	11	20	25	25	13	2	0	0	100
Days Maximum Temp. ≤ 32°F	2	1	0	0	0	0	0	0	0	0	0	1	4
Days Minimum Temp. ≤ 32°F	21	13	6	1	0	0	0	0	0	1	8	19	69
Days Minimum Temp. ≤ 0°F	0	0	0	0	0	0	0	0	0	0	0	0	0
Heating Degree Days (base 65°F)	669	476	297	109	18	2	0	0	21	110	369	617	2,688
Cooling Degree Days (base 65°F)	0	1	19	85	255	418	516	486	295	89	7	0	2,171
Mean Precipitation (in.)	0.66	0.98	0.84	1.45	2.45	1.80	1.81	2.24	3.13	1.88	0.80	0.81	18.85
Days With ≥ 0.1" Precipitation	2	2	2	2	4	3	3	4	4	3	2	2	33
Days With ≥ 1.0" Precipitation	0	0	0	0	1	0	1	1	1	1	0	0	5
Mean Snowfall (in.)	0.9	trace	trace	0.0	0.0	0.0	0.0	0.0	0.0	trace	0.3	0.1	1.3
Days With ≥ 1.0" Snow Depth	*0*	0	0	0	0	0	0	0	0	0	0	0	*0*

Blanco *Blanco County*   Elevation: 1,368 ft.   Latitude: 30° 06' N   Longitude: 98° 25' W

	JAN	FEB	MAR	APR	MAY	JUN	JUL	AUG	SEP	OCT	NOV	DEC	YEAR
Mean Maximum Temp. (°F)	58.8	63.4	70.8	77.7	83.5	89.6	93.6	94.1	88.2	79.7	68.8	61.4	77.5
Mean Temp. (°F)	46.3	50.5	57.8	64.8	72.1	78.5	81.8	81.7	76.2	66.8	56.3	48.9	65.1
Mean Minimum Temp. (°F)	33.7	37.5	44.8	51.8	60.7	67.4	69.9	69.2	64.2	53.9	43.7	36.4	52.8
Extreme Maximum Temp. (°F)	89	98	100	100	101	106	107	106	103	100	89	87	107
Extreme Minimum Temp. (°F)	6	2	14	27	34	46	58	53	38	22	15	0	0
Days Maximum Temp. ≥ 90°F	0	0	0	1	5	16	26	27	15	2	0	0	92
Days Maximum Temp. ≤ 32°F	1	1	0	0	0	0	0	0	0	0	0	0	2
Days Minimum Temp. ≤ 32°F	15	10	4	1	0	0	0	0	0	0	5	13	48
Days Minimum Temp. ≤ 0°F	0	0	0	0	0	0	0	0	0	0	0	0	0
Heating Degree Days (base 65°F)	575	410	247	93	12	0	0	0	8	74	283	496	2,198
Cooling Degree Days (base 65°F)	2	7	29	89	245	417	530	534	354	139	29	5	2,380
Mean Precipitation (in.)	1.81	2.12	2.69	2.67	4.62	4.05	2.04	2.36	3.39	3.92	2.37	2.30	34.34
Days With ≥ 0.1" Precipitation	4	4	5	4	6	5	3	3	5	4	4	4	51
Days With ≥ 1.0" Precipitation	0	0	1	1	2	1	1	1	1	1	1	1	11
Mean Snowfall (in.)	0.3	0.3	trace	0.0	0.0	0.0	0.0	0.0	0.0	0.0	trace	trace	0.6
Days With ≥ 1.0" Snow Depth	0	0	0	0	0	0	0	0	0	0	0	0	0

Boerne *Kendall County*   Elevation: 1,443 ft.   Latitude: 29° 48' N   Longitude: 98° 44' W

	JAN	FEB	MAR	APR	MAY	JUN	JUL	AUG	SEP	OCT	NOV	DEC	YEAR
Mean Maximum Temp. (°F)	59.8	64.6	71.9	78.3	83.6	89.3	92.5	93.2	88.4	80.2	69.7	62.2	77.8
Mean Temp. (°F)	47.0	51.2	58.3	65.2	72.2	78.2	80.9	80.8	76.2	67.1	56.8	49.5	65.3
Mean Minimum Temp. (°F)	34.2	37.8	44.8	52.1	60.8	67.1	69.2	68.4	64.0	53.9	43.8	36.8	52.7
Extreme Maximum Temp. (°F)	88	98	99	100	99	105	103	105	103	97	90	87	105
Extreme Minimum Temp. (°F)	8	5	14	27	34	45	56	55	37	21	16	2	2
Days Maximum Temp. ≥ 90°F	0	0	1	1	4	16	25	27	15	2	0	0	91
Days Maximum Temp. ≤ 32°F	0	0	0	0	0	0	0	0	0	0	0	0	0
Days Minimum Temp. ≤ 32°F	15	9	4	1	0	0	0	0	0	0	5	12	46
Days Minimum Temp. ≤ 0°F	0	0	0	0	0	0	0	0	0	0	0	0	0
Heating Degree Days (base 65°F)	553	390	233	84	11	0	0	0	6	69	269	477	2,092
Cooling Degree Days (base 65°F)	2	8	32	98	251	415	511	518	358	148	30	5	2,376
Mean Precipitation (in.)	1.82	2.31	2.62	2.87	4.73	4.63	2.23	2.99	3.77	3.56	2.83	2.31	36.67
Days With ≥ 0.1" Precipitation	5	4	5	4	6	5	3	4	5	5	4	4	54
Days With ≥ 1.0" Precipitation	0	1	1	1	2	2	1	1	1	1	1	1	13
Mean Snowfall (in.)	0.3	trace	0.0	0.0	0.0	0.0	0.0	0.0	0.0	0.0	trace	trace	0.3
Days With ≥ 1.0" Snow Depth	0	0	0	0	0	0	0	0	0	0	0	0	0

Bonham 3 NNE *Fannin County*   Elevation: 597 ft.   Latitude: 33° 38' N   Longitude: 96° 10' W

	JAN	FEB	MAR	APR	MAY	JUN	JUL	AUG	SEP	OCT	NOV	DEC	YEAR
Mean Maximum Temp. (°F)	52.6	58.3	66.7	74.7	81.5	89.2	93.9	94.0	86.4	76.4	64.1	55.6	74.4
Mean Temp. (°F)	41.7	46.8	54.9	62.8	70.8	78.4	82.6	82.2	74.9	64.3	52.8	44.7	63.1
Mean Minimum Temp. (°F)	30.8	35.3	43.0	50.9	59.9	67.6	71.4	70.4	63.5	52.2	41.6	33.8	51.7
Extreme Maximum Temp. (°F)	81	92	94	95	97	107	108	108	109	96	87	80	109
Extreme Minimum Temp. (°F)	2	3	13	26	38	48	52	53	35	23	8	-4	-4
Days Maximum Temp. ≥ 90°F	0	0	0	0	3	15	25	25	12	1	0	0	81
Days Maximum Temp. ≤ 32°F	2	1	0	0	0	0	0	0	0	0	0	1	4
Days Minimum Temp. ≤ 32°F	18	11	5	1	0	0	0	0	0	0	6	15	56
Days Minimum Temp. ≤ 0°F	0	0	0	0	0	0	0	0	0	0	0	0	0
Heating Degree Days (base 65°F)	715	508	325	123	20	1	0	0	17	105	371	624	2,809
Cooling Degree Days (base 65°F)	0	3	15	56	199	406	552	546	323	88	12	2	2,202
Mean Precipitation (in.)	2.35	3.22	3.75	3.38	5.58	4.29	3.48	2.22	3.72	5.41	3.69	3.40	44.49
Days With ≥ 0.1" Precipitation	4	5	6	5	7	5	4	3	5	5	4	5	58
Days With ≥ 1.0" Precipitation	1	1	1	1	2	1	1	1	1	2	1	1	14
Mean Snowfall (in.)	0.5	1.0	0.3	0.0	0.0	0.0	0.0	0.0	0.0	0.0	trace	0.3	2.1
Days With ≥ 1.0" Snow Depth	0	0	0	0	0	0	0	0	0	0	0	0	0

Borger *Hutchinson County*   Elevation: 3,139 ft.   Latitude: 35° 39' N   Longitude: 101° 27' W

	JAN	FEB	MAR	APR	MAY	JUN	JUL	AUG	SEP	OCT	NOV	DEC	YEAR
Mean Maximum Temp. (°F)	49.5	55.5	63.6	72.1	80.0	88.9	92.6	90.4	83.6	74.0	59.9	51.0	71.8
Mean Temp. (°F)	36.6	41.8	49.2	57.6	66.4	75.3	79.5	77.7	70.6	60.1	46.9	38.5	58.3
Mean Minimum Temp. (°F)	23.6	28.0	34.6	43.0	52.7	61.7	66.4	64.9	57.6	46.1	33.9	26.0	44.9
Extreme Maximum Temp. (°F)	79	85	95	97	103	108	106	104	105	95	88	79	108
Extreme Minimum Temp. (°F)	-6	-5	4	16	30	44	52	51	29	13	2	-7	-7
Days Maximum Temp. ≥ 90°F	0	0	0	1	4	15	22	19	8	1	0	0	70
Days Maximum Temp. ≤ 32°F	4	2	1	0	0	0	0	0	0	0	1	3	11
Days Minimum Temp. ≤ 32°F	26	19	13	3	0	0	0	0	0	2	13	24	100
Days Minimum Temp. ≤ 0°F	0	0	0	0	0	0	0	0	0	0	0	1	1
Heating Degree Days (base 65°F)	874	649	489	240	68	6	0	1	38	187	537	814	3,903
Cooling Degree Days (base 65°F)	0	0	4	23	113	313	456	404	214	37	2	0	1,566
Mean Precipitation (in.)	0.65	0.69	1.39	1.77	3.06	3.05	2.67	3.21	2.02	1.45	0.88	0.66	21.50
Days With ≥ 0.1" Precipitation	2	2	3	3	5	5	5	5	4	3	2	2	41
Days With ≥ 1.0" Precipitation	0	0	0	0	1	1	1	1	0	0	0	0	4
Mean Snowfall (in.)	5.7	5.5	4.0	1.0	trace	trace	0.0	trace	trace	0.7	2.8	4.2	23.9
Days With ≥ 1.0" Snow Depth	4	3	1	0	0	0	0	0	0	0	1	3	12

Bowie *Montague County*   Elevation: 1,079 ft.   Latitude: 33° 32' N   Longitude: 97° 51' W

	JAN	FEB	MAR	APR	MAY	JUN	JUL	AUG	SEP	OCT	NOV	DEC	YEAR
Mean Maximum Temp. (°F)	53.4	59.3	68.0	75.8	82.6	90.3	95.5	94.8	87.1	77.4	64.7	56.5	75.5
Mean Temp. (°F)	42.2	47.5	55.8	63.8	71.7	79.5	84.2	83.4	76.1	65.8	53.6	45.2	64.1
Mean Minimum Temp. (°F)	31.0	35.6	43.4	51.7	60.7	68.7	72.8	71.9	64.9	54.2	42.4	33.9	52.6
Extreme Maximum Temp. (°F)	88	94	100	99	102	115	113	108	108	101	89	83	115
Extreme Minimum Temp. (°F)	4	-1	10	22	40	51	59	53	37	23	16	-11	-11
Days Maximum Temp. ≥ 90°F	0	0	0	1	5	18	27	26	13	2	0	0	92
Days Maximum Temp. ≤ 32°F	2	1	0	0	0	0	0	0	0	0	0	1	4
Days Minimum Temp. ≤ 32°F	17	10	4	0	0	0	0	0	0	0	5	14	50
Days Minimum Temp. ≤ 0°F	0	0	0	0	0	0	0	0	0	0	0	0	0
Heating Degree Days (base 65°F)	702	493	305	112	17	1	0	0	15	87	352	608	2,692
Cooling Degree Days (base 65°F)	0	3	21	75	217	421	581	573	342	101	15	1	2,350
Mean Precipitation (in.)	1.43	2.23	2.62	2.88	5.10	3.39	1.82	2.27	3.79	3.99	2.03	1.91	33.46
Days With ≥ 0.1" Precipitation	3	4	4	5	6	5	3	3	5	4	4	3	50
Days With ≥ 1.0" Precipitation	0	1	1	1	2	1	1	1	1	1	1	0	11
Mean Snowfall (in.)	0.6	0.7	0.3	trace	0.0	0.0	0.0	0.0	0.0	0.0	0.2	0.4	2.2
Days With ≥ 1.0" Snow Depth	0	0	0	0	0	0	0	0	0	0	0	0	0

Brady *McCulloch County*   Elevation: 1,719 ft.   Latitude: 31° 07' N   Longitude: 99° 20' W

	JAN	FEB	MAR	APR	MAY	JUN	JUL	AUG	SEP	OCT	NOV	DEC	YEAR
Mean Maximum Temp. (°F)	58.1	62.8	70.7	78.8	84.7	91.0	94.9	94.3	88.3	79.7	68.2	60.4	77.7
Mean Temp. (°F)	44.9	49.5	57.0	64.8	72.2	78.7	82.1	81.5	75.6	66.1	55.1	47.4	64.6
Mean Minimum Temp. (°F)	31.6	36.1	43.3	50.8	59.6	66.4	69.2	68.6	62.9	52.4	42.0	34.4	51.4
Extreme Maximum Temp. (°F)	88	99	95	100	107	110	110	108	105	100	92	85	110
Extreme Minimum Temp. (°F)	5	3	11	27	37	47	56	51	40	24	13	-2	-2
Days Maximum Temp. ≥ 90°F	0	0	1	3	8	19	27	26	15	3	0	0	102
Days Maximum Temp. ≤ 32°F	1	1	0	0	0	0	0	0	0	0	0	1	3
Days Minimum Temp. ≤ 32°F	17	10	5	1	0	0	0	0	0	0	6	14	53
Days Minimum Temp. ≤ 0°F	0	0	0	0	0	0	0	0	0	0	0	0	0
Heating Degree Days (base 65°F)	618	436	269	94	15	1	0	0	13	80	309	540	2,375
Cooling Degree Days (base 65°F)	1	6	28	97	261	430	550	549	350	128	22	2	2,424
Mean Precipitation (in.)	1.00	1.73	1.68	1.93	3.60	3.15	2.69	2.62	3.35	2.51	1.37	1.57	27.20
Days With ≥ 0.1" Precipitation	3	4	3	4	6	5	3	3	4	4	3	3	45
Days With ≥ 1.0" Precipitation	0	0	0	1	1	1	1	1	1	1	0	0	7
Mean Snowfall (in.)	0.2	0.3	trace	0.0	0.0	0.0	0.0	0.0	0.0	0.0	0.0	0.0	0.5
Days With ≥ 1.0" Snow Depth	0	0	0	0	0	0	0	0	0	0	0	0	0

Bravo *Hartley County*   Elevation: 4,160 ft.   Latitude: 35° 39' N   Longitude: 103° 00' W

	JAN	FEB	MAR	APR	MAY	JUN	JUL	AUG	SEP	OCT	NOV	DEC	YEAR
Mean Maximum Temp. (°F)	51.0	56.4	64.3	71.9	79.7	88.1	91.2	89.1	82.6	73.5	60.6	52.6	71.8
Mean Temp. (°F)	35.7	40.5	47.2	55.0	63.8	72.7	76.6	75.0	67.9	57.2	44.9	37.4	56.2
Mean Minimum Temp. (°F)	20.3	24.7	30.1	38.0	47.9	57.2	61.8	60.8	53.2	40.9	29.1	22.1	40.5
Extreme Maximum Temp. (°F)	78	82	92	97	99	109	103	103	101	93	90	79	109
Extreme Minimum Temp. (°F)	-12	-11	4	17	26	39	48	47	25	10	-3	-12	-12
Days Maximum Temp. ≥ 90°F	0	0	0	0	3	14	20	16	6	1	0	0	60
Days Maximum Temp. ≤ 32°F	3	2	1	0	0	0	0	0	0	0	1	3	10
Days Minimum Temp. ≤ 32°F	28	23	19	8	1	0	0	0	0	5	19	28	131
Days Minimum Temp. ≤ 0°F	1	0	0	0	0	0	0	0	0	0	0	1	2
Heating Degree Days (base 65°F)	901	682	544	304	96	9	1	1	51	252	597	849	4,287
Cooling Degree Days (base 65°F)	0	0	1	8	63	240	374	323	148	14	0	0	1,171
Mean Precipitation (in.)	0.40	0.40	0.69	1.09	2.50	2.64	2.49	3.30	2.05	1.11	0.67	0.39	17.73
Days With ≥ 0.1" Precipitation	2	1	2	3	4	5	5	6	4	2	1	1	36
Days With ≥ 1.0" Precipitation	0	0	0	0	1	1	1	1	0	0	0	0	4
Mean Snowfall (in.)	0.6	0.3	trace	0.4	0.0	0.0	0.0	0.0	0.0	trace	0.4	0.4	2.1
Days With ≥ 1.0" Snow Depth	0	0	0	0	0	0	0	0	0	0	0	0	0

Brenham *Washington County*   Elevation: 311 ft.   Latitude: 30° 10' N   Longitude: 96° 24' W

	JAN	FEB	MAR	APR	MAY	JUN	JUL	AUG	SEP	OCT	NOV	DEC	YEAR
Mean Maximum Temp. (°F)	60.6	65.3	72.9	79.7	86.1	92.0	95.9	96.5	91.0	82.4	71.3	63.5	79.8
Mean Temp. (°F)	50.1	54.1	61.4	68.5	75.5	81.6	84.7	84.7	79.6	70.4	60.2	52.9	68.6
Mean Minimum Temp. (°F)	39.4	43.0	49.8	57.2	64.9	71.1	73.4	72.9	68.1	58.4	49.0	42.2	57.4
Extreme Maximum Temp. (°F)	86	94	94	94	101	105	106	107	105	98	90	85	107
Extreme Minimum Temp. (°F)	7	15	19	33	44	53	64	61	46	29	22	4	4
Days Maximum Temp. ≥ 90°F	0	0	0	1	9	23	29	28	20	6	0	0	116
Days Maximum Temp. ≤ 32°F	1	0	0	0	0	0	0	0	0	0	0	0	1
Days Minimum Temp. ≤ 32°F	8	4	1	0	0	0	0	0	0	0	1	5	19
Days Minimum Temp. ≤ 0°F	0	0	0	0	0	0	0	0	0	0	0	0	0
Heating Degree Days (base 65°F)	468	318	165	44	2	0	0	0	2	35	197	388	1,619
Cooling Degree Days (base 65°F)	10	20	62	157	350	516	626	639	462	220	63	21	3,146
Mean Precipitation (in.)	3.35	2.82	3.00	3.43	5.06	4.51	1.93	3.10	5.01	4.64	3.86	3.23	43.94
Days With ≥ 0.1" Precipitation	6	5	5	4	7	5	4	5	5	5	5	5	61
Days With ≥ 1.0" Precipitation	1	1	1	1	2	1	0	1	2	1	1	1	13
Mean Snowfall (in.)	0.2	trace	trace	0.0	0.0	0.0	0.0	0.0	0.0	0.0	0.1	trace	0.3
Days With ≥ 1.0" Snow Depth	0	0	0	0	0	0	0	0	0	0	0	0	0

Bridgeport *Wise County*   Elevation: 744 ft.   Latitude: 33° 12' N   Longitude: 97° 46' W

	JAN	FEB	MAR	APR	MAY	JUN	JUL	AUG	SEP	OCT	NOV	DEC	YEAR
Mean Maximum Temp. (°F)	55.6	60.5	68.8	77.2	83.9	91.6	97.5	96.9	89.3	79.2	66.6	58.7	77.2
Mean Temp. (°F)	42.6	47.3	55.2	63.6	71.5	79.1	83.8	82.8	75.6	64.9	53.6	45.5	63.8
Mean Minimum Temp. (°F)	29.6	33.9	41.6	49.9	59.0	66.6	70.1	68.5	62.0	50.5	40.5	32.4	50.4
Extreme Maximum Temp. (°F)	89	96	95	101	102	115	114	110	109	105	92	86	115
Extreme Minimum Temp. (°F)	2	3	9	24	37	48	54	52	33	21	14	-8	-8
Days Maximum Temp. ≥ 90°F	0	0	1	2	7	19	28	28	17	4	0	0	106
Days Maximum Temp. ≤ 32°F	2	1	0	0	0	0	0	0	0	0	0	1	4
Days Minimum Temp. ≤ 32°F	20	13	6	1	0	0	0	0	0	1	8	16	65
Days Minimum Temp. ≤ 0°F	0	0	0	0	0	0	0	0	0	0	0	0	0
Heating Degree Days (base 65°F)	689	498	318	115	20	1	0	0	16	101	352	598	2,708
Cooling Degree Days (base 65°F)	1	4	22	80	237	430	587	567	347	105	18	2	2,400
Mean Precipitation (in.)	1.52	2.17	2.57	2.87	5.48	3.37	2.28	2.03	3.34	4.24	2.11	1.95	33.93
Days With ≥ 0.1" Precipitation	3	4	4	5	6	5	3	3	4	5	3	4	49
Days With ≥ 1.0" Precipitation	0	0	1	1	2	1	1	1	1	1	1	0	10
Mean Snowfall (in.)	0.7	1.2	0.2	0.1	0.0	0.0	0.0	0.0	0.0	0.0	0.5	0.3	3.0
Days With ≥ 1.0" Snow Depth	0	0	0	0	0	0	0	0	0	0	0	0	0

Brownfield 2 *Terry County*   Elevation: 3,297 ft.   Latitude: 33° 11' N   Longitude: 102° 16' W

	JAN	FEB	MAR	APR	MAY	JUN	JUL	AUG	SEP	OCT	NOV	DEC	YEAR
Mean Maximum Temp. (°F)	53.8	59.6	67.6	75.9	83.7	90.8	92.5	90.7	84.3	76.2	64.3	56.0	74.6
Mean Temp. (°F)	39.7	44.4	51.4	59.7	68.6	76.3	78.9	77.4	71.0	61.3	49.6	41.8	60.0
Mean Minimum Temp. (°F)	25.6	29.2	35.0	43.3	53.3	61.7	65.2	64.0	57.5	46.3	34.9	27.5	45.3
Extreme Maximum Temp. (°F)	83	86	97	98	103	111	109	104	102	99	88	82	111
Extreme Minimum Temp. (°F)	-2	2	9	22	31	45	53	52	36	19	6	-1	-2
Days Maximum Temp. ≥ 90°F	0	0	0	2	8	18	23	20	10	2	0	0	83
Days Maximum Temp. ≤ 32°F	3	1	0	0	0	0	0	0	0	0	0	2	6
Days Minimum Temp. ≤ 32°F	26	19	11	2	0	0	0	0	0	1	11	23	93
Days Minimum Temp. ≤ 0°F	0	0	0	0	0	0	0	0	0	0	0	0	0
Heating Degree Days (base 65°F)	777	574	420	191	44	3	0	0	35	156	457	713	3,370
Cooling Degree Days (base 65°F)	0	1	4	35	169	357	456	408	224	50	2	0	1,706
Mean Precipitation (in.)	0.54	0.69	0.73	0.89	2.95	2.85	2.26	2.19	2.83	1.48	0.73	0.63	18.77
Days With ≥ 0.1" Precipitation	2	2	2	2	4	4	4	4	4	3	2	2	35
Days With ≥ 1.0" Precipitation	0	0	0	0	1	1	1	1	1	0	0	0	5
Mean Snowfall (in.)	2.3	2.1	0.8	0.2	0.0	0.0	0.0	0.0	0.0	trace	0.7	1.6	7.7
Days With ≥ 1.0" Snow Depth	1	1	0	0	0	0	0	0	0	0	0	0	2

Brownwood *Brown County*   Elevation: 1,384 ft.   Latitude: 31° 41' N   Longitude: 98° 58' W

	JAN	FEB	MAR	APR	MAY	JUN	JUL	AUG	SEP	OCT	NOV	DEC	YEAR
Mean Maximum Temp. (°F)	58.0	63.5	71.4	79.3	85.5	91.8	96.0	95.5	89.0	80.9	68.7	61.0	78.4
Mean Temp. (°F)	44.5	49.5	57.1	65.3	73.0	79.7	83.3	82.6	76.1	66.7	55.3	47.2	65.0
Mean Minimum Temp. (°F)	30.9	35.5	42.8	51.2	60.3	67.5	70.5	69.7	63.1	52.4	41.8	33.3	51.6
Extreme Maximum Temp. (°F)	87	95	95	100	105	107	109	109	107	100	91	85	109
Extreme Minimum Temp. (°F)	0	6	10	26	37	50	53	51	37	21	12	-6	-6
Days Maximum Temp. ≥ 90°F	0	0	1	3	9	21	28	27	17	4	0	0	110
Days Maximum Temp. ≤ 32°F	1	1	0	0	0	0	0	0	0	0	0	1	3
Days Minimum Temp. ≤ 32°F	18	11	5	1	0	0	0	0	0	0	6	15	56
Days Minimum Temp. ≤ 0°F	0	0	0	0	0	0	0	0	0	0	0	0	0
Heating Degree Days (base 65°F)	629	434	264	89	11	1	0	0	10	70	304	548	2,360
Cooling Degree Days (base 65°F)	1	3	22	99	264	435	568	566	353	123	20	1	2,455
Mean Precipitation (in.)	1.29	2.14	2.16	2.37	3.79	3.62	1.84	2.40	2.94	2.68	1.48	1.68	28.39
Days With ≥ 0.1" Precipitation	3	3	3	3	5	4	3	3	4	3	2	3	39
Days With ≥ 1.0" Precipitation	0	1	1	0	1	1	1	1	1	1	0	0	8
Mean Snowfall (in.)	0.9	0.1	trace	0.0	0.0	0.0	0.0	0.0	0.0	0.0	0.3	0.2	1.5
Days With ≥ 1.0" Snow Depth	*0*	0	0	0	0	0	0	0	0	0	0	0	*0*

Burnet *Burnet County*   Elevation: 1,272 ft.   Latitude: 30° 44' N   Longitude: 98° 14' W

	JAN	FEB	MAR	APR	MAY	JUN	JUL	AUG	SEP	OCT	NOV	DEC	YEAR
Mean Maximum Temp. (°F)	58.5	63.2	70.5	77.4	83.2	89.2	93.3	93.5	87.8	79.2	68.1	60.6	77.0
Mean Temp. (°F)	45.9	50.5	58.0	65.2	72.3	78.6	81.8	81.7	76.1	66.6	56.0	48.4	65.1
Mean Minimum Temp. (°F)	33.2	37.7	45.5	52.9	61.3	67.9	70.4	69.9	64.4	53.9	43.9	36.1	53.1
Extreme Maximum Temp. (°F)	87	97	100	97	101	106	104	105	104	102	92	84	106
Extreme Minimum Temp. (°F)	2	-1	12	27	38	49	54	53	38	22	15	-4	-4
Days Maximum Temp. ≥ 90°F	0	0	0	1	5	16	26	26	14	2	0	0	90
Days Maximum Temp. ≤ 32°F	1	0	0	0	0	0	0	0	0	0	0	1	2
Days Minimum Temp. ≤ 32°F	16	9	3	1	0	0	0	0	0	0	5	12	46
Days Minimum Temp. ≤ 0°F	0	0	0	0	0	0	0	0	0	0	0	0	0
Heating Degree Days (base 65°F)	586	411	242	85	12	0	0	0	9	74	285	510	2,214
Cooling Degree Days (base 65°F)	1	6	26	95	250	416	540	540	354	132	22	3	2,385
Mean Precipitation (in.)	1.60	2.16	2.34	2.50	4.64	4.03	2.04	2.03	3.21	3.40	2.10	2.10	32.15
Days With ≥ 0.1" Precipitation	4	4	4	4	6	5	3	3	5	5	4	4	51
Days With ≥ 1.0" Precipitation	0	1	1	1	2	2	1	0	1	1	1	1	12
Mean Snowfall (in.)	0.2	0.3	trace	0.0	0.0	0.0	0.0	0.0	0.0	0.0	trace	trace	0.5
Days With ≥ 1.0" Snow Depth	0	0	0	0	0	0	0	0	0	0	0	0	0

Cameron *Milam County*   Elevation: 360 ft.   Latitude: 30° 51' N   Longitude: 96° 58' W

	JAN	FEB	MAR	APR	MAY	JUN	JUL	AUG	SEP	OCT	NOV	DEC	YEAR
Mean Maximum Temp. (°F)	60.4	65.2	72.8	79.4	85.0	90.9	95.3	95.6	89.7	81.1	70.6	63.2	79.1
Mean Temp. (°F)	49.6	54.0	61.3	68.1	75.0	80.9	84.3	84.3	78.8	69.7	59.7	52.3	68.2
Mean Minimum Temp. (°F)	38.8	42.7	49.7	56.8	64.9	70.9	73.2	72.9	67.9	58.3	48.7	41.3	57.2
Extreme Maximum Temp. (°F)	90	98	98	98	100	105	104	106	106	97	90	85	106
Extreme Minimum Temp. (°F)	8	10	17	28	41	51	61	59	44	27	17	2	2
Days Maximum Temp. ≥ 90°F	0	0	0	1	6	20	28	28	18	4	0	0	105
Days Maximum Temp. ≤ 32°F	1	0	0	0	0	0	0	0	0	0	0	0	1
Days Minimum Temp. ≤ 32°F	9	5	2	0	0	0	0	0	0	0	2	6	24
Days Minimum Temp. ≤ 0°F	0	0	0	0	0	0	0	0	0	0	0	0	0
Heating Degree Days (base 65°F)	480	323	171	47	3	0	0	0	2	42	208	406	1,682
Cooling Degree Days (base 65°F)	10	21	63	152	331	494	615	618	435	203	60	19	3,021
Mean Precipitation (in.)	2.19	2.64	2.52	2.93	4.88	3.14	1.93	1.96	3.72	3.72	2.79	2.78	35.20
Days With ≥ 0.1" Precipitation	4	4	4	4	6	5	3	3	5	4	4	5	51
Days With ≥ 1.0" Precipitation	0	1	1	1	2	1	0	1	1	1	1	1	11
Mean Snowfall (in.)	0.1	trace	trace	0.0	0.0	0.0	0.0	0.0	0.0	0.0	0.0	0.0	0.1
Days With ≥ 1.0" Snow Depth	0	0	0	0	0	0	0	0	0	0	0	0	0

Camp Wood *Real County*   Elevation: 1,469 ft.   Latitude: 29° 41' N   Longitude: 100° 01' W

	JAN	FEB	MAR	APR	MAY	JUN	JUL	AUG	SEP	OCT	NOV	DEC	YEAR
Mean Maximum Temp. (°F)	61.5	66.2	73.4	80.0	86.0	91.1	94.3	94.1	89.3	*81.0*	70.7	63.5	*79.3*
Mean Temp. (°F)	47.4	51.8	59.3	66.3	73.9	79.6	82.1	81.7	76.9	*67.6*	57.1	49.5	*66.1*
Mean Minimum Temp. (°F)	33.3	37.4	45.1	52.6	61.8	68.0	70.0	69.2	64.5	*54.2*	43.4	35.4	*52.9*
Extreme Maximum Temp. (°F)	87	96	101	101	105	108	106	109	104	100	93	87	109
Extreme Minimum Temp. (°F)	10	5	16	25	38	45	55	59	41	*26*	15	5	*5*
Days Maximum Temp. ≥ 90°F	0	0	1	3	9	21	27	26	17	3	0	0	107
Days Maximum Temp. ≤ 32°F	0	0	0	0	0	0	0	0	0	0	0	0	0
Days Minimum Temp. ≤ 32°F	16	9	4	1	0	0	0	0	0	0	5	13	48
Days Minimum Temp. ≤ 0°F	0	0	0	0	0	0	0	0	0	0	0	0	0
Heating Degree Days (base 65°F)	540	370	207	70	5	0	0	0	6	*50*	256	476	*1,980*
Cooling Degree Days (base 65°F)	0	3	30	108	297	451	546	533	374	138	24	2	2,506
Mean Precipitation (in.)	1.12	1.47	1.54	2.43	3.15	3.68	2.11	3.25	3.03	3.24	1.65	1.36	28.03
Days With ≥ 0.1" Precipitation	2	3	3	3	5	5	3	3	4	4	3	3	41
Days With ≥ 1.0" Precipitation	0	0	0	1	1	1	1	1	1	1	0	0	7
Mean Snowfall (in.)	trace	0.2	0.0	0.0	0.0	0.0	0.0	0.0	0.0	0.0	trace	0.0	0.2
Days With ≥ 1.0" Snow Depth	0	0	0	0	0	0	0	0	0	0	0	0	0

Canadian *Hemphill County* Elevation: 2,349 ft. Latitude: 35° 55' N Longitude: 100° 23' W

	JAN	FEB	MAR	APR	MAY	JUN	JUL	AUG	SEP	OCT	NOV	DEC	YEAR
Mean Maximum Temp. (°F)	50.4	56.4	65.1	74.3	81.4	90.0	95.4	94.0	86.2	76.0	61.8	52.4	73.6
Mean Temp. (°F)	36.0	41.3	49.8	58.8	67.6	76.4	81.3	79.8	71.9	60.4	47.0	38.0	59.0
Mean Minimum Temp. (°F)	21.6	26.2	34.4	43.3	53.6	62.7	67.1	65.6	57.5	44.7	32.2	23.6	44.4
Extreme Maximum Temp. (°F)	85	89	95	99	105	112	109	108	107	101	89	83	112
Extreme Minimum Temp. (°F)	-11	-7	3	18	34	44	47	47	27	11	6	-13	-13
Days Maximum Temp. ≥ 90°F	0	0	0	2	6	16	26	24	13	3	0	0	90
Days Maximum Temp. ≤ 32°F	4	2	1	0	0	0	0	0	0	0	0	3	10
Days Minimum Temp. ≤ 32°F	28	21	13	3	0	0	0	0	0	3	15	26	109
Days Minimum Temp. ≤ 0°F	1	0	0	0	0	0	0	0	0	0	0	1	2
Heating Degree Days (base 65°F)	891	662	471	219	54	4	0	1	35	184	534	831	3,886
Cooling Degree Days (base 65°F)	0	0	4	38	140	339	509	473	249	43	2	0	1,797
Mean Precipitation (in.)	0.42	0.74	1.46	1.79	3.72	3.13	2.18	2.46	2.43	1.25	0.92	0.67	21.17
Days With ≥ 0.1" Precipitation	1	2	3	3	6	5	4	4	4	2	2	2	38
Days With ≥ 1.0" Precipitation	0	0	0	0	1	1	1	1	1	0	0	0	5
Mean Snowfall (in.)	*3.1*	na	2.1	0.6	0.0	0.0	0.0	0.0	0.0	0.1	1.2	*4.4*	na
Days With ≥ 1.0" Snow Depth	*1*	na	1	0	0	0	0	0	0	0	*0*	*1*	na

Candelaria *Presidio County* Elevation: 2,874 ft. Latitude: 30° 08' N Longitude: 104° 41' W

	JAN	FEB	MAR	APR	MAY	JUN	JUL	AUG	SEP	OCT	NOV	DEC	YEAR
Mean Maximum Temp. (°F)	66.2	72.7	80.6	88.5	95.7	101.6	99.6	97.2	92.5	85.3	74.3	66.8	85.1
Mean Temp. (°F)	48.8	53.8	60.4	67.8	75.7	83.1	83.5	81.4	76.7	67.4	55.8	49.4	67.0
Mean Minimum Temp. (°F)	31.3	35.0	40.1	47.1	55.7	64.5	67.4	65.5	61.0	49.5	37.3	31.9	48.9
Extreme Maximum Temp. (°F)	86	92	98	105	109	115	114	110	109	102	93	86	115
Extreme Minimum Temp. (°F)	9	14	17	21	34	46	56	42	37	22	15	6	6
Days Maximum Temp. ≥ 90°F	0	0	3	15	26	29	29	27	22	9	0	0	160
Days Maximum Temp. ≤ 32°F	0	0	0	0	0	0	0	0	0	0	0	0	0
Days Minimum Temp. ≤ 32°F	18	11	5	1	0	0	0	0	0	1	8	17	61
Days Minimum Temp. ≤ 0°F	0	0	0	0	0	0	0	0	0	0	0	0	0
Heating Degree Days (base 65°F)	495	311	160	41	1	0	0	0	5	42	274	478	1,807
Cooling Degree Days (base 65°F)	0	3	20	127	347	559	595	534	378	134	5	0	2,702
Mean Precipitation (in.)	0.32	0.34	0.24	0.39	0.74	1.81	2.14	2.60	2.48	1.18	0.36	0.51	13.11
Days With ≥ 0.1" Precipitation	1	1	1	1	2	3	5	5	5	2	1	1	28
Days With ≥ 1.0" Precipitation	0	0	0	0	0	0	0	1	1	0	0	0	2
Mean Snowfall (in.)	trace	trace	0.0	trace	0.0	0.0	0.0	0.0	0.0	0.0	trace	0.0	trace
Days With ≥ 1.0" Snow Depth	0	0	0	0	0	0	0	0	0	0	0	0	0

Canyon *Randall County* Elevation: 3,589 ft. Latitude: 34° 59' N Longitude: 101° 56' W

	JAN	FEB	MAR	APR	MAY	JUN	JUL	AUG	SEP	OCT	NOV	DEC	YEAR
Mean Maximum Temp. (°F)	52.0	57.6	65.5	73.9	81.7	90.1	92.5	90.0	84.3	75.2	61.8	53.6	73.2
Mean Temp. (°F)	37.8	42.8	49.9	58.2	67.1	75.8	79.2	77.2	70.6	60.3	47.6	39.8	58.9
Mean Minimum Temp. (°F)	23.5	27.9	34.3	42.5	52.4	61.5	66.0	64.3	57.0	45.4	33.3	25.9	44.5
Extreme Maximum Temp. (°F)	79	85	93	97	101	109	106	103	103	95	87	82	109
Extreme Minimum Temp. (°F)	-6	-11	7	19	27	43	51	51	29	15	4	-6	-11
Days Maximum Temp. ≥ 90°F	0	0	0	1	6	17	22	19	9	1	0	0	75
Days Maximum Temp. ≤ 32°F	3	2	0	0	0	0	0	0	0	0	0	2	7
Days Minimum Temp. ≤ 32°F	27	19	13	3	0	0	0	0	0	2	14	24	102
Days Minimum Temp. ≤ 0°F	0	0	0	0	0	0	0	0	0	0	0	0	0
Heating Degree Days (base 65°F)	838	621	464	223	58	4	0	0	36	177	516	773	3,710
Cooling Degree Days (base 65°F)	0	0	3	25	133	336	457	397	217	38	1	0	1,607
Mean Precipitation (in.)	0.46	0.53	0.92	1.09	2.91	2.88	2.39	2.90	1.99	1.74	0.65	0.61	19.07
Days With ≥ 0.1" Precipitation	2	1	2	3	5	5	4	4	3	3	2	2	36
Days With ≥ 1.0" Precipitation	0	0	0	0	1	1	1	1	1	1	0	0	6
Mean Snowfall (in.)	3.2	2.6	1.2	0.4	0.0	0.0	0.0	0.0	0.0	trace	1.3	2.7	11.4
Days With ≥ 1.0" Snow Depth	2	1	0	0	0	0	0	0	0	0	0	1	4

Carta Valley 4 W *Val Verde County* Elevation: 1,778 ft. Latitude: 29° 48' N Longitude: 100° 44' W

	JAN	FEB	MAR	APR	MAY	JUN	JUL	AUG	SEP	OCT	NOV	DEC	YEAR
Mean Maximum Temp. (°F)	*62.5*	*67.4*	75.0	81.9	87.3	91.8	94.4	94.3	89.6	80.9	*71.1*	64.3	*80.0*
Mean Temp. (°F)	*48.5*	*52.9*	60.8	68.0	75.3	80.5	82.9	82.7	77.9	68.3	*57.8*	50.3	*67.2*
Mean Minimum Temp. (°F)	*34.4*	*38.4*	46.4	54.2	63.3	69.2	71.4	71.0	66.3	55.8	*44.5*	36.3	*54.3*
Extreme Maximum Temp. (°F)	85	*94*	99	102	*106*	110	107	105	106	101	*93*	87	*110*
Extreme Minimum Temp. (°F)	9	*12*	16	25	*33*	44	*60*	59	41	25	*15*	4	*4*
Days Maximum Temp. ≥ 90°F	0	0	1	5	11	20	26	26	17	3	0	0	109
Days Maximum Temp. ≤ 32°F	0	0	0	0	0	0	0	0	0	0	0	0	0
Days Minimum Temp. ≤ 32°F	13	8	3	0	0	0	0	0	0	0	4	11	39
Days Minimum Temp. ≤ 0°F	0	0	0	0	0	0	0	0	0	0	0	0	0
Heating Degree Days (base 65°F)	*507*	*341*	171	50	4	0	0	0	4	49	*234*	450	*1,810*
Cooling Degree Days (base 65°F)	*1*	*4*	*40*	146	*354*	495	*587*	584	417	*162*	*26*	2	*2,818*
Mean Precipitation (in.)	0.84	1.12	1.32	1.90	2.80	2.40	2.66	2.91	2.30	2.10	1.17	0.76	22.28
Days With ≥ 0.1" Precipitation	2	2	2	3	4	3	3	3	4	3	2	2	33
Days With ≥ 1.0" Precipitation	0	0	0	1	1	1	1	1	1	0	0	0	6
Mean Snowfall (in.)	0.5	trace	0.0	0.0	0.0	0.0	0.0	0.0	0.0	0.0	trace	0.0	0.5
Days With ≥ 1.0" Snow Depth	0	0	0	0	0	0	0	0	0	0	0	0	0

Carthage *Panola County*   Elevation: 337 ft.   Latitude: 32° 08' N   Longitude: 94° 21' W

	JAN	FEB	MAR	APR	MAY	JUN	JUL	AUG	SEP	OCT	NOV	DEC	YEAR
Mean Maximum Temp. (°F)	56.7	62.3	70.0	77.0	83.5	90.0	93.9	93.7	88.1	78.8	67.6	60.0	76.8
Mean Temp. (°F)	45.5	50.2	57.6	64.6	72.1	78.9	82.4	81.7	76.0	65.7	55.5	48.5	64.9
Mean Minimum Temp. (°F)	34.3	38.0	45.2	52.0	60.7	67.6	70.8	69.6	63.8	52.6	43.3	36.9	52.9
Extreme Maximum Temp. (°F)	84	90	92	93	98	101	106	108	105	95	88	82	108
Extreme Minimum Temp. (°F)	5	10	18	28	40	45	56	50	38	26	12	1	1
Days Maximum Temp. ≥ 90°F	0	0	0	0	4	18	27	26	14	2	0	0	91
Days Maximum Temp. ≤ 32°F	1	0	0	0	0	0	0	0	0	0	0	1	2
Days Minimum Temp. ≤ 32°F	15	9	3	0	0	0	0	0	0	0	4	12	43
Days Minimum Temp. ≤ 0°F	0	0	0	0	0	0	0	0	0	0	0	0	0
Heating Degree Days (base 65°F)	601	419	254	95	11	0	0	0	8	87	302	512	2,289
Cooling Degree Days (base 65°F)	2	7	26	79	229	420	547	530	336	106	20	7	2,309
Mean Precipitation (in.)	4.75	4.03	3.86	4.28	4.82	4.79	3.40	2.95	3.88	4.88	4.57	4.87	51.08
Days With ≥ 0.1" Precipitation	7	6	6	5	6	6	5	4	5	5	6	6	67
Days With ≥ 1.0" Precipitation	1	2	1	1	2	1	1	1	1	2	2	2	17
Mean Snowfall (in.)	0.7	0.3	trace	trace	0.0	0.0	0.0	0.0	0.0	0.0	trace	0.2	1.2
Days With ≥ 1.0" Snow Depth	0	0	0	0	0	0	0	0	0	0	0	0	0

Center *Shelby County*   Elevation: 324 ft.   Latitude: 31° 48' N   Longitude: 94° 10' W

	JAN	FEB	MAR	APR	MAY	JUN	JUL	AUG	SEP	OCT	NOV	DEC	YEAR
Mean Maximum Temp. (°F)	56.7	62.1	69.3	76.5	83.2	89.7	93.7	93.6	88.0	78.7	67.9	60.3	76.7
Mean Temp. (°F)	45.2	49.5	56.4	63.6	71.5	78.4	82.1	81.3	75.5	64.9	55.0	48.2	64.3
Mean Minimum Temp. (°F)	33.7	36.9	43.4	50.7	59.7	66.9	70.4	68.9	63.0	51.1	42.0	35.9	51.9
Extreme Maximum Temp. (°F)	82	90	89	94	97	101	108	108	105	94	89	83	108
Extreme Minimum Temp. (°F)	5	12	15	28	40	45	55	52	40	26	12	2	2
Days Maximum Temp. ≥ 90°F	0	0	0	0	4	18	26	25	15	2	0	0	90
Days Maximum Temp. ≤ 32°F	1	0	0	0	0	0	0	0	0	0	0	0	1
Days Minimum Temp. ≤ 32°F	15	11	4	1	0	0	0	0	0	1	6	14	52
Days Minimum Temp. ≤ 0°F	0	0	0	0	0	0	0	0	0	0	0	0	0
Heating Degree Days (base 65°F)	610	438	284	112	14	0	0	0	10	100	317	523	2,408
Cooling Degree Days (base 65°F)	3	8	27	79	234	422	555	536	348	111	25	9	2,357
Mean Precipitation (in.)	5.03	4.26	4.10	4.18	4.90	4.86	3.17	3.84	4.19	4.83	4.32	4.89	52.57
Days With ≥ 0.1" Precipitation	7	6	6	5	7	6	5	5	6	5	6	7	71
Days With ≥ 1.0" Precipitation	2	1	1	1	2	2	1	1	1	2	2	2	18
Mean Snowfall (in.)	0.8	0.1	trace	0.0	0.0	0.0	0.0	0.0	0.0	0.0	0.1	trace	1.0
Days With ≥ 1.0" Snow Depth	1	0	0	0	0	0	0	0	0	0	0	0	1

Centerville *Leon County*   Elevation: 318 ft.   Latitude: 31° 15' N   Longitude: 95° 58' W

	JAN	FEB	MAR	APR	MAY	JUN	JUL	AUG	SEP	OCT	NOV	DEC	YEAR
Mean Maximum Temp. (°F)	57.6	62.5	70.2	77.2	83.6	90.1	94.3	94.6	88.8	79.6	68.6	61.0	77.3
Mean Temp. (°F)	46.0	50.3	57.9	65.0	72.4	79.1	82.7	82.3	76.6	66.4	56.3	49.1	65.3
Mean Minimum Temp. (°F)	34.3	38.1	45.4	52.7	61.2	68.1	71.0	69.9	64.5	53.1	43.9	37.1	53.3
Extreme Maximum Temp. (°F)	86	94	91	93	98	106	106	107	108	96	88	83	108
Extreme Minimum Temp. (°F)	5	12	17	26	39	48	55	52	42	27	15	1	1
Days Maximum Temp. ≥ 90°F	0	0	0	1	4	18	27	27	16	3	0	0	96
Days Maximum Temp. ≤ 32°F	1	0	0	0	0	0	0	0	0	0	0	0	1
Days Minimum Temp. ≤ 32°F	15	9	3	1	0	0	0	0	0	0	5	12	45
Days Minimum Temp. ≤ 0°F	0	0	0	0	0	0	0	0	0	0	0	0	0
Heating Degree Days (base 65°F)	588	415	249	91	11	0	0	0	7	78	285	497	2,221
Cooling Degree Days (base 65°F)	3	8	33	94	253	435	561	557	370	129	32	10	2,485
Mean Precipitation (in.)	3.39	3.25	3.43	3.37	4.58	4.09	2.50	2.63	3.69	4.93	3.40	3.51	42.77
Days With ≥ 0.1" Precipitation	6	5	5	5	6	6	4	4	5	5	5	5	61
Days With ≥ 1.0" Precipitation	1	1	1	1	2	1	1	1	1	2	1	1	14
Mean Snowfall (in.)	0.4	0.2	trace	0.0	0.0	0.0	0.0	0.0	0.0	0.0	trace	0.0	0.6
Days With ≥ 1.0" Snow Depth	0	0	0	0	0	0	0	0	0	0	0	0	0

Chapman Ranch *Nueces County*   Elevation: 22 ft.   Latitude: 27° 35' N   Longitude: 97° 27' W

	JAN	FEB	MAR	APR	MAY	JUN	JUL	AUG	SEP	OCT	NOV	DEC	YEAR
Mean Maximum Temp. (°F)	66.7	70.2	76.2	81.0	85.2	89.6	92.2	92.5	89.6	83.5	75.4	69.1	80.9
Mean Temp. (°F)	56.8	60.2	66.4	72.1	77.4	81.6	83.5	83.6	80.7	74.1	65.7	59.1	71.8
Mean Minimum Temp. (°F)	46.8	50.3	56.5	63.2	69.6	73.5	74.7	74.6	71.8	64.5	56.0	49.1	62.6
Extreme Maximum Temp. (°F)	91	94	102	98	102	98	99	101	101	97	96	89	102
Extreme Minimum Temp. (°F)	18	23	25	34	48	59	66	65	51	27	27	12	12
Days Maximum Temp. ≥ 90°F	0	0	1	1	3	16	27	26	17	3	0	0	94
Days Maximum Temp. ≤ 32°F	0	0	0	0	0	0	0	0	0	0	0	0	0
Days Minimum Temp. ≤ 32°F	3	1	0	0	0	0	0	0	0	0	0	2	6
Days Minimum Temp. ≤ 0°F	0	0	0	0	0	0	0	0	0	0	0	0	0
Heating Degree Days (base 65°F)	278	171	73	14	0	0	0	0	0	10	93	226	865
Cooling Degree Days (base 65°F)	26	45	110	228	401	515	590	590	488	299	127	50	3,469
Mean Precipitation (in.)	1.61	1.86	1.52	2.27	3.50	3.45	1.84	3.57	5.20	4.46	1.65	1.30	32.23
Days With ≥ 0.1" Precipitation	4	3	2	3	4	4	2	3	6	4	3	2	40
Days With ≥ 1.0" Precipitation	0	1	0	1	1	1	1	1	2	1	0	0	9
Mean Snowfall (in.)	0.0	trace	0.0	0.0	0.0	0.0	0.0	0.0	0.0	0.0	0.0	0.0	trace
Days With ≥ 1.0" Snow Depth	0	0	0	0	0	0	0	0	0	0	0	0	0

Charlotte 5 NNW *Atascosa County* Elevation: 439 ft. Latitude: 28° 56' N Longitude: 98° 45' W

	JAN	FEB	MAR	APR	MAY	JUN	JUL	AUG	SEP	OCT	NOV	DEC	YEAR
Mean Maximum Temp. (°F)	66.5	71.4	78.8	84.7	89.2	93.9	96.7	96.9	92.4	85.3	75.8	68.7	83.4
Mean Temp. (°F)	53.8	57.9	65.2	71.6	77.8	82.6	84.6	84.6	80.6	72.7	63.3	56.2	70.9
Mean Minimum Temp. (°F)	41.1	44.5	51.7	58.5	66.4	71.3	72.5	72.2	68.7	60.0	50.7	43.6	58.4
Extreme Maximum Temp. (°F)	93	99	100	107	104	109	105	105	105	102	97	90	109
Extreme Minimum Temp. (°F)	15	16	19	28	43	54	59	62	44	27	20	6	6
Days Maximum Temp. ≥ 90°F	0	1	2	7	15	25	29	29	22	9	1	0	140
Days Maximum Temp. ≤ 32°F	0	0	0	0	0	0	0	0	0	0	0	0	0
Days Minimum Temp. ≤ 32°F	7	4	1	0	0	0	0	0	0	0	0	0	0
Days Minimum Temp. ≤ 0°F	0	0	0	0	0	0	0	0	0	0	0	0	0
Heating Degree Days (base 65°F)	356	226	99	24	1	0	0	0	1	20	137	297	1,161
Cooling Degree Days (base 65°F)	16	35	104	229	422	553	634	635	483	274	97	33	3,515
Mean Precipitation (in.)	1.25	1.60	1.29	2.31	3.64	3.26	1.31	2.65	2.97	3.14	1.61	1.39	26.42
Days With ≥ 0.1" Precipitation	3	3	3	3	4	4	3	3	4	4	3	3	40
Days With ≥ 1.0" Precipitation	0	0	0	1	1	1	0	1	1	1	0	0	6
Mean Snowfall (in.)	0.0	trace	0.0	0.0	0.0	0.0	0.0	0.0	0.0	trace	0.0	0.0	trace
Days With ≥ 1.0" Snow Depth	0	0	0	0	0	0	0	0	0	0	0	0	0

Childress Municipal Airport *Childress County* Elevation: 1,948 ft. Latitude: 34° 26' N Longitude: 100° 17' W

	JAN	FEB	MAR	APR	MAY	JUN	JUL	AUG	SEP	OCT	NOV	DEC	YEAR
Mean Maximum Temp. (°F)	51.2	57.0	66.0	75.6	82.6	90.8	94.9	93.6	85.4	75.7	62.7	53.8	74.1
Mean Temp. (°F)	38.5	43.8	52.2	61.6	70.0	78.4	82.7	81.3	73.4	62.6	50.1	41.4	61.3
Mean Minimum Temp. (°F)	25.7	30.5	38.4	47.5	57.3	65.9	70.4	69.0	61.3	49.5	37.5	29.0	48.5
Extreme Maximum Temp. (°F)	84	93	100	102	107	117	109	108	106	103	89	91	117
Extreme Minimum Temp. (°F)	0	-5	13	23	37	50	57	55	34	21	13	-5	-5
Days Maximum Temp. ≥ 90°F	0	0	1	3	7	18	26	24	13	2	0	0	94
Days Maximum Temp. ≤ 32°F	4	2	0	0	0	0	0	0	0	0	0	2	8
Days Minimum Temp. ≤ 32°F	24	16	7	1	0	0	0	0	0	1	9	21	79
Days Minimum Temp. ≤ 0°F	0	0	0	0	0	0	0	0	0	0	0	0	0
Heating Degree Days (base 65°F)	815	593	402	158	33	2	0	0	27	138	445	723	3,336
Cooling Degree Days (base 65°F)	0	2	13	63	196	400	555	*536*	290	69	*6*	0	*2,130*
Mean Precipitation (in.)	0.55	0.89	1.31	1.87	3.64	3.46	2.10	2.18	2.63	2.00	1.04	0.84	22.51
Days With ≥ 0.1" Precipitation	2	3	3	4	6	5	4	4	4	3	2	2	42
Days With ≥ 1.0" Precipitation	0	0	0	0	1	1	0	0	1	0	0	0	3
Mean Snowfall (in.)	2.4	1.9	0.5	0.2	trace	trace	0.0	trace	trace	0.1	*1.1*	2.1	*8.3*
Days With ≥ 1.0" Snow Depth	2	2	0	0	0	0	0	0	0	0	*0*	2	6

Chisos Basin *Brewster County* Elevation: 5,298 ft. Latitude: 29° 16' N Longitude: 103° 18' W

	JAN	FEB	MAR	APR	MAY	JUN	JUL	AUG	SEP	OCT	NOV	DEC	YEAR
Mean Maximum Temp. (°F)	57.4	61.2	67.9	74.8	81.8	85.6	84.1	82.5	78.6	72.8	65.0	59.2	72.6
Mean Temp. (°F)	46.7	50.0	55.9	62.6	70.0	74.3	73.9	72.6	68.7	62.2	54.3	48.6	61.7
Mean Minimum Temp. (°F)	35.9	38.9	43.9	50.4	58.2	63.0	63.7	62.6	58.7	51.6	43.4	38.0	50.7
Extreme Maximum Temp. (°F)	77	84	96	94	98	103	101	99	96	94	82	87	103
Extreme Minimum Temp. (°F)	9	10	17	25	37	45	56	52	34	19	13	4	4
Days Maximum Temp. ≥ 90°F	0	0	0	0	3	8	4	1	1	0	0	0	17
Days Maximum Temp. ≤ 32°F	1	0	0	0	0	0	0	0	0	0	0	0	1
Days Minimum Temp. ≤ 32°F	10	6	3	1	0	0	0	0	0	0	4	8	32
Days Minimum Temp. ≤ 0°F	0	0	0	0	0	0	0	0	0	0	0	0	0
Heating Degree Days (base 65°F)	561	418	284	125	22	3	0	1	28	121	321	500	2,384
Cooling Degree Days (base 65°F)	0	1	10	54	186	294	292	252	145	39	5	0	1,278
Mean Precipitation (in.)	0.56	0.72	0.40	0.61	1.61	2.37	3.52	3.81	3.05	1.65	0.57	0.58	19.45
Days With ≥ 0.1" Precipitation	2	1	1	2	3	5	6	6	5	3	1	1	36
Days With ≥ 1.0" Precipitation	0	0	0	0	0	0	1	1	1	0	0	0	3
Mean Snowfall (in.)	0.9	0.2	trace	0.1	0.0	0.0	0.0	0.0	0.0	0.0	0.3	0.3	1.8
Days With ≥ 1.0" Snow Depth	0	0	0	0	0	0	0	0	0	0	0	0	0

Clarendon Municipal Airport *Donley County* Elevation: 2,870 ft. Latitude: 34° 57' N Longitude: 100° 56' W

	JAN	FEB	MAR	APR	MAY	JUN	JUL	AUG	SEP	OCT	NOV	DEC	YEAR
Mean Maximum Temp. (°F)	50.5	55.8	63.8	72.9	80.6	89.0	94.1	91.9	84.5	74.6	61.6	52.9	72.7
Mean Temp. (°F)	36.4	41.3	48.8	57.7	66.7	75.4	80.1	78.2	70.7	59.5	47.3	38.9	58.4
Mean Minimum Temp. (°F)	22.3	26.6	33.7	42.5	52.7	61.7	66.1	64.4	56.9	44.4	32.9	24.8	44.1
Extreme Maximum Temp. (°F)	84	89	98	100	105	112	109	107	106	100	92	83	112
Extreme Minimum Temp. (°F)	-3	-7	2	21	31	42	48	48	30	17	10	-11	-11
Days Maximum Temp. ≥ 90°F	0	0	0	1	5	15	24	21	11	2	0	0	79
Days Maximum Temp. ≤ 32°F	4	3	1	0	0	0	0	0	0	0	1	2	11
Days Minimum Temp. ≤ 32°F	28	21	13	3	0	0	0	0	0	2	15	26	108
Days Minimum Temp. ≤ 0°F	0	0	0	0	0	0	0	0	0	0	0	0	0
Heating Degree Days (base 65°F)	879	664	499	243	66	5	0	0	43	203	528	804	3,934
Cooling Degree Days (base 65°F)	0	0	4	27	127	319	481	430	228	38	3	0	1,657
Mean Precipitation (in.)	0.63	0.83	1.37	2.25	3.58	3.38	2.36	2.81	2.74	1.63	0.93	0.81	23.32
Days With ≥ 0.1" Precipitation	2	2	3	3	5	5	4	5	4	3	2	2	40
Days With ≥ 1.0" Precipitation	0	0	0	1	1	1	1	1	1	0	0	0	6
Mean Snowfall (in.)	2.2	*1.7*	1.1	0.3	0.0	0.0	0.0	0.0	0.0	trace	1.1	2.5	*8.9*
Days With ≥ 1.0" Snow Depth	1	2	0	0	0	0	0	0	0	0	0	1	4

Clarksville 2 NE *Red River County*   Elevation: 433 ft.   Latitude: 33° 37' N   Longitude: 95° 04' W

	JAN	FEB	MAR	APR	MAY	JUN	JUL	AUG	SEP	OCT	NOV	DEC	YEAR
Mean Maximum Temp. (°F)	52.1	57.9	65.8	74.0	80.4	87.8	92.4	92.6	86.0	76.2	64.4	55.6	73.8
Mean Temp. (°F)	40.8	45.8	53.6	61.7	69.6	77.4	81.4	81.0	74.4	63.4	52.4	44.2	62.1
Mean Minimum Temp. (°F)	29.3	33.7	41.3	49.3	58.8	66.8	70.3	69.3	62.7	50.5	40.4	32.8	50.4
Extreme Maximum Temp. (°F)	81	90	88	92	97	101	106	109	108	96	85	81	109
Extreme Minimum Temp. (°F)	1	3	12	26	37	45	55	52	37	23	8	2	1
Days Maximum Temp. ≥ 90°F	0	0	0	0	1	12	23	23	11	1	0	0	71
Days Maximum Temp. ≤ 32°F	2	1	0	0	0	0	0	0	0	0	0	1	4
Days Minimum Temp. ≤ 32°F	21	14	6	1	0	0	0	0	0	1	7	15	65
Days Minimum Temp. ≤ 0°F	0	0	0	0	0	0	0	0	0	0	0	0	0
Heating Degree Days (base 65°F)	747	538	363	142	26	1	0	0	18	122	378	640	2,975
Cooling Degree Days (base 65°F)	1	2	13	45	178	388	523	520	311	77	9	2	2,069
Mean Precipitation (in.)	2.58	3.24	4.51	4.02	5.26	3.68	3.23	2.10	3.85	5.10	4.91	4.35	46.83
Days With ≥ 0.1" Precipitation	5	5	6	5	7	5	4	3	5	5	5	6	61
Days With ≥ 1.0" Precipitation	1	1	1	1	2	1	1	1	1	2	2	1	15
Mean Snowfall (in.)	trace	0.2	trace	trace	0.0	0.0	0.0	0.0	0.0	0.0	trace	trace	0.2
Days With ≥ 1.0" Snow Depth	0	0	0	0	0	0	0	0	0	0	0	0	0

Claude *Armstrong County*   Elevation: 3,395 ft.   Latitude: 35° 07' N   Longitude: 101° 22' W

	JAN	FEB	MAR	APR	MAY	JUN	JUL	AUG	SEP	OCT	NOV	DEC	YEAR
Mean Maximum Temp. (°F)	48.5	53.1	61.6	70.4	78.3	86.9	91.0	89.0	81.9	72.0	58.9	50.4	70.2
Mean Temp. (°F)	34.6	38.8	46.7	55.2	64.3	73.4	77.7	76.1	69.0	57.7	45.1	36.8	56.3
Mean Minimum Temp. (°F)	20.8	24.9	31.5	40.0	50.1	59.8	64.3	63.1	55.8	43.4	31.2	23.2	42.3
Extreme Maximum Temp. (°F)	80	85	92	98	101	108	107	104	102	97	90	79	108
Extreme Minimum Temp. (°F)	-6	-7	3	16	30	42	50	50	29	10	5	-7	-7
Days Maximum Temp. ≥ 90°F	0	0	0	1	3	12	19	17	7	1	0	0	60
Days Maximum Temp. ≤ 32°F	5	3	1	0	0	0	0	0	0	0	1	4	14
Days Minimum Temp. ≤ 32°F	29	23	17	6	0	0	0	0	0	3	16	27	121
Days Minimum Temp. ≤ 0°F	0	1	0	0	0	0	0	0	0	0	0	1	2
Heating Degree Days (base 65°F)	933	731	561	305	100	11	1	1	52	244	590	867	4,396
Cooling Degree Days (base 65°F)	0	0	1	17	86	265	406	361	180	23	1	0	1,340
Mean Precipitation (in.)	0.49	0.58	1.24	1.58	3.33	3.23	3.05	3.07	2.39	1.74	0.82	0.60	22.12
Days With ≥ 0.1" Precipitation	1	2	3	3	5	5	4	5	4	3	2	2	39
Days With ≥ 1.0" Precipitation	0	0	0	0	1	1	1	1	1	0	0	0	5
Mean Snowfall (in.)	3.1	3.3	1.4	0.4	0.0	0.0	0.0	0.0	trace	0.1	0.9	2.8	12.0
Days With ≥ 1.0" Snow Depth	2	2	0	0	0	0	0	0	0	0	0	3	8

Cleburne *Johnson County*   Elevation: 780 ft.   Latitude: 32° 20' N   Longitude: 97° 24' W

	JAN	FEB	MAR	APR	MAY	JUN	JUL	AUG	SEP	OCT	NOV	DEC	YEAR
Mean Maximum Temp. (°F)	57.4	63.0	70.9	78.6	85.0	92.2	97.0	96.8	89.6	80.2	67.9	60.0	78.2
Mean Temp. (°F)	45.6	50.6	58.3	66.0	73.5	80.5	84.5	84.1	77.7	67.6	56.3	48.3	66.1
Mean Minimum Temp. (°F)	33.7	38.2	45.7	53.3	62.0	68.8	71.9	71.4	65.7	55.0	44.6	36.6	53.9
Extreme Maximum Temp. (°F)	85	98	101	99	103	113	111	111	108	102	91	84	113
Extreme Minimum Temp. (°F)	5	7	12	28	40	51	57	53	40	22	13	-5	-5
Days Maximum Temp. ≥ 90°F	0	0	0	1	7	21	29	27	17	4	0	0	106
Days Maximum Temp. ≤ 32°F	1	0	0	0	0	0	0	0	0	0	0	1	2
Days Minimum Temp. ≤ 32°F	15	8	3	0	0	0	0	0	0	0	4	11	41
Days Minimum Temp. ≤ 0°F	0	0	0	0	0	0	0	0	0	0	0	0	0
Heating Degree Days (base 65°F)	597	406	236	74	8	0	0	0	8	64	283	516	2,192
Cooling Degree Days (base 65°F)	2	8	34	112	288	474	617	613	397	151	29	5	2,730
Mean Precipitation (in.)	1.85	2.40	3.06	3.63	5.10	3.41	2.18	2.46	3.11	3.86	2.38	2.49	35.93
Days With ≥ 0.1" Precipitation	4	4	5	4	6	5	3	3	4	5	4	4	51
Days With ≥ 1.0" Precipitation	0	1	1	1	2	1	1	1	1	1	1	1	12
Mean Snowfall (in.)	0.7	0.6	0.2	0.0	0.0	0.0	0.0	0.0	0.0	trace	0.2	0.2	1.9
Days With ≥ 1.0" Snow Depth	0	0	0	0	0	0	0	0	0	0	0	0	0

Cleveland *Liberty County*   Elevation: 193 ft.   Latitude: 30° 22' N   Longitude: 95° 06' W

	JAN	FEB	MAR	APR	MAY	JUN	JUL	AUG	SEP	OCT	NOV	DEC	YEAR
Mean Maximum Temp. (°F)	59.5	64.3	71.6	77.4	83.7	89.2	92.4	92.8	88.2	79.5	69.0	62.3	77.5
Mean Temp. (°F)	48.7	52.6	59.8	66.2	73.4	79.2	81.9	81.9	77.3	67.7	57.9	51.3	66.5
Mean Minimum Temp. (°F)	38.0	40.8	48.0	54.9	63.0	69.2	71.4	70.8	66.3	55.8	46.7	40.2	55.4
Extreme Maximum Temp. (°F)	82	90	91	92	98	101	105	107	102	95	87	84	107
Extreme Minimum Temp. (°F)	11	16	20	29	43	50	59	54	46	28	19	5	5
Days Maximum Temp. ≥ 90°F	0	0	0	0	4	16	25	25	14	2	0	0	86
Days Maximum Temp. ≤ 32°F	0	0	0	0	0	0	0	0	0	0	0	0	0
Days Minimum Temp. ≤ 32°F	11	6	2	0	0	0	0	0	0	0	3	9	31
Days Minimum Temp. ≤ 0°F	0	0	0	0	0	0	0	0	0	0	0	0	0
Heating Degree Days (base 65°F)	506	358	197	67	6	0	0	0	3	61	247	433	1,878
Cooling Degree Days (base 65°F)	6	15	45	106	282	444	541	544	382	156	41	16	2,578
Mean Precipitation (in.)	4.79	3.85	4.11	3.73	5.84	5.27	3.67	3.35	4.79	5.52	4.87	4.78	54.57
Days With ≥ 0.1" Precipitation	7	6	6	5	6	7	6	5	6	6	6	7	73
Days With ≥ 1.0" Precipitation	1	1	1	1	2	2	1	1	1	2	2	2	17
Mean Snowfall (in.)	0.5	0.2	0.0	0.0	0.0	0.0	0.0	0.0	0.0	0.0	trace	trace	0.7
Days With ≥ 1.0" Snow Depth	0	0	0	0	0	0	0	0	0	0	0	0	0

Coldspring 5 SSW *San Jacinto County* Elevation: 354 ft. Latitude: 30° 32' N Longitude: 95° 09' W

	JAN	FEB	MAR	APR	MAY	JUN	JUL	AUG	SEP	OCT	NOV	DEC	YEAR
Mean Maximum Temp. (°F)	59.3	63.8	70.9	77.3	83.8	89.9	93.2	93.6	88.6	80.5	69.9	62.6	77.8
Mean Temp. (°F)	48.2	51.8	58.8	65.5	72.9	79.1	82.0	81.7	77.1	67.6	58.1	51.1	66.2
Mean Minimum Temp. (°F)	37.1	39.9	46.7	53.7	61.9	68.3	70.7	69.8	65.6	54.6	46.2	39.6	54.5
Extreme Maximum Temp. (°F)	83	90	90	94	99	103	105	110	106	96	89	83	110
Extreme Minimum Temp. (°F)	9	14	19	26	40	49	58	53	44	25	16	3	3
Days Maximum Temp. ≥ 90°F	0	0	0	0	4	17	26	25	15	3	0	0	90
Days Maximum Temp. ≤ 32°F	1	0	0	0	0	0	0	0	0	0	0	0	1
Days Minimum Temp. ≤ 32°F	12	8	3	0	0	0	0	0	0	0	3	9	35
Days Minimum Temp. ≤ 0°F	0	0	0	0	0	0	0	0	0	0	0	0	0
Heating Degree Days (base 65°F)	521	377	222	80	8	0	0	0	4	60	243	438	1,953
Cooling Degree Days (base 65°F)	6	13	39	104	271	*445*	543	548	393	158	46	16	*2,582*
Mean Precipitation (in.)	4.66	3.47	3.70	3.72	5.39	5.75	2.84	3.48	4.52	4.52	4.60	4.75	51.40
Days With ≥ 0.1" Precipitation	7	5	6	4	6	6	5	6	6	5	6	7	69
Days With ≥ 1.0" Precipitation	1	1	1	1	2	2	1	1	1	2	1	2	16
Mean Snowfall (in.)	0.1	trace	0.0	0.0	0.0	0.0	0.0	0.0	0.0	0.0	trace	trace	0.1
Days With ≥ 1.0" Snow Depth	0	0	0	0	0	0	0	0	0	0	0	0	0

Coleman *Coleman County* Elevation: 1,725 ft. Latitude: 32° 08' N Longitude: 99° 45' W

	JAN	FEB	MAR	APR	MAY	JUN	JUL	AUG	SEP	OCT	NOV	DEC	YEAR
Mean Maximum Temp. (°F)	58.5	63.6	71.7	79.4	85.4	91.3	95.2	94.5	88.5	80.0	68.1	60.4	78.1
Mean Temp. (°F)	45.7	50.5	57.9	65.7	72.9	79.1	82.5	81.8	75.8	66.7	55.5	48.0	65.2
Mean Minimum Temp. (°F)	32.9	37.2	44.1	51.8	60.2	66.8	69.7	69.0	63.1	53.4	42.8	35.4	52.2
Extreme Maximum Temp. (°F)	88	99	96	99	104	107	108	110	107	101	91	85	110
Extreme Minimum Temp. (°F)	3	8	9	26	39	50	54	55	36	25	17	-4	-4
Days Maximum Temp. ≥ 90°F	0	0	1	3	9	20	27	26	15	3	0	0	104
Days Maximum Temp. ≤ 32°F	1	1	0	0	0	0	0	0	0	0	0	1	3
Days Minimum Temp. ≤ 32°F	15	8	4	0	0	0	0	0	0	0	5	12	44
Days Minimum Temp. ≤ 0°F	0	0	0	0	0	0	0	0	0	0	0	0	0
Heating Degree Days (base 65°F)	591	410	246	81	11	0	0	0	10	66	297	523	2,235
Cooling Degree Days (base 65°F)	1	6	30	105	265	423	552	543	342	127	18	1	2,413
Mean Precipitation (in.)	1.03	1.82	1.88	2.22	4.20	3.65	1.77	2.63	3.29	2.94	1.41	1.44	28.28
Days With ≥ 0.1" Precipitation	3	3	3	3	6	4	3	4	4	4	3	3	43
Days With ≥ 1.0" Precipitation	0	1	0	1	1	1	0	1	1	1	0	0	7
Mean Snowfall (in.)	1.0	0.7	0.3	trace	0.0	0.0	0.0	0.0	0.0	trace	0.2	0.4	2.6
Days With ≥ 1.0" Snow Depth	0	*0*	0	0	0	0	0	0	0	0	0	0	*0*

College Station Easterwood *Brazos County* Elevation: 311 ft. Latitude: 30° 35' N Longitude: 96° 22' W

	JAN	FEB	MAR	APR	MAY	JUN	JUL	AUG	SEP	OCT	NOV	DEC	YEAR
Mean Maximum Temp. (°F)	58.8	*63.9*	71.6	78.3	84.4	90.8	94.3	95.0	89.3	80.8	70.1	62.2	*78.3*
Mean Temp. (°F)	49.0	*53.3*	60.9	67.7	74.7	81.1	83.9	84.1	78.9	69.7	59.5	52.1	*67.9*
Mean Minimum Temp. (°F)	39.0	*42.7*	50.1	57.1	65.0	71.3	73.5	73.2	68.4	58.6	48.9	41.8	*57.5*
Extreme Maximum Temp. (°F)	86	*99*	94	94	100	104	105	107	106	96	89	86	*107*
Extreme Minimum Temp. (°F)	7	*14*	19	28	45	53	63	60	44	29	19	2	*2*
Days Maximum Temp. ≥ 90°F	0	*0*	0	1	5	21	27	28	17	3	0	0	*102*
Days Maximum Temp. ≤ 32°F	0	*0*	0	0	0	0	0	0	0	0	0	0	*0*
Days Minimum Temp. ≤ 32°F	8	*4*	1	0	0	0	0	0	0	0	2	6	*21*
Days Minimum Temp. ≤ 0°F	0	*0*	0	0	0	0	0	0	0	0	0	0	*0*
Heating Degree Days (base 65°F)	499	*341*	176	52	3	0	0	0	2	41	212	411	*1,737*
Cooling Degree Days (base 65°F)	7	*20*	54	147	327	503	606	622	444	206	59	19	*3,014*
Mean Precipitation (in.)	3.20	*2.53*	2.86	3.09	5.16	3.82	2.03	2.62	4.02	4.01	2.86	3.06	*39.26*
Days With ≥ 0.1" Precipitation	5	*4*	5	4	6	5	3	4	5	5	4	5	*55*
Days With ≥ 1.0" Precipitation	1	*1*	1	1	2	1	1	1	1	1	1	1	*13*
Mean Snowfall (in.)	0.3	*0.1*	trace	trace	trace	0.0	trace	0.0	0.0	trace	trace	trace	*0.4*
Days With ≥ 1.0" Snow Depth	0	*0*	0	0	0	0	0	0	0	0	0	0	*0*

Columbus *Colorado County* Elevation: 196 ft. Latitude: 29° 43' N Longitude: 96° 32' W

	JAN	FEB	MAR	APR	MAY	JUN	JUL	AUG	SEP	OCT	NOV	DEC	YEAR
Mean Maximum Temp. (°F)	62.6	67.0	74.5	80.2	86.0	91.9	95.4	96.7	92.1	84.2	73.6	65.8	80.9
Mean Temp. (°F)	49.7	53.6	61.1	67.6	74.5	80.3	82.7	82.9	78.1	69.1	59.6	52.3	67.6
Mean Minimum Temp. (°F)	36.6	40.1	47.6	54.9	63.0	68.7	70.0	69.1	64.1	54.0	45.6	38.8	54.4
Extreme Maximum Temp. (°F)	87	97	93	95	102	106	107	109	107	100	93	88	109
Extreme Minimum Temp. (°F)	10	13	18	28	40	49	59	46	40	25	18	4	4
Days Maximum Temp. ≥ 90°F	0	0	1	2	9	23	29	29	22	8	0	0	123
Days Maximum Temp. ≤ 32°F	0	0	0	0	0	0	0	0	0	0	0	0	0
Days Minimum Temp. ≤ 32°F	12	7	2	0	0	0	0	0	0	0	4	10	35
Days Minimum Temp. ≤ 0°F	0	0	0	0	0	0	0	0	0	0	0	0	0
Heating Degree Days (base 65°F)	478	333	173	56	5	0	0	0	3	46	213	406	1,713
Cooling Degree Days (base 65°F)	9	19	58	140	319	473	558	570	417	189	61	21	2,834
Mean Precipitation (in.)	3.57	2.83	3.04	3.53	5.70	4.78	2.60	3.06	4.22	4.12	3.68	3.16	44.29
Days With ≥ 0.1" Precipitation	6	5	5	5	7	6	4	5	5	5	5	6	64
Days With ≥ 1.0" Precipitation	1	1	1	1	2	2	1	1	1	1	1	1	14
Mean Snowfall (in.)	trace	0.0	trace	0.0	0.0	0.0	0.0	0.0	0.0	0.0	trace	0.0	trace
Days With ≥ 1.0" Snow Depth	0	0	0	0	0	0	0	0	0	0	0	0	0

Conroe *Montgomery County*   Elevation: 242 ft.   Latitude: 30° 20' N   Longitude: 95° 29' W

	JAN	FEB	MAR	APR	MAY	JUN	JUL	AUG	SEP	OCT	NOV	DEC	YEAR
Mean Maximum Temp. (°F)	60.2	64.5	72.3	78.5	84.8	90.6	94.1	94.2	89.1	80.9	70.8	62.9	78.6
Mean Temp. (°F)	49.5	53.3	60.7	67.3	74.4	80.5	83.4	83.2	78.3	68.9	59.5	52.1	67.6
Mean Minimum Temp. (°F)	38.7	42.0	49.2	56.1	63.9	70.4	72.6	72.1	67.4	56.9	48.1	41.1	56.5
Extreme Maximum Temp. (°F)	84	91	90	93	100	104	104	106	103	96	89	83	106
Extreme Minimum Temp. (°F)	11	13	20	33	41	52	60	58	44	26	21	3	3
Days Maximum Temp. ≥ 90°F	0	0	0	1	6	20	27	27	17	3	0	0	101
Days Maximum Temp. ≤ 32°F	0	0	0	0	0	0	0	0	0	0	0	0	0
Days Minimum Temp. ≤ 32°F	9	5	1	0	0	0	0	0	0	0	2	6	23
Days Minimum Temp. ≤ 0°F	0	0	0	0	0	0	0	0	0	0	0	0	0
Heating Degree Days (base 65°F)	483	340	176	55	4	0	0	0	2	47	210	412	1,729
Cooling Degree Days (base 65°F)	6	16	53	133	314	488	593	587	416	179	50	15	2,850
Mean Precipitation (in.)	4.21	3.04	3.10	3.80	5.50	4.55	3.25	3.82	4.50	4.82	4.53	4.03	49.15
Days With ≥ 0.1" Precipitation	7	5	5	4	6	6	5	6	6	5	6	5	66
Days With ≥ 1.0" Precipitation	1	1	1	1	2	1	1	1	2	1	2	1	15
Mean Snowfall (in.)	trace	trace	0.0	0.0	0.0	0.0	0.0	0.0	0.0	0.0	0.0	trace	trace
Days With ≥ 1.0" Snow Depth	0	0	0	0	0	0	0	0	0	0	0	0	0

Cope Ranch *Reagan County*   Elevation: 2,568 ft.   Latitude: 31° 32' N   Longitude: 101° 17' W

	JAN	FEB	MAR	APR	MAY	JUN	JUL	AUG	SEP	OCT	NOV	DEC	YEAR
Mean Maximum Temp. (°F)	56.9	62.3	70.2	79.0	86.3	92.0	94.8	93.6	86.9	78.0	66.6	58.8	77.1
Mean Temp. (°F)	42.0	46.7	54.3	63.0	71.6	78.4	81.0	79.7	73.2	63.2	51.5	43.9	62.4
Mean Minimum Temp. (°F)	27.0	31.2	38.3	47.0	56.9	64.7	67.1	65.8	59.5	48.3	36.5	28.9	47.6
Extreme Maximum Temp. (°F)	84	93	95	98	109	115	110	105	105	102	89	84	115
Extreme Minimum Temp. (°F)	0	-9	2	18	33	45	48	49	32	20	10	-7	-9
Days Maximum Temp. ≥ 90°F	0	0	1	4	12	21	27	24	13	3	0	0	105
Days Maximum Temp. ≤ 32°F	2	1	0	0	0	0	0	0	0	0	0	1	4
Days Minimum Temp. ≤ 32°F	23	16	9	2	0	0	0	0	0	2	11	21	84
Days Minimum Temp. ≤ 0°F	0	0	0	0	0	0	0	0	0	0	0	0	0
Heating Degree Days (base 65°F)	708	511	341	133	25	2	0	0	23	128	405	648	2,924
Cooling Degree Days (base 65°F)	0	2	13	77	250	420	521	488	284	82	6	0	2,143
Mean Precipitation (in.)	0.66	0.91	0.84	1.14	2.65	2.48	1.81	2.13	3.11	1.89	0.74	0.96	19.32
Days With ≥ 0.1" Precipitation	2	2	2	2	4	3	3	4	4	3	1	2	32
Days With ≥ 1.0" Precipitation	0	0	0	0	1	1	0	1	1	1	0	0	5
Mean Snowfall (in.)	0.4	0.1	0.3	0.0	0.0	0.0	0.0	0.0	0.0	trace	0.0	0.3	1.1
Days With ≥ 1.0" Snow Depth	0	0	0	0	0	0	0	0	0	0	0	0	0

Corsicana *Navarro County*   Elevation: 410 ft.   Latitude: 32° 06' N   Longitude: 96° 28' W

	JAN	FEB	MAR	APR	MAY	JUN	JUL	AUG	SEP	OCT	NOV	DEC	YEAR
Mean Maximum Temp. (°F)	55.2	60.5	68.1	75.6	82.3	89.5	94.2	94.5	88.4	78.8	67.0	58.6	76.1
Mean Temp. (°F)	44.5	49.2	56.7	64.2	72.0	79.3	83.5	83.4	77.3	67.0	55.6	47.7	65.0
Mean Minimum Temp. (°F)	33.7	37.8	45.2	52.8	61.6	69.2	72.8	72.3	66.2	55.1	44.2	36.7	53.9
Extreme Maximum Temp. (°F)	84	96	94	92	100	108	107	108	109	97	89	81	109
Extreme Minimum Temp. (°F)	6	5	17	30	38	54	59	58	41	27	19	-1	-1
Days Maximum Temp. ≥ 90°F	0	0	0	0	3	16	27	26	16	3	0	0	91
Days Maximum Temp. ≤ 32°F	1	1	0	0	0	0	0	0	0	0	0	1	3
Days Minimum Temp. ≤ 32°F	15	8	3	0	0	0	0	0	0	0	3	10	39
Days Minimum Temp. ≤ 0°F	0	0	0	0	0	0	0	0	0	0	0	0	0
Heating Degree Days (base 65°F)	631	446	275	96	13	0	0	0	8	70	298	535	2,372
Cooling Degree Days (base 65°F)	2	6	23	76	238	437	585	590	391	135	23	5	2,511
Mean Precipitation (in.)	2.46	3.10	3.34	3.37	4.86	3.19	2.17	2.40	3.24	4.43	3.03	3.46	39.05
Days With ≥ 0.1" Precipitation	5	5	5	5	6	5	3	4	5	5	5	5	58
Days With ≥ 1.0" Precipitation	0	1	1	1	2	1	1	1	1	1	1	1	12
Mean Snowfall (in.)	0.3	*trace*	trace	0.0	0.0	0.0	0.0	0.0	0.0	0.0	trace	0.1	*0.4*
Days With ≥ 1.0" Snow Depth	0	0	0	0	0	0	0	0	0	0	0	0	0

Crane *Crane County*   Elevation: 2,627 ft.   Latitude: 31° 23' N   Longitude: 102° 20' W

	JAN	FEB	MAR	APR	MAY	JUN	JUL	AUG	SEP	OCT	NOV	DEC	YEAR
Mean Maximum Temp. (°F)	61.4	67.1	74.9	82.7	89.9	95.1	96.1	94.9	88.7	80.7	70.1	63.0	80.4
Mean Temp. (°F)	46.6	51.7	59.1	67.1	75.3	81.7	83.5	82.2	76.0	67.0	55.8	48.3	66.2
Mean Minimum Temp. (°F)	31.7	36.2	43.3	51.5	60.7	68.2	70.9	69.5	63.3	53.3	41.4	33.5	52.0
Extreme Maximum Temp. (°F)	88	91	95	102	108	115	111	107	103	103	91	86	115
Extreme Minimum Temp. (°F)	4	-6	12	25	36	46	57	57	37	26	11	3	-6
Days Maximum Temp. ≥ 90°F	0	0	1	7	17	25	27	26	16	4	0	0	123
Days Maximum Temp. ≤ 32°F	0	0	0	0	0	0	0	0	0	0	0	0	0
Days Minimum Temp. ≤ 32°F	17	10	4	1	0	0	0	0	0	0	6	14	52
Days Minimum Temp. ≤ 0°F	0	0	0	0	0	0	0	0	0	0	0	0	0
Heating Degree Days (base 65°F)	564	375	210	68	9	0	0	0	13	64	284	512	2,099
Cooling Degree Days (base 65°F)	1	6	37	143	353	518	595	555	365	145	17	0	2,735
Mean Precipitation (in.)	0.55	0.64	0.38	0.84	1.80	1.68	1.47	2.12	3.07	1.58	0.66	0.70	15.49
Days With ≥ 0.1" Precipitation	1	2	1	2	3	3	2	3	4	3	1	2	27
Days With ≥ 1.0" Precipitation	0	0	0	0	0	1	0	0	1	0	0	0	2
Mean Snowfall (in.)	*0.9*	trace	trace	trace	0.0	0.0	0.0	0.0	0.0	trace	0.5	0.7	*2.1*
Days With ≥ 1.0" Snow Depth	*0*	0	0	0	0	0	0	0	0	0	0	0	*0*

Crockett *Houston County*   Elevation: 344 ft.   Latitude: 31° 18' N   Longitude: 95° 27' W

	JAN	FEB	MAR	APR	MAY	JUN	JUL	AUG	SEP	OCT	NOV	DEC	YEAR
Mean Maximum Temp. (°F)	57.3	62.3	69.8	76.8	83.3	89.5	93.3	93.7	88.4	79.6	68.3	60.7	76.9
Mean Temp. (°F)	46.4	50.7	57.8	65.0	72.5	79.2	82.5	82.3	77.2	67.2	56.7	49.4	65.6
Mean Minimum Temp. (°F)	35.5	39.0	45.8	53.1	61.7	68.8	71.6	70.8	66.0	54.7	45.0	38.1	54.2
Extreme Maximum Temp. (°F)	84	95	89	93	98	104	105	107	106	94	88	84	107
Extreme Minimum Temp. (°F)	6	13	18	28	40	48	58	55	41	27	17	0	0
Days Maximum Temp. ≥ 90°F	0	0	0	0	3	16	26	26	15	2	0	0	88
Days Maximum Temp. ≤ 32°F	1	0	0	0	0	0	0	0	0	0	0	0	1
Days Minimum Temp. ≤ 32°F	13	8	3	0	0	0	0	0	0	0	0	4	38
Days Minimum Temp. ≤ 0°F	0	0	0	0	0	0	0	0	0	0	0	0	0
Heating Degree Days (base 65°F)	573	406	247	85	9	0	0	0	4	64	276	486	2,150
Cooling Degree Days (base 65°F)	4	9	30	92	257	443	556	557	386	140	33	9	2,516
Mean Precipitation (in.)	4.02	3.20	3.39	3.83	4.45	4.33	2.92	2.92	4.18	4.37	3.53	3.89	45.03
Days With ≥ 0.1" Precipitation	6	5	6	5	6	6	4	5	5	5	5	6	64
Days With ≥ 1.0" Precipitation	1	1	1	1	2	1	1	1	1	2	1	1	14
Mean Snowfall (in.)	0.5	trace	0.0	0.0	0.0	0.0	0.0	0.0	0.0	0.0	trace	trace	0.5
Days With ≥ 1.0" Snow Depth	0	0	0	0	0	0	0	0	0	0	0	0	0

Crosbyton *Crosby County*   Elevation: 3,008 ft.   Latitude: 33° 39' N   Longitude: 101° 15' W

	JAN	FEB	MAR	APR	MAY	JUN	JUL	AUG	SEP	OCT	NOV	DEC	YEAR
Mean Maximum Temp. (°F)	51.7	57.4	65.7	74.6	81.9	89.2	92.7	90.6	83.4	74.7	62.4	54.1	73.2
Mean Temp. (°F)	38.1	42.8	50.4	59.3	67.9	76.0	79.5	77.7	70.7	60.9	48.7	40.6	59.4
Mean Minimum Temp. (°F)	24.5	28.2	35.0	44.0	54.0	62.8	66.2	64.9	58.1	47.0	35.0	27.1	45.6
Extreme Maximum Temp. (°F)	82	89	96	99	105	113	108	104	103	100	89	81	113
Extreme Minimum Temp. (°F)	-2	-3	9	21	34	45	53	54	32	19	9	-6	-6
Days Maximum Temp. ≥ 90°F	0	0	0	2	7	16	23	20	9	1	0	0	78
Days Maximum Temp. ≤ 32°F	3	2	0	0	0	0	0	0	0	0	0	2	7
Days Minimum Temp. ≤ 32°F	26	19	11	2	0	0	0	0	0	1	11	24	94
Days Minimum Temp. ≤ 0°F	0	0	0	0	0	0	0	0	0	0	0	0	0
Heating Degree Days (base 65°F)	827	620	451	203	52	4	0	0	39	169	483	748	3,596
Cooling Degree Days (base 65°F)	0	0	5	38	152	337	460	419	220	48	2	0	1,681
Mean Precipitation (in.)	0.68	0.96	1.02	1.79	3.09	2.99	2.03	3.08	3.56	1.89	0.87	0.81	22.77
Days With ≥ 0.1" Precipitation	2	2	2	3	5	5	4	5	5	3	2	2	40
Days With ≥ 1.0" Precipitation	0	0	0	0	1	1	1	1	1	1	0	0	6
Mean Snowfall (in.)	3.0	2.3	0.6	trace	0.0	0.0	0.0	0.0	0.0	0.2	1.0	1.8	8.9
Days With ≥ 1.0" Snow Depth	0	0	0	0	0	0	0	0	0	0	0	0	0

Crystal City *Zavala County*   Elevation: 577 ft.   Latitude: 28° 41' N   Longitude: 99° 50' W

	JAN	FEB	MAR	APR	MAY	JUN	JUL	AUG	SEP	OCT	NOV	DEC	YEAR
Mean Maximum Temp. (°F)	65.8	71.3	79.2	84.8	89.6	94.4	96.8	96.7	91.9	84.3	74.3	67.5	83.1
Mean Temp. (°F)	54.2	59.0	66.6	73.0	79.1	84.0	85.9	85.8	81.5	73.4	63.3	56.1	71.8
Mean Minimum Temp. (°F)	42.6	46.8	53.9	61.1	68.6	73.5	75.0	74.9	71.1	62.4	52.1	44.7	60.6
Extreme Maximum Temp. (°F)	92	100	103	107	105	109	107	106	104	99	93	90	109
Extreme Minimum Temp. (°F)	18	17	22	32	42	57	65	67	52	29	24	11	11
Days Maximum Temp. ≥ 90°F	0	1	3	8	16	26	29	29	22	8	0	0	142
Days Maximum Temp. ≤ 32°F	0	0	0	0	0	0	0	0	0	0	0	0	0
Days Minimum Temp. ≤ 32°F	4	2	1	0	0	0	0	0	0	0	1	3	11
Days Minimum Temp. ≤ 0°F	0	0	0	0	0	0	0	0	0	0	0	0	0
Heating Degree Days (base 65°F)	341	200	78	16	1	0	0	0	1	16	131	289	1,073
Cooling Degree Days (base 65°F)	13	43	129	264	462	596	678	674	519	299	93	24	3,794
Mean Precipitation (in.)	0.97	1.05	1.09	1.72	2.55	3.21	1.69	2.11	2.24	2.35	1.03	0.79	20.80
Days With ≥ 0.1" Precipitation	2	2	2	3	4	4	2	3	4	3	2	2	33
Days With ≥ 1.0" Precipitation	0	0	0	1	1	1	0	1	1	1	0	0	6
Mean Snowfall (in.)	0.2	trace	0.0	0.0	0.0	0.0	0.0	0.0	0.0	trace	0.0	0.0	0.2
Days With ≥ 1.0" Snow Depth	0	0	0	0	0	0	0	0	0	0	0	0	0

Daingerfield 9 S *Morris County*   Elevation: 298 ft.   Latitude: 32° 55' N   Longitude: 94° 43' W

	JAN	FEB	MAR	APR	MAY	JUN	JUL	AUG	SEP	OCT	NOV	DEC	YEAR
Mean Maximum Temp. (°F)	56.6	62.4	70.3	77.5	84.2	90.8	94.7	95.0	88.8	79.2	67.8	59.9	77.3
Mean Temp. (°F)	46.1	51.2	58.7	66.1	73.7	80.7	84.3	84.0	78.0	67.6	56.9	49.4	66.4
Mean Minimum Temp. (°F)	35.7	39.9	47.2	54.6	63.2	70.4	73.8	73.0	67.2	55.9	46.1	38.8	55.5
Extreme Maximum Temp. (°F)	82	91	92	94	100	105	107	112	107	98	95	82	112
Extreme Minimum Temp. (°F)	10	9	17	32	43	54	60	56	44	26	17	5	5
Days Maximum Temp. ≥ 90°F	0	0	0	1	5	20	27	26	16	2	0	0	97
Days Maximum Temp. ≤ 32°F	1	0	0	0	0	0	0	0	0	0	0	1	2
Days Minimum Temp. ≤ 32°F	12	7	2	0	0	0	0	0	0	0	2	9	32
Days Minimum Temp. ≤ 0°F	0	0	0	0	0	0	0	0	0	0	0	0	0
Heating Degree Days (base 65°F)	581	393	226	72	6	0	0	0	5	61	264	484	2,092
Cooling Degree Days (base 65°F)	2	10	35	108	278	475	608	604	400	140	30	7	2,697
Mean Precipitation (in.)	3.48	3.48	4.54	4.36	4.26	4.06	3.01	2.44	3.20	4.41	4.46	4.22	45.92
Days With ≥ 0.1" Precipitation	6	5	6	6	6	5	4	4	4	5	6	6	63
Days With ≥ 1.0" Precipitation	1	1	1	1	2	1	1	1	1	2	2	1	15
Mean Snowfall (in.)	trace	trace	trace	0.0	0.0	0.0	0.0	0.0	0.0	0.0	trace	0.2	0.2
Days With ≥ 1.0" Snow Depth	0	0	0	0	0	0	0	0	0	0	0	0	0

Dalhart Municipal Airport *Dallam County* Elevation: 3,989 ft. Latitude: 36° 01' N Longitude: 102° 33' W

	JAN	FEB	MAR	APR	MAY	JUN	JUL	AUG	SEP	OCT	NOV	DEC	YEAR
Mean Maximum Temp. (°F)	48.7	53.6	61.4	69.3	77.6	87.2	90.7	88.2	81.1	71.2	58.6	50.1	69.8
Mean Temp. (°F)	34.2	38.7	45.8	54.0	63.3	72.8	76.9	75.0	67.4	56.2	43.9	35.8	55.3
Mean Minimum Temp. (°F)	19.7	23.7	30.2	38.7	48.9	58.4	63.1	61.7	53.6	41.2	29.1	21.4	40.8
Extreme Maximum Temp. (°F)	78	84	90	94	102	107	105	101	103	94	89	81	107
Extreme Minimum Temp. (°F)	-14	-10	4	16	27	42	49	43	27	9	-5	-10	-14
Days Maximum Temp. ≥ 90°F	0	0	0	1	3	12	20	15	6	1	0	0	58
Days Maximum Temp. ≤ 32°F	4	2	1	0	0	0	0	0	0	0	1	3	11
Days Minimum Temp. ≤ 32°F	29	24	19	7	0	0	0	0	0	4	20	28	131
Days Minimum Temp. ≤ 0°F	1	1	0	0	0	0	0	0	0	0	0	1	3
Heating Degree Days (base 65°F)	947	738	590	330	111	12	1	1	63	278	627	900	4,598
Cooling Degree Days (base 65°F)	0	0	1	8	67	251	380	328	147	13	0	0	1,195
Mean Precipitation (in.)	0.51	0.41	0.97	1.40	2.74	2.28	3.21	3.08	1.62	1.19	0.72	0.54	18.67
Days With ≥ 0.1" Precipitation	2	1	2	3	5	4	5	6	3	3	2	2	38
Days With ≥ 1.0" Precipitation	0	0	0	0	1	1	1	1	0	0	0	0	4
Mean Snowfall (in.)	4.6	3.6	3.3	1.0	0.3	trace	trace	trace	trace	0.7	2.0	3.5	19.0
Days With ≥ 1.0" Snow Depth	5	3	2	1	0	0	0	0	0	0	1	3	15

Dallas Love Field *Dallas County* Elevation: 439 ft. Latitude: 32° 51' N Longitude: 96° 51' W

	JAN	FEB	MAR	APR	MAY	JUN	JUL	AUG	SEP	OCT	NOV	DEC	YEAR
Mean Maximum Temp. (°F)	54.9	60.5	69.1	76.8	83.6	91.6	95.9	95.7	88.3	78.6	66.7	58.4	76.7
Mean Temp. (°F)	45.1	50.3	58.5	66.3	73.9	81.9	86.0	85.8	78.5	68.1	56.5	48.5	66.6
Mean Minimum Temp. (°F)	35.3	40.0	47.8	55.7	64.2	72.1	76.1	75.9	68.6	57.4	46.3	38.5	56.5
Extreme Maximum Temp. (°F)	84	95	97	97	103	112	110	108	105	100	89	85	112
Extreme Minimum Temp. (°F)	7	10	16	32	42	53	60	59	43	27	19	1	1
Days Maximum Temp. ≥ 90°F	0	0	0	1	6	21	28	27	15	3	0	0	101
Days Maximum Temp. ≤ 32°F	2	1	0	0	0	0	0	0	0	0	0	1	4
Days Minimum Temp. ≤ 32°F	12	7	2	0	0	0	0	0	0	0	2	8	31
Days Minimum Temp. ≤ 0°F	0	0	0	0	0	0	0	0	0	0	0	0	0
Heating Degree Days (base 65°F)	611	418	235	72	9	0	0	0	7	62	278	511	2,203
Cooling Degree Days (base 65°F)	3	9	38	117	297	517	667	670	427	164	33	5	2,947
Mean Precipitation (in.)	1.71	2.49	3.10	3.54	5.40	3.69	2.51	2.37	2.89	4.52	2.38	2.38	36.98
Days With ≥ 0.1" Precipitation	4	4	5	5	6	5	4	3	4	5	4	4	53
Days With ≥ 1.0" Precipitation	0	1	1	1	2	1	1	1	1	2	1	1	13
Mean Snowfall (in.)	*0.9*	*0.6*	*trace*	*trace*	*trace*	*trace*	0.0	0.0	0.0	trace	*0.2*	*0.2*	*1.9*
Days With ≥ 1.0" Snow Depth	*0*	*0*	*0*	*0*	*0*	*0*	0	0	0	0	*0*	*0*	*0*

Danevang 1 W *Wharton County* Elevation: 68 ft. Latitude: 29° 03' N Longitude: 96° 14' W

	JAN	FEB	MAR	APR	MAY	JUN	JUL	AUG	SEP	OCT	NOV	DEC	YEAR
Mean Maximum Temp. (°F)	63.0	67.0	73.8	79.8	85.0	90.0	92.7	93.5	89.9	83.2	73.5	66.1	79.8
Mean Temp. (°F)	53.2	56.4	63.3	69.5	75.6	80.8	82.7	83.1	79.7	71.9	62.7	55.9	69.6
Mean Minimum Temp. (°F)	43.3	45.8	52.7	59.2	66.2	71.5	72.7	72.7	69.4	60.5	51.9	45.6	59.3
Extreme Maximum Temp. (°F)	84	91	90	94	97	99	102	104	101	97	90	87	104
Extreme Minimum Temp. (°F)	12	19	23	30	42	56	63	58	47	25	25	8	8
Days Maximum Temp. ≥ 90°F	0	0	0	1	4	18	27	27	17	5	0	0	99
Days Maximum Temp. ≤ 32°F	0	0	0	0	0	0	0	0	0	0	0	0	0
Days Minimum Temp. ≤ 32°F	4	2	1	0	0	0	0	0	0	0	1	3	11
Days Minimum Temp. ≤ 0°F	0	0	0	0	0	0	0	0	0	0	0	0	0
Heating Degree Days (base 65°F)	375	256	122	32	1	0	0	0	1	22	144	307	1,260
Cooling Degree Days (base 65°F)	11	20	67	164	341	489	563	575	456	245	83	31	3,045
Mean Precipitation (in.)	3.27	2.68	2.87	2.63	5.36	4.75	3.43	3.85	5.74	4.75	3.36	3.00	45.69
Days With ≥ 0.1" Precipitation	6	5	4	3	5	6	5	6	7	5	5	5	62
Days With ≥ 1.0" Precipitation	1	1	1	1	2	2	1	1	2	1	1	1	15
Mean Snowfall (in.)	trace	trace	trace	0.0	0.0	0.0	0.0	0.0	0.0	0.0	trace	trace	trace
Days With ≥ 1.0" Snow Depth	0	0	0	0	0	0	0	0	0	0	0	0	0

Denison Dam *Grayson County* Elevation: 610 ft. Latitude: 33° 49' N Longitude: 96° 34' W

	JAN	FEB	MAR	APR	MAY	JUN	JUL	AUG	SEP	OCT	NOV	DEC	YEAR
Mean Maximum Temp. (°F)	50.7	56.5	65.3	73.4	80.4	88.5	93.7	93.1	85.5	76.0	63.4	54.6	73.4
Mean Temp. (°F)	40.2	45.4	54.0	62.3	70.2	78.3	82.9	81.8	74.6	64.2	52.9	44.2	62.6
Mean Minimum Temp. (°F)	29.7	34.2	42.7	51.1	60.0	68.1	72.0	70.4	63.7	52.3	42.4	33.7	51.7
Extreme Maximum Temp. (°F)	82	92	94	98	97	109	108	108	106	95	91	80	109
Extreme Minimum Temp. (°F)	4	6	15	25	41	47	56	51	41	24	16	-3	-3
Days Maximum Temp. ≥ 90°F	0	0	0	0	2	15	25	24	11	1	0	0	78
Days Maximum Temp. ≤ 32°F	3	2	0	0	0	0	0	0	0	0	0	1	6
Days Minimum Temp. ≤ 32°F	19	12	4	0	0	0	0	0	0	0	5	14	54
Days Minimum Temp. ≤ 0°F	0	0	0	0	0	0	0	0	0	0	0	0	0
Heating Degree Days (base 65°F)	763	549	349	136	24	0	0	0	17	110	368	639	2,955
Cooling Degree Days (base 65°F)	0	2	14	56	191	409	*567*	542	316	87	13	1	*2,198*
Mean Precipitation (in.)	1.78	2.62	3.25	3.74	5.20	4.12	2.90	2.56	4.58	4.40	3.45	2.42	41.02
Days With ≥ 0.1" Precipitation	4	4	5	5	7	6	3	4	5	5	5	5	58
Days With ≥ 1.0" Precipitation	0	1	1	1	2	1	1	1	2	2	1	1	14
Mean Snowfall (in.)	*0.2*	*0.6*	0.0	0.0	0.0	0.0	0.0	0.0	0.0	0.0	0.0	trace	*0.8*
Days With ≥ 1.0" Snow Depth	*0*	*0*	0	0	0	0	0	0	0	0	0	0	*0*

Denton 2 SE *Denton County* Elevation: 629 ft. Latitude: 33° 12' N Longitude: 97° 06' W

	JAN	FEB	MAR	APR	MAY	JUN	JUL	AUG	SEP	OCT	NOV	DEC	YEAR
Mean Maximum Temp. (°F)	54.7	60.4	68.8	75.9	82.6	90.0	94.7	94.1	87.0	77.6	65.6	57.7	75.8
Mean Temp. (°F)	43.8	48.8	57.0	64.5	72.1	79.6	84.0	83.1	76.3	66.1	54.7	47.2	64.8
Mean Minimum Temp. (°F)	32.7	37.3	45.1	52.9	61.6	69.2	73.2	72.0	65.5	54.6	43.8	36.2	53.7
Extreme Maximum Temp. (°F)	82	92	99	96	104	108	107	108	110	96	89	82	110
Extreme Minimum Temp. (°F)	4	6	13	28	40	50	58	58	40	24	12	0	0
Days Maximum Temp. ≥ 90°F	0	0	0	1	3	17	27	26	13	2	0	0	89
Days Maximum Temp. ≤ 32°F	2	1	0	0	0	0	0	0	0	0	0	1	4
Days Minimum Temp. ≤ 32°F	15	8	3	0	0	0	0	0	0	0	4	11	41
Days Minimum Temp. ≤ 0°F	0	0	0	0	0	0	0	0	0	0	0	0	0
Heating Degree Days (base 65°F)	652	455	270	94	12	0	0	0	11	79	320	549	2,442
Cooling Degree Days (base 65°F)	1	4	25	79	242	446	600	584	360	117	18	3	2,479
Mean Precipitation (in.)	1.89	2.70	2.87	3.40	5.51	3.18	2.55	2.31	3.79	4.57	2.64	2.57	37.98
Days With ≥ 0.1" Precipitation	4	4	5	5	6	5	3	3	4	5	4	4	52
Days With ≥ 1.0" Precipitation	0	1	1	1	2	1	1	1	1	1	1	1	12
Mean Snowfall (in.)	0.3	0.3	trace	0.0	0.0	0.0	0.0	0.0	0.0	0.0	trace	0.1	0.7
Days With ≥ 1.0" Snow Depth	0	0	0	0	0	0	0	0	0	0	0	0	0

Dilley *Frio County* Elevation: 547 ft. Latitude: 28° 41' N Longitude: 99° 11' W

	JAN	FEB	MAR	APR	MAY	JUN	JUL	AUG	SEP	OCT	NOV	DEC	YEAR
Mean Maximum Temp. (°F)	63.9	68.9	76.8	83.7	88.6	93.7	97.5	97.1	92.0	84.0	73.6	66.7	82.2
Mean Temp. (°F)	51.8	56.3	64.1	70.9	77.3	82.3	85.0	84.9	80.6	72.0	61.7	54.8	70.1
Mean Minimum Temp. (°F)	39.7	43.7	51.3	58.1	66.0	70.9	72.6	72.6	69.1	59.9	49.7	42.9	58.0
Extreme Maximum Temp. (°F)	94	99	102	109	106	109	107	108	105	104	93	91	109
Extreme Minimum Temp. (°F)	16	17	22	31	46	55	60	62	49	28	24	12	12
Days Maximum Temp. ≥ 90°F	0	0	2	8	15	24	29	29	22	8	1	0	138
Days Maximum Temp. ≤ 32°F	0	0	0	0	0	0	0	0	0	0	0	0	0
Days Minimum Temp. ≤ 32°F	6	3	1	0	0	0	0	0	0	0	1	4	15
Days Minimum Temp. ≤ 0°F	0	0	0	0	0	0	0	0	0	0	0	0	0
Heating Degree Days (base 65°F)	411	262	116	29	2	0	0	0	2	25	163	328	1,338
Cooling Degree Days (base 65°F)	8	29	88	212	408	542	653	648	493	265	76	21	3,443
Mean Precipitation (in.)	1.22	1.34	1.38	1.74	3.78	3.47	1.44	2.71	2.82	3.43	1.37	1.21	25.91
Days With ≥ 0.1" Precipitation	3	3	2	3	5	4	3	3	5	4	3	3	41
Days With ≥ 1.0" Precipitation	0	0	0	1	1	1	0	1	1	1	0	0	6
Mean Snowfall (in.)	trace	0.0	0.0	0.0	0.0	0.0	0.0	0.0	0.0	trace	0.0	0.0	trace
Days With ≥ 1.0" Snow Depth	0	0	0	0	0	0	0	0	0	0	0	0	0

Dimmitt 2 N *Castro County* Elevation: 3,848 ft. Latitude: 34° 36' N Longitude: 102° 19' W

	JAN	FEB	MAR	APR	MAY	JUN	JUL	AUG	SEP	OCT	NOV	DEC	YEAR
Mean Maximum Temp. (°F)	49.8	55.0	63.3	71.6	80.0	88.1	90.7	88.2	81.9	72.4	59.9	51.2	71.0
Mean Temp. (°F)	35.0	39.4	46.5	54.8	64.1	72.8	76.1	74.2	67.5	56.7	44.5	36.6	55.7
Mean Minimum Temp. (°F)	20.3	23.7	29.6	37.9	48.2	57.5	61.6	60.2	53.0	41.0	29.1	21.9	40.3
Extreme Maximum Temp. (°F)	80	84	92	98	102	108	111	103	102	96	87	78	111
Extreme Minimum Temp. (°F)	-9	-9	5	18	28	38	48	46	29	14	-2	-6	-9
Days Maximum Temp. ≥ 90°F	0	0	0	1	5	14	19	14	7	1	0	0	61
Days Maximum Temp. ≤ 32°F	5	2	1	0	0	0	0	0	0	0	1	3	12
Days Minimum Temp. ≤ 32°F	29	24	20	8	1	0	0	0	0	4	20	29	135
Days Minimum Temp. ≤ 0°F	0	0	0	0	0	0	0	0	0	0	0	1	1
Heating Degree Days (base 65°F)	922	716	567	311	103	12	1	2	63	266	608	874	4,445
Cooling Degree Days (base 65°F)	0	0	0	10	83	252	364	307	147	14	0	0	1,177
Mean Precipitation (in.)	0.50	0.52	0.78	0.97	2.74	3.06	2.42	3.12	2.60	1.56	0.69	0.69	19.65
Days With ≥ 0.1" Precipitation	1	2	2	2	5	5	4	5	4	3	2	2	37
Days With ≥ 1.0" Precipitation	0	0	0	0	1	1	1	1	1	0	0	0	5
Mean Snowfall (in.)	3.2	2.0	1.0	0.4	0.0	0.0	0.0	0.0	0.0	0.2	0.8	2.8	10.4
Days With ≥ 1.0" Snow Depth	2	1	1	0	0	0	0	0	0	0	0	2	6

Dublin *Erath County* Elevation: 1,499 ft. Latitude: 32° 06' N Longitude: 98° 20' W

	JAN	FEB	MAR	APR	MAY	JUN	JUL	AUG	SEP	OCT	NOV	DEC	YEAR
Mean Maximum Temp. (°F)	54.2	59.5	67.6	75.8	82.0	88.8	93.7	93.8	86.8	77.3	65.1	57.0	75.1
Mean Temp. (°F)	42.8	47.7	55.3	63.6	70.9	77.9	82.0	81.8	75.3	65.5	54.0	45.8	63.6
Mean Minimum Temp. (°F)	31.4	35.9	43.0	51.3	59.7	66.9	70.2	69.7	63.8	53.8	42.7	34.6	51.9
Extreme Maximum Temp. (°F)	87	96	93	97	104	107	107	107	108	100	92	82	108
Extreme Minimum Temp. (°F)	3	2	9	28	40	51	57	56	39	25	15	-7	-7
Days Maximum Temp. ≥ 90°F	0	0	0	1	4	14	25	25	13	2	0	0	84
Days Maximum Temp. ≤ 32°F	2	1	0	0	0	0	0	0	0	0	0	1	4
Days Minimum Temp. ≤ 32°F	17	10	4	0	0	0	0	0	0	0	5	12	48
Days Minimum Temp. ≤ 0°F	0	0	0	0	0	0	0	0	0	0	0	0	0
Heating Degree Days (base 65°F)	681	484	315	114	20	1	0	0	15	88	340	588	2,646
Cooling Degree Days (base 65°F)	0	4	20	77	215	392	537	547	336	107	16	1	2,252
Mean Precipitation (in.)	1.56	2.49	2.47	3.10	5.24	4.12	2.05	3.28	3.49	3.38	2.13	2.24	35.55
Days With ≥ 0.1" Precipitation	3	4	5	4	6	5	3	4	5	5	4	4	52
Days With ≥ 1.0" Precipitation	0	1	0	1	2	1	1	1	1	1	1	1	11
Mean Snowfall (in.)	1.1	0.8	0.1	trace	0.0	0.0	0.0	0.0	0.0	trace	0.5	0.3	2.8
Days With ≥ 1.0" Snow Depth	1	1	0	0	0	0	0	0	0	0	0	0	2

Dumas *Moore County*   Elevation: 3,654 ft.   Latitude: 35° 52' N   Longitude: 101° 58' W

	JAN	FEB	MAR	APR	MAY	JUN	JUL	AUG	SEP	OCT	NOV	DEC	YEAR
Mean Maximum Temp. (°F)	47.3	52.5	60.3	69.2	78.0	87.6	91.8	89.3	81.7	71.5	58.1	49.1	69.7
Mean Temp. (°F)	34.0	38.5	45.5	54.3	63.9	73.6	78.5	76.6	68.6	57.3	44.4	36.1	55.9
Mean Minimum Temp. (°F)	20.6	24.4	30.7	39.4	49.8	59.6	65.1	63.8	55.5	43.0	30.7	23.0	42.1
Extreme Maximum Temp. (°F)	79	85	92	96	102	109	108	103	103	95	87	76	109
Extreme Minimum Temp. (°F)	-11	-9	2	14	27	41	47	50	28	14	-2	-9	-11
Days Maximum Temp. ≥ 90°F	0	0	0	1	4	13	21	18	8	1	0	0	66
Days Maximum Temp. ≤ 32°F	5	3	1	0	0	0	0	0	0	0	1	4	14
Days Minimum Temp. ≤ 32°F	29	23	18	7	0	0	0	0	0	3	18	28	126
Days Minimum Temp. ≤ 0°F	1	1	0	0	0	0	0	0	0	0	0	1	3
Heating Degree Days (base 65°F)	955	743	599	329	110	14	1	2	62	257	612	890	4,574
Cooling Degree Days (base 65°F)	0	0	1	13	81	272	427	374	179	21	0	0	1,368
Mean Precipitation (in.)	0.46	0.57	1.01	1.38	2.68	2.35	2.44	2.54	1.96	1.02	0.66	0.50	17.57
Days With ≥ 0.1" Precipitation	1	2	2	3	5	4	4	5	4	2	2	2	36
Days With ≥ 1.0" Precipitation	0	0	0	0	1	1	1	1	1	0	0	0	5
Mean Snowfall (in.)	3.7	3.5	2.4	1.1	0.1	0.0	0.0	0.0	trace	0.3	1.7	1.8	14.6
Days With ≥ 1.0" Snow Depth	4	3	1	1	0	0	0	0	0	0	1	2	12

Eagle Pass *Maverick County*   Elevation: 807 ft.   Latitude: 28° 43' N   Longitude: 100° 29' W

	JAN	FEB	MAR	APR	MAY	JUN	JUL	AUG	SEP	OCT	NOV	DEC	YEAR
Mean Maximum Temp. (°F)	63.2	69.1	77.5	84.9	90.1	95.2	97.9	97.8	92.3	83.7	73.4	65.7	82.6
Mean Temp. (°F)	51.6	56.7	64.7	71.9	78.5	83.8	86.2	86.0	81.0	72.0	61.4	53.8	70.6
Mean Minimum Temp. (°F)	39.9	44.2	51.8	58.9	66.9	72.4	74.6	74.1	69.7	60.2	49.4	41.9	58.7
Extreme Maximum Temp. (°F)	89	100	104	108	108	114	110	108	104	104	95	94	114
Extreme Minimum Temp. (°F)	19	17	23	33	45	55	65	61	50	30	25	12	12
Days Maximum Temp. ≥ 90°F	0	1	3	10	17	26	29	29	23	8	1	0	147
Days Maximum Temp. ≤ 32°F	0	0	0	0	0	0	0	0	0	0	0	0	0
Days Minimum Temp. ≤ 32°F	6	3	0	0	0	0	0	0	0	0	1	4	14
Days Minimum Temp. ≤ 0°F	0	0	0	0	0	0	0	0	0	0	0	0	0
Heating Degree Days (base 65°F)	413	252	105	24	2	0	0	0	2	23	162	347	1,330
Cooling Degree Days (base 65°F)	5	28	104	240	448	595	690	684	509	264	69	7	3,643
Mean Precipitation (in.)	0.85	0.94	0.76	1.73	3.15	3.43	2.03	2.13	2.76	2.19	1.00	0.79	21.76
Days With ≥ 0.1" Precipitation	2	2	2	3	4	4	3	3	4	3	2	2	34
Days With ≥ 1.0" Precipitation	0	0	0	1	1	1	1	1	1	1	0	0	7
Mean Snowfall (in.)	0.7	trace	0.0	0.0	0.0	0.0	0.0	0.0	0.0	0.0	0.0	0.0	0.7
Days With ≥ 1.0" Snow Depth	0	0	0	0	0	0	0	0	0	0	0	0	0

Eastland *Eastland County*   Elevation: 1,430 ft.   Latitude: 32° 24' N   Longitude: 98° 49' W

	JAN	FEB	MAR	APR	MAY	JUN	JUL	AUG	SEP	OCT	NOV	DEC	YEAR
Mean Maximum Temp. (°F)	54.1	59.8	68.6	76.7	83.8	90.5	94.8	94.5	87.3	78.4	65.7	57.4	76.0
Mean Temp. (°F)	41.6	46.9	54.9	62.9	*71.0*	78.4	82.1	81.6	74.9	64.5	52.6	44.7	*63.0*
Mean Minimum Temp. (°F)	29.0	33.8	41.0	49.1	58.0	66.2	69.5	68.7	62.5	50.8	39.6	32.0	50.0
Extreme Maximum Temp. (°F)	83	95	94	101	*104*	109	110	106	110	103	93	83	*110*
Extreme Minimum Temp. (°F)	-6	-3	8	26	38	47	54	50	34	20	14	-1	-6
Days Maximum Temp. ≥ 90°F	0	0	1	2	8	18	26	26	14	3	0	0	98
Days Maximum Temp. ≤ 32°F	2	1	0	0	0	0	0	0	0	0	0	1	4
Days Minimum Temp. ≤ 32°F	20	12	6	1	0	0	0	0	0	1	8	17	65
Days Minimum Temp. ≤ 0°F	0	0	0	0	0	0	0	0	0	0	0	0	0
Heating Degree Days (base 65°F)	712	507	*324*	131	*26*	1	0	0	17	105	377	630	*2,830*
Cooling Degree Days (base 65°F)	0	2	15	66	*210*	388	523	517	311	91	14	0	*2,137*
Mean Precipitation (in.)	1.16	1.89	2.01	2.29	3.57	3.31	1.73	2.46	2.88	3.07	1.57	1.57	27.51
Days With ≥ 0.1" Precipitation	3	3	4	4	*5*	4	3	4	4	4	3	3	*44*
Days With ≥ 1.0" Precipitation	0	0	0	1	1	1	1	1	1	1	0	0	7
Mean Snowfall (in.)	1.3	0.6	0.7	trace	0.0	0.0	0.0	0.0	trace	trace	0.5	0.4	3.5
Days With ≥ 1.0" Snow Depth	*1*	1	0	0	0	0	0	0	0	0	0	*0*	2

Elgin *Bastrop County*   Elevation: 577 ft.   Latitude: 30° 21' N   Longitude: 97° 22' W

	JAN	FEB	MAR	APR	MAY	JUN	JUL	AUG	SEP	OCT	NOV	DEC	YEAR
Mean Maximum Temp. (°F)	61.2	66.1	73.8	80.1	85.7	91.7	95.5	95.8	90.3	82.0	71.3	63.8	79.8
Mean Temp. (°F)	50.5	54.8	62.1	68.7	75.3	81.2	84.2	84.2	79.3	70.5	60.4	53.1	68.7
Mean Minimum Temp. (°F)	39.7	43.5	50.3	57.3	64.9	70.6	72.8	72.6	68.1	59.0	49.4	42.3	57.6
Extreme Maximum Temp. (°F)	89	98	96	97	100	107	106	105	105	96	89	86	107
Extreme Minimum Temp. (°F)	7	10	17	33	45	55	62	59	44	29	21	0	0
Days Maximum Temp. ≥ 90°F	0	0	1	2	8	22	28	29	19	5	0	0	114
Days Maximum Temp. ≤ 32°F	0	0	0	0	0	0	0	0	0	0	0	0	0
Days Minimum Temp. ≤ 32°F	8	4	1	0	0	0	0	0	0	0	2	5	20
Days Minimum Temp. ≤ 0°F	0	0	0	0	0	0	0	0	0	0	0	0	0
Heating Degree Days (base 65°F)	454	303	152	41	3	0	0	0	2	34	191	381	1,561
Cooling Degree Days (base 65°F)	9	24	64	164	342	501	613	620	443	216	60	19	3,075
Mean Precipitation (in.)	2.24	2.22	2.47	2.48	4.86	3.78	1.97	1.96	3.06	3.85	2.92	2.37	34.18
Days With ≥ 0.1" Precipitation	4	4	5	4	6	5	3	3	5	5	4	4	52
Days With ≥ 1.0" Precipitation	1	1	1	1	2	1	1	0	1	1	1	1	12
Mean Snowfall (in.)	trace	0.2	trace	0.0	0.0	0.0	0.0	0.0	0.0	0.0	0.0	0.0	0.2
Days With ≥ 1.0" Snow Depth	0	0	0	0	0	0	0	0	0	0	0	0	0

Fairfield 3 W *Freestone County* Elevation: 429 ft. Latitude: 31° 44' N Longitude: 96° 12' W

	JAN	FEB	MAR	APR	MAY	JUN	JUL	AUG	SEP	OCT	NOV	DEC	YEAR
Mean Maximum Temp. (°F)	58.2	63.7	71.3	78.2	84.5	91.0	*95.6*	95.5	89.1	80.0	69.0	60.7	*78.1*
Mean Temp. (°F)	47.3	52.1	59.3	66.3	73.6	80.1	*83.8*	83.2	77.4	68.0	57.9	49.6	*66.6*
Mean Minimum Temp. (°F)	36.3	40.5	47.2	54.3	62.7	69.1	*72.0*	70.9	65.6	55.9	46.7	38.5	*55.0*
Extreme Maximum Temp. (°F)	84	94	93	97	99	105	*107*	109	108	99	*90*	88	109
Extreme Minimum Temp. (°F)	8	0	13	27	42	*49*	*56*	56	38	*30*	16	-2	-2
Days Maximum Temp. ≥ 90°F	0	0	0	1	6	19	*28*	28	16	3	*0*	0	*101*
Days Maximum Temp. ≤ 32°F	1	0	0	0	0	0	0	0	0	0	0	0	1
Days Minimum Temp. ≤ 32°F	12	7	3	0	0	0	0	0	0	0	0	0	0
Days Minimum Temp. ≤ 0°F	0	0	0	0	0	0	0	0	0	0	3	9	34
Heating Degree Days (base 65°F)	547	370	214	69	5	0	*0*	0	5	56	245	482	*1,993*
Cooling Degree Days (base 65°F)	5	14	41	112	288	465	593	589	388	*154*	*40*	12	*2,701*
Mean Precipitation (in.)	2.87	3.50	3.31	3.55	4.49	3.41	2.16	2.59	3.85	4.71	*3.85*	3.66	*41.95*
Days With ≥ 0.1" Precipitation	5	5	5	5	5	5	*3*	4	5	5	*5*	5	*57*
Days With ≥ 1.0" Precipitation	1	1	1	1	2	1	*1*	1	1	2	*1*	1	*14*
Mean Snowfall (in.)	0.5	0.3	trace	0.0	0.0	0.0	0.0	0.0	0.0	0.0	trace	0.1	0.9
Days With ≥ 1.0" Snow Depth	0	0	0	0	0	0	0	0	0	0	0	0	0

Falcon Dam *Starr County* Elevation: 318 ft. Latitude: 26° 33' N Longitude: 99° 08' W

	JAN	FEB	MAR	APR	MAY	JUN	JUL	AUG	SEP	OCT	NOV	DEC	YEAR
Mean Maximum Temp. (°F)	67.5	72.9	81.7	87.8	92.9	97.3	99.6	99.5	93.8	86.5	77.5	69.7	85.6
Mean Temp. (°F)	56.5	61.0	68.9	75.3	81.2	85.5	87.0	86.9	82.5	75.1	66.2	58.8	73.7
Mean Minimum Temp. (°F)	45.4	49.1	56.1	62.7	69.5	73.6	74.3	74.3	71.2	63.6	54.8	47.9	61.9
Extreme Maximum Temp. (°F)	97	102	105	109	114	116	110	111	108	101	97	94	116
Extreme Minimum Temp. (°F)	21	24	27	30	50	59	63	64	51	31	31	15	15
Days Maximum Temp. ≥ 90°F	0	2	7	14	23	27	30	30	23	12	3	0	171
Days Maximum Temp. ≤ 32°F	0	0	0	0	0	0	0	0	0	0	0	0	0
Days Minimum Temp. ≤ 32°F	2	1	0	0	0	0	0	0	0	0	0	0	0
Days Minimum Temp. ≤ 0°F	0	0	0	0	0	0	0	0	0	0	0	1	4
Heating Degree Days (base 65°F)	288	169	59	14	1	0	0	0	1	12	97	234	875
Cooling Degree Days (base 65°F)	29	72	187	325	528	647	714	702	554	354	152	52	4,316
Mean Precipitation (in.)	0.93	1.09	0.59	1.42	2.44	2.44	1.66	2.13	4.06	1.77	0.98	0.87	20.38
Days With ≥ 0.1" Precipitation	3	2	2	2	3	3	3	3	5	3	2	2	33
Days With ≥ 1.0" Precipitation	0	0	0	0	1	1	1	1	1	1	0	0	6
Mean Snowfall (in.)	trace	0.0	0.0	0.0	0.0	0.0	0.0	0.0	0.0	0.0	0.0	0.0	trace
Days With ≥ 1.0" Snow Depth	0	0	0	0	0	0	0	0	0	0	0	0	0

Falfurrias *Brooks County* Elevation: 118 ft. Latitude: 27° 13' N Longitude: 98° 08' W

	JAN	FEB	MAR	APR	MAY	JUN	JUL	AUG	SEP	OCT	NOV	DEC	YEAR
Mean Maximum Temp. (°F)	67.1	71.6	78.9	85.0	89.6	94.2	96.9	96.9	92.1	85.3	76.3	69.8	83.7
Mean Temp. (°F)	55.4	59.3	66.3	72.9	78.7	83.4	85.2	84.8	81.0	73.4	64.5	58.4	71.9
Mean Minimum Temp. (°F)	43.7	47.0	53.5	60.7	67.8	72.5	73.5	72.7	69.8	61.5	52.6	46.9	60.2
Extreme Maximum Temp. (°F)	96	99	103	108	109	115	107	107	104	99	96	97	115
Extreme Minimum Temp. (°F)	18	22	23	34	44	55	66	60	50	28	27	13	13
Days Maximum Temp. ≥ 90°F	0	1	3	10	17	25	28	29	22	10	1	0	146
Days Maximum Temp. ≤ 32°F	0	0	0	0	0	0	0	0	0	0	0	0	0
Days Minimum Temp. ≤ 32°F	4	2	1	0	0	0	0	0	0	0	0	0	0
Days Minimum Temp. ≤ 0°F	0	0	0	0	0	0	0	0	0	0	1	2	10
Heating Degree Days (base 65°F)	321	204	87	22	1	0	0	0	1	17	124	255	1,032
Cooling Degree Days (base 65°F)	29	55	134	262	455	577	646	642	502	301	128	58	3,789
Mean Precipitation (in.)	1.15	1.59	0.87	1.52	2.85	3.36	1.95	2.88	3.97	2.95	1.24	1.07	25.40
Days With ≥ 0.1" Precipitation	3	3	2	3	4	4	3	3	5	3	2	2	37
Days With ≥ 1.0" Precipitation	0	0	0	0	1	1	1	1	1	1	0	0	6
Mean Snowfall (in.)	0.0	0.0	0.0	0.0	0.0	0.0	0.0	0.0	0.0	0.0	0.0	0.0	0.0
Days With ≥ 1.0" Snow Depth	0	0	0	0	0	0	0	0	0	0	0	0	0

Ferris *Ellis County* Elevation: 469 ft. Latitude: 32° 31' N Longitude: 96° 40' W

	JAN	FEB	MAR	APR	MAY	JUN	JUL	AUG	SEP	OCT	NOV	DEC	YEAR
Mean Maximum Temp. (°F)	55.9	61.8	69.6	77.3	83.8	91.4	96.1	96.2	89.2	79.3	67.3	58.9	77.2
Mean Temp. (°F)	44.8	50.1	57.7	65.2	72.9	80.2	84.2	83.9	77.5	67.2	56.0	47.9	65.6
Mean Minimum Temp. (°F)	33.6	38.3	45.9	53.0	61.9	68.9	72.2	71.6	65.8	55.0	44.7	36.9	54.0
Extreme Maximum Temp. (°F)	82	96	94	94	102	110	110	111	110	97	89	81	111
Extreme Minimum Temp. (°F)	7	7	14	29	42	53	57	56	42	26	16	-1	-1
Days Maximum Temp. ≥ 90°F	0	0	0	1	5	20	28	27	17	3	0	0	101
Days Maximum Temp. ≤ 32°F	1	1	0	0	0	0	0	0	0	0	0	1	3
Days Minimum Temp. ≤ 32°F	15	8	3	0	0	0	0	0	0	0	0	0	0
Days Minimum Temp. ≤ 0°F	0	0	0	0	0	0	0	0	0	0	4	11	41
Heating Degree Days (base 65°F)	623	420	250	83	9	0	0	0	7	65	287	528	2,272
Cooling Degree Days (base 65°F)	1	6	26	85	254	448	598	601	392	134	25	4	2,574
Mean Precipitation (in.)	2.50	2.98	3.24	3.81	4.74	3.41	2.14	2.31	2.84	4.65	2.90	3.26	38.78
Days With ≥ 0.1" Precipitation	4	5	5	4	6	4	3	3	4	5	4	5	52
Days With ≥ 1.0" Precipitation	1	1	1	1	2	1	1	1	1	1	1	1	13
Mean Snowfall (in.)	0.6	0.6	0.1	0.0	0.0	0.0	0.0	0.0	0.0	0.0	0.1	0.3	1.7
Days With ≥ 1.0" Snow Depth	0	1	0	0	0	0	0	0	0	0	0	0	1

Flatonia *Fayette County*   Elevation: 518 ft.   Latitude: 29° 40' N   Longitude: 97° 07' W

	JAN	FEB	MAR	APR	MAY	JUN	JUL	AUG	SEP	OCT	NOV	DEC	YEAR
Mean Maximum Temp. (°F)	61.6	65.9	73.2	79.3	85.1	90.9	94.6	95.1	89.9	82.0	71.4	64.1	79.4
Mean Temp. (°F)	51.5	55.4	62.5	68.9	75.3	80.8	83.7	83.8	79.1	71.0	61.1	54.0	68.9
Mean Minimum Temp. (°F)	41.3	44.8	51.8	58.5	65.4	70.7	72.7	72.4	68.3	59.8	50.7	43.9	58.4
Extreme Maximum Temp. (°F)	90	99	98	94	98	102	104	104	103	97	89	85	104
Extreme Minimum Temp. (°F)	9	15	18	31	44	52	59	61	44	31	19	3	3
Days Maximum Temp. ≥ 90°F	0	0	0	1	7	19	28	28	18	4	0	0	105
Days Maximum Temp. ≤ 32°F	0	0	0	0	0	0	0	0	0	0	0	0	0
Days Minimum Temp. ≤ 32°F	6	3	1	0	0	0	0	0	0	0	1	5	16
Days Minimum Temp. ≤ 0°F	0	0	0	0	0	0	0	0	0	0	0	0	0
Heating Degree Days (base 65°F)	427	288	140	39	2	0	0	0	2	30	179	358	1,465
Cooling Degree Days (base 65°F)	11	25	64	161	333	482	590	600	440	223	68	24	3,021
Mean Precipitation (in.)	2.63	2.41	2.53	2.94	5.32	4.37	1.85	2.70	3.94	4.22	2.81	2.53	38.25
Days With ≥ 0.1" Precipitation	5	4	4	4	6	5	3	4	5	4	4	5	53
Days With ≥ 1.0" Precipitation	1	1	1	1	2	1	0	1	1	1	1	1	12
Mean Snowfall (in.)	0.3	0.1	trace	0.0	0.0	0.0	0.0	0.0	0.0	0.0	0.0	trace	0.4
Days With ≥ 1.0" Snow Depth	0	0	0	0	0	0	0	0	0	0	0	0	0

Floresville *Wilson County*   Elevation: 396 ft.   Latitude: 29° 08' N   Longitude: 98° 10' W

	JAN	FEB	MAR	APR	MAY	JUN	JUL	AUG	SEP	OCT	NOV	DEC	YEAR
Mean Maximum Temp. (°F)	63.8	68.6	76.0	82.0	87.4	93.0	96.3	96.6	91.8	84.2	74.4	67.3	81.8
Mean Temp. (°F)	50.7	55.1	62.8	69.5	76.4	82.0	84.8	84.7	79.9	71.0	61.3	53.8	69.3
Mean Minimum Temp. (°F)	37.4	41.4	49.5	57.0	65.3	71.0	73.3	72.7	67.9	57.7	48.0	39.9	56.8
Extreme Maximum Temp. (°F)	91	99	101	100	109	109	106	110	107	99	95	89	110
Extreme Minimum Temp. (°F)	5	10	19	30	37	46	62	58	43	26	20	7	5
Days Maximum Temp. ≥ 90°F	0	0	1	4	12	24	29	29	22	8	0	0	129
Days Maximum Temp. ≤ 32°F	0	0	0	0	0	0	0	0	0	0	0	0	0
Days Minimum Temp. ≤ 32°F	11	6	2	0	0	0	0	0	0	0	3	9	31
Days Minimum Temp. ≤ 0°F	0	0	0	0	0	0	0	0	0	0	0	0	0
Heating Degree Days (base 65°F)	447	294	139	40	2	0	0	0	2	35	176	365	1,500
Cooling Degree Days (base 65°F)	9	21	69	175	376	533	637	637	462	232	72	21	3,244
Mean Precipitation (in.)	1.50	1.68	1.62	2.51	3.83	3.09	1.61	2.62	2.71	2.64	2.03	1.38	27.22
Days With ≥ 0.1" Precipitation	4	4	3	3	4	4	3	3	4	4	3	3	42
Days With ≥ 1.0" Precipitation	0	0	0	1	1	1	0	1	1	1	1	0	7
Mean Snowfall (in.)	0.4	0.0	0.0	0.0	0.0	0.0	0.0	0.0	0.0	trace	0.0	0.0	0.4
Days With ≥ 1.0" Snow Depth	0	0	0	0	0	0	0	0	0	0	0	0	0

Floydada *Floyd County*   Elevation: 3,218 ft.   Latitude: 33° 58' N   Longitude: 101° 20' W

	JAN	FEB	MAR	APR	MAY	JUN	JUL	AUG	SEP	OCT	NOV	DEC	YEAR
Mean Maximum Temp. (°F)	50.1	55.6	63.8	72.9	80.8	88.8	92.1	89.9	82.8	73.7	60.8	52.1	71.9
Mean Temp. (°F)	36.6	41.4	48.7	57.8	66.8	75.5	79.1	77.2	70.0	59.7	47.2	38.8	58.2
Mean Minimum Temp. (°F)	23.0	27.1	33.5	42.7	52.8	62.2	66.1	64.3	57.1	45.6	33.6	25.5	44.5
Extreme Maximum Temp. (°F)	81	87	94	98	103	111	107	104	102	99	87	79	111
Extreme Minimum Temp. (°F)	-4	-5	3	19	29	43	55	50	34	16	2	-3	-5
Days Maximum Temp. ≥ 90°F	0	0	0	1	6	15	22	19	8	1	0	0	72
Days Maximum Temp. ≤ 32°F	4	2	1	0	0	0	0	0	0	0	1	3	11
Days Minimum Temp. ≤ 32°F	28	21	13	3	0	0	0	0	0	2	13	26	106
Days Minimum Temp. ≤ 0°F	0	0	0	0	0	0	0	0	0	0	0	0	0
Heating Degree Days (base 65°F)	873	661	503	238	66	5	0	1	44	196	529	804	3,920
Cooling Degree Days (base 65°F)	0	0	3	27	133	330	464	412	209	39	1	0	1,618
Mean Precipitation (in.)	0.45	0.70	0.95	1.50	3.04	3.66	1.96	2.56	3.00	1.60	0.82	0.64	20.88
Days With ≥ 0.1" Precipitation	1	2	2	3	5	5	4	4	5	3	2	2	38
Days With ≥ 1.0" Precipitation	0	0	0	0	1	1	1	1	1	0	0	0	5
Mean Snowfall (in.)	2.4	1.9	0.2	0.2	0.0	0.0	0.0	0.0	0.0	0.2	1.0	1.3	7.2
Days With ≥ 1.0" Snow Depth	2	1	0	0	0	0	0	0	0	0	0	1	4

Follett *Lipscomb County*   Elevation: 2,769 ft.   Latitude: 36° 26' N   Longitude: 100° 08' W

	JAN	FEB	MAR	APR	MAY	JUN	JUL	AUG	SEP	OCT	NOV	DEC	YEAR
Mean Maximum Temp. (°F)	45.3	51.5	59.0	69.0	77.1	86.4	91.6	90.2	81.9	71.2	57.4	47.9	69.1
Mean Temp. (°F)	32.7	38.1	45.5	55.2	64.4	74.0	78.8	77.7	69.2	57.7	44.7	35.7	56.1
Mean Minimum Temp. (°F)	20.0	24.6	31.9	41.3	51.6	61.5	66.1	65.1	56.4	44.2	31.9	23.4	43.2
Extreme Maximum Temp. (°F)	82	87	93	98	102	111	108	107	104	98	88	78	111
Extreme Minimum Temp. (°F)	-8	-11	-1	12	30	42	49	48	29	14	3	-13	-13
Days Maximum Temp. ≥ 90°F	0	0	0	1	3	12	20	19	8	1	0	0	64
Days Maximum Temp. ≤ 32°F	7	4	1	0	0	0	0	0	0	0	1	4	17
Days Minimum Temp. ≤ 32°F	29	22	16	5	0	0	0	0	0	3	16	27	118
Days Minimum Temp. ≤ 0°F	1	1	0	0	0	0	0	0	0	0	0	1	3
Heating Degree Days (base 65°F)	994	753	600	309	102	12	2	2	61	249	603	902	4,589
Cooling Degree Days (base 65°F)	0	0	1	18	84	276	425	400	188	24	1	0	1,417
Mean Precipitation (in.)	0.64	0.90	2.11	2.10	3.51	3.03	2.54	2.82	2.20	1.32	1.19	0.75	23.11
Days With ≥ 0.1" Precipitation	2	2	4	4	6	5	4	4	4	2	3	2	42
Days With ≥ 1.0" Precipitation	0	0	1	1	1	1	1	1	1	0	0	0	7
Mean Snowfall (in.)	4.2	4.4	4.0	1.2	trace	0.0	0.0	0.0	trace	0.3	2.7	3.6	20.4
Days With ≥ 1.0" Snow Depth	2	2	1	0	0	0	0	0	0	0	1	1	7

Fort Stockton *Pecos County*   Elevation: 2,979 ft.   Latitude: 30° 53' N   Longitude: 102° 52' W

	JAN	FEB	MAR	APR	MAY	JUN	JUL	AUG	SEP	OCT	NOV	DEC	YEAR
Mean Maximum Temp. (°F)	60.0	65.8	73.3	81.6	88.6	94.5	95.1	93.7	87.8	80.2	69.8	62.4	79.4
Mean Temp. (°F)	45.4	50.3	57.3	65.2	73.4	80.3	81.7	80.2	74.6	65.4	54.6	47.6	64.7
Mean Minimum Temp. (°F)	30.8	34.7	41.2	48.8	58.1	66.0	68.3	66.7	61.4	50.7	39.3	32.8	49.9
Extreme Maximum Temp. (°F)	87	92	96	103	108	117	112	107	104	105	92	85	117
Extreme Minimum Temp. (°F)	4	-6	12	23	37	41	59	56	39	25	13	1	-6
Days Maximum Temp. ≥ 90°F	0	0	1	7	15	24	26	24	15	5	0	0	117
Days Maximum Temp. ≤ 32°F	1	0	0	0	0	0	0	0	0	0	0	1	2
Days Minimum Temp. ≤ 32°F	18	11	5	1	0	0	0	0	0	0	6	15	56
Days Minimum Temp. ≤ 0°F	0	0	0	0	0	0	0	0	0	0	0	0	0
Heating Degree Days (base 65°F)	600	413	256	94	16	1	0	0	18	86	318	532	2,334
Cooling Degree Days (base 65°F)	1	4	26	117	307	492	552	506	333	119	16	1	2,474
Mean Precipitation (in.)	0.50	0.51	0.43	0.74	1.65	1.63	1.35	2.01	2.90	1.42	0.59	0.62	14.35
Days With ≥ 0.1" Precipitation	2	1	1	2	3	3	3	4	4	3	1	1	28
Days With ≥ 1.0" Precipitation	0	0	0	0	0	0	0	1	1	0	0	0	2
Mean Snowfall (in.)	0.8	0.0	trace	0.0	0.0	0.0	0.0	0.0	0.0	0.0	0.0	0.3	1.1
Days With ≥ 1.0" Snow Depth	0	0	0	0	0	0	0	0	0	0	0	0	0

Franklin *Robertson County*   Elevation: 469 ft.   Latitude: 31° 02' N   Longitude: 96° 29' W

	JAN	FEB	MAR	APR	MAY	JUN	JUL	AUG	SEP	OCT	NOV	DEC	YEAR
Mean Maximum Temp. (°F)	59.2	63.9	71.4	77.9	84.1	90.4	94.9	95.4	89.2	80.4	69.5	62.0	78.2
Mean Temp. (°F)	48.5	52.9	59.9	66.6	73.7	79.9	83.4	83.4	77.7	68.5	58.3	51.2	67.0
Mean Minimum Temp. (°F)	37.7	41.8	48.3	55.3	63.2	69.4	71.8	71.2	66.2	56.5	47.1	40.4	55.7
Extreme Maximum Temp. (°F)	86	97	93	92	100	108	107	108	109	96	89	85	109
Extreme Minimum Temp. (°F)	4	7	16	30	41	50	55	56	43	25	16	-1	-1
Days Maximum Temp. ≥ 90°F	0	0	0	1	4	18	28	27	15	3	0	0	96
Days Maximum Temp. ≤ 32°F	1	0	0	0	0	0	0	0	0	0	0	0	1
Days Minimum Temp. ≤ 32°F	10	5	2	0	0	0	0	0	0	0	3	7	27
Days Minimum Temp. ≤ 0°F	0	0	0	0	0	0	0	0	0	0	0	0	0
Heating Degree Days (base 65°F)	512	350	196	62	5	0	0	0	3	51	236	434	1,849
Cooling Degree Days (base 65°F)	7	14	42	115	289	461	587	588	398	167	42	12	2,722
Mean Precipitation (in.)	2.96	2.95	2.91	3.07	4.65	2.93	2.04	2.62	3.89	4.55	3.01	3.43	39.01
Days With ≥ 0.1" Precipitation	5	5	5	5	6	5	3	4	5	6	5	5	59
Days With ≥ 1.0" Precipitation	1	1	1	1	2	1	1	1	1	1	1	1	13
Mean Snowfall (in.)	0.4	0.5	0.0	0.0	0.0	0.0	0.0	0.0	0.0	0.0	trace	trace	0.9
Days With ≥ 1.0" Snow Depth	0	0	0	0	0	0	0	0	0	0	0	0	0

Fredericksburg *Gillespie County*   Elevation: 1,683 ft.   Latitude: 30° 14' N   Longitude: 98° 55' W

	JAN	FEB	MAR	APR	MAY	JUN	JUL	AUG	SEP	OCT	NOV	DEC	YEAR
Mean Maximum Temp. (°F)	60.3	64.9	72.2	78.9	84.1	89.6	92.9	93.0	87.7	79.7	69.0	62.1	77.9
Mean Temp. (°F)	48.1	52.3	59.5	66.3	73.0	78.5	81.1	80.8	75.9	67.4	57.0	50.1	65.8
Mean Minimum Temp. (°F)	35.9	39.7	46.9	53.7	61.7	67.4	69.4	68.6	64.1	55.0	45.0	38.0	53.8
Extreme Maximum Temp. (°F)	88	96	101	101	100	108	109	104	101	99	91	86	109
Extreme Minimum Temp. (°F)	3	0	12	24	38	50	58	55	37	24	14	1	0
Days Maximum Temp. ≥ 90°F	0	0	1	2	5	16	24	26	13	2	0	0	89
Days Maximum Temp. ≤ 32°F	0	0	0	0	0	0	0	0	0	0	0	1	1
Days Minimum Temp. ≤ 32°F	12	7	3	0	0	0	0	0	0	0	4	10	36
Days Minimum Temp. ≤ 0°F	0	0	0	0	0	0	0	0	0	0	0	0	0
Heating Degree Days (base 65°F)	519	359	203	67	7	0	0	0	6	59	259	463	1,942
Cooling Degree Days (base 65°F)	2	8	37	113	272	427	518	518	346	145	26	5	2,417
Mean Precipitation (in.)	1.35	1.87	1.93	2.35	4.48	3.91	2.03	2.76	3.04	3.60	1.99	2.11	31.42
Days With ≥ 0.1" Precipitation	3	4	4	4	6	5	3	4	4	4	3	3	47
Days With ≥ 1.0" Precipitation	0	0	0	1	1	1	1	1	1	1	1	1	9
Mean Snowfall (in.)	trace	trace	trace	0.0	0.0	0.0	0.0	0.0	0.0	0.0	trace	trace	trace
Days With ≥ 1.0" Snow Depth	0	0	0	0	0	0	0	0	0	0	0	0	0

Freeport 2 NW *Brazoria County*   Elevation: 6 ft.   Latitude: 28° 59' N   Longitude: 95° 23' W

	JAN	FEB	MAR	APR	MAY	JUN	JUL	AUG	SEP	OCT	NOV	DEC	YEAR
Mean Maximum Temp. (°F)	62.6	65.5	71.8	77.5	83.7	89.2	91.8	92.0	88.3	81.5	73.1	66.5	78.6
Mean Temp. (°F)	53.9	56.6	63.1	69.5	76.4	82.1	84.5	84.2	80.3	72.4	63.6	57.4	70.3
Mean Minimum Temp. (°F)	45.1	47.7	54.3	61.4	68.9	75.0	77.2	76.4	72.3	63.2	54.0	48.2	62.0
Extreme Maximum Temp. (°F)	82	83	88	95	98	101	100	101	100	96	90	84	101
Extreme Minimum Temp. (°F)	15	22	25	36	41	58	67	66	45	34	28	13	13
Days Maximum Temp. ≥ 90°F	0	0	0	0	2	14	26	25	14	1	0	0	82
Days Maximum Temp. ≤ 32°F	0	0	0	0	0	0	0	0	0	0	0	0	0
Days Minimum Temp. ≤ 32°F	3	2	0	0	0	0	0	0	0	0	0	1	6
Days Minimum Temp. ≤ 0°F	0	0	0	0	0	0	0	0	0	0	0	0	0
Heating Degree Days (base 65°F)	353	249	116	27	1	0	0	0	0	19	130	268	1,163
Cooling Degree Days (base 65°F)	11	19	60	169	369	528	616	612	471	255	96	39	3,245
Mean Precipitation (in.)	4.33	2.86	2.99	2.81	4.17	4.86	4.80	4.09	7.92	4.61	4.00	3.54	50.98
Days With ≥ 0.1" Precipitation	7	5	4	3	5	5	6	7	8	5	5	5	65
Days With ≥ 1.0" Precipitation	1	1	1	1	1	2	1	1	2	1	1	1	14
Mean Snowfall (in.)	trace	trace	0.0	0.0	0.0	0.0	0.0	0.0	0.0	0.0	trace	0.0	trace
Days With ≥ 1.0" Snow Depth	0	0	0	0	0	0	0	0	0	0	0	0	0

Friona *Parmer County*   Elevation: 4,009 ft.   Latitude: 34° 39' N   Longitude: 102° 43' W

	JAN	FEB	MAR	APR	MAY	JUN	JUL	AUG	SEP	OCT	NOV	DEC	YEAR
Mean Maximum Temp. (°F)	49.7	55.0	62.7	70.8	79.3	88.1	90.1	88.0	81.5	72.3	59.8	51.3	70.7
Mean Temp. (°F)	35.7	40.2	47.0	55.1	64.4	73.4	76.4	74.6	67.9	57.4	45.4	37.3	56.2
Mean Minimum Temp. (°F)	21.6	25.3	31.4	39.3	49.5	58.7	62.7	61.2	54.2	42.3	30.9	23.2	41.7
Extreme Maximum Temp. (°F)	80	83	91	96	99	108	105	103	99	96	86	79	108
Extreme Minimum Temp. (°F)	-10	-4	7	16	30	42	51	47	29	13	2	-9	-10
Days Maximum Temp. ≥ 90°F	0	0	0	0	4	14	19	14	7	1	0	0	59
Days Maximum Temp. ≤ 32°F	4	2	1	0	0	0	0	0	0	0	1	3	11
Days Minimum Temp. ≤ 32°F	29	23	17	6	0	0	0	0	0	3	17	27	122
Days Minimum Temp. ≤ 0°F	0	0	0	0	0	0	0	0	0	0	0	1	1
Heating Degree Days (base 65°F)	902	694	550	302	95	10	1	1	58	248	582	852	4,295
Cooling Degree Days (base 65°F)	0	0	1	9	80	262	360	313	149	15	0	0	1,189
Mean Precipitation (in.)	0.59	0.54	0.87	1.09	2.15	2.51	2.19	3.00	2.33	1.52	0.76	0.75	18.30
Days With ≥ 0.1" Precipitation	2	2	2	3	5	5	4	5	4	3	2	2	39
Days With ≥ 1.0" Precipitation	0	0	0	0	1	1	1	1	1	0	0	0	5
Mean Snowfall (in.)	4.5	3.6	1.4	0.9	trace	0.0	0.0	0.0	0.0	0.4	1.9	3.5	16.2
Days With ≥ 1.0" Snow Depth	3	2	1	0	0	0	0	0	0	0	1	2	9

Gail *Borden County*   Elevation: 2,526 ft.   Latitude: 32° 46' N   Longitude: 101° 27' W

	JAN	FEB	MAR	APR	MAY	JUN	JUL	AUG	SEP	OCT	NOV	DEC	YEAR
Mean Maximum Temp. (°F)	56.5	62.2	70.6	78.8	85.7	92.1	94.6	92.8	85.8	77.7	66.1	58.6	76.8
Mean Temp. (°F)	43.7	48.5	56.1	64.2	72.1	79.1	81.9	80.5	73.8	64.9	53.1	45.7	63.6
Mean Minimum Temp. (°F)	30.8	34.8	41.5	49.5	58.4	66.0	69.2	68.1	61.7	52.0	40.0	32.9	50.4
Extreme Maximum Temp. (°F)	84	89	98	101	107	116	113	107	104	100	91	83	116
Extreme Minimum Temp. (°F)	4	0	9	25	35	45	57	55	36	21	8	-1	-1
Days Maximum Temp. ≥ 90°F	0	0	1	4	11	20	26	23	11	2	0	0	98
Days Maximum Temp. ≤ 32°F	2	1	0	0	0	0	0	0	0	0	0	1	4
Days Minimum Temp. ≤ 32°F	17	11	5	1	0	0	0	0	0	0	6	15	55
Days Minimum Temp. ≤ 0°F	0	0	0	0	0	0	0	0	0	0	0	0	0
Heating Degree Days (base 65°F)	654	462	294	108	18	1	0	0	20	96	360	590	2,603
Cooling Degree Days (base 65°F)	0	4	21	90	253	426	547	512	297	98	7	0	2,255
Mean Precipitation (in.)	0.63	0.75	0.69	1.20	2.86	2.65	2.22	2.52	2.91	1.65	0.70	0.69	19.47
Days With ≥ 0.1" Precipitation	2	2	2	2	4	4	3	4	4	3	2	2	34
Days With ≥ 1.0" Precipitation	0	0	0	0	1	1	1	1	1	0	0	0	5
Mean Snowfall (in.)	na	0.6	trace	trace	0.0	0.0	0.0	0.0	0.0	0.0	0.1	trace	na
Days With ≥ 1.0" Snow Depth	0	0	0	0	0	0	0	0	0	0	0	0	0

Garden City 1 E *Glasscock County*   Elevation: 2,637 ft.   Latitude: 31° 52' N   Longitude: 101° 29' W

	JAN	FEB	MAR	APR	MAY	JUN	JUL	AUG	SEP	OCT	NOV	DEC	YEAR
Mean Maximum Temp. (°F)	56.4	61.8	70.4	78.1	85.8	91.7	94.1	92.6	86.2	77.7	66.5	58.7	76.7
Mean Temp. (°F)	41.5	46.4	54.2	61.9	71.0	78.2	80.9	79.7	73.3	63.5	51.6	43.8	62.2
Mean Minimum Temp. (°F)	26.5	30.9	37.9	45.8	56.2	64.6	67.8	66.7	60.3	49.3	36.6	28.9	47.6
Extreme Maximum Temp. (°F)	84	91	97	100	106	114	108	105	106	102	89	84	114
Extreme Minimum Temp. (°F)	0	5	10	18	34	45	55	54	35	22	10	-3	-3
Days Maximum Temp. ≥ 90°F	0	0	1	4	11	20	25	23	12	2	0	0	98
Days Maximum Temp. ≤ 32°F	2	1	0	0	0	0	0	0	0	0	0	1	4
Days Minimum Temp. ≤ 32°F	24	16	8	2	0	0	0	0	0	1	9	20	80
Days Minimum Temp. ≤ 0°F	0	0	0	0	0	0	0	0	0	0	0	0	0
Heating Degree Days (base 65°F)	720	521	341	150	24	2	0	0	22	120	398	649	2,947
Cooling Degree Days (base 65°F)	0	1	13	70	235	414	526	489	290	87	3	0	2,128
Mean Precipitation (in.)	0.71	0.73	0.62	1.14	2.25	1.88	1.86	2.10	3.04	1.60	0.70	0.69	17.32
Days With ≥ 0.1" Precipitation	2	2	1	2	3	3	3	3	4	3	2	2	30
Days With ≥ 1.0" Precipitation	0	0	0	0	1	1	1	1	1	0	0	0	5
Mean Snowfall (in.)	trace	trace	trace	0.0	0.0	0.0	0.0	0.0	0.0	0.0	0.0	0.4	0.4
Days With ≥ 1.0" Snow Depth	0	0	0	0	0	0	0	0	0	0	0	0	0

Gatesville 4 SSE *Coryell County*   Elevation: 757 ft.   Latitude: 31° 23' N   Longitude: 97° 43' W

	JAN	FEB	MAR	APR	MAY	JUN	JUL	AUG	SEP	OCT	NOV	DEC	YEAR
Mean Maximum Temp. (°F)	58.5	63.4	70.9	78.1	83.8	90.4	95.1	95.1	88.9	80.1	69.0	61.4	77.9
Mean Temp. (°F)	45.9	50.5	58.1	65.5	72.8	79.3	83.2	82.9	77.0	67.3	56.5	48.7	65.6
Mean Minimum Temp. (°F)	33.3	37.5	45.2	53.0	61.7	68.3	71.2	70.5	65.1	54.5	44.0	36.1	53.4
Extreme Maximum Temp. (°F)	86	100	96	98	101	105	109	108	105	101	93	85	109
Extreme Minimum Temp. (°F)	1	5	13	28	41	50	57	53	39	21	13	-4	-4
Days Maximum Temp. ≥ 90°F	0	0	0	1	5	18	28	27	16	3	0	0	98
Days Maximum Temp. ≤ 32°F	1	1	0	0	0	0	0	0	0	0	0	1	3
Days Minimum Temp. ≤ 32°F	15	9	4	1	0	0	0	0	0	0	5	12	46
Days Minimum Temp. ≤ 0°F	0	0	0	0	0	0	0	0	0	0	0	0	0
Heating Degree Days (base 65°F)	586	411	241	81	10	0	0	0	8	67	277	504	2,185
Cooling Degree Days (base 65°F)	3	9	37	110	274	447	580	579	384	153	33	6	2,615
Mean Precipitation (in.)	1.63	2.39	2.63	2.83	4.32	3.58	2.37	2.55	3.05	3.20	2.28	2.30	33.13
Days With ≥ 0.1" Precipitation	4	4	4	4	6	5	3	4	4	4	4	4	50
Days With ≥ 1.0" Precipitation	0	1	1	1	1	1	1	1	1	1	1	1	10
Mean Snowfall (in.)	0.3	0.2	trace	trace	0.0	0.0	0.0	0.0	0.0	0.0	0.0	0.1	0.6
Days With ≥ 1.0" Snow Depth	0	0	0	0	0	0	0	0	0	0	0	0	0

Gilmer 2 W *Upshur County*   Elevation: 387 ft.   Latitude: 32° 44' N   Longitude: 94° 59' W

	JAN	FEB	MAR	APR	MAY	JUN	JUL	AUG	SEP	OCT	NOV	DEC	YEAR
Mean Maximum Temp. (°F)	54.6	60.3	67.8	75.3	81.9	89.0	93.2	93.6	87.3	77.6	66.1	58.4	75.4
Mean Temp. (°F)	42.9	47.7	55.0	62.5	70.4	77.9	81.8	81.3	74.9	64.2	53.7	46.4	63.2
Mean Minimum Temp. (°F)	31.1	35.0	42.3	49.6	58.9	66.8	70.4	68.9	62.4	50.9	41.3	34.4	51.0
Extreme Maximum Temp. (°F)	84	90	90	92	100	102	107	108	106	96	88	82	108
Extreme Minimum Temp. (°F)	2	3	14	25	38	47	55	52	37	23	13	-4	-4
Days Maximum Temp. ≥ 90°F	0	0	0	0	2	15	25	25	13	2	0	0	82
Days Maximum Temp. ≤ 32°F	2	1	0	0	0	0	0	0	0	0	0	1	4
Days Minimum Temp. ≤ 32°F	19	13	6	1	0	0	0	0	0	0	1	7	15	62
Days Minimum Temp. ≤ 0°F	0	0	0	0	0	0	0	0	0	0	0	0	0
Heating Degree Days (base 65°F)	683	489	323	133	23	1	0	0	14	115	350	575	2,706
Cooling Degree Days (base 65°F)	1	5	20	63	205	402	545	531	327	98	18	6	2,221
Mean Precipitation (in.)	3.45	3.68	4.33	4.13	4.25	3.87	3.05	2.52	3.99	4.68	4.36	4.20	46.51
Days With ≥ 0.1" Precipitation	6	5	6	6	6	5	4	4	4	6	6	6	64
Days With ≥ 1.0" Precipitation	1	1	1	1	1	1	1	1	1	1	1	1	12
Mean Snowfall (in.)	0.6	0.6	trace	0.0	0.0	0.0	0.0	0.0	0.0	0.0	trace	0.3	1.5
Days With ≥ 1.0" Snow Depth	0	0	0	0	0	0	0	0	0	0	0	0	0

Glen Rose 2 W *Somervell County*   Elevation: 652 ft.   Latitude: 32° 14' N   Longitude: 97° 48' W

	JAN	FEB	MAR	APR	MAY	JUN	JUL	AUG	SEP	OCT	NOV	DEC	YEAR
Mean Maximum Temp. (°F)	58.3	64.0	72.0	79.6	85.8	92.7	97.6	97.5	90.0	80.9	68.8	60.9	79.0
Mean Temp. (°F)	43.4	48.7	56.8	64.5	72.2	79.5	83.3	82.3	75.7	65.6	53.9	45.9	64.3
Mean Minimum Temp. (°F)	28.5	33.3	41.6	49.4	58.6	66.2	68.9	67.2	61.3	50.2	39.2	31.2	49.6
Extreme Maximum Temp. (°F)	87	96	101	100	104	110	110	115	110	99	95	86	115
Extreme Minimum Temp. (°F)	-1	-8	7	16	29	47	45	41	30	9	5	-15	-15
Days Maximum Temp. ≥ 90°F	0	0	1	3	9	23	29	28	19	5	0	0	117
Days Maximum Temp. ≤ 32°F	1	0	0	0	0	0	0	0	0	0	0	1	2
Days Minimum Temp. ≤ 32°F	21	14	7	2	0	0	0	0	0	0	2	9	18	73
Days Minimum Temp. ≤ 0°F	0	0	0	0	0	0	0	0	0	0	0	0	0
Heating Degree Days (base 65°F)	663	459	281	104	16	0	0	0	13	98	346	588	2,568
Cooling Degree Days (base 65°F)	0	3	27	86	241	428	562	538	319	112	18	3	2,337
Mean Precipitation (in.)	1.61	2.39	2.84	3.01	5.20	3.76	2.20	2.19	3.32	3.78	2.09	2.30	34.69
Days With ≥ 0.1" Precipitation	4	4	4	4	6	5	3	3	5	5	4	4	51
Days With ≥ 1.0" Precipitation	0	1	1	1	2	1	1	1	1	1	1	1	12
Mean Snowfall (in.)	0.8	0.5	0.2	0.0	0.0	0.0	0.0	0.0	0.0	0.0	0.2	0.3	2.0
Days With ≥ 1.0" Snow Depth	1	0	0	0	0	0	0	0	0	0	0	0	1

Goldthwaite 1 WSW *Mills County*   Elevation: 1,499 ft.   Latitude: 31° 27' N   Longitude: 98° 35' W

	JAN	FEB	MAR	APR	MAY	JUN	JUL	AUG	SEP	OCT	NOV	DEC	YEAR
Mean Maximum Temp. (°F)	58.6	63.2	70.9	78.0	83.3	89.5	93.3	92.8	87.3	79.0	68.1	60.8	77.1
Mean Temp. (°F)	46.7	51.2	58.6	66.0	72.6	78.9	82.2	81.8	76.5	67.6	56.7	49.1	65.7
Mean Minimum Temp. (°F)	34.7	39.2	46.2	54.0	61.8	68.3	71.1	70.8	65.7	56.2	45.4	37.4	54.2
Extreme Maximum Temp. (°F)	84	98	98	97	103	*107*	106	105	104	97	89	84	*107*
Extreme Minimum Temp. (°F)	4	0	8	28	40	54	57	56	40	26	12	-7	-7
Days Maximum Temp. ≥ 90°F	0	0	0	2	5	14	25	25	12	2	0	0	85
Days Maximum Temp. ≤ 32°F	1	1	0	0	0	0	0	0	0	0	0	1	3
Days Minimum Temp. ≤ 32°F	13	7	3	0	0	0	0	0	0	0	3	10	36
Days Minimum Temp. ≤ 0°F	0	0	0	0	0	0	0	0	0	0	0	0	0
Heating Degree Days (base 65°F)	563	390	228	73	10	0	0	0	8	60	267	489	2,088
Cooling Degree Days (base 65°F)	1	7	32	110	256	423	540	538	360	151	28	2	2,448
Mean Precipitation (in.)	1.25	2.17	2.20	2.27	3.87	3.71	1.75	2.01	3.03	3.04	1.80	1.77	28.87
Days With ≥ 0.1" Precipitation	3	4	4	4	5	5	3	3	4	4	3	3	45
Days With ≥ 1.0" Precipitation	0	1	1	1	1	1	0	1	1	1	0	0	8
Mean Snowfall (in.)	*trace*	trace	trace	0.0	0.0	0.0	0.0	0.0	0.0	0.0	0.0	trace	*trace*
Days With ≥ 1.0" Snow Depth	*0*	0	0	0	0	0	0	0	0	0	0	0	*0*

Goliad *Goliad County*   Elevation: 141 ft.   Latitude: 28° 40' N   Longitude: 97° 24' W

	JAN	FEB	MAR	APR	MAY	JUN	JUL	AUG	SEP	OCT	NOV	DEC	YEAR
Mean Maximum Temp. (°F)	67.5	71.4	77.7	82.8	87.7	92.6	95.3	95.9	92.0	85.7	76.2	69.9	82.9
Mean Temp. (°F)	55.4	58.8	65.5	71.2	77.3	82.0	84.1	84.4	80.5	73.1	64.1	57.7	71.2
Mean Minimum Temp. (°F)	43.4	46.2	53.2	59.5	66.9	71.4	72.9	72.8	68.9	60.4	51.9	45.5	59.4
Extreme Maximum Temp. (°F)	90	97	99	101	102	112	109	109	106	101	91	88	112
Extreme Minimum Temp. (°F)	15	19	21	32	42	55	61	58	45	23	20	8	8
Days Maximum Temp. ≥ 90°F	0	0	1	4	11	23	29	29	22	9	1	0	129
Days Maximum Temp. ≤ 32°F	0	0	0	0	0	0	0	0	0	0	0	0	0
Days Minimum Temp. ≤ 32°F	6	3	1	0	0	0	0	0	0	0	0	0	0
Days Minimum Temp. ≤ 0°F	0	0	0	0	0	0	0	0	0	0	1	4	15
Heating Degree Days (base 65°F)	319	208	91	21	1	0	0	0	0	17	124	264	1,045
Cooling Degree Days (base 65°F)	29	44	108	220	413	542	620	636	491	292	113	53	3,561
Mean Precipitation (in.)	2.32	2.06	2.11	3.31	4.23	4.67	2.97	3.66	4.65	4.24	2.01	2.02	38.25
Days With ≥ 0.1" Precipitation	5	3	3	4	5	5	4	5	6	4	3	3	50
Days With ≥ 1.0" Precipitation	1	1	1	1	2	1	1	1	1	1	1	0	12
Mean Snowfall (in.)	0.2	0.1	0.0	0.0	0.0	0.0	0.0	0.0	0.0	0.0	trace	trace	0.3
Days With ≥ 1.0" Snow Depth	0	0	0	0	0	0	0	0	0	0	0	0	0

Gonzales 1 N *Gonzales County*   Elevation: 377 ft.   Latitude: 29° 32' N   Longitude: 97° 27' W

	JAN	FEB	MAR	APR	MAY	JUN	JUL	AUG	SEP	OCT	NOV	DEC	YEAR
Mean Maximum Temp. (°F)	61.0	65.7	73.1	79.7	85.4	91.3	94.9	95.3	90.2	82.3	71.8	64.1	79.6
Mean Temp. (°F)	49.9	54.0	61.3	68.0	75.1	81.0	83.9	83.8	79.1	70.1	60.0	52.7	68.3
Mean Minimum Temp. (°F)	38.6	42.2	49.5	56.4	64.8	70.7	72.8	72.3	67.8	57.9	48.2	41.2	56.9
Extreme Maximum Temp. (°F)	89	96	100	98	102	108	105	107	105	98	91	86	108
Extreme Minimum Temp. (°F)	12	15	18	31	44	50	64	59	47	28	21	4	4
Days Maximum Temp. ≥ 90°F	0	0	1	2	8	21	28	28	19	5	0	0	112
Days Maximum Temp. ≤ 32°F	0	0	0	0	0	0	0	0	0	0	0	0	0
Days Minimum Temp. ≤ 32°F	8	5	2	0	0	0	0	0	0	0	2	6	23
Days Minimum Temp. ≤ 0°F	0	0	0	0	0	0	0	0	0	0	0	0	0
Heating Degree Days (base 65°F)	472	322	169	51	4	0	0	0	2	38	199	393	1,650
Cooling Degree Days (base 65°F)	7	15	53	141	330	492	600	600	435	205	57	17	2,952
Mean Precipitation (in.)	2.32	2.08	2.26	2.98	5.44	4.10	1.61	2.71	3.32	3.84	2.59	2.36	35.61
Days With ≥ 0.1" Precipitation	4	4	4	4	6	5	3	4	5	4	4	4	51
Days With ≥ 1.0" Precipitation	1	1	1	1	2	1	1	1	1	1	1	1	13
Mean Snowfall (in.)	trace	0.0	0.0	0.0	0.0	0.0	0.0	0.0	0.0	0.0	0.0	trace	trace
Days With ≥ 1.0" Snow Depth	0	0	0	0	0	0	0	0	0	0	0	0	0

Graham *Young County*   Elevation: 1,049 ft.   Latitude: 33° 06' N   Longitude: 98° 35' W

	JAN	FEB	MAR	APR	MAY	JUN	JUL	AUG	SEP	OCT	NOV	DEC	YEAR
Mean Maximum Temp. (°F)	54.9	60.3	69.1	77.3	83.9	91.2	96.4	96.1	88.8	79.4	66.8	58.1	76.9
Mean Temp. (°F)	41.0	46.2	54.8	63.0	71.3	79.2	83.7	83.0	75.6	64.8	52.9	44.1	63.3
Mean Minimum Temp. (°F)	27.2	32.0	40.5	48.6	58.5	67.1	70.9	69.9	62.5	50.2	38.9	30.1	49.7
Extreme Maximum Temp. (°F)	89	97	98	101	107	112	110	109	108	105	93	87	112
Extreme Minimum Temp. (°F)	0	0	9	25	35	46	55	49	36	19	12	-8	-8
Days Maximum Temp. ≥ 90°F	0	0	1	3	8	19	27	26	16	4	0	0	104
Days Maximum Temp. ≤ 32°F	2	1	0	0	0	0	0	0	0	0	0	1	4
Days Minimum Temp. ≤ 32°F	23	15	6	1	0	0	0	0	0	1	9	19	74
Days Minimum Temp. ≤ 0°F	0	0	0	0	0	0	0	0	0	0	0	0	0
Heating Degree Days (base 65°F)	737	527	330	132	26	1	0	0	18	105	367	641	2,884
Cooling Degree Days (base 65°F)	0	2	19	71	229	434	592	579	345	99	11	1	2,382
Mean Precipitation (in.)	1.11	1.88	2.18	2.55	4.55	3.43	2.17	2.38	3.68	3.75	1.70	1.77	31.15
Days With ≥ 0.1" Precipitation	3	4	4	4	6	4	3	4	5	5	3	4	49
Days With ≥ 1.0" Precipitation	0	0	1	1	2	1	1	1	1	1	1	0	10
Mean Snowfall (in.)	0.7	0.9	0.5	trace	0.0	0.0	0.0	0.0	0.0	0.0	0.2	0.3	2.6
Days With ≥ 1.0" Snow Depth	*0*	*0*	0	0	0	0	0	0	0	0	0	0	*0*

Grapevine Dam *Tarrant County*   Elevation: 583 ft.   Latitude: 32° 57' N   Longitude: 97° 03' W

	JAN	FEB	MAR	APR	MAY	JUN	JUL	AUG	SEP	OCT	NOV	DEC	YEAR
Mean Maximum Temp. (°F)	53.6	59.4	67.4	75.2	82.4	90.4	95.3	95.2	88.1	78.3	65.8	57.4	75.7
Mean Temp. (°F)	42.1	47.5	55.3	63.4	71.6	79.4	83.9	83.3	76.4	65.8	54.3	45.9	64.1
Mean Minimum Temp. (°F)	30.6	35.5	43.2	51.5	60.6	68.4	72.4	71.4	64.7	53.1	42.7	34.3	52.4
Extreme Maximum Temp. (°F)	83	95	96	98	101	109	110	108	109	100	89	84	110
Extreme Minimum Temp. (°F)	6	4	13	29	42	50	56	55	38	22	17	-1	-1
Days Maximum Temp. ≥ 90°F	0	0	0	1	5	19	27	27	15	3	0	0	97
Days Maximum Temp. ≤ 32°F	2	1	0	0	0	0	0	0	0	0	0	1	4
Days Minimum Temp. ≤ 32°F	18	10	4	0	0	0	0	0	0	0	5	13	50
Days Minimum Temp. ≤ 0°F	0	0	0	0	0	0	0	0	0	0	0	0	0
Heating Degree Days (base 65°F)	703	493	312	113	18	1	0	0	12	87	333	588	2,660
Cooling Degree Days (base 65°F)	1	4	18	66	234	441	598	593	370	117	19	2	2,463
Mean Precipitation (in.)	1.73	2.44	2.71	3.33	4.71	3.32	2.22	1.87	3.09	3.99	2.49	2.61	34.51
Days With ≥ 0.1" Precipitation	3	4	5	5	6	4	3	4	4	5	4	5	52
Days With ≥ 1.0" Precipitation	0	1	1	1	2	1	1	1	1	1	1	1	12
Mean Snowfall (in.)	0.0	*trace*	0.0	0.0	0.0	0.0	0.0	0.0	0.0	0.0	0.0	0.1	*0.1*
Days With ≥ 1.0" Snow Depth	*0*	0	0	0	0	0	0	0	0	0	0	0	*0*

Greenville KGVL Radio *Hunt County*   Elevation: 544 ft.   Latitude: 33° 10' N   Longitude: 96° 06' W

	JAN	FEB	MAR	APR	MAY	JUN	JUL	AUG	SEP	OCT	NOV	DEC	YEAR
Mean Maximum Temp. (°F)	52.1	57.5	65.6	73.7	80.9	89.1	93.8	93.9	86.8	76.9	64.5	55.6	74.2
Mean Temp. (°F)	41.1	45.9	53.8	62.1	70.3	78.4	82.7	82.2	75.4	64.5	53.1	44.5	62.8
Mean Minimum Temp. (°F)	30.1	34.3	42.0	50.4	59.6	67.6	71.5	70.4	63.9	52.1	41.6	33.3	51.4
Extreme Maximum Temp. (°F)	80	93	90	93	96	105	106	108	107	97	87	81	108
Extreme Minimum Temp. (°F)	4	1	14	27	34	48	55	55	40	27	13	-3	-3
Days Maximum Temp. ≥ 90°F	0	0	0	0	2	15	25	25	12	2	0	0	81
Days Maximum Temp. ≤ 32°F	2	1	0	0	0	0	0	0	0	0	0	1	4
Days Minimum Temp. ≤ 32°F	20	12	5	1	0	0	0	0	0	0	6	15	59
Days Minimum Temp. ≤ 0°F	0	0	0	0	0	0	0	0	0	0	0	0	0
Heating Degree Days (base 65°F)	733	534	355	136	22	1	0	0	13	105	365	632	2,896
Cooling Degree Days (base 65°F)	1	3	13	54	198	415	565	559	341	96	14	3	2,262
Mean Precipitation (in.)	2.47	3.26	3.72	3.83	5.35	3.77	2.90	2.27	3.82	4.97	3.71	3.22	43.29
Days With ≥ 0.1" Precipitation	5	5	6	5	7	5	4	3	5	5	5	4	59
Days With ≥ 1.0" Precipitation	1	1	1	1	2	1	1	1	1	2	1	1	14
Mean Snowfall (in.)	0.9	1.3	0.2	0.0	0.0	0.0	0.0	0.0	0.0	0.0	0.1	0.3	2.8
Days With ≥ 1.0" Snow Depth	1	1	0	0	0	0	0	0	0	0	0	1	3

Groveton *Trinity County*   Elevation: 347 ft.   Latitude: 31° 04' N   Longitude: 95° 08' W

	JAN	FEB	MAR	APR	MAY	JUN	JUL	AUG	SEP	OCT	NOV	DEC	YEAR
Mean Maximum Temp. (°F)	60.7	65.6	73.0	79.5	85.6	91.2	94.7	95.0	89.7	81.6	70.9	63.4	79.2
Mean Temp. (°F)	48.8	53.0	59.8	66.5	73.7	79.8	83.0	82.6	77.4	67.9	58.0	50.9	66.8
Mean Minimum Temp. (°F)	36.9	40.4	46.4	53.5	61.7	68.4	71.2	70.2	65.0	54.2	45.1	38.4	54.3
Extreme Maximum Temp. (°F)	83	95	90	95	101	102	106	108	105	99	88	84	108
Extreme Minimum Temp. (°F)	6	14	18	28	41	49	56	55	40	27	16	1	1
Days Maximum Temp. ≥ 90°F	0	0	0	1	7	21	28	28	17	4	0	0	106
Days Maximum Temp. ≤ 32°F	0	0	0	0	0	0	0	0	0	0	0	0	0
Days Minimum Temp. ≤ 32°F	11	6	2	0	0	0	0	0	0	0	3	8	30
Days Minimum Temp. ≤ 0°F	0	0	0	0	0	0	0	0	0	0	0	0	0
Heating Degree Days (base 65°F)	502	343	198	57	3	0	0	0	2	51	234	438	1,828
Cooling Degree Days (base 65°F)	6	12	40	113	293	468	581	574	394	155	30	9	2,675
Mean Precipitation (in.)	4.12	3.29	3.58	3.14	5.13	4.91	3.57	3.41	4.00	4.30	3.96	4.35	47.76
Days With ≥ 0.1" Precipitation	6	5	5	4	6	6	5	5	5	5	5	6	63
Days With ≥ 1.0" Precipitation	1	1	1	1	2	2	1	1	1	1	1	2	15
Mean Snowfall (in.)	0.3	0.0	0.0	0.0	0.0	0.0	0.0	0.0	0.0	0.0	trace	0.0	0.3
Days With ≥ 1.0" Snow Depth	0	0	0	0	0	0	0	0	0	0	0	0	0

Gruver *Hansford County*   Elevation: 3,169 ft.   Latitude: 36° 15' N   Longitude: 101° 24' W

	JAN	FEB	MAR	APR	MAY	JUN	JUL	AUG	SEP	OCT	NOV	DEC	YEAR
Mean Maximum Temp. (°F)	48.2	54.6	63.0	72.0	80.0	89.8	94.2	91.9	84.3	73.9	59.1	49.8	71.7
Mean Temp. (°F)	34.0	39.4	47.1	56.1	65.3	74.9	79.4	77.5	69.6	58.1	44.6	36.0	56.8
Mean Minimum Temp. (°F)	19.8	24.1	31.2	40.2	50.5	60.0	64.7	63.1	54.9	42.3	30.1	22.2	41.9
Extreme Maximum Temp. (°F)	82	88	93	100	104	110	108	106	104	96	88	79	110
Extreme Minimum Temp. (°F)	-13	-13	0	12	27	42	48	49	27	10	-4	-12	-13
Days Maximum Temp. ≥ 90°F	0	0	0	1	5	16	25	22	10	2	0	0	81
Days Maximum Temp. ≤ 32°F	5	3	1	0	0	0	0	0	0	0	1	4	14
Days Minimum Temp. ≤ 32°F	29	23	17	6	0	0	0	0	0	4	18	28	125
Days Minimum Temp. ≤ 0°F	1	1	0	0	0	0	0	0	0	0	0	1	3
Heating Degree Days (base 65°F)	954	717	550	281	85	7	1	1	49	234	604	892	4,375
Cooling Degree Days (base 65°F)	0	0	2	17	88	292	439	390	187	22	0	0	1,437
Mean Precipitation (in.)	0.52	0.57	1.30	1.61	3.04	2.75	2.93	2.26	1.78	1.36	0.87	0.69	19.68
Days With ≥ 0.1" Precipitation	2	2	3	3	5	5	5	4	4	2	2	2	39
Days With ≥ 1.0" Precipitation	0	0	0	0	1	1	1	0	0	0	0	0	3
Mean Snowfall (in.)	3.2	3.0	2.6	1.0	0.2	0.0	0.0	0.0	0.0	0.5	1.9	3.5	15.9
Days With ≥ 1.0" Snow Depth	2	1	0	0	0	0	0	0	0	0	0	1	4

Guthrie *King County*   Elevation: 1,738 ft.   Latitude: 33° 37' N   Longitude: 100° 19' W

	JAN	FEB	MAR	APR	MAY	JUN	JUL	AUG	SEP	OCT	NOV	DEC	YEAR
Mean Maximum Temp. (°F)	54.4	59.9	68.6	78.2	85.9	93.2	97.2	95.5	88.1	78.8	65.9	56.4	76.8
Mean Temp. (°F)	39.6	44.5	52.3	61.5	70.7	78.8	82.9	81.4	74.0	63.2	50.6	41.6	61.8
Mean Minimum Temp. (°F)	24.8	29.1	36.2	44.7	55.5	64.3	68.5	67.2	59.8	47.6	35.2	26.8	46.7
Extreme Maximum Temp. (°F)	86	93	103	102	108	119	111	111	109	107	91	84	119
Extreme Minimum Temp. (°F)	0	-4	12	19	34	46	56	52	35	16	10	-10	-10
Days Maximum Temp. ≥ 90°F	0	0	1	4	11	22	28	26	16	4	0	0	112
Days Maximum Temp. ≤ 32°F	2	1	0	0	0	0	0	0	0	0	0	2	5
Days Minimum Temp. ≤ 32°F	25	18	10	2	0	0	0	0	0	1	11	24	91
Days Minimum Temp. ≤ 0°F	0	0	0	0	0	0	0	0	0	0	0	0	0
Heating Degree Days (base 65°F)	781	572	396	158	29	1	0	0	22	123	430	719	3,231
Cooling Degree Days (base 65°F)	0	1	12	58	218	420	569	538	302	77	5	0	2,200
Mean Precipitation (in.)	1.04	1.40	1.20	1.76	3.81	3.06	2.00	3.00	3.19	2.33	0.96	1.00	24.75
Days With ≥ 0.1" Precipitation	2	3	2	3	5	5	3	4	4	3	2	2	38
Days With ≥ 1.0" Precipitation	0	0	0	1	1	1	0	1	1	1	0	0	6
Mean Snowfall (in.)	2.0	1.4	0.1	trace	0.0	0.0	0.0	0.0	0.0	trace	0.7	0.6	4.8
Days With ≥ 1.0" Snow Depth	1	1	0	0	0	0	0	0	0	0	0	0	2

Hallettsville 2 N *Lavaca County*   Elevation: 272 ft.   Latitude: 29° 28' N   Longitude: 96° 57' W

	JAN	FEB	MAR	APR	MAY	JUN	JUL	AUG	SEP	OCT	NOV	DEC	YEAR
Mean Maximum Temp. (°F)	63.4	67.1	74.2	80.1	85.5	90.9	94.3	94.9	90.3	83.0	72.9	65.7	80.2
Mean Temp. (°F)	52.6	55.9	63.1	69.3	75.7	81.0	83.5	83.6	79.3	71.2	61.7	54.8	69.3
Mean Minimum Temp. (°F)	41.7	44.8	51.9	58.3	65.7	71.0	72.6	72.3	68.3	59.4	50.4	44.0	58.4
Extreme Maximum Temp. (°F)	90	92	98	93	99	109	111	104	102	98	89	85	111
Extreme Minimum Temp. (°F)	11	15	20	29	44	52	64	58	47	27	20	5	5
Days Maximum Temp. ≥ 90°F	0	0	0	1	6	20	28	28	19	5	0	0	107
Days Maximum Temp. ≤ 32°F	0	0	0	0	0	0	0	0	0	0	0	0	0
Days Minimum Temp. ≤ 32°F	6	4	1	0	0	0	0	0	0	0	2	5	18
Days Minimum Temp. ≤ 0°F	0	0	0	0	0	0	0	0	0	0	0	0	0
Heating Degree Days (base 65°F)	397	273	130	36	1	0	0	0	1	27	165	337	1,367
Cooling Degree Days (base 65°F)	14	25	68	166	350	491	586	595	443	232	75	30	3,075
Mean Precipitation (in.)	2.85	2.52	2.48	3.40	5.94	4.89	2.31	2.92	4.66	4.02	3.23	2.77	41.99
Days With ≥ 0.1" Precipitation	5	4	4	4	6	6	4	5	6	5	4	5	58
Days With ≥ 1.0" Precipitation	1	1	1	1	2	2	1	1	2	1	1	1	15
Mean Snowfall (in.)	0.1	trace	trace	0.0	0.0	0.0	0.0	0.0	0.0	0.0	0.0	trace	0.1
Days With ≥ 1.0" Snow Depth	0	0	0	0	0	0	0	0	0	0	0	0	0

Harlingen *Cameron County* Elevation: 36 ft. Latitude: 26° 12' N Longitude: 97° 40' W

	JAN	FEB	MAR	APR	MAY	JUN	JUL	AUG	SEP	OCT	NOV	DEC	YEAR
Mean Maximum Temp. (°F)	68.2	72.5	79.4	83.9	88.4	92.5	94.3	95.0	91.2	85.1	77.3	70.7	83.2
Mean Temp. (°F)	58.1	61.8	68.4	73.7	79.0	82.9	84.3	84.5	81.3	74.8	67.0	60.6	73.0
Mean Minimum Temp. (°F)	48.0	51.0	57.4	63.5	69.7	73.4	74.1	74.1	71.5	64.4	56.7	50.4	62.8
Extreme Maximum Temp. (°F)	90	95	104	103	105	104	101	103	100	96	97	92	105
Extreme Minimum Temp. (°F)	23	27	29	37	46	57	67	65	54	33	30	15	15
Days Maximum Temp. ≥ 90°F	0	0	2	6	14	24	28	28	21	7	1	0	131
Days Maximum Temp. ≤ 32°F	0	0	0	0	0	0	0	0	0	0	0	0	0
Days Minimum Temp. ≤ 32°F	2	1	0	0	0	0	0	0	0	0	0	1	4
Days Minimum Temp. ≤ 0°F	0	0	0	0	0	0	0	0	0	0	0	0	0
Heating Degree Days (base 65°F)	251	150	57	13	1	0	0	0	0	9	84	202	767
Cooling Degree Days (base 65°F)	49	73	167	281	456	571	628	631	514	331	168	76	3,945
Mean Precipitation (in.)	1.60	1.85	1.21	2.37	2.82	2.93	1.88	2.85	5.37	3.02	1.38	1.38	28.66
Days With ≥ 0.1" Precipitation	3	3	2	2	4	4	3	4	7	4	3	3	42
Days With ≥ 1.0" Precipitation	0	1	0	1	1	1	0	1	1	1	0	0	7
Mean Snowfall (in.)	trace	0.0	0.0	0.0	0.0	0.0	0.0	0.0	0.0	0.0	trace	trace	trace
Days With ≥ 1.0" Snow Depth	0	0	0	0	0	0	0	0	0	0	0	0	0

Haskell *Haskell County* Elevation: 1,597 ft. Latitude: 33° 09' N Longitude: 99° 45' W

	JAN	FEB	MAR	APR	MAY	JUN	JUL	AUG	SEP	OCT	NOV	DEC	YEAR
Mean Maximum Temp. (°F)	54.2	59.5	68.9	78.0	85.5	92.2	96.4	95.1	87.6	78.2	65.1	56.8	76.5
Mean Temp. (°F)	41.5	46.4	54.9	64.0	72.7	80.0	84.3	83.0	75.6	65.2	52.8	44.2	63.7
Mean Minimum Temp. (°F)	28.7	33.3	40.9	50.0	59.9	67.8	72.1	70.9	63.5	52.2	40.4	31.6	50.9
Extreme Maximum Temp. (°F)	84	93	99	102	108	115	112	108	107	105	90	82	115
Extreme Minimum Temp. (°F)	3	-6	8	26	38	47	59	53	37	25	2	-6	-6
Days Maximum Temp. ≥ 90°F	0	0	1	4	10	20	28	25	15	3	0	0	106
Days Maximum Temp. ≤ 32°F	3	1	0	0	0	0	0	0	0	0	0	2	6
Days Minimum Temp. ≤ 32°F	20	13	6	1	0	0	0	0	0	0	6	16	62
Days Minimum Temp. ≤ 0°F	0	0	0	0	0	0	0	0	0	0	0	0	0
Heating Degree Days (base 65°F)	723	521	327	117	19	1	0	0	19	99	370	638	2,834
Cooling Degree Days (base 65°F)	0	3	21	94	272	452	613	587	351	115	11	0	2,519
Mean Precipitation (in.)	0.94	1.50	1.44	1.96	3.37	3.01	1.58	2.80	3.02	2.47	1.14	1.33	24.56
Days With ≥ 0.1" Precipitation	2	3	3	4	5	5	3	4	5	4	2	3	43
Days With ≥ 1.0" Precipitation	0	0	0	1	1	1	0	1	1	1	0	0	6
Mean Snowfall (in.)	1.6	1.3	0.3	trace	0.0	0.0	0.0	0.0	0.0	trace	0.7	0.6	4.5
Days With ≥ 1.0" Snow Depth	1	1	0	0	0	0	0	0	0	0	0	0	2

Hebbronville *Jim Hogg County* Elevation: 577 ft. Latitude: 27° 19' N Longitude: 98° 41' W

	JAN	FEB	MAR	APR	MAY	JUN	JUL	AUG	SEP	OCT	NOV	DEC	YEAR
Mean Maximum Temp. (°F)	67.0	71.7	79.4	85.3	90.4	94.6	96.8	97.4	92.4	85.5	76.5	69.5	83.9
Mean Temp. (°F)	55.1	59.3	66.8	73.1	79.3	83.5	84.9	85.0	81.0	73.3	64.6	57.9	72.0
Mean Minimum Temp. (°F)	43.2	46.9	54.2	60.9	68.1	72.3	73.0	72.6	69.5	61.2	52.7	45.8	60.0
Extreme Maximum Temp. (°F)	95	98	102	106	110	111	109	108	103	100	95	93	111
Extreme Minimum Temp. (°F)	18	22	25	33	48	53	62	64	48	26	27	12	12
Days Maximum Temp. ≥ 90°F	0	1	3	9	18	26	29	29	23	10	1	0	149
Days Maximum Temp. ≤ 32°F	0	0	0	0	0	0	0	0	0	0	0	0	0
Days Minimum Temp. ≤ 32°F	4	2	1	0	0	0	0	0	0	0	1	3	11
Days Minimum Temp. ≤ 0°F	0	0	0	0	0	0	0	0	0	0	0	0	0
Heating Degree Days (base 65°F)	326	202	80	21	1	0	0	0	1	17	118	259	1,025
Cooling Degree Days (base 65°F)	24	51	134	265	457	579	647	647	504	295	117	45	3,765
Mean Precipitation (in.)	1.14	1.41	1.07	1.68	3.47	3.19	1.48	2.32	3.89	2.21	1.20	1.12	24.18
Days With ≥ 0.1" Precipitation	4	3	2	3	4	4	3	3	5	3	2	3	39
Days With ≥ 1.0" Precipitation	0	0	0	1	1	1	0	1	1	1	0	0	6
Mean Snowfall (in.)	trace	trace	0.0	0.0	0.0	0.0	0.0	0.0	0.0	0.0	0.0	trace	trace
Days With ≥ 1.0" Snow Depth	0	0	0	0	0	0	0	0	0	0	0	0	0

Henderson *Rusk County* Elevation: 419 ft. Latitude: 32° 11' N Longitude: 94° 48' W

	JAN	FEB	MAR	APR	MAY	JUN	JUL	AUG	SEP	OCT	NOV	DEC	YEAR
Mean Maximum Temp. (°F)	55.3	60.6	68.1	75.6	82.2	89.1	92.9	93.0	86.9	77.7	66.7	58.8	75.6
Mean Temp. (°F)	44.5	49.0	56.1	63.6	71.4	78.5	82.1	81.7	75.7	65.4	55.1	47.6	64.2
Mean Minimum Temp. (°F)	33.6	37.3	44.0	51.4	60.4	67.9	71.2	70.3	64.5	53.1	43.4	36.4	52.8
Extreme Maximum Temp. (°F)	83	93	88	93	101	104	108	110	105	96	87	82	110
Extreme Minimum Temp. (°F)	4	11	16	25	38	51	55	54	40	24	17	-1	-1
Days Maximum Temp. ≥ 90°F	0	0	0	0	3	16	25	24	13	1	0	0	82
Days Maximum Temp. ≤ 32°F	1	1	0	0	0	0	0	0	0	0	0	1	3
Days Minimum Temp. ≤ 32°F	15	10	4	1	0	0	0	0	0	0	4	12	46
Days Minimum Temp. ≤ 0°F	0	0	0	0	0	0	0	0	0	0	0	0	0
Heating Degree Days (base 65°F)	632	453	292	114	16	1	0	0	10	92	314	537	2,461
Cooling Degree Days (base 65°F)	2	7	22	76	225	417	542	538	342	111	21	6	2,309
Mean Precipitation (in.)	4.04	3.90	3.95	3.90	4.55	4.81	2.97	2.80	3.78	4.91	4.37	4.11	48.09
Days With ≥ 0.1" Precipitation	6	5	5	5	6	5	5	4	5	5	6	6	63
Days With ≥ 1.0" Precipitation	1	1	1	1	2	1	1	1	1	2	2	1	15
Mean Snowfall (in.)	0.5	0.4	trace	0.0	0.0	0.0	0.0	0.0	0.0	0.0	trace	0.2	1.1
Days With ≥ 1.0" Snow Depth	0	0	0	0	0	0	0	0	0	0	0	0	0

Henrietta *Clay County*   Elevation: 928 ft.   Latitude: 33° 49' N   Longitude: 98° 12' W

	JAN	FEB	MAR	APR	MAY	JUN	JUL	AUG	SEP	OCT	NOV	DEC	YEAR
Mean Maximum Temp. (°F)	52.4	58.2	66.7	75.3	82.5	90.4	96.5	95.7	87.5	77.6	64.8	55.9	75.3
Mean Temp. (°F)	39.5	44.9	53.2	61.9	70.3	78.5	83.6	82.6	74.8	64.0	51.7	43.0	62.3
Mean Minimum Temp. (°F)	26.6	31.5	39.7	48.5	58.0	66.5	70.7	69.4	62.1	50.3	38.6	30.1	49.3
Extreme Maximum Temp. (°F)	84	95	96	100	103	115	113	111	107	106	90	84	115
Extreme Minimum Temp. (°F)	1	-7	6	24	35	48	55	51	37	20	13	-8	-8
Days Maximum Temp. ≥ 90°F	0	0	0	1	6	18	27	26	15	3	0	0	96
Days Maximum Temp. ≤ 32°F	3	1	0	0	0	0	0	0	0	0	0	1	5
Days Minimum Temp. ≤ 32°F	23	15	7	1	0	0	0	0	0	1	8	20	75
Days Minimum Temp. ≤ 0°F	0	0	0	0	0	0	0	0	0	0	0	0	0
Heating Degree Days (base 65°F)	783	564	372	150	28	2	0	0	22	118	400	675	3,114
Cooling Degree Days (base 65°F)	0	2	12	58	200	411	588	569	333	90	8	1	2,272
Mean Precipitation (in.)	1.46	2.09	2.53	2.71	4.44	3.70	1.72	2.41	3.61	3.28	1.63	2.13	31.71
Days With ≥ 0.1" Precipitation	3	4	4	4	5	5	3	4	5	5	3	3	48
Days With ≥ 1.0" Precipitation	0	1	1	1	1	1	0	1	1	1	0	1	9
Mean Snowfall (in.)	0.2	*trace*	0.2	0.0	0.0	0.0	0.0	0.0	0.0	trace	trace	0.2	*0.6*
Days With ≥ 1.0" Snow Depth	0	*0*	0	0	0	0	0	0	0	0	0	0	*0*

Hereford *Deaf Smith County*   Elevation: 3,818 ft.   Latitude: 34° 49' N   Longitude: 102° 24' W

	JAN	FEB	MAR	APR	MAY	JUN	JUL	AUG	SEP	OCT	NOV	DEC	YEAR
Mean Maximum Temp. (°F)	49.3	54.5	62.7	71.2	79.6	88.3	90.8	88.5	81.7	72.3	59.7	50.9	70.8
Mean Temp. (°F)	35.3	39.7	46.9	55.3	64.7	73.7	77.2	75.3	68.1	57.4	45.1	37.0	56.3
Mean Minimum Temp. (°F)	21.2	24.9	31.1	39.4	49.8	59.0	63.4	62.1	54.4	42.4	30.5	23.1	41.8
Extreme Maximum Temp. (°F)	80	83	92	98	101	108	105	103	100	95	87	78	108
Extreme Minimum Temp. (°F)	-9	-9	5	18	30	40	53	50	31	15	0	-6	-9
Days Maximum Temp. ≥ 90°F	0	0	0	1	4	14	20	15	7	1	0	0	62
Days Maximum Temp. ≤ 32°F	4	2	1	0	0	0	0	0	0	0	1	3	11
Days Minimum Temp. ≤ 32°F	29	23	17	6	0	0	0	0	0	3	18	28	124
Days Minimum Temp. ≤ 0°F	0	0	0	0	0	0	0	0	0	0	0	1	1
Heating Degree Days (base 65°F)	916	707	555	299	93	10	1	1	59	248	587	862	4,338
Cooling Degree Days (base 65°F)	0	0	1	14	94	286	404	352	170	20	0	0	1,341
Mean Precipitation (in.)	0.50	0.51	0.92	1.00	2.09	2.78	2.08	3.26	2.28	1.56	0.71	0.70	18.39
Days With ≥ 0.1" Precipitation	1	2	2	2	4	5	4	5	4	3	2	2	36
Days With ≥ 1.0" Precipitation	0	0	0	0	0	1	0	1	0	0	0	0	2
Mean Snowfall (in.)	3.8	*2.8*	1.4	0.6	0.0	0.0	0.0	0.0	0.0	0.2	1.3	3.5	*13.6*
Days With ≥ 1.0" Snow Depth	4	2	1	0	0	0	0	0	0	0	1	3	11

Hico *Hamilton County*   Elevation: 1,023 ft.   Latitude: 31° 59' N   Longitude: 98° 02' W

	JAN	FEB	MAR	APR	MAY	JUN	JUL	AUG	SEP	OCT	NOV	DEC	YEAR
Mean Maximum Temp. (°F)	58.2	63.0	70.7	78.4	84.6	91.3	96.0	95.3	88.6	79.5	67.4	59.9	77.7
Mean Temp. (°F)	45.1	49.8	57.4	65.1	72.8	79.4	83.5	82.6	76.3	66.5	55.1	47.3	65.1
Mean Minimum Temp. (°F)	32.0	36.5	44.0	51.7	60.9	67.4	71.0	69.8	63.9	53.4	42.7	34.6	52.3
Extreme Maximum Temp. (°F)	87	98	99	98	102	111	111	107	107	99	89	86	111
Extreme Minimum Temp. (°F)	-3	0	14	25	40	46	55	50	38	21	16	-7	-7
Days Maximum Temp. ≥ 90°F	0	0	0	2	7	20	28	27	15	3	0	0	102
Days Maximum Temp. ≤ 32°F	1	1	0	0	0	0	0	0	0	0	0	1	3
Days Minimum Temp. ≤ 32°F	17	10	4	1	0	0	0	0	0	0	6	13	51
Days Minimum Temp. ≤ 0°F	0	0	0	0	0	0	0	0	0	0	0	0	0
Heating Degree Days (base 65°F)	611	430	260	86	10	0	0	0	11	77	310	545	2,340
Cooling Degree Days (base 65°F)	1	5	26	90	261	430	581	560	352	127	22	2	2,457
Mean Precipitation (in.)	1.66	2.38	2.69	3.01	4.90	3.32	2.15	2.48	3.35	3.40	2.05	2.05	33.44
Days With ≥ 0.1" Precipitation	4	4	4	4	6	5	3	4	5	5	4	4	52
Days With ≥ 1.0" Precipitation	0	1	1	1	2	1	1	1	1	1	1	0	11
Mean Snowfall (in.)	*0.8*	0.3	0.1	0.0	0.6	0.0	0.0	0.0	0.0	0.0	0.2	0.2	*2.2*
Days With ≥ 1.0" Snow Depth	0	0	0	0	0	0	0	0	0	0	0	0	0

Hillsboro *Hill County*   Elevation: 547 ft.   Latitude: 32° 01' N   Longitude: 97° 07' W

	JAN	FEB	MAR	APR	MAY	JUN	JUL	AUG	SEP	OCT	NOV	DEC	YEAR
Mean Maximum Temp. (°F)	56.8	62.1	69.8	77.2	83.4	90.5	95.0	95.2	88.8	79.6	67.9	59.9	77.2
Mean Temp. (°F)	45.5	50.4	58.0	65.5	72.9	80.0	83.9	83.8	77.6	67.7	56.5	48.6	65.9
Mean Minimum Temp. (°F)	34.1	38.8	46.0	53.8	62.3	69.5	72.7	72.4	66.3	55.7	45.1	37.3	54.5
Extreme Maximum Temp. (°F)	85	97	95	96	99	106	107	107	107	99	90	85	107
Extreme Minimum Temp. (°F)	2	4	13	26	39	51	58	53	39	21	14	-6	-6
Days Maximum Temp. ≥ 90°F	0	0	0	1	4	19	28	27	17	3	0	0	99
Days Maximum Temp. ≤ 32°F	1	1	0	0	0	0	0	0	0	0	0	1	3
Days Minimum Temp. ≤ 32°F	14	8	3	0	0	0	0	0	0	0	4	10	39
Days Minimum Temp. ≤ 0°F	0	0	0	0	0	0	0	0	0	0	0	0	0
Heating Degree Days (base 65°F)	600	412	243	80	10	0	0	0	8	66	277	506	2,202
Cooling Degree Days (base 65°F)	3	9	34	109	277	463	600	606	404	161	32	7	2,705
Mean Precipitation (in.)	2.15	2.80	3.25	3.22	4.56	3.66	2.10	2.19	3.09	4.15	2.53	3.03	36.73
Days With ≥ 0.1" Precipitation	5	5	5	4	6	5	3	3	4	5	4	5	54
Days With ≥ 1.0" Precipitation	1	1	1	1	1	1	1	1	1	1	1	1	12
Mean Snowfall (in.)	0.3	0.1	trace	0.0	0.0	0.0	0.0	0.0	0.0	0.0	0.1	trace	0.5
Days With ≥ 1.0" Snow Depth	0	0	0	0	0	0	0	0	0	0	0	0	0

Hords Creek Dam *Coleman County*   Elevation: 1,938 ft.   Latitude: 31° 51' N   Longitude: 99° 34' W

	JAN	FEB	MAR	APR	MAY	JUN	JUL	AUG	SEP	OCT	NOV	DEC	YEAR
Mean Maximum Temp. (°F)	55.5	60.6	68.7	77.0	83.5	89.8	93.5	93.0	86.7	78.4	66.1	58.2	75.9
Mean Temp. (°F)	42.3	47.1	55.0	63.2	70.8	77.6	81.1	80.4	73.9	64.7	53.0	45.0	62.8
Mean Minimum Temp. (°F)	28.9	33.5	41.1	49.2	58.0	65.3	68.6	67.8	61.1	51.0	39.9	31.6	49.7
Extreme Maximum Temp. (°F)	85	98	94	98	103	107	106	107	105	100	89	84	107
Extreme Minimum Temp. (°F)	3	-1	8	21	36	46	53	49	35	18	14	-9	-9
Days Maximum Temp. ≥ 90°F	0	0	0	2	7	17	25	24	13	2	0	0	90
Days Maximum Temp. ≤ 32°F	2	1	0	0	0	0	0	0	0	0	0	1	4
Days Minimum Temp. ≤ 32°F	20	13	5	1	0	0	0	0	0	1	7	16	63
Days Minimum Temp. ≤ 0°F	0	0	0	0	0	0	0	0	0	0	0	0	0
Heating Degree Days (base 65°F)	698	501	322	126	24	1	0	0	19	97	364	615	2,767
Cooling Degree Days (base 65°F)	0	3	18	76	217	382	511	500	296	93	13	0	2,109
Mean Precipitation (in.)	0.97	1.55	1.66	2.01	3.60	3.34	1.69	2.22	3.07	2.65	1.30	1.28	25.34
Days With ≥ 0.1" Precipitation	2	3	3	3	5	4	3	3	4	4	3	3	40
Days With ≥ 1.0" Precipitation	0	0	0	1	1	1	0	1	1	1	0	0	6
Mean Snowfall (in.)	0.0	trace	trace	0.0	0.0	0.0	0.0	0.0	0.0	0.0	trace	trace	trace
Days With ≥ 1.0" Snow Depth	0	0	0	0	0	0	0	0	0	0	0	0	0

Houston William P. Hobby Airport *Harris County*   Elevation: 49 ft.   Latitude: 29° 39' N   Longitude: 95° 17' W

	JAN	FEB	MAR	APR	MAY	JUN	JUL	AUG	SEP	OCT	NOV	DEC	YEAR
Mean Maximum Temp. (°F)	61.6	65.6	72.4	78.5	84.8	89.9	92.3	92.1	88.1	80.9	71.6	64.9	78.6
Mean Temp. (°F)	52.7	56.2	63.1	69.4	76.2	81.6	83.7	83.6	79.7	71.4	62.2	55.7	69.6
Mean Minimum Temp. (°F)	43.7	46.8	53.7	60.1	67.6	73.2	75.0	75.0	71.3	61.8	52.6	46.4	60.6
Extreme Maximum Temp. (°F)	85	87	91	92	100	101	103	101	98	95	90	84	103
Extreme Minimum Temp. (°F)	15	20	24	22	44	56	45	65	53	33	25	9	9
Days Maximum Temp. ≥ 90°F	0	0	0	1	5	18	26	25	14	2	0	0	91
Days Maximum Temp. ≤ 32°F	0	0	0	0	0	0	0	0	0	0	0	0	0
Days Minimum Temp. ≤ 32°F	4	2	1	0	0	0	0	0	0	0	1	2	10
Days Minimum Temp. ≤ 0°F	0	0	0	0	0	0	0	0	0	0	0	0	0
Heating Degree Days (base 65°F)	392	264	123	31	1	0	0	0	0	24	154	312	1,301
Cooling Degree Days (base 65°F)	11	24	69	167	365	510	593	594	453	233	77	32	3,128
Mean Precipitation (in.)	4.29	3.22	3.31	3.40	5.39	6.81	4.42	4.55	5.56	5.21	4.16	3.70	54.02
Days With ≥ 0.1" Precipitation	7	5	5	4	6	7	6	6	7	5	5	5	68
Days With ≥ 1.0" Precipitation	1	1	1	1	2	2	1	1	2	2	1	1	16
Mean Snowfall (in.)	trace	trace	trace	trace	trace	trace	0.0	trace	0.0	0.0	trace	trace	trace
Days With ≥ 1.0" Snow Depth	0	0	0	0	0	0	0	0	0	0	0	0	0

Huntsville *Walker County*   Elevation: 492 ft.   Latitude: 30° 43' N   Longitude: 95° 33' W

	JAN	FEB	MAR	APR	MAY	JUN	JUL	AUG	SEP	OCT	NOV	DEC	YEAR
Mean Maximum Temp. (°F)	58.1	63.1	70.8	77.8	84.4	90.7	94.2	94.1	88.5	79.7	69.1	61.3	77.7
Mean Temp. (°F)	48.5	52.8	60.2	67.3	74.4	80.6	83.6	83.3	78.0	68.9	59.0	41.6	67.3
Mean Minimum Temp. (°F)	38.8	42.5	49.7	56.8	64.2	70.5	72.9	72.4	67.4	58.0	48.9	41.6	57.0
Extreme Maximum Temp. (°F)	88	94	91	93	98	106	106	107	103	95	89	85	107
Extreme Minimum Temp. (°F)	7	14	18	31	45	54	60	59	41	28	19	2	2
Days Maximum Temp. ≥ 90°F	0	0	0	1	7	20	27	27	16	3	0	0	101
Days Maximum Temp. ≤ 32°F	1	0	0	0	0	0	0	0	0	0	0	0	1
Days Minimum Temp. ≤ 32°F	9	5	1	0	0	0	0	0	0	0	1	6	22
Days Minimum Temp. ≤ 0°F	0	0	0	0	0	0	0	0	0	0	0	0	0
Heating Degree Days (base 65°F)	513	351	191	58	6	0	0	0	4	50	223	426	1,822
Cooling Degree Days (base 65°F)	5	16	51	135	308	480	589	589	413	182	51	15	2,834
Mean Precipitation (in.)	4.27	3.17	3.50	3.53	4.90	4.48	2.63	3.70	4.72	4.31	4.37	4.02	47.60
Days With ≥ 0.1" Precipitation	6	5	6	4	6	6	5	5	6	5	6	6	66
Days With ≥ 1.0" Precipitation	1	1	1	1	2	1	1	1	2	1	1	1	14
Mean Snowfall (in.)	0.2	trace	trace	0.0	0.0	0.0	0.0	0.0	0.0	0.0	trace	trace	0.2
Days With ≥ 1.0" Snow Depth	0	0	0	0	0	0	0	0	0	0	0	0	0

Jacksboro *Jack County*   Elevation: 1,099 ft.   Latitude: 33° 14' N   Longitude: 98° 09' W

	JAN	FEB	MAR	APR	MAY	JUN	JUL	AUG	SEP	OCT	NOV	DEC	YEAR
Mean Maximum Temp. (°F)	55.3	60.9	68.9	76.7	83.4	90.7	95.5	95.0	87.8	78.6	66.4	58.4	76.5
Mean Temp. (°F)	43.3	48.5	56.4	64.4	72.0	79.7	83.9	83.4	76.3	66.4	54.6	46.1	64.6
Mean Minimum Temp. (°F)	31.2	36.1	43.7	52.0	60.6	68.6	72.6	71.6	64.8	54.1	42.7	33.8	52.7
Extreme Maximum Temp. (°F)	88	94	99	98	102	113	110	109	106	101	88	85	113
Extreme Minimum Temp. (°F)	4	4	9	27	39	50	58	55	39	22	16	-7	-7
Days Maximum Temp. ≥ 90°F	0	0	1	1	6	18	27	26	15	3	0	0	97
Days Maximum Temp. ≤ 32°F	2	1	0	0	0	0	0	0	0	0	0	1	4
Days Minimum Temp. ≤ 32°F	17	10	4	0	0	0	0	0	0	0	5	14	50
Days Minimum Temp. ≤ 0°F	0	0	0	0	0	0	0	0	0	0	0	0	0
Heating Degree Days (base 65°F)	668	466	295	105	17	0	0	0	13	81	326	580	2,551
Cooling Degree Days (base 65°F)	1	5	23	81	234	438	590	588	357	119	17	2	2,455
Mean Precipitation (in.)	1.24	1.85	2.40	2.60	4.96	3.02	2.28	2.16	3.28	3.72	1.86	1.80	31.17
Days With ≥ 0.1" Precipitation	3	4	4	4	6	4	3	3	4	5	3	3	46
Days With ≥ 1.0" Precipitation	0	0	1	1	2	1	1	1	1	1	1	0	10
Mean Snowfall (in.)	0.6	0.4	0.2	trace	0.0	0.0	0.0	0.0	0.0	0.0	trace	0.2	1.4
Days With ≥ 1.0" Snow Depth	0	0	0	0	0	0	0	0	0	0	0	0	0

Jayton *Kent County*   Elevation: 2,007 ft.   Latitude: 33° 15' N   Longitude: 100° 34' W

	JAN	FEB	MAR	APR	MAY	JUN	JUL	AUG	SEP	OCT	NOV	DEC	YEAR
Mean Maximum Temp. (°F)	53.5	58.8	67.5	76.9	84.3	91.7	95.9	93.7	86.1	76.9	64.6	56.1	75.5
Mean Temp. (°F)	39.7	44.6	52.3	61.5	70.3	78.5	82.6	80.8	73.3	63.0	50.6	42.2	61.6
Mean Minimum Temp. (°F)	25.9	30.2	37.1	46.1	56.2	65.2	69.4	67.8	60.5	49.1	36.5	28.3	47.7
Extreme Maximum Temp. (°F)	85	91	99	102	109	116	110	106	105	105	90	86	116
Extreme Minimum Temp. (°F)	2	-6	6	24	35	47	55	54	34	25	10	-5	-6
Days Maximum Temp. ≥ 90°F	0	0	1	4	9	19	26	24	12	3	0	0	98
Days Maximum Temp. ≤ 32°F	3	1	0	0	0	0	0	0	0	0	0	2	6
Days Minimum Temp. ≤ 32°F	24	17	9	2	0	0	0	0	0	0	10	22	85
Days Minimum Temp. ≤ 0°F	0	0	0	0	0	0	0	0	0	1	0	0	0
Heating Degree Days (base 65°F)	778	571	397	164	34	2	0	0	29	133	430	699	3,237
Cooling Degree Days (base 65°F)	0	2	10	62	207	405	562	516	295	81	4	0	2,144
Mean Precipitation (in.)	0.88	1.13	1.08	1.68	3.25	3.04	1.63	2.83	3.06	2.17	0.87	0.90	22.52
Days With ≥ 0.1" Precipitation	2	2	2	3	5	4	3	4	4	4	2	2	37
Days With ≥ 1.0" Precipitation	0	0	0	0	1	1	0	1	1	1	0	0	5
Mean Snowfall (in.)	na	0.4	0.1	trace	0.0	0.0	0.0	0.0	0.0	0.0	trace	0.1	na
Days With ≥ 1.0" Snow Depth	0	na	0	0	0	0	0	0	0	0	0	0	na

Johnson City *Blanco County*   Elevation: 1,230 ft.   Latitude: 30° 17' N   Longitude: 98° 25' W

	JAN	FEB	MAR	APR	MAY	JUN	JUL	AUG	SEP	OCT	NOV	DEC	YEAR
Mean Maximum Temp. (°F)	60.3	64.0	71.7	79.1	85.3	91.1	95.1	94.8	89.0	80.6	70.2	62.3	78.6
Mean Temp. (°F)	47.1	51.2	58.9	66.0	73.6	79.7	83.0	82.4	76.8	67.6	57.6	49.5	66.1
Mean Minimum Temp. (°F)	33.9	38.3	46.0	52.9	61.9	68.4	70.8	69.9	64.7	54.6	44.7	36.8	53.6
Extreme Maximum Temp. (°F)	88	100	102	101	102	110	108	105	103	98	93	89	110
Extreme Minimum Temp. (°F)	7	3	13	27	36	50	58	54	37	22	17	1	1
Days Maximum Temp. ≥ 90°F	0	0	1	2	8	21	28	27	16	4	0	0	107
Days Maximum Temp. ≤ 32°F	0	0	0	0	0	0	0	0	0	0	0	0	0
Days Minimum Temp. ≤ 32°F	15	9	4	1	0	0	0	0	0	0	0	0	46
Days Minimum Temp. ≤ 0°F	0	0	0	0	0	0	0	0	0	0	5	12	0
Heating Degree Days (base 65°F)	552	393	226	82	9	0	0	0	8	64	250	477	2,061
Cooling Degree Days (base 65°F)	2	10	40	118	291	454	569	565	379	156	33	7	2,624
Mean Precipitation (in.)	1.77	2.23	2.21	2.21	4.82	3.97	1.83	2.51	3.47	3.98	2.39	2.06	33.45
Days With ≥ 0.1" Precipitation	4	4	4	4	6	5	3	3	5	5	3	3	49
Days With ≥ 1.0" Precipitation	0	1	1	0	2	1	0	1	1	1	1	1	10
Mean Snowfall (in.)	0.4	0.3	trace	0.0	0.0	0.0	0.0	0.0	0.0	0.0	trace	trace	0.7
Days With ≥ 1.0" Snow Depth	0	0	0	0	0	0	0	0	0	0	0	0	0

Kaufman 3 SE *Kaufman County*   Elevation: 419 ft.   Latitude: 32° 34' N   Longitude: 96° 16' W

	JAN	FEB	MAR	APR	MAY	JUN	JUL	AUG	SEP	OCT	NOV	DEC	YEAR
Mean Maximum Temp. (°F)	54.3	59.6	67.4	75.3	82.4	90.1	95.0	95.3	88.7	78.8	66.4	57.8	75.9
Mean Temp. (°F)	43.5	48.3	56.0	63.7	71.9	79.4	83.7	83.5	77.1	66.4	55.1	46.7	64.6
Mean Minimum Temp. (°F)	32.6	36.9	44.5	52.1	61.3	68.8	72.4	71.7	65.5	54.1	43.7	35.7	53.3
Extreme Maximum Temp. (°F)	81	96	93	94	98	106	112	111	109	98	88	81	112
Extreme Minimum Temp. (°F)	2	2	13	28	40	51	56	54	40	21	14	-3	-3
Days Maximum Temp. ≥ 90°F	0	0	0	0	3	18	27	27	16	3	0	0	94
Days Maximum Temp. ≤ 32°F	2	1	0	0	0	0	0	0	0	0	0	1	4
Days Minimum Temp. ≤ 32°F	16	10	3	0	0	0	0	0	0	0	0	12	45
Days Minimum Temp. ≤ 0°F	0	0	0	0	0	0	0	0	0	0	4	0	0
Heating Degree Days (base 65°F)	661	471	294	107	13	0	0	0	9	79	308	563	2,505
Cooling Degree Days (base 65°F)	1	5	20	74	239	446	592	596	389	129	19	4	2,514
Mean Precipitation (in.)	2.71	3.04	3.43	3.17	4.31	3.13	2.12	2.01	3.05	4.93	3.59	3.35	38.84
Days With ≥ 0.1" Precipitation	4	4	5	4	5	4	3	3	4	5	4	4	49
Days With ≥ 1.0" Precipitation	1	1	1	1	2	1	1	0	1	2	1	1	13
Mean Snowfall (in.)	0.5	0.3	trace	0.0	0.0	0.0	0.0	0.0	0.0	0.0	0.1	0.3	1.2
Days With ≥ 1.0" Snow Depth	0	0	0	0	0	0	0	0	0	0	0	0	0

Kerrville 3 NNE *Kerr County*   Elevation: 1,781 ft.   Latitude: 30° 04' N   Longitude: 99° 07' W

	JAN	FEB	MAR	APR	MAY	JUN	JUL	AUG	SEP	OCT	NOV	DEC	YEAR
Mean Maximum Temp. (°F)	58.4	62.7	69.7	76.8	82.3	88.4	91.6	92.4	86.9	78.4	67.8	60.3	76.3
Mean Temp. (°F)	45.4	49.7	56.9	64.2	71.6	77.8	80.5	80.4	75.0	65.6	55.4	47.6	64.2
Mean Minimum Temp. (°F)	32.3	36.6	44.1	51.6	60.8	67.2	69.2	68.4	63.0	52.8	43.0	34.9	52.0
Extreme Maximum Temp. (°F)	87	97	95	98	101	105	104	103	101	95	91	84	105
Extreme Minimum Temp. (°F)	6	1	12	22	37	48	54	54	37	21	12	0	0
Days Maximum Temp. ≥ 90°F	0	0	0	1	4	12	22	25	11	1	0	0	76
Days Maximum Temp. ≤ 32°F	1	1	0	0	0	0	0	0	0	0	0	1	3
Days Minimum Temp. ≤ 32°F	17	10	5	1	0	0	0	0	0	0	1	14	54
Days Minimum Temp. ≤ 0°F	0	0	0	0	0	0	0	0	0	1	6	0	0
Heating Degree Days (base 65°F)	602	430	268	98	13	0	0	0	12	91	299	534	2,347
Cooling Degree Days (base 65°F)	0	4	25	87	235	402	498	497	326	122	20	3	2,219
Mean Precipitation (in.)	1.35	1.96	2.27	2.34	4.31	3.89	2.26	2.31	3.57	3.61	2.45	2.15	32.47
Days With ≥ 0.1" Precipitation	3	3	4	4	6	5	3	3	5	5	4	4	49
Days With ≥ 1.0" Precipitation	0	1	1	1	1	1	1	0	1	1	1	1	10
Mean Snowfall (in.)	0.7	0.1	trace	0.0	0.0	0.0	0.0	0.0	0.0	0.0	0.2	trace	1.0
Days With ≥ 1.0" Snow Depth	0	0	0	0	0	0	0	0	0	0	0	0	0

La Grange *Fayette County*   Elevation: 354 ft.   Latitude: 29° 55' N   Longitude: 96° 53' W

	JAN	FEB	MAR	APR	MAY	JUN	JUL	AUG	SEP	OCT	NOV	DEC	YEAR
Mean Maximum Temp. (°F)	62.4	66.8	74.2	80.5	86.1	91.8	95.9	96.2	90.6	82.9	72.2	65.0	80.4
Mean Temp. (°F)	51.7	55.4	62.7	69.1	75.8	81.5	84.6	84.6	79.5	71.1	61.1	54.0	69.3
Mean Minimum Temp. (°F)	40.8	44.0	51.1	57.8	65.4	71.2	73.2	72.9	68.3	59.2	50.0	43.0	58.1
Extreme Maximum Temp. (°F)	88	99	97	97	103	106	108	106	105	98	91	87	108
Extreme Minimum Temp. (°F)	9	15	19	28	45	54	60	59	45	27	21	3	3
Days Maximum Temp. ≥ 90°F	0	0	0	2	8	22	29	29	19	6	0	0	115
Days Maximum Temp. ≤ 32°F	0	0	0	0	0	0	0	0	0	0	0	0	0
Days Minimum Temp. ≤ 32°F	7	4	1	0	0	0	0	0	0	0	2	6	20
Days Minimum Temp. ≤ 0°F	0	0	0	0	0	0	0	0	0	0	0	0	0
Heating Degree Days (base 65°F)	422	285	138	36	1	0	0	0	1	31	177	357	1,448
Cooling Degree Days (base 65°F)	13	23	70	172	363	517	629	636	457	237	72	25	3,214
Mean Precipitation (in.)	2.96	2.92	2.63	3.04	4.92	4.25	2.25	2.84	3.98	4.57	3.08	2.93	40.37
Days With ≥ 0.1" Precipitation	5	5	5	4	6	5	4	4	5	5	5	5	58
Days With ≥ 1.0" Precipitation	1	1	1	1	2	1	1	1	1	1	1	1	13
Mean Snowfall (in.)	trace	trace	0.0	0.0	0.0	0.0	0.0	0.0	0.0	0.0	trace	trace	trace
Days With ≥ 1.0" Snow Depth	0	0	0	0	0	0	0	0	0	0	0	0	0

Lake Kemp *Baylor County*   Elevation: 1,164 ft.   Latitude: 33° 45' N   Longitude: 99° 09' W

	JAN	FEB	MAR	APR	MAY	JUN	JUL	AUG	SEP	OCT	NOV	DEC	YEAR
Mean Maximum Temp. (°F)	52.4	57.4	66.6	76.3	83.9	92.0	97.5	96.6	88.1	77.9	64.7	54.8	75.7
Mean Temp. (°F)	40.2	45.0	53.4	62.8	71.4	79.9	84.8	83.7	75.5	64.7	52.3	42.9	63.1
Mean Minimum Temp. (°F)	27.8	32.5	40.3	49.2	59.0	67.6	72.1	70.8	62.9	51.4	39.9	30.9	50.4
Extreme Maximum Temp. (°F)	83	92	96	98	107	115	113	108	108	106	89	82	115
Extreme Minimum Temp. (°F)	2	-2	9	28	33	50	58	55	36	22	13	-6	-6
Days Maximum Temp. ≥ 90°F	0	0	1	2	8	20	28	27	15	3	0	0	104
Days Maximum Temp. ≤ 32°F	3	2	0	0	0	0	0	0	0	0	0	2	7
Days Minimum Temp. ≤ 32°F	22	12	5	0	0	0	0	0	0	0	7	17	63
Days Minimum Temp. ≤ 0°F	0	0	0	0	0	0	0	0	0	0	0	0	0
Heating Degree Days (base 65°F)	761	559	367	130	24	1	0	0	16	104	383	680	3,025
Cooling Degree Days (base 65°F)	0	1	17	72	236	450	629	595	348	104	10	0	2,462
Mean Precipitation (in.)	0.99	1.66	1.74	1.66	3.73	3.63	1.38	2.39	3.13	2.33	1.35	1.36	25.35
Days With ≥ 0.1" Precipitation	2	3	4	3	5	5	3	4	4	4	2	3	42
Days With ≥ 1.0" Precipitation	0	0	0	0	1	1	0	1	1	1	0	0	5
Mean Snowfall (in.)	na	1.2	trace	0.0	0.0	0.0	0.0	0.0	0.0	0.0	trace	0.4	na
Days With ≥ 1.0" Snow Depth	na	na	0	0	0	0	0	0	0	0	0	0	na

Lamesa 1 SSE *Dawson County*   Elevation: 2,962 ft.   Latitude: 32° 43' N   Longitude: 101° 56' W

	JAN	FEB	MAR	APR	MAY	JUN	JUL	AUG	SEP	OCT	NOV	DEC	YEAR
Mean Maximum Temp. (°F)	54.3	60.5	68.9	77.4	85.5	92.1	94.2	92.6	85.6	77.2	65.4	56.7	75.9
Mean Temp. (°F)	40.0	45.2	52.5	61.1	70.2	77.6	80.4	78.9	72.4	62.4	50.5	42.4	61.1
Mean Minimum Temp. (°F)	25.7	29.8	36.0	44.6	54.8	63.1	66.5	65.2	59.1	47.6	35.6	28.0	46.3
Extreme Maximum Temp. (°F)	84	87	94	100	107	114	111	111	105	101	92	84	114
Extreme Minimum Temp. (°F)	-3	-9	13	25	35	45	54	52	36	22	6	-3	-9
Days Maximum Temp. ≥ 90°F	0	0	0	3	11	20	25	23	12	3	0	0	97
Days Maximum Temp. ≤ 32°F	2	1	0	0	0	0	0	0	0	0	0	1	4
Days Minimum Temp. ≤ 32°F	26	18	9	2	0	0	0	0	0	1	11	23	90
Days Minimum Temp. ≤ 0°F	0	0	0	0	0	0	0	0	0	0	0	0	0
Heating Degree Days (base 65°F)	767	554	386	162	30	2	0	0	25	132	429	695	3,182
Cooling Degree Days (base 65°F)	0	1	5	46	194	374	481	440	248	56	2	0	1,847
Mean Precipitation (in.)	0.58	0.77	0.79	0.89	2.37	2.71	2.19	2.01	3.52	1.66	0.78	0.75	19.02
Days With ≥ 0.1" Precipitation	2	2	2	2	4	4	4	3	4	3	2	2	34
Days With ≥ 1.0" Precipitation	0	0	0	0	1	1	1	1	1	0	0	0	5
Mean Snowfall (in.)	1.5	0.6	0.2	trace	0.0	0.0	0.0	0.0	0.0	0.0	0.5	0.7	3.5
Days With ≥ 1.0" Snow Depth	na	0	0	0	0	0	0	0	0	0	0	0	na

Lampasas *Lampasas County*   Elevation: 1,023 ft.   Latitude: 31° 03' N   Longitude: 98° 11' W

	JAN	FEB	MAR	APR	MAY	JUN	JUL	AUG	SEP	OCT	NOV	DEC	YEAR
Mean Maximum Temp. (°F)	57.5	62.2	69.7	77.2	83.0	89.5	94.1	94.2	88.1	79.2	67.9	60.0	76.9
Mean Temp. (°F)	43.8	48.2	55.8	63.4	71.0	78.0	81.7	81.3	75.4	65.3	54.2	46.4	63.7
Mean Minimum Temp. (°F)	30.1	34.3	41.9	49.6	59.0	66.5	69.2	68.3	62.6	51.4	40.4	32.7	50.5
Extreme Maximum Temp. (°F)	87	99	100	99	102	108	110	106	107	102	93	84	110
Extreme Minimum Temp. (°F)	3	1	12	24	34	48	54	50	35	20	12	-4	-4
Days Maximum Temp. ≥ 90°F	0	0	1	1	5	16	27	27	15	3	0	0	95
Days Maximum Temp. ≤ 32°F	1	1	0	0	0	0	0	0	0	0	0	1	3
Days Minimum Temp. ≤ 32°F	21	13	6	2	0	0	0	0	0	0	8	17	68
Days Minimum Temp. ≤ 0°F	0	0	0	0	0	0	0	0	0	0	0	0	0
Heating Degree Days (base 65°F)	650	470	301	119	20	0	0	0	13	95	335	572	2,575
Cooling Degree Days (base 65°F)	1	4	22	75	223	406	533	528	334	114	20	3	2,263
Mean Precipitation (in.)	1.49	2.40	2.45	2.50	4.41	3.28	1.68	2.48	2.85	3.32	2.18	2.18	31.22
Days With ≥ 0.1" Precipitation	4	4	4	4	7	5	3	3	5	4	4	4	51
Days With ≥ 1.0" Precipitation	0	1	1	1	1	1	0	1	1	1	1	1	10
Mean Snowfall (in.)	0.3	0.2	0.0	0.0	0.0	0.0	0.0	0.0	0.0	0.0	0.2	trace	0.7
Days With ≥ 1.0" Snow Depth	0	0	0	0	0	0	0	0	0	0	0	0	0

Langtry *Val Verde County*   Elevation: 1,289 ft.   Latitude: 29° 48' N   Longitude: 101° 34' W

	JAN	FEB	MAR	APR	MAY	JUN	JUL	AUG	SEP	OCT	NOV	DEC	YEAR
Mean Maximum Temp. (°F)	62.3	67.7	76.3	84.4	90.7	95.5	97.7	97.3	91.8	82.4	71.4	63.8	81.8
Mean Temp. (°F)	48.1	53.2	62.1	70.5	78.3	83.9	86.1	85.7	80.0	69.8	58.1	49.8	68.8
Mean Minimum Temp. (°F)	33.8	38.7	48.0	56.6	65.8	72.3	74.5	74.0	68.2	57.1	44.8	35.7	55.8
Extreme Maximum Temp. (°F)	89	98	100	110	110	113	111	111	107	104	97	90	113
Extreme Minimum Temp. (°F)	13	11	21	29	42	53	57	62	42	26	15	9	9
Days Maximum Temp. ≥ 90°F	0	0	2	8	19	26	29	29	22	6	0	0	141
Days Maximum Temp. ≤ 32°F	0	0	0	0	0	0	0	0	0	0	0	0	0
Days Minimum Temp. ≤ 32°F	15	7	2	0	0	0	0	0	0	0	0	0	0
Days Minimum Temp. ≤ 0°F	0	0	0	0	0	0	0	0	0	0	3	11	38
Heating Degree Days (base 65°F)	518	333	145	32	2	0	0	0	5	39	227	466	1,767
Cooling Degree Days (base 65°F)	0	8	63	206	443	599	692	683	481	214	34	1	3,424
Mean Precipitation (in.)	0.49	0.80	0.66	1.02	1.90	1.56	1.40	1.96	2.44	1.45	0.68	0.54	14.90
Days With ≥ 0.1" Precipitation	1	2	1	2	3	3	2	3	3	2	2	1	25
Days With ≥ 1.0" Precipitation	0	0	0	0	1	0	0	0	1	0	0	0	2
Mean Snowfall (in.)	0.2	0.2	0.0	0.0	0.0	0.0	0.0	0.0	0.0	0.0	trace	0.0	0.4
Days With ≥ 1.0" Snow Depth	0	0	0	0	0	0	0	0	0	0	0	0	0

Laredo 2 *Webb County*   Elevation: 429 ft.   Latitude: 27° 34' N   Longitude: 99° 30' W

	JAN	FEB	MAR	APR	MAY	JUN	JUL	AUG	SEP	OCT	NOV	DEC	YEAR
Mean Maximum Temp. (°F)	67.3	72.8	81.2	88.2	93.5	98.0	100.5	100.1	94.2	86.5	76.9	69.2	85.7
Mean Temp. (°F)	55.6	60.5	68.5	75.5	81.7	86.0	88.0	87.6	82.8	74.9	65.3	57.6	73.7
Mean Minimum Temp. (°F)	43.7	48.2	55.8	62.7	69.8	74.0	75.5	75.1	71.3	63.2	53.6	46.1	61.6
Extreme Maximum Temp. (°F)	95	103	105	110	114	114	113	111	108	104	96	95	114
Extreme Minimum Temp. (°F)	19	20	27	32	45	58	66	61	50	28	27	11	11
Days Maximum Temp. ≥ 90°F	0	1	6	15	22	28	30	30	24	12	2	0	170
Days Maximum Temp. ≤ 32°F	0	0	0	0	0	0	0	0	0	0	0	0	0
Days Minimum Temp. ≤ 32°F	4	2	0	0	0	0	0	0	0	0	0	0	0
Days Minimum Temp. ≤ 0°F	0	0	0	0	0	0	0	0	0	0	1	3	10
Heating Degree Days (base 65°F)	313	177	65	13	0	0	0	0	1	14	109	261	953
Cooling Degree Days (base 65°F)	25	62	171	336	547	670	745	738	563	344	129	40	4,370
Mean Precipitation (in.)	0.82	0.92	0.86	1.51	2.80	2.99	1.82	2.40	2.86	2.64	1.05	0.86	21.53
Days With ≥ 0.1" Precipitation	2	2	2	2	4	4	3	3	4	3	2	2	33
Days With ≥ 1.0" Precipitation	0	0	0	1	1	1	0	1	1	1	0	0	6
Mean Snowfall (in.)	trace	0.1	0.0	0.0	0.0	0.0	0.0	0.0	0.0	trace	0.0	trace	0.1
Days With ≥ 1.0" Snow Depth	0	0	0	0	0	0	0	0	0	0	0	0	0

Lavon Dam *Collin County*   Elevation: 508 ft.   Latitude: 33° 02' N   Longitude: 96° 29' W

	JAN	FEB	MAR	APR	MAY	JUN	JUL	AUG	SEP	OCT	NOV	DEC	YEAR
Mean Maximum Temp. (°F)	52.6	58.6	66.5	74.6	81.8	89.6	94.2	94.4	87.8	78.0	65.4	56.8	75.0
Mean Temp. (°F)	41.7	47.3	55.2	63.5	71.6	79.2	83.3	82.9	76.4	65.8	54.3	45.8	63.9
Mean Minimum Temp. (°F)	31.0	36.0	43.8	52.5	61.3	68.8	72.3	71.4	64.9	53.5	43.1	34.9	52.8
Extreme Maximum Temp. (°F)	82	96	93	94	98	106	106	107	105	98	91	82	107
Extreme Minimum Temp. (°F)	5	7	12	28	40	49	58	56	42	26	14	-3	-3
Days Maximum Temp. ≥ 90°F	0	0	0	0	3	17	27	27	14	2	0	0	90
Days Maximum Temp. ≤ 32°F	2	1	0	0	0	0	0	0	0	0	0	1	4
Days Minimum Temp. ≤ 32°F	17	10	3	0	0	0	0	0	0	0	4	12	46
Days Minimum Temp. ≤ 0°F	0	0	0	0	0	0	0	0	0	0	0	0	0
Heating Degree Days (base 65°F)	717	496	315	106	14	1	0	0	9	82	334	589	2,663
Cooling Degree Days (base 65°F)	0	3	15	70	228	437	576	576	360	108	16	2	2,391
Mean Precipitation (in.)	2.28	2.88	3.25	3.69	5.28	3.82	2.25	1.98	3.51	4.42	3.13	3.22	39.71
Days With ≥ 0.1" Precipitation	5	5	5	5	6	5	3	3	5	5	5	5	57
Days With ≥ 1.0" Precipitation	1	1	1	1	2	1	1	1	1	2	1	1	14
Mean Snowfall (in.)	0.0	0.0	trace	0.0	0.0	0.0	0.0	0.0	0.0	0.0	0.0	trace	trace
Days With ≥ 1.0" Snow Depth	0	0	0	0	0	0	0	0	0	0	0	0	0

Levelland *Hockley County*   Elevation: 3,549 ft.   Latitude: 33° 34' N   Longitude: 102° 23' W

	JAN	FEB	MAR	APR	MAY	JUN	JUL	AUG	SEP	OCT	NOV	DEC	YEAR
Mean Maximum Temp. (°F)	53.2	58.8	66.9	75.4	83.8	91.2	92.7	90.3	83.6	75.6	63.5	55.3	74.2
Mean Temp. (°F)	38.3	42.9	49.8	58.6	67.8	75.9	78.2	76.3	69.6	59.7	48.0	40.3	58.8
Mean Minimum Temp. (°F)	23.4	27.0	32.8	41.7	51.8	60.5	63.7	62.2	55.6	43.8	32.6	25.3	43.4
Extreme Maximum Temp. (°F)	82	87	95	100	106	115	111	106	105	99	87	80	115
Extreme Minimum Temp. (°F)	-10	2	6	20	30	44	54	50	33	18	0	-3	-10
Days Maximum Temp. ≥ 90°F	0	0	0	2	9	19	23	19	9	2	0	0	83
Days Maximum Temp. ≤ 32°F	3	1	0	0	0	0	0	0	0	0	0	2	6
Days Minimum Temp. ≤ 32°F	28	21	14	4	0	0	0	0	0	0	15	26	110
Days Minimum Temp. ≤ 0°F	0	0	0	0	0	0	0	0	0	0	0	0	0
Heating Degree Days (base 65°F)	820	617	465	216	51	4	0	1	42	190	503	757	3,666
Cooling Degree Days (base 65°F)	0	0	2	28	153	346	437	381	196	34	1	0	1,578
Mean Precipitation (in.)	0.59	0.64	0.59	1.00	2.40	2.65	2.22	2.90	3.28	1.53	0.78	0.79	19.37
Days With ≥ 0.1" Precipitation	2	2	2	3	4	5	4	5	4	3	2	2	38
Days With ≥ 1.0" Precipitation	0	0	0	0	1	1	1	1	1	0	0	0	5
Mean Snowfall (in.)	2.7	2.6	0.5	0.2	0.0	0.0	0.0	0.0	0.0	0.4	0.8	2.8	10.0
Days With ≥ 1.0" Snow Depth	2	1	1	0	0	0	0	0	0	0	0	2	6

Lexington *Lee County*   Elevation: 462 ft.   Latitude: 30° 25' N   Longitude: 97° 01' W

	JAN	FEB	MAR	APR	MAY	JUN	JUL	AUG	SEP	OCT	NOV	DEC	YEAR
Mean Maximum Temp. (°F)	58.3	63.4	70.7	77.5	83.5	89.8	93.8	94.1	88.8	80.3	69.4	61.7	77.6
Mean Temp. (°F)	47.5	52.3	59.7	66.7	73.8	79.9	83.4	83.3	78.1	68.7	58.6	50.8	66.9
Mean Minimum Temp. (°F)	36.7	41.1	48.7	55.8	64.0	70.3	72.9	72.4	67.4	57.1	47.7	39.9	56.2
Extreme Maximum Temp. (°F)	88	97	94	94	99	102	105	105	103	97	90	84	105
Extreme Minimum Temp. (°F)	8	12	18	32	42	52	61	59	43	25	19	2	2
Days Maximum Temp. ≥ 90°F	0	0	0	1	4	18	27	27	17	3	0	0	97
Days Maximum Temp. ≤ 32°F	1	0	0	0	0	0	0	0	0	0	0	1	2
Days Minimum Temp. ≤ 32°F	11	5	1	0	0	0	0	0	0	0	2	7	26
Days Minimum Temp. ≤ 0°F	0	0	0	0	0	0	0	0	0	0	0	0	0
Heating Degree Days (base 65°F)	540	364	201	63	6	0	0	0	4	50	230	445	1,903
Cooling Degree Days (base 65°F)	4	12	42	119	297	458	591	591	418	180	47	12	2,771
Mean Precipitation (in.)	2.50	2.26	2.59	2.53	4.89	3.70	1.65	2.10	3.35	4.65	2.98	2.67	35.87
Days With ≥ 0.1" Precipitation	5	4	4	4	6	5	3	3	5	5	4	4	52
Days With ≥ 1.0" Precipitation	1	1	1	1	2	1	0	1	1	2	1	1	13
Mean Snowfall (in.)	0.0	trace	0.0	0.0	0.0	0.0	0.0	0.0	0.0	0.0	0.0	0.0	trace
Days With ≥ 1.0" Snow Depth	0	0	0	0	0	0	0	0	0	0	0	0	0

Liberty *Liberty County*   Elevation: 32 ft.   Latitude: 30° 04' N   Longitude: 94° 48' W

	JAN	FEB	MAR	APR	MAY	JUN	JUL	AUG	SEP	OCT	NOV	DEC	YEAR
Mean Maximum Temp. (°F)	61.3	65.4	72.3	78.2	84.9	90.3	93.2	93.5	89.0	81.3	71.4	64.3	78.8
Mean Temp. (°F)	50.9	54.5	61.3	67.6	74.7	80.5	83.1	82.9	78.4	69.4	60.0	53.6	68.1
Mean Minimum Temp. (°F)	40.4	43.5	50.2	56.9	64.5	70.6	72.9	72.4	67.8	57.4	48.6	42.9	57.3
Extreme Maximum Temp. (°F)	86	87	93	93	97	100	103	103	102	95	90	86	103
Extreme Minimum Temp. (°F)	14	19	22	31	43	53	59	60	47	31	20	7	7
Days Maximum Temp. ≥ 90°F	0	0	0	1	5	20	27	27	17	3	0	0	100
Days Maximum Temp. ≤ 32°F	0	0	0	0	0	0	0	0	0	0	0	0	0
Days Minimum Temp. ≤ 32°F	7	4	1	0	0	0	0	0	0	0	2	6	20
Days Minimum Temp. ≤ 0°F	0	0	0	0	0	0	0	0	0	0	0	0	0
Heating Degree Days (base 65°F)	440	306	159	48	2	0	0	0	1	40	200	366	1,562
Cooling Degree Days (base 65°F)	8	19	58	138	330	491	586	582	427	202	64	25	2,930
Mean Precipitation (in.)	4.94	3.83	3.99	3.90	5.85	6.83	4.43	4.45	6.11	6.18	5.64	4.98	61.13
Days With ≥ 0.1" Precipitation	7	6	6	4	6	7	7	7	7	5	6	7	75
Days With ≥ 1.0" Precipitation	1	1	1	1	2	2	1	1	2	2	2	2	18
Mean Snowfall (in.)	0.2	trace	0.0	0.0	0.0	0.0	0.0	0.0	0.0	0.0	0.0	0.0	0.2
Days With ≥ 1.0" Snow Depth	0	0	0	0	0	0	0	0	0	0	0	0	0

Lipscomb *Lipscomb County*   Elevation: 2,447 ft.   Latitude: 36° 14' N   Longitude: 100° 16' W

	JAN	FEB	MAR	APR	MAY	JUN	JUL	AUG	SEP	OCT	NOV	DEC	YEAR
Mean Maximum Temp. (°F)	46.9	52.9	61.3	70.6	79.2	88.7	94.6	92.9	84.9	73.7	59.1	49.7	71.2
Mean Temp. (°F)	32.1	37.4	45.8	55.1	65.1	74.9	80.2	78.5	70.0	57.8	43.9	34.8	56.3
Mean Minimum Temp. (°F)	17.2	21.8	30.3	39.9	50.9	61.0	65.7	64.0	55.1	41.7	28.6	19.7	41.3
Extreme Maximum Temp. (°F)	84	88	95	100	105	113	114	108	106	100	90	79	114
Extreme Minimum Temp. (°F)	-18	-11	-2	14	30	42	45	44	27	10	1	-16	-18
Days Maximum Temp. ≥ 90°F	0	0	0	1	4	15	25	22	11	2	0	0	80
Days Maximum Temp. ≤ 32°F	6	4	1	0	0	0	0	0	0	0	1	4	16
Days Minimum Temp. ≤ 32°F	30	25	18	7	0	0	0	0	0	6	20	29	135
Days Minimum Temp. ≤ 0°F	2	1	0	0	0	0	0	0	0	0	0	1	4
Heating Degree Days (base 65°F)	1,013	773	591	312	97	10	1	2	54	249	628	930	4,660
Cooling Degree Days (base 65°F)	0	0	3	20	107	310	481	439	221	31	1	0	1,613
Mean Precipitation (in.)	0.54	0.76	1.83	1.99	3.77	3.17	2.32	2.49	2.06	1.29	1.10	0.79	22.11
Days With ≥ 0.1" Precipitation	2	2	3	4	6	5	4	4	4	2	3	2	41
Days With ≥ 1.0" Precipitation	0	0	0	0	1	1	1	1	1	0	0	0	5
Mean Snowfall (in.)	3.1	4.0	3.3	0.8	0.0	0.0	0.0	0.0	0.0	trace	1.8	4.8	17.8
Days With ≥ 1.0" Snow Depth	3	3	1	0	0	0	0	0	0	0	1	3	11

Littlefield 2 NW *Lamb County*   Elevation: 3,503 ft.   Latitude: 33° 56' N   Longitude: 102° 21' W

	JAN	FEB	MAR	APR	MAY	JUN	JUL	AUG	SEP	OCT	NOV	DEC	YEAR
Mean Maximum Temp. (°F)	51.6	57.3	65.4	73.5	81.9	89.9	91.8	89.1	83.0	74.3	62.1	53.8	72.8
Mean Temp. (°F)	37.1	41.9	48.9	57.5	66.9	75.4	78.2	76.0	69.3	59.1	47.4	39.3	58.1
Mean Minimum Temp. (°F)	22.5	26.4	32.5	41.4	51.8	60.9	64.6	62.8	55.6	43.8	32.6	24.7	43.3
Extreme Maximum Temp. (°F)	83	85	94	99	105	112	109	103	103	96	86	77	112
Extreme Minimum Temp. (°F)	-6	-4	6	19	31	44	54	47	32	16	2	-4	-6
Days Maximum Temp. ≥ 90°F	0	0	0	1	7	17	21	17	8	1	0	0	72
Days Maximum Temp. ≤ 32°F	4	2	0	0	0	0	0	0	0	0	0	2	8
Days Minimum Temp. ≤ 32°F	28	22	15	4	0	0	0	0	0	2	15	26	112
Days Minimum Temp. ≤ 0°F	0	0	0	0	0	0	0	0	0	0	0	1	1
Heating Degree Days (base 65°F)	859	646	493	243	61	5	0	1	44	204	522	791	3,869
Cooling Degree Days (base 65°F)	0	0	1	19	127	320	422	360	181	25	1	0	1,456
Mean Precipitation (in.)	0.57	0.53	0.73	1.17	2.29	2.88	2.43	2.78	2.36	1.48	0.71	0.69	18.62
Days With ≥ 0.1" Precipitation	2	2	2	3	4	5	4	5	4	3	2	2	38
Days With ≥ 1.0" Precipitation	0	0	0	0	1	1	1	1	1	0	0	0	5
Mean Snowfall (in.)	*1.7*	1.5	0.3	0.5	0.0	0.0	0.0	0.0	0.0	trace	0.8	*1.7*	*6.5*
Days With ≥ 1.0" Snow Depth	na	na	0	0	0	0	0	0	0	0	0	na	na

Livingston 2 NNE *Polk County*　　Elevation: 177 ft.　　Latitude: 30° 44' N　　Longitude: 94° 56' W

	JAN	FEB	MAR	APR	MAY	JUN	JUL	AUG	SEP	OCT	NOV	DEC	YEAR
Mean Maximum Temp. (°F)	58.9	63.6	71.0	77.6	84.2	90.4	93.9	94.2	88.6	80.1	69.9	62.3	77.9
Mean Temp. (°F)	47.7	51.3	58.4	65.3	72.9	79.4	82.6	82.1	76.8	67.0	57.7	50.3	66.0
Mean Minimum Temp. (°F)	36.4	38.9	45.8	52.8	61.5	68.3	71.2	70.0	65.0	53.8	45.4	38.3	54.0
Extreme Maximum Temp. (°F)	83	91	89	94	100	104	111	108	105	97	88	84	111
Extreme Minimum Temp. (°F)	9	16	18	25	40	47	57	54	42	25	17	3	3
Days Maximum Temp. ≥ 90°F	0	0	0	0	5	19	27	27	15	2	0	0	95
Days Maximum Temp. ≤ 32°F	0	0	0	0	0	0	0	0	0	0	0	0	0
Days Minimum Temp. ≤ 32°F	14	9	4	1	0	0	0	0	0	0	5	12	45
Days Minimum Temp. ≤ 0°F	0	0	0	0	0	0	0	0	0	0	0	0	0
Heating Degree Days (base 65°F)	537	393	236	89	8	0	0	0	5	72	257	463	2,060
Cooling Degree Days (base 65°F)	5	12	38	100	268	448	563	554	375	147	45	16	2,571
Mean Precipitation (in.)	4.66	3.49	3.95	3.85	5.47	5.00	3.48	3.45	4.72	4.08	4.52	4.80	51.47
Days With ≥ 0.1" Precipitation	7	5	6	5	6	6	6	5	5	5	6	6	68
Days With ≥ 1.0" Precipitation	1	1	1	1	2	2	1	1	2	1	1	2	16
Mean Snowfall (in.)	0.3	0.1	0.0	0.0	0.0	0.0	0.0	0.0	0.0	0.0	0.0	trace	0.4
Days With ≥ 1.0" Snow Depth	0	0	0	0	0	0	0	0	0	0	0	0	0

Llano *Llano County*　　Elevation: 1,017 ft.　　Latitude: 30° 45' N　　Longitude: 98° 39' W

	JAN	FEB	MAR	APR	MAY	JUN	JUL	AUG	SEP	OCT	NOV	DEC	YEAR
Mean Maximum Temp. (°F)	59.4	64.3	72.0	79.3	85.5	91.9	96.1	95.8	89.8	81.0	69.8	62.2	78.9
Mean Temp. (°F)	45.6	50.3	58.4	66.1	73.9	80.6	84.0	83.3	77.3	67.4	56.2	48.3	66.0
Mean Minimum Temp. (°F)	31.9	36.2	44.6	52.9	62.2	69.2	71.9	70.8	64.8	53.7	42.6	34.3	52.9
Extreme Maximum Temp. (°F)	88	100	100	101	105	112	110	109	106	103	94	86	112
Extreme Minimum Temp. (°F)	7	6	14	27	39	50	51	55	39	24	15	-1	-1
Days Maximum Temp. ≥ 90°F	0	0	1	3	9	22	28	28	19	5	0	0	115
Days Maximum Temp. ≤ 32°F	1	0	0	0	0	0	0	0	0	0	0	0	1
Days Minimum Temp. ≤ 32°F	17	10	3	1	0	0	0	0	0	0	6	14	51
Days Minimum Temp. ≤ 0°F	0	0	0	0	0	0	0	0	0	0	0	0	0
Heating Degree Days (base 65°F)	598	413	236	80	9	0	0	0	7	66	283	515	2,207
Cooling Degree Days (base 65°F)	1	5	35	118	307	483	608	602	398	157	30	4	2,748
Mean Precipitation (in.)	1.08	1.80	1.92	2.15	3.98	3.28	1.83	2.04	2.18	2.83	1.93	1.86	26.88
Days With ≥ 0.1" Precipitation	3	3	4	3	6	4	3	3	4	4	3	3	43
Days With ≥ 1.0" Precipitation	0	0	0	1	1	1	1	1	1	1	1	0	8
Mean Snowfall (in.)	0.5	0.2	trace	0.0	0.0	0.0	0.0	0.0	0.0	0.0	trace	trace	0.7
Days With ≥ 1.0" Snow Depth	0	0	0	0	0	0	0	0	0	0	0	0	0

Lufkin FAA Airport *Angelina County*　　Elevation: 275 ft.　　Latitude: 31° 19' N　　Longitude: 94° 43' W

	JAN	FEB	MAR	APR	MAY	JUN	JUL	AUG	SEP	OCT	NOV	DEC	YEAR
Mean Maximum Temp. (°F)	58.9	64.2	71.6	78.2	84.4	90.1	93.4	93.4	88.5	80.0	69.4	61.9	77.8
Mean Temp. (°F)	48.4	52.7	59.7	66.5	73.9	80.0	82.8	82.4	77.5	67.7	57.7	50.8	66.7
Mean Minimum Temp. (°F)	37.8	41.2	47.9	54.8	63.3	69.8	72.2	71.3	66.5	55.3	46.0	39.7	55.5
Extreme Maximum Temp. (°F)	85	92	90	93	99	103	107	108	104	96	89	83	108
Extreme Minimum Temp. (°F)	8	15	18	30	43	50	58	54	42	25	17	2	2
Days Maximum Temp. ≥ 90°F	0	0	0	1	5	18	27	26	16	3	0	0	96
Days Maximum Temp. ≤ 32°F	0	0	0	0	0	0	0	0	0	0	0	0	0
Days Minimum Temp. ≤ 32°F	11	6	2	0	0	0	0	0	0	0	3	9	31
Days Minimum Temp. ≤ 0°F	0	0	0	0	0	0	0	0	0	0	0	0	0
Heating Degree Days (base 65°F)	518	355	202	67	4	0	0	0	3	60	252	448	1,909
Cooling Degree Days (base 65°F)	6	14	41	112	285	455	559	550	380	143	39	14	2,598
Mean Precipitation (in.)	4.46	3.25	3.46	3.12	5.13	4.05	2.60	3.12	4.04	4.37	4.05	4.33	45.98
Days With ≥ 0.1" Precipitation	6	5	6	5	7	6	5	5	5	5	5	6	66
Days With ≥ 1.0" Precipitation	1	1	1	1	2	1	1	1	1	1	1	2	14
Mean Snowfall (in.)	0.4	trace	trace	trace	trace	trace	trace	trace	0.0	0.0	trace	trace	0.4
Days With ≥ 1.0" Snow Depth	0	0	0	0	0	0	0	0	0	0	0	0	0

Luling *Caldwell County*　　Elevation: 396 ft.　　Latitude: 29° 41' N　　Longitude: 97° 39' W

	JAN	FEB	MAR	APR	MAY	JUN	JUL	AUG	SEP	OCT	NOV	DEC	YEAR
Mean Maximum Temp. (°F)	61.1	65.7	73.4	79.9	85.6	91.8	95.4	96.5	91.1	82.9	71.9	64.1	79.9
Mean Temp. (°F)	49.2	53.4	61.0	67.7	74.7	81.0	83.7	83.9	78.7	69.7	59.5	52.0	67.9
Mean Minimum Temp. (°F)	37.3	41.1	48.6	55.4	63.8	70.1	71.9	71.2	66.4	56.5	46.9	39.9	55.8
Extreme Maximum Temp. (°F)	89	99	100	99	101	106	107	107	109	98	92	87	109
Extreme Minimum Temp. (°F)	10	15	18	26	41	53	61	56	41	26	20	4	4
Days Maximum Temp. ≥ 90°F	0	0	1	2	8	22	28	29	20	7	0	0	117
Days Maximum Temp. ≤ 32°F	0	0	0	0	0	0	0	0	0	0	0	0	0
Days Minimum Temp. ≤ 32°F	10	5	2	0	0	0	0	0	0	0	3	8	28
Days Minimum Temp. ≤ 0°F	0	0	0	0	0	0	0	0	0	0	0	0	0
Heating Degree Days (base 65°F)	488	335	175	56	5	0	0	0	3	42	213	411	1,728
Cooling Degree Days (base 65°F)	7	15	56	142	330	503	604	614	436	202	57	16	2,982
Mean Precipitation (in.)	2.26	2.28	2.21	3.07	5.34	4.17	1.74	2.34	3.84	4.22	2.72	2.22	36.41
Days With ≥ 0.1" Precipitation	5	4	4	4	6	5	3	4	5	4	4	4	52
Days With ≥ 1.0" Precipitation	1	0	1	1	2	1	1	1	1	1	1	0	11
Mean Snowfall (in.)	0.4	trace	0.0	0.0	0.0	0.0	0.0	0.0	0.0	0.0	trace	trace	0.4
Days With ≥ 1.0" Snow Depth	0	0	0	0	0	0	0	0	0	0	0	0	0

Lytle 3 W *Medina County*   Elevation: 721 ft.   Latitude: 29° 14' N   Longitude: 98° 51' W

	JAN	FEB	MAR	APR	MAY	JUN	JUL	AUG	SEP	OCT	NOV	DEC	YEAR
Mean Maximum Temp. (°F)	63.8	68.6	75.8	82.7	87.2	92.4	95.7	95.9	91.4	83.9	73.1	65.9	81.4
Mean Temp. (°F)	52.0	56.3	63.3	70.2	76.7	81.9	84.2	84.1	79.8	71.8	61.6	54.3	69.7
Mean Minimum Temp. (°F)	40.2	44.0	50.7	57.7	66.2	71.3	72.7	72.3	68.2	59.6	50.1	42.7	58.0
Extreme Maximum Temp. (°F)	89	97	99	106	103	107	106	104	103	101	95	88	107
Extreme Minimum Temp. (°F)	13	15	16	32	46	55	63	60	45	23	20	6	6
Days Maximum Temp. ≥ 90°F	0	0	1	5	10	22	28	29	21	7	0	0	123
Days Maximum Temp. ≤ 32°F	0	0	0	0	0	0	0	0	0	0	0	0	0
Days Minimum Temp. ≤ 32°F	7	3	1	0	0	0	0	0	0	0	2	5	18
Days Minimum Temp. ≤ 0°F	0	0	0	0	0	0	0	0	0	0	0	0	0
Heating Degree Days (base 65°F)	402	262	124	30	1	0	0	0	1	23	160	343	1,346
Cooling Degree Days (base 65°F)	8	25	81	197	371	515	601	604	455	240	67	19	3,183
Mean Precipitation (in.)	1.59	1.86	1.72	2.33	3.39	3.72	1.38	1.93	2.58	3.05	1.78	1.67	27.00
Days With ≥ 0.1" Precipitation	4	3	3	3	5	5	2	3	4	4	3	3	42
Days With ≥ 1.0" Precipitation	0	0	0	1	1	1	0	1	1	1	1	0	7
Mean Snowfall (in.)	0.6	trace	0.0	0.0	0.0	0.0	0.0	0.0	0.0	trace	0.0	0.0	0.6
Days With ≥ 1.0" Snow Depth	0	0	0	0	0	0	0	0	0	0	0	0	0

Madisonville *Madison County*   Elevation: 249 ft.   Latitude: 30° 57' N   Longitude: 95° 55' W

	JAN	FEB	MAR	APR	MAY	JUN	JUL	AUG	SEP	OCT	NOV	DEC	YEAR
Mean Maximum Temp. (°F)	60.9	65.6	73.0	79.5	85.8	91.7	95.4	96.1	90.5	81.9	70.9	63.6	79.6
Mean Temp. (°F)	49.9	54.0	61.0	67.6	74.8	80.9	83.9	83.9	78.7	69.2	59.3	52.3	68.0
Mean Minimum Temp. (°F)	38.8	42.3	49.0	55.7	63.8	70.0	72.4	71.8	66.9	56.5	47.7	41.0	56.3
Extreme Maximum Temp. (°F)	85	94	91	95	100	105	107	108	107	98	90	86	108
Extreme Minimum Temp. (°F)	7	14	19	29	40	51	59	57	43	27	18	3	3
Days Maximum Temp. ≥ 90°F	0	0	0	1	7	23	28	28	19	5	0	0	111
Days Maximum Temp. ≤ 32°F	0	0	0	0	0	0	0	0	0	0	0	0	0
Days Minimum Temp. ≤ 32°F	10	5	2	0	0	0	0	0	0	0	3	7	27
Days Minimum Temp. ≤ 0°F	0	0	0	0	0	0	0	0	0	0	0	0	0
Heating Degree Days (base 65°F)	472	320	173	54	3	0	0	0	2	44	216	404	1,688
Cooling Degree Days (base 65°F)	9	20	54	140	321	491	600	610	435	186	54	19	2,939
Mean Precipitation (in.)	3.79	2.90	3.29	3.29	4.83	3.86	2.73	2.96	4.34	4.54	3.79	3.53	43.85
Days With ≥ 0.1" Precipitation	5	5	5	4	6	5	4	4	5	5	5	5	58
Days With ≥ 1.0" Precipitation	1	1	1	1	2	1	1	1	1	2	1	1	14
Mean Snowfall (in.)	0.3	trace	0.0	0.0	0.0	0.0	0.0	0.0	0.0	0.0	trace	trace	0.3
Days With ≥ 1.0" Snow Depth	0	0	0	0	0	0	0	0	0	0	0	0	0

Marathon *Brewster County*   Elevation: 4,087 ft.   Latitude: 30° 13' N   Longitude: 103° 14' W

	JAN	FEB	MAR	APR	MAY	JUN	JUL	AUG	SEP	OCT	NOV	DEC	YEAR
Mean Maximum Temp. (°F)	61.6	66.2	73.0	80.0	86.4	90.7	90.2	88.9	84.3	78.4	69.2	63.8	77.7
Mean Temp. (°F)	45.4	49.1	55.2	62.3	69.8	75.5	76.3	75.2	70.5	62.4	52.7	47.4	61.8
Mean Minimum Temp. (°F)	29.1	31.8	37.4	44.4	53.2	60.2	62.3	61.5	56.9	46.5	36.2	30.9	45.9
Extreme Maximum Temp. (°F)	82	88	92	97	105	108	105	103	102	100	89	83	108
Extreme Minimum Temp. (°F)	-1	6	10	19	32	42	50	51	35	17	0	0	-1
Days Maximum Temp. ≥ 90°F	0	0	0	2	11	18	18	15	7	2	0	0	73
Days Maximum Temp. ≤ 32°F	0	0	0	0	0	0	0	0	0	0	0	0	0
Days Minimum Temp. ≤ 32°F	20	15	8	2	0	0	0	0	0	2	10	18	75
Days Minimum Temp. ≤ 0°F	0	0	0	0	0	0	0	0	0	0	0	0	0
Heating Degree Days (base 65°F)	601	445	303	121	18	1	0	0	23	118	364	539	2,533
Cooling Degree Days (base 65°F)	0	1	6	47	197	340	376	347	210	51	3	0	1,578
Mean Precipitation (in.)	0.38	0.41	0.26	0.63	1.64	1.90	2.36	2.14	2.82	1.47	0.35	0.54	14.90
Days With ≥ 0.1" Precipitation	1	1	1	1	3	4	4	4	5	3	1	1	29
Days With ≥ 1.0" Precipitation	0	0	0	0	0	0	1	1	1	0	0	0	3
Mean Snowfall (in.)	0.7	trace	trace	0.0	0.0	0.0	0.0	0.0	0.0	trace	0.3	trace	1.0
Days With ≥ 1.0" Snow Depth	0	0	0	0	0	0	0	0	0	0	0	0	0

Marfa 2 *Presidio County*   Elevation: 4,757 ft.   Latitude: 30° 18' N   Longitude: 104° 01' W

	JAN	FEB	MAR	APR	MAY	JUN	JUL	AUG	SEP	OCT	NOV	DEC	YEAR
Mean Maximum Temp. (°F)	59.9	65.0	71.5	78.6	85.8	91.6	89.6	87.6	83.6	77.3	67.7	61.2	76.6
Mean Temp. (°F)	42.9	46.9	52.8	59.9	68.1	74.7	75.0	73.5	69.0	60.8	50.4	44.3	59.9
Mean Minimum Temp. (°F)	25.9	28.8	34.1	41.1	50.3	57.8	60.3	59.3	54.4	44.3	33.2	27.3	43.0
Extreme Maximum Temp. (°F)	81	86	90	95	101	106	103	104	100	95	86	79	106
Extreme Minimum Temp. (°F)	-2	0	6	17	27	39	53	50	36	16	-1	2	-2
Days Maximum Temp. ≥ 90°F	0	0	0	1	9	20	16	12	6	1	0	0	65
Days Maximum Temp. ≤ 32°F	0	0	0	0	0	0	0	0	0	0	0	0	0
Days Minimum Temp. ≤ 32°F	25	20	13	4	0	0	0	0	0	2	13	24	101
Days Minimum Temp. ≤ 0°F	0	0	0	0	0	0	0	0	0	0	0	0	0
Heating Degree Days (base 65°F)	677	504	371	169	25	1	0	0	25	148	429	636	2,985
Cooling Degree Days (base 65°F)	0	0	0	18	134	309	327	284	155	24	0	0	1,251
Mean Precipitation (in.)	0.41	0.49	0.28	0.69	1.35	1.71	2.83	2.80	3.06	1.50	0.38	0.59	16.09
Days With ≥ 0.1" Precipitation	1	1	1	2	3	4	6	6	5	3	1	2	35
Days With ≥ 1.0" Precipitation	0	0	0	0	0	0	1	1	1	0	0	0	3
Mean Snowfall (in.)	0.9	0.5	trace	trace	0.0	0.0	0.0	0.0	0.0	trace	0.3	0.5	2.2
Days With ≥ 1.0" Snow Depth	0	0	0	0	0	0	0	0	0	0	0	0	0

Marlin 3 NE *Falls County*   Elevation: 387 ft.   Latitude: 31° 20' N   Longitude: 96° 51' W

	JAN	FEB	MAR	APR	MAY	JUN	JUL	AUG	SEP	OCT	NOV	DEC	YEAR
Mean Maximum Temp. (°F)	58.9	64.1	71.5	78.1	84.2	90.7	94.8	95.1	89.3	80.7	69.0	61.3	78.1
Mean Temp. (°F)	47.7	52.4	59.7	66.7	73.9	80.4	83.7	83.6	78.1	68.5	57.8	50.3	66.9
Mean Minimum Temp. (°F)	36.4	40.7	47.9	55.3	63.6	70.1	72.6	72.0	66.8	56.2	46.6	39.2	55.6
Extreme Maximum Temp. (°F)	88	98	95	96	98	105	107	105	104	98	89	85	107
Extreme Minimum Temp. (°F)	-1	10	17	29	40	50	59	55	41	25	15	6	-1
Days Maximum Temp. ≥ 90°F	0	0	0	1	5	20	28	28	17	3	0	0	102
Days Maximum Temp. ≤ 32°F	0	0	0	0	0	0	0	0	0	0	0	0	0
Days Minimum Temp. ≤ 32°F	12	6	2	0	0	0	0	0	0	0	3	9	32
Days Minimum Temp. ≤ 0°F	0	0	0	0	0	0	0	0	0	0	0	0	0
Heating Degree Days (base 65°F)	535	359	203	63	5	0	0	0	3	52	247	459	1,926
Cooling Degree Days (base 65°F)	5	12	42	120	296	470	587	590	406	166	40	10	2,744
Mean Precipitation (in.)	2.42	2.68	3.29	3.22	5.27	3.39	2.10	1.99	3.20	3.82	2.84	3.20	37.42
Days With ≥ 0.1" Precipitation	4	4	5	4	6	5	3	3	5	5	5	5	54
Days With ≥ 1.0" Precipitation	0	1	1	1	2	1	1	1	1	1	1	1	12
Mean Snowfall (in.)	0.2	0.1	trace	0.0	0.0	0.0	0.0	0.0	0.0	0.0	trace	trace	0.3
Days With ≥ 1.0" Snow Depth	0	0	0	0	0	0	0	0	0	0	0	0	0

Marshall *Harrison County*   Elevation: 351 ft.   Latitude: 32° 32' N   Longitude: 94° 21' W

	JAN	FEB	MAR	APR	MAY	JUN	JUL	AUG	SEP	OCT	NOV	DEC	YEAR
Mean Maximum Temp. (°F)	54.5	60.0	67.5	75.0	81.6	88.5	92.3	92.2	86.5	76.9	66.0	57.9	74.9
Mean Temp. (°F)	43.8	48.6	56.0	63.4	70.9	78.1	81.7	81.2	75.3	64.2	54.5	47.0	63.7
Mean Minimum Temp. (°F)	33.0	37.2	44.5	51.6	60.1	67.6	71.0	70.2	64.0	51.6	43.0	35.9	52.5
Extreme Maximum Temp. (°F)	82	90	88	92	97	100	104	107	104	95	88	80	107
Extreme Minimum Temp. (°F)	0	10	16	30	42	48	52	55	35	27	14	3	0
Days Maximum Temp. ≥ 90°F	0	0	0	0	2	14	24	23	12	1	0	0	76
Days Maximum Temp. ≤ 32°F	1	1	0	0	0	0	0	0	0	0	0	1	3
Days Minimum Temp. ≤ 32°F	16	10	3	0	0	0	0	0	0	1	5	12	47
Days Minimum Temp. ≤ 0°F	0	0	0	0	0	0	0	0	0	0	0	0	0
Heating Degree Days (base 65°F)	653	461	294	115	17	0	0	0	11	101	325	555	2,532
Cooling Degree Days (base 65°F)	2	6	24	72	213	408	534	524	328	89	20	5	2,225
Mean Precipitation (in.)	4.26	4.20	4.22	4.30	4.92	5.06	3.19	2.70	3.97	4.82	4.32	4.83	50.79
Days With ≥ 0.1" Precipitation	6	6	6	5	6	6	5	4	5	6	6	6	67
Days With ≥ 1.0" Precipitation	1	2	1	2	2	2	1	1	1	2	2	2	19
Mean Snowfall (in.)	0.5	0.2	0.0	0.0	0.0	0.0	0.0	0.0	0.0	0.0	trace	trace	0.7
Days With ≥ 1.0" Snow Depth	0	0	0	0	0	0	0	0	0	0	0	0	0

Mason *Mason County*   Elevation: 1,427 ft.   Latitude: 30° 45' N   Longitude: 99° 14' W

	JAN	FEB	MAR	APR	MAY	JUN	JUL	AUG	SEP	OCT	NOV	DEC	YEAR
Mean Maximum Temp. (°F)	na	64.3	72.0	na	84.3	90.6	na	94.2	na	na	na	na	na
Mean Temp. (°F)	na	49.9	na	na	71.9	78.7	na	80.8	na	na	na	na	na
Mean Minimum Temp. (°F)	na	35.6	na	na	59.3	66.3	na	67.4	62.5	na	na	na	na
Extreme Maximum Temp. (°F)	87	100	98	100	105	106	107	105	104	100	92	86	107
Extreme Minimum Temp. (°F)	5	3	11	25	36	48	54	52	36	26	14	3	3
Days Maximum Temp. ≥ 90°F	0	0	1	3	7	18	24	24	15	3	0	0	95
Days Maximum Temp. ≤ 32°F	1	0	0	0	0	0	0	0	0	0	0	0	1
Days Minimum Temp. ≤ 32°F	16	11	4	1	0	0	0	0	0	1	5	12	50
Days Minimum Temp. ≤ 0°F	0	0	0	0	0	0	0	0	0	0	0	0	0
Heating Degree Days (base 65°F)	na	423	na	na	16	1	na	0	na	na	na	na	na
Cooling Degree Days (base 65°F)	na	5	na	na	236	426	na	519	na	na	na	na	na
Mean Precipitation (in.)	0.93	2.06	1.84	1.97	3.32	3.94	2.03	2.56	3.03	2.97	1.75	1.35	27.75
Days With ≥ 0.1" Precipitation	2	3	3	2	5	4	3	3	3	3	2	2	35
Days With ≥ 1.0" Precipitation	0	0	0	0	1	1	1	1	1	1	0	0	6
Mean Snowfall (in.)	0.2	0.4	trace	trace	0.0	0.0	0.0	0.0	0.0	0.0	trace	trace	0.6
Days With ≥ 1.0" Snow Depth	0	0	0	0	0	0	0	0	0	0	0	0	0

Matador *Motley County*   Elevation: 2,290 ft.   Latitude: 34° 01' N   Longitude: 100° 50' W

	JAN	FEB	MAR	APR	MAY	JUN	JUL	AUG	SEP	OCT	NOV	DEC	YEAR
Mean Maximum Temp. (°F)	52.8	58.2	66.2	75.4	82.5	90.6	95.1	92.8	85.1	76.1	63.7	55.4	74.5
Mean Temp. (°F)	40.0	44.9	52.2	61.2	69.5	78.1	82.4	80.6	73.0	63.0	50.9	42.7	61.5
Mean Minimum Temp. (°F)	27.1	31.6	38.2	47.0	56.4	65.4	69.8	68.2	60.8	49.9	38.0	30.0	48.5
Extreme Maximum Temp. (°F)	85	93	100	103	105	116	111	108	106	105	91	84	116
Extreme Minimum Temp. (°F)	2	0	7	22	34	47	57	54	37	22	12	-5	-5
Days Maximum Temp. ≥ 90°F	0	0	1	3	7	17	25	23	12	2	0	0	90
Days Maximum Temp. ≤ 32°F	3	2	0	0	0	0	0	0	0	0	0	2	7
Days Minimum Temp. ≤ 32°F	22	15	8	1	0	0	0	0	0	1	8	19	74
Days Minimum Temp. ≤ 0°F	0	0	0	0	0	0	0	0	0	0	0	0	0
Heating Degree Days (base 65°F)	770	564	402	170	40	2	0	0	32	135	423	684	3,222
Cooling Degree Days (base 65°F)	0	3	13	60	189	396	551	505	282	81	8	0	2,088
Mean Precipitation (in.)	0.66	0.90	1.10	1.79	3.20	3.43	2.05	2.43	3.16	2.08	0.93	0.83	22.56
Days With ≥ 0.1" Precipitation	2	2	3	4	5	5	3	4	4	3	2	2	39
Days With ≥ 1.0" Precipitation	0	0	0	1	1	1	1	1	1	1	0	0	6
Mean Snowfall (in.)	3.3	2.5	0.5	trace	0.0	0.0	0.0	0.0	0.0	trace	1.3	1.9	9.5
Days With ≥ 1.0" Snow Depth	2	2	0	0	0	0	0	0	0	0	1	1	6

Matagorda 2 *Matagorda County*   Elevation: 9 ft.   Latitude: 28° 41' N   Longitude: 95° 58' W

	JAN	FEB	MAR	APR	MAY	JUN	JUL	AUG	SEP	OCT	NOV	DEC	YEAR
Mean Maximum Temp. (°F)	63.8	66.8	72.4	78.1	83.5	88.5	90.9	92.0	88.9	82.7	74.3	67.2	79.1
Mean Temp. (°F)	54.9	57.8	63.8	70.2	76.6	81.9	84.1	84.2	80.6	73.2	64.7	57.8	70.8
Mean Minimum Temp. (°F)	45.9	48.7	55.2	62.2	69.6	75.2	77.2	76.3	72.2	63.7	55.1	48.3	62.5
Extreme Maximum Temp. (°F)	82	82	86	92	98	99	99	101	99	97	89	82	101
Extreme Minimum Temp. (°F)	16	21	23	35	49	59	66	63	50	32	26	9	9
Days Maximum Temp. ≥ 90°F	0	0	0	0	1	10	24	26	15	2	0	0	78
Days Maximum Temp. ≤ 32°F	0	0	0	0	0	0	0	0	0	0	0	0	0
Days Minimum Temp. ≤ 32°F	3	2	0	0	0	0	0	0	0	0	1	2	8
Days Minimum Temp. ≤ 0°F	0	0	0	0	0	0	0	0	0	0	0	0	0
Heating Degree Days (base 65°F)	324	220	105	23	1	0	0	0	0	15	111	255	1,054
Cooling Degree Days (base 65°F)	14	23	71	186	377	524	609	616	488	288	116	43	3,355
Mean Precipitation (in.)	3.65	2.78	2.55	2.54	4.71	4.51	3.42	3.27	6.64	3.87	3.90	2.55	44.39
Days With ≥ 0.1" Precipitation	6	4	4	3	5	5	4	5	7	4	5	5	57
Days With ≥ 1.0" Precipitation	1	1	1	1	1	1	1	1	2	1	1	0	12
Mean Snowfall (in.)	trace	trace	trace	0.0	0.0	0.0	0.0	0.0	0.0	0.0	trace	trace	trace
Days With ≥ 1.0" Snow Depth	0	0	0	0	0	0	0	0	0	0	0	0	0

Mathis 4 SSW *Jim Wells County*   Elevation: 137 ft.   Latitude: 28° 02' N   Longitude: 97° 52' W

	JAN	FEB	MAR	APR	MAY	JUN	JUL	AUG	SEP	OCT	NOV	DEC	YEAR
Mean Maximum Temp. (°F)	65.1	69.4	76.5	82.2	87.0	92.1	95.3	95.8	91.1	84.4	74.8	68.1	81.8
Mean Temp. (°F)	54.3	58.1	65.0	71.1	77.0	82.0	84.0	84.4	80.6	73.1	63.9	57.1	70.9
Mean Minimum Temp. (°F)	43.5	46.7	53.4	60.1	67.0	71.8	72.7	72.9	70.0	61.7	52.9	46.1	59.9
Extreme Maximum Temp. (°F)	92	97	101	105	101	110	105	104	105	102	95	91	110
Extreme Minimum Temp. (°F)	18	22	24	35	47	56	62	66	51	33	27	11	11
Days Maximum Temp. ≥ 90°F	0	0	2	4	10	23	29	29	21	8	1	0	127
Days Maximum Temp. ≤ 32°F	0	0	0	0	0	0	0	0	0	0	0	0	0
Days Minimum Temp. ≤ 32°F	4	2	0	0	0	0	0	0	0	0	0	2	8
Days Minimum Temp. ≤ 0°F	0	0	0	0	0	0	0	0	0	0	0	0	0
Heating Degree Days (base 65°F)	348	225	99	24	1	0	0	0	1	14	127	277	1,116
Cooling Degree Days (base 65°F)	20	38	97	208	394	526	605	616	485	280	107	43	3,419
Mean Precipitation (in.)	1.90	1.75	1.78	2.11	3.96	4.35	2.29	3.07	4.40	3.96	1.68	1.43	32.68
Days With ≥ 0.1" Precipitation	4	3	3	3	5	5	3	4	6	4	3	3	46
Days With ≥ 1.0" Precipitation	0	0	1	1	1	1	1	1	1	1	0	0	8
Mean Snowfall (in.)	0.0	trace	0.0	0.0	0.0	0.0	0.0	0.0	0.0	0.0	0.0	trace	trace
Days With ≥ 1.0" Snow Depth	0	0	0	0	0	0	0	0	0	0	0	0	0

McAllen Miller Int'l Airport *Hidalgo County*   Elevation: 98 ft.   Latitude: 26° 11' N   Longitude: 98° 14' W

	JAN	FEB	MAR	APR	MAY	JUN	JUL	AUG	SEP	OCT	NOV	DEC	YEAR
Mean Maximum Temp. (°F)	68.9	73.6	81.6	86.5	90.2	94.3	96.1	96.8	92.5	86.8	78.6	71.9	84.8
Mean Temp. (°F)	59.2	63.1	70.6	76.2	80.8	84.4	85.8	86.3	82.7	76.4	68.3	62.0	74.7
Mean Minimum Temp. (°F)	49.4	52.7	59.6	65.9	71.4	74.5	75.4	75.7	73.0	66.0	58.0	52.1	64.5
Extreme Maximum Temp. (°F)	94	99	105	107	110	107	106	108	105	103	102	96	110
Extreme Minimum Temp. (°F)	22	24	31	42	52	59	68	68	55	44	32	18	18
Days Maximum Temp. ≥ 90°F	0	1	5	11	19	26	29	29	22	12	3	1	158
Days Maximum Temp. ≤ 32°F	0	0	0	0	0	0	0	0	0	0	0	0	0
Days Minimum Temp. ≤ 32°F	1	0	0	0	0	0	0	0	0	0	0	1	2
Days Minimum Temp. ≤ 0°F	0	0	0	0	0	0	0	0	0	0	0	0	0
Heating Degree Days (base 65°F)	232	134	39	7	0	0	0	0	0	6	69	175	662
Cooling Degree Days (base 65°F)	53	95	221	361	517	617	683	696	563	389	195	95	4,485
Mean Precipitation (in.)	1.39	1.32	0.68	1.31	2.92	2.78	1.79	2.58	4.14	2.20	0.82	1.20	23.13
Days With ≥ 0.1" Precipitation	3	3	1	2	4	4	3	4	5	3	2	3	37
Days With ≥ 1.0" Precipitation	0	0	0	0	1	1	0	1	1	1	0	0	5
Mean Snowfall (in.)	0.0	trace	0.0	trace	0.0	0.0	0.0	0.0	0.0	0.0	0.0	0.0	trace
Days With ≥ 1.0" Snow Depth	0	0	0	0	0	0	0	0	0	0	0	0	0

McCamey *Upton County*   Elevation: 2,447 ft.   Latitude: 31° 08' N   Longitude: 102° 12' W

	JAN	FEB	MAR	APR	MAY	JUN	JUL	AUG	SEP	OCT	NOV	DEC	YEAR
Mean Maximum Temp. (°F)	59.6	65.1	73.4	81.6	88.9	94.3	95.4	94.2	88.1	79.7	68.7	61.3	79.2
Mean Temp. (°F)	45.6	50.7	58.6	67.1	75.1	81.7	83.8	82.6	76.4	67.0	55.2	47.4	65.9
Mean Minimum Temp. (°F)	31.4	36.2	43.7	52.5	61.3	69.0	72.1	71.0	64.7	54.3	41.7	33.4	52.6
Extreme Maximum Temp. (°F)	86	92	97	102	108	113	110	107	104	103	92	88	113
Extreme Minimum Temp. (°F)	6	-1	12	27	35	44	61	58	38	26	12	6	-1
Days Maximum Temp. ≥ 90°F	0	0	1	6	15	23	27	26	16	3	0	0	117
Days Maximum Temp. ≤ 32°F	1	0	0	0	0	0	0	0	0	0	0	0	1
Days Minimum Temp. ≤ 32°F	17	9	3	0	0	0	0	0	0	0	5	14	48
Days Minimum Temp. ≤ 0°F	0	0	0	0	0	0	0	0	0	0	0	0	0
Heating Degree Days (base 65°F)	596	401	223	69	9	0	0	0	13	65	301	539	2,216
Cooling Degree Days (base 65°F)	0	4	35	142	348	524	609	574	380	148	15	0	2,779
Mean Precipitation (in.)	0.47	0.60	0.44	0.94	1.63	1.51	0.94	1.99	2.80	2.05	0.55	0.70	14.62
Days With ≥ 0.1" Precipitation	1	2	1	2	3	3	2	3	4	2	1	2	26
Days With ≥ 1.0" Precipitation	0	0	0	0	0	0	0	1	1	0	0	0	2
Mean Snowfall (in.)	0.6	0.1	trace	trace	0.0	0.0	0.0	0.0	0.0	trace	0.3	0.1	1.1
Days With ≥ 1.0" Snow Depth	0	0	0	0	0	0	0	0	0	0	0	0	0

McCook *Hidalgo County* Elevation: 219 ft. Latitude: 26° 29' N Longitude: 98° 23' W

	JAN	FEB	MAR	APR	MAY	JUN	JUL	AUG	SEP	OCT	NOV	DEC	YEAR
Mean Maximum Temp. (°F)	68.2	73.0	80.7	86.1	89.9	94.5	96.7	97.6	92.9	86.1	77.5	70.6	84.5
Mean Temp. (°F)	57.1	61.2	68.5	74.4	79.4	83.6	85.1	85.3	81.6	74.6	66.3	59.7	73.1
Mean Minimum Temp. (°F)	46.0	49.4	56.2	62.7	69.0	72.6	73.4	73.0	70.2	63.1	55.0	48.7	61.6
Extreme Maximum Temp. (°F)	96	100	104	108	109	113	109	109	104	99	97	97	113
Extreme Minimum Temp. (°F)	19	25	28	36	48	56	65	62	51	38	30	14	14
Days Maximum Temp. ≥ 90°F	0	1	5	10	18	26	29	29	23	12	3	1	157
Days Maximum Temp. ≤ 32°F	0	0	0	0	0	0	0	0	0	0	0	0	0
Days Minimum Temp. ≤ 32°F	3	1	0	0	0	0	0	0	0	0	0	1	5
Days Minimum Temp. ≤ 0°F	0	0	0	0	0	0	0	0	0	0	0	0	0
Heating Degree Days (base 65°F)	282	169	63	14	1	0	0	0	1	12	97	225	864
Cooling Degree Days (base 65°F)	44	77	177	308	475	594	661	665	523	338	162	74	4,098
Mean Precipitation (in.)	1.10	1.24	0.82	1.21	2.75	3.08	1.69	1.91	3.73	2.73	0.92	1.04	22.22
Days With ≥ 0.1" Precipitation	3	3	2	2	3	4	3	3	5	3	2	3	36
Days With ≥ 1.0" Precipitation	0	0	0	0	1	1	0	1	1	1	0	0	5
Mean Snowfall (in.)	0.0	0.0	trace	0.0	0.0	0.0	0.0	0.0	0.0	0.0	0.0	trace	trace
Days With ≥ 1.0" Snow Depth	0	0	0	0	0	0	0	0	0	0	0	0	0

McGregor *McLennan County* Elevation: 721 ft. Latitude: 31° 26' N Longitude: 97° 24' W

	JAN	FEB	MAR	APR	MAY	JUN	JUL	AUG	SEP	OCT	NOV	DEC	YEAR
Mean Maximum Temp. (°F)	55.6	60.9	68.6	76.6	83.6	90.5	95.5	95.4	88.6	78.9	66.8	58.7	76.6
Mean Temp. (°F)	44.7	49.5	57.0	65.0	72.7	79.8	83.9	83.8	77.3	67.2	55.9	47.9	65.4
Mean Minimum Temp. (°F)	33.6	38.1	45.5	53.4	61.9	69.0	72.4	72.0	65.9	55.4	45.0	37.0	54.1
Extreme Maximum Temp. (°F)	87	95	98	96	100	109	108	107	106	101	89	83	109
Extreme Minimum Temp. (°F)	5	10	14	29	37	52	58	53	40	27	19	-1	-1
Days Maximum Temp. ≥ 90°F	0	0	0	1	5	18	28	27	16	3	0	0	98
Days Maximum Temp. ≤ 32°F	1	1	0	0	0	0	0	0	0	0	0	1	3
Days Minimum Temp. ≤ 32°F	15	8	3	0	0	0	0	0	0	0	3	10	39
Days Minimum Temp. ≤ 0°F	0	0	0	0	0	0	0	0	0	0	0	0	0
Heating Degree Days (base 65°F)	624	438	269	89	12	0	0	0	8	69	290	529	2,328
Cooling Degree Days (base 65°F)	1	7	28	92	263	449	601	602	389	141	26	6	2,605
Mean Precipitation (in.)	2.03	2.58	2.64	2.89	4.31	3.39	2.02	2.31	2.83	3.71	2.44	2.71	33.86
Days With ≥ 0.1" Precipitation	4	4	5	5	6	5	3	3	4	5	4	4	52
Days With ≥ 1.0" Precipitation	0	1	1	1	1	1	1	1	1	1	1	1	11
Mean Snowfall (in.)	0.5	trace	0.0	0.0	0.0	0.0	0.0	0.0	0.0	0.0	trace	trace	0.5
Days With ≥ 1.0" Snow Depth	0	0	0	0	0	0	0	0	0	0	0	0	0

McKinney 3 S *Collin County* Elevation: 593 ft. Latitude: 33° 10' N Longitude: 96° 37' W

	JAN	FEB	MAR	APR	MAY	JUN	JUL	AUG	SEP	OCT	NOV	DEC	YEAR
Mean Maximum Temp. (°F)	54.9	60.6	68.9	76.5	82.9	90.5	95.4	95.2	88.1	78.6	66.2	57.8	76.3
Mean Temp. (°F)	44.0	48.9	57.1	64.5	72.0	79.7	84.0	83.2	76.5	66.4	55.1	46.9	64.8
Mean Minimum Temp. (°F)	33.0	37.2	45.1	52.5	61.1	68.8	72.3	71.0	64.8	54.2	44.0	36.0	53.3
Extreme Maximum Temp. (°F)	82	86	96	93	99	108	109	107	109	97	87	82	109
Extreme Minimum Temp. (°F)	5	2	13	28	40	50	53	54	39	24	15	-4	-4
Days Maximum Temp. ≥ 90°F	0	0	0	1	3	18	28	27	14	2	0	0	93
Days Maximum Temp. ≤ 32°F	1	1	0	0	0	0	0	0	0	0	0	0	3
Days Minimum Temp. ≤ 32°F	15	9	3	0	0	0	0	0	0	0	5	12	44
Days Minimum Temp. ≤ 0°F	0	0	0	0	0	0	0	0	0	0	0	0	0
Heating Degree Days (base 65°F)	646	450	266	92	12	0	0	0	10	76	312	558	2,422
Cooling Degree Days (base 65°F)	1	3	24	81	242	451	603	594	367	125	21	3	2,515
Mean Precipitation (in.)	2.39	3.02	3.40	3.75	5.60	4.02	2.35	2.27	3.43	4.33	3.42	3.08	41.06
Days With ≥ 0.1" Precipitation	4	5	5	5	6	5	3	3	4	4	4	4	52
Days With ≥ 1.0" Precipitation	1	1	1	1	2	1	1	1	1	1	1	1	13
Mean Snowfall (in.)	0.8	1.0	0.2	0.0	0.0	0.0	0.0	0.0	0.0	0.0	0.2	0.2	2.4
Days With ≥ 1.0" Snow Depth	1	1	0	0	0	0	0	0	0	0	0	1	3

Medina 2 W *Bandera County* Elevation: 1,702 ft. Latitude: 29° 47' N Longitude: 99° 17' W

	JAN	FEB	MAR	APR	MAY	JUN	JUL	AUG	SEP	OCT	NOV	DEC	YEAR
Mean Maximum Temp. (°F)	61.6	66.4	73.5	80.3	85.2	90.9	93.8	94.2	89.3	80.6	70.5	63.4	79.1
Mean Temp. (°F)	47.2	51.5	59.1	66.0	73.2	79.1	81.4	81.1	76.4	67.1	56.9	49.8	65.7
Mean Minimum Temp. (°F)	32.8	36.6	44.6	51.7	61.1	67.2	68.8	68.0	63.5	53.6	43.2	36.1	52.3
Extreme Maximum Temp. (°F)	88	98	100	101	102	109	107	106	104	99	93	87	109
Extreme Minimum Temp. (°F)	9	7	15	22	35	47	55	54	39	23	15	5	5
Days Maximum Temp. ≥ 90°F	0	0	1	3	7	20	27	27	17	3	0	0	105
Days Maximum Temp. ≤ 32°F	0	0	0	0	0	0	0	0	0	0	0	0	0
Days Minimum Temp. ≤ 32°F	17	10	4	1	0	0	0	0	0	0	5	12	49
Days Minimum Temp. ≤ 0°F	0	0	0	0	0	0	0	0	0	0	0	0	0
Heating Degree Days (base 65°F)	547	379	215	72	7	0	0	0	7	70	262	469	2,028
Cooling Degree Days (base 65°F)	2	5	35	110	282	456	534	533	370	147	29	4	2,507
Mean Precipitation (in.)	1.70	1.97	2.52	2.67	4.45	4.16	2.57	3.15	3.86	4.16	2.60	2.25	36.06
Days With ≥ 0.1" Precipitation	4	3	4	4	6	5	4	3	4	4	4	4	49
Days With ≥ 1.0" Precipitation	0	1	1	1	2	1	1	1	1	1	1	0	11
Mean Snowfall (in.)	1.0	0.2	trace	0.0	0.0	0.0	0.0	0.0	0.0	trace	trace	trace	1.2
Days With ≥ 1.0" Snow Depth	0	0	0	0	0	0	0	0	0	0	0	0	0

Memphis *Hall County*   Elevation: 2,089 ft.   Latitude: 34° 44' N   Longitude: 100° 32' W

	JAN	FEB	MAR	APR	MAY	JUN	JUL	AUG	SEP	OCT	NOV	DEC	YEAR
Mean Maximum Temp. (°F)	51.5	57.3	65.8	75.0	82.6	91.0	95.7	93.9	86.0	75.9	63.1	54.0	74.3
Mean Temp. (°F)	38.3	43.3	51.2	60.2	69.3	77.7	82.5	80.7	72.9	61.8	49.2	40.7	60.6
Mean Minimum Temp. (°F)	24.9	29.3	36.5	45.4	56.0	64.6	69.3	67.4	59.8	47.6	35.4	27.4	47.0
Extreme Maximum Temp. (°F)	85	92	99	100	108	116	110	107	107	100	89	82	116
Extreme Minimum Temp. (°F)	0	0	12	24	38	47	58	56	35	19	13	-6	-6
Days Maximum Temp. ≥ 90°F	0	0	1	3	7	18	26	24	13	3	0	0	95
Days Maximum Temp. ≤ 32°F	3	2	0	0	0	0	0	0	0	0	0	2	7
Days Minimum Temp. ≤ 32°F	26	18	9	2	0	0	0	0	0	1	12	23	91
Days Minimum Temp. ≤ 0°F	0	0	0	0	0	0	0	0	0	0	0	0	0
Heating Degree Days (base 65°F)	822	605	430	184	37	2	0	0	29	152	469	746	3,476
Cooling Degree Days (base 65°F)	0	2	9	46	186	393	562	511	286	62	3	0	2,060
Mean Precipitation (in.)	0.59	0.86	1.35	1.93	3.92	3.22	1.85	2.33	2.52	1.71	0.91	0.73	21.92
Days With ≥ 0.1" Precipitation	2	2	2	3	5	5	3	3	4	3	2	2	36
Days With ≥ 1.0" Precipitation	0	0	0	1	1	1	1	1	1	0	0	0	6
Mean Snowfall (in.)	1.1	0.9	0.3	trace	0.0	0.0	0.0	0.0	0.0	trace	0.4	0.7	3.4
Days With ≥ 1.0" Snow Depth	1	0	0	0	0	0	0	0	0	0	0	1	2

Menard *Menard County*   Elevation: 1,948 ft.   Latitude: 30° 55' N   Longitude: 99° 47' W

	JAN	FEB	MAR	APR	MAY	JUN	JUL	AUG	SEP	OCT	NOV	DEC	YEAR
Mean Maximum Temp. (°F)	60.1	65.3	72.9	80.6	86.2	91.2	94.5	93.8	88.1	80.1	68.9	62.0	78.7
Mean Temp. (°F)	45.3	50.0	57.6	65.2	72.6	78.4	81.2	80.2	74.6	65.5	54.5	47.3	64.4
Mean Minimum Temp. (°F)	30.5	34.5	42.2	49.6	58.9	65.6	67.9	66.6	61.1	50.7	40.0	32.6	50.0
Extreme Maximum Temp. (°F)	88	97	97	101	107	108	109	109	105	99	91	84	109
Extreme Minimum Temp. (°F)	1	-1	7	20	32	44	53	50	33	21	9	-2	-2
Days Maximum Temp. ≥ 90°F	0	0	1	4	10	20	26	24	14	3	0	0	102
Days Maximum Temp. ≤ 32°F	1	0	0	0	0	0	0	0	0	0	0	1	2
Days Minimum Temp. ≤ 32°F	19	12	7	2	0	0	0	0	0	1	9	16	66
Days Minimum Temp. ≤ 0°F	0	0	0	0	0	0	0	0	0	0	0	0	0
Heating Degree Days (base 65°F)	604	422	253	91	13	0	0	0	12	88	326	542	2,351
Cooling Degree Days (base 65°F)	1	4	28	102	266	423	526	508	315	116	17	1	2,307
Mean Precipitation (in.)	0.96	1.52	1.66	1.75	3.37	3.27	2.07	2.43	2.71	2.38	1.25	1.23	24.60
Days With ≥ 0.1" Precipitation	3	3	3	3	5	4	3	3	4	4	2	3	40
Days With ≥ 1.0" Precipitation	0	0	0	0	1	1	1	1	1	1	0	0	6
Mean Snowfall (in.)	1.2	0.3	trace	0.0	0.0	0.0	0.0	0.0	0.0	0.0	trace	0.2	1.7
Days With ≥ 1.0" Snow Depth	0	0	0	0	0	0	0	0	0	0	0	0	0

Mexia *Limestone County*   Elevation: 534 ft.   Latitude: 31° 41' N   Longitude: 96° 29' W

	JAN	FEB	MAR	APR	MAY	JUN	JUL	AUG	SEP	OCT	NOV	DEC	YEAR
Mean Maximum Temp. (°F)	57.1	62.3	70.1	77.5	83.8	91.4	95.8	96.3	90.4	80.7	68.8	60.1	77.9
Mean Temp. (°F)	45.4	50.1	57.6	65.3	72.3	79.7	83.4	83.3	77.4	67.3	56.4	48.3	65.6
Mean Minimum Temp. (°F)	33.6	37.9	45.2	52.9	60.7	68.0	71.1	70.2	64.3	53.9	44.1	36.4	53.2
Extreme Maximum Temp. (°F)	83	95	91	98	99	107	108	108	110	101	91	82	110
Extreme Minimum Temp. (°F)	6	5	13	30	41	50	55	54	40	28	15	-5	-5
Days Maximum Temp. ≥ 90°F	0	0	0	1	6	20	27	28	18	5	0	0	105
Days Maximum Temp. ≤ 32°F	1	1	0	0	0	0	0	0	0	0	0	1	3
Days Minimum Temp. ≤ 32°F	15	8	3	0	0	0	0	0	0	0	4	10	40
Days Minimum Temp. ≤ 0°F	0	0	0	0	0	0	0	0	0	0	0	0	0
Heating Degree Days (base 65°F)	603	420	250	77	9	0	0	0	6	65	275	516	2,221
Cooling Degree Days (base 65°F)	2	6	28	91	243	439	576	575	389	142	25	6	2,522
Mean Precipitation (in.)	2.41	3.15	3.53	3.14	4.84	3.62	1.99	2.60	4.40	4.39	3.37	3.73	41.17
Days With ≥ 0.1" Precipitation	5	5	5	4	6	5	3	3	5	5	5	5	56
Days With ≥ 1.0" Precipitation	0	1	1	1	2	1	1	1	1	2	1	1	13
Mean Snowfall (in.)	0.2	0.5	trace	0.0	0.0	0.0	0.0	0.0	0.0	0.0	trace	trace	0.7
Days With ≥ 1.0" Snow Depth	0	0	0	0	0	0	0	0	0	0	0	0	0

Miami *Roberts County*   Elevation: 2,752 ft.   Latitude: 35° 42' N   Longitude: 100° 38' W

	JAN	FEB	MAR	APR	MAY	JUN	JUL	AUG	SEP	OCT	NOV	DEC	YEAR
Mean Maximum Temp. (°F)	47.1	52.5	60.5	70.2	78.3	87.3	92.6	90.9	82.8	72.1	58.6	49.8	70.2
Mean Temp. (°F)	33.8	38.7	46.5	55.9	65.2	74.5	79.4	77.8	69.7	57.8	45.0	36.3	56.7
Mean Minimum Temp. (°F)	20.4	24.8	32.4	41.5	52.1	61.6	66.3	64.7	56.7	43.5	31.4	22.8	43.2
Extreme Maximum Temp. (°F)	83	86	97	97	104	110	111	106	105	97	90	81	111
Extreme Minimum Temp. (°F)	-8	-10	4	18	30	41	48	48	28	14	6	-11	-11
Days Maximum Temp. ≥ 90°F	0	0	0	1	4	13	22	20	9	1	0	0	70
Days Maximum Temp. ≤ 32°F	6	3	1	0	0	0	0	0	0	0	1	4	15
Days Minimum Temp. ≤ 32°F	29	22	15	5	0	0	0	0	0	3	17	27	118
Days Minimum Temp. ≤ 0°F	1	1	0	0	0	0	0	0	0	0	0	1	3
Heating Degree Days (base 65°F)	962	737	570	291	92	10	1	2	56	246	594	881	4,442
Cooling Degree Days (base 65°F)	0	0	3	21	104	297	458	419	208	29	1	0	1,540
Mean Precipitation (in.)	0.68	0.80	1.78	2.17	3.66	2.98	2.39	2.45	2.45	1.59	1.13	0.85	22.93
Days With ≥ 0.1" Precipitation	2	2	3	3	6	5	4	5	4	3	3	2	42
Days With ≥ 1.0" Precipitation	0	0	1	1	1	1	1	1	1	0	0	0	7
Mean Snowfall (in.)	3.1	4.0	3.2	1.0	0.0	0.0	0.0	0.0	trace	trace	1.7	3.7	16.7
Days With ≥ 1.0" Snow Depth	3	2	1	0	0	0	0	0	0	0	0	2	9

Midland 4 ENE *Midland County* Elevation: 2,739 ft. Latitude: 32° 01' N Longitude: 102° 01' W

	JAN	FEB	MAR	APR	MAY	JUN	JUL	AUG	SEP	OCT	NOV	DEC	YEAR
Mean Maximum Temp. (°F)	58.8	65.1	72.6	81.3	88.3	94.2	95.2	93.7	87.6	79.6	67.8	60.8	78.7
Mean Temp. (°F)	44.3	49.4	56.6	64.9	73.4	80.0	82.0	80.7	74.5	65.3	53.4	46.2	64.2
Mean Minimum Temp. (°F)	29.7	33.6	40.6	48.4	58.3	65.8	68.6	67.7	61.4	50.9	38.9	31.5	49.6
Extreme Maximum Temp. (°F)	84	89	96	100	105	116	110	106	103	100	90	82	116
Extreme Minimum Temp. (°F)	2	2	10	22	28	46	56	52	37	24	11	-2	-2
Days Maximum Temp. ≥ 90°F	0	0	1	5	14	24	27	25	14	2	0	0	112
Days Maximum Temp. ≤ 32°F	1	0	0	0	0	0	0	0	0	0	0	1	2
Days Minimum Temp. ≤ 32°F	20	13	6	1	0	0	0	0	0	1	7	17	65
Days Minimum Temp. ≤ 0°F	0	0	0	0	0	0	0	0	0	0	0	0	0
Heating Degree Days (base 65°F)	636	436	273	91	11	0	0	0	15	82	347	578	2,469
Cooling Degree Days (base 65°F)	0	3	16	94	294	475	558	517	320	107	7	0	2,391
Mean Precipitation (in.)	0.57	0.52	0.51	0.78	1.89	1.34	1.49	2.22	3.02	1.31	0.69	0.57	14.91
Days With ≥ 0.1" Precipitation	1	1	1	1	3	2	3	4	3	2	1	1	23
Days With ≥ 1.0" Precipitation	0	0	0	0	1	0	0	1	1	0	0	0	3
Mean Snowfall (in.)	1.3	0.3	0.2	0.0	0.0	0.0	0.0	0.0	0.0	trace	0.4	0.5	2.7
Days With ≥ 1.0" Snow Depth	0	0	0	0	0	0	0	0	0	0	0	0	0

Mineola 8 ENE *Wood County* Elevation: 383 ft. Latitude: 32° 43' N Longitude: 95° 22' W

	JAN	FEB	MAR	APR	MAY	JUN	JUL	AUG	SEP	OCT	NOV	DEC	YEAR
Mean Maximum Temp. (°F)	54.6	60.2	67.7	75.2	82.0	89.1	93.3	93.7	87.4	78.0	66.2	58.2	75.5
Mean Temp. (°F)	42.9	47.7	55.1	62.4	70.7	78.1	81.7	81.3	75.0	64.4	53.7	46.3	63.3
Mean Minimum Temp. (°F)	31.1	35.1	42.4	49.5	59.3	66.9	70.1	68.8	62.5	50.7	41.1	34.3	51.0
Extreme Maximum Temp. (°F)	84	93	90	93	99	106	107	108	107	95	86	82	108
Extreme Minimum Temp. (°F)	3	9	15	24	38	45	53	50	35	22	9	1	1
Days Maximum Temp. ≥ 90°F	0	0	0	0	2	16	25	25	14	2	0	0	84
Days Maximum Temp. ≤ 32°F	2	0	0	0	0	0	0	0	0	0	0	1	3
Days Minimum Temp. ≤ 32°F	19	13	7	2	0	0	0	0	0	1	7	15	64
Days Minimum Temp. ≤ 0°F	0	0	0	0	0	0	0	0	0	0	0	0	0
Heating Degree Days (base 65°F)	682	488	323	138	22	1	0	0	15	109	349	580	2,707
Cooling Degree Days (base 65°F)	2	5	19	58	205	401	526	520	318	93	16	7	2,170
Mean Precipitation (in.)	3.38	3.51	4.06	3.82	4.69	3.81	3.00	2.30	3.73	4.95	4.15	4.04	45.44
Days With ≥ 0.1" Precipitation	6	6	6	5	7	5	4	4	5	5	5	5	63
Days With ≥ 1.0" Precipitation	1	1	1	1	2	1	1	1	1	2	1	1	14
Mean Snowfall (in.)	0.7	0.3	trace	trace	0.0	0.0	0.0	0.0	0.0	0.0	trace	0.3	1.3
Days With ≥ 1.0" Snow Depth	0	0	0	0	0	0	0	0	0	0	0	0	0

Mineral Wells Municipal Airport *Palo Pinto County* Elevation: 928 ft. Latitude: 32° 47' N Longitude: 98° 04' W

	JAN	FEB	MAR	APR	MAY	JUN	JUL	AUG	SEP	OCT	NOV	DEC	YEAR
Mean Maximum Temp. (°F)	56.8	63.0	70.3	78.1	84.6	92.5	97.0	95.8	89.5	79.9	67.6	60.4	78.0
Mean Temp. (°F)	44.9	50.1	57.4	65.5	72.9	80.7	84.6	83.6	77.5	67.2	55.6	48.0	65.7
Mean Minimum Temp. (°F)	33.0	37.3	44.6	52.8	61.1	68.8	72.3	71.4	65.4	54.4	43.4	35.5	53.3
Extreme Maximum Temp. (°F)	88	97	96	100	102	114	109	109	109	101	93	84	114
Extreme Minimum Temp. (°F)	5	8	12	29	42	51	58	56	42	23	17	7	5
Days Maximum Temp. ≥ 90°F	0	0	1	2	8	21	27	27	17	4	0	0	107
Days Maximum Temp. ≤ 32°F	1	0	0	0	0	0	0	0	0	0	0	1	2
Days Minimum Temp. ≤ 32°F	16	9	3	0	0	0	0	0	0	0	4	13	45
Days Minimum Temp. ≤ 0°F	0	0	0	0	0	0	0	0	0	0	0	0	0
Heating Degree Days (base 65°F)	627	418	257	84	13	0	0	0	8	72	297	524	2,300
Cooling Degree Days (base 65°F)	na	6	32	107	na	478	631	593	386	na	22	4	na
Mean Precipitation (in.)	1.48	2.00	2.80	3.00	5.00	2.99	2.56	2.36	2.78	3.75	1.93	1.79	32.44
Days With ≥ 0.1" Precipitation	3	4	5	4	6	4	3	4	4	4	3	3	47
Days With ≥ 1.0" Precipitation	0	0	1	2	1	1	1	1	1	1	0	0	10
Mean Snowfall (in.)	0.6	0.9	0.4	trace	trace	trace	0.0	0.0	0.0	trace	0.1	0.2	2.2
Days With ≥ 1.0" Snow Depth	0	0	0	0	0	0	0	0	0	0	0	0	0

Monahans *Ward County* Elevation: 2,657 ft. Latitude: 31° 35' N Longitude: 102° 53' W

	JAN	FEB	MAR	APR	MAY	JUN	JUL	AUG	SEP	OCT	NOV	DEC	YEAR
Mean Maximum Temp. (°F)	61.3	66.4	75.2	83.1	90.6	97.2	98.5	96.9	90.2	82.3	70.2	62.1	81.2
Mean Temp. (°F)	44.7	49.8	57.8	65.5	74.2	81.7	83.7	82.4	75.7	65.9	53.8	46.1	65.1
Mean Minimum Temp. (°F)	28.1	33.1	40.3	47.9	57.7	66.1	68.9	67.9	61.1	49.6	37.4	30.0	49.0
Extreme Maximum Temp. (°F)	87	91	100	106	111	120	115	110	108	104	92	86	120
Extreme Minimum Temp. (°F)	4	-8	12	25	35	45	55	50	33	22	10	5	-8
Days Maximum Temp. ≥ 90°F	0	0	2	8	18	25	28	27	19	7	0	0	134
Days Maximum Temp. ≤ 32°F	0	0	0	0	0	0	0	0	0	0	0	0	0
Days Minimum Temp. ≤ 32°F	22	13	5	1	0	0	0	0	0	1	8	20	70
Days Minimum Temp. ≤ 0°F	0	0	0	0	0	0	0	0	0	0	0	0	0
Heating Degree Days (base 65°F)	621	424	237	84	10	0	0	0	16	81	334	579	2,386
Cooling Degree Days (base 65°F)	0	1	20	101	308	526	598	561	356	119	6	0	2,596
Mean Precipitation (in.)	0.49	0.64	0.36	0.56	1.82	1.36	1.33	1.68	2.63	1.34	0.49	0.69	13.39
Days With ≥ 0.1" Precipitation	1	2	1	1	3	2	2	3	4	2	1	2	24
Days With ≥ 1.0" Precipitation	0	0	0	0	1	0	0	0	1	0	0	0	2
Mean Snowfall (in.)	0.4	0.2	0.1	0.0	0.0	0.0	0.0	0.0	0.0	trace	0.2	0.5	1.4
Days With ≥ 1.0" Snow Depth	0	0	0	0	0	0	0	0	0	0	0	0	0

Morton *Cochran County*   Elevation: 3,759 ft.   Latitude: 33° 43' N   Longitude: 102° 46' W

	JAN	FEB	MAR	APR	MAY	JUN	JUL	AUG	SEP	OCT	NOV	DEC	YEAR
Mean Maximum Temp. (°F)	52.4	57.8	65.5	73.8	82.1	89.9	91.2	88.9	82.5	74.1	62.5	54.2	72.9
Mean Temp. (°F)	37.8	42.2	48.9	57.2	66.7	75.0	77.5	75.4	68.9	58.9	47.4	39.5	58.0
Mean Minimum Temp. (°F)	23.0	26.5	32.3	40.5	51.1	60.0	63.7	62.0	55.2	43.7	32.4	24.8	42.9
Extreme Maximum Temp. (°F)	82	85	92	98	104	110	107	104	101	97	85	79	110
Extreme Minimum Temp. (°F)	-8	0	9	21	31	40	53	49	32	16	5	-6	-8
Days Maximum Temp. ≥ 90°F	0	0	0	1	6	17	20	16	7	1	0	0	68
Days Maximum Temp. ≤ 32°F	3	1	0	0	0	0	0	0	0	0	0	2	6
Days Minimum Temp. ≤ 32°F	28	22	15	5	0	0	0	0	0	2	15	26	113
Days Minimum Temp. ≤ 0°F	0	0	0	0	0	0	0	0	0	0	0	1	1
Heating Degree Days (base 65°F)	837	637	492	248	63	5	0	1	45	208	521	786	3,843
Cooling Degree Days (base 65°F)	0	0	1	19	124	320	406	346	174	27	0	0	1,417
Mean Precipitation (in.)	0.50	0.59	0.63	0.87	1.96	2.44	2.59	2.87	2.79	1.55	0.70	0.62	18.11
Days With ≥ 0.1" Precipitation	1	2	2	2	4	4	5	5	4	3	2	2	36
Days With ≥ 1.0" Precipitation	0	0	0	0	0	1	1	1	1	0	0	0	4
Mean Snowfall (in.)	2.2	1.6	0.1	0.2	trace	0.0	0.0	0.0	0.0	0.1	0.8	2.7	7.7
Days With ≥ 1.0" Snow Depth	*0*	*0*	0	0	0	0	0	0	0	0	0	*0*	*0*

Mount Locke *Jeff Davis County*   Elevation: 6,788 ft.   Latitude: 30° 40' N   Longitude: 104° 00' W

	JAN	FEB	MAR	APR	MAY	JUN	JUL	AUG	SEP	OCT	NOV	DEC	YEAR
Mean Maximum Temp. (°F)	53.6	57.5	64.1	70.9	78.5	84.5	82.9	80.7	76.7	70.9	61.7	55.0	69.8
Mean Temp. (°F)	42.7	45.8	51.2	57.6	65.4	71.3	70.9	69.4	65.6	59.3	50.3	44.4	57.8
Mean Minimum Temp. (°F)	31.8	34.1	38.1	44.1	52.2	58.1	58.9	58.1	54.4	47.6	38.8	33.7	45.8
Extreme Maximum Temp. (°F)	73	78	88	94	96	104	100	96	95	89	81	80	104
Extreme Minimum Temp. (°F)	-2	0	7	11	31	36	40	40	32	13	8	-2	-2
Days Maximum Temp. ≥ 90°F	0	0	0	0	2	7	4	1	1	0	0	0	15
Days Maximum Temp. ≤ 32°F	1	0	0	0	0	0	0	0	0	0	0	1	2
Days Minimum Temp. ≤ 32°F	16	11	9	3	0	0	0	0	0	2	8	13	62
Days Minimum Temp. ≤ 0°F	0	0	0	0	0	0	0	0	0	0	0	0	0
Heating Degree Days (base 65°F)	684	535	423	231	71	13	6	12	62	196	435	632	3,300
Cooling Degree Days (base 65°F)	0	0	2	15	99	224	215	173	95	27	1	0	851
Mean Precipitation (in.)	0.55	0.55	0.40	0.59	1.73	2.45	3.87	4.06	3.47	1.63	0.54	0.73	20.57
Days With ≥ 0.1" Precipitation	2	2	1	2	4	5	7	8	6	3	1	2	43
Days With ≥ 1.0" Precipitation	0	0	0	0	0	1	1	1	1	0	0	0	4
Mean Snowfall (in.)	*0.4*	trace	trace	0.0	0.0	0.0	0.0	0.0	0.0	0.0	0.0	1.3	*1.7*
Days With ≥ 1.0" Snow Depth	*0*	0	0	0	0	0	0	0	0	0	0	1	*1*

Mount Pleasant *Titus County*   Elevation: 423 ft.   Latitude: 33° 10' N   Longitude: 95° 00' W

	JAN	FEB	MAR	APR	MAY	JUN	JUL	AUG	SEP	OCT	NOV	DEC	YEAR
Mean Maximum Temp. (°F)	54.5	59.5	67.6	75.7	82.6	90.1	94.4	94.4	87.8	78.5	66.0	57.8	75.7
Mean Temp. (°F)	42.3	46.4	54.4	62.4	70.4	78.4	82.3	81.6	74.9	63.8	53.0	45.4	62.9
Mean Minimum Temp. (°F)	30.0	33.3	41.3	49.0	58.2	66.6	70.2	68.8	61.9	49.2	40.0	32.9	50.1
Extreme Maximum Temp. (°F)	83	91	90	95	99	101	107	109	108	97	86	83	109
Extreme Minimum Temp. (°F)	3	2	11	27	35	48	52	51	36	23	9	-2	-2
Days Maximum Temp. ≥ 90°F	0	0	0	0	4	18	27	26	15	2	0	0	92
Days Maximum Temp. ≤ 32°F	1	1	0	0	0	0	0	0	0	0	0	1	3
Days Minimum Temp. ≤ 32°F	20	14	7	1	0	0	0	0	0	1	8	16	67
Days Minimum Temp. ≤ 0°F	0	0	0	0	0	0	0	0	0	0	0	0	0
Heating Degree Days (base 65°F)	700	522	341	136	22	1	0	0	16	118	365	606	2,827
Cooling Degree Days (base 65°F)	1	3	18	61	197	412	553	533	319	90	13	4	2,204
Mean Precipitation (in.)	3.22	3.65	4.47	3.89	4.91	4.62	3.73	2.16	3.59	4.95	4.76	4.36	48.31
Days With ≥ 0.1" Precipitation	5	5	6	6	6	5	4	4	4	5	5	5	60
Days With ≥ 1.0" Precipitation	1	1	1	1	2	2	1	1	1	2	2	2	17
Mean Snowfall (in.)	0.7	0.7	trace	0.0	0.0	0.0	0.0	0.0	0.0	0.0	trace	0.3	1.7
Days With ≥ 1.0" Snow Depth	1	1	0	0	0	0	0	0	0	0	0	0	2

Mount Vernon *Franklin County*   Elevation: 479 ft.   Latitude: 33° 12' N   Longitude: 95° 13' W

	JAN	FEB	MAR	APR	MAY	JUN	JUL	AUG	SEP	OCT	NOV	DEC	YEAR
Mean Maximum Temp. (°F)	52.7	58.5	66.3	74.2	80.9	88.4	92.9	93.1	86.5	76.5	64.6	56.1	74.2
Mean Temp. (°F)	42.1	47.3	55.0	62.8	70.5	78.2	82.4	81.9	75.2	64.6	53.8	45.8	63.3
Mean Minimum Temp. (°F)	31.4	36.1	43.7	51.3	60.1	68.0	71.8	70.6	63.9	52.7	42.9	35.4	52.3
Extreme Maximum Temp. (°F)	81	90	87	94	97	100	106	108	107	95	85	81	108
Extreme Minimum Temp. (°F)	2	4	11	27	40	50	56	53	41	27	13	-1	-1
Days Maximum Temp. ≥ 90°F	0	0	0	0	2	14	24	24	13	2	0	0	79
Days Maximum Temp. ≤ 32°F	2	1	0	0	0	0	0	0	0	0	0	1	4
Days Minimum Temp. ≤ 32°F	17	11	4	0	0	0	0	0	0	0	5	13	50
Days Minimum Temp. ≤ 0°F	0	0	0	0	0	0	0	0	0	0	0	0	0
Heating Degree Days (base 65°F)	705	498	322	124	22	1	0	0	16	107	347	593	2,735
Cooling Degree Days (base 65°F)	1	5	19	64	203	407	555	546	336	97	17	4	2,254
Mean Precipitation (in.)	2.75	3.48	4.22	3.67	4.61	4.27	3.70	2.34	3.79	4.88	4.79	4.37	46.87
Days With ≥ 0.1" Precipitation	5	5	6	5	7	5	4	4	5	5	5	6	62
Days With ≥ 1.0" Precipitation	1	1	1	1	2	1	1	1	1	2	2	1	15
Mean Snowfall (in.)	0.9	0.5	0.1	trace	0.0	0.0	0.0	0.0	0.0	0.0	trace	0.5	2.0
Days With ≥ 1.0" Snow Depth	0	1	0	0	0	0	0	0	0	0	0	1	2

Muleshoe 1 *Bailey County*   Elevation: 3,822 ft.   Latitude: 34° 14' N   Longitude: 102° 44' W

	JAN	FEB	MAR	APR	MAY	JUN	JUL	AUG	SEP	OCT	NOV	DEC	YEAR
Mean Maximum Temp. (°F)	51.2	56.9	64.8	73.1	81.6	89.8	91.7	89.5	82.9	73.9	61.6	53.1	72.5
Mean Temp. (°F)	35.6	40.4	47.5	56.0	65.3	74.2	77.2	75.3	68.3	57.3	45.3	37.3	56.7
Mean Minimum Temp. (°F)	19.9	23.8	30.1	39.0	49.0	58.6	62.6	61.1	53.7	40.7	29.0	21.4	40.8
Extreme Maximum Temp. (°F)	79	84	92	96	102	109	106	106	106	96	86	78	109
Extreme Minimum Temp. (°F)	-11	-1	5	19	29	41	50	41	28	14	-1	-9	-11
Days Maximum Temp. ≥ 90°F	0	0	0	1	6	16	21	17	8	1	0	0	70
Days Maximum Temp. ≤ 32°F	4	1	1	0	0	0	0	0	0	0	1	3	10
Days Minimum Temp. ≤ 32°F	30	24	19	6	0	0	0	0	0	4	20	28	131
Days Minimum Temp. ≤ 0°F	0	0	0	0	0	0	0	0	0	0	0	1	1
Heating Degree Days (base 65°F)	905	689	535	276	80	7	1	2	53	247	585	851	4,231
Cooling Degree Days (base 65°F)	0	0	0	11	100	297	407	351	168	16	0	0	1,350
Mean Precipitation (in.)	0.43	0.50	0.60	0.99	2.05	2.42	2.05	3.07	2.43	1.42	0.65	0.58	17.19
Days With ≥ 0.1" Precipitation	1	2	2	3	4	5	4	5	4	3	2	2	37
Days With ≥ 1.0" Precipitation	0	0	0	0	0	0	0	1	1	0	0	0	2
Mean Snowfall (in.)	2.2	2.2	0.7	0.5	0.0	0.0	0.0	0.0	0.0	0.2	1.0	2.8	9.6
Days With ≥ 1.0" Snow Depth	na	0	0	0	0	0	0	0	0	0	0	na	na

Munday *Knox County*   Elevation: 1,479 ft.   Latitude: 33° 27' N   Longitude: 99° 37' W

	JAN	FEB	MAR	APR	MAY	JUN	JUL	AUG	SEP	OCT	NOV	DEC	YEAR
Mean Maximum Temp. (°F)	56.6	62.2	70.8	79.8	86.5	93.4	97.5	96.1	88.8	79.9	67.7	59.0	78.2
Mean Temp. (°F)	42.7	47.9	55.9	64.7	72.9	80.4	84.4	83.0	75.9	65.9	54.1	45.4	64.4
Mean Minimum Temp. (°F)	28.8	33.5	40.9	49.5	59.2	67.3	71.2	70.0	62.9	51.8	40.4	31.9	50.6
Extreme Maximum Temp. (°F)	85	93	101	104	108	117	116	109	110	105	90	85	117
Extreme Minimum Temp. (°F)	-1	-8	7	26	37	49	55	54	35	23	14	-9	-9
Days Maximum Temp. ≥ 90°F	0	0	1	5	12	22	28	27	17	4	0	0	116
Days Maximum Temp. ≤ 32°F	2	1	0	0	0	0	0	0	0	0	0	1	4
Days Minimum Temp. ≤ 32°F	20	12	6	1	0	0	0	0	0	0	6	17	62
Days Minimum Temp. ≤ 0°F	0	0	0	0	0	0	0	0	0	0	0	0	0
Heating Degree Days (base 65°F)	685	479	301	99	14	0	0	0	15	81	332	601	2,607
Cooling Degree Days (base 65°F)	1	3	23	94	270	468	615	588	358	119	12	1	2,552
Mean Precipitation (in.)	0.98	1.57	1.67	1.85	3.86	3.34	1.68	2.75	3.34	2.66	1.19	1.18	26.07
Days With ≥ 0.1" Precipitation	2	3	3	3	5	5	3	4	4	4	2	3	41
Days With ≥ 1.0" Precipitation	0	0	0	0	1	1	0	1	1	1	0	0	5
Mean Snowfall (in.)	1.0	1.2	0.2	0.0	0.0	0.0	0.0	0.0	0.0	0.0	0.6	0.4	3.4
Days With ≥ 1.0" Snow Depth	1	0	0	0	0	0	0	0	0	0	0	0	1

Nacogdoches *Nacogdoches County*   Elevation: 433 ft.   Latitude: 31° 37' N   Longitude: 94° 39' W

	JAN	FEB	MAR	APR	MAY	JUN	JUL	AUG	SEP	OCT	NOV	DEC	YEAR
Mean Maximum Temp. (°F)	56.6	61.9	69.5	76.8	83.4	89.6	93.5	93.9	88.0	79.0	68.3	59.9	76.7
Mean Temp. (°F)	46.4	50.8	58.1	65.2	73.1	79.4	82.9	82.5	76.6	66.6	56.8	49.1	65.6
Mean Minimum Temp. (°F)	36.1	39.6	46.6	53.6	62.7	69.1	72.3	71.2	65.2	54.2	45.2	38.1	54.5
Extreme Maximum Temp. (°F)	84	92	90	93	100	108	106	108	104	98	88	84	108
Extreme Minimum Temp. (°F)	5	12	13	29	40	50	58	55	42	25	15	3	3
Days Maximum Temp. ≥ 90°F	0	0	0	1	4	17	26	26	15	2	0	0	91
Days Maximum Temp. ≤ 32°F	1	1	0	0	0	0	0	0	0	0	0	0	2
Days Minimum Temp. ≤ 32°F	12	7	3	0	0	0	0	0	0	0	4	11	37
Days Minimum Temp. ≤ 0°F	0	0	0	0	0	0	0	0	0	0	0	0	0
Heating Degree Days (base 65°F)	576	405	244	86	9	0	0	0	6	74	273	497	2,170
Cooling Degree Days (base 65°F)	4	11	35	102	271	454	575	571	381	135	32	11	2,582
Mean Precipitation (in.)	4.57	4.14	4.09	4.09	4.95	4.18	2.84	3.30	3.80	4.16	4.36	4.34	48.82
Days With ≥ 0.1" Precipitation	7	6	6	5	6	6	4	5	5	5	6	6	67
Days With ≥ 1.0" Precipitation	1	1	1	1	2	1	1	1	1	1	2	1	14
Mean Snowfall (in.)	0.2	trace	0.0	0.0	0.0	0.0	0.0	0.0	0.0	0.0	trace	trace	0.2
Days With ≥ 1.0" Snow Depth	0	0	0	0	0	0	0	0	0	0	0	0	0

Navarro Mills Dam *Navarro County*   Elevation: 452 ft.   Latitude: 31° 57' N   Longitude: 96° 42' W

	JAN	FEB	MAR	APR	MAY	JUN	JUL	AUG	SEP	OCT	NOV	DEC	YEAR
Mean Maximum Temp. (°F)	55.0	60.6	68.3	76.0	82.9	90.3	95.0	95.1	88.8	79.3	66.9	58.7	76.4
Mean Temp. (°F)	43.5	48.7	56.5	64.3	72.2	79.5	83.5	83.1	76.8	66.4	55.2	47.1	64.7
Mean Minimum Temp. (°F)	32.1	36.7	44.8	52.5	61.4	68.7	72.0	71.1	64.7	53.6	43.4	35.4	53.0
Extreme Maximum Temp. (°F)	84	95	93	93	101	107	109	108	108	98	92	82	109
Extreme Minimum Temp. (°F)	5	6	15	26	40	51	58	52	39	25	18	-5	-5
Days Maximum Temp. ≥ 90°F	0	0	0	1	4	18	28	27	17	3	0	0	98
Days Maximum Temp. ≤ 32°F	1	1	0	0	0	0	0	0	0	0	0	1	3
Days Minimum Temp. ≤ 32°F	17	10	3	0	0	0	0	0	0	0	4	12	46
Days Minimum Temp. ≤ 0°F	0	0	0	0	0	0	0	0	0	0	0	0	0
Heating Degree Days (base 65°F)	659	458	280	98	13	0	0	0	9	78	311	553	2,459
Cooling Degree Days (base 65°F)	1	5	25	81	245	438	584	580	371	126	23	4	2,483
Mean Precipitation (in.)	2.19	2.82	3.29	3.21	4.96	3.34	1.78	2.38	3.16	4.49	3.00	3.06	37.68
Days With ≥ 0.1" Precipitation	4	5	5	5	6	5	3	3	4	5	4	4	53
Days With ≥ 1.0" Precipitation	0	1	1	1	2	1	1	1	1	2	1	1	13
Mean Snowfall (in.)	0.5	0.0	0.0	0.0	0.0	0.0	0.0	0.0	0.0	0.0	0.0	0.0	0.5
Days With ≥ 1.0" Snow Depth	0	0	0	0	0	0	0	0	0	0	0	0	0

Navasota *Grimes County*   Elevation: 219 ft.   Latitude: 30° 23' N   Longitude: 96° 07' W

	JAN	FEB	MAR	APR	MAY	JUN	JUL	AUG	SEP	OCT	NOV	DEC	YEAR
Mean Maximum Temp. (°F)	59.3	63.8	71.4	78.1	84.6	90.7	94.6	95.2	89.3	80.9	70.2	62.4	78.4
Mean Temp. (°F)	48.7	52.9	60.3	67.1	74.4	80.5	83.4	83.5	78.0	68.7	59.1	51.5	67.3
Mean Minimum Temp. (°F)	38.0	42.0	49.2	56.1	64.1	70.3	72.2	71.7	66.7	56.4	47.9	40.5	56.3
Extreme Maximum Temp. (°F)	88	90	94	93	99	104	105	110	105	98	89	84	110
Extreme Minimum Temp. (°F)	9	16	19	30	43	52	62	60	43	28	21	3	3
Days Maximum Temp. ≥ 90°F	0	0	0	1	6	20	27	28	16	3	0	0	101
Days Maximum Temp. ≤ 32°F	1	0	0	0	0	0	0	0	0	0	0	0	1
Days Minimum Temp. ≤ 32°F	9	5	2	0	0	0	0	0	0	0	2	7	25
Days Minimum Temp. ≤ 0°F	0	0	0	0	0	0	0	0	0	0	0	0	0
Heating Degree Days (base 65°F)	509	347	189	61	5	0	0	0	3	51	222	427	1,814
Cooling Degree Days (base 65°F)	7	12	46	127	303	474	580	587	409	173	52	15	2,785
Mean Precipitation (in.)	3.51	2.80	3.21	3.06	4.24	4.33	2.20	2.80	4.53	4.48	3.35	3.19	41.70
Days With ≥ 0.1" Precipitation	5	5	5	4	6	5	4	4	6	5	5	5	59
Days With ≥ 1.0" Precipitation	1	1	1	1	1	1	0	1	1	1	1	1	11
Mean Snowfall (in.)	0.1	trace	0.0	0.0	0.0	0.0	0.0	0.0	0.0	0.0	trace	trace	0.1
Days With ≥ 1.0" Snow Depth	0	0	0	0	0	0	0	0	0	0	0	0	0

New Braunfels *Comal County*   Elevation: 708 ft.   Latitude: 29° 44' N   Longitude: 98° 07' W

	JAN	FEB	MAR	APR	MAY	JUN	JUL	AUG	SEP	OCT	NOV	DEC	YEAR
Mean Maximum Temp. (°F)	60.8	65.7	73.4	79.7	85.4	91.1	94.9	95.4	90.2	81.7	71.3	63.4	79.4
Mean Temp. (°F)	49.0	53.1	60.6	67.3	74.6	80.5	83.5	83.6	78.7	69.3	59.5	51.7	67.6
Mean Minimum Temp. (°F)	37.2	40.5	47.8	54.9	63.7	69.8	72.2	71.7	67.1	56.9	47.6	39.9	55.8
Extreme Maximum Temp. (°F)	89	98	100	100	100	110	105	107	105	98	90	86	110
Extreme Minimum Temp. (°F)	9	11	17	29	37	46	61	58	43	24	21	2	2
Days Maximum Temp. ≥ 90°F	0	0	1	2	8	21	28	29	19	4	0	0	112
Days Maximum Temp. ≤ 32°F	0	0	0	0	0	0	0	0	0	0	0	0	0
Days Minimum Temp. ≤ 32°F	11	6	2	0	0	0	0	0	0	0	2	8	29
Days Minimum Temp. ≤ 0°F	0	0	0	0	0	0	0	0	0	0	0	0	0
Heating Degree Days (base 65°F)	495	341	181	55	4	0	0	0	3	45	208	417	1,749
Cooling Degree Days (base 65°F)	6	11	45	125	314	467	581	593	421	182	52	11	2,808
Mean Precipitation (in.)	1.94	2.07	1.99	2.75	5.42	4.58	2.03	2.52	3.59	4.39	2.48	2.41	36.17
Days With ≥ 0.1" Precipitation	4	4	4	4	6	5	3	4	4	4	4	4	50
Days With ≥ 1.0" Precipitation	0	0	0	1	2	2	1	1	1	1	1	1	11
Mean Snowfall (in.)	0.4	0.0	0.0	0.0	0.0	0.0	0.0	0.0	0.0	0.0	0.0	0.0	0.4
Days With ≥ 1.0" Snow Depth	0	0	0	0	0	0	0	0	0	0	0	0	0

New Gulf *Wharton County*   Elevation: 68 ft.   Latitude: 29° 16' N   Longitude: 95° 54' W

	JAN	FEB	MAR	APR	MAY	JUN	JUL	AUG	SEP	OCT	NOV	DEC	YEAR
Mean Maximum Temp. (°F)	62.7	66.3	72.9	78.8	85.0	90.5	93.1	93.1	89.4	82.6	73.1	65.9	79.5
Mean Temp. (°F)	52.4	56.0	62.8	69.0	75.6	81.1	83.3	83.0	79.1	71.1	62.4	55.4	69.3
Mean Minimum Temp. (°F)	42.1	45.6	52.6	59.2	66.1	71.7	73.4	72.9	68.7	59.6	51.7	44.9	59.0
Extreme Maximum Temp. (°F)	83	89	95	92	98	100	103	104	100	96	90	86	104
Extreme Minimum Temp. (°F)	12	18	22	37	45	55	63	60	47	29	22	7	7
Days Maximum Temp. ≥ 90°F	0	0	0	0	5	20	27	27	18	4	0	0	101
Days Maximum Temp. ≤ 32°F	0	0	0	0	0	0	0	0	0	0	0	0	0
Days Minimum Temp. ≤ 32°F	6	3	1	0	0	0	0	0	0	0	1	3	14
Days Minimum Temp. ≤ 0°F	0	0	0	0	0	0	0	0	0	0	0	0	0
Heating Degree Days (base 65°F)	400	270	132	36	2	0	0	0	2	28	153	322	1,345
Cooling Degree Days (base 65°F)	15	25	70	154	343	499	582	574	438	230	86	35	3,051
Mean Precipitation (in.)	3.36	2.60	2.98	3.11	4.63	4.35	3.76	3.61	6.11	4.83	4.10	3.24	46.68
Days With ≥ 0.1" Precipitation	5	4	4	4	4	5	6	6	6	4	5	4	57
Days With ≥ 1.0" Precipitation	1	1	1	1	2	1	1	1	2	1	1	1	14
Mean Snowfall (in.)	trace	trace	0.0	0.0	0.0	0.0	0.0	0.0	0.0	0.0	trace	0.0	trace
Days With ≥ 1.0" Snow Depth	0	0	0	0	0	0	0	0	0	0	0	0	0

Nixon *Gonzales County*   Elevation: 396 ft.   Latitude: 29° 16' N   Longitude: 97° 45' W

	JAN	FEB	MAR	APR	MAY	JUN	JUL	AUG	SEP	OCT	NOV	DEC	YEAR
Mean Maximum Temp. (°F)	63.3	67.8	74.8	80.7	86.2	91.6	94.7	95.4	90.6	83.2	73.1	65.7	80.6
Mean Temp. (°F)	52.1	56.1	63.0	69.3	75.6	81.1	83.6	83.6	79.3	71.2	61.7	54.5	69.3
Mean Minimum Temp. (°F)	40.9	44.4	51.1	57.8	65.0	70.6	72.3	71.9	68.0	59.1	50.2	43.3	57.9
Extreme Maximum Temp. (°F)	90	95	100	98	99	109	104	106	103	97	89	88	109
Extreme Minimum Temp. (°F)	11	15	24	32	45	54	63	*58*	47	27	22	5	*5*
Days Maximum Temp. ≥ 90°F	0	0	1	2	8	22	28	29	20	7	0	0	117
Days Maximum Temp. ≤ 32°F	0	0	0	0	0	0	0	0	0	0	0	0	0
Days Minimum Temp. ≤ 32°F	6	3	1	0	0	0	0	0	0	0	1	5	16
Days Minimum Temp. ≤ 0°F	0	0	0	0	0	0	0	0	0	0	0	0	0
Heating Degree Days (base 65°F)	407	267	131	37	1	0	0	0	1	28	167	342	1,381
Cooling Degree Days (base 65°F)	9	22	66	169	345	499	589	596	443	227	75	24	3,064
Mean Precipitation (in.)	2.03	2.37	2.01	2.95	4.91	3.99	1.92	3.04	3.66	3.42	2.30	2.07	34.67
Days With ≥ 0.1" Precipitation	4	4	3	4	5	5	3	4	5	5	4	4	50
Days With ≥ 1.0" Precipitation	0	0	1	1	2	1	0	1	1	1	1	0	9
Mean Snowfall (in.)	0.3	trace	0.0	0.0	0.0	0.0	0.0	0.0	0.0	0.0	trace	0.0	0.3
Days With ≥ 1.0" Snow Depth	0	0	0	0	0	0	0	0	0	0	0	0	0

O C Fisher Dam *Tom Green County*   Elevation: 1,961 ft.   Latitude: 31° 28' N   Longitude: 100° 29' W

	JAN	FEB	MAR	APR	MAY	JUN	JUL	AUG	SEP	OCT	NOV	DEC	YEAR
Mean Maximum Temp. (°F)	56.9	62.7	70.5	79.2	na	91.4	95.2	94.5	88.1	79.0	67.3	59.4	na
Mean Temp. (°F)	43.2	48.6	56.1	64.7	na	79.3	83.0	82.1	75.4	65.2	53.7	45.7	na
Mean Minimum Temp. (°F)	29.5	34.4	41.7	50.2	na	67.0	70.7	69.6	62.6	51.4	40.0	31.9	na
Extreme Maximum Temp. (°F)	86	97	95	99	106	111	109	108	105	101	91	85	111
Extreme Minimum Temp. (°F)	4	3	9	27	38	51	56	55	35	26	12	-2	-2
Days Maximum Temp. ≥ 90°F	0	0	0	5	11	20	26	25	14	3	0	0	104
Days Maximum Temp. ≤ 32°F	1	1	0	0	0	0	0	0	0	0	0	1	3
Days Minimum Temp. ≤ 32°F	20	12	5	1	0	0	0	0	0	1	7	17	63
Days Minimum Temp. ≤ 0°F	0	0	0	0	0	0	0	0	0	0	0	0	0
Heating Degree Days (base 65°F)	669	461	289	99	na	1	0	0	12	96	347	593	na
Cooling Degree Days (base 65°F)	0	4	22	98	262	435	568	541	325	107	14	1	2,377
Mean Precipitation (in.)	0.85	1.39	1.23	1.94	3.38	2.96	1.72	1.97	2.87	2.25	1.20	1.12	22.88
Days With ≥ 0.1" Precipitation	2	3	3	3	5	4	3	4	3	3	2	2	37
Days With ≥ 1.0" Precipitation	0	0	0	1	1	1	0	1	1	1	0	0	6
Mean Snowfall (in.)	na	0.2	trace	0.0	0.0	0.0	0.0	0.0	0.0	0.0	0.1	trace	na
Days With ≥ 1.0" Snow Depth	na	0	0	0	0	0	0	0	0	0	0	0	na

Olton *Lamb County*   Elevation: 3,608 ft.   Latitude: 34° 11' N   Longitude: 102° 08' W

	JAN	FEB	MAR	APR	MAY	JUN	JUL	AUG	SEP	OCT	NOV	DEC	YEAR
Mean Maximum Temp. (°F)	50.5	56.1	64.2	72.5	80.5	88.2	90.2	87.9	81.6	73.1	60.6	52.7	71.5
Mean Temp. (°F)	36.0	40.7	47.9	56.7	65.7	73.9	76.6	74.7	67.8	57.8	45.9	38.2	56.8
Mean Minimum Temp. (°F)	21.6	25.2	31.6	40.8	50.8	59.5	63.0	61.4	54.3	42.4	31.1	23.8	42.1
Extreme Maximum Temp. (°F)	81	85	91	96	103	108	107	104	102	95	86	78	108
Extreme Minimum Temp. (°F)	-7	-4	6	20	30	41	52	50	29	15	-1	-6	-7
Days Maximum Temp. ≥ 90°F	0	0	0	1	5	14	18	13	6	1	0	0	58
Days Maximum Temp. ≤ 32°F	4	2	1	0	0	0	0	0	0	0	1	2	10
Days Minimum Temp. ≤ 32°F	29	23	16	4	0	0	0	0	0	4	16	27	119
Days Minimum Temp. ≤ 0°F	0	0	0	0	0	0	0	0	0	0	0	1	1
Heating Degree Days (base 65°F)	890	681	524	262	77	8	1	1	54	236	566	823	4,123
Cooling Degree Days (base 65°F)	0	0	1	17	106	276	383	330	155	20	0	0	1,288
Mean Precipitation (in.)	0.48	0.49	0.77	1.10	2.49	2.69	1.99	2.59	2.19	1.46	0.74	0.66	17.65
Days With ≥ 0.1" Precipitation	2	2	2	3	4	4	4	5	4	3	2	2	37
Days With ≥ 1.0" Precipitation	0	0	0	0	1	1	1	1	1	0	0	0	5
Mean Snowfall (in.)	2.3	1.5	0.9	0.2	0.0	0.0	0.0	0.0	0.0	0.1	0.5	2.3	7.8
Days With ≥ 1.0" Snow Depth	1	1	0	0	0	0	0	0	0	0	0	0	2

Ozona 1 SSW *Crockett County*   Elevation: 2,339 ft.   Latitude: 30° 41' N   Longitude: 101° 12' W

	JAN	FEB	MAR	APR	MAY	JUN	JUL	AUG	SEP	OCT	NOV	DEC	YEAR
Mean Maximum Temp. (°F)	58.7	63.5	71.7	79.3	85.7	90.5	92.8	92.4	86.6	78.0	67.3	60.2	77.2
Mean Temp. (°F)	44.3	48.7	56.7	64.4	72.4	78.3	80.6	80.0	74.1	64.4	53.3	45.7	63.6
Mean Minimum Temp. (°F)	29.9	33.7	41.6	49.5	59.1	66.2	68.4	67.5	61.6	50.9	39.3	31.2	49.9
Extreme Maximum Temp. (°F)	85	93	96	102	104	107	107	106	104	98	88	85	107
Extreme Minimum Temp. (°F)	0	9	8	19	35	45	50	51	34	20	11	-2	-2
Days Maximum Temp. ≥ 90°F	0	0	1	3	10	17	23	24	12	1	0	0	91
Days Maximum Temp. ≤ 32°F	1	0	0	0	0	0	0	0	0	0	0	1	2
Days Minimum Temp. ≤ 32°F	19	13	6	1	0	0	0	0	0	1	8	18	66
Days Minimum Temp. ≤ 0°F	0	0	0	0	0	0	0	0	0	0	0	0	0
Heating Degree Days (base 65°F)	635	456	271	103	14	0	0	0	17	103	349	590	2,538
Cooling Degree Days (base 65°F)	0	1	17	78	261	414	500	483	304	95	10	0	2,163
Mean Precipitation (in.)	0.79	0.86	1.14	1.39	2.47	1.79	1.59	2.27	2.98	2.09	0.91	0.66	18.94
Days With ≥ 0.1" Precipitation	2	2	2	2	4	3	3	3	3	3	2	1	30
Days With ≥ 1.0" Precipitation	0	0	0	0	1	1	0	1	1	1	0	0	5
Mean Snowfall (in.)	0.1	trace	trace	0.0	0.0	0.0	0.0	0.0	0.0	trace	0.1	trace	0.2
Days With ≥ 1.0" Snow Depth	0	0	0	0	0	0	0	0	0	0	0	0	0

Paducah *Cottle County*   Elevation: 1,899 ft.   Latitude: 34° 00' N   Longitude: 100° 18' W

	JAN	FEB	MAR	APR	MAY	JUN	JUL	AUG	SEP	OCT	NOV	DEC	YEAR
Mean Maximum Temp. (°F)	52.5	57.9	66.8	76.2	83.4	91.4	96.2	94.4	86.2	76.6	63.9	55.7	75.1
Mean Temp. (°F)	39.3	44.3	52.2	61.2	69.9	78.3	82.8	81.2	73.4	62.7	50.5	42.5	61.5
Mean Minimum Temp. (°F)	26.1	30.6	37.6	46.2	56.4	65.2	69.3	68.0	60.6	48.7	37.1	29.2	47.9
Extreme Maximum Temp. (°F)	86	93	102	104	107	118	112	109	106	105	90	87	118
Extreme Minimum Temp. (°F)	1	-2	7	24	36	49	57	55	32	21	13	-7	-7
Days Maximum Temp. ≥ 90°F	0	0	1	3	8	19	27	25	13	3	0	0	99
Days Maximum Temp. ≤ 32°F	3	2	0	0	0	0	0	0	0	0	0	2	7
Days Minimum Temp. ≤ 32°F	24	16	8	1	0	0	0	0	0	1	9	20	79
Days Minimum Temp. ≤ 0°F	0	0	0	0	0	0	0	0	0	0	0	0	0
Heating Degree Days (base 65°F)	789	581	401	164	33	2	0	0	27	137	432	691	3,257
Cooling Degree Days (base 65°F)	0	2	13	55	194	404	562	529	294	74	6	0	2,133
Mean Precipitation (in.)	0.81	1.11	1.21	1.91	3.82	3.51	1.66	2.67	2.97	2.01	1.06	0.98	23.72
Days With ≥ 0.1" Precipitation	2	3	3	3	5	5	3	4	4	3	2	2	39
Days With ≥ 1.0" Precipitation	0	0	0	1	1	1	0	1	1	0	0	0	5
Mean Snowfall (in.)	2.5	2.3	0.3	0.1	0.0	0.0	0.0	0.0	0.0	trace	0.9	1.5	7.6
Days With ≥ 1.0" Snow Depth	2	2	0	0	0	0	0	0	0	0	0	1	5

Paint Rock *Concho County*   Elevation: 1,624 ft.   Latitude: 31° 30' N   Longitude: 99° 55' W

	JAN	FEB	MAR	APR	MAY	JUN	JUL	AUG	SEP	OCT	NOV	DEC	YEAR
Mean Maximum Temp. (°F)	61.0	66.4	74.4	82.7	88.8	94.0	97.4	96.4	89.7	81.7	70.2	63.0	80.5
Mean Temp. (°F)	46.3	51.3	59.1	67.1	74.7	80.8	83.9	83.1	76.5	67.3	55.9	48.3	66.2
Mean Minimum Temp. (°F)	31.6	36.2	43.7	51.4	60.6	67.6	70.5	69.6	63.3	52.9	41.7	33.7	51.9
Extreme Maximum Temp. (°F)	89	98	98	102	107	109	111	110	110	103	92	86	111
Extreme Minimum Temp. (°F)	2	-8	8	22	36	47	56	51	36	23	12	-4	-8
Days Maximum Temp. ≥ 90°F	0	0	1	7	14	24	29	27	17	5	0	0	124
Days Maximum Temp. ≤ 32°F	1	0	0	0	0	0	0	0	0	0	0	1	2
Days Minimum Temp. ≤ 32°F	17	10	5	1	0	0	0	0	0	1	7	15	56
Days Minimum Temp. ≤ 0°F	0	0	0	0	0	0	0	0	0	0	0	0	0
Heating Degree Days (base 65°F)	574	385	218	68	8	0	0	0	9	60	288	512	2,122
Cooling Degree Days (base 65°F)	1	6	36	132	324	484	599	585	366	147	25	2	2,707
Mean Precipitation (in.)	1.05	1.57	1.48	1.59	3.41	3.43	1.84	2.07	3.71	2.74	1.28	1.29	25.46
Days With ≥ 0.1" Precipitation	3	3	3	3	5	4	3	4	4	4	2	3	41
Days With ≥ 1.0" Precipitation	0	0	0	0	1	1	1	1	1	1	0	0	6
Mean Snowfall (in.)	2.3	0.8	0.2	0.0	0.0	0.0	0.0	0.0	0.0	0.0	0.4	0.4	4.1
Days With ≥ 1.0" Snow Depth	0	0	0	0	0	0	0	0	0	0	0	0	0

Palacios Municipal Airport *Matagorda County*   Elevation: 13 ft.   Latitude: 28° 43' N   Longitude: 96° 15' W

	JAN	FEB	MAR	APR	MAY	JUN	JUL	AUG	SEP	OCT	NOV	DEC	YEAR
Mean Maximum Temp. (°F)	62.4	65.7	71.9	77.5	83.3	88.1	90.1	90.9	87.8	81.4	72.5	65.5	78.1
Mean Temp. (°F)	53.4	56.5	62.9	69.3	76.0	81.4	83.6	83.4	79.5	71.7	62.9	56.2	69.7
Mean Minimum Temp. (°F)	44.3	47.3	53.9	61.0	68.7	74.6	77.1	75.9	71.1	62.1	53.2	46.8	61.3
Extreme Maximum Temp. (°F)	79	84	88	93	98	96	97	99	97	95	90	83	99
Extreme Minimum Temp. (°F)	15	20	23	32	37	58	65	60	49	30	26	9	9
Days Maximum Temp. ≥ 90°F	0	0	0	0	1	9	21	24	12	1	0	0	68
Days Maximum Temp. ≤ 32°F	0	0	0	0	0	0	0	0	0	0	0	0	0
Days Minimum Temp. ≤ 32°F	4	2	1	0	0	0	0	0	0	0	1	2	10
Days Minimum Temp. ≤ 0°F	0	0	0	0	0	0	0	0	0	0	0	0	0
Heating Degree Days (base 65°F)	366	251	121	32	1	0	0	0	0	22	141	298	1,232
Cooling Degree Days (base 65°F)	12	19	62	164	363	507	591	590	452	246	89	34	3,129
Mean Precipitation (in.)	3.22	2.47	2.82	2.87	4.51	4.38	4.05	3.48	6.77	5.14	3.29	3.01	46.01
Days With ≥ 0.1" Precipitation	5	4	4	3	5	5	4	5	7	5	4	5	56
Days With ≥ 1.0" Precipitation	1	1	1	1	1	1	1	1	2	2	1	1	14
Mean Snowfall (in.)	trace	trace	trace	0.0	trace	0.0	0.0	0.0	trace	0.0	trace	trace	trace
Days With ≥ 1.0" Snow Depth	0	0	0	0	0	0	0	0	0	0	0	0	0

Palestine *Anderson County*   Elevation: 479 ft.   Latitude: 31° 45' N   Longitude: 95° 40' W

	JAN	FEB	MAR	APR	MAY	JUN	JUL	AUG	SEP	OCT	NOV	DEC	YEAR
Mean Maximum Temp. (°F)	57.1	62.1	69.9	76.6	83.0	89.3	93.6	93.9	88.2	79.6	68.0	60.0	76.8
Mean Temp. (°F)	46.5	51.0	58.3	65.4	72.6	79.0	82.6	82.3	76.8	67.3	56.9	49.3	65.7
Mean Minimum Temp. (°F)	35.8	39.7	46.8	54.1	62.1	68.5	71.7	70.7	65.3	55.0	45.8	38.6	54.5
Extreme Maximum Temp. (°F)	85	92	90	90	99	103	106	106	105	96	88	82	106
Extreme Minimum Temp. (°F)	2	10	14	28	40	37	54	53	40	27	18	-1	-1
Days Maximum Temp. ≥ 90°F	0	0	0	0	3	16	26	26	15	2	0	1	88
Days Maximum Temp. ≤ 32°F	1	1	0	0	0	0	0	0	0	0	0	1	3
Days Minimum Temp. ≤ 32°F	13	8	3	0	0	0	0	0	0	0	3	9	36
Days Minimum Temp. ≤ 0°F	0	0	0	0	0	0	0	0	0	0	0	0	0
Heating Degree Days (base 65°F)	573	401	234	79	10	0	0	0	5	63	268	490	2,123
Cooling Degree Days (base 65°F)	5	13	38	100	259	434	564	561	376	140	33	11	2,534
Mean Precipitation (in.)	3.52	3.42	3.83	3.96	4.38	4.49	2.58	3.30	3.67	4.64	4.02	4.03	45.84
Days With ≥ 0.1" Precipitation	6	5	6	5	6	5	4	4	5	5	6	6	63
Days With ≥ 1.0" Precipitation	1	1	1	1	2	1	1	1	1	2	1	1	14
Mean Snowfall (in.)	0.6	0.2	trace	0.0	0.0	0.0	0.0	0.0	0.0	0.0	trace	trace	0.8
Days With ≥ 1.0" Snow Depth	0	0	0	0	0	0	0	0	0	0	0	0	0

Pampa 2 *Gray County*   Elevation: 3,149 ft.   Latitude: 35° 34' N   Longitude: 100° 58' W

	JAN	FEB	MAR	APR	MAY	JUN	JUL	AUG	SEP	OCT	NOV	DEC	YEAR
Mean Maximum Temp. (°F)	47.1	52.4	60.5	69.6	77.6	86.7	91.5	89.4	81.9	71.9	58.2	49.4	69.7
Mean Temp. (°F)	34.3	39.1	46.3	55.3	64.5	73.8	78.7	77.0	69.4	58.3	45.3	36.9	56.6
Mean Minimum Temp. (°F)	21.5	25.7	32.1	41.0	51.3	60.8	65.8	64.6	56.8	44.7	32.3	24.3	43.4
Extreme Maximum Temp. (°F)	82	86	93	98	102	111	108	103	104	99	88	80	111
Extreme Minimum Temp. (°F)	-5	-7	3	17	30	43	51	50	31	12	5	-8	-8
Days Maximum Temp. ≥ 90°F	0	0	0	1	3	12	21	18	8	1	0	0	64
Days Maximum Temp. ≤ 32°F	5	3	1	0	0	0	0	0	0	0	1	4	14
Days Minimum Temp. ≤ 32°F	28	21	16	4	0	0	0	0	0	2	15	26	112
Days Minimum Temp. ≤ 0°F	1	1	0	0	0	0	0	0	0	0	0	1	3
Heating Degree Days (base 65°F)	945	725	575	304	100	12	1	2	57	233	586	865	4,405
Cooling Degree Days (base 65°F)	0	0	2	18	91	282	436	397	196	28	1	0	1,451
Mean Precipitation (in.)	0.57	0.83	1.45	1.93	3.26	3.19	2.94	2.47	2.38	1.41	1.19	0.66	22.28
Days With ≥ 0.1" Precipitation	2	2	3	4	6	6	5	5	4	3	3	2	45
Days With ≥ 1.0" Precipitation	0	0	0	0	1	1	1	1	1	0	0	0	5
Mean Snowfall (in.)	4.2	5.1	3.4	0.8	trace	0.0	0.0	0.0	trace	0.4	2.3	4.1	20.3
Days With ≥ 1.0" Snow Depth	5	4	2	0	0	0	0	0	0	0	2	4	17

Panhandle *Carson County*   Elevation: 3,530 ft.   Latitude: 35° 25' N   Longitude: 101° 22' W

	JAN	FEB	MAR	APR	MAY	JUN	JUL	AUG	SEP	OCT	NOV	DEC	YEAR
Mean Maximum Temp. (°F)	49.8	55.1	63.5	72.1	80.0	88.2	92.2	90.1	83.6	73.7	60.0	50.9	71.6
Mean Temp. (°F)	35.8	40.7	48.1	56.7	65.5	74.2	78.4	76.6	69.7	59.0	46.2	37.6	57.4
Mean Minimum Temp. (°F)	21.8	26.1	32.6	41.2	50.9	60.1	64.5	63.1	55.9	44.2	32.3	24.3	43.1
Extreme Maximum Temp. (°F)	80	85	92	98	102	108	107	103	101	97	88	78	108
Extreme Minimum Temp. (°F)	-9	-9	2	16	29	40	51	52	29	15	4	-8	-9
Days Maximum Temp. ≥ 90°F	0	0	0	1	4	13	21	18	9	1	0	0	67
Days Maximum Temp. ≤ 32°F	4	2	1	0	0	0	0	0	0	0	1	3	11
Days Minimum Temp. ≤ 32°F	28	21	15	5	0	0	0	0	0	2	15	26	112
Days Minimum Temp. ≤ 0°F	1	1	0	0	0	0	0	0	0	0	0	1	3
Heating Degree Days (base 65°F)	896	681	519	264	79	8	1	1	46	211	557	843	4,106
Cooling Degree Days (base 65°F)	0	0	2	20	100	281	424	378	193	26	1	0	1,425
Mean Precipitation (in.)	0.62	0.78	1.35	1.76	3.02	3.37	2.63	2.87	2.26	1.82	0.96	0.63	22.07
Days With ≥ 0.1" Precipitation	2	2	3	3	5	5	5	6	4	3	2	2	42
Days With ≥ 1.0" Precipitation	0	0	0	0	1	1	1	1	1	0	0	0	5
Mean Snowfall (in.)	4.6	5.4	2.5	0.8	trace	0.0	0.0	0.0	0.0	0.9	2.1	3.9	20.2
Days With ≥ 1.0" Snow Depth	6	4	1	0	0	0	0	0	0	0	2	4	17

Panther Junction *Brewster County*   Elevation: 3,740 ft.   Latitude: 29° 20' N   Longitude: 103° 12' W

	JAN	FEB	MAR	APR	MAY	JUN	JUL	AUG	SEP	OCT	NOV	DEC	YEAR
Mean Maximum Temp. (°F)	61.0	66.1	74.1	81.9	89.0	93.5	92.3	90.7	86.3	79.0	69.8	62.3	78.8
Mean Temp. (°F)	48.0	52.4	59.7	67.1	74.8	79.8	80.3	78.8	74.1	66.0	56.7	49.6	65.6
Mean Minimum Temp. (°F)	34.9	38.7	45.3	52.4	60.4	66.0	68.2	66.9	61.9	52.9	43.6	36.9	52.3
Extreme Maximum Temp. (°F)	83	91	95	99	105	109	107	105	101	99	89	82	109
Extreme Minimum Temp. (°F)	10	11	19	30	40	49	51	57	40	24	14	4	4
Days Maximum Temp. ≥ 90°F	0	0	1	6	16	23	23	20	12	2	0	0	103
Days Maximum Temp. ≤ 32°F	1	0	0	0	0	0	0	0	0	0	0	0	1
Days Minimum Temp. ≤ 32°F	11	6	2	0	0	0	0	0	0	0	3	8	30
Days Minimum Temp. ≤ 0°F	0	0	0	0	0	0	0	0	0	0	0	0	0
Heating Degree Days (base 65°F)	521	354	191	66	6	0	0	0	14	70	259	470	1,951
Cooling Degree Days (base 65°F)	0	7	35	132	329	461	495	450	306	110	17	0	2,342
Mean Precipitation (in.)	0.44	0.52	0.34	0.55	1.50	1.92	2.26	2.42	2.08	1.39	0.50	0.50	14.42
Days With ≥ 0.1" Precipitation	1	1	1	1	3	4	4	5	4	3	1	1	29
Days With ≥ 1.0" Precipitation	0	0	0	0	0	1	0	1	1	0	0	0	3
Mean Snowfall (in.)	0.8	trace	0.0	trace	0.0	0.0	0.0	0.0	0.0	0.0	0.2	0.1	1.1
Days With ≥ 1.0" Snow Depth	0	0	0	0	0	0	0	0	0	0	0	0	0

Paris *Lamar County*   Elevation: 541 ft.   Latitude: 33° 40' N   Longitude: 95° 34' W

	JAN	FEB	MAR	APR	MAY	JUN	JUL	AUG	SEP	OCT	NOV	DEC	YEAR
Mean Maximum Temp. (°F)	51.0	57.3	65.4	74.1	81.3	89.5	94.3	94.3	87.0	76.6	63.5	54.5	74.1
Mean Temp. (°F)	40.7	46.2	54.5	62.9	71.1	79.2	83.7	83.1	75.9	64.8	53.1	44.3	63.3
Mean Minimum Temp. (°F)	30.2	35.1	43.6	51.7	60.8	68.9	73.0	71.8	64.8	53.1	42.6	34.0	52.5
Extreme Maximum Temp. (°F)	79	90	88	94	100	103	108	110	110	98	87	80	110
Extreme Minimum Temp. (°F)	3	2	12	27	42	52	57	54	40	22	16	0	0
Days Maximum Temp. ≥ 90°F	0	0	0	0	3	16	26	25	14	2	0	0	86
Days Maximum Temp. ≤ 32°F	3	1	0	0	0	0	0	0	0	0	0	1	5
Days Minimum Temp. ≤ 32°F	19	11	4	0	0	0	0	0	0	0	5	14	53
Days Minimum Temp. ≤ 0°F	0	0	0	0	0	0	0	0	0	0	0	0	0
Heating Degree Days (base 65°F)	749	527	336	125	22	1	0	0	14	101	365	638	2,878
Cooling Degree Days (base 65°F)	1	3	19	68	216	437	595	585	356	100	13	2	2,395
Mean Precipitation (in.)	2.52	3.18	4.12	3.66	5.41	4.06	3.81	2.45	4.52	5.09	4.40	4.08	47.30
Days With ≥ 0.1" Precipitation	5	5	6	6	7	6	4	4	5	5	5	5	63
Days With ≥ 1.0" Precipitation	1	1	1	1	2	1	1	1	1	2	1	1	14
Mean Snowfall (in.)	0.9	1.2	trace	0.0	0.0	0.0	0.0	0.0	0.0	0.0	0.2	0.5	2.8
Days With ≥ 1.0" Snow Depth	1	1	0	0	0	0	0	0	0	0	0	0	2

Pecos *Reeves County*   Elevation: 2,608 ft.   Latitude: 31° 25' N   Longitude: 103° 30' W

	JAN	FEB	MAR	APR	MAY	JUN	JUL	AUG	SEP	OCT	NOV	DEC	YEAR
Mean Maximum Temp. (°F)	60.3	66.8	75.3	83.5	91.2	97.9	98.5	96.9	90.3	81.8	70.2	62.2	81.2
Mean Temp. (°F)	44.4	49.4	57.0	65.0	73.8	81.7	83.7	82.2	75.7	65.4	53.3	45.7	64.8
Mean Minimum Temp. (°F)	28.4	32.0	38.6	46.4	56.3	65.4	68.9	67.6	61.0	48.9	36.2	29.2	48.2
Extreme Maximum Temp. (°F)	89	93	101	106	111	117	113	113	108	106	94	88	117
Extreme Minimum Temp. (°F)	3	-8	12	24	34	48	60	58	41	25	8	1	-8
Days Maximum Temp. ≥ 90°F	0	0	2	10	20	26	29	27	19	7	0	0	140
Days Maximum Temp. ≤ 32°F	1	0	0	0	0	0	0	0	0	0	0	1	2
Days Minimum Temp. ≤ 32°F	22	15	6	1	0	0	0	0	0	1	10	21	76
Days Minimum Temp. ≤ 0°F	0	0	0	0	0	0	0	0	0	0	0	0	0
Heating Degree Days (base 65°F)	633	435	260	93	12	1	0	0	16	85	352	591	2,478
Cooling Degree Days (base 65°F)	0	2	16	93	299	509	594	550	346	105	8	0	2,522
Mean Precipitation (in.)	0.46	0.50	0.39	0.48	1.25	1.23	1.35	1.64	2.32	1.12	0.45	0.62	11.81
Days With ≥ 0.1" Precipitation	1	1	1	1	2	2	3	3	4	2	1	2	23
Days With ≥ 1.0" Precipitation	0	0	0	0	0	0	0	0	1	0	0	0	1
Mean Snowfall (in.)	1.9	0.8	0.1	trace	0.0	0.0	0.0	0.0	0.0	trace	0.6	1.0	4.4
Days With ≥ 1.0" Snow Depth	1	0	0	0	0	0	0	0	0	0	0	0	1

Penwell *Ector County*   Elevation: 2,939 ft.   Latitude: 31° 44' N   Longitude: 102° 35' W

	JAN	FEB	MAR	APR	MAY	JUN	JUL	AUG	SEP	OCT	NOV	DEC	YEAR
Mean Maximum Temp. (°F)	58.0	63.6	71.7	79.7	87.7	93.6	95.3	94.3	87.3	79.0	68.0	59.3	78.1
Mean Temp. (°F)	43.2	48.4	56.0	64.2	73.0	79.9	82.3	81.2	74.5	64.8	53.4	44.7	63.8
Mean Minimum Temp. (°F)	28.4	33.2	40.2	48.7	58.2	66.2	69.3	68.0	61.8	50.6	38.7	30.2	49.5
Extreme Maximum Temp. (°F)	90	90	95	101	107	116	111	106	103	100	91	82	116
Extreme Minimum Temp. (°F)	0	-12	8	23	34	47	56	57	38	22	8	1	-12
Days Maximum Temp. ≥ 90°F	0	0	1	4	14	23	27	26	14	4	0	0	113
Days Maximum Temp. ≤ 32°F	1	1	0	0	0	0	0	0	0	0	0	1	3
Days Minimum Temp. ≤ 32°F	22	12	5	1	0	0	0	0	0	1	7	18	66
Days Minimum Temp. ≤ 0°F	0	0	0	0	0	0	0	0	0	0	0	0	0
Heating Degree Days (base 65°F)	666	463	286	107	15	1	0	0	18	96	348	621	2,621
Cooling Degree Days (base 65°F)	0	1	13	82	278	464	556	518	319	102	7	0	2,340
Mean Precipitation (in.)	0.42	0.62	0.50	0.60	2.10	1.47	1.31	1.50	2.43	1.15	0.59	0.60	13.29
Days With ≥ 0.1" Precipitation	1	2	1	1	3	3	3	3	4	2	1	1	25
Days With ≥ 1.0" Precipitation	0	0	0	0	1	0	0	0	1	0	0	0	2
Mean Snowfall (in.)	0.5	0.3	0.2	0.0	0.0	0.0	0.0	0.0	0.0	0.0	0.0	0.4	1.4
Days With ≥ 1.0" Snow Depth	0	0	0	0	0	0	0	0	0	0	0	0	0

Perryton *Ochiltree County*   Elevation: 2,939 ft.   Latitude: 36° 23' N   Longitude: 100° 49' W

	JAN	FEB	MAR	APR	MAY	JUN	JUL	AUG	SEP	OCT	NOV	DEC	YEAR
Mean Maximum Temp. (°F)	45.7	51.6	59.3	69.0	77.3	87.3	92.9	91.0	82.9	72.4	57.7	48.0	69.6
Mean Temp. (°F)	31.5	36.6	44.0	53.4	63.1	73.0	78.3	76.8	68.7	56.9	43.2	33.8	54.9
Mean Minimum Temp. (°F)	17.2	21.5	28.6	37.8	48.9	58.7	63.8	62.5	54.4	41.3	28.7	19.8	40.3
Extreme Maximum Temp. (°F)	81	87	95	101	106	111	108	106	105	95	88	78	111
Extreme Minimum Temp. (°F)	-17	-15	-2	14	27	41	47	46	29	11	-4	-12	-17
Days Maximum Temp. ≥ 90°F	0	0	0	1	3	13	22	20	10	1	0	0	70
Days Maximum Temp. ≤ 32°F	6	4	1	0	0	0	0	0	0	0	1	5	17
Days Minimum Temp. ≤ 32°F	30	25	20	8	1	0	0	0	0	4	20	29	137
Days Minimum Temp. ≤ 0°F	2	1	0	0	0	0	0	0	0	0	0	1	4
Heating Degree Days (base 65°F)	1,032	794	647	353	125	16	2	2	66	272	647	960	4,916
Cooling Degree Days (base 65°F)	0	0	1	11	72	257	418	381	188	22	1	0	1,351
Mean Precipitation (in.)	0.46	0.62	1.65	1.87	3.31	2.73	2.72	2.27	1.86	1.22	1.08	0.64	20.43
Days With ≥ 0.1" Precipitation	1	2	3	4	5	4	4	4	3	2	2	2	36
Days With ≥ 1.0" Precipitation	0	0	0	0	1	1	1	1	1	0	0	0	5
Mean Snowfall (in.)	3.7	4.6	4.3	1.2	0.1	0.0	0.0	0.0	trace	0.6	2.4	4.0	20.9
Days With ≥ 1.0" Snow Depth	4	3	1	0	0	0	0	0	0	0	1	3	12

Pilot Point *Denton County*   Elevation: 688 ft.   Latitude: 33° 23' N   Longitude: 96° 58' W

	JAN	FEB	MAR	APR	MAY	JUN	JUL	AUG	SEP	OCT	NOV	DEC	YEAR
Mean Maximum Temp. (°F)	52.7	58.6	67.1	75.4	83.1	90.8	96.6	96.0	88.5	78.3	65.2	56.6	75.7
Mean Temp. (°F)	41.2	46.3	54.0	62.7	71.5	79.7	84.9	84.1	76.8	65.8	53.1	44.7	63.7
Mean Minimum Temp. (°F)	29.7	33.9	41.1	50.0	59.8	68.6	73.3	72.2	64.9	53.3	41.0	32.8	51.7
Extreme Maximum Temp. (°F)	81	93	94	98	103	104	111	109	109	99	89	82	111
Extreme Minimum Temp. (°F)	1	3	10	28	39	49	57	57	40	24	15	-2	-2
Days Maximum Temp. ≥ 90°F	0	0	0	1	6	20	28	27	16	3	0	0	101
Days Maximum Temp. ≤ 32°F	2	1	0	0	0	0	0	0	0	0	0	1	4
Days Minimum Temp. ≤ 32°F	19	11	5	1	0	0	0	0	0	0	5	14	55
Days Minimum Temp. ≤ 0°F	0	0	0	0	0	0	0	0	0	0	0	0	0
Heating Degree Days (base 65°F)	731	524	346	125	19	1	0	0	10	85	361	621	2,823
Cooling Degree Days (base 65°F)	0	3	14	62	233	457	641	628	393	124	13	1	2,569
Mean Precipitation (in.)	2.42	3.23	3.88	3.53	6.27	4.45	2.69	2.87	4.11	4.79	3.20	2.95	44.39
Days With ≥ 0.1" Precipitation	5	5	6	6	8	6	4	4	5	6	5	5	65
Days With ≥ 1.0" Precipitation	1	1	1	1	2	2	1	1	2	2	1	1	16
Mean Snowfall (in.)	*0.1*	*0.4*	0.2	0.0	0.0	0.0	0.0	0.0	0.0	0.0	0.1	trace	*0.8*
Days With ≥ 1.0" Snow Depth	0	*0*	0	0	0	0	0	0	0	0	0	0	*0*

Plainview *Hale County*   Elevation: 3,369 ft.   Latitude: 34° 11' N   Longitude: 101° 42' W

	JAN	FEB	MAR	APR	MAY	JUN	JUL	AUG	SEP	OCT	NOV	DEC	YEAR
Mean Maximum Temp. (°F)	50.3	55.9	63.9	72.4	80.7	88.7	91.4	89.0	82.3	73.6	60.7	52.4	71.8
Mean Temp. (°F)	37.6	42.5	49.7	58.2	67.4	75.9	79.1	77.1	70.2	60.1	47.8	39.8	58.8
Mean Minimum Temp. (°F)	25.0	29.1	35.4	43.9	54.0	63.0	66.7	65.1	58.1	46.5	34.8	27.1	45.7
Extreme Maximum Temp. (°F)	81	85	92	96	104	111	107	102	102	97	86	78	111
Extreme Minimum Temp. (°F)	-1	-1	8	20	34	46	54	51	34	17	3	-3	-3
Days Maximum Temp. ≥ 90°F	0	0	0	1	6	15	21	17	8	1	0	0	69
Days Maximum Temp. ≤ 32°F	4	2	1	0	0	0	0	0	0	0	1	2	10
Days Minimum Temp. ≤ 32°F	26	18	10	2	0	0	0	0	0	1	12	24	93
Days Minimum Temp. ≤ 0°F	0	0	0	0	0	0	0	0	0	0	0	0	0
Heating Degree Days (base 65°F)	841	636	471	228	58	5	0	1	42	182	509	775	3,748
Cooling Degree Days (base 65°F)	0	0	3	29	138	327	451	394	205	37	1	0	1,585
Mean Precipitation (in.)	0.59	0.63	0.80	1.49	2.94	2.92	2.41	2.42	2.30	1.68	0.81	0.71	19.70
Days With ≥ 0.1" Precipitation	2	2	2	3	5	5	4	5	4	3	2	2	39
Days With ≥ 1.0" Precipitation	0	0	0	0	1	1	1	1	1	0	0	0	5
Mean Snowfall (in.)	3.4	2.7	0.6	0.2	trace	0.0	0.0	0.0	0.0	trace	1.3	2.8	11.0
Days With ≥ 1.0" Snow Depth	3	2	0	0	0	0	0	0	0	0	1	2	8

Point Comfort *Calhoun County*   Elevation: 19 ft.   Latitude: 28° 39' N   Longitude: 96° 33' W

	JAN	FEB	MAR	APR	MAY	JUN	JUL	AUG	SEP	OCT	NOV	DEC	YEAR
Mean Maximum Temp. (°F)	64.1	67.8	73.7	79.0	84.4	89.3	91.7	91.7	89.0	82.4	73.8	67.1	79.5
Mean Temp. (°F)	54.8	58.3	64.4	70.4	76.7	82.1	84.6	84.3	80.6	73.2	64.4	57.6	70.9
Mean Minimum Temp. (°F)	45.3	48.7	55.2	61.8	68.9	74.9	77.4	76.8	71.7	63.5	54.7	48.1	62.3
Extreme Maximum Temp. (°F)	84	87	95	98	99	106	103	106	102	96	88	86	106
Extreme Minimum Temp. (°F)	14	18	23	34	42	52	60	64	47	35	27	9	9
Days Maximum Temp. ≥ 90°F	0	0	0	0	3	13	25	25	15	2	0	0	83
Days Maximum Temp. ≤ 32°F	0	0	0	0	0	0	0	0	0	0	0	0	0
Days Minimum Temp. ≤ 32°F	3	2	0	0	0	0	0	0	0	0	0	0	0
Days Minimum Temp. ≤ 0°F	0	0	0	0	0	0	0	0	0	0	0	2	7
Heating Degree Days (base 65°F)	325	207	94	20	1	0	0	0	0	17	112	259	1,035
Cooling Degree Days (base 65°F)	15	26	83	199	390	547	635	625	490	292	113	39	3,454
Mean Precipitation (in.)	2.95	2.60	2.86	2.98	4.56	4.44	3.51	3.45	5.90	4.75	3.57	2.82	44.39
Days With ≥ 0.1" Precipitation	5	4	3	3	5	5	4	5	7	5	5	5	56
Days With ≥ 1.0" Precipitation	1	1	1	1	2	2	1	1	2	1	1	1	15
Mean Snowfall (in.)	0.0	0.0	0.0	0.0	0.0	0.0	0.0	0.0	0.0	0.0	trace	0.0	trace
Days With ≥ 1.0" Snow Depth	0	0	0	0	0	0	0	0	0	0	0	0	0

Port Mansfield *Willacy County*   Elevation: 6 ft.   Latitude: 26° 33' N   Longitude: 97° 26' W

	JAN	FEB	MAR	APR	MAY	JUN	JUL	AUG	SEP	OCT	NOV	DEC	YEAR
Mean Maximum Temp. (°F)	64.5	67.7	73.4	77.9	82.4	86.8	88.3	88.5	86.1	81.1	74.1	67.4	78.2
Mean Temp. (°F)	56.5	60.0	66.7	72.0	77.3	81.5	82.7	82.5	79.7	74.0	66.6	59.5	71.6
Mean Minimum Temp. (°F)	48.5	52.2	59.9	66.1	72.3	76.1	77.0	76.5	73.2	66.9	59.0	51.6	64.9
Extreme Maximum Temp. (°F)	87	95	101	98	101	101	96	99	99	96	98	88	101
Extreme Minimum Temp. (°F)	23	26	29	38	52	49	65	67	55	32	32	15	15
Days Maximum Temp. ≥ 90°F	0	0	1	1	1	3	9	11	4	1	0	0	31
Days Maximum Temp. ≤ 32°F	0	0	0	0	0	0	0	0	0	0	0	0	0
Days Minimum Temp. ≤ 32°F	2	1	0	0	0	0	0	0	0	0	0	0	0
Days Minimum Temp. ≤ 0°F	0	0	0	0	0	0	0	0	0	0	0	1	4
Heating Degree Days (base 65°F)	285	179	66	15	1	0	0	0	0	12	86	219	863
Cooling Degree Days (base 65°F)	25	44	120	221	396	511	551	549	439	299	146	61	3,362
Mean Precipitation (in.)	1.65	1.70	1.12	1.56	3.22	2.53	1.29	1.77	5.16	3.27	2.13	1.31	26.71
Days With ≥ 0.1" Precipitation	3	3	2	2	4	3	2	3	6	4	3	3	38
Days With ≥ 1.0" Precipitation	0	0	0	1	1	1	0	0	2	1	1	0	7
Mean Snowfall (in.)	0.0	0.0	0.0	0.0	0.0	0.0	0.0	0.0	0.0	0.0	0.0	0.0	0.0
Days With ≥ 1.0" Snow Depth	0	0	0	0	0	0	0	0	0	0	0	0	0

Post *Garza County*   Elevation: 2,618 ft.   Latitude: 33° 11' N   Longitude: 101° 23' W

	JAN	FEB	MAR	APR	MAY	JUN	JUL	AUG	SEP	OCT	NOV	DEC	YEAR
Mean Maximum Temp. (°F)	54.1	59.8	68.0	76.7	84.1	91.1	94.1	92.4	85.4	76.8	64.7	56.5	75.3
Mean Temp. (°F)	40.6	45.5	52.9	61.4	70.0	77.9	81.4	79.9	73.0	63.2	50.9	43.1	61.7
Mean Minimum Temp. (°F)	27.1	31.2	37.8	46.0	56.0	64.7	68.9	67.4	60.5	49.5	37.1	29.6	48.0
Extreme Maximum Temp. (°F)	84	89	99	101	107	115	108	106	104	103	90	82	115
Extreme Minimum Temp. (°F)	0	-1	5	22	36	45	56	51	37	22	8	-1	-1
Days Maximum Temp. ≥ 90°F	0	0	1	3	9	18	25	22	11	2	0	0	91
Days Maximum Temp. ≤ 32°F	2	1	0	0	0	0	0	0	0	0	0	2	5
Days Minimum Temp. ≤ 32°F	23	16	8	2	0	0	0	0	0	1	9	20	79
Days Minimum Temp. ≤ 0°F	0	0	0	0	0	0	0	0	0	0	0	0	0
Heating Degree Days (base 65°F)	749	545	380	163	33	2	0	0	27	129	420	672	3,120
Cooling Degree Days (base 65°F)	0	2	12	58	198	393	530	496	285	84	5	0	2,063
Mean Precipitation (in.)	0.58	0.98	0.81	1.41	3.03	2.70	2.02	2.93	3.04	1.92	0.89	0.78	21.09
Days With ≥ 0.1" Precipitation	1	2	2	3	5	4	4	4	4	2	2	2	35
Days With ≥ 1.0" Precipitation	0	0	0	0	1	1	0	1	1	0	0	0	4
Mean Snowfall (in.)	1.3	1.6	0.4	0.1	0.0	0.0	0.0	0.0	0.0	trace	1.0	0.9	5.3
Days With ≥ 1.0" Snow Depth	0	0	0	0	0	0	0	0	0	0	0	0	0

Poteet *Atascosa County*   Elevation: 479 ft.   Latitude: 29° 02' N   Longitude: 98° 35' W

	JAN	FEB	MAR	APR	MAY	JUN	JUL	AUG	SEP	OCT	NOV	DEC	YEAR
Mean Maximum Temp. (°F)	63.5	68.0	75.8	82.0	87.3	92.9	95.7	96.1	91.8	83.8	74.1	66.2	81.4
Mean Temp. (°F)	51.2	55.0	62.8	69.3	76.2	81.6	84.0	84.2	80.1	71.3	61.5	53.7	69.2
Mean Minimum Temp. (°F)	38.8	41.9	49.8	56.5	65.1	70.3	72.4	72.2	68.4	58.9	49.0	41.1	57.0
Extreme Maximum Temp. (°F)	96	98	100	101	103	107	107	107	107	103	98	88	107
Extreme Minimum Temp. (°F)	12	17	19	31	45	52	60	60	46	26	22	9	9
Days Maximum Temp. ≥ 90°F	0	0	1	5	11	23	28	29	21	7	0	0	125
Days Maximum Temp. ≤ 32°F	0	0	0	0	0	0	0	0	0	0	0	0	0
Days Minimum Temp. ≤ 32°F	8	4	1	0	0	0	0	0	0	0	0	0	0
Days Minimum Temp. ≤ 0°F	0	0	0	0	0	0	0	0	0	0	2	7	22
Heating Degree Days (base 65°F)	430	292	134	39	2	0	0	0	1	30	167	363	1,458
Cooling Degree Days (base 65°F)	9	17	67	164	368	512	611	611	471	237	69	22	3,158
Mean Precipitation (in.)	1.27	1.90	1.61	2.58	4.20	3.71	1.69	2.76	2.93	3.01	1.61	1.57	28.84
Days With ≥ 0.1" Precipitation	3	3	3	4	5	5	3	3	4	4	3	3	43
Days With ≥ 1.0" Precipitation	0	1	1	1	1	1	0	1	1	1	0	0	8
Mean Snowfall (in.)	0.0	trace	0.0	0.0	0.0	0.0	0.0	0.0	0.0	0.0	0.0	0.0	trace
Days With ≥ 1.0" Snow Depth	0	0	0	0	0	0	0	0	0	0	0	0	0

Presidio *Presidio County* Elevation: 2,582 ft. Latitude: 29° 33' N Longitude: 104° 23' W

	JAN	FEB	MAR	APR	MAY	JUN	JUL	AUG	SEP	OCT	NOV	DEC	YEAR
Mean Maximum Temp. (°F)	68.7	75.1	82.9	90.4	97.2	102.4	100.6	98.8	94.8	87.6	77.3	69.0	87.1
Mean Temp. (°F)	51.5	57.1	64.3	71.9	80.1	86.9	87.1	85.5	80.8	71.7	60.0	52.2	70.8
Mean Minimum Temp. (°F)	34.2	39.1	45.5	53.4	62.8	71.4	73.5	72.2	66.8	55.8	42.7	35.4	54.4
Extreme Maximum Temp. (°F)	87	94	100	106	111	115	113	110	108	100	95	88	115
Extreme Minimum Temp. (°F)	16	17	21	27	34	55	62	56	42	27	13	13	13
Days Maximum Temp. ≥ 90°F	0	1	6	19	28	29	30	29	24	13	1	0	180
Days Maximum Temp. ≤ 32°F	0	0	0	0	0	0	0	0	0	0	0	0	0
Days Minimum Temp. ≤ 32°F	13	5	1	0	0	0	0	0	0	0	3	12	34
Days Minimum Temp. ≤ 0°F	0	0	0	0	0	0	0	0	0	0	0	0	0
Heating Degree Days (base 65°F)	413	227	87	18	0	0	0	0	3	20	170	390	1,328
Cooling Degree Days (base 65°F)	0	14	76	245	508	690	713	670	515	254	35	1	3,721
Mean Precipitation (in.)	0.31	0.47	0.19	0.38	0.67	1.45	2.05	1.83	1.92	0.95	0.34	0.52	11.08
Days With ≥ 0.1" Precipitation	1	1	0	1	2	2	4	4	3	2	1	1	22
Days With ≥ 1.0" Precipitation	0	0	0	0	0	0	1	0	0	0	0	0	1
Mean Snowfall (in.)	trace	trace	0.0	0.0	0.0	0.0	0.0	0.0	0.0	0.0	0.0	trace	trace
Days With ≥ 1.0" Snow Depth	0	0	0	0	0	0	0	0	0	0	0	0	0

Proctor Reservoir *Comanche County* Elevation: 1,220 ft. Latitude: 31° 58' N Longitude: 98° 30' W

	JAN	FEB	MAR	APR	MAY	JUN	JUL	AUG	SEP	OCT	NOV	DEC	YEAR
Mean Maximum Temp. (°F)	56.2	61.2	69.1	76.9	83.4	90.6	95.0	94.6	87.8	79.1	67.3	59.4	76.7
Mean Temp. (°F)	43.4	48.3	56.3	64.4	72.1	79.2	82.9	82.2	75.7	65.9	54.8	46.6	64.3
Mean Minimum Temp. (°F)	30.5	35.3	43.5	51.9	60.6	67.8	70.7	69.7	63.5	52.6	42.2	33.9	51.9
Extreme Maximum Temp. (°F)	88	96	95	98	105	107	106	107	106	100	92	84	107
Extreme Minimum Temp. (°F)	3	3	12	28	41	50	57	53	38	26	16	-8	-8
Days Maximum Temp. ≥ 90°F	0	0	1	2	7	19	28	26	15	4	0	0	102
Days Maximum Temp. ≤ 32°F	2	1	0	0	0	0	0	0	0	0	0	1	4
Days Minimum Temp. ≤ 32°F	19	11	4	0	0	0	0	0	0	0	5	14	53
Days Minimum Temp. ≤ 0°F	0	0	0	0	0	0	0	0	0	0	0	0	0
Heating Degree Days (base 65°F)	663	469	287	104	16	1	0	0	14	83	319	564	2,520
Cooling Degree Days (base 65°F)	1	3	24	90	246	431	563	557	347	116	20	2	2,400
Mean Precipitation (in.)	1.29	2.13	2.23	2.88	4.84	3.82	1.70	2.28	3.28	3.17	1.86	1.74	31.22
Days With ≥ 0.1" Precipitation	3	4	4	4	6	5	3	4	5	4	3	3	48
Days With ≥ 1.0" Precipitation	0	1	1	1	2	1	1	1	1	1	1	0	11
Mean Snowfall (in.)	trace	trace	0.0	0.0	0.0	0.0	0.0	0.0	0.0	0.0	0.0	0.0	trace
Days With ≥ 1.0" Snow Depth	0	0	0	0	0	0	0	0	0	0	0	0	0

Putnam *Callahan County* Elevation: 1,587 ft. Latitude: 32° 22' N Longitude: 99° 11' W

	JAN	FEB	MAR	APR	MAY	JUN	JUL	AUG	SEP	OCT	NOV	DEC	YEAR
Mean Maximum Temp. (°F)	56.8	62.2	70.6	78.6	85.1	91.6	95.6	95.0	87.9	79.2	66.9	58.9	77.4
Mean Temp. (°F)	44.8	49.9	57.5	65.4	72.9	79.8	83.6	82.9	76.1	67.0	55.2	47.2	65.2
Mean Minimum Temp. (°F)	32.8	37.6	44.4	52.2	60.6	67.9	71.5	70.7	64.2	54.7	43.5	35.5	53.0
Extreme Maximum Temp. (°F)	86	96	97	100	104	107	109	108	107	101	91	89	109
Extreme Minimum Temp. (°F)	2	0	6	25	36	48	56	52	37	20	16	-8	-8
Days Maximum Temp. ≥ 90°F	0	0	1	3	9	21	27	26	15	3	0	0	105
Days Maximum Temp. ≤ 32°F	2	1	0	0	0	0	0	0	0	0	0	1	4
Days Minimum Temp. ≤ 32°F	15	9	4	1	0	0	0	0	0	0	5	12	46
Days Minimum Temp. ≤ 0°F	0	0	0	0	0	0	0	0	0	0	0	0	0
Heating Degree Days (base 65°F)	619	427	260	90	13	1	0	0	13	72	308	548	2,351
Cooling Degree Days (base 65°F)	1	8	34	113	274	449	592	588	362	146	23	3	2,593
Mean Precipitation (in.)	1.16	1.61	1.82	1.89	3.20	3.04	1.96	2.06	2.82	2.96	1.50	1.38	25.40
Days With ≥ 0.1" Precipitation	3	3	3	3	5	4	3	3	4	4	3	3	41
Days With ≥ 1.0" Precipitation	0	0	0	1	1	1	1	1	1	1	0	0	7
Mean Snowfall (in.)	2.2	1.4	0.8	0.2	0.0	0.0	0.0	0.0	0.0	0.0	0.6	0.9	6.1
Days With ≥ 1.0" Snow Depth	1	0	0	0	0	0	0	0	0	0	0	0	1

Quanah 5 SE *Hardeman County* Elevation: 1,492 ft. Latitude: 34° 15' N Longitude: 99° 41' W

	JAN	FEB	MAR	APR	MAY	JUN	JUL	AUG	SEP	OCT	NOV	DEC	YEAR
Mean Maximum Temp. (°F)	51.5	57.2	65.7	75.1	82.9	91.5	96.4	94.4	86.2	76.4	63.4	54.8	74.6
Mean Temp. (°F)	38.1	43.6	51.9	61.0	70.3	79.2	83.9	82.0	73.9	62.5	50.0	41.3	61.5
Mean Minimum Temp. (°F)	24.6	29.8	38.0	46.9	57.6	66.9	71.4	69.5	61.6	48.5	36.5	27.7	48.3
Extreme Maximum Temp. (°F)	87	92	102	103	105	119	111	108	107	106	89	85	119
Extreme Minimum Temp. (°F)	-2	-8	1	22	35	46	52	53	29	16	11	-15	-15
Days Maximum Temp. ≥ 90°F	0	0	1	2	7	19	27	24	13	2	0	0	95
Days Maximum Temp. ≤ 32°F	3	2	0	0	0	0	0	0	0	0	0	2	7
Days Minimum Temp. ≤ 32°F	26	17	8	2	0	0	0	0	0	1	10	23	87
Days Minimum Temp. ≤ 0°F	0	0	0	0	0	0	0	0	0	0	0	0	0
Heating Degree Days (base 65°F)	827	601	412	169	32	2	0	0	27	145	449	729	3,393
Cooling Degree Days (base 65°F)	0	1	11	51	202	427	590	543	307	72	5	0	2,209
Mean Precipitation (in.)	0.96	1.18	1.57	2.05	3.93	3.60	2.40	2.64	3.54	2.31	1.33	1.14	26.65
Days With ≥ 0.1" Precipitation	2	3	3	4	5	5	3	4	4	3	2	2	40
Days With ≥ 1.0" Precipitation	0	0	0	1	1	1	1	1	1	1	0	0	7
Mean Snowfall (in.)	2.0	1.9	0.3	trace	0.0	0.0	0.0	0.0	0.0	trace	0.6	1.0	5.8
Days With ≥ 1.0" Snow Depth	2	2	0	0	0	0	0	0	0	0	0	1	5

Raymondville *Willacy County* Elevation: 29 ft. Latitude: 26° 29' N Longitude: 97° 49' W

	JAN	FEB	MAR	APR	MAY	JUN	JUL	AUG	SEP	OCT	NOV	DEC	YEAR
Mean Maximum Temp. (°F)	69.2	73.4	80.3	85.5	89.5	93.6	96.3	96.8	92.3	86.8	78.7	71.9	84.5
Mean Temp. (°F)	58.2	61.7	68.4	74.1	79.4	83.3	85.0	85.3	81.7	75.2	67.2	60.6	73.3
Mean Minimum Temp. (°F)	47.1	49.9	56.4	62.7	69.2	72.9	73.7	73.8	71.0	63.5	55.7	49.3	62.1
Extreme Maximum Temp. (°F)	92	97	104	106	107	108	107	106	103	100	99	94	108
Extreme Minimum Temp. (°F)	22	24	28	33	47	57	63	67	53	33	31	15	15
Days Maximum Temp. ≥ 90°F	0	1	4	9	16	26	28	28	23	12	3	0	150
Days Maximum Temp. ≤ 32°F	0	0	0	0	0	0	0	0	0	0	0	0	0
Days Minimum Temp. ≤ 32°F	2	1	0	0	0	0	0	0	0	0	0	0	5
Days Minimum Temp. ≤ 0°F	0	0	0	0	0	0	0	0	0	0	0	2	0
Heating Degree Days (base 65°F)	253	157	64	13	1	0	0	0	1	10	86	204	789
Cooling Degree Days (base 65°F)	48	75	167	291	464	576	651	652	516	343	168	77	4,028
Mean Precipitation (in.)	1.45	1.59	1.39	1.58	2.99	3.30	1.96	3.10	5.60	3.07	1.38	1.11	28.52
Days With ≥ 0.1" Precipitation	3	3	2	2	3	4	4	4	7	4	2	2	40
Days With ≥ 1.0" Precipitation	0	0	0	0	1	1	0	1	2	1	0	0	6
Mean Snowfall (in.)	0.0	0.0	0.0	0.0	0.0	0.0	0.0	0.0	0.0	0.0	0.0	0.0	0.0
Days With ≥ 1.0" Snow Depth	0	0	0	0	0	0	0	0	0	0	0	0	0

Red Rock *Bastrop County* Elevation: 518 ft. Latitude: 29° 58' N Longitude: 97° 27' W

	JAN	FEB	MAR	APR	MAY	JUN	JUL	AUG	SEP	OCT	NOV	DEC	YEAR
Mean Maximum Temp. (°F)	60.1	64.6	72.6	78.8	84.5	91.3	95.6	96.4	90.6	82.0	71.0	63.0	79.2
Mean Temp. (°F)	48.1	52.3	60.3	66.6	73.7	80.2	83.4	83.4	77.8	68.8	58.5	50.7	67.0
Mean Minimum Temp. (°F)	36.1	39.9	47.9	54.4	62.8	69.0	71.1	70.3	64.9	55.5	45.9	38.4	54.7
Extreme Maximum Temp. (°F)	88	100	97	96	102	109	106	107	106	99	92	88	109
Extreme Minimum Temp. (°F)	8	9	18	22	34	50	57	50	36	19	10	-3	-3
Days Maximum Temp. ≥ 90°F	0	0	0	1	6	21	29	29	19	6	0	0	111
Days Maximum Temp. ≤ 32°F	0	0	0	0	0	0	0	0	0	0	0	0	0
Days Minimum Temp. ≤ 32°F	12	7	3	1	0	0	0	0	0	0	4	10	37
Days Minimum Temp. ≤ 0°F	0	0	0	0	0	0	0	0	0	0	0	0	0
Heating Degree Days (base 65°F)	523	365	192	70	8	0	0	0	5	57	235	449	1,904
Cooling Degree Days (base 65°F)	6	11	47	116	286	467	580	589	397	177	47	12	2,735
Mean Precipitation (in.)	2.43	2.56	2.23	3.30	4.95	3.58	1.70	2.34	3.57	4.43	3.03	2.50	36.62
Days With ≥ 0.1" Precipitation	4	5	4	4	6	5	3	4	5	5	5	4	54
Days With ≥ 1.0" Precipitation	1	1	1	1	2	1	0	1	1	2	1	1	13
Mean Snowfall (in.)	0.4	*trace*	0.0	0.0	0.0	0.0	0.0	0.0	0.0	0.0	0.0	trace	*0.4*
Days With ≥ 1.0" Snow Depth	0	0	0	0	0	0	0	0	0	0	0	0	0

Rio Grande City 1 SE *Starr County* Elevation: 170 ft. Latitude: 26° 23' N Longitude: 98° 49' W

	JAN	FEB	MAR	APR	MAY	JUN	JUL	AUG	SEP	OCT	NOV	DEC	YEAR
Mean Maximum Temp. (°F)	68.7	73.9	82.2	88.2	92.0	96.7	98.9	99.2	93.9	86.7	78.1	70.8	85.8
Mean Temp. (°F)	56.5	60.8	68.7	75.3	80.7	85.0	86.6	86.7	82.3	74.6	65.9	58.7	73.5
Mean Minimum Temp. (°F)	44.3	47.8	55.0	62.4	69.3	73.3	74.3	74.0	70.7	62.3	53.7	46.5	61.1
Extreme Maximum Temp. (°F)	97	100	105	108	111	116	111	110	105	101	97	97	116
Extreme Minimum Temp. (°F)	18	23	25	34	46	53	59	65	49	29	24	15	15
Days Maximum Temp. ≥ 90°F	1	2	7	14	21	28	30	30	24	12	3	1	173
Days Maximum Temp. ≤ 32°F	0	0	0	0	0	0	0	0	0	0	0	0	0
Days Minimum Temp. ≤ 32°F	4	2	0	0	0	0	0	0	0	0	1	3	10
Days Minimum Temp. ≤ 0°F	0	0	0	0	0	0	0	0	0	0	0	0	0
Heating Degree Days (base 65°F)	291	176	66	13	1	0	0	0	1	14	106	242	910
Cooling Degree Days (base 65°F)	36	71	182	327	510	629	707	703	550	335	156	59	4,265
Mean Precipitation (in.)	0.97	1.14	0.73	1.26	2.47	3.07	1.32	2.03	4.60	2.40	0.88	0.91	21.78
Days With ≥ 0.1" Precipitation	3	2	1	2	3	4	2	3	5	3	2	2	32
Days With ≥ 1.0" Precipitation	0	0	0	0	1	1	0	1	2	1	0	0	6
Mean Snowfall (in.)	trace	trace	0.0	0.0	0.0	0.0	0.0	0.0	0.0	0.0	0.0	0.0	trace
Days With ≥ 1.0" Snow Depth	0	0	0	0	0	0	0	0	0	0	0	0	0

Rising Star 1 S *Eastland County* Elevation: 1,630 ft. Latitude: 32° 05' N Longitude: 98° 58' W

	JAN	FEB	MAR	APR	MAY	JUN	JUL	AUG	SEP	OCT	NOV	DEC	YEAR
Mean Maximum Temp. (°F)	54.9	60.0	68.3	76.6	83.0	89.4	93.8	93.6	86.7	78.1	65.9	57.8	75.7
Mean Temp. (°F)	42.2	47.1	54.8	63.1	71.0	78.0	81.7	81.2	74.6	64.9	53.2	45.1	63.1
Mean Minimum Temp. (°F)	29.5	34.2	41.3	49.6	59.0	66.5	69.6	68.8	62.5	51.7	40.5	32.4	50.5
Extreme Maximum Temp. (°F)	86	97	93	98	104	106	107	109	106	101	92	84	109
Extreme Minimum Temp. (°F)	0	-2	8	25	37	50	54	49	39	21	15	-8	-8
Days Maximum Temp. ≥ 90°F	0	0	1	2	6	16	25	25	13	3	0	0	91
Days Maximum Temp. ≤ 32°F	2	1	0	0	0	0	0	0	0	0	0	1	4
Days Minimum Temp. ≤ 32°F	19	12	5	1	0	0	0	0	0	1	7	16	61
Days Minimum Temp. ≤ 0°F	0	0	0	0	0	0	0	0	0	0	0	0	0
Heating Degree Days (base 65°F)	700	500	325	126	21	1	0	0	17	100	360	611	2,761
Cooling Degree Days (base 65°F)	0	2	14	72	216	394	524	524	321	107	14	1	2,189
Mean Precipitation (in.)	1.28	1.96	2.28	2.50	4.39	4.16	1.96	2.35	2.99	3.22	1.68	1.54	30.31
Days With ≥ 0.1" Precipitation	3	4	4	4	5	5	3	4	4	4	3	3	46
Days With ≥ 1.0" Precipitation	0	0	1	1	1	1	1	0	1	1	1	0	8
Mean Snowfall (in.)	1.9	1.5	0.7	trace	0.0	0.0	0.0	0.0	0.0	0.0	0.5	0.5	5.1
Days With ≥ 1.0" Snow Depth	1	0	0	0	0	0	0	0	0	0	0	0	1

Robert Lee *Coke County*   Elevation: 1,778 ft.   Latitude: 31° 54' N   Longitude: 100° 29' W

	JAN	FEB	MAR	APR	MAY	JUN	JUL	AUG	SEP	OCT	NOV	DEC	YEAR
Mean Maximum Temp. (°F)	57.3	62.9	71.2	79.9	86.8	92.9	96.4	95.2	88.4	79.6	67.9	59.6	78.2
Mean Temp. (°F)	43.4	48.4	56.2	64.7	73.2	80.2	83.7	82.4	75.7	65.7	54.0	45.7	64.4
Mean Minimum Temp. (°F)	29.4	33.8	41.1	49.5	59.6	67.5	70.9	69.6	63.0	51.7	40.1	31.8	50.7
Extreme Maximum Temp. (°F)	86	98	98	101	109	111	110	110	107	103	92	85	111
Extreme Minimum Temp. (°F)	3	-1	8	26	38	50	57	52	39	24	14	-2	-2
Days Maximum Temp. ≥ 90°F	0	0	1	6	12	22	28	26	16	4	0	0	115
Days Maximum Temp. ≤ 32°F	1	1	0	0	0	0	0	0	0	0	0	1	3
Days Minimum Temp. ≤ 32°F	21	13	6	1	0	0	0	0	0	1	7	18	67
Days Minimum Temp. ≤ 0°F	0	0	0	0	0	0	0	0	0	0	0	0	0
Heating Degree Days (base 65°F)	664	467	292	106	15	1	0	0	14	86	339	591	2,575
Cooling Degree Days (base 65°F)	0	4	22	104	285	468	601	572	349	119	17	1	2,542
Mean Precipitation (in.)	0.81	1.26	1.15	1.76	3.25	2.89	1.40	2.28	3.69	2.56	1.07	0.99	23.11
Days With ≥ 0.1" Precipitation	2	3	3	3	5	4	3	4	5	4	2	2	40
Days With ≥ 1.0" Precipitation	0	0	0	1	1	1	0	1	1	1	0	0	6
Mean Snowfall (in.)	0.1	0.0	0.3	0.0	0.0	0.0	0.0	0.0	0.0	0.0	0.1	0.0	0.5
Days With ≥ 1.0" Snow Depth	0	0	0	0	0	0	0	0	0	0	0	0	0

Robstown *Nueces County*   Elevation: 82 ft.   Latitude: 27° 47' N   Longitude: 97° 40' W

	JAN	FEB	MAR	APR	MAY	JUN	JUL	AUG	SEP	OCT	NOV	DEC	YEAR
Mean Maximum Temp. (°F)	65.4	69.6	76.7	82.3	86.7	92.0	94.8	95.1	91.1	84.3	75.9	68.6	81.9
Mean Temp. (°F)	55.1	58.8	66.0	72.2	77.8	82.7	84.8	85.1	81.3	73.9	65.3	58.1	71.8
Mean Minimum Temp. (°F)	44.8	47.9	55.3	62.0	68.9	73.4	74.7	75.0	71.5	63.4	54.7	47.7	61.6
Extreme Maximum Temp. (°F)	92	95	104	104	104	108	103	113	109	100	98	91	113
Extreme Minimum Temp. (°F)	19	20	23	37	50	60	63	67	50	32	25	12	12
Days Maximum Temp. ≥ 90°F	0	0	1	4	9	24	29	29	20	6	1	0	123
Days Maximum Temp. ≤ 32°F	0	0	0	0	0	0	0	0	0	0	0	0	0
Days Minimum Temp. ≤ 32°F	3	2	0	0	0	0	0	0	0	0	0	2	7
Days Minimum Temp. ≤ 0°F	0	0	0	0	0	0	0	0	0	0	0	0	0
Heating Degree Days (base 65°F)	327	205	83	17	0	0	0	0	1	13	104	253	1,003
Cooling Degree Days (base 65°F)	25	37	115	236	416	552	628	641	510	304	128	50	3,642
Mean Precipitation (in.)	1.85	1.91	1.80	1.97	3.44	3.58	2.33	3.79	5.06	3.88	1.81	1.54	32.96
Days With ≥ 0.1" Precipitation	4	3	3	3	4	4	3	4	6	4	3	3	44
Days With ≥ 1.0" Precipitation	0	1	1	1	1	1	1	1	2	1	1	0	11
Mean Snowfall (in.)	trace	trace	0.0	0.0	0.0	0.0	0.0	0.0	0.0	0.0	trace	0.0	trace
Days With ≥ 1.0" Snow Depth	0	0	0	0	0	0	0	0	0	0	0	0	0

Rockport *Aransas County*   Elevation: 6 ft.   Latitude: 28° 02' N   Longitude: 97° 03' W

	JAN	FEB	MAR	APR	MAY	JUN	JUL	AUG	SEP	OCT	NOV	DEC	YEAR
Mean Maximum Temp. (°F)	64.3	67.7	73.4	78.2	83.5	88.4	90.5	90.9	88.6	82.4	74.1	67.0	79.1
Mean Temp. (°F)	55.3	58.8	65.2	70.8	77.1	82.4	84.1	84.0	81.0	73.7	65.3	57.9	71.3
Mean Minimum Temp. (°F)	46.2	49.9	57.0	63.4	70.8	76.3	77.6	77.1	73.3	65.3	56.4	48.8	63.5
Extreme Maximum Temp. (°F)	87	90	91	96	100	99	100	98	99	97	96	87	100
Extreme Minimum Temp. (°F)	18	22	23	38	52	58	64	64	50	29	27	12	12
Days Maximum Temp. ≥ 90°F	0	0	0	0	1	10	23	25	14	1	0	0	74
Days Maximum Temp. ≤ 32°F	0	0	0	0	0	0	0	0	0	0	0	2	6
Days Minimum Temp. ≤ 32°F	3	1	0	0	0	0	0	0	0	0	0	0	0
Days Minimum Temp. ≤ 0°F	0	0	0	0	0	0	0	0	0	0	0	0	0
Heating Degree Days (base 65°F)	309	194	78	18	0	0	0	0	0	14	102	249	964
Cooling Degree Days (base 65°F)	16	27	89	198	401	546	615	612	504	302	125	38	3,473
Mean Precipitation (in.)	2.35	2.19	2.18	2.03	3.76	3.50	2.58	3.18	5.75	4.46	2.27	1.86	36.11
Days With ≥ 0.1" Precipitation	4	4	2	3	4	4	3	4	7	5	4	4	48
Days With ≥ 1.0" Precipitation	1	1	1	1	1	1	1	1	2	1	1	0	12
Mean Snowfall (in.)	0.0	0.0	0.0	0.0	0.0	0.0	0.0	0.0	0.0	0.0	trace	0.0	trace
Days With ≥ 1.0" Snow Depth	0	0	0	0	0	0	0	0	0	0	0	0	0

Roscoe *Nolan County*   Elevation: 2,378 ft.   Latitude: 32° 27' N   Longitude: 100° 32' W

	JAN	FEB	MAR	APR	MAY	JUN	JUL	AUG	SEP	OCT	NOV	DEC	YEAR
Mean Maximum Temp. (°F)	55.5	61.6	70.3	78.8	85.1	91.0	93.8	92.2	85.3	77.4	66.0	57.9	76.2
Mean Temp. (°F)	42.8	48.1	55.8	64.2	72.0	78.8	81.9	80.5	73.9	64.8	53.5	45.2	63.5
Mean Minimum Temp. (°F)	30.0	34.5	41.2	49.5	58.9	66.7	69.9	68.7	62.3	52.3	40.9	32.4	50.6
Extreme Maximum Temp. (°F)	85	91	98	99	108	113	108	104	105	102	90	82	113
Extreme Minimum Temp. (°F)	0	-9	7	22	36	43	57	56	35	26	12	-6	-9
Days Maximum Temp. ≥ 90°F	0	0	1	4	9	19	26	23	10	2	0	0	94
Days Maximum Temp. ≤ 32°F	2	1	0	0	0	0	0	0	0	0	0	1	4
Days Minimum Temp. ≤ 32°F	19	11	6	1	0	0	0	0	0	0	6	16	59
Days Minimum Temp. ≤ 0°F	0	0	0	0	0	0	0	0	0	0	0	0	0
Heating Degree Days (base 65°F)	681	474	302	107	20	1	0	0	19	95	351	610	2,660
Cooling Degree Days (base 65°F)	0	3	20	86	249	418	539	505	295	100	12	0	2,227
Mean Precipitation (in.)	1.02	1.23	1.13	1.54	3.10	2.99	1.89	2.61	3.62	2.45	0.91	1.01	23.50
Days With ≥ 0.1" Precipitation	2	3	3	3	5	4	3	4	5	4	2	2	40
Days With ≥ 1.0" Precipitation	0	0	0	0	1	1	0	1	1	1	0	0	5
Mean Snowfall (in.)	1.9	1.0	0.6	0.0	0.0	0.0	0.0	0.0	0.0	trace	0.8	0.8	5.1
Days With ≥ 1.0" Snow Depth	1	0	0	0	0	0	0	0	0	0	0	0	1

Rusk *Cherokee County*   Elevation: 718 ft.   Latitude: 31° 49' N   Longitude: 95° 09' W

	JAN	FEB	MAR	APR	MAY	JUN	JUL	AUG	SEP	OCT	NOV	DEC	YEAR
Mean Maximum Temp. (°F)	55.1	60.7	67.9	75.3	81.9	88.5	92.7	93.1	87.3	77.8	66.6	58.6	75.5
Mean Temp. (°F)	45.3	50.2	57.3	64.5	71.8	78.4	82.0	81.9	76.3	66.5	56.2	48.6	64.9
Mean Minimum Temp. (°F)	35.3	39.6	46.6	53.8	61.7	68.2	71.2	70.6	65.4	55.2	45.7	38.5	54.3
Extreme Maximum Temp. (°F)	82	93	88	93	98	103	105	106	107	95	86	82	107
Extreme Minimum Temp. (°F)	0	10	14	29	40	50	59	55	43	26	15	1	0
Days Maximum Temp. ≥ 90°F	0	0	0	0	2	13	24	24	13	1	0	0	77
Days Maximum Temp. ≤ 32°F	1	1	0	0	0	0	0	0	0	0	0	1	3
Days Minimum Temp. ≤ 32°F	12	7	2	0	0	0	0	0	0	0	2	8	31
Days Minimum Temp. ≤ 0°F	0	0	0	0	0	0	0	0	0	0	0	0	0
Heating Degree Days (base 65°F)	608	420	261	89	11	0	0	0	7	74	281	507	2,258
Cooling Degree Days (base 65°F)	1	7	27	81	231	410	541	545	362	124	23	5	2,357
Mean Precipitation (in.)	4.41	3.67	4.10	3.91	4.49	4.20	2.97	2.42	4.20	5.01	4.29	4.42	48.09
Days With ≥ 0.1" Precipitation	6	5	6	5	6	5	4	4	5	6	6	6	64
Days With ≥ 1.0" Precipitation	1	2	1	1	2	1	1	1	1	2	2	2	17
Mean Snowfall (in.)	0.3	trace	trace	0.0	0.0	0.0	0.0	0.0	0.0	0.0	trace	trace	0.3
Days With ≥ 1.0" Snow Depth	0	0	0	0	0	0	0	0	0	0	0	0	0

Sam Rayburn Dam *Jasper County*   Elevation: 187 ft.   Latitude: 31° 04' N   Longitude: 94° 06' W

	JAN	FEB	MAR	APR	MAY	JUN	JUL	AUG	SEP	OCT	NOV	DEC	YEAR
Mean Maximum Temp. (°F)	57.4	62.2	69.8	76.9	84.0	90.2	93.2	93.2	88.4	79.2	68.5	61.1	77.0
Mean Temp. (°F)	46.5	50.5	58.1	65.0	72.7	79.0	81.7	81.2	76.7	66.4	57.0	49.9	65.4
Mean Minimum Temp. (°F)	35.7	38.9	46.3	53.0	61.5	67.9	70.2	69.2	64.8	53.5	45.4	38.5	53.7
Extreme Maximum Temp. (°F)	83	88	91	93	101	103	105	107	104	95	87	85	107
Extreme Minimum Temp. (°F)	11	14	19	24	38	50	59	52	39	20	18	7	7
Days Maximum Temp. ≥ 90°F	0	0	0	0	4	19	26	25	15	2	0	0	91
Days Maximum Temp. ≤ 32°F	0	0	0	0	0	0	0	0	0	0	0	0	0
Days Minimum Temp. ≤ 32°F	13	8	3	0	0	0	0	0	0	0	4	10	38
Days Minimum Temp. ≤ 0°F	0	0	0	0	0	0	0	0	0	0	0	0	0
Heating Degree Days (base 65°F)	570	411	240	92	9	0	0	0	4	76	267	472	2,141
Cooling Degree Days (base 65°F)	2	9	32	89	257	429	525	515	355	124	31	9	2,377
Mean Precipitation (in.)	5.97	4.61	5.25	4.42	5.60	5.76	4.33	3.91	3.94	5.02	5.43	6.03	60.27
Days With ≥ 0.1" Precipitation	7	6	7	5	7	7	7	6	5	5	6	7	75
Days With ≥ 1.0" Precipitation	2	2	2	2	2	2	1	1	1	2	2	2	21
Mean Snowfall (in.)	trace	0.0	0.0	0.0	0.0	0.0	0.0	0.0	0.0	0.0	0.0	trace	trace
Days With ≥ 1.0" Snow Depth	0	0	0	0	0	0	0	0	0	0	0	0	0

San Marcos *Hays County*   Elevation: 610 ft.   Latitude: 29° 51' N   Longitude: 97° 57' W

	JAN	FEB	MAR	APR	MAY	JUN	JUL	AUG	SEP	OCT	NOV	DEC	YEAR
Mean Maximum Temp. (°F)	60.9	65.6	73.2	79.6	85.5	91.6	95.0	95.3	90.3	82.4	71.5	63.6	79.5
Mean Temp. (°F)	49.3	53.2	60.6	67.5	74.8	81.0	83.8	83.8	78.9	69.7	59.3	51.7	67.8
Mean Minimum Temp. (°F)	37.5	40.6	48.0	55.3	64.0	70.3	72.6	72.2	67.3	57.1	47.1	39.8	56.0
Extreme Maximum Temp. (°F)	89	99	99	98	100	109	105	107	102	97	91	87	109
Extreme Minimum Temp. (°F)	11	17	17	30	42	51	60	60	42	28	17	4	4
Days Maximum Temp. ≥ 90°F	0	0	0	2	8	22	28	28	20	5	0	0	113
Days Maximum Temp. ≤ 32°F	0	0	0	0	0	0	0	0	0	0	0	0	0
Days Minimum Temp. ≤ 32°F	9	6	2	0	0	0	0	0	0	0	3	8	28
Days Minimum Temp. ≤ 0°F	0	0	0	0	0	0	0	0	0	0	0	0	0
Heating Degree Days (base 65°F)	485	341	178	53	4	0	0	0	2	38	209	417	1,727
Cooling Degree Days (base 65°F)	6	15	49	140	340	510	616	622	447	206	50	12	3,013
Mean Precipitation (in.)	2.05	2.21	2.09	2.87	5.52	4.62	2.15	2.69	3.65	3.82	2.96	2.36	36.99
Days With ≥ 0.1" Precipitation	4	4	5	4	6	5	3	3	5	4	4	4	51
Days With ≥ 1.0" Precipitation	0	1	1	1	2	1	1	1	1	1	1	1	12
Mean Snowfall (in.)	trace	trace	0.0	0.0	0.0	0.0	0.0	0.0	0.0	0.0	trace	trace	trace
Days With ≥ 1.0" Snow Depth	0	0	0	0	0	0	0	0	0	0	0	0	0

San Saba *San Saba County*   Elevation: 1,194 ft.   Latitude: 31° 11' N   Longitude: 98° 43' W

	JAN	FEB	MAR	APR	MAY	JUN	JUL	AUG	SEP	OCT	NOV	DEC	YEAR
Mean Maximum Temp. (°F)	58.4	63.0	70.9	78.7	84.9	91.4	95.7	95.1	89.1	80.4	68.9	61.0	78.1
Mean Temp. (°F)	45.6	50.3	58.1	66.0	73.4	79.9	83.4	82.5	76.9	67.3	56.4	48.2	65.7
Mean Minimum Temp. (°F)	32.8	37.6	45.3	53.2	61.9	68.4	71.0	69.8	64.7	54.2	43.8	35.3	53.2
Extreme Maximum Temp. (°F)	86	100	96	102	109	110	112	109	106	100	94	85	112
Extreme Minimum Temp. (°F)	0	4	11	25	38	51	54	51	39	23	13	-1	-1
Days Maximum Temp. ≥ 90°F	0	0	1	3	8	21	28	26	17	5	0	0	109
Days Maximum Temp. ≤ 32°F	1	1	0	0	0	0	0	0	0	0	0	1	3
Days Minimum Temp. ≤ 32°F	16	9	3	1	0	0	0	0	0	0	5	13	47
Days Minimum Temp. ≤ 0°F	0	0	0	0	0	0	0	0	0	0	0	0	0
Heating Degree Days (base 65°F)	596	415	245	84	12	0	0	0	9	70	279	518	2,228
Cooling Degree Days (base 65°F)	1	8	36	120	297	466	588	572	385	160	31	4	2,668
Mean Precipitation (in.)	1.08	1.99	2.05	2.12	3.95	3.41	1.86	2.29	2.49	2.86	1.83	1.65	27.58
Days With ≥ 0.1" Precipitation	3	4	3	4	6	5	2	4	4	4	3	3	45
Days With ≥ 1.0" Precipitation	0	0	1	1	1	1	1	1	1	1	0	0	9
Mean Snowfall (in.)	0.4	0.3	trace	trace	0.0	0.0	0.0	0.0	0.0	trace	trace	trace	0.7
Days With ≥ 1.0" Snow Depth	0	0	0	0	0	0	0	0	0	0	0	0	0

Sanderson *Terrell County*   Elevation: 2,837 ft.   Latitude: 30° 09' N   Longitude: 102° 24' W

	JAN	FEB	MAR	APR	MAY	JUN	JUL	AUG	SEP	OCT	NOV	DEC	YEAR
Mean Maximum Temp. (°F)	60.4	64.8	72.6	80.4	86.7	91.0	91.9	91.5	86.2	77.8	68.7	61.7	77.8
Mean Temp. (°F)	45.4	49.6	57.4	65.5	73.2	78.8	80.4	79.7	74.1	64.2	54.2	47.0	64.1
Mean Minimum Temp. (°F)	30.4	34.4	42.1	50.6	59.7	66.6	68.8	67.9	62.0	50.5	39.6	32.2	50.4
Extreme Maximum Temp. (°F)	86	94	96	101	105	108	106	106	106	102	94	85	108
Extreme Minimum Temp. (°F)	8	5	13	22	37	46	57	55	40	21	12	3	3
Days Maximum Temp. ≥ 90°F	0	0	1	5	12	19	22	22	11	2	0	0	94
Days Maximum Temp. ≤ 32°F	1	0	0	0	0	0	0	0	0	0	0	0	1
Days Minimum Temp. ≤ 32°F	19	12	4	0	0	0	0	0	0	0	0	6	16	57
Days Minimum Temp. ≤ 0°F	0	0	0	0	0	0	0	0	0	0	0	0	0
Heating Degree Days (base 65°F)	600	430	249	83	12	1	0	0	16	99	325	552	2,367
Cooling Degree Days (base 65°F)	0	3	21	102	287	432	499	483	309	90	8	0	2,234
Mean Precipitation (in.)	0.39	0.61	0.43	0.87	1.80	2.11	1.51	1.98	2.60	1.59	0.76	0.50	15.15
Days With ≥ 0.1" Precipitation	1	2	1	2	3	3	3	3	4	3	2	1	28
Days With ≥ 1.0" Precipitation	0	0	0	0	0	1	0	0	1	0	0	0	2
Mean Snowfall (in.)	0.4	0.0	0.0	0.0	0.0	0.0	0.0	0.0	0.0	0.0	0.0	0.1	0.5
Days With ≥ 1.0" Snow Depth	0	0	0	0	0	0	0	0	0	0	0	0	0

Seminole *Gaines County*   Elevation: 3,339 ft.   Latitude: 32° 43' N   Longitude: 102° 33' W

	JAN	FEB	MAR	APR	MAY	JUN	JUL	AUG	SEP	OCT	NOV	DEC	YEAR
Mean Maximum Temp. (°F)	54.8	60.6	68.8	77.5	85.3	92.4	94.0	92.0	85.6	77.2	65.3	57.0	75.9
Mean Temp. (°F)	40.5	45.2	52.4	60.9	69.7	77.5	79.9	78.2	71.8	61.9	50.1	42.3	60.9
Mean Minimum Temp. (°F)	26.0	29.7	35.9	44.1	54.0	62.5	65.8	64.4	58.0	46.5	34.9	27.6	45.8
Extreme Maximum Temp. (°F)	83	85	95	99	106	114	110	108	104	102	88	82	114
Extreme Minimum Temp. (°F)	-1	-2	8	20	33	44	55	51	36	20	5	-1	-2
Days Maximum Temp. ≥ 90°F	0	0	0	3	11	21	25	22	12	3	0	0	97
Days Maximum Temp. ≤ 32°F	2	1	0	0	0	0	0	0	0	0	0	1	4
Days Minimum Temp. ≤ 32°F	25	19	10	2	0	0	0	0	0	1	12	23	92
Days Minimum Temp. ≤ 0°F	0	0	0	0	0	0	0	0	0	0	0	0	0
Heating Degree Days (base 65°F)	755	553	389	165	34	2	0	0	30	143	441	696	3,208
Cooling Degree Days (base 65°F)	0	0	5	45	195	388	482	430	240	54	2	0	1,841
Mean Precipitation (in.)	0.63	0.73	0.67	0.88	2.44	2.41	2.46	2.31	2.77	1.38	0.80	0.69	18.17
Days With ≥ 0.1" Precipitation	2	2	2	2	4	4	4	4	4	3	2	2	35
Days With ≥ 1.0" Precipitation	0	0	0	0	1	1	1	1	1	0	0	0	5
Mean Snowfall (in.)	2.8	2.0	0.8	0.4	0.0	0.0	0.0	0.0	0.0	0.1	1.0	1.8	8.9
Days With ≥ 1.0" Snow Depth	2	1	0	0	0	0	0	0	0	0	1	1	5

Seymour *Baylor County*   Elevation: 1,282 ft.   Latitude: 33° 35' N   Longitude: 99° 16' W

	JAN	FEB	MAR	APR	MAY	JUN	JUL	AUG	SEP	OCT	NOV	DEC	YEAR
Mean Maximum Temp. (°F)	52.5	57.9	66.7	75.8	83.4	91.2	96.2	95.4	87.1	77.2	64.0	55.5	75.2
Mean Temp. (°F)	39.8	44.7	53.2	62.0	70.8	79.2	83.8	82.9	74.9	64.0	51.2	42.6	62.4
Mean Minimum Temp. (°F)	27.0	31.5	39.6	48.2	58.2	67.1	71.4	70.3	62.6	50.8	38.3	29.6	49.6
Extreme Maximum Temp. (°F)	83	93	99	101	107	115	113	110	106	105	89	83	115
Extreme Minimum Temp. (°F)	1	-9	7	23	35	47	56	51	35	20	14	-8	-9
Days Maximum Temp. ≥ 90°F	0	0	1	2	7	19	27	26	14	3	0	0	99
Days Maximum Temp. ≤ 32°F	3	2	0	0	0	0	0	0	0	0	0	2	7
Days Minimum Temp. ≤ 32°F	23	15	7	1	0	0	0	0	0	1	9	20	76
Days Minimum Temp. ≤ 0°F	0	0	0	0	0	0	0	0	0	0	0	0	0
Heating Degree Days (base 65°F)	775	567	375	151	30	1	0	0	23	121	415	688	3,146
Cooling Degree Days (base 65°F)	0	1	15	63	220	435	597	583	335	99	8	0	2,356
Mean Precipitation (in.)	1.01	1.58	1.79	1.88	4.13	3.44	1.85	2.60	3.63	2.82	1.20	1.40	27.33
Days With ≥ 0.1" Precipitation	3	3	3	4	5	5	3	4	4	4	3	3	44
Days With ≥ 1.0" Precipitation	0	0	0	0	1	1	0	1	1	1	0	0	5
Mean Snowfall (in.)	*0.9*	*0.3*	trace	0.0	0.0	0.0	0.0	0.0	0.0	0.0	0.3	0.4	*1.9*
Days With ≥ 1.0" Snow Depth	*0*	*0*	0	0	0	0	0	0	0	0	0	0	*0*

Shamrock 2 *Wheeler County*   Elevation: 2,358 ft.   Latitude: 35° 13' N   Longitude: 100° 15' W

	JAN	FEB	MAR	APR	MAY	JUN	JUL	AUG	SEP	OCT	NOV	DEC	YEAR
Mean Maximum Temp. (°F)	49.1	54.9	62.9	72.5	80.0	88.7	94.1	92.4	84.6	74.1	60.8	51.7	72.2
Mean Temp. (°F)	36.0	41.2	48.7	58.4	67.1	76.0	81.2	79.6	71.7	60.2	47.6	38.8	58.9
Mean Minimum Temp. (°F)	22.9	27.6	34.5	44.2	54.1	63.3	68.1	66.8	58.7	46.2	34.3	25.8	45.5
Extreme Maximum Temp. (°F)	83	90	97	100	104	113	109	107	104	100	87	81	113
Extreme Minimum Temp. (°F)	-13	-5	1	21	31	45	53	53	30	16	10	-8	-13
Days Maximum Temp. ≥ 90°F	0	0	0	1	5	14	24	22	11	2	0	0	79
Days Maximum Temp. ≤ 32°F	4	3	1	0	0	0	0	0	0	0	1	3	12
Days Minimum Temp. ≤ 32°F	27	19	12	2	0	0	0	0	0	1	12	25	98
Days Minimum Temp. ≤ 0°F	0	0	0	0	0	0	0	0	0	0	0	0	0
Heating Degree Days (base 65°F)	889	665	503	226	60	5	0	1	38	187	517	806	3,897
Cooling Degree Days (base 65°F)	0	0	3	30	127	332	509	466	247	41	2	0	1,757
Mean Precipitation (in.)	0.55	0.77	1.70	2.22	3.88	3.49	2.17	2.31	2.74	1.66	1.15	0.77	23.41
Days With ≥ 0.1" Precipitation	2	2	3	4	6	5	3	4	5	3	2	2	41
Days With ≥ 1.0" Precipitation	0	0	0	1	1	1	1	1	1	0	0	0	6
Mean Snowfall (in.)	1.8	2.2	0.2	0.1	0.0	0.0	0.0	0.0	0.0	0.0	0.8	1.4	6.5
Days With ≥ 1.0" Snow Depth	1	*0*	0	0	0	0	0	0	0	0	1	*1*	3

Sheffield *Pecos County*   Elevation: 2,168 ft.   Latitude: 30° 42' N   Longitude: 101° 50' W

	JAN	FEB	MAR	APR	MAY	JUN	JUL	AUG	SEP	OCT	NOV	DEC	YEAR
Mean Maximum Temp. (°F)	61.5	66.9	75.4	83.0	89.5	94.1	95.8	95.2	89.1	80.4	69.7	62.5	80.3
Mean Temp. (°F)	46.1	51.0	59.4	66.8	75.1	81.5	83.7	82.8	76.4	66.2	54.9	47.4	65.9
Mean Minimum Temp. (°F)	30.6	35.0	43.3	50.6	60.7	68.7	71.5	70.4	63.7	51.9	39.9	32.2	51.5
Extreme Maximum Temp. (°F)	87	96	97	101	108	110	111	106	104	100	92	89	111
Extreme Minimum Temp. (°F)	5	6	9	22	37	44	57	50	35	20	13	-2	-2
Days Maximum Temp. ≥ 90°F	0	0	1	6	15	24	28	27	16	4	0	0	121
Days Maximum Temp. ≤ 32°F	0	0	0	0	0	0	0	0	0	0	0	0	0
Days Minimum Temp. ≤ 32°F	19	11	4	1	0	0	0	0	0	1	7	16	59
Days Minimum Temp. ≤ 0°F	0	0	0	0	0	0	0	0	0	0	0	0	0
Heating Degree Days (base 65°F)	577	391	199	67	5	0	0	0	10	72	307	538	2,166
Cooling Degree Days (base 65°F)	0	3	33	135	346	513	606	572	374	126	12	1	2,721
Mean Precipitation (in.)	0.53	0.68	0.52	0.95	2.22	1.44	1.18	1.82	2.58	1.69	0.78	0.63	15.02
Days With ≥ 0.1" Precipitation	1	1	1	1	3	2	2	3	3	2	1	1	21
Days With ≥ 1.0" Precipitation	0	0	0	0	1	0	0	0	1	1	0	0	3
Mean Snowfall (in.)	0.0	0.0	0.0	0.0	0.0	0.0	0.0	0.0	0.0	0.0	0.0	0.0	0.0
Days With ≥ 1.0" Snow Depth	0	0	0	0	0	0	0	0	0	0	0	0	0

Sherman *Grayson County*   Elevation: 757 ft.   Latitude: 33° 42' N   Longitude: 96° 38' W

	JAN	FEB	MAR	APR	MAY	JUN	JUL	AUG	SEP	OCT	NOV	DEC	YEAR
Mean Maximum Temp. (°F)	51.6	56.9	65.4	73.8	81.0	89.2	94.2	93.8	86.1	75.9	63.4	54.6	73.8
Mean Temp. (°F)	41.2	46.2	54.3	62.7	70.7	78.9	83.4	82.7	75.4	64.6	52.8	44.3	63.1
Mean Minimum Temp. (°F)	30.8	35.3	43.2	51.6	60.3	68.5	72.6	71.5	64.5	53.1	42.2	34.1	52.3
Extreme Maximum Temp. (°F)	82	91	92	97	100	110	109	106	107	98	89	84	110
Extreme Minimum Temp. (°F)	4	4	15	28	39	49	53	56	39	24	13	-2	-2
Days Maximum Temp. ≥ 90°F	0	0	0	0	3	16	26	25	12	1	0	0	83
Days Maximum Temp. ≤ 32°F	3	1	0	0	0	0	0	0	0	0	0	1	5
Days Minimum Temp. ≤ 32°F	18	11	4	0	0	0	0	0	0	0	5	14	52
Days Minimum Temp. ≤ 0°F	0	0	0	0	0	0	0	0	0	0	0	0	0
Heating Degree Days (base 65°F)	737	527	340	126	23	1	0	0	16	104	371	634	2,879
Cooling Degree Days (base 65°F)	0	2	16	62	209	429	586	576	345	99	13	1	2,338
Mean Precipitation (in.)	2.06	2.79	3.42	3.55	5.44	4.18	2.37	2.32	4.29	5.13	3.61	2.83	41.99
Days With ≥ 0.1" Precipitation	4	5	5	5	7	6	4	3	5	5	4	4	58
Days With ≥ 1.0" Precipitation	0	1	1	1	2	1	1	1	2	2	1	1	14
Mean Snowfall (in.)	*0.4*	1.2	0.1	0.0	0.0	0.0	0.0	0.0	0.0	0.0	0.2	0.3	*2.2*
Days With ≥ 1.0" Snow Depth	*0*	0	0	0	0	0	0	0	0	0	0	0	*0*

Sierra Blanca 2 E *Hudspeth County*   Elevation: 4,534 ft.   Latitude: 31° 11' N   Longitude: 105° 19' W

	JAN	FEB	MAR	APR	MAY	JUN	JUL	AUG	SEP	OCT	NOV	DEC	YEAR
Mean Maximum Temp. (°F)	58.0	63.9	70.8	78.5	86.7	93.9	92.7	90.2	85.4	77.7	67.4	59.1	77.0
Mean Temp. (°F)	42.2	47.0	53.2	60.2	68.9	76.9	77.9	75.8	70.5	60.9	50.2	43.0	60.6
Mean Minimum Temp. (°F)	26.4	30.1	35.6	41.8	51.1	60.0	63.2	61.3	55.6	44.0	33.0	26.8	44.1
Extreme Maximum Temp. (°F)	77	89	96	96	101	109	108	102	99	94	89	82	109
Extreme Minimum Temp. (°F)	0	-10	*6*	19	26	40	53	49	36	19	9	1	*-10*
Days Maximum Temp. ≥ 90°F	0	0	0	1	10	24	23	19	9	1	0	0	87
Days Maximum Temp. ≤ 32°F	0	0	0	0	0	0	0	0	0	0	0	0	0
Days Minimum Temp. ≤ 32°F	24	18	11	4	0	0	0	0	0	2	14	24	97
Days Minimum Temp. ≤ 0°F	0	0	0	0	0	0	0	0	0	0	0	0	0
Heating Degree Days (base 65°F)	698	502	361	163	25	1	0	0	22	151	437	675	3,035
Cooling Degree Days (base 65°F)	0	0	2	26	170	373	417	348	199	28	0	0	1,563
Mean Precipitation (in.)	0.52	0.42	0.28	0.28	0.53	1.11	2.17	2.33	2.33	1.18	0.40	0.65	12.20
Days With ≥ 0.1" Precipitation	2	*1*	1	1	1	3	4	5	5	3	1	2	*29*
Days With ≥ 1.0" Precipitation	0	0	0	0	0	0	1	0	1	0	0	0	*2*
Mean Snowfall (in.)	na	*trace*	trace	0.0	0.0	0.0	0.0	0.0	0.0	0.0	trace	trace	2
Days With ≥ 1.0" Snow Depth	*0*	0	0	0	0	0	0	0	0	0	0	0	*na*

Silverton *Briscoe County*   Elevation: 3,277 ft.   Latitude: 34° 28' N   Longitude: 101° 18' W

	JAN	FEB	MAR	APR	MAY	JUN	JUL	AUG	SEP	OCT	NOV	DEC	YEAR
Mean Maximum Temp. (°F)	49.5	54.7	62.5	71.4	78.9	87.4	90.9	88.7	81.9	73.0	60.3	51.8	70.9
Mean Temp. (°F)	35.4	40.0	47.2	56.0	65.1	74.0	77.8	75.9	68.9	58.3	46.0	37.7	56.9
Mean Minimum Temp. (°F)	21.2	25.3	31.9	40.7	51.1	60.6	64.6	63.1	56.0	43.6	31.6	23.6	42.8
Extreme Maximum Temp. (°F)	80	87	94	98	103	109	106	102	102	97	88	80	109
Extreme Minimum Temp. (°F)	-6	-7	4	19	30	43	53	50	30	16	1	-6	-7
Days Maximum Temp. ≥ 90°F	0	0	0	1	4	13	20	16	7	1	0	0	62
Days Maximum Temp. ≤ 32°F	4	3	1	0	0	0	0	0	0	0	1	3	12
Days Minimum Temp. ≤ 32°F	29	23	16	5	0	0	0	0	0	3	17	27	120
Days Minimum Temp. ≤ 0°F	0	0	0	0	0	0	0	0	0	0	0	0	0
Heating Degree Days (base 65°F)	911	699	546	280	90	8	0	1	53	227	565	838	4,218
Cooling Degree Days (base 65°F)	0	0	2	17	103	287	419	367	186	26	1	0	1,408
Mean Precipitation (in.)	0.56	0.78	1.13	1.53	3.21	3.72	2.32	2.81	2.71	1.63	0.87	0.71	21.98
Days With ≥ 0.1" Precipitation	2	2	3	4	6	6	4	6	4	3	2	2	44
Days With ≥ 1.0" Precipitation	0	0	0	0	1	1	1	1	1	0	0	0	5
Mean Snowfall (in.)	3.0	3.0	1.1	0.3	0.0	0.0	0.0	0.0	0.0	0.2	1.5	2.6	11.7
Days With ≥ 1.0" Snow Depth	*0*	*0*	*0*	0	0	0	0	0	0	0	0	*0*	*0*

Smithville *Bastrop County*   Elevation: 337 ft.   Latitude: 30° 01' N   Longitude: 97° 09' W

	JAN	FEB	MAR	APR	MAY	JUN	JUL	AUG	SEP	OCT	NOV	DEC	YEAR
Mean Maximum Temp. (°F)	60.5	64.8	72.6	79.7	85.0	91.8	95.5	96.4	90.9	82.1	71.2	63.9	*79.5*
Mean Temp. (°F)	48.3	52.2	59.7	67.3	*74.0*	*80.6*	*83.5*	83.3	78.3	68.8	58.6	51.6	*67.2*
Mean Minimum Temp. (°F)	35.9	39.6	46.8	54.7	*62.9*	69.3	*71.5*	70.0	65.6	55.4	46.0	39.3	*54.8*
Extreme Maximum Temp. (°F)	88	96	98	*95*	*100*	*106*	*105*	108	107	*100*	91	85	*108*
Extreme Minimum Temp. (°F)	9	13	19	25	*45*	*50*	*52*	50	43	*27*	20	10	*9*
Days Maximum Temp. ≥ 90°F	0	0	0	2	7	22	28	28	20	6	0	0	113
Days Maximum Temp. ≤ 32°F	0	0	0	0	0	0	0	0	0	0	0	0	0
Days Minimum Temp. ≤ 32°F	13	7	3	0	0	*0*	*0*	0	0	0	3	9	*35*
Days Minimum Temp. ≤ 0°F	0	0	0	0	0	0	0	0	0	0	0	0	0
Heating Degree Days (base 65°F)	517	*366*	201	60	7	*0*	*0*	0	3	54	229	423	*1,860*
Cooling Degree Days (base 65°F)	6	10	44	134	303	479	585	582	406	184	50	14	2,797
Mean Precipitation (in.)	2.81	2.60	2.66	3.02	5.20	3.48	2.04	2.18	3.58	4.77	3.09	2.98	38.41
Days With ≥ 0.1" Precipitation	5	4	5	4	6	5	3	3	5	4	4	5	53
Days With ≥ 1.0" Precipitation	1	1	1	1	2	1	1	1	1	1	1	1	13
Mean Snowfall (in.)	trace	0.0	0.0	0.0	0.0	0.0	0.0	0.0	0.0	0.0	0.0	trace	trace
Days With ≥ 1.0" Snow Depth	0	0	0	0	0	0	0	0	0	0	0	0	0

Somerville Dam *Burleson County*   Elevation: 262 ft.   Latitude: 30° 20' N   Longitude: 96° 32' W

	JAN	FEB	MAR	APR	MAY	JUN	JUL	AUG	SEP	OCT	NOV	DEC	YEAR
Mean Maximum Temp. (°F)	58.8	63.2	70.7	77.5	83.8	90.5	94.4	95.0	89.7	80.8	69.9	62.3	78.0
Mean Temp. (°F)	47.9	52.1	59.7	66.8	74.0	80.7	84.0	83.8	78.3	68.8	58.7	51.0	67.2
Mean Minimum Temp. (°F)	37.0	41.0	48.7	56.1	64.1	70.9	73.5	72.6	66.9	56.8	47.5	39.8	56.2
Extreme Maximum Temp. (°F)	84	96	91	94	100	106	106	108	104	96	90	84	108
Extreme Minimum Temp. (°F)	8	13	19	32	43	55	57	59	42	28	18	3	3
Days Maximum Temp. ≥ 90°F	0	0	0	0	4	19	28	28	18	3	0	0	1
Days Maximum Temp. ≤ 32°F	1	0	0	0	0	0	0	0	0	0	0	0	1
Days Minimum Temp. ≤ 32°F	11	5	2	0	0	0	0	0	0	0	2	8	28
Days Minimum Temp. ≤ 0°F	0	0	0	0	0	0	0	0	0	0	0	0	0
Heating Degree Days (base 65°F)	526	366	198	60	6	0	0	0	4	50	225	436	1,871
Cooling Degree Days (base 65°F)	3	9	40	123	299	494	609	609	423	179	47	11	2,846
Mean Precipitation (in.)	2.87	2.59	2.65	2.94	4.54	4.10	1.80	2.44	3.75	4.43	3.35	3.03	38.49
Days With ≥ 0.1" Precipitation	5	5	5	4	6	5	4	4	5	5	5	5	58
Days With ≥ 1.0" Precipitation	1	1	1	1	2	1	1	1	1	1	1	1	13
Mean Snowfall (in.)	0.0	trace	0.0	0.0	0.0	0.0	0.0	0.0	0.0	0.0	0.0	0.0	0
Days With ≥ 1.0" Snow Depth	0	0	0	0	0	0	0	0	0	0	0	0	0

Spearman *Hansford County*   Elevation: 3,093 ft.   Latitude: 36° 11' N   Longitude: 101° 11' W

	JAN	FEB	MAR	APR	MAY	JUN	JUL	AUG	SEP	OCT	NOV	DEC	YEAR
Mean Maximum Temp. (°F)	50.1	56.2	64.6	73.5	81.0	90.2	94.2	92.1	85.3	75.2	61.1	51.8	72.9
Mean Temp. (°F)	36.1	41.3	49.0	57.8	66.5	75.7	80.0	78.3	71.1	60.0	46.8	38.2	58.4
Mean Minimum Temp. (°F)	22.1	26.3	33.2	42.0	52.0	61.3	65.8	64.5	56.8	44.7	32.6	24.5	43.8
Extreme Maximum Temp. (°F)	80	92	95	100	105	110	107	108	106	96	87	79	110
Extreme Minimum Temp. (°F)	-11	-9	3	16	29	42	50	47	30	13	0	-9	-11
Days Maximum Temp. ≥ 90°F	0	0	0	1	5	17	25	22	11	2	0	0	83
Days Maximum Temp. ≤ 32°F	4	2	1	0	0	0	0	0	0	0	1	3	11
Days Minimum Temp. ≤ 32°F	27	21	14	4	0	0	0	0	0	2	15	26	109
Days Minimum Temp. ≤ 0°F	1	0	0	0	0	0	0	0	0	0	0	1	2
Heating Degree Days (base 65°F)	888	663	495	239	67	6	0	0	36	191	539	824	3,948
Cooling Degree Days (base 65°F)	0	0	4	27	124	335	483	433	238	45	1	0	1,690
Mean Precipitation (in.)	0.53	0.60	1.41	1.58	2.81	2.87	2.81	2.50	2.09	1.21	0.99	0.65	20.05
Days With ≥ 0.1" Precipitation	2	2	3	3	6	5	4	5	3	2	2	2	39
Days With ≥ 1.0" Precipitation	0	0	0	0	1	1	1	1	1	0	0	0	5
Mean Snowfall (in.)	5.0	4.4	3.8	1.4	0.2	0.0	0.0	0.0	trace	0.7	2.3	4.7	22.5
Days With ≥ 1.0" Snow Depth	4	2	1	0	0	0	0	0	0	0	1	3	11

Stillhouse Hollow Dam *Bell County*   Elevation: 705 ft.   Latitude: 31° 02' N   Longitude: 97° 32' W

	JAN	FEB	MAR	APR	MAY	JUN	JUL	AUG	SEP	OCT	NOV	DEC	YEAR
Mean Maximum Temp. (°F)	57.7	63.0	70.2	77.5	83.9	90.4	94.9	95.1	89.1	80.3	68.8	61.0	77.7
Mean Temp. (°F)	46.0	50.8	58.1	65.7	73.1	79.8	83.4	83.2	77.5	68.0	57.1	49.3	66.0
Mean Minimum Temp. (°F)	34.2	38.6	45.9	53.9	62.3	69.1	71.9	71.3	65.9	55.6	45.4	37.6	54.3
Extreme Maximum Temp. (°F)	84	98	97	97	100	106	107	105	105	99	92	83	107
Extreme Minimum Temp. (°F)	6	12	15	31	41	52	52	57	39	22	19	-5	-5
Days Maximum Temp. ≥ 90°F	0	0	0	1	6	19	28	28	17	4	0	0	103
Days Maximum Temp. ≤ 32°F	1	0	0	0	0	0	0	0	0	0	0	1	2
Days Minimum Temp. ≤ 32°F	14	7	2	0	0	0	0	0	0	0	3	9	35
Days Minimum Temp. ≤ 0°F	0	0	0	0	0	0	0	0	0	0	0	0	0
Heating Degree Days (base 65°F)	585	403	238	75	9	0	0	0	6	59	257	486	2,118
Cooling Degree Days (base 65°F)	2	10	30	103	278	456	586	589	396	161	33	8	2,652
Mean Precipitation (in.)	1.85	2.69	2.61	2.89	4.94	3.78	1.90	2.24	3.77	3.83	2.67	2.56	35.73
Days With ≥ 0.1" Precipitation	4	4	5	4	7	5	3	4	5	5	4	4	54
Days With ≥ 1.0" Precipitation	0	1	1	1	2	1	1	1	1	1	1	1	12
Mean Snowfall (in.)	0.0	*0.0*	trace	0.0	0.0	0.0	0.0	0.0	0.0	0.0	0.0	trace	*trace*
Days With ≥ 1.0" Snow Depth	0	*0*	0	0	0	0	0	0	0	0	0	0	*0*

Stratford *Sherman County*   Elevation: 3,690 ft.   Latitude: 36° 21' N   Longitude: 102° 05' W

	JAN	FEB	MAR	APR	MAY	JUN	JUL	AUG	SEP	OCT	NOV	DEC	YEAR
Mean Maximum Temp. (°F)	47.0	52.5	60.3	69.1	77.5	86.8	91.3	89.1	81.6	71.6	58.5	48.7	69.5
Mean Temp. (°F)	32.7	37.5	44.6	53.3	62.6	72.2	77.0	75.3	67.4	56.0	43.4	34.6	54.7
Mean Minimum Temp. (°F)	18.4	22.5	28.8	37.5	47.7	57.5	62.7	61.4	53.0	40.3	28.3	20.5	39.9
Extreme Maximum Temp. (°F)	82	86	91	95	103	107	106	102	104	95	88	82	107
Extreme Minimum Temp. (°F)	-14	-10	2	13	27	41	48	43	26	8	-10	-11	-14
Days Maximum Temp. ≥ 90°F	0	0	0	0	3	12	20	17	7	1	0	0	60
Days Maximum Temp. ≤ 32°F	5	3	1	0	0	0	0	0	0	0	1	4	14
Days Minimum Temp. ≤ 32°F	30	25	20	8	1	0	0	0	0	5	21	29	139
Days Minimum Temp. ≤ 0°F	1	1	0	0	0	0	0	0	0	0	0	1	3
Heating Degree Days (base 65°F)	993	770	626	352	126	16	2	2	68	288	640	935	4,818
Cooling Degree Days (base 65°F)	0	0	1	7	55	227	378	330	144	12	0	0	1,154
Mean Precipitation (in.)	0.47	0.44	1.05	1.52	2.86	2.11	2.31	2.77	1.76	0.99	0.79	0.55	17.62
Days With ≥ 0.1" Precipitation	1	1	3	3	4	4	5	4	3	2	2	1	33
Days With ≥ 1.0" Precipitation	0	0	0	0	1	0	1	1	0	0	0	0	3
Mean Snowfall (in.)	4.4	2.9	3.5	1.7	0.4	0.0	0.0	0.0	0.0	0.7	2.1	4.0	19.7
Days With ≥ 1.0" Snow Depth	2	1	0	0	0	0	0	0	0	0	1	1	5

Sugar Land *Fort Bend County*   Elevation: 82 ft.   Latitude: 29° 37' N   Longitude: 95° 38' W

	JAN	FEB	MAR	APR	MAY	JUN	JUL	AUG	SEP	OCT	NOV	DEC	YEAR
Mean Maximum Temp. (°F)	61.5	65.5	72.1	79.1	85.4	90.7	93.5	93.5	88.9	81.6	72.0	64.8	79.0
Mean Temp. (°F)	51.5	55.0	61.8	68.9	76.0	81.5	83.9	83.6	79.1	70.5	61.4	54.3	69.0
Mean Minimum Temp. (°F)	41.5	44.5	51.4	58.6	66.5	72.3	74.3	73.7	69.3	59.4	50.7	43.7	58.8
Extreme Maximum Temp. (°F)	84	89	92	94	99	101	103	103	100	95	90	86	103
Extreme Minimum Temp. (°F)	12	19	21	32	47	56	63	64	47	30	22	6	6
Days Maximum Temp. ≥ 90°F	0	0	0	1	6	20	27	26	16	3	0	0	99
Days Maximum Temp. ≤ 32°F	0	0	0	0	0	0	0	0	0	0	0	0	0
Days Minimum Temp. ≤ 32°F	6	3	1	0	0	0	0	0	0	0	0	0	0
Days Minimum Temp. ≤ 0°F	0	0	0	0	0	0	0	0	0	0	1	4	15
Heating Degree Days (base 65°F)	426	295	152	40	2	0	0	0	1	33	175	349	1,473
Cooling Degree Days (base 65°F)	12	21	59	159	362	512	605	600	442	218	73	24	3,087
Mean Precipitation (in.)	4.03	3.03	3.36	3.38	4.97	5.40	3.40	4.35	6.16	4.42	4.21	3.29	50.00
Days With ≥ 0.1" Precipitation	6	5	5	4	5	6	6	6	7	5	5	5	66
Days With ≥ 1.0" Precipitation	1	1	1	1	2	2	1	1	2	1	1	1	15
Mean Snowfall (in.)	trace	trace	trace	0.0	0.0	0.0	0.0	0.0	0.0	0.0	trace	trace	trace
Days With ≥ 1.0" Snow Depth	0	0	0	0	0	0	0	0	0	0	0	0	0

Sulphur Springs *Hopkins County*   Elevation: 501 ft.   Latitude: 33° 08' N   Longitude: 95° 36' W

	JAN	FEB	MAR	APR	MAY	JUN	JUL	AUG	SEP	OCT	NOV	DEC	YEAR
Mean Maximum Temp. (°F)	53.4	58.7	66.4	74.6	81.6	89.1	93.6	94.3	87.5	77.5	65.0	56.6	74.9
Mean Temp. (°F)	42.1	47.2	54.9	62.7	70.8	78.5	82.5	82.3	75.5	64.7	53.6	45.5	63.4
Mean Minimum Temp. (°F)	30.8	35.6	43.3	50.9	60.0	67.8	71.4	70.3	63.5	51.9	42.2	34.3	51.8
Extreme Maximum Temp. (°F)	82	91	89	91	97	104	107	109	110	98	87	81	110
Extreme Minimum Temp. (°F)	4	2	14	27	39	48	53	52	40	23	14	-4	-4
Days Maximum Temp. ≥ 90°F	0	0	0	0	2	16	25	26	14	2	0	0	85
Days Maximum Temp. ≤ 32°F	2	1	0	0	0	0	0	0	0	0	0	1	4
Days Minimum Temp. ≤ 32°F	18	11	4	1	0	0	0	0	0	0	5	14	53
Days Minimum Temp. ≤ 0°F	0	0	0	0	0	0	0	0	0	0	0	0	0
Heating Degree Days (base 65°F)	704	502	324	126	20	1	0	0	15	105	350	600	2,747
Cooling Degree Days (base 65°F)	0	5	17	64	212	423	563	565	344	98	14	4	2,309
Mean Precipitation (in.)	2.83	3.28	4.22	4.40	4.89	4.18	3.22	2.45	3.55	5.27	4.28	4.32	46.89
Days With ≥ 0.1" Precipitation	5	5	6	5	7	6	4	4	5	6	5	6	64
Days With ≥ 1.0" Precipitation	1	1	1	2	2	1	1	1	1	2	1	1	15
Mean Snowfall (in.)	trace	0.1	0.3	0.0	0.0	0.0	0.0	0.0	0.0	0.0	0.0	0.2	0.6
Days With ≥ 1.0" Snow Depth	0	0	0	0	0	0	0	0	0	0	0	0	0

Tahoka *Lynn County*   Elevation: 3,120 ft.   Latitude: 33° 10' N   Longitude: 101° 48' W

	JAN	FEB	MAR	APR	MAY	JUN	JUL	AUG	SEP	OCT	NOV	DEC	YEAR
Mean Maximum Temp. (°F)	53.2	59.1	67.3	75.9	83.3	90.1	92.0	90.3	83.7	75.6	63.6	55.8	74.2
Mean Temp. (°F)	39.0	44.0	51.2	60.0	68.8	76.5	79.2	77.6	71.0	61.3	49.3	41.6	60.0
Mean Minimum Temp. (°F)	24.9	28.8	35.0	44.1	54.3	62.9	66.4	64.8	58.2	47.0	35.0	27.4	45.7
Extreme Maximum Temp. (°F)	83	88	96	99	104	111	107	105	104	101	89	82	111
Extreme Minimum Temp. (°F)	-2	-2	8	20	33	46	56	52	33	19	4	-3	-3
Days Maximum Temp. ≥ 90°F	0	0	0	2	8	17	22	19	9	2	0	0	79
Days Maximum Temp. ≤ 32°F	3	1	0	0	0	0	0	0	0	0	0	2	6
Days Minimum Temp. ≤ 32°F	26	19	11	3	0	0	0	0	0	1	11	24	95
Days Minimum Temp. ≤ 0°F	0	0	0	0	0	0	0	0	0	0	0	0	0
Heating Degree Days (base 65°F)	798	587	427	186	43	2	0	1	36	158	464	718	3,420
Cooling Degree Days (base 65°F)	0	1	5	41	176	362	466	418	226	51	2	0	1,748
Mean Precipitation (in.)	0.64	0.78	0.74	1.41	2.75	3.04	2.57	2.22	2.87	1.68	0.78	0.81	20.29
Days With ≥ 0.1" Precipitation	2	2	2	3	4	4	4	4	5	3	2	2	37
Days With ≥ 1.0" Precipitation	0	0	0	0	1	1	1	1	1	0	0	0	5
Mean Snowfall (in.)	3.1	2.5	0.7	0.3	0.0	0.0	0.0	0.0	0.0	0.1	0.9	1.8	9.4
Days With ≥ 1.0" Snow Depth	2	1	0	0	0	0	0	0	0	0	0	1	4

Taylor *Williamson County* Elevation: 564 ft. Latitude: 30° 34' N Longitude: 97° 25' W

	JAN	FEB	MAR	APR	MAY	JUN	JUL	AUG	SEP	OCT	NOV	DEC	YEAR
Mean Maximum Temp. (°F)	58.7	63.5	71.7	78.6	84.7	90.9	95.0	95.6	90.0	81.1	69.5	61.6	78.4
Mean Temp. (°F)	47.0	51.3	59.1	66.2	73.6	79.9	83.5	83.5	78.0	68.4	57.3	49.8	66.4
Mean Minimum Temp. (°F)	35.2	39.0	46.4	53.7	62.4	69.0	71.9	71.2	65.8	55.6	45.0	37.9	54.4
Extreme Maximum Temp. (°F)	89	99	98	99	100	105	105	106	105	98	89	86	106
Extreme Minimum Temp. (°F)	7	7	15	29	41	51	59	57	42	27	17	0	0
Days Maximum Temp. ≥ 90°F	0	0	0	2	6	20	28	29	19	5	0	0	109
Days Maximum Temp. ≤ 32°F	1	1	0	0	0	0	0	0	0	0	0	0	2
Days Minimum Temp. ≤ 32°F	13	7	2	0	0	0	0	0	0	0	4	9	35
Days Minimum Temp. ≤ 0°F	0	0	0	0	0	0	0	0	0	0	0	0	0
Heating Degree Days (base 65°F)	556	390	220	69	7	0	0	0	5	55	259	474	2,035
Cooling Degree Days (base 65°F)	4	10	41	108	289	459	589	590	406	173	36	10	2,715
Mean Precipitation (in.)	2.02	2.49	2.69	2.62	5.27	3.69	1.59	2.11	3.41	3.85	2.65	2.47	34.86
Days With ≥ 0.1" Precipitation	4	5	5	4	6	5	3	3	5	5	4	4	53
Days With ≥ 1.0" Precipitation	0	1	1	1	2	1	1	1	1	1	1	1	12
Mean Snowfall (in.)	trace	0.1	0.0	0.0	0.0	0.0	0.0	0.0	0.0	0.0	0.0	0.0	0.1
Days With ≥ 1.0" Snow Depth	0	0	0	0	0	0	0	0	0	0	0	0	0

Texarkana *Bowie County* Elevation: 387 ft. Latitude: 33° 25' N Longitude: 94° 05' W

	JAN	FEB	MAR	APR	MAY	JUN	JUL	AUG	SEP	OCT	NOV	DEC	YEAR
Mean Maximum Temp. (°F)	52.9	58.7	66.9	75.2	81.9	89.1	93.2	93.1	86.5	76.6	64.6	56.7	74.6
Mean Temp. (°F)	42.4	47.1	55.0	63.2	71.2	78.8	82.6	82.0	75.4	64.6	53.4	46.0	63.5
Mean Minimum Temp. (°F)	31.8	35.5	43.0	51.1	60.5	68.6	72.0	70.8	64.2	52.5	42.1	35.3	52.3
Extreme Maximum Temp. (°F)	81	90	89	95	98	101	105	105	104	94	86	80	105
Extreme Minimum Temp. (°F)	3	8	15	28	40	52	57	55	38	27	16	-6	-6
Days Maximum Temp. ≥ 90°F	0	0	0	0	3	16	25	24	12	1	0	0	81
Days Maximum Temp. ≤ 32°F	2	1	0	0	0	0	0	0	0	0	0	0	3
Days Minimum Temp. ≤ 32°F	18	11	4	1	0	0	0	0	0	0	5	13	52
Days Minimum Temp. ≤ 0°F	0	0	0	0	0	0	0	0	0	0	0	0	0
Heating Degree Days (base 65°F)	697	503	321	118	17	0	0	0	11	103	356	585	2,711
Cooling Degree Days (base 65°F)	1	3	18	70	219	430	564	547	334	97	14	4	2,301
Mean Precipitation (in.)	3.92	3.87	4.59	4.19	4.83	4.73	3.63	2.77	3.71	4.73	5.28	4.76	51.01
Days With ≥ 0.1" Precipitation	7	6	6	6	7	6	5	4	5	6	6	6	70
Days With ≥ 1.0" Precipitation	1	1	1	1	2	1	1	1	1	2	2	2	16
Mean Snowfall (in.)	0.3	0.3	trace	0.0	0.0	0.0	0.0	0.0	0.0	0.0	0.0	trace	0.6
Days With ≥ 1.0" Snow Depth	0	0	0	0	0	0	0	0	0	0	0	0	0

Thompsons 3 WSW *Fort Bend County* Elevation: 68 ft. Latitude: 29° 29' N Longitude: 95° 38' W

	JAN	FEB	MAR	APR	MAY	JUN	JUL	AUG	SEP	OCT	NOV	DEC	YEAR
Mean Maximum Temp. (°F)	61.8	65.5	72.6	79.1	85.4	90.9	93.3	93.8	89.6	82.3	72.5	65.3	79.3
Mean Temp. (°F)	51.9	55.2	62.4	68.8	75.6	81.2	83.3	83.5	79.4	70.8	62.0	55.0	69.1
Mean Minimum Temp. (°F)	42.3	45.1	52.2	58.5	65.6	71.4	73.2	73.1	68.9	59.5	51.6	44.9	58.9
Extreme Maximum Temp. (°F)	85	88	92	*94*	*96*	101	*102*	104	100	95	*91*	85	*104*
Extreme Minimum Temp. (°F)	14	20	22	35	46	45	64	60	51	32	21	8	8
Days Maximum Temp. ≥ 90°F	0	0	0	1	6	21	26	27	18	4	0	0	103
Days Maximum Temp. ≤ 32°F	0	0	0	0	0	0	0	0	0	0	0	0	0
Days Minimum Temp. ≤ 32°F	5	3	1	0	0	0	0	0	0	0	1	3	13
Days Minimum Temp. ≤ 0°F	0	0	0	0	0	0	0	0	0	0	0	0	0
Heating Degree Days (base 65°F)	412	290	138	37	2	0	0	0	1	29	163	329	1,401
Cooling Degree Days (base 65°F)	11	21	65	159	352	510	*589*	598	447	226	87	31	*3,096*
Mean Precipitation (in.)	4.00	2.63	3.08	3.37	4.50	4.78	3.38	4.23	5.39	3.61	4.03	3.35	46.35
Days With ≥ 0.1" Precipitation	6	5	5	4	5	6	5	6	6	5	4	5	62
Days With ≥ 1.0" Precipitation	1	1	1	1	2	1	1	1	2	1	1	1	14
Mean Snowfall (in.)	trace	trace	0.0	0.0	0.0	0.0	0.0	0.0	0.0	0.0	0.0	0.0	trace
Days With ≥ 1.0" Snow Depth	0	0	0	0	0	0	0	0	0	0	0	0	0

Throckmorton *Throckmorton County* Elevation: 1,368 ft. Latitude: 33° 11' N Longitude: 99° 11' W

	JAN	FEB	MAR	APR	MAY	JUN	JUL	AUG	SEP	OCT	NOV	DEC	YEAR
Mean Maximum Temp. (°F)	53.7	59.1	67.8	76.1	83.4	91.4	96.1	95.1	87.4	77.7	65.0	56.5	75.8
Mean Temp. (°F)	40.8	45.9	54.3	62.6	70.9	79.1	83.5	82.4	75.0	64.5	52.3	43.8	62.9
Mean Minimum Temp. (°F)	27.8	32.7	40.7	49.1	58.3	66.8	70.8	69.7	62.5	51.2	39.6	31.0	50.0
Extreme Maximum Temp. (°F)	85	96	99	101	111	114	111	108	108	105	91	86	114
Extreme Minimum Temp. (°F)	1	-5	5	21	35	49	56	54	36	20	13	-11	-11
Days Maximum Temp. ≥ 90°F	0	0	1	2	7	19	27	26	15	3	0	0	100
Days Maximum Temp. ≤ 32°F	3	2	0	0	0	0	0	0	0	0	1	1	6
Days Minimum Temp. ≤ 32°F	21	13	6	1	0	0	0	0	0	0	7	18	66
Days Minimum Temp. ≤ 0°F	0	0	0	0	0	0	0	0	0	0	0	0	0
Heating Degree Days (base 65°F)	744	535	345	139	26	1	0	0	20	109	386	651	2,956
Cooling Degree Days (base 65°F)	0	3	18	70	218	431	588	566	336	103	13	1	2,347
Mean Precipitation (in.)	0.98	1.49	1.55	2.17	3.30	3.20	1.74	2.64	3.48	2.87	1.45	1.47	26.34
Days With ≥ 0.1" Precipitation	2	3	3	4	5	5	3	3	5	4	3	3	43
Days With ≥ 1.0" Precipitation	0	0	0	1	1	1	1	1	1	1	0	0	7
Mean Snowfall (in.)	1.1	1.2	0.3	trace	0.0	0.0	0.0	0.0	0.0	trace	0.5	0.6	3.7
Days With ≥ 1.0" Snow Depth	1	1	0	0	0	0	0	0	0	0	0	1	3

Tilden 4 SSE *McMullen County* Elevation: 344 ft. Latitude: 28° 25' N Longitude: 98° 32' W

	JAN	FEB	MAR	APR	MAY	JUN	JUL	AUG	SEP	OCT	NOV	DEC	YEAR
Mean Maximum Temp. (°F)	65.3	70.3	78.0	84.3	89.7	95.0	97.9	98.3	93.3	85.4	75.3	68.2	83.4
Mean Temp. (°F)	52.9	57.5	64.9	71.5	78.1	83.1	85.4	85.4	80.9	72.5	62.8	55.8	70.9
Mean Minimum Temp. (°F)	40.5	44.6	51.8	58.7	66.4	71.3	72.8	72.6	68.5	59.4	50.2	43.3	58.3
Extreme Maximum Temp. (°F)	95	100	104	108	109	113	109	107	106	103	96	92	113
Extreme Minimum Temp. (°F)	16	19	20	33	43	54	57	60	44	26	24	5	5
Days Maximum Temp. ≥ 90°F	0	1	3	8	16	26	30	30	24	11	1	0	150
Days Maximum Temp. ≤ 32°F	0	0	0	0	0	0	0	0	0	0	0	0	0
Days Minimum Temp. ≤ 32°F	6	3	1	0	0	0	0	0	0	0	0	0	0
Days Minimum Temp. ≤ 0°F	0	0	0	0	0	0	0	0	0	0	1	4	15
Heating Degree Days (base 65°F)	381	241	104	27	2	0	0	0	1	25	150	310	1,241
Cooling Degree Days (base 65°F)	13	38	103	229	432	571	660	657	497	277	97	31	3,605
Mean Precipitation (in.)	1.19	1.29	1.31	1.93	3.29	3.26	1.59	2.62	3.01	1.99	1.25	1.18	23.91
Days With ≥ 0.1" Precipitation	3	3	2	3	5	4	3	3	4	3	2	2	37
Days With ≥ 1.0" Precipitation	0	0	0	1	1	1	0	1	1	0	0	0	5
Mean Snowfall (in.)	0.0	trace	0.0	0.0	0.0	0.0	0.0	0.0	0.0	trace	0.0	0.0	trace
Days With ≥ 1.0" Snow Depth	0	0	0	0	0	0	0	0	0	0	0	0	0

Toledo Bend Dam *Newton County* Elevation: 187 ft. Latitude: 31° 11' N Longitude: 93° 34' W

	JAN	FEB	MAR	APR	MAY	JUN	JUL	AUG	SEP	OCT	NOV	DEC	YEAR
Mean Maximum Temp. (°F)	56.1	60.9	68.6	75.9	83.4	89.6	93.1	92.6	87.5	78.1	67.6	59.8	76.1
Mean Temp. (°F)	45.8	49.9	57.2	64.2	72.1	78.6	81.8	81.3	76.1	65.7	56.3	49.0	64.8
Mean Minimum Temp. (°F)	35.4	39.0	45.7	52.4	60.9	67.7	70.5	70.0	64.6	53.1	44.9	38.1	53.5
Extreme Maximum Temp. (°F)	79	86	88	92	100	104	108	109	100	94	85	83	109
Extreme Minimum Temp. (°F)	9	12	14	30	40	50	58	54	42	30	20	7	7
Days Maximum Temp. ≥ 90°F	0	0	0	0	4	17	25	24	14	1	0	0	85
Days Maximum Temp. ≤ 32°F	0	0	0	0	0	0	0	0	0	0	0	0	0
Days Minimum Temp. ≤ 32°F	14	9	3	0	0	0	0	0	0	0	0	0	0
Days Minimum Temp. ≤ 0°F	0	0	0	0	0	0	0	0	0	0	4	11	41
Heating Degree Days (base 65°F)	592	428	263	99	10	0	0	0	7	88	282	500	2,269
Cooling Degree Days (base 65°F)	3	9	28	80	242	418	530	518	346	121	27	10	2,332
Mean Precipitation (in.)	5.74	4.58	4.78	3.84	4.77	5.32	3.70	3.50	3.64	4.27	4.75	5.62	54.51
Days With ≥ 0.1" Precipitation	7	6	6	5	6	6	6	6	5	5	6	7	71
Days With ≥ 1.0" Precipitation	2	1	2	1	2	2	1	1	1	1	2	2	18
Mean Snowfall (in.)	trace	trace	0.0	0.0	0.0	0.0	0.0	0.0	0.0	0.0	0.0	trace	trace
Days With ≥ 1.0" Snow Depth	0	0	0	0	0	0	0	0	0	0	0	0	0

Town Bluff Dam *Tyler County* Elevation: 213 ft. Latitude: 30° 48' N Longitude: 94° 11' W

	JAN	FEB	MAR	APR	MAY	JUN	JUL	AUG	SEP	OCT	NOV	DEC	YEAR
Mean Maximum Temp. (°F)	58.3	63.6	70.5	77.1	83.5	89.2	92.2	92.5	87.9	79.3	69.0	62.0	77.1
Mean Temp. (°F)	47.8	52.0	59.3	65.9	73.2	79.1	81.8	81.6	77.2	67.3	58.1	51.1	66.2
Mean Minimum Temp. (°F)	37.3	40.5	48.1	54.7	62.8	69.0	71.3	70.6	66.4	55.4	47.1	40.2	55.3
Extreme Maximum Temp. (°F)	82	89	90	93	99	102	105	106	103	95	87	84	106
Extreme Minimum Temp. (°F)	11	16	21	29	42	50	57	54	45	28	23	6	6
Days Maximum Temp. ≥ 90°F	0	0	0	0	3	16	25	24	14	1	0	0	83
Days Maximum Temp. ≤ 32°F	0	0	0	0	0	0	0	0	0	0	0	0	0
Days Minimum Temp. ≤ 32°F	11	7	2	0	0	0	0	0	0	0	0	0	0
Days Minimum Temp. ≤ 0°F	0	0	0	0	0	0	0	0	0	0	3	9	32
Heating Degree Days (base 65°F)	532	372	208	73	6	0	0	0	3	64	242	437	1,937
Cooling Degree Days (base 65°F)	4	14	40	103	272	435	528	528	375	143	41	14	2,497
Mean Precipitation (in.)	5.20	4.10	4.54	4.39	5.68	5.59	3.48	3.48	4.12	3.93	4.76	5.54	54.81
Days With ≥ 0.1" Precipitation	7	5	6	5	7	7	6	6	6	5	5	6	71
Days With ≥ 1.0" Precipitation	2	1	1	1	2	2	1	1	1	1	2	2	17
Mean Snowfall (in.)	trace	0.0	0.0	0.0	0.0	0.0	0.0	0.0	0.0	0.0	0.0	trace	trace
Days With ≥ 1.0" Snow Depth	0	0	0	0	0	0	0	0	0	0	0	0	0

Truscott 3 W *Knox County* Elevation: 1,568 ft. Latitude: 33° 45' N Longitude: 99° 52' W

	JAN	FEB	MAR	APR	MAY	JUN	JUL	AUG	SEP	OCT	NOV	DEC	YEAR
Mean Maximum Temp. (°F)	53.0	58.3	67.1	76.7	84.6	92.9	97.3	95.5	87.4	77.8	64.6	55.8	75.9
Mean Temp. (°F)	40.0	44.9	53.0	62.6	71.3	80.0	84.3	82.6	74.9	64.2	51.4	42.7	62.7
Mean Minimum Temp. (°F)	26.9	31.5	38.9	48.4	58.0	67.1	71.3	69.6	62.3	50.5	38.2	29.7	49.4
Extreme Maximum Temp. (°F)	84	93	102	104	107	118	113	108	107	106	89	85	118
Extreme Minimum Temp. (°F)	0	-6	6	21	37	49	54	55	38	27	14	-10	-10
Days Maximum Temp. ≥ 90°F	0	0	1	4	10	21	28	25	15	4	0	0	108
Days Maximum Temp. ≤ 32°F	3	2	0	0	0	0	0	0	0	0	0	2	7
Days Minimum Temp. ≤ 32°F	23	14	6	1	0	0	0	0	0	0	8	19	71
Days Minimum Temp. ≤ 0°F	0	0	0	0	0	0	0	0	0	0	0	0	0
Heating Degree Days (base 65°F)	770	562	379	140	26	1	0	0	21	110	406	686	3,101
Cooling Degree Days (base 65°F)	1	2	14	70	232	453	609	573	336	92	8	0	2,390
Mean Precipitation (in.)	0.94	1.44	1.60	1.90	4.21	3.14	1.76	2.51	3.35	2.58	1.19	0.91	25.53
Days With ≥ 0.1" Precipitation	2	3	3	3	6	4	3	4	5	3	2	2	40
Days With ≥ 1.0" Precipitation	0	0	0	0	1	1	0	1	1	1	0	0	5
Mean Snowfall (in.)	0.7	0.2	trace	0.0	0.0	0.0	0.0	0.0	0.0	0.0	trace	0.3	1.2
Days With ≥ 1.0" Snow Depth	0	0	0	0	0	0	0	0	0	0	0	0	0

Tulia *Swisher County*   Elevation: 3,467 ft.   Latitude: 34° 32' N   Longitude: 101° 46' W

	JAN	FEB	MAR	APR	MAY	JUN	JUL	AUG	SEP	OCT	NOV	DEC	YEAR
Mean Maximum Temp. (°F)	50.3	55.6	63.6	72.3	80.0	88.5	91.2	89.0	82.5	73.4	60.6	52.0	71.6
Mean Temp. (°F)	36.2	40.7	47.7	56.3	65.4	74.3	77.9	76.0	69.2	58.6	46.2	38.1	57.2
Mean Minimum Temp. (°F)	22.1	25.8	31.8	40.3	50.6	60.1	64.4	63.0	55.9	43.8	31.7	24.1	42.8
Extreme Maximum Temp. (°F)	82	86	94	98	103	110	105	102	104	98	87	79	110
Extreme Minimum Temp. (°F)	-3	-6	7	19	28	44	50	52	32	16	-3	-4	-6
Days Maximum Temp. ≥ 90°F	0	0	0	1	5	15	21	17	9	1	0	0	69
Days Maximum Temp. ≤ 32°F	4	2	1	0	0	0	0	0	0	0	1	3	11
Days Minimum Temp. ≤ 32°F	29	22	16	5	0	0	0	0	0	3	16	27	118
Days Minimum Temp. ≤ 0°F	0	0	0	0	0	0	0	0	0	0	0	1	1
Heating Degree Days (base 65°F)	885	679	530	274	84	8	0	1	52	219	560	828	4,120
Cooling Degree Days (base 65°F)	0	0	1	18	100	287	410	359	185	26	0	0	1,386
Mean Precipitation (in.)	0.59	0.72	1.04	1.29	3.00	3.14	2.24	2.66	2.41	1.59	0.82	0.73	20.23
Days With ≥ 0.1" Precipitation	2	2	2	3	5	5	4	5	4	3	2	2	39
Days With ≥ 1.0" Precipitation	0	0	0	0	1	1	1	1	0	0	0	0	4
Mean Snowfall (in.)	3.8	4.0	1.3	0.4	0.0	0.0	0.0	0.0	0.0	0.3	1.7	3.5	15.0
Days With ≥ 1.0" Snow Depth	3	2	1	0	0	0	0	0	0	0	0	1	2	9

Turkey *Hall County*   Elevation: 2,329 ft.   Latitude: 34° 24' N   Longitude: 100° 54' W

	JAN	FEB	MAR	APR	MAY	JUN	JUL	AUG	SEP	OCT	NOV	DEC	YEAR
Mean Maximum Temp. (°F)	53.9	60.2	68.5	77.2	84.2	91.8	95.6	93.8	86.2	77.6	64.8	55.9	75.8
Mean Temp. (°F)	40.7	46.0	53.6	62.2	70.6	78.5	82.7	81.0	73.5	63.6	51.4	43.0	62.2
Mean Minimum Temp. (°F)	27.5	31.9	38.6	47.2	56.9	65.3	69.7	68.2	60.8	49.7	38.1	29.9	48.6
Extreme Maximum Temp. (°F)	84	93	99	102	107	115	110	108	106	100	92	82	115
Extreme Minimum Temp. (°F)	1	-1	7	22	35	46	55	53	35	20	11	-3	-3
Days Maximum Temp. ≥ 90°F	0	0	1	3	8	19	27	25	12	3	0	0	98
Days Maximum Temp. ≤ 32°F	3	1	0	0	0	0	0	0	0	0	0	1	5
Days Minimum Temp. ≤ 32°F	21	14	7	1	0	0	0	0	0	1	8	18	70
Days Minimum Temp. ≤ 0°F	0	0	0	0	0	0	0	0	0	0	0	0	0
Heating Degree Days (base 65°F)	744	530	364	145	28	1	0	0	25	121	405	676	3,039
Cooling Degree Days (base 65°F)	0	2	12	64	200	394	553	507	294	78	7	0	2,111
Mean Precipitation (in.)	0.64	1.03	1.26	1.78	3.06	3.50	2.19	2.55	2.79	1.54	0.94	0.84	22.12
Days With ≥ 0.1" Precipitation	2	2	2	3	5	6	3	5	4	3	2	2	39
Days With ≥ 1.0" Precipitation	0	0	0	0	1	1	1	1	1	0	0	0	5
Mean Snowfall (in.)	3.2	2.4	0.3	trace	0.0	0.0	0.0	0.0	0.0	0.1	0.9	1.5	8.4
Days With ≥ 1.0" Snow Depth	2	2	0	0	0	0	0	0	0	0	1	1	6

Vernon *Wilbarger County*   Elevation: 1,227 ft.   Latitude: 34° 09' N   Longitude: 99° 20' W

	JAN	FEB	MAR	APR	MAY	JUN	JUL	AUG	SEP	OCT	NOV	DEC	YEAR
Mean Maximum Temp. (°F)	53.7	59.7	68.6	76.8	84.7	92.7	97.8	96.0	88.0	78.3	65.1	56.2	76.5
Mean Temp. (°F)	40.5	45.8	54.2	62.6	71.8	80.1	84.9	83.2	75.5	64.6	52.0	43.0	63.2
Mean Minimum Temp. (°F)	27.1	31.8	39.8	48.4	58.8	67.5	72.1	70.4	63.0	50.9	38.8	29.7	49.9
Extreme Maximum Temp. (°F)	86	93	103	102	106	118	113	109	107	105	90	85	118
Extreme Minimum Temp. (°F)	-4	3	12	23	36	49	57	54	35	21	16	-9	-9
Days Maximum Temp. ≥ 90°F	0	0	1	2	9	21	28	26	15	3	0	0	105
Days Maximum Temp. ≤ 32°F	2	1	0	0	0	0	0	0	0	0	0	2	5
Days Minimum Temp. ≤ 32°F	23	14	6	1	0	0	0	0	0	1	8	21	74
Days Minimum Temp. ≤ 0°F	0	0	0	0	0	0	0	0	0	0	0	0	0
Heating Degree Days (base 65°F)	754	537	344	137	19	0	0	0	17	105	393	675	2,981
Cooling Degree Days (base 65°F)	0	2	13	60	228	451	618	580	338	94	8	0	2,392
Mean Precipitation (in.)	1.09	1.33	2.01	2.35	4.10	3.64	1.92	3.10	3.66	2.50	1.27	1.09	28.06
Days With ≥ 0.1" Precipitation	2	3	4	4	5	4	3	4	4	4	3	2	42
Days With ≥ 1.0" Precipitation	0	0	1	1	1	1	1	1	1	1	0	0	8
Mean Snowfall (in.)	1.6	0.8	0.2	0.0	0.0	0.0	0.0	0.0	0.0	trace	0.1	trace	2.7
Days With ≥ 1.0" Snow Depth	*0*	*0*	0	0	0	0	0	0	0	0	0	0	*0*

Waco Dam *McLennan County*   Elevation: 492 ft.   Latitude: 31° 36' N   Longitude: 97° 13' W

	JAN	FEB	MAR	APR	MAY	JUN	JUL	AUG	SEP	OCT	NOV	DEC	YEAR
Mean Maximum Temp. (°F)	*55.5*	*61.0*	69.2	76.7	83.0	90.5	95.1	95.2	89.0	*79.1*	67.6	59.4	*76.8*
Mean Temp. (°F)	*44.0*	*49.2*	57.5	65.3	72.9	80.4	84.5	84.1	77.5	*67.2*	56.2	47.8	*65.6*
Mean Minimum Temp. (°F)	*32.5*	37.4	45.6	53.7	62.8	70.3	73.8	73.0	66.0	*55.0*	*44.9*	36.2	*54.3*
Extreme Maximum Temp. (°F)	86	97	96	94	98	109	109	107	107	100	89	84	109
Extreme Minimum Temp. (°F)	6	4	15	28	42	54	56	55	41	26	17	-4	-4
Days Maximum Temp. ≥ 90°F	0	0	0	1	4	19	26	26	15	3	0	0	94
Days Maximum Temp. ≤ 32°F	1	1	0	0	0	0	0	0	0	0	0	1	3
Days Minimum Temp. ≤ 32°F	15	8	3	0	0	0	0	0	0	0	3	10	39
Days Minimum Temp. ≤ 0°F	0	0	0	0	0	0	0	0	0	0	0	0	0
Heating Degree Days (base 65°F)	*644*	*445*	253	82	11	0	0	0	8	*69*	*283*	528	*2,323*
Cooling Degree Days (base 65°F)	*0*	*4*	27	93	268	471	622	617	394	*145*	*30*	3	*2,674*
Mean Precipitation (in.)	2.02	2.63	2.89	3.05	4.60	3.19	2.55	2.10	3.38	3.77	2.69	2.78	35.65
Days With ≥ 0.1" Precipitation	4	4	5	4	6	5	3	3	4	5	4	4	51
Days With ≥ 1.0" Precipitation	0	1	1	1	1	1	1	1	1	1	1	1	11
Mean Snowfall (in.)	trace	*trace*	trace	0.0	0.0	0.0	0.0	0.0	0.0	0.0	0.0	trace	*trace*
Days With ≥ 1.0" Snow Depth	*0*	0	0	0	0	0	0	0	0	0	0	0	*0*

Water Valley *Tom Green County*   Elevation: 2,119 ft.   Latitude: 31° 40' N   Longitude: 100° 44' W

	JAN	FEB	MAR	APR	MAY	JUN	JUL	AUG	SEP	OCT	NOV	DEC	YEAR
Mean Maximum Temp. (°F)	58.2	63.4	71.4	79.6	86.1	91.4	94.8	93.5	87.1	79.0	68.3	60.0	77.7
Mean Temp. (°F)	43.1	47.8	55.7	63.8	72.0	78.7	82.0	80.6	74.2	64.5	53.2	45.0	63.4
Mean Minimum Temp. (°F)	27.9	32.1	39.8	48.0	57.8	65.8	69.1	67.7	61.3	49.9	38.0	29.9	48.9
Extreme Maximum Temp. (°F)	87	97	97	101	107	112	109	106	105	102	90	85	112
Extreme Minimum Temp. (°F)	3	5	5	19	35	46	54	51	33	23	10	-4	-4
Days Maximum Temp. ≥ 90°F	0	0	1	5	11	19	26	25	13	3	0	0	103
Days Maximum Temp. ≤ 32°F	2	1	0	0	0	0	0	0	0	0	0	1	4
Days Minimum Temp. ≤ 32°F	22	15	7	2	0	0	0	0	0	0	1	10	76
Days Minimum Temp. ≤ 0°F	0	0	0	0	0	0	0	0	0	0	0	0	0
Heating Degree Days (base 65°F)	673	482	301	117	20	1	0	0	17	104	357	615	2,687
Cooling Degree Days (base 65°F)	0	3	16	87	256	426	549	513	310	98	10	0	2,268
Mean Precipitation (in.)	0.69	1.15	1.07	1.59	3.16	2.81	1.51	2.90	3.23	2.50	0.95	1.01	22.57
Days With ≥ 0.1" Precipitation	2	2	2	3	5	4	3	4	4	3	2	2	36
Days With ≥ 1.0" Precipitation	0	0	0	1	1	1	0	1	1	1	0	0	6
Mean Snowfall (in.)	1.1	trace	0.3	trace	0.0	0.0	0.0	0.0	0.0	0.0	0.4	trace	1.8
Days With ≥ 1.0" Snow Depth	0	0	0	0	0	0	0	0	0	0	0	0	0

Waxahachie *Ellis County*   Elevation: 629 ft.   Latitude: 32° 25' N   Longitude: 96° 51' W

	JAN	FEB	MAR	APR	MAY	JUN	JUL	AUG	SEP	OCT	NOV	DEC	YEAR
Mean Maximum Temp. (°F)	56.7	62.4	70.3	77.5	84.1	91.5	96.0	95.8	89.2	80.0	67.7	59.5	77.6
Mean Temp. (°F)	45.7	50.8	58.5	65.9	73.3	80.5	84.6	84.1	77.8	68.0	56.7	48.8	66.2
Mean Minimum Temp. (°F)	34.7	39.2	46.6	54.2	62.4	69.4	73.1	72.3	66.4	55.9	45.7	38.0	54.8
Extreme Maximum Temp. (°F)	84	96	94	95	103	114	109	109	109	106	91	83	114
Extreme Minimum Temp. (°F)	5	7	13	28	43	52	59	55	43	24	17	-4	-4
Days Maximum Temp. ≥ 90°F	0	0	0	1	5	21	29	27	17	3	0	0	103
Days Maximum Temp. ≤ 32°F	1	1	0	0	0	0	0	0	0	0	0	1	3
Days Minimum Temp. ≤ 32°F	13	8	3	0	0	0	0	0	0	0	3	9	36
Days Minimum Temp. ≤ 0°F	0	0	0	0	0	0	0	0	0	0	0	0	0
Heating Degree Days (base 65°F)	594	402	231	72	8	0	0	0	6	58	272	502	2,145
Cooling Degree Days (base 65°F)	1	8	31	100	271	471	616	607	396	152	30	5	2,688
Mean Precipitation (in.)	2.09	2.96	3.25	3.96	4.70	3.11	2.29	2.31	3.38	4.49	2.82	3.18	38.54
Days With ≥ 0.1" Precipitation	4	5	5	5	6	5	4	3	5	5	5	5	57
Days With ≥ 1.0" Precipitation	1	1	1	1	2	1	1	1	1	1	1	1	13
Mean Snowfall (in.)	trace	0.2	0.0	0.0	0.0	0.0	0.0	0.0	0.0	0.0	trace	trace	0.2
Days With ≥ 1.0" Snow Depth	0	0	0	0	0	0	0	0	0	0	0	0	0

Weatherford *Parker County*   Elevation: 954 ft.   Latitude: 32° 45' N   Longitude: 97° 46' W

	JAN	FEB	MAR	APR	MAY	JUN	JUL	AUG	SEP	OCT	NOV	DEC	YEAR
Mean Maximum Temp. (°F)	53.7	59.2	67.5	75.8	82.6	90.3	95.2	95.1	87.8	78.1	65.6	57.5	75.7
Mean Temp. (°F)	41.2	46.5	54.4	62.8	70.9	78.8	83.3	82.6	75.4	64.6	52.9	44.8	63.2
Mean Minimum Temp. (°F)	28.6	33.8	41.2	49.7	59.3	67.2	71.3	70.0	63.0	51.2	40.2	32.0	50.6
Extreme Maximum Temp. (°F)	85	95	96	97	101	119	109	114	107	101	92	83	119
Extreme Minimum Temp. (°F)	2	-1	9	24	36	48	54	55	36	20	13	-10	-10
Days Maximum Temp. ≥ 90°F	0	0	0	1	5	18	27	26	15	3	0	0	95
Days Maximum Temp. ≤ 32°F	2	1	0	0	0	0	0	0	0	0	0	1	4
Days Minimum Temp. ≤ 32°F	20	13	6	1	0	0	0	0	0	0	0	1	66
Days Minimum Temp. ≤ 0°F	0	0	0	0	0	0	0	0	0	1	8	17	0
Heating Degree Days (base 65°F)	733	519	340	130	25	1	0	0	17	106	369	620	2,860
Cooling Degree Days (base 65°F)	0	2	14	66	221	422	577	569	341	100	14	1	2,327
Mean Precipitation (in.)	1.47	2.46	2.79	2.81	4.77	3.56	2.13	2.68	3.03	4.05	2.50	2.09	34.34
Days With ≥ 0.1" Precipitation	3	4	5	4	6	5	3	4	4	5	4	4	51
Days With ≥ 1.0" Precipitation	0	1	1	1	2	1	1	1	1	1	1	0	11
Mean Snowfall (in.)	trace	0.5	0.3	0.0	0.0	0.0	0.0	0.0	0.0	0.0	0.2	0.3	1.3
Days With ≥ 1.0" Snow Depth	0	0	0	0	0	0	0	0	0	0	0	0	0

Wellington *Collingsworth County*   Elevation: 2,037 ft.   Latitude: 34° 50' N   Longitude: 100° 13' W

	JAN	FEB	MAR	APR	MAY	JUN	JUL	AUG	SEP	OCT	NOV	DEC	YEAR
Mean Maximum Temp. (°F)	52.4	57.3	66.7	76.6	83.2	91.5	96.3	94.5	87.2	77.0	63.5	54.4	75.1
Mean Temp. (°F)	39.0	43.6	51.8	61.3	69.6	78.2	82.9	81.3	74.0	62.9	50.0	41.4	61.3
Mean Minimum Temp. (°F)	25.5	29.9	36.9	45.9	56.0	64.9	69.3	68.1	60.8	48.8	36.5	28.3	47.6
Extreme Maximum Temp. (°F)	85	93	100	102	107	113	112	108	108	100	89	84	113
Extreme Minimum Temp. (°F)	-3	0	6	23	36	47	56	54	37	20	13	-6	-6
Days Maximum Temp. ≥ 90°F	0	0	1	3	7	19	27	25	14	2	0	0	98
Days Maximum Temp. ≤ 32°F	3	2	0	0	0	0	0	0	0	0	0	2	7
Days Minimum Temp. ≤ 32°F	25	16	9	1	0	0	0	0	0	0	0	1	84
Days Minimum Temp. ≤ 0°F	0	0	0	0	0	0	0	0	0	1	11	21	0
Heating Degree Days (base 65°F)	800	598	410	159	33	1	0	0	19	124	446	726	3,316
Cooling Degree Days (base 65°F)	0	1	9	55	195	416	574	535	311	69	5	0	2,170
Mean Precipitation (in.)	0.64	0.69	1.35	1.97	3.92	3.24	2.19	1.92	2.74	2.19	0.85	0.57	22.27
Days With ≥ 0.1" Precipitation	2	1	2	2	5	4	3	3	4	3	2	1	32
Days With ≥ 1.0" Precipitation	0	0	0	1	1	1	1	0	1	1	0	0	6
Mean Snowfall (in.)	1.8	1.9	0.4	0.0	0.0	0.0	0.0	0.0	0.0	0.0	0.5	1.0	5.6
Days With ≥ 1.0" Snow Depth	1	0	0	0	0	0	0	0	0	0	0	1	2

Weslaco 2 E *Hidalgo County*   Elevation: 72 ft.   Latitude: 26° 09' N   Longitude: 97° 58' W

	JAN	FEB	MAR	APR	MAY	JUN	JUL	AUG	SEP	OCT	NOV	DEC	YEAR
Mean Maximum Temp. (°F)	70.0	74.3	81.2	85.4	89.4	93.3	95.4	96.1	92.1	86.7	78.8	72.3	84.6
Mean Temp. (°F)	59.7	63.5	70.2	75.2	80.0	83.8	85.1	85.4	82.1	76.0	68.4	62.0	74.3
Mean Minimum Temp. (°F)	49.4	52.7	59.1	64.8	70.6	74.1	74.7	74.7	72.0	65.1	57.9	51.7	63.9
Extreme Maximum Temp. (°F)	93	98	104	102	105	105	103	103	102	100	99	94	105
Extreme Minimum Temp. (°F)	25	28	30	41	50	59	66	64	56	33	31	16	16
Days Maximum Temp. ≥ 90°F	0	1	4	8	16	26	29	29	22	11	2	0	148
Days Maximum Temp. ≤ 32°F	0	0	0	0	0	0	0	0	0	0	0	0	0
Days Minimum Temp. ≤ 32°F	1	0	0	0	0	0	0	0	0	0	0	1	2
Days Minimum Temp. ≤ 0°F	0	0	0	0	0	0	0	0	0	0	0	0	0
Heating Degree Days (base 65°F)	213	120	42	8	0	0	0	0	0	7	67	174	631
Cooling Degree Days (base 65°F)	53	87	194	313	478	586	647	650	528	358	192	87	4,173
Mean Precipitation (in.)	1.39	1.46	0.97	1.45	2.66	2.93	2.31	2.62	4.93	2.44	1.28	1.15	25.59
Days With ≥ 0.1" Precipitation	3	3	2	2	3	4	3	4	7	4	3	3	41
Days With ≥ 1.0" Precipitation	0	0	0	0	1	1	1	1	1	1	0	0	6
Mean Snowfall (in.)	0.0	trace	0.0	0.0	0.0	0.0	0.0	0.0	0.0	0.0	0.0	0.0	trace
Days With ≥ 1.0" Snow Depth	0	0	0	0	0	0	0	0	0	0	0	0	0

Whitney Dam *Bosque County*   Elevation: 574 ft.   Latitude: 31° 51' N   Longitude: 97° 22' W

	JAN	FEB	MAR	APR	MAY	JUN	JUL	AUG	SEP	OCT	NOV	DEC	YEAR
Mean Maximum Temp. (°F)	56.1	61.3	69.2	76.9	83.9	91.3	96.1	96.1	89.3	79.7	67.5	59.3	77.2
Mean Temp. (°F)	44.3	49.1	57.1	64.9	72.9	80.0	83.9	83.4	77.3	66.9	55.7	47.6	65.3
Mean Minimum Temp. (°F)	32.4	36.8	45.0	52.8	61.8	68.7	71.4	70.7	65.2	54.1	43.9	35.8	53.2
Extreme Maximum Temp. (°F)	83	97	97	97	101	110	109	108	105	101	90	86	110
Extreme Minimum Temp. (°F)	4	7	15	29	42	52	59	56	38	26	16	-3	-3
Days Maximum Temp. ≥ 90°F	0	0	0	1	6	20	28	27	17	4	0	0	103
Days Maximum Temp. ≤ 32°F	1	1	0	0	0	0	0	0	0	0	0	1	3
Days Minimum Temp. ≤ 32°F	17	9	3	0	0	0	0	0	0	0	4	12	45
Days Minimum Temp. ≤ 0°F	0	0	0	0	0	0	0	0	0	0	0	0	0
Heating Degree Days (base 65°F)	637	448	265	89	11	0	0	0	7	71	294	538	2,360
Cooling Degree Days (base 65°F)	2	5	27	94	274	458	600	593	389	137	24	5	2,608
Mean Precipitation (in.)	1.90	2.49	2.85	3.15	4.31	3.59	2.04	2.38	2.90	4.01	2.40	2.65	34.67
Days With ≥ 0.1" Precipitation	4	4	5	5	6	5	3	4	4	5	4	4	53
Days With ≥ 1.0" Precipitation	0	1	1	1	1	1	1	1	1	1	1	1	11
Mean Snowfall (in.)	trace	trace	0.0	0.0	0.0	0.0	0.0	0.0	0.0	0.0	0.0	trace	trace
Days With ≥ 1.0" Snow Depth	0	0	0	0	0	0	0	0	0	0	0	0	0

Wills Point *Van Zandt County*   Elevation: 521 ft.   Latitude: 32° 42' N   Longitude: 96° 01' W

	JAN	FEB	MAR	APR	MAY	JUN	JUL	AUG	SEP	OCT	NOV	DEC	YEAR
Mean Maximum Temp. (°F)	53.2	58.8	66.6	74.6	81.6	88.9	93.8	94.2	87.5	77.5	65.3	56.8	74.9
Mean Temp. (°F)	43.2	48.1	55.6	63.4	71.4	78.7	83.0	82.8	76.4	66.1	54.6	46.6	64.2
Mean Minimum Temp. (°F)	33.0	37.3	44.6	52.1	61.2	68.5	72.1	71.4	65.3	54.5	43.9	36.3	53.4
Extreme Maximum Temp. (°F)	80	93	90	92	98	105	109	108	107	95	86	80	109
Extreme Minimum Temp. (°F)	6	9	17	28	37	50	59	58	42	24	13	-2	-2
Days Maximum Temp. ≥ 90°F	0	0	0	0	2	14	26	25	14	2	0	0	83
Days Maximum Temp. ≤ 32°F	2	1	0	0	0	0	0	0	0	0	0	1	4
Days Minimum Temp. ≤ 32°F	16	9	3	0	0	0	0	0	0	0	4	11	43
Days Minimum Temp. ≤ 0°F	0	0	0	0	0	0	0	0	0	0	0	0	0
Heating Degree Days (base 65°F)	671	476	304	111	15	1	0	0	10	82	324	568	2,562
Cooling Degree Days (base 65°F)	1	5	20	68	225	423	567	573	367	118	20	4	2,391
Mean Precipitation (in.)	3.06	3.33	3.81	3.77	4.75	4.18	2.17	2.34	3.57	4.86	3.91	3.82	43.57
Days With ≥ 0.1" Precipitation	6	5	6	5	6	5	4	4	5	5	5	5	61
Days With ≥ 1.0" Precipitation	1	1	1	1	2	2	1	1	1	1	1	1	14
Mean Snowfall (in.)	0.9	1.0	trace	0.0	0.0	0.0	0.0	0.0	0.0	0.0	trace	0.4	2.3
Days With ≥ 1.0" Snow Depth	1	1	0	0	0	0	0	0	0	0	0	0	2

Wink Winkler Co. Airport *Winkler County*   Elevation: 2,805 ft.   Latitude: 31° 47' N   Longitude: 103° 12' W

	JAN	FEB	MAR	APR	MAY	JUN	JUL	AUG	SEP	OCT	NOV	DEC	YEAR
Mean Maximum Temp. (°F)	59.1	65.4	72.9	81.5	89.3	95.9	96.2	94.6	88.2	80.1	68.7	61.1	79.4
Mean Temp. (°F)	43.6	49.0	56.5	64.8	73.7	81.4	83.1	81.6	75.0	64.9	52.6	45.1	64.3
Mean Minimum Temp. (°F)	28.1	32.6	40.0	48.0	58.1	66.8	69.9	68.5	61.7	49.8	36.7	28.8	49.1
Extreme Maximum Temp. (°F)	87	89	94	102	107	117	111	108	104	102	92	82	117
Extreme Minimum Temp. (°F)	2	-6	9	23	33	45	57	56	33	22	7	2	-6
Days Maximum Temp. ≥ 90°F	0	0	1	7	16	24	27	25	17	5	0	0	122
Days Maximum Temp. ≤ 32°F	1	0	0	0	0	0	0	0	0	0	0	0	1
Days Minimum Temp. ≤ 32°F	21	15	6	1	0	0	0	0	0	1	9	20	73
Days Minimum Temp. ≤ 0°F	0	0	0	0	0	0	0	0	0	0	0	0	0
Heating Degree Days (base 65°F)	657	447	273	95	12	0	0	0	16	92	370	611	2,573
Cooling Degree Days (base 65°F)	0	2	15	92	303	513	586	541	335	105	8	0	2,500
Mean Precipitation (in.)	0.42	0.49	0.38	0.54	1.35	1.87	1.96	1.31	2.22	1.49	0.50	0.57	13.10
Days With ≥ 0.1" Precipitation	1	2	1	1	3	3	3	3	3	2	1	1	24
Days With ≥ 1.0" Precipitation	0	0	0	0	0	0	0	1	0	1	0	0	3
Mean Snowfall (in.)	2.0	0.4	0.3	trace	trace	trace	0.0	0.0	0.0	trace	0.4	0.7	3.8
Days With ≥ 1.0" Snow Depth	1	0	0	0	0	0	0	0	0	0	0	0	1

Winters 1 NNE *Runnels County*   Elevation: 1,860 ft.   Latitude: 31° 58' N   Longitude: 99° 57' W

	JAN	FEB	MAR	APR	MAY	JUN	JUL	AUG	SEP	OCT	NOV	DEC	YEAR
Mean Maximum Temp. (°F)	57.5	62.6	71.0	79.8	86.0	91.9	95.2	94.4	88.0	79.4	67.5	59.8	77.8
Mean Temp. (°F)	43.9	48.8	56.6	65.0	72.9	79.5	82.9	81.9	75.6	66.3	54.4	46.4	64.5
Mean Minimum Temp. (°F)	30.3	34.9	42.2	50.2	59.7	67.1	70.3	69.4	63.2	53.1	41.3	33.0	51.2
Extreme Maximum Temp. (°F)	85	95	95	100	105	109	109	107	107	103	91	84	109
Extreme Minimum Temp. (°F)	-5	6	8	26	37	48	59	54	39	28	15	-5	-5
Days Maximum Temp. ≥ 90°F	0	0	0	4	10	21	27	26	14	3	0	0	105
Days Maximum Temp. ≤ 32°F	1	1	0	0	0	0	0	0	0	0	0	1	3
Days Minimum Temp. ≤ 32°F	18	11	5	1	0	0	0	0	0	0	6	15	56
Days Minimum Temp. ≤ 0°F	0	0	0	0	0	0	0	0	0	0	0	0	0
Heating Degree Days (base 65°F)	647	453	275	91	14	0	0	0	11	74	324	570	2,459
Cooling Degree Days (base 65°F)	0	3	22	100	286	455	580	563	351	133	14	1	2,508
Mean Precipitation (in.)	0.88	1.32	1.66	1.93	3.03	3.35	1.92	1.94	3.74	2.83	1.14	1.09	24.83
Days With ≥ 0.1" Precipitation	2	3	3	3	5	4	3	3	4	4	2	2	38
Days With ≥ 1.0" Precipitation	0	0	0	1	1	1	1	1	1	1	0	0	7
Mean Snowfall (in.)	1.0	0.3	0.3	0.0	0.0	0.0	0.0	0.0	0.0	0.0	0.2	trace	1.8
Days With ≥ 1.0" Snow Depth	1	0	0	0	0	0	0	0	0	0	0	0	1

Yoakum *Lavaca County*   Elevation: 324 ft.   Latitude: 29° 16' N   Longitude: 97° 07' W

	JAN	FEB	MAR	APR	MAY	JUN	JUL	AUG	SEP	OCT	NOV	DEC	YEAR
Mean Maximum Temp. (°F)	62.3	66.9	74.0	80.1	86.0	91.4	94.5	95.3	90.8	83.2	72.8	65.5	80.2
Mean Temp. (°F)	51.2	55.4	62.7	68.9	75.6	81.1	83.3	83.6	79.4	71.0	61.4	54.3	69.0
Mean Minimum Temp. (°F)	40.2	43.9	51.3	57.7	65.2	70.7	72.1	71.9	67.9	58.9	50.0	43.1	57.7
Extreme Maximum Temp. (°F)	89	93	99	97	98	111	104	105	103	97	92	85	111
Extreme Minimum Temp. (°F)	11	16	19	31	44	52	62	62	46	28	20	6	6
Days Maximum Temp. ≥ 90°F	0	0	0	2	8	21	28	29	20	6	0	0	114
Days Maximum Temp. ≤ 32°F	0	0	0	0	0	0	0	0	0	0	0	0	0
Days Minimum Temp. ≤ 32°F	7	4	1	0	0	0	0	0	0	0	1	5	18
Days Minimum Temp. ≤ 0°F	0	0	0	0	0	0	0	0	0	0	0	0	0
Heating Degree Days (base 65°F)	433	286	139	38	1	0	0	0	1	29	172	350	1,449
Cooling Degree Days (base 65°F)	9	17	60	153	340	492	577	587	440	217	70	23	2,985
Mean Precipitation (in.)	2.51	2.27	2.62	3.50	4.99	4.67	2.59	3.48	4.02	4.63	2.88	2.34	40.50
Days With ≥ 0.1" Precipitation	5	4	4	4	5	6	4	5	5	5	4	5	56
Days With ≥ 1.0" Precipitation	1	1	1	1	2	1	1	1	1	1	1	1	13
Mean Snowfall (in.)	trace	trace	0.0	0.0	0.0	0.0	0.0	0.0	0.0	0.0	trace	trace	trace
Days With ≥ 1.0" Snow Depth	0	0	0	0	0	0	0	0	0	0	0	0	0

Ysleta *El Paso County*   Elevation: 3,667 ft.   Latitude: 31° 42' N   Longitude: 106° 19' W

	JAN	FEB	MAR	APR	MAY	JUN	JUL	AUG	SEP	OCT	NOV	DEC	YEAR
Mean Maximum Temp. (°F)	60.2	66.0	73.4	81.1	89.7	98.8	98.6	95.5	90.2	81.3	70.0	na	na
Mean Temp. (°F)	44.7	49.9	56.7	63.9	72.7	81.7	83.5	81.1	75.2	64.8	53.3	na	na
Mean Minimum Temp. (°F)	29.2	33.7	40.0	46.7	55.7	64.5	68.4	66.6	60.2	48.3	36.4	na	na
Extreme Maximum Temp. (°F)	82	85	93	102	109	115	112	110	108	98	88	82	115
Extreme Minimum Temp. (°F)	5	12	15	25	34	46	47	55	44	26	8	8	5
Days Maximum Temp. ≥ 90°F	0	0	0	3	17	28	29	27	19	4	0	0	127
Days Maximum Temp. ≤ 32°F	0	0	0	0	0	0	0	0	0	0	0	0	0
Days Minimum Temp. ≤ 32°F	21	12	4	1	0	0	0	0	0	0	0	0	0
Days Minimum Temp. ≤ 0°F	0	0	0	0	0	0	0	0	0	1	8	15	62
Heating Degree Days (base 65°F)	621	420	259	94	9	0	0	0	8	81	345	na	na
Cooling Degree Days (base 65°F)	0	0	10	80	285	531	604	530	344	93	3	na	na
Mean Precipitation (in.)	0.55	0.44	0.25	0.26	0.46	0.70	1.34	1.77	1.86	0.97	0.44	0.67	9.71
Days With ≥ 0.1" Precipitation	2	1	1	1	1	2	4	4	4	2	1	2	25
Days With ≥ 1.0" Precipitation	0	0	0	0	0	0	0	0	0	0	0	0	0
Mean Snowfall (in.)	trace	trace	0.0	0.0	0.0	0.0	0.0	0.0	0.0	0.0	trace	0.0	trace
Days With ≥ 1.0" Snow Depth	0	0	0	0	0	0	0	0	0	0	0	0	0

Zapata 3 SW *Zapata County*   Elevation: 318 ft.   Latitude: 26° 53' N   Longitude: 99° 18' W

	JAN	FEB	MAR	APR	MAY	JUN	JUL	AUG	SEP	OCT	NOV	DEC	YEAR
Mean Maximum Temp. (°F)	69.5	74.6	83.1	89.0	93.9	97.7	99.1	99.3	94.3	87.2	78.2	70.3	86.4
Mean Temp. (°F)	58.0	62.4	70.0	76.4	82.1	85.9	87.2	87.3	83.0	75.7	66.8	59.3	74.5
Mean Minimum Temp. (°F)	46.3	49.9	56.9	63.8	70.3	74.1	75.1	75.1	71.7	64.2	55.3	48.1	62.6
Extreme Maximum Temp. (°F)	98	101	105	110	114	116	110	110	106	100	98	95	116
Extreme Minimum Temp. (°F)	21	24	30	38	50	50	42	64	52	30	31	15	15
Days Maximum Temp. ≥ 90°F	0	2	7	16	25	28	29	29	25	12	3	0	176
Days Maximum Temp. ≤ 32°F	0	0	0	0	0	0	0	0	0	0	0	0	0
Days Minimum Temp. ≤ 32°F	2	1	0	0	0	0	0	0	0	0	0	2	5
Days Minimum Temp. ≤ 0°F	0	0	0	0	0	0	0	0	0	0	0	0	0
Heating Degree Days (base 65°F)	249	140	44	9	0	0	0	0	1	8	83	217	751
Cooling Degree Days (base 65°F)	35	74	202	350	549	655	723	723	572	359	154	45	4,441
Mean Precipitation (in.)	0.73	1.05	0.79	1.40	2.34	2.73	1.61	1.85	3.89	1.74	0.96	0.86	19.95
Days With ≥ 0.1" Precipitation	2	2	1	2	3	3	3	3	5	3	2	2	31
Days With ≥ 1.0" Precipitation	0	0	0	1	1	0	0	1	1	0	0	4
Mean Snowfall (in.)	trace	trace	0.0	0.0	0.0	0.0	0.0	0.0	0.0	0.0	0.0	trace	trace
Days With ≥ 1.0" Snow Depth	0	0	0	0	0	0	0	0	0	0	0	0	0

Note: See Appendix D for explanation of data.

UTAH

PHYSICAL FEATURES. The topography of Utah is extremely varied, with most of the State being mountainous. A series of mountains (including the Wasatch Range), which runs generally north and south through the middle of Utah, and the Uinta Mountains, which extend east and west through the northeast portion, are the principal ranges. Crest lines of these mountains are mostly above 10,000 feet. Less extensive ranges are scattered over the remainder of the State. The lowest area is the Virgin River Valley in the southwestern part with elevations between 2,500 and 3,500 feet, while the highest point is Kings Peak in the Uinta Mountains (13,498 feet).

Practically all of eastern Utah is drained by the Colorado River and its principal tributary within the State, the Green River, although neither rises within its borders. Western Utah is almost entirely within the Great Basin, with no outlet to the sea. The largest rivers in this area are the Bear, Weber, Jordan, Provo, and Sevier, the first three of which empty into Great Salt Lake. The Sevier River drains the west-central area and empties into Sevier Lake, a brackish saline basin in southwest Utah. The main streams in the eastern portion of the State flow through canyons or very narrow, confined mountain valleys and finally into desert canyons. Highest flow occurs in this region in May and June during spring runoff from melting snow.

Great Salt Lake, in northwestern Utah, lies in the Great Basin, the largest closed basin in North America. Part of this drainage area is below 4,500 feet in elevation, with the Lake being about 4,200 feet. Great Salt Lake is the largest lake at the highest elevation in the world. In glacial times it was a fresh water lake occupying an area 346 miles long and 145 miles wide; due to increased evaporation and/or reduced precipitation, it gradually shrank in size and the salinity increased. Since this large body of water now has no drainage outlet, the salt content is high, averaging about 25 percent. Thus the Lake, which never freezes over, provides a moderating effect throughout the year on temperatures in the immediate vicinity.

GENERAL CLIMATE. Utah's climate is determined by its distance from the equator, its elevation above sea level, the location of the State with respect to the average storm paths over the Intermountain Region, and its distance from the principal moisture sources of the area, namely, the Pacific Ocean and the Gulf of Mexico. Also, the mountain ranges over the western United States, particularly the Sierra Nevada and Cascade Ranges and the Rocky Mountains, have a marked influence on the climate of the State. Pacific storms, before reaching Utah, must first cross the Sierras or Cascades. As the moist air is forced to rise over these high mountains, a large portion of the original moisture falls as precipitation. Thus, the prevailing westerly air currents reaching Utah are comparatively dry, resulting in light precipitation over most of the State.

TEMPERATURE. There are definite variations in temperature with altitude and with latitude. Naturally, the mountains and the elevated valleys have the cooler climates, with the lower areas of the State having the higher temperatures. There is about a 3°F. decrease in mean annual temperature for each 1,000-foot increase in altitude, and approximately 1.5 to 2°F. decrease in average yearly temperature for each one degree increase in latitude.

Temperatures over 100°F. occur occasionally in summer in nearly all parts of the State. However, low humidity makes these high temperatures more bearable than in more humid regions. Temperatures below zero during winter and early spring are uncommon in most areas of the State, and prolonged periods of extremely cold weather are rare. This is primarily due to the mountains east and north of the State, which act as a barrier to intensely cold continental Arctic air masses. Utah experiences relatively strong insolation during the day and rapid nocturnal cooling, resulting in wide daily ranges in temperature. Even after the hottest days, nights are usually cool over the State. On clear nights the colder air accumulates, by drainage, on the valley bottoms, while the foothills and bench areas remain relatively warm.

PRECIPITATION. Precipitation varies greatly, from an average of less than five inches annually over the Great Salt Lake Desert (west of Great Salt Lake), to more than 40 inches in some parts of the Wasatch Mountains. In the mountains, winter snows form the chief reservoirs of moisture. The areas of the State below an elevation of 4,000 feet, all in the southern part, generally receive less than 10 inches of moisture annually.

Northwestern Utah, over and along the mountains, receives appreciably more precipitation in a year than is received at similar elevations over the rest of the State, primarily due to terrain and the direction of normal storm tracks. The bulk of the moisture falling over that area can be attributed to the movement of Pacific storms through the region during the winter and spring months. In summer northwestern Utah is comparatively dry. The eastern portion receives appreciable rain from summer thunderstorms, which are usually associated with moisture-laden air masses from the Gulf of Mexico.

Snowfall is moderately heavy in the mountains, especially over the northern part. A deep snow cover seldom remains long on the ground. Runoff from melting mountain snow usually reaches a peak in April, May or early June, and sometimes causes flooding along the lower streams. However, damaging floods of this kind are infrequent. Flash floods from summer thunderstorms are more frequent, but they affect only small, local areas.

OTHER CLIMATIC ELEMENTS. Sunny skies prevail most of the year in Utah. There is an average of about 65 to 75 percent of the possible amount of sunshine at Salt Lake City during spring, summer, and fall. In winter Salt Lake City has about 50 percent of the possible sunshine.

During the late fall and winter months, anticyclones tend to settle over the Great Basin for as long as several weeks at a time. Under these conditions, smoke and haze accumulate in the lower levels of the stagnant air over the valleys of northwestern Utah, frequently becoming an obstruction to visibility. This is also true of fog which may persist for several weeks at a time.

Wind speeds are usually light to moderate, ranging below 20 miles per hour. There are only a few tornadoes in Utah as a rule, and those reported usually cause only slight damage. However, strong winds occur occasionally, each year sometimes attaining damaging proportions in local areas, particularly in the vicinity of the canyon mouths along the western slopes of the Wasatch Mountains. Duststorms occur occasionally, principally over western Utah. These storms are associated with the movement of low pressure disturbances through the area during the spring months.

Hailstorms may occur in limited areas during spring and summer, although the hail is usually small.

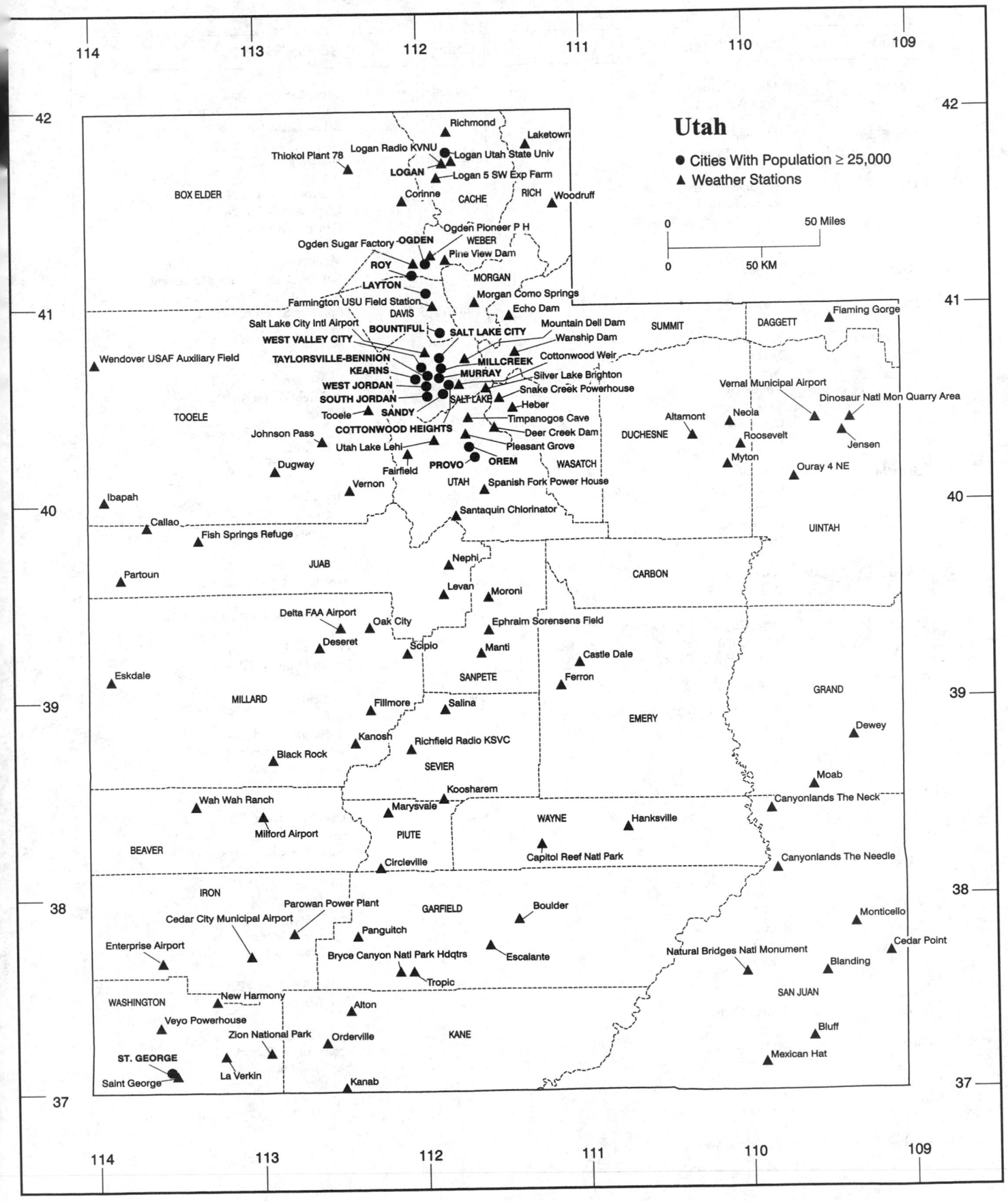

Utah

● Cities With Population ≥ 25,000
▲ Weather Stations

Richmond
Laketown
Thiokol Plant 78
Logan Radio KVNU
Logan Utah State Univ
LOGAN
Logan 5 SW Exp Farm
BOX ELDER
Corinne
CACHE
RICH
Woodruff
Ogden Pioneer P H
WEBER
Ogden Sugar Factory **OGDEN**
Pine View Dam
ROY
MORGAN
LAYTON
Morgan Como Springs
Farmington USU Field Station
Echo Dam
Salt Lake City Intl Airport
DAVIS
BOUNTIFUL
SALT LAKE CITY
Mountain Dell Dam
SUMMIT
DAGGETT
Flaming Gorge
WEST VALLEY CITY
Wanship Dam
Wendover USAF Auxiliary Field
TAYLORSVILLE-BENNION
MILLCREEK
Cottonwood Weir
KEARNS
MURRAY
Silver Lake Brighton
Vernal Municipal Airport
Dinosaur Natl Mon Quarry Area
WEST JORDAN
Snake Creek Powerhouse
SOUTH JORDAN
SALT LAKE
Altamont
Neola
TOOELE
Tooele **SANDY**
Heber
Roosevelt
Jensen
Johnson Pass
COTTONWOOD HEIGHTS
Timpanogos Cave
DUCHESNE
Myton
Ouray 4 NE
Utah Lake Lehi
Deer Creek Dam
Dugway
Fairfield
Pleasant Grove
PROVO
OREM
WASATCH
Ibapah
Vernon
UTAH
Spanish Fork Power House
UINTAH
Callao
Santaquin Chlorinator
Fish Springs Refuge
Nephi
CARBON
Partoun
JUAB
Levan
Moroni
Delta FAA Airport
Oak City
Ephraim Sorensens Field
Deseret
Scipio
Manti
Castle Dale
GRAND
Eskdale
SANPETE
Ferron
Dewey
Fillmore
Salina
MILLARD
EMERY
Kanosh
Richfield Radio KSVC
Black Rock
SEVIER
Moab
Koosharem
Canyonlands The Neck
Wah Wah Ranch
Marysvale
WAYNE
Hanksville
Milford Airport
PIUTE
Canyonlands The Needle
BEAVER
Circleville
Capitol Reef Natl Park
IRON
GARFIELD
Boulder
Monticello
Parowan Power Plant
Cedar City Municipal Airport
Panguitch
Cedar Point
Enterprise Airport
Bryce Canyon Natl Park Hdqtrs
Escalante
Natural Bridges Natl Monument
Blanding
Tropic
New Harmony
WASHINGTON
Alton
SAN JUAN
Veyo Powerhouse
Zion National Park
Orderville
Bluff
KANE
ST. GEORGE
Mexican Hat
Saint George
La Verkin
Kanab

0   50 Miles
0   50 KM

Utah Weather Stations by County

County	Station Name
Beaver	Milford Airport
	Wah Wah Ranch
Box Elder	Corinne
	Thiokol Plant 78
Cache	Logan 5 SW Exp. Farm
	Logan Radio KVNU
	Logan Utah State University
	Richmond
Daggett	Flaming Gorge
Davis	Farmington USU Field Station
Duchesne	Altamont
	Myton
	Neola
	Roosevelt
Emery	Castle Dale
	Ferron
Garfield	Boulder
	Bryce Canyon Nat'l Park Hdqtrs.
	Escalante
	Panguitch
	Tropic
Grand	Dewey
	Moab
Iron	Cedar City Municipal Airport
	Enterprise Airport
	Parowan Power Plant
Juab	Callao
	Fish Springs Refuge
	Levan
	Nephi
	Partoun
Kane	Alton
	Kanab
	Orderville
Millard	Black Rock
	Delta FAA Airport
	Deseret
	Eskdale
	Fillmore
	Kanosh
	Oak City
	Scipio
Morgan	Morgan Como Springs
Piute	Circleville
	Marysvale
Rich	Laketown
	Woodruff
Salt Lake	Cottonwood Weir

County	Station Name
Salt Lake (cont.)	Mountain Dell Dam
	Salt Lake City Int'l Airport
	Silver Lake Brighton
San Juan	Blanding
	Bluff
	Canyonlands The Neck
	Canyonlands The Needle
	Cedar Point
	Mexican Hat
	Monticello
	Natural Bridges Nat'l Monument
Sanpete	Ephraim Sorensens Field
	Manti
	Moroni
Sevier	Koosharem
	Richfield Radio KSVC
	Salina
Summit	Echo Dam
	Wanship Dam
Tooele	Dugway
	Ibapah
	Johnson Pass
	Tooele
	Vernon
	Wendover USAF Auxiliary Field
Uintah	Dinosaur Nat'l Mon. Quarry Area
	Jensen
	Ouray 4 NE
	Vernal Municipal Airport
Utah	Fairfield
	Pleasant Grove
	Santaquin Chlorinator
	Spanish Fork Power House
	Timpanogos Cave
	Utah Lake Lehi
Wasatch	Deer Creek Dam
	Heber
	Snake Creek Powerhouse
Washington	La Verkin
	New Harmony
	Saint George
	Veyo Powerhouse
	Zion National Park
Wayne	Capitol Reef Nat'l Park
	Hanksville
Weber	Ogden Pioneer P H
	Ogden Sugar Factory
	Pine View Dam

Utah Weather Stations by City

City	Station Name	Miles
Bountiful	Cottonwood Weir	19
	Farmington USU Field Station	10
	Morgan Como Springs	16
	Mountain Dell Dam	12
	Salt Lake City Int'l Airport	8
Cottonwood Heights	Cottonwood Weir	2
	Mountain Dell Dam	11
	Pleasant Grove	18
	Salt Lake City Int'l Airport	14
	Silver Lake Brighton	12
	Snake Creek Powerhouse	17
	Timpanogos Cave	13
	Utah Lake Lehi	18
Kearns	Cottonwood Weir	12
	Mountain Dell Dam	17
	Salt Lake City Int'l Airport	9
	Tooele	17
Layton	Farmington USU Field Station	5
	Morgan Como Springs	16
	Ogden Pioneer P H	12
	Ogden Sugar Factory	11
	Pine View Dam	13
Logan	Corinne	19
	Logan Radio KVNU	1
	Logan Utah State University	1
	Logan 5 SW Exp. Farm	6
	Richmond	11
Millcreek	Cottonwood Weir	7
	Mountain Dell Dam	9
	Salt Lake City Int'l Airport	8
	Silver Lake Brighton	16
	Timpanogos Cave	19
Murray	Cottonwood Weir	6
	Mountain Dell Dam	11
	Salt Lake City Int'l Airport	10
	Silver Lake Brighton	17
	Timpanogos Cave	17
	Utah Lake Lehi	20
Ogden	Farmington USU Field Station	15
	Ogden Pioneer P H	1
	Ogden Sugar Factory	4
	Pine View Dam	7
Orem	Deer Creek Dam	11
	Pleasant Grove	5
	Spanish Fork Power House	16
	Timpanogos Cave	10
	Utah Lake Lehi	12
Provo	Deer Creek Dam	12
	Pleasant Grove	9
	Spanish Fork Power House	12
	Timpanogos Cave	14
	Utah Lake Lehi	15
Roy	Farmington USU Field Station	13
	Ogden Pioneer P H	7

City	Station Name	Miles
Roy *(cont.)*	Ogden Sugar Factory	4
	Pine View Dam	12
Salt Lake City	Cottonwood Weir	11
	Farmington USU Field Station	18
	Mountain Dell Dam	8
	Salt Lake City Int'l Airport	5
	Silver Lake Brighton	19
Sandy	Cottonwood Weir	5
	Mountain Dell Dam	14
	Pleasant Grove	16
	Salt Lake City Int'l Airport	16
	Silver Lake Brighton	14
	Snake Creek Powerhouse	19
	Timpanogos Cave	12
	Utah Lake Lehi	14
South Jordan	Cottonwood Weir	10
	Mountain Dell Dam	18
	Pleasant Grove	19
	Salt Lake City Int'l Airport	15
	Silver Lake Brighton	20
	Timpanogos Cave	16
	Tooele	18
	Utah Lake Lehi	14
St. George	La Verkin	19
	Saint George	1
	Veyo Powerhouse	18
Taylorsville-Bennion	Cottonwood Weir	9
	Mountain Dell Dam	14
	Salt Lake City Int'l Airport	9
	Silver Lake Brighton	20
	Timpanogos Cave	19
West Jordan	Cottonwood Weir	9
	Mountain Dell Dam	16
	Salt Lake City Int'l Airport	12
	Silver Lake Brighton	20
	Timpanogos Cave	18
	Tooele	19
	Utah Lake Lehi	17
West Valley City	Cottonwood Weir	12
	Mountain Dell Dam	15
	Salt Lake City Int'l Airport	7
	Tooele	20

Note: Miles is the distance between the geographic center of the city and the weather station.

Utah Weather Stations by Elevation

Feet	Station Name	Feet	Station Name
8,740	Silver Lake Brighton	4,996	Canyonlands The Needle
7,913	Bryce Canyon Nat'l Park Hdqtrs.	4,990	Kanosh
7,037	Alton	4,977	Eskdale
6,929	Koosharem	4,957	Cottonwood Weir
6,817	Monticello	4,937	Kanab
6,758	Cedar Point	4,937	Pine View Dam
6,679	Boulder	4,895	Black Rock
6,607	Panguitch	4,878	Fairfield
6,499	Natural Bridges Nat'l Monument	4,878	Wah Wah Ranch
6,368	Altamont	4,790	Logan Utah State University
6,312	Woodruff	4,776	Partoun
6,279	Tropic	4,767	Dinosaur Nat'l Mon. Quarry Area
6,269	Flaming Gorge	4,763	Delta FAA Airport
6,049	Circleville	4,760	Pleasant Grove
6,040	Blanding	4,747	Jensen
6,007	Snake Creek Powerhouse	4,717	Spanish Fork Power House
5,997	Parowan Power Plant	4,678	Richmond
5,977	Laketown	4,668	Ouray 4 NE
5,948	Neola	4,599	Thiokol Plant 78
5,938	Wanship Dam	4,599	Veyo Powerhouse
5,928	Canyonlands The Neck	4,589	Deseret
5,928	Ferron	4,498	Logan Radio KVNU
5,908	Marysvale	4,494	Utah Lake Lehi
5,807	Escalante	4,488	Logan 5 SW Exp. Farm
5,738	Manti	4,353	Bluff
5,639	Timpanogos Cave	4,347	Ogden Pioneer P H
5,629	Heber	4,337	Dugway
5,629	Johnson Pass	4,337	Farmington USU Field Station
5,620	Castle Dale	4,333	Fish Springs Refuge
5,606	Cedar City Municipal Airport	4,327	Callao
5,557	Moroni	4,307	Hanksville
5,508	Ephraim Sorensens Field	4,278	Ogden Sugar Factory
5,498	Capitol Reef Nat'l Park	4,235	Wendover USAF Auxiliary Field
5,482	Vernon	4,219	Corinne
5,469	Echo Dam	4,219	Salt Lake City Int'l Airport
5,459	Orderville	4,127	Mexican Hat
5,419	Mountain Dell Dam	4,117	Dewey
5,314	Scipio	4,048	Zion National Park
5,298	Richfield Radio KSVC	4,041	Moab
5,288	Levan	3,218	La Verkin
5,278	Ibapah	2,769	Saint George
5,269	Deer Creek Dam		
5,262	New Harmony		
5,259	Vernal Municipal Airport		
5,200	Enterprise Airport		
5,164	Santaquin Chlorinator		
5,127	Nephi		
5,127	Salina		
5,118	Fillmore		
5,104	Roosevelt		
5,078	Morgan Como Springs		
5,078	Myton		
5,068	Oak City		
5,068	Tooele		
5,029	Milford Airport		

Milford Airport

Milford is located in Beaver County in the west-central portion of the state. The city is situated in a flat to gently sloping valley 15 to 20 miles in width. The Mineral Mountains, 10 miles to the east of the station, and the San Francisco Range, 15 miles to the northwest, rise about 5,000 feet above the valley floor.

The station is in the Sevier River Basin, and drainage is toward the north. The Beaver River just to the east extends north-south through the valley, but no significant body of water is reached by it. The river is dry most of the time due to the low annual rainfall in the area, and to the Minersville Reservoir 6 miles east of Minersville, which regulates the flow of water in the stream. Water for the irrigation of agricultural land in the valley is obtained from the diversion of surface water from this reservoir and from numerous deep wells.

The climate is temperate and dry. Irrigation water is necessary for the economic production of most crops.

Snowfall is rather evenly distributed during the season. The snow is usually light and powdery with below average moisture content. January, the coldest month of the year, has the greatest average monthly total.

Relative humidity is rather low during the summer months. It increases considerably in the change from summer to winter, and winters are cold and uncomfortable. In four out of five years the temperature can be expected to drop to -10 degrees or lower.

Summers are characterized by warm days and cool nights. Temperatures of 100 degrees or more occur about once in every two years.

Diurnal heating is a factor in producing strong southerly winds during the spring and summer months. Winter winds may cause considerable drifting snow, with resultant hazards to stock and transportation in the area.

Low pressure storm systems are rare during the summer months. Precipitation during this period occurs as showers or thundershowers and rainfall amounts from these storms are quite variable. As winter approaches, the number of atmospheric disturbances increases.

Based on the 1951-1980 period, the average first occurrence of 32 degrees Fahrenheit in the fall is September 22 and the average last occurrence in the spring is May 25.

Milford Airport *Beaver County*   Elevation: 5,029 ft.   Latitude: 38° 26' N   Longitude: 113° 01' W

	JAN	FEB	MAR	APR	MAY	JUN	JUL	AUG	SEP	OCT	NOV	DEC	YEAR
Mean Maximum Temp. (°F)	39.6	46.4	55.2	63.5	73.4	85.5	92.2	*89.8*	*80.0*	67.3	52.6	41.2	*65.6*
Mean Temp. (°F)	26.8	32.7	40.3	47.0	55.8	66.1	73.7	*72.0*	*62.1*	49.8	37.8	27.6	*49.3*
Mean Minimum Temp. (°F)	14.0	19.0	25.3	30.6	38.2	46.7	55.2	*54.0*	*44.2*	32.3	23.0	13.8	*33.0*
Extreme Maximum Temp. (°F)	68	75	80	86	*94*	105	107	*102*	*96*	88	*77*	68	*107*
Extreme Minimum Temp. (°F)	-25	-29	-13	9	*17*	24	34	*35*	*23*	-2	*-12*	-35	*-35*
Days Maximum Temp. ≥ 90°F	0	0	0	0	1	10	23	*18*	*3*	0	0	0	*55*
Days Maximum Temp. ≤ 32°F	8	2	1	0	0	0	0	*0*	*0*	0	1	6	*18*
Days Minimum Temp. ≤ 32°F	29	26	26	18	6	1	0	*0*	*3*	15	25	30	*179*
Days Minimum Temp. ≤ 0°F	5	2	0	0	0	0	0	*0*	*0*	0	0	3	*10*
Heating Degree Days (base 65°F)	1,178	905	760	532	283	64	2	*5*	*129*	463	810	1,154	*6,285*
Cooling Degree Days (base 65°F)	0	0	0	0	6	106	274	*238*	*53*	0	0	0	*677*
Mean Precipitation (in.)	0.72	0.70	1.19	0.96	0.89	0.42	0.83	*1.03*	*1.01*	1.00	0.75	0.60	*10.10*
Maximum Precipitation (in.)	1.9	1.7	2.0	2.3	1.9	2.4	1.4	2.5	2.6	2.6	2.2	2.4	13.1
Minimum Precipitation (in.)	0	trace	0	trace	trace	trace	trace	trace	trace	0	0	0	4.5
Maximum 24-hr. Precipitation (in.)	0.9	0.7	0.9	0.8	0.9	0.9	0.8	1.0	1.3	1.2	0.8	1.0	1.3
Days With ≥ 0.1" Precipitation	2	2	4	3	3	1	3	*2*	*3*	3	2	2	*30*
Days With ≥ 1.0" Precipitation	0	0	0	0	0	0	0	*0*	*0*	0	0	0	*0*
Mean Snowfall (in.)	6.7	5.6	8.4	4.8	1.6	0.0	0.0	*0.0*	*0.1*	2.0	3.6	5.3	*38.1*
Maximum Snowfall (in.)	30	19	20	24	11	trace	0	0	8	17	14	31	78
Maximum 24-hr. Snowfall (in.)	12	9	9	7	8	trace	0	0	6	6	8	13	13
Days With ≥ 1.0" Snow Depth	13	10	4	2	0	0	0	*0*	*0*	0	3	9	*41*
Thunderstorm Days	< 1	< 1	< 1	3	3	4	9	6	3	< 1	< 1	< 1	28
Foggy Days	6	6	3	1	1	0	0	0	< 1	1	2	9	29
Predominant Sky Cover	OVR	OVR	OVR	OVR	SCT	CLR	SCT	CLR	CLR	CLR	CLR	OVR	CLR
Mean Relative Humidity 5am (%)	83	83	73	68	65	54	56	57	55	67	78	82	66
Mean Relative Humidity 5pm (%)	60	53	37	27	23	18	20	22	20	28	46	61	35
Mean Dewpoint (°F)	18	20	22	23	29	31	40	40	33	28	23	19	27
Prevailing Wind Direction	SSW	SSW	SSW	SSW	SSW	SSW	SSW	SSW	SSW	SSW	SSW	SSW	SSW
Prevailing Wind Speed (mph)	16	15	17	17	17	16	15	15	15	14	15	15	16
Maximum Wind Gust (mph)	53	59	69	67	68	75	64	77	56	63	60	56	77

Salt Lake City Int'l Airport

Salt Lake City is located in a northern Utah valley surrounded by mountains on three sides and the Great Salt Lake to the northwest. The city varies in altitude from near 4,200 to 5,000 feet above sea level.

The Wasatch Mountains to the east have peaks to nearly 12,000 feet above sea level. Their orographic effects cause more precipitation in the eastern part of the city than over the western part.

The Oquirrh Mountains to the southwest of the city have several peaks to above 10,000 feet above sea level. The Traverse Mountain Range at the south end of the Salt Lake Valley rises to above 6,000 feet above sea level. These mountain ranges help to shelter the valleys from storms from the southwest in the winter, but are instrumental in developing thunderstorms which can drift over the valley in the summer.

Besides the mountain ranges, the most influential natural condition affecting the climate of Salt Lake City is the Great Salt Lake. This large inland body of water, which never freezes over due to its high salt content, can moderate the temperatures of cold winter winds blowing from the northwest and helps drive a lake/valley wind system. The warmer lake water during the winter and spring also contributes to increased precipitation in the valley downwind from the lake.

Salt Lake City normally has a semi-arid continental climate with four well-defined seasons. Summers are characterized by hot, dry weather, but the high temperatures are usually not oppressive since the relative humidity is generally low and the nights usually cool. July is the hottest month with temperature readings in the 90s.

The mean diurnal temperature range is about 30 degrees in the summer and 18 degrees during the winter. Temperatures above 102 degrees in the summer or colder than -10 degrees in the winter are likely to occur one season out of four.

Winters are cold, but usually not severe. Mountains to the north and east act as a barrier to frequent invasions of cold continental air. The average annual snowfall is under 60 inches at the airport but much higher amounts fall in higher bench locations. Heavy fog can develop under temperature inversions in the winter and persist for several days.

Precipitation, generally light during the summer and early fall, is heavy in the spring.

The growing season is over five months in length. The last freezing temperature in the spring averages late April and the first freeze of the fall is mid-October.

Salt Lake City Int'l Airport *Salt Lake County*   Elevation: 4,219 ft.   Latitude: 40° 47' N   Longitude: 111° 58' W

	JAN	FEB	MAR	APR	MAY	JUN	JUL	AUG	SEP	OCT	NOV	DEC	YEAR
Mean Maximum Temp. (°F)	37.7	44.2	53.6	61.3	71.5	83.4	92.1	90.5	79.0	65.3	50.2	38.7	64.0
Mean Temp. (°F)	29.5	34.9	43.5	50.0	59.2	69.5	77.7	76.4	65.6	53.1	40.5	30.6	52.5
Mean Minimum Temp. (°F)	21.3	25.5	33.3	38.7	46.7	55.6	63.2	62.3	52.1	40.8	30.8	22.4	41.1
Extreme Maximum Temp. (°F)	62	69	76	86	95	104	106	106	100	88	75	69	106
Extreme Minimum Temp. (°F)	-13	-14	3	19	28	38	47	42	30	16	3	-15	-15
Days Maximum Temp. ≥ 90°F	0	0	0	0	0	9	22	20	4	0	0	0	55
Days Maximum Temp. ≤ 32°F	9	3	0	0	0	0	0	0	0	0	1	8	21
Days Minimum Temp. ≤ 32°F	27	22	13	6	0	0	0	0	0	4	18	27	117
Days Minimum Temp. ≤ 0°F	1	0	0	0	0	0	0	0	0	0	0	1	2
Heating Degree Days (base 65°F)	1,095	844	660	446	209	46	2	3	88	368	728	1,061	5,550
Cooling Degree Days (base 65°F)	0	0	0	5	40	188	401	383	121	7	0	0	1,145
Mean Precipitation (in.)	1.34	1.31	1.91	2.10	2.06	0.82	0.73	0.72	1.36	1.56	1.43	1.28	16.62
Maximum Precipitation (in.)	3.2	2.8	4.0	4.6	4.8	2.8	2.6	3.7	7.0	3.9	3.0	4.4	24.3
Minimum Precipitation (in.)	0.1	0.1	0.1	0.4	0.1	trace	trace	trace	trace	0	trace	0.1	8.7
Maximum 24-hr. Precipitation (in.)	1.4	0.9	0.9	1.6	1.3	1.8	2.3	1.6	2.3	1.5	1.1	1.2	2.3
Days With ≥ 0.1" Precipitation	4	4	6	6	5	2	2	2	3	4	4	4	46
Days With ≥ 1.0" Precipitation	0	0	0	0	0	0	0	0	0	0	0	0	0
Mean Snowfall (in.)	14.1	10.2	9.2	6.5	0.7	trace	trace	trace	0.2	2.1	7.3	12.6	62.9
Maximum Snowfall (in.)	50	28	42	26	8	trace	0	0	4	20	33	35	100
Maximum 24-hr. Snowfall (in.)	10	11	12	12	5	trace	0	0	4	14	10	13	14
Days With ≥ 1.0" Snow Depth	18	11	4	1	0	0	0	0	0	1	4	13	52
Thunderstorm Days	< 1	1	2	2	6	5	7	7	4	2	1	< 1	37
Foggy Days	13	8	3	1	1	< 1	< 1	< 1	< 1	1	5	13	45
Predominant Sky Cover	OVR	OVR	OVR	OVR	OVR	CLR	CLR	CLR	CLR	CLR	OVR	OVR	OVR
Mean Relative Humidity 5am (%)	79	78	71	67	66	60	53	54	60	68	75	80	68
Mean Relative Humidity 5pm (%)	69	59	47	39	33	26	22	23	28	41	59	71	43
Mean Dewpoint (°F)	20	24	27	31	37	41	45	45	40	34	28	22	33
Prevailing Wind Direction	SSE	SSE	SSE	SSE	SSE	SSE	SSE	SSE	SSE	SSE	SSE	SSE	SSE
Prevailing Wind Speed (mph)	9	10	10	10	10	10	10	12	10	9	9	9	10
Maximum Wind Gust (mph)	69	54	62	69	69	94	74	74	71	71	59	60	94

Altamont *Duchesne County*   Elevation: 6,368 ft.   Latitude: 40° 21' N   Longitude: 110° 17' W

	JAN	FEB	MAR	APR	MAY	JUN	JUL	AUG	SEP	OCT	NOV	DEC	YEAR
Mean Maximum Temp. (°F)	31.5	36.5	47.1	56.6	66.0	76.0	82.7	81.2	71.9	59.2	43.6	33.1	57.1
Mean Temp. (°F)	19.2	24.0	34.4	42.6	51.5	60.5	67.3	65.9	56.9	45.3	31.5	21.3	43.4
Mean Minimum Temp. (°F)	6.8	11.5	21.5	28.5	37.0	45.1	51.7	50.6	41.9	31.4	19.2	9.5	29.6
Extreme Maximum Temp. (°F)	59	69	74	86	87	93	97	94	90	80	69	64	97
Extreme Minimum Temp. (°F)	-24	-29	-6	5	16	26	34	28	19	0	-6	-32	-32
Days Maximum Temp. ≥ 90°F	0	0	0	0	0	1	2	1	0	0	0	0	4
Days Maximum Temp. ≤ 32°F	16	9	2	0	0	0	0	0	0	0	4	14	45
Days Minimum Temp. ≤ 32°F	31	28	29	21	8	1	0	0	3	16	29	31	197
Days Minimum Temp. ≤ 0°F	8	4	0	0	0	0	0	0	0	0	1	5	18
Heating Degree Days (base 65°F)	1,414	1,151	943	668	412	157	26	37	245	604	998	1,349	8,004
Cooling Degree Days (base 65°F)	0	0	0	0	1	29	105	76	9	0	0	0	220
Mean Precipitation (in.)	0.70	0.62	0.66	0.72	1.00	0.77	0.88	0.85	1.04	1.04	0.63	0.56	9.47
Days With ≥ 0.1" Precipitation	3	2	3	2	3	2	3	3	3	3	2	2	31
Days With ≥ 1.0" Precipitation	0	0	0	0	0	0	0	0	0	0	0	0	0
Mean Snowfall (in.)	10.2	7.3	4.4	2.0	trace	trace	0.0	0.0	0.0	1.0	5.5	8.2	38.6
Days With ≥ 1.0" Snow Depth	*19*	*15*	6	*1*	0	0	0	0	0	1	*4*	na	na

Alton *Kane County*   Elevation: 7,037 ft.   Latitude: 37° 26' N   Longitude: 112° 29' W

	JAN	FEB	MAR	APR	MAY	JUN	JUL	AUG	SEP	OCT	NOV	DEC	YEAR
Mean Maximum Temp. (°F)	40.2	43.7	49.0	58.0	67.8	78.1	83.3	81.1	73.9	63.2	49.6	41.5	60.8
Mean Temp. (°F)	27.9	30.9	35.8	42.7	51.0	60.0	66.3	64.8	57.6	47.8	36.2	29.0	45.8
Mean Minimum Temp. (°F)	15.5	18.1	22.6	27.4	34.2	41.8	49.2	48.4	41.3	32.4	22.8	16.4	30.8
Extreme Maximum Temp. (°F)	64	68	72	81	88	95	99	94	89	83	71	65	99
Extreme Minimum Temp. (°F)	-20	-13	-3	1	9	25	34	32	22	-2	-2	-24	-24
Days Maximum Temp. ≥ 90°F	0	0	0	0	0	1	3	1	0	0	0	0	5
Days Maximum Temp. ≤ 32°F	6	3	1	0	0	0	0	0	0	0	2	5	17
Days Minimum Temp. ≤ 32°F	31	28	30	24	12	2	0	0	3	15	28	31	204
Days Minimum Temp. ≤ 0°F	2	1	0	0	0	0	0	0	0	0	0	1	4
Heating Degree Days (base 65°F)	1,143	955	897	662	426	163	30	49	220	526	857	1,110	7,038
Cooling Degree Days (base 65°F)	0	0	0	0	0	16	72	49	4	0	0	0	141
Mean Precipitation (in.)	1.74	1.82	1.78	0.96	0.96	0.54	1.42	1.63	1.53	1.43	1.49	1.25	16.55
Days With ≥ 0.1" Precipitation	4	4	5	3	3	2	4	5	4	3	3	3	43
Days With ≥ 1.0" Precipitation	0	0	0	0	0	0	0	0	0	0	0	0	0
Mean Snowfall (in.)	23.5	19.3	16.8	5.5	0.4	0.4	0.0	0.0	0.0	1.2	9.5	*15.9*	*92.5*
Days With ≥ 1.0" Snow Depth	22	*20*	14	5	0	0	0	0	0	0	6	*13*	*80*

Black Rock *Millard County*   Elevation: 4,895 ft.   Latitude: 38° 43' N   Longitude: 112° 57' W

	JAN	FEB	MAR	APR	MAY	JUN	JUL	AUG	SEP	OCT	NOV	DEC	YEAR
Mean Maximum Temp. (°F)	40.7	48.4	57.7	65.7	75.2	86.0	92.5	90.1	80.4	68.0	53.1	41.8	66.6
Mean Temp. (°F)	27.6	33.9	41.7	48.1	56.6	65.7	72.9	71.0	61.4	49.7	37.9	28.1	49.6
Mean Minimum Temp. (°F)	14.4	19.3	25.7	30.4	37.9	45.4	53.2	51.9	42.4	31.3	22.7	14.4	32.4
Extreme Maximum Temp. (°F)	68	75	83	88	96	103	105	102	97	89	80	67	105
Extreme Minimum Temp. (°F)	-29	-28	-12	7	19	25	32	29	22	-6	-22	-37	-37
Days Maximum Temp. ≥ 90°F	0	0	0	0	1	12	23	18	3	0	0	0	57
Days Maximum Temp. ≤ 32°F	7	2	0	0	0	0	0	0	0	0	1	5	15
Days Minimum Temp. ≤ 32°F	29	26	25	19	7	1	0	0	4	18	25	29	183
Days Minimum Temp. ≤ 0°F	5	2	0	0	0	0	0	0	0	0	1	4	12
Heating Degree Days (base 65°F)	1,154	873	715	502	261	66	4	7	140	468	805	1,137	6,132
Cooling Degree Days (base 65°F)	0	0	0	1	8	95	254	210	41	0	0	0	609
Mean Precipitation (in.)	0.54	0.52	1.10	0.92	0.98	0.51	0.70	0.89	0.85	0.94	0.74	0.53	9.22
Days With ≥ 0.1" Precipitation	2	2	4	3	3	2	2	2	2	2	2	2	28
Days With ≥ 1.0" Precipitation	0	0	0	0	0	0	0	0	0	0	0	0	0
Mean Snowfall (in.)	*7.0*	*6.0*	*6.5*	*2.4*	0.5	trace	0.0	0.0	0.1	0.2	*3.8*	*5.0*	*31.5*
Days With ≥ 1.0" Snow Depth	12	8	2	0	0	0	0	0	0	0	3	8	33

Blanding *San Juan County*   Elevation: 6,040 ft.   Latitude: 37° 37' N   Longitude: 109° 29' W

	JAN	FEB	MAR	APR	MAY	JUN	JUL	AUG	SEP	OCT	NOV	DEC	YEAR
Mean Maximum Temp. (°F)	40.2	46.6	54.0	62.3	72.9	84.7	89.5	87.1	78.6	65.7	51.0	41.8	64.5
Mean Temp. (°F)	29.2	35.0	41.5	48.3	57.8	68.2	73.8	72.0	63.8	52.1	39.3	31.1	51.0
Mean Minimum Temp. (°F)	18.2	23.5	28.9	34.2	42.7	51.7	58.0	56.8	49.0	38.5	27.6	20.2	37.4
Extreme Maximum Temp. (°F)	61	70	76	86	93	102	102	101	97	87	74	63	102
Extreme Minimum Temp. (°F)	-14	-8	-3	16	23	33	42	42	23	10	0	-13	-14
Days Maximum Temp. ≥ 90°F	0	0	0	0	0	8	17	11	1	0	0	0	37
Days Maximum Temp. ≤ 32°F	5	1	0	0	0	0	0	0	0	0	0	3	9
Days Minimum Temp. ≤ 32°F	30	26	22	12	2	0	0	0	0	6	22	30	150
Days Minimum Temp. ≤ 0°F	1	0	0	0	0	0	0	0	0	0	0	1	2
Heating Degree Days (base 65°F)	1,103	839	723	496	228	42	1	4	91	394	763	1,045	5,729
Cooling Degree Days (base 65°F)	0	0	0	1	17	158	294	248	74	2	0	0	794
Mean Precipitation (in.)	1.49	1.07	1.01	0.92	0.80	0.49	1.31	1.20	1.30	1.51	1.10	1.02	13.22
Days With ≥ 0.1" Precipitation	4	3	3	3	2	1	3	3	3	4	3	3	35
Days With ≥ 1.0" Precipitation	0	0	0	0	0	0	0	0	0	0	0	0	0
Mean Snowfall (in.)	14.2	7.1	4.1	2.9	0.2	0.0	0.0	0.0	0.0	0.4	4.0	8.2	41.1
Days With ≥ 1.0" Snow Depth	*15*	*9*	2	0	0	0	0	0	0	0	2	7	*35*

Bluff *San Juan County*   Elevation: 4,353 ft.   Latitude: 37° 17' N   Longitude: 109° 34' W

	JAN	FEB	MAR	APR	MAY	JUN	JUL	AUG	SEP	OCT	NOV	DEC	YEAR
Mean Maximum Temp. (°F)	42.8	51.9	62.1	70.6	79.9	90.8	95.4	93.0	84.6	71.2	55.6	44.4	70.2
Mean Temp. (°F)	29.9	37.4	46.0	53.3	62.2	71.0	77.5	75.9	66.6	53.2	40.3	30.7	53.7
Mean Minimum Temp. (°F)	16.9	22.9	29.9	36.0	44.5	51.1	59.5	58.7	48.5	35.2	25.0	17.1	37.1
Extreme Maximum Temp. (°F)	65	76	85	92	96	105	108	105	100	91	76	66	108
Extreme Minimum Temp. (°F)	-15	-11	10	19	26	33	40	37	25	10	-2	-22	-22
Days Maximum Temp. ≥ 90°F	0	0	0	0	3	18	28	24	8	0	0	0	81
Days Maximum Temp. ≤ 32°F	5	1	0	0	0	0	0	0	0	0	0	2	8
Days Minimum Temp. ≤ 32°F	29	24	20	11	1	0	0	0	1	13	24	30	153
Days Minimum Temp. ≤ 0°F	2	0	0	0	0	0	0	0	0	0	0	1	3
Heating Degree Days (base 65°F)	1,081	772	582	346	120	14	0	0	51	360	734	1,054	5,114
Cooling Degree Days (base 65°F)	0	0	0	3	47	209	401	361	113	2	0	0	1,136
Mean Precipitation (in.)	0.86	0.65	0.66	0.50	0.53	0.22	0.75	0.73	0.73	1.01	0.73	0.64	8.01
Days With ≥ 0.1" Precipitation	3	2	2	2	2	1	2	2	2	3	2	2	25
Days With ≥ 1.0" Precipitation	0	0	0	0	0	0	0	0	0	0	0	0	0
Mean Snowfall (in.)	3.9	1.9	trace	*0.1*	0.0	0.0	0.0	0.0	0.0	0.1	0.5	3.3	*9.8*
Days With ≥ 1.0" Snow Depth	na	*1*	0	*0*	0	0	0	0	0	0	0	*2*	na

Boulder *Garfield County*   Elevation: 6,679 ft.   Latitude: 37° 54' N   Longitude: 111° 25' W

	JAN	FEB	MAR	APR	MAY	JUN	JUL	AUG	SEP	OCT	NOV	DEC	YEAR
Mean Maximum Temp. (°F)	39.6	44.4	51.5	59.2	68.3	79.1	84.5	82.0	74.3	63.3	49.4	41.0	61.4
Mean Temp. (°F)	28.4	33.0	39.6	46.3	54.9	65.3	71.4	69.4	61.7	51.0	38.0	29.9	49.1
Mean Minimum Temp. (°F)	17.2	21.6	27.6	33.3	41.5	51.5	58.2	56.7	49.0	38.6	26.5	18.7	36.7
Extreme Maximum Temp. (°F)	63	69	72	82	87	95	96	94	90	83	70	64	96
Extreme Minimum Temp. (°F)	-15	-17	2	8	20	32	39	40	24	4	-1	-11	-17
Days Maximum Temp. ≥ 90°F	0	0	0	0	0	2	5	2	0	0	0	0	9
Days Maximum Temp. ≤ 32°F	6	2	0	0	0	0	0	0	0	0	1	5	14
Days Minimum Temp. ≤ 32°F	31	26	23	14	4	0	0	0	1	7	23	30	159
Days Minimum Temp. ≤ 0°F	1	0	0	0	0	0	0	0	0	0	0	1	2
Heating Degree Days (base 65°F)	1,127	897	781	556	312	76	5	13	132	430	804	1,082	6,215
Cooling Degree Days (base 65°F)	0	0	0	0	7	90	208	159	39	1	0	0	504
Mean Precipitation (in.)	0.95	0.90	1.02	0.50	0.76	0.33	1.11	1.52	1.20	1.09	0.81	0.59	10.78
Days With ≥ 0.1" Precipitation	3	3	3	1	2	1	3	4	3	2	2	31
Days With ≥ 1.0" Precipitation	0	0	0	0	0	0	0	0	0	0	0	0	0
Mean Snowfall (in.)	na	*8.6*	*3.0*	*1.3*	trace	trace	0.0	0.0	trace	0.4	*2.8*	*5.6*	na
Days With ≥ 1.0" Snow Depth	*17*	10	2	0	0	0	0	0	0	0	2	7	*38*

Bryce Canyon Nat'l Park Hdqtrs. *Garfield County*   Elevation: 7,913 ft.   Latitude: 37° 38' N   Longitude: 112° 10' W

	JAN	FEB	MAR	APR	MAY	JUN	JUL	AUG	SEP	OCT	NOV	DEC	YEAR
Mean Maximum Temp. (°F)	36.0	38.9	44.8	52.6	62.9	73.9	79.4	76.9	69.4	58.4	44.2	36.8	56.2
Mean Temp. (°F)	22.9	25.6	31.8	38.3	47.1	56.7	62.8	60.9	53.1	42.7	31.0	23.6	41.4
Mean Minimum Temp. (°F)	9.8	12.2	18.7	23.8	31.3	39.5	46.3	44.9	36.9	27.0	17.9	10.3	26.5
Extreme Maximum Temp. (°F)	59	64	67	75	82	92	95	90	86	79	68	60	95
Extreme Minimum Temp. (°F)	-25	-26	-10	-3	13	21	28	28	16	0	-9	-23	-26
Days Maximum Temp. ≥ 90°F	0	0	0	0	0	0	0	0	0	0	0	0	0
Days Maximum Temp. ≤ 32°F	11	6	3	1	0	0	0	0	0	1	4	9	35
Days Minimum Temp. ≤ 32°F	31	28	30	27	18	5	0	0	8	25	29	31	232
Days Minimum Temp. ≤ 0°F	6	3	1	0	0	0	0	0	0	0	1	5	16
Heating Degree Days (base 65°F)	1,297	1,106	1,023	796	548	250	85	132	349	684	1,012	1,277	8,559
Cooling Degree Days (base 65°F)	0	0	0	0	0	9	24	11	1	0	0	0	45
Mean Precipitation (in.)	1.48	1.58	1.61	0.85	1.07	0.64	1.42	2.18	1.65	1.49	1.23	1.00	16.20
Days With ≥ 0.1" Precipitation	3	4	4	2	3	2	4	5	3	4	3	3	40
Days With ≥ 1.0" Precipitation	0	0	0	0	0	0	0	0	0	0	0	0	0
Mean Snowfall (in.)	17.8	18.1	15.7	*7.5*	*1.3*	0.2	0.0	0.0	trace	1.9	11.7	14.4	*88.6*
Days With ≥ 1.0" Snow Depth	27	25	21	7	1	0	0	0	0	1	10	20	112

Callao *Juab County*   Elevation: 4,327 ft.   Latitude: 39° 54' N   Longitude: 113° 43' W

	JAN	FEB	MAR	APR	MAY	JUN	JUL	AUG	SEP	OCT	NOV	DEC	YEAR
Mean Maximum Temp. (°F)	38.9	46.0	56.2	63.9	72.3	82.5	90.1	88.8	79.0	65.8	51.2	40.6	64.6
Mean Temp. (°F)	26.9	33.1	42.1	48.9	57.2	66.3	73.4	71.9	61.8	49.6	37.5	27.9	49.7
Mean Minimum Temp. (°F)	14.7	20.1	28.0	33.8	42.1	50.2	56.6	55.0	44.6	33.4	23.7	15.2	34.8
Extreme Maximum Temp. (°F)	68	74	80	86	92	99	102	101	97	88	76	72	102
Extreme Minimum Temp. (°F)	-18	-23	6	12	21	30	40	28	24	12	-2	-23	-23
Days Maximum Temp. ≥ 90°F	0	0	0	0	0	7	19	*16*	3	0	0	0	*45*
Days Maximum Temp. ≤ 32°F	10	3	0	0	0	0	0	0	0	0	1	6	20
Days Minimum Temp. ≤ 32°F	30	26	22	13	3	0	0	0	2	14	26	29	165
Days Minimum Temp. ≤ 0°F	3	1	0	0	0	0	0	0	0	0	0	2	6
Heating Degree Days (base 65°F)	1,178	895	702	479	253	72	5	9	143	473	820	1,143	6,172
Cooling Degree Days (base 65°F)	0	0	0	2	21	118	273	246	56	1	0	0	717
Mean Precipitation (in.)	0.40	0.33	0.45	0.53	0.91	0.58	0.55	0.64	0.54	0.73	0.38	0.24	6.28
Days With ≥ 0.1" Precipitation	1	1	1	2	3	2	2	2	1	2	1	1	19
Days With ≥ 1.0" Precipitation	0	0	0	0	0	0	0	0	0	0	0	0	0
Mean Snowfall (in.)	4.3	1.8	0.9	0.3	trace	trace	0.0	0.0	0.0	*trace*	1.5	*1.8*	*10.6*
Days With ≥ 1.0" Snow Depth	*6*	4	*1*	0	0	0	0	0	0	*0*	1	*1*	*13*

Canyonlands The Neck *San Juan County*   Elevation: 5,928 ft.   Latitude: 38° 27' N   Longitude: 109° 49' W

	JAN	FEB	MAR	APR	MAY	JUN	JUL	AUG	SEP	OCT	NOV	DEC	YEAR
Mean Maximum Temp. (°F)	36.7	44.1	53.2	61.8	72.7	84.3	90.2	88.0	78.5	64.8	48.7	37.7	63.4
Mean Temp. (°F)	28.4	35.0	42.9	50.2	60.5	71.8	77.6	75.7	66.6	53.9	39.7	29.6	52.7
Mean Minimum Temp. (°F)	20.0	25.9	32.4	38.5	48.2	59.2	65.0	63.3	54.7	43.0	30.6	21.5	41.8
Extreme Maximum Temp. (°F)	58	67	75	84	97	102	104	101	98	89	72	62	104
Extreme Minimum Temp. (°F)	-7	-13	8	15	22	26	44	42	25	13	6	-10	-13
Days Maximum Temp. ≥ 90°F	0	0	0	0	0	8	19	13	2	0	0	0	42
Days Maximum Temp. ≤ 32°F	9	2	0	0	0	0	0	0	0	0	1	7	19
Days Minimum Temp. ≤ 32°F	29	22	16	9	1	0	0	0	0	4	18	29	128
Days Minimum Temp. ≤ 0°F	0	0	0	0	0	0	0	0	0	0	0	0	0
Heating Degree Days (base 65°F)	1,128	842	679	442	178	29	1	1	65	348	753	1,090	5,556
Cooling Degree Days (base 65°F)	0	0	0	4	44	231	390	337	117	9	0	0	1,132
Mean Precipitation (in.)	0.56	0.38	0.86	0.84	0.81	0.44	0.99	0.77	0.87	1.26	0.77	0.55	9.10
Days With ≥ 0.1" Precipitation	2	1	3	3	2	1	3	2	3	3	2	2	27
Days With ≥ 1.0" Precipitation	0	0	0	0	0	0	0	0	0	0	0	0	0
Mean Snowfall (in.)	6.0	2.6	3.9	1.9	0.1	0.0	0.0	0.0	0.0	1.1	2.4	5.2	23.2
Days With ≥ 1.0" Snow Depth	16	9	3	1	0	0	0	0	0	0	2	10	41

Canyonlands The Needle *San Juan County*   Elevation: 4,996 ft.   Latitude: 38° 09' N   Longitude: 109° 47' W

	JAN	FEB	MAR	APR	MAY	JUN	JUL	AUG	SEP	OCT	NOV	DEC	YEAR
Mean Maximum Temp. (°F)	40.5	49.0	58.8	67.0	77.6	89.2	95.0	92.5	83.4	69.7	53.9	42.5	68.3
Mean Temp. (°F)	28.2	35.8	44.6	51.7	61.6	72.0	78.3	76.4	66.8	53.7	40.3	30.2	53.3
Mean Minimum Temp. (°F)	15.9	22.6	30.3	36.4	45.6	54.8	61.6	60.2	50.1	37.7	26.6	17.8	38.3
Extreme Maximum Temp. (°F)	63	73	80	89	97	106	107	104	99	90	76	66	107
Extreme Minimum Temp. (°F)	-16	-14	7	12	27	29	42	41	27	15	-4	-15	-16
Days Maximum Temp. ≥ 90°F	0	0	0	0	2	17	26	24	6	0	0	0	75
Days Maximum Temp. ≤ 32°F	6	1	0	0	0	0	0	0	0	0	0	3	10
Days Minimum Temp. ≤ 32°F	30	25	20	10	1	0	0	0	0	8	23	30	147
Days Minimum Temp. ≤ 0°F	3	1	0	0	0	0	0	0	0	0	0	1	5
Heating Degree Days (base 65°F)	1,134	817	627	396	146	21	1	0	56	348	735	1,074	5,355
Cooling Degree Days (base 65°F)	0	0	0	4	50	240	411	360	114	5	0	0	1,184
Mean Precipitation (in.)	0.57	0.43	0.80	0.76	0.66	0.33	0.91	0.96	0.82	1.17	0.64	0.50	8.55
Days With ≥ 0.1" Precipitation	2	2	*2*	2	2	1	3	3	3	3	2	2	*27*
Days With ≥ 1.0" Precipitation	0	0	0	0	0	0	0	0	0	0	0	0	0
Mean Snowfall (in.)	*4.1*	*2.4*	*2.5*	0.6	trace	0.0	0.0	0.0	0.0	0.3	*0.9*	*3.2*	*14.0*
Days With ≥ 1.0" Snow Depth	*9*	3	*1*	0	0	0	0	0	0	0	*1*	5	*19*

Capitol Reef Nat'l Park *Wayne County*   Elevation: 5,498 ft.   Latitude: 38° 17' N   Longitude: 111° 16' W

	JAN	FEB	MAR	APR	MAY	JUN	JUL	AUG	SEP	OCT	NOV	DEC	YEAR
Mean Maximum Temp. (°F)	40.5	47.6	57.5	65.8	75.8	87.0	91.9	89.2	81.1	67.9	52.1	41.9	66.5
Mean Temp. (°F)	29.9	36.4	45.0	52.2	61.7	72.0	77.7	75.6	67.4	55.4	40.9	31.6	53.8
Mean Minimum Temp. (°F)	19.1	25.3	32.5	38.7	47.6	57.0	63.4	62.0	53.7	42.9	29.7	21.2	41.1
Extreme Maximum Temp. (°F)	69	71	79	89	95	104	104	102	98	91	77	69	104
Extreme Minimum Temp. (°F)	-9	-7	10	18	29	35	48	47	32	17	5	-7	-9
Days Maximum Temp. ≥ 90°F	0	0	0	0	1	13	22	16	4	0	0	0	56
Days Maximum Temp. ≤ 32°F	6	1	0	0	0	0	0	0	0	0	0	4	11
Days Minimum Temp. ≤ 32°F	30	23	16	7	0	0	0	0	0	3	20	30	129
Days Minimum Temp. ≤ 0°F	1	0	0	0	0	0	0	0	0	0	0	0	1
Heating Degree Days (base 65°F)	1,083	800	612	380	141	20	0	0	46	303	716	1,029	5,130
Cooling Degree Days (base 65°F)	0	0	0	6	46	230	390	328	120	12	0	0	1,132
Mean Precipitation (in.)	0.52	0.38	0.63	0.54	0.64	0.37	0.99	1.21	0.82	0.68	0.62	0.26	7.66
Days With ≥ 0.1" Precipitation	1	1	2	2	2	1	3	4	2	2	2	1	23
Days With ≥ 1.0" Precipitation	0	0	0	0	0	0	0	0	0	0	0	0	0
Mean Snowfall (in.)	5.4	1.8	2.8	0.7	trace	0.0	0.0	0.0	0.0	0.6	2.1	2.3	15.7
Days With ≥ 1.0" Snow Depth	8	4	0	0	0	0	0	0	0	0	1	1	14

Castle Dale *Emery County*   Elevation: 5,620 ft.   Latitude: 39° 12' N   Longitude: 111° 01' W

	JAN	FEB	MAR	APR	MAY	JUN	JUL	AUG	SEP	OCT	NOV	DEC	YEAR
Mean Maximum Temp. (°F)	36.1	43.3	54.2	62.7	72.5	83.4	89.1	87.0	78.4	66.0	50.1	39.5	63.5
Mean Temp. (°F)	22.2	29.2	39.2	46.5	55.7	65.1	71.2	69.3	60.6	48.9	35.5	25.6	47.4
Mean Minimum Temp. (°F)	8.2	15.0	24.2	30.3	38.9	46.8	53.3	51.6	42.7	31.7	21.0	11.6	31.3
Extreme Maximum Temp. (°F)	62	70	77	85	91	103	103	101	94	87	75	67	103
Extreme Minimum Temp. (°F)	-24	-21	3	11	18	25	35	33	22	3	-4	-28	-28
Days Maximum Temp. ≥ 90°F	0	0	0	0	0	7	16	10	2	0	0	0	35
Days Maximum Temp. ≤ 32°F	11	3	0	0	0	0	0	0	0	0	1	6	21
Days Minimum Temp. ≤ 32°F	31	28	28	19	6	0	0	0	3	17	28	31	191
Days Minimum Temp. ≤ 0°F	8	3	0	0	0	0	0	0	0	0	0	3	14
Heating Degree Days (base 65°F)	1,321	1,005	792	548	286	72	4	10	151	493	877	1,216	6,775
Cooling Degree Days (base 65°F)	0	0	0	0	5	76	190	144	24	0	0	0	439
Mean Precipitation (in.)	0.64	0.53	0.68	0.53	0.62	0.44	0.82	0.97	0.86	0.82	0.53	0.36	7.80
Days With ≥ 0.1" Precipitation	2	2	2	2	2	2	2	3	2	2	2	1	24
Days With ≥ 1.0" Precipitation	0	0	0	0	0	0	0	0	0	0	0	0	0
Mean Snowfall (in.)	7.3	4.5	1.5	0.6	trace	0.0	0.0	0.0	0.0	0.3	1.3	4.1	19.6
Days With ≥ 1.0" Snow Depth	*16*	8	1	0	0	0	0	0	0	0	1	5	*31*

Cedar City Municipal Airport *Iron County*   Elevation: 5,606 ft.   Latitude: 37° 43' N   Longitude: 113° 06' W

	JAN	FEB	MAR	APR	MAY	JUN	JUL	AUG	SEP	OCT	NOV	DEC	YEAR
Mean Maximum Temp. (°F)	42.6	47.7	54.4	61.7	72.0	84.1	90.3	88.0	79.5	66.9	52.6	43.4	65.3
Mean Temp. (°F)	30.6	35.3	41.4	47.7	56.7	67.0	74.1	72.4	63.5	51.4	39.4	31.1	50.9
Mean Minimum Temp. (°F)	18.6	22.9	28.4	33.6	41.3	50.0	57.8	56.8	47.5	35.9	26.2	18.7	36.5
Extreme Maximum Temp. (°F)	70	73	76	83	96	101	105	100	96	88	75	68	105
Extreme Minimum Temp. (°F)	-16	-24	4	6	21	30	40	37	24	-7	-6	-23	-24
Days Maximum Temp. ≥ 90°F	0	0	0	0	0	8	19	13	2	0	0	0	42
Days Maximum Temp. ≤ 32°F	5	2	0	0	0	0	0	0	0	0	1	4	12
Days Minimum Temp. ≤ 32°F	29	24	22	14	3	0	0	0	0	10	23	29	155
Days Minimum Temp. ≤ 0°F	2	1	0	0	0	0	0	0	0	0	0	2	5
Heating Degree Days (base 65°F)	1,059	831	725	513	260	57	2	3	99	416	760	1,045	5,770
Cooling Degree Days (base 65°F)	0	0	0	0	10	123	284	245	62	0	0	0	724
Mean Precipitation (in.)	0.85	0.92	1.33	1.01	0.88	0.48	1.02	1.16	0.83	1.21	1.02	0.64	11.35
Days With ≥ 0.1" Precipitation	3	3	4	3	3	2	3	3	2	3	3	2	34
Days With ≥ 1.0" Precipitation	0	0	0	0	0	0	0	0	0	0	0	0	0
Mean Snowfall (in.)	8.9	8.9	8.6	5.3	1.4	0.1	trace	trace	trace	2.2	6.1	6.9	48.4
Days With ≥ 1.0" Snow Depth	13	9	4	2	0	0	0	0	0	1	4	9	42

Cedar Point *San Juan County*   Elevation: 6,758 ft.   Latitude: 37° 43' N   Longitude: 109° 05' W

	JAN	FEB	MAR	APR	MAY	JUN	JUL	AUG	SEP	OCT	NOV	DEC	YEAR
Mean Maximum Temp. (°F)	36.8	41.7	48.3	57.3	68.2	80.3	85.8	83.0	74.4	62.0	47.1	38.3	60.3
Mean Temp. (°F)	25.6	30.1	36.7	44.1	53.4	63.6	69.8	67.8	59.8	48.5	35.7	27.3	46.9
Mean Minimum Temp. (°F)	14.4	18.4	25.0	30.8	38.6	46.9	53.8	52.4	45.1	35.0	24.3	16.3	33.4
Extreme Maximum Temp. (°F)	58	66	72	80	89	98	100	98	92	81	71	62	100
Extreme Minimum Temp. (°F)	-15	-18	-2	10	21	27	38	37	26	10	-6	-20	-20
Days Maximum Temp. ≥ 90°F	0	0	0	0	0	3	8	4	0	0	0	0	15
Days Maximum Temp. ≤ 32°F	9	4	1	0	0	0	0	0	0	0	2	7	23
Days Minimum Temp. ≤ 32°F	31	28	27	18	5	0	0	0	1	10	27	31	178
Days Minimum Temp. ≤ 0°F	3	1	0	0	0	0	0	0	0	0	0	1	5
Heating Degree Days (base 65°F)	1,214	979	872	621	353	96	6	19	170	505	872	1,162	6,869
Cooling Degree Days (base 65°F)	0	0	0	0	2	57	159	116	19	0	0	0	353
Mean Precipitation (in.)	1.45	1.31	1.39	1.09	1.07	0.45	1.35	1.33	1.66	2.02	1.56	1.16	15.84
Days With ≥ 0.1" Precipitation	4	3	4	3	3	1	4	4	4	4	4	3	41
Days With ≥ 1.0" Precipitation	0	0	0	0	0	0	0	0	0	0	0	0	0
Mean Snowfall (in.)	20.1	15.4	10.5	5.4	1.0	trace	0.0	0.0	0.0	2.4	9.9	12.1	76.8
Days With ≥ 1.0" Snow Depth	21	17	10	2	0	0	0	0	0	1	5	13	69

Circleville *Piute County*   Elevation: 6,049 ft.   Latitude: 38° 10' N   Longitude: 112° 17' W

	JAN	FEB	MAR	APR	MAY	JUN	JUL	AUG	SEP	OCT	NOV	DEC	YEAR
Mean Maximum Temp. (°F)	41.7	47.1	53.4	60.9	70.7	82.1	88.0	85.7	77.5	65.8	52.3	43.3	64.1
Mean Temp. (°F)	27.6	32.8	38.3	44.7	53.7	63.4	69.9	67.9	59.4	48.1	36.8	28.6	47.6
Mean Minimum Temp. (°F)	13.5	18.4	23.2	28.4	36.6	44.7	51.7	50.1	41.2	30.5	21.3	13.9	31.1
Extreme Maximum Temp. (°F)	66	70	77	83	91	100	103	99	95	85	73	67	103
Extreme Minimum Temp. (°F)	-23	-26	-3	8	15	24	32	29	18	-12	-10	-31	-31
Days Maximum Temp. ≥ 90°F	0	0	0	0	0	6	13	8	1	0	0	0	28
Days Maximum Temp. ≤ 32°F	5	1	0	0	0	0	0	0	0	0	1	4	11
Days Minimum Temp. ≤ 32°F	30	27	27	20	8	2	0	0	4	19	27	30	194
Days Minimum Temp. ≤ 0°F	4	1	0	0	0	0	0	0	0	0	1	3	9
Heating Degree Days (base 65°F)	1,152	902	820	604	346	103	7	18	179	516	841	1,121	6,609
Cooling Degree Days (base 65°F)	0	0	0	0	2	55	152	110	16	0	0	0	335
Mean Precipitation (in.)	0.59	0.54	0.78	0.65	0.88	0.57	0.91	1.36	0.96	0.83	0.55	0.42	9.04
Days With ≥ 0.1" Precipitation	2	2	3	2	3	2	3	4	3	3	2	2	31
Days With ≥ 1.0" Precipitation	0	0	0	0	0	0	0	0	0	0	0	0	0
Mean Snowfall (in.)	6.7	3.4	3.6	1.3	0.2	0.0	0.0	0.0	trace	0.8	2.9	4.3	23.2
Days With ≥ 1.0" Snow Depth	8	4	1	0	0	0	0	0	0	0	2	4	19

Corinne *Box Elder County*   Elevation: 4,219 ft.   Latitude: 41° 33' N   Longitude: 112° 06' W

	JAN	FEB	MAR	APR	MAY	JUN	JUL	AUG	SEP	OCT	NOV	DEC	YEAR
Mean Maximum Temp. (°F)	34.2	41.2	51.6	60.7	70.9	81.5	89.9	88.5	77.7	64.4	47.2	36.4	62.0
Mean Temp. (°F)	25.1	30.6	40.7	47.8	57.0	66.0	73.2	71.9	61.8	49.8	36.8	27.3	49.0
Mean Minimum Temp. (°F)	16.2	20.0	29.7	34.9	43.2	50.4	56.4	55.2	45.8	35.2	26.4	18.1	36.0
Extreme Maximum Temp. (°F)	59	65	74	86	91	101	103	104	97	88	*75*	64	*104*
Extreme Minimum Temp. (°F)	-20	-23	0	15	23	33	40	37	22	15	-3	-19	-23
Days Maximum Temp. ≥ 90°F	0	0	0	0	0	6	19	14	2	0	0	0	41
Days Maximum Temp. ≤ 32°F	12	5	0	0	0	0	0	0	0	0	1	9	27
Days Minimum Temp. ≤ 32°F	29	25	21	11	2	0	0	0	1	11	24	29	153
Days Minimum Temp. ≤ 0°F	4	2	0	0	0	0	0	0	0	0	0	2	8
Heating Degree Days (base 65°F)	1,230	965	745	509	256	71	8	9	140	464	839	1,163	6,399
Cooling Degree Days (base 65°F)	0	0	0	1	18	103	249	228	54	0	0	0	653
Mean Precipitation (in.)	1.57	1.49	1.75	1.81	2.19	1.24	0.85	0.86	1.59	1.70	1.48	1.48	18.01
Days With ≥ 0.1" Precipitation	5	4	5	5	5	3	2	2	3	4	4	5	47
Days With ≥ 1.0" Precipitation	0	0	0	0	0	0	0	0	0	0	0	0	0
Mean Snowfall (in.)	na	*6.1*	*3.1*	*2.3*	0.2	0.0	0.0	0.0	0.0	0.5	na	na	na
Days With ≥ 1.0" Snow Depth	*21*	*12*	*4*	0	0	0	0	0	0	0	na	na	na

Cottonwood Weir *Salt Lake County*   Elevation: 4,957 ft.   Latitude: 40° 37' N   Longitude: 111° 47' W

	JAN	FEB	MAR	APR	MAY	JUN	JUL	AUG	SEP	OCT	NOV	DEC	YEAR
Mean Maximum Temp. (°F)	38.9	45.3	53.6	61.2	71.7	82.8	90.8	89.2	78.5	65.5	50.2	39.9	64.0
Mean Temp. (°F)	30.5	35.9	43.7	50.6	59.9	70.3	78.4	77.0	66.6	54.5	41.1	31.4	53.3
Mean Minimum Temp. (°F)	22.0	26.5	33.6	40.0	48.1	57.6	65.9	64.6	54.6	43.5	31.9	22.8	42.6
Extreme Maximum Temp. (°F)	64	69	75	89	92	102	106	102	96	89	77	69	106
Extreme Minimum Temp. (°F)	-8	-8	7	20	28	35	47	41	30	15	2	-12	-12
Days Maximum Temp. ≥ 90°F	0	0	0	0	0	8	20	17	2	0	0	0	47
Days Maximum Temp. ≤ 32°F	8	2	0	0	0	0	0	0	0	0	1	7	18
Days Minimum Temp. ≤ 32°F	27	21	14	7	1	0	0	0	0	3	16	27	116
Days Minimum Temp. ≤ 0°F	0	0	0	0	0	0	0	0	0	0	0	1	1
Heating Degree Days (base 65°F)	1,064	815	654	434	201	48	1	3	81	334	711	1,036	5,382
Cooling Degree Days (base 65°F)	0	0	0	13	56	211	415	395	145	16	0	0	1,251
Mean Precipitation (in.)	2.02	2.14	2.95	3.14	3.06	1.32	1.13	1.13	2.18	2.63	2.50	2.07	26.27
Days With ≥ 0.1" Precipitation	5	5	7	7	6	3	2	3	4	5	6	5	58
Days With ≥ 1.0" Precipitation	0	0	0	0	1	0	0	0	1	0	0	0	2
Mean Snowfall (in.)	22.4	19.6	13.6	8.0	0.9	0.0	0.0	0.0	0.1	3.5	13.2	23.4	104.7
Days With ≥ 1.0" Snow Depth	24	18	8	3	0	0	0	0	0	1	7	21	82

Deer Creek Dam *Wasatch County*   Elevation: 5,269 ft.   Latitude: 40° 24' N   Longitude: 111° 32' W

	JAN	FEB	MAR	APR	MAY	JUN	JUL	AUG	SEP	OCT	NOV	DEC	YEAR
Mean Maximum Temp. (°F)	32.8	38.0	48.0	57.4	67.2	77.7	85.5	84.4	74.8	63.1	47.5	36.0	59.4
Mean Temp. (°F)	20.8	24.4	34.7	42.8	51.2	59.4	66.2	64.9	56.3	45.9	34.5	24.8	43.8
Mean Minimum Temp. (°F)	8.7	10.8	21.2	28.1	35.1	41.1	46.9	45.3	37.7	28.8	21.4	13.4	28.2
Extreme Maximum Temp. (°F)	58	65	73	80	87	97	96	96	92	83	72	64	97
Extreme Minimum Temp. (°F)	-28	-39	-16	10	16	28	33	29	19	8	-8	-30	-39
Days Maximum Temp. ≥ 90°F	0	0	0	0	0	2	8	5	0	0	0	0	15
Days Maximum Temp. ≤ 32°F	14	7	1	0	0	0	0	0	0	0	2	10	34
Days Minimum Temp. ≤ 32°F	30	28	29	22	10	2	0	0	7	22	27	30	207
Days Minimum Temp. ≤ 0°F	8	6	1	0	0	0	0	0	0	0	0	3	18
Heating Degree Days (base 65°F)	1,364	1,139	934	660	422	177	31	48	259	583	909	1,241	7,767
Cooling Degree Days (base 65°F)	0	0	0	0	0	14	71	53	5	0	0	0	143
Mean Precipitation (in.)	3.05	2.71	2.40	1.78	1.88	1.07	0.94	1.11	1.62	2.04	2.39	2.36	23.35
Days With ≥ 0.1" Precipitation	6	5	5	5	6	3	3	3	4	4	5	5	54
Days With ≥ 1.0" Precipitation	1	1	0	0	0	0	0	0	0	0	0	0	2
Mean Snowfall (in.)	23.4	na	na	1.6	0.0	0.0	0.0	0.0	0.0	0.6	na	na	na
Days With ≥ 1.0" Snow Depth	24	22	12	na	0	0	0	0	0	0	na	na	na

Delta FAA Airport *Millard County*   Elevation: 4,763 ft.   Latitude: 39° 23' N   Longitude: 112° 31' W

	JAN	FEB	MAR	APR	MAY	JUN	JUL	AUG	SEP	OCT	NOV	DEC	YEAR
Mean Maximum Temp. (°F)	38.0	46.0	56.2	64.1	73.8	85.1	92.6	90.9	80.5	67.2	51.3	39.2	65.4
Mean Temp. (°F)	25.9	32.7	41.6	48.3	57.4	67.2	74.5	72.9	62.8	50.5	37.3	26.8	49.8
Mean Minimum Temp. (°F)	13.8	19.3	27.0	32.4	41.0	49.2	56.4	54.9	45.1	33.8	23.4	14.3	34.2
Extreme Maximum Temp. (°F)	62	74	84	89	94	105	108	105	98	92	77	70	108
Extreme Minimum Temp. (°F)	-25	-27	-2	12	21	25	37	35	24	-2	-3	-30	-30
Days Maximum Temp. ≥ 90°F	0	0	0	0	1	11	23	20	4	0	0	0	59
Days Maximum Temp. ≤ 32°F	9	3	0	0	0	0	0	0	0	0	1	7	20
Days Minimum Temp. ≤ 32°F	30	26	24	15	3	0	0	0	2	13	26	30	169
Days Minimum Temp. ≤ 0°F	5	2	0	0	0	0	0	0	0	0	0	3	10
Heating Degree Days (base 65°F)	1,205	907	718	497	242	59	3	5	118	444	822	1,179	6,199
Cooling Degree Days (base 65°F)	0	0	0	1	14	125	301	270	64	2	0	0	777
Mean Precipitation (in.)	0.59	0.61	0.86	0.83	0.98	0.51	0.56	0.64	0.80	0.91	0.64	0.45	8.38
Days With ≥ 0.1" Precipitation	2	2	3	3	3	1	2	2	2	3	2	2	27
Days With ≥ 1.0" Precipitation	0	0	0	0	0	0	0	0	0	0	0	0	0
Mean Snowfall (in.)	7.1	4.8	4.7	1.8	0.7	trace	0.0	0.0	0.2	0.9	3.5	4.6	28.3
Days With ≥ 1.0" Snow Depth	12	7	1	0	0	0	0	0	0	0	2	8	30

Deseret *Millard County*   Elevation: 4,589 ft.   Latitude: 39° 17' N   Longitude: 112° 39' W

	JAN	FEB	MAR	APR	MAY	JUN	JUL	AUG	SEP	OCT	NOV	DEC	YEAR
Mean Maximum Temp. (°F)	38.1	46.1	56.7	64.9	75.1	86.9	94.4	91.9	81.1	67.3	51.6	39.3	66.1
Mean Temp. (°F)	25.8	32.5	41.4	48.1	57.2	67.3	74.8	72.5	62.1	49.6	37.3	26.7	49.6
Mean Minimum Temp. (°F)	13.4	18.8	26.0	31.2	39.4	47.6	55.1	53.1	43.0	32.0	22.9	13.9	33.0
Extreme Maximum Temp. (°F)	62	74	83	90	99	106	109	107	100	93	77	69	109
Extreme Minimum Temp. (°F)	-24	-27	0	11	21	25	35	28	22	-3	-6	-29	-29
Days Maximum Temp. ≥ 90°F	0	0	0	0	1	13	26	22	5	0	0	0	67
Days Maximum Temp. ≤ 32°F	9	3	0	0	0	0	0	0	0	0	1	7	20
Days Minimum Temp. ≤ 32°F	30	26	25	17	5	0	0	0	4	16	26	30	179
Days Minimum Temp. ≤ 0°F	5	2	0	0	0	0	0	0	0	0	0	3	10
Heating Degree Days (base 65°F)	1,209	913	725	503	246	59	3	5	133	470	825	1,182	6,273
Cooling Degree Days (base 65°F)	0	0	0	1	13	127	307	256	53	0	0	0	757
Mean Precipitation (in.)	0.64	0.57	0.78	0.88	1.05	0.47	0.57	0.68	0.84	0.97	0.75	0.49	8.69
Days With ≥ 0.1" Precipitation	2	2	2	3	3	1	2	2	2	3	2	2	26
Days With ≥ 1.0" Precipitation	0	0	0	0	0	0	0	0	0	0	0	0	0
Mean Snowfall (in.)	5.1	2.9	2.1	1.4	0.6	0.0	0.0	0.0	0.2	0.5	2.0	3.5	18.3
Days With ≥ 1.0" Snow Depth	11	6	1	0	0	0	0	0	0	0	2	6	26

Dewey *Grand County*   Elevation: 4,117 ft.   Latitude: 38° 49' N   Longitude: 109° 18' W

	JAN	FEB	MAR	APR	MAY	JUN	JUL	AUG	SEP	OCT	NOV	DEC	YEAR
Mean Maximum Temp. (°F)	39.6	49.7	61.8	70.8	81.4	93.2	99.6	97.3	87.4	72.8	55.5	43.0	71.0
Mean Temp. (°F)	26.2	34.9	45.6	53.5	63.2	72.9	79.6	77.8	67.6	54.0	40.2	29.6	53.8
Mean Minimum Temp. (°F)	12.9	20.1	29.4	36.2	44.9	52.5	59.6	58.2	47.8	35.1	24.9	16.1	36.5
Extreme Maximum Temp. (°F)	64	73	84	95	100	111	113	110	107	93	80	71	113
Extreme Minimum Temp. (°F)	-25	-24	4	16	28	33	44	38	23	9	-5	-13	-25
Days Maximum Temp. ≥ 90°F	0	0	0	0	5	21	29	28	13	1	0	0	97
Days Maximum Temp. ≤ 32°F	7	2	0	0	0	0	0	0	0	0	0	4	13
Days Minimum Temp. ≤ 32°F	30	26	21	10	1	0	0	0	1	12	25	30	156
Days Minimum Temp. ≤ 0°F	5	2	0	0	0	0	0	0	0	0	0	1	8
Heating Degree Days (base 65°F)	1,196	843	595	341	103	9	0	0	44	337	738	1,092	5,298
Cooling Degree Days (base 65°F)	0	0	0	5	59	254	452	410	132	2	0	0	1,314
Mean Precipitation (in.)	0.79	0.59	0.93	0.82	0.95	0.45	0.67	0.63	0.72	1.34	0.90	0.67	9.46
Days With ≥ 0.1" Precipitation	2	2	3	3	3	1	2	2	2	3	3	2	28
Days With ≥ 1.0" Precipitation	0	0	0	0	0	0	0	0	0	0	0	0	0
Mean Snowfall (in.)	*5.5*	*0.5*	*trace*	0.0	0.0	0.0	0.0	0.0	0.0	0.0	1.0	*3.1*	*10.1*
Days With ≥ 1.0" Snow Depth	na	na	*0*	0	0	0	0	0	0	0	0	na	na

Dinosaur Nat'l Mon. Quarry Area *Uintah County*   Elevation: 4,767 ft.   Latitude: 40° 26' N   Longitude: 109° 18' W

	JAN	FEB	MAR	APR	MAY	JUN	JUL	AUG	SEP	OCT	NOV	DEC	YEAR
Mean Maximum Temp. (°F)	31.0	39.3	54.4	65.4	76.0	88.0	94.4	92.4	82.2	67.4	48.4	35.5	64.5
Mean Temp. (°F)	17.9	25.4	39.7	49.1	58.7	68.3	74.8	72.7	63.0	49.7	35.0	23.1	48.1
Mean Minimum Temp. (°F)	4.8	11.5	25.0	32.8	41.3	48.5	55.1	52.9	43.7	32.0	21.6	10.1	31.6
Extreme Maximum Temp. (°F)	60	66	77	89	94	105	107	105	99	93	74	61	107
Extreme Minimum Temp. (°F)	-39	-40	-3	10	20	30	38	36	20	2	-10	-33	-40
Days Maximum Temp. ≥ 90°F	0	0	0	0	1	15	26	24	6	0	0	0	72
Days Maximum Temp. ≤ 32°F	17	7	1	0	0	0	0	0	0	0	2	10	37
Days Minimum Temp. ≤ 32°F	31	28	26	14	2	0	0	0	2	16	27	30	176
Days Minimum Temp. ≤ 0°F	12	6	0	0	0	0	0	0	0	0	0	5	23
Heating Degree Days (base 65°F)	1,454	1,113	777	470	202	37	1	2	109	467	891	1,292	6,815
Cooling Degree Days (base 65°F)	0	0	0	1	16	143	308	257	58	0	0	0	783
Mean Precipitation (in.)	0.62	0.64	0.73	0.84	1.05	0.61	0.72	0.66	0.93	1.16	0.64	0.52	9.12
Days With ≥ 0.1" Precipitation	2	2	2	3	3	2	2	2	3	3	2	2	28
Days With ≥ 1.0" Precipitation	0	0	0	0	0	0	0	0	0	0	0	0	0
Mean Snowfall (in.)	6.3	4.2	1.4	0.6	0.1	0.0	0.0	0.0	0.0	0.5	2.4	6.4	21.9
Days With ≥ 1.0" Snow Depth	23	18	5	0	0	0	0	0	0	0	2	14	62

Dugway *Tooele County*   Elevation: 4,337 ft.   Latitude: 40° 11' N   Longitude: 112° 55' W

	JAN	FEB	MAR	APR	MAY	JUN	JUL	AUG	SEP	OCT	NOV	DEC	YEAR
Mean Maximum Temp. (°F)	37.7	45.8	54.7	63.0	73.5	85.7	94.5	92.5	80.9	66.0	50.7	39.5	65.4
Mean Temp. (°F)	26.4	34.0	41.9	48.9	58.4	69.1	77.4	75.4	64.0	50.3	38.0	27.8	51.0
Mean Minimum Temp. (°F)	15.0	22.2	29.1	34.7	43.3	52.4	60.2	58.2	47.2	34.6	25.3	16.1	36.5
Extreme Maximum Temp. (°F)	63	71	80	88	99	106	109	108	102	91	78	69	109
Extreme Minimum Temp. (°F)	-25	-29	4	11	21	31	42	33	22	9	-2	-27	-29
Days Maximum Temp. ≥ 90°F	0	0	0	0	1	12	25	23	7	0	0	0	68
Days Maximum Temp. ≤ 32°F	10	3	0	0	0	0	0	0	0	0	1	7	21
Days Minimum Temp. ≤ 32°F	29	24	21	12	2	0	0	0	1	13	25	29	156
Days Minimum Temp. ≤ 0°F	4	1	0	0	0	0	0	0	0	0	0	3	8
Heating Degree Days (base 65°F)	1,190	868	708	479	226	50	2	3	111	449	803	1,145	6,034
Cooling Degree Days (base 65°F)	0	0	0	3	30	177	385	346	96	1	0	0	1,038
Mean Precipitation (in.)	0.58	0.64	0.95	0.84	1.19	0.52	0.61	0.56	0.70	0.85	0.64	0.52	8.60
Days With ≥ 0.1" Precipitation	2	2	3	3	4	2	2	1	2	3	2	2	28
Days With ≥ 1.0" Precipitation	0	0	0	0	0	0	0	0	0	0	0	0	0
Mean Snowfall (in.)	4.0	2.5	2.1	0.9	trace	0.0	0.0	0.0	trace	0.1	1.5	3.6	14.7
Days With ≥ 1.0" Snow Depth	na	3	*1*	0	0	0	0	0	0	0	0	*0*	na

Echo Dam *Summit County*   Elevation: 5,469 ft.   Latitude: 40° 58' N   Longitude: 111° 26' W

	JAN	FEB	MAR	APR	MAY	JUN	JUL	AUG	SEP	OCT	NOV	DEC	YEAR
Mean Maximum Temp. (°F)	34.0	39.5	49.0	57.8	67.6	78.6	86.9	85.9	76.2	63.7	46.5	35.7	60.1
Mean Temp. (°F)	22.7	26.8	36.3	43.9	52.4	61.0	68.3	67.1	57.8	46.8	34.1	24.5	45.1
Mean Minimum Temp. (°F)	11.3	14.0	23.7	29.9	37.2	43.3	49.6	48.3	39.3	29.8	21.6	13.2	30.1
Extreme Maximum Temp. (°F)	58	65	72	80	87	97	99	98	94	85	73	65	99
Extreme Minimum Temp. (°F)	-28	-34	-15	9	16	26	33	27	16	6	-14	-32	-34
Days Maximum Temp. ≥ 90°F	0	0	0	0	0	3	10	7	1	0	0	0	21
Days Maximum Temp. ≤ 32°F	13	6	1	0	0	0	0	0	0	0	3	11	34
Days Minimum Temp. ≤ 32°F	30	27	27	20	7	1	0	0	6	21	27	30	196
Days Minimum Temp. ≤ 0°F	7	5	1	0	0	0	0	0	0	0	1	4	18
Heating Degree Days (base 65°F)	1,306	1,073	882	627	383	142	17	25	222	558	921	1,249	7,405
Cooling Degree Days (base 65°F)	0	0	0	0	1	26	115	98	12	0	0	0	252
Mean Precipitation (in.)	1.10	1.00	1.37	1.56	1.94	1.11	0.85	0.74	1.38	1.58	1.60	1.07	15.30
Days With ≥ 0.1" Precipitation	4	4	4	5	6	3	3	2	4	4	5	4	48
Days With ≥ 1.0" Precipitation	0	0	0	0	0	0	0	0	0	0	0	0	0
Mean Snowfall (in.)	15.0	12.6	10.0	6.1	2.1	0.2	0.0	0.0	0.2	2.3	11.9	13.5	73.9
Days With ≥ 1.0" Snow Depth	25	22	8	1	0	0	0	0	0	1	9	22	88

Enterprise Airport *Iron County*   Elevation: 5,200 ft.   Latitude: 37° 41' N   Longitude: 113° 39' W

	JAN	FEB	MAR	APR	MAY	JUN	JUL	AUG	SEP	OCT	NOV	DEC	YEAR
Mean Maximum Temp. (°F)	41.7	47.2	55.9	63.9	73.4	84.0	90.3	88.3	80.0	68.2	53.3	42.9	65.8
Mean Temp. (°F)	27.2	32.8	39.6	45.5	54.5	63.2	70.1	68.7	60.0	48.5	36.4	27.6	47.8
Mean Minimum Temp. (°F)	12.7	18.2	23.3	27.1	35.5	42.3	49.9	49.1	39.9	28.8	19.5	12.3	29.9
Extreme Maximum Temp. (°F)	70	77	79	86	97	100	104	102	95	88	78	72	104
Extreme Minimum Temp. (°F)	-26	-33	-2	7	10	26	27	30	18	-5	-11	-34	-34
Days Maximum Temp. ≥ 90°F	0	0	0	0	1	8	18	14	2	0	0	0	43
Days Maximum Temp. ≤ 32°F	6	2	0	0	0	0	0	0	0	0	1	4	13
Days Minimum Temp. ≤ 32°F	30	26	27	23	11	1	0	0	5	22	28	30	203
Days Minimum Temp. ≤ 0°F	5	2	0	0	0	0	0	0	0	0	1	4	12
Heating Degree Days (base 65°F)	1,163	904	780	577	323	101	9	19	166	506	851	1,151	6,550
Cooling Degree Days (base 65°F)	0	0	0	0	5	55	173	144	23	0	0	0	400
Mean Precipitation (in.)	0.72	0.87	1.35	0.79	0.78	0.49	1.11	1.12	0.90	0.98	0.84	0.58	10.53
Days With ≥ 0.1" Precipitation	2	3	4	2	2	1	3	3	2	3	2	2	29
Days With ≥ 1.0" Precipitation	0	0	0	0	0	0	0	0	0	0	0	0	0
Mean Snowfall (in.)	6.6	5.0	5.0	2.0	0.9	0.0	0.0	0.0	trace	0.8	4.6	5.1	30.0
Days With ≥ 1.0" Snow Depth	12	7	1	0	0	0	0	0	0	0	3	7	30

Ephraim Sorensens Field *Sanpete County*   Elevation: 5,508 ft.   Latitude: 39° 22' N   Longitude: 111° 35' W

	JAN	FEB	MAR	APR	MAY	JUN	JUL	AUG	SEP	OCT	NOV	DEC	YEAR
Mean Maximum Temp. (°F)	35.9	41.9	50.8	59.1	69.8	81.6	89.2	87.4	77.4	64.8	48.9	37.6	62.0
Mean Temp. (°F)	24.7	30.3	38.6	45.5	54.5	64.3	71.6	69.9	60.7	49.2	36.5	26.2	47.7
Mean Minimum Temp. (°F)	13.6	18.7	26.3	31.8	39.3	47.0	53.9	52.4	44.0	33.6	24.0	14.8	33.3
Extreme Maximum Temp. (°F)	59	70	76	85	94	101	108	102	96	90	76	66	108
Extreme Minimum Temp. (°F)	-28	-22	-9	9	20	26	34	37	20	12	-5	-34	-34
Days Maximum Temp. ≥ 90°F	0	0	0	0	0	6	17	13	2	0	0	0	38
Days Maximum Temp. ≤ 32°F	10	4	1	0	0	0	0	0	0	0	2	9	26
Days Minimum Temp. ≤ 32°F	31	27	25	16	5	1	0	0	2	13	26	30	176
Days Minimum Temp. ≤ 0°F	4	1	0	0	0	0	0	0	0	0	0	3	8
Heating Degree Days (base 65°F)	1,242	972	812	580	322	91	5	11	155	483	849	1,194	6,716
Cooling Degree Days (base 65°F)	0	0	0	0	4	78	217	179	35	0	0	0	513
Mean Precipitation (in.)	0.97	1.02	1.40	1.16	1.26	0.74	0.80	0.83	1.18	1.31	1.11	0.87	12.65
Days With ≥ 0.1" Precipitation	3	4	5	4	4	2	2	3	4	4	3	3	41
Days With ≥ 1.0" Precipitation	0	0	0	0	0	0	0	0	0	0	0	0	0
Mean Snowfall (in.)	na	na	na	na	0.0	0.0	0.0	0.0	0.0	0.0	na	na	na
Days With ≥ 1.0" Snow Depth	na	na	na	na	0	0	0	0	0	0	na	na	na

Escalante *Garfield County*   Elevation: 5,807 ft.   Latitude: 37° 46' N   Longitude: 111° 36' W

	JAN	FEB	MAR	APR	MAY	JUN	JUL	AUG	SEP	OCT	NOV	DEC	YEAR
Mean Maximum Temp. (°F)	41.8	47.5	55.7	63.8	74.1	85.2	90.4	87.2	78.9	67.2	52.8	43.3	65.7
Mean Temp. (°F)	28.8	34.6	41.7	48.4	57.4	66.7	72.7	70.4	62.1	51.3	39.1	30.5	50.3
Mean Minimum Temp. (°F)	15.8	21.7	27.7	33.0	40.6	48.2	54.9	53.4	45.3	35.4	25.3	17.6	34.9
Extreme Maximum Temp. (°F)	68	70	80	85	95	103	103	100	95	87	76	69	103
Extreme Minimum Temp. (°F)	-14	-13	6	15	25	31	42	40	23	10	0	-11	-14
Days Maximum Temp. ≥ 90°F	0	0	0	0	0	9	19	12	2	0	0	0	42
Days Maximum Temp. ≤ 32°F	4	1	0	0	0	0	0	0	0	0	0	3	8
Days Minimum Temp. ≤ 32°F	30	27	24	14	3	0	0	0	1	9	26	30	164
Days Minimum Temp. ≤ 0°F	2	1	0	0	0	0	0	0	0	0	0	1	4
Heating Degree Days (base 65°F)	1,115	851	715	491	238	49	1	6	116	416	770	1,063	5,831
Cooling Degree Days (base 65°F)	0	0	0	0	10	108	249	189	39	0	0	0	595
Mean Precipitation (in.)	0.90	0.79	0.92	0.49	0.64	0.38	0.82	1.57	1.11	1.05	0.80	0.55	10.02
Days With ≥ 0.1" Precipitation	2	2	3	1	2	1	3	4	3	3	2	2	28
Days With ≥ 1.0" Precipitation	0	0	0	0	0	0	0	0	0	0	0	0	0
Mean Snowfall (in.)	9.7	5.1	4.2	1.7	0.0	0.0	0.0	0.0	0.0	0.4	3.2	4.9	29.2
Days With ≥ 1.0" Snow Depth	14	6	1	0	0	0	0	0	0	0	2	5	28

Eskdale *Millard County*   Elevation: 4,977 ft.   Latitude: 39° 07' N   Longitude: 113° 57' W

	JAN	FEB	MAR	APR	MAY	JUN	JUL	AUG	SEP	OCT	NOV	DEC	YEAR
Mean Maximum Temp. (°F)	41.9	48.3	56.9	64.7	74.4	85.3	92.7	90.8	80.8	68.2	53.3	42.5	66.7
Mean Temp. (°F)	28.0	33.9	42.4	49.0	57.7	67.5	74.8	73.0	62.8	50.9	38.6	28.5	50.6
Mean Minimum Temp. (°F)	14.0	19.5	27.7	33.4	41.0	49.7	56.8	55.1	44.8	33.6	23.8	14.3	34.5
Extreme Maximum Temp. (°F)	69	75	81	87	94	102	105	101	98	89	79	71	105
Extreme Minimum Temp. (°F)	-23	-31	-8	11	21	25	32	35	20	-3	-5	-20	-31
Days Maximum Temp. ≥ 90°F	0	0	0	0	1	11	24	20	5	0	0	0	61
Days Maximum Temp. ≤ 32°F	7	2	0	0	0	0	0	0	0	0	1	5	15
Days Minimum Temp. ≤ 32°F	29	25	22	14	4	0	0	0	2	14	25	29	164
Days Minimum Temp. ≤ 0°F	4	1	0	0	0	0	0	0	0	0	0	3	8
Heating Degree Days (base 65°F)	1,141	870	693	474	235	56	3	4	121	432	788	1,126	5,943
Cooling Degree Days (base 65°F)	0	0	0	0	3	19	139	314	275	69	2	0	821
Mean Precipitation (in.)	0.28	0.35	0.71	0.61	0.83	0.61	0.60	0.56	0.76	0.64	0.41	0.18	6.54
Days With ≥ 0.1" Precipitation	1	1	2	2	2	2	2	2	2	2	1	1	20
Days With ≥ 1.0" Precipitation	0	0	0	0	0	0	0	0	0	0	0	0	0
Mean Snowfall (in.)	3.8	2.7	2.6	1.1	0.6	0.0	0.0	0.0	0.0	0.4	1.0	2.3	14.5
Days With ≥ 1.0" Snow Depth	4	3	1	0	0	0	0	0	0	0	1	na	na

Fairfield *Utah County*   Elevation: 4,878 ft.   Latitude: 40° 16' N   Longitude: 112° 05' W

	JAN	FEB	MAR	APR	MAY	JUN	JUL	AUG	SEP	OCT	NOV	DEC	YEAR
Mean Maximum Temp. (°F)	37.6	43.9	53.2	61.7	71.2	81.7	88.6	87.5	78.8	66.1	50.4	39.2	63.3
Mean Temp. (°F)	24.9	30.5	39.2	45.6	54.1	62.9	69.8	68.4	59.2	47.8	35.9	26.2	47.0
Mean Minimum Temp. (°F)	12.2	17.0	25.0	29.5	36.9	44.0	50.8	49.2	39.7	29.4	21.4	13.1	30.7
Extreme Maximum Temp. (°F)	63	70	77	85	91	99	100	100	95	88	76	70	100
Extreme Minimum Temp. (°F)	-28	-36	-2	11	17	23	32	28	18	4	-9	-29	-36
Days Maximum Temp. ≥ 90°F	0	0	0	0	0	5	15	11	2	0	0	0	33
Days Maximum Temp. ≤ 32°F	8	3	0	0	0	0	0	0	0	0	1	7	19
Days Minimum Temp. ≤ 32°F	30	27	26	20	8	1	0	0	6	22	27	30	197
Days Minimum Temp. ≤ 0°F	6	3	0	0	0	0	0	0	0	0	1	4	14
Heating Degree Days (base 65°F)	1,236	968	792	575	334	108	9	16	188	526	867	1,197	6,816
Cooling Degree Days (base 65°F)	0	0	0	0	3	50	163	140	24	0	0	0	380
Mean Precipitation (in.)	1.14	1.12	1.18	1.17	1.28	0.75	1.14	1.04	1.07	1.25	1.06	0.87	13.07
Days With ≥ 0.1" Precipitation	4	4	4	4	4	2	3	3	3	4	3	3	41
Days With ≥ 1.0" Precipitation	0	0	0	0	0	0	0	0	0	0	0	0	0
Mean Snowfall (in.)	10.7	7.0	4.7	2.2	0.3	0.0	trace	0.0	trace	1.1	4.6	7.6	38.2
Days With ≥ 1.0" Snow Depth	19	14	4	0	0	0	0	0	0	0	4	14	55

Farmington USU Field Station *Davis County*   Elevation: 4,337 ft.   Latitude: 41° 01' N   Longitude: 111° 55' W

	JAN	FEB	MAR	APR	MAY	JUN	JUL	AUG	SEP	OCT	NOV	DEC	YEAR
Mean Maximum Temp. (°F)	38.2	44.7	54.2	62.7	72.6	83.7	91.7	90.2	79.7	66.3	50.4	39.3	64.5
Mean Temp. (°F)	29.3	34.5	42.7	50.0	58.7	68.4	75.9	74.4	64.5	52.5	39.9	30.4	51.8
Mean Minimum Temp. (°F)	20.4	24.3	31.2	37.2	44.8	53.0	59.9	58.4	49.2	38.6	29.4	21.4	39.0
Extreme Maximum Temp. (°F)	60	69	78	87	92	102	105	104	99	89	77	68	105
Extreme Minimum Temp. (°F)	-14	-9	5	16	25	32	41	39	28	14	3	-12	-14
Days Maximum Temp. ≥ 90°F	0	0	0	0	0	9	21	18	3	0	0	0	51
Days Maximum Temp. ≤ 32°F	8	2	0	0	0	0	0	0	0	0	1	6	17
Days Minimum Temp. ≤ 32°F	28	24	18	9	1	0	0	0	0	6	20	28	134
Days Minimum Temp. ≤ 0°F	1	0	0	0	0	0	0	0	0	0	0	1	2
Heating Degree Days (base 65°F)	1,098	855	684	448	217	51	2	3	94	385	745	1,067	5,649
Cooling Degree Days (base 65°F)	0	0	0	6	35	170	359	328	97	3	0	0	998
Mean Precipitation (in.)	2.18	1.99	2.60	2.78	2.99	1.31	0.92	0.78	1.66	2.16	2.09	1.94	23.40
Days With ≥ 0.1" Precipitation	6	5	6	6	6	3	2	2	3	4	5	5	53
Days With ≥ 1.0" Precipitation	0	0	0	0	1	0	0	0	0	0	0	0	1
Mean Snowfall (in.)	15.5	8.9	4.5	2.2	0.3	0.0	0.0	0.0	0.1	0.6	5.2	16.0	53.3
Days With ≥ 1.0" Snow Depth	22	14	4	1	0	0	0	0	0	0	4	16	61

Ferron *Emery County*   Elevation: 5,928 ft.   Latitude: 39° 05' N   Longitude: 111° 08' W

	JAN	FEB	MAR	APR	MAY	JUN	JUL	AUG	SEP	OCT	NOV	DEC	YEAR
Mean Maximum Temp. (°F)	36.3	42.7	52.6	60.6	70.8	81.8	87.5	85.5	77.2	65.2	49.6	38.8	62.4
Mean Temp. (°F)	23.9	30.4	39.6	47.0	56.5	66.6	72.5	70.5	61.9	50.2	36.4	26.4	48.5
Mean Minimum Temp. (°F)	11.4	18.0	26.6	33.3	42.2	51.3	57.5	55.5	46.4	35.1	23.2	14.0	34.5
Extreme Maximum Temp. (°F)	59	68	77	85	91	100	102	99	94	84	71	62	102
Extreme Minimum Temp. (°F)	-17	-15	4	13	22	28	39	37	22	8	-4	-21	-21
Days Maximum Temp. ≥ 90°F	0	0	0	0	0	5	13	8	1	0	0	0	27
Days Maximum Temp. ≤ 32°F	10	3	0	0	0	0	0	0	0	0	1	6	20
Days Minimum Temp. ≤ 32°F	31	27	25	14	3	0	0	0	1	11	27	31	170
Days Minimum Temp. ≤ 0°F	4	1	0	0	0	0	0	0	0	0	0	1	6
Heating Degree Days (base 65°F)	1,269	971	780	534	267	66	5	9	133	454	851	1,189	6,528
Cooling Degree Days (base 65°F)	0	0	0	1	15	122	250	198	49	0	0	0	635
Mean Precipitation (in.)	0.66	0.60	0.74	0.53	0.71	0.43	1.08	0.98	1.02	0.91	0.57	0.40	8.63
Days With ≥ 0.1" Precipitation	3	2	2	2	2	1	3	3	3	2	2	2	27
Days With ≥ 1.0" Precipitation	0	0	0	0	0	0	0	0	0	0	0	0	0
Mean Snowfall (in.)	9.8	7.0	3.8	1.5	trace	0.0	0.0	0.0	0.0	0.8	2.6	4.8	30.3
Days With ≥ 1.0" Snow Depth	19	12	3	1	0	0	0	0	0	0	2	9	46

Fillmore *Millard County*   Elevation: 5,118 ft.   Latitude: 38° 58' N   Longitude: 112° 20' W

	JAN	FEB	MAR	APR	MAY	JUN	JUL	AUG	SEP	OCT	NOV	DEC	YEAR
Mean Maximum Temp. (°F)	39.4	46.1	55.0	62.9	72.8	84.0	91.1	88.9	79.7	66.6	51.0	39.9	64.8
Mean Temp. (°F)	28.7	34.5	42.4	49.0	57.8	67.8	75.0	73.4	64.2	52.1	39.3	29.3	51.1
Mean Minimum Temp. (°F)	18.1	23.0	29.8	35.1	42.7	51.5	58.8	57.8	48.7	37.5	27.5	18.6	37.4
Extreme Maximum Temp. (°F)	65	72	78	86	92	104	103	102	97	87	79	69	104
Extreme Minimum Temp. (°F)	-21	-15	-6	12	22	24	40	38	20	1	-2	-19	-21
Days Maximum Temp. ≥ 90°F	0	0	0	0	0	7	20	15	2	0	0	0	44
Days Maximum Temp. ≤ 32°F	8	3	0	0	0	0	0	0	0	0	1	7	19
Days Minimum Temp. ≤ 32°F	29	24	20	13	3	0	0	0	1	8	22	29	149
Days Minimum Temp. ≤ 0°F	2	1	0	0	0	0	0	0	0	0	0	2	5
Heating Degree Days (base 65°F)	1,118	852	694	473	238	57	2	3	98	397	764	1,100	5,796
Cooling Degree Days (base 65°F)	0	0	0	3	23	140	304	273	82	3	0	0	828
Mean Precipitation (in.)	1.36	1.32	2.00	1.84	1.63	0.73	0.82	0.80	1.05	1.61	1.54	1.23	15.93
Days With ≥ 0.1" Precipitation	4	4	6	5	4	2	3	3	3	4	4	4	46
Days With ≥ 1.0" Precipitation	0	0	0	0	0	0	0	0	0	0	0	0	0
Mean Snowfall (in.)	15.0	13.3	14.6	8.0	2.1	0.1	0.0	0.0	0.2	3.4	10.9	14.0	81.6
Days With ≥ 1.0" Snow Depth	20	14	5	2	0	0	0	0	0	1	7	17	66

Fish Springs Refuge *Juab County*   Elevation: 4,333 ft.   Latitude: 39° 50' N   Longitude: 113° 24' W

	JAN	FEB	MAR	APR	MAY	JUN	JUL	AUG	SEP	OCT	NOV	DEC	YEAR
Mean Maximum Temp. (°F)	39.2	46.2	56.3	64.1	74.4	86.0	94.4	92.8	81.7	67.1	51.7	40.6	66.2
Mean Temp. (°F)	28.4	34.6	44.0	50.8	60.7	71.3	79.1	77.4	66.3	52.5	39.6	29.6	52.9
Mean Minimum Temp. (°F)	17.6	23.0	31.6	37.5	46.9	56.5	63.6	61.9	50.8	37.8	27.4	18.6	39.5
Extreme Maximum Temp. (°F)	69	74	80	88	97	104	109	105	101	92	78	74	109
Extreme Minimum Temp. (°F)	-19	-18	6	14	27	32	44	40	29	9	1	-18	-19
Days Maximum Temp. ≥ 90°F	0	0	0	0	1	13	26	24	7	0	0	0	71
Days Maximum Temp. ≤ 32°F	9	3	0	0	0	0	0	0	0	0	1	7	20
Days Minimum Temp. ≤ 32°F	29	24	17	8	1	0	0	0	0	8	22	29	138
Days Minimum Temp. ≤ 0°F	2	1	0	0	0	0	0	0	0	0	0	1	4
Heating Degree Days (base 65°F)	1,128	851	645	425	180	37	2	2	79	388	756	1,090	5,583
Cooling Degree Days (base 65°F)	0	0	0	7	53	220	434	398	125	7	0	0	1,244
Mean Precipitation (in.)	0.46	0.53	0.85	1.01	1.07	0.61	0.53	0.63	0.75	0.85	0.59	0.36	8.24
Days With ≥ 0.1" Precipitation	2	2	3	3	3	2	2	2	2	3	2	1	27
Days With ≥ 1.0" Precipitation	0	0	0	0	0	0	0	0	0	0	0	0	0
Mean Snowfall (in.)	3.4	2.2	2.4	1.0	0.3	trace	0.0	0.0	trace	0.1	1.9	2.7	14.0
Days With ≥ 1.0" Snow Depth	8	4	1	0	0	0	0	0	0	0	1	3	17

Flaming Gorge *Daggett County*   Elevation: 6,269 ft.   Latitude: 40° 56' N   Longitude: 109° 25' W

	JAN	FEB	MAR	APR	MAY	JUN	JUL	AUG	SEP	OCT	NOV	DEC	YEAR
Mean Maximum Temp. (°F)	35.4	40.1	47.8	56.4	67.1	78.1	85.2	83.6	74.2	61.6	45.0	36.0	59.2
Mean Temp. (°F)	22.5	26.4	34.6	42.1	51.3	60.4	67.3	65.8	56.7	45.5	32.6	23.7	44.1
Mean Minimum Temp. (°F)	9.5	12.5	21.3	27.7	35.4	42.7	49.3	47.9	39.2	29.5	20.1	11.4	28.9
Extreme Maximum Temp. (°F)	59	66	71	80	88	96	100	98	91	83	71	64	100
Extreme Minimum Temp. (°F)	-29	-31	-10	-1	14	26	30	26	15	-4	-13	-36	-36
Days Maximum Temp. ≥ 90°F	0	0	0	0	0	2	7	4	0	0	0	0	13
Days Maximum Temp. ≤ 32°F	11	6	2	0	0	0	0	0	0	0	4	11	34
Days Minimum Temp. ≤ 32°F	30	27	28	23	10	2	0	0	6	20	27	30	203
Days Minimum Temp. ≤ 0°F	7	5	1	0	0	0	0	0	0	0	1	5	19
Heating Degree Days (base 65°F)	1,311	1,085	937	681	420	157	23	40	250	597	966	1,274	7,741
Cooling Degree Days (base 65°F)	0	0	0	0	1	25	102	71	9	0	0	0	208
Mean Precipitation (in.)	0.50	0.56	1.12	1.64	1.76	1.19	1.07	1.34	1.14	1.35	0.85	0.59	13.11
Days With ≥ 0.1" Precipitation	2	2	4	4	4	3	3	3	3	3	3	2	36
Days With ≥ 1.0" Precipitation	0	0	0	0	0	0	0	0	0	0	0	0	0
Mean Snowfall (in.)	9.5	8.1	11.2	8.5	0.9	0.3	0.0	0.0	0.2	3.4	9.0	9.4	60.5
Days With ≥ 1.0" Snow Depth	22	18	8	2	0	0	0	0	0	2	9	18	79

Hanksville *Wayne County*   Elevation: 4,307 ft.   Latitude: 38° 22' N   Longitude: 110° 43' W

	JAN	FEB	MAR	APR	MAY	JUN	JUL	AUG	SEP	OCT	NOV	DEC	YEAR
Mean Maximum Temp. (°F)	41.3	50.6	61.8	70.7	81.7	93.8	99.2	96.3	86.1	71.9	55.0	43.4	71.0
Mean Temp. (°F)	26.3	34.9	45.2	53.5	63.4	73.5	79.5	77.1	67.1	53.4	38.9	28.8	53.5
Mean Minimum Temp. (°F)	11.2	19.2	28.6	36.3	45.1	53.2	59.7	58.0	48.0	34.9	22.8	14.1	35.9
Extreme Maximum Temp. (°F)	69	74	85	98	103	110	114	110	105	95	82	70	114
Extreme Minimum Temp. (°F)	-26	-33	4	16	26	31	40	35	25	-6	-7	-22	-33
Days Maximum Temp. ≥ 90°F	0	0	0	1	7	22	29	27	12	1	0	0	99
Days Maximum Temp. ≤ 32°F	7	1	0	0	0	0	0	0	0	0	0	3	11
Days Minimum Temp. ≤ 32°F	30	26	22	10	2	0	0	0	1	12	27	30	160
Days Minimum Temp. ≤ 0°F	7	2	0	0	0	0	0	0	0	0	0	2	11
Heating Degree Days (base 65°F)	1,193	844	607	346	111	14	0	0	55	356	777	1,115	5,418
Cooling Degree Days (base 65°F)	0	0	0	9	72	283	457	388	129	3	0	0	1,341
Mean Precipitation (in.)	0.50	0.25	0.55	0.46	0.51	0.24	0.52	0.57	0.79	0.69	0.40	0.27	5.75
Days With ≥ 0.1" Precipitation	1	1	2	2	2	1	1	2	2	2	1	1	18
Days With ≥ 1.0" Precipitation	0	0	0	0	0	0	0	0	0	0	0	0	0
Mean Snowfall (in.)	1.6	0.8	0.6	0.1	trace	0.0	0.0	0.0	0.0	0.4	0.7	0.8	5.0
Days With ≥ 1.0" Snow Depth	11	5	0	0	0	0	0	0	0	0	1	5	22

Heber *Wasatch County*   Elevation: 5,629 ft.   Latitude: 40° 30' N   Longitude: 111° 25' W

	JAN	FEB	MAR	APR	MAY	JUN	JUL	AUG	SEP	OCT	NOV	DEC	YEAR
Mean Maximum Temp. (°F)	35.1	40.6	50.0	59.5	69.3	79.8	87.2	86.1	77.0	65.0	48.5	37.1	61.3
Mean Temp. (°F)	22.7	27.4	36.9	44.4	52.6	61.0	67.9	66.7	58.2	47.5	35.2	24.8	45.4
Mean Minimum Temp. (°F)	10.3	14.1	23.7	29.2	35.9	42.2	48.5	47.2	39.5	29.9	21.9	12.5	29.6
Extreme Maximum Temp. (°F)	59	68	74	85	90	97	102	101	95	88	78	68	102
Extreme Minimum Temp. (°F)	-29	-36	-8	9	15	18	33	29	17	6	-11	-34	-36
Days Maximum Temp. ≥ 90°F	0	0	0	0	0	3	11	9	1	0	0	0	24
Days Maximum Temp. ≤ 32°F	11	5	0	0	0	0	0	0	0	0	2	9	27
Days Minimum Temp. ≤ 32°F	30	28	28	21	9	2	0	0	5	21	27	30	201
Days Minimum Temp. ≤ 0°F	7	4	0	0	0	0	0	0	0	0	1	5	17
Heating Degree Days (base 65°F)	1,304	1,057	865	612	378	139	17	30	210	537	887	1,238	7,274
Cooling Degree Days (base 65°F)	0	0	0	0	1	27	117	99	16	0	0	0	260
Mean Precipitation (in.)	1.85	1.64	1.48	1.29	1.47	0.88	0.87	0.95	1.29	1.61	1.56	1.44	16.33
Days With ≥ 0.1" Precipitation	5	4	4	5	5	3	2	3	4	4	4	4	47
Days With ≥ 1.0" Precipitation	0	0	0	0	0	0	0	0	0	0	0	0	0
Mean Snowfall (in.)	21.1	15.6	5.9	3.4	1.3	trace	0.0	0.0	0.1	1.7	8.3	14.3	71.7
Days With ≥ 1.0" Snow Depth	26	22	9	0	0	0	0	0	0	0	6	18	81

Ibapah *Tooele County*   Elevation: 5,278 ft.   Latitude: 40° 02' N   Longitude: 113° 59' W

	JAN	FEB	MAR	APR	MAY	JUN	JUL	AUG	SEP	OCT	NOV	DEC	YEAR
Mean Maximum Temp. (°F)	42.5	47.4	55.7	62.7	71.8	82.2	91.3	90.5	80.5	67.9	52.9	42.9	65.7
Mean Temp. (°F)	27.0	31.5	39.3	45.0	53.0	61.2	68.8	67.6	58.1	47.2	36.0	27.0	46.8
Mean Minimum Temp. (°F)	11.5	15.6	22.7	27.2	34.1	40.2	46.2	44.7	35.5	26.5	19.1	11.1	27.9
Extreme Maximum Temp. (°F)	68	75	81	88	94	101	105	103	102	94	79	73	105
Extreme Minimum Temp. (°F)	-30	-31	-9	2	16	22	29	22	12	-3	-6	-31	-31
Days Maximum Temp. ≥ 90°F	0	0	0	0	0	7	22	20	5	0	0	0	54
Days Maximum Temp. ≤ 32°F	5	2	0	0	0	0	0	0	0	0	0	4	11
Days Minimum Temp. ≤ 32°F	30	28	28	23	12	3	0	1	11	25	28	30	219
Days Minimum Temp. ≤ 0°F	6	2	0	0	0	0	0	0	0	0	1	5	14
Heating Degree Days (base 65°F)	1,171	938	791	594	362	143	19	30	220	544	862	1,171	6,845
Cooling Degree Days (base 65°F)	0	0	0	0	3	34	140	111	21	0	0	0	309
Mean Precipitation (in.)	0.74	0.63	0.99	1.17	1.32	0.95	0.91	0.72	0.87	1.01	0.55	0.51	10.37
Days With ≥ 0.1" Precipitation	2	2	3	3	4	2	2	2	2	2	2	1	27
Days With ≥ 1.0" Precipitation	0	0	0	0	0	0	0	0	0	0	0	0	0
Mean Snowfall (in.)	8.4	6.1	5.0	3.6	1.2	0.0	0.0	0.0	0.1	0.9	3.4	5.0	33.7
Days With ≥ 1.0" Snow Depth	14	10	3	1	0	0	0	0	0	0	3	10	41

Jensen *Uintah County*   Elevation: 4,747 ft.   Latitude: 40° 22' N   Longitude: 109° 21' W

	JAN	FEB	MAR	APR	MAY	JUN	JUL	AUG	SEP	OCT	NOV	DEC	YEAR
Mean Maximum Temp. (°F)	29.7	38.1	53.2	64.0	74.2	84.6	90.7	88.9	79.2	65.8	47.5	33.7	62.5
Mean Temp. (°F)	16.7	24.1	38.1	47.3	57.0	65.6	71.8	69.7	60.4	48.2	33.6	21.0	46.1
Mean Minimum Temp. (°F)	3.7	10.1	22.9	30.6	39.7	46.6	52.8	50.5	41.6	30.6	19.7	8.2	29.7
Extreme Maximum Temp. (°F)	57	67	77	87	95	106	105	102	98	85	74	60	106
Extreme Minimum Temp. (°F)	-36	-40	-5	8	18	30	38	27	20	0	-12	-36	-40
Days Maximum Temp. ≥ 90°F	0	0	0	0	0	9	20	15	2	0	0	0	46
Days Maximum Temp. ≤ 32°F	18	9	1	0	0	0	0	0	0	0	2	13	43
Days Minimum Temp. ≤ 32°F	31	28	28	18	4	0	0	0	4	19	29	31	192
Days Minimum Temp. ≤ 0°F	12	7	0	0	0	0	0	0	0	0	0	7	26
Heating Degree Days (base 65°F)	1,491	1,150	827	523	247	59	2	8	154	515	936	1,359	7,271
Cooling Degree Days (base 65°F)	0	0	0	0	6	87	224	176	30	0	0	0	523
Mean Precipitation (in.)	0.53	0.52	0.67	0.80	0.91	0.60	0.70	0.62	0.90	1.14	0.59	0.47	8.45
Days With ≥ 0.1" Precipitation	2	2	2	3	3	2	2	2	3	3	2	2	28
Days With ≥ 1.0" Precipitation	0	0	0	0	0	0	0	0	0	0	0	0	0
Mean Snowfall (in.)	6.0	4.0	1.9	1.1	0.3	0.0	0.0	0.0	0.0	1.0	2.7	5.6	22.6
Days With ≥ 1.0" Snow Depth	na	na	3	0	0	0	0	0	0	0	0	1	na	na

Johnson Pass *Tooele County*   Elevation: 5,629 ft.   Latitude: 40° 20' N   Longitude: 112° 37' W

	JAN	FEB	MAR	APR	MAY	JUN	JUL	AUG	SEP	OCT	NOV	DEC	YEAR
Mean Maximum Temp. (°F)	38.8	43.7	50.8	58.8	69.1	80.9	89.6	87.7	77.3	63.9	48.9	39.7	62.4
Mean Temp. (°F)	28.2	32.9	39.4	46.2	55.5	65.4	74.0	72.6	63.1	51.1	37.7	29.1	49.6
Mean Minimum Temp. (°F)	17.6	22.1	28.0	33.6	41.9	49.9	58.4	57.4	48.6	38.1	26.5	18.6	36.7
Extreme Maximum Temp. (°F)	62	67	74	84	93	101	105	101	98	87	74	66	105
Extreme Minimum Temp. (°F)	-12	-14	2	11	20	23	38	36	23	13	-2	-19	-19
Days Maximum Temp. ≥ 90°F	0	0	0	0	0	6	18	13	2	0	0	0	39
Days Maximum Temp. ≤ 32°F	8	3	0	0	0	0	0	0	0	0	2	7	20
Days Minimum Temp. ≤ 32°F	30	24	21	14	4	0	0	0	1	7	22	29	152
Days Minimum Temp. ≤ 0°F	1	0	0	0	0	0	0	0	0	0	0	1	2
Heating Degree Days (base 65°F)	1,129	902	787	554	302	93	7	9	124	429	813	1,105	6,254
Cooling Degree Days (base 65°F)	0	0	0	1	17	115	296	264	72	4	0	0	769
Mean Precipitation (in.)	1.51	1.56	1.93	1.65	2.12	1.00	1.27	1.04	1.29	1.41	1.33	1.32	17.43
Days With ≥ 0.1" Precipitation	5	4	5	4	5	3	3	3	3	3	4	4	46
Days With ≥ 1.0" Precipitation	0	0	0	0	0	0	0	0	0	0	0	0	0
Mean Snowfall (in.)	15.0	13.7	12.3	6.9	1.1	trace	0.0	0.0	0.3	1.9	7.8	13.4	72.4
Days With ≥ 1.0" Snow Depth	26	19	8	2	0	0	0	0	0	1	6	19	81

Kanab *Kane County*   Elevation: 4,937 ft.   Latitude: 37° 02' N   Longitude: 112° 31' W

	JAN	FEB	MAR	APR	MAY	JUN	JUL	AUG	SEP	OCT	NOV	DEC	YEAR
Mean Maximum Temp. (°F)	48.1	53.6	59.5	67.1	76.7	87.6	92.4	90.0	82.9	72.1	58.3	49.4	69.8
Mean Temp. (°F)	35.6	40.4	45.4	51.6	60.0	69.4	75.3	73.7	66.5	55.9	44.2	36.7	54.6
Mean Minimum Temp. (°F)	23.0	27.1	31.3	36.0	43.3	51.2	58.2	57.3	50.1	39.7	30.0	23.8	39.2
Extreme Maximum Temp. (°F)	72	77	81	90	97	106	108	105	99	94	80	71	108
Extreme Minimum Temp. (°F)	-9	-3	6	12	22	33	39	43	33	13	5	-10	-10
Days Maximum Temp. ≥ 90°F	0	0	0	0	1	13	23	17	5	0	0	0	59
Days Maximum Temp. ≤ 32°F	1	0	0	0	0	0	0	0	0	0	0	1	2
Days Minimum Temp. ≤ 32°F	28	22	18	8	1	0	0	0	0	4	20	28	129
Days Minimum Temp. ≤ 0°F	0	0	0	0	0	0	0	0	0	0	0	0	0
Heating Degree Days (base 65°F)	905	688	601	397	168	24	0	0	42	281	618	872	4,596
Cooling Degree Days (base 65°F)	0	0	0	2	24	172	335	294	101	7	0	0	935
Mean Precipitation (in.)	1.85	1.66	1.90	0.95	0.67	0.40	1.06	1.46	1.37	1.22	1.21	1.03	14.78
Days With ≥ 0.1" Precipitation	4	4	5	3	2	1	3	4	3	3	3	3	38
Days With ≥ 1.0" Precipitation	0	0	0	0	0	0	0	0	0	0	0	0	0
Mean Snowfall (in.)	9.0	5.0	2.6	2.2	trace	0.0	0.0	0.0	0.0	0.2	2.1	4.0	25.1
Days With ≥ 1.0" Snow Depth	7	3	0	0	0	0	0	0	0	0	1	3	14

Kanosh *Millard County*   Elevation: 4,990 ft.   Latitude: 38° 48' N   Longitude: 112° 26' W

	JAN	FEB	MAR	APR	MAY	JUN	JUL	AUG	SEP	OCT	NOV	DEC	YEAR
Mean Maximum Temp. (°F)	40.6	47.4	55.5	63.1	72.9	84.7	92.2	89.9	80.9	67.4	52.8	41.4	65.7
Mean Temp. (°F)	29.5	35.7	43.2	49.6	58.8	69.4	77.3	75.4	66.0	53.7	40.7	30.3	52.5
Mean Minimum Temp. (°F)	18.5	23.8	30.7	36.2	44.6	54.0	62.3	60.8	51.0	39.8	28.5	19.1	39.1
Extreme Maximum Temp. (°F)	65	74	79	85	96	102	107	106	98	91	76	71	107
Extreme Minimum Temp. (°F)	-16	-16	5	15	22	29	41	35	26	6	1	-20	-20
Days Maximum Temp. ≥ 90°F	0	0	0	0	1	10	22	18	4	0	0	0	55
Days Maximum Temp. ≤ 32°F	7	2	0	0	0	0	0	0	0	0	1	6	16
Days Minimum Temp. ≤ 32°F	28	23	18	11	2	0	0	0	1	7	21	28	139
Days Minimum Temp. ≤ 0°F	2	1	0	0	0	0	0	0	0	0	0	2	5
Heating Degree Days (base 65°F)	1,094	823	671	459	221	46	1	3	75	355	721	1,069	5,538
Cooling Degree Days (base 65°F)	0	0	0	5	36	181	388	348	114	11	0	0	1,083
Mean Precipitation (in.)	1.30	1.19	1.91	1.83	1.53	0.69	0.92	1.09	1.03	1.56	1.51	1.23	15.79
Days With ≥ 0.1" Precipitation	4	4	5	5	4	2	2	3	3	4	4	4	44
Days With ≥ 1.0" Precipitation	0	0	0	0	0	0	0	0	0	0	0	0	0
Mean Snowfall (in.)	15.1	13.8	*11.0*	9.0	1.2	0.1	0.0	0.0	0.1	4.2	12.1	15.8	*82.4*
Days With ≥ 1.0" Snow Depth	18	13	5	1	0	0	0	0	0	1	6	18	62

Koosharem *Sevier County*   Elevation: 6,929 ft.   Latitude: 38° 31' N   Longitude: 111° 53' W

	JAN	FEB	MAR	APR	MAY	JUN	JUL	AUG	SEP	OCT	NOV	DEC	YEAR
Mean Maximum Temp. (°F)	39.0	42.7	49.0	57.1	*67.1*	78.4	84.4	82.2	74.8	63.0	48.8	40.4	*60.6*
Mean Temp. (°F)	24.3	28.3	34.9	41.1	*49.7*	59.0	65.2	63.6	55.9	44.9	33.5	25.5	*43.8*
Mean Minimum Temp. (°F)	9.6	13.8	20.8	25.1	32.2	*39.6*	46.1	44.9	37.0	26.9	18.1	10.7	*27.1*
Extreme Maximum Temp. (°F)	64	69	73	79	88	95	98	95	90	83	73	63	98
Extreme Minimum Temp. (°F)	-24	-24	-9	2	12	18	29	26	14	-6	-15	-32	-32
Days Maximum Temp. ≥ 90°F	0	0	0	0	0	1	4	2	0	0	0	0	7
Days Maximum Temp. ≤ 32°F	7	3	1	0	0	0	0	0	0	0	2	6	19
Days Minimum Temp. ≤ 32°F	31	27	30	26	15	4	0	1	7	24	27	30	222
Days Minimum Temp. ≤ 0°F	7	3	1	0	0	0	0	0	0	0	1	5	17
Heating Degree Days (base 65°F)	1,255	1,030	927	708	*467*	*186*	38	69	268	616	939	1,218	*7,721*
Cooling Degree Days (base 65°F)	0	0	0	0	*0*	na	51	30	2	0	0	0	na
Mean Precipitation (in.)	0.63	0.55	0.80	0.60	0.90	0.61	1.07	1.28	1.01	0.92	0.58	0.51	9.46
Days With ≥ 0.1" Precipitation	2	2	3	2	3	2	3	4	3	3	2	2	31
Days With ≥ 1.0" Precipitation	0	0	0	0	0	0	0	0	0	0	0	0	0
Mean Snowfall (in.)	9.1	6.8	6.5	2.6	1.4	0.2	0.0	0.0	0.1	1.5	4.2	5.7	38.1
Days With ≥ 1.0" Snow Depth	20	15	5	0	0	0	0	0	0	0	4	10	54

La Verkin *Washington County*   Elevation: 3,218 ft.   Latitude: 37° 12' N   Longitude: 113° 16' W

	JAN	FEB	MAR	APR	MAY	JUN	JUL	AUG	SEP	OCT	NOV	DEC	YEAR
Mean Maximum Temp. (°F)	53.2	59.9	66.4	74.4	83.9	94.2	98.8	96.6	89.4	77.6	63.0	53.8	75.9
Mean Temp. (°F)	40.2	46.0	52.0	58.5	67.1	76.4	82.0	80.4	72.7	61.1	48.3	40.3	60.4
Mean Minimum Temp. (°F)	27.2	32.1	37.6	42.6	50.3	58.5	65.2	64.2	56.1	44.5	33.5	26.8	44.9
Extreme Maximum Temp. (°F)	74	80	88	95	103	108	113	111	105	97	85	73	113
Extreme Minimum Temp. (°F)	2	2	18	21	27	34	46	47	36	17	12	1	1
Days Maximum Temp. ≥ 90°F	0	0	0	2	8	23	30	28	16	3	0	0	110
Days Maximum Temp. ≤ 32°F	0	0	0	0	0	0	0	0	0	0	0	0	0
Days Minimum Temp. ≤ 32°F	24	14	7	2	0	0	0	0	0	2	13	25	87
Days Minimum Temp. ≤ 0°F	0	0	0	0	0	0	0	0	0	0	0	0	0
Heating Degree Days (base 65°F)	761	529	399	213	59	4	0	0	11	158	495	758	3,387
Cooling Degree Days (base 65°F)	0	0	3	35	149	368	552	519	273	47	0	0	1,946
Mean Precipitation (in.)	1.55	1.50	1.78	0.76	0.55	0.28	0.75	1.09	0.88	0.86	1.11	0.78	11.89
Days With ≥ 0.1" Precipitation	4	3	4	2	2	1	2	3	2	2	3	2	30
Days With ≥ 1.0" Precipitation	0	0	0	0	0	0	0	0	0	0	0	0	0
Mean Snowfall (in.)	1.7	0.9	0.2	trace	0.0	0.0	0.0	0.0	0.0	trace	0.1	0.3	3.2
Days With ≥ 1.0" Snow Depth	*0*	0	0	0	0	0	0	0	0	0	0	0	*0*

Laketown *Rich County*   Elevation: 5,977 ft.   Latitude: 41° 50' N   Longitude: 111° 19' W

	JAN	FEB	MAR	APR	MAY	JUN	JUL	AUG	SEP	OCT	NOV	DEC	YEAR
Mean Maximum Temp. (°F)	31.9	34.8	43.2	53.6	64.0	74.1	82.0	81.0	71.2	58.8	43.1	33.9	56.0
Mean Temp. (°F)	21.9	23.2	31.9	40.8	49.8	58.2	65.0	64.0	55.2	44.6	32.8	24.1	42.6
Mean Minimum Temp. (°F)	11.8	11.6	20.6	28.0	35.5	42.2	48.0	46.8	39.1	30.4	22.5	14.3	29.2
Extreme Maximum Temp. (°F)	59	60	69	80	82	96	94	94	90	82	66	62	96
Extreme Minimum Temp. (°F)	-30	-34	-13	0	16	26	31	29	18	8	-10	-27	-34
Days Maximum Temp. ≥ 90°F	0	0	0	0	0	0	2	1	0	0	0	0	3
Days Maximum Temp. ≤ 32°F	16	9	2	0	0	0	0	0	0	0	4	13	44
Days Minimum Temp. ≤ 32°F	30	28	29	22	9	2	0	0	5	20	27	30	202
Days Minimum Temp. ≤ 0°F	6	6	1	0	0	0	0	0	0	0	1	3	17
Heating Degree Days (base 65°F)	1,330	1,173	1,018	720	466	210	50	67	292	624	958	1,260	8,168
Cooling Degree Days (base 65°F)	0	0	0	0	0	0	13	60	45	5	0	0	123
Mean Precipitation (in.)	1.05	0.88	1.12	1.29	1.43	1.07	0.84	0.88	1.23	1.30	1.18	1.04	13.31
Days With ≥ 0.1" Precipitation	3	3	4	4	5	3	2	2	4	3	3	4	40
Days With ≥ 1.0" Precipitation	0	0	0	0	0	0	0	0	0	0	0	0	0
Mean Snowfall (in.)	*11.6*	9.4	*7.1*	5.0	0.8	trace	0.0	0.0	0.5	1.4	6.7	11.6	*54.1*
Days With ≥ 1.0" Snow Depth	*23*	*19*	*7*	1	0	0	0	0	0	0	*6*	17	*73*

Levan *Juab County*   Elevation: 5,288 ft.   Latitude: 39° 33' N   Longitude: 111° 52' W

	JAN	FEB	MAR	APR	MAY	JUN	JUL	AUG	SEP	OCT	NOV	DEC	YEAR
Mean Maximum Temp. (°F)	37.9	44.6	53.7	61.7	71.5	82.9	90.3	88.9	79.8	66.7	51.1	39.2	64.0
Mean Temp. (°F)	26.5	32.3	40.3	47.0	55.8	65.7	73.0	71.7	62.7	50.9	38.4	27.9	49.4
Mean Minimum Temp. (°F)	15.1	19.9	26.9	32.4	40.1	48.5	55.7	54.5	45.6	35.0	25.5	16.5	34.6
Extreme Maximum Temp. (°F)	60	71	77	85	95	101	105	102	100	90	75	70	105
Extreme Minimum Temp. (°F)	-21	-22	-2	11	21	26	39	36	20	5	-6	-21	-22
Days Maximum Temp. ≥ 90°F	0	0	0	0	0	8	19	15	3	0	0	0	45
Days Maximum Temp. ≤ 32°F	8	2	0	0	0	0	0	0	0	0	1	7	18
Days Minimum Temp. ≤ 32°F	30	27	24	16	5	0	0	0	2	11	25	30	170
Days Minimum Temp. ≤ 0°F	4	1	0	0	0	0	0	0	0	0	0	2	7
Heating Degree Days (base 65°F)	1,187	916	759	533	285	76	4	5	119	432	793	1,143	6,252
Cooling Degree Days (base 65°F)	0	0	0	1	9	102	256	233	62	2	0	0	665
Mean Precipitation (in.)	1.32	1.29	1.65	1.53	1.56	0.86	0.82	0.84	1.23	1.52	1.27	1.15	15.04
Days With ≥ 0.1" Precipitation	4	4	6	5	4	2	3	3	3	4	4	4	46
Days With ≥ 1.0" Precipitation	0	0	0	0	0	0	0	0	0	0	0	0	0
Mean Snowfall (in.)	12.4	8.3	6.8	3.3	1.3	0.0	0.0	0.0	0.2	2.3	6.1	10.4	51.1
Days With ≥ 1.0" Snow Depth	*15*	*12*	*4*	*0*	0	0	0	0	0	1	*3*	na	na

Logan 5 SW Exp. Farm *Cache County*   Elevation: 4,488 ft.   Latitude: 41° 40' N   Longitude: 111° 53' W

	JAN	FEB	MAR	APR	MAY	JUN	JUL	AUG	SEP	OCT	NOV	DEC	YEAR
Mean Maximum Temp. (°F)	32.4	38.2	48.7	57.8	67.6	78.4	87.2	86.5	75.7	62.8	46.3	34.3	59.7
Mean Temp. (°F)	21.7	26.5	37.2	45.2	53.4	62.3	69.4	68.3	58.1	46.8	34.5	23.0	45.5
Mean Minimum Temp. (°F)	10.9	14.8	25.7	32.5	39.3	46.2	51.6	49.9	40.4	30.6	22.7	11.7	31.4
Extreme Maximum Temp. (°F)	57	63	73	83	88	99	101	102	94	86	72	65	102
Extreme Minimum Temp. (°F)	-30	-35	-10	12	21	27	35	33	20	0	-16	-44	-44
Days Maximum Temp. ≥ 90°F	0	0	0	0	0	3	13	11	1	0	0	0	28
Days Maximum Temp. ≤ 32°F	14	7	1	0	0	0	0	0	0	0	2	12	36
Days Minimum Temp. ≤ 32°F	30	27	25	16	4	0	0	0	4	19	27	30	182
Days Minimum Temp. ≤ 0°F	8	5	1	0	0	0	0	0	0	0	1	6	21
Heating Degree Days (base 65°F)	1,338	1,081	854	588	355	130	18	27	221	559	909	1,295	7,375
Cooling Degree Days (base 65°F)	0	0	0	0	4	50	158	139	23	0	0	0	374
Mean Precipitation (in.)	1.70	1.64	1.85	1.97	2.18	1.32	0.93	0.89	1.45	1.95	1.64	1.51	19.03
Days With ≥ 0.1" Precipitation	5	5	5	6	6	4	2	2	3	5	5	5	53
Days With ≥ 1.0" Precipitation	0	0	0	0	0	0	0	0	0	0	0	0	0
Mean Snowfall (in.)	11.0	9.7	6.2	3.7	0.4	0.0	0.0	0.0	trace	0.9	5.6	12.6	50.1
Days With ≥ 1.0" Snow Depth	23	20	8	2	0	0	0	0	0	0	5	20	78

Logan Radio KVNU *Cache County*   Elevation: 4,498 ft.   Latitude: 41° 45' N   Longitude: 111° 50' W

	JAN	FEB	MAR	APR	MAY	JUN	JUL	AUG	SEP	OCT	NOV	DEC	YEAR
Mean Maximum Temp. (°F)	31.1	37.0	48.7	58.4	68.4	79.1	88.3	87.3	76.2	63.1	45.8	33.4	59.7
Mean Temp. (°F)	21.9	26.9	37.6	45.8	54.7	63.5	71.2	70.0	59.8	48.1	35.1	23.9	46.5
Mean Minimum Temp. (°F)	12.6	16.7	26.5	33.1	40.9	47.7	54.0	52.7	43.4	33.0	24.3	14.3	33.3
Extreme Maximum Temp. (°F)	59	65	74	84	90	97	100	102	96	86	71	67	102
Extreme Minimum Temp. (°F)	-25	-29	-6	16	25	29	40	35	22	6	-10	-31	-31
Days Maximum Temp. ≥ 90°F	0	0	0	0	0	4	14	12	1	0	0	0	31
Days Maximum Temp. ≤ 32°F	15	9	2	0	0	0	0	0	0	0	3	14	43
Days Minimum Temp. ≤ 32°F	30	27	25	15	3	0	0	0	2	14	26	30	172
Days Minimum Temp. ≤ 0°F	7	4	0	0	0	0	0	0	0	0	1	4	16
Heating Degree Days (base 65°F)	1,330	1,071	842	571	320	108	10	17	176	518	890	1,269	7,122
Cooling Degree Days (base 65°F)	0	0	0	0	7	63	203	184	32	0	0	0	489
Mean Precipitation (in.)	1.36	1.36	1.85	2.00	2.11	1.31	0.90	0.87	1.53	1.79	1.47	1.39	17.94
Days With ≥ 0.1" Precipitation	4	4	5	6	6	3	3	2	4	4	5	5	51
Days With ≥ 1.0" Precipitation	0	0	0	0	0	0	0	0	0	0	0	0	0
Mean Snowfall (in.)	na	na	na	na	*trace*	0.0	0.0	0.0	trace	*0.5*	na	na	na
Days With ≥ 1.0" Snow Depth	na	na	na	*1*	0	0	0	0	0	*0*	na	na	na

Logan Utah State University *Cache County*   Elevation: 4,790 ft.   Latitude: 41° 45' N   Longitude: 111° 48' W

	JAN	FEB	MAR	APR	MAY	JUN	JUL	AUG	SEP	OCT	NOV	DEC	YEAR
Mean Maximum Temp. (°F)	32.0	37.4	47.6	56.7	66.8	77.6	86.5	85.7	74.4	61.1	44.8	33.7	58.7
Mean Temp. (°F)	24.4	28.9	38.5	46.4	55.4	64.8	72.7	72.0	61.6	49.9	36.6	25.9	48.1
Mean Minimum Temp. (°F)	16.8	20.4	29.3	36.0	44.0	51.9	59.0	58.2	48.7	38.6	28.3	18.0	37.4
Extreme Maximum Temp. (°F)	60	63	74	82	86	98	101	100	97	85	70	66	101
Extreme Minimum Temp. (°F)	-16	-19	3	17	27	33	42	41	26	14	-2	-21	-21
Days Maximum Temp. ≥ 90°F	0	0	0	0	0	3	11	9	1	0	0	0	24
Days Maximum Temp. ≤ 32°F	15	8	2	0	0	0	0	0	0	0	3	14	42
Days Minimum Temp. ≤ 32°F	29	25	20	10	2	0	0	0	1	6	20	29	142
Days Minimum Temp. ≤ 0°F	4	2	0	0	0	0	0	0	0	0	0	2	8
Heating Degree Days (base 65°F)	1,251	1,012	816	553	304	95	9	11	148	463	846	1,206	6,714
Cooling Degree Days (base 65°F)	0	0	0	1	16	92	255	246	56	2	0	0	668
Mean Precipitation (in.)	1.58	1.59	2.15	2.14	2.41	1.38	1.01	0.92	1.56	2.12	1.65	1.64	20.15
Days With ≥ 0.1" Precipitation	5	5	6	6	6	4	3	2	4	5	5	5	56
Days With ≥ 1.0" Precipitation	0	0	0	0	0	0	0	0	0	0	0	0	0
Mean Snowfall (in.)	12.4	11.2	9.6	4.9	0.8	trace	0.0	0.0	trace	2.3	7.4	15.7	64.3
Days With ≥ 1.0" Snow Depth	24	18	8	2	0	0	0	0	0	1	6	21	80

Manti *Sanpete County*   Elevation: 5,738 ft.   Latitude: 39° 15' N   Longitude: 111° 38' W

	JAN	FEB	MAR	APR	MAY	JUN	JUL	AUG	SEP	OCT	NOV	DEC	YEAR
Mean Maximum Temp. (°F)	36.9	42.4	51.2	59.3	68.8	79.6	86.0	84.3	75.6	63.9	48.9	38.3	61.3
Mean Temp. (°F)	26.2	31.2	39.0	45.8	54.4	63.7	70.4	68.8	60.3	49.3	37.0	27.6	47.8
Mean Minimum Temp. (°F)	15.4	19.8	26.8	32.3	39.9	47.8	54.7	53.3	44.9	34.6	25.0	16.7	34.3
Extreme Maximum Temp. (°F)	60	69	73	83	87	97	98	98	92	84	73	66	98
Extreme Minimum Temp. (°F)	-20	-19	1	10	19	30	38	37	22	8	-6	-24	-24
Days Maximum Temp. ≥ 90°F	0	0	0	0	0	2	8	5	0	0	0	0	15
Days Maximum Temp. ≤ 32°F	9	4	1	0	0	0	0	0	0	0	2	8	24
Days Minimum Temp. ≤ 32°F	30	27	25	16	4	0	0	0	1	11	25	30	169
Days Minimum Temp. ≤ 0°F	3	1	0	0	0	0	0	0	0	0	0	2	6
Heating Degree Days (base 65°F)	1,196	949	799	569	325	95	6	12	159	480	834	1,155	6,579
Cooling Degree Days (base 65°F)	0	0	0	0	3	63	182	146	26	0	0	0	420
Mean Precipitation (in.)	1.05	1.01	1.50	1.34	1.48	0.79	0.83	0.90	1.30	1.43	1.19	0.91	13.73
Days With ≥ 0.1" Precipitation	3	4	5	5	4	2	3	3	3	4	3	3	42
Days With ≥ 1.0" Precipitation	0	0	0	0	0	0	0	0	0	0	0	0	0
Mean Snowfall (in.)	12.3	10.4	9.0	5.2	1.1	trace	0.0	0.0	0.1	1.9	8.4	11.2	59.6
Days With ≥ 1.0" Snow Depth	22	16	4	1	0	0	0	0	0	0	5	16	64

Marysvale *Piute County*   Elevation: 5,908 ft.   Latitude: 38° 27' N   Longitude: 112° 14' W

	JAN	FEB	MAR	APR	MAY	JUN	JUL	AUG	SEP	OCT	NOV	DEC	YEAR
Mean Maximum Temp. (°F)	41.6	47.2	54.4	62.2	72.0	83.0	88.7	86.7	78.7	66.8	52.2	42.7	64.7
Mean Temp. (°F)	28.1	33.4	39.9	46.1	54.6	63.5	69.6	68.0	60.0	48.9	37.5	28.8	48.2
Mean Minimum Temp. (°F)	14.5	19.7	25.4	30.0	37.2	44.0	50.5	49.2	41.3	31.0	22.7	14.9	31.7
Extreme Maximum Temp. (°F)	64	73	78	84	92	99	101	102	95	87	76	66	102
Extreme Minimum Temp. (°F)	-18	-28	-11	7	17	23	33	30	20	1	-4	-35	-35
Days Maximum Temp. ≥ 90°F	0	0	0	0	0	6	15	9	1	0	0	0	31
Days Maximum Temp. ≤ 32°F	5	2	0	0	0	0	0	0	0	0	1	4	12
Days Minimum Temp. ≤ 32°F	30	26	25	19	8	1	0	0	3	19	26	29	186
Days Minimum Temp. ≤ 0°F	3	1	0	0	0	0	0	0	0	0	0	3	7
Heating Degree Days (base 65°F)	1,137	885	771	561	318	91	6	14	161	491	819	1,116	6,370
Cooling Degree Days (base 65°F)	0	0	0	0	4	53	149	112	18	0	0	0	336
Mean Precipitation (in.)	0.59	0.53	0.80	0.63	0.76	0.43	0.79	0.99	0.81	0.81	0.60	0.45	8.19
Days With ≥ 0.1" Precipitation	2	2	3	2	3	2	3	3	3	2	2	2	29
Days With ≥ 1.0" Precipitation	0	0	0	0	0	0	0	0	0	0	0	0	0
Mean Snowfall (in.)	*5.1*	*2.1*	*1.7*	*1.5*	0.3	0.0	0.0	0.0	0.0	0.2	*2.1*	*2.9*	*15.9*
Days With ≥ 1.0" Snow Depth	*7*	3	1	0	0	0	0	0	0	0	*2*	5	*18*

Mexican Hat *San Juan County*   Elevation: 4,127 ft.   Latitude: 37° 09' N   Longitude: 109° 52' W

	JAN	FEB	MAR	APR	MAY	JUN	JUL	AUG	SEP	OCT	NOV	DEC	YEAR
Mean Maximum Temp. (°F)	44.6	52.8	61.8	70.3	80.8	92.6	97.7	95.0	86.5	73.3	57.6	46.0	71.6
Mean Temp. (°F)	32.3	39.1	46.8	54.5	64.6	75.0	81.5	79.2	69.8	56.6	43.3	33.3	56.3
Mean Minimum Temp. (°F)	19.9	25.4	31.8	38.7	48.3	57.4	65.3	63.5	53.1	39.8	28.9	20.5	41.1
Extreme Maximum Temp. (°F)	69	76	84	92	99	108	110	106	103	92	79	68	110
Extreme Minimum Temp. (°F)	-11	-8	9	11	27	38	50	47	29	19	8	-16	-16
Days Maximum Temp. ≥ 90°F	0	0	0	0	5	21	29	26	11	1	0	0	93
Days Maximum Temp. ≤ 32°F	4	0	0	0	0	0	0	0	0	0	0	2	6
Days Minimum Temp. ≤ 32°F	30	24	17	6	0	0	0	0	0	4	22	29	132
Days Minimum Temp. ≤ 0°F	0	0	0	0	0	0	0	0	0	0	0	1	1
Heating Degree Days (base 65°F)	1,007	725	558	314	87	6	0	0	29	264	644	976	4,610
Cooling Degree Days (base 65°F)	0	0	0	7	87	320	521	457	190	9	0	0	1,591
Mean Precipitation (in.)	0.61	0.50	0.52	0.46	0.51	0.19	0.59	0.61	0.70	0.93	0.54	0.49	6.65
Days With ≥ 0.1" Precipitation	2	2	2	2	2	1	2	2	2	2	2	2	23
Days With ≥ 1.0" Precipitation	0	0	0	0	0	0	0	0	0	0	0	0	0
Mean Snowfall (in.)	na	na	*trace*	trace	0.0	0.0	0.0	0.0	0.0	0.0	0.1	*1.5*	na
Days With ≥ 1.0" Snow Depth	na	na	*0*	0	0	0	0	0	0	0	0	na	na

Moab *Grand County*   Elevation: 4,041 ft.   Latitude: 38° 34' N   Longitude: 109° 33' W

	JAN	FEB	MAR	APR	MAY	JUN	JUL	AUG	SEP	OCT	NOV	DEC	YEAR
Mean Maximum Temp. (°F)	43.5	52.3	63.8	72.3	83.0	94.2	99.9	97.6	88.3	74.9	57.8	46.2	72.8
Mean Temp. (°F)	31.5	39.0	49.4	57.0	66.4	75.9	82.0	80.5	70.7	57.7	43.8	33.8	57.3
Mean Minimum Temp. (°F)	19.5	25.6	35.0	41.5	49.9	57.6	64.1	63.3	53.1	40.4	29.7	21.4	41.8
Extreme Maximum Temp. (°F)	67	75	86	96	100	109	114	110	108	95	80	69	114
Extreme Minimum Temp. (°F)	-13	-10	15	19	33	38	47	45	30	17	7	-2	-13
Days Maximum Temp. ≥ 90°F	0	0	0	1	7	23	30	29	14	2	0	0	106
Days Maximum Temp. ≤ 32°F	4	1	0	0	0	0	0	0	0	0	0	1	6
Days Minimum Temp. ≤ 32°F	29	23	13	4	0	0	0	0	0	4	20	28	121
Days Minimum Temp. ≤ 0°F	1	0	0	0	0	0	0	0	0	0	0	0	1
Heating Degree Days (base 65°F)	1,031	729	477	254	65	4	0	0	24	237	630	959	4,410
Cooling Degree Days (base 65°F)	0	0	1	22	124	349	534	496	209	17	0	0	1,752
Mean Precipitation (in.)	0.64	0.49	0.90	0.99	0.81	0.39	0.89	0.80	0.75	1.23	0.76	0.64	9.29
Days With ≥ 0.1" Precipitation	2	2	3	3	2	1	2	2	2	3	2	2	26
Days With ≥ 1.0" Precipitation	0	0	0	0	0	0	0	0	0	0	0	0	0
Mean Snowfall (in.)	na	*0.5*	0.4	trace	0.0	0.0	0.0	0.0	0.0	trace	trace	*1.6*	na
Days With ≥ 1.0" Snow Depth	na	*2*	0	0	0	0	0	0	0	0	0	na	na

Monticello San Juan County   Elevation: 6,817 ft.   Latitude: 37° 52' N   Longitude: 109° 18' W

	JAN	FEB	MAR	APR	MAY	JUN	JUL	AUG	SEP	OCT	NOV	DEC	YEAR
Mean Maximum Temp. (°F)	34.8	40.1	48.6	57.8	67.7	79.0	84.1	81.4	73.5	61.2	46.0	36.6	59.2
Mean Temp. (°F)	24.1	29.1	36.6	43.9	52.8	62.4	68.5	66.5	58.5	47.1	34.5	25.9	45.8
Mean Minimum Temp. (°F)	13.4	18.0	24.6	30.1	37.9	45.7	52.8	51.6	43.5	33.0	23.1	15.1	32.4
Extreme Maximum Temp. (°F)	56	72	69	78	88	94	96	95	89	82	69	58	96
Extreme Minimum Temp. (°F)	-18	-19	-1	5	19	27	33	35	24	5	-5	-22	-22
Days Maximum Temp. ≥ 90°F	0	0	0	0	0	2	4	1	0	0	0	0	7
Days Maximum Temp. ≤ 32°F	12	5	1	0	0	0	0	0	0	0	3	9	30
Days Minimum Temp. ≤ 32°F	31	27	27	19	6	1	0	0	2	14	26	31	184
Days Minimum Temp. ≤ 0°F	3	1	0	0	0	0	0	0	0	0	0	2	6
Heating Degree Days (base 65°F)	1,261	1,009	875	625	372	115	10	27	197	547	907	1,206	7,151
Cooling Degree Days (base 65°F)	0	0	0	0	1	39	120	81	10	0	0	0	251
Mean Precipitation (in.)	1.76	1.29	1.20	0.99	1.02	0.65	1.33	1.84	1.55	1.83	1.43	1.29	16.18
Days With ≥ 0.1" Precipitation	4	3	3	3	3	2	4	5	4	4	3	3	41
Days With ≥ 1.0" Precipitation	0	0	0	0	0	0	0	0	0	0	0	0	0
Mean Snowfall (in.)	20.2	12.5	9.2	4.2	0.8	trace	0.0	0.0	trace	1.0	7.9	13.6	69.4
Days With ≥ 1.0" Snow Depth	22	18	10	2	0	0	0	0	0	1	5	16	74

Morgan Como Springs Morgan County   Elevation: 5,078 ft.   Latitude: 41° 02' N   Longitude: 111° 39' W

	JAN	FEB	MAR	APR	MAY	JUN	JUL	AUG	SEP	OCT	NOV	DEC	YEAR
Mean Maximum Temp. (°F)	35.4	41.3	51.0	60.1	70.3	81.5	88.9	87.7	77.9	65.3	48.0	37.2	62.1
Mean Temp. (°F)	24.1	28.9	38.2	45.6	54.1	63.0	69.9	68.4	59.1	48.1	35.4	25.4	46.7
Mean Minimum Temp. (°F)	12.7	16.4	25.3	31.0	37.9	44.4	50.7	49.0	40.3	30.8	22.7	13.6	31.2
Extreme Maximum Temp. (°F)	57	65	74	84	90	99	100	100	95	88	75	68	100
Extreme Minimum Temp. (°F)	-27	-32	-6	5	20	29	35	27	19	8	-12	-33	-33
Days Maximum Temp. ≥ 90°F	0	0	0	0	0	5	16	13	2	0	0	0	36
Days Maximum Temp. ≤ 32°F	11	5	1	0	0	0	0	0	0	0	2	9	28
Days Minimum Temp. ≤ 32°F	30	26	25	18	6	1	0	0	5	19	25	29	184
Days Minimum Temp. ≤ 0°F	6	3	0	0	0	0	0	0	0	0	1	4	14
Heating Degree Days (base 65°F)	1,262	1,014	824	575	332	104	9	21	191	519	881	1,220	6,952
Cooling Degree Days (base 65°F)	0	0	0	0	2	47	168	146	23	0	0	0	386
Mean Precipitation (in.)	1.88	1.72	1.88	2.19	1.99	1.15	0.73	0.80	1.55	1.78	1.93	1.63	19.23
Days With ≥ 0.1" Precipitation	6	5	6	6	6	3	2	2	3	4	6	5	54
Days With ≥ 1.0" Precipitation	0	0	0	0	0	0	0	0	0	0	0	0	0
Mean Snowfall (in.)	17.6	14.6	6.7	5.6	1.4	0.0	0.0	0.0	0.1	1.7	9.3	18.1	75.1
Days With ≥ 1.0" Snow Depth	na	na	3	0	0	0	0	0	0	0	4	na	na

Moroni Sanpete County   Elevation: 5,557 ft.   Latitude: 39° 32' N   Longitude: 111° 35' W

	JAN	FEB	MAR	APR	MAY	JUN	JUL	AUG	SEP	OCT	NOV	DEC	YEAR
Mean Maximum Temp. (°F)	35.9	42.1	51.9	60.5	70.2	81.5	88.5	86.8	78.3	65.1	48.9	37.8	62.3
Mean Temp. (°F)	23.6	29.4	37.9	44.7	53.3	62.1	69.0	67.8	59.3	48.0	35.4	25.4	46.3
Mean Minimum Temp. (°F)	11.4	16.7	24.0	28.8	36.3	42.7	49.4	48.6	40.4	30.9	21.8	12.8	30.3
Extreme Maximum Temp. (°F)	58	69	75	83	91	98	102	102	97	89	77	66	102
Extreme Minimum Temp. (°F)	-27	-25	-4	10	20	24	33	32	15	8	-9	-26	-27
Days Maximum Temp. ≥ 90°F	0	0	0	0	0	6	15	11	2	0	0	0	34
Days Maximum Temp. ≤ 32°F	10	4	0	0	0	0	0	0	0	0	2	8	24
Days Minimum Temp. ≤ 32°F	31	28	28	22	8	1	0	0	4	19	28	31	200
Days Minimum Temp. ≤ 0°F	5	2	0	0	0	0	0	0	0	0	0	4	11
Heating Degree Days (base 65°F)	1,275	998	831	603	358	118	10	17	177	520	882	1,222	7,011
Cooling Degree Days (base 65°F)	0	0	0	0	1	38	139	113	16	0	0	0	307
Mean Precipitation (in.)	0.88	0.83	0.90	0.69	0.84	0.58	0.77	0.73	0.94	1.01	0.87	0.83	9.87
Days With ≥ 0.1" Precipitation	2	2	3	2	3	2	2	2	3	3	2	2	28
Days With ≥ 1.0" Precipitation	0	0	0	0	0	0	0	0	0	0	0	0	0
Mean Snowfall (in.)	12.8	9.4	5.6	2.8	1.1	trace	0.0	0.0	trace	1.2	7.4	11.0	51.3
Days With ≥ 1.0" Snow Depth	na	na	na	0	0	0	0	0	0	0	na	na	na

Mountain Dell Dam Salt Lake County   Elevation: 5,419 ft.   Latitude: 40° 45' N   Longitude: 111° 43' W

	JAN	FEB	MAR	APR	MAY	JUN	JUL	AUG	SEP	OCT	NOV	DEC	YEAR
Mean Maximum Temp. (°F)	37.1	42.0	49.6	57.9	68.0	79.7	87.9	86.1	75.9	62.7	47.4	37.9	61.0
Mean Temp. (°F)	25.7	29.8	37.1	44.4	53.2	62.6	70.2	68.6	59.4	48.1	36.3	27.0	46.9
Mean Minimum Temp. (°F)	14.3	17.5	24.4	30.8	38.3	45.6	52.5	51.1	43.0	33.4	25.0	16.1	32.7
Extreme Maximum Temp. (°F)	64	65	75	80	89	98	98	98	94	86	71	61	98
Extreme Minimum Temp. (°F)	-21	-21	-9	4	18	27	36	33	22	7	-3	-25	-25
Days Maximum Temp. ≥ 90°F	0	0	0	0	0	4	13	8	1	0	0	0	26
Days Maximum Temp. ≤ 32°F	9	4	1	0	0	0	0	0	0	0	2	8	24
Days Minimum Temp. ≤ 32°F	30	27	26	18	6	0	0	0	3	12	24	29	175
Days Minimum Temp. ≤ 0°F	4	2	1	0	0	0	0	0	0	0	0	3	10
Heating Degree Days (base 65°F)	1,211	989	859	612	363	120	7	16	184	519	856	1,171	6,907
Cooling Degree Days (base 65°F)	0	0	0	0	3	56	182	146	28	0	0	0	415
Mean Precipitation (in.)	2.01	1.89	2.51	2.53	2.68	1.45	1.16	1.12	2.19	2.58	2.18	2.10	24.40
Days With ≥ 0.1" Precipitation	6	6	7	6	6	4	3	3	4	5	5	5	60
Days With ≥ 1.0" Precipitation	0	0	0	0	0	0	0	0	1	0	0	0	1
Mean Snowfall (in.)	na	16.7	na	na	0.8	0.2	trace	0.0	0.3	3.2	10.9	na	na
Days With ≥ 1.0" Snow Depth	27	24	11	3	0	0	0	0	0	1	7	21	94

Myton *Duchesne County* Elevation: 5,078 ft. Latitude: 40° 12' N Longitude: 110° 04' W

	JAN	FEB	MAR	APR	MAY	JUN	JUL	AUG	SEP	OCT	NOV	DEC	YEAR
Mean Maximum Temp. (°F)	30.5	37.8	52.6	63.0	72.3	82.9	89.3	87.4	78.1	64.6	47.3	34.3	61.7
Mean Temp. (°F)	17.1	23.8	37.8	47.0	56.1	65.4	71.8	70.0	60.7	48.1	33.6	21.1	46.1
Mean Minimum Temp. (°F)	3.6	9.8	23.1	31.0	39.9	47.9	54.1	52.6	43.3	31.6	19.9	7.9	30.4
Extreme Maximum Temp. (°F)	62	70	77	87	93	100	104	99	94	85	71	68	104
Extreme Minimum Temp. (°F)	-33	-39	-6	1	17	28	34	37	22	3	-5	-28	-39
Days Maximum Temp. ≥ 90°F	0	0	0	0	0	7	18	12	2	0	0	0	39
Days Maximum Temp. ≤ 32°F	17	8	1	0	0	0	0	0	0	0	2	12	40
Days Minimum Temp. ≤ 32°F	30	28	28	17	4	0	0	0	2	17	29	31	186
Days Minimum Temp. ≤ 0°F	11	5	0	0	0	0	0	0	0	0	0	4	20
Heating Degree Days (base 65°F)	1,478	1,157	834	532	275	72	5	10	154	517	934	1,346	7,314
Cooling Degree Days (base 65°F)	0	0	0	0	7	89	222	183	32	0	0	0	533
Mean Precipitation (in.)	0.34	0.32	0.51	0.69	0.91	0.60	0.65	0.73	0.78	0.86	0.40	0.26	7.05
Days With ≥ 0.1" Precipitation	1	1	2	2	2	2	2	2	2	2	1	1	20
Days With ≥ 1.0" Precipitation	0	0	0	0	0	0	0	0	0	0	0	0	0
Mean Snowfall (in.)	3.9	2.6	2.1	0.2	trace	0.0	0.0	0.0	0.0	0.5	1.5	3.2	14.0
Days With ≥ 1.0" Snow Depth	na	na	na	0	0	0	0	0	0	0	na	na	na

Natural Bridges Nat'l Monument *San Juan County* Elevation: 6,499 ft. Latitude: 37° 37' N Longitude: 109° 59' W

	JAN	FEB	MAR	APR	MAY	JUN	JUL	AUG	SEP	OCT	NOV	DEC	YEAR
Mean Maximum Temp. (°F)	39.7	45.0	52.0	60.9	71.8	83.8	89.0	86.2	77.4	64.4	49.7	40.8	63.4
Mean Temp. (°F)	29.0	34.1	40.2	47.5	57.4	68.1	74.0	71.8	63.6	51.6	38.7	30.3	50.5
Mean Minimum Temp. (°F)	18.4	23.1	28.5	34.0	42.9	52.5	58.9	57.3	49.7	38.6	27.7	19.8	37.6
Extreme Maximum Temp. (°F)	60	68	77	85	90	101	103	99	95	86	78	61	103
Extreme Minimum Temp. (°F)	-11	-13	6	6	22	32	41	42	22	6	-2	-14	-14
Days Maximum Temp. ≥ 90°F	0	0	0	0	0	7	16	9	1	0	0	0	33
Days Maximum Temp. ≤ 32°F	5	2	0	0	0	0	0	0	0	0	1	5	13
Days Minimum Temp. ≤ 32°F	30	26	22	13	3	0	0	0	0	7	21	30	152
Days Minimum Temp. ≤ 0°F	1	0	0	0	0	0	0	0	0	0	0	0	1
Heating Degree Days (base 65°F)	1,108	867	762	518	242	45	2	5	96	410	781	1,070	5,906
Cooling Degree Days (base 65°F)	0	0	0	1	12	137	269	217	58	1	0	0	695
Mean Precipitation (in.)	1.00	0.73	1.15	0.87	0.80	0.48	1.16	1.55	1.25	1.45	0.97	0.83	12.24
Days With ≥ 0.1" Precipitation	3	2	4	3	3	1	3	4	3	3	2	3	34
Days With ≥ 1.0" Precipitation	0	0	0	0	0	0	0	0	0	0	0	0	0
Mean Snowfall (in.)	11.7	5.7	6.1	3.2	0.2	0.0	0.0	0.0	0.0	1.0	4.7	8.0	40.6
Days With ≥ 1.0" Snow Depth	18	12	4	1	0	0	0	0	0	0	3	13	51

Neola *Duchesne County* Elevation: 5,948 ft. Latitude: 40° 25' N Longitude: 110° 03' W

	JAN	FEB	MAR	APR	MAY	JUN	JUL	AUG	SEP	OCT	NOV	DEC	YEAR
Mean Maximum Temp. (°F)	30.9	37.4	49.2	58.8	68.0	78.3	84.5	82.6	73.8	60.7	43.9	32.6	58.4
Mean Temp. (°F)	19.5	25.2	36.7	44.8	53.9	63.2	69.3	67.8	58.9	46.9	32.6	21.7	45.1
Mean Minimum Temp. (°F)	8.2	13.1	24.0	30.9	39.7	48.0	54.1	52.9	44.1	33.0	21.2	10.7	31.7
Extreme Maximum Temp. (°F)	54	63	72	83	86	96	96	95	92	80	66	59	96
Extreme Minimum Temp. (°F)	-27	-26	-2	2	18	30	34	33	21	0	-6	-26	-27
Days Maximum Temp. ≥ 90°F	0	0	0	0	0	1	4	2	0	0	0	0	7
Days Maximum Temp. ≤ 32°F	17	7	1	0	0	0	0	0	0	0	3	14	42
Days Minimum Temp. ≤ 32°F	31	28	28	18	5	0	0	0	2	13	28	31	184
Days Minimum Temp. ≤ 0°F	7	4	0	0	0	0	0	0	0	0	0	4	15
Heating Degree Days (base 65°F)	1,403	1,117	872	598	339	102	11	18	191	554	966	1,337	7,508
Cooling Degree Days (base 65°F)	0	0	0	0	2	54	161	118	17	0	0	0	352
Mean Precipitation (in.)	0.58	0.49	0.63	0.80	1.17	0.71	0.72	0.85	1.03	1.12	0.59	0.43	9.12
Days With ≥ 0.1" Precipitation	2	2	2	3	4	2	2	3	3	3	2	2	30
Days With ≥ 1.0" Precipitation	0	0	0	0	0	0	0	0	0	0	0	0	0
Mean Snowfall (in.)	na	na	na	1.1	trace	0.0	0.0	0.0	0.0	1.0	2.1	na	na
Days With ≥ 1.0" Snow Depth	na	16	5	0	0	0	0	0	0	1	2	na	na

Nephi *Juab County* Elevation: 5,127 ft. Latitude: 39° 42' N Longitude: 111° 50' W

	JAN	FEB	MAR	APR	MAY	JUN	JUL	AUG	SEP	OCT	NOV	DEC	YEAR
Mean Maximum Temp. (°F)	39.8	45.9	55.1	63.3	73.3	84.9	92.1	90.4	80.8	67.7	51.9	40.8	65.5
Mean Temp. (°F)	28.5	33.7	41.7	48.4	57.4	67.2	74.4	72.9	63.6	51.7	39.3	29.5	50.7
Mean Minimum Temp. (°F)	17.2	21.5	28.2	33.5	41.4	49.5	56.7	55.5	46.4	35.6	26.5	18.1	35.8
Extreme Maximum Temp. (°F)	66	74	80	91	96	110	106	102	99	93	76	70	110
Extreme Minimum Temp. (°F)	-17	-20	0	16	20	28	38	37	25	12	-2	-21	-21
Days Maximum Temp. ≥ 90°F	0	0	0	0	0	11	22	19	4	0	0	0	56
Days Maximum Temp. ≤ 32°F	6	2	0	0	0	0	0	0	0	0	1	6	15
Days Minimum Temp. ≤ 32°F	30	25	23	15	3	0	0	0	1	11	23	29	160
Days Minimum Temp. ≤ 0°F	3	1	0	0	0	0	0	0	0	0	0	2	6
Heating Degree Days (base 65°F)	1,124	877	716	492	244	61	2	4	103	408	766	1,094	5,891
Cooling Degree Days (base 65°F)	0	0	0	1	17	129	289	264	69	2	0	0	771
Mean Precipitation (in.)	1.33	1.28	1.76	1.59	1.54	0.86	0.87	0.97	1.16	1.50	1.43	1.18	15.47
Days With ≥ 0.1" Precipitation	5	4	6	5	5	2	3	3	3	4	4	4	48
Days With ≥ 1.0" Precipitation	0	0	0	0	0	0	0	0	0	0	0	0	0
Mean Snowfall (in.)	13.5	10.5	7.2	3.4	1.0	trace	0.0	0.0	0.0	1.4	6.7	12.1	55.8
Days With ≥ 1.0" Snow Depth	15	10	4	1	0	0	0	0	0	0	4	11	45

New Harmony *Washington County*   Elevation: 5,262 ft.   Latitude: 37° 29' N   Longitude: 113° 19' W

	JAN	FEB	MAR	APR	MAY	JUN	JUL	AUG	SEP	OCT	NOV	DEC	YEAR
Mean Maximum Temp. (°F)	44.4	49.3	55.1	62.6	72.5	83.2	88.6	86.6	79.1	67.8	54.3	45.6	65.8
Mean Temp. (°F)	32.6	36.9	42.3	48.5	57.2	67.1	73.3	71.7	63.9	53.0	41.2	33.5	51.8
Mean Minimum Temp. (°F)	20.8	24.5	29.4	34.2	41.8	50.8	58.0	56.8	48.7	38.2	28.0	21.4	37.7
Extreme Maximum Temp. (°F)	67	76	78	85	92	99	104	101	94	88	77	69	104
Extreme Minimum Temp. (°F)	-9	-20	0	12	23	29	40	40	23	6	4	-19	-20
Days Maximum Temp. ≥ 90°F	0	0	0	0	0	6	14	9	1	0	0	0	30
Days Maximum Temp. ≤ 32°F	3	1	0	0	0	0	0	0	0	0	0	3	7
Days Minimum Temp. ≤ 32°F	30	24	21	13	3	0	0	0	1	7	22	29	150
Days Minimum Temp. ≤ 0°F	1	0	0	0	0	0	0	0	0	0	0	1	2
Heating Degree Days (base 65°F)	997	786	698	490	247	51	1	3	87	367	708	970	5,405
Cooling Degree Days (base 65°F)	0	0	0	0	15	121	267	231	64	2	0	0	700
Mean Precipitation (in.)	2.02	2.35	2.53	1.11	0.95	0.52	1.32	1.54	1.36	1.40	1.66	1.37	18.13
Days With ≥ 0.1" Precipitation	4	4	5	3	3	1	3	4	3	3	3	3	39
Days With ≥ 1.0" Precipitation	1	1	1	0	0	0	0	0	0	0	0	0	3
Mean Snowfall (in.)	na	na	4.7	2.0	trace	trace	0.0	0.0	0.0	0.2	na	na	na
Days With ≥ 1.0" Snow Depth	na	5	1	1	0	0	0	0	0	0	1	3	na

Oak City *Millard County*   Elevation: 5,068 ft.   Latitude: 39° 23' N   Longitude: 112° 20' W

	JAN	FEB	MAR	APR	MAY	JUN	JUL	AUG	SEP	OCT	NOV	DEC	YEAR
Mean Maximum Temp. (°F)	39.7	46.4	55.4	63.1	74.2	86.3	94.1	92.6	82.7	68.6	51.8	40.8	66.3
Mean Temp. (°F)	29.7	35.4	43.3	49.6	59.6	70.4	78.5	76.8	66.9	54.3	40.2	30.0	52.9
Mean Minimum Temp. (°F)	19.6	24.3	31.1	36.0	44.9	54.5	62.9	61.1	51.2	40.0	28.6	19.5	39.5
Extreme Maximum Temp. (°F)	68	73	78	87	95	105	108	105	100	91	75	68	108
Extreme Minimum Temp. (°F)	-14	-18	1	13	24	30	43	40	26	6	1	-23	-23
Days Maximum Temp. ≥ 90°F	0	0	0	0	1	12	26	22	6	0	0	0	67
Days Maximum Temp. ≤ 32°F	7	2	0	0	0	0	0	0	0	0	1	6	16
Days Minimum Temp. ≤ 32°F	28	23	19	12	2	0	0	0	1	6	21	28	140
Days Minimum Temp. ≤ 0°F	2	0	0	0	0	0	0	0	0	0	0	1	3
Heating Degree Days (base 65°F)	1,088	830	666	459	200	43	1	1	67	335	736	1,080	5,506
Cooling Degree Days (base 65°F)	0	0	0	3	42	204	421	382	133	9	0	0	1,194
Mean Precipitation (in.)	1.21	1.14	1.60	1.54	1.51	0.82	0.52	0.74	1.06	1.53	1.31	1.07	14.05
Days With ≥ 0.1" Precipitation	4	4	5	4	4	2	2	2	3	4	3	3	40
Days With ≥ 1.0" Precipitation	0	0	0	0	0	0	0	0	0	0	0	0	0
Mean Snowfall (in.)	11.3	7.6	7.7	4.3	1.3	0.0	0.0	0.0	0.2	2.0	6.7	9.0	50.1
Days With ≥ 1.0" Snow Depth	14	11	2	1	0	0	0	0	0	0	4	13	45

Ogden Pioneer P H *Weber County*   Elevation: 4,347 ft.   Latitude: 41° 15' N   Longitude: 111° 57' W

	JAN	FEB	MAR	APR	MAY	JUN	JUL	AUG	SEP	OCT	NOV	DEC	YEAR
Mean Maximum Temp. (°F)	36.8	43.3	52.9	61.5	71.1	82.1	90.3	88.9	78.1	65.1	49.2	38.4	63.1
Mean Temp. (°F)	28.9	34.0	42.7	50.3	59.2	69.0	76.5	75.3	65.0	53.0	40.0	30.3	52.0
Mean Minimum Temp. (°F)	20.9	24.6	32.6	39.0	47.1	55.8	62.7	61.6	51.9	40.9	30.7	22.2	40.8
Extreme Maximum Temp. (°F)	65	68	76	85	92	101	102	102	96	86	75	66	102
Extreme Minimum Temp. (°F)	-7	-11	9	20	21	33	45	42	29	11	7	-12	-12
Days Maximum Temp. ≥ 90°F	0	0	0	0	0	7	19	16	3	0	0	0	45
Days Maximum Temp. ≤ 32°F	9	3	0	0	0	0	0	0	0	0	1	8	21
Days Minimum Temp. ≤ 32°F	28	23	15	7	1	0	0	0	0	4	17	28	123
Days Minimum Temp. ≤ 0°F	1	0	0	0	0	0	0	0	0	0	0	1	2
Heating Degree Days (base 65°F)	1,113	870	683	442	213	51	2	4	92	369	745	1,068	5,652
Cooling Degree Days (base 65°F)	0	0	0	8	43	176	361	344	108	6	0	0	1,046
Mean Precipitation (in.)	2.36	2.07	2.41	2.56	2.91	1.56	0.96	0.96	1.81	2.22	2.08	2.01	23.91
Days With ≥ 0.1" Precipitation	6	5	6	6	7	3	2	2	4	4	5	5	55
Days With ≥ 1.0" Precipitation	0	0	0	0	0	0	0	0	0	1	0	0	1
Mean Snowfall (in.)	na	na	na	0.7	trace	0.0	0.0	0.0	trace	0.4	2.9	na	na
Days With ≥ 1.0" Snow Depth	19	12	3	0	0	0	0	0	0	0	3	10	47

Ogden Sugar Factory *Weber County*   Elevation: 4,278 ft.   Latitude: 41° 14' N   Longitude: 112° 02' W

	JAN	FEB	MAR	APR	MAY	JUN	JUL	AUG	SEP	OCT	NOV	DEC	YEAR
Mean Maximum Temp. (°F)	36.0	43.2	53.2	62.1	72.0	83.2	91.7	90.3	79.5	65.8	49.4	38.2	63.7
Mean Temp. (°F)	27.1	33.1	42.1	49.6	58.6	68.3	75.6	74.1	63.9	51.8	38.9	29.3	51.0
Mean Minimum Temp. (°F)	18.1	23.0	31.0	37.1	45.1	53.3	59.5	57.8	48.2	37.7	28.4	20.2	38.3
Extreme Maximum Temp. (°F)	59	67	75	87	92	102	103	104	100	88	75	64	104
Extreme Minimum Temp. (°F)	-14	-14	5	18	25	34	44	40	28	18	-1	-18	-18
Days Maximum Temp. ≥ 90°F	0	0	0	0	0	9	22	19	4	0	0	0	54
Days Maximum Temp. ≤ 32°F	11	4	0	0	0	0	0	0	0	0	1	8	24
Days Minimum Temp. ≤ 32°F	29	24	18	9	1	0	0	0	1	7	21	28	138
Days Minimum Temp. ≤ 0°F	2	1	0	0	0	0	0	0	0	0	0	1	4
Heating Degree Days (base 65°F)	1,169	894	703	454	220	51	3	4	105	404	775	1,100	5,882
Cooling Degree Days (base 65°F)	0	0	0	4	33	158	342	314	88	2	0	0	941
Mean Precipitation (in.)	1.70	1.48	1.91	2.00	2.25	1.38	0.63	0.78	1.48	1.88	1.64	1.42	18.55
Days With ≥ 0.1" Precipitation	5	4	4	5	5	2	2	2	3	3	4	4	43
Days With ≥ 1.0" Precipitation	0	0	0	0	0	0	0	0	0	0	0	0	0
Mean Snowfall (in.)	na	4.4	na	0.2	0.0	0.0	0.0	0.0	0.0	trace	na	na	na
Days With ≥ 1.0" Snow Depth	na	na	na	0	0	0	0	0	0	0	na	na	na

Orderville *Kane County* Elevation: 5,459 ft. Latitude: 37° 16' N Longitude: 112° 38' W

	JAN	FEB	MAR	APR	MAY	JUN	JUL	AUG	SEP	OCT	NOV	DEC	YEAR
Mean Maximum Temp. (°F)	47.8	52.3	57.9	65.7	75.1	86.1	91.2	88.9	81.5	70.6	57.5	49.1	68.6
Mean Temp. (°F)	33.2	38.0	43.0	49.1	57.7	67.2	73.2	71.6	64.3	53.1	41.5	34.3	52.2
Mean Minimum Temp. (°F)	18.6	23.6	27.7	32.3	40.2	48.3	55.2	54.3	47.1	35.7	25.4	19.5	35.7
Extreme Maximum Temp. (°F)	71	76	80	87	95	106	106	103	100	92	80	72	106
Extreme Minimum Temp. (°F)	-25	-12	9	12	15	32	39	35	28	10	-5	-20	-25
Days Maximum Temp. ≥ 90°F	0	0	0	0	1	11	21	16	4	0	0	0	53
Days Maximum Temp. ≤ 32°F	1	1	0	0	0	0	0	0	0	0	0	1	3
Days Minimum Temp. ≤ 32°F	30	25	24	16	4	0	0	0	0	10	25	29	163
Days Minimum Temp. ≤ 0°F	1	0	0	0	0	0	0	0	0	0	0	1	2
Heating Degree Days (base 65°F)	978	757	676	473	230	43	1	3	72	365	698	944	5,240
Cooling Degree Days (base 65°F)	0	0	0	1	12	117	265	234	64	3	0	0	696
Mean Precipitation (in.)	1.81	1.84	2.06	0.99	0.88	0.52	1.21	1.68	1.18	1.17	1.28	1.12	15.74
Days With ≥ 0.1" Precipitation	4	4	5	3	3	2	3	4	3	3	3	3	40
Days With ≥ 1.0" Precipitation	0	0	0	0	0	0	0	0	0	0	0	0	0
Mean Snowfall (in.)	13.2	7.2	4.4	1.4	trace	0.0	0.0	0.0	0.0	0.3	3.5	*4.1*	*34.1*
Days With ≥ 1.0" Snow Depth	11	*6*	*1*	0	0	0	0	0	0	0	2	na	na

Ouray 4 NE *Uintah County* Elevation: 4,668 ft. Latitude: 40° 08' N Longitude: 109° 39' W

	JAN	FEB	MAR	APR	MAY	JUN	JUL	AUG	SEP	OCT	NOV	DEC	YEAR
Mean Maximum Temp. (°F)	29.0	37.6	54.1	65.6	76.4	87.8	94.0	91.7	81.4	66.9	47.7	*33.5*	*63.8*
Mean Temp. (°F)	16.2	23.7	39.4	49.6	59.6	69.1	75.3	73.1	63.2	49.7	34.3	*20.8*	*47.8*
Mean Minimum Temp. (°F)	3.3	9.7	24.7	33.6	42.7	50.3	56.5	54.5	44.8	32.4	20.9	*8.2*	*31.8*
Extreme Maximum Temp. (°F)	62	68	79	90	96	106	107	105	99	88	70	63	107
Extreme Minimum Temp. (°F)	-43	-41	-10	6	21	30	38	36	20	-1	-6	-40	-43
Days Maximum Temp. ≥ 90°F	0	0	0	0	1	14	25	*22*	5	0	0	0	*67*
Days Maximum Temp. ≤ 32°F	18	10	1	0	0	0	0	0	0	0	2	13	44
Days Minimum Temp. ≤ 32°F	31	28	26	*13*	2	0	0	0	2	*15*	28	30	*175*
Days Minimum Temp. ≤ 0°F	13	7	1	0	0	0	0	0	0	0	0	6	27
Heating Degree Days (base 65°F)	1,521	1,161	783	456	176	32	1	3	105	*463*	916	*1,365*	*6,982*
Cooling Degree Days (base 65°F)	0	0	0	1	24	159	327	269	60	0	0	*0*	*840*
Mean Precipitation (in.)	0.39	0.31	0.57	0.77	0.80	0.50	0.71	0.73	0.71	0.99	0.48	0.35	7.31
Days With ≥ 0.1" Precipitation	1	1	2	2	3	2	2	2	2	3	1	1	22
Days With ≥ 1.0" Precipitation	0	0	0	0	0	0	0	0	0	0	0	0	0
Mean Snowfall (in.)	*5.1*	*3.0*	*1.5*	0.6	trace	0.0	0.0	0.0	0.0	0.6	*1.9*	*3.6*	*16.3*
Days With ≥ 1.0" Snow Depth	13	8	1	0	0	0	0	0	0	0	*2*	*4*	28

Panguitch *Garfield County* Elevation: 6,607 ft. Latitude: 37° 49' N Longitude: 112° 26' W

	JAN	FEB	MAR	APR	MAY	JUN	JUL	AUG	SEP	OCT	NOV	DEC	YEAR
Mean Maximum Temp. (°F)	40.2	45.2	52.4	60.4	70.1	80.9	86.2	83.6	76.6	65.6	51.1	41.9	62.9
Mean Temp. (°F)	24.8	29.8	36.6	42.7	51.3	59.9	66.2	64.3	56.6	46.0	34.5	26.1	44.9
Mean Minimum Temp. (°F)	9.2	14.3	20.7	24.8	32.4	38.9	46.2	45.0	36.5	26.3	17.8	10.2	26.9
Extreme Maximum Temp. (°F)	63	69	76	82	91	98	101	98	94	85	73	63	101
Extreme Minimum Temp. (°F)	-30	-31	-5	3	16	23	30	25	17	-10	-13	-30	-31
Days Maximum Temp. ≥ 90°F	0	0	0	0	0	3	9	4	1	0	0	0	17
Days Maximum Temp. ≤ 32°F	5	2	1	0	0	0	0	0	0	0	1	5	14
Days Minimum Temp. ≤ 32°F	31	28	30	26	16	4	0	1	9	25	29	31	230
Days Minimum Temp. ≤ 0°F	7	3	0	0	0	0	0	0	0	0	1	6	17
Heating Degree Days (base 65°F)	1,241	988	875	664	420	164	31	61	250	583	909	1,200	7,386
Cooling Degree Days (base 65°F)	0	0	0	0	1	19	81	51	5	0	0	0	157
Mean Precipitation (in.)	0.57	0.66	0.76	0.63	0.74	0.58	1.24	1.84	0.99	0.95	0.74	0.43	10.13
Days With ≥ 0.1" Precipitation	2	2	3	2	2	2	4	5	3	3	2	1	31
Days With ≥ 1.0" Precipitation	0	0	0	0	0	0	0	0	0	0	0	0	0
Mean Snowfall (in.)	na	na	na	na	0.3	0.0	0.0	0.0	0.0	0.3	na	na	na
Days With ≥ 1.0" Snow Depth	na	na	na	*0*	0	0	0	0	0	0	na	na	na

Parowan Power Plant *Iron County* Elevation: 5,997 ft. Latitude: 37° 50' N Longitude: 112° 50' W

	JAN	FEB	MAR	APR	MAY	JUN	JUL	AUG	SEP	OCT	NOV	DEC	YEAR
Mean Maximum Temp. (°F)	42.1	46.5	52.7	60.2	70.1	82.0	87.8	85.7	78.2	66.0	51.5	43.4	63.9
Mean Temp. (°F)	28.3	32.7	38.9	45.6	54.5	64.7	71.2	69.2	61.1	49.6	37.2	29.5	48.5
Mean Minimum Temp. (°F)	14.5	18.7	25.1	30.9	38.9	47.3	54.4	52.7	44.0	33.2	22.8	15.6	33.2
Extreme Maximum Temp. (°F)	68	74	75	82	90	98	102	99	94	87	76	67	102
Extreme Minimum Temp. (°F)	-18	-21	-2	2	17	25	39	35	25	-2	-6	-22	-22
Days Maximum Temp. ≥ 90°F	0	0	0	0	0	5	13	8	1	0	0	0	27
Days Maximum Temp. ≤ 32°F	5	2	0	0	0	0	0	0	0	0	1	4	12
Days Minimum Temp. ≤ 32°F	31	27	27	18	6	0	0	0	2	14	27	31	183
Days Minimum Temp. ≤ 0°F	3	1	0	0	0	0	0	0	0	0	0	2	6
Heating Degree Days (base 65°F)	1,130	907	802	577	322	83	6	11	140	470	829	1,093	6,370
Cooling Degree Days (base 65°F)	0	0	0	0	5	80	203	155	32	1	0	0	476
Mean Precipitation (in.)	0.96	1.09	1.44	1.27	0.95	0.52	1.16	1.46	0.98	1.35	1.21	0.79	13.18
Days With ≥ 0.1" Precipitation	3	3	4	4	3	2	3	4	2	4	3	3	38
Days With ≥ 1.0" Precipitation	0	0	0	0	0	0	0	0	0	0	0	0	0
Mean Snowfall (in.)	13.2	12.2	11.6	7.5	1.5	0.1	0.0	0.0	trace	2.7	10.0	10.9	69.7
Days With ≥ 1.0" Snow Depth	18	12	5	2	0	0	0	0	0	1	6	13	57

Partoun *Juab County*   Elevation: 4,776 ft.   Latitude: 39° 38' N   Longitude: 113° 53' W

	JAN	FEB	MAR	APR	MAY	JUN	JUL	AUG	SEP	OCT	NOV	DEC	YEAR
Mean Maximum Temp. (°F)	40.5	47.1	56.5	64.3	74.2	86.2	94.1	92.1	81.8	67.7	52.4	41.8	66.5
Mean Temp. (°F)	27.2	33.1	41.6	48.3	57.4	67.8	75.0	73.1	63.1	50.5	38.1	28.1	50.3
Mean Minimum Temp. (°F)	13.9	19.2	26.6	32.3	40.5	49.2	55.9	54.0	44.3	33.2	23.6	14.4	33.9
Extreme Maximum Temp. (°F)	66	74	79	86	97	105	107	104	100	90	78	66	107
Extreme Minimum Temp. (°F)	-23	-29	2	11	20	21	39	31	21	2	-2	-27	-29
Days Maximum Temp. ≥ 90°F	0	0	0	0	1	12	26	22	6	0	0	0	67
Days Maximum Temp. ≤ 32°F	7	3	0	0	0	0	0	0	0	0	1	5	16
Days Minimum Temp. ≤ 32°F	30	26	24	15	4	0	0	0	2	14	26	30	171
Days Minimum Temp. ≤ 0°F	4	1	0	0	0	0	0	0	0	0	0	3	8
Heating Degree Days (base 65°F)	1,163	893	719	495	244	51	2	4	118	445	802	1,137	6,073
Cooling Degree Days (base 65°F)	0	0	0	0	16	139	312	266	67	1	0	0	801
Mean Precipitation (in.)	0.46	0.44	0.60	0.71	0.98	0.58	0.63	0.56	0.70	0.72	0.47	0.26	7.11
Days With ≥ 0.1" Precipitation	2	2	2	2	3	2	2	2	2	2	1	1	23
Days With ≥ 1.0" Precipitation	0	0	0	0	0	0	0	0	0	0	0	0	0
Mean Snowfall (in.)	na	na	na	0.3	trace	0.0	0.0	0.0	0.0	trace	0.3	na	na
Days With ≥ 1.0" Snow Depth	10	na	1	0	0	0	0	0	0	0	1	3	na

Pine View Dam *Weber County*   Elevation: 4,937 ft.   Latitude: 41° 15' N   Longitude: 111° 50' W

	JAN	FEB	MAR	APR	MAY	JUN	JUL	AUG	SEP	OCT	NOV	DEC	YEAR
Mean Maximum Temp. (°F)	30.7	35.7	45.9	55.7	65.9	76.9	85.5	84.4	73.8	60.9	44.1	32.4	57.7
Mean Temp. (°F)	19.2	23.0	33.9	42.9	51.7	60.3	67.7	66.6	57.0	45.8	33.1	22.1	43.6
Mean Minimum Temp. (°F)	7.8	10.2	21.9	30.1	37.3	43.7	49.9	48.9	40.2	30.6	22.1	11.7	29.5
Extreme Maximum Temp. (°F)	57	61	71	81	88	96	97	98	92	83	70	61	98
Extreme Minimum Temp. (°F)	-29	-39	-15	9	20	27	37	30	22	11	-9	-36	-39
Days Maximum Temp. ≥ 90°F	0	0	0	0	0	2	9	6	0	0	0	0	17
Days Maximum Temp. ≤ 32°F	16	9	2	0	0	0	0	0	0	0	4	15	46
Days Minimum Temp. ≤ 32°F	31	28	29	20	7	1	0	0	4	20	28	30	198
Days Minimum Temp. ≤ 0°F	9	7	1	0	0	0	0	0	0	0	0	5	22
Heating Degree Days (base 65°F)	1,413	1,180	956	656	408	160	24	35	243	589	950	1,324	7,938
Cooling Degree Days (base 65°F)	0	0	0	0	1	27	113	98	11	0	0	0	250
Mean Precipitation (in.)	3.88	3.10	3.44	3.02	3.45	1.81	1.14	1.03	2.07	2.93	3.27	3.45	32.59
Days With ≥ 0.1" Precipitation	8	7	8	7	7	3	2	2	4	5	7	7	67
Days With ≥ 1.0" Precipitation	1	1	1	0	1	0	0	0	1	1	1	1	8
Mean Snowfall (in.)	32.1	24.4	13.9	6.8	1.1	0.0	0.0	0.0	trace	2.3	14.9	29.5	125.0
Days With ≥ 1.0" Snow Depth	30	28	22	6	1	0	0	0	0	1	11	26	125

Pleasant Grove *Utah County*   Elevation: 4,760 ft.   Latitude: 40° 22' N   Longitude: 111° 43' W

	JAN	FEB	MAR	APR	MAY	JUN	JUL	AUG	SEP	OCT	NOV	DEC	YEAR
Mean Maximum Temp. (°F)	38.4	45.1	54.5	62.3	72.2	82.7	89.8	88.4	78.9	66.2	50.7	39.8	64.1
Mean Temp. (°F)	29.3	34.6	42.8	49.6	58.3	67.6	74.7	73.3	64.1	52.4	40.2	30.8	51.5
Mean Minimum Temp. (°F)	20.1	24.1	31.2	36.7	44.2	52.4	59.5	58.1	49.2	38.6	29.7	21.7	38.8
Extreme Maximum Temp. (°F)	62	70	79	87	94	101	102	100	96	90	77	66	102
Extreme Minimum Temp. (°F)	-14	-17	9	20	25	32	26	42	29	16	5	-14	-17
Days Maximum Temp. ≥ 90°F	0	0	0	0	0	7	18	14	2	0	0	0	41
Days Maximum Temp. ≤ 32°F	8	2	0	0	0	0	0	0	0	0	1	6	17
Days Minimum Temp. ≤ 32°F	29	24	18	9	1	0	0	0	0	6	20	28	135
Days Minimum Temp. ≤ 0°F	1	0	0	0	0	0	0	0	0	0	0	1	2
Heating Degree Days (base 65°F)	1,101	852	680	459	223	53	2	3	96	385	737	1,056	5,647
Cooling Degree Days (base 65°F)	0	0	0	3	24	142	311	288	83	3	0	0	854
Mean Precipitation (in.)	1.80	1.65	1.82	1.69	1.84	0.93	0.90	0.83	1.35	1.73	1.54	1.46	17.54
Days With ≥ 0.1" Precipitation	5	5	6	5	5	3	3	3	3	4	4	5	51
Days With ≥ 1.0" Precipitation	0	0	0	0	0	0	0	0	0	0	0	0	0
Mean Snowfall (in.)	12.1	7.7	3.9	3.7	0.3	0.0	0.0	0.0	trace	1.1	5.6	9.4	43.8
Days With ≥ 1.0" Snow Depth	16	8	1	0	0	0	0	0	0	0	3	10	38

Richfield Radio KSVC *Sevier County*   Elevation: 5,298 ft.   Latitude: 38° 46' N   Longitude: 112° 05' W

	JAN	FEB	MAR	APR	MAY	JUN	JUL	AUG	SEP	OCT	NOV	DEC	YEAR
Mean Maximum Temp. (°F)	40.5	47.2	55.7	63.4	72.4	83.0	89.0	87.3	79.4	67.8	52.0	42.1	65.0
Mean Temp. (°F)	27.9	33.6	41.0	47.2	55.4	64.4	70.8	69.1	60.8	49.6	37.6	28.9	48.9
Mean Minimum Temp. (°F)	15.2	20.0	26.3	31.0	38.4	45.7	52.4	50.9	42.1	31.4	23.1	15.6	32.7
Extreme Maximum Temp. (°F)	67	72	78	84	92	100	102	101	95	87	76	68	102
Extreme Minimum Temp. (°F)	-22	-33	-11	10	21	25	34	29	21		-8	-32	-33
Days Maximum Temp. ≥ 90°F	0	0	0	0	0	6	16	11	2	0	0	0	35
Days Maximum Temp. ≤ 32°F	7	2	0	0	0	0	0	0	0	0	2	5	16
Days Minimum Temp. ≤ 32°F	30	26	25	17	5	0	0	0	4	18	26	30	181
Days Minimum Temp. ≤ 0°F	4	1	0	0	0	0	0	0	0	0	0	3	8
Heating Degree Days (base 65°F)	1,145	878	736	528	293	78	4	10	148	471	815	1,113	6,219
Cooling Degree Days (base 65°F)	0	0	0	0	4	68	185	147	28	0	0	0	432
Mean Precipitation (in.)	0.59	0.50	0.80	0.64	1.01	0.59	0.74	0.68	0.85	0.98	0.69	0.45	8.52
Days With ≥ 0.1" Precipitation	2	2	3	2	3	2	2	2	2	3	2	2	27
Days With ≥ 1.0" Precipitation	0	0	0	0	0	0	0	0	0	0	0	0	0
Mean Snowfall (in.)	3.3	3.8	1.8	0.3	0.4	trace	0.0	0.0	trace	0.8	2.1	na	na
Days With ≥ 1.0" Snow Depth	na	3	1	0	0	0	0	0	0	0	2	5	na

Richmond *Cache County*   Elevation: 4,678 ft.   Latitude: 41° 54' N   Longitude: 111° 49' W

	JAN	FEB	MAR	APR	MAY	JUN	JUL	AUG	SEP	OCT	NOV	DEC	YEAR
Mean Maximum Temp. (°F)	31.9	38.5	49.3	59.2	69.3	80.8	90.3	89.1	77.8	63.2	45.5	33.4	60.7
Mean Temp. (°F)	23.2	28.3	37.9	45.9	54.4	63.8	71.5	70.8	60.8	48.7	35.4	24.6	47.1
Mean Minimum Temp. (°F)	14.5	18.1	26.5	32.5	39.4	46.7	52.7	52.4	43.8	34.2	25.3	15.7	33.5
Extreme Maximum Temp. (°F)	54	63	73	89	89	101	103	103	99	88	72	67	103
Extreme Minimum Temp. (°F)	-23	-27	-4	12	20	31	37	34	22	7	-8	-28	-28
Days Maximum Temp. ≥ 90°F	0	0	0	0	0	5	19	16	3	0	0	0	43
Days Maximum Temp. ≤ 32°F	14	7	1	0	0	0	0	0	0	0	3	13	38
Days Minimum Temp. ≤ 32°F	30	26	25	16	5	0	0	0	2	12	25	29	170
Days Minimum Temp. ≤ 0°F	6	3	0	0	0	0	0	0	0	0	1	3	13
Heating Degree Days (base 65°F)	1,290	1,030	833	568	327	103	10	12	159	498	881	1,245	6,956
Cooling Degree Days (base 65°F)	0	0	0	1	5	70	221	215	45	0	0	0	557
Mean Precipitation (in.)	1.70	1.60	2.18	2.23	2.65	1.34	1.01	0.99	1.48	2.00	1.72	1.59	20.49
Days With ≥ 0.1" Precipitation	5	5	7	6	7	3	2	2	3	5	5	5	55
Days With ≥ 1.0" Precipitation	0	0	0	0	0	0	0	0	0	0	0	0	0
Mean Snowfall (in.)	12.9	12.0	10.9	5.5	1.1	trace	0.0	0.0	0.1	2.2	9.2	14.9	68.8
Days With ≥ 1.0" Snow Depth	26	20	8	1	0	0	0	0	0	0	7	21	83

Roosevelt *Duchesne County*   Elevation: 5,104 ft.   Latitude: 40° 18' N   Longitude: 109° 59' W

	JAN	FEB	MAR	APR	MAY	JUN	JUL	AUG	SEP	OCT	NOV	DEC	YEAR
Mean Maximum Temp. (°F)	30.0	38.0	53.4	64.4	74.4	85.1	91.0	89.2	79.6	65.6	47.5	34.3	62.7
Mean Temp. (°F)	17.1	24.2	38.3	47.7	57.3	66.4	72.4	70.7	61.3	48.7	33.8	21.3	46.6
Mean Minimum Temp. (°F)	4.1	10.3	23.1	30.9	40.1	47.7	53.7	52.2	43.0	31.7	20.0	8.2	30.4
Extreme Maximum Temp. (°F)	60	68	75	88	94	102	105	102	97	85	70	61	105
Extreme Minimum Temp. (°F)	-29	-47	-6	8	18	29	37	32	21	2	-6	-40	-47
Days Maximum Temp. ≥ 90°F	0	0	0	0	0	11	20	16	3	0	0	0	50
Days Maximum Temp. ≤ 32°F	17	9	1	0	0	0	0	0	0	0	3	12	42
Days Minimum Temp. ≤ 32°F	31	28	28	17	4	0	0	0	3	17	28	31	187
Days Minimum Temp. ≤ 0°F	12	6	0	0	0	0	0	0	0	0	0	6	24
Heating Degree Days (base 65°F)	1,480	1,147	822	513	239	55	3	5	140	498	930	1,349	7,181
Cooling Degree Days (base 65°F)	0	0	0	0	8	95	227	189	34	0	0	0	553
Mean Precipitation (in.)	0.56	0.42	0.54	0.66	0.89	0.51	0.50	0.64	0.74	1.03	0.47	0.36	7.32
Days With ≥ 0.1" Precipitation	2	2	2	2	3	1	2	2	3	3	2	1	25
Days With ≥ 1.0" Precipitation	0	0	0	0	0	0	0	0	0	0	0	0	0
Mean Snowfall (in.)	7.4	3.8	1.5	0.4	trace	0.0	0.0	0.0	0.0	0.3	2.1	3.9	19.4
Days With ≥ 1.0" Snow Depth	12	11	3	0	0	0	0	0	0	0	2	7	35

Saint George *Washington County*   Elevation: 2,769 ft.   Latitude: 37° 06' N   Longitude: 113° 34' W

	JAN	FEB	MAR	APR	MAY	JUN	JUL	AUG	SEP	OCT	NOV	DEC	YEAR
Mean Maximum Temp. (°F)	54.2	61.2	68.6	76.9	86.7	97.2	102.4	100.2	92.8	80.6	64.7	54.7	78.3
Mean Temp. (°F)	41.4	47.2	53.9	61.1	70.7	80.1	86.1	84.2	75.9	63.4	49.9	41.6	62.9
Mean Minimum Temp. (°F)	28.8	33.1	39.1	45.2	54.6	62.9	69.8	68.1	59.1	46.2	35.2	28.4	47.5
Extreme Maximum Temp. (°F)	71	84	89	97	105	115	117	112	109	99	83	73	117
Extreme Minimum Temp. (°F)	1	6	20	28	34	43	53	47	37	20	15	3	1
Days Maximum Temp. ≥ 90°F	0	0	0	2	13	25	31	30	21	5	0	0	127
Days Maximum Temp. ≤ 32°F	0	0	0	0	0	0	0	0	0	0	0	0	0
Days Minimum Temp. ≤ 32°F	22	12	5	1	0	0	0	0	0	1	10	23	74
Days Minimum Temp. ≤ 0°F	0	0	0	0	0	0	0	0	0	0	0	0	0
Heating Degree Days (base 65°F)	724	497	341	154	29	1	0	0	5	108	445	726	3,030
Cooling Degree Days (base 65°F)	0	0	3	54	237	478	680	634	363	66	0	0	2,515
Mean Precipitation (in.)	1.28	1.07	1.22	0.52	0.40	0.22	0.60	0.76	0.63	0.70	0.81	0.60	8.81
Days With ≥ 0.1" Precipitation	3	3	4	1	1	1	2	2	2	2	2	2	25
Days With ≥ 1.0" Precipitation	0	0	0	0	0	0	0	0	0	0	0	0	0
Mean Snowfall (in.)	1.4	0.4	trace	trace	0.0	0.0	0.0	0.0	0.0	trace	0.1	0.1	2.0
Days With ≥ 1.0" Snow Depth	0	0	0	0	0	0	0	0	0	0	0	0	0

Salina *Sevier County*   Elevation: 5,127 ft.   Latitude: 38° 58' N   Longitude: 111° 52' W

	JAN	FEB	MAR	APR	MAY	JUN	JUL	AUG	SEP	OCT	NOV	DEC	YEAR
Mean Maximum Temp. (°F)	39.1	46.2	55.3	64.6	74.1	85.3	91.4	89.3	80.5	67.6	51.5	41.3	65.5
Mean Temp. (°F)	25.9	32.3	40.6	48.0	56.5	66.1	72.6	70.6	61.5	49.9	37.2	27.8	49.1
Mean Minimum Temp. (°F)	12.5	18.4	25.9	31.2	38.8	46.8	53.7	51.8	42.4	32.0	22.8	14.2	32.6
Extreme Maximum Temp. (°F)	65	74	77	89	98	102	105	105	102	89	76	66	105
Extreme Minimum Temp. (°F)	-23	-27	-8	11	20	25	35	28	20	-3	-8	-32	-32
Days Maximum Temp. ≥ 90°F	0	0	0	0	1	10	21	16	4	0	0	0	52
Days Maximum Temp. ≤ 32°F	8	2	0	0	0	0	0	0	0	0	1	6	17
Days Minimum Temp. ≤ 32°F	31	27	26	18	6	1	0	0	4	17	26	30	186
Days Minimum Temp. ≤ 0°F	5	2	0	0	0	0	0	0	0	0	0	3	10
Heating Degree Days (base 65°F)	1,207	916	749	505	264	67	4	8	138	463	828	1,148	6,297
Cooling Degree Days (base 65°F)	0	0	0	0	5	94	210	172	33	0	na	0	na
Mean Precipitation (in.)	0.64	0.59	1.22	0.93	1.06	0.53	0.68	0.80	0.94	1.06	0.85	0.61	9.91
Days With ≥ 0.1" Precipitation	2	2	4	3	3	2	2	3	3	3	3	2	32
Days With ≥ 1.0" Precipitation	0	0	0	0	0	0	0	0	0	0	0	0	0
Mean Snowfall (in.)	na	na	na	na	trace	trace	0.0	0.0	0.0	na	na	na	na
Days With ≥ 1.0" Snow Depth	na	na	na	na	0	0	0	0	0	na	na	na	na

Santaquin Chlorinator *Utah County*   Elevation: 5,164 ft.   Latitude: 39° 57' N   Longitude: 111° 47' W

	JAN	FEB	MAR	APR	MAY	JUN	JUL	AUG	SEP	OCT	NOV	DEC	YEAR
Mean Maximum Temp. (°F)	38.0	43.7	52.3	60.0	70.6	81.8	89.9	88.7	78.4	65.0	49.5	38.8	63.1
Mean Temp. (°F)	27.7	32.8	40.5	47.2	57.0	66.9	74.6	73.1	62.7	51.0	38.2	28.7	50.0
Mean Minimum Temp. (°F)	17.4	21.8	29.0	34.5	43.1	51.9	59.3	57.4	47.0	36.9	26.8	18.5	37.0
Extreme Maximum Temp. (°F)	60	71	78	86	94	102	102	104	98	88	78	69	104
Extreme Minimum Temp. (°F)	-17	-19	2	14	23	29	37	35	24	12	-2	-20	-20
Days Maximum Temp. ≥ 90°F	0	0	0	0	0	6	19	15	2	0	0	0	42
Days Maximum Temp. ≤ 32°F	9	3	0	0	0	0	0	0	0	0	2	8	22
Days Minimum Temp. ≤ 32°F	28	25	21	13	3	0	0	0	1	8	23	29	151
Days Minimum Temp. ≤ 0°F	2	0	0	0	0	0	0	0	0	0	0	1	3
Heating Degree Days (base 65°F)	1,148	903	751	526	263	75	7	7	129	430	801	1,119	6,159
Cooling Degree Days (base 65°F)	0	0	0	3	22	120	297	280	72	3	0	0	797
Mean Precipitation (in.)	1.50	1.52	1.92	1.98	2.05	0.87	0.79	0.99	1.45	2.01	1.85	1.37	18.30
Days With ≥ 0.1" Precipitation	4	4	5	6	4	2	2	3	3	4	4	4	45
Days With ≥ 1.0" Precipitation	0	0	0	0	0	0	0	0	0	0	0	0	0
Mean Snowfall (in.)	12.8	11.7	6.5	4.0	1.1	trace	0.0	0.0	0.0	2.0	8.3	11.1	57.5
Days With ≥ 1.0" Snow Depth	na	na	na	1	0	0	0	0	0	0	na	na	na

Scipio *Millard County*   Elevation: 5,314 ft.   Latitude: 39° 15' N   Longitude: 112° 06' W

	JAN	FEB	MAR	APR	MAY	JUN	JUL	AUG	SEP	OCT	NOV	DEC	YEAR
Mean Maximum Temp. (°F)	38.2	45.0	53.8	62.5	72.8	83.0	90.1	87.8	79.1	66.8	51.0	39.8	64.1
Mean Temp. (°F)	25.0	31.4	39.3	46.3	55.0	64.3	72.3	70.0	60.3	48.9	36.8	26.1	48.0
Mean Minimum Temp. (°F)	11.8	17.7	24.7	29.9	37.1	45.3	54.5	52.2	41.5	30.9	22.5	12.4	31.7
Extreme Maximum Temp. (°F)	65	70	78	89	92	100	105	100	96	87	75	69	105
Extreme Minimum Temp. (°F)	-34	-38	-17	3	15	22	35	28	15	0	-24	-36	-38
Days Maximum Temp. ≥ 90°F	0	0	0	0	0	7	18	12	2	0	0	0	39
Days Maximum Temp. ≤ 32°F	8	2	0	0	0	0	0	0	0	0	2	6	18
Days Minimum Temp. ≤ 32°F	30	26	25	19	9	1	0	0	5	19	26	30	190
Days Minimum Temp. ≤ 0°F	7	2	0	0	0	0	0	0	0	0	1	5	15
Heating Degree Days (base 65°F)	1,233	944	791	556	310	95	4	12	167	493	840	1,199	6,644
Cooling Degree Days (base 65°F)	0	0	0	1	7	87	251	202	34	1	0	0	583
Mean Precipitation (in.)	1.25	1.22	1.33	1.23	1.34	0.78	0.89	1.10	1.07	1.52	1.31	1.06	14.10
Days With ≥ 0.1" Precipitation	4	4	5	4	4	2	3	3	3	4	4	4	44
Days With ≥ 1.0" Precipitation	0	0	0	0	0	0	0	0	0	0	0	0	0
Mean Snowfall (in.)	na	na	na	1.0	0.0	0.0	0.0	0.0	0.0	0.1	5.2	na	na
Days With ≥ 1.0" Snow Depth	na	na	na	na	0	0	0	0	0	0	na	na	na

Silver Lake Brighton *Salt Lake County*   Elevation: 8,740 ft.   Latitude: 40° 36' N   Longitude: 111° 35' W

	JAN	FEB	MAR	APR	MAY	JUN	JUL	AUG	SEP	OCT	NOV	DEC	YEAR
Mean Maximum Temp. (°F)	30.7	33.5	37.3	43.5	52.4	63.5	71.6	70.4	61.4	49.8	36.7	30.9	48.5
Mean Temp. (°F)	19.9	21.8	26.0	31.9	40.7	50.3	58.0	56.9	48.7	38.1	26.3	20.1	36.6
Mean Minimum Temp. (°F)	9.1	10.1	14.7	20.3	28.9	37.1	44.3	43.4	36.0	26.3	15.8	9.2	24.6
Extreme Maximum Temp. (°F)	55	57	58	66	73	83	87	85	78	71	62	56	87
Extreme Minimum Temp. (°F)	-28	-27	-17	-10	4	18	28	25	10	-2	-18	-29	-29
Days Maximum Temp. ≥ 90°F	0	0	0	0	0	0	0	0	0	0	0	0	0
Days Maximum Temp. ≤ 32°F	18	13	9	4	1	0	0	0	0	2	11	17	75
Days Minimum Temp. ≤ 32°F	31	28	30	28	21	8	1	1	9	24	29	31	241
Days Minimum Temp. ≤ 0°F	7	5	2	1	0	0	0	0	0	0	2	6	23
Heating Degree Days (base 65°F)	1,390	1,214	1,201	986	749	434	214	245	481	829	1,155	1,385	10,283
Cooling Degree Days (base 65°F)	0	0	0	0	0	0	3	2	0	0	0	0	5
Mean Precipitation (in.)	5.10	4.77	5.35	4.28	3.43	1.62	1.69	1.79	2.58	3.61	4.91	4.72	43.85
Days With ≥ 0.1" Precipitation	10	9	11	10	8	4	4	5	6	6	10	10	93
Days With ≥ 1.0" Precipitation	1	1	1	1	0	0	0	0	0	1	1	1	7
Mean Snowfall (in.)	68.7	63.8	68.1	49.7	20.2	2.8	trace	trace	3.2	25.7	61.0	65.4	428.6
Days With ≥ 1.0" Snow Depth	31	28	31	30	25	4	0	0	1	13	28	31	222

Snake Creek Powerhouse *Wasatch County*   Elevation: 6,007 ft.   Latitude: 40° 33' N   Longitude: 111° 30' W

	JAN	FEB	MAR	APR	MAY	JUN	JUL	AUG	SEP	OCT	NOV	DEC	YEAR
Mean Maximum Temp. (°F)	34.1	39.2	47.3	56.9	66.9	77.1	84.5	83.3	74.1	62.2	45.9	35.5	58.9
Mean Temp. (°F)	22.5	26.3	34.7	42.3	50.6	58.5	65.2	64.3	55.8	45.6	33.5	23.9	43.6
Mean Minimum Temp. (°F)	10.8	13.4	22.1	27.6	34.2	39.9	45.9	45.2	37.4	29.0	21.0	12.2	28.2
Extreme Maximum Temp. (°F)	56	61	72	81	85	96	99	98	94	85	71	65	99
Extreme Minimum Temp. (°F)	-25	-34	-7	-4	14	24	31	27	16	5	-11	-29	-34
Days Maximum Temp. ≥ 90°F	0	0	0	0	0	1	5	4	0	0	0	0	10
Days Maximum Temp. ≤ 32°F	12	6	1	0	0	0	0	0	0	0	3	11	33
Days Minimum Temp. ≤ 32°F	31	28	29	24	12	3	0	1	7	22	28	31	216
Days Minimum Temp. ≤ 0°F	7	4	0	0	0	0	0	0	0	0	1	5	17
Heating Degree Days (base 65°F)	1,313	1,086	932	675	440	199	42	60	275	595	938	1,267	7,822
Cooling Degree Days (base 65°F)	0	0	0	0	0	14	64	54	7	0	0	0	139
Mean Precipitation (in.)	2.89	2.60	1.95	1.66	1.84	0.96	1.13	1.17	1.52	1.93	2.31	2.37	22.33
Days With ≥ 0.1" Precipitation	7	6	6	5	5	3	3	3	4	5	6	6	59
Days With ≥ 1.0" Precipitation	0	0	0	0	0	0	0	0	0	0	0	0	0
Mean Snowfall (in.)	32.5	na	na	2.9	1.6	0.0	0.0	0.0	trace	2.0	na	24.5	na
Days With ≥ 1.0" Snow Depth	29	26	na	4	0	0	0	0	0	1	10	24	na

Spanish Fork Power House *Utah County*   Elevation: 4,717 ft.   Latitude: 40° 05' N   Longitude: 111° 36' W

	JAN	FEB	MAR	APR	MAY	JUN	JUL	AUG	SEP	OCT	NOV	DEC	YEAR
Mean Maximum Temp. (°F)	36.6	43.7	54.1	63.1	73.6	84.8	92.0	89.9	79.8	66.0	49.3	37.7	64.2
Mean Temp. (°F)	28.4	34.0	42.8	50.1	59.2	68.6	75.7	74.0	64.7	53.0	39.8	29.7	51.6
Mean Minimum Temp. (°F)	20.2	24.2	31.3	37.1	44.8	52.3	59.3	58.0	49.5	39.9	30.1	21.6	39.0
Extreme Maximum Temp. (°F)	59	72	80	86	97	101	105	103	96	87	74	65	105
Extreme Minimum Temp. (°F)	-10	-20	9	15	26	29	41	40	27	13	1	-14	-20
Days Maximum Temp. ≥ 90°F	0	0	0	0	1	10	23	18	3	0	0	0	55
Days Maximum Temp. ≤ 32°F	10	3	0	0	0	0	0	0	0	0	2	8	23
Days Minimum Temp. ≤ 32°F	28	23	18	8	1	0	0	0	0	5	18	28	129
Days Minimum Temp. ≤ 0°F	1	0	0	0	0	0	0	0	0	0	0	1	2
Heating Degree Days (base 65°F)	1,127	871	683	443	202	48	2	3	85	367	750	1,089	5,670
Cooling Degree Days (base 65°F)	0	0	0	3	33	162	334	300	87	3	0	0	922
Mean Precipitation (in.)	1.86	2.03	2.34	2.29	2.22	1.10	0.96	1.07	1.52	2.20	2.30	1.85	21.74
Days With ≥ 0.1" Precipitation	5	5	6	6	5	3	3	3	3	5	6	5	55
Days With ≥ 1.0" Precipitation	0	0	0	0	0	0	0	0	0	0	0	0	0
Mean Snowfall (in.)	*17.9*	*13.8*	*7.5*	*4.0*	0.2	0.0	0.0	0.0	0.0	0.8	9.1	*14.2*	*67.5*
Days With ≥ 1.0" Snow Depth	*21*	na	*3*	1	0	0	0	0	0	0	5	*19*	na

Thiokol Plant 78 *Box Elder County*   Elevation: 4,599 ft.   Latitude: 41° 43' N   Longitude: 112° 26' W

	JAN	FEB	MAR	APR	MAY	JUN	JUL	AUG	SEP	OCT	NOV	DEC	YEAR
Mean Maximum Temp. (°F)	33.2	40.1	50.5	60.5	70.7	82.3	91.3	90.4	79.1	64.5	47.1	35.4	62.1
Mean Temp. (°F)	22.9	28.5	38.2	46.0	55.0	64.8	72.6	71.5	60.9	48.1	35.1	24.7	47.4
Mean Minimum Temp. (°F)	12.5	17.0	26.0	31.4	39.2	47.2	53.8	52.7	42.7	31.6	23.1	14.0	32.6
Extreme Maximum Temp. (°F)	52	65	73	85	89	103	103	104	98	88	72	60	104
Extreme Minimum Temp. (°F)	-28	-29	-2	11	16	29	35	31	20	10	-17	-27	-29
Days Maximum Temp. ≥ 90°F	0	0	0	0	0	7	21	19	4	0	0	0	51
Days Maximum Temp. ≤ 32°F	13	6	1	0	0	0	0	0	0	0	2	10	32
Days Minimum Temp. ≤ 32°F	30	27	26	18	5	0	0	0	3	17	27	30	183
Days Minimum Temp. ≤ 0°F	7	3	0	0	0	0	0	0	0	0	1	4	15
Heating Degree Days (base 65°F)	1,300	1,024	823	565	311	90	8	9	157	518	890	1,242	6,937
Cooling Degree Days (base 65°F)	0	0	0	1	8	86	249	230	47	0	0	0	621
Mean Precipitation (in.)	1.20	1.09	1.28	1.34	1.99	1.18	0.94	0.87	1.22	1.35	1.24	0.97	14.67
Days With ≥ 0.1" Precipitation	4	4	4	4	5	3	2	2	3	3	4	3	41
Days With ≥ 1.0" Precipitation	0	0	0	0	0	0	0	0	0	0	0	0	0
Mean Snowfall (in.)	*6.4*	4.3	0.7	trace	0.0	trace	0.0	0.0	0.0	trace	3.2	7.0	*21.6*
Days With ≥ 1.0" Snow Depth	22	14	4	0	0	0	0	0	0	0	4	14	58

Timpanogos Cave *Utah County*   Elevation: 5,639 ft.   Latitude: 40° 27' N   Longitude: 111° 42' W

	JAN	FEB	MAR	APR	MAY	JUN	JUL	AUG	SEP	OCT	NOV	DEC	YEAR
Mean Maximum Temp. (°F)	33.3	40.5	50.0	60.2	70.8	82.3	91.3	90.5	79.0	62.4	43.2	34.1	61.5
Mean Temp. (°F)	26.3	31.7	39.2	47.1	56.2	65.9	74.0	73.2	63.3	50.1	35.7	27.4	49.2
Mean Minimum Temp. (°F)	19.3	22.9	28.4	34.0	41.7	49.5	56.7	55.7	47.6	37.9	28.1	20.7	36.9
Extreme Maximum Temp. (°F)	53	63	77	85	90	101	104	106	98	88	69	64	106
Extreme Minimum Temp. (°F)	-11	-10	1	12	24	28	39	33	26	13	2	-14	-14
Days Maximum Temp. ≥ 90°F	0	0	0	0	0	7	21	19	4	0	0	0	51
Days Maximum Temp. ≤ 32°F	13	5	0	0	0	0	0	0	0	0	4	13	35
Days Minimum Temp. ≤ 32°F	30	*25*	*21*	12	3	0	0	0	1	6	20	29	*147*
Days Minimum Temp. ≤ 0°F	1	0	0	0	0	0	0	0	0	0	0	1	2
Heating Degree Days (base 65°F)	1,191	933	793	531	276	77	4	5	112	454	874	1,160	6,410
Cooling Degree Days (base 65°F)	0	0	0	1	14	105	280	274	71	1	0	0	746
Mean Precipitation (in.)	2.30	2.24	2.93	2.32	3.05	1.57	1.15	1.40	2.09	2.52	2.09	2.00	25.66
Days With ≥ 0.1" Precipitation	6	5	6	6	7	3	3	4	4	5	5	5	59
Days With ≥ 1.0" Precipitation	0	0	0	0	1	0	0	0	0	1	0	0	2
Mean Snowfall (in.)	*19.9*	*14.2*	*9.2*	*4.1*	0.3	0.1	0.0	0.0	trace	1.8	10.0	16.1	*75.7*
Days With ≥ 1.0" Snow Depth	30	26	18	3	0	0	0	0	0	1	*9*	25	*112*

Tooele *Tooele County*   Elevation: 5,068 ft.   Latitude: 40° 32' N   Longitude: 112° 18' W

	JAN	FEB	MAR	APR	MAY	JUN	JUL	AUG	SEP	OCT	NOV	DEC	YEAR
Mean Maximum Temp. (°F)	38.4	44.1	52.3	60.5	70.3	81.1	89.0	87.6	77.1	64.0	48.9	39.1	62.7
Mean Temp. (°F)	29.1	33.9	41.6	48.8	57.9	67.9	75.5	74.0	63.8	51.7	38.9	29.9	51.1
Mean Minimum Temp. (°F)	19.7	23.8	30.8	37.1	45.4	54.7	61.9	60.3	50.5	39.3	28.8	20.7	39.4
Extreme Maximum Temp. (°F)	63	70	76	85	91	101	102	102	98	87	74	70	102
Extreme Minimum Temp. (°F)	-9	-7	3	18	25	27	39	38	28	11	2	-16	-16
Days Maximum Temp. ≥ 90°F	0	0	0	0	0	6	16	13	2	0	0	0	37
Days Maximum Temp. ≤ 32°F	9	3	0	0	0	0	0	0	0	0	1	7	20
Days Minimum Temp. ≤ 32°F	28	24	19	10	2	0	0	0	0	6	20	28	137
Days Minimum Temp. ≤ 0°F	1	0	0	0	0	0	0	0	0	0	0	1	2
Heating Degree Days (base 65°F)	1,106	871	719	484	246	65	5	5	111	410	778	1,080	5,880
Cooling Degree Days (base 65°F)	0	0	0	7	35	161	344	314	93	5	0	0	959
Mean Precipitation (in.)	1.37	1.55	2.48	2.41	2.24	1.05	0.90	0.90	1.50	1.92	1.99	1.51	19.82
Days With ≥ 0.1" Precipitation	4	4	6	6	5	3	2	3	3	4	5	4	49
Days With ≥ 1.0" Precipitation	0	0	0	0	0	0	0	0	0	0	0	0	0
Mean Snowfall (in.)	14.4	14.4	14.3	8.4	1.5	trace	0.0	0.0	0.1	3.9	12.3	17.2	86.5
Days With ≥ 1.0" Snow Depth	21	17	8	2	0	0	0	0	0	1	9	22	80

Tropic *Garfield County* Elevation: 6,279 ft. Latitude: 37° 38' N Longitude: 112° 05' W

	JAN	FEB	MAR	APR	MAY	JUN	JUL	AUG	SEP	OCT	NOV	DEC	YEAR
Mean Maximum Temp. (°F)	41.3	45.5	52.3	59.8	69.2	79.4	85.3	82.6	74.4	63.7	50.5	42.4	62.2
Mean Temp. (°F)	28.6	32.5	38.7	44.6	52.9	61.8	68.4	66.3	58.5	48.7	37.2	29.5	47.3
Mean Minimum Temp. (°F)	15.9	19.5	24.9	29.5	36.5	44.1	51.4	50.1	42.6	33.6	23.8	16.5	32.4
Extreme Maximum Temp. (°F)	66	71	76	89	92	96	99	96	93	85	70	66	99
Extreme Minimum Temp. (°F)	-14	-10	5	6	18	27	29	32	21	9	-5	-18	-18
Days Maximum Temp. ≥ 90°F	0	0	0	0	0	2	7	4	0	0	0	0	13
Days Maximum Temp. ≤ 32°F	5	2	0	0	0	0	0	0	0	0	1	4	12
Days Minimum Temp. ≤ 32°F	31	27	28	21	8	1	0	0	2	14	27	30	189
Days Minimum Temp. ≤ 0°F	2	1	0	0	0	0	0	0	0	0	0	1	4
Heating Degree Days (base 65°F)	1,121	911	810	604	371	130	18	43	200	498	828	1,095	6,629
Cooling Degree Days (base 65°F)	0	0	0	0	3	39	135	96	14	0	0	0	287
Mean Precipitation (in.)	0.89	1.07	1.15	0.69	0.66	0.49	1.09	1.52	1.26	1.31	1.01	0.86	12.00
Days With ≥ 0.1" Precipitation	3	2	3	2	2	2	4	4	3	3	3	2	33
Days With ≥ 1.0" Precipitation	0	0	0	0	0	0	0	0	0	0	0	0	0
Mean Snowfall (in.)	*6.2*	*5.6*	3.8	0.7	trace	0.0	0.0	0.0	0.0	0.1	*1.5*	*5.1*	*23.0*
Days With ≥ 1.0" Snow Depth	*13*	*9*	3	0	0	0	0	0	0	0	*3*	*6*	*34*

Utah Lake Lehi *Utah County* Elevation: 4,494 ft. Latitude: 40° 22' N Longitude: 111° 54' W

	JAN	FEB	MAR	APR	MAY	JUN	JUL	AUG	SEP	OCT	NOV	DEC	YEAR
Mean Maximum Temp. (°F)	36.2	42.2	51.0	60.7	70.8	82.4	90.0	88.0	77.8	64.5	48.1	38.3	62.5
Mean Temp. (°F)	25.8	31.0	39.4	47.3	56.1	65.8	73.2	71.1	61.1	49.3	36.7	27.8	48.7
Mean Minimum Temp. (°F)	15.3	19.7	27.7	33.8	41.2	49.2	56.4	54.2	44.5	34.0	25.3	17.2	34.9
Extreme Maximum Temp. (°F)	57	69	78	87	90	99	103	100	99	87	75	61	103
Extreme Minimum Temp. (°F)	-22	-28	1	15	24	29	39	35	27	7	-5	-19	-28
Days Maximum Temp. ≥ 90°F	0	0	0	0	0	5	18	13	1	0	0	0	37
Days Maximum Temp. ≤ 32°F	10	3	0	0	0	0	0	0	0	0	1	7	21
Days Minimum Temp. ≤ 32°F	30	27	24	13	3	0	0	0	2	12	25	30	166
Days Minimum Temp. ≤ 0°F	3	1	0	0	0	0	0	0	0	0	0	2	6
Heating Degree Days (base 65°F)	1,209	954	787	526	276	62	3	6	141	481	841	1,147	6,433
Cooling Degree Days (base 65°F)	0	0	0	1	8	97	274	224	34	0	0	0	638
Mean Precipitation (in.)	0.98	0.96	1.12	1.31	1.36	0.66	0.68	0.91	1.18	1.31	1.20	*0.69*	*12.36*
Days With ≥ 0.1" Precipitation	*4*	3	4	4	4	2	2	3	3	4	4	3	*40*
Days With ≥ 1.0" Precipitation	0	0	0	0	0	0	0	0	0	0	0	0	0
Mean Snowfall (in.)	*8.6*	*4.6*	*1.6*	1.0	trace	0.0	0.0	0.0	0.0	0.5	4.1	na	na
Days With ≥ 1.0" Snow Depth	na	na	na	0	0	0	0	0	0	0	4	na	na

Vernal Municipal Airport *Uintah County* Elevation: 5,259 ft. Latitude: 40° 26' N Longitude: 109° 31' W

	JAN	FEB	MAR	APR	MAY	JUN	JUL	AUG	SEP	OCT	NOV	DEC	YEAR
Mean Maximum Temp. (°F)	29.6	37.3	51.6	62.1	72.5	83.5	89.8	87.8	77.3	62.9	45.6	32.9	61.1
Mean Temp. (°F)	18.3	25.0	37.9	46.7	56.0	65.4	71.5	69.6	60.0	47.4	33.2	21.5	46.0
Mean Minimum Temp. (°F)	6.9	12.7	24.1	31.3	39.6	47.2	53.2	51.4	42.6	31.9	20.9	10.1	31.0
Extreme Maximum Temp. (°F)	56	64	76	85	92	101	102	100	95	89	68	65	102
Extreme Minimum Temp. (°F)	-26	-38	1	10	20	28	37	32	22	6	-12	-30	-38
Days Maximum Temp. ≥ 90°F	0	0	0	0	0	8	18	13	2	0	0	0	41
Days Maximum Temp. ≤ 32°F	18	9	1	0	0	0	0	0	0	0	3	14	45
Days Minimum Temp. ≤ 32°F	31	28	28	17	5	0	0	0	3	17	28	31	188
Days Minimum Temp. ≤ 0°F	9	4	0	0	0	0	0	0	0	0	0	5	18
Heating Degree Days (base 65°F)	1,442	1,124	834	542	276	68	5	10	167	539	946	1,342	7,295
Cooling Degree Days (base 65°F)	0	0	0	0	5	78	202	158	23	0	0	0	466
Mean Precipitation (in.)	0.44	0.48	0.67	0.87	1.04	0.72	0.66	0.73	0.88	1.23	0.58	0.47	8.77
Days With ≥ 0.1" Precipitation	2	2	2	2	3	2	2	2	3	3	2	2	27
Days With ≥ 1.0" Precipitation	0	0	0	0	0	0	0	0	0	0	0	0	0
Mean Snowfall (in.)	na	na	na	*0.0*	0.0	0.0	0.0	0.0	0.0	0.3	*0.6*	na	na
Days With ≥ 1.0" Snow Depth	na	na	na	*0*	0	0	0	0	0	0	0	na	na

Vernon *Tooele County* Elevation: 5,482 ft. Latitude: 40° 05' N Longitude: 112° 27' W

	JAN	FEB	MAR	APR	MAY	JUN	JUL	AUG	SEP	OCT	NOV	DEC	YEAR
Mean Maximum Temp. (°F)	39.2	44.3	51.1	59.2	69.3	80.7	89.3	87.5	77.6	64.7	49.6	40.2	62.7
Mean Temp. (°F)	26.3	31.2	38.1	44.6	53.4	63.5	71.4	70.0	60.3	48.5	36.0	26.9	47.5
Mean Minimum Temp. (°F)	13.3	18.0	25.0	29.9	37.5	46.1	53.5	52.5	43.0	32.2	22.4	13.6	32.3
Extreme Maximum Temp. (°F)	61	67	73	85	91	101	103	102	96	88	77	66	103
Extreme Minimum Temp. (°F)	-22	-25	-7	8	16	23	35	31	20	-4	-9	-26	-26
Days Maximum Temp. ≥ 90°F	0	0	0	0	0	5	17	13	2	0	0	0	37
Days Maximum Temp. ≤ 32°F	7	3	1	0	0	0	0	0	0	0	2	6	19
Days Minimum Temp. ≤ 32°F	30	27	26	20	8	1	0	0	3	16	26	30	187
Days Minimum Temp. ≤ 0°F	5	2	0	0	0	0	0	0	0	0	1	4	12
Heating Degree Days (base 65°F)	1,194	948	828	605	356	111	8	13	166	505	863	1,174	6,771
Cooling Degree Days (base 65°F)	0	0	0	0	4	72	214	187	35	0	0	0	512
Mean Precipitation (in.)	0.73	0.81	1.07	0.86	1.21	0.75	0.90	0.84	0.90	1.09	0.92	0.64	10.72
Days With ≥ 0.1" Precipitation	3	3	4	3	4	2	3	2	2	3	3	2	34
Days With ≥ 1.0" Precipitation	0	0	0	0	0	0	0	0	0	0	0	0	0
Mean Snowfall (in.)	*8.6*	*7.9*	5.7	2.4	0.2	0.2	0.0	0.0	0.2	1.2	5.0	*6.6*	*38.0*
Days With ≥ 1.0" Snow Depth	na	na	na	1	0	0	0	0	0	0	1	*4*	*6*	na

Veyo Powerhouse *Washington County*   Elevation: 4,599 ft.   Latitude: 37° 21' N   Longitude: 113° 40' W

	JAN	FEB	MAR	APR	MAY	JUN	JUL	AUG	SEP	OCT	NOV	DEC	YEAR
Mean Maximum Temp. (°F)	46.9	51.8	57.5	65.0	74.9	86.1	92.1	90.1	82.6	71.0	56.9	48.3	68.6
Mean Temp. (°F)	36.3	40.5	45.5	51.9	60.6	70.5	76.4	74.7	67.6	56.9	44.5	37.2	55.2
Mean Minimum Temp. (°F)	25.6	29.2	33.4	38.7	46.2	54.7	60.5	59.2	52.6	42.8	32.1	26.1	41.8
Extreme Maximum Temp. (°F)	69	75	78	85	95	105	107	103	98	90	79	66	107
Extreme Minimum Temp. (°F)	2	3	10	18	25	32	40	40	25	12	9	-3	-3
Days Maximum Temp. ≥ 90°F	0	0	0	0	1	11	23	18	4	0	0	0	57
Days Maximum Temp. ≤ 32°F	1	1	0	0	0	0	0	0	0	0	0	2	4
Days Minimum Temp. ≤ 32°F	27	20	*13*	5	1	0	0	0	0	3	15	26	*110*
Days Minimum Temp. ≤ 0°F	0	0	0	0	0	0	0	0	0	0	0	0	0
Heating Degree Days (base 65°F)	883	685	598	389	166	24	1	0	40	261	608	856	4,511
Cooling Degree Days (base 65°F)	0	0	0	2	38	190	353	312	125	17	0	0	1,037
Mean Precipitation (in.)	1.54	1.70	2.39	1.08	0.81	0.43	1.08	1.23	1.13	1.19	1.26	1.06	14.90
Days With ≥ 0.1" Precipitation	4	4	5	3	2	1	3	3	2	3	3	3	36
Days With ≥ 1.0" Precipitation	0	0	1	0	0	0	0	0	0	0	0	0	1
Mean Snowfall (in.)	*0.5*	*1.6*	1.0	0.2	0.0	0.0	0.0	0.0	0.0	0.0	*0.5*	*0.7*	*4.5*
Days With ≥ 1.0" Snow Depth	na	*1*	*0*	0	0	0	0	0	0	0	0	*1*	na

Wah Wah Ranch *Beaver County*   Elevation: 4,878 ft.   Latitude: 38° 29' N   Longitude: 113° 26' W

	JAN	FEB	MAR	APR	MAY	JUN	JUL	AUG	SEP	OCT	NOV	DEC	YEAR
Mean Maximum Temp. (°F)	43.2	49.7	58.5	66.0	75.8	87.5	94.2	92.1	83.1	70.4	55.0	44.1	68.3
Mean Temp. (°F)	29.2	35.1	42.7	49.1	58.2	68.6	76.1	74.2	64.5	52.0	39.3	29.3	51.5
Mean Minimum Temp. (°F)	15.2	20.4	26.9	32.2	40.5	49.8	57.9	56.2	45.8	33.6	23.6	14.4	34.7
Extreme Maximum Temp. (°F)	70	76	85	89	97	106	106	104	100	92	82	71	106
Extreme Minimum Temp. (°F)	-25	-29	-3	10	18	25	35	34	21	-5	-11	-30	-30
Days Maximum Temp. ≥ 90°F	0	0	0	0	1	14	25	22	7	0	0	0	69
Days Maximum Temp. ≤ 32°F	5	1	0	0	0	0	0	0	0	0	1	4	11
Days Minimum Temp. ≤ 32°F	29	25	23	16	5	0	0	0	2	14	25	29	168
Days Minimum Temp. ≤ 0°F	3	1	0	0	0	0	0	0	0	0	0	4	8
Heating Degree Days (base 65°F)	1,104	838	685	471	223	47	2	2	93	399	764	1,100	5,728
Cooling Degree Days (base 65°F)	0	0	0	1	19	158	348	306	88	2	0	0	922
Mean Precipitation (in.)	0.33	0.31	0.62	0.60	0.74	0.37	0.68	0.95	0.80	0.72	0.48	0.21	6.81
Days With ≥ 0.1" Precipitation	1	1	2	2	2	1	3	3	2	3	2	1	23
Days With ≥ 1.0" Precipitation	0	0	0	0	0	0	0	0	0	0	0	0	0
Mean Snowfall (in.)	na	*1.0*	*0.4*	*trace*	0.0	0.0	0.0	0.0	trace	trace	*0.4*	*trace*	na
Days With ≥ 1.0" Snow Depth	*4*	3	1	0	0	0	0	0	0	0	2	3	*13*

Wanship Dam *Summit County*   Elevation: 5,938 ft.   Latitude: 40° 47' N   Longitude: 111° 24' W

	JAN	FEB	MAR	APR	MAY	JUN	JUL	AUG	SEP	OCT	NOV	DEC	YEAR
Mean Maximum Temp. (°F)	35.6	40.4	48.2	57.7	67.9	78.7	86.3	85.8	76.2	63.4	47.0	37.3	60.4
Mean Temp. (°F)	23.4	27.4	35.4	42.9	51.4	59.8	66.4	65.4	56.7	45.7	33.8	24.9	44.4
Mean Minimum Temp. (°F)	11.1	14.3	22.5	28.0	34.9	40.8	46.4	45.0	37.1	28.0	20.5	12.5	28.4
Extreme Maximum Temp. (°F)	57	65	73	81	88	97	98	97	93	85	72	65	98
Extreme Minimum Temp. (°F)	-25	-37	-13	4	15	24	26	23	12	2	-21	-28	-37
Days Maximum Temp. ≥ 90°F	0	0	0	0	0	2	9	8	1	0	0	0	20
Days Maximum Temp. ≤ 32°F	10	5	1	0	0	0	0	0	0	0	3	9	28
Days Minimum Temp. ≤ 32°F	30	27	27	22	11	3	1	1	9	22	26	29	208
Days Minimum Temp. ≤ 0°F	7	4	1	0	0	0	0	0	0	0	1	5	18
Heating Degree Days (base 65°F)	1,283	1,056	912	657	415	171	33	45	252	593	930	1,237	7,584
Cooling Degree Days (base 65°F)	0	0	0	0	0	21	86	70	8	0	0	0	185
Mean Precipitation (in.)	1.22	1.07	1.50	1.79	1.99	1.05	1.11	0.99	1.48	1.70	1.66	1.06	16.62
Days With ≥ 0.1" Precipitation	4	4	5	6	6	3	3	3	4	5	5	4	52
Days With ≥ 1.0" Precipitation	0	0	0	0	0	0	0	0	0	0	0	0	0
Mean Snowfall (in.)	na	na	na	na	*0.5*	trace	0.0	0.0	trace	na	na	na	na
Days With ≥ 1.0" Snow Depth	na	na	na	*1*	0	0	0	0	0	na	na	na	na

Wendover USAF Auxiliary Field *Tooele County*   Elevation: 4,235 ft.   Latitude: 40° 44' N   Longitude: 114° 02' W

	JAN	FEB	MAR	APR	MAY	JUN	JUL	AUG	SEP	OCT	NOV	DEC	YEAR
Mean Maximum Temp. (°F)	34.8	42.1	52.6	61.1	71.0	82.1	90.8	88.8	77.0	61.9	46.2	35.5	62.0
Mean Temp. (°F)	27.1	33.5	43.1	50.8	60.5	70.8	79.2	76.8	65.7	51.7	37.8	27.8	52.1
Mean Minimum Temp. (°F)	19.3	24.7	33.4	40.5	50.0	59.6	67.4	64.8	54.2	41.3	29.4	20.0	42.1
Extreme Maximum Temp. (°F)	62	66	75	87	94	105	105	102	98	88	78	64	105
Extreme Minimum Temp. (°F)	-16	-12	13	20	26	39	49	44	33	19	6	-18	-18
Days Maximum Temp. ≥ 90°F	0	0	0	0	1	7	20	16	2	0	0	0	46
Days Maximum Temp. ≤ 32°F	13	4	0	0	0	0	0	0	0	0	1	11	29
Days Minimum Temp. ≤ 32°F	29	24	14	4	0	0	0	0	0	3	20	29	123
Days Minimum Temp. ≤ 0°F	1	0	0	0	0	0	0	0	0	0	0	1	2
Heating Degree Days (base 65°F)	1,168	885	673	424	180	38	1	2	81	410	808	1,148	5,818
Cooling Degree Days (base 65°F)	0	0	0	6	52	211	441	381	112	2	0	0	1,205
Mean Precipitation (in.)	0.26	0.25	0.44	0.49	0.82	0.42	0.30	0.40	0.43	0.53	0.32	0.18	4.84
Days With ≥ 0.1" Precipitation	1	1	1	2	2	2	1	1	1	2	1	1	16
Days With ≥ 1.0" Precipitation	0	0	0	0	0	0	0	0	0	0	0	0	0
Mean Snowfall (in.)	na	na	*0.2*	0.1	trace	0.0	0.0	0.0	0.0	trace	0.3	*0.5*	na
Days With ≥ 1.0" Snow Depth	na	na	0	0	0	0	0	0	0	0	0	*1*	na

Woodruff *Rich County*   Elevation: 6,312 ft.   Latitude: 41° 32' N   Longitude: 111° 09' W

	JAN	FEB	MAR	APR	MAY	JUN	JUL	AUG	SEP	OCT	NOV	DEC	YEAR
Mean Maximum Temp. (°F)	28.2	32.7	43.3	54.0	63.8	73.4	81.2	80.5	71.4	59.3	41.6	30.0	54.9
Mean Temp. (°F)	15.6	19.3	30.4	39.0	47.9	56.3	62.5	61.1	52.1	41.3	28.2	17.2	39.3
Mean Minimum Temp. (°F)	3.1	5.9	17.6	24.1	31.9	39.0	43.8	41.6	32.8	23.3	14.7	4.4	23.5
Extreme Maximum Temp. (°F)	52	59	69	79	83	93	94	94	90	82	69	60	94
Extreme Minimum Temp. (°F)	-43	-46	-29	-1	10	25	28	20	8	-16	-30	-46	-46
Days Maximum Temp. ≥ 90°F	0	0	0	0	0	0	1	1	0	0	0	0	2
Days Maximum Temp. ≤ 32°F	18	12	4	0	0	0	0	0	0	1	7	17	59
Days Minimum Temp. ≤ 32°F	31	28	31	27	16	4	0	3	15	27	29	31	242
Days Minimum Temp. ≤ 0°F	13	10	2	0	0	0	0	0	0	0	3	12	40
Heating Degree Days (base 65°F)	1,525	1,285	1,065	773	523	259	88	126	381	728	1,098	1,475	9,326
Cooling Degree Days (base 65°F)	0	0	0	0	0	4	21	13	1	0	0	0	39
Mean Precipitation (in.)	0.52	0.50	0.63	0.95	1.17	1.02	0.80	0.77	1.22	1.09	0.71	0.47	9.85
Days With ≥ 0.1" Precipitation	2	2	2	3	4	3	3	2	3	3	3	2	32
Days With ≥ 1.0" Precipitation	0	0	0	0	0	0	0	0	0	0	0	0	0
Mean Snowfall (in.)	8.3	8.3	6.0	4.7	0.9	0.1	0.0	0.0	0.5	3.1	6.5	7.2	45.6
Days With ≥ 1.0" Snow Depth	*13*	na	*6*	1	0	0	0	0	0	1	5	*12*	na

Zion National Park *Washington County*   Elevation: 4,048 ft.   Latitude: 37° 13' N   Longitude: 112° 59' W

	JAN	FEB	MAR	APR	MAY	JUN	JUL	AUG	SEP	OCT	NOV	DEC	YEAR
Mean Maximum Temp. (°F)	52.4	58.0	64.1	72.3	82.7	94.1	99.3	96.8	89.4	77.6	62.2	53.1	75.2
Mean Temp. (°F)	40.7	45.8	50.9	57.7	67.2	77.7	83.8	81.9	74.6	63.2	49.5	41.3	61.2
Mean Minimum Temp. (°F)	29.0	33.7	37.7	43.0	51.7	61.3	68.3	66.9	59.7	48.7	36.6	29.5	47.2
Extreme Maximum Temp. (°F)	73	81	86	93	102	112	113	110	104	99	83	74	113
Extreme Minimum Temp. (°F)	0	0	12	21	26	36	52	52	34	17	6	-5	-5
Days Maximum Temp. ≥ 90°F	0	0	0	1	7	23	30	28	16	4	0	0	109
Days Maximum Temp. ≤ 32°F	0	0	0	0	0	0	0	0	0	0	0	0	0
Days Minimum Temp. ≤ 32°F	20	12	8	4	0	0	0	0	0	0	0	0	0
Days Minimum Temp. ≤ 0°F	0	0	0	0	0	0	0	0	0	2	10	19	75
Heating Degree Days (base 65°F)	746	535	431	236	65	5	0	0	8	133	461	727	3,347
Cooling Degree Days (base 65°F)	0	0	2	28	143	390	583	535	303	80	1	0	2,065
Mean Precipitation (in.)	1.89	1.84	2.35	1.15	0.93	0.45	1.37	1.57	1.05	1.06	1.43	1.13	16.22
Days With ≥ 0.1" Precipitation	5	4	6	3	3	1	3	4	2	3	3	3	40
Days With ≥ 1.0" Precipitation	0	0	0	0	0	0	0	0	0	0	0	0	0
Mean Snowfall (in.)	2.7	1.2	0.4	0.2	trace	0.0	0.0	0.0	0.0	0.1	0.8	1.4	6.8
Days With ≥ 1.0" Snow Depth	1	1	0	0	0	0	0	0	0	0	0	0	2

Note: See Appendix D for explanation of data.

VERMONT

PHYSICAL FEATURES. The Green Mountain State occupies 9,609 square miles. Though Vermont is the only New England state without a coastline on the Atlantic Ocean, most of its boundary is water. The Connecticut River forms the entire eastern border. Lake Champlain marks over 100 miles of the western boundary. Vermont extends southward from near the 45 parallel of latitude almost 160 miles to about 20 miles south of the 43rd parallel. Vermont widens northward from about 40 to 90 miles across.

The terrain is hilly to mountainous. The Green Mountains extend the length of the State. They rise to their highest elevation at Mt. Mansfield, 4,393 feet above sea level. Many peaks in this range rise to over 3,000 feet, as do several others in eastern Vermont. Elevations of less than 500 feet above sea level are mostly confined to the lowlands paralleling Lake Champlain in the west and to the central and southern portions of the Connecticut Valley in the east. Much of the State ranges from 500 to 2,000 feet in elevation. The glacier of the great Ice Age accounts for many topographical features, lakes, and soils. Inland waters cover more than 300 square miles.

GENERAL CLIMATE. Vermont shares with the other New England states in the chief climatic characteristics. These include: (1) changeableness of the weather; (2) large range of temperature, both daily and annual; (3) great differences between the same seasons in different years; (4) equable distribution of precipitation; and (5) considerable diversity from place to place. The regional climatic influences are modified in Vermont by varying elevations, types of terrain, and distances from the Atlantic Ocean and from Lake Champlain. The State has been divided into three climatological divisions- (Western, Northeastern, and Southeastern).

Vermont lies in the "prevailing westerlies," the belt of generally eastward air movement which encircles the globe in middle latitudes. Embedded in this circulation are extensive masses of air originating in higher or lower latitudes and interacting to produce low-pressure storm systems. Relative to most other sections of the country, a large number of such storms pass over or near Vermont. The majority of air masses affecting this State belong to three types: (1) cold, dry air pouring down from subarctic North America; (2) warm, moist air streaming up on a long overland journey from the Gulf of Mexico and other subtropical waters; and (3) cool, damp air moving in from the North Atlantic. Because the atmospheric flow is usually from a westerly direction, Vermont is more influenced by the first two types than it is by the third.

The procession of contrasting air masses and the relatively frequent passage of low pressure systems resulting an average of a twice-weekly alternation from fair to cloudy or stormy conditions, attended by often abrupt changes in temperature, moisture, sunshine, wind direction and speed. There is no regular or persistent rhythm to this sequence, and it is interrupted by periods during which the weather patterns continue the same for several days, infrequently for several weeks.

TEMPERATURE. The annual mean temperature is near 43°F. in the Northeastern Division, 44°F. in the Southeastern, and 46°F. in the Western. Summer temperatures are comfortable as a rule. They are also reasonably uniform over the State, excepting topographical extremes. Long-period means for July average near 70°F. in the western division and near 68°F. in the other Divisions. Average daily minima in July are in the 50s over nearly the entire State. The average daily maxima reach only near 80°F. Hot days with maxima of 90°F. or higher average less than 10 per year at most weather stations. Even after one of these hot days the temperature is likely to fall to 60°F. or lower during the night.

Temperatures from place to place vary more in winter than in summer. The Northeastern Division average in January is near 17°F. The Southeastern Division average is nearly 19°F. and the Western Division, 21°F. Days with subzero readings are common at most stations in winter. They number from 10 to 40 per year in the southern portion and from 20 to 50 in the north. The growing season for vegetation subject to injury from freezing temperature averages 130 to 150 days in much of the Western Division and along the Connecticut River in the Southeastern Division. Elsewhere, and including the extreme southern portion of the Western Division, the season varies from 100 to 130 days.

PRECIPITATION. Vermont's precipitation, fortunately, is well distributed through the year. Winter precipitation is noticeably less than summer rainfall in the northern and western portions of the State. This difference is greater in those areas than in any other part of New England. New England as a whole is noted for the even distribution of its precipitation throughout the year, an effect due to the influence of the Atlantic Ocean. This ocean influence is still strongly felt in southeastern Vermont, but it becomes weaker with increasing distance from the ocean. Low-pressure, or frontal, storm systems are the principal year-round moisture producers. When this activity ebbs somewhat in summer, bands or patches of thunderstorms increase in activity, more than making up the difference. Though brief and often of small extent, the thunderstorms produce the heaviest local rainfall intensities.

Floods occur most often in the spring when they are caused by rainfall and melting snow. Stages of spring over-bank flooding are frequently increased by ice jams. Local flash floods result on occasions from short period summer storms between May and November. The Connecticut River and its tributaries drain the major portion of Vermont. In the northwest portion, rivers drain into Lake Champlain or directly to the St. Lawrence. A small area in southwest Vermont drains to the Hudson River.

Occasionally freezing rain occurs, coating exposed surfaces with troublesome ice. Most areas can expect at least one such occurrence in a winter. Frequency of days with measurable precipitation is between 120 and 160 days per year.

SNOWFALL. Average annual total snowfall is from 55 to 65 inches in much of the Western Division and also in parts of the Connecticut River Valley. Elsewhere the annual averages vary greatly. They range upward to as much as 100 inches. Topographical differences cause large variations in a short distance. The average number of days with 1 inch or more of snowfall in a season varies from 20 to 40. The frequency increases with elevation. Most winters have several snowstorms of five inches or more per year. Snow cover is continuous throughout the winter season as a rule. Depth of snow on the ground reaches its maximum for much of the State in the latter part of February. At the highest elevations, however, the date falls in the middle of March. Water stored in the snow is an important contribution to the water supply. Spring melting is usually too gradual to produce serious flooding.

OTHER CLIMATIC ELEMENTS. Sunshine averages near 50 percent of possible on a year-round basis, but varies with topography. Higher elevations and peaks are much more cloudy, especially in winter. Sunshine is most abundant during the summer season. Persistent fogs are sometimes experienced on the higher elevations. The duration of fog diminishes over flatland valley locations; short duration, heavy ground fogs of early morning do occur frequently at susceptible places in these areas. The number of days with fog varies from 10 to 60 per year over the State.

WINDS AND STORMS. Vermont lies in the region of prevailing westerlies — wind from the northwest in winter, and from the southwest in the warmer part of the year. But because the rugged topography has a strong influence on the direction of the wind, many areas have prevailing winds paralleling a valley. The major valleys tend to lie in a north-south direction. Thus prevailing winds may be from the north in winter and from the south in the warmer seasons in those areas.

Coastal storms, or "northeasters," are well known to New England. Their influence on Vermont is minimized by its inland location. They remain a factor, however, especially in the Southeastern Division. They generate very strong winds and heavy rain or snow. Storms of tropical origin may occasionally affect Vermont in summer or fall, but only rarely contain destructive winds. Vermont is far enough inland so that, usually, winds are considerably weakened by the time tropical storms reach the State. Rainfall associated with these storms may, however, remain heavy.

Tornadoes are not common phenomena, yet one or more of these most violent storms may occur in a year. The peak months are June and July. Thunder and hailstorms have a frequency maximum from midspring to early fall. Thunderstorms occur on 20 to 30 days per year. The most severe are attended by hail. The size of an area struck by a hailstorm, however, is usually small.

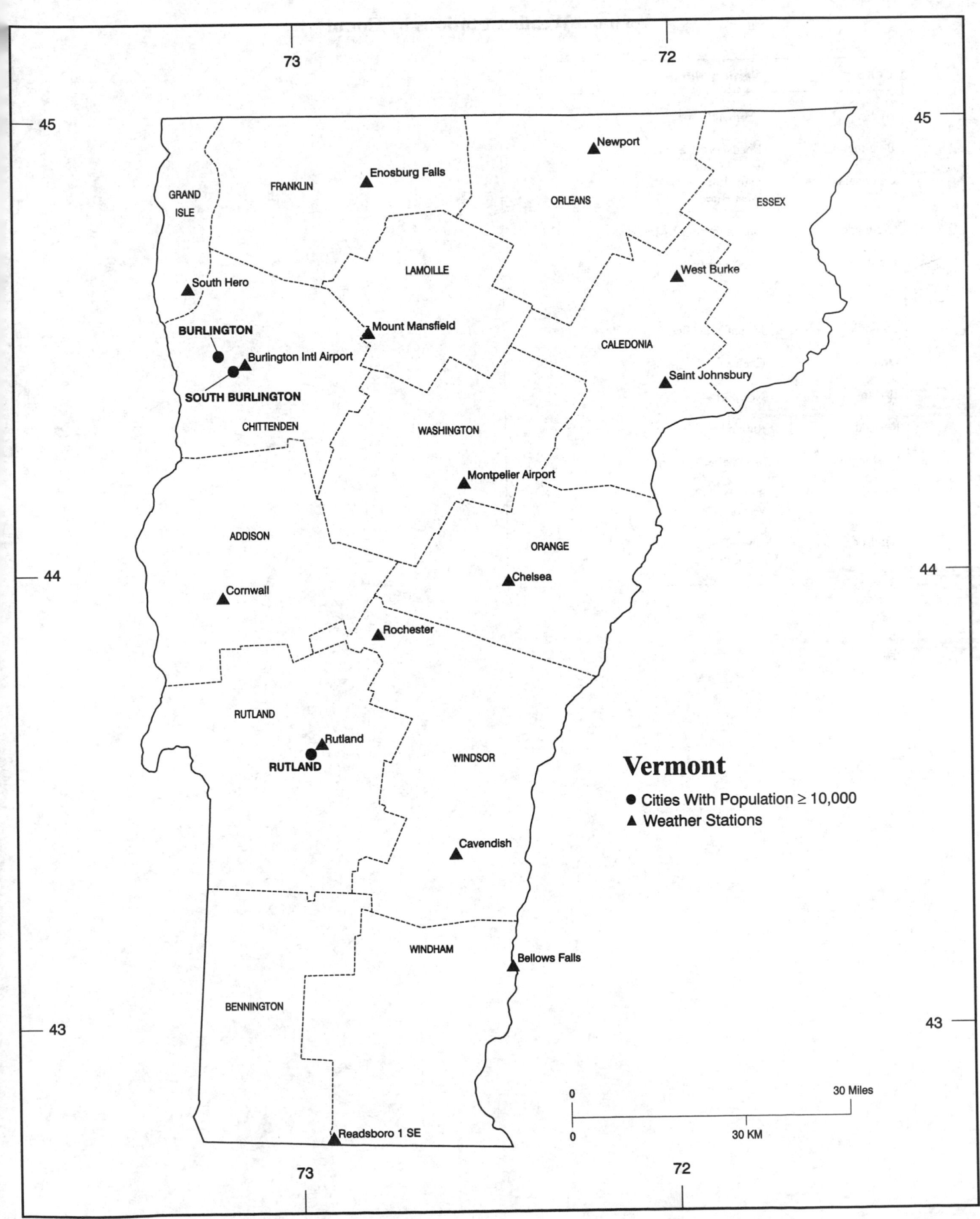

73

72

45

Newport

FRANKLIN

Enosburg Falls

GRAND
ISLE

ORLEANS

ESSEX

LAMOILLE

West Burke

South Hero

BURLINGTON

Mount Mansfield

CALEDONIA

Burlington Intl Airport

Saint Johnsbury

SOUTH BURLINGTON

CHITTENDEN

WASHINGTON

Montpelier Airport

ADDISON

ORANGE

44

Chelsea

Cornwall

Rochester

Vermont

● Cities With Population ≥ 10,000
▲ Weather Stations

RUTLAND

Rutland

RUTLAND

WINDSOR

Cavendish

WINDHAM

Bellows Falls

BENNINGTON

43

0   30 Miles

0   30 KM

73

72

Vermont Weather Stations by County

County	Station Name
Addison	Cornwall
Bennington	Readsboro 1 SE
Caledonia	Saint Johnsbury West Burke
Chittenden	Burlington Int'l Airport
Franklin	Enosburg Falls
Grand Isle	South Hero
Lamoille	Mount Mansfield
Orange	Chelsea
Orleans	Newport
Rutland	Rutland
Washington	Montpelier Airport
Windham	Bellows Falls Vernon
Windsor	Cavendish Rochester

Vermont Weather Stations by City

City	Station Name	Miles
Burlington	Peru 2 WSW, NY	18
	Burlington Int'l Airport	4
	South Hero	11
Rutland	Rochester	20
	Rutland	1
South Burlington	Burlington Int'l Airport	2
	Mount Mansfield	19
	South Hero	14

Note: Miles is the distance between the geographic center of the city and the weather station.

Vermont Weather Stations by Elevation

Feet	Station Name
3,950	Mount Mansfield
1,125	Montpelier Airport
1,118	Readsboro 1 SE
898	West Burke
830	Rochester
797	Cavendish
797	Chelsea
767	Newport
698	Saint Johnsbury
620	Rutland
488	Cornwall
419	Enosburg Falls
328	Burlington Int'l Airport
298	Bellows Falls
223	Vernon
108	South Hero

Burlington Int'l Airport

Burlington is located on the eastern shore of Lake Champlain at the widest part of the lake. About 35 miles to the west lie the highest peaks of the Adirondacks, while the foothills of the Green Mountains begin 10 miles to the east and southeast.

Its northerly latitude assures the variety and vigor of a true New England climate, while thanks to the modifying influence of the lake, the many rapid and marked weather changes are tempered in severity. Due to its location in the path of the St. Lawrence Valley storm track and the lake effects, the city is one of the cloudiest in the United States.

Lake Champlain exercises a tempering influence on the local temperature. During the winter months and prior to the lake freezing, temperatures along the lake shore are often five to 10 degrees warmer than at the airport three and a half miles inland. At the airport the average occurrence of the last freeze in spring is around May 10th and that of the first in fall is early October, giving a growing season of 145 days. On average, there are few days a year with maxima of 90 degrees or higher. This moderate summer heat gives way to a cooler, but none the less pleasant fall period, usually extending well into October. High pressure systems moving down rapidly from central Canada or Hudson Bay produce the coldest temperatures during the winter months, but extended periods of very cold weather are rare.

Precipitation, although generally plentiful and well distributed throughout the year, is less in the Champlain Valley than in other areas of Vermont due to the shielding effect of the mountain barriers to the east and west. The heaviest rainfall usually occurs during summer thunderstorms, but excessively heavy rainfall is quite uncommon. Droughts are infrequent.

Because of the trend of the Champlain Valley between the Adirondack and Green Mountain ranges, most winds have a northerly or southerly component. The prevailing direction most of the year is from the south. Winds of damaging force are very uncommon.

Smoke pollution is nearly non-existent since there is no concentration of heavy industry here, however, haze has been on the increase over the years due to the large increase in industry to the north and south. During the spring and fall months, fog occasionally forms along the Winooski River to the north and east and may drift over the airport with favorable winds. In spite of the high percentage of cloudiness, periods of low aircraft ceilings and visibilities are usually of short duration, allowing this area to have one of the highest percentages of flying weather in New England.

Burlington Int'l Airport *Chittenden County*   Elevation: 328 ft.   Latitude: 44° 28' N   Longitude: 73° 09' W

	JAN	FEB	MAR	APR	MAY	JUN	JUL	AUG	SEP	OCT	NOV	DEC	YEAR
Mean Maximum Temp. (°F)	26.3	29.0	39.4	53.5	67.5	76.2	81.2	78.4	69.0	56.7	44.3	32.3	54.5
Mean Temp. (°F)	17.6	19.8	30.6	43.7	56.5	65.6	70.7	68.3	59.5	47.8	37.3	24.7	45.2
Mean Minimum Temp. (°F)	8.7	10.7	21.7	33.9	45.5	55.0	60.0	58.1	49.9	38.9	30.2	17.0	35.8
Extreme Maximum Temp. (°F)	66	62	84	91	93	100	100	99	93	82	74	67	100
Extreme Minimum Temp. (°F)	-29	-30	-18	2	27	33	40	35	28	15	2	-26	-30
Days Maximum Temp. ≥ 90°F	0	0	0	0	1	1	3	1	0	0	0	0	6
Days Maximum Temp. ≤ 32°F	21	17	8	1	0	0	0	0	0	0	4	15	66
Days Minimum Temp. ≤ 32°F	29	26	25	14	2	0	0	0	1	9	18	27	151
Days Minimum Temp. ≤ 0°F	10	8	2	0	0	0	0	0	0	0	0	4	24
Heating Degree Days (base 65°F)	1,466	1,270	1,061	635	279	75	15	36	196	528	824	1,244	7,629
Cooling Degree Days (base 65°F)	0	0	0	2	19	98	200	146	39	1	0	0	505
Mean Precipitation (in.)	2.16	1.64	2.33	2.80	3.22	3.46	3.93	4.00	3.86	3.14	3.04	2.24	35.82
Maximum Precipitation (in.)	4.7	5.4	3.6	6.5	6.3	7.7	6.1	11.5	6.3	6.2	6.8	5.9	50.2
Minimum Precipitation (in.)	0.4	0.2	0.4	0.9	0.3	0.8	1.2	0.7	0.9	0.5	0.6	0.6	26.2
Maximum 24-hr. Precipitation (in.)	1.3	1.8	1.4	1.4	2.3	2.6	2.7	3.6	3.1	1.6	2.5	2.6	3.6
Days With ≥ 0.1" Precipitation	5	4	6	7	8	8	8	8	7	7	7	6	81
Days With ≥ 1.0" Precipitation	0	0	0	0	0	1	1	1	1	1	0	0	5
Mean Snowfall (in.)	20.6	15.3	15.0	5.6	trace	0.0	trace	0.0	trace	0.2	7.0	17.9	81.6
Maximum Snowfall (in.)	42	34	40	21	4	0	0	0	trace	5	19	57	130
Maximum 24-hr. Snowfall (in.)	15	17	16	13	4	0	0	0	trace	5	10	17	17
Days With ≥ 1.0" Snow Depth	25	24	17	3	0	0	0	0	0	0	5	18	92
Thunderstorm Days	< 1	0	< 1	1	2	5	6	5	2	1	< 1	< 1	22
Foggy Days	8	7	10	10	10	10	9	12	12	11	11	10	120
Predominant Sky Cover	OVR	OVR	OVR	OVR	OVR	OVR	OVR	OVR	OVR	OVR	OVR	OVR	OVR
Mean Relative Humidity 7am (%)	73	74	75	74	73	76	78	83	85	82	78	76	77
Mean Relative Humidity 4pm (%)	65	61	58	52	51	54	53	56	60	61	67	69	59
Mean Dewpoint (°F)	9	11	20	31	43	54	58	58	51	39	29	16	35
Prevailing Wind Direction	S	S	S	S	S	S	S	S	S	S	S	S	S
Prevailing Wind Speed (mph)	13	12	12	13	12	10	10	10	12	12	12	13	12
Maximum Wind Gust (mph)	51	54	56	52	71	52	60	59	52	51	62	52	71

Bellows Falls *Windham County*   Elevation: 298 ft.   Latitude: 43° 08' N   Longitude: 72° 27' W

	JAN	FEB	MAR	APR	MAY	JUN	JUL	AUG	SEP	OCT	NOV	DEC	YEAR
Mean Maximum Temp. (°F)	29.6	33.0	42.4	54.8	68.3	76.7	81.7	79.6	70.4	59.2	46.6	34.0	56.4
Mean Temp. (°F)	19.4	22.0	32.3	44.2	56.4	65.1	70.2	68.3	59.4	48.2	38.0	25.6	45.8
Mean Minimum Temp. (°F)	9.2	10.9	22.2	33.6	44.6	53.5	58.7	57.0	48.3	37.2	29.3	17.1	35.1
Extreme Maximum Temp. (°F)	61	62	78	91	92	98	100	98	91	85	76	68	100
Extreme Minimum Temp. (°F)	-23	-22	-6	12	27	35	42	36	29	19	6	-21	-23
Days Maximum Temp. ≥ 90°F	0	0	0	0	0	1	4	2	0	0	0	0	7
Days Maximum Temp. ≤ 32°F	18	13	4	0	0	0	0	0	0	0	1	12	48
Days Minimum Temp. ≤ 32°F	30	27	27	14	1	0	0	0	1	10	20	29	159
Days Minimum Temp. ≤ 0°F	8	6	1	0	0	0	0	0	0	0	0	3	18
Heating Degree Days (base 65°F)	1,407	1,209	1,006	617	278	75	14	32	194	515	804	1,216	7,367
Cooling Degree Days (base 65°F)	0	0	0	1	18	83	189	149	33	2	0	0	475
Mean Precipitation (in.)	3.13	2.64	3.26	3.32	3.57	3.19	3.66	3.85	3.40	3.41	3.49	3.41	40.33
Days With ≥ 0.1" Precipitation	7	6	7	7	8	7	7	6	6	6	7	7	81
Days With ≥ 1.0" Precipitation	1	1	1	1	1	1	1	1	1	1	1	1	12
Mean Snowfall (in.)	19.1	14.1	10.7	2.6	trace	0.0	0.0	0.0	0.0	trace	4.0	16.2	66.7
Days With ≥ 1.0" Snow Depth	24	23	15	1	0	0	0	0	0	0	3	18	84

Cavendish *Windsor County*   Elevation: 797 ft.   Latitude: 43° 23' N   Longitude: 72° 36' W

	JAN	FEB	MAR	APR	MAY	JUN	JUL	AUG	SEP	OCT	NOV	DEC	YEAR
Mean Maximum Temp. (°F)	28.4	32.4	41.1	53.9	68.1	76.1	81.0	78.7	69.6	58.1	45.1	33.1	55.5
Mean Temp. (°F)	17.1	19.9	30.1	42.0	54.7	63.1	68.0	66.0	57.3	45.9	35.9	23.5	43.6
Mean Minimum Temp. (°F)	5.7	7.5	19.0	30.1	41.4	50.1	54.9	53.2	45.0	33.6	26.6	13.9	31.7
Extreme Maximum Temp. (°F)	59	60	80	91	92	98	97	97	92	84	75	71	98
Extreme Minimum Temp. (°F)	-36	-32	-17	6	22	29	37	31	24	13	-2	-25	-36
Days Maximum Temp. ≥ 90°F	0	0	0	0	0	1	3	1	0	0	0	0	5
Days Maximum Temp. ≤ 32°F	19	14	5	0	0	0	0	0	0	0	2	14	54
Days Minimum Temp. ≤ 32°F	31	28	29	19	5	0	0	0	3	16	23	30	184
Days Minimum Temp. ≤ 0°F	11	10	3	0	0	0	0	0	0	0	0	5	29
Heating Degree Days (base 65°F)	1,479	1,267	1,077	684	324	110	34	58	245	586	868	1,279	8,011
Cooling Degree Days (base 65°F)	0	0	0	0	10	59	133	93	20	1	0	0	316
Mean Precipitation (in.)	3.63	2.77	3.78	3.93	4.17	4.17	3.73	4.09	3.90	3.91	4.04	3.53	45.65
Days With ≥ 0.1" Precipitation	7	6	7	7	8	8	7	7	7	6	8	7	85
Days With ≥ 1.0" Precipitation	1	1	1	1	1	1	1	1	1	1	1	1	12
Mean Snowfall (in.)	23.6	17.3	17.4	5.9	trace	0.0	0.0	0.0	trace	0.3	6.8	18.7	90.0
Days With ≥ 1.0" Snow Depth	30	28	30	10	0	0	0	0	0	0	6	25	129

Chelsea *Orange County*   Elevation: 797 ft.   Latitude: 43° 59' N   Longitude: 72° 27' W

	JAN	FEB	MAR	APR	MAY	JUN	JUL	AUG	SEP	OCT	NOV	DEC	YEAR
Mean Maximum Temp. (°F)	27.0	30.7	39.6	52.6	66.6	75.1	79.9	77.7	68.8	57.1	43.8	31.6	54.2
Mean Temp. (°F)	13.9	16.4	27.0	39.9	52.3	61.1	65.8	63.9	55.4	44.2	33.8	20.8	41.2
Mean Minimum Temp. (°F)	0.7	2.1	14.3	27.2	38.0	47.0	51.8	50.1	42.0	31.3	23.7	9.8	28.2
Extreme Maximum Temp. (°F)	61	62	79	90	93	95	98	99	90	82	73	68	99
Extreme Minimum Temp. (°F)	-36	-34	-21	2	20	28	33	31	22	10	-3	-32	-36
Days Maximum Temp. ≥ 90°F	0	0	0	0	0	1	2	1	0	0	0	0	4
Days Maximum Temp. ≤ 32°F	20	15	7	0	0	0	0	0	0	0	3	16	61
Days Minimum Temp. ≤ 32°F	31	28	30	22	9	1	0	0	5	18	25	30	199
Days Minimum Temp. ≤ 0°F	16	14	5	0	0	0	0	0	0	0	0	8	43
Heating Degree Days (base 65°F)	1,581	1,366	1,172	747	392	151	59	95	294	637	930	1,365	8,789
Cooling Degree Days (base 65°F)	0	0	0	0	4	34	83	62	11	0	0	0	194
Mean Precipitation (in.)	2.98	2.13	2.77	2.88	3.41	3.50	3.73	4.02	3.55	3.36	3.28	2.79	38.40
Days With ≥ 0.1" Precipitation	6	5	7	7	8	8	7	8	7	7	7	7	84
Days With ≥ 1.0" Precipitation	1	0	0	1	0	1	1	1	1	1	1	0	8
Mean Snowfall (in.)	20.1	15.0	15.2	5.1	trace	0.0	0.0	0.0	0.0	0.2	6.1	18.6	80.3
Days With ≥ 1.0" Snow Depth	29	28	27	6	0	0	0	0	0	0	7	24	121

Cornwall *Addison County*   Elevation: 488 ft.   Latitude: 43° 57' N   Longitude: 73° 13' W

	JAN	FEB	MAR	APR	MAY	JUN	JUL	AUG	SEP	OCT	NOV	DEC	YEAR
Mean Maximum Temp. (°F)	27.8	31.0	41.8	55.6	69.2	76.9	81.8	79.2	70.2	58.1	45.9	33.0	55.9
Mean Temp. (°F)	18.7	21.3	32.1	44.7	57.3	65.3	70.2	67.9	59.5	48.2	37.9	24.9	45.7
Mean Minimum Temp. (°F)	9.6	11.5	22.4	33.9	45.4	53.7	58.6	56.6	48.8	38.3	29.8	16.7	35.4
Extreme Maximum Temp. (°F)	64	61	82	90	92	97	97	100	95	81	75	66	100
Extreme Minimum Temp. (°F)	-30	-29	-15	2	21	31	39	32	23	13	4	-23	-30
Days Maximum Temp. ≥ 90°F	0	0	0	0	0	1	2	1	0	0	0	0	4
Days Maximum Temp. ≤ 32°F	20	15	5	0	0	0	0	0	0	0	2	14	56
Days Minimum Temp. ≤ 32°F	29	26	26	14	1	0	0	0	1	8	18	29	152
Days Minimum Temp. ≤ 0°F	9	6	1	0	0	0	0	0	0	0	0	4	20
Heating Degree Days (base 65°F)	1,428	1,229	1,012	604	255	74	16	37	193	515	807	1,236	7,406
Cooling Degree Days (base 65°F)	0	0	0	3	20	82	183	131	35	0	0	0	455
Mean Precipitation (in.)	2.19	1.90	2.34	2.68	3.41	3.21	3.28	4.17	3.78	3.38	3.11	2.59	36.04
Days With ≥ 0.1" Precipitation	5	4	6	6	8	8	7	7	7	7	7	6	78
Days With ≥ 1.0" Precipitation	0	0	0	0	1	0	0	1	1	1	1	0	5
Mean Snowfall (in.)	16.6	13.1	10.8	3.4	trace	0.0	0.0	0.0	0.0	0.2	4.7	14.3	63.1
Days With ≥ 1.0" Snow Depth	na	na	na	na	0	0	0	0	0	0	na	na	na

Enosburg Falls *Franklin County*   Elevation: 419 ft.   Latitude: 44° 52' N   Longitude: 72° 49' W

	JAN	FEB	MAR	APR	MAY	JUN	JUL	AUG	SEP	OCT	NOV	DEC	YEAR
Mean Maximum Temp. (°F)	27.5	30.8	41.2	55.2	68.9	76.2	80.4	77.9	69.3	58.4	44.8	32.8	55.3
Mean Temp. (°F)	16.3	18.8	30.0	43.2	55.8	64.0	68.5	66.2	58.2	47.5	36.1	23.2	44.0
Mean Minimum Temp. (°F)	5.0	6.8	18.7	31.2	42.7	51.7	56.6	54.5	47.0	36.5	27.4	13.5	32.6
Extreme Maximum Temp. (°F)	67	62	82	88	92	94	95	95	92	84	74	66	95
Extreme Minimum Temp. (°F)	-41	-38	-28	-2	22	27	34	31	22	11	-9	-37	-41
Days Maximum Temp. ≥ 90°F	0	0	0	0	0	1	2	1	0	0	0	0	4
Days Maximum Temp. ≤ 32°F	20	15	7	1	0	0	0	0	0	0	4	14	61
Days Minimum Temp. ≤ 32°F	29	27	26	17	5	0	0	0	2	11	21	28	166
Days Minimum Temp. ≤ 0°F	12	10	4	0	0	0	0	0	0	0	0	6	32
Heating Degree Days (base 65°F)	1,504	1,299	1,079	649	296	97	30	58	225	537	860	1,291	7,925
Cooling Degree Days (base 65°F)	0	0	0	1	15	73	147	106	27	2	0	0	371
Mean Precipitation (in.)	2.76	2.08	2.90	3.24	3.89	3.92	4.48	4.68	4.40	3.92	4.16	3.05	43.48
Days With ≥ 0.1" Precipitation	8	6	8	9	10	9	10	9	8	9	10	9	105
Days With ≥ 1.0" Precipitation	0	0	0	0	1	1	1	1	1	1	1	0	7
Mean Snowfall (in.)	22.3	18.4	15.8	5.3	trace	0.0	0.0	0.0	trace	0.4	8.8	20.9	91.9
Days With ≥ 1.0" Snow Depth	na	na	na	1	0	0	0	0	0	0	na	na	na

Montpelier Airport *Washington County*   Elevation: 1,125 ft.   Latitude: 44° 12' N   Longitude: 72° 34' W

	JAN	FEB	MAR	APR	MAY	JUN	JUL	AUG	SEP	OCT	NOV	DEC	YEAR
Mean Maximum Temp. (°F)	24.8	27.7	37.8	50.9	65.3	73.3	78.5	75.7	66.7	55.2	42.5	29.8	52.3
Mean Temp. (°F)	15.9	18.4	28.9	41.6	54.3	62.5	67.6	65.1	56.5	45.7	35.1	21.8	42.8
Mean Minimum Temp. (°F)	6.9	9.0	19.9	32.2	43.2	51.5	56.6	54.4	46.3	36.1	27.6	13.7	33.1
Extreme Maximum Temp. (°F)	64	61	77	90	90	95	97	97	88	80	73	64	97
Extreme Minimum Temp. (°F)	-34	-28	-17	7	25	32	38	35	26	14	-4	-27	-34
Days Maximum Temp. ≥ 90°F	0	0	0	0	0	1	1	1	0	0	0	0	3
Days Maximum Temp. ≤ 32°F	22	19	10	1	0	0	0	0	0	0	6	18	76
Days Minimum Temp. ≤ 32°F	30	27	27	17	3	0	0	0	1	11	21	29	166
Days Minimum Temp. ≤ 0°F	10	8	2	0	0	0	0	0	0	0	0	6	26
Heating Degree Days (base 65°F)	1,516	1,312	1,113	699	339	124	38	77	265	592	892	1,334	8,301
Cooling Degree Days (base 65°F)	0	0	0	1	10	53	121	81	16	1	0	0	283
Mean Precipitation (in.)	2.54	2.00	2.41	2.60	3.30	3.34	3.11	3.99	3.42	3.14	3.04	2.61	35.50
Days With ≥ 0.1" Precipitation	6	5	6	7	8	7	7	7	7	7	7	7	81
Days With ≥ 1.0" Precipitation	0	0	0	0	1	1	1	1	0	1	0	0	5
Mean Snowfall (in.)	22.8	17.5	16.6	6.7	trace	0.0	0.0	0.0	trace	0.8	10.4	23.1	97.9
Days With ≥ 1.0" Snow Depth	29	26	24	8	0	0	0	0	0	0	7	24	118

Mount Mansfield *Lamoille County*   Elevation: 3,950 ft.   Latitude: 44° 32' N   Longitude: 72° 49' W

	JAN	FEB	MAR	APR	MAY	JUN	JUL	AUG	SEP	OCT	NOV	DEC	YEAR
Mean Maximum Temp. (°F)	17.2	19.1	27.3	38.7	53.5	61.6	65.5	63.4	55.3	44.1	32.0	22.1	41.6
Mean Temp. (°F)	9.2	11.3	19.8	31.4	45.5	54.1	58.5	56.7	48.7	37.4	25.7	14.7	34.4
Mean Minimum Temp. (°F)	1.1	3.4	12.4	24.2	37.4	46.5	51.5	50.0	41.9	30.6	19.3	7.3	27.1
Extreme Maximum Temp. (°F)	49	51	64	74	77	84	82	79	78	68	60	51	84
Extreme Minimum Temp. (°F)	-37	-33	-29	-13	7	20	24	28	20	9	-10	-38	-38
Days Maximum Temp. ≥ 90°F	0	0	0	0	0	0	0	0	0	0	0	0	0
Days Maximum Temp. ≤ 32°F	28	24	22	10	1	0	0	0	0	5	17	26	133
Days Minimum Temp. ≤ 32°F	31	28	29	24	10	1	0	0	4	18	27	31	203
Days Minimum Temp. ≤ 0°F	15	12	6	0	0	0	0	0	0	0	1	9	43
Heating Degree Days (base 65°F)	1,726	1,513	1,394	1,000	601	326	206	255	484	852	1,173	1,553	11,083
Cooling Degree Days (base 65°F)	0	0	0	0	0	7	12	5	1	0	0	0	25
Mean Precipitation (in.)	5.78	4.33	5.81	6.07	5.92	6.99	7.34	8.02	7.59	6.36	7.36	6.31	77.88
Days With ≥ 0.1" Precipitation	16	12	13	12	11	11	12	11	12	11	14	16	151
Days With ≥ 1.0" Precipitation	1	0	1	1	2	2	2	2	2	2	2	1	18
Mean Snowfall (in.)	43.6	32.4	36.6	23.4	3.7	trace	trace	trace	0.3	8.2	32.2	41.6	222.0
Days With ≥ 1.0" Snow Depth	31	28	31	30	23	1	0	0	0	7	23	31	205

Newport *Orleans County*   Elevation: 767 ft.   Latitude: 44° 56' N   Longitude: 72° 12' W

	JAN	FEB	MAR	APR	MAY	JUN	JUL	AUG	SEP	OCT	NOV	DEC	YEAR
Mean Maximum Temp. (°F)	25.0	29.6	39.6	52.9	67.6	75.4	79.8	77.5	68.4	56.1	42.2	30.1	53.7
Mean Temp. (°F)	14.7	18.1	28.7	41.8	55.1	63.7	68.2	66.0	57.5	46.2	34.6	21.3	43.0
Mean Minimum Temp. (°F)	4.3	6.5	17.7	30.6	42.5	51.9	56.6	54.4	46.5	36.4	26.8	12.5	32.2
Extreme Maximum Temp. (°F)	64	61	83	87	92	95	95	95	96	84	72	66	96
Extreme Minimum Temp. (°F)	-37	-38	-21	0	23	28	36	34	23	13	-4	-28	-38
Days Maximum Temp. ≥ 90°F	0	0	0	0	0	1	2	1	0	0	0	0	4
Days Maximum Temp. ≤ 32°F	22	16	8	1	0	0	0	0	0	0	5	17	69
Days Minimum Temp. ≤ 32°F	30	27	28	19	4	0	0	0	1	11	22	29	171
Days Minimum Temp. ≤ 0°F	13	11	3	0	0	0	0	0	0	0	0	7	34
Heating Degree Days (base 65°F)	1,555	1,320	1,119	692	317	100	29	60	241	576	907	1,348	8,264
Cooling Degree Days (base 65°F)	0	0	0	1	13	68	138	98	22	1	0	0	341
Mean Precipitation (in.)	2.87	2.17	2.96	2.83	3.61	3.86	4.14	4.24	3.88	3.45	3.44	3.10	40.55
Days With ≥ 0.1" Precipitation	8	6	8	8	9	9	9	8	8	8	8	8	97
Days With ≥ 1.0" Precipitation	0	0	0	0	0	1	1	1	1	1	0	0	5
Mean Snowfall (in.)	23.5	16.9	18.7	6.4	trace	0.0	0.0	0.0	trace	1.0	9.9	21.5	97.9
Days With ≥ 1.0" Snow Depth	30	28	28	7	0	0	0	0	0	0	9	25	127

Readsboro 1 SE *Bennington County*   Elevation: 1,118 ft.   Latitude: 42° 45' N   Longitude: 72° 56' W

	JAN	FEB	MAR	APR	MAY	JUN	JUL	AUG	SEP	OCT	NOV	DEC	YEAR
Mean Maximum Temp. (°F)	29.3	32.0	40.5	52.6	66.0	74.4	79.4	77.4	68.7	57.9	45.2	33.5	54.8
Mean Temp. (°F)	19.2	21.0	30.3	41.8	53.8	62.2	67.2	65.4	56.9	46.3	36.3	24.7	43.8
Mean Minimum Temp. (°F)	9.0	9.9	20.1	30.8	41.6	50.0	54.9	53.3	45.2	34.6	27.4	15.9	32.7
Extreme Maximum Temp. (°F)	61	63	81	88	90	92	96	98	92	84	78	65	98
Extreme Minimum Temp. (°F)	-25	-25	-12	9	25	29	38	33	25	16	0	-20	-25
Days Maximum Temp. ≥ 90°F	0	0	0	0	0	1	2	1	0	0	0	0	4
Days Maximum Temp. ≤ 32°F	19	14	6	0	0	0	0	0	0	0	3	14	56
Days Minimum Temp. ≤ 32°F	30	27	28	18	3	0	0	0	2	14	22	29	173
Days Minimum Temp. ≤ 0°F	9	7	1	0	0	0	0	0	0	0	0	4	21
Heating Degree Days (base 65°F)	1,416	1,235	1,069	692	349	123	39	64	254	574	853	1,241	7,909
Cooling Degree Days (base 65°F)	0	0	0	0	9	44	112	80	17	1	0	0	263
Mean Precipitation (in.)	3.84	3.32	4.18	4.36	4.79	4.42	4.19	4.55	4.05	4.21	4.73	4.33	50.97
Days With ≥ 0.1" Precipitation	8	7	8	8	8	7	7	8	8	7	8	8	92
Days With ≥ 1.0" Precipitation	1	1	1	1	2	1	1	1	1	1	1	1	13
Mean Snowfall (in.)	20.9	14.9	14.5	4.5	trace	0.0	0.0	0.0	0.0	0.1	6.0	18.0	78.9
Days With ≥ 1.0" Snow Depth	23	23	22	7	0	0	0	0	0	0	3	18	96

Rochester *Windsor County*   Elevation: 830 ft.   Latitude: 43° 52' N   Longitude: 72° 48' W

	JAN	FEB	MAR	APR	MAY	JUN	JUL	AUG	SEP	OCT	NOV	DEC	YEAR
Mean Maximum Temp. (°F)	28.5	32.1	40.5	53.2	67.3	75.0	79.7	77.5	69.5	58.5	45.3	33.4	55.0
Mean Temp. (°F)	16.8	19.2	28.6	41.2	53.5	61.9	66.6	64.9	57.0	46.2	35.6	23.4	42.9
Mean Minimum Temp. (°F)	5.0	6.2	16.7	29.2	39.8	48.7	53.5	52.3	44.5	33.9	25.9	13.3	30.7
Extreme Maximum Temp. (°F)	62	64	81	91	92	93	95	98	94	84	75	67	98
Extreme Minimum Temp. (°F)	-32	-28	-17	1	24	30	36	33	23	12	-1	-30	-32
Days Maximum Temp. ≥ 90°F	0	0	0	0	0	1	1	1	0	0	0	0	3
Days Maximum Temp. ≤ 32°F	19	14	7	0	0	0	0	0	0	0	3	14	57
Days Minimum Temp. ≤ 32°F	30	28	29	21	7	0	0	0	2	15	22	29	183
Days Minimum Temp. ≤ 0°F	12	11	4	0	0	0	0	0	0	0	0	6	33
Heating Degree Days (base 65°F)	1,491	1,288	1,121	707	359	134	47	74	250	578	875	1,285	8,209
Cooling Degree Days (base 65°F)	0	0	0	0	7	41	101	76	18	1	0	0	244
Mean Precipitation (in.)	3.72	2.84	3.55	3.74	4.19	4.27	4.03	4.90	4.34	4.21	3.99	3.64	47.42
Days With ≥ 0.1" Precipitation	7	6	7	8	9	8	8	9	7	8	8	8	93
Days With ≥ 1.0" Precipitation	1	1	1	1	1	1	1	1	1	1	1	1	12
Mean Snowfall (in.)	22.6	17.6	16.9	4.6	trace	0.0	0.0	0.0	0.0	0.3	6.4	19.4	87.8
Days With ≥ 1.0" Snow Depth	27	26	21	5	0	0	0	0	0	0	5	21	105

Rutland *Rutland County*   Elevation: 620 ft.   Latitude: 43° 37' N   Longitude: 72° 58' W

	JAN	FEB	MAR	APR	MAY	JUN	JUL	AUG	SEP	OCT	NOV	DEC	YEAR
Mean Maximum Temp. (°F)	30.3	33.5	43.5	56.9	70.1	77.9	82.1	79.5	70.7	59.6	46.9	35.0	57.2
Mean Temp. (°F)	20.6	23.1	33.0	45.2	57.2	65.5	70.0	68.0	59.5	48.7	38.2	26.3	46.3
Mean Minimum Temp. (°F)	10.8	12.7	22.4	33.4	44.3	52.9	57.8	56.3	48.4	37.8	29.5	17.6	35.3
Extreme Maximum Temp. (°F)	66	67	86	92	93	95	96	98	91	83	79	68	98
Extreme Minimum Temp. (°F)	-36	-26	-17	9	26	33	39	36	26	17	3	-23	-36
Days Maximum Temp. ≥ 90°F	0	0	0	0	0	1	2	1	0	0	0	0	4
Days Maximum Temp. ≤ 32°F	18	13	5	0	0	0	0	0	0	0	2	12	50
Days Minimum Temp. ≤ 32°F	29	26	26	15	3	0	0	0	1	10	19	28	157
Days Minimum Temp. ≤ 0°F	8	6	1	0	0	0	0	0	0	0	0	3	18
Heating Degree Days (base 65°F)	1,371	1,175	985	590	256	68	15	33	189	500	798	1,192	7,172
Cooling Degree Days (base 65°F)	0	0	0	1	17	82	171	122	29	2	0	0	424
Mean Precipitation (in.)	2.60	1.92	2.59	2.75	3.48	3.79	4.40	4.15	4.03	3.20	3.06	2.66	38.63
Days With ≥ 0.1" Precipitation	6	5	6	7	8	8	7	8	7	7	7	6	82
Days With ≥ 1.0" Precipitation	0	0	0	0	0	1	1	1	1	1	0	0	5
Mean Snowfall (in.)	16.3	13.8	12.5	3.4	trace	0.0	0.0	0.0	trace	0.4	5.4	13.6	65.4
Days With ≥ 1.0" Snow Depth	24	21	12	1	0	0	0	0	0	0	4	18	80

Saint Johnsbury *Caledonia County*   Elevation: 698 ft.   Latitude: 44° 25' N   Longitude: 72° 01' W

	JAN	FEB	MAR	APR	MAY	JUN	JUL	AUG	SEP	OCT	NOV	DEC	YEAR
Mean Maximum Temp. (°F)	27.5	31.9	42.0	56.0	70.5	78.2	82.3	79.7	70.8	58.6	44.0	31.7	56.1
Mean Temp. (°F)	17.0	20.3	30.8	43.6	56.7	65.2	69.7	67.6	59.2	47.6	35.9	22.8	44.7
Mean Minimum Temp. (°F)	6.5	8.6	19.7	31.2	42.9	52.2	57.1	55.4	47.5	36.5	27.8	13.8	33.3
Extreme Maximum Temp. (°F)	63	62	84	92	93	98	99	93	91	84	73	67	99
Extreme Minimum Temp. (°F)	-32	-32	-20	7	21	30	37	34	25	13	-6	-31	-32
Days Maximum Temp. ≥ 90°F	0	0	0	0	1	2	3	1	0	0	0	0	7
Days Maximum Temp. ≤ 32°F	20	15	6	0	0	0	0	0	0	0	3	16	60
Days Minimum Temp. ≤ 32°F	30	27	27	17	4	0	0	0	1	12	20	29	167
Days Minimum Temp. ≤ 0°F	12	9	3	0	0	0	0	0	0	0	0	6	30
Heating Degree Days (base 65°F)	1,483	1,258	1,052	636	270	75	18	38	200	535	865	1,303	7,733
Cooling Degree Days (base 65°F)	0	0	0	1	18	85	171	122	30	1	0	0	428
Mean Precipitation (in.)	2.78	2.03	2.56	2.63	3.26	3.98	3.81	4.24	3.42	3.17	3.25	3.02	38.15
Days With ≥ 0.1" Precipitation	7	5	7	7	8	8	8	7	7	7	7	7	85
Days With ≥ 1.0" Precipitation	0	0	0	0	1	1	1	1	1	1	0	0	6
Mean Snowfall (in.)	22.6	16.4	15.2	5.2	trace	0.0	0.0	0.0	trace	0.4	6.7	21.8	88.3
Days With ≥ 1.0" Snow Depth	29	27	22	3	0	0	0	0	0	0	6	24	111

South Hero *Grand Isle County*   Elevation: 108 ft.   Latitude: 44° 38' N   Longitude: 73° 18' W

	JAN	FEB	MAR	APR	MAY	JUN	JUL	AUG	SEP	OCT	NOV	DEC	YEAR
Mean Maximum Temp. (°F)	26.6	29.4	39.5	52.9	66.9	75.8	80.9	78.5	69.3	57.1	44.5	32.5	54.5
Mean Temp. (°F)	18.3	20.5	30.7	43.7	56.7	65.9	71.2	69.2	60.7	49.3	38.2	25.5	45.8
Mean Minimum Temp. (°F)	9.9	11.7	22.0	34.4	46.4	56.0	61.6	59.9	52.0	41.6	31.8	18.5	37.1
Extreme Maximum Temp. (°F)	61	60	79	88	90	96	98	99	96	81	71	65	99
Extreme Minimum Temp. (°F)	-31	-27	-15	8	26	34	37	41	29	21	7	-22	-31
Days Maximum Temp. ≥ 90°F	0	0	0	0	0	1	2	1	0	0	0	0	4
Days Maximum Temp. ≤ 32°F	21	17	8	1	0	0	0	0	0	0	3	14	64
Days Minimum Temp. ≤ 32°F	30	26	26	13	1	0	0	0	0	4	16	27	143
Days Minimum Temp. ≤ 0°F	8	6	1	0	0	0	0	0	0	0	0	3	18
Heating Degree Days (base 65°F)	1,443	1,250	1,056	633	270	63	11	24	163	480	798	1,217	7,408
Cooling Degree Days (base 65°F)	0	0	0	1	15	98	210	158	40	1	0	0	523
Mean Precipitation (in.)	1.89	1.35	2.07	2.44	2.84	3.24	3.40	3.95	3.47	3.09	2.91	1.94	32.59
Days With ≥ 0.1" Precipitation	5	3	6	6	7	7	8	8	7	6	6	5	74
Days With ≥ 1.0" Precipitation	0	0	0	0	0	1	1	1	1	1	0	0	5
Mean Snowfall (in.)	13.5	10.0	9.9	2.7	trace	0.0	0.0	0.0	0.0	trace	3.6	10.9	50.6
Days With ≥ 1.0" Snow Depth	24	23	17	3	0	0	0	0	0	0	3	15	85

Vernon *Windham County*   Elevation: 223 ft.   Latitude: 42° 46' N   Longitude: 72° 31' W

	JAN	FEB	MAR	APR	MAY	JUN	JUL	AUG	SEP	OCT	NOV	DEC	YEAR
Mean Maximum Temp. (°F)	31.7	35.2	44.6	57.2	70.3	78.7	83.8	81.8	73.0	61.5	48.4	36.2	58.5
Mean Temp. (°F)	20.9	23.6	34.0	45.4	57.5	66.2	71.3	69.5	60.8	49.2	38.8	26.8	47.0
Mean Minimum Temp. (°F)	10.0	12.1	23.4	33.5	44.7	53.6	58.7	57.1	48.5	37.0	29.1	17.4	35.4
Extreme Maximum Temp. (°F)	62	65	83	97	95	100	99	99	95	88	78	68	100
Extreme Minimum Temp. (°F)	-25	-21	-7	14	25	34	41	36	28	17	7	-20	-25
Days Maximum Temp. ≥ 90°F	0	0	0	0	1	3	6	4	1	0	0	0	15
Days Maximum Temp. ≤ 32°F	16	11	3	0	0	0	0	0	0	0	1	10	41
Days Minimum Temp. ≤ 32°F	30	27	26	14	2	0	0	0	1	11	21	29	161
Days Minimum Temp. ≤ 0°F	8	6	0	0	0	0	0	0	0	0	0	3	17
Heating Degree Days (base 65°F)	1,362	1,161	953	584	251	62	10	25	164	486	780	1,176	7,014
Cooling Degree Days (base 65°F)	0	0	0	2	26	108	218	176	46	3	0	0	579
Mean Precipitation (in.)	3.74	3.13	3.88	4.01	4.33	3.98	3.86	4.31	3.71	4.01	4.23	3.85	47.04
Days With ≥ 0.1" Precipitation	7	6	7	7	8	7	7	7	6	6	8	7	83
Days With ≥ 1.0" Precipitation	1	1	1	1	1	1	1	1	1	1	1	1	12
Mean Snowfall (in.)	*15.8*	12.4	9.7	2.3	trace	0.0	0.0	0.0	0.0	trace	3.8	12.6	*56.6*
Days With ≥ 1.0" Snow Depth	*24*	*22*	*15*	*1*	0	0	0	0	0	0	3	17	*82*

West Burke *Caledonia County*   Elevation: 898 ft.   Latitude: 44° 39' N   Longitude: 71° 59' W

	JAN	FEB	MAR	APR	MAY	JUN	JUL	AUG	SEP	OCT	NOV	DEC	YEAR
Mean Maximum Temp. (°F)	23.5	27.3	37.4	50.9	65.8	74.5	79.1	77.0	67.0	54.1	40.7	28.4	52.1
Mean Temp. (°F)	10.9	13.2	24.4	38.3	51.3	60.3	65.1	63.0	53.8	42.4	31.3	17.7	39.3
Mean Minimum Temp. (°F)	-1.8	-1.0	11.3	25.7	36.7	46.1	50.9	49.0	40.6	30.7	21.9	7.0	26.4
Extreme Maximum Temp. (°F)	61	59	75	90	92	95	95	96	89	80	70	59	96
Extreme Minimum Temp. (°F)	-38	-37	-27	0	18	26	31	29	20	9	-11	-35	-38
Days Maximum Temp. ≥ 90°F	0	0	0	0	0	1	2	1	0	0	0	0	4
Days Maximum Temp. ≤ 32°F	23	18	10	1	0	0	0	0	0	0	6	19	77
Days Minimum Temp. ≤ 32°F	31	28	30	24	12	2	0	1	7	19	25	30	209
Days Minimum Temp. ≤ 0°F	18	16	8	0	0	0	0	0	0	0	1	10	53
Heating Degree Days (base 65°F)	1,674	1,460	1,254	794	425	171	74	117	338	692	1,004	1,462	9,465
Cooling Degree Days (base 65°F)	0	0	0	0	4	34	81	61	8	0	0	0	188
Mean Precipitation (in.)	3.00	2.26	2.81	2.80	3.61	4.28	4.36	4.88	3.76	3.55	3.48	3.33	42.12
Days With ≥ 0.1" Precipitation	7	6	8	7	9	9	9	9	8	8	8	9	97
Days With ≥ 1.0" Precipitation	0	0	0	0	0	1	1	1	1	1	0	0	5
Mean Snowfall (in.)	23.1	18.2	16.8	5.6	trace	0.0	0.0	0.0	trace	0.5	7.5	23.7	95.4
Days With ≥ 1.0" Snow Depth	30	28	29	10	0	0	0	0	0	0	10	28	135

Note: See Appendix D for explanation of data.

VIRGINIA

PHYSICAL FEATURES. Virginia is located on the east coast of the North American continent between latitudes 36.5° and 39.5° N. The State is triangular in shape with the longest north-south distance of about 200 miles and the longest east-west distance more than 400 miles. There are 40,815 square miles of area within the State of which 1,200 square miles are inland waters.

The State is composed of three natural topographic regions, namely: the Tidewater or coastal plains area, the Piedmont plateau or middle Virginia; and the western mountain region. Tidewater Virginia extends westward from the Atlantic Coast and west shore of the Chesapeake Bay to the "Fall Line." The "Fall Line" extends from Great Falls in the north, southward through Richmond to Emporia. It is divided into necks, or peninsulas, by four principal rivers and by numerous estuaries that open into the Chesapeake Bay. The principal rivers include the Potomac, Rappahannock, York, and the James. The Piedmont region is more than 200 miles wide in southern Virginia, but the Virginia section becomes quite narrow in the north. This region from east to west becomes more rolling and hilly with a few isolated mountains and ridges appearing a few miles east of the Blue Ridge. Elevations in general range from about 300 feet above sea level in the east to about 1,000 feet in the west. The James, the largest river crossing this region, divides it into two parts.

West of the Piedmont, the Blue Ridge Mountains traverse the State from southwest to northeast. They range from narrow ridges in the north to a high, wide plateau southwest from Roanoke. Elevations range generally from 1,500 to 3,500 feet. Mt. Rogers, in western Grayson County, towers to 5,719 feet, the highest point in the State. A great valley west of the Blue Ridge extends from Tennessee through Scott and Washington Counties in the south, northeastward to the northern-most point of the State. This great valley of Virginia is well drained. The north is drained by the north and south forks of the Shenandoah River, thence into the Potomac; the central portion by the Cow Pasture and Jackson Rivers flowing southeastward into the James; and the southwestern half of the valley is drained by the Roanoke River, the New River, and three forks of the Holston River.

GENERAL CLIMATE. The climate of Virginia is determined by its proximity to the Atlantic Ocean, latitude, and topography. The State is in the zone of prevailing westerly movement of the earth's atmosphere, in or near the mean path of winter storm tracks, and in the mean path of tropical, moist air from the southwest Atlantic and Gulf of Mexico much of the summer and early fall seasons. The mountains provide the usual elevation effects on temperatures, which are distinctly lower in this section, and there are wide variations over short distances as elevations change. Summers in the mountains are comparatively cool, and winters are more severe. In addition, these mountains produce various steering, blocking, and modifying effects on storms and general air movements in their vicinity. Temperature variations within the State due to latitude alone are very small. The longitudinal variations, however, show a sharper contrast, from the mountain extremes in the west toward an ocean influence in the east. The prevalence of winds with a westerly component prevents the extension of ocean influences very far westward from the coast.

Virginia lies in the zone of prevailing westerlies where the general motion is from west to east. Southerly and northerly winds are about equally frequent, reflecting the progression of weather systems over the State. The Appalachian mountains, however, act to deflect these winds to some extent with northeasterly and southwesterly directions occurring frequently. During the cold season a more intense circulation is present with frequent storms and outbreaks of cold polar air. Northerly winds are most common during this season. The storm track is well north of the State during the warm season and southerly winds with light speeds prevail.

Summers in Virginia are usually warm and humid, and several hot and humid periods usually occur each year. Principal sources of moisture are the Gulf of Mexico and the Atlantic Ocean. Relative humidity varies inversely with temperature — high in the morning and low in the afternoon. Tidewater locations have a much higher frequency of humidity and uncomfortable temperatures.

PRECIPITATION. The annual precipitation ranges from about 35 to 50 inches. The heaviest amounts occur in the extreme southwest, the southeast, and the south-central areas. Minimum amounts are found in the sheltered valleys west of the Blue Ridge Mountains. Precipitation is well distributed throughout the year without distinct wet and dry periods. Maximum rainfall occurs in the summer months and minimum in the fall months. Precipitation during the cold season is associated with migratory low-pressure storms. The amounts are quite evenly distributed during this season in comparison to the warm season when showers and thundershowers account for most of the rainfall. Excessive rainfall usually occurs in the fall season with the passage of hurricanes. Snow is common in winter. Average seasonal amounts range from less than 10 inches in Tidewater Virginia to around 20 inches west of the Blue Ridge, and up to 30 inches on the mountains. Occasionally, a major snowstorm will occur with snow depths greater than 10 inches.

The greater portion of the State lies in the Atlantic drainage. The extreme southwestern portion drains to the Ohio Basin. Floods occur in all months of the year. The greatest frequency occurs in late winter and early spring; snowmelt occasionally is a factor. July is the month of least flooding. A second period of high water shows up in late summer and fall in the Piedmont and Tidewater sections associated mainly with tropical storms. Intense convectional storms in summer occasionally cause local flash floods.

Virginia is also subject to drought periods. Drought may be defined broadly as a prolonged and abnormal moisture deficiency. Some portions of Virginia sustain real damage from drought on the average of one year out of three. Equitable distribution of ample precipitation has seldom, if ever, occurred over all of Virginia for an entire season. Almost every year some sections undergo periods of insufficient rainfall.

STORMS. Thunderstorms occur on the average of 32 to 50 days each year, the greater number occurring in the mountains of extreme southwestern Virginia, decreasing in number toward the northeastern part of the State. About 85 percent of the annual total occur during the period May to September. Only a small percentage of these can be classed as severe, however. Thunderstorms exact a sizable annual toll of damage when accompanied by severe lightning, wind, or hail. Tornadoes are local storms of short duration and usually small dimensions, formed of winds rotating at high speeds. Approximately four tornadoes are reported in Virginia each year. These tornadoes occur mainly east of the Blue Ridge, but a few have been observed in the mountains.

A hurricane is a tropical storm with winds of at least 74 m.p.h., which blow in a large spiral around a relatively calm center. Virginia has been affected by hurricanes since the early settlement days, but most have decreased in intensity before entering the State. Even though a hurricane may not enter the State, it can be much more destructive by passing closely offshore and maintaining its intense circulation. High tides along with waves and currents, and flooding from the torrential rains, cause damage. About 80 percent of the hurricanes occur during August, September, and October. An average of about two hurricanes each year come close enough to affect Virginia, but less than one enters the State.

Middle latitude storms sometimes develop south of Virginia and move northward along the Virginia coast. These storms, although usually weaker than hurricanes, produce similar type of damage. This type of storm, often referred to as a "Northeaster," generally occurs from late fall through the spring months. They often account for considerable damage from high tides, strong east or northeast winds, and heavy rain, mainly in Tidewater Virginia.

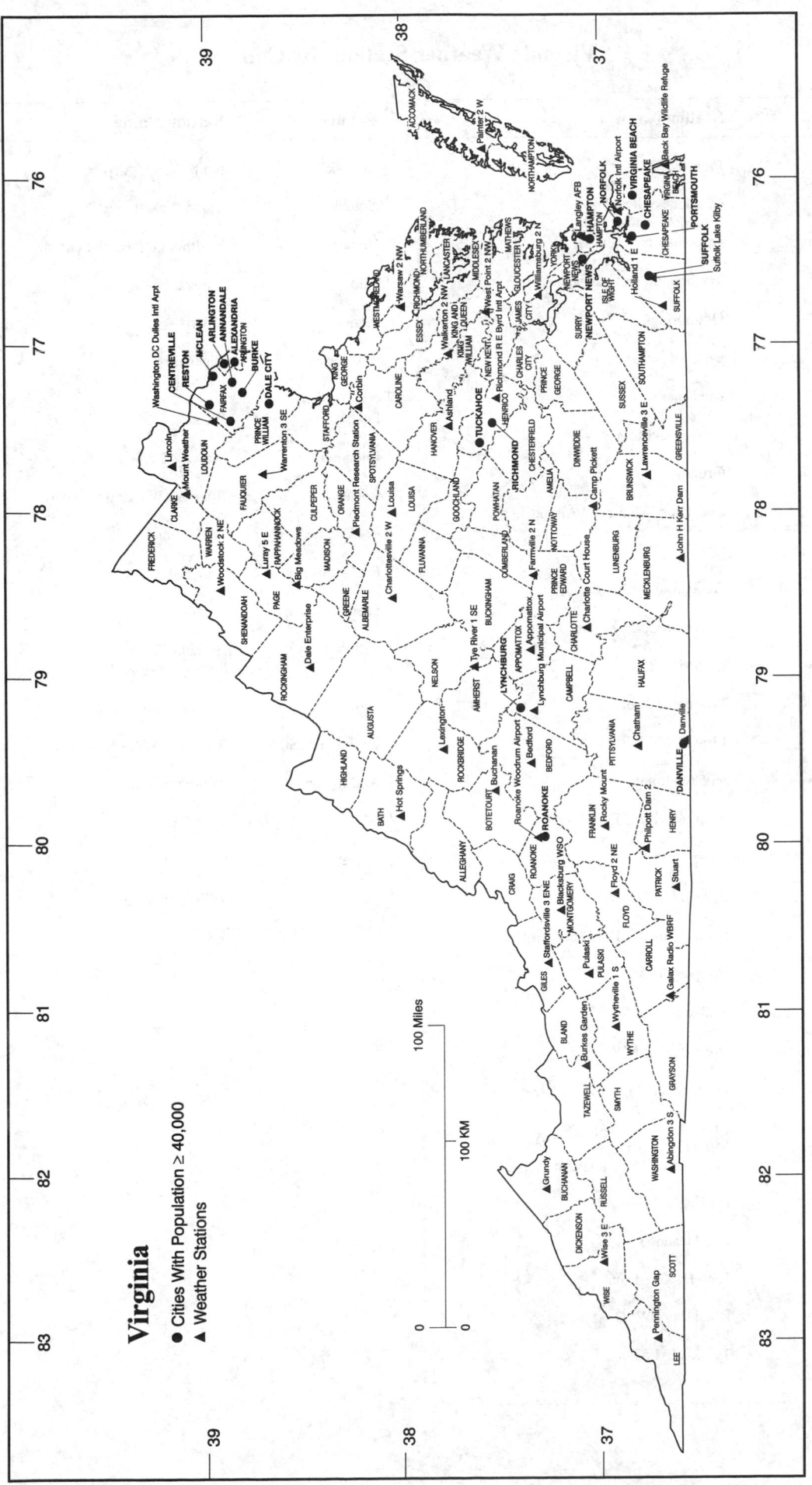

Virginia

- ● Cities With Population ≥ 40,000
- ▲ Weather Stations

100 Miles

100 KM

Virginia Weather Stations by County

County	Station Name
Accomack	Painter 2 W
Albemarle	Charlottesville 2 W
Appomattox	Appomattox
Arlington	Washington DC National Airport
Bath	Hot Springs
Bedford	Bedford
Botetourt	Buchanan
Brunswick	Lawrenceville 3 E
Buchanan	Grundy
Campbell	Lynchburg Municipal Airport
Caroline	Corbin
Carroll	Galax Radio WBRF
Charlotte	Charlotte Court House
Cumberland	Farmville 2 N
Fauquier	Warrenton 3 SE
Floyd	Floyd 2 NE
Franklin	Rocky Mount
Giles	Staffordsville 3 ENE
Hampton (City)	Langley AFB
Hanover	Ashland
Henrico	Richmond R.E. Byrd Int'l Airport
Henry	Philpott Dam 2
King And Queen	Walkerton 2 NW
King William	West Point 2 NW
Lee	Pennington Gap
Loudoun	Lincoln Mount Weather Washington DC Dulles Int'l Arpt.
Louisa	Louisa
Madison	Big Meadows
Mecklenburg	John H. Kerr Dam
Montgomery	Blacksburg WSO
Nelson	Tye River 1 SE

County	Station Name
Norfolk	Norfolk Int'l Airport
Nottoway	Camp Pickett
Orange	Piedmont Research Station
Page	Luray 5 E
Patrick	Stuart
Pittsylvania	Chatham Danville
Pulaski	Pulaski
Richmond	Warsaw 2 NW
Roanoke	Roanoke Woodrum Airport
Rockbridge	Lexington
Rockingham	Dale Enterprise
Shenandoah	Woodstock 2 NE
Suffolk (City)	Holland 1 E Suffolk Lake Kilby
Tazewell	Burkes Garden
Virginia Beach	Back Bay Wildlife Refuge
Washington	Abingdon 3 S
Wise	Wise 3 E
Wythe	Wytheville 1 S
York	Williamsburg 2 N

Virginia Weather Stations by City

City	Station Name	Miles
Alexandria	Beltsville, MD	18
	College Park, MD	14
	Dalecarlia Reservoir, MD	8
	Glenn Dale Bell Station, MD	19
	National Arboretum, MD	8
	Rockville 1 NE, MD	19
	Upper Marlboro 3 NNW, MD	17
	Washington DC National Airport	4
Annandale	College Park, MD	17
	Dalecarlia Reservoir, MD	9
	National Arboretum, MD	13
	Rockville 1 NE, MD	19
	Washington DC Dulles Int'l Arpt.	15
	Washington DC National Airport	10
Arlington	Beltsville, MD	16
	College Park, MD	11
	Dalecarlia Reservoir, MD	4
	Glenn Dale Bell Station, MD	17
	Laurel 3 W, MD	19
	National Arboretum, MD	7
	Rockville 1 NE, MD	16
	Upper Marlboro 3 NNW, MD	17
	Washington DC Dulles Int'l Arpt.	19
	Washington DC National Airport	4
Burke	Dalecarlia Reservoir, MD	13
	National Arboretum, MD	18
	Washington DC Dulles Int'l Arpt.	14
	Washington DC National Airport	14
Centreville	Dalecarlia Reservoir, MD	19
	Washington DC Dulles Int'l Arpt.	6
Chesapeake	Norfolk Int'l Airport	10
	Suffolk Lake Kilby	18
Danville	Chatham	16
	Danville	1
Hampton	Langley AFB	3
	Norfolk Int'l Airport	13
Lynchburg	Appomattox	20
	Bedford	19
	Lynchburg Municipal Airport	5
McLean	Beltsville, MD	17
	College Park, MD	13
	Dalecarlia Reservoir, MD	3
	Laurel 3 W, MD	19
	National Arboretum, MD	11
	Rockville 1 NE, MD	12
	Washington DC Dulles Int'l Arpt.	15
	Washington DC National Airport	9
Newport News	Langley AFB	8
	Williamsburg 2 N	19
Norfolk	Langley AFB	14
	Norfolk Int'l Airport	3
Portsmouth	Langley AFB	17

City	Station Name	Miles
Portsmouth (cont.)	Norfolk Int'l Airport	10
	Suffolk Lake Kilby	15
Reston	Dalecarlia Reservoir, MD	12
	National Arboretum, MD	20
	Rockville 1 NE, MD	17
	Washington DC Dulles Int'l Arpt.	6
	Washington DC National Airport	18
Richmond	Ashland	15
	Richmond R.E. Byrd Int'l Airport	8
Roanoke	Roanoke Woodrum Airport	3
Suffolk	Holland 1 E	11
	Suffolk Lake Kilby	1
Tuckahoe	Ashland	12
	Richmond R.E. Byrd Int'l Airport	16
Virginia Beach	Back Bay Wildlife Refuge	15
	Norfolk Int'l Airport	7

Note: Miles is the distance between the geographic center of the city and the weather station.

Virginia Weather Stations by Elevation

Feet	Station Name
3,536	Big Meadows
3,297	Burkes Garden
2,624	Floyd 2 NE
2,545	Wise 3 E
2,447	Wytheville 1 S
2,381	Galax Radio WBRF
2,234	Hot Springs
2,007	Blacksburg WSO
1,948	Staffordsville 3 ENE
1,919	Abingdon 3 S
1,847	Pulaski
1,719	Mount Weather
1,499	Pennington Gap
1,397	Dale Enterprise
1,374	Stuart
1,312	Rocky Mount
1,299	Luray 5 E
1,167	Grundy
1,148	Roanoke Woodrum Airport
1,122	Philpott Dam 2
1,059	Lexington
974	Bedford
938	Lynchburg Municipal Airport
908	Appomattox
879	Buchanan
869	Charlottesville 2 W
718	Tye River 1 SE
659	Woodstock 2 NE
639	Chatham
587	Charlotte Court House
518	Piedmont Research Station
498	Lincoln
498	Warrenton 3 SE
449	Farmville 2 N
419	Louisa
410	Danville
328	Camp Pickett
324	Lawrenceville 3 E
288	Washington DC Dulles Int'l Arpt.
249	John H. Kerr Dam
219	Ashland
219	Corbin
164	Richmond R.E. Byrd Int'l Airport
137	Warsaw 2 NW
78	Holland 1 E
68	Williamsburg 2 N
49	Walkerton 2 NW
29	Painter 2 W
22	Norfolk Int'l Airport
19	Suffolk Lake Kilby
19	West Point 2 NW
9	Back Bay Wildlife Refuge
9	Langley AFB
9	Washington DC National Airport

Lynchburg Municipal Airport

Lynchburg is situated in the valley of the James River, and on the eastern edge of the Blue Ridge Mountains. The terrain is definitely hilly, with sheltered valleys which are visited by early autumn and late spring frosts. The climate is usually a pleasant one, being neither too hot in the summer, nor too cold in the winter. Rainfall is fairly evenly distributed throughout the year, but there is a distinct summertime rainfall, occasioned by afternoon thunderstorms.

Spring makes itself felt in March, when the mean monthly temperature increases about seven degrees over the February temperature. Autumn rapidly comes in October, which shows about a 10 degree drop below the September mean. The approaching autumn season brings periods of two to three days of cloudy, cool weather, with high humidity and light rain or drizzle. In midwinter, however, after the passage of a cold front, dry invigorating air, with clear skies, is the rule in Lynchburg. There are occasional snow showers, but the mountains to the immediate west act as a barrier and shelter the area from many storms and high winds.

The mountains also act as a barrier to extremely cold weather. Temperatures have fallen below zero only on a few days, and 100 degree heat is almost as rare, although this mark has been exceeded in the months of May through September.

Great variation in temperature is quite frequently noted during clear, still nights in the winter months. On some such nights, differences of as much as 10-15 degrees occur between the low valleys and the higher terrain.

Based on the 1951-1980 period, the average first occurrence of 32 degrees Fahrenheit in the fall is October 23 and the average last occurrence in the spring is April 13.

Lynchburg Municipal Airport *Campbell County*   Elevation: 938 ft.   Latitude: 37° 20' N   Longitude: 79° 12' W

	JAN	FEB	MAR	APR	MAY	JUN	JUL	AUG	SEP	OCT	NOV	DEC	YEAR
Mean Maximum Temp. (°F)	44.4	48.4	57.2	68.1	75.4	82.5	86.6	85.1	78.7	68.3	58.1	48.7	66.8
Mean Temp. (°F)	35.2	38.4	46.5	56.1	64.1	71.9	76.2	74.9	68.5	57.1	47.5	39.3	56.3
Mean Minimum Temp. (°F)	26.0	28.4	35.7	44.1	52.8	61.2	65.8	64.6	58.2	45.8	37.0	29.9	45.8
Extreme Maximum Temp. (°F)	75	79	87	92	92	97	101	102	97	90	83	79	102
Extreme Minimum Temp. (°F)	-10	-10	7	20	31	40	49	47	36	23	8	-4	-10
Days Maximum Temp. ≥ 90°F	0	0	0	0	0	4	10	7	3	0	0	0	24
Days Maximum Temp. ≤ 32°F	4	2	0	0	0	0	0	0	0	0	0	2	8
Days Minimum Temp. ≤ 32°F	23	19	12	3	0	0	0	0	0	2	10	19	88
Days Minimum Temp. ≤ 0°F	1	0	0	0	0	0	0	0	0	0	0	0	1
Heating Degree Days (base 65°F)	917	743	570	282	98	12	0	1	40	259	519	790	4,231
Cooling Degree Days (base 65°F)	0	0	4	21	81	239	375	315	146	22	1	0	1,204
Mean Precipitation (in.)	3.46	3.12	3.82	3.41	4.11	3.63	4.31	3.35	3.77	3.57	3.27	3.28	43.10
Maximum Precipitation (in.)	8.0	5.7	9.2	7.9	9.1	10.0	10.3	11.4	9.9	11.4	8.8	7.1	59.7
Minimum Precipitation (in.)	0.5	0.3	0.7	0.3	1.4	0.5	1.1	0.7	trace	0.4	0.9	0.3	26.6
Maximum 24-hr. Precipitation (in.)	2.3	2.2	2.4	3.7	3.3	6.0	3.6	3.1	3.6	5.0	2.3	2.7	6.0
Days With ≥ 0.1" Precipitation	7	6	7	6	8	6	7	6	6	5	6	6	76
Days With ≥ 1.0" Precipitation	1	1	1	1	1	1	1	1	1	1	1	1	12
Mean Snowfall (in.)	5.6	6.0	2.7	0.3	trace	0.0	0.0	0.0	0.0	trace	0.6	2.4	17.6
Maximum Snowfall (in.)	32	19	25	5	0	0	0	0	0	2	12	18	56
Maximum 24-hr. Snowfall (in.)	12	13	13	3	0	0	0	0	0	2	6	10	13
Days With ≥ 1.0" Snow Depth	5	4	1	0	0	0	0	0	0	0	0	2	12
Thunderstorm Days	< 1	< 1	2	4	7	8	10	7	3	1	1	< 1	43
Foggy Days	13	13	13	11	16	13	16	19	16	13	12	12	167
Predominant Sky Cover	OVR	OVR	OVR	OVR	OVR	SCT	OVR	SCT	OVR	CLR	OVR	OVR	OVR
Mean Relative Humidity 7am (%)	72	72	73	72	80	83	86	88	88	85	78	74	79
Mean Relative Humidity 4pm (%)	51	49	46	43	51	54	56	57	56	51	50	53	52
Mean Dewpoint (°F)	22	24	31	39	52	61	65	65	58	46	35	26	44
Prevailing Wind Direction	SW	SW	SW	SW	SW	SW	SW	SW	NE	NE	SW	SW	SW
Prevailing Wind Speed (mph)	8	9	10	10	9	8	8	7	9	10	8	8	9
Maximum Wind Gust (mph)	56	58	56	58	59	74	64	75	41	51	64	47	75

Norfolk Int'l Airport

The city of Norfolk, Virginia, is located near the coast and the southern border of the state. It is almost surrounded by water, with the Chesapeake Bay immediately to the north, Hampton Roads to the west, and the Atlantic Ocean only 18 miles to the east. It is traversed by numerous rivers and waterways and its average elevation above sea level is 13 feet. There are no nearby hilly areas and the land is low and level throughout the city. The climate is generally marine. The geographic location of the city with respect to the principal storm tracks, is especially favorable, being south of the average path of storms originating in the higher latitudes and north of the usual tracks of hurricanes and other tropical storms.

The winters are usually mild, while the autumn and spring seasons usually are delightful. Summers, though warm and long, frequently are tempered by cool periods, often associated with northeasterly winds off the Atlantic. Temperatures of 100 degrees or higher occur infrequently. Extreme cold waves seldom penetrate the area and temperatures of zero or below are almost nonexistent. Winters pass, on occasion, without a measurable amount of snowfall. Most of the snowfall in Norfolk is light and generally melts within 24 hours.

Based on the 1951-1980 period, the average first occurrence of 32 degrees Fahrenheit in the fall is November 17 and the average last occurrence in the spring is March 23.

Norfolk Int'l Airport *Norfolk County*   Elevation: 22 ft.   Latitude: 36° 54' N   Longitude: 76° 12' W

	JAN	FEB	MAR	APR	MAY	JUN	JUL	AUG	SEP	OCT	NOV	DEC	YEAR
Mean Maximum Temp. (°F)	48.5	51.2	58.5	68.1	75.8	83.7	87.9	85.9	80.7	70.4	61.9	53.4	68.8
Mean Temp. (°F)	40.4	42.4	49.4	58.1	66.8	75.0	79.6	78.0	72.8	61.9	53.1	45.1	60.2
Mean Minimum Temp. (°F)	32.2	33.6	40.3	48.2	57.7	66.2	71.3	70.1	64.9	53.3	44.2	36.6	51.6
Extreme Maximum Temp. (°F)	78	82	88	94	100	100	103	104	99	94	86	80	104
Extreme Minimum Temp. (°F)	-3	9	18	28	39	49	54	49	47	27	24	7	-3
Days Maximum Temp. ≥ 90°F	0	0	0	0	1	7	13	9	3	0	0	0	33
Days Maximum Temp. ≤ 32°F	3	1	0	0	0	0	0	0	0	0	0	1	5
Days Minimum Temp. ≤ 32°F	15	14	5	0	0	0	0	0	0	0	3	11	48
Days Minimum Temp. ≤ 0°F	0	0	0	0	0	0	0	0	0	0	0	0	0
Heating Degree Days (base 65°F)	758	634	485	235	62	4	0	0	7	142	363	614	3,304
Cooling Degree Days (base 65°F)	1	1	9	37	130	321	486	410	244	56	10	2	1,707
Mean Precipitation (in.)	3.84	3.43	4.11	3.36	3.69	3.63	5.09	4.58	3.91	3.51	3.00	3.09	45.24
Maximum Precipitation (in.)	9.9	6.2	10.4	7.3	10.1	9.7	14.4	14.3	13.8	10.1	7.0	6.1	65.0
Minimum Precipitation (in.)	1.0	0.8	0.8	0.4	0.6	0.4	0.4	0.7	0.3	0.6	0.5	0.7	26.5
Maximum 24-hr. Precipitation (in.)	3.7	2.7	3.8	5.9	3.4	5.8	4.7	7.4	6.5	3.7	3.3	2.5	7.4
Days With ≥ 0.1" Precipitation	7	7	7	6	7	6	7	6	6	5	6	6	76
Days With ≥ 1.0" Precipitation	1	1	1	1	1	1	2	1	1	1	1	1	13
Mean Snowfall (in.)	2.3	3.7	1.2	trace	trace	trace	0.0	trace	0.0	0.0	trace	0.4	7.6
Maximum Snowfall (in.)	14	24	14	1	0	0	0	0	0	0	1	15	42
Maximum 24-hr. Snowfall (in.)	9	14	8	1	0	0	0	0	0	0	1	10	14
Days With ≥ 1.0" Snow Depth	2	2	0	0	0	0	0	0	0	0	0	0	4
Thunderstorm Days	< 1	1	2	3	5	6	9	7	3	1	1	< 1	38
Foggy Days	13	12	12	11	13	12	12	15	14	14	13	12	153
Predominant Sky Cover	OVR	OVR	OVR	OVR	OVR	OVR	SCT	SCT	OVR	OVR	OVR	OVR	OVR
Mean Relative Humidity 7am (%)	74	74	74	73	77	79	81	84	83	82	79	75	78
Mean Relative Humidity 4pm (%)	59	56	53	50	56	57	60	63	62	60	58	59	58
Mean Dewpoint (°F)	30	30	36	44	55	63	69	68	63	52	42	33	49
Prevailing Wind Direction	N	N	N	SW	SW	SW	SW	SW	NE	NE	SW	SW	SW
Prevailing Wind Speed (mph)	13	14	14	13	12	12	10	9	13	13	10	12	12
Maximum Wind Gust (mph)	69	59	66	62	66	69	63	63	67	75	55	53	75

Richmond R.E. Byrd Int'l Airport

Richmond is located in east-central Virginia at the head of navigation on the James River and along a line separating the Coastal Plains (Tidewater Virginia) from the Piedmont. The Blue Ridge Mountains lie about 90 miles to the west and the Chesapeake Bay 60 miles to the east. Elevations range from a few feet above sea level along the river to a little over 300 feet in parts of the western section of the city.

The climate might be classified as modified continental. Summers are warm and humid and winters generally mild. The mountains to the west act as a partial barrier to outbreaks of cold, continental air in winter. The cold winter air is delayed long enough to be modified, then further warmed as it subsides in its approach to Richmond. The open waters of the Chesapeake Bay and Atlantic Ocean contribute to the humid summers and mild winters. The coldest weather normally occurs in late December and January, when low temperatures usually average in the upper 20s, and the high temperatures in the upper 40s. Temperatures seldom lower to zero, but there have been several occurrences of below zero temperatures. Summertime high temperatures above 100 degrees are not uncommon, but do not occur every year.

Precipitation is rather uniformly distributed throughout the year. However, dry periods lasting several weeks do occur, especially in autumn when long periods of pleasant, mild weather are most common. There is considerable variability in total monthly amounts from year to year. Snow usually remains on the ground only one or two days at a time. Ice storms (freezing rain or glaze) are not uncommon, but they are seldom severe.

The James River reaches tidewater at Richmond where flooding may occur in every month of the year, most frequently in March and least in July. Hurricanes and tropical storms have been responsible for most of the flooding during the summer and early fall months. Hurricanes passing near Richmond have produced record rainfalls. In 1955, three hurricanes brought record rainfall to Richmond within a six-week period. The most noteworthy of these were Hurricanes Connie and Diane that brought heavy rains five days apart.

Damaging storms occur mainly from snow and freezing rain in winter and from hurricanes, tornadoes, and severe thunderstorms in other seasons. Damage may be from wind, flooding, or rain, or from any combination of these.

Based on the 1951-1980 period, the average first occurrence of 32 degrees Fahrenheit in the fall is October 26 and the average last occurrence in the spring is April 10.

Richmond R.E. Byrd Int'l Airport *Henrico County*   Elevation: 164 ft.   Latitude: 37° 31' N   Longitude: 77° 19' W

	JAN	FEB	MAR	APR	MAY	JUN	JUL	AUG	SEP	OCT	NOV	DEC	YEAR
Mean Maximum Temp. (°F)	46.5	50.5	59.4	70.3	77.7	85.2	89.2	87.3	81.3	70.5	61.0	51.2	69.2
Mean Temp. (°F)	37.0	40.0	48.1	57.8	66.2	74.2	78.8	77.1	70.7	59.0	49.8	41.3	58.3
Mean Minimum Temp. (°F)	27.3	29.4	36.8	45.3	54.6	63.2	68.4	66.8	60.0	47.4	38.5	31.3	47.4
Extreme Maximum Temp. (°F)	77	82	91	96	98	101	105	102	100	94	86	81	105
Extreme Minimum Temp. (°F)	-6	-8	13	23	32	44	52	47	35	22	14	3	-8
Days Maximum Temp. ≥ 90°F	0	0	0	1	2	8	15	11	4	0	0	0	41
Days Maximum Temp. ≤ 32°F	4	2	0	0	0	0	0	0	0	0	0	1	7
Days Minimum Temp. ≤ 32°F	22	18	11	2	0	0	0	0	0	1	9	18	81
Days Minimum Temp. ≤ 0°F	0	0	0	0	0	0	0	0	0	0	0	0	0
Heating Degree Days (base 65°F)	863	700	523	243	71	6	0	1	25	215	457	730	3,834
Cooling Degree Days (base 65°F)	0	0	8	33	116	303	455	378	198	36	3	1	1,531
Mean Precipitation (in.)	3.47	3.01	4.09	3.11	3.92	3.38	4.69	3.96	3.90	3.65	3.11	3.14	43.43
Maximum Precipitation (in.)	10.1	6.0	8.6	7.3	8.9	9.3	16.1	14.1	11.0	9.4	7.6	7.1	61.3
Minimum Precipitation (in.)	0.6	0.3	0.9	0.5	0.4	0.4	0.5	0.6	0.3	0.3	0.2	0.4	26.8
Maximum 24-hr. Precipitation (in.)	3.3	2.6	3.1	2.8	3.0	3.9	7.2	8.8	4.9	4.8	3.0	2.5	8.8
Days With ≥ 0.1" Precipitation	7	6	7	6	7	6	8	6	6	5	6	6	76
Days With ≥ 1.0" Precipitation	1	1	1	1	1	1	1	1	1	1	1	1	12
Mean Snowfall (in.)	3.9	4.6	1.4	trace	trace	0.0	0.0	0.0	0.0	trace	0.3	1.5	11.7
Maximum Snowfall (in.)	26	21	20	3	0	0	0	0	0	trace	9	13	47
Maximum 24-hr. Snowfall (in.)	13	13	11	2	0	0	0	0	0	trace	7	8	13
Days With ≥ 1.0" Snow Depth	3	3	1	0	0	0	0	0	0	0	0	1	8
Thunderstorm Days	< 1	< 1	2	3	6	8	10	8	3	1	1	< 1	42
Foggy Days	11	9	10	9	13	12	14	16	15	14	11	10	144
Predominant Sky Cover	OVR	OVR	OVR	OVR	OVR	OVR	OVR	OVR	OVR	CLR	OVR	OVR	OVR
Mean Relative Humidity 7am (%)	80	79	78	76	81	82	85	89	90	89	84	80	83
Mean Relative Humidity 4pm (%)	55	50	46	43	51	53	56	58	57	53	51	55	52
Mean Dewpoint (°F)	26	27	34	42	54	63	68	67	61	49	38	30	47
Prevailing Wind Direction	N	N	SSW	SSW	S	S	SSW	S	N	N	S	SSW	S
Prevailing Wind Speed (mph)	8	9	10	10	8	7	8	7	8	8	8	8	8
Maximum Wind Gust (mph)	104	60	67	64	79	67	93	128	51	104	54	54	128

Roanoke Woodrum Airport

The climate of Roanoke is relatively mild. Roanoke is nestled among mountains which interrupt the Great Valley, extending from northernmost Virginia southwestward into east Tennessee. This location, at a point where the valley is pinched between the Blue Ridges and the Alleghenies, offers a natural barrier to the winter cold as it moves southward. It is also far enough inland that hurricanes lose much of their destructive force before reaching Roanoke. Finally, the rough terrain is an inhospitable breeding ground for tornadic activity. The elevation in the vicinity usually produces cool summer nights that make a light cover comfortable for sleeping. Although past records show extremes over 100 degrees and below zero, many years pass without either extreme being threatened.

Roanoke is located near the headwaters of the Roanoke River, which flows in a general southeasterly direction. Numerous creeks and small streams from nearby mountainous areas empty into the Roanoke River. The usual low water stage is one to 1.5 feet, and flood stage is 10 feet. Some low-lying streets in Roanoke and nearby Salem have to be blocked off during seven to eight foot stages, but damage is minor until the river overflows its banks. The highest stage on record exceeds 19 feet. Damage has been widespread on occasion and has amounted to several million dollars in the city of Roanoke alone.

The growing season averages 190 days. The average date of the last freezing temperature in spring is mid-April and the average date of the first freezing date in the fall is late October.

Rainfall is well apportioned throughout the year. Droughts are so infrequent that quoting actual records would be difficult. Snow usually falls each winter, ranging from only a trace to more than 60 inches.

Roanoke Woodrum Airport *Roanoke County*   Elevation: 1,148 ft.   Latitude: 37° 19' N   Longitude: 79° 58' W

	JAN	FEB	MAR	APR	MAY	JUN	JUL	AUG	SEP	OCT	NOV	DEC	YEAR
Mean Maximum Temp. (°F)	44.6	48.7	57.3	67.8	75.4	82.8	87.1	85.6	78.7	68.2	57.9	48.7	66.9
Mean Temp. (°F)	35.5	38.6	46.7	56.0	64.1	71.9	76.4	74.9	68.1	56.8	47.4	39.3	56.3
Mean Minimum Temp. (°F)	26.3	28.4	35.9	44.2	52.6	60.9	65.7	64.2	57.5	45.3	37.0	29.9	45.7
Extreme Maximum Temp. (°F)	75	80	87	92	93	97	102	105	97	89	82	80	105
Extreme Minimum Temp. (°F)	-11	-1	9	20	32	39	47	42	34	22	11	-4	-11
Days Maximum Temp. ≥ 90°F	0	0	0	0	1	5	11	8	3	0	0	0	28
Days Maximum Temp. ≤ 32°F	4	2	0	0	0	0	0	0	0	0	0	2	8
Days Minimum Temp. ≤ 32°F	22	19	12	3	0	0	0	0	0	2	10	19	87
Days Minimum Temp. ≤ 0°F	0	0	0	0	0	0	0	0	0	0	0	0	0
Heating Degree Days (base 65°F)	909	739	566	284	102	12	1	2	45	267	522	789	4,238
Cooling Degree Days (base 65°F)	0	0	5	22	81	237	382	318	143	21	1	0	1,210
Mean Precipitation (in.)	3.20	3.11	3.81	3.52	4.21	3.68	3.87	3.84	3.72	3.40	3.26	2.90	42.52
Maximum Precipitation (in.)	7.3	7.2	7.9	11.3	8.4	10.3	10.1	9.5	11.1	9.9	12.4	7.1	58.9
Minimum Precipitation (in.)	0.3	0.1	0.4	0.5	1.3	0.6	0.4	0.7	0.1	trace	0.4	0.2	25.7
Maximum 24-hr. Precipitation (in.)	2.7	2.4	2.8	5.0	3.9	3.4	2.4	3.3	6.6	4.9	6.6	3.4	6.6
Days With ≥ 0.1" Precipitation	6	6	7	6	8	6	7	6	6	5	6	6	75
Days With ≥ 1.0" Precipitation	1	1	1	1	1	1	1	1	1	1	1	0	11
Mean Snowfall (in.)	5.9	6.7	3.0	0.7	trace	trace	0.0	0.0	0.0	trace	1.2	3.0	20.5
Maximum Snowfall (in.)	41	28	30	7	trace	0	0	0	0	1	14	23	73
Maximum 24-hr. Snowfall (in.)	14	15	14	4	trace	0	0	0	0	1	8	15	15
Days With ≥ 1.0" Snow Depth	4	4	1	0	0	0	0	0	0	0	0	2	11
Thunderstorm Days	< 1	< 1	1	3	6	7	8	6	3	1	< 1	< 1	35
Foggy Days	10	9	10	7	11	10	12	14	13	10	9	9	124
Predominant Sky Cover	OVR	OVR	OVR	OVR	OVR	OVR	SCT	SCT	OVR	CLR	OVR	OVR	OVR
Mean Relative Humidity 7am (%)	70	70	70	71	79	81	83	86	88	83	75	72	77
Mean Relative Humidity 4pm (%)	51	48	45	44	51	53	54	54	54	49	50	52	51
Mean Dewpoint (°F)	23	24	30	39	51	60	64	64	57	45	34	26	43
Prevailing Wind Direction	WNW	WNW	NW	NW	SE	W	W	SE	SE	NW	NW	NW	WNW
Prevailing Wind Speed (mph)	15	15	14	14	9	8	8	7	7	10	13	13	12
Maximum Wind Gust (mph)	60	60	66	77	59	74	81	62	54	59	55	61	81

Washington DC Dulles Int'l Arpt.

Dulles International Airport is located in the Virginia Piedmont about 23 miles east of the Blue Ridge Mountains and 12 miles east of the Bull Run and Catoctin Mountains. The Blue Ridge rises to about 2,500 feet above sea level and the Bull Run Mountains to about 1,500 feet at their nearest points. Field elevation is 313 feet. The terrain near the airport is mostly low rolling hills about one-fourth wooded. Ponds located on and near the airport, along with poor air drainage contribute to the formation of local ground fog. Easterly winds cause an upslope effect from the Atlantic Ocean, 140 miles east, and from the Chesapeake Bay, about 55 miles east. Westerly winds create a slight foehn effect.

Its location in the middle latitudes, where the general atmospheric flow is from west to east, favors a continental climate with four well defined seasons. Summers are warm and at times humid, Winters are mild. Generally pleasant weather prevails in spring and autumn. The coldest period, when temperatures average 21 degrees, occurs in late January. The warmest period, averaging 88 degrees, occurs in the last half of July.

Precipitation is rather evenly distributed through the year. Annual precipitation has ranged from about 25 inches to more than 55 inches. Rainfalls of over 10 inches in a 24-hour period have been recorded during the passage of tropical storms. The seasonal snowfall is nearly 24 inches, but varies greatly from season to season. Snowfalls of four inches or more occur only twice each winter on average. Accumulations of over 20 inches from a single storm are extremely rare.

Storm damage results mainly from heavy snows and freezing rains in winter and from hurricanes and severe thunderstorms during the other seasons. Damage may result from wind, flooding or rain.

Prevailing winds are from the south except during the winter months when they are from the northwest. The windiest period is late winter and early spring. Winds are generally less during the night and early morning hours and increase to a high in the afternoon. Winds may reach 50 to 60 miles per hour or even higher during severe summer thunderstorms, hurricanes, and winter storms.

The growing season averages 169 days. The average date for the last freeze in spring is late April and the average date for the first freeze in the fall is mid October.

Washington DC Dulles Int'l Arpt. *Loudoun County*   Elevation: 288 ft.   Latitude: 38° 56' N   Longitude: 77° 27' W

	JAN	FEB	MAR	APR	MAY	JUN	JUL	AUG	SEP	OCT	NOV	DEC	YEAR
Mean Maximum Temp. (°F)	41.1	45.3	54.6	65.9	74.6	82.7	87.5	86.1	79.1	67.6	56.6	46.2	65.6
Mean Temp. (°F)	31.7	35.0	43.4	53.3	62.5	71.1	76.0	74.6	67.5	55.1	45.5	36.6	54.4
Mean Minimum Temp. (°F)	22.2	24.6	32.1	40.6	50.4	59.3	64.5	63.0	55.9	42.6	34.4	26.8	43.0
Extreme Maximum Temp. (°F)	75	79	89	92	95	99	104	104	99	90	84	79	104
Extreme Minimum Temp. (°F)	-18	-14	-1	19	28	36	41	38	30	19	9	-4	-18
Days Maximum Temp. ≥ 90°F	0	0	0	0	1	5	12	9	3	0	0	0	30
Days Maximum Temp. ≤ 32°F	6	4	1	0	0	0	0	0	0	0	0	3	14
Days Minimum Temp. ≤ 32°F	26	22	17	6	0	0	0	0	0	5	14	23	113
Days Minimum Temp. ≤ 0°F	1	0	0	0	0	0	0	0	0	0	0	0	1
Heating Degree Days (base 65°F)	1,025	842	668	355	134	19	1	3	57	315	582	875	4,876
Cooling Degree Days (base 65°F)	0	0	5	12	68	221	372	310	137	18	2	0	1,145
Mean Precipitation (in.)	3.01	2.79	3.53	3.22	4.23	4.02	3.62	3.67	3.71	3.46	3.46	3.13	41.85
Maximum Precipitation (in.)	6.6	5.8	7.6	7.3	10.3	8.6	7.2	10.7	11.3	9.2	7.8	6.7	55.4
Minimum Precipitation (in.)	0.4	0.2	1.0	0.3	0.8	0.5	0.9	0.8	0.6	trace	0.2	0.4	28.9
Maximum 24-hr. Precipitation (in.)	1.6	2.1	2.2	2.4	3.1	4.3	3.5	4.7	5.5	4.1	2.6	2.9	5.5
Days With ≥ 0.1" Precipitation	6	5	7	7	8	7	7	6	6	5	6	6	76
Days With ≥ 1.0" Precipitation	1	1	1	1	1	1	1	1	1	1	1	1	12
Mean Snowfall (in.)	7.5	6.2	3.5	0.4	trace	trace	0.0	trace	0.0	trace	0.8	2.4	20.8
Maximum Snowfall (in.)	29	28	16	4	trace	0	0	0	0	1	11	24	55
Maximum 24-hr. Snowfall (in.)	11	23	14	3	trace	0	0	0	0	1	11	11	23
Days With ≥ 1.0" Snow Depth	8	5	2	0	0	0	0	0	0	0	0	2	17
Thunderstorm Days	< 1	< 1	1	2	4	6	6	5	2	1	1	< 1	28
Foggy Days	13	10	12	10	14	16	19	20	18	14	12	12	170
Predominant Sky Cover	OVR	OVR	OVR	OVR	OVR	OVR	OVR	OVR	OVR	OVR	OVR	OVR	OVR
Mean Relative Humidity 7am (%)	77	77	78	77	82	84	86	89	89	88	82	78	82
Mean Relative Humidity 4pm (%)	57	52	49	46	53	54	54	55	55	52	54	57	53
Mean Dewpoint (°F)	21	22	30	39	52	61	65	64	58	45	35	26	43
Prevailing Wind Direction	NW	NW	NW	NW	S	S	S	S	S	S	NW	NW	NW
Prevailing Wind Speed (mph)	13	13	13	13	8	7	7	7	7	7	12	13	10
Maximum Wind Gust (mph)	62	53	61	68	59	78	78	68	54	52	56	62	78

Washington DC National Airport

Washington lies at the western edge of the mid Atlantic Coastal Plain, about 50 miles east of the Blue Ridge Mountains and 35 miles west of Chesapeake Bay, adjacent to the Potomac and Anacostia Rivers. Elevations range from a few feet above sea level to about 400 feet in parts of the northwest section of the city.

Observations have been kept continuously since November 1870. Since June 1941 the official observations have been taken at Washington National Airport.

National Airport is located at the center of the urban heat island. As a result, low temperatures are the highest for the area. Differences between the airport and suburban locations are often 10 to 15 degrees. There is less variation in the high temperatures.

Summers are warm and humid and winters are cold, but not severe. Periods of pleasant weather often occur in the spring and fall. The summertime temperature is in the upper 80s and the winter is in the upper 20s. Precipitation is rather uniformly distributed throughout the year.

Thunderstorms can occur at any time but are most frequent during the late spring and summer. The storms are most often accompanied by downpours and gusty winds, but are not usually severe.

Tornadoes, which infrequently occur, have resulted in significant damage. Severe hailstorms have occurred in the spring.

Tropical storms can bring heavy rain, high winds and flooding, but extensive damage from wind and tidal flooding is rare. Wind gusts of nearly 100 mph and rainfall over seven inches have occurred during the passage of tropical storms and hurricanes.

Major flooding of the Potomac River can result from heavy rains over the basin, occasionally augmented by snowmelt, and above normal tides associated with hurricanes or severe storms along the coast. Flooding may also occur after a cold winter when the Potomac may be blocked with ice.

Although a snowfall of 10 inches or more in 24 hours is unusual, several notable falls of more than 25 inches have occurred. Normal snowfall during the winter season is 18 inches.

The average date of the last freezing temperature in the spring is April 1 and the average date for the first freezing temperature in the fall is November 10.

Washington DC National Airport *Arlington County*   Elevation: 9 ft.   Latitude: 38° 52' N   Longitude: 77° 02' W

	JAN	FEB	MAR	APR	MAY	JUN	JUL	AUG	SEP	OCT	NOV	DEC	YEAR
Mean Maximum Temp. (°F)	43.1	47.1	56.0	66.8	75.9	84.3	88.7	86.9	80.1	68.7	58.1	48.1	67.0
Mean Temp. (°F)	35.6	38.7	46.9	56.7	66.3	75.1	80.0	78.2	71.5	59.7	49.6	40.6	58.2
Mean Minimum Temp. (°F)	28.0	30.3	37.7	46.6	56.6	65.9	71.2	69.6	62.9	50.6	41.1	33.1	49.5
Extreme Maximum Temp. (°F)	76	79	89	95	99	101	104	105	101	91	86	79	105
Extreme Minimum Temp. (°F)	-5	5	14	24	38	47	54	49	44	30	18	3	-5
Days Maximum Temp. ≥ 90°F	0	0	0	0	2	7	15	10	4	0	0	0	38
Days Maximum Temp. ≤ 32°F	5	2	0	0	0	0	0	0	0	0	0	2	9
Days Minimum Temp. ≤ 32°F	21	17	8	1	0	0	0	0	0	0	4	13	64
Days Minimum Temp. ≤ 0°F	0	0	0	0	0	0	0	0	0	0	0	0	0
Heating Degree Days (base 65°F)	904	736	559	264	68	4	0	1	18	193	459	748	3,954
Cooling Degree Days (base 65°F)	0	0	5	21	117	320	488	414	213	35	2	0	1,615
Mean Precipitation (in.)	3.12	2.65	3.56	2.78	3.81	3.06	3.74	3.35	3.68	3.29	3.17	3.09	39.30
Maximum Precipitation (in.)	7.1	5.7	8.4	6.9	10.7	11.5	12.9	14.3	12.4	8.6	6.7	6.5	57.5
Minimum Precipitation (in.)	0.3	0.4	0.7	trace	0.8	0.9	0.9	0.5	0.2	trace	0.3	0.2	26.9
Maximum 24-hr. Precipitation (in.)	1.8	1.9	2.3	3.0	3.2	6.1	4.7	5.4	4.8	3.4	2.6	2.8	6.1
Days With ≥ 0.1" Precipitation	6	6	7	6	7	6	7	5	5	5	6	6	72
Days With ≥ 1.0" Precipitation	1	0	1	0	1	1	1	1	1	1	1	1	10
Mean Snowfall (in.)	5.6	5.2	1.6	trace	trace	trace	trace	trace	0.0	trace	0.7	1.5	14.6
Maximum Snowfall (in.)	21	31	17	1	0	0	0	0	0	trace	12	16	44
Maximum 24-hr. Snowfall (in.)	12	16	7	1	0	0	0	0	0	trace	12	11	16
Days With ≥ 1.0" Snow Depth	5	4	1	0	0	0	0	0	0	0	0	1	11
Thunderstorm Days	< 1	< 1	1	3	5	6	7	5	2	1	1	< 1	31
Foggy Days	11	10	10	9	12	10	10	11	12	13	11	11	130
Predominant Sky Cover	OVR	OVR	OVR	OVR	OVR	OVR	OVR	OVR	OVR	OVR	OVR	OVR	OVR
Mean Relative Humidity 7am (%)	71	70	70	70	75	76	77	81	82	81	76	72	75
Mean Relative Humidity 4pm (%)	55	50	47	46	51	52	53	54	55	53	53	55	52
Mean Dewpoint (°F)	23	24	31	40	52	61	66	65	59	48	37	27	45
Prevailing Wind Direction	NW	NW	NW	S	S	S	S	S	S	S	S	NW	S
Prevailing Wind Speed (mph)	14	14	14	9	9	9	9	9	9	9	9	14	10
Maximum Wind Gust (mph)	71	69	73	66	64	66	83	67	64	70	66	67	83

Abingdon 3 S *Washington County*   Elevation: 1,919 ft.   Latitude: 36° 40' N   Longitude: 81° 58' W

	JAN	FEB	MAR	APR	MAY	JUN	JUL	AUG	SEP	OCT	NOV	DEC	YEAR
Mean Maximum Temp. (°F)	45.2	49.6	58.7	67.9	75.4	82.1	85.4	84.3	78.4	68.9	57.9	48.7	66.9
Mean Temp. (°F)	34.8	38.0	45.8	53.8	61.8	69.4	73.0	71.8	65.5	55.1	45.6	37.8	54.4
Mean Minimum Temp. (°F)	24.4	26.4	32.8	39.6	48.2	56.5	60.5	59.2	52.5	41.2	33.2	26.9	41.8
Extreme Maximum Temp. (°F)	75	78	85	91	91	96	99	100	97	86	81	78	100
Extreme Minimum Temp. (°F)	-21	-17	-6	12	28	35	42	37	28	18	6	-12	-21
Days Maximum Temp. ≥ 90°F	0	0	0	0	0	2	6	4	1	0	0	0	13
Days Maximum Temp. ≤ 32°F	4	2	1	0	0	0	0	0	0	0	0	3	10
Days Minimum Temp. ≤ 32°F	24	21	16	8	1	0	0	0	0	6	15	21	112
Days Minimum Temp. ≤ 0°F	1	0	0	0	0	0	0	0	0	0	0	0	1
Heating Degree Days (base 65°F)	930	757	590	337	137	21	2	3	71	311	577	836	4,572
Cooling Degree Days (base 65°F)	0	0	1	8	48	169	274	225	96	11	0	0	832
Mean Precipitation (in.)	4.10	4.06	4.46	3.75	4.95	4.01	4.78	3.65	3.69	2.84	3.26	4.01	47.56
Days With ≥ 0.1" Precipitation	9	9	10	8	10	8	9	7	7	6	7	8	98
Days With ≥ 1.0" Precipitation	1	1	1	1	1	1	1	1	1	1	1	1	12
Mean Snowfall (in.)	5.9	4.9	1.8	0.2	0.0	0.0	0.0	0.0	0.0	trace	0.5	2.1	15.4
Days With ≥ 1.0" Snow Depth	5	4	1	0	0	0	0	0	0	0	0	2	12

Appomattox *Appomattox County*   Elevation: 908 ft.   Latitude: 37° 21' N   Longitude: 78° 50' W

	JAN	FEB	MAR	APR	MAY	JUN	JUL	AUG	SEP	OCT	NOV	DEC	YEAR
Mean Maximum Temp. (°F)	44.7	48.4	57.1	67.9	75.4	83.0	87.2	85.5	79.2	68.6	58.6	49.1	67.1
Mean Temp. (°F)	34.5	37.5	45.4	55.1	63.3	71.5	76.0	74.5	68.0	56.0	47.1	38.6	55.6
Mean Minimum Temp. (°F)	24.3	26.5	33.7	42.3	51.0	60.0	64.8	63.4	56.8	43.4	35.6	28.1	44.2
Extreme Maximum Temp. (°F)	73	79	89	93	93	97	103	103	98	90	83	79	103
Extreme Minimum Temp. (°F)	-14	-7	5	23	27	39	45	44	34	23	9	-8	-14
Days Maximum Temp. ≥ 90°F	0	0	0	1	0	5	11	8	3	0	0	0	28
Days Maximum Temp. ≤ 32°F	4	2	0	0	0	0	0	0	0	0	0	2	8
Days Minimum Temp. ≤ 32°F	25	21	14	4	0	0	0	0	0	3	12	21	100
Days Minimum Temp. ≤ 0°F	1	0	0	0	0	0	0	0	0	0	0	0	1
Heating Degree Days (base 65°F)	939	772	606	307	114	16	1	2	42	286	531	811	4,427
Cooling Degree Days (base 65°F)	0	0	4	15	68	231	372	307	142	18	1	0	1,158
Mean Precipitation (in.)	3.45	3.11	4.30	3.58	4.61	3.29	4.58	3.84	4.30	3.91	3.66	3.05	45.68
Days With ≥ 0.1" Precipitation	6	6	7	7	8	6	7	6	5	6	6	6	76
Days With ≥ 1.0" Precipitation	1	1	1	1	1	1	1	1	1	1	1	1	12
Mean Snowfall (in.)	5.5	4.9	1.3	0.1	0.0	0.0	0.0	0.0	0.0	0.0	0.3	1.3	13.4
Days With ≥ 1.0" Snow Depth	4	2	0	0	0	0	0	0	0	0	0	0	6

Ashland *Hanover County*   Elevation: 219 ft.   Latitude: 37° 45' N   Longitude: 77° 29' W

	JAN	FEB	MAR	APR	MAY	JUN	JUL	AUG	SEP	OCT	NOV	DEC	YEAR
Mean Maximum Temp. (°F)	45.6	50.0	59.4	70.1	76.3	83.4	87.3	85.5	79.5	68.5	59.4	49.8	67.9
Mean Temp. (°F)	35.6	39.0	47.3	56.8	64.6	72.5	76.9	75.3	69.0	57.3	48.1	39.7	56.9
Mean Minimum Temp. (°F)	25.6	28.0	35.1	43.4	52.9	61.6	66.5	65.1	58.5	46.1	36.8	29.6	45.8
Extreme Maximum Temp. (°F)	76	82	90	94	95	100	100	103	102	91	84	80	103
Extreme Minimum Temp. (°F)	-9	-11	9	18	31	40	49	43	34	25	11	-1	-11
Days Maximum Temp. ≥ 90°F	0	0	0	1	1	5	11	7	3	0	0	0	28
Days Maximum Temp. ≤ 32°F	4	2	0	0	0	0	0	0	0	0	0	2	8
Days Minimum Temp. ≤ 32°F	24	20	14	4	0	0	0	0	0	2	11	20	95
Days Minimum Temp. ≤ 0°F	0	0	0	0	0	0	0	0	0	0	0	0	0
Heating Degree Days (base 65°F)	904	728	549	266	91	10	0	2	36	256	504	777	4,123
Cooling Degree Days (base 65°F)	0	0	6	25	92	252	390	323	161	26	2	1	1,278
Mean Precipitation (in.)	3.65	3.28	4.25	3.18	4.18	3.22	4.23	3.85	3.97	3.54	3.35	3.38	44.08
Days With ≥ 0.1" Precipitation	7	7	8	6	7	6	7	6	6	5	6	6	77
Days With ≥ 1.0" Precipitation	1	1	1	1	1	1	1	1	1	1	1	1	12
Mean Snowfall (in.)	6.3	6.2	1.8	0.2	trace	0.0	0.0	0.0	0.0	trace	0.7	2.8	18.0
Days With ≥ 1.0" Snow Depth	5	4	1	0	0	0	0	0	0	0	0	2	12

Back Bay Wildlife Refuge *Virginia Beach County*   Elevation: 9 ft.   Latitude: 36° 40' N   Longitude: 75° 55' W

	JAN	FEB	MAR	APR	MAY	JUN	JUL	AUG	SEP	OCT	NOV	DEC	YEAR
Mean Maximum Temp. (°F)	na	52.1	58.4	67.4	74.9	83.1	87.1	85.5	81.5	na	na	na	na
Mean Temp. (°F)	na	42.5	49.0	57.4	66.1	74.5	na	77.7	73.6	na	na	na	na
Mean Minimum Temp. (°F)	na	33.4	39.7	47.6	57.3	65.9	na	69.8	65.8	na	na	na	na
Extreme Maximum Temp. (°F)	75	81	87	94	98	98	100	102	99	93	83	81	102
Extreme Minimum Temp. (°F)	-11	10	15	26	32	47	52	46	44	30	22	5	-11
Days Maximum Temp. ≥ 90°F	0	0	0	0	1	6	12	7	2	0	0	0	28
Days Maximum Temp. ≤ 32°F	1	0	0	0	0	0	0	0	0	0	0	0	1
Days Minimum Temp. ≤ 32°F	13	12	4	1	0	0	0	0	0	0	2	7	39
Days Minimum Temp. ≤ 0°F	0	0	0	0	0	0	0	0	0	0	0	0	0
Heating Degree Days (base 65°F)	na	627	491	244	63	3	0	0	4	na	na	na	na
Cooling Degree Days (base 65°F)	na	1	na	24	na	311	na	397	na	na	na	na	na
Mean Precipitation (in.)	4.20	3.51	3.95	2.77	3.91	3.34	4.51	5.17	4.38	3.60	3.16	3.16	45.66
Days With ≥ 0.1" Precipitation	6	5	6	4	5	5	6	6	5	4	5	5	62
Days With ≥ 1.0" Precipitation	1	1	1	0	1	1	1	1	1	1	1	1	11
Mean Snowfall (in.)	1.4	1.9	0.3	trace	0.0	0.0	0.0	0.0	0.0	0.0	trace	trace	3.6
Days With ≥ 1.0" Snow Depth	0	0	0	0	0	0	0	0	0	0	0	0	0

Bedford *Bedford County*   Elevation: 974 ft.   Latitude: 37° 21' N   Longitude: 79° 31' W

	JAN	FEB	MAR	APR	MAY	JUN	JUL	AUG	SEP	OCT	NOV	DEC	YEAR
Mean Maximum Temp. (°F)	45.5	49.3	59.1	69.6	75.5	82.1	85.8	84.1	77.9	67.7	58.5	49.5	67.1
Mean Temp. (°F)	36.3	39.0	47.5	57.0	64.2	71.6	75.6	74.1	68.0	57.1	47.5	40.2	56.5
Mean Minimum Temp. (°F)	27.1	28.7	35.8	44.3	52.8	61.0	65.4	63.9	58.0	46.4	37.6	30.8	46.0
Extreme Maximum Temp. (°F)	74	79	87	94	94	96	99	100	97	86	84	83	100
Extreme Minimum Temp. (°F)	-10	-1	7	22	33	39	45	42	34	22	14	-6	-10
Days Maximum Temp. ≥ 90°F	0	0	0	0	0	3	8	5	1	0	0	0	17
Days Maximum Temp. ≤ 32°F	3	2	0	0	0	0	0	0	0	0	0	2	7
Days Minimum Temp. ≤ 32°F	22	19	11	2	0	0	0	0	0	2	10	17	83
Days Minimum Temp. ≤ 0°F	0	0	0	0	0	0	0	0	0	0	0	0	0
Heating Degree Days (base 65°F)	883	728	540	257	93	11	1	3	42	255	503	763	4,079
Cooling Degree Days (base 65°F)	0	0	4	25	72	225	356	290	130	16	1	0	1,119
Mean Precipitation (in.)	3.43	3.19	3.72	3.73	4.60	4.14	4.41	3.56	3.80	3.81	3.34	3.13	44.86
Days With ≥ 0.1" Precipitation	7	6	7	6	8	7	8	6	6	6	6	6	79
Days With ≥ 1.0" Precipitation	1	1	1	1	1	1	1	1	1	1	1	1	12
Mean Snowfall (in.)	5.5	5.4	2.3	trace	0.0	0.0	0.0	0.0	0.0	trace	0.4	1.5	15.1
Days With ≥ 1.0" Snow Depth	na	na	0	0	0	0	0	0	0	0	0	0	na

Big Meadows *Madison County*   Elevation: 3,536 ft.   Latitude: 38° 31' N   Longitude: 78° 26' W

	JAN	FEB	MAR	APR	MAY	JUN	JUL	AUG	SEP	OCT	NOV	DEC	YEAR
Mean Maximum Temp. (°F)	34.6	37.4	45.1	55.9	64.3	71.5	75.5	73.6	67.8	57.7	48.1	39.4	55.9
Mean Temp. (°F)	25.6	28.2	35.5	45.5	54.4	62.1	66.2	64.5	58.7	48.1	39.2	30.7	46.6
Mean Minimum Temp. (°F)	16.6	18.9	25.9	35.1	44.5	52.6	56.8	55.4	49.5	38.5	30.3	21.9	37.2
Extreme Maximum Temp. (°F)	62	65	77	85	88	87	95	92	86	84	72	67	95
Extreme Minimum Temp. (°F)	-29	-11	-6	9	18	31	34	31	27	12	-1	-15	-29
Days Maximum Temp. ≥ 90°F	0	0	0	0	0	0	0	0	0	0	0	0	0
Days Maximum Temp. ≤ 32°F	13	10	5	1	0	0	0	0	0	0	3	9	41
Days Minimum Temp. ≤ 32°F	28	24	22	13	3	0	0	0	1	9	18	25	143
Days Minimum Temp. ≤ 0°F	3	2	0	0	0	0	0	0	0	0	0	1	6
Heating Degree Days (base 65°F)	1,214	1,033	907	577	331	118	43	66	204	517	768	1,057	6,835
Cooling Degree Days (base 65°F)	0	0	0	1	10	41	92	54	20	1	0	0	219
Mean Precipitation (in.)	4.09	3.44	3.91	4.12	5.09	5.03	4.99	4.32	5.78	5.39	4.99	3.92	55.07
Days With ≥ 0.1" Precipitation	7	6	7	7	8	7	8	7	6	6	6	6	81
Days With ≥ 1.0" Precipitation	1	1	1	1	1	1	1	1	1	2	1	1	13
Mean Snowfall (in.)	11.9	11.2	7.1	2.0	trace	0.0	0.0	0.0	0.0	0.9	3.4	6.4	42.9
Days With ≥ 1.0" Snow Depth	13	14	9	2	0	0	0	0	0	0	2	8	48

Blacksburg WSO *Montgomery County*   Elevation: 2,007 ft.   Latitude: 37° 12' N   Longitude: 80° 24' W

	JAN	FEB	MAR	APR	MAY	JUN	JUL	AUG	SEP	OCT	NOV	DEC	YEAR
Mean Maximum Temp. (°F)	40.9	45.0	53.3	63.4	71.7	78.7	82.8	81.6	75.9	65.4	55.0	44.8	63.2
Mean Temp. (°F)	30.6	33.9	41.6	50.7	59.2	67.1	71.3	69.9	63.6	52.2	43.1	34.3	51.5
Mean Minimum Temp. (°F)	20.2	22.6	29.9	38.0	46.6	55.3	59.7	58.3	51.4	38.9	31.1	23.6	39.6
Extreme Maximum Temp. (°F)	73	75	85	86	89	94	97	99	94	85	78	75	99
Extreme Minimum Temp. (°F)	-18	-12	3	14	23	30	41	36	22	18	0	-10	-18
Days Maximum Temp. ≥ 90°F	0	0	0	0	0	0	3	2	1	0	0	0	6
Days Maximum Temp. ≤ 32°F	7	4	1	0	0	0	0	0	0	0	1	5	18
Days Minimum Temp. ≤ 32°F	28	24	19	9	2	0	0	0	0	9	18	26	135
Days Minimum Temp. ≤ 0°F	2	1	0	0	0	0	0	0	0	0	0	1	4
Heating Degree Days (base 65°F)	1,062	874	720	426	199	44	8	11	101	394	653	948	5,440
Cooling Degree Days (base 65°F)	0	0	1	5	27	125	233	174	67	5	0	0	637
Mean Precipitation (in.)	3.24	3.03	3.89	3.83	4.39	3.70	4.26	3.72	3.37	3.35	3.05	2.92	42.75
Days With ≥ 0.1" Precipitation	7	7	9	8	9	8	9	7	6	6	7	7	90
Days With ≥ 1.0" Precipitation	1	0	1	1	1	1	1	1	1	1	1	0	10
Mean Snowfall (in.)	7.0	6.3	3.6	1.2	trace	0.0	0.0	0.0	0.0	trace	0.8	3.5	22.4
Days With ≥ 1.0" Snow Depth	8	7	2	0	0	0	0	0	0	0	1	4	22

Buchanan *Botetourt County*   Elevation: 879 ft.   Latitude: 37° 32' N   Longitude: 79° 41' W

	JAN	FEB	MAR	APR	MAY	JUN	JUL	AUG	SEP	OCT	NOV	DEC	YEAR
Mean Maximum Temp. (°F)	45.2	50.7	59.6	71.2	78.1	84.3	88.1	86.9	80.4	70.3	58.7	49.4	68.6
Mean Temp. (°F)	35.5	39.2	47.1	56.6	64.7	72.0	76.1	75.0	68.6	57.6	46.9	39.1	56.5
Mean Minimum Temp. (°F)	25.7	27.6	34.5	41.9	51.3	59.7	64.1	63.0	56.7	44.8	35.0	28.8	44.4
Extreme Maximum Temp. (°F)	76	80	90	95	95	98	104	102	98	88	85	80	104
Extreme Minimum Temp. (°F)	-11	-13	1	22	24	37	48	41	33	22	10	-5	-13
Days Maximum Temp. ≥ 90°F	0	0	0	1	2	6	13	10	4	0	0	0	36
Days Maximum Temp. ≤ 32°F	3	2	0	0	0	0	0	0	0	0	0	1	6
Days Minimum Temp. ≤ 32°F	24	20	13	5	0	0	0	0	0	3	13	20	98
Days Minimum Temp. ≤ 0°F	0	0	0	0	0	0	0	0	0	0	0	0	0
Heating Degree Days (base 65°F)	908	724	551	263	86	10	0	1	39	241	539	796	4,158
Cooling Degree Days (base 65°F)	0	0	3	20	91	250	380	327	156	21	0	0	1,248
Mean Precipitation (in.)	3.62	3.15	3.93	3.37	4.07	3.72	4.56	3.35	3.75	3.60	3.05	2.96	43.13
Days With ≥ 0.1" Precipitation	7	6	8	7	8	7	8	6	6	6	6	6	81
Days With ≥ 1.0" Precipitation	1	1	1	1	1	1	1	1	1	1	1	1	12
Mean Snowfall (in.)	4.6	4.6	2.5	0.3	0.0	0.0	0.0	0.0	0.0	trace	1.0	2.9	15.9
Days With ≥ 1.0" Snow Depth	4	4	1	0	0	0	0	0	0	0	0	2	11

Burkes Garden *Tazewell County*   Elevation: 3,297 ft.   Latitude: 37° 05' N   Longitude: 81° 20' W

	JAN	FEB	MAR	APR	MAY	JUN	JUL	AUG	SEP	OCT	NOV	DEC	YEAR
Mean Maximum Temp. (°F)	39.2	42.6	51.4	60.9	68.6	75.2	78.9	77.7	72.2	62.3	52.1	43.5	60.4
Mean Temp. (°F)	29.7	32.3	40.4	48.3	56.6	63.8	67.7	66.2	60.3	49.6	40.8	33.5	49.1
Mean Minimum Temp. (°F)	20.1	22.0	29.4	35.6	44.5	52.5	56.5	54.7	48.3	36.9	29.7	23.5	37.8
Extreme Maximum Temp. (°F)	64	72	78	81	83	89	93	94	90	78	73	70	94
Extreme Minimum Temp. (°F)	-26	-24	-2	3	19	29	34	31	21	11	-1	-22	-26
Days Maximum Temp. ≥ 90°F	0	0	0	0	0	0	0	0	0	0	0	0	0
Days Maximum Temp. ≤ 32°F	9	6	2	0	0	0	0	0	0	1	2	5	25
Days Minimum Temp. ≤ 32°F	26	23	20	12	3	0	0	0	1	11	18	25	139
Days Minimum Temp. ≤ 0°F	3	1	0	0	0	0	0	0	0	0	0	1	5
Heating Degree Days (base 65°F)	1,089	916	755	497	263	75	22	33	157	470	718	970	5,965
Cooling Degree Days (base 65°F)	0	0	0	1	8	52	124	79	23	1	0	0	288
Mean Precipitation (in.)	3.87	3.40	4.09	3.56	4.86	4.29	4.25	4.03	3.44	3.23	3.17	3.44	45.63
Days With ≥ 0.1" Precipitation	8	7	9	8	10	9	8	8	7	6	7	7	94
Days With ≥ 1.0" Precipitation	1	1	1	1	1	1	1	1	1	1	1	1	12
Mean Snowfall (in.)	14.8	13.9	8.2	2.9	trace	0.0	0.0	0.0	0.0	0.4	2.9	8.7	51.8
Days With ≥ 1.0" Snow Depth	12	11	4	1	0	0	0	0	0	0	2	7	37

Camp Pickett *Nottoway County*   Elevation: 328 ft.   Latitude: 37° 02' N   Longitude: 77° 58' W

	JAN	FEB	MAR	APR	MAY	JUN	JUL	AUG	SEP	OCT	NOV	DEC	YEAR
Mean Maximum Temp. (°F)	47.1	51.0	59.4	69.6	77.1	84.4	88.5	86.8	80.9	70.3	61.2	50.9	68.9
Mean Temp. (°F)	35.6	38.4	46.3	55.6	64.0	72.2	76.9	75.1	68.5	56.6	48.0	39.1	56.4
Mean Minimum Temp. (°F)	24.1	25.9	33.1	41.5	50.9	59.9	65.2	63.5	56.2	42.8	34.7	27.3	43.8
Extreme Maximum Temp. (°F)	78	82	89	95	95	99	102	103	101	91	86	80	103
Extreme Minimum Temp. (°F)	-12	-9	6	11	31	37	41	41	35	22	13	-1	-12
Days Maximum Temp. ≥ 90°F	0	0	0	1	1	7	14	10	3	0	0	0	36
Days Maximum Temp. ≤ 32°F	3	2	0	0	0	0	0	0	0	0	0	2	7
Days Minimum Temp. ≤ 32°F	25	22	16	6	0	0	0	0	0	5	14	23	111
Days Minimum Temp. ≤ 0°F	1	0	0	0	0	0	0	0	0	0	0	0	1
Heating Degree Days (base 65°F)	903	743	578	298	107	14	0	3	42	275	506	797	4,266
Cooling Degree Days (base 65°F)	0	0	5	21	84	243	393	319	155	23	2	1	1,246
Mean Precipitation (in.)	4.37	3.21	4.43	3.58	3.94	3.51	4.46	4.22	4.18	3.74	3.23	3.29	46.16
Days With ≥ 0.1" Precipitation	8	6	8	6	7	6	7	7	6	5	6	6	78
Days With ≥ 1.0" Precipitation	1	1	1	1	1	1	1	1	1	1	1	1	12
Mean Snowfall (in.)	3.3	3.3	0.9	trace	0.0	0.0	0.0	0.0	0.0	0.0	0.1	1.1	8.7
Days With ≥ 1.0" Snow Depth	3	2	0	0	0	0	0	0	0	0	0	2	7

Charlotte Court House *Charlotte County*   Elevation: 587 ft.   Latitude: 37° 04' N   Longitude: 78° 42' W

	JAN	FEB	MAR	APR	MAY	JUN	JUL	AUG	SEP	OCT	NOV	DEC	YEAR
Mean Maximum Temp. (°F)	46.2	49.9	58.1	69.0	76.2	83.7	87.6	86.4	80.4	69.7	60.2	50.5	68.2
Mean Temp. (°F)	35.7	38.5	46.3	55.9	63.9	72.2	76.4	75.0	68.9	57.0	48.2	39.8	56.5
Mean Minimum Temp. (°F)	25.2	27.1	34.3	42.8	51.7	60.5	65.2	63.8	57.3	44.2	36.1	29.0	44.8
Extreme Maximum Temp. (°F)	78	79	86	94	93	99	103	103	100	91	87	80	103
Extreme Minimum Temp. (°F)	-8	-3	10	19	30	36	44	39	34	20	9	-1	-8
Days Maximum Temp. ≥ 90°F	0	0	0	1	1	5	11	9	4	0	0	0	31
Days Maximum Temp. ≤ 32°F	3	2	0	0	0	0	0	0	0	0	0	2	7
Days Minimum Temp. ≤ 32°F	24	21	13	4	0	0	0	0	0	4	12	20	98
Days Minimum Temp. ≤ 0°F	0	0	0	0	0	0	0	0	0	0	0	0	0
Heating Degree Days (base 65°F)	901	741	576	288	104	13	1	3	40	265	500	776	4,208
Cooling Degree Days (base 65°F)	0	0	4	23	83	248	384	319	163	27	1	0	1,252
Mean Precipitation (in.)	3.99	3.36	4.15	3.48	4.04	3.30	4.30	3.82	4.18	4.10	3.44	3.31	45.47
Days With ≥ 0.1" Precipitation	7	7	8	6	7	6	7	6	6	5	5	6	76
Days With ≥ 1.0" Precipitation	1	1	1	1	1	1	1	1	1	1	1	1	12
Mean Snowfall (in.)	2.5	2.3	1.9	trace	0.0	0.0	0.0	0.0	0.0	trace	0.2	1.1	8.0
Days With ≥ 1.0" Snow Depth	1	1	0	0	0	0	0	0	0	0	0	1	3

Charlottesville 2 W *Albemarle County*   Elevation: 869 ft.   Latitude: 38° 02' N   Longitude: 78° 31' W

	JAN	FEB	MAR	APR	MAY	JUN	JUL	AUG	SEP	OCT	NOV	DEC	YEAR
Mean Maximum Temp. (°F)	44.3	48.2	57.0	68.5	75.6	83.2	87.3	85.5	79.3	68.6	58.5	48.2	67.0
Mean Temp. (°F)	35.2	38.3	46.4	56.8	64.8	72.5	76.7	74.9	68.9	57.9	48.6	39.2	56.7
Mean Minimum Temp. (°F)	26.1	28.4	35.7	45.1	54.0	61.8	65.9	64.2	58.5	47.3	38.7	30.2	46.3
Extreme Maximum Temp. (°F)	78	81	92	94	96	100	103	105	98	91	85	83	105
Extreme Minimum Temp. (°F)	-10	1	10	22	35	44	49	44	35	26	14	-3	-10
Days Maximum Temp. ≥ 90°F	0	0	0	1	1	5	11	8	4	0	0	0	30
Days Maximum Temp. ≤ 32°F	5	3	0	0	0	0	0	0	0	0	0	2	10
Days Minimum Temp. ≤ 32°F	24	19	11	2	0	0	0	0	0	1	8	19	84
Days Minimum Temp. ≤ 0°F	0	0	0	0	0	0	0	0	0	0	0	0	0
Heating Degree Days (base 65°F)	917	750	578	269	92	11	1	2	37	237	492	793	4,179
Cooling Degree Days (base 65°F)	0	0	7	30	93	254	384	308	155	26	2	1	1,260
Mean Precipitation (in.)	3.69	3.38	4.13	3.30	4.85	4.14	5.08	4.11	4.72	4.50	3.87	3.21	48.98
Days With ≥ 0.1" Precipitation	6	6	7	6	8	6	8	7	6	5	6	6	77
Days With ≥ 1.0" Precipitation	1	1	1	1	1	1	1	1	1	1	1	1	12
Mean Snowfall (in.)	5.3	6.0	3.0	0.3	0.0	0.0	0.0	0.0	0.0	0.1	0.9	3.1	18.7
Days With ≥ 1.0" Snow Depth	6	5	2	0	0	0	0	0	0	0	0	1	14

Chatham *Pittsylvania County*   Elevation: 639 ft.   Latitude: 36° 49' N   Longitude: 79° 25' W

	JAN	FEB	MAR	APR	MAY	JUN	JUL	AUG	SEP	OCT	NOV	DEC	YEAR
Mean Maximum Temp. (°F)	46.3	50.5	58.8	69.2	76.5	83.6	87.4	85.9	79.9	69.5	60.1	50.7	68.2
Mean Temp. (°F)	34.6	37.2	44.8	53.7	62.1	70.4	74.7	72.9	66.7	54.8	45.8	38.1	54.6
Mean Minimum Temp. (°F)	22.6	23.9	30.7	38.2	47.8	57.0	61.9	60.1	53.2	39.9	31.6	25.4	41.0
Extreme Maximum Temp. (°F)	76	81	88	92	99	99	102	102	99	92	85	79	102
Extreme Minimum Temp. (°F)	-9	-3	0	17	25	33	43	38	26	19	10	-3	-9
Days Maximum Temp. ≥ 90°F	0	0	0	0	1	5	12	9	3	0	0	0	30
Days Maximum Temp. ≤ 32°F	3	2	0	0	0	0	0	0	0	0	0	1	6
Days Minimum Temp. ≤ 32°F	26	23	19	10	2	0	0	0	0	9	18	23	130
Days Minimum Temp. ≤ 0°F	1	0	0	0	0	0	0	0	0	0	0	0	1
Heating Degree Days (base 65°F)	935	780	624	345	136	22	2	6	62	320	571	827	4,630
Cooling Degree Days (base 65°F)	0	0	2	9	54	190	319	254	104	11	0	0	943
Mean Precipitation (in.)	3.74	3.26	4.39	3.67	4.06	3.66	4.17	3.41	4.34	3.82	3.34	3.32	45.18
Days With ≥ 0.1" Precipitation	7	7	8	7	8	6	7	6	5	5	6	6	78
Days With ≥ 1.0" Precipitation	1	1	1	1	1	1	1	1	1	1	1	1	12
Mean Snowfall (in.)	2.7	2.0	0.9	trace	0.0	0.0	0.0	0.0	0.0	trace	0.2	0.6	6.4
Days With ≥ 1.0" Snow Depth	2	1	0	0	0	0	0	0	0	0	0	0	3

Corbin *Caroline County*   Elevation: 219 ft.   Latitude: 38° 12' N   Longitude: 77° 22' W

	JAN	FEB	MAR	APR	MAY	JUN	JUL	AUG	SEP	OCT	NOV	DEC	YEAR
Mean Maximum Temp. (°F)	43.8	47.5	56.1	66.9	75.1	82.9	87.2	85.7	79.6	68.5	58.6	48.5	66.7
Mean Temp. (°F)	33.9	37.2	45.2	54.7	63.5	71.9	76.4	74.9	68.6	56.7	47.5	38.7	55.8
Mean Minimum Temp. (°F)	23.9	26.8	34.2	42.4	51.9	60.8	65.6	64.2	57.5	45.0	36.5	28.8	44.8
Extreme Maximum Temp. (°F)	76	80	90	93	96	99	103	104	100	92	86	80	104
Extreme Minimum Temp. (°F)	-8	-11	9	21	29	36	43	43	32	23	11	-1	-11
Days Maximum Temp. ≥ 90°F	0	0	0	0	1	5	11	9	3	0	0	0	29
Days Maximum Temp. ≤ 32°F	5	3	0	0	0	0	0	0	0	0	0	2	10
Days Minimum Temp. ≤ 32°F	25	21	14	5	0	0	0	0	0	3	12	21	101
Days Minimum Temp. ≤ 0°F	1	0	0	0	0	0	0	0	0	0	0	0	1
Heating Degree Days (base 65°F)	958	780	613	323	119	17	1	3	45	272	521	810	4,462
Cooling Degree Days (base 65°F)	0	0	7	19	82	238	378	311	154	25	3	1	1,218
Mean Precipitation (in.)	3.66	3.22	4.24	3.23	4.00	3.45	4.32	3.70	3.83	3.99	3.46	3.32	44.42
Days With ≥ 0.1" Precipitation	7	6	8	6	7	6	7	5	6	6	6	6	76
Days With ≥ 1.0" Precipitation	1	1	1	1	1	1	1	1	1	1	1	1	12
Mean Snowfall (in.)	5.1	4.5	1.8	0.2	0.0	0.0	0.0	0.0	0.0	trace	0.5	1.6	13.7
Days With ≥ 1.0" Snow Depth	5	3	1	0	0	0	0	0	0	0	0	2	11

Dale Enterprise *Rockingham County*   Elevation: 1,397 ft.   Latitude: 38° 27' N   Longitude: 78° 56' W

	JAN	FEB	MAR	APR	MAY	JUN	JUL	AUG	SEP	OCT	NOV	DEC	YEAR
Mean Maximum Temp. (°F)	41.5	45.8	54.8	65.5	74.3	82.2	86.1	84.3	77.8	66.7	55.5	45.9	65.0
Mean Temp. (°F)	31.8	35.2	43.2	52.6	61.6	69.9	74.0	72.2	65.8	54.4	44.8	36.0	53.5
Mean Minimum Temp. (°F)	22.1	24.4	31.7	39.5	49.0	57.6	61.9	60.1	53.8	42.1	33.9	26.2	41.9
Extreme Maximum Temp. (°F)	72	78	85	91	96	98	105	102	98	90	79	76	105
Extreme Minimum Temp. (°F)	-13	-13	1	14	28	34	44	39	26	19	10	-11	-13
Days Maximum Temp. ≥ 90°F	0	0	0	0	1	4	9	6	2	0	0	0	22
Days Maximum Temp. ≤ 32°F	6	4	1	0	0	0	0	0	0	0	0	3	14
Days Minimum Temp. ≤ 32°F	26	22	17	7	1	0	0	0	0	5	14	23	115
Days Minimum Temp. ≤ 0°F	1	0	0	0	0	0	0	0	0	0	0	0	1
Heating Degree Days (base 65°F)	1,022	837	668	374	148	23	2	6	75	332	601	891	4,979
Cooling Degree Days (base 65°F)	0	0	2	8	52	189	309	246	105	12	0	0	923
Mean Precipitation (in.)	2.59	2.15	2.85	2.63	3.63	3.38	3.73	3.49	3.43	2.88	2.75	2.38	35.89
Days With ≥ 0.1" Precipitation	6	5	6	6	8	7	8	6	5	5	6	5	73
Days With ≥ 1.0" Precipitation	1	0	1	0	1	1	1	1	1	1	1	0	9
Mean Snowfall (in.)	7.3	6.4	4.0	0.7	0.0	0.0	0.0	0.0	0.0	0.3	1.6	4.2	24.5
Days With ≥ 1.0" Snow Depth	8	6	2	0	0	0	0	0	0	0	1	3	20

Danville *Pittsylvania County*   Elevation: 410 ft.   Latitude: 36° 35' N   Longitude: 79° 23' W

	JAN	FEB	MAR	APR	MAY	JUN	JUL	AUG	SEP	OCT	NOV	DEC	YEAR
Mean Maximum Temp. (°F)	47.2	51.5	60.6	71.3	78.9	86.1	90.1	88.4	82.3	71.2	61.2	51.7	70.1
Mean Temp. (°F)	36.9	40.1	48.1	57.5	66.2	74.4	78.9	77.3	70.8	58.5	48.9	41.0	58.2
Mean Minimum Temp. (°F)	26.7	28.6	35.5	43.7	53.4	62.6	67.6	66.0	59.3	45.7	36.6	30.2	46.3
Extreme Maximum Temp. (°F)	77	85	91	95	97	102	105	105	101	94	86	81	105
Extreme Minimum Temp. (°F)	-5	4	11	25	29	40	50	47	38	25	15	2	-5
Days Maximum Temp. ≥ 90°F	0	0	0	1	2	11	18	15	6	0	0	0	53
Days Maximum Temp. ≤ 32°F	2	1	0	0	0	0	0	0	0	0	0	1	4
Days Minimum Temp. ≤ 32°F	23	20	12	3	0	0	0	0	0	2	12	20	92
Days Minimum Temp. ≤ 0°F	0	0	0	0	0	0	0	0	0	0	0	0	0
Heating Degree Days (base 65°F)	863	697	523	247	71	7	0	1	25	224	479	737	3,874
Cooling Degree Days (base 65°F)	0	0	5	29	118	309	458	389	200	32	2	1	1,543
Mean Precipitation (in.)	3.94	3.48	4.23	3.76	3.98	3.56	4.46	3.54	3.94	3.84	3.10	3.19	45.02
Days With ≥ 0.1" Precipitation	7	7	8	6	7	6	7	6	6	5	6	6	77
Days With ≥ 1.0" Precipitation	1	1	1	1	1	1	1	1	1	1	1	1	12
Mean Snowfall (in.)	na	0.7	0.4	trace	0.0	0.0	0.0	0.0	0.0	0.0	trace	0.7	na
Days With ≥ 1.0" Snow Depth	2	1	0	0	0	0	0	0	0	0	0	0	3

Farmville 2 N *Cumberland County*   Elevation: 449 ft.   Latitude: 37° 20' N   Longitude: 78° 23' W

	JAN	FEB	MAR	APR	MAY	JUN	JUL	AUG	SEP	OCT	NOV	DEC	YEAR
Mean Maximum Temp. (°F)	47.5	51.7	60.5	71.1	77.9	85.2	89.1	87.1	81.1	71.2	61.1	51.3	69.5
Mean Temp. (°F)	36.4	39.5	47.4	56.7	65.0	73.0	77.3	75.4	69.1	57.7	48.4	40.2	57.2
Mean Minimum Temp. (°F)	25.2	27.3	34.2	42.3	52.1	60.9	65.5	63.7	57.0	44.3	35.6	29.0	44.8
Extreme Maximum Temp. (°F)	77	80	89	95	96	100	102	105	100	91	87	82	105
Extreme Minimum Temp. (°F)	-8	-9	9	16	30	38	47	43	35	21	9	-2	-9
Days Maximum Temp. ≥ 90°F	0	0	0	1	2	8	15	11	4	0	0	0	41
Days Maximum Temp. ≤ 32°F	2	1	0	0	0	0	0	0	0	0	0	1	4
Days Minimum Temp. ≤ 32°F	24	20	15	5	0	0	0	0	0	4	13	20	101
Days Minimum Temp. ≤ 0°F	0	0	0	0	0	0	0	0	0	0	0	0	0
Heating Degree Days (base 65°F)	882	714	545	269	85	9	0	1	37	244	495	763	4,044
Cooling Degree Days (base 65°F)	0	0	6	24	93	267	406	331	161	28	2	1	1,319
Mean Precipitation (in.)	3.92	3.37	4.22	3.32	4.20	3.10	4.29	3.83	3.86	3.94	3.50	3.23	44.78
Days With ≥ 0.1" Precipitation	7	6	8	6	7	6	7	6	6	6	6	6	77
Days With ≥ 1.0" Precipitation	1	1	1	1	1	1	1	1	1	1	1	1	12
Mean Snowfall (in.)	4.6	5.3	1.7	trace	0.0	0.0	0.0	0.0	0.0	trace	0.6	1.9	14.1
Days With ≥ 1.0" Snow Depth	4	4	1	0	0	0	0	0	0	0	0	2	11

Floyd 2 NE *Floyd County*   Elevation: 2,624 ft.   Latitude: 36° 56' N   Longitude: 80° 18' W

	JAN	FEB	MAR	APR	MAY	JUN	JUL	AUG	SEP	OCT	NOV	DEC	YEAR
Mean Maximum Temp. (°F)	42.6	46.9	55.2	65.0	72.1	78.2	82.0	81.0	75.3	65.8	55.2	46.5	63.8
Mean Temp. (°F)	32.1	35.1	42.7	51.1	59.0	66.0	70.2	68.8	62.8	52.3	43.1	35.5	51.6
Mean Minimum Temp. (°F)	21.5	23.4	30.3	37.1	45.9	53.8	58.4	56.5	50.3	38.6	30.9	24.5	39.3
Extreme Maximum Temp. (°F)	70	75	83	87	90	91	95	97	92	84	78	74	97
Extreme Minimum Temp. (°F)	-19	-15	-7	0	22	30	37	32	24	16	2	-11	-19
Days Maximum Temp. ≥ 90°F	0	0	0	0	0	0	2	1	0	0	0	0	3
Days Maximum Temp. ≤ 32°F	6	3	1	0	0	0	0	0	0	0	0	3	13
Days Minimum Temp. ≤ 32°F	27	23	19	11	3	0	0	0	1	10	18	24	136
Days Minimum Temp. ≤ 0°F	1	1	0	0	0	0	0	0	0	0	0	1	3
Heating Degree Days (base 65°F)	1,013	837	683	413	196	48	10	16	110	391	653	907	5,277
Cooling Degree Days (base 65°F)	0	0	0	2	18	97	198	144	52	3	0	0	514
Mean Precipitation (in.)	3.05	2.89	3.78	3.76	4.11	3.83	3.34	3.04	3.64	3.56	3.48	2.52	41.00
Days With ≥ 0.1" Precipitation	5	5	6	6	8	7	7	5	5	5	6	5	70
Days With ≥ 1.0" Precipitation	1	1	1	1	1	1	1	1	1	1	1	1	12
Mean Snowfall (in.)	6.4	6.2	2.7	1.1	0.0	0.0	0.0	0.0	0.0	trace	0.8	3.2	20.4
Days With ≥ 1.0" Snow Depth	*0*	na	0	0	0	0	0	0	0	0	0	*0*	na

Galax Radio WBRF *Carroll County*   Elevation: 2,381 ft.   Latitude: 36° 40' N   Longitude: 80° 55' W

	JAN	FEB	MAR	APR	MAY	JUN	JUL	AUG	SEP	OCT	NOV	DEC	YEAR
Mean Maximum Temp. (°F)	42.3	47.1	55.9	65.6	73.1	79.3	82.9	81.3	75.4	65.6	54.9	46.2	64.1
Mean Temp. (°F)	32.4	35.9	43.6	51.9	60.2	67.2	71.2	69.8	63.7	52.9	43.6	36.0	52.4
Mean Minimum Temp. (°F)	22.4	24.6	31.3	38.2	47.2	55.1	59.5	58.3	52.1	40.2	32.3	25.7	40.6
Extreme Maximum Temp. (°F)	69	78	83	88	91	92	96	97	90	85	76	71	97
Extreme Minimum Temp. (°F)	-18	-13	-9	16	26	34	40	35	29	19	5	-8	-18
Days Maximum Temp. ≥ 90°F	0	0	0	0	0	0	2	1	0	0	0	0	3
Days Maximum Temp. ≤ 32°F	6	3	1	0	0	0	0	0	0	0	0	3	13
Days Minimum Temp. ≤ 32°F	26	22	18	9	2	0	0	0	0	8	17	24	126
Days Minimum Temp. ≤ 0°F	1	0	0	0	0	0	0	0	0	0	0	0	1
Heating Degree Days (base 65°F)	1,004	816	657	386	168	33	4	9	93	371	635	893	5,069
Cooling Degree Days (base 65°F)	0	0	0	2	27	114	218	164	59	3	0	0	587
Mean Precipitation (in.)	3.24	3.22	3.97	3.69	4.64	4.02	3.93	3.42	3.71	3.69	3.47	2.93	43.93
Days With ≥ 0.1" Precipitation	6	5	7	6	9	7	8	7	5	5	6	5	76
Days With ≥ 1.0" Precipitation	1	1	1	1	1	1	1	1	1	1	1	1	12
Mean Snowfall (in.)	6.7	5.6	2.4	0.8	0.0	0.0	0.0	0.0	0.0	trace	0.2	3.4	19.1
Days With ≥ 1.0" Snow Depth	na	na	0	0	0	0	0	0	0	0	0	*0*	na

Grundy *Buchanan County*   Elevation: 1,167 ft.   Latitude: 37° 17' N   Longitude: 82° 05' W

	JAN	FEB	MAR	APR	MAY	JUN	JUL	AUG	SEP	OCT	NOV	DEC	YEAR
Mean Maximum Temp. (°F)	45.5	50.2	59.4	69.2	76.5	83.5	87.3	86.2	80.4	70.4	60.2	49.9	68.2
Mean Temp. (°F)	34.4	37.7	45.7	54.1	62.8	70.7	75.1	74.1	68.0	55.9	46.6	38.1	55.3
Mean Minimum Temp. (°F)	23.2	25.2	32.0	39.1	49.0	57.9	62.9	62.1	55.2	41.5	32.9	26.2	42.3
Extreme Maximum Temp. (°F)	78	80	88	92	95	99	101	99	102	90	85	80	102
Extreme Minimum Temp. (°F)	-14	-12	-3	21	25	40	40	45	34	20	9	-11	-14
Days Maximum Temp. ≥ 90°F	0	0	0	0	1	5	11	8	3	0	0	0	28
Days Maximum Temp. ≤ 32°F	5	3	0	0	0	0	0	0	0	0	0	2	10
Days Minimum Temp. ≤ 32°F	26	21	17	9	0	0	0	0	0	5	16	23	117
Days Minimum Temp. ≤ 0°F	1	0	0	0	0	0	0	0	0	0	0	0	1
Heating Degree Days (base 65°F)	946	766	592	331	125	16	1	2	46	292	547	828	4,492
Cooling Degree Days (base 65°F)	0	0	1	12	69	210	339	295	137	18	1	0	1,082
Mean Precipitation (in.)	3.44	3.16	4.01	3.99	4.85	4.46	4.76	3.85	3.47	3.24	3.24	3.26	45.73
Days With ≥ 0.1" Precipitation	7	7	8	8	10	9	9	7	7	6	7	7	92
Days With ≥ 1.0" Precipitation	1	0	1	1	1	1	1	1	1	1	0	1	10
Mean Snowfall (in.)	6.8	5.3	3.2	1.1	0.0	0.0	0.0	0.0	0.0	0.0	0.7	2.9	20.0
Days With ≥ 1.0" Snow Depth	7	5	2	0	0	0	0	0	0	0	1	3	18

Holland 1 E *Suffolk (City) County*   Elevation: 78 ft.   Latitude: 36° 41' N   Longitude: 76° 46' W

	JAN	FEB	MAR	APR	MAY	JUN	JUL	AUG	SEP	OCT	NOV	DEC	YEAR
Mean Maximum Temp. (°F)	49.0	52.1	60.2	70.0	77.5	85.0	88.7	87.1	82.0	71.8	63.0	53.6	70.0
Mean Temp. (°F)	38.6	41.2	48.7	57.4	65.9	73.8	78.0	76.3	70.7	59.5	51.1	42.6	58.6
Mean Minimum Temp. (°F)	28.1	30.2	37.0	44.7	54.3	62.5	67.3	65.4	59.4	47.0	39.1	31.7	47.2
Extreme Maximum Temp. (°F)	79	81	88	94	97	99	101	104	99	93	88	81	104
Extreme Minimum Temp. (°F)	-5	-5	15	21	31	39	51	45	37	25	16	4	-5
Days Maximum Temp. ≥ 90°F	0	0	0	1	2	8	14	11	4	0	0	0	40
Days Maximum Temp. ≤ 32°F	2	1	0	0	0	0	0	0	0	0	0	1	4
Days Minimum Temp. ≤ 32°F	21	18	11	3	0	0	0	0	0	2	9	18	82
Days Minimum Temp. ≤ 0°F	0	0	0	0	0	0	0	0	0	0	0	0	0
Heating Degree Days (base 65°F)	813	668	506	252	75	9	0	1	23	202	418	687	3,654
Cooling Degree Days (base 65°F)	0	1	6	29	112	287	426	349	189	38	6	1	1,444
Mean Precipitation (in.)	4.29	3.51	4.41	3.38	3.98	3.46	5.31	5.21	4.75	3.98	3.12	3.38	48.78
Days With ≥ 0.1" Precipitation	8	7	8	6	7	6	8	6	5	5	6	7	79
Days With ≥ 1.0" Precipitation	1	1	1	1	1	1	2	2	1	1	1	1	14
Mean Snowfall (in.)	1.8	2.8	1.2	trace	0.0	0.0	0.0	0.0	0.0	0.0	trace	0.5	6.3
Days With ≥ 1.0" Snow Depth	1	2	1	0	0	0	0	0	0	0	0	0	4

Hot Springs *Bath County*   Elevation: 2,234 ft.   Latitude: 38° 00' N   Longitude: 79° 50' W

	JAN	FEB	MAR	APR	MAY	JUN	JUL	AUG	SEP	OCT	NOV	DEC	YEAR
Mean Maximum Temp. (°F)	39.8	43.7	52.9	63.6	72.9	79.8	83.4	82.6	75.9	65.0	53.9	44.3	63.2
Mean Temp. (°F)	30.1	32.8	41.1	50.7	59.8	67.3	71.3	70.4	63.7	52.7	42.9	34.3	51.4
Mean Minimum Temp. (°F)	20.3	21.9	29.3	37.7	46.6	54.7	59.1	58.0	51.5	40.4	31.7	24.2	39.6
Extreme Maximum Temp. (°F)	67	75	83	89	93	97	98	100	95	85	78	75	*100*
Extreme Minimum Temp. (°F)	-20	-10	2	14	26	34	38	35	30	19	5	-15	-20
Days Maximum Temp. ≥ 90°F	0	0	0	0	0	1	4	3	0	0	0	0	8
Days Maximum Temp. ≤ 32°F	9	5	2	0	0	0	0	0	0	0	1	5	22
Days Minimum Temp. ≤ 32°F	27	24	20	9	2	0	0	0	0	7	17	25	131
Days Minimum Temp. ≤ 0°F	2	1	0	0	0	0	0	0	0	0	0	1	4
Heating Degree Days (base 65°F)	1,076	903	733	430	188	44	7	10	102	379	657	945	5,474
Cooling Degree Days (base 65°F)	*0*	0	0	5	37	127	224	183	65	*6*	0	0	*647*
Mean Precipitation (in.)	3.61	2.93	3.77	3.31	4.31	3.56	4.12	3.42	3.49	3.76	3.65	2.67	42.60
Days With ≥ 0.1" Precipitation	7	6	7	7	8	7	8	6	6	6	6	6	80
Days With ≥ 1.0" Precipitation	1	1	1	1	1	1	1	1	1	1	1	1	12
Mean Snowfall (in.)	8.5	7.1	4.3	1.2	0.0	0.0	0.0	0.0	0.0	0.2	1.8	*5.3*	*28.4*
Days With ≥ 1.0" Snow Depth	7	8	2	0	0	0	0	0	0	0	1	*3*	*21*

John H. Kerr Dam *Mecklenburg County*   Elevation: 249 ft.   Latitude: 36° 36' N   Longitude: 78° 17' W

	JAN	FEB	MAR	APR	MAY	JUN	JUL	AUG	SEP	OCT	NOV	DEC	YEAR
Mean Maximum Temp. (°F)	48.0	51.6	59.9	70.2	77.7	85.3	89.3	87.8	82.0	71.6	62.0	52.4	69.8
Mean Temp. (°F)	37.7	40.3	47.9	57.3	65.8	73.9	78.4	77.0	70.7	59.0	50.1	41.8	58.3
Mean Minimum Temp. (°F)	27.3	29.0	35.9	44.3	53.8	62.5	67.6	66.2	59.4	46.4	38.2	31.1	46.8
Extreme Maximum Temp. (°F)	77	81	90	94	99	101	102	105	100	93	84	81	105
Extreme Minimum Temp. (°F)	-5	1	12	21	30	37	47	44	33	24	14	5	-5
Days Maximum Temp. ≥ 90°F	0	0	0	1	2	8	16	13	5	0	0	0	45
Days Maximum Temp. ≤ 32°F	3	1	0	0	0	0	0	0	0	0	0	1	5
Days Minimum Temp. ≤ 32°F	22	19	12	3	0	0	0	0	0	2	10	18	86
Days Minimum Temp. ≤ 0°F	0	0	0	0	0	0	0	0	0	0	0	0	0
Heating Degree Days (base 65°F)	841	691	527	252	80	8	0	2	26	213	446	714	3,800
Cooling Degree Days (base 65°F)	0	0	6	26	113	294	445	383	206	39	3	1	1,516
Mean Precipitation (in.)	3.81	3.04	4.27	3.22	3.91	3.49	4.58	4.01	3.73	3.77	3.17	3.03	44.03
Days With ≥ 0.1" Precipitation	7	6	8	6	7	6	7	6	5	5	5	6	74
Days With ≥ 1.0" Precipitation	1	1	1	1	1	1	1	1	1	1	1	1	12
Mean Snowfall (in.)	na	*0.4*	0.5	0.0	0.0	0.0	0.0	0.0	0.0	0.0	trace	0.3	na
Days With ≥ 1.0" Snow Depth	na	*0*	0	0	0	0	0	0	0	0	0	0	na

Langley AFB *Hampton (City) County*   Elevation: 9 ft.   Latitude: 37° 05' N   Longitude: 76° 21' W

	JAN	FEB	MAR	APR	MAY	JUN	JUL	AUG	SEP	OCT	NOV	DEC	YEAR
Mean Maximum Temp. (°F)	47.3	49.9	57.3	66.9	74.5	82.5	86.7	85.1	79.4	69.2	60.5	52.0	67.6
Mean Temp. (°F)	39.6	41.8	48.9	57.7	66.3	74.6	79.3	77.9	72.3	61.0	52.2	44.1	59.6
Mean Minimum Temp. (°F)	31.9	33.6	40.4	48.5	58.1	66.8	71.8	70.7	65.2	52.9	43.8	36.1	51.6
Extreme Maximum Temp. (°F)	77	81	87	94	96	100	101	105	99	91	85	79	105
Extreme Minimum Temp. (°F)	-3	7	12	29	39	48	54	54	45	33	21	8	-3
Days Maximum Temp. ≥ 90°F	0	0	0	0	1	5	11	7	2	0	0	0	26
Days Maximum Temp. ≤ 32°F	3	2	0	0	0	0	0	0	0	0	0	1	6
Days Minimum Temp. ≤ 32°F	16	14	6	0	0	0	0	0	0	0	3	11	50
Days Minimum Temp. ≤ 0°F	0	0	0	0	0	0	0	0	0	0	0	0	0
Heating Degree Days (base 65°F)	781	650	501	242	67	5	0	0	11	164	387	643	3,451
Cooling Degree Days (base 65°F)	0	1	8	34	119	311	472	403	231	54	6	1	1,640
Mean Precipitation (in.)	4.00	3.71	4.70	3.30	3.99	3.39	4.83	4.56	4.77	3.49	3.38	3.51	47.63
Days With ≥ 0.1" Precipitation	7	7	7	6	7	5	7	6	6	5	6	7	76
Days With ≥ 1.0" Precipitation	1	1	2	1	1	1	1	1	1	1	1	1	13
Mean Snowfall (in.)	2.3	2.9	1.2	0.2	0.0	0.0	0.0	0.0	0.0	trace	trace	0.5	7.1
Days With ≥ 1.0" Snow Depth	2	2	0	0	0	0	0	0	0	0	0	0	4

Lawrenceville 3 E *Brunswick County*   Elevation: 324 ft.   Latitude: 36° 46' N   Longitude: 77° 47' W

	JAN	FEB	MAR	APR	MAY	JUN	JUL	AUG	SEP	OCT	NOV	DEC	YEAR
Mean Maximum Temp. (°F)	49.0	53.4	61.3	71.2	78.4	85.1	89.0	87.3	81.9	71.6	62.6	53.2	70.4
Mean Temp. (°F)	37.9	41.0	48.3	57.0	65.0	72.7	76.9	75.3	69.4	58.3	49.7	41.7	57.8
Mean Minimum Temp. (°F)	26.7	28.5	35.3	42.7	51.6	60.1	64.8	63.2	56.8	44.9	36.7	30.1	45.1
Extreme Maximum Temp. (°F)	77	83	89	96	98	98	101	102	100	91	86	81	102
Extreme Minimum Temp. (°F)	-10	-6	8	17	28	36	46	40	35	22	9	1	-10
Days Maximum Temp. ≥ 90°F	0	0	0	1	1	7	15	11	4	0	0	0	39
Days Maximum Temp. ≤ 32°F	2	1	0	0	0	0	0	0	0	0	0	1	4
Days Minimum Temp. ≤ 32°F	22	19	13	5	0	0	0	0	0	3	12	19	93
Days Minimum Temp. ≤ 0°F	0	0	0	0	0	0	0	0	0	0	0	0	0
Heating Degree Days (base 65°F)	834	673	516	258	83	9	0	1	31	230	458	717	3,810
Cooling Degree Days (base 65°F)	0	1	6	23	94	261	401	330	164	30	4	1	1,315
Mean Precipitation (in.)	3.87	3.32	4.43	3.16	3.80	3.51	4.64	4.23	4.57	3.79	3.49	3.18	45.99
Days With ≥ 0.1" Precipitation	7	6	8	6	7	7	7	6	5	5	6	6	76
Days With ≥ 1.0" Precipitation	1	1	1	1	1	1	1	1	2	1	1	1	13
Mean Snowfall (in.)	2.7	3.8	1.3	trace	0.0	0.0	0.0	0.0	0.0	0.0	trace	1.0	8.8
Days With ≥ 1.0" Snow Depth	2	1	0	0	0	0	0	0	0	0	0	0	3

Lexington *Rockbridge County*   Elevation: 1,059 ft.   Latitude: 37° 47' N   Longitude: 79° 26' W

	JAN	FEB	MAR	APR	MAY	JUN	JUL	AUG	SEP	OCT	NOV	DEC	YEAR
Mean Maximum Temp. (°F)	44.8	49.3	58.7	69.7	76.6	83.0	86.6	85.0	78.6	68.4	57.9	48.8	67.3
Mean Temp. (°F)	34.3	37.6	45.9	55.3	63.4	70.8	75.0	73.7	67.2	55.8	46.0	38.0	55.3
Mean Minimum Temp. (°F)	23.9	25.9	33.1	40.8	50.2	58.6	63.3	62.3	55.7	43.2	34.1	27.2	43.2
Extreme Maximum Temp. (°F)	75	78	86	92	95	99	100	100	96	89	84	79	100
Extreme Minimum Temp. (°F)	-12	-15	0	15	29	36	45	42	32	21	8	-9	-15
Days Maximum Temp. ≥ 90°F	0	0	0	1	1	4	10	6	2	0	0	0	24
Days Maximum Temp. ≤ 32°F	3	1	0	0	0	0	0	0	0	0	0	1	5
Days Minimum Temp. ≤ 32°F	25	21	15	6	1	0	0	0	0	5	14	22	109
Days Minimum Temp. ≤ 0°F	1	0	0	0	0	0	0	0	0	0	0	0	1
Heating Degree Days (base 65°F)	943	767	586	297	103	13	1	2	53	290	563	828	4,446
Cooling Degree Days (base 65°F)	0	0	2	13	62	200	328	276	117	14	0	0	1,012
Mean Precipitation (in.)	2.96	2.77	3.51	3.13	3.92	3.98	3.81	3.01	3.27	3.27	3.11	2.92	39.66
Days With ≥ 0.1" Precipitation	6	6	7	6	8	6	7	5	5	5	6	6	73
Days With ≥ 1.0" Precipitation	1	1	1	1	1	1	1	1	1	1	1	1	12
Mean Snowfall (in.)	4.8	4.4	2.0	0.2	0.0	0.0	0.0	0.0	0.0	trace	0.7	2.1	14.2
Days With ≥ 1.0" Snow Depth	6	4	1	0	0	0	0	0	0	0	0	2	13

Lincoln *Loudoun County*   Elevation: 498 ft.   Latitude: 39° 08' N   Longitude: 77° 43' W

	JAN	FEB	MAR	APR	MAY	JUN	JUL	AUG	SEP	OCT	NOV	DEC	YEAR
Mean Maximum Temp. (°F)	43.6	47.9	56.7	67.8	76.4	84.0	88.2	86.6	80.5	69.6	58.5	47.9	67.3
Mean Temp. (°F)	33.7	36.8	44.8	54.9	63.9	72.2	76.5	74.7	68.5	57.1	47.5	37.8	55.7
Mean Minimum Temp. (°F)	23.7	25.6	33.0	41.8	51.3	60.3	64.8	62.8	56.2	44.5	36.3	27.8	44.0
Extreme Maximum Temp. (°F)	76	81	88	94	96	98	105	102	100	94	84	79	105
Extreme Minimum Temp. (°F)	-10	-8	7	20	30	39	48	41	35	21	11	-3	-10
Days Maximum Temp. ≥ 90°F	0	0	0	0	2	6	13	10	3	0	0	0	34
Days Maximum Temp. ≤ 32°F	4	2	0	0	0	0	0	0	0	0	0	2	8
Days Minimum Temp. ≤ 32°F	26	22	16	4	0	0	0	0	0	3	12	22	105
Days Minimum Temp. ≤ 0°F	0	0	0	0	0	0	0	0	0	0	0	0	0
Heating Degree Days (base 65°F)	963	800	624	313	106	12	0	2	43	257	524	835	4,479
Cooling Degree Days (base 65°F)	0	0	5	16	79	237	382	305	143	19	2	0	1,188
Mean Precipitation (in.)	3.21	2.53	3.38	3.51	4.47	4.12	3.75	3.81	3.78	3.39	3.64	3.14	42.73
Days With ≥ 0.1" Precipitation	6	5	6	6	8	6	6	6	5	5	6	5	70
Days With ≥ 1.0" Precipitation	1	1	1	1	1	1	1	1	1	1	1	1	12
Mean Snowfall (in.)	6.7	5.7	4.1	0.2	0.0	0.0	0.0	0.0	0.0	0.2	0.6	1.9	19.4
Days With ≥ 1.0" Snow Depth	9	7	3	0	0	0	0	0	0	0	0	2	21

Louisa *Louisa County*   Elevation: 419 ft.   Latitude: 38° 02' N   Longitude: 78° 00' W

	JAN	FEB	MAR	APR	MAY	JUN	JUL	AUG	SEP	OCT	NOV	DEC	YEAR
Mean Maximum Temp. (°F)	45.3	49.8	58.9	69.9	76.7	83.7	87.4	85.6	79.9	69.6	59.3	49.3	67.9
Mean Temp. (°F)	34.9	38.2	46.2	55.7	63.9	71.8	76.1	74.4	68.2	56.8	47.4	38.7	56.0
Mean Minimum Temp. (°F)	24.4	26.5	33.5	41.4	51.2	59.8	64.8	63.1	56.4	44.0	35.5	28.2	44.1
Extreme Maximum Temp. (°F)	77	81	89	95	96	98	102	102	100	89	88	79	102
Extreme Minimum Temp. (°F)	-13	-21	2	13	26	38	42	38	29	21	11	-9	-21
Days Maximum Temp. ≥ 90°F	0	0	0	0	1	5	11	8	3	0	0	0	28
Days Maximum Temp. ≤ 32°F	4	2	0	0	0	0	0	0	0	0	0	2	8
Days Minimum Temp. ≤ 32°F	24	21	15	6	0	0	0	0	0	5	13	21	105
Days Minimum Temp. ≤ 0°F	1	0	0	0	0	0	0	0	0	0	0	0	1
Heating Degree Days (base 65°F)	927	752	579	292	103	14	1	3	48	269	525	808	4,321
Cooling Degree Days (base 65°F)	0	0	5	18	80	233	367	295	143	23	2	0	1,166
Mean Precipitation (in.)	3.44	3.02	3.86	3.06	3.88	3.56	4.51	3.57	3.89	3.97	3.95	3.14	43.85
Days With ≥ 0.1" Precipitation	6	6	7	6	7	6	7	6	5	5	6	6	73
Days With ≥ 1.0" Precipitation	1	1	1	1	1	1	1	1	1	1	1	1	12
Mean Snowfall (in.)	5.9	5.2	2.0	0.4	trace	0.0	0.0	0.0	0.0	trace	0.8	2.5	16.8
Days With ≥ 1.0" Snow Depth	6	3	1	0	0	0	0	0	0	0	0	2	12

Luray 5 E *Page County*   Elevation: 1,299 ft.   Latitude: 38° 40' N   Longitude: 78° 22' W

	JAN	FEB	MAR	APR	MAY	JUN	JUL	AUG	SEP	OCT	NOV	DEC	YEAR
Mean Maximum Temp. (°F)	42.8	46.7	55.2	66.8	75.0	82.2	86.0	84.3	78.4	68.0	58.2	47.8	65.9
Mean Temp. (°F)	31.4	34.4	42.5	52.6	61.4	68.9	73.1	71.5	65.2	54.2	45.3	36.3	53.1
Mean Minimum Temp. (°F)	19.9	22.1	29.7	38.4	47.6	55.6	60.2	58.7	52.1	40.5	32.5	24.7	40.2
Extreme Maximum Temp. (°F)	76	78	90	94	97	99	105	100	96	91	84	78	105
Extreme Minimum Temp. (°F)	-10	-14	-2	15	26	31	39	37	28	19	6	-7	-14
Days Maximum Temp. ≥ 90°F	0	0	0	0	1	4	9	6	2	0	0	0	22
Days Maximum Temp. ≤ 32°F	6	4	1	0	0	0	0	0	0	0	0	3	14
Days Minimum Temp. ≤ 32°F	27	24	20	9	1	0	0	0	0	7	16	25	129
Days Minimum Temp. ≤ 0°F	2	0	0	0	0	0	0	0	0	0	0	0	2
Heating Degree Days (base 65°F)	1,036	859	695	376	157	31	4	9	80	339	584	883	5,053
Cooling Degree Days (base 65°F)	0	0	3	11	51	165	280	220	95	16	0	0	841
Mean Precipitation (in.)	3.09	2.64	3.34	3.13	3.89	3.80	3.88	3.45	4.19	3.59	3.60	2.93	41.53
Days With ≥ 0.1" Precipitation	6	5	7	6	7	7	7	6	6	5	6	5	73
Days With ≥ 1.0" Precipitation	1	1	1	1	1	1	1	1	1	1	1	1	12
Mean Snowfall (in.)	6.7	5.2	4.4	0.6	0.0	0.0	0.0	0.0	0.0	0.2	1.1	2.8	21.0
Days With ≥ 1.0" Snow Depth	6	4	2	0	0	0	0	0	0	0	0	1	13

Mount Weather *Loudoun County*   Elevation: 1,719 ft.   Latitude: 39° 04' N   Longitude: 77° 53' W

	JAN	FEB	MAR	APR	MAY	JUN	JUL	AUG	SEP	OCT	NOV	DEC	YEAR
Mean Maximum Temp. (°F)	35.7	38.6	47.1	58.9	68.1	76.2	80.5	78.8	72.0	60.5	50.1	40.7	58.9
Mean Temp. (°F)	28.3	30.8	38.6	49.6	59.5	68.0	72.4	70.9	64.2	52.8	43.0	33.5	51.0
Mean Minimum Temp. (°F)	20.8	23.0	30.1	40.2	50.8	59.7	64.3	63.0	56.5	45.0	35.8	26.3	42.9
Extreme Maximum Temp. (°F)	71	74	84	88	91	92	99	96	91	85	78	71	99
Extreme Minimum Temp. (°F)	-15	-4	-3	15	30	38	48	44	31	21	7	-8	-15
Days Maximum Temp. ≥ 90°F	0	0	0	0	0	0	2	1	0	0	0	0	3
Days Maximum Temp. ≤ 32°F	13	9	4	0	0	0	0	0	0	0	1	7	34
Days Minimum Temp. ≤ 32°F	27	23	19	6	0	0	0	0	0	2	12	23	112
Days Minimum Temp. ≤ 0°F	1	1	0	0	0	0	0	0	0	0	0	0	2
Heating Degree Days (base 65°F)	1,132	960	813	466	206	44	6	11	97	381	654	970	5,740
Cooling Degree Days (base 65°F)	0	0	2	9	46	152	265	208	85	10	1	0	778
Mean Precipitation (in.)	3.08	2.41	3.45	3.52	4.48	4.11	4.02	3.55	4.15	3.79	3.57	3.02	43.15
Days With ≥ 0.1" Precipitation	6	5	6	6	8	7	7	6	7	6	6	6	76
Days With ≥ 1.0" Precipitation	1	0	1	1	1	1	1	1	1	1	1	1	11
Mean Snowfall (in.)	*7.3*	*2.6*	*3.4*	0.6	0.0	0.0	0.0	0.0	0.0	0.3	*1.5*	*2.2*	*17.9*
Days With ≥ 1.0" Snow Depth	10	9	4	0	0	0	0	0	0	0	1	4	28

Painter 2 W *Accomack County*   Elevation: 29 ft.   Latitude: 37° 35' N   Longitude: 75° 49' W

	JAN	FEB	MAR	APR	MAY	JUN	JUL	AUG	SEP	OCT	NOV	DEC	YEAR
Mean Maximum Temp. (°F)	46.9	49.2	56.7	66.4	74.8	82.5	87.1	85.3	80.1	69.8	60.4	51.5	67.5
Mean Temp. (°F)	38.4	40.2	47.2	56.0	64.9	73.1	78.1	76.2	70.8	60.0	51.2	42.9	58.2
Mean Minimum Temp. (°F)	29.8	31.1	37.7	45.5	55.0	63.7	69.0	67.1	61.4	50.1	42.0	34.2	48.9
Extreme Maximum Temp. (°F)	74	78	85	91	95	97	99	98	98	91	82	77	99
Extreme Minimum Temp. (°F)	1	-1	11	26	34	43	47	44	41	24	19	7	-1
Days Maximum Temp. ≥ 90°F	0	0	0	0	1	4	11	6	2	0	0	0	24
Days Maximum Temp. ≤ 32°F	3	2	0	0	0	0	0	0	0	0	0	1	6
Days Minimum Temp. ≤ 32°F	19	16	10	2	0	0	0	0	0	1	6	14	68
Days Minimum Temp. ≤ 0°F	0	0	0	0	0	0	0	0	0	0	0	0	0
Heating Degree Days (base 65°F)	818	695	550	283	87	10	0	1	19	187	413	678	3,741
Cooling Degree Days (base 65°F)	0	0	5	19	98	277	441	357	202	41	4	1	1,445
Mean Precipitation (in.)	3.94	3.34	4.50	3.08	3.43	3.10	4.28	3.76	3.61	3.55	3.13	3.34	43.06
Days With ≥ 0.1" Precipitation	7	6	8	5	6	5	6	6	5	5	5	7	71
Days With ≥ 1.0" Precipitation	1	1	1	1	1	1	1	1	1	1	1	1	12
Mean Snowfall (in.)	2.4	3.1	1.1	0.2	0.0	0.0	0.0	0.0	0.0	0.0	trace	0.7	7.5
Days With ≥ 1.0" Snow Depth	2	1	0	0	0	0	0	0	0	0	0	1	4

Pennington Gap *Lee County*   Elevation: 1,499 ft.   Latitude: 36° 44' N   Longitude: 83° 00' W

	JAN	FEB	MAR	APR	MAY	JUN	JUL	AUG	SEP	OCT	NOV	DEC	YEAR
Mean Maximum Temp. (°F)	44.8	49.9	59.3	69.3	76.6	83.1	86.4	85.7	80.5	70.3	59.5	49.5	67.9
Mean Temp. (°F)	34.1	37.5	45.9	54.5	62.7	70.3	74.2	73.2	67.3	55.7	46.3	38.1	55.0
Mean Minimum Temp. (°F)	23.2	25.0	32.4	39.7	48.8	57.4	61.9	60.6	54.2	41.0	32.9	26.6	42.0
Extreme Maximum Temp. (°F)	76	80	86	89	90	97	98	101	97	87	80	78	101
Extreme Minimum Temp. (°F)	-25	-21	-8	16	24	35	43	36	28	16	5	-8	-25
Days Maximum Temp. ≥ 90°F	0	0	0	0	0	3	8	6	2	0	0	0	19
Days Maximum Temp. ≤ 32°F	4	3	0	0	0	0	0	0	0	0	0	2	9
Days Minimum Temp. ≤ 32°F	24	21	16	7	1	0	0	0	0	7	16	22	114
Days Minimum Temp. ≤ 0°F	1	1	0	0	0	0	0	0	0	0	0	0	2
Heating Degree Days (base 65°F)	952	771	585	316	117	16	1	2	50	293	556	828	4,487
Cooling Degree Days (base 65°F)	0	0	1	7	51	192	302	264	116	10	0	0	943
Mean Precipitation (in.)	4.11	4.27	4.36	4.32	4.91	4.27	4.40	3.90	3.48	3.14	3.88	4.37	49.41
Days With ≥ 0.1" Precipitation	*8*	8	8	7	9	8	7	7	6	5	7	7	*87*
Days With ≥ 1.0" Precipitation	1	1	1	1	1	1	1	1	1	1	1	1	12
Mean Snowfall (in.)	6.6	4.0	1.9	0.7	0.0	0.0	0.0	0.0	0.0	0.0	0.5	2.6	16.3
Days With ≥ 1.0" Snow Depth	na	*1*	*0*	0	0	0	0	0	0	0	0	*1*	na

Philpott Dam 2 *Henry County* Elevation: 1,122 ft. Latitude: 36° 47' N Longitude: 80° 02' W

	JAN	FEB	MAR	APR	MAY	JUN	JUL	AUG	SEP	OCT	NOV	DEC	YEAR
Mean Maximum Temp. (°F)	45.8	50.1	58.1	68.5	76.0	83.0	87.0	85.5	79.7	70.0	59.9	50.1	67.8
Mean Temp. (°F)	35.4	38.6	45.8	55.1	63.4	71.4	75.8	74.4	68.3	57.1	48.0	39.4	56.1
Mean Minimum Temp. (°F)	25.0	26.7	33.5	41.8	50.8	59.7	64.5	63.3	56.8	44.2	36.1	28.7	44.2
Extreme Maximum Temp. (°F)	76	80	87	92	94	97	100	102	97	90	85	78	102
Extreme Minimum Temp. (°F)	-10	-1	6	21	31	35	48	44	35	22	12	-2	-10
Days Maximum Temp. ≥ 90°F	0	0	0	0	1	5	11	7	3	0	0	0	27
Days Maximum Temp. ≤ 32°F	4	2	0	0	0	0	0	0	0	0	0	2	8
Days Minimum Temp. ≤ 32°F	25	21	15	4	0	0	0	0	0	3	12	21	101
Days Minimum Temp. ≤ 0°F	1	0	0	0	0	0	0	0	0	0	0	0	1
Heating Degree Days (base 65°F)	910	740	590	305	110	13	1	2	40	255	505	787	4,258
Cooling Degree Days (base 65°F)	0	0	3	17	73	231	367	309	146	20	1	0	1,167
Mean Precipitation (in.)	3.90	3.57	4.56	3.84	5.02	4.44	5.29	4.78	4.65	4.25	3.41	3.38	51.09
Days With ≥ 0.1" Precipitation	7	6	7	7	8	7	8	7	6	6	6	6	81
Days With ≥ 1.0" Precipitation	1	1	1	1	2	1	2	1	1	1	1	1	14
Mean Snowfall (in.)	0.7	2.3	1.3	0.1	0.0	0.0	0.0	0.0	0.0	0.0	trace	0.6	5.0
Days With ≥ 1.0" Snow Depth	3	2	1	0	0	0	0	0	0	0	0	1	7

Piedmont Research Station *Orange County* Elevation: 518 ft. Latitude: 38° 13' N Longitude: 78° 07' W

	JAN	FEB	MAR	APR	MAY	JUN	JUL	AUG	SEP	OCT	NOV	DEC	YEAR
Mean Maximum Temp. (°F)	43.1	46.7	55.3	66.5	74.5	82.5	86.5	84.7	78.7	67.9	57.5	47.5	65.9
Mean Temp. (°F)	33.3	36.4	44.4	54.7	63.5	71.9	76.2	74.5	68.1	56.4	46.9	37.9	55.4
Mean Minimum Temp. (°F)	23.6	26.0	33.5	42.8	52.5	61.3	65.9	64.2	57.4	44.8	36.3	28.3	44.7
Extreme Maximum Temp. (°F)	77	79	88	93	95	98	103	99	99	89	85	79	103
Extreme Minimum Temp. (°F)	-9	-11	7	18	30	42	47	44	36	22	10	-4	-11
Days Maximum Temp. ≥ 90°F	0	0	0	0	1	5	10	7	3	0	0	0	26
Days Maximum Temp. ≤ 32°F	5	3	1	0	0	0	0	0	0	0	0	2	11
Days Minimum Temp. ≤ 32°F	26	22	15	4	0	0	0	0	0	2	11	22	102
Days Minimum Temp. ≤ 0°F	1	0	0	0	0	0	0	0	0	0	0	0	1
Heating Degree Days (base 65°F)	973	802	634	321	114	13	1	2	43	278	538	833	4,552
Cooling Degree Days (base 65°F)	0	0	5	17	77	238	372	301	142	19	1	0	1,172
Mean Precipitation (in.)	3.28	2.84	3.74	3.18	4.37	3.90	4.90	3.72	3.74	4.05	3.81	3.08	44.61
Days With ≥ 0.1" Precipitation	6	6	7	6	8	6	8	6	6	5	6	6	76
Days With ≥ 1.0" Precipitation	1	1	1	1	1	1	1	1	1	1	1	1	12
Mean Snowfall (in.)	6.5	5.1	2.7	0.3	0.0	0.0	0.0	0.0	0.0	0.1	0.9	2.7	18.3
Days With ≥ 1.0" Snow Depth	6	4	1	0	0	0	0	0	0	0	0	2	13

Pulaski *Pulaski County* Elevation: 1,847 ft. Latitude: 37° 04' N Longitude: 80° 47' W

	JAN	FEB	MAR	APR	MAY	JUN	JUL	AUG	SEP	OCT	NOV	DEC	YEAR
Mean Maximum Temp. (°F)	43.1	47.3	56.1	66.3	73.8	80.2	84.0	82.8	77.0	66.9	56.5	47.4	65.1
Mean Temp. (°F)	33.0	36.0	43.8	52.5	60.5	67.9	72.0	70.7	64.5	53.5	44.5	36.7	53.0
Mean Minimum Temp. (°F)	22.9	24.7	31.5	38.5	47.2	55.6	59.8	58.5	51.9	40.1	32.5	26.0	40.8
Extreme Maximum Temp. (°F)	69	79	84	91	96	96	99	98	93	89	79	73	99
Extreme Minimum Temp. (°F)	-16	-13	0	14	25	32	39	33	30	19	3	-12	-16
Days Maximum Temp. ≥ 90°F	0	0	0	0	0	1	4	3	0	0	0	0	8
Days Maximum Temp. ≤ 32°F	5	3	1	0	0	0	0	0	0	0	0	3	12
Days Minimum Temp. ≤ 32°F	26	22	17	8	2	0	0	0	0	7	16	23	121
Days Minimum Temp. ≤ 0°F	1	0	0	0	0	0	0	0	0	0	0	0	1
Heating Degree Days (base 65°F)	985	811	649	374	164	35	5	8	86	354	609	870	4,950
Cooling Degree Days (base 65°F)	0	0	1	5	34	136	243	191	71	5	0	0	686
Mean Precipitation (in.)	2.88	2.76	3.30	3.06	4.04	3.85	3.68	2.93	2.97	3.03	2.55	2.61	37.66
Days With ≥ 0.1" Precipitation	6	6	6	6	8	7	7	6	6	5	5	6	74
Days With ≥ 1.0" Precipitation	1	0	1	1	1	1	1	1	1	1	1	0	10
Mean Snowfall (in.)	4.6	5.7	1.7	0.5	0.0	0.0	0.0	0.0	0.0	trace	0.4	2.6	15.5
Days With ≥ 1.0" Snow Depth	na	na	1	0	0	0	0	0	0	0	0	1	na

Rocky Mount *Franklin County* Elevation: 1,312 ft. Latitude: 36° 59' N Longitude: 79° 54' W

	JAN	FEB	MAR	APR	MAY	JUN	JUL	AUG	SEP	OCT	NOV	DEC	YEAR
Mean Maximum Temp. (°F)	44.5	48.8	56.9	67.6	75.2	82.4	86.6	85.2	78.7	68.4	58.4	48.8	66.8
Mean Temp. (°F)	34.9	38.0	45.4	54.8	63.0	71.0	75.5	74.0	67.5	56.2	47.1	38.8	55.5
Mean Minimum Temp. (°F)	25.3	27.2	34.0	42.0	50.7	59.6	64.3	62.7	56.3	43.8	35.7	28.8	44.2
Extreme Maximum Temp. (°F)	75	79	86	91	93	97	102	101	98	89	83	78	102
Extreme Minimum Temp. (°F)	-11	-2	8	20	28	38	48	40	31	23	12	-4	-11
Days Maximum Temp. ≥ 90°F	0	0	0	0	1	4	10	8	3	0	0	0	26
Days Maximum Temp. ≤ 32°F	4	3	0	0	0	0	0	0	0	0	0	2	9
Days Minimum Temp. ≤ 32°F	23	21	15	5	0	0	0	0	0	4	12	20	100
Days Minimum Temp. ≤ 0°F	1	0	0	0	0	0	0	0	0	0	0	0	1
Heating Degree Days (base 65°F)	926	755	602	315	121	15	1	2	48	283	532	805	4,405
Cooling Degree Days (base 65°F)	0	0	3	17	69	220	356	289	128	18	1	0	1,101
Mean Precipitation (in.)	3.70	3.24	4.18	4.13	4.31	4.02	4.92	3.84	4.19	3.75	3.31	3.14	46.73
Days With ≥ 0.1" Precipitation	7	6	8	7	8	7	7	6	6	5	6	6	79
Days With ≥ 1.0" Precipitation	1	1	1	1	1	1	1	1	1	1	1	1	12
Mean Snowfall (in.)	5.6	5.5	2.6	0.3	0.0	0.0	0.0	0.0	0.0	trace	0.5	2.4	16.9
Days With ≥ 1.0" Snow Depth	5	4	1	0	0	0	0	0	0	0	0	2	12

Staffordsville 3 ENE *Giles County*   Elevation: 1,948 ft.   Latitude: 37° 16' N   Longitude: 80° 43' W

	JAN	FEB	MAR	APR	MAY	JUN	JUL	AUG	SEP	OCT	NOV	DEC	YEAR
Mean Maximum Temp. (°F)	42.8	46.9	56.5	66.1	73.4	80.2	84.0	82.8	76.8	67.3	56.8	47.3	65.1
Mean Temp. (°F)	33.0	36.3	44.8	53.0	60.6	68.0	72.3	70.9	64.8	54.0	44.9	37.1	53.3
Mean Minimum Temp. (°F)	23.2	25.7	33.0	39.9	47.8	55.8	60.5	59.0	52.9	40.6	32.9	26.8	41.5
Extreme Maximum Temp. (°F)	72	76	82	90	90	96	100	100	95	85	79	74	100
Extreme Minimum Temp. (°F)	-18	-13	-5	15	26	34	40	39	29	16	8	-12	-18
Days Maximum Temp. ≥ 90°F	0	0	0	0	0	1	4	3	1	0	0	0	9
Days Maximum Temp. ≤ 32°F	6	3	1	0	0	0	0	0	0	0	0	3	13
Days Minimum Temp. ≤ 32°F	26	21	16	7	1	0	0	0	0	7	16	22	116
Days Minimum Temp. ≤ 0°F	1	0	0	0	0	0	0	0	0	0	0	0	1
Heating Degree Days (base 65°F)	985	804	620	360	163	30	4	6	79	341	599	859	4,850
Cooling Degree Days (base 65°F)	0	0	1	6	37	138	260	204	85	8	1	0	740
Mean Precipitation (in.)	3.13	2.86	3.48	3.45	4.11	3.88	3.85	3.23	3.15	2.80	2.83	2.61	39.38
Days With ≥ 0.1" Precipitation	6	6	8	7	9	7	8	6	6	5	6	6	80
Days With ≥ 1.0" Precipitation	1	0	1	1	1	1	1	1	1	1	0	0	9
Mean Snowfall (in.)	6.3	6.2	3.4	1.0	trace	0.0	0.0	0.0	0.0	trace	0.8	3.5	21.2
Days With ≥ 1.0" Snow Depth	5	5	2	0	0	0	0	0	0	0	1	3	16

Stuart *Patrick County*   Elevation: 1,374 ft.   Latitude: 36° 38' N   Longitude: 80° 16' W

	JAN	FEB	MAR	APR	MAY	JUN	JUL	AUG	SEP	OCT	NOV	DEC	YEAR
Mean Maximum Temp. (°F)	44.5	49.0	57.9	68.3	75.4	82.0	85.8	84.3	78.2	67.9	58.3	49.2	66.7
Mean Temp. (°F)	35.5	38.8	46.7	56.0	63.7	71.0	75.0	73.7	67.6	56.6	47.9	39.8	56.0
Mean Minimum Temp. (°F)	26.5	28.6	35.5	43.6	52.0	59.9	64.0	63.1	57.0	45.3	37.4	30.3	45.3
Extreme Maximum Temp. (°F)	75	80	85	91	95	96	99	*100*	95	89	81	77	*100*
Extreme Minimum Temp. (°F)	-13	0	2	18	30	40	50	*48*	35	24	8	-3	*-13*
Days Maximum Temp. ≥ 90°F	0	0	0	0	1	3	8	5	2	0	0	0	19
Days Maximum Temp. ≤ 32°F	4	2	0	0	0	0	0	0	0	0	0	1	7
Days Minimum Temp. ≤ 32°F	23	19	12	3	0	0	0	0	0	2	10	19	88
Days Minimum Temp. ≤ 0°F	0	0	0	0	0	0	0	0	0	0	0	0	0
Heating Degree Days (base 65°F)	907	732	562	284	102	14	1	1	44	269	510	775	4,201
Cooling Degree Days (base 65°F)	0	0	2	18	74	218	344	*296*	138	19	1	0	*1,110*
Mean Precipitation (in.)	3.97	3.43	4.56	4.50	5.06	4.64	5.41	4.58	4.58	4.05	3.61	3.62	52.01
Days With ≥ 0.1" Precipitation	7	7	7	7	8	8	8	7	6	6	6	6	83
Days With ≥ 1.0" Precipitation	1	1	1	1	2	1	2	1	1	1	1	1	14
Mean Snowfall (in.)	4.2	4.4	1.6	0.2	0.0	0.0	0.0	0.0	0.0	0.0	0.3	*1.4*	*12.1*
Days With ≥ 1.0" Snow Depth	na	na	*0*	0	0	0	0	0	0	0	0	na	na

Suffolk Lake Kilby *Suffolk (City) County*   Elevation: 19 ft.   Latitude: 36° 44' N   Longitude: 76° 36' W

	JAN	FEB	MAR	APR	MAY	JUN	JUL	AUG	SEP	OCT	NOV	DEC	YEAR
Mean Maximum Temp. (°F)	48.6	52.1	60.0	69.5	76.9	84.2	88.1	86.2	80.7	70.7	62.0	53.2	69.3
Mean Temp. (°F)	39.4	42.1	49.4	58.1	66.4	74.1	78.5	76.8	71.4	60.5	51.6	43.6	59.3
Mean Minimum Temp. (°F)	30.0	32.0	38.6	46.7	55.9	64.0	68.9	67.4	61.9	50.2	41.2	33.9	49.2
Extreme Maximum Temp. (°F)	77	81	88	94	98	98	100	100	98	91	84	80	100
Extreme Minimum Temp. (°F)	-5	4	14	26	35	46	52	48	41	29	20	4	-5
Days Maximum Temp. ≥ 90°F	0	0	0	0	1	6	13	9	3	0	0	0	32
Days Maximum Temp. ≤ 32°F	2	1	0	0	0	0	0	0	0	0	0	1	4
Days Minimum Temp. ≤ 32°F	19	16	8	1	0	0	0	0	0	0	6	15	65
Days Minimum Temp. ≤ 0°F	0	0	0	0	0	0	0	0	0	0	0	0	0
Heating Degree Days (base 65°F)	789	643	485	232	64	4	0	1	15	175	403	659	3,470
Cooling Degree Days (base 65°F)	1	1	7	30	119	290	443	359	201	42	5	1	1,499
Mean Precipitation (in.)	3.95	3.68	4.39	3.27	3.75	3.88	5.12	5.41	4.82	3.70	3.11	3.31	48.39
Days With ≥ 0.1" Precipitation	7	6	7	6	7	6	8	6	6	5	6	6	76
Days With ≥ 1.0" Precipitation	1	1	1	1	1	1	2	2	1	1	1	1	14
Mean Snowfall (in.)	1.7	3.0	1.1	0.0	0.0	0.0	0.0	0.0	0.0	0.0	trace	0.4	6.2
Days With ≥ 1.0" Snow Depth	1	1	0	0	0	0	0	0	0	0	0	0	2

Tye River 1 SE *Nelson County*   Elevation: 718 ft.   Latitude: 37° 38' N   Longitude: 78° 56' W

	JAN	FEB	MAR	APR	MAY	JUN	JUL	AUG	SEP	OCT	NOV	DEC	YEAR
Mean Maximum Temp. (°F)	45.8	49.8	58.3	69.3	76.1	83.4	87.3	86.0	79.9	70.3	60.5	50.3	68.1
Mean Temp. (°F)	35.4	38.2	46.1	55.8	63.7	71.7	76.3	74.8	68.5	57.2	48.0	39.4	56.3
Mean Minimum Temp. (°F)	24.9	26.7	33.6	42.2	51.2	60.0	65.2	63.5	57.0	44.1	35.5	28.4	44.4
Extreme Maximum Temp. (°F)	77	80	89	95	95	98	103	105	101	91	86	82	105
Extreme Minimum Temp. (°F)	-10	-5	9	18	30	39	51	44	32	23	11	-3	-10
Days Maximum Temp. ≥ 90°F	0	0	0	1	1	6	12	9	4	0	0	0	33
Days Maximum Temp. ≤ 32°F	3	2	0	0	0	0	0	0	0	0	0	1	6
Days Minimum Temp. ≤ 32°F	24	21	15	5	0	0	0	0	0	4	13	21	103
Days Minimum Temp. ≤ 0°F	1	0	0	0	0	0	0	0	0	0	0	0	1
Heating Degree Days (base 65°F)	911	749	585	291	109	14	0	2	41	256	506	788	4,252
Cooling Degree Days (base 65°F)	0	0	4	21	74	229	372	307	143	24	1	1	1,176
Mean Precipitation (in.)	3.69	3.30	4.07	3.46	4.78	3.40	4.43	3.42	4.24	4.07	3.58	3.39	45.83
Days With ≥ 0.1" Precipitation	7	7	8	6	8	6	8	6	6	5	6	6	79
Days With ≥ 1.0" Precipitation	1	1	1	1	1	1	1	1	1	1	1	1	12
Mean Snowfall (in.)	na	*1.0*	*0.8*	0.1	0.0	0.0	0.0	0.0	0.0	0.0	0.3	0.2	na
Days With ≥ 1.0" Snow Depth	*2*	3	1	0	0	0	0	0	0	0	0	1	*7*

Walkerton 2 NW *King And Queen County*   Elevation: 49 ft.   Latitude: 37° 45' N   Longitude: 77° 03' W

	JAN	FEB	MAR	APR	MAY	JUN	JUL	AUG	SEP	OCT	NOV	DEC	YEAR
Mean Maximum Temp. (°F)	47.2	51.4	60.2	71.2	78.0	85.1	88.7	87.2	81.6	70.8	61.1	51.6	69.5
Mean Temp. (°F)	36.6	39.8	47.7	57.4	65.9	73.8	77.9	76.3	70.2	58.5	49.2	40.8	57.9
Mean Minimum Temp. (°F)	26.1	28.2	35.2	43.5	53.8	62.4	67.1	65.4	58.7	46.2	37.3	29.9	46.2
Extreme Maximum Temp. (°F)	76	82	91	97	96	99	101	101	102	93	85	83	102
Extreme Minimum Temp. (°F)	-12	-9	10	21	33	37	48	45	36	22	12	-4	-12
Days Maximum Temp. ≥ 90°F	0	0	0	1	1	7	14	11	4	0	0	0	38
Days Maximum Temp. ≤ 32°F	3	1	0	0	0	0	0	0	0	0	0	1	5
Days Minimum Temp. ≤ 32°F	23	20	14	4	0	0	0	0	0	3	11	19	94
Days Minimum Temp. ≤ 0°F	1	0	0	0	0	0	0	0	0	0	0	0	1
Heating Degree Days (base 65°F)	873	706	535	252	71	7	0	1	27	224	471	744	3,911
Cooling Degree Days (base 65°F)	0	0	8	30	111	287	427	358	190	32	4	1	1,448
Mean Precipitation (in.)	3.65	3.14	4.20	2.98	4.02	3.45	4.47	3.38	3.93	3.41	3.22	3.25	43.10
Days With ≥ 0.1" Precipitation	7	7	8	6	7	6	7	6	6	5	6	7	78
Days With ≥ 1.0" Precipitation	1	1	1	1	1	1	1	1	1	1	1	1	12
Mean Snowfall (in.)	3.9	4.1	0.9	trace	0.0	0.0	0.0	0.0	0.0	0.0	0.2	1.4	10.5
Days With ≥ 1.0" Snow Depth	4	3	0	0	0	0	0	0	0	0	0	2	9

Warrenton 3 SE *Fauquier County*   Elevation: 498 ft.   Latitude: 38° 41' N   Longitude: 77° 46' W

	JAN	FEB	MAR	APR	MAY	JUN	JUL	AUG	SEP	OCT	NOV	DEC	YEAR
Mean Maximum Temp. (°F)	42.3	45.9	54.5	65.7	74.0	81.7	86.1	84.9	79.1	67.9	57.1	46.9	65.5
Mean Temp. (°F)	32.7	35.5	43.6	53.8	62.6	70.8	75.3	73.9	67.5	55.8	46.7	37.4	54.6
Mean Minimum Temp. (°F)	22.9	25.1	32.6	41.8	51.1	59.8	64.4	62.9	55.9	43.6	36.1	27.8	43.7
Extreme Maximum Temp. (°F)	75	80	90	94	94	99	103	104	101	91	86	79	104
Extreme Minimum Temp. (°F)	-11	-7	7	15	30	39	48	44	27	16	10	-2	-11
Days Maximum Temp. ≥ 90°F	0	0	0	0	1	4	10	8	4	0	0	0	27
Days Maximum Temp. ≤ 32°F	5	3	1	0	0	0	0	0	0	0	0	3	12
Days Minimum Temp. ≤ 32°F	26	22	16	4	0	0	0	0	0	3	11	22	104
Days Minimum Temp. ≤ 0°F	1	0	0	0	0	0	0	0	0	0	0	0	1
Heating Degree Days (base 65°F)	994	826	662	344	133	18	1	4	53	294	547	850	4,726
Cooling Degree Days (base 65°F)	0	0	4	13	66	207	343	280	133	17	1	0	1,064
Mean Precipitation (in.)	3.34	2.77	3.58	3.31	4.25	3.88	4.18	3.75	3.86	3.58	3.64	3.28	43.42
Days With ≥ 0.1" Precipitation	7	5	7	6	8	7	7	6	6	5	6	6	76
Days With ≥ 1.0" Precipitation	1	1	1	1	1	1	1	1	1	1	1	1	12
Mean Snowfall (in.)	6.7	5.0	2.8	0.3	0.0	0.0	0.0	0.0	0.0	trace	0.8	2.1	17.7
Days With ≥ 1.0" Snow Depth	9	7	2	0	0	0	0	0	0	0	1	2	21

Warsaw 2 NW *Richmond County*   Elevation: 137 ft.   Latitude: 37° 59' N   Longitude: 76° 46' W

	JAN	FEB	MAR	APR	MAY	JUN	JUL	AUG	SEP	OCT	NOV	DEC	YEAR
Mean Maximum Temp. (°F)	46.1	50.0	58.7	69.2	77.3	84.8	88.8	87.0	81.4	70.6	60.4	50.8	68.8
Mean Temp. (°F)	36.8	39.9	47.5	56.9	65.8	73.7	78.0	76.2	70.3	59.1	50.0	41.4	58.0
Mean Minimum Temp. (°F)	27.5	29.7	36.3	44.6	54.1	62.5	67.2	65.4	59.2	47.5	39.4	31.9	47.1
Extreme Maximum Temp. (°F)	76	80	88	94	99	99	102	103	102	93	85	82	103
Extreme Minimum Temp. (°F)	-6	-4	10	25	33	40	48	44	37	26	15	-1	-6
Days Maximum Temp. ≥ 90°F	0	0	0	0	2	7	14	10	4	0	0	0	37
Days Maximum Temp. ≤ 32°F	3	2	0	0	0	0	0	0	0	0	0	1	6
Days Minimum Temp. ≤ 32°F	21	18	12	3	0	0	0	0	0	2	9	17	82
Days Minimum Temp. ≤ 0°F	0	0	0	0	0	0	0	0	0	0	0	0	0
Heating Degree Days (base 65°F)	866	703	541	264	78	7	0	1	28	212	451	727	3,878
Cooling Degree Days (base 65°F)	0	0	7	28	115	288	430	351	190	38	5	1	1,453
Mean Precipitation (in.)	3.39	2.83	3.92	2.87	4.51	3.36	4.57	3.91	4.29	3.57	3.16	3.08	43.46
Days With ≥ 0.1" Precipitation	6	6	7	6	8	7	7	6	5	5	6	6	75
Days With ≥ 1.0" Precipitation	1	1	1	1	1	1	1	1	1	1	1	1	12
Mean Snowfall (in.)	5.2	5.2	1.7	0.1	0.0	0.0	0.0	0.0	0.0	0.0	0.4	2.4	15.0
Days With ≥ 1.0" Snow Depth	5	3	1	0	0	0	0	0	0	0	0	2	11

West Point 2 NW *King William County*   Elevation: 19 ft.   Latitude: 37° 34' N   Longitude: 76° 48' W

	JAN	FEB	MAR	APR	MAY	JUN	JUL	AUG	SEP	OCT	NOV	DEC	YEAR
Mean Maximum Temp. (°F)	47.5	51.3	60.2	71.0	78.6	85.8	89.5	87.4	81.7	71.0	61.2	51.9	69.8
Mean Temp. (°F)	37.6	40.5	48.4	57.9	66.5	74.2	78.3	76.4	70.5	59.3	50.2	41.8	58.4
Mean Minimum Temp. (°F)	27.5	29.6	36.5	44.7	54.3	62.6	67.0	65.3	59.2	47.6	39.1	31.7	47.1
Extreme Maximum Temp. (°F)	77	83	90	95	98	100	102	104	101	94	85	83	104
Extreme Minimum Temp. (°F)	-7	-1	14	26	35	40	48	45	37	23	12	2	-7
Days Maximum Temp. ≥ 90°F	0	0	0	1	2	9	16	11	4	0	0	0	43
Days Maximum Temp. ≤ 32°F	3	1	0	0	0	0	0	0	0	0	0	1	5
Days Minimum Temp. ≤ 32°F	22	18	13	3	0	0	0	0	0	2	9	17	84
Days Minimum Temp. ≤ 0°F	0	0	0	0	0	0	0	0	0	0	0	0	0
Heating Degree Days (base 65°F)	844	687	517	242	67	6	0	1	24	206	445	713	3,752
Cooling Degree Days (base 65°F)	0	1	9	35	128	307	445	362	195	40	6	1	1,529
Mean Precipitation (in.)	3.89	3.19	4.46	3.11	3.93	3.51	4.42	3.95	4.54	3.62	3.26	3.22	45.10
Days With ≥ 0.1" Precipitation	7	6	8	6	7	6	7	6	6	5	6	6	76
Days With ≥ 1.0" Precipitation	1	0	1	1	1	1	1	1	1	1	1	1	11
Mean Snowfall (in.)	3.9	3.5	1.3	trace	0.0	0.0	0.0	0.0	0.0	0.0	0.2	1.2	10.1
Days With ≥ 1.0" Snow Depth	4	2	0	0	0	0	0	0	0	0	0	1	7

Williamsburg 2 N *York County*   Elevation: 68 ft.   Latitude: 37° 18' N   Longitude: 76° 42' W

	JAN	FEB	MAR	APR	MAY	JUN	JUL	AUG	SEP	OCT	NOV	DEC	YEAR
Mean Maximum Temp. (°F)	48.7	52.2	60.6	71.1	78.1	85.2	89.0	87.3	81.8	71.5	62.6	53.3	70.1
Mean Temp. (°F)	38.3	41.0	48.5	57.7	66.1	73.7	78.1	76.6	71.0	59.8	51.0	42.7	58.7
Mean Minimum Temp. (°F)	27.9	29.7	36.4	44.2	54.0	62.2	67.2	65.8	60.0	48.1	39.4	32.1	47.3
Extreme Maximum Temp. (°F)	77	83	90	94	98	100	103	104	100	93	85	82	104
Extreme Minimum Temp. (°F)	-7	1	12	22	32	41	51	46	38	26	16	0	-7
Days Maximum Temp. ≥ 90°F	0	0	0	1	2	8	15	10	3	0	0	0	39
Days Maximum Temp. ≤ 32°F	2	1	0	0	0	0	0	0	0	0	0	1	4
Days Minimum Temp. ≤ 32°F	22	18	12	3	0	0	0	0	0	1	8	17	81
Days Minimum Temp. ≤ 0°F	0	0	0	0	0	0	0	0	0	0	0	0	0
Heating Degree Days (base 65°F)	821	671	512	242	67	6	0	1	18	190	420	686	3,634
Cooling Degree Days (base 65°F)	0	0	8	30	112	283	430	360	196	35	4	1	1,459
Mean Precipitation (in.)	4.10	3.48	4.62	3.21	4.49	3.36	5.35	4.76	4.79	3.66	3.48	3.32	48.62
Days With ≥ 0.1" Precipitation	8	6	8	6	8	6	8	7	5	5	6	7	80
Days With ≥ 1.0" Precipitation	1	1	1	1	1	1	2	1	1	1	1	1	13
Mean Snowfall (in.)	2.5	2.7	0.9	trace	0.0	0.0	0.0	0.0	0.0	0.0	0.3	0.4	6.8
Days With ≥ 1.0" Snow Depth	2	1	0	0	0	0	0	0	0	0	0	1	4

Wise 3 E *Wise County*   Elevation: 2,545 ft.   Latitude: 37° 00' N   Longitude: 82° 32' W

	JAN	FEB	MAR	APR	MAY	JUN	JUL	AUG	SEP	OCT	NOV	DEC	YEAR
Mean Maximum Temp. (°F)	42.0	46.3	55.6	65.1	71.9	78.2	81.4	80.3	75.1	66.1	55.8	46.1	63.7
Mean Temp. (°F)	33.1	36.7	45.1	53.7	61.2	68.0	71.6	70.5	65.0	55.1	46.1	37.4	53.6
Mean Minimum Temp. (°F)	24.2	27.1	34.6	42.5	50.4	57.8	61.7	60.5	54.9	44.1	36.4	28.7	43.6
Extreme Maximum Temp. (°F)	68	74	80	87	90	92	93	94	90	82	77	72	94
Extreme Minimum Temp. (°F)	-24	-15	-5	17	28	36	44	42	32	20	4	-13	-24
Days Maximum Temp. ≥ 90°F	0	0	0	0	0	0	1	1	0	0	0	0	2
Days Maximum Temp. ≤ 32°F	7	4	1	0	0	0	0	0	0	0	0	4	16
Days Minimum Temp. ≤ 32°F	23	19	14	6	1	0	0	0	0	4	12	19	98
Days Minimum Temp. ≤ 0°F	1	1	0	0	0	0	0	0	0	0	0	1	3
Heating Degree Days (base 65°F)	984	792	611	342	148	26	3	5	72	305	560	850	4,698
Cooling Degree Days (base 65°F)	0	0	1	11	39	136	234	189	78	8	0	0	696
Mean Precipitation (in.)	3.86	3.76	4.37	3.96	4.59	3.93	4.67	3.81	3.67	3.08	3.66	3.60	46.96
Days With ≥ 0.1" Precipitation	8	8	9	8	10	9	9	7	6	6	8	8	96
Days With ≥ 1.0" Precipitation	1	1	1	1	1	1	1	1	1	1	1	1	12
Mean Snowfall (in.)	14.0	13.0	8.8	2.8	0.1	0.0	0.0	0.0	0.0	0.3	3.0	9.0	51.0
Days With ≥ 1.0" Snow Depth	10	8	2	0	0	0	0	0	0	0	1	5	26

Woodstock 2 NE *Shenandoah County*   Elevation: 659 ft.   Latitude: 38° 54' N   Longitude: 78° 28' W

	JAN	FEB	MAR	APR	MAY	JUN	JUL	AUG	SEP	OCT	NOV	DEC	YEAR
Mean Maximum Temp. (°F)	43.3	47.6	56.6	67.5	76.2	83.9	88.0	86.5	80.3	69.4	58.0	47.8	67.1
Mean Temp. (°F)	32.7	35.9	44.1	53.6	62.8	70.9	75.2	73.6	67.1	55.5	45.8	37.1	54.5
Mean Minimum Temp. (°F)	22.0	24.3	31.5	39.6	49.3	57.8	62.3	60.6	53.8	41.6	33.6	26.4	41.9
Extreme Maximum Temp. (°F)	76	80	89	92	96	99	105	105	99	93	86	79	105
Extreme Minimum Temp. (°F)	-17	-13	-1	16	26	37	40	33	29	19	6	-10	-17
Days Maximum Temp. ≥ 90°F	0	0	0	0	1	6	12	10	4	0	0	0	33
Days Maximum Temp. ≤ 32°F	5	2	1	0	0	0	0	0	0	0	0	2	10
Days Minimum Temp. ≤ 32°F	27	23	17	7	1	0	0	0	0	6	14	24	119
Days Minimum Temp. ≤ 0°F	1	0	0	0	0	0	0	0	0	0	0	0	1
Heating Degree Days (base 65°F)	995	814	644	348	126	17	1	4	59	299	570	858	4,735
Cooling Degree Days (base 65°F)	0	0	2	9	62	200	334	270	120	15	0	0	1,012
Mean Precipitation (in.)	2.81	2.42	3.08	2.67	3.73	3.68	3.74	3.25	3.52	3.19	2.94	2.50	37.53
Days With ≥ 0.1" Precipitation	6	6	7	6	8	8	8	7	6	5	6	5	78
Days With ≥ 1.0" Precipitation	0	0	1	0	1	1	1	1	1	1	1	0	8
Mean Snowfall (in.)	7.8	6.3	4.3	0.4	0.0	0.0	0.0	0.0	0.0	0.1	1.1	2.9	22.9
Days With ≥ 1.0" Snow Depth	7	5	2	0	0	0	0	0	0	0	0	2	16

Wytheville 1 S *Wythe County*   Elevation: 2,447 ft.   Latitude: 36° 56' N   Longitude: 81° 06' W

	JAN	FEB	MAR	APR	MAY	JUN	JUL	AUG	SEP	OCT	NOV	DEC	YEAR
Mean Maximum Temp. (°F)	42.8	47.3	56.3	66.0	73.8	80.2	84.3	83.3	77.6	67.9	56.5	46.9	65.2
Mean Temp. (°F)	32.5	35.6	43.4	51.7	60.1	67.5	71.8	70.6	64.6	53.5	44.0	36.1	52.6
Mean Minimum Temp. (°F)	22.2	23.9	30.5	37.2	46.4	54.7	59.3	57.8	51.6	39.1	31.5	25.3	40.0
Extreme Maximum Temp. (°F)	72	78	83	88	89	93	98	97	95	86	79	76	98
Extreme Minimum Temp. (°F)	-20	-9	1	12	24	32	39	36	25	14	4	-13	-20
Days Maximum Temp. ≥ 90°F	0	0	0	0	0	1	4	3	1	0	0	0	9
Days Maximum Temp. ≤ 32°F	5	3	1	0	0	0	0	0	0	0	0	3	12
Days Minimum Temp. ≤ 32°F	26	23	19	10	3	0	0	0	0	9	17	23	131
Days Minimum Temp. ≤ 0°F	1	0	0	0	0	0	0	0	0	0	0	1	2
Heating Degree Days (base 65°F)	1,000	823	662	396	173	35	4	9	84	353	623	888	5,050
Cooling Degree Days (base 65°F)	0	0	0	2	28	117	235	185	70	5	0	0	642
Mean Precipitation (in.)	2.90	2.84	3.19	3.14	4.28	3.25	3.73	3.20	3.00	3.01	2.67	2.44	37.65
Days With ≥ 0.1" Precipitation	6	6	7	6	8	7	7	6	6	5	6	6	76
Days With ≥ 1.0" Precipitation	1	0	1	1	1	1	1	1	1	1	0	0	9
Mean Snowfall (in.)	6.8	5.7	3.0	1.2	0.0	0.0	0.0	0.0	0.0	trace	0.6	3.5	20.8
Days With ≥ 1.0" Snow Depth	7	6	2	0	0	0	0	0	0	0	0	4	19

Note: See Appendix D for explanation of data.

WASHINGTON

PHYSICAL FEATURES. Washington's western boundary is formed by the Pacific Ocean. There are two ranges of mountains parallel to the coast. The Cascade Mountains, 90 to 125 miles inland and 4,000 to 10,000 feet in elevation, are a topographic and climatic barrier separating the State into eastern and western Washington. The higher, wider and more rugged sections are in the northern part of the State. Some of the highest isolated volcanic peaks are Mt. Rainier (14,408 ft.), Mt. Adams (12,307 ft.), and Mt. Baker (10,730 ft.). These and other high peaks are snowcapped throughout the year. The only break in the Cascade Range is the narrow Columbia River gorge.

GENERAL CLIMATE. The location of the State of Washington on the windward coast in mid-latitudes is such that the climatic elements combine to produce a predominantly marine-type climate west of the Cascade Mountains, while east of the Cascades, the climate possesses both continental and marine characteristics. Considering its northerly latitude, 46 to 49°, Washington's climate is mild. There are several climatic controls which have a definite influence on the climate: (a) terrain; (b) Pacific Ocean; and (c) semi-permanent high and low pressure regions located over the north Pacific Ocean. The effect of these various controls combine to produce entirely different conditions within short distances.

The seasonal change in the temperature of the ocean is less than the seasonal change in the temperature of the land, thus the ocean is warmer in winter and cooler in summer than the adjoining land surfaces. The average temperature of the water along the coast and in the Strait of Juan de Fuca ranges from 45°F. in January to 53°F. in July; however, during the summer, some of the shallow bays and protected coves are five to 10 degrees warmer.

The first orographic lifting and major release of moisture occurs along the western slope of the Coastal Range. The second area of heavy orographic precipitation is along the windward slopes of the Cascade Range. Warming and drying of air as it descends along the lee (eastern) slopes of the Cascade Range results in near desert conditions in the lowest section of the Columbia Basin. Another orographic lifting of the air occurs as it flows eastward from the lowest elevations of the Inland Basin toward the Rocky Mountains. This lifting of air results in a gradual increase in precipitation from the lowest section of the basin to the higher elevations along the eastern border of the State.

The location and intensity of the semi-permanent high and low pressure areas over the north Pacific Ocean have a definite influence on the climate. Air circulates in a clockwise direction around the semi-permanent high pressure cell and in a counter-clockwise direction around the semi-permanent low pressure cell. During the spring and summer, the low pressure cell becomes weak and moves north of the Aleutian Islands. At the same time, the high pressure area spreads over most of the north Pacific Ocean. A circulation of air around the high pressure center brings a prevailing westerly and northwesterly flow of comparatively dry, cool and stable air into the Pacific Northwest. As the air moves inland, it becomes warmer and drier which results in a dry season beginning in the late spring and reaching a peak in midsummer.

In the fall and winter, the Aleutian low pressure center intensifies and moves southward reaching a maximum intensity in midwinter. At the same time, the high pressure area becomes weaker and moves southward. A circulation of air around these two pressure centers over the ocean brings a prevailing southwesterly and westerly flow of air into the Pacific Northwest. This air from over the ocean is moist and near the temperature of the water. Condensation occurs as the air moves inland over the cooler land and rises along the windward slopes of the mountains. This results in a wet season beginning in October, reaching a peak in winter, then gradually decreasing in the spring.

WESTERN WASHINGTON. West of the Cascade mountains, summers are cool and comparatively dry and winters are mild, wet and cloudy. The average number of clear or only partly cloudy days each month varies from four to eight in winter, eight to 15 in spring and fall, and 15 to 20 in summer. The percent of possible sunshine received each month ranges from approximately 25 percent in winter to 60 percent in summer. In the interior valleys, measurable rainfall is recorded on 150 days each year, and on 190 days in the mountains and along the coast. Thunderstorms over the lower elevations occur on four to eight days each year and over the mountains on seven to 15 days. Damaging hail storms rarely, if ever, occur in most localities of western Washington. During July and August, the driest months, it is not unusual for 2 to 4 weeks to pass with only a few showers; however, in December and January, the wettest months, precipitation is frequently recorded on 20 to 25 days or more each month. The range in annual precipitation is from approximately 20 inches in an area northeast of the Olympic Mountains to 150 inches along the southwestern slopes of these mountains. Snowfall is light in the lower elevations and heavy in the mountains.

During the wet season, rainfall is usually of light to moderate intensity and continuous over a period of time rather than heavy downpours for brief periods. The heavier intensities occur along the windward slopes of the mountains. During the latter half of the summer and early fall, the lower valleys are sometimes filled with fog or low clouds until noon, while at the same time, the higher elevations are sunny. The strongest winds are generally from the south or southwest and occur during the late fall and winter. In the interior valleys, wind velocities can be expected to reach 40 to 50 m.p.h. each winter. The daily variation in relative humidity in January is from approximately 87 percent at 4 a.m. to 78 percent at 4 p.m., and in July, from 85 percent at 4 a.m. to 47 percent at 4 p.m. During periods of easterly winds, the relative humidity occasionally drops to 25 percent or lower. The highest summer and lowest winter temperatures are usually recorded during periods of easterly winds.

The Olympic Mountains, located on the northern section of the Olympic Peninsula, tower to nearly 8,000 feet. This area receives the full force of storms moving inland from over the ocean, thus heavy precipitation and winds of gale force occur frequently during the winter season. The "rainforest" area along the southwestern and western slopes of the Olympic Mountains receives the heaviest precipitation in the continental United States. A belt on the northeastern slope of the Olympic Mountains in the "rain shadow" of the Olympic Mountains is the driest area in western Washington. This area frequently receives drizzle or light rain while other localities are experiencing light to moderate rainfall, and has slightly more sunshine and slightly less cloudiness than other localities in Puget Sound..

EASTERN WASHINGTON. This section of the State is part of the large inland basin between the Cascade and Rocky Mountains. In an easterly and northerly direction, the Rocky Mountains shield the inland basin from the winter season's cold air masses traveling southward across Canada. In a westerly direction, the Cascade range forms a barrier to the easterly movement of moist and comparatively mild air in winter and cool air in summer. Some of the air from each of these source regions reaches this section of the State and produces a climate which has some of the characteristics of both continental and marine types. Most of the air masses and weather systems crossing eastern Washington are traveling under the influence of the prevailing westerly winds. Infrequently, dry continental air masses enter the inland basin from the north or east. In the summer season, this air from over the continent results in low relative humidity and high temperatures while in winter, clear cold weather prevails. Extremes in both summer and winter temperatures generally occur when the inland basin is under the influence of air from over the continent.

East of the Cascades, summers are warmer, winters are colder, and precipitation is less than in western Washington. The average number of clear or only partly cloudy days each month varies from five to 10 in winter, 12 to 18 in spring and fall, and 20 to 28 in summer. The percent of possible sunshine received each month is from 20 to 30 percent in winter, 50 to 60 percent in spring and fall, and 80 to 85 percent in summer. The number of hours of sunshine possible on a clear day ranges from approximately 8 in December to 16 in June. In the driest areas, rainfall is recorded on 70 days each year .

Annual precipitation ranges from seven to nine inches near the confluence of the Snake and Columbia Rivers, 15 to 30 inches along the eastern border, and 75 to 90 inches near the summit of the Cascade Mountains. During July and August, it is not unusual for four to eight weeks to pass with only a few scattered showers. Thunderstorms can be expected on one to three days each month from April through September. Most thunderstorms in the warmest months occur as isolated cells covering only a few square miles. A few damaging hail storms are reported each summer.

During the coldest months, a loss of heat by radiation at night and moist air crossing the Cascades and mixing with the colder air in the inland basin results in cloudiness, fog, and occasional freezing drizzle. A "chinook" wind which produces a rapid rise in temperature occurs a few times each winter. During most of the year, the prevailing direction of the wind is from the southwest or west. The frequency of northeasterly winds is greatest in the fall and winter.

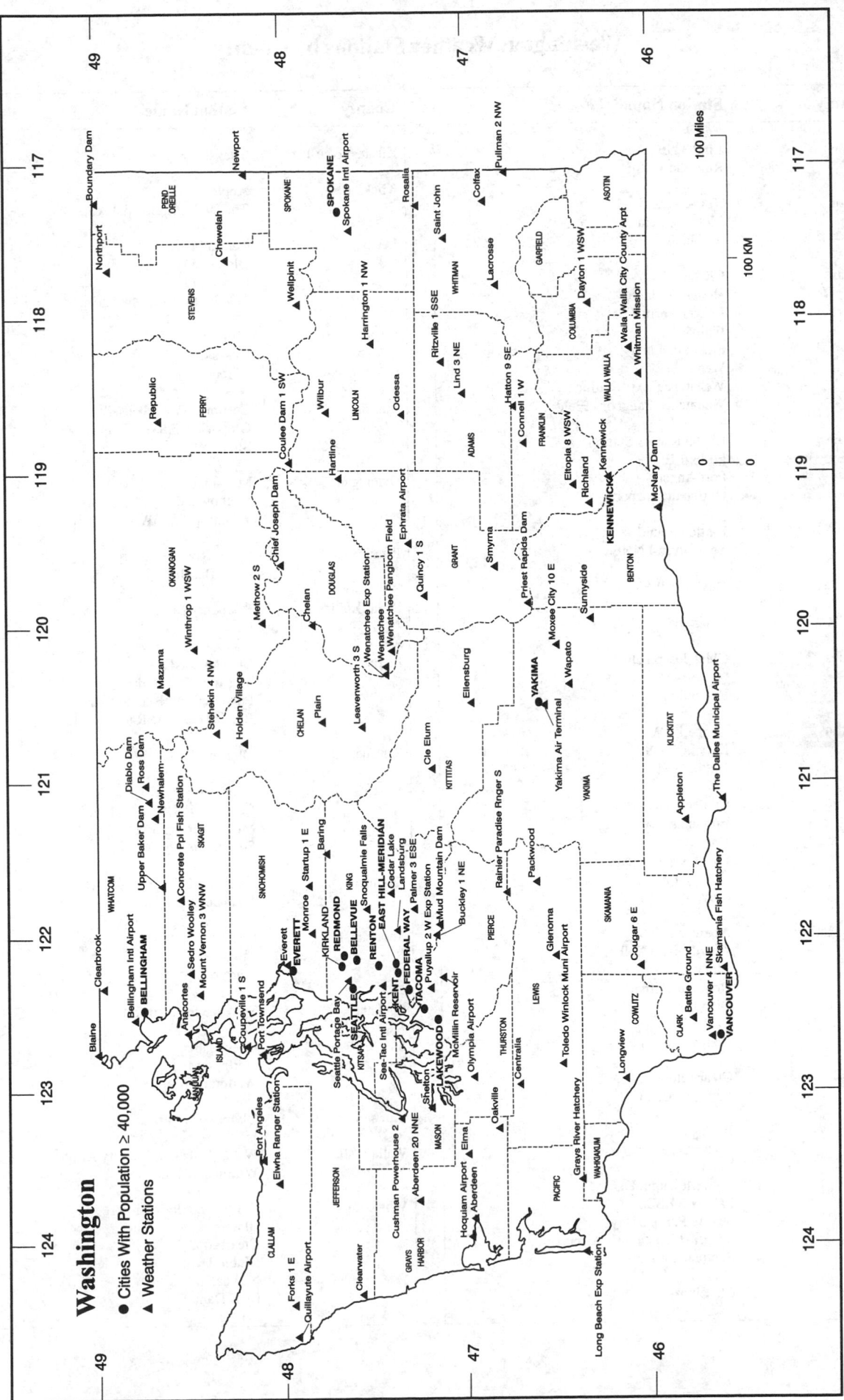

Washington

- ● Cities With Population ≥ 40,000
- ▲ Weather Stations

Washington Weather Stations by County

County	Station Name
Adams	Lind 3 NE
	Ritzville 1 SSE
Benton	Kennewick
	McNary Dam
	Richland
Chelan	Chelan
	Holden Village
	Leavenworth 3 S
	Plain
	Stehekin 4 NW
	Wenatchee
	Wenatchee Exp. Station
	Wenatchee Pangborn Field
Clallam	Elwha Ranger Station
	Forks 1 E
	Port Angeles
	Quillayute Airport
Clark	Battle Ground
	Vancouver 4 NNE
Columbia	Dayton 1 WSW
Cowlitz	Longview
Douglas	Chief Joseph Dam
Ferry	Republic
Franklin	Connell 1 W
	Eltopia 8 WSW
	Hatton 9 SE
Grant	Coulee Dam 1 SW
	Ephrata Airport
	Hartline
	Priest Rapids Dam
	Quincy 1 S
	Smyrna
Grays Harbor	Aberdeen
	Aberdeen 20 NNE
	Elma
	Hoquiam Airport
	Oakville
Island	Coupeville 1 S
Jefferson	Clearwater
	Port Townsend
King	Baring
	Cedar Lake
	Landsburg
	Mud Mountain Dam
	Palmer 3 ESE
	Seattle Portage Bay
	Seattle-Tacoma Int'l Airport
	Snoqualmie Falls
Kittitas	Cle Elum

County	Station Name
Kittitas (cont.)	Ellensburg
Klickitat	Appleton
	The Dalles Municipal Airport
Lewis	Centralia
	Glenoma
	Packwood
	Toledo Winlock Muni Airport
Lincoln	Harrington 1 NW
	Odessa
	Wilbur
Mason	Cushman Powerhouse 2
	Grapeview 3 SW
	Shelton
Okanogan	Mazama
	Methow 2 S
	Winthrop 1 WSW
Pacific	Grays River Hatchery
	Long Beach Exp. Station
Pend Oreille	Boundary Dam
	Newport
Pierce	Buckley 1 NE
	McMillin Reservoir
	Puyallup 2 W Exp. Station
	Rainier Paradise Ranger Station
San Juan	Olga 2 SE
Skagit	Anacortes
	Concrete Ppl. Fish Station
	Mount Vernon 3 WNW
	Sedro Woolley
Skamania	Cougar 6 E
	Skamania Fish Hatchery
Snohomish	Everett
	Monroe
	Startup 1 E
Spokane	Spokane Int'l Airport
Stevens	Chewelah
	Northport
	Wellpinit
Thurston	Olympia Airport
Walla Walla	Walla Walla City County Airport
	Whitman Mission
Whatcom	Bellingham Int'l Airport
	Blaine
	Clearbrook
	Diablo Dam
	Newhalem
	Ross Dam

County	Station Name
Whatcom *(cont.)*	Upper Baker Dam
Whitman	Colfax
	Lacrosse
	Pullman 2 NW
	Rosalia
	Saint John
Yakima	Moxee City 10 E
	Sunnyside
	Wapato
	Yakima Air Terminal

Washington Weather Stations by City

City	Station Name	Miles
Bellevue	Landsburg, WA	18
	Monroe, WA	19
	Seattle Portage Bay, WA	7
	Seattle-Tacoma Int'l Airport, WA	12
	Snoqualmie Falls, WA	15
Bellingham	Anacortes, WA	17
	Bellingham Int'l Airport, WA	5
	Clearbrook, WA	16
	Olga 2 SE, WA	17
East Hill-Meridian	Buckley 1 NE, WA	18
	Landsburg, WA	10
	McMillin Reservoir, WA	18
	Palmer 3 ESE, WA	17
	Puyallup 2 W Exp. Station, WA	15
	Seattle Portage Bay, WA	19
	Seattle-Tacoma Int'l Airport, WA	8
	Snoqualmie Falls, WA	19
Everett	Everett, WA	3
	Monroe, WA	13
Federal Way	Buckley 1 NE, WA	19
	Landsburg, WA	18
	McMillin Reservoir, WA	13
	Puyallup 2 W Exp. Station, WA	8
	Seattle-Tacoma Int'l Airport, WA	10
Kennewick	Eltopia 8 WSW, WA	14
	Kennewick, WA	3
	McNary Dam, WA	19
	Richland, WA	9
Kent	Buckley 1 NE, WA	18
	Landsburg, WA	13
	McMillin Reservoir, WA	17
	Palmer 3 ESE, WA	19
	Puyallup 2 W Exp. Station, WA	13
	Seattle Portage Bay, WA	19
	Seattle-Tacoma Int'l Airport, WA	7
Kirkland	Monroe, WA	15
	Seattle Portage Bay, WA	6
	Seattle-Tacoma Int'l Airport, WA	16
	Snoqualmie Falls, WA	19
Lakewood	Grapeview 3 SW, WA	18
	McMillin Reservoir, WA	13
	Puyallup 2 W Exp. Station, WA	10
Redmond	Monroe, WA	14
	Seattle Portage Bay, WA	8
	Seattle-Tacoma Int'l Airport, WA	17
	Snoqualmie Falls, WA	16
Renton	Landsburg, WA	13
	Seattle Portage Bay, WA	12
	Seattle-Tacoma Int'l Airport, WA	6
	Snoqualmie Falls, WA	17
Seattle	Seattle Portage Bay, WA	2
	Seattle-Tacoma Int'l Airport, WA	11

City	Station Name	Miles
Spokane	Spokane Int'l Airport, WA	7
Tacoma	Grapeview 3 SW, WA	19
	McMillin Reservoir, WA	12
	Puyallup 2 W Exp. Station, WA	7
	Seattle-Tacoma Int'l Airport, WA	17
Vancouver	Beaverton 2 SSW, OR	15
	Hillsboro, OR	18
	Oregon City, OR	20
	Portland KGW TV, OR	9
	Portland Int'l Airport, OR	3
	Troutdale Airport, OR	13
	Battle Ground, WA	11
	Vancouver 4 NNE, WA	3
Yakima	Moxee City 10 E, WA	19
	Wapato, WA	12
	Yakima Air Terminal, WA	2

Note: Miles is the distance between the geographic center of the city and the weather station.

Washington Weather Stations by Elevation

Feet	Station Name	Feet	Station Name
5,426	Rainier Paradise Ranger Station	656	Cougar 6 E
3,218	Holden Village	639	Wenatchee
2,608	Republic	629	Whitman Mission
2,542	Pullman 2 NW	577	McMillin Reservoir
2,490	Wellpinit	557	Smyrna
2,398	Rosalia	534	Landsburg
2,355	Spokane Int'l Airport	524	Newhalem
2,335	Appleton	459	Priest Rapids Dam
2,227	Wilbur	439	Skamania Fish Hatchery
2,188	Harrington 1 NW	439	Snoqualmie Falls
2,168	Mazama	433	Aberdeen 20 NNE
2,132	Newport	396	Seattle-Tacoma Int'l Airport
1,978	Colfax	387	Kennewick
1,942	Saint John	377	Toledo Winlock Muni Airport
1,938	Plain	370	Richland
1,919	Cle Elum	360	McNary Dam
1,909	Hartline	357	Elwha Ranger Station
1,827	Ritzville 1 SSE	347	Forks 1 E
1,797	Boundary Dam	282	Battle Ground
1,751	Winthrop 1 WSW	239	The Dalles Municipal Airport
1,699	Coulee Dam 1 SW	209	Vancouver 4 NNE
1,669	Chewelah	203	Olympia Airport
1,627	Lind 3 NE	193	Concrete Ppl. Fish Station
1,558	Cedar Lake	183	Centralia
1,555	Dayton 1 WSW	177	Quillayute Airport
1,548	Moxee City 10 E	167	Startup 1 E
1,528	Odessa	147	Bellingham Int'l Airport
1,509	Hatton 9 SE	118	Monroe
1,479	Ellensburg	98	Grays River Hatchery
1,450	Lacrosse	88	Port Angeles
1,348	Northport	78	Clearwater
1,305	Mud Mountain Dam	78	Oakville
1,272	Quincy 1 S	78	Olga 2 SE
1,269	Stehekin 4 NW	68	Elma
1,256	Ephrata Airport	68	Port Townsend
1,233	Ross Dam	62	Clearbrook
1,227	Wenatchee Pangborn Field	59	Blaine
1,167	Methow 2 S	59	Everett
1,164	Walla Walla City County Airport	59	Sedro Woolley
1,125	Leavenworth 3 S	49	Coupeville 1 S
1,118	Chelan	49	Grapeview 3 SW
1,062	Yakima Air Terminal	49	Puyallup 2 W Exp. Station
1,059	Packwood	29	Long Beach Exp. Station
1,017	Connell 1 W	19	Anacortes
918	Palmer 3 ESE	19	Cushman Powerhouse 2
889	Diablo Dam	19	Shelton
839	Glenoma	16	Seattle Portage Bay
839	Wapato	13	Mount Vernon 3 WNW
816	Chief Joseph Dam	9	Aberdeen
797	Wenatchee Exp. Station	9	Hoquiam Airport
770	Baring	9	Longview
744	Sunnyside		
698	Eltopia 8 WSW		
688	Upper Baker Dam		
682	Buckley 1 NE		

Olympia Airport

The climate of Olympia and vicinity is characterized by warm, generally dry summers and wet, mild winters.

Fall rains usually begin about mid-October, borne inland to the Cascade Mountains by frequent maritime disturbances originating in the Pacific Ocean. These rains continue with few interruptions through spring. Daytime temperatures will be in the 40s and low 50s, with nighttime temperatures in the 30s. The progression of the wet and mild Pacific disturbances is usually broken once or twice each winter by the formation of large anticyclones, which originate in Alaska and northwestern Canada, and move southward over the state of Washington. These southerly migrations of polar-continental air from the interior will normally lower daytime temperatures to about freezing and nighttime temperatures to 10 - 20 degrees. Often the onset of the cold weather is accompanied by a little snow, but during these cold snaps the air is dry and skies are clear.

During the spring months, the track of the Pacific storms moves gradually farther north, and the semi-permanent Pacific anticyclone also moves northward. The effects of the maritime disturbances lessen, and the periods of improving weather between storms lengthen. During the spring and early fall, clearing skies at night will usually be followed by fog or low stratus clouds in the early morning, which normally dissipate by noon.

Daily high temperatures average 70 to 80 degrees during July, August, and September. The temperature will equal or exceed 90 degrees about 6 days each summer, but as the warm weather is usually accompanied by lowering humidity, it is seldom uncomfortably hot. Rainfall is near one inch per month during July and August and about two inches per month during the transitional period of May, June, and September. About two-thirds of the days are sunny in July, August, and September, and about half are sunny during May and June.

Olympia and vicinity are quite well protected by the Coast Range from the strong south and southwest winds accompanying many of the Pacific storms during the fall and winter. Winds which reach hurricane force along the coast, only 45 miles away, will reach only 50 or 55 mph in gusts in this vicinity. The prevailing wind in Olympia is southerly during most of the year, but during the fair weather in the summers the wind is gentle and from the north to east.

The length of the growing season in the vicinity of Olympia varies with distance from the waterfront and elevation above sea level. The average length of the growing season is 166 days.

Olympia Airport *Thurston County*   Elevation: 203 ft.   Latitude: 46° 58' N   Longitude: 122° 54' W

	JAN	FEB	MAR	APR	MAY	JUN	JUL	AUG	SEP	OCT	NOV	DEC	YEAR
Mean Maximum Temp. (°F)	45.3	49.5	54.3	59.2	65.7	70.9	76.8	77.6	72.0	60.8	50.2	44.4	60.6
Mean Temp. (°F)	38.6	41.1	44.2	47.9	53.8	58.7	63.4	63.7	58.6	50.0	42.8	38.2	50.1
Mean Minimum Temp. (°F)	31.8	32.6	34.1	36.5	41.9	46.5	49.8	49.8	45.2	39.0	35.4	32.0	39.6
Extreme Maximum Temp. (°F)	61	73	76	87	96	98	102	104	98	90	72	63	104
Extreme Minimum Temp. (°F)	-8	-1	9	23	26	30	37	33	25	20	0	-7	-8
Days Maximum Temp. ≥ 90°F	0	0	0	0	0	1	2	2	1	0	0	0	6
Days Maximum Temp. ≤ 32°F	1	0	0	0	0	0	0	0	0	0	0	1	2
Days Minimum Temp. ≤ 32°F	15	14	13	8	1	0	0	0	1	6	11	15	84
Days Minimum Temp. ≤ 0°F	0	0	0	0	0	0	0	0	0	0	0	0	0
Heating Degree Days (base 65°F)	812	669	637	507	342	193	85	73	192	460	659	823	5,452
Cooling Degree Days (base 65°F)	0	0	0	0	3	11	40	46	9	0	0	0	109
Mean Precipitation (in.)	7.68	6.12	5.22	3.66	2.20	1.70	0.82	1.09	2.07	4.14	8.26	8.24	51.20
Maximum Precipitation (in.)	19.8	13.2	10.1	7.8	5.8	3.7	3.0	5.4	7.6	10.1	15.5	14.3	66.7
Minimum Precipitation (in.)	0.3	0.2	0.5	0.4	0.2	0	trace	trace	trace	0.4	1.4	2.5	29.9
Maximum 24-hr. Precipitation (in.)	3.8	3.6	3.4	3.1	1.5	1.6	1.3	1.4	1.5	2.9	4.3	3.5	4.3
Days With ≥ 0.1" Precipitation	14	12	13	10	7	5	2	3	5	8	15	14	108
Days With ≥ 1.0" Precipitation	2	1	1	0	0	0	0	0	0	1	2	2	9
Mean Snowfall (in.)	4.2	3.7	1.0	0.1	trace	trace	0.0	0.0	trace	trace	1.5	3.8	14.3
Maximum Snowfall (in.)	59	27	21	2	trace	trace	0	0	0	trace	15	21	60
Maximum 24-hr. Snowfall (in.)	14	11	9	2	trace	trace	0	0	0	trace	10	10	14
Days With ≥ 1.0" Snow Depth	2	2	0	0	0	0	0	0	0	0	1	2	7
Thunderstorm Days	< 1	< 1	< 1	1	1	< 1	1	1	1	< 1	< 1	< 1	5
Foggy Days	25	21	20	16	11	9	10	15	21	26	25	26	225
Predominant Sky Cover	OVR	OVR	OVR	OVR	OVR	OVR	CLR	OVR	OVR	OVR	OVR	OVR	OVR
Mean Relative Humidity 7am (%)	91	91	91	88	83	82	83	87	92	94	92	92	89
Mean Relative Humidity 4pm (%)	80	71	61	55	52	53	49	50	54	68	79	84	63
Mean Dewpoint (°F)	34	36	36	39	44	49	52	52	50	45	39	36	43
Prevailing Wind Direction	SSW	SSW	SSW	SSW	SSW	SSW	SSW	SSW	SSW	SSW	SSW	SSW	SSW
Prevailing Wind Speed (mph)	10	10	10	9	9	8	8	8	8	9	10	10	9
Maximum Wind Gust (mph)	58	53	51	43	44	38	32	39	38	45	64	56	64

Quillayute Airport

Quillayute Airport, located on the coastal plain between the Pacific Ocean and the Olympic Mountains, is three miles inland from the coast, and 10 miles west of the city of Forks. The terrain is slightly rolling with a gradual increase in elevation from sea level to 180 feet at the station, to 350 feet in the vicinity of Forks. Foothills of the Olympic Mountains begin near the eastern edge of Forks.

In the late fall and winter, storm systems crossing the Pacific follow a more southerly path striking the coast at frequent intervals. The wet season begins in September or October. From October through January, rain may be expected on about 26 days per month, from February through March, on 20 days, from April to June, on 15 days, and from July to September, on 10 days. As the weather systems move inland, rainfall is usually of moderate intensity and continuous, rather than heavy downpours for brief periods. Gale force winds are not unusual. Most of the winter precipitation over the coastal plains falls as rain, however, snow can be expected each year.

Annual precipitation increases from approximately 90 inches near the coast, to amounts in excess of 120 inches over the coastal plains, to 200 inches or more on the wettest slopes of the Olympic Mountains.

During the rainy season, temperatures show little diurnal or day-to-day change. Maximums are in the 40s and minimums in the mid-30s. A few brief outbreaks of cold air from the interior of Canada can be expected each winter. Clear, dry, cold weather generally prevails during periods of easterly winds.

The dry season begins in May with the driest period between mid-July and mid-August. The total rainfall for July is less than .5 inch in one summer out of ten. It also exceeds five inches in one summer out of ten. During the warmest months, afternoon temperatures are in the upper 60s and lower 70s, reaching the upper 70s and the lower 80s on a few days. Occasionally, hot, dry air from the east of the Cascade Mountains reaches this area and temperatures are in the mid- or upper-90s for one to three days.

In summer and early fall, fog or low clouds form over the ocean and frequently move inland at night, but generally disappear by midday. In winter, under the influence of a surface high pressure system, centered off the coast, fog, low clouds, and drizzle are a daily occurence as long as this type of pressure continues.

Quillayute Airport *Clallam County*   Elevation: 177 ft.   Latitude: 47° 56' N   Longitude: 124° 34' W

	JAN	FEB	MAR	APR	MAY	JUN	JUL	AUG	SEP	OCT	NOV	DEC	YEAR
Mean Maximum Temp. (°F)	46.6	49.3	51.9	55.5	60.4	63.8	68.2	69.2	67.2	59.2	50.8	46.4	57.4
Mean Temp. (°F)	40.6	42.3	43.9	46.7	51.4	55.3	59.0	59.6	56.7	50.2	44.1	40.4	49.2
Mean Minimum Temp. (°F)	34.6	35.1	35.8	37.7	42.3	46.8	49.8	50.0	46.2	41.0	37.5	34.4	40.9
Extreme Maximum Temp. (°F)	65	73	72	83	92	96	97	99	97	83	69	63	99
Extreme Minimum Temp. (°F)	9	11	19	23	29	33	38	36	28	24	18	7	7
Days Maximum Temp. ≥ 90°F	0	0	0	0	0	0	0	0	0	0	0	0	0
Days Maximum Temp. ≤ 32°F	0	0	0	0	0	0	0	0	0	0	0	1	1
Days Minimum Temp. ≤ 32°F	12	10	9	6	0	0	0	0	0	3	7	13	60
Days Minimum Temp. ≤ 0°F	0	0	0	0	0	0	0	0	0	0	0	0	0
Heating Degree Days (base 65°F)	748	635	649	544	416	287	187	168	245	453	619	755	5,706
Cooling Degree Days (base 65°F)	0	0	0	0	1	4	7	8	3	0	0	0	23
Mean Precipitation (in.)	14.13	12.24	10.90	7.67	5.30	3.35	2.33	2.64	4.21	9.83	15.01	14.83	102.44
Maximum Precipitation (in.)	24.0	20.6	21.9	13.9	12.4	8.5	11.0	15.1	10.9	27.2	29.1	27.8	132.
Minimum Precipitation (in.)	1.2	0.9	1.8	2.9	1.0	0.4	0.4	0.3	0.1	1.4	4.4	3.6	60.2
Maximum 24-hr. Precipitation (in.)	7.2	5.1	4.0	2.6	3.5	1.6	5.3	4.3	3.3	4.9	5.3	6.7	7.2
Days With ≥ 0.1" Precipitation	18	16	16	14	10	7	4	4	7	13	19	18	146
Days With ≥ 1.0" Precipitation	5	4	3	2	1	1	0	1	3	5	5	31
Mean Snowfall (in.)	3.7	2.9	1.6	0.3	trace	trace	0.0	0.0	trace	trace	1.2	2.9	12.6
Maximum Snowfall (in.)	40	16	10	3	trace	0	0	0	trace	trace	16	12	58
Maximum 24-hr. Snowfall (in.)	8	7	8	2	trace	0	0	0	trace	trace	8	7	8
Days With ≥ 1.0" Snow Depth	2	1	1	0	0	0	0	0	0	0	1	1	6
Thunderstorm Days	1	< 1	< 1	< 1	< 1	< 1	1	< 1	1	1	2	1	7
Foggy Days	21	19	20	17	17	18	19	20	20	22	21	22	236
Predominant Sky Cover	OVR	OVR	OVR	OVR	OVR	OVR	OVR	OVR	OVR	OVR	OVR	OVR	OVR
Mean Relative Humidity 7am (%)	92	91	92	92	90	90	91	94	94	94	93	92	92
Mean Relative Humidity 4pm (%)	83	77	72	68	66	67	65	67	67	75	84	87	73
Mean Dewpoint (°F)	37	38	39	40	45	49	52	53	50	46	41	38	44
Prevailing Wind Direction	NE	ENE	S	S	S	WNW	NW	S	S	S	ENE	ENE	S
Prevailing Wind Speed (mph)	8	6	9	8	8	8	8	7	7	8	6	6	7
Maximum Wind Gust (mph)	55	58	49	40	41	44	32	48	36	53	54	58	58

Seattle Portage Bay

Seattle is located on a hill between the salt waters of Puget Sound to the west and the fresh waters of Lake Washington to the east. The lake shore roughly parallels the shore of Puget Sound at distances varying from about two and a half to six miles. Hills rise abruptly from both shorelines and reach elevations of more than 300 feet in the central area to more than 500 feet in the northern and the southwestern sections. The north-south orientation of the city is matched on the east by the Cascade Mountains and the Olympic Mountains to the west and northwest.

The climate of Seattle is mild and moist, the result of the prevailing westerly winds off the Pacific Ocean approximately 90 miles to the west, and the Cascade Mountains which tend to shield the city from the cold continental air from the east. Winters are comparatively warm and summers cool because of the steady influx of marine air.

An average year will have less than three days during the summer with a high temperature of 90 degrees or more with the maximum temperature rarely reaching 100 degrees. Nighttime temperatures during the warmest months seldom remain above 65 degrees. Daily highs during the winter fail to rise above 32 degrees on an average of about two days per year, while the number of days with minimum temperatures of 32 degrees or less averages only 15 days per year.

The city lies within the lee side dry area caused by the Olympic Mountains. As a result, the normal precipitation of less than 36 inches is relatively light when compared to the 50 inches or more that falls on the nearby Cascade foothills. The western slopes of these hills and mountains lift the moist marine air, causing very heavy precipitation on the seaward slopes and significantly less at the summits. The winter wet season, usually from October to March, is the result of the air flowing around the Aleutian low pressure system, but, in the summer the Eastern Pacific high pressure system moves north and forces the moist marine air to the north of Washington and brings relatively dry and cool air to the state. The warmest temperatures of the summer usually occur when the Pacific high extends into southwest Canada creating a hot and dry flow of continental air across the Cascade Mountains into the Puget Sound area. Less than 20 percent of the annual rainfall occurs during the summer dry season, April through September.

The average winter snowfall is about nine inches but the snow seldom remains on the ground for more than two days at a time. Fog is a frequent occurrence during the late fall and winter months.

Seattle Portage Bay *King County*   Elevation: 16 ft.   Latitude: 47° 39' N   Longitude: 122° 18' W

	JAN	FEB	MAR	APR	MAY	JUN	JUL	AUG	SEP	OCT	NOV	DEC	YEAR
Mean Maximum Temp. (°F)	47.2	50.7	54.8	59.4	65.1	69.8	74.4	74.6	70.0	60.4	51.4	46.7	60.4
Mean Temp. (°F)	42.0	44.3	47.4	51.5	57.0	61.5	65.6	66.0	61.6	53.7	46.1	41.9	53.2
Mean Minimum Temp. (°F)	36.8	37.8	40.0	43.5	48.8	53.2	56.7	57.3	53.2	46.9	40.7	36.9	46.0
Extreme Maximum Temp. (°F)	64	70	74	85	88	93	96	94	91	82	71	65	96
Extreme Minimum Temp. (°F)	16	11	23	32	38	42	47	48	41	31	13	12	11
Days Maximum Temp. ≥ 90°F	0	0	0	0	0	0	1	0	0	0	0	0	1
Days Maximum Temp. ≤ 32°F	0	0	0	0	0	0	0	0	0	0	0	1	1
Days Minimum Temp. ≤ 32°F	8	5	2	0	0	0	0	0	0	0	3	7	25
Days Minimum Temp. ≤ 0°F	0	0	0	0	0	0	0	0	0	0	0	0	0
Heating Degree Days (base 65°F)	707	579	538	400	247	117	37	33	113	345	561	710	4,387
Cooling Degree Days (base 65°F)	0	0	0	0	7	21	65	78	19	1	0	0	191
Mean Precipitation (in.)	5.01	3.92	3.80	2.81	1.99	1.52	0.95	1.30	1.61	3.35	5.63	6.03	37.92
Maximum Precipitation (in.)	10.9	8.1	7.2	5.3	4.7	3.7	2.2	5.5	5.6	8.0	11.2	15.3	48.1
Minimum Precipitation (in.)	0.6	0.3	0.4	0.2	0.3	trace	0	trace	trace	0.2	0.5	1.0	19.5
Maximum 24-hr. Precipitation (in.)	4.2	2.2	2.6	2.0	1.1	1.4	0.9	1.5	1.7	2.6	2.7	3.4	4.2
Days With ≥ 0.1" Precipitation	11	10	11	8	6	4	3	3	5	8	13	12	94
Days With ≥ 1.0" Precipitation	1	0	0	0	0	0	0	0	0	1	1	1	4
Mean Snowfall (in.)	1.4	0.7	0.3	trace	trace	0.0	0.0	0.0	0.0	trace	0.7	1.8	4.9
Maximum Snowfall (in.)	31	35	9	2	0	0	0	0	0	trace	10	14	64
Maximum 24-hr. Snowfall (in.)	12	22	6	2	0	0	0	0	0	trace	6	10	22
Days With ≥ 1.0" Snow Depth	1	1	0	0	0	0	0	0	0	0	1	1	4
Thunderstorm Days	< 1	< 1	< 1	< 1	< 1	< 1	< 1	1	< 1	< 1	< 1	< 1	1
Foggy Days	3	2	1	1	1	1	1	3	4	3	3	3	26
Predominant Sky Cover	na	na	na	na	na	na	na	na	na	na	na	na	na
Mean Relative Humidity 7am (%)	na	na	na	na	na	na	na	na	na	na	na	na	na
Mean Relative Humidity 4pm (%)	na	na	na	na	na	na	na	na	na	na	na	na	na
Mean Dewpoint (°F)	na	na	na	na	na	na	na	na	na	na	na	na	na
Prevailing Wind Direction	na	na	na	na	na	na	na	na	na	na	na	na	na
Prevailing Wind Speed (mph)	na	na	na	na	na	na	na	na	na	na	na	na	na
Maximum Wind Gust (mph)	44	48	49	43	40	35	41	43	39	43	47	51	51

Seattle-Tacoma Int'l Airport

The Seattle-Tacoma International Airport is located 6 miles south of the Seattle city limits and 14 miles north of Tacoma. It is situated on a low ridge lying between Puget Sound on the west and the Green River valley on the east with terrain sloping moderately to the shores of Puget Sound some two miles to the west. The Olympic Mountains, rising sharply from Puget Sound, are about 50 miles to the northwest. Rather steep bluffs border the Green River Valley about 2.5 miles to the east and the foothills of the Cascade Range begin 10 to 15 miles to the east of the airport.

The mild climate of the Pacific Coast is modified by the Cascade Mountains and, to a lesser extent, by the Olympic Mountains. The climate is characterized by mild temperatures, a pronounced though not sharply defined rainy season, and considerable cloudiness, particularly during the winter months. The Cascades are very effective in shielding the Seattle-Tacoma area from the cold, dry continental air during the winter and the hot, dry continental air during the summer months. Southwesterly circulation keeps the average winter daytime temperatures in the 40s and the nighttime readings in the 30s. During the summer, daytime temperatures are usually in the 70s with nighttime lows in the 50s. Extremes of temperatures, both in the winter and summer, are usually of short duration. The dry season is centered around July and early August with July being the driest month of the year. The rainy season extends from October to March with December normally the wettest month, however, precipitation is rather evenly distributed through the winter and early spring months with more than 75 percent of the yearly precipitation falling during the winter wet season.

The occurrence of snow in the Seattle-Tacoma area is extremely variable and usually melts before accumulating measurable depths. There are winters on record with only a trace of snow, but at the other extreme, over 21 inches has fallen in a 24-hour period.

The highest winds recorded in the Seattle-Tacoma area were associated with strong storms crossing the state from the southwest. Prevailing winds are from the southwest but occasional severe winter storms will produce strong northerly winds. Winds during the summer months are relatively light with occasional land-sea breeze effects creating afternoon northerly winds of eight to 15 miles an hour. Fog or low clouds that form over the southern Puget Sound area in the late summer, fall, and early winter months, often dominate the weather conditions during the late night and early morning hours.

Based on the 1951-1980 period, the average first occurrence of 32 degrees Fahrenheit in the fall is November 11 and the average last occurrence in the spring is March 24.

Seattle-Tacoma Int'l Airport *King County*   Elevation: 396 ft.   Latitude: 47° 28' N   Longitude: 122° 19' W

	JAN	FEB	MAR	APR	MAY	JUN	JUL	AUG	SEP	OCT	NOV	DEC	YEAR
Mean Maximum Temp. (°F)	45.8	49.6	53.3	58.0	64.4	69.7	75.3	75.5	70.0	59.6	50.6	45.3	59.7
Mean Temp. (°F)	40.9	43.5	46.2	50.0	55.8	60.7	65.3	65.6	61.0	52.6	45.3	40.6	52.3
Mean Minimum Temp. (°F)	36.0	37.3	39.2	42.0	47.1	51.7	55.3	55.7	51.9	45.6	40.0	35.9	44.8
Extreme Maximum Temp. (°F)	64	68	75	85	92	96	100	99	98	89	72	64	100
Extreme Minimum Temp. (°F)	12	7	20	29	36	42	45	46	35	30	10	9	7
Days Maximum Temp. ≥ 90°F	0	0	0	0	0	0	1	1	0	0	0	0	2
Days Maximum Temp. ≤ 32°F	1	0	0	0	0	0	0	0	0	0	0	1	2
Days Minimum Temp. ≤ 32°F	9	6	2	0	0	0	0	0	0	0	3	9	29
Days Minimum Temp. ≤ 0°F	0	0	0	0	0	0	0	0	0	0	0	0	0
Heating Degree Days (base 65°F)	739	602	575	443	285	143	51	41	134	377	584	748	4,722
Cooling Degree Days (base 65°F)	0	0	0	0	6	19	64	71	21	0	0	0	181
Mean Precipitation (in.)	5.28	4.08	3.76	2.65	1.70	1.45	0.80	1.02	1.66	3.18	5.96	5.81	37.35
Maximum Precipitation (in.)	12.9	9.1	8.4	6.5	4.8	3.8	2.4	4.6	5.9	7.8	10.7	11.8	55.1
Minimum Precipitation (in.)	0.6	0.3	0.6	0.3	0.1	0.1	trace	trace	trace	0.3	0.7	1.4	23.7
Maximum 24-hr. Precipitation (in.)	3.0	3.0	2.7	2.6	1.8	1.8	0.8	1.6	1.6	2.7	3.4	2.1	3.4
Days With ≥ 0.1" Precipitation	12	10	11	7	5	4	3	3	5	8	13	12	93
Days With ≥ 1.0" Precipitation	1	0	0	0	0	0	0	0	0	0	1	1	3
Mean Snowfall (in.)	2.3	1.2	0.6	trace	trace	0.0	0.0	0.0	trace	trace	1.1	1.9	7.1
Maximum Snowfall (in.)	57	13	18	2	trace	0	0	0	0	2	18	22	61
Maximum 24-hr. Snowfall (in.)	20	7	6	1	trace	0	0	0	0	2	8	9	20
Days With ≥ 1.0" Snow Depth	1	1	0	0	0	0	0	0	0	0	1	1	4
Thunderstorm Days	< 1	< 1	1	1	1	1	1	1	1	< 1	1	< 1	8
Foggy Days	18	15	13	10	8	8	8	11	16	19	19	19	164
Predominant Sky Cover	OVR	OVR	OVR	OVR	OVR	OVR	CLR	OVR	OVR	OVR	OVR	OVR	OVR
Mean Relative Humidity 7am (%)	83	83	84	83	80	79	79	83	88	88	86	85	83
Mean Relative Humidity 4pm (%)	75	69	63	57	54	53	49	51	56	68	76	79	62
Mean Dewpoint (°F)	33	35	36	39	44	48	52	53	50	45	39	35	43
Prevailing Wind Direction	S	S	SSW	SSW	SSW	SSW	SW	SSW	N	S	S	S	SSW
Prevailing Wind Speed (mph)	12	10	13	12	10	9	9	9	9	10	12	12	10
Maximum Wind Gust (mph)	64	60	53	44	46	33	29	38	39	45	67	60	67

Spokane Int'l Airport

Spokane lies on the eastern edge of the broad Columbia Basin area of Washington which is bounded by the Cascade Range on the west and the Rocky Mountains on the east. The elevations in eastern Washington vary from less than 400 feet above sea level near Pasco where the Columbia River flows out of Washington to over 5,000 feet in the mountain areas of the extreme eastern edge of the State. Spokane is located on the upper plateau area where the long gradual slope from the Columbia River meets the sharp rise of the Rocky Mountain Ranges.

Much of the urban area of Spokane lies along both sides of the Spokane River at an elevation of approximately 2,000 feet, but the residential areas have spread to the crests of the plateaus on either side of the river with elevations up to 2,500 feet above sea level. Spokane International Airport is situated on the plateau area 6 miles west-southwest and some 400 feet higher than the downtown business district.

The climate of Spokane combines some of the characteristics of damp coastal type weather and arid interior conditions. Most of the air masses which reach Spokane are brought in by the prevailing westerly and southwesterly circulations. Annual precipitation totals in the Spokane area are generally less than 20 inches. The lifting action of the air masses as they move up the east slope of the Columbia Basin frequently produces the cooling and condensation necessary for formation of clouds and precipitation.

Infrequently, the Spokane area comes under the influence of dry continental air masses from the north or east. On occasions when these air masses penetrate into eastern Washington the result is high temperatures and very low humidity in the summer and sub-zero temperatures in the winter.

In general, Spokane weather has the characteristics of a mild, arid climate during the summer months and a cold, coastal type in the winter. Approximately 70 percent of the total annual precipitation falls between the first of October and the end of March and about half of that falls as snow. The growing season usually extends over nearly six months from mid-April to mid-October. Winter weather includes many cloudy or foggy days and below freezing temperatures with occasional snowfall of several inches in depth. Sub-zero temperatures and traffic-stopping snowfalls are infrequent.

Based on the 1951-1980 period, the average first occurrence of 32 degrees Fahrenheit in the fall is October 6 and the average last occurrence in the spring is May 4.

Spokane Int'l Airport *Spokane County*   Elevation: 2,355 ft.   Latitude: 47° 37' N   Longitude: 117° 32' W

	JAN	FEB	MAR	APR	MAY	JUN	JUL	AUG	SEP	OCT	NOV	DEC	YEAR
Mean Maximum Temp. (°F)	32.9	39.5	48.6	57.2	66.3	74.2	82.7	82.8	72.5	58.4	41.4	33.0	57.5
Mean Temp. (°F)	27.3	32.7	39.5	46.4	54.5	61.8	68.8	68.7	59.2	47.1	35.2	27.4	47.4
Mean Minimum Temp. (°F)	21.6	25.8	30.3	35.4	42.6	49.3	54.8	54.6	45.8	35.8	28.8	21.7	37.2
Extreme Maximum Temp. (°F)	59	63	70	90	96	101	103	103	98	86	67	56	103
Extreme Minimum Temp. (°F)	-22	-24	-7	21	25	33	37	37	24	10	-21	-22	-24
Days Maximum Temp. ≥ 90°F	0	0	0	0	0	2	8	8	1	0	0	0	19
Days Maximum Temp. ≤ 32°F	13	5	1	0	0	0	0	0	0	0	4	14	37
Days Minimum Temp. ≤ 32°F	26	22	20	10	2	0	0	0	1	10	20	27	138
Days Minimum Temp. ≤ 0°F	2	1	0	0	0	0	0	0	0	0	0	2	5
Heating Degree Days (base 65°F)	1,163	906	784	554	330	143	40	39	195	548	890	1,160	6,752
Cooling Degree Days (base 65°F)	0	0	0	0	14	46	153	156	32	1	0	0	402
Mean Precipitation (in.)	1.90	1.52	1.52	1.24	1.56	1.20	0.77	0.68	0.74	1.11	2.27	2.26	16.77
Maximum Precipitation (in.)	5.0	3.9	3.8	3.1	5.7	3.1	2.3	1.8	2.0	4.0	5.1	5.1	26.1
Minimum Precipitation (in.)	0.4	0.3	0.3	0.1	0.2	0.2	trace	trace	trace	trace	0.2	0.6	11.2
Maximum 24-hr. Precipitation (in.)	1.3	0.8	1.0	0.9	1.6	1.5	1.1	1.0	1.0	0.9	1.4	1.4	1.6
Days With ≥ 0.1" Precipitation	6	5	5	4	5	4	2	2	2	3	7	7	52
Days With ≥ 1.0" Precipitation	0	0	0	0	0	0	0	0	0	0	0	0	0
Mean Snowfall (in.)	12.3	7.7	2.9	0.8	trace	trace	0.0	0.0	trace	0.4	6.6	13.1	43.8
Maximum Snowfall (in.)	57	29	15	7	4	trace	0	0	0	6	25	42	99
Maximum 24-hr. Snowfall (in.)	13	11	5	4	4	trace	0	0	0	6	9	11	13
Days With ≥ 1.0" Snow Depth	17	9	2	0	0	0	0	0	0	0	5	16	49
Thunderstorm Days	< 1	< 1	< 1	1	2	3	2	2	1	< 1	< 1	0	11
Foggy Days	19	14	9	4	3	2	1	1	2	8	17	21	101
Predominant Sky Cover	OVR	OVR	OVR	OVR	OVR	OVR	CLR	CLR	CLR	OVR	OVR	OVR	OVR
Mean Relative Humidity 7am (%)	86	85	81	73	68	64	56	59	69	81	88	88	75
Mean Relative Humidity 4pm (%)	79	69	55	43	40	37	27	28	34	50	75	83	52
Mean Dewpoint (°F)	22	26	28	32	38	43	44	43	40	35	30	24	34
Prevailing Wind Direction	NE	NE	SW	SW	SW	SW	SW	SW	SW	NE	NE	NE	SW
Prevailing Wind Speed (mph)	7	8	14	14	12	12	10	10	12	7	7	7	10
Maximum Wind Gust (mph)	67	55	64	62	53	49	51	54	47	62	58	55	67

Yakima Air Terminal

Yakima is located in a small east-west valley in the upper (northwestern) part of the Yakima Valley. Local topography is complex with a number of minor valleys and ridges giving a local relief of as much as 1,000 feet. This complex topography results in marked variations in air drainage, winds, and low temperatures within short distances.

The climate of the Yakima Valley is relatively mild and dry. It has characteristics of both maritime and continental climates, modified by the Cascade and the Rocky Mountains, respectively. Summers are dry and rather hot, and winters cool with only light snowfall. The maritime influence is strongest in winter when the prevailing westerlies are the strongest and most steady. The Selkirk and Rocky Mountains in British Columbia and Idaho shield the area from most of the very cold air masses that sweep down from Canada into the Great Plains and eastern United States. Sometimes a strong polar high pressure area over western Canada will occur at the same time that a low pressure area covers the southwestern United States. On these occasions, the cold arctic air will pour through the passes and down the river valleys of British Columbia, bringing very cold temperatures to Yakima. However, over one-half of the winters remain above zero.

The modifying influence of the Pacific Ocean is much less in summer. Afternoons are hot, but the dry air results in a rapid temperature fall after sunset, and nights are pleasantly cool with summertime low temperatures, usually in the 50s. Spells of four to 11 days of 100 degrees or more have occurred.

Temperatures below 32 degrees are infrequent during the period from mid-May through September. Temperatures below 40 degrees during July and August have occurred in about half of the years.

Precipitation follows a West Coast marine climate with the typical late fall and early winter high. However, since Yakima lies in the rain shadow of the Cascades, total amounts are small. The three months, November to January, total nearly half of the annual fall.

Irrigation is necessary for nearly all crops. Ample water supplies are available from the snowmelt in the Cascade Mountains which is collected in storage reservoirs for summer use.

Snowfall in the Yakima area is light, averaging 20 to 25 inches.

Summers are sunny, with about 85 percent of the possible sunshine. Winters are generally cloudy, with only a third of the possible sunshine.

Winds are mostly light, averaging about seven mph for the year, being somewhat stronger in late spring and weaker in winter. Speeds of 30 to 35 mph are reached at least once in about half the months and speeds over 40 mph occur in about one out of five months. The most common wind direction in downtown Yakima is northwest, while at the airport the wind is from the west in winter and the west-northwest in summer.

Yakima Air Terminal *Yakima County*   Elevation: 1,062 ft.   Latitude: 46° 34' N   Longitude: 120° 33' W

	JAN	FEB	MAR	APR	MAY	JUN	JUL	AUG	SEP	OCT	NOV	DEC	YEAR
Mean Maximum Temp. (°F)	37.6	45.8	56.1	63.9	72.5	79.7	87.2	86.6	77.5	64.3	47.9	37.2	63.0
Mean Temp. (°F)	29.8	36.1	43.4	49.5	57.4	64.2	70.3	69.4	60.7	49.3	37.9	29.5	49.8
Mean Minimum Temp. (°F)	22.0	26.4	30.7	35.1	42.2	48.6	53.2	52.2	43.9	34.2	27.9	21.7	36.5
Extreme Maximum Temp. (°F)	68	68	77	92	102	105	108	110	100	88	73	67	110
Extreme Minimum Temp. (°F)	-17	-17	10	20	25	30	34	36	24	11	-13	-16	-17
Days Maximum Temp. ≥ 90°F	0	0	0	0	1	5	13	11	2	0	0	0	32
Days Maximum Temp. ≤ 32°F	10	3	0	0	0	0	0	0	0	0	2	10	25
Days Minimum Temp. ≤ 32°F	27	23	20	12	3	0	0	0	1	13	22	28	149
Days Minimum Temp. ≤ 0°F	2	1	0	0	0	0	0	0	0	0	0	1	4
Heating Degree Days (base 65°F)	1,083	810	663	459	249	93	25	25	152	480	805	1,094	5,938
Cooling Degree Days (base 65°F)	0	0	0	2	22	66	184	161	34	0	0	0	469
Mean Precipitation (in.)	1.24	0.78	0.69	0.52	0.50	0.61	0.22	0.36	0.39	0.54	1.07	1.41	8.33
Maximum Precipitation (in.)	3.7	2.5	2.6	1.8	2.8	2.5	0.7	2.1	2.1	2.2	2.8	4.2	13.9
Minimum Precipitation (in.)	0.1	trace	trace	trace	trace	trace	trace	0	0	0	trace	0.1	4.2
Maximum 24-hr. Precipitation (in.)	1.4	0.9	0.7	1.1	0.8	1.5	0.7	1.6	1.4	1.0	1.0	1.4	1.6
Days With ≥ 0.1" Precipitation	4	3	2	2	2	2	1	1	2	4	4	28
Days With ≥ 1.0" Precipitation	0	0	0	0	0	0	0	0	0	0	0	0	0
Mean Snowfall (in.)	6.9	3.2	1.3	trace	trace	0.0	0.0	0.0	0.0	0.2	3.3	9.3	24.2
Maximum Snowfall (in.)	27	17	11	trace	trace	0	0	0	0	3	21	38	53
Maximum 24-hr. Snowfall (in.)	14	8	7	trace	trace	0	0	0	0	2	11	14	14
Days With ≥ 1.0" Snow Depth	16	6	0	0	0	0	0	0	0	0	2	13	37
Thunderstorm Days	0	< 1	< 1	< 1	1	2	1	1	1	< 1	0	0	6
Foggy Days	15	8	3	< 1	< 1	< 1	< 1	< 1	< 1	2	11	17	56
Predominant Sky Cover	OVR	OVR	OVR	OVR	OVR	CLR	CLR	CLR	CLR	OVR	OVR	OVR	OVR
Mean Relative Humidity 7am (%)	84	83	77	64	56	54	54	61	72	81	85	85	71
Mean Relative Humidity 4pm (%)	72	59	41	33	30	30	26	28	32	43	63	75	44
Mean Dewpoint (°F)	22	27	28	31	37	43	46	47	43	36	30	25	34
Prevailing Wind Direction	W	W	W	W	W	NW	W	W	WNW	WNW	W	W	W
Prevailing Wind Speed (mph)	6	7	8	8	8	10	8	7	8	8	7	6	8
Maximum Wind Gust (mph)	66	59	61	56	69	69	59	44	55	54	59	61	69

Aberdeen *Grays Harbor County*   Elevation: 9 ft.   Latitude: 46° 58' N   Longitude: 123° 49' W

	JAN	FEB	MAR	APR	MAY	JUN	JUL	AUG	SEP	OCT	NOV	DEC	YEAR
Mean Maximum Temp. (°F)	46.7	49.8	53.5	56.5	61.2	64.5	68.3	69.3	69.1	61.1	52.0	46.6	58.2
Mean Temp. (°F)	41.2	43.1	45.7	48.5	53.5	57.3	60.7	61.4	59.5	52.6	45.8	41.3	50.9
Mean Minimum Temp. (°F)	35.6	36.2	37.9	40.6	45.7	50.0	53.1	53.5	50.0	44.0	39.6	35.9	43.5
Extreme Maximum Temp. (°F)	58	73	79	85	91	98	98	105	100	86	70	62	105
Extreme Minimum Temp. (°F)	14	12	23	29	33	37	41	42	34	26	14	10	10
Days Maximum Temp. ≥ 90°F	0	0	0	0	0	0	0	0	0	0	0	0	0
Days Maximum Temp. ≤ 32°F	0	0	0	0	0	0	0	0	0	0	0	1	1
Days Minimum Temp. ≤ 32°F	10	8	5	1	0	0	0	0	0	1	4	10	39
Days Minimum Temp. ≤ 0°F	0	0	0	0	0	0	0	0	0	0	0	0	0
Heating Degree Days (base 65°F)	731	613	591	488	355	232	140	119	172	380	569	729	5,119
Cooling Degree Days (base 65°F)	0	0	0	0	5	6	14	17	14	1	0	0	57
Mean Precipitation (in.)	13.03	10.88	9.12	6.46	3.54	2.53	1.54	1.50	2.98	7.28	12.93	13.52	85.31
Days With ≥ 0.1" Precipitation	17	15	15	13	9	7	3	3	6	11	18	18	135
Days With ≥ 1.0" Precipitation	5	3	3	1	0	0	0	0	1	2	4	4	23
Mean Snowfall (in.)	1.2	0.3	0.1	0.0	0.0	0.0	0.0	0.0	0.0	0.0	trace	*0.3*	*1.9*
Days With ≥ 1.0" Snow Depth	1	1	0	0	0	0	0	0	0	0	0	*0*	*2*

Aberdeen 20 NNE *Grays Harbor County*   Elevation: 433 ft.   Latitude: 47° 16' N   Longitude: 123° 42' W

	JAN	FEB	MAR	APR	MAY	JUN	JUL	AUG	SEP	OCT	NOV	DEC	YEAR
Mean Maximum Temp. (°F)	43.2	46.5	51.1	55.4	62.2	66.3	71.7	72.3	67.5	57.7	47.9	42.2	57.0
Mean Temp. (°F)	38.1	40.0	43.0	46.3	52.1	56.4	60.7	61.4	57.1	49.3	42.3	37.6	48.7
Mean Minimum Temp. (°F)	33.0	33.4	34.8	37.1	41.9	46.4	49.6	50.4	46.6	40.9	36.7	33.0	40.3
Extreme Maximum Temp. (°F)	57	66	74	85	98	95	95	100	93	79	71	58	100
Extreme Minimum Temp. (°F)	8	7	17	26	29	32	36	36	30	24	10	3	3
Days Maximum Temp. ≥ 90°F	0	0	0	0	0	0	1	1	0	0	0	0	2
Days Maximum Temp. ≤ 32°F	1	0	0	0	0	0	0	0	0	0	0	1	2
Days Minimum Temp. ≤ 32°F	16	14	13	8	1	0	0	0	0	3	10	16	81
Days Minimum Temp. ≤ 0°F	0	0	0	0	0	0	0	0	0	0	0	0	0
Heating Degree Days (base 65°F)	826	700	676	556	396	259	151	126	234	479	675	842	5,920
Cooling Degree Days (base 65°F)	0	0	0	0	3	8	24	23	3	0	0	0	61
Mean Precipitation (in.)	19.61	17.23	14.49	10.15	5.97	3.95	2.80	2.74	5.51	11.41	20.46	21.95	136.27
Days With ≥ 0.1" Precipitation	18	16	17	15	10	8	5	5	7	12	19	19	151
Days With ≥ 1.0" Precipitation	7	6	5	3	2	1	1	1	2	4	8	8	48
Mean Snowfall (in.)	5.3	5.1	2.4	0.3	trace	0.0	0.0	0.0	0.0	trace	1.1	3.3	17.5
Days With ≥ 1.0" Snow Depth	6	5	2	0	0	0	0	0	0	0	1	4	18

Anacortes *Skagit County*   Elevation: 19 ft.   Latitude: 48° 31' N   Longitude: 122° 37' W

	JAN	FEB	MAR	APR	MAY	JUN	JUL	AUG	SEP	OCT	NOV	DEC	YEAR
Mean Maximum Temp. (°F)	45.4	48.8	52.4	57.2	62.8	67.4	71.7	72.1	67.1	58.6	50.5	45.6	58.3
Mean Temp. (°F)	40.0	42.6	45.5	49.5	54.6	58.9	62.3	62.6	58.5	51.3	44.9	40.4	50.9
Mean Minimum Temp. (°F)	34.5	36.3	38.5	41.8	46.4	50.3	52.8	52.9	49.9	44.0	39.2	35.2	43.5
Extreme Maximum Temp. (°F)	61	69	68	76	86	88	93	88	86	77	66	61	93
Extreme Minimum Temp. (°F)	9	9	18	30	34	38	41	37	34	27	10	8	8
Days Maximum Temp. ≥ 90°F	0	0	0	0	0	0	0	0	0	0	0	0	0
Days Maximum Temp. ≤ 32°F	1	0	0	0	0	0	0	0	0	0	0	1	2
Days Minimum Temp. ≤ 32°F	11	7	4	0	0	0	0	0	0	1	5	10	38
Days Minimum Temp. ≤ 0°F	0	0	0	0	0	0	0	0	0	0	0	0	0
Heating Degree Days (base 65°F)	769	627	598	457	317	183	97	88	192	417	598	755	5,098
Cooling Degree Days (base 65°F)	0	0	0	0	1	7	19	23	4	0	0	0	54
Mean Precipitation (in.)	3.77	2.50	2.18	1.87	1.60	1.44	1.02	1.01	1.41	2.28	4.25	3.81	27.14
Days With ≥ 0.1" Precipitation	10	8	8	6	5	4	3	2	4	7	11	11	79
Days With ≥ 1.0" Precipitation	0	0	0	0	0	0	0	0	0	0	1	0	1
Mean Snowfall (in.)	1.8	0.4	0.0	0.0	0.0	0.0	0.0	0.0	0.0	0.0	0.8	*1.2*	*4.2*
Days With ≥ 1.0" Snow Depth	*1*	0	0	0	0	0	0	0	0	0	0	*0*	*1*

Appleton *Klickitat County*   Elevation: 2,335 ft.   Latitude: 45° 49' N   Longitude: 121° 17' W

	JAN	FEB	MAR	APR	MAY	JUN	JUL	AUG	SEP	OCT	NOV	DEC	YEAR
Mean Maximum Temp. (°F)	35.6	40.1	47.4	54.4	63.2	70.4	78.9	79.4	70.9	58.4	42.9	35.5	56.4
Mean Temp. (°F)	29.8	33.3	38.8	44.1	51.2	57.6	64.2	64.5	57.0	47.0	36.5	30.0	46.2
Mean Minimum Temp. (°F)	24.0	26.5	30.2	33.7	39.1	44.8	49.5	49.5	43.0	35.5	30.0	24.4	35.9
Extreme Maximum Temp. (°F)	58	60	73	83	95	98	105	102	99	85	67	59	105
Extreme Minimum Temp. (°F)	-19	-18	6	20	24	22	30	31	23	12	-15	-19	-19
Days Maximum Temp. ≥ 90°F	0	0	0	0	0	1	6	5	1	0	0	0	13
Days Maximum Temp. ≤ 32°F	10	5	0	0	0	0	0	0	0	0	3	9	27
Days Minimum Temp. ≤ 32°F	26	22	21	14	4	1	0	0	2	10	19	26	145
Days Minimum Temp. ≤ 0°F	1	1	0	0	0	0	0	0	0	0	0	1	3
Heating Degree Days (base 65°F)	1,084	889	805	623	426	237	105	96	249	552	850	1,077	6,993
Cooling Degree Days (base 65°F)	0	0	0	0	5	23	87	88	21	0	0	0	224
Mean Precipitation (in.)	5.98	4.46	3.28	2.06	1.21	0.88	0.34	0.50	1.11	2.33	5.41	6.27	33.83
Days With ≥ 0.1" Precipitation	10	9	8	6	4	2	1	1	3	5	11	11	71
Days With ≥ 1.0" Precipitation	1	1	0	0	0	0	0	0	0	0	1	1	4
Mean Snowfall (in.)	21.9	14.1	8.3	1.2	trace	0.0	0.0	0.0	0.0	0.4	10.5	23.3	79.7
Days With ≥ 1.0" Snow Depth	21	16	8	0	0	0	0	0	0	0	5	16	66

Baring *King County*   Elevation: 770 ft.   Latitude: 47° 46' N   Longitude: 121° 29' W

	JAN	FEB	MAR	APR	MAY	JUN	JUL	AUG	SEP	OCT	NOV	DEC	YEAR
Mean Maximum Temp. (°F)	40.6	45.8	51.8	58.3	64.8	68.7	74.3	74.4	69.4	58.6	45.7	39.7	57.7
Mean Temp. (°F)	35.7	38.9	42.9	47.9	53.9	58.3	62.9	63.2	58.4	49.8	40.4	35.4	49.0
Mean Minimum Temp. (°F)	30.6	32.0	33.9	37.5	43.0	47.7	51.4	51.9	47.4	40.8	35.0	31.0	40.2
Extreme Maximum Temp. (°F)	60	73	80	91	100	98	97	98	98	86	70	58	100
Extreme Minimum Temp. (°F)	3	6	16	27	30	31	37	38	30	23	8	1	1
Days Maximum Temp. ≥ 90°F	0	0	0	0	0	0	1	1	0	0	0	0	2
Days Maximum Temp. ≤ 32°F	3	1	0	0	0	0	0	0	0	0	1	3	8
Days Minimum Temp. ≤ 32°F	19	15	12	6	0	0	0	0	0	2	10	19	83
Days Minimum Temp. ≤ 0°F	0	0	0	0	0	0	0	0	0	0	0	0	0
Heating Degree Days (base 65°F)	902	730	679	506	342	207	98	88	198	466	732	911	5,859
Cooling Degree Days (base 65°F)	0	0	0	0	5	11	41	43	8	0	0	0	108
Mean Precipitation (in.)	16.27	12.04	10.16	8.10	5.30	3.91	2.42	2.43	4.98	9.89	18.16	16.96	110.62
Days With ≥ 0.1" Precipitation	17	15	na	14	12	9	5	5	na	12	18	17	na
Days With ≥ 1.0" Precipitation	5	4	2	2	1	1	0	0	1	3	6	6	31
Mean Snowfall (in.)	18.3	9.5	3.6	0.8	trace	0.0	0.0	trace	0.0	trace	6.0	16.9	55.1
Days With ≥ 1.0" Snow Depth	18	13	5	0	0	0	0	0	0	0	0	13	53

Battle Ground *Clark County*   Elevation: 282 ft.   Latitude: 45° 47' N   Longitude: 122° 32' W

	JAN	FEB	MAR	APR	MAY	JUN	JUL	AUG	SEP	OCT	NOV	DEC	YEAR
Mean Maximum Temp. (°F)	45.9	50.7	55.3	59.5	65.9	71.2	77.6	78.9	74.5	63.7	52.0	45.2	61.7
Mean Temp. (°F)	38.9	42.3	45.7	49.2	54.8	59.7	64.2	64.6	60.3	51.9	44.5	39.0	51.3
Mean Minimum Temp. (°F)	31.9	33.7	36.1	38.8	43.6	48.1	50.9	50.2	46.2	40.0	36.8	32.7	40.8
Extreme Maximum Temp. (°F)	68	72	80	90	101	100	101	105	105	93	72	65	105
Extreme Minimum Temp. (°F)	6	5	17	27	29	33	38	37	29	23	8	-1	-1
Days Maximum Temp. ≥ 90°F	0	0	0	0	0	1	3	4	2	0	0	0	10
Days Maximum Temp. ≤ 32°F	1	0	0	0	0	0	0	0	0	0	0	1	2
Days Minimum Temp. ≤ 32°F	16	12	10	5	0	0	0	0	0	4	9	14	70
Days Minimum Temp. ≤ 0°F	0	0	0	0	0	0	0	0	0	0	0	0	0
Heating Degree Days (base 65°F)	801	633	591	469	318	175	79	71	155	401	609	799	5,101
Cooling Degree Days (base 65°F)	0	0	0	1	9	19	61	69	21	1	0	0	181
Mean Precipitation (in.)	7.13	5.95	5.48	4.36	3.24	2.47	1.02	1.27	2.49	4.13	8.14	8.22	53.90
Days With ≥ 0.1" Precipitation	15	13	14	12	8	6	2	2	6	9	16	15	118
Days With ≥ 1.0" Precipitation	1	1	0	0	0	0	0	0	0	1	1	2	6
Mean Snowfall (in.)	2.2	1.5	0.1	trace	0.0	0.0	0.0	0.0	0.0	0.0	trace	1.1	4.9
Days With ≥ 1.0" Snow Depth	1	0	0	0	0	0	0	0	0	0	0	0	1

Bellingham Int'l Airport *Whatcom County*   Elevation: 147 ft.   Latitude: 48° 48' N   Longitude: 122° 32' W

	JAN	FEB	MAR	APR	MAY	JUN	JUL	AUG	SEP	OCT	NOV	DEC	YEAR
Mean Maximum Temp. (°F)	43.9	47.9	51.9	56.6	62.2	66.5	70.9	71.3	67.0	58.1	49.3	44.0	57.5
Mean Temp. (°F)	38.0	41.2	44.5	48.8	54.2	58.8	62.5	62.7	58.0	50.2	43.3	38.5	50.1
Mean Minimum Temp. (°F)	32.1	34.5	37.1	41.0	46.2	51.0	54.0	54.1	48.8	42.3	37.1	32.9	42.6
Extreme Maximum Temp. (°F)	65	68	72	78	90	89	92	94	89	78	68	63	94
Extreme Minimum Temp. (°F)	1	5	15	26	34	38	42	40	28	20	4	6	1
Days Maximum Temp. ≥ 90°F	0	0	0	0	0	0	0	0	0	0	0	0	0
Days Maximum Temp. ≤ 32°F	2	0	0	0	0	0	0	0	0	0	1	3	6
Days Minimum Temp. ≤ 32°F	15	11	7	2	0	0	0	0	0	2	8	14	59
Days Minimum Temp. ≤ 0°F	0	0	0	0	0	0	0	0	0	0	0	0	0
Heating Degree Days (base 65°F)	828	665	629	479	327	188	93	87	208	451	645	816	5,416
Cooling Degree Days (base 65°F)	0	0	0	0	1	8	22	24	3	0	0	0	58
Mean Precipitation (in.)	4.69	3.53	2.81	2.85	2.23	1.93	1.37	1.29	1.63	3.07	5.43	4.74	35.57
Days With ≥ 0.1" Precipitation	11	9	9	8	6	5	3	3	5	8	13	12	92
Days With ≥ 1.0" Precipitation	1	0	0	0	0	0	0	0	0	0	1	1	3
Mean Snowfall (in.)	4.5	2.1	0.6	0.2	trace	0.0	0.0	0.0	0.0	trace	1.4	3.7	12.5
Days With ≥ 1.0" Snow Depth	3	1	0	0	0	0	0	0	0	0	1	2	7

Blaine *Whatcom County*   Elevation: 59 ft.   Latitude: 49° 00' N   Longitude: 122° 45' W

	JAN	FEB	MAR	APR	MAY	JUN	JUL	AUG	SEP	OCT	NOV	DEC	YEAR
Mean Maximum Temp. (°F)	42.8	47.1	51.6	57.1	63.3	67.9	71.7	71.6	66.4	57.0	48.3	42.6	57.3
Mean Temp. (°F)	37.3	40.5	43.8	48.3	54.1	58.7	61.9	61.9	56.9	49.2	42.4	37.5	49.4
Mean Minimum Temp. (°F)	31.7	33.8	35.9	39.5	44.8	49.5	52.1	52.1	47.4	41.4	36.5	32.3	41.4
Extreme Maximum Temp. (°F)	61	68	66	80	84	85	87	90	84	78	65	62	90
Extreme Minimum Temp. (°F)	1	5	14	25	30	35	40	37	28	19	6	3	1
Days Maximum Temp. ≥ 90°F	0	0	0	0	0	0	0	0	0	0	0	0	0
Days Maximum Temp. ≤ 32°F	2	1	0	0	0	0	0	0	0	0	1	3	7
Days Minimum Temp. ≤ 32°F	15	12	10	4	0	0	0	0	0	4	9	15	69
Days Minimum Temp. ≤ 0°F	0	0	0	0	0	0	0	0	0	0	0	0	0
Heating Degree Days (base 65°F)	853	686	651	494	332	183	99	102	236	483	671	845	5,635
Cooling Degree Days (base 65°F)	0	0	0	0	1	3	12	11	1	0	0	0	28
Mean Precipitation (in.)	5.36	4.18	3.52	2.93	2.49	2.09	1.51	1.50	1.89	3.71	6.36	5.83	41.37
Days With ≥ 0.1" Precipitation	13	11	10	9	7	5	4	4	4	9	14	14	104
Days With ≥ 1.0" Precipitation	1	0	0	0	0	0	0	0	0	0	1	1	3
Mean Snowfall (in.)	5.1	2.4	0.5	trace	0.0	0.0	0.0	0.0	0.0	trace	1.2	5.3	14.5
Days With ≥ 1.0" Snow Depth	4	1	0	0	0	0	0	0	0	0	1	3	9

Boundary Dam *Pend Oreille County*　Elevation: 1,797 ft.　Latitude: 48° 59' N　Longitude: 117° 21' W

	JAN	FEB	MAR	APR	MAY	JUN	JUL	AUG	SEP	OCT	NOV	DEC	YEAR
Mean Maximum Temp. (°F)	31.5	37.8	47.3	57.7	65.1	70.9	80.1	81.8	71.7	56.1	40.2	31.7	56.0
Mean Temp. (°F)	24.6	29.4	36.9	45.3	52.7	59.1	65.4	65.4	56.7	45.1	33.8	25.6	45.0
Mean Minimum Temp. (°F)	17.6	21.2	26.3	32.8	40.3	47.2	50.8	48.9	41.6	34.0	27.4	19.6	34.0
Extreme Maximum Temp. (°F)	48	57	72	90	96	99	104	101	98	80	61	52	104
Extreme Minimum Temp. (°F)	-20	-11	-2	15	28	31	37	32	22	9	-19	-23	-23
Days Maximum Temp. ≥ 90°F	0	0	0	0	0	1	7	7	1	0	0	0	16
Days Maximum Temp. ≤ 32°F	14	5	0	0	0	0	0	0	0	0	3	15	37
Days Minimum Temp. ≤ 32°F	31	27	26	15	2	0	0	0	2	13	23	30	169
Days Minimum Temp. ≤ 0°F	3	2	0	0	0	0	0	0	0	0	0	2	7
Heating Degree Days (base 65°F)	1,247	998	865	586	378	190	69	64	251	611	930	1,212	7,401
Cooling Degree Days (base 65°F)	0	0	0	0	6	22	93	83	9	0	0	0	213
Mean Precipitation (in.)	2.78	2.31	2.12	2.11	2.78	2.77	1.87	1.62	1.50	1.92	3.21	3.36	28.35
Days With ≥ 0.1" Precipitation	9	7	7	7	8	8	6	5	4	6	10	10	87
Days With ≥ 1.0" Precipitation	0	0	0	0	0	0	0	0	0	0	0	0	0
Mean Snowfall (in.)	18.6	9.7	2.8	0.1	0.0	0.0	0.0	0.0	0.0	trace	7.4	21.3	59.9
Days With ≥ 1.0" Snow Depth	30	27	17	1	0	0	0	0	0	0	7	26	108

Buckley 1 NE *Pierce County*　Elevation: 682 ft.　Latitude: 47° 10' N　Longitude: 122° 00' W

	JAN	FEB	MAR	APR	MAY	JUN	JUL	AUG	SEP	OCT	NOV	DEC	YEAR
Mean Maximum Temp. (°F)	45.7	49.9	54.2	59.3	65.7	70.7	76.5	77.4	71.8	60.6	50.3	44.8	60.6
Mean Temp. (°F)	39.5	42.2	45.2	49.0	54.7	59.3	63.7	64.1	59.4	51.0	43.7	38.8	50.9
Mean Minimum Temp. (°F)	33.2	34.6	36.1	38.7	43.6	47.9	50.8	50.8	47.0	41.3	37.0	32.8	41.2
Extreme Maximum Temp. (°F)	65	72	74	86	95	95	98	103	97	89	70	63	103
Extreme Minimum Temp. (°F)	7	7	13	25	31	35	37	36	29	25	5	0	0
Days Maximum Temp. ≥ 90°F	0	0	0	0	0	1	2	2	0	0	0	0	5
Days Maximum Temp. ≤ 32°F	1	0	0	0	0	0	0	0	0	0	0	1	2
Days Minimum Temp. ≤ 32°F	13	10	8	4	0	0	0	0	0	2	7	14	58
Days Minimum Temp. ≤ 0°F	0	0	0	0	0	0	0	0	0	0	0	0	0
Heating Degree Days (base 65°F)	784	636	607	474	318	182	84	70	175	429	632	804	5,195
Cooling Degree Days (base 65°F)	0	0	0	1	5	18	50	53	15	1	0	0	143
Mean Precipitation (in.)	6.10	4.82	4.60	4.13	3.34	2.84	1.60	1.71	2.42	3.99	7.18	6.14	48.87
Days With ≥ 0.1" Precipitation	13	12	13	12	10	7	4	4	6	10	15	14	120
Days With ≥ 1.0" Precipitation	1	1	0	0	0	0	0	0	0	0	2	1	5
Mean Snowfall (in.)	3.2	1.8	0.8	trace	0.0	0.0	0.0	0.0	0.0	trace	1.1	2.7	9.6
Days With ≥ 1.0" Snow Depth	1	1	0	0	0	0	0	0	0	0	0	1	3

Cedar Lake *King County*　Elevation: 1,558 ft.　Latitude: 47° 25' N　Longitude: 121° 44' W

	JAN	FEB	MAR	APR	MAY	JUN	JUL	AUG	SEP	OCT	NOV	DEC	YEAR
Mean Maximum Temp. (°F)	40.5	44.5	48.5	53.4	60.2	65.4	71.7	72.7	66.8	57.3	45.7	40.1	55.6
Mean Temp. (°F)	35.5	38.2	40.8	44.7	50.7	55.6	60.7	61.6	56.5	48.8	40.2	35.4	47.4
Mean Minimum Temp. (°F)	30.5	31.9	33.1	35.9	41.2	45.7	49.5	50.4	46.2	40.2	34.7	30.7	39.2
Extreme Maximum Temp. (°F)	58	67	76	85	96	92	97	98	101	89	68	58	101
Extreme Minimum Temp. (°F)	-16	3	14	24	29	32	37	37	29	22	7	2	-16
Days Maximum Temp. ≥ 90°F	0	0	0	0	0	0	1	1	0	0	0	0	2
Days Maximum Temp. ≤ 32°F	4	1	0	0	0	0	0	0	0	0	1	3	9
Days Minimum Temp. ≤ 32°F	19	15	15	8	1	0	0	0	0	2	11	19	90
Days Minimum Temp. ≤ 0°F	0	0	0	0	0	0	0	0	0	0	0	0	0
Heating Degree Days (base 65°F)	906	749	743	604	439	286	160	134	258	499	736	910	6,424
Cooling Degree Days (base 65°F)	0	0	0	0	4	9	33	35	9	1	0	0	91
Mean Precipitation (in.)	13.19	10.17	9.87	8.51	6.40	5.26	2.99	2.51	4.87	8.20	14.96	13.07	100.00
Days With ≥ 0.1" Precipitation	17	14	16	15	12	10	6	5	8	12	18	17	150
Days With ≥ 1.0" Precipitation	5	3	3	2	1	1	1	1	1	2	5	5	30
Mean Snowfall (in.)	12.4	10.4	7.6	3.2	0.2	0.0	0.0	0.0	0.0	0.3	5.7	13.8	53.6
Days With ≥ 1.0" Snow Depth	14	9	7	2	0	0	0	0	0	0	4	12	48

Centralia *Lewis County*　Elevation: 183 ft.　Latitude: 46° 43' N　Longitude: 122° 57' W

	JAN	FEB	MAR	APR	MAY	JUN	JUL	AUG	SEP	OCT	NOV	DEC	YEAR
Mean Maximum Temp. (°F)	46.3	50.5	55.4	60.9	67.4	72.5	78.1	78.7	73.3	62.2	51.5	45.6	61.9
Mean Temp. (°F)	40.4	43.1	46.5	50.5	56.4	61.2	65.7	66.1	61.3	52.6	45.3	40.3	52.5
Mean Minimum Temp. (°F)	34.4	35.6	37.4	40.1	45.3	49.9	53.4	53.5	49.2	43.1	39.1	35.0	43.0
Extreme Maximum Temp. (°F)	64	73	79	89	98	98	103	103	100	92	73	65	103
Extreme Minimum Temp. (°F)	1	0	17	27	30	34	38	38	30	21	7	0	0
Days Maximum Temp. ≥ 90°F	0	0	0	0	0	1	3	3	1	0	0	0	8
Days Maximum Temp. ≤ 32°F	1	0	0	0	0	0	0	0	0	0	0	0	2
Days Minimum Temp. ≤ 32°F	12	9	8	4	0	0	0	0	0	1	6	11	51
Days Minimum Temp. ≤ 0°F	0	0	0	0	0	0	0	0	0	0	0	0	0
Heating Degree Days (base 65°F)	756	611	568	427	268	133	47	40	127	376	583	760	4,696
Cooling Degree Days (base 65°F)	0	0	0	1	10	26	80	92	27	1	0	0	237
Mean Precipitation (in.)	6.61	5.54	4.81	3.52	2.47	1.88	0.80	1.12	2.03	3.96	7.40	7.61	47.75
Days With ≥ 0.1" Precipitation	13	13	13	10	8	5	2	3	5	9	15	14	110
Days With ≥ 1.0" Precipitation	1	1	0	0	0	0	0	0	0	1	1	2	6
Mean Snowfall (in.)	1.2	0.8	trace	trace	0.0	0.0	0.0	0.0	0.0	0.0	0.2	0.7	2.9
Days With ≥ 1.0" Snow Depth	1	0	0	0	0	0	0	0	0	0	0	0	1

Chelan *Chelan County*   Elevation: 1,118 ft.   Latitude: 47° 50' N   Longitude: 120° 02' W

	JAN	FEB	MAR	APR	MAY	JUN	JUL	AUG	SEP	OCT	NOV	DEC	YEAR
Mean Maximum Temp. (°F)	32.6	39.9	51.1	61.2	70.4	77.5	84.5	84.9	74.8	61.2	44.0	33.8	59.7
Mean Temp. (°F)	27.5	33.2	41.9	50.4	59.1	66.2	72.2	72.1	62.5	50.4	37.9	29.1	50.2
Mean Minimum Temp. (°F)	22.4	26.4	32.6	39.6	47.6	54.7	59.8	59.3	50.1	39.7	31.7	24.3	40.7
Extreme Maximum Temp. (°F)	62	63	72	88	96	98	106	105	97	80	72	59	106
Extreme Minimum Temp. (°F)	-5	-2	11	26	32	33	37	43	26	13	-3	-8	-8
Days Maximum Temp. ≥ 90°F	0	0	0	0	0	3	9	9	1	0	0	0	22
Days Maximum Temp. ≤ 32°F	14	5	0	0	0	0	0	0	0	0	2	13	34
Days Minimum Temp. ≤ 32°F	28	22	15	3	0	0	0	0	0	3	16	26	113
Days Minimum Temp. ≤ 0°F	0	0	0	0	0	0	0	0	0	0	0	0	0
Heating Degree Days (base 65°F)	1,155	892	710	431	199	60	13	9	116	444	808	1,107	5,944
Cooling Degree Days (base 65°F)	0	0	0	0	23	94	233	231	54	0	0	0	635
Mean Precipitation (in.)	1.56	1.18	0.98	0.71	0.79	0.80	0.39	0.45	0.47	0.59	1.62	1.78	11.32
Days With ≥ 0.1" Precipitation	5	4	3	2	2	2	1	1	1	2	5	5	33
Days With ≥ 1.0" Precipitation	0	0	0	0	0	0	0	0	0	0	0	0	0
Mean Snowfall (in.)	9.7	4.7	1.4	trace	0.0	0.0	0.0	0.0	0.0	trace	2.8	12.7	31.3
Days With ≥ 1.0" Snow Depth	17	10	2	0	0	0	0	0	0	0	3	11	43

Chewelah *Stevens County*   Elevation: 1,669 ft.   Latitude: 48° 17' N   Longitude: 117° 43' W

	JAN	FEB	MAR	APR	MAY	JUN	JUL	AUG	SEP	OCT	NOV	DEC	YEAR
Mean Maximum Temp. (°F)	33.6	41.0	51.4	61.0	70.0	77.3	85.2	86.4	76.1	61.3	42.8	33.9	60.0
Mean Temp. (°F)	25.9	31.8	39.6	47.0	55.1	61.7	67.2	67.1	57.6	46.0	35.0	27.0	46.7
Mean Minimum Temp. (°F)	18.3	22.5	27.8	33.0	40.1	46.0	49.2	47.7	39.1	30.7	27.2	20.0	33.5
Extreme Maximum Temp. (°F)	54	62	75	91	100	106	105	105	104	92	67	58	106
Extreme Minimum Temp. (°F)	-28	-20	-10	17	23	30	32	29	20	10	-19	-29	-29
Days Maximum Temp. ≥ 90°F	0	0	0	0	1	3	12	13	3	0	0	0	32
Days Maximum Temp. ≤ 32°F	12	4	0	0	0	0	0	0	0	0	2	11	29
Days Minimum Temp. ≤ 32°F	29	25	24	16	4	0	0	0	4	19	22	28	171
Days Minimum Temp. ≤ 0°F	4	1	0	0	0	0	0	0	0	0	0	2	7
Heating Degree Days (base 65°F)	1,204	932	780	535	311	138	48	47	230	582	895	1,172	6,874
Cooling Degree Days (base 65°F)	0	0	0	0	14	47	134	128	19	0	0	0	342
Mean Precipitation (in.)	2.30	2.01	1.98	1.60	2.11	1.76	1.16	1.01	1.02	1.26	2.73	3.04	21.98
Days With ≥ 0.1" Precipitation	7	6	6	5	6	5	3	3	3	4	8	8	64
Days With ≥ 1.0" Precipitation	0	0	0	0	0	0	0	0	0	0	0	0	0
Mean Snowfall (in.)	11.4	6.0	1.9	trace	trace	0.0	0.0	0.0	0.0	0.1	5.4	13.7	38.5
Days With ≥ 1.0" Snow Depth	24	15	5	0	0	0	0	0	0	0	4	18	66

Chief Joseph Dam *Douglas County*   Elevation: 816 ft.   Latitude: 48° 00' N   Longitude: 119° 39' W

	JAN	FEB	MAR	APR	MAY	JUN	JUL	AUG	SEP	OCT	NOV	DEC	YEAR
Mean Maximum Temp. (°F)	33.5	40.6	53.6	64.5	73.4	80.8	89.0	89.3	79.0	63.6	45.4	34.2	62.2
Mean Temp. (°F)	26.9	32.9	42.9	51.4	59.6	66.9	73.7	73.5	63.7	50.6	37.9	28.1	50.7
Mean Minimum Temp. (°F)	20.2	25.1	32.2	38.1	45.8	53.0	58.4	57.8	48.3	37.6	30.4	21.9	39.1
Extreme Maximum Temp. (°F)	57	63	77	93	103	108	110	110	103	86	75	58	110
Extreme Minimum Temp. (°F)	-13	-15	4	22	26	35	35	35	30	12	-9	-14	-15
Days Maximum Temp. ≥ 90°F	0	0	0	0	2	6	16	16	4	0	0	0	44
Days Maximum Temp. ≤ 32°F	13	4	0	0	0	0	0	0	0	0	2	12	31
Days Minimum Temp. ≤ 32°F	28	23	16	6	0	0	0	0	0	7	17	27	124
Days Minimum Temp. ≤ 0°F	2	1	0	0	0	0	0	0	0	0	0	1	4
Heating Degree Days (base 65°F)	1,176	901	677	404	188	52	9	7	103	440	807	1,139	5,903
Cooling Degree Days (base 65°F)	0	0	0	1	36	117	285	282	81	1	0	0	803
Mean Precipitation (in.)	1.28	1.05	0.94	0.65	0.91	0.83	0.58	0.44	0.48	0.56	1.45	1.71	10.88
Days With ≥ 0.1" Precipitation	4	4	3	2	3	2	2	1	1	2	5	5	34
Days With ≥ 1.0" Precipitation	0	0	0	0	0	0	0	0	0	0	0	0	0
Mean Snowfall (in.)	na	na	0.6	trace	0.0	0.0	0.0	0.0	0.0	0.1	2.8	na	na
Days With ≥ 1.0" Snow Depth	na	na	1	0	0	0	0	0	0	0	na	na	na

Cle Elum *Kittitas County*   Elevation: 1,919 ft.   Latitude: 47° 11' N   Longitude: 120° 57' W

	JAN	FEB	MAR	APR	MAY	JUN	JUL	AUG	SEP	OCT	NOV	DEC	YEAR
Mean Maximum Temp. (°F)	35.2	40.9	49.5	56.8	65.2	71.7	79.6	80.1	72.4	59.8	42.9	34.9	57.4
Mean Temp. (°F)	28.1	32.5	39.1	45.2	52.8	59.4	65.7	65.6	57.1	46.5	35.8	28.6	46.4
Mean Minimum Temp. (°F)	21.0	24.2	28.7	33.5	40.2	47.1	51.8	51.0	41.7	33.1	28.7	22.3	35.3
Extreme Maximum Temp. (°F)	57	62	74	88	99	100	103	102	97	86	66	54	103
Extreme Minimum Temp. (°F)	-24	-20	0	17	22	30	31	30	21	13	-14	-23	-24
Days Maximum Temp. ≥ 90°F	0	0	0	0	0	1	6	6	1	0	0	0	14
Days Maximum Temp. ≤ 32°F	10	4	0	0	0	0	0	0	0	0	2	10	26
Days Minimum Temp. ≤ 32°F	27	24	23	13	3	0	0	0	4	15	20	28	157
Days Minimum Temp. ≤ 0°F	2	1	0	0	0	0	0	0	0	0	0	1	4
Heating Degree Days (base 65°F)	1,137	911	797	588	378	189	70	69	243	568	869	1,121	6,940
Cooling Degree Days (base 65°F)	0	0	0	0	6	25	95	92	16	0	0	0	234
Mean Precipitation (in.)	3.90	2.57	1.63	1.18	0.92	0.93	0.44	0.57	0.86	1.75	3.98	4.27	23.00
Days With ≥ 0.1" Precipitation	9	7	6	4	3	3	1	2	3	5	11	10	64
Days With ≥ 1.0" Precipitation	0	0	0	0	0	0	0	0	0	0	1	1	2
Mean Snowfall (in.)	24.8	14.2	6.2	0.8	0.2	0.0	0.0	0.0	0.0	0.5	12.1	27.2	86.0
Days With ≥ 1.0" Snow Depth	26	19	8	0	0	0	0	0	0	0	8	22	83

Clearbrook *Whatcom County* Elevation: 62 ft. Latitude: 48° 58' N Longitude: 122° 20' W

	JAN	FEB	MAR	APR	MAY	JUN	JUL	AUG	SEP	OCT	NOV	DEC	YEAR
Mean Maximum Temp. (°F)	42.2	47.3	53.1	59.2	65.6	70.0	75.1	75.8	70.5	59.4	48.3	42.4	59.1
Mean Temp. (°F)	36.9	40.5	44.6	49.3	55.1	59.5	63.1	63.2	58.4	50.3	42.4	37.3	50.1
Mean Minimum Temp. (°F)	31.6	33.7	36.0	39.4	44.6	48.9	51.1	50.5	46.3	41.2	36.4	32.1	41.0
Extreme Maximum Temp. (°F)	65	64	76	85	98	93	95	95	95	81	68	65	98
Extreme Minimum Temp. (°F)	6	2	15	22	29	33	38	35	28	19	6	5	0
Days Maximum Temp. ≥ 90°F	0	0	0	0	0	0	1	1	0	0	0	0	2
Days Maximum Temp. ≤ 32°F	4	1	0	0	0	0	0	0	0	0	1	3	9
Days Minimum Temp. ≤ 32°F	15	11	8	3	1	0	0	0	0	4	8	15	65
Days Minimum Temp. ≤ 0°F	0	0	0	0	0	0	0	0	0	0	0	0	0
Heating Degree Days (base 65°F)	864	685	627	464	303	169	83	80	196	448	672	853	5,444
Cooling Degree Days (base 65°F)	0	0	0	0	5	11	33	34	6	0	0	0	89
Mean Precipitation (in.)	5.29	4.16	3.97	3.68	3.17	2.66	1.84	1.62	2.59	4.35	6.35	5.82	45.50
Days With ≥ 0.1" Precipitation	12	10	11	10	8	7	4	4	6	10	13	13	108
Days With ≥ 1.0" Precipitation	1	1	0	0	0	0	0	0	0	1	1	1	5
Mean Snowfall (in.)	5.1	2.2	0.6	trace	0.0	0.0	0.0	0.0	0.0	trace	1.2	2.8	11.9
Days With ≥ 1.0" Snow Depth	na	0	0	0	0	0	0	0	0	0	0	0	na

Clearwater *Jefferson County* Elevation: 78 ft. Latitude: 47° 35' N Longitude: 124° 18' W

	JAN	FEB	MAR	APR	MAY	JUN	JUL	AUG	SEP	OCT	NOV	DEC	YEAR
Mean Maximum Temp. (°F)	46.3	50.2	53.5	57.6	62.8	65.8	70.3	71.2	69.3	60.8	51.0	45.4	58.7
Mean Temp. (°F)	40.4	42.6	44.8	47.9	52.6	56.2	59.7	60.2	57.6	51.2	44.2	39.9	49.8
Mean Minimum Temp. (°F)	34.5	34.9	36.0	38.2	42.4	46.4	49.2	49.1	45.8	41.5	37.3	34.3	40.8
Extreme Maximum Temp. (°F)	63	76	76	85	90	96	92	98	93	84	74	59	98
Extreme Minimum Temp. (°F)	5	7	21	25	29	31	36	31	27	23	11	4	4
Days Maximum Temp. ≥ 90°F	0	0	0	0	0	0	0	0	0	0	0	0	0
Days Maximum Temp. ≤ 32°F	0	0	0	0	0	0	0	0	0	0	0	1	1
Days Minimum Temp. ≤ 32°F	13	12	11	6	1	0	0	0	0	4	8	14	69
Days Minimum Temp. ≤ 0°F	0	0	0	0	0	0	0	0	0	0	0	0	0
Heating Degree Days (base 65°F)	756	626	620	506	379	262	165	150	219	424	619	772	5,498
Cooling Degree Days (base 65°F)	0	0	0	0	1	3	8	10	3	0	0	0	25
Mean Precipitation (in.)	15.51	13.51	12.31	8.76	6.02	3.57	2.84	2.95	5.07	10.43	16.69	16.97	114.63
Days With ≥ 0.1" Precipitation	18	16	16	14	10	8	4	5	7	13	19	19	149
Days With ≥ 1.0" Precipitation	5	5	4	3	2	1	1	1	2	4	6	6	40
Mean Snowfall (in.)	0.1	0.4	0.5	trace	0.0	0.0	0.0	0.0	0.0	0.0	trace	0.9	1.9
Days With ≥ 1.0" Snow Depth	1	0	0	0	0	0	0	0	0	0	0	0	1

Colfax *Whitman County* Elevation: 1,978 ft. Latitude: 46° 53' N Longitude: 117° 21' W

	JAN	FEB	MAR	APR	MAY	JUN	JUL	AUG	SEP	OCT	NOV	DEC	YEAR
Mean Maximum Temp. (°F)	36.8	43.2	50.9	58.7	67.0	74.3	82.7	83.3	73.8	62.5	45.4	37.3	59.6
Mean Temp. (°F)	30.1	35.4	41.0	47.3	54.2	60.7	66.6	66.5	57.6	48.0	37.7	30.9	48.0
Mean Minimum Temp. (°F)	23.5	27.6	31.1	35.8	41.3	47.1	50.4	49.5	41.4	33.5	29.9	24.4	36.3
Extreme Maximum Temp. (°F)	62	67	73	93	95	99	101	103	101	91	73	60	103
Extreme Minimum Temp. (°F)	-17	-11	8	19	19	30	34	33	22	11	-10	-16	-17
Days Maximum Temp. ≥ 90°F	0	0	0	0	1	2	8	8	1	0	0	0	20
Days Maximum Temp. ≤ 32°F	9	3	0	0	0	0	0	0	0	0	2	8	22
Days Minimum Temp. ≤ 32°F	24	21	19	9	2	0	0	0	2	13	18	24	132
Days Minimum Temp. ≤ 0°F	2	1	0	0	0	0	0	0	0	0	0	1	4
Heating Degree Days (base 65°F)	1,073	830	737	527	339	163	56	56	230	520	814	1,051	6,396
Cooling Degree Days (base 65°F)	0	0	0	2	13	na	na	na	na	na	na	na	na
Mean Precipitation (in.)	2.42	1.82	2.07	1.64	1.76	1.34	0.80	0.81	0.75	1.03	2.43	2.83	19.70
Days With ≥ 0.1" Precipitation	7	6	7	6	5	4	2	2	2	4	8	8	61
Days With ≥ 1.0" Precipitation	0	0	0	0	0	0	0	0	0	0	0	0	0
Mean Snowfall (in.)	9.0	5.5	1.9	0.2	trace	0.0	0.0	0.0	0.0	0.1	3.3	8.8	28.8
Days With ≥ 1.0" Snow Depth	13	6	1	0	0	0	0	0	0	0	3	11	34

Concrete Ppl. Fish Station *Skagit County* Elevation: 193 ft. Latitude: 48° 33' N Longitude: 121° 46' W

	JAN	FEB	MAR	APR	MAY	JUN	JUL	AUG	SEP	OCT	NOV	DEC	YEAR
Mean Maximum Temp. (°F)	42.2	46.8	52.3	58.3	64.8	69.1	74.7	75.4	70.4	60.2	48.1	42.0	58.7
Mean Temp. (°F)	37.0	39.9	43.9	48.8	54.7	59.3	63.5	64.1	59.7	51.5	42.5	37.3	50.2
Mean Minimum Temp. (°F)	31.7	33.0	35.5	39.2	44.5	49.4	52.3	52.8	48.9	42.8	36.9	32.4	41.6
Extreme Maximum Temp. (°F)	60	70	80	86	95	99	97	98	98	82	67	63	99
Extreme Minimum Temp. (°F)	6	4	17	28	32	38	40	41	32	25	11	4	4
Days Maximum Temp. ≥ 90°F	0	0	0	0	0	0	1	1	0	0	0	0	2
Days Maximum Temp. ≤ 32°F	1	0	0	0	0	0	0	0	0	0	0	2	3
Days Minimum Temp. ≤ 32°F	15	11	8	2	0	0	0	0	0	1	6	14	57
Days Minimum Temp. ≤ 0°F	0	0	0	0	0	0	0	0	0	0	0	0	0
Heating Degree Days (base 65°F)	862	702	647	480	318	181	84	69	168	411	667	853	5,442
Cooling Degree Days (base 65°F)	0	0	0	0	6	15	43	49	17	0	0	0	130
Mean Precipitation (in.)	10.08	7.55	6.82	4.96	3.57	2.90	1.82	1.69	3.31	6.28	11.54	11.27	71.79
Days With ≥ 0.1" Precipitation	16	13	14	12	9	8	4	4	7	12	18	17	134
Days With ≥ 1.0" Precipitation	3	2	1	1	0	0	0	0	1	1	3	4	16
Mean Snowfall (in.)	6.5	4.6	1.1	0.2	trace	0.0	0.0	0.0	0.0	0.0	1.7	6.3	20.4
Days With ≥ 1.0" Snow Depth	8	4	1	0	0	0	0	0	0	0	1	5	19

Connell 1 W *Franklin County*   Elevation: 1,017 ft.   Latitude: 46° 40' N   Longitude: 118° 53' W

	JAN	FEB	MAR	APR	MAY	JUN	JUL	AUG	SEP	OCT	NOV	DEC	YEAR
Mean Maximum Temp. (°F)	37.3	45.8	55.9	64.8	73.9	81.2	89.2	88.6	78.7	64.8	47.3	37.5	63.7
Mean Temp. (°F)	31.0	37.3	44.4	51.1	58.9	65.6	72.4	71.7	62.6	51.3	39.5	31.4	51.4
Mean Minimum Temp. (°F)	24.5	28.8	32.8	37.4	43.9	50.1	55.5	54.6	46.4	37.6	31.7	25.3	39.1
Extreme Maximum Temp. (°F)	67	70	76	93	100	103	110	107	100	86	75	66	110
Extreme Minimum Temp. (°F)	-17	-19	4	20	26	33	37	37	27	11	-15	-14	-19
Days Maximum Temp. ≥ 90°F	0	0	0	0	1	5	15	13	3	0	0	0	37
Days Maximum Temp. ≤ 32°F	10	3	0	0	0	0	0	0	0	0	2	9	24
Days Minimum Temp. ≤ 32°F	25	19	15	7	1	0	0	0	1	8	15	24	115
Days Minimum Temp. ≤ 0°F	1	0	0	0	0	0	0	0	0	0	0	1	2
Heating Degree Days (base 65°F)	1,049	776	632	412	210	68	10	12	115	418	757	1,034	5,493
Cooling Degree Days (base 65°F)	0	0	0	2	32	79	231	230	50	1	0	0	625
Mean Precipitation (in.)	0.97	0.81	0.87	0.67	0.80	0.44	0.33	0.32	0.38	0.68	1.15	1.18	8.60
Days With ≥ 0.1" Precipitation	4	3	3	2	2	1	1	1	1	2	4	4	28
Days With ≥ 1.0" Precipitation	0	0	0	0	0	0	0	0	0	0	0	0	0
Mean Snowfall (in.)	2.3	0.7	0.2	0.0	0.0	0.0	0.0	0.0	0.0	trace	0.9	1.4	5.5
Days With ≥ 1.0" Snow Depth	2	1	0	0	0	0	0	0	0	0	0	2	5

Cougar 6 E *Skamania County*   Elevation: 656 ft.   Latitude: 46° 04' N   Longitude: 122° 12' W

	JAN	FEB	MAR	APR	MAY	JUN	JUL	AUG	SEP	OCT	NOV	DEC	YEAR
Mean Maximum Temp. (°F)	42.6	46.5	52.1	57.3	65.1	71.1	78.1	78.5	72.7	61.9	49.0	42.6	59.8
Mean Temp. (°F)	37.8	40.5	44.3	48.4	54.9	60.2	65.6	65.9	61.5	53.2	43.7	38.1	51.2
Mean Minimum Temp. (°F)	33.1	34.4	36.5	39.4	44.7	49.3	53.1	53.3	50.3	44.5	38.4	33.6	42.5
Extreme Maximum Temp. (°F)	60	68	78	91	100	103	105	104	104	92	69	59	105
Extreme Minimum Temp. (°F)	9	5	15	28	29	33	34	38	34	28	12	2	2
Days Maximum Temp. ≥ 90°F	0	0	0	0	1	1	5	4	2	0	0	0	13
Days Maximum Temp. ≤ 32°F	2	1	0	0	0	0	0	0	0	0	0	1	4
Days Minimum Temp. ≤ 32°F	13	9	6	2	0	0	0	0	0	0	4	12	46
Days Minimum Temp. ≤ 0°F	0	0	0	0	0	0	0	0	0	0	0	0	0
Heating Degree Days (base 65°F)	835	685	635	493	322	175	75	67	145	363	632	827	5,254
Cooling Degree Days (base 65°F)	0	0	0	2	21	39	108	114	58	5	0	0	347
Mean Precipitation (in.)	17.61	15.02	12.18	8.87	5.36	3.76	1.58	1.88	4.43	8.43	18.71	19.68	117.51
Days With ≥ 0.1" Precipitation	17	16	16	13	10	7	3	4	7	11	18	18	140
Days With ≥ 1.0" Precipitation	6	6	4	3	1	1	0	0	1	3	7	7	39
Mean Snowfall (in.)	na	5.2	1.1	0.1	0.0	0.0	0.0	0.0	0.0	0.0	2.0	3.1	na
Days With ≥ 1.0" Snow Depth	5	4	0	0	0	0	0	0	0	0	1	3	13

Coulee Dam 1 SW *Grant County*   Elevation: 1,699 ft.   Latitude: 47° 57' N   Longitude: 119° 00' W

	JAN	FEB	MAR	APR	MAY	JUN	JUL	AUG	SEP	OCT	NOV	DEC	YEAR
Mean Maximum Temp. (°F)	32.6	40.2	51.2	61.3	70.4	78.5	86.4	86.4	76.1	61.4	43.4	33.7	60.1
Mean Temp. (°F)	27.1	33.3	41.7	49.9	58.2	65.8	72.6	72.5	63.0	50.8	37.5	28.7	50.1
Mean Minimum Temp. (°F)	21.7	26.4	32.2	38.4	45.9	53.0	58.8	58.5	49.9	40.2	31.5	23.6	40.0
Extreme Maximum Temp. (°F)	61	61	73	91	100	102	107	104	103	84	69	58	107
Extreme Minimum Temp. (°F)	-13	-10	5	23	30	37	41	39	30	10	-10	-13	-13
Days Maximum Temp. ≥ 90°F	0	0	0	0	1	4	12	12	2	0	0	0	31
Days Maximum Temp. ≤ 32°F	14	5	0	0	0	0	0	0	0	0	3	13	35
Days Minimum Temp. ≤ 32°F	27	22	16	6	0	0	0	0	0	4	15	26	116
Days Minimum Temp. ≤ 0°F	1	1	0	0	0	0	0	0	0	0	0	1	3
Heating Degree Days (base 65°F)	1,168	889	714	448	227	71	14	12	118	435	819	1,120	6,035
Cooling Degree Days (base 65°F)	0	0	0	1	26	96	254	253	73	2	0	0	705
Mean Precipitation (in.)	1.02	1.00	0.96	0.82	1.27	0.94	0.66	0.48	0.55	0.61	1.34	1.50	11.15
Days With ≥ 0.1" Precipitation	4	4	3	3	4	3	2	1	2	2	5	5	38
Days With ≥ 1.0" Precipitation	0	0	0	0	0	0	0	0	0	0	0	0	0
Mean Snowfall (in.)	na	1.1	0.2	trace	0.0	0.0	0.0	0.0	0.0	trace	0.7	na	na
Days With ≥ 1.0" Snow Depth	na	na	0	0	0	0	0	0	0	0	1	na	na

Coupeville 1 S *Island County*   Elevation: 49 ft.   Latitude: 48° 12' N   Longitude: 122° 42' W

	JAN	FEB	MAR	APR	MAY	JUN	JUL	AUG	SEP	OCT	NOV	DEC	YEAR
Mean Maximum Temp. (°F)	45.3	48.6	52.6	56.9	62.6	66.5	70.8	71.9	67.2	58.2	49.9	45.0	57.9
Mean Temp. (°F)	40.1	42.1	45.1	48.5	53.7	57.4	60.7	61.4	57.0	50.1	44.0	40.0	50.0
Mean Minimum Temp. (°F)	34.8	35.6	37.5	40.1	44.7	48.3	50.7	51.0	46.8	41.9	38.2	35.0	42.0
Extreme Maximum Temp. (°F)	61	69	70	79	83	90	90	90	90	79	67	61	90
Extreme Minimum Temp. (°F)	8	5	14	27	33	37	40	38	29	20	6	6	5
Days Maximum Temp. ≥ 90°F	0	0	0	0	0	0	0	0	0	0	0	0	0
Days Maximum Temp. ≤ 32°F	1	0	0	0	0	0	0	0	0	0	0	1	2
Days Minimum Temp. ≤ 32°F	10	9	6	2	0	0	0	0	0	2	6	10	45
Days Minimum Temp. ≤ 0°F	0	0	0	0	0	0	0	0	0	0	0	0	0
Heating Degree Days (base 65°F)	766	641	612	488	345	222	132	113	233	456	622	768	5,398
Cooling Degree Days (base 65°F)	0	0	0	0	0	0	2	7	1	0	0	0	18
Mean Precipitation (in.)	2.55	1.81	1.89	1.67	1.74	1.31	0.99	0.90	1.25	1.77	2.91	2.73	21.52
Days With ≥ 0.1" Precipitation	8	6	6	5	5	4	3	3	4	5	9	9	67
Days With ≥ 1.0" Precipitation	0	0	0	0	0	0	0	0	0	0	0	0	0
Mean Snowfall (in.)	2.4	0.8	0.2	trace	0.0	0.0	0.0	0.0	0.0	trace	0.9	1.7	6.0
Days With ≥ 1.0" Snow Depth	1	1	0	0	0	0	0	0	0	0	0	1	3

Cushman Powerhouse 2 *Mason County*   Elevation: 19 ft.   Latitude: 47° 22' N   Longitude: 123° 10' W

	JAN	FEB	MAR	APR	MAY	JUN	JUL	AUG	SEP	OCT	NOV	DEC	YEAR
Mean Maximum Temp. (°F)	45.6	48.7	54.1	59.6	66.2	71.1	76.2	76.7	71.3	60.4	50.0	44.7	60.4
Mean Temp. (°F)	40.1	42.0	45.4	49.6	55.3	60.0	64.2	64.6	60.1	51.8	44.0	39.7	51.4
Mean Minimum Temp. (°F)	34.6	35.2	36.7	39.5	44.4	48.7	52.1	52.3	48.8	43.2	38.1	34.7	42.4
Extreme Maximum Temp. (°F)	60	71	77	83	92	94	95	97	91	82	68	66	97
Extreme Minimum Temp. (°F)	11	14	21	28	31	34	41	39	34	28	13	11	11
Days Maximum Temp. ≥ 90°F	0	0	0	0	0	0	1	1	0	0	0	0	2
Days Maximum Temp. ≤ 32°F	0	0	0	0	0	0	0	0	0	0	0	1	1
Days Minimum Temp. ≤ 32°F	12	10	7	3	0	0	0	0	0	0	6	12	50
Days Minimum Temp. ≤ 0°F	0	0	0	0	0	0	0	0	0	0	0	0	0
Heating Degree Days (base 65°F)	765	643	599	456	295	160	65	55	149	402	622	777	4,988
Cooling Degree Days (base 65°F)	0	0	0	0	4	15	48	53	9	0	0	0	129
Mean Precipitation (in.)	13.42	12.37	9.50	5.81	3.33	1.82	1.19	1.54	2.88	7.62	15.69	15.74	90.91
Days With ≥ 0.1" Precipitation	14	14	13	10	6	5	3	3	5	9	16	16	114
Days With ≥ 1.0" Precipitation	5	5	3	1	1	0	0	0	1	3	5	6	30
Mean Snowfall (in.)	1.9	na	0.3	trace	0.0	0.0	0.0	0.0	0.0	0.0	0.3	1.8	na
Days With ≥ 1.0" Snow Depth	na	1	0	0	0	0	0	0	0	0	1	1	na

Dayton 1 WSW *Columbia County*   Elevation: 1,555 ft.   Latitude: 46° 19' N   Longitude: 118° 00' W

	JAN	FEB	MAR	APR	MAY	JUN	JUL	AUG	SEP	OCT	NOV	DEC	YEAR
Mean Maximum Temp. (°F)	40.4	46.1	53.7	60.9	69.1	77.2	86.6	86.5	76.8	64.3	49.1	40.9	62.6
Mean Temp. (°F)	33.2	37.7	43.8	49.7	56.9	63.9	70.9	70.7	61.9	51.2	40.9	33.8	51.2
Mean Minimum Temp. (°F)	25.9	29.3	33.9	38.5	44.5	50.5	55.2	54.9	46.9	38.1	32.6	26.7	39.8
Extreme Maximum Temp. (°F)	65	74	77	93	101	105	109	110	102	90	79	68	110
Extreme Minimum Temp. (°F)	-16	-17	5	23	26	31	38	38	26	16	-10	-21	-21
Days Maximum Temp. ≥ 90°F	0	0	0	0	1	4	13	12	3	0	0	0	33
Days Maximum Temp. ≤ 32°F	8	3	0	0	0	0	0	0	0	0	2	7	20
Days Minimum Temp. ≤ 32°F	22	17	12	5	0	0	0	0	1	6	14	23	100
Days Minimum Temp. ≤ 0°F	2	1	0	0	0	0	0	0	0	0	0	1	4
Heating Degree Days (base 65°F)	978	764	649	454	268	109	24	24	141	423	717	960	5,511
Cooling Degree Days (base 65°F)	0	0	0	2	26	76	206	207	59	2	0	0	578
Mean Precipitation (in.)	2.40	1.87	1.99	1.71	1.53	1.20	0.59	0.73	0.88	1.52	2.72	2.48	19.62
Days With ≥ 0.1" Precipitation	7	6	7	5	5	4	2	2	2	4	8	8	60
Days With ≥ 1.0" Precipitation	0	0	0	0	0	0	0	0	0	0	0	0	0
Mean Snowfall (in.)	6.3	3.1	1.1	trace	0.0	0.0	0.0	0.0	0.0	trace	1.3	6.1	17.9
Days With ≥ 1.0" Snow Depth	8	4	1	0	0	0	0	0	0	0	2	5	20

Diablo Dam *Whatcom County*   Elevation: 889 ft.   Latitude: 48° 43' N   Longitude: 121° 09' W

	JAN	FEB	MAR	APR	MAY	JUN	JUL	AUG	SEP	OCT	NOV	DEC	YEAR
Mean Maximum Temp. (°F)	38.3	43.2	49.8	57.0	64.9	70.3	76.8	77.8	70.8	58.0	44.4	38.3	57.5
Mean Temp. (°F)	33.4	36.7	41.5	47.1	54.0	59.4	64.5	65.4	59.2	49.4	39.4	34.0	48.7
Mean Minimum Temp. (°F)	28.5	30.2	33.3	37.1	43.1	48.4	52.1	52.9	47.5	40.7	34.2	29.7	39.8
Extreme Maximum Temp. (°F)	58	63	72	90	103	100	102	105	101	87	61	58	105
Extreme Minimum Temp. (°F)	0	1	11	25	31	36	39	40	31	18	13	-2	-2
Days Maximum Temp. ≥ 90°F	0	0	0	0	1	2	4	4	1	0	0	0	12
Days Maximum Temp. ≤ 32°F	5	1	0	0	0	0	0	0	0	0	1	3	10
Days Minimum Temp. ≤ 32°F	21	18	12	4	0	0	0	0	0	2	10	20	87
Days Minimum Temp. ≤ 0°F	0	0	0	0	0	0	0	0	0	0	0	0	0
Heating Degree Days (base 65°F)	973	792	720	532	341	188	86	68	188	477	763	954	6,082
Cooling Degree Days (base 65°F)	0	0	0	0	10	24	77	87	23	0	0	0	221
Mean Precipitation (in.)	11.91	8.39	7.09	4.90	3.14	2.39	1.89	1.71	3.21	7.39	14.53	13.04	79.59
Days With ≥ 0.1" Precipitation	15	12	13	11	8	7	4	4	6	11	17	16	124
Days With ≥ 1.0" Precipitation	4	3	2	1	0	0	0	0	1	2	4	5	22
Mean Snowfall (in.)	17.5	11.4	2.1	trace	0.0	0.0	0.0	0.0	0.0	trace	2.9	12.5	46.4
Days With ≥ 1.0" Snow Depth	16	12	3	0	0	0	0	0	0	0	2	12	45

Ellensburg *Kittitas County*   Elevation: 1,479 ft.   Latitude: 46° 58' N   Longitude: 120° 32' W

	JAN	FEB	MAR	APR	MAY	JUN	JUL	AUG	SEP	OCT	NOV	DEC	YEAR
Mean Maximum Temp. (°F)	34.2	41.8	52.6	60.4	68.7	75.7	83.3	83.7	75.0	62.1	44.8	34.4	59.7
Mean Temp. (°F)	26.9	32.7	40.7	47.2	55.2	62.1	68.1	67.9	58.9	47.4	35.9	27.1	47.5
Mean Minimum Temp. (°F)	19.4	23.5	28.7	34.0	41.8	48.3	52.8	52.1	42.7	32.6	26.9	19.7	35.2
Extreme Maximum Temp. (°F)	64	64	74	94	99	100	104	103	97	86	66	59	104
Extreme Minimum Temp. (°F)	-23	-21	7	17	21	32	35	37	23	13	-17	-28	-28
Days Maximum Temp. ≥ 90°F	0	0	0	0	1	3	9	9	1	0	0	0	23
Days Maximum Temp. ≤ 32°F	13	4	0	0	0	0	0	0	0	0	2	12	31
Days Minimum Temp. ≤ 32°F	29	25	22	13	2	0	0	0	2	16	23	29	161
Days Minimum Temp. ≤ 0°F	2	1	0	0	0	0	0	0	0	0	0	2	5
Heating Degree Days (base 65°F)	1,173	906	748	527	306	134	42	39	198	540	867	1,169	6,649
Cooling Degree Days (base 65°F)	0	0	0	1	13	45	138	129	24	0	0	0	350
Mean Precipitation (in.)	1.33	0.89	0.77	0.58	0.59	0.64	0.36	0.36	0.43	0.57	1.18	1.50	9.20
Days With ≥ 0.1" Precipitation	4	4	3	2	2	2	1	1	1	2	4	5	31
Days With ≥ 1.0" Precipitation	0	0	0	0	0	0	0	0	0	0	0	0	0
Mean Snowfall (in.)	8.7	3.1	1.2	0.2	0.0	0.0	0.0	0.0	0.0	trace	3.5	9.9	26.6
Days With ≥ 1.0" Snow Depth	19	10	1	0	0	0	0	0	0	0	4	14	48

Elma *Grays Harbor County*   Elevation: 68 ft.   Latitude: 47° 00' N   Longitude: 123° 24' W

	JAN	FEB	MAR	APR	MAY	JUN	JUL	AUG	SEP	OCT	NOV	DEC	YEAR
Mean Maximum Temp. (°F)	46.9	50.9	55.8	60.9	67.4	71.9	77.1	78.4	73.9	63.3	51.8	45.9	62.0
Mean Temp. (°F)	40.4	42.8	46.0	49.7	55.3	59.7	63.8	64.8	60.4	52.3	44.6	40.0	51.7
Mean Minimum Temp. (°F)	33.9	34.7	36.1	38.4	43.1	47.4	50.5	51.2	47.0	41.2	37.4	34.1	41.3
Extreme Maximum Temp. (°F)	61	73	80	89	99	98	102	103	100	91	74	61	103
Extreme Minimum Temp. (°F)	5	7	18	25	28	31	38	37	28	20	4	2	2
Days Maximum Temp. ≥ 90°F	0	0	0	0	0	1	3	3	1	0	0	0	8
Days Maximum Temp. ≤ 32°F	0	0	0	0	0	0	0	0	0	0	0	1	1
Days Minimum Temp. ≤ 32°F	13	11	10	6	1	0	0	0	0	4	8	13	66
Days Minimum Temp. ≤ 0°F	0	0	0	0	0	0	0	0	0	0	0	0	0
Heating Degree Days (base 65°F)	754	619	584	453	300	170	78	56	148	388	605	768	4,923
Cooling Degree Days (base 65°F)	0	0	0	0	6	17	47	62	19	1	0	0	152
Mean Precipitation (in.)	10.23	8.49	7.31	5.04	3.13	2.17	1.20	1.38	2.95	5.65	10.51	11.54	69.60
Days With ≥ 0.1" Precipitation	16	14	15	12	8	6	3	4	6	10	17	17	128
Days With ≥ 1.0" Precipitation	3	2	1	1	0	0	0	0	1	2	3	4	17
Mean Snowfall (in.)	3.0	1.2	0.4	trace	0.0	0.0	0.0	0.0	0.0	0.0	0.7	1.3	6.6
Days With ≥ 1.0" Snow Depth	1	1	0	0	0	0	0	0	0	0	1	1	4

Eltopia 8 WSW *Franklin County*   Elevation: 698 ft.   Latitude: 46° 24' N   Longitude: 119° 09' W

	JAN	FEB	MAR	APR	MAY	JUN	JUL	AUG	SEP	OCT	NOV	DEC	YEAR
Mean Maximum Temp. (°F)	38.3	46.5	57.0	64.5	71.9	78.6	85.2	84.4	76.8	63.8	48.1	38.3	62.8
Mean Temp. (°F)	31.7	37.7	45.1	51.2	58.1	64.5	70.0	69.6	62.4	51.4	40.1	32.1	51.2
Mean Minimum Temp. (°F)	25.0	28.9	33.1	37.8	44.3	50.4	54.8	54.6	48.0	39.1	32.0	25.9	39.5
Extreme Maximum Temp. (°F)	66	71	75	86	97	101	102	103	97	86	74	62	103
Extreme Minimum Temp. (°F)	-16	-16	8	21	27	32	39	40	29	19	-10	-11	-16
Days Maximum Temp. ≥ 90°F	0	0	0	0	1	2	10	8	1	0	0	0	22
Days Maximum Temp. ≤ 32°F	9	3	0	0	0	0	0	0	0	0	2	9	23
Days Minimum Temp. ≤ 32°F	24	19	15	7	1	0	0	0	0	5	15	25	111
Days Minimum Temp. ≤ 0°F	1	0	0	0	0	0	0	0	0	0	0	1	2
Heating Degree Days (base 65°F)	1,027	764	610	408	226	75	17	16	111	415	741	1,013	5,423
Cooling Degree Days (base 65°F)	0	0	0	1	24	65	178	167	41	1	0	0	477
Mean Precipitation (in.)	1.05	0.95	0.84	0.75	0.71	0.50	0.35	0.37	0.37	0.65	1.17	1.14	8.85
Days With ≥ 0.1" Precipitation	4	4	3	3	2	2	1	1	1	2	4	4	31
Days With ≥ 1.0" Precipitation	0	0	0	0	0	0	0	0	0	0	0	0	0
Mean Snowfall (in.)	na	1.9	trace	0.0	0.0	trace	0.0	0.0	0.0	0.0	0.4	na	na
Days With ≥ 1.0" Snow Depth	na	1	0	0	0	0	0	0	0	0	0	na	na

Elwha Ranger Station *Clallam County*   Elevation: 357 ft.   Latitude: 48° 02' N   Longitude: 123° 35' W

	JAN	FEB	MAR	APR	MAY	JUN	JUL	AUG	SEP	OCT	NOV	DEC	YEAR
Mean Maximum Temp. (°F)	40.9	44.5	50.3	56.4	62.9	67.1	72.7	73.9	67.7	56.7	46.0	41.2	56.7
Mean Temp. (°F)	36.3	38.6	42.3	47.0	52.5	56.9	61.4	62.6	57.6	48.9	40.9	36.7	48.5
Mean Minimum Temp. (°F)	31.6	32.6	34.2	37.4	42.1	46.7	50.1	51.3	47.4	40.9	35.7	32.2	40.2
Extreme Maximum Temp. (°F)	60	62	68	78	87	91	95	97	91	75	70	65	97
Extreme Minimum Temp. (°F)	9	8	19	26	31	32	40	36	32	21	10	8	8
Days Maximum Temp. ≥ 90°F	0	0	0	0	0	0	1	1	0	0	0	0	2
Days Maximum Temp. ≤ 32°F	2	1	0	0	0	0	0	0	0	0	1	2	6
Days Minimum Temp. ≤ 32°F	16	13	11	4	0	0	0	0	0	1	7	16	68
Days Minimum Temp. ≤ 0°F	0	0	0	0	0	0	0	0	0	0	0	0	0
Heating Degree Days (base 65°F)	883	740	697	535	381	245	136	105	221	494	717	869	6,023
Cooling Degree Days (base 65°F)	0	0	0	0	1	9	31	37	5	0	0	0	83
Mean Precipitation (in.)	8.64	7.18	6.05	3.42	1.89	1.22	0.82	1.25	1.72	4.84	9.47	9.69	56.19
Days With ≥ 0.1" Precipitation	12	11	11	7	6	4	2	3	4	8	14	13	95
Days With ≥ 1.0" Precipitation	3	2	1	1	0	0	0	0	0	1	3	3	14
Mean Snowfall (in.)	3.2	2.3	1.0	trace	0.0	0.0	0.0	0.0	0.0	trace	1.9	2.2	10.6
Days With ≥ 1.0" Snow Depth	4	1	1	0	0	0	0	0	0	0	1	2	9

Ephrata Airport *Grant County*   Elevation: 1,256 ft.   Latitude: 47° 18' N   Longitude: 119° 31' W

	JAN	FEB	MAR	APR	MAY	JUN	JUL	AUG	SEP	OCT	NOV	DEC	YEAR
Mean Maximum Temp. (°F)	34.1	42.2	53.6	63.3	72.9	80.6	88.3	87.6	78.0	63.2	45.1	34.3	62.0
Mean Temp. (°F)	27.9	34.5	43.4	51.4	60.4	67.9	74.8	74.0	64.6	51.6	37.8	28.3	51.4
Mean Minimum Temp. (°F)	21.5	26.8	33.2	39.4	47.8	55.1	61.3	60.3	51.1	40.0	30.4	22.2	40.8
Extreme Maximum Temp. (°F)	61	65	75	94	101	105	108	107	106	86	72	63	108
Extreme Minimum Temp. (°F)	-18	-19	5	22	30	33	40	37	30	14	-15	-21	-21
Days Maximum Temp. ≥ 90°F	0	0	0	0	2	5	15	13	3	0	0	0	38
Days Maximum Temp. ≤ 32°F	13	4	0	0	0	0	0	0	0	0	3	12	32
Days Minimum Temp. ≤ 32°F	28	21	14	5	0	0	0	0	0	4	18	27	117
Days Minimum Temp. ≤ 0°F	2	1	0	0	0	0	0	0	0	0	0	1	4
Heating Degree Days (base 65°F)	1,145	854	662	405	180	47	9	7	93	411	810	1,131	5,754
Cooling Degree Days (base 65°F)	0	0	0	3	45	124	301	281	90	4	0	0	848
Mean Precipitation (in.)	0.88	0.76	0.73	0.42	0.61	0.50	0.44	0.25	0.37	0.47	1.04	1.23	7.70
Days With ≥ 0.1" Precipitation	3	3	3	1	2	2	1	1	1	2	4	4	27
Days With ≥ 1.0" Precipitation	0	0	0	0	0	0	0	0	0	0	0	0	0
Mean Snowfall (in.)	5.2	2.8	0.9	trace	0.0	0.0	0.0	0.0	0.0	trace	2.6	7.3	18.8
Days With ≥ 1.0" Snow Depth	17	8	1	0	0	0	0	0	0	0	3	12	41

Everett *Snohomish County*   Elevation: 59 ft.   Latitude: 47° 59' N   Longitude: 122° 11' W

	JAN	FEB	MAR	APR	MAY	JUN	JUL	AUG	SEP	OCT	NOV	DEC	YEAR
Mean Maximum Temp. (°F)	45.7	49.3	53.3	58.1	63.8	68.4	72.9	73.8	68.5	59.5	50.6	45.1	59.1
Mean Temp. (°F)	39.7	42.2	45.3	49.5	55.0	59.8	63.5	63.9	58.6	51.0	44.0	39.6	51.0
Mean Minimum Temp. (°F)	33.6	35.0	37.3	41.0	46.2	51.1	54.1	53.9	48.6	42.4	37.5	34.0	42.9
Extreme Maximum Temp. (°F)	67	74	76	85	85	94	91	92	89	83	74	66	94
Extreme Minimum Temp. (°F)	4	6	14	28	33	39	39	40	31	22	0	6	0
Days Maximum Temp. ≥ 90°F	0	0	0	0	0	0	0	0	0	0	0	0	0
Days Maximum Temp. ≤ 32°F	1	0	0	0	0	0	0	0	0	0	0	1	2
Days Minimum Temp. ≤ 32°F	12	10	7	2	0	0	0	0	0	2	8	12	53
Days Minimum Temp. ≤ 0°F	0	0	0	0	0	0	0	0	0	0	0	0	0
Heating Degree Days (base 65°F)	778	639	603	458	305	161	77	69	190	428	622	781	5,111
Cooling Degree Days (base 65°F)	0	0	0	0	2	11	41	46	6	0	0	0	106
Mean Precipitation (in.)	4.41	3.36	3.78	2.97	2.54	2.23	1.33	1.34	2.11	3.28	5.18	5.11	37.64
Days With ≥ 0.1" Precipitation	11	10	11	9	7	6	3	3	5	9	12	13	99
Days With ≥ 1.0" Precipitation	0	0	0	0	0	0	0	0	0	0	1	1	2
Mean Snowfall (in.)	1.2	0.5	trace	trace	0.0	0.0	0.0	0.0	0.0	0.0	0.3	0.3	2.3
Days With ≥ 1.0" Snow Depth	0	0	0	0	0	0	0	0	0	0	0	0	0

Forks 1 E *Clallam County*   Elevation: 347 ft.   Latitude: 47° 57' N   Longitude: 124° 22' W

	JAN	FEB	MAR	APR	MAY	JUN	JUL	AUG	SEP	OCT	NOV	DEC	YEAR
Mean Maximum Temp. (°F)	45.9	49.8	53.2	58.2	63.8	67.5	72.8	74.0	71.0	61.0	50.4	45.1	59.4
Mean Temp. (°F)	40.0	42.4	44.5	48.1	53.3	57.2	61.3	62.2	59.0	51.6	43.9	39.7	50.3
Mean Minimum Temp. (°F)	34.2	35.0	35.7	37.9	42.7	46.8	49.7	50.4	47.1	42.1	37.5	34.2	41.1
Extreme Maximum Temp. (°F)	64	75	77	84	96	98	99	102	100	88	71	62	102
Extreme Minimum Temp. (°F)	9	12	12	26	30	34	37	36	27	24	8	9	8
Days Maximum Temp. ≥ 90°F	0	0	0	0	0	1	1	1	1	0	0	0	4
Days Maximum Temp. ≤ 32°F	0	0	0	0	0	0	0	0	0	0	0	1	1
Days Minimum Temp. ≤ 32°F	14	10	10	5	1	0	0	0	0	2	7	14	63
Days Minimum Temp. ≤ 0°F	0	0	0	0	0	0	0	0	0	0	0	0	0
Heating Degree Days (base 65°F)	767	630	629	501	360	236	132	105	183	410	624	779	5,356
Cooling Degree Days (base 65°F)	0	0	0	0	3	9	24	27	10	0	0	0	73
Mean Precipitation (in.)	16.62	15.42	13.44	9.23	5.92	3.69	2.73	2.76	4.42	11.08	17.98	18.85	122.14
Days With ≥ 0.1" Precipitation	18	16	17	14	12	9	5	5	7	13	19	19	154
Days With ≥ 1.0" Precipitation	6	6	5	3	2	0	1	1	1	4	7	6	42
Mean Snowfall (in.)	3.0	2.0	1.1	0.1	trace	0.0	0.0	0.0	0.0	trace	0.7	2.3	9.2
Days With ≥ 1.0" Snow Depth	2	1	0	0	0	0	0	0	0	0	1	2	6

Glenoma *Lewis County*   Elevation: 839 ft.   Latitude: 46° 31' N   Longitude: 122° 08' W

	JAN	FEB	MAR	APR	MAY	JUN	JUL	AUG	SEP	OCT	NOV	DEC	YEAR
Mean Maximum Temp. (°F)	45.2	50.1	53.9	58.8	65.3	70.6	76.8	77.9	72.6	62.6	50.9	45.2	60.8
Mean Temp. (°F)	38.1	41.2	44.2	48.0	53.9	58.8	63.6	63.8	58.8	50.6	42.9	38.2	50.2
Mean Minimum Temp. (°F)	30.9	32.4	34.4	37.2	42.5	46.9	50.2	49.6	45.0	38.6	34.9	31.2	39.5
Extreme Maximum Temp. (°F)	68	78	76	90	103	100	102	104	108	99	77	65	108
Extreme Minimum Temp. (°F)	4	2	11	25	28	30	38	35	27	20	6	-2	-2
Days Maximum Temp. ≥ 90°F	0	0	0	0	0	1	3	3	1	0	0	0	8
Days Maximum Temp. ≤ 32°F	1	0	0	0	0	0	0	0	0	0	0	1	2
Days Minimum Temp. ≤ 32°F	17	14	12	6	1	0	0	0	1	5	10	18	84
Days Minimum Temp. ≤ 0°F	0	0	0	0	0	0	0	0	0	0	0	0	0
Heating Degree Days (base 65°F)	827	665	638	504	345	198	91	81	194	442	656	823	5,464
Cooling Degree Days (base 65°F)	0	0	0	1	8	18	54	53	12	2	0	0	148
Mean Precipitation (in.)	9.97	7.38	6.42	5.50	3.85	2.93	1.31	1.40	3.08	5.16	9.99	10.62	67.61
Days With ≥ 0.1" Precipitation	16	13	15	13	11	8	3	3	6	10	16	16	130
Days With ≥ 1.0" Precipitation	3	2	1	1	0	0	0	0	0	1	2	3	13
Mean Snowfall (in.)	7.0	4.2	1.2	0.4	0.0	0.0	0.0	0.0	0.0	0.0	1.5	3.1	17.4
Days With ≥ 1.0" Snow Depth	3	3	1	0	0	0	0	0	0	0	1	3	11

Grapeview 3 SW *Mason County*   Elevation: 49 ft.   Latitude: 47° 18' N   Longitude: 122° 52' W

	JAN	FEB	MAR	APR	MAY	JUN	JUL	AUG	SEP	OCT	NOV	DEC	YEAR
Mean Maximum Temp. (°F)	45.2	48.9	53.9	58.8	65.7	70.4	75.2	75.7	69.9	59.8	49.8	44.9	59.9
Mean Temp. (°F)	39.8	42.4	45.6	49.3	55.2	59.8	63.6	64.4	59.4	51.5	44.3	40.0	51.3
Mean Minimum Temp. (°F)	34.4	35.9	37.3	39.7	44.6	49.0	52.0	53.0	48.9	43.3	38.7	35.0	42.6
Extreme Maximum Temp. (°F)	60	67	70	83	91	92	98	98	95	80	68	58	98
Extreme Minimum Temp. (°F)	9	12	20	28	31	35	38	41	31	24	14	9	9
Days Maximum Temp. ≥ 90°F	0	0	0	0	0	0	1	1	0	0	0	0	2
Days Maximum Temp. ≤ 32°F	0	0	0	0	0	0	0	0	0	0	0	1	1
Days Minimum Temp. ≤ 32°F	13	9	6	2	0	0	0	0	0	1	5	11	47
Days Minimum Temp. ≤ 0°F	0	0	0	0	0	0	0	0	0	0	0	0	0
Heating Degree Days (base 65°F)	774	633	595	466	300	164	75	56	168	411	616	770	5,028
Cooling Degree Days (base 65°F)	0	0	0	0	4	15	38	47	8	0	0	0	112
Mean Precipitation (in.)	7.50	6.40	5.80	3.73	2.16	1.68	0.94	1.15	2.15	4.15	8.17	8.47	52.30
Days With ≥ 0.1" Precipitation	13	12	12	9	5	4	3	3	5	8	15	14	103
Days With ≥ 1.0" Precipitation	2	1	1	0	0	0	0	0	0	1	2	2	9
Mean Snowfall (in.)	1.6	1.2	0.4	trace	0.0	0.0	0.0	0.0	0.0	0.0	1.0	1.1	5.3
Days With ≥ 1.0" Snow Depth	1	1	0	0	0	0	0	0	0	0	1	na	na

Grays River Hatchery *Pacific County*   Elevation: 98 ft.   Latitude: 46° 23' N   Longitude: 123° 34' W

	JAN	FEB	MAR	APR	MAY	JUN	JUL	AUG	SEP	OCT	NOV	DEC	YEAR
Mean Maximum Temp. (°F)	47.5	50.8	54.3	57.9	63.4	67.5	72.6	73.8	71.4	62.5	52.4	47.0	60.1
Mean Temp. (°F)	40.3	42.3	44.7	47.7	52.7	57.0	61.1	61.5	58.3	51.1	44.4	40.2	50.1
Mean Minimum Temp. (°F)	32.9	33.8	35.1	37.4	42.0	46.4	49.5	49.2	45.2	39.7	36.5	33.3	40.1
Extreme Maximum Temp. (°F)	63	73	81	88	97	100	99	105	101	87	72	66	105
Extreme Minimum Temp. (°F)	4	3	19	22	29	32	35	34	29	23	9	2	2
Days Maximum Temp. ≥ 90°F	0	0	0	0	0	1	2	1	1	0	0	0	5
Days Maximum Temp. ≤ 32°F	0	0	0	0	0	0	0	0	0	0	0	1	1
Days Minimum Temp. ≤ 32°F	15	12	11	6	1	0	0	0	0	4	10	14	73
Days Minimum Temp. ≤ 0°F	0	0	0	0	0	0	0	0	0	0	0	0	0
Heating Degree Days (base 65°F)	761	634	622	513	378	243	139	124	205	423	610	762	5,414
Cooling Degree Days (base 65°F)	0	0	0	0	3	8	25	25	10	0	0	0	71
Mean Precipitation (in.)	15.89	13.31	11.91	8.13	5.00	3.69	2.02	2.16	4.43	9.43	16.72	18.16	110.85
Days With ≥ 0.1" Precipitation	18	16	17	15	11	8	4	5	7	12	19	18	150
Days With ≥ 1.0" Precipitation	6	5	4	2	1	0	0	1	1	3	6	6	35
Mean Snowfall (in.)	2.3	1.2	0.2	trace	trace	0.0	0.0	0.0	0.0	trace	0.8	1.3	5.8
Days With ≥ 1.0" Snow Depth	1	0	0	0	0	0	0	0	0	0	0	*0*	*1*

Harrington 1 NW *Lincoln County*   Elevation: 2,188 ft.   Latitude: 47° 30' N   Longitude: 118° 15' W

	JAN	FEB	MAR	APR	MAY	JUN	JUL	AUG	SEP	OCT	NOV	DEC	YEAR
Mean Maximum Temp. (°F)	32.0	39.1	49.2	58.6	67.7	75.4	83.6	83.4	73.7	59.6	41.8	32.5	58.1
Mean Temp. (°F)	26.2	32.2	39.5	45.8	53.2	59.9	66.1	65.9	57.5	46.2	34.7	26.6	46.2
Mean Minimum Temp. (°F)	20.4	25.2	29.7	32.8	38.6	44.2	48.5	48.4	41.2	32.8	27.6	20.7	34.2
Extreme Maximum Temp. (°F)	57	62	71	89	95	99	101	103	98	86	65	57	103
Extreme Minimum Temp. (°F)	-20	-24	-1	16	17	24	27	28	22	9	-20	-23	-24
Days Maximum Temp. ≥ 90°F	0	0	0	0	0	2	9	8	1	0	0	0	20
Days Maximum Temp. ≤ 32°F	14	5	1	0	0	0	0	0	0	0	4	14	38
Days Minimum Temp. ≤ 32°F	28	23	22	15	7	1	0	0	4	15	21	28	164
Days Minimum Temp. ≤ 0°F	2	1	0	0	0	0	0	0	0	0	0	2	5
Heating Degree Days (base 65°F)	1,195	920	783	571	366	179	64	66	235	576	902	1,183	7,040
Cooling Degree Days (base 65°F)	0	0	0	0	8	24	92	98	19	1	0	0	242
Mean Precipitation (in.)	1.37	1.20	1.22	0.96	1.26	0.94	0.67	0.49	0.59	0.91	1.67	1.84	13.12
Days With ≥ 0.1" Precipitation	5	4	4	3	4	3	2	2	2	3	6	7	45
Days With ≥ 1.0" Precipitation	0	0	0	0	0	0	0	0	0	0	0	0	0
Mean Snowfall (in.)	8.1	4.5	1.3	0.3	trace	0.0	0.0	0.0	0.0	0.2	3.7	9.4	27.5
Days With ≥ 1.0" Snow Depth	18	7	2	0	0	0	0	0	0	0	3	14	44

Hartline *Grant County*   Elevation: 1,909 ft.   Latitude: 47° 41' N   Longitude: 119° 06' W

	JAN	FEB	MAR	APR	MAY	JUN	JUL	AUG	SEP	OCT	NOV	DEC	YEAR
Mean Maximum Temp. (°F)	32.7	40.4	51.5	61.5	71.0	78.9	87.2	86.7	77.2	62.1	43.1	33.1	60.5
Mean Temp. (°F)	26.5	32.9	41.3	48.7	56.8	63.9	71.3	70.9	62.2	49.6	35.7	26.9	48.9
Mean Minimum Temp. (°F)	20.2	25.2	31.0	35.9	42.6	48.9	55.3	55.2	47.2	37.1	28.2	20.7	37.3
Extreme Maximum Temp. (°F)	52	60	73	93	100	103	107	104	101	85	67	56	107
Extreme Minimum Temp. (°F)	-18	-16	5	18	25	28	34	36	28	11	-8	-19	-19
Days Maximum Temp. ≥ 90°F	0	0	0	0	1	4	13	12	2	0	0	0	32
Days Maximum Temp. ≤ 32°F	13	4	0	0	0	0	0	0	0	0	3	13	33
Days Minimum Temp. ≤ 32°F	29	24	19	10	2	0	0	0	1	8	21	27	141
Days Minimum Temp. ≤ 0°F	2	1	0	0	0	0	0	0	0	0	0	1	4
Heating Degree Days (base 65°F)	1,188	901	728	483	266	101	21	21	136	472	873	1,174	6,364
Cooling Degree Days (base 65°F)	0	0	0	1	23	66	216	209	64	2	0	*0*	*581*
Mean Precipitation (in.)	0.94	0.99	1.00	0.77	1.04	0.80	0.68	0.49	0.50	0.61	1.42	na	na
Days With ≥ 0.1" Precipitation	3	3	3	2	3	3	1	1	1	2	4	*4*	*30*
Days With ≥ 1.0" Precipitation	0	0	0	0	0	0	0	0	0	0	0	*0*	*0*
Mean Snowfall (in.)	6.9	3.5	0.6	0.2	0.0	0.0	0.0	0.0	0.0	0.2	3.1	*9.9*	*24.4*
Days With ≥ 1.0" Snow Depth	na	na	0	0	0	0	0	0	0	0	na	na	na

Hatton 9 SE *Franklin County*   Elevation: 1,509 ft.   Latitude: 46° 43' N   Longitude: 118° 39' W

	JAN	FEB	MAR	APR	MAY	JUN	JUL	AUG	SEP	OCT	NOV	DEC	YEAR
Mean Maximum Temp. (°F)	36.6	44.3	54.3	63.1	72.5	81.2	88.8	88.0	78.1	63.6	46.1	36.7	62.8
Mean Temp. (°F)	30.6	36.8	43.9	50.3	58.2	65.8	72.6	71.9	63.0	50.8	39.0	31.0	51.2
Mean Minimum Temp. (°F)	24.6	29.2	33.4	37.5	43.9	50.5	56.3	55.8	47.9	38.0	31.8	25.3	39.5
Extreme Maximum Temp. (°F)	63	69	75	94	100	104	108	109	100	90	73	63	109
Extreme Minimum Temp. (°F)	-21	-19	6	17	26	32	31	33	24	7	-12	-15	-21
Days Maximum Temp. ≥ 90°F	0	0	0	0	1	6	16	14	3	0	0	0	40
Days Maximum Temp. ≤ 32°F	10	3	0	0	0	0	0	0	0	0	3	10	26
Days Minimum Temp. ≤ 32°F	24	18	15	8	2	0	0	0	1	8	16	24	116
Days Minimum Temp. ≤ 0°F	1	0	0	0	0	0	0	0	0	0	0	1	2
Heating Degree Days (base 65°F)	1,059	791	648	437	231	74	14	13	121	436	774	1,048	5,646
Cooling Degree Days (base 65°F)	0	0	0	2	33	98	250	239	76	3	0	0	701
Mean Precipitation (in.)	1.29	0.96	1.05	0.84	0.90	0.55	0.37	0.43	0.50	0.81	1.37	1.45	10.52
Days With ≥ 0.1" Precipitation	4	4	4	3	3	2	1	1	2	2	5	5	36
Days With ≥ 1.0" Precipitation	0	0	0	0	0	0	0	0	0	0	0	0	0
Mean Snowfall (in.)	4.4	2.0	0.4	trace	0.0	0.0	0.0	0.0	0.0	trace	1.3	4.7	12.8
Days With ≥ 1.0" Snow Depth	7	3	0	0	0	0	0	0	0	0	1	7	18

Holden Village *Chelan County* Elevation: 3,218 ft. Latitude: 48° 12' N Longitude: 120° 47' W

	JAN	FEB	MAR	APR	MAY	JUN	JUL	AUG	SEP	OCT	NOV	DEC	YEAR
Mean Maximum Temp. (°F)	30.4	35.8	43.6	51.8	61.7	68.8	76.7	77.2	68.5	54.5	36.9	29.4	52.9
Mean Temp. (°F)	22.7	26.6	32.9	39.8	47.9	54.5	60.2	60.5	52.8	42.2	30.0	22.1	41.0
Mean Minimum Temp. (°F)	15.0	17.5	22.2	27.8	34.0	40.2	43.7	43.8	37.1	29.9	23.0	15.1	29.1
Extreme Maximum Temp. (°F)	58	57	64	85	91	94	99	97	96	82	65	58	99
Extreme Minimum Temp. (°F)	-22	-19	-7	9	20	23	28	28	22	6	-10	-25	-25
Days Maximum Temp. ≥ 90°F	0	0	0	0	0	0	3	3	0	0	0	0	6
Days Maximum Temp. ≤ 32°F	17	7	1	0	0	0	0	0	0	0	7	20	52
Days Minimum Temp. ≤ 32°F	30	28	30	26	13	3	0	1	7	21	28	31	218
Days Minimum Temp. ≤ 0°F	4	2	0	0	0	0	0	0	0	0	0	3	9
Heating Degree Days (base 65°F)	1,306	1,076	987	748	524	312	169	159	363	699	1,043	1,321	8,707
Cooling Degree Days (base 65°F)	0	0	0	0	0	5	27	25	4	0	0	0	61
Mean Precipitation (in.)	6.66	5.10	3.00	1.54	1.10	1.16	0.76	1.06	1.68	3.26	6.76	7.55	39.63
Days With ≥ 0.1" Precipitation	11	10	6	4	3	3	2	3	4	7	12	13	78
Days With ≥ 1.0" Precipitation	2	1	1	0	0	0	0	0	0	1	2	2	9
Mean Snowfall (in.)	60.6	43.0	23.2	6.1	0.3	trace	0.0	0.0	0.0	5.6	41.3	74.2	254.3
Days With ≥ 1.0" Snow Depth	31	28	31	24	5	0	0	0	0	2	20	30	171

Hoquiam Airport *Grays Harbor County* Elevation: 9 ft. Latitude: 46° 59' N Longitude: 123° 56' W

	JAN	FEB	MAR	APR	MAY	JUN	JUL	AUG	SEP	OCT	NOV	DEC	YEAR
Mean Maximum Temp. (°F)	46.8	49.7	52.7	56.1	60.3	63.6	67.3	68.3	67.7	60.2	51.7	46.6	57.6
Mean Temp. (°F)	42.1	43.9	46.1	49.0	53.3	56.9	60.1	61.0	59.5	52.9	46.3	42.0	51.1
Mean Minimum Temp. (°F)	37.3	38.1	39.4	41.9	46.2	50.0	52.8	53.6	51.2	45.7	40.8	37.2	44.5
Extreme Maximum Temp. (°F)	59	72	77	83	88	96	95	98	96	83	70	59	98
Extreme Minimum Temp. (°F)	16	13	22	29	32	37	35	42	32	28	18	9	9
Days Maximum Temp. ≥ 90°F	0	0	0	0	0	0	0	0	0	0	0	0	0
Days Maximum Temp. ≤ 32°F	0	0	0	0	0	0	0	0	0	0	0	1	1
Days Minimum Temp. ≤ 32°F	7	6	4	1	0	0	0	0	0	0	3	7	28
Days Minimum Temp. ≤ 0°F	0	0	0	0	0	0	0	0	0	0	0	0	0
Heating Degree Days (base 65°F)	703	589	579	474	358	241	153	127	170	368	554	707	5,023
Cooling Degree Days (base 65°F)	0	0	0	0	2	4	8	11	11	1	0	0	37
Mean Precipitation (in.)	9.81	8.44	7.21	5.06	3.27	2.20	1.34	1.47	2.96	5.96	10.42	10.78	68.92
Days With ≥ 0.1" Precipitation	16	15	15	12	8	6	3	3	6	11	17	16	128
Days With ≥ 1.0" Precipitation	3	2	1	1	0	0	0	0	1	2	2	3	15
Mean Snowfall (in.)	1.8	0.7	0.1	trace	trace	0.0	0.0	0.0	trace	trace	0.3	0.6	3.5
Days With ≥ 1.0" Snow Depth	1	0	0	0	0	0	0	0	0	0	0	0	1

Kennewick *Benton County* Elevation: 387 ft. Latitude: 46° 13' N Longitude: 119° 06' W

	JAN	FEB	MAR	APR	MAY	JUN	JUL	AUG	SEP	OCT	NOV	DEC	YEAR
Mean Maximum Temp. (°F)	40.4	48.0	58.4	66.8	75.0	82.5	90.2	89.6	79.7	66.2	50.4	41.1	65.7
Mean Temp. (°F)	33.8	39.2	46.9	54.0	61.5	68.6	75.0	74.4	65.0	53.4	42.6	34.7	54.1
Mean Minimum Temp. (°F)	27.1	30.4	35.4	41.1	48.0	54.6	59.8	59.2	50.4	40.5	34.8	28.2	42.5
Extreme Maximum Temp. (°F)	68	74	78	91	104	107	108	110	100	89	79	68	110
Extreme Minimum Temp. (°F)	-11	-11	13	24	30	38	42	45	30	17	-8	-7	-11
Days Maximum Temp. ≥ 90°F	0	0	0	0	2	7	17	16	4	0	0	0	46
Days Maximum Temp. ≤ 32°F	7	2	0	0	0	0	0	0	0	1	7		17
Days Minimum Temp. ≤ 32°F	21	16	10	3	0	0	0	0	0	4	11	21	86
Days Minimum Temp. ≤ 0°F	0	0	0	0	0	0	0	0	0	0	0	1	1
Heating Degree Days (base 65°F)	962	721	553	327	149	31	3	3	75	356	664	933	4,777
Cooling Degree Days (base 65°F)	0	0	0	4	52	141	319	306	93	4	0	0	919
Mean Precipitation (in.)	1.08	0.78	0.75	0.56	0.63	0.37	0.25	0.39	0.35	0.57	1.08	1.15	7.96
Days With ≥ 0.1" Precipitation	4	3	3	2	2	1	1	1	1	2	4	4	28
Days With ≥ 1.0" Precipitation	0	0	0	0	0	0	0	0	0	0	0	0	0
Mean Snowfall (in.)	na	0.4	trace	trace	0.0	0.0	0.0	0.0	0.0	trace	0.2	*1.0*	na
Days With ≥ 1.0" Snow Depth	na	*0*	0	0	0	0	0	0	0	0	0	*0*	na

Lacrosse *Whitman County* Elevation: 1,450 ft. Latitude: 46° 49' N Longitude: 117° 53' W

	JAN	FEB	MAR	APR	MAY	JUN	JUL	AUG	SEP	OCT	NOV	DEC	YEAR
Mean Maximum Temp. (°F)	37.7	45.0	53.9	62.2	71.2	79.5	88.3	87.8	77.6	63.9	46.8	37.8	62.6
Mean Temp. (°F)	31.0	36.6	42.7	49.1	56.3	63.5	70.2	69.6	60.4	49.3	38.7	31.3	49.9
Mean Minimum Temp. (°F)	24.3	28.1	31.5	35.9	41.3	47.4	52.1	51.5	43.3	34.7	30.6	24.9	37.1
Extreme Maximum Temp. (°F)	61	70	77	95	100	103	106	108	102	90	76	62	108
Extreme Minimum Temp. (°F)	-30	-24	0	16	21	26	30	28	19	9	-17	-21	-30
Days Maximum Temp. ≥ 90°F	0	0	0	0	1	5	15	14	3	0	0	0	38
Days Maximum Temp. ≤ 32°F	9	3	0	0	0	0	0	0	0	0	2	9	23
Days Minimum Temp. ≤ 32°F	24	19	17	10	4	0	0	0	2	11	17	25	129
Days Minimum Temp. ≤ 0°F	2	1	0	0	0	0	0	0	0	0	0	1	4
Heating Degree Days (base 65°F)	1,046	797	684	473	276	104	23	25	164	480	780	1,037	5,889
Cooling Degree Days (base 65°F)	0	0	0	2	17	58	179	176	37	1	0	0	470
Mean Precipitation (in.)	1.82	1.48	1.43	1.21	1.16	0.94	0.47	0.48	0.57	1.00	1.97	2.18	14.71
Days With ≥ 0.1" Precipitation	6	5	5	4	4	3	1	2	2	3	7	7	49
Days With ≥ 1.0" Precipitation	0	0	0	0	0	0	0	0	0	0	0	0	0
Mean Snowfall (in.)	5.3	2.7	0.8	trace	trace	0.0	0.0	0.0	0.0	trace	1.9	5.4	16.1
Days With ≥ 1.0" Snow Depth	9	3	1	0	0	0	0	0	0	0	2	7	21

Landsburg *King County*   Elevation: 534 ft.   Latitude: 47° 23' N   Longitude: 121° 58' W

	JAN	FEB	MAR	APR	MAY	JUN	JUL	AUG	SEP	OCT	NOV	DEC	YEAR
Mean Maximum Temp. (°F)	43.7	48.2	52.5	57.7	64.5	69.4	75.4	75.4	69.6	59.0	48.7	42.9	58.9
Mean Temp. (°F)	37.9	40.6	43.5	47.6	53.5	58.4	63.1	62.9	57.5	49.3	42.2	37.3	49.5
Mean Minimum Temp. (°F)	32.0	33.0	34.5	37.5	42.6	47.3	50.8	50.3	45.3	39.6	35.7	31.7	40.0
Extreme Maximum Temp. (°F)	61	68	71	85	102	99	99	102	95	84	72	61	102
Extreme Minimum Temp. (°F)	4	0	12	24	28	34	38	35	28	23	14	4	0
Days Maximum Temp. ≥ 90°F	0	0	0	0	0	1	1	1	0	0	0	0	3
Days Maximum Temp. ≤ 32°F	1	0	0	0	0	0	0	0	0	0	0	1	2
Days Minimum Temp. ≤ 32°F	15	13	11	6	1	0	0	0	0	4	9	16	75
Days Minimum Temp. ≤ 0°F	0	0	0	0	0	0	0	0	0	0	0	0	0
Heating Degree Days (base 65°F)	834	683	659	515	352	205	94	98	224	479	677	852	5,672
Cooling Degree Days (base 65°F)	0	0	0	0	4	12	43	43	6	0	0	0	108
Mean Precipitation (in.)	7.64	6.04	5.60	4.67	3.56	3.05	1.73	1.62	2.72	4.73	8.47	7.83	57.66
Days With ≥ 0.1" Precipitation	14	13	13	12	9	7	4	4	6	10	16	15	123
Days With ≥ 1.0" Precipitation	2	1	1	0	0	1	0	0	0	1	2	2	10
Mean Snowfall (in.)	*1.8*	1.6	*0.1*	trace	0.0	0.0	0.0	0.0	0.0	trace	1.5	1.8	*6.8*
Days With ≥ 1.0" Snow Depth	*4*	2	0	0	0	0	0	0	0	0	1	3	*10*

Leavenworth 3 S *Chelan County*   Elevation: 1,125 ft.   Latitude: 47° 34' N   Longitude: 120° 41' W

	JAN	FEB	MAR	APR	MAY	JUN	JUL	AUG	SEP	OCT	NOV	DEC	YEAR
Mean Maximum Temp. (°F)	33.8	42.2	52.4	62.4	71.7	79.0	87.1	87.5	78.1	63.9	43.6	33.5	61.3
Mean Temp. (°F)	25.8	32.1	39.8	47.9	55.9	62.7	68.9	68.8	59.9	48.3	35.6	26.7	47.7
Mean Minimum Temp. (°F)	17.6	22.1	27.2	33.4	40.0	46.3	50.7	50.1	41.7	32.8	27.7	19.8	34.1
Extreme Maximum Temp. (°F)	64	64	76	92	101	105	107	107	102	89	68	54	107
Extreme Minimum Temp. (°F)	-24	-18	-1	19	27	26	34	30	24	14	-7	-26	-26
Days Maximum Temp. ≥ 90°F	0	0	0	0	1	4	13	14	4	0	0	0	36
Days Maximum Temp. ≤ 32°F	12	3	0	0	0	0	0	0	0	0	2	12	29
Days Minimum Temp. ≤ 32°F	31	26	25	14	3	0	0	0	2	15	23	30	169
Days Minimum Temp. ≤ 0°F	3	1	0	0	0	0	0	0	0	0	0	1	5
Heating Degree Days (base 65°F)	1,210	921	774	507	287	119	36	33	175	510	875	1,183	6,630
Cooling Degree Days (base 65°F)	0	0	0	0	14	54	163	159	36	0	0	0	426
Mean Precipitation (in.)	4.55	3.24	2.10	1.10	0.84	0.82	0.38	0.58	0.72	1.72	4.27	5.07	25.39
Days With ≥ 0.1" Precipitation	10	8	6	3	2	2	1	2	2	4	10	10	60
Days With ≥ 1.0" Precipitation	1	1	0	0	0	0	0	0	0	0	1	1	4
Mean Snowfall (in.)	29.5	13.6	4.6	0.2	0.0	0.0	0.0	0.0	0.0	0.3	11.4	32.0	91.6
Days With ≥ 1.0" Snow Depth	28	24	13	0	0	0	0	0	0	0	7	24	96

Lind 3 NE *Adams County*   Elevation: 1,627 ft.   Latitude: 47° 00' N   Longitude: 118° 34' W

	JAN	FEB	MAR	APR	MAY	JUN	JUL	AUG	SEP	OCT	NOV	DEC	YEAR
Mean Maximum Temp. (°F)	35.9	43.7	53.6	62.5	71.7	79.7	88.2	87.6	77.8	63.5	45.6	35.9	62.1
Mean Temp. (°F)	29.6	35.8	42.7	48.9	56.6	63.6	70.4	70.0	61.3	49.6	37.9	29.8	49.7
Mean Minimum Temp. (°F)	23.3	27.9	31.8	35.3	41.4	47.4	52.7	52.3	44.7	35.7	30.2	23.7	37.2
Extreme Maximum Temp. (°F)	62	67	74	92	99	103	107	106	102	89	72	60	107
Extreme Minimum Temp. (°F)	-20	-22	1	17	24	31	32	32	24	8	-16	-15	-22
Days Maximum Temp. ≥ 90°F	0	0	0	0	1	5	14	14	3	0	0	0	37
Days Maximum Temp. ≤ 32°F	11	4	0	0	0	0	0	0	0	0	2	10	27
Days Minimum Temp. ≤ 32°F	25	20	18	11	3	0	0	0	1	11	17	26	132
Days Minimum Temp. ≤ 0°F	2	1	0	0	0	0	0	0	0	0	0	1	4
Heating Degree Days (base 65°F)	1,090	818	684	478	273	105	25	26	150	471	806	1,085	6,011
Cooling Degree Days (base 65°F)	0	0	0	2	23	64	193	189	51	2	0	0	524
Mean Precipitation (in.)	1.11	0.84	1.01	0.84	0.85	0.57	0.42	0.39	0.49	0.76	1.34	1.34	9.96
Days With ≥ 0.1" Precipitation	4	3	4	3	3	2	1	1	2	2	5	5	35
Days With ≥ 1.0" Precipitation	0	0	0	0	0	0	0	0	0	0	0	0	0
Mean Snowfall (in.)	5.4	2.4	0.6	0.2	trace	0.0	0.0	0.0	0.0	trace	2.2	5.0	15.8
Days With ≥ 1.0" Snow Depth	9	3	0	0	0	0	0	0	0	0	2	8	22

Long Beach Exp. Station *Pacific County*   Elevation: 29 ft.   Latitude: 46° 22' N   Longitude: 124° 02' W

	JAN	FEB	MAR	APR	MAY	JUN	JUL	AUG	SEP	OCT	NOV	DEC	YEAR
Mean Maximum Temp. (°F)	48.9	51.2	53.4	55.6	59.6	62.6	65.7	66.8	67.1	61.0	53.3	49.0	57.8
Mean Temp. (°F)	42.4	44.0	45.9	48.1	52.2	55.7	58.6	59.1	57.3	51.6	46.4	42.5	50.3
Mean Minimum Temp. (°F)	35.8	36.7	38.3	40.6	44.8	48.9	51.5	51.4	47.5	42.2	39.5	36.0	42.8
Extreme Maximum Temp. (°F)	65	73	72	82	91	93	95	99	92	90	71	64	99
Extreme Minimum Temp. (°F)	8	9	25	26	30	33	38	36	29	21	15	0	0
Days Maximum Temp. ≥ 90°F	0	0	0	0	0	0	0	0	0	0	0	0	0
Days Maximum Temp. ≤ 32°F	0	0	0	0	0	0	0	0	0	0	0	1	1
Days Minimum Temp. ≤ 32°F	10	8	6	2	0	0	0	0	0	2	6	10	44
Days Minimum Temp. ≤ 0°F	0	0	0	0	0	0	0	0	0	0	0	0	0
Heating Degree Days (base 65°F)	695	587	587	501	391	274	193	179	229	408	550	690	5,284
Cooling Degree Days (base 65°F)	0	0	0	0	1	2	2	4	5	1	0	0	15
Mean Precipitation (in.)	11.52	9.84	8.93	6.15	3.82	2.86	1.70	1.75	3.42	6.87	12.06	12.80	81.72
Days With ≥ 0.1" Precipitation	17	16	16	13	9	7	4	4	7	11	18	18	140
Days With ≥ 1.0" Precipitation	3	3	2	1	1	0	0	0	1	2	3	4	20
Mean Snowfall (in.)	0.6	0.4	trace	0.0	0.0	0.0	0.0	0.0	0.0	0.0	trace	0.5	1.5
Days With ≥ 1.0" Snow Depth	0	0	0	0	0	0	0	0	0	0	0	0	0

Longview *Cowlitz County*   Elevation: 9 ft.   Latitude: 46° 09' N   Longitude: 122° 55' W

	JAN	FEB	MAR	APR	MAY	JUN	JUL	AUG	SEP	OCT	NOV	DEC	YEAR
Mean Maximum Temp. (°F)	45.9	50.7	55.7	60.2	66.7	71.3	76.7	77.9	73.3	63.0	51.8	45.5	61.6
Mean Temp. (°F)	39.8	42.8	46.4	49.8	55.4	60.0	64.4	65.1	61.1	53.1	45.2	40.1	51.9
Mean Minimum Temp. (°F)	33.7	34.9	37.0	39.3	44.1	48.6	52.1	52.2	48.9	43.2	38.6	34.6	42.3
Extreme Maximum Temp. (°F)	62	72	80	88	96	99	104	108	100	90	72	62	108
Extreme Minimum Temp. (°F)	7	5	22	27	31	36	40	38	33	24	12	4	4
Days Maximum Temp. ≥ 90°F	0	0	0	0	0	1	2	2	1	0	0	0	6
Days Maximum Temp. ≤ 32°F	1	0	0	0	0	0	0	0	0	0	0	1	2
Days Minimum Temp. ≤ 32°F	12	10	7	3	0	0	0	0	0	1	5	11	49
Days Minimum Temp. ≤ 0°F	0	0	0	0	0	0	0	0	0	0	0	0	0
Heating Degree Days (base 65°F)	773	620	570	449	298	163	65	53	134	363	586	766	4,840
Cooling Degree Days (base 65°F)	0	0	0	1	9	18	59	66	29	1	0	0	183
Mean Precipitation (in.)	6.51	5.22	4.60	3.76	2.74	2.15	1.07	1.24	2.27	3.70	7.53	7.50	48.29
Days With ≥ 0.1" Precipitation	14	12	13	11	8	6	3	3	6	9	15	15	115
Days With ≥ 1.0" Precipitation	1	1	0	0	0	0	0	0	0	0	1	1	4
Mean Snowfall (in.)	1.4	0.7	trace	trace	trace	0.0	0.0	0.0	0.0	0.0	0.3	0.9	3.3
Days With ≥ 1.0" Snow Depth	1	1	0	0	0	0	0	0	0	0	0	1	3

Mazama *Okanogan County*   Elevation: 2,168 ft.   Latitude: 48° 37' N   Longitude: 120° 27' W

	JAN	FEB	MAR	APR	MAY	JUN	JUL	AUG	SEP	OCT	NOV	DEC	YEAR
Mean Maximum Temp. (°F)	28.7	36.3	46.1	57.3	66.8	74.0	81.9	82.2	72.6	56.6	37.6	27.3	55.6
Mean Temp. (°F)	20.7	27.0	35.3	44.2	53.2	60.2	66.5	66.4	56.9	43.9	30.7	20.4	43.8
Mean Minimum Temp. (°F)	12.7	17.6	24.5	31.0	39.6	46.3	51.1	50.6	41.2	31.2	23.8	13.4	31.9
Extreme Maximum Temp. (°F)	58	55	74	90	97	98	103	103	101	84	65	51	103
Extreme Minimum Temp. (°F)	-28	-21	-8	10	20	26	27	32	19	9	-14	-30	-30
Days Maximum Temp. ≥ 90°F	0	0	0	0	0	2	7	8	1	0	0	0	18
Days Maximum Temp. ≤ 32°F	20	7	1	0	0	0	0	0	0	0	6	22	56
Days Minimum Temp. ≤ 32°F	31	28	28	19	5	1	0	0	4	19	26	31	192
Days Minimum Temp. ≤ 0°F	6	2	0	0	0	0	0	0	0	0	1	5	14
Heating Degree Days (base 65°F)	1,366	1,067	912	619	363	170	59	59	251	648	1,022	1,377	7,913
Cooling Degree Days (base 65°F)	0	0	0	0	5	27	105	108	20	0	0	0	265
Mean Precipitation (in.)	3.81	2.61	1.66	1.07	1.04	1.05	0.81	0.80	0.85	1.48	3.53	4.21	22.92
Days With ≥ 0.1" Precipitation	9	7	5	3	3	3	2	2	2	4	9	9	58
Days With ≥ 1.0" Precipitation	1	0	0	0	0	0	0	0	0	0	0	1	2
Mean Snowfall (in.)	35.3	20.3	7.5	0.3	trace	0.0	0.0	0.0	0.0	2.3	17.4	39.7	122.8
Days With ≥ 1.0" Snow Depth	31	28	28	6	0	0	0	0	0	1	15	30	139

McMillin Reservoir *Pierce County*   Elevation: 577 ft.   Latitude: 47° 08' N   Longitude: 122° 16' W

	JAN	FEB	MAR	APR	MAY	JUN	JUL	AUG	SEP	OCT	NOV	DEC	YEAR
Mean Maximum Temp. (°F)	44.9	48.5	52.8	57.6	63.8	68.9	74.7	75.7	69.9	59.7	50.0	44.4	59.2
Mean Temp. (°F)	38.3	40.9	44.1	47.9	53.6	58.5	63.0	63.5	58.4	50.2	43.0	38.2	50.0
Mean Minimum Temp. (°F)	31.7	33.2	35.3	38.2	43.4	47.9	51.1	51.4	46.8	40.6	36.1	32.0	40.6
Extreme Maximum Temp. (°F)	64	67	72	83	92	95	98	100	95	86	72	64	100
Extreme Minimum Temp. (°F)	1	4	13	25	30	32	39	37	29	21	2	-1	-1
Days Maximum Temp. ≥ 90°F	0	0	0	0	0	0	1	1	0	0	0	0	2
Days Maximum Temp. ≤ 32°F	1	0	0	0	0	0	0	0	0	0	0	1	2
Days Minimum Temp. ≤ 32°F	16	12	10	5	0	0	0	0	0	3	10	16	72
Days Minimum Temp. ≤ 0°F	0	0	0	0	0	0	0	0	0	0	0	0	0
Heating Degree Days (base 65°F)	820	674	641	505	349	202	96	81	198	453	652	823	5,494
Cooling Degree Days (base 65°F)	0	0	0	0	3	13	40	44	9	0	0	0	109
Mean Precipitation (in.)	5.70	4.57	4.30	3.46	2.56	2.14	1.14	1.22	2.02	3.37	6.55	6.07	43.10
Days With ≥ 0.1" Precipitation	13	11	13	10	8	6	3	3	5	9	14	14	109
Days With ≥ 1.0" Precipitation	1	1	0	0	0	0	0	0	0	0	1	1	4
Mean Snowfall (in.)	1.4	1.2	0.9	trace	trace	0.0	0.0	0.0	0.0	trace	1.0	2.1	6.6
Days With ≥ 1.0" Snow Depth	2	1	1	0	0	0	0	0	0	0	1	2	7

McNary Dam *Benton County*   Elevation: 360 ft.   Latitude: 45° 57' N   Longitude: 119° 18' W

	JAN	FEB	MAR	APR	MAY	JUN	JUL	AUG	SEP	OCT	NOV	DEC	YEAR
Mean Maximum Temp. (°F)	40.0	46.4	56.0	64.2	72.6	79.9	88.1	87.6	77.9	65.2	50.1	41.4	64.1
Mean Temp. (°F)	34.1	38.7	45.9	52.8	60.4	67.3	74.4	74.1	65.1	54.2	43.1	35.6	53.8
Mean Minimum Temp. (°F)	28.4	30.9	35.8	41.3	48.0	54.5	60.4	60.6	52.3	43.0	36.0	29.9	43.4
Extreme Maximum Temp. (°F)	67	70	73	90	104	104	107	106	99	87	75	67	107
Extreme Minimum Temp. (°F)	-4	-7	12	29	34	35	44	47	34	20	1	-9	-9
Days Maximum Temp. ≥ 90°F	0	0	0	0	1	4	14	13	2	0	0	0	34
Days Maximum Temp. ≤ 32°F	7	3	0	0	0	0	0	0	0	0	1	5	16
Days Minimum Temp. ≤ 32°F	20	15	7	1	0	0	0	0	0	2	8	19	72
Days Minimum Temp. ≤ 0°F	0	0	0	0	0	0	0	0	0	0	0	1	1
Heating Degree Days (base 65°F)	952	738	585	360	168	43	3	3	69	332	651	904	4,808
Cooling Degree Days (base 65°F)	0	0	0	2	36	109	292	287	88	4	0	0	818
Mean Precipitation (in.)	1.06	0.76	0.74	0.64	0.63	0.43	0.25	0.37	0.38	0.56	1.19	1.12	8.13
Days With ≥ 0.1" Precipitation	4	3	3	2	2	1	1	1	1	2	4	4	28
Days With ≥ 1.0" Precipitation	0	0	0	0	0	0	0	0	0	0	0	0	0
Mean Snowfall (in.)	na	0.9	trace	0.0	0.0	0.0	0.0	0.0	0.0	0.0	0.3	na	na
Days With ≥ 1.0" Snow Depth	na	0	0	0	0	0	0	0	0	0	0	na	na

Methow 2 S *Okanogan County*   Elevation: 1,167 ft.   Latitude: 48° 06' N   Longitude: 120° 01' W

	JAN	FEB	MAR	APR	MAY	JUN	JUL	AUG	SEP	OCT	NOV	DEC	YEAR
Mean Maximum Temp. (°F)	31.5	39.8	52.4	63.3	72.0	79.7	87.8	88.1	78.2	63.0	43.6	31.6	60.9
Mean Temp. (°F)	23.6	30.6	40.3	48.9	56.9	64.0	70.7	70.3	60.9	48.1	34.6	24.1	47.7
Mean Minimum Temp. (°F)	15.6	21.3	28.1	34.4	41.9	48.4	53.5	52.6	43.6	33.1	25.6	16.4	34.5
Extreme Maximum Temp. (°F)	55	69	76	87	100	105	107	105	102	88	72	53	107
Extreme Minimum Temp. (°F)	-20	-15	0	21	25	33	35	35	24	11	-12	-21	-21
Days Maximum Temp. ≥ 90°F	0	0	0	0	1	5	14	14	3	0	0	0	37
Days Maximum Temp. ≤ 32°F	15	5	0	0	0	0	0	0	0	0	3	16	39
Days Minimum Temp. ≤ 32°F	30	27	24	12	2	0	0	0	1	15	24	30	165
Days Minimum Temp. ≤ 0°F	3	1	0	0	0	0	0	0	0	0	1	2	7
Heating Degree Days (base 65°F)	1,278	966	761	478	259	96	20	22	153	518	905	1,263	6,719
Cooling Degree Days (base 65°F)	0	0	0	1	19	66	194	192	44	1	0	0	517
Mean Precipitation (in.)	1.56	1.39	1.13	0.83	1.14	0.89	0.46	0.61	0.59	0.71	1.84	2.03	13.18
Days With ≥ 0.1" Precipitation	5	4	4	3	3	3	1	2	2	2	5	5	39
Days With ≥ 1.0" Precipitation	0	0	0	0	0	0	0	0	0	0	0	0	0
Mean Snowfall (in.)	*10.4*	*6.5*	2.7	0.3	0.0	0.0	0.0	0.0	0.0	0.2	*3.6*	na	na
Days With ≥ 1.0" Snow Depth	28	21	9	0	0	0	0	0	0	0	6	*23*	*87*

Monroe *Snohomish County*   Elevation: 118 ft.   Latitude: 47° 51' N   Longitude: 121° 59' W

	JAN	FEB	MAR	APR	MAY	JUN	JUL	AUG	SEP	OCT	NOV	DEC	YEAR
Mean Maximum Temp. (°F)	45.7	50.2	54.3	59.6	65.9	70.7	76.0	76.7	71.2	60.6	50.4	44.5	60.5
Mean Temp. (°F)	39.4	42.4	45.6	49.9	55.5	60.2	64.3	64.9	60.0	51.6	44.0	39.0	51.4
Mean Minimum Temp. (°F)	33.1	34.4	36.8	40.1	45.2	49.6	52.6	53.1	48.8	42.7	37.5	33.4	42.3
Extreme Maximum Temp. (°F)	67	75	75	84	93	94	100	97	97	88	77	62	100
Extreme Minimum Temp. (°F)	1	1	12	26	31	36	40	39	30	21	1	1	1
Days Maximum Temp. ≥ 90°F	0	0	0	0	0	0	1	1	0	0	0	0	2
Days Maximum Temp. ≤ 32°F	1	0	0	0	0	0	0	0	0	0	0	1	2
Days Minimum Temp. ≤ 32°F	14	10	8	3	0	0	0	0	0	2	7	13	57
Days Minimum Temp. ≤ 0°F	0	0	0	0	0	0	0	0	0	0	0	0	0
Heating Degree Days (base 65°F)	785	633	594	447	289	149	63	50	155	408	623	800	4,996
Cooling Degree Days (base 65°F)	0	0	0	0	3	14	51	61	13	0	0	0	142
Mean Precipitation (in.)	6.21	4.51	5.04	3.79	3.13	2.46	1.46	1.76	2.71	4.31	6.98	6.74	49.10
Days With ≥ 0.1" Precipitation	14	12	13	10	9	6	4	4	6	10	15	14	117
Days With ≥ 1.0" Precipitation	1	0	1	0	0	0	0	0	1	1	2	1	6
Mean Snowfall (in.)	1.8	0.8	0.1	trace	0.0	0.0	0.0	0.0	0.0	0.0	0.8	2.0	5.5
Days With ≥ 1.0" Snow Depth	1	1	0	0	0	0	0	0	0	0	1	1	4

Mount Vernon 3 WNW *Skagit County*   Elevation: 13 ft.   Latitude: 48° 27' N   Longitude: 122° 22' W

	JAN	FEB	MAR	APR	MAY	JUN	JUL	AUG	SEP	OCT	NOV	DEC	YEAR
Mean Maximum Temp. (°F)	45.5	49.2	53.1	57.5	63.6	68.0	72.6	73.8	68.5	59.4	50.4	45.3	58.9
Mean Temp. (°F)	39.6	42.3	45.3	48.8	54.3	58.5	61.8	62.5	57.9	50.5	44.3	39.8	50.5
Mean Minimum Temp. (°F)	33.7	35.4	37.4	40.1	45.0	48.9	51.0	51.2	47.2	41.7	38.1	34.2	42.0
Extreme Maximum Temp. (°F)	66	71	72	80	88	92	94	93	89	83	71	63	94
Extreme Minimum Temp. (°F)	1	8	9	25	33	38	39	36	30	19	7	5	1
Days Maximum Temp. ≥ 90°F	0	0	0	0	0	0	0	0	0	0	0	0	0
Days Maximum Temp. ≤ 32°F	1	0	0	0	0	0	0	0	0	0	0	2	3
Days Minimum Temp. ≤ 32°F	13	10	7	2	0	0	0	0	0	3	7	13	55
Days Minimum Temp. ≤ 0°F	0	0	0	0	0	0	0	0	0	0	0	0	0
Heating Degree Days (base 65°F)	780	634	604	478	324	192	106	89	210	441	615	775	5,248
Cooling Degree Days (base 65°F)	0	0	0	0	1	4	15	19	2	0	0	0	41
Mean Precipitation (in.)	4.22	2.83	2.73	2.47	2.31	1.92	1.22	1.31	1.76	2.94	4.87	3.95	32.53
Days With ≥ 0.1" Precipitation	11	9	9	8	7	5	3	3	5	8	12	11	91
Days With ≥ 1.0" Precipitation	1	0	0	0	0	0	0	0	0	0	1	0	2
Mean Snowfall (in.)	1.3	0.3	trace	trace	0.0	0.0	0.0	0.0	0.0	0.0	0.2	*0.8*	*2.6*
Days With ≥ 1.0" Snow Depth	*1*	0	0	0	0	0	0	0	0	0	*0*	1	2

Moxee City 10 E *Yakima County*   Elevation: 1,548 ft.   Latitude: 46° 30' N   Longitude: 120° 10' W

	JAN	FEB	MAR	APR	MAY	JUN	JUL	AUG	SEP	OCT	NOV	DEC	YEAR
Mean Maximum Temp. (°F)	36.3	43.8	53.6	61.9	70.5	78.2	85.6	84.8	75.9	62.5	46.2	35.9	61.3
Mean Temp. (°F)	29.7	35.5	42.4	48.7	55.9	63.0	69.1	68.4	60.7	49.6	38.0	29.5	49.2
Mean Minimum Temp. (°F)	23.0	27.1	31.1	35.6	41.4	47.7	52.6	52.0	45.4	36.7	29.9	22.9	37.1
Extreme Maximum Temp. (°F)	65	68	74	87	99	102	104	102	97	86	72	60	104
Extreme Minimum Temp. (°F)	-15	-15	7	20	25	30	36	37	25	15	-7	-12	-15
Days Maximum Temp. ≥ 90°F	0	0	0	0	1	3	11	9	2	0	0	0	26
Days Maximum Temp. ≤ 32°F	11	4	0	0	0	0	0	0	0	0	3	11	29
Days Minimum Temp. ≤ 32°F	28	23	19	11	4	0	0	0	1	9	19	27	141
Days Minimum Temp. ≤ 0°F	1	0	0	0	0	0	0	0	0	0	0	1	2
Heating Degree Days (base 65°F)	1,089	829	695	482	287	113	31	33	157	470	802	1,095	6,083
Cooling Degree Days (base 65°F)	0	0	0	*1*	17	59	171	153	41	1	0	0	*443*
Mean Precipitation (in.)	1.01	0.63	0.71	0.68	0.73	0.63	0.28	0.52	0.42	0.59	0.99	1.07	8.26
Days With ≥ 0.1" Precipitation	4	2	3	2	2	2	1	1	1	2	4	4	28
Days With ≥ 1.0" Precipitation	0	0	0	0	0	0	0	0	0	0	0	0	0
Mean Snowfall (in.)	4.6	1.9	0.8	trace	trace	0.0	0.0	0.0	0.0	0.1	1.7	5.0	14.1
Days With ≥ 1.0" Snow Depth	na	*3*	0	0	0	0	0	0	0	0	*1*	na	na

Mud Mountain Dam *King County* Elevation: 1,305 ft. Latitude: 47° 09' N Longitude: 121° 56' W

	JAN	FEB	MAR	APR	MAY	JUN	JUL	AUG	SEP	OCT	NOV	DEC	YEAR
Mean Maximum Temp. (°F)	44.7	47.7	50.8	55.1	61.0	66.1	72.3	73.3	68.4	59.2	49.3	44.4	57.7
Mean Temp. (°F)	38.3	40.3	42.7	46.2	51.8	56.6	61.6	62.2	57.6	49.7	42.3	38.1	48.9
Mean Minimum Temp. (°F)	31.7	32.8	34.6	37.3	42.4	47.1	50.9	51.0	46.8	40.3	35.2	31.6	40.1
Extreme Maximum Temp. (°F)	64	71	72	83	92	93	97	98	94	90	70	66	98
Extreme Minimum Temp. (°F)	5	2	14	24	29	33	40	39	31	24	7	3	2
Days Maximum Temp. ≥ 90°F	0	0	0	0	0	0	1	1	0	0	0	0	2
Days Maximum Temp. ≤ 32°F	1	0	0	0	0	0	0	0	0	0	0	2	3
Days Minimum Temp. ≤ 32°F	16	13	11	6	1	0	0	0	0	0	1	1	76
Days Minimum Temp. ≤ 0°F	0	0	0	0	0	0	0	0	0	2	10	17	0
Heating Degree Days (base 65°F)	822	691	683	558	408	258	138	119	228	467	675	829	5,876
Cooling Degree Days (base 65°F)	0	0	0	0	5	12	40	41	12	1	0	0	111
Mean Precipitation (in.)	6.85	5.24	5.34	5.17	4.40	3.86	2.18	2.13	2.99	4.61	8.23	6.87	57.87
Days With ≥ 0.1" Precipitation	13	12	13	13	11	9	5	5	7	10	15	13	126
Days With ≥ 1.0" Precipitation	1	1	1	0	0	1	0	0	0	1	2	1	8
Mean Snowfall (in.)	*3.1*	2.7	1.3	0.4	0.0	0.0	0.0	0.0	0.0	trace	0.5	*4.1*	*12.1*
Days With ≥ 1.0" Snow Depth	*3*	2	1	0	0	0	0	0	0	0	1	3	*10*

Newhalem *Whatcom County* Elevation: 524 ft. Latitude: 48° 41' N Longitude: 121° 15' W

	JAN	FEB	MAR	APR	MAY	JUN	JUL	AUG	SEP	OCT	NOV	DEC	YEAR
Mean Maximum Temp. (°F)	39.3	43.2	49.8	57.2	64.9	70.0	76.2	76.8	70.0	57.3	45.1	39.2	57.4
Mean Temp. (°F)	35.2	37.8	42.5	48.1	54.7	59.6	64.4	65.1	59.7	50.1	40.6	35.4	49.4
Mean Minimum Temp. (°F)	30.9	32.3	35.1	38.8	44.5	49.2	52.7	53.3	49.4	42.8	36.0	31.6	41.4
Extreme Maximum Temp. (°F)	63	60	73	89	101	95	100	103	97	80	70	58	103
Extreme Minimum Temp. (°F)	2	2	16	25	32	35	41	40	33	20	7	2	2
Days Maximum Temp. ≥ 90°F	0	0	0	0	0	1	3	3	0	0	0	0	7
Days Maximum Temp. ≤ 32°F	3	1	0	0	0	0	0	0	0	0	0	3	8
Days Minimum Temp. ≤ 32°F	17	*12*	8	2	0	0	0	0	0	0	1	3	8
Days Minimum Temp. ≤ 0°F	0	0	0	0	0	0	0	0	0	1	7	*16*	63
Heating Degree Days (base 65°F)	917	762	691	503	321	182	84	69	179	456	725	910	5,799
Cooling Degree Days (base 65°F)	0	0	0	0	12	24	71	79	26	0	0	0	212
Mean Precipitation (in.)	11.87	8.86	6.96	4.90	3.33	2.71	2.08	1.79	3.29	7.33	13.61	13.25	79.98
Days With ≥ 0.1" Precipitation	14	*12*	13	11	*8*	7	4	4	7	*12*	*16*	15	*123*
Days With ≥ 1.0" Precipitation	4	*2*	2	1	0	0	0	0	1	2	4	5	*21*
Mean Snowfall (in.)	12.5	9.6	1.6	trace	trace	0.0	0.0	0.0	0.0	trace	2.7	*9.0*	*35.4*
Days With ≥ 1.0" Snow Depth	12	*9*	2	0	0	0	0	0	0	0	1	8	32

Newport *Pend Oreille County* Elevation: 2,132 ft. Latitude: 48° 11' N Longitude: 117° 03' W

	JAN	FEB	MAR	APR	MAY	JUN	JUL	AUG	SEP	OCT	NOV	DEC	YEAR
Mean Maximum Temp. (°F)	32.0	38.4	48.6	59.1	69.0	76.1	83.8	83.8	73.0	57.6	39.8	32.1	57.8
Mean Temp. (°F)	25.8	30.6	37.7	45.5	54.2	60.8	66.2	65.4	56.1	44.8	33.8	26.5	45.6
Mean Minimum Temp. (°F)	19.6	22.8	26.7	31.9	39.2	45.4	48.5	46.9	39.1	32.1	27.8	20.9	33.4
Extreme Maximum Temp. (°F)	56	59	75	89	96	99	104	102	98	84	62	55	104
Extreme Minimum Temp. (°F)	-30	-19	-8	14	21	29	29	28	20	7	-13	-33	-33
Days Maximum Temp. ≥ 90°F	0	0	0	0	0	2	9	8	1	0	0	0	20
Days Maximum Temp. ≤ 32°F	13	5	0	0	0	0	0	0	0	0	4	15	37
Days Minimum Temp. ≤ 32°F	28	25	24	17	6	1	0	0	5	16	22	28	172
Days Minimum Temp. ≤ 0°F	3	1	0	0	0	0	0	0	0	0	0	2	6
Heating Degree Days (base 65°F)	1,209	964	839	578	336	152	55	65	268	618	931	1,186	7,201
Cooling Degree Days (base 65°F)	0	0	0	0	7	30	98	82	9	0	0	0	226
Mean Precipitation (in.)	2.95	2.47	2.22	1.85	2.24	1.94	1.36	1.16	1.19	1.60	3.45	4.16	26.59
Days With ≥ 0.1" Precipitation	8	6	7	6	6	5	4	3	4	5	9	9	72
Days With ≥ 1.0" Precipitation	0	0	0	0	0	0	0	0	0	0	0	1	1
Mean Snowfall (in.)	17.1	11.2	3.2	0.2	trace	0.0	0.0	0.0	0.0	0.1	5.5	19.8	57.1
Days With ≥ 1.0" Snow Depth	*22*	18	11	1	0	0	0	0	0	0	5	18	*75*

Northport *Stevens County* Elevation: 1,348 ft. Latitude: 48° 55' N Longitude: 117° 47' W

	JAN	FEB	MAR	APR	MAY	JUN	JUL	AUG	SEP	OCT	NOV	DEC	YEAR
Mean Maximum Temp. (°F)	32.5	39.7	51.8	63.3	73.0	79.7	86.9	87.0	76.0	59.2	41.7	32.7	60.3
Mean Temp. (°F)	26.6	32.1	40.3	48.9	57.3	63.7	69.5	69.0	59.6	47.2	35.3	32.7	48.1
Mean Minimum Temp. (°F)	20.8	24.5	28.8	34.5	41.5	47.7	51.7	51.0	43.2	35.1	28.9	22.3	35.8
Extreme Maximum Temp. (°F)	54	60	76	92	102	100	107	105	100	81	69	55	107
Extreme Minimum Temp. (°F)	-16	-11	3	17	20	26	30	35	24	12	-11	-18	-18
Days Maximum Temp. ≥ 90°F	0	0	0	0	1	5	13	14	2	0	0	0	35
Days Maximum Temp. ≤ 32°F	13	4	0	0	0	0	0	0	0	0	3	13	33
Days Minimum Temp. ≤ 32°F	28	24	22	12	3	0	0	0	2	11	20	27	149
Days Minimum Temp. ≤ 0°F	2	1	0	0	0	0	0	0	0	0	0	1	4
Heating Degree Days (base 65°F)	1,182	922	758	476	245	90	21	24	174	546	886	1,156	6,480
Cooling Degree Days (base 65°F)	0	0	0	0	14	48	156	147	22	0	0	0	387
Mean Precipitation (in.)	1.84	1.53	1.54	1.58	2.21	2.29	1.60	1.32	1.20	1.25	2.15	2.52	21.03
Days With ≥ 0.1" Precipitation	7	5	6	5	6	6	5	4	3	4	7	8	66
Days With ≥ 1.0" Precipitation	0	0	0	0	0	0	0	0	0	0	0	0	0
Mean Snowfall (in.)	14.7	8.4	1.9	0.2	0.0	0.0	0.0	0.0	0.0	trace	7.8	19.2	52.2
Days With ≥ 1.0" Snow Depth	27	21	7	0	0	0	0	0	0	0	6	22	83

Oakville *Grays Harbor County*   Elevation: 78 ft.   Latitude: 46° 50' N   Longitude: 123° 14' W

	JAN	FEB	MAR	APR	MAY	JUN	JUL	AUG	SEP	OCT	NOV	DEC	YEAR
Mean Maximum Temp. (°F)	46.5	50.6	55.7	60.5	66.7	71.5	*76.6*	77.6	72.6	62.2	51.8	45.7	*61.5*
Mean Temp. (°F)	39.5	42.0	45.4	49.0	54.6	59.3	*63.4*	*64.1*	59.4	51.3	44.2	39.4	*51.0*
Mean Minimum Temp. (°F)	32.4	33.3	35.0	37.4	42.4	47.1	*50.3*	*50.6*	46.1	40.3	36.5	33.2	*40.4*
Extreme Maximum Temp. (°F)	61	75	76	86	98	100	*100*	105	100	90	72	61	*105*
Extreme Minimum Temp. (°F)	-1	3	15	20	27	33	*36*	*33*	23	16	2	-6	*-6*
Days Maximum Temp. ≥ 90°F	0	0	0	0	0	1	*2*	2	0	0	0	0	*5*
Days Maximum Temp. ≤ 32°F	0	0	0	0	0	0	*0*	0	0	0	0	1	*1*
Days Minimum Temp. ≤ 32°F	15	13	11	7	2	0	*0*	0	1	5	9	14	*77*
Days Minimum Temp. ≤ 0°F	0	0	0	0	0	0	*0*	0	0	0	0	0	*0*
Heating Degree Days (base 65°F)	784	644	602	475	322	180	*86*	72	173	419	619	786	*5,162*
Cooling Degree Days (base 65°F)	0	0	0	0	6	*16*	49	57	*13*	0	0	0	*141*
Mean Precipitation (in.)	8.39	6.84	5.97	4.23	2.68	2.07	*0.91*	*1.23*	2.59	4.62	8.72	9.37	*57.62*
Days With ≥ 0.1" Precipitation	15	12	14	12	8	6	*3*	*3*	6	9	16	15	*119*
Days With ≥ 1.0" Precipitation	2	2	1	0	0	0	*0*	0	0	1	2	3	*11*
Mean Snowfall (in.)	2.7	0.6	0.7	trace	0.0	0.0	*0.0*	0.0	0.0	0.0	trace	1.2	*5.2*
Days With ≥ 1.0" Snow Depth	*0*	0	0	0	0	0	*0*	0	0	0	0	*0*	*0*

Odessa *Lincoln County*   Elevation: 1,528 ft.   Latitude: 47° 20' N   Longitude: 118° 42' W

	JAN	FEB	MAR	APR	MAY	JUN	JUL	AUG	SEP	OCT	NOV	DEC	YEAR
Mean Maximum Temp. (°F)	35.5	43.0	53.2	62.5	71.0	78.6	86.2	86.0	76.9	63.3	45.8	35.9	61.5
Mean Temp. (°F)	27.6	33.6	41.0	48.1	55.6	62.8	69.0	68.4	59.5	47.9	36.4	27.9	48.2
Mean Minimum Temp. (°F)	19.7	24.2	28.9	33.7	40.0	46.9	51.7	50.7	42.0	32.7	27.0	19.9	34.8
Extreme Maximum Temp. (°F)	62	67	75	91	100	103	107	106	101	88	71	58	107
Extreme Minimum Temp. (°F)	-29	-22	4	11	20	27	32	32	21	7	-16	-24	-29
Days Maximum Temp. ≥ 90°F	0	0	0	0	1	3	11	11	2	0	0	0	28
Days Maximum Temp. ≤ 32°F	11	4	0	0	0	0	0	0	0	0	2	10	27
Days Minimum Temp. ≤ 32°F	28	24	22	13	4	0	0	0	3	15	21	28	158
Days Minimum Temp. ≤ 0°F	2	1	0	0	0	0	0	0	0	0	0	2	5
Heating Degree Days (base 65°F)	1,152	880	737	500	300	117	35	40	186	524	850	1,143	6,464
Cooling Degree Days (base 65°F)	0	0	0	2	17	47	153	144	30	1	0	0	394
Mean Precipitation (in.)	1.25	1.06	1.01	0.75	0.88	0.61	0.51	0.35	0.49	0.70	1.42	1.69	10.72
Days With ≥ 0.1" Precipitation	5	4	4	2	3	2	2	1	2	2	5	6	38
Days With ≥ 1.0" Precipitation	0	0	0	0	0	0	0	0	0	0	0	0	0
Mean Snowfall (in.)	4.8	2.0	0.4	trace	0.0	0.0	0.0	0.0	0.0	trace	1.2	5.9	14.3
Days With ≥ 1.0" Snow Depth	na	*2*	0	0	0	0	0	0	0	0	*1*	7	na

Olga 2 SE *San Juan County*   Elevation: 78 ft.   Latitude: 48° 37' N   Longitude: 122° 48' W

	JAN	FEB	MAR	APR	MAY	JUN	JUL	AUG	SEP	OCT	NOV	DEC	YEAR
Mean Maximum Temp. (°F)	45.2	48.1	52.2	57.0	62.8	66.6	69.9	70.2	66.3	57.8	49.6	45.2	57.6
Mean Temp. (°F)	40.3	42.4	45.4	49.1	53.9	57.4	60.2	60.6	57.4	51.1	44.3	40.4	50.2
Mean Minimum Temp. (°F)	35.3	36.7	38.5	41.1	45.0	48.2	50.5	50.9	48.5	44.3	39.0	35.6	42.8
Extreme Maximum Temp. (°F)	62	66	67	76	87	87	85	89	85	77	67	65	89
Extreme Minimum Temp. (°F)	13	-1	20	29	34	38	41	38	36	29	4	10	-1
Days Maximum Temp. ≥ 90°F	0	0	0	0	0	0	0	0	0	0	0	0	0
Days Maximum Temp. ≤ 32°F	1	0	0	0	0	0	0	0	0	0	1	2	4
Days Minimum Temp. ≤ 32°F	10	6	3	0	0	0	0	0	0	0	4	9	32
Days Minimum Temp. ≤ 0°F	0	0	0	0	0	0	0	0	0	0	0	0	0
Heating Degree Days (base 65°F)	760	632	603	471	338	223	147	136	222	424	614	755	5,325
Cooling Degree Days (base 65°F)	0	0	0	0	1	3	6	6	1	0	0	0	17
Mean Precipitation (in.)	3.93	2.79	2.25	1.92	1.63	1.35	0.94	1.03	1.35	2.45	4.34	4.10	28.08
Days With ≥ 0.1" Precipitation	11	8	8	7	5	4	3	3	4	7	11	11	82
Days With ≥ 1.0" Precipitation	1	0	0	0	0	0	0	0	0	0	1	1	3
Mean Snowfall (in.)	1.8	1.0	0.5	trace	0.0	0.0	0.0	0.0	0.0	0.1	0.5	2.0	5.9
Days With ≥ 1.0" Snow Depth	1	0	0	0	0	0	0	0	0	0	1	1	3

Packwood *Lewis County*   Elevation: 1,059 ft.   Latitude: 46° 37' N   Longitude: 121° 40' W

	JAN	FEB	MAR	APR	MAY	JUN	JUL	AUG	SEP	OCT	NOV	DEC	YEAR
Mean Maximum Temp. (°F)	42.9	48.0	53.3	59.4	66.4	71.5	78.3	79.0	73.6	62.2	47.8	42.1	60.4
Mean Temp. (°F)	36.1	39.1	43.3	47.9	54.2	59.4	64.8	65.0	59.1	50.1	40.8	35.8	49.6
Mean Minimum Temp. (°F)	29.2	30.2	32.9	36.3	41.9	47.3	51.3	51.0	44.5	37.8	33.7	29.6	38.8
Extreme Maximum Temp. (°F)	64	77	79	90	102	100	103	105	105	97	72	62	105
Extreme Minimum Temp. (°F)	-3	-2	14	20	24	28	32	30	23	18	-3	-8	-8
Days Maximum Temp. ≥ 90°F	0	0	0	0	1	1	4	4	2	0	0	0	12
Days Maximum Temp. ≤ 32°F	2	0	0	0	0	0	0	0	0	0	0	2	4
Days Minimum Temp. ≤ 32°F	18	16	14	7	2	0	0	0	2	8	11	19	97
Days Minimum Temp. ≤ 0°F	0	0	0	0	0	0	0	0	0	0	0	0	0
Heating Degree Days (base 65°F)	891	725	665	509	335	184	71	64	185	455	720	898	5,702
Cooling Degree Days (base 65°F)	0	0	0	1	8	22	75	76	18	1	0	0	201
Mean Precipitation (in.)	9.59	7.01	5.31	3.79	2.53	2.00	1.00	1.13	2.35	4.66	9.46	9.57	58.40
Days With ≥ 0.1" Precipitation	13	12	12	9	8	6	3	3	5	9	15	*14*	*109*
Days With ≥ 1.0" Precipitation	3	2	1	0	0	0	0	0	0	1	2	3	12
Mean Snowfall (in.)	*10.4*	7.0	*1.9*	0.2	0.0	0.0	0.0	0.0	0.0	0.0	2.4	6.0	*27.9*
Days With ≥ 1.0" Snow Depth	*10*	*5*	1	0	0	0	0	0	0	0	1	*7*	*24*

Palmer 3 ESE *King County*   Elevation: 918 ft.   Latitude: 47° 18' N   Longitude: 121° 51' W

	JAN	FEB	MAR	APR	MAY	JUN	JUL	AUG	SEP	OCT	NOV	DEC	YEAR
Mean Maximum Temp. (°F)	43.1	47.1	51.3	56.3	62.7	67.5	73.3	74.0	68.8	59.2	47.9	42.7	57.8
Mean Temp. (°F)	37.7	40.4	43.2	47.1	52.7	57.5	62.3	62.8	58.4	50.5	42.1	37.5	49.3
Mean Minimum Temp. (°F)	32.2	33.6	35.1	37.8	42.8	47.5	51.2	51.6	47.8	41.9	36.3	32.3	40.8
Extreme Maximum Temp. (°F)	61	68	75	85	100	95	97	99	97	90	68	62	100
Extreme Minimum Temp. (°F)	8	-3	15	29	31	34	41	41	32	27	9	4	-3
Days Maximum Temp. ≥ 90°F	0	0	0	0	0	0	1	1	0	0	0	0	2
Days Maximum Temp. ≤ 32°F	2	1	0	0	0	0	0	0	0	0	1	2	6
Days Minimum Temp. ≤ 32°F	15	11	8	3	0	0	0	0	0	1	8	15	61
Days Minimum Temp. ≤ 0°F	0	0	0	0	0	0	0	0	0	0	0	0	0
Heating Degree Days (base 65°F)	840	689	669	532	379	233	119	103	207	443	679	846	5,739
Cooling Degree Days (base 65°F)	0	0	0	0	0	6	13	40	42	14	1	0	116
Mean Precipitation (in.)	11.04	8.89	8.66	7.47	5.91	5.03	3.02	2.66	4.33	6.79	12.13	11.18	87.11
Days With ≥ 0.1" Precipitation	16	14	16	15	13	10	6	5	8	12	18	17	150
Days With ≥ 1.0" Precipitation	3	3	2	1	1	1	1	1	1	2	4	3	23
Mean Snowfall (in.)	7.3	5.3	2.7	0.5	trace	0.0	0.0	0.0	0.0	0.2	1.9	7.5	25.4
Days With ≥ 1.0" Snow Depth	6	3	2	0	0	0	0	0	0	0	2	5	18

Plain *Chelan County*   Elevation: 1,938 ft.   Latitude: 47° 47' N   Longitude: 120° 39' W

	JAN	FEB	MAR	APR	MAY	JUN	JUL	AUG	SEP	OCT	NOV	DEC	YEAR
Mean Maximum Temp. (°F)	34.2	40.4	49.3	58.1	67.0	73.6	81.1	81.5	73.4	59.7	41.4	33.0	57.7
Mean Temp. (°F)	27.1	31.7	38.1	44.7	52.4	58.8	64.6	64.7	56.8	46.1	34.6	27.1	45.6
Mean Minimum Temp. (°F)	19.9	23.0	26.8	31.2	37.8	44.0	48.0	47.9	40.1	32.4	27.8	21.1	33.3
Extreme Maximum Temp. (°F)	59	61	74	88	98	98	101	100	98	86	64	55	101
Extreme Minimum Temp. (°F)	-24	-17	-1	17	24	26	29	30	21	13	-7	-22	-24
Days Maximum Temp. ≥ 90°F	0	0	0	0	0	2	7	6	1	0	0	0	16
Days Maximum Temp. ≤ 32°F	12	4	0	0	0	0	0	0	0	0	3	13	32
Days Minimum Temp. ≤ 32°F	30	27	27	19	6	1	0	0	5	16	24	30	185
Days Minimum Temp. ≤ 0°F	3	1	0	0	0	0	0	0	0	0	0	1	5
Heating Degree Days (base 65°F)	1,169	933	827	602	385	195	78	73	247	580	905	1,169	7,163
Cooling Degree Days (base 65°F)	0	0	0	0	4	15	68	70	9	0	0	0	166
Mean Precipitation (in.)	4.95	3.56	2.18	1.33	1.07	0.98	0.48	0.66	0.75	1.95	4.78	5.47	28.16
Days With ≥ 0.1" Precipitation	11	8	7	5	3	2	2	2	3	5	12	12	72
Days With ≥ 1.0" Precipitation	1	1	0	0	0	0	0	0	0	0	1	1	4
Mean Snowfall (in.)	40.6	22.9	10.2	1.3	trace	0.0	0.0	0.0	0.0	1.6	20.3	43.4	140.3
Days With ≥ 1.0" Snow Depth	15	13	10	1	0	0	0	0	0	0	7	15	61

Port Angeles *Clallam County*   Elevation: 88 ft.   Latitude: 48° 07' N   Longitude: 123° 26' W

	JAN	FEB	MAR	APR	MAY	JUN	JUL	AUG	SEP	OCT	NOV	DEC	YEAR
Mean Maximum Temp. (°F)	45.5	47.8	51.2	55.2	60.6	64.5	68.5	68.9	65.9	57.6	49.8	45.6	56.8
Mean Temp. (°F)	39.9	41.6	44.1	47.5	52.7	56.7	60.1	60.4	57.3	50.4	44.0	40.3	49.6
Mean Minimum Temp. (°F)	34.3	35.4	37.0	39.8	44.7	48.8	51.6	51.9	48.6	43.2	38.1	34.9	42.4
Extreme Maximum Temp. (°F)	64	64	65	82	86	87	91	94	83	73	66	63	94
Extreme Minimum Temp. (°F)	10	10	20	25	30	36	40	40	31	29	6	12	6
Days Maximum Temp. ≥ 90°F	0	0	0	0	0	0	0	0	0	0	0	0	0
Days Maximum Temp. ≤ 32°F	0	0	0	0	0	0	0	0	0	0	0	1	1
Days Minimum Temp. ≤ 32°F	11	7	5	2	0	0	0	0	0	1	5	11	42
Days Minimum Temp. ≤ 0°F	0	0	0	0	0	0	0	0	0	0	0	0	0
Heating Degree Days (base 65°F)	771	653	641	518	376	247	159	147	228	446	623	760	5,569
Cooling Degree Days (base 65°F)	0	0	0	0	1	4	11	12	2	0	0	0	30
Mean Precipitation (in.)	3.86	2.78	2.10	1.36	1.06	0.85	0.61	0.76	1.08	2.46	4.40	4.50	25.82
Days With ≥ 0.1" Precipitation	9	8	6	4	3	3	2	2	3	7	10	10	67
Days With ≥ 1.0" Precipitation	1	0	0	0	0	0	0	0	0	0	1	1	3
Mean Snowfall (in.)	0.5	trace	trace	trace	0.0	0.0	0.0	0.0	0.0	0.0	0.2	0.3	1.0
Days With ≥ 1.0" Snow Depth	0	0	0	0	0	0	0	0	0	0	0	0	0

Port Townsend *Jefferson County*   Elevation: 68 ft.   Latitude: 48° 07' N   Longitude: 122° 45' W

	JAN	FEB	MAR	APR	MAY	JUN	JUL	AUG	SEP	OCT	NOV	DEC	YEAR
Mean Maximum Temp. (°F)	45.7	48.5	52.5	57.1	62.8	67.0	71.7	72.4	67.8	58.4	49.8	45.7	58.3
Mean Temp. (°F)	41.4	43.4	46.1	49.9	54.8	58.6	62.2	62.8	59.1	52.0	45.4	41.6	51.4
Mean Minimum Temp. (°F)	37.1	38.2	39.7	42.6	46.8	50.1	52.7	53.1	50.4	45.6	40.9	37.5	44.6
Extreme Maximum Temp. (°F)	62	65	67	76	86	90	90	93	85	75	66	61	93
Extreme Minimum Temp. (°F)	14	12	20	33	35	42	44	37	38	22	16	11	11
Days Maximum Temp. ≥ 90°F	0	0	0	0	0	0	0	0	0	0	0	0	0
Days Maximum Temp. ≤ 32°F	1	0	0	0	0	0	0	0	0	0	0	1	2
Days Minimum Temp. ≤ 32°F	6	3	2	0	0	0	0	0	0	0	2	5	18
Days Minimum Temp. ≤ 0°F	0	0	0	0	0	0	0	0	0	0	0	0	0
Heating Degree Days (base 65°F)	724	603	579	447	309	191	100	85	176	397	582	717	4,910
Cooling Degree Days (base 65°F)	0	0	0	0	1	7	20	25	5	0	0	0	58
Mean Precipitation (in.)	2.16	1.61	1.65	1.52	1.59	1.28	1.02	0.90	1.06	1.40	2.66	2.64	19.49
Days With ≥ 0.1" Precipitation	7	6	5	5	5	4	3	3	3	5	8	8	62
Days With ≥ 1.0" Precipitation	0	0	0	0	0	0	0	0	0	0	0	0	0
Mean Snowfall (in.)	1.1	0.6	trace	0.0	0.0	0.0	0.0	0.0	0.0	0.0	0.7	0.6	3.0
Days With ≥ 1.0" Snow Depth	0	0	0	0	0	0	0	0	0	0	0	0	0

Priest Rapids Dam *Grant County*   Elevation: 459 ft.   Latitude: 46° 39' N   Longitude: 119° 54' W

	JAN	FEB	MAR	APR	MAY	JUN	JUL	AUG	SEP	OCT	NOV	DEC	YEAR
Mean Maximum Temp. (°F)	40.2	47.1	57.5	66.1	75.3	82.9	91.0	90.2	79.9	66.2	50.0	40.5	65.6
Mean Temp. (°F)	33.3	38.8	47.2	54.7	63.4	70.6	77.6	77.1	67.6	54.8	42.2	33.8	55.1
Mean Minimum Temp. (°F)	26.4	30.5	36.8	43.3	51.3	58.3	64.2	63.9	55.1	43.4	34.3	27.1	44.6
Extreme Maximum Temp. (°F)	71	72	80	94	105	109	112	110	105	87	76	71	112
Extreme Minimum Temp. (°F)	-12	-10	11	26	30	35	47	42	33	18	-7	-4	-12
Days Maximum Temp. ≥ 90°F	0	0	0	0	2	7	18	17	4	0	0	0	48
Days Maximum Temp. ≤ 32°F	7	2	0	0	0	0	0	0	0	0	1	6	16
Days Minimum Temp. ≤ 32°F	23	15	7	2	0	0	0	0	0	2	12	23	84
Days Minimum Temp. ≤ 0°F	1	0	0	0	0	0	0	0	0	0	0	0	1
Heating Degree Days (base 65°F)	977	735	546	307	109	21	2	2	47	317	678	961	4,702
Cooling Degree Days (base 65°F)	0	0	0	5	68	187	389	374	130	9	0	0	1,162
Mean Precipitation (in.)	0.85	0.64	0.64	0.44	0.43	0.39	0.19	0.27	0.35	0.46	1.02	1.21	6.89
Days With ≥ 0.1" Precipitation	3	2	2	1	1	1	0	1	1	2	3	4	21
Days With ≥ 1.0" Precipitation	0	0	0	0	0	0	0	0	0	0	0	0	0
Mean Snowfall (in.)	3.1	0.6	trace	0.0	0.0	0.0	0.0	0.0	0.0	0.0	0.7	na	na
Days With ≥ 1.0" Snow Depth	na	1	0	0	0	0	0	0	0	0	0	2	na

Pullman 2 NW *Whitman County*   Elevation: 2,542 ft.   Latitude: 46° 46' N   Longitude: 117° 10' W

	JAN	FEB	MAR	APR	MAY	JUN	JUL	AUG	SEP	OCT	NOV	DEC	YEAR
Mean Maximum Temp. (°F)	35.1	40.7	47.9	55.6	64.0	71.3	80.9	82.5	72.7	59.9	43.3	35.4	57.4
Mean Temp. (°F)	29.5	34.0	39.7	45.7	52.8	59.0	65.6	66.5	58.3	48.3	37.0	29.9	47.2
Mean Minimum Temp. (°F)	23.8	27.3	31.4	35.7	41.6	46.6	50.2	50.5	43.9	36.6	30.6	24.3	36.9
Extreme Maximum Temp. (°F)	57	66	73	88	92	98	102	103	100	90	71	59	103
Extreme Minimum Temp. (°F)	-21	-24	2	17	25	32	33	33	20	14	-9	-20	-24
Days Maximum Temp. ≥ 90°F	0	0	0	0	0	1	6	8	1	0	0	0	16
Days Maximum Temp. ≤ 32°F	11	4	1	0	0	0	0	0	0	0	3	10	29
Days Minimum Temp. ≤ 32°F	25	21	18	10	3	0	0	0	2	9	17	25	130
Days Minimum Temp. ≤ 0°F	1	1	0	0	0	0	0	0	0	0	0	1	3
Heating Degree Days (base 65°F)	1,093	868	777	575	378	201	75	66	221	514	834	1,083	6,685
Cooling Degree Days (base 65°F)	0	0	0	1	10	24	97	122	34	3	0	0	291
Mean Precipitation (in.)	2.61	2.08	1.97	1.72	1.72	1.31	0.83	0.90	0.86	1.49	2.86	2.78	21.13
Days With ≥ 0.1" Precipitation	8	7	7	6	5	4	3	2	3	4	9	8	66
Days With ≥ 1.0" Precipitation	0	0	0	0	0	0	0	0	0	0	0	0	0
Mean Snowfall (in.)	10.2	5.8	2.5	0.9	trace	0.0	0.0	0.0	0.0	0.5	4.6	10.3	34.8
Days With ≥ 1.0" Snow Depth	13	7	3	0	0	0	0	0	0	0	4	11	38

Puyallup 2 W Exp. Station *Pierce County*   Elevation: 49 ft.   Latitude: 47° 12' N   Longitude: 122° 20' W

	JAN	FEB	MAR	APR	MAY	JUN	JUL	AUG	SEP	OCT	NOV	DEC	YEAR
Mean Maximum Temp. (°F)	46.9	50.9	55.6	60.7	67.7	72.6	77.9	78.5	72.6	62.3	51.4	46.0	61.9
Mean Temp. (°F)	39.7	42.5	45.8	49.8	55.9	60.5	64.8	65.0	59.8	51.8	44.0	39.4	51.6
Mean Minimum Temp. (°F)	32.6	34.0	36.0	38.8	44.0	48.4	51.5	51.4	46.9	41.3	36.4	32.7	41.2
Extreme Maximum Temp. (°F)	65	69	73	83	92	95	99	99	94	85	71	67	99
Extreme Minimum Temp. (°F)	1	5	13	25	26	33	37	35	29	20	2	3	1
Days Maximum Temp. ≥ 90°F	0	0	0	0	0	1	2	2	0	0	0	0	5
Days Maximum Temp. ≤ 32°F	0	0	0	0	0	0	0	0	0	0	0	1	1
Days Minimum Temp. ≤ 32°F	14	11	10	5	0	0	0	0	0	3	9	15	67
Days Minimum Temp. ≤ 0°F	0	0	0	0	0	0	0	0	0	0	0	0	0
Heating Degree Days (base 65°F)	776	630	587	450	280	145	54	49	161	403	624	787	4,946
Cooling Degree Days (base 65°F)	0	0	0	0	6	17	54	64	14	0	0	0	155
Mean Precipitation (in.)	5.40	4.46	4.07	3.12	2.00	1.77	0.88	1.17	1.79	3.02	5.85	5.96	39.49
Days With ≥ 0.1" Precipitation	12	11	11	9	6	5	2	3	5	7	13	13	97
Days With ≥ 1.0" Precipitation	1	1	0	0	0	0	0	0	0	0	1	1	4
Mean Snowfall (in.)	1.8	0.9	0.2	0.0	0.0	0.0	0.0	0.0	0.0	trace	1.0	1.4	5.3
Days With ≥ 1.0" Snow Depth	1	1	0	0	0	0	0	0	0	0	1	1	4

Quincy 1 S *Grant County*   Elevation: 1,272 ft.   Latitude: 47° 13' N   Longitude: 119° 51' W

	JAN	FEB	MAR	APR	MAY	JUN	JUL	AUG	SEP	OCT	NOV	DEC	YEAR
Mean Maximum Temp. (°F)	35.1	43.2	55.0	63.9	72.6	79.4	86.4	85.7	77.1	63.2	46.0	35.3	61.9
Mean Temp. (°F)	27.7	34.4	43.3	50.7	59.1	65.6	71.4	70.7	62.2	50.0	37.5	28.1	50.1
Mean Minimum Temp. (°F)	20.2	25.6	31.5	37.5	45.5	51.8	56.4	55.7	47.3	36.8	29.0	20.8	38.2
Extreme Maximum Temp. (°F)	62	68	74	92	99	101	105	102	98	84	72	64	105
Extreme Minimum Temp. (°F)	-15	-22	8	17	27	33	38	38	26	13	-15	-17	-22
Days Maximum Temp. ≥ 90°F	0	0	0	0	1	4	12	10	2	0	0	0	29
Days Maximum Temp. ≤ 32°F	12	4	0	0	0	0	0	0	0	0	2	12	30
Days Minimum Temp. ≤ 32°F	28	23	18	8	1	0	0	0	1	9	20	28	136
Days Minimum Temp. ≤ 0°F	2	1	0	0	0	0	0	0	0	0	0	2	5
Heating Degree Days (base 65°F)	1,150	857	667	423	205	67	15	16	126	458	818	1,138	5,940
Cooling Degree Days (base 65°F)	0	0	0	2	33	84	218	199	54	1	0	0	591
Mean Precipitation (in.)	0.94	0.73	0.67	0.46	0.63	0.48	0.30	0.34	0.44	0.53	1.24	1.37	8.13
Days With ≥ 0.1" Precipitation	3	3	2	2	2	2	1	1	2	2	4	5	28
Days With ≥ 1.0" Precipitation	0	0	0	0	0	0	0	0	0	0	0	0	0
Mean Snowfall (in.)	na	0.9	trace	0.0	0.0	0.0	0.0	0.0	0.0	trace	1.2	na	na
Days With ≥ 1.0" Snow Depth	na	na	0	0	0	0	0	0	0	0	0	na	na

Rainier Paradise Ranger Station *Pierce County*   Elevation: 5,426 ft.   Latitude: 46° 47' N   Longitude: 121° 44' W

	JAN	FEB	MAR	APR	MAY	JUN	JUL	AUG	SEP	OCT	NOV	DEC	YEAR
Mean Maximum Temp. (°F)	32.2	34.0	36.0	40.2	47.3	53.1	60.7	62.0	56.1	47.0	35.2	32.2	44.7
Mean Temp. (°F)	26.5	27.8	29.4	32.8	39.1	44.7	51.4	52.7	47.7	39.7	29.5	26.3	37.3
Mean Minimum Temp. (°F)	20.7	21.7	22.7	25.3	30.8	36.2	42.0	43.5	39.2	32.2	23.8	20.3	29.9
Extreme Maximum Temp. (°F)	56	60	65	78	83	85	86	85	89	81	64	60	89
Extreme Minimum Temp. (°F)	-10	-18	2	3	14	20	23	26	20	11	-3	-17	-18
Days Maximum Temp. ≥ 90°F	0	0	0	0	0	0	0	0	0	0	0	0	0
Days Maximum Temp. ≤ 32°F	17	14	11	7	1	0	0	0	0	3	12	16	81
Days Minimum Temp. ≤ 32°F	29	26	29	25	20	11	3	2	7	17	27	29	225
Days Minimum Temp. ≤ 0°F	1	0	0	0	0	0	0	0	0	0	0	1	2
Heating Degree Days (base 65°F)	1,186	1,043	1,098	961	798	604	425	385	517	779	1,058	1,195	10,049
Cooling Degree Days (base 65°F)	0	0	0	0	0	1	8	10	4	0	0	0	23
Mean Precipitation (in.)	17.88	13.84	12.58	9.04	5.40	3.84	2.11	2.27	4.72	8.54	19.26	19.95	119.43
Days With ≥ 0.1" Precipitation	18	15	18	15	12	9	5	5	8	12	20	19	156
Days With ≥ 1.0" Precipitation	7	5	4	2	1	1	0	1	1	3	7	7	39
Mean Snowfall (in.)	124.9	105.8	102.4	75.8	27.3	6.5	0.7	trace	3.3	26.0	103.3	126.7	702.7
Days With ≥ 1.0" Snow Depth	31	28	31	30	30	28	14	2	1	9	27	31	262

Republic *Ferry County*   Elevation: 2,608 ft.   Latitude: 48° 39' N   Longitude: 118° 44' W

	JAN	FEB	MAR	APR	MAY	JUN	JUL	AUG	SEP	OCT	NOV	DEC	YEAR
Mean Maximum Temp. (°F)	29.4	37.6	47.4	57.3	65.8	72.7	80.4	81.0	71.2	56.8	38.3	29.0	55.6
Mean Temp. (°F)	22.3	28.6	36.2	43.8	51.7	58.2	63.9	63.8	54.9	43.5	31.3	22.5	43.4
Mean Minimum Temp. (°F)	15.1	19.6	25.1	30.3	37.6	43.6	47.3	46.5	38.6	30.2	24.2	16.0	31.2
Extreme Maximum Temp. (°F)	51	58	72	87	96	96	103	100	97	84	64	50	103
Extreme Minimum Temp. (°F)	-27	-18	-6	13	21	28	30	32	19	1	-20	-29	-29
Days Maximum Temp. ≥ 90°F	0	0	0	0	0	1	6	6	1	0	0	0	14
Days Maximum Temp. ≤ 32°F	17	6	1	0	0	0	0	0	0	0	6	19	49
Days Minimum Temp. ≤ 32°F	30	26	27	19	7	1	0	0	5	19	24	30	188
Days Minimum Temp. ≤ 0°F	5	2	0	0	0	0	0	0	0	0	1	3	11
Heating Degree Days (base 65°F)	1,319	1,020	884	629	408	213	90	92	299	659	1,006	1,311	7,930
Cooling Degree Days (base 65°F)	0	0	0	0	3	13	59	60	5	0	0	0	140
Mean Precipitation (in.)	1.41	1.30	1.30	1.32	2.03	1.76	1.24	1.09	0.91	0.88	1.73	1.89	16.86
Days With ≥ 0.1" Precipitation	5	4	4	4	6	5	3	3	3	3	6	6	52
Days With ≥ 1.0" Precipitation	0	0	0	0	0	0	0	0	0	0	0	0	0
Mean Snowfall (in.)	11.9	6.6	2.5	0.4	trace	0.0	0.0	0.0	0.0	0.4	7.4	16.0	45.2
Days With ≥ 1.0" Snow Depth	29	25	10	0	0	0	0	0	0	0	7	25	96

Richland *Benton County*   Elevation: 370 ft.   Latitude: 46° 19' N   Longitude: 119° 16' W

	JAN	FEB	MAR	APR	MAY	JUN	JUL	AUG	SEP	OCT	NOV	DEC	YEAR
Mean Maximum Temp. (°F)	40.1	47.8	57.9	65.9	74.4	81.6	89.1	88.7	79.0	66.2	50.0	40.6	65.1
Mean Temp. (°F)	33.2	39.0	46.7	53.5	61.2	68.1	74.3	73.8	64.6	53.3	41.9	34.1	53.6
Mean Minimum Temp. (°F)	26.3	30.2	35.4	41.0	47.9	54.6	59.4	58.8	50.2	40.3	33.8	27.5	42.1
Extreme Maximum Temp. (°F)	71	73	77	92	104	103	109	106	100	88	77	66	109
Extreme Minimum Temp. (°F)	-6	-10	11	23	32	38	42	39	31	18	-6	-6	-10
Days Maximum Temp. ≥ 90°F	0	0	0	0	2	6	15	15	3	0	0	0	41
Days Maximum Temp. ≤ 32°F	8	2	0	0	0	0	0	0	0	0	1	7	18
Days Minimum Temp. ≤ 32°F	22	16	10	2	0	0	0	0	0	4	12	22	88
Days Minimum Temp. ≤ 0°F	0	0	0	0	0	0	0	0	0	0	0	1	1
Heating Degree Days (base 65°F)	979	728	561	343	153	37	5	3	83	359	686	952	4,889
Cooling Degree Days (base 65°F)	0	0	0	4	46	124	287	276	76	2	0	0	815
Mean Precipitation (in.)	1.04	0.75	0.68	0.55	0.59	0.39	0.25	0.32	0.32	0.50	1.05	1.04	7.48
Days With ≥ 0.1" Precipitation	4	3	2	2	2	1	1	1	1	1	4	4	26
Days With ≥ 1.0" Precipitation	0	0	0	0	0	0	0	0	0	0	0	0	0
Mean Snowfall (in.)	2.6	2.3	0.3	trace	0.0	0.0	0.0	0.0	0.0	trace	1.2	3.1	9.5
Days With ≥ 1.0" Snow Depth	7	3	0	0	0	0	0	0	0	0	1	5	16

Ritzville 1 SSE *Adams County*   Elevation: 1,827 ft.   Latitude: 47° 07' N   Longitude: 118° 22' W

	JAN	FEB	MAR	APR	MAY	JUN	JUL	AUG	SEP	OCT	NOV	DEC	YEAR
Mean Maximum Temp. (°F)	34.2	41.6	51.2	60.0	68.6	76.7	85.4	85.4	75.6	62.0	44.4	34.9	60.0
Mean Temp. (°F)	28.0	33.7	40.5	46.7	54.3	61.6	68.7	68.7	60.0	48.6	36.4	28.6	48.0
Mean Minimum Temp. (°F)	21.7	25.8	29.8	33.4	39.9	46.4	52.0	51.9	44.3	35.1	28.5	22.2	35.9
Extreme Maximum Temp. (°F)	60	66	74	92	99	102	107	105	103	88	70	58	107
Extreme Minimum Temp. (°F)	-21	-21	0	19	22	29	33	32	23	11	-14	-15	-21
Days Maximum Temp. ≥ 90°F	0	0	0	0	1	3	12	11	2	0	0	0	29
Days Maximum Temp. ≤ 32°F	12	5	0	0	0	0	0	0	0	0	3	11	31
Days Minimum Temp. ≤ 32°F	28	24	22	14	4	0	0	0	1	11	21	28	153
Days Minimum Temp. ≤ 0°F	2	1	0	0	0	0	0	0	0	0	0	1	4
Heating Degree Days (base 65°F)	1,141	878	752	543	339	151	45	41	185	504	850	1,123	6,552
Cooling Degree Days (base 65°F)	0	0	0	1	16	50	160	160	46	2	0	0	435
Mean Precipitation (in.)	1.37	1.17	1.18	0.94	0.99	0.72	0.53	0.45	0.57	0.91	1.67	1.77	12.27
Days With ≥ 0.1" Precipitation	5	4	4	3	3	3	1	1	2	3	6	6	41
Days With ≥ 1.0" Precipitation	0	0	0	0	0	0	0	0	0	0	0	0	0
Mean Snowfall (in.)	6.6	2.9	0.6	trace	0.0	0.0	0.0	0.0	0.0	trace	2.7	6.5	19.3
Days With ≥ 1.0" Snow Depth	13	5	0	0	0	0	0	0	0	0	2	11	32

Rosalia *Whitman County*   Elevation: 2,398 ft.   Latitude: 47° 14' N   Longitude: 117° 22' W

	JAN	FEB	MAR	APR	MAY	JUN	JUL	AUG	SEP	OCT	NOV	DEC	YEAR
Mean Maximum Temp. (°F)	34.9	40.9	48.8	57.0	65.5	72.7	81.9	83.3	73.6	60.8	43.6	35.3	58.2
Mean Temp. (°F)	28.6	33.6	39.7	45.8	53.1	59.4	66.0	66.6	57.9	47.3	36.3	29.0	46.9
Mean Minimum Temp. (°F)	22.3	26.3	30.7	34.4	40.6	46.0	50.0	49.8	42.1	33.7	28.9	22.7	35.6
Extreme Maximum Temp. (°F)	60	66	74	94	95	100	104	104	101	90	72	59	104
Extreme Minimum Temp. (°F)	-24	-25	0	18	24	27	31	31	20	12	-15	-18	-25
Days Maximum Temp. ≥ 90°F	0	0	0	0	0	2	8	8	2	0	0	0	20
Days Maximum Temp. ≤ 32°F	11	5	1	0	0	0	0	0	0	0	2	10	29
Days Minimum Temp. ≤ 32°F	26	22	20	12	3	0	0	0	3	13	21	27	147
Days Minimum Temp. ≤ 0°F	2	1	0	0	0	0	0	0	0	0	0	1	4
Heating Degree Days (base 65°F)	1,121	881	776	572	372	196	69	63	231	544	855	1,109	6,789
Cooling Degree Days (base 65°F)	0	0	0	1	12	32	110	122	30	2	0	0	309
Mean Precipitation (in.)	2.24	1.69	1.68	1.43	1.70	1.33	0.80	0.70	0.83	1.23	2.43	2.50	18.56
Days With ≥ 0.1" Precipitation	8	6	6	5	5	4	3	2	3	4	9	9	64
Days With ≥ 1.0" Precipitation	0	0	0	0	0	0	0	0	0	0	0	0	0
Mean Snowfall (in.)	6.3	2.9	1.0	0.2	trace	0.0	0.0	0.0	0.0	0.2	3.1	8.0	21.7
Days With ≥ 1.0" Snow Depth	*10*	*4*	0	0	0	0	0	0	0	0	*2*	7	*23*

Ross Dam *Whatcom County*   Elevation: 1,233 ft.   Latitude: 48° 44' N   Longitude: 121° 03' W

	JAN	FEB	MAR	APR	MAY	JUN	JUL	AUG	SEP	OCT	NOV	DEC	YEAR
Mean Maximum Temp. (°F)	37.5	41.6	48.1	55.6	63.6	69.6	76.4	77.2	69.4	57.0	43.8	37.9	56.5
Mean Temp. (°F)	33.1	36.0	40.7	46.5	53.7	59.4	65.0	66.0	59.4	49.5	39.3	33.9	48.6
Mean Minimum Temp. (°F)	28.7	30.4	33.3	37.4	43.6	49.3	53.6	54.8	49.4	42.0	34.8	29.9	40.6
Extreme Maximum Temp. (°F)	57	61	69	80	97	100	101	100	97	86	62	57	101
Extreme Minimum Temp. (°F)	-1	-2	10	28	31	36	41	40	34	16	2	-4	-4
Days Maximum Temp. ≥ 90°F	0	0	0	0	0	1	4	3	0	0	0	0	8
Days Maximum Temp. ≤ 32°F	5	2	0	0	0	0	0	0	0	0	1	4	12
Days Minimum Temp. ≤ 32°F	20	17	12	4	0	0	0	0	0	1	8	19	81
Days Minimum Temp. ≤ 0°F	0	0	0	0	0	0	0	0	0	0	0	0	0
Heating Degree Days (base 65°F)	982	812	746	548	350	189	82	63	186	473	765	956	6,152
Cooling Degree Days (base 65°F)	0	0	0	0	8	29	93	101	29	0	0	0	260
Mean Precipitation (in.)	8.90	6.62	5.04	3.15	2.03	1.57	1.36	1.20	2.22	5.23	10.61	9.79	57.72
Days With ≥ 0.1" Precipitation	13	11	11	8	5	4	3	3	5	9	15	14	101
Days With ≥ 1.0" Precipitation	3	2	1	0	0	0	0	0	0	1	3	3	13
Mean Snowfall (in.)	*15.6*	*11.1*	3.3	0.2	0.0	0.0	0.0	0.0	0.0	trace	4.0	na	na
Days With ≥ 1.0" Snow Depth	18	14	5	0	0	0	0	0	0	0	2	14	53

Saint John *Whitman County*   Elevation: 1,942 ft.   Latitude: 47° 06' N   Longitude: 117° 35' W

	JAN	FEB	MAR	APR	MAY	JUN	JUL	AUG	SEP	OCT	NOV	DEC	YEAR
Mean Maximum Temp. (°F)	37.3	44.0	52.2	60.3	68.9	76.4	84.8	85.3	75.9	62.9	45.9	37.2	60.9
Mean Temp. (°F)	30.5	35.7	41.5	47.5	54.6	61.0	67.2	67.3	59.1	47.9	37.8	30.5	48.4
Mean Minimum Temp. (°F)	23.6	27.4	30.8	34.5	40.2	45.6	49.6	49.2	41.9	33.0	29.8	23.9	35.8
Extreme Maximum Temp. (°F)	61	67	77	92	99	100	107	103	101	91	72	59	107
Extreme Minimum Temp. (°F)	-28	-22	7	12	19	25	26	26	17	11	-18	-16	-28
Days Maximum Temp. ≥ 90°F	0	0	0	0	1	2	10	10	2	0	0	0	25
Days Maximum Temp. ≤ 32°F	9	3	0	0	0	0	0	0	0	0	2	8	22
Days Minimum Temp. ≤ 32°F	24	20	19	12	5	1	0	0	3	14	18	25	141
Days Minimum Temp. ≤ 0°F	2	1	0	0	0	0	0	0	0	0	0	1	4
Heating Degree Days (base 65°F)	1,064	821	722	521	326	152	46	47	194	525	811	1,063	6,292
Cooling Degree Days (base 65°F)	0	0	0	1	11	34	118	129	28	1	0	0	322
Mean Precipitation (in.)	1.80	1.51	1.50	1.42	1.59	1.23	0.77	0.69	0.79	1.28	2.23	2.32	17.13
Days With ≥ 0.1" Precipitation	6	5	5	4	5	3	2	2	3	4	7	7	53
Days With ≥ 1.0" Precipitation	0	0	0	0	0	0	0	0	0	0	0	0	0
Mean Snowfall (in.)	8.5	3.8	1.2	0.4	trace	0.0	0.0	0.0	trace	0.2	2.8	7.7	24.6
Days With ≥ 1.0" Snow Depth	*3*	*1*	0	0	0	0	0	0	0	0	1	*3*	*8*

Sedro Woolley *Skagit County*   Elevation: 59 ft.   Latitude: 48° 30' N   Longitude: 122° 14' W

	JAN	FEB	MAR	APR	MAY	JUN	JUL	AUG	SEP	OCT	NOV	DEC	YEAR
Mean Maximum Temp. (°F)	45.5	49.4	53.6	58.4	64.3	68.8	73.6	74.8	69.3	60.2	50.5	45.1	59.5
Mean Temp. (°F)	39.3	42.1	45.6	49.7	54.9	59.2	62.7	63.4	58.7	51.2	44.1	39.4	50.9
Mean Minimum Temp. (°F)	33.2	34.7	37.5	40.9	45.5	49.6	51.8	52.1	48.0	42.1	37.7	33.7	42.2
Extreme Maximum Temp. (°F)	66	74	74	81	91	95	91	92	89	86	70	65	95
Extreme Minimum Temp. (°F)	10	8	19	27	30	37	39	39	30	25	9	8	8
Days Maximum Temp. ≥ 90°F	0	0	0	0	0	0	0	0	0	0	0	0	0
Days Maximum Temp. ≤ 32°F	1	0	0	0	0	0	0	0	0	0	0	2	3
Days Minimum Temp. ≤ 32°F	13	10	5	1	0	0	0	0	0	2	7	12	50
Days Minimum Temp. ≤ 0°F	0	0	0	0	0	0	0	0	0	0	0	0	0
Heating Degree Days (base 65°F)	789	640	595	454	309	175	91	73	189	423	620	786	5,144
Cooling Degree Days (base 65°F)	0	0	0	0	0	3	10	27	34	5	0	0	79
Mean Precipitation (in.)	5.72	4.11	4.00	3.75	2.92	2.78	1.70	1.55	2.79	4.01	6.96	5.96	46.25
Days With ≥ 0.1" Precipitation	12	11	11	10	8	6	4	3	6	9	14	13	107
Days With ≥ 1.0" Precipitation	1	0	0	0	0	0	0	0	1	1	1	1	5
Mean Snowfall (in.)	1.7	1.0	0.5	trace	0.0	0.0	0.0	0.0	0.0	trace	0.8	2.6	6.6
Days With ≥ 1.0" Snow Depth	2	1	0	0	0	0	0	0	0	0	1	1	5

Shelton *Mason County*   Elevation: 19 ft.   Latitude: 47° 12' N   Longitude: 123° 06' W

	JAN	FEB	MAR	APR	MAY	JUN	JUL	AUG	SEP	OCT	NOV	DEC	YEAR
Mean Maximum Temp. (°F)	45.1	49.0	54.2	59.7	66.8	71.7	77.2	77.5	71.9	60.9	50.1	44.3	60.7
Mean Temp. (°F)	39.7	41.9	45.5	49.6	56.0	60.7	65.1	65.5	60.3	51.7	44.1	39.3	51.6
Mean Minimum Temp. (°F)	34.1	34.8	36.7	39.5	45.1	49.6	53.1	53.3	48.6	42.4	38.0	34.1	42.5
Extreme Maximum Temp. (°F)	60	72	75	89	98	96	100	107	99	87	70	64	107
Extreme Minimum Temp. (°F)	7	10	19	26	30	35	42	39	30	24	6	6	6
Days Maximum Temp. ≥ 90°F	0	0	0	0	0	1	3	2	0	0	0	0	6
Days Maximum Temp. ≤ 32°F	1	0	0	0	0	0	0	0	0	0	0	1	2
Days Minimum Temp. ≤ 32°F	12	11	8	4	0	0	0	0	0	2	7	13	57
Days Minimum Temp. ≤ 0°F	0	0	0	0	0	0	0	0	0	0	0	0	0
Heating Degree Days (base 65°F)	779	644	599	455	279	146	54	46	150	407	621	791	4,971
Cooling Degree Days (base 65°F)	0	0	0	0	8	22	67	72	18	1	0	0	188
Mean Precipitation (in.)	10.02	8.47	6.86	4.61	2.56	1.73	1.00	1.24	2.64	5.29	10.58	11.28	66.28
Days With ≥ 0.1" Precipitation	15	14	13	10	7	5	3	3	5	9	16	16	116
Days With ≥ 1.0" Precipitation	3	2	1	1	0	0	0	0	1	1	3	4	16
Mean Snowfall (in.)	1.4	0.3	trace	0.0	0.0	0.0	0.0	0.0	0.0	0.0	0.9	1.6	4.2
Days With ≥ 1.0" Snow Depth	1	0	0	0	0	0	0	0	0	0	0	1	2

Skamania Fish Hatchery *Skamania County*   Elevation: 439 ft.   Latitude: 45° 37' N   Longitude: 122° 13' W

	JAN	FEB	MAR	APR	MAY	JUN	JUL	AUG	SEP	OCT	NOV	DEC	YEAR
Mean Maximum Temp. (°F)	44.9	49.4	55.0	59.6	66.6	72.0	78.6	79.8	74.5	64.0	51.2	44.5	61.7
Mean Temp. (°F)	37.5	40.6	44.3	47.6	53.3	58.1	62.7	62.9	58.3	50.6	43.0	37.7	49.7
Mean Minimum Temp. (°F)	30.1	31.8	33.5	35.6	40.0	44.3	46.8	45.9	42.1	37.1	34.7	30.8	37.7
Extreme Maximum Temp. (°F)	64	72	82	89	100	104	103	107	105	93	71	64	107
Extreme Minimum Temp. (°F)	7	3	15	21	22	29	32	33	26	17	11	2	2
Days Maximum Temp. ≥ 90°F	0	0	0	0	1	1	4	5	2	0	0	0	13
Days Maximum Temp. ≤ 32°F	2	0	0	0	0	0	0	0	0	0	0	1	3
Days Minimum Temp. ≤ 32°F	19	15	14	9	3	0	0	0	2	7	11	18	98
Days Minimum Temp. ≤ 0°F	0	0	0	0	0	0	0	0	0	0	0	0	0
Heating Degree Days (base 65°F)	845	682	634	516	362	215	110	103	207	441	655	840	5,610
Cooling Degree Days (base 65°F)	0	0	0	0	6	16	44	44	13	1	0	0	124
Mean Precipitation (in.)	12.25	9.84	8.67	7.06	5.25	4.14	1.48	1.78	4.00	6.43	12.91	13.21	87.02
Days With ≥ 0.1" Precipitation	16	14	15	14	10	7	3	4	7	11	17	17	135
Days With ≥ 1.0" Precipitation	4	3	2	1	1	1	0	0	1	2	4	5	24
Mean Snowfall (in.)	2.7	2.3	0.6	trace	0.0	0.0	0.0	0.0	0.0	0.0	1.1	2.2	8.9
Days With ≥ 1.0" Snow Depth	4	2	1	0	0	0	0	0	0	0	1	3	11

Smyrna *Grant County*   Elevation: 557 ft.   Latitude: 46° 50' N   Longitude: 119° 40' W

	JAN	FEB	MAR	APR	MAY	JUN	JUL	AUG	SEP	OCT	NOV	DEC	YEAR
Mean Maximum Temp. (°F)	38.8	46.5	57.7	66.5	75.4	82.8	90.7	90.4	80.4	66.6	49.3	38.7	65.3
Mean Temp. (°F)	30.8	36.6	45.1	52.5	60.7	68.0	74.4	73.5	63.6	51.5	39.6	31.0	52.3
Mean Minimum Temp. (°F)	22.8	26.8	32.4	38.5	46.0	53.2	58.0	56.6	46.8	36.3	29.9	23.2	39.2
Extreme Maximum Temp. (°F)	69	71	79	96	105	105	113	109	103	88	75	70	113
Extreme Minimum Temp. (°F)	-24	-24	3	21	29	34	41	39	26	15	-19	-19	-24
Days Maximum Temp. ≥ 90°F	0	0	0	0	3	7	18	17	5	0	0	0	50
Days Maximum Temp. ≤ 32°F	9	2	0	0	0	0	0	0	0	0	1	8	20
Days Minimum Temp. ≤ 32°F	27	21	16	6	0	0	0	0	1	10	18	26	125
Days Minimum Temp. ≤ 0°F	1	1	0	0	0	0	0	0	0	0	0	1	3
Heating Degree Days (base 65°F)	1,053	796	610	371	165	34	6	5	99	413	755	1,048	5,355
Cooling Degree Days (base 65°F)	0	0	0	3	40	131	298	269	69	1	0	0	811
Mean Precipitation (in.)	0.98	0.77	0.71	0.44	0.54	0.48	0.38	0.34	0.39	0.52	1.15	1.30	8.00
Days With ≥ 0.1" Precipitation	4	3	3	2	2	1	1	1	1	2	4	4	28
Days With ≥ 1.0" Precipitation	0	0	0	0	0	0	0	0	0	0	0	0	0
Mean Snowfall (in.)	na	trace	trace	trace	0.0	0.0	0.0	0.0	0.0	trace	0.2	na	na
Days With ≥ 1.0" Snow Depth	na	1	0	0	0	0	0	0	0	0	1	na	na

Snoqualmie Falls *King County*   Elevation: 439 ft.   Latitude: 47° 33' N   Longitude: 121° 50' W

	JAN	FEB	MAR	APR	MAY	JUN	JUL	AUG	SEP	OCT	NOV	DEC	YEAR
Mean Maximum Temp. (°F)	45.9	49.8	53.4	58.1	63.8	68.4	74.3	75.2	69.9	60.0	50.4	45.0	59.5
Mean Temp. (°F)	39.7	42.1	44.6	48.4	53.9	58.5	63.0	63.4	58.2	50.3	43.7	39.1	50.4
Mean Minimum Temp. (°F)	33.4	34.5	35.7	38.6	43.9	48.5	51.7	51.6	46.4	40.6	36.8	33.2	41.2
Extreme Maximum Temp. (°F)	65	74	79	86	97	99	97	97	98	95	74	67	99
Extreme Minimum Temp. (°F)	0	1	17	27	30	32	40	39	30	24	5	3	0
Days Maximum Temp. ≥ 90°F	0	0	0	0	0	0	1	1	0	0	0	0	2
Days Maximum Temp. ≤ 32°F	1	0	0	0	0	0	0	0	0	0	0	2	3
Days Minimum Temp. ≤ 32°F	13	11	9	4	0	0	0	0	0	3	8	14	62
Days Minimum Temp. ≤ 0°F	0	0	0	0	0	0	0	0	0	0	0	0	0
Heating Degree Days (base 65°F)	779	640	627	493	343	201	96	84	207	449	634	795	5,348
Cooling Degree Days (base 65°F)	0	0	0	1	4	13	42	43	9	1	0	0	113
Mean Precipitation (in.)	8.55	6.32	6.17	4.75	3.68	2.92	1.63	1.50	2.80	5.09	9.53	9.29	62.23
Days With ≥ 0.1" Precipitation	14	13	14	12	10	7	4	4	6	10	16	14	124
Days With ≥ 1.0" Precipitation	2	1	1	1	0	0	0	0	0	1	3	3	12
Mean Snowfall (in.)	2.6	1.7	0.9	trace	trace	0.0	0.0	0.0	0.0	0.0	1.2	2.9	9.3
Days With ≥ 1.0" Snow Depth	1	1	0	0	0	0	0	0	0	0	0	1	3

Startup 1 E *Snohomish County* Elevation: 167 ft. Latitude: 47° 52' N Longitude: 121° 43' W

	JAN	FEB	MAR	APR	MAY	JUN	JUL	AUG	SEP	OCT	NOV	DEC	YEAR
Mean Maximum Temp. (°F)	46.1	50.1	54.0	58.8	65.2	69.7	75.4	76.4	71.2	61.3	50.8	45.2	60.4
Mean Temp. (°F)	39.7	42.5	45.1	49.0	54.8	59.3	63.5	63.9	59.1	51.1	44.0	39.4	51.0
Mean Minimum Temp. (°F)	33.2	34.7	36.3	39.1	44.4	48.8	51.6	51.3	46.9	40.8	37.2	33.6	41.5
Extreme Maximum Temp. (°F)	65	74	79	86	102	98	98	98	98	92	74	67	102
Extreme Minimum Temp. (°F)	5	2	19	17	31	31	37	36	30	20	6	3	2
Days Maximum Temp. ≥ 90°F	0	0	0	0	0	0	2	1	1	0	0	0	4
Days Maximum Temp. ≤ 32°F	1	0	0	0	0	0	0	0	0	0	0	1	2
Days Minimum Temp. ≤ 32°F	14	10	8	4	1	0	0	0	0	5	7	13	62
Days Minimum Temp. ≤ 0°F	0	0	0	0	0	0	0	0	0	0	0	0	0
Heating Degree Days (base 65°F)	778	630	610	474	318	182	86	75	181	424	624	786	5,168
Cooling Degree Days (base 65°F)	0	0	0	1	8	17	45	51	12	1	0	0	135
Mean Precipitation (in.)	8.48	5.78	6.16	5.49	4.75	3.69	2.25	2.16	3.48	5.33	8.97	8.68	65.22
Days With ≥ 0.1" Precipitation	15	13	14	13	11	9	5	5	7	10	16	15	133
Days With ≥ 1.0" Precipitation	2	1	1	1	1	1	0	0	1	1	2	2	13
Mean Snowfall (in.)	2.5	1.8	0.4	0.1	0.0	0.0	0.0	0.0	0.0	trace	0.8	1.4	7.0
Days With ≥ 1.0" Snow Depth	2	0	0	0	0	0	0	0	0	0	0	1	3

Stehekin 4 NW *Chelan County* Elevation: 1,269 ft. Latitude: 48° 21' N Longitude: 120° 43' W

	JAN	FEB	MAR	APR	MAY	JUN	JUL	AUG	SEP	OCT	NOV	DEC	YEAR
Mean Maximum Temp. (°F)	33.1	38.6	48.0	58.9	69.1	76.3	83.8	83.3	72.9	57.5	41.0	33.1	58.0
Mean Temp. (°F)	28.6	32.4	39.1	47.5	56.2	63.0	69.1	69.0	59.6	47.5	35.9	29.1	48.1
Mean Minimum Temp. (°F)	23.9	26.2	30.0	36.2	43.2	49.7	54.4	54.5	46.2	37.4	30.8	25.1	38.1
Extreme Maximum Temp. (°F)	55	57	70	84	101	103	107	105	98	84	65	55	107
Extreme Minimum Temp. (°F)	-8	-4	7	23	26	30	39	39	25	21	6	-8	-8
Days Maximum Temp. ≥ 90°F	0	0	0	0	0	3	9	8	1	0	0	0	21
Days Maximum Temp. ≤ 32°F	12	4	0	0	0	0	0	0	0	0	2	11	29
Days Minimum Temp. ≤ 32°F	30	26	22	7	1	0	0	0	0	7	19	29	141
Days Minimum Temp. ≤ 0°F	0	0	0	0	0	0	0	0	0	0	0	0	0
Heating Degree Days (base 65°F)	1,123	913	797	517	279	109	32	30	183	537	865	1,106	6,491
Cooling Degree Days (base 65°F)	0	0	0	0	15	57	170	162	35	0	0	0	439
Mean Precipitation (in.)	6.38	4.19	2.74	1.56	0.98	0.86	0.60	0.82	1.16	2.93	6.57	7.36	36.15
Days With ≥ 0.1" Precipitation	12	9	7	4	3	3	2	2	3	6	13	13	77
Days With ≥ 1.0" Precipitation	2	1	0	0	0	0	0	0	0	1	2	2	8
Mean Snowfall (in.)	45.9	22.4	7.1	0.3	0.0	0.0	0.0	0.0	0.0	0.4	13.6	46.5	136.2
Days With ≥ 1.0" Snow Depth	31	27	23	5	0	0	0	0	0	0	8	28	122

Sunnyside *Yakima County* Elevation: 744 ft. Latitude: 46° 19' N Longitude: 120° 00' W

	JAN	FEB	MAR	APR	MAY	JUN	JUL	AUG	SEP	OCT	NOV	DEC	YEAR
Mean Maximum Temp. (°F)	39.4	47.7	58.5	66.4	75.1	82.2	89.4	88.9	79.6	67.3	50.4	39.7	65.4
Mean Temp. (°F)	32.0	38.1	46.2	52.7	60.6	67.3	72.9	71.9	63.3	52.2	40.7	32.4	52.5
Mean Minimum Temp. (°F)	24.5	28.5	33.8	39.0	46.0	52.4	56.3	54.9	47.0	37.1	31.0	25.1	39.6
Extreme Maximum Temp. (°F)	68	72	78	93	104	107	110	106	103	89	77	66	110
Extreme Minimum Temp. (°F)	-11	-11	10	21	30	35	41	40	29	16	-5	-12	-12
Days Maximum Temp. ≥ 90°F	0	0	0	0	2	7	16	15	4	0	0	0	44
Days Maximum Temp. ≤ 32°F	8	3	0	0	0	0	0	0	0	0	1	8	20
Days Minimum Temp. ≤ 32°F	26	20	14	5	0	0	0	0	0	8	18	26	117
Days Minimum Temp. ≤ 0°F	1	0	0	0	0	0	0	0	0	0	0	1	2
Heating Degree Days (base 65°F)	1,017	754	577	366	172	49	10	8	103	392	721	1,003	5,172
Cooling Degree Days (base 65°F)	0	0	0	6	51	125	265	236	70	3	0	0	756
Mean Precipitation (in.)	0.95	0.58	0.60	0.52	0.54	0.41	0.19	0.30	0.48	0.52	0.95	1.15	7.19
Days With ≥ 0.1" Precipitation	3	2	2	2	2	1	1	1	1	2	3	3	23
Days With ≥ 1.0" Precipitation	0	0	0	0	0	0	0	0	0	0	0	0	0
Mean Snowfall (in.)	3.0	1.4	0.2	trace	trace	0.0	0.0	0.0	0.0	trace	1.4	4.8	10.8
Days With ≥ 1.0" Snow Depth	5	1	0	0	0	0	0	0	0	0	1	4	11

The Dalles Municipal Airport *Klickitat County* Elevation: 239 ft. Latitude: 45° 37' N Longitude: 121° 09' W

	JAN	FEB	MAR	APR	MAY	JUN	JUL	AUG	SEP	OCT	NOV	DEC	YEAR
Mean Maximum Temp. (°F)	41.2	47.9	57.2	64.8	73.8	80.4	88.1	88.0	80.5	66.7	50.2	41.7	65.0
Mean Temp. (°F)	35.3	40.0	46.8	53.2	61.1	67.6	74.2	73.8	66.0	54.6	43.0	36.0	54.3
Mean Minimum Temp. (°F)	29.4	32.1	36.4	41.5	48.4	54.8	60.1	59.6	51.3	42.4	35.7	30.3	43.5
Extreme Maximum Temp. (°F)	68	69	80	95	107	108	111	110	105	90	72	66	111
Extreme Minimum Temp. (°F)	-6	-4	11	25	31	39	40	42	31	19	-1	-9	-9
Days Maximum Temp. ≥ 90°F	0	0	0	0	2	6	14	13	6	0	0	0	41
Days Maximum Temp. ≤ 32°F	6	2	0	0	0	0	0	0	0	0	1	4	13
Days Minimum Temp. ≤ 32°F	18	13	9	3	0	0	0	0	0	3	9	18	73
Days Minimum Temp. ≤ 0°F	0	0	0	0	0	0	0	0	0	0	0	1	1
Heating Degree Days (base 65°F)	914	699	557	352	155	40	5	3	61	323	653	892	4,654
Cooling Degree Days (base 65°F)	0	0	0	0	4	46	119	291	285	103	6	0	0	854
Mean Precipitation (in.)	2.77	1.77	1.16	0.74	0.55	0.43	0.17	0.32	0.51	1.01	2.23	2.72	14.38
Days With ≥ 0.1" Precipitation	7	5	4	2	2	1	1	1	2	3	7	7	42
Days With ≥ 1.0" Precipitation	0	0	0	0	0	0	0	0	0	0	0	0	0
Mean Snowfall (in.)	6.3	2.8	0.5	trace	0.0	0.0	0.0	trace	0.0	trace	2.5	5.0	17.1
Days With ≥ 1.0" Snow Depth	9	3	0	0	0	0	0	0	0	0	2	5	19

Toledo Winlock Muni Airport *Lewis County*   Elevation: 377 ft.   Latitude: 46° 29' N   Longitude: 122° 49' W

	JAN	FEB	MAR	APR	MAY	JUN	JUL	AUG	SEP	OCT	NOV	DEC	YEAR
Mean Maximum Temp. (°F)	45.7	50.8	56.0	60.9	67.6	72.4	78.3	79.6	74.6	63.1	51.0	44.9	62.1
Mean Temp. (°F)	39.5	42.6	46.3	49.8	55.6	60.1	64.5	65.0	60.4	52.1	44.3	39.5	51.6
Mean Minimum Temp. (°F)	33.2	34.3	36.6	38.7	43.6	47.8	50.7	50.4	46.1	41.0	37.7	34.0	41.2
Extreme Maximum Temp. (°F)	62	72	80	89	93	97	102	104	100	96	71	62	104
Extreme Minimum Temp. (°F)	0	3	12	23	28	31	33	31	25	20	9	-2	-2
Days Maximum Temp. ≥ 90°F	0	0	0	0	0	1	3	4	1	0	0	0	9
Days Maximum Temp. ≤ 32°F	1	0	0	0	0	0	0	0	0	0	0	1	2
Days Minimum Temp. ≤ 32°F	14	11	10	5	1	0	0	0	0	1	4	8	12	66
Days Minimum Temp. ≤ 0°F	0	0	0	0	0	0	0	0	0	0	0	0	0
Heating Degree Days (base 65°F)	784	626	572	449	291	158	*68*	58	148	395	613	784	*4,946*
Cooling Degree Days (base 65°F)	0	0	0	0	7	20	*58*	*71*	19	1	0	0	*176*
Mean Precipitation (in.)	na	na	*5.07*	na	na	na	na	na	na	na	*6.34*	na	na
Days With ≥ 0.1" Precipitation	13	12	12	9	7	6	2	3	5	8	13	14	104
Days With ≥ 1.0" Precipitation	1	1	0	0	0	0	0	0	0	0	1	1	4
Mean Snowfall (in.)	na	na	na	na	na	na	na	na	na	na	na	na	na
Days With ≥ 1.0" Snow Depth	na	na	na	na	na	na	na	na	na	na	na	na	na

Upper Baker Dam *Whatcom County*   Elevation: 688 ft.   Latitude: 48° 39' N   Longitude: 121° 41' W

	JAN	FEB	MAR	APR	MAY	JUN	JUL	AUG	SEP	OCT	NOV	DEC	YEAR
Mean Maximum Temp. (°F)	39.1	43.7	49.5	56.1	63.0	67.4	73.3	74.2	68.9	57.9	45.2	38.9	56.4
Mean Temp. (°F)	33.8	36.6	40.8	46.0	52.4	57.3	62.1	62.8	58.0	49.3	39.9	34.4	47.8
Mean Minimum Temp. (°F)	28.4	29.5	32.1	35.9	41.9	47.2	50.8	51.4	47.0	40.7	34.6	29.9	39.1
Extreme Maximum Temp. (°F)	57	68	76	92	102	98	98	97	100	84	66	60	102
Extreme Minimum Temp. (°F)	0	4	10	24	30	35	39	39	30	22	5	-3	-3
Days Maximum Temp. ≥ 90°F	0	0	0	0	0	0	1	1	0	0	0	0	2
Days Maximum Temp. ≤ 32°F	3	1	0	0	0	0	0	0	0	0	1	3	8
Days Minimum Temp. ≤ 32°F	22	20	17	8	0	0	0	0	0	2	10	21	100
Days Minimum Temp. ≤ 0°F	0	0	0	0	0	0	0	0	0	0	0	0	0
Heating Degree Days (base 65°F)	961	795	743	562	385	233	118	97	212	480	747	941	6,274
Cooling Degree Days (base 65°F)	0	0	0	0	4	10	36	39	9	0	0	0	98
Mean Precipitation (in.)	14.39	11.03	9.62	6.60	4.88	3.54	2.70	2.07	4.35	9.12	16.61	15.99	100.90
Days With ≥ 0.1" Precipitation	17	15	15	13	10	8	5	4	7	12	18	18	142
Days With ≥ 1.0" Precipitation	5	4	3	1	1	1	1	1	1	3	6	6	33
Mean Snowfall (in.)	15.4	10.8	4.0	0.6	trace	0.0	0.0	0.0	0.0	trace	3.5	15.2	49.5
Days With ≥ 1.0" Snow Depth	19	14	6	0	0	0	0	0	0	0	3	13	55

Vancouver 4 NNE *Clark County*   Elevation: 209 ft.   Latitude: 45° 41' N   Longitude: 122° 39' W

	JAN	FEB	MAR	APR	MAY	JUN	JUL	AUG	SEP	OCT	NOV	DEC	YEAR
Mean Maximum Temp. (°F)	45.7	50.0	55.1	59.5	66.0	71.5	77.3	78.2	73.7	63.3	51.9	45.4	61.5
Mean Temp. (°F)	38.6	41.6	45.7	49.3	55.2	60.3	64.9	65.1	60.2	51.8	44.4	38.9	51.3
Mean Minimum Temp. (°F)	31.6	33.2	36.3	39.1	44.3	49.1	52.5	51.9	46.7	40.2	36.8	32.4	41.2
Extreme Maximum Temp. (°F)	62	69	77	87	99	103	100	103	103	90	70	64	103
Extreme Minimum Temp. (°F)	0	5	19	25	28	34	37	35	28	21	8	-2	-2
Days Maximum Temp. ≥ 90°F	0	0	0	0	0	1	3	3	1	0	0	0	8
Days Maximum Temp. ≤ 32°F	1	0	0	0	0	0	0	0	0	0	0	1	2
Days Minimum Temp. ≤ 32°F	16	13	10	4	0	0	0	0	0	4	8	15	70
Days Minimum Temp. ≤ 0°F	0	0	0	0	0	0	0	0	0	0	0	0	0
Heating Degree Days (base 65°F)	811	654	592	464	307	158	66	65	158	404	611	801	5,091
Cooling Degree Days (base 65°F)	0	0	0	1	11	27	75	80	26	1	0	0	221
Mean Precipitation (in.)	6.03	4.83	4.17	3.10	2.59	1.72	0.80	1.04	1.83	3.26	6.41	6.52	42.30
Days With ≥ 0.1" Precipitation	13	12	12	10	7	5	2	3	5	8	14	13	104
Days With ≥ 1.0" Precipitation	1	1	0	0	0	0	0	0	0	0	1	1	4
Mean Snowfall (in.)	*2.3*	*1.1*	*0.3*	0.0	0.0	0.0	0.0	0.0	0.0	0.0	0.2	*0.9*	*4.8*
Days With ≥ 1.0" Snow Depth	*1*	*1*	*0*	0	0	0	0	0	0	0	0	*1*	*3*

Walla Walla City County Arpt. *Walla Walla County*   Elevation: 1,164 ft.   Latitude: 46° 06' N   Longitude: 118° 17' W

	JAN	FEB	MAR	APR	MAY	JUN	JUL	AUG	SEP	OCT	NOV	DEC	YEAR
Mean Maximum Temp. (°F)	39.3	46.0	*55.2*	63.1	*71.3*	80.2	*89.3*	88.4	77.9	*64.9*	48.6	*39.9*	63.7
Mean Temp. (°F)	33.9	39.4	*46.4*	52.6	*59.8*	67.5	75.0	74.8	65.2	*54.3*	42.1	34.6	53.8
Mean Minimum Temp. (°F)	28.5	32.7	*37.5*	42.0	48.3	54.8	60.6	61.2	52.5	43.6	35.6	29.2	43.9
Extreme Maximum Temp. (°F)	67	75	77	*96*	*100*	107	*114*	110	102	88	80	68	*114*
Extreme Minimum Temp. (°F)	-10	-13	*4*	*22*	34	39	40	42	32	19	*-11*	*-15*	*-15*
Days Maximum Temp. ≥ 90°F	0	0	*0*	*0*	*1*	7	*16*	14	*4*	0	*0*	*0*	*42*
Days Maximum Temp. ≤ 32°F	9	4	*0*	*0*	0	0	0	0	0	0	2	*9*	24
Days Minimum Temp. ≤ 32°F	18	12	*5*	*1*	0	0	0	0	0	2	8	19	65
Days Minimum Temp. ≤ 0°F	1	0	*0*	*0*	0	0	0	0	0	0	0	1	2
Heating Degree Days (base 65°F)	958	716	*571*	*370*	191	*55*	*7*	*7*	*83*	*330*	680	*937*	4,905
Cooling Degree Days (base 65°F)	*0*	*0*	*0*	*5*	*44*	*131*	*310*	*316*	*104*	*7*	*0*	*0*	*917*
Mean Precipitation (in.)	2.28	1.87	2.17	1.78	1.89	1.20	0.75	0.90	0.90	1.63	2.77	2.38	20.52
Days With ≥ 0.1" Precipitation	7	6	7	*5*	*5*	3	2	2	*3*	4	8	7	59
Days With ≥ 1.0" Precipitation	0	0	*0*	*0*	*0*	0	0	0	*0*	0	0	0	0
Mean Snowfall (in.)	5.6	3.8	*1.2*	trace	trace	0.0	trace	0.0	0.0	0.3	2.4	5.9	19.2
Days With ≥ 1.0" Snow Depth	8	4	*1*	0	0	0	0	0	0	0	2	7	22

Wapato *Yakima County*   Elevation: 839 ft.   Latitude: 46° 26' N   Longitude: 120° 25' W

	JAN	FEB	MAR	APR	MAY	JUN	JUL	AUG	SEP	OCT	NOV	DEC	YEAR
Mean Maximum Temp. (°F)	38.8	47.3	57.7	65.8	75.0	82.1	89.4	88.8	79.8	66.7	49.7	38.7	65.0
Mean Temp. (°F)	31.1	37.5	45.6	52.5	60.8	67.7	74.0	73.1	64.0	51.9	40.0	30.9	52.4
Mean Minimum Temp. (°F)	23.2	27.6	33.3	39.2	46.5	53.3	58.6	57.4	48.1	37.1	30.2	23.1	39.8
Extreme Maximum Temp. (°F)	68	70	78	94	102	104	107	106	99	89	73	66	107
Extreme Minimum Temp. (°F)	-14	-19	6	23	26	33	40	35	29	15	-9	-18	-19
Days Maximum Temp. ≥ 90°F	0	0	0	0	2	7	16	15	4	0	0	0	44
Days Maximum Temp. ≤ 32°F	9	2	0	0	0	0	0	0	0	0	1	9	21
Days Minimum Temp. ≤ 32°F	27	21	14	5	1	0	0	0	0	8	19	27	122
Days Minimum Temp. ≤ 0°F	1	1	0	0	0	0	0	0	0	0	0	1	3
Heating Degree Days (base 65°F)	1,045	771	596	372	173	52	12	9	96	401	744	1,049	5,320
Cooling Degree Days (base 65°F)	0	0	0	4	49	122	274	249	73	3	0	0	774
Mean Precipitation (in.)	1.21	0.67	0.68	0.55	0.53	0.57	0.32	0.34	0.41	0.53	1.06	1.25	8.12
Days With ≥ 0.1" Precipitation	4	3	2	2	2	2	1	1	1	2	3	4	27
Days With ≥ 1.0" Precipitation	0	0	0	0	0	0	0	0	0	0	0	0	0
Mean Snowfall (in.)	4.8	2.1	0.5	trace	0.0	0.0	0.0	0.0	0.0	0.1	1.9	5.9	15.3
Days With ≥ 1.0" Snow Depth	11	4	0	0	0	0	0	0	0	0	2	10	27

Wellpinit *Stevens County*   Elevation: 2,490 ft.   Latitude: 47° 54' N   Longitude: 118° 00' W

	JAN	FEB	MAR	APR	MAY	JUN	JUL	AUG	SEP	OCT	NOV	DEC	YEAR
Mean Maximum Temp. (°F)	32.1	38.1	48.4	57.9	66.8	74.6	83.8	83.8	72.3	58.5	40.3	32.0	57.4
Mean Temp. (°F)	26.4	31.2	39.1	46.6	54.5	61.5	68.6	68.4	58.7	47.1	34.4	26.9	46.9
Mean Minimum Temp. (°F)	20.6	24.3	29.8	35.2	42.1	48.0	53.5	52.9	45.0	35.6	28.6	21.7	36.4
Extreme Maximum Temp. (°F)	56	64	72	88	98	98	104	101	104	84	65	53	104
Extreme Minimum Temp. (°F)	-22	-25	2	18	24	32	33	36	20	12	1	-18	-25
Days Maximum Temp. ≥ 90°F	0	0	0	0	0	2	9	9	1	0	0	0	21
Days Maximum Temp. ≤ 32°F	14	7	1	0	0	0	0	0	0	0	5	15	42
Days Minimum Temp. ≤ 32°F	30	24	20	11	3	0	0	0	1	11	21	28	149
Days Minimum Temp. ≤ 0°F	2	1	0	0	0	0	0	0	0	0	0	1	4
Heating Degree Days (base 65°F)	1,193	948	797	549	332	153	42	42	213	550	912	1,178	6,909
Cooling Degree Days (base 65°F)	0	0	0	2	15	51	158	150	38	0	0	0	414
Mean Precipitation (in.)	1.87	1.86	1.79	1.44	1.83	1.41	0.87	0.76	0.89	1.16	2.79	3.06	19.73
Days With ≥ 0.1" Precipitation	5	4	4	4	4	3	2	2	2	3	6	6	45
Days With ≥ 1.0" Precipitation	0	0	0	0	0	0	0	0	0	0	0	0	0
Mean Snowfall (in.)	na	na	2.5	0.3	trace	0.0	0.0	0.0	0.0	0.6	na	na	na
Days With ≥ 1.0" Snow Depth	na	na	4	0	0	0	0	0	0	0	na	na	na

Wenatchee *Chelan County*   Elevation: 639 ft.   Latitude: 47° 26' N   Longitude: 120° 19' W

	JAN	FEB	MAR	APR	MAY	JUN	JUL	AUG	SEP	OCT	NOV	DEC	YEAR
Mean Maximum Temp. (°F)	35.7	43.5	55.5	64.7	73.6	80.8	88.3	87.7	78.0	63.9	46.6	36.1	62.9
Mean Temp. (°F)	29.8	35.8	44.8	52.6	60.9	68.0	74.4	73.7	64.4	52.2	39.5	30.8	52.2
Mean Minimum Temp. (°F)	23.9	28.0	34.1	40.5	48.3	55.1	60.4	59.6	50.7	40.4	32.4	25.4	41.6
Extreme Maximum Temp. (°F)	65	66	75	93	104	107	106	106	101	84	74	65	107
Extreme Minimum Temp. (°F)	-9	-4	14	27	33	39	40	41	31	19	0	-9	-9
Days Maximum Temp. ≥ 90°F	0	0	0	0	1	5	15	13	2	0	0	0	36
Days Maximum Temp. ≤ 32°F	10	3	0	0	0	0	0	0	0	0	1	9	23
Days Minimum Temp. ≤ 32°F	27	21	12	2	0	0	0	0	0	3	15	25	105
Days Minimum Temp. ≤ 0°F	1	0	0	0	0	0	0	0	0	0	0	0	1
Heating Degree Days (base 65°F)	1,084	818	618	368	157	37	5	6	86	393	758	1,054	5,384
Cooling Degree Days (base 65°F)	0	0	0	3	44	129	299	282	87	2	0	0	846
Mean Precipitation (in.)	1.41	0.91	0.65	0.52	0.51	0.68	0.30	0.40	0.40	0.49	1.38	1.55	9.20
Days With ≥ 0.1" Precipitation	5	3	2	2	2	2	1	1	1	1	4	5	29
Days With ≥ 1.0" Precipitation	0	0	0	0	0	0	0	0	0	0	0	0	0
Mean Snowfall (in.)	8.6	3.9	0.5	0.0	0.0	0.0	0.0	0.0	0.0	trace	2.6	10.4	26.0
Days With ≥ 1.0" Snow Depth	20	7	0	0	0	0	0	0	0	0	2	12	41

Wenatchee Exp. Station *Chelan County*   Elevation: 797 ft.   Latitude: 47° 26' N   Longitude: 120° 21' W

	JAN	FEB	MAR	APR	MAY	JUN	JUL	AUG	SEP	OCT	NOV	DEC	YEAR
Mean Maximum Temp. (°F)	35.9	43.4	55.5	64.3	72.9	79.4	87.2	86.9	77.8	63.7	45.5	35.2	62.3
Mean Temp. (°F)	28.6	34.3	43.4	51.0	59.0	65.7	71.8	71.1	61.7	49.6	37.1	28.6	50.1
Mean Minimum Temp. (°F)	21.2	25.3	31.3	37.6	45.0	51.9	56.3	55.2	45.6	35.5	28.6	21.8	37.9
Extreme Maximum Temp. (°F)	64	66	78	94	102	102	107	105	99	87	73	65	107
Extreme Minimum Temp. (°F)	-14	-12	9	23	29	36	38	38	24	17	-7	-20	-20
Days Maximum Temp. ≥ 90°F	0	0	0	0	1	5	13	12	3	0	0	0	34
Days Maximum Temp. ≤ 32°F	10	3	0	0	0	0	0	0	0	0	2	11	26
Days Minimum Temp. ≤ 32°F	28	24	18	7	1	0	0	0	1	11	21	28	139
Days Minimum Temp. ≤ 0°F	2	0	0	0	0	0	0	0	0	0	0	1	3
Heating Degree Days (base 65°F)	1,122	860	662	415	204	64	12	13	132	470	831	1,123	5,908
Cooling Degree Days (base 65°F)	0	0	0	1	26	89	220	197	43	1	0	0	577
Mean Precipitation (in.)	1.58	1.06	0.73	0.59	0.50	0.69	0.35	0.41	0.48	0.59	1.55	1.94	10.47
Days With ≥ 0.1" Precipitation	5	4	2	2	2	2	1	1	1	2	5	6	33
Days With ≥ 1.0" Precipitation	0	0	0	0	0	0	0	0	0	0	0	0	0
Mean Snowfall (in.)	10.5	5.4	1.0	trace	trace	0.0	0.0	0.0	0.0	0.1	5.1	13.9	36.0
Days With ≥ 1.0" Snow Depth	23	13	1	0	0	0	0	0	0	0	4	17	58

Wenatchee Pangborn Field *Chelan County*   Elevation: 1,227 ft.   Latitude: 47° 24' N   Longitude: 120° 12' W

	JAN	FEB	MAR	APR	MAY	JUN	JUL	AUG	SEP	OCT	NOV	DEC	YEAR
Mean Maximum Temp. (°F)	33.9	41.7	53.5	62.6	71.6	78.8	86.8	86.2	76.4	61.7	44.1	33.5	60.9
Mean Temp. (°F)	27.9	34.2	43.6	51.2	59.4	66.4	73.4	72.9	63.7	50.9	37.4	28.2	50.8
Mean Minimum Temp. (°F)	21.8	26.7	33.5	39.8	47.3	54.0	59.9	59.7	50.9	40.0	30.5	22.8	40.6
Extreme Maximum Temp. (°F)	60	65	78	93	103	105	108	104	101	87	70	62	108
Extreme Minimum Temp. (°F)	-12	-15	10	27	33	38	43	42	32	16	2	-15	-15
Days Maximum Temp. ≥ 90°F	0	0	0	0	1	4	12	12	2	0	0	0	31
Days Maximum Temp. ≤ 32°F	14	5	0	0	0	0	0	0	0	0	3	14	36
Days Minimum Temp. ≤ 32°F	28	22	13	3	0	0	0	0	0	4	18	28	116
Days Minimum Temp. ≤ 0°F	1	0	0	0	0	0	0	0	0	0	0	1	2
Heating Degree Days (base 65°F)	1,144	863	658	408	198	61	11	8	105	433	823	1,135	5,847
Cooling Degree Days (base 65°F)	0	0	0	2	38	105	267	256	80	2	0	0	750
Mean Precipitation (in.)	1.20	0.82	0.66	0.47	0.61	0.64	0.30	0.35	0.42	0.45	1.20	1.46	8.58
Days With ≥ 0.1" Precipitation	4	3	2	2	2	2	1	1	1	1	4	5	28
Days With ≥ 1.0" Precipitation	0	0	0	0	0	0	0	0	0	0	0	0	0
Mean Snowfall (in.)	10.7	4.3	1.3	trace	0.0	trace	trace	0.0	0.0	0.2	4.6	12.5	33.6
Days With ≥ 1.0" Snow Depth	22	11	1	0	0	0	0	0	0	0	4	16	54

Whitman Mission *Walla Walla County*   Elevation: 629 ft.   Latitude: 46° 03' N   Longitude: 118° 27' W

	JAN	FEB	MAR	APR	MAY	JUN	JUL	AUG	SEP	OCT	NOV	DEC	YEAR
Mean Maximum Temp. (°F)	40.4	47.3	56.7	64.2	72.2	80.3	88.9	88.6	79.0	65.7	50.2	41.5	64.6
Mean Temp. (°F)	33.1	38.2	45.0	51.0	57.9	64.8	70.9	70.0	61.0	50.2	41.2	34.1	51.5
Mean Minimum Temp. (°F)	25.8	29.1	33.3	37.7	43.6	49.3	52.7	51.3	43.0	34.7	32.2	26.7	38.3
Extreme Maximum Temp. (°F)	69	76	78	89	98	104	110	110	103	88	82	70	110
Extreme Minimum Temp. (°F)	-22	-21	4	19	28	32	34	33	18	14	-13	-21	-22
Days Maximum Temp. ≥ 90°F	0	0	0	0	1	6	15	15	3	0	0	0	40
Days Maximum Temp. ≤ 32°F	8	3	0	0	0	0	0	0	0	0	2	8	21
Days Minimum Temp. ≤ 32°F	23	18	15	7	1	0	0	0	0	3	13	23	118
Days Minimum Temp. ≤ 0°F	1	1	0	0	0	0	0	0	0	0	0	1	3
Heating Degree Days (base 65°F)	983	750	612	416	233	82	18	22	149	453	706	952	5,376
Cooling Degree Days (base 65°F)	0	0	0	2	22	78	197	177	40	0	0	0	516
Mean Precipitation (in.)	1.63	1.28	1.41	1.35	1.31	0.94	0.48	0.66	0.68	1.11	1.89	1.66	14.40
Days With ≥ 0.1" Precipitation	5	4	5	4	4	3	1	2	2	3	6	5	44
Days With ≥ 1.0" Precipitation	0	0	0	0	0	0	0	0	0	0	0	0	0
Mean Snowfall (in.)	*3.8*	2.2	0.3	0.0	0.0	0.0	0.0	0.0	0.0	0.0	0.3	*3.4*	*10.0*
Days With ≥ 1.0" Snow Depth	7	3	1	0	0	0	0	0	0	0	1	4	16

Wilbur *Lincoln County*   Elevation: 2,227 ft.   Latitude: 47° 45' N   Longitude: 118° 41' W

	JAN	FEB	MAR	APR	MAY	JUN	JUL	AUG	SEP	OCT	NOV	DEC	YEAR
Mean Maximum Temp. (°F)	31.9	38.9	49.1	59.0	68.1	75.8	83.9	84.2	74.3	60.3	41.9	32.7	58.4
Mean Temp. (°F)	25.3	31.1	38.8	45.7	53.6	60.4	67.0	67.1	58.2	46.6	34.1	26.2	46.2
Mean Minimum Temp. (°F)	18.6	23.3	28.4	32.4	39.0	44.9	50.0	49.9	41.9	32.7	26.3	19.6	33.9
Extreme Maximum Temp. (°F)	53	60	70	89	96	101	104	103	100	85	69	55	104
Extreme Minimum Temp. (°F)	-21	-20	1	18	20	27	29	32	24	11	-18	-23	-23
Days Maximum Temp. ≥ 90°F	0	0	0	0	0	2	9	9	1	0	0	0	21
Days Maximum Temp. ≤ 32°F	14	6	0	0	0	0	0	0	0	0	4	14	38
Days Minimum Temp. ≤ 32°F	29	25	24	17	6	1	0	0	3	15	23	29	172
Days Minimum Temp. ≤ 0°F	2	1	0	0	0	0	0	0	0	0	0	1	4
Heating Degree Days (base 65°F)	1,225	949	807	573	355	169	58	56	219	565	919	1,197	7,092
Cooling Degree Days (base 65°F)	0	0	0	1	10	32	126	128	26	0	0	0	323
Mean Precipitation (in.)	1.21	1.18	1.17	0.87	1.32	0.95	0.89	0.55	0.62	0.84	1.63	1.76	12.99
Days With ≥ 0.1" Precipitation	4	4	4	3	4	3	2	2	2	3	5	6	42
Days With ≥ 1.0" Precipitation	0	0	0	0	0	0	0	0	0	0	0	0	0
Mean Snowfall (in.)	5.9	3.7	1.3	0.2	0.0	0.0	0.0	0.0	0.0	0.1	2.7	8.1	22.0
Days With ≥ 1.0" Snow Depth	na	na	1	0	0	0	0	0	0	0	*0*	na	na

Winthrop 1 WSW *Okanogan County*   Elevation: 1,751 ft.   Latitude: 48° 28' N   Longitude: 120° 11' W

	JAN	FEB	MAR	APR	MAY	JUN	JUL	AUG	SEP	OCT	NOV	DEC	YEAR
Mean Maximum Temp. (°F)	29.5	38.4	50.5	62.0	71.3	78.3	85.7	86.0	76.9	62.4	41.0	28.9	59.2
Mean Temp. (°F)	21.0	28.0	37.8	46.7	55.0	61.7	67.4	67.2	58.2	46.4	32.5	21.2	45.3
Mean Minimum Temp. (°F)	12.4	17.5	25.0	31.3	38.8	45.2	49.0	48.4	39.5	30.4	24.0	13.5	31.2
Extreme Maximum Temp. (°F)	57	62	77	89	100	100	104	103	100	86	68	54	104
Extreme Minimum Temp. (°F)	-28	-20	-6	16	21	28	31	30	18	10	-16	-30	-30
Days Maximum Temp. ≥ 90°F	0	0	0	0	1	3	11	11	2	0	0	0	28
Days Maximum Temp. ≤ 32°F	18	5	0	0	0	0	0	0	0	0	4	19	46
Days Minimum Temp. ≤ 32°F	31	27	27	18	6	1	0	0	5	19	25	31	190
Days Minimum Temp. ≤ 0°F	6	2	0	0	0	0	0	0	0	0	1	5	14
Heating Degree Days (base 65°F)	1,359	1,039	837	544	308	131	39	41	211	570	968	1,351	7,398
Cooling Degree Days (base 65°F)	0	0	0	0	7	33	110	114	19	0	0	0	283
Mean Precipitation (in.)	2.04	1.44	1.06	0.78	1.01	1.07	0.74	0.74	0.61	0.91	2.04	2.71	15.15
Days With ≥ 0.1" Precipitation	6	5	3	3	3	3	2	2	2	2	6	7	44
Days With ≥ 1.0" Precipitation	0	0	0	0	0	0	0	0	0	0	0	0	0
Mean Snowfall (in.)	17.8	8.6	3.7	trace	trace	0.0	0.0	0.0	0.0	0.9	9.4	25.0	65.4
Days With ≥ 1.0" Snow Depth	31	27	18	1	0	0	0	0	0	0	*10*	29	*116*

Note: See Appendix D for explanation of data.

WEST VIRGINIA

PHYSICAL FEATURES. West Virginia has an area of over 24,000 square miles. From southwest to northeast, the State is about 200 miles in length; width averages a little over one-half the length. There are two projections: the Northeastern Panhandle juts eastward between Maryland and Virginia; and the Northern Panhandle, a narrow strip stretching northward along the Ohio River between Ohio and Pennsylvania. The easternmost extremity of the State is about 150 miles from the Atlantic Ocean and the southwestern corner adjacent to Kentucky is nearly 400 miles away from the ocean. As a result, West Virginia lies beyond the immediate climatic effect of the Atlantic, and its climate is much more continental than maritime type. The most important aspect of this type of climate is the marked temperature contrast between summer and winter.

The physical configuration of the State accentuates its interior location. Excluding the Northeastern Panhandle, the State lies in the Allegheny Plateau. The eastern third of the plateau is part of the Appalachian Mountain chain and contains the highest land in the State. Peak elevations in this area range from about 2,500 feet to 4,860 feet (above sea level) at Spruce Knob, the highest point in West Virginia. The central and western thirds of the plateau slope generally westward to the Ohio River which lies at about 550 to 650 feet above sea level.

The Northeastern Panhandle is marked by long ridges and valleys, oriented southwest-northeast, intersected by the winding courses of the Potomac River and its tributaries. The main stream of the Potomac with its North Branch forms the northern border of this part of the State. Summit elevations exceed 4,000 feet (above sea level), but the land in general slopes eastward away from the main ridgeline to the west and finally reaches the lowest elevation in the State of 274 feet at Harpers Ferry. This section lies in the Atlantic Ocean drainage and is drained by the Potomac River. The remainder of the State drains into the Ohio River.

GENERAL CLIMATE. Physical features considerably modify the effects of the major climatic controls. The State's latitudinal position (from about 37° 15' N. latitude in the south to 40° in the north) places it in the zone of prevailing westerly winds, which are frequently interrupted by northward and southward surges of relatively warm and cold air, respectively. These atmospheric movements are accompanied by the passage of high and low-pressure areas; the latter are the large-dimension storms, known as extratropical cyclones, which are most common in the United States in the colder half-year. West Virginia lies near the average path of the extratropical cyclones that move in a general easterly direction across the United States. In the warmer half-year, the State is affected by the showers and thunderstorms that occur in the broad current of air that tends to sweep northeastward from the Gulf of Mexico.

The State has a moderately severe winter climate, accentuated and prolonged in the mountains, with frequent alternations of fair and stormy weather. Summer is marked by hot and showery weather; the heat is less pronounced in the mountains, which are more subject to thunderstorms and have fewer clear days the year-round. There are marked variations in temperature, precipitation, and the other weather elements, due to the rugged topography occurring not only between the mountains and plateau areas but also between different parts of the same county.

TEMPERATURE. Locations in the mountainous belt, regardless of their latitude, tend to have lower temperatures than those in the rest of the State. Average winter minimum temperatures range from the low 20s in the mountains of the Central and Northeastern Divisions and in the Northern Panhandle, to near 30°F. in the extreme southern and southwestern corners of the State. Average winter maximum readings are in the middle and upper 40s, except in the mountains and in the Northern Panhandle where they are close to 40°F. In summer, maximum temperatures average over 85°F. everywhere except in the mountains, where they are 5 to 10°F. cooler; average minimum temperatures during this season range from the middle 50s in the mountains to the middle 60s elsewhere. Spring and autumn mean temperatures average in the 50s, with similar geographical variations. The average date of the last freezing temperature in spring ranges from mid-April in the southwest to mid-May in the mountains; the average first occurrence of 32°F. in the fall similarly varies from late October to late September.

Despite the coolness of the mountains, they can on occasion be as hot as any other part of West Virginia. Temperatures near or over 100°F. have been recorded at all weather stations in the State. On the other hand, very low temperatures (below -30°F.) have been observed only in the mountains and in the North Central Division. These are extremes, and do not represent usual winter conditions. Cold waves, with near or subzero temperatures, occur on average three times a winter, but as a rule do not last more than two or three days.

Fog conditions over the State are complicated as to their causes and distribution. The valley fogs are usually of the radiation type, and occur characteristically when a high-pressure area is centered over or near the State. This situation is most common in late summer and fall. Low cloudiness and fog in the mountains are generally orographic in nature, the result of moist winds moving upslope, so that there is usually a great difference in cloud and fog conditions on opposite sides of a ridge.

PRECIPITATION. The precipitation pattern can be directly related to the rain and snow-producing atmospheric currents generally move across West Virginia on an eastward course. As they approach the mountains, these air currents are subject to orographic lifting, which acts to trigger potential precipitation or to intensify the rain or snow that may already be falling. As a result, average annual precipitation increases from the Ohio eastward to the Appalachians. On the other side of the mountains, there is the well-marked "rain shadow" where the air currents descend the leeward slopes and precipitation is correspondingly reduced, to increase only when more favorable topographic influences are encountered farther eastward and where the influence of the ocean and coastal storms is more pronounced.

Mean annual snowfall exhibits the same features, but to a more remarkable degree. The mountain belt receives over 60 inches of snow a year, on the average. Amounts over 20 inches have been experienced everywhere in of the State except west of longitude 81° 30' W. which usually receives about 15 inches. It is very unusual for a relatively small and compact area the size of West Virginia to exhibit such great differences in snowfall. Furthermore, the heavy snowfall at elevations under 5,000 feet (above sea level) is unusual in the East, for an area located south of 40° N. latitude. The snow, as a general rule, does not remain on the ground for extended periods over most of the State. Except in the higher portions of the plateau and in the mountains themselves. Snowstorms are usually followed by thawing periods and there is no large-scale melting in the spring of a seasonally accumulated snowpack.

SUNSHINE AND CLOUDINESS. West Virginia lies in a cloudy belt. Percentage of possible sunshine is only about 40 in winter, increasing to somewhat over 60 percent in early autumn. Cloudiness is most pronounced over the mountains. The average annual number of clear days ranges from about 80 in the mountains to about 120 in the western portion. In addition to cloudiness, the hours of sunshine are reduced by fog, particularly in the river valleys.

WINDS AND STORMS. The prevailing winds blow from westerly directions. There is a tendency outside of the mountain belt for southerly or southwesterly winds during summer and fall. Thunderstorms occur on an average of 40 to 50 days per year, being more frequent in the mountains and during June and July. Violent local winds accompanying thunderstorms are experienced every year in some part of the State, but tornadoes are rare. Destructive hailstorms occur on an average of about three per year. Though hurricanes have damaged the State, principally as a result of heavy rains, it is uncommon for this type of storm to strike West Virginia with full force. The remnants of the hurricanes which have affected the State have been more noted for their accompanying heavy rainfalls than for any high winds produced. Much more frequent and costly is the damage from intense large-area storms — that is, from exceptionally strong specimens of the ordinary lows that affect the State quite frequently during the colder half of the year. Such storms produce high winds and heavy rain or snow.

Warm-season thunderstorms, mostly those of June and July, often yield intense local rainfall and cause flash flooding in the narrow valleys that cut through the plateau and mountain districts. This kind of severe local flood is likely to occur in some part of the State every year. In contrast to flash flooding on the smaller streams, flooding in the larger streams is almost exclusively a cold season phenomenon. The ideal setup for the cold season floods is soil well saturated from previous rains, a good snow cover, and a more-or-less stationary front lying northeast-southwest across the State. Along this front separating two contrasting air masses, a succession of "waves" may move northeastward, resulting in copious warm rains for a period of at least several days and a rapid melting of the snow cover.

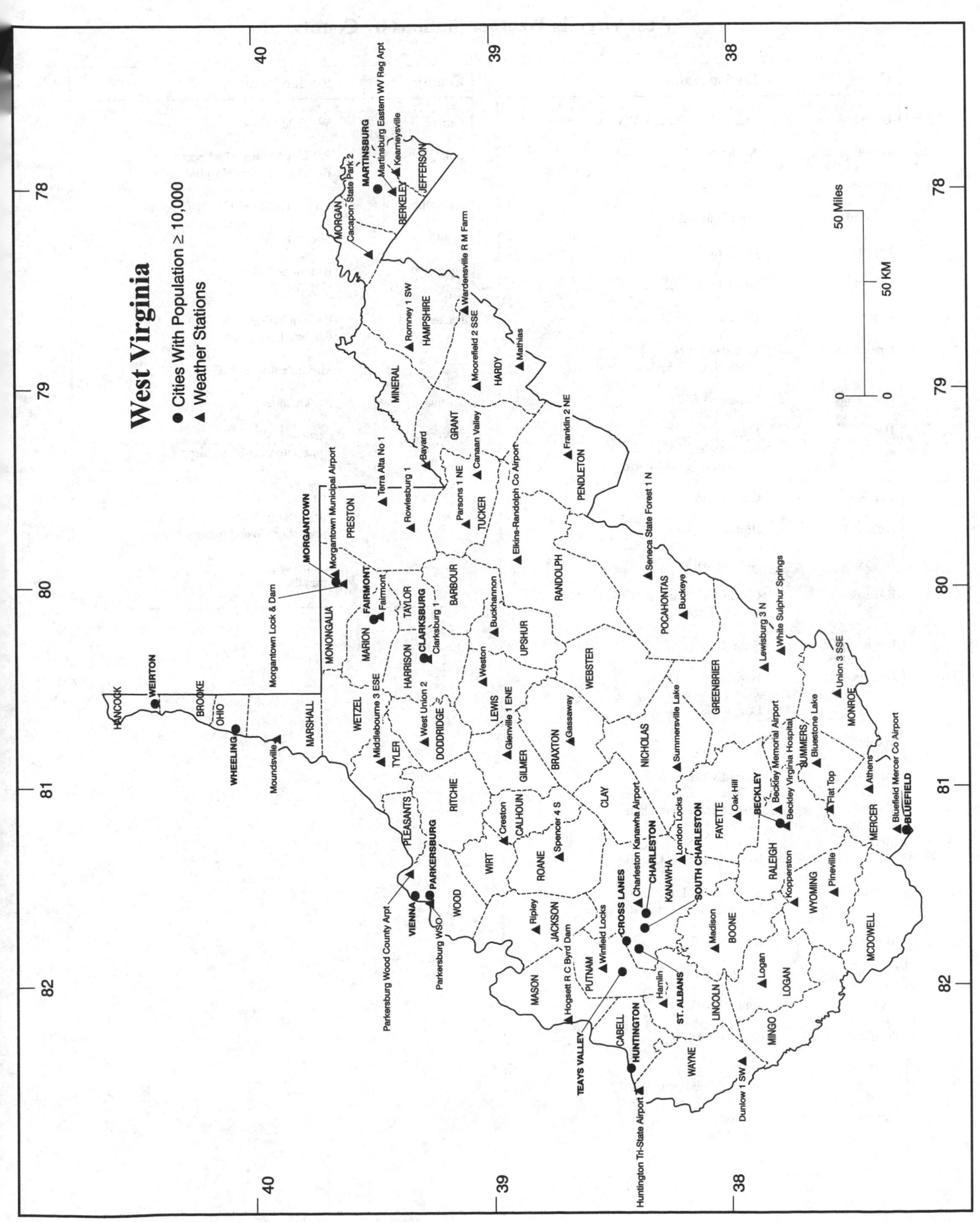

West Virginia

- ● Cities With Population ≥ 10,000
- ▲ Weather Stations

50 Miles

50 KM

MORGAN
Cacapon State Park 2
MARTINSBURG
Martinsburg Eastern WV Reg Arpt
Kearneysville
BERKELEY
JEFFERSON
Wardensville R M Farm
Romney 1 SW
HAMPSHIRE
Moorefield 2 SSE
HARDY
Mathias
MINERAL
GRANT
Bayard
Canaan Valley
Parsons 1 NE
TUCKER
Elkins-Randolph Co Airport
Franklin 2 NE
PENDLETON
Terra Alta No 1
Rowlesburg 1
PRESTON
MORGANTOWN
Morgantown Municipal Airport
Seneca State Forest 1 N
Morgantown Lock & Dam
RANDOLPH
WEIRTON
BROOKE
OHIO
HANCOCK
MONONGALIA
MARION
FAIRMONT
Fairmont
TAYLOR
CLARKSBURG
Clarksburg 1
BARBOUR
Buckhannon
UPSHUR
Pocahontas
Buckeye
POCAHONTAS
Lewisburg 3 N
White Sulphur Springs
WHEELING
Moundsville
MARSHALL
WETZEL
Middlebourne 3 ESE
TYLER
West Union 2
DODDRIDGE
HARRISON
Weston
LEWIS
WEBSTER
GREENBRIER
Union 3 SSE
MONROE
RITCHIE
Creston
CALHOUN
Glenville 1 ENE
GILMER
Gassaway
BRAXTON
NICHOLAS
Summersville Lake
Beckley Memorial Airport
BECKLEY
Beckley Virginia Hospital
Bluestone Lake
SUMMERS
Flat Top
Athens
PLEASANTS
WOOD
PARKERSBURG
Parkersburg Wood County Arpt
Parkersburg WSO
VIENNA
WIRT
Ripley
JACKSON
ROANE
Spencer 4 S
CLAY
Charleston Kanawha Airport
London Locks
FAYETTE
Oak Hill
RALEIGH
Kopperston
Pineville
WYOMING
MERCER
Bluefield Mercer Co Airport
BLUEFIELD
MCDOWELL
Bluefield Mercer Co Airport
Hogsett R C Byrd Dam
Winfield Locks
PUTNAM
CROSS LANES
CHARLESTON
KANAWHA
SOUTH CHARLESTON
Madison
BOONE
Logan
LOGAN
MASON
Hamlin
ST. ALBANS
LINCOLN
MINGO
TEAYS VALLEY
CABELL
HUNTINGTON
Huntington Tri-State Airport
WAYNE
Dunlow 1 SW

West Virginia Weather Stations by County

County	Station Name
Berkeley	Martinsburg Eastern WV Reg. Arpt.
Boone	Madison
Braxton	Gassaway
Doddridge	West Union 2
Fayette	Oak Hill
Gilmer	Glenville 1 ENE
Grant	Bayard
Greenbrier	Lewisburg 3 N
	White Sulphur Springs
Hampshire	Romney 1 SW
Hardy	Mathias
	Moorefield 2 SSE
	Wardensville R M Farm
Harrison	Clarksburg 1
Jackson	Ripley
Jefferson	Kearneysville
Kanawha	Charleston Kanawha Airport
	London Locks
Lewis	Weston
Lincoln	Hamlin
Logan	Logan
Marion	Fairmont
Marshall	Moundsville
Mason	Hogsett R.C. Byrd Dam
Mercer	Athens
	Bluefield Mercer Co. Airport
Monongalia	Morgantown Lock & Dam
	Morgantown Municipal Airport
Monroe	Union 3 SSE
Morgan	Cacapon State Park 2
Nicholas	Summersville Lake
Pendleton	Franklin 2 NE
Pocahontas	Buckeye
	Seneca State Forest 1 N
Preston	Rowlesburg 1
	Terra Alta 1

County	Station Name
Putnam	Winfield Locks
Raleigh	Beckley Memorial Airport
	Beckley Virginia Hospital
Randolph	Elkins-Randolph Co. Airport
Roane	Spencer 4 S
Summers	Bluestone Lake
	Flat Top
Tucker	Canaan Valley
	Parsons 1 NE
Tyler	Middlebourne 3 ESE
Upshur	Buckhannon
Wayne	Dunlow 1 SW
	Huntington Tri-State Airport
Wirt	Creston
Wood	Parkersburg WSO
	Parkersburg Wood County Airport
Wyoming	Kopperston
	Pineville

West Virginia Weather Stations by City

City	Station Name	Miles
Beckley	Beckley Virginia Hospital	1
	Beckley Memorial Airport	4
	Bluestone Lake	19
	Flat Top	14
	Oak Hill	13
Bluefield	Burkes Garden, VA	14
	Athens	16
	Bluefield Mercer Co. Airport	3
Charleston	Charleston Kanawha Airport	4
	London Locks	18
	Winfield Locks	20
Clarksburg	Clarksburg 1	1
	Fairmont	17
	Weston	18
Cross Lanes	Charleston Kanawha Airport	11
	Winfield Locks	10
Fairmont	Clarksburg 1	18
	Fairmont	1
	Morgantown Municipal Airport	17
	Morgantown Lock & Dam	13
Huntington	Ashland, KY	10
	Huntington Tri-State Airport	7
Martinsburg	Cacapon State Park 2	18
	Kearneysville	7
	Martinsburg Eastern WV Reg. Arpt.	4
Morgantown	Fairmont	15
	Morgantown Municipal Airport	2
	Morgantown Lock & Dam	2
Parkersburg	Marietta WWTP, OH	12
	Parkersburg Wood County Airport	8
	Parkersburg WSO	1
South Charleston	Charleston Kanawha Airport	7
	Winfield Locks	17
St. Albans	Charleston Kanawha Airport	13
	Hamlin	17
	Winfield Locks	12
Teays Valley	Charleston Kanawha Airport	19
	Hamlin	15
	Winfield Locks	6
Vienna	Marietta WWTP, OH	9
	Parkersburg Wood County Airport	6
	Parkersburg WSO	4
Weirton	Steubenville, OH	4
	Montgomery Lock & Dam, PA	19
	Pittsburgh Int'l Airport, PA	19
Wheeling	Moundsville	12

Note: Miles is the distance between the geographic center of the city and the weather station.

West Virginia Weather Stations by Elevation

Feet	Station Name
3,248	Canaan Valley
3,234	Flat Top
2,890	Bluefield Mercer Co. Airport
2,627	Terra Alta 1
2,562	Athens
2,503	Beckley Memorial Airport
2,447	Seneca State Forest 1 N
2,372	Bayard
2,329	Beckley Virginia Hospital
2,303	Lewisburg 3 N
2,148	Buckeye
2,109	Union 3 SSE
1,988	Oak Hill
1,945	Elkins-Randolph Co. Airport
1,919	White Sulphur Springs
1,899	Franklin 2 NE
1,768	Parsons 1 NE
1,758	Summersville Lake
1,660	Kopperston
1,538	Mathias
1,453	Buckhannon
1,420	Rowlesburg 1
1,387	Bluestone Lake
1,299	Fairmont
1,279	Pineville
1,240	Morgantown Municipal Airport
1,197	Dunlow 1 SW
1,013	Charleston Kanawha Airport
987	Clarksburg 1
958	Wardensville R M Farm
948	Cacapon State Park 2
921	Weston
889	Moorefield 2 SSE
859	Spencer 4 S
839	Gassaway
830	Huntington Tri-State Airport
830	Parkersburg Wood County Airport
823	Morgantown Lock & Dam
787	West Union 2
780	Middlebourne 3 ESE
708	Glenville 1 ENE
672	Madison
669	Romney 1 SW
649	Creston
639	Hamlin
639	Logan
620	London Locks
620	Moundsville
613	Parkersburg WSO
587	Ripley
570	Winfield Locks
567	Hogsett R.C. Byrd Dam
547	Kearneysville
534	Martinsburg Eastern WV Reg. Arpt.

Beckley Memorial Airport

The city of Beckley is located in the Appalachian Mountains about 30 miles northwest of the high ridges through eastern West Virginia. The Raleigh County Memorial Airport is on a plateau about 2.5 miles east of the city. Beckley is almost surrounded by distant peaks. The entire area is on a broad plateau composed of rough, hilly ground and lush valleys. The generalized 2,000-foot contour line is about 25 miles to the northwest and runs from southwest to northeast. The generalized 3,000-foot contour is about 10 miles to the southeast and follows the general configuration of the Appalachians.

Due to the configuration the weather often remains clear over Beckley even though the low stratus clouds to the east may obscure the ridges and be solid to the east of these ridges. To a lesser degree, this location is largely responsible for the formation of heavy fogs at the Beckley Airport.

Beckley has a climate characterized by sharp temperature contrasts, both seasonal and day to day. The months of May through September are moderately cold, with April and October months of fairly rapid transition. Cold waves occur on an average of two or three times during the winter, but severe cold spells are seldom of more than two or three days duration. Below-zero temperatures, as well as temperatures in the 70s have been recorded during winter months. A low of -13 degrees may be expected once every 10 years and -16 degrees once every 25 years. Summer highs near 90 degrees have occurred, contrasting with lows in the 30s during the same months. Highs seldom reach above the mid-80s. Cool nights are common throughout the summer, with lowest temperatures usually ranging from the 50s to the low 60s.

Ample precipitation is well distributed throughout the year. July has the highest monthly average while October has the lowest average. Summer rainfall occurs mostly during thunderstorms or showery precipitation, while the heaviest winter precipitation usually is associated with storms originating to the southwest and moving northeastward over the Ohio Valley. The formation of storms in the eastern Gulf of Mexico which move up the east coast will sometimes bring heavy snow to the Beckley area. Snowfall occurs chiefly from November through March and occasionally in October and April. The average seasonal snowfall is greater than snowfall at stations to the west at lower elevations, and considerably less than the totals for stations at higher elevations to the east and northeast.

Beckley Memorial Airport *Raleigh County*   Elevation: 2,503 ft.   Latitude: 37° 48' N   Longitude: 81° 07' W

	JAN	FEB	MAR	APR	MAY	JUN	JUL	AUG	SEP	OCT	NOV	DEC	YEAR
Mean Maximum Temp. (°F)	38.8	42.7	51.6	62.4	70.1	76.5	80.0	78.8	72.7	62.8	52.4	43.5	61.0
Mean Temp. (°F)	30.4	33.7	41.9	51.6	59.6	66.7	70.6	69.3	63.2	52.7	43.5	35.2	51.5
Mean Minimum Temp. (°F)	21.9	24.6	32.2	40.7	49.1	56.9	61.2	59.8	53.6	42.6	34.5	26.9	42.0
Extreme Maximum Temp. (°F)	69	74	81	86	89	89	94	96	92	81	78	73	96
Extreme Minimum Temp. (°F)	-22	-16	-5	11	26	32	41	36	30	18	4	-18	-22
Days Maximum Temp. ≥ 90°F	0	0	0	0	0	0	1	0	0	0	0	0	1
Days Maximum Temp. ≤ 32°F	10	7	2	0	0	0	0	0	0	0	2	6	27
Days Minimum Temp. ≤ 32°F	25	21	17	7	1	0	0	0	0	5	14	22	112
Days Minimum Temp. ≤ 0°F	2	1	0	0	0	0	0	0	0	0	0	1	4
Heating Degree Days (base 65°F)	1,067	878	709	406	192	45	9	14	109	378	639	917	5,363
Cooling Degree Days (base 65°F)	0	0	2	8	33	114	208	160	61	6	0	0	592
Mean Precipitation (in.)	3.24	2.97	3.63	3.41	4.32	3.89	4.71	3.48	3.12	2.70	2.89	3.14	41.50
Maximum Precipitation (in.)	6.4	6.0	9.2	7.6	7.1	7.0	9.6	5.9	8.3	5.9	6.3	6.4	57.1
Minimum Precipitation (in.)	0.5	0.5	1.7	0.3	1.0	1.5	1.6	1.7	0.5	0.1	1.0	0.6	32.6
Maximum 24-hr. Precipitation (in.)	2.1	2.1	2.0	3.6	2.1	2.5	2.9	2.5	4.3	3.1	2.5	1.8	4.3
Days With ≥ 0.1" Precipitation	8	8	9	8	9	8	8	7	6	6	7	8	92
Days With ≥ 1.0" Precipitation	0	0	0	0	1	1	1	1	1	0	0	0	5
Mean Snowfall (in.)	17.8	15.3	9.2	2.8	trace	trace	0.0	0.0	0.0	0.6	3.6	10.8	60.1
Maximum Snowfall (in.)	36	31	13	19	1	0	0	0	trace	7	13	27	94
Maximum 24-hr. Snowfall (in.)	12	9	7	13	1	0	0	0	trace	7	6	14	14
Days With ≥ 1.0" Snow Depth	13	12	5	1	0	0	0	0	0	0	2	8	41
Thunderstorm Days	< 1	1	2	4	6	8	10	7	3	1	< 1	< 1	42
Foggy Days	14	12	14	12	16	19	23	24	21	14	13	13	195
Predominant Sky Cover	OVR	OVR	OVR	OVR	OVR	OVR	OVR	OVR	OVR	OVR	OVR	OVR	OVR
Mean Relative Humidity 7am (%)	80	79	77	74	81	86	89	91	91	86	79	79	83
Mean Relative Humidity 4pm (%)	65	61	54	48	54	59	61	62	62	55	58	65	59
Mean Dewpoint (°F)	22	23	30	37	48	57	62	61	55	42	33	26	41
Prevailing Wind Direction	WNW	WNW	WNW	WNW	SSE	WSW	WSW	SE	SE	SE	SSE	WNW	SSE
Prevailing Wind Speed (mph)	13	13	13	13	10	9	8	9	9	12	12	12	12
Maximum Wind Gust (mph)	61	62	70	60	58	55	61	46	48	49	60	56	70

Charleston Kanawha Airport

Charleston lies at the junction of the Kanawha and Elk Rivers in the western foothills of the Appalachian Mountains. The hilltops are around 1,100 feet above sea level, about 500 feet higher than the valleys. The Kanawha Airport is just over two miles northeast of the center-city area, on an artificial plateau constructed from several hilltops.

Weather records are maintained at the Kanawha Airport by National Weather Service personnel. This site tends to be slightly cooler than the river valleys during the afternoons. Conversely, the valleys can become cooler than the hilltops during clear, calm nights. The weather at Charleston is highly changeable, especially from mid-autumn through the spring.

Winters can vary greatly from one season to the next. Snow does not favor any given winter month, heavy snowstorms are infrequent, and most snowfalls are in the four inch or less category. Snow and ice usually do not persist on valley roads, but can linger longer on nearby hills and outlying rural roads.

Afternoon temperatures in the 40s and morning readings in the 20s are common during the winter. Yet, every winter typically has two or three extended cold spells when temperatures stay below freezing for a few consecutive days. Northwesterly winds are associated with the cold weather. Air reaching Charleston from the northwest can cause cloudiness and flurries, even when there is no nearby organized storm system. Winter conditions are much more severe over the higher mountains less than 50 miles to the northeast through the southeast. Temperatures warm rapidly in the spring and are accompanied by low daytime humidities.

Summer and early autumn have more day-to-day consistency in the weather. Sunshine is more abundant than in winter. Summer precipitation falls mostly in brief, but sometimes heavy, showers. Flash flooding can occur along small streams, but flooding is rare on the dam-controlled Kanawha and Elk Rivers.

Afternoon summer temperatures are mostly in the 80s. Readings above 95 degrees are rare. However, during a hot spell, haze and humidity can add to the unpleasantness and indoor air conditioning is recommended. Cooler and less humid air often penetrates the area from the north to end a hot spell.

Early morning fog is common from late June into October. By the end of October, the first 32 degree temperature has usually arrived.

Ample precipitation is well distributed throughout the year. July is quite often the wettest month of the year, while October averages the least rain. Droughts severe enough to limit water use are scarce. Any dry spells during the spring or autumn can cause conditions favorable for brush fires in outlying areas.

Charleston Kanawha Airport   *Kanawha County*   Elevation: 1,013 ft.   Latitude: 38° 23' N   Longitude: 81° 35' W

	JAN	FEB	MAR	APR	MAY	JUN	JUL	AUG	SEP	OCT	NOV	DEC	YEAR
Mean Maximum Temp. (°F)	42.1	46.6	56.6	67.6	75.5	82.5	86.0	84.3	78.1	67.4	56.7	47.0	65.9
Mean Temp. (°F)	33.4	36.9	45.7	55.3	63.7	71.3	75.4	73.9	67.4	56.0	46.5	38.1	55.3
Mean Minimum Temp. (°F)	24.5	27.1	34.7	43.1	51.8	60.1	64.8	63.5	56.7	44.4	36.3	29.1	44.7
Extreme Maximum Temp. (°F)	76	78	89	94	93	98	104	101	96	87	85	80	104
Extreme Minimum Temp. (°F)	-16	-12	0	19	29	33	47	42	34	21	9	-12	-16
Days Maximum Temp. ≥ 90°F	0	0	0	0	1	4	9	5	1	0	0	0	20
Days Maximum Temp. ≤ 32°F	7	5	1	0	0	0	0	0	0	0	0	4	17
Days Minimum Temp. ≤ 32°F	23	20	14	5	0	0	0	0	0	3	12	20	97
Days Minimum Temp. ≤ 0°F	1	0	0	0	0	0	0	0	0	0	0	0	1
Heating Degree Days (base 65°F)	974	787	599	310	117	16	1	2	53	291	551	828	4,529
Cooling Degree Days (base 65°F)	0	0	7	27	83	221	354	293	129	21	3	1	1,139
Mean Precipitation (in.)	3.25	3.17	3.96	3.20	4.18	4.06	4.77	4.12	3.47	2.81	3.70	3.38	44.07
Maximum Precipitation (in.)	9.1	6.9	7.7	6.5	6.8	7.5	13.5	10.4	7.6	6.5	8.4	8.0	60.6
Minimum Precipitation (in.)	1.1	0.5	1.3	0.5	0.8	0.7	2.0	0.7	0.6	0.1	0.6	0.4	30.3
Maximum 24-hr. Precipitation (in.)	1.9	1.9	2.8	2.5	2.3	2.2	5.6	4.1	2.4	2.1	2.5	2.4	5.6
Days With ≥ 0.1" Precipitation	8	8	9	8	9	8	8	7	7	6	8	8	94
Days With ≥ 1.0" Precipitation	0	0	1	0	1	1	1	1	1	0	1	0	7
Mean Snowfall (in.)	13.4	9.8	6.5	1.3	trace	trace	trace	trace	trace	0.1	1.9	5.5	38.5
Maximum Snowfall (in.)	40	22	20	21	1	0	0	0	0	3	26	22	68
Maximum 24-hr. Snowfall (in.)	16	10	17	11	1	0	0	0	0	3	13	11	17
Days With ≥ 1.0" Snow Depth	11	8	3	0	0	0	0	0	0	0	1	5	28
Thunderstorm Days	1	1	2	4	7	8	10	7	3	1	1	< 1	45
Foggy Days	15	13	13	13	22	25	28	29	26	23	16	15	238
Predominant Sky Cover	OVR	OVR	OVR	OVR	OVR	OVR	OVR	OVR	OVR	OVR	OVR	OVR	OVR
Mean Relative Humidity 7am (%)	77	77	75	75	83	87	90	92	91	88	80	78	83
Mean Relative Humidity 4pm (%)	60	55	49	44	50	53	56	57	55	51	54	60	54
Mean Dewpoint (°F)	24	25	31	39	51	60	65	64	58	46	35	28	44
Prevailing Wind Direction	WSW	WSW	WSW	WSW	SW	SW	SW	SW	NE	SW	SW	WSW	SW
Prevailing Wind Speed (mph)	10	10	12	10	8	8	8	7	6	8	9	10	9
Maximum Wind Gust (mph)	76	68	60	66	58	49	67	64	44	46	49	62	76

Elkins-Randolph Co. Airport

Elkins, West Virginia, is located near the principal storm tracks and is therefore subjected to frequent weather changes throughout the year. While changes may be rigorous, they bring relief from summer heat waves and winter cold waves. The airport and city are located near the middle of a valley with a narrow floor and ridges at or near 3,000 feet. The ridges are oriented north northeast to south southwest, three to four miles to the east and west. The valley is located on the general northwest slope of the Appalachian Mountains which crest about 20 miles to the southeast at about 4,500 feet, with some higher peaks.

The seasonal climates vary greatly from year to year. When the Atlantic High extends westward, warm weather with high humidities occur in both summer and winter. Conversely, if the Atlantic High is displaced eastward and the circulation is principally from the northwest, weather is colder than normal.

Summers are characterized by warm, humid, showery weather, but the heat is moderated by elevation and orographically induced cloudiness. A daily high temperature of 90 or above may occasionally be expected during the summer months. Winters are moderately severe with rapid changes. Snowfall may be frequent, and at times, heavy. However, it seldom remains on the ground for extended periods. Snows often fall upon warm ground thereby causing preliminary melting, then freezing, resulting in slippery road conditions. Glaze formation upon the ground or upon wires and trees is rare. Cold spells alternate frequently with thaws, and snow is subject to frequent complete melting during the winter. Severe cold spells occur occasionally but they seldom last more than two or three days. A daily low of zero degrees or below can be expected several times annually.

Significant climatic characteristics are associated with air currents rising and descending over the mountains. During the winter when low clouds and snow flurries sometimes persist for 24 hours or more. Easterly and southerly winds, tend to diminish existing low cloud layers and keep ceilings higher than otherwise anticipated. Night time fog is common during the summer and the autumn but it usually dissipates rapidly after sunrise.

Tornadoes are rare in this area, and severe thunderstorms are very infrequent. However, occasionally intense local rainfall from warm-season thunderstorms causes flash flooding in the narrow valleys of the area. Due to the remote location of the city with respect to concentrated industry, the air is usually relatively unpolluted. The average last occurrence in the spring of temperatures as low as 32 is early to mid-May, and the first occurrence in the autumn is early October. The length of the growing season averages about 148 days.

Elkins-Randolph Co. Airport *Randolph County*   Elevation: 1,945 ft.   Latitude: 38° 53' N   Longitude: 79° 51' W

	JAN	FEB	MAR	APR	MAY	JUN	JUL	AUG	SEP	OCT	NOV	DEC	YEAR
Mean Maximum Temp. (°F)	38.6	42.4	51.8	62.2	70.9	77.7	81.1	79.9	73.8	63.8	52.7	43.6	61.5
Mean Temp. (°F)	28.2	31.0	39.4	48.5	57.5	65.2	69.4	68.3	62.0	50.5	41.1	32.9	49.5
Mean Minimum Temp. (°F)	17.8	19.6	27.0	34.8	44.2	52.6	57.7	56.7	50.2	37.2	29.4	22.2	37.4
Extreme Maximum Temp. (°F)	70	72	83	89	93	91	99	94	93	84	79	74	99
Extreme Minimum Temp. (°F)	-24	-22	-15	3	20	25	32	38	29	13	2	-24	-24
Days Maximum Temp. ≥ 90°F	0	0	0	0	0	0	1	1	0	0	0	0	2
Days Maximum Temp. ≤ 32°F	10	7	2	0	0	0	0	0	0	0	2	6	27
Days Minimum Temp. ≤ 32°F	27	24	22	13	3	0	0	0	1	11	20	25	146
Days Minimum Temp. ≤ 0°F	4	2	1	0	0	0	0	0	0	0	0	2	9
Heating Degree Days (base 65°F)	1,134	952	788	489	242	67	14	21	128	446	712	988	5,981
Cooling Degree Days (base 65°F)	0	0	0	2	19	84	174	135	42	3	0	0	459
Mean Precipitation (in.)	3.42	3.12	3.91	3.54	4.67	4.59	4.87	4.29	3.64	2.90	3.44	3.56	45.95
Maximum Precipitation (in.)	6.1	6.5	8.8	6.9	7.7	8.3	8.3	10.4	7.5	6.3	11.1	6.7	58.7
Minimum Precipitation (in.)	1.0	0.8	1.4	1.0	1.4	1.7	1.3	1.1	0.3	0.3	1.2	0.9	34.1
Maximum 24-hr. Precipitation (in.)	1.4	1.8	2.9	1.9	2.6	2.1	2.7	2.8	2.7	3.3	5.0	1.9	5.0
Days With ≥ 0.1" Precipitation	9	9	10	9	10	9	9	8	8	7	8	9	105
Days With ≥ 1.0" Precipitation	0	0	0	0	1	1	1	1	1	0	1	0	6
Mean Snowfall (in.)	24.1	17.0	12.6	5.0	trace	trace	0.0	0.0	0.0	0.6	6.2	14.3	79.8
Maximum Snowfall (in.)	54	32	34	25	1	0	0	0	0	4	38	37	125
Maximum 24-hr. Snowfall (in.)	16	13	17	9	1	0	0	0	0	3	12	18	18
Days With ≥ 1.0" Snow Depth	15	13	6	1	0	0	0	0	0	0	3	9	47
Thunderstorm Days	< 1	1	2	4	7	8	9	6	3	1	1	< 1	42
Foggy Days	14	13	15	15	21	24	27	29	27	23	16	16	240
Predominant Sky Cover	OVR	OVR	OVR	OVR	OVR	OVR	OVR	OVR	OVR	OVR	OVR	OVR	OVR
Mean Relative Humidity 7am (%)	81	81	82	83	87	92	94	96	95	90	83	82	87
Mean Relative Humidity 4pm (%)	64	60	55	50	54	58	61	62	61	54	58	64	58
Mean Dewpoint (°F)	22	23	29	37	48	57	62	61	54	42	32	25	42
Prevailing Wind Direction	WNW	WNW	WNW	WNW	NW	NW	NW	NW	NW	NW	WNW	WNW	WNW
Prevailing Wind Speed (mph)	12	12	12	12	9	8	7	7	7	8	10	12	9
Maximum Wind Gust (mph)	59	49	63	69	60	69	52	46	44	46	59	54	69

Huntington Tri-State Airport

The Tri-State Airport is near the confluence of the Ohio and Big Sandy Rivers, located on a man-made plateau constructed by cutting the tops off several hills and filling intervening valleys. The elevation of the ground at the National Weather Service Office is 260 feet higher than at the Federal Building in downtown Huntington.

The temperature record for the valley locations is not compatible with that for the airport, which is generally cooler throughout the year. The summer season is moderately warm and humid, with the valley locations considerably warmer and more humid than the Tri-State Airport site. The winter months are moderately cold, with an occasional severe cold wave lasting a few days. The four seasons are nearly equal in length and autumn is the most pleasant, with warm days and cool nights.

The heaviest rainfall occurs in July and August, mostly in thunderstorms, and flash floods are common in the area. The winter rainfall occurs mostly prior to and with a frontal passage and frequently lasts from two to four days, causing frequent general flooding on all streams.

Snow seldom remains on the ground more than two days in the valleys. However, at higher elevations surrounding the airport, roads are frequently blocked for several days during the winter months.

Huntington Tri-State Airport *Wayne County* Elevation: 830 ft. Latitude: 38° 23' N Longitude: 82° 33' W

	JAN	FEB	MAR	APR	MAY	JUN	JUL	AUG	SEP	OCT	NOV	DEC	YEAR
Mean Maximum Temp. (°F)	41.1	46.0	56.2	67.2	75.2	82.4	86.0	84.8	78.3	67.3	56.0	46.2	65.6
Mean Temp. (°F)	32.9	36.8	45.9	55.6	64.0	71.8	75.9	74.6	67.9	56.3	46.6	37.9	55.5
Mean Minimum Temp. (°F)	24.6	27.5	35.5	44.0	52.7	61.2	65.8	64.4	57.4	45.2	37.1	29.5	45.4
Extreme Maximum Temp. (°F)	76	79	86	92	93	100	102	100	97	87	82	80	102
Extreme Minimum Temp. (°F)	-21	-9	-2	20	30	40	47	43	31	23	10	-13	-21
Days Maximum Temp. ≥ 90°F	0	0	0	0	1	4	9	7	2	0	0	0	23
Days Maximum Temp. ≤ 32°F	8	5	1	0	0	0	0	0	0	0	0	4	18
Days Minimum Temp. ≤ 32°F	23	19	13	4	0	0	0	0	0	3	11	19	92
Days Minimum Temp. ≤ 0°F	1	0	0	0	0	0	0	0	0	0	0	0	1
Heating Degree Days (base 65°F)	990	791	594	301	112	13	1	2	51	283	549	835	4,522
Cooling Degree Days (base 65°F)	0	0	7	26	87	232	362	310	140	21	3	1	1,189
Mean Precipitation (in.)	3.18	3.01	3.85	3.32	4.39	3.86	4.41	3.87	2.78	2.88	3.36	3.39	42.30
Maximum Precipitation (in.)	6.4	8.7	8.6	6.6	9.3	7.6	8.6	6.9	6.3	5.7	7.4	8.7	60.0
Minimum Precipitation (in.)	0.6	0.5	1.1	0.7	0.9	0.4	1.4	0.7	0.3	trace	0.7	0.3	30.0
Maximum 24-hr. Precipitation (in.)	2.5	2.7	2.6	1.9	3.7	2.8	3.1	2.9	2.2	2.7	2.5	3.0	3.7
Days With ≥ 0.1" Precipitation	8	7	8	8	8	8	8	6	6	6	7	7	87
Days With ≥ 1.0" Precipitation	0	0	1	0	1	1	1	1	1	1	1	1	9
Mean Snowfall (in.)	8.9	7.6	4.8	0.7	trace	trace	0.0	trace	0.0	trace	1.0	3.2	26.2
Maximum Snowfall (in.)	30	24	24	14	trace	0	0	0	0	2	5	13	51
Maximum 24-hr. Snowfall (in.)	10	10	21	7	trace	0	0	0	0	2	4	7	21
Days With ≥ 1.0" Snow Depth	9	7	2	0	0	0	0	0	0	0	0	3	21
Thunderstorm Days	< 1	1	3	4	6	7	9	7	3	1	1	< 1	42
Foggy Days	12	11	12	11	18	20	24	26	23	16	13	12	198
Predominant Sky Cover	OVR	OVR	OVR	OVR	OVR	OVR	OVR	OVR	OVR	OVR	OVR	OVR	OVR
Mean Relative Humidity 7am (%)	78	77	76	76	85	88	90	92	92	87	80	79	83
Mean Relative Humidity 4pm (%)	61	56	50	45	51	55	57	57	57	51	56	62	55
Mean Dewpoint (°F)	23	24	32	40	52	61	66	65	58	45	35	28	44
Prevailing Wind Direction	W	WSW	WSW	WSW	SW	SW	SW	SW	SW	ESE	SW	SW	SW
Prevailing Wind Speed (mph)	10	9	10	10	7	7	7	7	7	5	8	8	8
Maximum Wind Gust (mph)	60	53	54	56	55	56	56	49	46	39	55	62	62

Athens *Mercer County*   Elevation: 2,562 ft.   Latitude: 37° 25' N   Longitude: 81° 01' W

	JAN	FEB	MAR	APR	MAY	JUN	JUL	AUG	SEP	OCT	NOV	DEC	YEAR
Mean Maximum Temp. (°F)	42.0	46.0	55.3	65.2	73.1	78.6	82.1	81.1	75.4	66.0	55.5	46.3	63.9
Mean Temp. (°F)	32.0	35.1	43.2	52.3	60.3	67.0	70.9	69.5	63.7	53.5	44.3	36.3	52.3
Mean Minimum Temp. (°F)	22.0	24.1	30.9	39.3	47.6	55.4	59.5	57.8	52.0	40.9	33.0	26.4	40.7
Extreme Maximum Temp. (°F)	69	75	82	85	91	91	97	95	94	89	80	74	97
Extreme Minimum Temp. (°F)	-22	-12	-3	10	24	34	40	36	25	16	3	-22	-22
Days Maximum Temp. ≥ 90°F	0	0	0	0	0	0	1	1	0	0	0	0	2
Days Maximum Temp. ≤ 32°F	6	4	1	0	0	0	0	0	0	0	0	3	14
Days Minimum Temp. ≤ 32°F	25	22	17	8	2	0	0	0	0	7	15	22	118
Days Minimum Temp. ≤ 0°F	2	1	0	0	0	0	0	0	0	0	0	1	4
Heating Degree Days (base 65°F)	1,017	838	672	381	168	38	6	11	97	355	615	880	5,078
Cooling Degree Days (base 65°F)	0	0	1	7	33	114	212	159	63	5	0	0	594
Mean Precipitation (in.)	2.99	2.71	3.25	3.25	3.77	3.17	3.77	2.98	2.96	2.58	2.77	2.70	36.90
Days With ≥ 0.1" Precipitation	7	7	7	7	8	6	8	6	6	5	6	6	79
Days With ≥ 1.0" Precipitation	0	0	1	0	1	1	1	1	1	0	0	0	6
Mean Snowfall (in.)	*10.6*	*9.8*	4.3	0.9	0.0	0.0	0.0	0.0	0.0	0.1	1.2	4.8	*31.7*
Days With ≥ 1.0" Snow Depth	na	7	2	0	0	0	0	0	0	0	1	2	na

Bayard *Grant County*   Elevation: 2,372 ft.   Latitude: 39° 16' N   Longitude: 79° 22' W

	JAN	FEB	MAR	APR	MAY	JUN	JUL	AUG	SEP	OCT	NOV	DEC	YEAR
Mean Maximum Temp. (°F)	35.4	38.7	48.3	60.0	69.0	76.0	79.2	77.4	70.5	60.7	49.3	40.1	58.7
Mean Temp. (°F)	26.3	28.8	37.1	47.0	56.1	63.7	67.7	66.0	59.4	48.8	39.3	31.0	47.6
Mean Minimum Temp. (°F)	17.2	18.9	25.9	33.9	43.1	51.3	56.3	54.5	48.3	36.8	29.3	21.8	36.4
Extreme Maximum Temp. (°F)	67	69	81	88	87	90	94	94	92	80	75	68	94
Extreme Minimum Temp. (°F)	-23	-18	-13	3	23	30	33	31	24	11	-2	-20	-23
Days Maximum Temp. ≥ 90°F	0	0	0	0	0	0	1	1	0	0	0	0	2
Days Maximum Temp. ≤ 32°F	12	9	4	0	0	0	0	0	0	0	3	8	36
Days Minimum Temp. ≤ 32°F	29	25	24	14	4	0	0	0	1	12	19	26	154
Days Minimum Temp. ≤ 0°F	3	2	0	0	0	0	0	0	0	0	0	1	6
Heating Degree Days (base 65°F)	1,193	1,015	858	535	279	87	29	46	184	497	763	1,048	6,534
Cooling Degree Days (base 65°F)	0	0	0	1	11	59	135	90	23	1	0	0	320
Mean Precipitation (in.)	3.84	3.43	4.24	4.22	4.82	4.64	5.21	4.55	3.69	3.26	3.71	3.81	49.42
Days With ≥ 0.1" Precipitation	10	9	11	10	10	9	9	8	8	8	9	10	111
Days With ≥ 1.0" Precipitation	0	0	1	1	1	1	1	1	1	0	1	1	9
Mean Snowfall (in.)	26.6	21.8	17.3	4.4	trace	0.0	0.0	0.0	0.0	0.3	7.3	17.0	94.7
Days With ≥ 1.0" Snow Depth	23	21	13	2	0	0	0	0	0	0	6	14	79

Beckley Virginia Hospital *Raleigh County*   Elevation: 2,329 ft.   Latitude: 37° 46' N   Longitude: 81° 12' W

	JAN	FEB	MAR	APR	MAY	JUN	JUL	AUG	SEP	OCT	NOV	DEC	YEAR
Mean Maximum Temp. (°F)	39.8	44.5	53.4	64.3	71.8	76.7	79.6	78.6	72.5	63.2	53.3	44.3	61.8
Mean Temp. (°F)	30.0	33.5	41.3	50.6	58.7	65.3	68.9	67.8	61.7	51.3	42.2	34.4	50.5
Mean Minimum Temp. (°F)	20.1	22.4	29.3	36.8	45.6	53.9	58.2	57.0	50.8	39.4	31.0	24.3	39.1
Extreme Maximum Temp. (°F)	69	75	82	88	89	89	93	96	90	81	80	75	96
Extreme Minimum Temp. (°F)	-23	-22	-10	9	22	29	37	35	27	14	2	-22	-23
Days Maximum Temp. ≥ 90°F	0	0	0	0	0	0	1	1	0	0	0	0	2
Days Maximum Temp. ≤ 32°F	9	6	2	0	0	0	0	0	0	0	1	6	24
Days Minimum Temp. ≤ 32°F	26	23	20	11	3	0	0	0	1	9	18	24	135
Days Minimum Temp. ≤ 0°F	3	2	0	0	0	0	0	0	0	0	0	1	6
Heating Degree Days (base 65°F)	1,079	885	726	429	207	56	14	22	129	421	678	943	5,589
Cooling Degree Days (base 65°F)	0	0	0	4	19	79	157	119	36	4	0	0	418
Mean Precipitation (in.)	3.13	2.64	3.20	3.34	4.15	3.37	4.46	3.61	3.14	2.60	2.84	2.91	39.39
Days With ≥ 0.1" Precipitation	8	7	8	8	9	8	8	7	6	6	7	7	89
Days With ≥ 1.0" Precipitation	0	0	0	1	1	1	1	1	1	0	0	0	6
Mean Snowfall (in.)	11.3	*8.6*	5.6	0.7	0.0	0.0	0.0	0.0	0.0	trace	1.7	6.8	*34.7*
Days With ≥ 1.0" Snow Depth	12	9	4	1	0	0	0	0	0	0	1	7	34

Bluefield Mercer Co. Airport *Mercer County*   Elevation: 2,890 ft.   Latitude: 37° 18' N   Longitude: 81° 13' W

	JAN	FEB	MAR	APR	MAY	JUN	JUL	AUG	SEP	OCT	NOV	DEC	YEAR
Mean Maximum Temp. (°F)	39.8	43.7	52.7	63.0	70.0	75.8	79.3	78.4	72.6	63.2	53.3	44.5	61.4
Mean Temp. (°F)	31.8	35.0	43.6	53.2	60.7	67.3	71.0	70.0	64.3	54.2	45.0	36.7	52.7
Mean Minimum Temp. (°F)	23.9	26.6	34.4	43.3	51.4	58.7	62.7	61.6	55.9	45.2	36.8	28.8	44.1
Extreme Maximum Temp. (°F)	72	75	83	88	88	91	96	95	92	82	81	74	96
Extreme Minimum Temp. (°F)	-21	-9	-2	15	28	37	44	39	30	22	7	-13	-21
Days Maximum Temp. ≥ 90°F	0	0	0	0	0	0	1	1	0	0	0	0	2
Days Maximum Temp. ≤ 32°F	9	6	2	0	0	0	0	0	0	0	1	6	24
Days Minimum Temp. ≤ 32°F	24	19	14	5	0	0	0	0	0	2	11	20	95
Days Minimum Temp. ≤ 0°F	1	0	0	0	0	0	0	0	0	0	0	0	1
Heating Degree Days (base 65°F)	1,021	842	659	365	167	37	7	10	90	335	593	872	4,998
Cooling Degree Days (base 65°F)	0	0	3	15	41	123	218	181	74	10	1	0	666
Mean Precipitation (in.)	3.05	2.87	3.59	3.42	4.34	3.76	3.89	3.20	3.17	2.70	2.69	2.86	39.54
Days With ≥ 0.1" Precipitation	7	7	8	7	9	8	8	7	6	5	6	7	85
Days With ≥ 1.0" Precipitation	0	0	1	1	1	1	1	1	1	1	0	0	8
Mean Snowfall (in.)	9.1	8.4	4.3	1.8	trace	0.0	trace	trace	0.0	0.3	1.9	5.6	31.4
Days With ≥ 1.0" Snow Depth	10	10	3	1	0	0	0	0	0	0	1	6	31

Bluestone Lake *Summers County*   Elevation: 1,387 ft.   Latitude: 37° 38' N   Longitude: 80° 53' W

	JAN	FEB	MAR	APR	MAY	JUN	JUL	AUG	SEP	OCT	NOV	DEC	YEAR
Mean Maximum Temp. (°F)	40.4	45.2	54.6	65.6	73.8	80.6	84.5	83.2	77.0	66.3	55.0	44.4	64.2
Mean Temp. (°F)	31.4	34.8	43.0	52.4	61.0	69.1	73.5	72.5	66.2	54.5	44.2	35.2	53.2
Mean Minimum Temp. (°F)	22.4	24.3	31.3	39.2	48.3	57.6	62.5	61.7	55.4	42.6	33.4	26.0	42.1
Extreme Maximum Temp. (°F)	72	77	85	88	90	96	98	99	96	86	80	75	99
Extreme Minimum Temp. (°F)	-17	-13	0	20	28	37	45	41	31	24	10	-9	-17
Days Maximum Temp. ≥ 90°F	0	0	0	0	0	1	5	3	1	0	0	0	10
Days Maximum Temp. ≤ 32°F	7	4	1	0	0	0	0	0	0	0	0	4	16
Days Minimum Temp. ≤ 32°F	25	23	18	7	1	0	0	0	0	4	15	23	116
Days Minimum Temp. ≤ 0°F	1	0	0	0	0	0	0	0	0	0	0	0	1
Heating Degree Days (base 65°F)	1,035	848	675	376	157	26	2	3	63	327	617	916	5,045
Cooling Degree Days (base 65°F)	0	0	1	6	44	163	291	239	99	9	0	0	852
Mean Precipitation (in.)	3.00	2.68	3.41	3.27	3.90	3.34	4.03	3.28	2.75	2.70	2.53	2.60	37.49
Days With ≥ 0.1" Precipitation	7	6	8	7	9	8	8	7	6	6	6	6	84
Days With ≥ 1.0" Precipitation	0	0	1	1	1	1	1	1	1	1	0	0	8
Mean Snowfall (in.)	7.6	5.7	3.2	0.4	trace	0.0	0.0	0.0	0.0	trace	0.7	3.5	21.1
Days With ≥ 1.0" Snow Depth	8	6	2	0	0	0	0	0	0	0	0	3	19

Buckeye *Pocahontas County*   Elevation: 2,148 ft.   Latitude: 38° 11' N   Longitude: 80° 08' W

	JAN	FEB	MAR	APR	MAY	JUN	JUL	AUG	SEP	OCT	NOV	DEC	YEAR
Mean Maximum Temp. (°F)	37.0	42.5	52.0	63.0	71.8	78.7	82.0	80.6	74.7	64.3	51.9	41.8	61.7
Mean Temp. (°F)	26.6	30.8	39.0	48.5	57.8	65.8	70.0	68.6	62.5	50.8	40.1	31.4	49.3
Mean Minimum Temp. (°F)	16.1	19.1	25.9	34.0	43.8	52.9	57.8	56.5	50.3	37.2	28.2	21.0	36.9
Extreme Maximum Temp. (°F)	68	72	82	91	95	92	96	95	93	83	77	72	96
Extreme Minimum Temp. (°F)	-26	-17	-9	9	18	29	41	38	27	*14*	-7	-19	*-26*
Days Maximum Temp. ≥ 90°F	0	0	0	0	0	0	2	1	0	0	0	0	3
Days Maximum Temp. ≤ 32°F	10	5	2	0	0	0	0	0	0	0	1	6	24
Days Minimum Temp. ≤ 32°F	29	25	24	13	4	0	0	0	1	11	21	27	155
Days Minimum Temp. ≤ 0°F	4	2	0	0	0	0	0	0	0	0	0	2	8
Heating Degree Days (base 65°F)	1,186	960	800	488	234	55	11	17	117	436	742	1,034	6,080
Cooling Degree Days (base 65°F)	0	0	0	1	19	91	183	139	47	4	0	0	484
Mean Precipitation (in.)	3.92	3.30	4.42	3.54	4.35	3.67	4.58	3.82	3.20	3.43	3.61	3.84	45.68
Days With ≥ 0.1" Precipitation	8	7	9	8	9	8	9	7	6	6	7	8	92
Days With ≥ 1.0" Precipitation	1	1	1	1	1	1	1	1	1	1	1	1	12
Mean Snowfall (in.)	12.4	9.1	8.0	2.3	trace	0.0	0.0	0.0	trace	0.2	2.1	7.1	41.2
Days With ≥ 1.0" Snow Depth	15	13	5	1	0	0	0	0	0	0	2	8	44

Buckhannon *Upshur County*   Elevation: 1,453 ft.   Latitude: 38° 59' N   Longitude: 80° 13' W

	JAN	FEB	MAR	APR	MAY	JUN	JUL	AUG	SEP	OCT	NOV	DEC	YEAR
Mean Maximum Temp. (°F)	39.5	44.0	53.7	64.7	73.8	80.4	83.4	82.3	76.7	66.3	54.5	45.6	63.7
Mean Temp. (°F)	29.6	32.7	41.4	50.8	60.0	67.7	71.7	70.2	64.3	52.9	43.2	35.6	51.7
Mean Minimum Temp. (°F)	19.6	21.4	29.1	36.8	46.3	54.9	59.9	58.0	51.6	39.6	31.8	25.6	39.6
Extreme Maximum Temp. (°F)	71	74	84	90	90	95	96	96	95	83	80	76	96
Extreme Minimum Temp. (°F)	-30	-20	-13	12	23	29	39	37	28	15	3	-13	-30
Days Maximum Temp. ≥ 90°F	0	0	0	0	0	1	3	2	1	0	0	0	7
Days Maximum Temp. ≤ 32°F	10	6	2	0	0	0	0	0	0	0	1	5	24
Days Minimum Temp. ≤ 32°F	26	23	20	11	2	0	0	0	0	8	17	23	130
Days Minimum Temp. ≤ 0°F	3	2	0	0	0	0	0	0	0	0	0	1	6
Heating Degree Days (base 65°F)	1,092	907	725	425	181	38	6	11	92	371	648	904	5,400
Cooling Degree Days (base 65°F)	0	0	0	5	34	131	235	*178*	*69*	5	0	0	*657*
Mean Precipitation (in.)	3.82	3.25	4.36	3.80	4.50	4.79	4.84	4.48	3.86	3.20	3.83	4.16	48.89
Days With ≥ 0.1" Precipitation	9	8	9	9	9	9	9	8	7	7	8	10	102
Days With ≥ 1.0" Precipitation	0	0	1	1	1	1	1	1	1	1	1	1	10
Mean Snowfall (in.)	17.9	12.4	8.1	1.4	trace	0.0	0.0	0.0	0.0	0.1	3.4	8.4	51.7
Days With ≥ 1.0" Snow Depth	15	11	5	0	0	0	0	0	0	0	2	6	39

Cacapon State Park 2 *Morgan County*   Elevation: 948 ft.   Latitude: 39° 30' N   Longitude: 78° 18' W

	JAN	FEB	MAR	APR	MAY	JUN	JUL	AUG	SEP	OCT	NOV	DEC	YEAR
Mean Maximum Temp. (°F)	38.1	42.5	51.4	63.2	72.6	*80.9*	85.4	*83.5*	76.2	65.0	54.2	42.9	*63.0*
Mean Temp. (°F)	29.1	32.8	40.7	51.7	61.2	*69.4*	74.1	*72.0*	64.6	53.1	44.1	33.9	*52.2*
Mean Minimum Temp. (°F)	20.1	22.9	30.1	40.1	49.8	*57.8*	62.8	*60.5*	52.9	41.1	34.0	24.8	*41.4*
Extreme Maximum Temp. (°F)	*73*	80	88	94	97	*98*	104	*101*	97	92	84	75	*104*
Extreme Minimum Temp. (°F)	*-26*	-6	0	*17*	*29*	*37*	*44*	36	28	23	4	-8	*-26*
Days Maximum Temp. ≥ 90°F	0	0	0	0	1	*4*	8	*5*	2	0	0	0	*20*
Days Maximum Temp. ≤ 32°F	10	6	2	0	0	*0*	0	*0*	0	0	0	5	*23*
Days Minimum Temp. ≤ 32°F	28	23	19	*6*	0	*0*	0	*0*	0	5	*14*	25	*120*
Days Minimum Temp. ≤ 0°F	2	1	0	0	0	*0*	0	*0*	0	0	0	0	*3*
Heating Degree Days (base 65°F)	1,106	904	749	407	169	*34*	4	*12*	94	370	621	958	*5,428*
Cooling Degree Days (base 65°F)	0	0	3	11	56	181	304	232	91	10	0	0	888
Mean Precipitation (in.)	2.77	2.20	3.18	3.08	3.88	*3.64*	4.16	*3.56*	3.40	3.43	3.03	2.50	*38.83*
Days With ≥ 0.1" Precipitation	*6*	5	7	6	8	*7*	7	*6*	6	5	6	5	*74*
Days With ≥ 1.0" Precipitation	0	0	1	1	1	*1*	1	*1*	1	1	1	0	*9*
Mean Snowfall (in.)	na	*7.3*	*5.1*	0.2	0.0	*0.0*	0.0	*0.0*	0.0	0.0	0.9	*2.2*	na
Days With ≥ 1.0" Snow Depth	*9*	*8*	*4*	0	0	*0*	0	*0*	0	0	1	*3*	25

Canaan Valley *Tucker County*   Elevation: 3,248 ft.   Latitude: 39° 03' N   Longitude: 79° 25' W

	JAN	FEB	MAR	APR	MAY	JUN	JUL	AUG	SEP	OCT	NOV	DEC	YEAR
Mean Maximum Temp. (°F)	35.1	38.5	47.8	58.4	67.5	74.3	77.7	76.6	70.6	60.7	49.6	40.1	58.1
Mean Temp. (°F)	25.5	28.3	36.6	46.0	55.0	61.9	65.9	64.4	58.6	48.5	39.2	30.5	46.7
Mean Minimum Temp. (°F)	15.9	18.1	25.3	33.5	42.4	49.4	54.1	52.3	46.5	36.3	28.8	20.8	35.3
Extreme Maximum Temp. (°F)	64	66	77	83	84	86	96	97	86	80	73	68	97
Extreme Minimum Temp. (°F)	-27	-23	-10	-2	20	24	27	25	18	7	-5	-21	-27
Days Maximum Temp. ≥ 90°F	0	0	0	0	0	0	0	0	0	0	0	0	0
Days Maximum Temp. ≤ 32°F	12	9	4	1	0	0	0	0	0	0	2	8	36
Days Minimum Temp. ≤ 32°F	28	24	23	15	5	1	0	0	3	12	20	26	157
Days Minimum Temp. ≤ 0°F	4	3	1	0	0	0	0	0	0	0	0	2	10
Heating Degree Days (base 65°F)	1,217	1,029	875	565	310	120	47	66	203	504	766	1,062	6,764
Cooling Degree Days (base 65°F)	0	0	0	1	8	36	95	63	18	1	0	0	222
Mean Precipitation (in.)	4.08	3.66	4.46	4.07	5.03	4.88	5.02	4.70	3.86	3.67	4.15	4.13	51.71
Days With ≥ 0.1" Precipitation	11	9	11	10	11	10	10	9	8	8	10	10	117
Days With ≥ 1.0" Precipitation	0	0	1	0	1	1	1	1	1	1	1	0	8
Mean Snowfall (in.)	34.7	28.2	23.1	10.3	0.2	0.0	0.0	0.0	trace	2.3	13.0	23.0	134.8
Days With ≥ 1.0" Snow Depth	22	na	na	3	0	0	0	0	0	0	6	na	na

Clarksburg 1 *Harrison County*   Elevation: 987 ft.   Latitude: 39° 16' N   Longitude: 80° 21' W

	JAN	FEB	MAR	APR	MAY	JUN	JUL	AUG	SEP	OCT	NOV	DEC	YEAR
Mean Maximum Temp. (°F)	38.9	42.8	52.9	64.2	73.5	81.4	84.4	82.9	76.5	65.4	53.9	43.8	63.4
Mean Temp. (°F)	29.8	32.4	41.1	50.8	60.4	69.0	73.0	71.7	65.1	53.1	43.2	34.8	52.0
Mean Minimum Temp. (°F)	20.7	22.0	29.2	37.5	47.3	56.6	61.6	60.4	53.6	40.6	32.5	25.7	40.6
Extreme Maximum Temp. (°F)	78	74	84	93	92	97	97	98	94	86	80	75	98
Extreme Minimum Temp. (°F)	-24	-11	-6	18	26	35	47	40	32	21	9	-11	-24
Days Maximum Temp. ≥ 90°F	0	0	0	0	0	2	6	3	1	0	0	0	12
Days Maximum Temp. ≤ 32°F	9	6	2	0	0	0	0	0	0	0	1	5	23
Days Minimum Temp. ≤ 32°F	26	23	21	9	1	0	0	0	0	6	16	23	125
Days Minimum Temp. ≤ 0°F	2	1	0	0	0	0	0	0	0	0	0	0	3
Heating Degree Days (base 65°F)	1,084	913	735	425	180	31	4	7	84	370	648	930	5,411
Cooling Degree Days (base 65°F)	0	0	1	7	45	168	281	225	89	7	0	0	823
Mean Precipitation (in.)	3.48	2.96	4.13	3.47	4.47	4.19	4.37	4.46	3.28	3.06	3.74	3.46	45.07
Days With ≥ 0.1" Precipitation	8	8	9	9	9	9	8	8	7	7	8	8	98
Days With ≥ 1.0" Precipitation	1	0	1	0	1	1	1	1	1	1	0	1	9
Mean Snowfall (in.)	11.6	7.3	3.9	0.3	trace	0.0	0.0	0.0	0.0	trace	0.7	3.5	27.3
Days With ≥ 1.0" Snow Depth	14	9	3	0	0	0	0	0	0	0	1	5	32

Creston *Wirt County*   Elevation: 649 ft.   Latitude: 38° 57' N   Longitude: 81° 16' W

	JAN	FEB	MAR	APR	MAY	JUN	JUL	AUG	SEP	OCT	NOV	DEC	YEAR
Mean Maximum Temp. (°F)	40.5	45.3	55.5	67.0	76.1	83.3	86.8	85.4	79.2	68.0	56.5	45.8	65.8
Mean Temp. (°F)	29.9	33.2	41.9	51.6	61.3	69.6	74.2	72.9	66.1	53.7	43.8	34.9	52.7
Mean Minimum Temp. (°F)	19.2	21.1	28.2	36.2	46.5	55.8	61.5	60.3	53.0	39.3	31.1	23.9	39.7
Extreme Maximum Temp. (°F)	76	78	90	95	96	103	106	105	95	90	85	80	106
Extreme Minimum Temp. (°F)	-30	-20	-6	15	21	33	42	41	29	18	3	-19	-30
Days Maximum Temp. ≥ 90°F	0	0	0	0	2	5	11	7	2	0	0	0	27
Days Maximum Temp. ≤ 32°F	8	5	1	0	0	0	0	0	0	0	0	4	18
Days Minimum Temp. ≤ 32°F	27	24	22	12	2	0	0	0	0	8	18	24	137
Days Minimum Temp. ≤ 0°F	3	2	0	0	0	0	0	0	0	0	0	1	6
Heating Degree Days (base 65°F)	1,082	892	712	405	164	29	3	5	73	356	631	928	5,280
Cooling Degree Days (base 65°F)	0	0	1	10	61	192	324	269	116	14	1	0	988
Mean Precipitation (in.)	3.62	3.15	4.03	3.35	4.50	4.30	4.85	4.18	3.50	3.23	3.58	3.68	45.97
Days With ≥ 0.1" Precipitation	9	8	9	8	9	8	8	7	6	7	8	8	95
Days With ≥ 1.0" Precipitation	1	0	1	1	1	1	1	1	1	1	1	1	11
Mean Snowfall (in.)	7.7	5.0	3.4	0.4	0.0	0.0	0.0	0.0	0.0	trace	0.6	na	na
Days With ≥ 1.0" Snow Depth	9	6	2	0	0	0	0	0	0	0	0	2	19

Dunlow 1 SW *Wayne County*   Elevation: 1,197 ft.   Latitude: 37° 57' N   Longitude: 82° 24' W

	JAN	FEB	MAR	APR	MAY	JUN	JUL	AUG	SEP	OCT	NOV	DEC	YEAR
Mean Maximum Temp. (°F)	41.8	46.4	56.4	67.0	74.1	80.6	84.2	82.6	76.7	66.4	56.0	45.8	64.8
Mean Temp. (°F)	32.8	36.2	45.0	54.6	62.2	69.7	73.7	72.2	65.7	54.8	45.8	36.5	54.1
Mean Minimum Temp. (°F)	23.8	26.0	33.5	42.2	50.4	58.8	63.2	61.7	54.6	43.2	35.6	27.1	43.3
Extreme Maximum Temp. (°F)	73	80	87	90	90	94	100	100	97	86	82	78	100
Extreme Minimum Temp. (°F)	-20	-10	2	11	26	36	43	33	27	19	1	-15	-20
Days Maximum Temp. ≥ 90°F	0	0	0	0	0	1	4	3	1	0	0	0	9
Days Maximum Temp. ≤ 32°F	7	4	1	0	0	0	0	0	0	0	0	5	17
Days Minimum Temp. ≤ 32°F	24	19	16	6	1	0	0	0	0	4	13	21	104
Days Minimum Temp. ≤ 0°F	1	1	0	0	0	0	0	0	0	0	0	1	3
Heating Degree Days (base 65°F)	992	807	619	330	140	25	2	7	79	324	569	880	4,774
Cooling Degree Days (base 65°F)	0	0	4	21	57	171	281	221	93	12	1	1	862
Mean Precipitation (in.)	3.42	3.25	3.98	3.78	4.95	4.12	4.65	3.81	3.41	3.11	3.82	3.64	45.94
Days With ≥ 0.1" Precipitation	8	7	9	8	10	7	8	6	6	6	8	7	90
Days With ≥ 1.0" Precipitation	0	1	1	1	1	1	1	1	1	1	1	0	10
Mean Snowfall (in.)	7.8	4.8	3.0	0.7	0.0	0.0	0.0	0.0	0.0	trace	0.8	3.1	20.2
Days With ≥ 1.0" Snow Depth	na	6	2	0	0	0	0	0	0	0	0	3	na

Fairmont *Marion County*   Elevation: 1,299 ft.   Latitude: 39° 28' N   Longitude: 80° 08' W

	JAN	FEB	MAR	APR	MAY	JUN	JUL	AUG	SEP	OCT	NOV	DEC	YEAR
Mean Maximum Temp. (°F)	37.9	42.2	52.6	64.1	72.7	80.1	83.5	82.3	75.8	64.6	53.1	42.8	62.6
Mean Temp. (°F)	29.3	32.4	41.5	51.6	60.6	68.3	72.4	71.1	64.6	53.1	43.4	34.3	51.9
Mean Minimum Temp. (°F)	20.6	22.5	30.4	39.0	48.4	56.6	61.2	59.8	53.3	41.5	33.7	25.7	41.1
Extreme Maximum Temp. (°F)	73	75	84	92	90	94	100	98	95	84	81	74	100
Extreme Minimum Temp. (°F)	-21	-8	-1	16	25	35	42	36	29	17	6	-16	-21
Days Maximum Temp. ≥ 90°F	0	0	0	0	0	1	5	3	1	0	0	0	10
Days Maximum Temp. ≤ 32°F	11	7	2	0	0	0	0	0	0	0	1	6	27
Days Minimum Temp. ≤ 32°F	26	23	19	8	1	0	0	0	0	5	15	24	121
Days Minimum Temp. ≤ 0°F	2	1	0	0	0	0	0	0	0	0	0	1	4
Heating Degree Days (base 65°F)	1,101	915	724	408	177	36	4	9	91	371	642	945	5,423
Cooling Degree Days (base 65°F)	0	0	3	10	44	142	249	201	78	7	1	0	735
Mean Precipitation (in.)	3.46	2.82	4.14	3.58	4.75	4.23	4.94	4.24	3.47	3.10	3.68	3.40	45.81
Days With ≥ 0.1" Precipitation	8	7	8	8	9	9	8	8	7	7	8	8	95
Days With ≥ 1.0" Precipitation	1	0	1	0	1	1	1	1	0	1	1	0	8
Mean Snowfall (in.)	13.3	9.2	6.5	1.2	0.0	0.0	0.0	0.0	0.0	trace	2.2	5.3	37.7
Days With ≥ 1.0" Snow Depth	12	9	4	0	0	0	0	0	0	0	2	6	33

Flat Top *Summers County*   Elevation: 3,234 ft.   Latitude: 37° 35' N   Longitude: 81° 07' W

	JAN	FEB	MAR	APR	MAY	JUN	JUL	AUG	SEP	OCT	NOV	DEC	YEAR
Mean Maximum Temp. (°F)	35.2	38.9	47.6	58.3	66.2	73.1	76.8	75.8	70.0	60.0	49.0	39.8	57.6
Mean Temp. (°F)	27.2	30.2	38.4	48.3	56.8	64.5	68.6	67.4	61.5	50.8	40.6	31.8	48.8
Mean Minimum Temp. (°F)	19.1	21.5	29.0	38.2	47.4	55.8	60.2	58.9	52.9	41.6	32.3	23.9	40.1
Extreme Maximum Temp. (°F)	67	69	79	81	87	89	92	90	90	79	78	72	92
Extreme Minimum Temp. (°F)	-28	-12	-5	10	23	33	44	38	30	18	1	-21	-28
Days Maximum Temp. ≥ 90°F	0	0	0	0	0	0	0	0	0	0	0	0	0
Days Maximum Temp. ≤ 32°F	13	9	5	1	0	0	0	0	0	0	3	9	40
Days Minimum Temp. ≤ 32°F	27	23	20	10	1	0	0	0	0	6	16	24	127
Days Minimum Temp. ≤ 0°F	3	2	0	0	0	0	0	0	0	0	0	1	6
Heating Degree Days (base 65°F)	1,165	976	817	499	261	74	20	27	140	435	724	1,021	6,159
Cooling Degree Days (base 65°F)	0	0	0	4	16	76	159	118	43	3	0	0	419
Mean Precipitation (in.)	3.79	3.37	4.19	3.99	4.88	3.94	4.62	3.72	3.38	3.32	3.09	3.48	45.77
Days With ≥ 0.1" Precipitation	8	8	9	9	10	8	8	7	7	7	7	8	96
Days With ≥ 1.0" Precipitation	1	1	1	1	1	1	1	1	1	1	0	1	11
Mean Snowfall (in.)	18.4	16.7	9.9	2.8	trace	0.0	0.0	0.0	0.0	0.7	3.7	11.2	63.4
Days With ≥ 1.0" Snow Depth	16	15	7	2	0	0	0	0	0	0	3	10	53

Franklin 2 NE *Pendleton County*   Elevation: 1,899 ft.   Latitude: 38° 40' N   Longitude: 79° 19' W

	JAN	FEB	MAR	APR	MAY	JUN	JUL	AUG	SEP	OCT	NOV	DEC	YEAR
Mean Maximum Temp. (°F)	42.5	46.0	54.9	65.2	73.5	80.0	83.8	82.4	76.3	66.8	55.7	46.6	64.5
Mean Temp. (°F)	31.5	34.1	42.0	51.1	59.8	66.9	71.0	69.5	63.3	52.9	43.5	35.5	51.8
Mean Minimum Temp. (°F)	20.4	22.3	29.2	37.0	46.0	53.7	58.2	56.6	50.3	39.0	31.2	24.4	39.0
Extreme Maximum Temp. (°F)	71	74	87	89	95	94	101	98	95	86	81	76	101
Extreme Minimum Temp. (°F)	-20	-16	-5	11	25	29	34	33	26	14	5	-16	-20
Days Maximum Temp. ≥ 90°F	0	0	0	0	0	1	4	3	1	0	0	0	9
Days Maximum Temp. ≤ 32°F	6	4	1	0	0	0	0	0	0	0	0	3	14
Days Minimum Temp. ≤ 32°F	27	24	21	10	2	0	0	0	1	9	17	25	136
Days Minimum Temp. ≤ 0°F	2	1	0	0	0	0	0	0	0	0	0	1	4
Heating Degree Days (base 65°F)	1,033	865	706	413	183	43	8	15	106	371	639	908	5,290
Cooling Degree Days (base 65°F)	0	0	1	3	29	115	218	165	59	4	0	0	594
Mean Precipitation (in.)	2.43	1.91	2.97	2.71	3.70	3.18	4.05	3.56	3.08	2.85	2.77	2.17	35.38
Days With ≥ 0.1" Precipitation	6	5	7	6	7	7	8	7	5	5	5	5	73
Days With ≥ 1.0" Precipitation	0	0	1	0	1	1	1	1	1	1	0	0	7
Mean Snowfall (in.)	8.6	7.3	4.3	1.0	0.0	0.0	0.0	0.0	0.0	0.3	1.9	5.2	28.6
Days With ≥ 1.0" Snow Depth	na	na	na	0	0	0	0	0	0	0	0	na	na

Gassaway *Braxton County*   Elevation: 839 ft.   Latitude: 38° 40' N   Longitude: 80° 46' W

	JAN	FEB	MAR	APR	MAY	JUN	JUL	AUG	SEP	OCT	NOV	DEC	YEAR
Mean Maximum Temp. (°F)	43.4	48.0	58.5	69.2	77.1	82.9	86.2	84.6	78.8	69.3	58.4	47.8	67.0
Mean Temp. (°F)	33.0	36.1	44.9	54.1	62.8	70.1	74.3	72.9	66.8	55.8	46.0	37.2	54.5
Mean Minimum Temp. (°F)	22.6	24.1	31.4	39.0	48.6	57.4	62.5	61.2	54.8	42.3	33.5	26.5	42.0
Extreme Maximum Temp. (°F)	76	78	88	91	95	97	102	98	95	87	83	76	102
Extreme Minimum Temp. (°F)	-22	-14	-3	17	26	35	40	40	34	18	8	-10	-22
Days Maximum Temp. ≥ 90°F	0	0	0	0	1	3	8	6	1	0	0	0	19
Days Maximum Temp. ≤ 32°F	6	3	1	0	0	0	0	0	0	0	0	3	13
Days Minimum Temp. ≤ 32°F	25	22	17	8	1	0	0	0	0	0	14	22	114
Days Minimum Temp. ≤ 0°F	2	1	0	0	0	0	0	0	0	5	0	0	3
Heating Degree Days (base 65°F)	984	811	618	331	122	18	1	2	53	293	564	856	4,653
Cooling Degree Days (base 65°F)	0	0	2	12	65	187	317	262	110	18	0	0	973
Mean Precipitation (in.)	3.48	3.35	4.26	3.75	4.45	4.75	5.45	4.67	3.85	3.19	3.96	3.90	49.06
Days With ≥ 0.1" Precipitation	9	8	10	9	10	9	9	8	7	7	8	9	103
Days With ≥ 1.0" Precipitation	0	0	1	1	1	1	1	1	1	1	1	1	10
Mean Snowfall (in.)	8.0	5.8	3.4	0.6	0.0	0.0	0.0	0.0	0.0	trace	0.9	3.4	22.1
Days With ≥ 1.0" Snow Depth	8	6	2	0	0	0	0	0	0	0	0	1	4	21

Glenville 1 ENE *Gilmer County*   Elevation: 708 ft.   Latitude: 38° 56' N   Longitude: 80° 50' W

	JAN	FEB	MAR	APR	MAY	JUN	JUL	AUG	SEP	OCT	NOV	DEC	YEAR
Mean Maximum Temp. (°F)	41.1	45.5	55.1	66.2	75.2	82.3	85.8	84.7	78.8	67.9	56.3	46.2	65.4
Mean Temp. (°F)	30.3	33.4	41.8	51.6	61.1	69.2	73.7	72.5	65.8	53.7	43.6	35.5	52.7
Mean Minimum Temp. (°F)	19.5	21.2	28.5	36.9	46.7	56.1	61.6	60.3	52.8	39.4	30.8	24.7	39.9
Extreme Maximum Temp. (°F)	76	78	87	91	94	99	104	101	97	87	85	79	104
Extreme Minimum Temp. (°F)	-25	-19	-10	15	23	31	40	41	30	16	3	-14	-25
Days Maximum Temp. ≥ 90°F	0	0	0	0	1	3	8	6	2	0	0	0	20
Days Maximum Temp. ≤ 32°F	8	4	1	0	0	0	0	0	0	0	0	4	17
Days Minimum Temp. ≤ 32°F	26	23	21	11	2	0	0	0	0	8	18	23	132
Days Minimum Temp. ≤ 0°F	3	2	0	0	0	0	0	0	0	0	0	1	6
Heating Degree Days (base 65°F)	1,069	888	713	405	164	30	3	5	72	353	636	908	5,246
Cooling Degree Days (base 65°F)	0	0	1	8	53	174	302	256	104	11	0	0	909
Mean Precipitation (in.)	3.33	3.00	4.18	3.66	4.30	4.04	5.25	4.26	3.36	3.14	3.83	3.46	45.81
Days With ≥ 0.1" Precipitation	8	7	9	9	8	8	8	7	6	6	8	8	92
Days With ≥ 1.0" Precipitation	0	0	1	0	1	1	1	1	1	1	1	0	8
Mean Snowfall (in.)	9.0	5.2	4.6	0.6	trace	0.0	0.0	0.0	0.0	trace	0.9	3.2	23.5
Days With ≥ 1.0" Snow Depth	9	6	3	0	0	0	0	0	0	0	1	3	22

Hamlin *Lincoln County*   Elevation: 639 ft.   Latitude: 38° 17' N   Longitude: 82° 06' W

	JAN	FEB	MAR	APR	MAY	JUN	JUL	AUG	SEP	OCT	NOV	DEC	YEAR
Mean Maximum Temp. (°F)	42.4	46.8	56.7	67.4	76.1	83.1	86.9	85.5	79.5	68.8	57.7	47.9	66.6
Mean Temp. (°F)	31.6	34.7	43.5	52.8	62.2	70.1	74.7	73.2	66.4	54.2	44.7	36.5	53.7
Mean Minimum Temp. (°F)	20.5	22.6	30.4	38.3	48.2	57.1	62.4	60.8	53.0	39.2	31.4	24.9	40.7
Extreme Maximum Temp. (°F)	78	80	89	92	94	99	103	101	100	88	85	82	103
Extreme Minimum Temp. (°F)	-28	-19	-8	15	27	34	40	40	31	18	7	-17	-28
Days Maximum Temp. ≥ 90°F	0	0	0	0	1	5	11	8	2	0	0	0	27
Days Maximum Temp. ≤ 32°F	7	4	1	0	0	0	0	0	0	0	0	3	15
Days Minimum Temp. ≤ 32°F	26	23	19	10	1	0	0	0	0	9	17	23	128
Days Minimum Temp. ≤ 0°F	2	1	0	0	0	0	0	0	0	0	0	1	4
Heating Degree Days (base 65°F)	1,028	848	660	371	147	26	2	4	69	340	603	875	4,973
Cooling Degree Days (base 65°F)	0	0	2	12	71	195	330	271	114	12	0	0	1,007
Mean Precipitation (in.)	3.19	3.15	3.87	3.42	4.46	3.98	4.72	4.24	3.28	3.07	3.56	3.55	44.49
Days With ≥ 0.1" Precipitation	7	7	9	8	9	8	8	7	6	6	7	7	89
Days With ≥ 1.0" Precipitation	0	0	1	0	1	1	1	1	1	1	1	0	8
Mean Snowfall (in.)	8.3	7.1	3.6	0.7	trace	0.0	0.0	0.0	0.0	trace	0.6	3.4	23.7
Days With ≥ 1.0" Snow Depth	9	7	2	0	0	0	0	0	0	0	0	3	21

Hogsett R.C. Byrd Dam *Mason County*   Elevation: 567 ft.   Latitude: 38° 41' N   Longitude: 82° 11' W

	JAN	FEB	MAR	APR	MAY	JUN	JUL	AUG	SEP	OCT	NOV	DEC	YEAR
Mean Maximum Temp. (°F)	40.6	44.7	54.8	66.2	74.9	82.5	86.7	85.2	79.0	67.9	56.3	46.0	65.4
Mean Temp. (°F)	30.8	33.9	42.7	52.6	61.9	70.2	74.7	73.4	66.8	55.2	45.1	36.0	53.6
Mean Minimum Temp. (°F)	20.9	22.9	30.5	38.9	48.8	57.9	62.7	61.5	54.5	42.4	33.5	25.9	41.7
Extreme Maximum Temp. (°F)	75	77	88	91	93	100	102	102	97	86	81	78	102
Extreme Minimum Temp. (°F)	-24	-12	-6	15	28	31	45	41	34	17	11	-15	-24
Days Maximum Temp. ≥ 90°F	0	0	0	0	1	4	10	7	2	0	0	0	24
Days Maximum Temp. ≤ 32°F	8	5	1	0	0	0	0	0	0	0	0	4	18
Days Minimum Temp. ≤ 32°F	26	23	20	7	1	0	0	0	0	4	15	23	119
Days Minimum Temp. ≤ 0°F	2	1	0	0	0	0	0	0	0	0	0	0	3
Heating Degree Days (base 65°F)	1,055	874	685	376	149	23	1	3	60	311	592	892	5,021
Cooling Degree Days (base 65°F)	0	0	2	11	60	195	332	278	119	15	1	0	1,013
Mean Precipitation (in.)	3.10	2.90	3.70	3.24	3.94	3.64	4.46	3.82	2.92	2.85	3.14	3.22	40.93
Days With ≥ 0.1" Precipitation	7	7	8	8	8	7	8	7	6	6	7	7	86
Days With ≥ 1.0" Precipitation	0	0	1	0	1	1	1	1	1	1	1	1	9
Mean Snowfall (in.)	na	na	na	trace	0.0	0.0	0.0	0.0	0.0	trace	trace	1.4	na
Days With ≥ 1.0" Snow Depth	9	6	2	0	0	0	0	0	0	0	0	1	18

Kearneysville *Jefferson County*   Elevation: 547 ft.   Latitude: 39° 23' N   Longitude: 77° 53' W

	JAN	FEB	MAR	APR	MAY	JUN	JUL	AUG	SEP	OCT	NOV	DEC	YEAR
Mean Maximum Temp. (°F)	38.7	42.6	52.3	63.5	73.0	81.2	85.6	83.9	77.4	65.7	55.2	43.9	63.6
Mean Temp. (°F)	29.3	32.3	41.2	51.3	60.7	69.0	73.6	71.7	64.8	52.7	44.1	34.4	52.1
Mean Minimum Temp. (°F)	19.8	21.9	30.0	39.0	48.5	56.8	61.6	59.4	52.1	39.6	33.0	24.9	40.6
Extreme Maximum Temp. (°F)	75	80	86	91	92	98	105	103	98	93	84	77	105
Extreme Minimum Temp. (°F)	-21	-10	-1	18	28	34	40	35	27	15	7	-4	-21
Days Maximum Temp. ≥ 90°F	0	0	0	0	1	3	8	5	2	0	0	0	19
Days Maximum Temp. ≤ 32°F	9	6	1	0	0	0	0	0	0	0	0	4	20
Days Minimum Temp. ≤ 32°F	28	24	20	8	1	0	0	0	0	8	15	25	129
Days Minimum Temp. ≤ 0°F	2	0	0	0	0	0	0	0	0	0	0	0	2
Heating Degree Days (base 65°F)	1,101	917	734	414	176	34	4	12	96	382	620	942	5,432
Cooling Degree Days (base 65°F)	0	0	2	9	54	172	306	223	93	9	1	0	869
Mean Precipitation (in.)	2.67	2.54	3.22	3.44	4.21	3.79	3.96	3.46	3.21	3.58	3.25	3.03	40.36
Days With ≥ 0.1" Precipitation	6	6	7	7	8	7	7	6	5	6	6	6	77
Days With ≥ 1.0" Precipitation	0	0	0	1	1	1	1	1	1	1	1	1	9
Mean Snowfall (in.)	7.3	6.3	3.1	0.5	0.0	0.0	0.0	0.0	0.0	trace	0.5	2.1	19.8
Days With ≥ 1.0" Snow Depth	10	7	2	0	0	0	0	0	0	0	1	na	na

Kopperston *Wyoming County* Elevation: 1,660 ft. Latitude: 37° 44' N Longitude: 81° 35' W

	JAN	FEB	MAR	APR	MAY	JUN	JUL	AUG	SEP	OCT	NOV	DEC	YEAR
Mean Maximum Temp. (°F)	39.9	45.0	56.0	66.7	74.5	80.2	83.3	81.8	74.9	64.1	54.3	44.4	63.8
Mean Temp. (°F)	31.0	34.6	44.1	52.9	61.2	67.7	71.6	70.4	64.1	52.6	44.0	35.3	52.4
Mean Minimum Temp. (°F)	22.1	24.1	32.2	39.1	47.8	55.2	60.0	58.9	53.2	41.0	33.6	26.4	41.1
Extreme Maximum Temp. (°F)	71	75	84	89	90	95	98	97	92	81	78	74	98
Extreme Minimum Temp. (°F)	-19	-8	-6	15	27	32	41	39	28	20	6	-15	-19
Days Maximum Temp. ≥ 90°F	0	0	0	0	0	1	2	2	0	0	0	0	5
Days Maximum Temp. ≤ 32°F	7	5	1	0	0	0	0	0	0	0	1	4	18
Days Minimum Temp. ≤ 32°F	26	22	17	8	1	0	0	0	0	7	15	22	118
Days Minimum Temp. ≤ 0°F	2	0	0	0	0	0	0	0	0	0	0	1	3
Heating Degree Days (base 65°F)	1,046	853	641	363	148	30	3	7	93	382	624	915	5,105
Cooling Degree Days (base 65°F)	0	0	1	7	34	116	222	173	64	4	0	na	na
Mean Precipitation (in.)	3.90	3.64	4.67	4.39	5.04	4.38	5.17	4.51	3.61	3.52	3.76	4.40	50.99
Days With ≥ 0.1" Precipitation	9	9	10	9	10	8	9	8	6	7	8	9	102
Days With ≥ 1.0" Precipitation	1	1	1	1	1	1	1	1	1	1	1	1	12
Mean Snowfall (in.)	na	na	na	0.1	0.0	0.0	0.0	0.0	0.0	trace	1.4	na	na
Days With ≥ 1.0" Snow Depth	11	9	na	0	0	0	0	0	0	0	1	5	na

Lewisburg 3 N *Greenbrier County* Elevation: 2,303 ft. Latitude: 37° 51' N Longitude: 80° 24' W

	JAN	FEB	MAR	APR	MAY	JUN	JUL	AUG	SEP	OCT	NOV	DEC	YEAR
Mean Maximum Temp. (°F)	40.2	44.8	54.1	64.4	73.0	79.8	83.5	82.2	76.2	66.0	54.1	44.6	63.6
Mean Temp. (°F)	30.6	34.1	42.1	51.1	60.0	67.6	71.7	70.3	64.2	52.9	42.9	34.9	51.9
Mean Minimum Temp. (°F)	21.0	23.5	30.0	37.7	46.9	55.4	59.8	58.4	52.2	39.7	31.7	25.0	40.1
Extreme Maximum Temp. (°F)	68	75	83	91	90	95	98	97	93	88	80	75	98
Extreme Minimum Temp. (°F)	-20	-10	-6	15	25	32	41	39	27	14	6	-22	-22
Days Maximum Temp. ≥ 90°F	0	0	0	0	0	1	3	2	0	0	0	0	6
Days Maximum Temp. ≤ 32°F	7	4	1	0	0	0	0	0	0	0	1	5	18
Days Minimum Temp. ≤ 32°F	27	23	19	10	2	0	0	0	0	9	17	24	131
Days Minimum Temp. ≤ 0°F	1	1	0	0	0	0	0	0	0	0	0	1	3
Heating Degree Days (base 65°F)	1,058	865	704	416	180	39	6	9	94	378	657	927	5,333
Cooling Degree Days (base 65°F)	0	0	0	4	31	127	233	178	67	10	0	0	650
Mean Precipitation (in.)	3.21	2.91	3.68	3.41	4.13	3.73	4.13	3.58	2.80	2.92	3.05	3.19	40.74
Days With ≥ 0.1" Precipitation	7	7	8	7	8	7	8	6	5	5	6	8	82
Days With ≥ 1.0" Precipitation	0	1	1	1	1	1	1	1	1	1	1	1	11
Mean Snowfall (in.)	8.5	6.9	5.8	0.7	0.0	0.0	0.0	0.0	trace	0.2	1.4	5.0	28.5
Days With ≥ 1.0" Snow Depth	na	na	3	0	0	0	0	0	0	0	1	5	na

Logan *Logan County* Elevation: 639 ft. Latitude: 37° 52' N Longitude: 82° 00' W

	JAN	FEB	MAR	APR	MAY	JUN	JUL	AUG	SEP	OCT	NOV	DEC	YEAR
Mean Maximum Temp. (°F)	43.8	48.4	57.9	69.1	77.1	83.9	87.6	86.2	80.2	68.9	57.6	47.5	67.3
Mean Temp. (°F)	34.8	37.9	46.0	55.5	64.1	72.4	76.7	75.4	69.1	56.9	46.7	38.5	56.2
Mean Minimum Temp. (°F)	25.8	27.3	34.1	41.9	51.1	60.9	65.8	64.6	57.9	45.0	35.8	29.6	45.0
Extreme Maximum Temp. (°F)	76	80	90	94	96	98	101	100	101	88	83	78	101
Extreme Minimum Temp. (°F)	-15	-8	-2	22	30	40	46	45	36	22	11	-8	-15
Days Maximum Temp. ≥ 90°F	0	0	0	1	2	7	13	9	3	0	0	0	35
Days Maximum Temp. ≤ 32°F	5	3	1	0	0	0	0	0	0	0	0	3	12
Days Minimum Temp. ≤ 32°F	23	19	14	5	0	0	0	0	0	2	12	19	94
Days Minimum Temp. ≤ 0°F	1	0	0	0	0	0	0	0	0	0	0	0	1
Heating Degree Days (base 65°F)	928	761	585	300	106	14	1	1	39	265	543	813	4,356
Cooling Degree Days (base 65°F)	0	0	4	26	92	255	382	338	163	21	1	0	1,282
Mean Precipitation (in.)	3.42	3.59	4.15	3.58	5.13	4.46	5.07	4.03	3.43	3.02	3.36	3.84	47.08
Days With ≥ 0.1" Precipitation	8	8	10	8	9	8	9	7	7	6	7	8	95
Days With ≥ 1.0" Precipitation	0	1	1	0	1	1	1	1	1	1	1	1	10
Mean Snowfall (in.)	6.4	5.6	2.3	trace	0.0	0.0	0.0	0.0	0.0	0.0	0.2	2.4	16.9
Days With ≥ 1.0" Snow Depth	6	5	1	0	0	0	0	0	0	0	0	2	14

London Locks *Kanawha County* Elevation: 620 ft. Latitude: 38° 12' N Longitude: 81° 22' W

	JAN	FEB	MAR	APR	MAY	JUN	JUL	AUG	SEP	OCT	NOV	DEC	YEAR
Mean Maximum Temp. (°F)	42.5	46.6	56.1	66.9	74.9	82.1	85.8	84.2	78.2	67.7	56.9	47.2	65.8
Mean Temp. (°F)	33.6	36.6	44.9	54.2	63.0	71.3	75.6	74.4	68.4	56.8	46.6	38.2	55.3
Mean Minimum Temp. (°F)	24.8	26.6	33.5	41.5	51.1	60.4	65.3	64.6	58.4	46.0	36.3	29.1	44.8
Extreme Maximum Temp. (°F)	78	78	88	92	95	97	98	101	97	88	84	79	101
Extreme Minimum Temp. (°F)	-16	-7	-1	22	31	39	48	45	38	22	10	-7	-16
Days Maximum Temp. ≥ 90°F	0	0	0	0	1	4	8	6	2	0	0	0	21
Days Maximum Temp. ≤ 32°F	6	4	1	0	0	0	0	0	0	0	0	3	14
Days Minimum Temp. ≤ 32°F	24	20	15	5	0	0	0	0	0	1	11	20	96
Days Minimum Temp. ≤ 0°F	1	0	0	0	0	0	0	0	0	0	0	0	1
Heating Degree Days (base 65°F)	965	796	619	330	125	15	1	2	43	267	547	823	4,533
Cooling Degree Days (base 65°F)	0	0	2	15	72	223	358	304	147	23	0	0	1,144
Mean Precipitation (in.)	3.33	2.97	3.86	3.63	4.74	4.15	4.83	4.21	3.44	2.63	3.48	3.55	44.82
Days With ≥ 0.1" Precipitation	9	8	9	9	10	8	8	7	7	6	8	7	96
Days With ≥ 1.0" Precipitation	0	0	1	1	1	1	1	1	1	0	1	1	9
Mean Snowfall (in.)	na	na	0.7	0.0	0.0	0.0	0.0	0.0	0.0	0.0	trace	na	na
Days With ≥ 1.0" Snow Depth	na	6	1	0	0	0	0	0	0	0	0	na	na

Madison *Boone County*   Elevation: 672 ft.   Latitude: 38° 04' N   Longitude: 81° 49' W

	JAN	FEB	MAR	APR	MAY	JUN	JUL	AUG	SEP	OCT	NOV	DEC	YEAR
Mean Maximum Temp. (°F)	42.3	47.5	57.8	69.0	76.7	83.5	87.1	85.6	79.7	68.7	57.4	47.2	66.9
Mean Temp. (°F)	31.9	35.6	44.3	53.9	62.7	70.7	75.0	73.6	67.2	54.9	44.9	36.5	54.3
Mean Minimum Temp. (°F)	21.5	23.6	30.8	38.8	48.6	57.9	62.8	61.6	54.6	41.1	32.3	25.9	41.6
Extreme Maximum Temp. (°F)	77	80	89	93	93	100	101	100	96	88	84	77	101
Extreme Minimum Temp. (°F)	-25	-13	-8	21	28	36	40	42	32	18	7	-16	-25
Days Maximum Temp. ≥ 90°F	0	0	0	1	1	5	11	8	3	0	0	0	29
Days Maximum Temp. ≤ 32°F	7	4	1	0	0	0	0	0	0	0	0	3	15
Days Minimum Temp. ≤ 32°F	26	22	19	8	1	0	0	0	0	6	17	23	122
Days Minimum Temp. ≤ 0°F	2	1	0	0	0	0	0	0	0	0	0	0	3
Heating Degree Days (base 65°F)	1,020	824	636	341	135	20	1	3	54	318	598	877	4,827
Cooling Degree Days (base 65°F)	0	0	2	15	72	209	336	279	120	16	0	0	1,049
Mean Precipitation (in.)	3.48	3.24	3.96	3.89	5.12	4.40	5.04	4.49	3.77	3.06	3.61	3.66	47.72
Days With ≥ 0.1" Precipitation	8	8	9	9	10	9	8	7	7	6	8	8	97
Days With ≥ 1.0" Precipitation	0	1	1	1	1	1	1	1	1	1	1	1	11
Mean Snowfall (in.)	8.0	5.0	3.0	1.0	0.0	0.0	0.0	0.0	0.0	0.0	0.5	2.2	19.7
Days With ≥ 1.0" Snow Depth	6	5	2	0	0	0	0	0	0	0	0	2	15

Martinsburg Eastern WV Reg. Arpt. *Berkeley County*   Elevation: 534 ft.   Latitude: 39° 24' N   Longitude: 77° 59' W

	JAN	FEB	MAR	APR	MAY	JUN	JUL	AUG	SEP	OCT	NOV	DEC	YEAR
Mean Maximum Temp. (°F)	39.5	43.8	53.4	64.8	74.3	82.8	87.2	85.3	78.1	66.3	55.0	44.6	64.6
Mean Temp. (°F)	30.8	34.3	42.9	53.2	62.6	71.2	76.0	74.1	66.8	54.8	45.0	35.9	54.0
Mean Minimum Temp. (°F)	22.1	24.7	32.5	41.5	51.0	59.6	64.8	62.8	55.5	43.2	34.9	27.1	43.3
Extreme Maximum Temp. (°F)	76	83	88	93	96	100	107	103	100	89	86	78	107
Extreme Minimum Temp. (°F)	-18	-5	-3	19	30	39	47	40	31	19	11	-12	-18
Days Maximum Temp. ≥ 90°F	0	0	0	0	1	6	11	8	3	0	0	0	29
Days Maximum Temp. ≤ 32°F	8	4	1	0	0	0	0	0	0	0	0	4	17
Days Minimum Temp. ≤ 32°F	26	22	16	5	0	0	0	0	0	4	13	22	108
Days Minimum Temp. ≤ 0°F	1	0	0	0	0	0	0	0	0	0	0	0	1
Heating Degree Days (base 65°F)	1,053	862	680	360	134	16	1	4	64	322	596	895	4,987
Cooling Degree Days (base 65°F)	0	0	4	9	67	215	368	289	123	14	0	1	1,090
Mean Precipitation (in.)	2.66	2.41	3.47	3.23	4.15	3.57	3.69	3.36	3.32	3.54	3.23	2.78	39.41
Days With ≥ 0.1" Precipitation	6	6	7	6	8	7	7	6	6	5	6	6	76
Days With ≥ 1.0" Precipitation	0	0	1	1	1	1	1	1	1	1	1	0	9
Mean Snowfall (in.)	8.3	7.3	4.7	0.5	0.0	trace	0.0	0.0	trace	trace	1.5	3.5	25.8
Days With ≥ 1.0" Snow Depth	11	8	3	0	0	0	0	0	0	0	1	3	26

Mathias *Hardy County*   Elevation: 1,538 ft.   Latitude: 38° 52' N   Longitude: 78° 52' W

	JAN	FEB	MAR	APR	MAY	JUN	JUL	AUG	SEP	OCT	NOV	DEC	YEAR
Mean Maximum Temp. (°F)	40.4	44.2	53.0	64.5	73.1	80.3	83.9	82.3	76.3	65.4	53.7	44.6	63.5
Mean Temp. (°F)	30.1	33.1	40.9	50.5	59.6	67.1	71.0	69.5	63.5	52.4	42.6	34.5	51.2
Mean Minimum Temp. (°F)	19.8	21.9	28.7	36.6	46.1	53.8	58.2	56.7	50.7	39.4	31.4	24.3	39.0
Extreme Maximum Temp. (°F)	72	77	84	90	95	95	106	100	95	88	80	76	106
Extreme Minimum Temp. (°F)	-20	-20	0	11	25	30	37	31	25	16	5	-15	-20
Days Maximum Temp. ≥ 90°F	0	0	0	0	0	2	5	3	1	0	0	0	11
Days Maximum Temp. ≤ 32°F	8	5	1	0	0	0	0	0	0	0	0	4	18
Days Minimum Temp. ≤ 32°F	28	24	20	11	3	0	0	0	1	9	18	25	139
Days Minimum Temp. ≤ 0°F	2	1	0	0	0	0	0	0	0	0	0	1	4
Heating Degree Days (base 65°F)	1,074	896	742	431	193	44	8	17	107	388	666	939	5,505
Cooling Degree Days (base 65°F)	0	*0*	0	3	36	*118*	*213*	*161*	67	7	0	0	*605*
Mean Precipitation (in.)	2.31	2.28	3.01	2.82	4.12	3.35	3.97	3.84	3.31	3.11	3.15	2.37	37.64
Days With ≥ 0.1" Precipitation	6	5	7	6	9	7	8	7	6	5	6	5	77
Days With ≥ 1.0" Precipitation	0	1	1	0	1	1	1	1	1	1	1	0	9
Mean Snowfall (in.)	9.4	9.1	6.8	1.7	trace	0.0	0.0	0.0	0.0	0.5	2.5	6.2	36.2
Days With ≥ 1.0" Snow Depth	10	9	3	0	0	0	0	0	0	0	1	4	27

Middlebourne 3 ESE *Tyler County*   Elevation: 780 ft.   Latitude: 39° 28' N   Longitude: 80° 52' W

	JAN	FEB	MAR	APR	MAY	JUN	JUL	AUG	SEP	OCT	NOV	DEC	YEAR
Mean Maximum Temp. (°F)	39.1	43.7	54.1	65.3	73.9	81.2	84.6	83.1	77.2	66.2	54.4	44.1	63.9
Mean Temp. (°F)	29.7	32.9	41.9	51.6	60.9	69.0	73.4	72.0	65.6	53.5	43.5	34.8	52.4
Mean Minimum Temp. (°F)	20.2	22.1	29.7	37.8	47.8	56.9	62.2	60.8	54.0	40.8	32.6	25.5	40.9
Extreme Maximum Temp. (°F)	74	76	85	91	92	98	103	100	95	85	80	78	103
Extreme Minimum Temp. (°F)	-34	-18	-8	16	22	32	37	38	30	18	7	-21	-34
Days Maximum Temp. ≥ 90°F	0	0	0	0	0	2	5	3	1	0	0	0	11
Days Maximum Temp. ≤ 32°F	9	5	1	0	0	0	0	0	0	0	0	5	20
Days Minimum Temp. ≤ 32°F	26	23	20	10	2	0	0	0	0	7	16	23	127
Days Minimum Temp. ≤ 0°F	2	2	0	0	0	0	0	0	0	0	0	1	5
Heating Degree Days (base 65°F)	1,088	900	709	404	167	29	3	7	78	358	638	929	5,310
Cooling Degree Days (base 65°F)	0	0	1	8	44	159	281	226	95	10	0	0	824
Mean Precipitation (in.)	3.33	2.88	3.89	3.47	4.61	4.22	4.85	4.22	3.66	3.23	3.63	3.32	45.31
Days With ≥ 0.1" Precipitation	9	7	9	9	10	8	9	8	6	7	8	9	99
Days With ≥ 1.0" Precipitation	1	0	1	1	1	1	1	1	1	1	1	1	11
Mean Snowfall (in.)	10.9	6.0	4.0	0.6	0.0	0.0	0.0	0.0	0.0	trace	0.8	2.6	24.9
Days With ≥ 1.0" Snow Depth	11	8	2	0	0	0	0	0	0	0	1	3	25

Moorefield 2 SSE *Hardy County*   Elevation: 889 ft.   Latitude: 39° 03' N   Longitude: 78° 58' W

	JAN	FEB	MAR	APR	MAY	JUN	JUL	AUG	SEP	OCT	NOV	DEC	YEAR
Mean Maximum Temp. (°F)	42.3	46.7	56.3	67.7	76.6	84.1	87.4	86.1	80.0	69.6	57.3	46.9	66.8
Mean Temp. (°F)	31.8	35.3	43.7	53.5	63.0	71.0	74.6	73.2	66.9	55.7	45.3	36.4	54.2
Mean Minimum Temp. (°F)	21.2	23.7	31.0	39.3	49.4	57.8	61.8	60.3	53.7	41.8	33.2	25.9	41.6
Extreme Maximum Temp. (°F)	75	82	89	95	98	99	106	103	98	90	84	78	106
Extreme Minimum Temp. (°F)	-20	-17	-9	15	26	33	39	38	28	18	8	-10	-20
Days Maximum Temp. ≥ 90°F	0	0	0	0	1	6	11	9	3	0	0	0	30
Days Maximum Temp. ≤ 32°F	6	3	1	0	0	0	0	0	0	0	0	3	13
Days Minimum Temp. ≤ 32°F	26	22	18	8	1	0	0	0	0	6	15	24	120
Days Minimum Temp. ≤ 0°F	2	1	0	0	0	0	0	0	0	0	0	0	3
Heating Degree Days (base 65°F)	1,023	833	657	352	126	17	2	4	61	297	586	879	4,837
Cooling Degree Days (base 65°F)	0	0	3	13	71	207	319	266	120	18	1	0	1,018
Mean Precipitation (in.)	1.98	1.69	2.57	2.36	3.53	3.50	3.62	3.38	2.89	2.81	2.54	1.98	32.85
Days With ≥ 0.1" Precipitation	5	4	6	6	8	7	7	7	6	5	5	4	70
Days With ≥ 1.0" Precipitation	0	0	1	0	1	1	1	1	1	1	1	0	8
Mean Snowfall (in.)	*9.3*	5.4	4.2	0.4	0.0	0.0	0.0	0.0	0.0	0.0	1.1	3.3	*23.7*
Days With ≥ 1.0" Snow Depth	na	na	*2*	0	0	0	0	0	0	0	0	2	na

Morgantown Lock & Dam *Monongalia County*   Elevation: 823 ft.   Latitude: 39° 37' N   Longitude: 79° 58' W

	JAN	FEB	MAR	APR	MAY	JUN	JUL	AUG	SEP	OCT	NOV	DEC	YEAR
Mean Maximum Temp. (°F)	39.1	43.1	53.2	64.6	73.2	80.4	83.9	82.5	76.4	65.4	54.2	44.2	63.3
Mean Temp. (°F)	30.2	33.1	41.9	51.9	60.9	68.8	73.0	71.5	65.4	53.9	44.1	35.2	52.5
Mean Minimum Temp. (°F)	21.1	23.1	30.7	39.1	48.6	57.2	62.1	60.4	54.3	42.3	33.9	26.2	41.6
Extreme Maximum Temp. (°F)	73	74	83	91	90	95	98	100	99	84	81	78	100
Extreme Minimum Temp. (°F)	-21	-11	-3	14	23	31	42	36	34	15	6	-15	-21
Days Maximum Temp. ≥ 90°F	0	0	0	0	0	2	5	3	1	0	0	0	11
Days Maximum Temp. ≤ 32°F	9	6	1	0	0	0	0	0	0	0	0	5	21
Days Minimum Temp. ≤ 32°F	26	22	18	8	1	0	0	0	0	4	14	23	116
Days Minimum Temp. ≤ 0°F	2	1	0	0	0	0	0	0	0	0	0	0	3
Heating Degree Days (base 65°F)	1,073	894	709	394	163	30	4	7	77	346	622	917	5,236
Cooling Degree Days (base 65°F)	0	0	1	7	43	159	281	224	97	9	0	0	821
Mean Precipitation (in.)	3.26	2.74	3.87	3.73	4.25	4.03	4.24	3.94	3.38	2.92	3.56	3.33	43.25
Days With ≥ 0.1" Precipitation	8	7	9	9	9	8	8	7	7	7	8	8	95
Days With ≥ 1.0" Precipitation	0	0	1	1	1	1	1	1	1	1	0	0	8
Mean Snowfall (in.)	na	na	*1.5*	trace	0.0	0.0	0.0	0.0	0.0	trace	0.2	*1.1*	na
Days With ≥ 1.0" Snow Depth	9	6	2	0	0	0	0	0	0	0	0	3	20

Morgantown Municipal Arpt. *Monongalia County*   Elevation: 1,240 ft.   Latitude: 39° 39' N   Longitude: 79° 55' W

	JAN	FEB	MAR	APR	MAY	JUN	JUL	AUG	SEP	OCT	NOV	DEC	YEAR
Mean Maximum Temp. (°F)	38.2	42.0	52.0	63.3	72.8	80.0	83.7	82.3	75.6	64.5	53.2	43.2	62.6
Mean Temp. (°F)	30.3	33.3	42.0	52.1	61.6	69.1	73.4	72.1	65.4	54.1	44.6	35.4	52.8
Mean Minimum Temp. (°F)	22.3	24.5	32.0	40.8	50.4	58.3	63.0	61.7	55.2	43.8	35.9	27.5	42.9
Extreme Maximum Temp. (°F)	73	75	83	92	91	97	100	99	95	84	80	77	100
Extreme Minimum Temp. (°F)	-20	-10	4	14	27	30	41	38	30	18	9	-13	-20
Days Maximum Temp. ≥ 90°F	0	0	0	0	0	2	6	3	1	0	0	0	12
Days Maximum Temp. ≤ 32°F	11	7	2	0	0	0	0	0	0	0	1	6	27
Days Minimum Temp. ≤ 32°F	25	21	17	6	1	0	0	0	0	3	13	21	107
Days Minimum Temp. ≤ 0°F	2	1	0	0	0	0	0	0	0	0	0	1	4
Heating Degree Days (base 65°F)	1,069	890	708	397	162	40	4	7	83	341	609	913	5,223
Cooling Degree Days (base 65°F)	0	0	2	14	61	169	288	233	93	11	2	0	873
Mean Precipitation (in.)	2.88	2.58	3.78	3.55	4.11	4.12	4.36	4.05	3.59	2.96	3.37	3.24	42.59
Days With ≥ 0.1" Precipitation	8	7	9	8	9	8	8	7	7	6	8	7	92
Days With ≥ 1.0" Precipitation	0	0	0	1	1	1	1	1	1	0	0	0	6
Mean Snowfall (in.)	10.9	6.7	6.2	0.9	trace	trace	trace	0.0	0.0	trace	1.3	4.4	30.4
Days With ≥ 1.0" Snow Depth	12	9	4	0	0	0	0	0	0	0	1	6	32

Moundsville *Marshall County*   Elevation: 620 ft.   Latitude: 39° 54' N   Longitude: 80° 45' W

	JAN	FEB	MAR	APR	MAY	JUN	JUL	AUG	SEP	OCT	NOV	DEC	YEAR
Mean Maximum Temp. (°F)	*38.1*	42.1	52.5	64.9	74.5	82.1	85.7	84.4	78.2	66.4	53.8	43.7	*63.9*
Mean Temp. (°F)	*28.9*	31.8	41.0	51.8	61.4	69.7	73.9	72.7	66.2	54.0	43.7	35.0	*52.5*
Mean Minimum Temp. (°F)	*19.7*	21.5	29.5	38.6	48.4	57.4	62.1	61.0	54.1	41.6	33.6	26.2	*41.1*
Extreme Maximum Temp. (°F)	74	75	*84*	92	*91*	98	99	99	96	87	81	*78*	*99*
Extreme Minimum Temp. (°F)	-20	-13	-3	*16*	26	36	44	40	31	19	6	-11	*-20*
Days Maximum Temp. ≥ 90°F	0	0	0	0	1	4	8	6	2	0	0	0	21
Days Maximum Temp. ≤ 32°F	10	6	1	0	0	0	0	0	0	0	0	4	21
Days Minimum Temp. ≤ 32°F	26	23	20	*9*	1	0	0	0	0	4	15	23	*121*
Days Minimum Temp. ≤ 0°F	2	2	0	0	0	0	0	0	0	0	0	0	4
Heating Degree Days (base 65°F)	*1,111*	931	738	400	160	27	3	6	75	343	632	924	*5,350*
Cooling Degree Days (base 65°F)	*0*	*0*	*1*	*9*	55	183	300	254	111	10	0	0	*923*
Mean Precipitation (in.)	2.87	2.20	3.31	3.49	4.03	4.51	4.37	4.10	3.31	2.77	3.59	3.05	41.60
Days With ≥ 0.1" Precipitation	*8*	6	8	9	8	8	8	7	6	7	8	8	*91*
Days With ≥ 1.0" Precipitation	0	0	1	1	1	1	1	1	1	0	0	0	7
Mean Snowfall (in.)	na	na	na	*trace*	0.0	0.0	0.0	0.0	0.0	trace	*0.3*	*1.4*	na
Days With ≥ 1.0" Snow Depth	na	na	na	*0*	0	0	0	0	0	0	*0*	na	na

Oak Hill *Fayette County*   Elevation: 1,988 ft.   Latitude: 37° 58' N   Longitude: 81° 09' W

	JAN	FEB	MAR	APR	MAY	JUN	JUL	AUG	SEP	OCT	NOV	DEC	YEAR
Mean Maximum Temp. (°F)	39.4	43.6	52.8	63.5	71.6	78.6	82.3	81.1	75.1	64.7	54.1	44.5	62.6
Mean Temp. (°F)	30.1	33.4	41.7	51.4	59.5	67.0	71.1	70.0	63.9	52.9	43.7	35.1	51.7
Mean Minimum Temp. (°F)	20.7	23.0	30.6	39.3	47.4	55.6	59.9	58.8	52.7	41.1	33.4	25.6	40.7
Extreme Maximum Temp. (°F)	73	76	86	89	89	93	95	94	92	84	85	79	95
Extreme Minimum Temp. (°F)	-20	-11	-1	13	28	34	40	39	30	18	6	-15	-20
Days Maximum Temp. ≥ 90°F	0	0	0	0	0	0	2	1	0	0	0	0	3
Days Maximum Temp. ≤ 32°F	9	6	2	0	0	0	0	0	0	0	1	6	24
Days Minimum Temp. ≤ 32°F	26	22	18	8	1	0	0	0	0	6	15	23	119
Days Minimum Temp. ≤ 0°F	2	1	0	0	0	0	0	0	0	0	0	0	3
Heating Degree Days (base 65°F)	1,076	888	716	408	196	45	7	13	99	373	635	920	5,376
Cooling Degree Days (base 65°F)	0	0	1	6	32	116	216	170	66	6	0	0	613
Mean Precipitation (in.)	3.62	3.19	3.99	3.84	4.39	4.18	5.21	4.07	3.53	3.10	3.33	3.52	45.97
Days With ≥ 0.1" Precipitation	9	8	10	10	10	9	9	7	7	7	8	9	103
Days With ≥ 1.0" Precipitation	0	0	1	1	1	1	1	1	1	0	0	0	7
Mean Snowfall (in.)	15.6	10.5	6.4	1.3	0.0	0.0	0.0	0.0	0.0	trace	2.4	7.1	43.3
Days With ≥ 1.0" Snow Depth	14	11	4	1	0	0	0	0	0	0	2	7	39

Parkersburg WSO *Wood County*   Elevation: 613 ft.   Latitude: 39° 16' N   Longitude: 81° 34' W

	JAN	FEB	MAR	APR	MAY	JUN	JUL	AUG	SEP	OCT	NOV	DEC	YEAR
Mean Maximum Temp. (°F)	38.9	43.4	53.7	65.1	74.6	82.2	85.9	84.7	78.0	66.4	54.6	44.3	64.3
Mean Temp. (°F)	30.6	34.0	43.0	53.0	62.8	70.9	75.2	73.8	66.9	55.0	44.9	35.9	53.8
Mean Minimum Temp. (°F)	22.2	24.5	32.2	41.0	51.0	59.6	64.4	62.8	55.8	43.5	35.2	27.6	43.3
Extreme Maximum Temp. (°F)	76	78	85	94	96	102	105	103	98	90	82	78	105
Extreme Minimum Temp. (°F)	-26	-5	1	17	29	36	45	42	34	22	10	-10	-26
Days Maximum Temp. ≥ 90°F	0	0	0	0	1	4	9	7	2	0	0	0	23
Days Maximum Temp. ≤ 32°F	10	6	2	0	0	0	0	0	0	0	1	5	24
Days Minimum Temp. ≤ 32°F	25	22	17	6	0	0	0	0	0	4	13	22	109
Days Minimum Temp. ≤ 0°F	1	0	0	0	0	0	0	0	0	0	0	0	1
Heating Degree Days (base 65°F)	1,059	869	680	368	137	19	2	4	62	319	598	894	5,011
Cooling Degree Days (base 65°F)	0	0	2	15	73	214	342	287	123	17	1	1	1,075
Mean Precipitation (in.)	2.75	2.55	3.59	3.18	4.11	4.03	4.55	3.93	3.13	2.73	3.04	3.04	40.63
Days With ≥ 0.1" Precipitation	7	6	8	8	9	7	8	7	6	6	7	7	86
Days With ≥ 1.0" Precipitation	0	0	1	0	1	1	1	1	1	1	0	0	7
Mean Snowfall (in.)	7.3	4.1	2.6	0.9	0.0	0.0	0.0	0.0	0.0	trace	0.8	1.9	17.6
Days With ≥ 1.0" Snow Depth	7	6	1	0	0	0	0	0	0	0	0	1	15

Parkersburg Wood County Airport *Wood County*   Elevation: 830 ft.   Latitude: 39° 21' N   Longitude: 81° 26' W

	JAN	FEB	MAR	APR	MAY	JUN	JUL	AUG	SEP	OCT	NOV	DEC	YEAR
Mean Maximum Temp. (°F)	38.5	42.8	53.9	64.8	73.9	81.4	84.5	83.1	76.5	65.8	54.3	44.0	63.6
Mean Temp. (°F)	30.5	33.8	43.7	53.4	62.8	70.7	74.7	73.4	66.6	55.4	45.4	36.1	53.9
Mean Minimum Temp. (°F)	22.4	24.7	33.6	42.0	51.6	60.0	64.9	63.7	56.6	44.9	36.4	28.0	44.1
Extreme Maximum Temp. (°F)	74	74	85	94	92	100	102	101	93	88	81	79	102
Extreme Minimum Temp. (°F)	-24	-10	-5	17	28	37	44	40	32	22	8	-16	-24
Days Maximum Temp. ≥ 90°F	0	0	0	0	1	3	6	4	1	0	0	0	15
Days Maximum Temp. ≤ 32°F	10	7	1	0	0	0	0	0	0	0	0	5	23
Days Minimum Temp. ≤ 32°F	25	21	15	5	0	0	0	0	0	3	12	20	101
Days Minimum Temp. ≤ 0°F	1	1	0	0	0	0	0	0	0	0	0	0	2
Heating Degree Days (base 65°F)	1,061	875	656	359	139	19	2	4	65	309	584	890	4,963
Cooling Degree Days (base 65°F)	0	0	3	18	74	203	321	275	113	19	3	1	1,030
Mean Precipitation (in.)	2.95	2.71	3.92	3.33	4.18	3.85	4.33	4.49	3.23	3.12	3.34	3.39	42.84
Days With ≥ 0.1" Precipitation	8	7	9	8	9	7	8	7	6	6	8	8	91
Days With ≥ 1.0" Precipitation	0	0	1	1	1	1	1	1	1	1	0	1	9
Mean Snowfall (in.)	10.1	5.6	4.1	0.8	trace	trace	0.0	trace	trace	trace	1.2	2.8	24.6
Days With ≥ 1.0" Snow Depth	11	8	2	0	0	0	0	0	0	0	0	3	24

Parsons 1 NE *Tucker County*   Elevation: 1,768 ft.   Latitude: 39° 06' N   Longitude: 79° 40' W

	JAN	FEB	MAR	APR	MAY	JUN	JUL	AUG	SEP	OCT	NOV	DEC	YEAR
Mean Maximum Temp. (°F)	37.9	41.4	50.7	61.6	71.0	78.2	81.8	80.7	74.5	63.8	52.2	42.5	61.4
Mean Temp. (°F)	28.2	30.8	39.2	48.8	58.5	66.3	70.7	69.5	63.0	51.2	41.4	32.9	50.0
Mean Minimum Temp. (°F)	18.4	20.1	27.6	36.0	45.8	54.5	59.5	58.2	51.4	38.5	30.6	23.3	38.7
Extreme Maximum Temp. (°F)	72	73	85	89	91	93	101	95	92	82	78	74	101
Extreme Minimum Temp. (°F)	-20	-16	-7	11	23	30	36	38	31	19	7	-17	-20
Days Maximum Temp. ≥ 90°F	0	0	0	0	0	1	2	1	0	0	0	0	4
Days Maximum Temp. ≤ 32°F	10	7	3	0	0	0	0	0	0	0	2	7	29
Days Minimum Temp. ≤ 32°F	27	24	22	12	2	0	0	0	0	9	19	25	140
Days Minimum Temp. ≤ 0°F	3	2	0	0	0	0	0	0	0	0	0	1	6
Heating Degree Days (base 65°F)	1,135	960	795	484	224	57	11	16	115	424	701	987	5,909
Cooling Degree Days (base 65°F)	0	0	0	4	29	107	208	163	56	4	0	0	571
Mean Precipitation (in.)	3.84	3.39	4.14	4.33	5.10	5.33	5.55	4.99	4.10	3.46	3.91	4.00	52.14
Days With ≥ 0.1" Precipitation	9	9	10	10	10	10	10	8	7	7	8	10	108
Days With ≥ 1.0" Precipitation	1	0	1	1	1	1	1	1	1	1	1	0	10
Mean Snowfall (in.)	17.3	12.6	9.8	2.0	0.0	0.0	0.0	0.0	0.0	0.1	3.7	8.8	54.3
Days With ≥ 1.0" Snow Depth	17	13	7	1	0	0	0	0	0	0	3	9	50

Pineville *Wyoming County* Elevation: 1,279 ft. Latitude: 37° 34' N Longitude: 81° 32' W

	JAN	FEB	MAR	APR	MAY	JUN	JUL	AUG	SEP	OCT	NOV	DEC	YEAR
Mean Maximum Temp. (°F)	41.3	46.1	55.9	67.0	75.3	82.1	85.2	84.3	78.3	67.5	56.3	45.8	65.4
Mean Temp. (°F)	31.6	34.9	43.2	52.7	61.6	69.7	73.8	72.9	66.6	54.4	44.5	35.8	53.5
Mean Minimum Temp. (°F)	21.9	23.6	30.5	38.2	47.9	57.2	62.4	61.3	54.8	41.4	32.7	25.8	41.5
Extreme Maximum Temp. (°F)	76	78	86	92	93	96	98	100	97	86	82	80	100
Extreme Minimum Temp. (°F)	-17	-16	-6	19	27	37	42	43	33	20	7	-13	-17
Days Maximum Temp. ≥ 90°F	0	0	0	0	0	2	7	5	1	0	0	0	15
Days Maximum Temp. ≤ 32°F	7	4	1	0	0	0	0	0	0	0	0	4	16
Days Minimum Temp. ≤ 32°F	26	23	19	9	1	0	0	0	0	5	16	23	122
Days Minimum Temp. ≤ 0°F	2	1	0	0	0	0	0	0	0	0	0	0	3
Heating Degree Days (base 65°F)	1,028	844	669	371	148	22	2	3	57	331	609	897	4,981
Cooling Degree Days (base 65°F)	0	0	1	8	53	180	306	256	108	11	0	0	923
Mean Precipitation (in.)	3.84	3.24	3.94	3.88	4.95	3.97	4.91	3.80	3.53	3.19	3.29	3.50	46.04
Days With ≥ 0.1" Precipitation	8	8	9	8	9	9	9	7	7	6	7	8	95
Days With ≥ 1.0" Precipitation	1	0	1	1	1	1	1	1	1	1	1	0	10
Mean Snowfall (in.)	8.4	5.8	3.5	0.8	trace	0.0	0.0	0.0	0.0	trace	0.7	3.7	22.9
Days With ≥ 1.0" Snow Depth	9	6	2	0	0	0	0	0	0	0	1	4	22

Ripley *Jackson County* Elevation: 587 ft. Latitude: 38° 49' N Longitude: 81° 43' W

	JAN	FEB	MAR	APR	MAY	JUN	JUL	AUG	SEP	OCT	NOV	DEC	YEAR
Mean Maximum Temp. (°F)	42.0	47.0	57.0	68.0	77.0	83.7	87.5	85.6	79.9	68.9	57.0	46.9	66.7
Mean Temp. (°F)	31.8	35.6	44.3	53.8	63.3	70.9	75.2	73.4	67.0	55.3	45.3	36.8	54.4
Mean Minimum Temp. (°F)	21.8	24.3	31.5	39.5	49.4	58.0	62.9	61.1	54.0	41.6	33.3	26.8	42.0
Extreme Maximum Temp. (°F)	75	77	89	95	95	102	107	103	100	88	83	82	107
Extreme Minimum Temp. (°F)	-28	-16	-11	11	25	35	39	37	29	17	6	-17	-28
Days Maximum Temp. ≥ 90°F	0	0	0	1	2	6	11	8	3	0	0	0	31
Days Maximum Temp. ≤ 32°F	7	3	1	0	0	0	0	0	0	0	0	3	14
Days Minimum Temp. ≤ 32°F	25	21	17	8	1	0	0	0	0	6	15	22	115
Days Minimum Temp. ≤ 0°F	2	1	0	0	0	0	0	0	0	0	0	1	4
Heating Degree Days (base 65°F)	1,022	822	638	344	122	17	1	4	61	308	586	866	4,791
Cooling Degree Days (base 65°F)	0	0	3	14	69	200	331	265	114	13	0	0	1,009
Mean Precipitation (in.)	3.31	3.17	3.98	3.50	4.44	4.27	4.87	3.78	3.33	3.29	3.58	3.58	45.10
Days With ≥ 0.1" Precipitation	9	8	9	8	9	8	8	7	7	7	8	8	96
Days With ≥ 1.0" Precipitation	1	0	1	1	1	1	1	1	1	1	1	1	11
Mean Snowfall (in.)	7.4	5.0	2.4	0.7	0.0	0.0	0.0	0.0	0.0	0.1	0.7	2.0	18.3
Days With ≥ 1.0" Snow Depth	9	6	2	0	0	0	0	0	0	0	0	3	20

Romney 1 SW *Hampshire County* Elevation: 669 ft. Latitude: 39° 20' N Longitude: 78° 46' W

	JAN	FEB	MAR	APR	MAY	JUN	JUL	AUG	SEP	OCT	NOV	DEC	YEAR
Mean Maximum Temp. (°F)	39.3	44.1	53.3	65.4	74.9	82.9	86.8	85.0	78.5	67.4	55.4	44.4	64.8
Mean Temp. (°F)	29.6	32.9	41.3	51.7	61.3	69.8	74.2	72.5	65.6	53.8	43.6	34.6	52.6
Mean Minimum Temp. (°F)	19.9	21.7	29.3	37.9	47.7	56.6	61.5	59.9	52.7	40.1	31.7	24.7	40.3
Extreme Maximum Temp. (°F)	74	81	90	94	98	97	103	103	97	89	85	78	103
Extreme Minimum Temp. (°F)	-17	-9	1	16	25	32	41	38	30	19	8	-7	-17
Days Maximum Temp. ≥ 90°F	0	0	0	0	1	6	11	7	3	0	0	0	28
Days Maximum Temp. ≤ 32°F	8	4	1	0	0	0	0	0	0	0	0	4	17
Days Minimum Temp. ≤ 32°F	28	24	20	9	1	0	0	0	0	7	17	25	131
Days Minimum Temp. ≤ 0°F	2	1	0	0	0	0	0	0	0	0	0	0	3
Heating Degree Days (base 65°F)	1,089	900	730	403	163	26	3	7	80	350	635	937	5,323
Cooling Degree Days (base 65°F)	0	0	2	9	56	179	305	242	100	10	0	0	903
Mean Precipitation (in.)	2.53	2.01	3.05	2.98	3.59	3.28	3.89	3.36	3.16	2.69	2.71	2.39	35.64
Days With ≥ 0.1" Precipitation	6	5	7	7	8	7	8	7	6	5	6	6	78
Days With ≥ 1.0" Precipitation	0	0	1	0	1	1	1	1	1	1	1	0	8
Mean Snowfall (in.)	9.3	7.2	5.9	0.3	0.0	0.0	0.0	0.0	0.0	trace	1.4	3.4	27.5
Days With ≥ 1.0" Snow Depth	12	7	4	0	0	0	0	0	0	0	1	4	28

Rowlesburg 1 *Preston County* Elevation: 1,420 ft. Latitude: 39° 20' N Longitude: 79° 41' W

	JAN	FEB	MAR	APR	MAY	JUN	JUL	AUG	SEP	OCT	NOV	DEC	YEAR
Mean Maximum Temp. (°F)	37.6	41.3	51.0	62.2	71.6	78.4	81.9	81.0	75.0	64.2	52.8	42.3	61.6
Mean Temp. (°F)	28.5	31.1	39.8	49.3	58.9	66.7	71.0	70.1	63.8	52.1	42.5	33.3	50.6
Mean Minimum Temp. (°F)	19.3	20.9	28.3	36.5	46.2	54.9	60.1	59.2	52.6	40.1	31.9	24.3	39.5
Extreme Maximum Temp. (°F)	73	74	84	90	91	95	101	98	94	83	80	77	101
Extreme Minimum Temp. (°F)	-21	-19	-5	12	25	32	40	38	30	18	4	-13	-21
Days Maximum Temp. ≥ 90°F	0	0	0	0	0	1	2	2	0	0	0	0	5
Days Maximum Temp. ≤ 32°F	11	7	2	0	0	0	0	0	0	0	1	6	27
Days Minimum Temp. ≤ 32°F	27	24	22	10	2	0	0	0	0	6	16	25	132
Days Minimum Temp. ≤ 0°F	3	2	0	0	0	0	0	0	0	0	0	1	6
Heating Degree Days (base 65°F)	1,125	951	777	467	213	48	7	13	98	397	668	975	5,739
Cooling Degree Days (base 65°F)	0	0	0	4	31	108	212	179	67	4	0	0	605
Mean Precipitation (in.)	4.37	3.93	4.72	4.71	5.16	5.48	5.90	4.73	4.13	3.80	4.43	4.52	55.88
Days With ≥ 0.1" Precipitation	11	10	11	11	10	10	10	8	8	8	9	10	116
Days With ≥ 1.0" Precipitation	1	0	1	1	1	2	2	1	1	1	1	1	13
Mean Snowfall (in.)	19.1	13.3	9.1	1.3	0.0	0.0	0.0	0.0	0.0	trace	2.9	9.8	55.5
Days With ≥ 1.0" Snow Depth	16	13	6	1	0	0	0	0	0	0	3	9	48

Seneca State Forest 1 N *Pocahontas County*   Elevation: 2,447 ft.   Latitude: 38° 20' N   Longitude: 79° 56' W

	JAN	FEB	MAR	APR	MAY	JUN	JUL	AUG	SEP	OCT	NOV	DEC	YEAR
Mean Maximum Temp. (°F)	38.1	42.9	51.3	62.2	71.3	78.1	81.9	80.3	74.0	63.8	52.0	42.3	61.5
Mean Temp. (°F)	26.6	30.2	37.9	46.9	56.2	63.9	68.2	67.0	60.5	49.1	39.2	30.8	48.0
Mean Minimum Temp. (°F)	14.9	17.2	24.4	31.5	41.1	49.6	54.5	53.6	46.9	34.3	26.2	19.2	34.5
Extreme Maximum Temp. (°F)	64	72	82	88	91	92	99	96	93	84	77	75	99
Extreme Minimum Temp. (°F)	-24	-21	-13	1	18	24	29	32	18	10	-2	-25	-25
Days Maximum Temp. ≥ 90°F	0	0	0	0	0	1	2	1	0	0	0	0	4
Days Maximum Temp. ≤ 32°F	9	6	2	0	0	0	0	0	0	0	1	6	24
Days Minimum Temp. ≤ 32°F	29	26	25	17	6	1	0	0	2	15	23	27	171
Days Minimum Temp. ≤ 0°F	5	3	0	0	0	0	0	0	0	0	0	2	10
Heating Degree Days (base 65°F)	1,185	976	834	538	276	83	21	30	158	488	769	1,052	6,410
Cooling Degree Days (base 65°F)	0	0	0	1	14	63	142	100	27	1	0	0	348
Mean Precipitation (in.)	3.91	3.41	4.44	3.58	4.64	4.09	4.87	4.28	3.55	3.48	3.89	4.00	48.14
Days With ≥ 0.1" Precipitation	9	7	9	8	9	9	9	8	6	6	7	8	95
Days With ≥ 1.0" Precipitation	1	1	1	1	1	1	1	1	1	1	1	1	12
Mean Snowfall (in.)	17.5	14.5	12.1	2.9	trace	0.0	0.0	0.0	trace	0.6	5.1	11.4	64.1
Days With ≥ 1.0" Snow Depth	19	16	8	1	0	0	0	0	0	0	4	10	58

Spencer 4 S *Roane County*   Elevation: 859 ft.   Latitude: 38° 43' N   Longitude: 81° 21' W

	JAN	FEB	MAR	APR	MAY	JUN	JUL	AUG	SEP	OCT	NOV	DEC	YEAR
Mean Maximum Temp. (°F)	41.3	45.7	55.5	66.8	75.5	82.6	86.1	84.6	78.8	67.9	56.2	45.6	65.5
Mean Temp. (°F)	31.0	33.8	42.3	52.3	61.6	69.6	73.8	72.0	65.6	53.9	44.1	35.3	52.9
Mean Minimum Temp. (°F)	20.6	21.9	29.1	37.7	47.4	56.6	61.5	59.4	52.3	39.9	31.9	24.9	40.3
Extreme Maximum Temp. (°F)	76	77	87	92	96	99	103	101	97	86	84	81	103
Extreme Minimum Temp. (°F)	-31	-22	-10	15	26	31	38	35	29	16	7	-22	-31
Days Maximum Temp. ≥ 90°F	0	0	0	0	1	4	8	6	2	0	0	0	21
Days Maximum Temp. ≤ 32°F	7	4	1	0	0	0	0	0	0	0	0	4	16
Days Minimum Temp. ≤ 32°F	26	23	20	10	2	0	0	0	1	9	16	23	130
Days Minimum Temp. ≤ 0°F	3	2	0	0	0	0	0	0	0	0	0	1	6
Heating Degree Days (base 65°F)	1,048	876	701	390	158	28	3	8	81	349	623	916	5,181
Cooling Degree Days (base 65°F)	0	0	2	12	59	177	300	225	96	11	1	1	884
Mean Precipitation (in.)	3.55	3.15	4.02	3.39	4.21	3.87	5.09	3.95	3.97	3.18	3.79	3.56	45.73
Days With ≥ 0.1" Precipitation	8	8	9	8	9	8	9	7	7	6	8	8	95
Days With ≥ 1.0" Precipitation	1	0	1	0	1	1	1	1	1	1	1	1	10
Mean Snowfall (in.)	*11.3*	*8.2*	*4.4*	0.6	0.0	0.0	0.0	0.0	0.0	trace	0.6	3.1	*28.2*
Days With ≥ 1.0" Snow Depth	*11*	na	*3*	0	0	0	0	0	0	0	0	4	na

Summersville Lake *Nicholas County*   Elevation: 1,758 ft.   Latitude: 38° 13' N   Longitude: 80° 54' W

	JAN	FEB	MAR	APR	MAY	JUN	JUL	AUG	SEP	OCT	NOV	DEC	YEAR
Mean Maximum Temp. (°F)	39.1	42.8	51.9	62.8	71.0	77.6	81.4	80.2	74.6	64.2	53.6	44.0	61.9
Mean Temp. (°F)	29.6	32.3	40.6	50.4	59.0	66.5	70.7	69.4	63.7	52.5	43.2	34.5	51.0
Mean Minimum Temp. (°F)	20.0	21.8	29.3	38.0	46.9	55.3	60.0	58.7	52.7	40.8	32.7	25.0	40.1
Extreme Maximum Temp. (°F)	70	78	83	92	89	93	94	94	92	85	80	75	94
Extreme Minimum Temp. (°F)	-20	-16	-9	14	27	33	41	39	32	15	5	-16	-20
Days Maximum Temp. ≥ 90°F	0	0	0	0	0	1	2	1	0	0	0	0	4
Days Maximum Temp. ≤ 32°F	10	7	3	0	0	0	0	0	0	0	1	6	27
Days Minimum Temp. ≤ 32°F	26	23	20	10	1	0	0	0	0	6	16	24	126
Days Minimum Temp. ≤ 0°F	3	2	0	0	0	0	0	0	0	0	0	1	6
Heating Degree Days (base 65°F)	1,092	918	750	438	210	53	11	14	101	386	649	938	5,560
Cooling Degree Days (base 65°F)	0	0	0	7	28	105	209	156	63	6	0	0	574
Mean Precipitation (in.)	3.62	3.05	3.92	3.75	4.73	4.25	5.58	4.58	3.56	3.34	3.32	3.54	47.24
Days With ≥ 0.1" Precipitation	9	8	9	9	10	9	9	7	7	7	7	8	99
Days With ≥ 1.0" Precipitation	0	0	1	1	1	1	2	1	1	1	0	1	10
Mean Snowfall (in.)	*16.5*	10.5	6.3	1.5	0.0	0.0	0.0	0.0	0.0	0.2	1.9	7.2	*44.1*
Days With ≥ 1.0" Snow Depth	14	10	5	1	0	0	0	0	0	0	2	7	39

Terra Alta 1 *Preston County*   Elevation: 2,627 ft.   Latitude: 39° 27' N   Longitude: 79° 33' W

	JAN	FEB	MAR	APR	MAY	JUN	JUL	AUG	SEP	OCT	NOV	DEC	YEAR
Mean Maximum Temp. (°F)	34.0	37.8	47.0	58.4	67.1	74.1	77.6	76.6	70.6	60.4	49.3	39.2	57.7
Mean Temp. (°F)	26.0	29.0	37.4	47.9	57.1	64.4	68.6	67.4	61.3	50.7	40.9	31.3	48.5
Mean Minimum Temp. (°F)	18.1	20.2	27.9	37.4	47.0	54.7	59.4	58.0	52.0	41.1	32.4	23.4	39.3
Extreme Maximum Temp. (°F)	67	69	81	88	88	88	95	94	87	80	77	71	95
Extreme Minimum Temp. (°F)	-25	-12	-6	10	23	33	39	34	28	18	2	-22	-25
Days Maximum Temp. ≥ 90°F	0	0	0	0	0	0	0	0	0	0	0	0	0
Days Maximum Temp. ≤ 32°F	14	10	5	1	0	0	0	0	0	0	3	10	43
Days Minimum Temp. ≤ 32°F	28	24	21	11	1	0	0	0	0	5	16	25	131
Days Minimum Temp. ≤ 0°F	3	2	0	0	0	0	0	0	0	0	0	1	6
Heating Degree Days (base 65°F)	1,202	1,011	849	511	258	76	20	29	143	437	717	1,038	6,291
Cooling Degree Days (base 65°F)	0	0	1	3	18	69	148	111	37	1	0	0	388
Mean Precipitation (in.)	4.63	3.93	4.94	4.84	4.87	5.24	5.99	4.71	3.94	3.54	4.45	4.80	55.88
Days With ≥ 0.1" Precipitation	12	10	11	11	10	10	10	9	8	8	10	12	121
Days With ≥ 1.0" Precipitation	1	0	1	1	1	1	2	1	1	1	1	1	12
Mean Snowfall (in.)	42.6	31.1	27.4	12.1	0.3	0.0	0.0	0.0	0.0	1.7	15.3	27.3	157.8
Days With ≥ 1.0" Snow Depth	22	18	12	3	0	0	0	0	0	0	5	15	75

Union 3 SSE *Monroe County* Elevation: 2,109 ft. Latitude: 37° 33' N Longitude: 80° 32' W

	JAN	FEB	MAR	APR	MAY	JUN	JUL	AUG	SEP	OCT	NOV	DEC	YEAR
Mean Maximum Temp. (°F)	41.2	45.2	54.1	64.1	72.4	79.1	82.9	81.6	75.7	65.7	54.6	45.3	63.5
Mean Temp. (°F)	31.1	34.3	42.0	50.7	59.2	66.8	70.9	69.6	63.4	52.2	42.9	34.9	51.5
Mean Minimum Temp. (°F)	20.9	23.3	29.9	37.2	46.0	54.5	58.9	57.6	51.0	38.7	31.1	24.4	39.5
Extreme Maximum Temp. (°F)	71	74	83	88	90	92	96	96	92	84	82	73	96
Extreme Minimum Temp. (°F)	-23	-26	-11	11	21	31	36	35	24	13	4	-22	-26
Days Maximum Temp. ≥ 90°F	0	0	0	0	0	0	2	2	1	0	0	0	5
Days Maximum Temp. ≤ 32°F	7	5	1	0	0	0	0	0	0	0	1	4	18
Days Minimum Temp. ≤ 32°F	26	23	19	10	3	0	0	0	1	9	17	24	132
Days Minimum Temp. ≤ 0°F	2	1	0	0	0	0	0	0	0	0	0	1	4
Heating Degree Days (base 65°F)	1,030	861	705	427	196	43	8	12	104	393	657	928	5,364
Cooling Degree Days (base 65°F)	0	0	1	3	25	112	217	166	59	5	0	0	588
Mean Precipitation (in.)	2.59	2.55	3.12	3.19	3.92	3.30	3.55	3.10	3.05	2.59	2.62	2.32	35.90
Days With ≥ 0.1" Precipitation	6	6	7	7	8	7	8	6	6	5	5	5	76
Days With ≥ 1.0" Precipitation	0	0	1	1	1	1	1	1	1	1	0	0	8
Mean Snowfall (in.)	8.2	6.6	4.3	1.1	trace	0.0	0.0	0.0	0.0	0.2	1.0	4.0	25.4
Days With ≥ 1.0" Snow Depth	9	6	3	1	0	0	0	0	0	0	1	4	24

Wardensville R M Farm *Hardy County* Elevation: 958 ft. Latitude: 39° 06' N Longitude: 78° 35' W

	JAN	FEB	MAR	APR	MAY	JUN	JUL	AUG	SEP	OCT	NOV	DEC	YEAR
Mean Maximum Temp. (°F)	40.7	44.1	52.7	64.0	73.3	81.5	85.7	84.2	77.9	66.8	55.8	45.5	64.4
Mean Temp. (°F)	29.5	32.4	40.5	50.4	60.0	68.5	72.9	71.2	64.4	52.5	43.3	34.5	51.7
Mean Minimum Temp. (°F)	18.3	20.6	28.2	36.8	46.7	55.5	60.0	58.1	50.8	38.1	30.8	23.4	38.9
Extreme Maximum Temp. (°F)	75	81	86	91	96	97	105	103	98	92	87	78	105
Extreme Minimum Temp. (°F)	-17	-16	-4	14	24	35	39	36	27	16	7	-6	-17
Days Maximum Temp. ≥ 90°F	0	0	0	0	1	3	9	6	2	0	0	0	21
Days Maximum Temp. ≤ 32°F	8	5	1	0	0	0	0	0	0	0	0	4	18
Days Minimum Temp. ≤ 32°F	29	25	21	10	1	0	0	0	1	10	18	26	141
Days Minimum Temp. ≤ 0°F	2	1	0	0	0	0	0	0	0	0	0	1	4
Heating Degree Days (base 65°F)	1,093	915	753	437	189	36	5	11	98	388	644	939	5,508
Cooling Degree Days (base 65°F)	0	0	1	5	43	154	275	212	87	8	0	0	785
Mean Precipitation (in.)	2.31	1.98	2.88	2.77	3.50	3.47	3.69	3.39	3.11	3.08	3.01	2.22	35.41
Days With ≥ 0.1" Precipitation	6	5	6	6	7	7	7	6	5	6	5	5	71
Days With ≥ 1.0" Precipitation	0	0	0	1	1	1	1	1	1	1	1	1	9
Mean Snowfall (in.)	9.2	6.5	5.1	0.6	0.0	0.0	0.0	0.0	0.0	trace	1.5	4.3	27.2
Days With ≥ 1.0" Snow Depth	8	5	2	0	0	0	0	0	0	0	1	2	18

West Union 2 *Doddridge County* Elevation: 787 ft. Latitude: 39° 17' N Longitude: 80° 46' W

	JAN	FEB	MAR	APR	MAY	JUN	JUL	AUG	SEP	OCT	NOV	DEC	YEAR
Mean Maximum Temp. (°F)	39.6	43.2	53.3	64.2	73.1	80.7	84.1	83.2	77.1	66.0	54.7	44.5	63.6
Mean Temp. (°F)	29.3	31.5	40.8	50.4	59.6	68.2	72.2	71.3	64.6	52.4	42.5	34.2	51.4
Mean Minimum Temp. (°F)	18.9	19.7	28.2	36.5	46.0	55.7	60.3	59.4	52.3	38.8	30.3	23.7	39.2
Extreme Maximum Temp. (°F)	74	75	86	90	92	97	103	101	96	85	81	78	103
Extreme Minimum Temp. (°F)	-33	-17	-7	15	25	32	38	40	28	18	7	-18	-33
Days Maximum Temp. ≥ 90°F	0	0	0	0	0	2	5	4	1	0	0	0	12
Days Maximum Temp. ≤ 32°F	9	6	2	0	0	0	0	0	0	0	0	5	22
Days Minimum Temp. ≤ 32°F	26	24	21	11	2	0	0	0	0	9	19	25	137
Days Minimum Temp. ≤ 0°F	3	2	0	0	0	0	0	0	0	0	0	1	6
Heating Degree Days (base 65°F)	1,100	941	744	439	199	39	7	9	91	388	667	949	5,573
Cooling Degree Days (base 65°F)	0	0	1	5	35	141	244	208	80	5	0	0	719
Mean Precipitation (in.)	3.53	2.95	4.31	3.66	4.90	4.28	5.01	4.23	3.62	3.10	3.34	3.48	46.41
Days With ≥ 0.1" Precipitation	8	7	9	9	9	8	9	7	6	7	7	8	94
Days With ≥ 1.0" Precipitation	1	0	1	1	1	1	1	1	1	1	1	1	11
Mean Snowfall (in.)	na	na	3.4	0.3	0.0	0.0	0.0	0.0	0.0	trace	0.5	2.6	na
Days With ≥ 1.0" Snow Depth	12	9	3	0	0	0	0	0	0	0	1	4	29

Weston *Lewis County* Elevation: 921 ft. Latitude: 39° 02' N Longitude: 80° 28' W

	JAN	FEB	MAR	APR	MAY	JUN	JUL	AUG	SEP	OCT	NOV	DEC	YEAR
Mean Maximum Temp. (°F)	40.4	44.3	54.2	65.8	74.8	82.3	85.8	84.5	78.3	67.2	55.7	45.5	64.9
Mean Temp. (°F)	30.1	32.6	41.2	51.2	60.4	68.8	73.1	71.8	65.4	53.3	43.6	35.2	52.2
Mean Minimum Temp. (°F)	19.8	20.8	28.2	36.5	45.9	55.2	60.4	59.1	52.3	39.4	31.5	24.9	39.5
Extreme Maximum Temp. (°F)	75	78	88	92	95	98	104	100	99	87	82	77	104
Extreme Minimum Temp. (°F)	-24	-11	-6	15	18	33	39	38	30	19	5	-14	-24
Days Maximum Temp. ≥ 90°F	0	0	0	0	1	5	9	6	2	0	0	0	23
Days Maximum Temp. ≤ 32°F	9	5	1	0	0	0	0	0	0	0	0	4	19
Days Minimum Temp. ≤ 32°F	27	24	21	10	2	0	0	0	0	7	17	24	132
Days Minimum Temp. ≤ 0°F	2	2	0	0	0	0	0	0	0	0	0	1	5
Heating Degree Days (base 65°F)	1,075	908	731	416	179	36	5	8	77	364	636	917	5,352
Cooling Degree Days (base 65°F)	0	0	1	8	43	161	280	228	87	8	1	0	817
Mean Precipitation (in.)	4.04	3.39	4.67	3.87	4.80	4.97	5.22	4.61	4.04	3.26	4.00	3.99	50.86
Days With ≥ 0.1" Precipitation	10	9	10	9	10	9	9	8	7	7	9	9	106
Days With ≥ 1.0" Precipitation	1	0	1	0	1	1	1	1	1	1	1	1	10
Mean Snowfall (in.)	14.0	9.4	6.9	1.1	0.1	0.0	0.0	0.0	0.0	trace	2.3	6.4	40.2
Days With ≥ 1.0" Snow Depth	12	9	4	0	0	0	0	0	0	0	1	6	32

White Sulphur Springs *Greenbrier County*   Elevation: 1,919 ft.   Latitude: 37° 47' N   Longitude: 80° 19' W

	JAN	FEB	MAR	APR	MAY	JUN	JUL	AUG	SEP	OCT	NOV	DEC	YEAR
Mean Maximum Temp. (°F)	41.3	46.3	55.8	66.3	74.5	80.4	84.2	83.3	77.5	67.6	55.5	45.5	64.9
Mean Temp. (°F)	31.2	34.6	42.9	51.6	60.4	67.6	72.1	71.1	64.9	53.5	43.4	34.9	52.3
Mean Minimum Temp. (°F)	21.0	22.9	29.6	36.8	46.2	54.7	59.9	58.8	52.2	39.3	31.3	24.3	39.8
Extreme Maximum Temp. (°F)	70	79	85	92	93	99	98	100	97	85	81	76	100
Extreme Minimum Temp. (°F)	-19	-16	-6	14	25	31	39	36	27	16	4	-20	-20
Days Maximum Temp. ≥ 90°F	0	0	0	0	0	1	4	4	2	0	0	0	11
Days Maximum Temp. ≤ 32°F	6	4	1	0	0	0	0	0	0	0	0	4	15
Days Minimum Temp. ≤ 32°F	27	23	19	11	2	0	0	0	0	9	17	24	132
Days Minimum Temp. ≤ 0°F	2	1	0	0	0	0	0	0	0	0	0	1	4
Heating Degree Days (base 65°F)	1,040	851	680	401	172	37	4	8	85	359	640	927	5,204
Cooling Degree Days (base 65°F)	0	0	1	4	32	115	226	182	67	7	0	0	634
Mean Precipitation (in.)	3.35	2.92	3.67	3.23	4.24	3.41	4.21	3.27	3.08	3.01	2.88	3.00	40.27
Days With ≥ 0.1" Precipitation	7	7	8	7	9	7	8	7	6	5	6	7	84
Days With ≥ 1.0" Precipitation	1	1	1	1	1	1	1	1	1	1	0	1	11
Mean Snowfall (in.)	*6.9*	*5.8*	3.6	0.6	0.0	0.0	0.0	0.0	0.0	trace	1.0	3.4	*21.3*
Days With ≥ 1.0" Snow Depth	na	*6*	*2*	0	0	0	0	0	0	0	*0*	*4*	na

Winfield Locks *Putnam County*   Elevation: 570 ft.   Latitude: 38° 32' N   Longitude: 81° 55' W

	JAN	FEB	MAR	APR	MAY	JUN	JUL	AUG	SEP	OCT	NOV	DEC	YEAR
Mean Maximum Temp. (°F)	41.6	45.5	55.3	66.7	75.1	82.3	86.2	84.9	78.9	68.3	57.0	47.0	65.7
Mean Temp. (°F)	32.4	35.2	43.7	53.3	62.5	70.7	75.3	74.3	67.9	56.4	46.2	37.5	54.6
Mean Minimum Temp. (°F)	23.1	24.9	32.0	40.0	49.9	59.2	64.5	63.6	56.8	44.4	35.3	28.0	43.5
Extreme Maximum Temp. (°F)	77	78	86	91	96	102	101	101	98	89	84	79	102
Extreme Minimum Temp. (°F)	-18	-7	1	20	31	37	48	43	35	25	9	-11	-18
Days Maximum Temp. ≥ 90°F	0	0	0	0	0	3	9	6	2	0	0	0	20
Days Maximum Temp. ≤ 32°F	7	4	1	0	0	0	0	0	0	0	0	3	15
Days Minimum Temp. ≤ 32°F	25	21	17	6	0	0	0	0	0	2	13	20	104
Days Minimum Temp. ≤ 0°F	1	0	0	0	0	0	0	0	0	0	0	0	1
Heating Degree Days (base 65°F)	1,005	835	656	357	133	18	1	2	48	277	558	844	4,734
Cooling Degree Days (base 65°F)	0	0	2	11	62	205	348	301	132	17	1	0	1,079
Mean Precipitation (in.)	2.93	2.78	3.72	3.18	4.01	3.57	4.57	4.23	3.55	2.81	3.24	3.16	41.75
Days With ≥ 0.1" Precipitation	7	7	8	8	8	7	8	7	6	6	7	7	86
Days With ≥ 1.0" Precipitation	0	0	1	0	1	1	1	1	1	1	1	1	9
Mean Snowfall (in.)	*4.7*	3.8	2.9	0.9	0.0	0.0	0.0	0.0	0.0	trace	0.2	1.6	*14.1*
Days With ≥ 1.0" Snow Depth	7	5	1	0	0	0	0	0	0	0	0	1	14

Note: See Appendix D for explanation of data.

WISCONSIN

PHYSICAL FEATURES. Wisconsin lies in the upper Midwest between Lake Superior, Upper Michigan, Lake Michigan, and the Mississippi and St. Croix Rivers. Its greatest length is 320 miles, greatest width 295 miles, and total area 56,066 square miles. Glaciation has largely determined the topography and soils of the State. The various glaciations created a rolling terrain with nearly 9,000 lakes and several areas of marshes and swamps. Elevations range from about 600 feet above sea level along the Lake Superior and Lake Michigan shores and in the Mississippi flood plain in southwestern Wisconsin, to nearly 1,950 feet above sea level at Rib and Strawberry Hills.

The Northern Highlands, a plateau extending across northern Wisconsin, is an area of about 15,000 square miles with elevations from 1,000 to 1,800 feet above sea level. This area is the location of many lakes and the origin of most of the major streams in the State. The slope down to the narrow Lake Superior plain is quite steep. A comparatively flat, crescent shaped lowland lies immediately south of the Northern Highlands, embodying nearly one-fourth of Wisconsin. The eastern ridges and lowlands lie to the southeast of the central plains. The western uplands of southwestern Wisconsin west of the ridges and lowlands and south of the central plains contains approximately one-fourth of the State. This area is the roughest section of the State, rising 200 to 350 feet above the central plains and 100 to 200 feet above the Eastern Ridges and Lowlands. The Mississippi River bluffs rise 230 to 650 feet.

GENERAL CLIMATE. The Wisconsin climate is typically continental with some modification by Lakes Michigan and Superior. The winters are cold and snowy, and the summers are warm. About two-thirds of the annual precipitation falls during the growing season (freeze-free period). The rapid succession of storms moving from west to east and southwest to northeast account for the stimulating climate.

TEMPERATURE. The average annual temperature varies from 39°F. to 49.5°F. During more than one-half of the winters temperatures fall to -40°F. or lower, and almost every winter -30°F. or colder is reported from northern Wisconsin. Summer temperatures above 90°F. or higher average two to four days in northern counties to about 14 days in southern districts. During marked cool outbreaks in the summer months, the central lowlands occasionally report freezing temperatures. The freeze-free season averages around 80 days per year in the upper northeast and north-central lowlands, to about 180 days in the Milwaukee area. The pronounced moderating effect of Lake Michigan is well illustrated by the fact that the growing season of 140 to 150 days along the east-central coastal area is of the same duration as in the southwestern Wisconsin valleys. The short growing season in the central portion of the State is attributed to a number of factors, among them being an inward cold air drainage and the low heat capacities of the peat and sandy soils. The average date of last spring freeze ranges from early May along the Lake Michigan coastal area and southern counties to early June in the northernmost counties. The first autumn freezes occur in late August and early September in northern and central lowlands to mid-October along the Lake Michigan coast line. However, July freeze is not unusual in the north and central Wisconsin lowlands.

PRECIPITATION. The mean annual precipitation totals 30 to 34 inches over most of the Western Uplands and Northern Highlands, diminishing to about 28 inches along most of the Wisconsin coastal area bordering Lake Michigan and 28 to 30 inches over most of the Wisconsin Central Plain and Lake Superior Coastal area. The higher average annual precipitation coincides generally with the highest elevations, particularly to the windward slopes of the Western Uplands and Northern Highlands. Thunderstorms average about 30 per year in northern Wisconsin to about 40 per year in southern counties, occurring mostly in the summer. Occasional hail, wind, and lightning damage are reported.

The average seasonal snowfall varies from about 30 inches to well over 100 inches along the steep western slope of the Gogebic Range. The heavy snowfall along the Gogebic Range is a result of the prevailing cold northerly winter winds blowing across the relatively warm Lake Superior. Relatively greater average snowfall is recorded over the Western Uplands and Eastern Ridges than in adjacent lowland areas. The mean dates of the first snowfall of consequence, an inch or more, varies from early November in northern localities to around December 1 in southern Wisconsin counties. Average annual duration of snowcover ranges from 85 days in southern-most Wisconsin to more than 140 days along Lake Superior.

The drainage of Wisconsin is into Lake Superior, Lake Michigan, and the Mississippi River. The Mississippi and St. Croix Rivers form most of the western boundary. About one-half of the northwestern portion of the State is drained through the Chippewa River, while the remainder of this region drains directly into the Mississippi or the St. Croix and into Lake Superior. The Wisconsin River has its source at a small lake nearly 1,600 feet above mean sea level on the Upper Michigan boundary and drains most of central Wisconsin. Most of the Wisconsin

River tributaries also spring from the many lakes in the north. Except for the Rock River, a Mississippi River tributary which flows through northern Illinois, eastern Wisconsin drains into Lake Michigan, a large part through Green Bay.

Most of the streams and lakes in Wisconsin are ice-covered from late November to late March. Snow covers the ground in practically all the winter months, except in the extreme southern areas. Flooding is most frequent, and most serious, during April due to the melting of snow associated with spring rains. During this period, flood conditions are often aggravated by ice jams which back up the flood waters. Excessive rains of the thunderstorm type sometimes produce tributary flooding or flash flooding along the smaller streams and creeks. Major flooding occurs on the Mississippi River, on the average, about three years in 10.

Tornadoes occur in Wisconsin. Most of the very destructive tornadoes occur in the northwestern quarter of the State. Wisconsin tornado frequency is highest in June and July, followed in order by April, May, and September.

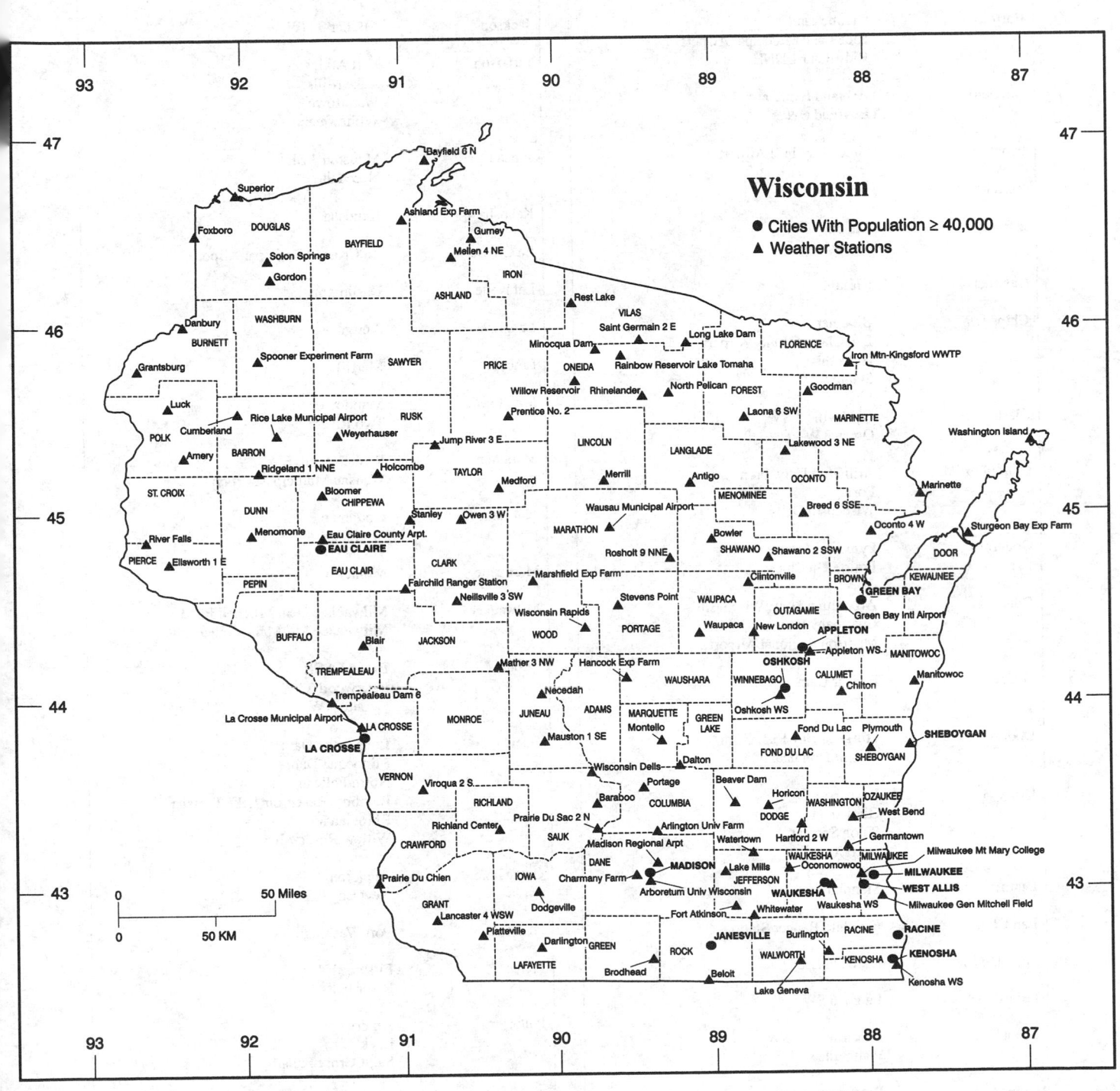

Wisconsin

● Cities With Population ≥ 40,000
▲ Weather Stations

Wisconsin Weather Stations by County

County	Station Name
Ashland	Mellen 4 NE
Barron	Cumberland
	Rice Lake Municipal Airport
	Ridgeland 1 NNE
Bayfield	Ashland Exp. Farm
	Bayfield 6 N
Brown	Green Bay Int'l Airport
Buffalo	Alma Dam 4
Burnett	Danbury
	Grantsburg
Calumet	Chilton
Chippewa	Bloomer
	Eau Claire County Airport
	Holcombe
	Stanley
Clark	Neillsville 3 SW
	Owen 3 W
Columbia	Arlington Univ. Farm
	Portage
	Wisconsin Dells
Crawford	Lynxville Dam 9
	Prairie Du Chien
Dane	Arboretum Univ. Wisconsin
	Charmany Farm
	Madison Regional Airport
Dodge	Beaver Dam
	Horicon
Door	Sturgeon Bay Exp. Farm
	Washington Island
Douglas	Foxboro
	Gordon
	Solon Springs
	Superior
Dunn	Menomonie
Eau Claire	Fairchild Ranger Station
Fond Du Lac	Fond Du Lac
Forest	Laona 6 SW
Grant	Lancaster 4 WSW
	Platteville
Green	Brodhead
Green Lake	Dalton
Iowa	Dodgeville

County	Station Name
Iron	Gurney
Jackson	Mather 3 NW
Jefferson	Fort Atkinson
	Lake Mills
	Watertown
	Whitewater
Juneau	Mauston 1 SE
	Necedah
Kenosha	Kenosha
La Crosse	La Crosse Municipal Airport
Lafayette	Darlington
Langlade	Antigo
Lincoln	Merrill
Manitowoc	Manitowoc
	Two Rivers
Marathon	Rosholt 9 NNE
	Wausau Municipal Airport
Marinette	Goodman
	Marinette
Marquette	Montello
Milwaukee	Milwaukee Gen. Mitchell Field
	Milwaukee Mt. Mary College
Oconto	Breed 6 SSE
	Lakewood 3 NE
	Oconto 4 W
Oneida	Long Lake Dam
	Minocqua Dam
	North Pelican
	Rainbow Reservoir Lake Tomaha
	Rhinelander
	Willow Reservoir
Outagamie	Appleton
	New London
Ozaukee	Port Washington
Pierce	Ellsworth 1 E
	River Falls
Polk	Amery
	Luck
	Saint Croix Falls
Portage	Stevens Point
Price	Prentice 2

County	Station Name
Racine	Burlington
	Racine
Richland	Richland Center
Rock	Beloit
Rusk	Weyerhauser
Sauk	Baraboo
	Prairie Du Sac 2 N
Shawano	Bowler
	Shawano 2 SSW
Sheboygan	Plymouth
	Sheboygan
Taylor	Jump River 3 E
	Medford
Trempealeau	Blair
	Trempealeau Dam 6
Vernon	Genoa Dam 8
	Viroqua 2 S
Vilas	Rest Lake
	Saint Germain 2 E
Walworth	Lake Geneva
Washburn	Spooner Experiment Farm
Washington	Germantown
	Hartford 2 W
	West Bend
Waukesha	Oconomowoc
	Waukesha
Waupaca	Clintonville
	Waupaca
Waushara	Hancock Exp. Farm
Winnebago	Oshkosh
Wood	Marshfield Exp. Farm
	Wisconsin Rapids

Wisconsin Weather Stations by City

City	Station Name	Miles
Appleton	Appleton	2
	New London	17
	Oshkosh	19
Eau Claire	Bloomer	20
	Eau Claire County Airport	4
Green Bay	Green Bay Int'l Airport	6
Janesville	Beloit	13
	Brodhead	19
	Fort Atkinson	17
	Whitewater	18
Kenosha	Waukegan, IL	16
	Kenosha	2
	Racine	9
La Crosse	Caledonia, MN	18
	Genoa Dam 8	17
	La Crosse Municipal Airport	4
	Trempealeau Dam 6	17
Madison	Arboretum Univ. Wisconsin	2
	Arlington Univ. Farm	16
	Charmany Farm	4
	Madison Regional Airport	5
Milwaukee	Germantown	14
	Milwaukee Mt. Mary College	4
	Milwaukee Gen. Mitchell Field	8
	Waukesha	14
Oshkosh	Appleton	18
	Chilton	20
	Fond Du Lac	16
	Oshkosh	0
Racine	Kenosha	11
	Milwaukee Gen. Mitchell Field	16
	Racine	2
Sheboygan	Plymouth	12
	Sheboygan	0
Waukesha	Germantown	16
	Milwaukee Mt. Mary College	11
	Milwaukee Gen. Mitchell Field	18
	Oconomowoc	15
	Waukesha	1
Wauwatosa	Germantown	12
	Milwaukee Mt. Mary College	1
	Milwaukee Gen. Mitchell Field	10
	Waukesha	11
West Allis	Germantown	15
	Milwaukee Mt. Mary College	4
	Milwaukee Gen. Mitchell Field	7
	Waukesha	11

Note: Miles is the distance between the geographic center of the city and the weather station.

Wisconsin Weather Stations by Elevation

Feet	Station Name
1,643	Saint Germain 2 E
1,627	Long Lake Dam
1,607	North Pelican
1,607	Rest Lake
1,597	Rainbow Reservoir Lake Tomaha
1,578	Minocqua Dam
1,578	Rhinelander
1,558	Willow Reservoir
1,538	Prentice 2
1,522	Laona 6 SW
1,519	Antigo
1,469	Medford
1,427	Goodman
1,299	Mellen 4 NE
1,289	Lakewood 3 NE
1,263	Jump River 3 E
1,250	Marshfield Exp. Farm
1,250	Merrill
1,240	Cumberland
1,240	Owen 3 W
1,217	Luck
1,197	Wausau Municipal Airport
1,194	Weyerhauser
1,158	Rosholt 9 NNE
1,158	Viroqua 2 S
1,108	Dodgeville
1,102	Rice Lake Municipal Airport
1,099	Spooner Experiment Farm
1,089	Stanley
1,079	Arlington Univ. Farm
1,079	Bowler
1,079	Fairchild Ranger Station
1,079	Solon Springs
1,076	Hancock Exp. Farm
1,076	Stevens Point
1,069	Amery
1,040	Gordon
1,040	Lancaster 4 WSW
1,040	Wisconsin Rapids
1,033	Neillsville 3 SW
1,026	Ellsworth 1 E
1,023	Holcombe
1,003	Platteville
977	Bloomer
977	Hartford 2 W
967	Gurney
967	Mather 3 NW
958	Ridgeland 1 NNE
938	West Bend
931	Foxboro
928	Darlington
921	Danbury
921	Necedah
912	River Falls
908	Charmany Farm

Feet	Station Name
898	Grantsburg
889	Eau Claire County Airport
879	Horicon
879	Lake Geneva
872	Whitewater
862	Arboretum Univ. Wisconsin
862	Mauston 1 SE
859	Blair
859	Breed 6 SSE
859	Dalton
856	Madison Regional Airport
853	Oconomowoc
849	Germantown
849	Lake Mills
839	Beaver Dam
839	Chilton
839	Waupaca
833	Plymouth
833	Wisconsin Dells
830	Waukesha
823	Watertown
820	Baraboo
816	Bayfield 6 N
807	Shawano 2 SSW
803	New London
797	Clintonville
797	Fort Atkinson
787	Brodhead
784	Montello
777	Beloit
777	Menomonie
777	Prairie Du Sac 2 N
774	Portage
767	Saint Croix Falls
757	Fond Du Lac
748	Appleton
748	Burlington
748	Oshkosh
725	Milwaukee Mt. Mary College
721	Richland Center
685	Green Bay Int'l Airport
669	Alma Dam 4
669	Milwaukee Gen. Mitchell Field
659	Manitowoc
659	Oconto 4 W
659	Trempealeau Dam 6
656	Prairie Du Chien
652	Sturgeon Bay Exp. Farm
649	Ashland Exp. Farm
649	La Crosse Municipal Airport
646	Sheboygan
636	Genoa Dam 8
629	Lynxville Dam 9
629	Superior
610	Washington Island

Feet	Station Name
606	Marinette
597	Kenosha
597	Port Washington
597	Two Rivers
593	Racine

Green Bay Int'l Airport

The Green Bay climate is modified by surrounding topography. The modification is caused by the Bay of Green Bay, Lakes Michigan, and Superior, and to a lesser extent, the slightly higher surrounding terrain terminating in the Fox River Valley. The city of Green Bay is located at the mouth of the Fox River, one of the largest rivers flowing northward in the United States. It empties into the south end of the Bay.

The modified continental climate of Green Bay is shown by the few occurrences of 90 degree temperatures in the summer season and the few occurrences of sub-zero temperatures in the winter season. The narrow temperature range stems from the lake effects and the limited hours of sunshine caused by cloudiness.

Precipitation normally falls in the five-month period May through September. Three-fifths of the annual total is in the growing season, most often falling during thunderstorms. During the winter months, snowfall is less than in nearby communities where the ground is slightly higher.

The comparatively low range in temperature along with the greater portion of the precipitation falling during the growing season is conducive to the development of the dairy industry. Cherry and apple orchards are important crops in nearby lake communities. The growing of potatoes and canning vegetables are predominant inland. Paper products are the major manufacturing industry.

High winds, excessive precipitation, and electrical storms cause occasional damage. Snowstorms are the principal winter hazard. While the winters are long in Green Bay, the extremes are never as severe as the northern latitude location would indicate.

Based on the 1951-1980 period, the average first occurrence of 32 degrees Fahrenheit in the fall is October 2 and the average last occurrence in the spring is May 12.

Green Bay Int'l Airport *Brown County*   Elevation: 685 ft.   Latitude: 44° 29' N   Longitude: 88° 08' W

	JAN	FEB	MAR	APR	MAY	JUN	JUL	AUG	SEP	OCT	NOV	DEC	YEAR
Mean Maximum Temp. (°F)	23.4	28.2	39.0	54.1	67.5	76.7	81.3	78.4	69.9	57.4	42.0	28.9	53.9
Mean Temp. (°F)	15.2	19.9	30.6	44.0	56.0	65.4	70.2	67.9	59.3	47.7	34.2	21.4	44.3
Mean Minimum Temp. (°F)	6.9	11.6	22.2	33.9	44.5	54.0	59.0	57.3	48.7	38.0	26.4	14.0	34.7
Extreme Maximum Temp. (°F)	49	58	77	89	90	98	103	99	92	85	74	62	103
Extreme Minimum Temp. (°F)	-28	-28	-12	11	24	35	43	39	27	16	-9	-27	-28
Days Maximum Temp. ≥ 90°F	0	0	0	0	0	2	3	1	0	0	0	0	6
Days Maximum Temp. ≤ 32°F	23	17	8	0	0	0	0	0	0	0	5	18	71
Days Minimum Temp. ≤ 32°F	31	27	26	14	2	0	0	0	1	9	23	29	162
Days Minimum Temp. ≤ 0°F	11	6	1	0	0	0	0	0	0	0	0	5	23
Heating Degree Days (base 65°F)	1,540	1,267	1,060	628	296	81	17	35	201	530	917	1,345	7,917
Cooling Degree Days (base 65°F)	0	0	0	4	23	100	179	134	38	1	0	0	479
Mean Precipitation (in.)	1.20	0.98	2.06	2.54	2.80	3.29	3.36	3.70	3.18	2.26	2.32	1.41	29.10
Maximum Precipitation (in.)	2.6	3.6	4.7	5.9	8.2	10.3	7.0	9.0	7.8	5.0	5.3	3.1	38.4
Minimum Precipitation (in.)	0.1	trace	0.3	0.5	0.1	0.3	0.8	0.9	0.3	trace	0.2	0.1	17.8
Maximum 24-hr. Precipitation (in.)	1.0	1.8	1.3	1.9	2.2	4.9	2.9	3.8	3.0	3.4	2.2	1.2	4.9
Days With ≥ 0.1" Precipitation	4	3	5	6	6	6	6	7	6	5	5	4	63
Days With ≥ 1.0" Precipitation	0	0	0	0	1	1	1	1	1	0	0	0	5
Mean Snowfall (in.)	13.8	8.3	9.5	2.8	0.2	trace	0.0	trace	trace	0.2	5.4	12.0	52.2
Maximum Snowfall (in.)	30	21	24	12	4	0	0	0	trace	2	17	27	92
Maximum 24-hr. Snowfall (in.)	9	9	13	10	4	0	0	0	trace	1	10	14	14
Days With ≥ 1.0" Snow Depth	27	22	14	2	0	0	0	0	0	0	4	20	89
Thunderstorm Days	< 1	< 1	1	2	4	6	7	6	4	2	1	< 1	33
Foggy Days	9	10	11	10	9	9	11	14	12	11	12	11	129
Predominant Sky Cover	OVR	OVR	OVR	OVR	OVR	OVR	OVR	OVR	OVR	OVR	OVR	OVR	OVR
Mean Relative Humidity 6am (%)	78	79	81	79	79	82	86	90	89	85	82	81	83
Mean Relative Humidity 3pm (%)	68	65	63	54	52	55	55	58	59	59	67	71	60
Mean Dewpoint (°F)	9	12	22	32	43	54	60	59	51	40	27	15	35
Prevailing Wind Direction	W	W	NE	NE	NE	SW	SW	SW	SSW	SW	W	W	SW
Prevailing Wind Speed (mph)	12	10	12	13	12	10	9	9	10	12	12	10	10
Maximum Wind Gust (mph)	69	55	58	68	81	70	60	54	48	46	54	53	81

La Crosse Municipal Airport

The city of La Crosse is situated on the east bank of the Mississippi River at the confluence of the Mississippi, Black, and La Crosse Rivers. The official records are taken at the La Crosse Municipal Airport which is six and a half miles north of the main Post Office, on the north end of French Island. This island is about six miles long from north to south and two to four miles wide with the Mississippi River to the west and the old channel of the Black River to the east. A sandy plain exists on each side of the river extending between the Wisconsin and Minnesota bluffs which rise 450 to 500 feet above the valley floor. The distance from bluff to bluff averages about five miles.

The prevailing winds in the area are from the northwest from January through April and southerly during the remainder of the year. The situation of the city and airport in a natural bowl between the hills results in somewhat colder temperatures at night due to the settling of cooler air. Valley fogs often persist to mid-forenoon. Steepsided hills with narrow valleys are characteristic of most of the surrounding area.

The flow of the Mississippi River is regulated by dams built for the purpose of navigation, but the reservoirs have limited storage capacity. La Crosse is in the area of Pool No. eight with a mean sea level elevation of 631 feet. When the river reaches an elevation of 639 feet, with open gate operation, there is considerable flooding of land near the river and some industrial sections of the city.

The invigorating continental-type climate results in wide and frequent variations in temperature. General storms moving eastward or northeastward into the area bring warmer weather and supply most of our moisture. These are usually followed by cooler air from Canada. The winters are cold and humid. The summers are warm with moderate humidities, while periods of hot and humid weather occur occasionally, usually lasting from a few days to a week at a time.

Sixty percent of the precipitation falls during the main growing season, extending from May through September. Most of the summer rainfall occurs during scattered thunderstorms. Some damage from heavy rains, high winds, and hail occurs each year, but tornadoes are infrequent and cover very small areas. Snow is frequent and is the predominant form of precipitation in winter. Heavy snow sometimes falls with larger amounts over the ridges.

Based on the 1951-1980 period, the average first occurrence of 32 degrees Fahrenheit in the fall is October 13 and the average last occurrence in the spring is April 29.

La Crosse Municipal Airport *La Crosse County*   Elevation: 649 ft.   Latitude: 43° 52' N   Longitude: 91° 15' W

	JAN	FEB	MAR	APR	MAY	JUN	JUL	AUG	SEP	OCT	NOV	DEC	YEAR
Mean Maximum Temp. (°F)	23.8	30.7	42.7	58.5	71.4	80.4	84.4	81.6	72.8	60.1	42.9	29.4	56.6
Mean Temp. (°F)	14.9	21.6	33.5	47.8	60.0	69.2	73.6	71.1	62.3	50.2	35.3	21.9	46.8
Mean Minimum Temp. (°F)	5.9	12.4	24.1	37.1	48.7	58.0	62.8	60.6	51.7	40.2	27.5	14.4	36.9
Extreme Maximum Temp. (°F)	57	64	80	93	94	102	108	105	100	92	75	67	108
Extreme Minimum Temp. (°F)	-33	-36	-12	7	26	37	45	43	29	14	-9	-30	-36
Days Maximum Temp. ≥ 90°F	0	0	0	0	1	4	8	4	1	0	0	0	18
Days Maximum Temp. ≤ 32°F	22	14	6	0	0	0	0	0	0	0	5	17	64
Days Minimum Temp. ≤ 32°F	30	26	24	9	1	0	0	0	0	6	21	29	146
Days Minimum Temp. ≤ 0°F	12	7	1	0	0	0	0	0	0	0	0	5	25
Heating Degree Days (base 65°F)	1,548	1,222	970	518	198	35	5	15	149	460	885	1,329	7,334
Cooling Degree Days (base 65°F)	0	0	0	8	51	178	290	225	76	6	0	0	834
Mean Precipitation (in.)	1.18	1.00	2.03	3.42	3.38	3.83	4.25	4.24	3.52	2.24	2.07	1.19	32.35
Maximum Precipitation (in.)	2.9	2.6	3.8	7.3	8.8	10.8	9.3	9.8	10.5	5.1	6.2	2.9	44.1
Minimum Precipitation (in.)	0.1	0	0.3	0.6	0.9	1.3	0.2	0.5	0.4	trace	trace	0.3	16.6
Maximum 24-hr. Precipitation (in.)	1.3	1.3	1.6	3.9	2.7	3.9	5.2	2.8	3.3	2.0	2.8	1.4	5.2
Days With ≥ 0.1" Precipitation	4	3	5	7	7	7	7	7	6	5	5	4	67
Days With ≥ 1.0" Precipitation	0	0	0	1	1	1	1	1	1	0	0	0	6
Mean Snowfall (in.)	13.0	8.0	7.2	2.0	trace	trace	0.0	trace	trace	0.2	4.5	9.1	44.0
Maximum Snowfall (in.)	30	31	34	17	1	0	0	0	trace	2	30	30	91
Maximum 24-hr. Snowfall (in.)	10	10	13	10	1	0	0	0	trace	2	13	14	14
Days With ≥ 1.0" Snow Depth	27	22	11	1	0	0	0	0	0	0	4	20	85
Thunderstorm Days	< 1	< 1	1	3	5	8	8	7	5	2	1	< 1	40
Foggy Days	11	11	12	9	8	8	10	14	13	10	12	13	131
Predominant Sky Cover	OVR	OVR	OVR	OVR	OVR	OVR	OVR	OVR	OVR	OVR	OVR	OVR	OVR
Mean Relative Humidity 6am (%)	78	79	81	79	79	84	88	90	90	83	82	81	83
Mean Relative Humidity 3pm (%)	64	61	57	49	49	52	54	55	56	53	63	68	57
Mean Dewpoint (°F)	8	13	22	34	46	57	62	61	52	40	27	15	37
Prevailing Wind Direction	NW	NW	NW	NW	S	S	S	S	S	S	S	S	S
Prevailing Wind Speed (mph)	12	12	13	14	12	10	10	9	10	12	10	10	12
Maximum Wind Gust (mph)	na	na	na	na	na	na	na	na	na	na	na	na	na

Madison Regional Airport

Madison is set on a narrow isthmus of land between Lakes Mendota and Monona. Lake Mendota (15 square miles) lies northwest of Lake Monona (five square miles) and the lakes are only two-thirds of a mile apart at one point. Drainage at Madison is southeast through two other lakes into the Rock River, which flows south into Illinois, and then west to the Mississippi. The westward flowing Wisconsin River is only 20 miles northwest of Madison. Madison lakes are normally frozen from mid-December to early April.

Madison has the typical continental climate of interior North America with a large annual temperature range and with frequent short period temperature changes. The range of extreme temperatures is from about 110 to -40 degrees. Winter temperatures (December-February) average near 20 degrees and the summer average (June-August) is in the upper 60s. Daily temperatures average below 32 degrees about 120 days and above 40 degrees for about 210 days of the year.

Madison lies in the path of the frequent cyclones and anticyclones which move eastward over this area during fall, winter and spring. In summer, the cyclones have diminished intensity and tend to pass farther north. The most frequent air masses are of polar origin. Occasional outbreaks of arctic air affect this area during the winter months. Although northward moving tropical air masses contribute considerable cloudiness and precipitation, the true Gulf air mass does not reach this area in winter, and only occasionally at other seasons. Summers are pleasant, with only occasional periods of extreme heat or high humidity.

There are no dry and wet seasons, but about 60 percent of the annual precipitation falls in the five months of May through September. Cold season precipitation is lighter, but lasts longer. Soil moisture is usually adequate in the first part of the growing season. During July, August, and September, the crops depend on current rainfall, which is mostly from thunderstorms and tends to be erratic and variable. Average occurrence of thunderstorms is just under 7 days per month during this period.

March and November are the windiest months. Tornadoes are infrequent. Dane County has about one tornado in every three to five years.

The ground is covered with one inch or more of snow about 60 percent of the time from about December 10 to near February 25 in an average winter. The soil is usually frozen from the first of December through most of March with an average frost penetration of 25 to 30 inches. The growing season averages 175 days.

Farming is diversified with the main emphasis on dairying. Field crops are mainly corn, oats, clover, and alfalfa, but barley, wheat, rye, and tobacco are also raised. Canning factories pack peas, sweet corn, and lima beans. Fruits are mainly apples, strawberries, and raspberries.

Madison Regional Airport *Dane County*   Elevation: 856 ft.   Latitude: 43° 08' N   Longitude: 89° 21' W

	JAN	FEB	MAR	APR	MAY	JUN	JUL	AUG	SEP	OCT	NOV	DEC	YEAR
Mean Maximum Temp. (°F)	25.3	31.1	43.1	57.5	70.2	79.3	83.0	80.2	72.0	60.0	43.9	31.0	56.4
Mean Temp. (°F)	16.7	22.1	33.4	46.1	57.7	67.0	71.5	68.9	60.5	49.0	35.3	23.2	46.0
Mean Minimum Temp. (°F)	8.1	13.2	23.7	34.6	45.2	54.7	59.9	57.6	49.0	37.9	26.8	15.2	35.5
Extreme Maximum Temp. (°F)	56	61	82	94	93	101	104	102	97	90	74	62	104
Extreme Minimum Temp. (°F)	-28	-29	-8	0	19	31	40	37	25	13	-6	-25	-29
Days Maximum Temp. ≥ 90°F	0	0	0	0	0	3	5	3	1	0	0	0	12
Days Maximum Temp. ≤ 32°F	21	14	5	1	0	0	0	0	0	0	4	15	60
Days Minimum Temp. ≤ 32°F	30	27	25	13	3	0	0	0	1	9	21	29	158
Days Minimum Temp. ≤ 0°F	10	6	1	0	0	0	0	0	0	0	0	5	22
Heating Degree Days (base 65°F)	1,492	1,205	972	567	254	60	11	31	179	494	883	1,291	7,439
Cooling Degree Days (base 65°F)	0	0	0	6	31	131	225	165	51	3	0	0	612
Mean Precipitation (in.)	1.24	1.22	2.28	3.33	3.13	3.84	3.90	4.23	3.26	2.24	2.28	1.68	32.63
Maximum Precipitation (in.)	2.4	2.8	5.0	7.1	6.3	9.9	10.9	9.5	9.2	5.6	5.1	4.1	43.3
Minimum Precipitation (in.)	0.1	0.1	0.3	1.1	0.6	0.8	1.5	0.7	0.1	0.1	0.1	0.3	21.1
Maximum 24-hr. Precipitation (in.)	1.1	1.6	1.9	1.9	3.6	3.7	3.9	3.0	2.7	2.8	2.3	2.2	3.9
Days With ≥ 0.1" Precipitation	3	3	5	7	7	7	6	7	6	5	5	4	65
Days With ≥ 1.0" Precipitation	0	0	0	1	1	1	1	1	1	0	0	0	6
Mean Snowfall (in.)	12.8	8.3	7.2	3.4	0.1	trace	trace	trace	trace	0.4	4.4	12.0	48.6
Maximum Snowfall (in.)	28	37	25	17	3	0	0	0	trace	3	18	33	83
Maximum 24-hr. Snowfall (in.)	13	12	12	13	3	0	0	0	trace	3	8	17	17
Days With ≥ 1.0" Snow Depth	24	21	9	2	0	0	0	0	0	0	4	18	78
Thunderstorm Days	< 1	< 1	2	4	5	7	8	7	5	2	1	< 1	41
Foggy Days	13	11	13	11	11	10	11	14	14	12	13	14	147
Predominant Sky Cover	OVR	OVR	OVR	OVR	OVR	OVR	OVR	OVR	OVR	OVR	OVR	OVR	OVR
Mean Relative Humidity 6am (%)	78	80	81	80	79	81	85	89	90	85	83	82	83
Mean Relative Humidity 3pm (%)	67	63	59	51	49	51	53	55	56	54	64	69	57
Mean Dewpoint (°F)	10	14	23	34	45	55	61	60	51	40	28	17	37
Prevailing Wind Direction	WNW	WNW	NW	S	S	S	S	S	S	S	S	WNW	S
Prevailing Wind Speed (mph)	12	12	13	12	10	9	9	9	10	10	10	12	10
Maximum Wind Gust (mph)	58	62	67	63	64	83	83	64	64	62	55	58	83

Milwaukee Gen. Mitchell Field

Milwaukee possesses a continental climate characterized by a wide range of temperatures between summer and winter. Precipitation is moderate and occurs mostly in the spring, less in the autumn, and very little in the wintertime. Rainfall is well distributed for agricultural purposes, although spring planting is sometimes delayed by wet ground and cold weather.

Milwaukee is in a region of frequently changeable weather and its climate is influenced by general easterly-moving storms which traverse the nations midsection. The most severe winter storms, which produce in excess of 10 inches of snow, develop in the southern Great Plains and move northeast across Illinois and Indiana.

Occasionally during the cold season, frigid air masses from Canada push southeast across the Great Lakes region. These arctic air masses account for the coldest winter temperatures. If northwesterly wind circulation persists, repeated incursions of arctic air will result in a period of bitterly cold weather lasting several days.

Summer temperatures, which reach into the 90s but rarely exceed 100 degrees, occur with brisk southwest winds that carry hot air from the plains and lower Mississippi River Valley across the city. A combination of high temperatures and humidity occasionally develops, usually building up over a period of several days when persistent southerly winds transport moisture from the Gulf of Mexico into the area.

The Gulf is a major source of moisture for Milwaukee in all seasons. Cold-season precipitation (rain, snow, or a mixture) is usually of relatively long duration and low intensity, and occasionally persists for two days or more, whereas in the warm season, relatively short-duration and high-intensity showery rainfall, usually lasting a few hours or less, predominates.

The Great Lakes significantly influence the local climate. Temperature extremes are modified by Lake Michigan and, to a lesser extent, the other Great Lakes. In late autumn and winter, air masses that are initially very cold often reach the city only after being tempered by passage over one or more of the lakes. Similarly, air masses that approach from the northeast in the spring and summer are cooler because of movement over the Great Lakes.

Lake-induced snows usually occur a few times each winter, but snow accumulation is rarely heavy.

Milwaukee Gen. Mitchell Field *Milwaukee County*   Elevation: 669 ft.   Latitude: 42° 57' N   Longitude: 87° 54' W

	JAN	FEB	MAR	APR	MAY	JUN	JUL	AUG	SEP	OCT	NOV	DEC	YEAR
Mean Maximum Temp. (°F)	27.2	31.7	41.5	53.3	65.2	75.6	80.6	78.5	71.2	59.4	45.1	32.8	55.2
Mean Temp. (°F)	20.2	24.9	34.3	44.9	55.7	65.9	71.8	70.3	62.6	51.0	38.1	26.3	47.2
Mean Minimum Temp. (°F)	13.1	18.0	27.0	36.4	46.0	56.2	63.0	62.1	54.0	42.5	31.0	19.7	39.1
Extreme Maximum Temp. (°F)	60	68	82	91	93	101	103	103	96	88	75	64	103
Extreme Minimum Temp. (°F)	-26	-26	-4	12	29	39	45	44	28	18	-3	-20	-26
Days Maximum Temp. ≥ 90°F	0	0	0	0	0	2	4	2	1	0	0	0	9
Days Maximum Temp. ≤ 32°F	20	14	6	1	0	0	0	0	0	0	3	13	57
Days Minimum Temp. ≤ 32°F	29	25	23	8	1	0	0	0	0	3	17	27	133
Days Minimum Temp. ≤ 0°F	6	3	0	0	0	0	0	0	0	0	0	3	12
Heating Degree Days (base 65°F)	1,384	1,127	946	602	311	83	11	17	130	434	801	1,195	7,041
Cooling Degree Days (base 65°F)	0	0	1	0	33	128	240	199	69	5	0	0	681
Mean Precipitation (in.)	1.82	1.60	2.61	3.75	2.89	3.58	3.40	3.88	3.29	2.54	2.69	2.24	34.29
Maximum Precipitation (in.)	4.0	3.9	6.9	7.3	7.6	8.3	7.7	9.0	9.4	7.0	7.1	5.4	42.2
Minimum Precipitation (in.)	0.3	0	0.3	1.3	0.5	0.7	1.0	0.5	trace	0.1	0.6	0.3	19.1
Maximum 24-hr. Precipitation (in.)	1.5	1.7	2.3	3.0	2.1	3.0	3.0	6.8	2.5	2.3	1.8	2.2	6.8
Days With ≥ 0.1" Precipitation	5	4	6	7	6	6	6	7	6	5	6	5	69
Days With ≥ 1.0" Precipitation	0	0	0	1	1	1	1	1	1	0	1	0	7
Mean Snowfall (in.)	14.9	10.9	7.7	2.5	0.1	trace	trace	trace	trace	0.4	3.6	10.7	50.8
Maximum Snowfall (in.)	34	42	27	16	3	0	0	0	0	6	16	28	88
Maximum 24-hr. Snowfall (in.)	14	17	11	12	3	0	0	0	0	4	10	13	17
Days With ≥ 1.0" Snow Depth	22	18	8	1	0	0	0	0	0	0	2	13	64
Thunderstorm Days	< 1	< 1	2	4	4	6	7	6	4	2	1	< 1	36
Foggy Days	11	11	12	11	11	10	10	13	12	11	12	13	137
Predominant Sky Cover	OVR	OVR	OVR	OVR	OVR	OVR	OVR	OVR	OVR	OVR	OVR	OVR	OVR
Mean Relative Humidity 6am (%)	76	77	79	78	77	79	82	86	85	82	80	79	80
Mean Relative Humidity 3pm (%)	68	66	64	58	57	58	59	62	61	60	66	69	62
Mean Dewpoint (°F)	13	16	24	34	44	55	61	61	53	41	30	19	38
Prevailing Wind Direction	WNW	WNW	WNW	NNE	NNE	NNE	SW	SW	SSW	SSW	WNW	WNW	WNW
Prevailing Wind Speed (mph)	13	13	13	14	14	12	10	10	12	12	13	13	13
Maximum Wind Gust (mph)	66	67	77	67	74	76	81	64	62	53	56	61	81

Alma Dam 4 *Buffalo County*   Elevation: 669 ft.   Latitude: 44° 20' N   Longitude: 91° 56' W

	JAN	FEB	MAR	APR	MAY	JUN	JUL	AUG	SEP	OCT	NOV	DEC	YEAR
Mean Maximum Temp. (°F)	24.0	30.1	41.2	57.5	70.3	79.1	82.8	80.5	71.7	59.5	42.0	28.9	55.6
Mean Temp. (°F)	15.5	21.5	32.7	47.2	59.5	68.5	72.9	70.8	62.0	50.1	34.5	21.5	46.4
Mean Minimum Temp. (°F)	7.0	12.8	24.1	37.0	48.7	57.9	62.8	61.1	52.2	40.7	26.9	14.2	37.1
Extreme Maximum Temp. (°F)	55	61	80	89	90	97	100	99	97	91	73	64	100
Extreme Minimum Temp. (°F)	-38	-35	-15	7	24	38	43	43	25	18	-5	-32	-38
Days Maximum Temp. ≥ 90°F	0	0	0	0	0	2	4	2	0	0	0	0	8
Days Maximum Temp. ≤ 32°F	22	14	6	0	0	0	0	0	0	0	6	18	66
Days Minimum Temp. ≤ 32°F	30	27	24	9	1	0	0	0	0	6	21	30	148
Days Minimum Temp. ≤ 0°F	11	6	1	0	0	0	0	0	0	0	0	5	23
Heating Degree Days (base 65°F)	1,529	1,225	996	532	204	40	4	15	147	459	911	1,342	7,404
Cooling Degree Days (base 65°F)	0	0	0	6	43	153	258	204	66	4	0	0	734
Mean Precipitation (in.)	0.97	0.66	1.76	3.33	3.94	4.27	5.18	4.68	4.09	2.51	2.27	0.92	34.58
Days With ≥ 0.1" Precipitation	3	2	4	7	8	8	8	8	7	5	4	3	67
Days With ≥ 1.0" Precipitation	0	0	0	1	1	1	1	1	1	0	0	0	6
Mean Snowfall (in.)	*10.8*	5.9	7.4	1.3	trace	0.0	0.0	0.0	0.0	trace	3.7	8.4	*37.5*
Days With ≥ 1.0" Snow Depth	29	23	13	1	0	0	0	0	0	0	4	20	90

Amery *Polk County*   Elevation: 1,069 ft.   Latitude: 45° 18' N   Longitude: 92° 22' W

	JAN	FEB	MAR	APR	MAY	JUN	JUL	AUG	SEP	OCT	NOV	DEC	YEAR
Mean Maximum Temp. (°F)	19.2	26.4	37.7	54.3	67.9	76.4	80.9	78.5	69.1	56.5	38.6	24.8	52.5
Mean Temp. (°F)	9.0	15.8	28.1	43.4	56.3	65.2	69.9	67.3	58.0	45.8	30.4	15.9	42.1
Mean Minimum Temp. (°F)	-1.3	5.3	18.5	32.6	44.7	53.9	58.7	56.1	46.8	35.1	22.1	6.9	31.6
Extreme Maximum Temp. (°F)	54	57	80	90	90	101	101	101	97	85	73	61	101
Extreme Minimum Temp. (°F)	-46	-38	-17	-5	20	34	39	35	23	8	-21	-43	-46
Days Maximum Temp. ≥ 90°F	0	0	0	0	0	1	3	2	0	0	0	0	6
Days Maximum Temp. ≤ 32°F	26	18	9	1	0	0	0	0	0	0	9	23	86
Days Minimum Temp. ≤ 32°F	31	28	27	15	3	0	0	0	2	12	26	31	175
Days Minimum Temp. ≤ 0°F	17	11	4	0	0	0	0	0	0	0	1	10	43
Heating Degree Days (base 65°F)	1,734	1,384	1,136	643	288	83	21	47	238	589	1,032	1,519	8,714
Cooling Degree Days (base 65°F)	0	0	0	3	23	102	180	133	35	2	0	0	478
Mean Precipitation (in.)	1.02	0.69	1.72	2.64	3.23	4.62	3.96	4.67	3.80	2.58	2.05	1.13	32.11
Days With ≥ 0.1" Precipitation	3	2	4	6	7	8	7	7	6	6	4	3	63
Days With ≥ 1.0" Precipitation	0	0	0	0	1	1	1	1	1	0	0	0	5
Mean Snowfall (in.)	11.3	6.4	8.5	2.1	0.0	0.0	0.0	0.0	0.0	0.5	7.0	*9.5*	*45.3*
Days With ≥ 1.0" Snow Depth	30	27	20	2	0	0	0	0	0	0	8	25	112

Antigo *Langlade County*   Elevation: 1,519 ft.   Latitude: 45° 09' N   Longitude: 89° 07' W

	JAN	FEB	MAR	APR	MAY	JUN	JUL	AUG	SEP	OCT	NOV	DEC	YEAR
Mean Maximum Temp. (°F)	20.5	26.5	36.5	53.1	67.0	74.8	*79.4*	76.6	67.6	55.6	38.7	25.0	*51.8*
Mean Temp. (°F)	10.4	15.6	26.4	42.0	54.3	62.6	*67.3*	64.9	56.2	45.1	30.6	16.4	*41.0*
Mean Minimum Temp. (°F)	0.3	4.7	16.3	30.8	41.5	50.3	*55.2*	53.2	44.8	34.6	22.5	7.7	*30.1*
Extreme Maximum Temp. (°F)	51	54	70	87	*88*	*94*	96	95	94	87	*71*	59	96
Extreme Minimum Temp. (°F)	-39	-38	-23	-1	*20*	*30*	*30*	32	21	8	*-10*	*-35*	*-39*
Days Maximum Temp. ≥ 90°F	0	0	0	0	0	1	2	1	0	0	0	0	4
Days Maximum Temp. ≤ 32°F	27	19	11	1	0	0	0	0	0	0	9	23	90
Days Minimum Temp. ≤ 32°F	31	28	29	18	6	0	0	0	3	13	26	30	184
Days Minimum Temp. ≤ 0°F	15	11	5	0	0	0	0	0	0	0	1	9	41
Heating Degree Days (base 65°F)	1,688	1,391	1,189	687	344	123	*42*	75	278	610	1,025	1,502	*8,954*
Cooling Degree Days (base 65°F)	0	0	0	*3*	*12*	*52*	*108*	75	*17*	0	0	0	*267*
Mean Precipitation (in.)	0.89	0.81	1.69	2.53	3.04	3.57	3.92	4.16	4.16	2.66	2.12	1.22	30.77
Days With ≥ 0.1" Precipitation	3	2	5	6	6	8	7	7	7	6	5	4	66
Days With ≥ 1.0" Precipitation	0	0	0	0	1	1	1	1	1	1	0	0	6
Mean Snowfall (in.)	13.6	8.9	9.8	4.0	0.5	0.0	0.0	0.0	trace	1.0	7.6	14.2	59.6
Days With ≥ 1.0" Snow Depth	30	28	25	5	0	0	0	0	0	1	8	27	124

Appleton *Outagamie County*   Elevation: 748 ft.   Latitude: 44° 15' N   Longitude: 88° 22' W

	JAN	FEB	MAR	APR	MAY	JUN	JUL	AUG	SEP	OCT	NOV	DEC	YEAR
Mean Maximum Temp. (°F)	23.9	29.1	39.8	54.4	68.4	77.2	81.6	78.7	70.2	57.4	41.9	28.9	54.3
Mean Temp. (°F)	15.8	20.7	31.2	44.6	57.5	66.8	71.8	69.3	60.8	48.6	34.6	21.6	45.3
Mean Minimum Temp. (°F)	7.7	12.3	22.5	34.8	46.7	56.3	61.9	59.9	51.3	39.7	27.3	14.3	36.2
Extreme Maximum Temp. (°F)	50	58	78	89	94	101	102	103	91	84	73	61	103
Extreme Minimum Temp. (°F)	-29	-29	-9	7	25	35	43	42	25	15	-7	-23	-29
Days Maximum Temp. ≥ 90°F	0	0	0	0	0	2	3	1	0	0	0	0	6
Days Maximum Temp. ≤ 32°F	23	16	7	1	0	0	0	0	0	0	5	18	70
Days Minimum Temp. ≤ 32°F	31	27	26	12	1	0	0	0	0	6	21	30	154
Days Minimum Temp. ≤ 0°F	10	6	1	0	0	0	0	0	0	0	0	5	22
Heating Degree Days (base 65°F)	1,519	1,245	1,042	608	262	63	10	23	171	505	905	1,340	7,693
Cooling Degree Days (base 65°F)	0	0	0	5	39	131	232	170	56	2	0	0	635
Mean Precipitation (in.)	1.18	1.03	2.05	2.81	3.11	3.45	3.35	3.84	3.29	2.28	2.25	1.28	29.92
Days With ≥ 0.1" Precipitation	3	3	5	6	6	6	6	7	6	5	5	3	61
Days With ≥ 1.0" Precipitation	0	0	0	0	1	1	1	1	1	0	0	0	5
Mean Snowfall (in.)	12.2	8.0	8.0	2.5	0.2	0.0	0.0	0.0	0.0	0.2	4.3	10.3	45.7
Days With ≥ 1.0" Snow Depth	26	22	13	2	0	0	0	0	0	0	4	20	87

Arboretum Univ. Wisconsin *Dane County*   Elevation: 862 ft.   Latitude: 43° 03' N   Longitude: 89° 24' W

	JAN	FEB	MAR	APR	MAY	JUN	JUL	AUG	SEP	OCT	NOV	DEC	YEAR
Mean Maximum Temp. (°F)	26.6	32.2	43.7	57.2	70.3	79.6	83.8	81.6	73.7	61.5	45.4	32.1	57.3
Mean Temp. (°F)	16.2	21.3	32.8	45.3	57.3	66.3	70.9	68.7	60.3	48.9	35.3	22.4	45.5
Mean Minimum Temp. (°F)	5.8	10.4	21.8	33.4	44.2	53.1	58.0	55.7	46.9	35.8	25.2	12.7	33.6
Extreme Maximum Temp. (°F)	55	62	82	95	93	104	101	108	99	93	77	65	108
Extreme Minimum Temp. (°F)	-33	-38	-12	4	22	29	36	32	20	7	-14	-28	-38
Days Maximum Temp. ≥ 90°F	0	0	0	0	0	3	6	4	1	0	0	0	14
Days Maximum Temp. ≤ 32°F	20	14	5	0	0	0	0	0	0	0	3	15	57
Days Minimum Temp. ≤ 32°F	31	28	27	15	3	0	0	0	2	13	23	30	172
Days Minimum Temp. ≤ 0°F	12	8	2	0	0	0	0	0	0	0	1	6	29
Heating Degree Days (base 65°F)	1,508	1,227	992	590	266	67	16	33	179	496	883	1,313	7,570
Cooling Degree Days (base 65°F)	0	0	0	6	30	121	207	161	45	3	0	0	573
Mean Precipitation (in.)	1.34	1.17	2.44	3.94	3.62	4.45	4.48	4.12	3.74	2.70	2.70	1.75	36.45
Days With ≥ 0.1" Precipitation	4	3	5	7	7	7	6	7	6	6	6	4	68
Days With ≥ 1.0" Precipitation	0	0	0	1	1	1	1	1	1	1	1	0	8
Mean Snowfall (in.)	na	na	na	na	0.0	0.0	0.0	0.0	0.0	trace	na	na	na
Days With ≥ 1.0" Snow Depth	na	na	na	na	0	0	0	0	0	0	na	na	na

Arlington Univ. Farm *Columbia County*   Elevation: 1,079 ft.   Latitude: 43° 18' N   Longitude: 89° 21' W

	JAN	FEB	MAR	APR	MAY	JUN	JUL	AUG	SEP	OCT	NOV	DEC	YEAR
Mean Maximum Temp. (°F)	24.7	30.4	41.9	57.3	70.4	79.4	82.7	80.3	72.6	60.3	43.2	30.3	56.1
Mean Temp. (°F)	16.2	21.7	32.8	46.1	58.1	67.3	71.3	69.1	61.2	49.6	35.1	22.5	45.9
Mean Minimum Temp. (°F)	7.6	13.0	23.6	34.9	45.8	55.1	59.9	57.9	49.7	38.9	26.9	14.6	35.7
Extreme Maximum Temp. (°F)	55	60	81	90	91	100	100	102	96	87	75	62	102
Extreme Minimum Temp. (°F)	-36	-30	-9	7	23	34	44	34	25	14	-9	-26	-36
Days Maximum Temp. ≥ 90°F	0	0	0	0	0	3	4	2	0	0	0	0	9
Days Maximum Temp. ≤ 32°F	22	15	6	0	0	0	0	0	0	0	5	17	65
Days Minimum Temp. ≤ 32°F	31	27	26	12	2	0	0	0	1	8	22	30	159
Days Minimum Temp. ≤ 0°F	10	6	1	0	0	0	0	0	0	0	0	5	22
Heating Degree Days (base 65°F)	1,507	1,216	992	564	240	51	10	26	164	475	891	1,312	7,448
Cooling Degree Days (base 65°F)	0	0	0	5	30	128	211	163	56	4	0	0	597
Mean Precipitation (in.)	1.05	1.07	1.97	3.21	3.25	3.88	3.85	4.17	3.88	2.47	2.38	1.33	32.51
Days With ≥ 0.1" Precipitation	4	3	5	7	7	7	7	7	7	6	6	4	70
Days With ≥ 1.0" Precipitation	0	0	0	1	1	1	1	1	1	0	0	0	6
Mean Snowfall (in.)	9.7	6.7	5.3	2.2	0.1	0.0	0.0	0.0	0.0	0.3	3.8	8.7	36.8
Days With ≥ 1.0" Snow Depth	25	22	10	1	0	0	0	0	0	0	4	19	81

Ashland Exp. Farm *Bayfield County*   Elevation: 649 ft.   Latitude: 46° 34' N   Longitude: 90° 58' W

	JAN	FEB	MAR	APR	MAY	JUN	JUL	AUG	SEP	OCT	NOV	DEC	YEAR
Mean Maximum Temp. (°F)	*22.1*	28.4	38.0	51.8	*65.7*	75.1	80.3	78.4	*68.8*	56.8	*39.5*	26.6	*52.6*
Mean Temp. (°F)	*11.5*	17.1	27.5	40.1	*52.4*	62.0	67.7	66.0	*57.2*	45.7	*31.3*	17.6	*41.3*
Mean Minimum Temp. (°F)	1.2	5.7	16.9	28.4	*38.9*	48.9	55.0	53.8	45.5	34.6	23.1	8.6	*30.0*
Extreme Maximum Temp. (°F)	52	59	80	89	93	97	103	97	100	88	74	60	103
Extreme Minimum Temp. (°F)	-41	-40	-30	-2	16	28	34	34	24	10	-16	-28	-41
Days Maximum Temp. ≥ 90°F	0	0	0	0	0	1	3	2	0	0	0	0	6
Days Maximum Temp. ≤ 32°F	23	17	9	1	0	0	0	0	0	0	7	20	77
Days Minimum Temp. ≤ 32°F	29	27	28	20	8	1	0	0	2	13	24	28	180
Days Minimum Temp. ≤ 0°F	14	11	4	0	0	0	0	0	0	0	1	8	38
Heating Degree Days (base 65°F)	*1,655*	1,349	1,158	742	*399*	136	40	63	*254*	594	*1,004*	1,463	*8,857*
Cooling Degree Days (base 65°F)	*0*	0	0	2	*15*	54	128	*105*	*21*	2	*0*	*0*	*327*
Mean Precipitation (in.)	1.26	0.77	1.82	2.11	2.91	3.60	4.05	3.96	3.79	2.61	2.33	1.19	30.40
Days With ≥ 0.1" Precipitation	3	2	4	5	6	7	7	6	7	5	4	3	59
Days With ≥ 1.0" Precipitation	0	0	0	0	0	1	1	1	1	0	0	0	4
Mean Snowfall (in.)	14.5	8.5	9.7	4.2	trace	0.0	0.0	0.0	0.0	0.3	7.9	12.4	57.5
Days With ≥ 1.0" Snow Depth	27	25	19	4	0	0	0	0	0	0	8	23	106

Baraboo *Sauk County*   Elevation: 820 ft.   Latitude: 43° 27' N   Longitude: 89° 44' W

	JAN	FEB	MAR	APR	MAY	JUN	JUL	AUG	SEP	OCT	NOV	DEC	YEAR
Mean Maximum Temp. (°F)	25.6	31.7	42.8	56.9	69.6	78.7	82.5	80.0	71.7	59.7	43.7	31.2	56.2
Mean Temp. (°F)	14.8	20.5	31.8	44.6	56.8	66.0	70.2	67.4	58.9	47.2	33.7	21.3	44.4
Mean Minimum Temp. (°F)	4.0	9.3	20.7	32.4	43.9	53.2	57.8	54.8	46.1	34.8	23.7	11.4	32.7
Extreme Maximum Temp. (°F)	57	63	84	92	92	102	102	102	96	89	76	64	102
Extreme Minimum Temp. (°F)	-36	-41	-16	-2	22	31	38	34	22	10	-17	-35	-41
Days Maximum Temp. ≥ 90°F	0	0	0	0	0	2	5	2	0	0	0	0	9
Days Maximum Temp. ≤ 32°F	21	14	6	0	0	0	0	0	0	0	4	16	61
Days Minimum Temp. ≤ 32°F	31	27	27	17	4	0	0	0	3	14	24	30	177
Days Minimum Temp. ≤ 0°F	13	8	2	0	0	0	0	0	0	0	1	7	31
Heating Degree Days (base 65°F)	1,551	1,250	1,023	610	278	71	20	47	216	549	932	1,349	7,896
Cooling Degree Days (base 65°F)	0	0	0	6	28	110	193	131	38	2	0	0	508
Mean Precipitation (in.)	1.06	1.00	2.08	3.57	3.43	3.89	4.33	4.34	3.67	2.56	2.34	1.11	33.38
Days With ≥ 0.1" Precipitation	3	3	4	7	7	7	7	7	7	6	5	3	66
Days With ≥ 1.0" Precipitation	0	0	0	1	1	1	1	1	1	0	0	0	6
Mean Snowfall (in.)	10.7	7.8	6.4	2.3	trace	0.0	0.0	0.0	0.0	0.4	4.5	9.0	41.1
Days With ≥ 1.0" Snow Depth	26	23	12	2	0	0	0	0	0	0	4	19	86

Bayfield 6 N *Bayfield County* Elevation: 816 ft. Latitude: 46° 53' N Longitude: 90° 49' W

	JAN	FEB	MAR	APR	MAY	JUN	JUL	AUG	SEP	OCT	NOV	DEC	YEAR
Mean Maximum Temp. (°F)	21.7	27.4	36.9	50.5	63.8	72.8	77.6	75.8	66.4	54.8	38.8	26.8	51.1
Mean Temp. (°F)	13.2	17.9	27.6	40.2	51.8	60.9	66.7	65.6	56.9	45.8	31.8	19.4	41.5
Mean Minimum Temp. (°F)	4.6	8.3	18.2	29.9	39.7	48.9	55.8	55.3	47.3	36.8	24.9	12.0	31.8
Extreme Maximum Temp. (°F)	53	61	78	88	91	96	101	98	99	85	76	61	101
Extreme Minimum Temp. (°F)	-29	-34	-17	2	22	22	36	36	28	15	-4	-24	-34
Days Maximum Temp. ≥ 90°F	0	0	0	0	0	0	1	1	0	0	0	0	2
Days Maximum Temp. ≤ 32°F	26	19	10	1	0	0	0	0	0	0	8	21	85
Days Minimum Temp. ≤ 32°F	31	28	28	19	5	0	0	0	1	9	25	30	176
Days Minimum Temp. ≤ 0°F	12	9	3	0	0	0	0	0	0	0	0	6	30
Heating Degree Days (base 65°F)	1,602	1,325	1,152	737	412	157	49	66	257	589	988	1,408	8,742
Cooling Degree Days (base 65°F)	0	0	0	1	11	39	101	89	17	1	0	0	259
Mean Precipitation (in.)	1.78	0.95	2.14	2.26	3.26	3.76	4.10	3.93	3.84	2.94	2.84	1.72	33.52
Days With ≥ 0.1" Precipitation	6	3	5	5	6	8	7	7	7	7	6	6	73
Days With ≥ 1.0" Precipitation	0	0	0	0	1	1	1	1	1	1	1	0	7
Mean Snowfall (in.)	26.3	11.5	13.5	5.4	0.7	0.0	0.0	0.0	trace	0.6	13.4	25.0	96.4
Days With ≥ 1.0" Snow Depth	31	28	28	9	0	0	0	0	0	0	10	28	134

Beaver Dam *Dodge County* Elevation: 839 ft. Latitude: 43° 27' N Longitude: 88° 51' W

	JAN	FEB	MAR	APR	MAY	JUN	JUL	AUG	SEP	OCT	NOV	DEC	YEAR
Mean Maximum Temp. (°F)	25.5	31.0	42.5	57.4	70.5	79.4	82.8	80.4	72.7	60.7	44.0	30.9	56.5
Mean Temp. (°F)	17.2	22.5	33.6	46.6	58.5	67.6	71.6	69.3	61.6	50.1	36.1	23.3	46.5
Mean Minimum Temp. (°F)	8.8	13.9	24.6	35.8	46.4	55.8	60.3	58.3	50.4	39.4	28.1	15.8	36.5
Extreme Maximum Temp. (°F)	55	61	80	90	92	98	98	100	96	88	73	63	100
Extreme Minimum Temp. (°F)	-31	-29	-11	6	24	35	42	40	26	16	-7	-24	-31
Days Maximum Temp. ≥ 90°F	0	0	0	0	0	2	4	2	0	0	0	0	8
Days Maximum Temp. ≤ 32°F	21	15	5	0	0	0	0	0	0	0	4	16	61
Days Minimum Temp. ≤ 32°F	30	27	25	11	1	0	0	0	0	7	21	29	151
Days Minimum Temp. ≤ 0°F	9	6	1	0	0	0	0	0	0	0	0	4	20
Heating Degree Days (base 65°F)	1,480	1,196	972	553	235	47	9	21	153	464	864	1,288	7,282
Cooling Degree Days (base 65°F)	0	0	0	5	33	132	219	161	55	3	0	0	608
Mean Precipitation (in.)	1.33	1.18	2.22	3.35	3.14	3.89	4.24	3.72	3.84	2.58	2.28	1.65	33.42
Days With ≥ 0.1" Precipitation	4	4	5	7	7	7	7	7	6	6	5	4	69
Days With ≥ 1.0" Precipitation	0	0	0	1	1	1	1	1	1	0	0	0	6
Mean Snowfall (in.)	10.7	7.3	5.8	1.5	trace	0.0	0.0	0.0	0.0	0.2	2.5	10.1	38.1
Days With ≥ 1.0" Snow Depth	25	21	10	1	0	0	0	0	0	0	3	18	78

Beloit *Rock County* Elevation: 777 ft. Latitude: 42° 30' N Longitude: 89° 02' W

	JAN	FEB	MAR	APR	MAY	JUN	JUL	AUG	SEP	OCT	NOV	DEC	YEAR
Mean Maximum Temp. (°F)	27.1	32.2	44.1	58.9	71.3	80.5	83.9	81.4	74.3	62.6	46.0	32.8	57.9
Mean Temp. (°F)	19.1	24.2	35.1	48.3	59.9	69.2	73.3	71.0	63.4	51.6	38.0	25.2	48.2
Mean Minimum Temp. (°F)	11.1	16.2	26.1	37.6	48.4	57.9	62.6	60.6	52.4	41.1	29.9	17.7	38.5
Extreme Maximum Temp. (°F)	60	61	84	92	95	101	102	102	98	89	76	65	102
Extreme Minimum Temp. (°F)	-26	-25	-3	7	25	38	42	43	30	17	-5	-23	-26
Days Maximum Temp. ≥ 90°F	0	0	0	0	0	4	6	4	1	0	0	0	15
Days Maximum Temp. ≤ 32°F	20	14	5	0	0	0	0	0	0	0	3	13	55
Days Minimum Temp. ≤ 32°F	30	26	24	8	0	0	0	0	0	5	18	28	139
Days Minimum Temp. ≤ 0°F	7	4	0	0	0	0	0	0	0	0	0	4	15
Heating Degree Days (base 65°F)	1,417	1,145	920	506	205	36	6	14	123	417	803	1,228	6,820
Cooling Degree Days (base 65°F)	0	0	0	8	44	163	262	205	73	6	0	0	761
Mean Precipitation (in.)	1.32	1.22	2.15	3.69	3.36	4.37	3.90	4.28	3.84	2.45	2.80	1.87	35.25
Days With ≥ 0.1" Precipitation	4	3	5	7	7	7	6	6	5	5	6	4	65
Days With ≥ 1.0" Precipitation	0	0	0	1	1	1	1	1	1	1	1	0	8
Mean Snowfall (in.)	*8.8*	*6.5*	*3.6*	1.0	trace	0.0	0.0	0.0	0.0	trace	*1.5*	*6.7*	*28.1*
Days With ≥ 1.0" Snow Depth	na	*16*	*4*	0	0	0	0	0	0	0	*2*	na	na

Blair *Trempealeau County* Elevation: 859 ft. Latitude: 44° 18' N Longitude: 91° 14' W

	JAN	FEB	MAR	APR	MAY	JUN	JUL	AUG	SEP	OCT	NOV	DEC	YEAR
Mean Maximum Temp. (°F)	23.0	29.9	41.2	56.7	69.5	78.3	82.2	79.9	71.1	59.0	41.8	28.4	55.1
Mean Temp. (°F)	11.6	18.0	30.4	44.6	56.6	65.7	69.9	67.6	58.6	46.7	32.3	18.3	43.4
Mean Minimum Temp. (°F)	0.1	6.1	19.6	32.4	43.6	53.0	57.5	55.4	46.0	34.4	22.6	8.2	31.6
Extreme Maximum Temp. (°F)	56	61	82	91	90	100	105	101	96	90	75	64	105
Extreme Minimum Temp. (°F)	-41	-45	-21	-4	21	28	36	35	24	8	-14	-39	-45
Days Maximum Temp. ≥ 90°F	0	0	0	0	0	2	4	2	0	0	0	0	8
Days Maximum Temp. ≤ 32°F	23	15	7	0	0	0	0	0	0	0	6	19	70
Days Minimum Temp. ≤ 32°F	31	28	27	16	4	0	0	0	2	15	25	30	178
Days Minimum Temp. ≤ 0°F	15	10	3	0	0	0	0	0	0	0	1	9	38
Heating Degree Days (base 65°F)	1,654	1,322	1,066	610	282	78	19	42	223	562	976	1,442	8,276
Cooling Degree Days (base 65°F)	0	0	0	5	26	107	180	136	36	1	0	0	491
Mean Precipitation (in.)	0.94	0.95	1.93	3.19	4.00	3.84	4.40	4.61	4.23	2.58	2.24	1.13	34.04
Days With ≥ 0.1" Precipitation	3	3	5	7	7	7	7	7	7	5	4	3	65
Days With ≥ 1.0" Precipitation	0	0	0	0	1	1	1	1	1	1	0	0	6
Mean Snowfall (in.)	10.9	6.5	7.6	1.7	trace	0.0	0.0	0.0	0.0	0.2	4.2	9.2	40.3
Days With ≥ 1.0" Snow Depth	30	27	18	2	0	0	0	0	0	0	6	25	108

Bloomer *Chippewa County*   Elevation: 977 ft.   Latitude: 45° 06' N   Longitude: 91° 29' W

	JAN	FEB	MAR	APR	MAY	JUN	JUL	AUG	SEP	OCT	NOV	DEC	YEAR
Mean Maximum Temp. (°F)	21.2	28.4	39.9	56.8	70.1	78.5	82.7	80.1	70.8	58.0	40.0	26.1	54.4
Mean Temp. (°F)	11.4	18.1	29.9	45.0	57.5	66.3	70.7	68.3	59.2	47.1	31.7	17.6	43.6
Mean Minimum Temp. (°F)	1.5	7.7	19.9	33.1	44.7	54.1	58.8	56.5	47.5	36.0	23.3	9.1	32.7
Extreme Maximum Temp. (°F)	51	57	81	90	92	99	103	104	94	88	72	60	104
Extreme Minimum Temp. (°F)	-43	-36	-17	4	20	32	41	34	22	6	-18	-35	-43
Days Maximum Temp. ≥ 90°F	0	0	0	0	0	2	5	2	0	0	0	0	9
Days Maximum Temp. ≤ 32°F	25	17	7	0	0	0	0	0	0	0	7	22	78
Days Minimum Temp. ≤ 32°F	31	28	27	15	3	0	0	0	2	12	25	30	173
Days Minimum Temp. ≤ 0°F	15	9	3	0	0	0	0	0	0	0	1	9	37
Heating Degree Days (base 65°F)	1,658	1,321	1,081	599	260	67	16	36	209	551	993	1,463	8,254
Cooling Degree Days (base 65°F)	0	0	0	5	33	121	207	157	45	1	0	0	569
Mean Precipitation (in.)	0.97	0.70	1.81	2.79	3.68	4.41	3.80	4.95	3.79	2.48	2.12	1.02	32.52
Days With ≥ 0.1" Precipitation	3	2	4	6	7	7	8	7	7	5	4	3	63
Days With ≥ 1.0" Precipitation	0	0	0	1	1	1	1	2	1	1	1	0	9
Mean Snowfall (in.)	12.0	6.1	7.5	1.1	trace	0.0	0.0	0.0	trace	0.3	5.9	9.6	42.5
Days With ≥ 1.0" Snow Depth	29	27	18	1	0	0	0	0	0	0	6	23	104

Bowler *Shawano County*   Elevation: 1,079 ft.   Latitude: 44° 51' N   Longitude: 88° 59' W

	JAN	FEB	MAR	APR	MAY	JUN	JUL	AUG	SEP	OCT	NOV	DEC	YEAR
Mean Maximum Temp. (°F)	22.0	27.6	38.6	54.2	67.4	76.1	80.6	77.8	67.9	56.5	40.9	26.3	53.0
Mean Temp. (°F)	11.3	16.3	28.0	42.5	54.2	63.1	68.0	65.4	55.9	44.7	31.9	na	na
Mean Minimum Temp. (°F)	0.6	4.9	17.3	30.6	40.9	49.9	55.3	52.9	43.9	33.0	22.7	na	na
Extreme Maximum Temp. (°F)	53	58	74	92	90	95	100	99	92	87	74	59	100
Extreme Minimum Temp. (°F)	-41	-36	-20	1	20	28	34	34	20	11	-12	-26	-41
Days Maximum Temp. ≥ 90°F	0	0	0	0	0	1	2	1	0	0	0	0	4
Days Maximum Temp. ≤ 32°F	25	17	8	1	0	0	0	0	0	0	6	18	75
Days Minimum Temp. ≤ 32°F	29	27	28	18	6	0	0	0	2	14	22	26	172
Days Minimum Temp. ≤ 0°F	14	11	4	0	0	0	0	0	0	0	1	7	37
Heating Degree Days (base 65°F)	1,661	1,370	1,141	673	344	115	35	68	282	615	987	na	na
Cooling Degree Days (base 65°F)	0	0	0	3	13	65	136	97	16	0	0	na	na
Mean Precipitation (in.)	1.01	0.86	1.75	2.77	3.66	3.55	3.91	4.08	3.71	2.62	2.06	1.35	31.33
Days With ≥ 0.1" Precipitation	3	2	3	6	6	6	6	6	6	5	4	3	56
Days With ≥ 1.0" Precipitation	0	0	0	1	1	1	1	1	1	1	0	0	7
Mean Snowfall (in.)	na	5.9	7.0	1.6	trace	0.0	0.0	0.0	0.0	0.2	4.2	10.2	na
Days With ≥ 1.0" Snow Depth	na	na	na	1	0	0	0	0	0	0	na	na	na

Breed 6 SSE *Oconto County*   Elevation: 859 ft.   Latitude: 44° 59' N   Longitude: 88° 23' W

	JAN	FEB	MAR	APR	MAY	JUN	JUL	AUG	SEP	OCT	NOV	DEC	YEAR
Mean Maximum Temp. (°F)	24.2	29.6	39.8	55.1	68.9	77.8	81.7	79.2	70.1	57.9	41.0	28.6	54.5
Mean Temp. (°F)	13.3	18.1	28.9	42.6	54.9	64.2	68.6	66.4	57.7	46.3	32.2	19.8	42.7
Mean Minimum Temp. (°F)	2.3	6.5	17.9	30.0	40.7	50.5	55.5	53.6	45.2	34.6	23.4	10.8	30.9
Extreme Maximum Temp. (°F)	56	57	72	91	91	100	101	99	95	87	74	59	101
Extreme Minimum Temp. (°F)	-41	-44	-26	-3	15	26	28	31	16	8	-16	-29	-44
Days Maximum Temp. ≥ 90°F	0	0	0	0	0	2	4	2	0	0	0	0	8
Days Maximum Temp. ≤ 32°F	24	16	7	1	0	0	0	0	0	0	6	20	74
Days Minimum Temp. ≤ 32°F	31	28	28	19	7	1	0	0	3	14	25	30	186
Days Minimum Temp. ≤ 0°F	14	10	4	0	0	0	0	0	0	0	1	7	36
Heating Degree Days (base 65°F)	1,598	1,321	1,113	669	328	96	30	56	240	575	976	1,396	8,398
Cooling Degree Days (base 65°F)	0	0	0	3	19	80	146	113	23	1	0	0	385
Mean Precipitation (in.)	1.35	0.95	2.16	2.85	3.66	3.53	3.53	3.93	3.70	2.61	2.54	1.64	32.45
Days With ≥ 0.1" Precipitation	4	3	5	6	7	7	7	7	7	6	5	5	69
Days With ≥ 1.0" Precipitation	0	0	0	1	1	1	1	1	1	1	0	0	7
Mean Snowfall (in.)	14.3	8.5	10.4	4.0	0.3	0.0	0.0	0.0	trace	0.2	5.8	12.9	56.4
Days With ≥ 1.0" Snow Depth	21	19	15	4	0	0	0	0	0	0	4	18	81

Brodhead *Green County*   Elevation: 787 ft.   Latitude: 42° 37' N   Longitude: 89° 23' W

	JAN	FEB	MAR	APR	MAY	JUN	JUL	AUG	SEP	OCT	NOV	DEC	YEAR
Mean Maximum Temp. (°F)	26.2	31.7	43.5	57.7	70.4	80.0	83.5	81.0	73.5	61.4	45.2	31.9	57.2
Mean Temp. (°F)	16.5	22.0	33.5	46.3	58.2	67.7	71.7	69.2	60.8	49.1	35.7	22.9	46.1
Mean Minimum Temp. (°F)	6.7	12.0	23.4	34.8	46.0	55.4	59.9	57.4	48.1	36.7	26.1	13.9	35.0
Extreme Maximum Temp. (°F)	59	65	83	91	93	101	101	102	99	89	75	65	102
Extreme Minimum Temp. (°F)	-30	-34	-10	7	24	35	41	38	24	14	-9	-26	-34
Days Maximum Temp. ≥ 90°F	0	0	0	0	0	3	6	3	1	0	0	0	13
Days Maximum Temp. ≤ 32°F	21	13	5	0	0	0	0	0	0	0	3	15	57
Days Minimum Temp. ≤ 32°F	31	27	26	12	2	0	0	0	2	11	23	29	163
Days Minimum Temp. ≤ 0°F	11	7	1	0	0	0	0	0	0	0	0	6	25
Heating Degree Days (base 65°F)	1,498	1,208	971	562	245	49	10	26	169	492	873	1,298	7,401
Cooling Degree Days (base 65°F)	0	0	0	5	33	133	220	160	47	3	0	0	601
Mean Precipitation (in.)	1.34	1.32	2.28	3.45	3.62	4.54	3.94	4.15	3.63	2.75	2.36	1.80	35.18
Days With ≥ 0.1" Precipitation	4	4	5	7	7	7	7	6	6	6	5	4	68
Days With ≥ 1.0" Precipitation	0	0	0	1	1	1	1	1	1	1	0	0	7
Mean Snowfall (in.)	10.5	6.2	5.2	1.4	trace	0.0	0.0	0.0	0.0	trace	2.1	8.0	33.4
Days With ≥ 1.0" Snow Depth	na	na	na	1	0	0	0	0	0	0	1	na	na

Burlington *Racine County*   Elevation: 748 ft.   Latitude: 42° 39' N   Longitude: 88° 15' W

	JAN	FEB	MAR	APR	MAY	JUN	JUL	AUG	SEP	OCT	NOV	DEC	YEAR
Mean Maximum Temp. (°F)	26.1	31.4	42.1	55.6	68.4	78.1	82.1	79.9	72.4	60.3	45.2	32.6	56.2
Mean Temp. (°F)	17.7	22.8	33.2	45.5	56.9	66.6	71.2	69.3	61.1	49.3	36.8	24.8	46.3
Mean Minimum Temp. (°F)	9.3	14.2	24.2	35.3	45.4	55.0	60.2	58.6	49.9	38.3	28.2	16.9	36.3
Extreme Maximum Temp. (°F)	59	66	77	90	94	102	105	102	100	90	76	63	105
Extreme Minimum Temp. (°F)	-27	-27	-7	3	23	32	39	40	23	18	-9	-18	-27
Days Maximum Temp. ≥ 90°F	0	0	0	0	0	3	4	3	1	0	0	0	11
Days Maximum Temp. ≤ 32°F	21	14	6	0	0	0	0	0	0	0	3	14	58
Days Minimum Temp. ≤ 32°F	30	27	25	12	2	0	0	0	0	9	21	29	155
Days Minimum Temp. ≤ 0°F	9	5	1	0	0	0	0	0	0	0	0	4	19
Heating Degree Days (base 65°F)	1,460	1,183	980	585	278	69	15	27	163	484	840	1,241	7,325
Cooling Degree Days (base 65°F)	0	0	0	7	32	127	213	169	52	3	0	0	603
Mean Precipitation (in.)	1.56	1.24	2.27	3.66	3.04	3.98	3.74	4.07	3.36	2.37	2.56	1.92	33.77
Days With ≥ 0.1" Precipitation	4	3	5	7	7	7	6	6	6	5	6	5	67
Days With ≥ 1.0" Precipitation	0	0	0	1	0	1	1	1	1	1	0	0	6
Mean Snowfall (in.)	12.5	6.8	5.6	1.1	trace	0.0	0.0	0.0	0.0	trace	1.8	8.0	35.8
Days With ≥ 1.0" Snow Depth	na	na	na	1	0	0	0	0	0	0	1	na	na

Charmany Farm *Dane County*   Elevation: 908 ft.   Latitude: 43° 04' N   Longitude: 89° 29' W

	JAN	FEB	MAR	APR	MAY	JUN	JUL	AUG	SEP	OCT	NOV	DEC	YEAR
Mean Maximum Temp. (°F)	24.8	30.6	42.0	56.2	68.9	78.2	82.0	79.6	71.4	59.6	43.8	30.8	55.7
Mean Temp. (°F)	16.1	21.9	32.8	45.7	57.7	67.0	71.1	68.8	60.6	48.9	35.2	22.5	45.7
Mean Minimum Temp. (°F)	7.4	13.1	23.5	35.1	46.4	55.6	60.2	58.1	49.8	38.1	26.4	14.2	35.7
Extreme Maximum Temp. (°F)	53	61	80	93	90	101	100	102	95	88	74	65	102
Extreme Minimum Temp. (°F)	-34	-27	-6	4	25	33	42	37	24	17	-9	-30	-34
Days Maximum Temp. ≥ 90°F	0	0	0	0	0	2	4	2	0	0	0	0	8
Days Maximum Temp. ≤ 32°F	22	15	6	0	0	0	0	0	0	0	4	16	63
Days Minimum Temp. ≤ 32°F	31	27	26	11	2	0	0	0	1	9	22	30	159
Days Minimum Temp. ≤ 0°F	10	6	1	0	0	0	0	0	0	0	0	5	22
Heating Degree Days (base 65°F)	1,511	1,211	986	577	252	55	12	27	177	495	889	1,312	7,504
Cooling Degree Days (base 65°F)	0	0	0	4	28	118	204	146	46	2	0	0	548
Mean Precipitation (in.)	1.12	1.06	2.16	3.60	3.37	4.25	4.05	3.87	3.45	2.46	2.34	1.32	33.05
Days With ≥ 0.1" Precipitation	4	3	5	7	7	7	7	7	6	6	5	4	68
Days With ≥ 1.0" Precipitation	0	0	0	1	1	1	1	1	1	0	1	0	7
Mean Snowfall (in.)	11.2	6.7	5.0	1.5	trace	0.0	0.0	0.0	0.0	trace	2.3	8.6	35.3
Days With ≥ 1.0" Snow Depth	14	11	3	1	0	0	0	0	0	0	2	9	40

Chilton *Calumet County*   Elevation: 839 ft.   Latitude: 44° 02' N   Longitude: 88° 09' W

	JAN	FEB	MAR	APR	MAY	JUN	JUL	AUG	SEP	OCT	NOV	DEC	YEAR
Mean Maximum Temp. (°F)	24.3	29.3	40.1	55.5	69.0	78.4	82.3	79.9	71.8	59.1	42.9	29.8	55.2
Mean Temp. (°F)	16.2	21.0	31.4	44.9	56.8	66.7	71.0	69.1	60.9	49.2	35.3	22.6	45.4
Mean Minimum Temp. (°F)	8.1	12.8	22.8	34.3	44.8	54.7	59.7	58.1	50.0	39.2	27.7	15.3	35.6
Extreme Maximum Temp. (°F)	53	61	78	89	92	99	103	100	93	86	73	62	103
Extreme Minimum Temp. (°F)	-30	-28	-11	8	23	33	37	40	26	17	-5	-21	-30
Days Maximum Temp. ≥ 90°F	0	0	0	0	0	2	4	2	0	0	0	0	8
Days Maximum Temp. ≤ 32°F	23	16	7	0	0	0	0	0	0	0	4	18	68
Days Minimum Temp. ≤ 32°F	31	27	26	14	3	0	0	0	1	7	21	30	160
Days Minimum Temp. ≤ 0°F	10	6	1	0	0	0	0	0	0	0	0	5	22
Heating Degree Days (base 65°F)	1,507	1,237	1,035	601	280	63	14	26	167	486	883	1,309	7,608
Cooling Degree Days (base 65°F)	0	0	0	4	30	123	201	160	51	2	0	0	571
Mean Precipitation (in.)	1.38	1.18	2.16	2.70	3.00	3.74	3.55	3.70	3.62	2.48	2.30	1.56	31.37
Days With ≥ 0.1" Precipitation	4	3	5	6	7	7	7	7	6	6	6	4	68
Days With ≥ 1.0" Precipitation	0	0	0	0	1	1	1	1	1	0	0	0	5
Mean Snowfall (in.)	12.4	9.5	7.7	2.3	0.3	0.0	0.0	0.0	0.0	0.4	4.5	9.7	46.8
Days With ≥ 1.0" Snow Depth	26	21	11	1	0	0	0	0	0	0	4	18	81

Clintonville *Waupaca County*   Elevation: 797 ft.   Latitude: 44° 37' N   Longitude: 88° 45' W

	JAN	FEB	MAR	APR	MAY	JUN	JUL	AUG	SEP	OCT	NOV	DEC	YEAR
Mean Maximum Temp. (°F)	23.9	29.4	39.7	54.9	68.3	77.3	81.5	78.8	70.3	58.3	42.1	28.8	54.5
Mean Temp. (°F)	14.2	19.3	29.9	43.8	56.0	65.3	69.8	67.1	58.4	47.0	33.3	20.3	43.7
Mean Minimum Temp. (°F)	4.4	9.2	20.1	32.6	43.7	53.3	58.1	55.3	46.5	35.6	24.4	11.7	32.9
Extreme Maximum Temp. (°F)	51	57	77	92	91	101	106	103	95	87	73	61	106
Extreme Minimum Temp. (°F)	-35	-31	-13	7	23	31	38	35	22	15	-10	-23	-35
Days Maximum Temp. ≥ 90°F	0	0	0	0	0	2	3	1	0	0	0	0	6
Days Maximum Temp. ≤ 32°F	23	16	7	1	0	0	0	0	0	0	5	19	71
Days Minimum Temp. ≤ 32°F	31	28	28	16	3	0	0	0	2	12	25	30	175
Days Minimum Temp. ≤ 0°F	13	8	2	0	0	0	0	0	0	0	0	6	29
Heating Degree Days (base 65°F)	1,571	1,285	1,080	634	296	82	18	43	221	554	944	1,380	8,108
Cooling Degree Days (base 65°F)	0	0	0	3	23	99	168	116	28	1	0	0	438
Mean Precipitation (in.)	1.26	0.95	2.12	2.60	3.66	3.37	4.01	3.97	3.58	2.53	2.28	1.42	31.75
Days With ≥ 0.1" Precipitation	4	3	5	6	7	7	7	7	7	5	5	5	68
Days With ≥ 1.0" Precipitation	0	0	0	0	1	1	1	1	1	1	1	0	7
Mean Snowfall (in.)	13.0	7.5	8.0	2.3	trace	0.0	0.0	0.0	0.0	0.2	4.1	10.5	45.6
Days With ≥ 1.0" Snow Depth	27	22	14	2	0	0	0	0	0	0	4	19	88

Cumberland *Barron County*   Elevation: 1,240 ft.   Latitude: 45° 32' N   Longitude: 92° 01' W

	JAN	FEB	MAR	APR	MAY	JUN	JUL	AUG	SEP	OCT	NOV	DEC	YEAR
Mean Maximum Temp. (°F)	20.7	28.0	39.2	56.1	70.1	78.1	82.0	79.5	69.8	57.1	38.7	25.0	53.7
Mean Temp. (°F)	10.5	17.0	28.7	44.3	57.8	66.5	70.9	68.4	58.9	46.8	30.7	16.5	43.1
Mean Minimum Temp. (°F)	0.2	6.1	18.2	32.5	45.3	54.7	59.7	57.2	47.9	36.4	22.6	7.9	32.4
Extreme Maximum Temp. (°F)	52	57	80	92	96	97	103	101	95	88	71	60	103
Extreme Minimum Temp. (°F)	-40	-38	-22	1	18	36	42	37	24	8	-16	-39	-40
Days Maximum Temp. ≥ 90°F	0	0	0	0	0	2	4	2	0	0	0	0	8
Days Maximum Temp. ≤ 32°F	26	17	8	1	0	0	0	0	0	0	9	23	84
Days Minimum Temp. ≤ 32°F	31	27	28	15	2	0	0	0	1	10	26	31	171
Days Minimum Temp. ≤ 0°F	15	9	4	0	0	0	0	0	0	0	1	9	38
Heating Degree Days (base 65°F)	1,686	1,351	1,118	617	249	59	12	30	211	560	1,023	1,498	8,414
Cooling Degree Days (base 65°F)	0	0	0	4	28	107	198	146	35	1	0	0	519
Mean Precipitation (in.)	1.18	0.84	1.82	2.72	3.40	4.49	4.37	4.47	4.24	2.84	2.19	1.13	33.69
Days With ≥ 0.1" Precipitation	4	3	5	6	7	8	7	7	7	6	5	4	69
Days With ≥ 1.0" Precipitation	0	0	0	0	1	1	1	1	1	1	1	0	7
Mean Snowfall (in.)	13.1	8.0	10.0	3.7	trace	0.0	0.0	0.0	trace	0.6	7.9	10.9	54.2
Days With ≥ 1.0" Snow Depth	23	19	14	3	0	0	0	0	0	0	5	18	82

Dalton *Green Lake County*   Elevation: 859 ft.   Latitude: 43° 39' N   Longitude: 89° 12' W

	JAN	FEB	MAR	APR	MAY	JUN	JUL	AUG	SEP	OCT	NOV	DEC	YEAR
Mean Maximum Temp. (°F)	25.7	31.5	42.7	57.8	70.8	79.8	83.3	80.9	72.5	60.5	43.7	30.9	56.7
Mean Temp. (°F)	16.7	22.2	33.0	46.2	58.3	67.4	71.6	69.4	61.2	49.8	35.3	22.7	46.2
Mean Minimum Temp. (°F)	7.7	12.9	23.2	34.6	45.8	54.9	59.8	57.9	49.8	39.0	26.9	14.4	35.6
Extreme Maximum Temp. (°F)	56	63	83	91	92	102	103	103	95	88	76	64	103
Extreme Minimum Temp. (°F)	-29	-34	-10	4	22	33	41	33	22	11	-7	-28	-34
Days Maximum Temp. ≥ 90°F	0	0	0	0	0	3	5	2	1	0	0	0	11
Days Maximum Temp. ≤ 32°F	21	14	5	0	0	0	0	0	0	0	4	16	60
Days Minimum Temp. ≤ 32°F	31	27	25	13	3	0	0	0	1	8	21	30	159
Days Minimum Temp. ≤ 0°F	10	6	1	0	0	0	0	0	0	0	0	5	22
Heating Degree Days (base 65°F)	1,491	1,203	987	562	239	52	10	25	165	470	883	1,305	7,392
Cooling Degree Days (base 65°F)	0	0	0	5	36	135	223	176	59	5	0	0	639
Mean Precipitation (in.)	1.25	1.09	2.26	3.07	3.58	3.95	4.15	3.75	3.70	2.43	2.40	1.39	33.02
Days With ≥ 0.1" Precipitation	4	3	5	7	7	7	7	7	6	6	5	4	68
Days With ≥ 1.0" Precipitation	0	0	0	1	1	1	1	1	1	0	0	0	6
Mean Snowfall (in.)	12.5	7.8	8.3	2.9	0.1	0.0	0.0	0.0	trace	0.5	4.6	10.2	46.9
Days With ≥ 1.0" Snow Depth	25	23	11	1	0	0	0	0	0	0	3	18	81

Danbury *Burnett County*   Elevation: 921 ft.   Latitude: 46° 00' N   Longitude: 92° 22' W

	JAN	FEB	MAR	APR	MAY	JUN	JUL	AUG	SEP	OCT	NOV	DEC	YEAR
Mean Maximum Temp. (°F)	20.2	27.6	38.9	55.2	68.8	76.2	80.1	77.5	68.2	56.3	38.3	25.0	52.7
Mean Temp. (°F)	9.3	16.3	28.4	42.9	55.5	63.9	68.6	66.2	57.1	45.6	30.0	15.7	41.6
Mean Minimum Temp. (°F)	-1.6	5.0	17.8	30.6	42.1	51.6	57.0	54.9	46.0	34.9	21.7	6.4	30.6
Extreme Maximum Temp. (°F)	53	57	80	92	92	96	101	98	96	87	73	57	101
Extreme Minimum Temp. (°F)	-44	-43	-24	-1	19	29	37	31	21	8	-25	-42	-44
Days Maximum Temp. ≥ 90°F	0	0	0	0	0	1	2	1	0	0	0	0	4
Days Maximum Temp. ≤ 32°F	26	17	8	1	0	0	0	0	0	0	9	23	84
Days Minimum Temp. ≤ 32°F	31	28	28	17	5	0	0	0	3	13	26	31	182
Days Minimum Temp. ≤ 0°F	17	11	4	0	0	0	0	0	0	0	2	11	45
Heating Degree Days (base 65°F)	1,722	1,370	1,129	658	309	99	30	61	258	596	1,043	1,523	8,798
Cooling Degree Days (base 65°F)	0	0	0	2	21	77	150	112	29	2	0	0	393
Mean Precipitation (in.)	0.98	0.77	1.68	2.15	3.30	4.13	4.36	4.36	3.41	2.48	1.91	0.97	30.50
Days With ≥ 0.1" Precipitation	3	2	4	6	7	8	7	7	7	6	4	3	64
Days With ≥ 1.0" Precipitation	0	0	0	0	1	1	1	1	1	0	1	0	6
Mean Snowfall (in.)	12.1	7.5	8.8	3.1	0.2	0.0	0.0	0.0	trace	0.7	8.2	9.9	50.5
Days With ≥ 1.0" Snow Depth	24	21	18	5	0	0	0	0	0	0	7	20	95

Darlington *Lafayette County*   Elevation: 928 ft.   Latitude: 42° 41' N   Longitude: 90° 06' W

	JAN	FEB	MAR	APR	MAY	JUN	JUL	AUG	SEP	OCT	NOV	DEC	YEAR
Mean Maximum Temp. (°F)	25.9	32.2	43.9	58.2	70.6	79.3	83.3	80.7	72.8	60.8	44.6	31.1	56.9
Mean Temp. (°F)	16.5	22.6	34.0	46.7	58.5	67.5	72.1	69.5	61.0	49.2	35.5	22.5	46.3
Mean Minimum Temp. (°F)	7.1	12.9	24.0	35.3	46.4	55.6	60.8	58.2	49.2	37.7	26.3	13.8	35.6
Extreme Maximum Temp. (°F)	59	62	84	93	92	101	101	102	96	91	74	65	102
Extreme Minimum Temp. (°F)	-30	-29	-10	-1	24	36	42	37	25	11	-14	-27	-30
Days Maximum Temp. ≥ 90°F	0	0	0	0	0	2	5	3	1	0	0	0	11
Days Maximum Temp. ≤ 32°F	21	14	5	0	0	0	0	0	0	0	4	15	59
Days Minimum Temp. ≤ 32°F	31	27	25	12	2	0	0	0	1	10	23	30	161
Days Minimum Temp. ≤ 0°F	11	6	1	0	0	0	0	0	0	0	0	6	24
Heating Degree Days (base 65°F)	1,498	1,191	957	548	235	50	9	24	171	488	879	1,312	7,362
Cooling Degree Days (base 65°F)	0	0	1	7	35	130	241	167	55	3	0	0	639
Mean Precipitation (in.)	1.18	1.31	2.35	3.44	3.49	4.58	4.15	4.32	3.82	2.32	2.44	1.62	35.02
Days With ≥ 0.1" Precipitation	4	4	5	7	7	7	6	7	6	5	5	4	67
Days With ≥ 1.0" Precipitation	0	0	0	1	1	1	1	1	1	0	0	0	6
Mean Snowfall (in.)	9.9	7.4	6.3	2.9	0.2	0.0	0.0	0.0	0.0	0.4	3.0	8.1	38.2
Days With ≥ 1.0" Snow Depth	22	20	8	1	0	0	0	0	0	0	3	14	68

Dodgeville *Iowa County*   Elevation: 1,108 ft.   Latitude: 42° 59' N   Longitude: 90° 07' W

	JAN	FEB	MAR	APR	MAY	JUN	JUL	AUG	SEP	OCT	NOV	DEC	YEAR
Mean Maximum Temp. (°F)	24.8	30.1	42.5	57.0	69.0	78.2	81.8	79.4	71.4	59.3	42.4	30.3	55.5
Mean Temp. (°F)	16.0	21.0	33.0	45.9	57.4	66.7	70.8	68.6	60.4	48.4	34.1	22.0	45.4
Mean Minimum Temp. (°F)	7.1	11.9	23.4	34.8	45.7	55.2	59.8	57.8	49.4	37.5	25.7	13.7	35.2
Extreme Maximum Temp. (°F)	54	61	83	93	89	100	99	101	96	91	70	64	101
Extreme Minimum Temp. (°F)	-33	-32	-7	10	24	33	42	39	26	12	-9	-21	-33
Days Maximum Temp. ≥ 90°F	0	0	0	0	0	1	4	2	0	0	0	0	7
Days Maximum Temp. ≤ 32°F	22	15	6	0	0	0	0	0	0	0	5	18	66
Days Minimum Temp. ≤ 32°F	31	28	26	13	2	0	0	0	1	10	23	30	164
Days Minimum Temp. ≤ 0°F	11	7	1	0	0	0	0	0	0	0	1	5	25
Heating Degree Days (base 65°F)	1,516	1,235	986	571	261	58	14	30	178	511	920	1,326	7,606
Cooling Degree Days (base 65°F)	0	0	0	6	27	113	186	140	42	2	0	0	516
Mean Precipitation (in.)	1.34	1.36	2.65	3.57	3.43	4.32	4.47	4.79	3.65	2.38	2.48	1.51	35.95
Days With ≥ 0.1" Precipitation	4	4	5	8	7	7	7	8	7	5	6	4	72
Days With ≥ 1.0" Precipitation	0	0	0	1	1	1	1	1	1	0	0	0	6
Mean Snowfall (in.)	10.4	7.2	6.2	2.4	trace	0.0	0.0	0.0	0.0	0.5	4.6	9.9	41.2
Days With ≥ 1.0" Snow Depth	24	20	8	1	0	0	0	0	0	0	4	18	75

Eau Claire County Airport *Chippewa County*   Elevation: 889 ft.   Latitude: 44° 52' N   Longitude: 91° 29' W

	JAN	FEB	MAR	APR	MAY	JUN	JUL	AUG	SEP	OCT	NOV	DEC	YEAR
Mean Maximum Temp. (°F)	20.9	28.0	39.9	56.6	70.1	78.6	82.7	79.9	70.4	57.8	40.1	26.3	54.3
Mean Temp. (°F)	11.6	18.2	30.2	45.1	57.9	66.9	71.5	69.0	59.4	47.3	31.8	18.0	43.9
Mean Minimum Temp. (°F)	2.2	8.3	20.5	33.5	45.6	55.2	60.2	58.0	48.4	36.7	23.5	9.7	33.5
Extreme Maximum Temp. (°F)	54	59	84	90	93	100	104	104	97	89	76	63	104
Extreme Minimum Temp. (°F)	-39	-35	-13	6	22	33	42	39	25	11	-12	-32	-39
Days Maximum Temp. ≥ 90°F	0	0	0	0	1	3	5	3	1	0	0	0	13
Days Maximum Temp. ≤ 32°F	24	17	8	1	0	0	0	0	0	0	7	21	78
Days Minimum Temp. ≤ 32°F	30	27	27	14	2	0	0	0	1	10	24	30	165
Days Minimum Temp. ≤ 0°F	14	9	3	0	0	0	0	0	0	0	1	8	35
Heating Degree Days (base 65°F)	1,653	1,318	1,071	597	251	60	11	29	207	545	990	1,451	8,183
Cooling Degree Days (base 65°F)	0	0	0	5	36	129	221	167	48	2	0	0	608
Mean Precipitation (in.)	1.00	0.77	1.87	2.89	3.73	4.11	4.01	4.69	3.61	2.39	1.93	1.02	32.02
Days With ≥ 0.1" Precipitation	3	2	5	6	7	8	7	7	7	5	4	3	64
Days With ≥ 1.0" Precipitation	0	0	0	0	1	1	1	1	1	0	0	0	5
Mean Snowfall (in.)	13.7	7.3	9.3	2.3	trace	trace	trace	trace	trace	0.3	6.5	10.3	49.7
Days With ≥ 1.0" Snow Depth	30	26	17	2	0	0	0	0	0	0	6	23	104

Ellsworth 1 E *Pierce County*   Elevation: 1,026 ft.   Latitude: 44° 44' N   Longitude: 92° 28' W

	JAN	FEB	MAR	APR	MAY	JUN	JUL	AUG	SEP	OCT	NOV	DEC	YEAR
Mean Maximum Temp. (°F)	21.7	29.3	40.8	57.4	70.2	78.9	82.7	79.8	71.2	59.3	40.4	26.5	54.8
Mean Temp. (°F)	12.1	19.5	30.9	45.5	58.1	67.1	71.1	68.3	59.4	48.0	31.9	18.0	44.1
Mean Minimum Temp. (°F)	2.4	9.6	21.0	33.6	46.0	55.2	59.5	56.8	47.7	36.7	23.3	9.4	33.4
Extreme Maximum Temp. (°F)	53	59	80	88	90	98	105	97	94	89	77	63	105
Extreme Minimum Temp. (°F)	-37	-37	-15	3	21	33	38	36	22	12	-15	-40	-40
Days Maximum Temp. ≥ 90°F	0	0	0	0	0	2	4	1	0	0	0	0	7
Days Maximum Temp. ≤ 32°F	24	15	7	0	0	0	0	0	0	0	7	21	74
Days Minimum Temp. ≤ 32°F	31	28	27	14	2	0	0	0	1	11	25	31	170
Days Minimum Temp. ≤ 0°F	14	8	2	0	0	0	0	0	0	0	1	8	33
Heating Degree Days (base 65°F)	1,636	1,279	1,049	582	239	57	12	34	199	522	987	1,453	8,049
Cooling Degree Days (base 65°F)	0	0	0	3	24	114	187	129	42	3	0	0	502
Mean Precipitation (in.)	1.05	0.72	2.00	3.10	4.05	4.46	4.69	4.47	4.09	2.74	2.43	1.13	34.93
Days With ≥ 0.1" Precipitation	3	2	5	6	8	8	7	7	7	6	5	4	68
Days With ≥ 1.0" Precipitation	0	0	0	0	1	1	1	1	1	1	0	0	6
Mean Snowfall (in.)	13.2	7.2	10.5	2.2	trace	0.0	0.0	0.0	0.0	0.4	7.5	10.4	51.4
Days With ≥ 1.0" Snow Depth	na	na	na	1	0	0	0	0	0	0	na	na	na

Fairchild Ranger Station *Eau Claire County*   Elevation: 1,079 ft.   Latitude: 44° 36' N   Longitude: 90° 58' W

	JAN	FEB	MAR	APR	MAY	JUN	JUL	AUG	SEP	OCT	NOV	DEC	YEAR
Mean Maximum Temp. (°F)	19.3	27.4	39.5	55.1	68.3	76.8	81.0	78.5	69.9	57.1	40.7	na	na
Mean Temp. (°F)	na	17.6	29.9	44.4	56.8	65.5	69.9	67.6	58.7	46.5	32.8	na	na
Mean Minimum Temp. (°F)	na	7.1	20.2	33.7	45.3	54.0	58.8	56.4	47.2	36.0	24.5	8.7	na
Extreme Maximum Temp. (°F)	55	58	81	90	93	100	103	102	95	92	73	62	103
Extreme Minimum Temp. (°F)	-35	-35	-16	5	22	29	38	35	25	10	-13	-30	-35
Days Maximum Temp. ≥ 90°F	0	0	0	0	0	1	3	2	0	0	0	0	6
Days Maximum Temp. ≤ 32°F	23	16	8	1	0	0	0	0	0	0	6	18	72
Days Minimum Temp. ≤ 32°F	28	26	26	14	2	0	0	0	1	11	22	26	156
Days Minimum Temp. ≤ 0°F	14	9	3	0	0	0	0	0	0	0	1	7	34
Heating Degree Days (base 65°F)	na	1,336	1,082	615	277	78	22	41	222	570	948	na	na
Cooling Degree Days (base 65°F)	na	0	0	4	28	101	186	132	na	1	na	na	na
Mean Precipitation (in.)	1.13	0.82	2.00	2.93	3.70	4.16	4.37	4.41	4.39	2.65	2.20	1.22	33.98
Days With ≥ 0.1" Precipitation	3	2	4	6	7	7	6	6	6	5	4	4	60
Days With ≥ 1.0" Precipitation	0	0	0	0	1	1	1	1	1	1	0	0	6
Mean Snowfall (in.)	11.4	7.3	8.6	2.7	trace	0.0	0.0	0.0	trace	0.5	5.3	10.4	46.2
Days With ≥ 1.0" Snow Depth	26	25	20	3	0	0	0	0	0	0	5	21	100

Fond Du Lac *Fond Du Lac County*   Elevation: 757 ft.   Latitude: 43° 48' N   Longitude: 88° 27' W

	JAN	FEB	MAR	APR	MAY	JUN	JUL	AUG	SEP	OCT	NOV	DEC	YEAR
Mean Maximum Temp. (°F)	24.4	29.4	40.3	54.4	68.2	77.4	81.6	78.8	70.7	58.5	42.9	30.1	54.7
Mean Temp. (°F)	16.5	21.5	32.0	45.3	57.9	67.2	71.9	69.6	61.4	49.7	35.6	22.9	46.0
Mean Minimum Temp. (°F)	8.6	13.4	23.7	36.1	47.5	57.0	62.2	60.4	52.1	40.8	28.3	15.6	37.1
Extreme Maximum Temp. (°F)	55	62	81	90	92	100	103	102	94	87	74	64	103
Extreme Minimum Temp. (°F)	-32	-29	-8	9	28	37	46	41	30	18	-5	-24	-32
Days Maximum Temp. ≥ 90°F	0	0	0	0	0	2	4	2	0	0	0	0	8
Days Maximum Temp. ≤ 32°F	22	16	7	1	0	0	0	0	0	0	5	16	67
Days Minimum Temp. ≤ 32°F	30	27	26	10	1	0	0	0	0	5	20	29	148
Days Minimum Temp. ≤ 0°F	10	5	1	0	0	0	0	0	0	0	0	5	21
Heating Degree Days (base 65°F)	1,497	1,220	1,014	592	255	57	8	20	158	473	875	1,299	7,468
Cooling Degree Days (base 65°F)	0	0	0	0	7	39	134	227	172	59	3	0	641
Mean Precipitation (in.)	1.06	0.94	1.82	2.73	2.94	3.34	3.49	4.12	3.51	2.46	1.96	1.38	29.75
Days With ≥ 0.1" Precipitation	3	3	5	6	6	6	7	7	6	6	5	4	64
Days With ≥ 1.0" Precipitation	0	0	0	1	1	1	1	1	1	0	0	0	6
Mean Snowfall (in.)	11.1	7.4	7.0	1.8	0.1	0.0	0.0	0.0	0.0	0.1	3.3	9.4	40.2
Days With ≥ 1.0" Snow Depth	25	21	10	1	0	0	0	0	0	0	3	18	78

Fort Atkinson *Jefferson County*   Elevation: 797 ft.   Latitude: 42° 54' N   Longitude: 88° 51' W

	JAN	FEB	MAR	APR	MAY	JUN	JUL	AUG	SEP	OCT	NOV	DEC	YEAR
Mean Maximum Temp. (°F)	25.6	31.3	43.1	57.4	69.9	79.6	83.3	80.7	73.1	60.9	44.9	31.7	56.8
Mean Temp. (°F)	16.6	22.2	33.9	46.8	58.2	67.8	72.0	69.5	61.3	49.7	36.3	23.6	46.5
Mean Minimum Temp. (°F)	7.5	13.0	24.6	36.2	46.4	55.9	60.6	58.2	49.5	38.5	27.7	15.4	36.1
Extreme Maximum Temp. (°F)	58	67	83	90	93	101	102	102	98	88	78	65	102
Extreme Minimum Temp. (°F)	-30	-39	-9	-4	26	35	42	37	28	11	-7	-29	-39
Days Maximum Temp. ≥ 90°F	0	0	0	0	1	3	6	3	1	0	0	0	14
Days Maximum Temp. ≤ 32°F	21	14	5	0	0	0	0	0	0	0	4	14	58
Days Minimum Temp. ≤ 32°F	30	27	24	11	1	0	0	0	1	9	21	29	153
Days Minimum Temp. ≤ 0°F	10	6	1	0	0	0	0	0	0	0	0	5	22
Heating Degree Days (base 65°F)	1,496	1,204	958	547	246	51	10	26	163	472	854	1,277	7,304
Cooling Degree Days (base 65°F)	0	0	0	0	7	37	138	226	167	53	4	0	632
Mean Precipitation (in.)	1.38	1.25	2.10	3.43	3.21	3.74	3.95	4.04	3.51	2.63	2.48	1.66	33.38
Days With ≥ 0.1" Precipitation	4	4	5	7	7	6	6	7	6	5	5	4	66
Days With ≥ 1.0" Precipitation	0	0	0	1	1	1	1	1	1	1	0	0	7
Mean Snowfall (in.)	12.4	6.7	5.4	1.9	0.2	0.0	0.0	0.0	0.0	trace	2.8	8.7	38.1
Days With ≥ 1.0" Snow Depth	23	17	7	1	0	0	0	0	0	0	3	15	66

Foxboro *Douglas County*   Elevation: 931 ft.   Latitude: 46° 29' N   Longitude: 92° 17' W

	JAN	FEB	MAR	APR	MAY	JUN	JUL	AUG	SEP	OCT	NOV	DEC	YEAR
Mean Maximum Temp. (°F)	20.3	27.3	37.3	52.4	66.2	74.7	79.8	77.4	68.2	55.9	37.5	24.9	51.8
Mean Temp. (°F)	8.6	15.3	26.4	39.8	51.2	60.1	66.3	64.6	56.1	44.5	28.6	14.6	39.7
Mean Minimum Temp. (°F)	-3.1	3.3	15.3	27.1	36.2	45.5	52.8	51.9	44.1	33.0	19.7	4.2	27.5
Extreme Maximum Temp. (°F)	54	59	75	89	91	98	104	99	100	88	75	57	104
Extreme Minimum Temp. (°F)	-45	-42	-35	-4	16	21	32	29	19	-1	-24	-43	-45
Days Maximum Temp. ≥ 90°F	0	0	0	0	0	1	3	2	0	0	0	0	6
Days Maximum Temp. ≤ 32°F	26	18	9	1	0	0	0	0	0	0	10	22	86
Days Minimum Temp. ≤ 32°F	31	28	29	22	10	1	0	0	4	15	26	30	196
Days Minimum Temp. ≤ 0°F	18	12	5	0	0	0	0	0	0	0	2	13	50
Heating Degree Days (base 65°F)	1,745	1,397	1,193	750	428	176	56	84	281	630	1,085	1,560	9,385
Cooling Degree Days (base 65°F)	0	0	0	0	7	31	89	77	18	1	0	0	223
Mean Precipitation (in.)	0.95	0.67	1.40	2.12	3.27	4.20	4.48	4.22	3.93	2.66	2.10	0.90	30.90
Days With ≥ 0.1" Precipitation	3	2	4	5	6	7	7	7	7	5	5	3	61
Days With ≥ 1.0" Precipitation	0	0	0	0	1	1	1	1	1	0	0	0	5
Mean Snowfall (in.)	na	na	na	na	na	na	na	na	na	na	na	na	na
Days With ≥ 1.0" Snow Depth	na	na	na	na	na	na	na	na	na	na	na	na	na

Genoa Dam 8 *Vernon County*   Elevation: 636 ft.   Latitude: 43° 34' N   Longitude: 91° 14' W

	JAN	FEB	MAR	APR	MAY	JUN	JUL	AUG	SEP	OCT	NOV	DEC	YEAR
Mean Maximum Temp. (°F)	24.6	30.9	42.6	57.9	70.6	79.4	83.1	80.7	72.2	60.3	43.2	30.1	56.3
Mean Temp. (°F)	16.0	22.2	33.9	47.9	59.9	69.0	73.1	71.0	62.5	51.0	35.7	22.9	47.1
Mean Minimum Temp. (°F)	7.4	13.4	25.1	37.8	49.1	58.6	63.2	61.2	52.8	41.5	28.2	15.6	37.8
Extreme Maximum Temp. (°F)	55	62	81	93	90	101	109	100	94	90	73	65	109
Extreme Minimum Temp. (°F)	-34	-38	-10	6	27	38	46	42	28	15	-9	-24	-38
Days Maximum Temp. ≥ 90°F	0	0	0	0	0	2	4	2	1	0	0	0	9
Days Maximum Temp. ≤ 32°F	22	14	5	0	0	0	0	0	0	0	5	17	63
Days Minimum Temp. ≤ 32°F	31	26	24	8	0	0	0	0	0	5	20	29	143
Days Minimum Temp. ≤ 0°F	10	6	1	0	0	0	0	0	0	0	0	4	21
Heating Degree Days (base 65°F)	1,513	1,204	958	513	196	31	5	13	137	434	872	1,300	7,176
Cooling Degree Days (base 65°F)	0	0	0	8	44	164	271	216	72	4	0	0	779
Mean Precipitation (in.)	0.99	0.83	1.83	3.59	3.56	3.79	4.64	4.48	3.70	2.33	2.26	1.09	33.09
Days With ≥ 0.1" Precipitation	3	2	4	7	7	7	7	7	6	5	5	3	63
Days With ≥ 1.0" Precipitation	0	0	0	1	1	1	1	1	1	0	0	0	6
Mean Snowfall (in.)	9.9	5.1	4.2	0.9	0.0	0.0	0.0	0.0	0.0	trace	3.6	7.2	30.9
Days With ≥ 1.0" Snow Depth	25	20	10	1	0	0	0	0	0	0	4	19	79

Germantown *Washington County*   Elevation: 849 ft.   Latitude: 43° 13' N   Longitude: 88° 07' W

	JAN	FEB	MAR	APR	MAY	JUN	JUL	AUG	SEP	OCT	NOV	DEC	YEAR
Mean Maximum Temp. (°F)	25.2	30.3	40.6	54.0	66.8	76.6	81.0	78.8	71.2	59.0	44.2	31.4	54.9
Mean Temp. (°F)	16.5	21.5	31.8	43.9	55.2	64.6	69.6	67.7	59.8	48.2	35.6	23.2	44.8
Mean Minimum Temp. (°F)	7.7	12.7	22.9	33.8	43.5	52.7	58.1	56.5	48.4	37.3	26.9	14.9	34.6
Extreme Maximum Temp. (°F)	56	64	83	89	92	99	102	102	95	88	74	64	102
Extreme Minimum Temp. (°F)	-40	-28	-9	7	21	27	38	36	22	14	-15	-25	-40
Days Maximum Temp. ≥ 90°F	0	0	0	0	0	2	4	2	1	0	0	0	9
Days Maximum Temp. ≤ 32°F	22	15	7	1	0	0	0	0	0	0	4	15	64
Days Minimum Temp. ≤ 32°F	30	27	26	14	4	0	0	0	1	10	22	29	163
Days Minimum Temp. ≤ 0°F	10	6	1	0	0	0	0	0	0	0	0	5	22
Heating Degree Days (base 65°F)	1,498	1,220	1,023	631	324	96	29	45	194	519	876	1,292	7,747
Cooling Degree Days (base 65°F)	0	0	0	5	25	90	175	133	42	2	0	0	472
Mean Precipitation (in.)	1.34	1.16	2.03	3.24	2.93	3.75	4.04	4.19	3.57	2.51	2.55	1.68	32.99
Days With ≥ 0.1" Precipitation	4	3	5	6	6	6	7	7	6	5	5	4	64
Days With ≥ 1.0" Precipitation	0	0	0	1	0	1	1	1	1	0	0	0	5
Mean Snowfall (in.)	14.1	8.0	6.7	2.2	0.3	0.0	0.0	0.0	0.0	0.1	3.6	9.4	44.4
Days With ≥ 1.0" Snow Depth	22	17	11	2	0	0	0	0	0	0	3	16	71

Goodman *Marinette County*   Elevation: 1,427 ft.   Latitude: 45° 38' N   Longitude: 88° 21' W

	JAN	FEB	MAR	APR	MAY	JUN	JUL	AUG	SEP	OCT	NOV	DEC	YEAR
Mean Maximum Temp. (°F)	20.7	27.3	37.1	52.0	66.2	73.7	78.3	75.1	66.0	54.7	39.2	26.6	51.4
Mean Temp. (°F)	10.2	16.6	26.4	40.4	53.1	61.4	66.4	63.8	54.9	44.3	30.9	17.9	40.5
Mean Minimum Temp. (°F)	0.0	5.7	15.7	28.8	39.9	49.0	54.5	52.6	43.8	33.8	22.4	9.1	29.6
Extreme Maximum Temp. (°F)	53	56	72	91	89	94	96	96	92	84	73	60	96
Extreme Minimum Temp. (°F)	-39	-35	-20	-3	18	28	34	32	21	11	-13	-28	-39
Days Maximum Temp. ≥ 90°F	0	0	0	0	0	1	1	1	0	0	0	0	3
Days Maximum Temp. ≤ 32°F	24	18	10	1	0	0	0	0	0	0	8	20	81
Days Minimum Temp. ≤ 32°F	28	26	28	21	7	0	0	0	3	14	24	27	178
Days Minimum Temp. ≤ 0°F	14	10	4	0	0	0	0	0	0	0	1	8	37
Heating Degree Days (base 65°F)	1,696	1,369	1,188	733	378	150	54	91	311	638	1,018	1,456	9,082
Cooling Degree Days (base 65°F)	na	0	0	2	11	49	na	61	11	1	0	na	na
Mean Precipitation (in.)	1.12	0.91	1.91	2.04	3.37	3.65	3.77	3.57	3.94	2.76	1.98	1.28	30.30
Days With ≥ 0.1" Precipitation	3	3	4	5	6	7	6	6	6	5	4	4	59
Days With ≥ 1.0" Precipitation	0	0	0	0	1	1	1	1	1	1	0	0	6
Mean Snowfall (in.)	13.9	7.4	10.3	3.5	0.6	0.0	0.0	0.0	0.0	1.2	5.0	12.2	54.1
Days With ≥ 1.0" Snow Depth	27	25	24	8	0	0	0	0	0	1	7	21	113

Gordon *Douglas County*   Elevation: 1,040 ft.   Latitude: 46° 15' N   Longitude: 91° 48' W

	JAN	FEB	MAR	APR	MAY	JUN	JUL	AUG	SEP	OCT	NOV	DEC	YEAR
Mean Maximum Temp. (°F)	19.4	27.1	38.1	53.8	68.0	76.5	80.7	77.5	67.8	55.0	37.4	24.3	52.1
Mean Temp. (°F)	6.8	13.7	26.0	40.6	53.7	62.6	67.2	64.5	55.2	43.5	27.9	13.8	39.6
Mean Minimum Temp. (°F)	-5.8	0.4	13.9	27.4	39.3	48.6	53.9	51.5	42.5	31.6	18.5	3.2	27.1
Extreme Maximum Temp. (°F)	51	58	73	92	93	97	101	98	98	86	71	59	101
Extreme Minimum Temp. (°F)	-48	-46	-30	-8	13	26	34	26	20	4	-31	-44	-48
Days Maximum Temp. ≥ 90°F	0	0	0	0	0	2	3	1	0	0	0	0	6
Days Maximum Temp. ≤ 32°F	26	18	9	1	0	0	0	0	0	0	10	23	87
Days Minimum Temp. ≤ 32°F	31	28	29	22	8	1	0	0	5	18	27	31	200
Days Minimum Temp. ≤ 0°F	19	14	6	0	0	0	0	0	0	0	2	13	54
Heating Degree Days (base 65°F)	1,804	1,445	1,202	726	373	128	49	88	307	663	1,097	1,582	9,464
Cooling Degree Days (base 65°F)	0	0	0	2	16	59	117	79	15	0	0	0	288
Mean Precipitation (in.)	1.08	0.80	1.67	2.16	3.37	3.75	4.89	4.38	3.86	2.72	1.89	1.00	31.57
Days With ≥ 0.1" Precipitation	4	2	4	6	6	8	8	7	7	6	5	4	67
Days With ≥ 1.0" Precipitation	0	0	0	0	1	1	1	1	1	1	0	0	6
Mean Snowfall (in.)	13.2	7.7	9.5	3.7	0.2	0.0	0.0	0.0	trace	0.8	9.1	11.4	55.6
Days With ≥ 1.0" Snow Depth	31	28	26	8	0	0	0	0	0	1	13	29	136

Grantsburg *Burnett County*   Elevation: 898 ft.   Latitude: 45° 46' N   Longitude: 92° 40' W

	JAN	FEB	MAR	APR	MAY	JUN	JUL	AUG	SEP	OCT	NOV	DEC	YEAR
Mean Maximum Temp. (°F)	19.3	26.9	38.4	55.4	68.8	76.2	80.5	78.0	68.2	56.0	38.6	24.6	52.6
Mean Temp. (°F)	8.5	15.6	27.8	43.4	56.2	64.5	69.0	66.7	57.1	45.3	29.9	14.9	41.6
Mean Minimum Temp. (°F)	-2.4	4.4	17.2	31.3	43.6	52.8	57.6	55.4	45.9	34.6	21.1	5.2	30.6
Extreme Maximum Temp. (°F)	51	54	72	95	92	95	100	96	94	86	72	60	100
Extreme Minimum Temp. (°F)	-42	-42	-18	-2	21	33	36	32	24	10	-18	-36	-42
Days Maximum Temp. ≥ 90°F	0	0	0	0	0	1	2	1	0	0	0	0	4
Days Maximum Temp. ≤ 32°F	26	18	9	1	0	0	0	0	0	0	9	23	86
Days Minimum Temp. ≤ 32°F	31	28	29	17	3	0	0	0	2	14	27	31	182
Days Minimum Temp. ≤ 0°F	18	12	4	0	0	0	0	0	0	0	2	12	48
Heating Degree Days (base 65°F)	1,749	1,390	1,146	645	291	86	24	49	257	604	1,047	1,547	8,835
Cooling Degree Days (base 65°F)	0	0	0	3	25	81	159	114	24	1	0	0	407
Mean Precipitation (in.)	1.14	0.80	1.76	2.21	3.49	4.64	4.22	4.52	3.48	2.64	2.04	1.08	32.02
Days With ≥ 0.1" Precipitation	4	2	4	6	7	8	7	7	7	5	5	3	65
Days With ≥ 1.0" Precipitation	0	0	0	0	1	1	1	1	1	1	0	0	6
Mean Snowfall (in.)	13.5	6.8	8.5	2.3	trace	0.0	0.0	0.0	trace	0.3	na	10.4	na
Days With ≥ 1.0" Snow Depth	21	19	17	3	0	0	0	0	0	0	na	na	na

Gurney *Iron County*   Elevation: 967 ft.   Latitude: 46° 28' N   Longitude: 90° 31' W

	JAN	FEB	MAR	APR	MAY	JUN	JUL	AUG	SEP	OCT	NOV	DEC	YEAR
Mean Maximum Temp. (°F)	21.9	28.1	38.1	51.5	65.3	73.8	78.1	76.1	67.0	56.0	39.3	26.9	51.8
Mean Temp. (°F)	12.1	17.3	27.4	40.5	52.7	61.6	66.7	65.0	56.5	46.1	31.6	18.4	41.3
Mean Minimum Temp. (°F)	2.1	6.5	16.8	29.4	40.2	49.4	55.1	53.8	45.8	36.2	23.9	9.8	30.7
Extreme Maximum Temp. (°F)	58	63	72	92	92	97	99	99	99	87	75	60	99
Extreme Minimum Temp. (°F)	-36	-37	-28	-4	20	27	33	32	26	12	-8	-30	-37
Days Maximum Temp. ≥ 90°F	0	0	0	0	0	1	2	1	0	0	0	0	4
Days Maximum Temp. ≤ 32°F	25	18	9	1	0	0	0	0	0	0	8	21	82
Days Minimum Temp. ≤ 32°F	31	27	28	20	7	1	0	0	2	11	25	30	182
Days Minimum Temp. ≤ 0°F	14	10	4	0	0	0	0	0	0	0	1	8	37
Heating Degree Days (base 65°F)	1,638	1,342	1,158	732	393	153	57	82	276	580	996	1,440	8,847
Cooling Degree Days (base 65°F)	0	0	0	3	18	59	111	88	25	2	0	0	306
Mean Precipitation (in.)	1.84	1.08	1.96	2.11	3.01	4.01	4.12	4.19	4.17	3.50	2.80	1.77	34.56
Days With ≥ 0.1" Precipitation	6	3	5	6	7	8	8	7	8	8	7	5	78
Days With ≥ 1.0" Precipitation	0	0	0	0	0	1	1	1	1	1	0	0	5
Mean Snowfall (in.)	35.4	20.0	21.3	7.8	1.2	0.0	0.0	0.0	0.2	1.9	20.1	30.8	138.7
Days With ≥ 1.0" Snow Depth	*29*	25	28	13	0	0	0	0	0	1	*12*	*26*	*134*

Hancock Exp. Farm *Waushara County*   Elevation: 1,076 ft.   Latitude: 44° 07' N   Longitude: 89° 32' W

	JAN	FEB	MAR	APR	MAY	JUN	JUL	AUG	SEP	OCT	NOV	DEC	YEAR
Mean Maximum Temp. (°F)	24.2	30.4	41.4	57.7	70.9	79.1	82.4	79.9	71.8	59.7	42.5	28.9	55.7
Mean Temp. (°F)	14.6	20.3	31.3	45.7	58.2	66.9	70.8	68.6	60.4	48.9	34.0	20.4	45.0
Mean Minimum Temp. (°F)	4.9	10.1	21.2	33.6	45.3	54.7	59.1	57.3	49.1	38.1	25.4	11.9	34.2
Extreme Maximum Temp. (°F)	54	62	84	90	91	100	105	102	96	91	75	61	105
Extreme Minimum Temp. (°F)	-34	-37	-17	-1	20	33	39	33	16	9	-12	-32	-37
Days Maximum Temp. ≥ 90°F	0	0	0	0	0	2	5	2	0	0	0	0	9
Days Maximum Temp. ≤ 32°F	23	16	6	0	0	0	0	0	0	0	5	19	69
Days Minimum Temp. ≤ 32°F	31	27	26	14	3	0	0	0	1	9	23	30	164
Days Minimum Temp. ≤ 0°F	12	8	3	0	0	0	0	0	0	0	1	7	31
Heating Degree Days (base 65°F)	1,559	1,256	1,037	580	246	59	16	31	182	496	924	1,375	7,761
Cooling Degree Days (base 65°F)	0	0	0	6	36	126	202	155	53	4	0	0	582
Mean Precipitation (in.)	0.93	0.87	1.99	2.87	3.51	3.65	4.20	4.18	3.74	2.37	2.15	1.02	31.48
Days With ≥ 0.1" Precipitation	3	3	5	6	7	7	7	7	7	6	5	3	66
Days With ≥ 1.0" Precipitation	0	0	0	0	1	1	1	1	1	0	0	0	5
Mean Snowfall (in.)	13.3	9.2	10.5	3.3	trace	0.0	0.0	0.0	trace	0.6	5.4	11.2	53.5
Days With ≥ 1.0" Snow Depth	28	26	17	2	0	0	0	0	0	0	5	23	101

Hartford 2 W *Washington County*   Elevation: 977 ft.   Latitude: 43° 20' N   Longitude: 88° 25' W

	JAN	FEB	MAR	APR	MAY	JUN	JUL	AUG	SEP	OCT	NOV	DEC	YEAR
Mean Maximum Temp. (°F)	25.5	30.7	41.7	55.8	68.8	78.2	82.2	79.7	71.9	59.7	44.0	31.0	55.8
Mean Temp. (°F)	16.3	21.5	32.7	44.9	56.7	65.9	70.3	68.1	60.0	48.7	35.5	22.8	45.3
Mean Minimum Temp. (°F)	7.1	12.3	23.5	33.9	44.4	53.4	58.3	56.4	48.1	37.7	26.9	14.5	34.7
Extreme Maximum Temp. (°F)	55	62	81	88	94	100	105	101	96	89	75	63	105
Extreme Minimum Temp. (°F)	-35	-29	-12	1	20	31	40	36	23	15	-11	-29	-35
Days Maximum Temp. ≥ 90°F	0	0	0	0	0	2	4	2	1	0	0	0	9
Days Maximum Temp. ≤ 32°F	21	15	6	0	0	0	0	0	0	0	4	15	61
Days Minimum Temp. ≤ 32°F	31	27	26	13	3	0	0	0	1	9	21	29	160
Days Minimum Temp. ≤ 0°F	11	7	1	0	0	0	0	0	0	0	0	5	24
Heating Degree Days (base 65°F)	1,504	1,222	994	602	281	75	19	38	187	502	880	1,303	7,607
Cooling Degree Days (base 65°F)	0	0	0	5	27	107	187	140	42	3	0	0	511
Mean Precipitation (in.)	1.30	1.01	1.93	2.96	3.02	3.77	4.17	4.07	3.76	2.70	2.21	1.59	32.49
Days With ≥ 0.1" Precipitation	4	3	5	7	6	7	7	7	6	6	5	5	68
Days With ≥ 1.0" Precipitation	0	0	0	0	0	1	1	1	1	1	0	0	5
Mean Snowfall (in.)	11.4	6.8	6.0	2.0	0.4	0.0	0.0	0.0	0.0	0.1	2.5	7.8	37.0
Days With ≥ 1.0" Snow Depth	23	20	9	1	0	0	0	0	0	0	2	16	71

Holcombe *Chippewa County*   Elevation: 1,023 ft.   Latitude: 45° 13' N   Longitude: 91° 08' W

	JAN	FEB	MAR	APR	MAY	JUN	JUL	AUG	SEP	OCT	NOV	DEC	YEAR
Mean Maximum Temp. (°F)	22.1	29.2	40.0	56.4	70.1	77.8	82.0	79.4	70.6	58.3	41.1	27.1	54.5
Mean Temp. (°F)	11.1	17.9	29.8	44.6	57.3	65.6	70.1	67.8	59.0	47.5	32.3	17.9	43.4
Mean Minimum Temp. (°F)	-0.1	6.5	19.2	32.7	44.5	53.3	58.2	56.0	47.4	36.7	24.0	8.9	32.3
Extreme Maximum Temp. (°F)	52	58	81	90	91	95	99	100	95	89	71	60	100
Extreme Minimum Temp. (°F)	-44	-45	-22	1	23	30	39	34	24	11	-16	-39	-45
Days Maximum Temp. ≥ 90°F	0	0	0	0	0	1	3	1	0	0	0	0	5
Days Maximum Temp. ≤ 32°F	24	16	7	0	0	0	0	0	0	0	6	20	73
Days Minimum Temp. ≤ 32°F	30	28	26	15	2	0	0	0	1	10	23	29	164
Days Minimum Temp. ≤ 0°F	15	9	3	0	0	0	0	0	0	0	1	8	36
Heating Degree Days (base 65°F)	1,670	1,334	1,084	613	256	65	16	38	212	537	970	*1,462*	*8,257*
Cooling Degree Days (base 65°F)	0	0	0	3	25	92	177	*136*	34	1	0	*0*	*468*
Mean Precipitation (in.)	1.01	0.77	1.71	2.64	3.40	4.09	3.61	4.66	3.95	2.52	2.12	1.04	31.52
Days With ≥ 0.1" Precipitation	3	3	4	5	6	7	6	7	5	5	4	3	59
Days With ≥ 1.0" Precipitation	0	0	0	1	1	1	1	1	1	1	0	0	7
Mean Snowfall (in.)	na	na	na	*0.7*	trace	0.0	0.0	0.0	0.0	trace	na	na	na
Days With ≥ 1.0" Snow Depth	na	na	na	2	0	0	0	0	0	0	na	na	na

Horicon *Dodge County*   Elevation: 879 ft.   Latitude: 43° 26' N   Longitude: 88° 38' W

	JAN	FEB	MAR	APR	MAY	JUN	JUL	AUG	SEP	OCT	NOV	DEC	YEAR
Mean Maximum Temp. (°F)	25.4	30.2	41.8	56.3	69.3	78.4	82.2	79.6	71.9	59.8	43.9	30.8	55.8
Mean Temp. (°F)	16.2	21.1	32.6	45.7	57.6	66.7	70.9	68.3	60.3	48.8	35.3	22.5	45.5
Mean Minimum Temp. (°F)	6.9	11.9	23.4	35.1	45.9	54.8	59.5	57.0	48.6	37.7	26.6	14.1	35.1
Extreme Maximum Temp. (°F)	55	61	80	89	93	99	101	100	95	87	74	64	101
Extreme Minimum Temp. (°F)	-36	-30	-10	9	25	33	42	38	24	14	-10	-25	-36
Days Maximum Temp. ≥ 90°F	0	0	0	0	0	2	4	2	0	0	0	0	8
Days Maximum Temp. ≤ 32°F	21	15	6	0	0	0	0	0	0	0	4	16	62
Days Minimum Temp. ≤ 32°F	31	27	26	12	1	0	0	0	1	9	22	30	159
Days Minimum Temp. ≤ 0°F	11	7	1	0	0	0	0	0	0	0	0	5	24
Heating Degree Days (base 65°F)	1,510	1,234	998	577	258	62	13	32	179	500	885	1,311	7,559
Cooling Degree Days (base 65°F)	0	0	0	5	31	112	192	132	41	3	0	0	516
Mean Precipitation (in.)	1.17	1.10	2.11	3.34	3.03	3.88	4.32	4.10	3.75	2.69	2.11	1.47	33.07
Days With ≥ 0.1" Precipitation	4	3	5	7	7	7	7	7	6	6	5	4	68
Days With ≥ 1.0" Precipitation	0	0	0	1	0	1	1	1	1	0	0	0	5
Mean Snowfall (in.)	11.8	6.8	5.5	1.7	0.2	0.0	0.0	0.0	0.0	0.1	2.5	9.1	37.7
Days With ≥ 1.0" Snow Depth	25	21	10	1	0	0	0	0	0	0	3	20	80

Jump River 3 E *Taylor County*   Elevation: 1,263 ft.   Latitude: 45° 22' N   Longitude: 90° 46' W

	JAN	FEB	MAR	APR	MAY	JUN	JUL	AUG	SEP	OCT	NOV	DEC	YEAR
Mean Maximum Temp. (°F)	20.9	27.6	38.9	54.9	68.5	75.7	79.6	77.3	68.3	56.4	38.5	25.4	52.7
Mean Temp. (°F)	10.0	16.4	27.9	42.7	54.9	62.8	66.8	64.9	56.4	45.4	30.0	16.3	41.2
Mean Minimum Temp. (°F)	-1.0	5.1	16.9	30.5	41.2	49.7	54.0	52.4	44.5	34.3	21.5	7.1	29.7
Extreme Maximum Temp. (°F)	54	61	79	88	91	93	98	99	95	87	71	61	99
Extreme Minimum Temp. (°F)	-47	-44	-27	-10	12	23	27	24	14	-3	-31	-47	-47
Days Maximum Temp. ≥ 90°F	0	0	0	0	0	1	1	1	0	0	0	0	3
Days Maximum Temp. ≤ 32°F	26	18	8	1	0	0	0	0	0	0	9	23	85
Days Minimum Temp. ≤ 32°F	31	28	27	18	7	1	0	1	4	14	26	31	188
Days Minimum Temp. ≤ 0°F	16	10	5	0	0	0	0	0	0	0	2	10	43
Heating Degree Days (base 65°F)	1,703	1,369	1,144	665	324	122	50	82	277	603	1,042	1,506	8,887
Cooling Degree Days (base 65°F)	0	0	0	4	16	66	116	90	26	1	0	0	319
Mean Precipitation (in.)	1.02	0.78	1.68	2.48	3.48	4.16	4.50	4.44	3.99	2.80	2.22	1.16	32.71
Days With ≥ 0.1" Precipitation	3	2	4	6	7	7	7	7	7	5	5	4	64
Days With ≥ 1.0" Precipitation	0	0	0	0	1	1	1	1	1	1	0	0	6
Mean Snowfall (in.)	15.0	8.9	9.5	2.2	trace	0.0	0.0	0.0	trace	0.9	6.7	12.2	55.4
Days With ≥ 1.0" Snow Depth	30	27	23	3	0	0	0	0	0	0	8	26	117

Kenosha *Kenosha County*   Elevation: 597 ft.   Latitude: 42° 34' N   Longitude: 87° 49' W

	JAN	FEB	MAR	APR	MAY	JUN	JUL	AUG	SEP	OCT	NOV	DEC	YEAR
Mean Maximum Temp. (°F)	28.5	32.8	41.7	51.7	62.4	73.0	79.1	77.9	70.7	59.5	46.2	34.3	54.8
Mean Temp. (°F)	20.7	25.4	34.2	43.8	53.9	64.0	70.4	69.6	62.1	50.9	38.5	26.9	46.7
Mean Minimum Temp. (°F)	12.7	18.0	26.6	35.8	45.3	54.9	61.6	61.2	53.4	42.3	30.7	19.5	38.5
Extreme Maximum Temp. (°F)	63	69	83	90	94	101	104	100	96	88	76	66	104
Extreme Minimum Temp. (°F)	-31	-23	-2	10	26	36	41	40	30	20	-5	-29	-31
Days Maximum Temp. ≥ 90°F	0	0	0	0	0	1	3	2	0	0	0	0	6
Days Maximum Temp. ≤ 32°F	18	12	5	0	0	0	0	0	0	0	2	10	47
Days Minimum Temp. ≤ 32°F	29	26	23	9	1	0	0	0	0	4	17	27	136
Days Minimum Temp. ≤ 0°F	7	3	0	0	0	0	0	0	0	0	0	2	12
Heating Degree Days (base 65°F)	1,370	1,112	949	631	353	106	16	18	133	434	788	1,173	7,083
Cooling Degree Days (base 65°F)	0	0	0	2	17	86	199	174	54	4	0	0	536
Mean Precipitation (in.)	1.63	1.24	2.32	3.82	3.26	3.53	3.61	4.13	3.69	2.52	2.66	2.05	34.46
Days With ≥ 0.1" Precipitation	4	3	6	7	7	6	6	6	6	5	6	5	67
Days With ≥ 1.0" Precipitation	0	0	0	1	1	1	1	1	1	0	0	0	6
Mean Snowfall (in.)	12.4	9.0	6.0	1.5	trace	0.0	0.0	0.0	0.0	trace	1.4	7.1	37.4
Days With ≥ 1.0" Snow Depth	20	14	6	1	0	0	0	0	0	0	1	9	51

Lake Geneva *Walworth County*   Elevation: 879 ft.   Latitude: 42° 36' N   Longitude: 88° 26' W

	JAN	FEB	MAR	APR	MAY	JUN	JUL	AUG	SEP	OCT	NOV	DEC	YEAR
Mean Maximum Temp. (°F)	27.7	33.4	44.2	58.3	71.2	81.0	85.1	82.5	74.7	62.0	45.9	33.1	58.3
Mean Temp. (°F)	19.8	25.1	35.2	47.6	59.4	69.1	73.9	71.7	63.7	51.8	38.0	25.9	48.5
Mean Minimum Temp. (°F)	11.9	16.8	26.2	36.9	47.6	57.2	62.7	60.9	52.7	41.6	30.1	18.7	38.6
Extreme Maximum Temp. (°F)	58	65	81	90	94	104	104	106	98	87	75	64	106
Extreme Minimum Temp. (°F)	-27	-25	-4	9	27	35	44	40	28	17	-5	-23	-27
Days Maximum Temp. ≥ 90°F	0	0	0	0	1	4	8	4	1	0	0	0	18
Days Maximum Temp. ≤ 32°F	20	12	4	0	0	0	0	0	0	0	3	13	52
Days Minimum Temp. ≤ 32°F	30	26	24	9	1	0	0	0	0	5	18	28	141
Days Minimum Temp. ≤ 0°F	7	4	0	0	0	0	0	0	0	0	0	3	14
Heating Degree Days (base 65°F)	1,396	1,121	918	522	216	39	5	12	118	411	804	1,205	6,767
Cooling Degree Days (base 65°F)	0	0	0	7	48	177	297	235	87	6	0	0	857
Mean Precipitation (in.)	2.02	1.60	2.67	3.76	3.44	3.96	3.81	3.99	3.74	2.73	2.80	2.33	36.85
Days With ≥ 0.1" Precipitation	6	4	6	7	7	7	7	6	6	5	6	5	72
Days With ≥ 1.0" Precipitation	0	0	0	1	1	1	1	1	1	1	0	0	7
Mean Snowfall (in.)	14.2	9.2	7.3	2.5	trace	0.0	0.0	0.0	0.0	0.1	3.5	11.2	48.0
Days With ≥ 1.0" Snow Depth	23	18	7	1	0	0	0	0	0	0	3	15	67

Lake Mills *Jefferson County*   Elevation: 849 ft.   Latitude: 43° 05' N   Longitude: 88° 55' W

	JAN	FEB	MAR	APR	MAY	JUN	JUL	AUG	SEP	OCT	NOV	DEC	YEAR
Mean Maximum Temp. (°F)	26.6	32.5	44.1	58.9	71.9	80.9	84.8	81.7	74.1	61.5	44.9	32.0	57.8
Mean Temp. (°F)	17.6	23.0	34.3	47.6	59.4	68.6	73.1	70.3	62.5	50.7	36.6	24.0	47.3
Mean Minimum Temp. (°F)	8.6	13.5	24.5	36.3	46.8	56.2	61.4	58.8	50.9	39.8	28.3	16.0	36.8
Extreme Maximum Temp. (°F)	55	64	81	89	93	103	102	104	98	87	73	66	104
Extreme Minimum Temp. (°F)	-29	-25	-11	8	21	34	45	41	26	15	-13	-24	-29
Days Maximum Temp. ≥ 90°F	0	0	0	0	1	3	7	4	1	0	0	0	16
Days Maximum Temp. ≤ 32°F	21	13	4	0	0	0	0	0	0	0	3	15	56
Days Minimum Temp. ≤ 32°F	31	27	25	11	1	0	0	0	1	7	20	29	152
Days Minimum Temp. ≤ 0°F	9	6	1	0	0	0	0	0	0	0	0	4	20
Heating Degree Days (base 65°F)	1,464	1,179	944	522	211	38	4	17	135	442	844	1,263	7,063
Cooling Degree Days (base 65°F)	0	0	0	7	42	155	268	194	67	5	0	0	738
Mean Precipitation (in.)	1.38	1.20	2.26	3.31	3.24	3.87	4.23	4.46	3.68	2.50	2.37	1.74	34.24
Days With ≥ 0.1" Precipitation	4	4	5	7	7	7	7	6	6	5	6	4	68
Days With ≥ 1.0" Precipitation	0	0	0	1	1	1	1	1	1	0	0	0	6
Mean Snowfall (in.)	10.9	7.3	5.4	2.0	0.1	0.0	0.0	0.0	0.0	trace	3.2	9.8	38.7
Days With ≥ 1.0" Snow Depth	23	19	8	1	0	0	0	0	0	0	3	16	70

Lakewood 3 NE *Oconto County*   Elevation: 1,289 ft.   Latitude: 45° 19' N   Longitude: 88° 30' W

	JAN	FEB	MAR	APR	MAY	JUN	JUL	AUG	SEP	OCT	NOV	DEC	YEAR
Mean Maximum Temp. (°F)	22.9	28.9	39.5	54.4	68.7	76.7	80.5	77.8	68.3	56.0	39.5	27.3	53.4
Mean Temp. (°F)	12.3	17.3	28.0	41.6	54.2	62.9	67.2	65.0	56.1	44.7	30.9	18.3	41.5
Mean Minimum Temp. (°F)	1.6	5.6	16.4	28.8	39.7	48.9	53.8	52.0	43.8	33.4	22.3	9.3	29.6
Extreme Maximum Temp. (°F)	52	59	72	93	92	97	100	96	94	84	73	61	100
Extreme Minimum Temp. (°F)	-43	-36	-24	-7	18	27	30	31	20	8	-13	-27	-43
Days Maximum Temp. ≥ 90°F	0	0	0	0	0	1	3	1	0	0	0	0	5
Days Maximum Temp. ≤ 32°F	26	18	7	1	0	0	0	0	0	0	8	21	81
Days Minimum Temp. ≤ 32°F	31	28	29	20	8	1	0	0	3	16	26	31	193
Days Minimum Temp. ≤ 0°F	15	11	4	0	0	0	0	0	0	0	1	9	40
Heating Degree Days (base 65°F)	1,630	1,342	1,140	697	343	119	43	74	277	623	1,017	1,440	8,745
Cooling Degree Days (base 65°F)	0	0	0	2	15	64	115	85	17	0	0	0	298
Mean Precipitation (in.)	1.38	0.99	2.29	2.94	3.55	3.74	3.35	3.86	3.95	2.82	2.46	1.67	33.00
Days With ≥ 0.1" Precipitation	4	3	5	6	7	7	7	7	7	6	6	5	70
Days With ≥ 1.0" Precipitation	0	0	1	1	1	1	1	1	1	1	1	0	9
Mean Snowfall (in.)	16.6	9.0	12.0	4.4	0.6	0.0	0.0	0.0	trace	0.3	6.5	15.3	64.7
Days With ≥ 1.0" Snow Depth	31	28	27	7	0	0	0	0	0	0	8	28	129

Lancaster 4 WSW *Grant County*   Elevation: 1,040 ft.   Latitude: 42° 50' N   Longitude: 90° 47' W

	JAN	FEB	MAR	APR	MAY	JUN	JUL	AUG	SEP	OCT	NOV	DEC	YEAR
Mean Maximum Temp. (°F)	24.0	30.6	42.3	57.3	69.3	78.5	82.1	79.9	71.7	59.9	43.0	29.9	55.7
Mean Temp. (°F)	15.6	22.0	33.5	46.7	58.4	67.6	71.6	69.6	61.2	49.6	34.8	22.0	46.1
Mean Minimum Temp. (°F)	7.1	13.4	24.5	36.0	47.5	56.7	61.0	59.3	50.8	39.2	26.6	14.1	36.3
Extreme Maximum Temp. (°F)	57	61	79	95	91	100	100	103	94	89	74	62	103
Extreme Minimum Temp. (°F)	-28	-31	-11	6	25	37	43	40	27	15	-15	-27	-31
Days Maximum Temp. ≥ 90°F	0	0	0	0	0	1	4	2	0	0	0	0	7
Days Maximum Temp. ≤ 32°F	23	15	6	0	0	0	0	0	0	0	6	18	68
Days Minimum Temp. ≤ 32°F	31	27	25	10	1	0	0	0	1	8	22	30	155
Days Minimum Temp. ≤ 0°F	11	6	1	0	0	0	0	0	0	0	0	5	23
Heating Degree Days (base 65°F)	1,527	1,208	971	549	232	46	10	22	164	475	898	1,327	7,429
Cooling Degree Days (base 65°F)	0	0	0	5	29	127	220	169	56	4	0	0	610
Mean Precipitation (in.)	0.79	0.96	2.22	3.31	3.68	4.47	4.26	4.58	3.39	2.46	2.46	1.18	33.76
Days With ≥ 0.1" Precipitation	3	3	5	7	8	7	7	7	6	5	5	3	66
Days With ≥ 1.0" Precipitation	0	0	0	1	1	1	1	1	1	1	0	0	8
Mean Snowfall (in.)	10.8	7.2	6.3	2.6	0.2	0.0	0.0	0.0	0.0	0.3	4.2	8.9	40.5
Days With ≥ 1.0" Snow Depth	24	19	10	1	0	0	0	0	0	0	4	16	74

Laona 6 SW *Forest County*   Elevation: 1,522 ft.   Latitude: 45° 30' N   Longitude: 88° 46' W

	JAN	FEB	MAR	APR	MAY	JUN	JUL	AUG	SEP	OCT	NOV	DEC	YEAR
Mean Maximum Temp. (°F)	20.7	26.9	37.3	52.6	66.2	72.6	75.7	72.9	64.5	53.9	37.0	24.8	50.4
Mean Temp. (°F)	11.7	16.9	27.0	40.8	53.3	61.1	65.1	63.0	54.9	44.4	29.7	17.1	40.4
Mean Minimum Temp. (°F)	2.6	6.8	16.6	29.1	40.3	49.5	54.6	53.1	45.3	34.8	22.4	9.4	30.4
Extreme Maximum Temp. (°F)	50	57	72	90	88	92	92	90	90	82	70	58	92
Extreme Minimum Temp. (°F)	-39	-36	-24	-4	16	26	29	32	22	8	-17	-29	-39
Days Maximum Temp. ≥ 90°F	0	0	0	0	0	0	1	0	0	0	0	0	1
Days Maximum Temp. ≤ 32°F	27	19	10	1	0	0	0	0	0	0	11	25	93
Days Minimum Temp. ≤ 32°F	31	28	29	20	7	1	0	0	2	13	26	31	188
Days Minimum Temp. ≤ 0°F	13	10	5	0	0	0	0	0	0	0	1	8	37
Heating Degree Days (base 65°F)	1,649	1,355	1,172	720	369	151	69	105	310	634	1,052	1,478	9,064
Cooling Degree Days (base 65°F)	0	0	0	3	10	39	72	51	12	1	0	0	188
Mean Precipitation (in.)	1.28	0.93	1.97	2.61	3.36	3.70	3.62	3.63	3.77	2.80	2.29	1.48	31.44
Days With ≥ 0.1" Precipitation	4	3	5	6	7	8	8	8	7	6	5	5	72
Days With ≥ 1.0" Precipitation	0	0	0	0	1	1	1	1	1	1	0	0	6
Mean Snowfall (in.)	16.8	9.8	12.5	6.0	0.8	0.0	0.0	0.0	trace	1.9	9.2	15.7	72.7
Days With ≥ 1.0" Snow Depth	31	28	28	10	0	0	0	0	0	1	12	29	139

Long Lake Dam *Oneida County*   Elevation: 1,627 ft.   Latitude: 45° 54' N   Longitude: 89° 08' W

	JAN	FEB	MAR	APR	MAY	JUN	JUL	AUG	SEP	OCT	NOV	DEC	YEAR
Mean Maximum Temp. (°F)	21.1	26.8	37.6	51.6	66.1	74.0	78.1	75.8	65.8	53.8	37.5	25.0	51.1
Mean Temp. (°F)	9.3	13.5	24.7	38.6	52.0	60.9	65.5	63.4	54.1	42.9	28.7	15.2	39.1
Mean Minimum Temp. (°F)	-2.7	0.1	11.8	25.5	37.9	47.8	52.9	50.9	42.3	31.9	19.9	5.3	27.0
Extreme Maximum Temp. (°F)	52	59	71	89	90	97	98	95	95	88	72	58	98
Extreme Minimum Temp. (°F)	-43	-45	-27	-10	16	25	33	31	20	9	-14	-35	-45
Days Maximum Temp. ≥ 90°F	0	0	0	0	0	1	1	0	0	0	0	0	2
Days Maximum Temp. ≤ 32°F	27	19	10	1	0	0	0	0	0	0	10	24	91
Days Minimum Temp. ≤ 32°F	31	28	30	24	11	1	0	0	5	18	28	31	207
Days Minimum Temp. ≤ 0°F	17	14	8	1	0	0	0	0	0	0	2	11	53
Heating Degree Days (base 65°F)	1,725	1,452	1,242	788	408	161	67	106	337	678	1,082	1,540	9,586
Cooling Degree Days (base 65°F)	0	0	0	2	10	47	88	69	12	0	0	0	228
Mean Precipitation (in.)	1.30	0.94	1.84	2.38	3.30	3.79	3.57	4.12	4.22	2.81	2.37	1.42	32.06
Days With ≥ 0.1" Precipitation	5	3	5	6	7	8	8	7	8	7	6	4	74
Days With ≥ 1.0" Precipitation	0	0	0	0	1	1	1	1	1	1	0	0	6
Mean Snowfall (in.)	15.2	9.5	11.4	5.2	0.4	0.0	0.0	0.0	trace	0.8	9.7	14.5	66.7
Days With ≥ 1.0" Snow Depth	na	na	na	na	0	0	0	0	0	0	7	na	na

Luck *Polk County*   Elevation: 1,217 ft.   Latitude: 45° 34' N   Longitude: 92° 28' W

	JAN	FEB	MAR	APR	MAY	JUN	JUL	AUG	SEP	OCT	NOV	DEC	YEAR
Mean Maximum Temp. (°F)	20.7	27.6	39.4	56.1	69.5	76.9	81.1	78.5	69.3	57.5	38.6	24.9	53.3
Mean Temp. (°F)	10.7	17.3	29.4	44.3	57.1	65.2	69.5	67.4	58.4	47.0	30.6	16.4	42.8
Mean Minimum Temp. (°F)	0.8	7.0	19.4	32.6	44.7	53.4	57.9	56.3	47.4	36.4	22.5	7.8	32.2
Extreme Maximum Temp. (°F)	52	56	80	89	89	96	101	100	96	84	71	61	101
Extreme Minimum Temp. (°F)	-43	-38	-22	0	20	32	39	33	22	9	-21	-44	-44
Days Maximum Temp. ≥ 90°F	0	0	0	0	0	1	3	1	0	0	0	0	5
Days Maximum Temp. ≤ 32°F	25	17	8	0	0	0	0	0	0	0	9	23	82
Days Minimum Temp. ≤ 32°F	31	28	27	15	3	0	0	0	2	11	25	31	173
Days Minimum Temp. ≤ 0°F	15	10	3	0	0	0	0	0	0	0	1	10	39
Heating Degree Days (base 65°F)	1,679	1,342	1,096	616	265	78	21	46	228	552	1,026	1,502	8,451
Cooling Degree Days (base 65°F)	0	0	0	3	25	95	172	134	37	2	0	0	468
Mean Precipitation (in.)	0.96	0.71	1.72	2.42	3.60	4.29	4.06	4.48	3.97	2.69	1.96	0.92	31.78
Days With ≥ 0.1" Precipitation	3	2	4	6	7	8	7	7	7	6	4	3	64
Days With ≥ 1.0" Precipitation	0	0	0	1	1	1	1	1	1	0	0	0	6
Mean Snowfall (in.)	13.8	7.8	10.5	3.4	trace	0.0	0.0	0.0	0.0	0.7	10.9	11.6	58.7
Days With ≥ 1.0" Snow Depth	30	25	17	2	0	0	0	0	0	0	10	26	110

Lynxville Dam 9 *Crawford County*   Elevation: 629 ft.   Latitude: 43° 13' N   Longitude: 91° 06' W

	JAN	FEB	MAR	APR	MAY	JUN	JUL	AUG	SEP	OCT	NOV	DEC	YEAR
Mean Maximum Temp. (°F)	25.6	32.0	43.6	58.9	71.6	80.4	84.2	81.4	72.9	60.9	44.0	30.9	57.2
Mean Temp. (°F)	16.9	22.9	34.7	48.7	60.8	69.8	74.2	71.8	63.3	51.5	36.4	23.5	47.9
Mean Minimum Temp. (°F)	8.1	13.8	25.7	38.5	49.9	59.2	64.1	62.1	53.7	42.1	28.8	16.1	38.5
Extreme Maximum Temp. (°F)	56	63	82	93	92	100	101	101	95	92	75	64	101
Extreme Minimum Temp. (°F)	-33	-34	-13	11	27	40	46	44	29	18	-8	-21	-34
Days Maximum Temp. ≥ 90°F	0	0	0	0	0	2	6	3	1	0	0	0	12
Days Maximum Temp. ≤ 32°F	21	13	4	0	0	0	0	0	0	0	4	16	58
Days Minimum Temp. ≤ 32°F	31	27	24	7	0	0	0	0	0	4	19	29	141
Days Minimum Temp. ≤ 0°F	10	6	1	0	0	0	0	0	0	0	0	4	21
Heating Degree Days (base 65°F)	1,487	1,182	932	491	175	26	3	8	120	417	851	1,279	6,971
Cooling Degree Days (base 65°F)	0	0	0	8	48	180	301	232	77	5	0	0	851
Mean Precipitation (in.)	1.02	0.96	1.94	3.58	3.83	4.02	4.04	4.30	3.14	2.31	2.34	1.20	32.68
Days With ≥ 0.1" Precipitation	3	3	5	8	8	7	7	7	6	5	5	4	68
Days With ≥ 1.0" Precipitation	0	0	0	1	1	1	1	1	1	0	1	0	7
Mean Snowfall (in.)	10.2	7.0	4.3	1.2	0.0	0.0	0.0	0.0	0.0	trace	3.7	7.7	34.1
Days With ≥ 1.0" Snow Depth	27	23	12	1	0	0	0	0	0	0	3	22	88

Manitowoc *Manitowoc County*   Elevation: 659 ft.   Latitude: 44° 05' N   Longitude: 87° 41' W

	JAN	FEB	MAR	APR	MAY	JUN	JUL	AUG	SEP	OCT	NOV	DEC	YEAR
Mean Maximum Temp. (°F)	26.2	30.3	39.4	52.3	65.1	74.8	79.6	77.8	69.8	57.4	43.5	31.7	54.0
Mean Temp. (°F)	18.4	22.6	31.7	43.3	54.7	64.2	69.9	68.5	60.7	49.1	36.4	24.5	45.3
Mean Minimum Temp. (°F)	10.5	14.9	23.9	34.1	44.2	53.5	60.1	59.2	51.6	40.8	29.2	17.2	36.6
Extreme Maximum Temp. (°F)	53	57	77	90	90	97	101	96	97	87	74	62	101
Extreme Minimum Temp. (°F)	-26	-27	-4	3	26	35	43	40	29	19	-7	-21	-27
Days Maximum Temp. ≥ 90°F	0	0	0	0	0	1	2	1	0	0	0	0	4
Days Maximum Temp. ≤ 32°F	20	15	6	0	0	0	0	0	0	0	3	14	58
Days Minimum Temp. ≤ 32°F	30	27	26	12	2	0	0	0	0	5	19	28	149
Days Minimum Temp. ≤ 0°F	8	4	0	0	0	0	0	0	0	0	0	4	16
Heating Degree Days (base 65°F)	1,440	1,191	1,025	647	324	95	16	25	160	487	853	1,250	7,513
Cooling Degree Days (base 65°F)	0	0	0	1	14	78	170	146	41	1	0	0	451
Mean Precipitation (in.)	1.51	1.22	1.93	2.82	2.79	3.21	3.30	3.63	3.16	2.31	2.32	1.75	29.95
Days With ≥ 0.1" Precipitation	4	4	5	6	6	6	6	7	6	5	5	4	64
Days With ≥ 1.0" Precipitation	0	0	0	1	1	1	1	1	1	0	0	0	6
Mean Snowfall (in.)	na	na	na	0.5	trace	0.0	0.0	0.0	0.0	trace	1.5	na	na
Days With ≥ 1.0" Snow Depth	16	13	6	1	0	0	0	0	0	0	1	na	na

Marinette *Marinette County* Elevation: 606 ft. Latitude: 45° 05' N Longitude: 87° 38' W

	JAN	FEB	MAR	APR	MAY	JUN	JUL	AUG	SEP	OCT	NOV	DEC	YEAR
Mean Maximum Temp. (°F)	25.7	30.4	40.4	54.1	67.7	77.4	82.4	79.7	70.5	57.8	43.3	30.9	55.0
Mean Temp. (°F)	17.1	21.5	31.2	43.7	56.0	65.7	70.8	68.8	60.2	48.5	35.5	23.2	45.2
Mean Minimum Temp. (°F)	8.5	12.6	21.8	33.1	44.2	53.9	59.2	57.7	49.8	39.2	27.6	15.6	35.3
Extreme Maximum Temp. (°F)	50	62	75	89	97	100	102	99	94	84	74	62	102
Extreme Minimum Temp. (°F)	-30	-30	-8	5	23	35	40	34	23	16	-7	-22	-30
Days Maximum Temp. ≥ 90°F	0	0	0	0	1	2	5	2	0	0	0	0	10
Days Maximum Temp. ≤ 32°F	22	16	6	0	0	0	0	0	0	0	3	16	63
Days Minimum Temp. ≤ 32°F	31	27	27	13	3	0	0	0	1	7	21	29	159
Days Minimum Temp. ≤ 0°F	9	5	1	0	0	0	0	0	0	0	0	4	19
Heating Degree Days (base 65°F)	1,478	1,222	1,043	635	300	77	13	28	180	505	879	1,288	7,648
Cooling Degree Days (base 65°F)	0	0	0	1	24	99	191	152	41	1	0	0	509
Mean Precipitation (in.)	1.98	1.29	2.34	2.78	3.22	3.51	3.41	3.29	3.59	2.56	2.71	1.82	32.50
Days With ≥ 0.1" Precipitation	5	4	5	6	6	7	7	7	7	6	6	5	71
Days With ≥ 1.0" Precipitation	0	0	0	1	1	1	1	0	1	0	1	0	6
Mean Snowfall (in.)	16.4	9.9	9.5	2.7	0.1	0.0	0.0	0.0	0.0	trace	*3.4*	12.7	*54.7*
Days With ≥ 1.0" Snow Depth	*22*	na	*14*	2	0	0	0	0	0	0	*2*	*14*	na

Marshfield Exp. Farm *Wood County* Elevation: 1,250 ft. Latitude: 44° 38' N Longitude: 90° 08' W

	JAN	FEB	MAR	APR	MAY	JUN	JUL	AUG	SEP	OCT	NOV	DEC	YEAR
Mean Maximum Temp. (°F)	22.7	29.1	40.0	56.5	69.7	78.3	82.2	79.8	70.9	58.6	41.0	27.6	54.7
Mean Temp. (°F)	13.3	19.4	30.2	44.7	56.9	65.7	69.9	67.9	59.0	47.5	32.6	19.2	43.9
Mean Minimum Temp. (°F)	3.8	9.7	20.3	32.9	44.0	53.1	57.6	55.7	47.2	36.4	24.2	10.7	33.0
Extreme Maximum Temp. (°F)	55	55	80	91	91	97	104	102	97	90	73	63	104
Extreme Minimum Temp. (°F)	-33	-33	-14	5	22	32	38	35	20	14	-12	-27	-33
Days Maximum Temp. ≥ 90°F	0	0	0	0	0	2	4	2	0	0	0	0	8
Days Maximum Temp. ≤ 32°F	24	17	7	0	0	0	0	0	0	0	6	20	74
Days Minimum Temp. ≤ 32°F	31	28	27	15	3	0	0	0	1	11	25	31	172
Days Minimum Temp. ≤ 0°F	13	8	2	0	0	0	0	0	0	0	1	7	31
Heating Degree Days (base 65°F)	1,599	1,282	1,071	606	272	71	18	37	210	537	965	1,415	8,083
Cooling Degree Days (base 65°F)	0	0	0	2	26	107	182	146	39	1	0	0	503
Mean Precipitation (in.)	0.98	0.87	1.94	2.94	3.86	3.94	4.10	4.22	4.05	2.64	2.31	1.29	33.14
Days With ≥ 0.1" Precipitation	3	3	4	6	7	7	8	7	7	6	5	4	67
Days With ≥ 1.0" Precipitation	0	0	0	1	1	1	1	1	1	1	1	0	8
Mean Snowfall (in.)	11.9	7.9	9.6	3.0	trace	0.0	0.0	0.0	0.0	0.6	5.4	10.9	49.3
Days With ≥ 1.0" Snow Depth	21	*16*	*12*	*1*	0	0	0	0	0	0	*3*	*18*	*71*

Mather 3 NW *Jackson County* Elevation: 967 ft. Latitude: 44° 11' N Longitude: 90° 22' W

	JAN	FEB	MAR	APR	MAY	JUN	JUL	AUG	SEP	OCT	NOV	DEC	YEAR
Mean Maximum Temp. (°F)	22.7	29.4	40.1	55.3	68.5	77.5	81.5	79.0	70.3	58.1	41.7	28.0	54.3
Mean Temp. (°F)	12.6	18.9	29.9	43.9	55.9	65.0	69.4	66.9	58.1	46.7	32.7	19.0	43.2
Mean Minimum Temp. (°F)	2.6	8.4	19.7	32.4	43.3	52.6	57.2	54.8	45.8	35.1	23.7	9.8	32.1
Extreme Maximum Temp. (°F)	58	58	84	90	92	100	103	103	96	91	75	62	103
Extreme Minimum Temp. (°F)	-36	-37	-18	7	22	31	39	30	25	8	-12	-29	-37
Days Maximum Temp. ≥ 90°F	0	0	0	0	0	2	4	2	0	0	0	0	8
Days Maximum Temp. ≤ 32°F	24	16	8	1	0	0	0	0	0	0	6	20	75
Days Minimum Temp. ≤ 32°F	31	27	27	16	3	0	0	0	2	13	25	30	174
Days Minimum Temp. ≤ 0°F	14	9	3	0	0	0	0	0	0	0	1	8	35
Heating Degree Days (base 65°F)	1,619	1,298	1,081	631	301	86	24	48	235	564	962	1,422	8,271
Cooling Degree Days (base 65°F)	0	0	0	4	21	92	161	116	31	2	0	0	427
Mean Precipitation (in.)	1.11	0.83	2.01	3.03	3.60	3.97	4.60	4.55	3.80	2.42	2.38	1.32	33.62
Days With ≥ 0.1" Precipitation	4	3	5	7	7	8	7	8	7	5	6	4	71
Days With ≥ 1.0" Precipitation	0	0	0	0	1	1	1	1	1	0	0	0	5
Mean Snowfall (in.)	14.0	8.2	8.8	2.1	trace	0.0	0.0	0.0	0.0	0.4	5.5	10.3	49.3
Days With ≥ 1.0" Snow Depth	14	na	10	2	0	0	0	0	0	0	3	*12*	na

Mauston 1 SE *Juneau County* Elevation: 862 ft. Latitude: 43° 47' N Longitude: 90° 04' W

	JAN	FEB	MAR	APR	MAY	JUN	JUL	AUG	SEP	OCT	NOV	DEC	YEAR
Mean Maximum Temp. (°F)	25.5	31.8	42.8	57.9	70.5	79.3	82.8	80.0	71.9	60.3	43.5	30.9	56.4
Mean Temp. (°F)	15.0	20.8	32.1	45.9	57.6	66.5	70.8	68.0	59.9	48.4	34.1	21.9	45.1
Mean Minimum Temp. (°F)	4.4	9.7	21.4	33.8	44.7	53.7	58.8	55.9	47.8	36.5	24.9	12.8	33.7
Extreme Maximum Temp. (°F)	56	64	84	91	94	100	103	102	97	90	75	63	103
Extreme Minimum Temp. (°F)	-35	-34	-13	5	18	32	41	35	20	9	-18	-30	-35
Days Maximum Temp. ≥ 90°F	0	0	0	0	0	3	5	2	1	0	0	0	11
Days Maximum Temp. ≤ 32°F	22	14	5	0	0	0	0	0	0	0	4	16	61
Days Minimum Temp. ≤ 32°F	31	27	27	14	3	0	0	0	2	11	23	30	168
Days Minimum Temp. ≤ 0°F	13	8	2	0	0	0	0	0	0	0	1	6	30
Heating Degree Days (base 65°F)	1,545	1,243	1,016	573	254	61	14	34	189	510	919	1,330	7,688
Cooling Degree Days (base 65°F)	0	0	0	6	29	119	208	136	41	1	0	0	540
Mean Precipitation (in.)	1.12	0.95	2.02	3.42	3.58	3.74	4.03	4.18	4.01	2.38	2.35	1.21	32.99
Days With ≥ 0.1" Precipitation	3	2	5	7	7	7	7	7	6	5	5	3	64
Days With ≥ 1.0" Precipitation	0	0	0	1	1	1	1	1	1	0	0	0	6
Mean Snowfall (in.)	13.5	8.9	8.3	2.8	trace	0.0	0.0	0.0	0.0	0.4	5.2	10.4	49.5
Days With ≥ 1.0" Snow Depth	26	22	11	1	0	0	0	0	0	0	4	19	83

Medford *Taylor County*   Elevation: 1,469 ft.   Latitude: 45° 08' N   Longitude: 90° 21' W

	JAN	FEB	MAR	APR	MAY	JUN	JUL	AUG	SEP	OCT	NOV	DEC	YEAR
Mean Maximum Temp. (°F)	19.6	26.0	36.5	52.5	66.5	74.6	78.9	76.7	67.3	54.9	37.9	24.7	51.3
Mean Temp. (°F)	9.6	15.5	26.9	41.9	54.8	63.4	67.9	65.8	56.5	44.7	30.1	16.2	41.1
Mean Minimum Temp. (°F)	-0.4	5.0	17.3	31.3	43.0	52.2	56.9	54.9	45.7	34.5	22.2	7.5	30.8
Extreme Maximum Temp. (°F)	50	55	74	87	88	97	98	98	93	89	71	59	98
Extreme Minimum Temp. (°F)	-38	-37	-20	1	20	30	38	32	23	8	-19	-29	-38
Days Maximum Temp. ≥ 90°F	0	0	0	0	0	0	1	1	0	0	0	0	2
Days Maximum Temp. ≤ 32°F	27	20	11	1	0	0	0	0	0	0	10	24	93
Days Minimum Temp. ≤ 32°F	31	28	28	17	4	0	0	0	2	14	26	31	181
Days Minimum Temp. ≤ 0°F	16	11	4	0	0	0	0	0	0	0	1	10	42
Heating Degree Days (base 65°F)	1,715	1,393	1,174	688	329	112	34	61	273	624	1,041	1,509	8,953
Cooling Degree Days (base 65°F)	0	0	0	2	16	74	130	97	25	0	0	0	344
Mean Precipitation (in.)	1.14	0.89	1.89	2.50	3.25	4.30	4.05	4.43	4.53	2.72	2.13	1.29	33.12
Days With ≥ 0.1" Precipitation	4	3	5	6	7	7	8	7	8	6	5	5	71
Days With ≥ 1.0" Precipitation	0	0	0	0	0	1	1	1	1	1	0	0	5
Mean Snowfall (in.)	*11.2*	6.1	*7.7*	*1.8*	trace	0.0	0.0	0.0	0.0	0.4	*4.2*	*9.6*	*41.0*
Days With ≥ 1.0" Snow Depth	na	*26*	*19*	2	0	0	0	0	0	0	5	*21*	na

Mellen 4 NE *Ashland County*   Elevation: 1,299 ft.   Latitude: 46° 22' N   Longitude: 90° 39' W

	JAN	FEB	MAR	APR	MAY	JUN	JUL	AUG	SEP	OCT	NOV	DEC	YEAR
Mean Maximum Temp. (°F)	20.2	26.8	36.8	51.6	65.7	74.3	78.7	76.3	66.9	54.6	37.7	24.8	51.2
Mean Temp. (°F)	9.2	14.7	25.6	39.8	52.7	61.9	66.9	64.7	55.6	44.2	29.6	15.5	40.0
Mean Minimum Temp. (°F)	-1.9	2.7	14.2	27.9	39.7	49.5	55.0	53.0	44.3	33.8	21.4	6.1	28.8
Extreme Maximum Temp. (°F)	55	63	73	89	90	96	97	98	98	87	73	61	98
Extreme Minimum Temp. (°F)	-41	-46	-32	-6	18	27	34	32	25	6	-20	-36	-46
Days Maximum Temp. ≥ 90°F	0	0	0	0	0	1	2	1	0	0	0	0	4
Days Maximum Temp. ≤ 32°F	26	19	11	1	0	0	0	0	0	0	10	23	90
Days Minimum Temp. ≤ 32°F	31	28	29	21	8	1	0	0	3	15	26	31	193
Days Minimum Temp. ≤ 0°F	17	13	6	0	0	0	0	0	0	0	2	11	49
Heating Degree Days (base 65°F)	1,729	1,415	1,216	752	394	147	54	87	297	638	1,058	1,530	9,317
Cooling Degree Days (base 65°F)	0	0	0	2	18	60	110	87	20	1	0	0	298
Mean Precipitation (in.)	1.60	0.96	2.00	2.29	3.20	3.89	4.19	3.81	3.88	3.24	2.74	1.57	33.37
Days With ≥ 0.1" Precipitation	5	3	5	6	7	8	8	7	8	7	6	5	75
Days With ≥ 1.0" Precipitation	0	0	0	0	1	1	1	1	1	1	0	0	6
Mean Snowfall (in.)	25.8	13.3	16.6	5.9	0.6	0.0	0.0	0.0	0.1	2.2	14.5	21.9	100.9
Days With ≥ 1.0" Snow Depth	31	28	29	13	0	0	0	0	0	1	15	30	147

Menomonie *Dunn County*   Elevation: 777 ft.   Latitude: 44° 53' N   Longitude: 91° 56' W

	JAN	FEB	MAR	APR	MAY	JUN	JUL	AUG	SEP	OCT	NOV	DEC	YEAR
Mean Maximum Temp. (°F)	23.6	30.6	42.1	59.0	71.5	79.4	83.5	81.0	72.3	60.4	42.3	28.5	56.2
Mean Temp. (°F)	13.6	20.1	31.7	46.6	58.5	67.1	71.6	69.3	60.5	49.0	33.6	19.8	45.1
Mean Minimum Temp. (°F)	3.6	9.6	21.3	33.9	45.5	54.8	59.7	57.5	48.7	37.5	24.8	11.1	34.0
Extreme Maximum Temp. (°F)	55	60	82	90	91	98	100	100	96	90	76	64	100
Extreme Minimum Temp. (°F)	-39	-40	-15	5	23	30	41	39	28	12	-13	-36	-40
Days Maximum Temp. ≥ 90°F	0	0	0	0	0	2	5	3	1	0	0	0	11
Days Maximum Temp. ≤ 32°F	23	14	6	0	0	0	0	0	0	0	6	19	68
Days Minimum Temp. ≤ 32°F	31	27	26	14	2	0	0	0	1	10	23	30	164
Days Minimum Temp. ≤ 0°F	13	8	2	0	0	0	0	0	0	0	1	8	32
Heating Degree Days (base 65°F)	1,590	1,263	1,025	552	231	54	11	26	180	494	937	1,396	7,759
Cooling Degree Days (base 65°F)	0	0	0	5	31	120	213	163	51	2	0	0	585
Mean Precipitation (in.)	0.81	0.61	1.66	2.57	3.55	4.42	4.13	4.06	3.67	2.32	1.89	0.86	30.55
Days With ≥ 0.1" Precipitation	3	2	4	6	7	7	7	7	6	5	4	3	61
Days With ≥ 1.0" Precipitation	0	0	0	0	1	1	1	1	1	0	0	0	5
Mean Snowfall (in.)	*12.3*	6.7	8.3	1.1	trace	0.0	0.0	trace	trace	trace	*5.0*	*7.9*	*41.3*
Days With ≥ 1.0" Snow Depth	29	26	18	1	0	0	0	0	0	0	6	23	103

Merrill *Lincoln County*   Elevation: 1,250 ft.   Latitude: 45° 10' N   Longitude: 89° 40' W

	JAN	FEB	MAR	APR	MAY	JUN	JUL	AUG	SEP	OCT	NOV	DEC	YEAR
Mean Maximum Temp. (°F)	21.4	27.7	38.4	53.8	67.9	76.2	80.0	77.6	68.2	55.7	39.2	26.1	52.7
Mean Temp. (°F)	10.5	16.0	27.4	41.9	54.6	63.5	67.6	65.2	56.0	44.5	30.4	16.9	41.2
Mean Minimum Temp. (°F)	-0.5	4.1	16.3	29.8	41.2	50.8	55.1	52.7	43.8	33.3	21.6	7.6	29.7
Extreme Maximum Temp. (°F)	54	56	77	88	89	97	100	98	91	88	72	61	100
Extreme Minimum Temp. (°F)	-45	-41	-20	0	20	28	33	31	18	8	-15	-31	-45
Days Maximum Temp. ≥ 90°F	0	0	0	0	0	1	2	1	0	0	0	0	4
Days Maximum Temp. ≤ 32°F	26	18	9	0	0	0	0	0	0	0	8	22	84
Days Minimum Temp. ≤ 32°F	31	28	28	19	6	1	0	0	4	16	26	30	189
Days Minimum Temp. ≤ 0°F	16	11	5	0	0	0	0	0	0	0	1	10	43
Heating Degree Days (base 65°F)	1,687	1,378	1,160	689	334	113	40	72	285	629	1,031	1,488	8,906
Cooling Degree Days (base 65°F)	0	0	0	3	15	73	122	88	20	0	0	0	321
Mean Precipitation (in.)	1.10	0.87	1.81	2.62	3.34	3.65	3.94	4.25	4.34	2.72	2.35	1.39	32.38
Days With ≥ 0.1" Precipitation	4	3	4	6	7	7	8	8	8	6	5	4	70
Days With ≥ 1.0" Precipitation	0	0	0	0	1	1	1	1	1	1	0	0	6
Mean Snowfall (in.)	na	*6.7*	na	*2.5*	trace	0.0	0.0	0.0	trace	0.6	*6.4*	*11.4*	na
Days With ≥ 1.0" Snow Depth	*29*	*27*	*20*	*3*	0	0	0	0	0	0	na	*26*	na

Milwaukee Mt. Mary College *Milwaukee County*   Elevation: 725 ft.   Latitude: 43° 04' N   Longitude: 88° 02' W

	JAN	FEB	MAR	APR	MAY	JUN	JUL	AUG	SEP	OCT	NOV	DEC	YEAR
Mean Maximum Temp. (°F)	27.9	33.2	44.0	57.2	70.0	80.1	84.7	82.1	74.2	61.1	46.0	33.7	57.8
Mean Temp. (°F)	20.6	25.8	35.6	47.4	58.9	68.8	74.1	72.1	64.2	52.0	38.7	26.9	48.8
Mean Minimum Temp. (°F)	13.3	18.3	27.2	37.5	47.8	57.4	63.5	62.1	54.0	42.8	31.3	20.1	39.6
Extreme Maximum Temp. (°F)	57	67	85	90	95	104	108	108	98	88	74	64	108
Extreme Minimum Temp. (°F)	-26	-25	-2	12	27	37	46	43	30	19	-4	-22	-26
Days Maximum Temp. ≥ 90°F	0	0	0	0	1	4	8	5	1	0	0	0	19
Days Maximum Temp. ≤ 32°F	19	12	4	0	0	0	0	0	0	0	2	12	49
Days Minimum Temp. ≤ 32°F	29	25	22	8	1	0	0	0	0	4	17	27	133
Days Minimum Temp. ≤ 0°F	6	3	0	0	0	0	0	0	0	0	0	3	12
Heating Degree Days (base 65°F)	1,369	1,102	905	530	231	43	5	9	106	405	783	1,173	6,661
Cooling Degree Days (base 65°F)	0	0	1	8	51	171	301	246	91	7	0	0	876
Mean Precipitation (in.)	1.56	1.30	1.94	3.37	2.79	3.64	3.38	3.87	3.34	2.34	2.32	1.80	31.65
Days With ≥ 0.1" Precipitation	4	3	4	6	6	6	6	6	5	5	5	5	61
Days With ≥ 1.0" Precipitation	0	0	0	1	1	1	1	1	1	0	0	0	6
Mean Snowfall (in.)	12.1	8.1	5.5	1.9	trace	0.0	0.0	0.0	0.0	0.1	2.6	8.0	38.3
Days With ≥ 1.0" Snow Depth	22	16	5	1	0	0	0	0	0	0	2	11	57

Minocqua Dam *Oneida County*   Elevation: 1,578 ft.   Latitude: 45° 52' N   Longitude: 89° 43' W

	JAN	FEB	MAR	APR	MAY	JUN	JUL	AUG	SEP	OCT	NOV	DEC	YEAR
Mean Maximum Temp. (°F)	19.7	26.5	36.7	51.2	65.9	73.6	77.6	75.5	65.9	53.6	36.8	24.0	50.6
Mean Temp. (°F)	9.2	14.3	24.8	39.2	53.0	61.6	65.9	63.7	54.8	43.3	28.6	14.9	39.4
Mean Minimum Temp. (°F)	-1.7	2.1	12.8	27.1	40.0	49.6	54.1	51.9	43.7	33.1	20.4	5.8	28.2
Extreme Maximum Temp. (°F)	52	57	69	89	90	95	97	95	95	86	70	57	97
Extreme Minimum Temp. (°F)	-39	-48	-26	-9	20	28	34	34	21	12	-18	-36	-48
Days Maximum Temp. ≥ 90°F	0	0	0	0	0	1	1	0	0	0	0	0	2
Days Maximum Temp. ≤ 32°F	27	19	11	2	0	0	0	0	0	0	11	25	95
Days Minimum Temp. ≤ 32°F	31	28	29	22	8	0	0	0	3	16	27	31	195
Days Minimum Temp. ≤ 0°F	16	13	7	0	0	0	0	0	0	0	2	11	49
Heating Degree Days (base 65°F)	1,728	1,428	1,242	768	382	145	59	94	314	666	1,085	1,548	9,459
Cooling Degree Days (base 65°F)	0	0	0	1	13	50	88	60	12	0	0	0	224
Mean Precipitation (in.)	1.23	0.85	1.79	2.29	3.42	3.74	3.87	4.42	3.92	2.75	2.29	1.29	31.86
Days With ≥ 0.1" Precipitation	4	3	4	6	7	8	8	7	8	6	6	4	71
Days With ≥ 1.0" Precipitation	0	0	0	0	1	1	1	1	1	0	0	0	5
Mean Snowfall (in.)	24.5	15.8	18.2	9.7	1.4	0.0	0.0	0.0	trace	2.7	14.3	23.9	110.5
Days With ≥ 1.0" Snow Depth	31	28	29	11	0	0	0	0	0	1	14	30	144

Montello *Marquette County*   Elevation: 784 ft.   Latitude: 43° 47' N   Longitude: 89° 19' W

	JAN	FEB	MAR	APR	MAY	JUN	JUL	AUG	SEP	OCT	NOV	DEC	YEAR
Mean Maximum Temp. (°F)	24.9	30.7	42.0	57.2	70.1	79.4	82.9	80.1	72.1	60.2	43.5	30.1	56.1
Mean Temp. (°F)	15.2	20.7	32.2	45.9	58.2	67.5	71.5	68.8	60.6	48.8	34.5	21.4	45.4
Mean Minimum Temp. (°F)	5.8	10.8	22.3	34.4	46.1	55.6	60.1	57.4	48.8	37.3	25.3	12.8	34.7
Extreme Maximum Temp. (°F)	52	65	84	92	92	102	104	103	97	86	76	65	104
Extreme Minimum Temp. (°F)	-35	-33	-8	10	25	31	41	39	25	11	-12	-34	-35
Days Maximum Temp. ≥ 90°F	0	0	0	0	0	3	5	2	1	0	0	0	11
Days Maximum Temp. ≤ 32°F	22	15	6	0	0	0	0	0	0	0	5	17	65
Days Minimum Temp. ≤ 32°F	31	28	26	14	2	0	0	0	1	10	23	29	164
Days Minimum Temp. ≤ 0°F	12	8	2	0	0	0	0	0	0	0	1	7	30
Heating Degree Days (base 65°F)	1,539	1,248	1,011	573	245	50	11	30	175	498	909	1,345	7,634
Cooling Degree Days (base 65°F)	0	0	0	8	37	130	204	149	46	2	0	0	576
Mean Precipitation (in.)	1.28	1.10	2.27	3.27	3.52	4.02	4.16	4.14	3.98	2.30	2.42	1.36	33.82
Days With ≥ 0.1" Precipitation	4	3	5	7	7	7	7	7	6	6	5	4	68
Days With ≥ 1.0" Precipitation	0	0	0	1	1	1	1	1	1	0	0	0	6
Mean Snowfall (in.)	*12.1*	7.8	*7.4*	2.3	trace	0.0	0.0	0.0	0.0	0.2	na	*8.9*	na
Days With ≥ 1.0" Snow Depth	28	25	17	2	0	0	0	0	0	0	5	21	98

Necedah *Juneau County*   Elevation: 921 ft.   Latitude: 44° 02' N   Longitude: 90° 05' W

	JAN	FEB	MAR	APR	MAY	JUN	JUL	AUG	SEP	OCT	NOV	DEC	YEAR
Mean Maximum Temp. (°F)	25.4	32.2	43.4	58.9	72.1	80.7	84.6	81.7	73.1	61.0	43.3	30.2	57.2
Mean Temp. (°F)	14.9	21.0	32.0	45.9	58.3	67.2	71.8	69.1	60.5	49.1	34.1	21.0	45.4
Mean Minimum Temp. (°F)	4.4	9.8	20.6	32.8	44.5	53.7	59.0	56.4	47.9	37.0	24.8	11.8	33.6
Extreme Maximum Temp. (°F)	58	64	85	93	93	101	104	105	98	92	75	63	105
Extreme Minimum Temp. (°F)	-39	-41	-17	1	19	30	38	30	18	5	-19	-31	-41
Days Maximum Temp. ≥ 90°F	0	0	0	0	1	4	7	3	1	0	0	0	16
Days Maximum Temp. ≤ 32°F	22	14	5	0	0	0	0	0	0	0	5	17	63
Days Minimum Temp. ≤ 32°F	31	27	26	15	4	0	0	0	2	11	23	30	169
Days Minimum Temp. ≤ 0°F	13	9	3	0	0	0	0	0	0	0	1	7	33
Heating Degree Days (base 65°F)	1,548	1,236	1,017	572	237	56	11	30	182	492	922	1,358	7,661
Cooling Degree Days (base 65°F)	0	0	0	7	39	138	232	174	58	5	0	0	653
Mean Precipitation (in.)	0.95	0.88	1.95	2.97	3.55	3.47	4.23	4.60	3.84	2.33	2.17	1.16	32.10
Days With ≥ 0.1" Precipitation	4	3	5	7	6	7	7	7	6	6	5	4	68
Days With ≥ 1.0" Precipitation	0	0	0	1	1	1	1	1	1	0	0	0	6
Mean Snowfall (in.)	8.1	5.3	4.9	1.7	trace	0.0	0.0	0.0	0.0	0.3	3.3	7.7	31.3
Days With ≥ 1.0" Snow Depth	26	23	14	1	0	0	0	0	0	0	4	20	88

Neillsville 3 SW *Clark County*   Elevation: 1,033 ft.   Latitude: 44° 32' N   Longitude: 90° 38' W

	JAN	FEB	MAR	APR	MAY	JUN	JUL	AUG	SEP	OCT	NOV	DEC	YEAR
Mean Maximum Temp. (°F)	22.8	29.5	40.7	56.4	69.5	77.6	81.6	79.2	70.2	58.4	40.7	27.6	54.5
Mean Temp. (°F)	12.5	19.0	30.2	44.2	56.4	64.6	68.9	66.9	58.0	46.9	31.8	18.4	43.2
Mean Minimum Temp. (°F)	2.3	8.5	19.6	32.0	43.1	51.6	56.1	54.5	45.8	35.3	22.7	9.2	31.7
Extreme Maximum Temp. (°F)	57	59	83	89	90	99	102	101	94	92	73	63	102
Extreme Minimum Temp. (°F)	-38	-37	-15	3	15	22	35	34	21	8	-16	-33	-38
Days Maximum Temp. ≥ 90°F	0	0	0	0	0	2	3	2	0	0	0	0	7
Days Maximum Temp. ≤ 32°F	24	16	7	0	0	0	0	0	0	0	7	20	74
Days Minimum Temp. ≤ 32°F	31	28	28	17	4	0	0	0	3	13	26	31	181
Days Minimum Temp. ≤ 0°F	14	8	3	0	0	0	0	0	0	0	1	8	34
Heating Degree Days (base 65°F)	1,622	1,294	1,072	620	283	86	25	47	233	557	991	1,439	8,269
Cooling Degree Days (base 65°F)	0	0	0	4	18	82	149	112	30	1	0	0	396
Mean Precipitation (in.)	0.87	0.80	1.68	2.73	3.48	4.15	4.55	4.56	4.07	2.41	2.05	0.99	32.34
Days With ≥ 0.1" Precipitation	3	2	4	6	7	7	7	7	7	5	4	3	62
Days With ≥ 1.0" Precipitation	0	0	0	0	1	1	1	1	1	1	0	0	6
Mean Snowfall (in.)	11.0	7.2	8.7	1.7	trace	0.0	0.0	0.0	0.0	0.3	4.5	9.0	42.4
Days With ≥ 1.0" Snow Depth	28	25	18	2	0	0	0	0	0	0	5	23	101

New London *Outagamie County*   Elevation: 803 ft.   Latitude: 44° 21' N   Longitude: 88° 43' W

	JAN	FEB	MAR	APR	MAY	JUN	JUL	AUG	SEP	OCT	NOV	DEC	YEAR
Mean Maximum Temp. (°F)	24.5	30.3	40.9	56.4	69.7	78.8	82.5	79.7	71.8	59.2	42.7	29.6	55.5
Mean Temp. (°F)	14.9	20.3	30.8	45.1	57.6	66.5	70.6	68.1	59.8	48.1	34.0	21.1	44.7
Mean Minimum Temp. (°F)	5.1	10.1	20.6	33.7	45.1	54.2	58.8	56.5	47.7	37.0	25.3	12.5	33.9
Extreme Maximum Temp. (°F)	53	60	81	92	92	99	105	99	95	88	74	63	105
Extreme Minimum Temp. (°F)	-33	-32	-16	8	25	35	42	35	22	11	-9	-27	-33
Days Maximum Temp. ≥ 90°F	0	0	0	0	0	2	5	2	1	0	0	0	10
Days Maximum Temp. ≤ 32°F	23	15	6	0	0	0	0	0	0	0	5	17	66
Days Minimum Temp. ≤ 32°F	30	28	26	14	2	0	0	0	1	10	23	30	164
Days Minimum Temp. ≤ 0°F	12	8	2	0	0	0	0	0	0	0	0	6	28
Heating Degree Days (base 65°F)	1,550	1,257	1,055	596	258	64	16	35	194	520	921	1,356	7,822
Cooling Degree Days (base 65°F)	0	0	0	5	*31*	107	179	131	39	2	0	0	*494*
Mean Precipitation (in.)	*1.40*	1.07	2.01	2.58	3.40	3.47	3.93	4.06	3.19	2.40	2.10	1.38	*30.99*
Days With ≥ 0.1" Precipitation	4	3	5	6	7	6	7	7	6	5	4	4	64
Days With ≥ 1.0" Precipitation	0	0	0	0	1	1	1	1	1	1	0	0	6
Mean Snowfall (in.)	11.3	6.8	*8.5*	*2.0*	trace	0.0	0.0	0.0	0.0	0.1	3.9	*8.8*	*41.4*
Days With ≥ 1.0" Snow Depth	*25*	na	*13*	2	0	0	0	0	0	0	3	*15*	na

North Pelican *Oneida County*   Elevation: 1,607 ft.   Latitude: 45° 38' N   Longitude: 89° 15' W

	JAN	FEB	MAR	APR	MAY	JUN	JUL	AUG	SEP	OCT	NOV	DEC	YEAR
Mean Maximum Temp. (°F)	20.5	27.3	37.3	52.3	66.8	73.7	76.9	74.2	65.1	53.9	37.2	25.1	50.9
Mean Temp. (°F)	9.6	15.0	25.3	39.8	53.0	61.3	65.2	63.0	54.3	43.8	29.1	15.9	39.6
Mean Minimum Temp. (°F)	-1.3	2.6	13.1	27.3	39.2	48.9	53.4	51.7	43.6	33.6	21.0	6.5	28.3
Extreme Maximum Temp. (°F)	49	58	69	88	91	96	96	93	93	86	70	58	96
Extreme Minimum Temp. (°F)	-46	-47	-30	-7	15	25	28	29	19	10	-17	-35	-47
Days Maximum Temp. ≥ 90°F	0	0	0	0	0	1	1	0	0	0	0	0	2
Days Maximum Temp. ≤ 32°F	26	18	10	1	0	0	0	0	0	0	10	23	88
Days Minimum Temp. ≤ 32°F	31	28	29	21	9	1	0	0	4	15	27	31	196
Days Minimum Temp. ≤ 0°F	16	13	7	0	0	0	0	0	0	0	1	10	47
Heating Degree Days (base 65°F)	1,714	1,407	1,225	751	378	148	67	107	327	652	1,070	1,518	9,364
Cooling Degree Days (base 65°F)	0	0	0	2	10	45	76	57	13	0	0	0	203
Mean Precipitation (in.)	1.22	0.89	1.72	2.37	3.40	3.43	3.95	4.08	3.92	2.63	2.10	1.31	31.02
Days With ≥ 0.1" Precipitation	4	3	5	6	7	8	8	7	8	6	5	4	71
Days With ≥ 1.0" Precipitation	0	0	0	0	1	0	1	1	1	0	0	0	4
Mean Snowfall (in.)	14.7	8.3	10.0	4.1	0.4	0.0	0.0	0.0	trace	1.1	7.6	*14.1*	*60.3*
Days With ≥ 1.0" Snow Depth	31	28	26	8	0	0	0	0	0	1	10	28	132

Oconomowoc *Waukesha County*   Elevation: 853 ft.   Latitude: 43° 06' N   Longitude: 88° 30' W

	JAN	FEB	MAR	APR	MAY	JUN	JUL	AUG	SEP	OCT	NOV	DEC	YEAR
Mean Maximum Temp. (°F)	25.8	31.0	42.4	56.4	69.2	78.4	82.6	80.0	72.0	59.9	44.5	31.9	56.2
Mean Temp. (°F)	17.0	22.3	33.4	46.3	57.9	67.1	71.9	69.5	61.0	49.3	36.2	24.0	46.3
Mean Minimum Temp. (°F)	8.1	13.5	24.4	36.0	46.7	55.8	61.1	59.0	50.0	38.7	27.9	16.0	36.4
Extreme Maximum Temp. (°F)	59	64	81	88	94	100	100	101	95	87	74	64	101
Extreme Minimum Temp. (°F)	-29	-29	-10	4	26	34	42	40	27	14	-10	-19	-29
Days Maximum Temp. ≥ 90°F	0	0	0	0	0	2	5	2	0	0	0	0	9
Days Maximum Temp. ≤ 32°F	21	14	5	0	0	0	0	0	0	0	4	15	59
Days Minimum Temp. ≤ 32°F	30	27	25	11	1	0	0	0	1	8	20	29	152
Days Minimum Temp. ≤ 0°F	10	6	1	0	0	0	0	0	0	0	0	5	22
Heating Degree Days (base 65°F)	1,484	1,201	973	563	254	57	10	23	166	484	857	1,264	7,336
Cooling Degree Days (base 65°F)	0	0	0	7	35	129	226	174	54	4	0	0	629
Mean Precipitation (in.)	1.31	1.15	1.94	3.20	2.99	3.91	4.18	4.46	3.82	2.70	2.27	1.70	33.63
Days With ≥ 0.1" Precipitation	4	3	5	7	7	7	7	7	6	5	5	4	67
Days With ≥ 1.0" Precipitation	0	0	0	1	0	1	1	1	1	1	0	0	6
Mean Snowfall (in.)	11.1	7.3	5.9	2.0	0.3	0.0	0.0	0.0	trace	trace	3.1	10.0	39.7
Days With ≥ 1.0" Snow Depth	25	19	8	1	0	0	0	0	0	0	3	17	73

Oconto 4 W *Oconto County*   Elevation: 659 ft.   Latitude: 44° 53' N   Longitude: 87° 57' W

	JAN	FEB	MAR	APR	MAY	JUN	JUL	AUG	SEP	OCT	NOV	DEC	YEAR
Mean Maximum Temp. (°F)	23.6	28.6	38.6	52.8	66.5	75.6	80.5	77.9	69.5	57.5	42.3	29.4	53.6
Mean Temp. (°F)	13.8	18.4	28.8	42.1	54.5	63.9	68.8	66.3	57.8	46.6	33.4	20.7	42.9
Mean Minimum Temp. (°F)	4.2	8.0	18.8	31.3	42.4	52.1	57.1	54.8	46.0	35.5	24.5	11.9	32.2
Extreme Maximum Temp. (°F)	51	57	74	90	91	95	98	98	94	85	74	62	98
Extreme Minimum Temp. (°F)	-35	-35	-12	7	22	30	37	37	23	14	-8	-22	-35
Days Maximum Temp. ≥ 90°F	0	0	0	0	0	1	3	1	0	0	0	0	5
Days Maximum Temp. ≤ 32°F	24	17	8	1	0	0	0	0	0	0	5	18	73
Days Minimum Temp. ≤ 32°F	31	28	28	18	4	0	0	0	2	12	24	30	177
Days Minimum Temp. ≤ 0°F	13	9	2	0	0	0	0	0	0	0	0	6	30
Heating Degree Days (base 65°F)	1,581	1,310	1,117	682	339	102	27	51	235	566	941	1,368	8,319
Cooling Degree Days (base 65°F)	0	0	0	2	20	75	144	102	25	1	0	0	369
Mean Precipitation (in.)	1.90	1.18	2.30	2.61	3.21	3.41	3.86	3.41	3.31	2.41	2.49	1.63	31.72
Days With ≥ 0.1" Precipitation	5	4	5	6	6	7	7	6	6	5	5	5	67
Days With ≥ 1.0" Precipitation	0	0	0	0	1	1	1	1	1	1	1	0	7
Mean Snowfall (in.)	14.6	8.5	9.2	3.4	trace	0.0	0.0	0.0	0.0	0.3	4.0	12.3	52.3
Days With ≥ 1.0" Snow Depth	28	23	14	2	0	0	0	0	0	0	4	20	91

Oshkosh *Winnebago County*   Elevation: 748 ft.   Latitude: 44° 01' N   Longitude: 88° 33' W

	JAN	FEB	MAR	APR	MAY	JUN	JUL	AUG	SEP	OCT	NOV	DEC	YEAR
Mean Maximum Temp. (°F)	24.4	29.6	40.1	54.5	68.3	77.7	82.1	79.4	71.1	58.5	42.8	29.9	54.9
Mean Temp. (°F)	15.9	20.8	31.2	44.6	57.6	67.2	71.8	69.3	61.0	49.1	35.0	22.2	45.5
Mean Minimum Temp. (°F)	7.3	12.0	22.3	34.8	46.8	56.7	61.4	59.2	50.8	39.6	27.2	14.5	36.0
Extreme Maximum Temp. (°F)	52	60	80	91	91	98	101	100	94	86	74	63	101
Extreme Minimum Temp. (°F)	-29	-30	-8	10	22	33	44	41	25	16	-8	-27	-30
Days Maximum Temp. ≥ 90°F	0	0	0	0	0	2	4	2	0	0	0	0	8
Days Maximum Temp. ≤ 32°F	23	16	7	0	0	0	0	0	0	0	5	17	68
Days Minimum Temp. ≤ 32°F	31	27	26	12	1	0	0	0	1	7	21	30	156
Days Minimum Temp. ≤ 0°F	11	6	1	0	0	0	0	0	0	0	0	5	23
Heating Degree Days (base 65°F)	1,518	1,240	1,040	609	259	58	9	24	168	490	892	1,321	7,628
Cooling Degree Days (base 65°F)	0	0	0	5	33	134	222	163	53	3	0	0	613
Mean Precipitation (in.)	1.33	1.06	2.18	2.84	2.99	3.54	3.64	4.03	3.44	2.29	2.50	1.55	31.39
Days With ≥ 0.1" Precipitation	4	3	5	6	6	7	7	7	6	5	5	4	65
Days With ≥ 1.0" Precipitation	0	0	0	1	1	1	1	1	1	0	0	0	6
Mean Snowfall (in.)	12.4	7.1	8.0	1.5	0.0	0.0	0.0	0.0	0.0	trace	3.9	10.5	43.4
Days With ≥ 1.0" Snow Depth	na	na	9	1	0	0	0	0	0	0	1	na	na

Owen 3 W *Clark County*   Elevation: 1,240 ft.   Latitude: 44° 58' N   Longitude: 90° 36' W

	JAN	FEB	MAR	APR	MAY	JUN	JUL	AUG	SEP	OCT	NOV	DEC	YEAR
Mean Maximum Temp. (°F)	19.0	25.3	36.4	52.5	66.6	75.1	79.3	77.1	68.0	55.3	38.5	24.7	51.5
Mean Temp. (°F)	9.1	15.1	27.0	42.3	55.0	63.8	68.2	65.9	56.7	44.9	30.4	16.0	41.2
Mean Minimum Temp. (°F)	-0.8	4.8	17.5	31.9	43.3	52.5	57.1	54.8	45.4	34.5	22.2	7.3	30.9
Extreme Maximum Temp. (°F)	52	54	78	87	90	94	99	101	94	82	72	60	101
Extreme Minimum Temp. (°F)	-42	-38	-19	2	13	28	36	32	23	8	-18	-33	-42
Days Maximum Temp. ≥ 90°F	0	0	0	0	0	1	2	1	0	0	0	0	4
Days Maximum Temp. ≤ 32°F	26	19	10	1	0	0	0	0	0	0	9	23	88
Days Minimum Temp. ≤ 32°F	31	28	28	16	3	0	0	0	2	14	26	31	179
Days Minimum Temp. ≤ 0°F	16	11	4	0	0	0	0	0	0	0	1	10	42
Heating Degree Days (base 65°F)	1,729	1,406	1,172	678	325	105	32	61	268	617	1,031	1,514	8,938
Cooling Degree Days (base 65°F)	0	0	0	3	20	80	139	101	26	1	0	0	370
Mean Precipitation (in.)	1.00	0.85	1.85	2.49	3.65	4.22	4.27	4.39	4.15	2.63	2.15	1.18	32.83
Days With ≥ 0.1" Precipitation	3	3	5	6	7	8	8	7	7	6	5	4	69
Days With ≥ 1.0" Precipitation	0	0	0	0	1	1	1	1	1	1	0	0	6
Mean Snowfall (in.)	12.1	8.1	8.9	2.8	trace	0.0	0.0	0.0	trace	0.5	5.7	*10.7*	*48.8*
Days With ≥ 1.0" Snow Depth	31	28	23	4	0	0	0	0	0	0	7	27	120

Platteville *Grant County*   Elevation: 1,003 ft.   Latitude: 42° 45' N   Longitude: 90° 29' W

	JAN	FEB	MAR	APR	MAY	JUN	JUL	AUG	SEP	OCT	NOV	DEC	YEAR
Mean Maximum Temp. (°F)	25.3	31.7	43.7	58.7	70.6	79.7	83.4	81.1	73.1	61.2	44.0	31.0	57.0
Mean Temp. (°F)	16.8	23.1	34.3	47.4	59.0	68.3	72.4	70.3	61.9	50.4	35.7	23.1	46.9
Mean Minimum Temp. (°F)	8.3	14.4	24.9	36.1	47.4	56.8	61.5	59.5	50.7	39.7	27.4	15.2	36.8
Extreme Maximum Temp. (°F)	58	62	85	94	91	101	100	103	95	90	75	64	103
Extreme Minimum Temp. (°F)	-28	-32	-9	3	26	36	42	38	25	13	-14	-26	-32
Days Maximum Temp. ≥ 90°F	0	0	0	0	0	2	5	2	1	0	0	0	10
Days Maximum Temp. ≤ 32°F	21	14	5	0	0	0	0	0	0	0	4	15	59
Days Minimum Temp. ≤ 32°F	31	26	24	11	2	0	0	0	1	8	21	29	153
Days Minimum Temp. ≤ 0°F	10	5	1	0	0	0	0	0	0	0	0	5	21
Heating Degree Days (base 65°F)	1,489	1,178	944	529	222	43	8	18	152	454	872	1,292	7,201
Cooling Degree Days (base 65°F)	0	0	0	8	38	148	248	194	66	6	0	0	708
Mean Precipitation (in.)	1.09	1.26	2.24	3.50	3.97	4.79	4.50	4.39	3.61	2.64	2.42	1.42	35.83
Days With ≥ 0.1" Precipitation	3	3	5	7	7	7	7	7	7	6	5	4	67
Days With ≥ 1.0" Precipitation	0	0	0	1	1	1	1	1	1	1	0	0	7
Mean Snowfall (in.)	11.0	7.5	5.6	2.2	0.1	0.0	0.0	0.0	trace	0.3	3.3	9.6	39.6
Days With ≥ 1.0" Snow Depth	23	20	8	1	0	0	0	0	0	0	4	18	74

Plymouth *Sheboygan County*   Elevation: 833 ft.   Latitude: 43° 44' N   Longitude: 87° 58' W

	JAN	FEB	MAR	APR	MAY	JUN	JUL	AUG	SEP	OCT	NOV	DEC	YEAR
Mean Maximum Temp. (°F)	25.7	30.6	40.8	54.8	67.7	77.2	81.7	79.3	71.4	58.8	43.5	31.1	55.2
Mean Temp. (°F)	17.8	22.4	32.3	44.7	56.3	65.9	71.0	69.1	61.0	49.3	36.0	23.9	45.8
Mean Minimum Temp. (°F)	9.8	14.2	23.7	34.6	44.7	54.6	60.3	58.8	50.6	39.7	28.4	16.7	36.3
Extreme Maximum Temp. (°F)	58	62	80	89	92	99	102	101	92	88	74	63	102
Extreme Minimum Temp. (°F)	-29	-27	-7	11	22	33	41	40	26	15	-7	-20	-29
Days Maximum Temp. ≥ 90°F	0	0	0	0	0	2	4	2	0	0	0	0	8
Days Maximum Temp. ≤ 32°F	21	15	6	1	0	0	0	0	0	0	4	16	63
Days Minimum Temp. ≤ 32°F	30	27	26	13	2	0	0	0	1	6	21	29	155
Days Minimum Temp. ≤ 0°F	8	5	1	0	0	0	0	0	0	0	0	4	18
Heating Degree Days (base 65°F)	1,458	1,195	1,007	606	293	76	16	27	164	484	864	1,266	7,456
Cooling Degree Days (base 65°F)	0	0	0	4	29	113	207	165	50	3	0	0	571
Mean Precipitation (in.)	1.42	1.19	2.41	3.43	3.75	3.84	3.93	4.44	4.11	3.00	2.90	1.89	36.31
Days With ≥ 0.1" Precipitation	4	3	5	7	7	7	7	7	7	7	6	4	71
Days With ≥ 1.0" Precipitation	0	0	0	1	1	1	1	1	1	1	1	0	8
Mean Snowfall (in.)	15.1	11.9	10.6	3.6	0.2	0.0	0.0	0.0	0.0	0.2	5.4	13.4	60.4
Days With ≥ 1.0" Snow Depth	26	24	13	2	0	0	0	0	0	0	3	16	84

Port Washington *Ozaukee County*   Elevation: 597 ft.   Latitude: 43° 23' N   Longitude: 87° 52' W

	JAN	FEB	MAR	APR	MAY	JUN	JUL	AUG	SEP	OCT	NOV	DEC	YEAR
Mean Maximum Temp. (°F)	27.4	31.8	40.4	50.6	61.8	72.0	78.3	77.0	69.7	58.0	44.6	32.8	53.7
Mean Temp. (°F)	19.8	24.3	33.1	43.0	53.3	63.2	69.6	68.9	61.2	49.8	37.4	25.7	45.8
Mean Minimum Temp. (°F)	12.1	16.8	25.8	35.2	44.7	54.2	60.9	60.7	52.7	41.6	30.2	18.5	37.8
Extreme Maximum Temp. (°F)	57	61	78	92	90	102	106	103	96	88	76	65	106
Extreme Minimum Temp. (°F)	-25	-29	-4	11	25	38	45	42	28	16	-10	-20	-29
Days Maximum Temp. ≥ 90°F	0	0	0	0	0	1	3	2	0	0	0	0	6
Days Maximum Temp. ≤ 32°F	19	13	6	0	0	0	0	0	0	0	3	12	53
Days Minimum Temp. ≤ 32°F	29	26	24	10	1	0	0	0	0	4	18	27	139
Days Minimum Temp. ≤ 0°F	7	3	0	0	0	0	0	0	0	0	0	3	13
Heating Degree Days (base 65°F)	1,396	1,145	984	654	367	118	20	22	150	465	822	1,214	7,357
Cooling Degree Days (base 65°F)	0	0	0	1	11	73	170	158	46	1	0	0	460
Mean Precipitation (in.)	1.48	1.12	1.87	3.08	2.80	3.63	3.78	4.14	3.41	2.34	2.21	1.81	31.67
Days With ≥ 0.1" Precipitation	4	3	5	6	6	6	6	7	6	5	5	4	63
Days With ≥ 1.0" Precipitation	0	0	0	1	0	1	1	1	1	1	0	0	6
Mean Snowfall (in.)	12.0	8.0	6.0	1.6	trace	0.0	0.0	0.0	0.0	0.2	1.6	7.0	36.4
Days With ≥ 1.0" Snow Depth	23	17	8	1	0	0	0	0	0	0	2	12	63

Portage *Columbia County*   Elevation: 774 ft.   Latitude: 43° 32' N   Longitude: 89° 26' W

	JAN	FEB	MAR	APR	MAY	JUN	JUL	AUG	SEP	OCT	NOV	DEC	YEAR
Mean Maximum Temp. (°F)	25.7	31.9	42.9	57.9	70.6	79.6	83.2	80.9	72.8	60.7	44.4	31.2	56.8
Mean Temp. (°F)	16.3	22.2	33.1	46.4	58.1	67.1	71.3	68.9	60.7	49.0	35.4	22.8	45.9
Mean Minimum Temp. (°F)	6.8	12.3	23.2	34.8	45.5	54.6	59.3	57.0	48.5	37.5	26.6	14.4	35.0
Extreme Maximum Temp. (°F)	55	63	83	92	91	101	102	103	95	89	76	64	103
Extreme Minimum Temp. (°F)	-32	-30	-14	5	21	29	37	35	17	11	-10	-24	-32
Days Maximum Temp. ≥ 90°F	0	0	0	0	0	3	6	3	1	0	0	0	13
Days Maximum Temp. ≤ 32°F	22	14	5	0	0	0	0	0	0	0	4	16	61
Days Minimum Temp. ≤ 32°F	31	27	25	12	3	0	0	0	2	10	22	29	161
Days Minimum Temp. ≤ 0°F	11	7	1	0	0	0	0	0	0	0	0	5	24
Heating Degree Days (base 65°F)	1,505	1,201	983	559	245	59	14	32	176	493	881	1,303	7,451
Cooling Degree Days (base 65°F)	0	0	0	8	36	138	222	173	53	3	0	0	633
Mean Precipitation (in.)	1.24	1.17	2.25	3.45	3.49	4.01	4.48	4.28	3.69	2.45	2.44	1.37	34.32
Days With ≥ 0.1" Precipitation	4	3	5	7	7	7	7	7	7	5	5	4	68
Days With ≥ 1.0" Precipitation	0	0	0	1	1	1	1	1	1	0	0	0	6
Mean Snowfall (in.)	11.0	7.8	5.9	2.0	trace	0.0	0.0	0.0	0.0	0.3	3.5	7.6	38.1
Days With ≥ 1.0" Snow Depth	23	19	8	1	0	0	0	0	0	0	4	16	71

Prairie Du Chien *Crawford County*   Elevation: 656 ft.   Latitude: 43° 02' N   Longitude: 91° 09' W

	JAN	FEB	MAR	APR	MAY	JUN	JUL	AUG	SEP	OCT	NOV	DEC	YEAR
Mean Maximum Temp. (°F)	27.1	33.9	45.9	60.9	72.9	81.9	85.7	83.3	75.4	63.5	45.9	32.5	59.1
Mean Temp. (°F)	17.8	24.3	35.7	49.2	60.7	70.0	74.1	72.0	63.7	52.2	37.2	24.3	48.4
Mean Minimum Temp. (°F)	8.3	14.5	25.6	37.4	48.5	58.0	62.4	60.6	52.0	40.9	28.4	16.0	37.7
Extreme Maximum Temp. (°F)	57	64	86	96	93	102	103	104	98	92	82	65	104
Extreme Minimum Temp. (°F)	-29	-36	-12	0	22	37	43	41	27	13	-17	-25	-36
Days Maximum Temp. ≥ 90°F	0	0	0	0	1	4	9	6	2	0	0	0	22
Days Maximum Temp. ≤ 32°F	19	12	4	0	0	0	0	0	0	0	3	14	52
Days Minimum Temp. ≤ 32°F	30	26	23	9	1	0	0	0	1	7	19	29	145
Days Minimum Temp. ≤ 0°F	10	6	1	0	0	0	0	0	0	0	0	5	22
Heating Degree Days (base 65°F)	1,460	1,145	900	479	182	26	5	11	122	401	828	1,256	6,815
Cooling Degree Days (base 65°F)	0	0	0	10	51	182	295	237	88	9	0	0	872
Mean Precipitation (in.)	1.00	1.15	2.04	3.56	3.85	4.22	3.69	4.59	3.21	2.40	2.34	1.27	33.32
Days With ≥ 0.1" Precipitation	3	3	5	8	8	7	7	7	6	5	5	4	68
Days With ≥ 1.0" Precipitation	0	0	0	1	1	1	1	1	1	0	1	0	7
Mean Snowfall (in.)	13.1	8.0	4.8	1.8	0.0	0.0	0.0	0.0	0.0	0.2	3.5	8.8	40.2
Days With ≥ 1.0" Snow Depth	na	na	na	1	0	0	0	0	0	0	0	1	na

Prairie Du Sac 2 N *Sauk County*   Elevation: 777 ft.   Latitude: 43° 19' N   Longitude: 89° 44' W

	JAN	FEB	MAR	APR	MAY	JUN	JUL	AUG	SEP	OCT	NOV	DEC	YEAR
Mean Maximum Temp. (°F)	25.3	31.2	42.1	56.5	69.5	79.0	82.7	80.0	71.3	59.4	42.9	*30.1*	*55.8*
Mean Temp. (°F)	16.2	21.9	33.1	46.5	58.9	68.2	72.4	69.9	61.4	49.5	34.9	*22.3*	*46.3*
Mean Minimum Temp. (°F)	7.1	12.8	24.0	36.5	48.3	57.4	62.0	59.7	51.1	39.6	26.9	*14.3*	*36.6*
Extreme Maximum Temp. (°F)	57	63	81	94	92	101	103	102	98	88	78	64	103
Extreme Minimum Temp. (°F)	-31	-31	-10	9	25	38	45	38	26	14	-9	-23	-31
Days Maximum Temp. ≥ 90°F	0	0	0	0	0	3	5	2	0	0	0	0	10
Days Maximum Temp. ≤ 32°F	21	14	6	0	0	0	0	0	0	0	4	15	60
Days Minimum Temp. ≤ 32°F	30	27	24	10	1	0	0	0	1	7	21	28	149
Days Minimum Temp. ≤ 0°F	10	6	1	0	0	0	0	0	0	0	0	5	22
Heating Degree Days (base 65°F)	1,508	1,212	983	555	224	41	6	21	161	478	895	*1,319*	7,403
Cooling Degree Days (base 65°F)	0	0	0	6	40	149	248	187	60	4	0	*0*	694
Mean Precipitation (in.)	1.02	1.05	1.96	3.15	3.02	3.71	3.82	4.19	3.36	2.27	2.08	1.22	30.85
Days With ≥ 0.1" Precipitation	3	3	5	7	6	6	6	7	6	5	5	3	62
Days With ≥ 1.0" Precipitation	0	0	0	1	1	1	1	1	1	0	0	0	6
Mean Snowfall (in.)	7.7	5.5	3.3	1.1	0.0	0.0	0.0	0.0	0.0	trace	2.0	5.8	25.4
Days With ≥ 1.0" Snow Depth	*19*	16	7	1	0	0	0	0	0	0	2	11	*56*

Prentice 2 *Price County*   Elevation: 1,538 ft.   Latitude: 45° 31' N   Longitude: 90° 17' W

	JAN	FEB	MAR	APR	MAY	JUN	JUL	AUG	SEP	OCT	NOV	DEC	YEAR
Mean Maximum Temp. (°F)	19.7	26.4	37.1	52.4	66.3	73.8	77.8	75.7	66.7	54.6	37.4	24.4	51.0
Mean Temp. (°F)	8.4	14.3	26.1	40.8	53.4	61.5	65.8	63.9	55.1	43.9	29.0	14.9	39.8
Mean Minimum Temp. (°F)	-3.0	2.2	15.0	29.2	40.5	49.2	53.8	52.0	43.5	33.2	20.6	5.4	28.5
Extreme Maximum Temp. (°F)	54	59	72	87	88	91	99	95	93	89	70	64	99
Extreme Minimum Temp. (°F)	-45	-47	-28	-6	15	24	28	26	16	-1	-27	-43	-47
Days Maximum Temp. ≥ 90°F	0	0	0	0	0	0	1	0	0	0	0	0	1
Days Maximum Temp. ≤ 32°F	27	19	11	2	0	0	0	0	0	0	10	24	93
Days Minimum Temp. ≤ 32°F	31	28	28	19	7	1	0	0	4	15	27	31	191
Days Minimum Temp. ≤ 0°F	17	12	6	0	0	0	0	0	0	0	2	11	48
Heating Degree Days (base 65°F)	1,753	1,427	1,201	721	365	149	62	94	309	648	1,074	1,548	9,351
Cooling Degree Days (base 65°F)	0	0	0	2	12	52	95	67	18	0	0	0	246
Mean Precipitation (in.)	0.91	0.63	1.46	2.21	3.43	3.91	4.07	4.12	4.35	2.80	1.99	1.06	30.94
Days With ≥ 0.1" Precipitation	3	2	4	5	7	8	8	7	8	6	5	4	67
Days With ≥ 1.0" Precipitation	0	0	0	0	1	1	1	1	1	1	0	0	6
Mean Snowfall (in.)	13.4	8.3	9.7	3.5	0.2	0.0	0.0	0.0	trace	1.1	6.9	11.8	54.9
Days With ≥ 1.0" Snow Depth	na	na	*16*	4	0	0	0	0	0	0	6	20	na

Racine *Racine County*   Elevation: 593 ft.   Latitude: 42° 42' N   Longitude: 87° 47' W

	JAN	FEB	MAR	APR	MAY	JUN	JUL	AUG	SEP	OCT	NOV	DEC	YEAR
Mean Maximum Temp. (°F)	27.8	32.2	41.1	51.9	62.7	73.7	79.2	78.1	70.7	58.9	45.6	33.8	54.6
Mean Temp. (°F)	20.1	25.1	34.1	44.4	54.5	64.9	71.1	70.5	62.8	51.0	38.7	26.8	47.0
Mean Minimum Temp. (°F)	12.4	18.0	27.2	36.8	46.2	56.0	63.0	62.8	54.9	43.1	31.7	19.8	39.3
Extreme Maximum Temp. (°F)	58	67	83	91	92	100	104	100	95	90	75	65	104
Extreme Minimum Temp. (°F)	-31	-24	-2	12	29	39	42	40	33	21	-5	-23	-31
Days Maximum Temp. ≥ 90°F	0	0	0	0	0	2	4	2	0	0	0	0	8
Days Maximum Temp. ≤ 32°F	19	14	6	0	0	0	0	0	0	0	3	12	54
Days Minimum Temp. ≤ 32°F	29	25	22	7	0	0	0	0	0	3	16	27	129
Days Minimum Temp. ≤ 0°F	7	3	0	0	0	0	0	0	0	0	0	3	13
Heating Degree Days (base 65°F)	1,383	1,121	951	615	336	89	12	13	122	430	783	1,178	7,033
Cooling Degree Days (base 65°F)	0	0	0	1	14	80	196	185	58	3	0	0	537
Mean Precipitation (in.)	1.67	1.40	2.42	4.00	3.13	3.61	3.48	4.01	3.90	2.52	2.90	2.02	35.06
Days With ≥ 0.1" Precipitation	4	4	5	7	6	6	7	6	6	6	6	5	68
Days With ≥ 1.0" Precipitation	0	0	0	1	1	1	1	1	1	0	0	0	6
Mean Snowfall (in.)	15.4	8.9	6.1	1.5	trace	0.0	0.0	0.0	0.0	0.2	2.1	7.4	41.6
Days With ≥ 1.0" Snow Depth	*20*	*15*	*5*	0	0	0	0	0	0	0	*1*	na	na

Rainbow Reservoir Lake Tomaha *Oneida County*   Elevation: 1,597 ft.   Latitude: 45° 50' N   Longitude: 89° 33' W

	JAN	FEB	MAR	APR	MAY	JUN	JUL	AUG	SEP	OCT	NOV	DEC	YEAR
Mean Maximum Temp. (°F)	20.1	25.7	36.4	50.9	65.4	73.3	77.2	75.1	65.3	53.4	36.9	24.2	50.3
Mean Temp. (°F)	8.9	13.0	24.1	38.3	52.0	60.9	65.3	63.5	54.3	43.1	28.6	14.9	38.9
Mean Minimum Temp. (°F)	-2.4	0.3	11.8	25.8	38.6	48.4	53.3	51.9	43.3	32.8	20.2	5.5	27.5
Extreme Maximum Temp. (°F)	54	58	70	90	89	96	96	94	94	87	72	59	96
Extreme Minimum Temp. (°F)	-41	-42	-29	-9	19	28	33	34	23	9	-16	-30	-42
Days Maximum Temp. ≥ 90°F	0	0	0	0	0	1	1	0	0	0	0	0	2
Days Maximum Temp. ≤ 32°F	27	20	11	2	0	0	0	0	0	0	11	25	96
Days Minimum Temp. ≤ 32°F	31	28	30	23	10	0	0	0	3	17	27	31	200
Days Minimum Temp. ≤ 0°F	17	14	7	0	0	0	0	0	0	0	2	12	52
Heating Degree Days (base 65°F)	1,737	1,465	1,261	795	408	159	67	99	329	672	1,086	1,549	9,627
Cooling Degree Days (base 65°F)	0	0	0	1	8	42	*74*	63	12	*0*	*0*	*0*	*200*
Mean Precipitation (in.)	1.07	0.85	1.73	2.31	3.24	3.81	3.73	4.50	4.47	2.88	2.33	1.34	32.26
Days With ≥ 0.1" Precipitation	3	3	5	6	7	8	8	8	9	7	6	4	74
Days With ≥ 1.0" Precipitation	0	0	0	0	1	1	1	1	1	1	0	0	6
Mean Snowfall (in.)	*12.5*	*9.2*	9.6	4.5	0.5	0.0	*0.0*	0.0	trace	*1.3*	*7.8*	*12.7*	*58.1*
Days With ≥ 1.0" Snow Depth	*31*	28	29	12	0	0	0	0	0	1	*13*	*30*	*144*

Rest Lake *Vilas County*   Elevation: 1,607 ft.   Latitude: 46° 07' N   Longitude: 89° 52' W

	JAN	FEB	MAR	APR	MAY	JUN	JUL	AUG	SEP	OCT	NOV	DEC	YEAR
Mean Maximum Temp. (°F)	19.7	26.0	36.6	52.4	66.8	73.7	77.1	74.8	65.6	53.9	36.5	24.2	50.6
Mean Temp. (°F)	9.6	14.9	25.5	40.3	54.0	62.2	66.2	64.1	55.3	44.1	29.1	15.8	40.1
Mean Minimum Temp. (°F)	-0.6	3.8	14.4	28.1	41.1	50.6	55.3	53.3	45.0	34.2	21.7	7.4	29.5
Extreme Maximum Temp. (°F)	49	57	72	89	90	96	97	92	92	84	70	58	97
Extreme Minimum Temp. (°F)	-40	-49	-35	-11	19	27	35	32	23	6	-21	-36	-49
Days Maximum Temp. ≥ 90°F	0	0	0	0	0	0	1	0	0	0	0	0	1
Days Maximum Temp. ≤ 32°F	27	20	11	1	0	0	0	0	0	0	12	25	96
Days Minimum Temp. ≤ 32°F	31	28	29	21	7	0	0	0	2	14	26	31	189
Days Minimum Temp. ≤ 0°F	15	11	6	0	0	0	0	0	0	0	1	9	42
Heating Degree Days (base 65°F)	1,715	1,410	1,216	737	353	132	57	86	304	643	1,070	1,519	9,242
Cooling Degree Days (base 65°F)	0	0	0	1	14	53	97	63	16	0	0	0	244
Mean Precipitation (in.)	1.22	0.78	1.58	2.19	3.69	3.91	4.27	4.44	3.99	3.03	2.10	1.33	32.53
Days With ≥ 0.1" Precipitation	3	2	3	5	7	8	8	7	8	6	5	4	66
Days With ≥ 1.0" Precipitation	0	0	0	0	1	1	1	1	1	1	0	0	6
Mean Snowfall (in.)	20.5	11.8	12.3	5.2	0.4	0.0	0.0	0.0	trace	1.3	11.4	18.1	81.0
Days With ≥ 1.0" Snow Depth	29	26	25	10	0	0	0	0	0	1	11	26	128

Rhinelander *Oneida County*   Elevation: 1,578 ft.   Latitude: 45° 37' N   Longitude: 89° 25' W

	JAN	FEB	MAR	APR	MAY	JUN	JUL	AUG	SEP	OCT	NOV	DEC	YEAR
Mean Maximum Temp. (°F)	21.2	27.4	37.9	52.7	66.8	74.8	79.0	76.4	67.0	54.7	38.0	25.4	51.8
Mean Temp. (°F)	10.1	15.6	26.7	41.0	54.2	62.9	67.5	65.3	56.1	44.5	29.8	16.2	40.8
Mean Minimum Temp. (°F)	-1.0	3.7	15.4	29.3	41.5	50.8	55.9	54.1	45.1	34.3	21.6	6.9	29.8
Extreme Maximum Temp. (°F)	53	59	75	89	90	98	100	97	95	92	73	62	100
Extreme Minimum Temp. (°F)	-40	-42	-23	-4	22	30	37	36	24	11	-16	-34	-42
Days Maximum Temp. ≥ 90°F	0	0	0	0	0	1	2	1	0	0	0	0	4
Days Maximum Temp. ≤ 32°F	27	19	9	1	0	0	0	0	0	0	10	24	90
Days Minimum Temp. ≤ 32°F	31	28	29	20	6	0	0	0	3	15	27	31	190
Days Minimum Temp. ≤ 0°F	16	12	5	0	0	0	0	0	0	0	1	11	45
Heating Degree Days (base 65°F)	1,698	1,389	1,181	715	345	121	40	69	283	628	1,049	1,508	9,026
Cooling Degree Days (base 65°F)	0	0	0	2	15	67	121	90	21	1	0	0	317
Mean Precipitation (in.)	1.22	0.82	1.55	2.33	3.44	3.79	3.82	4.27	4.25	2.74	2.07	1.35	31.65
Days With ≥ 0.1" Precipitation	4	3	4	6	8	8	8	7	8	6	5	5	72
Days With ≥ 1.0" Precipitation	0	0	0	0	1	1	1	1	1	1	0	0	6
Mean Snowfall (in.)	*11.4*	*5.2*	*7.2*	*1.9*	0.2	0.0	0.0	0.0	trace	0.1	na	na	na
Days With ≥ 1.0" Snow Depth	30	27	20	4	0	0	0	0	0	0	8	26	115

Rice Lake Municipal Airport *Barron County*   Elevation: 1,102 ft.   Latitude: 45° 25' N   Longitude: 91° 46' W

	JAN	FEB	MAR	APR	MAY	JUN	JUL	AUG	SEP	OCT	NOV	DEC	YEAR
Mean Maximum Temp. (°F)	20.1	27.3	38.6	55.7	69.0	77.0	81.0	78.5	69.3	57.1	38.4	24.8	53.1
Mean Temp. (°F)	9.6	16.6	28.6	43.8	56.6	65.1	69.5	67.1	58.1	46.4	30.3	16.0	42.3
Mean Minimum Temp. (°F)	-0.9	5.8	18.6	31.9	44.2	53.1	58.0	55.7	46.9	35.7	22.1	7.3	31.5
Extreme Maximum Temp. (°F)	52	55	80	90	89	95	100	100	95	87	71	59	100
Extreme Minimum Temp. (°F)	-43	-37	-24	2	21	28	37	34	22	9	-22	-40	-43
Days Maximum Temp. ≥ 90°F	0	0	0	0	0	1	3	1	0	0	0	0	5
Days Maximum Temp. ≤ 32°F	26	17	8	1	0	0	0	0	0	0	9	23	84
Days Minimum Temp. ≤ 32°F	31	28	27	16	4	0	0	0	2	12	26	31	177
Days Minimum Temp. ≤ 0°F	16	10	4	0	0	0	0	0	0	0	1	10	41
Heating Degree Days (base 65°F)	1,713	1,362	1,119	632	279	81	22	46	234	569	1,036	1,514	8,607
Cooling Degree Days (base 65°F)	0	0	0	4	27	98	174	126	36	1	0	0	466
Mean Precipitation (in.)	1.05	0.72	1.82	2.65	3.23	4.18	3.96	4.47	4.25	2.67	2.01	1.06	32.07
Days With ≥ 0.1" Precipitation	3	2	4	6	7	7	7	7	7	6	4	3	63
Days With ≥ 1.0" Precipitation	0	0	0	1	1	1	1	1	1	1	1	0	8
Mean Snowfall (in.)	12.3	6.7	9.3	2.7	trace	0.0	0.0	0.0	trace	0.6	7.0	9.8	48.4
Days With ≥ 1.0" Snow Depth	30	26	19	2	0	0	0	0	0	0	7	24	*108*

Richland Center *Richland County*   Elevation: 721 ft.   Latitude: 43° 19' N   Longitude: 90° 22' W

	JAN	FEB	MAR	APR	MAY	JUN	JUL	AUG	SEP	OCT	NOV	DEC	YEAR
Mean Maximum Temp. (°F)	26.3	32.5	43.7	58.1	71.0	80.0	84.3	81.5	73.0	61.2	44.3	31.5	57.3
Mean Temp. (°F)	15.7	21.8	33.3	46.1	57.7	66.9	71.5	69.0	60.6	48.8	34.5	22.1	45.7
Mean Minimum Temp. (°F)	5.1	11.0	22.7	34.0	44.4	53.8	58.6	56.5	48.0	36.2	24.6	12.5	34.0
Extreme Maximum Temp. (°F)	56	63	84	93	91	103	102	102	96	91	75	64	103
Extreme Minimum Temp. (°F)	-38	-38	-9	0	25	33	38	33	26	13	-13	-30	-38
Days Maximum Temp. ≥ 90°F	0	0	0	0	1	3	7	3	1	0	0	0	15
Days Maximum Temp. ≤ 32°F	21	14	5	0	0	0	0	0	0	0	4	15	59
Days Minimum Temp. ≤ 32°F	31	27	25	13	3	0	0	0	1	12	24	30	166
Days Minimum Temp. ≤ 0°F	12	7	1	0	0	0	0	0	0	0	1	6	27
Heating Degree Days (base 65°F)	1,524	1,216	978	568	249	57	11	28	177	502	908	1,325	7,543
Cooling Degree Days (base 65°F)	0	0	0	5	22	113	202	152	44	2	0	0	540
Mean Precipitation (in.)	1.17	1.12	2.20	3.95	3.81	4.07	4.75	4.19	3.87	2.31	2.52	1.28	35.24
Days With ≥ 0.1" Precipitation	4	3	5	8	7	7	7	7	7	5	5	4	69
Days With ≥ 1.0" Precipitation	0	0	1	1	1	1	2	1	1	0	0	0	7
Mean Snowfall (in.)	11.8	7.8	6.0	2.4	trace	0.0	0.0	0.0	0.0	0.1	4.8	8.8	41.7
Days With ≥ 1.0" Snow Depth	26	21	10	1	0	0	0	0	0	0	4	18	80

Ridgeland 1 NNE *Barron County*   Elevation: 958 ft.   Latitude: 45° 13' N   Longitude: 91° 53' W

	JAN	FEB	MAR	APR	MAY	JUN	JUL	AUG	SEP	OCT	NOV	DEC	YEAR
Mean Maximum Temp. (°F)	21.1	27.7	39.2	56.3	69.4	77.4	81.3	78.8	69.8	57.7	39.8	26.0	53.7
Mean Temp. (°F)	10.2	16.6	28.7	43.6	56.4	65.0	69.3	67.0	58.0	46.3	31.1	16.7	42.4
Mean Minimum Temp. (°F)	-0.7	5.4	18.0	31.1	43.2	52.8	57.2	55.0	46.2	34.9	22.3	7.4	31.1
Extreme Maximum Temp. (°F)	54	59	80	91	92	96	100	101	96	88	71	61	101
Extreme Minimum Temp. (°F)	-47	-38	-25	2	20	29	37	32	22	6	-18	-42	-47
Days Maximum Temp. ≥ 90°F	0	0	0	0	0	1	3	1	0	0	0	0	5
Days Maximum Temp. ≤ 32°F	25	17	8	1	0	0	0	0	0	0	8	22	81
Days Minimum Temp. ≤ 32°F	31	28	28	17	5	0	0	0	2	13	25	31	180
Days Minimum Temp. ≤ 0°F	16	10	4	0	0	0	0	0	0	0	0	2	10	42
Heating Degree Days (base 65°F)	1,695	1,362	1,121	640	286	82	25	49	236	575	1,012	1,491	8,574
Cooling Degree Days (base 65°F)	0	0	0	4	23	91	159	118	31	1	0	0	427
Mean Precipitation (in.)	1.08	0.75	2.12	2.75	3.48	4.18	3.89	4.89	3.82	2.66	1.92	1.09	32.63
Days With ≥ 0.1" Precipitation	3	2	5	6	6	8	7	7	7	6	4	3	64
Days With ≥ 1.0" Precipitation	0	0	0	0	1	1	1	2	1	1	0	0	7
Mean Snowfall (in.)	10.9	6.1	9.3	1.7	trace	0.0	0.0	0.0	trace	0.3	5.4	8.5	42.2
Days With ≥ 1.0" Snow Depth	29	26	21	3	0	0	0	0	0	0	7	23	109

River Falls *Pierce County*   Elevation: 912 ft.   Latitude: 44° 51' N   Longitude: 92° 37' W

	JAN	FEB	MAR	APR	MAY	JUN	JUL	AUG	SEP	OCT	NOV	DEC	YEAR
Mean Maximum Temp. (°F)	22.0	28.8	40.6	57.7	70.5	79.0	82.9	80.2	71.1	58.9	40.5	27.0	54.9
Mean Temp. (°F)	12.5	19.2	31.1	46.0	58.4	67.4	71.7	69.3	60.4	48.6	32.4	18.8	44.6
Mean Minimum Temp. (°F)	3.0	9.5	21.4	34.2	46.3	55.8	60.4	58.4	49.5	38.1	24.3	10.6	34.3
Extreme Maximum Temp. (°F)	51	57	81	92	91	99	102	101	95	90	77	66	102
Extreme Minimum Temp. (°F)	-36	-35	-15	5	23	33	39	35	23	12	-15	-36	-36
Days Maximum Temp. ≥ 90°F	0	0	0	0	0	2	4	2	1	0	0	0	9
Days Maximum Temp. ≤ 32°F	23	16	7	0	0	0	0	0	0	0	7	20	73
Days Minimum Temp. ≤ 32°F	31	27	26	13	2	0	0	0	1	9	23	30	162
Days Minimum Temp. ≤ 0°F	14	9	2	0	0	0	0	0	0	0	1	8	34
Heating Degree Days (base 65°F)	1,623	1,286	1,046	569	237	53	11	25	185	506	972	1,426	7,939
Cooling Degree Days (base 65°F)	0	0	0	6	37	134	222	169	54	3	0	0	625
Mean Precipitation (in.)	0.82	0.63	1.57	2.47	3.56	4.32	4.32	4.50	3.46	2.60	1.69	0.82	30.76
Days With ≥ 0.1" Precipitation	3	2	4	6	8	8	7	7	6	5	4	3	63
Days With ≥ 1.0" Precipitation	0	0	0	0	1	1	1	1	1	0	0	0	5
Mean Snowfall (in.)	11.0	6.5	9.5	2.6	trace	trace	0.0	0.0	trace	0.5	7.6	8.5	46.2
Days With ≥ 1.0" Snow Depth	26	23	16	1	0	0	0	0	0	0	7	22	95

Rosholt 9 NNE *Marathon County*   Elevation: 1,158 ft.   Latitude: 44° 45' N   Longitude: 89° 15' W

	JAN	FEB	MAR	APR	MAY	JUN	JUL	AUG	SEP	OCT	NOV	DEC	YEAR
Mean Maximum Temp. (°F)	23.1	28.9	39.4	55.3	68.9	77.2	80.8	*78.9*	*69.8*	*58.0*	40.7	27.6	*54.0*
Mean Temp. (°F)	12.8	18.5	28.7	43.2	55.8	64.3	68.4	*66.7*	*57.6*	*46.6*	31.8	18.7	*42.8*
Mean Minimum Temp. (°F)	2.5	8.1	18.0	31.1	42.7	51.4	56.1	54.3	45.4	35.1	22.9	9.8	31.4
Extreme Maximum Temp. (°F)	53	58	78	89	91	97	103	98	94	90	73	60	103
Extreme Minimum Temp. (°F)	-41	-38	-30	2	15	26	35	31	19	10	-12	-35	-41
Days Maximum Temp. ≥ 90°F	0	0	0	0	0	2	3	2	0	0	0	0	7
Days Maximum Temp. ≤ 32°F	24	17	8	0	0	0	0	0	0	0	6	20	75
Days Minimum Temp. ≤ 32°F	31	28	27	17	4	0	0	0	2	12	26	30	177
Days Minimum Temp. ≤ 0°F	14	9	4	0	0	0	0	0	0	0	1	8	36
Heating Degree Days (base 65°F)	1,615	1,306	1,120	651	302	96	30	*52*	*245*	*567*	989	1,418	*8,391*
Cooling Degree Days (base 65°F)	0	0	0	2	17	74	123	99	25	1	0	0	341
Mean Precipitation (in.)	1.09	0.89	1.66	2.89	3.91	3.57	3.99	4.43	3.87	2.65	2.37	1.37	32.69
Days With ≥ 0.1" Precipitation	4	3	5	6	7	7	8	7	7	6	5	4	69
Days With ≥ 1.0" Precipitation	0	0	0	1	1	1	1	1	1	1	0	0	7
Mean Snowfall (in.)	11.6	8.4	10.2	2.9	0.2	0.0	0.0	0.0	0.0	0.4	6.7	11.7	52.1
Days With ≥ 1.0" Snow Depth	30	28	21	3	0	0	0	0	0	0	6	26	114

Saint Croix Falls *Polk County*   Elevation: 767 ft.   Latitude: 45° 25' N   Longitude: 92° 39' W

	JAN	FEB	MAR	APR	MAY	JUN	JUL	AUG	SEP	OCT	NOV	DEC	YEAR
Mean Maximum Temp. (°F)	21.6	28.9	40.6	57.2	70.8	79.2	83.4	80.6	71.1	58.7	40.3	26.6	54.9
Mean Temp. (°F)	10.2	17.3	29.8	45.1	58.1	66.9	71.5	69.3	59.7	47.6	31.5	17.1	43.7
Mean Minimum Temp. (°F)	-1.2	5.8	18.9	32.9	45.3	54.6	59.5	57.8	48.3	36.6	22.7	7.6	32.4
Extreme Maximum Temp. (°F)	56	57	83	93	96	99	105	102	98	90	76	66	105
Extreme Minimum Temp. (°F)	-42	-43	-19	-1	23	30	38	41	26	11	-17	-39	-43
Days Maximum Temp. ≥ 90°F	0	0	0	0	1	3	6	3	1	0	0	0	14
Days Maximum Temp. ≤ 32°F	23	16	7	0	0	0	0	0	0	0	7	21	74
Days Minimum Temp. ≤ 32°F	31	27	27	15	2	0	0	0	1	11	25	31	170
Days Minimum Temp. ≤ 0°F	17	10	3	0	0	0	0	0	0	0	1	10	41
Heating Degree Days (base 65°F)	1,695	1,342	1,086	595	246	58	12	26	198	535	998	1,479	8,270
Cooling Degree Days (base 65°F)	0	0	0	4	39	128	224	175	51	3	0	0	624
Mean Precipitation (in.)	0.82	0.61	1.57	2.59	3.42	4.46	4.12	4.74	3.66	2.66	1.67	0.76	31.08
Days With ≥ 0.1" Precipitation	3	2	4	6	7	8	7	7	7	6	4	3	64
Days With ≥ 1.0" Precipitation	0	0	0	0	1	1	1	1	1	1	0	0	6
Mean Snowfall (in.)	11.1	5.6	7.4	1.4	0.0	0.0	0.0	0.0	0.0	0.4	7.5	7.3	40.7
Days With ≥ 1.0" Snow Depth	29	26	19	2	0	0	0	0	0	0	7	24	107

Saint Germain 2 E *Vilas County* Elevation: 1,643 ft. Latitude: 45° 55' N Longitude: 89° 26' W

	JAN	FEB	MAR	APR	MAY	JUN	JUL	AUG	SEP	OCT	NOV	DEC	YEAR
Mean Maximum Temp. (°F)	19.5	25.0	35.5	50.2	64.9	71.7	75.4	72.8	63.9	52.2	36.7	24.0	49.3
Mean Temp. (°F)	9.7	14.3	25.4	39.4	53.0	61.2	65.8	63.5	54.8	43.3	29.4	15.8	39.6
Mean Minimum Temp. (°F)	-0.2	3.6	15.1	28.5	41.1	50.7	56.1	54.2	45.6	34.3	22.1	7.6	29.9
Extreme Maximum Temp. (°F)	48	54	66	89	87	93	97	95	92	83	70	58	97
Extreme Minimum Temp. (°F)	-40	-43	-25	-8	19	32	35	35	24	7	-18	-33	-43
Days Maximum Temp. ≥ 90°F	0	0	0	0	0	0	1	0	0	0	0	0	1
Days Maximum Temp. ≤ 32°F	27	20	12	2	0	0	0	0	0	1	11	25	98
Days Minimum Temp. ≤ 32°F	31	28	29	20	6	0	0	0	1	14	27	31	187
Days Minimum Temp. ≤ 0°F	15	12	5	0	0	0	0	0	0	0	1	9	42
Heating Degree Days (base 65°F)	1,712	1,427	1,223	764	378	150	59	98	314	666	1,061	1,519	9,371
Cooling Degree Days (base 65°F)	0	0	0	2	10	50	89	62	15	0	0	0	228
Mean Precipitation (in.)	1.28	0.81	1.67	2.25	3.49	3.63	3.78	4.50	4.12	2.67	2.14	1.32	31.66
Days With ≥ 0.1" Precipitation	5	3	4	6	7	8	8	8	8	7	5	4	73
Days With ≥ 1.0" Precipitation	0	0	0	0	1	1	1	1	1	0	0	0	5
Mean Snowfall (in.)	16.9	8.6	10.9	3.6	0.4	0.0	0.0	0.0	trace	0.7	*8.0*	14.1	*63.2*
Days With ≥ 1.0" Snow Depth	*24*	*20*	*19*	*4*	0	0	0	0	0	0	na	*22*	na

Shawano 2 SSW *Shawano County* Elevation: 807 ft. Latitude: 44° 45' N Longitude: 88° 37' W

	JAN	FEB	MAR	APR	MAY	JUN	JUL	AUG	SEP	OCT	NOV	DEC	YEAR
Mean Maximum Temp. (°F)	23.5	29.2	40.0	55.9	69.0	78.1	82.1	79.3	70.8	58.3	41.7	28.5	54.7
Mean Temp. (°F)	13.6	18.8	30.0	44.2	56.1	65.3	69.7	67.2	58.5	47.1	33.1	20.0	43.6
Mean Minimum Temp. (°F)	3.6	8.3	20.0	32.5	43.1	52.5	57.2	55.1	46.1	35.8	24.4	11.3	32.5
Extreme Maximum Temp. (°F)	53	55	77	93	92	99	104	100	95	88	74	60	104
Extreme Minimum Temp. (°F)	-35	-33	-16	4	23	31	33	34	20	12	-10	-26	-35
Days Maximum Temp. ≥ 90°F	0	0	0	0	0	3	4	2	0	0	0	0	9
Days Maximum Temp. ≤ 32°F	24	17	7	0	0	0	0	0	0	0	5	19	72
Days Minimum Temp. ≤ 32°F	31	28	27	16	4	0	0	0	2	12	24	30	174
Days Minimum Temp. ≤ 0°F	13	9	2	0	0	0	0	0	0	0	1	7	32
Heating Degree Days (base 65°F)	1,590	1,299	1,079	621	296	83	22	46	223	552	952	1,391	8,154
Cooling Degree Days (base 65°F)	0	0	0	5	27	104	177	132	35	2	0	0	482
Mean Precipitation (in.)	1.28	0.93	1.83	2.71	3.73	3.20	3.99	3.85	3.57	2.49	2.39	1.29	31.26
Days With ≥ 0.1" Precipitation	4	3	5	6	7	6	7	7	6	5	5	4	65
Days With ≥ 1.0" Precipitation	0	0	0	0	1	1	1	1	1	1	1	0	7
Mean Snowfall (in.)	14.0	7.8	8.6	2.5	0.2	0.0	0.0	0.0	0.0	0.2	4.8	12.1	50.2
Days With ≥ 1.0" Snow Depth	30	25	*15*	2	0	0	0	0	0	0	5	22	*99*

Sheboygan *Sheboygan County* Elevation: 646 ft. Latitude: 43° 45' N Longitude: 87° 43' W

	JAN	FEB	MAR	APR	MAY	JUN	JUL	AUG	SEP	OCT	NOV	DEC	YEAR
Mean Maximum Temp. (°F)	28.2	32.8	41.4	52.3	64.1	74.8	80.8	79.3	71.7	59.2	45.1	33.3	55.2
Mean Temp. (°F)	20.7	25.3	33.9	44.1	54.6	64.7	71.2	70.4	62.7	51.0	38.3	26.6	46.9
Mean Minimum Temp. (°F)	13.0	17.8	26.4	35.8	45.2	54.6	61.6	61.3	53.6	42.7	31.4	19.7	38.6
Extreme Maximum Temp. (°F)	58	63	77	92	92	99	108	99	96	89	76	65	108
Extreme Minimum Temp. (°F)	-26	-25	-6	14	28	39	48	43	32	21	-5	-21	-26
Days Maximum Temp. ≥ 90°F	0	0	0	0	0	2	4	3	1	0	0	0	10
Days Maximum Temp. ≤ 32°F	19	13	5	0	0	0	0	0	0	0	2	12	51
Days Minimum Temp. ≤ 32°F	30	26	23	8	0	0	0	0	0	3	16	27	133
Days Minimum Temp. ≤ 0°F	6	3	0	0	0	0	0	0	0	0	0	3	12
Heating Degree Days (base 65°F)	1,368	1,115	958	623	327	88	10	11	121	431	796	1,185	7,033
Cooling Degree Days (base 65°F)	0	0	0	1	16	91	212	196	63	3	0	0	582
Mean Precipitation (in.)	1.63	1.26	2.23	2.93	2.89	3.23	3.09	3.90	3.34	2.57	2.44	1.86	31.37
Days With ≥ 0.1" Precipitation	5	4	5	6	6	6	6	7	6	6	6	5	68
Days With ≥ 1.0" Precipitation	0	0	0	1	1	0	1	1	1	0	0	0	5
Mean Snowfall (in.)	14.4	9.8	7.9	1.9	trace	0.0	0.0	0.0	0.0	0.1	3.0	9.2	46.3
Days With ≥ 1.0" Snow Depth	21	19	10	1	0	0	0	0	0	0	1	13	65

Solon Springs *Douglas County* Elevation: 1,079 ft. Latitude: 46° 21' N Longitude: 91° 49' W

	JAN	FEB	MAR	APR	MAY	JUN	JUL	AUG	SEP	OCT	NOV	DEC	YEAR
Mean Maximum Temp. (°F)	19.9	27.5	38.3	54.4	69.2	77.6	81.9	79.5	69.1	56.1	37.5	24.1	52.9
Mean Temp. (°F)	8.0	14.9	26.6	41.0	54.1	63.1	68.2	66.0	56.2	44.4	28.5	13.8	40.4
Mean Minimum Temp. (°F)	-3.8	2.2	14.8	27.6	39.0	48.6	54.4	52.4	43.3	32.7	19.6	3.9	27.9
Extreme Maximum Temp. (°F)	53	61	76	92	94	97	102	100	99	90	73	58	102
Extreme Minimum Temp. (°F)	-47	-46	-31	0	19	29	34	34	23	6	-26	-41	-47
Days Maximum Temp. ≥ 90°F	0	0	0	0	0	2	4	2	0	0	0	0	8
Days Maximum Temp. ≤ 32°F	27	18	9	1	0	0	0	0	0	0	11	24	90
Days Minimum Temp. ≤ 32°F	31	28	29	22	8	1	0	0	4	16	27	31	197
Days Minimum Temp. ≤ 0°F	18	12	6	0	0	0	0	0	0	0	2	12	50
Heating Degree Days (base 65°F)	1,764	1,412	1,184	714	351	113	35	64	282	633	1,089	1,584	9,225
Cooling Degree Days (base 65°F)	0	0	0	1	17	64	133	95	19	0	0	0	329
Mean Precipitation (in.)	1.00	0.77	1.65	2.23	3.24	3.90	4.81	4.21	3.62	2.71	2.04	0.96	31.14
Days With ≥ 0.1" Precipitation	3	2	4	*5*	*6*	*7*	7	7	7	*6*	4	3	*61*
Days With ≥ 1.0" Precipitation	0	0	0	0	1	1	1	1	1	0	0	0	5
Mean Snowfall (in.)	13.0	8.2	9.0	3.7	0.2	0.0	0.0	0.0	0.0	0.6	8.8	11.1	54.6
Days With ≥ 1.0" Snow Depth	30	28	26	0	0	0	0	0	0	0	11	28	129

Spooner Experiment Farm *Washburn County*   Elevation: 1,099 ft.   Latitude: 45° 49' N   Longitude: 91° 53' W

	JAN	FEB	MAR	APR	MAY	JUN	JUL	AUG	SEP	OCT	NOV	DEC	YEAR
Mean Maximum Temp. (°F)	21.2	28.7	40.1	56.6	70.1	77.7	81.5	79.0	69.7	57.7	39.1	25.6	53.9
Mean Temp. (°F)	10.4	17.3	29.1	44.1	56.6	65.0	69.5	67.0	58.2	46.8	30.9	16.6	42.6
Mean Minimum Temp. (°F)	-0.5	5.8	18.1	31.5	43.1	52.3	57.3	55.0	46.7	35.9	22.7	7.5	31.3
Extreme Maximum Temp. (°F)	57	58	79	90	90	94	101	97	95	86	74	60	101
Extreme Minimum Temp. (°F)	-43	-42	-26	0	20	29	37	31	23	8	-22	-44	-44
Days Maximum Temp. ≥ 90°F	0	0	0	0	0	1	3	1	0	0	0	0	5
Days Maximum Temp. ≤ 32°F	26	17	7	1	0	0	0	0	0	0	9	22	82
Days Minimum Temp. ≤ 32°F	31	28	27	17	5	0	0	0	2	12	25	31	178
Days Minimum Temp. ≤ 0°F	15	10	4	0	0	0	0	0	0	0	1	10	40
Heating Degree Days (base 65°F)	1,690	1,343	1,105	624	282	80	23	50	231	560	1,015	1,497	8,500
Cooling Degree Days (base 65°F)	0	0	0	3	26	92	169	127	35	1	0	0	453
Mean Precipitation (in.)	0.85	0.63	1.39	2.19	3.09	3.88	4.14	4.54	3.80	2.73	1.85	0.85	29.94
Days With ≥ 0.1" Precipitation	3	2	4	5	6	8	7	7	7	6	4	3	62
Days With ≥ 1.0" Precipitation	0	0	0	0	1	1	1	2	1	1	0	0	7
Mean Snowfall (in.)	14.2	6.9	8.6	2.5	trace	0.0	0.0	0.0	0.0	0.7	7.7	10.7	51.3
Days With ≥ 1.0" Snow Depth	30	26	18	3	0	0	0	0	0	0	8	24	109

Stanley *Chippewa County*   Elevation: 1,089 ft.   Latitude: 44° 58' N   Longitude: 90° 56' W

	JAN	FEB	MAR	APR	MAY	JUN	JUL	AUG	SEP	OCT	NOV	DEC	YEAR
Mean Maximum Temp. (°F)	21.5	27.5	39.7	55.5	68.8	76.7	81.0	78.6	69.6	57.4	39.7	26.1	53.5
Mean Temp. (°F)	11.6	17.2	29.8	43.9	56.2	64.7	69.4	67.0	57.9	46.4	31.2	17.3	42.7
Mean Minimum Temp. (°F)	1.7	6.8	19.9	32.2	43.6	52.6	57.7	55.2	46.2	35.2	22.6	8.4	31.8
Extreme Maximum Temp. (°F)	53	57	84	89	90	94	99	101	97	91	75	60	101
Extreme Minimum Temp. (°F)	-36	-34	-17	4	21	29	38	33	23	9	-13	-39	-39
Days Maximum Temp. ≥ 90°F	0	0	0	0	0	1	3	1	0	0	0	0	5
Days Maximum Temp. ≤ 32°F	25	17	8	1	0	0	0	0	0	0	7	22	80
Days Minimum Temp. ≤ 32°F	30	27	27	16	4	0	0	0	2	13	25	30	174
Days Minimum Temp. ≤ 0°F	15	10	3	0	0	0	0	0	0	0	1	9	38
Heating Degree Days (base 65°F)	1,651	1,343	1,084	629	289	86	22	45	237	573	1,008	1,475	8,442
Cooling Degree Days (base 65°F)	0	0	0	3	19	83	155	109	28	1	0	0	398
Mean Precipitation (in.)	0.94	0.77	1.63	2.66	3.67	4.01	4.06	4.47	3.64	2.37	2.17	1.13	31.52
Days With ≥ 0.1" Precipitation	3	2	4	6	7	7	7	7	7	6	5	4	65
Days With ≥ 1.0" Precipitation	0	0	0	0	1	1	1	1	1	1	0	0	6
Mean Snowfall (in.)	12.9	7.3	8.3	2.5	trace	0.0	0.0	0.0	trace	0.5	6.5	11.4	49.4
Days With ≥ 1.0" Snow Depth	na	na	13	1	0	0	0	0	0	0	3	16	na

Stevens Point *Portage County*   Elevation: 1,076 ft.   Latitude: 44° 30' N   Longitude: 89° 35' W

	JAN	FEB	MAR	APR	MAY	JUN	JUL	AUG	SEP	OCT	NOV	DEC	YEAR
Mean Maximum Temp. (°F)	23.0	28.9	39.6	55.2	68.3	77.1	80.9	78.5	69.7	57.7	41.4	28.2	54.0
Mean Temp. (°F)	13.9	19.4	30.3	44.6	56.9	65.9	70.2	68.0	59.3	47.8	33.4	20.2	44.2
Mean Minimum Temp. (°F)	4.8	9.9	21.0	33.9	45.5	54.6	59.5	57.5	48.8	37.8	25.3	12.2	34.2
Extreme Maximum Temp. (°F)	54	58	81	88	90	96	102	100	93	90	73	61	102
Extreme Minimum Temp. (°F)	-32	-32	-14	6	24	33	41	37	26	12	-10	-26	-32
Days Maximum Temp. ≥ 90°F	0	0	0	0	0	2	3	1	0	0	0	0	6
Days Maximum Temp. ≤ 32°F	24	17	8	0	0	0	0	0	0	0	6	19	74
Days Minimum Temp. ≤ 32°F	31	28	26	14	2	0	0	0	1	9	23	30	164
Days Minimum Temp. ≤ 0°F	12	8	3	0	0	0	0	0	0	0	1	6	30
Heating Degree Days (base 65°F)	1,578	1,282	1,068	612	276	73	16	35	206	531	943	1,383	8,003
Cooling Degree Days (base 65°F)	0	0	0	5	30	109	182	140	41	2	0	0	509
Mean Precipitation (in.)	1.07	0.96	1.94	2.80	3.77	3.43	4.28	4.00	3.82	2.43	2.28	1.33	32.11
Days With ≥ 0.1" Precipitation	4	3	5	7	7	7	8	7	7	6	5	4	70
Days With ≥ 1.0" Precipitation	0	0	0	0	1	1	1	1	1	0	0	0	5
Mean Snowfall (in.)	11.3	7.8	7.2	1.9	trace	0.0	0.0	0.0	0.0	0.1	4.1	11.0	43.4
Days With ≥ 1.0" Snow Depth	29	27	19	2	0	0	0	0	0	0	5	24	106

Sturgeon Bay Exp. Farm *Door County*   Elevation: 652 ft.   Latitude: 44° 52' N   Longitude: 87° 20' W

	JAN	FEB	MAR	APR	MAY	JUN	JUL	AUG	SEP	OCT	NOV	DEC	YEAR
Mean Maximum Temp. (°F)	24.8	29.0	38.5	51.6	64.9	74.5	79.3	77.5	69.3	56.6	42.4	30.5	53.2
Mean Temp. (°F)	17.0	20.9	30.4	42.3	53.9	63.5	68.9	67.7	59.8	48.3	35.9	24.1	44.4
Mean Minimum Temp. (°F)	9.1	12.7	22.3	33.0	42.9	52.5	58.6	57.7	50.3	40.0	29.4	17.6	35.5
Extreme Maximum Temp. (°F)	49	54	70	85	90	96	99	96	92	84	74	59	99
Extreme Minimum Temp. (°F)	-29	-28	-13	8	25	32	39	39	27	20	-1	-19	-29
Days Maximum Temp. ≥ 90°F	0	0	0	0	0	1	1	1	0	0	0	0	3
Days Maximum Temp. ≤ 32°F	23	17	7	1	0	0	0	0	0	0	4	16	68
Days Minimum Temp. ≤ 32°F	31	28	26	14	3	0	0	0	0	5	19	29	155
Days Minimum Temp. ≤ 0°F	9	6	1	0	0	0	0	0	0	0	0	3	19
Heating Degree Days (base 65°F)	1,483	1,240	1,065	675	347	104	22	36	183	511	867	1,261	7,794
Cooling Degree Days (base 65°F)	0	0	0	0	0	12	69	148	131	35	0	0	395
Mean Precipitation (in.)	1.77	1.08	2.13	2.67	3.01	3.43	3.40	3.47	3.47	2.77	2.52	1.73	31.45
Days With ≥ 0.1" Precipitation	5	4	5	7	7	7	7	7	7	6	6	5	73
Days With ≥ 1.0" Precipitation	0	0	0	0	1	1	1	1	1	0	0	0	5
Mean Snowfall (in.)	15.5	7.9	7.9	2.2	trace	0.0	0.0	0.0	trace	trace	3.2	10.7	47.4
Days With ≥ 1.0" Snow Depth	28	26	21	4	0	0	0	0	0	0	4	18	101

Superior *Douglas County*   Elevation: 629 ft.   Latitude: 46° 42' N   Longitude: 92° 01' W

	JAN	FEB	MAR	APR	MAY	JUN	JUL	AUG	SEP	OCT	NOV	DEC	YEAR
Mean Maximum Temp. (°F)	20.2	25.9	34.6	46.8	58.3	68.3	76.4	74.0	65.9	53.7	38.1	25.3	49.0
Mean Temp. (°F)	10.6	16.5	26.6	38.5	49.0	58.4	66.3	65.0	56.6	45.1	30.8	16.8	40.0
Mean Minimum Temp. (°F)	1.0	7.1	18.6	30.1	39.6	48.3	56.1	56.1	47.3	36.4	23.5	8.4	31.0
Extreme Maximum Temp. (°F)	53	59	72	85	94	98	100	99	97	89	74	57	100
Extreme Minimum Temp. (°F)	-37	-37	-19	0	22	21	40	35	24	12	-11	-32	-37
Days Maximum Temp. ≥ 90°F	0	0	0	0	0	1	2	1	0	0	0	0	4
Days Maximum Temp. ≤ 32°F	27	19	12	1	0	0	0	0	0	0	9	22	90
Days Minimum Temp. ≤ 32°F	31	28	29	18	3	0	0	0	1	9	24	30	173
Days Minimum Temp. ≤ 0°F	16	10	2	0	0	0	0	0	0	0	1	10	39
Heating Degree Days (base 65°F)	1,683	1,365	1,183	790	495	220	62	78	263	610	1,019	1,488	9,256
Cooling Degree Days (base 65°F)	0	0	0	0	5	29	112	95	19	0	0	0	260
Mean Precipitation (in.)	1.00	0.74	1.85	2.19	3.15	3.96	4.28	4.02	4.23	2.49	2.01	0.94	30.86
Days With ≥ 0.1" Precipitation	3	2	4	5	7	8	7	7	7	6	5	3	64
Days With ≥ 1.0" Precipitation	0	0	0	0	1	1	1	1	1	0	0	0	5
Mean Snowfall (in.)	13.9	7.5	8.3	2.3	trace	0.0	0.0	0.0	0.0	0.3	7.7	10.9	50.9
Days With ≥ 1.0" Snow Depth	30	26	22	4	0	0	0	0	0	0	8	23	113

Trempealeau Dam 6 *Trempealeau County*   Elevation: 659 ft.   Latitude: 44° 00' N   Longitude: 91° 26' W

	JAN	FEB	MAR	APR	MAY	JUN	JUL	AUG	SEP	OCT	NOV	DEC	YEAR
Mean Maximum Temp. (°F)	23.8	30.6	42.0	58.0	70.4	79.3	83.3	80.6	71.9	59.8	42.0	28.9	55.9
Mean Temp. (°F)	14.4	20.9	32.8	47.4	59.4	68.6	72.8	70.2	61.6	49.8	34.3	21.0	46.1
Mean Minimum Temp. (°F)	5.1	11.1	23.5	36.9	48.3	57.8	62.2	59.8	51.3	39.7	26.5	13.0	36.3
Extreme Maximum Temp. (°F)	56	62	83	93	90	98	103	100	98	89	75	63	103
Extreme Minimum Temp. (°F)	-39	-41	-11	8	25	38	43	40	23	13	-9	-32	-41
Days Maximum Temp. ≥ 90°F	0	0	0	0	0	2	5	3	0	0	0	0	10
Days Maximum Temp. ≤ 32°F	22	14	6	0	0	0	0	0	0	0	6	18	66
Days Minimum Temp. ≤ 32°F	31	27	25	10	1	0	0	0	1	7	22	30	154
Days Minimum Temp. ≤ 0°F	12	7	2	0	0	0	0	0	0	0	0	6	27
Heating Degree Days (base 65°F)	1,563	1,241	992	527	207	35	6	18	153	470	915	1,358	7,485
Cooling Degree Days (base 65°F)	0	0	0	7	38	150	253	187	57	3	0	0	695
Mean Precipitation (in.)	1.06	0.86	2.01	3.23	3.78	3.68	4.32	4.51	3.96	2.49	2.17	1.09	33.16
Days With ≥ 0.1" Precipitation	3	2	4	7	7	7	7	8	7	5	5	3	65
Days With ≥ 1.0" Precipitation	0	0	0	1	1	1	1	1	1	1	0	0	7
Mean Snowfall (in.)	na	5.9	na	0.9	0.0	0.0	0.0	0.0	0.0	0.0	2.7	8.2	na
Days With ≥ 1.0" Snow Depth	na	na	7	1	0	0	0	0	0	0	2	11	na

Two Rivers *Manitowoc County*   Elevation: 597 ft.   Latitude: 44° 08' N   Longitude: 87° 34' W

	JAN	FEB	MAR	APR	MAY	JUN	JUL	AUG	SEP	OCT	NOV	DEC	YEAR
Mean Maximum Temp. (°F)	26.1	29.9	38.4	49.2	60.1	69.4	75.1	74.7	67.2	55.4	42.5	31.4	51.6
Mean Temp. (°F)	18.7	22.8	31.5	41.7	51.6	60.6	66.7	66.8	59.4	48.3	36.1	24.7	44.1
Mean Minimum Temp. (°F)	11.2	15.6	24.4	34.3	43.1	51.8	58.2	58.9	51.5	41.1	29.7	18.0	36.5
Extreme Maximum Temp. (°F)	52	57	71	82	89	95	97	94	91	86	73	62	97
Extreme Minimum Temp. (°F)	-25	-26	-3	12	24	36	44	42	29	19	-6	-21	-26
Days Maximum Temp. ≥ 90°F	0	0	0	0	0	0	1	0	0	0	0	0	1
Days Maximum Temp. ≤ 32°F	20	15	6	0	0	0	0	0	0	0	3	14	58
Days Minimum Temp. ≤ 32°F	30	27	24	10	1	0	0	0	0	4	18	28	142
Days Minimum Temp. ≤ 0°F	7	4	1	0	0	0	0	0	0	0	0	3	15
Heating Degree Days (base 65°F)	1,431	1,186	1,033	691	411	155	34	34	183	513	860	1,242	7,773
Cooling Degree Days (base 65°F)	0	0	0	0	2	36	96	109	22	0	0	0	265
Mean Precipitation (in.)	1.58	1.27	2.35	2.81	2.80	3.08	2.78	3.54	3.38	2.38	2.31	1.74	30.02
Days With ≥ 0.1" Precipitation	4	4	5	7	6	6	6	6	6	6	6	5	67
Days With ≥ 1.0" Precipitation	0	0	0	0	1	1	1	1	1	0	0	0	5
Mean Snowfall (in.)	10.3	6.4	6.0	1.0	trace	0.0	0.0	0.0	0.0	trace	2.0	7.2	32.9
Days With ≥ 1.0" Snow Depth	25	24	13	1	0	0	0	0	0	0	2	16	81

Viroqua 2 S *Vernon County*   Elevation: 1,158 ft.   Latitude: 43° 32' N   Longitude: 90° 52' W

	JAN	FEB	MAR	APR	MAY	JUN	JUL	AUG	SEP	OCT	NOV	DEC	YEAR
Mean Maximum Temp. (°F)	23.0	29.7	41.3	56.9	68.9	77.5	81.4	78.9	70.4	58.8	41.8	28.1	54.7
Mean Temp. (°F)	13.4	19.9	31.5	45.2	56.8	65.8	70.0	67.7	59.0	47.7	33.1	19.6	44.1
Mean Minimum Temp. (°F)	3.9	10.2	21.6	33.4	44.7	54.1	58.6	56.4	47.6	36.6	24.3	11.2	33.6
Extreme Maximum Temp. (°F)	54	60	83	89	90	97	98	100	95	89	72	63	100
Extreme Minimum Temp. (°F)	-34	-37	-15	-8	23	32	36	32	20	10	-17	-36	-37
Days Maximum Temp. ≥ 90°F	0	0	0	0	0	1	3	1	0	0	0	0	5
Days Maximum Temp. ≤ 32°F	24	15	7	0	0	0	0	0	0	0	6	20	72
Days Minimum Temp. ≤ 32°F	31	28	26	15	3	0	0	0	2	12	24	30	171
Days Minimum Temp. ≤ 0°F	13	8	2	0	0	0	0	0	0	0	1	7	31
Heating Degree Days (base 65°F)	1,600	1,269	1,033	595	274	70	20	39	216	533	951	1,403	8,003
Cooling Degree Days (base 65°F)	0	0	0	5	20	95	167	123	33	2	0	0	445
Mean Precipitation (in.)	0.85	0.73	1.56	3.47	3.52	3.79	4.99	4.52	3.74	2.34	2.03	17.79	49.33
Days With ≥ 0.1" Precipitation	3	2	4	7	8	7	7	7	6	6	5	3	65
Days With ≥ 1.0" Precipitation	0	0	0	1	1	1	2	1	1	0	1	0	8
Mean Snowfall (in.)	11.8	6.7	6.3	2.5	0.0	0.0	0.0	0.0	0.0	0.5	4.7	9.3	41.8
Days With ≥ 1.0" Snow Depth	26	22	12	2	0	0	0	0	0	0	5	22	89

Washington Island *Door County*   Elevation: 610 ft.   Latitude: 45° 22' N   Longitude: 86° 56' W

	JAN	FEB	MAR	APR	MAY	JUN	JUL	AUG	SEP	OCT	NOV	DEC	YEAR
Mean Maximum Temp. (°F)	25.4	28.6	37.1	48.4	60.8	69.8	76.1	75.2	67.0	55.4	42.4	31.1	51.4
Mean Temp. (°F)	17.8	20.1	28.8	39.5	50.5	59.8	66.5	66.0	58.4	47.8	36.0	25.0	43.0
Mean Minimum Temp. (°F)	9.9	11.7	20.5	30.6	40.1	49.7	56.9	56.7	49.8	40.2	29.7	18.8	34.6
Extreme Maximum Temp. (°F)	47	52	65	76	87	92	94	93	87	77	71	57	94
Extreme Minimum Temp. (°F)	-27	-26	-15	2	21	29	35	37	26	18	2	-21	-27
Days Maximum Temp. ≥ 90°F	0	0	0	0	0	0	0	0	0	0	0	0	0
Days Maximum Temp. ≤ 32°F	23	17	8	1	0	0	0	0	0	0	3	15	67
Days Minimum Temp. ≤ 32°F	31	28	28	17	5	0	0	0	1	5	19	29	163
Days Minimum Temp. ≤ 0°F	7	6	1	0	0	0	0	0	0	0	0	2	16
Heating Degree Days (base 65°F)	1,457	1,262	1,115	758	445	172	39	50	209	526	862	1,235	8,130
Cooling Degree Days (base 65°F)	0	0	0	0	2	27	100	98	22	0	0	0	249
Mean Precipitation (in.)	1.56	0.81	1.63	2.24	2.68	3.13	3.03	3.24	3.36	2.87	2.43	1.45	28.43
Days With ≥ 0.1" Precipitation	5	3	4	5	6	6	6	6	7	6	6	5	65
Days With ≥ 1.0" Precipitation	0	0	0	0	0	1	1	1	1	1	0	0	5
Mean Snowfall (in.)	15.5	8.4	9.8	2.8	0.2	0.0	0.0	0.0	0.0	0.1	4.0	11.6	52.4
Days With ≥ 1.0" Snow Depth	19	14	13	3	0	0	0	0	0	0	3	10	62

Watertown *Jefferson County*   Elevation: 823 ft.   Latitude: 43° 11' N   Longitude: 88° 44' W

	JAN	FEB	MAR	APR	MAY	JUN	JUL	AUG	SEP	OCT	NOV	DEC	YEAR
Mean Maximum Temp. (°F)	25.6	30.8	42.4	56.8	70.1	79.7	83.3	80.9	72.9	60.5	44.4	31.4	56.6
Mean Temp. (°F)	17.0	22.3	33.6	46.5	58.6	68.1	72.4	70.0	61.8	50.2	36.5	23.7	46.7
Mean Minimum Temp. (°F)	8.4	13.6	24.8	36.1	47.0	56.5	61.4	59.1	50.7	39.7	28.6	15.9	36.8
Extreme Maximum Temp. (°F)	57	64	81	91	94	101	101	102	96	89	74	64	102
Extreme Minimum Temp. (°F)	-31	-27	-5	10	25	35	43	41	26	16	-6	-27	-31
Days Maximum Temp. ≥ 90°F	0	0	0	0	1	3	5	3	1	0	0	0	13
Days Maximum Temp. ≤ 32°F	21	14	5	0	0	0	0	0	0	0	4	15	59
Days Minimum Temp. ≤ 32°F	30	27	24	10	1	0	0	0	1	7	20	29	149
Days Minimum Temp. ≤ 0°F	10	6	1	0	0	0	0	0	0	0	0	4	21
Heating Degree Days (base 65°F)	1,483	1,201	968	555	236	46	7	20	151	459	849	1,274	7,249
Cooling Degree Days (base 65°F)	0	0	0	7	37	142	236	179	58	4	0	0	663
Mean Precipitation (in.)	1.31	1.18	2.14	3.11	2.99	4.18	4.41	4.36	3.76	2.62	2.38	1.71	34.15
Days With ≥ 0.1" Precipitation	4	3	5	7	7	6	7	7	6	5	5	4	66
Days With ≥ 1.0" Precipitation	0	0	0	1	0	1	1	1	1	0	0	0	5
Mean Snowfall (in.)	12.4	7.4	5.3	1.8	0.2	0.0	0.0	0.0	trace	0.1	2.8	9.0	39.0
Days With ≥ 1.0" Snow Depth	21	18	8	1	0	0	0	0	0	0	3	14	65

Waukesha *Waukesha County*   Elevation: 830 ft.   Latitude: 43° 01' N   Longitude: 88° 14' W

	JAN	FEB	MAR	APR	MAY	JUN	JUL	AUG	SEP	OCT	NOV	DEC	YEAR
Mean Maximum Temp. (°F)	25.8	32.1	42.6	56.1	69.2	78.8	83.3	80.5	72.6	60.4	44.5	32.5	56.5
Mean Temp. (°F)	18.1	24.5	34.3	46.4	58.3	67.9	72.9	70.7	62.6	51.0	37.1	25.5	47.4
Mean Minimum Temp. (°F)	10.4	16.9	25.9	36.7	47.4	56.9	62.5	60.8	52.5	41.5	29.5	18.4	38.3
Extreme Maximum Temp. (°F)	58	66	82	91	93	100	109	98	97	88	74	65	109
Extreme Minimum Temp. (°F)	-27	-28	-5	7	26	35	44	40	29	19	-7	-23	-28
Days Maximum Temp. ≥ 90°F	0	0	0	0	1	3	6	3	1	0	0	0	14
Days Maximum Temp. ≤ 32°F	21	14	6	0	0	0	0	0	0	0	4	14	59
Days Minimum Temp. ≤ 32°F	30	26	24	9	1	0	0	0	0	4	19	28	141
Days Minimum Temp. ≤ 0°F	8	4	0	0	0	0	0	0	0	0	0	3	15
Heating Degree Days (base 65°F)	1,449	1,137	946	560	241	53	7	16	137	434	833	1,219	7,032
Cooling Degree Days (base 65°F)	0	0	0	6	37	156	271	215	75	7	0	0	767
Mean Precipitation (in.)	1.54	1.36	2.22	3.63	2.98	3.85	3.79	4.60	3.52	2.63	2.57	1.86	34.55
Days With ≥ 0.1" Precipitation	4	4	5	7	7	6	7	7	6	5	5	5	68
Days With ≥ 1.0" Precipitation	0	0	0	1	1	1	1	1	1	1	0	0	7
Mean Snowfall (in.)	12.8	7.7	7.4	2.7	trace	0.0	0.0	0.0	0.0	0.1	3.0	9.5	43.2
Days With ≥ 1.0" Snow Depth	23	19	7	1	0	0	0	0	0	0	3	16	69

Waupaca *Waupaca County*   Elevation: 839 ft.   Latitude: 44° 21' N   Longitude: 89° 04' W

	JAN	FEB	MAR	APR	MAY	JUN	JUL	AUG	SEP	OCT	NOV	DEC	YEAR
Mean Maximum Temp. (°F)	24.8	30.5	41.0	56.1	69.4	78.2	82.2	79.6	71.3	59.1	43.0	29.8	55.4
Mean Temp. (°F)	15.7	21.1	31.8	45.4	57.6	66.6	71.2	68.8	60.4	48.7	34.8	21.8	45.3
Mean Minimum Temp. (°F)	6.6	11.6	22.5	34.6	45.7	54.9	60.1	57.9	49.5	38.3	26.5	13.7	35.1
Extreme Maximum Temp. (°F)	58	60	84	92	92	99	105	100	95	89	75	64	105
Extreme Minimum Temp. (°F)	-32	-30	-10	8	20	33	42	39	24	15	-8	-28	-32
Days Maximum Temp. ≥ 90°F	0	0	0	0	0	3	4	2	0	0	0	0	9
Days Maximum Temp. ≤ 32°F	23	15	6	0	0	0	0	0	0	0	5	18	67
Days Minimum Temp. ≤ 32°F	31	27	26	12	2	0	0	0	1	8	22	30	159
Days Minimum Temp. ≤ 0°F	11	7	1	0	0	0	0	0	0	0	0	5	24
Heating Degree Days (base 65°F)	1,523	1,235	1,024	589	259	65	13	29	180	501	901	1,334	7,653
Cooling Degree Days (base 65°F)	0	0	0	6	33	117	205	155	47	2	0	0	565
Mean Precipitation (in.)	1.34	1.02	2.25	2.99	3.85	3.74	4.40	4.05	3.69	2.48	2.41	1.35	33.57
Days With ≥ 0.1" Precipitation	4	3	5	6	7	7	7	7	6	5	5	4	66
Days With ≥ 1.0" Precipitation	0	0	0	0	1	1	1	1	1	0	1	0	6
Mean Snowfall (in.)	12.8	7.0	9.4	2.4	0.1	0.0	0.0	0.0	0.0	0.2	4.4	10.8	47.1
Days With ≥ 1.0" Snow Depth	28	25	17	2	0	0	0	0	0	0	5	21	98

Wausau Municipal Airport *Marathon County*   Elevation: 1,197 ft.   Latitude: 44° 55' N   Longitude: 89° 38' W

	JAN	FEB	MAR	APR	MAY	JUN	JUL	AUG	SEP	OCT	NOV	DEC	YEAR
Mean Maximum Temp. (°F)	21.9	28.1	38.9	54.3	67.9	76.3	80.4	77.7	68.3	55.9	39.4	26.6	53.0
Mean Temp. (°F)	12.8	18.6	29.5	43.8	56.5	65.3	69.9	67.6	58.3	46.7	32.1	19.0	43.4
Mean Minimum Temp. (°F)	3.7	9.1	20.1	33.3	45.0	54.2	59.4	57.4	48.3	37.5	24.8	11.3	33.7
Extreme Maximum Temp. (°F)	52	55	79	88	94	97	102	99	94	91	73	61	102
Extreme Minimum Temp. (°F)	-36	-33	-15	4	23	35	40	39	25	16	-11	-26	-36
Days Maximum Temp. ≥ 90°F	0	0	0	0	0	2	3	1	0	0	0	0	6
Days Maximum Temp. ≤ 32°F	25	17	8	1	0	0	0	0	0	0	8	22	81
Days Minimum Temp. ≤ 32°F	31	27	27	14	2	0	0	0	1	9	24	30	165
Days Minimum Temp. ≤ 0°F	13	8	2	0	0	0	0	0	0	0	0	7	30
Heating Degree Days (base 65°F)	1,614	1,304	1,093	632	284	80	19	39	227	562	979	1,422	8,255
Cooling Degree Days (base 65°F)	0	0	0	4	25	100	177	132	33	1	0	0	472
Mean Precipitation (in.)	1.07	0.88	1.94	2.80	3.68	4.02	4.24	4.36	4.06	2.81	2.22	1.35	33.43
Days With ≥ 0.1" Precipitation	3	3	5	6	7	7	7	7	8	6	5	4	68
Days With ≥ 1.0" Precipitation	0	0	0	0	1	1	1	1	1	0	1	0	6
Mean Snowfall (in.)	13.3	8.6	10.7	3.7	0.1	trace	0.0	trace	trace	1.0	6.9	12.9	57.2
Days With ≥ 1.0" Snow Depth	31	27	20	3	0	0	0	0	0	0	6	26	113

West Bend *Washington County*   Elevation: 938 ft.   Latitude: 43° 22' N   Longitude: 88° 05' W

	JAN	FEB	MAR	APR	MAY	JUN	JUL	AUG	SEP	OCT	NOV	DEC	YEAR
Mean Maximum Temp. (°F)	25.8	30.7	41.0	54.7	67.8	77.3	81.5	79.0	71.2	59.2	43.9	31.5	55.3
Mean Temp. (°F)	17.9	22.8	32.7	44.7	56.0	65.5	70.5	68.4	60.5	49.3	36.1	24.2	45.7
Mean Minimum Temp. (°F)	9.9	14.9	24.3	34.7	44.2	53.7	59.4	57.8	49.7	39.4	28.3	16.9	36.1
Extreme Maximum Temp. (°F)	57	63	82	88	91	100	103	105	95	87	74	64	105
Extreme Minimum Temp. (°F)	-30	-25	-11	2	21	33	37	38	25	14	-8	-24	-30
Days Maximum Temp. ≥ 90°F	0	0	0	0	0	2	4	2	0	0	0	0	8
Days Maximum Temp. ≤ 32°F	21	15	6	1	0	0	0	0	0	0	4	15	62
Days Minimum Temp. ≤ 32°F	30	27	26	12	2	0	0	0	1	7	20	29	154
Days Minimum Temp. ≤ 0°F	9	5	1	0	0	0	0	0	0	0	0	4	19
Heating Degree Days (base 65°F)	1,456	1,185	995	608	300	79	17	32	174	483	860	1,258	7,447
Cooling Degree Days (base 65°F)	0	0	0	5	26	104	190	148	44	3	0	0	520
Mean Precipitation (in.)	1.47	1.07	1.98	3.06	2.96	3.77	3.95	4.02	3.58	2.61	2.49	1.68	32.64
Days With ≥ 0.1" Precipitation	5	3	5	7	6	7	7	7	6	6	6	4	69
Days With ≥ 1.0" Precipitation	0	0	0	1	1	1	1	1	1	0	0	0	6
Mean Snowfall (in.)	15.4	10.3	8.1	3.2	0.1	0.0	0.0	0.0	0.0	0.2	3.9	12.2	53.4
Days With ≥ 1.0" Snow Depth	26	22	12	1	0	0	0	0	0	0	3	18	82

Weyerhauser *Rusk County*   Elevation: 1,194 ft.   Latitude: 45° 25' N   Longitude: 91° 23' W

	JAN	FEB	MAR	APR	MAY	JUN	JUL	AUG	SEP	OCT	NOV	DEC	YEAR
Mean Maximum Temp. (°F)	21.4	28.9	40.8	57.2	70.4	77.6	81.1	79.0	70.0	57.8	39.6	26.1	54.2
Mean Temp. (°F)	10.3	17.2	29.3	44.0	56.2	64.2	68.3	66.1	57.6	45.6	30.3	16.4	42.1
Mean Minimum Temp. (°F)	-0.9	5.4	17.7	30.7	41.9	50.9	55.3	53.2	45.0	33.5	20.9	6.6	30.0
Extreme Maximum Temp. (°F)	51	56	81	88	92	96	100	100	96	87	71	58	100
Extreme Minimum Temp. (°F)	-39	-39	-17	2	18	22	37	25	20	8	-22	-32	-39
Days Maximum Temp. ≥ 90°F	0	0	0	0	0	1	3	2	0	0	0	0	6
Days Maximum Temp. ≤ 32°F	25	16	7	1	0	0	0	0	0	0	8	21	78
Days Minimum Temp. ≤ 32°F	31	28	28	18	6	1	0	0	3	15	26	31	187
Days Minimum Temp. ≤ 0°F	16	10	4	0	0	0	0	0	0	0	2	10	42
Heating Degree Days (base 65°F)	1,693	1,347	1,100	627	286	88	31	58	242	594	1,035	1,503	8,604
Cooling Degree Days (base 65°F)	0	0	0	3	17	77	138	104	25	1	0	0	365
Mean Precipitation (in.)	1.16	0.89	2.05	2.48	3.55	4.13	4.46	4.36	4.31	2.84	2.04	1.07	33.34
Days With ≥ 0.1" Precipitation	4	3	5	7	7	7	8	8	8	6	5	4	72
Days With ≥ 1.0" Precipitation	0	0	0	0	1	1	1	1	1	1	0	0	6
Mean Snowfall (in.)	12.9	7.3	9.1	1.9	trace	0.0	0.0	0.0	0.0	0.5	7.3	9.2	48.2
Days With ≥ 1.0" Snow Depth	30	27	21	3	0	0	0	0	0	0	7	24	112

Whitewater *Jefferson County*   Elevation: 872 ft.   Latitude: 42° 51' N   Longitude: 88° 44' W

	JAN	FEB	MAR	APR	MAY	JUN	JUL	AUG	SEP	OCT	NOV	DEC	YEAR
Mean Maximum Temp. (°F)	26.4	31.9	43.5	57.8	70.7	79.9	83.5	81.0	73.7	61.6	45.5	32.5	57.3
Mean Temp. (°F)	17.9	23.2	34.1	46.6	58.3	67.7	71.7	69.4	61.7	50.3	36.9	24.5	46.9
Mean Minimum Temp. (°F)	9.3	14.4	24.7	35.3	45.8	55.4	59.9	57.8	49.6	39.0	28.3	16.5	36.3
Extreme Maximum Temp. (°F)	58	66	82	90	93	99	100	100	97	89	75	64	100
Extreme Minimum Temp. (°F)	-27	-27	-6	0	21	30	41	37	26	13	-7	-24	-27
Days Maximum Temp. ≥ 90°F	0	0	0	0	0	3	6	3	1	0	0	0	13
Days Maximum Temp. ≤ 32°F	20	14	5	0	0	0	0	0	0	0	3	14	56
Days Minimum Temp. ≤ 32°F	30	27	25	12	2	0	0	0	1	8	20	29	154
Days Minimum Temp. ≤ 0°F	10	6	1	0	0	0	0	0	0	0	0	4	21
Heating Degree Days (base 65°F)	1,454	1,175	950	554	244	53	12	30	155	454	837	1,249	7,167
Cooling Degree Days (base 65°F)	0	0	0	7	36	134	217	172	58	4	0	0	628
Mean Precipitation (in.)	1.24	1.08	2.03	3.37	3.15	3.72	4.02	4.48	3.48	2.65	2.48	1.55	33.25
Days With ≥ 0.1" Precipitation	4	3	5	7	7	6	6	7	6	5	5	4	65
Days With ≥ 1.0" Precipitation	0	0	0	1	1	1	1	1	1	1	0	0	7
Mean Snowfall (in.)	9.7	6.1	4.2	1.3	trace	0.0	0.0	0.0	0.0	trace	1.6	7.6	30.5
Days With ≥ 1.0" Snow Depth	22	17	7	1	0	0	0	0	0	0	2	13	62

Willow Reservoir *Oneida County*   Elevation: 1,558 ft.   Latitude: 45° 42' N   Longitude: 89° 51' W

	JAN	FEB	MAR	APR	MAY	JUN	JUL	AUG	SEP	OCT	NOV	DEC	YEAR
Mean Maximum Temp. (°F)	18.8	25.4	35.5	50.5	65.1	73.1	77.4	75.1	65.8	53.3	37.0	24.3	50.1
Mean Temp. (°F)	8.0	13.4	24.1	39.0	52.5	61.5	65.8	63.5	54.7	43.3	29.0	15.3	39.2
Mean Minimum Temp. (°F)	-2.9	1.4	12.6	27.5	39.7	49.8	54.3	51.8	43.5	33.4	21.0	6.3	28.2
Extreme Maximum Temp. (°F)	51	59	70	87	88	93	97	94	93	85	71	59	97
Extreme Minimum Temp. (°F)	-45	-43	-29	-14	16	27	33	31	18	7	-22	-35	-45
Days Maximum Temp. ≥ 90°F	0	0	0	0	0	0	1	0	0	0	0	0	1
Days Maximum Temp. ≤ 32°F	28	20	11	2	0	0	0	0	0	1	10	24	96
Days Minimum Temp. ≤ 32°F	31	28	28	22	7	1	0	0	4	15	26	30	192
Days Minimum Temp. ≤ 0°F	17	14	7	0	0	0	0	0	0	0	2	10	50
Heating Degree Days (base 65°F)	1,766	1,452	1,263	774	393	146	57	99	320	665	1,073	1,534	9,542
Cooling Degree Days (base 65°F)	0	0	0	*0*	1	8	47	82	61	14	0	0	*213*
Mean Precipitation (in.)	1.09	0.76	1.57	2.17	3.24	3.89	3.80	4.26	4.18	2.61	2.04	1.13	30.74
Days With ≥ 0.1" Precipitation	4	3	4	6	7	8	8	7	8	6	4	4	69
Days With ≥ 1.0" Precipitation	0	0	0	0	1	1	1	1	1	1	0	0	6
Mean Snowfall (in.)	13.6	7.1	*9.1*	3.1	0.4	0.0	0.0	0.0	trace	0.6	*4.6*	10.5	*49.0*
Days With ≥ 1.0" Snow Depth	na	na	na	na	0	0	0	0	0	0	0	na	na	na

Wisconsin Dells *Columbia County*   Elevation: 833 ft.   Latitude: 43° 37' N   Longitude: 89° 46' W

	JAN	FEB	MAR	APR	MAY	JUN	JUL	AUG	SEP	OCT	NOV	DEC	YEAR
Mean Maximum Temp. (°F)	24.6	31.0	42.2	56.6	69.6	78.0	81.7	79.3	70.9	59.2	42.8	30.4	55.5
Mean Temp. (°F)	15.0	20.6	32.1	45.0	57.3	66.2	70.5	68.2	59.7	48.1	34.0	21.7	44.9
Mean Minimum Temp. (°F)	5.5	10.2	21.8	33.3	44.9	54.4	59.3	57.0	48.5	36.8	25.1	13.0	34.2
Extreme Maximum Temp. (°F)	56	64	84	91	93	98	101	98	94	87	75	63	101
Extreme Minimum Temp. (°F)	-36	-37	-13	5	22	31	41	37	25	9	-11	-24	-37
Days Maximum Temp. ≥ 90°F	0	0	0	0	0	2	3	2	0	0	0	0	7
Days Maximum Temp. ≤ 32°F	22	15	6	0	0	0	0	0	0	0	5	17	65
Days Minimum Temp. ≤ 32°F	30	27	26	15	3	0	0	0	1	11	23	30	166
Days Minimum Temp. ≤ 0°F	12	8	2	0	0	0	0	0	0	0	1	6	29
Heating Degree Days (base 65°F)	1,545	1,242	1,014	600	263	65	15	35	197	522	925	1,337	7,760
Cooling Degree Days (base 65°F)	0	0	0	6	30	111	197	146	44	3	0	0	537
Mean Precipitation (in.)	0.94	0.95	2.09	3.43	3.54	4.05	4.07	4.41	3.57	2.37	2.01	1.19	32.62
Days With ≥ 0.1" Precipitation	3	3	5	7	7	7	7	7	6	5	4	4	65
Days With ≥ 1.0" Precipitation	0	0	0	1	1	1	1	1	1	0	0	0	6
Mean Snowfall (in.)	11.8	6.8	6.7	2.5	trace	0.0	0.0	0.0	0.0	0.4	4.1	9.0	41.3
Days With ≥ 1.0" Snow Depth	23	22	11	1	0	0	0	0	0	0	3	18	78

Wisconsin Rapids *Wood County*   Elevation: 1,040 ft.   Latitude: 44° 23' N   Longitude: 89° 48' W

	JAN	FEB	MAR	APR	MAY	JUN	JUL	AUG	SEP	OCT	NOV	DEC	YEAR
Mean Maximum Temp. (°F)	23.2	29.9	40.8	56.3	69.7	78.3	82.3	79.6	70.3	57.8	41.4	28.4	54.8
Mean Temp. (°F)	13.4	19.3	30.3	44.4	56.9	65.9	70.5	67.9	58.8	46.9	32.5	19.8	43.9
Mean Minimum Temp. (°F)	3.7	8.7	19.8	32.4	44.0	53.4	58.5	56.2	47.2	35.9	23.6	11.2	32.9
Extreme Maximum Temp. (°F)	57	61	81	92	93	100	107	103	96	91	74	64	107
Extreme Minimum Temp. (°F)	-38	-32	-16	2	22	34	41	34	21	9	-11	-26	-38
Days Maximum Temp. ≥ 90°F	0	0	0	0	1	3	5	2	1	0	0	0	12
Days Maximum Temp. ≤ 32°F	24	16	7	0	0	0	0	0	0	0	6	20	73
Days Minimum Temp. ≤ 32°F	31	28	28	16	3	0	0	0	2	12	25	30	175
Days Minimum Temp. ≤ 0°F	13	9	3	0	0	0	0	0	0	0	1	8	34
Heating Degree Days (base 65°F)	1,594	1,284	1,068	617	277	72	18	38	219	557	968	1,395	8,107
Cooling Degree Days (base 65°F)	0	0	0	5	28	107	192	139	37	1	0	0	509
Mean Precipitation (in.)	1.14	1.00	2.03	2.94	3.54	3.60	4.20	4.20	3.64	2.59	2.11	1.38	32.37
Days With ≥ 0.1" Precipitation	4	3	5	7	7	7	7	7	7	6	5	4	69
Days With ≥ 1.0" Precipitation	0	0	0	0	1	1	1	1	1	0	0	0	5
Mean Snowfall (in.)	12.0	8.5	10.6	2.6	trace	0.0	0.0	0.0	0.0	0.3	3.7	*9.6*	*47.3*
Days With ≥ 1.0" Snow Depth	27	25	15	1	0	0	0	0	0	0	5	*22*	*95*

Note: See Appendix D for explanation of data.

WYOMING

PHYSICAL FEATURES AND GENERAL CLIMATE. Wyoming is a name of Delaware Indian origin and is variously interpreted as "large plains" or "end of the plains." Thus, the name describes the State's outstanding topographic feature. There are, of course, several mountain ranges, but the mountains themselves cover less area than the high plains. The topography and variations in elevation make it difficult to divide the State into homogeneous, climatological areas.

The mean elevation is about 6,700 feet above sea level. Even excluding the mountain ranges, the average elevation over the southern portion is well over 6,000 feet, while much of the northern portion is some 2,500 feet lower. The lowest point, 3,125 feet, is near the northeast corner where the Belle Fourche River crosses the State line to South Dakota. The highest point is Gannett Peak at 13,785 feet, which is part of the Wind River Range in the west-central portion. Since the mountain ranges lie in a general north to south direction, they are perpendicular to the prevailing westerlies. Therefore, the mountain ranges provide effective barriers which force the air currents moving in from the Pacific Ocean to drop much of their moisture. It naturally follows that the mountain ranges and the western slopes receive the greatest amount of precipitation. Outside of the mountains, the State is considered semiarid.

The Continental Divide splits the State from near the northwest corner to a point along the southern border about midway. This leaves most of the drainage areas to the east. Precipitation drains into three great river systems: the Columbia; the Colorado; and the Missouri. The Snake with its tributaries in the northwest portion flows to the Columbia; the Green River draining most of the Southwest portion joins the Colorado; the Yellowstone, Wind River, Big Horn, Tongue, and Powder drainage areas cover most of the north portion and flow northward into Montana, entering the Missouri there; the Belle Fourche, Cheyenne, and Niobrara covering the east-central portion flow eastward; and the Platte (mostly North Platte), draining all of the southeast, flows eastward over Nebraska. There is a relatively small area along the southwest border that is drained by the Bear going to the Great Salt Lake. In the south-central portion west of Rawlins, there is an area called the Great Divide Basin which extends from near Rawlins to nearly 100 miles westward and about 50 miles in a north to south direction. Part of this is often referred to as the Red Desert. There is no drainage from the Great Divide Basin. Precipitation here, which averages only seven to 10 inches annually, follows usually dry creekbeds to ponds or small lakes, also often dry.

Rapid runoff from heavy thunderstorm rains causes flash flooding on the headwater streams of the State, and when the time of these storms coincides with the melting of the snowpack, the flooding is intensified.

PRECIPITATION. Like the other states in the western part of the country, precipitation varies considerably from one location to another. The period of maximum precipitation occurs in the spring and early summer for most of the State. It is greater over the mountain ranges and usually at the higher elevations, although elevation alone is not the only influence. Mountain ranges block the flow of moisture laden air from the east as well as from the west. During the summer months showers are quite frequent but light and often amount to only a few hundredths of an inch. Occasionally there will be some very heavy rain associated with thunderstorms covering a few square miles. There are usually several local storms each year with one to two inches of rain in a 24-hour period. On rarer occasions 24-hour amounts range from three to five inches.

SNOWFALL. Snow falls frequently from November through May. Generally snowfall at lower elevations is light to moderate. About five times a year on the average, weather stations at the lower elevations will have snowfall exceeding five inches. Wind will frequently accompany or follow a snowstorm and pile the snow into drifts several feet deep, often causing blizzard or near blizzard conditions in parts of the State for a few hours; however, it is uncommon for a severe blizzard to last long.

The total annual amount of snow varies considerably over the State as does the rainfall. At the lower elevations of the east portion, the range is mostly from 60 to 70 inches annually. Over the drier southwest portion, amounts vary from 45 to 55 inches at most places. Snow is very light in the Big Horn Basin with annual averages from 15 to 20 inches over the lower portion to 30 to 40 inches on the sides of the Basin where elevations range from 5,000 to 6,000 feet. The mountains receive a great deal more and over the higher ranges annual amounts are well over 200 inches.

TEMPERATURES. Because of the elevation, Wyoming has a relatively cool climate. Above the 6,000-foot level the temperature rarely exceeds 100°F. The warmest parts of the State are the lower portion of the Big Horn Basin, the lower elevations of the central and northeast portions, and along the east border. With increasing elevation, average values drop rapidly. A few places in the mountains, at about 9,000-feet level, show an average high in July close to 70°F. Summer nights are almost invariably cool, even though daytime readings may be quite high at times. For most places outside of the mountains, the mean low temperature in July is in the range from 50 to 60°F. The mountains and high valleys are much cooler, with average lows in the middle of the summer in the 30s and low 40s with occasional drops below freezing.

In the wintertime it is characteristic to have rapid and frequent changes between mild and cold spells. Usually there are less than 10 cold waves during a winter, and frequently less than half that number for most of the State. The majority of cold waves move southward on the east side of the Divide, with only an occasional cold wave for the west side. Sometimes only the northeast portion will be affected by the cold air as it slides on to the east over the plains. Many of the cold waves are not accompanied by enough snow to cause severe conditions. Numerous valleys provide ideal pockets for the collection of cold air drainage at night. Protecting mountain ranges prevent the wind from stirring the air, and the colder heavier air continues to deepen in valleys, often sending readings well below zero. It is common to have temperatures in the valleys considerably lower than on the nearby mountain sides. Except for the occasional cold waves and an infrequent blizzard, the winters are not severe. Even January, the coldest month, has occasional mild periods when maximum readings will reach the 50s and 60s.

Early freezes in the fall and late in the spring are characteristic of the Wyoming climate. This has the effect of seemingly long winters and short growing seasons.

SUNSHINE. For most of the State, sunshine ranges from approximately 60 percent of the possible amount during the winter to about 75 percent during the summer. Mountain areas receive less, and in the wintertime the estimated amount over the northwestern mountains is about 45 percent. Although the average amount of sunshine is less in winter, the low point on the annual variations is not during the coldest month (January or February). One low period of sunshine comes in November or December, and another in April or May. These periods of low sunshine correspond fairly closely to the periods of greatest temperature changes, i.e., in the late fall when average temperatures are dropping rapidly and in the spring when the average is climbing rapidly. To be sure, sunshine will not be much higher during the coldest months, but cold air masses are apt to be more stable at that time, and frontal activity is followed by a slightly longer period of sunshine. In the summertime when sunshine is greatest—not only in time but also intensity—it is characteristic for the forenoons to be mostly clear. Cumulus clouds develop nearly every day and frequently blot out the sun for a portion of the afternoons. Because of the altitude—providing less atmosphere for the sun's rays to penetrate—and because of the very small amount of fog, haze, and smoke, the intensity of sunshine is unusually high.

OTHER CLIMATIC ELEMENTS. Hailstorms are the most destructive type of local storm for this State. Tornadoes occur over Wyoming, but they are small and have a short duration. Many of them touch the ground for only a few minutes before receding into the clouds. The season for these local storms extends from April through September. June has the greatest number on the average, with May next.

Wind is an important factor of the Wyoming climate. This is largely due to the high elevation and the enormous stretches of rolling plains. Most of Wyoming is quite windy, and during the colder months from November through March there are frequent periods when the wind reaches 30 to 40 m.p.h., with occasional gusts much higher. Prevailing directions in the different localities vary from west-southwest through west to northwest. In many localities winds are so strong and constant from those directions that trees show a definite lean toward the east or southeast.

The average relative humidity is quite low and, while this has a distinct advantage in providing comfortable summer weather, it is related to the rather low amount of moisture. During the warmer part of the summer days, the average drops to about 25 to 30 percent. Late at night when the temperature is lowest the humidity will generally be up to 65 to 75 percent. Low relative humidity, high percentage of sunshine, and rather high average winds add their influence in causing a large amount of evaporation.

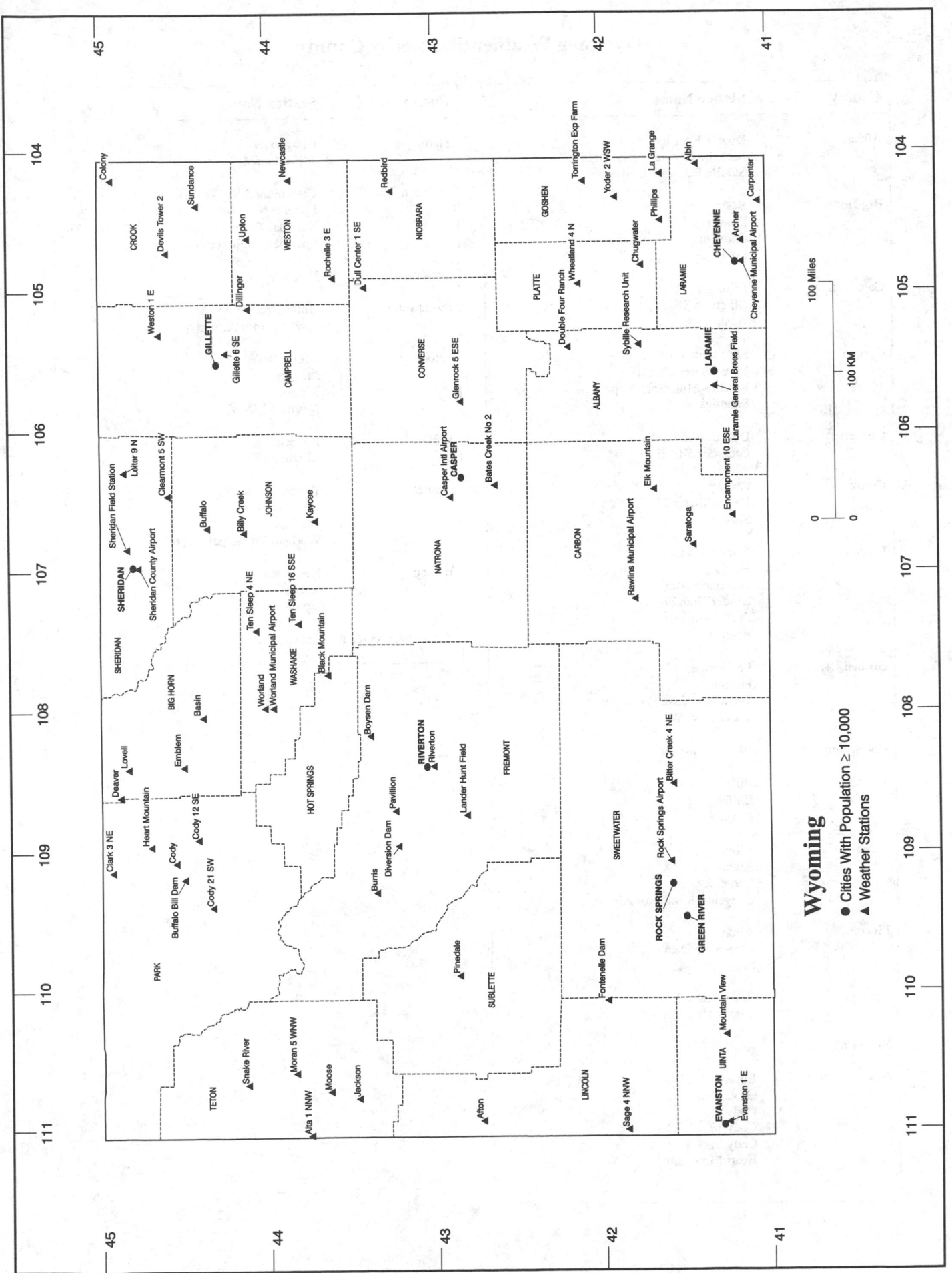

Wyoming

- ● Cities With Population ≥ 10,000
- ▲ Weather Stations

Wyoming Weather Stations by County

County	Station Name
Albany	Double Four Ranch
	Laramie General Brees Field
	Sybille Research Unit
Big Horn	Basin
	Deaver
	Emblem
	Lovell
Campbell	Dillinger
	Gillette 6 SE
	Weston 1 E
Carbon	Elk Mountain
	Encampment 10 ESE
	Rawlins Municipal Airport
	Saratoga
Converse	Dull Center 1 SE
	Glenrock 5 ESE
Crook	Colony
	Devils Tower 2
	Sundance
Fremont	Boysen Dam
	Burris
	Diversion Dam
	Lander Hunt Field
	Pavillion
	Riverton
Goshen	La Grange
	Phillips
	Torrington Exp. Farm
	Yoder 2 WSW
Hot Springs	Black Mountain
Johnson	Billy Creek
	Buffalo
	Kaycee
Laramie	Albin
	Archer
	Carpenter
	Cheyenne Municipal Airport
Lincoln	Afton
	Fontenelle Dam
	Sage 4 NNW
Natrona	Bates Creek 2
	Casper Int'l Airport
Niobrara	Redbird
Park	Buffalo Bill Dam
	Clark 3 NE
	Cody
	Cody 12 SE
	Cody 21 SW
	Heart Mountain

County	Station Name
Platte	Chugwater
	Wheatland 4 N
Sheridan	Clearmont 5 SW
	Leiter 9 N
	Sheridan County Airport
	Sheridan Field Station
Sublette	Pinedale
Sweetwater	Bitter Creek 4 NE
	Rock Springs Airport
Teton	Alta 1 NNW
	Jackson
	Moose
	Moran 5 WNW
Uinta	Evanston 1 E
	Mountain View
Washakie	Ten Sleep 16 SSE
	Ten Sleep 4 NE
	Worland
	Worland Municipal Airport
Weston	Newcastle
	Rochelle 3 E
	Upton
Yellowstone National	Snake River

Wyoming Weather Stations by City

City	Station Name	Miles
Casper	Bates Creek 2	14
	Casper Int'l Airport	9
Cheyenne	Archer	8
	Cheyenne Municipal Airport	0
Evanston	Evanston 1 E	1
Gillette	Gillette 6 SE	5
Laramie	Laramie General Brees Field	5
Riverton	Riverton	0
Rock Springs	Rock Springs Airport	8
Sheridan	Sheridan County Airport	2
	Sheridan Field Station	7

Note: Miles is the distance between the geographic center of the city and the weather station.

Wyoming Weather Stations by Elevation

Feet	Station Name
7,381	Encampment 10 ESE
7,263	Elk Mountain
7,263	Laramie General Brees Field
7,171	Pinedale
6,879	Snake River
6,824	Evanston 1 E
6,797	Moran 5 WNW
6,797	Mountain View
6,788	Saratoga
6,738	Rock Springs Airport
6,735	Rawlins Municipal Airport
6,719	Bitter Creek 4 NE
6,479	Fontenelle Dam
6,469	Moose
6,427	Alta 1 NNW
6,227	Jackson
6,207	Afton
6,207	Sage 4 NNW
6,197	Double Four Ranch
6,125	Cheyenne Municipal Airport
6,118	Burris
6,099	Sybille Research Unit
6,007	Archer
6,007	Bates Creek 2
5,839	Cody 21 SW
5,633	Black Mountain
5,574	Diversion Dam
5,554	Lander Hunt Field
5,439	Pavillion
5,387	Carpenter
5,344	Albin
5,337	Casper Int'l Airport
5,301	Chugwater
5,246	Cody 12 SE
5,154	Buffalo Bill Dam
4,990	Cody
4,980	Phillips
4,973	Billy Creek
4,954	Riverton
4,947	Glenrock 5 ESE
4,809	Boysen Dam
4,799	Ten Sleep 4 NE
4,790	Heart Mountain
4,747	Sundance
4,691	Buffalo
4,678	Ten Sleep 16 SSE
4,658	Kaycee
4,639	Gillette 6 SE
4,635	Wheatland 4 N
4,589	La Grange
4,494	Rochelle 3 E
4,445	Emblem
4,412	Dull Center 1 SE
4,379	Newcastle
4,317	Upton

Feet	Station Name
4,307	Dillinger
4,288	Yoder 2 WSW
4,199	Leiter 9 N
4,169	Worland Municipal Airport
4,104	Deaver
4,097	Torrington Exp. Farm
4,087	Clark 3 NE
4,058	Worland
3,992	Clearmont 5 SW
3,963	Sheridan County Airport
3,887	Redbird
3,861	Devils Tower 2
3,835	Basin
3,835	Lovell
3,750	Sheridan Field Station
3,569	Colony
3,523	Weston 1 E

Casper Int'l Airport

Casper is located in the central portion of Wyoming in the North Platte River Valley at an elevation of about 5,300 feet. The country immediately surrounding Casper is mostly rolling and hilly with considerable flat prairie land in each direction except toward the south where Casper Mountain rises some 3,500 feet above the valley floor. The prairie land is used mainly for grazing.

The National Weather Service Office is located at Natrona County International Airport, some eight miles west-northwest of the Casper Post Office and about 200 feet higher in elevation.

The climate of Casper is semi-arid. Most of the air masses reaching this area move in from the Pacific and the mountains to the west are effective moisture barriers. About 70 percent of the annual precipitation occurs during the growing season of late spring and summer, mostly in thunderstorms. Monthly snowfall amounts are unusually uniform from November through February, and a bit heavier in March and April. Snow has occurred as early in the season as September and as late as early June.

Casper experiences large diurnal and annual temperature ranges. This is due to the advent of both warm and cold air masses and the relatively high elevation which permits rapid incoming and outgoing radiation. The mean daily temperature averages about 71 degrees in summer and 22 degrees in winter. Temperatures during winter months average a few degrees higher and summer temperatures average several degrees cooler than locations in the Missouri Valley to the east.

Windy days are quite frequent during winter and spring months. Usually the stronger winds are from the southwest and this tends to raise the temperature because the air is moving downslope.

Based on the 1951-1980 period, the average first occurrence of 32 degrees Fahrenheit in the fall is September 22 and the average last occurrence in the spring is May 22.

Casper Int'l Airport *Natrona County*   Elevation: 5,337 ft.   Latitude: 42° 54' N   Longitude: 106° 28' W

	JAN	FEB	MAR	APR	MAY	JUN	JUL	AUG	SEP	OCT	NOV	DEC	YEAR
Mean Maximum Temp. (°F)	33.1	37.9	47.1	56.1	66.7	79.3	87.4	86.2	74.3	60.2	43.9	34.7	58.9
Mean Temp. (°F)	22.8	27.2	35.1	42.9	52.5	63.3	70.6	69.3	58.2	46.1	33.1	24.7	45.5
Mean Minimum Temp. (°F)	12.5	16.5	23.0	29.5	38.2	47.2	53.7	52.3	42.1	32.0	22.2	14.6	32.0
Extreme Maximum Temp. (°F)	60	68	74	84	92	102	103	102	97	87	72	63	103
Extreme Minimum Temp. (°F)	-40	-29	-15	-6	19	31	30	33	16	-3	-21	-41	-41
Days Maximum Temp. ≥ 90°F	0	0	0	0	0	5	13	11	2	0	0	0	31
Days Maximum Temp. ≤ 32°F	13	8	4	1	0	0	0	0	0	1	6	12	45
Days Minimum Temp. ≤ 32°F	29	26	26	19	6	0	0	0	4	15	25	28	178
Days Minimum Temp. ≤ 0°F	7	4	1	0	0	0	0	0	0	0	2	5	19
Heating Degree Days (base 65°F)	1,302	1,060	921	658	385	112	14	22	227	579	951	1,244	7,475
Cooling Degree Days (base 65°F)	0	0	0	0	4	66	195	174	31	1	0	0	471
Mean Precipitation (in.)	0.59	0.63	0.93	1.53	2.34	1.47	1.30	0.70	0.93	1.16	0.84	0.63	13.05
Maximum Precipitation (in.)	1.4	1.4	2.4	3.9	6.5	4.1	3.0	2.7	3.4	4.2	2.7	3.7	20.5
Minimum Precipitation (in.)	trace	0.1	0.3	0.1	0.3	trace	0.1	trace	0.1	trace	trace	trace	6.6
Maximum 24-hr. Precipitation (in.)	0.5	0.6	1.0	1.8	2.1	2.1	1.8	1.3	2.0	1.9	1.0	1.3	2.1
Days With ≥ 0.1" Precipitation	2	2	3	5	6	4	3	2	2	3	3	2	37
Days With ≥ 1.0" Precipitation	0	0	0	0	0	0	0	0	0	0	0	0	0
Mean Snowfall (in.)	11.0	10.5	12.9	13.5	5.0	trace	trace	trace	1.6	7.5	11.8	11.8	85.6
Maximum Snowfall (in.)	39	24	36	56	25	3	0	0	12	22	37	63	138
Maximum 24-hr. Snowfall (in.)	10	10	15	17	13	3	0	0	7	13	12	24	24
Days With ≥ 1.0" Snow Depth	18	13	7	4	1	0	0	0	0	0	3	9	69
Thunderstorm Days	0	< 1	< 1	1	6	8	9	7	3	< 1	< 1	0	34
Foggy Days	3	3	4	4	4	2	1	1	2	3	3	3	33
Predominant Sky Cover	OVR	OVR	OVR	OVR	OVR	CLR	CLR	CLR	CLR	CLR	OVR	OVR	OVR
Mean Relative Humidity 6am (%)	67	71	74	74	74	68	63	63	65	66	69	68	68
Mean Relative Humidity 3pm (%)	54	52	45	38	36	29	23	22	28	34	48	54	38
Mean Dewpoint (°F)	13	16	20	25	34	40	43	41	33	27	20	15	27
Prevailing Wind Direction	SW	SW	SW	SW	SW	WSW	WSW	SW	SW	SW	SW	SW	SW
Prevailing Wind Speed (mph)	20	18	17	15	15	14	12	13	15	16	18	20	16
Maximum Wind Gust (mph)	67	67	64	69	64	64	67	67	63	62	60	67	69

Lander Hunt Field

Lander, located in the central Wyoming valley of the Popo Agie River, lies at the foot and east of the Wind River Range. Situated on a flat-topped mesa, the airport station is one and a half miles south-southeast and approximately 200 feet above the town.

The terrain to the north, east and south varies from rolling to broken with some grass covered hills two to five miles distant, rising approximately 400 feet above the station elevation. To the west and southwest the foothills of the Wind River Range begin about three miles from the station, sloping upward to over 12,000 feet above sea level along the Continental Divide, 20 miles distant.

Because Lander is in a pocket, winds from all directions except northeast are downslope and produce a Chinook effect, most noticable in winds from westerly quadrants. The airport, on its mesa, receives more wind than the town of Lander. Because of light winds, steep temperature inversions are the rule during winter nights and early mornings. Temperatures in the valley will be as much as 15 degrees lower than at the airport on calm, clear nights when there is a snow cover. However, when the wind is calm and the humidities low, the chilling effect is much less than is usual in extreme cold. For several days each winter, temperatures are 20 to 30 degrees lower than in the surrounding areas where higher wind speeds occur. The sheltered location, however, offers protection from most severe storms that sweep down from Canada.

Lander does not have a true spring season, and snow has been recorded in June.

Usually on 15 to 20 days a year the temperature reaches or exceeds 90 degrees. Even the warmest days are not oppressive, the humidity being low, and the nights being cool. The normal daily range of summer temperature is near 30 degrees.

Mountains block moisture from the Pacific, creating a semi-arid climate. The heaviest and most persistent precipitation comes when the wind in the lower levels is from easterly quadrants, through a combination of low pressure to the south, usually over Colorado, and high pressure to the north over Montana or the western Dakotas. More than a third of the annual precipitation occurs in April and May, with another but lesser peak in September and October. Summer moisture comes from occasional showers but is very erratic and spotty. Since about one-third of the annual snowfall comes in March and April, when the temperature is comparatively high, the snow soon melts.

Hardier plants and vegetables do well in this area. The average first occurrence of 32 degrees Fahrenheit in the fall is September 24 and the average last occurrence in the spring is May 22.

Lander Hunt Field *Fremont County* Elevation: 5,554 ft. Latitude: 42° 49' N Longitude: 108° 44' W

	JAN	FEB	MAR	APR	MAY	JUN	JUL	AUG	SEP	OCT	NOV	DEC	YEAR
Mean Maximum Temp. (°F)	31.6	37.2	46.9	55.6	66.0	77.9	85.8	84.5	72.6	59.2	42.3	32.6	57.7
Mean Temp. (°F)	20.1	25.6	35.1	43.4	53.1	63.5	70.7	69.3	58.5	46.2	30.8	21.3	44.8
Mean Minimum Temp. (°F)	8.6	13.9	23.3	31.0	40.2	48.9	55.4	54.1	44.3	33.0	19.3	10.0	31.9
Extreme Maximum Temp. (°F)	63	65	73	82	90	99	100	101	94	84	70	64	101
Extreme Minimum Temp. (°F)	-31	-24	-9	-2	21	31	39	37	20	-3	-18	-37	-37
Days Maximum Temp. ≥ 90°F	0	0	0	0	0	3	10	7	1	0	0	0	21
Days Maximum Temp. ≤ 32°F	15	9	3	1	0	0	0	0	0	1	7	15	51
Days Minimum Temp. ≤ 32°F	31	28	27	17	4	0	0	0	3	14	27	31	182
Days Minimum Temp. ≤ 0°F	8	4	0	0	0	0	0	0	0	0	2	6	20
Heating Degree Days (base 65°F)	1,386	1,107	919	643	364	113	15	22	219	577	1,018	1,348	7,731
Cooling Degree Days (base 65°F)	0	0	0	0	4	74	204	177	33	0	0	0	492
Mean Precipitation (in.)	0.52	0.53	1.29	2.10	2.34	1.20	0.85	0.56	1.13	1.38	1.00	0.61	13.51
Maximum Precipitation (in.)	1.3	2.2	3.3	5.5	6.0	5.3	2.5	2.3	4.7	4.9	3.4	1.6	21.9
Minimum Precipitation (in.)	trace	trace	0.3	0.2	0.1	trace	0	trace	trace	trace	trace	trace	6.4
Maximum 24-hr. Precipitation (in.)	0.7	0.8	1.3	2.1	2.5	2.2	2.1	1.0	1.7	1.7	1.1	1.0	2.5
Days With ≥ 0.1" Precipitation	2	2	4	6	5	3	2	2	3	4	3	2	38
Days With ≥ 1.0" Precipitation	0	0	0	0	0	0	0	0	0	0	0	0	0
Mean Snowfall (in.)	9.9	9.2	18.4	21.9	6.9	0.3	trace	trace	3.1	10.4	15.6	11.2	106.9
Maximum Snowfall (in.)	27	44	52	66	34	18	0	0	33	40	49	28	200
Maximum 24-hr. Snowfall (in.)	14	20	16	22	16	16	0	0	14	19	23	16	23
Days With ≥ 1.0" Snow Depth	25	21	12	6	1	0	0	0	0	3	13	23	104
Thunderstorm Days	0	0	< 1	1	5	7	10	7	3	< 1	< 1	0	33
Foggy Days	2	2	1	2	1	< 1	< 1	< 1	1	1	2	2	14
Predominant Sky Cover	OVR	OVR	OVR	OVR	OVR	SCT	CLR	CLR	CLR	CLR	OVR	CLR	CLR
Mean Relative Humidity 6am (%)	69	69	67	65	66	60	55	55	59	64	69	69	64
Mean Relative Humidity 3pm (%)	57	51	42	36	36	30	26	25	31	36	49	54	39
Mean Dewpoint (°F)	8	13	18	24	33	39	42	40	34	27	17	10	26
Prevailing Wind Direction	SW	SW	SW	SW	WSW	SW	WSW	WSW	SW	SW	WSW	SE	SW
Prevailing Wind Speed (mph)	9	9	9	10	9	10	9	9	9	9	9	7	9
Maximum Wind Gust (mph)	86	69	63	63	69	63	66	67	67	53	68	75	86

Sheridan County Airport

Sheridan is located east of the Rocky Mountains at an elevation of a little less than 4,000 feet. To the northwest, east, and southeast are rolling hills, but to the southwest and west the Bighorn Mountains rise abruptly, oriented generally northwest-southeast. The foothills are only about 15 miles from Sheridan, and within 30 miles to the southwest the average elevation is near 10,000 feet, with Cloud Peak rising to 13,175 feet.

During the winter months, a few days after the outbreak of cold arctic air from Canada, the winds generally shift to the west or southwest and increase in velocity. These downslope winds produce a pronounced warming or Chinook. At other times, a gentle downslope flow will persist for several days and result in a prolonged period of mild weather. The Chinook is very effective in moderating the weather of the winter season, which otherwise would be more severe. On the other hand, winds from the east or northeast blowing toward the mountains are upslope and usually cause cooling, persistent low clouds, and often heavy precipitation. The upslope precipitation occurs at times all through the year, but most frequently during the winter and spring. In the summer, the mountains act as a breeding ground for thunderstorms that frequently move away from the mountains toward the northeast and give afternoon or evening showers to Sheridan.

Based on the 1951-1980 period, the average first occurrence of 32 degrees Fahrenheit in the fall is September 20 and the average last occurrence in the spring is May 20.

The climate of Sheridan can be described generally as semi-arid with long cold winters and short hot summers. However, during all of the winter months, more than 50 percent of the possible sunshine is received, while the hot days in the summer are marked by very low humidity and nights are cool. During July, the warmest month, even though temperatures of 90 degrees or above occur frequently, the nights are cool. January is usually the coldest month.

The yearly precipitation pattern for Sheridan is heavy in the spring and early summer. The three winter months constitute the period with the least moisture. Amounts of snowfall are quite generous during the winter, but the water content of the snow is usually low. This dry snow is ordinarily not injurious to livestock and does not result in serious inconvenience or discomfort to the public. During the spring months of March and April, however, precipitation often begins as rain, gradually turning to rain and snow mixed or to heavy wet snow. These snowstorms are frequently accompanied by strong winds and drifting. As a result, these two months are considered to have the most disagreeable weather of the year and are most likely to cause livestock loss. March has more snow than any other month.

Sheridan County Airport *Sheridan County*   Elevation: 3,963 ft.   Latitude: 44° 46' N   Longitude: 106° 58' W

	JAN	FEB	MAR	APR	MAY	JUN	JUL	AUG	SEP	OCT	NOV	DEC	YEAR
Mean Maximum Temp. (°F)	33.2	39.0	47.4	57.0	66.8	77.2	85.8	85.7	73.8	60.9	44.9	35.6	58.9
Mean Temp. (°F)	21.4	27.0	35.0	43.9	53.1	62.4	69.4	69.0	58.0	46.2	32.5	23.3	45.1
Mean Minimum Temp. (°F)	9.5	14.9	22.5	30.8	39.4	47.6	53.1	52.2	42.1	31.5	19.9	10.9	31.2
Extreme Maximum Temp. (°F)	70	76	77	86	93	105	106	106	103	92	81	72	106
Extreme Minimum Temp. (°F)	-35	-32	-20	-2	20	31	35	33	6	-9	-20	-37	-37
Days Maximum Temp. ≥ 90°F	0	0	0	0	0	3	11	12	3	0	0	0	29
Days Maximum Temp. ≤ 32°F	13	8	4	1	0	0	0	0	0	1	6	11	44
Days Minimum Temp. ≤ 32°F	30	27	27	18	5	0	0	0	3	16	27	30	183
Days Minimum Temp. ≤ 0°F	9	5	1	0	0	0	0	0	0	0	0	2	24
Heating Degree Days (base 65°F)	1,346	1,068	924	626	366	124	25	30	236	577	971	1,289	7,582
Cooling Degree Days (base 65°F)	0	0	0	1	5	56	180	177	36	2	0	0	457
Mean Precipitation (in.)	0.72	0.56	1.05	1.78	2.47	2.03	1.12	0.79	1.39	1.40	0.84	0.66	14.81
Maximum Precipitation (in.)	1.9	2.7	3.0	4.8	6.8	6.1	3.8	3.0	3.1	3.4	2.4	2.4	23.8
Minimum Precipitation (in.)	0.1	0	0.1	0.2	0.3	0.3	0.1	trace	0.1	trace	0.1	0.1	8.2
Maximum 24-hr. Precipitation (in.)	0.9	1.0	0.9	2.8	1.8	1.9	2.0	1.0	1.2	1.6	0.8	0.7	2.8
Days With ≥ 0.1" Precipitation	3	2	4	5	6	5	3	2	4	4	3	2	43
Days With ≥ 1.0" Precipitation	0	0	0	0	0	0	0	0	0	0	0	0	0
Mean Snowfall (in.)	12.2	9.3	12.6	10.3	2.0	trace	trace	0.0	2.0	5.8	9.5	11.9	75.6
Maximum Snowfall (in.)	33	35	37	40	13	4	0	0	21	18	26	44	158
Maximum 24-hr. Snowfall (in.)	12	10	10	23	7	3	0	0	13	13	10	12	23
Days With ≥ 1.0" Snow Depth	24	18	11	3	1	0	0	0	1	2	10	21	91
Thunderstorm Days	0	<1	<1	1	4	9	9	7	3	<1	<1	0	33
Foggy Days	2	3	3	3	2	1	<1	<1	1	2	2	2	21
Predominant Sky Cover	OVR	OVR	OVR	OVR	OVR	BRK	SCT	SCT	CLR	OVR	OVR	OVR	OVR
Mean Relative Humidity 5am (%)	71	73	75	74	77	78	72	68	71	71	73	71	73
Mean Relative Humidity 5pm (%)	64	61	52	45	46	45	34	30	37	46	62	66	49
Mean Dewpoint (°F)	11	16	21	28	38	46	48	45	38	30	21	14	30
Prevailing Wind Direction	NW	NW	NW	NW	NW	NW	NW	NW	NW	NW	NW	NW	NW
Prevailing Wind Speed (mph)	13	13	15	15	14	13	12	12	13	13	13	13	13
Maximum Wind Gust (mph)	71	69	68	69	66	58	64	60	67	64	73	69	73

Afton *Lincoln County*   Elevation: 6,207 ft.   Latitude: 42° 44' N   Longitude: 110° 56' W

	JAN	FEB	MAR	APR	MAY	JUN	JUL	AUG	SEP	OCT	NOV	DEC	YEAR
Mean Maximum Temp. (°F)	29.0	34.0	42.5	52.1	63.5	73.4	80.9	80.6	71.0	59.4	*40.7*	29.7	*54.7*
Mean Temp. (°F)	16.9	20.8	29.5	38.0	47.6	55.5	61.7	60.9	52.1	42.2	*28.5*	17.7	*39.3*
Mean Minimum Temp. (°F)	4.7	7.5	16.5	23.9	31.6	37.5	42.4	41.1	33.1	24.9	16.0	5.6	23.7
Extreme Maximum Temp. (°F)	54	54	68	77	80	94	95	95	90	83	70	58	95
Extreme Minimum Temp. (°F)	-46	-40	-22	-3	9	19	26	21	11	-2	-22	-38	-46
Days Maximum Temp. ≥ 90°F	0	0	0	0	0	0	2	1	0	0	0	0	3
Days Maximum Temp. ≤ 32°F	17	10	2	0	0	0	0	0	0	0	6	17	52
Days Minimum Temp. ≤ 32°F	30	28	30	27	16	6	1	2	14	26	28	30	238
Days Minimum Temp. ≤ 0°F	12	9	2	0	0	0	0	0	0	0	3	12	38
Heating Degree Days (base 65°F)	1,480	1,244	1,094	803	533	284	116	136	382	701	*1,089*	1,461	*9,323*
Cooling Degree Days (base 65°F)	0	0	0	0	0	4	23	16	2	0	0	0	45
Mean Precipitation (in.)	1.54	1.18	1.41	1.71	2.16	1.47	1.46	1.23	1.65	1.52	1.51	1.46	18.30
Days With ≥ 0.1" Precipitation	6	4	4	5	7	4	4	3	4	5	5	5	56
Days With ≥ 1.0" Precipitation	0	0	0	0	0	0	0	0	0	0	0	0	0
Mean Snowfall (in.)	*15.7*	11.6	*11.7*	*5.3*	1.1	trace	0.0	0.0	0.3	*2.3*	*11.8*	*15.6*	*75.4*
Days With ≥ 1.0" Snow Depth	29	25	22	na	0	0	0	0	0	*1*	*11*	*24*	na

Albin *Laramie County*   Elevation: 5,344 ft.   Latitude: 41° 25' N   Longitude: 104° 06' W

	JAN	FEB	MAR	APR	MAY	JUN	JUL	AUG	SEP	OCT	NOV	DEC	YEAR
Mean Maximum Temp. (°F)	38.1	42.7	49.3	57.7	67.7	79.0	85.2	84.1	75.4	63.2	47.4	39.6	60.8
Mean Temp. (°F)	26.5	30.7	36.4	44.1	53.9	64.2	70.1	69.0	60.2	48.7	35.4	28.1	47.3
Mean Minimum Temp. (°F)	14.9	18.7	23.5	30.4	40.1	49.4	54.9	53.9	44.9	34.1	23.3	16.5	33.7
Extreme Maximum Temp. (°F)	70	70	77	86	90	99	102	100	96	85	77	72	102
Extreme Minimum Temp. (°F)	-21	-28	-10	-7	20	32	41	35	11	-4	-18	-31	-31
Days Maximum Temp. ≥ 90°F	0	0	0	0	0	3	9	6	2	0	0	0	20
Days Maximum Temp. ≤ 32°F	9	6	3	1	0	0	0	0	0	1	4	8	32
Days Minimum Temp. ≤ 32°F	29	26	26	18	4	0	0	0	2	12	25	29	171
Days Minimum Temp. ≤ 0°F	5	3	1	0	0	0	0	0	0	0	1	3	13
Heating Degree Days (base 65°F)	1,186	963	879	622	341	89	14	19	178	501	883	1,139	6,814
Cooling Degree Days (base 65°F)	0	0	0	0	5	72	179	156	40	1	0	0	453
Mean Precipitation (in.)	0.79	0.61	1.60	1.95	2.84	2.51	2.27	1.64	1.46	1.19	0.98	0.79	18.63
Days With ≥ 0.1" Precipitation	3	2	4	5	7	5	5	4	4	3	3	3	48
Days With ≥ 1.0" Precipitation	0	0	0	0	0	0	0	0	0	0	0	0	0
Mean Snowfall (in.)	13.1	8.6	16.8	11.5	1.3	trace	0.0	0.0	1.0	5.0	12.4	13.5	83.2
Days With ≥ 1.0" Snow Depth	16	11	9	4	0	0	0	0	0	2	8	14	64

Alta 1 NNW *Teton County*   Elevation: 6,427 ft.   Latitude: 43° 46' N   Longitude: 111° 02' W

	JAN	FEB	MAR	APR	MAY	JUN	JUL	AUG	SEP	OCT	NOV	DEC	YEAR
Mean Maximum Temp. (°F)	28.9	33.9	39.9	48.1	59.5	69.7	78.3	77.4	67.6	54.9	38.2	29.4	52.2
Mean Temp. (°F)	19.0	23.0	29.0	36.6	46.4	55.5	*62.4*	61.3	52.6	41.6	28.1	19.4	*39.6*
Mean Minimum Temp. (°F)	8.9	12.0	18.1	25.0	33.4	41.2	*46.9*	45.4	37.5	28.6	18.0	9.4	*27.0*
Extreme Maximum Temp. (°F)	56	60	64	79	81	92	91	92	90	78	69	57	92
Extreme Minimum Temp. (°F)	-30	-30	-18	-14	8	20	30	20	10	-5	-28	-40	-40
Days Maximum Temp. ≥ 90°F	0	0	0	0	0	0	1	1	0	0	0	0	2
Days Maximum Temp. ≤ 32°F	20	12	5	1	0	0	0	0	0	1	9	19	67
Days Minimum Temp. ≤ 32°F	31	28	30	24	15	4	0	1	8	20	28	31	220
Days Minimum Temp. ≤ 0°F	8	5	2	0	0	0	0	0	0	0	2	7	24
Heating Degree Days (base 65°F)	1,421	1,180	1,109	847	571	289	*111*	128	369	720	1,097	1,400	*9,242*
Cooling Degree Days (base 65°F)	0	0	0	0	0	10	39	21	2	0	0	0	72
Mean Precipitation (in.)	2.35	1.74	1.96	2.17	3.49	2.16	1.85	1.54	1.86	2.02	2.11	2.11	25.36
Days With ≥ 0.1" Precipitation	7	5	7	7	9	6	5	5	5	5	7	6	74
Days With ≥ 1.0" Precipitation	0	0	0	0	0	0	0	0	0	0	0	0	0
Mean Snowfall (in.)	22.5	15.0	14.2	10.2	4.8	0.3	0.0	0.0	0.7	6.8	16.0	18.9	109.4
Days With ≥ 1.0" Snow Depth	29	26	29	22	3	0	0	0	0	4	16	30	159

Archer *Laramie County*   Elevation: 6,007 ft.   Latitude: 41° 09' N   Longitude: 104° 39' W

	JAN	FEB	MAR	APR	MAY	JUN	JUL	AUG	SEP	OCT	NOV	DEC	YEAR
Mean Maximum Temp. (°F)	39.1	42.8	48.3	56.0	65.9	76.9	84.3	83.0	74.3	62.2	47.7	40.6	60.1
Mean Temp. (°F)	26.3	29.7	34.9	41.9	51.6	61.5	68.1	66.9	57.9	46.7	34.3	27.5	45.6
Mean Minimum Temp. (°F)	13.4	16.5	21.3	27.8	37.1	46.1	51.8	50.7	41.4	31.0	20.9	14.5	31.1
Extreme Maximum Temp. (°F)	69	70	75	82	90	100	102	102	99	86	78	69	102
Extreme Minimum Temp. (°F)	-22	-28	-13	-8	18	29	37	35	8	-4	-17	-30	-30
Days Maximum Temp. ≥ 90°F	0	0	0	0	0	2	8	5	2	0	0	0	17
Days Maximum Temp. ≤ 32°F	8	6	4	1	0	0	0	0	0	1	4	8	32
Days Minimum Temp. ≤ 32°F	30	26	28	21	7	1	0	0	4	16	27	30	190
Days Minimum Temp. ≤ 0°F	5	3	1	0	0	0	0	0	0	0	1	4	14
Heating Degree Days (base 65°F)	1,193	992	927	685	412	140	30	36	231	561	914	1,156	7,277
Cooling Degree Days (base 65°F)	0	0	0	0	2	39	127	102	23	0	0	0	293
Mean Precipitation (in.)	0.41	0.42	1.13	1.63	2.73	2.56	2.20	1.95	1.54	0.91	0.65	0.43	16.56
Days With ≥ 0.1" Precipitation	2	1	3	4	6	5	5	5	4	3	2	2	42
Days With ≥ 1.0" Precipitation	0	0	0	0	1	0	0	0	0	0	0	0	1
Mean Snowfall (in.)	6.7	5.8	9.6	7.1	1.3	0.0	0.0	0.0	0.9	3.6	7.8	6.8	49.6
Days With ≥ 1.0" Snow Depth	13	10	8	4	1	0	0	0	0	2	8	12	58

Basin *Big Horn County*   Elevation: 3,835 ft.   Latitude: 44° 23' N   Longitude: 108° 02' W

	JAN	FEB	MAR	APR	MAY	JUN	JUL	AUG	SEP	OCT	NOV	DEC	YEAR
Mean Maximum Temp. (°F)	28.5	38.4	51.2	61.8	71.8	82.7	90.0	88.9	76.6	62.7	44.3	32.1	60.8
Mean Temp. (°F)	15.3	24.5	37.0	46.9	56.8	66.5	72.7	70.8	59.1	46.6	31.2	19.2	45.6
Mean Minimum Temp. (°F)	2.1	10.6	22.8	31.9	41.7	50.3	55.4	52.7	41.6	30.5	18.0	6.1	30.3
Extreme Maximum Temp. (°F)	59	73	80	89	96	110	105	115	100	88	77	67	115
Extreme Minimum Temp. (°F)	-42	-41	-25	5	18	30	39	34	16	-1	-27	-43	-43
Days Maximum Temp. ≥ 90°F	0	0	0	0	1	8	18	16	4	0	0	0	47
Days Maximum Temp. ≤ 32°F	17	7	2	0	0	0	0	0	0	0	5	14	45
Days Minimum Temp. ≤ 32°F	31	28	28	15	3	0	0	0	4	18	29	31	187
Days Minimum Temp. ≤ 0°F	14	6	1	0	0	0	0	0	0	0	2	9	32
Heating Degree Days (base 65°F)	1,536	1,137	861	538	264	68	10	17	204	563	1,008	1,415	7,621
Cooling Degree Days (base 65°F)	0	0	0	1	20	114	247	211	38	0	0	0	631
Mean Precipitation (in.)	0.25	0.16	0.34	0.73	1.30	0.99	0.62	0.42	0.81	0.59	0.28	0.27	6.76
Days With ≥ 0.1" Precipitation	1	1	1	2	4	3	2	1	2	2	1	1	21
Days With ≥ 1.0" Precipitation	0	0	0	0	0	0	0	0	0	0	0	0	0
Mean Snowfall (in.)	4.1	2.8	2.7	1.4	0.1	trace	0.0	0.0	0.9	0.5	2.6	4.2	19.3
Days With ≥ 1.0" Snow Depth	21	11	2	0	0	0	0	0	0	0	3	13	50

Bates Creek 2 *Natrona County*   Elevation: 6,007 ft.   Latitude: 42° 38' N   Longitude: 106° 23' W

	JAN	FEB	MAR	APR	MAY	JUN	JUL	AUG	SEP	OCT	NOV	DEC	YEAR
Mean Maximum Temp. (°F)	34.3	38.1	45.6	54.4	65.1	76.5	83.4	82.4	71.8	59.4	44.0	35.6	57.5
Mean Temp. (°F)	22.9	26.6	34.2	42.1	51.9	62.0	68.5	67.5	57.5	45.9	32.8	24.6	44.7
Mean Minimum Temp. (°F)	11.4	15.1	22.6	29.8	38.7	47.5	53.7	52.5	43.1	32.4	21.6	13.5	31.8
Extreme Maximum Temp. (°F)	60	62	72	78	87	97	98	98	92	84	71	63	98
Extreme Minimum Temp. (°F)	-26	-29	-11	-3	17	29	32	35	14	1	-16	-38	-38
Days Maximum Temp. ≥ 90°F	0	0	0	0	0	2	4	2	0	0	0	0	8
Days Maximum Temp. ≤ 32°F	12	7	3	1	0	0	0	0	0	1	5	11	40
Days Minimum Temp. ≤ 32°F	30	27	27	19	6	1	0	0	3	15	25	30	183
Days Minimum Temp. ≤ 0°F	6	3	1	0	0	0	0	0	0	0	1	4	15
Heating Degree Days (base 65°F)	1,300	1,078	950	680	401	136	24	32	242	585	959	1,246	7,633
Cooling Degree Days (base 65°F)	0	0	0	0	3	51	135	120	22	0	0	0	331
Mean Precipitation (in.)	0.60	0.66	1.09	1.65	2.35	1.41	1.09	0.93	0.79	1.34	0.69	0.59	13.19
Days With ≥ 0.1" Precipitation	2	2	3	5	6	4	3	3	3	3	2	2	38
Days With ≥ 1.0" Precipitation	0	0	0	0	0	0	0	0	0	0	0	0	0
Mean Snowfall (in.)	11.5	12.1	15.7	14.5	2.6	0.0	0.0	0.0	0.4	6.6	8.4	12.0	83.8
Days With ≥ 1.0" Snow Depth	26	22	12	4	1	0	0	0	0	2	7	20	94

Billy Creek *Johnson County*   Elevation: 4,973 ft.   Latitude: 44° 08' N   Longitude: 106° 43' W

	JAN	FEB	MAR	APR	MAY	JUN	JUL	AUG	SEP	OCT	NOV	DEC	YEAR
Mean Maximum Temp. (°F)	35.6	40.2	47.0	55.4	65.0	75.8	83.7	83.3	72.2	59.8	45.2	38.3	58.4
Mean Temp. (°F)	22.3	27.3	34.3	42.3	51.7	61.5	68.2	67.3	56.8	45.3	32.3	24.8	44.5
Mean Minimum Temp. (°F)	8.9	14.4	21.5	29.2	38.3	47.1	52.6	51.3	41.3	30.9	19.3	11.2	30.5
Extreme Maximum Temp. (°F)	66	71	75	85	90	100	104	105	98	87	81	72	105
Extreme Minimum Temp. (°F)	-32	-41	-19	-1	20	27	35	31	11	-12	-26	-39	-41
Days Maximum Temp. ≥ 90°F	0	0	0	0	0	3	8	8	2	0	0	0	21
Days Maximum Temp. ≤ 32°F	11	7	4	1	0	0	0	0	0	1	5	10	39
Days Minimum Temp. ≤ 32°F	30	27	28	20	7	1	0	0	5	18	27	30	193
Days Minimum Temp. ≤ 0°F	8	4	1	0	0	0	0	0	0	0	2	5	20
Heating Degree Days (base 65°F)	1,320	1,057	946	674	410	153	40	49	269	603	974	1,242	7,737
Cooling Degree Days (base 65°F)	0	0	0	1	6	54	150	134	30	0	0	0	375
Mean Precipitation (in.)	0.28	0.33	0.65	1.52	2.27	2.08	1.61	1.06	1.12	1.05	0.44	0.33	12.74
Days With ≥ 0.1" Precipitation	1	1	2	4	6	5	4	3	3	3	1	1	34
Days With ≥ 1.0" Precipitation	0	0	0	0	0	0	0	0	0	0	0	0	0
Mean Snowfall (in.)	5.6	6.1	7.7	8.1	1.7	trace	0.0	0.0	0.8	3.6	5.5	5.8	44.9
Days With ≥ 1.0" Snow Depth	17	12	8	3	0	0	0	0	0	1	6	11	58

Bitter Creek 4 NE *Sweetwater County*   Elevation: 6,719 ft.   Latitude: 41° 35' N   Longitude: 108° 31' W

	JAN	FEB	MAR	APR	MAY	JUN	JUL	AUG	SEP	OCT	NOV	DEC	YEAR
Mean Maximum Temp. (°F)	31.9	35.8	44.6	54.4	65.2	76.5	83.5	82.5	72.5	58.9	42.7	33.4	56.8
Mean Temp. (°F)	19.5	23.3	32.2	39.8	49.1	58.5	65.1	63.8	54.3	42.7	30.1	21.1	41.6
Mean Minimum Temp. (°F)	7.0	10.8	19.8	25.1	33.0	40.5	46.6	44.9	36.0	26.4	17.4	8.7	26.4
Extreme Maximum Temp. (°F)	57	58	67	78	85	97	96	97	90	78	68	57	97
Extreme Minimum Temp. (°F)	-46	-42	-11	-10	10	18	27	17	10	-9	-29	-37	-46
Days Maximum Temp. ≥ 90°F	0	0	0	0	0	1	3	2	0	0	0	0	6
Days Maximum Temp. ≤ 32°F	14	9	2	1	0	0	0	0	0	0	5	13	44
Days Minimum Temp. ≤ 32°F	31	28	29	25	15	3	0	1	10	24	28	30	224
Days Minimum Temp. ≤ 0°F	8	6	1	0	0	0	0	0	0	0	3	8	26
Heating Degree Days (base 65°F)	1,403	1,171	1,010	750	485	203	51	73	321	684	1,042	1,355	8,548
Cooling Degree Days (base 65°F)	0	0	0	0	0	16	69	45	6	0	0	0	136
Mean Precipitation (in.)	0.38	0.45	0.32	0.49	1.30	0.68	0.73	0.58	0.74	0.72	0.44	na	na
Days With ≥ 0.1" Precipitation	na	na	1	2	4	2	2	2	2	2	2	na	na
Days With ≥ 1.0" Precipitation	0	0	0	0	0	0	0	0	0	0	0	0	0
Mean Snowfall (in.)	na	na	1.7	2.1	trace	trace	0.0	0.0	trace	1.0	na	na	na
Days With ≥ 1.0" Snow Depth	na	na	na	0	0	0	0	0	0	0	na	na	na

Black Mountain *Hot Springs County* Elevation: 5,633 ft. Latitude: 43° 39' N Longitude: 107° 44' W

	JAN	FEB	MAR	APR	MAY	JUN	JUL	AUG	SEP	OCT	NOV	DEC	YEAR
Mean Maximum Temp. (°F)	34.3	38.7	44.5	53.3	63.7	76.5	85.5	84.4	71.5	58.1	43.2	35.5	57.5
Mean Temp. (°F)	24.1	28.5	34.1	42.4	52.1	63.3	71.0	70.2	57.8	45.8	33.2	26.0	45.7
Mean Minimum Temp. (°F)	14.3	18.2	23.7	31.4	40.5	49.9	56.6	55.6	44.2	33.5	23.1	16.5	34.0
Extreme Maximum Temp. (°F)	60	65	73	81	89	102	101	100	95	86	71	61	102
Extreme Minimum Temp. (°F)	-24	-36	-12	4	19	28	37	35	10	0	-19	-34	-36
Days Maximum Temp. ≥ 90°F	0	0	0	0	0	3	11	9	1	0	0	0	24
Days Maximum Temp. ≤ 32°F	11	6	5	1	0	0	0	0	0	1	5	11	40
Days Minimum Temp. ≤ 32°F	29	26	26	18	6	0	0	0	4	14	24	29	176
Days Minimum Temp. ≤ 0°F	5	3	1	0	0	0	0	0	0	0	1	3	13
Heating Degree Days (base 65°F)	1,262	1,024	951	674	400	130	25	25	252	588	948	1,203	7,482
Cooling Degree Days (base 65°F)	0	0	0	1	7	77	213	196	42	1	0	0	537
Mean Precipitation (in.)	0.57	0.48	1.17	1.80	2.38	1.71	1.07	0.76	1.29	1.49	0.82	0.61	14.15
Days With ≥ 0.1" Precipitation	2	2	4	5	5	4	3	2	3	4	3	2	39
Days With ≥ 1.0" Precipitation	0	0	0	0	0	0	0	0	0	0	0	0	0
Mean Snowfall (in.)	8.8	5.7	11.3	8.5	3.7	0.6	0.0	0.0	1.5	5.6	7.9	8.4	62.0
Days With ≥ 1.0" Snow Depth	25	18	14	6	1	0	0	0	1	2	12	21	100

Boysen Dam *Fremont County* Elevation: 4,809 ft. Latitude: 43° 24' N Longitude: 108° 10' W

	JAN	FEB	MAR	APR	MAY	JUN	JUL	AUG	SEP	OCT	NOV	DEC	YEAR
Mean Maximum Temp. (°F)	28.9	36.9	49.8	60.0	70.4	81.8	89.8	88.2	75.9	61.8	43.3	30.4	59.8
Mean Temp. (°F)	17.7	24.4	37.1	47.0	57.1	67.4	74.7	73.3	61.7	49.0	33.3	20.1	46.9
Mean Minimum Temp. (°F)	6.3	11.8	24.3	33.8	43.7	52.9	59.5	58.3	47.5	36.0	23.1	9.8	33.9
Extreme Maximum Temp. (°F)	62	65	75	84	93	103	105	104	99	89	70	65	105
Extreme Minimum Temp. (°F)	-39	-32	-10	2	21	32	40	42	22	8	-15	-36	-39
Days Maximum Temp. ≥ 90°F	0	0	0	0	0	7	18	15	2	0	0	0	42
Days Maximum Temp. ≤ 32°F	16	8	2	0	0	0	0	0	0	0	4	15	45
Days Minimum Temp. ≤ 32°F	29	26	25	12	2	0	0	0	1	8	25	29	157
Days Minimum Temp. ≤ 0°F	9	5	0	0	0	0	0	0	0	0	1	6	21
Heating Degree Days (base 65°F)	1,462	1,141	859	535	257	61	5	6	152	491	947	1,388	7,304
Cooling Degree Days (base 65°F)	0	0	0	1	20	134	310	278	62	1	0	0	806
Mean Precipitation (in.)	0.27	0.29	0.65	1.19	1.93	1.19	0.78	0.54	0.91	0.95	0.38	0.30	9.38
Days With ≥ 0.1" Precipitation	1	1	2	3	5	3	2	2	2	2	1	1	25
Days With ≥ 1.0" Precipitation	0	0	0	0	0	0	0	0	0	0	0	0	0
Mean Snowfall (in.)	na	na	na	na	0.0	0.0	0.0	0.0	0.0	0.2	na	na	na
Days With ≥ 1.0" Snow Depth	na	na	na	1	0	0	0	0	0	0	na	na	na

Buffalo *Johnson County* Elevation: 4,691 ft. Latitude: 44° 21' N Longitude: 106° 41' W

	JAN	FEB	MAR	APR	MAY	JUN	JUL	AUG	SEP	OCT	NOV	DEC	YEAR
Mean Maximum Temp. (°F)	35.3	39.8	48.0	56.9	66.9	77.6	85.4	84.8	73.5	60.9	45.1	37.5	59.3
Mean Temp. (°F)	22.5	27.1	35.1	44.1	53.5	63.4	70.3	69.2	58.3	46.5	32.7	24.8	45.6
Mean Minimum Temp. (°F)	9.6	14.4	22.2	31.1	40.1	49.2	55.1	53.5	43.0	32.1	20.3	12.1	31.9
Extreme Maximum Temp. (°F)	64	74	78	88	92	102	105	106	101	89	80	68	106
Extreme Minimum Temp. (°F)	-29	-32	-22	7	13	30	36	35	13	-8	-20	-35	-35
Days Maximum Temp. ≥ 90°F	0	0	0	0	0	4	11	9	2	0	0	0	26
Days Maximum Temp. ≤ 32°F	11	7	4	1	0	0	0	0	0	1	5	9	38
Days Minimum Temp. ≤ 32°F	31	27	28	18	5	0	0	0	3	15	27	30	184
Days Minimum Temp. ≤ 0°F	8	4	1	0	0	0	0	0	0	0	1	5	19
Heating Degree Days (base 65°F)	1,314	1,064	921	623	357	117	23	28	229	567	963	1,241	7,447
Cooling Degree Days (base 65°F)	0	0	0	1	10	81	204	179	35	1	0	0	511
Mean Precipitation (in.)	0.45	0.39	0.77	1.62	2.44	2.15	1.48	0.88	1.37	1.04	0.49	0.45	13.53
Days With ≥ 0.1" Precipitation	2	2	2	4	5	5	4	3	4	3	2	2	38
Days With ≥ 1.0" Precipitation	0	0	0	0	0	0	0	0	0	0	0	0	0
Mean Snowfall (in.)	na	na	na	2.8	0.6	0.0	0.0	0.0	0.1	2.3	5.3	na	na
Days With ≥ 1.0" Snow Depth	na	na	na	1	0	0	0	0	0	1	na	na	na

Buffalo Bill Dam *Park County* Elevation: 5,154 ft. Latitude: 44° 30' N Longitude: 109° 11' W

	JAN	FEB	MAR	APR	MAY	JUN	JUL	AUG	SEP	OCT	NOV	DEC	YEAR
Mean Maximum Temp. (°F)	35.6	39.3	45.5	52.7	60.4	68.4	74.4	75.5	68.2	58.4	na	na	na
Mean Temp. (°F)	27.3	31.1	37.0	44.0	51.8	59.1	65.1	65.8	58.6	49.3	na	na	na
Mean Minimum Temp. (°F)	19.5	23.1	28.6	35.1	43.0	49.8	55.8	56.0	48.9	40.1	na	na	na
Extreme Maximum Temp. (°F)	60	63	76	76	82	93	93	92	90	80	72	65	93
Extreme Minimum Temp. (°F)	-28	-36	-17	12	24	29	39	34	22	7	-16	-27	-36
Days Maximum Temp. ≥ 90°F	0	0	0	0	0	0	1	0	0	0	0	0	1
Days Maximum Temp. ≤ 32°F	9	6	3	1	0	0	0	0	0	0	3	8	30
Days Minimum Temp. ≤ 32°F	23	19	19	10	2	0	0	0	1	5	16	21	116
Days Minimum Temp. ≤ 0°F	4	2	1	0	0	0	0	0	0	0	1	2	10
Heating Degree Days (base 65°F)	1,162	950	859	623	403	185	54	40	210	481	na	na	na
Cooling Degree Days (base 65°F)	na	0	0	0	1	15	56	73	23	na	na	na	na
Mean Precipitation (in.)	0.41	0.34	0.63	1.34	2.11	1.69	0.94	0.73	1.13	0.88	0.49	0.28	10.97
Days With ≥ 0.1" Precipitation	1	1	2	3	5	4	3	3	3	2	2	1	30
Days With ≥ 1.0" Precipitation	0	0	0	0	0	0	0	0	0	0	0	0	0
Mean Snowfall (in.)	5.3	na	5.4	4.0	trace	0.0	0.0	0.0	0.3	0.9	na	3.5	na
Days With ≥ 1.0" Snow Depth	9	na	4	2	0	0	0	0	0	1	na	5	na

Burris *Fremont County*   Elevation: 6,118 ft.   Latitude: 43° 22' N   Longitude: 109° 17' W

	JAN	FEB	MAR	APR	MAY	JUN	JUL	AUG	SEP	OCT	NOV	DEC	YEAR
Mean Maximum Temp. (°F)	36.6	41.0	47.3	55.2	64.4	74.1	80.8	79.6	69.7	59.8	44.5	37.2	57.5
Mean Temp. (°F)	23.6	27.4	33.9	41.4	50.3	59.0	64.8	63.5	54.3	45.2	32.0	24.4	43.3
Mean Minimum Temp. (°F)	10.6	13.8	20.4	27.6	36.2	43.8	48.8	47.3	38.9	30.5	19.5	11.6	29.1
Extreme Maximum Temp. (°F)	62	66	72	84	89	95	95	93	88	84	72	64	95
Extreme Minimum Temp. (°F)	-38	-32	-19	-4	13	29	31	32	11	-5	-21	-45	-45
Days Maximum Temp. ≥ 90°F	0	0	0	0	0	1	2	0	0	0	0	0	3
Days Maximum Temp. ≤ 32°F	10	5	3	1	0	0	0	0	0	0	5	9	33
Days Minimum Temp. ≤ 32°F	30	26	29	21	9	1	0	0	6	18	27	29	196
Days Minimum Temp. ≤ 0°F	7	4	1	0	0	0	0	0	0	0	0	2	6	20
Heating Degree Days (base 65°F)	1,276	1,056	959	701	449	194	63	78	318	608	983	1,252	7,937
Cooling Degree Days (base 65°F)	0	0	0	0	1	18	63	38	5	0	0	0	125
Mean Precipitation (in.)	0.17	0.20	0.53	1.23	1.78	1.21	1.02	0.70	1.02	0.68	0.37	0.20	9.11
Days With ≥ 0.1" Precipitation	1	1	2	3	5	3	3	2	3	2	1	1	27
Days With ≥ 1.0" Precipitation	0	0	0	0	0	0	0	0	0	0	0	0	0
Mean Snowfall (in.)	3.6	2.9	na	6.7	1.5	0.2	0.0	0.0	1.0	1.5	4.2	na	na
Days With ≥ 1.0" Snow Depth	na	3	na	na	0	0	0	0	0	1	4	5	na

Carpenter *Laramie County*   Elevation: 5,387 ft.   Latitude: 41° 03' N   Longitude: 104° 22' W

	JAN	FEB	MAR	APR	MAY	JUN	JUL	AUG	SEP	OCT	NOV	DEC	YEAR
Mean Maximum Temp. (°F)	39.8	44.4	50.4	58.9	69.1	79.8	86.5	85.1	76.2	64.0	48.8	41.3	62.0
Mean Temp. (°F)	26.6	30.7	36.4	44.2	54.1	63.9	70.2	68.9	59.9	48.3	35.2	27.9	47.2
Mean Minimum Temp. (°F)	13.3	17.0	22.3	29.4	39.0	48.0	53.9	52.6	43.5	32.5	21.6	14.5	32.3
Extreme Maximum Temp. (°F)	70	71	78	88	92	101	103	103	98	87	76	70	103
Extreme Minimum Temp. (°F)	-29	-28	-8	-9	18	31	39	36	15	-6	-14	-31	-31
Days Maximum Temp. ≥ 90°F	0	0	0	0	0	4	12	9	2	0	0	0	27
Days Maximum Temp. ≤ 32°F	8	5	3	1	0	0	0	0	0	0	4	7	28
Days Minimum Temp. ≤ 32°F	30	27	28	19	5	0	0	0	3	14	27	29	182
Days Minimum Temp. ≤ 0°F	5	3	1	0	0	0	0	0	0	0	1	4	14
Heating Degree Days (base 65°F)	1,185	962	880	617	336	92	13	18	180	512	886	1,144	6,825
Cooling Degree Days (base 65°F)	0	0	0	0	5	66	180	151	35	0	0	0	437
Mean Precipitation (in.)	0.32	0.19	0.90	1.31	2.29	2.44	2.57	1.52	1.43	0.68	0.45	0.33	14.43
Days With ≥ 0.1" Precipitation	1	1	3	4	6	6	5	4	4	2	1	1	38
Days With ≥ 1.0" Precipitation	0	0	0	0	0	0	0	0	0	0	0	0	0
Mean Snowfall (in.)	5.3	3.2	7.8	4.6	0.6	trace	trace	0.0	0.6	2.3	4.9	5.4	34.7
Days With ≥ 1.0" Snow Depth	7	5	4	1	0	0	0	0	0	1	4	6	28

Cheyenne Municipal Airport *Laramie County*   Elevation: 6,125 ft.   Latitude: 41° 09' N   Longitude: 104° 48' W

	JAN	FEB	MAR	APR	MAY	JUN	JUL	AUG	SEP	OCT	NOV	DEC	YEAR
Mean Maximum Temp. (°F)	37.7	41.0	46.3	54.0	64.1	75.1	82.1	80.5	71.3	59.2	45.8	39.0	58.0
Mean Temp. (°F)	26.8	29.8	34.9	42.0	51.8	61.8	68.2	66.9	57.7	46.3	34.6	28.1	45.7
Mean Minimum Temp. (°F)	15.8	18.5	23.4	30.0	39.4	48.5	54.3	53.2	44.0	33.5	23.3	17.2	33.4
Extreme Maximum Temp. (°F)	66	67	74	83	87	96	98	96	95	83	75	66	98
Extreme Minimum Temp. (°F)	-29	-25	-9	-8	18	32	40	36	8	-1	-16	-28	-29
Days Maximum Temp. ≥ 90°F	0	0	0	0	0	1	5	2	0	0	0	0	8
Days Maximum Temp. ≤ 32°F	9	6	4	2	0	0	0	0	0	1	5	9	36
Days Minimum Temp. ≤ 32°F	29	26	27	19	4	0	0	0	2	13	25	29	174
Days Minimum Temp. ≤ 0°F	4	2	1	0	0	0	0	0	0	0	1	3	11
Heating Degree Days (base 65°F)	1,178	988	927	683	404	132	26	35	235	572	905	1,137	7,222
Cooling Degree Days (base 65°F)	0	0	0	0	1	44	136	105	22	0	0	0	308
Mean Precipitation (in.)	0.45	0.42	1.05	1.56	2.54	2.19	2.20	1.76	1.38	0.77	0.64	0.45	15.41
Days With ≥ 0.1" Precipitation	1	1	3	4	6	5	5	5	3	3	2	2	40
Days With ≥ 1.0" Precipitation	0	0	0	0	0	0	0	0	0	0	0	0	0
Mean Snowfall (in.)	7.2	6.5	12.6	9.3	2.5	trace	trace	trace	1.2	4.3	8.5	7.5	59.6
Days With ≥ 1.0" Snow Depth	12	8	8	5	1	0	0	0	0	2	8	12	56

Chugwater *Platte County*   Elevation: 5,301 ft.   Latitude: 41° 45' N   Longitude: 104° 49' W

	JAN	FEB	MAR	APR	MAY	JUN	JUL	AUG	SEP	OCT	NOV	DEC	YEAR
Mean Maximum Temp. (°F)	38.9	42.8	49.6	57.9	67.9	79.1	86.1	84.7	75.8	63.4	48.1	40.7	61.3
Mean Temp. (°F)	27.3	30.6	36.3	43.4	52.9	62.8	69.0	67.5	58.2	47.2	35.3	28.8	46.6
Mean Minimum Temp. (°F)	15.8	18.3	22.9	28.9	37.9	46.4	51.8	50.3	40.5	30.9	22.5	16.7	31.9
Extreme Maximum Temp. (°F)	69	70	76	84	89	101	101	100	98	85	77	69	101
Extreme Minimum Temp. (°F)	-34	-28	-16	-16	14	25	35	31	10	-5	-26	-35	-35
Days Maximum Temp. ≥ 90°F	0	0	0	0	0	4	11	8	2	0	0	0	25
Days Maximum Temp. ≤ 32°F	9	5	3	1	0	0	0	0	0	1	4	7	30
Days Minimum Temp. ≤ 32°F	28	25	26	20	7	1	0	0	5	17	25	28	182
Days Minimum Temp. ≤ 0°F	5	3	1	0	0	0	0	0	0	0	1	4	14
Heating Degree Days (base 65°F)	1,161	966	883	641	370	114	21	28	221	546	883	1,118	6,952
Cooling Degree Days (base 65°F)	0	0	0	0	3	50	149	117	22	0	0	0	341
Mean Precipitation (in.)	0.59	0.54	1.02	1.57	2.92	2.14	1.92	1.53	1.20	0.96	0.71	0.62	15.72
Days With ≥ 0.1" Precipitation	2	2	3	4	7	5	5	4	3	3	2	2	42
Days With ≥ 1.0" Precipitation	0	0	0	0	1	0	0	0	0	0	0	0	1
Mean Snowfall (in.)	10.4	8.8	11.9	10.2	3.0	0.0	0.0	0.0	1.5	5.2	11.0	10.7	72.7
Days With ≥ 1.0" Snow Depth	15	11	9	4	0	0	0	0	0	2	9	14	64

Clark 3 NE *Park County* Elevation: 4,087 ft. Latitude: 44° 56' N Longitude: 109° 08' W

	JAN	FEB	MAR	APR	MAY	JUN	JUL	AUG	SEP	OCT	NOV	DEC	YEAR
Mean Maximum Temp. (°F)	35.7	43.9	51.3	60.3	69.2	79.0	85.2	84.9	74.3	62.6	47.1	37.7	60.9
Mean Temp. (°F)	21.2	28.6	36.0	44.7	54.0	63.3	68.8	67.8	57.2	46.0	32.5	23.1	45.3
Mean Minimum Temp. (°F)	6.7	13.3	20.6	29.1	38.7	47.5	52.4	50.6	40.1	29.3	17.9	8.4	29.5
Extreme Maximum Temp. (°F)	67	70	79	89	95	104	105	102	103	87	78	67	105
Extreme Minimum Temp. (°F)	-37	-38	-25	1	14	27	36	28	16	-12	-30	-44	-44
Days Maximum Temp. ≥ 90°F	0	0	0	0	0	4	10	9	2	0	0	0	25
Days Maximum Temp. ≤ 32°F	11	5	2	0	0	0	0	0	0	0	4	10	32
Days Minimum Temp. ≤ 32°F	30	26	28	20	7	0	0	0	6	20	28	30	195
Days Minimum Temp. ≤ 0°F	10	4	1	0	0	0	0	0	0	0	2	8	25
Heating Degree Days (base 65°F)	1,354	1,023	894	604	343	111	29	33	248	585	969	1,294	7,487
Cooling Degree Days (base 65°F)	0	0	0	2	9	64	147	135	24	1	0	0	382
Mean Precipitation (in.)	0.29	0.18	0.29	0.54	1.30	1.27	0.96	0.71	0.81	0.61	0.31	0.20	7.47
Days With ≥ 0.1" Precipitation	*1*	1	1	2	4	4	3	2	2	2	1	1	*24*
Days With ≥ 1.0" Precipitation	0	0	0	0	0	0	0	0	0	0	0	0	0
Mean Snowfall (in.)	6.9	*2.3*	4.0	2.2	0.3	0.0	0.0	0.0	0.8	1.5	*3.0*	4.1	*25.1*
Days With ≥ 1.0" Snow Depth	*8*	na	*2*	1	0	0	0	0	0	1	*2*	*7*	na

Clearmont 5 SW *Sheridan County* Elevation: 3,992 ft. Latitude: 44° 35' N Longitude: 106° 27' W

	JAN	FEB	MAR	APR	MAY	JUN	JUL	AUG	SEP	OCT	NOV	DEC	YEAR
Mean Maximum Temp. (°F)	30.8	37.0	46.7	57.3	67.1	77.1	84.4	83.3	71.5	59.7	43.1	33.0	57.6
Mean Temp. (°F)	17.7	24.1	33.8	43.1	52.5	62.0	68.1	66.4	55.3	44.1	30.0	19.9	43.1
Mean Minimum Temp. (°F)	4.6	11.2	20.7	28.8	37.9	46.9	51.7	49.5	39.0	28.5	16.9	6.8	28.5
Extreme Maximum Temp. (°F)	59	68	76	86	91	99	103	104	98	86	83	67	104
Extreme Minimum Temp. (°F)	-46	-37	-24	1	14	24	32	30	6	-16	-29	-48	-48
Days Maximum Temp. ≥ 90°F	0	0	0	0	0	3	8	7	1	0	0	0	19
Days Maximum Temp. ≤ 32°F	14	8	3	1	0	0	0	0	0	1	6	13	46
Days Minimum Temp. ≤ 32°F	31	28	29	20	7	1	0	0	6	21	29	31	203
Days Minimum Temp. ≤ 0°F	11	6	1	0	0	0	0	0	0	0	2	8	28
Heating Degree Days (base 65°F)	1,462	1,150	961	652	383	132	29	49	295	641	1,043	1,391	8,188
Cooling Degree Days (base 65°F)	0	0	0	0	4	49	130	105	12	0	0	0	300
Mean Precipitation (in.)	0.63	0.40	0.88	1.66	2.35	2.08	1.60	1.14	1.40	1.21	0.67	0.47	14.49
Days With ≥ 0.1" Precipitation	2	2	3	4	6	5	4	3	4	3	2	2	40
Days With ≥ 1.0" Precipitation	0	0	0	0	0	0	0	0	0	0	0	0	0
Mean Snowfall (in.)	8.5	5.5	6.9	6.1	0.6	trace	0.0	0.0	0.9	2.5	6.5	8.1	45.6
Days With ≥ 1.0" Snow Depth	22	17	9	2	0	0	0	0	0	1	7	18	76

Cody *Park County* Elevation: 4,990 ft. Latitude: 44° 33' N Longitude: 109° 04' W

	JAN	FEB	MAR	APR	MAY	JUN	JUL	AUG	SEP	OCT	NOV	DEC	YEAR
Mean Maximum Temp. (°F)	35.1	40.6	48.3	56.3	65.9	76.3	83.6	82.3	71.8	60.3	45.0	37.0	58.5
Mean Temp. (°F)	24.2	29.2	36.5	44.1	53.2	62.6	69.1	67.8	57.9	47.6	34.5	26.3	46.1
Mean Minimum Temp. (°F)	13.2	17.8	24.7	31.9	40.5	48.9	54.5	53.3	43.9	34.8	24.0	15.6	33.6
Extreme Maximum Temp. (°F)	64	66	75	82	89	99	100	100	96	83	74	65	100
Extreme Minimum Temp. (°F)	-28	-37	-15	4	21	30	36	33	14	-4	-17	-34	-37
Days Maximum Temp. ≥ 90°F	0	0	0	0	0	2	7	5	1	0	0	0	15
Days Maximum Temp. ≤ 32°F	11	6	3	1	0	0	0	0	0	1	4	10	36
Days Minimum Temp. ≤ 32°F	28	25	24	16	5	0	0	0	3	12	23	28	164
Days Minimum Temp. ≤ 0°F	7	3	1	0	0	0	0	0	0	0	1	4	16
Heating Degree Days (base 65°F)	1,260	1,004	876	620	364	124	26	36	239	535	908	1,194	7,186
Cooling Degree Days (base 65°F)	0	0	0	0	7	54	150	131	33	1	0	0	376
Mean Precipitation (in.)	0.42	0.24	0.52	1.18	1.93	1.57	1.20	0.89	1.20	0.88	0.48	0.32	10.83
Days With ≥ 0.1" Precipitation	1	1	2	3	6	5	4	3	3	3	2	1	34
Days With ≥ 1.0" Precipitation	0	0	0	0	0	0	0	0	0	0	0	0	0
Mean Snowfall (in.)	9.5	5.6	*6.5*	*5.3*	0.4	0.0	0.0	0.0	0.4	4.4	6.1	8.3	*46.5*
Days With ≥ 1.0" Snow Depth	na	na	na	na	0	0	0	0	0	*1*	na	na	na

Cody 12 SE *Park County* Elevation: 5,246 ft. Latitude: 44° 25' N Longitude: 108° 54' W

	JAN	FEB	MAR	APR	MAY	JUN	JUL	AUG	SEP	OCT	NOV	DEC	YEAR
Mean Maximum Temp. (°F)	36.1	40.2	46.4	55.0	64.4	75.6	83.5	82.6	70.8	58.3	44.3	38.0	57.9
Mean Temp. (°F)	23.3	27.6	34.2	42.4	51.5	61.2	68.1	66.8	55.4	44.0	31.7	24.7	44.2
Mean Minimum Temp. (°F)	9.8	14.7	21.9	29.8	38.5	46.8	52.6	51.0	40.0	29.7	19.1	11.4	30.4
Extreme Maximum Temp. (°F)	65	68	75	84	88	98	102	102	97	85	73	69	102
Extreme Minimum Temp. (°F)	-30	-40	-18	0	18	29	30	31	7	-5	-23	-41	-41
Days Maximum Temp. ≥ 90°F	0	0	0	0	0	2	8	6	1	0	0	0	17
Days Maximum Temp. ≤ 32°F	10	6	4	1	0	0	0	0	0	1	5	8	35
Days Minimum Temp. ≤ 32°F	29	27	27	19	6	0	0	0	6	19	27	29	189
Days Minimum Temp. ≤ 0°F	8	5	1	0	0	0	0	0	0	0	3	6	23
Heating Degree Days (base 65°F)	1,288	1,049	949	671	416	157	39	52	299	645	993	1,242	7,800
Cooling Degree Days (base 65°F)	0	0	0	0	4	46	137	121	20	0	0	0	328
Mean Precipitation (in.)	0.38	0.23	0.50	1.02	1.99	1.78	1.05	0.82	0.99	0.67	0.42	0.32	10.17
Days With ≥ 0.1" Precipitation	*1*	1	2	*3*	5	5	3	3	3	2	2	1	*31*
Days With ≥ 1.0" Precipitation	*0*	0	0	0	0	0	0	0	0	0	0	0	*0*
Mean Snowfall (in.)	na	na	na	na	0.2	0.0	0.0	0.0	0.2	0.67	0.42	na	na
Days With ≥ 1.0" Snow Depth	na	na	na	na	0	0	0	0	0	*0.4*	*1.4*	na	na

Cody 21 SW *Park County*   Elevation: 5,839 ft.   Latitude: 44° 20' N   Longitude: 109° 23' W

	JAN	FEB	MAR	APR	MAY	JUN	JUL	AUG	SEP	OCT	NOV	DEC	YEAR
Mean Maximum Temp. (°F)	37.7	40.9	46.8	54.3	63.1	73.8	81.7	81.0	70.1	59.3	44.9	38.3	57.6
Mean Temp. (°F)	26.0	28.9	34.4	41.3	49.6	58.4	64.8	64.0	54.5	45.2	33.3	27.0	43.9
Mean Minimum Temp. (°F)	14.3	16.8	22.0	28.2	36.0	42.9	47.8	46.9	38.8	30.9	21.8	15.6	30.2
Extreme Maximum Temp. (°F)	67	68	73	87	87	97	99	97	93	86	74	63	99
Extreme Minimum Temp. (°F)	-29	-47	-23	-2	12	27	30	28	8	-12	-24	-40	-47
Days Maximum Temp. ≥ 90°F	0	0	0	0	0	1	4	3	1	0	0	0	9
Days Maximum Temp. ≤ 32°F	9	6	3	1	0	0	0	0	0	1	4	9	33
Days Minimum Temp. ≤ 32°F	27	25	27	21	10	2	0	0	6	17	25	27	187
Days Minimum Temp. ≤ 0°F	6	4	2	0	0	0	0	0	0	0	0	2	5	19
Heating Degree Days (base 65°F)	1,202	1,013	941	704	473	213	68	80	319	609	943	1,173	7,738
Cooling Degree Days (base 65°F)	0	0	0	0	1	20	70	56	11	1	0	0	159
Mean Precipitation (in.)	0.47	0.46	0.88	1.52	2.01	1.48	1.35	1.00	1.44	1.28	0.73	0.54	13.16
Days With ≥ 0.1" Precipitation	2	1	3	4	5	4	4	3	4	3	3	2	38
Days With ≥ 1.0" Precipitation	0	0	0	0	0	0	0	0	0	0	0	0	0
Mean Snowfall (in.)	5.6	5.0	7.4	8.1	1.2	trace	0.0	0.0	1.8	6.6	7.5	6.9	50.1
Days With ≥ 1.0" Snow Depth	15	10	6	4	0	0	0	0	0	2	9	13	59

Colony *Crook County*   Elevation: 3,569 ft.   Latitude: 44° 55' N   Longitude: 104° 12' W

	JAN	FEB	MAR	APR	MAY	JUN	JUL	AUG	SEP	OCT	NOV	DEC	YEAR
Mean Maximum Temp. (°F)	32.0	37.7	45.4	57.5	68.7	79.4	87.4	86.8	75.1	60.6	43.6	34.4	59.1
Mean Temp. (°F)	21.9	27.3	34.2	45.1	55.8	65.8	72.7	71.9	60.9	48.2	33.6	24.5	46.8
Mean Minimum Temp. (°F)	11.4	16.9	23.0	32.7	42.8	52.1	58.0	56.9	46.6	35.8	23.6	14.5	34.5
Extreme Maximum Temp. (°F)	69	75	80	90	98	109	112	107	108	91	79	67	112
Extreme Minimum Temp. (°F)	-23	-36	-21	3	21	30	42	39	20	-6	-17	-32	-36
Days Maximum Temp. ≥ 90°F	0	0	0	0	1	4	13	13	4	0	0	0	35
Days Maximum Temp. ≤ 32°F	14	9	6	1	0	0	0	0	0	0	7	12	49
Days Minimum Temp. ≤ 32°F	29	25	26	15	3	0	0	0	2	10	24	29	163
Days Minimum Temp. ≤ 0°F	8	4	1	0	0	0	0	0	0	0	1	5	19
Heating Degree Days (base 65°F)	1,330	1,057	947	594	299	76	12	17	184	518	936	1,250	7,220
Cooling Degree Days (base 65°F)	0	0	0	4	23	106	263	245	69	4	0	0	714
Mean Precipitation (in.)	0.35	0.40	0.83	1.57	2.62	2.63	1.75	1.27	1.19	1.31	0.55	0.46	14.93
Days With ≥ 0.1" Precipitation	1	2	2	4	6	5	4	3	3	3	2	1	36
Days With ≥ 1.0" Precipitation	0	0	0	0	0	1	0	0	0	0	0	0	1
Mean Snowfall (in.)	5.1	4.4	7.4	5.8	0.4	0.0	0.0	0.0	0.1	1.5	5.3	6.4	36.4
Days With ≥ 1.0" Snow Depth	22	14	12	3	0	0	0	0	0	1	8	20	80

Deaver *Big Horn County*   Elevation: 4,104 ft.   Latitude: 44° 53' N   Longitude: 108° 36' W

	JAN	FEB	MAR	APR	MAY	JUN	JUL	AUG	SEP	OCT	NOV	DEC	YEAR
Mean Maximum Temp. (°F)	30.4	39.2	50.6	61.4	70.9	80.6	87.8	86.9	75.5	62.3	43.7	32.9	60.2
Mean Temp. (°F)	17.3	25.1	35.7	45.3	55.2	64.3	70.5	69.0	58.0	46.0	30.6	20.0	44.8
Mean Minimum Temp. (°F)	4.6	11.0	20.8	29.3	39.5	47.9	53.1	51.1	40.5	29.7	17.4	7.0	29.3
Extreme Maximum Temp. (°F)	63	74	76	87	95	102	105	104	98	89	72	63	105
Extreme Minimum Temp. (°F)	-36	-36	-15	6	15	30	35	25	17	-6	-23	-38	-38
Days Maximum Temp. ≥ 90°F	0	0	0	0	0	5	14	13	2	0	0	0	34
Days Maximum Temp. ≤ 32°F	16	7	2	0	0	0	0	0	0	0	5	13	43
Days Minimum Temp. ≤ 32°F	31	28	29	20	5	0	0	0	4	19	29	31	196
Days Minimum Temp. ≤ 0°F	11	5	1	0	0	0	0	0	0	0	0	2	7	26
Heating Degree Days (base 65°F)	1,473	1,119	901	584	304	93	15	26	230	582	1,025	1,391	7,743
Cooling Degree Days (base 65°F)	0	0	0	0	10	74	188	161	26	0	0	0	459
Mean Precipitation (in.)	0.16	0.11	0.21	0.37	1.06	1.04	0.74	0.56	0.60	0.35	0.16	0.13	5.49
Days With ≥ 0.1" Precipitation	0	0	1	1	3	3	2	2	2	1	1	1	17
Days With ≥ 1.0" Precipitation	0	0	0	0	0	0	0	0	0	0	0	0	0
Mean Snowfall (in.)	3.6	*1.1*	*1.2*	0.9	0.1	0.0	0.0	0.0	0.5	0.3	1.4	*1.8*	*10.9*
Days With ≥ 1.0" Snow Depth	na	na	*2*	0	0	0	0	0	0	0	0	*6*	na

Devils Tower 2 *Crook County*   Elevation: 3,861 ft.   Latitude: 44° 35' N   Longitude: 104° 43' W

	JAN	FEB	MAR	APR	MAY	JUN	JUL	AUG	SEP	OCT	NOV	DEC	YEAR
Mean Maximum Temp. (°F)	33.8	40.0	48.6	59.3	69.3	79.2	86.6	86.3	75.6	62.4	45.1	36.0	60.2
Mean Temp. (°F)	19.1	25.4	33.9	43.8	53.7	63.2	69.6	68.3	57.6	45.4	31.2	21.7	44.4
Mean Minimum Temp. (°F)	4.4	10.7	19.1	28.2	38.0	47.2	52.6	50.3	39.4	28.3	17.3	7.4	28.6
Extreme Maximum Temp. (°F)	65	71	80	90	93	102	108	102	103	90	80	67	108
Extreme Minimum Temp. (°F)	-40	-44	-29	-12	15	26	31	29	14	-20	-27	-48	-48
Days Maximum Temp. ≥ 90°F	0	0	0	0	0	4	12	12	3	0	0	0	31
Days Maximum Temp. ≤ 32°F	11	7	4	1	0	0	0	0	0	1	5	10	39
Days Minimum Temp. ≤ 32°F	31	28	29	21	8	1	0	0	7	22	28	31	206
Days Minimum Temp. ≤ 0°F	11	6	2	0	0	0	0	0	0	0	2	8	29
Heating Degree Days (base 65°F)	1,417	1,111	959	631	353	117	27	35	248	602	1,007	1,335	7,842
Cooling Degree Days (base 65°F)	0	0	0	1	10	68	180	152	30	0	0	0	441
Mean Precipitation (in.)	0.60	0.57	1.02	1.84	2.62	3.11	2.06	1.53	1.29	1.54	0.73	0.72	17.63
Days With ≥ 0.1" Precipitation	2	2	3	5	6	6	5	3	3	3	3	3	44
Days With ≥ 1.0" Precipitation	0	0	0	0	0	1	0	0	0	0	0	0	1
Mean Snowfall (in.)	9.2	7.7	9.2	6.2	0.5	trace	0.0	0.0	0.2	2.8	6.7	10.6	53.1
Days With ≥ 1.0" Snow Depth	28	23	14	3	0	0	0	0	0	2	9	21	100

Dillinger *Campbell County*   Elevation: 4,307 ft.   Latitude: 44° 06' N   Longitude: 105° 07' W

	JAN	FEB	MAR	APR	MAY	JUN	JUL	AUG	SEP	OCT	NOV	DEC	YEAR
Mean Maximum Temp. (°F)	32.5	38.3	46.2	56.3	66.9	78.5	86.8	85.9	74.4	60.3	44.3	34.9	58.8
Mean Temp. (°F)	19.8	25.5	33.3	42.6	52.8	63.0	70.1	68.9	57.6	45.0	31.0	21.8	44.3
Mean Minimum Temp. (°F)	7.0	12.7	20.4	28.8	38.7	47.5	53.3	51.7	40.8	29.6	17.7	8.5	29.7
Extreme Maximum Temp. (°F)	66	70	78	87	93	103	105	104	102	90	77	70	105
Extreme Minimum Temp. (°F)	-35	-38	-25	-5	19	30	32	30	12	-16	-26	-45	-45
Days Maximum Temp. ≥ 90°F	0	0	0	0	0	4	13	12	3	0	0	0	32
Days Maximum Temp. ≤ 32°F	14	8	4	1	0	0	0	0	0	1	6	12	46
Days Minimum Temp. ≤ 32°F	30	28	28	21	6	0	0	0	5	19	28	30	195
Days Minimum Temp. ≤ 0°F	10	5	2	0	0	0	0	0	0	0	3	7	27
Heating Degree Days (base 65°F)	1,396	1,110	976	667	375	121	24	31	249	616	1,013	1,334	7,912
Cooling Degree Days (base 65°F)	0	0	0	1	6	68	195	174	36	1	0	0	481
Mean Precipitation (in.)	0.40	0.52	0.83	1.69	2.58	2.20	1.90	1.13	1.13	1.23	0.54	0.54	14.69
Days With ≥ 0.1" Precipitation	2	2	3	4	7	5	4	3	3	3	2	2	40
Days With ≥ 1.0" Precipitation	0	0	0	0	0	0	0	0	0	0	0	0	0
Mean Snowfall (in.)	6.0	6.6	7.2	5.6	0.6	0.1	0.0	0.0	trace	2.0	5.6	8.2	41.9
Days With ≥ 1.0" Snow Depth	na	na	na	1	0	0	0	0	0	0	4	13	na

Diversion Dam *Fremont County*   Elevation: 5,574 ft.   Latitude: 43° 14' N   Longitude: 108° 57' W

	JAN	FEB	MAR	APR	MAY	JUN	JUL	AUG	SEP	OCT	NOV	DEC	YEAR
Mean Maximum Temp. (°F)	34.7	41.5	49.8	57.6	66.3	77.2	84.8	83.4	73.1	61.8	44.4	36.5	59.3
Mean Temp. (°F)	21.0	27.3	35.6	43.4	52.3	61.8	68.2	66.7	56.9	46.3	30.9	22.4	44.4
Mean Minimum Temp. (°F)	7.5	12.5	21.3	29.3	38.4	46.4	51.6	50.0	40.8	30.8	17.3	8.2	29.5
Extreme Maximum Temp. (°F)	66	67	76	86	88	105	115	106	101	96	72	72	115
Extreme Minimum Temp. (°F)	-36	-39	-23	-6	18	29	33	32	10	-5	-23	-44	-44
Days Maximum Temp. ≥ 90°F	0	0	0	0	0	3	8	5	1	0	0	0	17
Days Maximum Temp. ≤ 32°F	12	6	2	1	0	0	0	0	0	1	5	11	38
Days Minimum Temp. ≤ 32°F	30	27	28	20	7	1	0	0	5	18	27	30	193
Days Minimum Temp. ≤ 0°F	9	5	1	0	0	0	0	0	0	0	3	8	26
Heating Degree Days (base 65°F)	1,358	1,058	907	641	393	141	31	38	251	576	1,018	1,315	7,727
Cooling Degree Days (base 65°F)	0	0	0	1	7	57	143	110	17	2	0	0	337
Mean Precipitation (in.)	0.17	0.16	0.49	1.28	1.96	1.23	0.97	0.64	1.11	0.74	0.36	0.20	9.31
Days With ≥ 0.1" Precipitation	1	1	2	3	4	3	3	2	2	2	1	1	25
Days With ≥ 1.0" Precipitation	0	0	0	0	0	0	0	0	0	0	0	0	0
Mean Snowfall (in.)	na	2.0	3.8	2.6	0.9	trace	0.0	0.0	0.4	0.7	3.4	na	na
Days With ≥ 1.0" Snow Depth	na	4	2	1	0	0	0	0	0	0	4	5	na

Double Four Ranch *Albany County*   Elevation: 6,197 ft.   Latitude: 42° 11' N   Longitude: 105° 24' W

	JAN	FEB	MAR	APR	MAY	JUN	JUL	AUG	SEP	OCT	NOV	DEC	YEAR
Mean Maximum Temp. (°F)	34.2	37.8	45.2	53.5	63.2	74.3	81.4	80.2	70.9	58.8	43.8	35.4	56.6
Mean Temp. (°F)	23.8	26.9	33.2	40.2	49.1	58.0	64.3	62.8	53.7	43.5	32.6	25.0	42.8
Mean Minimum Temp. (°F)	13.4	15.9	21.2	26.8	34.9	41.6	47.1	45.3	36.5	28.2	21.4	14.6	28.9
Extreme Maximum Temp. (°F)	57	61	69	81	88	96	99	96	94	87	72	61	99
Extreme Minimum Temp. (°F)	-33	-37	-24	-16	15	25	29	25	-1	-2	-22	-41	-41
Days Maximum Temp. ≥ 90°F	0	0	0	0	0	1	3	1	0	0	0	0	5
Days Maximum Temp. ≤ 32°F	12	7	4	1	0	0	0	0	0	1	5	10	40
Days Minimum Temp. ≤ 32°F	30	27	28	23	11	2	0	1	9	22	26	29	208
Days Minimum Temp. ≤ 0°F	5	3	1	0	0	0	0	0	0	0	1	4	14
Heating Degree Days (base 65°F)	1,270	1,069	979	738	487	215	66	93	335	659	965	1,233	8,109
Cooling Degree Days (base 65°F)	0	0	0	0	0	9	43	29	3	0	0	0	84
Mean Precipitation (in.)	0.42	0.50	0.94	1.96	2.81	2.23	1.74	1.40	1.16	0.99	0.76	0.56	15.47
Days With ≥ 0.1" Precipitation	2	2	3	5	7	5	5	4	3	3	3	2	44
Days With ≥ 1.0" Precipitation	0	0	0	0	0	0	0	0	0	0	0	0	0
Mean Snowfall (in.)	8.7	8.5	11.5	11.7	3.6	0.3	0.0	0.0	1.2	4.5	10.8	11.3	72.1
Days With ≥ 1.0" Snow Depth	19	16	11	5	1	0	0	0	0	2	10	17	81

Dull Center 1 SE *Converse County*   Elevation: 4,412 ft.   Latitude: 43° 25' N   Longitude: 104° 58' W

	JAN	FEB	MAR	APR	MAY	JUN	JUL	AUG	SEP	OCT	NOV	DEC	YEAR
Mean Maximum Temp. (°F)	34.6	40.6	48.9	58.3	69.0	80.7	89.3	88.4	76.9	63.0	45.7	36.6	61.0
Mean Temp. (°F)	22.9	28.3	35.8	44.7	54.8	65.0	72.2	71.2	60.1	47.7	33.7	24.8	46.8
Mean Minimum Temp. (°F)	11.1	16.1	22.7	30.9	40.7	49.4	55.0	53.9	43.3	32.4	21.7	12.9	32.5
Extreme Maximum Temp. (°F)	68	71	77	87	92	106	107	107	103	87	76	69	107
Extreme Minimum Temp. (°F)	-28	-35	-18	-8	17	30	29	38	14	-8	-21	-42	-42
Days Maximum Temp. ≥ 90°F	0	0	0	0	0	6	15	15	4	0	0	0	40
Days Maximum Temp. ≤ 32°F	12	7	3	1	0	0	0	0	0	1	5	10	39
Days Minimum Temp. ≤ 32°F	29	26	27	17	4	0	0	0	3	14	25	29	174
Days Minimum Temp. ≤ 0°F	8	4	1	0	0	0	0	0	0	0	2	5	20
Heating Degree Days (base 65°F)	1,300	1,029	898	604	317	86	11	13	187	528	932	1,242	7,147
Cooling Degree Days (base 65°F)	0	0	0	1	10	86	232	216	46	0	0	0	591
Mean Precipitation (in.)	0.24	0.41	0.75	1.60	2.37	2.12	1.71	1.27	1.01	1.00	0.56	0.39	13.43
Days With ≥ 0.1" Precipitation	1	2	2	4	5	5	4	3	3	3	2	1	35
Days With ≥ 1.0" Precipitation	0	0	0	0	0	0	0	0	0	0	0	0	0
Mean Snowfall (in.)	5.9	6.3	9.6	8.3	1.3	trace	0.0	0.0	0.4	3.4	7.0	8.2	50.4
Days With ≥ 1.0" Snow Depth	17	10	7	3	0	0	0	0	0	2	7	14	60

Elk Mountain *Carbon County*   Elevation: 7,263 ft.   Latitude: 41° 41' N   Longitude: 106° 25' W

	JAN	FEB	MAR	APR	MAY	JUN	JUL	AUG	SEP	OCT	NOV	DEC	YEAR
Mean Maximum Temp. (°F)	32.0	35.0	41.4	49.2	60.3	72.0	79.0	77.0	67.8	55.6	40.7	33.6	53.6
Mean Temp. (°F)	22.9	25.4	31.4	37.9	47.5	57.4	63.4	61.8	53.2	43.1	31.0	24.3	41.6
Mean Minimum Temp. (°F)	13.8	15.7	21.5	26.5	34.6	42.7	47.7	46.5	38.4	30.5	21.3	14.9	29.5
Extreme Maximum Temp. (°F)	55	56	69	75	79	89	92	92	89	78	67	58	92
Extreme Minimum Temp. (°F)	-36	-34	-17	-5	15	24	34	29	6	-10	-19	-35	-36
Days Maximum Temp. ≥ 90°F	0	0	0	0	0	0	0	0	0	0	0	0	0
Days Maximum Temp. ≤ 32°F	15	10	5	2	0	0	0	0	0	1	7	13	53
Days Minimum Temp. ≤ 32°F	30	27	28	22	11	2	0	0	7	18	25	29	199
Days Minimum Temp. ≤ 0°F	4	3	1	0	0	0	0	0	0	0	1	3	12
Heating Degree Days (base 65°F)	1,297	1,113	1,033	807	537	233	79	112	351	673	1,014	1,256	8,505
Cooling Degree Days (base 65°F)	0	0	0	0	0	9	31	18	1	0	0	0	59
Mean Precipitation (in.)	0.71	0.65	1.07	1.44	1.84	1.06	0.96	0.93	1.00	0.98	0.98	0.78	12.40
Days With ≥ 0.1" Precipitation	3	2	3	4	4	3	2	3	3	3	3	2	35
Days With ≥ 1.0" Precipitation	0	0	0	0	0	0	0	0	0	0	0	0	0
Mean Snowfall (in.)	12.1	10.8	14.0	11.3	4.6	0.5	0.0	0.0	1.0	6.3	12.5	13.3	86.4
Days With ≥ 1.0" Snow Depth	26	24	17	7	1	0	0	0	0	3	13	19	110

Emblem *Big Horn County*   Elevation: 4,445 ft.   Latitude: 44° 30' N   Longitude: 108° 23' W

	JAN	FEB	MAR	APR	MAY	JUN	JUL	AUG	SEP	OCT	NOV	DEC	YEAR
Mean Maximum Temp. (°F)	29.6	37.7	49.1	59.1	69.1	79.5	86.5	85.5	73.3	60.0	42.9	32.1	58.7
Mean Temp. (°F)	18.1	25.6	36.2	45.4	55.3	64.4	70.3	68.9	58.0	46.1	31.4	20.6	45.0
Mean Minimum Temp. (°F)	6.7	13.5	23.2	31.6	41.4	49.2	54.1	52.2	42.6	32.3	19.9	9.1	31.3
Extreme Maximum Temp. (°F)	61	69	78	89	91	101	105	103	97	85	72	64	105
Extreme Minimum Temp. (°F)	-34	-34	-14	5	21	32	36	34	16	-7	-20	-37	-37
Days Maximum Temp. ≥ 90°F	0	0	0	0	0	5	11	10	1	0	0	0	27
Days Maximum Temp. ≤ 32°F	16	8	2	0	0	0	0	0	0	0	5	14	45
Days Minimum Temp. ≤ 32°F	31	28	27	17	3	0	0	0	3	15	27	31	182
Days Minimum Temp. ≤ 0°F	9	4	1	0	0	0	0	0	0	0	2	6	22
Heating Degree Days (base 65°F)	1,448	1,107	886	582	303	93	17	25	230	578	1,002	1,370	7,641
Cooling Degree Days (base 65°F)	0	0	0	1	12	77	189	163	28	0	0	0	470
Mean Precipitation (in.)	0.25	0.19	0.47	0.77	1.38	1.16	0.82	0.52	0.88	0.67	0.29	0.25	7.65
Days With ≥ 0.1" Precipitation	1	1	2	2	4	3	2	2	2	2	1	1	23
Days With ≥ 1.0" Precipitation	0	0	0	0	0	0	0	0	0	0	0	0	0
Mean Snowfall (in.)	*2.6*	1.7	*1.8*	1.4	0.3	0.0	0.0	0.0	0.3	1.6	1.8	*2.7*	*14.2*
Days With ≥ 1.0" Snow Depth	na	na	na	0	0	0	0	0	0	0	0	na	na

Encampment 10 ESE *Carbon County*   Elevation: 7,381 ft.   Latitude: 41° 11' N   Longitude: 106° 37' W

	JAN	FEB	MAR	APR	MAY	JUN	JUL	AUG	SEP	OCT	NOV	DEC	YEAR
Mean Maximum Temp. (°F)	32.8	36.5	42.9	52.2	62.5	72.4	78.4	77.5	69.4	57.8	42.2	34.5	54.9
Mean Temp. (°F)	21.5	24.4	30.5	38.0	47.5	55.9	61.9	60.9	52.6	42.1	29.6	22.6	40.6
Mean Minimum Temp. (°F)	10.0	12.2	18.0	23.8	32.3	39.3	45.3	44.1	35.8	26.3	17.0	10.7	26.3
Extreme Maximum Temp. (°F)	58	58	66	73	80	90	96	92	99	81	69	60	99
Extreme Minimum Temp. (°F)	-35	-32	-20	-13	9	9	24	27	3	-13	-24	-44	-44
Days Maximum Temp. ≥ 90°F	0	0	0	0	0	0	0	0	0	0	0	0	0
Days Maximum Temp. ≤ 32°F	13	9	4	1	0	0	0	0	0	1	6	12	46
Days Minimum Temp. ≤ 32°F	31	28	30	26	16	5	0	1	10	24	29	31	231
Days Minimum Temp. ≤ 0°F	7	4	2	0	0	0	0	0	0	0	2	6	21
Heating Degree Days (base 65°F)	1,343	1,141	1,063	803	536	271	107	131	366	704	1,056	1,307	8,828
Cooling Degree Days (base 65°F)	0	0	0	0	0	3	15	8	1	0	0	0	27
Mean Precipitation (in.)	0.72	0.84	1.22	1.51	1.74	1.21	1.31	1.14	1.11	1.40	1.12	0.84	14.16
Days With ≥ 0.1" Precipitation	3	3	4	5	6	4	4	4	4	4	4	3	48
Days With ≥ 1.0" Precipitation	0	0	0	0	0	0	0	0	0	0	0	0	0
Mean Snowfall (in.)	10.1	*11.5*	12.7	8.8	1.9	0.8	0.0	0.0	0.4	4.9	*12.1*	*10.7*	*73.9*
Days With ≥ 1.0" Snow Depth	na	na	na	na	0	0	0	0	0	2	na	na	na

Evanston 1 E *Uinta County*   Elevation: 6,824 ft.   Latitude: 41° 16' N   Longitude: 110° 57' W

	JAN	FEB	MAR	APR	MAY	JUN	JUL	AUG	SEP	OCT	NOV	DEC	YEAR
Mean Maximum Temp. (°F)	31.4	35.5	42.9	52.8	62.7	73.5	81.5	80.3	70.8	58.3	42.0	33.2	55.4
Mean Temp. (°F)	20.6	23.7	31.0	39.6	48.0	56.7	63.5	62.5	53.8	43.1	30.1	21.7	41.2
Mean Minimum Temp. (°F)	9.8	11.7	19.2	26.2	33.2	39.9	45.4	44.7	36.8	27.9	18.1	10.1	26.9
Extreme Maximum Temp. (°F)	57	60	75	77	82	94	99	94	88	80	69	59	99
Extreme Minimum Temp. (°F)	-31	-30	-14	0	13	24	31	25	14	-8	-19	-31	-31
Days Maximum Temp. ≥ 90°F	0	0	0	0	0	0	2	1	0	0	0	0	3
Days Maximum Temp. ≤ 32°F	16	10	3	1	0	0	0	0	0	1	6	14	51
Days Minimum Temp. ≤ 32°F	30	28	30	24	14	4	0	1	8	23	28	31	221
Days Minimum Temp. ≤ 0°F	7	5	1	0	0	0	0	0	0	0	2	6	21
Heating Degree Days (base 65°F)	1,371	1,160	1,046	754	520	248	73	91	331	672	1,042	1,336	8,644
Cooling Degree Days (base 65°F)	0	0	0	1	0	8	35	24	2	0	0	0	70
Mean Precipitation (in.)	0.68	0.61	0.89	1.15	1.48	0.99	0.88	0.86	1.21	1.19	0.84	0.65	11.43
Days With ≥ 0.1" Precipitation	2	2	3	4	5	3	3	3	3	4	3	2	37
Days With ≥ 1.0" Precipitation	0	0	0	0	0	0	0	0	0	0	0	0	0
Mean Snowfall (in.)	na	na	na	na	*1.0*	0.2	trace	0.0	*trace*	2.2	na	na	na
Days With ≥ 1.0" Snow Depth	na	na	na	na	0	0	0	0	0	1	na	na	na

Fontenelle Dam *Lincoln County* Elevation: 6,479 ft. Latitude: 41° 59' N Longitude: 110° 04' W

	JAN	FEB	MAR	APR	MAY	JUN	JUL	AUG	SEP	OCT	NOV	DEC	YEAR
Mean Maximum Temp. (°F)	25.8	31.1	40.9	51.6	61.8	73.1	81.4	80.1	69.1	56.4	37.9	27.3	53.0
Mean Temp. (°F)	11.8	16.5	27.5	36.7	46.3	55.9	62.8	61.0	50.4	38.6	23.9	13.3	37.1
Mean Minimum Temp. (°F)	-2.2	1.8	14.0	21.7	30.8	38.6	44.1	41.8	31.6	20.8	9.9	-0.8	21.0
Extreme Maximum Temp. (°F)	52	57	66	79	83	94	95	95	88	79	67	57	95
Extreme Minimum Temp. (°F)	-43	-46	-33	-9	8	19	21	17	4	-8	-29	-46	-46
Days Maximum Temp. ≥ 90°F	0	0	0	0	0	1	3	1	0	0	0	0	5
Days Maximum Temp. ≤ 32°F	21	14	6	1	0	0	0	0	0	1	9	20	72
Days Minimum Temp. ≤ 32°F	30	28	31	28	19	5	1	3	16	30	29	31	251
Days Minimum Temp. ≤ 0°F	17	12	3	0	0	0	0	0	0	0	6	17	55
Heating Degree Days (base 65°F)	1,643	1,366	1,157	843	573	277	102	138	433	811	1,225	1,598	10,166
Cooling Degree Days (base 65°F)	0	0	0	0	0	9	38	18	1	0	0	0	66
Mean Precipitation (in.)	0.27	0.26	0.37	0.75	1.22	0.82	0.82	0.72	0.93	0.66	0.40	0.21	7.43
Days With ≥ 0.1" Precipitation	1	1	2	3	4	3	3	2	2	2	1	1	25
Days With ≥ 1.0" Precipitation	0	0	0	0	0	0	0	0	0	0	0	0	0
Mean Snowfall (in.)	na	na	na	na	*0.3*	0.0	0.0	0.0	trace	*1.4*	na	na	na
Days With ≥ 1.0" Snow Depth	na	na	na	na	0	0	0	0	0	*1*	na	na	na

Gillette 6 SE *Campbell County* Elevation: 4,639 ft. Latitude: 44° 14' N Longitude: 105° 26' W

	JAN	FEB	MAR	APR	MAY	JUN	JUL	AUG	SEP	OCT	NOV	DEC	YEAR
Mean Maximum Temp. (°F)	31.6	37.2	45.4	55.1	65.4	76.5	85.1	84.3	72.7	59.2	43.0	34.0	57.4
Mean Temp. (°F)	21.3	26.7	34.1	43.0	52.8	62.9	70.0	69.2	58.3	46.2	32.3	23.7	45.0
Mean Minimum Temp. (°F)	11.0	16.2	22.7	30.8	40.1	49.1	54.9	54.0	43.8	33.2	21.6	13.4	32.6
Extreme Maximum Temp. (°F)	67	70	76	88	91	101	107	104	102	87	75	66	107
Extreme Minimum Temp. (°F)	-31	-35	-20	-5	20	32	36	36	18	-9	-23	-37	-37
Days Maximum Temp. ≥ 90°F	0	0	0	0	0	3	10	9	2	0	0	0	24
Days Maximum Temp. ≤ 32°F	14	9	5	1	0	0	0	0	0	1	6	13	49
Days Minimum Temp. ≤ 32°F	30	27	27	18	5	0	0	0	3	13	25	29	177
Days Minimum Temp. ≤ 0°F	8	4	1	0	0	0	0	0	0	0	2	5	20
Heating Degree Days (base 65°F)	1,348	1,075	951	655	378	125	24	31	232	576	974	1,275	7,644
Cooling Degree Days (base 65°F)	0	0	0	1	7	66	189	173	36	1	0	0	473
Mean Precipitation (in.)	0.55	0.53	1.03	1.92	3.01	2.66	1.80	1.31	1.46	1.56	0.67	0.66	17.16
Days With ≥ 0.1" Precipitation	2	2	4	5	7	6	4	3	3	4	2	2	44
Days With ≥ 1.0" Precipitation	0	0	0	0	1	0	0	0	0	0	0	0	1
Mean Snowfall (in.)	8.7	7.7	11.7	10.5	2.4	0.1	0.0	0.0	0.8	4.8	8.1	10.5	65.3
Days With ≥ 1.0" Snow Depth	20	13	10	3	1	0	0	0	0	2	8	18	75

Glenrock 5 ESE *Converse County* Elevation: 4,947 ft. Latitude: 42° 50' N Longitude: 105° 47' W

	JAN	FEB	MAR	APR	MAY	JUN	JUL	AUG	SEP	OCT	NOV	DEC	YEAR
Mean Maximum Temp. (°F)	37.4	41.8	49.4	58.3	68.8	80.9	88.7	86.8	76.2	62.4	46.3	38.3	61.3
Mean Temp. (°F)	26.7	30.8	37.4	45.2	54.9	65.4	72.2	70.6	59.9	48.0	35.4	28.0	47.9
Mean Minimum Temp. (°F)	16.0	19.7	25.5	32.0	40.9	49.8	55.7	54.2	43.8	33.5	24.4	17.7	34.4
Extreme Maximum Temp. (°F)	65	68	80	86	92	105	107	107	98	86	74	67	107
Extreme Minimum Temp. (°F)	-34	-25	-11	1	21	32	34	35	17	-9	-20	-40	-40
Days Maximum Temp. ≥ 90°F	0	0	0	0	0	7	15	12	2	0	0	0	36
Days Maximum Temp. ≤ 32°F	9	6	3	1	0	0	0	0	0	0	4	9	32
Days Minimum Temp. ≤ 32°F	27	23	24	16	4	0	0	0	3	14	23	27	161
Days Minimum Temp. ≤ 0°F	5	3	0	0	0	0	0	0	0	0	1	3	12
Heating Degree Days (base 65°F)	1,180	961	848	589	313	80	9	13	187	523	882	1,140	6,725
Cooling Degree Days (base 65°F)	0	0	0	1	8	93	236	195	42	1	0	0	576
Mean Precipitation (in.)	0.37	0.43	0.81	1.77	2.33	1.43	1.18	0.70	1.09	1.11	0.69	0.40	12.31
Days With ≥ 0.1" Precipitation	1	2	2	4	5	3	3	2	3	3	2	1	31
Days With ≥ 1.0" Precipitation	0	0	0	0	0	0	0	0	0	0	0	0	0
Mean Snowfall (in.)	*3.8*	*3.5*	na	*0.6*	0.1	trace	0.0	0.0	trace	1.3	*3.6*	na	na
Days With ≥ 1.0" Snow Depth	na	na	na	*0*	0	0	0	0	0	0	0	na	na

Heart Mountain *Park County* Elevation: 4,790 ft. Latitude: 44° 42' N Longitude: 108° 57' W

	JAN	FEB	MAR	APR	MAY	JUN	JUL	AUG	SEP	OCT	NOV	DEC	YEAR
Mean Maximum Temp. (°F)	32.6	40.0	49.2	58.9	68.1	78.2	84.1	83.1	72.7	60.5	43.6	34.3	58.8
Mean Temp. (°F)	20.7	27.4	35.8	44.7	53.9	62.6	67.9	66.7	56.9	46.1	31.9	22.7	44.8
Mean Minimum Temp. (°F)	8.8	14.8	22.3	30.5	39.6	46.9	51.5	50.2	41.1	31.7	20.1	11.1	30.7
Extreme Maximum Temp. (°F)	67	71	80	87	93	99	100	100	95	85	74	68	100
Extreme Minimum Temp. (°F)	-30	-38	-18	5	22	30	36	32	12	-10	-22	-36	-38
Days Maximum Temp. ≥ 90°F	0	0	0	0	0	3	7	5	1	0	0	0	16
Days Maximum Temp. ≤ 32°F	13	7	3	1	0	0	0	0	0	1	5	12	42
Days Minimum Temp. ≤ 32°F	30	27	27	18	5	0	0	0	5	16	26	30	184
Days Minimum Temp. ≤ 0°F	9	4	1	0	0	0	0	0	0	0	2	6	22
Heating Degree Days (base 65°F)	1,368	1,054	900	602	345	120	29	41	254	579	988	1,304	7,584
Cooling Degree Days (base 65°F)	0	0	0	1	8	52	125	105	19	0	0	0	310
Mean Precipitation (in.)	0.27	0.22	0.61	0.90	1.89	1.35	1.09	0.58	0.93	0.74	0.39	0.26	9.23
Days With ≥ 0.1" Precipitation	1	1	2	3	5	4	3	2	3	2	1	1	28
Days With ≥ 1.0" Precipitation	0	0	0	0	0	0	0	0	0	0	0	0	0
Mean Snowfall (in.)	na	*3.3*	na	3.5	0.1	0.0	0.0	0.0	0.6	3.2	*3.9*	*5.3*	na
Days With ≥ 1.0" Snow Depth	na	na	na	1	0	0	0	0	0	1	6	*11*	na

Jackson *Teton County*   Elevation: 6,227 ft.   Latitude: 43° 29' N   Longitude: 110° 46' W

	JAN	FEB	MAR	APR	MAY	JUN	JUL	AUG	SEP	OCT	NOV	DEC	YEAR
Mean Maximum Temp. (°F)	28.0	33.1	42.6	52.4	62.8	73.3	81.7	80.8	70.8	58.2	39.6	28.3	54.3
Mean Temp. (°F)	16.5	20.5	30.1	38.3	46.7	55.2	61.3	60.0	51.0	40.7	27.9	17.2	38.8
Mean Minimum Temp. (°F)	5.0	7.9	17.5	24.2	30.6	37.0	40.9	39.2	31.2	23.2	16.0	6.1	23.2
Extreme Maximum Temp. (°F)	55	58	68	79	81	95	95	98	90	87	66	55	98
Extreme Minimum Temp. (°F)	-50	-37	-23	-5	5	19	25	20	8	2	-21	-49	-50
Days Maximum Temp. ≥ 90°F	0	0	0	0	0	1	2	1	0	0	0	0	4
Days Maximum Temp. ≤ 32°F	19	12	3	0	0	0	0	0	0	1	7	20	62
Days Minimum Temp. ≤ 32°F	30	27	29	26	19	8	3	5	18	26	27	30	248
Days Minimum Temp. ≤ 0°F	12	10	3	0	0	0	0	0	0	0	0	3	13	41
Heating Degree Days (base 65°F)	1,495	1,250	1,077	794	561	293	124	159	412	746	1,105	1,475	9,491
Cooling Degree Days (base 65°F)	0	0	0	0	0	5	20	14	1	0	0	0	40
Mean Precipitation (in.)	1.41	1.03	1.18	1.20	2.22	1.64	1.28	1.29	1.33	1.20	1.66	1.53	16.97
Days With ≥ 0.1" Precipitation	5	4	4	4	6	5	4	4	4	4	5	5	54
Days With ≥ 1.0" Precipitation	0	0	0	0	0	0	0	0	0	0	0	0	0
Mean Snowfall (in.)	19.7	11.5	7.8	3.2	0.9	0.2	0.0	0.0	trace	1.1	12.6	18.5	75.5
Days With ≥ 1.0" Snow Depth	28	24	22	4	0	0	0	0	0	1	10	24	113

Kaycee *Johnson County*   Elevation: 4,658 ft.   Latitude: 43° 43' N   Longitude: 106° 38' W

	JAN	FEB	MAR	APR	MAY	JUN	JUL	AUG	SEP	OCT	NOV	DEC	YEAR
Mean Maximum Temp. (°F)	37.1	42.0	49.6	57.8	67.7	79.6	87.4	86.6	75.4	62.6	47.0	39.3	61.0
Mean Temp. (°F)	22.0	27.7	35.5	43.4	53.2	63.6	70.4	68.9	57.9	46.3	32.6	24.4	45.5
Mean Minimum Temp. (°F)	6.8	13.3	21.4	29.0	38.6	47.6	53.3	51.1	40.4	29.9	18.2	9.5	29.9
Extreme Maximum Temp. (°F)	71	70	76	87	92	103	105	107	101	88	78	70	107
Extreme Minimum Temp. (°F)	-37	-37	-16	-5	18	31	31	33	15	-5	-24	-40	-40
Days Maximum Temp. ≥ 90°F	0	0	0	0	0	5	14	12	3	0	0	0	34
Days Maximum Temp. ≤ 32°F	10	6	3	1	0	0	0	0	0	0	4	8	32
Days Minimum Temp. ≤ 32°F	31	27	28	20	6	0	0	0	5	19	28	30	194
Days Minimum Temp. ≤ 0°F	10	5	1	0	0	0	0	0	0	0	2	7	25
Heating Degree Days (base 65°F)	1,328	1,048	907	641	364	107	17	23	230	574	965	1,251	7,455
Cooling Degree Days (base 65°F)	0	0	0	0	5	78	203	169	28	0	0	0	483
Mean Precipitation (in.)	0.42	0.39	0.82	1.48	2.52	2.12	1.26	0.85	1.11	1.27	0.55	0.40	13.19
Days With ≥ 0.1" Precipitation	2	1	3	4	6	5	3	2	3	3	2	1	35
Days With ≥ 1.0" Precipitation	0	0	0	0	0	0	0	0	0	0	0	0	0
Mean Snowfall (in.)	6.2	5.6	8.0	6.8	0.8	trace	0.0	0.0	0.4	2.4	5.3	6.9	42.4
Days With ≥ 1.0" Snow Depth	16	10	5	2	0	0	0	0	0	1	6	13	53

La Grange *Goshen County*   Elevation: 4,589 ft.   Latitude: 41° 38' N   Longitude: 104° 10' W

	JAN	FEB	MAR	APR	MAY	JUN	JUL	AUG	SEP	OCT	NOV	DEC	YEAR
Mean Maximum Temp. (°F)	39.3	44.1	50.8	59.9	70.1	81.3	88.3	86.8	76.8	64.5	48.8	40.7	62.6
Mean Temp. (°F)	26.2	30.6	36.8	45.1	54.8	64.8	71.3	69.5	59.4	47.8	35.0	27.6	47.4
Mean Minimum Temp. (°F)	13.0	17.1	22.7	30.2	39.4	48.4	54.1	52.2	42.0	31.1	21.1	14.4	32.2
Extreme Maximum Temp. (°F)	70	73	82	88	92	102	106	109	100	89	83	70	109
Extreme Minimum Temp. (°F)	-28	-32	-13	-13	11	29	37	34	9	-5	-26	-35	-35
Days Maximum Temp. ≥ 90°F	0	0	0	0	0	6	14	12	3	0	0	0	35
Days Maximum Temp. ≤ 32°F	9	5	3	0	0	0	0	0	0	1	4	7	29
Days Minimum Temp. ≤ 32°F	29	26	27	18	5	0	0	0	4	17	26	29	181
Days Minimum Temp. ≤ 0°F	6	3	1	0	0	0	0	0	0	0	1	4	15
Heating Degree Days (base 65°F)	1,199	965	867	591	318	87	12	17	197	527	894	1,154	6,828
Cooling Degree Days (base 65°F)	0	0	0	0	9	87	209	169	35	2	0	0	511
Mean Precipitation (in.)	0.54	0.52	1.32	1.89	2.77	2.36	2.15	1.45	1.26	1.12	0.81	0.67	16.86
Days With ≥ 0.1" Precipitation	2	2	3	5	6	5	5	4	3	3	3	2	43
Days With ≥ 1.0" Precipitation	0	0	0	0	1	0	0	0	0	0	0	0	1
Mean Snowfall (in.)	8.0	6.8	12.9	9.3	0.7	0.0	0.0	0.0	0.9	4.1	9.7	9.7	62.1
Days With ≥ 1.0" Snow Depth	11	7	7	3	0	0	0	0	0	1	6	10	45

Laramie General Brees Field *Albany County*   Elevation: 7,263 ft.   Latitude: 41° 19' N   Longitude: 105° 41' W

	JAN	FEB	MAR	APR	MAY	JUN	JUL	AUG	SEP	OCT	NOV	DEC	YEAR
Mean Maximum Temp. (°F)	32.3	35.7	42.1	50.2	61.1	72.9	79.4	77.8	68.4	56.0	41.3	33.3	54.2
Mean Temp. (°F)	20.7	23.7	30.1	37.2	47.2	57.4	63.5	62.0	53.0	41.8	29.1	21.8	40.6
Mean Minimum Temp. (°F)	9.1	11.7	18.0	24.1	33.3	41.9	47.6	46.1	37.5	27.4	16.9	10.3	27.0
Extreme Maximum Temp. (°F)	59	60	68	76	84	92	94	94	90	77	70	61	94
Extreme Minimum Temp. (°F)	-38	-37	-21	-14	15	22	32	28	-2	-18	-26	-34	-38
Days Maximum Temp. ≥ 90°F	0	0	0	0	0	0	1	0	0	0	0	0	1
Days Maximum Temp. ≤ 32°F	14	11	6	2	0	0	0	0	0	1	8	14	56
Days Minimum Temp. ≤ 32°F	31	28	30	26	14	2	0	0	7	22	28	30	218
Days Minimum Temp. ≤ 0°F	8	5	2	0	0	0	0	0	0	0	3	7	25
Heating Degree Days (base 65°F)	1,367	1,160	1,076	829	544	229	70	100	356	713	1,070	1,332	8,846
Cooling Degree Days (base 65°F)	0	0	0	0	0	8	29	13	2	0	0	0	52
Mean Precipitation (in.)	0.37	0.46	0.82	1.03	1.55	1.37	1.54	1.21	0.98	0.81	0.68	0.46	11.28
Days With ≥ 0.1" Precipitation	1	1	2	3	5	4	4	4	3	3	2	1	33
Days With ≥ 1.0" Precipitation	0	0	0	0	0	0	0	0	0	0	0	0	0
Mean Snowfall (in.)	5.3	5.7	9.6	8.1	3.2	0.4	trace	trace	1.0	4.3	7.9	7.3	52.8
Days With ≥ 1.0" Snow Depth	17	14	10	5	1	0	0	0	0	3	10	15	75

Leiter 9 N *Sheridan County*   Elevation: 4,199 ft.   Latitude: 44° 51' N   Longitude: 106° 17' W

	JAN	FEB	MAR	APR	MAY	JUN	JUL	AUG	SEP	OCT	NOV	DEC	YEAR
Mean Maximum Temp. (°F)	32.4	38.8	47.5	57.5	67.8	78.5	87.7	87.5	74.6	61.1	44.0	34.9	59.3
Mean Temp. (°F)	21.7	27.8	35.8	44.9	54.7	64.4	72.3	71.8	60.0	47.6	33.2	24.4	46.5
Mean Minimum Temp. (°F)	11.0	16.7	24.1	32.3	41.6	50.3	56.9	55.9	45.3	34.1	22.4	13.8	33.7
Extreme Maximum Temp. (°F)	63	71	78	88	94	105	108	105	104	90	77	68	108
Extreme Minimum Temp. (°F)	-34	-35	-17	6	22	33	38	36	12	-13	-20	-36	-36
Days Maximum Temp. ≥ 90°F	0	0	0	0	0	4	14	14	3	0	0	0	35
Days Maximum Temp. ≤ 32°F	13	8	4	1	0	0	0	0	0	1	6	11	44
Days Minimum Temp. ≤ 32°F	30	27	26	16	4	0	0	0	2	12	26	30	173
Days Minimum Temp. ≤ 0°F	8	4	1	0	0	0	0	0	0	0	1	5	19
Heating Degree Days (base 65°F)	1,337	1,045	898	596	323	98	15	16	200	534	948	1,254	7,264
Cooling Degree Days (base 65°F)	0	0	0	1	13	89	253	248	59	1	0	0	664
Mean Precipitation (in.)	0.53	0.40	0.91	1.83	2.55	2.42	1.48	1.04	1.42	1.47	0.78	0.56	15.39
Days With ≥ 0.1" Precipitation	2	1	3	5	6	6	4	3	4	4	3	2	43
Days With ≥ 1.0" Precipitation	0	0	0	0	0	0	0	0	0	0	0	0	0
Mean Snowfall (in.)	8.6	6.3	10.5	8.9	1.3	trace	0.0	0.0	1.4	4.2	8.1	8.6	57.9
Days With ≥ 1.0" Snow Depth	24	15	8	2	0	0	0	0	0	1	9	20	79

Lovell *Big Horn County*   Elevation: 3,835 ft.   Latitude: 44° 50' N   Longitude: 108° 24' W

	JAN	FEB	MAR	APR	MAY	JUN	JUL	AUG	SEP	OCT	NOV	DEC	YEAR
Mean Maximum Temp. (°F)	29.1	37.9	48.8	58.7	68.4	78.9	86.6	85.7	73.5	60.6	43.9	32.6	58.7
Mean Temp. (°F)	16.9	24.9	35.6	44.9	54.9	64.3	70.4	68.7	57.1	45.6	31.4	20.5	44.6
Mean Minimum Temp. (°F)	4.6	11.8	22.4	31.1	41.4	49.7	54.3	51.7	40.7	30.5	19.0	8.3	30.4
Extreme Maximum Temp. (°F)	61	71	78	88	95	103	103	105	99	87	72	66	105
Extreme Minimum Temp. (°F)	-39	-35	-20	7	19	30	38	34	17	-8	-21	-38	-39
Days Maximum Temp. ≥ 90°F	0	0	0	0	0	5	12	10	2	0	0	0	29
Days Maximum Temp. ≤ 32°F	17	8	3	0	0	0	0	0	0	1	5	14	48
Days Minimum Temp. ≤ 32°F	31	28	28	17	3	0	0	0	4	18	28	31	188
Days Minimum Temp. ≤ 0°F	11	5	1	0	0	0	0	0	0	0	2	7	26
Heating Degree Days (base 65°F)	1,486	1,126	904	597	317	99	22	30	253	595	1,000	1,375	7,804
Cooling Degree Days (base 65°F)	0	0	0	1	12	79	186	152	23	0	0	0	453
Mean Precipitation (in.)	0.23	0.15	0.31	0.61	1.20	1.00	0.75	0.60	0.79	0.65	0.25	0.22	6.76
Days With ≥ 0.1" Precipitation	1	1	1	2	4	3	3	2	2	2	1	1	23
Days With ≥ 1.0" Precipitation	0	0	0	0	0	0	0	0	0	0	0	0	0
Mean Snowfall (in.)	5.0	3.1	2.9	0.8	trace	0.0	0.0	0.0	0.7	0.8	1.6	3.9	18.8
Days With ≥ 1.0" Snow Depth	na	3	na	0	0	0	0	0	0	0	2	na	na

Moose *Teton County*   Elevation: 6,469 ft.   Latitude: 43° 39' N   Longitude: 110° 43' W

	JAN	FEB	MAR	APR	MAY	JUN	JUL	AUG	SEP	OCT	NOV	DEC	YEAR
Mean Maximum Temp. (°F)	25.7	30.9	39.6	48.7	60.5	70.5	79.0	78.5	68.8	55.3	37.6	25.8	51.7
Mean Temp. (°F)	13.2	16.7	26.1	35.1	45.6	53.7	60.1	59.1	50.3	39.0	25.5	13.6	36.5
Mean Minimum Temp. (°F)	0.6	2.5	12.6	21.5	30.7	36.9	41.2	39.7	31.8	22.7	13.3	1.2	21.2
Extreme Maximum Temp. (°F)	50	53	61	75	81	90	93	93	88	82	67	53	93
Extreme Minimum Temp. (°F)	-46	-42	-23	-10	7	21	26	22	9	-3	-20	-43	-46
Days Maximum Temp. ≥ 90°F	0	0	0	0	0	0	1	1	0	0	0	0	2
Days Maximum Temp. ≤ 32°F	23	14	5	0	0	0	0	0	0	0	9	23	74
Days Minimum Temp. ≤ 32°F	31	28	30	28	19	7	1	3	17	28	29	31	252
Days Minimum Temp. ≤ 0°F	15	13	5	0	0	0	0	0	0	0	5	17	55
Heating Degree Days (base 65°F)	1,602	1,358	1,197	890	595	333	155	184	433	798	1,178	1,590	10,313
Cooling Degree Days (base 65°F)	0	0	0	0	0	2	11	8	0	0	0	0	21
Mean Precipitation (in.)	2.59	1.97	1.66	1.48	2.04	1.73	1.43	1.42	1.32	1.25	2.27	2.53	21.69
Days With ≥ 0.1" Precipitation	8	6	5	5	6	5	4	4	4	4	6	8	65
Days With ≥ 1.0" Precipitation	0	0	0	0	0	0	0	0	0	0	0	0	0
Mean Snowfall (in.)	40.7	28.9	18.7	9.6	3.0	trace	0.0	trace	0.3	4.9	25.8	38.9	170.8
Days With ≥ 1.0" Snow Depth	31	28	31	21	3	0	0	0	0	3	18	30	165

Moran 5 WNW *Teton County*   Elevation: 6,797 ft.   Latitude: 43° 51' N   Longitude: 110° 35' W

	JAN	FEB	MAR	APR	MAY	JUN	JUL	AUG	SEP	OCT	NOV	DEC	YEAR
Mean Maximum Temp. (°F)	25.6	32.0	39.7	47.7	58.1	69.2	77.8	77.2	66.8	53.8	36.1	25.9	50.8
Mean Temp. (°F)	13.7	17.9	26.1	34.5	44.2	53.3	59.9	58.9	49.8	39.3	25.7	14.8	36.5
Mean Minimum Temp. (°F)	1.7	3.8	12.4	21.2	30.3	37.4	42.0	40.5	32.8	24.7	15.2	3.8	22.1
Extreme Maximum Temp. (°F)	51	53	59	73	80	90	91	90	85	78	64	50	91
Extreme Minimum Temp. (°F)	-42	-43	-26	-11	8	25	23	23	8	-5	-19	-45	-45
Days Maximum Temp. ≥ 90°F	0	0	0	0	0	0	0	0	0	0	0	0	0
Days Maximum Temp. ≤ 32°F	24	14	5	1	0	0	0	0	0	1	10	24	79
Days Minimum Temp. ≤ 32°F	31	28	31	28	20	6	1	2	16	27	29	31	250
Days Minimum Temp. ≤ 0°F	15	11	6	1	0	0	0	0	0	0	3	14	50
Heating Degree Days (base 65°F)	1,586	1,324	1,200	909	637	346	158	188	449	791	1,174	1,549	10,311
Cooling Degree Days (base 65°F)	0	0	0	0	0	2	8	6	0	0	0	0	16
Mean Precipitation (in.)	3.31	2.33	2.22	2.05	2.30	1.52	1.41	1.27	1.45	1.58	3.00	3.06	25.50
Days With ≥ 0.1" Precipitation	10	7	8	7	7	5	4	4	5	5	9	9	80
Days With ≥ 1.0" Precipitation	0	0	0	0	0	0	0	0	0	0	0	0	0
Mean Snowfall (in.)	na	na	na	8.6	1.6	0.1	0.0	0.0	0.5	3.2	na	na	na
Days With ≥ 1.0" Snow Depth	31	28	31	26	5	0	0	0	0	2	18	31	172

Mountain View *Uinta County*   Elevation: 6,797 ft.   Latitude: 41° 17' N   Longitude: 110° 19' W

	JAN	FEB	MAR	APR	MAY	JUN	JUL	AUG	SEP	OCT	NOV	DEC	YEAR
Mean Maximum Temp. (°F)	32.3	35.5	44.1	52.7	63.4	73.5	80.0	79.3	70.4	58.1	42.0	33.6	55.4
Mean Temp. (°F)	21.7	24.0	32.1	39.3	48.6	57.6	63.7	62.6	54.0	43.6	30.2	22.5	41.7
Mean Minimum Temp. (°F)	11.1	12.6	20.0	25.9	33.9	41.7	47.2	45.8	37.6	29.0	18.5	11.4	27.9
Extreme Maximum Temp. (°F)	57	62	70	79	83	90	93	92	88	82	74	62	93
Extreme Minimum Temp. (°F)	-26	-33	-10	-3	15	22	30	28	9	-8	-19	-31	-33
Days Maximum Temp. ≥ 90°F	0	0	0	0	0	0	1	0	0	0	0	0	1
Days Maximum Temp. ≤ 32°F	14	9	3	1	0	0	0	0	0	1	6	14	48
Days Minimum Temp. ≤ 32°F	30	27	30	25	13	3	0	0	7	20	29	31	215
Days Minimum Temp. ≤ 0°F	6	4	1	0	0	0	0	0	0	0	1	5	17
Heating Degree Days (base 65°F)	1,335	1,150	1,013	763	500	223	69	91	326	656	1,036	1,311	8,473
Cooling Degree Days (base 65°F)	0	0	0	0	0	11	41	28	3	0	0	0	83
Mean Precipitation (in.)	0.41	0.37	0.52	0.93	1.25	1.00	0.97	0.85	1.01	0.95	0.60	0.41	9.27
Days With ≥ 0.1" Precipitation	1	1	2	3	5	3	3	3	3	3	2	1	30
Days With ≥ 1.0" Precipitation	0	0	0	0	0	0	0	0	0	0	0	0	0
Mean Snowfall (in.)	5.7	5.0	4.6	6.1	2.7	0.4	0.0	trace	0.2	4.1	5.8	5.0	39.6
Days With ≥ 1.0" Snow Depth	na	na	na	na	0	0	0	0	0	1	5	13	na

Newcastle *Weston County*   Elevation: 4,379 ft.   Latitude: 43° 51' N   Longitude: 104° 12' W

	JAN	FEB	MAR	APR	MAY	JUN	JUL	AUG	SEP	OCT	NOV	DEC	YEAR
Mean Maximum Temp. (°F)	33.5	39.3	47.6	58.4	69.3	80.1	87.7	85.9	74.7	60.9	44.4	35.4	59.8
Mean Temp. (°F)	22.3	27.5	35.6	45.5	55.9	65.9	72.9	71.1	60.3	47.6	33.4	24.3	46.8
Mean Minimum Temp. (°F)	11.0	15.6	23.4	32.5	42.4	51.6	58.1	56.3	45.9	34.2	22.3	13.1	33.9
Extreme Maximum Temp. (°F)	64	69	78	86	94	104	104	103	100	90	78	65	104
Extreme Minimum Temp. (°F)	-26	-31	-16	-5	22	32	39	37	18	1	-21	-35	-35
Days Maximum Temp. ≥ 90°F	0	0	0	0	0	5	13	10	2	0	0	0	30
Days Maximum Temp. ≤ 32°F	12	7	3	1	0	0	0	0	0	0	5	11	39
Days Minimum Temp. ≤ 32°F	31	27	26	16	3	0	0	0	2	12	25	31	173
Days Minimum Temp. ≤ 0°F	7	4	1	0	0	0	0	0	0	0	1	5	18
Heating Degree Days (base 65°F)	1,319	1,053	906	580	290	81	10	18	187	534	942	1,257	7,177
Cooling Degree Days (base 65°F)	0	0	0	2	16	110	256	225	61	2	0	0	672
Mean Precipitation (in.)	0.43	0.56	0.79	1.58	2.54	2.42	2.10	1.79	1.15	1.33	0.68	0.59	15.96
Days With ≥ 0.1" Precipitation	2	2	3	4	7	5	5	4	3	3	3	2	43
Days With ≥ 1.0" Precipitation	0	0	0	0	0	0	0	0	0	0	0	0	0
Mean Snowfall (in.)	6.3	6.6	7.1	4.0	0.3	0.0	0.0	0.0	0.2	1.4	5.5	8.3	39.7
Days With ≥ 1.0" Snow Depth	18	11	6	1	0	0	0	0	0	1	6	15	58

Pavillion *Fremont County*   Elevation: 5,439 ft.   Latitude: 43° 15' N   Longitude: 108° 42' W

	JAN	FEB	MAR	APR	MAY	JUN	JUL	AUG	SEP	OCT	NOV	DEC	YEAR
Mean Maximum Temp. (°F)	32.2	38.6	48.9	58.2	66.7	77.5	84.8	83.2	72.0	59.5	na	na	na
Mean Temp. (°F)	20.0	25.9	35.6	44.1	52.5	62.2	68.8	67.4	56.7	45.4	na	na	na
Mean Minimum Temp. (°F)	7.6	13.2	22.2	29.9	38.3	47.0	52.6	51.5	41.4	31.3	na	na	na
Extreme Maximum Temp. (°F)	62	67	74	81	87	94	97	98	92	83	69	65	98
Extreme Minimum Temp. (°F)	-36	-27	-15	0	17	20	35	35	15	-5	-22	-40	-40
Days Maximum Temp. ≥ 90°F	0	0	0	0	0	2	5	2	0	0	0	0	9
Days Maximum Temp. ≤ 32°F	12	7	2	0	0	0	0	0	0	0	5	11	37
Days Minimum Temp. ≤ 32°F	27	27	27	19	6	0	0	0	3	15	24	25	173
Days Minimum Temp. ≤ 0°F	8	5	1	0	0	0	0	0	0	0	2	6	22
Heating Degree Days (base 65°F)	1,390	1,098	906	621	383	124	17	24	255	600	na	na	na
Cooling Degree Days (base 65°F)	na	0	0	0	1	41	135	102	10	0	na	na	na
Mean Precipitation (in.)	0.19	0.19	0.36	1.01	1.76	1.00	0.81	0.56	0.91	0.57	0.36	0.21	7.93
Days With ≥ 0.1" Precipitation	1	1	1	3	3	2	2	2	1	1	1	1	20
Days With ≥ 1.0" Precipitation	0	0	0	0	0	0	0	0	0	0	0	0	0
Mean Snowfall (in.)	na	2.6	na	2.7	0.3	0.2	0.0	0.0	0.4	1.6	na	na	na
Days With ≥ 1.0" Snow Depth	na	na	1	1	0	0	0	0	0	1	na	na	na

Phillips *Goshen County*   Elevation: 4,980 ft.   Latitude: 41° 38' N   Longitude: 104° 30' W

	JAN	FEB	MAR	APR	MAY	JUN	JUL	AUG	SEP	OCT	NOV	DEC	YEAR
Mean Maximum Temp. (°F)	40.4	44.4	50.9	59.0	68.7	79.5	86.7	85.3	76.3	64.4	49.7	42.2	62.3
Mean Temp. (°F)	28.4	31.9	37.7	45.1	54.6	64.3	70.7	69.1	59.9	48.8	36.7	29.9	48.1
Mean Minimum Temp. (°F)	16.3	19.3	24.5	31.1	40.5	49.0	54.6	52.8	43.3	33.1	23.6	17.5	33.8
Extreme Maximum Temp. (°F)	71	73	80	88	93	104	103	102	100	89	82	73	104
Extreme Minimum Temp. (°F)	-29	-26	-12	-12	12	30	36	25	11	-4	-20	-33	-33
Days Maximum Temp. ≥ 90°F	0	0	0	0	0	4	12	8	2	0	0	0	26
Days Maximum Temp. ≤ 32°F	7	5	3	1	0	0	0	0	0	0	3	6	25
Days Minimum Temp. ≤ 32°F	28	25	26	17	5	0	0	0	3	13	24	28	169
Days Minimum Temp. ≤ 0°F	5	3	1	0	0	0	0	0	0	0	1	3	13
Heating Degree Days (base 65°F)	1,129	929	838	591	321	92	11	20	186	497	843	1,082	6,539
Cooling Degree Days (base 65°F)	0	0	0	0	8	78	192	159	39	1	0	0	477
Mean Precipitation (in.)	0.40	0.38	0.85	1.54	2.76	2.39	2.18	1.68	1.22	0.90	0.68	0.44	15.42
Days With ≥ 0.1" Precipitation	2	1	3	5	6	5	5	4	3	3	2	2	41
Days With ≥ 1.0" Precipitation	0	0	0	0	0	0	0	0	0	0	0	0	0
Mean Snowfall (in.)	8.4	6.0	9.7	6.8	1.0	0.0	0.0	0.0	0.6	4.1	8.6	8.6	53.8
Days With ≥ 1.0" Snow Depth	11	7	6	3	0	0	0	0	0	2	6	11	46

Pinedale *Sublette County*   Elevation: 7,171 ft.   Latitude: 42° 52' N   Longitude: 109° 53' W

	JAN	FEB	MAR	APR	MAY	JUN	JUL	AUG	SEP	OCT	NOV	DEC	YEAR
Mean Maximum Temp. (°F)	26.3	30.4	38.7	49.4	61.0	70.6	77.4	76.8	67.4	55.1	36.9	27.3	51.4
Mean Temp. (°F)	13.0	16.3	25.2	35.3	44.9	53.8	59.5	57.4	49.0	38.5	24.1	14.4	36.0
Mean Minimum Temp. (°F)	-0.3	2.1	11.7	21.0	28.8	36.9	41.6	38.1	30.4	22.0	11.3	1.5	20.4
Extreme Maximum Temp. (°F)	55	51	59	75	81	87	88	91	85	78	67	54	91
Extreme Minimum Temp. (°F)	-39	-42	-23	-12	9	18	26	20	8	-6	-28	-49	-49
Days Maximum Temp. ≥ 90°F	0	0	0	0	0	0	0	0	0	0	0	0	0
Days Maximum Temp. ≤ 32°F	22	15	6	1	0	0	0	0	0	1	10	21	76
Days Minimum Temp. ≤ 32°F	31	28	31	28	22	7	1	6	19	28	30	31	262
Days Minimum Temp. ≤ 0°F	16	12	5	1	0	0	0	0	0	0	5	14	53
Heating Degree Days (base 65°F)	1,606	1,370	1,227	886	616	331	166	229	474	814	1,220	1,563	10,502
Cooling Degree Days (base 65°F)	0	0	0	0	0	1	4	2	0	0	0	0	7
Mean Precipitation (in.)	0.71	0.51	0.76	0.92	1.74	1.07	1.23	1.06	1.21	0.83	0.78	0.59	11.41
Days With ≥ 0.1" Precipitation	3	2	2	3	5	3	4	3	3	3	3	2	36
Days With ≥ 1.0" Precipitation	0	0	0	0	0	0	0	0	0	0	0	0	0
Mean Snowfall (in.)	13.8	10.5	10.1	6.2	3.0	0.5	0.0	0.0	0.9	4.0	10.1	10.8	69.9
Days With ≥ 1.0" Snow Depth	30	27	24	6	0	0	0	0	0	2	14	26	129

Rawlins Municipal Airport *Carbon County*   Elevation: 6,735 ft.   Latitude: 41° 48' N   Longitude: 107° 12' W

	JAN	FEB	MAR	APR	MAY	JUN	JUL	AUG	SEP	OCT	NOV	DEC	YEAR
Mean Maximum Temp. (°F)	30.5	34.4	42.7	52.3	63.3	75.4	82.8	81.1	70.3	56.8	40.5	32.0	55.2
Mean Temp. (°F)	21.4	24.8	32.5	40.1	49.8	60.3	67.1	65.6	55.7	44.1	30.7	23.0	42.9
Mean Minimum Temp. (°F)	12.4	15.1	22.1	27.9	36.4	45.1	51.4	50.0	41.1	31.4	20.8	14.0	30.6
Extreme Maximum Temp. (°F)	56	57	68	77	82	94	97	95	95	81	70	56	97
Extreme Minimum Temp. (°F)	-36	-36	-23	-11	13	26	32	33	8	-7	-23	-35	-36
Days Maximum Temp. ≥ 90°F	0	0	0	0	0	1	3	2	0	0	0	0	6
Days Maximum Temp. ≤ 32°F	16	11	5	1	0	0	0	0	0	1	8	15	57
Days Minimum Temp. ≤ 32°F	30	27	28	21	8	1	0	0	5	17	26	30	193
Days Minimum Temp. ≤ 0°F	5	4	1	0	0	0	0	0	0	0	1	4	15
Heating Degree Days (base 65°F)	1,344	1,130	1,002	740	463	162	27	43	282	640	1,023	1,295	8,151
Cooling Degree Days (base 65°F)	0	0	0	0	0	0	27	104	11	0	0	0	218
Mean Precipitation (in.)	0.56	0.47	0.66	1.06	1.45	0.98	0.92	0.82	0.83	0.88	0.65	0.50	9.78
Days With ≥ 0.1" Precipitation	2	2	2	4	4	3	3	2	3	3	3	1	32
Days With ≥ 1.0" Precipitation	0	0	0	0	0	0	0	0	0	0	0	0	0
Mean Snowfall (in.)	8.8	6.3	6.5	6.8	1.5	0.3	trace	trace	0.8	4.0	8.3	7.0	50.3
Days With ≥ 1.0" Snow Depth	21	16	9	4	1	0	0	0	0	2	11	17	81

Redbird *Niobrara County*   Elevation: 3,887 ft.   Latitude: 43° 15' N   Longitude: 104° 17' W

	JAN	FEB	MAR	APR	MAY	JUN	JUL	AUG	SEP	OCT	NOV	DEC	YEAR
Mean Maximum Temp. (°F)	34.6	41.2	50.3	60.2	70.4	81.3	89.4	88.4	77.5	64.3	46.4	37.1	61.8
Mean Temp. (°F)	21.1	27.7	36.0	45.7	55.8	65.8	72.8	71.2	59.9	47.4	32.6	22.9	46.6
Mean Minimum Temp. (°F)	7.6	13.9	21.7	31.0	41.2	50.2	56.2	53.9	42.2	30.3	18.6	8.7	31.3
Extreme Maximum Temp. (°F)	69	71	80	90	94	105	110	106	102	91	80	77	110
Extreme Minimum Temp. (°F)	-42	-38	-22	2	18	31	36	32	11	-16	-26	-47	-47
Days Maximum Temp. ≥ 90°F	0	0	0	0	1	6	16	15	4	0	0	0	42
Days Maximum Temp. ≤ 32°F	12	7	3	1	0	0	0	0	0	0	5	10	38
Days Minimum Temp. ≤ 32°F	30	27	27	16	4	0	0	0	5	18	27	30	184
Days Minimum Temp. ≤ 0°F	10	5	1	0	0	0	0	0	0	0	2	8	26
Heating Degree Days (base 65°F)	1,357	1,048	892	575	289	75	9	15	195	542	967	1,299	7,263
Cooling Degree Days (base 65°F)	0	0	0	1	14	103	265	235	52	1	0	0	671
Mean Precipitation (in.)	0.31	0.39	0.77	1.90	2.60	2.42	2.01	1.54	1.39	1.08	0.64	0.33	15.38
Days With ≥ 0.1" Precipitation	1	1	3	5	6	5	4	3	3	3	2	1	37
Days With ≥ 1.0" Precipitation	0	0	0	0	0	0	0	0	0	0	0	0	0
Mean Snowfall (in.)	6.9	6.5	10.4	6.8	0.5	trace	0.0	0.0	0.3	2.8	7.8	8.1	50.1
Days With ≥ 1.0" Snow Depth	16	9	6	2	0	0	0	0	0	1	7	14	55

Riverton *Fremont County*   Elevation: 4,954 ft.   Latitude: 43° 02' N   Longitude: 108° 23' W

	JAN	FEB	MAR	APR	MAY	JUN	JUL	AUG	SEP	OCT	NOV	DEC	YEAR
Mean Maximum Temp. (°F)	28.9	36.8	49.0	58.7	69.0	80.5	88.3	87.0	75.0	61.2	42.8	30.0	58.9
Mean Temp. (°F)	14.1	21.5	34.1	43.5	53.5	63.4	69.8	67.9	56.8	44.3	28.3	15.6	42.7
Mean Minimum Temp. (°F)	-0.7	6.1	19.2	28.2	37.9	46.1	51.3	48.7	38.5	27.3	13.7	1.2	26.5
Extreme Maximum Temp. (°F)	61	70	78	87	96	102	104	103	98	90	73	65	104
Extreme Minimum Temp. (°F)	-46	-37	-19	-7	19	28	30	31	13	-7	-28	-46	-46
Days Maximum Temp. ≥ 90°F	0	0	0	0	0	6	15	13	2	0	0	0	36
Days Maximum Temp. ≤ 32°F	17	9	3	1	0	0	0	0	0	0	6	17	53
Days Minimum Temp. ≤ 32°F	30	28	29	21	6	1	0	0	6	24	29	30	204
Days Minimum Temp. ≤ 0°F	16	9	1	0	0	0	0	0	0	0	4	13	43
Heating Degree Days (base 65°F)	1,573	1,224	950	639	352	112	21	27	257	637	1,094	1,526	8,412
Cooling Degree Days (base 65°F)	0	0	0	0	5	67	173	134	21	0	0	0	400
Mean Precipitation (in.)	0.28	0.22	0.48	1.01	1.74	1.21	0.75	0.48	0.88	0.81	0.46	0.37	8.69
Days With ≥ 0.1" Precipitation	1	1	1	3	4	3	2	1	2	2	1	1	22
Days With ≥ 1.0" Precipitation	0	0	0	0	0	0	0	0	0	0	0	0	0
Mean Snowfall (in.)	5.2	4.5	4.9	4.0	0.4	trace	0.0	0.0	0.5	2.8	5.2	5.9	33.4
Days With ≥ 1.0" Snow Depth	na	na	4	2	0	0	0	0	0	1	3	na	na

Rochelle 3 E *Weston County*   Elevation: 4,494 ft.   Latitude: 43° 36' N   Longitude: 104° 54' W

	JAN	FEB	MAR	APR	MAY	JUN	JUL	AUG	SEP	OCT	NOV	DEC	YEAR
Mean Maximum Temp. (°F)	32.2	38.4	46.8	56.4	67.7	79.8	88.1	86.8	76.2	64.0	44.8	34.2	59.6
Mean Temp. (°F)	20.0	25.7	33.9	42.4	52.8	63.5	71.1	69.6	57.9	46.3	31.8	21.6	44.7
Mean Minimum Temp. (°F)	7.8	13.0	20.9	28.5	37.8	47.2	54.0	52.4	39.5	28.6	18.8	8.9	29.8
Extreme Maximum Temp. (°F)	63	70	80	91	93	105	107	105	103	90	79	65	107
Extreme Minimum Temp. (°F)	-35	-39	-22	-14	17	29	31	31	11	-11	-29	-47	-47
Days Maximum Temp. ≥ 90°F	0	0	0	0	0	5	14	12	3	0	0	0	34
Days Maximum Temp. ≤ 32°F	14	7	3	0	0	0	0	0	0	0	5	12	41
Days Minimum Temp. ≤ 32°F	31	28	28	21	6	1	0	0	6	22	29	31	203
Days Minimum Temp. ≤ 0°F	10	6	2	0	0	0	0	0	0	0	3	9	30
Heating Degree Days (base 65°F)	1,389	1,103	958	672	375	103	14	26	235	573	991	1,341	7,780
Cooling Degree Days (base 65°F)	0	0	0	1	3	62	208	182	27	0	0	0	483
Mean Precipitation (in.)	0.26	0.35	0.77	1.66	2.60	1.97	1.82	1.19	0.99	1.05	0.56	0.39	13.61
Days With ≥ 0.1" Precipitation	1	1	3	5	6	5	4	3	3	3	2	2	38
Days With ≥ 1.0" Precipitation	0	0	0	0	0	0	0	0	0	0	0	0	0
Mean Snowfall (in.)	5.1	5.6	7.2	6.0	0.8	0.0	0.0	0.0	0.2	2.8	6.1	7.1	40.9
Days With ≥ 1.0" Snow Depth	18	12	10	3	1	0	0	0	0	1	8	18	71

Rock Springs Airport *Sweetwater County*   Elevation: 6,738 ft.   Latitude: 41° 36' N   Longitude: 109° 04' W

	JAN	FEB	MAR	APR	MAY	JUN	JUL	AUG	SEP	OCT	NOV	DEC	YEAR
Mean Maximum Temp. (°F)	29.2	34.2	43.3	53.2	63.6	75.1	82.7	80.9	70.1	56.9	40.1	30.5	55.0
Mean Temp. (°F)	20.4	24.4	33.0	41.1	50.5	60.7	67.6	65.9	55.8	44.2	30.2	21.3	42.9
Mean Minimum Temp. (°F)	11.6	14.6	22.6	29.0	37.3	46.2	52.6	50.8	41.4	31.5	20.3	12.1	30.8
Extreme Maximum Temp. (°F)	54	60	67	79	83	95	96	93	89	78	66	57	96
Extreme Minimum Temp. (°F)	-26	-29	-7	2	18	28	35	34	15	3	-13	-29	-29
Days Maximum Temp. ≥ 90°F	0	0	0	0	0	1	3	1	0	0	0	0	5
Days Maximum Temp. ≤ 32°F	18	12	4	1	0	0	0	0	0	1	8	17	61
Days Minimum Temp. ≤ 32°F	31	28	29	21	8	1	0	0	4	17	28	31	198
Days Minimum Temp. ≤ 0°F	5	3	0	0	0	0	0	0	0	0	1	5	14
Heating Degree Days (base 65°F)	1,375	1,140	986	710	444	161	24	41	278	637	1,038	1,348	8,182
Cooling Degree Days (base 65°F)	0	0	0	0	0	35	115	76	10	0	0	0	236
Mean Precipitation (in.)	0.62	0.49	0.77	1.06	1.38	0.75	0.92	0.55	0.76	0.90	0.64	0.62	9.46
Days With ≥ 0.1" Precipitation	2	2	3	3	4	2	2	2	2	3	2	2	29
Days With ≥ 1.0" Precipitation	0	0	0	0	0	0	0	0	0	0	0	0	0
Mean Snowfall (in.)	7.5	5.0	7.2	7.2	2.4	0.2	trace	trace	0.4	4.8	6.3	6.7	47.7
Days With ≥ 1.0" Snow Depth	23	16	8	2	0	0	0	0	0	1	8	17	75

Sage 4 NNW *Lincoln County*   Elevation: 6,207 ft.   Latitude: 41° 52' N   Longitude: 111° 00' W

	JAN	FEB	MAR	APR	MAY	JUN	JUL	AUG	SEP	OCT	NOV	DEC	YEAR
Mean Maximum Temp. (°F)	26.6	31.3	42.5	*54.4*	64.2	74.3	81.8	81.5	71.8	59.9	41.4	28.1	*54.8*
Mean Temp. (°F)	12.5	16.3	28.9	*38.7*	47.6	56.0	61.7	60.1	50.8	40.1	26.9	13.8	*37.8*
Mean Minimum Temp. (°F)	-1.7	1.3	15.3	*22.9*	30.9	37.7	41.5	38.6	29.7	20.3	12.3	-0.6	*20.7*
Extreme Maximum Temp. (°F)	55	56	70	*79*	85	91	93	94	90	84	74	61	*94*
Extreme Minimum Temp. (°F)	-51	-51	-30	*-3*	8	21	26	15	3	-4	-34	-48	*-51*
Days Maximum Temp. ≥ 90°F	0	0	0	0	0	1	2	1	0	0	0	0	*64*
Days Maximum Temp. ≤ 32°F	20	13	3	*0*	0	0	0	0	0	1	7	20	*64*
Days Minimum Temp. ≤ 32°F	31	28	*31*	*28*	18	6	3	6	19	29	29	31	*259*
Days Minimum Temp. ≤ 0°F	17	13	3	*0*	0	0	0	0	0	0	5	17	*55*
Heating Degree Days (base 65°F)	1,625	1,369	1,112	*783*	532	268	114	154	421	765	1,136	1,583	*9,862*
Cooling Degree Days (base 65°F)	0	0	0	*0*	0	0	3	17	7	1	0	0	28
Mean Precipitation (in.)	*0.59*	na	*0.63*	*1.05*	1.21	1.03	0.98	0.79	1.20	1.05	*0.69*	*0.44*	na
Days With ≥ 0.1" Precipitation	na	na	na	*3*	4	3	3	2	3	3	*2*	*1*	na
Days With ≥ 1.0" Precipitation	na	na	na	*0*	0	0	0	0	0	0	0	*0*	na
Mean Snowfall (in.)	na	na	na	*2.1*	0.6	0.2	0.0	0.0	*0.2*	*1.5*	*3.2*	na	na
Days With ≥ 1.0" Snow Depth	na	na	na	na	*0*	0	0	0	0	*0*	na	na	na

Saratoga *Carbon County*   Elevation: 6,788 ft.   Latitude: 41° 27' N   Longitude: 106° 49' W

	JAN	FEB	MAR	APR	MAY	JUN	JUL	AUG	SEP	OCT	NOV	DEC	YEAR
Mean Maximum Temp. (°F)	33.0	37.3	45.1	54.4	65.2	76.1	82.3	80.9	71.7	59.3	43.0	34.8	56.9
Mean Temp. (°F)	21.9	25.5	33.2	40.9	50.5	60.1	66.1	64.4	55.4	44.3	31.3	23.3	43.1
Mean Minimum Temp. (°F)	10.8	13.7	21.3	27.4	35.7	44.0	49.8	47.8	38.9	29.2	19.7	11.8	29.2
Extreme Maximum Temp. (°F)	56	58	69	76	83	97	98	95	89	81	70	58	98
Extreme Minimum Temp. (°F)	-36	-39	-19	-12	12	26	33	31	10	-8	-20	-33	-39
Days Maximum Temp. ≥ 90°F	0	0	0	0	0	1	2	1	0	0	0	0	4
Days Maximum Temp. ≤ 32°F	13	8	3	1	0	0	0	0	0	1	6	12	44
Days Minimum Temp. ≤ 32°F	30	28	29	22	9	1	0	0	7	20	27	30	203
Days Minimum Temp. ≤ 0°F	6	4	1	0	0	0	0	0	0	0 .	2	6	. 19
Heating Degree Days (base 65°F)	1,329	1,108	980	716	444	164	34	56	288	635	1,004	1,286	8,044
Cooling Degree Days (base 65°F)	0	0	0	0	0	21	71	45	5	0	0	0	142
Mean Precipitation (in.)	0.46	0.45	0.73	1.01	1.56	0.98	1.18	0.90	0.87	1.02	0.66	0.46	10.28
Days With ≥ 0.1" Precipitation	1	2	3	3	5	3	3	3	3	3	2	2	33
Days With ≥ 1.0" Precipitation	0	0	0	0	0	0	0	0	0	0	0	0	0
Mean Snowfall (in.)	9.8	8.5	9.4	7.0	1.9	0.2	0.0	0.0	0.7	4.6	10.4	9.8	62.3
Days With ≥ 1.0" Snow Depth	22	19	9	3	0	0	0	0	0	2	13	20	88

Sheridan Field Station — *Sheridan County*   Elevation: 3,750 ft.   Latitude: 44° 50' N   Longitude: 106° 50' W

	JAN	FEB	MAR	APR	MAY	JUN	JUL	AUG	SEP	OCT	NOV	DEC	YEAR
Mean Maximum Temp. (°F)	32.7	38.4	47.0	57.4	67.6	77.6	86.6	86.8	74.8	61.3	44.9	35.5	59.2
Mean Temp. (°F)	19.0	24.9	33.8	43.4	53.0	62.5	69.4	68.2	57.0	45.0	31.2	21.7	44.1
Mean Minimum Temp. (°F)	5.3	11.3	20.5	29.4	38.5	47.4	52.1	49.7	39.1	28.8	17.5	7.8	28.9
Extreme Maximum Temp. (°F)	68	74	80	88	96	104	106	105	102	92	80	70	106
Extreme Minimum Temp. (°F)	-40	-37	-24	-1	7	28	32	30	4	-18	-26	-44	-44
Days Maximum Temp. ≥ 90°F	0	0	0	0	0	3	13	13	4	0	0	0	33
Days Maximum Temp. ≤ 32°F	13	8	4	1	0	0	0	0	0	1	5	11	43
Days Minimum Temp. ≤ 32°F	31	28	29	20	7	1	0	0	6	21	28	31	202
Days Minimum Temp. ≤ 0°F	11	6	2	0	0	0	0	0	0	0	3	8	30
Heating Degree Days (base 65°F)	1,420	1,127	961	642	370	129	30	39	263	612	1,006	1,338	7,937
Cooling Degree Days (base 65°F)	0	0	0	1	7	63	176	155	30	1	0	0	433
Mean Precipitation (in.)	0.49	0.39	0.90	1.58	2.66	2.48	1.26	0.83	1.41	1.30	0.72	0.51	14.53
Days With ≥ 0.1" Precipitation	2	2	3	5	6	5	3	2	4	4	2	2	40
Days With ≥ 1.0" Precipitation	0	0	0	0	0	0	0	0	0	0	0	0	0
Mean Snowfall (in.)	na	4.5	na	4.7	0.2	0.0	0.0	0.0	0.2	1.1	na	7.3	na
Days With ≥ 1.0" Snow Depth	na	na	na	2	0	0	0	0	0	1	na	na	na

Snake River — *Yellowstone National County*   Elevation: 6,879 ft.   Latitude: 44° 08' N   Longitude: 110° 40' W

	JAN	FEB	MAR	APR	MAY	JUN	JUL	AUG	SEP	OCT	NOV	DEC	YEAR
Mean Maximum Temp. (°F)	26.1	31.5	37.9	46.2	56.8	67.9	76.7	76.2	66.1	52.6	35.6	26.3	50.0
Mean Temp. (°F)	12.5	15.9	23.2	32.0	41.7	50.7	56.9	55.6	46.3	35.7	22.6	12.5	33.8
Mean Minimum Temp. (°F)	-1.2	0.3	8.4	17.7	26.6	33.3	37.1	34.9	26.5	18.8	9.6	-1.5	17.5
Extreme Maximum Temp. (°F)	51	51	59	74	80	92	90	93	89	76	63	51	93
Extreme Minimum Temp. (°F)	-43	-44	-31	-11	1	20	22	16	7	-12	-30	-46	-46
Days Maximum Temp. ≥ 90°F	0	0	0	0	0	0	0	0	0	0	0	0	0
Days Maximum Temp. ≤ 32°F	24	15	7	1	0	0	0	0	0	1	12	24	84
Days Minimum Temp. ≤ 32°F	31	28	31	30	27	15	7	11	25	30	30	31	296
Days Minimum Temp. ≤ 0°F	17	13	9	2	0	0	0	0	0	1	7	17	66
Heating Degree Days (base 65°F)	1,624	1,382	1,291	985	716	427	244	289	555	901	1,265	1,624	11,303
Cooling Degree Days (base 65°F)	0	0	0	0	0	0	1	0	0	0	0	0	1
Mean Precipitation (in.)	4.04	2.98	2.70	2.34	2.67	2.36	1.70	1.68	1.79	2.04	3.43	4.16	31.89
Days With ≥ 0.1" Precipitation	12	9	9	7	8	6	5	5	6	9	11	11	92
Days With ≥ 1.0" Precipitation	0	0	0	0	0	0	0	0	0	0	0	0	0
Mean Snowfall (in.)	56.9	43.4	36.2	20.5	7.6	0.5	0.0	0.0	0.5	8.5	41.6	60.2	275.9
Days With ≥ 1.0" Snow Depth	31	28	31	29	16	0	0	0	0	6	25	31	197

Sundance — *Crook County*   Elevation: 4,747 ft.   Latitude: 44° 24' N   Longitude: 104° 23' W

	JAN	FEB	MAR	APR	MAY	JUN	JUL	AUG	SEP	OCT	NOV	DEC	YEAR
Mean Maximum Temp. (°F)	31.7	36.5	44.5	54.5	64.8	75.3	82.7	82.0	71.7	58.6	42.2	33.5	56.5
Mean Temp. (°F)	20.9	25.6	32.9	42.2	52.3	62.1	68.6	67.7	57.6	45.6	31.7	23.2	44.2
Mean Minimum Temp. (°F)	10.0	14.6	21.3	29.8	39.6	48.8	54.4	53.4	43.5	32.6	21.3	12.8	31.8
Extreme Maximum Temp. (°F)	65	65	74	84	90	98	101	100	96	88	74	62	101
Extreme Minimum Temp. (°F)	-25	-33	-21	-2	19	30	30	33	16	0	-20	-40	-40
Days Maximum Temp. ≥ 90°F	0	0	0	0	0	2	6	4	1	0	0	0	13
Days Maximum Temp. ≤ 32°F	14	8	5	1	0	0	0	0	0	1	7	13	49
Days Minimum Temp. ≤ 32°F	30	27	27	19	6	0	0	0	4	14	26	30	183
Days Minimum Temp. ≤ 0°F	8	4	2	0	0	0	0	0	0	0	1	5	20
Heating Degree Days (base 65°F)	1,363	1,107	988	679	392	139	35	40	245	594	992	1,291	7,865
Cooling Degree Days (base 65°F)	0	0	0	0	6	60	161	140	32	0	0	0	399
Mean Precipitation (in.)	0.70	0.67	0.98	2.29	2.83	3.04	2.10	1.67	1.30	1.56	0.83	0.73	18.70
Days With ≥ 0.1" Precipitation	2	2	3	6	7	6	5	4	3	4	3	3	48
Days With ≥ 1.0" Precipitation	0	0	0	0	0	1	0	0	0	0	0	0	1
Mean Snowfall (in.)	12.7	11.0	12.5	13.7	2.4	0.1	0.0	0.0	0.5	6.3	10.1	13.2	82.5
Days With ≥ 1.0" Snow Depth	28	22	13	5	0	0	0	0	0	3	11	21	103

Sybille Research Unit — *Albany County*   Elevation: 6,099 ft.   Latitude: 41° 46' N   Longitude: 105° 23' W

	JAN	FEB	MAR	APR	MAY	JUN	JUL	AUG	SEP	OCT	NOV	DEC	YEAR
Mean Maximum Temp. (°F)	35.9	39.7	47.7	56.1	66.4	78.1	84.4	83.4	74.3	62.1	45.6	37.2	59.2
Mean Temp. (°F)	25.8	29.1	35.6	43.3	52.5	62.7	69.0	68.0	59.0	48.0	34.9	27.2	46.3
Mean Minimum Temp. (°F)	15.8	18.5	23.6	30.4	38.5	47.2	53.6	52.5	43.5	33.9	24.0	17.1	33.2
Extreme Maximum Temp. (°F)	62	64	73	81	87	98	99	98	93	85	75	68	99
Extreme Minimum Temp. (°F)	-22	-28	-11	-2	17	28	37	34	9	-2	-17	-30	-30
Days Maximum Temp. ≥ 90°F	0	0	0	0	0	2	7	3	0	0	0	0	12
Days Maximum Temp. ≤ 32°F	10	7	3	1	0	0	0	0	0	0	5	9	35
Days Minimum Temp. ≤ 32°F	29	25	26	18	6	1	0	0	3	13	24	28	173
Days Minimum Temp. ≤ 0°F	4	2	1	0	0	0	0	0	0	0	1	3	11
Heating Degree Days (base 65°F)	1,207	1,007	904	645	384	119	20	25	204	519	898	1,165	7,097
Cooling Degree Days (base 65°F)	0	0	0	0	2	56	149	128	30	1	0	0	366
Mean Precipitation (in.)	0.65	0.56	1.03	1.92	2.63	2.04	1.71	1.50	1.20	1.20	0.94	0.60	15.98
Days With ≥ 0.1" Precipitation	3	2	3	5	6	4	5	3	3	3	3	2	42
Days With ≥ 1.0" Precipitation	0	0	0	0	0	0	0	0	0	0	0	0	0
Mean Snowfall (in.)	11.6	8.6	13.0	10.7	3.0	0.1	0.0	0.0	1.5	6.6	12.4	10.8	78.3
Days With ≥ 1.0" Snow Depth	15	10	8	4	1	0	0	0	0	2	8	11	59

Ten Sleep 16 SSE *Washakie County*   Elevation: 4,678 ft.   Latitude: 43° 49' N   Longitude: 107° 22' W

	JAN	FEB	MAR	APR	MAY	JUN	JUL	AUG	SEP	OCT	NOV	DEC	YEAR
Mean Maximum Temp. (°F)	31.6	38.7	47.3	56.9	66.8	78.3	87.0	85.8	73.4	60.3	44.5	34.2	58.7
Mean Temp. (°F)	14.6	22.3	33.1	42.1	51.7	61.9	68.7	66.6	54.9	43.0	29.2	17.6	42.1
Mean Minimum Temp. (°F)	-2.5	5.9	18.9	27.3	36.6	45.4	50.3	47.5	36.4	25.7	13.8	1.0	25.5
Extreme Maximum Temp. (°F)	61	66	77	85	91	100	103	103	97	88	74	65	103
Extreme Minimum Temp. (°F)	-44	-46	-24	-1	18	27	31	30	12	-8	-31	-51	-51
Days Maximum Temp. ≥ 90°F	0	0	0	0	0	4	14	10	2	0	0	0	30
Days Maximum Temp. ≤ 32°F	14	7	3	1	0	0	0	0	0	1	5	12	43
Days Minimum Temp. ≤ 32°F	31	28	30	23	8	0	0	0	9	27	30	31	217
Days Minimum Temp. ≤ 0°F	17	10	2	0	0	0	0	0	0	0	4	14	47
Heating Degree Days (base 65°F)	1,558	1,201	982	681	406	138	29	40	307	675	1,069	1,463	8,549
Cooling Degree Days (base 65°F)	0	0	0	0	1	41	134	92	10	0	0	0	278
Mean Precipitation (in.)	0.62	0.50	1.09	1.52	2.25	1.69	0.99	0.70	1.30	1.28	0.75	0.67	13.36
Days With ≥ 0.1" Precipitation	2	2	4	4	5	4	3	2	3	4	3	2	38
Days With ≥ 1.0" Precipitation	0	0	0	0	0	0	0	0	0	0	0	0	0
Mean Snowfall (in.)	10.8	8.3	10.9	6.1	1.8	trace	0.0	0.0	0.5	4.4	8.8	10.8	62.4
Days With ≥ 1.0" Snow Depth	29	27	16	3	1	0	0	0	0	2	13	24	115

Ten Sleep 4 NE *Washakie County*   Elevation: 4,799 ft.   Latitude: 44° 04' N   Longitude: 107° 25' W

	JAN	FEB	MAR	APR	MAY	JUN	JUL	AUG	SEP	OCT	NOV	DEC	YEAR
Mean Maximum Temp. (°F)	36.0	41.0	49.9	59.1	69.2	79.5	86.9	86.0	75.1	62.3	46.0	38.1	60.8
Mean Temp. (°F)	24.2	29.4	38.0	46.4	55.7	65.1	71.6	70.5	60.1	48.5	34.8	26.6	47.6
Mean Minimum Temp. (°F)	12.4	17.7	26.0	33.6	42.1	50.6	56.2	55.0	44.9	34.7	23.6	15.0	34.3
Extreme Maximum Temp. (°F)	64	66	79	84	91	100	102	99	95	87	74	66	102
Extreme Minimum Temp. (°F)	-25	-31	-12	10	24	31	38	38	15	4	-16	-34	-34
Days Maximum Temp. ≥ 90°F	0	0	0	0	0	3	12	10	1	0	0	0	26
Days Maximum Temp. ≤ 32°F	11	5	2	0	0	0	0	0	0	0	4	8	30
Days Minimum Temp. ≤ 32°F	30	27	24	14	3	0	0	0	2	12	25	29	166
Days Minimum Temp. ≤ 0°F	6	3	0	0	0	0	0	0	0	0	1	3	13
Heating Degree Days (base 65°F)	1,258	999	831	553	295	85	11	17	186	506	899	1,185	6,825
Cooling Degree Days (base 65°F)	0	0	0	2	14	87	217	200	46	1	0	0	567
Mean Precipitation (in.)	0.57	0.38	0.96	1.38	2.34	1.84	0.98	0.67	1.44	1.25	0.80	0.62	13.23
Days With ≥ 0.1" Precipitation	2	2	3	5	5	5	3	2	4	4	3	2	40
Days With ≥ 1.0" Precipitation	0	0	0	0	0	0	0	0	0	0	0	0	0
Mean Snowfall (in.)	10.8	6.7	8.9	5.5	2.0	0.0	0.0	0.0	0.8	3.4	8.0	10.9	57.0
Days With ≥ 1.0" Snow Depth	25	19	8	1	0	0	0	0	0	1	9	19	82

Torrington Exp. Farm *Goshen County*   Elevation: 4,097 ft.   Latitude: 42° 05' N   Longitude: 104° 13' W

	JAN	FEB	MAR	APR	MAY	JUN	JUL	AUG	SEP	OCT	NOV	DEC	YEAR
Mean Maximum Temp. (°F)	39.6	45.4	52.0	61.2	71.3	82.6	89.1	87.5	78.1	65.4	49.9	41.4	63.6
Mean Temp. (°F)	25.0	30.2	37.2	45.9	56.2	66.3	72.2	70.2	59.9	47.4	34.6	26.4	47.6
Mean Minimum Temp. (°F)	10.3	15.0	22.4	30.5	41.1	50.2	55.2	52.8	41.6	29.3	19.3	11.4	31.6
Extreme Maximum Temp. (°F)	69	75	81	91	95	105	111	104	100	91	83	72	111
Extreme Minimum Temp. (°F)	-30	-32	-20	-17	11	30	39	35	14	-9	-23	-43	-43
Days Maximum Temp. ≥ 90°F	0	0	0	0	1	8	16	14	5	0	0	0	44
Days Maximum Temp. ≤ 32°F	9	5	3	0	0	0	0	0	0	0	3	7	27
Days Minimum Temp. ≤ 32°F	30	27	27	18	4	0	0	0	4	20	28	30	188
Days Minimum Temp. ≤ 0°F	7	4	1	0	0	0	0	0	0	0	2	6	20
Heating Degree Days (base 65°F)	1,235	974	855	566	278	67	9	17	186	541	904	1,192	6,824
Cooling Degree Days (base 65°F)	0	0	0	0	16	108	229	186	40	0	0	0	579
Mean Precipitation (in.)	0.30	0.38	0.69	1.65	2.53	2.22	1.81	1.17	1.19	0.99	0.53	0.36	13.82
Days With ≥ 0.1" Precipitation	1	1	2	4	5	5	5	3	3	2	2	1	34
Days With ≥ 1.0" Precipitation	0	0	0	0	0	0	0	0	0	0	0	0	0
Mean Snowfall (in.)	5.3	4.7	*5.6*	3.1	0.1	trace	0.0	0.0	0.3	2.3	5.0	6.6	*33.0*
Days With ≥ 1.0" Snow Depth	*13*	8	*5*	2	0	0	0	0	0	1	5	11	*45*

Upton *Weston County*   Elevation: 4,317 ft.   Latitude: 44° 06' N   Longitude: 104° 37' W

	JAN	FEB	MAR	APR	MAY	JUN	JUL	AUG	SEP	OCT	NOV	DEC	YEAR
Mean Maximum Temp. (°F)	30.4	36.3	46.0	56.8	67.8	78.5	86.5	85.3	74.2	60.1	42.6	32.7	58.1
Mean Temp. (°F)	17.9	24.2	33.2	43.1	53.8	63.9	70.9	69.5	58.3	45.5	30.8	20.5	44.3
Mean Minimum Temp. (°F)	5.5	12.0	20.5	29.3	39.7	49.2	55.2	53.6	42.4	30.9	18.9	8.4	30.5
Extreme Maximum Temp. (°F)	65	68	78	88	93	102	105	102	100	87	76	66	105
Extreme Minimum Temp. (°F)	-34	-33	-19	-11	18	30	30	32	15	-6	-33	-42	-42
Days Maximum Temp. ≥ 90°F	0	0	0	0	0	4	12	10	2	0	0	0	28
Days Maximum Temp. ≤ 32°F	15	9	5	1	0	0	0	0	0	1	6	14	51
Days Minimum Temp. ≤ 32°F	31	27	29	20	5	1	0	0	4	17	27	31	192
Days Minimum Temp. ≤ 0°F	10	5	2	0	0	0	0	0	0	0	2	8	27
Heating Degree Days (base 65°F)	1,454	1,147	977	652	348	107	17	26	231	604	1,019	1,372	7,954
Cooling Degree Days (base 65°F)	0	0	0	1	9	80	218	193	40	0	0	0	541
Mean Precipitation (in.)	0.41	0.42	0.70	1.54	2.49	2.44	2.04	1.40	1.03	1.36	0.60	0.54	14.97
Days With ≥ 0.1" Precipitation	1	2	3	4	6	6	4	3	3	3	2	2	39
Days With ≥ 1.0" Precipitation	0	0	0	0	0	0	0	0	0	0	0	0	0
Mean Snowfall (in.)	*7.8*	6.4	8.2	5.1	trace	0.1	0.0	0.0	trace	2.5	*7.3*	9.5	*46.9*
Days With ≥ 1.0" Snow Depth	*23*	17	*8*	*2*	0	0	0	0	0	1	na	*19*	na

Weston 1 E *Campbell County* Elevation: 3,523 ft. Latitude: 44° 38' N Longitude: 105° 18' W

	JAN	FEB	MAR	APR	MAY	JUN	JUL	AUG	SEP	OCT	NOV	DEC	YEAR
Mean Maximum Temp. (°F)	34.1	40.4	48.2	58.1	68.4	79.0	87.2	86.9	75.5	62.2	46.2	36.1	60.2
Mean Temp. (°F)	20.8	27.0	35.0	44.2	54.1	63.8	70.4	69.4	58.4	46.3	32.8	22.8	45.4
Mean Minimum Temp. (°F)	7.5	13.5	21.7	30.3	39.7	48.4	53.4	51.9	41.2	30.3	19.4	9.6	30.6
Extreme Maximum Temp. (°F)	70	79	79	88	94	104	108	104	103	90	77	68	108
Extreme Minimum Temp. (°F)	-35	-47	-29	-4	11	30	35	30	15	-17	-28	-47	-47
Days Maximum Temp. ≥ 90°F	0	0	0	0	0	5	13	13	3	0	0	0	34
Days Maximum Temp. ≤ 32°F	12	7	4	1	0	0	0	0	0	0	4	10	38
Days Minimum Temp. ≤ 32°F	31	27	27	18	6	0	0	0	5	18	27	30	189
Days Minimum Temp. ≤ 0°F	10	5	2	0	0	0	0	0	0	0	2	7	26
Heating Degree Days (base 65°F)	1,363	1,068	924	617	337	103	22	29	225	573	959	1,301	7,521
Cooling Degree Days (base 65°F)	0	0	0	1	8	73	198	179	36	1	0	0	496
Mean Precipitation (in.)	0.32	0.31	0.61	1.31	2.56	2.46	1.48	1.07	1.15	1.27	0.46	0.34	13.34
Days With ≥ 0.1" Precipitation	1	1	2	4	7	5	4	3	3	3	2	1	36
Days With ≥ 1.0" Precipitation	0	0	0	0	0	0	0	0	0	0	0	0	0
Mean Snowfall (in.)	6.0	5.5	8.1	5.3	1.1	0.0	0.0	0.0	0.4	2.2	4.9	7.2	40.7
Days With ≥ 1.0" Snow Depth	20	13	9	2	0	0	0	0	0	1	6	17	68

Wheatland 4 N *Platte County* Elevation: 4,635 ft. Latitude: 42° 07' N Longitude: 104° 57' W

	JAN	FEB	MAR	APR	MAY	JUN	JUL	AUG	SEP	OCT	NOV	DEC	YEAR
Mean Maximum Temp. (°F)	41.0	44.9	52.7	61.0	70.7	81.8	88.6	87.2	77.8	65.8	50.3	42.3	63.7
Mean Temp. (°F)	28.7	32.1	38.9	46.2	55.7	65.7	71.9	70.2	60.5	49.7	37.6	30.1	49.0
Mean Minimum Temp. (°F)	15.8	19.4	25.1	31.3	40.7	49.5	55.1	53.1	43.2	33.5	25.0	17.8	34.1
Extreme Maximum Temp. (°F)	70	72	81	88	95	104	107	103	100	89	81	72	107
Extreme Minimum Temp. (°F)	-36	-30	-16	-22	13	31	38	36	12	-9	-18	-39	-39
Days Maximum Temp. ≥ 90°F	0	0	0	0	0	7	14	12	3	0	0	0	36
Days Maximum Temp. ≤ 32°F	7	5	2	0	0	0	0	0	0	0	3	6	23
Days Minimum Temp. ≤ 32°F	27	23	24	16	4	0	0	0	3	14	22	26	159
Days Minimum Temp. ≤ 0°F	6	3	0	0	0	0	0	0	0	0	1	4	14
Heating Degree Days (base 65°F)	1,118	924	801	559	289	68	8	11	168	470	814	1,075	6,305
Cooling Degree Days (base 65°F)	0	0	0	1	11	99	233	197	46	3	0	0	590
Mean Precipitation (in.)	0.23	0.26	0.67	1.43	2.41	2.13	1.77	1.22	1.24	0.90	0.50	0.27	13.03
Days With ≥ 0.1" Precipitation	1	1	2	4	6	4	4	3	3	2	2	1	33
Days With ≥ 1.0" Precipitation	0	0	0	0	0	0	0	0	0	0	0	0	0
Mean Snowfall (in.)	6.2	5.1	7.0	4.4	0.9	0.0	0.0	0.0	0.7	3.0	6.4	6.7	40.4
Days With ≥ 1.0" Snow Depth	7	5	4	1	0	0	0	0	0	1	4	7	29

Worland *Washakie County* Elevation: 4,058 ft. Latitude: 44° 01' N Longitude: 107° 58' W

	JAN	FEB	MAR	APR	MAY	JUN	JUL	AUG	SEP	OCT	NOV	DEC	YEAR
Mean Maximum Temp. (°F)	28.5	38.2	50.0	60.3	70.4	81.9	89.4	88.1	75.6	61.8	44.1	31.3	60.0
Mean Temp. (°F)	15.4	24.4	36.4	46.1	56.3	66.4	72.2	70.3	58.6	46.4	31.2	18.6	45.2
Mean Minimum Temp. (°F)	2.2	10.5	22.7	31.8	42.2	50.9	55.1	52.4	41.5	31.1	18.2	6.0	30.4
Extreme Maximum Temp. (°F)	61	72	81	89	96	104	106	105	100	90	77	68	106
Extreme Minimum Temp. (°F)	-42	-36	-24	8	26	34	36	35	21	-3	-26	-44	-44
Days Maximum Temp. ≥ 90°F	0	0	0	0	1	8	18	15	3	0	0	0	45
Days Maximum Temp. ≤ 32°F	17	7	3	0	0	0	0	0	0	0	5	15	47
Days Minimum Temp. ≤ 32°F	31	28	28	16	3	0	0	0	3	17	29	31	186
Days Minimum Temp. ≤ 0°F	12	5	1	0	0	0	0	0	0	0	2	8	28
Heating Degree Days (base 65°F)	1,533	1,141	881	562	278	69	14	19	220	570	1,009	1,434	7,730
Cooling Degree Days (base 65°F)	0	0	0	1	19	115	248	205	39	0	0	0	627
Mean Precipitation (in.)	0.27	0.20	0.42	0.84	1.60	1.09	0.71	0.57	0.87	0.73	0.36	0.26	7.92
Days With ≥ 0.1" Precipitation	1	1	2	2	4	3	2	2	3	2	1	1	24
Days With ≥ 1.0" Precipitation	0	0	0	0	0	0	0	0	0	0	0	0	0
Mean Snowfall (in.)	na	*3.0*	na	*0.7*	0.0	0.0	0.0	0.0	trace	*0.2*	na	na	na
Days With ≥ 1.0" Snow Depth	na	na	na	*0*	0	0	0	0	0	*0*	na	na	na

Worland Municipal Airport *Washakie County* Elevation: 4,169 ft. Latitude: 43° 58' N Longitude: 107° 58' W

	JAN	FEB	MAR	APR	MAY	JUN	JUL	AUG	SEP	OCT	NOV	DEC	YEAR
Mean Maximum Temp. (°F)	29.5	38.7	50.5	60.8	71.1	82.5	89.6	88.2	75.5	62.2	44.6	32.1	60.4
Mean Temp. (°F)	16.4	25.3	37.1	46.8	56.9	66.8	73.1	71.5	59.7	47.4	31.6	19.1	46.0
Mean Minimum Temp. (°F)	3.2	11.7	23.6	32.7	42.6	51.1	56.6	54.7	43.9	32.5	18.6	6.1	31.4
Extreme Maximum Temp. (°F)	61	70	81	88	95	107	106	106	100	90	77	67	107
Extreme Minimum Temp. (°F)	-36	-37	-28	9	24	34	38	36	15	-3	-26	-50	-50
Days Maximum Temp. ≥ 90°F	0	0	0	0	1	8	18	16	3	0	0	0	46
Days Maximum Temp. ≤ 32°F	17	7	2	0	0	0	0	0	0	0	5	14	45
Days Minimum Temp. ≤ 32°F	31	28	27	15	2	0	0	0	2	15	29	31	180
Days Minimum Temp. ≤ 0°F	11	5	1	0	0	0	0	0	0	0	2	8	27
Heating Degree Days (base 65°F)	1,501	1,117	857	542	263	63	9	14	193	539	996	1,417	7,511
Cooling Degree Days (base 65°F)	0	0	0	1	20	119	263	231	45	0	0	0	679
Mean Precipitation (in.)	0.28	0.19	0.47	0.83	1.59	1.10	0.70	0.54	0.83	0.71	0.39	0.26	7.89
Days With ≥ 0.1" Precipitation	1	1	2	3	4	3	2	1	2	2	1	1	23
Days With ≥ 1.0" Precipitation	0	0	0	0	0	0	0	0	0	0	0	1	0
Mean Snowfall (in.)	5.6	3.6	4.6	3.1	0.5	trace	trace	0.0	0.8	2.5	4.7	6.2	31.6
Days With ≥ 1.0" Snow Depth	25	18	6	1	0	0	0	0	0	1	7	16	74

Yoder 2 WSW *Goshen County* Elevation: 4,288 ft. Latitude: 41° 54' N Longitude: 104° 20' W

	JAN	FEB	MAR	APR	MAY	JUN	JUL	AUG	SEP	OCT	NOV	DEC	YEAR
Mean Maximum Temp. (°F)	40.7	46.2	53.1	61.8	71.6	82.9	89.6	88.1	78.7	66.0	50.1	42.2	64.3
Mean Temp. (°F)	27.4	31.9	38.3	46.1	55.9	66.0	72.1	70.4	60.5	49.0	36.1	28.8	48.5
Mean Minimum Temp. (°F)	14.1	17.5	23.4	30.3	40.2	49.0	54.5	52.5	42.2	31.9	22.1	15.4	32.8
Extreme Maximum Temp. (°F)	71	78	81	90	95	104	109	105	101	90	81	72	109
Extreme Minimum Temp. (°F)	-32	-28	-16	-22	9	30	38	33	14	-14	-21	-40	-40
Days Maximum Temp. ≥ 90°F	0	0	0	0	0	8	17	15	4	0	0	0	44
Days Maximum Temp. ≤ 32°F	8	4	2	0	0	0	0	0	0	0	3	6	23
Days Minimum Temp. ≤ 32°F	29	26	26	18	4	0	0	0	3	16	26	29	177
Days Minimum Temp. ≤ 0°F	6	3	1	0	0	0	0	0	0	0	1	4	15
Heating Degree Days (base 65°F)	1,158	930	823	562	284	68	7	11	169	491	860	1,116	6,479
Cooling Degree Days (base 65°F)	0	0	0	0	10	101	226	186	41	2	0	0	567
Mean Precipitation (in.)	0.32	0.31	0.92	1.79	2.82	2.27	1.75	1.13	1.34	1.01	0.61	0.34	14.61
Days With ≥ 0.1" Precipitation	1	1	3	5	7	5	4	4	3	3	2	1	39
Days With ≥ 1.0" Precipitation	0	0	0	0	1	1	0	0	0	0	0	0	2
Mean Snowfall (in.)	7.2	5.7	8.5	6.1	0.4	0.0	0.0	0.0	0.5	3.4	8.1	8.1	48.0
Days With ≥ 1.0" Snow Depth	12	7	5	2	0	0	0	0	0	1	6	10	43

Note: See Appendix D for explanation of data.

Appendix A: National, Regional, and State Climate Centers

National Climate Centers

National Oceanic and Atmospheric Administration
14th Street & Constitution Avenue, NW
Room 6013
Washington, DC 20230
Tel: 202-482-6090
Fax: 202-482-3154
WWW: http://www.noaa.gov/

National Climatic Data Center
Federal Building
151 Patton Avenue
Asheville NC 28801-5001
Tel: 828-271-4800
Fax: 828-271-4876
WWW: http://www.ncdc.noaa.gov/

Climate Prediction Center
World Weather Building
5200 Auth Road
Camp Springs, MD 20746
Tel: 301-763-8000
WWW: http://www.cpc.ncep.noaa.gov/

Office of Oceanic and Atmospheric Research
Silver Spring Metro Center
Building 3, Room 11627
1315 East-West Highway
Silver Spring, MD 20910
Tel: 301-713-2458
WWW: http://www.oar.noaa.gov/

National Weather Service Headquarters
1325 East-West Highway
Silver Spring, MD 20910
WWW: http://www.nws.noaa.gov

National Huricane Center/
Tropical Prediction Center
11691 S.W. 17th Street
Miami, Florida 33165-2149
Tel: 305-229-4470
http://www.nhc.noaa.gov/

Storm Prediction Center
1313 Halley Avenue
Norman, Oklahoma 73069
Tel: 405-579-0771
http://www.spc.noaa.gov/

Aviation Weather Center
7220 NW 101st Terrace, Room 101
Kansas City, Missouri 64153-2371
Tel: 816-584-7200
WWW: http://www.awc-kc.noaa.gov/

Regional Climate Centers

High Plains

Dr. Kenneth G. Hubbard, Director
High Plains Regional Climate Center
Dept of Agricultural Meteorology
Room 242, L.W. Chase Hall
University of Nebraska
Lincoln, NE 68583-0728
Tel: 402-472-6706
Fax: 402-472-6338
Internet Email: khubbard@hpccsun.unl.edu
WWW: http://hpccsun.unl.edu/

Midwest

Steven D. Hilberg, Director
Midwestern Regional Climate Center
Illinois State Water Survey
2204 Griffith Drive
Champaign, IL 61820
Tel: 217-333-8495
Fax: 217-244-0220
Internet Email: hberg@uiuc.edu
WWW: http://mcc.sws.uiuc.edu/

Northeast

Dr Warren Knapp, Director
Northeast Regional Climate Center
1107 Bradfield Hall
Cornell University
Ithaca, NY 14853
Tel: 607-255-1751
Fax: 607-255-2106
Internet Email: nrcc@cornell.edu
WWW: http://met-www.cit.cornell.edu/nrcc_home.html

Southeast

Michael J. Janis, Interim Director
Southeast Regional Climate Center
SC Dept of Natural Resources
Land, Water & Conservation Division
1201 Main Street, Suite 1100
Columbia, SC 29201
Tel: 803-737-0800
Fax: 803-765-9080
Internet Email: janis@water.dnr.state.sc.us
WWW: http://water.dnr.state.sc.us/water/
climate/sercc/index.html

South

Dr. Kevin Robbins, Director
Southern Regional Climate Center
Louisiana State University
260 Howe-Russell Building
Baton Rouge, LA 70803-4105
Tel: 225-388-5021
Fax: 225-388-2912
Internet Email: krobbins@mistral.srcc.lsu.edu
WWW: http://www.srcc.lsu.edu/srcc.html

West

Dr. Richard Reinhardt, Director
Western Regional Climate Center
Desert Research Institute
2215 Raggio Parkway
Reno, NV 89512-1095
Tel: 775-674-7010
Fax: 775-674-7016
Internet Email: rrwrcc@dri.edu
WWW: http://www.wrcc.dri.edu/

State Climate Centers

Alabama

Dr. Richard McNider
Earth Systems Science Laboratory
University of Alabama in Huntsville
Huntsville AL 35899
Tel: 256-922-5756
Fax: 256-922-5755
Internet Email: mcnider@atmos.uah.edu
WWW: http://alclimate.atmos.uah.edu

Alaska

Dr. Dwight D. Pollard
Alaska State Climate Center
ENRI University of Alaska-Anchorage
707 A Street
Anchorage AK 99501
Tel: 907-257-2737
Fax: 907-257-2707
Internet Email: auclima@uaa.alaska.edu
WWW: http://www.uaa.alaska.edu/
enri/ascc_web/ascc_home.html

Arizona

Russell S. Vose
Office of Climatology
PO Box 871508
Arizona State University
Tempe AZ 85287-1508
Tel: 480-965-6265
Fax: 480-965-1473
Internet Email: azclimate@geography.asu.edu
WWW: http://geography.asu.edu/azclimate/

Arkansas

Dr. John G. Hehr
Department of Geography
104 Carnall Hall
University of Arkansas
Fayetteville AR 72701
Tel: 501-575-3159
Fax: 501-575-2642

California

Mr. William A. Mork
CA Dept of Water Resources
Division of Flood Management
P.O. BOX 219000
Sacramento CA 95821-9000
Tel: 916-574-2614
Fax: 916-574-2767
Internet Email: morkb@water.ca.gov

Colorado

Dr. Roger A. Pielke, Sr.
Colorado Climate Center
Dept of Atmospheric Science
Colorado State University
Fort Collins CO 80523
Tel: 970-491-8545
Fax: 970-491-8449
Internet Email: pielke@hercules.atmos.colostate.edu
WWW: http://ulysses.atmos.colostate.edu

Connecticut

Dr. David R. Miller
Dept of Natural Resources-U87
1376 Storrs Road
University of Connecticut
Storrs CT 06269-4087
Tel: 860-486-2840
Fax: 860-486-5408
Internet Email: dmiller@canr.uconn.edu

Delaware

Dr. Daniel J. Leathers
Center for Climatic Research
210 Newark Hall
Department of Geography
University of Delaware
Newark DE 19716
Tel: 302-831-2294
Fax: 302-831-6654
Internet Email: cxl30950@udelvm.udel.edu
WWW: http://www.udel.edu/leathers/stclim.html

Florida

Dr. James J. O'Brien
Florida Climate Center
Department of Meteorology
Florida State University
Johnson Building Room 223
Tallahassee, Fl 32306-2840
Tel: 850-644-3417
Fax: 850-644-5092
Internet Email: obrien@coaps.fsu.edu
WWW: http://www.coaps.fsu.edu/climate_center

Georgia

David E. Stooksbury, PhD
Georgia State Climatologist
Bioligical & Agricultural Engineering Dept.
Driftmier Engineering Center
University of Georgia
Athens GA 30602
Tel: 706-583-0156
Fax: 706-542-8806
Internet Email: climate@bae.uga.edu
WWW: http://www.bae.uga.edu/climate/

Hawaii

Pao-Shin Chu, Ph.D.
Associate Professor
Department of Meteorology
University of Hawaii at Manoa
2525 Correa Road
Honolulu HI 96822
Tel: 808-956-2324
Fax: 808-956-2877
Internet Email: chu@soest.hawaii.edu

Idaho

Dr. Russell Qualls
State Climate Services
Biological & Agricultural Engineering Dept.
425 Engineering/Physics Bldg.
University of Idaho
Moscow ID 83844-0904
Tel: 208-885-6184 or 208-885-7004
Fax: 208-885-7908
Internet Email: climate@uidaho.edu
WWW: http://www.uidaho.edu/~climate

Illinois

Dr. Jim Angel
Illinois State Water Survey
2204 Griffith Drive
Champaign IL 61820-7495
Tel: 217-333-0729
Fax: 217-244-0220
Internet Email: j-angel@uiuc.edu
WWW: http://www.sws.uiuc.edu/atmos/statecli/index.htm

Indiana

Mr. Ken Scheeringa
1150 Lilly Bldg.
Purdue University
West Lafayette IN 47907-1150
Tel: 765-494-8105
Fax: 765-496-2926
Internet Email: kens@purdue.edu or pbeneker@purdue.edu
WWW: http://shadow.agry.purdue.edu

Iowa

Mr. Harry J. Hillaker, Jr.
State Climatologist
Iowa Dept. of Agriculture
9607 NW Beaver Drive
Johnston, IA 50131-1908
Tel: 515-270-6907
Internet Email: iastatec@netins.net

Kansas

Ms Mary Knapp
Dept of Communications
Weather Data Library
211 Umberger Hall
Kansas State University
Manhattan KS 66506-3402
Tel: 785-532-7019
Fax: 785-532-6487
Internet Email: mknapp@oz.oznet.ksu.edu
WWW: http://www.oznet.ksu.edu/wdl/

Kentucky

Mr. Glen Conner
Kentucky Climate Center
Dept of Geography & Geology
Western Kentucky University
Bowling green KY 42164
Tel: 270-745-5983
Internet Email: glen.conner@wku.edu
WWW:
http://www2.wku.edu/~gg024004/ky-climate-center.html

Louisiana

Mr. John M. Grymes, III
Louisiana Office of State Climatology
LSU Southern Regional Climate Center
254 Howe-Russell Complex
Baton Rouge LA 70803-4105
Tel: 504-388-6870
Fax: 504-388-2912
Internet Email: jgrymes@maestro.srcc.lsu.edu
WWW: http://www.srcc.lsu.edu/LOSC/index.html

Maine

No state climate center at this time.

Maryland

Dr. Kenneth E. Pickering
Acting State Climatologist
Department of Meteorology
University of Maryland
College Park, MD 20742
Tel. 301-405-7223
FAX 301-314-9482
Internet Email: climate@atmos.umd.edu
WWW: http://meto.umd.edu/SC/sc.html

Massachusetts

Dr. David Taylor
State Climatologist
Mass Dept of Water Resources
496 Park Street
North Reading MA 01864
Tel: 617-275-8860 EXT 138
Fax: 617-271-0178
Internet Email: climat@wx.com

Michigan

Dr. Fred V. Nurnberger
MSU/State Climatology
417 Natural Sciences Bldg.
Michigan State University
East Lansing MI 48824-1115
Tel: 517-355-0231
Fax: 517-432-1076
Internet Email: scmifred@pilot.msu.edu
WWW: http://climate.geo.msu.edu

Minnesota

Mr. Jim Zandlo
State Climatology Office
University of Minnesota
S-325 Borlaug Hall
St. Paul MN 55108
Tel: 651-296-4214
Fax: 651-625-2208
Internet Email: mcwg@soils.umn.edu
WWW: http://www.soils.agri.umn.edu/re search/climatology/

Mississippi

Dr. Charles L. Wax
MS State Climatologist
Drawer 5448
Mississippi State Univ/Geosciences
Mississippi State MS 39762
Tel: 601-325-3915
Internet Email: wax@geosci.msstate.edu
WWW: http://www.msstate.edu/Dept/GeoSciences/climate/

Missouri

Dr. F. Adnan Akyuz
Missouri State Climatologist
Missouri Climate Center
100 Gentry Hall
University of Missouri-Columbia
Columbia, MO 65211
Tel: 573-882-8599
Fax: 573-884-5133
Internet Email: AkyuzF@missouri.edu
WWW: http://www.missouri.edu/~moclimat

Montana

No state climate center at this time.

Nebraska

Mr. Allen Dutcher
Nebraska State Climatologist
15 L.W. Chase Hall
University of Nebraska
Lincoln NE 68583-0728
Tel: 402-472-5206
Fax: 402-472-8763
Internet Email: adutcher@hpccsun.unl.edu
WWW: http://hpccsun.unl.edu/st_climate_ne

Nevada

Professor John W. James
Department of Geography
College of Ats & Sciences
University of Nevada/Reno
Reno NV 89557-0048
Tel: 702-784-6921

New Hampshire

Dr. Barry Keim
Dept of Geography/James Hall
University of New Hampshire
Durham NH 03824
Tel: 603-862-3136
Fax: 603-862-2649
Internet Email: bdk@hopper.unh.edu
WWW: http://www.unh.edu/geography/climate.html

New Jersey

Dr. David A. Robinson
New Jersey State Climatologist
Department of Geography
Rutgers University
54 Joyce Kilmer Avenue
Piscataway NJ 08854-8054
Tel: 732-445-4741
Fax: 732-445-0006
Internet Email: drobins@rci.rutgers.edu
WWW: http://climate.rutgers.edu/stateclim/

New Mexico

Dr. Ted Sammis
New Mexico State Climatologist
Dept. of Agronomy & Horticulture
New Mexico State University
P.O. Box 3001/Dept. 3Q
Las Cruces, NM 88003-8003
Tel: 505-646-2104
Fax: 505-646-6041
Internet Email: tsammis@nmsu.edu
WWW: http://weather.nmsu.edu/

New York

Mr. Keith L. Eggleston
1117 Bradfield Hall
Cornell University
Ithaca NY 14853
Tel: 607-255-1749
Fax: 607-255-2106
Internet Email: KLE1@cornell.edu

North Carolina

Dr. Sethu Raman
State Climate Office of North Carolina
Campus Box 7236
NC State University
Raleigh NC 27695-7236
Tel: 919-515-1440
Fax: 919-515-1446
Internet Email: sethu_raman@ncsu.edu
Internet Email: sco@cumulus.meas.ncsu.edu
WWW: http://www.nc-climate.ncsu.edu

North Dakota

John W. Enz
Agricultural Climatology
State Climatologist for North Dakota
Dept of Soil Science, Box 5638
North Dakota State University
Fargo ND 58105
Tel: 701-231-8576
Fax: 701-231-7861
Internet Email: jenz@badlands.nodak.edu

Ohio

Dr. Jeffrey C. Rogers
Department of Geography
Ohio State University
103 Bricker Hall
Columbus OH 43210-1361
Tel: 614-422-2514
Internet Email: jcrogers@magnus.acs.ohio-state.edu
WWW: http://www.geography.ohio-state.edu/
faculty/rogers/statclim.html

Oklahoma

Dr. Ken Crawford
Oklahoma Climatological Survey
University of Oklahoma
Sarkey's Energy Center
100 East Boyd, Suite 1210
Norman OK 73019-0628
Tel: 405-325-2541
Fax: 405-325-2550
Internet Email: ocs@ou.edu
WWW: http://www.ocs.ou.edu

Oregon

George H. Taylor
Oregon Climate Service
316 Strand Ag Hall
Oregon State University
Corvallis OR 97331-2209
Tel: 541-737-5705
Fax: 541-737-5710
Internet Email: oregon@oce.orst.edu
WWW: http://www.ocs.orst.edu/

Pennsylvania

Mr. Paul Knight
Department of Meteorology
503 Walker Building
University Park, PA 16802
Tel: 814-865-3197 OR 814-863-8732
Fax: 814-865-3663
Internet Email: knight@psumeteo.psu.edu
WWW: http://www.ems.psu.edu/PA_Climatologist/

Puerto Rico

Dr. Amos Winter
Dept of Marine Sciences
College of Arts and Sciences
University of Puerto Rico
Mayaguez, PR 00681-9013
Tel: 787-265-5416
Fax: 787-265-2195
Internet Email: a_winter@rumac.uprm.edu

Rhode Island

Mr. Carl D. Sawyer
Dept of Plant Sciences
Room 333, Woodward Hall
University of Rhode Island
Kingston RI 02881
Tel: 401-792-2937
Internet Email: ltn101@uriacc.uri.edu

South Carolina

Dr. Michael R. Helfert
State Climatology Office
SC Dept of Natural Resources
Land, Water & Conservation Division
1201 Main Street, Suite 1100
Columbia SC 29201
Tel: 803-737-0849
Fax: 803-765-9080
Internet Email: helfert@water.dnr.state.sc.us
WWW: http://water.dnr.state.sc.us/climate/sco

South Dakota

Dr. Alan R. Bender
Agricultural Engineering Department
South Dakota State University
Brookings SD 57007
Tel: 605-688-5678
Fax: 605-688-4917
Internet Email: bender.al@ces.sdstate.edu
WWW: http://www.abs.sdstate.edu/ae/weather/weather.htm

Tennessee

Mr. Wayne Hamberger
Tennessee Valley Authority
400 West Summit Hill Dr
Knoxville TN 37902-1499
Tel: 615-632-4222
Internet Email: whamberger@tva.gov

Texas

John Nielsen-Gammon
Texas State Climatologist
Department of Atmospheric Sciences
Texas A&M University
College Station TX 77843-3150
Tel: 979-845-5044
Fax: 979-862-4466
Internet Email: n-g@tamu.edu
WWW: http://www.met.tamu.edu/met/osc/osc.html

Utah

Dr. Don T. Jensen
Utah State Climatologist
Utah Climate Center
Utah State University
4825 Old Main Hill
Logan UT 84322-4825
Tel: 435-797-2190
Fax: 435-797-2117
Internet Email: djensen@cc.usu.edu
WWW: http://climate.usu.edu/

Vermont

Dr. Lesley-Ann Dupigny-Giroux
Department of Geography
Old Mill Bldg
University of Vermont
P.O. Box 54170
Burlington VT 05405-4170
Tel: 802-656-3060
Fax: 802-656-3042
Internet Email: State.Climatologist@uvm.edu
WWW: http://www.uvm.edu/~ldupigny/sc

Virginia

Dr. Patrick J. Michaels
Virginia State Climate Office
Clark Hall
University of Virginia
Charlottesville VA 22903
Tel: 804-924-0549 OR 7761
WWW: http://wsrv.clas.virginia.edu/~climate/

Washington

Mr. Mark Albright (Acting)
Atmospheric Sciences Dept.
Univ of Washington, AK-40
Seattle WA 98195
Tel: 206-543-0448
Fax: 206-543-0308
Internet Email: marka@atmos.washington.edu

West Virginia

No state climate center at this time.

Wisconsin

Vacant
State Climatologist Office
University of Wisconsin
1225 West Dayton Street
Madison WI 53706-1612
Tel: 608-263-2374
Fax: 608-262-5964
Internet Email: stclim@macc.wisc.edu
WWW: http://www.uwex.edu/sco/

Wyoming

Dr. Larry Pochop
Wyoming State Climatologist
Dept. Of Civil & Architectural Engr.
P.o. Box 3295
University of Wyoming
Laramie WY 82071-3295
Tel: 307-766-3326
Fax: 307-766-4444
Internet Email: pochop@uwyo.edu
WWW: http://www-wwrc.uwyo.edu/wrds/wsc/wsc.html

Appendix B: Periods of Record

Station Name	Period of Record
Aberdeen Regional Airport, SD	1948-1995
Abilene Municipal Airport, TX	1948-1995
Akron-Canton Regional Airport, OH	1948-1995
Alamosa Bergman Field, CO	1948-1995
Albany County Airport, NY	1946-1995
Albuquerque Int'l Airport, NM	1948-1995
Allentown A-B-E Int'l Airport, PA	1948-1995
Alpena Phelps Collins Airport, MI	1959-1995
Amarillo Int'l Airport, TX	1948-1995
Anchorage Int'l Airport, AK	1953-1995
Apalachicola Municipal Airport, FL	1948-1992
Asheville Regional Airport, NC	1948-1995
Astoria Clatsop County Airport, OR	1953-1995
Athens Municipal Airport, GA	1948-1995
Atlanta Hartsfield Int'l Arpt., GA	1945-1995
Atlantic City Int'l Airport, NJ	1958-1995
Atlantic City State Marina, NJ	1948-1995
Augusta Bush Field, GA	1949-1995
Austin Municipal Airport, TX	1948-1995
Bakersfield Meadows Field, CA	1948-1995
Baltimore-Washington Int'l Arpt., MD	1950-1995
Barrow W. Post-W. Rogers Airport, AK	1949-1995
Baton Rouge Ryan Airport, LA	1948-1995
Beckley Memorial Airport, WV	1963-1995
Billings Logan Int'l Airport, MT	1948-1995
Binghamton Edwin A. Link Field, NY	1948-1995
Birmingham Municipal Airport, AL	1948-1995
Bishop Airport, CA	1948-1995
Bismarck Municipal Airport, ND	1948-1995
Boise Air Terminal, ID	1948-1995
Boston Logan Int'l Airport, MA	1945-1995
Bridgeport Sikorsky Memorial, CT	1948-1995
Bristol Tri-City Airport, TN	1948-1995
Brownsville Int'l Airport, TX	1948-1995
Buffalo Int'l Airport, NY	1946-1995
Burlington Int'l Airport, VT	1948-1995
Cape Hatteras NWS Bldg, NC	1957-1995
Caribou Municipal Airport, ME	1948-1995
Casper Int'l Airport, WY	1949-1995
Charleston Int'l Airport, SC	1945-1995
Charleston Kanawha Airport, WV	1949-1995
Charlotte Douglas Int'l Airport, NC	1948-1995
Chattanooga Lovell Field, TN	1948-1995
Chicago O'Hare Int'l Airport, IL	1958-1995
Cincinnati Covington Airport, KY	1948-1995
Clayton Municipal Airpark, NM	1948-1985
Cleveland Hopkins Int'l Airport, OH	1948-1995
Colorado Springs Muni Airport, CO	1978-1995
Columbia Metro Airport, SC	1948-1995
Columbia Regional Airport, MO	1969-1995

Station Name	Period of Record
Columbus Metropolitan Airport, GA	1948-1995
Columbus-Port Columbus Int'l, OH	1948-1995
Concord Municipal Airport, NH	1948-1995
Concordia Blosser Muni Airport, KS	1948-1995
Corpus Christi Int'l Airport, TX	1948-1995
Dallas-Fort Worth Int'l Airport, TX	1948-1995
Dayton Int'l Airport, OH	1948-1995
Daytona Beach Regional Airport, FL	1948-1995
Del Rio Int'l Airport, TX	1951-1979
Denver Stapleton Int'l Airport, CO	1948-1995
Des Moines Airport, IL	1945-1995
Detroit Metropolitan Airport, MI	1958-1995
Dodge City Municipal Airport, KS	1948-1995
Dubuque Regional Airport, IA	1951-1995
Duluth Int'l Airport, MN	1948-1995
El Paso Int'l Airport, TX	1948-1995
Elkins-Randolph Co. Airport, WV	1948-1995
Elko Municipal Airport, NV	1948-1995
Ely Yelland Field, NV	1948-1995
Erie Int'l Airport, PA	1948-1995
Eugene Mahlon Sweet Airport, OR	1948-1995
Eureka, CA	1941-1995
Evansville Regional Airport, IN	1948-1995
Fairbanks Int'l Airport, AK	1948-1995
Fargo Hector Field, ND	1948-1995
Flagstaff Pulliam Airport, AZ	1950-1995
Flint Bishop Airport, MI	1949-1995
Fort Myers Page Field, FL	1948-1995
Fort Smith Regional Airport, AR	1948-1995
Fort Wayne Baer Field, IN	1948-1995
Fresno Air Terminal, CA	1949-1995
Gainesville Regional Airport, FL	1962-1995
Galveston, TX	1963-1995
Glasgow Int'l Airport, MT	1948-1995
Goodland Renner Field, KS	1949-1995
Grand Island Airport, NE	1948-1995
Grand Junction Walker Field, CO	1948-1995
Grand Rapids Int'l Airport, MI	1948-1995
Great Falls Int'l Airport, MT	1948-1995
Greater Peoria Airport, IL	1948-1995
Green Bay Int'l Airport, WI	1949-1995
Greensboro Airport, NC	1948-1995
Greenville-Spartanbrg Airport, SC	1962-1995
Harrisburg Capital City Airport, PA	1948-1991
Hartford Bradley Int'l Airport, CT	1949-1995
Havre City-County Airport, MT	1961-1994
Helena Airport ASOS, MT	1948-1995
Hilo International Airport, HI	1949-1995
Honolulu Int'l Airport, HI	1949-1995
Houghton Lake Airport, MI	1964-1995

Station Name	Period of Record	Station Name	Period of Record
Houston Bush Intercontinental, TX	1969-1995	New York JFK Int'l Airport, NY	1948-1995
Huntington Tri-State Airport, WV	1961-1995	New York Laguardia Airport, NY	1947-1995
Huntsville Airport, AL	1958-1995	Newark Int'l Airport, NJ	1935-1995
Huron Regional Airport, SD	1900-1995	Nome Municipal Airport, AK	1948-1995
Indianapolis Int'l Airport, IN	1948-1995	Norfolk Int'l Airport, VA	1948-1995
International Falls Int'l Arpt., MI	1948-1995	Norfolk Karl Stefan Mem. Arpt., NE	1948-1995
Islip Macarthur Airport, NY	1984-1995	North Platte Lee Bird Field, NE	1948-1995
Jackson Julian Carroll Airport, KY	1981-1995	Oak Ridge, TN	1962-1995
Jackson Thompson Field, MS	1963-1995	Oklahoma City Int'l Airport, OK	1945-1995
Jacksonville Int'l Airport, FL	1948-1995	Olympia Airport, WA	1948-1995
Juneau Int'l Airport, AK	1948-1995	Omaha Eppley Airfield, NE	1948-1995
Kahului Airport, HI	1958-1995	Omaha WSFO, NE	1984-1993
Kalispell Airport, MT	1948-1995	Orlando Int'l Airport, FL	1974-1995
Kansas City Int'l Airport, MO	1948-1988	Pendleton Municipal Airport, OR	1948-1995
Key West Int'l Airport, FL	1948-1995	Pensacola Regional Airport, FL	1948-1995
Knoxville McGhee Tyson Airport, TN	1948-1995	Philadelphia Int'l Airport, PA	1948-1995
La Crosse Municipal Airport, WI	1948-1995	Phoenix Sky Harbor Int'l Arpt., AZ	1948-1995
Lake Charles Municipal Airport, LA	1961-1995	Pittsburgh Int'l Airport, PA	1948-1995
Lander Hunt Field, WY	1948-1995	Pocatello Municipal Airport, ID	1948-1995
Lansing Capital City Airport, MI	1948-1995	Port Arthur Jefferson County, TX	1948-1995
Las Vegas McCarran Int'l Arpt., NV	1948-1995	Portland Int'l Airport, OR	1926-1995
Lewiston Airport, ID	1948-1995	Portland Int'l Jetport, ME	1948-1995
Lexington Bluegrass Field, KY	1948-1995	Providence T F Green State Arpt., RI	1948-1995
Lihue Airport, HI	1950-1995	Pueblo Memorial Airport, CO	1954-1995
Lincoln Municipal Airport, NE	1948-1995	Quillayute Airport, WA	1966-1995
Little Rock Adams Field, AR	1948-1995	Raleigh-Durham Airport, NC	1948-1995
Long Beach Daugherty Field, CA	1949-1995	Rapid City Regional Airport, SD	1949-1995
Los Angeles Civic Center, CA	1921-1963	Reno Cannon Int'l Airport, NV	1945-1995
Los Angeles Int'l Airport, CA	1948-1995	Richmond R.E. Byrd Int'l Airport, VA	1948-1995
Louisville Standiford Field, KY	1948-1995	Roanoke Woodrum Airport, VA	1948-1995
Lubbock Regional Airport, TX	1948-1995	Rochester Int'l Airport, NY	1948-1995
Lynchburg Municipal Airport, VA	1948-1995	Rochester Municipal Airport, MN	1948-1995
Macon Regional Airport, GA	1948-1995	Rockford Greater Rockford Arpt., IL	1951-1995
Madison Regional Airport, WI	1948-1995	Roswell Industrial Airpark, NM	1946-1995
Mansfield Lahm Municipal Airport, OH	1948-1995	Sacramento Executive Airport, CA	1947-1995
Marquette County Airport, MI	1963-1995	Saint Cloud Municipal Airport, MN	1948-1995
Medford Jackson County Airport, OR	1948-1995	Saint Louis Lambert Int'l Arpt., MO	1945-1995
Memphis Int'l Airport, TN	1948-1995	Salem McNary Field, OR	1948-1995
Meridian Key Field, MS	1948-1995	Salt Lake City Int'l Airport, UT	1948-1995
Miami Int'l Airport, FL	1948-1995	San Angelo Mathis Field, TX	1948-1995
Midland Regional Air Terminal, TX	1948-1995	San Antonio Int'l Airport, TX	1948-1995
Miles City Municipal Airport, MT	1948-1989	San Diego Lindbergh Field, CA	1948-1995
Milford Airport, UT	1948-1989	San Francisco Int'l Airport, CA	1945-1995
Milton Blue Hill Observatory, MA	1962-1995	San Francisco Mission, CA	1921-1992
Milwaukee Gen. Mitchell Field, WI	1948-1995	Santa Maria Public Airport, CA	1954-1995
Minneapolis-St Paul Int'l Arpt., MN	1945-1995	Sault Ste Marie Sanderson Field, MI	1947-1995
Missoula Johnson-Bell Field, MT	1948-1995	Savannah Int'l Airport, GA	1950-1995
Mobile Regional Airport, AL	1948-1995	Scottsbluff County Airport, NE	1948-1995
Moline Quad City Airport, IL	1943-1995	Seattle Portage Bay, WA	1900-1992
Montgomery Dannelly Field, AL	1948-1995	Seattle-Tacoma Int'l Airport, WA	1948-1995
Mount Washington, NH	1948-1995	Sheridan County Airport, WY	1948-1995
Muskegon County Airport, MI	1948-1995	Shreveport Regional Airport, LA	1948-1995
Nashville Int'l Airport, TN	1948-1995	Sioux City Municipal Airport, IA	1948-1995
New Orleans Int'l Airport, LA	1948-1995	Sioux Falls Foss Field, SD	1932-1995
New York Central Park Observatory, NY	1965-1995	South Bend Michiana Regional, IN	1948-1995

Station Name	Period of Record
Spokane Int'l Airport, WA	1948-1995
Springfield Capital Airport, IL	1948-1995
Springfield Regional Airport, MO	1948-1995
Stockton Metropolitan Airport, CA	1948-1995
Syracuse Hancock Int'l Airport, NY	1945-1995
Tallahassee Municipal Airport, FL	1948-1995
Tampa Int'l Airport, FL	1948-1995
Toledo Express Airport, OH	1955-1995
Topeka Municipal Airport, KS	1948-1995
Tucson Int'l Airport, AZ	1946-1995
Tulsa Int'l Airport, OK	1948-1995
Tupelo C D Lemons Airport, MS	1983-1995
Valentine Miller Field, NE	1948-1995
Vero Beach, FL	1949-1995
Victoria Regional Airport, TX	1953-1995
Waco Madison Cooper Airport, TX	1948-1995
Washington DC Dulles Int'l Arpt., VA	1962-1995
Washington DC National Airport, DC	1945-1995
Waterloo Municipal Airport, IA	1960-1995
West Palm Beach Int'l Airport, FL	1948-1995
Wichita Falls Municipal Airport, TX	1948-1995
Wichita Mid-Continent Airport, KS	1948-1995
Wilkes-Barre Scranton Airport, PA	1949-1995
Williamsport Airport, PA	1948-1995
Williston Sloulin Int'l Airport, ND	1962-1995
Wilmington Airport, DE	1948-1995
Wilmington Airport, NC	1948-1995
Winnemucca Municipal Airport, NV	1949-1995
Winslow Municipal Airport, AZ	1948-1979
Worcester Municipal Airport, MA	1949-1995
Yakima Air Terminal, WA	1948-1995
Youngstown Municipal Airport, OH	1948-1995
Yuma Int'l Airport, AZ	1948-1979
All Cooperative Stations	1970-1999

Note: The National Weather Service station tables contain data from two different sources: The International Station Meteorological Climate Summary (ISMCS), with various periods of record as outlined in Appendix B; and the NCDC TD-3220 data tapes, which cover the years 1970-1999.

The following elements are from the ISMCS: maximum precipitation, minimum precipitation, maximum 24-hour precipitation, maximum snowfall, maximum 24-hour snowfall, thunderstorm days, foggy days, predominant sky cover, relative humidity, dewpoint, wind speed and direction, and maximum wind gust.

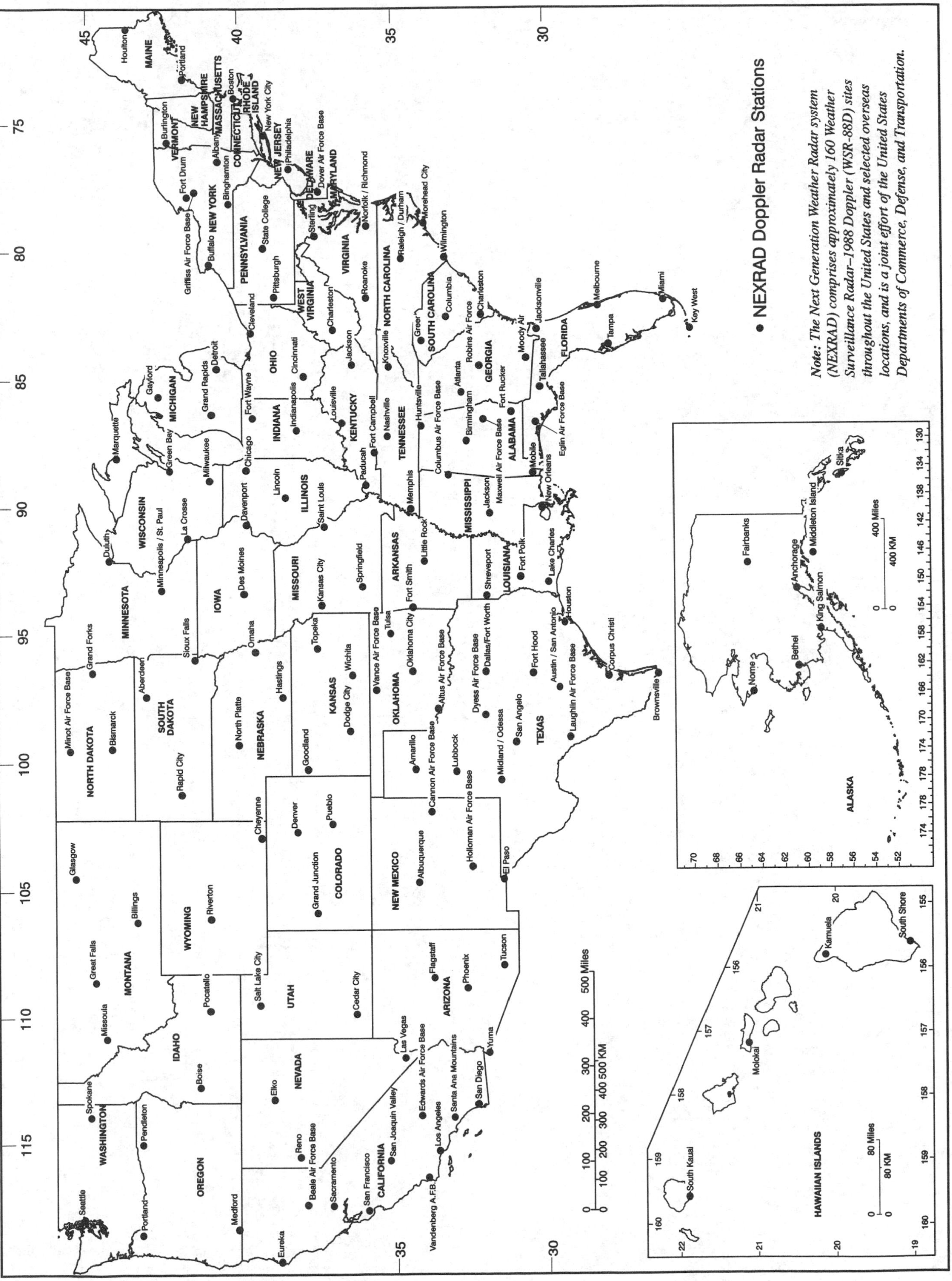

NEXRAD Doppler Radar Stations

Note: The Next Generation Weather Radar system (NEXRAD) comprises approximately 160 Weather Surveillance Radar–1988 Doppler (WSR-88D) sites throughout the United States and selected overseas locations, and is a joint effort of the United States Departments of Commerce, Defense, and Transportation.

MAINE — Houlton, Portland

NEW HAMPSHIRE — Burlington

VERMONT

MASSACHUSETTS — Boston

RHODE ISLAND

CONNECTICUT — Albany, New York City

NEW JERSEY — Philadelphia

DELAWARE

MARYLAND — Sterling, Dover Air Force Base

NEW YORK — Fort Drum, Griffiss Air Force Base, Buffalo, Binghamton, State College

PENNSYLVANIA — Pittsburgh

WEST VIRGINIA — Charleston

VIRGINIA — Roanoke, Norfolk / Richmond

NORTH CAROLINA — Raleigh / Durham, Morehead City, Wilmington, Greer

SOUTH CAROLINA — Columbia, Charleston

GEORGIA — Atlanta, Robins Air Force Base, Fort Rucker

FLORIDA — Jacksonville, Melbourne, Tampa, Miami, Key West, Tallahassee

ALABAMA — Birmingham, Huntsville, Maxwell Air Force Base, Mobile, Eglin Air Force Base

MISSISSIPPI — Jackson

LOUISIANA — New Orleans, Shreveport, Fort Polk, Lake Charles

TENNESSEE — Nashville, Memphis, Knoxville

KENTUCKY — Louisville, Fort Campbell, Paducah

OHIO — Cleveland, Cincinnati, Fort Wayne

INDIANA — Indianapolis

MICHIGAN — Detroit, Grand Rapids, Gaylord, Marquette, Green Bay

WISCONSIN — Milwaukee, La Crosse, Duluth

ILLINOIS — Chicago, Lincoln, Saint Louis, Springfield

MISSOURI — Davenport, Kansas City

IOWA — Des Moines

MINNESOTA — Minneapolis / St. Paul

ARKANSAS — Little Rock, Fort Smith

OKLAHOMA — Tulsa, Oklahoma City, Vance Air Force Base

KANSAS — Topeka, Wichita, Dodge City, Goodland

NEBRASKA — Omaha, Hastings, North Platte

SOUTH DAKOTA — Sioux Falls, Aberdeen, Rapid City

NORTH DAKOTA — Grand Forks, Minot Air Force Base, Bismarck

TEXAS — Dallas/Fort Worth, Houston, Fort Hood, San Angelo, Austin / San Antonio, Laughlin Air Force Base, Corpus Christi, Brownsville, Amarillo, Lubbock, Midland / Odessa, Dyess Air Force Base, Altus Air Force Base, Cannon Air Force Base, El Paso

NEW MEXICO — Albuquerque, Holloman Air Force Base

COLORADO — Denver, Pueblo, Grand Junction

WYOMING — Cheyenne, Riverton

MONTANA — Glasgow, Billings, Great Falls, Missoula

IDAHO — Pocatello, Boise, Spokane

WASHINGTON — Seattle, Pendleton

OREGON — Portland, Medford

CALIFORNIA — Eureka, San Francisco, Sacramento, San Joaquin Valley, Beale Air Force Base, Los Angeles, Santa Ana Mountains, San Diego, Vandenberg A.F.B., Edwards Air Force Base

NEVADA — Reno, Elko, Las Vegas

UTAH — Salt Lake City, Cedar City

ARIZONA — Flagstaff, Phoenix, Tucson, Yuma

ALASKA — Fairbanks, Anchorage, Middleton Island, Sitka, King Salmon, Bethel, Nome

HAWAIIAN ISLANDS — South Kauai, South Shore, Kamuela, Molokai

400 Miles
400 KM

80 Miles
80 KM

100 200 300 400 500 Miles
100 200 300 400 500 KM

Appendix D: Explanation of Data

Weather Station Tables

The weather station tables are grouped by type (National Weather Service and Cooperative) and then arranged alphabetically within each state section. The station name is almost always a place name, and is shown here just as it appears in NCDC data. The station name is followed by the county in which the station is located (or by county equivalent name, or by the NOAA division name, as in Alaska), the elevation of the station (at the time beginning of the thirty year period) and the latitude and longitude.

The National Weather Service Station tables contain 30 data elements which were compiled from two different sources, the International Station Meteorological Climate Summary (ISMCS) and NCDC TD-3220 data tapes. The following 14 elements are from the ISMCS: maximum precipitation, minimum precipitation, maximum 24-hour precipitation, maximum snowfall, maximum 24-hour snowfall, thunderstorm days, foggy days, predominant sky cover, relative humidity (morning and afternoon), dewpoint, wind speed and direction, and maximum wind gust. The remaining 16 elements come from the TD-3220 data tapes. The period of record (POR) for data from the TD-3220 data tapes is 1970-1999. The POR for ISMCS data varies from station to station. See Appendix B for a listing of the POR for each station.

The Cooperative Station tables contain 16 data elements which were all compiled from the TD-3220 data tapes with a POR of 1970-1999.

Weather Elements (National Weather Service and Cooperative Stations)

The following elements were compiled by the editor from the NCDC TD-3220 data tapes using a period of record of 1970-1999.

The average temperatures (maximum, minimum, and mean) are the average (see Methodology below) of those temperatures for all available values for a given month. For example, for a given station the average maximum temperature for July is the arithmetic average of all available maximum July temperatures for that station. (Maximum means the highest recorded temperature, minimum means the lowest recorded temperature, and mean means an arithmetic average temperature.)

The extreme maximum temperature is the highest temperature recorded in each month over the period 1970-1999. The extreme minimum temperature is the lowest temperature recorded in each month over the same time period.

The days for maximum temperature and minimum temperature are the average number of days those criteria were met for all available instances. The symbol >= means greater than or equal to, the symbol <= means less than or equal to. For example, for a given station, the number of days the maximum temperature was greater than or equal to 90°F in July, is just an arithmetic average of the number of days in all the available Julys for that station.

Heating and cooling degree days are based on the median temperature for a given day and its variance from 65°F. For example, for a given station if the day's high temperature was 50°F and the day's low temperature was 30°F, the median (midpoint) temperature was 40°F. 40°F is 25 degrees below 65°F, hence on this day there would be 25 heating degree days. The also applies for cooling degree days. For example, for a given station if the day's high temperature was 80°F and the day's low temperature was 70°F, the median (midpoint) temperature was 75°F. 75°F is 10 degrees above 65°F, hence on this day there would be 10 cooling degree days. All heating and/or cooling degree days in a month are summed for the month giving respective totals for each element for that month. These sums for a given month for a given station over the past thirty years are again summed and then arithmetically averaged. It should be noted that the heating and cooling degree days do not cancel each other out. It is possible to have both for a given station in the same month.

Precipitation data is computed the same as heating and cooling degree days. Mean precipitation and mean snowfall are arithmetic averages of cumulative totals for the month. All available values for the thirty year period for a given month for a given station are summed and then divided by the number of values. The same is true for days of greater than or equal to 0.1" and 1.0" of precipitation, and days of greater than or equal to 1.0" of snow depth on the ground. The word trace appears for precipitation and snowfall amounts that are too small to measure.

Finally, remember that all values presented in the tables and the rankings are averages of available data (see Methodology below) for that specific data element for the last thirty years (1970-1999).

Weather Elements (National Weather Service Stations Only)

The following elements were taken directly from the International Station Meteorological Climate Summary. The periods of records vary per station and are shown in Appendix B.

Maximum precipitation, minimum precipitation, maximum 24-hour precipitation, maximum snowfall, maximum 24-hour snowfall, thunderstorm days, foggy days, relative humidity (morning and afternoon), dewpoint, prevailing wind speed and direction, and maximum wind gust are all self-explanatory.

The word trace appears for precipitation and snowfall amounts that are too small to measure.

Predominant sky cover contains four possible entries: CLR (clear); SCT (scattered); BRK (broken); and OVR (overcast).

How Cooperative Stations Were Selected

The basic criteria is that a station must have data for temperature, precipitation, heating and cooling degree days of sufficient quantity in order to create a meaningful average. More specifically, the definition of sufficiency here has two parts. First, there must be 22 values for a given data element (with the exception of cooling degree days which required only 14 values in order to be considered sufficient- more about this later), and second, eight of the sixteen elements included in the table must pass this sufficiency test. For example, in regard to average maximum temperature (the first element on every data table), a given station needs to have a value for every month of at least 22 of the last thirty years in order to meet the criteria, and, in addition, every station included must have at least eight of the sixteen elements at least this minimal level of completeness in order to fulfill the criteria. By using this procedure, 3,933 stations met these requirements and are included here.

Methodology

The following discussion applies only to data compiled from the NCDC TD-3220 data tapes.

Weather America is based on an arithmetic average of all available data for a specific data element at a given station. For example, the average maximum daily high temperature during July for Alma, Michigan, was abstracted from NCDC source tapes for the thirty Julys, starting in July, 1970 and ending in July, 1999. These thirty figures were then summed and divided by thirty to produce an arithmetic average. As might be expected, there were not thirty values for every data element on every table. For a variety of reasons, NCDC data is sometimes incomplete. Thus the following standards were established.

For those data elements where there were 26-30 values, the data was taken to be essentially complete and an average was computed. For data elements where there were 22-25 values, the data was taken as being partly complete but still valid enough to use to compute an average. Such averages are shown in ***bold italic*** type to indicate that there was less than 26 values. For the few data elements where there were not even 22 values, no average was computed and 'na' appears in the space. If any of the twelve months for a given data element reported a value of 'na', no annual average was computed and the annual average was reported as 'na' as well.

This procedure was followed for 15 of the 16 data elements. The one exception is cooling degree days. The collection of this data began in 1980 so the following standards were adopted: for those data elements where there were 17-20 values, the data was taken to be essentially complete and an average was computed. For data elements where there were 14-16 values, the data was taken as being partly complete but still valid enough to use to compute an average. Such averages are shown in ***bold italic*** type to indicate that there was 14-16 values. For the few data elements where there were not even 14 values, no average was computed and 'na' appears in the space. If any of the twelve months for a given data element reported a value of 'na', no annual average was computed and the annual average was reported as 'na' as well.

Thus the basic computational methodology of *Weather America* is to provide an arithmetic average. Because of this, such a pure arithmetic average is somewhat different from the special type of average (called a "normal") which NCDC procedures produces and appears in federal publications.

Perhaps the best outline of the contrasting normalization methodology is found in the following paragraph (which appears as part of an NCDC technical document titled, CLIM81 1961-1990 NORMALS TD-9641 prepared by Lewis France of NCDC in May, 1992):

> Normals have been defined as the arithmetic mean of a climatological element computed over a long time period. International agreements eventually led to the decision that the appropriate time period would be three consecutive decades (Guttman, 1989). The data record should be consistent (have no changes in location, instruments, observation practices, etc.; these are identified here as "exposure changes") and have no missing values so a normal will reflect the actual average climatic conditions. If any significant exposure changes have occurred, the data record is said to be "inhomogeneous," and the normal may not reflect a true climatic average. Such data need to be adjusted to remove the nonclimatic inhomogeneities. The resulting (adjusted) record is then said to be "homogeneous." If no exposure changes have occurred at a station, the normal is calculated simply by averaging the appropriate 30 values from the 1961-1990 record.

In the main, there are two "inhomogeneities" that NCDC is correcting for with normalization: adjusting for variances in time of day of observation (at the so-called First Order stations data is based on midnight to midnight observation times and this practice is not necessarily followed at cooperative stations which are staffed by volunteers), and second, estimating data that is either missing or incongruent.

A long discussion of the normalization process is not required here but a short note concerning comparative results of the two methodologies is appropriate.

When the editors first started compiling *Weather America* a concern arose because the normalization process would not be replicated: would our methodology produce strikingly different results than NCDC's? To allay concerns, results of the two processes were compared for the time period normalized results are available (1961-1990). In short, what was found was that the answer to this question is no. Never-the-less, users should be aware that because of both the time period covered (1970-1999) and the methodology used, data in *Weather America* is not compatible with data from other sources.

Grey House Publishing
Statistical & Demographic Reference Books

Grey House Publishing is proud to announce that our business, health and education directories will be available in Online Databases by Fall 2000. Subscribers can access their subscription to our comprehensive databases via the Internet and do customized searches that instantly target the segment of each market that is right for them. Visit www.greyhouse.com and explore the subscription site, free of charge, or call 800-562-2139 for more information.

America's Top-Rated Cities, 2000

America's Top-Rated Cities provides current, comprehensive statistical information in one easy-to-use source on 76 cities which have been cited as the best for business and living in the U.S. Previously published by Universal Reference, this four-volume set offers a concise social, business, economic, demographic and environmental profile of each city, including brief evaluative comments. Comparisons with MSA and U.S. figures are shown and a special section with comparative statistics is also included. Each of the four volumes covers a specific region of the country: Southern, Western, Central and Eastern. This outstanding source of information will be widely used in any reference collection.

4 Volume Set	*ISBN 1-891482-50-5*	*1,528 pages*	*softcover*	*$195.00*
Vol. 1: Southern	*ISBN 1-891482-51-3*	*387 pages*	*softcover*	*$59.95*
Vol. 2: Western	*ISBN 1-891482-52-1*	*383 pages*	*softcover*	*$59.95*
Vol. 3: Central	*ISBN 1-891482-53-X*	*375 pages*	*softcover*	*$59.95*
Vol. 4: Eastern	*ISBN 1-891482-54-8*	*383 pages*	*softcover*	*$59.95*

Crime in America's Top-Rated Cities, 2000

This brand new volume includes over 20 years of crime statistics in all major crime categories: violent crimes, property crimes and total crime. *Crime in America's Top-Rated Cities* is arranged alphabetically by city and covers the 76 cities listed in *America's Top-Rated Cities, 2000*. It offers details that compare the number of crimes and crime rates for the city, suburbs and metro area and national crime trends for violent, property and total crimes. This handbook also contains important statistics on Anti-Crime Programs, Crime Risk, Crime Statistics, Hate Crimes, Illegal Drugs, Law Enforcement, Correctional Facilities and much more. Designed for people who are relocating, business professionals, general researchers, the press, law enforcement officials and students of criminal justice, this would be a well-used addition to the reference collection of public, academic and special libraries.

ISBN 1-891482-84-X	*841 pages*	*softcover*	*$155.00*
ISBN 1-891482-85-8	*841 pages*	*hardcover*	*$180.00*

America's Top-Rated Smaller Cities, 2000

A perfect companion to *America's Top-Rated Cities*, *America's Top-Rated Smaller Cities* provides a current, comprehensive business and living profile of smaller cities (population 25,000-99,999) that have been cited as the best for business and living in the United States. This one volume provides important statistical data on the Business and Living Environment of 60 "top" cities. Presented with each-of-use in mind, *America's Top-Rated Smaller Cities*, is arranged alphabetically by city. Each city report includes a Historical Background, an Overview of the State Finances and statistical details on Employment and Earnings, Household Income, Unemployment Rate, Population Characteristics, Taxes, Cost of Living, Education, Health Care, Public Safety, Recreation, Media, Air and Water Quality, and much more. *America's Top-Rated Smaller Cities* offers a reliable, one-stop source for statistical data that, before now, could only be found scattered in hundreds of sources.

ISBN 1-891482-65-3	*968 pages*	*softcover*	*$160.00*
ISBN 1-891482-66-1	*968 pages*	*hardcover*	*$185.00*

Health & Environment in America's Top-Rated Cities, 2001

This comprehensive publication provides critical health and environmental statistics for the 76 top-rated cities listed in *America's Top-Rated Cities*. Diverse topics are covered for each city, such as children's well being, infant mortality, air pollutants and death rates. From health and environmental protection agencies to school classrooms and libraries, this fact-filled handbook continues to educate the public through providing the most accurate and current health and environmental statistics for 76 top-rated cities.

ISBN 1-891482-92-0	*800 pages*	*softcover*	*$155.00*
ISBN 1-891482-93-9	*800 pages*	*hardcover*	*$180.00*

Working Americans, 1880-1999 Volume I: The Working Class

This brand new reference work focuses on the lifestyles and economic life of the American working class from 1880 to 1999. Family Profiles include real data on Income & Job Descriptions, Selected Prices of the Times, Annual Income, Annual Budget of Individuals, Family Finances & Budget, Life at Work, Life at Home, Life in the Community, Working Conditions, Cost of Living, Amusements and much more. You'll also find Economic Profiles with Average Wages of other Professions, a selection of Typical Pricing, Key Events and Inventions, Historical Snapshots, News Profiles, Articles from Local Media and Illustrations. This volume contains 72 Family Profiles that cover 34 occupations, and more than 25 ethnic groups. Geographically, the text travels the entire country, from the East Coast to Hawaii, to provide comprehensive coverage of the social and economic life of working class families available nowhere else. This interesting and useful compilation of portraits of the working class during the last 120 years will be an important addition to any high school, public or academic library reference collection.

ISBN 1-891482-81-5   *558 pages*   *hardcover*   *$125.00*

Working Americans, 1880-1999 Volume II: The Middle Class
ISBN 1-891482-72-6   *600 pages*   *hardcover*   *$125.00*

The Value of a Dollar – Millennium Edition

A guide to practical economy, *The Value of a Dollar* records the actual prices of thousands of items that consumers purchased from the Civil War to the present, along with facts about investment options and income opportunities. The first edition, published by Gale Research in 1994, covered the period of 1860 to 1989. This second edition has been completely redesigned and revised and now contains two new chapters, 1990-1994 and 1995-1999. Each 5-year chapter includes a Historical Snapshot, Consumer Expenditures, Investments, Selected Income, Income/Standard Jobs, Food Basket, Standard Prices and Miscellany. This interesting and useful publication will be widely used in any reference collection.

ISBN 1-891482-49-1   *660 pages*   *hardcover*   *$125.00*

The Comparative Guide to American Elementary & Secondary Schools

This comprehensive volume offers a snapshot profile of each public school district in the United States that serves 2,500 or more students. You'll find important contact information for each school district (name, address, phone number and web site) plus Grades Served, the Numbers of Students and Teachers and the Number of Regular, Special Education, Alternative and Vocational Schools in the district. Also, *The Comparative Guide to Elementary & Secondary Schools* provides important statistics to help evaluate educational programs, including Student/Classroom Teacher Ratios, Number of Librarians, Number of Guidance Counselors, District Expenditures per student and a National Socioeconomic Indicator for the district.

ISBN 1-884925-63-4   *774 pages*   *softcover*   *$85.00*

The Comparative Guide to American Suburbs

This unique reference focuses on the individual and suburban communities within each of the 50 largest metro areas. You'll find profiles of over 1,800 suburban communities with a 10,000+ population, a selection of Statistics on Population, Geography, the Economy, Safety, Housing and Education, plus details on Local Newspapers, Chambers of Commerce, School Districts and Place Name Origins. For each metro area, a Ranking Table is included that compares the suburbs in six critical indicators: Per Capita Income, Unemployment Rate, New Housing Permits, Median Home Prices and Crime Rates for Violent and Property Crimes. *The Comparative Guide to American Suburbs* is conveniently arranged by metro area. For anyone looking to relocate, as well as those doing preliminary market research, this volume is a must-have reference.

ISBN 1-884925-61-8   *816 pages*   *softcover*   *$85.00*

To preview any of our Directories for 30 days, please call toll-free
(800) 562-2139 or fax to (860) 435-3004

NOTES

NOTES

NOTES

NOTES

NOTES

NOTES

NOTES